WEBSTER'S
NEW W🌍RLD™

Concise French
Dictionary

WILEY

Wiley Publishing, Inc.

Webster's New World™ Concise French Dictionary

Copyright © 2004 by Chambers Harrap Publishers Ltd. All rights reserved.

Published by Wiley Publishing, Inc., Indianapolis, Indiana
Published simultaneously in Canada

For general information on our other products and services or to obtain technical support please con- tact our Customer Care Department within the U.S. at 800-762-2974, outside the U.S. at 317-572-3993 or fax 317-572-4002.

Wiley also publishes its books in a variety of electronic formats. Some content that appears in print may not be available in electronic books.

ISBN: 0-7645-4158-7

Cataloging-in-Publication information is available from the Library of Congress.

Designed and typeset by Chambers Harrap Publishers Ltd, Edinburgh.

Manufactured in the United States of America.

10 9 8 7 6 5 4 3 2 1

Project Editor / Directeur de projet
Gearóid Cronin

Editors / Rédacteurs
Isabelle Elkaim
Laurence Larroche

with / avec
Pat Dunn
Georges Pilard
Anna Stevenson

Publishing Manager / Direction éditoriale
Patrick White

Prepress / Prépresse
Clair Good
Marina Karapanovic

Contributors to the first edition / Ont participé à la première édition

Editor–in–Chief / Rédacteur en chef
Patrick White

Editors / Rédacteurs
Stuart Fortey   Isabelle Elkaim
Anna Stevenson   Laurence Larroche
                  Georges Pilard

with / avec
Ruth Blackmore   Sophie Marin
Lynda Carey   Martine Pierquin
Lesley Johnston   Catherine Roux
Irene Lakhani   Cécile Vanwalleghem
Ruth Noble

Trademarks

Words considered to be trademarks have been designated in this dictionary by the symbol ®. However, no judgement is implied concerning the legal status of any trademark by virtue of the presence or absence of such a symbol.

Marques déposées

Les termes considérés comme des marques déposées sont signalés dans ce dictionnaire par le symbole ®. Cependant, la présence ou l'absence de ce symbole ne constitue nullement une indication quant à la valeur juridique de ces termes.

Contents

Table des Matières

Preface

Webster's New World Concise French Dictionary provides comprehensive coverage of the basic vocabulary of both languages, while also including a wide range of neologisms. In this dictionary such new words as **arobase, boy band, clonage humain, e-cash, nethead** and **Webcam** have therefore been included. The *Concise* also contains a wide variety of idiomatic expressions, and provides coverage not only of American English on the English-French side but also of Canadian, Belgian and Swiss French terms on the French-English side.

As the dictionary will have a wide variety of users, and will find a place in school and workplace alike, it contains a broad range of vocabulary. In addition to good coverage of the French and English spoken today, including slang, technical terms from computing, finance, education, the media and business will all be found alongside encyclopedic information such as proper and geographical names.

The cultural boxes in the text are a novel feature of this dictionary. These notes focus on culture-specific topics which require more explanation than a simple translation can provide. There are a hundred and eighty boxed notes of this type in the dictionary, covering subjects as diverse as **devolution, Thanksgiving** and **vegetarianism** in Britain and the United States, and in the French context **bizutage, Canal +,** and **verlan,** to give but a few examples.

Finally, the supplement in the middle of the book contains a bilingual Communication Guide. The guide contains model letters and advice on how to correspond in the foreign language, as well as a section on e-mails and another on small ads, which can often be indecipherable to non-native speakers due to their extensive use of abbreviations.

Préface

Le *Webster's New World Concise French Dictionary,* sorti en 1997. Cet ouvrage présente un panorama très complet du vocabulaire de base de l'anglais et du français ainsi que de nombreux néologismes. Des termes désormais d'usage courant tels qu'**arobase, boys band, clonage humain, e-cash, nethead** et **Webcam** ont donc trouvé place dans ce dictionnaire. Le *Concise* contient également une abondance d'expressions idiomatiques, de nombreux américanismes et des termes de français du Canada, de Belgique et de Suisse.

Afin de satisfaire aux besoins des utilisateurs au collège et au lycée comme au bureau, cet ouvrage offre au lecteur un très large éventail de vocabulaire. Le français et l'anglais parlés aujourd'hui y sont traités en profondeur et l'argot y est bien représenté. On y trouvera également un abondant vocabulaire de spécialité (informatique, finance, enseignement, médias, monde des affaires) ainsi que des noms propres et des noms de lieux.

Cet ouvrage propose des encadrés culturels intégrés an texte. Ils concernent le plus souvent des thèmes propres à une culture ou à un pays particuliers, qui ne sont pas nécessairement connus en dehors du pays en question. Des explications y sont données lorsqu'une traduction ou une glose ne suffisent pas à fournir les informations nécessaires. Au total, cent-quatre-vingts encadrés figurent dans cet ouvrage, qui traitent de sujets tels que la **devolution, Thanksgiving** et le **végétarisme** pour la partie anglaise et le **bizutage, Canal+** et le **verlan** pour la partie française.

Enfin, le supplément qui se trouve en milieu d'ouvrage contient un guide de correspondance bilingue. Ce guide comprend des modèles de lettres et des conseils pour correspondre de façon efficace dans l'autre langue, un chapitre sur le courrier électronique et un autre sur les petites annonces, si souvent source de difficultés de compréhension en raison des nombreuses abréviations qui y sont utilisées.

Structure of Entries
Structure des Entrées

Indicateurs de champ sémantique pour les termes spécialisés
Field labels indicate senses belonging to a particular subject area

major ['meɪdʒə(r)] **1** *n* (**a**) *Mil (in air force)* ≃ commandant *m, Can & Belg* ≃ major *m*; *(in infantry)* chef *m* de bataillon; *(in cavalry)* chef *m* d'escadron; **m. general** général *m* de division (**b**) *Am Univ (subject)* matière *f* principale
2 *adj* (**a**) *(important)* majeur(e); *(most important)* principal(e); *(accident, illness)* très grave; **of m. importance** de la plus haute importance (**b**) *Mus* majeur(e)
3 *vi Am Univ* **to m. in sth** se spécialiser en qch

Anglais d'Amérique du Nord
American English senses indicated

Seule l'initiale du mot traité apparaît dans l'exemple
Headword abbreviated to first letter only

La phonétique complète est donnée pour chaque entrée
IPA shown in full for all headwords

management ['mænɪdʒmənt] *n* (**a**) *(activity) (of company, project)* gestion *f*, direction *f*; *(of economy, resources, shop, hotel)* gestion; **m. consultant** conseiller(ère) *m,f* en gestion; **m. studies** études *fpl* de gestion (**b**) *(managers, employers)* direction *f*; **under new m.** *(sign)* changement de propriétaire; **m. buyout** = rachat d'une société par la direction; **m. team** équipe *f* dirigeante

Les composés sont traités sous le premier élément et classés alphabétiquement
Compounds placed under first element; listed in alphabetical order

Chaque nouvelle catégorie grammaticale est traitée à la ligne et précédée d'un numéro en gras
New grammatical category introduced by bold numeral, placed on new line

managing director ['mænɪdʒɪŋdaɪ'rektə(r)] *n* directeur(trice) *m,f* général(e)

Indique que la traduction fonctionne aussi au sens figuré
This label means that the translation also works in figurative contexts

melt [melt] **1** *vt also Fig* faire fondre
2 *vi* fondre; **to m. into thin air** s'évaporer, disparaître; **to m. into the crowd** se fondre dans la foule
▶**melt away** *vi (of snow)* fondre; *(of clouds, vapour)* se dissiper; *(of crowd)* se disperser; *(of objections, opposition)* s'évanouir
▶**melt down** *vt sep (metal)* fondre

Les verbes à particule sont précédés du signe ▶
Phrasal verbs introduced by ▶

Le genre des noms donnés en traduction est indiqué en italiques
Gender of noun translations shown in italic

Les homographes sont numérotés
Superscript number marks homographs

minute¹ ['mɪnɪt] **1** *n* (**a**) *(of time)* minute *f*; **ten minutes past/to three** trois heures dix/moins dix; **wait a m.!** attendez une minute!; **go downstairs this m.!** descends immédiatement!; **just a m.** une minute; **the m. my back was turned** dès que j'ai eu le dos tourné; **any m.** d'une minute à l'autre; **in a m.** dans une minute; **at the last m.** à la dernière minute; **m. hand** *(of watch)* grande aiguille *f*; **m. steak** steak *m* minute (**b**) *(note)* note *f*; **minutes** *(of meeting)* compte rendu *m*
2 *vt (make note of)* inscrire au procès-verbal
minute² [maɪ'njuːt] *adj* (**a**) *(small)* infime, minuscule (**b**) *(detailed)* minutieux(euse)

Les indicateurs sémantiques apparaissent en italiques et entre parenthèses
Sense indicators shown in italic in brackets

Le féminin est donné systématiquement
Feminine inflections shown consistently

La forme développée des abréviations est donnée systématiquement; chaque abréviation est traduite
Full form of abbreviation given consistently; all abbreviations have translations

MOD [eməʊ'diː] *n Br Pol (abbr* **Ministry of Defence**) ministère *m* de la Défense

mollusc, *Am* **mollusk** ['mɒləsk] *n* mollusque *m*

Les variantes orthographiques américaines sont données
American spelling variants shown

académie [akademi] *nf* (**a**) *(des lettres, des sciences, d'art)* academy; **l'A. française** = learned society responsible for promoting the French language and imposing standards (**b**) *(école)* school, academy; **a. de musique/dessin** music/art school (**c**) *(dans l'Éducation nationale)* Br ≃ local education authority, Am ≃ school district

académique [akademik] *adj* (**a**) *Scol* = relating to a local education authority (**b**) *Péj (style)* conventional (**c**) *Belg, Suisse & Can* **l'année a.** the academic year

acquiescer [16] [akjese] *vi* to acquiesce (**à** to); **a. d'un signe de tête** to nod in agreement

aider [ede] **1** *vt* to help; *(sujet: gouvernement)* to aid; **que puis-je faire pour vous a.?** how may I help you?; **je me suis fait a. par un ami** I got a friend to help me; **a. qn à faire qch** to help sb to do sth; **a. qn à monter/sortir** to help sb up/out; *Ironique* **tu veux que je t'aide?** stop that!; **elle n'aide jamais** she never helps (out)
  2 aider à *vt ind* to contribute towards; **a. à faire qch** to help to do sth
  3 s'aider *vpr* (**a**) *(soi-même)* **s'a. de qch** to use sth; **marcher en s'aidant d'une canne/de béquilles** to walk with the aid of a stick/crutches; *Prov* **aide-toi et le ciel t'aidera** God helps those who help themselves (**b**) *(l'un l'autre)* to help each other

amnistier [66] [amnistje] *vt* to grant an amnesty to

arrière-plan (*pl* **arrière-plans**) [arjɛrplɑ̃] *nm aussi Fig* background; **à l'a.** in the background

arrière-saison (*pl* **arrière-saisons**) [arjɛrsɛzɔ̃] *nf Br* late autumn, *Am* late fall

arrière-train (*pl* **arrière-trains**) [arjɛrtrɛ̃] *nm (d'un animal)* (hind)quarters; *Fam (d'une personne)* rump, rear

artériosclérose [arterjɔsklerɔz] *nf* hardening of the arteries, *Spéc* arteriosclerosis

athlétisme [atletism] *nm* athletics *(singulier)*; **épreuves d'a.** athletic events

avril [avril] *nm* April; **le premier a.** *(jour des farces)* April Fools' Day; *Prov* **en a., ne te découvre pas d'un fil** ne'er cast a clout till May is out; *voir aussi* **janvier**

English Phonetic Symbols
Symboles Phonétiques de l'Anglais

Consonnes/Consonants

[b] but [bʌt]

[d] dab [dæb]

[dʒ] jam [dʒæm]; gem [dʒem]

[f] fat [fæt]

[g] go [gəʊ]

[h] hat [hæt]

[j] yet [jet]

[k] cat [kæt]

[l] lad [læd]

[m] mat [mæt]

[n] no [nəʊ]

[ŋ] bang [bæŋ]

[p] pat [pæt]

[r] rat [ræt]

[(r)] (*seulement prononcé en cas de liaison avec le mot suivant*) far [fɑː(r)]

[s] sat [sæt]

[ʃ] sham [ʃæm]

[t] tap [tæp]

[tʃ] chat [tʃæt]

[θ] thatch [θætʃ]

[ð] that [ðæt]

[v] vat [væt]

[w] wall [wɔːl]

[z] zinc [zɪŋk]

[ʒ] pleasure [pleʒə(r)]

[χ] loch [lɒχ]

Voyelles/Vowels

[æ] bat [bæt]

[ɑː] art [ɑːt]

[e] bet [bet]

[ɜː] curl [kɜːl]

[ə] amend [ə'mend]

[iː] bee [biː]

[ɪ] bit [bɪt]

[ɒ] wad [wɒd]

[ɔː] all [ɔːl]

[ʊ] put [pʊt]

[uː] shoe [ʃuː]

[ʌ] cut [kʌt]

Diphtongues/Diphthongs

[aɪ] life [laɪf]

[aʊ] house [haʊs]

[eə] there [ðeə(r)]

[eɪ] date [deɪt]

[əʊ] low [ləʊ]

[ɪə] beer [bɪə(r)]

[ɔɪ] boil [bɔɪl]

[ʊə] poor [pʊə(r)]

Symboles Phonétiques du Français
French Phonetic Symbols

Consonants/Consonnes

[b] beau [bo]
[d] donner [dɔne]
[f] feu [fø]
[g] garde [gard]
[ʒ] gilet [ʒilɛ]
[k] camp [kɑ̃]
[l] lait [lɛ]
[m] mon [mɔ̃]
[n] né [ne]
[ŋ] parking [parkiŋ]
[ɲ] campagne [kɑ̃paɲ]
[p] pain [pɛ̃]
[r] rare [rar]
[s] six [sis]
[ʃ] chose [ʃoz]
[t] table [tabl]
[v] vie [vi]
[z] zéro [zero]

Vowels/Voyelles

[a] chat [ʃa]
[ɑ] âge [ɑʒ]
[e] été [ete]
[ə] le [lə]; devin [dəvɛ̃]
[ø] feu [fø]
[œ] seul [sœl]
[ɛ] père [pɛr]
[i] vite [vit]
[ɔ] donner [dɔne]
[o] chaud [ʃo]
[u] tout [tu]
[y] cru [kry]
[ɑ̃] enfant [ɑ̃fɑ̃]
[ɛ̃] vin [vɛ̃]
[ɔ̃] bon [bɔ̃]
[œ̃] un [œ̃]

Semi-vowels/Semi-voyelles

[w] noir [nwar]
[j] yoga [jɔga]; rail [raj]
[ɥ] huit [ɥit]

Abbreviations
Abréviations

gloss [introduces an explanation]	=	glose [introduit une explication]
cultural equivalent [introduces a translation which has a roughly equivalent status in the target language]	≃	équivalent culturel [introduit une traduction dont les connotations dans la langue cible sont comparables]
abbreviation	*abbr, abrév*	abréviation
adjective	*adj*	adjectif
adverb	*adv*	adverbe
agriculture	*Agr*	agriculture
American English	*Am*	anglais d'Amérique du Nord
anatomy	*Anat*	anatomie
architecture	*Archit*	architecture
article	*art*	article
astrology	*Astrol*	astrologie
astronomy	*Astron*	astronomie
cars	*Aut*	automobile
auxiliary	*aux*	auxiliaire
aviation	*Aviat*	aviation
Belgian French	*Belg*	belgicisme
botany	*Bot*	botanique
British English	*Br*	anglais britannique
Canadian French	*Can*	canadianisme
chemistry	*Chem, Chim*	chimie
cinema	*Cin*	cinéma
commerce	*Com*	commerce
computing	*Comput*	informatique
conjunction	*conj*	conjonction
construction	*Constr*	construction
cooking	*Culin*	cuisine
economics	*Econ, Écon*	économie
electricity, electronics	*Elec, Élec*	électricité, électronique
European Union	*EU*	Union européenne
euphemism	*Euph*	euphémisme
exclamation	*exclam*	exclamation
feminine	*f*	féminin
familiar	*Fam*	familier
figurative	*Fig*	figuré
finance	*Fin*	finance
geography	*Geog, Géog*	géographie
geology	*Geol, Géol*	géologie
grammar	*Gram*	grammaire

history	*Hist*	histoire
humorous	*Hum*	humoristique
industry	*Ind*	industrie
invariable	*inv*	invariable
Irish English	*Ir*	anglais d'Irlande
journalism	*Journ*	journalisme
law	*Jur*	droit
linguistics	*Ling*	linguistique
literary	*Lit, Litt*	littéraire
masculine	*m*	masculin
medicine	*Med, Méd*	médecine
weather	*Met, Météo*	météorologie
military	*Mil*	militaire
music	*Mus*	musique
noun	*n*	nom
shipping	*Naut*	nautisme
feminine noun	*nf*	nom féminin
feminine plural noun	*nfpl*	nom féminin pluriel
masculine noun	*nm*	nom masculin
masculine and feminine noun [same form for both genders]	*nmf*	nom masculin et féminin [formes identiques]
masculine and feminine noun [different form in the feminine]	*nm,f*	nom masculin et féminin [formes différentes]
masculine plural noun	*nmpl*	nom masculin pluriel
plural noun	*npl*	nom pluriel
proper noun	*npr*	nom propre
officially approved term	*Offic*	recommandation officielle
computing	*Ordinat*	informatique
parliament	*Parl*	parlement
pejorative	*Pej, Péj*	péjoratif
photography	*Phot*	photographie
physics	*Phys*	physique
plural	*pl*	pluriel
politics	*Pol*	politique
past participle	*pp*	participe passé
prefix	*pref, préf*	préfixe
preposition	*prep, prép*	préposition
pronoun	*pron*	pronom
proverb	*Prov*	proverbe
psychology	*Psy*	psychologie, psychiatrie
past tense	*pt*	prétérit
something	*qch*	quelque chose
somebody	*qn*	quelqu'un
registered trademark	®	marque déposée
radio	*Rad*	radio
rail	*Rail*	chemins de fer
religion	*Rel*	religion
somebody	*sb*	quelqu'un
school	*Sch, Scol*	domaine scolaire

Scottish English	*Scot*	anglais d'Écosse
specialist term	*Spec, Spéc*	vocabulaire de spécialité
something	*sth*	quelque chose
suffix	*suff*	suffixe
technical term	*Tech*	terme technique
telecommunications	*Tel, Tél*	télécommunications
textiles	*Tex*	textile
theatre	*Theat, Théât*	théâtre
television	*TV*	télévision
typography, printing	*Typ*	typographie, imprimerie
European Union	*UE*	Union européenne
university	*Univ*	domaine universitaire
verb	*v*	verbe
intransitive verb	*vi*	verbe intransitif
reflexive verb	*vpr*	verbe pronominal
transitive verb	*vt*	verbe transitif
transitive verb used with a preposition [e.g. **parvenir à** (to reach); ils sont **parvenus à** un accord (they reached an agreement)]	*vt ind*	verbe transitif indirect [par exemple: **parvenir à**; ils sont **parvenus à** un accord]
inseparable transitive verb [phrasal verb where the verb and the adverb or preposition cannot be separated, e.g. **look after**; he **looked after** the children]	*vt insep*	verbe transitif à particule inséparable [par exemple: **look after** (s'occuper de); he **looked after** the children (il s'occupait des enfants)]
separable transitive verb [phrasal verb where the verb and the adverb or preposition can be separated, e.g. **send back**; she sent the present **back** or she sent **back** the present]	*vt sep*	verbe transitif à particule séparable [par exemple; **send back** (rendre); she **sent** the present back *ou* she **sent back** the present (elle a rendu le cadeau)]
vulgar	*Vulg*	vulgaire
zoology	*Zool*	zoologie

All other labels are written in full.
Toutes les autres indications d'usage sont données en entier.

English-French
Anglais-Français

A

A, a¹ [eɪ] *n* (**a**) *(letter)* A, a *m inv*; **to get from A to B** aller d'un point à un autre; **from A to Z** de A à Z; **A bomb** bombe *f* A; *Br Sch* **A level** = diplôme de fin d'études secondaires sanctionnant une matière déterminée; *Br Sch* **A levels** ≃ baccalauréat *m*; *Br* **A road** ≃ (route *f*) nationale *f*; **A side** *(of record)* face *f* A; **A-Z** *(street guide)* index *m* des rues; **an A-Z of gardening** le jardinage de A à Z
 (**b**) *Sch (grade)* **to get an A** *(in exam)* avoir mention bien ou très bien; *(in homework, essay)* ≃ avoir entre 14 et 20
 (**c**) *Mus* la *m inv*

> ### A levels
> Cet examen, qui ouvre l'accès aux études supérieures en Grande-Bretagne, est beaucoup plus spécialisé que le baccalauréat français; il ne comprend que deux ou trois matières (exceptionellement quatre). D'autre part, les mentions sont très importantes pour pouvoir choisir l'université où l'on souhaite faire ses études. En Écosse l'examen équivalent aux **A levels** s'appelle le "Higher" ou "Higher Grade".

a² [ə, *stressed* eɪ]

> a devient **an** [ən, *stressed* æn] devant voyelle ou h muet.

indefinite art (**a**) *(in general)* un (une); **a man** un homme; **a woman** une femme; **an hour** une heure; **he's got a red nose** il a le nez rouge; **I haven't got a car** je n'ai pas de voiture; **what a day!** quelle journée!
 (**b**) *(with professions, nationalities)* **he's an Englishman/a father/a lawyer** il est anglais/père/avocat
 (**c**) *(with prices, rates)* **30 pence a kilo** 30 pence le kilo; **three times a week** trois fois par semaine; **50 kilometres an hour** 50 kilomètres (à l')heure
 (**d**) *(a certain)* **a Mr Watkins phoned** un certain M. Watkins a appelé

AA [eɪ'eɪ] *n* (**a**) *(abbr* **Automobile Association***)* = club automobile britannique offrant notamment des services de dépannage (**b**) *(abbr* **Alcoholics Anonymous***)* AA *mpl*

AAA *n* (**a**) ['θriː'eɪz] *Br (abbr* **Amateur Athletics Association***)* = fédération britannique d'athlétisme (**b**) [eɪeɪ'eɪ] *Am (abbr* **American Automobile Association***)* = club automobile américain

A&E [eɪænd'iː] *Br Med (abbr* **accident and emergency***)* service *m* des urgences, urgences *fpl*

AB [eɪ'biː] *n Am (abbr* **Artium Baccalaureus***) (diploma)* ≃ licence *f* de lettres; *(graduate)* ≃ licencié(e) *m,f* ès lettres

abaci ['æbəsaɪ] *pl of* **abacus**

aback [ə'bæk] *adv* **taken a. (by)** déconcerté(e) (par)

abacus ['æbəkəs] *(pl* **abaci** ['æbəsaɪ] *or* **abacuses** ['æbəkəsɪz] *) n* boulier *m*

abandon [ə'bændən] **1** *n* **with a.** avec abandon; **to drive with reckless a.** conduire avec insouciance
 2 *vt* abandonner; *(match)* interrompre; **to a. ship** abandonner le navire

abase [ə'beɪs] *vt* **to a. oneself** s'abaisser, s'humilier

abashed [ə'bæʃt] *adj* penaud(e); **to be** *or* **feel a. (at sth)** avoir honte (de qch)

abate [ə'beɪt] *vi (of storm, pain)* se calmer; *(of noise)* diminuer

abattoir ['æbətwɑː(r)] *n* abattoir *m*

abbess ['æbɪs] *n* abbesse *f*

abbey ['æbɪ] *(pl* **abbeys***) n* abbaye *f*

abbot ['æbət] *n* abbé *m*

abbreviate [ə'briːvɪeɪt] *vt* abréger

abbreviation [əbriːvɪ'eɪʃən] *n* abréviation *f*

ABC [eɪbiː'siː] *n* (**a**) *(alphabet)* alphabet *m*; **an ABC of gardening** un ABC du jardinage (**b**) *(abbr* **American Broadcasting Corporation***)* = chaîne de télévision américaine (**c**) *(abbr* **Australian Broadcasting Corporation***)* = chaîne de télévision australienne

abdicate ['æbdɪkeɪt] **1** *vt* **to a. the throne** abdiquer; **to a. responsibility** abdiquer devant ses responsabilités
 2 *vi (of monarch)* abdiquer

abdication [æbdɪ'keɪʃən] *n (of throne)* abdication *f*; *(of responsibilities)* abandon *m*

abdomen ['æbdəmən] *n Anat & Zool* abdomen *m*

abdominal [æb'dɒmɪnəl] *adj Anat* abdominal(e)

abdominals [æb'dɒmɪnəlz] *npl (exercises)* abdominaux *mpl*

abduct [əb'dʌkt] *vt* enlever

abduction [əb'dʌkʃən] *n* enlèvement *m*

aberration [æbə'reɪʃən] *n* aberration *f*; **in a moment of a.** dans un moment de folie

abet [ə'bet] *(pt & pp* **abetted***) vt Law* **to aid and a. sb** être le complice de qn

abetting [ə'betɪŋ] *n Law* **aiding and a.** complicité *f*

abeyance [ə'beɪəns] *n* **in a.** *(of law, custom)* en désuétude

abhor [əb'hɔː(r)] *(pt & pp* **abhorred***) vt* détester, avoir horreur de

abhorrence [əb'hɒrəns] *n* horreur *f*

abhorrent [əb'hɒrənt] *adj* odieux(euse)

abide [ə'baɪd] *vt (tolerate)* **I can't a. him** je ne peux pas le supporter

▶**abide by** vt insep (promise) tenir; (rule, decision) se plier à, se soumettre à; **I a. by what I said** je maintiens ce que j'ai dit

abiding [ə'baɪdɪŋ] adj (impression) durable; **my a. memory of him is his generosity** je garde de lui le souvenir de quelqu'un de très généreux

ability [ə'bɪlɪtɪ] (pl **abilities**) n (**a**) (talent, skill) capacités fpl (**in** en), compétence f (**in** en) (**b**) (capability) capacité f (**to** à); **to the best of one's a.** de son mieux

abject ['æbdʒekt] adj (miserable) malheureux(euse); (contemptible) abject(e); **to make an a. apology** s'excuser platement; **a. poverty** misère f noire

ablaze [ə'bleɪz] adj en feu, en flammes; **to set sth a.** embraser qch; Fig **her eyes were a. with anger** ses yeux brillaient de colère

able ['eɪbəl] adj (**a**) (competent) (person, performance) compétent(e) (**b**) **to be a. to do sth** (be physically capable) pouvoir faire qch; (know how to) savoir faire qch; **I won't be a. to come** je ne pourrai pas venir; **we waited all afternoon, but we weren't a. to see him** nous avons attendu tout l'après-midi mais nous n'avons pas réussi à le voir

able-bodied ['eɪbəl'bɒdɪd] adj robuste; Naut **a. seaman** matelot m de deuxième classe

ably ['eɪblɪ] adv de façon compétente; **a. assisted by** efficacement assisté par

abnormal [æb'nɔːməl] adj anormal(e)

abnormality [æbnɔː'mælɪtɪ] (pl **abnormalities**) n (irregularity) anomalie f; (physical) malformation f

abnormally [æb'nɔːməlɪ] adv anormalement

aboard [ə'bɔːd] **1** adv (on ship, aeroplane) à bord; **to go a.** monter à bord
2 prep (ship, aeroplane) à bord de; (bus, train) dans

abode [ə'bəʊd] n Lit demeure f; Law **of no fixed a.** sans domicile fixe; Law **right of a.** droit m de séjour

abolish [ə'bɒlɪʃ] vt abolir; (law) abroger

abolition [æbə'lɪʃən] n abolition f; (of law) abrogation f

abominable [ə'bɒmɪnəbəl] adj abominable; **the a. snowman** l'abominable homme m des neiges

abomination [əbɒmɪ'neɪʃən] n abomination f

aborigine [æbə'rɪdʒɪnɪ] n aborigène mf

abort [ə'bɔːt] **1** vt (**a**) Med (woman) avorter; **the foetus was aborted** la grossesse a été interrompue (**b**) (project) & Comput abandonner
2 vi Med avorter, faire une fausse couche

abortion [ə'bɔːʃən] n avortement m, IVG f; **to have an a.** se faire avorter

abortive [ə'bɔːtɪv] adj (attempt, plan) avorté(e)

abound [ə'baʊnd] vi abonder (**in** or **with** en)

about [ə'baʊt] **1** prep (**a**) (regarding) **a book a. France** un livre sur la France; **the good/bad thing a....** ce qu'il y a de bien/de mauvais dans...; **what's it a.?** de quoi s'agit-il?; **to talk a. sth** parler de qch; **to argue a. sth** se disputer au sujet de qch; **we must do something a. this problem** il faut faire quelque chose à ce sujet
(**b**) (in various parts of) **to walk a. the town** se promener dans la ville; **to look a. the room** parcourir la pièce du regard
2 adv (**a**) (in different directions, places) **to walk a.** se promener; **to run a.** courir à droite et à gauche; **to be lying a.** traîner
(**b**) (in the general area) **is Jack a.?** est-ce que Jack est dans les environs ou parages?; **there was nobody a.** il n'y avait personne

(**c**) (approximately) environ, à peu près; **a. thirty** environ trente, une trentaine; **a. ten years** environ dix ans, une dizaine d'années; **at a. one o'clock** vers une heure; **she's a. as tall as you** elle est grande à peu près comme toi; **I've just a. finished** j'ai pratiquement terminé; **a. time!** ce n'est pas trop tôt!
(**d**) (on the point of) **to be a. to do sth** aller faire qch, être sur le point de faire qch; **I'm not a. to...** (have no intention of) je n'ai pas l'intention de...

about-face [ə'baʊt'feɪs], **about-turn** [ə'baʊt'tɜːn] n (radical change) volte-face f inv

above [ə'bʌv] **1** prep (**a**) (physically) au-dessus de; **the Seine a. Paris** la Seine en amont de Paris
(**b**) (with numbers) plus de; **the temperature didn't rise a. 10°C** la température n'a pas dépassé 10°C
(**c**) (in rank) **he is a. me** il est mon supérieur
(**d**) (not subject to) **to be a. suspicion** être au-dessus de tout soupçon; **her behaviour is a. criticism** il n'y a rien à redire à son attitude
(**e**) (superior to) **he thinks he's a. all that** il se croit au-dessus de tout ça; **she's not a. telling lies** elle est capable de mentir; **to get a. oneself** se donner des airs
(**f**) **a. all** surtout; **they value friendship a. all else** ils font passer l'amitié avant tout le reste
2 adv (**a**) (in general) au-dessus; **the tenants (of the flat) a.** les locataires du dessus; **from a.** (from one's superiors) d'en haut
(**b**) (in book, document) ci-dessus

above-board [ə'bʌvbɔːd] adj (honest) franc (franche), honnête

above-mentioned [əbʌv'menʃənd], **above-named** [əbʌv'neɪmd] adj susdit(e), susnommé(e)

abrasion [ə'breɪʒən] n (on skin) écorchure f

abrasive [ə'breɪsɪv] **1** n (substance) abrasif m
2 adj (surface, substance) abrasif(ive); (person, manner) caustique

abreast [ə'brest] adv de front; **to come a. of** arriver à la hauteur de; **to keep a. of** (events, progress) se tenir au courant de

abridged [ə'brɪdʒd] adj abrégé(e)

abroad [ə'brɔːd] adv à l'étranger; **our colleagues from a.** nos collègues étrangers; **to get a.** (of news) se répandre

abrupt [ə'brʌpt] adj (**a**) (sudden) brusque, soudain(e); **the train came to an a. halt** le train s'est brusquement ou soudainement arrêté (**b**) (curt) abrupt(e), brusque

abruptly [ə'brʌptlɪ] adv (**a**) (suddenly) brusquement, soudainement (**b**) (curtly) de façon abrupte, avec brusquerie

abscess ['æbses] n abcès m

abscond [əb'skɒnd] vi Formal s'enfuir, prendre la fuite

abseil ['æbseɪl] vi descendre en rappel; **to a. down sth** descendre qch en rappel

abseiling ['æbseɪlɪŋ] n rappel m, descente f en rappel; **to go a.** faire du rappel

absence ['æbsəns] n absence f; **in the a. of** (person) en l'absence de; (thing) faute de; Law **sentenced in one's a.** condamné(e) par contumace; Prov **a. makes the heart grow fonder** l'éloignement renforce l'affection

absent 1 adj ['æbsənt] (pupil, expression) absent(e); Mil **a. without leave** porté(e) manquant(e)
2 vt [æb'sent] **to a. oneself (from)** s'absenter (de)

absentee [æbsən'tiː] n absent(e) m,f; **a. landlord** propriétaire m absentéiste

absenteeism [æbsən'tiːɪzm] n absentéisme m
absent-minded [æbsənt'maɪndɪd] adj distrait(e)
absent-mindedness [æbsənt'maɪndɪdnɪs] n dis-traction f
absolute ['æbsəluːt] adj (**a**) (total) absolu(e); **a. majority** majorité f absolue; **a. monarch** monarque m absolu (**b**) (emphatic) **he's an a. fool!** il est complètement idiot!; **a. rubbish!** n'importe quoi!; **an a. disgrace/disaster** un véritable scandale/désastre
absolutely [æbsə'luːtlɪ] adv absolument; **you're a. right** vous avez absolument ou tout à fait raison; **do you support him? – a./a. not** vous le soutenez? – absolument/absolument pas
absolution [æbsə'luːʃən] n Rel absolution f
absolve [əb'zɒlv] vt Rel absoudre (**from** or **of** de); (from duty) dispenser (**from** or **of** de); **to be absolved from blame** être innocenté(e)
absorb [əb'zɔːb] vt (liquid) absorber; (losses) essuyer; **to be absorbed in sth** être absorbé(e) par qch
absorbent [əb'zɔːbənt] adj absorbant(e)
absorbing [əb'zɔːbɪŋ] adj (work) absorbant(e); (book, question) passionnant(e)
abstain [əb'steɪn] vi s'abstenir (**from** de)
abstemious [əb'stiːmɪəs] adj sobre
abstention [əb'stenʃən] n Pol abstention f
abstinence ['æbstɪnəns] n abstinence f
abstract ['æbstrækt] **1** n (**a**) (concept) **the a.** l'abstrait m (**b**) (of article) résumé m
 2 adj abstrait(e)
 3 vt [æb'strækt] Formal (remove) extraire (**from** de)
abstraction [æb'strækʃən] n abstraction f
abstruse [əb'struːs] adj obscur(e)
absurd [əb'sɜːd] adj absurde
absurdity [əb'sɜːdɪtɪ] (pl **absurdities**) n absurdité f
ABTA ['æbtə] n (abbr **Association of British Travel Agents**) = association d'agences de voyage britanniques
abundance [ə'bʌndəns] n abondance f; **an a. of talent** un grand talent; **in a.** en abondance
abundant [ə'bʌndənt] adj abondant(e); **to be a. in sth** abonder en qch
abundantly [ə'bʌndəntlɪ] adv en abondance; **a. clear** tout à fait clair(e)
abuse 1 n [ə'bjuːs] (**a**) (of power) abus m (**b**) (insults) injures fpl, insultes fpl; **term of a.** injure f, insulte f (**c**) (cruelty) mauvais traitements mpl, maltraitance f; (**sexual**) **a.** sévices mpl sexuels
 2 vt [ə'bjuːz] (**a**) (misuse) abuser de (**b**) (insult) injurier, insulter (**c**) (ill-treat) (physically) maltraiter; (sexually) faire subir des sévices sexuels à
abusive [ə'bjuːsɪv] adj (person, language) grossier (ère)
abysmal [ə'bɪzməl] adj (ignorance) sans bornes; (performance, quality) épouvantable
abyss [ə'bɪs] n also Fig abîme m, gouffre m
AC ['eɪ'siː] n Elec (abbr **alternating current**) courant m alternatif
a/c n (abbr **account**) compte m
academic [ækə'demɪk] **1** n (university teacher) universitaire mf; (intellectual) intellectuel(elle) m,f
 2 adj (**a**) (of school) scolaire; (of university) universitaire; **her a. achievements are impressive** elle a fait de brillantes études; **a. year** année f universitaire (**b**) (intellectual) intellectuel(elle) (**c**) (theoretical)

théorique; **it's entirely a. whether he did it or not** qu'il l'ait fait ou non n'a aucune importance
academy [ə'kædəmɪ] (pl **academies**) n académie f; **a. of music** conservatoire m (de musique)
ACAS ['eɪkæs] n (abbr **Advisory, Conciliation and Arbitration Service**) = organisme britannique indépendant d'arbitrage des conflits du travail
accede [æk'siːd] vi Formal (**a**) **to a. to** (request, demand) accéder à; (agreement, changes) accepter (**b**) (of monarch) **to a. to the throne** accéder au trône
accelerate [ək'seləreɪt] **1** vt (progress) accélérer; (downfall) précipiter
 2 vi (of car, driver) accélérer; (of pace) s'accélérer
acceleration [əkselə'reɪʃən] n accélération f
accelerator [ək'seləreɪtə(r)] n accélérateur m
accent ['æksənt] n accent m; **to put the a. on sth** (emphasize) mettre l'accent sur qch
accentuate [æk'sentʃʊeɪt] vt accentuer
accept [ək'sept] vt (**a**) (gift, apology, defeat) accepter; (responsibility) assumer (**for** de); (concede) admettre; **to a. (that)...** admettre que... (**b**) (into university) admettre
acceptable [ək'septəbəl] adj acceptable; **to be a. to sb** (suit) convenir à qn
acceptance [ək'septəns] n (**a**) (of invitation, apology, defeat) acceptation f; **to find a.** être reconnu(e) (**b**) (to university) admission f; **a. speech** = discours prononcé par le lauréat d'un prix
access ['ækses] **1** n accès m (**to** à); **to have a. to sth** avoir accès à qch; **to gain a. to** (get inside) s'introduire dans; (reach) accéder à; **a. ramp** bretelle f d'accès; **a. road** route f d'accès; (of motorway) bretelle f d'accès; Comput **a. code** code m d'accès; Comput **a. provider** fournisseur m d'accès; Comput **a. time** temps m d'accès
 2 vt Comput accéder à
accessible [ək'sesəbəl] adj (place, explanation) accessible; (person) joignable
accession [ək'seʃən] n (to power, throne) accession f; (library book) acquisition f
accessory [ək'sesərɪ] (pl **accessories**) n (**a**) (extra) accessoire m (**b**) Law complice mf (**to** de)
accident ['æksɪdənt] n accident m; **by a.** par accident ou hasard; **to have an a.** avoir un accident; Br Med **a. and emergency (unit)** service m des urgences, urgences fpl; **a. insurance** assurance f accidents
accidental [æksɪ'dentəl] adj accidentel(elle); Law **a. death** mort f accidentelle
accidentally [æksɪ'dentəlɪ] adv accidentellement
accident-prone ['æksɪdəntprəʊn] adj prédisposé(e) aux accidents
acclaim [ə'kleɪm] **1** n louanges fpl; **to meet with great critical a.** être salué(e) par la critique
 2 vt (person) acclamer; (performance, film) applaudir
acclamation [æklə'meɪʃən] n (cheering) acclamations fpl
acclimatize [ə'klaɪmətaɪz] **1** vt (animal, plant) acclimater; **to become acclimatized to** (person) s'habituer à, s'accoutumer à
 2 vi s'acclimater (**to** à)
accolade ['ækəleɪd] n honneur m
accommodate [ə'kɒmədeɪt] vt (**a**) (provide room for) loger (**b**) (satisfy) satisfaire
accommodating [ə'kɒmədeɪtɪŋ] adj (helpful) obligeant(e); (easy to please) accommodant(e)

accommodation [əkɒmə'deɪʃən] *n* (**a**) *(lodging)* logement *m*; *(in hotel)* chambre *f* (d'hôtel) (**b**) *Formal (agreement)* compromis *m*

accompaniment [ə'kʌmpənɪmənt] *n Mus* accompagnement *m*; *Culin* garniture *f*

accompany [ə'kʌmpənɪ] *(pt & pp* **accompanied**) *vt* accompagner; **to be accompanied by sth** s'accompagner de qch

accomplice [ə'kʌmplɪs] *n* complice *mf*

accomplish [ə'kʌmplɪʃ] *vt (task)* accomplir; *(aim)* atteindre

accomplished [ə'kʌmplɪʃt] *adj (musician, cook)* accompli(e); *(actor)* doué(e); *(performance)* très au point

accord [ə'kɔːd] **1** *n* accord *m*; **in a. with** en accord avec; **with one a.** d'un commun accord; **of one's own a.** de son plein gré
   2 *vt* accorder (**to** à)

▸**accord with** *vt insep* concorder avec

accordance [ə'kɔːdəns] *n* **in a. with** en accord avec; **his statement is not in a. with the facts** sa déclaration ne concorde pas avec les faits

according to [ə'kɔːdɪŋtuː] *prep* (**a**) *(depending on)* selon; **a. whether one is rich or poor** selon que l'on est riche ou pauvre; **a. which method you use** selon la méthode utilisée (**b**) *(in conformity with)* selon; **to go a. plan** se dérouler comme prévu (**c**) *(citing a source)* selon, d'après

accordingly [ə'kɔːdɪŋlɪ] *adv* (**a**) *(appropriately)* en conséquence (**b**) *(therefore)* par conséquent

accordion [ə'kɔːdɪən] *n* accordéon *m*

accost [ə'kɒst] *vt* accoster, aborder

account [ə'kaʊnt] *n* (**a**) *(at bank)* compte *m*; *Com* **accounts department** comptabilité *f*
   (**b**) *(reckoning)* **to keep (an) a. of sth** tenir un compte de qch; **to take sth into a., to take a. of sth** *(consider)* tenir compte de qch, prendre qch en compte; **taking everything into a.** *(after all)* au bout du compte; **to call sb to a.** demander des comptes à qn; **to be brought to a.** avoir des comptes à rendre (**c**) *(importance)* **of no a.** sans importance (**d**) **on a. of** *(because of)* à cause de; **on no a., not on any a.** en aucun cas, surtout pas; **to set up in business on one's own a.** s'installer à son compte; **don't do it on my a.!** ne le faites surtout pas pour moi! (**e**) *(report)* description *f*; **to give an a. of sth** faire le récit de qch; *Fig* **to give a good a. of oneself** *(in fight, contest)* bien se défendre; **by all accounts** au dire de tous

▸**account for** *vt insep* (**a**) *(explain, justify)* expliquer; **five people have still not been accounted for** *(are still missing)* cinq personnes n'ont toujours pas été retrouvées; **there's no accounting for taste** chacun ses goûts (**b**) *(constitute)* constituer

accountability [ə'kaʊntəbɪlɪtɪ] *n* responsabilité *f* (**to** envers)

accountable [ə'kaʊntəbəl] *adj* responsable (**to sb** envers qn; **for sth** de qch); *(for sum of money)* redevable (**for** de); **to hold sb a.** tenir qn pour responsable

accountancy [ə'kaʊntənsɪ] *n* comptabilité *f*

accountant [ə'kaʊntənt] *n* comptable *mf*

accounting [ə'kaʊntɪŋ] *n* comptabilité *f*; **a. period** période *f* comptable

accrue [ə'kruː] *vi Fin (of interest)* s'accumuler; **to a. to sb** *(of interest, benefits)* revenir à qn

accumulate [ə'kjuːmjʊleɪt] **1** *vt* accumuler
   2 *vi* s'accumuler

accumulation [əkjuːmjʊ'leɪʃən] *n* accumulation *f*

accuracy ['ækjʊrəsɪ] *n (of calculation, translation)* exactitude *f*, précision *f*; *(of firearm, shot)* précision; *(of portrayal)* fidélité *f*

accurate ['ækjʊrət] *adj (calculation, translation)* exact(e), précis(e); *(firearm, shot)* précis(e); *(portrayal)* fidèle

accurately ['ækjʊrətlɪ] *adv (calculate, translate)* avec exactitude *ou* précision; *(aim)* avec précision; *(portray)* fidèlement

accusation [ækjʊ'zeɪʃən] *n* accusation *f*; **to make an a. (against sb)** porter *ou* lancer une accusation (contre qn)

accuse [ə'kjuːz] *vt* **to a. sb (of sth/of doing sth)** accuser qn (de qch/de faire qch)

accused [ə'kjuːzd] *(pl* **accused**) *n Law* **the a.** l'inculpé(e) *m,f*

accuser [ə'kjuːzə(r)] *n* accusateur(trice) *m,f*

accusing [ə'kjuːzɪŋ] *adj (look, tone)* accusateur(trice)

accustom [ə'kʌstəm] *vt* accoutumer, habituer; **to be accustomed to sth/to doing sth** être habitué à qch/à faire qch; **to get** *or* **grow accustomed to sth/to doing sth** s'accoutumer *ou* s'habituer à qch/à faire qch

AC/DC ['eɪsiː'diːsiː] **1** *n Elec (abbr* **alternating current/direct current**) courant alternatif/courant continu
   2 *adj Fam (bisexual)* **to be A.** marcher à voile et à vapeur

ace [eɪs] **1** *n* (**a**) *(in cards)* as *m*; **a. of spades** as de pique; *Fig* **to have an a. up one's sleeve** avoir un atout en réserve; **to come within an a. of doing sth** être à deux doigts de faire qch (**b**) *(tennis)* ace *m* (**c**) *Fam (expert)* as *m*; **flying a.** as de l'aviation
   2 *adj Fam (very good)* super *inv*

acerbic [ə'sɜːbɪk] *adj* acerbe

acetate ['æsɪteɪt] *n Chem* acétate *m*

acetic acid [æ'siːtɪk'æsɪd] *n* acide *m* acétique

ache [eɪk] **1** *n* douleur *f*; **aches and pains** douleurs *fpl*
   2 *vi (of person)* avoir mal; **my head aches** j'ai mal à la tête; **my leg aches** j'ai mal à la jambe, ma jambe me fait mal; *Fig* **to be aching to do sth** mourir d'envie de faire qch

achieve [ə'tʃiːv] *vt (aim)* atteindre, parvenir à; **to a. success** réussir; **to a. a lot** faire beaucoup de chemin

achievement [ə'tʃiːvmənt] *n (action)* réalisation *f*; *(thing achieved)* réussite *f*

Achilles' heel [əkɪliː'hiːl] *n* talon *m* d'Achille

acid ['æsɪd] **1** *n* (**a**) *(chemical)* acide *m* (**b**) *Fam (LSD)* acide *m*; **a. house** *(music)* acid house *m*
   2 *adj* (**a**) *(chemical, taste)* acide; **a. rain** pluies *fpl* acides; *Fig* **a. test** test *m* décisif (**b**) *(tone, remark)* aigre

acidic [ə'sɪdɪk] *adj* acide; *(tone, remark)* aigre

acidity [ə'sɪdɪtɪ] *n (of chemical, taste)* acidité *f*; *(of tone, remark)* aigreur *f*

acknowledge [ək'nɒlɪdʒ] *vt (mistake, debt, truth)* admettre, reconnaître; **to a. (receipt of) a letter** accuser réception d'une lettre; **this restaurant is acknowledged to be the best in the city** ce restaurant est considéré comme le meilleur de la ville; **she didn't a. me** *or* **my presence** elle m'a ignoré

acknowledg(e)ment [ək'nɒlɪdʒmənt] *n (of mistake, debt, truth)* reconnaissance *f*; **in a. of** *(service, achievement)* en reconnaissance de; *(letter)* en

réponse à; **acknowledgements** (in book) remerciements mpl; **a. slip** (for letter) accusé m de réception
ACLU ['eɪsiːelju:] n (abbr **American Civil Liberties Union**) = organisme américain qui milite pour les droits civiques
acne ['ækni] n acné f
acolyte ['ækəlaɪt] n disciple mf
acorn ['eɪkɔːn] n gland m
acoustic [ə'kuːstɪk] adj acoustique; **a. guitar** guitare f acoustique
acoustics [ə'kuːstɪks] npl acoustique f
acquaint [ə'kweɪnt] vt (a) (with person) **to be acquainted with sb** connaître qn; **to become** or **get acquainted (with)** faire ou lier connaissance (avec) (b) (with facts, situation) **to be acquainted with sth** connaître qch; **to a. sb with sth** mettre qn au courant de qch; **to a. oneself with sth** se familiariser avec qch
acquaintance [ə'kweɪntəns] n (a) (person) connaissance f (b) (familiarity) (with person, facts) familiarité f; **to make sb's a.** faire la connaissance de qn
acquiesce [ækwɪ'es] vi consentir (**in/to** à)
acquiescence [ækwɪ'esəns] n consentement m (**in/to** à)
acquiescent [ækwɪ'esənt] adj consentant(e)
acquire [ə'kwaɪə(r)] vt (knowledge, reputation, property) acquérir; (habit, accent, air) prendre; **to a. a taste for sth** prendre goût à qch; **it's an acquired taste** c'est quelque chose que l'on apprend à aimer
acquisition [ækwɪ'zɪʃən] n acquisition f
acquisitive [ə'kwɪzɪtɪv] adj matérialiste
acquit [ə'kwɪt] (pt & pp **acquitted**) vt (a) Law acquitter (b) **to a. oneself well/badly** s'en sortir ou s'en tirer bien/mal
acquittal [ə'kwɪtəl] n Law acquittement m
acre ['eɪkə(r)] n = 4047 m², ≃ demi-hectare m; **acres of forest** des hectares de forêt; Fam **acres of space** plein de place
acrid ['ækrɪd] adj âcre
acrimonious [ækrɪ'məʊnɪəs] adj (person, remark) hargneux(euse); (discussion) virulent(e)
acrimony ['ækrɪmənɪ] n acrimonie f, hargne f
acrobat ['ækrəbæt] n acrobate mf
acrobatic [ækrə'bætɪk] adj acrobatique
acrobatics [ækrəʊ'bætɪks] **1** n acrobatie f
 2 npl Fig **mental a.** gymnastique f intellectuelle
acronym ['ækrənɪm] n sigle m
across [ə'krɒs] **1** prep (a) (from one side to the other of) **to go a. sth** traverser qch; **to run a. the road** traverser la route en courant; **to swim a. a river** traverser une rivière à la nage; **the bridge a. the river** le pont sur la rivière; **she threw it a. the room** elle l'a lancé à l'autre bout de la pièce
 (b) (on the other side of) de l'autre côté de; **she lives a. the road** elle habite en face; **the woman (from) a. the road** la femme d'en face
 (c) (throughout) **a. the country** dans tout le pays; **a. the political spectrum** dans l'ensemble de la classe politique
 2 adv (a) (from one side to the other) **to run/swim a.** traverser en courant/à la nage; **go a. and see her** traverse et va la voir
 (b) (with distance) **it's 10 cm/2 km a.** ça fait 10 cm/2 km de large
 (c) **a. from me/my house** en face de moi/de chez moi
 (d) (in crosswords) horizontalement

across-the-board [ə'krɒsðə'bɔːd] adj général(e), systématique
acrylic [ə'krɪlɪk] **1** n (fabric) acrylique m
 2 adj (paint, fibre) acrylique; (garment) en acrylique
act [ækt] **1** n (a) (thing done) acte m; **to be in the a. of doing sth** être en train de faire qch; **to catch sb in the a. of doing sth** surprendre qn en train de faire qch; **to catch sb in the a.** prendre qn sur le fait ou en flagrant délit; Fam **to get in on the a.** (get involved) se mettre dans le coup; **a. of war** acte m de guerre; Law **a. of God** catastrophe f naturelle
 (b) (of play) acte m; (in cabaret, circus) numéro m; Fig **to put on an a.** faire semblant; Fig **to get one's a. together** se secouer; Fig **it's all an a.** c'est du cinéma
 (c) Law **a. (of parliament)** loi f
 2 vt (a) (character) jouer (le rôle de), tenir le rôle de; (play) jouer; Fig **to a. the part** se conduire comme il convient
 (b) (behave like) **to a. the fool** or **the goat** faire l'imbécile; Fam **a. your age (not your shoe size)!** arrête de faire l'enfant!
 3 vi (a) (take action) agir; **to a. for sb** (of lawyer) représenter qn; **to a. as secretary/chairperson** remplir les fonctions de secrétaire/président; **to a. as a warning** servir d'avertissement; **to a. as an incentive** être une motivation
 (b) (behave) agir, se comporter; **to a. stupid** faire l'idiot
 (c) (of actor) jouer; **I always wanted to a.** j'ai toujours voulu être acteur
▸**act on** vt insep (advice, suggestion) suivre; **she acted on the information we gave her** elle a suivi les indications que nous lui avons données
▸**act out** vt sep (fantasy) vivre; (scene) jouer
▸**act up** vi (of car, child, injury) faire des siennes
acting ['æktɪŋ] **1** n (performance) jeu m; (profession) métier m d'acteur
 2 adj (temporary) par intérim
action ['ækʃən] n (a) (individual act) acte m, action f; Prov **actions speak louder than words** les actes en disent plus long que les paroles (b) (activity) action f; **to take a.** prendre des mesures; **to go into a.** passer à l'action; **to be out of a.** (machine, car) être en panne; (person) être hors service; Fam **where's the a. round here?** où est-ce que ça bouge par ici?; Com **a. plan** objectifs mpl (c) Mil combats mpl; **to see a.** combattre; **missing in a.** porté(e) disparu(e) (d) (of film, novel) action f; TV **a. replay** = répétition d'une séquence précédente (e) Law action f, procès m; **to bring an a. against sb** intenter un procès à qn
activate ['æktɪveɪt] vt déclencher
active ['æktɪv] adj (a) (person, mind, imagination) actif(ive); (interest, dislike) vif (vive); (volcano) en activité; **to be a. in doing sth** s'employer activement à faire qch; Mil **on a. service** en service actif (b) Gram actif(ive)
actively ['æktɪvlɪ] adv activement; **to a. dislike sb** détester cordialement qn
activist ['æktɪvɪst] n Pol militant(e) m,f
activity [æk'tɪvɪtɪ] (pl **activities**) n activité f; (in street) animation f; **a. book** livre jeu m; **a. centre** centre m aéré
actor ['æktə(r)] n acteur m
actress ['æktrɪs] n actrice f
actual ['æktʃʊəl] adj (a) (real) réel(elle); (example) concret(ète); **in a. fact** en fait (b) (specific) **I can't**

remember her a. words je ne me rappelle pas ses paroles exactes; although the garden is big, the a. house is small le jardin est grand, mais la maison elle-même est petite

actually ['æktʃʊəlɪ] adv (a) (really) réellement, vraiment; what a. happened? qu'est-ce qui s'est passé au juste?; what she a. means is... en réalité, ce qu'elle veut dire c'est... (b) (in fact) en fait; I'm not sure, a. en fait, je ne suis pas sûr

actuary ['æktʃʊərɪ] (pl actuaries) n actuaire mf

acumen ['ækjʊmən] n flair m; business a. sens m des affaires

acupuncture ['ækjʊpʌŋktʃə(r)] n acuponcture f

acute [ə'kjuːt] adj (a) (pain) aigu(ë); (remorse, embarrassment) vif (vive); (problem, shortage) grave (b) (eyesight) perçant(e) (c) (accent, angle) aigu(ë)

acutely [ə'kjuːtlɪ] adv (painful, embarrassing) extrêmement; (aware) profondément

AD [eɪ'diː] adv (abbr Anno Domini) apr. J.-C.

ad [æd] n Fam (classified) petite annonce f; (on radio, TV) pub f

Adam ['ædəm] n Fam I wouldn't know him from A. je ne le connais ni d'Éve ni d'Adam; A.'s apple pomme f d'Adam

adamant ['ædəmənt] adj formel(elle), catégorique (about sur); to be a. that... soutenir que...

adapt [ə'dæpt] 1 vt adapter; to a. oneself to sth s'adapter à qch
2 vi s'adapter

adaptable [ə'dæptəbəl] adj (instrument, tool) adaptable; (person) souple

adaptation [ædæp'teɪʃən] n (of book, play) adaptation f; (of machine, design) modification f

adapter [ə'dæptə(r)] n (for several plugs) prise f multiple; (for foreign plugs) adaptateur m

ADC [eɪdiː'siː] n Mil (abbr aide-de-camp) aide m de camp

add [æd] vt ajouter (to à); (figures) additionner; this book adds little to the debate ce livre n'apporte pas grand-chose au débat

▶**add up 1** vt sep (figures) additionner
2 vi (give correct total) être juste ou exact(e); (make sense) tenir debout

▶**add up to** vt insep (amount to) it adds up to £126 ça fait 126 livres au total ou en tout; it all adds up to an enjoyable day out tout cela fera de cette excursion un moment bien agréable; it doesn't a. up to much ça ne fait pas grand-chose au bout du compte

adder ['ædə(r)] n (snake) vipère f

addict ['ædɪkt] n (drug) a. toxicomane mf; heroin a. héroïnomane mf; to be a TV a. être accro à la télé

addicted [ə'dɪktɪd] adj to be a. to sth (drugs) être dépendant(e) de qch; (TV programme) être accro à qch

addiction [ə'dɪkʃən] n (to drugs) dépendance f (to à), accoutumance f (to à); (to chocolate, films) passion f (to pour)

addictive [ə'dɪktɪv] adj (substance) qui crée une dépendance ou accoutumance; soap operas are very a. on devient vite accro aux feuilletons

Addis Ababa ['ædɪs'æbəbə] n Addis-Abeba

addition [ə'dɪʃən] n (action) addition f; (thing added) ajout m (to à); (person) nouveau venu (nouvelle venue) m,f; she's the latest a. to the team c'est la dernière arrivée dans l'équipe; in a. (to) en plus (de)

additional [ə'dɪʃənəl] adj supplémentaire

additive ['ædɪtɪv] n additif m

addled ['ædəld] adj (egg) pourri(e); (brain) confus(e)

add-on ['ædɒn] n Comput produit m supplémentaire ou complémentaire

address [ə'dres] 1 n (a) (of person, letter) adresse f; a. book carnet m d'adresses (b) (speech) discours m, allocution f
2 vt (a) (letter, remarks, criticism) adresser (to à) (b) (speak to) (person, crowd) s'adresser à; he addressed her as "Your Majesty" il l'a appelée "Votre Majesté" (c) (question, problem) aborder; to a. oneself to sth (problem) aborder qch; (task) entreprendre qch

adenoids ['ædɪnɔɪdz] npl Anat végétations fpl

adept [ə'dept] adj habile (at à); to be a. at doing sth être habile à faire qch

adequate ['ædɪkwət] adj (enough) suffisant(e); (satisfactory) satisfaisant(e), adéquat(e); you were given a. warning on vous a prévenu suffisamment à l'avance

adequately ['ædɪkwɪtlɪ] adv (sufficiently) suffisamment; (suitably) convenablement

adhere [əd'hɪə(r)] vi (stick) adhérer (to à); to a. to (rule) observer; (belief) adhérer à; (plan) se conformer à

adherence [əd'hɪərəns] n (to rule) observation f (to de); (to belief, plan) adhésion f (to à)

adherent [əd'hɪərənt] n adhérent(e) m,f

adhesion [əd'hiːʒən] n (a) (stickiness) adhérence f (b) (to belief, plan) adhésion f (to à)

adhesive [əd'hiːsɪv] 1 n adhésif m, colle f
2 adj adhésif(ive), collant(e); a. tape ruban m adhésif

ad hoc ['æd'hɒk] adj (measure) ad hoc inv; (arrangement) temporaire; a. committee comité m spécial ou ad hoc; on an a. basis au coup par coup

ad infinitum ['ædɪnfɪ'naɪtəm] adv à l'infini; and so on a. et ainsi de suite à n'en plus finir

adjacent [ə'dʒeɪsənt] adj adjacent(e); (street) voisin(e); (room) contigu(ë)

adjective ['ædʒɪktɪv] n adjectif m

adjoin [ə'dʒɔɪn] vt être contigu(ë) ou attenant(e) à

adjoining [ə'dʒɔɪnɪŋ] adj attenant(e)

adjourn [ə'dʒɜːn] 1 vt (meeting, trial) ajourner, remettre à plus tard
2 vi (of meeting, trial) être ajourné(e); to a. to another room passer dans une autre pièce

adjournment [ə'dʒɜːnmənt] n ajournement m

adjudge [ə'dʒʌdʒ] vt to a. sb guilty/the winner déclarer qn coupable/vainqueur

adjudicate [ə'dʒuːdɪkeɪt] vt juger

adjudication [ədʒuːdɪ'keɪʃən] n jugement m, décision f

adjudicator [ə'dʒuːdɪkeɪtə(r)] n (in dispute) arbitre m; (in competition) juge m

adjunct ['ædʒʌŋkt] n (thing) accessoire m

adjust [ə'dʒʌst] 1 vt (machine, mechanism) régler, ajuster; (pay, figures) ajuster; (clothes) rajuster; to a. oneself to sth s'adapter à qch
2 vi (of person) s'adapter (to à)

adjustable [ə'dʒʌstəbəl] adj ajustable, réglable; a. spanner clé f à molette

adjustment [ə'dʒʌstmənt] n (of machine, mechanism) réglage m; (to pay, figures) réajustement m; to make an a. to sth régler qch; a period of a. une période d'adaptation

ad-lib ['æd'lɪb] **1** *adv* en improvisant, de manière improvisée

2 *vi* (*pt & pp* **ad-libbed**) improviser

ad-man ['ædmæn] *n Fam* publicitaire *m*

admin ['ædmɪn] *n Fam* (*work*) travail *m* administratif; (*department*) administration *f*

administer [əd'mɪnɪstə(r)] *vt* (**a**) (*estate, funds*) administrer, gérer; (*territory*) administrer (**b**) (*give*) (*punishment, medication*) administrer; (*blow*) donner

administration [ədmɪnɪ'streɪʃən] *n* (**a**) (*work*) administration *f* (**b**) (*government*) gouvernement *m*

administrative [əd'mɪnɪstrətɪv] *adj* administratif(ive)

administrator [əd'mɪnɪstreɪtə(r)] *n* administrateur (trice) *m,f*

admirable ['ædmərəbəl] *adj* admirable

admiral ['ædmərəl] *n* amiral *m*

Admiralty ['ædmərəltɪ] *n* **the A.** ≃ le ministère de la Marine

admiration [ædmə'reɪʃən] *n* admiration *f* (**for** pour)

admire [əd'maɪə(r)] *vt* admirer

admirer [əd'maɪərə(r)] *n* admirateur(trice) *m,f*

admiring [əd'maɪərɪŋ] *adj* (*look, glance*) admiratif(ive)

admissible [əd'mɪsɪbəl] *adj* (*behaviour, error*) admissible, acceptable; *Law* recevable

admission [əd'mɪʃən] *n* (**a**) (*entry*) (*to school, hospital*) admission *f*; (*to museum, exhibition*) entrée *f*; (*price*) (prix *m* d')entrée *f*; **no a.** (*sign*) entrée interdite (**b**) (*acknowledgement*) (*of guilt*) aveu *m*; (*of crime*) confession *f*; **by his own a.** de son propre aveu

admit [əd'mɪt] (*pt & pp* **admitted**) **1** *vt* (**a**) (*allow to enter*) laisser entrer; (*to hospital, college*) admettre; **to be admitted to hospital** être admis(e) à l'hôpital; **children not admitted** (*sign*) les enfants ne sont pas admis; **a. one** (*on ticket*) entrée valable pour une personne (**b**) (*acknowledge*) (*fact, mistake, guilt*) admettre, reconnaître; (*crime*) avouer; **I must a. you're right** je dois reconnaître que vous avez raison; **to a. defeat** s'avouer vaincu(e)

2 *vi* **to a. to** (*mistake*) reconnaître; **I a. to being in a bad mood yesterday** je dois admettre que j'étais de mauvaise humeur hier

admittance [əd'mɪtəns] *n* (*entry*) accès *m*; **to gain a.** parvenir à entrer; **to refuse sb a.** refuser de laisser entrer qn; **no a.** (*sign*) entrée interdite

admittedly [əd'mɪtɪdlɪ] *adv* de l'aveu général; **a., it was dark when I saw him** je dois convenir qu'il faisait sombre quand je l'ai vu

admonish [əd'mɒnɪʃ] *vt* (*reprimand*) admonester, faire des remontrances à (**for** pour)

ad nauseam [æd'nɔːsɪæm] *adv* à n'en plus finir

ado [ə'duː] *n* **without more** *or* **further a.** sans plus de cérémonie *ou* de manières; **much a. about nothing** beaucoup de bruit pour rien

adobe [ə'dəʊbɪ] *n* (*clay*) adobe *m*

adolescence [ædə'lesəns] *n* adolescence *f*

adolescent [ædə'lesənt] *n* adolescent(e) *m,f*

adopt [ə'dɒpt] *vt* (*child, custom, approach, measures*) adopter; (*career, candidate*) choisir; (*tone, attitude*) prendre

adopted [ə'dɒptɪd] *adj* (*child*) adopté(e); (*son, daughter*) adoptif(ive); **my a. country** mon pays d'adoption

adoption [ə'dɒpʃən] *n* adoption *f*

adorable [ə'dɔːrəbəl] *adj* adorable

adoration [ædə'reɪʃən] *n* adoration *f*

adore [ə'dɔː(r)] *vt* adorer

adorn [ə'dɔːn] *vt* orner, parer (**with** de)

adornment [ə'dɔːnmənt] *n* (*decorations*) ornements *mpl*, parure *f*

ADP [eɪdiː'piː] *n Comput* (*abbr* **automatic data processing**) traitement *m* automatique des données

adrenalin(e) [ə'drenəlɪn] *n* adrénaline *f*

Adriatic [eɪdrɪ'ætɪk] *n* **the A. (Sea)** la mer Adriatique, l'Adriatique *f*

adrift [ə'drɪft] *adv & adj* **to be a.** (*of boat*) aller à la dérive; **to go a.** (*of plan*) tomber à l'eau; **to come a.** (*come apart*) se défaire

adroit [ə'drɔɪt] *adj* habile (**at doing sth** à faire qch)

adulation [ædjʊ'leɪʃən] *n* adulation *f*

adult ['ædʌlt, ə'dʌlt] **1** *n* adulte *mf*

2 *adj* adulte; (*film*) pour adultes; **a. education** enseignement *m* pour adultes

adulterate [ə'dʌltəreɪt] *vt* (*food*) empoisonner; (*wine*) frelater; (*language*) corrompre

adulteration [ədʌltə'reɪʃən] *n* (*of food*) empoisonnement *m*; (*of wine*) frelatage *m*

adulterer [ə'dʌltərə(r)] *n* adultère *mf*

adulterous [ə'dʌltərəs] *adj* adultère

adultery [ə'dʌltərɪ] *n* adultère *m*; **to commit a.** commettre l'adultère

adulthood ['ædʌlthʊd] *n* âge *m* adulte

advance [əd'vɑːns] **1** *n* (**a**) (*forward movement*) avance *f*; (*progress*) progrès *m*; **to make advances to sb** faire des avances à qn; **in a.** (*book, apply, inform*) à l'avance; (*pay*) d'avance; **six weeks in a.** six semaines à l'avance; **a. booking** réservation *f* à l'avance; **a. notice** *or* **warning** préavis *m* (**b**) (*loan*) avance *f*

2 *vt* (**a**) (*move forward*) faire avancer; (*chess piece*) avancer; (*science, knowledge*) faire progresser, faire avancer (**b**) (*idea, opinion*) avancer, mettre en avant (**c**) (*loan*) avancer

3 *vi* (*move forward*) s'avancer (**towards** vers); (*make progress*) avancer

advanced [əd'vɑːnst] *adj* avancé(e); **she's very a. for her age** elle est très en avance pour son âge

advantage [əd'vɑːntɪdʒ] *n* avantage *m* (**over** sur); **to take a. of** profiter de; **to turn a situation to one's a.** tourner une situation à son avantage; **it would be to your a. to...** il serait dans votre intérêt de...; **a. Sampras** (*in tennis*) avantage Sampras

advantageous [ædvən'teɪdʒəs] *adj* avantageux(euse) (**to** pour)

advent ['ædvənt] *n* (*arrival*) arrivée *f*; *Rel* **A.** l'Avent *m*

adventure [əd'ventʃə(r)] *n* aventure *f*; **a. playground** terrain *m* de jeux (*spécialement aménagé*); **a. story** récit *m* d'aventures; (*novel*) roman *m* d'aventure(s)

adventurer [əd'ventʃərə(r)] *n* aventurier(ère) *m,f*

adventurous [əd'ventʃərəs] *adj* (*person*) aventureux(euse); (*plan*) audacieux(euse)

adverb ['ædvɜːb] *n* adverbe *m*

adversary ['ædvəsərɪ] (*pl* **adversaries**) *n* adversaire *mf*

adverse ['ædvɜːs] *adj* défavorable

adversely ['ædvɜːslɪ] *adv* **to influence sb a.** exercer une influence défavorable sur qn; **a. affected** affecté(e)

adversity [əd'vɜːsɪtɪ] *n* adversité *f*; **in a.** dans l'adversité

advert ['ædvɜːt] *n* (*for product*) pub *f*; (*for job, event*) annonce *f*

advertise ['ædvətaɪz] **1** vt (**a**) (product, service) faire de la réclame ou de la publicité pour; (job) mettre une annonce pour; **advertised on TV** vu(e) à la télé (**b**) (call attention to) **he didn't want to a. his presence** il ne voulait pas se faire remarquer **2** vi (for job) mettre une annonce; (to sell product) faire de la publicité ou de la réclame; **to a. for sb** passer une annonce pour trouver qn

advertisement [əd'vɜːtɪsmənt] n (for product, service) publicité f, réclame f; (for job, event) annonce f; Fig **you're not a good a. for your school** vous ne faites pas honneur à votre école

advertiser ['ædvətaɪzə(r)] n annonceur(euse) m,f

advertising ['ædvətaɪzɪŋ] n publicité f; **a. agency** agence f de publicité; **a. campaign** campagne f de publicité

advice [əd'vaɪs] n conseil(s) m(pl) (**on** sur); **a piece of a.** un conseil; **that's good a.** c'est un bon conseil; **to give sb a.** donner des conseils à qn; **to ask sb's a.** demander conseil à qn; **to take sb's a.** suivre le conseil ou les conseils de qn

advisable [əd'vaɪzəbəl] adj recommandé(e)

advise [əd'vaɪz] vt (**a**) (give advice to) conseiller; **to a. sb to do sth** conseiller à qn de faire qch; **to a. sb against doing sth** déconseiller à qn de faire qch; **I wouldn't a. it** je ne le conseillerais ou recommanderais pas (**b**) (inform) **to a. sb that...** aviser qn que...

adviser, advisor [əd'vaɪzə(r)] n conseiller(ère) m,f

advisory [əd'vaɪzərɪ] adj consultatif(ive); **in an a. capacity** en tant que conseiller

advocate 1 n ['ædvəkət] (**a**) Scot Law avocat(e) m,f; **the Lord A.** ≃ le procureur général (**b**) (of cause, doctrine) partisan(e) m,f **2** vt ['ædvəkeɪt] (policy, plan) préconiser, conseiller

AEA [eiː'eɪ] n Br (abbr **Atomic Energy Authority**) ≃ Commissariat m à l'énergie atomique

AEC [eiː'siː] n Am (abbr **Atomic Energy Commission**) ≃ Commissariat m à l'énergie atomique

Aegean [ɪ'dʒiːən] n **the A. (Sea)** la mer Égée

aegis ['iːdʒɪs] n Formal **under the a. of...** sous l'égide de...

aeon, Am **eon** ['iːən] n Fig éternité f; **aeons ago** il y a une éternité

aerate ['eəreɪt] vt (water) gazéifier

aerial ['eərɪəl] **1** n (of radio, TV) antenne f **2** adj aérien(enne)

aerobics [eə'rəʊbɪks] n aérobic m

aerodrome ['eərədrəʊm] n aérodrome m

aerodynamic [eərəʊdaɪ'næmɪk] adj aérodynamique

aerogram(me) ['eərəgræm] n aérogramme m

aeronautic(al) [eərə'nɔːtɪk(əl)] adj aéronautique

aeroplane ['eərəpleɪn] n avion m

aerosol ['eərəsɒl] n aérosol m; **a. spray** atomiseur m

aesthetic, Am **esthetic** [ɪs'θetɪk] adj esthétique

aesthetics, Am **esthetics** [ɪs'θetɪks] npl esthétique f

afar [ə'faː(r)] adv Lit **from a.** de loin

affable ['æfəbəl] adj affable, courtois(e)

affair [ə'feə(r)] n (**a**) (matter, concern) affaire f; **that's my a.!** c'est mes affaires!; **to put one's affairs in order** mettre de l'ordre dans ses affaires; **current affairs** les questions fpl d'actualité; **foreign affairs** les affaires étrangères; **affairs of state** les affaires de l'État; **in the present state of affairs** dans l'état actuel des choses (**b**) (sexual) liaison f; **to have an a. with sb** avoir une liaison avec qn (**c**) (event) affaire f; **the wedding was a quiet a.** le mariage fut célébré dans l'intimité; **what kind of a. was it?** c'était comment?

affect¹ [ə'fekt] vt (**a**) (have effect on) (person, organ, health) affecter; (decision) influencer; (of issue, law) concerner (**b**) (move emotionally) affecter, toucher; **to be deeply affected by sth** être très affecté(e) par qch

affect² vt (indifference, interest) affecter, feindre; **to a. an accent** prendre un accent

affectation [æfek'teɪʃən] n affectation f

affected [ə'fektɪd] adj (unnatural) affecté(e), maniéré(e)

affection [ə'fekʃən] n affection f

affectionate [ə'fekʃənət] adj affectueux(euse) (**towards** avec ou envers)

affidavit [æfɪ'deɪvɪt] n Law déclaration f par écrit et sous serment

affiliate 1 n [ə'fɪlɪət] (person) affilié(e) m,f **2** vt [ə'fɪlɪeɪt] affilier (**to** or **with** à); **affiliated company** filiale f

affiliation [əfɪlɪ'eɪʃən] n affiliation f

affinity [ə'fɪnɪtɪ] (pl **affinities**) n (**a**) (liking, attraction) affinité f (**for** or **with/between** avec/entre); **to have an a. with sb/sth** avoir des affinités avec qn/qch (**b**) (relationship, connection) lien m (**between/with** entre/avec)

affirm [ə'fɜːm] vt (**a**) (state) affirmer (**b**) (confirm) confirmer

affirmation [æfə'meɪʃən] n (**a**) (statement) affirmation f, assertion f (**b**) (confirmation) confirmation f

affirmative [ə'fɜːmətɪv] **1** n **to answer in the a.** répondre affirmativement ou par l'affirmative **2** adj affirmatif(ive); Am **a. action** mesures fpl d'embauche antidiscriminatoires (en faveur des minorités)

affix 1 n ['æfɪks] Ling affixe m **2** vt [ə'fɪks] attacher (**to** à); (notice, poster) fixer (**to** à)

afflict [ə'flɪkt] vt affliger; **afflicted with rheumatism** affligé(e) de rhumatismes

affliction [ə'flɪkʃən] n (illness) affection f; (misfortune) malheur m

affluent ['æflʊənt] adj riche; **the a. society** la société d'abondance

afford [ə'fɔːd] vt (**a**) (financially) **to be able to a. sth** avoir les moyens d'acheter qch; **I can't a. it** mes moyens ne me le permettent pas; **we can't a. a new car** nous ne pouvons pas nous offrir une nouvelle voiture; **she can a. to eat out twice a week** elle peut se permettre d'aller au restaurant deux fois par semaine (**b**) (non-financial use) **I can't a. to wait** je ne peux pas attendre; **can you a. the time?** est-ce que vous avez le temps?; **I can't a. not to** je n'ai pas le choix; **we can't a. another mistake** nous ne pouvons pas nous permettre une nouvelle erreur (**c**) Formal (give) offrir, procurer

affordable [ə'fɔːdəbəl] adj (price, purchase) abordable; (house) (d'un prix) abordable

affray [ə'freɪ] n Law & Formal rixe f

affront [ə'frʌnt] **1** n affront m, offense f **2** vt offenser, faire (un) affront à; **to be/feel affronted** être/se sentir offensé(e)

Afghan ['æfgæn] **1** n (**a**) (person) Afghan(e) m,f (**b**) (dog) lévrier m afghan
2 adj afghan(e); **A. hound** lévrier m afghan
Afghanistan [æf'gænɪstɑːn] n l'Afghanistan m
afield [ə'fiːld] adv further a. plus loin
AFL/CIO [eɪef'elsiːaɪ'əʊ] n (abbr**American Federa-tion of Labor and Congress of Industrial Organizations**) = confédération syndicale américaine
afloat [ə'fləʊt] adv & adj à flot; **to stay a.** (of boat, company) se maintenir à flot
afoot [ə'fʊt] adv **there's something a.** il se prépare ou se trame quelque chose
aforementioned [ə'fɔːmenʃənd] adj susmention-né(e)
afraid [ə'freɪd] adj (**a**) (scared) **to be a. (of)** avoir peur (de); **that's (exactly) what I was a. of!** c'est bien ce que je craignais!; **I was a. there would be an accident** je craignais un accident (**b**) (sorry) **I'm a. so/not** je crains que oui/que non; **I'm a. she's out** je regrette, mais elle est sortie; **I'm a. I can't help you** j'ai bien peur de ne pouvoir vous aider
afresh [ə'freʃ] adv de nouveau, à nouveau; **to start a.** recommencer
Africa ['æfrɪkə] n l'Afrique f
African ['æfrɪkən] **1** n Africain(e) m,f; **A. American** Noir(e) m,f américain(e)
2 adj africain(e)
Afrikaans [æfrɪ'kɑːnz] n afrikaans m
aft [ɑːft] adv Naut à l'arrière
after ['ɑːftə(r)] **1** prep (**a**) (with time) après; **a. dinner** après dîner; **a. three days** au bout de trois jours; **the day a. the battle** le lendemain de la bataille; **it's a. five** il est cinq heures passées; Am **it's twenty a. six** il est six heures vingt; **a. all** (all things considered) après tout; (despite everything) finalement
(**b**) (with motion) après; **to run a. sb** courir après qn; **close the door a. you** fermez la porte derrière vous; **a. you!** après vous!
(**c**) (in search of) **to be a. sb/sth** chercher qn/qch
(**d**) (expressing sequence) après; **a. her, he is the best** après elle, c'est lui le meilleur
(**e**) (expressing repetition) après; **day a. day** jour après jour; **year a. year** d'une année sur l'autre, tous les ans; **time a. time** cent fois; **it's one thing a. another** j'ai/nous avons/etc des problèmes à n'en plus finir
(**f**) (in honour of) **to name sb/sth a. sb** donner le nom de qn à qn/qch
2 adv après; **soon/long a.** peu/longtemps après; **the week a.** la semaine d'après; **the day a.** le lendemain
3 conj (when subject changes) après que + indicative or Fam subjunctive; (when subject stays the same) après + infinitive; **I came a. he left** je suis arrivé après qu'il est ou Fam soit parti; **a. I saw him I went out** je suis sorti après l'avoir vu; **a. doing sth** après avoir fait qch
afterbirth ['ɑːftəbɜːθ] n placenta m
aftercare ['ɑːftəkeə(r)] n (after operation) soins mpl postopératoires; (of convalescent, delinquent) surveillance f
after-effect ['ɑːftərəfekt] n (of drug) effet m secondaire; Fig (of event) répercussion f, contrecoup m
afterlife ['ɑːftəlaɪf] n vie f après la mort
aftermath ['ɑːftəmæθ] n suites fpl, conséquences fpl

afternoon [ɑːftə'nuːn] n après-midi m inv or f inv; **in the a.** (pendant) l'après-midi; **at two o'clock in the a.** à deux heures de l'après-midi; **good a.!** bonjour!
aftersales service ['ɑːftə'seɪlz'sɜːvɪs] n Com service m après-vente
aftershave ['ɑːftəʃeɪv] n **a. (lotion)** (lotion f) après-rasage m
aftersun ['ɑːftəsʌn] n (cream) crème f après-soleil; (lotion) lotion f après-soleil
aftertaste ['ɑːftəteɪst] n also Fig arrière-goût m
afterthought ['ɑːftəθɔːt] n réflexion f après coup; **as an a.** après coup
afterwards ['ɑːftəwədz] adv après; **I regretted it a.** par la suite, je l'ai regretté
Aga® ['ɑːgə] n = cuisinière en fonte à l'ancienne
again [ə'gen] adv (**a**) (in general) de nouveau, encore; **to begin a.** recommencer; **he never came back a.** il n'est plus jamais revenu; **don't do it a.!** ne recommence pas!; **not you a.!** encore toi!; **once a.** encore une fois, une fois de plus; **a. and a.** à maintes reprises; **now and a.** de temps en temps, de temps à autre; **half as much a.** moitié plus; **I'd like half as much a.** je voudrais encore la moitié de ça; **what did you say a.?** qu'avez-vous dit déjà? (**b**) (besides) en outre; (then) **a.** (on the other hand) d'un autre côté; **a., I may have imagined it** cela dit, il se peut aussi que je l'aie imaginé
against [ə'genst] prep (**a**) (in opposition to) contre; **to be a. sb/sth** être contre qn/qch, être opposé(e) à qn/qch; **to have something/nothing a. sb/sth** avoir quelque chose/ne rien avoir contre qn/qch; **a. the law** contraire à la loi, illégal(e)
(**b**) (as protection from) contre; **to warn sb a. sth** mettre qn en garde contre qn/qch
(**c**) (in contact with) contre; **to lean a. sth** s'appuyer contre qch
(**d**) (in comparison with) contre; **three deaths this year (as) a. thirty in 1990** trois morts cette année contre trente en 1990; **the pound rose/fell a. the dollar** la livre a augmenté/chuté par rapport au dollar
age [eɪdʒ] **1** n (**a**) (of person) âge m; **to be twenty years of a.** avoir vingt ans, être âgé(e) de vingt ans; **what a. is she?, what's her a.?** quel âge a-t-elle?; **he doesn't look his a.** il ne fait pas son âge; **people of all ages** des gens de tout âge; **a. group** tranche f d'âge; **a. of consent** = âge légal où on peut avoir des rapports sexuels; **a. limit** limite f d'âge
(**b**) (old) **a.** vieillesse f
(**c**) (adulthood) **to come of a.** atteindre sa majorité; **to be under a.** Law être mineur(e); (not old enough to buy alcohol etc) ne pas avoir l'âge
(**d**) (era) âge m, époque f
(**e**) Fam (long time) **it's ages since I saw him** il y a une éternité que je ne l'ai pas vu; **I've been waiting (for) ages** ça fait une éternité que j'attends
2 vt & vi (continuous **aging** or **ageing**) vieillir
aged adj (**a**) [eɪdʒd] (of the age of) **a. twenty** âgé(e) de vingt ans (**b**) ['eɪdʒɪd] (old) âgé(e), vieux (vieille)
ageing ['eɪdʒɪŋ] **1** n (of person, wine) vieillissement m; **a. process** processus m de vieillissement
2 adj (becoming older) vieillissant(e); (old) vieux (vieille)
ageism ['eɪdʒɪzəm] n âgisme m
agency ['eɪdʒənsɪ] (pl **agencies**) n (**a**) Com agence f; **advertising/travel a.** agence de publicité/de

voyages (**b**) **through the a. of** par l'entremise *ou* l'intermédiaire de

agenda [ə'dʒendə] *n* (*of meeting*) ordre *m* du jour; *Fig* programme *m*; **what's on today's a.?** (*for meeting*) quel est l'ordre du jour?; (*for activities*) qu'est-ce qu'il y a au programme pour aujourd'hui?; *Fig* **to set the a.** mener le jeu

agent ['eɪdʒənt] *n* (**a**) (*representative, spy*) agent *m* (**b**) (*instrument*) agent *m*; **to be the a. of sth** être l'instrument de qch

age-old ['eɪdʒəʊld] *adj* séculaire

aggravate ['æɡrəveɪt] *vt* (**a**) (*worsen*) aggraver (**b**) *Fam* (*annoy*) agacer, exaspérer

aggravating ['æɡrəveɪtɪŋ] *adj* (**a**) *Law* aggravant(e) (**b**) *Fam* (*annoying*) agaçant(e), exaspérant(e)

aggravation [æɡrə'veɪʃən] *n* (**a**) (*worsening*) aggravation *f* (**b**) *Fam* (*annoyance*) embêtements *mpl*

aggregate ['æɡrɪɡət] **1** *n* total *m*, ensemble *m*; **on a.** au total
2 *adj* collectif(ive); **a. scores** résultats *mpl* globaux

aggression [ə'ɡreʃən] *n* agressivité *f*; **an act of a.** une agression

aggressive [ə'ɡresɪv] *adj* agressif(ive)

aggressively [ə'ɡresɪvlɪ] *adv* (*violently*) d'une manière agressive; (*speak*) d'un ton agressif; (*vigorously*) énergiquement, avec dynamisme

aggressor [ə'ɡresə(r)] *n* agresseur *m*

aggrieved [ə'ɡriːvd] *adj* (*expression, tone*) vexé(e); **to be** *or* **feel a.** se sentir lésé(e)

aggro ['æɡrəʊ] *n Br Fam* (*violence*) grabuge *m*, bagarre(s) *f(pl)*; (*trouble*) enquiquinement *m*

aghast [ə'ɡɑːst] *adj* horrifié(e) (**at** par)

agile ['ædʒaɪl] *adj* agile

agility [ə'dʒɪlɪtɪ] *n* agilité *f*

agitate ['ædʒɪteɪt] **1** *vt* (*liquid, person*) agiter
2 *vi* **to a. for/against sth** mener une campagne en faveur de/contre qch

agitated ['ædʒɪteɪtɪd] *adj* (*person*) agité(e)

agitation [ædʒɪ'teɪʃən] *n* agitation *f*

agitator ['ædʒɪteɪtə(r)] *n Pol* agitateur(trice) *m,f*

aglow [ə'ɡləʊ] *adj* (*sky*) embrasé(e); **to be a. with** (*of person*) rayonner de

AGM [eɪdʒiː'em] *n Com* (*abbr* **annual general meeting**) AGA *f*

agnostic [æɡ'nɒstɪk] *n & adj* agnostique *mf*

ago [ə'ɡəʊ] *adv* **ten years a.** il y a dix ans; **long a.** il y a longtemps; **not long a.** il n'y a pas longtemps; **as long a. as 1840** déjà en 1840, dès 1840; **a short time a., a little while a.** il y a peu de temps, tout à l'heure; **how long a. was that?** c'était il y a combien de temps?

agog [ə'ɡɒɡ] *adj* en émoi; **he was a. to hear the latest news** il brûlait d'apprendre les dernières nouvelles

agonize ['æɡənaɪz] *vi* se ronger les sangs, se tourmenter (**over** à propos de)

agonizing ['æɡənaɪzɪŋ] *adj* (*pain, death*) atroce; (*silence, wait*) angoissant(e); (*decision, dilemma*) pénible, déchirant(e)

agony ['æɡənɪ] (*pl* **agonies**) *n* (*physical pain*) douleur *f* atroce; (*mental pain*) angoisse *f*; **to be in a.** être au supplice *ou* au martyre; **it's a. walking in these shoes!** c'est un véritable supplice de marcher avec ces chaussures!; **a. aunt** (*in newspaper*) = responsable de la rubrique courrier du cœur; **a. column** (*in newspaper*) courrier *m* du cœur

agoraphobia [æɡərə'fəʊbɪə] *n* agoraphobie *f*

agrarian [ə'ɡreərɪən] *adj* agraire

agree [ə'ɡriː] **1** *vt* (**a**) (*reach agreement on*) (*price, time, conditions*) se mettre d'accord sur; **to a. to do sth** convenir de faire qch; (**are we**) **agreed?** (nous sommes) d'accord?
(**b**) (*concur*) **to a. (that)...** s'accorder à dire que...; **I a. that's expensive, but...** c'est cher, j'en conviens, mais...; **everyone agrees (that) he's the best** tout le monde s'accorde à dire qu'il est le meilleur
(**c**) (*consent*) **to a. to do sth** accepter de faire qch, consentir à faire qch; **we'll have to a. to differ on that** je crois qu'ici il va nous falloir accepter nos différences d'opinion; **it is generally agreed that...** il est généralement admis que...
2 *vi* (**a**) (*be of same opinion, concur*) être d'accord (**about/with** sur/avec); (*after discussion*) se mettre d'accord; **I quite** *or* **entirely a.** je suis entièrement d'accord; **I'm afraid I can't a.** j'ai bien peur de ne pas être du même avis; **I couldn't a. more!** ça c'est bien dit!; **I don't a. with all this violence on television** je n'approuve pas toute cette violence à la télévision
(**b**) (*match*) (*of statements, facts, opinions*) concorder, coïncider (**with** avec); *Gram* s'accorder (**with** avec)
(**c**) (*accept*) consentir (**to** à); **to a. to a condition/proposal** accepter une condition/une proposition

▸**agree on** *vt insep* être d'accord sur; (*after discussion*) se mettre d'accord sur

▸**agree with** *vt insep* (*of food*) réussir à

agreeable [ə'ɡriːəbəl] *adj* (**a**) (*pleasant*) agréable; (*person*) aimable (**b**) (*acceptable*) **if that is a. to you** si cela vous convient

agreed [ə'ɡriːd] *adj* (*price, time*) convenu(e)

agreement [ə'ɡriːmənt] *n* (**a**) (*contract, assent*) & *Gram* accord *m* (**on** *or* **about** sur); **to come to an a.** tomber *ou* se mettre d'accord; **by mutual a.** d'un commun accord; **the proposal met with unanimous a.** la proposition a été reçue à l'unanimité; **to be in a. with sb** être d'accord avec qn; **to be in a. with a decision** approuver une décision (**b**) (*of facts, account*) **to be in a. with** concorder avec

agricultural [æɡrɪ'kʌltʃərəl] *adj* agricole; **a. college** = école supérieure d'agriculture et d'agronomie; **a. labourer** ouvrier *m* agricole

agriculture ['æɡrɪkʌltʃə(r)] *n* agriculture *f*

agronomy [ə'ɡrɒnəmɪ] *n* agronomie *f*

aground [ə'ɡraʊnd] *adv* **to run a.** (*of ship*) s'échouer; (*of project, government*) échouer

ahead [ə'hed] *adv* (**a**) (*in space*) devant; **to go on a.** partir devant; **the road a. was clear** devant nous/moi/*etc* la route était libre; **a. of** devant (**b**) (*winning*) **to be a.** être en tête; **to get a.** (*in career*) avancer; **to get a. of sb** dépasser qn (**c**) (*in time*) **to plan a.** faire des projets; **in the years a.** dans les années à venir; **a. of** (*prior to*) avant; **a. of schedule** (*flight, train*) en avance sur l'horaire; (*project*) en avance sur les prévisions; **to be a. of one's time** être en avance sur son temps

ahoy [ə'hɔɪ] *exclam* **a. there!** oh(é)!; **ship a.!** ohé du bateau!

AI [eɪ'aɪ] *n* (**a**) *Comput* (*abbr* **artificial intelligence**) IA *f* (**b**) *Biol* (*abbr* **artificial insemination**) insémination *f* artificielle (**c**) *Pol* (*abbr* **Amnesty International**) Amnesty International *f*

aid [eɪd] **1** *n* (**a**) (*help, for disaster relief*) aide *f*, secours *m*; **with the a. of sb** avec l'aide de qn; **with the a. of**

sth à l'aide de qch; **to go to sb's a.** aller *ou* se porter au secours de qn; **in a. of** *(fund-raising event)* au profit de; *Fam* **what's (all) this in a. of?** c'est en quel honneur?; **a. worker** *(voluntary)* volontaire *mf*; *(paid)* employé(e) *m,f* d'une organisation humanitaire (**b**) *(device)* outil *m*; **teaching aids** matériel *m* pédagogique, supports *mpl* pédagogiques

2 *vt* aider; *Law* **to a. and abet sb** être le complice de qn

aide [eɪd] *n* assistant(e) *m,f*, conseiller(ère) *m,f*

aide-de-camp [ˈeɪdˈdəkɒŋ] *(pl* **aides-de-camp***) n Mil* aide *m* de camp

aiding [ˈeɪdɪŋ] *n Law* **a. and abetting** complicité *f*

AIDS [eɪdz] *n* sida *m*; **A. clinic** = clinique spécialisée dans le traitement du sida; **A. sufferer** sidéen(enne) *m,f*, malade *mf* du sida; **A. virus** virus *m* du sida

ailing [ˈeɪlɪŋ] *adj (person)* souffrant(e); *(company, economy)* qui bat de l'aile

ailment [ˈeɪlmənt] *n* mal *m*

aim [eɪm] **1** *n* (**a**) *(at target)* **to take a. (at)** viser; **her a. was good** elle visait bien (**b**) *(goal)* but *m*, dessein *m*; **with the a. of doing sth** dans le but *ou* dessein de faire qch

2 *vt (stone)* lancer (**at** à); *(camera)* braquer (**at** sur); **to a. a gun at sb/sth** mettre qn/qch en joue; **to a. a blow at sb** chercher à frapper qn; **to be aimed at sb** *(of remarks, TV programme)* être destiné(e) à qn

3 *vi* **to a. at** *(with gun)* viser; **to a. to do sth** *(intend)* avoir l'intention de faire qch

aimless [ˈeɪmlɪs] *adj (existence, remark)* sans but

ain't [eɪnt] *very Fam* (**a**) = **is not, am not, are not** (**b**) = **has not, have not**

air [eər] **1** *n* (**a**) *(in general)* air *m*; **by a.** par avion; **to be on the a.** *(of person)* être à l'antenne; *(of programme)* être diffusé(e); **to throw sth (up) in the a.** lancer qch en l'air; **our plans are up in the a.** *(undecided)* nos projets n'ont toujours pas de forme précise; **to be in the a.** *(of rumour)* circuler; *(of feeling, idea)* être dans l'air; **a. bag** Air Bag® *m*; **a. bed** matelas *m* pneumatique; **a. filter** filtre *m* à air; **the A. Force** l'Armée *f* de l'air; **a. freight** fret *m* aérien; **a. freshener** désodorisant *m*; **a. hostess** hôtesse *f* de l'air; **a. rage** = comportement agressif de certains passagers d'avion; **a. raid** raid *m* aérien; **a. rifle** fusil *m* à air comprimé; **a. show** salon *m* de l'aéronautique; **a. steward** steward *m*; **a. stewardess** hôtesse *f* de l'air; **a. terminal** aérogare *f*; **a. traffic control** contrôle *m* aérien; **a. traffic controller** contrôleur *m* aérien, aiguilleur *m* du ciel (**b**) *(melody)* air *m* (**c**) *(look)* air *m*, apparence *f*; **he has a certain a. about him** c'est quelqu'un qui en impose; **to give oneself** *or* **to put on airs** se donner des airs

2 *vt* (**a**) *(room, clothing, bedding)* aérer (**b**) *(opinions, grievances)* exposer

airborne [ˈeəbɔːn] *adj (seeds, particles)* en suspension dans l'air; *(troops)* aéroporté(e); **once we are a.** une fois que nous aurons décollé

air-conditioned [ˈeəkənˈdɪʃənd] *adj* climatisé(e), à air conditionné

air-conditioning [ˈeəkənˈdɪʃənɪŋ] *n* climatisation *f*

air-cooled [ˈeəkuːld] *adj* refroidi(e) par air

aircraft [ˈeəkrɑːft] *(pl* **aircraft***) n* avion *m*; **a. carrier** porte-avions *m inv*

air-crew [ˈeəkruː] *n Aviat* équipage *m*

airfield [ˈeəfiːld] *n* champ *m ou* terrain *m* d'aviation

airing [ˈeərɪŋ] *n* **to give sth an a.** *(room, clothes, bedding)* aérer qch; *(opinions, grievances)* exposer; **a. cupboard** = placard où se trouve le chauffe-eau

airless [ˈeəlɪs] *adj (room)* qui sent le renfermé; *(evening, atmosphere)* lourd(e)

airlift [ˈeəlɪft] **1** *n* pont *m* aérien

2 *vt (supplies, troops)* transporter par avion; *(refugees)* évacuer par avion

airline [ˈeəlaɪn] *n* ligne *f ou* compagnie *f* aérienne; **a. pilot** pilote *m* de ligne

airlock [ˈeəlɒk] *n* (**a**) *(in submarine, spacecraft)* sas *m* (**b**) *(in pipe)* poche *f* d'air

airmail [ˈeəmeɪl] **1** *n (service)* poste *f* aérienne; **a. letter** aérogramme *m*

2 *adv* **to send sth a.** envoyer qch par avion

3 *vt (letter)* envoyer par avion

airplane [ˈeəpleɪn] *n Am* avion *m*

airport [ˈeəpɔːt] *n* aéroport *m*

air-sea rescue [ˈeəsiːˈreskjuː] *n* sauvetage *m* aérien en mer

airship [ˈeəʃɪp] *n* dirigeable *m*

airsick [ˈeəsɪk] *adj* **to be a.** avoir le mal de l'air

airspace [ˈeəspeɪs] *n* espace *m* aérien

airstrip [ˈeəstrɪp] *n* piste *f* d'atterrissage

airtight [ˈeətaɪt] *adj* hermétique

airtime [ˈeətaɪm] *n Rad & TV* temps *m* d'antenne

airwaves [ˈeəweɪvz] *npl* ondes *fpl* (hertziennes)

airworthy [ˈeəwɜːðɪ] *adj (aircraft)* en état de voler

airy [ˈeərɪ] *adj* (**a**) *(room, house)* clair(e) et spacieux(-euse) (**b**) *(person, attitude)* insouciant(e), désinvolte

airy-fairy [ˈeərɪˈfeərɪ] *adj Fam (idea, scheme)* farfelu(e)

aisle [aɪl] *n (in supermarket, cinema)* allée *f*; *(in church)* *(at side)* bas-côté *m*; *(central)* allée; *(in plane, bus)* couloir *m*; *Fam* **she had them rolling in the aisles** *(of comedian)* elle a fait mourir le public de rire; **a. seat** *(in plane)* place *f* côté couloir

ajar [əˈdʒɑː(r)] *adv & adj* entrouvert(e)

aka [eɪkeɪˈeɪ] *adv (abbr* **also known as***)* alias

akin [əˈkɪn] *adv & adj* **to be a. to** être apparenté(e) à

alabaster [ˈæləbæstə(r)] *n* albâtre *m*

alacrity [əˈlækrɪtɪ] *n* empressement *m*

alarm [əˈlɑːm] **1** *n* (**a**) *(signal, device)* alarme *f*; **to raise** *or* **give the a.** donner l'alarme; **a. clock** réveil *m*, réveille-matin *m inv*; **a. signal** signal *m* d'alarme (**b**) *(fright, anxiety)* alarme *f*, frayeur *f*; **there's no cause for a.** il n'y a aucune raison de s'alarmer

2 *vt* effrayer, alarmer; **to be alarmed at sth** s'alarmer *ou* s'effrayer de qch

alarming [əˈlɑːmɪŋ] *adj* alarmant(e), inquiétant(e)

alarmist [əˈlɑːmɪst] *n & adj* alarmiste *mf*

alas [əˈlæs] *exclam* hélas!

Albania [ælˈbeɪnɪə] *n* l'Albanie *f*

Albanian [ælˈbeɪnɪən] **1** *n* (**a**) *(person)* Albanais(e) *m,f* (**b**) *(language)* albanais *m*

2 *adj* albanais(e)

albatross [ˈælbətrɒs] *n* albatros *m*

albeit [ɔːlˈbiːɪt] *conj* quoique, bien que

albino [ælˈbiːnəʊ] *(pl* **albinos***) n* albinos *mf*

album [ˈælbəm] *n (record, for photos, stamps)* album *m*

albumen [ˈælbjʊmɪn] *n* (**a**) *(in egg)* albumen *m* (**b**) *(in blood)* albumine *f*

alchemy [ˈælkəmɪ] *n* alchimie *f*

alcohol [ˈælkəhɒl] *n* alcool *m*

alcoholic [ælkə'hɒlɪk] **1** n (person) alcoolique mf
2 adj alcoolique; (drink) alcoolisé(e)
alcoholism ['ælkəhɒlɪzəm] n alcoolisme m
alcopop ['ælkəʊpɒp] n prémix m
alcove ['ælkəʊv] n (in wall) niche f; (larger) renfoncement m
alder ['ɔːldə(r)] n au(l)ne m
ale [eɪl] n = bière anglaise au malt
alert [ə'lɜːt] **1** n alerte f; **to be on the a.** être en état
d'alerte, être sur le qui-vive
2 adj (watchful) éveillé(e); (lively) vif (vive); **to be a.
to sth** (aware of) être conscient(e) de qch
3 vt alerter; **to a. sb to a danger** alerter ou avertir qn
d'un danger
Aleutian Islands [æl'uːʃən'aɪləndz] npl **the A.** les îles
fpl Aléoutiennes
Alexandria [ælɪg'zɑːndrɪə] n Alexandrie
alfalfa [æl'fælfə] n Bot luzerne f
alfresco [æl'freskəʊ] adv & adj en plein air
algae ['ældʒiː] npl algues fpl
algebra ['ældʒɪbrə] n algèbre f
Algeria [æl'dʒɪərɪə] n l'Algérie f
Algerian [æl'dʒɪərɪən] **1** n Algérien(enne) m,f
2 adj algérien(enne)
Algiers [æl'dʒɪəz] n Alger
algorithm ['ælgərɪðəm] n Comput algorithme m
alias ['eɪlɪəs] (pl **aliases**) **1** n nom m d'emprunt, faux
nom
2 adv alias
alibi ['ælɪbaɪ] n Law alibi m
alien ['eɪlɪən] **1** n (a) Formal (foreigner) étranger(ère)
m,f (b) (from outer space) extraterrestre mf
2 adj (a) (strange) étranger(ère); **violence is completely a. to his nature** il n'est pas du tout d'un naturel violent (b) (from outer space) extraterrestre
alienate ['eɪlɪəneɪt] vt (supporters, readers) s'aliéner;
they feel alienated from society ils se sentent ex-
clus ou mis à l'écart de la société
alight¹ [ə'laɪt] adj (burning) en flammes, en feu; **to set
sth a.** mettre le feu à qch
alight² (pt & pp **alighted** or **alit** [ə'lɪt]) vi (a) Formal
(from train, car) descendre (b) (of bird, eyes, glance)
se poser (**on** sur)
align [ə'laɪn] vt aligner; **to a. oneself with sb** s'aligner
sur qn
alignment [ə'laɪnmənt] n alignement m; **out of a.** dé-
saligné(e); **in a. (with)** aligné(e) (sur)
alike [ə'laɪk] **1** adj semblable, pareil(eille); **to look a.**
se ressembler
2 adv (dress, think) de la même façon; **old and
young a.** les vieux comme les jeunes
alimentary canal [ælɪ'mentərɪkə'næl] n Anat tube m
digestif
alimony ['ælɪmənɪ] n Law pension f alimentaire
alit [ə'lɪt] pt & pp of alight
alive [ə'laɪv] adj (a) (living) **to be a.** être vivant(e); **to
keep sb a.** maintenir qn en vie; **to keep a memory/
custom a.** entretenir un souvenir/une tradition; **to
stay a.** survivre; **to be a. and well** bien se porter;
the oldest woman a. la doyenne du monde (b)
(aware) **to be a. to sth** avoir parfaitement conscience de qch (c) (full of vitality) **I've never felt so
a.** je ne me suis jamais senti aussi bien de ma vie; **to
come a.** s'animer (d) (teeming) **to be a. with sth**
grouiller de qch

alkali ['ælkəlaɪ] n alcali m
alkaline ['ælkəlaɪn] adj alcalin(e)
all [ɔːl] **1** adj (a) (every one of) tous (toutes); **a. men**
tous les hommes; **a. the girls** toutes les filles; **a. the
others** tous les autres; **a. four of them** tous les quatre; **at a. hours** à des heures impossibles
(b) (the whole of) tout(e); **a. the wine** tout le vin; **a.
day** toute la journée; **a. her life** toute sa vie; **a. the
time** tout le temps
(c) (for emphasis) **a. sorts of things** toutes sortes de
choses; **what's a. that noise?** c'est quoi, tout ce
bruit?; **in a. honesty** en toute honnêteté; **for a. his
wealth...** il a beau être riche...; **it's not a. that easy**
ce n'est pas si facile (que ça); **you, of a. people,
should understand** si quelqu'un doit comprendre
ça, c'est bien toi; **of a. the stupid things to say!** ce
n'est vraiment pas malin de dire un truc pareil!
2 pron (a) (everyone) tous (toutes) mpl, fpl; **a. of us**
nous tous; **a. of them say that..., they a. say that...**
ils disent tous que...; **a. together** tous ensemble
(b) (everything) tout m; **that's a.** c'est tout; **he ate a.
of it, he ate it a.** il a tout mangé; **a. I said was...** tout
ce que j'ai dit, c'est...; **I did a. I could** j'ai fait tout ce que
j'ai pu; **it was a. I could do not to laugh** j'ai bien failli
rire; **best/worst of a., ...** le mieux/le pire, c'est que...;
I like this best of a. c'est ça que je préfère; **most of a.**
surtout; **when a. is said and done** au bout du compte;
it's a. the same to me ça m'est égal; **thirty men in a.**
trente hommes en tout ou au total; **a. in a.** dans l'ensemble; **it cost £260, a. in a.** ça a coûté 260 livres tout
compris; Ironic **it cost a. of £2** ça a coûté la coquette
somme de 2 livres
3 adv (a) (entirely) tout; **a. alone** tout(e) seul(e); **to
be a. in black** être tout en noir; **to be a. for sth** être
pour qch; **a. ears/smiles** tout ouïe/sourire; **I forgot a.
about it** j'ai complètement oublié; **he's not a. bad** il
n'a pas que de mauvais côtés; **a. over Spain/the
world** dans toute l'Espagne/le monde entier; **a. over
(the place)** partout; **a. too soon** trop tôt; **a. along** depuis le début; **a. but** (almost) presque, pratiquement;
it's/he's a. yours il est à vous; Fam **a. in** (exhausted)
crevé(e)
(b) **at a.** (in the slightest) du tout; **do you know her
at a.?** tu la connais?; **if it's at a. possible** si c'était possible; **not at a.** pas du tout; (when thanked) je t'en prie
(c) (with comparatives) **a. the better/worse** d'autant mieux/plus mal; **a. the easier/faster** d'autant
plus facile/rapide
(d) (in games) **2 a.** 2 partout; **4 (games) a.** (in tennis)
4 jeux partout; **15 a.** (in tennis) 15 partout
4 n **to give one's a.** se donner à fond
Allah ['ælə] n Allah
allay [ə'leɪ] vt (doubts, suspicions) dissiper; (fear, pain)
soulager
all-clear ['ɔːl'klɪə(r)] n (after air-raid) (signal m de) fin f
d'alerte; Fig (for project) feu m vert
allegation [ælɪ'geɪʃən] n allégation f
allege [ə'ledʒ] vt alléguer, prétendre; **it is alleged
that...** on prétend que...
alleged [ə'ledʒd] adj (thief, culprit) présumé(e)
allegedly [ə'ledʒɪdlɪ] adv prétendument; **he a. stole
£500** il aurait volé 500 livres
allegiance [ə'liːdʒəns] n (to party, cause) fidélité f; (to
king) allégeance f
allegory ['ælɪgərɪ] (pl **allegories**) n allégorie f

all-embracing [ɔːlɪm'breɪsɪŋ] *adj (term, category)* large
allergenic [ælə'dʒenɪk] *adj Med* allergisant(e)
allergic [ə'lɜːdʒɪk] *adj* allergique (**to** à)
allergy ['ælədʒɪ] *(pl* **allergies)** *n* allergie *f* (**to** à)
alleviate [ə'liːvɪeɪt] *vt* soulager, calmer
alley ['ælɪ] *(pl* **alleys)** *n (street)* ruelle *f*; **a. cat** chat *m* de gouttière
alleyway ['ælɪweɪ] *n (street)* ruelle *f*
alliance [ə'laɪəns] *n* alliance *f*; **to enter into an a. with sb** former une alliance avec qn
allied ['ælaɪd] *adj (countries)* allié(e); *(issues, phenomena)* lié(e)
alligator ['ælɪɡeɪtə(r)] *n* alligator *m*; **a. shoes/handbag** chaussures *fpl*/sac *m* en crocodile
all-important ['ɔːlɪm'pɔːtənt] *adj* essentiel(elle), capital(e)
all-in ['ɔːlɪn] *adj (price)* tout compris; **a. wrestling** lutte *f* libre, catch *m*
alliteration [əlɪtə'reɪʃən] *n* allitération *f*
all-night ['ɔːlnaɪt] *adj (party, session)* qui dure toute la nuit
allocate ['æləkeɪt] *vt (resources, money)* affecter, attribuer (**to** à); *(duties)* assigner (**to** à); *(time)* prévoir (**to** pour)
allocation [ælə'keɪʃən] *n (distribution)* affectation *f*; *(share)* part *f*
allot [ə'lɒt] *(pt & pp* **allotted)** *vt (resources, money)* attribuer (**to** à); *(duties, job)* assigner (**to** à); **in the allotted time** dans le temps imparti
allotment [ə'lɒtmənt] *n* (**a**) *(land)* jardin *m* ouvrier (**b**) *(distribution) (of money)* affectation *f*; *(share)* part *f*
all-out ['ɔː'laʊt] *adj (resistance, effort)* acharné(e); *(strike, war)* total(e)
allow [ə'laʊ] *vt* (**a**) *(permit)* permettre; **to a. sb to do sth** permettre à qn de faire qch; **a. me!** *(offering help)* permettez(-moi)!; **smoking is not allowed** il est interdit de fumer; **I'm not allowed to do it** je n'ai pas l'autorisation de le faire; **to a. oneself to be deceived/persuaded** se laisser abuser/convaincre (**b**) *(allocate, grant)* accorder; *(time)* compter, prévoir
▶**allow for** *vt insep* tenir compte de; **add another hour to a. for delays** il faut prévoir une heure de plus au cas où il y aurait des retards
allowable [ə'laʊəbəl] *adj (error, delay)* admissible
allowance [ə'laʊəns] *n* (**a**) *(money given)* rente *f*, pension *f*; *(pocket money)* argent *m* de poche; **travel a.** indemnité *f* de transport (**b**) **to make a. for sth** tenir compte de qch; **I'm tired of making allowances for him** j'en ai assez de lui trouver des excuses
alloy ['ælɔɪ] *n* alliage *m*
all-powerful ['ɔːl'paʊəfʊl] *adj* tout-puissant (toute-puissante)
all-purpose ['ɔːl'pɜːpəs] *adj* universel(elle); **a. cleaner/adhesive** détachant *m*/colle *f* tous usages
all right [ɔːl'raɪt] **1** *adj* **are you a.?** ça va?; **he was in a car crash but he's a.** il a eu un accident de voiture mais il n'a rien; **it's a.** *(acceptable)* ce n'est pas mal; *(not a problem)* ce n'est pas grave; **to be a. for money** avoir suffisamment d'argent; **to be a. at maths/French** se débrouiller en maths/français.
2 *adv (yes)* oui; **is it a. if I smoke?** ça ne vous dérange pas si je fume?; **a., let's get started** bon, commençons

all-round ['ɔːl'raʊnd] *adj (education, improvement)* général(e); **an a. athlete** un athlète complet
all-rounder ['ɔːl'raʊndə(r)] *n* **she's a good a.** elle est bonne en tout
allspice ['ɔːlspaɪs] *n* poivre *m* de la Jamaïque
all-star ['ɔːl'stɑː(r)] *adj* **an a. cast** une distribution prestigieuse
all-time ['ɔːl'taɪm] *adj (record)* absolu(e); **unemployment has reached an a. high/low** le chômage n'a jamais été aussi élevé/bas
allude [ə'luːd] *vi* **to a. to** faire allusion à
allure [ə'lʊə(r)] *n* attrait *m*
allusion [ə'luːʒən] *n* allusion *f*; **to make an a. to sth** faire allusion à qch
ally 1 *n* ['ælaɪ] *(pl* **allies)** allié(e) *m,f*
2 *vt* [ə'laɪ] *(pt & pp* **allied)** **to a. oneself with** s'allier à *ou* avec
almanac ['ɔːlmənæk] *n* almanach *m*
almighty [ɔːl'maɪtɪ] **1** *n* **the A.** le Tout-Puissant
2 *adj Fam (fuss, row)* terrible
almond ['ɑːmənd] *n* amande *f*; **a. tree** amandier *m*
almost ['ɔːlməʊst] *adv* presque; **it's a. six o'clock** il est presque six heures; **we're a. there** *(in journey)* nous sommes presque arrivés; *(in task)* nous avons presque fini; **she a. missed the bus** elle a failli rater l'autobus
alms [ɑːmz] *npl* aumône *f*
aloft [ə'lɒft] *adv* en l'air
alone [ə'ləʊn] *adv & adj* seul(e); **to leave sb a.** laisser qn tranquille; **to leave sth a.** ne pas toucher à qch; **I did it a.** je l'ai fait tout seul; **to go it a.** faire cavalier seul; **we are not a. in thinking that...** nous ne sommes pas les seuls à penser que...; **you a. can help me** vous seul pouvez m'aider; **I can't afford a bicycle, let a. a car!** je n'ai pas assez d'argent pour m'acheter une bicyclette, encore moins une voiture!
along [ə'lɒŋ] **1** *prep* le long de; **to walk a. the shore** marcher le long de la côte; **to sail a. the coast** longer la côte; **I was walking a. the street** je marchais dans la rue; *Fig* **somewhere a. the way** à un moment donné
2 *adv* **to move a.** avancer; **she'll be a. in ten minutes** elle sera là dans dix minutes; **to bring sth a.** apporter qch; **to bring sb a.** amener qn; **he knew all a.** il le savait depuis le début; **a. with** *(as well as)* ainsi que
alongside [ə'lɒŋ'saɪd] *prep (next to)* à côté de; *(along)* le long de; *Naut* **to come a. a ship/quay** accoster un bateau/quai
aloof [ə'luːf] **1** *adj* distant(e)
2 *adv* **to remain a. (from sth)** rester à l'écart (de qch)
aloud [ə'laʊd] *adv* à haute voix; **I was thinking a.** je pensais tout haut
alpha ['ælfə] *n* alpha *m*; *Phys* **a. rays** rayons *mpl* alpha
alphabet ['ælfəbet] *n* alphabet *m*
alphabetical [ælfə'betɪkəl] *adj* alphabétique; **in a. order** dans l'ordre alphabétique
alphabetically [ælfə'betɪklɪ] *adv* alphabétiquement
alphasort ['ælfəsɔːt] *vt Comput* trier par order alphabétique
Alpine ['ælpaɪn] *adj* alpin(e); **an A. village** un village des Alpes
Alps [ælps] *npl* **the A.** les Alpes *fpl*

already [ɔːl'redɪ] *adv* déjà; **have you finished a.?** vous avez déjà fini?; *Am Fam* **enough, a.!** ça suffit comme ça!

alright = all right

Alsatian [æl'seɪʃən] **1** *n* (**a**) *(dog)* berger *m* allemand (**b**) *(person from Alsace)* Alsacien(enne) *m,f*
2 *adj* alsacien(enne)

also ['ɔːlsəʊ] *adv* aussi; **not only...but a....** non seulement... mais en plus...

also-ran ['ɔːlsəʊræn] *n (in horse race)* cheval *m* non classé; *Fig (person)* perdant(e) *m,f*

altar ['ɔːltə(r)] *n* autel *m*; **a. boy** enfant *m* de chœur

alter ['ɔːltə(r)] **1** *vt* changer; *(garment)* faire des retouches à; **he altered his opinion later** il a changé d'avis plus tard; **that doesn't a. the fact that...** cela ne change rien au fait que...
2 *vi* changer

alteration [ɔːltə'reɪʃən] *n (to design, plan)* modification *f*, changement *m*; *(to timetable)* changement; *(to garment)* retouche *f*

altercation [ɔːltə'keɪʃən] *n* altercation *f*

alter ego ['æltə'riːgəʊ] *n* alter ego *m*

alternate 1 *adj* [ɔːl'tɜːnət] alterné(e); **on a. days** un jour sur deux
2 ['ɔːltəneɪt] *vt* employer tour à tour
3 ['ɔːltəneɪt] *vi* alterner (**with** avec)

alternately [ɔːl'tɜːnətlɪ] *adv* tour à tour, alternativement

alternating ['ɔːltəneɪtɪŋ] *adj* alterné(e); *Elec* **a. current** courant *m* alternatif

alternative [ɔːl'tɜːnətɪv] **1** *n (choice)* choix *m*, solution *f*; **there is no a.** il n'y a pas le choix; **she had no a. but to obey** elle n'a pu faire autrement que d'obéir
2 *adj* (**a**) *(plan, route)* de remplacement; **an a. proposal** une contre-proposition (**b**) *(music, comedy)* alternatif(ive); **a. energy** énergies *fpl* de substitution; **a. medicine** médecine *f* douce

alternatively [ɔːl'tɜːnətɪvlɪ] *adv* (**a**) *(on the other hand)* sinon; **you could travel by train or a. by bus** vous pourriez voyager en train ou bien en autobus (**b**) *(in a different way)* autrement

alternator ['ɔːltəneɪtə(r)] *n* alternateur *m*

although [ɔːl'ðəʊ] *conj* bien que + *subjunctive*; **a. it's late** bien qu'il soit tard

altitude ['æltɪtjuːd] *n* altitude *f*

alto ['æltəʊ] *(pl* **altos)** *n (male voice)* haute-contre *f*; *(female voice)* contralto *m*; **a. clef** clef *f* d'ut; **a. saxophone** saxophone *m* alto

altogether [ɔːltə'geðə(r)] **1** *adv* (**a**) *(entirely)* complètement; **I was not a. pleased** je n'étais pas ravi (**b**) *(in total)* en tout; **the bill came to £63** en tout l'addition s'élevait à 63 livres
2 *n Fam* **in the a.** *(naked)* nu(e) comme un ver

altruism ['æltrʊɪzəm] *n* altruisme *m*

altruistic [æltrʊ'ɪstɪk] *adj* altruiste

aluminium [æljʊ'mɪnɪəm], *Am* **aluminum** [ə'luːmɪnəm] *n* aluminium *m*; **a. foil** papier *m* d'aluminium

always ['ɔːlweɪz] *adv* toujours; **I can a. try** je peux toujours essayer

AM ['eɪ'em] *n Rad (abbr* **amplitude modulation)** AM

am [æm] *1st pers singular of* be

a.m. ['eɪ'em] *adv (abbr* **ante meridiem)** du matin; **five a.m.** cinq heures du matin

amalgam [ə'mælgəm] *n* amalgame *m*

amalgamate [ə'mælgəmeɪt] **1** *vt (metals, ideas)* amalgamer; *(companies)* fusionner
2 *vi (of companies)* fusionner

amass [ə'mæs] *vt* amasser, accumuler

amateur ['æmətə(r)] **1** *n* amateur *m*
2 *adj (painter, musician)* amateur; *Pej (work, performance)* d'amateur; **a. dramatics** théâtre *m* amateur

amateurish [æmə'tɜːrɪʃ] *adj Pej* d'amateur

amaze [ə'meɪz] *vt* stupéfier; **I was amazed by his courage** son courage m'a stupéfié

amazement [ə'meɪzmənt] *n* stupéfaction *f*, stupeur *f*; **in a.** avec stupéfaction *ou* stupeur

amazing [ə'meɪzɪŋ] *adj* (**a**) *(surprising)* stupéfiant(e); **it's a. that no one helped her** il est incroyable que personne ne lui soit venu en aide (**b**) *(excellent)* formidable

Amazon ['æməzən] *n* (**a**) **the A.** *(river)* l'Amazone *f*; *(region)* l'Amazonie *f* (**b**) *(female warrior)* Amazone *f*

ambassador [æm'bæsədə(r)] *n* ambassadeur(drice) *m,f*

amber ['æmbə(r)] **1** *n (colour, stone)* ambre *m*; *(of traffic light)* orange *m*
2 *adj (jewellery)* d'ambre; *(colour)* couleur d'ambre, ambré(e)

ambience, ambiance ['æmbɪəns] *n* ambiance *f*

ambiguity [æmbɪ'gjuːɪtɪ] *(pl* **ambiguities)** *n* ambiguïté *f*

ambiguous [æm'bɪgjʊəs] *adj* ambigu(ë)

ambition [æm'bɪʃən] *n* ambition *f*

ambitious [æm'bɪʃəs] *adj* ambitieux(euse)

ambivalent [æm'bɪvələnt] *adj* ambivalent(e)

amble ['æmbəl] *vi* marcher d'un pas tranquille

ambulance ['æmbjʊləns] *n* ambulance *f*; **a. man** ambulancier *m*; **a. woman** ambulancière *f*

ambush ['æmbʊʃ] **1** *n also Fig* embuscade *f*
2 *vt also Fig* tendre une embuscade à; **to be ambushed** tomber dans une embuscade

ameba *Am* = amoeba

amen ['ɑː'men] *exclam* amen!, ainsi soit-il!

amenable [ə'miːnəbəl] *adj* souple; **to prove a. to a suggestion** approuver une proposition

amend [ə'mend] *vt (text, law)* modifier, amender; *(error)* corriger

amendment [ə'mendmənt] *n (to law, proposal)* amendement *m*

amends [ə'mendz] *npl* **to make a. (for sth)** faire amende honorable (pour qch); **to make a. to sb for sth** dédommager qn de qch

amenities [ə'miːnɪtɪz] *npl (shops)* commerces *mpl*; *(facilities)* équipements *mpl* collectifs

America [ə'merɪkə] *n* l'Amérique *f*

American [ə'merɪkən] **1** *n* Américain(e) *m,f*
2 *adj* américain(e); **the A. Civil War** la guerre de Sécession; **A. football** football *m* américain; **A. Indian** Indien(enne) *m,f* d'Amérique

amethyst ['æmɪθɪst] *n* améthyste *f*

amiable ['eɪmɪəbəl] *adj* aimable

amicable ['æmɪkəbəl] *adj* amical(e); **an a. agreement** un arrangement à l'amiable

amid [ə'mɪd], **amidst** [ə'mɪdst] *prep* au milieu de

amino acid [æ'miːnəʊ'æsɪd] *n* acide *m* aminé

amiss [ə'mɪs] *adv & adj* **there's something a.** il y a quelque chose qui ne va pas; **to take sth a.** prendre qch de travers, mal prendre qch; **a cup of coffee wouldn't go a.** une tasse de café serait bienvenue

ammeter ['æmi:tə(r)] *n Elec* ampèremètre *m*

ammonia [ə'məʊnɪə] *n* ammoniac *m*

ammunition [æmjʊ'nɪʃən] *n (for guns)* munitions *fpl*; *Fig (in debate, argument)* arguments *mpl*

amnesia [æm'ni:zɪə] *n* amnésie *f*

amnesty ['æmnɪstɪ] *(pl* **amnesties***) n* amnistie *f*

amoeba, *Am* **ameba** [ə'mi:bə] *n* amibe *f*

amok [ə'mɒk] *adv* **to run a.** être pris(e) de folie furieuse

among [ə'mʌŋ], **amongst** [ə'mʌŋst] *prep* parmi; **a. the crowd** au milieu de la foule; **we are a. friends** nous sommes entre amis; **they quarrel a. themselves** ils se disputent entre eux; **the money was divided a. them** l'argent a été divisé entre eux; **a. the best** parmi les meilleurs; **a. other things** entre autres choses

amoral [eɪ'mɒrəl] *adj* amoral(e)

amorphous [ə'mɔ:fəs] *adj (mass, lump)* informe; *(ideas, beliefs)* confus(e)

amount [ə'maʊnt] *n* **(a)** *(sum of money)* somme *f* **(b)** *(quantity)* quantité *f*; **a large a. of time/effort** beaucoup de temps/d'énergie; **a certain a. of discomfort** un certain manque de confort; **in large amounts** en grande quantité; **in small amounts** en petites quantités

▶**amount to** *vt insep* **(a)** *(add up to)* s'élever à; **her debts a. to £700** ses dettes s'élèvent à 700 livres **(b)** *(mean)* **it amounts to the same thing** cela revient au même; *Fig* **he'll never a. to much** il n'arrivera jamais à rien

amp [æmp] *n* **(a)** *Elec. (unit)* ampère *m*; **a 13-a. plug** une prise de 13 ampères **(b)** *Fam (amplifier)* ampli *m*

ampere ['æmpeə(r)] *n Elec* ampère *m*

ampersand ['æmpəsænd] *n* esperluette *f*

amphetamine [æm'fetəmin] *n* amphétamine *f*

amphibian [æm'fɪbɪən] **1** *n* amphibie *m*
    2 *adj* amphibie

amphibious [æm'fɪbɪəs] *adj* amphibie

amphitheatre, *Am* **amphitheater** ['æmfɪθɪətə(r)] *n* amphithéâtre *m*

ample ['æmpəl] *adj* **(a)** *(large) (woman, bosom)* fort(e) **(b)** *(plentiful)* abondant(e); **to have a. time to do sth** avoir largement le temps de faire qch; **to have a. opportunity to do sth** avoir tout loisir de faire qch; **this will be a.** ce sera largement suffisant

amplifier ['æmplɪfaɪə(r)] *n* amplificateur *m*

amplify ['æmplɪfaɪ] *(pt & pp* **amplified***) vt (essay, remarks)* développer; *(current, volume)* amplifier

amply ['æmplɪ] *adv* amplement, largement

amputate ['æmpjʊteɪt] *vt* amputer

amputation [æmpjʊ'teɪʃən] *n* amputation *f*

Amsterdam ['æmstə'dæm] *n* Amsterdam

amuck [ə'mʌk] = **amok**

amulet ['æmjʊlet] *n* amulette *f*

amuse [ə'mju:z] *vt* **(a)** *(make laugh)* amuser **(b)** *(occupy)* occuper; **to a. oneself by doing sth** se distraire en faisant qch; **to keep sb amused** distraire qn

amusement [ə'mju:zmənt] *n* **(a)** *(enjoyment)* amusement *m*; **much to everyone's a.** au grand amusement de tous **(b)** *(pastime)* distraction *f*; **a. arcade** galerie *f* de jeux; **a. park** parc *m* d'attractions

amusing [ə'mju:zɪŋ] *adj* amusant(e)

an [ən, *stressed* æn] *see* **a²**

anabolic steroid [ænə'bɒlɪk'sterɔɪd] *n* stéroïde *m* anabolisant

anachronism [ə'nækrənɪzəm] *n* anachronisme *m*; **to be an a.** faire figure d'anachronisme

anaconda [ænə'kɒndə] *n* anaconda *m*

anaemia, *Am* **anemia** [ə'ni:mɪə] *n* anémie *f*

anaemic, *Am* **anemic** [ə'ni:mɪk] *adj* anémique

anaesthetic, *Am* **anesthetic** [ænəs'θetɪk] *n (substance)* anesthésique *m*; *(process)* anesthésie *f*; **under a.** sous anesthésie; **local/general a.** anesthésie locale/générale

anaesthetist, *Am* **anesthetist** [ə'ni:sθətɪst] *n* anesthésiste *mf*

anaesthetize, *Am* **anesthetize** [ə'ni:sθətaɪz] *vt* anesthésier

anagram ['ænəgræm] *n* anagramme *f*

anal ['eɪnəl] *adj* anal(e)

analgesic [ænəl'dʒi:zɪk] **1** *n* analgésique *m*
    2 *adj* analgésique

analog *Am* = **analogue**

analogous [ə'næləgəs] *adj* analogue (**to** à)

analogue, *Am* **analog** ['ænəlɒg] *n* analogue *m*; **a. clock** horloge *f* à affichage analogique

analogy [ə'nælədʒɪ] *(pl* **analogies***) n* analogie *f*

analyse, *Am* **analyze** ['ænəlaɪz] *vt* analyser; *Psy* psychanalyser

analysis [ə'næləsɪs] *(pl* **analyses** [ə'næləsi:z] *) n* analyse *f*; *Psy* psychanalyse *f*; *Fig* **in the final a.** en fin de compte, au bout du compte

analyst ['ænəlɪst] *n* analyste *mf*; *Psy* (psych)analyste *mf*

analytic(al) [ænə'lɪtɪk(əl)] *adj* analytique

analyze *Am* = **analyse**

anarchist ['ænəkɪst] *n* anarchiste *mf*

anarchy ['ænəkɪ] *n* anarchie *f*

anathema [ə'næθəmə] *n* **(a)** *Rel* anathème *m* **(b)** *(repellent)* **the very idea was a. to her** l'idée même lui faisait horreur

anatomical [ænə'tɒmɪkəl] *adj* anatomique

anatomy [ə'nætəmɪ] *n* anatomie *f*

ANC [eɪen'si:] *n (abbr* **African National Congress***)* ANC *m*

ancestor ['ænsestə(r)] *n* ancêtre *mf*

ancestral [æn'sestrəl] *adj* ancestral(e); **a. home** demeure *f* ancestrale

ancestry ['ænsestrɪ] *n (descent)* ascendance *f*

anchor ['æŋkə(r)] **1** *n Naut* ancre *f*; *Fig* planche *f* de salut; **at a.** au mouillage; **to drop a.** jeter l'ancre; **to weigh a.** lever l'ancre
    2 *vt* **(a)** *Naut* ancrer **(b)** *(fix securely)* ancrer (**to** à) **(c)** *(radio, TV programme)* présenter
    3 *vi Naut* jeter l'ancre

anchorman ['æŋkəmən] *n (of radio, TV programme)* présentateur *m* principal

anchorwoman ['æŋkəwʊmən] *n (of radio, TV programme)* présentatrice *f* principale

anchovy ['æntʃəvɪ] *(pl* **anchovies***) n* anchois *m*

ancient ['eɪnʃənt] **1** *adj* ancien(enne); *Fig (person, car)* très vieux (vieille); **a. history** histoire *f* ancienne; **A. Rome** la Rome antique
    2 *n* **the ancients** les anciens *mpl*

ancillary [æn'sɪlərɪ] *adj* auxiliaire

and [ænd, *unstressed* ənd, ən] *conj* **(a)** *(in general)* et; **she can read a. write** elle sait lire et écrire; **my mother a. father** mon père et ma mère; **chicken a. chips** du poulet-frites; **a vodka a. orange** une vodka orange; **do that again a. I'll hit you!** si tu recommences, je te frappe!; **wait a. see** tu verras bien; **nice a. warm** bien chaud(e)

(**b**) *(to)* **go a. look for it** va le chercher; **come a. see me** viens me voir; **try a. help me** essaie de m'aider

(**c**) *(in numbers)* **two hundred a. two** deux cent deux; **four a. a half** quatre et demi; **an hour a. twenty minutes** une heure vingt; **four a. five make nine** quatre et *ou* plus cinq font neuf

(**d**) *(expressing repetition)* **hours a. hours** pendant des heures et des heures; **better a. better** de mieux en mieux; **smaller a. smaller** de plus en plus petit(e); **she talked a. talked** elle n'arrêtait pas de parler

(**e**) **a. so on a. so forth** et ainsi de suite

Andalusia [ændə'luːsɪə] *n* l'Andalousie *f*

Andes ['ændiːz] *npl* **the A.** les Andes *fpl*

Andorra [æn'dɔːrə] *n* l'Andorre *f*

Andorran [æn'dɔːrən] **1** *n* Andorran(e) *m,f*
 2 *adj* andorran(e)

androgynous [æn'drɒdʒɪnəs] *adj* androgyne

anecdotal [ænɪk'dəʊtəl] *adj* anecdotique

anecdote ['ænɪkdəʊt] *n* anecdote *f*

anemia, anemic *Am* = anaemia, anaemic

anemone [ə'nemənɪ] *n (flower)* anémone *f*; **sea a.** anémone de mer

anesthetic, anesthetist *etc Am* = anaesthetic, anaesthetist *etc*

anew [ə'njuː] *adv* encore, de nouveau; **to start a.** recommencer

angel ['eɪndʒəl] *n* ange *m*; *Fam* **you're an a.!** tu es un ange!

Angeleno [ændʒə'liːnəʊ] *(pl* **Angelenos**) *n* = personne née à ou habitant Los Angeles

angelic [æn'dʒelɪk] *adj* angélique

anger ['æŋɡə(r)] **1** *n* colère *f*; **a fit of a.** un accès de colère; **to speak in a.** parler sous le coup de la colère
 2 *vt* mettre en colère
 3 *vi* **to be slow/quick to a.** ne pas se mettre facilement/se mettre facilement en colère

angina [æn'dʒaɪnə] *n* angine *f* de poitrine

angle ['æŋɡəl] **1** *n* (**a**) *Math* angle *m*; **at an a. of...** formant un angle de...; **the car hit them at an a.** la voiture les a heurtés de biais; **the shop stands at an a. to the street** le magasin fait l'angle (**b**) *(viewpoint)* point *m* de vue; **seen from this a.** vu sous cet angle
 2 *vi* (**a**) *(fish)* pêcher à la ligne (**b**) *Fam* **to a. for an invitation** chercher à se faire inviter

angler ['æŋɡlə(r)] *n (person)* pêcheur(euse) *m,f* à la ligne; **a. fish** baudroie *f*, lotte *f* de mer

Anglican ['æŋɡlɪkən] *n & adj* anglican(e) *m,f*

angling ['æŋɡlɪŋ] *n (fishing)* pêche *f* à la ligne

Anglo-American ['æŋɡləʊə'merɪkən] *adj* anglo-américain(e)

Anglo-Saxon ['æŋɡləʊ'sæksən] **1** *n* (**a**) *(person)* Anglo-Saxon(onne) *m,f* (**b**) *(language)* anglo-saxon *m*
 2 *adj* anglo-saxon(onne)

Angola [æŋ'ɡəʊlə] *n* l'Angola *m*

Angolan [æŋ'ɡəʊlən] **1** *n* Angolais(e) *m,f*
 2 *adj* angolais(e)

angora [æŋ'ɡɔːrə] *n* angora *m*; **a. jumper** pull *m* en angora; **a. cat/rabbit** chat *m*/lapin *m* angora

angrily ['æŋɡrɪlɪ] *adv* avec colère

angry ['æŋɡrɪ] *adj (person)* en colère, fâché(e); *(voice, speech, letter)* furieux(euse); **to get a. (with)** se fâcher (contre), se mettre en colère (contre); **to make sb a.** mettre qn en colère

anguish ['æŋɡwɪʃ] *n* angoisse *f*

anguished ['æŋɡwɪʃt] *adj (look, cry)* d'angoisse; *(person)* tourmenté(e)

angular ['æŋɡjʊlə(r)] *adj* anguleux(euse)

animal ['ænɪməl] *n* animal *m*; **the a. kingdom** le règne animal; **a. lover** = personne qui aime les animaux; **a. rights** les droits *mpl* des animaux; **he's an a.** *(uncivilized person)* c'est une brute

animate 1 *adj* ['ænɪmɪt] animé(e)
 2 *vt* ['ænɪmeɪt] animer

animated ['ænɪmeɪtɪd] *adj (expression, discussion)* animé(e); **to become a.** s'animer; **a. cartoon** dessin *m* animé

animation [ænɪ'meɪʃən] *n* animation *f*

animator ['ænɪmeɪtə(r)] *n Cin* animateur(trice) *m,f*

animism ['ænɪmɪzəm] *n* animisme *m*

animosity [ænɪ'mɒsɪtɪ] *n* animosité *f*

aniseed ['ænɪsiːd] *n (flavour)* anis *m*; *(seed)* graine *f* d'anis

Ankara ['æŋkərə] *n* Ankara

ankle ['æŋkəl] *n* cheville *f*; **a. boots** chaussures *fpl* montantes; **a. socks** socquettes *fpl*

anklet ['æŋklət] *n (ankle bracelet)* bracelet *m* de cheville

annals ['ænəlz] *npl* annales *fpl*

annex 1 *vt* [æ'neks] annexer
 2 *n* ['æneks] *Am* = annexe

annexation [ænek'seɪʃən] *n* annexion *f*

annexe, *Am* **annex** ['æneks] *n (of building, document)* annexe *f*

annihilate [ə'naɪəleɪt] *vt* anéantir

annihilation [ənaɪə'leɪʃən] *n* anéantissement *m*

anniversary [ænɪ'vɜːsərɪ] *(pl* **anniversaries**) *n* anniversaire *m*; **wedding a.** anniversaire de mariage

anno Domini ['ænəʊ'dɒmɪnaɪ] *adv* en l'an de grâce

annotate ['ænəteɪt] *vt* annoter

announce [ə'naʊns] *vt* annoncer

announcement [ə'naʊnsmənt] *n (of news)* annonce *f*; *(formal statement)* avis *m*

announcer [ə'naʊnsə(r)] *n (on radio, TV programme)* annonceur(euse) *m,f*, speaker (speakerine) *m,f*

annoy [ə'nɔɪ] *vt* agacer; **to get annoyed** se mettre en colère, se fâcher; **to be annoyed with sb** être en colère contre qn

annoyance [ə'nɔɪəns] *n (feeling)* agacement *m*; *(annoying thing)* ennui *m*

annoying [ə'nɔɪɪŋ] *adj* agaçant(e), ennuyeux(euse); **how a.!** comme c'est ennuyeux!

annual ['ænjʊəl] **1** *n* (**a**) *(plant)* plante *f* annuelle (**b**) *(book)* publication *f* annuelle; *(for children)* album *m* *(publié une fois par an)*
 2 *adj* annuel(elle); **a. general meeting** assemblée *f* générale annuelle

annually ['ænjʊəlɪ] *adv (every year)* tous les ans; *(per year)* par an

annul [ə'nʌl] *(pt & pp* **annulled**) *vt Law (contract, marriage)* annuler

anode ['ænəʊd] *n* anode *f*

anodyne ['ænəʊdaɪn] *adj (bland)* anodin(e)

anoint [ə'nɔɪnt] *vt* oindre (**with** de); **to a. sb king** sacrer qn roi

anomalous [ə'nɒmələs] *adj* anormal(e)

anomaly [ə'nɒmɔlɪ] *(pl* **anomalies**) *n* anomalie *f*

anon¹ [ə'nɒn] *adv Lit (soon)* bientôt

anon² *adj (abbr* **anonymous**) anonyme

anonymity [ænə'nɪmɪtɪ] n anonymat m
anonymous [ə'nɒnɪməs] adj anonyme; **to remain a.** garder l'anonymat
anorak ['ænəræk] n anorak m
anorexia [ænə'reksɪə] n anorexie f; **a. nervosa** anorexie mentale
anorexic [ænə'reksɪk] adj anorexique
another [ə'nʌðə(r)] adj & pron (**a**) (additional) un (une) autre m,f; **a. cup of tea** une autre tasse de thé; **in a. ten years** dans dix ans; **don't say a. word** plus un mot; **a. Picasso/Vietnam** un nouveau Picasso/Viêt Nam
  (**b**) (different) un (une) autre m,f; **that's quite a. matter** c'est une toute autre affaire; **a. time, perhaps** (declining invitation) une autre fois, peut-être; **what with one thing and a., I forgot** avec tout ce qui s'est passé, j'ai oublié; **one way or a.** d'une façon ou d'une autre
  (**c**) (reciprocal) **they saw one a.** ils se sont vus
answer ['ɑːnsə(r)] **1** n (to question, letter) réponse f; (to problem) solution f; **I knocked but there was no a.** j'ai frappé mais personne n'a répondu; **there's no a.** (on telephone) ça ne répond pas; **he has an a. to everything** il a réponse à tout; Formal **in a. to your letter** en réponse à votre lettre
  2 vt répondre à; **"I'll do it tomorrow," he answered** "je le ferai demain", a-t-il répondu; **to a. the telephone** répondre au téléphone; **to a. the door** ouvrir (la porte)
  3 vi (of person) répondre
▸**answer back** vi (be impertinent) répondre
▸**answer for** vt insep répondre de; **he has a lot to a. for** il a beaucoup de comptes à rendre
▸**answer to** vt insep (**a**) (be accountable to) **to a. to sb** être responsable devant qn; **she answers to no one** elle n'a de comptes à rendre à personne (**b**) (correspond to) (description) répondre à (**c**) **the dog answers to the name of Rover** le chien répond au nom de Rover
answerable ['ɑːnsərəbəl] adj **to be a. to sb** être responsable devant qn; **he is a. to nobody** il n'a de comptes à rendre à personne
answering machine ['ɑːnsərɪŋməʃiːn], **answerphone** ['ɑːnsəfəʊn] n répondeur m (téléphonique)
ant [ænt] n fourmi f; **a. hill** fourmilière f
antagonism [æn'tægənɪzəm] n antagonisme m
antagonist [æn'tægənɪst] n antagoniste mf
antagonize [æn'tægənaɪz] vt rendre hostile
Antarctica [æn'tɑːktɪkə] n l'Antarctique m
ante ['æntɪ] n Fam **to up the a.** (in gambling, conflict) augmenter la mise
anteater ['æntiːtə(r)] n fourmilier m
antecedents [æntɪ'siːdəns] npl antécédents mpl
antelope ['æntɪləʊp] n antilope f
antenatal [æntɪ'neɪtəl] adj prénatal(e); **a. clinic** cours m de préparation à l'accouchement
antenna [æn'tenə] n (**a**) (pl **antennae** [æn'teniː]) (of insect, snail) antenne f (**b**) (pl **antennas**) (of radio, TV) antenne f
anterior [æn'tɪərɪə(r)] adj Formal & Anat antérieur(e) (**to** à)
anteroom ['æntɪruːm] n antichambre f
anthem ['ænθəm] n hymne m; **national a.** hymne national

anthology [æn'θɒlədʒɪ] (pl **anthologies**) n anthologie f
anthracite ['ænθrəsaɪt] n anthracite m
anthrax ['ænθræks] n (disease) anthrax m
anthropologist [ænθrə'pɒlədʒɪst] n anthropologue mf
anthropology [ænθrə'pɒlədʒɪ] n anthropologie f
anti- ['æntɪ] pref anti-; **a.-American** antiaméricain(e)
anti-aircraft ['æntɪ'eəkrɑːft] adj (gun, defences) anti-aérien(enne)
antibiotic [æntɪbaɪ'ɒtɪk] n antibiotique m
antibody ['æntɪbɒdɪ] (pl **antibodies**) n Med anticorps m
Antichrist ['æntɪkraɪst] n Antéchrist m
anticipate [æn'tɪsɪpeɪt] vt (**a**) (expect) prévoir, s'attendre à; (foresee) anticiper; **we hadn't anticipated such stiff resistance** nous ne nous attendions pas à une telle résistance; **as anticipated, there was trouble** comme on s'y attendait, il y eut des problèmes (**b**) (foreshadow) préfigurer, annoncer
anticipation [æntɪsɪ'peɪʃən] n (**a**) (foresight) prévoyance f; **in a. of trouble** en prévision de troubles; **thanking you in a.** en vous remerciant d'avance, avec mes remerciements anticipés (**b**) (eagerness) impatience f
anticlimax [æntɪ'klaɪmæks] n déception f
anti-clockwise [æntɪ'klɒkwaɪz], Am **counter-clockwise** ['kaʊntə'klɒkwaɪz] **1** adj **in an a. direction** dans le sens inverse des aiguilles d'une montre
  2 adv dans le sens inverse des aiguilles d'une montre
antics ['æntɪks] npl bouffonneries fpl; **he's been up to his usual a.** il a encore fait des siennes
anticyclone [æntɪ'saɪkləʊn] n Met anticyclone m
antidepressant [æntɪdɪ'presənt] n antidépresseur m
antidote ['æntɪdəʊt] n also Fig antidote m (**to** contre)
antifreeze ['æntɪfriːz] n antigel m
Antigua and Barbuda [æn'tiːgənbɑː'bjuːdə] n Antigua-et-Barbuda
antipathy [æn'tɪpəθɪ] n antipathie f (**towards** pour)
antiperspirant [æntɪ'pɜːspɪrənt] n déodorant m
Antipodes [æn'tɪpədiːz] npl **the A.** l'Australie f et la Nouvelle-Zélande
antiquarian [æntɪ'kweərɪən] **1** n (dealer) antiquaire mf; (collector) collectionneur(euse) m,f d'antiquités
  2 adj (book) ancien(enne); **a. bookshop** = librairie spécialisée dans les livres anciens
antiquated ['æntɪkweɪtɪd] adj (building, installation) vétuste; (idea, method) vieillot(otte)
antique [æn'tiːk] **1** n antiquité f; **a. dealer** antiquaire mf; **a. shop** magasin m d'antiquités
  2 adj ancien(enne); **an a. clock** une pendule ancienne ou d'époque; **a. furniture** meubles mpl anciens
antiquity [æn'tɪkwɪtɪ] (pl **antiquities**) n (historical period, ruin) antiquité f
antiracist [æntɪ'reɪsɪst] adj antiraciste
anti-Semitic [æntɪsɪ'mɪtɪk] adj antisémite
antiseptic [æntɪ'septɪk] **1** n antiseptique m
  2 adj (**a**) (anti-bacterial) antiseptique (**b**) Fig (lacking character or warmth) (place) aseptisé(e); (person) froid(e)
antisocial [æntɪ'səʊʃəl] adj (**a**) (disruptive) asocial(e) (**b**) (unsociable) peu sociable
antithesis [æn'tɪθɪsɪs] (pl **antitheses** [æn'tɪθɪsiːz]) n (opposite) opposé m, antithèse f

antlers ['æntləz] *npl* bois *mpl*

antonym ['æntənɪm] *n* antonyme *m*

Antwerp ['æntwɜːp] *n* Anvers

anus ['eɪnəs] *n* anus *m*

anvil ['ænvɪl] *n* enclume *f*

anxiety [æŋ'zaɪətɪ] *(pl* **anxieties)** *n* (**a**) *(worry, concern)* inquiétude *f*; *(stronger)* anxiété *f*; **my main a. is...** mon principal souci est...; **there is no cause for a.** il n'y a pas de quoi s'inquiéter; **to feel a.** être anxieux(euse) (**b**) *(eagerness)* désir *m*, souci *m*; **in her a. to help** dans son désir *ou* souci de se rendre utile

anxious ['æŋkʃəs] *adj* (**a**) *(worried)* inquiet(ète); *(stronger)* anxieux(euse); **to be a. for sb** être inquiet *ou* s'inquiéter pour qn; **to be a. about sth** être inquiet *ou* s'inquiéter pour qch (**b**) *(worrying) (moment)* d'angoisse; *(period)* angoissant(e) (**c**) **to be a. to do sth** *(impatient)* être impatient(e) de faire qch; *(eager)* tenir à faire qch

anxiously ['æŋkʃəslɪ] *adv* (**a**) *(worriedly)* avec inquiétude; *(stronger)* anxieusement (**b**) *(with impatience)* impatiemment, avec impatience

any ['enɪ] **1** *pron* (**a**) *(some)* **have you got a.?** en avez-vous?; **is/are there a. left?** en reste-t-il?; **can a. of them speak English?** y en a-t-il parmi eux qui parlent anglais?
(**b**) *(in negatives)* **I haven't got a.** je n'en ai pas; **there was nothing in a. of the boxes** il n'y avait rien dans aucune des boîtes; **few, if a., can read** aucun, ou presque aucun, ne sait lire
(**c**) *(no particular one)* n'importe lequel (laquelle) *m,f*; **a. of us** n'importe lequel d'entre nous
(**d**) *(every one)* tous ceux (toutes celles) *mpl, fpl*; **keep a. you find** garde tous ceux que tu trouveras
2 *adj* (**a**) *(some) (singular)* du (de la); *(plural)* des; **have you a. milk/flour/apples?** avez-vous du lait/de la farine/des pommes?
(**b**) *(in negatives)* **he hasn't got a. money** il n'a pas d'argent; **without a. doubt** sans aucun doute; **that won't do a. good** ça ne servira à rien
(**c**) *(no particular)* n'importe quel (quelle); **come a. day** venez n'importe quel jour; **a. minute now** d'une minute à l'autre
(**d**) *(every)* tout(e); **a. pupil who forgets his books will be punished** tout élève qui oubliera ses livres sera puni; **at a. rate, in a. case** en tout cas
3 *adv* (**a**) *(with comparative)* **I'm not a. better** je ne vais pas mieux; **does that make it a. easier?** est-ce que c'est plus facile comme ça?; **we don't see them a. longer** *or* **more** nous ne les voyons plus; **do you want a. more tea?** veux-tu encore du thé?; **I don't like her a. more than you do** je ne l'aime pas plus que toi
(**b**) *Fam* **a. old how** n'importe comment; **that didn't help us a.** ça ne nous a été d'aucun secours

anybody ['enɪbɒdɪ] *pron* (**a**) *(indeterminate)* quelqu'un; **would a. like some more cake?** quelqu'un veut-il encore du gâteau?; **she'll know if a. does** si quelqu'un doit le savoir, c'est bien elle
(**b**) *(in negatives)* **not a.** ne... personne; **there isn't a. here** il n'y a personne ici; **there was hardly a.** il n'y avait presque personne
(**c**) *(no matter who)* n'importe qui; **a. will tell you so** n'importe qui *ou* tout le monde vous le dira; **bring along a. you like** amenez qui vous voudrez; **a. else or but her would have refused** tout autre qu'elle aurait refusé; **it's a.'s guess** Dieu seul le sait; **he's not just a.!** ce n'est pas n'importe qui!

(**d**) *(person with status)* **he'll never be a.** il ne fera jamais rien dans la vie

anyhow ['enɪhaʊ] *adv* (**a**) *(however)* de toute façon *ou* manière; **a., let's get back to what we were saying** bref, revenons à ce que nous disions; **I don't care, I'm going a.** ça m'est égal, j'y vais quand même (**b**) *Fam (carelessly)* n'importe comment

anyone ['enɪwʌn] = **anybody**

anyplace ['enɪpleɪs] *Am* = **anywhere**

anything ['enɪθɪŋ] **1** *pron* (**a**) *(indeterminate)* quelque chose; **is there a. I can do?** est-ce que je peux faire quelque chose?; **have you a. to write with?** as-tu de quoi écrire?; **will there be a. else?** *(in shop)* et avec ceci?; **have you a. smaller?** avez-vous quelque chose de plus petit?; *(money)* vous n'avez pas plus petit?; **if a. should happen to me** s'il m'arrivait quelque chose *ou* quoi que ce soit; **is (there) a. the matter?** il y a quelque chose qui ne va pas?
(**b**) *(in negatives)* **not a.** ne... rien; **he doesn't do a.** il ne fait rien; **hardly a.** presque rien
(**c**) *(no matter what)* n'importe quoi; **he eats a.** il mange de tout; **I love a. French** j'aime tout ce qui est français; **she would do a. for me** elle ferait n'importe quoi pour moi; **he was a. but friendly** il était tout sauf amical; **are you angry? – a. but** tu es fâché? – non, loin de là
2 *adv* **is it a. like the other one?** est-ce qu'il ressemble un peu à l'autre ou pas du tout?; **she doesn't look a. like her sister** elle ne ressemble pas du tout à sa sœur; **the food wasn't a. like as bad as they said** la nourriture était loin d'être aussi mauvaise que ce qu'on m'avait dit; *Fam* **as funny/strong as a.** drôle/fort(e) comme tout; *Fam* **to work like a.** travailler comme un fou (une folle); *Fam* **it's not that you're wrong or a.** ce n'est pas que tu aies tort

anyway ['enɪweɪ] = **anyhow** (**a**)

anywhere ['enɪweə(r)] *adv* (**a**) *(in questions)* quelque part; **did you go a. yesterday?** êtes-vous allé quelque part hier?; **can you see it a.?** tu le vois?
(**b**) *(in negatives)* **not a.** ne... nulle part; **I can't find it a.** je ne le trouve nulle part; **we're not getting a.** nous n'avançons pas; **he isn't a. near as clever as her** il est loin d'être aussi intelligent qu'elle
(**c**) *(no matter where)* n'importe où; **put it a.** mets-le n'importe où; **I'd know her a.** je la reconnaîtrais entre mille; **it's miles from a.** c'est loin de tout; **a. else** n'importe où

AO(C)B [eɪəʊ(siː)'biː] *(abbr* **any other (competent) business)** divers

aorta [eɪ'ɔːtə] *n* aorte *f*

apart [ə'pɑːt] *adv* (**a**) *(at a distance)* à l'écart *(from* de); **to stand a.** *(of person)* se tenir à l'écart; **the garage stands a. from the house** le garage est séparé de la maison
(**b**) *(separated)* **they are far a.** ils sont éloignés l'un de l'autre; **the two towns are 10 kilometres a.** les deux villes sont à 10 kilomètres l'une de l'autre; **they're never a.** ils ne se séparent jamais; **with one's legs a.** les jambes écartées; **two years a.** à deux ans d'intervalle; **to set sth a. for sth** réserver qch à qch; **to live a.** vivre séparément; **it's difficult to tell them a.** il est difficile de les distinguer l'un de l'autre; **joking a., ...** blague à part, ...
(**c**) *(to pieces)* **to take sth a.** *(machine)* démonter qch; **to come a.** *(of garment)* se découdre
(**d**) *(excepting)* **a. from** à part; **a. from the fact that...** indépendamment du fait que...

apartheid [ə'pɑːtaɪt] *n* apartheid *m*

apartment [ə'pɑːtmənt] *n Am* appartement *m*; **a. block**, **a. building** immeuble *m* d'habitation, *Can* bloc-appartement *m*

apathetic [æpə'θetɪk] *adj* qui manque d'enthousiasme; **to be a. about sth** être indifférent(e) à qch

apathy ['æpəθɪ] *n* manque *m* d'enthousiasme

ape [eɪp] **1** *n (animal)* grand singe *m*; *Fam* **to go a.** piquer une crise
  2 *vt (imitate)* singer

aperitif [əperɪ'tiːf] *n* apéritif *m*

aperture ['æpətjʊə(r)] *n* ouverture *f*

APEX ['eɪpeks] *adj* **A. ticket** = billet d'avion ou de train à tarif réduit, soumis à certaines restrictions

apex ['eɪpeks] *n* sommet *m*

aphasia [ə'feɪzɪə] *n Med* aphasie *f*

aphid ['eɪfɪd] *n* puceron *m*

aphorism ['æfərɪzəm] *n* aphorisme *m*

aphrodisiac [æfrəʊ'dɪzɪæk] **1** *n* aphrodisiaque *m*
  2 *adj* aphrodisiaque

apiece [ə'piːs] *adv* chacun(e); **they cost £3 a.** ils valent 3 livres pièce *ou* chacun

aplenty [ə'plentɪ] *adv* en abondance

aplomb [ə'plɒm] *n* sang-froid *m*

apocalypse [ə'pɒkəlɪps] *n* apocalypse *f*

apocalyptic [əpɒkə'lɪptɪk] *adj* apocalyptique

apocryphal [ə'pɒkrɪfəl] *adj* apocryphe; **the story is a.** c'est une histoire inventée

apolitical [eɪpə'lɪtɪkəl] *adj* apolitique

apologetic [əpɒlə'dʒetɪk] *adj (tone, smile)* désolé(e); **to be a. about sth** s'excuser de qch; **she was quite a. about it** elle s'est répandue en excuses

apologize [ə'pɒlədʒaɪz] *vi* s'excuser; **to a. to sb for sth** s'excuser de qch auprès de qn, présenter ses excuses à qn pour qch; **she apologized for being late/for not telling him earlier** elle s'est excusée d'être en retard/de ne pas le lui avoir dit plus tôt

apology [ə'pɒlədʒɪ] *(pl* **apologies***) n* excuses *fpl*; **to make/offer an a.** faire/présenter des excuses; **I owe you an a.** je vous dois des excuses; *Pej* **an a. for a dinner** un semblant de dîner

apoplectic [æpə'plektɪk] *adj Fig (angry)* furieux(-euse); **to be a. with rage** s'étrangler de rage

apoplexy ['æpəpleksɪ] *n Med* apoplexie *f*; *Fig (anger)* rage *f*

apostle [ə'pɒsəl] *n* apôtre *m*

apostolic(al) [æpɒs'tɒlɪk(əl)] *adj* apostolique

apostrophe [ə'pɒstrəfɪ] *n* apostrophe *f*

appal, *Am* **appall** [ə'pɔːl] *(pt & pp* **appalled***) vt (shock)* choquer, scandaliser; *(fill with horror)* horrifier; **to be appalled at** *or* **by sth** être choqué(e)/horrifié(e) par qch; **it appals me to think that...** je suis horrifié(e) à la pensée que...

appalling [ə'pɔːlɪŋ] *adj (behaviour)* scandaleux(-euse); *(conditions, smell, weather, film)* épouvantable

apparatus [æpə'reɪtəs] *n (machine)* appareil *m*; *(set of machines, in laboratory)* équipement *m*; *(in gym)* agrès *mpl*; **a piece of a.** un appareil

apparel [ə'pærəl] *n Formal or Literary* mise *f*

apparent [ə'pærənt] *adj* **(a)** *(obvious)* clair(e), évident(e); **it soon became a. that...** il est vite devenu évident que... **(b)** *(seeming)* apparent(e)

apparently [ə'pærəntlɪ] *adv* apparemment; **a. he's going to Venice** il paraît qu'il va à Venise

apparition [æpə'rɪʃən] *n* apparition *f*

appeal [ə'piːl] **1** *n* **(a)** *(call)* appel *m* (**for** à); **to make an a. for help** lancer un appel à l'aide; **charity a.** = appel aux dons lancé par une organisation caritative **(b)** *Law* appel *m*; **on a.** en seconde instance; **A. Court, Court of A.** cour *f* d'appel **(c)** *(attraction)* attrait *m*; **to have great a.** *(of idea)* être très attrayant(e); *(of person)* avoir beaucoup de charme; **their music has a wide a.** leur musique attire un public très varié
  2 *vt Am Law* **to a. a decision** faire appel d'une décision
  3 *vi* **(a)** *(make a plea)* **to a. (to sb) for help/money** demander de l'aide/de l'argent (à qn); **to a. to sb's generosity** faire appel à la générosité de qn **(b) to a. to sb** *(attract)* attirer qn **(c)** *Law* se pourvoir en appel; **to a. against a decision** faire appel d'une décision

appealing [ə'piːlɪŋ] *adj (idea)* séduisant(e); *(person, manner)* sympathique

appear [ə'pɪə(r)] *vi* **(a)** *(come into view)* apparaître; *(of publication)* paraître; **where did you a. from?** d'où sors-tu?; **to a. from nowhere** sortir de nulle part; **to a. on TV** passer à la télé **(b)** *Law* comparaître **(c)** *(look, seem)* sembler; **to a. to be lost** avoir l'air d'être perdu(e); **there appears to be a mistake** il semble qu'il y ait une erreur; **so it would a.** c'est ce qu'on dirait

appearance [ə'pɪərəns] *n* **(a)** *(arrival)* apparition *f*, arrivée *f*; **to put in an a.** faire acte de présence **(b)** *(of actor)* **to make a television a.** passer à la télévision **(c)** *(of publication)* parution *f* **(d)** *Law (in court)* comparution *f* **(e)** *(looks, demeanour)* apparence *f*; **it's wrong to judge by appearances** il ne faut pas se fier aux apparences; **appearances can be deceptive** les apparences peuvent être trompeuses; **to keep up appearances** sauver les apparences

appease [ə'piːz] *vt (anger, person)* apaiser, calmer; *Pol* composer avec

appeasement [ə'piːzmənt] *n (of person, anger)* apaisement *m*; *Pol* conciliation *f*

append [ə'pend] *vt (list, document)* joindre (**to** à); *(one's signature)* apposer (**to** à)

appendage [ə'pendɪdʒ] *n* appendice *m*; **she was tired of being treated as her husband's a.** elle en avait assez de n'être traitée que comme la femme de son mari

appendicitis [əpendɪ'saɪtɪs] *n* appendicite *f*

appendix [ə'pendɪks] *(pl* **appendices** [ə'pendɪsiːz] *) n* **(a)** *Anat* appendice *m*; **to have one's a. (taken) out** se faire opérer de l'appendicite **(b)** *(of book)* appendice *m*

appetite ['æpɪtaɪt] *n* **(a)** *(for food)* appétit *m*; **to have a good a.** avoir bon appétit; **to spoil sb's a.** couper l'appétit à qn; **to give sb an a.** donner faim à qn; *(of fresh air, walk)* creuser qn **(b)** *(enthusiasm)* *(for knowledge, travel)* soif *f* (**for** de); *(for music, cinema)* goût *m* (**for** pour)

appetizer ['æpɪtaɪzə(r)] *n also Fig* amuse-gueule *m*

appetizing ['æpɪtaɪzɪŋ] *adj* appétissant(e)

applaud [ə'plɔːd] *vt & vi* applaudir

applause [ə'plɔːz] *n (clapping)* applaudissements *mpl*; *(approval)* approbation *f*

apple ['æpəl] *n* pomme *f*; **he was the a. of her eye** *(her favourite)* elle tenait à lui comme à la prunelle de ses yeux; **a. core** trognon *m* de pomme; **a. juice** jus *m* de pomme; **a. pie** *(without top crust)* tarte *f* aux pommes; *(with top crust)* tourte *f* aux pommes; **as American as**

a. pie typiquement américain(e); **a. tree** pommier *m*
applecart ['æpəlkɑːt] *n* **to upset the a.** *(spoil plan)* tout chambouler
apple-pie ['æpəlpaɪ] *adj* **in a. order** parfaitement en ordre
appliance [ə'plaɪəns] *n* appareil *m*; **electrical/domestic a.** appareil électrique/ménager
applicable [ə'plɪkəbəl] *adj* applicable; **the rule is a. to everybody** la règle s'applique à tous; **delete where not a.** *(on form)* rayer les mentions inutiles
applicant ['æplɪkənt] *n (for job)* candidat(e) *m,f* (**for** à)
application [æplɪ'keɪʃən] *n* (**a**) *(for job)* candidature *f* (**for** à); *(for passport, patent)* demande *f* (**for** de); **a. form** *(for job)* formulaire *m* de candidature; *(detailed)* dossier *m* de candidature; *(for grant, benefits)* formulaire de demande (**b**) *(of rule, theory, paint)* application *f* (**c**) *(effort)* application *f*, assiduité *f*
applied [ə'plaɪd] *adj (maths, physics)* appliqué(e)
apply [ə'plaɪ] *(pt & pp* **applied**) **1** *vt* (**a**) *(put on)* appliquer (**to** sur) (**b**) *(use) (system, theory)* appliquer (**to** à); **to a. one's mind to sth** concentrer ses efforts sur qch; **to a. oneself (to one's work)** s'appliquer
2 *vi* (**a**) **to a. to sb for sth** s'adresser à qn pour obtenir qch; **to a. for a job** poser sa candidature pour un poste; **to a. for a grant** faire une demande de bourse (**b**) *(of law, rule)* s'appliquer (**to** à)
appoint [ə'pɔɪnt] *vt (person)* nommer; *(committee)* constituer; **to a. sb to a post** nommer qn à un poste; **to a. sb (as) manager** nommer qn directeur(trice)
appointed [ə'pɔɪntɪd] *adj Formal (agreed) (place, hour)* convenu(e), dit(e)
appointment [ə'pɔɪntmənt] *n* (**a**) *(meeting, with doctor)* rendez-vous *m*; **to make an a. with sb** prendre rendez-vous avec qn; *(with dentist, doctor)* prendre rendez-vous chez qn (**b**) *(to job)* nomination *f*; *(of committee)* constitution *f*; **to make an a.** pourvoir un poste; *Com* **by a. to His/Her Majesty** *(sign)* fournisseur de la Couronne; **appointments** *(in newspaper)* offres d'emploi
apportion [ə'pɔːʃən] *vt* répartir
appraisal [ə'preɪzəl] *n (of standards, personnel)* évaluation *f*
appraise [ə'preɪz] *vt (performance, situation)* évaluer; *(value)* estimer
appreciable [ə'priːʃɪəbəl] *adj (change, difference)* appréciable, sensible
appreciate [ə'priːʃɪeɪt] **1** *vt* (**a**) *(be grateful for) (help)* être reconnaissant(e) de; *(kindness)* être sensible à; **I a. your helping me** je vous suis reconnaissant de m'avoir aidé (**b**) *(grasp, understand)* être conscient(e) de; **he doesn't a. how lucky he is** il ne se rend pas compte de la chance qu'il a (**c**) *(acknowledge)* apprécier
2 *vi (of goods, investment)* prendre de la valeur; *(of value)* augmenter
appreciation [əpriːʃɪ'eɪʃən] *n* (**a**) *(gratitude)* gratitude *f*, reconnaissance *f*; **in a. of** en reconnaissance de (**b**) *(understanding)* conscience *f*; **she has no a. of what is involved** elle ne se rend pas compte de ce que cela implique (**c**) *(review, assessment)* critique *f*; **a musical/wine a. society** une société d'amateurs de musique/de vin (**d**) *Fin* **a. of assets** plus-value *f* d'actif
appreciative [ə'priːʃɪətɪv] *adj* (**a**) *(grateful)* reconnaissant(e); **to be a. of sb's help/efforts** être recon-

naissant à qn de son aide/des ses efforts (**b**) *(review)* élogieux(euse); *(response)* favorable; **the audience were very a.** le public a beaucoup aimé; **to be a. of sth** apprécier qch
apprehend [æprɪ'hend] *vt* (**a**) *Law (arrest)* appréhender (**b**) *Formal (understand)* comprendre
apprehension [æprɪ'henʃən] *n* (**a**) *(fear)* appréhension *f* (**b**) *Law (arrest)* arrestation *f*
apprehensive [æprɪ'hensɪv] *adj* inquiet(ète); **to be a. about sth/doing sth** appréhender qch/de faire qch
apprentice [ə'prentɪs] **1** *n* apprenti(e) *m,f*
2 *vt* **to a. sb to sb** placer qn en apprentissage chez qn
apprenticeship [ə'prentɪʃɪp] *n also Fig* apprentissage *m*; **to serve one's a.** faire ses premières armes
approach [ə'prəʊtʃ] **1** *n* (**a**) *(coming) (of person, season)* approche *f*; **to make an a. to sb** *(proposal)* faire une proposition à qn (**b**) *(method)* approche *f* (**to** de); **let's try a different a.** essayons d'aborder le problème différemment (**c**) *(route of access)* voie *f* d'accès; **the approaches to a town** les abords *mpl* d'une ville; **a. road** voie d'accès
2 *vt* (**a**) *(get nearer to)* approcher de; **I'm approaching forty-five** je vais sur mes quarante-cinq ans (**b**) *(go up to)* aborder; *(organization)* approcher; **to be easy/difficult to a.** être d'un abord facile/difficile (**c**) *(problem)* aborder
3 *vi* approcher
approachable [ə'prəʊtʃəbəl] *adj (person)* d'un abord facile
approaching [ə'prəʊtʃɪŋ] *adj (holiday, season)* qui approche; *(car)* qui vient en sens inverse
appropriate¹ [ə'prəʊprɪət] *adj (suitable)* approprié(e) (**to** à); *(moment)* opportun(e)
appropriate² [ə'prəʊprɪeɪt] *vt* (**a**) *(take, steal)* s'approprier (**b**) *(set aside) (money, funds)* affecter (**to** à)
appropriately [ə'prəʊprɪətlɪ] *adv (suitably)* de manière appropriée; *(properly)* convenablement
appropriation [əprəʊprɪ'eɪʃən] *n (of funds)* affectation *f*
approval [ə'pruːvəl] *n* approbation *f*; **to meet with sb's a.** obtenir l'approbation de qn; *Com* **on a.** à l'essai
approve [ə'pruːv] *vt (action, proposal)* approuver; *(treaty)* ratifier
►**approve of** *vt insep* approuver; **I don't a. of your friends** tes amis ne me plaisent pas; **she doesn't a. of them smoking** elle n'aime pas qu'ils fument
approving [ə'pruːvɪŋ] *adj* approbateur(trice)
approx *(abbr* **approximately)** env.
approximate 1 *adj* [ə'prɒksɪmɪt] approximatif(ive)
2 *vi* [ə'prɒksɪmeɪt] **to a. to sth** se rapprocher de qch
approximately [ə'prɒksɪmətlɪ] *adv* approximativement, environ
approximation [əprɒksɪ'meɪʃən] *n* approximation *f*
Apr *(abbr* **April)** avril
APR [eɪpiː'ɑː(r)] *n Fin (abbr* **annual percentage rate)** TEG *m*
apricot ['eɪprɪkɒt] *n (fruit)* abricot *m*; **a. tree** abricotier *m*
April ['eɪprɪl] *n* avril *m*; **A. showers** ≃ giboulées *fpl* de mars; **A. Fool's Day** le premier avril; *see also* **May**

> **April Fool's Day**
> En Grande-Bretagne, le premier avril est l'occasion de farces en tous genres; en revanche, la tradition du poisson en papier n'existe pas.

apron ['eɪprən] n (a) (clothing) tablier m; **he's still tied to his mother's a. strings** (dependent on her) il est toujours pendu aux jupes de sa mère (b) Aviat aire f de stationnement

apt [æpt] adj (a) (word, description) juste (b) (likely) **to be a. to do sth** avoir tendance à faire qch

aptitude ['æptɪtjuːd] n aptitude f, don m; **to have an a. for sth** avoir une aptitude ou un don pour qch; **a. test** test m d'aptitude

aptly ['æptlɪ] adv (described) justement; (chosen) bien

aquamarine [ækwəmə'riːn] **1** n (gem) aigue-marine f **2** adj (colour) bleu vert inv

aquarium [ə'kweərɪəm] n aquarium m

Aquarius [ə'kweərɪəs] n le Verseau; **to be (an) A.** être (du) Verseau

aquarobics [ækwə'rəʊbɪks] n aquagym f

aquatic [ə'kwætɪk] adj aquatique

aqueduct ['ækwɪdʌkt] n aqueduc m

aquiline ['ækwɪlaɪn] adj aquilin(e)

Arab ['ærəb] **1** n Arabe mf **2** adj arabe

> ### Arab
> En anglais le mot "Arab" désigne l'ensemble des ressortissants des pays de culture arabe, et surtout de l'Arabie Saoudite. Il n'a pas le sens restreint de "Maghrébin" que l'on rencontre souvent en français: "the firm was bought by a wealthy Arab family".

Arabia [ə'reɪbɪə] n l'Arabie f

Arabian [ə'reɪbɪən] adj arabe; **the A. Sea** la mer d'Oman

Arabic ['ærəbɪk] **1** n (language) arabe m **2** adj arabe; **A. numerals** chiffres mpl arabes

arable ['ærəbəl] adj arable

arachnid [ə'ræknɪd] n Zool arachnide m

arbiter ['ɑːbɪtə(r)] n (in dispute) arbitre m; **the a. of taste** l'arbitre des élégances

arbitrary ['ɑːbɪtrərɪ] adj arbitraire

arbitrate ['ɑːbɪtreɪt] **1** vt arbitrer **2** vi servir d'arbitre (**between** entre)

arbitration [ɑːbɪ'treɪʃən] n arbitrage m; **to go to a.** (of parties) avoir recours à l'arbitrage

arbitrator ['ɑːbɪtreɪtə(r)] n médiateur(trice) m,f

arc [ɑːk] n arc m; **a. lamp** lampe f à arc

arcade [ɑː'keɪd] n (a) (for shopping) galerie f marchande (b) Archit galerie f

arch¹ [ɑːtʃ] **1** n (a) Archit arche f (b) (of foot) voûte f plantaire; **to have fallen arches** avoir les pieds plats **2** vt **to a. one's back** (inwards) se cambrer; (outwards) se voûter

arch² adj **a. enemy** ennemi(e) m,f juré(e)

arch³ adj (mischievous) espiègle

archaeological, Am **archeological** [ɑːkɪə'lɒdʒɪkəl] adj archéologique

archaeologist, Am **archeologist** [ɑːkɪ'ɒlədʒɪst] n archéologue mf

archaeology, Am **archeology** [ɑːkɪ'ɒlədʒɪ] adj archéologie f

archaic [ɑː'keɪɪk] adj archaïque

archangel ['ɑːkeɪndʒəl] n archange m

archbishop [ɑːtʃ'bɪʃəp] n archevêque m

archduke [ɑːtʃ'djuːk] n archiduc m

archeological, archeologist etc Am = archaeological, archaeologist etc

archer ['ɑːtʃə(r)] n archer m

archery ['ɑːtʃərɪ] n tir m à l'arc

archetypal [ɑːkɪ'taɪpəl] adj **the a. English village** l'archétype m du village anglais

archetype ['ɑːkɪtaɪp] n archétype m

Archimedes [ɑːkɪ'miːdɪz] n Archimède m

archipelago [ɑːkɪ'peləgəʊ] (pl **archipelagoes** or **archipelagos**) n archipel m

architect ['ɑːkɪtekt] n architecte mf; **he was the a. of his own downfall** il a été l'artisan de sa propre ruine

architecture ['ɑːkɪtektʃə(r)] n architecture f

archives ['ɑːkaɪvz] npl archives fpl

archway ['ɑːtʃweɪ] n arche f

arctic ['ɑːktɪk] **1** n **the A.** l'Arctique m; **the A. Circle** le cercle (polaire) arctique; **the A. Ocean** l'océan m Arctique **2** adj (a) (climate) arctique (b) Fam (very cold) **a spell of a. weather** un froid polaire

ardent ['ɑːdənt] adj (desire, love) ardent(e); (admirer, believer) fervent(e)

ardour ['ɑːdə(r)] n (of desire, love) ardeur f; (religious) ferveur f

arduous ['ɑːdjʊəs] adj ardu(e), pénible

are [ɑː(r)] plural and 2nd pers singular of **be**

area ['eərɪə] n (a) (surface) superficie f, surface f; **the room is 24 square metres in a.** la pièce a une surface de 24 mètres carrés (b) (region) région f; (of countryside, forest) zone f; (in building) partie f; (of town, city) quartier m; (of knowledge) domaine m; **the London a.** la région de Londres; **an a. of agreement** un terrain d'entente; Am Tel **a. code** indicatif m; Com **a. manager** directeur(trice) m,f régional(e)

arena [ə'riːnə] n (a) (Roman) arène f; (stadium) stade m (b) (area of activity) (economic, international) scène f

aren't [ɑːnt] (a) = are not (b) **a. I?** = am I not?

Argentina [ɑːdʒən'tiːnə] n l'Argentine f

Argentine ['ɑːdʒəntaɪn] **1** n (person) Argentin(e) m,f; Old-fashioned **the A.** (country) l'Argentine f **2** adj argentin(e)

Argentinian [ɑːdʒən'tɪnɪən] **1** n Argentin(e) m,f **2** adj argentin(e)

arguable ['ɑːgjʊəbəl] adj (a) (questionable) discutable; **it is a. whether it would have made any difference** on peut se demander si ça aurait changé quoi que ce soit (b) (conceivable) défendable; **it is a. that...** on pourrait soutenir que...

arguably ['ɑːgjʊəblɪ] adv **it's a. the city's best restaurant** on peut dire que c'est le meilleur restaurant de la ville

argue ['ɑːgjuː] **1** vt (position) défendre; **to a. the case for sth** plaider en faveur de qch; **to a. that...** soutenir que... **2** vi (quarrel) se disputer (**about** à propos de); **to a. for sth** plaider en faveur de qch; **to a. against sb/sth** s'opposer à qn/qch; **don't a.!** ne discute pas!, pas de discussion!

argument ['ɑːgjʊmənt] n (a) (quarrel) dispute f; (debate) discussion f; **to have an a. about sth** (quarrel) se disputer à propos de qch; (debate) discuter de qch; **to get into an a.** se disputer; **and I don't want any arguments!** et pas de discussion! (b) (reason) **an a. for/against doing sth** une raison de faire/de ne pas faire qch (**c**) *(point)* argument *m* (**for/against** en faveur de/contre); **for a.'s sake** à titre d'exemple

argumentative [ɑːgjʊ'mentətɪv] *adj (person)* qui a l'esprit de contradiction; *(tone)* agressif(ive)

aria ['ɑːrɪə] *n* aria *f*

arid ['ærɪd] *adj* aride

Aries ['eəriːz] *n* le Bélier; **to be (an) A.** être (du) Bélier

arise [e'raɪz] *(pt* **arose** [ə'rəʊz]*, pp* **arisen** [ə'rɪzən]) *vi (of problem, possibility)* surgir; *(of situation)* naître; *(of question)* se poser; *(of storm)* se lever; **if the need arises** si le besoin s'en fait sentir

aristocracy [ærɪs'tɒkrəsɪ] *n* aristocratie *f*

aristocrat ['ærɪstəkræt] *n* aristocrate *mf*

aristocratic [ærɪstə'krætɪk] *adj* aristocratique

Aristotle [ærɪs'tɒtəl] *n* Aristote

arithmetic [ə'rɪθmətɪk] *n (calculations)* calculs *mpl; (subject)* calcul *m,* arithmétique *f*

arithmetical [ærɪθ'metɪkəl] *adj* arithmétique; **an a. error** une erreur de calcul

ark [ɑːk] *n* arche *f*

arm [ɑːm] **1** *n* (**a**) *(of person, chair, garment)* bras *m;* **to carry sb/sth in one's arms** porter qn/qch dans ses bras; **to take sb's a.** prendre qn par le bras; **a. in a.** bras dessus bras dessous; **to receive sb with open arms** *(warmly welcome)* recevoir qn à bras ouverts; *Fig* **to keep sb at a.'s length** tenir qn à distance (**b**) **arms** *(weapons)* armement *m;* **arms race** course *f* aux armements (**c**) *(in heraldry)* **(coat of) arms** armoiries *fpl*
2 *vt (person, country)* armer; **to a. oneself with the facts** s'armer de faits

armadillo [ɑːmə'dɪləʊ] *(pl* **armadillos**) *n* tatou *m*

Armageddon [ɑːmə'gedən] *n* l'Apocalypse *f; Fig* apocalypse *f*

armaments ['ɑːməmənts] *npl* armement *m,* armes *fpl*

armband ['ɑːmbænd] *n (at funeral, for swimming)* brassard *m*

armchair ['ɑːmtʃeə(r)] *n* fauteuil *m;* **an a. sportsman** un sportif en chambre

armed [ɑːmd] *adj* armé(e) (**with** de); **a. forces** forces *fpl* armées; **a. robbery** vol *m* à main armée

Armenia [ɑː'miːnɪə] *n* l'Arménie *f*

Armenian [ɑː'miːnɪən] **1** *n* Arménien(enne) *m,f*
2 *adj* arménien(enne)

armhole ['ɑːmhəʊl] *n* emmanchure *f*

armistice ['ɑːmɪstɪs] *n* armistice *m;* **A. day** l'Armistice

armour ['ɑːmə(r)] *n* (**a**) *(of knight)* armure *f;* **suit of a.** armure complète (**b**) *Mil (of tank)* blindage *m; (tanks)* blindés *mpl*

armoured car ['ɑːməd'kɑː(r)] *n* voiture *f* blindée

armoury ['ɑːmərɪ] *(pl* **armouries**) *n (store)* arsenal *m*

armpit ['ɑːmpɪt] *n* aisselle *f*

army ['ɑːmɪ] *(pl* **armies**) *n* armée *f; (land forces)* armée de terre; **to be in the a.** être dans l'armée, être militaire

aroma [ə'rəʊmə] *n* arôme *m*

aromatic [ærəʊ'mætɪk] *adj* aromatique

arose [ə'rəʊz] *pt of* **arise**

around [ə'raʊnd] **1** *prep* (**a**) *(position)* autour de; **a. the table** autour de la table; **there were hills all a. the town** il y avait des collines tout autour de la ville; **there were posters all a. the walls** il y avait des posters partout sur les murs; **a. here** par ici
(**b**) *(motion)* autour de; **to look a. a room** jeter un coup d'œil à une pièce; **to travel a. the world** faire

le tour du monde; **to walk a. the town/the streets** se promener en ville/dans les rues
2 *adv* (**a**) *(surrounding)* autour; **a garden with a fence a.** un jardin avec une clôture autour; **all a.** tout autour; **for miles a.** à des kilomètres à la ronde
(**b**) *(in different directions)* **to walk a.** se promener; **there were books lying all a.** il y avait des livres qui traînaient partout
(**c**) *(in the general area)* dans le coin; **is Jack a.?** est-ce que Jack est dans le coin?; **there was nobody a.** il n'y avait personne
(**d**) *(approximately)* environ; **at a. one o'clock** vers une heure

arousal [ə'raʊzəl] *n (sexual)* excitation *f; (of interest, suspicion)* éveil *m*

arouse [ə'raʊz] *vt (sleeping person)* réveiller; *(emotion, desire, suspicion)* éveiller; *(enthusiasm, opposition)* soulever; *(sexually)* exciter

arraign [ə'reɪn] *vt Law* traduire en justice

arraignment [ə'reɪnmənt] *n Law* lecture *f* de l'acte d'accusation

arrange [ə'reɪndʒ] **1** *vt* (**a**) *(put in order)* arranger; *(classify)* ranger (**b**) *(organize) (wedding, meeting)* arranger; *(time, date)* fixer; *(accommodation)* s'occuper de; *(outing)* organiser; *(one's affairs)* mettre en ordre; **to a. where to go/what to do** prévoir où aller/quoi faire; **it was arranged that...** il a été prévu que...; **an arranged marriage** un mariage arrangé
2 *vi* **to a. to do sth** s'arranger pour faire qch; *(with someone else)* convenir *ou* prévoir de faire qch; **they arranged for a taxi to meet me** ils se sont arrangés pour qu'un taxi vienne me chercher

arrangement [ə'reɪndʒmənt] *n* (**a**) *(of objects, furniture)* disposition *f* (**b**) *(plan)* arrangement *m;* **to make arrangements** prendre des dispositions, faire le nécessaire; **I've made all the arrangements** j'ai tout arrangé (**c**) *(agreement)* arrangement *m;* **the a. was that...** il avait été convenu que...; **viewing by a.** *(sign)* visites sur rendez-vous; **to come to an a. with sb** parvenir à un arrangement avec qn (**d**) *Mus* arrangement *m*

array [ə'reɪ] *n (collection)* collection *f,* éventail *m*

arrears [ə'rɪəz] *npl* arriéré *m;* **to be two months in a. with the rent** devoir deux mois de loyer; **to be in a. with one's work** avoir du travail en retard; **to be paid monthly in a.** être payé(e) à la fin du mois

arrest [ə'rest] **1** *n* arrestation *f;* **to be under a.** être en état d'arrestation; **to make an a.** procéder à une arrestation
2 *vt (capture, stop)* arrêter; *(attention)* attirer

arresting [ə'restɪŋ] *adj (striking)* saisissant(e)

arrival [ə'raɪvəl] *n* arrivée *f;* **on a.** à l'arrivée; **a new a.** *(at work, in club)* un nouveau venu (une nouvelle venue); *(baby)* un nouveau-né (une nouveau-née)

arrive [ə'raɪv] *vi* (**a**) *(at place)* arriver; **to a. at** *(solution, decision)* arriver à, parvenir à (**b**) *Fam (attain success)* réussir, arriver

arrogance ['ærəgəns] *n* arrogance *f*

arrogant ['ærəgənt] *adj* arrogant(e)

arrow ['ærəʊ] *n* flèche *f*

arrowhead ['ærəʊhed] *n* pointe *f* de flèche

arrowroot ['ærəʊruːt] *n Culin* arrow-root *m*

arse [ɑːs] *n Br Vulg* (**a**) *(buttocks)* cul *m;* **to make an a. of sth** saloper qch (**b**) *(stupid person)* connard (connasse) *m,f;* **to make an a. of oneself** se couvrir de ridicule

▸**arse about, arse around** *vi Vulg* déconner

arsehole ['ɑːshəʊl] *n Vulg* (**a**) *(anus)* trou *m* du cul (**b**) *(stupid person)* connard (connasse) *m,f*; **don't be such an a.!** ne fais pas le salaud (la salope)!

arsenal ['ɑːsənəl] *n* arsenal *m*; *(of devices, arguments)* panoplie *f*

arsenic ['ɑːsnɪk] *n* arsenic *m*

arson ['ɑːsən] *n* incendie *m* criminel *ou* volontaire

arsonist ['ɑːsənɪst] *n* incendiaire *mf*

art [ɑːt] *n* (**a**) *(in general)* art *m*; *(school subject)* arts *mpl* plastiques; *(college course)* beaux-arts *mpl*; **the arts in Great Britain** la création artistique en Grande-Bretagne; **arts and crafts** artisanat *m*; **a gallery** *(museum)* musée *m* d'art; *(shop)* galerie *f* d'art; **a. school** école *f* des beaux-arts, beaux-arts *mpl* (**b**) *Univ* **arts** lettres *fpl* (**c**) *(technique)* art *m*; **there's an a. to making pastry** la pâtisserie, c'est tout un art

artefact ['ɑːtɪfækt] *n (manufactured object)* objet *m*

arteriosclerosis [ɑːˈtɪərɪəʊskləˈrəʊsɪs] *n Med* artériosclérose *f*

artery ['ɑːtərɪ] *(pl* **arteries)** *n* artère *f*

artful ['ɑːtfʊl] *adj* (**a**) *(skilful) (person)* habile; *(solution, reply)* astucieux(euse) (**b**) *(cunning)* malin(igne)

arthritic [ɑːˈθrɪtɪk] *adj* arthritique

arthritis [ɑːˈraɪtɪs] *n* arthrite *f*

arthropod ['ɑːθrəppd] *n Zool* arthropode *m*

arthrosis [ɑːˈθrəʊsɪs] *n Med* arthrose *f*

artichoke ['ɑːtɪtʃəʊk] *n* (**globe**) **a.** artichaut *m*

article ['ɑːtɪkəl] **1** *n* article *m*; **a. of clothing** vêtement *m*; *Gram* **definite/indefinite a.** article défini/indéfini **2** *vt Law* mettre en apprentissage (**to** chez)

articulate¹ [ɑːˈtɪkjʊlət] *adj (person)* qui s'exprime avec facilité; *(account)* clair(e)

articulate² [ɑːˈtɪkjʊleɪt] *vt* (**a**) *(word)* articuler; **to a. one's words** articuler (**b**) *(idea, feeling)* exprimer

articulated lorry [ɑːˈtɪkjʊleɪtɪdˈlɒrɪ] *n* semi-remorque *m*

articulation [ɑːtɪkjʊˈleɪʃən] *n* articulation *f*

artificial [ɑːtɪˈfɪʃəl] *adj* artificiel(elle); **a. insemination** insémination *f* artificielle; *Comput* **a. intelligence** intelligence *f* artificielle; **a. respiration** respiration *f* artificielle; **a. sweetener** édulcorant *m* (de synthèse)

artificially [ɑːtɪˈfɪʃəlɪ] *adv* artificiellement

artillery [ɑːˈtɪlərɪ] *n* artillerie *f*

artisan [ɑːtɪˈzæn] *n* artisan *m*

artist ['ɑːtɪst] *n* artiste *mf*

artistic [ɑːˈtɪstɪk] *adj* artistique; *(temperament, person)* artiste

artistry ['ɑːtɪstrɪ] *n (of painting, game)* qualité *f* artistique; *(of painter, footballer)* art *m*

artless ['ɑːtlɪs] *adj (simple)* naturel(elle); *(clumsy)* maladroit(e)

artwork ['ɑːtwɜːk] *n (in book, magazine)* illustrations *fpl*

arty ['ɑːtɪ] *adj Fam (person)* prétentieux(euse) *(et passionné d'art)*

arum lily ['eərəmˈlɪlɪ] *n Bot* calla *f*

Aryan ['eərɪən] **1** *n* Aryen(enne) *m,f* **2** *adj* aryen(enne)

as [əz, *stressed* æz] **1** *adv* (**a**) *(with manner)* **as promised/planned** comme promis/prévu; **A as in Anne** A comme Anne

(**b**) *(in comparisons)* **as tall as me** aussi grand(e) que moi; **as white as a sheet** blanc (blanche) comme un linge; **twice as big as** deux fois plus grand que; **I came as fast as I could** je suis venu aussi vite que j'ai pu; **as much money/many people as** autant d'argent/de gens que; **as much/many as you want** autant que tu veux; **as soon as possible** dès que possible; **as recently as last week** pas plus tard que la semaine dernière

(**c**) **as if** comme si; **it isn't as if** *or* **though it's difficult** ce n'est pourtant pas compliqué; **she looked as if** *or* **though she was angry** elle avait l'air fâché; **it looks as if** *or* **though he's already left** on dirait qu'il est déjà parti

(**d**) **as well** aussi, également; **he has two cars as well as a motorbike** il a une moto et aussi deux voitures

(**e**) **as for** quant à

2 *conj* (**a**) *(with time)* **he went out as I came in** il sortit au moment où j'entrais; **as the day went on** à mesure que la journée passait; **we'll see as we go along** nous verrons au fur et à mesure; **as you get older** en vieillissant, avec l'âge; **as always** comme toujours

(**b**) *(with manner)* comme; **as I was saying** comme je disais; **do as you're told** fais ce qu'on te dit; **as often happens,...** comme c'est souvent le cas,...; **it's hard/far enough as it is** c'est assez difficile/loin comme ça; **as it were** pour ainsi dire

(**c**) *(concessive)* **late as it was,...** bien qu'il fût tard,...; **try as she might,...** elle avait beau essayer,...; **strange as it may seem,...** aussi étrange que cela puisse paraître,...; **much as I like her,...** je l'aime bien, mais...

(**d**) *(because)* puisque, comme

(**e**) *(in addition)* **mother is well, as are the children** maman va bien, et les enfants aussi

3 *prep* comme; **to work as a team** travailler en équipe; **to regard sb as a friend** considérer qn comme un ami; **I meant it as a compliment** c'était un compliment; **she used it as a bandage** elle s'en est servi comme d'un bandage; **as a woman, I think that...** en tant que femme, je pense que...

asap [eɪeseɪˈpiː] *adv (abbr* **as soon as possible)** dès que possible

asbestos [æsˈbestəs] *n* amiante *f*

asbestosis [æsbesˈtəʊsɪs] *n Med* asbestose *f*

ascend [əˈsend] **1** *vt (mountain)* gravir, faire l'ascension de; *(throne)* accéder à; *(stairs)* gravir **2** *vi* monter

ascendancy, ascendency [əˈsendənsɪ] *n* ascendant *m*

ascendant, ascendent [əˈsendənt] *n* **to be in the a.** prospérer

Ascension [əˈsenʃən] *n Rel* l'Ascension *f*

ascent [əˈsent] *n also Fig* ascension *f*

ascertain [æsəˈteɪn] *vt* établir

ascetic [əˈsetɪk] **1** *n* ascète *mf* **2** *adj* ascétique

ASCII ['æskɪ] *n (abbr* **American Standard Code for Information Interchange)** ASCII *m*

ascribe [əˈskraɪb] *vt* attribuer (**to** à)

ASEAN ['æzɪæn] *n (abbr* **Association of South-East Asian Nations)** ANASE *f*

aseptic [eɪˈseptɪk] *adj* aseptique

asexual [eɪˈseksjʊəl] *adj* asexué(e)

ash¹ [æʃ] *n (tree)* frêne *m*

ash² *n (from fire, cigarette)* cendre *f*; *Rel* **A. Wednesday** mercredi *m* des Cendres

ashamed [ə'ʃeɪmd] *adj* honteux(euse); **to feel a.** avoir honte; **to be a. of** avoir honte de; **I am a. to say that...** j'avoue à ma grande honte que...; **there is nothing to be a. of** il n'y a pas de quoi avoir honte; **you ought to be a. of yourself!** tu devrais avoir honte!

ashen ['æʃən] *adj* blême

ashore [ə'ʃɔː(r)] *adv (on land)* à terre; **to go a.** débarquer

ashtray ['æʃtreɪ] *n* cendrier *m*

Asia ['eɪʒə] *n* l'Asie *f*; **A. Minor** l'Asie mineure

Asian ['eɪʒən] **1** *n* Asiatique *mf*; *Br (from Indian sub-continent)* = personne originaire du sous-continent indien
 2 *adj* asiatique; *Br (from Indian sub-continent)* du sous-continent indien; *Am* **A. American** Américain(e) *m,f* d'origine asiatique

> **Asian**
> Pour les Britanniques, "Asian" désigne le plus souvent les habitants de l'Inde et des pays limitrophes: ainsi, l'expression "the Asian community in Edinburgh" fait référence aux personnes d'origine indienne, pakistanaise et bangladaise qui habitent Édimbourg.

Asiatic [eɪʒɪ'ætɪk] **1** *n* Asiatique *mf*
 2 *adj* asiatique

aside [ə'saɪd] **1** *adv* **to stand a.** s'écarter; **to take sb a.** prendre qn à part; **to put** *or* **set sth a.** *(reserve)* mettre qch de côté; **politics a.,...** toute question de politique mise à part,...; **a. from** à part
 2 *n* aparté *m*

asinine ['æsɪnaɪn] *adj* stupide

ask [ɑːsk] **1** *vt* (**a**) *(enquire about)* demander; **to a. (sb) a question** poser une question (à qn); **to a. sb sth** demander qch à qn; **to a. sb the time** demander l'heure à qn; **to a. sb the way** demander son chemin à qn; **don't a. me!** je n'en ai pas la moindre idée!
 (**b**) *(request)* demander; **to a. sb for sth** demander qch à qn; **to a. to do sth** demander à faire qch; **to a. sb to do sth** demander à qn de faire qch; **to a. a favour of sb, to a. sb a favour** demander un service à qn; **if it isn't asking too much** si ce n'est pas trop demander; **to a. sb's permission to do sth** demander à qn la permission de faire qch
 (**c**) *(invite)* inviter; **to a. sb to lunch** inviter qn à déjeuner
 2 *vi* (**a**) *(enquire)* se renseigner (**about** sur)
 (**b**) *(request)* demander; **you only have to a.!** il n'y a qu'à demander!; **to a. for sth** demander qch; *Fam* **he was asking for it** il l'a cherché

▸**ask after** *vt insep* demander des nouvelles de

askance [ə'skæns] *adv* **to look a. at sb** regarder qn de travers

askew [ə'skjuː] *adv* de travers

asking ['ɑːskɪŋ] *n* **it's yours for the a.** il suffit de le demander pour l'obtenir; **a. price** prix *m* demandé

ASL [eɪes'el] *n (abbr* **American Sign Language)** = langage par signes d'origine américaine

asleep [ə'sliːp] *adj* **to be a.** dormir; **to fall a.** s'endormir; **to be fast** *or* **sound a.** dormir profondément

asocial [eɪ'səʊʃəl] *adj* asocial(e)

asparagus [ə'spærəgəs] *n* asperge *f*

aspect ['æspekt] *n* (**a**) *(of problem, subject)* aspect *m*
 (**b**) *(of building)* exposition *f*

asperity [æ'sperɪtɪ] *n (of character, voice)* rudesse *f*

aspersions [ə'spɜːʃənz] *npl* **to cast a. on sth** dénigrer qch; **to cast a. on sb's honour** porter atteinte à l'honneur de qn

asphalt ['æsfælt] *n* asphalte *m*

asphyxiate [æs'fɪksɪeɪt] *vt* asphyxier

asphyxiation [æsfɪksɪ'eɪʃən] *n* asphyxie *f*

aspic ['æspɪk] *n Culin* gelée *f*; **it was as if the house had been preserved in a.** la maison donnait l'impression de n'avoir pas subi le passage du temps

aspirate ['æspərət] *adj Ling* aspiré(e)

aspiration [æspɪ'reɪʃən] *n (ambition)* aspiration *f*

aspire [ə'spaɪə(r)] *vi* **to a. to do sth** aspirer à faire qch

aspirin ['æsprɪn] *n* aspirine *f*

aspiring [ə'spaɪərɪŋ] *adj* **to be an a. actor/writer** aspirer à devenir acteur/écrivain

ass¹ [æs] *n* (**a**) *(animal)* âne *m* (**b**) *Fam (idiot)* imbécile *mf*; **to make an a. of oneself** se ridiculiser

ass² *n Am very Fam (behind)* cul *m*

assail [ə'seɪl] *vt* (**a**) *(attack)* attaquer (**b**) **to a. sb with questions** assaillir qn de questions; **assailed by doubts** en proie au doute

assailant [ə'seɪlənt] *n* agresseur *m*

assassin [ə'sæsɪn] *n* assassin *m*

assassinate [ə'sæsɪneɪt] *vt* assassiner

assassination [əsæsɪ'neɪʃən] *n* assassinat *m*

assault [ə'sɔːlt] **1** *n Mil* assaut *m* (**on** de); *Law* agression *f* (**on** contre); *(criticism)* attaque *f* (**on** contre); *Mil* **a. course** parcours *m* du combattant
 2 *vt Law* agresser; **to be sexually assaulted** être victime d'une agression sexuelle

assemble [ə'sembəl] **1** *vt (people)* rassembler, réunir; *(facts, objects)* rassembler; *(machine, furniture)* assembler, monter
 2 *vi (of people)* se rassembler, se réunir

assembly [ə'semblɪ] *(pl* **assemblies)** *n* (**a**) *(gathering)* assemblée *f*; *Br Sch* = rassemblement des élèves d'une école avant d'entrer en classe; **a. hall** *(in school)* = salle où se réunissent les élèves d'une école (**b**) *(of machine, furniture)* assemblage *m*, montage *m*; **a. instructions** instructions *fpl* de montage; *Ind* **a. line** chaîne *f* de montage

assent [ə'sent] **1** *n* assentiment *m*
 2 *vi* donner son assentiment (**to** à)

assert [ə'sɜːt] *vt (one's rights, point of view)* faire valoir; **to a. one's authority** asseoir son autorité; **to a. oneself** s'imposer; **to a. that...** affirmer que...

assertion [ə'sɜːʃən] *n (statement)* déclaration *f*; *(of right)* revendication *f*

assertive [ə'sɜːtɪv] *adj* assuré(e); **he's not a. enough** ne s'affirme pas assez

assertiveness [ə'sɜːtɪvnɪs] *n* assurance *f*; **a. training** = cours pour adultes visant à améliorer la confiance en soi des participants

assess [ə'ses] *vt* (**a**) *(value, damage)* estimer; **to a. sb's income** *(for tax purposes)* évaluer les revenus de qn (**b**) *(situation, impact)* étudier, analyser; *(performance, ability, quality)* évaluer

assessment [ə'sesmənt] *n* (**a**) *(of value)* estimation *f*; *(for insurance or tax purposes)* évaluation *f* (**b**) *(of situation)* étude *f*, analyse *f*; *(of performance, ability, quality)* évaluation *f*

assessor [ə'sesə(r)] *n Fin* contrôleur *m*

asset ['æset] *n* (**a**) *(advantage)* atout *m*; **she is a great a. to the firm** c'est quelqu'un de très précieux pour l'entreprise (**b**) *Fin* **assets** actif *m*, avoir *m*; *(personal)* patrimoine *m*; **assets and liabilities** l'actif et le passif; *Fin* **a. stripper** = personne qui rachète une société pour profiter de la réalisation de l'actif; *Fin* **a. stripping** démembrement *m (suite au rachat d'une société)*

assiduous [ə'sɪdjʊəs] *adj* assidu(e)

assign [ə'saɪn] *vt (task)* assigner (**to** à); *(funds)* affecter (**to** à); *(importance)* attacher (**to** à); **to a. sb to do sth** charger qn de faire qch

assignation [æsɪg'neɪʃən] *n Formal or Hum (meeting)* rendez-vous *m*

assignment [ə'saɪnmənt] *n* (**a**) *(of funds)* affectation *f*; *(of tasks)* distribution *f* (**b**) *(task) Sch* devoir *m*; *Journ* reportage *m*; *(of soldier, politician)* mission *f*

assimilate [ə'sɪmɪleɪt] **1** *vt* assimiler **2** *vi (of immigrants)* s'assimiler, s'intégrer

assimilation [əsɪmɪ'leɪʃən] *n* assimilation *f*

assist [ə'sɪst] **1** *vt (person)* aider, assister; *(process, development)* faciliter; **to a. sb in doing** *or* **to do sth** aider qn à faire qch **2** *vi* aider

assistance [ə'sɪstəns] *n* aide *f*, secours *m*; **to come to sb's a.** venir en aide à qn; **can I be of any a.?** puis-je être utile à quelque chose?

assistant [ə'sɪstənt] *n* assistant(e) *m,f*; **(shop) a.** vendeur(euse) *m,f*; **a. manager** sous-directeur(trice) *m,f*

assizes [ə'saɪzɪz] *npl Law* assises *fpl*

associate 1 *n* [ə'səʊsɪət] *(in business)* associé(e) *m,f*; *(in crime)* complice *mf* **2** *adj* [ə'səʊsɪət] *(company)* associé(e) **3** *vt* [ə'səʊsɪeɪt] (**a**) *(mentally)* associer (**with** à) (**b**) **to be associated with** avoir des liens avec **4** *vi* [ə'səʊsɪeɪt] **to a. with sb** fréquenter qn

associated [ə'səʊsɪeɪtɪd] *adj* associé(e); **a. company** société *f* affiliée

association [əsəʊsɪ'eɪʃən] *n* association *f*; **the name has unfortunate associations for her** ce nom lui évoque des souvenirs désagréables; **in a. with** en association avec

assorted [ə'sɔːtɪd] *adj (colours, flavours)* variés(ées); *(biscuits, sweets)* assortis(ies)

assortment [ə'sɔːtmənt] *n* assortiment *m*

assuage [ə'sweɪdʒ] *vt Lit* apaiser

assume [ə'sjuːm] *vt* (**a**) *(suppose)* supposer; **I a. he'll come** je suppose qu'il viendra; **he was assumed to be rich** on le supposait riche; **let us a. that...** supposons *ou* mettons que... (**b**) *(power, control)* prendre; *(name)* adopter; **to a. responsibility for sth** devenir responsable de qch; **an assumed name** un nom d'emprunt (**c**) *(appearance, shape)* prendre

assumption [ə'sʌmpʃən] *n* (**a**) *(supposition)* supposition *f*; **to work on the a. that...** se fonder sur l'hypothèse que... (**b**) *(of power)* prise *f* (**c**) *Rel* **the A.** l'Assomption *f*

assurance [ə'ʃʊərəns] *n* (**a**) *(guarantee)* assurance *f*; **he gave me his a.** il me l'a assuré (**b**) *(confidence)* assurance *f* (**c**) *Br (insurance)* assurance *f*

assure [ə'ʃʊə(r)] *vt* assurer; **to a. sb of sth** assurer qn de qch

assured [ə'ʃʊəd] *adj (victory, success)* assuré(e), certain(e); *(person, performance)* plein(e) d'assurance

assuredly [ə'ʃʊərɪdlɪ] *adv* assurément

asterisk ['æstərɪsk] *n* astérisque *m*

asteroid ['æstərɔɪd] *n* astéroïde *m*

asthma ['æsmə] *n* asthme *m*

asthmatic [æs'mætɪk] *n & adj* asthmatique *mf*

astonish [ə'stɒnɪʃ] *vt* étonner; **to be astonished at** *or* **by sth** être étonné(e) par qch

astonishing [ə'stɒnɪʃɪŋ] *adj (amazing)* incroyable; *(performance)* extraordinaire; **I find it a. that...** je m'étonne que... + *subjunctive*

astonishment [ə'stɒnɪʃmənt] *n* étonnement *m*; **to my a.** à mon grand étonnement

astound [ə'staʊnd] *vt* stupéfier

astounding [ə'staʊndɪŋ] *adj* stupéfiant(e), incroyable

astral ['æstrəl] *adj* astral(e)

astray [ə'streɪ] *adv* **to go a.** *(become lost)* s'égarer; **to lead sb a.** *(morally)* détourner qn du droit chemin

astride [ə'straɪd] *prep* à cheval sur, à califourchon sur

astringent [ə'strɪndʒənt] **1** *n Med* astringent *m* **2** *adj Med* astringent(e); *Fig (person, voice)* caustique

astrologer [ə'strɒlədʒə(r)] *n* astrologue *mf*

astrological [æstrə'lɒdʒɪkəl] *adj* astrologique

astrology [ə'strɒlədʒɪ] *n* astrologie *f*

astronaut ['æstrənɔːt] *n* astronaute *mf*

astronomer [ə'strɒnəmə(r)] *n* astronome *mf*

astronomic(al) [æstrə'nɒmɪk(əl)] *adj* astronomique

astronomy [ə'strɒnəmɪ] *n* astronomie *f*

astrophysics [æstrəʊ'fɪzɪks] *n* astrophysique *f*

Astroturf® ['æstrəʊtɜːf] *n* gazon *m* artificiel

astute [ə'stjuːt] *adj* astucieux(euse)

astutely [ə'stjuːtlɪ] *adv* astucieusement

asunder [ə'sʌndə(r)] *adv Lit* **to tear sth a.** mettre qch en pièces

asylum [ə'saɪləm] *n* asile *m*; **(mental) a.** asile d'aliénés

asylum-seeker [ə'saɪləm'siːkə(r)] *n* demandeur(euse) *m,f* d'asile

asymmetric(al) [eɪsɪ'metrɪk(əl)] *adj* asymétrique

asymmetry [eɪ'sɪmɪtrɪ] *n* asymétrie *f*

at [æt, *unstressed* ət] *prep* (**a**) *(with place)* à; **at the office** au bureau; **at university** à l'université; **at the station** à la gare; **at the top/bottom (of)** en haut/bas (de); **at John's (house)** chez John; **at home** chez soi, à la maison

(**b**) *(with time)* à; **at six o'clock** à six heures; **at night** la nuit; **at Christmas** à Noël; **at the beginning** au début; **at (the age of) twenty** à (l'âge de) vingt ans

(**c**) *(with price, speed)* à; **at 60 mph** ≃ à 90 km/h; **at 50p a pound** à 50 pence la livre

(**d**) *(with direction)* **to look at sb/sth** regarder qn/qch; **to shout at sb** crier après qn; **to throw sth at sb** jeter qch à qn

(**e**) *(with cause)* **to be angry at sb** être fâché(e) contre qn; **to be surprised at sth** être surpris(e) de *ou* par qch; **to be shocked at sth** être choqué(e) par qch

(**f**) *(with activity)* **to be at work/lunch** être en train de travailler/déjeuner; **she's been at it all weekend** elle n'a pas arrêté du week-end; **while you're at it** tant que tu y es; **to be good/bad at sth** *(subject)* être bon (bonne)/mauvais(e) en qch; **to be good/bad at doing sth** être/ne pas être doué(e) pour faire qch

atavistic [ætə'vɪstɪk] *adj* atavique

ate [eɪt] *pt of* **eat**

atheism ['eɪθɪɪzəm] *n* athéisme *m*

atheist ['eɪθɪɪst] *n* athée *mf*

Athens ['æθənz] *n* Athènes

athlete ['æθliːt] *n* athlète *mf*; **a.'s foot** mycose *f*

athletic [æθ'letɪk] *adj (fit)* athlétique

athletics [æθ'letɪks] *npl* athlétisme *m*

Atlantic [ət'læntık] **1** *n* **the A.** l'Atlantique *m*
2 *adj (coast)* atlantique; *(island)* de l'Atlantique; **the A. Ocean** l'océan Atlantique
atlas ['ætləs] *n* atlas *m*
ATM [eıtiː'em] *n Fin (abbr* **automated teller machine**) DAB *m*
atmosphere ['ætməsfıə(r)] *n* atmosphère *f*; *Fig* atmosphère, ambiance *f*
atmospheric [ætməs'ferık] *adj (pressure)* atmosphérique; *Fig (music, lighting)* d'ambiance
atoll ['ætɒl] *n Geog* atoll *m*
atom ['ætəm] *n* atome *m*; **a. bomb** bombe *f* atomique
atomic [ə'tɒmık] *adj* atomique; **a. bomb** bombe *f* atomique; **a. energy** énergie *f* atomique; **a. warfare** guerre *f* atomique *ou* nucléaire
▸**atone for** [ə'təʊn] *vt insep (sin, crime)* expier; *(mistake)* racheter, réparer
atonement [ə'təʊnmənt] *n (for sin, crime)* expiation *f*; *(for mistake, behaviour)* réparation *f*
atrocious [ə'trəʊʃəs] *adj (crime)* atroce; *(behaviour)* ignoble; *(meal)* infect(e); *(decision, joke)* très mauvais(e); *(weather, conditions, journey)* épouvantable
atrocity [ə'trɒsıtı] *(pl* **atrocities**) *n* atrocité *f*
atrophy ['ætrəfı] *(pt & pp* **atrophied**) *vi* s'atrophier
at-sign ['æt'saın] *n Comput & Typ* arrobas *m*
attach [ə'tætʃ] *vt (label, importance)* attacher (**to** à); *(blame, responsibility)* imputer (**to** à); *(document)* joindre (**to** à); *(employee)* détacher (**to** à); **to a. oneself to sb** ne pas lâcher qn d'une semelle; **to be attached to** *(like)* être attaché(e) à
attachment [ə'tætʃmənt] *n* (**a**) *(device)* accessoire *m* (**b**) *(secondment)* détachement *m* (**c**) *(fondness)* attachement *m*; **to form an a. to sb** s'attacher à qn (**d**) *Comput (of e-mail)* fichier *m* joint
attack [ə'tæk] **1** *n* attaque *f*; **to be** *or* **come under a.** être attaqué(e); **to launch an a. on** attaquer; **an a. of nerves** une crise de nerfs; **to have an a. of doubt** être assailli(e) par le doute
2 *vt* attaquer; *(rights)* porter atteinte à; *(problem, task)* s'attaquer à; **to be attacked** se faire attaquer
attacker [ə'tækə(r)] *n (assailant)* agresseur *m*; *(in sport)* attaquant(e) *m,f*
attain [ə'teın] *vt (goal, ambition)* réaliser; *(rank, age)* atteindre
attainable [ə'teınəbəl] *adj (goal, ambition)* réalisable
attainment [ə'teınmənt] *n (of goal, ambition)* réalisation *f*
attempt [ə'tempt] **1** *n* tentative *f*; **to make an a. at doing sth** *or* **to do sth** essayer *ou* tâcher de faire qch; **they made no a. to help** ils n'ont pas essayé d'aider; **to make an a. on sb's life** attenter à la vie de qn; **at the first a.** du premier coup
2 *vt* **to a. to do sth** essayer *ou* tenter de faire qch; **to a. a smile** essayer de sourire; *Law* **attempted murder** tentative *f* d'assassinat
attend [ə'tend] **1** *vt (meeting)* assister à; *(school)* aller à; *(of doctor)* suivre
2 *vi (be present)* être présent(e)
▸**attend to** *vt insep (matter, problem, customer)* s'occuper de
attendance [ə'tendəns] *n (presence)* présence *f*; **to be in a. on sb** s'occuper de qn; **there was a good/poor a.** il y avait beaucoup de/peu de monde; **a. register** registre *m* des présences

attendant [ə'tendənt] *n (in museum, car park)* gardien(enne) *m,f*; *(in cloakroom)* préposé(e) *m,f*; *(at petrol pump)* pompiste *mf*
attention [ə'tenʃən] *n* (**a**) *(in general)* attention *f*; **to pay a. to** *(listen to)* écouter attentivement; *(watch)* regarder attentivement; **to pay a. to detail** faire attention aux détails; **to give sb/sth one's full a.** consacrer toute son attention à qn/qch; **to attract** *or* **catch sb's a.** attirer l'attention de qn; **to draw a. to oneself** se faire remarquer; **your a. please, ladies and gentlemen** mesdames et messieurs, votre attention s'il vous plaît; **for the a. of Mr Harvey** *(in letter)* à l'attention de M. Harvey; *Med* **a. deficit disorder** troubles *mpl* de l'attention; **a. span** capacité *f* de concentration (**b**) *(repairs)* **the engine needs some a.** le moteur a besoin d'être réparé (**c**) *Mil* **a.!** garde-à-vous!; **to stand at** *or* **to a.** être au garde-à-vous
attentive [ə'tentıv] *adj (paying attention)* attentif(-ive); *(considerate)* attentionné(e) (**to** pour)
attentively [ə'tentıvlı] *adv* attentivement
attest [ə'test] **1** *vt* attester
2 *vi* **to a. to** témoigner de
attic ['ætık] *n* grenier *m*
attire [ə'taıə(r)] *n* tenue *f*
attitude ['ætıtjuːd] *n* (**a**) *(behaviour)* attitude *f* (**b**) *(opinion)* opinion *f*; **attitudes have changed** les mentalités ont changé; **what's your a. to abortion?** quelle est votre position sur l'avortement?; **to take the a. that...** considérer que...; *Com* **a. survey** enquête *f* d'attitudes (**c**) *(pose)* pose *f*; **to strike an a.** prendre une pose affectée
attn *Com (abbr* **for the attention of**) à l'attention de
attorney [ə'tɜːnı] *(pl* **attorneys**) *n Am (lawyer)* avocat(e) *m,f*
attract [ə'trækt] *vt* attirer; **I'm extremely attracted to her** elle me plaît énormément; **the thought of working for him doesn't a. me** la perspective de travailler pour lui ne m'attire guère
attraction [ə'trækʃən] *n* (**a**) *(power)* attirance *f*; **the prospect holds little a. for me** cette perspective ne m'attire guère (**b**) *(attractive aspect)* attrait *m*
attractive [ə'træktıv] *adj (person, offer)* séduisant(e); *(prospect)* attrayant(e); **do you find her a.?** est-ce qu'elle te plaît?
attribute 1 *n* ['ætrıbjuːt] attribut *m*
2 *vt* [ə'trıbjuːt] attribuer (**to** à)
attrition [ə'trıʃən] *n* usure *f*; **war of a.** guerre *f* d'usure
attuned [ə'tjuːnd] *adj* **to be a. to sth** être accoutumé(e) à qch
atypical [eı'tıpıkəl] *adj* atypique
aubergine ['əʊbəʒiːn] *n Br* aubergine *f*
auburn ['ɔːbən] *adj (hair)* auburn *inv*
auction ['ɔːkʃən] **1** *n* vente *f* aux enchères; **to put sth up for a.** mettre qch aux enchères; **a. room** salle *f* des ventes
2 *vt* vendre aux enchères
▸**auction off** *vt sep* vendre aux enchères
auctioneer [ɔːkʃə'nıə(r)] *n* commissaire-priseur *m*
audacious [ɔː'deıʃəs] *adj* audacieux(euse)
audacity [ɔː'dæsıtı] *n* audace *f*
audible ['ɔːdıbəl] *adj* audible
audience ['ɔːdıəns] *n* (**a**) *(spectators, listeners)* public *m*; **a. participation** participation *f* du public (**b**) *(meeting with monarch, Pope)* audience *f*; **to grant sb an a.** accorder une audience à qn

audio ['ɔːdɪəʊ] *adj* **a. cassette** cassette *f* audio; **a. equipment** équipement *m* sonore

audiotypist [ɔːdɪəʊ'taɪpɪst] *n* audiotypiste *mf*

audiovisual [ɔːdɪəʊ'vɪzjʊəl] *adj* audiovisuel(elle)

audit ['ɔːdɪt] *Fin* **1** *n* audit *m*
2 *vt* vérifier

audition [ɔː'dɪʃən] **1** *n* audition *f*
2 *vt & vi* auditionner

auditor ['ɔːdɪtə(r)] *n Fin* commissaire *m* aux comptes

auditorium [ɔːdɪ'tɔːrɪəm] *n (of theatre, concert hall)* salle *f*; *(lecture theatre)* amphithéâtre *m*

auditory ['ɔːdɪtrɪ] *adj* auditif(ive)

Aug *(abbr* **August***)* août

augment [ɔːg'ment] *vt* augmenter, accroître

augur ['ɔːgə(r)] *vi* **to a. well/badly** être de bon/mauvais augure

August ['ɔːgəst] *n* août *m*; *see also* **May**

august [ɔː'gʌst] *adj Lit (distinguished)* auguste

aunt [ɑːnt] *n* tante *f*

auntie, aunty ['ɑːntɪ] *(pl* **aunties***) n Fam* tata *f*, tantine *f*

au pair [əʊ'peə(r)] *n* (jeune fille *f*) au pair *f*

aura ['ɔːrə] *n* aura *f*; *(of place)* atmosphère *f*

aural ['ɔːrəl] *adj* auditif(ive)

auspices ['ɔːspɪsɪz] *npl* **under the a. of** sous l'égide de

auspicious [ɔː'spɪʃəs] *adj* prometteur(euse)

Aussie ['ɒzɪ] *n Fam* Australien(enne) *m,f*

austere [ɒ'stɪə(r)] *adj* austère

austerity [ɒ'sterɪtɪ] *n* austérité *f*

Australasia [ɒstrə'leɪʒə] *n* l'Australasie *f*

Australasian [ɒstrə'leɪʒən] *adj* d'Australasie

Australia [ɒ'streɪlɪə] *n* l'Australie *f*

Australian [ɒ'streɪlɪən] **1** *n* Australien(enne) *m,f*
2 *adj* australien(enne)

Austria ['ɒstrɪə] *n* l'Autriche *f*

Austrian ['ɒstrɪən] **1** *n* Autrichien(enne) *m,f*
2 *adj* autrichien(enne)

autarchy ['ɔːtɑːkɪ] *n* autocratie *f*

authentic [ɔː'θentɪk] *adj* authentique

authenticate [ɔː'θentɪkeɪt] *vt* authentifier

authenticity [ɔːθen'tɪsɪtɪ] *n* authenticité *f*

author ['ɔːθə(r)] *n* auteur *m*

authoritarian [ɔːθɒrɪ'teərɪən] *adj* autoritaire

authoritative [ɔː'θɒrɪtətɪv] *adj* **(a)** *(voice, manner)* autoritaire **(b)** *(work, document)* qui fait autorité

authority [ɔː'θɒrɪtɪ] *(pl* **authorities***) n* **(a)** *(power)* autorité *f*; **the authorities** les autorités *fpl*; **I'd like to speak to someone in a.** je voudrais parler à un responsable **(b)** *(authorization)* autorisation *f*; **to give sb a. to do sth** autoriser qn à faire qch; **on one's own a.** de son propre chef **(c)** *(expert)* **to be an a. on sth** faire autorité en matière de qch; **to have sth on good a.** tenir qch de source sûre

authorization [ɔːθəraɪ'zeɪʃən] *n* autorisation *f*

authorize ['ɔːθəraɪz] *vt* autoriser; **to a. sb to do sth** autoriser qn à faire qch

autism ['ɔːtɪzəm] *n* autisme *m*

autistic [ɔː'tɪstɪk] *adj* autiste

auto ['ɔːtəʊ] *(pl* **autos***) n Am* voiture *f*, auto(mobile) *f*

auto- [ɔːtəʊ] *pref* auto-

autobiographical [ɔːtəʊbaɪə'græfɪkəl] *adj* autobiographique

autobiography [ɔːtəʊbaɪ'ɒgrəfɪ] *(pl* **autobiographies***) n* autobiographie *f*

autocrat ['ɔːtəkræt] *n* autocrate *m*

autocratic [ɔːtə'krætɪk] *adj* autocratique

Autocue® ['ɔːtəkjuː] *n* téléprompteur *m*

autograph ['ɔːtəgrɑːf] **1** *n* autographe *m*; **a. album** album *m* d'autographes
2 *vt* signer, dédicacer

automat ['ɔːtəmæt] *n Am* = cafétéria équipée de distributeurs automatiques

automate ['ɔːtəmeɪt] *vt* automatiser

automatic [ɔːtə'mætɪk] **1** *n (car)* (voiture *f*) automatique *f*; *(pistol)* (pistolet *m*) automatique *m*; *(washing machine)* machine *f* à laver automatique
2 *adj* automatique; *Comput* **a. data processing** traitement *m* automatique des données; *Aviat* **a. pilot** pilote *m* automatique; *Fig* **to be on a. pilot** marcher au radar

automatically [ɔːtə'mætɪklɪ] *adv* automatiquement

automation [ɔːtə'meɪʃən] *n* automatisation *f*

automaton [ɔː'tɒmətən] *n* automate *m*

automobile ['ɔːtəməʊbiːl] *n Am* voiture *f*, auto(mobile) *f*

autonomous [ɔː'tɒnəməs] *adj* autonome

autonomy [ɔː'tɒnəmɪ] *n* autonomie *f*

autopsy ['ɔːtɒpsɪ] *(pl* **autopsies***) n* autopsie *f*

autumn ['ɔːtəm] *n* automne *m*; **in (the) a.** en automne

autumnal [ɔː'tʌmnəl] *adj* automnal(e)

auxiliary [ɔːg'zɪlɪərɪ] **1** *(pl* **auxiliaries***) (person)* auxiliaire *mf*; *Ling* auxiliaire *m*
2 *adj* auxiliaire

avail [ə'veɪl] **1** *n* **of no a.** *(not effective)* inutile; **to no a.** *(in vain)* en vain
2 *vt* **to a. oneself of sth** profiter de qch

availability [əveɪlə'bɪlɪtɪ] *n* disponibilité *f*

available [ə'veɪləbəl] *adj* disponible; **tickets are still a.** il reste des tickets; **this model is a. in black and in green** ce modèle existe en noir et en vert

avalanche ['ævəlɑːntʃ] *n also Fig* avalanche *f*

avant-garde [ævɒŋ'gɑːd] *adj* d'avant-garde, avant-gardiste

avarice ['ævərɪs] *n* avarice *f*

Ave *(abbr* **avenue***)* av.

avenge [ə'vendʒ] *vt* venger; **to a. oneself on sb** se venger sur qn

avenue ['ævɪnjuː] *n* avenue *f*; *Fig* possibilité *f*

aver [ə'vɜː(r)] *(pt & pp* **averred***) vt Lit* déclarer, affirmer

average ['ævərɪdʒ] **1** *n* moyenne *f*; **on a.** en moyenne; **above/below a.** supérieur(e)/inférieur(e) à la moyenne
2 *adj* moyen(enne)
3 *vt* atteindre la moyenne de; **to a. eight hours' work a day** travailler en moyenne huit heures par jour

▸**average out** *vi* **it'll a. out over a month** sur un mois ça s'équilibrera

▸**average out at** *vt insep* **my expenses a. out at £400 per month** mes dépenses s'élèvent en moyenne à 400 livres par mois

averse [ə'vɜːs] *adj* opposé(e) (**to** à) ; **he is not a. to a glass of wine** il prend volontiers un verre de vin

aversion [ə'vɜːʃən] *n* aversion *f*; **to have an a. to sb/sth** avoir qn/qch en aversion

avert [ə'vɜːt] *vt* **(a)** *(turn away) (eyes, thoughts)* détourner (**from** de) **(b)** *(prevent) (misfortune, accident)* éviter, prévenir

aviary ['eɪvɪərɪ] *(pl* **aviaries***) n* volière *f*

aviation [eɪvɪ'eɪʃən] *n* aviation *f*
avid ['ævɪd] *adj* avide (**for** de)
avidly ['ævɪdlɪ] *adv* avidement, avec avidité
avocado [ævə'kɑːdəʊ] *(pl* **avocados**) *n* avocat *m*
avoid [ə'vɔɪd] *vt* éviter; *(question)* esquiver; **to a. doing sth** éviter de faire qch; **to a. sb/sth like the plague** fuir qn/qch comme la peste
avoidable [ə'vɔɪdəbəl] *adj* évitable
avowed [ə'vaʊd] *adj* déclaré(e)
AWACS ['eɪwæks] *n* Mil *(abbr* **Airborne Warning and Control System**) AWACS *m*
await [ə'weɪt] *vt* attendre; *Law* **to be awaiting trial** être en instance de jugement
awake [ə'weɪk] **1** *adj* éveillé(e); **he lay a. for hours worrying** l'inquiétude l'a tenu éveillé pendant des heures; *Fig* **he was a. to the danger** il avait conscience du danger
  2 *vt (pt* **awoke** [ə'wəʊk], *pp* **awoken** [ə'wəʊkən]) réveiller
  3 *vi* s'éveiller, se réveiller; *Fig* **to a. to a danger** prendre conscience d'un danger
awaken [ə'weɪkən] *(pt* **awakened** [ə'weɪkənd], *pp* **awakened** *or* **awoken** [ə'wəʊkən]) **1** *vt* réveiller
  2 *vi* s'éveiller, se réveiller
awakening [ə'weɪkənɪŋ] *n* réveil *m*
award [ə'wɔːd] **1** *n (prize)* prix *m; Law* dommages-intérêts *mpl*
  2 *vt (prize, contract)* décerner; *(damages)* accorder; **to a. sb sth** décerner qch à qn
award-winning [ə'wɔːdwɪnɪŋ] *adj (film, book)* primé(e); *(writer, author)* lauréat(e)
aware [ə'weə(r)] *adj* **to be a. of sth** avoir conscience de qch; **to be a. that...** savoir que...; **not that I am a. of** pas que je sache; **as far as I'm a.** autant que je sache; **to become a. of sth** se rendre compte de qch; **politically a.** politisé(e)
awareness [ə'weənɪs] *n* conscience *f*
awash [ə'wɒʃ] *adj (flooded)* inondé(e)
away [ə'weɪ] *adv* (**a**) *(in space)* **a long way a.** très loin; **far a.** dans le lointain, au loin; **it's 10 kilometres a.** c'est à 10 kilomètres (d'ici); **to keep a. from** ne pas s'approcher de; **to go a.** partir, s'en aller; **go a.!** va-t'en!; **to put sth a.** ranger qch; **to take sth a. from sb** retirer qch à qn; **to stand a. from sth** se tenir à l'écart de qch; **to turn a.** se détourner
  (**b**) *(not at school, work)* **to be a.** être absent(e)
  (**c**) *(in time)* **Christmas is only two weeks a.** nous ne sommes qu'à deux semaines de Noël; **right a.** tout de suite

awe [ɔː] *n* crainte *f* mêlée de respect; **to be in a. of sb/ sth** éprouver pour qn/qch une crainte mêlée de respect
awe-inspiring ['ɔːɪnspaɪərɪŋ] *adj* imposant(e)
awesome ['ɔːsəm] *adj* (**a**) *(incredible)* impressionnant(e) (**b**) *Am Fam (wonderful)* super *inv*
awful ['ɔːfʊl] *adj* horrible, effroyable; **an a. lot of people** plein de monde; **it cost an a. lot** ça a coûté beaucoup d'argent
awfully ['ɔːflɪ] *adv* (**a**) *(very badly)* terriblement mal (**b**) *(very)* très; **I'm a. sorry** je regrette infiniment *ou* énormément; **I'm a. glad** je suis rudement content
awhile [ə'waɪl] *adv* **wait a.** attendez un moment *ou* un peu
awkward ['ɔːkwəd] *adj* (**a**) *(clumsy)* gauche, maladroit(e) (**b**) *(inconvenient) (situation)* embarrassant(e); *(silence)* gêné(e), embarrassé(e); *(location)* peu pratique; **don't be so a.** arrête de nous ennuyer; **to arrive at an a. moment** arriver au mauvais moment; *Fam* **he's an a. customer** il n'est pas commode
awl [ɔːl] *n* alène *f*, poinçon *m*
awning ['ɔːnɪŋ] *n (of shop)* store *m*
awoke [ə'wəʊk] *pt of* **awake**
awoken [ə'wəʊkən] *pp of* **awake**, **awaken**
AWOL ['eɪwɒl] *adj (abbr* **absent without leave**) **to go A.** s'absenter sans permission; *Fig* disparaître
awry [ə'raɪ] *adv* **to go a.** aller de travers
axe, *Am* **ax** [æks] **1** *n* hache *f*; *Fig* **to have an a. to grind** agir dans un but intéressé; *Fam* **two hospitals have been given the a.** on va fermer deux hôpitaux
  2 *vt Fam (jobs)* supprimer; *(costs)* réduire
axes ['æksiːz] *pl of* **axis**
axiom ['æksɪəm] *n* axiome *m*
axiomatic [æksɪə'mætɪk] *adj (evident)* évident(e)
axis ['æksɪs] *(pl* **axes** ['æksiːz]) *n Math* axe *m; Hist* **the A. powers** les puissances *fpl* de l'Axe
axle ['æksəl] *n (of vehicle)* essieu *m*
azalea [ə'zeɪlɪə] *n* azalée *f*
Azerbaijan [æzəbaɪ'dʒɑːn] *n* l'Azerbaïdjan *m*
Azerbaijani [æzəbaɪ'dʒɑːnɪ], **Azeri** [ə'zeərɪ] **1** *n* Azerbaïdjanais(e) *m,f*, Azéri(e) *m,f*
  2 *adj* azerbaïdjanais(e), azéri(e)
Azores [ə'zɔːz] *npl* **the A.** les Açores *fpl*
Aztec ['æztek] **1** *n* Aztèque *mf*
  2 *adj* aztèque
azure ['æʒə(r)] **1** *n* azur *m*
  2 *adj* d'azur, azuré(e)

B

B, b [biː] *n* (**a**) *(letter)* B, b *m inv*; **B-movie** (film *m* de) série *f* B; *Br* **B road** route *f* secondaire (**b**) *Mus* si *m* (**c**) *Sch (grade)* **to get a B** *(in exam)* avoir mention assez bien; *(in homework, essay)* ≃ avoir 12 ou 13 sur 20

b *(abbr* **born**) né(e)

BA [biːˈeɪ] *n (abbr* **Bachelor of Arts**) **to have a BA in history** ≃ avoir une licence en histoire; **John Smith BA** ≃ John Smith, licencié ès lettres/en histoire/*etc*

baa [baː] **1** *exclam* bêê!

2 *vi (pt & pp* **baaed** *or* **baa'd** [baːd]) bêler

babble ['hæbəl] **1** *vi* (**a**) *(of baby)* babiller; *(of adult)* bafouiller; **what are you babbling on about?** qu'est-ce que tu baragouines? (**b**) *(of water)* murmurer

2 *n* murmure *m*

babe [beɪb] *n* (**a**) *Lit (baby)* **b. (in arms)** bébé *m* (**b**) *Fam (woman)* belle nana *f*

baboon [bəˈbuːn] *n* babouin *m*

baby ['beɪbɪ] **1** *n (pl* **babies**) (**a**) *(child)* bébé *m*; **b. brother** petit frère *m*; **b. sister** petite sœur *f*; **b. boom** baby-boom *m*; *Am* **b. carriage** landau *m*; **b. grand** *(piano)* demi-queue *m*; **b. talk** langage *m* enfantin (**b**) *(idioms)* **to throw the b. out with the bathwater** jeter le bébé avec l'eau du bain; **to leave sb holding the b.** refiler le bébé à qn

2 *vt (pt & pp* **babied**) materner

baby-faced ['beɪbɪfeɪst] *adj* au visage poupin

babyhood ['beɪbɪhʊd] *n* petite enfance *f*

babyish ['beɪbɪʃ] *adj Pej* de bébé

baby-minder ['beɪbɪmaɪndə(r)] *n* nourrice *f*

baby-sit ['beɪbɪsɪt] *(pt & pp* **baby-sat** ['beɪbɪsæt]) *vi* faire du baby-sitting; **to b. for sb** garder l'enfant/les enfants de qn

baby-sitter ['beɪbɪsɪtə(r)] *n* baby-sitter *mf*

baby-walker ['beɪbɪwɔːkə(r)] *n* trotteur *m*

bachelor ['bætʃələ(r)] *n* célibataire *m*; **b. flat** garçonnière *f*; *Univ* **B. of Arts** *(qualification)* ≃ licence *f* ès lettres/en histoire/*etc*; *(person)* ≃ licencié(e) *m,f* ès lettres/en histoire/*etc*; *Univ* **B. of Science** *(qualification)* ≃ licence *f* ès sciences; *(person)* ≃ licencié(e) *m,f* ès sciences

bacillus [bəˈsɪləs] *(pl* **bacilli** [bəˈsɪlaɪ]) *n Biol* bacille *m*

back [bæk] **1** *n* (**a**) *(of person, animal)* dos *m*; *also Fig* **to turn one's b. on sb** tourner le dos à qn; **to sit/ stand with one's b. to sb** tourner le dos à qn; **b. pain** mal *m* de dos; **to have b. problems** avoir des problèmes de dos; **b. slapping** *(self-congratulatory)* félicitations *fpl* excessives

(**b**) *(of hand, book)* dos *m*; *(of page)* dos, verso *m*; *(of chair)* dossier *m*; *(of car)* arrière *m*; *(of throat)* fond *m*; **at the b. (of),** *Am* **in b. (of)** *(behind)* derrière; *(at far end of)* au fond (de); **the dress fastens at the b.** cette robe s'attache dans le dos; **at the b. of the book** à la fin du livre; **the b. of the neck** la nuque; **he knows London like the b. of his hand** il connaît Londres comme sa poche; *Fam* **in the b. of beyond** au diable; **b. to front** devant derrière, à l'envers

(**c**) *(in sport)* arrière *mf*

(**d**) *(idioms)* **to do sth behind sb's b.** faire qch derrière le dos de qn; **I'll be glad to see the b. of him** je serai content d'en être débarrassé; **with one's b. to the wall** *(in desperate situation)* le dos au mur; **put your b. into it!** il faut t'y mettre!; **to break the b. of the work** faire le plus gros du travail; *Fam* **the boss was on my b. all day** j'ai eu le patron sur le dos toute la journée; *Fam* **get off my b.!** fiche-moi la paix!; *Fam* **to put** *or* **get sb's b. up** braquer qn

2 *adj* (**a**) *(in space) (part, wheel)* arrière *inv*; *Fig* **to put sth on the b. burner** remettre qch à plus tard; **b. door** porte *f* de derrière; **b. garden** jardin *m* de derrière; *Fig* **he got it through the b. door** il a magouillé pour l'avoir; **the b. page** la dernière page; *Euph* **b. passage** rectum *m*; **b. road** petite route *f*; **b. room** chambre *f* du fond; *Fig* **to take a b. seat** rester discret(ète); **b. yard** *Br (enclosed area)* arrière-cour *f*; *Am (garden)* jardin *m* de derrière

(**b**) *(in time)* **b. number** *(of magazine, newspaper)* vieux numéro *m*; **b. pay** rappel *m* de salaire; **b. rent** arriéré(s) *m(pl)* de loyer

3 *adv* (**a**) *(in space)* en arrière; **to stand** *or* **step b.** reculer; **to jump b.** faire un bond en arrière; **we passed it 3 kilometres b.** nous l'avons dépassé à 3 kilomètres d'ici

(**b**) *(in return, retaliation)* **to hit sb b.** rendre son coup à qn; **to call sb b.** rappeler qn; **if you kick me I'll kick you b.** si tu me donnes un coup de pied, je te le rendrai; **to get one's own b. (on sb)** prendre sa revanche (sur qn); **to get b. at sb** prendre sa revanche sur qn

(**c**) *(to original starting point)* **to come b.** revenir; **to go b.** retourner; **when will she be b.?** quand sera-t-elle de retour?; **b. in Britain, the situation was getting serious** la situation s'aggravait en Grande-Bretagne; **(once) b. in London he phoned the hospital** de retour à Londres il a téléphoné à l'hôpital; **a few pages b.** quelques pages plus haut

(**d**) *(in time)* **a few years b.** il y a quelques années; **b. when...** à l'époque où...; **b. in 1982** en 1982; **as far b. as 1914** dès 1914

4 *vt* (**a**) *(support)* soutenir, appuyer; *(financially)* financer

(**b**) *(bet on)* parier *ou* miser sur

(**c**) *(move backwards)* **to b. one's car into the garage** entrer au garage en marche arrière; **to b. one's**

car into a lamppost rentrer dans un lampadaire en faisant marche arrière
5 *vi (move backwards)* reculer; *(in car)* faire marche arrière
▶back away *vi* reculer (**from** devant)
▶back down *vi (in argument)* céder; *(in conflict)* faire marche arrière
▶back off *vi* reculer
▶back on to *vt insep* donner sur
▶back out *vi* (**a**) *(move backwards)* sortir à reculons; *(in car)* sortir en marche arrière (**b**) *(from agreement)* se dédire
▶back up 1 *vt sep* (**a**) *(support)* soutenir, appuyer; *(story, account)* étayer (**b**) *Comput (data, file)* sauvegarder
  2 *vi* (**a**) *(move backwards)* reculer; *(in car)* faire marche arrière (**b**) *Comput* sauvegarder
backache ['bækeɪk] *n* mal *m* au dos
backbencher ['bæk'bentʃə(r)] *n Br Parl* député *m* de base

> **Backbencher**
> Les "backbenchers" sont assis aux derniers rangs de la Chambre des communes, tandis que les rangs de devant sont réservés aux ministres et aux membres du "**shadow cabinet**".

backbiting ['bækbaɪtɪŋ] *n Fam* médisance *f*
backbone ['bækbəʊn] *n* épine *f* dorsale, colonne *f* vertébrale; *Fig* **he's got no b.** il n'a rien dans le ventre
backbreaking ['bækbreɪkɪŋ] *adj (work)* éreintant(e)
backchat ['bæktʃæt], *Am* **backtalk** ['bæktɔːk] *n Fam* impertinence *f*
backcloth ['bækklɒθ] *Br* = **backdrop**
backdate ['bækdeɪt] *vt* antidater
backdrop ['bækdrɒp] *n Theat* toile *f* de fond; *Fig* **against a b. of continuing violence** avec, comme toile de fond, un climat de violence permanente
backer ['bækə(r)] *n (of political party)* partisan *m*; *(for project)* commanditaire *m*
backfire [bæk'faɪə(r)] *vi (of car)* pétarader; *Fig* **the plan backfired on them** leur plan s'est retourné contre eux
backgammon ['bækgæmən] *n* backgammon *m*
background ['bækgraʊnd] *n* (**a**) *(of scene)* arrière-plan *m*, fond *m*; **in the b.** à l'arrière-plan, dans le fond; *Fig* **to stay in the b.** rester dans l'ombre; **b. music** *(in restaurant)* musique *f* d'ambiance; **she likes b. music when she's working** elle aime travailler avec un fond sonore; **b. noise** bruit *m* de fond (**b**) *(social)* origines *fpl*; *(educational)* formation *f*; *(professional)* expérience *f*; **from a disadvantaged b.** d'un milieu défavorisé; **we need someone with a b. in computers** il nous faut quelqu'un qui s'y connaisse en informatique (**c**) *(circumstances)* contexte *m*; **against a b. of discord** dans un climat de mécontentement; **can you give me some b. information?** pouvez-vous me donner quelques renseignements?; **I need a bit more b.** il me faut plus de données; **b. reading** lectures *fpl* complémentaires
backhand ['bækhænd] *n (in tennis)* revers *m*
backhanded [bæk'hændɪd] *adj (compliment)* équivoque
backhander ['bækhændə(r)] *n Fam (bribe)* pot-de-vin *m*

backing ['bækɪŋ] *n (support)* soutien *m*; **financial b.** financement *m*
backlash ['bæklæʃ] *n (reaction)* contrecoup *m* (**against** à); *(political)* réaction *f* (**against** à)
backlit ['bæklɪt] *adj Comput* rétro-éclairé(e)
backlog ['bæklɒg] *n* retard *m*; **to have a b. of work** avoir du travail en retard
backpack ['bækpæk] **1** *n* sac *m* à dos
  2 *vi* faire de la randonnée; **she backpacked around Europe** elle a fait toute l'Europe, sac à dos
backpacker ['bækpækə(r)] *n* routard(e) *m,f*
back-pedal ['bæk'pedəl] *(pt & pp* **back-pedalled**, *Am* **back-pedaled)** *vi Fig* faire marche arrière
backrest ['bækrest] *n* dossier *m*
back-seat ['bæksiːt] *adj Fam* **b. driver** = personne qui donne des conseils au conducteur; **I don't want any b. driving** je n'ai besoin des conseils de personne quand je conduis
backside [bæk'saɪd] *n Fam* derrière *m*, postérieur *m*
backslash ['bækslæʃ] *n Comput* barre *f* oblique inversée
backsliding ['bækslaɪdɪŋ] *n Fam* rechute *f*; **she was on the lookout for any signs of b.** elle nous surveillait pour voir si nous nous relâchions
backspace ['bækspeɪs] *n Comput* retour *m* en arrière
backstage [bæk'steɪdʒ] *adv also Fig* dans les coulisses
backstairs [bæk'steəz] *n* escalier *m* de service
backstitch ['bækstɪtʃ] *n (in sewing)* point *m* de piqûre
backstreet ['bækstriːt] *n* petite rue *f*; **b. abortion** avortement *m* clandestin
backstroke ['bækstrəʊk] *n (in swimming)* dos *m* crawlé
backtalk ['bæktɔːk] *Am* = **backchat**
back-to-back [bæktə'bæk] **1** *adj (victories, meetings)* consécutifs(ives)
  2 *adv* (**a**) *(physically)* dos à dos (**b**) *(consecutively)* de suite
backtrack ['bæktræk] *vi* (**a**) *(retrace one's steps)* revenir sur ses pas (**b**) *(renege)* faire marche arrière; **to b. on a promise/decision** revenir sur une promesse/une décision
backup ['bækʌp] *n (support)* soutien *m*, appui *m*; *Mil* renforts *mpl*; *Comput* **b. copy/file** copie *f*/fichier *m* de sauvegarde; **b. system** système *m* de sauvegarde; **b. team** *(providing support)* équipe *f* technique; *(on standby)* équipe *f* de remplacement
backward ['bækwəd] **1** *adj* (**a**) *(direction)* en arrière; **she left without a b. glance** elle est partie sans se retourner (**b**) *(retarded) (child)* retardé(e), attardé(e); *(country)* en retard; *Br Fam* **he isn't b. in coming forward** il n'a pas peur de se mettre en avant
  2 *adv* = **backwards**
backwardness ['bækwədnɪs] *n (of child)* arriération *f* mentale; *(of country)* retard *m*
backwards ['bækwədz] *adv* en arrière; *(walk)* à reculons; *(fall)* à la renverse; *(read)* à l'envers; **to walk b. and forwards** aller et venir; *Fig* **to know sth b.** connaître qch à fond
backwash ['bækwɒʃ] *n (of boat)* remous *m*; *Fig* conséquences *fpl* néfastes
backwater ['bækwɔːtə(r)] *n* (**a**) *(of river)* bras *m* mort (**b**) *(isolated place)* trou *m* perdu
bacon ['beɪkən] *n* (**a**) *(food)* bacon *m* (**b**) *(idioms) Fam* **to save sb's b.** sauver la peau de qn; *Fam* **to bring**

home the b. *(earn wages)* faire bouillir la marmite; *(succeed)* réussir

bacteria [bæk'tɪərɪə] *npl* bactéries *fpl*

bacterial [bæk'tɪərɪəl] *adj* bactérien(enne)

bacteriological [bæktɪərɪə'lɒdʒɪkəl] *adj* bactériologique

bacteriology [bæktɪərɪ'ɒlədʒɪ] *n* bactériologie *f*

bad [bæd] *(comparative* **worse** [wɜːs]*, superlative* **worst** [wɜːst]) *adj* (**a**) *(of poor quality, unpleasant)* mauvais(e); **it's not b.** *(fair)* ce n'est pas mal; *(good)* ce n'est pas mal du tout; **to be b. at maths** être mauvais en maths; **to be b. at cooking** être mauvais(e) cuisinier(ère); **things are going from b. to worse** c'est de pire en pire *ou* de mal en pis; **it was a b. time to leave** ce n'était pas le moment de partir; **to have a b. time** passer un mauvais moment; **there's b. blood between them** il y a de la rancune entre eux; **to get into sb's b. books** se faire prendre en grippe par qn; **b. cheque** chèque *m* sans provision; *Fin* **b. debts** créances *fpl* douteuses; **in b. faith** de mauvaise foi; **b. feeling** animosité *f*; **I gave it up as a b. job** j'ai fini par laisser tomber; **to be a b. loser** être mauvais(e) perdant(e); **b. luck** malchance *f*; **b. manners** mauvaises manières *fpl*; **in a b. mood** de mauvaise humeur; *Fig* **she's b. news** elle ne t'/lui/*etc* apportera que des ennuis

(**b**) *(unfortunate)* **it's (really) too b.!, that's too b.!** c'est vraiment dommage!; **to have a b. effect on sth** nuire à qch; **he'll come to a b. end** il finira mal

(**c**) *(not healthy)* **to have a b. back/heart** avoir le dos/cœur fragile; **smoking is b. for you** fumer est mauvais pour la santé; **to be in a b. way** aller mal

(**d**) *(wicked)* *(person, behaviour)* méchant(e); **to use b. language** dire des gros mots

(**e**) *(serious)* *(mistake, accident)* grave; *(pain)* fort(e); **I've got a really b. headache** j'ai vraiment très mal à la tête; **to have a b. cold** avoir un gros rhume

(**f**) *(rotten)* mauvais(e); **to go b.** *(of fruit)* se gâter, pourrir; *(of milk)* tourner; *Fig* **a b. apple** une brebis galeuse

(**g**) *(guilty)* **to feel b. about sth** s'en vouloir de qch

baddie, baddy ['bædɪ] *(pl* **baddies**) *n Fam* méchant(e) *m,f*

badge [bædʒ] *n (of company, organization)* badge *m*; *(fashion accessory)* pin's *m*; *Mil* insigne *m*

badger ['bædʒə(r)] **1** *n (animal)* blaireau *m* **2** *vt* harceler; **to b. sb into doing sth** harceler qn jusqu'à ce qu'il fasse qch

bad-looking [bæd'lʊkɪŋ] *adj* **not b.** pas mal

badly ['bædlɪ] *adv (comparative* **worse** [wɜːs]*, superlative* **worst** [wɜːst]) (**a**) *(not well)* mal; **to do b.** *(in exam, competition)* avoir un mauvais résultat; **he didn't do b.** il ne s'en est pas mal tiré; **she took it very b.** elle a très mal pris la chose; **to be b. off for sth** *(lacking)* manquer de qch; **to be b. off for money** avoir des problèmes d'argent; **to get on b. (with sb)** ne pas s'entendre (avec qn) (**b**) *(seriously) (damaged, broken)* gravement; **to be b. beaten** *(physically)* être roué(e) de coups; *(in match, competition)* être battu(e) à plates coutures; **b. wounded** gravement *ou* grièvement blessé(e) (**c**) *(greatly)* **to want sth b.** avoir très envie de qch; **to be b. in need of sth** avoir grand besoin de qch

bad-mannered [bæd'mænəd] *adj* mal élevé(e)

badminton ['bædmɪntən] *n* badminton *m*

bad-mouth ['bædmaʊθ] *vt Fam* dire du mal de

badness ['bædnɪs] *n* (**a**) *(poor quality)* mauvaise qualité *f* (**b**) *(wickedness)* méchanceté *f*

bad-tempered [bæd'tempəd] *adj (person)* grincheux(euse); *(remark)* désagréable

BAF [biːr'ef] *n (abbr* **British Athletics Federation**) = fédération britannique d'athlétisme

baffle ['bæfəl] *vt* (**a**) *(confuse)* laisser perplexe; **to be baffled** être perplexe; **I'm baffled as to why she did it** je ne comprends vraiment pas pourquoi elle a fait cela (**b**) *(foil) (plot, attempt)* déjouer

baffling ['bæfəlɪŋ] *adj* déconcertant(e)

BAFTA ['bæftə] *n (abbr* **British Academy of Film and Television Arts**) = organisation qui décerne chaque année des récompenses aux personnalités du cinéma et de la télévision britanniques

bag [bæg] **1** *n* (**a**) *(of paper, plastic)* sac *m*; *(handbag)* sac à main; **bags under the eyes** des poches sous les yeux; *Fam* **to be a b. of bones** être un sac d'os; *Fig* **it's in the b.** *(of deal, victory)* c'est dans la poche (**b**) *Fam* **bags of** *(lots)* des masses de; **we've bags of time** nous avons tout le temps; **there's bags of room** il y a plein de place (**c**) *Br very Fam Pej (woman)* **old b.** vieille toupie *f*

2 *vt (pt & pp* **bagged**) (**a**) *(put in bag)* mettre en sac (**b**) *(in hunting)* abattre, tuer (**c**) *Fam (claim)* accaparer

bagel ['beɪgəl] *n* = petite couronne de pain, *Can* bagel *m*

baggage ['bægɪdʒ] *n* bagages *mpl*; *Aviat* **b. allowance** franchise *f* de bagages; *Aviat* **b. handler** bagagiste *mf*; *Aviat* **b. reclaim** retrait *m* des bagages

baggy ['bægɪ] *adj (garment) (by design)* large; *(out of shape)* déformé(e)

Baghdad [bæg'dæd] *n* Bagdad

bagpipes ['bægpaɪps] *npl* cornemuse *f*

bah [bɑː] *exclam* bah!

Bahamas [bə'hɑːməz] *npl* **the B.** les Bahamas *fpl*

Bahrain [bɑː'reɪn] *n* Bahreïn

Bahraini [bɑː'reɪnɪ] **1** *n* Bahreïni(e) *m,f* **2** *adj* bahreïni(e)

bail [beɪl] *n Law (guarantee)* caution *f*; **on b.** sous caution; **to grant sb b.** libérer qn sous caution; **to stand b. for sb** se porter garant(e) de qn

▸**bail out** *vt sep* **to b. sb out** *Law* se porter garant(e) de qn; *Fig* tirer qn d'affaire; *Fig* **to b. a company out** renflouer une entreprise

bailiff ['beɪlɪf] *n* (**a**) *Law* huissier *m* (**b**) *(on estate)* régisseur *m*

bait [beɪt] **1** *n also Fig* appât *m*; *Fig* **to rise to the b.** mordre à l'hameçon; *Fig* **to swallow** *or* **take the b.** mordre à l'hameçon **2** *vt* (**a**) *(torment)* harceler (**b**) *(attach bait to)* mettre l'appât à

baize [beɪz] *n* feutre *m*

bake [beɪk] **1** *vt (food)* (faire) cuire au four; *(clay)* cuire **2** *vi* (**a**) *(of food)* cuire (**b**) *Fam* **I'm baking** je crève de chaleur

baked [beɪkt] *adj* **b. beans** haricots *mpl* blancs à la tomate; **b. potato** pomme *f* de terre au four

baker ['beɪkə(r)] *n* boulanger(ère) *m,f*; **b.'s (shop)** boulangerie *f*; **b.'s dozen** treize à la douzaine

bakery ['beɪkərɪ] *(pl* **bakeries**) *n* boulangerie *f*

baking ['beɪkɪŋ] **1** *n* **to do some b.** *(bread)* faire du pain; *(cakes)* faire de la pâtisserie; **b. powder** levure *f* chimique; **b. sheet** *or* **tray** plaque *f* (du four); **b. soda** bicarbonate *m* de soude; **b. tin** *(for meat)* plat *m* à rôtir; *(for cakes)* moule *m* à gâteau

2 *adj Fam* **it's b. (hot)** on crève de chaleur

balaclava [bælə'klɑːvə] *n* passe-montagne *m*

balance ['bæləns] **1** *n* (**a**) *(equilibrium)* équilibre *m*; **to keep/lose one's b.** garder/perdre son équilibre; **to throw sb off b.** faire perdre son équilibre à qn; *Fig* **to catch sb off b.** prendre qn au dépourvu; **the b. of power** l'équilibre des pouvoirs; **on b.** tout compte fait; **to strike a b.** trouver le juste milieu

(**b**) *(of bank account)* solde *m*; *(in accounting)* bilan *m*; *Econ* **b. of trade/payments** balance *f* commerciale/des paiements; **b. sheet** bilan

(**c**) *(for weighing)* balance *f*; *Fig* **to hang** *or* **be in the b.** *(of decision, result)* être en jeu

2 *vt (object)* maintenir en équilibre; **he sought to b. the claims of the two parties** il a tenté de contenter les deux partis; **they b. each other well** *(of people)* ils sont complémentaires; *Fin* **to b. the books** arrêter les comptes

3 *vi* (**a**) *(physically)* tenir en équilibre

(**b**) **she couldn't get the accounts to b.** elle n'arrivait pas à équilibrer les comptes

balanced ['bælənst] *adj (account, reporting)* objectif(-ive); *(judgement)* pondéré(e); **b. diet** alimentation *f* équilibrée

balancing act ['bælənsɪŋ'ækt] *n Fig* **to do a b.** faire des acrobaties

balcony ['bælkənɪ] *(pl* **balconies***) n (in house, theatre)* balcon *m*

bald [bɔːld] *adj* (**a**) *(person)* chauve; *(tyre)* lisse; **to go b.** devenir chauve, perdre ses cheveux; *Fam* **as b. as a coot** chauve comme un œuf; **b. eagle** aigle *m* à tête blanche; **b. patch** tonsure *f* (**b**) *(plain)* **the b. truth** la vérité toute nue; **a b. statement of the facts** une simple exposition des faits

balderdash ['bɔːldədæ ʃ] *n Fam* bêtises *fpl*, balivernes *fpl*

balding ['bɔːldɪŋ] *adj* qui commence à perdre ses cheveux; **a b. man** un homme à la calvitie naissante

baldly ['bɔːldlɪ] *adv (reply)* sèchement

baldness ['bɔːldnɪs] *n* (**a**) *(of person)* calvitie *f* (**b**) *(of statement, demand)* sécheresse *f*

bale [beɪl] *n (of cloth, paper)* balle *f*; *(of hay)* botte *f*

▶**bale out** *vi (of pilot)* s'éjecter; *Fig (from difficult situation)* s'éclipser

Balearic [bælɪ'ærɪk] *n & adj* **the Balearics, the B. Islands** les (îles *fpl)* Baléares *fpl*

baleful ['beɪlfʊl] *adj* sinistre, maléfique; **she gave me a b. look** elle m'a lancé un regard noir

Bali ['bɑːlɪ] *n* Bali

Balinese [bælɪ'niːz] *adj* balinais(e)

balk [bɔːk] **1** *vt (runner, racehorse)* empêcher de passer

2 *vi* reculer (**at** devant)

Balkan ['bɔːlkən] **1** *n* **the Balkans** les Balkans *fpl*

2 *adj* balkanique

ball¹ [bɔːl] *n* (**a**) *(in game) (for football, rugby, basketball)* ballon *m*; *(for cricket, tennis, golf)* balle *f*; *(for billiards)* bille *f*, boule *f*; *(of paper, of fire)* boule *f*; *(of wool)* pelote *f*; **to roll sth (up) into a b.** mettre qch en boule; **b. bearing** *(ball)* bille *f*; *(device)* roulement *m* à billes; **b. boy/girl** *(in tennis)* ramasseur(euse) *m,f* de balles; **b. game** *(in general)* jeu *m* de balle; *Am (baseball match)* match *m* de baseball; *Fig* **that's a whole new b. game** *(irrelevant)* ça n'a rien à voir; *(different*

situation) c'est une autre paire de manches (**b**) *(of foot)* plante *f* (**c**) *Vulg* **balls** *(testicles)* couilles *fpl*; *(nonsense)* conneries *fpl*; *Fig* **to have a lot of balls** avoir des couilles (**d**) *(idioms)* **to be on the b.** *(alert)* avoir de la présence d'esprit; *(knowledgeable)* connaître son affaire; **to start the b. rolling** faire démarrer les choses; **the b. is in your court** la balle est dans votre camp; **to play b.** *(co-operate)* jouer le jeu

ball² *n (party)* bal *m*; *Fam* **to have a b.** s'éclater; **b. dress** *or* **gown** robe *f* de bal

ballad ['bæləd] *n* ballade *f*

ball-and-socket joint [bɔːlən'sɒkɪt'dʒɔɪnt] *n Anat* articulation *f* à emboîtement; *Tech* joint *m* à rotule

ballast ['bæləst] *n* (**a**) *Naut* lest *m* (**b**) *Rail* ballast *m*

ballcock ['bɔːlkɒk] *n* soupape *f* à flotteur

ballerina [bælə'riːnə] *n* ballerine *f*; **prima b.** danseuse *f* étoile

ballet ['bæleɪ] *n* danse *f* classique; *(work)* ballet *m*; **b. dancer** danseur(euse) *m,f* classique; **b. shoe** chausson *m* de danse

ballistic [bə'lɪstɪk] *adj (missile)* balistique; *Fam Fig* **to go b.** piquer une crise

ballistics [bə'lɪstɪks] *npl* balistique *f*

balloon [bə'luːn] **1** *n* (**a**) *(for party, travel)* ballon *m*; *Fam Fig* **when the b. goes up** quand il va y avoir du grabuge (**b**) *(in cartoon)* bulle *f*

2 *vi (swell)* gonfler

ballooning [bə'luːnɪŋ] *n* **to go b.** faire du ballon

balloonist [bə'luːnɪst] *n* aérostier *m*

ballot ['bælət] **1** *n (process)* tour *m* de scrutin; *(vote)* scrutin *m*, vote *m*; **to hold a b.** organiser des élections; **to put sth to a b.** soumettre qch à un vote; **b. box** urne *f*; **this matter should be decided at the b. box** c'est aux urnes que doit se décider cette question; **b. paper** bulletin *m* de vote; **b. rigging** fraude *f* électorale

2 *vt* consulter

ballpark ['bɔːlpɑːk] *Am* **1** *n* terrain *m* de base-ball

2 *adj* **a b. figure** une estimation

ballpoint ['bɔːlpɔɪnt] *n* **b. (pen)** stylo *m* (à) bille

ballroom ['bɔːlruːm] *n* salle *f* de bal; **b. dancing** danses *fpl* de salon

▶**balls up** *vt sep Br very Fam* foirer

balls-up ['bɔːlzʌp] *n Br very Fam* merdier *m*; **to make a b. of sth** foirer qch

ballyhoo [bælɪ'huː] *n Fam* battage *m* publicitaire

balm [bɑːm] *n* baume *m*

balmy ['bɑːmɪ] *adj (weather)* doux (douce)

baloney [bə'ləʊnɪ] *n Fam (nonsense)* bêtises *fpl*

balsa ['bɔːlsə] *n* balsa *m*

balsam ['bɔːlsəm] *n* balsam *m*

balsamic vinegar [bɔːl'sæmɪk'vɪnɪgə(r)] *n Culin* vinaigre *m* balsamique

Baltic ['bɔːltɪk] **1** *n* **the B.** la Baltique

2 *adj (state)* balte; **the B. Sea** la mer Baltique

balustrade [bælə'streɪd] *n* balustrade *f*

bamboo [bæm'buː] *n* bambou *m*; **b. shoots** pousses *fpl* de bambou

bamboozle [bæm'buːzəl] *vt Fam* embobiner

ban [bæn] **1** *n* interdiction *f*; **to impose a b. on sth** interdire qch

2 *vt (pt & pp* **banned***)* interdire; **to b. sb from doing sth** interdire à qn de faire qch

banal [bə'næl] *adj* banal(e)

banality [bə'nælɪtɪ] *(pl* **banalities***) n* banalité *f*

banana [bə'nɑːnə] *n* banane *f*; **b. tree** bananier *m*; *Fam* **to be/go bananas** *(mad)* être/devenir cinglé(e); *Fam* **b. republic** république *f* bananière; *also Fig* **b. skin** peau *f* de banane; **b. split** banana split *m inv*

band¹ [bænd] *n* (**a**) *(of metal)* bande *f*, bague *f*; *(around hat)* ruban *m*; *(around cigar)* bague; *(of colour)* bande, raie *f* (**b**) *Rad* bande *f* de fréquence (**c**) *(of ages, tax)* tranche *f*; *(of salaries)* catégorie *f*

band² *n* *(of friends)* groupe *m*, cercle *m*; *(of robbers)* bande *f*; *(of musicians) (rock)* groupe; *(jazz)* orchestre *m*, groupe

▶**band together** *vi* se liguer (**against** contre)

bandage ['bændɪdʒ] **1** *n* bandage *m*; *(for support)* bande *f*
  2 *vt* bander; **to b. sb's arm** bander le bras à qn

▶**bandage up** *vt sep* bander

Band-Aid® ['bændeɪd] *n Am* sparadrap *m*

B & B [biːən'biː] *n Br (abbr* **bed and breakfast***) (service)* ≃ chambre *f* avec petit déjeuner; **to stay at a B & B** ≃ prendre une chambre d'hôte

bandit ['bændɪt] *n* bandit *m*

bandmaster ['bændmɑːstə(r)] *n* chef *m* de musique

bandsman ['bændzmən] *n* musicien *m*

bandstand ['bændstænd] *n* kiosque *m* à musique

b & w *n Phot & Cin (abbr* **black and white***)* noir et blanc *inv*

bandwagon ['bændwægən] *n Fam* **to jump on the b.** prendre le train en marche

bandwidth ['bændwɪθ] *n Comput* bande *f* passante; *Rad* largeur *f* de bande

bandy¹ ['bændɪ] *adj* **to have b. legs** avoir les jambes arquées

bandy² *(pt & pp* **bandied***) vt (words, insults)* échanger; **her name was being bandied about as a possible candidate** son nom est revenu plusieurs fois parmi ceux des candidats possibles

bandy-legged [bændɪ'leg(ɪ)d] *adj* aux jambes arquées

bane [beɪn] *n* plaie *f*; **he's the b. of my life** il m'empoisonne l'existence

bang [bæŋ] **1** *n* (**a**) *(noise)* claquement *m*; *(explosion)* détonation *f*; **the door shut with a b.** la porte s'est refermée en claquant; *Fig* **to go with a b.** *(of party, event)* être un grand succès (**b**) *(blow)* coup *m* violent; **to get a b. on the head** recevoir un coup sur la tête
  2 *adv* (**a**) *Fam* **b. went my hopes of a quiet weekend** pour le week-end tranquille, c'était loupé (**b**) *Fam (exactly)* **b. in the middle** en plein milieu; **b. on time** pile à l'heure
  3 *exclam (sound of gun)* pan!; *(explosion)* boum!
  4 *vt (hit)* frapper (violemment); **to b. one's head** se cogner la tête
  5 *vi (of door, window)* claquer, battre; **the door banged shut** la porte se ferma en claquant; **to b. at** *or* **on the door** frapper à la porte à coups violents; **to b. into sth** se cogner à qch

▶**bang about, bang around** *vi (make noise)* faire du potin

▶**bang on** *vi Fam* **he's always banging on about it** il n'arrête pas de bassiner tout le monde avec cela

▶**bang up** *vt sep Br very Fam (imprison)* boucler

banger ['bæŋə(r)] *n Br* (**a**) *Fam (sausage)* saucisse *f* (**b**) *(firework)* pétard *m* (**c**) *Fam (car)* **old b.** vieille guimbarde *f*

Bangkok [bæŋ'kɒk] *n* Bangkok

Bangladesh [bæŋglə'deʃ] *n* le Bangladesh

Bangladeshi [bæŋglə'deʃɪ] **1** *n* Bangladeshi *mf*, Bangladais(e) *m,f*
  2 *adj* bangladeshi, bangladais(e)

bangle ['bæŋgəl] *n* bracelet *m*

bangs [bæŋz] *npl Am* frange *f*

banish ['bænɪʃ] *vt (exile)* bannir (**from** de); *Fig (thought, fear)* chasser

banishment ['bænɪʃmənt] *n* bannissement *m*

banister ['bænɪstə(r)] *n* rampe *f* d'escalier

banjo ['bændʒəʊ] *(pl* **banjos** *or* **banjoes***) n* banjo *m*

bank¹ [bæŋk] **1** *n* (**a**) *(of river)* berge *f*, bord *m*; *(of earth)* talus *m* (**b**) *(of clouds, fog)* banc *m* (**c**) *(of lights, switches)* rangée *f*
  2 *vt* **the road is banked by trees** la route est bordée d'arbres
  3 *vi* (**a**) *(of clouds, snow)* s'amonceler (**b**) *(of plane)* virer

bank² **1** *n* (**a**) *(financial institution)* banque *f*; **b. account** compte *m* en banque; **b. balance** solde *m*; **b. charges** frais *mpl* bancaires; **b. clerk** employé(e) *m,f* de banque; **b. draft** traite *f* bancaire; *Br* **b. holiday** jour *m* férié; **b. loan** prêt *m* bancaire; **b. manager** directeur(trice) *m,f* d'agence; *Fin* **b. rate** taux *m* de l'escompte; **b. statement** relevé *m* de banque (**b**) *(in gambling)* banque *f*; **to break the b.** faire sauter la banque; *Fig* **it won't break the b.** ça ne me/te/le/*etc* ruinera pas (**c**) *(store)* **blood b.** banque *f* du sang; **data b.** banque de données
  2 *vt (funds)* mettre *ou* déposer à la banque
  3 *vi* **to b. with sb** avoir un compte chez qn; **who do you b. with?** à quelle banque êtes-vous?

▶**bank on** *vt insep (outcome, success)* compter sur

bankbook ['bæŋkbʊk] *n* livret *m* *ou* carnet *m* de compte

banker ['bæŋkə(r)] *n Fin* banquier(ère) *m,f*; **b.'s draft** traite *f* bancaire

banking ['bæŋkɪŋ] *n (business)* opérations *fpl* bancaires; **she's in b.** elle travaille dans la banque

banknote ['bæŋknəʊt] *n* billet *m* de banque

bankroll ['bæŋkrəʊl] *vt Am (finance)* financer

bankrupt ['bæŋkrʌpt] **1** *n Fin* failli(e) *m,f*
  2 *adj* failli(e); **to be b.** être en faillite; **to go b.** faire faillite; *Fig* **to be morally b.** avoir perdu toute crédibilité
  3 *vt Law* mettre en faillite; *Fig (make poor)* ruiner

bankruptcy ['bæŋkrʌptsɪ] *n Law* faillite *f*; *Fig (poverty)* ruine *f*

banner ['bænə(r)] *n* (**a**) *(flag)* bannière *f*; **the Star-Spangled B.** la bannière étoilée; **b. headline** manchette *f* (**b**) *Comput (for advertising on the Internet)* bandeau *m*, bannière *f* publicitaire

bannister ['bænɪstə(r)] = **banister**

banns [bænz] *npl* bans *mpl*

banquet ['bæŋkwɪt] *n* banquet *m*

bantam ['bæntəm] *n* = poulet de petite taille

bantamweight ['bæntəmweɪt] *n (in boxing)* poids *m* coq

banter ['bæntə(r)] **1** *n* taquineries *fpl*
  2 *vi* plaisanter

bap [bæp] *n* petit pain *m* rond

baptism ['bæptɪzəm] *n* baptême *m*; *Fig* **a b. of fire** un baptême du feu

baptismal [bæp'tɪzməl] *adj (certificate)* de baptême; **b. font** fonts *mpl* baptismaux

Baptist ['bæptɪst] *n* baptiste *mf*

baptize [bæp'taɪz] *vt* baptiser

bar [bɑː(r)] **1** *n* (**a**) *(of metal)* barre *f*; *(of gold)* lingot *m*; *(of chocolate) (large)* tablette *f*; *(smaller)* barre; *(on window)* barreau *m*; *(of electric fire)* résistance *f*; **b. of soap** savonnette *f*, morceau *m* de savon; **to be behind bars** être derrière les barreaux; **b. chart** histogramme *m*; *Comput* **b. code** code-barres *m*
  (**b**) *(obstacle)* obstacle *m*; **to be a b. to sth** faire obstacle à qch; **to impose a b. on sth** interdire qch
  (**c**) *Law* **the B.** ≃ l'Ordre *m* des avocats, le barreau; **to be called to the B.** s'inscrire au barreau; **to read for the B.** faire son droit; **the prisoner at the b.** l'accusé(e) *m,f*
  (**d**) *(pub, in hotel)* bar *m*; *(pub counter)* comptoir *m*, bar
  (**e**) *Mus* mesure *f*
  2 *vt* (*pt & pp* **barred**) (**a**) *(door)* barrer; **to b. sb's way** barrer le passage à qn
  (**b**) *(ban) (from club, pub)* exclure; **to b. sb from doing sth** interdire à qn de faire qch
  3 *prep* sauf, à l'exception de; **the finest b. none** sans conteste le (la) meilleur(e)

barb [bɑːb] *n* (**a**) *(on hook, arrow)* barbillon *m* (**b**) *(remark)* pique *f*

Barbadian [bɑː'beɪdɪən] **1** *n* = personne née à ou habitant la Barbade
  2 *adj* de la Barbade

Barbados [bɑː'beɪdɒs] *n* la Barbade

barbarian [bɑː'beərɪən] *n & adj* barbare *mf*

barbaric [bɑː'bærɪk] *adj* barbare; *(manners, behaviour)* de barbare

barbarism ['bɑːbərɪzəm] *n* barbarie *f*

barbarity [bɑː'bærɪtɪ] (*pl* **barbarities**) *n* *(cruelty)* barbarie *f*; *(act)* atrocité *f*

barbarous ['bɑːbərəs] *adj* barbare

barbecue ['bɑːbɪkjuː] **1** *n* barbecue *m*; **to have a b.** faire un barbecue; **b. sauce** sauce *f* barbecue
  2 *vt* cuire au barbecue

barbed [bɑːbd] *adj* (**a**) *(hook)* barbelé(e); **b. wire** (fil *m* de fer) barbelé *m* (**b**) *(remark, comment)* acerbe

barber ['bɑːbə(r)] *n* coiffeur *m* pour hommes, *Can* barbier *m*; **to go to the b.'s** aller chez le coiffeur

barbershop ['bɑːbəʃɒp] *n* *Am* salon *m* de coiffure *(pour hommes)*; **b. quartet** = quatuor chantant en harmonie

barbiturate [bɑː'bɪtjʊreɪt] *n* barbiturique *m*

bard [bɑːd] *n* *Lit (poet)* barde *m*; **the B.** Shakespeare

bare ['beə(r)] **1** *adj* (**a**) *(not covered)* nu(e); *(countryside)* nu, dénudé(e); **in one's b. feet** (les) pieds nus; **to lay sth b.** mettre qch à nu, exposer qch (**b**) *(empty) (room, cupboard)* vide; **to strip a house b.** tout enlever dans une maison (**c**) *(just sufficient)* **the b. minimum** le strict minimum; **the b. bones of the case** les grandes lignes de l'affaire; **the b. necessities (of life)** le strict nécessaire; **a b. majority** une petite *ou* faible majorité
  2 *vt* mettre à nu, découvrir; **to b. one's teeth** montrer les dents; **to b. one's heart** *or* **soul to sb** ouvrir son cœur à qn

bareback ['beəbæk] **1** *adj* **b. rider** cavalier(ère) *m,f* qui monte à cru
  2 *adv* **to ride b.** monter à cru

barefaced ['beəfeɪst] *adj* *(impudence, lie, liar)* éhonté(e)

barefoot(ed) ['beəfʊt(ɪd)] **1** *adj* (aux) pieds nus
  2 *adv* nu-pieds, (les) pieds nus

bareheaded [beə'hedɪd] **1** *adj* nu-tête *inv*, à la tête nue
  2 *adv* nu-tête, (la) tête nue

bare-legged [beə'leg(ɪ)d] **1** *adj* aux jambes nues
  2 *adv* (les) jambes nues

barely ['beəlɪ] *adv* (**a**) *(scarcely)* à peine; **b. enough** tout juste assez (**b**) *(sparsely)* **b. furnished** avec très peu de meubles

barf [bɑːf] *vi Am Fam* vomir

bargain ['bɑːgɪn] **1** *n* (**a**) *(agreement)* marché *m*, affaire *f*; **to make** *or* **strike a b. with sb** conclure un marché avec qn; **you haven't kept your side** *or* **part of the b.** vous n'avez pas tenu votre part du marché; **to drive a hard b.** ne pas faire de cadeaux; **into the b.** *(in addition)* par-dessus le marché, en plus (**b**) *(good buy)* affaire *f*, occasion *f*; **b. basement** rayon *m* des soldes, solderie *f*; **b. hunter** acheteur(euse) *m,f* à la recherche de bonnes affaires; **b. price** prix *m* exceptionnel
  2 *vi* **to b. with sb** négocier avec qn

▸**bargain away** *vt sep* *(rights, privileges)* brader

▸**bargain for** *vt insep* *(reaction, question)* s'attendre à; **I didn't b. for that** je ne m'y attendais pas; **he got more than he bargained for** il ne s'attendait pas à cela

▸**bargain on** *vt insep* **I didn't b. on that** je ne m'y attendais pas

barge [bɑːdʒ] *n* péniche *f*

▸**barge in** *vi* *(enter)* faire irruption

bargepole ['bɑːdʒpəʊl] *n* gaffe *f*; **I wouldn't touch it with a b.** *(it's disgusting)* ça me dégoûte d'y toucher; *(it's risky for you)* si j'étais vous, je ne m'en mêlerais pas

baritone ['bærɪtəʊn] *n* baryton *m*

barium ['beərɪəm] *n Chem* baryum *m*; *Med* **b. meal** (bouillie *f* de) sulfate *m* de baryum

bark¹ [bɑːk] **1** *n* *(of tree)* écorce *f*
  2 *vt* **to b. one's shins** s'écorcher les jambes

bark² **1** *n* *(of dog)* aboiement *m*; *Fig* **his b. is worse than his bite** il n'est pas si méchant qu'il y paraît
  2 *vt* aboyer
  3 *vi* aboyer (**at** après); *(of person)* crier (**at** sur); *Fam Fig* **you're barking up the wrong tree** tu fais fausse route

barkeeper ['bɑːkiːpə(r)] *n Am* barman *m*

barley ['bɑːlɪ] *n* orge *m*; **b. sugar** sucre *m* d'orge

barmaid ['bɑːmeɪd] *n Br* serveuse *f* (de bar)

barman ['bɑːmən] *n Br* serveur *m*, barman *m*

barmy ['bɑːmɪ] *adj Br Fam* toqué(e), cinglé(e)

barn [bɑːn] *n* grange *f*; *(for cows)* étable *f*; *(for horses)* écurie *f*; **b. dance** bal *m* folklorique; **b. owl** effraie *f*

barnacle ['bɑːnəkəl] *n* bernacle *f*

barnstorming ['bɑːnstɔːmɪŋ] *adj* *(speech, performance)* plein(e) de brio

barnyard ['bɑːnjɑːd] *n* cour *f* de ferme

barometer [bə'rɒmɪtə(r)] *n* baromètre *m*

baron ['bærən] *n* baron *m*; *Fig* **press/oil b.** magnat *m* de la presse/du pétrole

baroness ['bærənes] *n* baronne *f*

baronet ['bærənet] *n* baronet *m*

baroque [bə'rɒk] **1** *n* baroque *m*
  2 *adj* baroque

barrack ['bærək] *vt* *(heckle)* chahuter

barracks ['bærəks] *npl* caserne *f*; **to be confined to b.** être consigné(e)

barracuda [bærə'kju:də] *n* barracuda *m*

barrage ['bæra:ʒ] **1** *n* (**a**) *(dam)* barrage *m* (**b**) *Mil* tir *m* de barrage; *Fig (of questions, abuse)* flot *m*
2 *vt* **to b. sb with** *(questions)* assaillir qn de; *(criticism)* accabler qn de

barrel ['bærəl] *n* (**a**) *(container)* tonneau *m*, fût *m*; *(of oil)* baril *m*; *Fam* **to have sb over a b.** tenir qn à sa merci; *Fam* **the party wasn't exactly a b. of laughs** cette soirée, ça n'a pas été une partie de rigolade; **b. organ** orgue *m* de Barbarie (**b**) *(of gun)* canon *m*

barren ['bærən] *adj (woman, land, discussion)* stérile; *(landscape)* désolé(e)

barrenness ['bærənnɪs] *n (of land, discussion)* stérilité *f*

barrette [bə'ret] *n Am* barrette *f*

barricade ['bærɪkeɪd] **1** *n* barricade *f*
2 *vt* barricader; **to b. oneself** se barricader

barrier ['bærɪə(r)] *n also Fig* barrière *f*; **the Great B. Reef** la Grande Barrière

barring ['ba:rɪŋ] *prep* sauf; **b. accidents** sauf imprévu; **b. a miracle** à moins d'un miracle

barrister ['bærɪstə(r)] *n Br Law* ≃ avocat(e) *m,f*

barrow ['bærəʊ] *n (wheelbarrow)* brouette *f*

bartender ['ba:tendə(r)] *n Am* serveur(euse) *m,f* (de bar)

barter ['ba:tə(r)] **1** *n* troc *m*
2 *vt* troquer (**for** contre)
3 *vi* marchander

basalt ['bæsɔ:lt] *n* basalte *m*

base [beɪs] **1** *n* (**a**) *(of cliff, column)* pied *m*; *(of lamp, statue)* socle *m*; *(of spine)* bas *m*; *(of jug)* cul *m*; *(of triangle, structure)* base *f*; *Fin* **b. rate** taux *m* de base (**b**) *(for expedition, campaign)* base *f*; *(for tourism)* point *m* de départ; **b. camp** camp *m* de base (**c**) *(in baseball)* base *f*; *Fig* **we didn't get past first b.** nous ne sommes pas arrivés à grand-chose; **to touch b. (with sb)** entrer en contact (avec qn)
2 *adj* (**a**) *Formal (motive, conduct)* bas (basse), vil(e) (**b**) **b. metals** métaux *mpl* vils
3 *vt (hopes, opinion)* fonder (**on** sur); **to be based on** *(of calculation, film)* être basé(e) sur; **to be based in** *(of job, troops, company)* être basé à

baseball ['beɪsbɔ:l] *n* base-ball *m*; **b. cap** casquette *f*; **b. mitt** gant *m* de base-ball

Basel ['ba:zəl] *n* Bâle

baseless ['beɪslɪs] *adj* sans fondement

baseline ['beɪslaɪn] *n (in tennis)* ligne *f* de fond

basement ['beɪsmənt] *n* sous-sol *m*; **b. flat** = appartement en partie en sous-sol

bases ['beɪsi:z] *pl of* **basis**

bash [bæʃ] *Fam* **1** *n* (**a**) *(blow)* coup *m*; *(with fist)* coup de poing; *Br* **to have a b. at sth/doing sth** essayer qch/de faire qch (**b**) *(party)* fête *f*
2 *vt* **to b. one's head** se cogner la tête

▸**bash in** *vt sep Br (door, headlight)* enfoncer; **I'll b. your face in!** je vais te défoncer la tête!

▸**bash up** *vt sep Br Fam (person)* tabasser; *(car)* esquinter

bashful ['bæʃfʊl] *adj* timide; *(modest)* modeste

bashfulness ['bæʃfʊlnɪs] *n* timidité *f*; *(modesty)* modestie *f*

BASIC ['beɪsɪk] *n Comput (abbr* **Beginners' All-purpose Symbolic Instruction Code)** basic *m*

basic ['beɪsɪk] **1** *n* **the basics** l'essentiel *m*; *(of language, science)* les rudiments *mpl*; **let's get down to basics** venons-en à l'essentiel; **to get back to basics** *(traditional values)* retrouver les vraies valeurs
2 *adj (principle, problem, vocabulary)* de base; *(accommodation, understanding)* rudimentaire; **I get the b. idea** je vois en gros de quoi il s'agit; **to be b. to sth** être essentiel(elle) à qch; **b. pay** salaire *m* de base

basically ['beɪsɪklɪ] *adv* (**a**) *(on the whole)* en gros; *(in fact)* en fait (**b**) *(fundamentally)* fondamentalement

basil ['bæzəl] *n* basilic *m*

basilica [bə'zɪlɪkə] *n* basilique *f*

basin ['beɪsən] *n* (**a**) *(for cooking)* bol *m*; *(for washing hands)* lavabo *m*; *(plastic, for washing up)* bassine *f*, cuvette *f* (**b**) *Geog* bassin *m*

basis ['beɪsɪs] *(pl* **bases** ['beɪsi:z] *)* *n (for discussion)* base *f*; *(for opinion, accusation)* fondement *m*; **to be paid on a weekly/monthly b.** être payé à la semaine/au mois; **on an informal b.** à titre non officiel; **to have a b. in fact** être fondé(e); **on the b. of what you've told me** d'après ce que tu m'as dit

bask [ba:sk] *vi* **to b. in the sun** se chauffer au soleil; **he basked in her approval** il se délectait à l'idée qu'il avait son approbation

basket ['ba:skɪt] *n (of fruit, for washing)* corbeille *f*; *(for shopping, in basketball)* panier *m*; *Fam* **he's a real b. case** il est complètement cinglé

basketball ['ba:skɪtbɔ:l] *n* basket(-ball) *m*; **b. player** basketteur(euse) *m,f*

basketful ['ba:skɪtfʊl] *n (plein)* panier *m*

Basle [ba:l] *n* Bâle

Basque [ba:sk] **1** *n* (**a**) *(person)* Basque *mf* (**b**) *(language)* basque *m*
2 *adj* basque; **the B. Country** le Pays basque

bas-relief [ba:rɪ'li:f] *n* bas-relief *m*

bass¹ [bæs] *n (seawater)* bar *m*; *(freshwater)* perche *f*

bass² [beɪs] **1** *n* (**a**) *(voice, singer, guitar)* basse *f*; *(on amplifier)* basses *fpl*; *(double-bass)* contrebasse *f*
2 *adj (voice)* de basse; *(guitar, clarinet)* bas (basse); **b. clef** clef *f* de fa; **b. drum** grosse caisse *f*

basset ['bæsɪt] *n* **b. (hound)** basset *m*

bassist ['beɪsɪst] *n* bassiste *mf*

bassoon [bə'su:n] *n* basson *m*

bastard ['ba:stəd] **1** *n* (**a**) *(illegitimate child)* bâtard(e) *m,f* (**b**) *Vulg (unpleasant man)* salaud *m*; **you lucky b.!** sacré veinard!; **a b. of a job** une vraie galère
2 *adj (child)* bâtard(e)

baste [beɪst] *vt (meat)* arroser de son jus

bastion ['bæstɪən] *n also Fig* bastion *m*

bat¹ [bæt] *n (animal)* chauve-souris *f*; *Fam* **like a b. out of hell** comme un fou (une folle)

bat² **1** *n (for cricket, baseball)* batte *f*; *(for table tennis)* raquette *f*; *Fam* **to do sth off one's own b.** faire qch de sa propre initiative
2 *vt (pt & pp* **batted)** **she didn't b. an eyelid** elle n'a pas sourcillé *ou* bronché
3 *vi (in cricket, baseball)* manier la batte

batch [bætʃ] *n (of bread)* fournée *f*; *(of people)* groupe *m*; *(of goods)* lot *m*; *Comput* **b. file** fichier *m* séquentiel; *Comput* **b. processing** traitement *m* par lots

bated ['beɪtɪd] *adj* **with b. breath** en retenant son souffle

bath [ba:θ] **1** *n* (**a**) *(action)* bain *m*; **to take** *or* **have a b.** prendre un bain; **to give sb a b.** baigner qn; *Br* **(swimming) baths** piscine *f*; **b. mat** tapis *m* de bain; **b. salts**

sels *mpl* de bain; **b. towel** drap *m* de bain (**b**) *(tub)* baignoire *f*, *Can* bain *m*
2 *vt* baigner
3 *vi* se baigner

bathe [beɪð] **1** *n Old-fashioned* **to go for a b.** (aller) se baigner
2 *vt (wound)* laver; **bathed in tears/sweat** baigné(e) de larmes/de sueur
3 *vi Old-fashioned (swim)* se baigner

bather ['beɪðə(r)] *n* baigneur(euse) *m,f*

bathing ['beɪðɪŋ] *n* **b. is prohibited** *(sign)* la baignade est interdite; **b. cap** bonnet *m* de bain; **b. costume** maillot *m* de bain; **b. trunks** slip *m* de bain

bathos ['beɪθɒs] *n* chute *f* du sublime au ridicule

bathrobe ['bɑːθrəʊb] *n* peignoir *m* de bain

bathroom ['bɑːθruːm] *n* salle *f* de bains; *Am (toilet)* toilettes *fpl*; **b. scales** pèse-personne *m*

bathtub ['bɑːθtʌb] *n* baignoire *f*, *Can* bain *m*

batik [bə'tiːk] *n* batik *m*

batman ['bætmən] *n Mil* ordonnance *f*

baton ['bætən] *n (in relay race)* témoin *m*; *(of conductor)* baguette *f*; *Br (of policeman)* matraque *f*; **b. charge** charge *f* à la matraque

batsman ['bætsmən] *n* batteur *m*

battalion [bə'tæljən] *n* bataillon *m*

▸**batten down** ['bætən] *vt insep* **to b. down the hatches** condamner les panneaux; *Fig* dresser ses batteries

batter¹ ['bætə(r)] *n (in baseball)* batteur *m*

batter² *n (in cooking)* pâte *f* à frire

batter³ *vt (beat)* cogner sur; *(person)* battre

battered ['bætəd] *adj* (**a**) **b. women** femmes *fpl* battues; **b. child** enfant *m* martyr (**b**) *(hat, saucepan, car)* cabossé(e); *(furniture, house)* délabré(e)

battering ram ['bætərɪŋræm] *n* bélier *m*

battery ['bætərɪ] *(pl* **batteries**) *n* (**a**) *(of radio, clock)* pile *f*; *(of car)* batterie *f*; **to be b. operated** *or* **powered** fonctionner sur piles; **b. charger** chargeur *m* de piles/batteries (**b**) *Mil* batterie *f*; *Fig (of criticism, complaints)* déluge *m* (**c**) **a b. of tests** une batterie de tests (**d**) **b. farming** élevage *m* en batterie; **b. hen** poule *f* de batterie

battle ['bætəl] **1** *n* bataille *f*; *Fig* combat *m*, lutte *f*; **it was a b. of wits between them** ils ont joué au plus fin; **to do b. with sb** être en conflit avec qn; **that's half the b.** la partie est à moitié gagnée; **b. cry** cri *m* de guerre; **b. royal** une violente empoignade
2 *vi* se battre, lutter

battleaxe ['bætəlæks] *n* hache *f* d'armes; *Fam Pej (woman)* virago *f*

battledress ['bætəldres] *n* tenue *f* de combat

battlefield ['bætəlfiːld], **battleground** ['bætəlgraʊnd] *n also Fig* champ *m* de bataille

battle-hardened ['bætəlhɑːdənd] *adj* aguerri(e)

battlements ['bætəlmənts] *npl* remparts *mpl*

battle-scarred ['bætəlskɑːd] *adj* marqué(e) par la guerre

battleship ['bætəlʃɪp] *n* cuirassé *m*

batty ['bætɪ] *adj Fam* dingue

bauble ['bɔːbəl] *n (on Christmas tree)* boule *f*; *(worthless thing)* babiole *f*

baud [bɔːd] *n Comput* baud *m*; **b. rate** débit *m* en bauds

baulk = **balk**

bauxite ['bɔːksaɪt] *n* bauxite *f*

Bavaria [bə'veərɪə] *n* la Bavière

Bavarian [bə'veərɪən] **1** *n* Bavarois(e) *m,f*
2 *adj* bavarois(e)

bawdy ['bɔːdɪ] *adj* grivois(e), paillard(e)

bawl [bɔːl] **1** *vt* brailler
2 *vi* brailler; **to b. at sb** hurler après qn

▸**bawl out** *vt sep* (**a**) *(shout)* hurler (**b**) *(reprimand)* passer un savon à

bay¹ [beɪ] *n (shrub)* laurier *m*; **b. leaf** feuille *f* de laurier

bay² **1** *n* (**a**) *(on coastline)* baie *f*; **the B. of Bengal** le golfe du Bengale; **the B. of Biscay** le golfe de Gascogne (**b**) *Archit* travée *f*; *(recess)* renfoncement *m*, niche *f*; **b. window** bow-window *m* (**c**) *Br (in bus station, car park)* **(parking) b.** aire *f* de stationnement; **loading b.** aire de chargement (**d**) **to keep** *or* **hold sb at b.** tenir qn à distance; **to keep** *or* **hold sth at b.** se préserver de qch
2 *vi (of dog, wolf)* hurler; **to b. for sb's blood** réclamer la tête de qn

bayonet ['beɪənɪt] **1** *n* baïonnette *f*
2 *vt* **to b. sb** passer qn à la baïonnette

bazaar [bə'zɑː(r)] *n* (**a**) *(in Middle East)* bazar *m* (**b**) *(in aid of charity)* vente *f* de charité

bazooka [bə'zuːkə] *n* bazooka *m*

BBC [biːbiː'siː] *n (abbr* **British Broadcasting Corporation)** BBC *f*

BC [biː'siː] *adv (abbr* **before Christ)** av. J.-C.

be [biː]

> À l'oral et dans un style familier à l'écrit, le verbe **be** peut être contracté: **I am** devient **I'm**, **he/she/it is** deviennent **he's/she's/it's** et **you/we/they are** deviennent **you're/we're/they're**. Les formes négatives **is not/are not/was not** et **were not** se contractent respectivement en **isn't/aren't/wasn't** et **weren't**.

1 *vi (present* **I am**, **you/we/they are**, **he/she/it is**; *pt* **were** [wɜː(r)]; *1st and 3rd person singular* **was** [wɒz]; *pp* **been** [biːn]) (**a**) *(with state, condition)* être; **she's clever/pretty** elle est intelligente/jolie; **I'm a doctor/lawyer** je suis médecin/avocat; **they're English/Spanish** ils sont anglais/espagnols; **to be hungry/thirsty** avoir faim/soif; **to be cold/hot** *(of person)* avoir froid/chaud; *(of thing)* être froid(e)/chaud(e); **it's cold/hot** *(weather)* il fait froid/chaud; **to be 2 metres long/wide** faire 2 mètres de long/de large; **three and two are five** trois et deux font cinq
(**b**) *(with location)* être; **where is the station?** où est *ou* se trouve la gare?; **here I am** me voici; **there you are!** te voilà!; **where was I?** *(after digression)* où en étais-je?
(**c**) *(with time, date)* **it's six o'clock** il est six heures; **what day is it today?** quel jour sommes-nous?; **today's Friday/the tenth** c'est vendredi/le dix; **when is the concert?** quand a lieu le concert?; **it's a fortnight since I saw him** je l'ai vu il y a quinze jours
(**d**) *(with age)* **to be twenty (years old)** avoir vingt ans; **how old is he?** quel âge a-t-il?
(**e**) *(with cost)* coûter, valoir; **how much is it?** combien ça coûte?; **the tickets are £5 each** les billets valent 5 livres
(**f**) *(with health)* aller; **how are you?** comment vas-tu?; **I'm fine** ça va; **he's better/worse** il va mieux/plus mal
(**g**) *(with imperatives)* **be good!** sois sage!; **don't be stupid!** ne sois pas ridicule!; **let's be reasonable!** soyons raisonnables!

(**h**) *(with question tags)* **she's beautiful, isn't she?** elle est belle, n'est-ce pas *ou* non?; **they're big, aren't they?** ils sont grands, n'est-ce pas *ou* non?; **he isn't English, is he?** il n'est pas anglais, si?

(**i**) *(as past participle of go)* **I've been to London/to the museum** je suis allé à Londres/au musée; **where have you been?** où étais-tu passé?

2 *v aux* (**a**) *(in continuous tenses)* **to be doing sth** faire qch; **I was reading when the phone rang** j'étais en train de lire quand le téléphone a sonné; **she is/ was laughing** elle rit/riait; **I'm leaving tomorrow** je pars demain; **it's raining** il pleut; **I've been waiting for hours** ça fait des heures que j'attends (**b**) *(with passives)* **he was killed** il a été tué; **he wasn't allowed to go** on ne l'a pas autorisé à y aller (**c**) *(followed by infinitive)* **the house is to be sold** la maison doit être vendue; **there is to be an election** des élections sont prévues; **she was never to see them again** elle ne devait jamais les revoir; **you are not to mention this to anyone** tu ne dois en parler à personne

beach [biːtʃ] **1** *n* plage *f*; **b. ball** gros ballon *m* en plastique; **b. hut** cabine *f* sur la plage
2 *vt (boat, ship)* échouer

beachcomber ['biːtʃkəʊmə(r)] *n* = personne qui ramasse des objets échoués ou abandonnés sur la plage

beachhead ['biːtʃhed] *n* tête *f* de pont

beacon ['biːkən] *n (signal, buoy)* balise *f*; *(lighthouse)* phare *m*; *(bonfire)* feu *m* d'alarme; *Fig* **a b. of hope** une source d'espoir

bead [biːd] *n* perle *f*; **a string of beads** un collier

beady ['biːdɪ] *adj* **to have one's b. eyes on sb/sth** surveiller qn/qch de près

beady-eyed ['biːdɪˈaɪd] *adj Pej* aux yeux de fouine; *Fig* au regard perçant

beagle ['biːgəl] *n* beagle *m*

beak [biːk] *n* (**a**) *(of bird)* bec *m*; *Fam (nose)* nez *m* crochu (**b**) *Br Fam (magistrate)* juge *m*

beaker ['biːkə(r)] *n* gobelet *m*

be-all and end-all ['biːɔːləˈnendɔːl] *n Fam* **winning isn't the b.** gagner n'est pas tout

beam [biːm] **1** *n* (**a**) *(in building, in gymnastics)* poutre *f* (**b**) *(of sun, moon)* rayon *m*; *(of torch, headlamp)* faisceau *m* lumineux; *Phys* faisceau (**c**) *(idioms) Fam* **to be off b.** être à côté de la plaque; *Fam* **broad in the b.** *(of person)* large de hanches
2 *vt (programme, information)* transmettre
3 *vi (shine) (of sun, moon)* briller; **to b. with pride/ pleasure** rayonner de fierté/de plaisir

bean [biːn] *n* (**a**) *(vegetable)* haricot *m*; *(of coffee)* grain *m*; **b. curd** pâte *f* de soja (**b**) *(idioms) Fam* **to be full of beans** être plein(e) d'énergie; *Fam* **it isn't worth a b.** ça ne vaut pas un radis; *Fam* **he hasn't a b.** il n'a pas un radis

beanbag ['biːnbæg] *n (for juggling)* balle *f* lestée; *(for sitting on)* fauteuil *m* poire

beanfeast ['biːnfiːst] *n Br Hum* grande fête *f*

beanpole ['biːnpəʊl] *n* (**a**) *(stick)* rame *f* (**b**) *Fam (thin person)* asperge *f*

beansprout ['biːnspraʊt] *n* germe *m* de soja

beanstalk ['biːnstɔːk] *n* tige *f* de haricot

bear¹ [beə(r)] *n (animal)* ours *m*; *(female)* ourse *f*; **b. cub** ourson *m*; **to give sb a b. hug** serrer qn très fort dans ses bras; *Fin* **b. market** marché *m* à la baisse

bear² (*pt* **bore** [bɔː(r)], *pp* **borne** [bɔːn]) *vt* (**a**) *(carry)* porter; *(weight, load)* supporter; *(bring)* apporter; **to b. sth away** emporter qch; **to b. sth in mind** *(remember)* se souvenir de qch; *(take into account)* tenir compte de qch; **it bears no relation to...** cela n'a aucun rapport avec...; **to b. the responsibility for sth** assumer la responsabilité de qch

(**b**) *(endure)* supporter; **I can't b. him** je ne peux pas le supporter; **I couldn't b. it any longer** je n'en pouvais plus; **he can't b. losing** il ne supporte pas de perdre; **it doesn't b. thinking about** l'idée même en est insupportable

(**c**) *(produce) (child)* donner naissance à; *Fin (interest)* rapporter; **she bore him three children** elle lui a donné trois enfants; **to b. fruit** *(of tree)* porter des fruits; *(of effort, plan)* porter ses fruits
2 *vi (move)* **to b. (to the) right/left** tourner à droite/ gauche

▸**bear down (up)on** *vt insep* foncer sur
▸**bear out** *vt sep* confirmer, corroborer
▸**bear up** *vi* tenir le coup; **b. up!** courage!
▸**bear with** *vt insep* supporter; **if you could b. with me** si vous voulez bien patienter

bearable ['beərəbəl] *adj* supportable

beard [bɪəd] *n* barbe *f*; **to have a b.** porter la barbe

bearded ['bɪədɪd] *adj* barbu(e)

bearer ['beərə(r)] *n (of news, cheque)* porteur(euse) *m,f*; *(of passport)* titulaire *mf*

bearing ['beərɪŋ] *n* (**a**) *(comportment)* port *m* (**b**) *(in mechanism, engine)* palier *m* (**c**) *(orientation)* **to take a (compass) b. (on sth)** relever la position (de qch) au compas; **to find** *or* **get one's bearings** s'orienter; *Fig* s'y retrouver; **to lose one's bearings** être désorienté(e) (**d**) *(relevance)* rapport *m* (**on** avec)

beast [biːst] *n* (**a**) *(animal)* bête *f*; **b. of burden** bête de somme (**b**) *Fam (unpleasant person)* peau *f* de vache; *(cruel person)* brute *f*; **a b. of a job** un travail pénible

beastly ['biːstlɪ] *adj Fam (unpleasant)* horrible

beat [biːt] **1** *n* (**a**) *(of heart)* battement *m*; *(in bar, of music)* temps *m*; *(rhythm)* rythme *m* (**b**) *Br (of policeman)* ronde *f*; **to be on the b.** faire sa ronde
2 *adj Fam (exhausted)* crevé(e); **dead b.** complètement crevé
3 *vt (pt* **beat,** *pp* **beaten** ['biːtən]) (**a**) *(person, eggs)* battre; **to b. a drum** battre du tambour; **to b. its wings** *(of bird)* battre des ailes; **to b. a path through the crowd** se frayer un chemin à travers la foule; *Fam* **b. it!** dégage! (**b**) *(defeat)* battre; **that will take some beating** c'est difficile de faire mieux; **I left early to b. the traffic** je suis parti tôt pour éviter les embouteillages; **he beat me to it** il a été plus rapide que moi; **you can't b. a good book** rien de tel qu'un bon livre; *Prov* **if you can't b. them, join them** il faut savoir hurler avec les loups; *Fam* **that beats everything!** ça c'est la meilleure!; *Fam* **it beats me why he did it** je ne pige vraiment pas pourquoi il a fait ça; *Fam* **it beats me!** ça me dépasse!
4 *vi* (**a**) *(of heart)* battre (**b**) **to b. about** *or* **around the bush** tourner autour du pot

▸**beat back** *vt sep* repousser
▸**beat down 1** *vt sep (price)* faire baisser; **I b. her down to £40** je lui ai fait baisser son prix à 40 livres
2 *vi (of rain)* tomber à verse; *(of sun)* taper
▸**beat off** *vt sep* repousser
▸**beat out** *vt sep (fire, flames)* étouffer
▸**beat up** *vt sep (assault)* tabasser

beaten ['biːtən] **1** *adj* **b. earth** terre *f* battue; *Fig* **off the b. track** à l'écart
2 *pp of* **beat**
beater ['biːtə(r)] *n* (**a**) *(in hunting)* rabatteur *m* (**b**) *(in cookery)* fouet *m*
beatification [biːætɪfɪ'keɪʃən] *n* béatification *f*
beating ['biːtɪŋ] *n (punishment)* correction *f*; *(in fight)* raclée *f*; *(defeat)* défaite *f*; **to give sb a b.** *(as punishment)* donner une correction à qn; *(beat up)* flanquer une raclée à qn
beat-up ['biːtʌp] *adj Fam (car)* tout(e) déglingué(e)
beaut [bjuːt] *n Fam* **what a b.!** quelle merveille!
beautician [bjuː'tɪʃən] *n* esthéticien(enne) *m,f*
beautiful ['bjuːtɪfəl] *adj (person, weather, music)* (très) beau (belle); *(smell, taste)* très bon (bonne)
beautifully ['bjuːtɪfəlɪ] *adv* merveilleusement bien
beautify ['bjuːtɪfaɪ] *(pt & pp* **beautified**) *vt* embellir
beauty ['bjuːtɪ] *(pl* **beauties**) *n (attribute, person)* beauté *f*; *(object)* bijou *m*; **that's the b. of it** c'est ça qui est bien; **b. contest** concours *m* de beauté; **b. parlour** *or* **salon** institut *m* de beauté; **b. queen** reine *f* de beauté; **b. spot** *(on face)* grain *m* de beauté; *(in country)* site *m* remarquable
beaver ['biːvə(r)] *n* castor *m*
▸**beaver away** *vi* travailler d'arrache-pied (**at** à)
becalmed [bɪ'kɑːmd] *adj* encalminé(e)
became [bɪ'keɪm] *pt of* **become**
because [bɪ'kɒz] *conj* parce que; **why? – (just) b.** pourquoi? – parce que; **b. of** à cause de
beck [bek] *n* **to be at sb's b. and call** être aux ordres de qn
beckon ['bekən] **1** *vt* faire signe à; **to b. sb in** faire signe à qn d'entrer
2 *vi (of prospect)* être attirant(e); **to b. to sb** faire signe à qn; **fame beckons for him** la gloire l'attend
become [bɪ'kʌm] *(pt* **became** [bɪ'keɪm], *pp* **become**) **1** *vt Formal (of behaviour)* être digne de; *(of clothes, colour)* aller bien à
2 *vi* (**a**) *(come to be)* devenir; **to b. old** vieillir; **to b. thin** maigrir; **to b. known** *(of truth)* être révélé(e) (**b**) **what will b. of him?** que va-t-il devenir?; **I don't know what has become of her** je ne sais pas ce qu'elle est devenue
becoming [bɪ'kʌmɪŋ] *adj (behaviour)* convenable; *(clothes, colour)* seyant(e)
BEd [biː'ed] *n Univ (abbr* **Bachelor of Education**) *(qualification)* = diplôme universitaire d'aptitude à l'enseignement; *(person)* = titulaire d'un BEd
bed [bed] **1** *n* (**a**) *(for sleeping)* lit *m*; **to be in b.** être au lit; **to go to b.** aller au lit; **to put a child to b.** coucher un enfant; **to go to b. with sb** coucher avec qn; *Fam* **to get out of b. on the wrong side** se lever du pied gauche; **b. and breakfast** *(accommodation)* chambre *f* avec petit déjeuner; **to stay in a b. and breakfast** ≃ prendre une chambre d'hôte; **b. linen** draps *mpl (et taies d'oreiller etc)* (**b**) *(of river)* lit *m* (**c**) *(of flowers)* parterre *m*; *(of vegetables)* carré *m* (**d**) *Culin* lit *m*; **on a b. of rice** garni(e) de riz (**e**) *Geol* couche *f*
2 *vt (pt & pp* **bedded**) *Fam Old-fashioned* coucher avec
▸**bed down** *vi* **to b. down (for the night)** s'installer (pour la nuit)
bedbug ['bedbʌg] *n* punaise *f*
bedclothes ['bedkləʊðz] *npl* draps *mpl* et couvertures *fpl*
bedding ['bedɪŋ] *n* draps *mpl* et couvertures *fpl*

bedevil [bɪ'devəl] *(pt & pp* **bedevilled**, *Am* **bedeviled**) *vt* **to be bedevilled by sth** *(complaints)* être assailli(e) de qch; *(problems) (of person)* être accablé(e) de qch; *(of project)* être sapé(e) par qch
bedfellow ['bedfeləʊ] *n Fig* **they make strange bedfellows** ils forment une drôle de paire
bedlam ['bedləm] *n (chaos)* bazar *m*
Bedouin ['beduːɪn] **1** *n* Bédouin(e) *m,f*
2 *adj* bédouin(e)
bedpan ['bedpæn] *n* bassin *m*
bedpost ['bedpəʊst] *n* colonne *f* de lit
bedraggled [bɪ'drægəld] *adj (person, clothes)* débraillé(e); *(hair)* échevelé(e)
bedridden ['bedrɪdən] *adj* alité(e); *(permanently)* grabataire
bedrock ['bedrɒk] *n Geol* substrat *m* rocheux; *Fig (of beliefs, faith)* fondement *m*
bed-roll ['bedrəʊl] *n* matériel *m* de couchage
bedroom ['bedruːm] *n* chambre *f* (à coucher)
bedside ['bedsaɪd] *n* chevet *m*; **b. lamp** lampe *f* de chevet; **to have a good b. manner** *(of doctor)* savoir s'y prendre avec les malades; **b. table** table *f* de nuit *ou* de chevet
bedsit ['bedsɪt] *n Br* chambre *f* meublée
bedsock ['bedsɒk] *n* chaussette *f* pour le lit
bedsore ['bedsɔː(r)] *n* escarre *f*
bedspread ['bedspred] *n* dessus-de-lit *m inv*
bedstead ['bedsted] *n* châlit *m*
bedtime ['bedtaɪm] *n* **b.!** c'est l'heure d'aller au lit!; **it's past my b.** je devrais déjà être couché; **b. story** histoire *f (pour endormir un enfant)*
bed-wetting ['bedwetɪŋ] *n* énurésie *f* nocturne
bee [biː] *n* abeille *f*; *Fam* **he's got a b. in his bonnet about it** c'est son idée fixe; *Br Fam* **she thinks she's the b.'s knees** elle ne se prend pas pour n'importe qui
beech [biːtʃ] *n* hêtre *m*
beechnut ['biːtʃnʌt] *n* faîne *f*
beef [biːf] **1** *n* (**a**) *(meat)* bœuf *m*; **b. stew** ragoût *m* de bœuf (**b**) *Fam (strength)* **to have plenty of b.** avoir du muscle; **give it some b.!** allez, du nerf! (**c**) *Fam (complaint)* **what's your b.?** c'est quoi ton problème?
2 *vi Fam (complain)* rouspéter (**about** contre)
▸**beef up** *vt sep Fam (text, resources)* étoffer
beefburger ['biːfbɜːgə(r)] *n* hamburger *m*
beefeater ['biːfiːtə(r)] *n* = garde de la Tour de Londres
beefsteak ['biːfsteɪk] *n* bifteck *m*
beefy ['biːfɪ] *adj Fam (muscular)* costaud(e)
beehive ['biːhaɪv] *n* (**a**) *(for bees)* ruche *f* (**b**) *(hairstyle)* ≃ choucroute *f*
beekeeper ['biːkiːpə(r)] *n* apiculteur(trice) *m,f*
beeline ['biːlaɪn] *n Fam* **to make a b. for** foncer droit sur
been [biːn] *pp of* **be**
beep [biːp] **1** *n (of computer, alarm clock)* bip *m*; *(of car)* coup *m* de Klaxon®; *(device)* bip
2 *vt* biper
3 *vi (of computer, alarm clock)* faire bip; *(of car)* klaxonner
beer [bɪə(r)] *n* bière *f*; **b. garden** = jardin ou terrasse où les clients d'un pub peuvent consommer; **b. glass** verre *m* à bière
beery ['bɪərɪ] *adj (smell, taste)* de bière; *(breath)* qui sent la bière
beeswax ['biːzwæks] *n* cire *f* d'abeille

beet [biːt] *n* betterave *f* (potagère); *Am* betterave (rouge)

beetle ['biːtəl] *n* scarabée *m*

beetroot ['biːtruːt] *n* betterave *f* (rouge); *Fam* **to go b.** devenir rouge comme une tomate

befall [bɪ'fɔːl] (*pt* **befell** [bɪ'fel], *pp* **befallen** [bɪ'fɔːlən]) *vt Lit* arriver à

befit [bɪ'fɪt] (*pt & pp* **befitted**) *vt Formal* convenir à

befitting [bɪ'fɪtɪŋ] *adj* convenable

before [bɪ'fɔː(r)] **1** *prep* (**a**) *(with time)* avant; **I got here b. you** je suis arrivé avant toi; **the day b. the battle** la veille de la bataille; **b. that,...** avant,...
(**b**) *(with place)* devant; **b. my very eyes** sous mes propres yeux
(**c**) *(in importance)* avant; **she puts her family b. everything else** pour elle, la famille passe avant tout le reste
2 *adv* (**a**) *(with time)* avant; **two days b.** deux jours avant; **the day b.** le jour précédent, la veille; **the year b.** l'année précédente; **I've seen her b.** je l'ai déjà vue; **I've told you b.** je te l'ai déjà dit
(**b**) *(in space)* **this page and the one b.** cette page et celle d'avant *ou* et la précédente
3 *conj* **b. doing sth** avant de faire qch; **come and see me b. you leave** venez me voir avant de partir; **give it to her b. she cries** donne-le-lui avant qu'elle (ne) se mette à pleurer

beforehand [bɪ'fɔːhænd] *adv* à l'avance; **check b.** vérifiez au préalable

befriend [bɪ'frend] *vt* **to b. sb** se prendre d'amitié pour qn

befuddled [bɪ'fʌdəld] *adj (person)* perdu(e); *(mind)* embrouillé(e); **b. with drink** abruti(e) par l'alcool

beg [beg] (*pt & pp* **begged**) **1** *vt* **to b. sb to do sth** supplier qn de faire qch; **he begged a favour of me** il m'a supplié de lui rendre un service; **to b. sb's forgiveness** implorer le pardon de qn; **I b. your pardon** *(I apologize)* (je vous demande) pardon; *(what did you say?)* pardon?; **I b. to differ** je me permets d'être d'un autre avis; **this begs the question why** on peut se demander pourquoi
2 *vi (for money)* mendier; **I b. of you!** je vous en supplie!; **to b. for sth** *(money)* mendier qch; *(help)* implorer qch; **to b. for mercy** demander grâce; **there are still a few tickets going begging** il reste encore quelques billets

began [bɪ'gæn] *pt of* **begin**

beggar ['begə(r)] **1** *n* mendiant(e) *m,f*; *Br Fam* **poor b.!** pauvre diable!; *Br Fam* **lucky b.!** veinard!; *Prov* **beggars can't be choosers** nécessité fait loi
2 *vt* **to b. belief** être incroyable; **to b. description** être indescriptible

begin [bɪ'gɪn] (*pt* **began** [bɪ'gæn], *pp* **begun** [bɪ'gʌn]) **1** *vt* commencer; *(piece of work, new chapter)* commencer, entamer; **to b. to do sth, to b. doing sth** commencer à faire qch; **he began laughing** il s'est mis à rire; **I couldn't (even) b. to explain** je ne peux (vraiment) pas expliquer
2 *vi* commencer; **to b. by doing sth** commencer par faire qch; **to b. again** recommencer; **to b. with,...** pour commencer,...

beginner [bɪ'gɪnə(r)] *n* débutant(e) *m,f*

beginning [bɪ'gɪnɪŋ] *n* début *m*, commencement *m*; **in** *or* **at the b.** au début, au commencement; **at the b. of the year/month** au début de l'année/du mois; **I knew from the b. something was wrong** j'ai su dès le début que quelque chose n'allait pas; **to start from the b.** commencer au commencement; **from b. to end** *(read)* du début à la fin

begonia [bɪ'gəʊnɪə] *n* bégonia *m*

begrudge [bɪ'grʌdʒ] *vt* (**a**) *(resent)* **to b. doing sth** faire qch à contrecœur, rechigner à faire qch (**b**) *(envy)* **to b. sb sth** envier qch à qn

beguile [bɪ'gaɪl] *vt* (**a**) *(enchant)* envoûter (**b**) *(deceive)* enjôler; **to b. sb into doing sth** faire faire qch à qn en le séduisant

beguiling [bɪ'gaɪlɪŋ] *adj* enjôleur(euse)

begun [bɪ'gʌn] *pp of* **begin**

behalf [bɪ'hɑːf] *n* **on b. of sb, on sb's b.** *(act, speak, accept award)* au nom de qn; *(come, convey message)* de la part de qn; **don't worry on my b.** ne vous inquiétez pas pour moi

behave [bɪ'heɪv] *vi (of person)* se conduire, se comporter; *(be good)* bien se tenir; *(of car, machine)* marcher, fonctionner; **b. yourself!** tiens-toi bien!; *(to child)* sois sage!

behavior, behavioral *etc Am* = **behaviour, behavioural** *etc*

behaviour, *Am* **behavior** [bɪ'heɪvjə(r)] *n* comportement *m*, conduite *f*; **to be on one's best b.** se tenir particulièrement bien

behavioural, *Am* **behavioral** [bɪ'heɪvjərəl] *adj* de comportement

behaviourism, *Am* **behaviorism** [bɪ'heɪvjərɪzəm] *n Psy* behaviorisme *m*

behead [bɪ'hed] *vt* décapiter

beheld [bɪ'held] *pt & pp of* **behold**

behest [bɪ'hest] *n* **at sb's b., at the b. of sb** sur ordre de qn

behind [bɪ'haɪnd] **1** *prep* derrière; **he hid b. it** il s'est caché derrière; **to be b. sb** *(support)* être avec qn; **to be b. schedule** avoir du retard; **to put sth b. one** *(forget)* ne plus penser à qch; **she's ten minutes b. them** elle a dix minutes de retard sur eux; **to be b. the times** *(old-fashioned)* retarder sur son temps; **the reasons b. sth** les raisons de qch; **what's b. all this?** qu'est-ce que ça cache?
2 *adv* derrière; **from b.** *(viewed)* de derrière; *(attacked)* par-derrière; **to stay** *or* **remain b.** *(not leave)* rester; **to be b. with one's work** être en retard dans son travail en retard; **to be b. with the rent** être en retard pour payer le loyer; **they are only three points b.** *(in contest)* ils ne sont qu'à trois points
3 *n Fam (buttocks)* derrière *m*

behindhand [bɪ'haɪndhænd] *adv* en retard; **to be b. with the rent** être en retard pour payer le loyer; **to be b. with one's work** avoir du travail en retard

behold [bɪ'həʊld] (*pt & pp* **beheld** [bɪ'held]) *vt Lit* voir; **a sight to b.** un spectacle

beholden [bɪ'həʊldən] *adj Formal* **to be b. to sb** être redevable à qn

beholder [bɪ'həʊldə(r)] *n Prov* **beauty is in the eye of the b.** ce qu'on aime est toujours beau

beige [beɪʒ] **1** *n* beige *m*
2 *adj* beige

Beijing [beɪ'ʒɪŋ] *n* Pékin, Beijing

being ['biːɪŋ] *n* (**a**) *(creature)* être *m* (**b**) *(existence)* **to come into b.** naître; **to be in b.** exister

Beirut [beɪ'ruːt] *n* Beyrouth

Belarus [belə'ruːs] *n* la Biélorussie

belated [bɪˈleɪtɪd] *adj* tardif(ive); **wishing you a b. happy birthday** je te souhaite un bon anniversaire avec un peu de retard

belch [beltʃ] **1** *n (burp)* rot *m*; **to give a (loud) b.** roter (bruyamment)
2 *vt* **to b. smoke/flames** *(of fire, chimney)* cracher de la fumée/des flammes
3 *vi (of person)* roter

beleaguered [bɪˈliːɡəd] *adj (city, army)* assiégé(e); *(government)* assailli(e) de toutes parts; *(person)* accablé(e)

Belfast [belˈfɑːst] *n* Belfast

belfry [ˈbelfrɪ] *(pl* **belfries***)* *n* beffroi *m*, clocher *m*

Belgian [ˈbeldʒən] **1** *n* Belge *mf*
2 *adj* belge

Belgium [ˈbeldʒəm] *n* la Belgique

Belgrade [belˈɡreɪd] *n* Belgrade

belie [bɪˈlaɪ] *vt (feelings, background)* ne pas refléter

belief [bɪˈliːf] *n* **(a)** *(conviction)* conviction *f*; *(religious)* croyance *f*; **in the b. that...** étant convaincu(e) que...; **it is my b. that...** je suis convaincu(e) que... **(b)** *(confidence)* foi *f* **(in** en)

believable [bɪˈliːvəbəl] *adj* crédible, plausible

believe [bɪˈliːv] **1** *vt* croire; **I b. (that) I'm right** je crois que j'ai raison; **I b. him to be alive** je crois qu'il est vivant; **she is believed to be in hiding** on pense qu'elle se cache; **I don't b. a word of it** je n'en crois pas un mot; **I could scarcely b. my eyes** j'en croyais à peine mes yeux; **I don't b. it!** c'est pas vrai!
2 *vi* **(a)** **to b. in sth** *(have faith in)* croire à qch; **to b. in God** croire en Dieu; **to b. in sb** *(have confidence in)* avoir foi en qn; **to b. in oneself** avoir confiance en soi **(b)** **to believe in sth** *(be in favour of)* croire à qch; **I don't b. in making promises** je n'aime pas faire de promesses **(c)** *(think, suppose)* croire; **I b. not** je ne crois pas, je crois que non; **I b. so** je crois (que oui)

believer [bɪˈliːvə(r)] *n* **(a)** *(religious person)* croyant(e) *m,f*; **to be a b.** être croyant(e) **(b)** *(supporter)* **to be a b. in sth** croire à qch

belittle [bɪˈlɪtəl] *vt* rabaisser; **to b. oneself** se rabaisser

Belize [beˈliːz] *n* le Belize

bell [bel] *n (of church)* cloche *f*; *(handbell, on cat)* clochette *f*; *(on door, bicycle)* sonnette *f*; **to ring the b.** *(on door)* sonner; *Br Fam* **to give sb a b.** passer un coup de fil à qn; **b. jar** cloche *f*; **b. tower** clocher *m*

belladonna [beləˈdɒnə] *n* belladone *f*

bell-bottoms [ˈbelbɒtəmz] *npl* pantalon *m* (à) pattes d'éléphant

bell-boy [ˈbelbɔɪ] *n Am Fam* groom *m*

belle [bel] *n* beauté *f*; **the b. of the ball** la reine du bal

bellhop [ˈbelhɒp] *n Am Fam* groom *m*

bellicose [ˈbelɪkəʊs] *adj* belliqueux(euse)

belligerence [beˈlɪdʒərəns] *n* agressivité *f*

belligerent [beˈlɪdʒərənt] **1** *n (in war)* belligérant(e) *m,f*; *(in dispute)* partie *f*
2 *adj (aggressive)* agressif(ive), belliqueux(euse); *(at war)* belligérant(e)

bellow [ˈbeləʊ] **1** *n (of bull)* beuglement *m*, mugissement *m*; *(of person)* braillement *m*
2 *vi (of bull)* beugler, mugir; *(of person)* brailler

bellows [ˈbeləʊz] *npl* **(pair of) b.** soufflet *m*

bell-ringer [ˈbelrɪŋə(r)] *n* carillonneur(euse) *m,f*

belly [ˈbelɪ] *(pl* **bellies***) n* ventre *m*; **to have a full/an empty b.** avoir le ventre plein/vide; **b. dance** danse *f* du ventre; **b. dancer** danseuse *f* du ventre *ou* orientale; **b. laugh** gros rire *m*

bellyache [ˈbelɪeɪk] *Fam* **1** *n* mal *m* au ventre
2 *vi (complain)* rouspéter, râler (**about sb/about sth** après qn/au sujet de qch)

belly-button [ˈbelɪbʌtən] *n Fam* nombril *m*

belly-flop [ˈbelɪflɒp] **1** *n* plat *m*
2 *vi (pt & pp* **belly-flopped***)* faire un plat

bellyful [ˈbelɪfʊl] *n Fam* **to have had a b. of sb/sth** en avoir marre *ou* ras le bol de qn/qch

belong [bɪˈlɒŋ] *vi* **(a)** **to b. to** *(be property of)* appartenir à; **that book belongs to me** ce livre m'appartient *ou* est à moi **(b)** **to b. to** *(club, party)* être membre de; *(category)* appartenir à **(c)** *(have a proper place)* aller; **to put sth back where it belongs** remettre qch à sa place; **the saucepans don't b. in that cupboard** les casseroles ne vont pas *ou* ne se rangent pas dans ce placard; **I feel I b. here** je me sens à ma place ici

belonging [bɪˈlɒŋɪŋ] *n* **to have a sense of b.** se sentir à sa place

belongings [bɪˈlɒŋɪŋz] *npl* affaires *fpl*

beloved **1** *n* [bɪˈlʌvɪd] *Lit* bien-aimé(e) *m,f*
2 *adj* [bɪˈlʌvd] bien-aimé(e)

below [bɪˈləʊ] **1** *prep* **(a)** *(line, age, temperature)* au-dessous de; *(bridge, ground)* sous **(b)** *(with numbers)* moins de
2 *adv* au-dessous, en bas; *(in text)* ci-dessous; **on the floor b.** à l'étage du dessous; **it's 10 degrees b.** il fait moins dix

belt [belt] **1** *n* **(a)** *(for trousers)* ceinture *f*; *Fig* **to tighten one's b.** se serrer la ceinture; *Fig* **to have sth under one's b.** *(driving licence, degree)* avoir qch en poche; *(experience)* avoir qch à son actif; *Fig* **that was a bit below the b.** *(of remark, criticism)* c'était un coup bas **(b)** *(of machine)* courroie *f* **(c)** *(of land)* région *f*, zone *f* **(d)** *Fam (blow)* coup *m*; **to give sb a b.** flanquer un gnon à qn
2 *vt (hit) (ball)* cogner dans; *(person)* flanquer un gnon à
3 *vi Fam (move quickly)* **to b. along** foncer; **she belted down the stairs** elle a descendu les escaliers quatre à quatre

▸**belt out** *vt sep Fam (song)* brailler

▸**belt up** *vi Br very Fam (be quiet)* la fermer; **b. up!** la ferme!

bemoan [bɪˈməʊn] *vt (loss, somebody's death)* pleurer; *(one's fate)* se lamenter sur

bemused [bɪˈmjuːzd] *adj* perplexe

bench [bentʃ] *n (seat) & Pol* banc *m*; *(worktable)* établi *m*; *Br Law* **the b.** *(magistrates)* la magistrature; *(court)* la cour; **to be on the b.** *(in football)* être remplaçant(e)

benchmark [ˈbentʃmɑːk] *n* repère *m*, (point *m* de) référence *f*

bend [bend] **1** *n* **(a)** *(of road)* virage *m*, tournant *m*; *(of river)* méandre *m*; *(of pipe)* coude *m*; *Fam* **round the b.** dingue **(b)** **the bends** *(decompression sickness)* la maladie des caissons
2 *vt (pt & pp* **bent** [bent] *) (leg, arm, wire)* plier; *(head)* baisser; *(light)* réfracter; **do not b.** *(on envelope)* ne pas plier; **on bended knee** à genoux; **to b. the rules** faire une entorse au règlement; *Br Fam* **to b. sb's ear** tenir la jambe à qn
3 *vi (of road)* tourner; *(of river)* faire un coude; *(of branch)* plier

▸**bend down** *vi* se pencher

▶**bend over** *vi* se pencher; *Fig* **to b. over backwards to do sth** se décarcasser pour faire qch

bender ['bendə(r)] *n Fam* beuverie *f*; **to go on a b.** prendre une cuite

beneath [bɪ'niːθ] **1** *prep* (**a**) *(physically)* sous (**b**) *(unworthy of)* **to marry b. one** faire une mésalliance; **she thinks it's b. her to work** elle pense que travailler est indigne d'elle; **b. contempt** parfaitement méprisable
2 *adv* dessous, au-dessous; **from b.** de dessous

Benedictine [benɪ'dɪktɪn] *adj Rel* bénédictin(e)

benediction [benɪ'dɪkʃən] *n Rel* bénédiction *f*

benefactor ['benɪfæktə(r)] *n* bienfaiteur *m*

benefactress ['benɪfæktrɪs] *n* bienfaitrice *f*

beneficent [bɪ'nefɪsənt] *adj (system)* bienfaisant(e); *(person)* bon (bonne)

beneficial [benɪ'fɪʃəl] *adj* bénéfique (**to** pour)

beneficiary [benɪ'fɪʃərɪ] *(pl* **beneficiaries**) *n* bénéficiaire *mf*

benefit ['benɪfɪt] **1** *n* (**a**) *(advantage)* profit *m*; **to have the b. of sth** pouvoir profiter de qch; **for sb's b., for the b. of sb** à l'intention de qn; **that remark was for my b.** cette remarque m'était destinée; **to give sb the b. of the doubt** accorder à qn le bénéfice du doute (**b**) *(charity event)* spectacle *m* de bienfaisance; **b. match** match *m* de bienfaisance (**c**) *(state payment)* allocation *f*; **to be on b.** toucher une aide dc l'État; **social security benefits** prestations *fpl* sociales
2 *vt (person, country)* profiter à; *(trade)* favoriser
3 *vi* **to b. from sth** tirer profit de qch; **you'll b. from a holiday** ça te fera du bien d'aller en vacances; **who stands to b. most?** à qui cela profitera-t-il le plus?

Benelux ['benɪlʌks] *n* Benelux *m*; **the B. countries** les pays du Benelux

benevolence [bɪ'nevələns] *n* bienveillance *f*

benevolent [bɪ'nevələnt] *adj* bienveillant(e); **b. society** association *f* de bienfaisance

Bengal [beŋ'gɔːl] *n* le Bengale

Bengali [beŋ'gɔːlɪ] **1** *n* (**a**) *(person)* Bengali *mf* (**b**) *(language)* bengali *m*
2 *adj* bengali

benign [bɪ'naɪn] *adj (attitude)* bienveillant(e); *(climate)* doux (douce); *(tumour)* bénin(igne)

Benin [be'niːn] *n* le Bénin

bent [bent] **1** *n (taste)* penchant *m*, inclination *f*; *(aptitude)* dispositions *fpl*; **to have a musical b.** avoir des dispositions pour la musique
2 *adj* (**a**) *(curved)* tordu(e); *(out of shape)* plié(e); *(person, back)* voûté(e) (**b**) *Br Fam (dishonest)* pourri(e); **b. copper** (flic *m*) ripou *m* (**c**) *Br very Fam (homosexual)* pédé, = terme injurieux qualifiant un homosexuel (**d**) **to be b. on doing sth** *(determined)* être résolu(e) à faire qch; **to be b. on sth** vouloir à tout prix qch
3 *pt & pp of* **bend**

benzene ['benziːn] *n Chem* benzène *m*

benzine ['benziːn] *n Chem* benzine *f*

bequeath [bɪ'kwiːð] *vt Formal* léguer (**to** à)

bequest [bɪ'kwest] *n Formal* legs *m*

berate [bɪ'reɪt] *vt* réprimander

Berber ['bɜːbə(r)] **1** *n* Berbère *mf*
2 *adj* berbère

bereaved [bɪ'riːvd] **1** *npl* **the b.** la famille du défunt (de la défunte)
2 *adj* en deuil; **recently b.** qui vient de perdre un être cher

bereavement [bɪ'riːvmənt] *n* deuil *m*; **b. counselling** = aide psychologique aux personnes en deuil

bereft [bɪ'reft] *adj* **to be b. of sth** être privé(e) de qch; **to feel b.** se sentir totalement seul(e)

beret ['bereɪ] *n* béret *m*

bergamot ['bɜːgəmɒt] *n* bergamote *f*

berk [bɜːk] *n Br Fam* andouille *f*; **to feel a right b.** se sentir idiot(e)

Berlin [bɜː'lɪn] *n* Berlin; **the B. Wall** le mur de Berlin

Berliner [bɜː'lɪnə(r)] *n* Berlinois(e) *m,f*

Bermuda [bə'mjuːdə] *n* les Bermudes *fpl*; **B. shorts** bermuda *m*

Bern(e) [bɜːn] *n* Berne

berry ['berɪ] *(pl* **berries**) *n* baie *f*

berserk [bə'zɜːk] *adj Fam* **to go b.** devenir fou furieux (folle furieuse)

berth [bɜːθ] **1** *n* (**a**) *(on train, ship)* couchette *f* (**b**) *(in harbour)* poste *m* à quai; *Fig* **to give sb a wide b.** éviter qn
2 *vt (boat)* amarrer à quai
3 *vi (of boat)* aborder *ou* se ranger à quai

beseech [bɪ'siːtʃ] *(pt & pp* **besought** [bɪ'sɔːt]) *vt Lit* supplier

beseeching [bɪ'siːtʃɪŋ] *adj* suppliant(e)

beset [bɪ'set] *(pt & pp* **beset**) *vt* assaillir; **to be beset by doubts** être assailli(e) par le doute; **to be beset with dangers/difficulties** être en proie à toutes sortes de dangers/difficultés

beside [bɪ'saɪd] *prep* (**a**) *(next to)* à côté de; *(sea, lake)* au bord de; **that's b. the point** cela n'a rien à voir; **to be b. oneself with joy/anger** être fou (folle) de joie/ de colère (**b**) *(compared to)* à côté de, par rapport à

besides [bɪ'saɪdz] **1** *prep* à part; **other people b. ourselves** d'autres gens que nous; **what else can you do b. type?** à part taper, que savez-vous faire?; **b. being an excellent singer, she also plays the violin** non seulement elle chante très bien, mais en plus elle joue du violon; **b. which she was unwell** sans compter qu'elle ne se sentait pas bien
2 *adv* en plus; **many more b.** bien d'autres encore

besiege [bɪ'siːdʒ] *vt (castle, town)* assiéger; *Fig* **to b. sb with complaints/requests** assaillir qn de plaintes/demandes

besmirch [bɪ'smɜːtʃ] *vt Lit* souiller

besotted [bɪ'sɒtɪd] *adj* **to be b. with** *(person, car)* s'être entiché(e) de; *(idea)* être obsédé(e) par

besought [bɪ'sɔːt] *pt & pp of* **beseech**

bespatter [bɪ'spætə(r)] *vt* éclabousser (**with** de)

bespectacled [bɪ'spektəkəld] *adj* qui porte des lunettes, à lunettes

bespoke [bɪ'spəʊk] *adj* (fait(e)) sur mesure; **b. tailor** tailleur *m* à façon

best [best] *(superlative of* **good, well**) **1** *n* **the b.** *(the best thing)* ce qu'il y a de mieux; **that's the b. I could find** c'est ce que j'ai trouvé de mieux; **at b.** au mieux; **the b. of it is...** le plus beau, c'est...; **at the b. of times** en temps normal; **to do one's b.** faire de son mieux (**to** pour); **to look one's b.** être à son avantage; **to be at one's b.** être au mieux de sa forme; **to bring out the b. in sb** révéler les qualités de qn; **to get the b. of the bargain** faire une bonne affaire; **to get the b. out of sth** tirer le meilleur parti de qch; **to make the b. of sth** s'accommoder de qch; **we are the b. of friends** nous sommes les meilleurs amis du monde; **to be in the b. of health** se porter à merveille; **to the b. of my knowledge** autant que je sache; **to the b. of**

one's ability de son mieux; **he can sing with the b. of them** il chante aussi bien que n'importe qui; **to hope for the b.** avoir espoir; **to have** or **get the b. of both worlds** gagner sur les deux tableaux; *Fam* **all the b.**! *(wishing somebody luck)* bonne chance!; *(at end of letter)* amitiés; **my brother sends his b.** mon frère vous fait ses amitiés

2 *adj* meilleur(e); **my b. dress** ma plus belle robe; **she is b. at French** *(of group of people)* c'est la meilleure en français; **to put one's b. foot forward** faire de son mieux; **the b. part of a year** pratiquement un an; **I'm acting in your b. interests** j'agis au mieux de vos intérêts; **it is b. to...** le mieux, c'est de...; *Com* **b. before date** date *f* limite de consommation; **the b. case scenario** le scénario le plus optimiste; **b. man** *(at wedding)* garçon *m* d'honneur; **may the b. man win** *(in contest)* que le meilleur gagne

3 *adv* le mieux; **as b. I could** du mieux que j'ai pu, de mon mieux; **you know b.** c'est vous qui êtes le mieux placé pour savoir; **do as you think b.** fais comme bon te semblera; **the b. dressed man** l'homme le mieux habillé; **she came off b.** *(in argument)* elle a eu le dessus

4 *vt (in contest, argument)* l'emporter sur

> **Best Man**
> Dans les pays anglo-saxons, le garçon d'honneur présente l'alliance au marié et prononce un discours lors de la réception de mariage.

bestial ['bestɪəl] *adj* bestial(e)
bestiality [bestɪ'ælɪtɪ] *n* bestialité *f*
bestow [bɪ'stəʊ] *vt* accorder (**on** à)
bestseller [best'selə(r)] *n* best-seller *m*
bestselling [best'selɪŋ] *adj (book, author)* à succès
bet [bet] **1** *n* pari *m*; **to make** or **place a b.** parier; *Fig* **my b. is that he'll come** je parie qu'il viendra; *Fig* **your best b. would be to...** ce que tu as de mieux à faire, c'est de...; *Fig* **it's a safe b.** il y a gros à parier
2 *vt (pt & pp* **bet** or **betted**) *also Fig* parier; *Fam Fig* **I b. you she'll win** je te parie qu'elle va gagner; *Fam Fig* **b. you I will!** chiche (que je le fais)!
3 *vi* parier (**on** sur); **to b. on a horse** miser sur un cheval; *Fig* **I wouldn't b. on it!** je n'y compterais pas trop!; *Fam* **you b.!** et comment!; *Fam* **John says he's sorry – I b. (he does)!** John dit qu'il regrette – tu parles!
betel ['biːtəl] *n* bétel *m*; **b. nut** noix *f* d'arec
Bethlehem ['beθlɪhem] *n* Bethléem
betide [bɪ'taɪd] *vt Lit* **woe b. him/you!** malheur à lui/à toi!
betray [bɪ'treɪ] *vt also Fig* trahir; **to b. sb to the enemy** livrer qn à l'ennemi
betrayal [bɪ'treɪəl] *n* (**a**) *(of person, country)* trahison *f*; **b. of trust** abus *m* de confiance (**b**) *(of emotion)* indice *m*
betrothal [bɪ'trəʊðəl] *n Lit* fiançailles *fpl*
betrothed [bɪ'trəʊðd] *n & adj Lit* fiancé(e) *m,f*
better ['betə(r)] *(comparative of* **good, well**) **1** *n* I expected **b. of you** j'attendais mieux de ta part; **you should respect your (elders and) betters** il faut respecter ses aînés; **to change for the b.** *(of person)* changer en bien; *(of situation)* s'améliorer; **to get the b. of sb** avoir le dessus sur qn; **her shyness got the b. of her** sa timidité a été trop forte; **the sooner/faster the b.** le plus tôt/vite possible sera le mieux
2 *adj* meilleur(e); **to be b.** *(after illness)* aller mieux;

to get b. *(of person, wound)* aller mieux; *(of situation, weather)* s'arranger; **he's b. at maths/running than his brother** il est meilleur en maths/à la course que son frère; **it would be b. for you to go** il vaudrait mieux que vous y alliez; **that's b.**! voilà qui est mieux!; **b. luck next time!** tu feras mieux la prochaine fois!; **the b. part of a week** pratiquement une semaine; *Br Fam* **my b. half** ma moitié
3 *adv* mieux; **to look b.** *(of ill person)* avoir meilleure mine; **b. and b.** de mieux en mieux; **so much the b., all the b.** d'autant mieux; **for b. or for worse** pour le meilleur et pour le pire; **you had b. not stay** tu ferais mieux de ne pas rester; **to think b. of it** se raviser; **to be b. off** *(financially)* être plus à l'aise; *(in situation)* être mieux
4 *vt (improve)* améliorer; *(surpass)* faire mieux que; **to b. oneself** améliorer sa situation
betterment ['betəmənt] *n* amélioration *f*; *(of mankind)* progrès *m*
betting ['betɪŋ] *n (bets)* paris *mpl*; *Fam Fig* **the b. is that...** il y a fort à parier que...; **what's the b. that...?** combien tu paries que...?; **b. slip** bulletin *m* de pari; **b. shop** ≃ PMU *m*
between [bɪ'twiːn] **1** *prep* entre; **(in) b. now and Monday** d'ici lundi; **we bought it b. us** nous l'avons acheté à nous deux/trois/etc; **this is strictly b. you and me** que cela reste entre nous; **b. you, me and the gatepost** (soit dit) entre nous
2 *adv* **(in) b.** au milieu
bevel ['bevəl] **1** *n* biseau *m*
2 *vt (pt & pp* **bevelled,** *Am* **beveled**) biseauter
beverage ['bevərɪdʒ] *n* boisson *f*; *Can* **b. room** bar *m*
bevvied ['bevɪd] *adj Br Fam (drunk)* bourré(e)
bevvy ['bevɪ] *(pl* **bevvies**) *n Br Fam (drink)* alcool *m*
bevy ['bevɪ] *(pl* **bevies**) *n (group) (of people)* bande *f*; *(of birds)* volée *f*
bewail [bɪ'weɪl] *vt (loss)* pleurer; *(one's fate)* se lamenter sur
beware [bɪ'weə(r)] *vi* se méfier (**of** de); **b.!** attention!; **b. of the dog** *(sign)* chien méchant
bewilder [bɪ'wɪldə(r)] *vt* dérouter, laisser perplexe
bewildered [bɪ'wɪldəd] *adj* dérouté(e), perplexe
bewildering [bɪ'wɪldərɪŋ] *adj* déroutant(e)
bewilderment [bɪ'wɪldəmənt] *n* perplexité *f*; **to his b.** à son grand étonnement
bewitch [bɪ'wɪtʃ] *vt* ensorceler
bewitching [bɪ'wɪtʃɪŋ] *adj (smile, beauty)* enchanteur(eresse)
beyond [bɪ'jɒnd] **1** *prep* (**a**) *(in space, time)* au-delà de; **the house is b. the church** la maison est après l'église (**b**) *(surpassing)* **to live b. one's means** vivre au-dessus de ses moyens; **it's b. me (how they can do it)** ça me dépasse (qu'ils puissent faire ça); **due to circumstances b. our control** en raison de circonstances indépendantes de notre volonté; **it's b. my power** ça n'est pas en mon pouvoir; **I'm b. caring** ça m'est complètement égal; **it's b. doubt** cela ne fait aucun doute; **it's b. question** c'est incontestable; **it's b. a joke** ce n'est plus drôle; **b. belief** incroyable; **b. reach** hors de portée; **b. repair** irréparable (**c**) *(except)* à part
2 *adv* au-delà
3 *n* **the b.** l'au-delà *m*
Bhutan [buː'tɑːn] *n* le Bhoutan
bias ['baɪəs] **1** *n* (**a**) *(inclination)* préjugé *m*, parti *m* pris (**against/towards** contre/en faveur de) (**b**) *(in sewing)* biais *m*

2 *vt* (*pt & pp* **bias(s)ed**) influencer (**against**/**towards** contre/en faveur de)

bias(s)ed ['baɪəst] *adj* (*article, account*) partial(e); (*person*) de parti pris; (*opinion*) préconçu(e); **to be b. in sb's favour** avoir un préjugé en faveur de qn

bib [bɪb] *n* (*for baby*) bavoir *m*, bavette *f*; (*of apron, dungarees*) bavette

bible ['baɪbəl] *n also Fig* bible *f*; **the B.** la Bible; *Fam* **b. basher** grenouille *f* de bénitier; *Am* **the B. Belt** = ensemble des États du sud des États-Unis où le fondamentalisme chrétien est très répandu

biblical ['bɪblɪkəl] *adj* biblique; *Fam Hum* **to know sb in the b. sense** connaître qn au sens biblique du terme

bibliography [bɪblɪ'ɒgrəfɪ] (*pl* **bibliographies**) *n* bibliographie *f*

bibliophile ['bɪblɪəfaɪl] *n* bibliophile *mf*

bicameral [baɪ'kæmərəl] *adj Pol* bicaméral(e)

bicarbonate [baɪ'kɑːbəneɪt] *n* bicarbonate *m*; **b. of soda** bicarbonate de soude

bicentenary [baɪsen'tiːnərɪ], *Am* **bicentennial** [baɪsen'tenɪəl] **1** *n* bicentenaire *m*
2 *adj* bicentenaire

biceps ['baɪseps] (*pl* **biceps**) *n Anat* biceps *m*

bicker ['bɪkə(r)] *vi* se chamailler

bickering ['bɪkərɪŋ] *n* chamailleries *fpl*

bicycle ['baɪsɪkəl] *n* bicyclette *f*, vélo *m*; **to ride a b.** faire de la bicyclette *ou* du vélo; **b. clip** pince *f* à vélo; **b. kick** (*in football*) retourné *m* bicyclette

bid¹ [bɪd] **1** *n* (**a**) (*offer*) offre *f*; (*at auction*) enchère *f*; **to make a b. (for sth)** faire une offre (pour qch); (*at auction*) faire une enchère (sur qch) (**b**) (*attempt*) tentative *f* (**for sth**/**to do sth** de qch/pour faire qch); **a rescue**/**suicide b.** une tentative de sauvetage/de suicide; **to make a b. for power** (*legally*) viser le pouvoir; (*illegally*) faire une tentative de coup d'État
2 *vt* (*pt & pp* **bid**) (*offer*) offrir; (*at auction*) faire une enchère de; **what am I bid for this table?** que m'offrez-vous pour cette table?
3 *vi* **to b. for sth** faire une offre pour qch; (*at auction*) faire une enchère sur qch

bid² (*pt* **bade** [bæd, beɪd] *or* **bid**, *pp* **bidden** [bɪdən] *or* **bid**) *vt Lit* **to b. sb welcome** souhaiter la bienvenue à qn; **to b. sb goodbye** faire ses adieux à qn

bidder ['bɪdə(r)] *n* (*at auction*) enchérisseur(euse) *m,f*; **the highest b.** le plus offrant

bidding¹ ['bɪdɪŋ] *n* (*at auction*) enchères *fpl*

bidding² *n Lit* (*command*) **at sb's b.** sur l'ordre de qn

bide [baɪd] *vt* **to b. one's time** attendre le bon moment

bidet ['biːdeɪ] *n* bidet *m*

biennial [baɪ'enɪəl] **1** *n* (*plant*) plante *f* bisannuelle
2 *adj* bisannuel(elle)

bier [bɪə(r)] *n* brancards *mpl*

biff [bɪf] *Fam* **1** *n* gnon *m*
2 *vt* flanquer un gnon à

bifocal [baɪ'fəʊkəl] **1** *n* **bifocals** lunettes *fpl* à double foyer
2 *adj* à double foyer

big [bɪg] **1** *adj* (**a**) (*tall, large*) grand(e); (*fat*) gros (grosse); (*drop, increase*) fort(e); (*fashionable*) à la mode; **to get big(ger)** (*taller*) grandir; (*fatter*) grossir; **my b. brother** mon grand frère; **a b. problem** un gros problème; **to be a b. eater** être un gros mangeur (une grosse mangeuse); **a b. hand for our guest!** on applaudit bien fort notre invité!; **the B. Apple** = surnom de New York; **b. business** les milieux d'affaires; *Aut* **b. end** tête *f* de bielle; **b. game** (*in hunting*) gros gibier *m*; **b. spender** panier *m* percé; **b. toe** gros orteil *m*; **b. top** (*of circus*) chapiteau *m*; **b. wheel** (*at fair*) grande roue *f*
(**b**) (*idioms*) **it's her b. day tomorrow** demain c'est son grand jour; **to have b. ideas** avoir de grands projets; **don't get any b. ideas!** ne t'excite pas trop!; *Fam* **what's the b. idea?** c'est quoi cette histoire?; **to earn b. money** gagner beaucoup d'argent; **to make it b.** réussir; **to go in for sth in a b. way** adorer qch; *Ironic* **that's b. of you!** tu es trop bon!; **to be too b. for one's boots** ne plus se sentir; **to be b. on sth** tenir à qch; **to have a b. mouth** (*be indiscreet*) parler trop; *Fam* **b. gun** gros bonnet *m*; *Fig* **a b. name** un grand nom; *Fam* **b. shot** *or* **noise** gros bonnet *m*; **the b. time** le succès
2 *adv* **to talk b.** faire l'important; **to think b.** voir grand

Big Ben
Nom de la cloche de la Tour de l'horloge à Westminster, souvent donné à tort à la tour elle-même. Elle est considérée comme un des monuments principaux de Londres.

bigamist ['bɪgəmɪst] *n* bigame *mf*

bigamous ['bɪgəməs] *adj* bigame

bigamy ['bɪgəmɪ] *n* bigamie *f*

biggie, biggy ['bɪgɪ] (*pl* **biggies**) *n Fam* **it's going to be a b.** (*storm, new film*) ça va faire mal; *Am* **no b.!** pas de problème!

bighead ['bɪghed] *n Fam* crâneur(euse) *m,f*

bigheaded [bɪg'hedɪd] *adj* crâneur(euse); **to get b.** commencer à avoir la grosse tête

big-hearted [bɪg'hɑːtɪd] *adj* **to be b.** avoir le cœur sur la main

bigot ['bɪgət] *n* sectaire *mf*

bigoted ['bɪgətɪd] *adj* sectaire (**against** à l'égard de)

bigotry ['bɪgətrɪ] *n* sectarisme *m*

bigwig ['bɪgwɪg] *n Fam* gros bonnet *m*

bike [baɪk] *n* vélo *m*; (*motorcycle*) moto *f*; *Br Fam* **on your b.!** (*go away*) dégage!; (*don't talk nonsense*) à d'autres!; **b. shed** remise *f* à vélos

biker ['baɪkə(r)] *n Fam* motard(e) *m,f*

bikini [bɪ'kiːnɪ] *n* bikini® *m*; **b. bottom** bas *m* de maillot; **b. top** haut *m* de maillot

bilateral [baɪ'lætərəl] *adj* bilatéral(e)

bilberry ['bɪlbərɪ] (*pl* **bilberries**) *n* myrtille *f*

bile [baɪl] *n* bile *f*; *Fig* (*bitterness*) hargne *f*

bilge [bɪldʒ] *n Fam* (*nonsense*) bêtises *fpl*

bilingual [baɪ'lɪŋgwəl] *adj* bilingue

bilious ['bɪlɪəs] *adj* (**a**) (*nauseous*) nauséeux(euse); **b. attack** crise *f* de foie; **b. yellow** jaunâtre (**b**) (*bad-tempered*) hargneux(euse)

Bill [bɪl] *n Br Fam* **the (Old) B.** (*the police*) les flics *mpl*

bill¹ [bɪl] **1** *n* (*of bird*) bec *m*
2 *vi Fam* **to b. and coo** roucouler

bill² **1** *n* (**a**) (*in restaurant*) addition *f*; (*for goods, services*) facture *f*; (*in hotel*) note *f*; *Fin* **b. of exchange** lettre *f* de change (**b**) *Am* (*banknote*) billet *m* (**c**) (*notice*) affiche *f*; **(stick) no bills** (*sign*) défense d'afficher; *Theat* **to head** *or* **top the b.** être en tête d'affiche (**d**) (*list*) **b. of fare** menu *m*; **to give sb a clean b. of health** trouver qn en parfaite santé; *Fam* **to fit the b.** faire l'affaire (**e**) *Pol* (*proposed law*) projet *m* de loi; **B.**

of Rights = les dix premiers amendements à la Constitution américaine
  2 *vt* (**a**) *(give invoice to)* envoyer la facture à (**b**) *(publicize)* annoncer
billboard ['bɪlbɔːd] *n* panneau *m* d'affichage
billet ['bɪlɪt] *Mil* **1** *n* cantonnement *m*
  2 *vt* cantonner
billfold ['bɪlfəʊld] *n Am* portefeuille *m*
billiard ['bɪljəd] *n* **billiards** billard *m*; **b. ball/table** boule *f*/table *f* de billard
billion ['bɪljən] *n* milliard *m*; *Old-fashioned* billion *m*; *Fam* **I've got billions of things to do!** j'ai des tonnes de choses à faire!
billionaire [bɪljə'neə(r)] *n* milliardaire *mf*
billow ['bɪləʊ] **1** *n (of smoke)* nuage *m*
  2 *vi* ondoyer
billowy ['bɪləʊɪ] *adj* ondoyant(e); *(sea)* houleux(euse)
billposter ['bɪlpəʊstə] *n* **billposters will be prosecuted** *(sign)* ≃ défense d'afficher
billy-can ['bɪlɪkæn] *n* gamelle *f*
billy-goat ['bɪlɪgəʊt] *n* bouc *m*
bimbo ['bɪmbəʊ] *(pl* **bimbos)** *n Fam Pej* minette *f*
bin [bɪn] **1** *n* poubelle *f*
  2 *vt (pt & pp* **binned)** *Fam* mettre à la poubelle
binary ['baɪnərɪ] *adj Math & Comput* binaire; **b. code/number** code *m*/nombre *m* binaire
bind [baɪnd] **1** *n Fam* plaie *f*; **to be in a b.** avoir un embêtement
  2 *vt (pt & pp* **bound** [baʊnd]) (**a**) *(tie)* attacher; **to be bound hand and foot** être pieds et poings liés; **they are bound together by ties of friendship** ils sont unis par les liens de l'amitié (**b**) *(bandage)* bander (**c**) *(book)* relier (**d**) *(cause to stick)* lier (**e**) *(oblige)* **to be bound by sth** être lié(e) par qch; **she bound me to secrecy** elle m'a fait jurer de garder le secret; **you are bound to report any change in your income** vous êtes tenu de signaler tout changement dans vos revenus
▸**bind over** *vt sep Law* sommer
▸**bind up** *vt sep* (**a**) *(cut, wound)* bander (**b**) **to be bound up with sth** *(involved)* être lié(e) à qch
binder ['baɪndə(r)] *n* (**a**) *(for papers)* classeur *m* (**b**) *(bookbinder)* relieur(euse) *m,f* (**c**) *(farm machinery)* lieuse *f*
binding ['baɪndɪŋ] **1** *n* reliure *f*
  2 *adj (contract, promise)* qui engage *ou* lie
binge [bɪndʒ] *Fam* **1** *n (drinking spree)* beuverie *f*; **to go on a b.** prendre une cuite; **to go on a shopping b.** aller claquer du fric dans les magasins; **to have a chocolate b.** faire une orgie de chocolat
  2 *vi* **to b. on sth** *(drink)* s'enfiler des litres de qch; *(food)* s'empiffrer de qch
bingo ['bɪŋgəʊ] **1** *n* ≃ loto *m*; **b. hall** = salle où l'on joue au "bingo"
  2 *exclam* et voilà!

βingo
Ce jeu d'argent très populaire en Grande-Bretagne et aux États-Unis consiste à cocher des chiffres sur une carte jusqu'à ce qu'elle soit remplie; il est souvent pratiqué dans d'anciens cinémas ou des salles municipales.

---

binman ['bɪnmæn] *n Br* éboueur *m*
binoculars [bɪ'nɒkjʊləz] *npl* jumelles *fpl*
bint [bɪnt] *n very Fam* pétasse *f*
biochemical [baɪəʊ'kemɪkəl] *adj* biochimique

biochemist [baɪəʊ'kemɪst] *n* biochimiste *mf*
biochemistry [baɪəʊ'kemɪstrɪ] *n* biochimie *f*
biodegradable [baɪəʊdɪ'greɪdəbəl] *adj* biodégradable
biodiversity [baɪəʊdaɪ'vɜːsɪtɪ] *n* biodiversité *f*
biographer [baɪ'ɒgrəfə(r)] *n* biographe *mf*
biographic(al) [baɪə'græfɪk(əl)] *adj* biographique
biography [baɪ'ɒgrəfɪ] *(pl* **biographies)** *n* biographie *f*
biological [baɪə'lɒdʒɪkəl] *adj* biologique; **b. clock** horloge *f* interne *ou* biologique; **my b. clock is ticking away** *(of woman)* mon temps est compté si je veux avoir des enfants; **b. warfare** guerre *f* bactériologique; **b. washing powder** lessive *f* aux enzymes
biologist [baɪ'ɒlədʒɪst] *n* biologiste *mf*
biology [baɪ'ɒlədʒɪ] *n* biologie *f*
biopsy ['baɪɒpsɪ] *(pl* **biopsies)** *n Med* biopsie *f*
biorhythm ['baɪəʊrɪðəm] *n* rythme *m* biologique
biosphere ['baɪəsfɪə(r)] *n* biosphère *f*
biotechnology [baɪəʊtek'nɒlədʒɪ] *n* biotechnologie *f*
bipartisan [baɪ'pɑːtɪzæn] *adj Pol* bipartite
biped ['baɪped] *n* bipède *m*
biplane ['baɪpleɪn] *n* biplan *m*
birch [bɜːtʃ] **1** *n* bouleau *m*; **to give sb the b.** fouetter qn
  2 *vt (beat)* fouetter
bird [bɜːd] *n* (**a**) *(in general)* oiseau *m*; *(poultry)* volaille *f*; **b. of paradise** oiseau de paradis; **b. of prey** oiseau de proie, rapace *m*; **b. sanctuary** réserve *f* ornithologique; **b. table** mangeoire *f* pour oiseaux (**b**) *Br Fam (woman)* nana *f* (**c**) *(idioms) Fam* **a little b. told me** c'est mon petit doigt qui me l'a dit; **the b. has flown** l'oiseau s'est envolé; *Prov* **a b. in the hand is worth two in the bush** un tiens vaut mieux que deux tu l'auras; *Prov* **birds of a feather flock together** qui se ressemble s'assemble; **to kill two birds with one stone** faire d'une pierre deux coups; *Euph* **it's time you told him about the birds and the bees** il serait temps de lui expliquer que les bébés ne naissent pas dans les choux
birdbath ['bɜːdbɑːθ] *n* vasque *f* pour les oiseaux
bird-brained ['bɜːdbreɪnd] *adj Fam (idea)* extravagant(e); **to be b.** *(of person)* avoir une cervelle d'oiseau
birdcage ['bɜːdkeɪdʒ] *n* cage *f* à oiseaux; *(in zoo)* volière *f*
birdie ['bɜːdɪ] *n* (**a**) *Fam (bird)* petit oiseau *m*; *Fig* **watch the b.!** *(when taking photo)* attention, le petit oiseau va sortir! (**b**) *(in golf)* birdie *m*
birdseed ['bɜːdsiːd] *n* graines *fpl* pour oiseaux
bird's-eye view ['bɜːdzaɪ'vjuː] *n* vue *f* d'ensemble
birdwatcher ['bɜːdwɒtʃə(r)] *n* ornithologue *mf* amateur
birdwatching ['bɜːdwɒtʃɪŋ] *n* **to go b.** aller observer les oiseaux
Birmingham ['bɜːmɪŋəm] *n* Birmingham
Biro® ['baɪrəʊ] *(pl* **Biros)** *n Br* stylo *m* (à) bille
birth [bɜːθ] *n* naissance *f*; **to give b. (to)** accoucher (de); **at b.** à la naissance; **by b.** de naissance; **from b.** *(blind, deaf)* de naissance; **b. certificate** acte *m* de naissance; **b. control** contrôle *m* des naissances; *Fig* **b. pangs** accouchement *m* douloureux; **b. rate** taux *m* de natalité
birthday ['bɜːθdeɪ] *n* anniversaire *m*; *Fam* **to be in one's b. suit** *(of man)* être en costume d'Adam; *(of*

woman) être en costume d'Éve; **b. card/present** carte *f*/cadeau *m* d'anniversaire

birthing pool ['bɜːθɪŋˈpuːl] *n* piscine *f* d'accouchement

birthmark ['bɜːθmɑːk] *n* tache *f* de naissance, envie *f*

birthplace ['bɜːθpleɪs] *n* lieu *m* de naissance

birthright ['bɜːθraɪt] *n* droit *m* acquis à la naissance; *Fig* droit élémentaire

Biscay ['bɪskeɪ] *n see* **bay**

biscuit ['bɪskɪt] *n* biscuit *m*; *Fam* **that really takes the b.!** ça, c'est le bouquet!

bisect [baɪ'sekt] *vt* couper en deux

bisexual [baɪ'seksjʊəl] *n & adj* bisexuel(elle) *m,f*

bishop ['bɪʃəp] *n* évêque *m*; *(in chess)* fou *m*

bishopric ['bɪʃəprɪk] *n* évêché *m*

bison ['baɪsən] *n* bison *m*

bistro ['biːstrəʊ] *(pl* **bistros***)* n* petit restaurant *m*

bit¹ [bɪt] *n* (**a**) *(in horseriding)* mors *m*; *Fig* **to get the b. between one's teeth** prendre le mors aux dents (**b**) *(for drill)* mèche *f*

bit² *n* (**a**) *(piece)* bout *m*; *(of film, book)* passage *m*; **a b. of news** une nouvelle; **to take sth to bits** démonter qch; **to tear sth to bits** déchirer qch en petits morceaux; **to smash sth to bits** briser qch en mille morceaux; **he has eaten every b.** il a mangé jusqu'à la dernière miette; **to do one's b.** participer; *Br Fam* **she's a b. of all right** c'est une belle nana; *Fam* **to have a b. on the side** *(have male lover)* avoir un amant; *(have female lover)* avoir une maîtresse; **bits and pieces** *(personal belongings)* affaires *fpl*; *(small items)* trucs *mpl*

(**b**) **a b. (of)** *(expressing degree)* un peu (de); **a b. late/heavy/tired** un peu en retard/lourd(e)/fatigué(e); **we had a b. of difficulty in finding him** nous avons eu quelque difficulté à le trouver; **he's a b. of a know-all** il a un côté je-sais-tout; **b. by b.** petit à petit; **not a b. of it!** pas du tout!; **wait a b.!** attends une minute!; **it takes a b. of getting used to** il faut un moment pour s'y habituer; **a good b. older** nettement plus âgé(e); **a little b. (of)** un tout petit peu (de); **every b. as good/interesting as** tout aussi bon (bonne)/intéressant(e) que; *Fam* **that's a b. much!** ça c'est un peu fort!; **b. part** *(in play, film)* petit rôle *m*

(**c**) *Comput* bit *m*

(**d**) *Fam (coin)* pièce *f*; *Am* **two bits** vingt-cinq cents *mpl*

bit³ *pt of* **bite**

bitch [bɪtʃ] *n* 1 (**a**) *(female dog)* chienne *f* (**b**) *very Fam Pej (woman)* garce *f*; **I've had a b. of a day!** j'ai eu une putain de journée!; **life's a b.!** chienne de vie!

2 *vi Fam (complain)* râler, rouspéter (**about** après)

bitchy ['bɪtʃɪ] *adj Fam* vache

bite [baɪt] 1 *n* (**a**) *(of person)* coup *m* de dent; *(of dog)* morsure *f*; *(of insect)* piqûre *f*; *(of snake)* morsure, piqûre

(**b**) *(mouthful)* bouchée *f*; **to take a b. out of sth** mordre dans qch; **I haven't had a b. to eat all day** je n'ai rien mangé de la journée

(**c**) *Fig (of speech, article)* mordant *m*; *(of sauce)* piquant *m*

2 *vt (pt* **bit** [bɪt], *pp* **bitten** ['bɪtən] *)* (**a**) *(of person, dog)* mordre; *(of insect)* piquer; *(of snake)* mordre, piquer; **the dog bit him in the leg** le chien l'a mordu à la jambe; **to b. one's nails** se ronger les ongles

(**b**) *(idioms)* **to b. one's tongue** *(stay silent)* se mordre la langue; *Fam* **to b. the bullet** faire contre

mauvaise fortune bon cœur; *Fam* **to b. the dust** *(of scheme, plan)* tomber à l'eau; **to b. the hand that feeds you** cracher dans la soupe; *Prov* **once bitten twice shy** chat échaudé craint l'eau froide

3 *vi* (**a**) *(of person, dog)* mordre; *(of insect)* piquer; *(of snake)* mordre, piquer; **to b. into sth** mordre dans qch

(**b**) *Fig (be felt)* se faire sentir

▶**bite off** *vt sep* couper d'un coup de dent; *Fig* **to b. off more than one can chew** avoir les yeux plus gros que le ventre; *Fam Fig* **to b. sb's head off** rembarrer qn

biting ['baɪtɪŋ] *adj (wind, satire)* cinglant(e)

bitmap ['bɪtmap] *n Comput* bitmap *m*

bitmapped ['bɪtmæpt] *adj Comput* pixélisé(e)

bitten ['bɪtən] *pp of* **bite**

bitter ['bɪtə(r)] 1 *n Br (beer)* = bière anglaise brune faite avec beaucoup de houblon

2 *adj* (**a**) *(taste)* amer(ère); *Fig* **it was a b. pill to swallow** la pilule était amère, c'était dur à avaler (**b**) *(harsh) (wind, cold)* glacial(e); *(weather)* rigoureux(-euse); *(opposition, resistance)* âpre; *(struggle)* implacable; *(tears, disappointment)* amer(ère); **to go on to the b. end** aller jusqu'au bout (**c**) *(resentful)* amer(-ère); *(words)* acerbe; **to feel** *or* **be b. about sth** éprouver de l'amertume à propos de qch

bitterly ['bɪtəlɪ] *adv* (**a**) *(extremely)* extrêmement; *(opposed)* résolument, farouchement; **to b. regret doing sth** regretter amèrement d'avoir fait qch; **it was b. cold** il faisait un froid de canard (**b**) *(resentfully)* avec amertume

bitterness ['bɪtənɪs] *n* amertume *f*

bittersweet ['bɪtəswiːt] *adj also Fig* doux-amer (douce-amère)

bitty ['bɪtɪ] *adj Fam (patchy)* décousu(e)

bitumen ['bɪtjʊmɪn] *n* bitume *m*

bivouac ['bɪvʊæk] 1 *n* bivouac *m*

2 *vi (pt & pp* **bivouacked***)* bivouaquer

bi-weekly [baɪ'wiːklɪ] 1 *adj (fortnightly)* bimensuel(elle); *(twice weekly)* bihebdomadaire

2 *adv (fortnightly)* deux fois par mois; *(twice weekly)* deux fois par semaine

bizarre [bɪ'zɑː(r)] *adj* bizarre

blab [blæb] *(pt & pp* **blabbed***) Fam* 1 *vt* dire

2 *vi (chatter)* bavarder; *(betray secret)* vendre la mèche; **don't go blabbing to everybody** ne va pas le dire à tout le monde

black [blæk] 1 *n* (**a**) *(colour)* noir *m*; **b. doesn't suit her** le noir ne lui va pas

(**b**) *(person)* Noir(e) *m,f*

(**c**) **in the b.** *(person)* solvable; *(account)* créditeur(-trice)

(**d**) *(idioms)* **it says here in b. and white** c'est écrit noir sur blanc; **he sees everything in b. and white** avec lui, c'est ou tout l'un ou tout l'autre

2 *adj* (**a**) *(colour)* noir(e); **a b. man** un Noir; **a b. woman** une Noire; **to be b. and blue** *(bruised)* être couvert(e) de bleus; **b. belt** *(in martial arts)* ceinture *f* noire; **b. box** *(flight recorder)* boîte *f* noire; **b. coffee** café *m* noir; **b. eye** œil *m* poché; *Astron* **b. hole** trou *m* noir; **b. humour** humour *m* noir; **b. ice** verglas *m*; **b. pudding** boudin *m* noir; **b. sheep** brebis *f* galeuse

(**b**) *(evil, unfavourable)* noir(e); **to give sb a b. look** jeter à qn un regard noir; **the future is looking b.** l'avenir est sombre; **b. magic** magie *f* noire; **it was a b. mark against him** c'était un mauvais point pour lui; **b. spot** *(for accidents)* point *m* noir (**c**) *(unofficial)* **b. economy** économie *f* souterraine; **b. market** marché *m* noir

(**d**) *(in proper names)* **the B. Country** = la région de Birmingham *(qui est très industrielle)*; **the B. Death** la peste noire; **the B. Forest** la Forêt-Noire; **B. Forest gateau** forêt-noire *f*; *Br* **B. Maria** panier *m* à salade; **the B. Sea** la mer Noire

3 *vt* (**a**) *(blacken)* noircir; **to b. one's face** se noircir le visage

(**b**) *(boycott)* mettre à l'index, boycotter

▶**black out 1** *vt sep* (**a**) *(censor)* rayer *(d'un gros trait noir)* (**b**) *(city)* plonger dans l'obscurité (**c**) *(TV programme)* interrompre

2 *vi (faint)* perdre connaissance, s'évanouir

black-and-white [blækən'waɪt] *adj (film, photograph)* (en) noir et blanc *inv*; *(TV)* noir et blanc *inv*

blackball ['blækbɔːl] *vt* blackbouler

blackberry ['blækbərɪ] *(pl* **blackberries***) n* mûre *f*

blackbird ['blækbɜːd] *n* merle *m* noir

blackboard ['blækbɔːd] *n* tableau *m* (noir)

blackcurrant ['blækkʌrənt] *n* cassis *m*

blacken ['blækən] *vt* noircir; *Fig* **to b. sb's character** calomnier qn

blackguard ['blægɑːd] *n Old-fashioned* fripouille *f*

blackhead ['blækhed] *n* point *m* noir

blackjack ['blækdʒæk] *n* (**a**) *Am (truncheon)* nerf *m* de bœuf (**b**) *(card game)* black jack *m*, ≃ vingt-et-un *m*

blackleg ['blækleg] *n Fam (strikebreaker)* jaune *m*

blacklist ['blæklɪst] **1** *n* liste *f* noire

2 *vt* mettre sur la liste noire

blackmail ['blækmeɪl] **1** *n* chantage *m*; **emotional b.** chantage affectif

2 *vt* faire chanter

blackness ['blæknɪs] *n* noirceur *f*

blackout ['blækaʊt] *n* (**a**) *(during air-raid)* black-out *m* *inv*; *Fig* **to impose a news b.** empêcher la divulgation d'une information (**b**) *(fainting fit)* évanouissement *m*

blacksmith ['blæksmɪθ] *n* forgeron *m*; *(who shoes horses)* maréchal-ferrant *m*

bladder ['blædə(r)] *n* vessie *f*

blade [bleɪd] *n (of knife, sword)* lame *f*; *(of propeller, oar)* pale *f*; *(of grass)* brin *m*

blame [bleɪm] **1** *n* responsabilité *f*, faute *f*; **to put the b. (for sth) on sb** faire porter à qn la responsabilité (de qch); **to take the b. for sth** endosser la responsabilité de qch

2 *vt* rendre responsable, faire porter la responsabilité à *(for* de); **to b. sb for doing sth** reprocher à qn d'avoir fait qch; **I am to b.** je suis fautif, c'est de ma faute; **the bad weather was to b.** c'était à cause du mauvais temps; **I b. myself for what happened** je m'en veux pour ce qui est arrivé; **I don't b. you for wanting to leave** je ne te reproche pas de vouloir partir; **she has nobody to b. but herself** elle n'a de reproche à faire qu'à elle-même

blameless ['bleɪmlɪs] *adj* irréprochable

blameworthy ['bleɪmwɜːðɪ] *adj (person)* coupable, blâmable; *(conduct)* répréhensible

blanch [blɑːntʃ] **1** *vt Culin* blanchir

2 *vi (go pale)* blêmir, pâlir

blancmange [blə'mɒnʒ] *n* blanc-manger *m*

bland [blænd] *adj (person, appearance)* terne; *(food)* insipide, fade; *(music)* sans intérêt; *(promise)* vain(e); **despite her b. assurances...** malgré ses protestations de politesse...

blandishments ['blændɪʃmənts] *npl* cajoleries *fpl*; **to resist sb's b.** ne pas se laisser amadouer par qn

blandly ['blændlɪ] *adv (speak, reply)* mielleusement

blank [blæŋk] **1** *n* (**a**) *(space)* blanc *m*; **fill in the blanks** remplissez les blancs ou les (espaces) vides; *Fig* **to draw a b.** faire chou blanc (**b**) *(rifle cartridge)* cartouche *f* à blanc; **to fire blanks** tirer à blanc; *Fam Fig* être stérile

2 *adj (paper, screen)* blanc (blanche), vierge; *(face)* sans expression; **with a b. expression on his face** le visage sans expression; **to look b.** avoir l'air déconcerté ou ahuri; **my mind went b.** j'ai eu un trou; **b. cassette** cassette *f* vierge; **b. cheque** chèque *m* en blanc; *Fig* **to give sb a b. cheque** donner carte blanche à qn; **b. verse** vers *mpl* blancs

▶**blank out** *vt sep also Fig* effacer

blanket ['blæŋkɪt] **1** *n* couverture *f*; *Fig (of fog, cloud)* manteau *m*

2 *adj (general)* général(e), global(e); **the government imposed a b. ban on demonstrations** le gouvernement a interdit toutes les manifestations; **b. term** terme *m* général

blankly ['blæŋklɪ] *adv (without expression)* sans expression; *(without understanding)* l'air déconcerté; **she stared b. into space** elle avait le regard perdu dans le vide

blare ['bleə(r)] **1** *n* beuglements *mpl*

2 *vi (of TV, radio)* beugler

▶**blare out 1** *vt sep* beugler

2 *vi* beugler; **the music was blaring out** la musique était à fond

blarney ['blɑːnɪ] *n Fam* boniments *mpl*

blasé ['blɑːzeɪ] *adj* blasé(e); **she was very b. about the accident** l'accident ne lui avait fait ni chaud ni froid

blaspheme [blæs'fiːm] *vi* blasphémer

blasphemous ['blæsfəməs] *adj* blasphématoire

blasphemy ['blæsfəmɪ] *n* blasphème *m*

blast [blɑːst] **1** *n* (**a**) *(of wind)* coup *m*, rafale *f*; *(of heat)* bouffée *f*; *(of steam)* jet *m*; *(of whistle, horn)* coup; **at full b.** *(radio, TV, heater)* à fond; **b. furnace** haut-fourneau *m* (**b**) *(explosion)* explosion *f*; *(shock wave)* souffle *m* d'une explosion; *Fam* **meeting her/hearing that song was a real b. from the past!** la rencontrer/cette chanson m'a ramené des années en arrière (**c**) *Am Fam (good time)* **it was a b.** c'était génial; **we had a b.** on s'est super marrés

2 *vt* (**a**) *(hole, tunnel)* creuser *(en dynamitant)*; **the building had been blasted by a bomb** le bâtiment avait été détruit par une bombe; *Fam* **to b. sb's head off** faire sauter la tête à qn (**b**) *Fam (criticize)* démolir (**c**) *Fam* **b. (it)!** zut alors!

▶**blast off** *vi (of space rocket)* décoller

blast-off ['blɑːstɒf] *n (of space rocket)* lancement *m*

blatant ['bleɪtənt] *adj* flagrant(e), manifeste; *(lie)* éhonté(e)

blatantly ['bleɪtəntlɪ] *adv* de façon flagrante; **b. obvious** tout à fait évident(e)

blather ['blæðə(r)] *vi Am Fam* parler à tort et à travers

blaze [bleɪz] **1** *n* (**a**) *(fire)* feu *m*; **many people died in the b.** beaucoup de gens ont péri dans les flammes (**b**) *(of colour, light)* éclat *m*; **the film was released in a b. of publicity** ils ont fait une publicité monstre pour la sortie du film; **to go out in a b. of glory** s'en aller plein(e) de gloire (**c**) *Fam* **what the blazes does he want?** mais qu'est-ce qu'il veut, bon sang?

2 *vt Fig* **to b. a trail** ouvrir la voie

3 *vi (of fire, sun)* flamboyer; *(of light)* êtreéclatant(e); **the house was blazing with lights** la maison était tout illuminée; **to b. with anger** *(of person)* fulminer; *(of eyes)* lancer des éclairs de colère

blazer ['bleɪzə(r)] *n* blazer *m*

blazing ['bleɪzɪŋ] *adj (burning)* en feu, enflammé(e); *Fig* **a b. row** une violente dispute

bleach [bliːtʃ] **1** *n* (eau *f* de) Javel *f*

2 *vt (clothes)* passer à l'eau de Javel *ou* à la Javel; *(hair)* décolorer

bleak [bliːk] *adj (landscape, weather)* morne, triste; *(outlook)* lugubre; *(prospect)* peu encourageant(e)

bleary ['blɪərɪ] *adj (eyes)* rouge

bleary-eyed [blɪərɪ'aɪd] *adj* **to be b.** *(from lack of sleep)* avoir de petits yeux; *(from hay fever, crying)* avoir les yeux rouges

bleat [bliːt] **1** *n (of sheep)* bêlement *m*

2 *vi (of sheep)* bêler; *Fig (complain)* ronchonner (**about** à propos de)

bleed [bliːd] *(pt & pp* bled [bled]) **1** *vt Med* saigner; *(radiator)* purger; *Fig* **to b. sb dry** saigner qn à blanc

2 *vi* saigner; **her nose is bleeding** elle saigne du nez; **to b. to death** saigner à mort

bleeder ['bliːdə(r)] *n Br very Fam* salaud *m*

bleeding ['bliːdɪŋ] **1** *n* saignement *m*; **has the b. stopped?** est-ce que tu saignes/est-ce qu'il saigne/ *etc* toujours?

2 *adj* (**a**) *(wound)* qui saigne (**b**) *Br very Fam (for emphasis)* **you b. liar!** sale menteur!; **you b. idiot!** espèce de con!

3 *adv Br very Fam (for emphasis)* foutrement; **that was b. stupid!** c'était vraiment con!

bleep [bliːp] **1** *n* bip *m*

2 *vi* faire bip

bleeper ['bliːpə(r)] *n (pager)* bip *m*

blemish ['blemɪʃ] **1** *n (mark)* marque *f*; *Fig* **it left a b. on her reputation** cela a entaché sa réputation

2 *vt Fig (reputation)* entacher

blench [blentʃ] *vi* avoir un mouvement de recul

blend [blend] **1** *n* mélange *m*

2 *vt* mélanger (**with** à *ou* avec)

3 *vi* se mélanger, se mêler; **the colours b. together well** ces couleurs se marient bien *ou* vont bien ensemble

▶**blend in** *vi (with surroundings)* se fondre (**with** dans)

▶**blend into** *vt insep (surroundings)* se fondre dans; **to b. into the background** se fondre dans le décor

blender ['blendə(r)] *n* mixer *m*, mixeur *m*

bless [bles] *(pt & pp* blessed *or* blest [blest]) *vt* (**a**) *(say blessing for)* bénir; **God b. you!** que Dieu te bénisse!; **b. you!** *(when somebody sneezes)* à tes souhaits! (**b**) **to be blessed with sth** *(talent, beauty)* être doté(e) de qch; **they have been blessed with two fine children** ils ont deux beaux enfants

blessed ['blesɪd] *adj* (**a**) *(holy)* béni(e) (**b**) *Fam (for emphasis)* **the whole b. day** toute la sainte journée; **the whole b. lot** tout le bazar, tout le bataclan; **it's a b. nuisance having to...** quelle barbe d'avoir à...; **I can't see a b. thing!** je n'y vois absolument rien!

blessing ['blesɪŋ] *n* (**a**) *(religious)* bénédiction *f*; *Fig* **to give sb/sth one's b.** donner à qn/qch sa bénédiction (**b**) *(benefit, advantage)* bienfait *m*; **it was a b. in disguise** finalement, ça a été une bonne chose; **it was a mixed b.** il y avait du bon et du mauvais; **to count one's blessings** s'estimer heureux de ce qu'on a

blest [blest] *pt & pp of* **bless**

blether ['bleðə(r)] *vi Fam (talk foolishly)* parler à tort et à travers; *Scot (chat)* papoter

blew [bluː] *pt of* **blow**

blight [blaɪt] **1** *n (on cereals)* rouille *f*; *(on potatoes)* brunissure *f*; *Fig* **to cast a b. over sth** jeter un froid sur qch

2 *vt Fig* assombrir; *(hopes)* anéantir

blighter ['blaɪtə(r)] *n Br Fam Old-fashioned* type *m*, gars *m*; **lucky b.** veinard *m*

blimey ['blaɪmɪ] *exclam Br Fam* zut alors!

blind¹ [blaɪnd] **1** *npl* **the b.** les aveugles *mpl*; **school for the b.** école *f* pour aveugles; **they don't know what they're doing, it's like the b. leading the b.** ils ne savent pas ce qu'ils font, ils sont aussi nuls l'un que l'autre

2 *adj* (**a**) *also Fig* aveugle; **a b. man** un aveugle; **a b. woman** une aveugle; **b. in one eye** borgne, aveugle d'un œil; **as b. as a bat** myope comme une taupe; **to be b. to sth** ne pas voir qch; **to turn a b. eye to sth** fermer les yeux sur qch; **b. with fury** aveuglé(e) par la colère; *also Fig* **b. alley** impasse *f*; **b. date** = rencontre arrangée avec quelqu'un que l'on ne connaît pas; **b. man's buff** (jeu *m* de) colin-maillard *m*; **b. spot** *(for driver)* angle *m* mort; *Fig* **to have a b. spot for maths** être nul (nulle) en maths (**b**) *Fam (for emphasis)* **he didn't take a b. bit of notice** il n'y a pas prêté la moindre attention; **it didn't make a b. bit of difference** ça n'a pas fait la moindre différence

3 *adv* **b. drunk** ivre mort(e)

4 *vt* aveugler; *Fig* **love blinded her to his faults** aveuglée par l'amour, elle n'a pas vu ses défauts

blind² *n Br (for windows)* store *m*

blindfold ['blaɪndfəʊld] **1** *n* bandeau *m*

2 *vt* **to b. sb** mettre un bandeau à qn; **to be blindfolded** avoir les yeux bandés

blinding ['blaɪndɪŋ] *adj* (**a**) *(light)* aveuglant(e); *Fig (intensity, realization)* affolant(e) (**b**) *Br Fam (excellent)* génial(e)

blindly ['blaɪndlɪ] *adv Fig* aveuglément

blindness ['blaɪndnɪs] *n* cécité *f*; *Fig* aveuglement *m*

blink [blɪŋk] **1** *n* (**a**) *(of eyes)* clignement *m* de paupières (**b**) *Br Fam* **to be on the b.** *(of TV, machine)* faire des siennes

2 *vt* **to b. one's eyes** cligner des yeux

3 *vi (of person)* cligner des yeux; *(of light)* clignoter

blinkered ['blɪŋkəd] *adj (approach, attitude)* borné(e); **to be b.** *(of person)* avoir des œillères

blinkers ['blɪŋkəz] *npl* (**a**) *(for horse)* œillères *fpl*; *Fig* **to be wearing b.** avoir des œillères (**b**) *Fam (indicators)* clignotants *mpl*

blinking ['blɪŋkɪŋ] *adj* (**a**) *(light)* clignotant(e) (**b**) *Br Fam (for emphasis)* sacré(e); **what a b. nuisance!** quelle barbe!; **you b. idiot!** espèce d'imbécile!

blip [blɪp] *n (on radar screen)* spot *m*; *Fam (temporary problem)* hic *m inv*, os *m*

bliss [blɪs] *n* bonheur *m*, béatitude *f*; **breakfast in bed, what b.!** le petit déjeuner au lit, quel bonheur!

blissful ['blɪsfʊl] *adj (person)* (bien)heureux(euse); *(holiday)* plein(e) de bonheur; **I'd rather remain in b. ignorance** j'aime autant ne pas savoir

blissfully ['blɪsfʊlɪ] *adv* merveilleusement; **b. happy** au comble du bonheur; **to be b. unaware that...** ne pas se douter le moins du monde que...

blister ['blɪstə(r)] **1** *n (on skin)* ampoule *f*, cloque *f*; *(on paint)* cloque

2 *vt (skin)* provoquer des ampoules sur; *(paint)* faire des cloques sur
3 *vi (of skin)* se couvrir d'ampoules; *(of paint)* cloquer
blistering ['blɪstərɪŋ] *adj (sun, heat)* brûlant(e); *(criticism, attack)* virulent(e)
blithe ['blaɪð] *adj (attitude, disregard)* désinvolte; *Lit (person)* joyeux(euse), allègre
blithely ['blaɪðlɪ] *adv (ignore, disregard)* avec une complète désinvolture; *Lit (happily)* joyeusement, allègrement
blithering ['blɪðərɪŋ] *adj* **a b. idiot** un(e) sombre idiot(e)
blitz [blɪts] *n (air bombardment)* blitz *m*, bombardement *m* aérien; *Hist* **the B.** le Blitz; *Fam* **to have a b. on sth** s'attaquer à qch
blizzard ['blɪzəd] *n* tempête *f* de neige
bloated ['bləʊtɪd] *adj (stomach, face)* gonflé(e); *(ego)* énorme
blob [blɒb] *n* **(a)** *(of cream, jam, paint)* tache *f*; *(of ink)* pâté *m* **(b)** *(indistinct shape)* silhouette *f*
bloc [blɒk] *n Pol* bloc *m*
block [blɒk] **1** *n* **(a)** *(of wood, stone)* bloc *m*; *(for execution, of butcher)* billot *m*; *Fam* **I'll knock your b. off!** je vais te casser la gueule!; **b. and tackle** *(for lifting)* palan *m*; **b. capitals** majuscules *fpl* en caractères d'imprimerie; **b. diagram** *(flow chart)* schéma *m* fonctionnel **(b)** *Br (building)* immeuble *m*; *Am (group of buildings)* pâté *m* de maisons; *Br* **b. of flats** immeuble **(c)** *(of shares)* paquet *m*; **b. of seats** bloc-sièges *m inv*; **b. booking** réservation *f ou* location *f* de groupe; **b. vote** vote *m* groupé
2 *vt* **(a)** *(pipe, road, proposal)* bloquer; *(view)* cacher; **to b. sb's way** barrer *ou* bloquer le passage à qn; *Fin* **to b. a cheque** faire opposition à un chèque **(b)** *Comput (text)* sélectionner
▶**block off** *vt sep (road, exit)* barrer
▶**block out** *vt sep (light)* empêcher d'entrer *ou* de passer; *(a memory)* refouler; *(music, noise)* faire abstraction de
▶**block up** *vt sep (tunnel, passageway)* boucher; *(door, window)* murer; **to have a blocked-up nose** avoir le nez bouché
blockade [blɒ'keɪd] **1** *n* blocus *m* (**on** à)
2 *vt* bloquer, faire le blocus de
blockage ['blɒkɪdʒ] *n* obstruction *f*
blockbuster ['blɒkbʌstə(r)] *n (film)* superproduction *f*; *(novel)* best-seller *m*
blockhead ['blɒkhed] *n Fam* lourdaud *m*
bloke [bləʊk] *n Br Fam* type *m*
blonde [blɒnd] *n & adj* blond(e) *m,f*
blood [blʌd] **1** *n* **(a)** *(substance)* sang *m*; **to give b.** donner du sang; **b. bank** banque *f* du sang; **b. cell** globule *m* sanguin; **b. clot** caillot *m*; **b. count** numération *f* globulaire; **b. donor** donneur(euse) *m,f* de sang; **b. group** groupe *m* sanguin; **b. poisoning** septicémie *f*, toxémie *f*; **b. pressure** tension *f* (artérielle); **to have low/high b. pressure** avoir la tension basse/ de la tension; **b. relation** parent(e) *m,f*; **b. sports** la chasse; **b. test** prise *f* de sang; **b. transfusion** transfusion *f* sanguine; **b. vessel** vaisseau *m* sanguin **(b)** *(idioms)* **to have b. on one's hands** avoir du sang sur les mains; **it makes my b. boil** ça me fait bouillir; **it makes my b. run cold** ça me glace le sang; **in cold b.** de sang-froid; **he's after your b.** il en a après toi; **to have sth in one's b.** avoir qch dans le sang; **it's like**

trying to get b. out of a stone c'est comme si on se heurtait à un mur; *Prov* **b. is thicker than water** la famille passe avant tout
2 *vt (initiate)* initier
bloodbath ['blʌdbɑːθ] *n* bain *m* de sang
bloodcurdling ['blʌdkɜːdlɪŋ] *adj* à vous tourner les sangs
bloodhound ['blʌdhaʊnd] *n* limier *m*
bloodless ['blʌdlɪs] *adj* **(a)** *(without bloodshed)* **it was a b. coup** le coup d'État s'est déroulé sans effusion de sang **(b)** *(pale)* exsangue
bloodletting ['blʌdletɪŋ] *n* **(a)** *Med* saignée *f* **(b)** *(slaughter, feud)* effusion *f* de sang
bloodshed ['blʌdʃed] *n* effusion *f* de sang; **without b.** sans verser le sang
bloodshot ['blʌdʃɒt] *adj (eyes)* injecté(e) de sang
bloodstain ['blʌdsteɪn] *n* tache *f* de sang
bloodstained ['blʌdsteɪnd] *adj* taché(e) de sang
bloodstream ['blʌdstriːm] *n* sang *m*
bloodsucker ['blʌdsʌkə(r)] *n also Fig* sangsue *f*
bloodthirsty ['blʌdθɜːstɪ] *adj (person)* sanguinaire; *(film)* sanglant(e)
bloody ['blʌdɪ] **1** *adj* **(a)** *(bleeding, bloodstained)* ensanglanté(e); *(battle, revolution)* sanglant(e); *Fig* **to give sb a b. nose** mettre une raclée à qn **(b)** *Br very Fam* foutu(e); **you b. fool!** connard!; **b. hell!** merde!
2 *adv Br very Fam* **it's b. hot!** il fait une putain de chaleur!; **I'm b. tired** putain, qu'est-ce que je suis crevé; **not b. likely!** putain, il n'y a pas de danger!; **he can b. well do it himself!** il peut parfaitement se démerder tout seul!
bloody-minded [blʌdɪ'maɪndɪd] *adj Br* **to be b.** être un(e) emmerdeur(euse); **don't be so b.!** arrête d'emmerder le monde!
bloom [bluːm] **1** *n* fleur *f*; **in (full) b.** *(tree)* en fleur(s); *(flower)* éclos(e); **in the b. of youth** à *ou* dans la fleur de l'âge
2 *vi (of garden, flower, talent)* fleurir; *Fig* **to be blooming with health** être resplendissant(e) *ou* éclatant(e) de santé
bloomer ['bluːmə(r)] *n* **(a)** *Fam (mistake)* bourde *f* **(b)** *(bread)* ≃ bâtard *m* court
bloomers ['bluːməz] *npl* culotte *f* bouffante
blooming ['bluːmɪŋ] *Br Fam (for emphasis)* **1** *adj* sacré(e); **you b. idiot!** espèce d'idiot!
2 *adv* **b. good** sacrément bon (bonne); **b. awful** carrément horrible; **he's b. useless!** il est totalement nul!
blossom ['blɒsəm] **1** *n* fleur *f*; **in b.** en fleur(s)
2 *vi* fleurir; *Fig* s'épanouir; *Fig* **she had blossomed into a charming young woman** elle était devenue une charmante jeune femme
blot [blɒt] **1** *n (of ink)* pâté *m*; *Fig* **a b. on sb's reputation** une tache faite à la réputation de qn; *Fig* **to be a b. on the landscape** gâcher le paysage
2 *vt (pt & pp blotted) (stain)* tacher; *(with ink)* faire un pâté/des pâtés sur; **to b. one's lipstick** fixer son rouge à lèvres *(en pressant les lèvres sur un mouchoir en papier)*; *Fig* **to b. one's copybook** ternir sa réputation
▶**blot out** *vt sep (sun, light)* masquer; *(memory)* effacer
blotch [blɒtʃ] *n (on skin)* tache *f*
blotchy ['blɒtʃɪ] *adj (skin)* couvert(e) de taches
blotter ['blɒtə(r)] *n* buvard *m*
blotting paper ['blɒtɪŋpeɪpə(r)] *n* buvard *m*; **a sheet of b.** un buvard

blotto ['blɒtəʊ] *adj Br Fam (drunk)* bourré(e)

blouse [blaʊz] *n* chemisier *m*, corsage *m*

blow¹ [bləʊ] *n* (a) *(hit)* coup *m*; **to come to blows (over sth)** en venir aux mains (pour *ou* au sujet de qch); *Fig* **to strike a b. for sth** remporter une victoire pour qch; *Fig* **to soften the b.** atténuer le choc (**b**) *(setback)* coup *m*; **this news was a b. to us** cette nouvelle a été pour nous un coup rude; **it was a b. to her pride** son orgueil en a pris un coup

blow² *(pt* **blew** [blu:]*, pp* **blown** [bləʊn]) **1** *vt* (a) *(of wind, person)* **the wind blew down the fence** le vent a renversé la barrière; **the wind blew the door open** le vent a fait s'ouvrir la porte; **to b. glass** souffler le verre; **to b. the horn** klaxonner; **to b. a whistle** donner un coup de sifflet; *Fig* **to b. the whistle on sb/sth** dénoncer qn/qch; **to b. the dust off sth** souffler sur qch pour en enlever la poussière; **to b. sb a kiss** envoyer un baiser à qn; **to b. bubbles** faire des bulles; **to b. one's nose** se moucher; *Fig* **to b. one's own trumpet** chanter ses propres louanges

(**b**) *Elec* **to b. a fuse** faire sauter un plomb; *Fig (of person)* disjoncter; *Fam Fig* **the Grand Canyon blew my mind!** quel pied, le Grand Canyon!; *Fam Fig* **the prices blew my mind!** j'ai été affolé par les prix!

(**c**) *Fam (waste) (chance)* gâcher; **that's blown it!** ça a tout gâché, ça a fait tout louper!

(**d**) *Fam (money)* claquer (**on sth** pour s'acheter qch) **2** *vi* (a) *(of wind, person)* souffler; **to b. down** *or* **over** *(of fence, tree)* se renverser; **the door blew open/ shut** le vent a ouvert/fermé la porte; **to b. on one's fingers** se souffler sur les doigts; *Fig* **to b. hot and cold** souffler le chaud et le froid

(**b**) *Elec (of fuse)* sauter

▸**blow away 1** *vt sep* **to b. sth away** *(of wind)* faire s'envoler qch; *Fam Fig* **to b. sb away** *(shoot dead)* descendre qn; *Fam Fig* **his latest film blew me away!** son dernier film, c'est le pied!

2 *vi (of paper, hat)* s'envoler

▸**blow off 1** *vt sep (of wind)* emporter; *Fam Fig* **to b. sb's head off** faire sauter la cervelle à qn

2 *vi (of hat)* s'envoler

▸**blow out** *vt sep (of wind)* éteindre; *(candle, match)* souffler

▸**blow over** *vi (of storm, argument)* se calmer; **the scandal soon blew over** le scandale fut vite oublié

▸**blow up 1** *vt sep* (a) *(balloon, tyre)* gonfler (**b**) *(explode)* faire sauter (**c**) *(enlarge) (photograph)* agrandir; *Fig* **the incident was blown up out of all proportion** on a fait une histoire incroyable autour de ce petit incident

2 *vi (of bomb)* exploser, sauter; *Fig (lose one's temper)* piquer une colère; **to b. up at sb/sth** se mettre en colère contre qn/qch

blow-by-blow ['bləʊbaɪ'bləʊ] *adj (account)* détaillé(e), minutieux(euse)

blow-dry ['bləʊdraɪ] **1** *n* brushing *m*

2 *vt* **to b. sb's hair** faire un brushing à qn

blower ['bləʊə(r)] *n Br Fam (telephone)* bigophone *m*

blowhole ['bləʊhəʊl] *n (of whale)* évent *m*

blowjob ['bləʊdʒɒb] *n Vulg* pipe *f*; **to give sb a b.** tailler une pipe à qn

blowlamp ['bləʊlæmp] = **blowtorch**

blown [bləʊn] *pp of* **blow**

blow-out ['bləʊaʊt] *n* (a) *(of tyre)* éclatement *m* (**b**) *Fam (big meal)* gueuleton *m*

blowpipe ['bləʊpaɪp] *n* sarbacane *f*

blowtorch ['bləʊtɔːtʃ] *n (for welding)* chalumeau *m*, lampe *f* à souder; *(for removing paint)* brûloir *m*

blowzy ['blaʊzɪ] *adj* négligé(e)

blub [blʌb] *(pt & pp* **blubbed**) *vi Fam* pleurer comme une madeleine

blubber ['blʌbə(r)] **1** *n (fat)* graisse *f*

2 *vi Fam (cry)* pleurer comme une madeleine

bludgeon ['blʌdʒən] *vt* matraquer; *Fig* **to b. sb into doing sth** obliger brutalement qn à faire qch

blue [blu:] **1** *n* (a) *(colour)* bleu *m*; *Fig* **out of the b.** à l'improviste; **her resignation came out of the b.** sa démission nous a pris par surprise (**b**) **the blues** *(music)* le blues; *Fam* **to have the blues** *(be depressed)* avoir le cafard

2 *adj* (a) *(colour)* bleu(e); **b. with cold** bleu de froid; *Fam* **she can complain until she's b. in the face** elle peut se plaindre autant qu'elle veut; **once in a b. moon** tous les trente-six du mois; *Fam* **to scream b. murder** crier comme un putois; **b. blood** sang *m* bleu; **b. cheese** bleu *m*; **b. whale** baleine *f* bleue (**b**) *Fam (sad)* **to feel b.** avoir le cafard (**c**) *Fam (obscene) (joke)* grivois(e), paillard(e); *(film)* porno; **to tell b. stories** en raconter des vertes et de pas mûres

bluebell ['blu:bel] *n* jacinthe *f* des bois

blueberry ['blu:bərɪ] *(pl* **blueberries***) n* airelle *f*, myrtille *f, Can* bleuet *m*

bluebird ['blu:bɜːd] *n* rouge-gorge *m* bleu

bluebottle ['blu:bɒtəl] *n* mouche *f* de la viande

blue-chip ['blu:tʃɪp] *adj Fin* **b. shares** valeurs *fpl* de père de famille; **b. company** affaire *f* de premier ordre

blue-collar ['blu:kɒlə(r)] *adj* **b. worker** col *m* bleu

blue-eyed ['blu:aɪd] *adj* aux yeux bleus; *Br Fam* **his mother's b. boy** le petit chéri de sa maman

blueprint ['blu:prɪnt] *n Archit & Ind* plan *m*; *Fig* projet *m*; **a b. for success** une garantie de succès

bluff¹ [blʌf] **1** *n (deception)* bluff *m*; **to call sb's b.** *(at cards)* inviter qn à mettre les cartes sur la table; *(in negotiation)* prendre qn au mot

2 *vt* **you're bluffing me** tu bluffes; **to b. one's way out of a tricky situation** se tirer d'affaire par un coup de bluff

3 *vi* bluffer

bluff² *n (cliff)* à-pic *m inv*

bluff³ *adj (manner)* direct(e)

blunder ['blʌndə(r)] **1** *n* gaffe *f*

2 *vi (make mistake)* faire une gaffe; **to b. along** *(move clumsily)* avancer d'un pas maladroit; **to b. against** *or* **into sb/sth** heurter qn/à qch

blunderbuss ['blʌndəbʌs] *n* tromblon *m*

blunt [blʌnt] **1** *adj* (a) *(blade)* émoussé(e); *(pencil)* mal taillé(e); *(manner)* brutal(e); *(question, statement)* direct(e); *(refusal)* net (nette); *(person)* brusque; **to be b., ...** pour parler franchement, ...

2 *vt (blade)* émousser; *(pencil)* épointer; *Fig (anger, enthusiasm)* émousser, atténuer

bluntly ['blʌntlɪ] *adv (frankly)* franchement; **I told him b. that...** je lui ai dit tout net que...

bluntness ['blʌntnɪs] *n* (a) *(of blade)* manque *m* de tranchant (**b**) *(of manner, statement)* rudesse *f*; *(of person)* franchise *f*

blur [blɜː(r)] **1** *n (vague shape)* forme *f* vague; *(unclear memory)* vague souvenir *m*; **without my glasses, everything is a b.** sans mes lunettes, je suis complètement dans le brouillard; **to go by in a b.** *(of time)* passer à toute vitesse

2 *vt* (*pt* & *pp* **blurred**) brouiller, troubler
3 *vi* se brouiller; (*of memories*) s'estomper
blurb [blɜːb] *n* (*on book cover*) notice *f* publicitaire
blurred [blɜːd] *adj* (*ink*) qui a bavé; (*writing*) flou(e); (*vision*) trouble
▶**blurt out** [blɜːt] *vt sep* laisser échapper; **"I love him!"** **she blurted out** "je l'aime!" lâcha-t-elle
blush [blʌʃ] 1 *n* rougeur *f*; **to spare sb's blushes** éviter à qn un embarras
2 *vi* rougir; **to b. with shame** rougir de honte; **to b. at the thought of sth** rougir en pensant à qch; **I b. to admit it** j'ai honte de l'admettre
blusher ['blʌʃə(r)] *n* blush *m*, fard *m* à joues
bluster ['blʌstə(r)] 1 *n* protestations *fpl* véhémentes
2 *vi* protester avec véhémence
blustery ['blʌstərɪ] *adj* (*day*) venteux(euse), de grand vent; (*wind*) violent(e)
BMA [biːe'meɪ] *n* (*abbr* **British Medical Association**) ≃ ordre *m* des médecins
BO [biː'əʊ] *n Fam* (*abbr* **body odour**) odeur *f* corporelle; **to have BO** sentir mauvais
boa ['bəʊə] *n* **b. (constrictor)** boa *m* (constricteur); **(feather) b.** boa *m*
boar ['bɔː(r)] *n* (*male pig*) verrat *m*; (*wild pig*) sanglier *m*
board [bɔːd] 1 *n* (**a**) (*of wood*) planche *f*; (*for notices*) panneau *m*; (*for chess*) échiquier *m*; (*for draughts*) damier *m*; (*for Monopoly*® *etc*) tableau *m*; (*blackboard*) tableau; **to go by the b.** (*of plan, system*) être abandonné(e); **across the b.** globalement; **b. game** jeu *m* de société (*avec des pions etc*)
(**b**) (*of company*) conseil *m*, comité *m*; **b. (of directors)** conseil d'administration; **b. of enquiry** commission *f* d'enquête; **b. of examiners** jury *m* d'examen; *Br* **B. of Trade** ≃ ministère *m* du Commerce; **b. meeting** réunion *f* du conseil
(**c**) (*meals*) **half b.** demi-pension *f*; **full b.** pension *f* complète; **b. and lodging** (*in hotel*) pension complète
(**d**) **on b.** à bord; **to go on b.** monter à bord; *Fig* **to take sth on b.** (*idea, proposal*) prendre qch en considération; (*problem*) tenir compte de qch
2 *vt* (*ship, plane*) embarquer; (*train, bus*) monter dans
3 *vi* (**a**) (*lodge*) être en pension (**with** chez); (*at school*) aller en pension
(**b**) *Aviat* **flight 123 is now boarding** l'embarquement du vol 123 a commencé
▶**board up** *vt sep* (*house, window*) condamner
boarder ['bɔːdə(r)] *n* (*lodger*) pensionnaire *mf*; (*at school*) interne *mf*, pensionnaire
boarding ['bɔːdɪŋ] *n* (**a**) **b. card** *or* **pass** carte *f* d'embarquement (**b**) **b. house** pension *f* de famille; **b. school** pensionnat *m*

> ## Boarding Schools
> Les "boarding schools", traditionnellement réservées à la progéniture de la haute bourgeoisie, existent en Grande-Bretagne depuis des siècles et furent pendant très longtemps caractérisées par une discipline stricte et un confort rudimentaire. Aujourd'hui, même si les "boarding schools" prônent toujours des valeurs traditionnelles elles ont dû s'adapter à la société moderne. Elles sont maintenant très souvent mixtes et acceptent des pensionnaires d'origine sociale un peu plus variée ainsi qu'un nombre croissant d'internes à la semaine.

boardroom ['bɔːdruːm] *n* salle *f* de réunion (*du conseil d'administration*)
boardwalk ['bɔːdwɔːk] *n Am* = passage en bois sur la plage
boast [bəʊst] 1 *n* vantardise *f*
2 *vt* **the school boasts a fine library** l'école est fière de posséder une belle bibliothèque
3 *vi* se vanter (**about** de); **it's nothing to b. about!** il n'y a pas de quoi se vanter!
boastful ['bəʊstfʊl] *adj* vantard(e), fanfaron(onne)
boasting ['bəʊstɪŋ] *n* vantardise *f*, fanfaronnade *f*
boat [bəʊt] *n* bateau *m*; (*small*) canot *m*, embarcation *f*; **to come by b.** venir en bateau, prendre le bateau; *Fig* **we're all in the same b.** nous sommes tous dans le même cas; *Fig* **to push the b. out** (*celebrate lavishly*) faire des frais; **the B. Race** = traditionnelle course d'aviron qui oppose chaque année sur la Tamise une équipe d'Oxford à une équipe de Cambridge
boat-builder ['bəʊtbɪldə(r)] *n* constructeur *m* de bateaux
boater ['bəʊtə(r)] *n* (*hat*) canotier *m*
boathouse ['bəʊthaʊs] *n* hangar *m* pour bateaux
boating ['bəʊtɪŋ] *n* canotage *m*; **to go b.** faire du canotage
boat-load ['bəʊtləʊd] *n* cargaison *f*; *Fig* **by the b.** par bateaux entiers
boatswain ['bəʊsən] *n Naut* maître *m* d'équipage
boatyard ['bəʊtjɑːd] *n* chantier *m* de construction pour canots et bateaux de plaisance
Bob [bɒb] *n Fam* **and B.'s your uncle!** et voilà le travail!
bob¹ [bɒb] 1 *n* (**a**) (*curtsey*) petite révérence *f* (**b**) (*hairstyle*) (*coupe f au*) carré *m* (**c**) (*bobsleigh*) bobsleigh *m*
2 *vt* (*pt* & *pp* **bobbed**) (**a**) **to b. one's head** hocher la tête (**b**) **to have one's hair bobbed** se faire faire un carré
3 *vi* **to b. up and down** s'agiter; **to b. about** (*on water*) se balancer
bob² [bɒb] (*pl* **bob**) *n Br Fam Old-fashioned* (*shilling*) shilling *m*; **that must cost a few b.** à mon avis, ce n'est pas donné; **he's not short of a b. or two** il a de quoi
bobbin ['bɒbɪn] *n* bobine *f*
bobble ['bɒbəl] *n* (*on hat*) pompon *m*
bobby ['bɒbɪ] (*pl* **bobbies**) *n Br Fam* (*policeman*) flic *m*
bobsled ['bɒbsled], **bobsleigh** ['bɒbsleɪ] *n* bobsleigh *m*
bod [bɒd] *n Fam* (**a**) *Br* (*man*) type *m*; (*woman*) femme *f* (**b**) (*body*) corps *m*; **he's got a nice b.** il est bien foutu
bode [bəʊd] *vi* **to b. well/ill (for)** être de bon/mauvais augure (pour)
bodice ['bɒdɪs] *n* corsage *m*
bodily ['bɒdɪlɪ] 1 *adj* corporel(elle), physique; **b. functions** fonctions *fpl* corporelles; **b. needs** besoins *mpl* physiques
2 *adv* (*grab*) à bras-le-corps; **he was carried b. to the door** on l'a saisi à bras-le-corps et puis on l'a transporté jusqu'à la porte
body ['bɒdɪ] (*pl* **bodies**) *n* (**a**) (*of person, animal*) corps *m*; (*dead*) cadavre *m*, corps; **to have enough to keep b. and soul together** avoir juste de quoi vivre; *Fam* **over my dead b.!** plutôt crever!; **b. bag** = sac servant au transport des dépouilles mortelles; *Fig* **to deliver a b. blow (to)** porter un coup terrible (à); **b. builder** culturiste *mf*; **b. building** culturisme *m*; **b. count** (*of casualties*) comptage *m* des morts; (*of those present*) comptage des présents; **b. language** (*of performer*)

gestuelle *f*; **I could tell by his b. language** je le savais d'après la façon dont il se tenait; **b. odour** odeur *f* corporelle; **b. piercing** piercing *m*; **b. stocking** *(without legs)* body *m*; *(with legs)* combinaison *f* collante; **b. warmer** petit gilet *m* chaud

(**b**) *(of wine)* corps *m*; *(of hair)* volume *m*

(**c**) *(group)* corps *m*; **a large b. of people** une foule nombreuse; **b. of evidence** ensemble *m* de preuves; **b. of water** masse *f* d'eau; **public b.** organisme *m* public; **the b. politic** le corps politique

(**d**) *(main part) (of car)* carrosserie *f*; *(of letter)* corps *m*; *(of argument)* essentiel *m*; **b. shop** atelier *m* de carrosserie

(**e**) *(garment)* body *m*

bodyguard ['bɒdɪgɑːd] *n* *(person)* garde *m* du corps; *(group)* gardes *mpl* du corps

bodywork ['bɒdɪwɜːk] *n* *(of car)* carrosserie *f*

Boer ['bəʊə(r)] *n* Boer *mf*; **the B. War** la guerre des Boers

boffin ['bɒfɪn] *n* *Br Fam Hum (scientist)* savant *m*

bog [bɒg] *n* (**a**) *(marsh)* marécage *m* (**b**) *Br very Fam (toilet)* chiottes *fpl*; **b. roll** *or* **paper** PQ *m*

▶**bog down** *(pt & pp bogged)* *vt sep* **to get bogged down (in)** *(mud)* s'enliser (dans), s'embourber (dans); *(details)* se perdre (dans)

bogey ['bəʊgɪ] *(pl bogeys) n* (**a**) *(cause of fear)* hantise *f* (**b**) *Fam (from nose)* crotte *f* de nez

bogeyman ['bəʊgɪmæn] *n* **the b.** le croque-mitaine, le Père fouettard

boggle ['bɒgəl] *vi Fam* **to b. at doing sth** rechigner à faire qch; **the mind boggles!** ça laisse rêveur!

Bogotá [bɒgəˈtɑː] *n* Bogotá

bogus ['bəʊgəs] *adj* faux (fausse); *Fam* **he's completely b.** c'est vraiment un faux jeton

Bohemian [bəʊˈhiːmɪən] **1** *n* *(native of Bohemia)* Bohémien(enne) *m,f, (artistic person)* bohème *mf*
2 *adj (person, lifestyle)* bohème; *(from Bohemia)* bohémien(enne)

boil¹ [bɔɪl] *n (on skin)* furoncle *m*

boil² **1** *n* **to come to the b.** arriver à ébullition; **to bring sth to the b.** amener qch à ébullition; *Fig* **to go off the b.** ne plus marcher très fort
2 *vt* faire bouillir; **to b. the kettle** mettre de l'eau à chauffer
3 *vi* bouillir; **the kettle's boiling** la bouilloire siffle; **the saucepan has boiled dry** l'eau de la casserole s'est complètement évaporée; **to b. with rage** bouillir (de colère)

▶**boil down to** *vt insep Fam* **it all boils down to...** ça revient à...

▶**boil over** *vi (of milk, soup)* déborder; *Fig (of situation)* empirer, s'aggraver

boil up *vt sep (water, milk)* faire bouillir

boiler ['bɔɪlə(r)] *n* chaudière *f*; **b. maker** chaudronnier *m*; **b. room** salle *f* des chaudières, chaufferie *f*; **b. suit** bleu *m* de chauffe

boiling ['bɔɪlɪŋ] **1** *adj* bouillant(e); *Fam* **I'm b.!** je crève de chaleur!; **b. point** point *m* d'ébullition; *Fig* **the situation has reached b. point** la situation est explosive
2 *adv* **it's b. hot** il fait une chaleur à crever

boisterous ['bɔɪstərəs] *adj* bruyant(e)

bold [bəʊld] *adj* (**a**) *(brave)* hardi(e), intrépide (**b**) *(shameless)* **as b. as brass** culotté(e) (**c**) *(striking) (colour)* vif (vive); *(handwriting)* vigoureux(euse); *Typ* **b. type** caractères *mpl* gras

boldly ['bəʊldlɪ] *adv (bravely)* hardiment

boldness ['bəʊldnɪs] *n (bravery)* hardiesse *f*

Bolivia [bəˈlɪvɪə] *n* la Bolivie

Bolivian [bəˈlɪvɪən] **1** *n* Bolivien(enne) *m,f*
2 *adj* bolivien(enne)

bollard ['bɒləd] *n Naut* bollard *m*; *Br (traffic barrier)* borne *f*

bollocking ['bɒləkɪŋ] *n very Fam* **to give sb a b.** engueuler qn

bollocks ['bɒləks] *npl Br Vulg (testicles)* couilles *fpl*; **b.!** *(nonsense)* c'est des conneries!

Bolshevik ['bɒlʃəvɪk] *n & adj* bolchevique *mf*

Bolshevism ['bɒlʃəvɪzəm] *n* bolchevisme *m*

bolshie, bolshy ['bɒlʃɪ] *adj Fam* râleur(euse)

bolster ['bəʊlstə(r)] **1** *n (pillow)* traversin *m*
2 *vt (confidence, pride)* renforcer, consolider

bolt [bəʊlt] **1** *n* (**a**) *(on door)* verrou *m*; *(metal fastening)* boulon *m*; *Fam* **he has shot his b.** il a échoué après avoir joué sa dernière carte (**b**) *Fam (dash)* **to make a b. for it** se sauver à toutes jambes; **she made a b. for the door** elle s'est précipitée vers la porte; **b. hole** refuge *m* (**c**) **b. of lightning** foudre *f*; *Fig* **it came like a b. from the blue** ça a été comme un coup de tonnerre
2 *adv* **b. upright** droit(e) comme un i
3 *vt* (**a**) *(lock)* verrouiller; *(fasten with bolts)* boulonner (**b**) *(food)* engloutir
4 *vi (of horse)* s'emballer; *(of person)* décamper, déguerpir

▶**bolt down** *vt sep (food)* engloutir

bomb [bɒm] **1** *n* bombe *f*; *Br Fam* **to go like a b.** foncer; *Fam* **to cost a b.** coûter les yeux de la tête; **b. disposal expert** démineur *m*; **b. scare** alerte *f* à la bombe
2 *vt* bombarder
3 *vi Am (fail)* faire un bide

▶**bomb along** *vi Fam (go quickly)* foncer

bombard [bɒmˈbɑːd] *vt* bombarder; *Fig* **to b. sb with questions** bombarder *ou* assaillir qn de questions

bombardment [bɒmˈbɑːdmənt] *n* bombardement *m*

bombast ['bɒmbæst] *n* emphase *f*

bombastic [bɒmˈbæstɪk] *adj* ampoulé(e), emphatique

bomber ['bɒmə(r)] *n (aircraft)* bombardier *m*; *(person)* poseur(euse) *m,f* de bombe; **b. jacket** blouson *m* d'aviateur

bombing ['bɒmɪŋ] *n (aerial)* bombardement *m*; *(by terrorists)* attentat *m* à la bombe

bombshell ['bɒmʃel] *n* obus *m*; *Fig* **to drop a b.** faire une révélation fracassante; *Fam Fig* **a blonde b.** une magnifique blonde

bombsite ['bɒmsaɪt] *n* zone *f* bombardée; *Fig* **your bedroom is (like) a b.!** quel capharnaüm, ta chambre!

bona fide ['bəʊnəˈfaɪdɪ] *adj* véritable

bonanza [bəˈnænzə] *n* aubaine *f*; **a b. year** une année exceptionnelle

bonbon ['bɒnbɒn] *n* bonbon *m*

bonce [bɒns] *n Fam (head)* caboche *f*

bond [bɒnd] **1** *n* (**a**) *(attachment)* lien *m*; **to feel a b. with sb** se sentir lié(e) à qn (**b**) *Fin* obligation *f* (**c**) *Law* caution *f*; *Formal* **my word is my b.** je n'ai qu'une parole (**d**) *Com* **in b.** en dépôt
2 *vt* (**a**) *(stick)* coller (**b**) *Fig (unite)* **to b. together** créer des liens entre

3 vi (**a**) (stick) adhérer (**b**) Fig (form attachment) créer des liens affectifs (**with sb** avec qn)

bondage ['bɒndɪdʒ] n (**a**) (slavery) esclavage m (**b**) (sexual) = pratique sexuelle où l'un des partenaires est attaché

bonding [bɒndɪŋ] n (emotional attachment) liens mpl affectifs; **male b.** amitié f virile; Fam Hum **they're doing some male b. in the pub** ils sont allés au pub entre hommes

bone [bəʊn] **1** n (**a**) (of person, animal) os m; (of fish) arête f; **b. china** porcelaine f tendre; **b. meal** engrais m (de cendre d'os); **b. marrow** moëlle f; Med **b. marrow transplant** greffe f de moëlle (**b**) (idioms) **to work one's fingers to the b.** se tuer au travail; **b. idle** or **lazy** paresseux(euse) comme une couleuvre; **I feel it in my bones** je le sens; **b. of contention** sujet m de dispute; Fam **to have a b. to pick with sb** avoir un compte à régler avec qn; **she made no bones about it** elle ne l'a pas caché; **close to the b.** (tactless, risqué) limite
2 vt (chicken, meat) désosser; (fish) ôter les arêtes de
▸**bone up on** vt insep Fam potasser

bone-dry ['bəʊn'draɪ] adj complètement sec (sèche)

bonfire ['bɒnfaɪə(r)] n (for burning rubbish) feu m; (for celebration) feu de joie; Br **B. Night** = soirée du 5 novembre, célébration de la tentative de Guy Fawkes de faire sauter le Parlement en 1605

bong [bɒŋ] n (sound) bong m

bonhomie ['bɒnɒmi:] n bonhomie f

bonk¹ [bɒŋk] vt Fam (hit) frapper

bonk² Br very Fam **1** n **to have a b.** s'envoyer en l'air
2 vt s'envoyer en l'air avec
3 vi s'envoyer en l'air

bonkers ['bɒŋkəz] adj Br Fam (mad) dingue

Bonn [bɒn] n Bonn

bonnet ['bɒnɪt] n (**a**) (hat) bonnet m (**b**) Br (of car) capot m

bonny ['bɒnɪ] adj Scot joli(e)

bonsai ['bɒnzaɪ] n bonsaï m

bonus ['bəʊnəs] (pl **bonuses**) n (**a**) (money) prime f; **b. scheme** système m de primes de rendement (**b**) (advantage) avantage m; **b. number** (in lottery) numéro m supplémentaire

bony ['bəʊnɪ] adj (person, limb) maigre, décharné(e); (fish) plein(e) d'arêtes

boo [bu:] **1** n (pl **boos**) huée f
2 vt (pt & pp **booed**) huer
3 exclam hou!; **he wouldn't say b. to a goose** c'est un grand timide

boob [bu:b] Br Fam **1** n (**a**) (mistake) gaffe f; **to make a b.** faire une gaffe (**b**) (breast) nichon m; **b. tube** (garment) bustier m
2 vi (make mistake) faire une gaffe

booby-prize ['bu:bɪpraɪz] n prix m décerné au dernier (en guise de plaisanterie)

booby-trap ['bu:bɪtræp] **1** n (explosive device) objet m piégé; (practical joke) piège m
2 vt (pt & pp **booby-trapped**) piéger (en guise de farce)

book [bʊk] **1** n (**a**) (in general) livre m; (of stamps) carnet m; (of matches) pochette f; Fin **the books** (of company) les comptes mpl; **b. club** club m du livre; **b. end** serre-livres m inv; **b. token** chèque-cadeau m pour des livres (**b**) (idioms) **physics is a closed b. to me** je ne comprends absolument rien à la physique; **in my b.** à mon avis; **to be in sb's good books** être dans les petits papiers de qn, être bien vu(e) par qn; **to be in sb's bad books** être mal vu(e) par qn; **to bring sb to b.** forcer qn à rendre des comptes; **by** or **according to the b.** selon la procédure; **to throw the b. at sb** infliger la peine maximale à qn
2 vt (**a**) (seat, room, table, ticket) réserver; (performer) engager; **to b. sb on a flight** réserver une place pour qn sur un vol; **fully booked** (hotel, flight) complet(ète) (**b**) (for traffic offence) dresser une contravention à; (in football match) donner un carton jaune à
▸**book in 1** vt sep **to b. sb in** (to hotel) réserver une chambre à qn
2 vi Br (take a room) prendre une chambre; (register) = inscrire son nom dans le registre d'un hôtel
▸**book up 1** vt sep **the hotel is fully booked up** l'hôtel est complet; **I'm booked up for this evening** je suis pris toute la soirée
2 vi (make reservation) réserver

bookable ['bʊkəbəl] adj (seat, flight) qui peut être réservé(e)

bookbinder ['bʊkbaɪndə(r)] n relieur(euse) m,f

bookbinding ['bʊkbaɪndɪŋ] n reliure f

bookcase ['bʊkkeɪs] n bibliothèque f

bookie ['bʊkɪ] n Fam (bookmaker) bookmaker m

booking ['bʊkɪŋ] n (**a**) (reservation) réservation f; **to make a b.** effectuer une réservation; **b. office** bureau m de location (**b**) (in football) **to receive a b.** recevoir un carton jaune

bookish ['bʊkɪʃ] adj (person) studieux(euse); Pej (approach, style) livresque

bookkeeping ['bʊkki:pɪŋ] n Fin comptabilité f

booklet ['bʊklɪt] n brochure f

bookmaker ['bʊkmeɪkə(r)] n (in betting) bookmaker m

bookmark ['bʊkmɑ:k] n (**a**) (for book) marque-page m inv (**b**) Comput (for Web page) signet m

bookmarker ['bʊkmɑ:kə(r)] = **bookmark** (**a**)

bookseller ['bʊkselə(r)] n libraire mf

bookshelf ['bʊkʃelf] (pl **bookshelves** ['bʊkʃelvz]) n étagère f; **bookshelves** (furniture) bibliothèque f

bookshop ['bʊkʃɒp] n librairie f

bookstall ['bʊkstɔ:l] n (in railway station, airport) kiosque m à journaux; (selling second-hand books) étalage m de bouquiniste

bookstore ['bʊkstɔ:(r)] n Am librairie f

bookworm ['bʊkwɜ:m] n Fig passionné(e) m,f de lecture

boom¹ [bu:m] n (**a**) Naut (barrier) estacade f; (for sail) bôme f (**b**) Cin & TV perche f

boom² **1** n (economic) boom m; **b. town** ville f en plein essor économique
2 vi (of business, trade) être florissant(e)

boom³ **1** n (sound) détonation f
2 vi (of thunder, gun) gronder; (of person) tonitruer

boomerang ['bu:məræŋ] n boomerang m

booming ['bu:mɪŋ] adj (voice) tonitruant(e)

boon [bu:n] n bénédiction f, aubaine f

boor ['bʊə(r)] n rustaud(e) m,f

boorish ['bʊərɪʃ] adj rustre, grossier(ère)

boost [bu:st] **1** n **to give sth a b.** (production, economy) relancer qch; **to give sb's confidence a b.** redonner confiance à qn; **to give sb's morale a b.** remonter le moral à qn

2 vt Tel (signal) régénérer; (production, economy) relancer; **to b. sb's hopes** redonner espoir à qn

booster ['bu:stə(r)] n (**a**) **b. (rocket)** fusée f de démarrage (**b**) Elec survolteur m (**c**) Med (injection) rappel m

boot [bu:t] **1** n (**a**) (footwear) (for walking) brodequin m; (for sport) chaussure f; (ankle-length) bottine f; (knee-length) botte f (**b**) Br (of car) coffre m (**c**) (idioms) **the b. is on the other foot** les rôles sont inversés; Fam **to give sb the b.** mettre qn à la porte; Fam **to get the b.** se faire mettre à la porte; Fam **they put** or **stuck the b. into him** (kicked) ils l'ont roué de coups de pied; (criticized) ils lui ont passé un savon; **he's a liar and a thief to b.** c'est un menteur et par-dessus le marché c'est un voleur

2 vt (**a**) Fam (kick) donner un coup de pied dans; **to b. sb out** mettre qn à la porte (**b**) Comput amorcer **3** vi Comput **to b. (up)** s'amorcer

bootee [bu:'ti:] n chausson m (de bébé)

booth [bu:ð] n (at fair) baraque f, stand m; (for telephone) cabine f; (in voting) isoloir m; (in restaurant) alcôve f

bootlace ['bu:tleɪs] n lacet m (de botte)

bootleg ['bu:tleg] adj (alcohol) de contrebande; (recording) pirate

bootstrap ['bu:tstræp] n (**a**) (part of boot) tirant m de botte; Fig **to pull oneself up by one's bootstraps** se faire tout(e) seul(e) (**b**) Comput routine f d'amorçage

booty ['bu:tɪ] n (loot) butin m

booze [bu:z] Fam **1** n alcool m **2** vi picoler

boozer ['bu:zə(r)] n Fam (person) poivrot(e) m,f; Br (pub) pub m

booze-up ['bu:zʌp] n Br Fam beuverie f; **to have a b.** prendre une cuite

boozy ['bu:zɪ] adj Fam (voice, breath) aviné(e)

bop¹ [bɒp] Fam **1** n (dance) danse f **2** vi (pt & pp bopped) (dance) danser

bop² Fam **1** n (blow) léger coup m **2** vt (pt & pp bopped) (hit) donner un léger coup à

boracic [bə'ræsɪk] adj Chem borique

border ['bɔ:də(r)] **1** n (**a**) (edge) bord m; (in garden) plate-bande f (**b**) (frontier) frontière f; **the Borders** = région vallonnée du sud-est de l'Écosse; **b. guard** garde-frontière m; **b. town** ville f frontière ou frontalière

2 vt (country) avoir une frontière commune avec; (road) border

border on vt insep (of country) avoir une frontière commune avec; **to b. on insanity/the ridiculous** friser la folie/le ridicule

borderland ['bɔ:dəlænd] n zone f frontalière

borderline ['bɔ:dəlaɪn] n frontière f, ligne f de démarcation; **a b. case** un cas limite

bore¹ ['bɔ:(r)] **1** n (person) raseur(euse) m,f; (thing) chose f ennuyeuse; **what a b.!** quelle barbe! **2** vt ennuyer

bore² **1** n (calibre) calibre m **2** vt (with drill) forer; **to b. a hole in sth** percer un trou dans qch

bore³ pt of bear²

bored [bɔ:d] adj (sigh, look) d'ennui; **to be b.** s'ennuyer; Fam **to be b. stiff** or **to tears** s'ennuyer à mourir

boredom ['bɔ:dəm] n ennui m

boring ['bɔ:rɪŋ] adj ennuyeux(euse)

born [bɔ:n] **1** adj **to be a b. writer/leader** être un écrivain/leader né

2 (pp of bear) **to be b.** naître; **I was b. in London/in 1975** je suis né à Londres/en 1975; Fam **I wasn't b. yesterday** je ne suis pas né de la dernière pluie

born-again ['bɔ:nəgen] adj **b. Christian** chrétien(-enne) m,f régénéré(e)

borne [bɔ:n] pp of bear²

Borneo ['bɔ:nɪəʊ] n Bornéo

borough ['bʌrə] n Br circonscription f électorale urbaine

borrow ['bɒrəʊ] **1** vt emprunter (**from sb** à qn); **to be living on borrowed time** (of ill person, government) ne plus en avoir pour longtemps

2 vi emprunter (**from sb** à qn)

borrower ['bɒrəʊə(r)] n emprunteur(euse) m,f

borstal ['bɔ:stəl] n Br Formerly maison f de redressement

Bosnia(-Herzegovina) ['bɒznɪə('hɜ:tsəgə'vi:nə)] n la Bosnie(-Herzégovine)

Bosnian ['bɒznɪən] **1** n Bosniaque mf **2** adj bosniaque; **B. Croat/Muslim/Serb** Croate mf/Musulman(e) m,f/Serbe mf de Bosnie

bosom ['bʊzəm] **1** n (of woman) poitrine f; Fig **in the b. of one's family** au sein de sa famille **2** adj **b. friend** ami(e) m,f intime

Bosphorus ['bɒsfərəs] n **the B.** le Bosphore

boss¹ [bɒs] n (on shield) ombon m, ombo m

boss² Fam **1** n (at work) patron(onne) m,f; **to be one's own b.** être son propre patron; **to show sb who's b.** montrer à qn qui commande

2 vt **to b. sb (about** or **around)** donner des ordres à qn

bossy ['bɒsɪ] adj autoritaire; Fam **a b. boots** un petit chef, un tyran

bosun ['bəʊsən] n Naut maître m d'équipage

botanic(al) [bə'tænɪk(əl)] adj botanique; **b. garden(s)** jardin m botanique

botanist ['bɒtənɪst] n botaniste mf

botany ['bɒtənɪ] n botanique f

botch [bɒtʃ] Fam **1** n travail m salopé; **to make a b. of sth** (job) saloper qch; (interview, exam) rater qch complètement

2 vt **to b. sth (up)** (job) saloper qch; (interview, exam) rater complètement

botched [bɒtʃt] adj Fam raté(e); **a b. job** un travail de sagouin

both [bəʊθ] **1** pron les deux; **b. (of them) are dead** ils sont morts tous les deux; **b. of us saw it** nous l'avons vu tous les deux

2 adj les deux; **b. (the) brothers** les deux frères; **b. my parents** mes deux parents; **on b. sides** des deux côtés; **you can't have it b. ways** on ne peut pas tout avoir

3 adv **b. in Britain and in France** aussi bien en Grande-Bretagne qu'en France; **she is b. intelligent and beautiful** elle est à la fois intelligente et belle

bother ['bɒðə(r)] **1** n (trouble) ennui m; **if it's not too much b.** si cela ne vous dérange pas trop; **to go to the b. of doing sth** prendre la peine de faire qch

2 vt (**a**) (annoy) déranger; **my back's still bothering me** j'ai toujours des problèmes de dos; **I hate to b. you but...** je suis désolé de vous déranger mais... (**b**) (care) **to be bothered about sth** s'inquiéter de qch; Fam **I can't be bothered** ça ne me dit rien; Fam **I'm not bothered** ça m'est égal

3 *vi (care)* s'inquiéter (**about** de); **he didn't even b. to apologize** il n'a même pas pris la peine de s'excuser; **don't b.!** ce n'est pas la peine!
4 *exclam* zut!

bothersome ['bɒðəsəm] *adj* ennuyeux(euse), gênant(e)

Botswana [bɒt'swɑːnə] *n* le Botswana

bottle ['bɒtəl] **1** *n* (**a**) *(container)* bouteille *f*; *(for perfume)* flacon *m*; *(for baby)* biberon *m*; *Fam* **to take to** or **hit the b.** se mettre à picoler; **b. bank** conteneur *m* pour la récupération du verre usagé; **b. green** vert bouteille *inv*; **b. opener** ouvre-bouteilles *m inv*, décapsuleur *m*; **b. party** = soirée où chacun apporte une bouteille (**b**) *Br Fam (courage)* cran *m*; **to lose one's b.** se dégonfler
2 *vt* mettre en bouteille

▶**bottle out** *vi Br very Fam* se dégonfler; **he bottled out of the fight** il a eu peur de se battre

▶**bottle up** *vt sep (emotions, anger)* refouler, ravaler

bottled ['bɒtəld] *adj* en bouteille; **b. water** eau *f* minérale

bottle-feed ['bɒtəlfiːd] *(pt & pp* **bottle-fed** ['bɒtəlfed]) *vt* nourrir au biberon

bottleneck ['bɒtəlnek] *n (in road)* rétrécissement *m* de la chaussée; *(in traffic)* embouteillage *m (dû à un rétrécissement de la chaussée)*; *(in production)* goulot *m* d'étranglement

bottom ['bɒtəm] **1** *n* (**a**) *(lowest part) (of well, box, sea)* fond *m*; *(of street)* bout *m*; *(of stairs, mountain, page)* bas *m*; *(of ship)* carène *f*, fond *m*; **from the b. of one's heart** du fond du cœur; **to be at the b. of the class** être le (la) dernier(ère) de la classe; **to touch b.** *(of boat)* toucher le fond (**b**) *(buttocks)* derrière *m* (**c**) *(idioms)* **to be at the b. of sth** être à l'origine de qch; **to get to the b. of sth** aller au fond des choses; **at b.** au fond; **the b. has fallen out of the market** le marché s'est effondré; *Fam* **bottoms up!** cul sec!
2 *adj* du bas; **b. deck** *(on bus)* niveau *m* inférieur; **b. floor** rez-de-chaussée *m inv*; *Fam* **you can bet your b. dollar that...** vous pouvez être sûr que...; **in b. gear** en première; **the b. line** *(financially)* le solde final; *Fig* **the b. line is that he is unsuited to the job** le fait est qu'il n'est pas fait pour ce travail

▶**bottom out** *vi (of recession, slump)* atteindre son maximum; *(of price)* atteindre son minimum

bottomless ['bɒtəmlɪs] *adj (abyss)* sans fond; *(reserve)* inépuisable; *Fig* **a b. pit** un gouffre

bottommost ['bɒtəmməʊst] *adj* le (la) plus bas (basse)

botulism ['bɒtjʊlɪzəm] *n* botulisme *m*

boudoir ['buːdwɑː(r)] *n* boudoir *m*

bouffant ['buːfɒn] *adj (hair)* bouffant(e)

bough [baʊ] *n* branche *f*

bought [bɔːt] *pt & pp of* **buy**

boulder ['bəʊldə(r)] *n* gros bloc *m* de roche

boulevard ['buːləvɑːd] *n* boulevard *m*

bounce [baʊns] **1** *n* (**a**) *(of ball)* rebond *m* (**b**) *Fig (energy)* entrain *m*
2 *vt* (**a**) *(ball)* faire rebondir; *Fig* **to b. an idea off sb** soumettre une idée à qn *(de manière informelle)* (**b**) *Fam (cheque)* refuser d'honorer
3 *vi* (**a**) *(of ball)* rebondir (**off** contre); **to b. into/out of a room** *(of person)* entrer/sortir d'une pièce en sautillant (**b**) *Fam* **the cheque bounced** le chèque a été refusé *(parce qu'il était sans provision)*

▶**bounce back** *vi (after illness, disappointment)* se remettre rapidement

bouncer ['baʊnsə(r)] *n Fam (doorman)* videur *m*

bouncing ['baʊnsɪŋ] *adj* **a b. baby** un bébé en pleine santé

bouncy ['baʊnsɪ] *adj* (**a**) *(ball)* qui rebondit bien; *(mattress)* élastique; **b. castle** château *m* gonflable (**b**) *Fig (person)* plein(e) d'entrain

bound¹ [baʊnd] **1** *n (leap)* bond *m*; **at one b.** d'un bond
2 *vi (leap)* bondir

bound² *adj* (**a**) *(destined)* **b. for** en route pour (**b**) *(in predictions)* **he's b. to come** il ne peut pas manquer de venir; **it was b. to happen** ça devait arriver

bound³ *pt & pp of* **bind**

boundary ['baʊndərɪ] *(pl* **boundaries**) *n* limite *f*

bounder ['baʊndə(r)] *n Fam Old-fashioned* goujat *m*

boundless ['baʊndlɪs] *adj* illimité(e), sans bornes

bounds [baʊndz] *npl (limit)* limites *fpl*; **out of b.** interdit(e); **it is not beyond the b. of possibility** c'est dans le domaine du possible; **to know no b.** *(of anger, ambition)* être sans bornes

bountiful ['baʊntɪfʊl] *adj* abondant(e)

bounty ['baʊntɪ] *(pl* **bounties**) *n* (**a**) *(reward)* récompense *f*; **b. hunter** chasseur *m* de primes (**b**) *(generosity)* générosité *f*

bouquet [buː'keɪ] *n (of flowers, wine)* bouquet *m*

bourbon ['bɜːbən] *n (whisky)* bourbon *m*

bourgeois ['bʊəʒwɑː] *adj* bourgeois(e)

bourgeoisie [bʊəʒwɑː'ziː] *n* bourgeoisie *f*

bout [baʊt] *n* (**a**) *(of illness)* accès *m*; *(of work, activity)* période *f* (**b**) *(boxing match)* combat *m*

boutique [buː'tiːk] *n* boutique *f*

bovine ['bəʊvaɪn] *adj* bovin(e)

bow¹ [bəʊ] *n* (**a**) *(weapon)* arc *m*; *(for violin)* archet *m* (**b**) *(in hair, on dress)* nœud *m*; **b. tie** nœud papillon

bow² [baʊ] *n (of ship)* proue *f*, avant *m*

bow³ **1** *n* salut *m*; **to take a b.** saluer
2 *vt* **to b. one's head** baisser la tête
3 *vi* (**a**) *(as greeting, sign of respect)* saluer; *Fig* **to b. down before sb** s'incliner devant qn (**b**) *Fig (yield)* **to b. to sb/sth** s'incliner devant qn/qch

▶**bow out** *vi (resign)* tirer sa révérence

bowdlerize ['baʊdləraɪz] *vt* expurger

bowed [baʊd] *adj (back)* voûté(e); *(head)* baissé(e); **b. with age** courbé(e) par le fardeau des ans

bowel ['baʊəl] *n* intestin *m*; *Lit* **the bowels of the earth** les entrailles *fpl* de la terre; **b. complaint** affection *f* intestinale

bower ['baʊə(r)] *n* tonnelle *f*

bowl¹ [bəʊl] *n* (**a**) *(small dish)* bol *m*; *(for salad)* saladier *m*; *(for soup)* assiette *f* creuse (**b**) *(of toilet)* cuvette *f*

bowl² **1** *n* bowls *(game)* boules *fpl*
2 *vi (in cricket)* lancer la balle

▶**bowl along** *vi (of car, bicycle)* rouler à toute vitesse

▶**bowl over** *vt sep (knock down)* renverser; *Fig (astound)* **to be bowled over by sth** être stupéfié(e) par qch

bow-legged [bəʊ'legɪd] *adj* aux jambes arquées

bowler ['bəʊlə(r)] *n* (**a**) *(hat)* chapeau *m* melon (**b**) *(in cricket)* lanceur *m*

bowling ['bəʊlɪŋ] *n (game)* jeu *m* de boules; **b. alley** piste *f* de bowling; *(building)* bowling *m*; **b. green** terrain *m* de boules *(gazonné)*

box 55 **brave**

box [bɒks] **1** *n* (**a**) *(container)* boîte *f*; *(larger)* caisse *f*; *(postal)* boîte postale; **b. camera** appareil *m* photo compact (**b**) *(on form)* case *f*; *(containing text)* encadré *m*; (**penalty**) **b.** *(in football)* surface *f* de réparation (**c**) *Br Fam* **the b.** *(television)* la télé (**d**) *(in theatre)* loge *f*
2 *vt* (**a**) *(place in box)* mettre en boîte/en caisse (**b**) **to b. sb's ears** gifler qn
3 *vi (fight)* boxer

boxer ['bɒksə(r)] *n* (**a**) *(fighter)* boxeur *m*; **b. shorts, boxers** *(underwear)* caleçon *m* (**b**) *(dog)* boxer *m*

boxing ['bɒksɪŋ] *n* boxe *f*; **b. glove/match** gant *m*/ match *m* de boxe; **b. ring** ring *m*

Boxing Day ['bɒksɪŋ'deɪ] *n Br* le lendemain de Noël

box-office ['bɒksɒfɪs] *n* bureau *m* de location; **a b. success** un succès au box-office

boxroom ['bɒksruːm] *n* petite chambre *f*

boy [bɔɪ] *n* garçon *m*; **a night out with the boys** une soirée avec les copains; *Fam* **oh b.!** ça alors!; *Fam* **boys will be boys** il faut bien que jeunesse se passe; **b. band** boys band *m*; *Br Fam* **b. racer** = jeune conducteur imprudent; **B. Scout** scout *m*

boycott ['bɔɪkɒt] **1** *n* boycott *m*
2 *vt* boycotter

boyfriend ['bɔɪfrend] *n* petit ami *m*

boyhood ['bɔɪhʊd] *n* enfance *f*

boyish ['bɔɪʃ] *adj (of man) (looks, behaviour)* de garçon; *(of woman) (looks)* de garçon; *(behaviour)* de garçon manqué

BR [biː'ɑː(r)] *n (abbr* **British Rail***)* ≃ la SNCF

bra [brɑː] *n* soutien-gorge *m*

brace [breɪs] **1** *n* (**a**) *(on teeth)* appareil *m* dentaire *ou* orthodontique (**b**) *Br* **braces** *(for trousers)* bretelles *fpl* (**c**) *(pair) (of birds, pistols)* paire *f* (**d**) **b. and bit** *(tool)* vilebrequin *m (avec mèche)*
2 *vt* (**a**) **to b. oneself** *(for impact)* s'accrocher; *Fig* **to b. oneself (for sth)** se préparer (à qch) (**b**) *(reinforce)* consolider

bracelet ['breɪslɪt] *n* bracelet *m*

bracing ['breɪsɪŋ] *adj (wind, weather)* vivifiant(e)

bracken ['brækən] *n* fougère *f*

bracket ['brækɪt] **1** *n* (**a**) *(for shelves)* équerre *f* (**b**) *(in writing)* parenthèse *f*, **in brackets** entre parenthèses (**c**) *(category) (of tax)* tranche *f*; *(of salaries)* fourchette *f*; **the fifteen to twenty age b.** les quinze à vingt ans
2 *vt* (**a**) *(word, phrase)* mettre entre parenthèses (**b**) *(classify)* associer; **to b. together** mettre dans la même catégorie

brackish ['brækɪʃ] *adj* saumâtre

brag [bræg] *(pt & pp* **bragged***) vi* se vanter (**about** de)

braggart ['brægət] *n* vantard(e) *m,f*

braid [breɪd] **1** *n (of hair)* tresse *f*, natte *f*; *(of cloth)* galon *m*
2 *vt (hair, thread)* tresser

Braille [breɪl] *n* braille *m*

brain [breɪn] **1** *n* cerveau *m*; **brains** *(as food)* cervelle *f*; *Fam* **to have brains** être intelligent(e); *Fam* **she's the brains of the business** c'est elle le cerveau de l'entreprise; *Fam* **to have money/sex on the b.** être obsédé(e) par l'argent/le sexe; **b. damage** lésions *fpl* cérébrales; **b. dead** dans un coma dépassé; **the b. drain** la fuite des cerveaux; **b. surgeon** neurochirurgien(enne) *m,f*; **b. tumour** tumeur *f* au cerveau; *Fam* **b. wave** *(brilliant idea)* idée *f* de génie
2 *vt Fam (hit)* assommer

brainbox ['breɪnbɒks] *n Fam* cerveau *m*

brainchild ['breɪntʃaɪld] *n (idea, project)* idée *f*, trouvaille *f*

brainless ['breɪnlɪs] *adj* stupide

brainpower ['breɪnpaʊə(r)] *n* intelligence *f*

brainstorm ['breɪnstɔːm] *n Fam* (**a**) *Br (mental confusion)* moment *m* d'égarement (**b**) *Am (brilliant idea)* idée *f* de génie

brainstorming ['breɪnstɔːmɪŋ] *n* brainstorming *m*, remue-méninges *m*

brainwash ['breɪnwɒʃ] *vt* faire un lavage de cerveau à; **to b. sb into doing sth** faire faire qch à qn à force d'endoctrinement

brainy ['breɪnɪ] *adj Fam* intelligent(e)

braise [breɪz] *vt* braiser

brake [breɪk] **1** *n* frein *m*; **to apply the brake(s)** freiner; *Fig* **to put the brakes on a project** ralentir l'exécution d'un projet; **b. fluid** liquide *m* de freins; **b. lights** feux *mpl* de stop; **b. pedal** pédale *f* de frein
2 *vi* freiner

braking distance ['breɪkɪŋ'dɪstəns] *n* distance *f* de freinage

bramble ['bræmbəl] *n* ronce *f*

bran [bræn] *n* son *m*

branch [brɑːntʃ] **1** *n* (**a**) *(of tree, family, subject)* branche *f*; *(of river)* bras *m*; *(of railway, road)* embranchement *m*; **b. line** *(of railway)* ligne *f* secondaire (**b**) *(of shop)* succursale *f*; *(of bank)* agence *f*
2 *vi* bifurquer

▶**branch off** *vi (of discussion)* bifurquer (**into** vers)

▶**branch out** *vi* se diversifier; **to b. out into** étendre ses activités à

brand [brænd] **1** *n* (**a**) *(of product)* marque *f*; *Fig* **she has her own b. of humour** elle a un sens de l'humour particulier; **b. image** image *f* de marque; **b. leader** marque la plus vendue; **b. name** marque (**b**) *(on cattle)* marque *f (au fer rouge)*
2 *vt (cattle)* marquer au fer rouge; *Fig* **the image was branded on her memory** l'image était gravée dans sa mémoire; *Fig* **to b. sb (as) a liar/coward** coller à qn l'étiquette de menteur/lâche

brandish ['brændɪʃ] *vt* brandir

brand-new ['bræn(d)'njuː] *adj* flambant neuf (neuve)

brandy ['brændɪ] *(pl* **brandies***) n (cognac)* cognac *m*; *(more generally)* eau-de-vie *f*; **cherry b.** cherry *m*

brash [bræʃ] *adj (person, behaviour)* effronté(e); *(colour, décor)* tape-à-l'œil *inv*

brass [brɑːs] *n* (**a**) *(metal)* laiton *m*; *Br Fam* **it's not worth a b. farthing** ça ne vaut pas un clou; **to get down to b. tacks** en venir aux faits; *Br Fam* **it's b. monkey weather** il fait un froid de canard (**b**) *Mus (brass instruments)* cuivres *mpl*; **b. band** fanfare *f* (**c**) *Br Fam (money)* oseille *f*, pognon *m* (**d**) *Br Fam (cheek, nerve)* culot *m*; **to have a b. neck** avoir du culot, être culotté(e)

▶**brass off** *vt sep Br Fam* **to be brassed off (with)** en avoir marre (de)

brassière ['bræzɪə(r)] *n* soutien-gorge *m*

brassy ['brɑːsɪ] *adj Fam (person, manner)* exubérant(e)

brat [bræt] *n Pej* morveux(euse) *m,f*

bravado [brə'vɑːdəʊ] *n* bravade *f*

brave [breɪv] **1** *n (native American)* brave *m*
2 *adj* courageux(euse); **a b. effort** un bel effort; **a b. new world** un paradis; *Pej & Ironic* un monde utopi-

que; **to put a b. face on it** faire bonne contenance
3 *vt* braver
bravely [ˈbreɪvlɪ] *adv* courageusement
bravery [ˈbreɪvərɪ] *n* courage *m*
bravo [brɑːˈvəʊ] *exclam* bravo!
brawl [brɔːl] **1** *n* bagarre *f*; **a drunken b.** une querelle d'ivrognes
2 *vi* se bagarrer
brawn [brɔːn] *n Fam (strength)* muscle *m*; **he's all b. and no brain** il a du muscle mais rien dans la tête
brawny [ˈbrɔːnɪ] *adj* musclé(e)
bray [breɪ] **1** *n (of donkey)* braiment *m*; *Fig (of person)* braillement *m*
2 *vi (of donkey)* braire; *Fig (of person)* brailler
brazen [ˈbreɪzən] *adj* effronté(e), impudent(e); *(lie)* éhonté(e)
▶**brazen out** *vt sep* **to b. it out** s'en tirer au culot
brazier [ˈbreɪzɪə(r)] *n* brasero *m*
Brazil [brəˈzɪl] *n* le Brésil
brazil [brəˈzɪl] *n* **b. (nut)** noix *f* du Brésil
Brazilian [brəˈzɪlɪən] **1** *n* Brésilien(enne) *m,f*
2 *adj* brésilien(enne)
breach [briːtʃ] **1** *n* **(a)** *(in wall)* brèche *f*; *Fig* **to step into the b.** *(in emergency)* intervenir au pied levé
(b) *(of agreement, contract)* rupture *f* (**of** de); *(of trust)* abus *m* (**of** de); *(of discipline)* manquement *m* (**of** à); *(of rules)* infraction *f* (**of** à); *Law* **b. of the peace** atteinte *f* à l'ordre public
(c) *(in relationship)* **it caused a b. in their relationship** cela les a conduits à se brouiller
2 *vt* **(a)** *(defences)* ouvrir une brèche dans
(b) *(agreement, contract)* rompre; *(rules)* enfreindre
bread [bred] *n* **(a)** *(food)* pain *m*; **a loaf of b.** un pain; **b. and butter** du pain beurré; *Fig* gagne-pain *m*; *Fig* **he knows which side his b. is buttered on** il sait où est son intérêt; **b. bin** boîte *f* à pain; **b. knife** couteau *m* à pain **(b)** *very Fam (money)* blé *m*, pognon *m*
bread-and-butter [bredənˈbʌtə(r)] *adj Fam* **b. issues** questions *fpl* essentielles; *Culin* **b. pudding** pudding *m* au pain
breadbasket [ˈbredbɑːskɪt] *n* corbeille *f* à pain
breadboard [ˈbredbɔːd] *n* planche *f* à pain
breadcrumb [ˈbredkrʌm] *n* miette *f* de pain; **breadcrumbs** *(in recipe)* chapelure *f*; **fried in breadcrumbs** pané(e)
breadline [ˈbredlaɪn] *n* **on the b.** indigent(e), sans ressources
breadth [bredθ] *n* **(a)** *(width)* largeur *f* **(b)** *(of mind, opinions)* largeur *f*; *(of outlook, understanding)* ampleur *f*
breadwinner [ˈbredwɪnə(r)] *n* **to be the b.** faire bouillir la marmite
break [breɪk] **1** *n* **(a)** *(in bone)* fracture *f*; *(in wall, fence)* brèche *f*; *(in clouds)* trouée *f*; *(in electric circuit)* rupture *f*; **at b. of day** au point du jour; *Elec* **b. switch** disjoncteur *m*
(b) *(interval, rest)* pause *f*; *(holidays)* vacances *fpl*; **(commercial) b.** *(on TV, radio)* page *f* de publicité; **without a b.** sans interruption; **a b. in the weather** un changement de temps; *Fam* **give me a b.!** fichemoi la paix deux minutes!
(c) *Fam (escape)* évasion *f*; **to make a b. for it** se faire la belle; **to make a b. for the exit** se précipiter vers la sortie
(d) *Fam (chance)* chance *f*; **to have a lucky b.** avoir de la veine; **this could be your big b.** ça pourrait être la chance de ta vie
2 *vt (pt* **broke** [brəʊk], *pp* **broken** [ˈbrəʊkən]) **(a)** *(in general)* casser; **to b. one's arm** se casser le bras; **to b. sth into pieces** mettre qch en morceaux; **to b. the sound barrier** franchir le mur du son; *Fig* **to b. the ice** briser la glace; **to b. one's journey** s'arrêter en route; *Fig* **b. a leg!** *(good luck!)* bonne chance!
(b) *(cushion)* *(fall, force)* amortir
(c) *(destroy)* *(person, resistance, strike)* briser; *(health)* ruiner; **to b. sb's heart** briser le cœur à qn; **to b. sb's serve** *(in tennis)* prendre le service de qn
(d) *(infringe)* *(agreement, promise)* rompre; *(rule, speed limit)* enfreindre
(e) *(news, story)* annoncer (**to** à)
3 *vi* **(a)** *(of glass, machine, bone)* se casser; *(of weather)* changer; *(of day)* se lever; *(of waves)* se briser; *(of voice)* *(with emotion)* se briser; *(at puberty)* muer; **to b. in two** se casser en deux; **to b. loose** se détacher
(b) *(of news, story)* éclater
▶**break away** *vi* **(a)** *(escape)* **to b. away from** *(person)* échapper à; *(place)* s'évader de **(b)** **to b. away from** *(cut ties with)* *(party, country)* quitter; *(family)* couper les ponts avec
▶**break down 1** *vt sep* **(a)** *(destroy)* *(resistance)* briser **(b)** *(analyze)* *(argument, figures)* décomposer (**into** en)
2 *vi* **(a)** *(of car, machine)* tomber en panne; *(of talks)* échouer; *(of argument)* s'effondrer; *(of person under pressure)* craquer; **to b. down (in tears)** fondre en larmes **(b)** *(change chemically)* se décomposer (**into** en)
▶**break even** *vi* rentrer dans ses frais
▶**break in 1** *vt sep (horse)* dresser; *(new shoes)* faire; *(new recruit)* former; **to b. oneself in to sth** se faire à qch
2 *vi (of burglar)* entrer par effraction
▶**break into** *vt insep* **(a)** *(of burglar)* entrer par effraction dans .**(b)** *(begin suddenly)* **to b. into laughter** éclater de rire; **to b. into song/a run** se mettre à chanter/courir **(c)** *(showbusiness)* percer dans; *(market)* percer sur
▶**break off 1** *vt sep* **(a)** *(detach)* *(twig, handle)* casser **(b)** *(terminate)* *(relations, engagement)* rompre
2 *vi* **(a)** *(become detached)* se casser **(b)** *(stop talking, working)* s'interrompre
▶**break open 1** *vt sep (door)* enfoncer; *(lock, safe)* forcer
2 *vi* s'ouvrir
▶**break out** *vi* **(a)** *(escape)* s'évader (**of** de) **(b)** *(of argument)* éclater; *(of disease)* se déclarer; **to b. out in a sweat** se mettre à transpirer; **to b. out in a rash** avoir une éruption de boutons
▶**break through 1** *vt insep (wall)* faire une brèche dans; *(barrier)* forcer; *Fig (someone's reserve, shyness)* vaincre
2 *vi (of sun)* percer les nuages
▶**break up 1** *vt sep* **(a)** *(reduce to pieces)* couper en morceaux **(b)** *(estate, company)* morceler; *(machine)* démonter **(c)** *(fight, quarrel)* faire cesser
2 *vi* **(a)** *(disintegrate)* se disloquer **(b)** *(end)* *(of talks)* cesser; *(of meeting, school term)* se terminer; *(of school)* fermer; *(of pupils)* être en vacances; **to b. up with sb** *(end relationship)* rompre avec qn
▶**break with** *vt insep* rompre avec

breakable ['breɪkəbəl] **1** *n* **breakables** objets *mpl* fragiles
 2 *adj* fragile
breakage ['breɪkɪdʒ] *n* **were there any breakages?** est-ce qu'il y a eu de la casse?; **all breakages must be paid for** *(sign)* tout article cassé doit être payé
breakaway ['breɪkəweɪ] *adj* dissident(e)
breakdown ['breɪkdaʊn] *n* (**a**) *(of car, machine, computer)* panne *f*; *(of talks, in communication)* rupture *f*; **to have a b.** *(of motorist)* tomber en panne; **b. truck** dépanneuse *f*, camion *m* de dépannage (**b**) *Psy* (**nervous) b.** dépression *f* nerveuse; **to have a b.** faire une dépression nerveuse (**c**) *(analysis) (of figures, costs)* détail *m*
breaker ['breɪkə(r)] *n (wave)* déferlante *f*
break-even point [breɪk'iːvənpɔɪnt] *n Fin* seuil *m* de rentabilité
breakfast ['brekfəst] **1** *n* petit déjeuner *m*; **to have b.** prendre son petit déjeuner, déjeuner; **b. cereal** céréales *fpl*; **b. television** émissions *fpl* (télévisées) du matin
 2 *vi* prendre son petit déjeuner, déjeuner; **to b. on sth** manger qch au petit déjeuner
break-in ['breɪkɪn] *n* cambriolage *m*
breaking ['breɪkɪŋ] *n* (**a**) *Law* **b. and entering** entrée *f* par effraction (**b**) **b. point** *(of patience)* limite *f*; **to reach b. point** *(of person)* être à bout; *(of marriage)* être au bord de la rupture
breakneck ['breɪknek] *adj* **at b. speed** à toute allure
break-out ['breɪkaʊt] *n (from prison)* évasion *f*
breakthrough ['breɪkθruː] *n (discovery)* découverte *f* majeure; **there has been a b. in talks** un pas décisif a été franchi dans les négociations; **to make a b.** *(discovery)* faire une découverte majeure; *(in talks)* faire un pas décisif
breakwater ['breɪkwɔːtə(r)] *n* brise-lames *m inv*
bream [briːm] *(pl* **bream)** *n* brème *f*
breast [brest] *n (of woman)* & *Lit (of man)* sein *m*; *(of chicken)* blanc *m*; **to make a clean b. of it** tout avouer, **b. cancer** cancer *m* du sein; **b. pocket** poche *f* de poitrine
breastbone ['brestbəʊn] *n* sternum *m*
breast-feed ['brestfiːd] *(pt & pp* **breast-fed** ['brestfed]) *vt & vi* allaiter
breastplate ['brestpleɪt] *n* plastron *m (de cuirasse)*
breaststroke ['bres(t)strəʊk] *n* brasse *f*
breath [breθ] *n* souffle *m*; **to take a deep b.** inspirer profondément; **to pause for b.** s'arrêter pour reprendre sa respiration; **bad b.** mauvaise haleine *f*; **they are not to be mentioned in the same b.** on ne saurait les comparer; **in the next b.** aussitôt après; *also Fig* **to hold one's b.** retenir son souffle; *Fam* **don't hold your b.!** c'est pas demain la veille!; **to waste one's b.** gaspiller sa salive; **out of b.** à bout de souffle, hors d'haleine; **to get short of b.** s'essouffler; **to get one's b. back** reprendre haleine, reprendre son souffle; **under one's b.** à voix basse; *Fig* **to take sb's b. away** couper le souffle à qn; **a b. of wind/of air** un souffle de vent/d'air; **to go out for a b. of fresh air** sortir prendre l'air; *Fig* **she's a real b. of fresh air** elle apporte une bouffée d'air frais; **b. test** Alcotest® *m*
breathalyse, breathalyze ['breθəlaɪz] *vt* faire passer l'Alcotest® à
breathalyser, breathalyzer ['breθəlaɪzə(r)] *n* Alcotest® *m*

breathe [briːð] **1** *vt* (**a**) *(inhale)* respirer (**b**) *(idioms)* **to b. a sigh of relief** pousser un soupir de soulagement; *Lit* **to b. one's last** rendre son dernier soupir; **don't b. a word (of it)!** pas un mot!; **to b. fire** *(in anger)* jeter feu et flammes; **to b. new life into sth** *(project, scheme)* insuffler une force nouvelle à qch
 2 *vi* respirer; *(exhale)* souffler; **to b. heavily** *(noisily)* respirer bruyamment; *(with difficulty)* respirer avec difficulté; *Fig* **to b. easily again** respirer; *Fig* **to b. down sb's neck** *(follow)* talonner qn; *(nag)* être tout le temps sur le dos de qn
▸**breathe in 1** *vt* inhaler
 2 *vi* inspirer
▸**breathe out** *vi* expirer
breather ['briːðə(r)] *n Fam (rest)* pause *f*; **to take a b.** faire une pause
breathing ['briːðɪŋ] *n* respiration *f*; **b. apparatus** bouteille *f* d'oxygène et masque; *Fig* **to give sb some b. space** laisser respirer qn
breathless ['breθlɪs] *adj (person)* hors d'haleine, essoufflé(e); *(calm)* plat(e); *(silence)* profond(e)
breathtaking ['breθteɪkɪŋ] *adj (beauty, scenery)* à couper le souffle; *(speed)* vertigineux(euse); *(audacity)* sidérant(e)
breathy ['breθɪ] *adj (voice)* haletant(e)
bred [bred] *pt & pp of* **breed**
breech [briːtʃ] *n* (**a**) *Med* **b. delivery** *or* **birth** (accouchement *m* par le) siège *m* (**b**) *(of gun)* culasse *f*
breeches ['brɪtʃɪz] *npl* **(pair of) b.** culotte *f*
breed [briːd] **1** *n also Fig* race *f*
 2 *vt (pt & pp* **bred** [bred]) *(animals)* élever; *Fig (discontent)* engendrer
 3 *vi* se reproduire
breeder ['briːdə(r)] *n (of animals)* éleveur(euse) *m,f*; *Phys* **b. reactor** surgénérateur *m*
breeding ['briːdɪŋ] *n* (**a**) *(of animals)* élevage *m*; **b. ground** lieu *m* de reproduction; *Fig (of discontent, revolution)* foyer *m* (**b**) *(of person)* **(good) b.** éducation *f*, manières *fpl*
breeze [briːz] **1** *n* brise *f*; *Am Fam* **it was a b.** c'était du gâteau
 2 *vi* **to b. in/out** *(quickly)* entrer/sortir en coup de vent; *(casually)* entrer/sortir avec désinvolture
breeze-block ['briːzblɒk] *n Br* parpaing *m*
breezy ['briːzɪ] *adj* (**a**) *(weather)* venteux(euse) (**b**) *(casual)* désinvolte
brethren ['breðrɪn] *npl Rel* frères *mpl*
Breton ['bretɒn] **1** *n* Breton(onne) *m,f*
 2 *adj* breton(onne)
breviary ['briːvɪərɪ] *(pl* **breviaries)** *n Rel* bréviaire *m*
brevity ['brevɪtɪ] *n* brièveté *f*
brew [bruː] **1** *n (beer)* bière *f*; *(tea)* thé *m*; *Fig (mixture)* mélange *m*
 2 *vt (beer)* brasser; *(tea)* faire infuser, préparer
 3 *vi (of beer)* fermenter; *(of tea)* infuser; **there's a storm brewing** il y a de l'orage dans l'air; *Fig* **there's something brewing** il se trame quelque chose; **there's trouble brewing** il va y avoir du grabuge
▸**brew up** *vi Br Fam* faire du thé
brewer ['bruːə(r)] *n* brasseur *m*
brewery ['brʊərɪ] *(pl* **breweries)** *n* brasserie *f (fabrique)*
briar ['braɪə(r)] *n (plant)* bruyère *f*; *(pipe)* pipe *f* de bruyère; **b. rose** églantine *f*

bribe [braɪb] **1** n pot-de-vin m
 2 vt acheter; **to b. sb into doing sth** acheter qn pour qu'il fasse qch
bribery ['braɪbərɪ] n corruption f
bric-à-brac ['brɪkəbræk] n bric-à-brac m
brick [brɪk] n (for building) brique f; Fig **to drop a b.** faire une gaffe; **b. wall** mur m en briques; **you're banging your head against a b. wall** tu perds ton temps
▶**brick up** vt sep murer
brickie ['brɪkɪ] n Br Fam maçon m
bricklayer ['brɪkleɪə(r)] n maçon m
brickwork ['brɪkwɜːk] n briquetage m
bridal ['braɪdəl] adj nuptial(e); **b. dress** or **gown** robe f de mariée; **b. suite** suite f nuptiale
bride [braɪd] n mariée f; **the b. and groom** les mariés mpl
bridegroom ['braɪdgruːm] n marié m
bridesmaid ['braɪdzmeɪd] n demoiselle f d'honneur
bridge¹ [brɪdʒ] **1** n (over river) pont m; (on ship) passerelle f; (on teeth) bridge m; (of nose) arête f; Fig **we'll cross that b. when we come to it** chaque chose en son temps; Fig **b. building** réconciliation f
 2 vt (river) construire un pont sur; **to b. a gap** (in knowledge) combler une lacune; **to b. the gap between rich and poor** combler le fossé entre les riches et les pauvres
bridge² n (card game) bridge m
bridgehead ['brɪdʒhed] n Mil tête f de pont
bridging loan ['brɪdʒɪŋləʊn] n Fin prêt-relais m
bridle ['braɪdəl] **1** n bride f; **b. path** piste f cavalière
 2 vt (horse) brider
 3 vi (with anger) s'indigner (**at** de)
brief [briːf] **1** n Law dossier m; (instructions) consignes fpl
 2 adj bref (brève); (garment) court(e); **in b.,..., to be b.,...** en bref,...
 3 vt (inform) mettre au courant (**on** de)
briefcase ['briːfkeɪs] n serviette f
briefing ['briːfɪŋ] n (meeting) briefing m; (information) instructions fpl
briefly ['briːflɪ] adv brièvement; (hesitate, smile) pendant un court instant; **(put) b.,...** en bref,...
briefs [briːfs] npl (underwear) slip m
brier = briar
brigade [brɪ'geɪd] n brigade f
brigadier [brɪgə'dɪə(r)] n général m de brigade
brigand ['brɪgənd] n Lit brigand m
bright [braɪt] **1** adj (**a**) (sun, light) brillant(e); (day) clair(e); (colour) vif (vive); **to go b. red** (blush) devenir rouge comme une tomate (**b**) (hopeful) **the future looks b.** l'avenir s'annonce bien; **the situation is looking a bit brighter** la situation commence à s'améliorer; Fig **the only b. spot is...** la seule chose positive est...; **to look on the b. side (of things)** prendre les choses du bon côté (**c**) (cheerful) vif (vive) (**d**) (clever) (person) intelligent(e); (idea) lumineux(-euse); **to be b. at sth** être doué(e) en qch
 2 adv **b. and early** de bon matin
brighten ['braɪtən] **1** vt (room, mood) égayer
 2 vi (of weather, sky) s'éclaircir; (of face, eyes) s'éclairer; (of prospects) s'améliorer
▶**brighten up 1** vt sep (room) égayer
 2 vi (of person) devenir plus gai(e); (of weather, sky) s'éclaircir; (of face) s'éclairer; (of prospects) s'améliorer

bright-eyed ['braɪtaɪd] adj aux yeux brillants; Fig (eager) enthousiaste; Fam **b. and bushy-tailed** frais (fraîche) et dispos(e)
brightly ['braɪtlɪ] adv (say) gaiement; (lit, coloured) vivement; **the sun was shining b.** il faisait un soleil radieux; **to smile b.** faire un sourire radieux
brightness ['braɪtnɪs] n (of light, sun, colour) éclat m; (of lighting) intensité f; (on TV) luminosité f
brilliance ['brɪljəns] n (**a**) (of light, colour) éclat m (**b**) (of person) intelligence f; (of idea) ingéniosité f
brilliant ['brɪljənt] adj (**a**) (light) éclatant(e); (sun, smile) radieux(euse) (**b**) (scientist, career, pupil) brillant(e) (**c**) (excellent) formidable
brilliantly ['brɪljəntlɪ] adv (**a**) (coloured, lit) vivement (**b**) (acted, played) brillamment
brim [brɪm] **1** n (of cup, glass, hat) bord m; **to be full to the b. (with)** être plein(e) à ras bord (de)
 2 vi (pt & pp brimmed) **to be brimming with sth** (liquid) être rempli(e) à ras bord de qch; (enthusiasm, ideas) déborder de qch; **eyes brimming with tears** yeux noyés de larmes
▶**brim over** vi also Fig déborder (**with** de)
brimful ['brɪmfʊl] adj plein(e) à ras bord; Fig **b. of health/life** débordant(e) de santé/vie
brimstone ['brɪmstəʊn] n Fig **to preach fire and b.** menacer les fidèles des feux de l'enfer
brine [braɪn] n saumure f
bring [brɪŋ] (pt & pp brought [brɔːt]) vt (**a**) (cause to come) (object, letter, news) apporter; (person, animal) amener; **to b. sth to sb's attention** signaler qch à l'attention de qn; **what brings you to London?** qu'est-ce qui vous amène à Londres?; **to b. sth out of sth** (box, bag) sortir qch de qch; **to b. a child into the world** mettre un enfant au monde; Law **to b. an action against sb** intenter un procès à qn
 (**b**) (cause) provoquer; **it has brought me great happiness** cela m'a procuré un grand bonheur; **to b. sb (good) luck/bad luck** porter bonheur/malheur à qn; **to b. new hope to sb** redonner de l'espoir à qn; **to b. tears to sb's eyes** faire venir les larmes aux yeux de qn
 (**c**) (to a particular condition) **to b. sth into disrepute** discréditer qch; **to b. sth into question** remettre qch en question; **to b. sth to an end** mettre fin à qch; **to b. sth to light** (crime, secret) révéler qch; **to b. sth to mind** faire penser à qch; **I couldn't bring myself to do it** je n'ai pas pu me décider ou me résoudre à le faire
 (**d**) (be sold for) rapporter
▶**bring about** vt sep (cause) entraîner, provoquer
▶**bring along** vt sep (person) amener; (object) apporter
▶**bring back** vt sep (**a**) (person) ramener; (gift) rapporter; **to b. sb back to life** ramener qn à la vie; **to b. sb back to health** rendre la santé à qn (**b**) (memory) rappeler (**c**) (law, practice) rétablir
▶**bring down** vt sep (**a**) (from shelf, attic) descendre (**b**) (soldier, plane) abattre; (government) faire tomber, renverser; Fam **her performance brought the house down** son interprétation lui a valu des applaudissements enthousiastes (**c**) (lower) (price, temperature) faire baisser
▶**bring forward** vt sep (**a**) (proposal) émettre; (plan) proposer; (reasons, evidence) avancer (**b**) (advance time of) avancer (**c**) Com (in bookkeeping) reporter

▸**bring in** *vt sep* (**a**) *(expert, consultant)* faire appel à; **the police brought him in for questioning** la police l'a emmené au poste pour l'interroger (**b**) *(earn) (of person)* gagner; *(of investment, sale)* rapporter (**c**) *(law, act)* introduire (**d**) *Law (verdict)* rendre

▸**bring off** *vt sep (accomplish)* réussir

▸**bring on** *vt sep (cause)* provoquer; **you've brought it on yourself** tu l'as cherché

▸**bring out** *vt sep* (**a**) *(publish)* sortir (**b**) *(cause to appear)* **to b. out the best/the worst in sb** faire ressortir les qualités/les défauts de qn; **strawberries b. her out in a rash** les fraises lui donnent de l'urticaire; **to b. sb out of their shell** faire sortir qn de sa coquille

▸**bring round** *vt sep* (**a**) *(revive)* ranimer, faire revenir à soi (**b**) *(persuade)* convaincre; **she brought him round to her point of view** elle l'a rallié à son point de vue (**c**) *(conversation)* amener (**to** sur)

▸**bring to** *vt sep (revive)* ranimer, faire revenir à soi

▸**bring together** *vt sep* réunir

▸**bring up** *vt sep* (**a**) *(subject)* soulever (**b**) *(child)* élever; **I was brought up to be polite** on m'a appris à être poli (**c**) *(vomit)* vomir

bring-and-buy [ˈbrɪŋənˈbaɪ] *n Br* **b. (sale)** vente *f* de charité

Bring-and-Buy

Ces brocantes sont en général destinées à réunir des fonds pour une œuvre de charité. On y vend des articles d'occasion et des produits faits maison.

---

brink [brɪŋk] *n also Fig* bord *m*; *Fig* **to be on the b. of sth** *(war, ruin, disaster)* être au bord de qch; *(death, success)* être à deux doigts de qch; **to be on the b. of doing sth** être à deux doigts de faire qch

brinkmanship [ˈbrɪŋkmənʃɪp] *n* politique *f* de la corde raide

brisk [brɪsk] *adj* (**a**) *(weather)* frais (fraîche); *(wind)* vivifiant(e) (**b**) *(person) (efficient)* énergique; *(dismissive)* vif (vive) (**c**) *(rapid)* **at a b. pace** *(work)* rapidement; *(walk)* d'un pas vif; **to go for a b. walk** se promener d'un pas vif; **business is b.** les affaires marchent bien

briskly [ˈbrɪsklɪ] *adv* (**a**) *(efficiently)* énergiquement; *(dismissively)* vivement (**b**) *(rapidly) (walk)* d'un pas vif

bristle [ˈbrɪsəl] **1** *n (of plant, brush, face)* poil *m*; *(of pig)* soie *f*
2 *vi* (**a**) *(of animal, animal's fur)* se hérisser; **to b. (with anger) (at)** se hérisser (à) (**b**) **to be bristling with** *(people)* grouiller de; *(difficulties)* être hérissé(e) de

Brit [brɪt] *n Fam* Britannique *mf*

Britain [ˈbrɪtən] *n* la Grande-Bretagne

British [ˈbrɪtɪʃ] **1** *npl* **the B.** les Britanniques *mpl*
2 *adj* britannique; **B. Columbia** la Colombie-Britannique; **the B. Isles** les îles *fpl* Britanniques; **B. Summer Time** heure *f* d'été *(en Grande-Bretagne)*

British Council

Le British Council est un organisme chargé de promouvoir la langue et la culture anglaises, et de renforcer les liens culturels avec les autres pays.

Briton [ˈbrɪtən] *n* Britannique *mf*; *Hist* **ancient B.** Breton(onne) *m,f (de la Grande-Bretagne)*

Brittany [ˈbrɪtənɪ] *n* la Bretagne

brittle [ˈbrɪtəl] *adj (object, hair, voice)* cassant(e); *(bones)* friable

broach [brəʊtʃ] *vt (subject)* aborder

broad¹ [brɔːd] *adj (road, smile, sense, mind)* large; *(accent)* fort(e), prononcé(e); *(humour)* grossier(ère); *(hint)* appuyé(e); **in b. daylight** en plein jour; *Fig* **au grand jour**; **to be in b. agreement** être d'accord sur l'essentiel; *Fig* **to be a b. church** admettre de nombreuses tendances; **a b. outline** les grandes lignes *fpl*; **b. bean** fève *f*

broad² *n Am Fam (woman)* gonzesse *f*

broadcast [ˈbrɔːdkɑːst] **1** *n* émission *f*
2 *vt (pt & pp* broadcast) diffuser; *Fam* **don't b. it!** ne va pas le crier sur les toits!
3 *vi (of station)* émettre

broadcaster [ˈbrɔːdkɑːstə(r)] *n (person) (on TV, radio)* présentateur(trice) *m,f*; *(TV station)* chaîne *f* de télévision; *(radio station)* station *f* de radio

broadcasting [ˈbrɔːdkɑːstɪŋ] *n (action)* diffusion *f*; **he works in b.** *(radio)* il travaille à la radio; *(TV)* il travaille à la télé

broaden [ˈbrɔːdən] **1** *vt* élargir; **to b. one's horizons** élargir son horizon
2 *vi* **to b. (out)** s'élargir

broadly [ˈbrɔːdlɪ] *adv (generally)* en gros; **to smile b.** faire un large sourire; **b. speaking** en gros

broad-minded [brɔːdˈmaɪndɪd] *adj (person)* large d'esprit; *(attitude)* ouvert(e)

broadsheet [ˈbrɔːdʃiːt] *n* journal *m* grand format *(synonyme de qualité)*

broad-shouldered [brɔːdˈʃəʊldəd] *adj* large d'épaules; *Fig* **to be b.** *(resilient)* bien encaisser

broadside [ˈbrɔːdsaɪd] *n Naut* **to fire a b.** tirer une bordée; *Fig* **to fire a b. at sb/sth** attaquer violemment qn/qch

brocade [brəʊˈkeɪd] *n* brocart *m*

broccoli [ˈbrɒkəlɪ] *n* brocolis *mpl*

brochure [ˈbrəʊʃə(r)] *n* brochure *f*

brogue [brəʊg] *n (accent)* accent *m*

brogues [brəʊgz] *npl (shoes)* = chaussures solides souvent ornées de petits trous

broil [brɔɪl] *vt & vi Am* griller

broke [brəʊk] **1** *adj Fam* fauché(e); **to go for b.** jouer le tout pour le tout
2 *pt of* **break**

broken [ˈbrəʊkən] **1** *adj (object, bone)* cassé(e); *(promise)* rompu(e); *(marriage, heart, person)* brisé(e); *(ground, surface)* irrégulier(ère); **to speak b. English** parler un mauvais anglais; **b. home** famille *f* désunie
2 *pp of* **break**

brokenhearted [brəʊkənˈhɑːtɪd] *adj* **to be b.** avoir le cœur brisé

broker [ˈbrəʊkə(r)] *n Fin (for shares, currency)* agent *m* de change; *Com (for goods, insurance)* courtier *m*

brolly [ˈbrɒlɪ] *(pl* brollies) *n Br Fam* pépin *m*, pébroc *m*

bromide [ˈbrəʊmaɪd] *n Chem* bromure *m*; *Fig* banalité *f*

bronchial [ˈbrɒŋkɪəl] *adj Anat* bronchique; **b. pneumonia** broncho-pneumonie *f*; **b. tubes** bronches *fpl*

bronchitic [brɒŋˈkɪtɪk] *adj* bronchitique

bronchitis [brɒŋˈkaɪtɪs] *n* bronchite *f*; **to have b.** avoir une bronchite

bronze [brɒnz] **1** *n* bronze *m*; **to win a b.** *(medal)* remporter une médaille de bronze; **the B. Age** l'âge *m* du bronze

2 *adj (material)* de *ou* en bronze; *(colour)* couleur bronze *inv*

bronzed [brɒnzd] *adj* bronzé(e)

brooch [brəʊtʃ] *n* broche *f*

brood [bruːd] **1** *n (of birds)* couvée *f*; *Hum (of children)* progéniture *f*
2 *vi (of hen)* couver; *Fig* **to b. (over** *or* **about sth)** ruminer (qch)

broody ['bruːdɪ] *adj (hen)* couveuse; *Fig (woman)* en mal d'enfant

brook¹ [brʊk] *n (stream)* ruisseau *m*

brook² *vt Formal (tolerate)* tolérer

broom [bruːm] *n* **(a)** *(plant)* genêt *m* **(b)** *(for cleaning)* balai *m*; *Fig* **a new b.** = un nouvel arrivant qui veut tout changer

broomstick ['bruːmstɪk] *n* manche *m* à balai

Bros *npl Com (abbr* **Brothers)** **Richardson B.** Richardson frères

broth [brɒθ] *n (soup) (thin)* bouillon *m*; *(thick)* potage *m*

brothel ['brɒθəl] *n* maison *f* close

brother ['brʌðə(r)] *n* frère *m*

brotherhood ['brʌðəhʊd] *n* fraternité *f*; *Rel* confrérie *f*; **the b. of man** la fraternité humaine

brother-in-law ['brʌðərɪnlɔː] *(pl* **brothers-in-law)** *n* beau-frère *m*

brought [brɔːt] *pt & pp of* **bring**

brow [braʊ] *n* **(a)** *(forehead)* front *m*; *(eyebrow)* sourcil *m* **(b)** *(of hill)* sommet *m*

browbeat ['braʊbiːt] *(pt* **browbeat,** *pp* **browbeaten** ['braʊbiːtən]) *vt* intimider; **to b. sb into doing sth** forcer qn à faire qch en usant d'intimidation

brown [braʊn] **1** *n* marron *m*
2 *adj* marron *inv*; *(hair)* brun(e); *(skin)* mat(e); *(tanned)* bronzé(e); *(bread, flour, rice)* complet(ète); **b. paper** papier *m* kraft; **b. sugar** sucre *m* roux, cassonade *f*
3 *vt (in cooking)* faire dorer
4 *vi (in cooking)* dorer

browned-off ['braʊnd'ɒf] *adj Br Fam* **to be b. (with)** en avoir marre (de); **to be b. with doing sth** en avoir marre de faire qch

brownfield site ['braʊnfiːld'saɪt] *n* terrain *m* à bâtir *(après démolition de bâtiments préexistants)*

Brownie ['braʊnɪ] *n* ≃ jeannette *f*; *Fig* **to win** *or* **get b. points** se faire bien voir

brownie ['braʊnɪ] *n (cake)* brownie *m (petit gâteau au chocolat et aux noix)*

brown-nose ['braʊnnəʊz] *vi Vulg* faire le lèche-cul

browse [braʊz] **1** *n* **to have a b.** *(in shop)* regarder; **to have a b. through sth** *(collection, shelves)* jeter un œil sur qch; *(magazine)* feuilleter qch
2 *vt Comput* **to b. the Web** naviguer sur le Web
3 *vi* **(a)** *(in shop)* regarder; **to b. through sth** *(collection, shelves)* jeter un œil sur qch; *(magazine)* feuilleter qch **(b)** *(of animal)* brouter

browser ['braʊzə(r)] *n Comput* logiciel *m* de navigation, navigateur *m*

bruise [bruːz] **1** *n (on body)* bleu *m*; *(on fruit)* meurtrissure *f*
2 *vt (person)* faire un bleu à; *Fig (feelings, pride)* blesser; **to b. one's arm** se faire un bleu au bras
3 *vi (of person)* se faire des bleus; *(of fruit)* s'abîmer

bruiser ['bruːzə(r)] *n Fam* grosse brute *f*

bruising ['bruːzɪŋ] **1** *n (bruises)* bleus *mpl*
2 *adj (encounter, experience)* douloureux(euse)

Brummie ['brʌmɪ] *n Fam* = personne née à ou habitant Birmingham

brunch [brʌntʃ] *n* brunch *m*

Brunei [bruː'naɪ] *n* le Brunei

brunette [bruː'net] *n* brune *f*

brunt [brʌnt] *n* **to bear** *or* **take the b. of sth** *(attack)* essuyer le plus fort de qch; *(anger)* faire les frais de qch

brush [brʌʃ] **1** *n* **(a)** *(for clothes, hair)* brosse *f*; *(for sweeping)* balai *m*; *(for painting)* pinceau *m* **(b)** *(action)* **to give sth a b.** donner un coup de brosse à qch; **to give the floor a b.** donner un coup de balai; **to give one's hair a b.** se donner un coup de brosse **(c)** *(light touch)* effleurement *m*; *Fam* **to have a b. with the law** avoir des démêlés avec la justice **(d)** *(of fox)* queue *f* **(e)** *(undergrowth)* broussailles *fpl*
2 *vt* **(a)** *(clothes, shoes)* brosser; **to b. one's hair/teeth** se brosser les cheveux/les dents; **to b. the floor** balayer **(b)** *(touch lightly)* effleurer
3 *vi* **to b. against sb/sth** effleurer qn/qch; **to brush past sb/sth** effleurer qn/qch en passant

▸**brush aside** *vt sep (objection, obstacle)* balayer; *(opponent)* écarter

▸**brush off** *vt sep* **(a)** *(from clothes, shoes)* enlever d'un coup de brosse **(b)** *(person)* envoyer promener; *(insult, incident)* ignorer

▸**brush up** *vt sep* **(a)** *(leaves, crumbs)* balayer **(b)** *(subject, language)* **to b. up (on)** se remettre (à)

brushed [brʌʃt] *adj (nylon)* gratté(e); **b. cotton** pilou *m*, finette *f*

brush-off ['brʌʃɒf] *n Fam* **to give sb the b.** envoyer promener qn

brush-up ['brʌʃʌp] *n* **to have a wash and b.** faire un brin de toilette

brushwood ['brʌʃwʊd] *n (as fuel)* petit bois *m*; *(undergrowth)* broussailles *fpl*

brushwork ['brʌʃwɜːk] *n Art* touche *f*

brusque [bruːsk] *adj* brusque

brusquely ['bruːsklɪ] *adv (behave)* avec brusquerie; *(say)* d'un ton brusque

Brussels ['brʌsəlz] *n* Bruxelles; **B. sprout** chou *m* de Bruxelles

brutal ['bruːtəl] *adj* brutal(e); *(attack, crime)* sauvage

brutality [bruː'tælɪtɪ] *n* brutalité *f*; *(of attack, crime)* sauvagerie *f*

brutalize ['bruːtəlaɪz] *vt (ill-treat)* brutaliser; *(make insensitive)* rendre insensible

brutally ['bruːtəlɪ] *adv* avec brutalité; *(beat, attack)* sauvagement

brute [bruːt] **1** *n (animal)* bête *f*; *(person)* brute *f*
2 *adj* **b. force** *or* **strength** force *f* brutale

brutish ['bruːtɪʃ] *adj* bestial(e)

BSc [biːes'siː] *n (abbr* **Bachelor of Science)** **to have a B. in computer science/physics** avoir une licence d'informatique/de physique; **John Smith B.** John Smith, licencié en chimie/informatique/*etc*

BSE [biːes'iː] *n (abbr* **bovine spongiform encephalopathy)** EBS *f*, maladie *f* de la vache folle

BSI [biːes'aɪ] *n (abbr* **British Standards Institution)** = association britannique de normalisation

BST [biːes'tiː] *n (abbr* **British Summer Time)** heure *f* d'été *(en Grande-Bretagne)*

bubble ['bʌbəl] **1** *n (of air, soap)* bulle *f*; *Fig* **the b. has burst** le rêve est terminé; **b. bath** bain *m* moussant; **b. gum** chewing-gum *m*; *Comput* **b. jet printer** imprimante *f* à bulles
  2 *vi (form bubbles)* bouillonner
▸**bubble over** *vi (of liquid)* déborder; *Fig* **to b. over with joy** ne plus se tenir de joie
bubbly ['bʌblɪ] **1** *n Fam (champagne)* champ *m*
  2 *adj* (**a**) *(liquid)* plein(e) de bulles (**b**) *(person)* débordant(e) de vitalité
bubonic [bjuː'bɒnɪk] *adj* **b. plague** peste *f* bubonique
buccaneer [bʌkə'nɪə(r)] *n* boucanier *m*
Bucharest [bʊkə'rest] *n* Bucarest
buck [bʌk] **1** *n* (**a**) *Am Fam (dollar)* dollar *m*; **to make a fast** *or* **quick b.** faire du fric (**b**) *(of deer, rabbit)* mâle *m* (**c**) *Fam (responsibility)* **to pass the b.** refiler le bébé; **the b. stops here** *(with me)* en dernier ressort, c'est moi le responsable; *(with you)* en dernier ressort, c'est toi le responsable
  2 *vt* **to b. the system/a trend** aller à l'encontre de l'ordre établi/d'une tendance
  3 *vi (of horse)* faire le saut de mouton
▸**buck up** *Fam* **1** *vt sep (encourage)* remonter le moral à; **to b. one's ideas up** se prendre en main
  2 *vi Fam (cheer up)* reprendre courage; *(hurry)* se grouiller
bucket ['bʌkɪt] **1** *n* seau *m*; *Br Fam* **it's raining buckets** il tombe des cordes; *Fam* **to cry buckets** pleurer comme une madeleine; *Fam* **b. shop** *(for air tickets)* agence *f* de voyages à prix réduits
  2 *vi Br Fam* **it's bucketing (down)** il tombe des cordes
buckle ['bʌkəl] **1** *n* boucle *f*
  2 *vt* (**a**) *(fasten)* boucler (**b**) *(deform)* déformer; *(wheel)* voiler
  3 *vi (deform)* se déformer; *(of wheel)* se voiler; *(of knees)* flancher; **she buckled at the knees** ses jambes ont cédé sous elle
▸**buckle down** *vi* s'y mettre; **to b. down to a task** s'atteler à une tâche
buckshot ['bʌkʃɒt] *n* chevrotine *f*
buckskin ['bʌkskɪn] *n* daim *m (peau)*
buckteeth [bʌk'tiːθ] *npl* dents *fpl* de lapin
bucktoothed [bʌk'tuːθt] *adj* **to be b.** avoir des dents de lapin
buckwheat ['bʌkwiːt] *n* sarrasin *m*
bucolic [bjuː'kɒlɪk] *adj Lit* bucolique
bud [bʌd] **1** *n (of leaf, branch)* bourgeon *m*; *(of flower)* bouton *m*
  2 *vi (pt & pp* **budded***) (of tree)* bourgeonner; *(of flowers)* être en boutons
Budapest ['bʊdəpest] *n* Budapest
Buddha ['bʊdə] *n* Bouddha
Buddhist ['bʊdɪst] **1** *n* bouddhiste *mf*
  2 *adj (priest, doctrine)* bouddhiste; *(art, temple)* bouddhique
budding ['bʌdɪŋ] *adj (genius, actor)* en herbe; *(talent)* naissant(e)
buddy ['bʌdɪ] *(pl* **buddies***) n Fam (friend)* pote *m*; **hey, b.!** dis donc, mec!
budge [bʌdʒ] **1** *vt (move)* bouger; *Fig (convince)* faire changer d'avis
  2 *vi (move)* bouger; *Fig (yield)* céder
budgerigar ['bʌdʒərɪgɑː(r)] *n* perruche *f*
budget ['bʌdʒɪt] **1** *n* budget *m*; *Br Pol* **the B.** le budget; **to go over b.** dépasser le budget; **to be within b.** être

dans les limites du budget; **b. deficit/surplus** déficit *m*/excédent *m* budgétaire
  2 *vt (time, money)* gérer
  3 *vi* **to b. for sth** prévoir qch
budgetary ['bʌdʒɪtərɪ] *adj Fin* budgétaire
budgie ['bʌdʒɪ] *n Fam* perruche *f*
Buenos Aires ['bwenɒs'aɪrɪz] *n* Buenos Aires
buff [bʌf] **1** *n* (**a**) *(colour)* couleur *f* chamois (**b**) *Fam* **in the b.** *(naked)* à poil (**c**) *(enthusiast)* mordu(e) *m,f*; **film b.** cinéphile *mf*
  2 *adj (couleur)* chamois *inv*; *(envelope)* en papier kraft
  3 *vt (polish)* lustrer
buffalo ['bʌfələʊ] *(pl* **buffalo** *or* **buffaloes***) n* buffle *m*
buffer¹ ['bʌfə(r)] *n (on railway track)* butoir *m*; *Comput* mémoire *f* tampon; **to act as a b.** faire tampon; **b. state** État *m* tampon; **b. zone** zone *f* tampon
buffer² *n Br Fam* **old b.** vieux schnock *m*
buffet¹ ['bʌfɪt] *vt (of wind)* secouer; *Fig* **to be buffeted by the waves/by events** être ballotté(e) par les vagues/par les événements
buffet² ['bʊfeɪ] *n* (**a**) *(sideboard)* buffet *m* (**b**) *(meal)* buffet *m*; **b. lunch/dinner** buffet (**c**) *(in station)* buffet *m*; **b. (car)** wagon-restaurant *m*, voiture-restaurant *f*
buffeting ['bʌfɪtɪŋ] *n* **to take a b.** *(of ship)* être violemment ballotté(e); *Fig (of person)* être fortement ébranlé(e)
buffoon [bə'fuːn] *n* bouffon *m*; **to play the b.** faire le pitre
bug [bʌg] **1** *n* (**a**) *(insect)* insecte *m*; *(bed bug)* punaise *f* (**b**) *Fam (illness)* virus *m*, microbe *m*; **a stomach b.** un embarras gastrique; **there's a b. going round** il y a un virus qui traîne; *Fig* **the travel b.** le virus des voyages (**c**) *Comput* bug *m*, bogue *m* (**d**) *(listening device)* micro *m*
  2 *vt (pt & pp* **bugged***)* (**a**) *(telephone)* mettre sur écoute; *(building, room)* cacher des micros dans (**b**) *Fam (annoy)* taper sur les nerfs à; *(nag)* embêter; **stop bugging me about it!** arrête de m'embêter avec ça!
bugbear ['bʌgbeə(r)] *n Fam* cauchemar *m*
bug-eyed [bʌg'aɪd] *adj* aux yeux exorbités
bug-free [bʌg'friː] *adj Comput* sans bug
bugger ['bʌgə(r)] **1** *n very Fam (unpleasant person)* connard(asse) *m,f*; **you silly b.!** espèce d'andouille!; **the poor b.!** le pauvre!; **it's a b. of a job** c'est une vraie galère; **b. all** que dalle; **he knows b. all about it** il y connaît que dalle
  2 *vt* (**a**) *(sodomize)* sodomiser (**b**) *Br very Fam* **b. (it)!** merde!; **I'll be buggered if I'm going to do it!** tu peux toujours courir pour que je le fasse!; **I'm buggered if I know** j'en sais foutre rien; **that's really buggered it!** ça a tout foutu en l'air!
▸**bugger about, bugger around** *Br very Fam* **1** *vt sep* **to b. sb about** se foutre de la gueule de qn
  2 *vi* glander
▸**bugger off** *vi Br very Fam* se casser, foutre le camp
▸**bugger up** *vt sep Br very Fam (plan)* foutre en l'air; *(TV, machine)* bousiller
buggered ['bʌgəd] *adj Br very Fam (broken)* foutu(e); *(exhausted)* nase
buggery ['bʌgərɪ] *n* (**a**) *Law* sodomie *f* (**b**) *Br very Fam* **to run like b.** prendre ses jambes à son cou
buggy ['bʌgɪ] *(pl* **buggies***) n* (**a**) *Br (pushchair)* poussette *f*; *Am (pram)* landau *m* (**b**) *(carriage)* boghei *m*, buggy *m*
bugle ['bjuːgəl] *n* clairon *m*

bugler ['bjuːglə(r)] *n* (sonneur *m* de) clairon *m*

build [bɪld] **1** *n* carrure *f*

2 *vt* (*pt & pp* **built** [bɪlt]) construire; **to be built (out) of sth** être construit(e) en qch; **to b. sth into sth** *(include)* inclure qch dans qch; **to b. one's hopes on sth** fonder ses espoirs sur qch

▸ **build on 1** *vt sep (add)* ajouter

2 *vt insep (success)* tirer parti de

▸ **build up 1** *vt sep* (**a**) *(resources)* accumuler; **to b. up speed/one's strength** prendre de la vitesse/des forces; **don't b. your hopes up** ne te fais pas d'illusions (**b**) *(custom)* se constituer; *(reputation)* se faire; *(company)* développer; **to b. up an immunity (to sth)** s'immuniser (contre qch) (**c**) *(hype)* faire du battage autour de

2 *vi (of clouds)* s'amasser; *(of hurricane, storm)* se préparer; *(of tension, pressure)* s'accumuler

builder ['bɪldə(r)] *n* maçon *m*; *(business owner)* entrepreneur *m* (dans le bâtiment)

building ['bɪldɪŋ] *n* (**a**) *(structure)* bâtiment *m*; immeuble *m* (**b**) *(action)* construction *f*; **the b. trade** le bâtiment; **b. block** cube *m*; *Fig* élément *m* essentiel; **b. site** chantier *m* (de construction); *Br* **b. society** ≃ société *f* de crédit immobilier

---

Building Societies

Les "building societies" fonctionnent comme des banques mais elles n'ont pas de système de compensation. Établissements consentant des prêts immobiliers aux particuliers, elles jouent un rôle important dans la vie en Grande-Bretagne. Au cours des dernières années, de nombreuses "building societies" ont abandonné leur statut de sociétés mutuelles pour devenir des banques cotées en Bourse.

---

build-up ['bɪldʌp] *n (of tension, forces)* accumulation *f*; *(hype)* battage *m*; **the b. to Christmas/the match** la période précédant Noël/le match

built [bɪlt] *pt & pp of* **build**

built-in ['bɪl'tɪn] *adj (cupboard)* encastré(e); *(included)* compris(e); **b. obsolescence** obsolescence *f* programmée

built-up ['bɪl'tʌp] *adj* **b. area** agglomération *f* urbaine

bulb [bʌlb] *n* (**a**) *(of plant)* bulbe *m* (**b**) *(light bulb)* ampoule *f*

bulbous ['bʌlbəs] *adj* bulbeux(euse); **a b. nose** un gros nez

Bulgaria [bʌl'geərɪə] *n* la Bulgarie

Bulgarian [bʌl'geərɪən] **1** *n* (**a**) *(person)* Bulgare *mf* (**b**) *(language)* bulgare *m*

2 *adj* bulgare

bulge [bʌldʒ] **1** *n* renflement *m*

2 *vi (of stomach)* être gonflé(e); *(of bag, pocket)* être bourré(e) (**with** de)

bulimia [bə'lɪmɪə] *n* boulimie *f*

bulk [bʌlk] **1** *n* (**a**) *(mass)* masse *f*; **the b. (of sth)** la majeure partie (de qch) (**b**) *Com* **in b.** en gros; **b. purchase** achat *m* en gros

2 *vt* **to b. sth out** étoffer qch

3 *vi* **to b. large** *(of problem)* occuper une place importante

bulkhead ['bʌlkhed] *n Naut* cloison *f*

bulky ['bʌlkɪ] *adj* volumineux(euse), encombrant(e)

bull¹ [bʊl] *n* (**a**) *(animal)* taureau *m*; **b. elephant** éléphant *m* mâle; *Fin* **b. market** marché *m* à la hausse

(**b**) *very Fam (nonsense)* conneries *fpl* (**c**) *(idioms)* **to take the b. by the horns** prendre le taureau par les cornes; **like a b. in a china shop** comme un éléphant dans un magasin de porcelaine

bull² *n Rel* bulle *f*

bulldog ['bʊldɒg] *n* bouledogue *m*; **b. clip** pince *f* à dessin

bulldoze ['bʊldəʊz] *vt (land)* aplanir au bulldozer; *(building)* démolir au bulldozer; *Fig* **to b. sb into doing sth** forcer qn à faire qch

bulldozer ['bʊldəʊzə(r)] *n* bulldozer *m*

bullet ['bʊlɪt] *n* balle *f*; **b. hole** impact *m* de balle; **b. wound** blessure *f* par balle

bulletin ['bʊlɪtɪn] *n* bulletin *m*; **b. board** *Am (notice-board)* panneau *m* d'affichage; *Comput* serveur *m* télématique, *Can* babillard *m*

bulletproof ['bʊlɪtpruːf] *adj (car, glass)* blindé(e); **b. vest** gilet *m* pare-balles

bullfight ['bʊlfaɪt] *n* corrida *f*, course *f* de taureaux; *(art)* tauromachie *f*

bullfighter ['bʊlfaɪtə(r)] *n* torero *m*

bullfighting ['bʊlfaɪtɪŋ] *n (bullfights)* courses *fpl* de taureaux; *(art)* tauromachie *f*

bullfinch ['bʊlfɪntʃ] *n* bouvreuil *m*

bullfrog ['bʊlfrɒg] *n* grenouille-taureau *f*, *Can* ouaouaron *m*

bullion ['bʊljən] *n* **gold b.** lingots *mpl* d'or

bullish ['bʊlɪʃ] *adj Fin (market)* à la hausse; *Fig (optimistic)* optimiste

bullock ['bʊlək] *n* bœuf *m*

bullring ['bʊlrɪŋ] *n* arène *f*

bull's-eye ['bʊlzaɪ] *n* mille *m*; *also Fig* **to hit the b.** mettre dans le mille

bullshit ['bʊlʃɪt] *Vulg* **1** *n (nonsense)* conneries *fpl*

2 *exclam* c'est des conneries tout ça!

3 *vt (pt & pp* **bullshitted**) **to b. sb** raconter des conneries à qn; **she bullshitted her way into the job** elle a bluffé pour avoir le poste

4 *vi (talk nonsense)* dire des conneries

bully ['bʊlɪ] **1** *n (pl* **bullies**) *(child)* petite brute *f*; *(adult)* tyran *m*; **don't be such a b.** ne sois pas si tyrannique

2 *vt (pt & pp* **bullied**) maltraiter; **to b. sb into doing sth** forcer qn à faire qch

3 *exclam Ironic* **b. for you!** bravo!

bully-boy ['bʊlɪbɔɪ] *n* voyou *m*; **b. tactics** manœuvres *fpl* d'intimidation

bullying ['bʊlɪŋ] **1** *n* brimades *fpl*

2 *adj* brutal(e)

bulrush ['bʊlrʌʃ] *n* jonc *m*

bulwark ['bʊlwɜːk] *n also Fig* rempart *m* (**against** contre)

bum [bʌm] *Fam* **1** *n* (**a**) *Br (buttocks)* derrière *m* (**b**) *Am (tramp)* clochard(e) *m,f*

2 *adj (of poor quality)* minable; **to get a b. deal** se faire avoir

3 *vt (pt & pp* **bummed**) **to b. a cigarette from** *or* **off sb** taxer une cigarette à qn; **to b. a ride** se faire prendre en stop

▸ **bum around** *vi Fam (be idle)* glander; *(travel)* vadrouiller

bumblebee ['bʌmbəlbiː] *n* bourdon *m*

bumbling ['bʌmbəlɪŋ] *adj* **b. fool** *or* **idiot** imbécile *mf*

bumf [bʌmf] *n Fam* paperasse *f*

bummer ['bʌmə(r)] *n Fam* **what a b.!** quelle poisse!

bump [bʌmp] **1** n (**a**) (jolt) secousse f; **to land with a b.** tomber violemment par terre; Fig **to come back down to earth with a b.** redescendre brusquement sur terre (**b**) (lump) bosse f
2 vt cogner; **to b. one's head** se cogner la tête
▸**bump into** vt insep (collide with) rentrer dans; Fam (meet by chance) tomber sur
▸**bump off** vt sep Fam (kill) liquider
▸**bump up** vt sep Fam (price) gonfler, augmenter
bumper ['bʌmpə(r)] **1** n Br (of car) pare-chocs m inv; **b. car** (at fairground) auto f tamponneuse
2 adj **b. crop** récolte f exceptionnelle; **b. issue** numéro m exceptionnel
bumpkin ['bʌmpkɪn] n (**country**) **b.** péquenaud(e) m,f
bump-start ['bʌmpstɑːt] vt **to b. a car** pousser une voiture pour la faire démarrer
bumptious ['bʌmpʃəs] adj suffisant(e)
bumpy ['bʌmpɪ] adj (road) cahoteux(euse); (journey) agité(e); (landing) violent(e); Fam Fig **to give sb/sth a b. ride** malmener qn/qch
bun [bʌn] n (**a**) (sweet) petit gâteau m brioché; (for burger) petit pain m rond (**b**) (hairstyle) chignon m
bunch [bʌntʃ] n (of flowers) bouquet m; (of bananas) régime m; (of grapes) grappe f; (of keys) trousseau m; (of people) bande f; (of cyclists) peloton m; **bunches** (hairstyle) couettes fpl; **he's the best of a bad b.** c'est le moins mauvais du lot; **she's the best** or **the pick of the b.** c'est la meilleure du lot; **a whole b. of things to do** tout un tas de choses à faire
▸**bunch together** vi (of people) se serrer
bundle ['bʌndəl] **1** n (of clothes) paquet m; (of banknotes, papers) liasse f; (of straw) botte f; Fam **I don't go a b. on horror films** je ne suis pas un fana de films d'horreur; Fam Ironic **you're a b. of laughs!** c'est fou ce que tu as l'air gai!; Fam **she's a b. of nerves** c'est un paquet de nerfs
2 vt **to b. sb out of the door** mettre qn dehors sans ménagement; **to b. sb into a car** embarquer qn dans une voiture
▸**bundle off** vt sep (send) expédier
bung [bʌŋ] **1** n (**a**) (plug) bonde f (**b**) Br Fam (bribe) bakchich m
2 vt Br Fam (put) mettre; (throw) balancer; **b. it there** mets-le là; **b. me over an orange** balance-moi une orange
▸**bung up** vt sep Fam boucher; **my nose is bunged up** j'ai le nez bouché
bungalow ['bʌŋɡələʊ] n pavillon m de plain-pied
bungee jumping ['bʌndʒiːdʒʌmpɪŋ] n saut m à l'élastique
bunghole ['bʌŋhəʊl] n bonde f
bungle ['bʌŋɡəl] **1** vt (attempt) rater; (job) gâcher
2 vi se tromper
bunion ['bʌnjən] n oignon m (au pied)
bunk¹ [bʌŋk] n (bed) lit m; (in train, ship) couchette f; **b. beds** lits superposés
bunk² n Br Fam **to do a b.** (run away) se faire la malle
▸**bunk off** vi Br Fam (from school) sécher (les cours)
bunker ['bʌŋkə(r)] n (**a**) (for coal) coffre m à charbon (**b**) Mil bunker m, blockhaus m; **nuclear b.** abri m antiatomique (**c**) Br (on golf course) bunker m
bunkum ['bʌŋkəm] n Fam âneries fpl
bunny ['bʌnɪ] (pl bunnies) n Fam **b. (rabbit)** petit lapin m

Bunsen burner ['bʌnsən'bɜːnə(r)] n bec m Bunsen
bunting ['bʌntɪŋ] n (decorations) guirlandes fpl de fanions
buoy [bɔɪ] n bouée f
▸**buoy up** vt sep (person, prices) soutenir
buoyancy ['bɔɪənsɪ] n (in water) flottabilité f; Fig (of market) stabilité f
buoyant ['bɔɪənt] adj (in water) qui flotte; Fig (economy, prices) stable; Fig (person, mood) plein(e) d'allant
burble ['bɜːbəl] vi (of stream) murmurer; (of person) marmonner
burden ['bɜːdən] **1** n also Fig fardeau m; **b. of taxation** pression f fiscale; Law **b. of proof** charge f de la preuve
2 vt Fig accabler (with de)
burdensome ['bɜːdənsəm] adj lourd(e)
bureau ['bjʊərəʊ] (pl bureaux ['bjʊərəʊz]) n (**a**) (desk) bureau m, secrétaire m; Am (chest of drawers) commode f (**b**) (office) bureau m; Am (government department) service m
bureaucracy [bjʊə'rɒkrəsɪ] n bureaucratie f
bureaucrat ['bjʊərəkræt] n bureaucrate mf
bureaucratic [bjʊərə'krætɪk] adj bureaucratique
bureaux ['bjʊərəʊz] pl of bureau
burgeon ['bɜːdʒən] vi (of trade) se développer; (of crime) augmenter; (of relationship) s'épanouir; **a burgeoning talent** un talent qui s'affirme
burger ['bɜːɡə(r)] n hamburger m
burglar ['bɜːɡlə(r)] n cambrioleur(euse) m,f; **b. alarm** alarme f (de sécurité)
burglarize ['bɜːɡləraɪz] vt Am cambrioler
burglar-proof ['bɜːɡləpruːf] adj inviolable
burglary ['bɜːɡlərɪ] (pl burglaries) n cambriolage m
burgle ['bɜːɡəl] vt cambrioler
Burgundy ['bɜːɡəndɪ] n la Bourgogne
burgundy ['bɜːɡəndɪ] adj (colour) bordeaux inv
burial ['berɪəl] n enterrement m; **b. ground** cimetière m
Burkina-Faso [bɜː'kiːnə'fæsəʊ] n le Burkina
burlesque [bɜː'lesk] **1** n (caricature) parodie f; (style) burlesque m
2 adj burlesque
burly ['bɜːlɪ] adj bien bâti(e)
Burma ['bɜːmə] n Formerly la Birmanie
Burmese [bɜː'miːz] **1** npl **the B.** les Birmans mpl
2 n (**a**) (person) Birman(e) m,f (**b**) (language) birman m
3 adj birman(e)
burn¹ [bɜːn] **1** n brûlure f
2 vt (pt & pp burnt [bɜːnt] or burned) (**a**) (fuel, building) brûler; **to b. one's hand/one's finger** se brûler la main/le doigt; **to b. a hole in sth** faire un trou dans qch (**b**) (idioms) **to have money to b.** avoir de l'argent à ne plus savoir quoi en faire; **to b. one's boats** or **one's bridges** brûler ses vaisseaux; **to b. the candle at both ends** brûler la chandelle par les deux bouts; **to b. the midnight oil** travailler tard
3 vi brûler; (of light) briller; **the fire is burning low** le feu baisse; Fig **to b. with desire** brûler de désir; **to b. with anger** bouillonner de colère; **to b. with enthusiasm** déborder d'enthousiasme
▸**burn down 1** vt sep incendier
2 vi être détruit(e) par le feu

▸**burn out 1** *vt sep* **to b. itself out** *(of fire)* s'éteindre; *Fig* **to b. oneself out** *(become exhausted)* s'épuiser
2 *vi (of fire)* s'éteindre
▸**burn up 1** *vt sep (energy)* dépenser
2 *vi (of rocket)* se désintégrer
burn² *n Scot (stream)* ruisseau *m*
burner ['bɜːnə(r)] *n* brûleur *m*
burning ['bɜːnɪŋ] *adj (on fire)* en feu; *(very hot)* brûlant(e); *(passion, ambition)* dévorant(e); **a b. issue** une question brûlante
burnish ['bɜːnɪʃ] *vt* polir, brunir
burnt [bɜːnt] **1** *adj* brûlé(e)
2 *pt & pp of* **burn¹**
burnt-out ['bɜːnt'aʊt] *adj (building, car)* calciné(e); *Fig (person)* usé(e)
burp [bɜːp] **1** *n* rot *m*
2 *vi* roter
burr¹ [bɜː(r)] *n (of plant)* bardane *f*; *(on tree trunk)* broussin *m*
burr² *n* **to speak with a b.** grasseyer
burrow ['bʌrəʊ] **1** *n (of animal)* terrier *m*
2 *vi (of animal)* creuser la terre
bursar ['bɜːsə(r)] *n Univ* intendant(e) *m,f*
bursary ['bɜːsərɪ] *(pl* **bursaries)** *n (grant)* bourse *f* (d'études)
burst [bɜːst] **1** *n (of laughter)* éclat *m*; *(of enthusiasm)* élan *m*; **a b. of activity** une poussée d'activité; **a b. of applause** une salve d'applaudissements; **a b. of gunfire** une rafale; **a b. of speed** une pointe de vitesse
2 *vt (pt & pp* **burst)** *(balloon, tyre)* faire éclater; **to b. its banks** *(of river)* déborder, sortir de son lit
3 *vi (of balloon, bubble, tyre, pipe)* éclater; *Fig* **to be bursting with pride** déborder de fierté; **to be bursting with impatience** bouillir d'impatience; **to be bursting to do sth** mourir d'envie de faire qch; **to be bursting (for the toilet)** avoir un besoin pressant; *Fig* **to be bursting at the seams** *(of room)* être plein(e) à craquer
▸**burst into** *vt insep* **(a)** *(enter)* faire irruption dans **(b)** *(suddenly start)* **to b. into flames** prendre feu; **to b. into song** se mettre à chanter; **to b. into laughter/ tears** éclater de rire/en sanglots
▸**burst open** *vi (of door)* s'ouvrir brusquement; *(of packet)* éclater
▸**burst out** *vi* **to b. out laughing** éclater de rire; **to b. out crying** éclater en sanglots
Burundi [bə'rʊndɪ] *n* le Burundi
bury ['berɪ] *(pt & pp* **buried)** *vt (body, treasure)* enterrer; *(of avalanche, mudslide) & Fig (hide)* ensevelir; **to b. oneself in one's work** se plonger dans son travail; **to b. one's face in one's hands** enfouir son visage dans ses mains; **to b. the hatchet** enterrer la hache de guerre
bus [bʌs] **1** *n (pl* **buses** *or* **busses)** **(a)** *(vehicle)* bus *m*, autobus *m*; **by b.** en bus; **b. conductor/driver** receveur *m*/chauffeur *m* de bus; **b. lane** couloir *m* de bus; **b. route** ligne *f* de bus; **b. shelter** Abribus® *m*; **b. station** gare *f* routière; **b. stop** arrêt *m* d'autobus **(b)** *Comput* bus *m*
2 *vt (pt & pp* **bused** *or* **bussed)** transporter en autobus
bush [bʊʃ] *n (plant)* buisson *m*; **the b.** *(in Africa, Australia)* la brousse; *Fam* **b. telegraph** téléphone *m* arabe
bushed [bʊʃt] *adj Fam (exhausted)* vanné(e), claqué(e)

bushel ['bʊʃəl] *n* boisseau *m*; *Fig* **don't hide your light under a b.** ne cache pas ton talent
bushfire ['bʊʃfaɪə(r)] *n* feu *m* de brousse
bushy ['bʊʃɪ] *adj* touffu(e)
busily ['bɪzɪlɪ] *adv* **to be b. doing sth** être très occupé(e) à faire qch
business ['bɪznɪs] *n* **(a)** *(task, concern)* affaire *f*; **it's none of your b.** cela ne te regarde pas, ce ne sont pas tes affaires; **it's/it's not my b. to...** c'est/ce n'est pas à moi de...; **mind your own b.!** occupe-toi de tes affaires *ou* de ce qui te regarde!; **to make it one's b. to do sth** prendre sur soi de faire qch; **to go about one's b.** vaquer à ses occupations; **to get down to b.** se mettre au travail; **to mean b.** ne pas plaisanter; **I'm sick of the whole b.** j'en ai assez de toute cette histoire; **he was working like nobody's b.** il travaillait très dur; **she can tell jokes like nobody's b.** elle raconte très bien les histoires drôles; *Br Fam* **it's the b.** *(excellent)* c'est génial
(b) *(individual company)* affaire *f*, entreprise *f*; *(commercial activity)* affaires; **to be in the entertainment b.** être dans le spectacle; **the travel b.** les métiers *ou* le secteur du tourisme; **I'm not in the b. of making compromises** ce n'est pas mon genre de faire des compromis; **to be in b.** être dans les affaires; **to set up in b.** s'établir *ou* s'installer à son compte; **to go into b.** s'installer; **to go into b. with sb** monter une affaire avec qn; **to go out of b.** fermer; **to go to London on b.** aller à Londres pour affaires; **how's b.?** comment vont les affaires?; **it's good/bad for b.** c'est bon/mauvais pour les affaires; **to talk b.** parler affaires; **to do b. with sb** traiter avec qn; *Fin* **b. account** compte *m* professionnel; **b. card** carte *f* de visite; **b. class** *(on plane)* classe *f* affaires; **b. hours** *(of shop)* heures *fpl* d'ouverture; *(of office)* heures de bureau; **b. lunch** déjeuner *m* d'affaires; **b. management** gestion *f* d'entreprise; **b. park** parc *m* d'activités; **b. school** école *f* de commerce; **b. studies** études *fpl* commerciales *ou* de commerce; **b. trip** voyage *m* d'affaires
businesslike ['bɪznɪslaɪk] *adj* professionnel(elle)
businessman ['bɪznɪsmæn] *n* homme *m* d'affaires; **to be a good b.** avoir le sens des affaires
businesswoman ['bɪznɪswʊmən] *n* femme *f* d'affaires; **to be a good b.** avoir le sens des affaires
busk [bʌsk] *vi Br* jouer de la musique *(dans les rues ou le métro)*
busker ['bʌskə(r)] *n Br* musicien(enne) *m,f (dans les rues ou le métro)*
busman ['bʌsmən] *n Fam* **a b.'s holiday** = vacances pendant lesquelles on fait la même chose qu'à son travail
bust¹ [bʌst] *n* **(a)** *(of woman)* poitrine *f*; **b. measurement** tour *m* de poitrine **(b)** *(statue)* buste *m*
bust² *Fam* **1** *adj* **(a)** *(broken)* fichu(e) **(b)** **to go b.** *(bankrupt)* faire faillite
2 *vt (pt & pp* **busted** *or* **bust)** **(a)** *(break)* bousiller **(b)** *(arrest)* coffrer
▸**bust out** *vi Fam (escape)* se tirer **(of** de)
▸**bust up** *vt sep Fam (disrupt) (event)* interrompre; *(relationship)* ficher en l'air
bustle ['bʌsəl] **1** *n (commotion)* animation *f*
2 *vi* **to b. (about)** s'activer, s'affairer
bust-up ['bʌstʌp] *n Fam (dispute)* engueulade *f*; *(of relationship)* fin *f*; **to have a b.** *(argue)* s'engueuler
busy ['bɪzɪ] **1** *adj* **(a)** *(person)* occupé(e); *(day, week)* chargé(e); *(road)* à grande circulation; **to keep sb b.**

occuper qn; **to keep oneself b.** s'occuper; **to be b. doing sth** être occupé à faire qch; **the train was very b.** il y avait beaucoup de monde dans le train (**b**) *Am (telephone line)* occupé(e); **I keep getting the b. signal** ça sonne toujours occupé
 2 *vt (pt & pp busied)* **to b. oneself with sth** s'occuper à qch

busybody ['bɪzɪbɒdɪ] *(pl busybodies) n Fam* fouineur(euse) *m,f*

but [bʌt] **1** *prep (except)* sauf, à part; **any day b. tomorrow** n'importe quand sauf demain; **it's nothing b. prejudice** ce ne sont rien que des préjugés; **she is anything b. stupid** elle est loin d'être bête; **b. for** sans; **the last b. one** l'avant-dernier(ère) *m,f*; **the next b. one** le (la) deuxième
 2 *adv Formal* seulement; **he is b. a child** ce n'est qu'un enfant; **had I b. known!** si (seulement) j'avais su!; **one can b. try** on peut toujours essayer
 3 *conj* mais; **not once b. twice** pas une fois, mais deux; **I told her to do it b. she refused** je lui ai dit de le faire mais elle a refusé; **b. I tell you I saw it!** mais puisque je te dis que je l'ai vu!; **I had no choice b. to go** je n'ai pas pu faire autrement que d'y aller; **what could I do b. invite him?** comment pouvais-je faire autrement que de l'inviter?
 4 *n* **no buts!** il n'y a pas de "mais" qui tienne!

butane ['bjuːteɪn] *n* butane *m*

butch [bʊtʃ] *adj Fam* hommasse

butcher ['bʊtʃə(r)] **1** *n also Fig* boucher(ère) *m,f*; **b.'s (shop)** boucherie *f*; **to go to the b.'s** aller chez le boucher *ou* à la boucherie
 2 *vt (animal)* abattre; *Fig (person, song)* massacrer

butchery ['bʊtʃərɪ] *n also Fig* boucherie *f*

butler ['bʌtlə(r)] *n* majordome *m*, maître *m* d'hôtel

butt [bʌt] **1** *n* (**a**) *(of rifle)* crosse *f*; *(of cigarette)* mégot *m*; *Fig* **to be the b. of a joke** être la cible d'une plaisanterie (**b**) *Am Fam (buttocks)* fesses *fpl*
 2 *vt (hit with head)* donner un coup de tête à
▸**butt in** *vi (interrupt)* intervenir

butter ['bʌtə(r)] **1** *n* beurre *m*; **she looks as if b. wouldn't melt in her mouth** on lui donnerait le bon Dieu sans confession; **b. bean** = gros haricot blanc; **b. dish** beurrier *m*; **b. knife** couteau *m* à beurre; **b. mountain** montagne *f* de beurre
 2 *vt* beurrer
▸**butter up** *vt sep Fam (flatter)* passer de la pommade à

buttercup ['bʌtəkʌp] *n* bouton *m* d'or

butterfingers ['bʌtəfɪŋɡəz] *n Fam* empoté(e) *m,f*

butterfly ['bʌtəflaɪ] *(pl butterflies) n* papillon *m*; *Fig* **to have butterflies (in one's stomach)** avoir l'estomac noué; **b. (stroke)** *(in swimming)* (brasse *f*) papillon *m*

buttermilk ['bʌtəmɪlk] *n* babeurre *m*

butterscotch ['bʌtəskɒtʃ] *n* caramel *m* dur au beurre

buttock ['bʌtək] *n* fesse *f*

button ['bʌtən] **1** *n* (**a**) *(on shirt, machine)* bouton *m*; **b. mushroom** petit champignon *m* de Paris (**b**) *Am (badge)* badge *m*
 2 *vt (shirt, dress)* boutonner; *Fam* **b. it!** la ferme!
▸**button up** *vt sep (shirt, dress)* boutonner

buttonhole ['bʌtənhəʊl] **1** *n* boutonnière *f*
 2 *vt (detain)* coincer

buttress ['bʌtrɪs] **1** *n Archit* contrefort *m*; *Fig* pilier *m*
 2 *vt Fig (support)* renforcer

buxom ['bʌksəm] *adj (plump)* plantureux(euse); *(full-bosomed)* à la poitrine généreuse

buy [baɪ] **1** *n* **a good/bad b.** une bonne/mauvaise affaire
 2 *vt (pt & pp bought* [bɔːt]) (**a**) *(purchase)* acheter; **to b. sb sth, to b. sth for sb** acheter qch à qn; **to b. sth from sb** acheter qch à qn; *Fig* **to b. time** gagner du temps; **he's bought it** *(has died)* il a passé l'arme à gauche (**b**) *Fam (believe)* avaler
▸**buy in** *vt sep (supplies)* faire des stocks de
▸**buy into** *vt insep (company, scheme)* acheter des parts de
▸**buy off** *vt sep Fam* acheter
▸**buy out** *vt sep Com* racheter la part de
▸**buy up** *vt sep (land, shares)* acheter; *(supplies)* faire des stocks de

buyer ['baɪə(r)] *n* acheteur(euse) *m,f*; **b.'s market** marché *m* demandeur

buy-out ['baɪaʊt] *n Com* rachat *m*

buzz [bʌz] **1** *n* (**a**) *(noise)* bourdonnement *m*; *(of plane)* vrombissement *m*; *Fam* **b. word** mot *m* à la mode (**b**) *Fam (phone call)* **to give sb a b.** passer un coup de fil à qn (**c**) *Fam (thrill)* **to get a b. out of doing sth** prendre son pied à faire qch
 2 *vt Fam (on intercom)* appeler à l'Interphone®; *(on pager)* biper
 3 *vi (make noise)* bourdonner; *Fig* **to b. with excitement** *(of town)* bourdonner d'excitation; **my head was buzzing** j'avais la tête lourde; *Fam* **now we're buzzing!** maintenant on est lancés!
▸**buzz off** *vi Br Fam* se tirer

buzzard ['bʌzəd] *n* buse *f*

buzzer ['bʌzə(r)] *n (on intercom)* bouton *m* de l'Interphone®; *(on clock, oven)* sonnerie *f*

buzzing ['bʌzɪŋ] *n* bourdonnement *m*

by [baɪ] **1** *prep* (**a**) *(agent)* par; **he was arrested by the police** il a été arrêté par la police, la police l'a arrêté; **made by hand** fait(e) (à la) main; **a play by Shakespeare** une pièce de Shakespeare
 (**b**) *(with manner, means)* **by train/car/plane** en train/voiture/avion; **by doing sth** en faisant qch; **to pay by credit card** payer par carte de crédit; **to have a child by sb** avoir un enfant de qn; **to take sb by the hand/arm** prendre qn par la main/le bras; **to know sb by name/sight** connaître qn de nom/de vue; **to earn one's living by teaching** gagner sa vie en enseignant
 (**c**) *(close to)* près de; **by the fire** près du feu; **by the sea** au bord de la mer; **by the side of the road** sur le bord de la route
 (**d**) *(via)* par; **by land/sea** par terre/mer
 (**e**) *(past)* **to walk by sb/sth** passer devant qn/qch; **to drive by sb/sth** passer devant qn/qch (en voiture)
 (**f**) *(at or before)* **she should be here by now** elle devrait être ici à l'heure qu'il est; **it'll be ready by tomorrow** ce sera prêt pour demain; **by 1980 they were all dead** en 1980 ils étaient déjà tous morts; **by then it was too late** il était déjà trop tard
 (**g**) *(during)* **by day/night** jour/nuit
 (**h**) *(with measurements, quantities, numbers)* **to divide/multiply by three** diviser/multiplier par trois; **3 metres by 2** 3 mètres sur 2; **to sell sth by weight** vendre qch au poids; **one by one** un par un
 (**i**) *(according to)* **to go by appearances** se fier aux apparences; **to call sb by their first name** appeler qn par son prénom; **what do you mean by that?** qu'est-ce que tu entends par là?

(**j**) *(with reflexive pronouns)* **by oneself** tout(e) seul(e)
(**k**) *(as a result of)* **by accident/chance/mistake** par accident/hasard/erreur
2 *adv* (**a**) **by and large** dans l'ensemble; **by the way,...** au fait,...
(**b**) *(past)* **to go/walk by** passer; **to drive by** passer (en voiture)

bye [baɪ] *exclam Fam* au revoir!, salut!; **b. for now!** à bientôt!

bye-bye ['baɪ'baɪ] *exclam Fam* au revoir!, salut!

by-election ['baɪɪlekʃən] *n Pol* élection *f* partielle

Byelorussia [bɪeləʊ'rʌʃə] = **Belarus**

Byelorussian [bɪeləʊ'rʌʃən] **1** *n* Biélorusse *mf*
2 *adj* biélorusse

bygone ['baɪgɒn] **1** *n* **let bygones be bygones** oublions le passé
2 *adj* révolu(e); **in b. days** autrefois

by-line ['baɪlaɪn] *n (in newspaper)* signature *f*

bypass ['baɪpɑːs] **1** *n* (**a**) *(road)* rocade *f* (**b**) *(heart operation)* pontage *m*
2 *vt (of road) also Fig* contourner; *(middleman)* court-circuiter

by-product ['baɪprɒdʌkt] *n* sous-produit *m*, dérivé *m*; *Fig* conséquence *f* indirecte

bystander ['baɪstændə(r)] *n* passant(e) *m,f*

byte [baɪt] *n Comput* octet *m*

byway ['baɪweɪ] *n (road)* petite route *f*

byword ['baɪwɜːd] *n* **to be a b. for** être synonyme de

Byzantine [bɪ'zæntaɪn] *adj also Fig* byzantin(e)

C

C, c [siː] n (**a**) (letter) C, c m inv (**b**) Mus do m, ut m (**c**) Sch (grade) **to get a C** (in exam) avoir mention passable; (in homework, essay) ≃ avoir 10 ou 11 sur 20

C (**a**) (abbr **centigrade**) C (**b**) (abbr **century**) s.; **C.16** XVIᵉ s.

c, ca (abbr **circa**) (approximately) env.; (with dates) vers

CAB [siːeɪˈbiː] n (abbr **Citizens' Advice Bureau**) = organisme bénévole britannique de conseil, notamment en matière juridique et sociale

cab [kæb] n (**a**) (taxi) taxi m; **c. driver** chauffeur m de taxi (**b**) (of train, lorry) cabine f

cabaret [ˈkæbəreɪ] n cabaret m; **c. artist** artiste mf de cabaret

cabbage [ˈkæbɪdʒ] n chou m; **red c.** chou rouge; **c. white** (butterfly) piéride f du chou

cabbie, cabby [ˈkæbɪ] (pl **cabbies**) n Fam (chauffeur m de) taxi m

cabin [ˈkæbɪn] n (of ship, plane) cabine f; (hut) cabane f; **c. boy** (on ship) mousse m; **c. crew** (on plane) équipage m

cabinet [ˈkæbɪnɪt] n (**a**) (piece of furniture) meuble m (à tiroirs); (with glass front) vitrine f (**b**) Pol cabinet m; **c. meeting** ≃ Conseil m des ministres; **c. minister** ministre m, membre m du cabinet

cabinet-maker [ˈkæbɪnɪtmeɪkə(r)] n ébéniste mf

cable [ˈkeɪbəl] 1 n (electrical) & Tel câble m; **c. car** téléphérique m; **c. (television)** (télévision f par) câble

2 vt (message) câbler; **to c. sb** envoyer un câble à qn

caboodle [kəˈbuːdəl] n Fam **the whole (kit and) c.** tout le bazar ou bataclan

cacao [kəˈkɑːəʊ] n (plant) cacaotier m, cacaoyer m; **c. bean** fève f de cacao

cache [kæʃ] n (**a**) (of drugs, arms) cache f (**b**) Comput mémoire-cache f

cack-handed [kækˈhændɪd] adj Fam maladroit(e)

cackle [ˈkækəl] 1 n (**a**) (of hen) caquet m (**b**) Fam (talking) caquetage m; (laugh) gloussement m; **cut the c.!** arrête de jacasser!

2 vi (**a**) (of hen) caqueter (**b**) Fam (laugh) glousser

cacophonous [kəˈkɒfənəs] adj cacophonique

cactus [ˈkæktəs] (pl **cacti** [ˈkæktaɪ] or **cactuses**) n cactus m

CAD [siːeɪˈdiː] n Comput (abbr **computer-aided design**) CAO f

cad [kæd] n Br Fam Old-fashioned mufle m

cadaver [kəˈdævə(r)] n Formal cadavre m

cadaverous [kəˈdævərəs] adj cadavérique

caddie [ˈkædɪ] n (in golf) caddie m

caddy [ˈkædɪ] (pl **caddies**) n **(tea) c.** boîte f à thé

cadence [ˈkeɪdəns] n cadence f, rythme m

cadet [kəˈdet] n Mil élève m officier; **c. corps** peloton m de préparation militaire

cadge [kædʒ] vt Fam quémander (**from** or **off** à); **to c. a meal off** or **from sb** se faire inviter à manger par qn; **can I c. a lift from you?** tu me déposes?

cadmium [ˈkædmɪəm] n Chem cadmium m

Caesarean, Caesarian [sɪˈzeərɪən] n **C. (section)** césarienne f

café, cafe [ˈkæfeɪ] n café m

> ### Café
> En Grande-Bretagne, le mot "café" désigne une sorte de snack où l'on peut prendre un repas léger et boire du thé ou du café.

cafeteria [kæfɪˈtɪərɪə] n cafétéria f

caff [kæf] n Br Fam bistro m

caffeine [ˈkæfiːn] n caféine f; **c. free** décaféiné(e)

cage [keɪdʒ] 1 n (for bird, animal) cage f; (of lift) cabine f

2 vt mettre en cage; **to feel caged in** se sentir prisonnier (ère)

cagey [ˈkeɪdʒɪ] adj (evasive) évasif(ive) (**about** sur); (cautious) prudent(e)

cagoule [kəˈguːl] n K-way® m inv

cahoots [kəˈhuːts] npl Fam **to be in c. (with sb)** être de mèche (avec qn)

CAI [siːeɪˈaɪ] n Comput (abbr **computer-aided instruction**) EAO m

cairn [keən] n cairn m

Cairo [ˈkaɪrəʊ] n Le Caire

cajole [kəˈdʒəʊl] vt enjôler; **to c. sb into doing sth** amadouer qn pour qu'il fasse qch

cake [keɪk] 1 n (**a**) (food) gâteau m; (pastry) petit gâteau; **c. shop** pâtisserie f; **c. tin** moule m à gâteau (**b**) (of soap) pain m (**c**) (idioms) **it's a piece of c.** c'est du gâteau; Prov **you can't have your c. and eat it** on ne peut pas avoir le beurre et l'argent du beurre

2 vt **her shoes were caked with mud** ses chaussures étaient couvertes de boue

CAL [kæl] n Comput (abbr **computer-aided learning**) EAO m

calamity [kəˈlæmɪtɪ] (pl **calamities**) n calamité f

calcium [ˈkælsɪəm] n calcium m

calculate [ˈkælkjʊleɪt] 1 vt calculer; (consequences, risk) évaluer; **his remark was calculated to shock** sa remarque était destinée à choquer

2 vi **to c. on sth** compter sur qch; **to c. on doing sth** compter faire qch

calculated [ˈkælkjʊleɪtɪd] adj (risk) calculé(e); (crime) prémédité(e)

calculating ['kælkjʊleɪtɪŋ] *adj* calculateur(trice)

calculation [kælkjʊ'leɪʃən] *n* calcul *m*

calculator ['kælkjʊleɪtə(r)] *n* calculatrice *f*

calculus ['kælkjʊləs] *n Math* calcul *m*

calendar ['kælɪndə(r)] *n* calendrier *m*; **c. month** mois *m* civil; **c. year** année *f* civile

calf¹ [kɑːf] (*pl* **calves** [kɑːvz]) *n (animal)* veau *m*; **the cow is in** *or* **with c.** la vache est pleine; *Fig* **to kill the fatted c.** tuer le veau gras

calf² (*pl* **calves** [kɑːvz]) *n (of leg)* mollet *m*

calfskin ['kɑːfskɪn] *n* veau *m*

caliber *Am* = **calibre**

calibrate ['kælɪbreɪt] *vt* étalonner, calibrer

calibre, *Am* **caliber** ['kælɪbə(r)] *n also Fig* calibre *m*

calico ['kælɪkəʊ] *n* calicot *m*

California [kælɪ'fɔːnɪə] *n* la Californie

call [kɔːl] **1** *n* (**a**) *(shout)* appel *m*, cri *m*
(**b**) *(appeal)* appel *m* (**for** à); **a c. to arms** un appel aux armes
(**c**) *(on phone)* appel *m*, coup *m* de téléphone; **to give sb a c.** passer un coup de téléphone à qn; **to make a c.** passer un coup de téléphone *ou* de fil; **to return sb's c.** rappeler qn; **c. centre** centre *m* d'appels; **c. girl** call-girl *f*
(**d**) *(visit)* visite *f*; **to pay a c. on sb** rendre visite à qn
(**e**) *(demand)* demande *f*; **there are a lot of calls on my time** je suis très pris; **there's not much c. for it** il n'y a pas beaucoup de demande; **there's no c. for that kind of language!** inutile d'être impoli!; **to be on c.** *(of doctor)* être de garde
2 *vt* (**a**) *(shout to)* appeler
(**b**) *(summon)* appeler; **he's been called away** il a dû s'absenter; **he called me over to show me something** il m'a appelé pour que je vienne voir quelque chose; **to c. a meeting** décider d'organiser une réunion; **to c. a strike** appeler à la grève; **to c. sb's attention to sth** attirer l'attention de qn sur qch
(**c**) *(on phone)* appeler, téléphoner à; *(taxi)* appeler
(**d**) *(name)* appeler; **she's called Katy** elle s'appelle Katy; **to c. sb names** injurier qn; **to c. sb a liar/a thief** traiter qn de menteur/de voleur; **c. yourself a computer expert!** et moi qui te croyais bon en informatique!; **let's c. it £10** disons (que ce sera) 10 livres; **do you c. that clean?** tu trouves vraiment que c'est propre?; **let's c. it a day** assez pour aujourd'hui
3 *vi* (**a**) *(shout)* appeler; **to c. to sb** appeler qn; **to c. for help** appeler au secours *ou* à l'aide
(**b**) *(on phone)* appeler, téléphoner; **to c. for an ambulance** appeler une ambulance; **who's calling?** qui est à l'appareil?
(**c**) *(visit)* passer; **this train will c. at York and Peterborough** ce train s'arrêtera à York et Peterborough

▸**call back** *vt sep & vi* rappeler

▸**call for** *vt insep* (**a**) *(require)* nécessiter; **this calls for a celebration!** il faut fêter ça!; **that wasn't called for!** c'était parfaitement déplacé! (**b**) *(demand)* réclamer (**c**) *Br (collect) (person)* passer chercher; *(object)* passer prendre

▸**call in 1** *vt sep (doctor, police)* appeler, faire venir; *(expert)* faire appel à
2 *vi (visit)* passer (**on sb** chez qn)

▸**call off** *vt sep (match, holiday)* annuler; *(search, strike)* mettre fin à; *(engagement)* rompre

▸**call on** *vt insep* (**a**) *(request)* **to c. on sb to do sth** *(urgently)* demander instamment à qn de faire qch; *(politely)* inviter qn à faire qch (**b**) *(visit)* rendre visite à

▸**call out 1** *vt sep* (**a**) *(doctor, plumber, troops)* appeler; **to c. sb out on strike** donner l'ordre de grève à qn (**b**) *(shout)* appeler
2 *vi (shout)* crier

▸**call up** *vt sep* (**a**) *(on phone)* appeler, téléphoner à (**b**) *(memory, image)* évoquer (**c**) *Mil* appeler (sous les drapeaux)

callbox ['kɔːlbɒks] *n* cabine *f* téléphonique

caller [kɔːlə(r)] *n (visitor)* visiteur(euse) *m,f*; *(on phone)* correspondant(e) *m,f*; **next c., please** appel suivant, s'il vous plaît

calligraphy [kə'lɪgrəfɪ] *n* calligraphie *f*

calling ['kɔːlɪŋ] *n (vocation)* vocation *f*

callipers ['kælɪpəz] *npl* (**a**) *(for legs)* attelles *fpl* (**b**) *(measuring device)* compas *m*

callisthenics [kælɪs'θenɪks] *n* gymnastique *f* rythmique

callous ['kæləs] *adj* dur(e)

call-up ['kɔːlʌp] *n Mil* appel *m* (sous les drapeaux); **c. papers** ordre *m* d'incorporation

callus ['kæləs] *n* cal *m*

calm [kɑːm] **1** *n* calme *m*; *also Fig* **a dead c.** un calme plat; *also Fig* **the c. before the storm** le calme qui précède la tempête
2 *adj* calme, tranquille; *(sea)* calme; **to keep c.** rester calme; **to grow calmer** se calmer
3 *vt* calmer, apaiser; **to c. one's nerves** se calmer

▸**calm down 1** *vt sep* calmer
2 *vi* se calmer

calmly ['kɑːmlɪ] *adv* calmement

Calor Gas® [kælə'gæs] *n* butane *m*

calorie ['kælərɪ] *n* calorie *f*

calumny ['kæləmnɪ] (*pl* **calumnies**) *n* calomnie *f*

calve [kɑːv] *vi (of cow)* vêler

calves [kɑːvz] *pl of* **calf**

calypso [kə'lɪpsəʊ] (*pl* **calypsos**) *n Mus* calypso *m*

CAM [siːeɪ'em] *n Comput (abbr* **computer-aided manufacture***)* FAO *f*

cam [kæm] *n Tech* came *f*

Cambodia [kæm'bəʊdɪə] *n* le Cambodge

Cambodian [kæm'bəʊdɪən] **1** *n* Cambodgien(enne) *m,f*
2 *adj* cambodgien(enne)

camcorder ['kæmkɔːdə(r)] *n* Caméscope® *m*

came [keɪm] *pt of* **come**

camel ['kæməl] *n* chameau *m*; *(female)* chamelle *f*; **c. coat** manteau *m* en poil de chameau; **c. driver** chamelier *m*

camelhair ['kæməlheə(r)] *n* poil *m* de chameau

camellia [kə'miːlɪə] *n* camélia *m*

cameo ['kæmɪəʊ] (*pl* **cameos**) *n* (**a**) *(jewellery)* camée *m*; **c. brooch** camée (**b**) *(in film)* **c. (role)** brève apparition *f* (d'un acteur connu)

camera ['kæmərə] *n* (**a**) *(photographic)* appareil photo *m*; *TV & Cin* caméra *f*; *TV* **off c.** hors champ; **on c.** à l'écran; *Law* **in c.** à huis clos; **c. crew** équipe *f* de prise de vue (**b**) *Law* **in c.** à huis clos

cameraman ['kæmərəmən] *n* cameraman *m*

Cameroon [kæmə'ruːn] *n* le Cameroun

camisole ['kæmɪsəʊl] *n* caraco *m*, *Can & Suisse* camisole *f*

camomile ['kæməmaɪl] *n* camomille *f*; **c. tea** camomille

camouflage ['kæməflɑːʒ] **1** *n also Fig* camouflage *m*
2 *vt also Fig* camoufler

camp¹ [kæmp] **1** *n* camp *m*, campement *m*; **c. bed** lit *m* de camp; **c. site** *(establishment)* (terrain *m* de) camping *m*; *(in general)* campement
2 *vi* **to c. (out)** camper
camp² *adj* (**a**) *(effeminate)* efféminé(e) (**b**) *(theatrical)* *(person)* cabotin(e); *(behaviour, manner)* théâtral(e) (**c**) *(in dubious taste)* kitsch *inv*
campaign [kæm'peɪn] **1** *n* campagne *f*
2 *vi* faire campagne (**for/against** pour/contre)
campaigner [kæm'peɪnə(r)] *n* militant(e) *m,f*; **to be a c. for/against sth** faire campagne pour/contre qch
camper ['kæmpə(r)] *n* *(person)* campeur(euse) *m,f*; *(vehicle)* camping-car *m*
campfire ['kæmpfaɪə(r)] *n* feu *m* de camp
camphor ['kæmfə(r)] *n* camphre *m*
camping ['kæmpɪŋ] *n* camping *m*; **to go c.** faire du camping; **c. site** (terrain *m* de) camping
campus ['kæmpəs] *n* campus *m*
camshaft ['kæmʃɑːft] *n Aut* arbre *m* à cames
can¹ [kæn] **1** *n* (**a**) *(of food)* boîte *f*; *(of drink)* can(n)ette *f*; *(for petrol)* bidon *m*; *(of paint)* pot *m*; *Fig* **to open a c. of worms** mettre à jour toutes sortes d'histoires désagréables; **c. opener** ouvre-boîte *m* (**b**) *Am very Fam (toilet)* chiottes *fpl*; *(prison)* taule *f*, tôle *f*
2 *vt (pt & pp* **canned**) (**a**) *(fruit, meat)* mettre en boîte *ou* en conserve; *Fig* **canned laughter** *(on radio, TV)* rires *mpl* préenregistrés (**b**) *Am Fam* **c. it!** *(keep quiet)* la ferme!
can² [kən, *stressed* kæn]

> Le verbe **can** n'a ni infinitif, ni gérondif, ni participe. Pour exprimer l'infinitif ou le participe on aura recours à la forme correspondante de **be able to** (he wanted to be able to speak English; she has always been able to swim). La forme négative est **can't**, qui s'écrit **cannot** dans la langue soutenue.

modal aux v (**a**) *(be able to)* pouvoir; **I c. go** je peux y aller; **I c. see/hear them** je les vois/entends; **we can't possibly do it** nous ne pouvons en aucun cas le faire; **he'll do what he c.** il fera ce qu'il pourra; **how c. you tell?** à quoi vois-tu ça?; **it can't be done** c'est impossible à faire
(**b**) *(know how to)* savoir; **I c. swim** je sais nager; **c. you speak English?** parles-tu anglais?
(**c**) *(indicating possibility)* pouvoir; **it c. get very hot here** il peut faire très chaud ici; **it can't have been easy for her** ça n'a pas dû être facile pour elle; **you CAN'T be serious!** tu n'es pas sérieux!; **what c. it be?** qu'est-ce que ça peut bien être?
(**d**) *(with requests, permission)* pouvoir; **c. I ask you something?** je peux vous demander quelque chose?; **you can't smoke in here** on ne peut pas fumer ici
Canada ['kænədə] *n* le Canada
Canadian [kə'neɪdɪən] **1** *n* Canadien(enne) *m,f*
2 *adj* canadien(enne)
canal [kə'næl] *n* canal *m*
Canary [kə'neərɪ] *n* **the C. Islands, the Canaries** les (îles *fpl*) Canaries *fpl*
canary [kə'neərɪ] *(pl* **canaries**) *n* canari *m*; **c. yellow** jaune canari *inv*
cancel ['kænsəl] *(pt & pp* **cancelled**, *Am* **canceled**) **1** *vt* annuler; *(cheque)* faire opposition à
2 *vi* se décommander
▶**cancel out** *vt sep* annuler; **to c. each other out** s'annuler

cancellation [kænsə'leɪʃən] *n* annulation *f*; **c. fee** frais *mpl* d'annulation
Cancer ['kænsə(r)] *n (sign of zodiac)* le Cancer; **to be (a) C.** être (du) Cancer; *Geog* **theTropic of C.** le tropique du Cancer
cancer ['kænsə(r)] *n (disease)* cancer *m*; **lung/skin c.** cancer du poumon/de la peau; **c. research** cancérologie *f*
cancerous ['kænsərəs] *adj Med* cancéreux(euse)
candelabra [kændɪ'lɑːbrə] *n* candélabre *m*
candid ['kændɪd] *adj* franc (franche)
candidacy ['kændɪdəsɪ] *n* candidature *f*
candidate ['kændɪdeɪt] *n* candidat(e) *m,f* (**for** à); **to stand as a c.** poser sa candidature, se présenter
candidature ['kændɪdətʃə(r)] = **candidacy**
candidly ['kændɪdlɪ] *adv* franchement
candied ['kændɪd] *adj* glacé(e), confit(e); **c. peel** zeste *m* confit
candle ['kændəl] *n* bougie *f*; **he can't hold a c. to you** il ne t'arrive pas à la cheville; **it's not worth the c.** le jeu n'en vaut pas la chandelle
candlelight ['kændəllaɪt] *n* lumière *f* d'une bougie; **by c.** à la chandelle *ou* bougie
candlelit ['kændəllɪt] *adj* aux chandelles
candlestick ['kændəlstɪk] *n* bougeoir *m*; *(taller)* chandelier *m*
can-do ['kænduː] *adj* dynamique, entreprenant(e); **c. attitude** *or* **spirit** esprit *m* de battant *ou* de gagneur
candour ['kændə(r)] *n* franchise *f*
candy ['kændɪ] *(pl* **candies**) *n Am (sweet)* bonbon *m*; *(sweets)* bonbons; **c. store** confiserie *f*
candyfloss ['kændɪflɒs] *n Br* barbe *f* à papa
cane [keɪn] **1** *n (of sugar, bamboo)* canne *f*, tige *f*; *(walking stick)* canne; *(for punishment)* verge *f*, baguette *f*; **to get the c.** recevoir des coups de verge *ou* de baguette; **c. furniture** meubles *mpl* en rotin; **c. sugar** sucre *m* de canne
2 *vt (beat)* frapper avec une verge *ou* une baguette
canine ['keɪnaɪn] **1** *n* (**a**) *(tooth)* canine *f* (**b**) *(animal)* canidé *m*
2 *adj* canin(e)
canister ['kænɪstə(r)] *n* boîte *f* (en métal); *(of gas)* bonbonne *f*
canker ['kæŋkə(r)] *n also Fig* chancre *m*
cannabis ['kænəbɪs] *n* cannabis *m*
cannery ['kænərɪ] *(pl* **canneries**) *n* conserverie *f*
cannibal ['kænɪbəl] *n* cannibale *mf*
cannibalize ['kænɪbəlaɪz] *vt* cannibaliser
cannon ['kænən] *(pl* **cannons** *or* **cannon**) *n* canon *m*; **c. fodder** chair *f* à canon
cannonball ['kænənbɔːl] *n* boulet *m* de canon
cannot ['kænɒt] = **can not**
canny ['kænɪ] *adj* rusé(e)
canoe [kə'nuː] *n* canoë *m*
canoeing [kə'nuːɪŋ] *n* canoë-kayak *m*; **to go c.** faire du canoë-kayak
canoeist [kə'nuːɪst] *n* canoëiste *mf*
canon ['kænən] *n* (**a**) *(religious decree)* & *Fig* canon *m*; **c. law** droit *m* canon (**b**) *(priest)* chanoine *m*
canonize ['kænənaɪz] *vt Rel* canoniser
canoodle [kə'nuːdəl] *vi Hum* se faire des mamours
canopy ['kænəpɪ] *(pl* **canopies**) *n (above bed)* baldaquin *m*; *(outside shop)* auvent *m*; *(parachute)* parachute *m*; *(of tree branches)* canopée *f*
cant [kænt] *n (hypocrisy)* langage *m* hypocrite

can't [kɑːnt] = can not

cantaloup(e) ['kæntəluːp] n melon m (cantaloup)

cantankerous [kæn'tæŋkərəs] adj revêche, acariâtre

canteen [kæn'tiːn] n (**a**) (restaurant) cantine f (**b**) (water bottle) gourde f (**c**) (of cutlery) ménagère f

canter ['kæntə(r)] **1** n (on horse) petit galop m
2 vi (of horse) aller au petit galop; Fig **to c. through a speech** expédier un discours; Fig **to c. through an exam** réussir un examen haut la main

cantilever ['kæntiliːvə(r)] n Tech poutre f en porte-à-faux; **c. bridge** pont m cantilever

Cantonese [kæntə'niːz] **1** n (language) cantonais m
2 adj cantonais(e)

canvas ['kænvəs] n (**a**) (cloth) (grosse) toile f; **under c.** (in tent) sous la tente; Naut sous voiles (**b**) Art toile f

canvass ['kænvəs] **1** vt (**a**) Pol **to c. sb** faire campagne auprès de qn (**b**) Com (consumers) sonder; Fig **to c. opinion** sonder l'opinion
2 vi (**a**) Pol faire du porte-à-porte (dans le cadre d'une campagne électorale) (**b**) Com faire du démarchage

canvasser ['kænvəsə(r)] n Pol = personne qui fait du porte-à-porte dans le cadre d'une campagne électorale

canyon ['kænjən] n canyon m, canon m

canyoning ['kænjənɪŋ] n Sport canyoning m

CAP [siːeɪ'piː] n (abbr **Common Agricultural Policy**) PAC f

cap [kæp] **1** n (**a**) (hat) (without peak) bonnet m; (with peak) casquette f; Sport **to win a c.** être sélectionné(e) dans l'équipe nationale; Fig **to go c. in hand to sb** se présenter chapeau bas devant qn; Prov **if the c. fits (wear it)** qui se sent morveux se mouche (**b**) (cover) (of bottle) capsule f; (of pen) capuchon m (**c**) (for toy gun) amorce f (**d**) (contraceptive) diaphragme m
2 vt (pt & pp **capped**) (**a**) (cover) recouvrir (**with** de) (**b**) **to have a tooth capped** se faire refaire l'émail d'une dent (**c**) (surpass, do better than) surpasser; **that caps the lot!** c'est le bouquet!; **to c. it all,...** pour couronner le tout,.. (**d**) (spending) limiter (**e**) Sport **to be capped for England** être sélectionné(e) dans l'équipe d'Angleterre

capability [keɪpə'bɪlɪtɪ] (pl **capabilities**) n capacité f (**to do sth** de faire qch); **it is beyond our capabilities** c'est au-dessus de nos moyens

capable ['keɪpəbəl] adj capable; **to be c. of doing sth** être capable de faire qch; **the business is in c. hands** l'affaire est entre de bonnes mains

capably ['keɪpəblɪ] adv avec compétence

capacious [kə'peɪʃəs] adj Formal vaste, spacieux(-euse)

capacitor [kə'pæsɪtə(r)] n Elec condensateur m

capacity [kə'pæsɪtɪ] (pl **capacities**) n (**a**) (of container, bus, theatre) & Elec capacité f; **the stadium has a c. of 50,000** le stade peut accueillir 50 000 spectateurs; **full to c.** plein(e); **there was a c. crowd at the match** le stade était bondé pour le match (**b**) (aptitude) **to have a c. for sth** être capable de qch; **to be beyond sb's c.** dépasser les compétences de qn; **to be within sb's c.** être dans les possibilités de qn; **c. for work** capacité f de travail (**c**) (output) capacité f; **at full c.** à plein (**d**) (role) **in my c. as...** en ma qualité de...; **they are here in an official c.** ils sont ici à titre officiel

cape¹ [keɪp] n (cloak) pèlerine f, cape f

cape² n Geog cap m; **the C. of Good Hope** le cap de Bonne-Espérance; **C. Town** Le Cap

caper¹ ['keɪpə(r)] n Culin câpre f

caper² **1** n (prank) cabriole f; **what a c.!** (fuss) quel cirque!
2 vi **to c. (about)** faire des cabrioles

Cape Verde [keɪp'vɜːd] n le Cap-Vert

capillary [kə'pɪlərɪ] **1** (pl **capillaries**) n capillaire m
2 adj capillaire

capital ['kæpɪtəl] **1** n (**a**) (letter) majuscule f, capitale f (**b**) **c. (city)** capitale f (**c**) Fin capital m; Fig **to make c. out of sth** tirer parti de qch; **c. assets** actif m immobilisé; **c. expenditure** dépenses fpl en capital; **c. gains tax** impôt m sur les plus-values (en capital); **c. goods** biens mpl d'équipement; **c. investment** investissement m de capitaux
2 adj (**a**) (letter) majuscule; **c. T** T majuscule; **he's rich with a c. R** il est vraiment très riche (**b**) Law **c. crime** or **offence** crime m capital ou puni de mort; **c. punishment** peine f capitale (**c**) (important) capital(e); **of c. importance** d'une importance capitale (**d**) Br Old-fashioned (splendid) extra inv

capitalism ['kæpɪtəlɪzəm] n capitalisme m

capitalist ['kæpɪtəlɪst] n & adj capitaliste mf

capitalization [kæpɪtəlaɪ'zeɪʃən] n Fin capitalisation f

capitalize ['kæpɪtəlaɪz] vt (**a**) Fin capitaliser (**b**) (initial letter) écrire avec une majuscule; (whole word) écrire en majuscules
▶**capitalize on** vt insep profiter de, tirer parti de

Capitol ['kæpɪtəl] n Am Pol **the C.** le Capitol

> ### Capitol Hill
> Ce nom désigne, par extension, le Congrès américain. Par exemple, "The proposed bill is in danger of being rejected on Capitol Hill." ("La proposition de loi risque d'être rejetée par le Congrès américain.")

capitulate [kə'pɪtjʊleɪt] vi capituler (**to** devant)

capon ['keɪpən] n Culin chapon m

cappuccino [kæpʊ'tʃiːnəʊ] (pl **cappuccinos**) n cappuccino m

caprice [kə'priːs] n caprice m

capricious [kə'prɪʃəs] adj capricieux(euse)

Capricorn ['kæprɪkɔːn] n (sign of zodiac) le Capricorne; **to be (a) C.** être (du) Capricorne; Geog **the Tropic of C.** le tropique du Capricorne

capsicum ['kæpsɪkəm] n Culin poivron m

capsize [kæp'saɪz] **1** vt faire chavirer
2 vi chavirer

capstan ['kæpstən] n Naut cabestan m

capsule ['kæpsjuːl] n (of medicine) gélule f; **(space) c.** capsule f spatiale

Capt (abbr **Captain**) Capt

captain ['kæptɪn] **1** n capitaine m
2 vt être le capitaine de; **he captained them to victory** il les a conduits à la victoire

captaincy ['kæptɪnsɪ] n (in sport) **during her c.** pendant qu'elle était capitaine

caption ['kæpʃən] n légende f

captivate ['kæptɪveɪt] vt fasciner

captivating ['kæptɪveɪtɪŋ] adj fascinant(e)

captive ['kæptɪv] n & adj captif(ive) m,f; **to be taken c.** être fait(e) prisonnier(ère); **he had a c. audience** (spellbound) son auditoire était subjugué; (had no *choice but to listen)* son auditoire était forcé de l'écouter

captivity ['kæp'tɪvɪtɪ] *n* captivité *f*; **in c.** en captivité

captor ['kæptə(r)] *n* ravisseur(euse) *m,f*

capture ['kæptʃə(r)] **1** *n* capture *f*; *(of town, enemy, position)* prise *f*
2 *vt (person, animal)* capturer; *(town, enemy, position)* prendre (**from** à); *(in chess)* prendre; *Fig (mood)* rendre; **to c. sb's imagination** parler à l'imagination de qn; **to c. the moment** saisir l'instant

car [kɑː(r)] *n* (**a**) *(automobile)* voiture *f*, automobile *f*; **by c.** en voiture; **c. bomb** voiture piégée; **c. boot sale** = vente à la brocante où les vendeurs exposent leurs marchandises à l'arrière de leur voiture; **c. crash** accident *m* de voiture; **c. door** portière *f* de voiture; *Br* **c. hire**, *Am* **c. rental** location *f* de voitures; **c. industry** industrie *f* automobile; *Br* **c. park** parc *m* de stationnement, parking *m*; **c. phone** téléphone *m* de voiture; **c. pool** = groupe de personnes effectuant régulièrement un trajet dans la même voiture; **c. pooling** covoiturage *m*; **c. radio** autoradio *m* (**b**) *Am (rail wagon)* voiture *f*, wagon *m*

carafe [kə'ræf] *n* carafe *f*

caramel ['kærəməl] *n* caramel *m*

carat ['kærət] *n* carat *m*; **18-c. gold** or *m* (à) 18 carats

caravan ['kærəvæn] *n* caravane *f*; *(pulled by horse)* roulotte *f*; **c. holiday** vacances *fpl* en caravane; **c. site** camping *m* (pour caravanes)

caraway ['kærəweɪ] *n* carvi *m*, cumin *m* des prés; **c. seeds** graines *fpl* de carvi

carbohydrate [kɑːbəʊ'haɪdreɪt] *n* hydrate *m* de carbone; *(in food)* glucide *m*; **low-/high-c. diet** régime *m* hypoglucidique/hyperglucidique

carbolic [kɑː'bɒlɪk] *adj Chem* **c. acid** phénol *m*; **c. soap** ≃ savon *m* de Marseille

carbon ['kɑːbən] *n* carbone *m*; **c. copy** copie *f* (au carbone); *Fig* **she is a c. copy of her mother** c'est la copie conforme de sa mère; **c. dioxide** dioxyde *m* de carbone, gaz *m* carbonique; **c. fibre** fibre *f* de carbone; **c. monoxide** monoxyde *m* de carbone; **c. paper** (papier *m*) carbone

carbonated ['kɑːbəneɪtɪd] *adj* gazéifié(e); *(naturally)* gazeux(euse)

carbonize ['kɑːbənaɪz] *vt* carboniser

carbuncle ['kɑːbʌŋkəl] *n Med* furoncle *m*

carburettor, *Am* **carburetor** ['kɑːbjʊretə(r)] *n* carburateur *m*

carcase, carcass ['kɑːkəs] *n (of animal)* carcasse *f*

carcinogenic [kɑːsɪnə'dʒenɪk] *adj Med* carcinogène

card [kɑːd] *n* (**a**) *(for card game)* carte *f*; **to play cards** jouer aux cartes; **c. game** jeu *m* de cartes; **c. table** table *f* de jeux; **c. trick** tour *m* de cartes (**b**) *(with printed information)* carte *f*; *(postcard)* carte (postale); *Pol* **c. vote** = scrutin où chaque délégué muni d'une carte vote pour la totalité des membres qu'il représente; **c. index** or **file** fichier *m* (**c**) *(plastic)* carte *f* (**d**) *(cardboard)* carton *m* (fin) (**e**) *Comput* carte *f* (**f**) *(idioms)* **play your cards right and you could get promoted** si tu mènes bien ton jeu, tu seras peut-être promu; **to put one's cards on the table** jouer cartes sur table; **to have a c. up one's sleeve** avoir un atout dans son jeu; **it is** *Br* **on** or *Am* **in the cards that...** il est bien possible que...; *Br Fam* **to get one's cards** se faire virer

cardamom ['kɑːdəməm] *n* cardamome *f*

cardboard ['kɑːdbɔːd] *n* carton *m*; **c. box** (boîte *f* en) carton; **c. city** = campement où les sans-abri vivent dans des cartons; *Fig & Pej* **c. characters** personnages *mpl* sans aucune profondeur

card-carrying ['kɑːdkærɪŋ] *adj* **c. member** adhérent(e) *m,f*

cardiac ['kɑːdɪæk] *adj* cardiaque; **c. arrest** arrêt *m* cardiaque

cardigan ['kɑːdɪgən] *n* cardigan *m*

cardinal ['kɑːdɪnəl] **1** *n Rel* cardinal *m*
2 *adj* cardinal(e); *Fig* **it's a c. sin** c'est impardonnable

cardiograph ['kɑːdɪəgræf] *n* cardiographe *m*

cardiologist [kɑːdɪ'ɒlədʒɪst] *n* cardiologue *mf*

cardiology [kɑːdɪ'ɒlədʒɪ] *n* cardiologie *f*

cardiovascular [kɑːdɪəʊ'væskjʊlə(r)] *adj* cardiovasculaire

cardphone ['kɑːdfəʊn] *n* téléphone *m* à carte

cardsharp ['kɑːdʃɑːp], **cardsharper** ['kɑːdʃɑːpə(r)] *n* tricheur(euse) *m,f* professionnel(elle)

care [keə(r)] **1** *n* (**a**) *(worry)* souci *m*; **she doesn't have a c. in the world** elle n'a pas le moindre souci
(**b**) *(attention)* soin *m*; *(medical treatment)* soins médicaux; **to put a lot of c. into sth** apporter beaucoup de soin à qch; **to drive without due c.** conduire imprudemment; **to take c. of sth** s'occuper de; **to take c. of oneself** savoir se débrouiller tout(e) seul(e); *(healthwise)* prendre soin de sa santé; **to take c. to do sth** faire bien attention à faire qch; **take c.!** *(goodbye)* à bientôt!; **take good c. of yourself** fais bien attention à toi; *Br* **c. in the community** = système de soins prodigués aux malades mentaux en dehors du milieu hospitalier
(**c**) *(protection)* soins *mpl*; *(of clothes, machine)* entretien *m*; **to put a child in c.** mettre un enfant à l'Assistance publique; **to be in** or **under sb's c.** avoir été confié(e) à qn; **write to me c. of Mrs Wallace** écrivez-moi chez Mme Wallace *ou* aux bons soins de Mme Wallace
2 *vt* (**a**) *(mind)* **I don't c. what he says** peu m'importe ce qu'il en dit; **I don't c. whether he likes it or not** peu m'importe que cela lui plaise ou non
(**b**) *(like)* **would you c. to come with me?** aimeriez-vous m'accompagner?
3 *vi* (**a**) *(be concerned)* se préoccuper, se soucier (**about** de); **that's all he cares about** c'est tout ce qui l'intéresse; **to c. about sb** *(be fond of)* aimer qn
(**b**) *(mind)* **I don't c.** ça m'est égal; **who cares?** qu'est-ce que ça peut faire?; **I could be dead for all they c.!** ils se moquent éperdument de ce qui peut m'arriver!; **I couldn't c. less** je m'en moque éperdument

▶**care for** *vt insep* (**a**) *(look after)* soigner (**b**) *(like)* aimer

career [kə'rɪə(r)] **1** *n* carrière *f*; **it's a good/bad c. move** c'est bon/mauvais pour ma/ta/*etc* carrière; **c. break** interruption *f* de carrière; **c. path** *(strategy)* plan *m* de carrière; *(prospects)* perspectives *fpl* de carrière; **careers officer** conseiller(ère) *m,f* d'orientation; **careers service** service *m* d'orientation professionnelle
2 *vi* **to c. (along)** aller à vive allure; **the car careered off the road** la voiture a quitté la route à vive allure

careerist [kə'rɪərɪst] *n Pej* carriériste *mf*

carefree ['keəfriː] *adj* insouciant(e)

careful ['keəfʊl] *adj* (**a**) *(cautious)* prudent(e); **be c. of that step** fais attention à la marche; **(be) c.!** fais attention!; **to be c. to do sth** faire bien attention à faire qch; **she was c. not to mention his name** elle a bien fait attention à ne pas mentionner son nom; **be c. what you say** fais attention à ce que tu dis; **you can't be too c. these days** on n'est jamais trop prudent de nos jours (**b**) *(thorough) (work, inspection)* minutieux(euse); **after c. consideration** après mûre réflexion

carefully ['keəfəlɪ] *adv* (**a**) *(cautiously)* prudemment (**b**) *(thoroughly)* soigneusement, avec soin; *(listen)* attentivement; **c. worded** aux termes choisis (avec soin)

careless ['keəlɪs] *adj* (**a**) *(negligent)* négligent(e); *(work)* négligé(e); **to be c. about one's appearance** être négligé; **a c. mistake** une faute d'inattention, une étourderie; **a c. remark** une remarque inconsidérée (**b**) *(unconcerned)* insouciant(e)

carelessly ['keəlɪslɪ] *adv (negligently)* négligemment

carelessness ['keəlɪsnɪs] *n (negligence)* négligence *f*

carer ['keərə(r)] *n (professional)* aide *mf* à domicile; *(relative)* = personne s'occupant d'un parent malade ou âgé

caress [kə'res] **1** *n* caresse *f*
2 *vt* caresser

caretaker ['keəteɪkə(r)] *n* concierge *mf*, gardien(-enne) *m,f*; **c. government** gouvernement *m* intérimaire

careworn ['keəwɔːn] *adj* usé(e) par les soucis

cargo ['kɑːgəʊ] *(pl* **cargoes** *or* **cargos**) *n* cargaison *f*; **c. boat** *or* **ship** cargo *m*; **c. plane** avion-cargo *m*

Caribbean [kærɪ'biːən, *Am* kə'rɪbɪən] **1** *n* **the C. (Sea)** la mer des Caraïbes; **the C.** *(region)* la Caraïbe
2 *adj* caraïbe

caribou ['kærɪbuː] *n* caribou *m*

caricature ['kærɪkətjʊə(r)] **1** *n* caricature *f*
2 *vt* caricaturer

caricaturist [kærɪkə'tjʊərɪst] *n* caricaturiste *mf*

caries ['keəriːz] *n Med* carie *f*

caring ['keərɪŋ] *adj (society, personality)* humain(e); *(parent)* aimant(e); *(atmosphere)* chaleureux(euse); **the c. professions** les professions *fpl* médicales et paramédicales

carnage ['kɑːnɪdʒ] *n* carnage *m*

carnal ['kɑːnəl] *adj* charnel(elle)

carnation [kɑː'neɪʃən] *n* œillet *m*

carnival ['kɑːnɪvəl] *n (celebration)* carnaval *m*; *(funfair)* fête *f* foraine

carnivore ['kɑːnɪvɔː(r)] *n* carnivore *m*

carnivorous [kɑː'nɪvərəs] *adj* carnivore

carob ['kærəb] *n (fruit)* caroube *f*; *(tree)* caroubier *m*

carol ['kærəl] *n* **(Christmas) c.** chant *m* de Noël; **c. service** = office religieux qui précède Noël

> **Carol Service**
> Le "Carol Service" se tient juste avant Noël et se compose surtout de chants de Noël et de lectures de la Bible.

carouse [kə'raʊz] *vi* faire la fête

carousel [kærə'sel] *n* (**a**) *Am (at funfair)* chevaux *mpl* de bois, manège *m* (**b**) *(at airport)* carrousel *m* (pour bagages) (**c**) *(for slides)* magasin *m*

carp¹ [kɑːp] *(pl* **carp**) *n (fish)* carpe *f*

carp² *vi* se plaindre (**at** de)

Carpathians [kɑː'peɪθɪənz] *npl* **the C.** les Carpates *fpl*

carpenter ['kɑːpɪntə(r)] *n* menuisier *m*; *(on building site)* charpentier *m*

carpentry ['kɑːpɪntrɪ] *n* menuiserie *f*; *(on building site)* charpenterie *f*

carpet ['kɑːpɪt] **1** *n* (**a**) *(rug)* & *Fig (of flowers, snow)* tapis *m*; *(fitted)* moquette *f*; **c. bombing** bombardement *m* intensif; **c. shampoo** shampooing *m* pour moquette; **c. slippers** pantoufles *fpl* (**b**) *(idioms)* **to pull the c. out from under sb** faire un tour de cochon à qn
2 *vt* (**a**) *(with rug)* recouvrir d'un tapis; *(with fitted carpet)* moquetter; *Fig* **to be carpeted with snow** être recouvert(e) de neige (**b**) *Fam (tell off)* sermonner

carpet-sweeper ['kɑːpɪtswiːpə(r)] *n* balai *m* mécanique

carport ['kɑːpɔːt] *n* abri *m* pour voiture

carriage ['kærɪdʒ] *n* (**a**) *(vehicle)* voiture *f* (**b**) *(of train)* voiture *f*, wagon *m* (**c**) *Br (of typewriter)* chariot *m*; **c. return** retour-chariot *m* (**d**) *Com (transport)* transport *m*; *(cost)* frais *mpl* de port; **c. forward** (en) port *m* dû; **c. free** franco de port; **c. paid** (en) port *m* payé (**e**) *(bearing) (of person)* port *m*

carriageway ['kærɪdʒweɪ] *n* chaussée *f*

carrier ['kærɪə(r)] *n* (**a**) *(of disease, germs)* porteur(-euse) *m,f* (**b**) *Com (company, airline)* transporteur *m* (**c**) *(on bicycle)* porte-bagages *m inv* (**d**) **c. (bag)** sac *m (en papier ou en plastique)*

carrion ['kærɪən] *n* charogne *f*

carrot ['kærət] *n also Fig* carotte *f*; **a c. and stick approach** la carotte et le bâton

carry ['kærɪ] *(pt & pp* **carried**) **1** *vt* (**a**) *(transport, convey)* porter; *(goods, passengers)* transporter; *(electricity, fuel)* acheminer; *(gun, money)* avoir sur soi; *(a scar)* avoir; *(disease)* être porteur(euse) de; **the current carried the raft out to sea** le courant a emporté le radeau au large; **to c. an image in one's head** avoir une image en tête; **to be carrying sb's child** *(be pregnant)* porter l'enfant de qn; *Fig* **to c. the can** porter le chapeau; *Fig* **she refused to c. the can for their mistake** elle refusa qu'ils lui fassent porter la responsabilité de leur erreur
(**b**) *(involve) (risk)* comporter; **to c. a fine/penalty** être passible d'une amende/d'une peine; **to c. weight/authority** avoir du poids/de l'autorité
(**c**) *(develop)* **to c. sth too far** pousser qch trop loin; **to c. an argument to its logical conclusion** aller au bout d'un raisonnement
(**d**) *(capture, win)* **to c. all before one** *(be successful)* remporter tous les prix; *(win support, approval)* vaincre toutes les résistances; **his argument carried the day** son argument l'a emporté
(**e**) *(proposal, motion)* voter
(**f**) *(of newspaper, news programme) (story)* faire état de; *(advertisement)* contenir
(**g**) *Com (keep in stock)* vendre
(**h**) **to c. oneself** *(behave)* se conduire
(**i**) *Math* **c. two** et je retiens deux
2 *vi (of sound)* porter; **her voice carries well** elle a une voix qui porte bien

▶**carry away** *vt sep* (**a**) *(take away)* emporter (**b**) **to get carried away** *(excited)* s'emballer

▶**carry forward** *vt sep Fin* reporter; **carried forward** report, à reporter

▶**carry off** *vt sep* (**a**) *(take away)* emporter; *(prize)* remporter (**b**) *(do successfully)* **she carried it off (well)** elle s'en est bien sortie

▶**carry on 1** *vt sep (tradition)* perpétuer; *(business, trade)* exercer; *(correspondence)* entretenir; *(conversation)* poursuivre
  2 *vi* (**a**) *(continue)* continuer, poursuivre; **to c. on doing sth** continuer de *ou* à faire qch (**b**) *Fam (behave badly)* mal se conduire; **I don't like the way she carries on** je n'aime pas ses façons (**c**) *Fam (have an affair)* avoir une liaison (**with** avec) (**d**) *(talk)* parler sans cesse (**about** de)
▶**carry out** *vt sep (plan, threat, decision)* mettre à exécution; *(experiment, test)* faire, effectuer; *(instructions)* exécuter

carrycot ['kærɪkɒt] *n* porte-bébé *m inv*
carry-on ['kærɪˈɒn] *n Fam* ramdam *m*; **what a c.!** quel cirque!
carry-out ['kærɪaʊt] *n Am & Scot (meal)* repas *m* à emporter; *(restaurant)* = boutique qui fait des plats à emporter
carsick ['kɑːsɪk] *adj* **to be c.** avoir mal au cœur en voiture
cart[1] [kɑːt] **1** *n (vehicle)* charrette *f*; *(trolley)* chariot *m*; *Fig* **to put the c. before the horse** mettre la charrue avant les bœufs
  2 *vt Fam (carry)* trimballer
▶**cart off** *vt sep Fam* **to c. sb off** emmener qn
cart[2] *n (abbr* **cartridge***)* cassette *f*
carte blanche ['kɑːt'blɑ̃ʃ] *n* **to give sb c. (to do sth)** donner carte blanche à qn (pour faire qch)
cartel [kɑːˈtel] *n Econ* cartel *m*
carthorse ['kɑːthɔːs] *n* cheval *m* de trait; *Fig* lourdaud *m*
cartilage ['kɑːtɪlɪdʒ] *n* cartilage *m*
cartographer [kɑːˈtɒɡrəfə(r)] *n* cartographe *mf*
cartography [kɑːˈtɒɡrəfɪ] *n* cartographie *f*
carton ['kɑːtən] *n (of yoghurt, cream)* pot *m*; *(of milk, fruit juice)* brique *f*; *(of cigarettes)* cartouche *f*
cartoon [kɑːˈtuːn] *n (drawing)* dessin *m* humoristique; *(film)* dessin animé; **c. (strip)** bande *f* dessinée
cartoonist [kɑːˈtuːnɪst] *n* dessinateur(trice) *m,f*
cartridge ['kɑːtrɪdʒ] *n* (**a**) *(for gun, pen, of film)* cartouche *f*; **c. belt** cartouchière *f* (**b**) **c. paper** papier *m* à cartouche
cartwheel ['kɑːtwiːl] *n* roue *f* de charrette; **to turn cartwheels** faire la roue
carve [kɑːv] *vt (wood, stone, statue)* sculpter; *(name)* graver; *(meat)* découper
▶**carve out** *vt sep* **to c. out a career for oneself** faire carrière; **the company carved out a niche for itself** la société s'est taillé une place sur le marché
▶**carve up** *vt sep Fig (territory)* découper
carving ['kɑːvɪŋ] *n* (**a**) *Art* sculpture *f* (**b**) **c. knife** *(for meat)* couteau *m* à découper
carwash ['kɑːwɒʃ] *n* = station de lavage automatique pour autos; *(sign)* lavage automatique
cascade [kæsˈkeɪd] **1** *n* cascade *f*
  2 *vi* tomber en cascade
case[1] [keɪs] *n* (**a**) *(instance, situation) & Med* cas *m*; **a c. in point** un cas d'espèce; **in c. of emergency/accident** en cas d'urgence/d'accident; **in c. he isn't there** au cas où il ne serait pas là; **I'll take it just in c.** je vais le prendre au cas où; **just in c. it rains** au cas où il pleuvrait; **in any c.** *(besides)* de toute façon; **in that c.** dans ce cas; **in such a c.** en pareil cas; **as the c. may be** suivant le cas; **if that's the c.** dans ce cas(-là), s'il en est ainsi; *Med* **c. history** antécédents *mpl*; **c. study** étude *f* de cas

(**b**) *Law* affaire *f*; **the c. will be heard on 5 January** l'audience aura lieu le 5 janvier; **the c. for the defence** la défense; **the c. for the prosecution** l'accusation *f*; *Fig* **the c. for sb/sth** les arguments *mpl* en faveur de qn/qch; *Fig* **she has a good c.** elle a de bons arguments; **c. law** droit *m* jurisprudentiel
case[2] *n* (**a**) *(container) (for spectacles, cigarettes, musical instrument)* étui *m*; *(for jewellery)* écrin *m*; **(packing) c.** caisse *f*; **a c. of wine** une caisse de vin; **(display** *or* **glass) c.** vitrine *f* (**b**) *(suitcase)* valise *f*; *(briefcase)* porte-documents *m inv* (**c**) *Typ* **lower/upper c.** bas *m*/haut *m* de casse
casement ['keɪsmənt] *n* **c. (window)** fenêtre *f* à deux battants
case-sensitive ['keɪsˈsensɪtɪv] *adj Comput* qui distingue les majuscules des minuscules
cash [kæʃ] **1** *n (coins, banknotes)* liquide *m*; *Fam (money in general)* sous *mpl*; **to pay (in) c.** payer en liquide *ou* en espèces; **c. on delivery** paiement *m* à la livraison; **c. and carry** *(shop)* magasin *m* de demi-gros; **c. in hand** fonds *m ou* argent *m* en caisse; **c. box** caisse *f*; **c. card** carte *f* de retrait; **c. crop** culture *f* commerciale; **c. desk** caisse *f*; **c. dispenser** *or* **machine** distributeur *m* automatique de billets; *Fin* **c. flow** trésorerie *f*; **c. price** prix *m* au comptant; **c. register** caisse enregistreuse
  2 *vt (cheque, postal order)* encaisser
▶**cash in on** *vt insep Fam* profiter de, tirer profit de
cashback ['kæʃbæk] *n Br (in supermarket)* = espèces retirées à la caisse d'un supermarché lors d'un paiement par carte de crédit
cash-book ['kæʃbʊk] *n* livre *m ou* journal *m* de caisse
cashew ['kæʃuː] *n* **c. (nut)** noix *f* de cajou
cashier [kæˈʃɪə(r)] *n* caissier(ère) *m,f*
cashmere ['kæʃmɪə(r)] *n* cachemire *m*
cashpoint ['kæʃpɔɪnt] *n* distributeur *m* automatique de billets
casing ['keɪsɪŋ] *n Tech* boîtier *m*; *(of sausage)* boyau *m*
casino [kəˈsiːnəʊ] *(pl* **casinos***) n* casino *m*
cask [kɑːsk] *n* fût *m*, tonneau *m*
casket ['kɑːskɪt] *n* (**a**) *(for jewellery)* coffret *m* (**b**) *(coffin)* cercueil *m*
Caspian Sea ['kæspɪənsiː] *n* **the C.** la mer Caspienne
cassava [kəˈsɑːvə] *n* manioc *m*
casserole ['kæsərəʊl] *n (pot)* cocotte *f*; *(food)* ragoût *m*
cassette [kæˈset] *n* cassette *f*; **c. player** lecteur *m* de cassettes; **c. recorder** magnétophone *m* à cassettes
cassock ['kæsək] *n* soutane *f*
cast [kɑːst] **1** *n* (**a**) *(of play, film) (actors)* acteurs *mpl*; *(list)* distribution *f*; *Cin & TV* **c. and credits** générique *f* (**b**) *(moulded object)* moulage *m*; *Med* **(plaster) c.** plâtre *m*; *Fig* **c. of mind** tournure *f* d'esprit (**c**) **to have a c. in one's eye** *(squint)* avoir une coquetterie dans l'œil
  2 *vt (pt & pp* **cast***)* (**a**) *(throw) (stone)* jeter, lancer; *(shadow, net, line)* jeter; **to c. one's eyes over sth** parcourir qch des yeux; **to c. doubt on sth** jeter un doute sur qch, faire planer un doute sur qch; *Fig* **to c. light on sth** permettre de comprendre qch; **to c. one's mind back to sth** revenir sur qch, se rappeler qch; **to c. its skin** *(of reptile)* muer; **to c. a spell over sb** envoûter qn (**b**) **to c. one's vote (for)** voter (pour) (**c**) *(film, play)* faire la distribution de; **she was cast as** *or* **in the role of Desdemona** on l'a choisie pour

le rôle de Desdémone (**d**) *(metal, statue)* couler; **c. iron** fonte *f*

▸**cast about, cast around** *vi* **to c. about** *or* **around for sth** chercher qch

▸**cast aside** *vt sep (idea, prejudice)* se défaire de

▸**cast away** *vt sep* **to be cast away** faire naufrage

▸**cast down** *vt sep* **to be cast down** être abattu(e) *ou* découragé(e)

▸**cast off 1** *vt sep (clothes, chains)* rejeter, enlever; *(chains)* se libérer de

2 *vi* (**a**) *Naut* larguer les amarres (**b**) *(in knitting)* arrêter les mailles

▸**cast on** *vi (in knitting)* monter les mailles

castanets [kæstə'nets] *npl* castagnettes *fpl*

castaway ['kɑːstəweɪ] *n* naufragé(e) *m,f*

caste [kɑːst] *n (social rank)* caste *f*

caster sugar ['kɑːstəʃʊgə(r)] *n* sucre *m* en poudre

castigate ['kæstɪgeɪt] *vt Formal* critiquer sévèrement

casting ['kɑːstɪŋ] **1** *n (of play, film)* distribution *f*, casting *m*

2 *adj* **c. vote** voix *f* prépondérante

cast-iron ['kɑːst'aɪən] *adj* en *ou* de fonte; *Fig (alibi, guarantee)* en béton

castle ['kɑːsəl] **1** *n* château *m*; *(in chess)* tour *f*; *Fig* **to build castles in the air** bâtir des châteaux en Espagne

2 *vi (in chess)* roquer

cast-off ['kɑːstɒf] **1** *n (garment)* vieux vêtement *m*; *(person)* laissé-pour-compte (laissée-pour-compte) *m,f*

2 *adj* **c. clothing** vieux vêtements *mpl*

castor ['kɑːstə(r)] *n (on furniture)* roulette *f*

castor oil [kɑːstə'rɔɪl] *n* huile *f* de ricin

castrate [kæs'treɪt] *vt* châtrer, castrer

castration [kæs'treɪʃən] *n* castration *f*

casual ['kæʒjʊəl] *adj* (**a**) *(offhand) (remark, glance)* en passant (**b**) *(relaxed, informal)* décontracté(e); *(conversation)* à bâtons rompus; *(clothes)* sport *inv* (**c**) *(careless)* désinvolte (**d**) *(meeting)* fortuit(e) (**e**) *(employment, worker)* temporaire

casualization ['kæʒʊəlaɪ'zeɪʃən] *Br* **the c. of labour** la précarisation de l'emploi

casually ['kæʒjʊəlɪ] *adv* (**a**) *(remark, glance)* en passant (**b**) *(informally)* avec décontraction; *(dress)* sport (**c**) *(carelessly)* avec désinvolture (**d**) *(meet)* par hasard

casualty ['kæʒjʊəltɪ] *(pl* **casualties**) *n* victime *f*; **c. (department)** (service *m* des) urgences *fpl*

cat [kæt] *n* (**a**) *(animal)* chat *m*; *(female)* chatte *f*; **the big cats** les grands fauves *mpl*; **c. burglar** monte-en-l'air *m inv*; **c.'s eye**® *(on road)* catadioptre *m*; **c. flap** chatière *f*; **c. litter** litière *f* pour chats (**b**) *(idioms)* **to play a c.-and-mouse game with sb** jouer au chat et à la souris avec qn; *Fam* **to be like a c. on a hot tin roof** *or* **on hot bricks** ne pas tenir en place; **to let the c. out of the bag** vendre la mèche; **to fight like c. and dog** être comme chien et chat; **to set the c. among the pigeons** jeter un pavé dans la mare; *Fam* **there isn't enough room to swing a c.** il n'y a même pas la place de se retourner; *Fam* **he thinks he's the cat's whiskers** il se croit sorti de la cuisse de Jupiter

cataclysm ['kætəklɪzəm] *n* cataclysme *m*

Catalan ['kætəlæn] **1** *n* (**a**) *(person)* Catalan(e) *m,f* (**b**) *(language)* catalan *m*

2 *adj* catalan(e)

catalogue, *Am* **catalog** ['kætəlɒg] **1** *n* catalogue *m*

2 *vt* inventorier

Catalonia [kætə'ləʊnɪə] *n* la Catalogne

catalyst ['kætəlɪst] *n also Fig* catalyseur *m*

catamaran [kætəmə'ræn] *n* catamaran *m*

catapult ['kætəpʌlt] **1** *n (hand-held)* fronde *f*, lance-pierre *m*; *(on aircraft carrier)* & *Hist (weapon)* catapulte *f*

2 *vt* catapulter; **to c. sb to stardom** propulser qn vers la gloire

cataract ['kætərækt] *n (in river)* & *Med* cataracte *f*

catarrh [kə'tɑː(r)] *n* inflammation *f* des muqueuses respiratoires

catastrophe [kə'tæstrəfɪ] *n* catastrophe *f*

catastrophic [kætə'strɒfɪk] *adj* catastrophique

catatonic [kætə'tɒnɪk] *adj Med* catatonique

catcall ['kætkɔːl] *n* sifflet *m*

catch [kætʃ] **1** *n* (**a**) *(of ball)* prise *f* au vol; **good c.!** bien attrapé!

(**b**) *(in fishing)* prise *f*; *(of a whole day)* pêche *f*

(**c**) *(fastening) (of door)* loquet *m*; *(of window)* loqueteau *m*; *(of bracelet)* fermoir *m*

(**d**) *(disadvantage)* **where's the c.?** c'est quoi le truc *ou* le piège?; **it's a c.-22 situation** c'est un cercle vicieux

2 *vt (pt & pp* **caught** [kɔːt]) (**a**) *(ball, thief)* attraper; *(fish)* prendre; **caught you!** je t'y prends!; **to c. sb doing sth** surprendre qn en train de *ou* à faire qch; **you won't c. me doing that again** on ne m'y reprendra plus; **to be caught in a storm** être surpris(e) par un orage; **to c. the sun** *(of room, garden)* être ensoleillé(e); *(of person)* prendre des couleurs

(**b**) *(bus, train)* prendre; *(film)* voir

(**c**) *(hear)* saisir

(**d**) *(manage to find)* trouver; **you've caught me at a bad time** tu arrives/me téléphones au mauvais moment; **I'll c. you later!** on se voit plus tard!

(**e**) *(clothes)* accrocher (**on** à); **to c. one's fingers in the door** se prendre *ou* se coincer les doigts dans la porte

(**f**) *(attention)* attirer; **to c. sb's eye** attirer l'attention de qn

(**g**) *(illness)* attraper; **I caught this cold from you** c'est toi qui m'as passé ce rhume; **you'll c. your death out there!** tu vas attraper la mort!; **to c. fire** *or* **light** prendre feu

(**h**) *(of blow, missile)* atteindre; **the stone caught her on the arm** la pierre l'a atteinte au bras; *Fam* **you'll c. it!** *(get into trouble)* ça va être ta fête!

3 *vi* (**a**) *(of fire)* prendre

(**b**) *(in door)* se prendre, se coincer; *(on a nail)* s'accrocher

(**c**) *(of person)* **to c. at sth** s'accrocher à qch

▸**catch on** *vi* (**a**) *(of fashion)* prendre (**b**) *Fam (understand)* piger

▸**catch out** *vt sep (of difficult question)* piéger; *(of situation)* surprendre

▸**catch up 1** *vt sep* (**a**) *(reach)* rattraper (**b**) **to get caught up in sth** *(discussion)* être entraîné(e) dans qch; *(book, film)* être absorbé(e) par qch; *(traffic jam)* être pris(e) dans qch

2 *vi (close gap, get closer)* **to c. up with sb** rattraper qn; **to c. up with sth** *(news, gossip)* se mettre au courant de qch; **to c. up with one's work** se mettre à jour dans son travail; **his past caught up with him** son passé a resurgi

catch-all ['kætʃɔːl] *adj Fam* fourre-tout *inv*

catching ['kætʃɪŋ] *adj (disease, habit)* contagieux(-euse)

catchment area ['kætʃmənteərɪə] *n (of school)* = zone desservie par une école; *(of hospital)* = zone desservie par un hôpital

catchphrase ['kætʃfreɪz] *n (political)* slogan *m*; *(of comedian)* formule *f* favorite

catchy ['kætʃɪ] *adj (tune, slogan)* facile à retenir

catechism ['kætəkɪzəm] *n* catéchisme *m*

categorical [kætɪ'gɒrɪkəl] *adj (denial, refusal)* catégorique; *(evidence)* formel(elle)

categorize ['kætɪgəraɪz] *vt* étiqueter (**as** comme)

category ['kætɪgərɪ] *(pl* **categories**) *n* catégorie *f*

cater ['keɪtə(r)] *vi* (**a**) *(provide food)* s'occuper de la nourriture; **to c. for** *(guests)* fournir le repas pour; *(event)* fournir le(s) repas de (**b**) **to c. for** *(needs, tastes)* satisfaire; **parties catered for** *(sign in restaurant)* noces et banquets

caterer ['keɪtərə(r)] *n* traiteur *m*

catering ['keɪtərɪŋ] *n (trade)* restauration *f*; **to do the c.** fournir les repas; **c. school** école *f* hôtelière

caterpillar ['kætəpɪlə(r)] *n* chenille *f*; **c. track** *(on tank, tractor)* chenille

catfish ['kætfɪʃ] *n* poisson-chat *m*

cathartic [kə'θɑːtɪk] *adj* cathartique

cathedral [kə'θiːdrəl] *n* cathédrale *f*; **c. city** ville *f* épiscopale, évêché *m*

catheter ['kæθɪtə(r)] *n Med* cathéter *m*

cathode ['kæθəʊd] *n Elec* cathode *f*; **c. ray tube** tube *m* cathodique

Catholic ['kæθlɪk] *Rel* **1** *n* catholique *mf*; **to be a C.** être catholique
   2 *adj* catholique

catholic ['kæθlɪk] *adj (wide-ranging)* éclectique

Catholicism [kə'θɒlɪsɪzəm] *n* catholicisme *m*

catkin ['kætkɪn] *n* chaton *m (d'arbre)*

catnap ['kætnæp] *n Fam* petit somme *m*

catsuit ['kætsuːt] *n* combinaison *f* collante

cattle ['kætəl] *npl* bétail *m*; **c. breeding** élevage *m* de bétail; **c. grid** = grille recouvrant une fosse et empêchant le passage du bétail; *also Fig* **c. market** marché *m* ou foire *f* aux bestiaux; **c. truck** bétaillère *f*

catty ['kætɪ] *adj Fam* vache; **c. remark** vacherie *f*

catwalk ['kætwɔːk] *n* podium *m*

Caucasian [kɔː'keɪʒən] **1** *n (white person)* Blanc (Blanche) *m,f (de type européen)*
   2 *adj (in ethnology)* blanc (blanche) *(de type européen)*

Caucasus ['kɔːkəsəs] *n* **the C.** le Caucase

caucus ['kɔːkəs] *n Pol Br* = comité à l'intérieur d'un parti politique; *Am* caucus *m*

caught [kɔːt] *pt & pp of* **catch**

cauldron ['kɔːldrən] *n* chaudron *m*

cauliflower ['kɒlɪflaʊə(r)] *n* chou-fleur *m*; **c. cheese** chou-fleur au gratin; *Fam* **c. ear** oreille *f* en chou-fleur

cause [kɔːz] **1** *n* (**a**) *(origin)* cause *f*; **c. and effect** la cause et l'effet (**b**) *(reason)* raison *f*, motif *m*; **to have good c. for doing sth** avoir de bonnes raisons de faire qch; **and with good c.** et pour cause; **to give c. for complaint** donner lieu à des plaintes; **to give c. for concern** être inquiétant(e) (**c**) *(purpose, mission)* cause *f*; **to make common c. (with sb)** faire cause commune (avec qn); **it's all in a good c.** *(for charity)* c'est pour une bonne cause; *Fig* c'est pour la bonne

cause
   2 *vt* provoquer; *(trouble)* causer; **to c. sb grief** faire de la peine à qn; **to c. sb to do sth** faire faire qch à qn; **he caused the plan to fail** il a fait échouer le plan

causeway ['kɔːzweɪ] *n* chaussée *f (sur un marécage)*

caustic ['kɔːstɪk] *adj also Fig* caustique; **c. soda** soude *f* caustique

cauterize ['kɔːtəraɪz] *vt Med* cautériser

caution ['kɔːʃən] **1** *n* (**a**) *(prudence)* prudence *f*; **c.!** *(sign)* attention!; **to exercise c.** être prudent(e); **to throw c. to the wind(s)** abandonner toute prudence (**b**) *(warning)* avertissement *m*
   2 *vt* (**a**) *(warn)* mettre en garde (**against sth** contre qch); **to c. sb against doing sth** déconseiller à qn de faire qch (**b**) *Sport* donner un avertissement à (**c**) *Law* **to c. sb** *(on arrest)* informer qn de ses droits; *(instead of prosecuting)* donner un avertissement à qn

cautionary ['kɔːʃənərɪ] *adj* **a c. tale** une histoire édifiante

cautious ['kɔːʃəs] *adj* prudent(e)

cautiously ['kɔːʃəslɪ] *adv* prudemment, avec prudence

cautiousness ['kɔːʃəsnɪs] *n* prudence *f*

cavalier [kævə'lɪə(r)] *adj* cavalier(ère)

cavalry ['kævəlrɪ] *n* cavalerie *f*

cave [keɪv] *n* grotte *f*; **c. dweller** *(contemporary)* troglodyte *m*; *(prehistoric)* homme *m* des cavernes; **c. paintings** peintures *fpl* rupestres

▸**cave in** *vi (of ground, structure)* s'affaisser; *Fig (stop resisting)* céder (**to** à)

caveman ['keɪvmæn] *n* homme *m* des cavernes

cavern ['kævən] *n* caverne *f*

cavernous ['kævənəs] *adj* immense

caviar(e) ['kævɪɑː(r)] *n* caviar *m*

cavity ['kævɪtɪ] *(pl* **cavities**) *n* cavité *f*; **c. wall insulation** isolation *f* des murs creux

cavort [kə'vɔːt] *vi* faire des cabrioles; *Fig* batifoler

caw [kɔː] **1** *n* croassement *m*
   2 *vi* croasser

cayenne [keɪ'en] *n* **c. (pepper)** (poivre *m* de) Cayenne *m*

CB [siː'biː] *n (abbr* **Citizens' Band**) CB *f*

CBE [siːbiː'iː] *n (abbr* **Commander of the (Order of the) British Empire**) = distinction honorifique britannique

CBI [siːbiː'aɪ] *n Br (abbr* **Confederation of British Industry**) = confédération du patronat britannique

cc [siː'siː] *n (abbr* **cubic centimetre(s)**) cm³

CD [siː'diː] *n* (**a**) *(abbr* **compact disc**) CD *m*, compact *m*; **CD burner** graveur *m* de CD; **CD player** lecteur *m* laser *ou* de CD (**b**) *(abbr* **Corps Diplomatique**) CD

CDI [siːdiː'aɪ] *n Comput (abbr* **compact disc interactive**) CD-I *m inv*

Cdr *n (abbr* **Commander**) commandant

Cdre *n (abbr* **Commodore**) contre-amiral

CD-ROM [siːdiː'rɒm] *n Comput (abbr* **compact disc read-only memory**) CD-ROM *m inv*

cease [siːs] **1** *vt* cesser; **to c. doing sth** cesser de faire qch; **to c. fire** cesser le feu
   2 *vi* cesser (**from doing sth** *or* **to do sth** de faire qch); **it never ceases to amaze me** ça ne laisse jamais de m'étonner

cease-fire ['siːsfaɪə(r)] *n* cessez-le-feu *m inv*

ceaseless ['siːslɪs] *adj* incessant(e), continuel(elle)

ceaselessly ['siːslɪslɪ] *adv* sans cesse, continuellement

cedar ['siːdə(r)] *n (tree, wood)* cèdre *m*

cede [siːd] *vt Law (territory, property)* céder; **to c. a
point** concéder un point

cedilla [sɪ'dɪlə] *n* cédille *f*

Ceefax® ['siːfæks] *n Br* = télétexte de la BBC

ceilidh ['keɪlɪ] *n* = bal folklorique écossais ou irlandais

ceiling ['siːlɪŋ] *n (of room) & Fig (limit)* plafond *m*; *Fig*
to hit the c. piquer une crise; **c. price** prix *m* plafond

celebrant ['selɪbrənt] *n Rel* officiant *m*

celebrate ['selɪbreɪt] **1** *vt (anniversary, win, occasion)*
célébrer, fêter; *(mass)* célébrer
2 *vi* faire la fête

celebrated ['selɪbreɪtɪd] *adj* célèbre

celebration [selɪ'breɪʃən] *n* célébration *f*; **celebrations** *(festivities)* festivités *fpl*; **in c. of sth** pour célébrer *ou* fêter qch; **this calls for a c.!** il faut fêter *ou*
arroser ça!

celebrity [sɪ'lebrɪtɪ] *(pl* **celebrities)** *n (person, fame)*
célébrité *f*

celery ['selərɪ] *n* céleri *m*

celestial [sɪ'lestɪəl] *adj* céleste

celibacy ['selɪbəsɪ] *n (chastity)* absence *f* de rapports
sexuels; *(by choice)* chasteté *f*; *Rel* célibat *m*

celibate ['selɪbət] *adj* **to be c.** ne pas avoir de rapports
sexuels; *(by choice)* être chaste; *Rel* être célibataire

cell [sel] *n* cellule *f*

cellar ['selə(r)] *n* cave *f*

cellist ['tʃelɪst] *n* violoncelliste *mf*

cello ['tʃeləʊ] *(pl* **cellos)** *n* violoncelle *m*

cellophane® ['seləfeɪn] *n Br* Cellophane® *f*

cellphone ['selfəʊn] *n Tel* téléphone *m* cellulaire, *Can*
cellulaire *m*

cellular ['seljʊlə(r)] *adj* cellulaire; **c. phone** téléphone
m cellulaire, *Can* cellulaire *m*

cellulite ['seljʊlaɪt] *n* cellulite *f*

celluloid® ['seljʊlɔɪd] *n* Celluloïd® *m*

cellulose ['seljʊləʊs] *n* cellulose *f*

Celsius ['selsɪəs] *adj* Celsius; **10 degrees C.** 10 degrés
Celsius

Celt [kelt] *n* Celte *mf*

Celtic ['keltɪk] *adj* celte, celtique

cement [sɪ'ment] **1** *n* ciment *m*; **c. mixer** bétonnière *f*
2 *vt also Fig* cimenter

cemetery ['semətrɪ] *(pl* **cemetaries)** *n* cimetière *m*

cenotaph ['senətɑːf] *n* cénotaphe *m*

censor ['sensə(r)] **1** *n* censeur *m*; **the censors banned
the film** la censure a interdit le film
2 *vt* censurer

censorious [sen'sɔːrɪəs] *adj* sévère (**of** vis-à-vis de)

censorship ['sensəʃɪp] *n* censure *f*

censure ['senʃə(r)] **1** *n* critique *f*; *Pol* **vote of c.** motion
f de censure
2 *vt* blâmer; *(officially)* donner un blâme à

census ['sensəs] *n* recensement *m*

cent [sent] *n* cent *m*; *Am Fam* **I haven't got a c.** je n'ai
pas un rond

centaur ['sentɔː(r)] *n* centaure *m*

centenarian [sentɪ'neərɪən] *n* centenaire *mf*

centenary [sen'tiːnərɪ], *Am* **centennial** [sen'tenɪəl]
1 *n* centenaire *m*
2 *adj* centenaire

center *Am* = **centre**

centigrade ['sentɪɡreɪd] *adj* centigrade; **10 degrees c.**
10 degrés centigrades

centigram(me) ['sentɪɡræm] *n* centigramme *m*

centilitre, *Am* **centiliter** ['sentɪliːtə(r)] *n* centilitre *m*

centime ['sɒntiːm] *n* centime *m*

centimetre, *Am* **centimeter** ['sentɪmiːtə(r)] *n* centimètre *m*

centipede ['sentɪpiːd] *n* mille-pattes *m inv*

central ['sentrəl] *adj* central(e); **C. London** le centre de
Londres; **our hotel is quite c.** notre hôtel est dans le
centre; **of c. importance** d'une importance capitale;
C. America l'Amérique *f* centrale; **C. American**
d'Amérique centrale; **c. bank** banque *f* centrale; **C.
Europe** l'Europe *f* centrale; **C. European** d'Europe
centrale; **C. European Time** heure *f* de l'Europe centrale; **c. government** gouvernement *m* central; **c.
heating** chauffage *m* central; *Aut* **c. locking** verrouillage *m* centralisé; **c. nervous system** système *m* nerveux central; *Comput* **c. processing unit** unité *f*
centrale; **c. reservation** *(on motorway)* terre-plein *m*
central; *Am* **C. Standard Time** heure *f* du centre de
l'Amérique du Nord

Central African Republic ['sentrəl'æfrɪkənrɪ-'pʌblɪk]
n République *f* centrafricaine

centralize ['sentrəlaɪz] *vt* centraliser

centrally ['sentrəlɪ] *adv (funded, administered)* de façon centralisée; **c. located** central(e); **the flat is c.
heated** l'appartement a le chauffage central

centre, *Am* **center** ['sentə(r)] **1** *n* centre *m*; **in the c.** au
centre; *Pol* **left/right of c.** du centre gauche/droit; **c.
of gravity** centre de gravité; **c. of attention** centre
d'attraction; **c. forward** *(in football)* avant-centre *m*
2 *vt (attention, interest)* concentrer (**on** sur)

▶**centre on,** *Am* **center on** *vt insep* se concentrer sur;
(conversation) tourner autour de

centrefold, *Am* **centerfold** ['sentəfəʊld] *n (in magazine)* double page *f* centrale détachable; *(nude photo)*
photo *f* de pin-up

centrepiece, *Am* **centerpiece** ['sentəpiːs] *n (on
table)* centre *m* de table; *(main attraction)* pièce *f* de
résistance

centrifugal [sentrɪ'fjuːɡəl] *adj* centrifuge

century ['sentʃərɪ] *(pl* **centuries)** *n* siècle *m*; **the 19th
c.** le 19ᵉ siècle

CEO [siːiː'əʊ] *n Com (abbr* **Chief Executive Officer)** D.G.
m; **President and C.** président(e)-directeur(trice) *m,f*
général(e), P.-D.G. *m,f*

ceramic [sə'ræmɪk] **1** *n (material)* céramique *f*; **ceramics** *(art)* céramique; *(objects)* céramiques *fpl*
2 *adj* en céramique

cereal ['sɪərɪəl] *n* céréale *f*; **(breakfast) c.** céréales

cerebellum [serɪ'beləm] *n Anat* cervelet *m*

cerebral ['serɪbrəl] *adj (intellectual)* & *Anat* céré-
bral(e); *Med* **c. palsy** paralysie *f* cérébrale

cerebrum ['serɪbrəm] *n Anat* cerveau *m*

ceremonial [serɪ'məʊnɪəl] **1** *n* cérémonial *m*
2 *adj* de cérémonie

ceremonious [serɪ'məʊnɪəs] *adj* cérémonieux(euse)

ceremony ['serɪmənɪ] *(pl* **ceremonies)** *n* cérémonie *f*;
without c. sans cérémonies; **to stand on c.** faire des
cérémonies

cert [sɜːt] *n Fam* **it's a (dead) c.** c'est garanti

certain ['sɜːtən] *adj* **(a)** *(sure) (failure, victory)* cer-
tain(e), assuré(e); *(cure, solution)* infaillible; **I can't
say for c.** je ne peux pas l'affirmer; **I'll tell you next**

week for **c**. je vous le dirai la semaine prochaine sans faute; **to know sth for c.** être certain(e) de qch; **to be c. of sth** être sûr(e) *ou* certain(e) de qch; **they're c. of winning** ils sont assurés de gagner; **to make c. of sth** *(find out)* s'assurer de qch; *(be sure to get)* s'assurer qch; **he is c. to come** il viendra à coup sûr (**b**) *(particular)* certain(e); **a c. PhilipThomas** un certain Philip Thomas

certainly ['sɜːtənlɪ] *adv* certainement; **c. not!** certainement pas!; **she's c. very clever, but…** certes elle est très intelligente, mais…

certainty ['sɜːtəntɪ] *(pl* **certainties***) n (strong likelihood)* certitude *f; (conviction)* conviction *f;* **there is no c. that we will win** il n'est pas certain que nous gagnions; **to know sth for a c.** être certain(e) de qch

certifiable ['sɜːtɪfaɪəbəl] *adj Fam (mad)* bon (bonne) pour l'asile

certificate [sə'tɪfɪkət] *n* certificat *m; (in education)* diplôme *m*

certify ['sɜːtɪfaɪ] *(pt & pp* **certified***) vt* (**a**) *(confirm)* certifier; **this is to c. that…** nous certifions par la présente que…; **to c. sb (insane)** déclarer que l'état de santé de qn nécessite l'internement psychiatrique (**b**) *(give certificate to)* délivrer un certificat à

certitude ['sɜːtɪtjuːd] *n* certitude *f*

cervical ['sɜːvɪkəl, sə'vaɪkəl] *adj* **c. cancer** cancer *m* du col de l'utérus; **c. smear** frottis *m* vaginal

cervix ['sɜːvɪks] *(pl* **cervices** ['sɜːvɪsiːz]) *n Anat* col *m* de l'utérus

cessation [se'seɪʃən] *n* cessation *f*

cesspit ['sespɪt], **cesspool** ['sespuːl] *n* fosse *f* d'aisances; *Fig* cloaque *m*

Ceylon [sɪ'lɒn] *n Formerly* Ceylan

cf [siː'ef] *(abbr* **confer, compare***)* cf

CFC [siːef'siː] *(pl* **CFCs***) n (abbr* **chlorofluorocarbon***)* CFC *m*

Chad [tʃæd] *n* leTchad

chafe [tʃeɪf] **1** *vt (skin)* irriter; *(of shoes)* blesser
2 *vi (of skin)* être irrité(e); *(of shoes)* frotter (**against** contre); *Fig* **to c. at** *or* **against sth** *(resent)* s'irriter de qch

chaff [tʃɑːf] **1** *n* balle *f; Fig* **to separate the wheat from the c.** séparer le bon grain de l'ivraie
2 *vt (tease)* taquiner

chaffinch ['tʃæfɪntʃ] *n* pinson *m*

chagrin ['ʃæɡrɪn] *n Formal* dépit *m*

chain [tʃeɪn] **1** *n* chaîne *f; (for medallion)* chaînette *f;* **in chains** enchaîné(e); **to pull the c.** *(in toilet)* tirer la chasse (d'eau); **c. gang** chaîne de forçats; **c. letter** = lettre faisant partie d'une chaîne; **c. mail** cotte *f* de mailles; **c. reaction** réaction *f* en chaîne; **c. saw** tronçonneuse *f;* **c. store** magasin *m* à succursales multiples
2 *vt (prisoner)* enchaîner; *(dog, bicycle)* attacher avec une chaîne (**to** à)

▶**chain up** *vt sep (prisoner)* enchaîner; *(dog, bicycle)* attacher avec une chaîne (**to** à)

chain-smoke ['tʃeɪnsməʊk] *vi* fumer cigarette sur cigarette

chair [tʃeə(r)] **1** *n* (**a**) *(seat)* chaise *f; (armchair)* fauteuil *m* (**b**) *(chairperson)* président(e) *m,f;* **to be in the c.** présider (**c**) *Univ (of professor)* chaire *f*
2 *vt (meeting)* présider

chairlift ['tʃeəlɪft] *n* télésiège *m*

chairman ['tʃeəmən] *n (of meeting, political party)* président *m; (of company)* président-directeur *m* général, P.-D.G. *m*

chairmanship ['tʃeəmənʃɪp] *n* présidence *f*

chairperson ['tʃeəpɜːsən] *n* président(e) *m,f*

chairwoman ['tʃeəwʊmən] *n* présidente *f*

chalet ['ʃæleɪ] *n* chalet *m*

chalice ['tʃælɪs] *n Rel* calice *m*

chalk [tʃɔːk] **1** *n* craie *f;* **they are like c. and cheese** c'est le jour et la nuit; *Fam* **not by a long c.** loin s'en faut
2 *vt (mark)* marquer à la craie; *(write)* écrire à la craie

▶**chalk up** *vt sep (victory)* remporter

chalkboard ['tʃɔːkbɔːd] *n Am* tableau *m* (noir)

chalky ['tʃɔːkɪ] *adj (soil, complexion)* crayeux(euse); *(taste, texture)* plâtreux(euse)

challenge ['tʃælɪndʒ] **1** *n* défi *m* (**to** à); **to launch a leadership c.** chercher à conquérir la direction du parti; **the job presents a real c.** ce travail est très stimulant
2 *vt* (**a**) *(of job)* mettre à l'épreuve, être stimulant(e) pour; **to c. sb to do sth** défier qn de faire qch; **he challenged me to a fight** il m'a défié de me battre contre lui (**b**) *(statement, authority)* contester (**c**) *Mil* interpeller

challenger ['tʃælɪndʒə(r)] *n Sport* challenger *m*

challenging ['tʃælɪndʒɪŋ] *adj (job)* stimulant(e)

chamber ['tʃeɪmbə(r)] *n* (**a**) *(hall)* chambre *f; Pol* **Lower/Upper C.** Chambre basse/haute; **C. of Commerce** Chambre de commerce; **c. music** musique *f* de chambre; **c. pot** *m* de chambre (**b**) *Law* **chambers** *(of barrister, judge)* cabinet *m (au tribunal)* (**c**) *(of heart)* cavité *f; (of revolver)* chambre *f*

chambermaid ['tʃeɪmbəmeɪd] *n* femme *f* de chambre

chameleon [kə'miːlɪən] *n* caméléon *m*

chamois *n* (**a**) ['ʃæmɪ] **c. (leather)** peau *f* de chamois (**b**) ['ʃæmwɑː] *(deer)* chamois *m*

champ¹ [tʃæmp] *n Fam* champion(onne) *m,f*

champ² *vi Fig* **to c. at the bit** ronger son frein

champagne [ʃæm'peɪn] *n* champagne *m*

champion ['tʃæmpɪən] **1** *n (in sport, of cause)* champion(onne) *m,f;* **world/European c.** champion(onne) du monde/d'Europe
2 *vt* défendre

championship ['tʃæmpɪənʃɪp] *n* championnat *m*

chance [tʃɑːns] **1** *n* (**a**) *(luck)* hasard *m;* **by c.** par hasard; **to leave nothing to c.** ne rien laisser au hasard; **by any c.** par hasard; *Fam* **c. would be a fine thing!** ça ne risque pas!
(**b**) *(opportunity)* occasion *f;* **to give sb a c.** donner une chance à qn; **she was trying to apologize but you didn't give her a c.** elle essayait de s'excuser mais tu ne lui en as pas laissé l'occasion; **now's your c.!** à toi de jouer!; **it's your last c.** c'est ta dernière chance; **to have an eye to the main c.** chercher à tirer profit de toutes les occasions
(**c**) *(likelihood)* chance *f* (**of** de); **to have** *or* **stand a c. of doing sth** avoir des chances de faire qch; **he never stood a c.** *(of escaping, surviving etc)* il n'avait aucune chance de s'en tirer; **there's no c. of that happening** il n'y a aucune chance que cela se produise; **(the) chances are (that)…** il y a fort à parier que…
(**d**) *(risk)* risque *m;* **to take a c.** prendre un risque
2 *adj (discovery)* accidentel(elle); *(meeting)* fortuit(e)
3 *vt* **to c. doing sth** prendre le risque de faire qch;

Fam **to c. one's arm** tenter le coup
4 *vi* **to c. to do sth** faire qch par hasard

▸**chance on, chance upon** *vt insep* tomber (par hasard) sur

chancellor ['tʃɑːnsələ(r)] *n* (**a**) *Univ Br* président(e) *m,f* honoraire; *Am* président(e) *m,f* (**b**) *Pol (in Austria, Germany)* chancelier *m*; *Br Pol* **C. (of the Exchequer)** Chancelier de l'Échiquier, ≃ ministre *m* des Finances

chancy ['tʃɑːnsɪ] *adj Fam (risky)* risqué(e)

chandelier [ʃændə'lɪə(r)] *n* lustre *m*

change [tʃeɪndʒ] **1** *n* (**a**) *(alteration)* changement *m*; **a c. for the better/worse** une amélioration/détérioration; **a c. of address** un changement d'adresse; **a c. of clothes** des vêtements *mpl* de rechange; **to have a c. of heart** changer d'avis; **for a c.** pour une fois; *Ironic* pour changer; **that makes a c.** ça change un peu; *Euph* **the c. (of life)** *(menopause)* le retour d'âge (**b**) *(money)* monnaie *f*; **small** *or* **loose c.** petite *ou* menue monnaie; **have you got c. for a £10 note?** avez-vous la monnaie de 10 livres *ou* sur un billet de 10 livres?
 2 *vt* (**a**) *(alter)* changer; *(transform)* transformer (**into** en); **to c. one's mind** changer d'avis; **to c. the subject** changer de sujet
 (**b**) *(exchange)* changer (**for** pour *ou* contre); **to c. hands** *(of money, car)* changer de mains; **to c. trains** changer de train; **to c. places with sb** changer de place avec qn; *Fig* **I wouldn't like to c. places with him** je ne voudrais pas être à sa place
 (**c**) *(money)* changer; **to c. dollars into francs** changer des dollars en francs
 (**d**) **to get changed** *(put on other clothes)* se changer
 3 *vi* (**a**) *(alter)* changer; **to c. into sth** se transformer en qch
 (**b**) *(put on other clothes)* se changer
 (**c**) *(of passenger)* changer

▸**change over** *vi* changer; **to c. over from sth to sth** passer de qch à qch; **to c. over to another channel** changer de chaîne

changeable ['tʃeɪndʒəbəl] *adj (person, mood)* changeant(e); *(weather)* variable

changeless ['tʃeɪndʒlɪs] *adj* immuable

changeover ['tʃeɪndʒəʊvə(r)] *n (to new system, currency)* passage *m* (**to** à); *(after election, appointment)* transition *f*

changing ['tʃeɪndʒɪŋ] *adj* changeant(e)

changing room ['tʃeɪndʒɪŋruːm] *n* vestiaire *m*; *(in shop)* cabine *f* d'essayage

channel ['tʃænəl] **1** *n* (**a**) *(waterway)* chenal *m*; *(of communication, distribution)* canal *m*; **to go through the proper channels** suivre la filière officielle (**b**) *TV* chaîne *f*; *Rad* bande *f* de fréquences; **C. 4** = chaîne de télévision britannique à vocation culturelle; **C. 5** = chaîne de télévision commerciale britannique (**c**) **the (English) C.** la Manche; **the C. Islands** les îles *fpl* Anglo-Normandes; **the C. Tunnel** le tunnel sous la Manche
 2 *vt (pt & pp* **channelled,** *Am* **channeled)** canaliser (**to** vers)

chant [tʃɑːnt] **1** *n* (**a**) *(of demonstrators)* slogan *m* (**b**) *Rel* psalmodie *f*
 2 *vt* scander
 3 *vi (of demonstrators)* scander des slogans; *Rel* psalmodier

chaos ['keɪɒs] *n* chaos *m*; **our plans were thrown into c.** nos projets ont été bouleversés; **c. theory** théorie *f* du chaos

chaotic [keɪ'ɒtɪk] *adj* chaotique

chap [tʃæp] *n Fam (man)* bonhomme *m*, type *m*; **a good c.** un brave type

chapel ['tʃæpəl] *n* chapelle *f*

chaperone ['ʃæpərəʊn] **1** *n* chaperon *m*
 2 *vt* chaperonner

chaplain ['tʃæplɪn] *n Rel* aumônier *m*

chaplaincy ['tʃæplɪnsɪ] *n* aumônerie *f*

chapped [tʃæpt] *adj (lips, skin)* gercé(e)

chapter ['tʃæptə(r)] *n* chapitre *m*; **a c. of accidents** une série noire; *Fig* **to quote c. and verse for sth** donner les références exactes de qch

char¹ [tʃɑː(r)] *(pt & pp* **charred)** *vt (burn)* carboniser

char² *Br Fam* **1** *n (cleaning lady)* femme *f* de ménage
 2 *vi (pt & pp* **charred)** *(clean)* faire des ménages

char³ *n Br Fam (tea)* thé *m*

character ['kærɪktə(r)] *n* (**a**) *(in novel, film, play)* personnage *m*; **c. actor/actress** acteur(trice) *m,f* de genre *(qui se spécialise dans les rôles secondaires de personnages qui sont souvent comiques ou excentriques)* (**b**) *(personality)* caractère *m*; **his remark was in/out of c.** ça lui ressemble bien/ça ne lui ressemble pas d'avoir fait une remarque pareille; **to have/lack c.** avoir du/manquer de caractère; **a person of good c.** une personne honorable; **c. assassination** diffamation *f*; **c. reference** *(when applying for job)* références *fpl*; *Law* **c. witness** témoin *m* de moralité (**c**) *(unusual person)* personnage *m*; **he's quite a c.!** c'est un personnage! (**d**) *(letter)* caractère *m*; *Comput* **c. set** jeu *m* de caractères

characteristic [kærɪktə'rɪstɪk] **1** *n* caractéristique *f*
 2 *adj* caractéristique; **it's c. of him** ça lui ressemble bien, c'est bien de lui

characterization [kærɪktəraɪ'zeɪʃən] *n (of problem, situation)* description *f*; *(in novel)* psychologie *f* des personnages

characterize ['kærɪktəraɪz] *vt (describe)* décrire; *(be characteristic of)* caractériser

charade [ʃə'rɑːd] *n (farce)* mascarade *f*; **charades** *(party game)* charades *fpl* mimées

charcoal ['tʃɑːkəʊl] *n* charbon *m* de bois; *Art* fusain *m*; **c. drawing** (dessin *m* au) fusain; **c. grey** anthracite *m inv*

charge [tʃɑːdʒ] **1** *n* (**a**) *(cost)* frais *mpl*; **free of c.** gratuitement; **c. account** compte *m* clients; **c. card** carte *f* de paiement *(de grand magasin)*
 (**b**) *Law* chef *m* d'accusation; **to be arrested on a c. of...** être arrêté(e) pour...; **to bring a c. against sb** accuser qn; **c. sheet** ≃ procès-verbal *m*
 (**c**) *(responsibility)* **to take c. of sth** prendre qch en charge; **to be in c. of** être responsable de; **I'm in c. here!** c'est moi le chef ici!
 (**d**) *(of explosive)* charge *f*
 2 *vt* (**a**) *(price)* faire payer, demander; **to c. sb £10** faire payer £10 à qn; **c. it to my account** mettez ça sur mon compte
 (**b**) *Law* inculper (**with** de)
 (**c**) *(attack)* attaquer
 (**d**) *Elec* charger; *Fig* **a highly charged atmosphere** une atmosphère très tendue
 3 *vi (rush)* charger; **to c. in/out** entrer/sortir en trombe

chariot ['tʃærɪət] *n* char *m*

charisma [kæ'rızmə] *n* charisme *m*
charismatic [kærız'mætık] *adj* charismatique
charitable ['tʃærɪtəbəl] *adj (person, action)* charitable; *(organization)* caritatif(ive); *(work)* pour une association caritative
charity ['tʃærɪtɪ] *(pl* **charities)** *n* (**a**) *(quality)* charité *f*; *Prov* **c.** begins at home charité bien ordonnée commence par soi-même (**b**) *(organization)* association *f* caritative
charlady ['tʃɑːleɪdɪ] *(pl* **charladies)** *n Br* femme *f* de ménage
charlatan ['ʃɑːlətən] *n* charlatan *m*
Charlie ['tʃɑːlɪ] *n Br Fam* **to feel a right** *or* **proper C.** se sentir vraiment bête
charm [tʃɑːm] **1** *n* (**a**) *(attractiveness)* charme *m*; **to turn on the c.** faire le charmeur/la charmeuse (**b**) *(spell)* charme *m*; **it worked like a c.** ça a marché comme sur des roulettes; **c. offensive** offensive *f* de charme (**c**) **(lucky) c.** amulette *f*
 2 *vt* charmer; **she charmed the money out of him** elle lui a extorqué son argent en lui faisant du charme; **to lead a charmed life** être né(e) sous une bonne étoile
charmer ['tʃɑːmə(r)] *n* charmeur(euse) *m,f*
charming ['tʃɑːmɪŋ] *adj also Ironic* charmant(e)
charred [tʃɑːd] *adj* carbonisé(e)
chart [tʃɑːt] **1** *n (graph)* diagramme *m*, graphique *m*; *(map)* carte *f*; **the charts** *(pop music)* le hit-parade
 2 *vt* (**a**) *(on map)* porter sur une carte (**b**) *Fig (progress, rise)* retracer
charter ['tʃɑːtə(r)] **1** *n (of town)* charte *f*; *(of university)* statuts *mpl*; **c. flight** (vol *m*) charter *m*
 2 *vt (plane, ship)* affréter
chartered accountant ['tʃɑːtədə'kaʊntənt] *n* expert-comptable *m*
charwoman ['tʃɑːwʊmən] *n Br* femme *f* de ménage
chary ['tʃeərɪ] *adj* circonspect(e); **to be c. of doing sth** hésiter à faire qch
chase [tʃeɪs] **1** *n (pursuit)* poursuite *f*; **to give c. to sb** donner la chasse à qn
 2 *vt (pursue)* poursuivre, donner la chasse à; *(sexually)* courir après
 3 *vi* **to c. after sb** *(pursue)* poursuivre qn, donner la chasse à qn; *(sexually)* courir après qn
▶**chase up** *vt sep (person)* relancer; *(letter)* retrouver la trace de
chaser ['tʃeɪsə(r)] *n* = alcool bu après une bière ou vice versa
chasm ['kæzəm] *n also Fig* gouffre *m*, abîme *m*
chassis ['ʃæsɪ] *n (of car)* châssis *m*
chaste [tʃeɪst] *adj* chaste
chasten ['tʃeɪsən] *vt* rendre plus humble
chastise [tʃæs'taɪz] *vt* châtier; *(criticize)* fustiger
chastisement [tʃæs'taɪzmənt] *n* châtiment *m*; *(criticism)* fustigation *f*
chastity ['tʃæstɪtɪ] *n* chasteté *f*; **c. belt** ceinture *f* de chasteté
chat [tʃæt] **1** *n* (**a**) *(conversation)* discussion *f*; **to have a c. (with sb)** discuter *ou* bavarder (avec qn); **c. show** *(on TV)* talk-show *m* (**b**) *Comput (on Internet)* bavardage *m*, chat *m*; **c. room** site *m* de bavardage, salon *m*, *Can* bavardoir *m*
 2 *vi (pt & pp* **chatted)** *also Comput* bavarder; **to c. about sth** discuter de qch
▶**chat up** *vt sep Br Fam* draguer

chattel ['tʃætəl] *n Law* bien *m* meuble
chatter ['tʃætər] **1** *n* bavardage *m*, papotage *m*
 2 *vi (talk)* bavarder, papoter; **my teeth were chattering** je claquais des dents
chatterbox ['tʃætəbɒks] *n Fam* pie *f*, moulin *m* à paroles
chatty ['tʃætɪ] *adj (person)* bavard(e); *(letter)* plein(e) de détails
chauffeur ['ʃəʊfə(r)] **1** *n* chauffeur *m*
 2 *vt* conduire
chauvinism ['ʃəʊvɪnɪzəm] *n (patriotism)* chauvinisme *m*; **(male) c.** machisme *m*
chauvinist ['ʃəʊvɪnɪst] *n & adj (patriotic)* chauvin(e) *m,f*; **(male) c.** *(sexist)* macho *m*
chauvinistic [ʃəʊvɪ'nɪstɪk] *adj (patriotic)* chauvin(e); *(sexist)* macho
cheap [tʃiːp] **1** *n* **to do sth on the c.** faire qch à peu de frais *ou* pour pas cher
 2 *adj* (**a**) *(inexpensive)* bon marché *inv*, pas cher (chère); **cheaper** meilleur marché *inv*, moins cher (chère); **c. rate** tarif *m* réduit (**b**) *(of little value)* de peu de valeur; *(vulgar)* de mauvais goût; **to feel c.** *(of person)* se sentir minable; **it's c. and nasty** c'est de la camelote
 3 *adv Fam* **it was going c.** c'était bon marché
cheapen ['tʃiːpən] *vt (degrade)* gâcher; **to c. oneself** s'abaisser
cheaply ['tʃiːplɪ] *adv (buy)* (à) bon marché, à bas prix; *(live, travel)* à peu de frais, pour pas cher
cheapskate ['tʃiːpskeɪt] *n Fam* radin(e) *m,f*
cheat [tʃiːt] **1** *n (dishonest person)* escroc *m*; *(at games)* tricheur(euse) *m,f*; *(deception, trick)* tricherie *f*, triche *f*
 2 *vt* duper, rouler; *(financially)* escroquer; **to c. sb out of sth** *(money)* escroquer qch à qn; *(chance)* priver qn de qch
 3 *vi* tricher
▶**cheat on** *vt insep (be unfaithful to)* tromper
cheating ['tʃiːtɪŋ] *n* tricherie *f*, triche *f*; **that's c.!** c'est de la triche!
Chechenia, Chechnya ['tʃetʃnɪə] *n* la Tchétchénie
check¹ [tʃek] **1** *n* (**a**) *(inspection)* vérification *f*, contrôle *m* (**on** de); **to run a c. on sb** enquêter sur qn
 (**b**) *(restraint)* **to keep sb in c.** tenir qn en échec; **to keep sth in c.** *(emotion, enemy advance)* contenir qch; *Pol* **checks and balances** équilibre *m* des pouvoirs
 (**c**) *(in chess)* échec *m*; **in c.** en échec
 (**d**) *Am (cheque)* chèque *m*; *(restaurant bill)* addition *f*
 2 *vt* (**a**) *(verify, examine) (information, statement)* vérifier; *(passport, ticket)* contrôler; **to c. that...** vérifier *ou* s'assurer que...
 (**b**) *(restrain) (inflation)* enrayer; *(emotion, impulse, enemy advance)* contenir
 (**c**) *Am (coat, hat)* mettre au vestiaire; *(bag, luggage)* mettre à la consigne
 3 *vi* vérifier; **to c. on sth** vérifier qch; **to c. on sb** surveiller qn; **you'd better c. with her** vous feriez mieux de lui demander
▶**check in 1** *vt sep (baggage)* enregistrer
 2 *vi (at hotel)* remplir le registre; *(at airport)* se présenter à l'enregistrement
▶**check out 1** *vt sep* (**a**) *(investigate) (person)* se renseigner sur; *(information)* vérifier (**b**) *Fam (look at)* viser
 2 *vi (leave hotel)* quitter l'hôtel
▶**check up** *vi* vérifier; **to c. up on sb** surveiller qn

check² **1** n *(pattern)* carreaux *mpl*
  2 *adj* à carreaux, *Can* carreauté(e)

checkers ['tʃekəz] *npl Am* jeu *m* de dames

check-in ['tʃekɪn] *n Aviat* **c. (desk)** (comptoir *m* d')enregistrement *m*

checkmate ['tʃekmeɪt] **1** *n (in chess)* échec *m* et mat
  2 *vt (in chess)* faire échec et mat à; *Fig (opponent)* faire échec à

checkout ['tʃekaʊt] *n (in supermarket)* caisse *f*

checkpoint ['tʃekpɔɪnt] *n* (poste *m* de) contrôle *m*

checkup ['tʃekʌp] *n Med* bilan *m* complet

cheek [tʃiːk] **1** *n* (**a**) *(of face)* joue *f*; **to dance c. to c.** danser joue contre joue; **c. by jowl (with sb)** coude à coude (avec qn); *Fig* **to turn the other c.** tendre l'autre joue (**b**) *(buttock)* fesse *f* (**c**) *Fam (impudence)* toupet *m*, culot *m*; **he's got a c.!** il est culotté *ou* gonflé!
  2 *vt Fam (be impudent to)* être insolent(e) avec

cheekbone ['tʃiːkbəʊn] *n* pommette *f*

cheeky ['tʃiːkɪ] *adj Fam* effronté(e)

cheep [tʃiːp] *vi (of bird)* piailler

cheer [tʃɪə(r)] **1** *n* (**a**) *(shout)* hourra *m*; **cheers** acclamations *fpl*, bravos *mpl*; **three cheers for Mary!** un ban pour Mary! (**b**) *Fam* **cheers!** *(when drinking)* (à votre) santé!; *Br (goodbye)* à bientôt!; *Br (thanks)* merci! (**c**) *Lit (good spirits)* **to be of good c.** être de bonne humeur
  2 *vt* (**a**) *(applaud)* acclamer (**b**) *(make happier)* remonter le moral à
  3 *vi (shout)* pousser des hourras *ou* des acclamations

▸**cheer on** *vt sep (support)* encourager

▸**cheer up 1** *vt sep (person)* remonter le moral à; *(room)* égayer
  2 *vi (of person)* reprendre courage; **c. up!** courage!

cheerful ['tʃɪəfʊl] *adj (person)* gai(e), de bonne humeur; *(room, music, mood)* gai; *(conversation)* enjoué(e)

cheerfully ['tʃɪəfʊlɪ] *adv* gaiement, avec entrain; *Fam* **I could c. strangle him!** je l'étranglerais volontiers!

cheerily ['tʃɪərɪlɪ] *adv* gaiement

cheerio [tʃɪərɪ'əʊ] *exclam* salut!

cheerleader ['tʃɪəliːdə(r)] *n* = majorette qui encourage les supporters d'une équipe sportive à manifester leur enthousiasme

cheerless ['tʃɪəlɪs] *adj* morne; *(room)* triste

cheery ['tʃɪərɪ] *adj* joyeux(euse), gai(e)

cheese [tʃiːz] *n* fromage *m*; *Fam* **(say) c.!** *(for photograph)* souriez!; **c. sandwich/omelette** sandwich *m*/omelette *f* au fromage

▸**cheese off** *vt sep Fam* **to be cheesed off (with)** en avoir marre (de)

cheeseboard ['tʃiːzbɔːd] *n (selection)* plateau *m* de fromages

cheeseburger ['tʃiːzbɜːgə(r)] *n* cheeseburger *m*

cheesecake ['tʃiːzkeɪk] *n* gâteau *m* au fromage blanc

cheetah ['tʃiːtə] *n* guépard *m*

chef [ʃef] *n* chef *m* (cuisinier)

chemical ['kemɪkəl] **1** *n* produit *m* chimique
  2 *adj* chimique; **c. warfare** guerre *f* chimique; **c. weapons** armes *fpl* chimiques

chemist ['kemɪst] *n* (**a**) *Br (pharmacist)* pharmacien(enne) *m,f*; **c.'s (shop)** pharmacie *f* (**b**) *(scientist)* chimiste *mf*

chemistry ['kemɪstrɪ] *n* chimie *f*; *Fig* **there was a certain c. between them** il y avait une certaine affinité entre eux

chemotherapy [kiːməʊ'θerəpɪ] *n Med* chimiothérapie *f*

cheque [tʃek] *n Fin* chèque *m*; **to make out** *or* **write a c. (to sb)** faire un chèque (à l'ordre de qn); **a c. for £10** un chèque de 10 livres; **c. card** carte *f* bancaire *(sans laquelle un chéquier n'est pas valable)*

chequebook ['tʃekbʊk] *n* carnet *m* de chèques, chéquier *m*; **c. journalism** = dans les milieux de la presse, pratique qui consiste à payer des sommes importantes pour le témoignage d'une personne impliquée dans une affaire

chequered ['tʃekəd] *adj (patterned)* à carreaux, *Can* carreauté(e); *Fig* **she's had a c. career** elle a eu une carrière en dents de scie

cherish ['tʃerɪʃ] *vt (memory, person)* chérir; *(hopes)* caresser, nourrir

cherry ['tʃerɪ] *(pl* **cherries**) *n (fruit)* cerise *f*; **c. (tree)** cerisier *m*; **c. orchard** cerisaie *f*

cherub ['tʃerəb] *(pl* **cherubs** *or* **cherubim** ['tʃerəbɪm]) *n* chérubin *m*

chess [tʃes] *n* échecs *mpl*; **a game of c.** une partie d'échecs; **c. player** joueur(euse) *m,f* d'échecs

chessboard ['tʃesbɔːd] *n* échiquier *m*

chessman ['tʃesmæn], **chesspiece** ['tʃespiːs] *n* pièce *f* (de jeu d'échecs)

chest [tʃest] *n* (**a**) *(of person)* poitrine *f*; *Fig* **to get it off one's c.** dire ce qu'on a sur le cœur (**b**) *(box)* coffre *m*, caisse *f*; **c. of drawers** commode *f*

chestnut ['tʃesnʌt] **1** *n* (**a**) *(nut)* châtaigne *f*; *(tree, wood)* châtaignier *m*; **(horse) c.** marron *m* d'Inde; *Fam* **an old c.** une plaisanterie usée
  2 *adj (hair)* châtain; *(horse)* alezan(e)

chew [tʃuː] *vt* mâcher, mastiquer; *(cigar, end of pen)* mâchonner; **to c. one's nails** se ronger les ongles

▸**chew over** *vt sep Fam* réfléchir à, cogiter sur

chewing gum ['tʃuːɪŋgʌm] *n* chewing-gum *m*

chewy ['tʃuːɪ] *adj (meat)* caoutchouteux(euse); *(sweet)* mou (molle)

chic [ʃiːk] *adj* élégant(e), chic

chick [tʃɪk] *n* (**a**) *(young bird)* oisillon *m*; *(young chicken)* poussin *m* (**b**) *Fam (woman)* nana *f*

chicken ['tʃɪkɪn] **1** *n* (**a**) *(bird)* poulet *m*; *Prov* **don't count your chickens (before they are hatched)** il ne faut pas vendre la peau de l'ours avant de l'avoir tué; **c. feed** *(food)* nourriture *f* pour volaille; *Fam Fig* **that's c. feed!** c'est une misère! (**b**) *Fam (coward)* lâche *mf*, froussard(e) *m,f*
  2 *adj Fam (cowardly)* froussard(e)

▸**chicken out** *vi Fam* se dégonfler

chickenpox ['tʃɪkɪnpɒks] *n* varicelle *f*

chickpea ['tʃɪkpiː] *n* pois *m* chiche

chicory ['tʃɪkərɪ] *n* endive *f*

chide [tʃaɪd] *(pt* **chided** *or* **chid** [tʃɪd], *pp* **chided** *or* **chidden** ['tʃɪdən]) *vt Lit* réprimander

chief [tʃiːf] **1** *n (of tribe)* chef *m*; *Fam* **the c.** *(boss)* le patron; *Mil* **c. of staff** chef d'état-major; **(White House) c. of staff** secrétaire *m* de la Maison-Blanche
  2 *adj (most important)* principal(e); **c. assistant** principal(e) collaborateur(trice) *m,f*; *Com* **c. executive** directeur(trice) *m,f* général(e); *Am* **c. executive officer** directeur(trice) *m,f* général(e)

chiefly ['tʃiːflɪ] *adv* principalement, surtout

chieftain ['tʃiːftən] *n (of clan)* chef *m*

chiffon ['ʃɪfɒn] *n* mousseline *f* de soie

chilblain ['tʃɪlbleɪn] *n* engelure *f*

child [tʃaɪld] *(pl* **children** ['tʃɪldrən]*) n* enfant *mf*; **it's c.'s play** c'est un jeu d'enfant; **children's literature** littérature *f* enfantine *ou* pour enfants; **c. abuse** mauvais traitements *mpl* à enfant; *(sexual)* sévices *mpl* sexuels infligés à un enfant; **c. benefit** ≃ allocations *fpl* familiales; **c. labour** travail *m* des enfants; **c. minder** nourrice *f*

child-bearing ['tʃaɪldbeərɪŋ] *n* maternité *f*; **of c. age** en âge d'avoir des enfants

childbirth ['tʃaɪldbɜːθ] *n* accouchement *m*; **to die in c.** mourir en couches

childhood ['tʃaɪldhʊd] *n* enfance *f*

childish ['tʃaɪldɪʃ] *adj Pej* puéril(e); **don't be so c.!** ne fais pas l'enfant!

childless ['tʃaɪldlɪs] *adj* sans enfant(s)

childlike ['tʃaɪldlaɪk] *adj* enfantin(e)

childproof ['tʃaɪldpruːf] *adj* **c. lock** *(in car)* = serrure de sécurité pour enfants; **c. bottle** = bouteille pourvue d'une capsule de sécurité

children ['tʃɪldrən] *pl of* **child**

Chile ['tʃɪlɪ] *n* le Chili

Chilean ['tʃɪlɪən] **1** *n* Chilien(enne) *m,f*
2 *adj* chilien(enne)

chill [tʃɪl] **1** *n* coup *m* de froid; **to catch a c.** prendre froid; **a c. of fear** un frisson de peur; **there's a c. in the air** le fond de l'air est frais
2 *adj* froid(e), glacé(e)
3 *vt (wine, food)* mettre au frais; *(of wind)* glacer; **serve chilled** *(on product)* servir frais

►**chill out** *vi Fam* se détendre; **c. out!** on se calme!

chilli ['tʃɪlɪ] *(pl* **chillis** or **chillies***) n (dish)* chili *m* con carne; **c. (pepper)** piment *m* (rouge); **c. powder** piment en poudre

chilling ['tʃɪlɪŋ] *adj (frightening)* à vous donner le frisson

chilly ['tʃɪlɪ] *adj also Fig* froid(e)

chime [tʃaɪm] **1** *n (of bells)* carillon *m*
2 *vt* **the clock chimed nine o'clock** le carillon de l'horloge sonna neuf heures
3 *vi (of clock, bells)* carillonner

►**chime in** *vi Fam (in conversation)* intervenir

chimney ['tʃɪmnɪ] *(pl* **chimneys***) n* cheminée *f*; *Fam* **to smoke like a c.** *(of person)* fumer comme un pompier; **c. sweep** ramoneur *m*

chimneypot ['tʃɪmnɪpɒt] *n* tuyau *m* de cheminée

chimpanzee [tʃɪmpæn'ziː], *Fam* **chimp** [tʃɪmp] *n* chimpanzé *m*

chin [tʃɪn] *n* menton *m*; *Fig* **to keep one's c. up** tenir bon, tenir le coup

China ['tʃaɪnə] *n* la Chine

china ['tʃaɪnə] *n* porcelaine *f*; **c. clay** kaolin *m*

Chinese [tʃaɪ'niːz] **1** *npl* **the C.** *(people)* les Chinois *mpl*
2 *n* (**a**) *(person)* Chinois(e) *m,f* (**b**) *(language)* chinois *m*
3 *adj* chinois(e)

Chink [tʃɪŋk] *n Fam* Chinetoque *mf*, = terme raciste désignant un Chinois

chink¹ [tʃɪŋk] *n (gap)* fente *f*, lézarde *f*; *Fig* **to find a c. in sb's armour** trouver le talon d'Achille de qn

chink² **1** *n (sound)* tintement *m*
2 *vt (coins, glasses)* faire tinter
3 *vi* tinter

chintz [tʃɪnts] *n* chintz *m*

chinwag ['tʃɪnwæg] *n Fam* **to have a c.** tailler une bavette

chip [tʃɪp] **1** *n* (**a**) *(of wood, glass)* éclat *m*; *(in plate, cup)* ébréchure *f*; **this cup has a c. in it** cette tasse est ébréchée
(**b**) **chips** *Br (French fries)* frites *fpl*; *Am (crisps)* (pommes *fpl*) chips *mpl*, *Can* croustilles *fpl*; *Br* **c. shop** = petite boutique où l'on vend du poisson pané et frit, accompagné de frites
(**c**) *(in gambling)* jeton *m*
(**d**) *Comput* puce *f*
(**e**) *(idioms)* **he's a c. off the old block** c'est son père tout craché; **to have a c. on one's shoulder** en vouloir à tout le monde; *Fam* **when the chips are down** dans les moments critiques; *Fam* **he's had his chips** *(it's too late for him)* il est cuit *ou* fichu
2 *vt (pt & pp* **chipped***)* (**a**) *(cut at) (stone, wood)* tailler; *(damage) (knife, plate)* ébrécher; *(furniture)* écorner; **to c. one's tooth** se casser un petit bout de dent
(**b**) *(in sport)* **to c. the ball** frapper la balle par en dessous
3 *vi (of plate, cup)* s'ébrécher

►**chip in** *vi Fam (give money)* participer; **to c. in with a suggestion** intervenir pour faire une suggestion

chipboard ['tʃɪpbɔːd] *n* aggloméré *m*

chipmunk ['tʃɪpmʌŋk] *n* tamia *m* rayé, *Can* suisse *m*

chiropodist [kɪ'rɒpədɪst] *n* pédicure *mf*

chiropody [kɪ'rɒpədɪ] *n* pédicurie *f*

chirp [tʃɜːp] **1** *n (of birds)* gazouillis *m*, pépiement *m*; *(of grasshopper)* chant *m*
2 *vt & vi (of bird)* gazouiller, pépier; *(of grasshopper)* chanter

chirpy ['tʃɜːpɪ] *adj* d'humeur joyeuse

chirrup ['tʃɪrəp] = **chirp**

chisel ['tʃɪzəl] **1** *n (tool)* ciseau *m*; *(for sculpture)* burin *m*
2 *vt (pt & pp* **chiselled**, *Am* **chiseled***)* (**a**) *(in woodwork, sculpture)* ciseler; *Fig* **chiselled features** visage délicatement ciselé (**b**) *very Fam (cheat)* rouler

chit [tʃɪt] *n* (**a**) *(memo, note)* note *f*; *(voucher)* bon *m* (**b**) *Fam Old-fashioned Pej* **a c. of a girl** une gamine

chitchat ['tʃɪttʃæt] *n Fam* bavardage *m*, papotage *m*

chivalrous ['ʃɪvəlrəs] *adj* chevaleresque; *(towards women)* galant(e)

chivalry ['ʃɪvəlrɪ] *n (courteous behaviour)* courtoisie *f*; *(towards women)* galanterie *f*; *Hist* chevalerie *f*

chives [tʃaɪvz] *npl* ciboulette *f*

chiv(v)y ['tʃɪvɪ] *(pt & pp* **chiv(v)ied***) vt Br Fam* harceler; **to c. sb into doing sth** harceler qn jusqu'à ce qu'il fasse qch; **to c. sb along** faire se presser qn

chloride ['klɔːraɪd] *n Chem* chlorure *m*

chlorinate ['klɔːrɪneɪt] *vt* chlorer

chlorine ['klɔːriːn] *n Chem* chlore *m*

chloroform ['klɒrəfɔːm] *n Chem* chloroforme *m*

chlorophyl(l) ['klɒrəfɪl] *n Biol* chlorophylle *f*

choc-ice ['tʃɒkaɪs] *n* = glace individuelle rectangulaire enrobée de chocolat

chock [tʃɒk] *n (for wheel of car, plane)* cale *f*

chock-a-block ['tʃɒkə'blɒk] *adj Br Fam* plein(e) à craquer

chocolate ['tʃɒklət] **1** *n* chocolat *m*; **hot c.** chocolat chaud
2 *adj (made of chocolate)* en chocolat; *(chocolate-flavoured)* au chocolat; **c. (coloured)** chocolat *inv*

choice [tʃɔɪs] **1** *n* choix *m*; **to make a c.** choisir, faire un choix; **you have no c.** vous n'avez pas le choix; **I had no c. but to leave** je ne pouvais que partir; **there isn't much c.** il n'y a pas grand choix; **available in a wide c. of colours** disponible dans une large gamme de coloris
2 *adj* (**a**) *(well chosen)* choisi(e); **she used some c. language** *(offensive)* elle a juré comme un charretier (**b**) *(food)* de choix; *(wine)* fin(e)

choir ['kwaɪə(r)] *n* chœur *m*

choirboy ['kwaɪəbɔɪ] *n* jeune choriste *m*

choke [tʃəʊk] **1** *n* *(of car)* starter *m*
2 *vt* (**a**) *(strangle)* étrangler (**b**) *(block) (sink, road)* boucher
3 *vi* s'étrangler; **to c. with anger** s'étrangler de colère; **she choked on a fishbone** elle a failli s'étouffer en avalant une arête

▶**choke back** *vt sep (tears, words, anger)* ravaler

choker ['tʃəʊkə(r)] *n (necklace)* collier *m* (court)

cholera ['kɒlərə] *n* choléra *m*

cholesterol [kə'lestərɒl] *n* cholestérol *m*

choose [tʃuːz] *(pt* **chose** [tʃəʊz], *pp* **chosen** ['tʃəʊzən])
1 *vt* choisir; **to c. to do sth** choisir de faire qch; **there's not much to c. between them** ils se valent
2 *vi* choisir (**between** entre); **I'll do as I c.** je ferai comme il me plaît

choosy ['tʃuːzɪ] *adj Fam* difficile

chop [tʃɒp] **1** *n* (**a**) *(with axe)* coup *m*; *Fam* **to get the c.** *(get sacked)* se faire sacquer (**b**) *(of lamb, pork)* côtelette *f*
2 *vt (pt & pp* **chopped***) (wood)* couper; *(meat, vegetables)* couper en morceaux; *(finely)* hacher
3 *vi* **to c. and change** changer sans cesse; **he's always chopping and changing** il change d'avis comme de chemise

▶**chop down** *vt sep (tree)* abattre

▶**chop off** *vt sep* trancher, couper; **to c. sb's head off** couper la tête à qn

chopper ['tʃɒpə(r)] *n* (**a**) *(cleaver)* couperet *m*; *(axe)* hachette *f* (**b**) *Fam (helicopter)* hélico *m*

chopping ['tʃɒpɪŋ] *n* **c. block** *(of butcher)* billot *m*; **c. board** planche *f* (à découper)

choppy ['tʃɒpɪ] *adj (sea, lake)* agité(e)

chopsticks ['tʃɒpstɪks] *npl* baguettes *fpl*

choral ['kɔːrəl] *adj* choral(e); **c. society** chorale *f*

chord [kɔːd] *n* (**a**) *Mus* accord *m*; *Fig* **her speech struck a c. with the electorate** son discours a trouvé un écho auprès des électeurs (**b**) *Math (of arc)* corde *f*

chore [tʃɔː(r)] *n* (**a**) **chores** *(in household)* travaux *mpl* ménagers (**b**) *(unwelcome task)* corvée *f*

choreograph ['kɒrɪəgrɑːf] *vt* faire la chorégraphie de; *Fig* orchestrer

choreographer [kɒrɪ'ɒgrəfə(r)] *n* chorégraphe *mf*

choreography [kɒrɪ'ɒgrəfɪ] *n* chorégraphie *f*

chorister ['kɒrɪstə(r)] *n* choriste *mf*

chortle ['tʃɔːtəl] **1** *n* gloussement *m* (de joie)
2 *vi* glousser (de joie)

chorus ['kɔːrəs] **1** *n* (**a**) *(of song)* refrain *m* (**b**) *(group of singers, actors)* chœur *m*; *Fig* **a c. of protest** un concert de protestations; **c. girl** danseuse *f* de revue
2 *vt* dire en chœur

chose [tʃəʊz] *pt of* **choose**

chosen ['tʃəʊzən] **1** *adj* choisi(e); **the c. few** les heureux élus *mpl*; **the C. people** le peuple élu
2 *pp of* **choose**

Christ [kraɪst] **1** *n* le Christ *m*, Jésus-Christ *m*
2 *exclam very Fam* bon Dieu!; **C. Almighty!** nom de Dieu!

christen ['krɪsən] *vt (name)* baptiser

christening ['krɪsənɪŋ] *n* baptême *m*

Christian ['krɪstʃən] **1** *n* chrétien(enne) *m,f*; **to be a C.** être chrétien
2 *adj* chrétien(enne); **C. name** prénom *m*

Christianity [krɪstɪ'ænɪtɪ] *n* christianisme *m*

Christmas ['krɪsməs] *n* Noël *m*; **at C.** à Noël; **Merry** *or* **Happy C.!** joyeux Noël!; **C. cake** gâteau *m* de Noël *(aux fruits secs)*; **C. card** carte *f* de Noël; **C. carol** chant *m* de Noël; **C. Day** jour *m* de Noël; **C. Eve** veille *f* de Noël; **C. pudding** pudding *m* (de Noël); **C. tree** sapin *m* de Noël

chrome [krəʊm] *adj* chromé(e)

chromium ['krəʊmɪəm] *n Chem* chrome *m*

chromosome ['krəʊməsəʊm] *n Biol* chromosome *m*

chronic ['krɒnɪk] *adj* (**a**) *(invalid, illness, unemployment)* chronique (**b**) *Fam (bad)* atroce

chronicle ['krɒnɪkəl] **1** *n* chronique *f*; *Fig (of disasters)* suite *f*
2 *vt* faire la chronique de

chronological [krɒnə'lɒdʒɪkəl] *adj* chronologique

chronology [krə'nɒlədʒɪ] *n* chronologie *f*

chrysalis ['krɪsəlɪs] *n Zool* chrysalide *f*

chrysanthemum [krɪ'sænθəməm] *n* chrysanthème *m*

chubby ['tʃʌbɪ] *adj* potelé(e), dodu(e); *(face)* joufflu(e); **c.-cheeked** joufflu

chuck [tʃʌk] *vt Fam* (**a**) *(throw)* lancer, balancer (**b**) *(boyfriend, girlfriend)* plaquer; **to get chucked** se faire plaquer

▶**chuck away** *vt sep Fam* balancer; *Fig (opportunity)* foutre en l'air

▶**chuck out** *vt sep Fam (throw away)* balancer; *(from house, school, club)* vider

chuckle ['tʃʌkəl] **1** *n* petit rire *m*
2 *vi* rire tout bas

chuffed [tʃʌft] *adj Br Fam* tout(e) content(e) (**about** de)

chug [tʃʌg] *(pt & pp* **chugged***) vi (train)* haleter; *Fam* **he's still chugging along in the same job** il a toujours le même boulot pépère

chum [tʃʌm] *n Fam* copain (copine) *m,f*

chummy ['tʃʌmɪ] *adj Fam* copain (copine); **to be a bit too c.** être un peu trop familier(ère)

chump [tʃʌmp] *n Fam* (**a**) *(foolish person)* idiot(e) *m,f* (**b**) **to be off one's c.** être timbré(e)

chunk [tʃʌŋk] *n* gros morceau *m*; *(of bread)* quignon *m*; *(of time)* partie *f*

chunky ['tʃʌŋkɪ] *adj* (**a**) *(well-built)* bien bâti(e); *(fat)* grassouillet(ette); *(sweater)* gros (grosse) (**b**) *(stew, soup)* avec des morceaux

church [tʃɜːtʃ] *n* (**a**) *(building)* église *f*; *(French Protestant)* temple *m*; **to go to c.** aller à l'église/au temple; **c. hall** salle *f* paroissiale (**b**) *(institution)* **the C. of England** l'Église *f* anglicane; **the C. of Scotland** l'Église d'Écosse

churchgoer ['tʃɜːtʃgəʊə(r)] *n* pratiquant(e) *m,f*

churchyard ['tʃɜːtʃjɑːd] *n* cimetière *m*

churlish ['tʃɜːlɪʃ] *adj (rude)* grossier(ère); *(surly)* revêche

churn [tʃɜːn] **1** *n (for making butter)* baratte *f*; *(for milk)* bidon *m* à lait

2 *vt (butter)* battre; **the propeller churned up the water** l'eau bouillonnait sous l'action des hélices

3 *vi* **my stomach's churning** *(because of nervousness)* j'ai l'estomac noué

►**churn out** *vt sep Fam (books)* pondre (en série); *(goods)* produire en série

chute [ʃuːt] *n* (**a**) *(for parcels)* glissière *f*; **(rubbish) c.** vide-ordures *m inv* (**b**) *(in swimming pool, playground)* toboggan *m* (**c**) *Fam (parachute)* parachute *m*

chutney ['tʃʌtnɪ] *n* chutney *m*

CIA [siːaɪ'eɪ] *n Am (abbr* **Central Intelligence Agency)** CIA *f*

cicada [sɪ'kɑːdə] *n* cigale *f*

CID [siːaɪ'diː] *n Br (abbr* **Criminal Investigation Department)** ≃ P.J.

cider ['saɪdə(r)] *n* cidre *m*; **c. apple** pomme *f* à cidre; **c. vinegar** vinaigre *m* de cidre

cigar [sɪ'gɑː(r)] *n* cigare *m*

cigarette [sɪgə'ret] *n* cigarette *f*; **c. ash** cendre *f* de cigarette; **c. butt** *or* **end** mégot *m*; **c. case** étui *m* à cigarettes; **c. holder** fume-cigarette *m inv*; **c. lighter** briquet *m*; *(in car)* allume-cigare *m*; **c. machine** distributeur *m* automatique de cigarettes; **c. packet** paquet *m* de cigarettes; **c. paper** papier *m* à cigarettes

C-in-C [siːɪn'siː] *n Mil & Naut (abbr* **Commander-in-Chief)** commandant *m* en chef

cinch [sɪntʃ] *n Fam* **it's a c.** c'est un jeu d'enfant

cinder ['sɪndə(r)] *n* **cinders** cendres *fpl*; **burnt to a c.** complètement carbonisé(e)

Cinderella [sɪndə'relə] *n* Cendrillon

cine ['sɪnɪ] *pref* **c. camera** caméra *f*; **c. film** pellicule *f*

cinema ['sɪnəmə] *n* cinéma *m*; **to go to the c.** aller au cinéma

cinnamon ['sɪnəmən] *n* cannelle *f*

cipher ['saɪfə(r)] *n (code)* chiffre *m*, code *m*; *Fig* **he's a mere c.** c'est un zéro

circa ['sɜːkə] *prep (of time)* aux alentours de; *(of amount)* environ

circle ['sɜːkəl] **1** *n* (**a**) *(shape)* cercle *m*; **to sit in a c.** s'asseoir en cercle; *Fig* **to go round in circles** tourner en rond (**b**) *(movement)* **to come full c.** revenir à son point de départ (**c**) *(in theatre)* balcon *m*; **lower/ upper c.** premier/deuxième balcon (**d**) *(group)* cercle *m*, groupe *m*; **in certain circles** dans certains milieux

2 *vt* (**a**) *(go round)* tourner autour de (**b**) *(surround)* entourer (**with** de)

3 *vi (of plane, birds)* tourner, décrire des cercles

circuit ['sɜːkɪt] *n* (**a**) *(electric)* circuit *m*; **c. breaker** disjoncteur *m* (**b**) *(in motor racing) (course)* circuit *m*; *(lap)* tour *m*

circuitous [sə'kjuːɪtəs] *adj (route)* détourné(e); *(reasoning)* alambiqué(e)

circular ['sɜːkjʊlə(r)] **1** *n (letter)* circulaire *f*; *(advertisement)* prospectus *m*

2 *adj (movement, argument)* circulaire

circulate ['sɜːkjʊleɪt] **1** *vt* faire circuler

2 *vi* circuler

circulation [sɜːkjʊ'leɪʃən] *n (of air, blood, money)* circulation *f*; *(of newspaper)* tirage *m*; **for internal c. only** *(document)* à usage interne uniquement; *Fig* **to be out of c.** *(of person)* disparaître de la circulation

circumcise ['sɜːkəmsaɪz] *vt (boy)* circoncire; *(girl)* exciser

circumcision [sɜːkəm'sɪʒən] *n* circoncision *f*; **female c.** excision *f*

circumference [sə'kʌmfərəns] *n* circonférence *f*

circumflex ['sɜːkəmfleks] *n* accent *m* circonflexe

circumlocution [sɜːkəmlə'kjuːʃən] *n* circonlocution *f*, périphrase *f*

circumnavigate [sɜːkəm'nævɪgeɪt] *vt* **to c. sth** faire le tour de qch en bateau

circumscribe ['sɜːkəmskraɪb] *vt (limit)* limiter

circumspect ['sɜːkəmspekt] *adj* circonspect(e)

circumstances ['sɜːkəmstənsɪz] *npl* circonstances *fpl*; **in** *or* **under the c.** étant donné les circonstances; **in** *or* **under no c.** en aucun cas, sous aucun prétexte; **due to c. beyond our control** en raison de circonstances indépendantes de notre volonté

circumstantial [sɜːkəm'stænʃəl] *adj* **c. evidence** preuves *fpl* indirectes

circumvent [sɜːkəm'vent] *vt (law, rule)* contourner

circus ['sɜːkəs] *n* cirque *m*

cirrhosis [sɪ'rəʊsɪs] *n Med* cirrhose *f*

cissy ['sɪsɪ] *(pl* **cissies)** *n Fam* poule *f* mouillée

cistern ['sɪstən] *n* citerne *f*; *(in lavatory)* réservoir *m* de chasse d'eau

citadel ['sɪtədel] *n* citadelle *f*

citation [saɪ'teɪʃən] *n* citation *f*

cite [saɪt] *vt* citer

citizen ['sɪtɪzən] *n* citoyen(enne) *m,f*; *(of city)* habitant(e) *m,f*; **c.'s band (radio)** citizen band *f*

citizenship ['sɪtɪzənʃɪp] *n* citoyenneté *f*

citric acid ['sɪtrɪk'æsɪd] *n* acide *m* citrique

citrus fruit ['sɪtrəsfruːt] *n* agrumes *mpl*; **a c.** un agrume

city ['sɪtɪ] *(pl* **cities)** *n* (grande) ville *f*; *Br* **the C.** la City *(quartier des affaires de Londres)*; **c. centre** centre-ville *m*

> ### City
> La City, quartier financier de la capitale, est une circonscription administrative autonome de Londres ayant sa propre police.

civic ['sɪvɪk] *adj (duty, pride)* civique; *(building, authorities)* municipal(e); **c. centre** salle *f* municipale

civil ['sɪvəl] *adj* (**a**) *(of society)* civil(e); **c. aviation** aviation *f* civile; **c. defence** protection *f* civile; **c. disobedience** résistance *f* passive; **c. engineering** génie *m* civil; **c. law** *(subject)* droit *m* civil; **c. liberties** libertés *fpl* civiques; *Law* **c. rights** droits civils; **c. servant** fonctionnaire *mf*; **the c. service** la fonction publique; **c. war** guerre *f* civile (**b**) *(polite)* poli(e)

civilian [sɪ'vɪljən] **1** *n* civil *m*

2 *adj* civil(e)

civility [sɪ'vɪlɪtɪ] *(pl* **civilities)** *n* politesse *f*

civilization [sɪvɪlaɪ'zeɪʃən] *n* civilisation *f*

civilize ['sɪvɪlaɪz] *vt* civiliser

civilized ['sɪvɪlaɪzd] *adj* civilisé(e); **their divorce was very c.** leur divorce s'est passé sans heurts

CJD [siːdʒeɪ'diː] *n Med (abbr* **Creutzfeld-Jakob disease)** MJC *f*; **new variant CJD** nouveau variant *m* de MJC

cl *(abbr* **centilitre)** cl

clad [klæd] *adj* **c. in** vêtu(e) de

claim [kleɪm] **1** *n* (**a**) *(demand) (for damages, compensation)* demande *f* d'indemnisation; *(as a right)* revendication *f*; **to lay c. to sth** revendiquer qch; **I have many claims on my time** je suis très pris; **it's his only**

c. to fame c'est la seule façon dont il se soit distingué; **the town's only c. to fame** la seule chose pour laquelle cette ville soit connue (**b**) *(assertion)* déclaration *f*; **she makes no c. to originality** elle ne prétend pas être originale **2** *vt* (**a**) *(as a right)* revendiquer; **to c. damages (from sb)** réclamer des dommages et intérêts (à qn); **to c. responsibility for sth** revendiquer qch (**b**) *(assert)* **to c. that...** affirmer que...; **he claims to be an expert** il prétend être un expert (**c**) *(lost property)* réclamer (**d**) *(life)* **the epidemic has claimed thousands of lives** l'épidémie a fait des milliers de victimes

claimant ['kleɪmənt] *n (to throne)* prétendant(e) *m,f*; *Law (for social security, insurance)* demandeur(-eresse) *m,f*

clairvoyant [kleə'vɔɪənt] **1** *n* voyant(e) *m,f* **2** *adj* extralucide

clam [klæm] *n* palourde *f*

▶**clam up** *(pt & pp* **clammed**) *vi Fam* se fermer comme une huître

clamber ['klæmbə(r)] *vi* **to c. up sth** escalader qch

clammy ['klæmɪ] *adj* moite

clamorous ['klæmərəs] *adj* bruyant(e)

clamour ['klæmə(r)] **1** *n (noise)* clameur *f*; *(protest)* tollé *m* **2** *vi* **to c. for sth** réclamer qch à grands cris

clamp [klæmp] **1** *n (tool)* serre-joint *m*; *(fixed to bench)* étau *m*; *Med* clamp *m*; **(wheel) c.** sabot *m* (de Denver) **2** *vt (fasten)* fixer; *(car)* mettre un sabot à

▶**clamp down on** *vt insep* faire la chasse à

clampdown ['klæmpdaʊn] *n* répression *f* (**on** de); **a c. on crime** un plan de lutte contre la criminalité

clan [klæn] *n also Fig* clan *m*

clandestine [klæn'destɪn] *adj* clandestin(e)

clang [klæŋ] **1** *n* bruit *m* métallique **2** *vi (of bell)* retentir; **the gate clanged shut** le portail se ferma avec un bruit métallique

clanger ['klæŋə(r)] *n Fam* gaffe *f*; **to drop a c.** faire une gaffe

clank [klæŋk] **1** *n* bruit *m* métallique **2** *vi* cliqueter

clap [klæp] **1** *n* (**a**) *(with hands)* **to give sb a c.** applaudir qn; **a c. of thunder** un coup de tonnerre (**b**) *very Fam* **the c.** la chaude-pisse **2** *vt (pt & pp* **clapped**) (**a**) *(applaud)* applaudir; **to c. one's hands** applaudir; *(once)* frapper dans ses mains; **to c. sb on the back** donner une tape sur le dos à qn (**b**) *(put)* **he clapped his hat on** il enfonça son chapeau sur sa tête; *Fam* **to c. sb in prison** coller qn en prison; *Fam* **to c. eyes on sb/sth** voir qn/qch; **I've never clapped eyes on her before** je ne l'ai jamais vue de ma vie **3** *vi (applaud)* applaudir

clapped-out ['klæpt'aʊt] *adj Fam (car, machine)* déglingué(e)

clapper ['klæpə(r)] *n (of bell)* battant *m*; *Fam* **to run like the clappers** courir à toutes jambes

clapping ['klæpɪŋ] *n (applause)* applaudissements *mpl*

claptrap ['klæptræp] *n Fam* bêtises *fpl*

claret ['klærət] *n* bordeaux *m* (rouge)

clarification [klærɪfɪ'keɪʃən] *n* clarification *f*, éclaircissement *m*

clarify ['klærɪfaɪ] *(pt & pp* **clarified**) *vt* clarifier, éclaircir

clarinet [klærɪ'net] *n* clarinette *f*

clarity ['klærɪtɪ] *n* clarté *f*

clash [klæʃ] **1** *n* (**a**) *(of opinions, interests)* conflit *m*; *(between people, armies)* affrontement *m* (**b**) *(of metal objects)* fracas *m* **2** *vi* (**a**) *(come into conflict)* s'affronter; **to c. with sb** affronter qn; **police clashed with protesters** il y a eu des heurts entre la police et les manifestants (**b**) *(of evidence, explanations)* ne pas correspondre; *(of colours)* jurer (**c**) *(of events)* **to c. with** tomber en même temps que (**d**) *(of metal objects)* s'entrechoquer

clasp [klɑːsp] **1** *n (on necklace, handbag)* fermoir *m*; **c. knife** canif *m* **2** *vt (grip)* serrer; *(embrace)* étreindre; **to c. sb's hand** serrer la main à qn

class [klɑːs] **1** *n (in school, category, social group)* classe *f*; **to be in a c. of one's own** être insurpassable; **c. struggle** lutte *f* des classes **2** *vt (classify)* classer (**as** parmi)

classic ['klæsɪk] **1** *n* (**a**) *(book, film etc)* classique *m* (**b**) *Sch & Univ* **classics** lettres *fpl* classiques **2** *adj* classique

classical ['klæsɪkəl] *adj* classique; **c. music** musique *f* classique

classification [klæsɪfɪ'keɪʃən] *n* classification *f*; *(of students)* classement *m*

classified ['klæsɪfaɪd] **1** *n* **the classifieds** *(in newspaper)* les petites annonces *fpl* **2** *adj* (**a**) *(secret)* confidentiel(elle) (**b**) **c. advertisements** *(in newspaper)* petites annonces *fpl*

classify ['klæsɪfaɪ] *(pt & pp* **classified**) *vt* classer

classmate ['klɑːsmeɪt] *n* camarade *mf* de classe

classroom ['klɑːsruːm] *n (salle f de)* classe *f*

classy ['klɑːsɪ] *adj Fam* qui a de la classe; *(bar)* chic

clatter ['klætə(r)] **1** *n (of shoes)* claquement *m*; *(of dishes)* fracas *m* **2** *vi* **the car clattered along the road** la voiture descendit la rue dans un bruit de ferraille; **to c. about** *(of person)* s'activer bruyamment

clause [klɔːz] *n (of contract)* clause *f*; *Gram* proposition *f*

claustrophobia [klɔːstrə'fəʊbɪə] *n* claustrophobie *f*

claustrophobic [klɔːstrə'fəʊbɪk] *adj (person)* claustrophobe; *(place, situation)* où l'on se sent claustrophobe

clavicle ['klævɪkəl] *n* clavicule *f*

claw [klɔː] **1** *n (of animal)* griffe *f*; *(of bird of prey)* serre *f*; *(of crab, lobster)* pince *f*; **c. hammer** arrache-clou *m* **2** *vt (scratch)* griffer; *Fig* **to c. one's way to the top** parvenir au sommet à force de travail

▶**claw back** *vt (money)* récupérer

clay [kleɪ] *n* argile *f*, *(terre f)* glaise *f*; **c. court** *(for tennis)* court *m* en terre battue; **c. pigeon** pigeon *m* d'argile; **c. pigeon shooting** ball-trap *m*

clean [kliːn] **1** *n* **to give sth a c.** nettoyer qch **2** *adj* (**a**) *(not dirty)* propre; *(piece of paper)* blanc (blanche); **a c. game/fight** un jeu/une bataille dans les règles; **c. living** vie *f* saine; **to have a c. driving licence** avoir tous ses points sur son permis de conduire (**b**) *(not obscene)* décent(e); **it's good c. fun** c'est innocent (**c**) *(clear) (shape, outline)* net (nette); **to make a c. break** *(of couple)* rompre une bonne fois pour toutes **3** *adv* (**a**) *(completely)* **to cut c. through sth** couper qch net; *Fam* **I c. forgot** j'ai complètement oublié (**b**) *Fam* **to come c.** dire la vérité

4 *vt* nettoyer; **to c. one's teeth/hands** se laver les dents/mains

▶**clean out** *vt sep* (**a**) *(cupboard, room)* nettoyer à fond (**b**) *Fam (leave without money)* nettoyer, plumer

▶**clean up 1** *vt sep* nettoyer
2 *vi* (**a**) *(tidy up)* nettoyer; *(wash oneself)* se laver (**b**) *Fam (win money)* toucher un gros paquet

clean-cut ['kli:n'kʌt] *adj (features)* net (nette), bien dessiné(e); *(person)* à l'apparence très soignée

cleaner ['kli:nə(r)] *n (person)* agent *m* de service; *(substance)* produit *m* de nettoyage; **c.'s** *(shop)* pressing *m*; *Fam Fig* **to take sb to the c.'s** *(cheat)* nettoyer *ou* plumer qn

cleaning ['kli:nɪŋ] *n* nettoyage *m*; *(housework)* ménage *m*; **c. lady** femme *f* de ménage

cleanliness ['klenlɪnɪs] *n (of place, person)* propreté *f*

cleanly ['kli:nlɪ] *adv* proprement; *(fight)* dans les règles

cleanse [klenz] *vt* nettoyer; *(skin)* démaquiller

cleanser ['klenzə(r)] *n (for skin)* démaquillant *m*

clean-shaven ['kli:n'ʃeɪvən] *adj* rasé(e) de près

cleansing lotion ['klenzɪŋləʊʃən] *n* lait *m* démaquillant

clear [klɪə(r)] **1** *n* **to be in the c.** *(not under suspicion)* être lavé(e) de tout soupçon; *(out of danger)* être hors de danger
2 *adj* (**a**) *(liquid, image, directions)* clair(e); *(picture)* net (nette); *(glass)* transparent(e); *(skin)* net; **on a c. day** par temps clair; **all c.!** la voie est libre!; **to have a c. conscience** avoir la conscience tranquille; **as c. as a bell** *(of voice, sound)* cristallin(e); **c. profit** bénéfice *m* net; **c. winner** vainqueur *m* incontesté
(**b**) *(obvious)* clair(e), évident(e); **to make it c. to sb that...** bien faire comprendre à qn que...; **it is c. that...** il est clair *ou* évident que...; **to make oneself c.** se faire comprendre; **I wasn't c. what she meant** je n'étais pas sûr d'avoir parfaitement compris ce qu'elle voulait dire
(**c**) *(space, road, passageway)* libre
(**d**) **to be c. of sth** *(rid of)* être débarrassé(e) de qch
3 *adv* **to steer c. of** éviter; **stand c. of the doors!** attention à la fermeture automatique des portières!
4 *vt* (**a**) *(road, area)* dégager; **the police cleared the square of demonstrators** la police a forcé les manifestants à évacuer la place; **to c. one's throat** se racler la gorge; **to c. the table** débarrasser la table; **to c. a debt** s'acquitter d'une dette; *Fig* **to c. the decks** déblayer le terrain; *Fig* **to c. the way for sth** ouvrir la voie à qch; *Fig* **to c. the air** *(ease tension)* détendre l'atmosphère; *(clarify matters)* mettre les choses au point
(**b**) *(exonerate)* disculper, innocenter; **to c. sb of blame** disculper qn; **to c. sb's name** blanchir (le nom de) qn
(**c**) *(jump over)* sauter, franchir
(**d**) *(authorize) (proposal, request)* approuver; **I'll need to c. it with the boss** il faut que j'obtienne la permission du patron
5 *vi* (**a**) *(of weather)* s'éclaircir; *(of sky)* se dégager; *(of fog)* se lever
(**b**) *(of cheque)* **the cheque hasn't cleared yet** le chèque n'a pas encore été viré

▶**clear away** *vt sep (dishes)* ranger; *(obstruction)* enlever

▶**clear off** *vi Br Fam (leave)* filer, se tirer

▶**clear out 1** *vt sep (cupboard)* vider; *(garage, shed)* débarrasser
2 *vi Fam (leave)* filer, se tirer

▶**clear up 1** *vt sep* (**a**) *(room)* ranger (**b**) *(doubt, misunderstanding)* dissiper; **to c. up a matter** tirer une affaire au clair
2 *vi (of weather)* s'éclaircir

clearance ['klɪərəns] *n* (**a**) *Com* **c. sale** liquidation *f* (**b**) *(authorization)* autorisation *f* (**c**) *(space)* espace *m* (libre)

clear-cut ['klɪə'kʌt] *adj (division, outline, feature)* net (nette); *(opinion)* tranché(e); **it's not as c. as that** ce n'est pas aussi simple que ça

clear-headed ['klɪə'hedɪd] *adj* lucide

clearing ['klɪərɪŋ] *n (in forest)* clairière *f*

clearing house ['klɪərɪŋhaʊs] *n Fin* chambre *f* de compensation

clearly ['klɪəlɪ] *adv* (**a**) *(explain, write)* clairement; *(see)* bien (**b**) *(obviously)* évidemment; **he is c. wrong** il est évident qu'il a tort

clearness ['klɪənɪs] *n* clarté *f*; *(of image)* netteté *f*

clearout ['klɪəraʊt] *n* **to have a c.** faire le nettoyage par le vide

clear-sighted ['klɪə'saɪtɪd] *adj (perceptive)* clairvoyant(e)

cleavage ['kli:vɪdʒ] *n (of woman)* décolleté *m*

cleave [kli:v] *(pt* **cleaved** *or* **cleft** [kleft] *or* **clove** [kləʊv], *pp* **cleaved** *or* **cleft** *or* **cloven** ['kləʊvən]) *vt Lit* fendre

▶**cleave to** *(pt & pp* **cleaved**) *vt insep Formal* être fidèle à

cleaver ['kli:və(r)] *n* hachoir *m*

clef [klef] *n Mus* clé *f*, clef *f*

cleft [kleft] **1** *n* fissure *f*
2 *adj* fendu(e); **c. palate** division *f* palatine; **to be caught in a c. stick** *(in awkward situation)* être entre le marteau et l'enclume
3 *pt & pp of* **cleave**

clemency ['klemənsɪ] *n* clémence *f*

clementine ['klemənti:n] *n* clémentine *f*

clench [klentʃ] *vt* **to c. one's fist/teeth** serrer le poing/les dents

Cleopatra ['kli:əʊ'pætrə] *n* Cléopâtre

clergy ['klɜ:dʒɪ] *n* clergé *m*

clergyman ['klɜ:dʒɪmən] *n* ecclésiastique *m*; *(Protestant)* pasteur *m*; *(Catholic)* prêtre *m*

cleric ['klerɪk] *n Rel* ecclésiastique *m*

clerical ['klerɪkəl] *adj* (**a**) *(administrative)* **c. assistant** employé(e) *m,f* de bureau; **c. work** travail *m* de bureau (**b**) *Rel* clérical(e)

clerk [klɑ:k, *Am* klɜ:rk] *n* (**a**) *(office worker)* employé(e) *m,f* de bureau (**b**) *Am (in shop)* vendeur(euse) *m,f*

clever ['klevə(r)] *adj (intelligent)* intelligent(e); *(plan, idea)* ingénieux(euse); **to be c. with one's hands** être adroit(e) de ses mains; *Br Fam* **to be too c. by half** être trop malin(igne); *Br Fam* **a c. Dick** un petit malin

cleverly ['klevəlɪ] *adv (intelligently)* intelligemment; *(planned)* ingénieusement

cleverness ['klevənɪs] *n (intelligence)* intelligence *f*; *(of plan)* ingéniosité *f*; *(skill)* adresse *f*

cliché ['kli:ʃeɪ] *n* cliché *m*

click [klɪk] **1** *n (sound)* petit bruit *m* sec
2 *vt* **to c. one's heels** claquer les talons; **to c. one's tongue** faire claquer sa langue
3 *vi* (**a**) *(make a sound)* faire un petit bruit sec (**b**)

Fam (become obvious) faire tilt; **it suddenly clicked** tout à coup ça a fait tilt (**c**) *Fam (of people)* **we clicked straight away** ça a accroché tout de suite entre nous

client ['klaɪənt] *n* client(e) *m,f*

clientele [kliːənˈtel] *n* clientèle *f*

cliff [klɪf] *n* falaise *f*

cliffhanger ['klɪfhæŋə(r)] *n* **it was a real c.** il y a eu du suspense jusqu'au bout

climactic [klaɪˈmæktɪk] *adj* qui constitue le point culminant

climate ['klaɪmət] *n* climat *m*

climatic [klaɪˈmætɪk] *adj* climatique

climax ['klaɪmæks] **1** *n (of series of events)* paroxysme *m; (of reign, career)* apogée *m; (of film, book)* point *m* culminant; *(sexual)* orgasme *m*
2 *vi (of series of events)* atteindre son paroxysme; *(of reign, career)* atteindre son apogée; *(of film, book)* atteindre son point culminant; *(sexually)* atteindre l'orgasme

climb [klaɪm] **1** *n* montée *f*, ascension *f*
2 *vt (tree)* grimper à; *(mountain)* faire l'ascension de; *(rock face)* escalader; *(stairs)* monter
3 *vi (of road, prices)* grimper; *(of plane)* prendre de l'altitude, monter; **to c. over sth** passer par-dessus qch
▶**climb down 1** *vt insep (descend)* descendre
2 *vi* (**a**) *(descend)* descendre (**b**) *Fig (in argument)* céder, en rabattre

climbdown ['klaɪmdaʊn] *n* dérobade *f*, reculade *f*

climber ['klaɪmə(r)] *n* (**a**) *(mountaineer)* alpiniste *mf* (**b**) *(plant)* plante *f* grimpante

climbing ['klaɪmɪŋ] **1** *n (hill-walking)* randonnée *f* en montagne; *(of rockface)* escalade *f; (mountaineering)* alpinisme *m*; **c. frame** cage *f* à poules
2 *adj (plant)* grimpant(e)

clinch [klɪntʃ] **1** *n (of fighters)* corps à corps *m; (of lovers)* étreinte *f*
2 *vt (settle) (deal)* conclure; *(argument)* résoudre; **that clinches it!** voilà qui règle le problème une fois pour toutes!

cling [klɪŋ] *(pt & pp* **clung** [klʌŋ] *)* **to c. to** *(rope, person)* s'accrocher à; *Fig (opinion)* persister dans; *(faith)* se raccrocher à

clingfilm ['klɪŋfɪlm] *n* film *m* alimentaire

clinic ['klɪnɪk] *n (part of hospital)* service *m; Br (private hospital)* clinique *f*

clinical ['klɪnɪkəl] *adj* (**a**) *Med* clinique (**b**) *(unemotional)* froid(e), aseptisé(e)

clink¹ [klɪŋk] **1** *n (sound)* tintement *m*
2 *vt* faire tinter; **to c. glasses with sb** trinquer avec qn
3 *vi (of glasses)* tinter

clink² *n very Fam (prison)* taule *f*

clip¹ [klɪp] **1** *n (for paper)* trombone *m; (for hair)* barrette *f*
2 *vt (pt & pp* **clipped**) *(paper)* attacher *(avec un trombone)* (**to** à)
3 *vi* **to c. together** s'emboîter

clip² *n* (**a**) *Fam (blow)* **to give sb a c. round the ear** flanquer une taloche à qn (**b**) *(of film, programme)* extrait *m; Comput* **c. art** clipart *m*
2 *(pt & pp* **clipped**) *vt* (**a**) *(hit)* **to c. sb round the ear** flanquer une taloche à qn (**b**) *(hedge)* tailler; *(ticket)* poinçonner; *(dog)* couper les poils à; *(hair, nails)* couper; *Fig* **to c. sb's wings** réduire la marge de manœuvre de qn

clipboard ['klɪpbɔːd] *n* planchette *f* porte-papiers *(à pince)*

clip-on ['klɪpɒn] *adj* **c. earring** clip *m*; **c. microphone** micro-cravate *m*; **c. sunglasses** = verres teintés que l'on fixe à une autre paire de lunettes

clipped [klɪpt] *adj (speech, tone)* saccadé(e)

clipper ['klɪpə(r)] *n (ship)* clipper *m*

clippers ['klɪpəz] *npl (for hair)* tondeuse *f; (for nails)* coupe-ongles *m inv; (for hedge)* cisaille *f*

clipping ['klɪpɪŋ] *n (from newspaper)* coupure *f*

clique [kliːk] *n* clique *f*

clitoris ['klɪtərɪs] *n* clitoris *m*

cloak [kləʊk] **1** *n* cape *f; Fig* **under the c. of darkness** sous le couvert de la nuit
2 *vt Fig* **cloaked in secrecy** enveloppé(e) de mystère

cloak-and-dagger [kləʊkənˈdæɡə(r)] *adj (film, book)* d'espionnage; *Fig (mysterious)* mystérieux(euse)

cloakroom ['kləʊkruːm] *n* vestiaire *m*

clobber¹ ['klɒbə(r)] *n Br Fam (clothes)* frusques *fpl*, fringues *fpl; (belongings)* barda *m*

clobber² *vt Fam (hit)* tabasser; *(defeat)* battre à plate couture

clock [klɒk] **1** *n* (**a**) *(large)* horloge *f; (small)* pendule *f*; **round the c.** vingt-quatre heures sur vingt-quatre; **a race against the c.** une course contre la montre; **to put the clocks forward/back** *(in spring, autumn)* avancer/retarder les pendules; *Fig* **to turn the c. back** revenir en arrière; **c. radio** radio-réveil *m* (**b**) *Fam (mileometer)* compteur *m* kilométrique
2 *vt (measure speed of)* chronométrer; *(reach speed of)* atteindre
▶**clock in** *vi* pointer *(en arrivant sur son lieu de travail)*
▶**clock off** *vi* pointer *(en quittant son lieu de travail)*
▶**clock on** = clock in
▶**clock out** = clock off
▶**clock up** *vt sep (profits)* réaliser; *(votes)* totaliser; **this car has clocked up 10,000 miles** cette voiture a 10 000 miles au compteur

clockmaker ['klɒkmeɪkə(r)] *n* horloger(ère) *m,f*

clockwise ['klɒkwaɪz] *adv* dans le sens des aiguilles d'une montre

clockwork ['klɒkwɜːk] **1** *n* **to go like c.** *(of interview, ceremony)* marcher comme sur des roulettes; **to run like c.** *(of office, system)* être réglé(e) comme du papier à musique
2 *adj (toy)* mécanique

clod [klɒd] *n (of earth)* motte *f*

clog [klɒɡ] **1** *n (shoe)* sabot *m*
2 *vt (pt & pp* **clogged**) *(block)* boucher
3 *vi* se boucher
▶**clog up 1** *vt sep* boucher
2 *vi* se boucher

cloister ['klɔɪstə(r)] *n* cloître *m*

cloistered ['klɔɪstəd] *adj* **to lead a c. life** mener une vie de reclus(e)

clone [kləʊn] **1** *n also Fig* clone *m*
2 *vt Biol* cloner

cloning ['kləʊnɪŋ] *n* clonage *m*

close¹ [kləʊs] **1** *adj* (**a**) *(in distance, time, relationship)* proche; **to be in c. contact with sb** être en contact étroit avec qn; **a c. friend** un ami intime; **a c. relative** un proche parent; **that was a c. call** *or* **shave** il s'en est fallu de peu; **at c. quarters** de près; **at c. range** de près; **c. combat** corps à corps *m*
(**b**) *(inspection)* minutieux(euse); *(attention)* soute-

nu(e); **to keep a c. watch on sb/sth** surveiller qn/qch de près
   (**c**) *(weather)* lourd(e); *(room)* qui sent le renfermé
   (**d**) *(contest, election)* serré(e)
   2 *n (cul-de-sac)* impasse *f*
   3 *adv (near)* près; **to hold sb c.** serrer qn; **c. to** près de; **c. to tears** au bord des larmes; **c. to victory** proche de la victoire; **to come c. to death** frôler la mort; **to be c. to sb** *(emotionally)* être proche de qn; **c. at hand** à proximité; **to follow c. behind sb** suivre qn de près; **to be c. on fifty** friser la cinquantaine; **c. up** de près
close² [kləʊz] **1** *n (end)* fin *f*; **to draw to a c.** tirer à sa fin; **to bring sth to a c.** clore qch
   2 *vt* (**a**) *(door, eyes, book, road)* fermer; *Fig* **to c. ranks around sb** faire bloc autour de qn (**b**) *(meeting, debate)* clore; *(account)* fermer; *(deal)* conclure (**c**) *(business, shop)* fermer
   3 *vi (of shop, business)* fermer; *(of door)* se fermer
▸**close down 1** *vt (production, operations)* cesser; *(business, factory)* fermer
   2 *vi (of business, factory)* fermer; **Channel 6 closes down at midnight** les émissions sur Channel 6 se terminent à minuit
▸**close in** *vi (of night)* tomber; **to c. in on sb** se rapprocher de qn
▸**close up 1** *vt sep (shop)* fermer
   2 *vi* (**a**) *(of wound, hole)* se refermer (**b**) *(of shopkeeper)* fermer
close-cropped [ˈkləʊsˈkrɒpt] *adj (hair)* coupé(e) ras
closed [kləʊzd] *adj* fermé(e); **c. circuit television** télévision *f* en circuit fermé; **behind c. doors** à huis clos; *Ind* **c. shop** – usine ou société qui n'embauche que des travailleurs syndiqués
close-fitting [ˈkləʊsˈfɪtɪŋ] *adj* bien ajusté(e)
close-knit [ˈkləʊsˈnɪt] *adj (community, group)* très soudé(e); *(family)* très uni(e)
closely [ˈkləʊslɪ] *adv* (**a**) *(examine, listen, watch)* attentivement; *(resemble)* beaucoup; **to be c. related** *(of concepts)* être étroitement liés(es); *(of people)* être proches parents; **c. contested** très serré(e) (**b**) *(populated)* densément; **c. packed** très serré(e)
closeness [ˈkləʊsnɪs] *n (physical proximity)* proximité *f*; *(of relationship, contact)* intimité *f*
close-run [ˈkləʊsˈrʌn] *adj (election, race)* serré(e)
close-set [ˈkləʊsˈset] *adj (eyes)* rapproché(e)
closet [ˈklɒzɪt] **1** *n* placard *m*; *Fig* **to come out of the c.** révéler son homosexualité
   2 *adj* **c. homosexual** = personne qui cache son homosexualité; *Hum* **he's a c. Gary Glitter fan** il n'ose pas avouer qu'il aime Gary Glitter
   3 *vt* enfermer; **to c. oneself away** s'enfermer, s'isoler
close-up [ˈkləʊsʌp] *n* gros plan *m*; **in c.** en gros plan
closing [ˈkləʊzɪŋ] *n* fermeture *f*; **c. date** date *f* limite; **c. prices** cours *mpl* de clôture; **c. speech** discours *m* de clôture; **c. time** heure *f* de fermeture
closure [ˈkləʊʒə(r)] *n (of company, shop)* fermeture *f* *(définitive)*
clot [klɒt] **1** *n* (**a**) *(of blood)* caillot *m* (**b**) *Fam (stupid person)* andouille *f*
   2 *vi (pt & pp* **clotted***) (of blood)* (se) coaguler
cloth [klɒθ] *n* (**a**) *(material)* tissu *m*; **a man of the c.** un membre du clergé (**b**) *(duster)* chiffon *m*
clothe [kləʊð] *(pt & pp* **clad** [klæd] *or* **clothed***) vt* vêtir, habiller

clothes [kləʊðz] *npl* vêtements *mpl*; **to put one's c. on** s'habiller; **to take one's c. off** se déshabiller; **c. brush** brosse *f* à habits; **c. hanger** cintre *m*; **c. horse** séchoir *m (à linge)*; **c. line** corde *f* à linge; **c. peg** pince *f* à linge; **c. rack** séchoir *m* (à linge)
clothing [ˈkləʊðɪŋ] *n (clothes)* vêtements *mpl*; **an article of c.** un vêtement; **the c. industry** l'industrie *f* du vêtement
clotted cream [ˈklɒtɪdˈkriːm] *n* = crème fraîche très épaisse, typique du sud-ouest de l'Angleterre
cloud [klaʊd] **1** *n* (**a**) *(in sky)* nuage *m*; *Fig (of insects)* nuée *f* (**b**) *(idioms)* **to be under a c.** être en disgrâce; **to have one's head in the clouds** être dans les nuages; *Fam* **to be on c. nine** être aux anges
   2 *vt* (**a**) *(mirror)* embuer (**b**) *(happiness)* jeter une ombre sur; *(judgement)* affecter; **to c. the issue** embrouiller la question
▸**cloud over** *vi (of sky)* se couvrir
cloudburst [ˈklaʊdbɜːst] *n* averse *f*
cloudless [ˈklaʊdlɪs] *adj* sans nuages
cloudy [ˈklaʊdɪ] *adj* (**a**) *(sky, day)* nuageux(euse) (**b**) *(liquid)* trouble
clout [klaʊt] *Fam* **1** *n* (**a**) *(blow)* coup *m*; **to give sb a c. (with sth)** frapper qn (avec qch) (**b**) *(power, influence)* influence *f*; **to have a lot of c.** avoir le bras long
   2 *vt (hit)* flanquer une taloche à
clove¹ [kləʊv] *n (of garlic)* gousse *f*
clove² *n (spice)* clou *m* de girofle
clove³ *pt of* **cleave**
cloven [ˈkləʊvən] **1** *adj* **c. hoof** sabot *m* fendu
   2 *pp of* **cleave**
clover [ˈkləʊvə(r)] *n* trèfle *m*; *Fig* **to be in c.** être comme un coq en pâte
clown [klaʊn] **1** *n* clown *m*; **to act the c.** faire le clown
   2 *vi* **to c. about** *or* **around** faire le clown
cloying [ˈklɔɪɪŋ] *adj (taste, smell)* écœurant(e)
club [klʌb] **1** *n* (**a**) *(society)* club *m*; *Fam Fig* **join the c.!** tu n'es pas le seul/la seule! (**b**) *(nightclub)* boîte *f* (de nuit) (**c**) *(weapon)* massue *f*, gourdin *m*; *(in golf)* club *m* (**d**) **clubs** *(in cards)* trèfle *m*; **ace of clubs** as *m* de trèfle
   2 *vt (pt & pp* **clubbed***) (hit)* frapper avec une massue
   3 *vi* **to go clubbing** aller en boîte
▸**club together** *vi* se cotiser (**to buy** pour acheter)

Clubs
Les "clubs" britanniques sont des lieux de rencontre et de détente très fermés, qui jouent un rôle important dans la vie sociale des milieux aisés en Grande-Bretagne. Traditionnellement ces institutions (notamment les "gentlemen's clubs" londoniens, tels que l'Athenaeum ou le Carlton Club) étaient interdites aux femmes, mais récemment cette tendance a commencé à changer.

---

clubhouse [ˈklʌbhaʊs] *n* pavillon *m*
cluck [klʌk] **1** *n* gloussement *m*
   2 *vi* glousser
clue [kluː] *n (in crime, mystery)* indice *m*; *(in crossword)* définition *f*; **to give sb a c.** donner un indice à qn, mettre qn sur la voie; **where's Lola? – I haven't a c.!** où est Lola? – je n'en ai pas la moindre idée!; *Fam* **he hasn't a c.** *(is incompetent)* il est vraiment nul
▸**clue up** *vt sep Fam* **to be clued up (on sth)** être très calé(e) (en qch)

clueless ['klu:lɪs] *adj Br Fam* nul (nulle)

clump [klʌmp] **1** *n* (**a**) *(of bushes)* massif *m*; *(of people)* groupe *m* (**b**) *(sound)* bruit *m* bref et sourd
2 *vi* **to c. about** marcher d'un pas lourd

clumsiness ['klʌmzɪnɪs] *n* *(of person, movement)* maladresse *f*

clumsy ['klʌmzɪ] *adj (person, movement)* maladroit(e)

clung [klʌŋ] *pt & pp of* **cling**

cluster ['klʌstə(r)] **1** *n* *(of grapes)* grappe *f*; *(of people, islands, houses)* groupe *m*
2 *vi* **to c. round sb/sth** se grouper autour de qn/qch

clutch¹ [klʌtʃ] **1** *n* (**a**) *(in car)* embrayage *m*; **to let the c. in/out** embrayer/débrayer; **c. pedal** pédale *f* d'embrayage (**b**) *(grasp)* **to fall into sb's clutches** tomber entre les griffes de qn
2 *vt* tenir fermement
3 *vi* **to c. at sth** s'agripper à qch; *Fig* **to c. at straws** se raccrocher à n'importe quoi

clutch² *n* *(of eggs)* couvée *f*

clutter ['klʌtə(r)] **1** *n* désordre *m*; **in a c.** en désordre
2 *vt* encombrer; **to be cluttered (up) with sth** être encombré(e) de qch

cluttered ['klʌtəd] *adj* encombré(e)

cm *n* *(abbr* **centimetre(s)**) cm

CNAA [si:eneɪ'eɪ] *n Br (abbr* **Council for National Academic Awards**) = organisme chargé de délivrer les diplômes dans les établissements d'enseignement supérieur non universitaires

CND [si:en'di:] *n Br (abbr* **Campaign for Nuclear Disarmament**) = mouvement prônant le désarmement nucléaire

CO [si:'əʊ] *n Mil (abbr* **Commanding Officer**) chef *m* de corps

Co, co [kəʊ] *n (abbr* **company**) Cie; *Fig* **Jane and co** Jane et compagnie

c/o [si:'əʊ] *(abbr* **care of**) chez, aux bons soins de

coach [kəʊtʃ] **1** *n* (**a**) *Br (bus)* car *m*; *(horse-drawn carriage)* carrosse *m*; *(section of train)* voiture *f*, wagon *m*; **c. party** excursionnistes *mpl (voyageant en car)*; **c. trip** excursion *f* en car (**b**) *(of athlete, team)* entraîneur(euse) *m,f*
2 *vt (athlete, team)* entraîner; **to c. sb for an exam** donner des leçons particulières à qn en préparation à un examen

coachbuilder ['kəʊtʃbɪldə(r)] *n Aut* carrossier *m*

coagulant [kəʊ'ægjʊlənt] *n Med* coagulant *m*

coagulate [kəʊ'ægjʊleɪt] *vi* coaguler

coal [kəʊl] *n* (**a**) charbon *m*; **c. bunker** coffre *m* à charbon; **c. merchant** négociant *m* en charbon; **c. mine** mine *f* de charbon; **c. miner** mineur *m*; **c. mining** extraction *f* du charbon; **c. tar** goudron *m* de houille (**b**) *(idioms)* **to carry coals to Newcastle** porter de l'eau à la rivière

coalesce [kəʊə'les] *vi* s'unir

coalfield ['kəʊlfi:ld] *n* bassin *m* houiller

coalition [kəʊə'lɪʃən] *n* coalition *f*

coalman ['kəʊlmæn] *n* charbonnier *m*

coarse [kɔ:s] *adj* (**a**) *(person, language)* grossier(ère), vulgaire (**b**) *(surface, texture)* grossier(ère); **to have c. hair** avoir le cheveu épais et rêche

coarsely ['kɔ:slɪ] *adv* (**a**) *(vulgarly)* vulgairement (**b**) *(roughly)* **c. chopped/ground** haché(e)/moulu(e) grossièrement

coarseness ['kɔ:snɪs] *n* (**a**) *(of person, language)* grossièreté *f*, vulgarité *f* (**b**) *(of surface, texture)* grossièreté *f*

coast [kəʊst] **1** *n* côte *f*; *Fig* **the c. is clear** la voie est libre
2 *vi (in car, on bicycle)* avancer en roue libre; *Fig* **she coasted through her exams** elle a eu ses examens haut la main

coastal ['kəʊstəl] *adj* côtier(ère)

coaster ['kəʊstə(r)] *n* (**a**) *(for glass)* dessous *m* de verre (**b**) *(ship)* caboteur *m*

coastguard ['kəʊstgɑ:d] *n* garde-côte *m*

coastline ['kəʊstlaɪn] *n* littoral *m*

coat [kəʊt] **1** *n* (**a**) *(garment)* manteau *m*; **c. hanger** cintre *m*; **c. hook** patère *f* (**b**) *(of horse)* robe *f*; *(of dog)* pelage *m* (**c**) *(of snow, paint)* couche *f* (**d**) *(in heraldry)* **c. of arms** armoiries *fpl*
2 *vt (with mud, paint)* couvrir (**with** de); *(with chocolate, sugar)* enrober (**with** de)

coating ['kəʊtɪŋ] *n* *(of paint, dust)* couche *f*; *(of chocolate)* enrobage *m*

co-author [kəʊ'ɔ:θə(r)] **1** *n* coauteur *m*
2 *vt* **to c. a book with sb** écrire un livre en collaboration avec qn

coax [kəʊks] *vt* enjôler; **to c. sb to do** *or* **into doing sth** amener qn à faire qch par des cajoleries; **to c. sth out of sb** obtenir qch de qn par des cajoleries

cob [kɒb] *n* (**a**) *(horse)* cob *m* (**b**) *(of corn)* épi *m*

cobalt ['kəʊbɔ:lt] *n* cobalt *m*; **c. blue** bleu *m* de cobalt

cobble ['kɒbəl] **1** *n* pavé *m*
2 *vt* paver

▸**cobble together** *vt sep* bricoler

cobbled ['kɒbəld] *adj (path, street)* pavé(e)

cobbler ['kɒblə(r)] *n* cordonnier *m*

cobblers ['kɒbləz] *npl Br* (**a**) *very Fam (nonsense)* conneries *fpl* (**b**) *Vulg (testicles)* couilles *fpl*

COBOL ['kəʊbɒl] *n Comput (abbr* **Common Business Oriented Language**) Cobol *m*

cobra ['kəʊbrə] *n* cobra *m*

cobweb ['kɒbweb] *n* toile *f* d'araignée; *Fig* **to brush the cobwebs off sth** ressortir qch

cocaine [kəʊ'keɪn] *n* cocaïne *f*

cock [kɒk] **1** *n* (**a**) *(male fowl)* coq *m*; **c. sparrow** moineau *m* mâle (**b**) *Vulg (penis)* bi(t)te *f*
2 *vt (gun)* armer; **to c. a snook at sb** faire la nique à qn; **to c. its ears** *(of horse, dog)* dresser les oreilles

▸**cock up** *vt sep Br very Fam (plan, arrangement)* faire foirer; *(exam)* se planter à

cockade [kɒ'keɪd] *n* cocarde *f*

cock-a-doodle-doo ['kɒkədu:dəl'du:] *exclam* cocorico!

cock-a-hoop ['kɒkə'hu:p] *adj* enchanté(e)

cockatoo [kɒkə'tu:] *n* cacatoès *m*

cocked [kɒkt] *adj* **to knock sb into a c. hat** *(outclass)* surpasser qn

cockerel ['kɒkərəl] *n* jeune coq *m*

cocker spaniel [kɒkə'spænjəl] *n* cocker *m*

cockeyed ['kɒkaɪd] *adj Fam (decision, plan)* farfelu(e)

cockfight ['kɒkfaɪt] *n* combat *m* de coqs

cockle ['kɒkəl] *n* (**a**) *(shellfish)* coque *f* (**b**) *Fam* **it warmed the cockles of his heart** ça lui a réchauffé le cœur

Cockney ['kɒknɪ] **1** *n* (**a**) *(person)* cockney *mf* (**b**) *(dialect)* cockney *m*
2 *adj* cockney

cockpit ['kɒkpɪt] *n* cabine *f* de pilotage, cockpit *m*
cockroach ['kɒkrəʊtʃ] *n* cafard *m*
cocksure ['kɒk'ʃʊə(r)] *adj (person, manner)* présomptueux(euse)
cocktail ['kɒkteɪl] *n also Fig* cocktail *m*; **c. dress** robe *f* de cocktail; **c. lounge** bar *m* confortable *(dans un pub, un hôtel)*; **c. party** cocktail; **c. shaker** shaker *m*; **c. stick** pique *f*
cocky ['kɒkɪ] *adj Fam* culotté(e)
cocoa ['kəʊkəʊ] *n (powder, drink)* cacao *m*; **c. butter** beurre *m* de cacao
coconut ['kəʊkənʌt] *n* noix *f* de coco; **c. milk** lait *m* de coco; **c. palm** cocotier *m*
cocoon [kə'kuːn] **1** *n also Fig* cocon *m*
　2 *vt Fig (protect)* couver
COD [siːəʊ'diː] *n Com (abbr* **cash on delivery**) paiement *m* à la livraison
cod [kɒd] *(pl* **cod**) *n* morue *f*; **c. liver oil** huile *f* de foie de morue
coddle ['kɒdəl] *vt (child)* dorloter
code [kəʊd] **1** *n* (**a**) *(cipher)* code *m*; **in c.** codé(e); **c. book** code *m*; **c. name** nom *m* de code; **c. number** numéro *m* de code (**b**) *(rules)* code *m*; **c. of conduct** déontologie *f*, code de conduite
　2 *vt (message)* coder
codeine ['kəʊdiːn] *n* codéine *f*
codify ['kəʊdɪfaɪ] *(pt & pp* **codified**) *vt* codifier
codswallop ['kɒdzwɒləp] *n Br Fam* foutaises *fpl*
coeducational [kəʊedjʊ'keɪʃənəl] *adj (school)* mixte
coefficient [kəʊɪ'fɪʃənt] *n Math* coefficient *m*
coerce [kəʊ'ɜːs] *vt* forcer, contraindre; **to c. sb into doing sth** contraindre qn à faire qch
coercion [kəʊ'ɜːʃən] *n* coercition *f*
coexist [kəʊɪg'zɪst] *vi* coexister
coexistence [kəʊɪg'zɪstəns] *n* coexistence *f*
C of E [siːəv'iː] *adj Rel (abbr* **Church of England**) anglican(e)
coffee ['kɒfɪ] *n* café *m*; **c. bar** café; **c. bean** grain *m* de café; **c. break** pause-café *f*; **c. cup** tasse *f* à café; **c. grinder** moulin *m* à café; **c. grounds** marc *m* de café; **c. machine** *(in café)* percolateur *m*; *(vending machine)* machine *f* à café; *(in home)* cafetière *f* électrique; **c. mill** moulin à café; **c. pot** cafetière *f*; **c. spoon** cuillère *f* à café; **c. table** table *f* basse; **c. table book** grand livre *m* illustré
coffer ['kɒfə(r)] *n (chest)* coffre *m*; *Fig* **the coffers** *(of company, country)* les caisses *fpl*
coffin ['kɒfɪn] *n* cercueil *m*
cog [kɒg] *n (tooth on gearwheel)* dent *f*; *(gearwheel)* roue *f* dentée, rouage *m*; *Fig* **a c. in the machinery** un rouage dans la machine
cogent ['kəʊdʒənt] *adj* convaincant(e)
cogitate ['kɒdʒɪteɪt] *vi Formal* méditer, réfléchir
cognac ['kɒnjæk] *n* cognac *m*
cognition [kɒg'nɪʃən] *n* cognition *f*
cohabit [kəʊ'hæbɪt] *vi* vivre en concubinage (**with** avec)
cohabitation [kəʊhæbɪ'teɪʃən] *n* concubinage *m*
coherence [kəʊ'hɪərəns] *n* cohérence *f*
coherent [kəʊ'hɪərənt] *adj* cohérent(e)
cohesion [kəʊ'hiːʒən] *n* cohésion *f*
cohesive [kəʊ'hiːsɪv] *adj* cohésif(ive)
coiffure [kwɑː'fjʊə(r)] *n* coiffure *f*
coil [kɔɪl] **1** *n* (**a**) *(of rope, wire)* rouleau *m*; *(electrical)* bobine *f*; *(contraceptive device)* stérilet *m* (**b**) *(single loop)* anneau *m*
　2 *vt* enrouler (**around** autour de)
▶**coil up** *vi (of snake)* se lover
coin [kɔɪn] **1** *n* pièce *f* (de monnaie); *Fig* **the other side of the c.** le revers de la médaille
　2 *vt (phrase, word)* inventer; **to c. money** battre monnaie; *Fam* **he's coining it** il se fait un fric fou; *Hum & Ironic* **..., to c. a phrase** ..., comme on dit
coinage ['kɔɪnɪdʒ] *n* (**a**) *(coins)* monnaie *f* (**b**) *(word)* mot *m* nouveau, néologisme *m*; *(phrase)* expression *f* nouvelle
coincide [kəʊɪn'saɪd] *vi* coïncider (**with** avec)
coincidence [kəʊ'ɪnsɪdəns] *n* coïncidence *f*
coincidental [kəʊɪnsɪ'dentəl] *adj* fortuit(e)
coin-operated ['kɔɪnɒpəreɪtɪd] *adj (machine)* à pièces
coitus ['kɔɪtəs] *n Formal* coït *m*; **c. interruptus** coït interrompu
coke [kəʊk] *n* (**a**) *(fuel)* coke *m* (**b**) *Fam (cocaine)* coke *f*
col *(abbr* **column**) col
colander ['kɒləndə(r)] *n* passoire *f*
cold [kəʊld] **1** *n* (**a**) *(low temperature)* froid *m*; **to feel the c.** être frileux(euse); *Fig* **to be left out in the c.** rester sur la touche (**b**) *(illness)* rhume *m*; **to have a c.** avoir un rhume; **to catch a c.** attraper un rhume
　2 *adj also Fig* froid(e); **I'm c.** j'ai froid; **it's c.** *(weather)* il fait froid; **to get c.** *(of food)* refroidir; *(of weather)* se refroidir; *also Fig* **to be in a c. sweat** avoir des sueurs froides; *Fam* **that leaves me c.** ça me laisse froid; **that's c. comfort** c'est une maigre consolation; *Fig* **to get c. feet (about sth)** hésiter (à faire qch) à la dernière minute; **to give sb the c. shoulder** snober qn; **c. cream** cold-cream *m*; *Met* **c. front** front *m* froid; **c. meats** viandes *fpl* froides; **c. sore** bouton *m* de fièvre, *Can* feu *m* sauvage; **c. start** *(of car)* démarrage *m* à froid; **c. storage** conservation *f* par le froid; **c. war** guerre *f* froide
　3 *adv* **to do sth c.** faire qch à froid; *Fam Fig* **to be out c.** être sans connaissance
cold-blooded ['kəʊld'blʌdɪd] *adj (animal)* à sang froid; *Fig (person)* froid(e), insensible; **c. murder** meurtre *m* commis de sang-froid
cold-hearted ['kəʊld'hɑːtɪd] *adj (person, decision)* impitoyable
coldly ['kəʊldlɪ] *adv* froidement
coldness ['kəʊldnɪs] *n* froideur *f*
cold-shoulder ['kəʊld'ʃəʊldə(r)] *vt* snober
coleslaw ['kəʊlslɔː] *n* = salade de chou blanc à la mayonnaise
colic ['kɒlɪk] *n* colique *f*
collaborate [kə'læbəreɪt] *vi also Pej* collaborer (**with** avec)
collaboration [kəlæbə'reɪʃən] *n also Pej* collaboration *f*
collaborator [kə'læbəreɪtə(r)] *n also Pej* collaborateur(trice) *m,f*
collage ['kɒlɑːʒ] *n* collage *m*
collapse [kə'læps] **1** *n (of building, prices)* effondrement *m*
　2 *vi (of person, building, prices)* s'effondrer, s'écrouler
collapsible [kə'læpsəbəl] *adj (table, bed)* pliant(e)
collar ['kɒlə(r)] **1** *n (of shirt)* col *m*; *(for dog)* collier *m*
　2 *vt Fam (seize)* pincer
collarbone ['kɒləbəʊn] *n* clavicule *f*

collate [kə'leɪt] *vt* rassembler
collateral [kə'lætərəl] **1** *n Fin* nantissement *m*
 2 *adj Euph Mil* **c. damage** dégâts *mpl* collatéraux
colleague ['kɒliːg] *n* collègue *mf*
collect [kə'lekt] **1** *adv Am* **to call sb c.** appeler qn en PCV, *Can* faire un appel à frais virés à qn
 2 *vt* (**a**) *(stamps, paintings)* collectionner, faire collection de (**b**) *(gather)* *(belongings)* rassembler; *(information, news)* recueillir; *(rubbish)* ramasser; *(taxes)* lever; **to c. the dust** *(of ornament)* prendre la poussière; **to c. sb** *(pick up)* passer prendre qn (**c**) *(compose)* **to c. one's thoughts** se concentrer; **to c. oneself** se calmer
 3 *vi (of people)* se rassembler; *(of things)* s'amasser; *(of dust)* s'accumuler
collected [kə'lektɪd] *adj* (**a**) *(calm)* calme (**b**) **c. works** œuvres *fpl* complètes
collection [kə'lekʃən] *n* (**a**) *(of stamps, paintings)* collection *f* (**b**) *(act of collecting)* *(of money)* recouvrement *m*; *(of rubbish)* ramassage *m*; *(of taxes)* levée *f*; **to take a c.** *(for charity)* faire une collecte; **c. plate** *(in church)* plat *m* de quête
collective [kə'lektɪv] **1** *n (group)* collectif *m*; *(farm)* coopérative *f* agricole
 2 *adj* collectif(ive); **c. bargaining** = négociations afin d'établir une convention collective; **c. noun** collectif *m*
collectively [kə'lektɪvlɪ] *adv* collectivement
collectivize [kə'lektɪvaɪz] *vt* collectiviser
collector [kə'lektə(r)] *n* (**a**) *(of stamps, paintings)* collectionneur(euse) *m,f*; **c.'s item** pièce *f* de collection (**b**) **c. of taxes** percepteur *m*
college ['kɒlɪdʒ] *n Br (of further education)* établissement *m* d'enseignement supérieur; *Br (part of university)* = association d'enseignants et d'étudiants au sein de certaines universités, disposant d'une semi-autonomie administrative; *Am (university)* université *f*; **to be at c.** être étudiant(e); **c. of education** ≃ école *f* normale
collide [kə'laɪd] *vi* entrer en collision (**with** avec)
collie ['kɒlɪ] *n* colley *m*
colliery ['kɒlɪərɪ] *(pl* **collieries***)* *n* houillère *f*, mine *f* de charbon
collision [kə'lɪʒən] *n* collision *f*; *Fig* **to be on a c. course** aller droit au conflit
colloquial [kə'ləʊkwɪəl] *adj* familier(ère)
colloquialism [kə'ləʊkwɪəlɪzəm] *n* expression *f* familière
collude [kə'luːd] *vi* être de connivence (**with** avec)
collusion [kə'luːʒən] *n* collusion *f*; **to be in c. with sb** être de connivence avec qn
collywobbles ['kɒlɪwɒbəlz] *npl Fam* **to have the c.** avoir la trouille
cologne [kə'ləʊn] *n* eau *f* de Cologne
Colombia [kə'lʌmbɪə] *n* la Colombie
Colombian [kə'lʌmbɪən] **1** *n* Colombien(enne) *m,f*
 2 *adj* colombien(enne)
colon ['kəʊlən] *n* (**a**) *Anat* côlon *m* (**b**) *(punctuation mark)* deux-points *m*
colonel ['kɜːnəl] *n* colonel *m*
colonial [kə'ləʊnɪəl] *adj* colonial(e)
colonialism [kə'ləʊnɪəlɪzəm] *n* colonialisme *m*
colonist ['kɒlənɪst] *n* colon *m*
colonize ['kɒlənaɪz] *vt* coloniser
colonnade [kɒlə'neɪd] *n Archit* colonnade *f*

colony ['kɒlənɪ] *(pl* **colonies***)* *n* colonie *f*
color, colored *etc Am* = **colour, coloured** *etc*
colossal [kə'lɒsəl] *adj* colossal(e)
colour ['kʌlə(r)] **1** *n* (**a**) *(red, blue etc)* couleur *f*; **what c. is it?** de quelle couleur est-ce?; **c. bar** *(racial discrimination)* discrimination *f* raciale; **c. blindness** daltonisme *m*; **c. scheme** coloris *mpl*, couleurs *fpl*; **c. supplement** *(of newspaper)* supplément *m* en couleurs; **c. television** télévision *f* couleur (**b**) *(idioms)* **to be off c.** *(of person)* ne pas être dans son assiette; **to give c. to a story** rendre un récit plus vivant; **let's see the c. of your money** voyons la couleur de ton argent; **to pass with flying colours** être reçu(e) brillamment *ou* haut la main; **to show one's true colours** se montrer sous son vrai jour; **to nail one's colours to the mast** afficher ses opinions
 2 *vt* (**a**) *(of chemical, dye)* colorer; *(with felt-tips, crayons)* colorier; **to c. one's hair** se faire une couleur (**b**) *Fig (judgement, view)* fausser
 3 *vi (blush)* rougir
▶**colour in** *vt sep* colorier
colour-blind ['kʌləblaɪnd] *adj* daltonien(enne)
colour-coded ['kʌləkəʊdɪd] *adj* différencié(e) par des couleurs
coloured ['kʌləd] *adj* (**a**) *(illustration)* en couleurs; *(pen, ink)* de couleur; **brightly c.** aux couleurs vives; *Fig* **a highly c. narrative** un récit haut en couleurs (**b**) *(person)* de couleur
colourful ['kʌləfʊl] *adj* coloré(e); *(vivid)* coloré, pittoresque; **a c. character** un personnage haut en couleurs
colouring ['kʌlərɪŋ] *n* (**a**) *(in food)* colorants *mpl* (**b**) *(complexion)* teint *m*; **to have dark/fair c.** avoir le teint mat/clair (**c**) **c. book** album *m* à colorier
colourless ['kʌləlɪs] *adj* (**a**) *(clear)* incolore (**b**) *Fig (dull)* insipide, fade
colt [kəʊlt] *n* poulain *m*
Columbus [kə'lʌmbəs] *n* **Christopher C.** Christophe Colomb
column ['kɒləm] *n* *(of troops, text, in building)* colonne *f*; *(newspaper feature)* rubrique *f*
columnist ['kɒləmɪst] *n* *(for newspaper, magazine)* chroniqueur(euse) *m,f*
coma ['kəʊmə] *n* coma *m*; **to go into a c.** tomber dans le coma; **to be in a c.** être dans le coma
comatose ['kəʊmətəʊs] *adj also Fig* comateux(euse)
comb [kəʊm] **1** *n* (**a**) *(for hair)* peigne *m*; **to give one's hair a c.** se donner un coup de peigne (**b**) *(of cock)* crête *f*
 2 *vt* (**a**) *(hair)* peigner; **to c. one's hair** se peigner (**b**) *(search)* ratisser, passer au peigne fin
combat ['kɒmbæt] **1** *n* combat *m*; **c. jacket** veste *f* de treillis; **c. trousers** battle-dress *m*, pantalon *m* multipoches; **c. zone** zone *f* de combat
 2 *vt (disease, prejudice, crime)* combattre
combatant ['kɒmbətənt] *n & adj* combattant(e) *m,f*
combination [kɒmbɪ'neɪʃən] *n* combinaison *f*; **a c. of circumstances** un concours de circonstances; **c. lock** serrure *f* à combinaison; **c. skin** peau *f* mixte; *Med* **c. therapy** trithérapie *f*
combine 1 *n* ['kɒmbaɪn] (**a**) **c. (harvester)** moissonneuse-batteuse *f* (**b**) *Econ* cartel *m*
 2 *vt* [kəm'baɪn] combiner, allier; **to c. business with pleasure** joindre l'utile à l'agréable
 3 *vi* [kəm'baɪn] *(of people)* s'associer; *(of companies)* fusionner; *(of chemical elements)* se combiner

combustible [kəmˈbʌstɪbəl] *adj* combustible

combustion [kəmˈbʌstʃən] *n* combustion *f*; **c. chamber** chambre *f* de combustion

come [kʌm] (*pt* **came** [keɪm], *pp* **come**) *vi* (**a**) *(move)* venir (**from** de); *(arrive)* arriver; **to c. from France/Edinburgh** venir de France/d'Édimbourg; **to c. to the end of sth** arriver à la fin de qch; **here he comes!** le voilà!; **coming!** j'arrive!; **c., c.!** allons, allons!; **she always comes to me for help** elle s'adresse toujours à moi quand elle a besoin d'aide; **she came running towards us** elle vint vers nous en courant, elle courut vers nous; **the rain came pouring down** il s'est mis à tomber des cordes; **nothing comes between her and her work** son travail passe avant tout; *Fig* **she has come a long way since then** elle a fait du chemin depuis; *Fam* **I don't know whether I'm coming or going!** je ne sais plus où j'en suis!

(**b**) *(in time)* **c. January** en janvier; **c. next summer** l'été prochain; **in the days/years to c.** dans les jours/années à venir; **it came as a shock/surprise to me** ça m'a fait un choc/une surprise; *Fam* **he had it coming (to him)** ça lui pendait au nez

(**c**) *(happen)* **to c. to do sth** finir par faire qch; **c. to think of it** maintenant que j'y pense; **to take things as they c.** prendre les choses comme elles viennent; **c. what may** quoi qu'il arrive; **how c....?** comment se fait-il que...? + *subjunctive*

(**d**) *(in sequence)* **to c. first/last** *(in race, competition)* finir premier/dernier; **October comes before November** octobre vient avant novembre; **what comes next?** qu'est-ce qui vient après?

(**e**) *(exist, be available)* **to c. in three sizes/colours** exister en trois tailles/couleurs; **work of that quality doesn't c. cheap** du travail de cette qualité, ça se paie; **he's as tough as they c.** il n'y a pas plus dur que lui

(**f**) *(become)* **to c. loose** se défaire; **to c. true** se réaliser; **to c. open** s'ouvrir; **to c. of age** devenir majeur(e)

(**g**) *(reach)* **to c. up/down to** arriver (jusqu')à

(**h**) *very Fam (reach orgasm)* jouir

▸**come about** *vi* se produire, arriver

▸**come across 1** *vt insep (find)* tomber sur
   2 *vi (make an impression)* **to c. across well/badly** bien/mal passer; **he comes across as a nice person** il a l'air gentil

▸**come after** *vt insep (chase)* poursuivre

▸**come along** *vi* (**a**) **c. along!** allons, pressons! (**b**) *(make progress) (of project, work)* avancer; **his French is coming along well** il fait des progrès en français (**c**) *(arrive)* venir

▸**come at** *vt insep (attack)* attaquer

▸**come away** *vi (become detached)* se détacher

▸**come back** *vi* revenir; **it's all coming back to me** ça me revient; **to c. back to what I was saying...** pour revenir à ce que je disais...

▸**come by 1** *vt insep (acquire)* obtenir, trouver
   2 *vi (visit)* passer

▸**come down** *vi* (**a**) *(descend)* descendre; *(of temperature, prices)* baisser; *Fig* **to c. down in the world** déchoir; **to c. down with the flu** attraper la grippe (**b**) *(decide)* **to c. down in favour of sb/sth** décider en faveur de qn/qch (**c**) **to c. down to** *(be a matter of)* se ramener à, se résumer à; **it comes down to the fact that...** le fait est que...

▸**come down on** *vt insep (reprimand)* passer un savon à

▸**come forward** *vi* se présenter; **no one has come forward with any suggestions** personne n'a fait de suggestions

▸**come in** *vi* (**a**) *(of person)* entrer; *(of tide)* monter; **c. in!** entrez!; **to c. in first/second** arriver premier/deuxième (**b**) *(have a role)* intervenir; **and where do I c. in?** et moi, qu'est-ce que je fais?; **to c. in useful** être utile

▸**come in for** *vt insep* **to c. in for criticism** faire l'objet de critiques

▸**come into** *vt insep* (**a**) *(room, city)* entrer dans; **to c. into the world** venir au monde; **to c. into existence** être créé(e); **to c. into force** *or* **effect** *(of law, ruling)* entrer en vigueur; **to c. into power** arriver au pouvoir; **luck didn't c. into it** la chance n'a rien à voir là-dedans (**b**) *(inherit)* hériter de

▸**come of** *vi (result from)* **no good will c. of it** cela n'amènera rien de bon; **that's what comes of being too ambitious** c'est ce qui arrive lorsqu'on est trop ambitieux

▸**come off 1** *vt insep* (**a**) *(fall from) (horse, bicycle)* tomber de (**b**) **c. off it!** arrête ton char!
   2 *vi* (**a**) *(be removed) (of button)* se détacher; *(of paint)* s'écailler; *(of stain)* partir (**b**) *(succeed)* réussir; **to c. off well/badly** *(in contest)* bien/mal s'en tirer

▸**come on** *vi* (**a**) **c. on!** allez! (**b**) *(make progress) (of project, work)* avancer; **his chess is coming on** il fait des progrès aux échecs; **I feel a cold coming on** je sens que je suis en train de m'enrhumer (**c**) *(of lights)* s'allumer; *(of heating)* se mettre en route

▸**come out** *vi* (**a**) *(of person, magazine, film)* sortir; *(of sun)* paraître; *(of truth)* se faire jour; **to c. out on strike** se mettre en grève; **to c. out in a rash** se couvrir de boutons; **to c. out in favour of/against sth** se prononcer pour/contre qch; **he came out of the deal well/badly** il a fait une bonne/mauvaise affaire; **to c. out with** *(remark, opinion)* sortir (**b**) *(of tooth, hair)* tomber; *(of screw)* se dévisser; *(of stain)* partir (**c**) *(as gay or lesbian)* déclarer son homosexualité

▸**come over 1** *vt insep (affect)* **a strange feeling came over me** j'ai eu une sensation étrange; **what's come over you?** qu'est-ce qui te prend?
   2 *vi* (**a**) *(visit)* passer (**b**) *(make impression)* **to c. over well/badly** bien/mal passer (**c**) *(feel)* **to c. over all funny** se sentir tout(e) drôle; **to c. over all dizzy** être pris(e) de vertiges

▸**come round** *vi* (**a**) *(visit)* passer (**b**) *(regain consciousness)* reprendre connaissance (**c**) *(accept)* accepter; **to c. round to sb's way of thinking** se rallier à l'opinion de qn

▸**come through 1** *vi (of message, news)* arriver
   2 *vt insep (survive) (war, crisis, illness)* survivre à

▸**come to 1** *vt insep* (**a**) *(amount to)* s'élever à; **the scheme never came to anything** le projet n'a jamais abouti (**b**) *(reach)* **to c. to the point** en venir au fait; **to c. to a conclusion** arriver à une conclusion; **what is the world coming to?** où va-t-on?; **I never thought it would c. to this** je ne me doutais pas qu'on en arriverait là (**c**) *(be a matter of)* **when it comes to...** pour ce qui est de...; **if it comes to that...** à ce compte-là...
   2 *vi (regain consciousness)* reprendre connaissance

▸**come together** *vi (gather)* se rassembler

▸**come up 1** *vt insep (stairs, hill)* monter
   2 *vi* (**a**) *(of sun)* se lever; *(of opportunity, question,*

problem) se présenter; **to c. up against a problem** rencontrer un problème; **there are some interesting films coming up on television** il y a quelques films intéressants qui vont bientôt passer à la télévision; **I'll let you know if anything comes up** je te préviendrai si quelque chose se présente; **the case comes up (for trial) tomorrow** le procès commence demain (**b**) **to c. up with** *(funding, solution)* trouver; *(idea, theory)* proposer

▸**come upon** *vt insep (find)* tomber sur

▸**come up to** *vt insep* (**a**) *(approach)* s'approcher de (**b**) *(equal)* **the film didn't c. up to my expectations** le film n'était pas à la hauteur de mes espérances

comeback ['kʌmbæk] *n* **to make a c.** *(of fashion)* revenir; *(of actor, sportsperson)* faire un come-back

COMECON ['kɒmɪkɒn] *n Formerly (abbr* **Council for Mutual Economic Assistance**) COMECON *m*

comedian [kə'miːdɪən] *n* comique *mf*; *Fig (practical joker)* farceur(euse) *m,f*

comedienne [kəmiːdɪ'en] *n* comique *f*

comedown ['kʌmdaʊn] *n Fam* régression *f*

comedy ['kɒmɪdɪ] (*pl* **comedies**) *n (play, film)* comédie *f*; *(of situation)* comique *m*; *(situation comedy)* sitcom *m*; **c. show** *(on TV)* spectacle *m* comique

come-on ['kʌmɒn] *n Fam (enticement)* appât *m*; **to give sb the c.** *(sexually)* faire du gringue à qn

comer ['kʌmə(r)] *n* **open to all comers** ouvert(e) à tous

comet ['kɒmɪt] *n* comète *f*

comeuppance [kʌm'ʌpəns] *n Fam* **to get one's c.** avoir ce qu'on mérite

comfort ['kʌmfət] **1** *n* (**a**) *(ease)* confort *m*; *(financial)* aisance *f*; **to do sth in the c. of one's own home** faire qch confortablement chez soi; **comforts** *(luxuries)* commodités *fpl*; **I like my home comforts** j'aime mon petit confort; **the bullets were too close for c.** les balles passaient un peu trop près à mon goût; *Am* **c. station** toilettes *fpl* publiques (**b**) *(consolation)* réconfort *m*, consolation *f*; **if it's any c.,...** si ça peut vous consoler,...; **to take c. from** *or* **in sth** trouver du réconfort dans qch

2 *vt (console)* réconforter, consoler

comfortable ['kʌmftəbəl] *adj* (**a**) *(place, bed, chair)* confortable; *(person)* bien *inv*, à l'aise; **to be c.** *(of patient)* ne pas souffrir; **to make oneself c.** se mettre à l'aise *ou* à son aise; **I wouldn't feel c. accepting that money** ça me mettrait mal à l'aise d'accepter cet argent (**b**) *(majority, income)* confortable; **to be in c. circumstances** mener une vie aisée

comfortably ['kʌmftəblɪ] *adv* (**a**) *(sit)* confortablement; **to be c. off** *(financially)* être à l'aise financièrement; **to live c.** mener une vie aisée (**b**) *(easily)* facilement; **to win c.** gagner avec une avance confortable

comforter ['kʌmfətə(r)] *n Am (quilt)* édredon *m*, *Can* confortable *m*

comforting ['kʌmfətɪŋ] *adj* réconfortant(e)

comfy ['kʌmfɪ] *adj Br Fam (place, bed, chair)* confortable; *(person)* bien *inv*, à l'aise

comic ['kɒmɪk] **1** *n* (**a**) *(performer)* comique *mf* (**b**) **c. (book)** bande *f* dessinée, BD *f*

2 *adj* comique; **c. opera** opéra-comique *m*; **to provide some c. relief** détendre l'atmosphère; **c. strip** bande *f* dessinée, BD *f*

comical ['kɒmɪkəl] *adj* comique

coming ['kʌmɪŋ] **1** *n (of person)* venue *f*, arrivée *f*; *(of*

night) approche *f*; **comings and goings** allées *fpl* et venues; **c. of age** majorité *f*; **on his c. of age** à sa majorité

2 *adj (year, week)* prochain(e); *(elections, difficulties)* à venir

Coming of Age

À sa majorité, c'est-à-dire à 18 ans, un(e) jeune Britannique acquiert le droit de voter, de faire partie d'un jury, de boire de l'alcool dans les pubs et de se marier sans le consentement de ses parents.

comma ['kɒmə] *n* virgule *f*

command [kə'mɑːnd] **1** *n* (**a**) *(order)* ordre *m*; *Comput* commande *f*; *Comput* **c. language** langage *m* de commandes (**b**) *(authority, control)* commandement *m*; **to be in c. (of sth)** *(army, ship)* commander (qch); **to be in c. of the situation** maîtriser la situation; **to be at sb's c.** être aux ordres de qn; **to have sth at one's c.** avoir qch à sa disposition; **she has a good c. of English** elle a une bonne maîtrise de l'anglais; **c. economy** économie *f* planifiée

2 *vt* (**a**) *(give order to)* **to c. sb to do sth** ordonner *ou* commander à qn de faire qch (**b**) *(ship, regiment)* commander (**c**) *(have at one's disposal)* avoir à sa disposition (**d**) *(respect, admiration, attention)* forcer; **to c. a high price** se vendre cher

commandant [kɒmən'dænt] *n Mil* commandant *m*

commandeer [kɒmən'dɪə(r)] *vt* réquisitionner

commander [kə'mɑːndə(r)] *n Mil* commandant *m*; *Naut* capitaine *m* de frégate; **c.-in-chief** commandant en chef

commanding [kə'mɑːndɪŋ] *adj* (**a**) *Mil* **c. officer** chef *m* de corps (**b**) *(voice)* impérieux(euse); *(appearance)* qui en impose; *(position)* dominant(e); *(lead)* considérable

commandment [kə'mɑːndmənt] *n Rel* commandement *m*

commando [kə'mɑːndəʊ] (*pl* **commandos** *or* **commandoes**) *n Mil (soldier, unit)* commando *m*

commemorate [kə'meməreɪt] *vt* commémorer

commemoration [kəmemə'reɪʃən] *n* commémoration *f*

commemorative [kə'memərətɪv] *adj* commémoratif(ive)

commence [kə'mens] *vt & vi Formal* commencer; **to c. doing sth** commencer à faire qch

commencement [kə'mensmənt] *n* (**a**) *Formal (beginning)* commencement *m*, début *m* (**b**) *Am Univ* remise *f* des diplômes

commend [kə'mend] *vt* (**a**) *(praise)* louer, féliciter; **to c. sb for bravery** louer qn pour sa bravoure (**b**) *(recommend)* recommander; **the train journey has little to c. it** je ne vous recommande pas le voyage en train (**c**) *Lit (entrust)* recommander (**to** à)

commendable [kə'mendəbəl] *adj* louable

commendation [kɒmen'deɪʃən] *n (praise)* éloges *mpl*; *(in competition)* mention *f* spéciale; *Mil* citation *f*

commensurate [kə'menʃərət] *adj Formal* proportionnel(elle) (**with** à)

comment ['kɒment] **1** *n* commentaire *m*, observation *f* (**on** sur); **no c.!** je n'ai rien à dire!

2 *vt* **to c. that...** faire remarquer *ou* observer que...; **"how interesting," he commented** "comme c'est

intéressant," remarqua-t-il *ou* observa-t-il
  3 *vi* faire des commentaires (**on** sur)
commentary ['kɒməntərɪ] (*pl* **commentaries**) *n* commentaire *m*
commentate ['kɒmənteɪt] *vi* faire le commentaire; **to c. on sth** commenter qch
commentator ['kɒmənteɪtə(r)] *n* commentateur(-trice) *m,f*
commerce ['kɒmɜːs] *n* commerce *m*
commercial [kə'mɜːʃəl] **1** *n* (*advertisement*) publicité *f*, pub *f*
  2 *adj also Pej* commercial(e); **c. artist** graphiste *mf*; *Fin* **c. bank** banque *f* commerciale; **c. break** page *f* de publicité; **c. law** droit *m* commercial; **c. traveller** voyageur *m* de commerce; **c. value** valeur *f* marchande; **c. vehicle** véhicule *m* de commerce
commercialism [kə'mɜːʃəlɪzəm] *n Pej* mercantilisme *m*
commercialized [kə'mɜːʃəlaɪzd] *adj Pej* commercial(e)
commercially [kə'mɜːʃəlɪ] *adv* commercialement; **c. available** disponible dans le commerce
commie ['kɒmɪ] *n & adj Fam Pej* coco *mf*
commiserate [kə'mɪzəreɪt] *vi* **to c. with sb** (*show sympathy*) témoigner de la sympathie à qn; (*feel sympathy*) éprouver de la compassion pour qn
commiseration [kəmɪzə'reɪʃən] *n* commisération *f*; **you have my commiserations** je suis désolé pour vous
commission [kə'mɪʃən] **1** *n* (**a**) *Com* (*payment*) commission *f* (**b**) (*of work, painting*) commande *f* (**c**) (*investigating body*) commission *f* (**d**) *Naut* **in c.** armé(e); **out of c.** désarmé(e) (**e**) *Mil* brevet *m* d'officier
  2 *vt* (**a**) (*order*) (*work, painting*) commander; **to c. sb to do sth** charger qn de faire qch (**b**) *Mil* **to be commissioned** être nommé(e) officier
commissionaire [kəmɪʃə'neə(r)] *n* portier *m*
commissioner [kə'mɪʃənə(r)] *n* membre *m* d'une commission; **c. of police** ≃ commissaire *m* de police; *Law* **c. for oaths** = homme de loi habilité à recevoir des déclarations sous serment
commit [kə'mɪt] (*pt & pp* **committed**) **1** *vt* (**a**) (*error, crime*) commettre; **to c. suicide** se suicider (**b**) **to c. oneself** (*promise*) s'engager; **to c. oneself to sth/doing sth** s'engager à qch/faire qch (**c**) (*entrust*) (*resources, troops*) engager qch dans qch (**c**) (*entrust*) confier (**to** à); **to c. sth to writing** coucher qch par écrit; **to c. sth to memory** apprendre qch par cœur (**d**) (*confine*) **to c. sb (to prison)** incarcérer qn; **to c. sb** (*to mental institution*) interner qn (**e**) *Law* **to c. sb for trial** mettre qn en accusation
  2 *vi* (*emotionally*) s'engager, s'investir
commitment [kə'mɪtmənt] *n* (**a**) (*obligation*) engagement *m*; **family/business commitments** obligations *fpl* familiales/professionnelles (**b**) (*dedication*) dévouement *m* (**to** à); **to make a c.** s'engager; **she lacks c.** elle ne s'investit pas assez
committed [kə'mɪtɪd] *adj* dévoué(e) (**to** à); (*Christian, socialist*) convaincu(e); **to be c. (to one's work)** beaucoup s'impliquer (dans son travail)
committee [kə'mɪtɪ] *n* comité *m*, commission *f*
commode [kə'məʊd] *n* (**a**) (*chest of drawers*) commode *f* (**b**) (*toilet*) chaise *f* percée
commodious [kə'məʊdɪəs] *adj Formal* spacieux(-euse)

commodity [kə'mɒdɪtɪ] (*pl* **commodities**) *n Econ* marchandise *f*, produit *m*; *Fin* matière *f* première; **to be a rare c.** être une denrée rare; **commodities market** marché *m* des matières premières
commodore ['kɒmədɔː(r)] *n Naut* ≃ contre-amiral *m*
common ['kɒmən] **1** *n* (**a**) **to have sth in c. (with)** avoir qch en commun (avec); **in c. with** (*similar to*) de même que
  (**b**) (*land*) terrain *m* communal
  2 *adj* (**a**) (*frequent*) commun(e), courant(e); **in c. use** d'usage courant
  (**b**) (*shared*) commun(e); **it is by c. consent the best** de l'avis de tous, c'est le meilleur; **C. Agricultural Policy** politique *f* agricole commune; *Fin* **c. currency** monnaie *f* unique; *also Fig* **c. denominator** dénominateur *m* commun; **the c. good** le bien commun; *Fig* **c. ground** terrain *m* d'entente; **it's c. knowledge (that)...** tout le monde sait que...; **the C. Market** le Marché commun; *Sch* **c. room** (*for pupils*) salle *f* commune; (*for teachers*) salle des professeurs
  (**c**) (*average*) **c. or garden** ordinaire, standard *inv*; **the c. cold** le rhume; **the c. man** l'homme *m* de la rue; **the c. people** les gens *mpl* ordinaires; **c. sense** bon sens *m*
  (**d**) *Pej* (*vulgar*) vulgaire
commoner ['kɒmənə(r)] *n* roturier(ère) *m,f*
common-law ['kɒmənlɔː] *adj* **c. husband** concubin *m*; **c. marriage** concubinage *m*; **c. wife** concubine *f*
commonly ['kɒmənlɪ] *adv* communément
commonplace ['kɒmənpleɪs] **1** *n* lieu *m* commun
  2 *adj* courant(e)
Commons ['kɒmənz] *npl* **the (House of) C.** la Chambre des communes
Commonwealth ['kɒmənwelθ] *n* **the C.** le Commonwealth; **the C. games** les jeux *mpl* du Commonwealth
commotion [kə'məʊʃən] *n* (*noise*) vacarme *m*; (*disruption*) agitation *f*
communal ['kɒmjʊnəl] *adj* (*bathroom, resource*) commun(e); (*life*) communautaire
commune 1 *n* ['kɒmjuːn] (*collective*) communauté *f*
  2 *vi* [kə'mjuːn] **to c. with nature** communier avec la nature
communicable [kə'mjuːnɪkəbəl] *adj* (*disease*) transmissible
communicant [kə'mjuːnɪkənt] *n Rel* communiant(e) *m,f*
communicate [kə'mjuːnɪkeɪt] **1** *vt* communiquer; (*illness*) transmettre
  2 *vi* communiquer (**with** avec)
communication [kəmjuːnɪ'keɪʃən] *n* communication *f*; **to be in c. with sb** être en contact avec qn; **c. cord** sonnette *f* d'alarme
communicative [kə'mjuːnɪkətɪv] *adj* communicatif(-ive)
communion [kə'mjuːnjən] *n Rel* communion *f*; **to take C.** communier
communism ['kɒmjʊnɪzəm] *n* communisme *m*
communist ['kɒmjʊnɪst] *n & adj* communiste *mf*
community [kə'mjuːnɪtɪ] (*pl* **communities**) *n* communauté *f*; **the business c.** le milieu des affaires; **c. centre** foyer *m* municipal; *Formerly* **c. charge** = en Grande-Bretagne, impôt regroupant taxe d'habitation et impôts locaux; **c. service** travail *m* d'intérêt général; **c. spirit** esprit *m* communautaire

commute [kə'mjuːt] **1** *vt Law* commuer (**to** en) **2** *vi* **to c.** (**to work**) faire la navette entre son domicile et son travail

commuter [kə'mjuːtə(r)] *n* banlieusard(e) *m,f (qui fait la navette entre son domicile et son travail)*; **c. train** train *m* de banlieue

Comoros ['kɒmərɒs] *n* **the C. (Islands)** les Comores *fpl*

compact 1 *n* ['kɒmpækt] (**a**) *(for powder)* poudrier *m* (**b**) *(treaty)* accord *m* (**c**) *Am (car)* petite voiture *f* **2** *adj* [kəm'pækt] compact(e); **c. disc** disque *m* compact; **c. disc player** lecteur *m* de disques compacts **3** *vt* [kəm'pækt] compacter

companion [kəm'pænjən] *n* (**a**) *(friend)* compagnon (compagne) *m,f*; *(of elderly woman)* dame *f* de compagnie; **travelling c.** compagnon de voyage (**b**) *(guidebook)* guide *m*

companionable [kəm'pænjənəbəl] *adj (person)* sociable; *(manner)* amical(e)

companionship [kəm'pænjənʃɪp] *n* compagnie *f*

company ['kʌmpənɪ] *(pl* **companies**) *n* (**a**) *(companionship)* compagnie *f*; **in his c.** en sa compagnie; **to keep sb c.** tenir compagnie à qn; **to be good c.** être d'agréable compagnie; **the dog is good c. for her** le chien lui fait de la compagnie; **to part c. with sb** *(split up)* se séparer de qn; *(disagree)* ne plus être d'accord avec qn; **to get into bad c.** avoir de mauvaises fréquentations; **to do sth in c.** *(in public)* faire qch en public; **to be expecting c.** *(guests)* attendre de la visite

(**b**) *(business)* société *f*; **publishing c.** maison *f* d'édition; **Hobbs and C.** Hobbs et Compagnie; *Fam Fig* **Vɪctor and c.** Vɪctor et compagnie; **c. car** voiture *f* de fonction; **c. policy** politique *f* de la société; *Com* **c. secretary** secrétaire *mf* général(e)

(**c**) *(army unit, theatre group)* compagnie *f*

comparable ['kɒmpərəbəl] *adj* comparable (**to** à)

comparative [kəm'pærətɪv] **1** *n Gram* comparatif *m* **2** *adj* (**a**) *(relative) (cost, comfort, wealth)* relatif(ive); **she's a c. stranger to me** je la connais relativement peu (**b**) *(study, research)* comparatif(ive); *(psychology, literature)* comparé(e)

compare [kəm'peə(r)] **1** *vt* comparer (**with** *or* **to** avec *ou* à); **compared with** *or* **to** par rapport à, à côté de; *Fig* **to c. notes** échanger ses impressions **2** *vi* être comparable (**with** à); **to c. favourably with sth** ne le céder en rien à qch **3** *n Lit* **beyond c.** sans pareil(eille)

comparison [kəm'pærɪsən] *n* comparaison *f*; **in** *or* **by c. (with)** en comparaison (avec); **there is no c.** il n'y a pas de comparaison; **to draw** *or* **make a c. between sth and sth** faire la comparaison entre qch et qch

compartment [kəm'pɑːtmənt] *n* compartiment *m*

compass ['kʌmpəs] *n* (**a**) *(for finding direction)* boussole *f*; *(of boat)* compas *m* (**b**) *Math* **(pair of) compasses** compas *m* (**c**) *(scope) (of mind)* portée *f*; *(of powers)* étendue *f*

compassion [kəm'pæʃən] *n* compassion *f*

compassionate [kəm'pæʃənət] *adj (person, attitude)* compatissant(e); *(by nature)* humain(e); **to be c. towards sb** éprouver de la compassion pour qn; **on c. grounds** pour raisons personnelles; **c. leave** congé *m* exceptionnel pour raisons personnelles

compatibility [kəmpætə'bɪlɪtɪ] *n* compatibilité *f*

compatible [kəm'pætəbəl] *adj* compatible (**with** avec)

compatriot [kəm'pætrɪət] *n* compatriote *mf*

compel [kəm'pel] *(pt & pp* **compelled**) *vt* forcer, obliger; **to c. sb to do sth** forcer *ou* obliger qn à faire qch; **to c. admiration/respect** forcer l'admiration/le respect

compelling [kəm'pelɪŋ] *adj (film, performance)* captivant(e); *(argument)* convaincant(e); *(urge)* irrésistible

compendium [kəm'pendɪəm] *n (book)* précis *m*; *(of games)* sélection *f*

compensate ['kɒmpenseɪt] **1** *vt* dédommager (**for** de) **2** *vi* **to c. for sth** compenser qch

compensation [kɒmpen'seɪʃən] *n* compensation *f*; *(money)* dédommagement *m*, indemnité *f*

compensatory [kɒmpen'seɪtərɪ] *adj* compensatoire

compere ['kɒmpeə(r)] **1** *n* animateur(trice) *m,f*, présentateur(trice) *m,f* **2** *vt* animer, présenter

compete [kəm'piːt] *vi* (**a**) *(contend)* rivaliser (**with** avec); *(of company)* être en concurrence (**with** avec); **to c. for sth** se disputer qch (**b**) *(in race, competition)* concourir (**for** pour)

competence ['kɒmpɪtəns] *n* (**a**) *(ability)* compétence *f*, compétences *fpl* (**b**) *Law* compétence *f*

competent ['kɒmpɪtənt] *adj (person)* compétent(e); **a c. piece of work** du bon travail

competition [kɒmpɪ'tɪʃən] *n* (**a**) *(contest)* concours *m*; *(in sport)* compétition *f* (**b**) *(rivalry)* rivalité *f*; *(between companies, candidates)* concurrence *f*; **to be in c. with sb** être en concurrence avec qn; **the c.** *(opponents) (in sport)* les adversaires *mpl*; *(in business)* la concurrence; **there's no c.!** il n'y a aucune comparaison!

competitive [kəm'petɪtɪv] *adj (person)* qui a l'esprit de compétition; *(atmosphere)* de compétition; *(price, company)* compétitif(ive); **c. sports** sports *mpl* de compétition; *Com* **c. tendering** appel *m* d'offres

competitor [kəm'petɪtə(r)] *n* concurrent(e) *m,f*

compilation [kɒmpɪ'leɪʃən] *n* compilation *f*

compile [kəm'paɪl] *vt (list)* dresser; *(dictionary)* rédiger

complacency [kəm'pleɪsənsɪ] *n* autosatisfaction *f*

complacent [kəm'pleɪsənt] *adj* content(e) de soi; **to be c. about sth** faire de l'autosatisfaction à propos de qch

complain [kəm'pleɪn] *vi* se plaindre (**about** de); **to c. of** *(illness)* se plaindre de; **I can't c. about the service** je n'ai pas à me plaindre du service; **how are things? – can't c.** comment ça va? – je n'ai pas à me plaindre

complaint [kəm'pleɪnt] *n* (**a**) *(grievance)* récrimination *f*; *(official)* plainte *f*, réclamation *f*; **to have cause** *or* **grounds for c.** avoir des raisons de se plaindre; **to lodge** *or* **make a c. against sb** porter plainte contre qn (**b**) *(illness)* maladie *f*

complement 1 *n* ['kɒmplɪmənt] (**a**) *Gram* complément *m* (**b**) *Naut & Fig* **the full c.** l'effectif *m* complet **2** *vt* ['kɒmplɪment] compléter

complementary [kɒmplɪ'mentərɪ] *adj* complémentaire; **c. medicine** médecines *fpl* alternatives *ou* parallèles

complete [kəm'pliːt] **1** *adj* (**a**) *(whole)* complet(ète); *(utter)* total(e); **he is a c. fool** il est complètement idiot (**b**) *(finished)* achevé(e) **2** *vt* (**a**) *(finish)* achever; *(fill in) (form)* compléter (**b**) *(make whole)* compléter

completely [kəm'pliːtlɪ] *adv* complètement

completion [kəm'pliːʃən] *n* achèvement *m*; **on c.** *(of work)* à l'achèvement; **to near c.** toucher à sa fin

complex ['kɒmpleks] **1** *n (of buildings, psychological)* complexe *m*; **to have a c. about sth** être complexé(e) par qch
2 *adj* complexe

complexion [kəm'plekʃən] *n* teint *m*; **to have a fair c.** avoir le teint clair; *Fig* **that puts a different c. on things** voilà qui change tout

complexity [kəm'pleksɪtɪ] *(pl* **complexities)** *n* complexité *f*

compliance [kəm'plaɪəns] *n* observation *f* (**with** de); **in c. with** conformément à

compliant [kəm'plaɪənt] *adj* complaisant(e), accommodant(e)

complicate ['kɒmplɪkeɪt] *vt* compliquer

complicated ['kɒmplɪkeɪtɪd] *adj* compliqué(e)

complication [kɒmplɪ'keɪʃən] *n* complication *f*

complicity [kəm'plɪsɪtɪ] *n* complicité *f* (**in** dans)

compliment 1 *n* ['kɒmplɪmənt] compliment *m*; **to pay sb a c.** faire un compliment à qn; **with compliments** avec nos compliments; **compliments of the season** meilleurs vœux; **compliments slip** papillon *m* à en-tête *(portant la mention "avec les compliments de...")*
2 *vt* ['kɒmplɪment] **to c. sb on sth** *(bravery, command of language)* féliciter qn pour qch; *(dress, haircut)* faire des compliments à qn sur qch

complimentary [kɒmplɪ'mentərɪ] *adj* **(a)** *(praising)* élogieux(euse) (**about** à l'égard de) **(b)** *(free)* gratuit(e); **c. ticket** billet *m* de faveur

comply [kəm'plaɪ] *(pt & pp* **complied)** *vi* **to c. with** *(rule)* se conformer à, se plier à; *(order)* obéir à; *(request)* accéder à

component [kəm'pəʊnənt] **1** *n (electrical, chemical)* composant *m*; *Fig* composante *f*
2 *adj* **c. part** pièce *f* détachée; *Fig* composante *f*

compose [kəm'pəʊz] *vt* **(a)** *(music, poetry)* composer **(b)** *(constitute)* **to be composed of** être composé(e) de, se composer de **(c)** *(calm)* **to c. oneself** se ressaisir

composed [kəm'pəʊzd] *adj* calme

composer [kəm'pəʊzə(r)] *n* compositeur(trice) *m,f*

composite ['kɒmpəzɪt] *adj (photograph)* composite

composition [kɒmpə'zɪʃən] *n* composition *f*; *(essay)* rédaction *f*

compositor [kəm'pɒzɪtə(r)] *n Typ* compositeur(trice) *m,f*

compost ['kɒmpɒst] *n* compost *m*; **c. heap** tas *m* de compost

composure [kəm'pəʊʒə(r)] *n* sang-froid *m*

compound¹ 1 *n* ['kɒmpaʊnd] *Chem & Gram* composé *m*
2 *adj* ['kɒmpaʊnd] composé(e); *Med* **c. fracture** fracture *f* compliquée; *Fin* **c. interest** intérêts *mpl* composés
3 *vt* [kəm'paʊnd] *(problem, difficulty)* aggraver

compound² ['kɒmpaʊnd] *n (enclosure)* enceinte *f*

comprehend [kɒmprɪ'hend] *vt* comprendre

comprehensible [kɒmprɪ'hensəbəl] *adj* compréhensible

comprehension [kɒmprɪ'henʃən] *n* compréhension *f*; **it is beyond my c.** cela dépasse mon entendement

comprehensive [kɒmprɪ'hensɪv] *adj (answer, programme)* complet(ète); *(study)* exhaustif(ive); *(view)* d'ensemble; *(defeat, victory)* écrasant(e); *Fin* **c. insur-**ance assurance *f* tous risques; *Br* **c. (school)** établissement *m* secondaire *(n'opérant pas de sélection à l'entrée)*

Comprehensive Schools

Les "comprehensive schools" ont été introduites en Grande-Bretagne dans les années 60 dans le but d'assurer l'égalité des chances pour tous les enfants, quel que soit leur origine sociale. Aujourd'hui 90 pour cent des élèves du secondaire fréquentent ce type d'établissement scolaire. Cependant l'insuffisance des crédits alloués à l'éducation ainsi que la persistance d'un système d'enseignement privé dont ne peuvent bénéficier que les classes aisées rendent très aléatoire la réalisation d'un projet de démocratisation de l'enseignement.

---

compress 1 *n* ['kɒmpres] *Med* compresse *f*
2 *vt* [kəm'pres] *(air, gas)* comprimer; *Fig (text)* condenser

compression [kəm'preʃən] *n (of air, gas)* compression *f*; *Fig* raccourcissement *m*

compressor [kəm'presə(r)] *n* compresseur *m*

comprise [kəm'praɪz] *vt* comprendre, se composer de; **to be comprised of** comprendre, se composer de

compromise ['kɒmprəmaɪz] **1** *n* compromis *m*; **c. solution** solution *f* de compromis
2 *vt (person, security)* compromettre; *(principles)* transiger sur; **to c. oneself** se compromettre
3 *vi* transiger (**on** sur)

compromising ['kɒmprəmaɪzɪŋ] *adj* compromettant(e)

compulsion [kəm'pʌlʃən] *n (urge)* besoin *m*; *(obligation)* contrainte *f*; **under c.** sous la contrainte; **to be under no c. to do sth** ne pas être obligé(e) de faire qch

compulsive [kəm'pʌlsɪv] *adj (smoker, gambler, liar)* invétéré(e); **c. eating** boulimie *f*; **it's c. viewing** c'est captivant

compulsory [kəm'pʌlsərɪ] *adj* obligatoire; **c. redundancy** ≃ licenciement *m* sec; **c. retirement** mise *f* à la retraite d'office

compunction [kəm'pʌŋkʃən] *n* remords *m*, scrupules *mpl*

computation [kɒmpjʊ'teɪʃən] *n* calcul *m*

compute [kəm'pjuːt] *vt* calculer

computer [kəm'pjuːtə(r)] *n* ordinateur *m*; **c. game** jeu *m* électronique; **to be c. literate** avoir des connaissances en informatique; **c. printout** impression *f*; **c. program** programme *m* informatique; **c. programmer** programmeur(euse) *m,f*; **c. programming** programmation *f*; **c. science** informatique *f*; **c. scientist** informaticien(enne) *m,f*; **c. simulation** simulation *f* par ordinateur

computer-aided [kəm'pjuːtər'eɪdɪd], **computer-assisted** [kəm'pjuːtərə'sɪstɪd] *adj* assisté(e) par ordinateur

computerization [kəmpjuːtəraɪ'zeɪʃən] *n* informatisation *f*

computerize [kəm'pjuːtəraɪz] *vt* informatiser

computing [kəm'pjuːtɪŋ] *n* informatique *f*

comrade ['kɒmreɪd] *n* camarade *mf*

comradeship ['kɒmreɪdʃɪp] *n* camaraderie *f*

con¹ [kɒn] *Fam* **1** *n (swindle)* arnaque *f*; **c. man** arnaqueur *m*

2 *vt* (*pt & pp* **conned**) *(swindle)* arnaquer; **to c. sth out of sb** arnaquer qn de qch; **to c. sb into doing sth** persuader qn de faire qch par la ruse

con² *n Fam (convict)* taulard(e) *m,f*

con³ *n (disadvantage) see* **pro**

concave [kɒn'keɪv] *adj* concave

conceal [kən'siːl] *vt* cacher, dissimuler (**from** à)

concealer [kən'siːlə(r)] *n (make-up)* camoufleur *m*

concede [kən'siːd] **1** *vt* concéder; **to c. defeat** s'avouer vaincu(e); **to c. that...** admettre que...
2 *vi* s'incliner

conceit [kən'siːt] *n (vanity)* vanité *f*, suffisance *f*

conceited [kən'siːtɪd] *adj* vaniteux(euse), suffisant(e)

conceivable [kən'siːvəbəl] *adj* concevable, imaginable; **it is c. that...** il est concevable que... + *subjunctive*

conceivably [kən'siːvəblɪ] *adv* **we might c. get there by six** il se peut que nous soyons arrivés pour six heures; **she couldn't c. have done it** il est inconcevable qu'elle ait fait ça

conceive [kən'siːv] **1** *vt* (**a**) *(child, idea)* concevoir (**b**) *(understand)* concevoir
2 *vi* **to c. of sth** concevoir qch

concentrate ['kɒnsəntreɪt] **1** *n* concentré *m*
2 *vt* concentrer (**on** sur)
3 *vi* se concentrer (**on** sur); **to c. on doing sth** s'appliquer à faire qch

concentration [kɒnsən'treɪʃən] *n* concentration *f*; **c. camp** camp *m* de concentration; **to have a short c. span** ne pas avoir une grande capacité de concentration

concentric [kɒn'sentrɪk] *adj Math* concentrique

concept ['kɒnsept] *n* concept *m*

conception [kən'sepʃən] *n* (**a**) *(of child, idea)* conception *f* (**b**) *(understanding)* **to have no c. of sth** n'avoir aucune idée *ou* notion de qch

conceptual [kən'septjʊəl] *adj* conceptuel(elle)

conceptualize [kən'septjʊəlaɪz] *vt* conceptualiser

concern [kən'sɜːn] **1** *n* (**a**) *(interest)* **it's no c. of mine/yours** cela ne me/vous regarde pas; **this is a matter of public c.** c'est une affaire qui nous concerne tous (**b**) *(worry, compassion)* inquiétude *f*, souci *m*; **to give cause for c.** être un sujet d'inquiétude; **there is no cause for c.** il n'y a pas de raison de s'inquiéter; **to show c.** se montrer inquiet(ète) (**c**) *(company)* entreprise *f*
2 *vt* (**a**) *(affect)* concerner; **to c. oneself with sth** se préoccuper *ou* se soucier de qch; **as far as I'm concerned,...** pour moi,..., en ce qui me concerne,...; **to whom it may c.** à qui de droit (**b**) *(worry)* inquiéter (**c**) *(be about) (of book)* traiter de; **it concerns your request for a transfer** c'est au sujet de votre demande de transfert

concerned [kən'sɜːnd] *adj (worried)* inquiet(ète) (**about** au sujet de)

concerning [kən'sɜːnɪŋ] *prep* au sujet de

concert ['kɒnsət] *n* (**a**) *(musical)* concert *m*; **c. hall** salle *f* de concert; **c. pianist** concertiste *mf* (**b**) *(cooperation)* **in c. (with)** de concert (avec)

concerted [kən'sɜːtɪd] *adj* concerté(e)

concertina [kɒnsə'tiːnə] *n* concertina *m*

concerto [kən'tʃɜːtəʊ] *(pl* **concertos**) *n* concerto *m*

concession [kən'seʃən] *n* (**a**) *(compromise, giving up)* concession *f* (**b**) *(discount)* tarif *m* réduit

concessionary [kən'seʃənərɪ] *adj (fare)* réduit(e)

conciliate [kən'sɪlɪeɪt] *vt* apaiser

conciliation [kənsɪlɪ'eɪʃən] *n* conciliation *f*; *(in dispute)* conciliation, arbitrage *m*; **the dispute went to c.** le conflit a été soumis à l'arbitrage

conciliatory [kən'sɪlɪətərɪ] *adj* conciliant(e)

concise [kən'saɪs] *adj* concis(e)

conclude [kən'kluːd] **1** *vt* (**a**) *(speech, book, treaty)* conclure; *(conference, festival)* clore (**b**) *(deduce)* **to c. that...** conclure que...
2 *vi* se conclure (**with** sur); *(of speaker)* conclure (**with** sur); *(of conference, festival)* se clore (**with** sur)

concluding [kən'kluːdɪŋ] *adj* final(e)

conclusion [kən'kluːʒən] *n* (**a**) *(inference)* conclusion *f*; **to come to** *or* **reach a c.** arriver à une conclusion (**b**) *(end)* conclusion *f*; **in c.** pour conclure, en conclusion

conclusive [kən'kluːsɪv] *adj* concluant(e)

concoct [kən'kɒkt] *vt also Fig* concocter

concoction [kən'kɒkʃən] *n (drink, dish)* mixture *f*

concord ['kɒŋkɔːd] *n (harmony)* entente *f*

concordance [kən'kɔːdəns] *n (agreement)* accord *m*; **to be in c. with sth** être en accord avec qch

concourse ['kɒnkɔːs] *n (in airport, railway station)* hall *m*

concrete ['kɒnkriːt] **1** *n* béton *m*; **c. jungle** univers *m* de béton; **c. mixer** bétonnière *f*
2 *adj* en béton; *Fig (definite)* concret(ète)

concubine ['kɒŋkjʊbaɪn] *n* concubine *f*

concur [kən'kɜː(r)] *(pt & pp* **concurred**) *vi (of person)* être d'accord (**with** avec); *(of findings, results)* concorder (**with** avec)

concurrent [kən'kʌrənt] *adj* simultané(e), concordant(e)

concurrently [kən'kʌrəntlɪ] *adv* simultanément

concussed [kən'kʌst] *adj* commotionné(e)

concussion [kən'kʌʃən] *n* commotion *f* cérébrale

condemn [kən'dem] *vt* (**a**) *(disapprove of)* condamner (**b**) *Law (sentence)* condamner (**to** à); **condemned cell** cellule *f* de condamné à mort (**c**) *(building)* déclarer inhabitable

condemnation [kɒndem'neɪʃən] *n* condamnation *f*

condensation [kɒnden'seɪʃən] *n* (**a**) *(moisture) (on glass)* buée *f*; *(on walls)* condensation *f* (**b**) *(process)* condensation *f*

condense [kən'dens] **1** *vt* condenser; **condensed milk** lait *m* condensé
2 *vi* se condenser

condenser [kən'densə(r)] *n Tech* condensateur *m*

condescend [kɒndɪ'send] *vi* **to c. to do sth** condescendre à faire qch; **to c. towards sb** se montrer condescendant(e) envers qn

condescending [kɒndɪ'sendɪŋ] *adj* condescendant(e)

condescension [kɒndɪ'senʃən] *n* condescendance *f*

condiment ['kɒndɪmənt] *n* condiment *m*

condition [kən'dɪʃən] **1** *n* (**a**) *(state)* état *m*; *(of person)* forme *f*; **in good/bad c.** *(of machine, road)* en bon/mauvais état; **you're in no c. to drive** tu n'es pas en état de conduire; **to be in good c./out of c.** *(of person)* être/ne pas être en forme
(**b**) **conditions** *(circumstances)* conditions *fpl*; **working conditions** conditions de travail; **driving conditions** état *m* des routes; *Law* **conditions of employment** contrat *m* de travail
(**c**) *(requirement)* condition *f*; **on (the) c. that...** à (la)

condition que... + *subjunctive*; **on no c.** sous aucun prétexte, en aucun cas
  (**d**) *(disease)* maladie *f*; **heart c.** maladie du cœur
  2 *vt* (**a**) *(influence)* conditionner; **to be conditioned by** *(depend on)* dépendre de; **we have been conditioned to believe that...** on nous a appris que...; *Psy* **conditioned reflex** réflexe *m* conditionné
  (**b**) *(hair)* mettre de l'après-shampo(o)ing sur
conditional [kən'dɪʃənəl] **1** *n Gram* **the c.** le conditionnel
  2 *adj* conditionnel(elle); **to be c. on** dépendre de; *Law* **c. discharge** liberté *f* conditionnelle
conditionally [kən'dɪʃənəlɪ] *adv (accept, grant)* sous certaines conditions
conditioner [kən'dɪʃənə(r)] *n (for hair)* après-shampo(o)ing *m*
conditioning [kən'dɪʃənɪŋ] *n (psychological)* conditionnement *m*
condo ['kɒndəʊ] *(pl* **condos**) *n Am Fam (abbr* **condominium**) appartement *m* en copropriété
condolences [kən'dəʊlənsɪz] *npl* condoléances *fpl*
condom ['kɒndəm] *n* préservatif *m*
condominium [kɒndə'mɪnɪəm] *n Am (apartment)* appartement *m* en copropriété
condone [kən'dəʊn] *vt* excuser
condor ['kɒndɔː(r)] *n* condor *m*
conducive [kən'djuːsɪv] *adj* **to be c. to** être favorable *ou* propice à
conduct 1 *n* ['kɒndʌkt] *(behaviour)* conduite *f*
  2 *vt* [kən'dʌkt] (**a**) *(business, orchestra)* diriger; *(campaign, inquiry, experiment)* mener; **to c. oneself** se conduire (**b**) *(guide)* guider; **we were conducted round the factory** on nous a fait visiter l'usine; **a conducted tour** une visite guidée (**c**) *(heat, electricity)* conduire
  3 *vi* [kən'dʌkt] *Mus* diriger
conductivity [kɒndʌk'tɪvɪtɪ] *n Phys* conductivité *f*
conductor [kən'dʌktə(r)] *n* (**a**) *Br (on bus)* receveur *m* (**b**) *(of orchestra)* chef *m* d'orchestre (**c**) *Phys* conducteur *m*
conductress [kən'dʌktrɪs] *n Br (on bus)* receveuse *f*
conduit ['kɒndɪt] *n* conduit *m*
cone [kəʊn] *n* (**a**) *(shape)* cône *m* (**b**) *(of pine)* pomme *f* de pin (**c**) *(for ice cream)* cornet *m* (**d**) *(for traffic)* cône *m* de signalisation
cone-shaped ['kəʊnʃeɪpt] *adj* conique
confab ['kɒnfæb] *n Fam* **to have a c. about sth** discuter de qch
confectioner [kən'fekʃənə(r)] *n* confiseur(euse) *m,f*; *Culin* **c.'s custard** crème *f* pâtissière; **c.'s (shop)** confiserie *f*
confectionery [kən'fekʃənɪ] *n (sweets)* confiserie *f*
confederacy [kən'fedərəsɪ] *n* confédération *f*
confederate [kən'fedərət] **1** *n (accomplice)* complice *mf*
  2 *adj Pol* confédéré(e)
confederation [kənfedə'reɪʃən] *n* confédération *f*
confer [kən'fɜː(r)] *(pt & pp* **conferred**) **1** *vt (title, degree, powers)* octroyer (**on** à)
  2 *vi (discuss) (of several people)* se consulter; **to c. with sb about sth** discuter de qch avec qn
conference ['kɒnfərəns] *n* conférence *f*, congrès *m*; *Com* **to be in c.** être en conférence; *Tel* **c. call** téléconférence *f*

confess [kən'fes] **1** *vt (crime, mistake)* confesser, avouer; *(feeling)* avouer; *Rel* confesser; **to c. that...** confesser *ou* avouer que...
  2 *vi* avouer; *Rel* se confesser; **to c. to sth** *(crime, mistake)* confesser *ou* avouer qch; *(feeling)* avouer qch
confession [kən'feʃən] *n* confession *f*, aveu *m*; *Rel* confession; **to go to c.** aller se confesser
confessional [kən'feʃənəl] *n Rel* confessionnal *m*
confessor [kən'fesə(r)] *n Rel* confesseur *m*
confetti [kən'fetɪ] *n* confettis *mpl*
confidante [kɒnfɪ'dænt] *n* confident(e) *m,f*
confide [kən'faɪd] **1** *vt* **to c. sth to sb** confier qch à qn
  2 *vi* **to c. in sb** se confier à qn
confidence ['kɒnfɪdəns] *n* (**a**) *(trust)* confiance *f* (**in** en); **I have every c. that...** je ne doute pas un instant que...; **to take sb into one's c.** se confier à qn; **c. trick** escroquerie *f* (**b**) *(self-assurance)* confiance *f* en soi (**c**) *(secret)* confidence *f*; **in c.** en confidence
confident ['kɒnfɪdənt] *adj* (**a**) *(self-assured) (person)* sûr(e) de soi; *(smile, exterior)* confiant(e) (**b**) *(certain)* certain(e); **to be c. of doing sth** être certain de faire qch
confidential [kɒnfɪ'denʃəl] *adj* confidentiel(elle)
confidentiality [kɒnfɪdenʃɪ'ælɪtɪ] *n* confidentialité *f*
confidentially [kɒnfɪ'denʃəlɪ] *adv* confidentiellement, en confidence
confidently ['kɒnfɪdəntlɪ] *adv* (**a**) *(with self-assurance)* avec assurance (**b**) *(with certainty)* avec confiance
configuration [kənfɪgjʊ'reɪʃən] *n* configuration *f*
confine [kən'faɪn] *vt* (**a**) *(imprison)* enfermer; **to be confined to bed** être alité(e); **to be confined to barracks** être consigné(e); **confined space** espace *m* restreint (**b**) *(limit)* **to c. oneself to sth/doing sth** se limiter *ou* s'en tenir à qch/à faire qch
confinement [kən'faɪnmənt] *n* (**a**) *(in prison)* emprisonnement *m* (**b**) *Old-fashioned Med (labour)* couches *fpl*
confines ['kɒnfaɪnz] *npl (of town)* confins *mpl*; *Fig (limits)* limites *fpl*; **within the c. of** dans les limites de
confirm [kən'fɜːm] *vt* confirmer; *(power, position)* consolider, renforcer
confirmation [kɒnfə'meɪʃən] *n also Rel* confirmation *f*
confirmed [kən'fɜːmd] *adj (smoker, liar)* invétéré(e); *(bachelor)* endurci
confiscate ['kɒnfɪskeɪt] *vt* confisquer (**from** à)
confiscation [kɒnfɪs'keɪʃən] *n* confiscation *f*
conflict 1 *n* ['kɒnflɪkt] conflit *m*; **to come into c. with** entrer en conflit avec
  2 *vi* [kən'flɪkt] être en contradiction (**with** avec)
conflicting [kən'flɪktɪŋ] *adj (opinions)* opposé(e); *(reports, evidence)* contradictoire
confluence ['kɒnflʊəns] *n (of rivers)* confluent *m*
conform [kən'fɔːm] *vi* se plier aux règles; **to c. to** *(rules)* obéir à, se plier à; *(standards)* être en conformité avec; **to c. with** être conforme à
conformist [kən'fɔːmɪst] *n & adj* conformiste *mf*
conformity [kən'fɔːmɪtɪ] *n* conformité *f*; **in c. with** en conformité *ou* en accord avec
confound [kən'faʊnd] *vt* (**a**) *(puzzle)* laisser perplexe (**b**) *(frustrate) (plans)* faire échouer (**c**) *(surprise)* confondre (**d**) *Fam (damn)* **c. it!** quelle barbe!; **c. him!** le diable l'emporte!

confront [kən'frʌnt] *vt* affronter, faire face à; **to be confronted by sth** être confronté(e) à qch; **to c. sb with sth** confronter qn à qch

confrontation [kɒnfrʌn'teɪʃən] *n* affrontement *m*

confuse [kən'fjuːz] *vt (bewilder)* embrouiller; *(mix up)* confondre (**with** avec)

confused [kən'fjuːzd] *adj (person)* perdu(e); *(instructions, account, mind)* confus(e); **I'm c.** je m'y perds; **to get c.** s'embrouiller

confusing [kən'fjuːzɪŋ] *adj (bewildering)* déroutant(e); *(muddled)* confus(e); **it's very c.** on s'y perd

confusion [kən'fjuːʒən] *n (bewilderment)* perplexité *f*; *(disorder, lack of clarity)* confusion *f*; **to throw sth into c.** chambouler qch

congeal [kən'dʒiːl] *vi (of blood)* (se) coaguler

congenial [kən'dʒiːnɪəl] *adj* agréable

congenital [kən'dʒenɪtəl] *adj* congénital(e); *Fig* **he's a c. liar** il ment tout le temps, c'est congénital

conger ['kɒŋɡə(r)] *n* **c. (eel)** congre *m*

congested [kən'dʒestɪd] *adj (road)* encombré(e); *(area, town)* surpeuplé(e); *Med (lungs)* congestionné(e); *(nose)* bouché(e)

congestion [kən'dʒestʃən] *n (of traffic)* encombrements *mpl*; *(of area, town)* surpeuplement *m*; *Med (of lungs)* congestion *f*

conglomerate [kən'ɡlɒmərət] *n* conglomérat *m*

Congo ['kɒŋɡəʊ] *n* **the C.** *(country)* le Congo

Congolese [kɒŋɡə'liːz] **1** *n* Congolais(e) *m,f*
2 *adj* congolais(e)

congratulate [kən'ɡrætjʊleɪt] *vt* féliciter (**on** de); **to c. oneself on having done sth** se féliciter d'avoir fait qch

congratulations [kənɡrætjʊ'leɪʃənz] *npl* félicitations *fpl*; **c. on your promotion/passing your exams** félicitations pour votre promotion/vos examens

congratulatory [kən'ɡrætjʊleɪtərɪ] *adj* de félicitations

congregate ['kɒŋɡrɪɡeɪt] *vi* se rassembler, s'assembler

congregation [kɒŋɡrɪ'ɡeɪʃən] *n (of church)* assemblée *f* des fidèles

congress ['kɒŋɡres] *n (conference)* congrès *m*; *Am Pol* **C.** le Congrès *(assemblée législative américaine)*

┌───┐
Congress
Le Congrès, organe législatif américain, est constitué du Sénat et de la Chambre des représentants. Une proposition de loi doit obligatoirement être approuvée séparément par ces deux Chambres.
└───┘

Congressman ['kɒŋɡresmən] *n Am Pol* membre *m* du Congrès

Congresswoman ['kɒŋɡreswʊmən] *n Am Pol* membre *m* du Congrès

conical ['kɒnɪkəl] *adj* conique

conifer ['kɒnɪfə(r)] *n* conifère *m*

coniferous [kə'nɪfərəs] *adj (forest)* de conifères; **c. tree** conifère *m*

conjecture [kən'dʒektʃə(r)] **1** *n* conjecture *f*; **it's sheer c.** ce ne sont que des suppositions
2 *vt* supposer
3 *vi* faire des conjectures

conjugal ['kɒndʒʊɡəl] *adj* conjugal(e)

conjugate ['kɒndʒʊɡeɪt] *Gram* **1** *vt* conjuguer
2 *vi* se conjuguer

conjugation [kɒndʒʊ'ɡeɪʃən] *n Gram* conjugaison *f*

conjunction [kən'dʒʌŋkʃən] *n* conjonction *f*; **in c. with** conjointement avec

conjunctivitis [kəndʒʌŋktɪ'vaɪtɪs] *n* conjonctivite *f*

conjure ['kʌndʒə(r)] *vi (do magic)* faire des tours de passe-passe; *Fig* **a name to c. with** un nom prestigieux

▶**conjure up** *vt sep* (**a**) *(produce)* faire apparaître; **she conjured up a meal** elle s'est débrouillée pour préparer un repas en un rien de temps; **to c. sth up out of nowhere** faire apparaître qch comme par magie (**b**) *(call to mind)* évoquer

conjurer ['kʌndʒərə(r)] *n* prestidigitateur *m*, illusionniste *mf*

conjuring ['kʌndʒərɪŋ] *n* prestidigitation *f*; **c. trick** tour *m* de prestidigitation *ou* de passe-passe

conjuror = **conjurer**

conk [kɒŋk] *n Fam (nose)* blair *m*, pif *m*

▶**conk out** *vi Fam* (**a**) *(stop working) (of machine, TV)* flancher; **the car conked out on me** la voiture m'a claqué entre les doigts (**b**) *(fall asleep)* se mettre à pioncer

conker ['kɒŋkə(r)] *n Fam (chestnut)* marron *m* d'Inde; *Br* **conkers** *(game)* = jeu qui consiste à faire éclater le marron que son adversaire tient au bout d'une ficelle

conman ['kɒnmæn] *n* escroc *m*

connect [kə'nekt] **1** *vt* (**a**) *(pipes, wires, circuits)* relier (**to** à); **to c. sth to the mains** brancher qch sur secteur (**b**) *(link, associate)* **to c. sb/sth to sb/sth** établir un lien entre qn/qch et qn/qch; **there is nothing to c. the two crimes** il n'y a aucun lien entre les deux crimes; **to be connected with** avoir un lien *ou* un rapport avec; **the two issues are not connected** les deux questions n'ont aucun rapport; **are they connected?** *(of people)* sont-ils parents?; **to be well connected** *(of person)* avoir des relations (**c**) *Tel* mettre en ligne *ou* en communication (**with** avec); **can you c. me with reservations?** pourriez-vous me passer le service des réservations?
2 *vi* (**a**) *(of pipes, wires, roads)* être relié(e) (**with** avec); *(of rooms)* communiquer (**with** avec) (**b**) *(of train, plane)* assurer la correspondance (**with** avec) (**c**) *(of blow)* atteindre son but; **the blow connected with his knee** le coup l'a atteint au genou

▶**connect up** *vt sep (pipes, wires)* raccorder

connection [kə'nekʃən] *n* (**a**) *(link, association)* lien *m*, rapport *m*; **in c. with** à propos de; **in this c.** à ce propos (**b**) *(acquaintance)* relation *f*; **to have important connections** avoir des relations en haut lieu (**c**) *(of pipes, wires)* raccordement *m* (**d**) *(train, plane)* correspondance *f*

connivance [kə'naɪvəns] *n* connivence *f*

connive [kə'naɪv] *vi* (**a**) *(conspire)* comploter; **to c. with sb** être de connivence avec qn (**b**) **to c. at sth** *(let happen)* laisser faire qch

conniving [kə'naɪvɪŋ] *adj* intrigant(e)

connoisseur [kɒnə'sɜː(r)] *n* connaisseur(euse) *m,f* (**of** en)

connotation [kɒnə'teɪʃən] *n* connotation *f*

conquer ['kɒŋkə(r)] *vt (country, someone's heart)* conquérir; *(difficulty, fears)* vaincre

conquering ['kɒŋkərɪŋ] *adj* victorieux(euse)

conqueror ['kɒŋkərə(r)] *n* vainqueur *m*

conquest ['kɒŋkwest] *n* conquête *f*; **to make a c. of sb** faire la conquête de qn

conscience ['kɒnʃəns] *n* conscience *f*; **to have a clear c.** avoir la conscience tranquille; **to have a guilty c.**

avoir mauvaise conscience; **to have sth on one's c.** avoir qch sur la conscience; **to have no c. about doing sth** ne pas avoir de scrupules à faire qch; **in all c.** raisonnablement

conscientious [kɒnʃɪ'enʃəs] *adj* consciencieux(-euse); **c. objector** objecteur *m* de conscience

conscious ['kɒnʃəs] *adj* (**a**) *(awake)* conscient(e) (**b**) *(aware)* **to be c. of sth/that...** être conscient(e) de qch/que...; **to become c. of sth** prendre conscience de qch, s'apercevoir de qch; *Psy* **the c. mind** la conscience (**c**) *(intentional)* conscient(e); **to make a c. effort to do sth** faire un effort particulier pour faire qch; **to make a c. decision to do sth** chercher délibérément à faire qch

consciousness ['kɒnʃəsnɪs] *n* (**a**) *(wakefulness)* conscience *f*; **to lose/regain c.** perdre/reprendre connaissance (**b**) *(awareness)* conscience *f* (**of** de); **to raise people's c. of sth** sensibiliser les gens à qch

conscript 1 *n* ['kɒnskrɪpt] conscrit *m*
2 *vt* [kən'skrɪpt] enrôler; **to be conscripted** être appelé(e) (sous les drapeaux)

conscription [kən'skrɪpʃən] *n* conscription *f*

consecrate ['kɒnsɪkreɪt] *vt Rel & Fig* consacrer

consecration [kɒnsɪ'kreɪʃən] *n* consécration *f*

consecutive [kən'sekjʊtɪv] *adj* consécutif(ive); **on three c. days** trois jours consécutifs, trois jours de suite

consensus [kən'sensəs] *n* consensus *m*

consent [kən'sent] **1** *n* consentement *m*, assentiment *m*
2 *vi* **to c. to sth/to do sth** consentir à qch/à faire qch

consequence ['kɒnsɪkwəns] *n* (**a**) *(result)* conséquence *f*; **as a c., in c.** par conséquent; **to take the consequences** subir les conséquences (**b**) *(importance)* importance *f*; **of little c.** de peu d'importance; **of no c.** sans importance

consequent ['kɒnsɪkwənt] *adj* résultant(e); **c. upon sth** qui résulte de qch; **the war and its c. loss of life** la guerre et les pertes en vies humaines qui en résultent

consequently ['kɒnsɪkwəntlɪ] *adv* par conséquent

conservation [kɒnsə'veɪʃən] *n* *(of environment)* protection *f*; *(of energy)* économies *fpl*; **c. area** *(of town, city)* quartier *m* préservé; *(nature reserve)* réserve *f* naturelle

conservationist [kɒnsə'veɪʃənɪst] *n* défenseur *m* de l'environnement

Conservative [kən'sɜːvətɪv] *Br Pol* **1** *n* conserva-teur(-trice) *m,f*
2 *adj* conservateur(trice); **the C. Party** le Parti conservateur

conservative [kən'sɜːvətɪv] **1** *n* conservateur(trice) *m,f*
2 *adj* conservateur(trice); *(conventional)* classique; **at a c. estimate** au bas mot

conservatory [kən'sɜːvətərɪ] *(pl* conservatories*)* *n* (**a**) *(room)* véranda *f* (**b**) *Mus* conservatoire *m*

conserve 1 *n* ['kɒnsɜːv] *(jam)* confiture *f*
2 *vt* [kən'sɜːv] *(monument, language, tradition)* préserver; *(water, energy)* faire des économies de

consider [kən'sɪdə(r)] *vt* (**a**) *(think over)* considérer; *(offer, matter)* étudier; **he was considering whether to go out when...** il était en train de se demander s'il allait sortir lorsque...; **to c. doing sth** envisager de faire qch; **to c. sb for a job** envisager qn pour un

poste (**b**) *(take into account)* penser, réfléchir à; *(possibility)* envisager; *(person's feelings)* tenir compte de; **all things considered** tout bien considéré (**c**) *(regard)* considérer; **I c. her a friend** je la considère comme une amie; **c. it done** considère que c'est déjà fait; **c. yourself dismissed** considère-toi comme renvoyé

considerable [kən'sɪdərəbəl] *adj* considérable; **after c. difficulty** après bien des difficultés

considerate [kən'sɪdərət] *adj* prévenant(e) (**towards** envers); **that wasn't very c. of you** ce n'était pas très aimable de ta part

consideration [kənsɪdə'reɪʃən] *n* (**a**) *(deliberation)* **to be under c.** être à l'étude; **after due c.** après mûre réflexion; **to take sth into c.** prendre qch en considération (**b**) *(factor)* facteur *m* (**c**) *(respect)* considération *f*; **show some c.!** tu pourrais faire preuve d'un peu de considération!; **out of c. for** par égard pour (**d**) *(payment)* contribution *f*; **for a small c.** en échange d'une modique somme

considering [kən'sɪdərɪŋ] **1** *prep* étant donné, vu
2 *conj* étant donné que; **c. (that) he is so young** étant donné son jeune âge
3 *adv* *(after all)* **not bad c.** pas mal après tout

consign [kən'saɪn] *vt* (**a**) *(dispose of)* reléguer (**to** à); **she was consigned to a life of loneliness** elle fut condamnée à une existence solitaire (**b**) *(entrust)* confier (**to** à) (**c**) *(send)* expédier (**to** à)

consignment [kən'saɪnmənt] *n* *(of goods)* envoi *m*, expédition *f*

►**consist in** [kən'sɪst] *vt insep* **to c. in doing sth** consister à faire qch; **to c. in sth** résider dans qch, se résumer à qch

►**consist of** *vt insep* consister en, se composer de

consistency [kən'sɪstənsɪ] *n* (**a**) *(of substance, liquid)* consistance *f* (**b**) *(of arguments, ideas)* cohérence *f*; *(of behaviour, person)* logique *f*; *(of performer, results)* régularité *f*

consistent [kən'sɪstənt] *adj* *(arguments, ideas)* cohérent(e); *(behaviour, person)* logique; *(quality, standard)* constant(e); *(performer, results)* régulier(ère); *(refusal, failure)* persistant(e); **to be c. with** concorder avec

consistently [kən'sɪstəntlɪ] *adv* *(play, perform)* avec régularité; *(fail, deny, oppose)* toujours

consolation [kɒnsə'leɪʃən] *n* consolation *f*; **if it's any c.** si ça peut te consoler; **c. prize** prix *m* de consolation

console¹ ['kɒnsəʊl] *n* *(control panel)* console *f*

console² [kən'səʊl] *vt* consoler (**for** de); *(bereaved person)* réconforter

consolidate [kən'sɒlɪdeɪt] **1** *vt* *also Fig* consolider; *(position)* renforcer; *(power)* asseoir
2 *vi* se consolider

consolidation [kənsɒlɪ'deɪʃən] *n* *also Fig* consolidation *f*; *(of position, power)* renforcement *m*

consoling [kən'səʊlɪŋ] *adj* réconfortant(e)

consonant ['kɒnsənənt] **1** *n* consonne *f*
2 *adj Formal* **c. with** en accord avec

consort ['kɒnsɔːt] *n* *(spouse of monarch)* époux (épouse) *m,f*; **(prince) c.** prince *m* consort

►**consort with** [kən'sɔːt] *vt insep* frayer avec, fréquenter

consortium [kən'sɔːtɪəm] *(pl* consortiums *or* consortia [kən'sɔːtɪə] *)* *n Com* consortium *m*

conspicuous [kən'spɪkjʊəs] *adj* *(easily visible)* bien visible; *(bravery)* remarquable; **to look c.** ne pas passer inaperçu(e); **to make oneself c.** se faire remarquer;

in a c. position bien en évidence; **to be c. by one's absence** briller par son absence; **c. consumption** consommation *f* ostentatoire

conspiracy [kən'spɪrəsɪ] (*pl* **conspiracies**) *n* conspiration *f*; **c. theory** = théorie postulant l'existence d'un complot pour expliquer des événements demeurés mystérieux

conspirator [kən'spɪrətə(r)] *n* conspirateur(trice) *m,f*

conspiratorial [kənspɪrə'tɔːrɪəl] *adj* de conspirateur; **a c. wink** un coup d'œil complice

conspire [kən'spaɪə(r)] *vi* (*of person*) se liguer (**against/with** contre/avec); (*for political reasons*) conspirer (**against/with** contre/avec); **circumstances conspired against me** les circonstances se sont liguées contre moi

constable ['kʌnstəbəl] *n Br* agent *m* de police; (*rural*) gendarme *m*; **chief c.** = commissaire *m* de police divisionnaire

constabulary [kən'stæbjʊlərɪ] (*pl* **constabularies**) *n* police *f*

constant ['kɒnstənt] **1** *n Math & Phys* constante *f*
2 *adj* (**a**) (*unchanging*) (*price, temperature*) constant(e); (*friend*) fidèle (**b**) (*continual*) (*attention, noise, care*) continuel(elle); (*questions, complaints*) incessant(e); **a c. stream of insults** un flot d'injures ininterrompu

constellation [kɒnstə'leɪʃən] *n* constellation *f*

consternation [kɒnstə'neɪʃən] *n* consternation *f*

constipated ['kɒnstɪpeɪtɪd] *adj also Fig* constipé(e)

constipation [kɒnstɪ'peɪʃən] *n* constipation *f*

constituency [kən'stɪtjʊənsɪ] (*pl* **constituencies**) *n* circonscription *f* (électorale)

constituent [kən'stɪtjʊənt] **1** *n* (**a**) *Pol* électeur(trice) *m,f* (**b**) (*part*) élément *m* constitutif
2 *adj* constitutif(ive); **c. part** élément *m* constitutif

constitute ['kɒnstɪtjuːt] *vt* constituer

constitution [kɒnstɪ'tjuːʃən] *n* (**a**) (*of state, organization*) constitution *f* (**b**) (*of person*) constitution *f*; **to have a strong c.** avoir une santé de fer; **to have a weak c.** être de santé fragile

constitutional [kɒnstɪ'tjuːʃənəl] **1** *n* (*walk*) (courte) promenade *f*
2 *adj* (*reform, decision, monarchy*) constitutionnel(elle)

constrain [kən'streɪn] *vt* contraindre, obliger (**to do** à faire); **to feel constrained to do sth** se sentir obligé(e) de faire qch

constraint [kən'streɪnt] *n* contrainte *f*; **to place constraints upon** imposer des contraintes à; **under c.** sous la contrainte

constrict [kən'strɪkt] *vt* (*blood vessel*) resserrer; (*movement*) gêner; **to feel constricted** se sentir à l'étroit

constriction [kən'strɪkʃən] *n* (*of blood vessel*) constriction *f*; (*of person*) gêne *f*

construct 1 *n* ['kɒnstrʌkt] (*idea*) concept *m*
2 *vt* [kən'strʌkt] construire

construction [kən'strʌkʃən] *n* (**a**) (*building*) & *Gram* construction *f*; **under c.** en construction; **the c. industry** l'industrie *f* du bâtiment, le bâtiment; **c. site** chantier *m* (de construction); **c. worker** ouvrier *m* du bâtiment (**b**) (*interpretation*) **to put a favourable/an unfavourable c. on sth** bien/mal interpréter qch

constructive [kən'strʌktɪv] *adj* constructif(ive)

construe [kən'struː] *vt* interpréter

consul ['kɒnsəl] *n* consul *m*

consular ['kɒnsjʊlə(r)] *adj* consulaire

consulate ['kɒnsjʊlət] *n* consulat *m*

consult [kən'sʌlt] **1** *vt* consulter (**on** sur *ou* à propos de)
2 *vi* consulter (**with sb/about sth** qn/à propos de qch)

consultancy [kən'sʌltənsɪ] (*pl* **consultancies**) *n* (**a**) (*of doctor*) poste *m* de spécialiste (*haut placé dans la hiérarchie hospitalière*) (**b**) *Com* conseil *m*; **to do c. work** être consultant(e)

consultant [kən'sʌltənt] *n* (**a**) (*doctor*) spécialiste *mf* (*pratiquant à l'hôpital*) (**b**) (*adviser*) consultant(e) *m,f*

consultation [kɒnsəl'teɪʃən] *n* (*reference*) consultation *f*; (*discussion*) délibération *f*; **to hold a c. with sb** s'entretenir avec qn; **in c. with sb** en consultation avec qn

consume [kən'sjuːm] *vt* (*food, fuel, power*) consommer; **to be consumed with jealousy/desire** brûler de jalousie/désir

consumer [kən'sjuːmə(r)] *n* (*of product*) consommateur(trice) *m,f*; **c. durables** biens *mpl* de consommation durables; **c. goods** biens de consommation; *Econ* **c. price index** indice *m* des prix de détails; **c. protection** la défense du consommateur; **c. research** étude *f* de marché; **c. society** société *f* de consommation; **c. spending** dépenses *fpl* de consommation

consumerism [kən'sjuːmərɪzəm] *n* consumérisme *m*

consummate 1 *adj* [kən'sʌmɪt] (*linguist, cook*) de premier ordre; (*snob, hypocrite*) parfait(e)
2 *vt* ['kɒnsəmeɪt] (*marriage, relationship*) consommer

consumption [kən'sʌmpʃən] *n* (**a**) (*of goods, resources*) consommation *f*; **unfit for human c.** impropre à la consommation (**b**) *Old-fashioned Med* (*tuberculosis*) consomption *f*

contact ['kɒntækt] **1** *n* (**a**) (*act of touching*) contact *m*; **to be in/come into c. with** être en/entrer en contact avec; **to make c. with sb** prendre contact avec qn; **to lose c. with sb** perdre contact avec qn; **to get in c. with sb** contacter qn; **c. lenses,** *Fam* **contacts** lentilles *fpl* (de contact) (**b**) (*acquaintance*) relation *f*; **he has lots of contacts** il connaît beaucoup de monde
2 *vt* se mettre en rapport avec, contacter

contagious [kən'teɪdʒəs] *adj* (*disease*) contagieux(-euse); (*laughter*) communicatif(ive)

contain [kən'teɪn] *vt* (**a**) (*hold*) contenir, renfermer; (*include*) contenir (**b**) (*control*) contenir; **to c. oneself** se contenir; **he was unable to c. his laughter** il ne put s'empêcher de rire

container [kən'teɪnə(r)] *n* (*for storage*) récipient *m*; (*for transport*) conteneur *m*; **c. lorry** camion *m* adapté au transport des conteneurs; **c. ship** (navire *m*) porte-conteneurs *m inv*; **c. terminal** terminal *m* à conteneurs

contaminate [kən'tæmɪneɪt] *vt also Fig* contaminer

contamination [kəntæmɪ'neɪʃən] *n* contamination *f*

contd (*abbr* **continued**) **c. on page 14** suite (à la) page 14

contemplate ['kɒntempleɪt] **1** *vt* (*look at*) contempler; (*consider*) réfléchir à; **to c. doing sth** envisager de *ou* songer à faire qch
2 *vi* (*consider*) méditer

contemplation [kɒntem'pleɪʃən] *n* contemplation *f*

contemplative [kən'templətɪv] *adj* contemplatif(ive)

contemporary (*pl* **contemporaries**) [kən'tempərərɪ] *n & adj* contemporain(e) *m,f*

contempt [kən'tempt] *n* mépris *m*; **to hold sb/sth in c.** avoir du mépris pour qn/qch, mépriser qn/qch; **to be beneath c.** être des plus méprisables; *Law* **c. of court** outrage *m* au tribunal

contemptible [kən'temptəbəl] *adj* méprisable

contemptuous [kən'temptjʊəs] *adj* méprisant(e); **to be c. of sth** mépriser qch

contend [kən'tend] **1** *vt (maintain)* **to c. that...** prétendre *ou* soutenir que...

2 *vi* (**a**) *(struggle)* **to c. with sth** lutter contre qch; *(difficulties)* affronter qch; **they still had the chairman to c. with** il leur restait à régler le problème du P.D.-G. (**b**) *(compete)* **to c. for sth** se battre pour qch; *(for job, contract)* être en concurrence pour qch

contender [kən'tendə(r)] *n (in sport)* concurrent(e) *m,f*; *(in election, for job)* candidat(e) *m,f*

content¹ ['kɒntent] *n* (**a**) *(quantity)* teneur *f*; *(of book, speech, essay)* fond *m*; **protein/fibre c.** teneur en protéines/fibres (**b**) **contents** *(of pockets, drawer, house)* contenu *m*; **contents page** *(of book)* table *f* des matières

content² [kən'tent] **1** *adj (happy)* content(e), satisfait(e) (**with** de); **to be c. with one's lot** se contenter de son sort

2 *vt* contenter; **to c. oneself with sth/with doing sth** se contenter de qch/de faire qch

contented [kən'tentɪd] *adj (person)* content(e), satisfait(e) (**with** de); *(smile, sigh)* de satisfaction

contention [kən'tenʃən] *n* (**a**) *(dispute)* dispute *f* (**b**) *(competition)* **to be in c. (for sth)** être en compétition (pour qch) (**c**) *(opinion)* affirmation *f*; **it is my c. that...** j'affirme que...

contentious [kən'tenʃəs] *adj (issue, views)* controversé(e); *(person)* querelleur(euse)

contentment [kən'tentmənt] *n* contentement *m*

contest 1 *n* ['kɒntest] *(competition)* concours *m*; *(for job, presidency)* lutte *f*; *(in boxing)* combat *m*

2 *vt* [kən'test] *(right, ability, will)* contester; **to c. a seat** se porter candidat(e); **a fiercely contested election** une élection très disputée

contestant [kən'testənt] *n (in competition, game)* concurrent(e) *m,f*; *(in election)* candidat(e) *m,f*

context ['kɒntekst] *n* contexte *m*; **in/out of c.** en/hors contexte; **to put sth into c.** replacer qch dans son contexte

continent¹ ['kɒntɪnənt] *n (land mass)* continent *m*; *Br* **the C.** l'Europe *f* (continentale)

continent² *adj Med* continent(e)

continental [kɒntɪ'nentəl] *adj* (**a**) *(in geography)* continental(e); **c. drift** dérive *f* des continents; **c. shelf** plate-forme *f* continentale (**b**) *Br (European)* européen(enne), d'outre Manche, d'Europe continentale; **c. breakfast** = petit déjeuner se composant de tartines et d'une boisson chaude; **c. quilt** couette *f*

> ### Continental Breakfast
> Ce terme désigne un petit déjeuner léger, par opposition au breakfast anglais, beaucoup plus copieux et comportant un plat chaud.

contingency [kən'tɪndʒənsɪ] *(pl* **contingencies**) *n* éventualité *f*; **to allow for every c.** parer à toute éventualité; **c. fund** caisse *f ou* fond *m* de prévoyance; **c. plan** plan *m* d'urgence

contingent [kən'tɪndʒənt] *adj* contingent(e); **to be c. upon sth** dépendre de qch

continual [kən'tɪnjʊəl] *adj* continuel(elle), incessant(e)

continuation [kəntɪnjʊ'eɪʃən] *n (of story)* suite *f*; *(of action, work)* prolongation *f*; *(of road)* prolongement *m*

continue [kən'tɪnjuː] **1** *vt (activity, journey)* continuer, poursuivre; *(after interruption)* reprendre, continuer; *(tradition)* perpétuer; **to c. to do** *or* **doing sth** continuer à *ou* de faire qch; **to be continued** à suivre; **continued on page 30** suite (à la) page 30

2 *vi* continuer; *(of situation)* se prolonger; **to c. on one's way** continuer *ou* poursuivre son chemin; **she will c. as director until December** elle continuera d'assumer ses fonctions de directrice jusqu'en décembre; **the situation cannot c.** cette situation ne peut pas durer

continuity [kɒntɪ'njuːɪtɪ] *n* continuité *f*; **c. announcer** *(on TV, radio)* speaker(ine) *m,f*; **c. girl** scripte *f*

continuous [kən'tɪnjʊəs] *adj* continu(e); *Sch & Univ* **c. assessment** contrôle *m* continu; *Comput* **c. paper** *or* **stationery** papier *m* (en) continu; *Cin* **c. performance** cinéma *m* permanent

contort [kən'tɔːt] **1** *vt* tordre

2 *vi* se tordre (**with** de)

contortion [kən'tɔːʃən] *n (of features)* crispation *f*; *(of body)* contorsion *f*

contour ['kɒntʊə(r)] *n* contour *m*; **c. (line)** courbe *f* de niveau; **c. map** carte *f* en courbes de niveau

contraband ['kɒntrəbænd] *n* contrebande *f*; **c. goods** marchandises *fpl* de contrebande

contraception [kɒntrə'sepʃən] *n* contraception *f*

contraceptive [kɒntrə'septɪv] **1** *n* contraceptif *m*

2 *adj* **c. pill** pilule *f* contraceptive

contract 1 *n* ['kɒntrækt] contrat *m*; **to be under c.** être sous contrat; **to enter into a c.** passer un contrat; **to take out a c. on sb** *(hire assassin)* engager un tueur à gages pour assassiner qn; **c. killer** tueur *m* à gages

2 *vt* [kən'trækt] *(illness, debt)* contracter; **to c. to do sth** s'engager (par contrat) à faire qch

3 *vi* [kən'trækt] *(shrink)* se contracter

▸**contract out 1** *vt sep (work)* sous-traiter

2 *vi Com (of insurance policy, pension plan)* arrêter de souscrire (**of** à)

contraction [kən'trækʃən] *n* contraction *f*

contractor [kən'træktə(r)] *n (businessman)* entrepreneur *m* (en bâtiment); *(worker)* ouvrier *m* (en bâtiment)

contractual [kən'træktjʊəl] *adj* contractuel(elle)

contradict [kɒntrə'dɪkt] *vt (disagree with)* contredire; *(deny)* démentir; **to c. oneself** se contredire

contradiction [kɒntrə'dɪkʃən] *n* contradiction *f*; **it's a c. in terms** c'est parfaitement contradictoire

contradictory [kɒntrə'dɪktərɪ] *adj* contradictoire

contraflow ['kɒntrəfləʊ] *n* **c. (system)** *(on motorway)* = circulation sur une voie unique, lors de travaux routiers

contralto [kən'træltəʊ] *(pl* **contraltos**) *n* contralto *mf*

contraption [kən'træpʃən] *n Fam* machin *m*, truc *m*

contrary ['kɒntrərɪ] **1** *n* contraire *m*; **on the c.** au contraire; **unless you hear to the c.** sauf avis contraire; **there was no evidence to the c.** il n'y avait pas de preuve du contraire

2 *adj* (**a**) *(opposite)* contraire (**to** à); *(ideas, interests)* opposé(e) (**to** à); **c. to my expectations** contre mon attente; **c. to popular belief** contrairement à ce que croient la plupart des gens (**b**) [kən'treərɪ] *(awkward)* contrariant(e)

contrast1 *n* ['kɒntrɑːst] contraste *m* (**between** entre); **in c. with** *or* **to** par opposition à; **by c.** par contraste 2 *vt* [kən'trɑːst] mettre en contraste (**with** avec) 3 *vi* [kən'trɑːst] faire contraste (**with** avec)

contrasting [kən'trɑːstɪŋ] *adj (attitudes, lifestyles)* qui fait contraste; *(colours)* opposé(e), contrasté(e)

contravene [kɒntrə'viːn] *vt* enfreindre

contravention [kɒntrə'venʃən] *n (of law)* infraction *f* (**of** à); **in c. of a treaty** en violation d'un traité

contribute [kən'trɪbjuːt] 1 *vt (money)* verser; *(time, clothes)* donner; **to c. an article to a newspaper** écrire un article pour un journal; **he didn't c. anything to the discussion** il n'a pas pris part à la discussion
  2 *vi* (**a**) *(give money, goods etc)* contribuer (**to** à); *(to charity)* donner (**to** à); *(to newspaper)* collaborer (**to** à); **to c. to a discussion** prendre part à une discussion (**b**) *Fin (to pension fund)* cotiser (**to** à)

contribution [kɒntrɪ'bjuːʃən] *n* (**a**) *(of money, goods etc)* contribution *f* (**to** à); **the chocolate mousse was David's c.** c'est David qu'il faut remercier pour la mousse au chocolat (**b**) *Fin (to pension fund)* cotisation *f*

contributor [kən'trɪbjʊtə(r)] *n (to charity)* dona-teur(-trice) *m,f; (to newspaper)* collaborateur(trice) *m,f* (**to** de)

contributory [kən'trɪbjʊtərɪ] *adj (cause, factor)* concourant(e); **to be a c. factor in sth** concourir à qch; *Law* **c. negligence** manque *m* de précautions; *Fin* **c. pension scheme** système *m* de retraite par répartition

contrite ['kɒntraɪt] *adj* contrit(e)

contrition [kən'trɪʃən] *n* contrition *f*

contrivance [kən'traɪvəns] *n (device)* appareil *m; (scheme, plan)* système *m*

contrive [kən'traɪv] *vt* inventer; **to c. to do sth** trouver le moyen de faire qch

contrived [kən'traɪvd] *adj* forcé(e), qui manque de naturel

control [kən'trəʊl] 1 *n* (**a**) *(power, restriction)* contrôle *m;* **to impose controls on prices** imposer le contrôle des prix; **to take c. (of the situation)** prendre les choses en main; **to have c. over** *(power)* contrôler; *(authority)* avoir de l'autorité sur; **to be in c. of sth** contrôler qch; **to be back in c.** avoir repris le contrôle; **to get out of c.** devenir incontrôlable; **to let sth get out of c.** perdre le contrôle de qch; **to bring a fire under c.** maîtriser un incendie; **to keep one's feelings under c.** maîtriser ses émotions; **everything is under c.** je domine/nous dominons/*etc* la situation; **to lose c. (of oneself)** ne plus être maître de soi; **to regain c. (of oneself)** se ressaisir; *Pej* **c. freak** = personne qui veut tout régenter; **c. group** groupe *m* témoin; **c. tower** *(at airport)* tour *f* de contrôle (**b**) *(device)* **the controls** les commandes *fpl;* **to be at the controls** être aux commandes; **c. panel** tableau *m* de bord
  2 *vt (pt & pp* **controlled***) (production, expenditure, prices)* contrôler; *(business)* diriger; *(child, pupils)* avoir de l'autorité sur; *(disease)* maintenir à un niveau raisonnable; *(vehicle)* garder le contrôle de; **to c. oneself** se maîtriser; **to c. one's anger** maîtriser sa colère

controlled [kən'trəʊld] *adj (person)* maître de soi, posé(e); *(experiment, explosion)* contrôlé(e)

controlling interest [kən'trəʊlɪŋ'ɪntrest] *n Fin* participation *f* majoritaire

controversial [kɒntrə'vɜːʃəl] *adj* **to be c.** *(of film, decision)* être controversé(e); *(of person)* être provocateur(trice)

controversy ['kɒntrəvɜːsɪ, kən'trɒvəsɪ] *(pl* **contro-versies***) n* controverse *f,* polémique *f;* **to cause a lot of c.** provoquer une grande controverse *ou* une vive polémique

conundrum [kə'nʌndrəm] *n (riddle)* devinette *f; (mystery)* énigme *f*

conurbation [kɒnɜː'beɪʃən] *n* conurbation *f*

convalesce [kɒnvə'les] *vi* être en convalescence

convalescence [kɒnvə'lesəns] *n* convalescence *f*

convalescent [kɒnvə'lesənt] *adj (patient)* convalescent(e); **c. home** maison *f* de repos

convection [kən'vekʃən] *n* convection *f;* **c. heater** convecteur *m*

convene [kən'viːn] 1 *vt (meeting)* convoquer
  2 *vi (of meeting, committee)* se réunir

convenience [kən'viːnɪəns] *n* commodité *f;* **at your c.** quand cela vous conviendra; *Formal* **at your earliest c.** dans les meilleurs délais; **(public) c.** *(toilet)* toilettes *fpl* publiques; **c. food** aliments *mpl* tout prêts; *Am* **c. store** = supérette de quartier qui reste ouverte tard le soir, *Can* dépanneur *m*

convenient [kən'viːnɪənt] *adj (arrangement, method)* commode, pratique; **to be c. (for sb)** *(of arrangement)* être commode *ou* pratique (pour qn); *(of time)* convenir (à qn)

convent ['kɒnvənt] *n Rel* couvent *m;* **c. school** école *f* tenue par des sœurs

convention [kən'venʃən] *n* (**a**) *(conference)* convention *f,* congrès *m* (**b**) *(agreement)* convention *f* (**c**) *(established practice)* usage *m;* **the c. is that...** l'usage veut que...

conventional [kən'venʃənəl] *adj (behaviour, ideas)* conventionnel(le); *(person)* conformiste; **c. warfare** guerre *f* conventionnelle; **c. weapon** arme *f* conventionnelle; **c. wisdom** sagesse *f* populaire

converge [kən'vɜːdʒ] *vi* converger (**on** sur)

convergence [kən'vɜːdʒəns] *n* convergence *f; EU* **c. criteria** critères *mpl* de convergence

conversant [kən'vɜːsənt] *adj* **to be c. with sth** s'y connaître en qch; *(with events, developments)* être au courant de qch

conversation [kɒnvə'seɪʃən] *n* conversation *f;* **to have a c. with sb** avoir une conversation avec qn; **to make c.** faire la conversation; **the vase is quite a c. piece** le vase suscite bien des commentaires; *Fam* **to be a c. stopper** *or* **killer** arrêter net la conversation

conversational [kɒnvə'seɪʃənəl] *adj (style)* de la conversation; *Comput (mode)* dialogue; **in a c. tone** sur le ton de la conversation

conversationalist [kɒnvə'seɪʃənəlɪst] *n* **to be a good c.** avoir de la conversation; **I'm not much of a c.** je ne suis pas brillant causeur

converse¹ [kən'vɜːs] *vi (talk)* converser (**about** sur), s'entretenir (**about** de)

converse² ['kɒnvɜːs] *n (opposite)* **the c.** le contraire

conversely [kən'vɜːslɪ] *adv* inversement

conversion [kən'vɜːʃən] *n* (**a**) *(transformation)* conversion *f; (of building)* aménagement *m;* **c. table** *(for measurements)* table *f* de conversion (**b**) *(in rugby)* transformation *f*

convert 1 n ['kɒnvɜːt] Rel & Fig converti(e) m,f (**to** à)
 2 vt [kən'vɜːt] (**a**) Rel & Fig convertir (**to** à); (building) aménager (**into** en) (**b**) (in rugby) **to c. a try** transformer un essai
 3 vi [kən'vɜːt] Rel & Fig se convertir (**to** à)
convertible [kən'vɜːtəbəl] **1** n (car) décapotable f
 2 adj (sofa) convertible; (car) décapotable; **c. currency** monnaie f ou devise f convertible
convex [kɒn'veks] adj convexe
convey [kən'veɪ] vt (**a**) (communicate) transmettre; **to c. one's meaning** communiquer sa pensée (**b**) (transport) transporter
conveyance [kən'veɪəns] n (**a**) (of goods, passengers) transport m (**b**) Old-fashioned (vehicle) véhicule m
conveyancing [kən'veɪənsɪŋ] n Law procédure f translative de propriété
conveyor belt [kən'veɪəbelt] n convoyeur m, tapis m roulant
convict 1 n ['kɒnvɪkt] détenu(e) m,f
 2 vt [kən'vɪkt] **to c. sb (of)** déclarer qn coupable (de)
conviction [kən'vɪkʃən] n (**a**) Law condamnation f; **to have no previous convictions** n'avoir jamais été condamné(e) (**b**) (belief) conviction f; **to lack c.** manquer de conviction
convince [kən'vɪns] vt convaincre (**of/that** de/que); **I was convinced I was right** j'étais convaincu d'avoir raison
convincing [kən'vɪnsɪŋ] adj convaincant(e); (defeat) décisif(ive)
convivial [kən'vɪvɪəl] adj (person) chaleureux(euse); (atmosphere) joyeux(euse)
convoluted ['kɒnvəluːtɪd] adj (argument, explanation) compliqué(e)
convoy ['kɒnvɔɪ] n convoi m
convulse [kən'vʌls] vt secouer; **to be convulsed with laughter/pain** se tordre de rire/de douleur
convulsions [kən'vʌlʃənz] npl Med convulsions fpl; Fig **to be in c.** (of laughter) se tordre
coo [kuː] (pt & pp **cooed**) vi (of dove) roucouler; Fam **to c. over sb/sth** s'extasier devant qn/qch
cook [kʊk] **1** n cuisinier(ère) m,f; Prov **too many cooks spoil the broth** on n'arrive jamais à rien quand tout le monde met son grain de sel
 2 vt (meal) préparer; (food) (faire) cuire; Fig **to c. the books** falsifier les comptes
 3 vi (of food) cuire; (of person) faire la cuisine; Fam **what's cooking?** qu'est-ce qui se passe?
▸**cook up** vt sep (excuse, story) inventer
cookbook ['kʊkbʊk] n livre m de cuisine
cooker ['kʊkə(r)] n (stove) cuisinière f
cookery ['kʊkərɪ] n cuisine f; **c. book** livre m de cuisine
cookie ['kʊkɪ] n (**a**) Am (biscuit) biscuit m; Fam **that's the way the c. crumbles!** c'est la vie(, que veux-tu)! (**b**) (person) **a tough c.** un(e) dur(e) à cuire; **a smart c.** un(e) malin(igne) (**c**) Comput cookie m, cafteur m, Can témoin m
cooking ['kʊkɪŋ] n (process) cuisson f; (activity) cuisine f; **to do the c.** faire la cuisine; **c. apple** pomme f à cuire; **c. chocolate** chocolat m à cuire; **c. foil** papier m alu; **c. time** temps m de cuisson; **c. utensils** ustensiles mpl de cuisine
cool [kuːl] **1** n (**a**) (coldness) fraîcheur f
 (**b**) (calm) **to keep/lose one's c.** garder/perdre son sang-froid
 2 adj (**a**) (wind, weather, drink) frais (fraîche); (cof-

fee, bathwater) tiède; **it's c. outside** il fait frais dehors; Fam **I lost a c. thousand** j'ai bien perdu mille livres/dollars/etc
 (**b**) (calm) calme; (unfriendly) froid(e); **c. as a cucumber** parfaitement calme; **keep c.!** ne t'angoisse pas!; **to keep a c. head** garder la tête froide; **to be a c. customer** (cheeky) être culotté(e); (self-possessed) avoir beaucoup de sang-froid
 (**c**) Fam (good) cool inv; (trendy) branché(e)
 3 adv Fam **to play it c.** rester calme
 4 vt rafraîchir, refroidir; Fam **c. it!** on se calme!; Fam **to c. one's heels** poireauter
 5 vi (of liquid) refroidir; (of anger) passer; (of passion, enthusiasm) se refroidir
▸**cool down 1** vt sep (**a**) (of cold drink) rafraîchir (**b**) (make calm) calmer
 2 vi (**a**) (of weather) se rafraîchir; (of liquid) refroidir (**b**) (become calm) se calmer
▸**cool off** vi (**a**) (of person) se rafraîchir (**b**) (of passion, enthusiasm) se refroidir; (of angry person) se calmer
coolant ['kuːlənt] n liquide m de refroidissement
cool-headed ['kuːl'hedɪd] adj calme; **to remain c.** garder la tête froide
cooling ['kuːlɪŋ] adj (drink) rafraîchissant(e); (agent) réfrigérant(e); Ind & Com **c. off period** période f de réflexion; **c. tower** tour f de réfrigération
coop [kuːp] n (for chickens) poulailler m; Fig **to fly the c.** se faire la malle
▸**coop up** vt sep **to keep sb cooped up** tenir qn enfermé(e); **to feel cooped up** se sentir à l'étroit
co-op ['kəʊɒp] n coopérative f
cooperate [kəʊ'ɒpəreɪt] vi coopérer (**with** avec)
cooperation [kəʊɒpə'reɪʃən] n coopération f
cooperative [kəʊ'ɒpərətɪv] **1** n coopérative f
 2 adj coopératif(ive)
coopt [kəʊ'ɒpt] vt coopter (**onto** à)
coordinate 1 n [kəʊ'ɔːdɪnət] (**a**) Math coordonnée f (**b**) **coordinates** (clothes) coordonnés mpl
 2 vt [kəʊ'ɔːdɪneɪt] coordonner
coordination [kəʊɔːdɪ'neɪʃən] n coordination f
coordinator [kəʊ'ɔːdɪneɪtə(r)] n coordinateur(trice) m,f
co-owner ['kəʊ'əʊnə(r)] n copropriétaire mf
cop [kɒp] **1** n Fam (**a**) (policeman) flic m; **to play cops and robbers** jouer aux gendarmes et aux voleurs (**b**) Br **it's not much c.** ça ne vaut pas grand-chose
 2 vt (pt & pp **copped**) **to c. it** (be punished) se faire pincer; (die) clamser
▸**cop out** vi Fam (avoid responsibility) se défiler; (choose easy solution) choisir la solution de facilité; **to c. out of doing sth** ne pas avoir le cran de faire qch
cope [kəʊp] vi se débrouiller, s'en tirer; **to c. with** (demand, situation) faire face à; (problem, difficulty) venir à bout de; **I just can't c.** je n'y arrive pas; **he can't c. with his job** il ne s'en sort pas dans son travail
Copenhagen [kəʊpən'heɪgən] n Copenhague
copier ['kɒpɪə(r)] n (photocopier) (photo)copieuse f
copilot ['kəʊpaɪlət] n copilote m
copious ['kəʊpɪəs] adj copieux(euse); (tears, notes, amounts) abondant(e)
cop-out ['kɒpaʊt] n Fam solution f de facilité
copper ['kɒpə(r)] **1** n (**a**) (metal) cuivre m; Fam **coppers** (coins) petite monnaie f (**b**) Fam (policeman) flic m
 2 adj **c.(-coloured)** (couleur) cuivre inv, cuivré(e)

copperplate [ˈkɒpəpleɪt] *n* **c.** **(writing)** écriture *f* moulée

coppice [ˈkɒpɪs] *n* taillis *m*

coproduction [kəʊprəˈdʌkʃən] *n* Cin coproduction *f*

copse [kɒps] *n* taillis *m*

copulate [ˈkɒpjʊleɪt] *vi* copuler

copulation [kɒpjʊˈleɪʃən] *n* copulation *f*

copy [ˈkɒpɪ] **1** (*pl* **copies**) *n* (**a**) *(reproduction)* copie *f* (**b**) *(of letter, document)* copie *f*, double *m*; **c. typist** dactylo *mf* (**c**) *(of book)* exemplaire *m*; *(of newspaper)* numéro *m* (**d**) Journ *(written material)* copie *f*; **the story made good c.** ça a fait un bon sujet d'article; **c. editor** *(in journalism)* secrétaire *mf* de rédaction; *(in publishing)* réviseur *m*
2 *vt* (*pt & pp* **copied**) *(painting, document, text)* & Comput copier; **to c. sth to disk** copier qch sur disquette; **to c. and paste sth** faire un copier-coller sur qch
3 *vi (in exam)* copier

copybook [ˈkɒpɪbʊk] *n* cahier *m* d'écriture; **c. example** exemple *m* classique

copycat [ˈkɒpɪkæt] Fam **1** *n* copieur(euse) *m,f*
2 *adj* **c. crime/murder** délit *m*/meurtre *m* inspiré par un autre

copyright [ˈkɒpɪraɪt] **1** *n* droit *m* d'auteur, copyright *m*; **to be out of c.** être tombé(e) dans le domaine public
2 *adj* protégé(e) par le droit d'auteur

copywriter [ˈkɒpɪraɪtə(r)] *n* rédacteur(trice) *m,f* publicitaire

coquette [kɒˈket] *n* Lit coquette *f*

coral [ˈkɒrəl] *n* corail *m*; **c. island** île *f* corallienne; **c. reef** récif *m* corallien; **the C. Sea** la mer de Corail

cord [kɔːd] *n* (**a**) *(string)* grosse ficelle *f*; *(for curtains, pyjamas)* cordon *m* (**b**) *(corduroy)* velours *m* côtelé; **a c. jacket** une veste en velours côtelé; **cords** pantalon *m* en velours côtelé

cordial [ˈkɔːdɪəl] **1** *n (drink)* sirop *m*
2 *adj (friendly)* cordial(e)

cordless [ˈkɔːdlɪs] *adj* sans fil; **c. telephone** (téléphone *m*) sans-fil *m*

cordon [ˈkɔːdən] *n* cordon *m*

▸**cordon off** *vt sep (road)* barrer; *(area)* boucler

corduroy [ˈkɔːdərɔɪ] *n* velours *m* côtelé; **c. trousers** pantalon *m* en velours côtelé

core [kɔː(r)] **1** *n (of apple)* trognon *m*; *(of earth, magnet)* noyau *m*; *(of nuclear reactor)* centre *m*; *(of argument, problem)* cœur *m*; **hard c.** noyau dur; **he's rotten to the c.** il est pourri jusqu'à la moelle; Sch **c. curriculum** tronc *m* commun
2 *vt (apple)* évider

Corfu [kɔːˈfuː] *n* Corfou

coriander [kɒrɪˈændə(r)] *n* coriandre *f*

cork [kɔːk] **1** *n (material)* liège *m*; *(stopper)* bouchon *m* (en liège)
2 *vt (bottle)* boucher

corked [kɔːkt] *adj (wine)* bouchonné(e)

corkscrew [ˈkɔːkskruː] *n* tire-bouchon *m*

cormorant [ˈkɔːmərənt] *n* cormoran *m*

corn¹ [kɔːn] *n* (**a**) Br *(wheat)* blé *m* (**b**) Am *(maize)* maïs *m*; **c. on the cob** maïs en épi; **c. bread** pain *m* à la farine de maïs; **c. meal** farine *f* de maïs; **c. oil** huile *f* de maïs

corn² *n (on foot)* cor *m*; **c. plaster** pansement *m* pour cors

cornea [ˈkɔːnɪə] *n* Anat cornée *f*

corned beef [ˈkɔːndˈbiːf] *n* corned-beef *m*

corner [ˈkɔːnə(r)] **1** *n* (**a**) *(of room, street, page, screen)* coin *m*; **out of the c. of one's eye** du coin de l'œil; **it's just round the c.** c'est juste au coin; Fig **Christmas is just round the c.** on est tout près de Noël; **to turn the c.** tourner au coin de la rue; Fig *(of economy, company)* passer la période critique; **c. shop** épicerie *f* du coin, Can dépanneur *m* (**b**) *(bend in road)* tournant *m*; Fig **to cut corners** *(with time)* faire les choses à la va-vite; *(with materials, money)* faire les choses à l'économie (**c**) *(in football)* **c. (kick)** corner *m*; **to take a c.** tirer un corner
2 *vt* (**a**) *(person, animal)* acculer (**b**) *(market)* accaparer
3 *vi (of car, driver)* prendre un virage

cornerstone [ˈkɔːnəstəʊn] *n also Fig* pierre *f* angulaire

cornet [ˈkɔːnɪt] *n* (**a**) *(musical instrument)* cornet *m* à pistons (**b**) **(ice-cream) c.** cornet *m*

cornfield [ˈkɔːnfiːld] *n (of wheat)* champ *m* de blé; *(of maize)* champ de maïs

cornflakes [ˈkɔːnfleɪks] *npl* corn flakes *mpl*

cornflour [ˈkɔːnflaʊə(r)] *n Br* farine *f* de maïs

cornflower [ˈkɔːnflaʊə(r)] *n (plant)* bleuet *m*; **c. blue** bleu barbeau *inv*

cornice [ˈkɔːnɪs] *n* corniche *f*

Cornish [ˈkɔːnɪʃ] **1** *npl* **the C.** *(people)* les Cornouaillais *mpl*
2 *n (language)* cornique *m*
3 *adj* cornouaillais(e); *Br* **C. pasty** feuilleté *m* à la viande

Cornwall [ˈkɔːnwəl] *n* Cornouailles *f*

corny [ˈkɔːnɪ] *adj Fam (joke)* nul (nulle); *(film, novel)* tarte

corollary [kəˈrɒlərɪ] (*pl* **corollaries**) *n* corollaire *m*

coronary [ˈkɒrənərɪ] Med **1** (*pl* **coronaries**) *n* infarctus *m* (du myocarde)
2 *adj* coronarien(enne); **c. thrombosis** infarctus *m* du myocarde

coronation [kɒrəˈneɪʃən] *n* couronnement *m*; **c. chicken** = morceaux de poulet préparés avec de la mayonnaise au curry

coroner [ˈkɒrənə(r)] *n Law* coroner *m*

corporal¹ [ˈkɔːpərəl] *adj* corporel(elle); **c. punishment** châtiment *m* corporel

corporal² *n Mil (in infantry)* caporal *m*; *(in cavalry, artillery)* brigadier *m*

corporate [ˈkɔːpərət] *adj* Com *(of companies in general)* d'entreprise; *(of a specific company)* d'une société; **c. culture** culture *f* d'entreprise; **c. image** image *f* de marque de l'entreprise

corporation [kɔːpəˈreɪʃən] *n* (**a**) Com société *f*; **c. tax** impôt *m* sur les sociétés (**b**) *(council)* conseil *m* municipal

corps [kɔː(r)] (*pl* **corps** [kɔːz]) *n Mil* corps *m*

corpse [kɔːps] *n* cadavre *m*; **a lifeless c.** un corps inerte

corpulent [ˈkɔːpjʊlənt] *adj* corpulent(e)

corpuscle [ˈkɔːpʌsəl] *n Anat* corpuscule *m*; **red/white (blood) corpuscles** globules *mpl* rouges/blancs

corral [kɒˈrɑːl] *n Am* corral *m*

correct [kəˈrekt] *adj* **1** (**a**) *(accurate)* exact(e); **to prove c.** se vérifier, s'avérer juste; **if my memory is c.** si j'ai bonne mémoire; **he is c.** *(right)* il a raison; **that's c.** c'est exact (**b**) *(person, behaviour)* correct(e), convenable; **it wasn't the c. thing to say/do** ce n'était pas la chose à dire/faire

2 *vt (homework, proofs, error)* corriger; *(misunderstanding)* dissiper; **c. me if I'm wrong, but...** reprenez-moi si je me trompe, mais...; **I stand corrected** j'avais tort

correction [kə'rekʃən] *n* correction *f*; **c. fluid** liquide *m* correcteur

corrective [kə'rektɪv] **1** *n* correctif *m*
2 *adj (action, measure)* rectificatif(ive), correctif(-ive); **c. surgery** chirurgie *f* réparatrice

correlate ['kɒrɪleɪt] **1** *vt* mettre en rapport *ou* en corrélation (**with** avec); **they are closely correlated** ils sont étroitement liés
2 *vi* être en rapport *ou* en corrélation (**with** avec)

correlation [kɒrɪ'leɪʃən] *n* corrélation *f*

correspond [kɒrɪs'pɒnd] *vi* (**a**) *(be in accordance)* correspondre (**with** *or* **to** à) (**b**) *(be equivalent)* correspondre (**to** à), être l'équivalent (**to** de) (**c**) *(write letters)* correspondre (**with** avec)

correspondence [kɒrɪs'pɒndəns] *n* (**a**) *(relationship)* rapport *m* (**between** entre) (**b**) *(letter-writing)* correspondance *f*; **I don't get much c.** je ne reçois pas beaucoup de courrier; **c. course** cours *m* par correspondance

correspondent [kɒrɪs'pɒndənt] *n* correspondant(e) *m,f*

corresponding [kɒrɪ'spɒndɪŋ] *adj* correspondant(e)

corridor ['kɒrɪdɔː(r)] *n* couloir *m*, corridor *m*; *Fig* **the corridors of power** les hautes sphères *fpl* du pouvoir

corroborate [kə'rɒbəreɪt] *vt* corroborer, confirmer

corroboration [kərɒbə'reɪʃən] *n* corroboration *f*, confirmation *f*

corrode [kə'rəʊd] **1** *vt (metal)* corroder, attaquer; *Fig (society)* miner; *(optimism, friendship)* entamer
2 *vi (of metal)* se corroder

corrosion [kə'rəʊʒən] *n* corrosion *f*

corrosive [kə'rəʊsɪv] **1** *n* corrosif *m*
2 *adj* corrosif(ive)

corrugated ['kɒrəgeɪtɪd] *adj (cardboard)* ondulé(e); **c. iron** tôle *f* ondulée

corrupt [kə'rʌpt] **1** *adj (dishonest)* corrompu(e)
2 *vt* corrompre; *Comput* altérer; **to c. sb's morals** dépraver qn

corruption [kə'rʌpʃən] *n* corruption *f*

corset ['kɔːsɪt] *n* corset *m*

Corsica ['kɔːsɪkə] *n* la Corse

Corsican ['kɔːsɪkən] **1** *n* Corse *mf*
2 *adj* corse

cortege [kɔː'teʒ] *n* cortège *m*

cortex ['kɔːteks] *(pl* **cortices** ['kɔːtɪsiːz] *) n* cortex *m*

cortisone ['kɔːtɪzəʊn] *n* cortisone *f*

cos¹ [kʊz] *conj Br Fam* parce que

cos² [kɒs] *n* **c. (lettuce)** romaine *f*

cosh [kɒʃ] *Br* **1** *n* matraque *f*
2 *vt* matraquer

cosmetic [kɒz'metɪk] **1** *n* cosmétique *m*, produit *m* de beauté; **to wear a lot of cosmetics** se maquiller beaucoup
2 *adj Fig (superficial)* superficiel(elle); **c. surgery** chirurgie *f* esthétique

cosmic ['kɒzmɪk] *adj* cosmique; *Fig* prodigieux(euse)

cosmonaut ['kɒzmənɔːt] *n* cosmonaute *mf*

cosmopolitan [kɒzmə'pɒlɪtən] *adj* cosmopolite

cosmos ['kɒzmɒs] *n* cosmos *m*

cosset ['kɒsɪt] *vt* couver, choyer

cost [kɒst] **1** *n* (**a**) *(price)* coût *m*; *Law* **costs** dépens *mpl*; *also Fig* **at little/great c.** à peu de/à grands frais; **at great c. to his health** au prix de sa santé; *Econ* **c. of living** coût de la vie; *Com* **c. of production** coût de production; *Fin* **c. accounting** comptabilité *f* analytique; *Econ* **c. benefit analysis** analyse *f* coûts-bénéfices; *Com* **c. price** prix *m* coûtant
(**b**) *(idioms)* **to count the c. of sth** tirer la leçon de qch; **at all costs** à tout prix; **as I found out to my c.** comme je l'ai appris à mes dépens
2 *vt* (**a**) *(pt & pp* **cost***) also Fig* coûter; **how much does it c.?** combien ça coûte?; **it costs £25** ça coûte *ou* c'est 25 livres; **whatever it costs** quel qu'en soit le prix; *Fam* **to c. a fortune** *or* **the earth** coûter les yeux de la tête; **the attempt cost him his life** cette tentative lui a coûté la vie
(**b**) *(pt & pp* **costed***) Com (budget)* évaluer le coût de

co-star ['kəʊstɑː(r)] **1** *n (in film)* partenaire *mf* à l'écran
2 *vt (pt & pp* **co-starred***)* **the film co-stars Harvey Keitel** Harvey Keitel joue aussi dans ce film; **co-starring Ewan McGregor** avec Ewan McGregor
3 *vi* jouer dans un des rôles principaux

Costa Rica ['kɒstə'riːkə] *n* le Costa Rica

Costa Rican ['kɒstə'riːkən] **1** *n* Costaricien(enne) *m,f*
2 *adj* costaricien(enne)

cost-effective [kɒstɪ'fektɪv] *adj* rentable

costing ['kɒstɪŋ] *n Com (of job)* évaluation *f* du coût; *(of article)* évaluation *f* du prix de revient

costly ['kɒstlɪ] *adj* cher (chère), coûteux(euse); **it was a c. mistake** c'est une erreur qui a coûté cher

costume ['kɒstjʊm] *n* costume *m*; **(swimming) c.** maillot *m* de bain; **c. drama** film *m*/pièce *f* en costumes d'époque; **c. jewellery** bijoux *mpl* fantaisie

cosy, *Am* **cozy** ['kəʊzɪ] *adj (room, atmosphere)* douillet(ette), confortable; *(armchair, pub)* confortable; **to feel c.** *(in room)* être confortablement installé(e); *Fig & Pej* **they have a c. relationship** ils sont un peu trop copain-copain

cot [kɒt] *n Br (for child)* lit *m* d'enfant, petit lit; *Am (folding bed)* lit pliant; **c. death** mort *f* subite du nourrisson

cottage ['kɒtɪdʒ] *n* = petite maison, généralement à la campagne; **thatched c.** chaumière *f*; **c. cheese** fromage *m* blanc (égoutté); **c. hospital** = hôpital de médecine générale en zone rurale; **c. industry** industrie *f* artisanale; *(at home)* industrie familiale; **c. pie** hachis *m* Parmentier

cotton ['kɒtən] *n* coton *m*; **a c. shirt** une chemise en coton; **c. bud** Coton-Tige® *m*; *Am* **c. candy** barbe *f* à papa; **c. wool** ouate *f*, coton hydrophile

▸**cotton on** *vi Fam* piger; **to c. on to sth** piger qch

couch [kaʊtʃ] **1** *n* divan *m*, canapé *m*; *(at doctor's)* lit *m*; *Fam* **to be a c. potato** passer sa vie devant la télé
2 *vt (express)* formuler

cougar ['kuːgə(r)] *n* couguar *m*, puma *m*

cough [kɒf] **1** *n* toux *f*; **to have a c.** tousser; **c. drop** pastille *f* pour la toux; **c. mixture** sirop *m* pour la toux
2 *vi* tousser

▸**cough up 1** *vt sep (phlegm, blood)* cracher; *Fam (money)* allonger
2 *vi Fam (pay)* allonger

could [kʊd]

La forme négative est **couldn't**. Dans les contextes où il est nécessaire d'utiliser une langue plus soignée, on écrit **could not**.

modal aux v (**a**) *(was able to)* **we couldn't do it** nous n'avons pas pu le faire; **he did what he c.** il a fait ce qu'il pouvait; **I c. hear them talking** je les entendais parler; **I c. have tried harder** j'aurais pu faire plus d'efforts; **he couldn't have been kinder** il a été on ne peut plus aimable; **how COULD you!** comment as-tu pu faire ça!; **I c. have hit him!** *(I was so angry)* je l'aurais battu!
(**b**) *(knew how to)* **I c. swim well at that age** à cet âge-là je savais déjà bien nager; **c. you speak French then?** tu parlais français à cette époque-là?
(**c**) *(indicating possibility)* **it c. be weeks before he's better** il pourrait se passer des semaines avant qu'il se rétablisse; **it c. have been worse** ça aurait pu être pire
(**d**) *(with requests)* **c. you get me some water?** est-ce que tu pourrais m'apporter de l'eau?
(**e**) *(in conditional, suggestions)* **(it) c. be** peut-être; **if I had more money I c. buy a new car** si j'avais plus d'argent je pourrais acheter une nouvelle voiture; **we c. always telephone** on pourrait toujours téléphoner

couldn't ['kʊdənt] = **could not**

couldn't-care-less ['kʊdəntkeə'les] *adj* **c. attitude** je-m'en-foutisme *m*

council ['kaʊnsəl] *n* (**a**) *(assembly)* conseil *m*; **C. of Europe** Conseil de l'Europe (**b**) *(local government)* municipalité *f*; **to be on the c.** être au conseil municipal; *Br* **c. house** ≃ habitation *f* à loyer modéré, H.L.M. *f*; **c. tax** = en Grande-Bretagne, impôt regroupant taxe d'habitation et impôts locaux

councillor ['kaʊnsɪlə(r)] *n* conseiller(ère) *m,f*, membre *m* du conseil

counsel ['kaʊnsəl] **1** *n* (**a**) *(advice)* conseil *m*, avis *m*; **to keep one's own c.** *(about plans)* garder ses projets pour soi; *(about opinions)* garder ses opinions pour soi (**b**) *Br (lawyer)* avocat(e) *m,f*; **c. for the defence** avocat *m* de la défense; **c. for the prosecution** procureur *m*; **King's/Queen's C.** = membre haut placé du barreau
2 *vt (pt & pp* **counselled**, *Am* **counseled**) *(caution, patience)* conseiller; **to c. sb** *(advise)* conseiller qn; *(give psychological help to)* apporter une aide psychologique à qn; **to c. sb to do sth** conseiller à qn de faire qch

counselling ['kaʊnsəlɪŋ] *n* assistance *f* psychosociale

counsellor ['kaʊnsələ(r)] *n* (**a**) *(adviser, therapist)* conseiller(ère) *m,f* (**b**) *Am Law* avocat(e) *m,f*

count¹ [kaʊnt] *n (nobleman)* comte *m*

count² **1** *n* (**a**) *(calculation)* compte *m*, comptage *m*; *(of ballot papers)* dépouillement *m*; **at the last c.** au dernier comptage; **to keep c. of sth** tenir le compte de qch; **to lose c.** se perdre dans ses calculs; **I've lost c. of how many times I've asked you to...** je t'ai demandé je ne sais combien de fois de...
(**b**) *(in boxing) & Fig* **to be out for the c.** être K.-O.
(**c**) *Law* chef *m* d'accusation; *Fig* **on a number of counts** à plusieurs égards
2 *vt* (**a**) *(enumerate)* compter; **there were four of us counting/not counting the dog** nous étions quatre en comptant/sans compter le chien
(**b**) *(consider)* considérer (**as** comme); **c. yourself lucky you weren't killed** estime-toi heureux de n'avoir pas été tué
3 *vi* (**a**) *(add up)* compter; **to c. (up) to ten** compter jusqu'à dix
(**b**) *(be important, valid)* compter; **that doesn't c.** ça

ne compte pas; **it counts as one of my worst experiences** ça a été une de mes pires expériences
▸**count against** *vt insep* jouer contre
▸**count down** *vi* faire le compte à rebours
▸**count in** *vt sep (include)* compter; **c. me in!** j'en suis!
▸**count on** *vt insep* compter sur; **to c. on sb to do sth** compter sur qn pour faire qch
▸**count out** *vt sep* (**a**) *(money)* compter (**b**) *(exclude)* **c. me out!** ne comptez pas sur moi! (**c**) *(in boxing)* **to be counted out** être (mis(e)) K.-O.
▸**count up** *vt sep* compter

countable ['kaʊntəbəl] *adj* comptable

countdown ['kaʊntdaʊn] *n* compte *m* à rebours

countenance ['kaʊntɪnəns] *Formal* **1** *n* (**a**) *(face)* visage *m* (**b**) *(support)* **to give c. to** *(rumours)* accréditer; *(plans)* approuver
2 *vt (support)* approuver

counter¹ ['kaʊntə(r)] *n* (**a**) *(in shop)* comptoir *m*; *(in supermarket)* rayon *m*; *(in bank)* guichet *m*; **available over the c.** *(medicine)* en vente libre; **to buy/sell sth under the c.** acheter/vendre qch au noir (**b**) *(token in game)* jeton *m* (**c**) *(counting device)* compteur *m*

counter² **1** *adv* **c. to** contrairement à; **to run c. to** aller à l'encontre de
2 *vt* contrer; **to c. that...** riposter que...
3 *vi* riposter

counteract [kaʊntə'rækt] *vt (influence)* contrecarrer; *(rumours, effects)* neutraliser

counterattack ['kaʊntərətæk] **1** *n* contre-attaque *f*
2 *vt & vi* contre-attaquer

counter-clockwise ['kaʊntə'klɒkwaɪz] *Am* **1** *adj* **in a c. direction** dans le sens inverse des aiguilles d'une montre
2 *adv* dans le sens inverse des aiguilles d'une montre

counterfeit ['kaʊntəfɪt] **1** *n* faux *m*
2 *adj* faux (fausse)
3 *vt* contrefaire

counterfoil ['kaʊntəfɔɪl] *n* talon *m*, souche *f*

counterintelligence ['kaʊntərɪn'telɪdʒəns] *n* contre-espionnage *m*

countermand ['kaʊntəmɑːnd] *vt* annuler

countermeasure ['kaʊntəmeʒə(r)] *n* contre-mesure *f*

counteroffensive ['kaʊntərə'fensɪv] *n* contre-offensive *f*

counterpane ['kaʊntəpeɪn] *n* couvre-lit *m*

counterpart ['kaʊntəpɑːt] *n (person)* homologue *mf*; *(system)* équivalent *m*

counterpoint ['kaʊntəpɔɪnt] *n Mus* contrepoint *m*

counterproductive ['kaʊntəprə'dʌktɪv] *adj* contre-productif(ive)

counterproposal ['kaʊntəprə'pəʊzəl] *n* contre-proposition *f*

counter-revolution ['kaʊntərevə'luːʃən] *n* contre-révolution *f*

counter-revolutionary ['kaʊntərevə'luːʃənərɪ] *n & adj* contre-révolutionnaire *mf*

countersign ['kaʊntəsaɪn] *vt* contresigner, viser

counterweight ['kaʊntəweɪt] *n* contrepoids *m*

countess ['kaʊntɪs] *n* comtesse *f*

countless ['kaʊntlɪs] *adj* innombrable; **on c. occasions** à maintes occasions; **c. times** un nombre incalculable de fois

country ['kʌntrɪ] *(pl* **countries**) *n* (**a**) *(land, nation)* pays *m*; *(homeland)* patrie *f*; **to go to the c.** *(call* *elections)* appeler le pays aux urnes (**b**) *(as opposed to town)* campagne *f*; **in the c.** à la campagne; **c. and western (music)** country *m ou f*

countryside ['kʌntrɪsaɪd] *n* campagne *f*

county ['kaʊntɪ] *(pl* **counties***) n* comté *m*; **c. council** ≃ conseil *m* général; **c. town** chef-lieu *m* de comté

coup [kuː] *n (surprising achievement)* (beau) coup *m*; *Pol* **c. (d'état)** coup *m* d'État

couple ['kʌpəl] **1** *n* (**a**) *(of things)* **a c. of** *(two)* deux; *(a few)* quelques (**b**) *(people)* couple *m*; **the happy c.** les heureux époux *mpl*
2 *vt* (**a**) *(associate)* associer (**with** à) (**b**) *(combine)* allier (**with** à)
3 *vi* s'accoupler

couplet ['kʌplɪt] *n* distique *m*

coupon ['kuːpɒn] *n (form)* coupon *m*; (**money-off**) **c.** *(for discount)* bon *m* de réduction

courage ['kʌrɪdʒ] *n* courage *m*; **to have the c. to do sth** avoir le courage de faire qch; **to have the c. of one's convictions** avoir le courage de ses opinions

courageous [kə'reɪdʒəs] *adj* courageux(euse)

courageously [kə'reɪdʒəslɪ] *adv* courageusement, avec courage

courgette [kʊə'ʒət] *n Br* courgette *f*

courier ['kʊrɪə(r)] *n (messenger)* messager *m*, coursier *m*; *(in tourism)* guide *mf*; *(drug smuggler)* passeur(-euse) *m,f*

course [kɔːs] **1** *n* (**a**) *(of river, time, events)* cours *m*; **to be on c.** *Naut* suivre le cap; *Fig* être en bonne voie; *Naut* **to be off c.** dévier de son cap; **in the c. of time** *(gradually)* à la longue; *(eventually)* finalement; **in the c. of the evening** au cours de la soirée; **c. of action** ligne *f* de conduite; **to be in the c. of doing sth** être en train de faire qch; **in the normal c. of events** en temps normal; **to let things take** *or* **run their c.** laisser les choses suivre leur cours normal
(**b**) **of c.** naturellement, bien sûr; **of c. not** bien sûr que non
(**c**) *(at college, university)* cours *m* (**in** de); **c. of lectures** série *f* de conférences
(**d**) *Med* **c. of treatment** traitement *m*
(**e**) *(of meal)* plat *m*
(**f**) *(for race)* parcours *m*; *(for horseracing)* champ *m* de courses; *(for golf)* terrain *m*
2 *vi (of liquid)* couler

court [kɔːt] **1** *n* (**a**) *Law* cour *f*, tribunal *m*; **to go to c.** aller en justice; **to take sb to c.** faire un procès à qn; **to settle a case out of c.** arranger une affaire à l'amiable; **c. of appeal** cour d'appel; **c. of inquiry** commission *f* d'enquête; **c. of law** cour, tribunal; **c. appearance** comparution *f* en justice; *Mil* **c. martial** cour martiale (**b**) *(for tennis, squash)* court *m* (**c**) *(royal)* cour *f*; *Fig* **to hold c.** tenir des discours à un entourage admiratif; **c. shoe** escarpin *m*
2 *vt* (**a**) *Old-fashioned (woo)* courtiser (**b**) *(seek) (friendship, favour)* rechercher; *(death)* braver; *(disaster, danger)* aller au-devant de
3 *vi Old-fashioned* **to be courting** *(of couple)* se fréquenter

courteous ['kɜːtɪəs] *adj* courtois(e), poli(e)

courtesy ['kɜːtəsɪ] *(pl* **courtesies***) n* courtoisie *f*, politesse *f*; **by c. of...** avec l'aimable autorisation de...; **to exchange courtesies** se faire des politesses; **c. call** visite *f* de politesse; **c. car** = voiture mise à la disposition d'un client par un hôtel ou un garage

courthouse ['kɔːthaʊs] *n Am* palais *m* de justice, tribunal *m*

courtier ['kɔːtɪə(r)] *n (man)* courtisan *m*; *(woman)* dame *f* de la cour

court-martial ['kɔːt'mɑːʃəl] *(pt & pp* **court-martialled**, *Am* **court-martialed***) vt* faire passer en cour martiale; **to be court-martialled** passer en cour martiale

courtroom ['kɔːtruːm] *n Law* salle *f* d'audience

courtship ['kɔːtʃɪp] *n (of people)* cour *f*; *(of animals)* période *f* nuptiale; **c. display** parade *f* nuptiale

courtyard ['kɔːtjɑːd] *n* cour *f*

cousin ['kʌzən] *n* cousin(e) *m,f*

cove [kəʊv] *n* crique *f*

covenant ['kʌvənənt] *Law* **1** *n* convention *f*, contrat *m*
2 *vt* promettre par contrat

Coventry ['kʌvəntrɪ, 'kɒvəntrɪ] *n Fig* **to send sb to C.** mettre qn en quarantaine

cover ['kʌvə(r)] **1** *n* (**a**) *(lid)* couvercle *m*
(**b**) *(soft covering) (for cushion, typewriter, chair)* housse *f*
(**c**) *(bedspread)* couvre-lit *m*; **covers** *(blankets)* couvertures *fpl*
(**d**) *(of book, magazine)* couverture *f*; **from c. to c.** de la première à la dernière page; **c. price** prix *m* de vente
(**e**) *(shelter)* **to take c.** s'abriter; **to break c.** sortir à découvert; *Fig* se manifester publiquement; **under c. of darkness** à la faveur de la nuit
(**f**) *Fin (in insurance)* couverture *f*
(**g**) *(song)* **c. (version)** reprise *f*
2 *vt* (**a**) *(person, object)* couvrir (**with/in** de); **to c. one's eyes** se couvrir les yeux; **to c. a wall with paint** recouvrir un mur de peinture; **to c. oneself with glory** se couvrir de gloire; **to c. one's costs** couvrir ses frais; **to c. a song** *(of musician)* reprendre une chanson
(**b**) *(hide) (one's embarrassment, confusion)* dissimuler; **to c. one's tracks** brouiller les pistes
(**c**) *(travel over)* parcourir; **we covered 100 km in one day** nous avons fait *ou* parcouru 100 km en un jour; *Fig* **to c. a lot of ground** traiter de nombreux problèmes
(**d**) *(include, deal with) (of book, lecture)* traiter de; **to c. a story** *(of journalist)* couvrir un sujet
(**e**) *Fin (with insurance)* couvrir (**for** *or* **against** contre); *Fig* **to c. oneself** *(take precautions)* se couvrir

▸**cover for** *vt insep (replace)* remplacer; *(provide excuses for)* couvrir

▸**cover up 1** *vt sep* (**a**) *(corruption, mistakes)* dissimuler; *(scandal)* étouffer (**b**) *(put cover on)* recouvrir
2 *vi (conceal the truth)* cacher la vérité (**for sb** pour protéger qn)

coverage ['kʌvərɪdʒ] *n (on TV, in newspapers)* couverture *f* médiatique

covering ['kʌvərɪŋ] *n (on furniture)* housse *f*; *(of snow, dust)* couche *f*; *(of chocolate)* nappage *m*

coverlet ['kʌvəlɪt] *n* dessus-de-lit *m inv*

covert ['kʌvət] *adj (operation)* secret(ète), clandestin(e); *(look)* furtif(ive)

cover-up ['kʌvərʌp] *n* **there was a c.** l'affaire a été étouffée

covet ['kʌvɪt] *vt Formal* convoiter

covetous ['kʌvɪtəs] *adj Formal* envieux(euse); **to be c. of sth** convoiter qch

cow[1] [kaʊ] *n* (**a**) *(animal)* vache *f*; *(female elephant, whale)* femelle *f*; **till the cows come home** *(wait)* jusqu'à la saint-glinglin; *(argue, talk)* à n'en plus finir (**b**) *very Fam Pej (woman)* peau *f* de vache

cow[2] *vt* intimider; **to look cowed** avoir un air de chien battu

coward ['kaʊəd] *n* lâche *mf*, poltron(onne) *m,f*

cowardice ['kaʊədɪs], **cowardliness** ['kaʊədlɪnəs] *n* lâcheté *f*, poltronnerie *f*

cowardly ['kaʊədlɪ] *adj* lâche

cowboy ['kaʊbɔɪ] *n* (**a**) *(cattle handler, in westerns)* cow-boy *m* (**b**) *Br Fam Pej (workman)* filou *m*

cower ['kaʊə(r)] *vi* se tapir; **to c. before sb** trembler devant qn

cowhide ['kaʊhaɪd] *n* peau *f* de vache

cowl [kaʊl] *n* *(on monk's habit, on chimney)* capuchon *m*; **c. neck** col *m* boule

coworker ['kaʊwɜːkə(r)] *n Am* collègue *mf*

cowshed ['kaʊʃed] *n* étable *f*

cox [kɒks] **1** *n* *(in rowing)* barreur(euse) *m,f*
2 *vt & vi* barrer

coy [kɔɪ] *adj (shy)* timide; *Pej (affectedly shy)* (faussement) timide (**about** à propos de)

coyote [kɔɪ'əʊtɪ] *n* coyote *m*

cozy *Am* = **cosy**

CPU [siːpiː'juː] *n Comput (abbr* **central processing unit**) unité *f* centrale

crab [kræb] *n* (**a**) *(crustacean)* crabe *m* (**b**) *Fam (pubic louse)* morpion *m* (**c**) **c. apple** pomme *f* sauvage

crabbed ['kræbɪd] *adj (writing)* en pattes de mouche

crabby ['kræbɪ] *adj Fam* maussade, grincheux(euse)

crack [kræk] **1** *n* (**a**) *(in glass, porcelain)* fêlure *f*; *(in wood)* fente *f*; *(in wall)* lézarde *f*; *(in ice, rock)* fissure *f*; **at the c. of dawn** à la pointe du jour
(**b**) *(sound)* *(of branches, ice)* craquement *m*; *(of whip)* claquement *m*; *(of gunfire)* détonation *f*; *Fig* **to give sb a fair c. of the whip** donner toutes ses chances à qn; *Fig* **to have a c. at sth** tenter sa chance à qch
(**c**) *(blow)* coup *m* (**on** sur)
(**d**) *Fam (joke, insult)* plaisanterie *f*
(**e**) *(drug)* crack *m*
2 *adj Fam (team, regiment)* d'élite; **c. shot** fin tireur *m*
3 *vt* (**a**) *(glass, porcelain)* fêler; *(wood)* fendre; *(wall)* lézarder; *(ice, rock)* fissurer
(**b**) *(make sound with)* *(whip)* faire claquer; *(fingers)* faire craquer
(**c**) *Fam (hit)* **to c. sb over the head** assommer qn; **she cracked her head against the wall** elle s'est cogné la tête contre le mur
(**d**) *(solve)* *(problem)* résoudre; *(code)* décrypter
(**e**) *(break into)* *(safe)* percer; *(nut)* casser
(**f**) *Fam (joke)* raconter
4 *vi* (**a**) *(of glass, porcelain)* se fêler; *(of wood)* se fendre; *(of wall)* se lézarder; *(of ice, rock)* se fissurer; *(of paint)* se craqueler
(**b**) *(of voice)* se casser
(**c**) *(of person under pressure)* craquer
(**d**) *(make sound)* *(of branches, ice)* craquer; *(of whip)* claquer; *(of gunfire)* retentir; *Fam Fig* **to get cracking** se grouiller
▸**crack down** *vi* **to c. down (on)** prendre des mesures énergiques (contre)
▸**crack up** *Fam* **1** *vt sep* **it's not all it's cracked up to be** ce n'est pas aussi bien qu'on le dit
2 *vi (go mad)* craquer

crackbrained ['krækbreɪnd] *adj Fam* dingue

crackdown ['krækdaʊn] *n* mesures *fpl* énergiques (**on** en matière de)

cracked [krækt] *adj Fam (mad)* dingue, cinglé(e)

cracker ['krækə(r)] *n* (**a**) *(biscuit)* biscuit *m* salé, cracker *m* (**b**) *(firework)* pétard *m*; *(at Christmas)* diablotin *m* (**c**) *Fam (excellent thing, person)* pure merveille *f*; **she's a c.** *(very attractive)* elle est canon

crackers ['krækəz] *adj Fam* dingue, cinglé(e)

crackle ['krækəl] **1** *n* *(of twigs)* craquement *m*; *(of shots, fire)* crépitement *m*; *(of frying)* grésillement *m*; *(of radio)* crachotement *m*
2 *vi (of twigs)* craquer; *(of shots, fire)* crépiter; *(of frying)* grésiller; *(of radio)* crachoter

crackling ['kræklɪŋ] *n* (**a**) *(of fire)* crépitement *m*; *(on radio)* crachotement *m* (**b**) *(pork skin)* couenne *f* grillée

crackpot ['krækpɒt] *Fam* **1** *n (person)* fêlé(e) *m,f*, cinglé(e) *m,f*
2 *adj (plan)* dingue

cradle ['kreɪdəl] **1** *n* (**a**) *(of child, civilization)* berceau *m*; **from the c. to the grave** du berceau à la tombe (**b**) *(for cleaning windows)* nacelle *f*
2 *vt (baby)* bercer *(dans ses bras)*; *(object)* tenir délicatement

craft[1] [krɑːft] *n* (**a**) *(skill)* habileté *f*; *(professional)* métier *m* (**b**) *(cunning)* ruse *f*

craft[2] *(pl* **craft**) *n (boat)* (petite) embarcation *f*

craftsman ['krɑːftsmən] *n* artisan *m*; **this is the work of a real c.** c'est l'œuvre d'un spécialiste

craftsmanship ['krɑːftsmənʃɪp] *n* habileté *f* (manuelle); **a wonderful piece of c.** un pur chef-d'œuvre; **the c. is magnificent** c'est vraiment du beau travail

crafty ['krɑːftɪ] *adj* malin(igne)

crag [kræg] *n* rocher *m* à pic

craggy ['krægɪ] *adj (rocky)* rocheux(euse); *(features)* anguleux(euse)

cram [kræm] *(pt & pp* **crammed**) **1** *vt* fourrer, entasser (**into** dans); **to c. food into one's mouth** se gaver, s'empiffrer; **to be crammed (with)** être bourré(e) (de)
2 *vi* (**a**) *(crowd)* s'entasser (**into** dans) (**b**) *Fam (study)* bûcher

cramp [kræmp] **1** *n* crampe *f*
2 *vt (restrict)* gêner; *Fam* **to c. sb's style** priver qn de ses moyens

cramped [kræmpt] *adj (surroundings)* exigu(ë); **to be c. for space** être à l'étroit

cranberry ['krænbərɪ] *(pl* **cranberries**) *n* canneberge *f*; **c. sauce** sauce *f* à la canneberge

crane [kreɪn] **1** *n (lifting device, bird)* grue *f*; **c. fly** *(insect)* tipule *f*
2 *vt* **to c. one's neck** tendre le cou
3 *vi* **to c. forward** tendre le cou

cranium ['kreɪnɪəm] *(pl* **crania** ['kreɪnɪə]) *n Anat* boîte *f* crânienne

crank[1] [kræŋk] *n (gear mechanism)* manivelle *f*

crank[2] *n Fam* (**a**) *Br (eccentric)* excentrique *mf*; **a religious c.** un fanatique religieux (**b**) *Am & Ir (bad-tempered person)* grognon(onne) *m,f*

crankshaft ['kræŋkʃɑːft] *n Aut* vilebrequin *m*

cranky ['kræŋkɪ] *adj Fam* (**a**) *Br (eccentric)* excentrique (**b**) *Am & Ir (bad-tempered)* grognon(onne)

crap [kræp] **1** *n* (**a**) *Vulg (excrement)* merde *f*; **to have or take a c.** chier (**b**) *very Fam (junk)* saloperies *fpl*; *(nonsense)* conneries *fpl*; *(disgusting substance)*

saloperie *f*; **don't talk c.!** ne dis pas de conneries!
2 *adj very Fam (bad)* nul (nulle)

crash [kræʃ] **1** *n* (**a**) *(noise)* fracas *m* (**b**) *(accident) (in car)* accident *m*; *(in train, plane)* catastrophe *f*; **c. barrier** glissière *f* de sécurité; **c. helmet** casque *m*; **c. landing** atterrissage *m* en catastrophe (**c**) *(financial)* krach *m*
2 *adj* **c. course** cours *m* intensif; **c. diet** régime *m* amaigrissant intensif
3 *vt* (**a**) **to c. one's car** avoir un accident de voiture (**b**) *Fam* **to c. a party** = aller à une fête sans y être invité
4 *vi* (**a**) *(make noise)* s'écraser avec fracas; **to c. to the ground** s'écrouler avec fracas; **he was crashing around in the kitchen** il s'agitait bruyamment dans la cuisine (**b**) *(of cars)* se percuter; **to c. into** rentrer dans (**c**) *(of business)* faire faillite; *(of economy)* s'effondrer (**d**) *Comput* tomber en panne (**e**) *Fam (go to sleep)* s'écrouler

▸**crash out** *vi Fam (go to sleep)* s'écrouler; **he was crashed out on the sofa** il roupillait sur le divan

crashing ['kræʃɪŋ] *adj* **a c. bore** *(person)* une personne assommante; *(task)* une besogne assommante

crash-land ['kræʃ'lænd] *vi* atterrir en catastrophe

crass [kræs] *adj* grossier(ère); **c. ignorance** ignorance *f* crasse; **c. stupidity** immense bêtise *f*

crate [kreɪt] *n (box)* caisse *f*; *(for fruit)* cageot *m*; *(for bottles)* casier *m*

crater ['kreɪtə(r)] *n* cratère *m*

cravat [krə'væt] *n* foulard *m*

crave [kreɪv] **1** *vt (cigarette)* avoir très envie de; *(affection)* être en manque de; *(opportunity)* attendre avec impatience
2 *vi* **to be craving for sth** *(cigarette)* avoir très envie de qch; *(affection)* être en manque de qch; *(opportunity)* attendre qch avec impatience

craving ['kreɪvɪŋ] *n* envie *f* irrésistible; **to have a c. for sth** *(cigarette)* avoir très envie de qch; *(affection)* être en manque de qch

crawl [krɔːl] **1** *n* (**a**) *(slow pace)* **to move at a c.** *(of car, driver)* rouler au pas; *(of person)* piétiner sur place (**b**) *(swimming stroke)* crawl *m*
2 *vi* (**a**) *(of person)* ramper; *(of baby)* marcher à quatre pattes; *(of car)* rouler au pas (**b**) *Fam (be infested)* **to be crawling with** grouiller de; **to make sb's skin c.** flanquer des boutons à qn (**c**) *Fam (be obsequious)* faire le lèche-bottes; **to c. to sb** lécher les bottes à qn

crawler ['krɔːlə(r)] *n Fam (obsequious person)* lèche-bottes *mf inv*

crayfish ['kreɪfɪʃ] *n* écrevisse *f*

crayon ['kreɪɒn] *n (wax)* crayon *m* gras; *(pencil)* crayon *m* de couleur

craze [kreɪz] *n* engouement *m* (**for** pour)

crazed [kreɪzd] *adj (look, person)* fou (folle)

crazy ['kreɪzɪ] *adj* fou (folle); **to go c.** devenir fou; **to drive sb c.** rendre qn fou; *Fam* **to be c. about sb/sth** être fou de qn/qch; *Fam* **like c.** *(run, work)* comme un fou (une folle); **c. paving** dallage *m* irrégulier en pierres plates

creak [kriːk] **1** *n (of hinge)* grincement *m*; *(of floor, shoes)* craquement *m*
2 *vi (of hinge)* grincer; *(of floor, shoes)* craquer

creaky ['kriːkɪ] *adj (hinge)* grinçant(e); *(floor)* qui craque; *Fig (plot, dialogue)* boiteux(euse)

cream [kriːm] **1** *n* (**a**) *(of milk)* crème *f*; **c. of tomato/ chicken soup** crème de tomates/volaille; **c. cake**

gâteau *m* à la crème; **c. cheese** fromage *m* frais à tartiner (**b**) *Fig* **the c.** *(best part)* la crème (de la crème) (**c**) *(lotion)* crème *f* (**d**) *(colour)* crème *m*
2 *adj* **c.(-coloured)** (de couleur) crème *inv*
3 *vt Culin (butter)* battre en crème

▸**cream off** *vt sep Fig (money, profits)* écrémer; **the universities c. off the best students** les universités sélectionnent les meilleurs étudiants

creamy ['kriːmɪ] *adj (taste, consistency)* crémeux(-euse); *(skin)* laiteux(euse)

crease [kriːs] **1** *n (in skin, fabric)* pli *m*
2 *vt (fabric)* froisser; **to c. one's brow** plisser le front
3 *vi (of fabric)* se froisser; *(of face, brow)* se plisser

▸**crease up** *vi Fam (laugh)* se tordre (de rire)

create [kriː'eɪt] **1** *vt* créer; **to c. a sensation/a good impression** faire sensation/bonne impression
2 *vi Fam (get angry)* faire une scène

creation [kriː'eɪʃən] *n* création *f*

creative [kriː'eɪtɪv] *adj (person, activity)* créatif(ive); *(process, imagination)* créateur(trice); *Fin* **c. accounting** manipulations *fpl* comptables; **c. writing** techniques *fpl* de l'écriture

creator [kriː'eɪtə(r)] *n* créateur(trice) *m,f*; *Rel* **the C.** le Créateur

creature ['kriːtʃə(r)] *n (person)* créature *f*, être *m*; *(animal)* bête *f*; **to be a c. of habit** avoir ses petites habitudes; **c. comforts** confort *m* matériel; **to like one's c. comforts** aimer son confort

crèche [kreʃ] *n (nursery)* crèche *f*; *(in shopping centre)* halte-garderie *f*

credence ['kriːdəns] *n* **to give c. to sth** ajouter foi à qch

credentials [krɪ'denʃəlz] *npl* (**a**) *(proof of identity)* pièces *fpl* justificatives d'identité; *(of ambassador)* lettres *fpl* de créance (**b**) *(proof of ability)* références *fpl*; *Fig* **to establish one's c.** faire ses preuves

credibility [kredɪ'bɪlɪtɪ] *n* crédibilité *f*; **c. gap** manque *m* de crédibilité

credible ['kredɪbəl] *adj* crédible; **it is hardly c. that...** il est difficile de croire que...

credit ['kredɪt] **1** *n* (**a**) *(financial)* crédit *m*; **to be in c.** *(of person)* avoir un compte créditeur; *(of account)* être créditeur(trice); **to give sb c.** faire crédit à qn; **to buy/sell sth on c.** acheter/vendre qch à crédit; **c. card** carte *f* de crédit; *Econ* **c. control** encadrement *m* du crédit; **c. limit** plafond *m* de crédit; **c. note** avoir *m*; *Fin* **c. rating** degré *m* de solvabilité; *Econ* **c. squeeze** restrictions *fpl* de crédit; **c. transfer** transfert *m*, virement *m*
(**b**) *(belief)* **to give c. to sth** ajouter foi à qch; **to gain c.** *(of theory)* être accepté(e)
(**c**) *(recognition)* mérite *m*; **you have to give him c. for his honesty** tu es bien forcé de reconnaître qu'il est honnête; **to take the c. for sth** s'attribuer le mérite de qch; **to do sb c.** faire honneur à qn; **it does you c.** c'est tout à ton honneur; **c. where c.'s due** il faut rendre à César ce qui est à César; **to her c. she refused** elle a refusé, ce qui est tout à son honneur; **she is a c. to the school** elle fait honneur à l'école
(**d**) **credits** *(of film)* générique *m*
2 *vt* (**a**) *(money)* virer (**to an account** sur un compte) (**b**) *(attribute)* **to c. sb with sth** attribuer qch à qn (**c**) *(believe)* croire; **would you c. it?** tu te rends compte?

creditable ['kredɪtəbəl] *adj (praiseworthy)* honorable; *(efforts, attempt)* louable

creditor ['kredɪtə(r)] *n Fin* créditeur(trice) *m,f*
credulity [krɪ'djuːlɪtɪ] *n* crédulité *f*
credulous ['kredjʊləs] *adj* crédule
creed [kriːd] *n also Fig* principes *mpl*; **political c.** credo *m* politique
creek [kriːk] *n (small bay)* crique *f*; *(stream)* ruisseau *m*; *Fam Fig* **to be up the c. (without a paddle)** être dans le pétrin
creep [kriːp] **1** *n Fam* (**a**) *(unpleasant man)* type *m* répugnant; *(obsequious person)* lèche-bottes *mf inv* (**b**) **to give sb the creeps** faire froid dans le dos à qn
  2 *vi (pt & pp* **crept** [krept]) *(of animal, person)* ramper; *(of plants)* ramper; *(vertically)* grimper; **to c. in/out** entrer/sortir à pas de loup; **to c. into bed** se glisser sous les draps; **old age has crept up on me** je me fais vieux; *Fam* **it makes my flesh c.** ça me flanque des boutons
creeper ['kriːpə(r)] *n (plant)* plante *f* rampante; *(climbing)* plante grimpante
creeping ['kriːpɪŋ] *adj (gradual)* progressif(ive)
creepy ['kriːpɪ] *adj Fam* sinistre
creepy-crawly ['kriːpɪ'krɔːlɪ] *(pl* **creepy-crawlies**) *n Fam* bestiole *f*, insecte *m*
cremate [krɪ'meɪt] *vt* incinérer
cremation [krɪ'meɪʃən] *n* incinération *f*
crematorium [kremə'tɔːrɪəm] *(pl* **crematoria** [kremə'tɔːrɪə]) *n* crématorium *m*
creole ['kriːəʊl] **1** *n* (**a**) *(person)* Créole *mf* (**b**) *(language)* créole *m*
  2 *adj* créole
creosote ['krɪəsəʊt] *n* créosote *f*
crêpe [kreɪp, krep] *n* (**a**) *(textile)* crêpe *m*; **c. bandage** bande *f* Velpeau®; **c. paper** papier *m* crépon; **c.(-rubber) soles** semelles *fpl* de crêpe (**b**) *(pancake)* crêpe *f*
crept [krept] *pt & pp of* **creep**
crescendo [krɪ'ʃendəʊ] *(pl* **crescendos**) *n Mus & Fig* crescendo *m inv*; **to rise to a c.** *(of music, complaints)* aller crescendo
crescent ['kresənt] **1** *n (shape)* croissant *m*; *(street)* rue *f* en croissant
  2 *adj* **c.(-shaped)** en forme de croissant *ou* de demi-lune; **c. moon** croissant *m* de lune
cress [kres] *n* cresson *m*
crest [krest] *n (of bird, wave, helmet)* crête *f*; *(of hill)* sommet *m*; *(coat of arms)* armoiries *fpl*; *Fig* **to be on the c. of a wave** être dans une période faste
crestfallen ['krestfɔːlən] *adj* abattu(e), découragé(e)
Cretan ['kriːtən] **1** *n* Crétois(e) *m,f*
  2 *adj* crétois(e)
Crete [kriːt] *n* la Crète
cretin ['kretɪn] *n Fam* crétin(e) *m,f*
crevice ['krevɪs] *n (in rock)* crevasse *f*, fissure *f*; *(in wall)* lézarde *f*
crew [kruː] **1** *n (of ship, plane)* équipage *m*; *(of ambulance)* équipe *f*; *Fam (gang, group)* bande *f*; **c. cut** *(hairstyle)* brosse *f*, cheveux *mpl* (coupés) en brosse
  2 *vt (ship)* **the ship was crewed by** le bateau avait un équipage de
crib [krɪb] **1** *n* (**a**) *(cradle)* berceau *m*; *(Nativity scene)* crèche *f* (**b**) *Fam* **c. (sheet)** *(in exam)* antisèche *f*
  2 *vt (pt & pp* **cribbed**) *Fam (copy)* pomper
crick [krɪk] **1** *n* **to have a c. in one's neck** avoir un torticolis
  2 *vt* **to c. one's neck** attraper un torticolis
cricket¹ ['krɪkɪt] *n (insect)* grillon *m*

cricket² *n (sport)* cricket *m*; *Fig* **that's not c.!** ce n'est pas du jeu!; **c. ball** balle *f* de cricket; **c. bat** batte *f* de cricket; **c. pitch** terrain *m* de cricket
crikey ['kraɪkɪ] *exclam Fam* mince alors!
crime [kraɪm] *n (act)* crime *m*; *Law* délit *m*; *(phenomenon)* criminalité *f*; **c. is on the increase** la criminalité augmente; *Fig* **it's a c. to waste money like that** c'est un crime de gaspiller de l'argent de cette façon; **c. wave** vague *f* de criminalité; **c. writer** auteur *m* de romans policiers
Crimea [kraɪ'mɪə] *n* la Crimée
Crimean [kraɪ'mɪən] *adj* de Crimée; **the C. War** la guerre de Crimée
criminal ['krɪmɪnəl] **1** *n* criminel(elle) *m,f*
  2 *adj* criminel(elle); *Fig* **it's c. to knock down that building** c'est un crime de démolir ce bâtiment; **to go to c. court** être jugé(e) au pénal; **c. law** droit *m* pénal; **c. lawyer** avocat *m* au pénal; **c. offence** délit *m*; *(more serious)* crime *m*; **c. record** casier *m* judiciaire
criminalize ['krɪmɪnəlaɪz] *vt* criminaliser
criminology [krɪmɪ'nɒlədʒɪ] *n* criminologie *f*
crimp [krɪmp] *vt (hair)* friser; *(pastry)* pincer
crimson ['krɪmzən] **1** *n* pourpre *m*
  2 *adj* pourpre; **to go c. with rage** devenir rouge de colère
cringe [krɪndʒ] *vi* (**a**) *(show fear)* avoir un mouvement de recul (**b**) *(be embarrassed)* avoir envie de rentrer sous terre; **it makes me c.** ça me donne envie de rentrer sous terre
cringing ['krɪndʒɪŋ] *adj (afraid)* craintif(ive); *(servile)* servile
crinkle ['krɪŋkəl] **1** *n (in paper, fabric)* pli *m*
  2 *vt (paper, fabric)* froisser; **to c. one's nose** froncer le nez
  3 *vi (of brow, nose)* se froncer; *(of face)* se rider
crinkly ['krɪŋklɪ] *adj (skin)* ridé(e); *(paper, fabric)* froissé(e)
cripple ['krɪpəl] **1** *n* estropié(e) *m,f*
  2 *vt* estropier; *Fig (industry, system)* paralyser
crippling ['krɪplɪŋ] *adj* (**a**) *(illness)* invalidant(e) (**b**) *(effect, strike)* paralysant(e); *(taxes)* écrasant(e)
crisis ['kraɪsɪs] *(pl* **crises** ['kraɪsiːz]) *n* crise *f*; **to be in c.** être en (pleine) crise; **c. management** habileté *f* à gérer les situations de crise; **c. point** point *m* critique
crisp [krɪsp] **1** *n Br* **(potato) crisps** (pommes *fpl*) chips *fpl*, *Can* croustilles *fpl*; **a c.** une chips, *Can* une croustille
  2 *adj (apple, lettuce)* croquant(e); *(pastry)* croustillant(e); *(bank note)* neuf (neuve); *(sheets)* frais (fraîche); *(snow)* qui crisse sous les pas; *(air, breeze)* vif (vive); *(style)* vif (vive) et précis(e); *(tone)* brusque, tranchant(e)
crispbread ['krɪspbred] *n* pain *m* suédois
crisply ['krɪsplɪ] *adv (say)* d'un ton brusque *ou* tranchant; *(write)* dans un style vif et précis
crispy ['krɪspɪ] *adj* croustillant(e)
criss-cross ['krɪskrɒs] **1** *vt* entrecroiser
  2 *vi* s'entrecroiser
criterion [kraɪ'tɪərɪən] *(pl* **criteria** [kraɪ'tɪərɪə]) *n* critère *m*
critic ['krɪtɪk] *n (reviewer)* critique *mf*; *(opponent)* détracteur(trice) *m,f*
critical ['krɪtɪkəl] *adj* (**a**) *(judgemental)* critique (**of** à l'égard de); **to be c. of sb/sth** critiquer qn/qch (**b**) *(essay, study)* critique; **to be a c. success** être acclamé(e)

par la critique (**c**) *(decisive)* critique; **the next few days will be c.** les prochains jours seront décisifs; **in a c. condition** *(of patient)* dans un état critique

criticism ['krɪtɪsɪzəm] *n* critique *f*

criticize ['krɪtɪsaɪz] **1** *vt* critiquer; **to c. sb for sth** reprocher qch à qn; **to c. sb for doing sth** reprocher à qn de faire/d'avoir fait qch
2 *vi* critiquer

critique [krɪ'tiːk] *n* critique *f*

croak [krəʊk] **1** *n* *(of frog)* coassement *m*; *(of raven)* croassement *m*
2 *vi* (**a**) *(of frog)* coasser; *(of raven)* croasser; *(of person)* parler d'une voix rauque (**b**) *Fam (die)* claquer

Croat ['krəʊæt] **1** *n* *(person)* Croate *mf*
2 *adj* croate

Croatia [krəʊ'eɪʃə] *n* la Croatie

Croatian [krəʊ'eɪʃən] = **Croat**

crochet ['krəʊʃeɪ] **1** *n* (travail *m* au) crochet *m*; **c. hook** crochet
2 *vt* *(shawl, blanket)* faire au crochet
3 *vi* faire du crochet

crock [krɒk] *n* (**a**) *(pot)* pot *m* de terre (**b**) *Fam* **old c.** *(person)* croulant(e) *m,f*

crockery ['krɒkərɪ] *n* vaisselle *f*

crocodile ['krɒkədaɪl] *n* (**a**) *(animal)* crocodile *m*; **c. tears** larmes *fpl* de crocodile (**b**) *(line of people)* **to walk in a c.** marcher en rangs par deux

crocus ['krəʊkəs] *n* crocus *m*

croft [krɒft] *n* petite ferme *f*

crone [krəʊn] *n* *Pej* **old c.** vieille bique *f*

crony ['krəʊnɪ] *(pl* **cronies***)* *n* copain (copine) *m,f*

crook [krʊk] **1** *n* (**a**) *(criminal)* escroc *m* (**b**) *(of shepherd)* houlette *f*; *(of bishop)* crosse *f* (**c**) *(curve)* coude *m*; **in the c. of one's arm** au creux du bras
2 *vt* *(finger, arm)* plier

crooked ['krʊkɪd] *adj* (**a**) *(not straight)* de travers; *(nose)* tordu(e); **a c. smile** un sourire en coin (**b**) *(dishonest, illegal)* malhonnête

croon [kruːn] *vt & vi* chantonner, fredonner

crop [krɒp] **1** *n* (**a**) *(of fruit, vegetables)* récolte *f*; *(of cereals)* moisson *f*; *Fig* **this year's c. of films** la production cinématographique de cette année (**b**) *(handle of whip)* **(riding) c.** cravache *f* (**c**) *(of bird)* jabot *m* (**d**) *(short haircut)* coupe *f* très courte
2 *vt* *(pt & pp* **cropped***)* (**a**) *(cut)* couper; *(hair)* couper ras; **cropped hair** cheveux *mpl* coupés ras (**b**) *(of cattle)* brouter

►**crop up** *vi* *(of issue, question)* surgir; *(of problem, opportunity)* se présenter; *(of name)* être mentionné(e)

cropper ['krɒpə(r)] *n Fam* **to come a c.** se prendre une gamelle

croquet ['krəʊkeɪ] *n* croquet *m*

croquette [krɒ'ket] *n Culin* croquette *f*

cross [krɒs] **1** *n* (**a**) *(sign, shape)* croix *f*; **to make the sign of the c.** faire le signe de croix
(**b**) *(hybrid) & Fig* croisement *m* (**between** entre)
(**c**) *(in boxing)* coup *m* croisé; *(in football)* centre *m*
2 *adj* *(annoyed)* fâché(e); **to get c. (with sb)** se fâcher (contre qn); **to be c. with oneself** s'en vouloir; **we've never had a c. word** nous n'avons jamais eu un mot plus haut que l'autre
3 *vt* (**a**) *(river, road)* traverser; **to c. sb's path** se trouver sur le chemin de qn; **it crossed my mind that...** il m'est venu à l'esprit que...
(**b**) *(make into shape of cross)* croiser; **to c. oneself** se signer; **to c. one's legs/arms** croiser les jambes/

bras; **to keep one's fingers crossed** croiser les doigts; **to c. one's eyes** loucher; *Fig* **to c. swords (with sb)** croiser le fer (avec qn); *Fig* **we must have got our wires crossed** nous avons dû mal nous comprendre; *Fam* **c. my heart (and hope to die)** croix de bois, croix de fer
(**c**) *(oppose)* contrecarrer
(**d**) *(animals, plants)* croiser (**with** avec)
(**e**) *(in writing)* **to c. a cheque** barrer un chèque; **to c. one's t's** mettre une barre à ses t
4 *vi* (**a**) *(of roads, lines)* se croiser; **our letters crossed in the post** nos lettres se sont croisées
(**b**) *(go across)* traverser; **to c. from Dover to Calais** faire la traversée de Douvres à Calais

►**cross off, cross out** *vt sep* barrer, rayer

crossbar ['krɒsbɑː(r)] *n* *(on bike)* barre *f*; *(of goalposts)* barre transversale

crossbow ['krɒsbəʊ] *n* arbalète *f*

crossbreed ['krɒsbriːd] *n* *(of animals)* croisement *m*; *(of plants)* hybride *m*

cross-Channel ['krɒs'tʃænəl] *adj* transmanche *inv*

crosscheck ['krɒs'tʃek] **1** *n* vérification *f* (par recoupement)
2 *vt* vérifier par recoupement

cross-country ['krɒs'kʌntrɪ] *adj* **c. runner** coureur(-euse) *m,f* de fond; **c. running** cross *m*

cross-examination ['krɒsɪgzæmɪ'neɪʃən] *n Law* contre-interrogatoire *m*; *Fig* interrogatoire *m* serré

cross-examine ['krɒsɪg'zæmɪn] *vt Law* soumettre à un contre-interrogatoire; *Fig* soumettre à un interrogatoire serré; **to c. sb about sth** interroger qn en détail sur qch

cross-eyed ['krɒsaɪd] *adj* **to be c.** loucher

crossfire ['krɒsfaɪə(r)] *n* feu *m* croisé; *Fig* **to be caught in the c.** être pris(e) entre deux feux

crossing ['krɒsɪŋ] *n* (**a**) *(of sea, river)* traversée *f* (**b**) *(in street)* passage *m* (pour) piétons, passage clouté

cross-legged ['krɒs'leg(ɪ)d] *adv* **to sit c.** être assis(e) en tailleur

cross-platform [krɒs'plætfɔːm] *adj Comput* multi-plate-forme

cross-purposes ['krɒs'pɜːpəsɪz] *npl* **to be at c.** ne pas parler de la même chose

cross-reference ['krɒs'refərəns] *n* renvoi *m*

crossroads ['krɒsrəʊdz] *(pl* **crossroads***)* *n* carrefour *m*, croisement *m*; *Fig (decisive moment)* point *m* crucial

cross-section ['krɒs'sekʃən] *n* coupe *f ou* section *f* transversale; *Fig (of population)* échantillon *m* représentatif

crosswind ['krɒswɪnd] *n* vent *m* de travers

crossword ['krɒswɜːd] *n* **c. (puzzle)** mots *mpl* croisés

crotch [krɒtʃ] *n* entrejambe *m*

crotchet ['krɒtʃɪt] *n Mus* noire *f*

crotchety ['krɒtʃətɪ] *adj Fam* grognon

crouch [kraʊtʃ] *vi* *(of animal)* se tapir; *(of person)* s'accroupir

croupier ['kruːpɪə(r)] *n* croupier *m*

crow [krəʊ] **1** *n* *(bird)* corbeau *m*; **as the c. flies** à vol d'oiseau; **c.'s feet** *(on face)* pattes *fpl* d'oie; **c.'s nest** *(on ship)* nid-de-pie *m*
2 *vi* (**a**) *(of cock)* chanter (**b**) *(exult)* se vanter (**about** de)

crowbar ['krəʊbɑː(r)] *n* levier *m*

crowd [kraʊd] **1** *n* (**a**) *(large number of people)* foule *f*; *(at sporting event)* public *m*; **there was a c. at the**

cinema il y avait beaucoup de monde au cinéma; *Fig* **to stand out from the c.** se distinguer de la masse; *Fig* **to follow the c.** suivre le mouvement; **to be a c. puller** attirer les foules (**b**) *Fam (group)* bande *f*
  2 *vt (people, objects)* entasser; *(streets, square)* envahir; **don't c. me!** laisse-moi respirer!
  3 *vi* **to c. (together)** s'entasser; **to c. round sb** se presser autour de qn
▸**crowd out** *vt sep (of deal, market)* exclure (**of** de)
crowded ['kraʊdɪd] *adj (place)* bondé(e); *(day, schedule)* chargé(e)
crown [kraʊn] **1** *n* (**a**) *(of monarch)* couronne *f*; **the C.** *(the monarchy)* la Couronne; *Br Law* **c. court** ≃ assises *fpl*, Cour *f* d'assises; **c. jewels** joyaux *mpl* de la Couronne; **c. prince** prince *m* héritier (**b**) *(top) (of head)* sommet *m* de la tête; *(of hat)* haut *m*; *(of hill)* sommet; *(of tooth)* couronne *f*
  2 *vt also Fig* couronner; *Fam* **I'll c. you!** *(hit on the head)* je vais te flanquer une calotte!; **and to c. it all...** et pour couronner le tout...
crowning ['kraʊnɪŋ] *adj (achievement)* suprême; **c. glory** couronnement *m*
crucial ['kruːʃəl] *adj* (**a**) *(very important)* crucial(e) (**b**) *very Fam (very good)* d'enfer
crucible ['kruːsɪbəl] *n* creuset *m*; *Fig (test)* épreuve *f*
crucifix ['kruːsɪfɪks] *n* crucifix *m*
crucifixion [kruːsɪ'fɪkʃən] *n* crucifixion *f*
crucify ['kruːsɪfaɪ] *(pt & pp* **crucified**) *vt* crucifier; *Fig (criticize)* descendre en flammes; *(defeat)* écraser
crude [kruːd] *adj* (**a**) *(unsophisticated, unrefined)* grossier(ère); **c. (oil)** pétrole *m* brut (**b**) *(rude, vulgar)* vulgaire
cruel ['kruːəl] *adj* cruel(elle); *(winter)* rude; **you have to be c. to be kind** qui aime bien châtie bien
cruelty ['kruːəltɪ] *n* cruauté *f*
cruet ['kruːɪt] *n Culin* **c. (stand** *or* **set)** service *m* à condiments
cruise [kruːz] **1** *n (on ship)* croisière *f*; **to go on a c.** faire une croisière; **c. missile** missile *m* de croisière
  2 *vi (of passengers)* être en croisière; *(of taxi)* être en maraude; *(of car)* rouler; *Fam (look for sexual partner)* draguer; **cruising speed** *(of ship, plane)* vitesse *f* de croisière
cruiser ['kruːzə(r)] *n (ship)* (**battle**) **c.** croiseur *m*; **(cabin) c.** yacht *m* de croisière
crumb [krʌm] *n also Fig* miette *f*; **my only c. of comfort is...** mon seul petit réconfort est...
crumble ['krʌmbəl] **1** *n (dessert)* crumble *m (dessert aux fruits recouvert de pâte sablée)*
  2 *vt (bread, cake)* émietter
  3 *vi (of stone)* s'effriter; *(of bread)* s'émietter; *Fig (of empire, hopes)* s'effondrer
crumbly ['krʌmblɪ] *adj* friable
crumpet ['krʌmpɪt] *n* (**a**) *(teacake)* = petite crêpe épaisse mangée avec du beurre, de la confiture etc (**b**) *very Fam (women)* nanas *fpl*; **a nice bit of c.** une belle nana
crumple ['krʌmpəl] **1** *vt (material, dress)* froisser, chiffonner; **to c. sth into a ball** mettre qch en boule
  2 *vi (of material, dress)* se froisser, se chiffonner; *Fig (of face)* se crisper
crunch [krʌntʃ] **1** *n (sound)* craquement *m*; *(of snow, gravel)* crissement *m*; *Fig* **when it comes to the c.** au moment crucial; *Fig* **if it comes to the c.** au pire
  2 *vt (with teeth)* croquer (dans)

3 *vi (of snow, gravel)* crisser; **to c. on sth** *(with teeth)* croquer (dans) qch
crunchy ['krʌntʃɪ] *adj* croquant(e); *(snow, gravel)* qui crisse sous les pas
crusade [kruː'seɪd] **1** *n also Fig* croisade *f*
  2 *vi* **to c. for/against sth** se battre pour/contre qch
crusader [kruː'seɪdə(r)] *n Hist* croisé *m*; *Fig* militant(e) *m,f* (**for/against** pour/contre)
crush [krʌʃ] **1** *n* (**a**) *(crowd)* foule *f*; *(confusion)* bousculade *f*; **c. barrier** barrière *f* de sécurité (**b**) *Br (drink)* **orange/lemon c.** = boisson gazeuse à l'orange/au citron (**c**) *Fam (infatuation)* béguin *m*; **to have a c. on sb** avoir le béguin *ou* en pincer pour qn
  2 *vt* écraser; *(grapes)* presser; *(ice)* piler; *(in a drawer, suitcase)* entasser; *Fig (opponent)* écraser; *(revolt)* étouffer, mater; *(hopes, person)* anéantir
  3 *vi (be crammed)* s'entasser; *(crease)* se froisser
crushing ['krʌʃɪŋ] *adj (defeat)* écrasant(e); *(blow)* terrible; *(remark)* cinglant(e)
crust [krʌst] *n (of bread, pie, the earth)* croûte *f*; *Fam* **to earn a c.** gagner sa croûte
crustacean [krʌs'teɪʃən] *n* crustacé *m*
crusty ['krʌstɪ] *adj* (**a**) *(bread, roll)* croustillant(e) (**b**) *(person)* acariâtre
crutch [krʌtʃ] *n* (**a**) *(for walking)* béquille *f*; *Fig (support)* soutien *m*; **to be on crutches** marcher avec des béquilles (**b**) *(crotch)* entrejambe *m*
crux [krʌks] *n (of matter, problem)* cœur *m*
cruzado [cruː'zɑːdəʊ] *(pl* **cruzados**) *n* cruzado *m*
cry [kraɪ] **1** *n (pl* **cries**) (**a**) *(call) (of person, animal)* cri *m*; *(in demonstration)* slogan *m*; **to give a c.** pousser un cri; **a c. for help** un appel au secours; **to be a far c. from sth** n'avoir rien à voir avec qch (**b**) *(weeping)* **to have a good c.** pleurer un bon coup
  2 *vt (pt & pp* **cried**) (**a**) *(exclaim)* crier (**b**) *(weep)* **to c. oneself to sleep** s'endormir en pleurant
  3 *vi* (**a**) *(weep)* pleurer; **to c. over sth** se lamenter sur qch; *Prov* **it's no use crying over spilt milk** ce qui est fait est fait (**b**) *(shout, call)* crier; **to c. for help** appeler à l'aide *ou* au secours
▸**cry off** *vi (from invitation)* se décommander
▸**cry out 1** *vt sep* (**a**) *(shout)* crier (**b**) *(weep)* **to c. one's eyes** *or* **heart out** pleurer toutes les larmes de son corps
  2 *vi (shout)* pousser un cri; *Fam* **for crying out loud!** mais bon sang!; *Fam* **that wall is crying out for a coat of paint** ce mur aurait grand besoin d'une couche de peinture
crybaby ['kraɪbeɪbɪ] *(pl* **crybabies**) *n Fam* pleurnicheur(euse) *m,f*
crying ['kraɪɪŋ] **1** *n (weeping)* pleurs *mpl*
  2 *adj (need)* urgent(e); **it's a c. shame that...** il est scandaleux que... + *subjunctive*
crypt [krɪpt] *n* crypte *f*
cryptic ['krɪptɪk] *adj* énigmatique; **c. crossword** = mots croisés dont les définitions sont des énigmes
crystal ['krɪstəl] **1** *n* cristal *m*; **c. ball** boule *f* de cristal; **c. vase** vase *m* de *ou* en cristal
  2 *adj (clear)* cristallin(e), limpide
crystal-clear ['krɪstəl'klɪə(r)] *adj (water)* limpide; *(explanation)* clair(e) comme de l'eau de roche
crystallize ['krɪstəlaɪz] **1** *vt Chem* cristalliser; **crystallized fruit** fruits *mpl* confits
  2 *vi Chem & Fig* se cristalliser

CSA [siːes'eɪ] *n Br (abbr* **Child Support Agency**) = organisme gouvernemental qui décide du montant des pensions alimentaires et les prélève au besoin

CSE [siːes'iː] *n Br Formerly (abbr* **Certificate of Secondary Education**) = diplôme de fin d'études du premier cycle de l'enseignement secondaire

CST [siːes'tiː] *n Am (abbr* **Central Standard Time**) = heure du centre de l'Amérique du Nord

cub [kʌb] *n (of fox)* renardeau *m; (of bear)* ourson *m; (of lion)* lionceau *m; (of wolf)* louveteau *m;* **C. (Scout)** louveteau *m*

Cuba ['kjuːbə] *n* Cuba

Cuban ['kjuːbən] **1** *n* Cubain(e) *m,f* **2** *adj* cubain(e)

cubbyhole ['kʌbɪhəʊl] *n* cagibi *m*

cube [kjuːb] **1** *n (shape)* cube *m; (of sugar)* morceau *m; Math* **c. root** racine *f* cubique
2 *vt Math* élever au cube

cubic ['kjuːbɪk] *adj* cubique; **c. capacity** volume *m;* **c. metre** mètre *m* cube

cubicle ['kjuːbɪkəl] *n (in hospital, dormitory)* box *m; (in swimming pool)* cabine *f; (in public toilet)* W.-C. *m*

cubism ['kjuːbɪzəm] *n Art* cubisme *m*

cuckold ['kʌkəld] **1** *n* cocu *m*
2 *vt* cocufier, faire cocu

cuckoo ['kʊkuː] **1** *n (bird)* coucou *m;* **c. clock** coucou
2 *adj Fam (mad)* dingue

cucumber ['kjuːkʌmbə(r)] *n* concombre *m*

cud [kʌd] *n* **to chew the c.** ruminer

cuddle ['kʌdəl] **1** *n* câlin *m;* **to give sb a c.** faire un câlin à qn
2 *vt* câliner, faire des câlins à
3 *vi* se câliner, se faire des câlins; **to c. up to sb** se pelotonner *ou* se blottir contre qn

cuddly ['kʌdlɪ] *adj Fam (child, animal)* mignon(onne) à croquer; *Euph (plump)* rond(e); **c. toy** peluche *f*

cudgel ['kʌdʒəl] **1** *n* gourdin *m*, trique *f; Fig* **to take up the cudgels on sb's behalf** prendre fait et cause pour qn
2 *vt (pt & pp* **cudgelled**, *Am* **cudgeled)** donner des coups de gourdin *ou* de trique à; **to c. one's brains** se creuser la cervelle

cue¹ [kjuː] *n (of actor)* réplique *f; Fig (signal)* signal *m;* **on c.** au bon moment; *Fig* **to take one's c. from sb** prendre exemple sur qn; **c. card** *(for public speaker)* aide-mémoire *m inv*

cue² *n (in billiards, pool)* queue *f;* **c. ball** boule *f* blanche

cuff¹ [kʌf] *n (of shirt)* poignet *m; Fam* **cuffs** *(handcuffs)* menottes *fpl; Fam* **off the c.** au pied levé; **c. links** boutons *mpl* de manchette

cuff² *Fam* **1** *n (blow)* calotte *f*
2 *vt (hit)* donner une calotte à

cuisine [kwɪ'ziːn] *n* cuisine *f*

cul-de-sac ['kʌldəsæk] *n also Fig* impasse *f*

culinary ['kʌlɪnərɪ] *adj* culinaire

cull [kʌl] **1** *n (of seals, deer)* abattage *m*
2 *vt (a) (herd)* réduire la taille de; *(animal)* abattre **(b)** *(select)* sélectionner (**from** parmi)

culminate ['kʌlmɪneɪt] *vi* **to c. in sth** aboutir à qch

culmination [kʌlmɪ'neɪʃən] *n* point *m* culminant

culottes [kuː'lɒts] *npl* jupe-culotte *f*

culpable ['kʌlpəbəl] *adj* coupable (**of** de); *Scot Law* **c. homicide** homicide *m* involontaire

culprit ['kʌlprɪt] *n* coupable *mf*

cult [kʌlt] *n* culte *m; (sect)* secte *f;* **c. figure** personnage *m* culte; **c. film** film *m* culte

cultivate ['kʌltɪveɪt] *vt also Fig* cultiver

cultivated ['kʌltɪveɪtɪd] *adj* cultivé(e)

cultivation [kʌltɪ'veɪʃən] *n* culture *f*

cultivator ['kʌltɪveɪtə(r)] *n (for farm)* cultivateur *m; (for garden)* motoculteur *m; (person)* cultivateur(-trice) *m,f*

cultural ['kʌltʃərəl] *adj* culturel(elle)

culture ['kʌltʃə(r)] *n* **(a)** *(artistic activity, refinement)* culture *f; Hum* **c. vulture** fou (folle) *m,f* de culture **(b)** *(society)* culture *f;* **c. shock** choc *m* culturel **(c)** *Biol* culture *f*

cultured ['kʌltʃəd] *adj (educated)* cultivé(e); **c. pearl** perle *f* de culture

cumbersome ['kʌmbəsəm] *adj (luggage, furniture)* encombrant(e); *(procedure, style)* lourd(e)

cumin ['kʌmɪn] *n* cumin *m*

cumulative ['kjuːmjʊlətɪv] *adj* cumulatif(ive)

cunning ['kʌnɪŋ] **1** *n (deviousness)* ruse *f; (ingenuity)* astuce *f*, ingéniosité *f*
2 *adj (devious)* rusé(e); *(ingenious)* astucieux(euse), ingénieux(euse)

cunt [kʌnt] *n Vulg (vagina)* chatte *f; (as insult)* enculé(e) *m,f*

cup [kʌp] **1** *n* **(a)** *(for drinking, measurement)* tasse *f; (plastic, paper)* gobelet *m; Fam Fig* **it's not my c. of tea** ce n'est pas ma tasse de thé; **it's not everyone's c. of tea** tout le monde n'aime pas **(b)** *(trophy)* coupe *f;* **c. final** finale *f* de coupe; **c. tie** match *m* éliminatoire de coupe **(c)** *(of bra)* bonnet *m*
2 *vt (pt & pp* **cupped)** **to c. one's hands round one's mouth** mettre ses mains en porte-voix; **to c. one's hand behind one's ear** mettre sa main en cornet

cupboard ['kʌbəd] *n* placard *m; Fam* **c. love** amour *m* intéressé; **c. space** rangements *mpl*

cupcake ['kʌpkeɪk] *n* = sorte de madeleine

Cupid ['kjuːpɪd] *n* Cupidon

cuppa ['kʌpə] *n Br Fam* tasse *f* de thé

curable ['kjʊərəbəl] *adj* guérissable

curate ['kjʊərət] *n Rel* vicaire *m;* **this book is a bit of a c.'s egg** il y a du bon et du mauvais dans ce livre

curator [kjʊə'reɪtə(r)] *n* conservateur(trice) *m,f*

curb [kɜːb] **1** *n* **(a)** *(limit)* **to put a c. on sth** mettre un frein à qch **(b)** *Am (of road)* bordure *f* de trottoir
2 *vt (spending)* réduire; *(emotions)* réfréner

curd [kɜːd] *n* **curd(s)** lait *m* caillé; **c. cheese** fromage *m* blanc battu

curdle ['kɜːdəl] **1** *vt* cailler
2 *vi* (se) cailler

cure ['kjʊə(r)] **1** *n* remède *m* (**for** contre); **there is no known c.** on n'a pas trouvé de remède; **beyond c.** *(person)* incurable; *(situation)* irrémédiable
2 *vt (a) (person)* guérir (**of** de) **(b)** *(preserve) (by salting)* saler; *(by smoking)* fumer; *(by drying)* sécher; *(hides)* traiter

cure-all ['kjʊərɔːl] *n* panacée *f*

curfew ['kɜːfjuː] *n* couvre-feu *m*

curio ['kjʊərɪəʊ] *(pl* **curios)** *n* curiosité *f*

curiosity [kjʊərɪ'ɒsɪtɪ] *(pl* **curiosities)** *n* curiosité *f; Prov* **c. killed the cat** la curiosité est un vilain défaut

curious ['kjʊərɪəs] *adj (inquisitive, strange)* curieux(euse); **to be c. to see/know** vouloir voir/savoir par curiosité

curl [kɜːl] **1** n (of hair) boucle f; (of smoke) volute f
2 vt (hair) boucler; (tightly) friser; **to c. one's lip** faire une moue dédaigneuse; **to c. oneself into a ball** se rouler en boule
3 vi (of hair) boucler; (tightly) friser; (of paper, leaves) se recroqueviller; (of smoke) s'élever en volutes
▸**curl up** vi (**a**) (make oneself comfortable) se pelotonner (**b**) (protect oneself) se rouler en boule (**c**) (of paper, leaves) se recroqueviller
curler ['kɜːlə(r)] n (for hair) bigoudi m
curlew ['kɜːljuː] n courlis m
curling ['kɜːlɪŋ] n (**a**) (sport) curling m (**b**) **c. tongs** fer m à friser
curly ['kɜːlɪ] adj (hair) bouclé(e); (tightly) frisé(e)
currant ['kʌrənt] n raisin m de Corinthe; **c. bun** petit pain m aux raisins
currency ['kʌrənsɪ] (pl **currencies**) n (**a**) (money) monnaie f; (foreign) devise f; **c. market** marché m monétaire (**b**) (acceptance) **to gain c.** (of theory) être accrédité(e); (of idea, belief) se répandre; **to give c. to a rumour** faire courir un bruit
current ['kʌrənt] **1** n (of river, electricity) & Fig (trend) courant m; Fig **to swim against the c.** aller à contre-courant
2 adj (**a**) (existing, present) actuel(elle); **c. affairs** actualité f; **c. issue** (of magazine) dernier numéro m (**b**) Br Fin **c. account** compte m courant; **c. assets** actif m de roulement; **c. expenditure** dépenses fpl courantes; **c. liabilities** passif m exigible (**c**) (common) courant(e)
currently ['kʌrəntlɪ] adv actuellement
curriculum [kə'rɪkjʊləm] (pl **curricula** [kə'rɪkjʊlə]) n Sch programme m; **c. vitae** curriculum vitae m inv
curry¹ ['kʌrɪ] **1** n (pl **curries**) curry m; **chicken c.** curry de poulet; **c. powder** curry
2 vt (pt & pp **curried**) **curried lamb** agneau m au curry
curry² vt **to c. favour with sb** s'insinuer dans les bonnes grâces de qn
curse [kɜːs] **1** n (**a**) (jinx, affliction) malédiction f, mauvais sort m; (swearword) juron m; **to put a c. on sb** jeter un sort à qn (**b**) (scourge) fléau m
2 vt maudire; **to be cursed with sth** être affligé(e) de qch
3 vi jurer
cursor ['kɜːsə(r)] n Comput curseur m; **c. key** touche f de déplacement
cursory ['kɜːsərɪ] adj superficiel(elle)
curt [kɜːt] adj sec (sèche)
curtail [kɜː'teɪl] vt (shorten) abréger, écourter; (limit) réduire
curtain ['kɜːtən] n rideau m; **to draw the curtains** (open) ouvrir les rideaux; (close) fermer ou tirer les rideaux; Fam Fig **it's curtains for her** elle est fichue; Theat **c. call** rappel m; **c. raiser** Theat lever m de rideau; Fig prélude m (**to** à); **c. ring** anneau m de rideau; **c. rail** or **rod** tringle f à rideau
▸**curtain off** vt sep séparer par un rideau
curts(e)y ['kɜːtsɪ] **1** n (pl **curtsies** or **curtseys**) révérence f
2 vi (pt & pp **curtsied** or **curtseyed**) faire la révérence (**to** à)
curvaceous [kɜː'veɪʃəs] adj pulpeux(euse)
curvature ['kɜːvətʃə(r)] n courbure f; **c. of the spine** scoliose f

curve [kɜːv] **1** n courbe f; (in road) tournant m, virage m; (in river) méandre m
2 vi (of spine) se courber; (of road) faire une courbe; (of river) serpenter
curved [kɜːvd] adj (line) courbe; (spine) courbé(e)
cushion ['kʊʃən] **1** n (on chair, of air) coussin m; (on billiard table) bande f
2 vt (blow, impact) amortir; **to c. sb against sth** protéger qn contre qch
cushy ['kʊʃɪ] adj Fam pépère, peinard(e); **a c. number** une bonne planque
custard ['kʌstəd] n crème f anglaise; **c. pie** (in slapstick comedy) tarte f à la crème; **c. powder** préparation f instantanée pour crème anglaise
custodial [kʌs'təʊdɪəl] adj Law **c. sentence** peine f de prison
custodian [kʌs'təʊdɪən] n gardien(enne) m,f
custody ['kʌstədɪ] n (**a**) (of children, important papers) garde f; **to have c. of sb** avoir la garde de qn; **in safe c.** sous bonne garde (**b**) Law garde f à vue; **to take sb into c.** placer qn en garde à vue
custom ['kʌstəm] n (**a**) (tradition, practice) coutume f; **it was his c. to rise early** il avait l'habitude de se lever tôt (**b**) Com clientèle f; **to take one's c. elsewhere** aller se fournir ailleurs
customary ['kʌstəmərɪ] adj (usual) habituel(elle); (traditional) traditionnel(elle); **it is c. to...** il est d'usage de...
custom-built ['kʌstəmbɪlt] adj (car, offices) construit(e) sur mesure; (kitchen units) fabriqué(e) sur mesure
customer ['kʌstəmə(r)] n client(e) m,f; Fam Fig **he's an awkward c.** c'est un type pas commode; Com **c. services (department)** service m clientèle
customize ['kʌstəmaɪz] vt (vehicle) customiser; (kitchen, computer) personnaliser
custom-made ['kʌstəm'meɪd] adj (fait(e)) sur mesure
customs ['kʌstəmz] npl douane f; **to go through c.** passer la douane; **c. declaration** déclaration f en douane; **c. duty** droits mpl de douane; **c. officer** douanier(ère) m,f
cut [kʌt] **1** n (**a**) (in flesh, text, film) coupure f; (in wood, cloth) entaille f; **c. of meat** morceau m (de viande); Fam **to be a c. above sb/sth** être un cran au-dessus de qn/qch
(**b**) (in wages, prices) réduction f
(**c**) (blow) coup m; **the c. and thrust of debate** les joutes fpl oratoires
(**d**) Fam (share) part f
(**e**) (style) (of clothes, hair) coupe f
2 adj Fig **c. and dried** (clear) simple; (decided) décidé(e); **c. flowers** fleurs fpl coupées; **c. glass** cristal m taillé
3 vt (pt & pp **cut**) (**a**) (in general) couper; (into slices) trancher, découper; **to c. one's finger/nails** se couper le doigt/les ongles; **to c. sb's hair** couper les cheveux à qn; **to have one's hair cut** se faire couper les cheveux; **to c. sth in two** or **in half** couper qch en deux; **to c. sth to pieces** couper qch en morceaux; **to c. oneself loose** or **free** se dégager, se libérer; **to c. a record** enregistrer un disque; Comput **to c. and paste sth** faire un couper-coller sur qch
(**b**) (wages, prices) réduire
(**c**) (idioms) **to c. one's losses** limiter les dégâts; **to c. one's teeth on sth** se faire les dents sur qch; **to c. sb**

(dead) faire semblant de ne pas voir qn; **it's cutting it** *or* **things (a bit) fine** ça fait (un peu) juste; **to c. sb short** couper la parole à qn; **to c. sth short** écourter qch; **to c. a long story short...** bref...

4 *vi* **(a)** *(of knife, scissors)* couper; *(of wind)* être cinglant(e); *Cin* **c.!** coupez!

(b) *(idioms)* **that's an argument that cuts both ways** c'est un argument à double tranchant; *Fam* **to c. and run** décamper

►**cut across** *vt insep* **(a)** *(field)* couper à travers **(b)** *(transcend)* transcender

►**cut back 1** *vt sep* **(a)** *(bush, tree)* tailler **(b)** *(costs, production)* réduire

2 *vi* **to c. back on sth** *(spending, time)* réduire qch; **to c. back on smoking/drinking** fumer/boire moins

►**cut down 1** *vt sep* **(a)** *(tree, soldier)* abattre; **to be c. down in one's prime** être fauché(e) à la fleur de l'âge **(b)** *(speech, text)* abréger; *(spending, time)* réduire; *Fig* **to c. sb down to size** rabattre son caquet à qn

2 *vi* = **cut back**

cut in *vi* **(a)** *(interrupt conversation)* intervenir **(b)** *(in car)* **to c. in in front of sb** faire une queue de poisson à qn

►**cut into** *vt insep* *(with knife)* entamer; *(of rope, handle)* blesser

cut off *vt sep* **(a)** *(remove)* couper; **to c. off sb's head** trancher la tête à qn, décapiter qn; *Fig* **that would be cutting off your nose to spite your face** ça va te retomber sur le nez **(b)** *(disconnect)* couper; **we've been cut off** *(had electricity disconnected)* on nous a coupé l'électricité; **I've been cut off** *(during phone conversation)* j'ai été coupé(e) **(c)** *(isolate)* isoler; **to be cut off from** être coupé(e) de

►**cut out 1** *vt sep* **(a)** *(picture, article)* découper; *(tumour)* enlever; *Fam* **to have got one's work c. out** avoir du pain sur la planche; **to be cut out for sth** être fait(e) pour qch **(b)** *(stop)* supprimer; **to c. out smoking/puddings** arrêter de fumer/de manger des desserts; *Fam* **c. it out!** ça va maintenant! **(c)** *(exclude)* **to c. sb out of one's will** déshériter qn; **to c. sb out of a deal** évincer qn

2 *vi (of engine)* caler; *(of machine)* s'arrêter

cut up 1 *vt sep* **(a)** *(food, paper)* couper; *(into slices)* découper **(b)** *Fam (upset)* **to be very cut up (about sth)** être complètement chamboulé(e) (par qch)

2 *vi Fam* **to c. up rough** *(of person)* devenir agressif(-ive)

cut-and-paste ['kʌtənd'peɪst] *n Comput* couper-coller *m*

cutback ['kʌtbæk] *n* réduction *f*

cute [kjuːt] *adj* mignon(onne)

cuticle ['kjuːtɪkəl] *n* cuticule *f*

cutlery ['kʌtləri] *n* couverts *mpl*; *Com* argenterie *f*

cutlet ['kʌtlɪt] *n* côtelette *f*

cutoff ['kʌtɒf] *n* **c. date** date *f* limite; **c. point** limite *f*; *(for tax)* seuil *m*

cutout ['kʌtaʊt] *n* **(a)** *(shape)* silhouette *f* **(b)** *Elec* disjoncteur *m*

cut-price ['kʌt'praɪs] *adj (goods)* à prix réduit; *(rate)* réduit(e)

cutthroat ['kʌtθrəʊt] **1** *n* assassin *m*

2 *adj (competition)* acharné(e); **c. razor** coupe-choux *m inv*

cutting ['kʌtɪŋ] **1** *n* **(a)** *(of plant)* bouture *f* **(b)** **(newspaper) c.** coupure *f* de journal *ou* de presse **(c)** **(railway) c.** voie *f* en déblai

2 *adj (wind, remark)* cinglant(e); **c. edge** tranchant *m*; *Fig* **to be at the c. edge of technology** être à la pointe du progrès

cuttlefish ['kʌtəlfɪʃ] *n* seiche *f*

CV [siː'viː] *n (abbr* **curriculum vitae)** CV *m*

cyanide ['saɪənaɪd] *n Chem* cyanure *m*

cybercafé [saɪbə'kæfeɪ] *n* cybercafé *m*

cybernetics [saɪbə'netɪks] *n Comput* cybernétique *f*

cybersex ['saɪbəseks] *n Comput* cybersexe *m*

cyberspace ['saɪbəspeɪs] *n Comput* cyberespace *m*

cybersquatting ['saɪbəskwɒtɪŋ] *n Comput* cybersquatting *m*, *Offic* cybersquattage *m*

cyclamen ['sɪkləmən] *(pl* **cyclamen)** *n* cyclamen *m*

cycle ['saɪkəl] **1** *n* **(a)** *(pattern)* cycle *m* **(b)** *(bicycle)* bicyclette *f*, vélo *m*; **c. lane** voie *f* réservée aux vélos; **c. path** piste *f* cyclable; **c. racing** course *f* cycliste

2 *vi* aller à bicyclette *ou* à vélo

cyclic(al) ['saɪklɪk(əl)] *adj* cyclique

cycling ['saɪklɪŋ] *n* cyclisme *m*; **to go on a c. holiday** faire du cyclotourisme; **c. shorts** cuissard *m*; **c. track** piste *f* cycliste

cyclist ['saɪklɪst] *n* cycliste *mf*

cyclone ['saɪkləʊn] *n Met* cyclone *m*

cygnet ['sɪgnɪt] *n* jeune cygne *m*

cylinder ['sɪlɪndə(r)] *n (shape)* cylindre *m*; *(gas container)* bouteille *f*; **four-/eight-c. engine** moteur *m* à quatre/huit cylindres; **c. block** bloc-cylindres *m*; **c. head** culasse *f*

cylindrical [sɪ'lɪndrɪkəl] *adj* cylindrique

cymbal ['sɪmbəl] *n* cymbale *f*

cynic ['sɪnɪk] *n* cynique *mf*

cynical ['sɪnɪkəl] *adj* cynique (**about** sur)

cypress ['saɪprəs] *n* cyprès *m*

Cypriot ['sɪprɪət] **1** *n* Chypriote *mf*, Cypriote *mf*

2 *adj* chypriote, cypriote

Cyprus ['saɪprəs] *n* Chypre

cyst [sɪst] *n Med* kyste *m*

cystitis [sɪs'taɪtɪs] *n Med* cystite *f*

czar [zɑː(r)] *n* tsar *m*, czar *m*

Czech [tʃek] **1** *n* **(a)** *(person)* Tchèque *mf* **(b)** *(language)* tchèque *m*

2 *adj* tchèque; **the C. Republic** la République tchèque

Czechoslovakia [tʃekəʊslə'vækɪə] *n Formerly* la Tchécoslovaquie

D

D, d [diː] *n* (**a**) *(letter)* D, d *m inv* (**b**) *Mus* ré *m* (**c**) *Sch (grade)* **to get a D** avoir entre 8 et 10 sur 20

D *Am Pol (abbr* **Democrat**) démocrate

DA [diːˈeɪ] *n Am Law (abbr* **district attorney**) ≃ procureur *m* de la République

dab [dæb] **1** *n (of paint)* petit coup *m*; *(of glue)* point *m*; *(of perfume)* goutte *f*; *Br Fam* **dabs** *(fingerprints)* empreintes *fpl* (digitales)
　2 *adj* **to be a d. hand at sth** être doué(e) pour qch
　3 *vt (pt & pp* **dabbed**) *(paint)* passer; *(eyes, wound)* tamponner

dabble [ˈdæbəl] **1** *vt* **to d. one's feet in the water** balancer ses pieds dans l'eau
　2 *vi* **to d. in politics/journalism** faire vaguement de la politique/du journalisme

dabbler [ˈdæblə(r)] *n* amateur(trice) *m,f*

dachshund [ˈdækʃʊnd] *n* teckel *m*

dad [dæd] *n Fam* papa *m*

daddy [ˈdædɪ] *(pl* **daddies**) *n Fam* papa *m*

daddy-longlegs [ˈdædɪˈlɒŋlegz] *(pl* **daddy-longlegs**) *n Fam* tipule *f*

daffodil [ˈdæfədɪl] *n* jonquille *f*

daft [dɑːft] *adj Br* idiot(e); **to be d. about sb/sth** être fou (folle) de qn/qch

dagger [ˈdægə(r)] *n* (**a**) *(weapon)* dague *f* (**b**) *(idioms)* **to be at daggers drawn (with sb)** être à couteaux tirés (avec qn); **to look daggers at sb** foudroyer qn du regard

dago [ˈdeɪgəʊ] *(pl* **dagoes** *or* **dagos**) *n very Fam* = terme injurieux désignant un Espagnol, un Portugais, un Italien ou un Latino-Américain

dahlia [ˈdeɪlɪə] *n* dahlia *m*

daily [ˈdeɪlɪ] **1** *n (pl* **dailies**) (**a**) *(newspaper)* quotidien *m* (**b**) *Br Fam (maid)* femme *f* de ménage *(qui vient tous les jours)*
　2 *adj* quotidien(enne); **on a d. basis** *(paid, calculated)* à la journée; *(used)* quotidiennement; *Fam* **the d. grind** le train-train quotidien; **d. paper** quotidien *m*
　3 *adv* tous les jours, quotidiennement; **twice d.** deux fois par jour

dainty [ˈdeɪntɪ] *adj* délicat(e)

dairy [ˈdeərɪ] *(pl* **dairies**) *n (shop)* crémerie *f*; *(factory)* laiterie *f*; **d. cow** vache *f* laitière; **d. farm** = ferme spécialisée dans la production laitière; **d. farming** élevage *m* de vaches laitières; **d. produce** produits *mpl* laitiers

dais [ˈdeɪɪs] *n* estrade *f*

daisy [ˈdeɪzɪ] *(pl* **daisies**) *n* pâquerette *f*; *(bigger)* marguerite *f*; *Fam* **to push up the daisies** manger les pis-

senlits par la racine; **d. chain** guirlande *f* de pâquerettes

daisywheel [ˈdeɪzɪwiːl] *n (on printer)* marguerite *f*

dale [deɪl] *n* vallée *f*

dalliance [ˈdælɪəns] *n Lit* badinage *m*

dally [ˈdælɪ] *(pt & pp* **dallied**) *vi (dawdle)* traîner, lambiner; **to d. over a decision** mettre du temps à se décider; **to d. with sb** flirter avec qn

Dalmatian [dælˈmeɪʃən] *n (dog)* dalmatien *m*

dam [dæm] **1** *n* barrage *m*
　2 *vt (pt & pp* **dammed**) *(river, lake)* construire un barrage sur

▶**dam up** *vt sep (river, lake)* construire un barrage sur

damage [ˈdæmɪdʒ] **1** *n* (**a**) *(to machine, building)* dégâts *mpl*; *(to health, reputation)* mal *m*; **to do** *or* **cause d. to** *(building)* faire des dégâts dans; *(health, reputation)* nuire à; *Fig* **the d. is done** le mal est fait; *Br Fam* **what's the d.?** ça fait combien?; **we have to do some d. limitation** il faut limiter les dégâts (**b**) **damages** *(compensation)* dommages-intérêts *mpl*
　2 *vt (machine, building)* abîmer, endommager; *(health, reputation)* nuire à; *(chances)* compromettre; *(person)* faire du tort à

damaging [ˈdæmɪdʒɪŋ] *adj* préjudiciable (**to** à)

Damascus [dəˈmæskəs] *n* Damas

damask [ˈdæməsk] *n* damas *m*

dame [deɪm] *n* (**a**) *Am Fam (woman)* pépée *f*; *Br (in pantomime)* = dans la "pantomime", personnage comique de vieille dame tenu par un homme (**b**) *Br (title)* = titre donné à une femme ayant reçu une distinction honorifique

damn [dæm] **1** *n very Fam* **I don't give a d.** j'en ai rien à fiche; **it's not worth a d.** ça ne vaut pas un clou
　2 *adj very Fam* fichu(e); **you d. fool!** espèce d'idiot(e)!; **he's a d. nuisance!** qu'est-ce qu'il peut être casse-pieds!
　3 *adv very Fam* sacrément; **d. all** que dalle; **you know d. well what I mean!** tu sais fichtrement bien ce que je veux dire!
　4 *exclam very Fam* **d.!** zut!, mince!
　5 *vt* (**a**) *(criticize severely)* éreinter; **to d. sb with faint praise** éreinter qn sous couleur d'éloge (**b**) *very Fam* **d. the expense!** au diable l'avarice!; **d. it!** zut!, mince!; **well I'll be damned!** ben mince alors!

damnation [dæmˈneɪʃən] **1** *n Rel* damnation *f*
　2 *exclam Fam* **d.!** bon sang!

damned [dæmd] **1** *npl Rel* **the d.** les damnés *mpl*
　2 *adj & adv very Fam* = **damn**

damning [ˈdæmɪŋ] *adj (admission, revelation)* accablant(e)

damp [dæmp] **1** n humidité f
  2 adj humide; (skin) moite; **d. course** isolant m contre l'humidité; Fig **d. squib** déception f
  3 vt (make wet) humecter; **to d. down a fire** couvrir un feu

dampen [dæmpən] vt (make wet) humecter; Fig **to d. sb's spirits** décourager qn

damper ['dæmpə(r)] n Mus étouffoir m; Fig **to put a d. on sth** jeter un froid sur qch

damsel ['dæmzəl] n Lit damoiselle f; Hum **a d. in distress** une belle éplorée

damson ['dæmzən] n (fruit) prune f de Damas; (tree) prunier m de Damas

dance [dɑːns] **1** n danse f; (event) soirée f dansante; (for young people) boum f; (formal) bal m; Fam **to lead sb a (merry) d.** donner du fil à retordre à qn; **d. band** orchestre m de danse; **d. floor** piste f de danse; **d. hall** salle f de bal; **d. music** (in clubs) dance (music) f
  2 vt (waltz, tango) danser
  3 vi danser; **they danced down the road** ils ont descendu la rue en dansant

dancer ['dɑːnsə(r)] n danseur(euse) m,f

dancing ['dɑːnsɪŋ] n danse f; **d. shoes** chaussons mpl de danse

dandelion ['dændɪlaɪən] n pissenlit m

dander ['dændə(r)] n Fam **to get sb's d. up** hérisser qn

dandruff ['dændrəf] n pellicules fpl

dandy ['dændɪ] **1** n (pl dandies) dandy m
  2 adj Fam génial(e); **everything's just (fine and) d.** tout marche comme sur des roulettes

Dane [deɪn] n Danois(e) m,f

danger ['deɪndʒə(r)] n danger m; **in d.** en danger; **out of d.** hors de danger; **to be in d. of doing sth** risquer de faire qch; **there's no d. that...** il n'y a pas de danger que... + subjunctive; **to be on the d. list** (of patient) être dans un état critique; **to be off the d. list** (of patient) être hors de danger, **d. money** prime f de risque; Fig **d. sign** signal m d'alarme

dangerous ['deɪndʒərəs] adj dangereux(euse)

dangerously ['deɪndʒərəslɪ] adv dangereusement; **they came d. close to losing** ils ont bien failli perdre

dangle ['dæŋgəl] **1** vt balancer; Fig **to d. sth in front of sb** faire miroiter qch à qn
  2 vi (of legs) pendre; (from rope, chain) se balancer; Fig **to keep sb dangling** laisser qn dans l'incertitude

Danish ['deɪnɪʃ] **1** n (language) danois m
  2 adj danois(e); **D. (pastry)** = sorte de chausson fourré

dank [dæŋk] adj humide et froid(e)

Danube ['dænjuːb] n the D. le Danube

dapper ['dæpə(r)] adj soigné(e)

dappled ['dæpəld] adj tacheté(e); (horse) pommelé(e)

dare ['deə(r)] **1** n défi m; **to do sth for a d.** faire qch par défi
  2 vt **to d. to do sth** oser faire qch; **to d. sb to do sth** défier qn de faire qch; **I d. you!** chiche!; **don't you d. (do that)!** ne t'avise pas de faire ça!; **how d. you!** comment oses-tu!; **I d. say** sans doute, c'est bien possible

daredevil ['deədevəl] **1** n casse-cou mf inv
  2 adj (person) casse-cou inv; (stunt, escape) audacieux(euse)

daring ['deərɪŋ] **1** n audace f
  2 adj audacieux(euse)

dark [dɑːk] **1** n (a) (darkness) obscurité f; **before/after d.** avant/après la tombée de la nuit; **in the d.** dans le noir (b) (idioms) **to be in the d. (about)** ne pas être au courant (de)
  2 adj (a) (not light) sombre; (skin, hair) foncé(e); **it's d. by six o'clock** il fait nuit à six heures; **it's getting d.** il commence à faire nuit; **d. glasses** lunettes fpl noires; Fig **d. horse** (competitor) outsider m; (in politics) candidat(e) m,f surprise; (secretive person) personne f pleine de mystère (b) Fig (thought) sombre, morose; (period) sombre; (look) noir(e); Hist **the D. Ages** le Haut Moyen Âge; Fig **to be in the D. Ages** être encore au Moyen Âge

darken ['dɑːkən] **1** vt (sky, colour) assombrir; **never d. my door again!** ne remettez plus les pieds chez moi!
  2 vi (of sky, colour, thoughts) s'assombrir

darkness ['dɑːknɪs] n obscurité f; **in d.** dans l'obscurité

darkroom ['dɑːkruːm] n chambre f noire

dark-skinned ['dɑːk'skɪnd] adj à la peau mate

darling ['dɑːlɪŋ] **1** n (term of address) (to woman) chérie f; (to man) chéri m; **she's the d. of the press** c'est la coqueluche des journaux
  2 adj (dear) cher (chère); (charming) adorable

darn¹ [dɑːn] vt (mend) repriser

darn² Fam **1** adj sacré(e); **it's a d. nuisance!** c'est vachement embêtant!
  2 exclam **d. (it)!** zut!

darning ['dɑːnɪŋ] n reprisage m; **d. needle** aiguille f à repriser

dart [dɑːt] **1** n (a) (missile) flèche f; **darts** (game) fléchettes fpl (b) (movement) **to make a d. for sth** se ruer vers qch
  2 vt **to d. a glance at sb** jeter un regard à qn
  3 vi **to d. in/out** entrer/sortir comme une flèche

dartboard ['dɑːtbɔːd] n cible f (de jeu de fléchettes)

dash [dæʃ] **1** n (a) (of liquid) goutte f; (of humour, colour) touche f (b) (hyphen, in Morse code) tiret m (c) (run) course f effrénée; **to make a d. for sth** se ruer vers qch; **to make a d. for it** s'enfuir (d) (style) panache m; **to cut a d.** avoir fière allure (e) (of car) tableau m de bord
  2 vt (a) (throw) jeter; **to d. sth to the ground** jeter qch par terre (b) (destroy) (hopes) réduire à néant; Fam **d. (it)!** zut!
  3 vi **to d. in/out** entrer/sortir comme une flèche; **I dashed about** or **around all day** j'ai couru toute la journée; Fam **I must d.** il faut que je file

▸**dash off 1** vt sep (letter) écrire en vitesse
  2 vi (leave) filer

dashboard ['dæʃbɔːd] n (of car) tableau m de bord

dashing ['dæʃɪŋ] adj (person) fringant(e); (appearance) élégant(e)

DAT [diːeɪ'tiː] n (abbr digital audio tape) DAT m

data ['deɪtə] n informations fpl; Comput données fpl; **an item** or **piece of d.** une information/donnée; **d. bank** banque f de données; Comput **d. processing** traitement m de l'information; **d. protection** protection f de l'information; Law **D. Protection Act** loi f sur la protection de l'information (en Grande-Bretagne)

database ['deɪtəbeɪs] n Comput base f de données

date¹ [deɪt] n (fruit) datte f; **d. palm** palmier m dattier

date² **1** n (a) (day) date f; **d. of birth** date de naissance; **what's the d. (today)?** le combien sommes-nous (aujourd'hui)?; **to d.** à ce jour; **up to d.** (with work) à jour; (with events, news) au courant; (in *fashion)* à la mode; **out of d.** périmé(e); **d. stamp** tampon *m ou* timbre *m* à date (**b**) *(with girlfriend, boyfriend)* rendez-vous *m*; **d. rape** = viol commis par une connaissance de la victime (**c**) *Am (girlfriend, boyfriend)* ami(e) *m,f*

2 *vt* (**a**) *(letter, ticket)* dater (**b**) *Am (go out with)* sortir avec

3 *vi* (**a**) **to d. from** *or* **back to** *(of custom, practice)* remonter à; *(of building)* dater de (**b**) *(go out of fashion)* dater

---

> **Date**
> Pour donner une date en anglais, on n'emploie pas l'article à l'écrit. En anglais britannique, on écrira donc "Monday 25th December 2000" ou, de plus en plus souvent, "Monday 25 December 2000", et, en abrégé, "25.12.00". Notez cependant qu'à l'oral, on prononce "Monday the twenty-fifth of December". En anglais américain, le mois est indiqué avant le jour. On écrira ainsi "Monday December 25 2000" et, en abrégé, "12.25.00", et on prononcera "December twenty-five".

---

dateline ['deɪtlaɪn] *n* date *f* et lieu de rédaction

dating agency ['deɪtɪŋeɪdʒənsɪ] *n* agence *f* matrimoniale

dative ['deɪtɪv] *n Gram* datif *m*

daub [dɔːb] *vt* barbouiller (**with** de)

daughter ['dɔːtə(r)] *n* fille *f*

daughter-in-law ['dɔːtərɪnlɔː] *(pl* **daughters-in-law**) *n* belle-fille *f*

daunt [dɔːnt] *vt* intimider; **nothing daunted** nullement decouragé(e)

daunting ['dɔːntɪŋ] *adj* intimidant(e)

dawdle ['dɔːdəl] *vi* traînasser, lambiner

dawn [dɔːn] **1** *n also Fig* aube *f*; **at d.** à l'aube; **from d. to dusk** du lever au coucher du soleil; **the d. chorus** le chant des oiseaux à l'aube

2 *vi (of day)* se lever; *Fig (of life, civilization)* naître

▸**dawn on** *vt insep* **the truth finally dawned on her** la vérité a fini par lui apparaître; **it dawned on me that...** je me suis rendu compte que...

day [deɪ] *n* (**a**) *(period of daylight, twenty-four hours)* jour *m*; *(referring to duration)* journée *f*; **once/twice a d.** une fois/deux fois par jour; **the d. before yesterday** avant-hier; **the d. after tomorrow** après-demain; **all d.** toute la journée; **d. after d.** jour après jour; **to change from d. to d.** changer d'un jour sur l'autre; **to live from d. to d.** vivre au jour le jour; **one d., one of these days** un de ces jours; **any d. now** d'un jour à l'autre; **the other d.** l'autre jour; **every other d.** tous les deux jours, un jour sur deux; **a year ago to the d.** il y a un an jour pour jour; **from d. one** dès le début; **to take a d. off** prendre un jour de congé; **to be paid by the d.** être payé(e) à la journée; **to work d. and night** travailler jour et nuit; *Fam* **he's sixty if he's a d.** il a soixante ans bien sonnés; **d. nursery** crèche *f*; **d. pupil** externe *mf*; **d. release** formation *f* continue en alternance; **d. return** *(train ticket)* aller et retour *m* valable pour la journée; **d. school** externat *m*; **d. shift** *(in factory)* équipe *f* de jour; **d. trip** excursion *f* d'une journée

(**b**) *(era)* **in my d.** de mon temps; **in this d. and age** à notre époque; **this government/TV has had its d.** ce gouvernement/cette télé a fait son temps; **in the days of...** du temps de...; **these days** de nos jours; **in those days** en ce temps-là; **those were the days!** c'était le

bon temps!; **in days to come** à l'avenir

(**c**) *(idioms)* **it's all in a d.'s work** c'est la routine; **to make sb's d.** mettre qn de bonne humeur; *Fam* **let's call it a d.** ça suffit pour aujourd'hui; *Fam* **that'll be the d.!** c'est pas demain la veille!; **to name the d.** *(of wedding)* choisir la date de son mariage; **to carry** *or* **win the d.** l'emporter

daybreak ['deɪbreɪk] *n* lever *m* du jour; **at d.** au lever du jour

daydream ['deɪdriːm] **1** *n* rêverie *f*; *Pej* rêvasserie *f*

2 *vi* rêver (**about** à); *Pej* rêvasser

daylight ['deɪlaɪt] *n* jour *m*, lumière *f*; **it was still d.** il faisait encore jour; *Fig* **it's d. robbery!** c'est du vol pur et simple!

daytime ['deɪtaɪm] *n* jour *m*, journée *f*; **in the d.** pendant la journée; **d. TV** = émissions de télévision diffusées pendant la journée

day-to-day ['deɪtə'deɪ] *adj* courant(e), quotidien(-enne); **on a d. basis** au jour le jour

daze [deɪz] **1** *n* **in a d.** *(from news)* abasourdi(e); *(from drug, blow)* étourdi(e)

2 *vt (of news)* abasourdir; *(of drug, blow)* étourdir

dazed [deɪzd] *adj (by news)* abasourdi(e); *(by drug, blow)* étourdi(e)

dazzle ['dæzəl] *vt also Fig* éblouir

dazzling ['dæzlɪŋ] *adj also Fig* éblouissant(e)

DC [diː'siː] *n* (**a**) *Elec (abbr* **direct current**) courant *m* continu (**b**) *(abbr* **District of Columbia**) DC

deacon ['diːkən] *n Rel* diacre *m*

deaconess [diːkə'nes] *n Rel* diaconesse *f*

dead [ded] **1** *adj* (**a**) *(not alive)* mort(e); **a d. man** un mort; **a d. woman** une morte; *Fig* **to be d. to the world** dormir d'un sommeil profond; *Fam* **over my d. body!** moi vivant, jamais!; *Fam* **I wouldn't be seen d. in that dress!** je ne porterais cette robe pour rien au monde!; *Fam* **as d. as a doornail** *or* **a dodo** mort et bien mort; *Fig* **d. and buried** mort et enterré; *Fam* **if Dad finds out, you're d.** si Papa l'apprend, il va te tuer; **the D. Sea** la mer Morte

(**b**) *(numb) (limb)* engourdi(e); **to go d.** s'engourdir

(**c**) *(voice, eyes)* éteint(e); *(phone)* sans tonalité; *(battery)* mort(e); **this place is d. in winter** cet endroit est mort en hiver; **d. ball** *(in football)* ballon *m* mort; *also Fig* **d. end** cul-de-sac *m*; *Fig* **d. weight** poids *m* mort; *Fig Pej* **d. wood** personnel *m* inutile

(**d**) *(absolute)* **d. calm** calme *m* plat; **d. heat** *(in race)* arrivée *f* ex aequo; *Fam* **it was a d. loss** ça n'a servi à rien; **he's a d. loss** c'est un bon à rien; *Fam* **to be a d. ringer for sb** être le sosie de qn

2 *adv* (**a**) *(completely)* **to be d. set against sth** être totalement opposé(e) à qch; **to stop d.** s'arrêter net; *Br Fam* **you're d. right** tu as parfaitement raison; *Fam* **d. beat** *or* **tired** crevé(e); **d. slow** *(sign)* roulez au pas

(**b**) *Fam (very)* vachement

(**c**) *(exactly)* **d. on six o'clock** à six heures précises; **d. on time** exactement à l'heure

3 *n* **at d. of night** au plus profond de la nuit; **in the d. of winter** au cœur de l'hiver

4 *npl* **the d.** les morts *mpl*; **to rise from the d.** ressusciter d'entre les morts

deadbeat ['dedbiːt] *n Fam* feignant(e) *m,f*

deaden ['dedən] *vt (blow, sound)* amortir; *(pain)* calmer; **to become deadened to sth** devenir insensible à qch

deadline ['dedlaɪn] *n (day)* date *f* limite; *(time)* heure *f* limite; **to work to a d.** avoir un délai à respecter

deadlock ['dedlɒk] **1** n impasse f
 2 vt **to be deadlocked** (of talks, negotiations) être au
point mort
deadly ['dedlɪ] **1** adj (**a**) (poison, blow, enemy) mor-
tel(elle); (weapon) meurtrier(ère); (silence) de mort;
d. nightshade belladone f (**b**) Fam (boring) mor-
tel(elle)
 2 adv (very) **d. accurate** extrêmement précis(e); **d.
boring** d'un ennui mortel; **to be d. serious** être on
ne peut plus sérieux(euse)
deadpan ['dedpæn] adj (expression) figé(e); (humour)
pince-sans-rire inv
deaf [def] **1** adj sourd(e); **d. and dumb** sourd-muet,
sourde-muette; **to go d.** devenir sourd; **as d. as a
post** sourd comme un pot; **to turn a d. ear to sb/
sth** faire la sourde oreille à qn/qch; **the appeal fell
on d. ears** l'appel n'a pas été entendu
 2 npl **the d.** les sourds mpl
deaf-aid ['defeɪd] n appareil m acoustique
deafen ['defən] vt (make deaf) rendre sourd(e); (temporarily) assourdir
deafening ['defənɪŋ] adj assourdissant(e)
deafness ['defnəs] n surdité f
deal¹ [diːl] n (wood) planche f
deal² **1** n (**a**) (agreement) affaire f, marché m; **to do a
d.** conclure un marché; **it's a d.!** marché conclu!; **to
get a good/bad d.** faire une bonne/mauvaise affaire; **he's had a raw d.** on ne lui a jamais fait de cadeaux; Fam Ironic **big d.!** la belle affaire! **it's no big d.**
ce n'est pas bien grave(**b**) (amount) **a good** or **great
d.** beaucoup; **not a great d.** peu; **to have a great d.
to do** avoir beaucoup à faire; **a good** or **great d. of
my time** une grande partie de mon temps; **a good d.
quicker/easier** beaucoup plus rapide/facile (**c**) (in
cards) **whose d. is it?** c'est à qui de donner?; **your d.!**
à vous de donner!
 2 vt (pt & pp **dealt** [delt]) (**a**) (cards) donner, distribuer (**b**) **to d. sb/sth a blow** donner un coup à qn/
qch (**c**) (drugs) vendre
 3 vi (**a**) (in card game) donner, distribuer (**b**) (trade)
to d. in leather faire le commerce des cuirs
▸**deal out** vt sep (cards) distribuer; **to d. out justice**
rendre la justice
▸**deal with** vt insep (subject) traiter de; (problem) s'occuper de; **I know how to d. with him** je sais m'y
prendre avec lui
dealer ['diːlə(r)] n (**a**) (in card game) donneur(euse)
m,f (**b**) Com marchand(e) m,f; (in cars) concessionnaire m; (in drugs) dealer m, revendeur(euse) m,f
dealings ['diːlɪŋz] npl rapports mpl, relations fpl; **to
have d. with sb** traiter avec qn
dealt [delt] pt & pp of **deal**
dean [diːn] n Rel & Univ doyen m
dear [dɪə(r)] **1** n **my d.** (to man) chéri; (to woman)
chérie; **poor d.** mon pauvre/ma pauvre; **be a d.
and...** sois un amour et...; Fam **an old d.** une grand-
mère
 2 adj (**a**) (loved) cher (chère); **to hold sb/sth d.** tenir
à qn/qch; **a d. friend** un bon ami/une bonne amie; **a
place d. to the hearts of...** un endroit cher à...; Fam
to run for d. life se sauver à toutes jambes (**b**) (in letter) **D. Sir** Monsieur; **D. Madam** Madame; **D. Sir or Madam, D. Sir/Madam** Monsieur, Madame; **D. Mr
Thomas** Cher M. Thomas; **D. Andrew** Cher Andrew;
My dearest Gertrude Ma chère Gertrude (**c**) (expensive) cher (chère)

 3 adv (buy, sell) cher; Fig **it cost me d.** ça m'a coûté
cher
 4 exclam **oh d.!** mon Dieu!
dearly ['dɪəlɪ] adv (very much) **to love sb d.** aimer qn
de tout son cœur; **I would d. love to know** j'aimerais
vraiment savoir; Fig **she paid d. for her mistake** elle a
payé très cher son erreur
dearth [dɜːθ] n pénurie f (**of** de)
death [deθ] n (**a**) (end of life) mort f; **to put sb to d.**
mettre qn à mort, exécuter qn; **a fight to the d.** une
lutte à mort; **d. camp** camp m de la mort; **d. certificate** acte m de décès; **d. mask** masque m mortuaire;
d. penalty peine f de mort; **d. rate** taux m de mortalité; Am **d. row**= quartier d'une prison où les con-
damnés attendent leur exécution; **d. sentence**
condamnation f à mort; **d. squad** escadron m de la
mort; **d. throes** agonie f; **d. toll** nombre m de morts;
D. Valley la Vallée de la Mort; **d. warrant** ordre m d'exécution
 (**b**) (idioms) **to look like d. (warmed up)** avoir l'air
d'un déterré/d'une déterrée; **to be sick to d. of sth**
en avoir marre de qch; **to be scared to d.** être mort(e)
de peur; **those children will be the d. of me!** ces enfants finiront par me tuer!; **you'll catch your d. (of
cold)!** tu vas attraper la crève!; **to be at d.'s door** être
à l'article de la mort; **to sound the d. knell for sth**
sonner le glas de qch
deathbed ['deθbed] n lit m de mort
deathly ['deθlɪ] adj (pallor) mortel(elle); (silence) de
mort
deathtrap ['deθtræp] n **this house/car is a d.** cette
maison/voiture est très dangereuse
deathwatch beetle ['deθwɒtʃ'biːtəl] n vrillette f
debacle [deɪ'bɑːkəl] n débâcle f
debar [diː'bɑː(r)] (pt & pp **debarred**) vt (from club) exclure; **to d. sb from doing sth** interdire à qn de faire
qch
debase [dɪ'beɪs] vt (person) rabaisser; (reputation) ternir; (currency) déprécier; **to d. oneself** se déprécier
debasement [dɪ'beɪsmənt] n (of person) rabaisse-
ment m; (of currency) dépréciation f
debatable [dɪ'beɪtəbəl] adj discutable
debate [dɪ'beɪt] **1** n discussion f; (organized) débat m;
after much d. après bien des discussions
 2 vt (issue) débattre de, discuter de; **he debated
whether to do it** il se demandait s'il le ferait ou non
 3 vi participer à des débats
debating society [dɪ'beɪtɪŋsəsaɪətɪ] n = société qui
organise des débats
debauched [dɪ'bɔːtʃt] adj débauché(e)
debauchery [dɪ'bɔːtʃərɪ] n débauche f
debilitate [dɪ'bɪlɪteɪt] vt débiliter
debilitating [dɪ'bɪlɪteɪtɪŋ] adj débilitant(e)
debility [dɪ'bɪlɪtɪ] n débilité f
debit ['debɪt] Fin **1** n débit m; Fig **on the d. side,...** l'inconvénient, c'est que...; **d. card** = carte de paiement
à débit immédiat, ≃ carte f Bleue®
 2 vt (person, account) débiter (**with** de)
debonair [debə'neə(r)] adj élégant(e) et raffiné(e)
debrief [diː'briːf] vt faire faire un compte rendu de fin
de mission à
debriefing [diː'briːfɪŋ] n compte m rendu de fin de
mission
debris ['debriː] n (of building) décombres mpl; (of
plane, car) débris mpl

debt [det] *n* dette *f*; **to be in d.** avoir des dettes; *Fig* **I shall always be in your d.** je vous serai toujours redevable; **to owe sb a d. of gratitude** être redevable à qn; **d. collector** agent *m* de recouvrement

debtor ['detə(r)] *n* débiteur(trice) *m,f*

debug [di:'bʌg] (*pt & pp* **debugged**) *vt Comput* (*program*) déboguer

debunk [di:'bʌŋk] *vt Fam* (*theory*) discréditer; (*myth*) détruire

debut ['deɪbju:] *n* début *m*; **to make one's d.** faire ses débuts

Dec (*abbr* **December**) décembre

decade ['dekeɪd] *n* décennie *f*

decadence ['dekədəns] *n* décadence *f*

decadent ['dekədənt] *adj* décadent(e)

decaf, decaff ['di:kæf] *n Fam* (*coffee*) déca *m*

decaffeinated [di:'kæfɪneɪtɪd] *adj* décaféiné(e)

decant [dɪ'kænt] *vt* décanter

decanter [dɪ'kæntə(r)] *n* carafe *f*

decapitate [dɪ'kæpɪteɪt] *vt* décapiter

decathlon [dɪ'kæθlɒn] *n* décathlon *m*

decay [dɪ'keɪ] **1** *n* (**a**) (*of wood*) pourriture *f*; (*of teeth*) carie *f* (**b**) (*of civilization*) déclin *m*; (*of building*) délabrement *m*
   2 *vi* (**a**) (*of wood*) pourrir; (*of teeth*) se carier (**b**) (*of civilization*) péricliter; (*of building*) se délabrer

decayed [dɪ'keɪd] *adj* (*food*) pourri(e); (*tooth*) carié(e); (*corpse*) décomposé(e)

decease [dɪ'si:s] *n Formal* décès *m*

deceased [dɪ'si:st] *Formal* **1** *n* **the d.** le défunt (la défunte)
   2 *adj* décédé(e)

deceit [dɪ'si:t] *n* tromperie *f*, supercherie *f*

deceitful [dɪ'si:tfʊl] *adj* (*person*) fourbe; (*behaviour*) malhonnête

deceive [dɪ'si:v] *vt* tromper, abuser; **to be deceived by appearances** se laisser abuser par les apparences; **to d. oneself** se mentir à soi-même; **to d. sb into doing sth** faire faire qch à qn en le manipulant; **I thought my eyes were deceiving me** je n'en croyais pas mes yeux

decelerate [di:'seləreɪt] *vi* ralentir

December [dɪ'sembə(r)] *n* décembre *m*; *see also* **May**

decency ['di:sənsɪ] *n* (*respectability*) décence *f*; **to have the common d. to do sth** avoir la décence de faire qch; **he didn't even have the d. to tell us first** il n'a même pas eu la politesse de nous avertir avant

decent ['di:sənt] *adj* (**a**) (*respectable*) respectable; *Fam* **are you d.?** es-tu visible? (**b**) (*of acceptable quality, size*) convenable, correct(e) (**c**) (*kind*) gentil(ille)

decently ['di:səntlɪ] *adv* (**a**) (*respectably*) convenablement; **to dress d.** s'habiller décemment (**b**) (*to an acceptable degree*) convenablement, correctement (**c**) (*kindly*) gentiment

decentralization [di:sentrəlaɪ'zeɪʃən] *n* décentralisation *f*

decentralize [di:'sentrəlaɪz] *vt* décentraliser

deception [dɪ'sepʃən] *n* tromperie *f*, supercherie *f*

deceptive [dɪ'septɪv] *adj* trompeur(euse)

deceptively [dɪ'septɪvlɪ] *adv* **it looks d. easy** c'est moins facile que ça en a l'air; **she looks d. shy** c'est une fausse timide

decibel ['desɪbel] *n* décibel *m*

decide [dɪ'saɪd] **1** *vt* (*outcome, match, future*) décider de; **to d. to do sth** décider de faire qch; **it was**

decided to wait for her reply il fut décidé d'attendre sa réponse; **that was what decided me** c'est ce qui m'a décidé; **that decides the matter** ça règle la question
   2 *vi* décider; **to d. on sth** choisir qch; **to d. against doing sth** décider de ne pas faire qch; **they decided against going out** ils décidèrent de ne pas sortir; **to d. in favour of doing sth** décider de faire qch

decided [dɪ'saɪdɪd] *adj* (**a**) (*person*) décidé(e); (*opinion*) ferme (**b**) (*difference, preference, improvement*) net (nette)

decidedly [dɪ'saɪdɪdlɪ] *adv* (**a**) (*answer, say*) d'un ton résolu (**b**) (*very*) franchement; **he was d. unhelpful** il n'a pas été serviable du tout

decider [dɪ'saɪdə(r)] *n* (*goal*) but *m* décisif; (*match*) match *m* décisif

deciding [dɪ'saɪdɪŋ] *adj* décisif(ive)

deciduous [dɪ'sɪdjʊəs] *adj* à feuilles caduques

decimal ['desɪməl] **1** *n* décimale *f*
   2 *adj* décimal(e); **d. point** virgule *f*; **correct to five d. places** exact(e) jusqu'à la cinquième décimale

decimalization [desɪməlaɪ'zeɪʃən] *n* décimalisation *f*

decimate ['desɪmeɪt] *vt* décimer

decipher [dɪ'saɪfə(r)] *vt* déchiffrer

decision [dɪ'sɪʒən] *n* (**a**) (*of question*) décision *f* (**b**) (*resolve*) fermeté *f*, résolution *f*

decision-making [dɪ'sɪʒənmeɪkɪŋ] *n* prise *f* de décision

decisive [dɪ'saɪsɪv] *adj* (**a**) (*person, manner*) résolu(e) (**b**) (*action, event*) décisif(ive)

deck [dek] **1** *n* (**a**) (*of ship*) pont *m*; (*of bus*) niveau *m*, étage *m*; **on d.** sur le pont; **d. chair** transat *m* (**b**) **d. (of cards)** jeu *m* (de cartes)
   2 *vt* **to d. oneself out in one's Sunday best** se mettre sur son trente et un

declaim [dɪ'kleɪm] *vt & vi* déclamer

declamatory [dɪ'klæmətərɪ] *adj* déclamatoire

declaration [deklə'reɪʃən] *n* déclaration *f*; **the D. of Independence** la Déclaration d'indépendance

declare [dɪ'kleə(r)] **1** *vt* déclarer; **to d. war (on)** déclarer la guerre (à); **have you anything to d.?** (*at customs*) avez-vous quelque chose à déclarer?
   2 *vi* **to d. for/against sth** se déclarer en faveur de/contre qch; *Old-fashioned* **I do d.!** ça alors!

declassify [di:'klæsɪfaɪ] (*pt & pp* **declassified**) *vt* (*document*) ne plus considérer comme confidentiel

declension [dɪ'klenʃən] *n Gram* déclinaison *f*

decline [dɪ'klaɪn] **1** *n* déclin *m*; **to go into d.** (*of person, company, industry*) dépérir; (*of economy*) perdre de sa vigueur; (*of health*) se détériorer; **to be on the d.** (*of inflation, crime*) être en baisse
   2 *vt* (**a**) (*offer, invitation*) décliner; **to d. to do sth** refuser de faire qch (**b**) *Gram* décliner
   3 *vi* (**a**) (*refuse*) refuser (**b**) (*of health, influence*) décliner, baisser; **to d. in importance** perdre de son importance

declining [dɪ'klaɪnɪŋ] *adj* (*decreasing*) en baisse; (*deteriorating*) déclinant(e)

decode [di:'kəʊd] *vt* décoder

decompose [di:kəm'pəʊz] *vi* se décomposer

decomposition [di:kɒmpə'zɪʃən] *n* décomposition *f*

decompression [di:kəm'preʃən] *n* décompression *f*; **d. chamber** chambre *f* de décompression; **d. sickness** maladie *f* des caissons

decongestant [diːkən'dʒestənt] n Med décongestionnant m

decontaminate [diːkən'tæmɪneɪt] vt décontaminer

decor ['deɪkɔː(r)] n décor m

decorate ['dekəreɪt] vt (a) (with decorations) décorer (with de) (b) (with paint) peindre; (with wallpaper) tapisser (c) (with medal) décorer

decoration [dekə'reɪʃən] n (a) (of room, cake) décoration f (b) (medal) décoration f, médaille f

decorative ['dekərətɪv] adj décoratif(ive)

decorator ['dekəreɪtə(r)] n (painter and) d. (peintre m) décorateur m

decorous ['dekərəs] adj Formal bienséant(e)

decorum [dɪ'kɔːrəm] n convenances fpl, décorum m

decoy 1 n ['diːkɔɪ] also Fig leurre m
2 vt [dɪ'kɔɪ] leurrer

decrease 1 n ['diːkriːs] diminution f, baisse f (in de); to be on the d. être en diminution
2 vt [dɪ'kriːs] réduire, baisser
3 vi [dɪ'kriːs] diminuer, baisser

decreasing [dɪ'kriːsɪŋ] adj décroissant(e), en baisse

decree [dɪ'kriː] 1 n décret m; Law d. absolute jugement m irrévocable; d. nisi jugement m provisoire
2 vt décréter

decrepit [dɪ'krepɪt] adj (person) décrépit(e); (thing) délabré(e)

decriminalize [diː'krɪmɪnəlaɪz] vt dépénaliser

decry [dɪ'kraɪ] (pt & pp decried) vt décrier

dedicate ['dedɪkeɪt] vt (book, song) dédier (to à); to d. oneself to sth se consacrer à qch; she dedicated her life to helping the poor elle a consacré sa vie aux pauvres

dedicated ['dedɪkeɪtɪd] adj (a) (committed) dévoué(e); to be d. to sth se consacrer à qch; she is d. to helping the poor elle se consacre aux pauvres; he is d. to his family il est entièrement dévoué à sa famille (b) Comput spécialisé(e); d. word processor machine f servant uniquement au traitement de texte

dedication [dedɪ'keɪʃən] n (a) (of book, song) dédicace f (b) (devotion) dévouement m

deduce [dɪ'djuːs] vt déduire (from de)

deduct [dɪ'dʌkt] vt déduire (from de)

deductible [dɪ'dʌktəbəl] adj déductible; Fin d. for tax purposes déductible des impôts

deduction [dɪ'dʌkʃən] n (a) (subtraction) déduction f; after deductions une fois les prélèvements effectués (b) (conclusion) déduction f; by a process of d. par déduction

deed [diːd] n (a) (action) acte m, action f; to do one's good d. for the day faire sa bonne action de la journée (b) Law (document) acte m notarié; d. of covenant = document par lequel on s'engage à verser régulièrement une somme à un organisme; to change one's name by d. poll changer légalement son nom

deem [diːm] vt Formal juger, estimer

deep [diːp] 1 n Lit the d. l'océan m
2 adj (a) (water, sleep, thinker, cut) profond(e); to be 10 metres d. faire 10 mètres de profondeur; two/four d. sur deux/quatre rangs; Fig to be in d. water être dans le pétrin; d. in debt criblé(e) de dettes; d. in thought plongé(e) dans ses pensées; d. end (of swimming pool) côté m le plus profond; Fig to go off the d. end (at sb) s'emporter (contre qn); Fig to be thrown in at the d. end être mis(e) dans le bain; the D. South (of United States) le Sud profond (b) (colour) foncé(e), sombre; (sound) grave
3 adv profondément; to walk d. into the forest pénétrer profondément dans la forêt; to look d. into sb's eyes pénétrer qn du regard; to work d. into the night travailler tard dans la nuit; d. down he's very kind au fond il est très gentil; to run d. (of emotions, prejudice, mistrust) être profond(e)

deepen ['diːpən] 1 vt (well, ditch) approfondir; (sorrow, interest) augmenter; to d. sb's understanding of sth permettre à qn de mieux comprendre qch
2 vi (a) (of river, silence) devenir plus profond(e); (of conviction, belief) augmenter; (of mystery) s'épaissir (b) (of sound, voice) devenir plus grave

deep-freeze ['diːp'friːz] n congélateur m

deep-fry ['diːp'fraɪ] vt faire cuire dans la friture

deep-fryer ['diːp'fraɪə(r)] n friteuse f

deep-rooted [diːp'ruːtɪd] adj profondément enraciné(e)

deep-sea ['diːp'siː] adj d. diver plongeur m sous-marin; d. fishing pêche f hauturière

deep-seated ['diːp'siːtɪd] adj (dislike) profond(e); (belief, prejudice) profondément enraciné(e)

deer ['dɪə(r)] (pl deer) n (male) daim m; (female) biche f

deerstalker ['dɪəstɔːkə(r)] n (hat) chapeau m de chasse (à la Sherlock Holmes)

deface [dɪ'feɪs] vt (monument, statue) dégrader; (poster, wall) barbouiller

de facto [deɪ'fæktəʊ] adj & adv de facto

defamation [defə'meɪʃən] n diffamation f

defamatory [dɪ'fæmətərɪ] adj diffamatoire

defame [dɪ'feɪm] vt diffamer

default [dɪ'fɔːlt] 1 n (a) Law (failure to appear in court) défaut m; Fig by d. par défaut (b) Comput d. drive lecteur m par défaut; d. font police f par défaut
2 vi Law (a) (fail to appear in court) ne pas comparaître (b) (fail to pay) to d. on alimony payments manquer au versement de la pension alimentaire

defaulter [dɪ'fɔːltə(r)] n Law contumace mf; (debtor) débiteur(trice) m,f défaillant(e)

defeat [dɪ'fiːt] 1 n défaite f
2 vt (army, opponent) vaincre; (government) mettre en minorité; that defeats the object or purpose ça va à l'encontre du but recherché

defeatism [dɪ'fiːtɪzəm] n défaitisme m

defeatist [dɪ'fiːtɪst] n & adj défaitiste mf

defecate ['defəkeɪt] vi déféquer

defect 1 n ['diːfekt] défaut m
2 vi [dɪ'fekt] to d. to the enemy passer à l'ennemi

defection [dɪ'fekʃən] n défection f

defective [dɪ'fektɪv] adj (machine, reasoning) défectueux(euse); (hearing) déficient(e)

defector [dɪ'fektə(r)] n transfuge mf

defence, Am **defense** [dɪ'fens] n défense f; to come to sb's d. venir à l'aide de qn; she said in her d. that... elle a dit à sa décharge que...; Law d. counsel avocat m de la défense; d. mechanism (psychological) mécanisme m de défense; Law witness for the d. témoin m à décharge

defenceless, Am **defenseless** [dɪ'fensləs] adj sans défense

defend [dɪ'fend] 1 vt défendre (from or against contre)
2 vi (in sport) défendre

defendant [dɪ'fendənt] n Law défendeur(eresse) m,f

defender [dɪ'fendə(r)] n défenseur m
defending [dɪ'fendɪŋ] adj d. **champion** champion(-onne) m,f en titre
defense, defenseless Am = **defence, defenceless**
defensible [dɪ'fensəbəl] adj défendable
defensive [dɪ'fensɪv] **1** n **on the d.** sur la défensive
  2 adj défensif(ive); **to be/get d.** être/se mettre sur la défensive
defer [dɪ'fɜː(r)] (pt & pp **deferred**) **1** vt (postpone) différer, remettre
  2 vi **to d. to** s'en remettre à
deference ['defərəns] n déférence f; **out of** or **in d. to** par déférence pour
deferential [defə'renʃəl] adj (person) déférent(e); (air, tone) de déférence, respectueux(euse)
deferment [dɪ'fɜːmənt] n ajournement m, report m
defiance [dɪ'faɪəns] n défi m; **in d. of** au mépris de
defiant [dɪ'faɪənt] adj (gesture, look) de défi; (person) provocant(e)
deficiency [dɪ'fɪʃənsɪ] (pl **deficiencies**) n (**a**) (lack) (of resources) manque m; (of vitamins, minerals) carence f (**b**) (flaw) défaut m
deficient [dɪ'fɪʃənt] adj insuffisant(e); **to be d. in** manquer de
deficit ['defɪsɪt] n Fin déficit m
defile [dɪ'faɪl] vt (memory) salir; (sacred place, tomb) profaner
definable [dɪ'faɪnəbəl] adj définissable
define [dɪ'faɪn] vt définir
definite ['defɪnɪt] adj (**a**) (precise) (views, plan, date, answer) précis(e); (decision) définitif(ive) (**b**) (noticeable) (advantage, improvement) net (nette) (**c**) (certain) certain(e); (insistent) catégorique; **I can't be d.** je n'en suis pas sûr (**d**) Gram **d. article** article m défini
definitely ['defɪnɪtlɪ] adv (**a**) (certainly) sans aucun doute; **I'll d. be there** c'est sûr que j'y serai; **are you going? – d.!** est-ce que vous y allez? – absolument!; **d. not!** certainement pas! **he told me very d. that he didn't want to go** il m'a dit très clairement qu'il ne voulait pas y aller (**b**) (noticeably) (improved, superior) nettement
definition [defɪ'nɪʃən] n (**a**) (of word) définition f; **by d.** par définition (**b**) (of image) définition f; (of binoculars) netteté f
definitive [dɪ'fɪnɪtɪv] adj (book) qui fait autorité; (version) définitif(ive); **she was the d. Juliet** elle était la Juliette idéale
deflate [diː'fleɪt] **1** vt (**a**) (ball, tyre) dégonfler (**b**) Econ **to d. the economy** pratiquer une politique déflationniste (**c**) (person) démonter
  2 vi (of tyre) se dégonfler
deflated [diː'fleɪtɪd] adj (person) déprimé(e)
deflation [diː'fleɪʃən] n Econ déflation f
deflationary [diː'fleɪʃənərɪ] adj Econ déflationniste
deflect [dɪ'flekt] **1** vt (ball, bullet) (faire) dévier; (sound) renvoyer; (criticism) détourner; Fig (person) détourner (**from** de)
  2 vi (of ball, bullet) dévier
deflection [dɪ'flekʃən] n (of ball, bullet) déviation f
deforestation [diːfɒrɪs'teɪʃən] n déboisement m
deform [dɪ'fɔːm] vt déformer
deformation [diːfɔː'meɪʃən] n déformation f
deformity [dɪ'fɔːmɪtɪ] (pl **deformities**) n difformité f
defraud [dɪ'frɔːd] vt (tax office) frauder; (employer) escroquer; **to d. sb of sth** escroquer qch à qn

defray [dɪ'freɪ] vt Formal **to d. sb's expenses** défrayer qn; **to d. the cost of sth** rembourser les frais de qch
defrost [diː'frɒst] **1** vt (fridge) dégivrer; (food) décongeler
  2 vi (of fridge) se dégivrer; (of food) se décongeler
deft [deft] adj adroit(e), habile
defunct [dɪ'fʌŋkt] adj (person) défunt(e); (organization) dissous(oute); (law) abandonné(e)
defuse [diː'fjuːz] vt also Fig désamorcer
defy [dɪ'faɪ] (pt & pp **defied**) vt (authority, law) braver; (logic, analysis) défier; **to d. description** défier toute description; **to d. sb to do sth** mettre qn au défi de faire qch
degenerate 1 n & adj [dɪ'dʒenərət] dégénéré(e) m,f
  2 vi [dɪ'dʒenəreɪt] dégénérer (**into** en)
degeneration [dɪdʒenə'reɪʃən] n dégénérescence f
degradation [degrə'deɪʃən] n avilissement m; (squalor) misère f
degrade [dɪ'greɪd] vt avilir; **I won't d. myself by answering that** je ne m'abaisserai pas à répondre à cela
degrading [dɪ'greɪdɪŋ] adj avilissant(e), dégradant(e)
degree [dɪ'griː] n (**a**) (extent) degré m, point m; **to a d., to some d.** jusqu'à un certain point; **to such a d. that...** à (un) tel point que...; **by degrees** petit à petit; **a d. of risk** un certain risque; **a d. of truth** une part de vérité (**b**) (of temperature, in geometry) degré m; **it's 25 degrees** (temperature) il fait 25 degrés (**c**) (at university) diplôme m universitaire; (bachelor's) ≃ licence f; (master's) ≃ maîtrise f; (PhD) doctorat m; **to take** or **do a d.** préparer un diplôme
dehumanize [diː'hjuːmənaɪz] vt déshumaniser
dehumidifier [diːhjuː'mɪdɪfaɪə(r)] n déshumidificateur m
dehydrated [diːhaɪ'dreɪtɪd] adj déshydraté(e); **to get d.** se déshydrater
dehydration [diːhaɪ'dreɪʃən] n déshydratation f
de-icer [diː'aɪsə(r)] n dégivreur m
deify ['diːɪfaɪ] (pt & pp **deified**) vt déifier
deign [deɪn] vt **to d. to do sth** condescendre à ou daigner faire qch
deindustrialization [diːɪndʌstrɪəlaɪ'zeɪʃən] n désindustrialisation f
deity ['diːɪtɪ] (pl **deities**) n divinité f, dieu (déesse) m,f
dejected [dɪ'dʒektɪd] adj abattu(e), découragé(e)
dejection [dɪ'dʒekʃən] n abattement m, découragement m
delay [dɪ'leɪ] **1** n retard m; **without d.** sans délai; **an hour's d.** une heure de retard; **all flights are subject to d.** tous les vols risquent d'avoir du retard
  2 vt (**a**) (project, decision, act) retarder; (traffic) ralentir; **to be delayed** (of train, plane) avoir du retard; **delaying tactics** manœuvres fpl dilatoires (**b**) (put off) (decision, publication) différer; **we can't d. telling her any longer** on ne peut plus attendre davantage, nous devons le lui dire
  3 vi tarder; **don't d.!** faites vite!
delayed-action [dɪleɪd'ækʃən] adj (drug, fuse, shutter) à retardement
delectable [dɪ'lektəbəl] adj délicieux(euse)
delegate 1 n ['delɪgət] délégué(e) m,f
  2 vt ['delɪgeɪt] (power, responsibility) déléguer (**to** à); **to d. sb to do sth** déléguer qn pour faire qch
  3 vi ['delɪgeɪt] déléguer
delegation [delɪ'geɪʃən] n délégation f

delete [dɪ'liːt] vt supprimer; **d. where inapplicable** rayer les mentions inutiles

deleterious [delɪ'tɪərɪəs] adj Formal délétère

deletion [dɪ'liːʃən] n suppression f

deli ['delɪ] n Fam (shop) épicerie f fine; (café) restaurant-traiteur m

deliberate 1 adj [dɪ'lɪbərət] (**a**) (intentional) délibéré(e); **it wasn't d.** ça n'était pas voulu (**b**) (unhurried) (movement) mesuré(e); (person) méticuleux(euse)
2 vi [dɪ'lɪbəreɪt] (think) réfléchir (**on** sur); (discuss) délibérer (**on** sur)

deliberately [dɪ'lɪbərətlɪ] adv (**a**) (intentionally) délibérément; **she did it d.** elle l'a fait exprès (**b**) (un-hurriedly) de façon mesurée

deliberation [dɪlɪbə'reɪʃən] n (**a**) (thought) réflexion f; (discussion) délibération f, débat m (**b**) (unhurriedness) mesure f; **with d.** posément

delicacy ['delɪkəsɪ] (pl **delicacies**) n (**a**) (quality) délicatesse f (**b**) (food) mets m délicat

delicate ['delɪkət] adj délicat(e)

delicately ['delɪkətlɪ] adv (**a**) (finely) délicatement (**b**) (tactfully) avec délicatesse

delicatessen [delɪkə'tesən] n (shop) épicerie f fine; (café) restaurant-traiteur m

delicious [dɪ'lɪʃəs] adj délicieux(euse)

delight [dɪ'laɪt] **1** n plaisir m, joie f; **to my/her d.** à mon/son grand plaisir; **to take d. in sth** se réjouir de qch; **the car is a d. to drive** conduire cette voiture est un plaisir; **the delights of camping** les joies du camping; **the delights of Blackpool** les charmes de Blackpool
2 vt ravir, réjouir
3 vi **to d. in doing sth** prendre plaisir à faire qch; Hum **he delights in the name of Fergus Fotherington** il répond au joli nom de Fergus Fotherington

delighted [dɪ'laɪtɪd] adj ravi(e), enchanté(e) (**with** de)

delightful [dɪ'laɪtfʊl] adj (person, smile) charmant(e); (meal, evening) délicieux(euse)

delightfully [dɪ'laɪtfʊlɪ] adv (sing, write) merveilleusement

delimit [diː'lɪmɪt] vt délimiter

delineate [dɪ'lɪnɪeɪt] vt (plan, proposal) définir

delinquency [dɪ'lɪŋkwənsɪ] n délinquance f

delinquent [dɪ'lɪŋkwənt] n & adj délinquant(e) m,f

delirious [dɪ'lɪrɪəs] adj also Fig délirant(e); **to be d.** délirer

deliriously [dɪ'lɪrɪəslɪ] adv follement; **d. happy** fou (folle) de joie

delirium [dɪ'lɪrɪəm] n also Fig délire m; Med **d. tremens** delirium tremens m

deliver [dɪ'lɪvə(r)] **1** vt (**a**) (letter, parcel) remettre, distribuer (**to** à); (water, electricity, gas) distribuer; (goods) livrer; **to have sth delivered** faire livrer qch; Fig **to d. the goods** tenir ses engagements (**b**) (blow) donner; Sport (pass) faire; (speech, verdict) prononcer; (ultimatum) poser; **to d. a service** proposer un service (**c**) (baby) mettre au monde
2 vi livrer; Fig (keep one's promise) tenir ses engagements; Com **we d.** nous livrons à domicile

deliverance [dɪ'lɪvərəns] n Formal délivrance f (**from** de)

delivery [dɪ'lɪvərɪ] (pl **deliveries**) n (**a**) (of letter, parcel) distribution f, remise f; (of goods) livraison f; **to take d. of sth** prendre livraison de qch; **d. date** date f de livraison; **d. man** livreur m; **d. van** camion m de

livraison (**b**) (way of speaking) diction f (**c**) (of baby) accouchement m

delta ['deltə] n (of river, Greek letter) delta m inv; **d. wing** (of plane) aile f delta

delude [dɪ'luːd] vt tromper; **to d. oneself** se faire des illusions

deluge ['deljuːdʒ] **1** n also Fig déluge m
2 vt inonder (**with** de)

delusion [dɪ'luːʒən] n illusion f; **to be under a d.** se faire des illusions; **delusions of grandeur** mégalomanie f

de luxe [dɪ'lʌks] adj de luxe, haut de gamme inv

delve [delv] vi also Fig **to d. into** fouiller dans

demagogue ['deməgɒg] n démagogue m

demand [dɪ'mɑːnd] **1** n (**a**) (request) demande f, exigence f; **to make demands on sb** exiger beaucoup de qn (**b**) (for goods) demande f (**for** de); **to be in d.** être demandé(e) ou recherché(e)
2 vt exiger, réclamer

demanding [dɪ'mɑːndɪŋ] adj (person) exigeant(e); (job) astreignant(e)

demarcation [diːmɑː'keɪʃən] n démarcation f; Ind **d. dispute** conflit m d'attributions; **d. line** ligne f de démarcation

demean [dɪ'miːn] vt humilier; **to d. oneself** s'abaisser

demeanour, Am **demeanor** [dɪ'miːnə(r)] n comportement m

demented [dɪ'mentɪd] adj fou (folle)

dementia [dɪ'menʃɪə] n démence f

demerara sugar [demə'reərə'ʃʊgə(r)] n cassonade f

demigod ['demɪgɒd] n demi-dieu m

demilitarize [diː'mɪlɪtəraɪz] vt démilitariser

demise [dɪ'maɪz] n also Fig disparition f

demister [diː'mɪstə(r)] n BrAut dispositif m antibuée

demo ['deməʊ] (pl **demos**) n Fam (**a**) (protest) manif f (**b**) **d. (tape)** maquette f

demob [diː'mɒb] (pt & pp **demobbed**) vt Br Fam démobiliser

demobilize [diː'məʊbɪlaɪz] vt démobiliser

democracy [dɪ'mɒkrəsɪ] (pl **democracies**) n démocratie f

Democrat ['deməkræt] n (US politician) démocrate mf

democrat ['deməkræt] n démocrate mf

democratic [demə'krætɪk] adj démocratique

democratically [demə'krætɪklɪ] adv démocratiquement

demographic [demə'græfɪk] adj démographique

demolish [dɪ'mɒlɪʃ] vt (building, theory) démolir; Fam (eat) engloutir; (in game) battre

demolition [demə'lɪʃən] n démolition f

demon ['diːmən] n démon m; Fam **he's a d. tennis player** c'est un as du tennis

demonic [dɪ'mɒnɪk] adj démoniaque

demonstrable [dɪ'mɒnstrəbəl] adj démontrable

demonstrate ['demənstreɪt] **1** vt (fact, theory) démontrer; **to d. how sth works** montrer comment qch fonctionne
2 vi (protest) manifester (**for/against** pour/contre)

demonstration [demən'streɪʃən] n (**a**) (of fact, theory) démonstration f (**b**) (political) manifestation f

demonstrative [dɪ'mɒnstrətɪv] adj also Gram démonstratif(ive)

demonstrator ['demənstreɪtə(r)] n (**a**) (protester) manifestant(e) m,f (**b**) (of machine) démonstrateur(trice) m,f

demoralize [dɪ'mɒrəlaɪz] *vt* démoraliser
demoralizing [dɪ'mɒrəlaɪzɪŋ] *adj* démoralisant(e)
demote [dɪ'məʊt] *vt* rétrograder
demotion [dɪ'məʊʃən] *n* rétrogradation *f*
demur [dɪ'mɜ:(r)] *(pt & pp* **demurred**) *vi* soulever une objection
demure [dɪ'mjʊə(r)] *adj* réservé(e)
demystify [di:'mɪstɪfaɪ] *(pt & pp* **demystified**) *vt* démystifier
den [den] *n* (**a**) *(of lion, fox, bear)* antre *m*, tanière *f*; *Fig* **a d. of iniquity** un lieu de perdition; **a d. of thieves** un repaire de voleurs (**b**) *(room)* ≃ bureau *m*
denationalize [di:'næʃənəlaɪz] *vt* dénationaliser
denature [di:'neɪtʃə(r)] *vt* dénaturer
denial [dɪ'naɪəl] *n* (**a**) *(of request)* refus *m*; *(of right)* atteinte *f*; **d. of justice** déni *m* de justice (**b**) *(of accusation, rumour, guilt)* démenti *m* (**c**) *(psychological)* dénégation *f*; **to be in d.** refuser de se rendre à l'évidence
denigrate ['denɪgreɪt] *vt* dénigrer
denim ['denɪm] *n* (toile *f* de) jean *m*, denim *m*; **denims** *(jeans)* un jean; **d. skirt/shirt** jupe *f*/chemise *f* en jean
Denmark ['denmɑ:k] *n* le Danemark
denomination [dɪnɒmɪ'neɪʃən] *n* (**a**) *(religious)* confession *f* (**b**) *Fin* valeur *f*
denominator [dɪ'nɒmɪneɪtə(r)] *n Math* dénominateur *m*
denote [dɪ'nəʊt] *vt* indiquer
dénouement [deɪ'nu:mɒŋ] *n* dénouement *m*
denounce [dɪ'naʊns] *vt* dénoncer
dense [dens] *adj* (**a**) *(smoke, fog, jungle, crowd)* dense (**b**) *Fam (stupid)* bouché(e)
densely ['densli] *adv* **d. populated** fortement peuplé(e); **d. wooded** très boisé(e)
density ['densɪti] *n* densité *f*
dent [dent] **1** *n* bosse *f*; *Fig* **the wedding put a d. in his savings** le mariage a fait un trou dans ses économies **2** *vt* cabosser; *Fig (confidence)* entamer
dental ['dentəl] *adj* dentaire; **d. appointment** rendez-vous *m* chez le dentiste; **d. floss** fil *m* dentaire; **d. hygiene** hygiène *f* dentaire; **d. nurse** assistant(e) *m,f* dentaire; **d. surgeon** chirurgien-dentiste *m*
dentist ['dentɪst] *n* dentiste *mf*; **to go to the d.'s** aller chez le dentiste
dentistry ['dentɪstrɪ] *n* dentisterie *f*
dentures ['dentʃəz] *npl* **(set of) d.** dentier *m*
denude [dɪ'nju:d] *vt* dénuder; **to be denuded of sth** être dépourvu(e) de qch
denunciation [dɪnʌnsɪ'eɪʃən] *n* dénonciation *f*
deny [dɪ'naɪ] *(pt & pp* **denied**) *vt* (**a**) *(request)* refuser; **to d. sb his rights** priver qn de ses droits; **to d. oneself sth** se priver de qch (**b**) *(fact)* nier; *(rumour)* démentir; **to d. responsibility for sth** nier être responsable de qch; **to d. doing sth** nier avoir fait qch; **there's no denying that...** il est indéniable que...; **to d. all knowledge of sth** nier avoir connaissance de qch
deodorant [di:'əʊdərənt] *n* déodorant *m*; *(for room)* désodorisant *m*
depart [dɪ'pɑ:t] *vi (leave)* partir (**from** de); **to d. from** *(tradition, subject, truth)* s'écarter de
department [dɪ'pɑ:tmənt] *n (in company)* service *m*; *(in shop)* rayon *m*; *Univ* département *m*; *(of government)* ministère *m*; *Fig* **that's my d.** c'est mon rayon; **d. store** grand magasin *m*

departmental [di:pɑ:t'mentəl] *adj (manager)* de service; *Univ* **d. head** chef *m* de département
departure [dɪ'pɑ:tʃə(r)] *n (from place)* départ *m*; *(from tradition)* écart *m*; *(from plan)* modification *f*; *Fig* **a new d.** un nouveau départ; **d. lounge** *(in airport)* salle *f* d'embarquement; **d. time** heure *f* de départ
depend [dɪ'pend] *vi* **to d. on** dépendre de; **that depends, it all depends** ça dépend; **to d. on sb** *(rely on)* compter sur qn; *(financially)* être à la charge de qn; **you can d. on it** tu peux compter là-dessus; **it depends on how much money I have** cela dépend de l'argent que j'ai; *Ironic* **you can d. on him to be late** tu peux compter sur lui pour être en retard
dependable [dɪ'pendəbəl] *adj (person, machine)* fiable; *(information)* sûr(e)
dependant [dɪ'pendənt] *n* personne *f* à charge
dependence [dɪ'pendəns] *n (reliance)* dépendance *f* (**on** à)
dependency [dɪ'pendənsɪ] *(pl* **dependencies**) *n* dépendance *f*; **d. culture** = situation d'une société dont les membres ont une mentalité d'assistés
dependent [dɪ'pendənt] *adj (child)* à charge; **to be d. on** dépendre de; **to be d. on sb** *(financially)* être à la charge de qn
depict [dɪ'pɪkt] *vt (of painting)* représenter; *(of film, book)* décrire
depiction [dɪ'pɪkʃən] *n (in painting)* représentation *f*; *(in film, book)* description *f*
depilatory [dɪ'pɪlətərɪ] *adj* dépilatoire
deplete [dɪ'pli:t] *vt* réduire, diminuer
depleted uranium [dɪ'pli:tɪdjʊ'reɪnjəm] *n* uranium *m* appauvri
depletion [dɪ'pli:ʃən] *n* réduction *f*, diminution *f*
deplorable [dɪ'plɔ:rəbəl] *adj* déplorable
deplore [dɪ'plɔ:(r)] *vt* déplorer
deploy [dɪ'plɔɪ] *vt* déployer
deployment [dɪ'plɔɪmənt] *n* déploiement *m*
depopulate [di:'pɒpjʊleɪt] *vt* dépeupler
depopulation [di:pɒpjʊ'leɪʃən] *n* dépeuplement *m*
deport [dɪ'pɔ:t] *vt (criminal)* déporter; *(immigrant)* expulser
deportation [di:pɔ:'teɪʃən] *n (of criminal)* déportation *f*; *(of immigrant)* expulsion *f*
deportment [dɪ'pɔ:tmənt] *n* (**a**) *(posture)* maintien *m* (**b**) *(behaviour)* comportement *m*
depose [dɪ'pəʊz] *vt* déposer
deposit [dɪ'pɒzɪt] **1** *n* (**a**) *(in bank)* dépôt *m*; *Br* **d. account** compte *m* de dépôt (**b**) *(returnable)* caution *f*; *(first payment)* acompte *m*, arrhes *fpl*; **to put down a d. on sth** verser un acompte pour qch (**c**) *(of minerals)* gisement *m*; *(of wine)* dépôt *m* (**d**) *Br Pol* **to lose one's d.** perdre son cautionnement **2** *vt* déposer
deposition [di:pə'zɪʃən] *n Law* déposition *f*
depositor [dɪ'pɒzɪtə(r)] *n Fin* déposant(e) *m,f*
depot ['depəʊ] *n Mil & Com* dépôt *m*; *Am (bus station)* gare *f* routière
depravation [deprə'veɪʃən] *n* dépravation *f*
depraved [dɪ'preɪvd] *adj* dépravé(e)
depravity [dɪ'prævɪtɪ] *n* dépravation *f*
deprecate ['deprɪkeɪt] *vt* dévaloriser
deprecating ['deprɪkeɪtɪŋ], **deprecatory** ['deprɪkeɪtərɪ] *adj* désapprobateur(trice); **to be d. about sb/sth** dévaloriser qn/qch
depreciate [dɪ'pri:ʃɪeɪt] *vi (in value)* se déprécier

depreciation [dɪpriːʃɪˈeɪʃən] n (in value) dépréciation f

depress [dɪˈpres] vt (**a**) (person) déprimer; Fig (prices) faire baisser; (economy, market) affaiblir (**b**) (press) (button, lever) appuyer sur

depressed [dɪˈprest] adj déprimé(e); Fig (economy, market, region) touché(e) par la crise; **to make sb d.** déprimer qn

depressing [dɪˈpresɪŋ] adj déprimant(e)

depression [dɪˈpreʃən] n (**a**) (of person, economy) dépression f (**b**) Met dépression f (**c**) (hollow) creux m; (in landscape) dépression f

deprivation [deprɪˈveɪʃən] n (hardship) privations fpl; emotional d. carence f affective

deprive [dɪˈpraɪv] vt **to d. sb of sth** priver qn de qch

deprived [dɪˈpraɪvd] adj défavorisé(e); (childhood) malheureux(euse)

dept (abbr department) dép.

depth [depθ] n profondeur f; **in d.** (investigate, discuss) en profondeur; **to be out of one's d.** (of swimmer) ne plus avoir pied; Fig ne pas être à la hauteur; **in the depths of winter** au cœur de l'hiver; **in the depths of despair** au plus profond du désespoir; Naut **d. charge** grenade f sous-marine; Phot **d. of field** profondeur de champ

deputation [depjʊˈteɪʃən] n délégation f

depute [dɪˈpjuːt] vt **to d. sb to do sth** charger qn de faire qch

deputize [ˈdepjʊtaɪz] vi **to d. for sb** remplacer qn

deputy [ˈdepjʊtɪ] (pl **deputies**) n (second-in-command) adjoint(e) m,f; (replacement) remplaçant(e) m,f; (political representative) député m; Am (policeman) shérif m adjoint; **d. head** (of school) directeur(-trice) m,f adjoint(e); **d. manager** directeur(trice) m,f adjoint(e); **d. prime minister** vice-Premier ministre m

derail [dɪˈreɪl] **1** vt Fig (project, plan) faire avorter; **to be derailed** (of train) dérailler
2 vi (of train) dérailler

derailment [dɪˈreɪlmənt] n déraillement m

deranged [dɪˈreɪndʒd] adj dérangé(e)

derby [ˈdɑːbɪ] (pl **derbies**) n (**a**) (football match) derby m (**b**) Am (hat) chapeau m melon

deregulate [diːˈregjʊleɪt] vt (economy, market) déréguler; (prices) libérer; (industry) déréglementer

deregulation [diːregjʊˈleɪʃən] n (of economy, market) dérégulation f; (of industry) déréglementation f

derelict [ˈderəlɪkt] adj abandonné(e); (ruined) en ruines

dereliction [derɪˈlɪkʃən] n abandon m; **d. of duty** manquement m au devoir

deride [dɪˈraɪd] vt ridiculiser

derision [dɪˈrɪʒən] n dérision f

derisive [dɪˈraɪsɪv] adj moqueur(euse)

derisory [dɪˈraɪsərɪ] adj dérisoire

derivation [derɪˈveɪʃən] n (source) origine f

derivative [dɪˈrɪvətɪv] **1** n Chem & Gram dérivé m
2 adj banal(e), sans originalité

derive [dɪˈraɪv] **1** vt dériver, provenir (**from** de); **to d. pleasure from sth** prendre plaisir à qch; **to be derived from** provenir de
2 vi **to d. from** provenir de

dermatitis [dɜːməˈtaɪtɪs] n Med dermite f, dermatite f

dermatology [dɜːməˈtɒlədʒɪ] n Med dermatologie f

derogatory [dɪˈrɒgətərɪ] adj désobligeant(e)

derrick [ˈderɪk] n derrick m

derv [dɜːv] n Br (fuel) gas-oil m, gazole m

desalination [diːsælɪˈneɪʃən] n dessalement m

descend [dɪˈsend] **1** vt (hill, stairs) descendre
2 vi (**a**) (go down) descendre; (of darkness, dusk) tomber; **in descending order** en ordre décroissant; **every summer tourists d. on the town** chaque été les touristes débarquent en ville; Fig **to d. to sb's level** s'abaisser au niveau de qn (**b**) **to d.** or **be descended from sb** (be related to) descendre de qn

descent [dɪˈsent] n (**a**) (of plane, from mountain) descente f (**b**) (ancestry) **to be of Norman d.** être d'origine normande

describe [dɪsˈkraɪb] vt décrire

description [dɪsˈkrɪpʃən] n description f; (issued by police) signalement m; **to answer** or **fit the d.** répondre au signalement; **beyond d.** indescriptible; **birds of all descriptions** des oiseaux de toutes sortes; **he's a journalist of some d.** il travaille dans le journalisme

descriptive [dɪsˈkrɪptɪv] adj descriptif(ive)

desecrate [ˈdesɪkreɪt] vt profaner

desecration [desɪˈkreɪʃən] n profanation f

desegregation [diːsegrɪˈgeɪʃən] n déségrégation f

desert[1] [ˈdezət] n désert m; **d. island** île f déserte

desert[2] [dɪˈzɜːt] **1** vt abandonner; **to d. one's post** (of soldier) déserter son poste
2 vi (from army) déserter

deserted [dɪˈzɜːtɪd] adj désert(e)

deserter [dɪˈzɜːtə(r)] n déserteur m

desertion [dɪˈzɜːʃən] n Law abandon m du domicile conjugal; Mil désertion f

deserts [dɪˈzɜːts] npl **he got his just d.** il a eu ce qu'il méritait

deserve [dɪˈzɜːv] vt mériter; **to d. to do sth** mériter de faire qch; **she deserves to be punished** elle mérite une punition

deserving [dɪˈzɜːvɪŋ] adj (person) méritant(e); (action, cause) méritoire; **to be d. of praise** être digne d'éloge

design [dɪˈzaɪn] **1** n (**a**) (pattern) (on fabric, wallpaper) motif m (**b**) (style) (of car, furniture) modèle m; (of clothes) coupe f (**c**) (drawing) (of building, machine) plan m (**d**) (subject) design m, stylisme m (**e**) (planning) (of product, machine) conception f (**f**) (intention) dessein m; **by d.** à dessein; **to have designs on** avoir des vues sur
2 vt (building, vehicle) concevoir; (clothes, furniture) créer; **to be designed for sth/to do sth** (intended) être destiné(e) à qch/à faire qch

designate [ˈdezɪgneɪt] **1** vt désigner; **to d. sb to do sth** désigner qn pour faire qch; **this area has been designated a national park** cette zone a été classée parc national
2 adj désigné(e)

designation [dezɪgˈneɪʃən] n (**a**) (appointment) nomination f; (of funds) affectation f (**b**) (title) désignation f

designer [dɪˈzaɪnə(r)] n concepteur(trice) m,f; (of building) architecte mf; (of clothes) styliste mf (de mode); (of theatre set) décorateur(trice) m,f; **d. clothes** vêtements mpl de marque; **d. drugs** drogues fpl de synthèse; **d. label** griffe f de grande marque

desirable [dɪˈzaɪərəbəl] adj souhaitable; (job, location) attrayant(e); (sexually) désirable; **a d. residence** une belle résidence

desire [dɪˈzaɪə(r)] **1** n désir m, envie f; **I have no d. to go** je n'ai aucune envie d'y aller

2 *vt* désirer; **to d. to do sth** désirer faire qch, avoir envie de faire qch; **it leaves a lot to be desired** ça laisse beaucoup à désirer

desirous [dɪˈzaɪərəs] *adj Formal* désireux(euse) (**of** de)

desist [dɪˈzɪst] *vi Formal* cesser; **to d. from doing sth** cesser de faire qch

desk [desk] *n (in school)* table *f*; *(with lid)* pupitre *m*; *(in office, home)* bureau *m*; *(hotel reception)* réception *f*; **d. diary** agenda *m*; **a d. job** un travail de bureau; **d. lamp** lampe *f* de bureau

desktop [ˈdesktɒp] *n Comput* **d. computer** ordinateur *m* de bureau; **d. publishing** publication *f* assistée par ordinateur

desolate [ˈdesələt] *adj (place)* désolé(e); *(future, prospect)* sombre; *(person)* abattu(e), affligé(e)

desolation [desəˈleɪʃən] *n* désolation *f*; *(of person)* affliction *f*

despair [dɪsˈpeə(r)] **1** *n* désespoir *m*; **to be in d.** être désespéré(e); **to drive sb to d.** désespérer qn
2 *vi* désespérer; **I d. of you** tu me désespères

despairing [dɪˈspeərɪŋ] *adj* désespéré(e)

despatch = dispatch

desperate [ˈdespərət] *adj* désespéré(e); **to be in d. need of sth** avoir désespérément besoin de qch; **to be d. to do sth** vouloir à tout prix faire qch; **to be d. for sth** avoir désespérément besoin de qch

desperately [ˈdespərətlɪ] *adv* désespérément; *(ill)* très gravement; **to be d. in love** être éperdument amoureux(euse); **to be d. sorry about sth** être affreusement désolé(e) de qch

desperation [despəˈreɪʃən] *n* désespoir *m*; **in d.** par désespoir

despicable [dɪˈspɪkəbəl] *adj* méprisable

despise [dɪˈspaɪz] *vt* mépriser

despite [dɪsˈpaɪt] *prep* malgré

despondency [dɪsˈpɒndənsɪ] *n* abattement *m*

despondent [dɪˈspɒndənt] *adj* abattu(e)

despot [ˈdespɒt] *n* despote *m*

despotic [dɪsˈpɒtɪk] *adj* despotique

despotism [ˈdespətɪzəm] *n* despotisme *m*

dessert [dɪˈzɜːt] *n* dessert *m*; **d. wine** vin *m* doux

dessertspoon [dɪˈzɜːtspuːn] *n* cuillère *f* à dessert

destabilize [diːˈsteɪbəlaɪz] *vt* déstabiliser

destination [destɪˈneɪʃən] *n* destination *f*; **to reach one's d.** arriver à destination; *Comput* **d. disk/drive** disquette *f*/lecteur *m* cible

destine [ˈdestɪn] *vt* destiner

destined [ˈdestɪnd] *adj* (**a**) *(meant)* destiné(e); **to be d. to do sth** être destiné à faire qch; **he was d. to become famous** *(by fate)* il était destiné à devenir célèbre; *(reporting a fact)* il devait plus tard devenir célèbre (**b**) *(of plane, ship)* **d. for** à destination de

destiny [ˈdestɪnɪ] *(pl* **destinies**) *n* destin *m*, destinée *f*

destitute [ˈdestɪtjuːt] *adj* sans ressources; **to be utterly d.** être dans la misère

destroy [dɪsˈtrɔɪ] *vt* (**a**) *(damage, ruin)* détruire (**b**) *(animal)* abattre; *(vermin)* éliminer

destroyer [dɪsˈtrɔɪə(r)] *n (ship)* contre-torpilleur *m*

destruction [dɪsˈtrʌkʃən] *n* destruction *f*; *(damage)* ravages *mpl*

destructive [dɪsˈtrʌktɪv] *adj* destructeur(trice)

desultory [ˈdesəltərɪ] *adj (conversation)* décousu(e); *(attempt)* peu convaincant(e)

detach [dɪˈtætʃ] *vt* détacher (**from** de); **to d. oneself (from)** s'éloigner (de)

detachable [dɪˈtætʃəbəl] *adj* amovible

detached [dɪˈtætʃt] *adj* (**a**) *(separate)* détaché(e), séparé(e); **to become** *or* **get d. from sth** se détacher de qch; **d. house** maison *f* individuelle, pavillon *m*; *Med* **d. retina** décollement *m* de la rétine (**b**) *(disinterested) (tone)* détaché(e); **he's rather d.** il sait garder ses distances

detachment [dɪˈtætʃmənt] *n* (**a**) *(military unit)* détachement *m* (**b**) *(objectivity)* détachement *m*

detail [ˈdiːteɪl] **1** *n* (**a**) *(item of information)* détail *m*; **to pay attention to d.** être minutieux(euse); **to go into detail(s)** entrer dans les détails; **in d.** en détail; **details** *(information)* renseignements *mpl*; *(address and phone number)* coordonnées *fpl* (**b**) *Mil* détachement *m*
2 *vt* (**a**) *(describe)* détailler (**b**) *Mil* **to d. sb to do sth** donner l'ordre à qn de faire qch

detailed [ˈdiːteɪld] *adj (account, description)* détaillé(e); *(work)* minutieux(euse)

detain [dɪˈteɪn] *vt (in prison)* placer en détention; *(in hospital)* garder; *(delay)* retenir; **such details need not d. us** ne nous laissons pas arrêter par de tels détails

detainee [diːteɪˈniː] *n* détenu(e) *m,f*

detect [dɪˈtekt] *vt (change, emotion, trace of substance)* déceler; *(error, pattern)* découvrir; *Med (disease)* dépister; *Mil (mines etc)* détecter

detection [dɪˈtekʃən] *n (of error)* découverte *f*; *Med (of disease)* dépistage *m*; *Mil (of mines etc)* détection *f*; **to escape d.** *(of mistake, change)* passer inaperçu(e); *(of burglar)* ne pas être découvert(e); **crime d.** le travail de détective

detective [dɪˈtektɪv] *n (private)* détective *m*; *(police officer)* ≃ inspecteur(trice) *m,f* de police; **d. story** roman *m* policier; **d. work** enquêtes *fpl*

detector [dɪˈtektə(r)] *n* détecteur *m*

détente [deɪˈtɒnt] *n* détente *f*

detention [dɪˈtenʃən] *n* (**a**) *Law* détention *f*; *Law* **d. centre** = centre de détention pour mineurs (**b**) *Sch* retenue *f*

deter [dɪˈtɜː(r)] *(pt & pp* **deterred**) *vt* dissuader; **to d. sb from doing sth** dissuader qn de faire qch

detergent [dɪˈtɜːdʒənt] *n (for cleaning)* produit *m* de nettoyage

deteriorate [dɪˈtɪərɪəreɪt] *vi* se détériorer

deterioration [dɪtɪərɪəˈreɪʃən] *n* détérioration *f*

determination [dɪtɜːmɪˈneɪʃən] *n* détermination *f*

determine [dɪˈtɜːmɪn] *vt* (**a**) *(decide)* **to d. to do sth** décider de faire qch; **to d. that...** décider que... (**b**) *(cause, date)* déterminer

determined [dɪˈtɜːmɪnd] *adj* déterminé(e), résolu(e); **to be d. to do sth** être déterminé *ou* résolu à faire qch; **I'm d. that we'll succeed** je suis déterminé à ce que nous réussissions

deterrent [dɪˈterənt] **1** *n* moyen *m* de dissuasion; **to act as a d.** avoir un effet dissuasif
2 *adj (effect)* dissuasif(ive)

detest [dɪˈtest] *vt* détester

dethrone [dɪˈθrəʊn] *vt* détrôner

detonate [ˈdetəneɪt] **1** *vt* faire exploser
2 *vi* exploser

detonation [detəˈneɪʃən] *n* explosion *f*, détonation *f*

detonator [ˈdetəneɪtə(r)] *n* détonateur *m*

detour ['di:tʊə(r)] n détour m

detoxification [di:tɒksıfı'keıʃən], Fam **detox** ['di:tɒks] n désintoxication f; **d. centre/programme** centre m/cure f de désintoxication

▸**detract from** [dı'trækt] vt insep diminuer; **I don't want to d. from her achievement, but...** je ne veux pas minimiser ce qu'elle a accompli, mais...

detractor [dı'træktə(r)] n détracteur(trice) m,f

detriment ['detrımənt] n **to the d. of** au détriment de; **without d. to** sans porter préjudice à

detrimental [detrı'mentəl] adj préjudiciable (**to** à); **to have a d. effect on** nuire à

detritus [dı'traıtəs] n détritus mpl

Dettol ® ['detɒl] n = solution antiseptique

deuce [dju:s] n (in tennis) égalité f

Deutschmark ['dɒıtʃma:k] n (deutsche) mark m

devaluation [di:væljʊ'eıʃən] n (**a**) (of currency) dévaluation f (**b**) (of person, achievement) dévalorisation f

devalue [di:'vælju:] vt (**a**) (currency) dévaluer (**b**) (person, achievement) dévaloriser

devastate ['devəsteıt] vt (crops, village) dévaster; (person) anéantir; **I was devastated by the news** la nouvelle m'a anéanti

devastating ['devəsteıtıŋ] adj (storm, bombardment) dévastateur(trice); (news, findings, argument) accablant(e); (criticism) cinglant(e); (charm, beauty) irrésistible

devastation [devəs'teıʃən] n dévastation f

develop [dı'veləp] **1** vt (**a**) (skills, theory, argument) développer; (product) mettre au point (**b**) (region) développer; (site) aménager; **developed countries** pays mpl développés (**c**) (acquire) (infection, illness) attraper; (habit) prendre; **to d. a liking** or **taste for sth** se mettre à aimer qch (**d**) (film) développer
2 vi (**a**) (grow) se développer; **to d. into** devenir (**b**) (become apparent) apparaître

developer [dı'veləpə(r)] n (**a**) (of land) promoteur m (**b**) Phot révélateur m

developing [dı'veləpıŋ] adj (region, country) en (voie de) développement; (crisis) en évolution

development [dı'veləpmənt] n (**a**) (growth) développement m; (of idea) évolution f; **d. aid** aide f au développement; Br **d. area** = zone à fort taux de chômage où l'État incite les industries à venir s'installer (**b**) (progress, change) développement m; **there have been some interesting developments** il y a eu quelques faits nouveaux intéressants; **the latest developments in medical research** les dernières découvertes médicales

deviant ['di:vıənt] adj déviant(e)

deviate ['di:vıeıt] vi dévier (**from** de); Fig s'écarter (**from** de)

deviation [di:vı'eıʃən] n déviation f (**from** par rapport à); Fig écart m (**from** par rapport à)

device [dı'vaıs] n (**a**) (mechanism) dispositif m; (gadget) appareil m; (**explosive) d.** engin m explosif (**b**) (method, scheme) stratagème m; **to leave sb to their own devices** laisser qn se débrouiller

devil ['devəl] n (**a**) (evil spirit) diable m; **the D.** le Diable (**b**) Fam (person) **poor d.!** pauvre diable!; **you little d.!** (to child) petit diable!; **you lucky d.!** veinard! (**c**) Fam (for emphasis) **what the d. are you doing?** mais qu'est-ce que tu fabriques?; **how the d....?** comment diable...?; **we had a d. of a job moving it** nous avons eu un mal de chien à le déplacer (**d**) (idioms) **he's a bit of a d.** c'est un sacré numéro;

go on, be a d.! allez, laisse-toi tenter!; **to work like the d.** travailler comme un(e) fou (folle); **to be (caught) between the d. and the deep blue sea** avoir à choisir entre la peste et le choléra; **talk of the d.!** quand on parle du loup!; Prov **better the d. you know (than the d. you don't)** on sait ce qu'on perd, on ne sait pas ce qu'on trouve; **to play d.'s advocate** se faire l'avocat du diable

devilish ['devəlıʃ] adj diabolique

devil-may-care ['devəlmeı'keə(r)] adj insouciant(e)

devious ['di:vıəs] adj (person, mind) retors(e); (scheme, route) tortueux(euse); (means) détourné(e)

devise [dı'vaız] vt imaginer, élaborer

devoid [dı'vɔıd] adj dénué(e), dépourvu(e) (**of** de)

devolution [di:və'lu:ʃən] n Pol décentralisation f

Devolution
Ce terme désigne la décentralisation parlementaire au sein du Royaume Uni, processus engagé depuis l'élection du gouvernement travailliste de Tony Blair en 1997. Après cette victoire, le nouveau gouvernement organisa des référendums en Écosse et au Pays de Galles, à la suite de quoi un parlement écossais fut instauré à Édimbourg et une assemblée nationale galloise à Cardiff, répondant ainsi aux attentes des nombreux Écossais et Gallois qui revendiquaient depuis longtemps un plus grand degré d'autonomie. (Voir aussi encadrés sous "**Scottish Parliament**" et "**Welsh Assembly**".)

devolve [dı'vɒlv] **1** vt déléguer
2 vi **to d. on** incomber à; **power devolves on the regional assembly** le pouvoir appartient à l'assemblée régionale

devote [dı'vəʊt] vt consacrer (**to** à); **to d. oneself to** se consacrer à

devoted [dı'vəʊtıd] adj (parent) dévoué(e); (admirer) fervent(e); **years of d. service** des années de bons et loyaux services; **they are d. to each other** ils sont très attachés l'un à l'autre

devotee [devəʊ'ti:] n (of writer, artist) admirateur(trice) m,f; (of idea) partisan m; (of sport, music) passionné(e) m,f

devotion [dı'vəʊʃən] n (to cause, friend, family) dévouement m; (to god, saint) dévotion f; **devotions** (prayers) prières fpl

devour [dı'vaʊə(r)] vt also Fig dévorer

devout [dı'vaʊt] adj (person) dévot(e); (wish) fervent(e)

dew [dju:] n rosée f

dewy-eyed [dju:ı'aıd] adj (loving) ému(e); (naive) ingénu(e)

dexterity [deks'terıtı] n dextérité f

dext(e)rous ['dekstrəs] adj adroit(e), habile

diabetes [daıə'bi:ti:z] n diabète m

diabetic [daıə'betık] n & adj diabétique mf; **d. chocolate** chocolat m pour diabétiques

diabolical [daıə'bɒlıkəl] adj (**a**) (evil) diabolique (**b**) Fam (very bad) épouvantable

diadem ['daıədem] n diadème m

diagnose ['daıəgnəʊz] vt also Fig diagnostiquer

diagnosis [daıəg'nəʊsıs] (pl **diagnoses** [daıəg'nəʊsi:z]) n also Fig diagnostic m

diagnostic [daıəg'nɒstık] adj diagnostique

diagonal [daı'ægənəl] **1** n diagonale f
2 adj diagonal(e)

diagram ['daıəgræm] n schéma m

dial ['daɪəl] **1** *n* *(of clock, phone)* cadran *m*; *(control knob)* bouton *m*
    2 *vt* *(pt & pp* **dialled,** *Am* **dialed)** *(phone number)* composer; *(operator, country)* appeler

dialect ['daɪəlekt] *n* dialecte *m*

dialectic(al) [daɪə'lektɪk(əl)] *adj* dialectique

dialling ['daɪəlɪŋ] *n Br* **d. code** indicatif *m*; **d. tone** tonalité *f*

dialogue, *Am* **dialog** ['daɪəlɒg] *n* dialogue *m*; *Comput* **d. box** boîte *f* de dialogue

dialysis [daɪ'ælɪsɪs] *n Med* dialyse *f*

diameter [daɪ'æmɪtə(r)] *n* diamètre *m*; **the wheel is 60 cm in d.** la roue a un diamètre de 60 cm

diametrically [daɪə'metrɪklɪ] *adv* diamétralement

diamond ['daɪəmənd] *n* *(gem)* diamant *m*; *(shape)* losange *m*; **diamonds** *(card suit)* carreau *m*; **d. jubilee** soixantième anniversaire *m*; **d. necklace/ring** collier *m*/bague *f* de *ou* en diamants

diaper ['daɪəpə(r)] *n Am* couche *f*

diaphanous [daɪ'æfənəs] *adj* diaphane

diaphragm ['daɪəfræm] *n* diaphragme *m*

diarrhoea, *Am* **diarrhea** [daɪə'rɪə] *n* diarrhée *f*

diary ['daɪərɪ] *(pl* **diaries)** *n* *(personal)* journal *m* (intime); *(for appointments)* agenda *m*

diatribe ['daɪətraɪb] *n* diatribe *f* (**against** contre)

dice [daɪs] **1** *n* *(pl* **dice)** dé *m*; **to play d.** jouer aux dés
    2 *vt (food)* couper en dés
    3 *vi* **to d. with death** jouer avec sa vie

dicey ['daɪsɪ] *adj Fam* risqué(e)

dichotomy [daɪ'kɒtəmɪ] *(pl* **dichotomies)** *n* dichotomie *f*

dick [dɪk] *n* **(a)** *Vulg (penis)* bite *f* **(b)** *Am Fam (detective)* privé *m*

dickens ['dɪkɪnz] *n Br Fam* **who/what/why the d....?** qui/que/pourquoi diable...?

dickhead ['dɪkhed] *n BrVulg (idiot)* tête *f* de nœud

dicky ['dɪkɪ] *adj Br Fam* **to have a d. heart** avoir le cœur fragile

dictate 1 *n* ['dɪkteɪt] ordre *m*; **she followed the dictates of her conscience** elle fit ce que lui dictait sa conscience
    2 *vt* [dɪk'teɪt] **(a)** *(letter, passage, conditions)* dicter **(b)** *(determine)* imposer; *(choice)* dicter
    3 *vi* [dɪk'teɪt] **(a)** *(dictate text)* dicter **(b)** *(give orders)* **to d. to sb** donner des ordres à qn; **I won't be dictated to!** je n'ai pas d'ordres à recevoir!

dictation [dɪk'teɪʃən] *n* dictée *f*; **to take d.** écrire sous la dictée

dictator [dɪk'teɪtə(r)] *n* dictateur *m*

dictatorial [dɪktə'tɔːrɪəl] *adj (power, regime)* dictatorial(e); *(manner, tone)* autoritaire

dictatorship [dɪk'teɪtəʃɪp] *n* dictature *f*

diction ['dɪkʃən] *n (pronunciation)* diction *f*; *(choice of words)* style *m*

dictionary ['dɪkʃənərɪ] *(pl* **dictionaries)** *n* dictionnaire *m*

did [dɪd] *pt of* **do**

didactic [dɪ'dæktɪk] *adj* didactique

diddle ['dɪdəl] *vt Fam* rouler; **he diddled me out of £500** il m'a escroqué 500 livres

didn't ['dɪdənt] = **did not**

die¹ [daɪ] *n* **(a)** *(pl* **dice** [daɪs]) *(in games)* dé *m*; **the d. is cast** les dés sont jetés **(b)** *(pl* **dies** [daɪz]) *(mould)* matrice *f*

die² *(pt & pp* **died,** *continuous* **dying)** **1** *vi* mourir (**from** or **of** de); **she is dying** elle est mourante; **to d. hard** *(of habit, rumour)* avoir la vie dure; *Fam* **never say d.!** il ne faut jamais désespérer!; *Fam* **I nearly died (of shame)** j'ai cru mourir de honte; *Fam* **to be dying to do sth** mourir d'envie de faire qch; *Fam* **I'm dying for a cigarette** je meurs d'envie de fumer une cigarette; **the engine died on me/us** le moteur a calé
    2 *vt* **to d. a natural/violent death** mourir de mort naturelle/violente; *Fig* **to d. a death** *(of proposal)* tomber à l'eau; *(of performer)* faire un bide

▸**die away** *vi (of sound, voice)* s'affaiblir

▸**die down** *vi (of fire)* baisser; *(of wind)* tomber; *(of sound)* s'affaiblir; *(of excitement, scandal)* se calmer

▸**die off** *vi* mourir

▸**die out** *vi (of family, species)* s'éteindre

diehard ['daɪhɑːd] **1** *n* réactionnaire *mf*
    2 *adj* pur(e) et dur(e)

diesel ['diːzəl] **1** *n (fuel)* gas-oil *m*, gazole *m*; *(car, railway engine)* diesel *m*
    2 *adj (engine, train)* diesel; **d. oil** *or* **fuel** gas-oil *m*, gazole *m*

diet ['daɪət] **1** *n (usual food)* alimentation *f*; *(restricted food)* régime *m*; **to be/go on a d.** être/se mettre au régime
    2 *vi* être au régime

dietary ['daɪətərɪ] *adj* alimentaire; **d. fibre** fibres *fpl* (alimentaires)

dietician [daɪə'tɪʃən] *n* diététicien(enne) *m,f*

differ ['dɪfə(r)] *vi* **(a)** *(be different)* différer (**from** de); **to d. in size/colour** être de taille/couleur différente **(b)** *(disagree)* ne pas être d'accord; **to d. with sb** ne pas être d'accord avec qn; **I beg to d.** permettez-moi d'être d'un autre avis; **to agree to d.** garder chacun son opinion

difference ['dɪfərəns] *n* **(a)** *(disparity)* différence *f* (**between/in** entre/de); **that doesn't make any d.** ça ne fait aucune différence; **it makes no d. to me** cela m'est égal; **that makes all the d.** voilà qui change tout; **a car with a d.** une voiture pas comme les autres **(b)** *(disagreement)* désaccord *m*, différend *m*; **d. of opinion** divergence *f* d'opinion; **we have to settle our differences** il faut nous mettre d'accord

different ['dɪfərənt] *adj* **(a)** *(not the same)* différent(e) (**from** de); **that's quite a d. matter** ça, c'est une autre affaire; **she feels a d. person** elle ne se sent plus la même; **he just wants to be d.** il veut se singulariser **(b)** *(various)* différents(es), divers(es)

differential [dɪfə'renʃəl] **1** *n (in wages, prices)* écart *m*; *Math* **d. calculus** calcul *m* différentiel; *Aut* **d. (gear)** différentiel *m*
    2 *adj* différentiel(elle)

differentiate [dɪfə'renʃɪət] **1** *vt* différencier (**from** de)
    2 *vi* faire la différence (**between** entre)

differently ['dɪfərəntlɪ] *adv* différemment

difficult ['dɪfɪkəlt] *adj* difficile; **to find it d. to do sth** avoir du mal à faire qch; **he's d. to get on with** il n'est pas commode; **you're just being d.** tu le fais exprès pour embêter le monde; **to make life d. for sb** compliquer la vie à qn

difficulty ['dɪfɪkəltɪ] *(pl* **difficulties)** *n* difficulté *f*; **to have d. in doing sth** avoir des difficultés *ou* du mal à faire qch; **to make difficulties for sb** créer des difficultés à qn

diffidence ['dɪfɪdəns] *n* manque *m* de confiance en soi

diffident ['dɪfɪdənt] *adj* peu sûr(e) de soi; **to be d. about doing sth** hésiter à faire qch

diffuse 1 *adj* [dɪ'fjuːs] diffus(e)
2 *vt* [dɪ'fjuːz] diffuser, répandre
3 *vi* [dɪ'fjuːz] se diffuser, se répandre

dig [dɪg] **1** *n* (**a**) *(in archaeology)* fouilles *fpl*
(**b**) *(poke)* **a d. in the ribs** un coup de coude dans les côtes (**c**) *(remark)* pique *f*; **to have a d. at sb** lancer une pique à qn
2 *vt (pt & pp dug* [dʌg] *)* (**a**) *(hole, grave, ditch)* creuser; *(garden)* bêcher; *Fig* **she is digging her own grave** elle est en train de creuser sa propre tombe
(**b**) *(thrust)* **to d. sth into sth** planter qch dans qch
(**c**) *Fam Old-fashioned (like)* **she really digs that kind of music** ce genre de musique, ça la botte
(**d**) *Fam Old-fashioned (look at)* mater; **d. that guy over there** mate un peu le mec, là-bas
(**e**) *Fam Old-fashioned (understand)* piger; **you d.?** tu piges?
3 *vi (of person, animal)* creuser; *(in archaeology)* faire des fouilles; **to d. for sth** creuser pour trouver qch

▸**dig in 1** *vt sep Fig* **to d. one's heels in** s'entêter
2 *vi* (**a**) *(of soldiers)* se retrancher (**b**) *Fam (eat)* attaquer

▸**dig out** *vt sep* (**a**) *(bullet, splinter)* extraire; *(person from ruins, snow drift)* dégager (**b**) *Fam (find) (information)* dénicher

▸**dig up** *vt sep* (**a**) *(plant)* arracher; *(treasure, body)* déterrer; *(road)* excaver (**b**) *Fam (find) (information, person)* dénicher

digest 1 *n* ['daɪdʒest] *(summary)* condensé *m*
2 *vt* [dɪ'dʒest] *also Fig* digérer

digestible [dɪ'dʒestəbəl] *adj* digeste

digestion [dɪ'dʒestʃən] *n* digestion *f*

digestive [dɪ'dʒestɪv] *adj* digestif(ive); **d. (biscuit)** = sorte de sablé; **d. system/tract** système *m*/tube *m* digestif

digger ['dɪgə(r)] *n (machine)* excavateur *m*

digit ['dɪdʒɪt] *n* (**a**) *(finger)* doigt *m*; *(toe)* orteil *m* (**b**) *(number)* chiffre *m*

digital ['dɪdʒɪtəl] *adj* numérique; **d. camera** appareil *m* photo numérique; **d. recording** enregistrement *m* numérique; **d. signature** signature *f* numérique *ou* électronique; **d. television** *(technique)* télévision *f* numérique; *(appliance)* téléviseur *m* numérique

digitally ['dɪdʒɪtəlɪ] *adv* numériquement, sous forme digitale; *Mus* **d. recorded** enregistré en numérique

dignified ['dɪgnɪfaɪd] *adj* digne

dignify ['dɪgnɪfaɪ] *(pt & pp dignified)* *vt* donner de la dignité à; **I won't d. that remark with a response!** je ne m'abaisserai pas à répondre à cette remarque!

dignitary ['dɪgnɪtərɪ] *(pl dignitaries)* *n* dignitaire *m*

dignity ['dɪgnɪtɪ] *n* dignité *f*; **she considered it beneath her d. to respond** elle estimait indigne d'elle de répondre

digress [daɪ'gres] *vi* faire une digression; **to d. from** s'écarter de; **..., but I d.** ..., mais je m'égare

digression [daɪ'greʃən] *n* digression *f*

digs [dɪgz] *npl Br Fam Old-fashioned* chambre *f* meublée

dike = **dyke**

dilapidated [dɪ'læpɪdeɪtɪd] *adj* délabré(e)

dilapidation [dɪlæpɪ'deɪʃən] *n* délabrement *m*

dilate [daɪ'leɪt] **1** *vt* dilater
2 *vi* se dilater

dilation [daɪ'leɪʃən] *n* dilatation *f*

dilatory ['dɪlətərɪ] *adj Formal (reply)* dilatoire; **to be d. in doing sth** tarder à faire qch

dilemma [daɪ'lemə] *n* dilemme *m*; **to be in a d.** être placé(e) devant un dilemme

dilettante [dɪlɪ'tɑːntɪ] *n* dilettante *mf*

diligence ['dɪlɪdʒəns] *n* application *f*, zèle *m*

diligent ['dɪlɪdʒənt] *adj* consciencieux(euse)

dill [dɪl] *n* aneth *m*

dilly-dally ['dɪlɪ'dælɪ] *(pt & pp dilly-dallied)* *vi Fam (loiter)* traînasser; *(hesitate)* tergiverser

dilute [daɪ'luːt] **1** *adj* dilué(e)
2 *vt (liquid)* diluer; *Fig (policy, proposal)* édulcorer

dilution [daɪ'luːʃən] *n Fig (of policy, proposal)* édulcoration *f*

dim [dɪm] **1** *adj* (**a**) *(light, chance, hope)* faible; *(outline, memory)* vague; *(eyesight)* faible, trouble; *(future)* sombre; **to take a d. view of sth** avoir une piètre opinion de qch (**b**) *(stupid)* bête
2 *vt (pt & pp dimmed)* *(light)* baisser, atténuer
3 *vi (of light)* baisser

dime [daɪm] *n Am* (pièce *f* de) 10 cents *mpl*; *Fam* **it's not worth a d.** ça ne vaut pas un clou; *Fam* **they're a d. a dozen** il y en a à la pelle

dimension [daɪ'menʃən] *n also Fig* dimension *f*

diminish [dɪ'mɪnɪʃ] *vt & vi* diminuer; *Law* **diminished responsibility** responsabilité *f* atténuée

diminishing [dɪ'mɪnɪʃɪŋ] *adj* décroissant(e); **the law of d. returns** la loi des rendements décroissants

diminutive [dɪ'mɪnjʊtɪv] **1** *n Gram* diminutif *m*
2 *adj* minuscule

dimly ['dɪmlɪ] *adv (lit)* faiblement; *(remember, see)* vaguement

dimmer ['dɪmə(r)] *n* **d. (switch)** variateur *m*

dimple ['dɪmpəl] *n* fossette *f*

dimwit ['dɪmwɪt] *n Fam* andouille *f*

din [dɪn] *n* vacarme *m*

dine [daɪn] *vi* dîner, *Belg, Can & Suisse* souper

▸**dine out** *vi* dîner dehors; **to d. out on a story** rabâcher une histoire

diner ['daɪnə(r)] *n* (**a**) *(person)* dîneur(euse) *m,f* (**b**) *Am (restaurant)* petit restaurant *m*

ding-dong ['dɪŋ'dɒŋ] **1** *n* (**a**) *(sound)* ding dong *m* (**b**) *Fam (fight)* bagarre *f*
2 *adj Fam (argument, contest)* acharné(e)

dinghy ['dɪŋ(g)ɪ] *(pl dinghies)* *n* **(rubber) d.** canot *m* pneumatique; **(sailing) d.** dériveur *m*

dingo ['dɪŋgəʊ] *(pl dingoes)* *n* dingo *m*

dingy ['dɪndʒɪ] *adj (room, street)* miteux(euse); *(colour)* terne

dining ['daɪnɪŋ] *n* **d. car** *(on train)* wagon-restaurant *m*; **d. hall** *(in school)* réfectoire *m*; **d. room** salle *f* à manger; **d. table** table *f* de salle à manger

dinner ['dɪnə(r)] *n (evening meal)* dîner *m*, *Belg, Can & Suisse* souper *m*; *(lunch)* déjeuner *m*; **what's for d.?** qu'est-ce qu'on mange?; **to have d.** *(in evening)* dîner; *(at midday)* déjeuner; **d. hour** *(at school)* heure *f* du déjeuner; **d. jacket** smoking *m*; **d. lady** = femme de service dans une cantine scolaire; **d. party** dîner; **d. service** service *m* de table; **d. time** *(in evening)* heure du dîner; *(lunchtime)* heure du déjeuner

dinosaur ['daɪnəsɔː(r)] *n also Fig* dinosaure *m*

dint [dɪnt] *n Formal* **by d. of** à force de; **by d. of her efforts** grâce à ses efforts

diocese ['daɪəsɪs] *n Rel* diocèse *m*

diode ['daɪəʊd] *n Elec* diode *f*

dioxide [daɪ'ɒksaɪd] *n Chem* dioxyde *m*

dip [dɪp] **1** *n* (**a**) *(slope)* descente *f*; *(hollow)* dépression *f*; *(in prices, figures)* baisse *f* (**b**) *Fam (swim)* baignade *f*; **to go for a d.** faire trempette (**c**) *(sauce)* = sauce dans laquelle on trempe des crudités, des biscuits salés etc
2 *vt* (*pt & pp* **dipped**) (**a**) *(immerse)* plonger (**b**) *(lower)* baisser; *Br* **to d. one's headlights** se mettre en codes *(quand on est en pleins phares)*
3 *vi (of ground)* descendre; *(of prices, temperature)* baisser; **the sun dipped below the horizon** le soleil descendit derrière l'horizon

▸**dip into** *vt insep (savings, capital)* puiser dans; *(book)* feuilleter

DipEd [dɪp'ed] *n Br (abbr* **Diploma in Education**) ≃ CAPES *m*

diphtheria [dɪf'θɪərɪə] *n Med* diphtérie *f*

diphthong ['dɪfθɒŋ] *n Ling* diphtongue *f*

diploma [dɪ'pləʊmə] *n* diplôme *m*

diplomacy [dɪ'pləʊməsɪ] *n also Fig* diplomatie *f*

diplomat ['dɪpləmæt] *n* diplomate *mf*

diplomatic [dɪplə'mætɪk] *adj* diplomatique; *Fig (person)* diplomate; **d. bag** valise *f* diplomatique; **d. corps** corps *m* diplomatique; **d. immunity** immunité *f* diplomatique

dipper ['dɪpə(r)] *n (ladle)* louche *f*; **the Big D.** *(constellation)* la Grande Ourse; **big d.** *(at fairground)* montagnes *fpl* russes

dipsomaniac [dɪpsə'meɪnɪæk] *n* dipsomane *mf*

dipstick ['dɪpstɪk] *n* (**a**) *Aut* jauge *f* de niveau d'huile (**b**) *Fam (idiot)* abruti(e) *m,f*

dire ['daɪə(r)] *adj (consequences)* tragique; *Fam (bad)* épouvantable; **d. poverty** misère *f* noire; **to be in d. need of sth** avoir un besoin urgent de qch; **to be in d. straits** être dans une mauvaise passe

direct [dɪ'rekt] **1** *adj* direct(e); *(refusal, denial)* catégorique; **the d. opposite** l'exact opposé; **to be a d. descendant of sb** descendre de qn en ligne directe; *Elec* **d. current** courant *m* continu; *Fin* **d. debit** prélèvement *m* automatique; **d. hit** coup *m* au but; **d. mail** publipostage *m*; *Gram* **d. object** complément *m* d'objet direct; *Pol* **d. rule** administration *f* centrale; *Com* **d. selling** vente *f* directe; *Gram* **d. speech** discours *m* direct; *Fin* **d. taxation** contributions *fpl* directes
2 *adv* directement; *(broadcast)* en direct (**from** de)
3 *vt* (**a**) *(remark)* adresser (**at** à); *(gaze, light)* diriger (**at** sur); *(funds, effort)* consacrer (**towards** à); **can you d. me to the station?** pouvez-vous m'indiquer le chemin de la gare?
(**b**) *(company, actors)* diriger; *(traffic)* régler; *(play)* mettre en scène; *(film)* réaliser
(**c**) *(instruct)* **to d. sb to do sth** ordonner à qn de faire qch; **as directed** selon les instructions

direction [dɪ'rekʃən] *n* (**a**) *(way)* direction *f*, sens *m*; **in the d. of** en direction de; **they ran off in all directions** ils sont partis en courant dans toutes les directions; **the town was surrounded by hills in all directions** la ville était entourée de tous côtés par des collines
(**b**) *(management) (of project)* direction *f*; *(of play)* mise *f* en scène; *(of film)* réalisation *f*; **under the d. of** *(orchestra)* sous la direction de

(**c**) **directions** *(to place)* indications *fpl*; *(for use)* instructions *fpl*; **to ask for directions** demander son chemin

directly [dɪ'rektlɪ] **1** *adv* (**a**) *(go, write)* directement; **to be d. descended from sb** descendre de qn en ligne directe
(**b**) *(exactly)* juste; **d. opposite** juste en face de
(**c**) *(frankly) (answer, speak)* ouvertement
(**d**) *(soon)* immédiatement; **I'll be there d.** j'arrive tout de suite
2 *conj* aussitôt que, dès que; **I'll come d. I've finished** je viendrai dès que j'aurai fini

director [dɪ'rektə(r)] *n (manager)* directeur(trice) *m,f*; *(board member)* administrateur(trice) *m,f*; *(of film)* réalisateur(trice) *m,f*; *(of play)* metteur *m* en scène; *Br Law* **D. of Public Prosecutions** = magistrat dont le rôle recouvre à la fois celui du procureur général et celui du procureur de la République

directorate [dɪ'rektər(e)ɪt] *n (board)* conseil *m* d'administration

directorship [dɪ'rektəʃɪp] *n* direction *f*

directory [dɪ'rektərɪ] *(pl* **directories**) *n (of phone numbers)* annuaire *m*; *Comput* répertoire *m*; **(street) d.** index *m* (des rues); *Br* **d. enquiries** renseignements *mpl* (téléphoniques)

dirge [dɜːdʒ] *n* chant *m* funèbre; *Fam Fig* chanson *f* lugubre

dirham [dɪ'ræm] *n* dirham *m*

dirt [dɜːt] *n* (**a**) *(on clothes, body)* saleté *f*; *(mud)* boue *f*; *(soil)* terre *f*; **to treat sb like d.** traiter qn comme un chien; *Fam* **dog d.** crotte *f* de chien; **d. road** chemin *m* de terre (**b**) *Fam (scandal)* cancans *mpl*, ragots *mpl*

dirt-cheap ['dɜːt'tʃiːp] *Fam* **1** *adj* donné(e)
2 *adv* pour trois fois rien

dirty ['dɜːtɪ] **1** *adj* (**a**) *(unclean) (person, hands, clothes)* sale; *(with mud)* crotté(e); **to get d.** se salir; *also Fig* **to get one's hands d.** se salir les mains; *Fig* **to wash one's d. linen in public** laver son linge sale en public
(**b**) *Fig (unpleasant, unsavoury)* **it's a d. business** c'est une activité peu reluisante; **to give sb a d. look** regarder qn d'un sale œil; **d. work** sale boulot *m* (**c**) *(book, film, joke)* cochon(onne); *(language, word)* grossier(ère); **d. old man** vieux cochon *m*; **d. weekend** week-end *m* coquin; **"communism" is a d. word nowadays** "communisme" est un mot tabou de nos jours
2 *adv* (**a**) *(fight)* déloyalement (**b**) *(obscenely)* **to talk d.** dire des cochonneries (**c**) *Fam (for emphasis)* vachement; **a d. big hole** un sacré grand trou
3 *vt (pt & pp* **dirtied**) salir
4 *n Br Fam* **to do the d. on sb** jouer un sale tour à qn

disability [dɪsə'bɪlɪtɪ] *(pl* **disabilities**) *n* handicap *m*, infirmité *f*; **d. allowance** pension *f* d'invalidité

disable [dɪ'seɪbəl] *vt (person)* rendre infirme; *(ship)* désemparer; *(alarm system)* désactiver

disabled [dɪ'seɪbəld] **1** *npl* **the d.** les handicapés *mpl*
2 *adj* handicapé(e); **d. toilet** toilettes *fpl* pour handicapés

disabuse [dɪsə'bjuːz] *vt Formal* **to d. sb (of an idea)** détromper qn

disadvantage [dɪsəd'vɑːntɪdʒ] **1** *n* désavantage *m*, inconvénient *m*; **to be at a d.** être désavantagé(e); **to put sb at a d.** désavantager qn
2 *vt* désavantager

disadvantaged [dɪsəd'vɑːntɪdʒd] *adj* défavorisé(e)

disaffected [dɪsə'fektɪd] *adj* mécontent(e); *(stronger)* révolté(e)

disaffection [dɪsə'fekʃən] *n* désaffection *f*

disagree [dɪsə'griː] *vi* (**a**) *(quarrel)* ne pas être d'accord; **to d. with sb (about)** ne pas être d'accord avec qn (sur) (**b**) *(of reports, figures)* ne pas concorder (**c**) *(of climate, food)* **to d. with sb** ne pas réussir à qn

disagreeable [dɪsə'griːəbəl] *adj* désagréable

disagreement [dɪsə'griːmənt] *n* (**a**) *(failure to agree)* désaccord *m*; **to be in d. with sb** être en désaccord avec qn (**b**) *(quarrel)* différend *m* (**c**) *(discrepancy)* différence *f*

disallow [dɪsə'laʊ] *vt Formal (objection, claim)* rejeter; *(goal, try)* refuser

disappear [dɪsə'pɪə(r)] *vi* disparaître

disappearance [dɪsə'pɪərəns] *n* disparition *f*

disappoint [dɪsə'pɔɪnt] *vt* décevoir

disappointed [dɪsə'pɔɪntɪd] *adj* déçu(e) (**in** *or* **with** par)

disappointing [dɪsə'pɔɪntɪŋ] *adj* décevant(e)

disappointment [dɪsə'pɔɪntmənt] *n* déception *f*; **to be a d.** être décevant(e)

disapproval [dɪsə'pruːvəl] *n* désapprobation *f*

disapprove [dɪsə'pruːv] *vi* désapprouver; **to d. of sth** désapprouver qch; **he disapproves of them** ils ne lui plaisent pas

disapproving [dɪsə'pruːvɪŋ] *adj (tone, look)* désapprobateur(trice); **to be d. of sth** désapprouver qch

disarm [dɪs'ɑːm] *vt & vi* désarmer

disarmament [dɪs'ɑːməmənt] *n* désarmement *m*; **d. talks** conférence *f* sur le désarmement

disarming [dɪs'ɑːmɪŋ] *adj (smile, honesty)* désarmant(e)

disarray [dɪsə'reɪ] *n* désordre *m*; **in d.** en désordre

disaster [dɪ'zɑːstə(r)] *n* désastre *m*; *(earthquake, fire, crash)* catastrophe *f*; **d. area** région *f* sinistrée; *Fam Fig (person)* maladroit(e) *m,f*; **d. movie** film *m* catastrophe

disastrous [dɪ'zɑːstrəs] *adj* désastreux(euse)

disband [dɪs'bænd] **1** *vt (regiment)* supprimer; *(organization)* dissoudre
2 *vi (of organization)* se dissoudre; *(of regiment)* être supprimé(e)

disbelief [dɪsbɪ'liːf] *n* incrédulité *f*; **in d.** *(listen, watch)* avec incrédulité

disbelieve [dɪsbɪ'liːv] *vt* ne pas croire

disburse [dɪs'bɜːs] *vt Formal* débourser

disc, *Am* **disk** [dɪsk] *n* disque *m*; *Aut* **d. brake** frein *m* à disque; **d. jockey** disc-jockey *m*

discard [dɪs'kɑːd] *vt (person)* laisser tomber; *(plan, proposal)* abandonner; *(object)* se débarrasser de

discern [dɪ'sɜːn] *vt (shape, object)* discerner; *(sound, difference)* percevoir

discernible [dɪ'sɜːnɪbəl] *adj (shape, object)* discernable; *(sound, difference)* perceptible

discerning [dɪ'sɜːnɪŋ] *adj (person)* perspicace; *(taste)* fin(e)

discharge 1 *n* ['dɪstʃɑːdʒ] (**a**) *(of patient)* sortie *f*; *(authorization)* autorisation *f* de sortie; *(of prisoner)* mise *f* en liberté, libération *f*; *(of soldier)* libération; *(for unfitness)* réforme *f* (**b**) *(of firearm)* décharge *f* (**c**) *(of gas, chemical)* dégagement *m*; *(of pus, fluid)* écoulement *m*
2 *vt* [dɪs'tʃɑːdʒ] (**a**) *(patient)* laisser sortir; *(prisoner)* libérer; *(employee)* congédier; *(soldier)* li-

bérer; *(for unfitness)* réformer (**b**) *(firearm)* décharger (**c**) *(gas, chemical)* dégager; *(fluid)* déverser; **to d. pus** suppurer (**d**) *(duty, debt)* s'acquitter de; *(fine)* payer

disciple [dɪ'saɪpəl] *n* disciple *mf*

disciplinarian [dɪsɪplɪ'neərɪən] *n* **to be a strict d.** être stricte en matière de discipline

disciplinary ['dɪsɪplɪnərɪ] *adj* disciplinaire

discipline ['dɪsɪplɪn] **1** *n* discipline *f*
2 *vt (punish)* punir; **to d. oneself** se discipliner

disclaim [dɪs'kleɪm] *vt (renounce)* renoncer à; *(deny)* démentir

disclaimer [dɪs'kleɪmə(r)] *n* démenti *m*

disclose [dɪs'kləʊz] *vt* révéler

disclosure [dɪs'kləʊʒə(r)] *n* révélation *f*

disco ['dɪskəʊ] *(pl* **discos***)* *n* discothèque *f*, boîte *f* (de nuit)

discolour, *Am* **discolor** [dɪs'kʌlə(r)] *vt (fade)* décolorer; *(stain) (with age)* jaunir; *(with smoke)* noircir; **to become discoloured** se décolorer

discomfiture [dɪs'kʌmfɪtʃə(r)] *n* embarras *m*

discomfort [dɪs'kʌmfət] *n (lack of comfort)* inconfort *m*; *(pain)* légère douleur *f*; **to be in some d.** éprouver une légère douleur

disconcert [dɪskən'sɜːt] *vt* déconcerter, décontenancer

disconcerted [dɪskən'sɜːtɪd] *adj* déconcerté

disconcerting [dɪskən'sɜːtɪŋ] *adj* déconcertant(e)

disconnect [dɪskə'nekt] *vt (gas, electricity, phone)* couper; *(machine, appliance)* débrancher

disconsolate [dɪs'kɒnsələt] *adj* désespéré(e) (**at** par)

discontent [dɪskən'tent] *n* mécontentement *m*

discontented [dɪskən'tentɪd] *adj* mécontent(e) (**with** de)

discontinue [dɪskən'tɪnjuː] *vt* interrompre; *Com* **discontinued line** fin *f* de série

discord ['dɪskɔːd] *n* discorde *f*

discordant [dɪs'kɔːdənt] *adj (opinions, sound)* discordant(e)

discotheque ['dɪskətek] *n* discothèque *f*, boîte *f* (de nuit)

discount 1 *n* ['dɪskaʊnt] remise *f*; **at a d.** au rabais
2 *vt* (**a**) ['dɪskaʊnt] *(price)* baisser; *(goods)* solder (**b**) [dɪs'kaʊnt] *(suggestion, rumours)* ignorer, ne pas tenir compte de; *(possibility, fact)* écarter

discourage [dɪs'kʌrɪdʒ] *vt* (**a**) *(dishearten)* décourager (**b**) *(dissuade)* **to d. sb from doing sth** dissuader qn de faire qch

discouragement [dɪs'kʌrɪdʒmənt] *n* (**a**) *(loss of enthusiasm)* découragement *m* (**b**) *(dissuasion)* **to act as** *or* **be a d. (to sth)** avoir un effet dissuasif (sur qch)

discouraging [dɪs'kʌrɪdʒɪŋ] *adj* décourageant(e)

discourse *Formal* **1** *n* ['dɪskɔːs] *(speech)* discours *m*; *(conversation)* conversation *f*
2 *vi* [dɪs'kɔːs] **to d. (up)on sth** discourir sur qch

discourteous [dɪs'kɜːtɪəs] *adj* discourtois(e)

discourtesy [dɪs'kɜːtəsɪ] *n* impolitesse *f*

discover [dɪs'kʌvə(r)] *vt* découvrir

discovery [dɪs'kʌvərɪ] *(pl* **discoveries***)* *n* découverte *f*

discredit [dɪs'kredɪt] **1** *n* discrédit *m*; **to be a d. to sb/sth** déshonorer qn/qch; **much to their d., they didn't even apologize** ils ne se sont même pas excusés, ce qui ne leur fait pas honneur
2 *vt (person, theory)* discréditer

discreet [dɪs'kriːt] *adj* discret(ète)

discrepancy [dɪs'krepənsɪ] (*pl* **discrepancies**) *n* décalage *m* (**between** entre)

discretion [dɪs'kreʃən] *n* (**a**) *(tact)* discrétion *f* (**b**) *(judgement)* jugement *m*; **at the manager's d.** à la discrétion du directeur; **to use one's own d.** juger par soi-même

discretionary [dɪs'kreʃənərɪ] *adj* discrétionnaire

discriminate [dɪs'krɪmɪneɪt] **1** *vt* distinguer (**from** de) **2** *vi* **to d. between** faire la différence entre; **to d. against** faire de la discrimination envers; **to be discriminated against** être victime de discrimination; **to d. in favour of** favoriser

discriminating [dɪs'krɪmɪneɪtɪŋ] *adj* perspicace

discrimination [dɪskrɪmɪ'neɪʃən] *n* (**a**) *(bias)* discrimination *f* (**b**) *(taste)* discernement *m* (**c**) *(differentiation)* différenciation *f*

discriminatory [dɪs'krɪmɪnətərɪ] *adj* discriminatoire

discursive [dɪs'kɜːsɪv] *adj* discursif(ive)

discus ['dɪskəs] *n* disque *m*

discuss [dɪs'kʌs] *vt* *(issue, problem)* discuter de; *(author, book, report)* examiner, parler de; **I don't wish to d. it** je ne veux pas en parler

discussion [dɪs'kʌʃən] *n* discussion *f*; **under d.** en discussion

disdain [dɪs'deɪn] **1** *n* dédain *m* **2** *vt* dédaigner; **to d. to do sth** dédaigner de faire qch

disdainful [dɪs'deɪnfʊl] *adj* dédaigneux(euse)

disease [dɪ'ziːz] *n* maladie *f*

diseased [dɪ'ziːzd] *adj* malade

disembark [dɪsem'bɑːk] *vt & vi* débarquer

disembodied [dɪsɪm'bɒdɪd] *adj* désincarné(e)

disenchanted [dɪsɪn'tʃɑːntɪd] *adj* désenchanté(e); **to be d. with sth** être déçu(e) par qch

disenchantment [dɪsɪn'tʃɑːntmənt] *n* désenchantement *m*

disengage [dɪsɪn'geɪdʒ] **1** *vt* dégager (**from** de); **to d. oneself from sth** se retirer de qch **2** *vi* se retirer (**from** de); *Mil* cesser le combat

disentangle [dɪsɪn'tæŋgəl] *vt* démêler

disfavour, *Am* **disfavor** [dɪs'feɪvə(r)] *n* **to be in d.** être en défaveur; **to fall into d. (with sb)** tomber en disgrâce (auprès de qn)

disfigure [dɪs'fɪgə(r)] *vt* défigurer

disfigurement [dɪs'fɪgəmənt] *n* défigurement *m*

disgrace [dɪs'greɪs] **1** *n* *(shame)* honte *f*; **to be in d. (with sb)** être en disgrâce (auprès de qn); **to be a d. to one's family/country** déshonorer sa famille/son pays; **it's a d.!** c'est une honte! **2** *vt* déshonorer, couvrir de honte; **to d. oneself** se déshonorer

disgraceful [dɪs'greɪsfʊl] *adj* honteux(euse); **it's d.!** c'est honteux *ou* scandaleux!

disgracefully [dɪs'greɪsfʊlɪ] *adv* scandaleusement, honteusement

disgruntled [dɪs'grʌntəld] *adj* mécontent(e)

disguise [dɪs'gaɪz] **1** *n* *(costume)* déguisement *m*; **in d.** déguisé(e) **2** *vt* déguiser; **to d. oneself as** se déguiser en; **there is no disguising the fact that...** on ne peut pas cacher le fait que...

disgust [dɪs'gʌst] **1** *n* dégoût *m*; **to fill sb with d.** remplir qn de dégoût, écœurer qn; **in d.** dégoûté(e), écœuré(e)

2 *vt* dégoûter; **to be disgusted with oneself** se dégoûter

disgusting [dɪs'gʌstɪŋ] *adj* répugnant(e)

dish [dɪʃ] **1** *n* *(bowl, food)* plat *m*; **d. of the day** plat du jour; **dishes** *(crockery)* vaisselle *f*; **to do the dishes** faire la vaisselle **2** *vt* *Fam* **to d. the dirt** tout raconter

▸**dish out** *vt sep* *(food)* servir; *(money, advice)* distribuer

▸**dish up** *vt sep* *(meal)* servir

disharmony [dɪs'hɑːmənɪ] *n* désaccord *m*

dishcloth ['dɪʃklɒθ] *n* *(for washing)* lavette *f*; *(for drying)* torchon *m*

disheartening [dɪs'hɑːtənɪŋ] *adj* décourageant(e)

dishevelled [dɪ'ʃevəld] *adj* *(person, appearance)* débraillé(e); *(hair)* ébouriffé(e); *(clothes)* en désordre

dishonest [dɪs'ɒnɪst] *adj* malhonnête

dishonesty [dɪs'ɒnɪstɪ] *n* malhonnêteté *f*

dishonour, *Am* **dishonor** [dɪs'ɒnə(r)] **1** *n* déshonneur *m* **2** *vt* déshonorer

dishonourable, *Am* **dishonorable** [dɪs'ɒnərəbəl] *adj* déshonorant(e)

dishtowel ['dɪʃtaʊəl] *n* torchon *m*

dishwasher ['dɪʃwɒʃə(r)] *n* *(person)* plongeur(euse) *m,f*; *(machine)* lave-vaisselle *m inv*

dishwater ['dɪʃwɔːtə(r)] *n also Fig* eau *f* de vaisselle

dishy ['dɪʃɪ] *adj Br Fam* mignon(onne)

disillusioned [dɪsɪ'luːʒənd] *adj* désillusionné(e); **to be d. with sb/sth** être déçu(e) par qn/qch; **to become d.** perdre ses illusions

disincentive [dɪsɪn'sentɪv] *n* **to be a d. (to sth)** avoir un effet dissuasif (sur qch)

disinclination [dɪsɪŋklɪ'neɪʃən] *n* manque *m* d'enthousiasme (**to do sth** à faire qch)

disinclined [dɪsɪn'klaɪnd] *adj* **to be d. to do sth** être peu disposé(e) à faire qch

disinfect [dɪsɪn'fekt] *vt* désinfecter

disinfectant [dɪsɪn'fektənt] *n* désinfectant *m*

disinformation [dɪsɪnfə'meɪʃən] *n* désinformation *f*

disingenuous [dɪsɪn'dʒenjʊəs] *adj* *(person, answer)* peu sincère; *(manner, smile)* faux (fausse)

disinherit [dɪsɪn'herɪt] *vt* déshériter

disintegrate [dɪs'ɪntɪgreɪt] *vi* se désintégrer; *(of confidence)* s'effriter; *(of marriage, relationship)* se désagréger

disintegration [dɪsɪntɪ'greɪʃən] *n* désintégration *f*; *(of marriage, relationship)* désagrégation *f*

disinterest [dɪs'ɪntrɪst] *n* *(impartiality)* impartialité *f*; *(lack of interest)* désintérêt *m*, indifférence *f*

disinterested [dɪs'ɪntrɪstɪd] *adj* *(unbiased)* impartial(e); *(uninterested)* indifférent(e)

disinvestment [dɪsɪn'vestmənt] *n Fin* désinvestissement *m*

disjointed [dɪs'dʒɔɪntɪd] *adj* *(style, speech)* décousu(e); *(movements)* saccadé(e)

disk [dɪsk] *n* (**a**) *Comput* disque *m*; *(floppy)* disquette *f*; **d. drive** unité *f* de disques (**b**) *Am* = **disc**

diskette [dɪs'ket] *n Comput* disquette *f*

dislike [dɪs'laɪk] **1** *n* aversion *f* (**of** *or* **for** pour); **we have the same likes and dislikes** nous avons les mêmes goûts; **to take a d. to sb/sth** prendre qn/qch en grippe **2** *vt* ne pas aimer; **I don't d. him** il ne me déplaît pas

dislocate ['dɪsləkeɪt] *vt* (**a**) *(shoulder, hip)* déboîter; **to d. one's shoulder** se déboîter l'épaule (**b**) *(plan, timetable)* perturber

dislocation [dɪslə'keɪʃən] *n* (**a**) *(of shoulder, hip)* déboîtement *m* (**b**) *(of plan, timetable)* perturbation *f*

dislodge [dɪs'lɒdʒ] *vt (opponent, leader)* déloger (**from** de); *(brick, slate)* arracher; *(obstacle)* déplacer; *(something stuck)* décoincer

disloyal [dɪs'lɔɪəl] *adj* déloyal(e)

disloyalty [dɪs'lɔɪəltɪ] *n* déloyauté *f*

dismal ['dɪzməl] *adj (face, countryside)* lugubre; *(failure, performance)* lamentable; *(future)* sombre

dismantle [dɪs'mæntəl] *vt (empire, network)* démanteler; *(machine)* démonter

dismay [dɪs'meɪ] **1** *n* consternation *f*; **in d.** consterné(e); **(much) to my d.** à ma grande consternation **2** *vt* consterner

dismember [dɪs'membə(r)] *vt also Fig* démembrer

dismiss [dɪs'mɪs] *vt* (**a**) *(from job)* renvoyer (**b**) *(send away)* congédier; *(pupils)* libérer; *Mil* **d.!** rompez! (**c**) *(thought, theory)* rejeter; *(proposal, suggestion)* écarter; *(danger, threat)* ignorer; **she is dismissed as an airhead** elle est considérée comme une évaporée (**d**) *Law (case)* classer; *(appeal, charge)* rejeter

dismissal [dɪs'mɪsəl] *n* (**a**) *(of employee)* renvoi *m*, licenciement *m* (**b**) *Law (of case)* fin *f* de non-recevoir; *(of appeal, charge)* rejet *m*

dismissive [dɪs'mɪsɪv] *adj* dédaigneux(euse); **to be d. of sb/sth** faire peu de cas de qn/qch

dismount [dɪs'maʊnt] *vi (from horse, bicycle)* descendre, mettre pied à terre

disobedience [dɪsə'hiːdɪəns] *n* désobéissance *f*

disobedient [dɪsə'biːdɪənt] *adj* désobéissant(e); **to be d. to sb** désobéir à qn

disobey [dɪsə'beɪ] *vt (person, order)* désobéir à; *(law)* enfreindre

disorder [dis'ɔːdə(r)] *n* (**a**) *(confusion, unrest)* désordre *m*; **in d.** en désordre (**b**) *Med* troubles *mpl*; **a nervous d.** des troubles nerveux

disordered [dis'ɔːdəd] *adj* désordonné(e)

disorderly [dɪs'ɔːdəlɪ] *adj (untidy, unruly)* désordonné(e); *(crowd)* agité(e); *Law* **d. conduct** atteinte *f* à l'ordre public

disorganization [dɪsɔːgənaɪ'zeɪʃən] *n* désorganisation *f*

disorganized [dɪs'ɔːgənaɪzd] *adj* désorganisé(e)

disorientate [dɪs'ɔːrɪənteɪt], **disorient** [dɪs'ɔːrɪənt] *vt* désorienter

disorienting [dɪs'ɔːrɪəntɪŋ] *adj* déroutant(e)

disown [dɪs'əʊn] *vt* désavouer, renier

disparage [dɪs'pærɪdʒ] *vt* dénigrer

disparaging [dɪs'pærɪdʒɪŋ] *adj* désobligeant(e)

disparate ['dɪspərɪt] *adj* disparate

disparity [dɪs'pærɪtɪ] *(pl* **disparities**) *n* disparité *f*

dispassionate [dɪs'pæʃənət] *adj (calm)* calme; *(impartial)* impartial(e)

dispatch [dɪs'pætʃ] **1** *n* (**a**) *(of letter, parcel)* expédition *f*, envoi *m* (**b**) *(message)* dépêche *f*; *Mil* **to be mentioned in dispatches** être cité(e) à l'ordre du jour; **d. rider** *Mil* estafette *f*; *(courier)* coursier(ère) *m,f* (**c**) *Formal (promptness)* promptitude *f*; **with d.** promptement **2** *vt* (**a**) *(send)* envoyer (**b**) *(kill)* liquider

dispel [dɪs'pel] *(pt & pp* **dispelled**) *vt* dissiper

dispensable [dɪs'pensəbəl] *adj* dont on peut se passer

dispensary [dɪs'pensərɪ] *(pl* **dispensaries**) *n Med (in pharmacy)* officine *f*; *(in hospital)* pharmacie *f*

dispensation [dɪspen'seɪʃən] *n Law & Rel (exemption)* dispense *f* (**from** de)

dispense [dɪs'pens] *vt (justice)* rendre; *(advice)* prodiguer; *(medication)* préparer; *(of vending machine)* distribuer

▶**dispense with** *vt insep* se passer de; **to d. with the need for sth** rendre qch superflu(e)

dispensing chemist [dɪs'pensɪŋ'kemɪst] *n* pharmacien(enne) *m,f*

dispersal [dɪs'pɜːsəl] *n* dispersion *f*

disperse [dɪs'pɜːs] **1** *vt (seeds, people)* disperser; *(knowledge, information)* propager **2** *vi (of crowd)* se disperser; *(of darkness, mist, clouds)* se dissiper

dispirited [dɪs'pɪrɪtɪd] *adj* découragé(e), abattu(e)

displace [dɪs'pleɪs] *vt* (**a**) *(shift)* déplacer; **displaced persons** personnes *fpl* déplacées (**b**) *(supplant)* remplacer, supplanter

displacement [dɪs'pleɪsmənt] *n* (**a**) *(of water, people)* déplacement *m* (**b**) *(substitution)* remplacement *m*

display [dɪs'pleɪ] **1** *n* (**a**) *(of goods)* étalage *m*; *(of handicrafts, paintings)* exposition *f*; **on d.** à l'étalage; *(sign, notice)* affiché(e); **d. cabinet** vitrine *f*; **d. copy** *(of book)* exemplaire *m* de démonstration; **d. window** vitrine *f* (**b**) *(demonstration)* démonstration *f* (**c**) *Comput* écran *m* **2** *vt* (**a**) *(goods)* exposer; *(sign, notice)* afficher (**b**) *(emotion)* manifester; *(talent, concern, ignorance)* faire preuve de

displease [dɪs'pliːz] *vt* mécontenter, contrarier; **to be displeased with sb/sth** ne pas être satisfait(e) de qn/qch

displeasure [dɪs'pleʒə(r)] *n* déplaisir *m*, mécontentement *m*

disposable [dɪs'pəʊzəbəl] *adj* (**a**) *(nappy, lighter)* jetable (**b**) *(funds, income)* disponible

disposal [dɪs'pəʊzəl] *n* (**a**) *(getting rid of)* enlèvement *m*, élimination *f* (**b**) *(of property)* cession *f*, vente *f* (**c**) *(availability)* **to have sth at one's d.** avoir qch à sa disposition

dispose [dɪs'pəʊz] *vt Formal (arrange)* disposer

▶**dispose of** *vt insep* (**a**) *(rubbish)* jeter, se débarrasser de; *(problem)* régler (**b**) *(kill)* se débarrasser de

disposed [dɪs'pəʊzd] *adj (willing)* **to be d. to do sth** être disposé(e) à faire qch

disposition [dɪspə'zɪʃən] *n* (**a**) *(temperament)* tempérament *m*, nature *f* (**b**) *(inclination)* tendance *f*; **to have a d. to do sth** avoir tendance à faire qch (**c**) *Formal (arrangement)* disposition *f*

dispossess [dɪspə'zes] *vt* déposséder (**of** de)

Disprin® ['dɪsprɪn] *n* = marque d'analgésique

disproportionate [dɪsprə'pɔːʃənət] *adj* disproportionné(e) (**to** à)

disprove [dɪs'pruːv] *(pp* **disproved**, *Law* **disproven** [dɪs'prəʊvən]*) vt* réfuter

dispute [dɪs'pjuːt] **1** *n (debate)* controverse *f*; *(argument)* dispute *f*; **the matter in d.** l'objet de la controverse; **it's beyond d.** c'est incontestable; **it's open to d.** c'est contestable; **(industrial) d.** conflit *m* social **2** *vt (discuss)* discuter; *(call into question)* contester **3** *vi* se quereller (**with/about** avec/à propos de)

disqualification [dɪskwɒlɪfɪ'keɪʃən] *n (from competition)* disqualification *f*; **d. from driving** retrait *m* de permis

disqualify [dɪsˈkwɒlɪfaɪ] (*pt & pp* **disqualified**) *vt* (*from competition*) disqualifier (**from** de); **to d. sb from driving** retirer le permis de conduire à qn

disquiet [dɪsˈkwaɪət] *n Formal* inquiétude *f*

disregard [dɪsrɪˈgɑːd] **1** *n* mépris *m*
2 *vt* ignorer, ne tenir aucun compte de

disrepair [dɪsrɪˈpeə(r)] *n* délabrement *m*; **in (a state of) d.** délabré(e); **to fall into d.** se délabrer

disreputable [dɪsˈrepjʊtəbəl] *adj* (*person*) peu recommandable; (*behaviour*) peu honorable; (*neighbourhood, pub*) mal famé(e)

disrepute [dɪsrɪˈpjuːt] *n* discrédit *m*; **to bring sb/sth into d.** discréditer qn/qch; **to fall into d.** tomber en discrédit

disrespect [dɪsrɪˈspekt] *n* irrespect *m*; **to treat sb with d.** manquer de respect à qn; **I meant no d.** je ne voulais pas être irrespectueux

disrespectful [dɪsrɪˈspektfʊl] *adj* irrespectueux(-euse); **to be d. to sb** manquer de respect à qn

disrupt [dɪsˈrʌpt] *vt* perturber

disruption [dɪsˈrʌpʃən] *n* (*of traffic, life, routine*) perturbation *f*; (*of meeting*) interruption *f*

disruptive [dɪsˈrʌptɪv] *adj* perturbateur(trice); **to be d.** faire du chahut

dissatisfaction [dɪsætɪsˈfækʃən] *n* mécontentement *m* (**with** envers)

dissatisfied [dɪˈsætɪsfaɪd] *adj* mécontent(e) (**with** de)

dissect [dɪˈsekt] *vt also Fig* disséquer

dissemble [dɪˈsembəl] *vt & vi* dissimuler

disseminate [dɪˈsemɪneɪt] **1** *vt* propager, répandre
2 *vi* se propager, se répandre

dissension [dɪˈsenʃən] *n* dissension *f*

dissent [dɪˈsent] **1** *n* désaccord *m*
2 *vi* être en désaccord (**from** avec)

dissenter [dɪˈsentə(r)] *n Pol* dissident(e) *m,f*

dissenting [dɪˈsentɪŋ] *adj* dissident(e)

dissertation [dɪsəˈteɪʃən] *n* mémoire *m*

disservice [dɪˈsɜːvɪs] *n* **to do sb/sth a d.** rendre un mauvais service à qn/qch

dissident [ˈdɪsɪdənt] *n & adj* dissident(e) *m,f*

dissimilar [dɪˈsɪmɪlə(r)] *adj* différent(e) (**to** de)

dissipate [ˈdɪsɪpeɪt] **1** *vt* (*fears, doubts*) dissiper; (*money, energy*) gaspiller
2 *vi* (*of mist, doubts*) se dissiper

dissipation [dɪsɪˈpeɪʃən] *n* (*debauchery*) débauche *f*

dissociate [dɪˈsəʊsɪeɪt] *vt* dissocier (**from** de); **to d. oneself from sb/sth** se dissocier *ou* se désolidariser de qn/qch

dissolute [ˈdɪsəluːt] *adj* dissolu(e)

dissolve [dɪˈzɒlv] **1** *vt* dissoudre
2 *vi* se dissoudre; **to d. into tears** fondre en larmes

dissuade [dɪˈsweɪd] *vt* **to d. sb from doing sth** dissuader qn de faire qch

distance [ˈdɪstəns] **1** *n* distance *f*; **from a d.** de loin; **in the d.** au loin; **within five minutes' walking d.** à cinq minutes de marche; **a short d. away** tout près; **some d. away** assez loin; **to keep one's d.** garder ses distances; **to keep sb at a d.** tenir qn à distance; *Sport & Fig* **to go the d.** tenir la distance; **d. learning** enseignement *m* à distance
2 *vt* **to d. oneself from sb/sth** prendre ses distances vis-à-vis de qn/qch

distant [ˈdɪstənt] *adj* (**a**) (*far-off*) lointain(e); **in the d. past** il y a très longtemps; **in the d. future** dans un avenir lointain; **3 kilometres d.** à 3 kilomètres de dis-

tance (**b**) (*reserved*) distant(e) (**c**) (*distracted*) distrait(e); **she had a d. look** son regard était perdu dans le vague

distantly [ˈdɪstəntlɪ] *adv* (**a**) **to be d. related to sb** être un parent éloigné de qn (**b**) (*distractedly*) distraitement

distaste [dɪsˈteɪst] *n* dégoût *m* (**for** pour)

distasteful [dɪsˈteɪstfʊl] *adj* déplaisant(e)

distemper¹ [dɪsˈtempə(r)] *n* (*animal disease*) maladie *f* de Carré

distemper² *n* (*paint*) détrempe *f*

distend [dɪsˈtend] **1** *vt* distendre
2 *vi* se distendre

distil, *Am* **distill** [dɪsˈtɪl] (*pt & pp* **distilled**) *vt* distiller

distillery [dɪsˈtɪlərɪ] (*pl* **distilleries**) *n* distillerie *f*

distinct [dɪsˈtɪŋkt] *adj* (**a**) (*different*) distinct(e) (**from** de); **as d. from** par opposition à (**b**) (*clear*) clair(e); (*preference, improvement, difference*) net (nette); **it's a d. possibility** c'est fort possible

distinction [dɪsˈtɪŋkʃən] *n* (**a**) (*difference*) distinction *f*; **to draw a d. between** faire une distinction entre (**b**) (*honour, excellence*) distinction *f*; *Ironic* **I had the d. of coming last** j'ai eu l'honneur de venir en dernier; **a writer/scientist of d.** un écrivain/scientifique réputé; **with d.** (*perform, serve*) brillamment (**c**) (*in exam*) mention *f* bien

distinctive [dɪsˈtɪŋktɪv] *adj* distinctif(ive)

distinctly [dɪsˈtɪŋktlɪ] *adv* (**a**) (*clearly*) (*speak, hear*) distinctement; (*remember*) très bien; **I d. told you not to do it** je t'ai clairement dit de ne pas le faire (**b**) (*decidedly*) (*better, easier*) nettement; (*stupid, ill-mannered*) vraiment

distinguish [dɪsˈtɪŋgwɪʃ] **1** *vt* (**a**) (*recognize*) distinguer (**b**) (*characterize, differentiate*) distinguer (**from** de); **distinguishing marks** (*on passport*) signes *mpl* particuliers (**c**) **to d. oneself (by sth/by doing sth)** se distinguer (par qch/en faisant qch)
2 *vi* **to d. between** faire la distinction entre

distinguished [dɪsˈtɪŋgwɪʃd] *adj* (*performance, career*) brillant(e); (*person, air*) distingué(e)

distort [dɪsˈtɔːt] *vt also Fig* déformer

distorted [dɪsˈtɔːtɪd] *adj also Fig* déformé(e)

distortion [dɪsˈtɔːʃən] *n also Fig* distorsion *f*, déformation *f*

distract [dɪsˈtrækt] *vt* distraire; **to d. sb's attention** détourner l'attention de qn; **to be easily distracted** se laisser facilement distraire

distracted [dɪsˈtræktɪd] *adj* (**a**) (*with thoughts elsewhere*) distrait(e) (**b**) (*distraught*) affolé(e)

distracting [dɪsˈtræktɪŋ] *adj* gênant(e), qui distrait

distraction [dɪsˈtrækʃən] *n* (**a**) (*interruption, amusement*) distraction *f* (**b**) (*madness*) **to drive sb to d.** rendre qn fou (folle)

distraught [dɪsˈtrɔːt] *adj* angoissé(e); **d. with grief** fou (folle) de douleur

distress [dɪsˈtres] **1** *n* (*mental*) désarroi *m*; (*physical*) douleur *f*; **to be in d.** (*mentally*) être bouleversé(e); (*physically*) souffrir; (*of ship*) être en détresse; **d. signal** signal *m* de détresse
2 *vt* (*upset*) bouleverser

distressed [dɪsˈtrest] *adj* bouleversé(e)

distressing [dɪsˈtresɪŋ] *adj* bouleversant(e)

distribute [dɪsˈtrɪbjuːt] *vt* (*give out*) & *Com* (*supply*) distribuer; (*spread out*) répartir

distribution [dɪstrɪ'bjuːʃən] *n (giving out)* & *Com (supplying)* distribution *f; (spreading out)* répartition *f;* **d. of wealth** distribution des richesses; *Com* **d. cost** coût *m* de distribution; **d. rights** droits *mpl* de distribution

distributor [dɪs'trɪbjʊtə(r)] *n* (**a**) *(person, company)* distributeur(trice) *m,f; (of cars)* concessionnaire *mf* (**b**) *Aut* distributeur *m*

district ['dɪstrɪkt] *n (of country)* région *f; (of town, city)* quartier *m; (administrative)* district *m; Am* **d. attorney** ≃ procureur *m* de la République; *Br* **d. council** conseil *m* municipal; **d. nurse** infirmière *f* visiteuse

distrust [dɪs'trʌst] **1** *n* méfiance *f* (**of** à l'égard de)
2 *vt* se méfier de

distrustful [dɪs'trʌstfʊl] *adj* méfiant(e); **to be d. of** se méfier de

disturb [dɪs'tɜːb] *vt* (**a**) *(interrupt)* déranger; *(criminal)* surprendre; *(someone's sleep)* troubler; *Law* **to d. the peace** troubler l'ordre public (**b**) *(worry)* perturber (**c**) *(disarrange) (papers, room)* déranger; *(surface of water)* agiter; *(ground)* remuer

disturbance [dɪs'tɜːbəns] *n* (**a**) *(nuisance)* dérangement *m* (**b**) *(atmospheric, emotional)* perturbation *f* (**c**) *(fight)* bagarre *f; (riot)* émeute *f;* **to cause** *or* **create a d.** semer le désordre; *Law* troubler l'ordre public

disturbed [dɪs'tɜːbd] *adj (night, sleep)* agité(e); *(mentally, emotionally)* perturbé(e)

disturbing [dɪs'tɜːbɪŋ] *adj* perturbant(e), troublant(e)

disunity [dɪs'juːnɪtɪ] *n* désunion *f*

disuse [dɪs'juːs] *n* **to fall into d.** tomber en désuétude

ditch [dɪtʃ] **1** *n (at roadside)* fossé *m; (as defence)* douve *f, (for drainage)* rigole *f*
2 *vt Fam (get rid of) (thing)* se débarrasser de; *(plan, idea)* abandonner; *(boyfriend, girlfriend)* plaquer

dither ['dɪðə(r)] *Fam* **1** *n* **to be in a d.** être dans tous ses états
2 *vi* hésiter, tergiverser; **stop dithering!** décide-toi!

ditto ['dɪtəʊ] *adv* idem; *Fam* **I'm hungry – d.** j'ai faim – itou *ou* moi aussi

ditty ['dɪtɪ] *(pl* **ditties**) *n Fam* chansonnette *f*

divan [dɪ'væn] *n* divan *m;* **d. bed** divan-lit *m*

dive [daɪv] **1** *n* (**a**) *(of swimmer)* plongeon *m; (of submarine, diver)* plongée *f;* **to make a d. for sth** *(rush)* se précipiter vers qch; **to go into a d.** *(of plane)* piquer du nez (**b**) *Fam Pej (place)* bouge *m*
2 *vi (Am pt* **dove** [dəʊv]) plonger; *(of plane)* piquer; **to d. for cover** plonger à couvert; **to d. for the exit/into the pub** se précipiter vers la sortie/au pub

diver ['daɪvə(r)] *n* plongeur(euse) *m,f; (deep sea)* scaphandrier *m*

diverge [daɪ'vɜːdʒ] *vi (of rays, opinions)* diverger; *(of roads)* se séparer; *(of people)* avoir des opinions divergentes

divergence [daɪ'vɜːdʒəns] *n* divergence *f*

divergent [daɪ'vɜːdʒənt], **diverging** [daɪ'vɜːdʒɪŋ] *adj* divergent(e)

diverse [daɪ'vɜːs] *adj* divers(e)

diversification [daɪvɜːsɪfɪ'keɪʃən] *n* diversification *f*

diversify [daɪ'vɜːsɪfaɪ] *(pt & pp* **diversified**) **1** *vt* diversifier
2 *vi* se diversifier

diversion [daɪ'vɜːʃən] *n* (**a**) *(of traffic)* déviation *f; (of plane, funds)* détournement *m;* **to create a d.** faire diversion (**b**) *(amusement)* distraction *f*

diversity [daɪ'vɜːsɪtɪ] *n* diversité *f*

divert [daɪ'vɜːt, dɪ'vɜːt] *vt* (**a**) *(traffic)* dévier; *(plane, funds, attention)* détourner (**b**) *(amuse)* **to d. oneself** se distraire

divest [daɪ'vest] *vt Formal* **to d. sb of sth** *(authority)* priver qn de qch; *(possession)* débarrasser qn de qch

divide [dɪ'vaɪd] **1** *vt* (**a**) *(money, food)* partager (**between/among** entre); **to d. sth in two/three** diviser qch en deux/trois (**b**) *Math* diviser (**by** par) (**c**) *(separate)* séparer (**from** de)
2 *vi (of road)* bifurquer; *(of group)* se diviser; **to d. and rule** diviser pour régner
3 *n* fossé *m*

▶**divide up** *vt sep* partager

divided [dɪ'vaɪdɪd] *adj* divisé(e)

dividend ['dɪvɪdend] *n* dividende *m; Fig* **to pay dividends** porter ses fruits

dividers [dɪ'vaɪdəz] *npl (mathematical instrument)* compas *m* à pointe sèche

dividing [dɪ'vaɪdɪŋ] *adj* **d. line** ligne *f* de démarcation; **d. wall** mur *m* de séparation

divine [dɪ'vaɪn] **1** *adj also Fig* divin(e)
2 *vt* deviner

diving ['daɪvɪŋ] *n (in swimming pool)* plongeon *m; (sub-aqua)* plongée *f;* **d. bell** cloche *f* à plongeur; **d. board** plongeoir *m;* **d. suit** scaphandre *m*

divinity [dɪ'vɪnɪtɪ] *(pl* **divinities**) *n* (**a**) *(divine nature, god)* divinité *f* (**b**) *(subject)* théologie *f; (in school)* instruction *f* religieuse

divisible [dɪ'vɪzɪbəl] *adj* divisible

division [dɪ'vɪʒən] *n* (**a**) *(separation)* partage *m* (**b**) *(distribution)* répartition *f,* partage *m;* **d. of labour** division *f* du travail (**c**) *(discord)* division *f* (**d**) *(unit)* division *f;* **first/second d.** *(in sporting league)* première/deuxième division

divisive [dɪ'vaɪsɪv] *adj* qui crée des divisions

divorce [dɪ'vɔːs] **1** *n* divorce *m;* **d. proceedings** procédure *f* de divorce
2 *vt* (**a**) *(husband, wife)* divorcer de; **to get divorced (from sb)** divorcer (de qn) (**b**) *Fig* séparer (**from** de)
3 *vi* divorcer

divorcee [dɪvɔː'siː] *n* divorcé(e) *m,f*

divulge [daɪ'vʌldʒ] *vt* divulguer

DIY [diːaɪ'waɪ] *n (abbr* **do-it-yourself**) bricolage *m*

dizzy ['dɪzɪ] *adj* (**a**) *(unsteady)* étourdi(e); **to feel d.** avoir le vertige; *Fig* **to reach the d. heights of...** atteindre les hauteurs vertigineuses de...; **d. spell** étourdissement *m* (**b**) *Fam (frivolous)* écervelé(e); **a d. blonde** une blonde évaporée

DJ ['diːdʒeɪ] *n* (**a**) *(abbr* **disc jockey**) DJ *m* (**b**) *Fam (abbr* **dinner jacket**) smoking *m*

Djibouti [dʒɪ'buːtɪ] *n* Djibouti

DNA [diːen'eɪ] *n (abbr* **deoxyribonucleic acid**) ADN *m*

do¹ [dəʊ] *n Mus* do *m*

do² [duː]

> Les formes négatives sont **don't/doesn't** et **didn't**, qui deviennent **do not/does not** et **did not** à l'écrit, dans un style plus soutenu.

1 *v aux (3rd person singular* **does** [dʌz], *pt* **did** [dɪd], *pp* **done** [dʌn]) (**a**) *(in negatives)* **I don't speak French** je ne parle pas français; **I didn't see him** je ne l'ai pas vu
(**b**) *(in questions)* **do you speak French?** (est-ce que) tu parles français?; **did you see him?** (est-ce que) tu l'as vu?; **don't you speak French?** tu ne parles pas français?; **didn't you see him?** tu ne l'as pas vu?
(**c**) *(for emphasis)* **he DOES speak French!** mais oui,

il parle français!; **I DIDN'T see him!** mais non, je ne l'ai pas vu!; **it doesn't matter – it DOES matter!** ce n'est pas grave – si, c'est grave!

(**d**) *(as substitute for main verb)* **she writes better than I do** elle écrit mieux que moi; **if you want to speak to her, do it now** si tu veux lui parler, fais-le tout de suite; **do you speak French? – yes, I do/no, I don't** parlez-vous français? – oui/non; **I like Paris – so do I** j'aime Paris – moi aussi; **you left the door unlocked – so I did** tu as laissé la porte ouverte – effectivement; **you said you would go – no, I didn't** tu as dit que tu irais – non, ce n'est pas vrai

(**e**) *(in tag questions)* **you speak French, don't you?** vous parlez français, n'est-ce pas *ou* non?; **John doesn't live there, does he?** John n'habite pas là, si?; **they said they'd come, didn't they?** ils ont bien dit qu'ils viendraient, non?; **you didn't see her, did you?** est-ce que tu l'as vue ou pas?

2 *vt* (**a**) *(in general)* faire; **what do you do?** *(what's your job?)* que faites-vous dans la vie?; **don't do that again!** ne refais jamais ça!; **what are you going to do about it?** qu'est-ce que tu vas faire?

(**b**) *(activity)* faire; **to do the housework/the dishes** faire le ménage/la vaisselle; **to do one's hair** se coiffer; **to do one's teeth** se brosser les dents; *Fam* **to do drugs** se droguer; **they do good food here** ils font de la bonne cuisine ici; **it just isn't done!** ça ne se fait pas, c'est tout!; *Fam* **let's do lunch!** on se fait une bouffe?

(**c**) *(have effect on)* **to do sb good** faire du bien à qn; **that hairstyle does nothing/does a lot for her** cette coiffure ne la flatte pas/la flatte; **this music does nothing for me** cette musique ne me plaît pas tellement

(**d**) *(be enough for)* **will £10 do you?** est-ce que 10 livres te suffiront?; **that'll do me** ça m'ira

(**e**) *(study)* faire; **to do French/physics** faire du français/de la physique

(**f**) *(with speed, distance)* **the car was doing 100 (miles per hour)** $\simeq$ la voiture faisait du 160 (à l'heure); **we did 500 km on the first day** nous avons fait 500 km le premier jour

(**g**) *Fam (cheat)* avoir; **I've been done!** je me suis fait avoir!

(**h**) *Fam (prosecute)* pincer; **to get done for speeding** se faire pincer pour excès de vitesse

3 *vi* (**a**) *(act)* **to do well/badly** bien/mal se débrouiller; **do as you're told** fais ce qu'on te dit; **you would do well to accept** tu ferais bien d'accepter; **how do you do?** enchanté(e); **how are you doing?** (comment) ça va?

(**b**) *(be enough)* **two bottles of wine will do** deux bouteilles de vin suffiront; **that'll do** *(is satisfactory)* ça ira; *(stop it)* ça suffit maintenant!

4 *n* (**a**) **the do's and don'ts** les choses *fpl* à faire et à ne pas faire

(**b**) *(pl* **dos**) *Fam (party)* fête *f*

►**do away with** *vt insep* (**a**) *(abolish)* supprimer (**b**) *Fam (kill)* zigouiller

►**do down** *vt sep* rabaisser; **to do oneself down** se rabaisser

►**do for** *vt insep Fam* **to be done for** être fichu(e)

►**do in** *vt sep Fam* (**a**) *(murder)* zigouiller (**b**) *(exhaust)* **to be done in** être complètement crevé(e) (**c**) *(injure)* **to do one's back/knee in** se bousiller le dos/genou

►**do out of** *vt sep Fam* **to do sb out of sth** *(job)* priver qn de qch; *(money)* faire perdre qch à qn

►**do over** *vt sep Fam (beat up)* **to d. sb over** tabasser qn

►**do up 1** *vt sep* (**a**) *(fasten)* fermer; *(shoelaces)* attacher (**b**) *(wrap)* envelopper (**c**) *(improve appearance of)* restaurer; *(room, house)* rénover; *Fam* **to do oneself up** *(dress smartly)* se faire beau (belle)
2 *vi (of clothes)* se fermer

►**do with** *vt insep* (**a**) *(benefit from)* **I could do with a cup of tea** je prendrais bien une tasse de thé; **you could do with a haircut** tu aurais bien besoin de te faire couper les cheveux

(**b**) *(be connected with)* **to have nothing to do with sb/sth** *(be unconnected to)* n'avoir rien à voir avec qn/qch; *(not get involved with)* n'avoir rien à faire avec qn/qch; **I had nothing to do with it** je n'ai rien à voir là-dedans; **it's nothing to do with you** *(not your business)* ça ne te regarde pas

(**c**) *(finish using)* **to have done with sth** avoir fini avec qch; **have you done with the scissors yet?** est-ce que tu as fini avec les ciseaux?; **it's all over and done with** c'est du passé

►**do without 1** *vt insep* se passer de
2 *vi* se priver

doc [dɒk] *n Fam (doctor)* toubib *m*

docile ['dəʊsaɪl] *adj* docile

dock¹ [dɒk] **1** *n (for ships)* dock *m*; **d. workers** dockers *mpl*
2 *vi (of ship)* accoster; *(of two spacecraft)* s'arrimer

dock² *n Law* banc *m* des accusés

dock³ *vt* (**a**) *(tail)* couper (**b**) *(wages)* faire une retenue sur

docker ['dɒkə(r)] *n* docker *m*

dockyard ['dɒkjɑːd] *n* chantier *m* naval

doctor ['dɒktə(r)] **1** *n* (**a**) *(medical)* docteur *m*, médecin *m*; **to go to the d.('s)** aller chez le médecin; *Fam Fig* **just what the d. ordered** exactement ce qu'il me fallait (**b**) *Univ* docteur *m*; **D. of Science** docteur ès sciences
2 *vt* (**a**) *Fam (accounts, evidence)* falsifier (**b**) *(cat)* castrer

doctorate ['dɒktərɪt] *n Univ* doctorat *m* (**in** en)

doctrinaire [dɒktrɪ'neə(r)] *adj* doctrinaire

doctrinal [dɒk'traɪnəl] *adj* doctrinal(e)

doctrine ['dɒktrɪn] *n* doctrine *f*

document 1 *n* ['dɒkjəmənt] document *m*; *Comput* **d. reader** lecteur *m* de documents
2 *vt* ['dɒkjʊment] (**a**) *(show in detail)* présenter (**b**) *(support)* étayer; **the first documented case** le premier cas établi

documentary [dɒkjʊ'mentərɪ] **1** *n (pl* **documentaries**) *(TV programme)* documentaire *m*
2 *adj (film)* documentaire; *(proof)* littéral(e)

documentation [dɒkjʊmen'teɪʃən] *n* documentation *f*

docusoap ['dɒkjʊsəʊp] *n TV* docu-soap *m*

dodder ['dɒdə(r)] *vi* marcher d'un pas hésitant

doddering ['dɒdərɪŋ] *adj (walk)* hésitant(e); **a d. old fool** un vieux gâteux (une vieille gâteuse)

doddle ['dɒdəl] *n Br Fam* **it's a d.** c'est simple comme bonjour

dodge [dɒdʒ] **1** *n* (**a**) *Fam (trick)* truc *m*, combine *f*; **tax d.** combine pour payer moins d'impôts (**b**) *(movement)* écart *m*
2 *vt (blow, responsibility, question)* esquiver; *(person)* éviter; *(police)* échapper à
3 *vi* **to d. (out of the way)** faire un bond de côté

dodgems ['dɒdʒəmz] *npl* autos *fpl* tamponneuses

dodgy ['dɒdʒɪ] *adj Br Fam (suspect)* louche; *(not working properly)* en mauvais état; *(risky)* risqué(e); *(milk, meat)* douteux(euse)

dodo ['dəʊdəʊ] *(pl* **dodoes** *or* **dodos)** *n* dodo *m*, dronte *m*; **(as) dead as a d.** mort(e) et enterré(e)

DOE [diːəʊ'iː] *n Br (abbr* **Department of the Environment)** ≃ ministère *m* de l'Environnement

doe [dəʊ] *n (deer)* biche *f*; *(rabbit)* lapine *f*

does [dʌz] *3rd person singular of* **do**

doesn't ['dʌzənt] = **does not**

doff [dɒf] *vt* **to d. one's cap to sb** se découvrir devant qn

dog [dɒg] **1** *n* **(a)** *(animal)* chien *m*; **d. biscuit** biscuit *m* pour chien; **d. collar** collier *m* de chien; *Fam (of cleric)* col *m* blanc *(d'un religieux)*; **d. food** nourriture *f* pour chien; **d. handler** maître-chien *m*; *Br* **d. licence** = permis nécessaire pour posséder un chien; **to do the d. paddle** nager comme un petit chien; **d. racing** courses *fpl* de lévriers; **d. tag** plaque *f* d'identité **(b)** *Fam (person)* **you lucky d.!** sacré veinard!; **dirty d.** sale type *m* **(c)** *Fam Pej (ugly woman)* cageot *m* **(d)** *Am (hot dog)* hot dog *m* **(e)** *(idioms) Fam* **to lead a d.'s life** avoir une vie de chien; *Fam* **to make a d.'s breakfast** *or* **dinner of sth** gâcher qch; *Fam* **it's a d.-eat-d. world** c'est un monde sans pitié; *Fam* **to go to the dogs** *(of place)* aller à vau-l'eau; *(of person)* filer un mauvais coton; *Fam* **to be a d. in the manger** être un empêcheur de tourner en rond; *Prov* **you can't teach an old d. new tricks** les vieilles habitudes ont la vie dure; *Prov* **every d. has his day** tout le monde a son heure de gloire **2** *vt (pt & pp* **dogged)** *(follow)* suivre de près; **to d. sb's footsteps** être sur les talons de qn; **to be dogged by scandal/misfortune** être poursuivi(e) par le scandale/la malchance

dog-eared ['dɒgɪəd] *adj (page)* corné(e); *(book)* aux pages cornées

dogfight ['dɒgfaɪt] *n (between planes)* combat *m* aérien; *(between people)* bagarre *f*

dogfish ['dɒgfɪʃ] *n* roussette *f*

dogged ['dɒgɪd] *adj* tenace

doggerel ['dɒgərəl] *n (comical)* poésie *f* burlesque; *(bad)* vers *mpl* de mirliton

doggy ['dɒgɪ] *(pl* **doggies)** *n Fam* toutou *m*; **d. bag** = petit sac fourni par certains restaurants pour que les clients puissent emporter les restes

doghouse ['dɒghaʊs] *n Fam* **to be in the d.** ne pas être en odeur de sainteté

dogma ['dɒgmə] *n* dogme *m*

dogmatic [dɒg'mætɪk] *adj* dogmatique

do-gooder ['duːgʊdə(r)] *n Fam Pej* âme *f* charitable

dogsbody ['dɒgzbɒdɪ] *(pl* **dogsbodies)** *n Br Fam* factotum *m*

dog-tired ['dɒg'taɪəd] *adj Fam* claqué(e), crevé(e)

dogwood ['dɒgwʊd] *n* cornouiller *m*

doh [dəʊ] *n Mus* do *m*

doily ['dɔɪlɪ] *(pl* **doilies)** *n* napperon *m*

doing ['duːɪŋ] *n* **(a)** **this is his d.** c'est son œuvre; **it was none of my d.** je n'y étais pour rien; **that takes some d.** il faut le faire **(b)** **doings** faits *mpl* et gestes *mpl*

do-it-yourself [duːɪtjɔː'self] *n* bricolage *m*; **a d. enthusiast** un(e) adepte du bricolage

doldrums ['dɒldrəmz] *npl* **to be in the d.** *(of person)* broyer du noir; *(of economy)* être en plein marasme

dole [dəʊl] *n Br Fam* (indemnités *fpl* de) chômage *m*; **to be on the d.** être au chômage; *Fig* **to join the d. queue** se retrouver au chômage

▸**dole out** *vt sep Fam* distribuer

doleful ['dəʊlfʊl] *adj* triste

doll [dɒl] *n* poupée *f*; **d.'s house** maison *f* de poupée

▸**doll up** *vt sep Fam* **to d. oneself up** se pomponner

dollar ['dɒlə(r)] *n* dollar *m*; **d. bill** billet *m* de un dollar

dollop ['dɒləp] *n Fam (of cream, mashed potato)* bonne cuillerée *f*; *(of mud, clay)* tas *m*

dolly ['dɒlɪ] *(pl* **dollies)** *n* **(a)** *Fam (toy)* poupée *f* **(b)** *(for camera)* chariot *m*

dolphin ['dɒlfɪn] *n* dauphin *m*

dolt [dəʊlt] *n Fam* andouille *f*

domain [də'meɪn] *n also Fig* domaine *m*; *Comput* **d. name** nom *m* de domaine

dome [dəʊm] *n* dôme *m*

domestic [də'mestɪk] *adj* **(a)** *(appliance, use, tasks)* ménager(ère); *(animal)* domestique; **d. bliss** bonheur *m* familial; *Br* **d. science** *(school subject)* cours *mpl* de couture et de cuisine; **d. servant** domestique *mf* **(b)** *(policy, flight, affairs)* intérieur(e); *(economy, currency)* national(e)

domesticate [də'mestɪkeɪt] *vt (animal)* domestiquer; *Hum* **to be domesticated** *(of person)* se débrouiller plutôt bien avec les travaux ménagers

domicile ['dɒmɪsaɪl] *n Law* domicile *m*

dominance ['dɒmɪnəns] *n (of disease, gene)* dominance *f*; *(of race, political party)* prédominance *f*; *(of person)* supériorité *f*

dominant ['dɒmɪnənt] *adj* dominant(e); *(person, character)* dominateur(trice)

dominate ['dɒmɪneɪt] *vt & vi* dominer

domination [dɒmɪ'neɪʃən] *n* domination *f*

domineering [dɒmɪ'nɪərɪŋ] *adj* dominateur(trice)

Dominica [də'mɪnɪkə] *n* la Dominique

Dominican [də'mɪnɪkən] **1** *n* Dominicain(e) *m,f* **2** *adj* dominicain(e); **the D. Republic** la République Dominicaine

dominion [də'mɪnjən] *n* domination *f*; *Can* **D. day** Fête *f* du Canada *(anniversaire de l'indépendance canadienne, le 1ᵉʳ juillet)*

domino ['dɒmɪnəʊ] *(pl* **dominoes)** *n* domino *m*; *Pol & Fig* **d. effect** effet *m* d'entraînement

don¹ [dɒn] *n Br Univ* professeur *m* d'université *(surtout à Oxford et Cambridge)*

don² *(pt & pp* **donned)** *vt Formal (clothing)* mettre, revêtir

donate [də'neɪt] *vt* faire don de; **to d. blood** donner son sang

donation [də'neɪʃən] *n* donation *f*; don *m*

done [dʌn] *pp of* **do**

donkey ['dɒŋkɪ] *(pl* **donkeys)** *n (animal) & Fam (person)* âne *m*; *Fam* **I haven't seen her for d.'s years** je ne l'ai pas vue depuis une éternité; *Fam* **to talk the hind legs off a d.** avoir la langue bien pendue; **d. jacket** ≃ caban *m*; *Fam* **d. work** travail *m* pénible

donor ['dəʊnə(r)] *n* donneur(euse) *m,f*; **d. card** carte *f* de donneur d'organe

don't [dəʊnt] = **do not**

donut *Am* = **doughnut**

doodle ['duːdəl] **1** *n* gribouillis *m*, gribouillage *m* **2** *vi* gribouiller

doom [duːm] **1** *n* destin *m* (funeste); **to be all d. and gloom** voir tout en noir

2 *vt* **to be doomed** *(of person) (unlucky)* être marqué(e) par le destin; *(about to die)* être perdu(e); **to be doomed (to failure)** *(of project)* être voué(e) à l'échec; **to be doomed to do sth** être condamné(e) à faire qch

doom-laden ['du:mleɪdən] *adj* funeste, sinistre

doomsday ['du:mzdeɪ] *n* jour *m* du Jugement dernier; *Fig* **till d.** indéfiniment

door [dɔ:(r)] *n* porte *f*; *(of train, car)* portière *f*; **to answer the d.** aller ouvrir (la porte); **to see sb to the d.** raccompagner qn à la porte; **to show sb the d.** mettre qn à la porte; **to shut the d. in sb's face** fermer la porte au nez de qn; **she lives two doors away** elle habite deux portes plus loin; *Fig* **to lay sth at sb's d.** imputer qch à qn; **out of doors** dehors, en plein air; **d. handle** poignée *f* de porte; **d. knocker** heurtoir *m*

doorbell ['dɔ:bel] *n* sonnette *f*

doorkeeper ['dɔ:ki:pə(r)] *n* portier *m*

doorknob ['dɔ:nɒb] *n* bouton *m* de porte

doorman ['dɔ:mən] *n* *(in hotel)* portier *m*; *(in block of flats)* concierge *m*

doormat ['dɔ:mæt] *n* paillasson *m*; *Fig* **to treat sb like a d.** traiter qn comme un moins que rien

doorpost ['dɔ:pəʊst] *n* montant *m* de porte

doorstep ['dɔ:step] *n* pas *m* de la porte, seuil *m*; *Fig* **on one's d.** à deux pas

doorstop ['dɔ:stɒp] *n* *(fixed)* butoir *m*; *(wedge)* cale-porte *m*

door-to-door ['dɔ:tə'dɔ:(r)] *adj* **d. canvassing** porte-à-porte *m* électoral; **d. salesman** démarcheur *m*

doorway ['dɔ:weɪ] *n* porte *f*; **in the d.** dans l'embrasure de la porte

dopamine ['dəʊpəmɪn] *n* dopamine *f*

dope [dəʊp] **1** *n* (**a**) *very Fam (cannabis)* shit *m*; *Fam* **d. test** *(for athlete)* contrôle *m* antidopage (**b**) *Fam (idiot)* andouille *f*
2 *vt (person, horse) (to make faster)* doper; *(to make slower)* droguer; *(food, drink)* mettre une drogue dans

dopey ['dəʊpɪ] *adj Fam* idiot(e)

dorm [dɔ:m] *n Fam (dormitory)* dortoir *m*

dormant ['dɔ:mənt] **1** *adj (volcano)* en sommeil; *(conflict, emotion)* latent(e); *(idea)* qui sommeille
2 *adv* **to lie d.** être en sommeil

dormer window ['dɔ:mə'wɪndəʊ] *n* lucarne *f*

dormitory ['dɔ:mɪtərɪ] *(pl* **dormitories**) *n* (**a**) dortoir *m*; **d. town** cité-dortoir *f* (**b**) *Am Univ* résidence *f* universitaire

dormouse ['dɔ:maʊs] *(pl* **dormice** ['dɔ:maɪs]) *n* loir *m*

dorsal ['dɔ:səl] *adj* dorsal(e)

DOS [dɒs] *n Comput (abbr* **disk operating system**) DOS *m*

dose [dəʊs] **1** *n (amount)* dose *f*; **a bad d. of (the) flu** une bonne grippe; **to have a d. of measles** avoir la rougeole
2 *vt Fam* bourrer (**with** de); **to d. oneself (up) with pills** se bourrer de médicaments

dosh [dɒʃ] *n Br Fam (money)* fric *m*

doss [dɒs] *vi Fam* **to d. (down)** crécher

dosser ['dɒsə(r)] *n Br very Fam (tramp)* clodo *mf*

doss-house ['dɒshaʊs] *n Br Fam* asile *m* de nuit

dossier ['dɒsɪeɪ] *n* dossier *m*

dot [dɒt] **1** *n* point *m*; **on the d.** à l'heure pile; **at three o'clock on the d.** à trois heures pile; *Com* **d. com (company)** start-up *f*, jeune pousse *f*; *Comput* **d. mat-**

rix printer imprimante *f* matricielle
2 *vt (pt & pp* **dotted**) parsemer (**with** de); **to d. an i/a j** mettre un point sur un i/un j; **dotted line** pointillé *m*; **to sign on the dotted line** ≃ signer à l'endroit indiqué; *Fig* **to d. the i's (and cross the t's)** peaufiner les détails

dotage ['dəʊtɪdʒ] *n* **to be in one's d.** être gâteux(euse)

▸**dote on, dote upon** [dəʊt] *vt insep* adorer

dotty ['dɒtɪ] *adj Fam (person, idea)* toqué(e); **to be d. about sb** être fou (folle) de qn

double ['dʌbəl] **1** *n* (**a**) *(of person)* double *m*, sosie *m* (**b**) *(hotel room)* chambre *f* pour deux personnes (**c**) **doubles** *(in tennis)* double *m*; **a doubles match** un double (**d**) **at** *or* **on the d.** à l'instant (**e**) *(measure of drink)* double *m*
2 *adj* double; **d. m** *(when spelling)* deux m; **d. five two one** *(figure)* deux fois cinq deux un; *(phone number)* cinquante-cinq, vingt et un; **a d. whisky** un double whisky; **d. agent** agent *m* double; **d. bass** contrebasse *f*; **d. bed** grand lit *m*, lit à deux personnes; **d. bill** *(at cinema)* double programme *m*; **d. chin** double menton *m*; **d. cream** ≃ crème *f* fraîche épaisse; *Br* **to talk d. Dutch** parler chinois; **d. fault** *(in tennis)* double faute *f*; **to be in d. figures** *(of statistic)* avoir atteint plus de dix; **inflation is now in d. figures** l'inflation a passé la barre des 10 pour cent; **to lead a d. life** mener une double vie; **d. meaning** double sens *m*; **d. room** chambre *f* pour deux personnes; **to have d. standards** faire deux poids, deux mesures; **to do a d. take** marquer un temps d'arrêt *(par surprise)*; *Br* **d. yellow line** = double ligne jaune indiquant une zone de stationnement interdit
3 *adv* **to see d.** voir double; **to fold sth d.** plier qch en deux; **to be bent d.** être plié(e) en deux
4 *vt* (**a**) *(multiply by two)* doubler (**b**) *(fold)* plier en deux
5 *vi* (**a**) *(increase twofold)* doubler (**b**) **to d. as sth** servir aussi de qch

▸**double back** *vi* rebrousser chemin

▸**double up** *vi (bend)* se plier en deux (**with** de)

double-barrelled ['dʌbəl'bærəld] *adj (shotgun)* à deux coups; *(surname)* à rallonge

double-breasted ['dʌbəl'brestɪd] *adj (jacket, suit)* croisé(e)

double-check ['dʌbəl'tʃek] *vt & vi* bien vérifier

double-cross ['dʌbəl'krɒs] *vt* trahir, doubler

double-dealing ['dʌbəl'di:lɪŋ] *n* fourberie *f*

double-decker ['dʌbəl'dekə(r)] *n Br (bus)* autobus *m* à impériale *ou* à étage

double-edged ['dʌbəl'edʒd] *adj also Fig* à double tranchant

double-glazing ['dʌbəl'gleɪzɪŋ] *n* double vitrage *m*

double-jointed [dʌbəl'dʒɔɪntəd] *adj* désarticulé(e)

double-lock ['dʌbəl'lɒk] *vt* fermer à double tour

double-park ['dʌbəl'pɑ:k] *vi* se garer en double file

double-quick ['dʌbəl'kwɪk] *adv* en vitesse

doubly ['dʌbəlɪ] *adv* doublement; **to make d. sure of sth** bien vérifier qch; **d. difficult** deux fois plus difficile; **to be d. careful** redoubler de prudence

doubt [daʊt] **1** *n* doute *m*; **to have doubts about sth** avoir des doutes sur qch; **to be in d.** *(of person)* douter (**about** de); *(of outcome)* être incertain(e); **when in d.** en cas de doute, dans le doute; **beyond d.** sans le moindre doute; **no d.** sans doute; **there is no d. that...** il ne fait aucun doute que...; **there is no d.**

about her guilt sa culpabilité ne fait aucun doute; **there is some d. about...** il y a des doutes quant à... **2** *vt* douter de; **I d. it** j'en doute; **I d. if it makes him happy** je doute que cela le rende heureux

doubtful ['daʊtfʊl] *adj* (**a**) *(uncertain) (person)* dubitatif(ive); *(outcome)* incertain(e); **to be d. about sth** avoir des doutes sur qch (**b**) *(questionable)* douteux(-euse)

dough [dəʊ] *n* (**a**) *(for bread)* pâte *f* (**b**) *Fam (money)* fric *m*

doughnut ['dəʊnʌt] *n* beignet *m*, *Can* beigne *m*

dour [dʊə(r)] *adj* austère

douse [daʊs] *vt* (**a**) *(soak)* arroser (**b**) *(extinguish)* éteindre

dove[1] [dʌv] *n* colombe *f*

dove[2] [dəʊv] *Am pt of* **dive**

dovecot(e) ['dʌvkɒt] *n* colombier *m*

Dover ['dəʊvər] *n* Douvres

dovetail ['dʌvteɪl] *vi (fit closely)* concorder, cadrer (**with** avec)

dowager ['daʊədʒə(r)] *n* douairière *f*

dowdy ['daʊdɪ] *adj (person)* inélégant(e); *(clothes, image)* démodé(e)

dowel ['daʊəl] *n* cheville *f*

down[1] [daʊn] *n (feathers)* duvet *m*

down[2] **1** *prep* **to go d. the stairs/the street** descendre les escaliers/la rue; **to run d. the stairs/the street** descendre les escaliers/la rue en courant; **to fall d. the stairs** dégringoler les escaliers; **the tears ran d. her cheeks** les larmes coulaient sur ses joues **2** *adv* (**a**) *(with motion)* **to come/go d.** descendre; **to fall d.** tomber; **to bend d.** se pencher; **petrol has come** *or* **gone d. in price** le prix de l'essence a baissé; **I'll be d. in a minute** je descends tout de suite; **d. with traitors!** à bas les traîtres!

(**b**) *(with position)* en bas; **d. here/there** ici/là en bas; **further d.** plus bas; **petrol is d. in price** le prix de l'essence a baissé; **one d., two to go!** et d'un! encore deux et c'est fini!; **everyone from the boss d.** tout le monde, même le chef

(**c**) *(in crosswords)* verticalement

(**d**) *(idioms)* **to be d. on sb/sth** avoir une dent contre qn/qch; **it's d. to her** *(her decision)* c'est à elle de décider; *(her achievement)* c'est grâce à elle; **I'm d. to my last pound/cigarette** il ne me reste plus qu'une livre/une cigarette

3 *n Fam* **to have a d. on sb/sth** avoir une dent contre qn/qch

4 *adj* (**a**) *(depressed)* déprimé(e) (**b**) **to be d.** *(of computer, telephones)* être en panne

5 *vt* (**a**) *(aircraft)* abattre (**b**) *(drink)* descendre; **to d. tools** *(of workers)* se mettre en grève

down-and-out ['daʊnən'aʊt] *Fam* **1** *n (tramp)* clochard(e) *m,f* **2** *adj* sans le sou

downbeat ['daʊnbiːt] *adj* (**a**) *(gloomy, pessimistic)* triste, pessimiste (**b**) *(restrained)* réservé(e) (**about** sur)

downcast ['daʊnkɑːst] *adj (eyes)* baissé(e); *(person)* abattu(e), découragé(e)

downer ['daʊnə(r)] *n Fam* (**a**) *(drug)* tranquillisant *m* (**b**) *(depressing situation)* situation *f* déprimante; *(depressing event)* événement *m* déprimant

downfall ['daʊnfɔːl] *n (of government)* chute *f*; *(of person)* ruine *f*

downgrade ['daʊngreɪd] *vt* rétrograder

downhearted [daʊn'hɑːtɪd] *adj* découragé(e)

downhill ['daʊn'hɪl] **1** *adj (slope)* en pente; **d. skiing** ski *m* alpin *ou* de descente **2** *adv* **to go d.** *(of road, car)* descendre; *Fig (of person, career)* être sur le déclin; *(of business)* péricliter

Downing Street ['daʊnɪŋ'striːt] *n* Downing Street, = rue de Londres où se trouve la résidence officielle du Premier ministre britannique

---

Downing Street

C'est à Downing Street à Londres que se trouvent les résidences officielles du Premier ministre, au nº 10, et du ministre des Finances, au nº 11. Le terme "Downing Street" est souvent employé pour désigner le gouvernement.

---

download [daʊn'ləʊd] *vt Comput* télécharger

downmarket [daʊn'mɑːkɪt] *adj (product)* bas de gamme *inv*; *(area, place)* populaire

down payment [daʊn'peɪmənt] *n* acompte *m*

downpour ['daʊnpɔː(r)] *n* averse *f*

downright ['daʊnraɪt] **1** *adj (stupidity, dishonesty)* véritable; **it's a d. lie!** c'est un mensonge flagrant! **2** *adv (stupid, untrue)* carrément

downsizing ['daʊnsaɪzɪŋ] *n* réduction *f* d'effectifs

Down's syndrome ['daʊnz'sɪndrəʊm] *n* trisomie *f* 21

downstairs 1 *adj* ['daʊnsteəz] *(on a lower floor)* de l'étage du dessous; *(on ground floor)* du rez-de-chaussée; **the d. flat** l'appartement du dessous; **the d. bathroom** la salle de bains du bas **2** *adv* [daʊn'steəz] en bas; **to come/go d.** descendre; **he lives d.** il habite à l'étage au-dessous

downstream [daʊn'striːm] *adv* en aval; *(with movement)* vers l'aval

downswing ['daʊnswɪŋ] *n Econ* tendance *f* à la baisse

down-to-earth ['daʊntə'ɜːθ] *adj* terre à terre *inv*

downtown ['daʊntaʊn] *Am* **1** *n (city centre)* centre-ville *m* **2** *adj* du centre-ville; **d. New York** le centre de New York **3** *adv* au centre-ville

downtrodden ['daʊntrɒdən] *adj* opprimé(e)

downturn ['daʊntɜːn] *n (in inflation)* baisse *f*; *(in economy)* ralentissement *m*

down under [daʊn'ʌndə(r)] *adv Br Fam (in Australia)* en Australie; *(in New Zealand)* en Nouvelle-Zélande

downward ['daʊnwəd] *adj* vers le bas; **a d. trend** une tendance à la baisse

downwards ['daʊnwədz] *adv* vers le bas

dowry ['daʊrɪ] *(pl* **dowries***) n* dot *f*

doze [dəʊz] **1** *n* somme *m*; **to have a d.** faire un somme **2** *vi* somnoler

▸**doze off** *vi* s'assoupir

dozen ['dʌzən] *n* douzaine *f*; **half a d./a d. eggs** une demi-douzaine/une douzaine d'œufs; *Fam* **dozens of times/people** des dizaines de fois/gens

dozy ['dəʊzɪ] *adj* (**a**) *(sleepy)* **to feel d.** avoir envie de dormir (**b**) *Fam (stupid)* abruti(e)

Dr *(abbr* **Doctor***)* Dr

drab [dræb] *adj (person, colour)* terne; *(atmosphere, city)* morne

drachma ['drækmə] *n* drachme *f*

draconian [drə'kəʊnɪən] *adj* draconien(enne)

draft[1] [drɑːft] **1** *n* (**a**) *(of letter)* brouillon *m*; *(of law, proposal)* avant-projet *m*; *(of novel)* jet *m* (**b**) *Fin* traite *f* (**c**) *Am (conscription)* conscription *f*; **d. dodger**

insoumis *m*

2 *vt* (**a**) *(letter)* faire le brouillon de; *(proposal)* rédiger; *(law, bill)* préparer (**b**) *(recruit)* **to d. sb in** détacher qn

draft² *Am* = **draught**

draftsman *Am* = **draughtsman**

drafty *Am* = **draughty**

drag [dræg] **1** *n* (**a**) *(air resistance)* traînée *f*; **d. racing** courses *fpl* de dragsters

(**b**) *Fam (person)* raseur(euse) *m,f*; *(task)* corvée *f*; **the party was a real d.** la soirée était vraiment rasante

(**c**) *Fam (on cigarette)* taffe *f*; **to take** *or* **have a d. on a cigarette** tirer une taffe sur une cigarette

(**d**) *Fam (women's clothing worn by man)* **to be in d.** être travesti; **d. artist** travesti *m*; **d. queen** travelo *m*

(**e**) *Am Fam (street)* **the main d.** la rue principale

2 *vt (pt & pp dragged)* (**a**) *(pull)* traîner; **to d. sb out of bed** tirer qn de son lit; *Fig* **to d. one's feet over doing sth** tarder à faire qch; *Fig* **to d. oneself away from sth** s'arracher à qch; **don't d. me into this!** ne me mêlez pas à vos histoires!; **to d. sb's name through the mud** traîner qn dans la boue

(**b**) *(pond, canal)* draguer

3 *vi (of film, day)* traîner en longueur; *(of conversation)* languir

▸**drag on** *vi (of meeting, film)* traîner en longueur, s'éterniser

▸**drag out** *vt sep (meeting, speech)* faire traîner

▸**drag up** *vt sep (refer to)* ressortir

drag-and-drop ['drægən'drɒp] *n Comput* glisser-lâcher *m*

dragnet ['drægnet] *n (in deep-sea fishing)* seine *f*, senne *f*; *Fig (to catch criminals)* rafle *f*

dragon ['drægən] *n also Fig* dragon *m*

dragonfly ['drægənflaɪ] *(pl dragonflies) n* libellule *f*

dragoon [drə'guːn] **1** *n (soldier)* dragon *m*

2 *vt* **to d. sb into doing sth** forcer qn à faire qch

drain [dreɪn] **1** *n* (**a**) *(for water, sewage)* égout *m*; *Fig* **to throw money down the d.** jeter l'argent par les fenêtres; **that's five years' work down the d.** voilà cinq années de travail perdues; **that's my holiday down the d.** ce sont mes vacances qui tombent à l'eau (**b**) *(on resources)* ponction *f* (**on** sur); *(on strength)* perte (**on** de)

2 *vt (liquid)* vider; *(vegetables)* égoutter; **to d. one's glass** finir son verre; *Fig* **to feel drained** être épuisé(e) *ou* vidé(e)

3 *vi (of liquid)* s'écouler; *(of dishes)* égoutter; *(of sink, washing machine)* se vider; *(of river)* se jeter; **the colour drained from her face** elle est devenue blême

▸**drain away** *vi (of liquid)* s'écouler; *Fig (of strength, enthusiasm)* s'épuiser; *(of fear, tension)* s'apaiser

drainage ['dreɪnɪdʒ] *n* drainage *m*

drainpipe ['dreɪnpaɪp] *n* tuyau *m* d'écoulement; **d. trousers, drainpipes** pantalon *m* cigarette

drake [dreɪk] *n* canard *m* (mâle)

dram [dræm] *n (of whisky)* goutte *f*

drama ['drɑːmə] *n* (**a**) *(art form)* théâtre *m*; *(play)* drame *m*; *Fig* **to make a d. out of sth** faire un drame de qch; **d. school** école *f* d'art dramatique (**b**) *(excitement)* action *f*

dramatic [drə'mætɪk] *adj* (**a**) *(work)* dramatique; *(actor)* de théâtre (**b**) *(significant)* spectaculaire (**c**) *(theatrical)* théâtral(e)

dramatically [drə'mætɪklɪ] *adv* (**a**) *(change, increase, drop)* de manière spectaculaire (**b**) *(theatrically) (act, speak)* de façon théâtrale

dramatist ['dræmətɪst] *n* auteur *m* dramatique, dramaturge *mf*

dramatize ['dræmətaɪz] *vt* (**a**) *(adapt) (for stage)* adapter pour la scène; *(for screen)* adapter pour l'écran (**b**) *(exaggerate)* dramatiser

drank [dræŋk] *pt of* **drink**

drape [dreɪp] **1** *npl Am* **drapes** *(curtains)* rideaux *mpl*

2 *vt (table, coffin)* draper (**with** de); **to d. sth over sth** draper qch sur qch

drastic ['dræstɪk] *adj (solution, change)* radical(e); *(improvement, decline)* spectaculaire; *(action)* énergique; *(shortage, difficulty)* dramatique

drat [dræt] *exclam Fam* **d. (it)!** nom de nom!

draught, *Am* **draft** [drɑːft] *n* (**a**) *(wind)* courant *m* d'air; **d. excluder** bourrelet *m* (**b**) *(of drink)* gorgée *f*; *(of air)* bouffée *f* (**c**) **on d.** *(beer)* à la pression; **d. beer** bière *f* pression

draughtboard ['drɑːftbɔːd] *n Br* damier *m*

draughts ['drɑːfts] *n Br (game)* (jeu *m* de) dames *fpl*

draughtsman, *Am* **draftsman** ['drɑːftsmən] *n* dessinateur(trice) *m,f*

draughty, *Am* **drafty** ['drɑːftɪ] *adj* plein(e) de courants d'air

draw [drɔː] **1** *n* (**a**) *(in match, argument)* match *m* nul

(**b**) *(lottery)* loterie *f*, tombola *f*; *(for sporting competition)* tirage *m* au sort

(**c**) *(attraction)* attraction *f*

2 *vt (pt* **drew** [druː]*, pp* **drawn** [drɔːn] *)* (**a**) *(picture, diagram, map)* dessiner; *(circle, line)* tracer; **to d. sb's picture** faire le portrait de qn

(**b**) *(pull) (cart)* tirer; *(person)* attirer (**towards** vers); **to d. the curtains** *(open or shut)* tirer les rideaux; **to d. breath** souffler

(**c**) *(extract)* retirer; *(pistol, sword)* dégainer; *(water, wine)* tirer; *Fig (strength, comfort)* retirer, puiser (**from** de); **to d. a knife on sb** menacer qn d'un couteau; **to d. a salary** toucher un salaire; **to d. blood** *(of dog)* mordre jusqu'au sang; *(of cat)* griffer jusqu'au sang; **to d. lots for sth** tirer qch au sort; **to d. a conclusion from sth** tirer une conclusion de qch; **she refused to be drawn on the issue** elle refusa de se laisser entraîner sur ce sujet; **they were drawn against the champions** *(in competition)* le tirage au sort a décidé qu'ils joueraient contre les champions

(**d**) *(attract)* attirer; **to d. a crowd** *(of incident)* créer un attroupement; *(of play)* attirer le public; **to feel drawn to sb/sth** se sentir attiré(e) par qn/qch; *Fig* **to d. sb's fire** s'attirer les foudres de qn

3 *vi* (**a**) *(make picture)* dessiner

(**b**) *(in game)* faire match nul (**with** avec)

(**c**) *(move)* **to d. ahead of sb** devancer qn; **to d. level with sb** rattraper qn; **to d. to an end** *or* **a close** tirer *ou* toucher à sa fin; **to d. near** (s')approcher; **to d. to a halt** s'arrêter

▸**draw back 1** *vt sep (sheet, veil)* retirer

2 *vi* reculer; **to d. back from doing sth** hésiter à faire qch

▸**draw in** *vi (of night)* raccourcir

▸**draw on 1** *vt insep (resources, savings)* tirer sur; *(experience)* se servir de

2 *vi (of evening)* approcher

▸**draw out** *vt sep* (**a**) *(encourage to talk)* faire parler (**b**) *(prolong)* faire durer

▶**draw up 1** *vt sep* (**a**) *(chair)* approcher; **she drew herself up to her full height** elle s'est dressée de toute sa hauteur (**b**) *(plan, document)* dresser; *(will)* rédiger **2** *vi (of vehicle)* s'arrêter

drawback ['drɔːbæk] *n* inconvénient *m*

drawbridge ['drɔːbrɪdʒ] *n* pont-levis *m*

drawer [drɔː(r)] *n* tiroir *m*

drawers [drɔːəz] *npl Old-fashioned (for women)* culotte *f*; *(for men)* caleçon *m*

drawing ['drɔːɪŋ] *n* dessin *m*; **d. board** planche *f* à dessin; *Fig* **it's back to the d. board!** retour à la case départ!; **d. paper** papier *m* à dessin; **d. pin** punaise *f*; **d. room** salon *m*

drawl [drɔːl] **1** *n* voix *f* traînante **2** *vi* parler d'une voix traînante

drawn [drɔːn] **1** *adj (face)* blême; *(features)* tiré(e); **to look d.** avoir les traits tirés **2** *pp of* **draw**

drawstring ['drɔːstrɪŋ] *n* cordon *m*

dread [dred] **1** *n* terreur *f*; **to have a d. of sth** avoir la hantise de qch **2** *vt* **to d. sth/doing sth** appréhender *ou* redouter qch/de faire qch; **I d. to think!** je n'ose pas imaginer!

dreaded ['dredɪd] *adj* redouté(e)

dreadful ['dredfʊl] *adj* (**a**) *(terrible)* épouvantable, affreux(euse); **to feel d.** se sentir vraiment mal; **I feel really d. about it!** quand j'y pense, je suis horriblement gêné! (**b**) *Fam (for emphasis)* terrible; **it's a d. bore/shame!** c'est vraiment rasant/dommage!

dreadfully ['dredfʊlɪ] *adv* (**a**) *(very badly)* affreusement (**b**) *Fam (extremely)* terriblement, horriblement

dreadlocks ['dredlɒks] *npl* petites nattes *fpl (des rastas)*

dream [driːm] **1** *n* rêve *m*; **to have a d. (about)** rêver (de); **to have a bad d.** faire un mauvais rêve; **a d. come true** un rêve devenu réalité; **it worked like a d.** ça a marché à merveille **2** *adj* de rêve; **my d. house** la maison de mes rêves; **d. world** monde *m* imaginaire; *Fig* **to live in a d. world** vivre en pleine utopie **3** *vt (pt & pp* dreamt [dremt] *or* dreamed) **to d. that...** rêver que...; *Fig* **I never dreamt you would take me seriously** je n'aurais jamais pensé que tu me prendrais au sérieux **4** *vi* rêver (**of** *or* **about** de); *Fam* **I wouldn't d. of it!** je n'y songerais même pas!

dream up *vt sep (scheme, excuse)* imaginer, inventer

dreamer ['driːmə(r)] *n* rêveur(euse) *m,f*

dreamt [dremt] *pt & pp of* **dream**

dreamy ['driːmɪ] *adj* rêveur(euse)

dreary ['drɪərɪ] *adj* morne

dredge [dredʒ] *vt (canal, harbour)* draguer; *Fig* **to d. one's memory** fouiller dans ses souvenirs

▸**dredge up** *vt sep (body, object)* repêcher; *Fig (scandal, memory)* déterrer

dredger ['dredʒə(r)] *n (boat)* dragueur *m*

dregs [dregz] *npl (of wine)* lie *f*; *(of coffee)* marc *m*; *(in cup)* fond *m* de tasse; *Fig* **the d. of society** les bas-fonds *mpl* de la société

drench [drentʃ] *vt* tremper (**with** *or* **in** de); **drenched to the skin** trempé(e) jusqu'aux os

dress [dres] **1** *n* (**a**) *(for woman)* robe *f* (**b**) *(clothing)* tenue *f*; **to have good d. sense/no d. sense** savoir/ne pas savoir s'habiller; **d. circle** premier balcon *m*; **d. rehearsal** (répétition *f*) générale *f*; **d. shirt** chemise *f* de soirée

2 *vt* (**a**) *(person)* habiller, vêtir; **to d. oneself, to get dressed** s'habiller; **to be dressed in black/in rags** être vêtu(e) de noir/de haillons; **well/badly dressed** bien/mal habillé(e) (**b**) *(wound)* panser (**c**) *(salad)* assaisonner; **dressed crab** chair *f* de crabe **3** *vi* s'habiller

▶**dress up** *vi (elegantly)* se faire beau (belle), s'habiller; *(in fancy dress)* se déguiser (**as** en)

dresser ['dresə(r)] *n* (**a**) *(in kitchen)* vaisselier *m* (**b**) *Am (dressing table)* coiffeuse *f* (**c**) *Theat (person)* habilleur(euse) *m,f*

dressing ['dresɪŋ] *n* (**a**) **d. gown** robe *f* de chambre; **d. room** *(in theatre)* loge *f*; *(in gym, sports centre)* vestiaire *m*; *(in home)* cabinet *m* de toilette; **d. table** coiffeuse *f* (**b**) *(for wound)* pansement *m* (**c**) *(for salad)* assaisonnement *m*

dressing down ['dresɪŋ'daʊn] *n Fam* savon *m*; **to give sb a d.** passer un savon à qn

dressmaker ['dresmeɪkə(r)] *n* couturière *f*

dressmaking ['dresmeɪkɪŋ] *n* couture *f*

dressy ['dresɪ] *adj (clothes, party)* habillé(e), élégant(e)

drew [druː] *pt of* **draw**

drib [drɪb] *n* **in dribs and drabs** au compte-gouttes

dribble ['drɪbəl] **1** *n* (*saliva)* bave *f*; *(of blood, oil)* filet *m* **2** *vi* (**a**) *(of person)* baver (**b**) *(of liquid)* dégouliner; *Fig* **to d. in/out** *(of people)* entrer/sortir au compte-gouttes (**c**) *(of footballer)* dribbler

drier ['draɪə(r)] *n (for clothes)* séchoir *m*; *(for hair)* (*on stand)* casque *m*; *(hand-held)* sèche-cheveux *m inv*

drift [drɪft] **1** *n* (**a**) *(of current)* direction *f*, sens *m*; *(of events)* cours *m*; **the d. towards home ownership** la tendance actuelle à l'accession à la propriété; **the d. from the land** l'exode *f* rurale; **d. net** *(for fishing)* filet *m* dérivant (**b**) *(meaning)* sens *m* général; *Fam* **I get the d.** j'ai compris (**c**) *(of snow)* congère *f*; *(of leaves)* amoncellement *m*; *(of fog, mist)* traînée *f* **2** *vi* (**a**) *(of boat)* dériver, aller à la dérive; *(of smoke)* flotter; *(of events)* tendre (**towards** vers); *(of person)* se laisser porter par les événements; **people drifted in and out** les gens entraient et sortaient nonchalamment; **to d. apart** *(of friends)* se perdre de vue; *(of couple)* devenir des étrangers l'un pour l'autre; **to d. into crime** sombrer peu à peu dans la délinquance (**b**) *(of sand, snow)* s'amonceler, s'entasser

drifter ['drɪftə(r)] *n (person)* **she's a bit of a d.** elle n'a pas vraiment de but dans la vie

driftwood ['drɪftwʊd] *n (in sea)* bois *m* flottant *ou* flotté; *(on shore)* bois rejeté par la mer

drill [drɪl] **1** *n* (**a**) *(tool)* foret *m*, mèche *f*; *(electric)* perceuse *f*; *(of dentist)* fraise *f*, roulette *f*; *(pneumatic)* marteau *m* piqueur; **d. bit** foret (**b**) *(training)* exercice *m* **2** *vt* (**a**) *(well)* forer; *(hole)* percer (**b**) *(train) (soldiers)* entraîner; *Fam* **to d. sth into sb** enfoncer qch dans la tête de qn **3** *vi* (**a**) *(for oil)* forer (**for** pour trouver); *(in wall, rock)* percer (**into** dans) (**b**) *(of troops)* faire l'exercice

drink [drɪŋk] **1** *n* boisson *f*; **to have a d.** prendre un verre, boire quelque chose; **to go for a d.** aller prendre un verre; **to pay for the drinks** payer les consommations; *Fam* **the d.** *(sea)* la baille; **to take to d.** se mettre à boire; **to have a d. problem** (trop) boire;

drinks machine distributeur *m* automatique de boissons

2 *vt* (*pt* **drank** [dræŋk], *pp* **drunk** [drʌŋk]) boire; **she drank us all under the table** nous avions tous roulé sous la table depuis longtemps qu'elle était encore debout

3 *vi* boire; **to d. like a fish** boire comme un trou; **to d. to sb** *or* **to sb's health** boire à la santé de qn; *Fig* **to d. to sth** arroser qch; **to d. in the atmosphere** se pénétrer de l'atmosphère

▸**drink up 1** *vt sep* finir (de boire)

2 *vi* vider son verre

drinkable ['drɪŋkəbəl] *adj* (*water*) potable; (*wine, beer*) buvable

drink-driving ['drɪŋk'draɪvɪŋ] *n* conduite *f* en état d'ivresse

drinker ['drɪŋkə(r)] *n* buveur(euse) *m,f*; **to be a heavy d.** boire beaucoup

drinking ['drɪŋkɪŋ] *n* **d. is bad for you** l'alcool est mauvais pour la santé; **d. chocolate** chocolat *m* en poudre; **d. fountain** fontaine *f* publique; **d. straw** paille *f*; **d. water** eau *f* potable

drip [drɪp] **1** *n* (**a**) (*drop*) goutte *f*; (*sound*) bruit *m* de l'eau qui goutte (**b**) (*in hospital*) goutte-à-goutte *m inv*; **to be on a d.** être sous perfusion (**c**) *Fam Pej* (*weak person*) mou (molle) *m,f*

2 *vt* (*pt & pp* **dripped**) laisser tomber goutte à goutte; **you're dripping water everywhere!** tu mets de l'eau partout!; **to be dripping with sweat/blood** ruisseler de sueur/sang; *Fig* **to be dripping with jewels** être couvert(e) de bijoux

3 *vi* (*of liquid*) tomber goutte à goutte, goutter; (*of tap*) fuire

drip-dry ['drɪp'draɪ] *adj* (*shirt, fabric*) ne nécessitant aucun repassage

dripping ['drɪpɪŋ] **1** *n* graisse *f* de rôti

2 *adj* (*tap*) qui fuit

3 *adv* **d. wet** trempé(e)

drive [draɪv] **1** *n* (**a**) (*trip*) promenade *f* en voiture; **it's an hour's d. away** c'est à une heure en voiture; **to go for** *or* **take a d.** aller faire une promenade en voiture (**b**) (*of car*) **left-hand d.** conduite *f* à gauche; **four-wheel d.** (*car*) quatre-quatre *m inv*; (*system*) propulsion *f* à quatre roues motrices; **front-wheel d.** (*car, system*) traction *f* avant; **rear-wheel d.** (*car, system*) traction *f* arrière

(**c**) *Comput* lecteur *m*, unité *f*

(**d**) (*in golf, tennis*) drive *m*

(**e**) (*initiative*) énergie *f*, dynamisme *m*

(**f**) (*of house*) allée *f*

(**g**) (*campaign*) **sales/membership d.** campagne *f* pour attirer les acheteurs/de nouveaux membres

2 *vt* (*pt* **drove** [drəʊv], *pp* **driven** ['drɪvən]) (**a**) (*car, train*) conduire; **to d. sb somewhere** conduire qn en voiture quelque part; **could you d. me home?** pourriez-vous me reconduire chez moi?

(**b**) (*direct, guide*) (*cattle*) mener, conduire; (*people*) chasser

(**c**) (*push*) **to d. sb to sth/to do sth** pousser qn à qch/à faire qch; **to d. sb mad** rendre qn fou (folle); **to d. oneself too hard** trop exiger de soi-même; **to d. a hard bargain** ne pas faire de cadeau; **to d. prices up/down** faire monter/baisser les prix

(**d**) (*machine*) actionner, faire marcher; **to be driven by electricity** marcher à l'électricité

3 *vi* (*in car*) conduire; **can you d.?** savez-vous con-

duire?; **I don't d.** je n'ai pas mon permis; **to d. to work** aller au travail en voiture

▸**drive at** *vt insep* **what are you driving at?** où voulez-vous en venir?

▸**drive away 1** *vt sep* (**a**) (*in car*) emmener en voiture (**b**) (*force to leave*) chasser

2 *vi* (*in car*) s'en aller en voiture

▸**drive off 1** *vt sep* (*repel*) (*attackers*) chasser

2 *vi* (*in car*) s'en aller en voiture

▸**drive on** *vi* (*in car*) continuer (sa route)

drive-in ['draɪvɪn] *n* (*cinema*) drive-in *m*, *Can* ciné-parc *m*; (*restaurant*) = restaurant où on est servi dans sa voiture

drivel ['drɪvəl] *n Fam* bêtises *fpl*, balivernes *fpl*; **to talk (a load of) d.** dire n'importe quoi

driven ['drɪvən] *pp of* **drive**

driver ['draɪvə(r)] *n* (**a**) (*of car, bus*) conducteur(trice) *m,f*; (*of lorry, taxi*) chauffeur(euse) *m,f*; (*of train*) mécanicien(enne) *m,f*; *Am* **d.'s license** permis *m* de conduire (**b**) (*golf club*) driver *m*

driveway ['draɪvweɪ] *n* allée *f*

driving ['draɪvɪŋ] **1** *n* (*in car*) conduite *f*; *Fig* **to be in the d. seat** être aux commandes; **d. instructor** moniteur(trice) *m,f* d'auto-école; **d. lessons** leçons *fpl* de conduite; *Br* **d. licence** permis *m* de conduire; **d. school** auto-école *f*; **d. test** (examen *m* du) permis de conduire

2 *adj* (*rain*) battant(e); *Fig* **d. force** moteur *m*

drizzle ['drɪzəl] **1** *n* crachin *m*

2 *vi* bruiner

droll [drəʊl] *adj* drôle, comique; *Ironic* **oh, very d.!** très drôle!

dromedary ['drɒmədəri] (*pl* **dromedaries**) *n* dromadaire *m*

drone [drəʊn] **1** *n* (**a**) (*bee*) faux-bourdon *m* (**b**) (*of conversation, traffic, plane*) bourdonnement *m*

2 *vi* (**a**) (*of bee*) bourdonner (**b**) (*of person*) parler d'un ton monotone

▸**drone on** *vi* parler ad nauseam (*d'une voix monotone*) (**about** de)

drool [druːl] *vi* (*dribble*) baver; *Fig* **to d. over sb/sth** baver d'admiration devant qn/qch; *Fig* **she was drooling at the idea** elle en salivait d'avance

droop [druːp] *vi* (*of head*) pencher; (*of shoulders*) tomber; (*of flower*) pencher la tête; *Fig* (*of person*) perdre ses forces

drop [drɒp] **1** *n* (**a**) (*of liquid*) goutte *f*; **drops** (*for eyes, nose*) gouttes; **you've had a d. too much** (*to drink*) tu as bu un coup de trop; *Fig* **it's only a d. in the ocean** ce n'est qu'une goutte d'eau dans l'océan

(**b**) (*fall*) (*in prices, numbers*) chute *f*, baisse *f* (**in** de); (*by parachute*) parachutage *m*; **a d. of 10 metres** un à-pic *ou* escarpement de 10 mètres; *Fig* **at the d. of a hat** sans la moindre hésitation

2 *vt* (*pt & pp* **dropped**) (**a**) (*allow to fall*) laisser tomber; (*bomb*) lâcher; **to d. sb a line/a card** envoyer *ou* écrire un mot/une carte à qn; **I'll d. you at the station** (*in car*) je te déposerai à la gare

(**b**) (*lower*) (*prices, one's eyes*) baisser

(**c**) (*abandon*) (*subject, idea, plan*) abandonner; **to d. sb** (*as friend*) laisser tomber qn; (*from team*) écarter qn; **to d. maths/French** (*of student*) arrêter les maths/le français; *Law* **to d. the charges** abandonner les poursuites

(**d**) (*omit*) (*letter, syllable*) omettre, supprimer; (*when speaking*) ne pas prononcer (**e**) *(lose) (points)* perdre

3 *vi* (**a**) *(of object)* tomber; *(of ground)* s'affaisser; **he dropped to sixth place** il est descendu à la sixième place; *Fam* **I'm ready to d.** *(with fatigue)* je tombe de fatigue; *Fam* **people are dropping like flies** les gens tombent comme des mouches; **to d. dead** tomber raide mort(e); *Fam* **d. dead!** va te faire voir!; *Fam* **let it d.!** laisse tomber!

(**b**) *(of prices, temperature, voice)* baisser; *(of wind)* tomber; *(of speed)* diminuer

▶**drop by** *vi (visit)* passer

▶**drop in** *vi* passer (**on sb** chez qn)

▶**drop off 1** *vt sep (person from car)* déposer

2 *vi* (**a**) **to d. off (to sleep)** s'assoupir, s'endormir (**b**) *(of membership, attendance)* diminuer

▶**drop out** *vi* (**a**) *(of object) (from pocket, bag)* tomber (**b**) *(of person) (from contest)* se retirer; *(from society)* devenir un(e) marginal(e); *(from university)* abandonner ses études

▶**drop round 1** *vt sep (deliver)* déposer

2 *vi (visit)* passer

droplet ['droplɪt] *n* gouttelette *f*

dropout ['drɒpaʊt] *n Fam (from society)* marginal(e) *m,f; (from university)* étudiant(e) *m,f* qui abandonne ses études

dropper ['drɒpə(r)] *n (for medicine)* compte-gouttes *m inv*

droppings ['drɒpɪŋz] *npl (of birds)* fiente *f; (of animals)* crottes *fpl*

dross [drɒs] *n Fam (rubbish)* rebut *m;* **I've never heard such d. in all my life** j'ai rarement entendu de telles bêtises

drought [draʊt] *n* sécheresse *f*

drove [drəʊv] **1** *n* **to arrive in droves** arriver en foule

2 *pt of* **drive**

drown [draʊn] **1** *vt* (**a**) *(in water)* noyer; **to d. oneself** se noyer; **to d. one's sorrows** noyer son chagrin dans l'alcool (**b**) *(sound)* couvrir

2 *vi (die)* se noyer

▶**drown out** *vt sep (sound)* couvrir; *(person)* couvrir la voix de

drowse [draʊz] *vi* somnoler

drowsiness ['draʊzɪnɪs] *n* somnolence *f*

drowsy ['draʊzɪ] *adj* **to be** *or* **feel d.** avoir envie de dormir

drudge [drʌdʒ] *n (man)* homme *m* de peine; *(woman)* bonne *f* à tout faire

drudgery ['drʌdʒərɪ] *n* travail *m* pénible *ou* ingrat

drug [drʌg] **1** *n (medicine)* médicament *m; (narcotic)* drogue *f;* **hard/soft drugs** drogues dures/douces; **to take drugs** se droguer; **d. abuse** usage *m* de stupéfiants; **d. addict** drogué(e) *m,f;* **d. dealer** *(large-scale)* trafiquant *m* de drogue; *(small-scale)* petit trafiquant de drogue, dealer *m;* **d. squad** brigade *f* des stupéfiants

2 *vt (pt & pp* **drugged***)* droguer

druggist ['drʌgɪst] *n Am* pharmacien(enne) *m,f*

drugstore ['drʌgstɔː(r)] *n Am* drugstore *m*

druid ['druːɪd] *n* druide *m*

drum [drʌm] **1** *n* (**a**) *(musical instrument)* tambour *m;* **d. kit, drums** batterie *f* (**b**) *(container)* fût *m; (for oil)* bidon *m*

2 *vt (pt & pp* **drummed***)* **to d. one's fingers** tambouriner de ses doigts; **to d. sth into sb** enfoncer qch dans la tête de qn

3 *vi (play drums)* jouer de la batterie; **the rain was drumming on the window panes** la pluie tambourinait contre les vitres

▶**drum up** *vt (support, enthusiasm)* chercher à susciter

drummer ['drʌmə(r)] *n (in pop band)* batteur(euse) *m,f; (in military band)* tambour *m*

drumstick ['drʌmstɪk] *n* (**a**) *(for playing drums)* baguette *f* de tambour (**b**) *(chicken leg)* pilon *m*

drunk [drʌŋk] **1** *n (man)* homme *m* soûl; *(woman)* femme *f* soûle; *(habitual)* ivrogne *mf*

2 *adj* ivre, soûl(e); **to get d.** se soûler; *Law* **d. and disorderly** = en état d'ivresse sur la voie publique; *Fig* **d. with joy/power** ivre de joie/puissance

3 *pp of* **drink**

drunkard ['drʌŋkəd] *n* ivrogne *mf*

drunken ['drʌŋkən] *adj (person)* ivre; *(party)* bien arrosé(e); **in a d. stupor** hébété(e) par l'alcool; **d. brawl** querelle *f* d'ivrognes

dry [draɪ] **1** *adj* (**a**) *(weather, clothing, skin, hair, wine)* sec (sèche); *(day)* sans pluie; **to run** *or* **go d.** *(of river)* s'assécher; *(of spring)* (se) tarir, s'épuiser; **d. as a bone** complètement sec; *Naut* **d. dock** cale *f* sèche; **d. ice** neige *f* carbonique; **d. land** terre *f* ferme; **d. rot** pourriture *f* sèche; **d. run** coup *m* d'essai, test *m* (**b**) *(boring) (style, person)* ennuyeux(euse) (**c**) *(humour)* pince-sans-rire *inv*

2 *vt (pt & pp* **dried***)* sécher; *(clothes)* faire sécher; *(skin)* dessécher; *(dishes)* essuyer; **to d. oneself** se sécher; **to d. one's hair** se sécher les cheveux

3 *vi* sécher

▶**dry out** *vi* (**a**) *(of alcoholic)* se faire désintoxiquer (**b**) *(of wood, ground)* sécher; *(of skin)* se dessécher

▶**dry up** *vi* (**a**) *(of well, pool)* se dessécher, tarir (**b**) *(of funds, conversation)* tarir; *(of inspiration)* se tarir (**c**) *(forget one's lines)* oublier son texte; *(have nothing more to say)* ne plus rien avoir à dire

dry-clean ['draɪ'kliːn] *vt* nettoyer à sec

dry-cleaner's ['draɪ'kliːnəz] *n* teinturerie *f,* pressing *m*

dry-cleaning [draɪ'kliːnɪŋ] *n* (**a**) *(process)* nettoyage *m* à sec (**b**) *(clothes)* vêtements *mpl* laissés chez le teinturier

dryer = **drier**

DSS [diːe'ses] *n Br (abbr* **Department of Social Security***)* ≃ Sécurité *f* sociale

DTI [diːtiː'aɪ] *n Br (abbr* **Department of Trade and Industry***)* ≃ ministère *m* du Commerce et de l'Industrie

DTP [diːtiː'piː] *n Comput (abbr* **desktop publishing***)* PAO *f*

DTs [diː'tiːz] *npl (abbr* **delirium tremens***)* **the D.** le delirium tremens

dual ['djuːəl] *adj* double; **d. carriageway** *(road)* route *f* à deux chaussées; **d. nationality** double nationalité *f;* **d. ownership** copropriété *f*

dual-purpose ['djuːəl'pɜːpəs] *adj* à double emploi

dub [dʌb] *(pt & pp* **dubbed***) vt* (**a**) *(film)* doubler (**into** en) (**b**) *(nickname)* surnommer

dubbing ['dʌbɪŋ] *n (of film)* doublage *m*

dubious ['djuːbɪəs] *adj* (**a**) *(uncertain)* incertain(e); **to be d. (about)** avoir quelques doutes (au sujet de) (**b**) *(questionable)* douteux(euse)

Dublin ['dʌblɪn] *n* Dublin

Dubliner ['dʌblɪnə(r)] *n* Dublinois(e) *m,f*

duchess ['dʌtʃɪs] *n* duchesse *f*

duchy ['dʌtʃɪ] *(pl* **duchies***) n* duché *m*

duck [dʌk] **1** *n* canard *m*; *(female)* cane *f*; **to take to sth like a d. to water** faire qch comme si on l'avait fait toute sa vie; **criticism runs off him like water off a d.'s back** les critiques glissent sur lui; **d. pond** mare *f* aux canards

2 *vt* (**a**) *(head)* baisser subitement; **to d. sb** *(under water)* faire faire le plongeon à qn (**b**) *(avoid) (obligations)* se dérober à; **to d. the issue/question** se dérober

3 *vi (lower head)* baisser la tête, se baisser; *(under water)* plonger sous l'eau; **to d. behind a tree** se cacher derrière un arbre

▶**duck out of** *vt insep* **to d. out of doing sth** éviter de faire qch; **he ducked out of the meeting** il s'est débrouillé pour ne pas assister à la réunion

duck-billed platypus [ˈdʌkbɪldˈplætɪpəs] *n* ornithorynque *m*

duckling [ˈdʌklɪŋ] *n (male)* caneton *m*; *(female)* canette *f*

duct [dʌkt] *n* conduit *m*

dud [dʌd] *Fam* **1** *n (person)* incapable *mf*; *(shell)* obus *m* qui n'a pas éclaté; *(banknote)* faux *m*

2 *adj (shell)* qui n'a pas éclaté; *(banknote)* faux (fausse); *(cheque)* en bois

dude [duːd] *n Am* type *m*

due [djuː] **1** *n* (**a**) *(what is owed)* dû *m*; **to give her her d., she did apologize** pour lui rendre justice, il faut reconnaître qu'elle s'est excusée

(**b**) **dues** *(membership fees)* cotisation *f*

2 *adj* (**a**) *(owed)* dû (due); **to fall d.** échoir, arriver à échéance; **are you d. any money from her?** vous doit-elle de l'argent?; **you're d. an apology** je vous dois/il vous doit/*etc* une excuse; **d. to** par suite de, en raison de; **what is it d. to?** c'est dû à quoi?; *Fin* **d. date** échéance *f*

(**b**) *(merited, proper)* dû (due), mérité(e); **to give sb d. warning** avertir qn dans les formes; **after d. consideration** après mûre réflexion; **with all d. respect,...** avec tout le respect que je vous dois,...; **in d. course** *(when appropriate)* en temps voulu; *(eventually)* le moment venu

(**c**) *(expected)* **the train is d. (in** or **to arrive)** le train doit arriver d'un moment à l'autre; **when is he due (in** or **to arrive)?** quand doit-il arriver?; **when is the baby d.?** pour quand la naissance est-elle prévue?; **she's d. back any minute** elle doit revenir d'un moment à l'autre; **the film/book is d. out soon** le film/livre va sortir sous peu

3 *adv* **d. north/south** plein nord/sud

duel [ˈdjʊəl] **1** *n* duel *m*; **to fight a d.** se battre en duel

2 *vi (pt & pp* **duelled**, *Am* **dueled)** se battre en duel

duet [djuːˈet] *n* duo *m*; *(for piano)* morceau *m* à quatre mains

duff [dʌf] *adj Fam* nul (nulle)

▶**duff up** *vt sep Fam* rosser, tabasser

duffel = **duffle**

duffer [ˈdʌfə(r)] *n Br Fam* (**a**) *(incompetent person)* nul (nulle) *m,f* (**b**) *(old man)* vieux bonhomme *m*

duffle [ˈdʌfəl] *n* **d. (coat)** duffle-coat *m*; **d. bag** sac *m* (de) marin

dug [dʌg] *pt & pp of* **dig**

dugout [ˈdʌgaʊt] *n* (**a**) *(canoe)* pirogue *f* (**b**) *(shelter)* *Mil* tranchée-abri *f*; *Sport* banc *m* de touche

duke [djuːk] *n* duc *m*

dull [dʌl] **1** *adj* (**a**) *(boring)* ennuyeux(euse), terne; **as d. as ditchwater** ennuyeux comme la pluie (**b**) *(un-*

intelligent) lent(e) (**c**) *(not sharp) (pain, sound)* sourd(e); *(blade, senses)* émoussé(e) (**d**) *(not bright) (colour, surface)* terne; *(eyes)* sans éclat; *(weather, sky)* sombre, maussade

2 *vt* (**a**) *(pleasure)* rendre moins vif (vive); *(pain)* endormir, calmer; *(sound)* amortir, assourdir; *(blade, senses)* émousser (**b**) *(make less bright)* ternir

duly [ˈdjuːlɪ] *adv* (**a**) *(properly)* dûment (**b**) *(as expected)* comme prévu

dumb [dʌm] *adj* (**a**) *(unable to speak)* muet(ette); **to be struck d.** *(with astonishment)* en rester muet; **d. animal** bête *f*; **d. insolence** silence *m* insolent (**b**) *Fam (stupid)* bête; **d. blonde** blonde *f* évaporée

▶**dumb down** *vt sep (population, electorate)* infantiliser; *(media, programme)* faire baisser le niveau de

dumbbell [ˈdʌmbel] *n* haltère *m*

dumbfounded [dʌmˈfaʊndɪd] *adj* abasourdi(e), ébahi(e)

dumbing down [ˈdʌmɪŋˈdaʊn] *n (of population, electorate)* infantilisation *f*; *(of media, programme)* baisse *f* de niveau

dumbstruck [ˈdʌmstrʌk] = **dumbfounded**

dumbwaiter [ˈdʌmweɪtə(r)] *n (lift)* monte-plats *m inv*

dummy [ˈdʌmɪ] **1** *n (pl* **dummies)** (**a**) *(in shop window)* mannequin *m*; *(of ventriloquist)* marionnette *f*; *(model, fake)* objet *m* factice (**b**) *(for baby)* tétine *f* (**c**) *Fam (idiot)* abruti(e) *m,f*

2 *adj (fake)* factice; **d. run** coup *m* d'essai

dump [dʌmp] **1** *n* (**a**) *(for refuse)* décharge *f*; *Fam Pej (town)* bled *m* paumé; *(house)* dépotoir *m*; **d. truck** tombereau *m*, dumper *m* (**b**) *Mil (store)* dépôt *m* (**c**) *Comput* vidage *m*

2 *vt* (**a**) *(put down)* déposer (**b**) *(dispose of)* se débarrasser de; *(waste)* déverser; *Fam (boyfriend, girlfriend)* plaquer (**c**) *Comput (memory)* vider

dumper [ˈdʌmpə(r)] *n* **d. (truck)** tombereau *m*, dumper *m*

dumping [ˈdʌmpɪŋ] *n* (**a**) **no d.** *(sign)* décharge interdite; **d. ground** décharge *f*; *Fig* dépotoir *m* (**b**) *Econ* dumping *m*

dumpling [ˈdʌmplɪŋ] *n (in stew)* boulette *f* de pâte; *Scot* = sorte de plum-pudding écossais

dumps [dʌmps] *npl Fam* **to be down in the d.** broyer du noir, avoir le cafard

dumpy [ˈdʌmpɪ] *adj Fam (person, appearance)* boulot(otte)

dunce [dʌns] *n (at school)* âne *m*, cancre *m*; **d.'s cap** bonnet *m* d'âne

dune [djuːn] *n* dune *f*

dung [dʌŋ] *n (of cow)* bouse *f*; *(of horse)* crottin *m*; *(of wild animal)* fumées *fpl*

dungarees [dʌŋgəˈriːz] *npl* **(a pair of) d.** une salopette *f*; *(of workman)* un bleu de travail

dungeon [ˈdʌndʒən] *n (underground)* cachot *m*; *Hist (tower)* donjon *m*

dunghill [ˈdʌŋhɪl] *n* tas *m* de fumier

dunk [dʌŋk] *vt* tremper

Dunkirk [dʌnˈkɜːk] *n* Dunkerque *m*

duo [ˈdjuːəʊ] *n (pl* **duos)** *(in music)* duo *m*; *(two people)* couple *m*

duodenal [djuːəʊˈdiːnəl] *adj (ulcer)* duodénal(e)

dupe [djuːp] **1** *n* dupe *f*

2 *vt* duper, tromper; **to d. sb into doing sth** faire faire qch à qn en le dupant

duplicate ['dju:plıkət] **1** *n (of key)* double *m*; *(of letter, receipt)* double, duplicata *m*; **in d.** en double, en deux exemplaires
  2 *adj* **a d. key** un double de la clé; **a d. copy** un duplicata
  3 *vt* ['dju:plıkeıt] **(a)** *(copy)* faire un double/duplicata de; *(on photocopier)* faire une photocopie de **(b)** *(do again)* refaire
duplication [dju:plı'keıʃən] *n* **(a)** *(copying)* reproduction *f* **(b)** *(repetition)* répétition *f*
duplicity [dju:'plısıtı] *n* duplicité *f*
durability [djʊərə'bılıtı] *n (of material)* résistance *f*; *(of friendship)* durabilité *f*
durable ['djʊərəbəl] **1** *n* **(consumer) durables** biens *mpl* durables
  2 *adj (material)* résistant(e); *(friendship)* durable
duration [djʊ'reıʃən] *n* durée *f*; **for the d.** pour longtemps
duress [djʊ'res] *n* **under d.** sous la contrainte
during ['djʊərıŋ] *prep* pendant, durant; *(in the course of)* au cours de
dusk [dʌsk] *n* crépuscule *m*; **at d.** au crépuscule, à la tombée de la nuit
dust [dʌst] **1** *n* **(a)** *(dirt, powder)* poussière *f*; **d. cover** *(for furniture)* housse *f*; **d. cover** *or* **jacket** *(for book)* chemise *f*, jaquette *f* **(b)** *(action)* **to give sth a d.** passer un coup de chiffon sur qch **(c)** *(idioms)* **once the d. has settled** une fois que les choses se seront calmées; *Fam* **you won't see me for d.!** vous ne me reverrez pas de sitôt!
  2 *vt* **(a)** *(clean)* dépoussiérer, épousseter **(b)** *(sprinkle) (with flour, sugar)* saupoudrer (**with** de)
  3 *vi (clean)* épousseter
dust down, dust off *vt sep (furniture)* épousseter; *Fig (legislation)* dépoussiérer; *(one's French)* se remettre à
dustbin ['dʌstbın] *n* poubelle *f*
dustcart ['dʌstkɑ:t] *n* benne *f* à ordures
duster |'dʌstə(r)] *n (cloth)* chiffon *m* (à poussière); *(for blackboard)* brosse *f*
dustman ['dʌstmən] *n* éboueur *m*
dustpan ['dʌstpæn] *n* pelle *f* (à poussière)
dustsheet ['dʌstʃi:t] *n* housse *f*
dust-up ['dʌstʌp] *n Fam (brawl)* bagarre *f*; **to have a d. with sb** se bagarrer avec qn
dusty ['dʌstı] *adj* poussiéreux(euse), couvert(e) de poussière; **to get d.** se couvrir de poussière
Dutch [dʌtʃ] **1** *npl* **the D.** *(people)* les Hollandais *mpl*
  2 *n (language)* hollandais *m*
  3 *adj* hollandais(e); *Fam* **I need some D. courage** j'ai besoin d'un verre pour me donner du courage; **D. cap** *(contraceptive)* diaphragme *m*
  4 *adv Fam* **to go D.** payer chacun sa part
Dutchman ['dʌtʃmən] *n* Hollandais *m*, Néerlandais *m*; *Fam* **if that's a real diamond, (then) I'm a D.** si ça c'est un vrai diamant, alors je mange mon chapeau
Dutchwoman ['dʌtʃwʊmən] *n* Hollandaise *f*, Néerlandaise *f*
dutiful ['dju:tıfəl] *adj (obedient)* obéissant(e)
duty ['dju:tı] *(pl* **duties)** *n* **(a)** *(obligation)* devoir *m* (**to** envers); **to do one's d.** faire son devoir; **to fail in one's d.** manquer à son devoir; **to make it one's d. to...** se

faire un devoir de...; **it's your d. to...** il est de votre devoir de...
  (b) *(task)* **duties** fonctions *fpl*; **to take up** *or* **assume one's duties** entrer en fonctions; **to carry out** *or* **perform one's duties** exercer ses fonctions
  (c) *(of soldier, employee)* **to be on/off d.** être/ne pas être de service; **d. roster** tableau *m* de service
  (d) *Fin (tax)* droit *m*; **to pay d. on sth** payer une taxe sur qch
duty-free ['dju:tı'fri:] **1** *n* marchandises *fpl* hors taxe
  2 *adj (cigarettes, wine, perfume)* hors taxe; **d. shop** magasin *m* hors taxe
duvet ['du:veı] *n* couette *f*; **d. cover** housse *f* decouette
DVD [di:vi:'di:] *n Comput (abbr* **Digital Versatile Disk, Digital Video Disk)** DVD *m*, disque *m* vidéo numérique
dwarf [dwɔ:f] *(pl* **dwarfs** *or* **dwarves** [dwɔ:vz]) **1** *n & adj* nain(e) *m,f*
  2 *vt (be taller than)* écraser; *Fig (achievements, success)* éclipser
dwell [dwel] *(pt & pp* **dwelled** *or* **dwelt** [dwelt]) *vi Lit (live)* demeurer
▸**dwell on, dwell upon** *vt insep* remâcher, ressasser; **let's not d. on it** n'y pensons plus
dwelling ['dwelıŋ] *n Lit* **d. (place)** demeure *f*, résidence *f*; **d. house** maison *f* d'habitation
dwelt [dwelt] *pt & pp of* **dwell**
dwindle ['dwındəl] *vi* diminuer; **to d. (away) to nothing** se réduire à rien
dwindling ['dwındəlıŋ] *adj (funds, membership)* en baisse; *(enthusiasm)* faiblissant(e)
dye [daı] **1** *n (for clothes, hair)* teinture *f*
  2 *vt* teindre; **to d. sth black/red** teindre qch en noir/ rouge; **to d. one's hair** se teindre les cheveux
dyed-in-the-wool ['daıdınðə'wʊl] *adj (conservative, Englishman)* bon teint *inv*
dying ['daıŋ] **1** *npl* **the d.** les mourants *mpl*, les moribonds *mpl*
  2 *adj (person)* mourant(e), agonisant(e); *(industry, tradition)* moribond(e); **to my d. day** jusqu'à ma mort; **d. wish** dernières volontés *fpl*; **d. words** dernières paroles *fpl*
dyke [daık] *n* **(a)** *(barrier)* digue *f* **(b)** *very Fam (lesbian)* gouine *f*, = terme injurieux désignant une lesbienne
dynamic [daı'næmık] **1** *n (driving force)* dynamique *f*
  2 *adj also Fig* dynamique
dynamics [daı'næmıks] *npl* dynamique *f*
dynamism ['daınəmızəm] *n (of person, society)* dynamisme *m*
dynamite ['daınəmaıt] **1** *n also Fig* dynamite *f*; *Fam* **it's d.!** *(marvellous)* c'est du tonnerre!
  2 *vt* dynamiter
dynamo ['daınəməʊ] *(pl* **dynamos)** *n* dynamo *f*
dynastic [dı'næstık] *adj* dynastique
dynasty ['dınəstı] *(pl* **dynasties)** *n* dynastie *f*
dysentery ['dısəntrı] *n* dysenterie *f*
dysfunctional [dıs'fʌŋkʃənəl] *adj* **a d. family** une famille à problèmes
dyslexia [dıs'leksıə] *n* dyslexie *f*
dyslexic [dıs'leksık] *adj* dyslexique
dystrophy ['dıstrəfı] *n Med* dystrophie *f*

E

E, e [iː] *n* (**a**) *(letter)* E, e *m inv* (**b**) *Mus* mi *m* (**c**) *(abbr east)* E (**d**) *(abbr* **ecstasy**) X *f*, ecsta *f*

each [iːtʃ] **1** *adj* chaque; **e. one of us** chacun(e) de nous *ou* d'entre nous

2 *pron* (**a**) *(both, all)* chacun(e) *m,f*; **e. of us** chacun(e) de nous *ou* d'entre nous; **we e. earn £300** nous gagnons chacun 300 livres; **peaches at 25 pence e.** pêches à 25 pence chacune *ou* 25 pence pièce; **a little of e.** un peu de chaque (**b**) *(reciprocal)* **e. other** *(two)* l'un l'autre (l'une l'autre); *(more than two)* les uns les autres (les unes les autres); **separated from e. other** séparé l'un de l'autre; **they hate e. other** ils se haïssent; **we write to e. other** nous nous écrivons

eager ['iːgə(r)] *adj (look, voice)* avide; *(supporter)* fervent(e); *(desire, hope)* ardent(e), vif (vive); **to be e. for sth/to do sth** désirer vivement qch/faire qch; **to be e. to please** être désireux(euse) de plaire; *Fam* **to be an e. beaver** être zélé(e)

eagerly ['iːgəlɪ] *adv (listen)* avidement; *(work, talk)* avec enthousiasme; **e. awaited** attendu(e) avec impatience

eagerness ['iːgənɪs] *n* impatience *f*; *(to learn, please)* vif désir *m*; **to show e. in doing sth** montrer un intérêt très vif à faire qch

eagle ['iːgəl] *n* aigle *m*

eagle-eyed [iːgə'laɪd] *adj* aux yeux d'aigle

ear ['ɪə(r)] *n* (**a**) *(part of body)* oreille *f*; **to have an e. for music** avoir l'oreille musicale; **to have an e. for languages** avoir une bonne oreille pour les langues; *Med* **e., nose and throat specialist** oto-rhino(-laryngologiste) *mf*; **e. lobe** lobe *m* de l'oreille

(**b**) *(of wheat)* épi *m*

(**c**) *(idioms)* **to play it by e.** *(improvise)* improviser; **to have sb's e.** avoir l'oreille de qn; **to keep one's e. to the ground** rester sur le qui-vive; **to go in one e. and out the other** *(of words, information)* entrer par une oreille et sortir par l'autre; *Fam* **to be up to one's ears in debt** être endetté(e) jusqu'au cou; *Fam* **to be up to one's ears in work** être accablé(e) de travail; *Fam* **to be thrown out on one's e.** se faire jeter dehors *ou* sur le pavé; **I'm all ears** je suis tout ouïe; **my ears were burning** j'avais les oreilles qui sifflaient; **the house was falling down around their ears** la maison s'écroulait tout autour d'eux

earache ['ɪəreɪk] *n* mal *m* d'oreille(s); **to have e.** avoir mal à l'oreille/aux oreilles

eardrum ['ɪədrʌm] *n* tympan *m*

earful ['ɪəfʊl] *n Fam* **to give sb an e.** passer un savon à qn; **to get an e.** se faire passer un savon

earl [ɜːl] *n* comte *m*

earlier ['ɜːlɪə(r)] **1** *adj (previous)* plus ancien(enne); **I caught an e. train** j'ai pris un train qui partait plus tôt; **her e. novels** ses romans précédents

2 *adv* **e. (on)** avant; **a few days e.** quelques jours plus tôt; **no e. than tomorrow** pas avant demain; **as we saw e.** comme nous l'avons vu auparavant

earliest ['ɜːlɪəst] **1** *n* **at the e.** au plus tôt; **the e. I can be there is four o'clock** je pourrai être là à quatre heures au plus tôt

2 *adj (opportunity, memory)* premier(ère); **from the e. times** depuis les temps les plus reculés; **at the e. possible moment** le plus tôt possible, dans les plus brefs délais

early ['ɜːlɪ] **1** *adj* (**a**) *(in the day)* matinal(e); **to have an e. night** se coucher tôt; **to have an e. breakfast** déjeuner de bonne heure; **to be an e. riser** être matinal, se lever de bon matin; *Prov* **the e. bird catches the worm** l'avenir appartient à ceux qui se lèvent tôt

(**b**) *(at beginning of period of time)* **in (the) e. summer** au début de l'été; **at an e. age** tout jeune; **he's in his e. thirties** il a la trentaine; **in the e. 1980s** au début des années 80; **an e. example of...** un des premiers exemples de...

(**c**) *(ahead of time)* en avance; **half an hour e.** en avance d'une demi-heure

(**d**) *(premature) (death)* prématuré(e); **e. retirement** préretraite *f*; *Mil* **e. warning system** système *m* radar de préalerte

(**e**) *(in future)* **at an e. date** prochainement

2 *adv* (**a**) *(in the day)* de bonne heure, tôt; **e. in the morning** le matin de bonne heure; **e. in the evening** tôt dans la soirée; **as e. as possible** le plus tôt possible

(**b**) *(at beginning of period of time)* **e. in the year** au début de l'année; **e. on** dès l'abord; **e. in one's life** dans sa jeunesse; **e. in one's career** au début de sa carrière

(**c**) *(ahead of time)* en avance; **too e.** trop tôt

(**d**) *(prematurely) (die)* prématurément; **to retire e.** prendre une retraite anticipée

earmark ['ɪəmɑːk] *vt (funds)* assigner, affecter (**for** à); **the building is earmarked for closure** il est prévu que ce bâtiment soit fermé

earn [ɜːn] *vt (money)* gagner; *(rest, respect)* mériter; **to e. sb's love** gagner le cœur de qn; **to e. sb's praise** valoir des éloges à qn; **to e. one's living** gagner sa vie

earner ['ɜːnə(r)] *n* (**wage**) **e.** salarié(e) *m,f*; **to be a big/small e.** gagner beaucoup/peu; *Br Fam* **a nice little e.** une bonne petite affaire

earnest ['ɜːnɪst] **1** *n* **in e.** sérieusement; **things have started in e.** les choses ont vraiment commencé

2 *adj (person, effort, discussion)* sérieux(euse);

(expression) pénétré(e), grave; *(voice)* pressant(e); *(desire)* profond(e)

earnestly [ˈɜːnɪstlɪ] *adv* sérieusement; *(desire)* profondément; *(hope, believe)* sincèrement

earning power [ˈɜːnɪŋˈpaʊə(r)] *n* revenu *m* potentiel

earnings [ˈɜːnɪŋz] *npl (of person)* salaire *m*; *(of company)* bénéfices *mpl*; **e. related** *(pensions, benefits)* proportionnel(elle) au salaire

earphones [ˈɪəfəʊnz] *npl* écouteurs *mpl*

earpiece [ˈɪəpiːs] *n (of telephone)* écouteur *m*

earplug [ˈɪəplʌg] *n* boule *f* Quiès®

earring [ˈɪərɪŋ] *n* boucle *f* d'oreille

earshot [ˈɪəʃɒt] *n* **within/out of e.** à portée/hors de portée de voix

ear-splitting [ˈɪəsplɪtɪŋ] *adj* à vous déchirer *ou* crever les tympans

earth [ɜːθ] **1** *n* **(a)** *(planet)* **the E.** laTerre; *Fam* **where/ why on e....?** où/pourquoi diable...?; **to cost the e.** coûter les yeux de la tête; **to promise sb the e.** promettre la lune à qn; **e. mother** *(in mythology)* déesse *f* de la terre; *Fam Fig* mère *f* nourricière; *Br* **e. tremor** secousse *f* sismique **(b)** *(ground)* sol *m*; *(soil)* terre *f*; *Fig* **to come back to e. (with a bump)** revenir (brutalement) sur terre; *Fig* **to go to e.** *(of fugitive)* se terrer **(c)** *Br Elec* terre *f*, masse *f*
2 *vt Br Elec* mettre à la terre

earthenware [ˈɜːθənweə(r)] **1** *n* poterie *f* (de terre) **2** *adj* en *ou* de terre cuite

earthling [ˈɜːθlɪŋ] *n* terrien(enne) *m,f*

earthly [ˈɜːθlɪ] *adj* **(a)** *(life, existence)* terrestre **(b)** *Fam (for emphasis)* **there's no e. reason why...** il n'y a absolument aucune raison pour que...; **she hasn't got an e. (chance)** elle n'a pas la moindre chance

earthquake [ˈɜːθkweɪk] *n* tremblement *m* de terre, séisme *m*

earth-shattering [ˈɜːθʃætərɪŋ] *adj Fam* stupéfiant(e)

earthworks [ˈɜːθwɜːks] *n* travaux *mpl* de terrassement; *Mil* fortifications *fpl* en terre

earthworm [ˈɜːθwɜːm] *n* ver *m* de terre

earthy [ˈɜːθɪ] *adj* **(a)** *(of or like earth)* terreux(euse), **to have an e. smell** sentir la terre **(b)** *(coarse)* truculent(e); *(uninhibited)* direct(e)

earwax [ˈɪəwæks] *n* cérumen *m*, cire *f*

earwig [ˈɪəwɪg] *n (insect)* perce-oreille *m*

ease [iːz] **1** *n* **(a)** *(facility)* facilité *f*, aisance *f*; **with e.** avec facilité *ou* aisance **(b)** *(comfort)* tranquillité *f*, bien-être *m*; **at e.** à l'aise; **to put sb at (their) e.** mettre qn à l'aise; **to put** *or* **set sb's mind at e.** rassurer qn; **a life of e.** une vie d'oisiveté
2 *vt* **(a)** *(alleviate) (pain)* calmer, soulager; **to e. sb's mind** rassurer qn **(b)** *(relax) (pressure)* soulager; *(tension)* réduire; *(restrictions)* assouplir **(c)** *(move carefully, slowly)* déplacer doucement
3 *vi (of pain, pressure)* s'atténuer; *(of wind, rain)* se calmer; *(of situation)* se détendre

ease off, ease up *vi (of pain, rain)* se calmer

easel [ˈiːzəl] *n* chevalet *m*

easily [ˈiːzɪlɪ] *adv* **(a)** *(without difficulty)* facilement, sans difficulté; **that's e. said** c'est facile à dire **(b)** *(undoubtedly)* **e. the best** de loin le meilleur/la meilleure; **he is e. forty** il a au moins quarante ans **(c)** *(comfortably)* à son aise

easiness [ˈiːzɪnɪs] *n* **(a)** *(of task)* facilité *f* **(b)** *(of manner)* décontraction *f*

east [iːst] **1** *n* est *m*; **to the e. (of)** à l'est (de); **the E.** *(the Orient)* l'Orient *m*; *(Eastern Europe)* l'Est
2 *adj (coast, side)* est *inv*; *(wind)* d'est; **E. Africa** l'Afrique *f* orientale; **the E. End** = les quartiers pauvres et populeux de l'est de Londres ou Glasgow; *Formerly* **E. Germany** l'Allemagne *f* de l'Est; *Old-fashioned* **the E. Indies** les Indes *fpl* orientales; **the E. Side** = les quartiers est de NewYork
3 *adv* à l'est; *(travel)* vers l'est; **e. of the Rhine** à l'est du Rhin; **to face e.** être orienté(e) à l'est

eastbound [ˈiːstbaʊnd] *adj (train, traffic)* en direction de l'est

Easter [ˈiːstə(r)] *n* Pâques *fpl*; **at E.** à Pâques; **E. egg** œuf *m* de Pâques; **E. Island** l'île *f* de Pâques; **E. Sunday** dimanche *m ou* jour *m* de Pâques; **E. week** *(following Easter)* semaine *f* de Pâques; *(Holy Week)* semaine sainte

easterly [ˈiːstəlɪ] **1** *n (wind)* vent *m* d'est
2 *adj (point)* à l'est; *(wind)* d'est, qui vient de l'est; **in an e. direction** vers l'est

eastern [ˈiːstən] *adj* est *inv*; *(of Far East)* oriental(e); **e. France** l'est *m* de la France; **E. Europe** l'Europe *f* de l'est; *Am* **E. Standard Time** heure *f* de la côte est de l'Amérique du Nord

eastward [ˈiːstwəd] **1** *adj (in the east)* à l'est, dans l'est
2 *adv* = **eastwards**

eastwards [ˈiːstwədz] *adv (face, point)* à l'est; *(go, travel)* vers l'est

easy [ˈiːzɪ] **1** *adj* **(a)** *(not difficult)* facile; *(solution)* simple; **to be e. to please** ne pas être difficile; **e. to get on with** facile à vivre; *Fam* **as e. as ABC** *or* **as pie** facile comme tout, simple comme bonjour; **the e. way out** la solution de facilité; *Fam* **e. money** argent *m* facile; **e. on the eye** agréable à regarder; *Com* **by e. payments, on e. terms** avec facilités de paiement; *Fam* **I'm e.** *(I don't mind)* ça m'est égal **(b)** *(comfortable, relaxed) (pace, life)* tranquille; *(manners)* libre, dégagé(e); *(style)* facile, naturel(elle); *Fam* **to be on e. street** ne pas avoir de problèmes financiers; **to have an e. time (of it)** avoir la vie facile; **e. chair** fauteuil *m*; *Mus* **e. listening** variété *f*
2 *adv* **to go e. on sb/sth** y aller doucement avec qn/qch; **to take things** *or* **it e.** *(lead a life of ease)* mener une vie tranquille; *(not overdo things)* ralentir; **take it e.!** *(calm down)* t'en fais pas!; **that's easier said than done** c'est plus facile à dire qu'à faire; **e. come, e. go** ça va, ça vient

easy-going [ˈiːzɪˈgəʊɪŋ] *adj (tolerant)* coulant(e), accommodant(e); *(calm)* décontracté(e)

eat [iːt] *(pt* **ate** [et, eɪt], *pp* **eaten** [ˈiːtən] *)* **1** *vt* **(a)** *(food)* manger; **to e. one's breakfast** prendre son petit déjeuner **(b)** *(idioms)* **to e. sb out of house and home** ruiner qn en nourriture; *Fam* **I could e. a horse!** j'ai une faim de loup!; *Fam* **he won't e. you!** il ne va pas te manger!; *Fam* **what's eating you?** qu'est-ce qui te tracasse?; **to e. one's words** se rétracter; *Fam* **if it works, I'll e. my hat** si ça réussit, je mange mon chapeau
2 *vi* manger; *Fig* **you'll have them eating out of your hand** ils te mangeront dans la main

▸**eat away at** *vt insep (erode) (rocks, self-confidence)* éroder, miner; *(foundations)* saper

▸**eat into** *vt insep (erode)* ronger; *Fig (time, savings)* entamer

▸**eat out** *vi* manger au restaurant

▸**eat up 1** *vt sep* (**a**) *(food)* manger jusqu'à la dernière miette, finir (**b**) *(petrol, money)* consommer beaucoup de
2 *vi* finir son assiette; **e. up!** mange!

eaten [ˈiːtən] *pp of* **eat**

eater [ˈiːtə(r)] *n* mangeur(euse) *m,f*; **to be a fussy e.** être difficile (sur la nourriture)

eatery [ˈiːtərɪ] *(pl* **eateries**) *n Am* (café-)restaurant *m*

eats [iːts] *npl Fam* bouffe *f*

eau de Cologne [ˈəʊdəkəˈləʊn] *n* eau *f* de Cologne

eaves [iːvz] *npl* avant-toit *m*

eavesdrop [ˈiːvzdrɒp] *(pt & pp* **eavesdropped**) *vi* **to e. (on sb/sth)** écouter (qn/qch) avec indiscrétion; **she was eavesdropping outside the door** elle écoutait à la porte

ebb [eb] **1** *n (of tide)* reflux *m*; **e. tide** marée *f* descendante; *Fig* **the e. and flow** *(of events)* les fluctuations *fpl*; *Fig* **to be at a low e.** *(of person)* ne pas avoir le moral; *(of spirits)* être bien bas; *(of finances, relations)* aller mal
2 *vi (of tide)* baisser

▸**ebb away** *vi (of water)* s'écouler; *(of strength, enthusiasm)* faiblir, baisser

ebony [ˈebənɪ] *n* ébène *f*

EBRD [iːbiːɑːˈdiː] *n (abbr* **European Bank for Reconstruction and Development**) BERD *f*

ebullience [ɪˈbʌlɪəns] *n* bouillonnement *m*, effervescence *f*

ebullient [ɪˈbʌlɪənt] *adj* bouillant(e), exubérant(e)

EC [iːˈsiː] *n (abbr* **European Community**) CE *f*

e-card [ˈiːkɑːd] *n* carte *f* électronique

e-cash [ˈiːkæʃ] *n* argent *m* électronique, argent virtuel, e-cash *m*

eccentric [ekˈsentrɪk] *n & adj* excentrique *mf*

eccentricity [eksenˈtrɪsɪtɪ] *n* excentricité *f*

ecclesiastic [ɪkliːzɪˈæstɪk] **1** *n* ecclésiastique *m*
2 *adj* ecclésiastique

ECG [iːsiːˈdʒiː] *n Med (abbr* **electrocardiograph**) électrocardiographe *m*

echelon [ˈeʃəlɒn] *n* échelon *m*

echo [ˈekəʊ] **1** *n (pl* **echoes**) *also Fig* écho *m*
2 *vt (pt & pp* **echoed**) *(words)* répéter; *(opinion)* se faire l'écho de
3 *vi* résonner (**with** de)

eclair [eɪˈkleə(r)] *n (pastry)* éclair *m*; **chocolate e.** éclair au chocolat

eclectic [əˈklektɪk] *adj (tastes, style)* éclectique; *(blend)* hétérogène

eclipse [ɪˈklɪps] *also Fig* **1** *n* éclipse *f*
2 *vt* éclipser

eco-friendly [ˈiːkəʊfrendlɪ] *adj (product)* écologique, vert(e); *(lifestyle, person)* qui respecte l'environnement

ecological [iːkəˈlɒdʒɪkəl] *adj (damage, balance)* écologique; *(campaign, activist)* écologiste

ecologist [ɪˈkɒlədʒɪst] *n* écologiste *mf*

ecology [ɪˈkɒlədʒɪ] *n* écologie *f*

e-commerce [ˈiːkɒmɜːs] *n* commerce *m* électronique

economic [iːkəˈnɒmɪk] *adj* (**a**) *Econ* économique (**b**) *(profitable)* rentable; **to make sth e.** rentabiliser qch

economical [iːkəˈnɒmɪkəl] *adj (cost-effective)* économique; *(style)* concis(e); **to be e. with the truth** ne dire la vérité qu'à moitié

economically [iːkəˈnɒmɪklɪ] *adv* économiquement; *(written)* dans un style concis

economics [iːkəˈnɒmɪks] **1** *n* économie *f*
2 *npl (financial aspects)* aspects *mpl* financiers

economist [ɪˈkɒnəmɪst] *n* économiste *mf*

economize [ɪˈkɒnəmaɪz] *vi* économiser (**on** sur)

economy [ɪˈkɒnəmɪ] *(pl* **economies**) *n* économie *f*; **economies of scale** économies d'échelle; *Aviat* **e. class** classe *f* économique; **e. drive** politique *f* de réduction des dépenses; **e. measure** mesure *f* d'économie; **e. size** *(of packet)* taille *f* économique

ecoterrorist [ˈiːkəʊterərɪst] *n* = militant ecologiste ayant recours à des actions violentes

ecstasy [ˈekstəsɪ] *(pl* **ecstasies**) *n* (**a**) *(emotional state)* extase *f*; **to go into ecstasies over sth** s'extasier devant qch (**b**) *(drug)* ecstasy *f*

ecstatic [ekˈstætɪk] *adj* fou (folle) de joie; **he was e. about** *or* **over the news** la nouvelle l'a rendu fou de joie

ECT [iːsiːˈtiː] *n Med (abbr* **electroconvulsive therapy**) traitement *m* par électrochocs

ECU, ecu [ˈekjuː, ˈiːkjuː] *n (abbr* **European Currency Unit**) ÉCU *m*, écu *m*

Ecuador [ˈekwədɔː(r)] *n* l'Équateur *m*

ecumenical [iːkjʊˈmenɪkəl] *adj Rel* œcuménique

eczema [ˈeksɪmə] *n* eczéma *m*; **to have e.** avoir de l'eczéma

ed [ed] (**a**) *(abbr* **edition**) éd(it) (**b**) *(abbr* **editor**) éd., édit

eddy [ˈedɪ] **1** *n (pl* **eddies**) tourbillon *m*
2 *vi (pt & pp* **eddied**) *(of water)* faire des remous; *(of wind, snow)* tourbillonner

Eden [ˈiːdən] *n* l'Éden *m*

edge [edʒ] **1** *n* (**a**) *(of table, road, river)* bord *m*; *(of wood)* lisière *f*; *(of book)* tranche *f*; **at the water's e.** au bord de l'eau; **to be on the e. of** *(new age)* être au seuil de; *(war)* être au bord de; *Fig* **to be on the e. of one's seat** retenir son souffle
(**b**) *(of blade, tool)* tranchant *m*; *(of stone)* arête *f*; **to take the e. off** *(blade, appetite)* émousser; *(enjoyment)* gâter; *Fig* **to be on e.** être énervé(e); *Fig* **to set sb on e.** énerver qn
(**c**) *(advantage)* **to have the e. (over sb)** être avantagé(e) (par rapport à qn)
2 *vt (in sewing)* border (**with** de)
3 *vi (move slowly)* **to e. past sb** passer lentement devant qn; **to e. towards** avancer lentement vers

▸**edge out** *vt sep (supplant)* évincer (**of** de)

edgeways [ˈedʒweɪz], **edgewise** [ˈedʒwaɪz] *adv (on its edge)* de chant; *(from side)* de côté; *Fam* **I can't get a word in e.** je ne peux pas en placer une

edgy [ˈedʒɪ] *adj* nerveux(euse); **to get e.** s'énerver

edible [ˈedɪbəl] *adj (safe to eat)* comestible; *(fit to eat)* mangeable

edict [ˈiːdɪkt] *n Formal* édit *m*

edification [edɪfɪˈkeɪʃən] *n* édification *f*

edifice [ˈedɪfɪs] *n also Fig* édifice *m*

edify [ˈedɪfaɪ] *(pt & pp* **edified**) *vt* édifier

edifying [ˈedɪfaɪɪŋ] *adj* édifiant(e)

Edinburgh [ˈedɪnbrə] *n* Édimbourg

Edinburgh Festival

Le festival international d'Édimbourg, créé en 1947, est aujourd'hui un des plus grands festivals de théâtre et de musique au monde; il se tient chaque année dans la capitale écossaise en août et en septembre. Le festival ''off'' (fringe) est une grande rencontre du théâtre expérimental.

edit ['edit] *vt* (**a**) *(correct)* réviser; *(prepare for publication)* préparer pour la publication; **edited by** *(coordinated by)* sous la direction de (**b**) *(film)* monter (**c**) *(manage) (newspaper, magazine)* diriger (**d**) *Comput* éditer

▸**edit out** *vt sep (scene)* couper

editing ['editiŋ] *n Cin* montage *m*

edition [i'diʃən] *n (of book, newspaper)* édition *f*; **in Tuesday's e. of the programme** dans l'émission de mardi

editor ['editə(r)] *n* (**a**) *(of published work) (author)* rédacteur(trice) *m,f*; *(in charge)* directeur(trice) *m,f* (**b**) *(of film)* monteur(euse) *m,f* (**c**) *(of newspaper, magazine)* rédacteur(trice) *m,f* en chef; *(of section)* rédacteur(trice) (**d**) *Comput (software)* éditeur *m*

editorial [edi'tɔ:riəl] **1** *n* éditorial *m*
  2 *adj* de rédaction

EDP [i:di:'pi:] *n Comput (abbr* **electronic data processing***)* traitement *m* électronique de l'information

educate ['edjʊkeit] *vt* éduquer, instruire; **he was educated at Oxford** il a fait ses études à Oxford

educated ['edjʊkeitid] *adj* instruit(e); **I made an e. guess** j'ai émis une hypothèse, mais je ne risquais guère de me tromper

education [edjʊ'keiʃən] *n (process of learning, knowledge)* éducation *f*; *(process of teaching)* enseignement *m*; **to get (oneself) an e.** faire des études; **to complete one's e.** terminer ses études; *Fig* **it was an e. working over there** c'était instructif de travailler là-bas

educational [edjʊ'keiʃənəl] *adj (system)* éducatif(-ive); *(establishment, publisher)* scolaire; *(qualification)* d'enseignement; *(experience, visit)* instructif(ive)

Edwardian [ed'wɔ:diən] *adj (architecture, furniture)* de l'époque d'Édouard VII; **the E. era** ≃ la Belle Époque

EEC [i:i:'si:] *n Formerly (abbr* **European Economic Community***)* CEE *f*

eel [i:l] *n* anguille *f*

eerie ['iəri] *adj (atmosphere, cry)* sinistre; *(silence)* de mort; *(feeling)* étrange

eerily ['iərili] *adv* étrangement

eff [ef] *vi Fam Euph* **to e. and blind** débiter des grossièretés

efface [i'feis] *vt* effacer

effect [i'fekt] **1** *n* (**a**) *(result)* effet *m* (**on** sur*)*; **to take e.** *(of drug, medicine)* faire effet, agir; *(of law)* prendre effet; **to put sth into e.** mettre qch en application; **in e.** en fait; **or words to that e.** ou quelque chose d'approchant (**b**) *(impression)* effet *m*; **for e.** pour faire de l'effet (**c**) *Formal* **personal effects** effets *mpl* personnels
  2 *vt Formal (cause) (change, rescue)* effectuer; *(saving, wish)* réaliser; *(solution)* apporter (**to** à)

effective [i'fektiv] *adj* (**a**) *(efficient, successful)* efficace; *(argument, speech)* convaincant(e) (**b**) *(actual, real) (profit, value)* réel(elle); **she will assume e. control of the business** c'est elle qui dirigera concrètement l'entreprise (**c**) *Law (in force)* **to be e.** prendre effet

effectively [i'fektivli] *adv* (**a**) *(efficiently)* avec efficacité; *(speak)* de façon convaincante (**b**) *(really)* en fait, en réalité; **they are e. the same** en fait, ils sont identiques

effectiveness [i'fektivnis] *n* efficacité *f*

effeminate [i'feminət] *adj* efféminé(e)

effervescent [efə'vesənt] *adj also Fig* effervescent(e)

effete [i'fi:t] *adj (person)* veule; *(gesture)* efféminé(e)

efficacious [efi'keiʃəs] *adj Formal* efficace

efficacy ['efikəsi] *n Formal* efficacité *f*

efficiency [i'fiʃənsi] *n* efficacité *f*; *(output, productivity)* rendement *m*

efficient [i'fiʃənt] *adj* efficace; *(productive)* performant(e); **to be e. at sth** faire qch avec compétence

efficiently [i'fiʃəntli] *adv* efficacement

effigy ['efidʒi] *(pl* **effigies***) n* effigie *f*

effing ['efiŋ] *adj Fam Euph* fichu(e)

effluent ['efluənt] *n* effluents *mpl*

effort ['efət] *n* (**a**) *(exertion)* effort *m*; **to make an e. (to do sth)** faire un effort (pour faire qch); **put some e. into it!** fais un effort!; **to be worth the e.** valoir la peine(**b**) *(attempt)* tentative *f* (**at doing sth** pour faire qch); **a good e.** un bel effort; **a poor e.** un effort insuffisant

effortless ['efətlis] *adj (victory, success)* facile; *(skill, grace)* naturel(elle)

effortlessly ['efətlisli] *adv* facilement, sans effort

effrontery [i'frʌntəri] *n* effronterie *f*

effusive [i'fju:siv] *adj (person)* démonstratif(ive), expansif(ive); *(welcome, speech)* enthousiaste

effusively [i'fju:sivli] *adv (praise, welcome)* avec un enthousiasme débordant; *(thank)* avec effusion

EFL [i:e'fel] *n (abbr* **English as a Foreign Language***)* anglais *m* langue étrangère

EFT [i:ef'ti:] *n Comput (abbr* **electronic funds transfer***)* transfert *m* de fonds électronique

EFTA ['eftə] *n (abbr* **European Free Trade Association***)* AELE *f*

EFTPOS ['eftpɒs] *n Comput (abbr* **electronic funds transfer at point of sale***)* transfert *m* de fonds électronique sur point de vente

eg [i:'dʒi:] *adv (abbr* **exempli gratia***)* p. ex.

egalitarian [igæli'teəriən] **1** *n* égalitariste *mf*
  2 *adj (society)* égalitaire

egalitarianism [igæli'teəriənizəm] *n* égalitarisme *m*

egg [eg] *n* (**a**) *(of bird, fish etc)* œuf *m*; **e. cup** coquetier *m*; **e. flip** *(with milk)* lait *m* de poule; *(with alcohol)* lait de poule alcoolisé; *Am Culin* **e. roll** pâté *m* impérial; **e. timer** sablier *m*; **e. white** blanc *m* d'œuf; **e. yolk** jaune *m* d'œuf (**b**) *(idioms)* **a good e.** *(man)* un brave type; *(woman)* une brave fille; **a bad e.** *(man)* un sale type; *(woman)* une sale bonne femme; **to have e. on one's face** être ridicule; *Prov* **don't put all your eggs in one basket** il ne faut pas mettre tous ses œufs dans le même panier

▸**egg on** *vt sep* encourager (**to do sth** à faire qch)

egghead ['eghed] *n Hum or Pej* intello *mf*

eggplant ['egplænt] *n Am* aubergine *f*

eggshell ['egʃel] *n* coquille *f* d'œuf

eggwhisk ['egwisk] *n* fouet *m*

egis *Am* = **aegis**

ego ['i:gəʊ] *(pl* **egos***) n* ego *m*; **to have a big e.** être très imbu(e) de soi-même; **to give sb's e. a boost** flatter l'ego de qn; *Fam* **he's on an e. trip** il fait ça uniquement parce que ça flatte son ego

egocentric [i:gəʊ'sentrik] *adj* égocentrique

egoist ['i:gəʊist] *n* égoïste *mf*

egotism ['i:gəʊtizəm] *n* égocentrisme *m*

egotist ['i:gəʊtist] *n* égocentrique *mf*

egotistic(al) [i:gəʊ'tistik(əl)] *adj* égocentrique

Egypt ['i:dʒipt] *n* l'Égypte *f*

Egyptian [ɪˈdʒɪpʃən] **1** n Égyptien(enne) m,f
2 adj égyptien(enne)
eiderdown [ˈaɪdədaʊn] n édredon m
eight [eɪt] **1** n huit m inv; **come at e.** venez à huit heures; **e. and e. are sixteen** huit et huit font seize; **there were e. of us** nous étions huit; **all e. of them left** tous les huit sont partis, ils sont partis tous les huit; **the e. of hearts** (in cards) le huit de cœur
2 adj huit; **e. cars** huit voitures; **e. pounds** huit livres; **on page e.** (à la) page huit; **to be e. (years old)** avoir huit ans; **they live at number e.** ils habitent au numéro huit; **e. o'clock** huit heures; **it's e. minutes to five** il est cinq heures moins huit; Am Tel **e. hundred number** ≃ numéro m vert
eighteen [eɪˈtiːn] **1** n dix-huit m inv
2 adj dix-huit; see also **eight**
eighteenth [eɪˈtiːnθ] **1** n (**a**) (fraction) dix-huitième m; (in series) dix-huitième mf (**b**) (of month) dix-huit m inv
2 adj dix-huitième; see also **eighth**
eighth [eɪtθ] **1** n (**a**) (fraction) huitième m; (in series) huitième mf; **Edward the E.** Édouard Huit (**b**) (of month) huit m inv; (**on) the e. of May** le huit mai; **we're leaving on the e.** nous partons le huit
2 adj huitième
eightieth [ˈeɪtɪθ] **1** n (fraction) quatre-vingtième m; (in series) quatre-vingtième mf
2 adj quatre-vingtième
eighty [ˈeɪtɪ] **1** n quatre-vingts m inv; **he was doing e.** (in car) il faisait du quatre-vingt (à l'heure); **in the eighties** (decade) dans les années quatre-vingt; **to be in one's eighties** avoir quatre-vingts ans passés; **the temperature was in the eighties** il faisait dans les vingt-cinq degrés
2 adj quatre-vingts; **e. cars/passengers** quatre-vingts voitures/passagers; **e. percent** quatre-vingt pour cent; **she's about e. (years old)** elle a dans les quatre-vingts ans
Eire [ˈeərə] n l'Eire f
either [ˈaɪðə(r), ˈiːðə(r)] **1** adj (**a**) (one or the other) l'un (l'une) ou l'autre; **I didn't like e. book** je n'ai aimé ni l'un ni l'autre de ces livres; **e. candidate may win** les deux candidats ont des chances de gagner (**b**) (both) les deux; **on e. side** des deux côtés; **in e. case** dans les deux cas
2 pron (one or the other) l'un (l'une) m,f ou l'autre; **e. (of them) will do** l'un ou l'autre fera l'affaire; **I don't want e. (of them)** je ne veux ni l'un ni l'autre; **I don't believe e. of you** je ne vous crois ni l'un ni l'autre
3 conj **e.... or...** ou... ou..., soit... soit...; **e. you or your brother** ou toi ou ton frère, soit toi soit ton frère; **she doesn't eat e. meat or fish** elle ne mange ni viande ni poisson; **e. come in or go out!** ou tu rentres ou tu sors!
4 adv **if you don't go, I won't go e.** si tu n'y vas pas, moi non plus; **I don't like him – I don't e.** je ne l'aime pas – moi non plus
either-or [ˈaɪðərɔː(r)] adj **it's an e. situation** c'est soit l'un soit l'autre
ejaculate [ɪˈdʒækjʊleɪt] vi (**a**) (of man) éjaculer (**b**) Old-fashioned (exclaim) s'écrier, s'exclamer
ejaculation [ɪdʒækjʊˈleɪʃən] n (**a**) (of semen) éjaculation f (**b**) Old-fashioned (exclamation) exclamation f
eject [ɪˈdʒekt] **1** vt (cassette) éjecter; (troublemaker) expulser
2 vi (from plane) s'éjecter

ejection [ɪˈdʒekʃən] n (of cassette, from plane) éjection f; (of troublemaker) expulsion f
ejector seat [ɪˈdʒektə(r)siːt] n siège m éjectable
►**eke out** [iːk] vt sep (money) dépenser avec parcimonie; (rations, supplies) consommer avec parcimonie; **to e. out a living** gagner péniblement sa vie
elaborate 1 adj [ɪˈlæbərət] (meal) élaboré(e); (drawing, description) détaillé(e); (excuse, scheme) compliqué(e)
2 vt [ɪˈlæbəreɪt] (formulate) élaborer; (flesh out) développer
3 vi être plus précis; **to e. on sth** donner plus de détails sur qch
elan [eɪˈlɑːn] n Lit impétuosité f
elapse [ɪˈlæps] vi s'écouler
elastic [ɪˈlæstɪk] **1** n élastique m
2 adj also Fig élastique; **e. band** élastique m, bracelet m en caoutchouc
elasticated [ɪˈlæstɪkeɪtɪd] adj (garment, material) extensible; (waist) élastique
elasticity [iːlæsˈtɪsɪtɪ] n also Fig élasticité f
Elastoplast® [ɪˈlæstəplɑːst] n Élastoplast® m
elated [ɪˈleɪtɪd] adj transporté(e) (de joie)
elation [ɪˈleɪʃən] n exaltation f
elbow [ˈelbəʊ] **1** n coude m; **out at the elbows** (of pullover, jacket) troué(e) aux coudes; Fig **to give sb the e.** (of employer) se débarrasser de qn; (of lover) plaquer qn; Fig **to use some e. grease** mettre de l'huile de coude
2 vt **to e. sb (in the ribs)** donner un coup de coude (dans les côtes) à qn; **to e. sb aside** écarter qn d'un coup de coude; Fig jouer des coudes pour évincer qn; **to e. one's way through** se frayer un passage en jouant des coudes
elbowroom [ˈelbəʊrʊm] n Fam Fig **to have enough e.** avoir assez de liberté
elder¹ [ˈeldə(r)] **1** n (**a**) (older person) aîné(e) m,f; **young people should respect their elders** les jeunes doivent le respect à leurs aînés (**b**) (of tribe) ancien(-enne) m,f; (of church) = membre d'une congrégation protestante chargé de seconder le ministre dans certaines tâches
2 adj (brother, sister) aîné(e); **e. statesman** grand homme m politique
elder² n (tree) sureau m
elderberry [ˈeldəberɪ] (pl **elderberries**) n baie f de sureau
elderly [ˈeldəlɪ] **1** npl **the e.** les personnes fpl âgées
2 adj âgé(e)
eldest [ˈeldɪst] **1** n **the e.** l'aîné(e) m,f
2 adj aîné(e)
elect [ɪˈlekt] **1** adj élu(e)
2 vt (**a**) (councillor, MP) élire (**b**) Formal (choose) **to e. to do sth** choisir de faire qch
election [ɪˈlekʃən] n élection f; **to hold an e.** procéder à une élection; **to stand for e.** se présenter aux élections; **e. campaign** campagne f électorale
electioneering [ɪlekʃəˈnɪərɪŋ] n propagande f électorale
elective [ɪˈlektɪv] **1** n Univ (course) option f
2 adj (assembly) électoral(e); Univ (course) optionnel(elle); Med **e. surgery** chirurgie f de confort
elector [ɪˈlektə(r)] n électeur(trice) m,f
electoral [ɪˈlektərəl] adj électoral(e); **e. reform** réforme f du mode de scrutin; **e. roll** liste f électorale
electorate [ɪˈlektərət] n électorat m

electric [ɪ'lektrɪk] *adj* électrique; *Fig (atmosphere)* chargé(e) d'électricité; *Br* **e. blanket** couverture *f* chauffante; **e. blue** bleu *m* électrique; **e. chair** chaise *f* électrique; **e. cooker** cuisinière *f* électrique; **e. light** *(appliance)* lumière *f* électrique; *(lighting)* éclairage *m ou* lumière électrique; **e. shock** décharge *f* électrique; *Med* électrochoc *m*

electrical [ɪ'lektrɪkəl] *adj* électrique; **e. engineering** électrotechnique *f*

electrically [ɪ'lektrɪkəlɪ] *adv* **e. powered/operated** qui fonctionne à l'électricité; **e. charged** chargé(e) d'électricité

electrician [ɪlek'trɪʃən] *n* électricien(enne) *m,f*

electricity [ɪlek'trɪsɪtɪ] *n* électricité *f*

electrification [ɪlektrɪfɪ'keɪʃən] *n* électrification *f*

electrify [ɪ'lektrɪfaɪ] *(pt & pp* **electrified**) *vt* électrifier; *Fig (excite)* électriser

electrifying [ɪ'lektrɪfaɪɪŋ] *adj Fig* électrisant(e)

electrocardiogram [ɪlektrəʊ'kɑːdɪəʊɡræm] *n Med* électrocardiogramme *m*

electrocardiograph [ɪlektrəʊ'kɑːdɪəʊɡræf] *n Med* électrocardiographe *m*

electrocute [ɪ'lektrəkjuːt] *vt* électrocuter; **to e. oneself** s'électrocuter

electrocution [ɪlektrə'kjuːʃən] *n* électrocution *f*

electrode [ɪ'lektrəʊd] *n* électrode *f*

electrolysis [ɪlek'trɒlɪsɪs] *n* électrolyse *f*

electromagnet [ɪlektrəʊ'mæɡnɪt] *n* électroaimant *m*

electron [ɪ'lektrɒn] *n* électron *m*; **e. microscope** microscope *m* électronique

electronic [ɪlek'trɒnɪk] *adj* électronique; *Fin* **e. banking** bancatique *f*; *Comput* **e. mail** courrier *m* électronique; *Comput* **e. office** bureau *m* informatisé

electronically [ɪlek'trɒnɪklɪ] *adv* électroniquement

electronics [ɪlek'trɒnɪks] **1** *n (subject)* électronique *f*; **e. company** société *f* d'électronique; **the e. industry** l'industrie *f* (de l')électronique
   2 *npl* **the e.** *(of machine)* le système électronique

electroplated [ɪ'lektrəpleɪtɪd] *adj* plaqué(e) *(par électrodéposition)*

electroshock [ɪlektrəʊ'ʃɒk] *adj* **e. therapy** *or* **treatment** traitement *m* par électrochocs

elegance ['elɪɡəns] *n* élégance *f*

elegant ['elɪɡənt] *adj (person, appearance, movement)* élégant(e); *(reasoning)* clair(e) et simple

elegantly ['elɪɡəntlɪ] *adv* avec élégance; **e. proportioned** aux proportions élégantes

elegy ['elɪdʒɪ] *(pl* **elegies**) *n* élégie *f*

element ['elɪmənt] *n* (**a**) *(constituent part)* part *f*; **an e. of danger/chance** une part de danger/chance; **this film has all the elements of a hit movie** ce film réunit tous les ingrédients d'un grand succès
   (**b**) *(factor)* **the e. of surprise** l'effet *m* de surprise; **the human/time e.** le facteur humain/temps
   (**c**) *(in society)* élément *m*; **undesirable elements** éléments indésirables; **the hooligan e.** la frange constituée par les hooligans
   (**d**) *Chem* élément *m*
   (**e**) *(of kettle, electric fire)* résistance *f*
   (**f**) *(force of nature)* **the four elements** les quatre éléments; *Fig* **to brave the elements** braver les éléments; **to be in one's e.** être dans son élément

elemental [elɪ'mentəl] *adj* (**a**) *(basic)* fondamental(e) (**b**) *(primitive)* élémentaire, primitif(ive)

elementary [elɪ'mentərɪ] *adj* élémentaire; *Am (education)* primaire; **my Arabic is rather e.** je parle un arabe assez rudimentaire; *Am* **e. school** école *f* primaire

elephant ['elɪfənt] *n* éléphant *m*

elephantine [elɪ'fæntaɪn] *adj (movements)* lourd(e) et gauche; *(proportions)* éléphantesque

elevate ['elɪveɪt] *vt* élever (**to** à); **to e. sb to the peerage** élever qn à la pairie

elevated ['elɪveɪtɪd] *adj (position, rank)* élevé(e); *(thoughts, discussion)* qui vole haut; *(language)* soutenu(e); **e. railway** métro *m* aérien

elevation [elɪ'veɪʃən] *n* (**a**) *(height)* altitude *f* (**b**) *(promotion)* élévation *f* (**to** à) (**c**) *Archit* élévation *f*

elevator ['elɪveɪtə(r)] *n* (**a**) *Am (lift)* ascenseur *m* (**b**) *(for goods)* élévateur *m* (**c**) *(on aeroplane wing)* gouvernail *m* de profondeur

eleven [ɪ'levən] **1** *n* onze *m inv*; **the French e.** *(football team)* le onze de France
   2 *adj* onze; *see also* **eight**

elevenses [ɪ'levənzɪz] *npl Br Fam* casse-croûte *m inv (vers onze heures du matin)*

eleventh [ɪ'levənθ] **1** *n* (**a**) *(fraction)* onzième *m*; *(in series)* onzième *mf* (**b**) *(of month)* onze *m inv*
   2 *adj* onzième; **at the e. hour** à la dernière minute; *see also* **eighth**

elf [elf] *(pl* **elves** [elvz]) *n* elfe *m*

elicit [ɪ'lɪsɪt] *vt (information, smile)* tirer (**from** de); *(reaction, response)* susciter (**from** de la part de)

eligibility [elɪdʒɪ'bɪlɪtɪ] *n (for grant, benefit)* droit *m* (**for** à); *(for job)* admissibilité *f*; *(to vote)* éligibilité *f*

eligible ['elɪdʒɪbəl] *adj (for job)* admissible; *(to vote)* eligible; **to be e. for a grant** avoir droit à une subvention; **e. bachelor** bon parti *m*

eliminate [ɪ'lɪmɪneɪt] *vt* éliminer

elimination [ɪlɪmɪ'neɪʃən] *n* élimination *f*; **by a process of e.** (en procédant) par élimination

elite [eɪ'liːt] **1** *n* élite *f*
   2 *adj* d'élite

elitism [eɪ'liːtɪzəm] *n* élitisme *m*

elitist [eɪ'liːtɪst] *n & adj* élitiste *mf*

elixir [ɪ'lɪksə(r)] *n Lit* élixir *m*

Elizabethan [ɪlɪzə'biːθən] **1** *n* = Anglais vivant sous le règne d'Élisabeth 1ère
   2 *adj* élisabéthain(e)

elk [elk] *n* élan *m*

ellipse [ɪ'lɪps] *n Math* ellipse *f*

ellipsis [ɪ'lɪpsɪs] *(pl* **ellipses** [ɪ'lɪpsiːz]) *n Gram* ellipse *f*

elliptical [ɪ'lɪptɪkəl] *adj* elliptique

elm [elm] *n* orme *m*

elocution [elə'kjuːʃən] *n* élocution *f*, diction *f*

elongate ['iːlɒŋɡeɪt] *vt* allonger

elope [ɪ'ləʊp] *vi* s'enfuir (pour se marier)

eloquence ['eləkwəns] *n* éloquence *f*

eloquent ['eləkwənt] *adj* éloquent(e)

else [els] *adv* **anyone e.** n'importe qui; *(in negative sentences)* personne d'autre; **is anyone e. interested?** quelqu'un d'autre est-il intéressé?; **someone e.** quelqu'un d'autre; **everyone e.** tous les autres; **no one e.** personne d'autre; **anything e.** n'importe quoi d'autre; *(in negative sentences)* rien d'autre; **have you anything e. to do?** as-tu autre chose à faire?; **something e.** autre chose, quelque chose d'autre; **everything e.** tout le reste; **nothing e.** rien d'autre; **somewhere e.** autre part, ailleurs; **anywhere e.** (n'importe où) ailleurs; *(in negative sentences)* nulle part ailleurs; **everywhere e.** partout ailleurs; **nowhere e.** nulle part ailleurs; **who e. was there?** qui d'autre était là?; **who broke it? – Peter, who e.?** qui l'a cassé? – Peter, qui d'autre veux-tu que ce soit!; **what e.?** quoi d'autre?; **when e.?** à quel autre moment/quelle autre date?; **where e. did you go?** où êtes-vous allés encore?; **how e.?** de quelle autre manière?; **why e.?** pour quelle autre raison?; **little e.** pas grand-chose d'autre; **there isn't much e. we can do** nous ne pouvons pas faire grand-chose d'autre; **or e.** *(otherwise)* sinon; **do what I tell you or e.!** fais ce que je te dis ou sinon...!

elsewhere ['elsweə(r)] *adv* ailleurs, autre part

ELT [i:el'ti:] *n (abbr* **English Language Teaching**) anglais *m* langue étrangère

elucidate [ɪ'lu:sɪdeɪt] *vt (mystery)* élucider; *(reasons)* expliquer

elude [ɪ'lu:d] *vt* échapper à

elusive [ɪ'lu:sɪv] *adj (person)* insaisissable; *(concept)* difficile à saisir

elver ['elvə(r)] *n* civelle *f*

elves [elvz] *pl of* **elf**

emaciated [ɪ'meɪsɪeɪtɪd] *adj* émacié(e)

e-mail ['i:meɪl] **1** *n* courrier *m* électronique, mél *m*, *Can* courriel *m;* **e. address** adresse *f* électronique

2 *vt (person)* envoyer un courrier électronique à; *(file, message)* envoyer par courrier électronique

emanate ['eməneɪt] **1** *vt* dégager

2 *vi* émaner (**from** de)

emancipate [ɪ'mænsɪpeɪt] *vt* émanciper

emancipated [ɪ'mænsɪpeɪtɪd] *adj* émancipé(e)

emancipation [ɪmænsɪ'peɪʃən] *n* émancipation *f*

emasculate [ɪ'mæskjʊleɪt] *vt Fig* amputer

embalm [ɪm'bɑ:m] *vt* embaumer

embankment [ɪm'bæŋkmənt] *n (beside railway)* talus *m; (beside river)* berge *f,* quai *m*

embargo [em'bɑ:gəʊ] *(pl* **embargoes**) **1** *n* embargo *m;* **to put an e. on** mettre un embargo sur

2 *vt* mettre un embargo sur

embark [ɪm'bɑ:k] *vi* embarquer; *Fig* **to e. (up)on sth** s'embarquer dans qch

embarrass [ɪm'bærəs] *vt* embarrasser, gêner; *(make ashamed)* faire honte à

embarrassed [ɪm'bærəst] *adj (ashamed, uncomfortable)* embarrassé(e), gêné(e); *(financially)* gêné(e) (financièrement)

embarrassing [ɪm'bærəsɪŋ] *adj* embarrassant(e), gênant(e); **how e.!** comme ça a dû être/c'est embarrassant!

embarrassment [ɪm'bærəsmənt] *n* embarras *m,* gêne *f;* **much to my e.** à mon grand embarras; **to be an e. to sb** être une source d'embarras pour qn

embassy ['embəsɪ] *(pl* **embassies**) *n* ambassade *f;* **the French E.** l'ambassade de France

embattled [ɪm'bætəld] *adj* assiégé(e) de toutes parts

embed [ɪm'bed] *(pt & pp* **embedded**) *vt* (**a**) **to be embedded in sth** être fiché(e) dans qch; *(with cement)* être scellé(e) dans qch; *Fig* **to be embedded in sb's memory** être gravé(e) dans la mémoire de qn (**b**) *Comput* intégrer

embellish [ɪm'belɪʃ] *vt (room)* embellir (**with** de); *(account)* enjoliver

embers ['embəz] *npl* braises *fpl*

embezzle [ɪm'bezəl] *vt* détourner (**from** de)

embezzlement [ɪm'bezəlmənt] *n* **e. (of funds)** détournement *m* de fonds

embezzler [ɪm'bezlə(r)] *n* escroc *m*

embitter [ɪm'bɪtə(r)] *vt (person)* aigrir, remplir d'amertume

embittered [ɪm'bɪtəd] *adj (person)* aigri(e)

emblazon [ɪm'bleɪzən] *vt (shield)* orner (**with** de); *Fig (name, headline)* étaler

emblem ['embləm] *n* emblème *m*

embodiment [ɪm'bɒdɪmənt] *n* incarnation *f*

embody [ɪm'bɒdɪ] *(pt & pp* **embodied**) *vt* incarner

embolden [ɪm'bəʊldən] *vt* enhardir; **to e. sb to do sth** donner à qn le courage de faire qch

embolism ['embəlɪzəm] *n Med* embolie *f*

embossed [ɪm'bɒst] *adj (metal, leather)* repoussé(e); *(letter, wallpaper, design)* en relief

embrace [ɪm'breɪs] **1** *n* étreinte *f*

2 *vt* (**a**) *(person)* étreindre; *Fig (belief, religion)* embrasser (**b**) *(include)* couvrir

3 *vi* s'étreindre

embroider [ɪm'brɔɪdə(r)] *vt (cloth)* broder; *Fig (account, report)* enjoliver

embroidery [ɪm'brɔɪdərɪ] *n* broderie *f*

embroil [ɪm'brɔɪl] *vt* entraîner (**in** dans); **to get embroiled in sth** se laisser entraîner dans qch

embryo ['embrɪəʊ] *(pl* **embryos**) *n* embryon *m; Fig* **in e.** *(plan, idea)* à l'état embryonnaire

embryonic [embrɪ'ɒnɪk] *adj Biol* embryonnaire; *(plan, idea)* à l'état embryonnaire

emend [ɪ'mend] *vt* corriger

emendation [i:men'deɪʃən] *n* correction *f*

emerald ['emərəld] *n* émeraude *f;* **an e. necklace** un collier d'émeraudes; **e. (green)** (vert *m*) émeraude *m;* **the E. Isle** la verte Érin

emerge [ɪ'mɜ:dʒ] *vi (of person, truth)* émerger (**from** de); **it later emerged that...** il est apparu par la suite que...

emergence [ɪ'mɜ:dʒəns] *n (from hiding)* apparition *f; (of truth)* révélation *f; (of new state, new leader)* émergence *f*

emergency [ɪ'mɜ:dʒənsɪ] *(pl* **emergencies**) *n* urgence *f;* **in an e., in case of e.** en cas d'urgence; **e. exit** sortie *f* de secours; **e. landing** atterrissage *m* forcé; *Pol* **e. powers** pouvoirs *mpl* extraordinaires; **e. services** services *mpl* d'urgence; **e. stop** arrêt *m* d'urgence; *Fin* **e. tax** impôt *m* extraordinaire

emergent [ɪ'mɜ:dʒənt] *adj (talent, ability)* naissant(e); *(nation)* en voie de développement

emery ['emərɪ] *n* émeri *m;* **e. board** lime *f* à ongles *(en papier émeri);* **e. paper** papier *m* émeri

emetic [ɪ'metɪk] **1** *n* émétique *m*

2 *adj* émétique

emigrant ['emɪgrənt] **1** *n* émigrant(e) *m,f; (when settled)* émigré(e) *m,f*

2 *adj* migrant(e); *(when settled)* émigré(e)

emigrate ['emɪgreɪt] *vi* émigrer

emigration [emɪ'greɪʃən] *n* émigration *f*

émigré ['emɪgreɪ] *n* émigré(e) *m,f*

eminence ['emɪnəns] *n* (**a**) *(importance)* position *f* éminente; *(of post)* distinction *f* (**b**) *(title of cardinal)* **Your E.** Votre Éminence

eminent ['emɪnənt] *adj* éminent(e)

eminently ['emɪnəntlɪ] *adv* éminemment

emirate ['emɪreɪt] *n* émirat *m*

emissary ['emɪsərɪ] *(pl* **emissaries**) *n* émissaire *m*

emission [ɪ'mɪʃən] *n (of gas, light, bank notes)* émission *f*

emit [ɪ'mɪt] *(pt & pp* **emitted**) *vt (heat, signal, sound)* émettre; *(smell)* dégager; *(sigh, cry)* pousser

emoticon [ɪ'məʊtɪkɒn] *n Comput* émoticon *m, Can* binette *f*

emotion [ɪ'məʊʃən] *n (strength of feeling)* émotion *f; (individual feeling)* sentiment *m;* **full of e.** ému(e)

emotional [ɪ'məʊʃənəl] *adj (person, reaction)* émotif(-ive); *(problem, shock)* émotionnel(elle); *(film, farewell)* émouvant(e); **to get e.** être ému(e)

emotionally [ɪ'məʊʃənəlɪ] *adv (thank, welcome)* avec effusion; **to be e. involved with sb** avoir une relation intime avec qn; **to get e. involved (with sb)** s'attacher (à qn); **e. deprived** en manque d'affection

emotive [ɪ'məʊtɪv] *adj (issue)* sensible; *(argument, words)* qui fait vibrer la corde sensible

empathize ['empəθaɪz] *vi* **to e. with** *(person)* comprendre; *(plight, problems)* compatir à

empathy ['empəθɪ] *n* affinité(s) *f(pl); (power, ability)* capacité *f* à s'identifier à autrui

emperor ['empərə(r)] *n* empereur *m*

emphasis ['emfəsɪs] *(pl* **emphases** ['emfəsɪːz]) *n* accent *m;* **to lay** *or* **place e. on sth** *(point, fact)* mettre l'accent sur qch; *(word, syllable)* appuyer sur qch

emphasize ['emfəsaɪz] *vt (point, fact)* insister sur; *(word, syllable)* appuyer sur

emphatic [ɪm'fætɪk] *adj (denial, response, person)* catégorique; *(gesture, tone)* énergique

emphatically [ɪm'fætɪkəlɪ] *adv (say)* énergiquement; *(refuse, deny)* catégoriquement; **most e.!** absolument!

empire ['empaɪə(r)] *n also Fig* empire *m*

empirical [em'pɪrɪkəl] *adj* empirique

empiricism [em'pɪrɪsɪzəm] *n* empirisme *m*

employ [ɪm'plɔɪ] **1** *n Formal* **to be in sb's e.** être employé(e) par qn
   2 *vt (workers, force, skills)* employer; *(tool, means)* utiliser

employee [em'plɔɪiː] *n* employé(e) *m,f;* **employees** *(staff)* personnel *m,* salariés *mpl*

employer [ɪm'plɔɪə(r)] *n* employeur(euse) *m,f*

employment [ɪm'plɔɪmənt] *n (a) (work)* emploi *m;* **to be in e.** avoir un emploi; **to be without e.** être sans emploi; **to give e. to sb** employer qn; **e. agency** *or* **bureau** bureau *m ou* agence *f* de placement **(b)** *(use) (of money, force)* emploi *m; (of tool)* utilisation *f*

empower [ɪm'paʊə(r)] *vt* **to e. sb to do sth** habiliter qn à faire qch

empowering [ɪm'paʊərɪŋ] *adj (role, effect)* émancipateur(trice)

empress ['emprɪs] *n* impératrice *f*

emptiness ['emptɪnɪs] *n* vide *m*

empty ['emptɪ] **1** *n (bottle)* bouteille *f* vide
   2 *adj (container, existence)* vide; *(promise, threat, words)* en l'air; **on an e. stomach** l'estomac vide, à jeun
   3 *vt* vider
   4 *vi* se vider

►**empty out** *vt sep (pockets)* vider

empty-handed ['emptɪ'hændɪd] *adv* les mains vides, bredouille

empty-headed ['emptɪ'hedɪd] *adj* sans cervelle; **to be e.** n'avoir rien dans la tête

EMS [iːem'es] *n (abbr* **European Monetary System**) SME *m*

EMU [iːem'juː] *n (abbr* **Economic and Monetary Union**) union *f* économique et monétaire

emu ['iːmjuː] *n* émeu *m*

emulate ['emjʊleɪt] *vt* imiter

emulsion [ɪ'mʌlʃən] *n* émulsion *f*

enable [ɪ'neɪbəl] *vt* **(a)** *(allow)* **to e. sb to do sth** permettre à qn de faire qch **(b)** *Comput (function, device)* mettre en service

enact [ɪ'nækt] *vt (tragedy, play)* jouer; *(law)* promulguer

enamel [ɪ'næməl] **1** *n* émail *m*
   2 *vt (pt & pp* **enamelled,** *Am* **enameled**) émailler

enamoured, *Am* **enamored** [ɪ'næməd] *adj* **to be e. of** être entiché(e) de; **I'm not exactly e. of the idea** je ne peux pas dire que cette idée me ravisse

encampment [ɪn'kæmpmənt] *n Mil* camp *m,* campement *m*

encapsulate [ɪn'kæpsjʊleɪt] *vt* résumer

encase [ɪn'keɪs] *vt* envelopper; *(in concrete)* noyer

enchant [ɪn'tʃɑːnt] *vt* **(a)** *(charm)* enchanter, ravir **(b)** *(put under a spell)* ensorceler

enchanting [ɪn'tʃɑːntɪŋ] *adj (idea)* très séduisant(e); *(voice, person, smile)* charmant(e), ravissant(e)

enchantment [ɪn'tʃɑːntmənt] *n* enchantement *m*

enchantress [ɪn'tʃɑːntrɪs] *n* enchanteresse *f*

encircle [ɪn'sɜːkəl] *vt (of road, walls)* entourer; *(of army, police)* encercler, cerner

enclave ['enkleɪv] *n* enclave *f*

enclose [ɪn'kləʊz] *vt* **(a)** *(surround)* entourer; **an enclosed space** un espace clos **(b)** *(include in letter)* joindre (**in** à); **enclosed please find..., please find enclosed...** veuillez trouver ci-joint *ou* ci-inclus...

enclosure [ɪn'kləʊʒə(r)] *n* **(a)** *(area)* enceinte *f; (for animals)* enclos *m; (in horseracing)* paddock *m* **(b)** *(in letter)* pièce *f* jointe

encode [en'kəʊd] *vt* coder, chiffrer; *Comput* encoder

encompass [ɪn'kʌmpəs] *vt* englober, couvrir

encore ['ɒŋkɔː(r)] *n =* chanson, morceau etc exécutés à la suite d'un rappel; **to call for an e.** bisser; **e.!** bis!

encounter [ɪn'kaʊntə(r)] **1** *n* rencontre *f*
   2 *vt (person, difficulty)* rencontrer; *(enemy)* affronter

encourage [ɪn'kʌrɪdʒ] *vt* encourager; **to e. sb to do sth** encourager qn à faire qch

encouragement [ɪn'kʌrɪdʒmənt] *n* encouragement *m;* **to give sb e.** encourager qn

encouraging [ɪn'kʌrɪdʒɪŋ] *adj* encourageant(e); *(smile)* d'encouragement

►**encroach on, encroach upon** [ɪn'krəʊtʃ] *vt insep* empiéter sur; **the sea is encroaching on the land** la mer gagne du terrain

encrusted [ɪn'krʌstɪd] *adj* **e. with** *(jewels)* incrusté(e) de; *(mud)* couvert(e) de

encrypt [en'krɪpt] *vt Comput* crypter, chiffrer

encumber [ɪn'kʌmbə(r)] *vt Formal* **to be encumbered with** être encombré(e) par

encumbrance [ɪn'kʌmbrəns] *n Formal* gêne *f,* embarras *m* (**to** pour)

encyclical [ɪn'sɪklɪkəl] *n Rel* encyclique *f*

encyclop(a)edia [ɪnsaɪklə'piːdɪə] *n* encyclopédie *f*

encyclop(a)edic [ɪnsaɪklə'piːdɪk] *adj* encyclopédique

end [end] **1** *n* **(a)** *(extremity)* bout *m,* extrémité *f;* **from one e. to the other** d'un bout à l'autre; **e. to e.** bout à bout; **to stand sth on e.** mettre qch debout; **his hair was standing on e.** ses cheveux se dressaient sur sa tête; *Fig* **to come to the e. of the road** *or* **line** être en fin de parcours

(**b**) *(of month, book, meeting)* fin *f*; **for days on e.** pendant des jours entiers; **to put an e. to sth** mettre fin à qch; **to come to an e.** prendre fin; *Fig* **at the e. of the day** au bout du compte; **in the e.** finalement; **she gave me the money back in the e.** elle a fini par me rembourser; **it's not the e. of the world** ce n'est pas la fin du monde; *Fam* **no e. of** énormément de; **e. product** produit *m* fini; *Fig* résultat *m*

(**c**) *(aim, purpose)* fin *f*, but *m*; **an e. in itself** une fin en soi; **to what e.?** à quelle fin?, dans quel but?; **with this e. in view** dans ce but, à cette fin; **the e. justifies the means** la fin justifie les moyens

(**d**) *(idioms) Fam* **to keep one's e. up** ne pas se laisser abattre; *Fam* **to make ends meet** joindre les deux bouts; *Fam* **this job will be the e. of me!** ce boulot, j'y laisserai ma peau!; *Fam* **to get hold of the wrong e. of the stick** mal comprendre; **we shall never hear the e. of it!** on n'a pas fini d'en entendre parler!

2 *vt* finir, terminer; *(argument, uncertainty)* mettre fin à; *Fam* **to e. it all** *(commit suicide)* en finir

3 *vi* finir, se terminer; *(of road, path)* s'arrêter; **it ended in a fight/a divorce** ça a fini en bagarre/par un divorce

▶**end up** *vi* finir; *(in particular place)* se retrouver; **to e. up doing sth** finir par faire qch

endanger [ɪn'deɪndʒə(r)] *vt (person, life)* mettre en danger; *(chances, future, health)* compromettre; **an endangered species** une espèce menacée

endear [ɪn'dɪə(r)] *vt* **to e. oneself to sb** se rendre sympathique aux yeux de qn; **these remarks did not e. her to the voters** ces réflexions ne lui ont pas gagné la faveur des électeurs

endearing [ɪn'dɪərɪŋ] *adj (person, personality)* attachant(e); *(smile, habit)* charmant(e)

endearment [ɪn'dɪəmənt] *n* **terms of e.** mots *mpl* tendres

endeavour, *Am* **endeavor** [ɪn'devə(r)] *Formal* **1** *n* effort *m*
2 *vt* **to e. to do sth** s'efforcer de faire qch

endemic [en'demɪk] *adj* endémique; *Fig* **e. to** propre à

ending ['endɪŋ] *n (of story)* fin *f*; *(of word)* terminaison *f*

endive ['endaɪv] *n* (**a**) **(curly) e.** (chicorée *f*) frisée *f* (**b**) *Am (chicory)* endive *f*

endless ['endlɪs] *adj (desert, number, possibilities)* infini(e); *(list, wait, task)* interminable

endocrine ['endəʊkraɪn] *adj Med* **e. gland** glande *f* endocrine

endocrinology [endəʊkraɪ'nɒlədʒɪ] *n* endocrinologie *f*

endorse [ɪn'dɔːs] *vt* (**a**) *(document, cheque)* endosser; *Br (driving licence)* décompter des points sur (**b**) *(approve) (action)* approuver; *(opinion)* souscrire *ou* adhérer à; *(candidature)* appuyer

endorsement [ɪn'dɔːsmənt] *n* (**a**) *(on document, cheque)* endos *m*; *Br (on driving licence)* = mention portée sur le permis de conduire à la suite d'une infraction (**b**) *(approval) (of action)* approbation *f* (**of** de); *(of opinion)* adhésion *f* (**of** à); *(of candidature)* appui *m* (**of** à)

endow [ɪn'daʊ] *vt* doter (**with** de)

endowment [ɪn'daʊmənt] *n* (**a**) *Fin* dotation *f*; **e. mortgage** = emprunt immobilier associé à une assurance-vie (**b**) *(talent)* don *m*, talent *m*

endurable [ɪn'djʊərəbəl] *adj* supportable

endurance [ɪn'djʊərəns] *n* endurance *f*; **beyond e.** au-delà des limites du supportable; **e. test** épreuve *f* d'endurance; *Fig* **this is a real e. test** ma patience est mise à rude épreuve

endure [ɪn'djʊə(r)] **1** *vt (violence, hardship)* endurer; *(person, insults)* supporter
2 *vi (last)* survivre

enduring [ɪn'djʊərɪŋ] *adj* durable

enema ['enəmə] *n* lavement *m*

enemy ['enəmɪ] **1** *n (pl* **enemies)** ennemi(e) *m,f*; **to make enemies** se faire des ennemis; **to be one's own worst e.** se desservir soi-même
2 *adj (army, ship)* ennemi(e)

energetic [enə'dʒetɪk] *adj* énergique

energetically [enə'dʒetɪklɪ] *adv* énergiquement

energy ['enədʒɪ] *n* énergie *f*; **to save e.** faire des économies d'énergie; **e. crisis** crise *f* de l'énergie

energy-saving ['enədʒɪseɪvɪŋ] *adj* qui économise l'énergie

enervating ['enəveɪtɪŋ] *adj* débilitant(e)

enfeeble [ɪn'fiːbəl] *vt* affaiblir

enfold [ɪn'fəʊld] *vt* envelopper (**in** dans); **to e. sb in one's arms** serrer qn dans ses bras

enforce [ɪn'fɔːs] *vt (regulation)* mettre en vigueur; *(rights)* faire valoir; **to e. the law** faire respecter la loi

enforcement [ɪn'fɔːsmənt] *n (of a law)* mise *f* en vigueur

enfranchise [ɪn'fræntʃaɪz] *vt* accorder le droit de vote à

engage [ɪn'geɪdʒ] **1** *vt* (**a**) *(employ)* engager; *(workmen)* embaucher (**b**) *(occupy) (person)* occuper; *(attention)* fixer; **to e. sb in conversation** engager la conversation avec qn; **to be engaged in doing sth** être occupé(e) à faire qch (**c**) *Mil (enemy)* attaquer (**d**) *(cog, gear)* mettre en prise; **to e. the clutch** embrayer
2 *vi* (**a**) **to e. in** *(activity, sport)* s'adonner à (**b**) *(of cog wheel)* (s')engager

engaged [ɪn'geɪdʒd] *adj* (**a**) *(to be married)* fiancé(e) (**b**) *(busy)* occupé(e) (**in** à); *Br (phone, public toilet)* occupé; **to be otherwise e.** avoir d'autres engagements

engagement [ɪn'geɪdʒmənt] *n* (**a**) *(to be married)* fiançailles *fpl*; **e. ring** bague *f* de fiançailles (**b**) *(appointment)* rendez-vous *m* (**c**) *(military action)* combat *m*, engagement *m*

engaging [ɪn'geɪdʒɪŋ] *adj* engageant(e), attrayant(e)

engender [ɪn'dʒendə(r)] *vt* faire naître, engendrer

engine ['endʒɪn] *n* (**a**) *(of car, plane, ship)* moteur *m*; **e. room** salle *f* des machines; **e. trouble** panne *f* de moteur (**b**) *(of train)* locomotive *f*; **e. driver** conducteur *m*, mécanicien *m*

engineer [endʒɪ'nɪə(r)] **1** *n (technical specialist)* ingénieur *m*; *(mechanic)* dépanneur *m*; *(on ship)* mécanicien *m*
2 *vt (cause) (plan, downfall, defeat)* machiner, manigancer; *(situation)* manigancer

engineering [endʒɪ'nɪərɪŋ] *n* ingénierie *f*

England ['ɪŋglənd] *n* l'Angleterre *f*

English ['ɪŋglɪʃ] **1** *n (language)* anglais *m*; **E. class/teacher** cours *m*/professeur *m* d'anglais

2 *npl* **the E.** les Anglais *mpl*
3 *adj* anglais(e); **the E. Channel** la Manche

English Breakfast

Le petit déjeuner traditionnel anglais se compose d'un plat chaud (des œufs au bacon, par exemple), de céréales ou de porridge, et de toasts à la marmelade d'oranges, le tout accompagné de café ou de thé; aujourd'hui il est généralement remplacé par une collation plus légère.

Englishman ['ɪŋglɪʃmən] *n* Anglais *m*
Englishwoman ['ɪŋglɪʃwʊmən] *n* Anglaise *f*
engrave [ɪn'greɪv] *vt* graver
engraver [ɪn'greɪvə(r)] *n* graveur *m*
engraving [ɪn'greɪvɪŋ] *n* gravure *f*
engrossed [ɪn'grəʊst] *adj* plongé(e) (**in** dans), absorbé(e) (**in** par)
engrossing [ɪn'grəʊsɪŋ] *adj* absorbant(e), captivant(e)
engulf [ɪn'gʌlf] *vt (of waves, flames)* engloutir; *(of feeling)* s'emparer de
enhance [ɪn'hɑːns] *vt (quality of life, chances)* améliorer; *(beauty, colour)* rehausser, mettre en valeur; *(ability, effect)* renforcer; *(reputation, pleasure)* accroître; *(value)* augmenter
enigma [ɪ'nɪgmə] *n* énigme *f*
enigmatic [enɪg'mætɪk] *adj* énigmatique
enjoy [ɪn'dʒɔɪ] *vt* (**a**) *(take pleasure from)* prendre plaisir à; *(film, book, concert)* aimer; *(food, drink)* savourer; **to e. doing sth** aimer faire qch; **to e. oneself** s'amuser (**b**) *(benefit from)* jouir de
enjoyable [ɪn'dʒɔɪəbəl] *adj* agréable
enjoyment [ɪn'dʒɔɪmənt] *n* plaisir *m*; **to get e. out of sth** retirer du plaisir de qch; **to get e. out of doing sth** prendre plaisir à faire qch
enlarge [ɪn'lɑːdʒ] **1** *vt* agrandir; *(hole)* élargir
2 *vi* s'agrandir; **to e. (up)on sth** s'étendre sur qch
enlargement [ɪn'lɑːdʒmənt] *n* agrandissement *m*; *(of hole)* élargissement *m*
enlighten [ɪn'laɪtən] *vt* éclairer (**on** sur)
enlightened [ɪn'laɪtənd] *adj* éclairé(e)
enlightenment [ɪn'laɪtənmənt] *n* *(clarification)* éclaircissement *m*; **for your e.** pour votre édification; *Hist* **the E.** le Siècle des Lumières
enlist [ɪn'lɪst] **1** *vt (support, help)* s'assurer; *(soldier)* enrôler, engager
2 *vi (of soldier)* s'engager
enliven [ɪn'laɪvən] *vt* animer; *(party)* égayer, animer
en masse [ɒn'mæs] *adv* en masse, tous ensemble
enmesh [ɪn'meʃ] *vt* **to be enmeshed in sth** être empêtré(e) dans qch
enmity ['enmɪtɪ] *n* inimitié *f*, hostilité *f*
enormity [ɪ'nɔːmɪtɪ] *n* énormité *f*
enormous [ɪ'nɔːməs] *adj (in physical size)* énorme; *(patience, gratitude, power, intelligence)* immense; *(strength)* colossal(e)
enormously [ɪ'nɔːməslɪ] *adv* énormément
enough [ɪ'nʌf] **1** *adj* assez de; **e. money/wine** assez d'argent/de vin; **more than e. food** plus de nourriture qu'il n'en faut
2 *pron* assez; **to be e.** suffire; **more than e.** plus qu'il n'en faut; **that's e.!** ça suffit!; **e. is e.** il ne faut pas exagérer; **to have e. to live on** avoir de quoi vivre; **e. said!** je vois!; **to have had e. of sb/sth** en avoir assez de qn/qch

3 *adv* (**a**) *(sufficiently)* assez; **good e.** assez bon (bonne); **he didn't try hard e.** il n'a pas vraiment essayé (**b**) *(reasonably)* assez; **she's a nice e. girl** c'est une fille assez sympa; **oddly** *or* **strangely e.,...** chose curieuse,...
enquire = **inquire**
enquiry = **inquiry**
enrage [ɪn'reɪdʒ] *vt* rendre furieux(euse)
enrapture [ɪn'ræptʃə(r)] *vt* éblouir, émerveiller
enraptured [ɪn'ræptʃəd] *adj* ébloui(e), émerveillé(e)
enrich [ɪn'rɪtʃ] *vt* enrichir
enrol, *Am* **enroll** [ɪn'rəʊl] *(pt & pp* **enrolled**) **1** *vt (soldier)* enrôler; *(student)* immatriculer; *(worker)* embaucher
2 *vi (of soldier)* s'enrôler; *(of students)* s'inscrire
enrolment, *Am* **enrollment** [ɪn'rəʊlmənt] *n (of soldier)* enrôlement *m*; *(of student)* immatriculation *f*; *(of worker)* embauche *f*
ensconce [ɪn'skɒns] *vt* **to e. oneself** s'installer confortablement (**in** dans)
ensemble [ɒn'sɒmbəl] *n* ensemble *m*
enshrine [ɪn'ʃraɪn] *vt* **to be enshrined in sth** *(of belief, principle)* être enraciné(e) dans qch
ensign ['ensaɪn] *n* (**a**) *(flag)* drapeau *m*; *Naut* pavillon *m* national (**b**) *Am (naval officer)* enseigne *m (de vaisseau de deuxième classe)*
enslave [ɪn'sleɪv] *vt* réduire à l'esclavage, asservir
ensnare [ɪn'sneə(r)] *vt (animal, criminal)* prendre au piège; *Fig (lover)* attirer dans ses filets
ensue [ɪn'sjuː] *vi* s'ensuivre
ensuing [ɪn'sjuːɪŋ] *adj (in the past)* qui a suivi; *(in the future)* qui suivra
en suite ['ɒn'swiːt] *adj* **e. bathroom** *(in hotel)* salle *f* de bains particulière; *(in house)* salle *f* de bains attenante
ensure [ɪn'ʃʊə(r)] *vt* assurer; **to e. that...** faire en sorte que... + *subjunctive*
ENT [iːen'tiː] *n (abbr* **Ear, Nose and Throat**) ORL *f*; **E. specialist** ORL *mf*
entail [en'teɪl] *vt* (**a**) *(involve)* entraîner, occasionner; *(difficulties)* comporter; **what does the job e.?** en quoi le travail consiste-t-il? (**b**) *Law* **to e. an estate** substituer un bien
entangle [ɪn'tæŋgəl] *vt* **to get** *or* **become entangled in sth** *(of person, animal)* s'empêtrer dans qch; *(of hair, string, wires)* s'emmêler dans qch; *Fig* **he got entangled in the dispute** il s'est retrouvé impliqué dans la dispute
entanglement [ɪn'tæŋgəlmənt] *n* enchevêtrement *m*; **emotional entanglements** complications *fpl* sentimentales
enter ['entə(r)] **1** *vt* (**a**) *(house, country, army)* entrer dans; *(university)* entrer à; *(race, exam, competition)* participer à; **to e. sb for an exam** inscrire qn à un examen; **to e. sb for a race** inscrire qn au nombre des participants d'une course; **it never entered my head that...** il ne m'est jamais venu à l'esprit que...; **to e. a protest** protester formellement (**b**) *Comput (data)* entrer, introduire
2 *vi (go in)* entrer; **to e. for a race** se faire inscrire pour une course
▸**enter into** *vt insep* (**a**) *(begin) (service, relationship)* entrer en; *(dispute)* entrer dans; *(negotiations)* entamer, engager; **to e. into partnership with sb** s'associer avec qn; **to e. into conversation with sb** engager une conversation avec qn (**b**) *(have a part in)* **money**

doesn't e. into it l'argent n'entre pas en ligne de compte

enterprise ['entəpraɪz] *n* (**a**) *(undertaking, company)* entreprise *f* (**b**) *(initiative)* initiative *f*

enterprising ['entəpraɪzɪŋ] *adj* entreprenant(e); *(imaginative)* plein(e) d'imagination; *(solution)* ingénieux(euse)

entertain [entə'teɪn] **1** *vt* (**a**) *(amuse)* divertir, amuser; **to e. guests** recevoir (des invités) (**b**) *(consider) (idea)* considérer; *(hope)* nourrir; *(fear, suspicion)* éprouver **2** *vi (receive guests)* recevoir

entertainer [entə'teɪnə(r)] *n* fantaisiste *mf*; *(comedian)* comique *mf*

entertaining [entə'teɪnɪŋ] **1** *n (of guests)* **to do a lot of e.** recevoir beaucoup **2** *adj (amusing)* divertissant(e), amusant(e)

entertainment [entə'teɪnmənt] *n* (**a**) *(amusement)* divertissement *m*, amusement *m*; *Com* **e. allowance** indemnité *f* de représentation (**b**) *(performances)* spectacle *m*, divertissement *m*; **the e. business** l'industrie *f* du spectacle; **entertainments guide** guide *m* des spectacles

enthral, *Am* **enthrall** [ɪn'θrɔːl] *(pt & pp* **enthralled)** *vt* captiver, passionner; *(of object, beauty)* fasciner; *(of prospect, idea)* enthousiasmer

enthralling [ɪn'θrɔːlɪŋ] *adj* captivant(e), passionnant(e); *(object, beauty)* fascinant(e); *(prospect, idea)* enthousiasmant(e)

enthuse [ɪn'θjuːz] **1** *vt* enthousiasmer **2** *vi* s'enthousiasmer (**about** *or* **over** pour)

enthusiasm [ɪn'θjuːzɪæzəm] *n* enthousiasme *m*

enthusiast [ɪn'θjuːzɪæst] *n* passionné(e) *m,f*; **a golf e.** un passionné de golf

enthusiastic [ɪnθjuːzɪ'æstɪk] *adj* enthousiaste

enthusiastically [ɪnθjuːzɪ'æstɪklɪ] *adv* avec enthousiasme

entice [ɪn'taɪs] *vt* attirer, séduire; **to e. sb to do sth** inciter qn à faire qch; **to e. sb away from sb/sth** appâter qn pour qu'il quitte qn/qch

enticing [ɪn'taɪsɪŋ] *adj (offer, idea)* séduisant(e), tentant(e); *(dish)* alléchant(e); *(smile)* charmeur(euse)

entire [ɪn'taɪə(r)] *adj* (**a**) *(whole)* entier(ère), tout(e); **the e. day** toute la journée, la journée entière (**b**) *(intact)* intact(e)

entirely [ɪn'taɪəlɪ] *adv* entièrement, complètement

entirety [ɪn'taɪərətɪ] *n* intégralité *f*; **in its e.** dans son intégralité, intégralement

entitle [ɪn'taɪtəl] *vt* (**a**) *(allow)* **to e. sb to sth** donner à qn droit à qch; **to e. sb to do sth** permettre à qn de faire qch; **to be entitled to sth** avoir droit à qch; **to be entitled to do sth** avoir le droit de faire qch (**b**) *(book, chapter, song)* intituler

entitlement [ɪn'taɪtəlmənt] *n* droit *m* (**to** à); **holiday e.** congé *m* annuel *(auquel on a droit)*

entity ['entɪtɪ] *(pl* **entities)** *n* entité *f*

entomologist [entə'mɒlədʒɪst] *n* entomologiste *mf*

entomology [entə'mɒlədʒɪ] *n* entomologie *f*

entourage ['ɒntʊraːʒ] *n* entourage *m*

entrails ['entreɪlz] *npl* entrailles *fpl*

entrance¹ ['entrəns] *n* (**a**) *(way in, act of entering)* entrée *f*; **to make one's e.** faire son entrée; **to gain e. to** s'introduire *ou* pénétrer dans (**b**) *(admission) (to club)* admission *f*; *(to cinema)* entrée *f*; **e. examination** examen *m* d'entrée; **e. hall** *(in house)* vestibule *m*; *(in hotel)* hall *m*

entrance² [ɪn'trɑːns] *vt (charm)* ravir, transporter

entrancing [ɪn'trɑːnsɪŋ] *adj* ravissant(e), enchanteur(eresse)

entrant ['entrənt] *n (in race, competition)* inscrit(e) *m,f*; *(in examination)* candidat(e) *m,f*

entreat [ɪn'triːt] *vt* **to e. sb to do sth** implorer qn de faire qch

entreaty [ɪn'triːtɪ] *(pl* **entreaties)** *n* prière *f*, supplication *f*

entrée ['ɒntreɪ] *n (dish before main course)* entrée *f*; *Am (main course)* plat *m* de résistance

entrenched [ɪn'trentʃd] *adj (views, ideas)* arrêté(e); *(customs)* enraciné(e)

entrepreneur [ɒntrəprə'nɜː(r)] *n* entrepreneur *m*

entrepreneurial [ɒntrəprə'nɜːrɪəl] *adj (person)* qui a l'esprit d'entreprise; *(skill, talents)* d'entrepreneur

entrust [ɪn'trʌst] *vt* **to e. sb with sth, to e. sth to sb** confier qch à qn

entry ['entrɪ] *(pl* **entries)** *n* (**a**) *(way in, act of entering)* entrée *f*; **to make one's e.** faire son entrée; **to gain e. to** s'introduire *ou* pénétrer dans (**b**) *(of competitor)* inscription *f*; **e. form** feuille *f* d'inscription (**c**) *(in encyclopedia)* article *m*; *(in dictionary)* entrée *f*; *(in diary)* note *f*

entryphone ['entrɪfəʊn] *n* Interphone® *m*

entwine [ɪn'twaɪn] **1** *vt* entrelacer **2** *vi* s'entrelacer

enumerate [ɪ'njuːməreɪt] *vt* énumérer, détailler

enunciate [ɪ'nʌnsɪeɪt] *vt (sound, word)* prononcer, articuler; *(opinion, view)* énoncer

envelop [ɪn'veləp] *vt* envelopper (**in** dans)

envelope ['envələʊp, 'ɒnvələʊp] *n* enveloppe *f*

enviable ['envɪəbəl] *adj* enviable

envious ['envɪəs] *adj* envieux(euse); **to be e. of sb** envier qn

enviously ['envɪəslɪ] *adv* avec envie

environment [ɪn'vaɪrənmənt] *n* (**a**) *(surroundings)* milieu *m*; **a pleasant working e.** des conditions *fpl* de travail agréables; **a hostile e.** un climat d'hostilité, une ambiance hostile (**b**) *(nature)* **the e.** l'environnement *m*; **Department** *or* **Ministry of the E.** ministère *m* de l'Environnement

environmental [ɪnvaɪrən'mentəl] *adj* **e. damage** dégâts *mpl* causés à l'environnement; **e. disaster** désastre *m* écologique; **e. policy** politique *f* de l'environnement

environmentalist [ɪnvaɪrən'mentəlɪst] *n* écologiste *mf*

environment-friendly [ɪn'vaɪrənmənt'frendlɪ], **environmentally-friendly** [ɪnvaɪrən'mentəlɪ'frendlɪ] *adj (policy)* respectueux(euse) de l'environnement; *(technology, product)* non polluant(e)

environs [ɪn'vaɪrənz] *npl* environs *mpl*, alentours *mpl*

envisage [ɪn'vɪzɪdʒ], *Am* **envision** [en'vɪʒən] *vt* envisager

envoy ['envɔɪ] *n* envoyé(e) *m,f*

envy ['envɪ] **1** *n* envie *f*, jalousie *f*; **to be the e. of sb** être un objet d'envie pour qn **2** *vt (pt & pp* **envied)** envier; **to e. sb sth** envier qch à qn

enzyme ['enzaɪm] *n* enzyme *f*

EOC [iːəʊ'siː] *Br (abbr* **Equal Opportunities Commission)** = organisme gouvernemental qui veille à l'égalité des chances sur le lieu de travail

eon *Am* = **aeon**

epaulette, *Am* **epaulet** ['epəlet] *n* épaulette *f*

ephemeral [ɪ'femərəl] *adj* éphémère

epic ['epɪk] **1** *n (poem, novel)* épopée *f; (film)* film *m* à grand spectacle
    2 *adj* épique

epicentre, Am epicenter ['episentə(r)] *n* épicentre *m*

epicurean [epɪkjʊ'rɪən] *n & adj* épicurien(enne) *m,f*

epidemic [epɪ'demɪk] *also Fig* **1** *n* épidémie *f*
    2 *adj* épidémique

epidermis [epɪ'dɜːmɪs] *n Anat* épiderme *m*

epidural [epɪ'djuːrəl] *n Med* péridurale *f*

epigram ['epɪgræm] *n* épigramme *f*

epilepsy ['epɪlepsɪ] *n* épilepsie *f*

epileptic [epɪ'leptɪk] **1** *n* épileptique *mf*
    2 *adj* épileptique; **e. fit** crise *f* d'épilepsie

epilogue ['epɪlɒg] *n* épilogue *m*

Epiphany [ɪ'pɪfənɪ] *n* Épiphanie *f*

episcopal [ɪ'pɪskəpəl] *adj* épiscopal(e); **e. palace** évêché *m*

episcopalian [ɪpɪskə'peɪlɪən] *n & adj* épiscopalien(-enne) *m,f*

episode ['epɪsəʊd] *n (part of story)* épisode *m; (incident)* incident *m*

epistle [ɪ'pɪsəl] *n also Hum* épître *f*

epitaph ['epɪtɑːf] *n* épitaphe *f*

epithet ['epɪθet] *n* épithète *f*

epitome [ɪ'pɪtəmɪ] *n* **to be the e. of sth** être l'exemple même de qch

epitomize [ɪ'pɪtəmaɪz] *vt* incarner

epoch ['iːpɒk] *n* époque *f*

epoch-making ['iːpɒkmeɪkɪŋ] *adj* qui fait date

eponymous [ɪ'pɒnɪməs] *adj* éponyme

EPS [iːpiː'es] *n (abbr* **earnings per share)** BPA *m*

equable ['ekwəbəl] *adj* constant(e); *(person)* à l'humeur égale

equal ['iːkwəl] **1** *n* égal(e) *m,f;* **to treat sb as an e.** traiter qn d'égal à égal
    2 *adj* (**a**) *(identical)* égal(e) (**to** à); **all things being e.** en principe; **in e. measure** en quantité égale; **on e. terms** sur un pied d'égalité; **e. opportunities** égalité *f* des chances; **e. pay** égalité des salaires; **e. rights** égalité des droits (**b**) *(good enough)* **to be e. to sth** être à la hauteur de qch
    3 *vt (pt & pp* **equalled,** *Am* **equaled)** égaler

equality [ɪ'kwɒlɪtɪ] *n* égalité *f*

equalize ['iːkwəlaɪz] **1** *vt* égaliser; *(chances, forces)* équilibrer
    2 *vi (in sport)* égaliser

equalizer ['iːkwəlaɪzə(r)] *n* (**a**) *(in sport)* but *m* égalisateur (**b**) *Elec* égaliseur *m* de potentiel

equally ['iːkwəlɪ] *adv* (**a**) *(to an equal degree)* tout aussi (**b**) *(in equal amounts) (share, divide)* en parts égales (**c**) *(likewise)* tout aussi bien, de la même manière

equanimity [ekwə'nɪmɪtɪ] *n* sérénité *f*

equate [ɪ'kweɪt] *vt* assimiler (**with** avec)

equation [ɪ'kweɪʒən] *n* équation *f; Fig* **money doesn't even enter the e.** les questions d'argent n'entrent même pas en ligne de compte

equator [ɪ'kweɪtə(r)] *n* équateur *m*

equatorial [ekwə'tɔːrɪəl] *adj* équatorial(e); **E. Guinea** la Guinée équatoriale

equestrian [ɪ'kwestrɪən] **1** *n* cavalier(ère) *m,f; (in circus)* écuyer(ère) *m,f*
    2 *adj (sport, ability)* équestre

equidistant [ekwɪ'dɪstənt] *adj* équidistant(e)

equilateral [ekwɪ'lætərəl] *adj* équilatéral(e)

equilibrium [ekwɪ'lɪbrɪəm] *n* équilibre *m*

equinox ['ekwɪnɒks] *n* équinoxe *m*

equip [ɪ'kwɪp] *(pt & pp* **equipped)** *vt* (**a**) *(provide with equipment)* équiper (**with** de); **the plane is equipped with the latest technology** l'avion est doté des équipements les plus modernes (**b**) *(prepare)* préparer (**for** pour)

equipment [ɪ'kwɪpmənt] *n* équipement *m; (in factory)* installations *fpl,* matériel *m;* **e. allowance** subvention *f* pour l'achat de matériel

equitable ['ekwɪtəbəl] *adj* équitable

Equity ['ekwɪtɪ] *n* = syndicat britannique des artistes de théâtre et de télévision

equity ['ekwɪtɪ] *(pl* **equities)** *n* (**a**) *(fairness)* équité *f* (**b**) *Fin (of shareholders)* fonds *mpl* ou capitaux *mpl* propres; *(of company)* capital *m* actions; **equities** actions *fpl* ordinaires

equivalent [ɪ'kwɪvələnt] **1** *n* équivalent *m*
    2 *adj* équivalent(e) (**to** à)

equivocal [ɪ'kwɪvəkəl] *adj* équivoque, ambigu(ë)

equivocate [ɪ'kwɪvəkeɪt] *vi* user d'équivoques *ou* de faux-fuyants

equivocation [ɪkwɪvə'keɪʃən] *n* paroles *fpl* équivoques, faux-fuyants *mpl*

ER [iː'ɑː(r)] *n* (**a**) *Br (abbr* **Elizabeth Regina)** la Reine Elizabeth (**b**) *Am (abbr* **Emergency Room)** urgences *fpl*

era ['ɪərə] *n* ère *f*

eradicate [ɪ'rædɪkeɪt] *vt* éradiquer

erase [ɪ'reɪz] *vt* effacer; *(with eraser)* gommer

eraser [ɪ'reɪzə(r)] *n* gomme *f*

erect [ɪ'rekt] **1** *adj* droit(e), debout; *(penis, nipples)* en érection
    2 *vt (building)* ériger; *(statue)* élever, ériger; *(scaffolding)* dresser

erection [ɪ'rekʃən] *n* (**a**) *(of building, statue)* construction *f,* érection *f* (**b**) *(erect penis)* érection *f*

ergonomic [ɜːgə'nɒmɪk] *adj* ergonomique

ergonomics [ɜːgə'nɒmɪks] *n* ergonomic *f*

Eritrea [erɪ'treɪə] *n* l'Érythrée *f*

Eritrean [erɪ'treɪən] **1** *n* Érythréen(enne) *m,f*
    2 *adj* érythréen(enne)

ERM [iːɑː'rem] *n (abbr* **Exchange Rate Mechanism)** mécanisme *m* de change *(du SME)*

ermine ['ɜːmɪn] *n* hermine *f*

erode [ɪ'rəʊd] **1** *vt (rock, soil)* éroder; *(metal)* corroder, ronger; *Fig (confidence, power)* miner
    2 *vi (of rock, soil)* s'éroder; *(of metal)* se corroder; *Fig (of confidence, power)* s'éroder peu à peu

erogenous [ɪ'rɒdʒɪnəs] *adj* érogène; **e. zone** zone *f* érogène

Eros ['ɪərɒs] *n* Éros

erosion [ɪ'rəʊʒən] *n (of rock, soil) & Fig (of confidence, power)* érosion *f; (of metal)* corrosion *f*

erotic [ɪ'rɒtɪk] *adj* érotique

eroticism [ɪ'rɒtɪsɪzəm] *n* érotisme *m*

err [ɜː(r)] *vi (make mistake)* faire erreur; **to e. on the side of caution** pécher par excès de prudence; *Prov* **to e. is human** l'erreur est humaine

errand ['erənd] *n* commission *f,* course *f;* **to run errands for sb** (aller) faire des commissions *ou* des courses pour qn; *Old-fashioned* **e. boy** garçon *m* de courses

erratic [ɪ'rætɪk] *adj (service, results, pulse)* irrégulier(-ère); *(playing, performance)* inégal(e); *(behaviour)* imprévisible; *(person)* lunatique; *(driving)* mal assuré(e)

erroneous [ɪˈrəʊnɪəs] *adj* erroné(e)

error [ˈerə(r)] *n (mistake)* erreur *f*, faute *f*; **to make an e.** faire une erreur; **in e.** par erreur; **an e. of judgement** une erreur de jugement; **to see the e. of one's ways** reconnaître ses erreurs

ersatz [ˈɜːzæts] *adj* **e. coffee** un succédané de café

erstwhile [ˈɜːstwaɪl] *adj Lit* ancien(enne)

erudite [ˈerʊdaɪt] *adj* érudit(e)

erudition [erʊˈdɪʃən] *n* érudition *f*

erupt [ɪˈrʌpt] *vi (of volcano)* entrer en éruption; *(of person)* exploser; *(of anger, violence)* éclater; *(of spot)* sortir

eruption [ɪˈrʌpʃən] *n* éruption *f*

escalate [ˈeskəleɪt] *vi (of prices)* monter en flèche; *(of conflict)* s'intensifier, s'aggraver

escalation [eskəˈleɪʃən] *n (of prices)* montée *f* en flèche; *(of conflict)* escalade *f*

escalator [ˈeskəleɪtə(r)] *n* escalier *m* roulant, Escalator® *m*

escalope [ˈeskəlɒp] *n* escalope *f*

escapade [ˈeskəpeɪd] *n* fredaine *f*, frasque *f*

escape [ɪsˈkeɪp] **1** *n (of person)* évasion *f*; *(of gas, water)* fuite *f*; **to make one's e.** s'échapper; *Com* **e. clause** clause *f* échappatoire; **e. route** *(from fire)* itinéraire *m* de sortie de secours; *(of criminal)* itinéraire emprunté pour s'échapper
2 *vt (danger, punishment)* échapper à; **to e. sb's notice** échapper à l'attention de qn; **her name escapes me** son nom m'échappe
3 *vi (of person, gas, water)* s'échapper (**from** de); *(from prison)* s'évader (**from** de); **to e. unhurt** s'en tirer indemne; **he escaped to Italy** il s'est enfui en Italie; **to e. from reality** s'évader de la réalité

escapee [eskeɪˈpiː] *n* évadé(e) *m,f*

escapism [ɪsˈkeɪpɪzəm] *n* évasion *f* (hors de la réalité)

escapist [ɪsˈkeɪpɪst] **1** *n* personne *f* qui cherche à s'évader de la réalité
2 *adj* d'évasion

escapologist [eskəˈpɒlədʒɪst] *n* prestidigitateur *m* spécialiste de l'évasion

escarpment [ɪsˈkɑːpmənt] *n* escarpement *m*

eschew [ɪsˈtʃuː] *vt* éviter; **to e. sb's company** fuir *ou* éviter qn

escort **1** *n* [ˈeskɔːt] **(a)** *(for convoy)* escorte *f*; *(for tourists)* guide *m*; *(ship)* bâtiment *m* d'escorte; **under e.** sous escorte; *Mil* **e. duty** service *m* d'escorte **(b)** *(from agency) (woman)* hôtesse *f*; *(man)* call boy *m*; **e. agency** agence *f* d'hôtesses
2 *vt* [ɪsˈkɔːt] escorter; *(prisoner)* conduire sous escorte

escudo [eˈskuːdəʊ] *(pl* **escudos***) n* escudo *m*

Eskimo [ˈeskɪməʊ] **1** *n (pl* **Eskimos***)* Esquimau(aude) *m,f*
2 *adj* esquimau(aude), eskimo *inv*

esophagus *Am* = **oesophagus**

esoteric [esəʊˈterɪk] *adj* ésotérique

ESP [iːesˈpiː] *n (abbr* **extrasensory perception***)* perception *f* extra-sensorielle

especially [ɪsˈpeʃəlɪ] *adv* **(a)** *(in particular)* surtout **(b)** *(more than normally)* particulièrement; **we were e. lucky with the weather** le temps nous a été particulièrement favorable **(c)** *(expressly)* (tout) spéciale-

ment, exprès; **I did it e. for you** je l'ai fait spécialement *ou* exprès pour vous

Esperanto [espəˈræntəʊ] *n* l'Espéranto *m*

espionage [ˈespɪənɑːʒ] *n* espionnage *m*

esplanade [espləˈneɪd] *n* esplanade *f*

espouse [ɪsˈpaʊz] *vt* épouser

espresso [esˈpresəʊ] *(pl* **espressos***) n* expresso *m*

Esq *(abbr* **Esquire***)* **Derek Wilson, E.** = Monsieur Derek Wilson

essay [ˈeseɪ] *n (at school)* composition *f*; *(for younger pupils)* rédaction *f*; *(at university)* dissertation *f*

essayist [ˈeseɪɪst] *n* essayiste *mf*

essence [ˈesəns] *n* **(a)** *(most important part or quality)* essence *f*; *(of speech)* essentiel *m*; *(of question)* fond *m*; **in e.** essentiellement, surtout; **the very e. of bravery** le courage même; **time is of the e.** le temps est le facteur prioritaire **(b)** *Culin (extract)* extrait *m*

essential [ɪˈsenʃəl] **1** *npl* **essentials** *(basic foodstuffs)* produits *mpl* de première nécessité; *(basic issues)* essentiel *m*; **just pack a few essentials** ne prends que l'essentiel
2 *adj* **(a)** *(basic)* essentiel(elle); **e. oil** huile *f* essentielle **(b)** *(indispensable)* essentiel(elle), indispensable (**to** *or* **for** à); **it is e. that...** il est essentiel que... + *subjunctive*

essentially [ɪˈsenʃəlɪ] *adv* essentiellement

Essex [ˈesɪks] *n* l'Essex *m*, = comté dans le sud-est de l'Angleterre; *Br Fam Pej* **E. girl** minette *f*; *Br Fam Pej* **E. man** = stéréotype du réactionnaire bête et vulgaire, originaire de l'Essex

---

Essex

Il s'agit de stéréotypes sociaux apparus au cours des années 80. L'"Essex Girl" (originaire de l'Essex, comté situé à l'est de Londres) est censée être une jeune femme d'origine modeste aux mœurs légères, vulgaire, bruyante, et peu intelligente. L'"Essex Man" est lui aussi vulgaire et bruyant; de plus, il est réactionnaire et inculte.

EST [iːesˈtiː] *n Am (abbr* **Eastern Standard Time***)* heure *f* de la côte est de l'Amérique du Nord

establish [ɪsˈtæblɪʃ] *vt* **(a)** *(set up) (company)* fonder; *(custom)* instaurer; *(system, organization)* établir; **to e. oneself in business** s'établir dans les affaires; **to e. a reputation** se faire une réputation; **the film established her as an important director** avec ce film, elle s'est affirmée comme un metteur en scène important **(b)** *(prove)* établir

established [ɪsˈtæblɪʃt] *adj* établi(e); *(fact)* acquis(e)

establishment [ɪsˈtæblɪʃmənt] *n* **(a)** **the E.** *(dominant group)* l'establishment *m*; *(prevailing values)* l'ordre *m* établi **(b)** *(hotel, restaurant)* établissement *m* **(c)** *(of company, organization)* constitution *f*; *(of fact)* constatation *f*

estate [ɪsˈteɪt] *n* **(a)** *Law (possessions)* biens *mpl* **(b)** *(land)* terre *f*, propriété *f*; *Br* **(housing) e.** lotissement *m*; *(with council houses)* cité *f* HLM.; *Br* **e. agency** agence *f* immobilière; *Br* **e. agent** agent *m* immobilier **(c)** *Br* **e. (car)** break *m*

esteem [ɪsˈtiːm] **1** *n* estime *f*, considération *f*; **to hold sb in high e.** avoir qn en haute estime; **to hold sb in low e.** avoir peu d'estime pour qn
2 *vt* **(a)** *(person)* estimer; *(thing)* priser **(b)** *Formal (consider)* considérer; **she esteemed it a great**

honour to be invited elle se sentit fort honorée d'avoir été invitée

esthetic *Am* = **aesthetic**

estimate 1 *n* ['estɪmət] *(calculation)* évaluation *f*, calcul *m*; *Com* devis *m*; **at a rough e.** à vue de nez
  2 *vt* ['estɪmeɪt] estimer, évaluer; *(value)* estimer

estimation [estɪ'meɪʃən] *n* (**a**) *(calculation)* estimation *f*, évaluation *f* (**b**) *(judgement)* jugement *m*, opinion *f*; **in my e.** à mon avis; **to go up/down in sb's e.** monter/descendre dans l'estime de qn

Estonia [es'təʊnɪə] *n* l'Estonie *f*

Estonian [es'təʊnɪən] **1** *n* (**a**) *(person)* Estonien(enne) *m,f* (**b**) *(language)* estonien *m*
  2 *adj* estonien(enne)

estranged [ɪs'treɪndʒd] *adj (couple)* séparé(e); **her e. husband** son mari, dont elle est séparée; **their e. son** leur fils, avec qui ils sont brouillés

estrogen *Am* = **oestrogen**

estuary ['estjʊərɪ] *(pl* **estuaries)** *n* estuaire *m*

ETA [i:ti:'eɪ] *n (abbr* **estimated time of arrival)** heure *f* d'arrivée prévue

et al [et'æl] *(abbr* **et alii)** et autres

etc [et'setrə] *adv (abbr* **et cetera)** etc

etch [etʃ] *vt* graver à l'eau-forte; *Fig* **to be etched in sb's memory** être gravé(e) dans la mémoire de qn

etching ['etʃɪŋ] *n* (gravure *f* à l')eau-forte *f*

eternal [ɪ'tɜːnəl] *adj* éternel(elle); *Fig (continual)* continuel(elle), sans fin

eternally [ɪ'tɜːnəlɪ] *adv* éternellement

eternity [ɪ'tɜːnɪtɪ] *n* éternité *f*; *Fam* **to wait/last an e.** attendre/durer une éternité; **e. ring** = bague entièrement sertie de pierres symbolisant l'éternité du mariage

ether ['iːθə(r)] *n* éther *m*

ethereal [ɪ'θɪərɪəl] *adj* éthéré(e); *(fragile)* léger(ère), impalpable

ethical ['eθɪkəl] *adj* éthique, moral(e)

ethically ['eθɪklɪ] *adv* sur le plan éthique; **to behave e.** suivre la déontologie

ethics ['eθɪks] *npl* éthique *f*, morale *f*; *(of profession)* déontologie *f*

Ethiopia [iːθɪ'əʊpɪə] *n* l'Éthiopie *f*

Ethiopian [iːθɪ'əʊpɪən] **1** *n (person)* Éthiopien(enne) *m,f*
  2 *adj* éthiopien(enne)

ethnic ['eθnɪk] *adj* ethnique; **e. cleansing** purification *f* ethnique; **e. minority** minorité *f* ethnique

ethnically ['eθnɪklɪ] *adv* du point de vue ethnique

ethnocentric [eθnəʊ'sentrɪk] *adj* ethnocentrique

ethnography [eθ'nɒɡrəfɪ] *n* ethnographie *f*

ethnology [eθ'nɒlədʒɪ] *n* ethnologie *f*

ethos ['iːθɒs] *n (of people)* génie *m*; *(of class)* culture *f*

etiquette ['etɪket] *n* étiquette *f*; **professional e.** usages *mpl* professionnels

Etruscan [ɪ'trʌskən] **1** *n* (**a**) *(person)* Étrusque *mf* (**b**) *(language)* étrusque *m*
  2 *adj* étrusque

etymological [etɪmə'lɒdʒɪkəl] *adj* étymologique

etymology [etɪ'mɒlədʒɪ] *n* étymologie *f*

EU [iː'juː] *n (abbr* **European Union)** UE *f*

eucalyptus [juːkə'lɪptəs] *n* eucalyptus *m*

Eucharist ['juːkərɪst] *n* **the E.** l'eucharistie *f*

eulogize ['juːlədʒaɪz] *vt* faire l'éloge de

eulogy ['juːlədʒɪ] *(pl* **eulogies)** *n* éloge *m*

eunuch ['juːnək] *n* eunuque *m*

euphemism ['juːfɪmɪzəm] *n* euphémisme *m*

euphemistic [juːfɪ'mɪstɪk] *adj* euphémique

euphoria [juː'fɔːrɪə] *n* euphorie *f*

euphoric [juː'fɔːrɪk] *adj* euphorique

Eurasian [jʊə'reɪʒən] **1** *n* Eurasien(enne) *m,f*
  2 *adj* eurasien(enne); *(continent)* eurasiatique

EURATOM [jʊə'rætəm] *n (abbr* **European Atomic Energy Community)** CEEA *f*, EURATOM *f*

eureka [jʊə'riːkə] *exclam* eureka!

Euro, euro ['jʊərəʊ] *(pl* **Euros, euros)** *n (European currency)* euro *m*; **E. area, E. zone** zone *f* euro

Eurocheque ['jʊərəʊtʃek] *n* Eurocheque *m*

Eurodollar ['jʊərəʊdɒlə(r)] *n* eurodollar *m*

Euro-election ['jʊərəʊɪ'lekʃən] *n* **the Euro-elections** les élections *fpl* européennes

Euroland ['jʊərəʊlænd] *n* Eurolande *f*

Euro-MP ['jʊərəʊempiː] *n* député(e) *m,f* européen(enne)

Europe ['jʊərəp] *n* l'Europe *f*

European [jʊərə'piːən] **1** *n* Européen(enne) *m,f*
  2 *adj* européen(enne); **E. Commission** Commission *f* européenne; **E. Community** Communauté *f* européenne; **E. Court of Human Rights** Cour *f* européenne des droits de l'homme; **E. Court of Justice** Cour de justice européenne; **E. Currency Unit** unité *f* monétaire européenne; **E. Economic Community** Communauté *f* économique européenne; **E. Free Trade Association** Association *f* européenne de libre-échange; **E. Monetary System** Système *m* monétaire européen; **E. Parliament** Parlement *m* européen; **E. Union** Union *f* européenne

Europhile ['jʊərəʊ'faɪl] *n* europhile *mf*, partisan *m* de l'Europe unie

Eurosceptic [jʊərəʊ'skeptɪk] *n* eurosceptique *mf*

Eurostar® ['jʊərəʊstɑː(r)] *n* Eurostar® *m*

Eustachian tube [juːs'teɪʃən'tjuːb] *n Anat* trompe *f* d'Eustache

euthanasia [juːθə'neɪzɪə] *n* euthanasie *f*

evacuate [ɪ'vækjʊeɪt] *vt* évacuer

evacuation [ɪvækjʊ'eɪʃən] *n* évacuation *f*

evacuee [ɪvækjʊ'iː] *n* évacué(e) *m,f*

evade [ɪ'veɪd] *vt (blow)* esquiver, éviter; *(question)* éluder; *(pursuer)* échapper à; *(responsibilities)* se soustraire à, se dérober à; **to e. tax** frauder le fisc

evaluate [ɪ'væljʊeɪt] *vt* évaluer

evaluation [ɪvæljʊ'eɪʃən] *n* évaluation *f*

evangelical [iːvæn'dʒelɪkəl] **1** *n* protestant(e) *m,f* évangélique
  2 *adj* évangélique

evangelism [ɪ'vændʒɪlɪzəm] *n* évangélisme *m*

evangelist [ɪ'vændʒɪlɪst] *n* évangéliste *mf*

evangelize [ɪ'vændʒɪlaɪz] **1** *vt* évangéliser; *(person)* prêcher l'Évangile à
  2 *vi* prêcher l'Évangile

evaporate [ɪ'væpəreɪt] **1** *vt* faire évaporer; **evaporated milk** lait *m* condensé
  2 *vi (of liquid)* s'évaporer; *Fig (of enthusiasm, hope)* s'envoler

evaporation [ɪvæpə'reɪʃən] *n* évaporation *f*

evasion [ɪ'veɪʒən] *n (escape)* évasion *f*, fuite *f*; *(of pursuer, responsibilities, question)* dérobade *f*; **(tax) e.** fraude *f* fiscale

evasive [ɪ'veɪsɪv] *adj (person, reply)* évasif(ive); **to take e. action** faire une manœuvre d'évitement

eve [iːv] *n (day before)* veille *f*; **on the e. of** à la veille de

even ['iːvən] **1** *adj* (**a**) *(flat)* égal(e); *(smooth)* uni(e) (**b**) *(regular) (breathing, pace)* régulier(ère), égal(e); *(temperature)* constant(e); **to have an e. temper** être d'humeur égale; **e. number** nombre *m* pair (**c**) *(equal)* **to have an e. chance (of doing sth)** avoir une chance sur deux (de faire qch); *Fig* **to get e. with sb** prendre sa revanche sur qn

2 *adv* (**a**) même; *(with comparatives)* encore; **without e. speaking** sans même dire un mot; **I never e. saw it** je ne l'ai même pas vu; **e. bigger/more interesting** encore plus gros (grosse)/intéressant(e); **e. as I speak** au moment même où je parle (**b**) *(in phrases)* **e. if** même si; **e. now** même maintenant, aujourd'hui encore; **e. so** cependant, quand même; **e. then** *(already)* déjà (à cette époque); *(all the same)* même dans ces conditions; **e. though** bien que + *subjunctive*

3 *vt (make equal)* rendre égal(e); **to e. the odds** égaliser les chances

▸**even out 1** *vt sep (differences)* niveler; *(workload)* répartir plus également; *(inequalities)* réduire; **to e. things out** rendre les choses équitables **2** *vi (of differences)* se niveler; *(of workload)* être réparti(e) plus également; *(of inequalities)* se réduire

▸**even up** *vt sep* égaliser; **to e. things up** équilibrer les choses

even-handed ['iːvən'hændɪd] *adj* juste, équitable

evening ['iːvnɪŋ] *n* soir *m*; *(referring to duration)* soirée *f*; **tomorrow e.** demain soir; **yesterday e.** hier soir; **good e.!**, *Fam* **e.!** bonsoir!; **in the e.** le soir; **a musical/cultural e.** une soirée musicale/culturelle; **e. class** cours *m* du soir; **e. dress** *(for men)* tenue *f* de soirée; *(for women)* robe *f* du soir; **e. paper** journal *m* du soir; **e. performance** *(of play)* représentation *f* en soirée

evenly ['iːvənlɪ] *adv* (**a**) *(uniformly)* uniformément (**b**) *(regularly) (breathe)* régulièrement, de façon régulière; *(speak)* calmement (**c**) *(equally) (divide, distribute)* également, de façon égale; **e. matched** *(in size)* de grandeur égale; *(in strength)* de force égale

evensong ['iːvənsɒŋ] *n Rel* office *m* du soir

event [ɪ'vent] *n* (**a**) *(occurrence)* événement *m*; **in any e.** en tout cas; **in the e. of fire** en cas d'incendie; **in the e. of her refusing** au cas où elle refuserait; **after the e.** après coup (**b**) *(in athletics)* épreuve *f*

even-tempered ['iːvən'tempəd] *adj* d'humeur égale

eventful [ɪ'ventfʊl] *adj (day, life)* mouvementé(e), riche en événements

eventual [ɪ'ventjʊəl] *adj* final(e), définitif(ive)

eventuality [ɪventjʊ'ælɪtɪ] *(pl* **eventualities**) *n* éventualité *f*; **in that e.** dans cette éventualité

eventually [ɪ'ventjʊəlɪ] *adv (in the end)* finalement, en fin de compte; *(at a future date)* par la suite; **they e. reached the castle** ils ont fini par arriver au château; **he'll do it e.** il le fera tôt ou tard

ever ['evə(r)] *adv* (**a**) *(at any time)* **have you e. been to Spain?** es-tu déjà allé en Espagne?; **do you e. see Alan these days?** ça t'arrive de voir Alan?; **the worst/best e.** le pire/meilleur qui soit; **more than e.** plus que jamais; **she's a liar/fool if e. there was one** c'est une menteuse/idiote de première (**b**) *(always)* **e. since (then)/1960** depuis (lors)/1960; **all she e. does is criticize** elle ne fait que critiquer; **she was as friendly as e.** elle était toujours aussi aimable; **e. the gentleman, he opened the door for her** toujours galant, il lui ouvrit la porte; **for e.** pour toujours

(**c**) *(with negative sense)* **not e.** jamais; **hardly e.** presque jamais; **nothing e. happens** il ne se passe jamais rien; **I don't think I'll e. see him again** je ne pense pas que je le reverrai; **I seldom if e. see her** je la vois peu ou pas du tout

(**d**) *(for emphasis)* **e. so pretty** si joli(e); **e. so much** *or* **such a lot of money** tant d'argent; **e. so slightly** très légèrement; **e. such a nice girl** une fille si sympathique

evergreen ['evəɡriːn] **1** *n (tree)* arbre *m* à feuilles persistantes; *(bush)* arbuste *m* à feuilles persistantes **2** *adj* à feuilles persistantes; *Fig* **e. topic** question *f* toujours d'actualité

everlasting [evə'lɑːstɪŋ] *adj (eternal)* éternel(elle); *(continual)* continuel(elle), sans fin

evermore [evə'mɔː(r)] *adv Formal* toujours; **for e.** à jamais

every ['evrɪ] *adj* (**a**) *(each)* chaque; **children of e. age** des enfants de tous âges; **at e. opportunity** à la moindre occasion; **from e. side** de tous côtés; **e. one of us** chacun(e) d'entre nous; **e. man for himself!** chacun pour soi! (**b**) *(indicating regular occurrence)* **e. week** chaque semaine, toutes les semaines; **e. ten years** tous les dix ans; **e. other** *or* **second day** tous les deux jours, un jour sur deux; **e. other line** une ligne sur deux; **e. so often**, **e. now and again** de temps en temps (**c**) *(for emphasis)* **you have e. right to be angry** vous avez tout lieu d'être mécontent; **e. bit as good/ intelligent as...** tout aussi bon (bonne)/intelligent(e) que...; **she has e. chance of winning** elle a de très fortes chances de gagner

everybody ['evrɪbɒdɪ] *pron* tout le monde, chacun(e) *m,f*; **e. I know was there** tous ceux que je connais se trouvaient là; **e. else** tous les autres; **e. who is anybody** les gens qui comptent

everyday ['evrɪdeɪ] *adj* (**a**) *(daily)* journalier(ère), quotidien(enne); **it's an e. occurrence** ça se produit tous les jours (**b**) *(used every day)* de tous les jours; **for e. wear/use** à porter/utiliser tous les jours; **e. expression** expression *f* courante (**c**) *(ordinary)* usuel(elle), ordinaire

everyone ['evrɪwʌn] = **everybody**

everything ['evrɪθɪŋ] *pron* tout; **e. I did seemed to go wrong** tout ce que je faisais semblait voué à l'échec; **he did e. possible** il a fait tout son possible; **money isn't e.** l'argent n'est pas tout

everywhere ['evrɪweə(r)] *adv* partout; **to look e.** regarder partout; **e. you go** où que vous alliez, partout où vous allez; **e. you look there is poverty** de quelque côté que l'on se tourne, on voit la misère

evict [ɪ'vɪkt] *vt* expulser

eviction [ɪ'vɪkʃən] *n* expulsion *f*; **e. order** avis *m* d'expulsion

evidence ['evɪdəns] **1** *n* (**a**) *(reason for belief)* évidence *f*; *(indication)* marque *f*, signe *m*; **to be in e.** être en évidence; **to show e. of** donner des signes de; **there was no e. of his stay in the house** rien ne montrait qu'il eût séjourné dans la maison (**b**) *(in court case)* preuve *f*; *(testimony)* témoignage *m*; **to give e.** témoigner; **to call sb in e.** appeler qn à la barre des témoins; **to turn** *Br* **King's/Queen's** *or Am* **State's e.** témoigner contre ses complices *(sous promesse de pardon)* **2** *vt Formal* **as evidenced by...** comme en témoigne...

evident ['evɪdənt] *adj* évident(e), manifeste

evidently ['evɪdəntlɪ] *adv* (**a**) *(clearly)* manifeste-ment, à l'évidence; **there have e. been some problems** il est clair *ou* évident qu'il y a eu des problèmes (**b**) *(apparently)* apparemment; **so she won't be coming? – e. not** alors elle ne vient pas? – il semble bien que non

evil ['iːvəl] **1** *n* mal *m*
2 *adj (person, look)* mauvais(e), malveillant(e); *(influence, effect)* maléfique; *(spirit)* malfaisant(e), malin(igne); *(temper)* coléreux(euse)

evildoer ['iːvəlduːə(r)] *n Lit* homme (femme) *m,f* méchant(e)

evil-looking ['iːvəlʊkɪŋ] *adj* à l'aspect malfaisant

evil-minded ['iːvəl'maɪndɪd] *adj* malintentionné(e)

evil-smelling ['iːvəl'smelɪŋ] *adj* nauséabond(e)

evince [ɪ'vɪns] *vt Formal* faire montre de

evocation [evə'keɪʃən] *n* évocation *f*

evocative [ɪ'vɒkətɪv] *adj* évocateur(trice) (**of** de)

evoke [ɪ'vəʊk] *vt* (**a**) *(conjure up)* évoquer (**b**) *(provoke)* provoquer, susciter

evolution [iːvə'luːʃən] *n* évolution *f*, développement *m*

evolutionary [iːvə'luːʃənərɪ] *adj* évolutif(ive)

evolve [ɪ'vɒlv] **1** *vt (theory, plan)* élaborer, mettre au point
2 *vi (of species, situation)* évoluer, se développer

ewe [juː] *n* brebis *f*

ex [eks] *n Fam (former husband, wife, girlfriend, boyfriend)* ex *mf*

ex- [eks] *pref (former)* ex-; **ex-minister/teacher** ancien ministre *m*/professeur *m*

exacerbate [eg'zæsəbeɪt] *vt* aggraver

exact [ɪg'zækt] **1** *adj* exact(e), précis(e); **at the e. moment when...** juste au moment où..., au moment précis où...; **those were her e. words** c'est ce qu'elle a dit mot pour mot; **the e. opposite** exactement le contraire; **on 5 January, to be e.** le 5 janvier, pour être précis
2 *vt (obedience, tax)* exiger (**from** de); *(promise)* extorquer (**from** à)

exacting [ɪg'zæktɪŋ] *adj* exigeant(e)

exactitude [ɪg'zæktɪtjuːd] *n Formal* exactitude *f*

exactly [ɪg'zæktlɪ] *adv* exactement; **not e.** pas tout à fait; *Ironic* pas vraiment

exaggerate [ɪg'zædʒəreɪt] *vt & vi* exagérer

exaggerated [ɪg'zædʒəreɪtɪd] *adj* exagéré(e)

exaggeration [ɪgzædʒə'reɪʃən] *n* exagération *f*

exalt [ɪg'zɔːlt] *vt Formal* exalter

exalted [ɪg'zɔːltɪd] *adj* (**a**) *(high) (rank)* élevé(e); *(person)* haut placé(e) (**b**) *Formal (joyful)* exalté(e)

exam [ɪg'zæm] *n* examen *m*; **to take** *or* **sit an e.** passer un examen; **e. result** résultat *m* d'examen

examination [ɪgzæmɪ'neɪʃən] *n* examen *m*; *Med* examen médical; **to take** *or* **sit an e.** passer un examen; **e. board** ≃ académie *f (division administrative de l'enseignement)*; **e. result** résultat *m* d'examen

examine [ɪg'zæmɪn] *vt (evidence, patient, question)* examiner; *(student)* faire passer un examen à; **to e. one's conscience** faire son examen de conscience

examinee [ɪgzæmɪ'niː] *n* candidat(e) *m,f*

examiner [ɪg'zæmɪnə(r)] *n* examinateur(trice) *m,f*

example [ɪg'zɑːmpəl] *n* exemple *m*; **for e.** par exemple; **to set an e. (to sb)** donner l'exemple (à qn); **to make an e. of sb** faire un exemple de qn; **to follow** **sb's e.** suivre l'exemple de qn; **to lead by e.** montrer l'exemple

exasperate [ɪg'zɑːspəreɪt] *vt* exaspérer; **to get exasperated** s'irriter

exasperating [ɪg'zɑːspəreɪtɪŋ] *adj* exaspérant(e)

exasperation [ɪgzɑːspə'reɪʃən] *n* exaspération *f*

excavate ['ekskəveɪt] *vt (hole, tunnel)* creuser; *(remains)* déterrer, exhumer; *(site)* faire des fouilles dans

excavation [ekskə'veɪʃən] *n* excavation *f*

excavator ['ekskəveɪtə(r)] *n (machine)* excavatrice *f*

exceed [ɪk'siːd] *vt* (**a**) *(limits)* excéder, dépasser; *(hopes, fears)* dépasser; *(one's authority)* outrepasser (**b**) *(number, amount)* dépasser

exceedingly [ɪk'siːdɪŋlɪ] *adv* extrêmement

excel [ɪk'sel] *(pt & pp* **excelled***)* **1** *vt also Ironic* **to e. oneself** se surpasser
2 *vi* exceller (**at** *or* **in** à *ou* en)

excellence ['eksələns] *n* excellence *f*

excellency ['eksələnsɪ] *n* **Your/His E.** Votre/Son Excellence *f*

excellent ['eksələnt] *adj* excellent(e)

except [ɪk'sept] **1** *prep* sauf, à l'exception de; **nobody e. him** personne excepté *ou* sauf lui; **I would go, e. I'm busy** j'irais bien, mais je suis occupé; **e. for** à part; **e. that** excepté que, si ce n'est que; **e. when** sauf *ou* à part quand
2 *vt* excepter, exclure (**from** de); **present company excepted** les personnes présentes exceptées; **not excepting...** sans excepter...

exception [ɪk'sepʃən] *n* (**a**) *(thing excepted)* exception *f*; **to make an e. of sth/for sb** faire une exception pour qch/qn; **with the e. of...** à l'exception de..., exception faite de...; **without e.** sans exception; **the e. proves the rule** c'est l'exception qui confirme la règle (**b**) **to take e. to sth** *(be offended)* se formaliser *ou* s'offenser de qch; *(object)* trouver à redire à qch

exceptionable [ɪk'sepʃənəbəl] *adj Formal* critiquable; *(offensive)* offensant(e)

exceptional [ɪk'sepʃənəl] *adj* exceptionnel(elle)

exceptionally [ɪk'sepʃənəlɪ] *adv* exceptionnellement; *(in exceptional cases)* à titre exceptionnel

excerpt ['eksɜːpt] *n* extrait *m* (**from** de)

excess [ɪk'ses] *n* excès *m*; **to do sth to e.** faire qch à l'excès; **to pay the e.** *(on ticket)* payer un supplément; **e. baggage** excédent *m* de bagages

excessive [ɪk'sesɪv] *adj* excessif(ive)

excessively [ɪk'sesɪvlɪ] *adv* extrêmement; *(eat, drink)* à l'excès

exchange [ɪks'tʃeɪndʒ] **1** *n* (**a**) *(of prisoners, ideas)* échange *m*; **in e. (for)** en échange (de); **a heated e.** un échange de paroles assez vives; **e. visit** échange (**b**) *Fin (of currency)* change *m*; **e. controls** contrôle *m* des changes; **e. rate** taux *m* de change; **e. rate mechanism** mécanisme *m* de change (**c**) **(Stock) E.** Bourse *f* (des valeurs) (**d**) **(telephone) e.** central *m* téléphonique
2 *vt* échanger; **to e. sth for sth** échanger qch contre qch

exchangeable [ɪks'tʃeɪndʒəbəl] *adj* échangeable (**for** contre)

exchequer [eks'tʃekə(r)] *n Br* **the E.** ≃ le Trésor Public; **the Chancellor of the E.** le Ministre des Finances

excise 1 *n* ['eksaɪz] **e. (duties)** *(tax)* droits *mpl* d'accise
2 *vt* [ɪk'saɪz] *(remove) (tumour)* exciser; *(piece of text)* couper

excitable [ɪkˈsaɪtəbəl] *adj* nerveux(euse)

excite [ɪkˈsaɪt] *vt* (**a**) *(get worked up)* énerver, surexciter; *(arouse enthusiasm in)* enthousiasmer; *(stimulate)* exciter (**b**) *(give rise to)* (admiration, desire) provoquer; *(envy, interest)* susciter; *(curiosity)* piquer

excited [ɪkˈsaɪtɪd] *adj* (worked up) énervé(e), excité(e); *(enthusiastic)* enthousiaste; **to get e. (about)** s'exciter (pour); *(angry)* s'énerver (contre)

excitedly [ɪkˈsaɪtɪdlɪ] *adv* (speak, laugh) avec animation; *(wait)* avec une impatience fébrile

excitement [ɪkˈsaɪtmənt] *n* (agitation) agitation *f*; *(enthusiasm)* animation *f*, enthousiasme *m*; **to cause great e.** faire sensation

exciting [ɪkˈsaɪtɪŋ] *adj* passionnant(e); *(idea, prospect)* enthousiasmant(e)

exclaim [ɪksˈkleɪm] **1** *vt* **"leave me alone,"** he **exclaimed** "laissez-moi," s'est-il écrié
  2 *vi* s'exclamer, s'écrier

exclamation [ekskləˈmeɪʃən] *n* exclamation *f*; *Br* **e. mark**, *Am* **e. point** point *m* d'exclamation

exclamatory [eksˈklæmətərɪ] *adj* exclamatif(ive)

exclude [ɪksˈkluːd] *vt* exclure (**from** de); *(doubt, suspicion)* écarter; **excluding...** à l'exclusion de...

exclusion [ɪksˈkluːʒən] *n* exclusion *f* (**from** de); **to the e. of...** à l'exclusion de...

exclusive [ɪksˈkluːsɪv] **1** *n* (in newspaper, on TV) exclusivité *f*
  2 *adj* (**a**) *(right, article, interview)* exclusif(ive) (**b**) *(chic)* huppé(e); *(club, social circle)* très fermé(e); *(clothing, jewellery)* de grande marque (**c**) *(only)* seul(e), unique
  3 *adv* **e. of delivery** frais de livraison non compris; **e. of tax** hors taxes

exclusively [ɪksˈkluːsɪvlɪ] *adv* exclusivement; *(in newspaper, on TV)* en exclusivité

excommunicate [ekskəˈmjuːnɪkeɪt] *vt* excommunier

excommunication [ekskəmjuːnɪˈkeɪʃən] *n* excommunication *f*

excrement [ˈekskrɪmənt] *n* excrément *m*

excrescence [eksˈkresəns] *n* excroissance *f*

excrete [ɪksˈkriːt] *vt Formal* excréter

excruciating [ɪksˈkruːʃɪeɪtɪŋ] *adj* (pain, embarrassment) atroce; **the whole evening was e.** (embarrassing) on a été gênés toute la soirée; *(boring)* on s'est horriblement ennuyés toute la soirée

excruciatingly [ɪksˈkruːʃɪeɪtɪŋlɪ] *adv* (painful, embarrassing) atrocement; *Fam* **e. funny** tordant(e)

excursion [ɪksˈkɜːʃən] *n* excursion *f*

excuse 1 *n* [ɪksˈkjuːs] excuse *f*; **that's no e.** ce n'est pas une excuse *ou* une raison; **a poor e. for a father/bus service** un père/un service d'autobus lamentable
  2 *vt* [ɪksˈkjuːz] (**a**) *(forgive)* excuser, pardonner; **e. me!** pardon!, excusez-moi!; **e. me?** (what did you say?) pardon? (**b**) *(exempt)* exempter, dispenser (**from** de) (**c**) **to e. oneself** s'excuser

ex-directory [eksdɪˈrektərɪ] *adj Br* **to be e.** (of person, number) être sur la liste rouge

execrable [ˈeksɪkrəbəl] *adj* exécrable, abominable

execute [ˈeksɪkjuːt] *vt* (prisoner, order) exécuter; *(plan, operation)* mettre à exécution

execution [eksɪˈkjuːʃən] *n* (of prisoner, order) exécution *f*; **in the e. of one's duty** dans l'exercice de ses fonctions

executioner [eksɪˈkjuːʃənə(r)] *n* bourreau *m*

executive [ɪgˈzekjʊtɪv] **1** *n* (businessman) cadre *m*; *(committee)* bureau *m*, comité *m* central
  2 *adj* (post) de cadre; *(car, suite)* de luxe; *Br* **e. director** directeur(trice) *m,f* administratif(ive)

executor [ɪgˈzekjʊtə(r)] *n Law* exécuteur(trice) *m,f* testamentaire

exemplary [ɪgˈzemplərɪ] *adj* exemplaire

exemplify [ɪgˈzemplɪfaɪ] *(pt & pp* **exemplified**) *vt* illustrer

exempt [ɪgˈzempt] **1** *adj* exempté(e), dispensé(e) (**from** de)
  2 *vt* exempter, dispenser (**from** de)

exemption [ɪgˈzem(p)ʃən] *n* exemption *f*, dispense *f* (**from** de)

exercise [ˈeksəsaɪz] **1** *n* exercice *m*; **to take e.** faire de l'exercice; **e. bike** vélo *m* d'appartement; **e. book** cahier *m*
  2 *vt* (**a**) *(body, mind)* exercer (**b**) *(right, influence)* exercer; *(caution, restraint)* user de
  3 *vi* faire de l'exercice; *(train)* s'entraîner

exert [ɪgˈzɜːt] *vt* (pressure, influence) exercer; *(force)* faire usage de; **to e. oneself** se remuer, se donner du mal

exertion [ɪgˈzɜːʃən] *n* (of force) usage *m*, emploi *m*; *(effort)* effort *m*

exfoliant [eksˈfəʊlɪənt] *n* exfoliant *m*

exhale [eksˈheɪl] *vi* expirer

exhaust [ɪgˈzɔːst] **1** *n* (on car) échappement *m*; **e. (fumes)** gaz *mpl* d'échappement; **e. pipe** tuyau *m* d'échappement
  2 *vt* (person, resources) épuiser

exhausted [ɪgˈzɔːstɪd] *adj* épuisé(e)

exhausting [ɪgˈzɔːstɪŋ] *adj* épuisant(e)

exhaustion [ɪgˈzɔːstʃən] *n* épuisement *m*

exhaustive [ɪgˈzɔːstɪv] *adj* (list) exhaustif(ive); *(analysis, description)* détaillé(e), minutieux(euse); *(enquiry, search)* approfondi(e)

exhibit [ɪgˈzɪbɪt] **1** *n* (in art exhibition) objet *m* exposé; *(in court case)* pièce *f* à conviction
  2 *vt* (**a**) *(object, goods)* exhiber, montrer (**b**) *(painting in exhibition)* exposer (**c**) *(show)* (courage, judgement) faire preuve de; **to e. signs of stress/wear** donner des signes de tension/d'usure

exhibition [eksɪˈbɪʃən] *n* (**a**) *(of paintings)* exposition *f*; *Fam Fig* **to make an e. of oneself** se donner en spectacle (**b**) *(of courage, bad manners)* démonstration *f*; **it was a disgraceful e.** ce fut un spectacle honteux

exhibitionist [eksɪˈbɪʃənɪst] *n* (**a**) *(show-off)* = personne qui aime se faire remarquer (**b**) *Psy* exhibitionniste *mf*

exhibitor [ɪgˈzɪbɪtə(r)] *n* exposant(e) *m,f*

exhilarated [ɪgˈzɪləreɪtɪd] *adj* grisé(e)

exhilarating [ɪgˈzɪləreɪtɪŋ] *adj* (air, walk) vivifiant(e); *(experience)* exaltant(e), grisant(e); *(news)* enthousiasmant(e)

exhort [ɪgˈzɔːt] *vt* exhorter, encourager (**to do sth** à faire qch)

exhortation [ɪgzɔːˈteɪʃən] *n* exhortation *f*

exhume [eksˈhjuːm] *vt* exhumer, déterrer

exigent [ˈeksɪdʒənt] *adj Formal* (**a**) *(urgent)* urgent(e), pressant(e) (**b**) *(demanding)* exigeant(e)

exile [ˈeksaɪl] **1** *n* (**a**) *(banishment)* exil *m*, bannissement *m*; **in e.** en exil (**b**) *(exiled person)* exilé(e) *m,f*
  2 *vt* exiler

exist [ɪgˈzɪst] *vi* (**a**) *(be in existence)* exister; *(of conditions)* régner (**b**) *(survive)* se maintenir en vie, survivre (**on** avec)
existence [ɪgˈzɪstəns] *n* existence *f*; **in e.** existant(e), qui existe; **to come into e.** naître; **to go out of e.** disparaître, cesser d'exister
existential [egzɪsˈtenʃəl] *adj* existentiel(elle)
existentialism [egzɪsˈtenʃəlɪzəm] *n* existentialisme *m*
existentialist [egzɪsˈtenʃəlɪst] *n & adj* existentialiste *mf*
existing [ɪgˈzɪstɪŋ] *adj* existant(e), actuel(elle)
exit [ˈeksɪt] **1** *n* sortie *f*; **to make an e.** sortir; *Pol* **e. poll** = sondage effectué auprès des électeurs immédiatement après qu'ils ont voté; **e. visa** visa *m* de sortie
2 *vi (leave) & Comput* sortir
exodus [ˈeksədəs] *n* exode *m*
ex officio [ˈeksəˈfɪʃɪəʊ] *adj (member)* de droit
exonerate [ɪgˈzɒnəreɪt] *vt (absolve)* disculper, innocenter (**from** *or* **of** de)
exorbitant [ɪgˈzɔːbɪtənt] *adj* exorbitant(e)
exorcism [ˈeksɔːsɪzəm] *n* exorcisme *m*
exorcist [ˈeksɔːsɪst] *n* exorciste *mf*
exorcize [ˈeksɔːsaɪz] *vt* exorciser
exotic [ɪgˈzɒtɪk] *adj* exotique
expand [ɪksˈpænd] **1** *vt (production, output)* accroître; *(empire, company)* agrandir; *(mind, circle of friends)* élargir; *(range, idea)* développer
2 *vi (of solid, gas)* se dilater; *(of company)* s'agrandir
▶**expand on, expand upon** *vt insep* développer
expanded [ɪksˈpændɪd] *adj* étendu(e); *Comput (memory)* expansé(e); **e. polystyrene** polystyrène *m* expansé
expanding [ɪksˈpændɪŋ] *adj (market, company)* en expansion, qui se développe; *(universe)* en expansion
expanse [eksˈpæns] *n* étendue *f*
expansion [ɪksˈpænʃən] *n* expansion *f*; *(of gas)* dilatation *f*; *Comput* **e. card** carte *f* d'extension
expansive [ɪksˈpænsɪv] *adj (gas)* dilatable; *(person)* expansif(ive); **in an e. mood** d'humeur expansive
expat [eksˈpæt] *n & adj Br Fam* expatrié(e) *m,f*
expatriate 1 *n* [eksˈpætrɪət] expatrié(e) *m,f*
2 *vt* [eksˈpætrɪeɪt] expatrier
expect [ɪksˈpekt] **1** *vt* (**a**) *(anticipate)* s'attendre à; **to e. to do sth** compter *ou* espérer faire qch; **to e. sb to do sth** s'attendre à ce que qn fasse qch; **I expected as much** je m'y attendais; **to e. the worst** s'attendre au pire; **to be expecting a baby** attendre un bébé
(**b**) *(require)* **to e. sb to do sth** attendre de qn qu'il/elle fasse qch; **to e. sth from sb** attendre qch de qn; **I know what is expected of me** je sais ce qu'on attend de moi; **to e. too much from sb/sth** trop attendre de qn/qch
(**c**) *(suppose)* **to e. (that)...** penser que...; **I e. so/not** je crois bien que oui/non
2 *vi (be pregnant)* **to be expecting** attendre un bébé
expectancy [ɪksˈpektənsɪ] *n* attente *f*; **an air of e.** l'air d'attendre quelque chose
expectant [ɪksˈpektənt] *adj* impatient(e); **e. mother** future maman *f*
expectation [ekspekˈteɪʃən] *n* espérance *f*; **in (the) e. of sth** dans l'attente de qch; **to have high expectations of sb/sth** attendre beaucoup de qn/qch; **to come up to expectations** se montrer à la hauteur; **to fall short of (sb's) expectations** décevoir (qn); **contrary to all expectations** contre toute attente

expected [ɪksˈpektɪd] *adj* attendu(e); *(hoped for)* espéré(e)
expectorant [ɪksˈpektərənt] **1** *n Med* expectorant *m*
2 *adj* expectorant(e)
expediency [ɪksˈpiːdɪənsɪ] *n* opportunité *f*; *Pej (opportunism)* opportunisme *m*
expedient [ɪksˈpiːdɪənt] **1** *n* expédient *m*
2 *adj* opportun(e), expédient(e)
expedite [ˈekspɪdaɪt] *vt Formal* activer, accélérer
expedition [ekspəˈdɪʃən] *n* expédition *f*; *Fam* **a shopping e.** une séance de shopping
expeditionary [ekspəˈdɪʃənərɪ] *adj Mil* **e. force/corps** force *f*/corps *m* expéditionnaire
expel [ɪksˈpel] *(pt & pp* **expelled***) vt* expulser; *(from school)* renvoyer
expendable [ɪksˈpendəbəl] *adj (person)* qui n'est pas irremplaçable; *(troops)* que l'on peut sacrifier
expenditure [ɪksˈpendɪtʃə(r)] *n (of money, energy)* dépense *f*
expense [ɪksˈpens] *n* (**a**) *(cost)* dépense *f*, frais *mpl*; **to go to great e. (to do sth)** faire de grosses dépenses (pour faire qch); **no e. was spared** on n'a pas regardé à la dépense; **at the e. of one's health/sanity** aux dépens de sa santé/santé mentale; **to make a joke at sb's e.** faire une plaisanterie aux dépens de qn (**b**) *Com* **expenses** frais *mpl*, dépenses *fpl*; **it's on expenses** ça va sur la note de frais; **all expenses paid** tous frais payés; **e. account** note *f* de frais
expensive [ɪksˈpensɪv] *adj (object, shop, restaurant)* cher (chère); *(procedure, habit)* coûteux(euse); *(tastes)* de luxe; *(mistake)* qui coûte cher
experience [ɪksˈpɪərɪəns] **1** *n* expérience *f*; **to learn from e.** tirer les leçons d'une expérience; **in my e.** d'après mon expérience
2 *vt (emotions, pain)* ressentir; *(hunger, success)* connaître, faire l'expérience de; *(difficulties, problems)* avoir; *(ill-treatment)* subir
experienced [ɪksˈpɪərɪənst] *adj* expérimenté(e); **to be e. in sth** avoir de l'expérience en qch; *(observer)* averti(e)
experiment [ɪksˈperɪmənt] **1** *n* expérience *f*; **as an e.** à titre d'essai
2 *vi* expérimenter (**on** sur); **to e. with** *(technique, drugs)* essayer
experimental [ɪksperɪˈmentəl] *adj* expérimental(e)
expert [ˈekspɜːt] **1** *n* expert *m*, spécialiste *mf*
2 *adj* expert(e), habile; *(advice, opinion)* d'un expert; **to be e. in** *or* **at sth** être expert en qch; *Comput* **e. system** système *m* expert; *Law* **e. witness** expert *m* cité comme témoin
expertise [ekspɜːˈtiːz] *n (technical, financial)* compétence *f*, connaissances *fpl*; *(as cook, carpenter)* savoir-faire *m*
expertly [ˈekspɜːtlɪ] *adv* de manière experte
expiate [ˈekspɪeɪt] *vt Formal* expier
expire [ɪksˈpaɪə(r)] *vi* (**a**) *(of law, deadline, passport)* expirer (**b**) *Lit (die)* expirer
expiry [ɪksˈpaɪərɪ] *n* expiration *f*, fin *f*; **e. date** (date *f* d')échéance *f*, date d'expiration
explain [ɪksˈpleɪn] **1** *vt* expliquer; **to e. oneself** *(make oneself clear)* s'expliquer; *(justify oneself)* se justifier
2 *vi* donner des explications, expliquer; *(make oneself clear)* s'expliquer
▶**explain away** *vt sep (give explanation for)* donner une explication satisfaisante à; *(justify)* justifier

explanation [eksplə'neɪʃən] *n* explication *f*; **to give an e. of sth** *(make clear)* expliquer qch; *(justify)* justifier qch

explanatory [ɪks'plænətərɪ] *adj* explicatif(ive)

expletive [ɪks'pliːtɪv] *n* juron *m*

explicable [eks'plɪkəbəl] *adj* explicable

explicit [eks'plɪsɪt] *adj* explicite

explicitly [eks'plɪsɪtlɪ] *adv* de manière explicite

explode [ɪks'pləʊd] **1** *vt (bomb)* faire exploser; *Fig (idea, theory)* démontrer la fausseté de
2 *vi (of bomb)* & *Fig (with anger)* exploser; *(of mine)* sauter; **to e. with laughter** éclater de rire

exploit 1 *n* ['eksplɔɪt] exploit *m*
2 *vt* [eks'plɔɪt] **(a)** *(take unfair advantage of)* exploiter **(b)** *(use) (resources, scandal)* exploiter; *(talents)* mettre à profit

exploitation [eksplɔɪ'teɪʃən] *n* exploitation *f*

exploration [eksplə'reɪʃən] *n* exploration *f*

exploratory [ɪks'plɒrətərɪ] *adj (trip)* d'exploration; *(surgery, discussions, talks)* exploratoire

explore [ɪks'plɔː(r)] **1** *vt (area, countryside)* explorer; *(possibility, idea)* étudier
2 *vi* partir en exploration

explorer [ɪks'plɒrə(r)] *n* explorateur(trice) *m,f*

explosion [ɪks'pləʊʒən] *n also Fig* explosion *f*

explosive [ɪks'pləʊsɪv] **1** *n* explosif *m*
2 *adj also Fig* explosif(ive)

exponent [ɪks'pəʊnənt] *n* **(a)** *(of theory, idea)* avocat(e) *m,f*; *(of piece of music)* interprète *mf* **(b)** *Math* exposant *m*

exponential [ekspəʊ'nenʃəl] *adj* exponentiel(elle)

export 1 *n* ['ekspɔːt] **(a)** *(product)* article *m* d'exportation; **exports** *(of country)* exportations *fpl* **(b)** *(activity)* exportation *f*; **e. duty** droit(s) *m(pl)* de sortie; **e. licence** licence *f* d'exportation; **e. trade** exportations *fpl*
2 *vt* [eks'pɔːt] *also Comput* exporter

exportation [ekspɔː'teɪʃən] *n* exportation *f*

exporter [eks'pɔːtə(r)] *n* exportateur(trice) *m,f*

expose [ɪks'pəʊz] *vt* **(a)** *(to air, cold, danger)* & *Phot* exposer **(to** à); *(wire)* mettre à jour; **to e. oneself to danger** s'exposer au danger **(b)** *(reveal) (secret)* éventer; *(crime)* dévoiler; *(criminal)* démasquer; *(feelings)* afficher; **to e. sb as a traitor/criminal** révéler que qn est un traître/criminel; **to e. oneself** *(of flasher)* s'exhiber

exposé [eks'pəʊzeɪ] *n (article, book)* exposé *m*; *(of scandal, corruption)* révélations *fpl*

exposed [ɪks'pəʊzd] *adj* exposé(e) **(to** à)

exposition [ekspə'zɪʃən] *n (explanation)* exposition *f*, exposé *m*

expostulate [ɪks'pɒstjʊleɪt] *vi Formal* vitupérer

exposure [ɪks'pəʊʒə(r)] *n* **(a)** *(to air, cold, danger)* exposition *f*; **to die of e.** mourir de froid **(b)** *(publicity)* couverture *f*; **to get a lot of e.** faire l'objet d'une importante couverture médiatique **(c)** *(of crime)* révélation *f*; *(of criminal, scandal)* dénonciation *f* **(d)** *Phot* pose *f*; **e. meter** posemètre *m*

expound [ɪks'paʊnd] *vt Formal* exposer

express [ɪks'pres] **1** *n (train)* express *m*, rapide *m*
2 *adj* **(a)** *(clear) (purpose, instruction)* exprès(esse); *(order)* formel(elle) **(b)** *(rapid) (letter, delivery)* exprès *inv*; *(train)* express *inv*
3 *adv* **to send sth e.** envoyer qch en exprès
4 *vt* exprimer; **to e. oneself** s'exprimer

expression [ɪks'preʃən] *n* expression *f*

expressionism [ɪks'preʃənɪzəm] *n* expressionnisme *m*

expressionist [ɪks'preʃənɪst] *n & adj* expressionniste *mf*

expressionless [ɪks'preʃənlɪs] *adj* sans expression

expressive [ɪks'presɪv] *adj* expressif(ive); *(gesture, silence)* éloquent(e)

expressly [ɪks'preslɪ] *adv* expressément

expropriate [eks'prəʊprɪeɪt] *vt* exproprier

expropriation [eksprəʊprɪ'eɪʃən] *n* expropriation *f*

expulsion [ɪks'pʌlʃən] *n* expulsion *f*; *(from school)* renvoi *m*

expunge [ɪks'pʌndʒ] *vt* effacer

expurgate ['ekspɜːgeɪt] *vt* expurger

exquisite ['ekskwɪzɪt] *adj* exquis(e); *(pleasure)* vif (vive)

exquisitely [eks'kwɪzɪtlɪ] *adv* d'une manière exquise

extant [eks'tænt] *adj* qui existe encore

extempore [ɪks'tempərɪ] **1** *adj (speech)* impromptu(e)
2 *adv* **to speak e.** improviser

extemporize [ɪks'tempəraɪz] *vi* improviser

extend [ɪks'tend] **1** *vt* **(a)** *(in space)* étendre, allonger; *(knowledge)* accroître; *(frontiers)* faire reculer; *(house)* agrandir **(b)** *(in time)* prolonger **(c)** *(give, offer) (one's hand)* tendre; *(thanks)* présenter; *(support)* offrir; *Fin* **to e. credit to sb** accorder un crédit à qn
2 *vi* **(a)** *(in space)* s'étendre **(b)** *(in time)* se prolonger, continuer

extended family [ɪks'tendɪd'fæmɪlɪ] *n* famille *f* élargie

extension [ɪks'tenʃən] *n* **(a)** *(to building)* annexe *f* **(b)** *(in time)* prolongation *f*; *(for essay)* délai *m* supplémentaire **(c)** *(for telephone)* poste *m* **(d)** **e. (cable)** rallonge *f*

extensive [ɪks'tensɪv] *adj (area, knowledge)* vaste, étendu(e); *(damage, repairs)* important(e); **to make e. use of sth** faire un usage considérable de qch

extensively [ɪks'tensɪvlɪ] *adv (travel, read)* énormément; *(revised, rewritten)* entièrement; *(damaged)* gravement; **to use sth e.** se servir beaucoup de qch

extent [ɪks'tent] *n* **(a)** *(of land, damage, knowledge)* étendue *f* **(b)** *(degree)* **to an e., to a certain e., to some e.** jusqu'à un certain point, dans une certaine mesure; **to a large e.** en grande partie, dans une large mesure; **to such an e. that...** à tel point que...; **to what e.?** jusqu'à quel point?

extenuating circumstances [ɪks'tenjʊeɪtɪŋ'sɜːkəmstænsɪz] *npl* circonstances *fpl* atténuantes

exterior [ɪks'tɪərɪə(r)] **1** *n (of building, car)* extérieur *m*; *(of person)* extérieur, dehors *mpl*
2 *adj* extérieur(e)

exterminate [ɪks'tɜːmɪneɪt] *vt* exterminer; *(disease)* éradiquer

extermination [ɪkstɜːmɪ'neɪʃən] *n* extermination *f*; *(of disease)* éradication *f*

external [ɪks'tɜːnəl] *adj (events, trade, debt)* extérieur(e); *(angle, damage, wall)* externe; *Univ (examiner)* de l'extérieur; *Pol* **e. affairs** affaires *fpl* étrangères *ou* extérieures; **for e. use only** *(on medicine)* à usage externe

extinct [ɪks'tɪŋkt] *adj (animal, species)* disparu(e), qui n'existe plus; *(volcano)* éteint(e)

extinction [ɪks'tɪŋkʃən] *n* extinction *f*; **to be threatened with e.** être en voie de disparition

extinguish [ɪks'tɪŋgwɪʃ] *vt (fire)* éteindre; *(hope)* anéantir

extinguisher [ɪks'tɪŋgwɪʃə(r)] *n* extincteur *m*

extirpate ['ekstɜːpeɪt] *vt Formal* extirper

extol, *Am* **extoll** [ɪks'təʊl] *(pt & pp* **extolled***) vt (virtues, merits)* exalter, vanter; *(beauty)* célébrer, chanter

extort [ɪks'tɔːt] *vt (money)* extorquer (**from** à); *(promise)* arracher (**from** à)

extortion [ɪks'tɔːʃən] *n* extorsion *f*

extortionate [ɪks'tɔːʃənɪt] *adj* exorbitant(e)

extra ['ekstrə] **1** *n (in film)* figurant(e) *m,f; (on bill)* supplément *m*
   2 *adj* (**a**) *(additional)* supplémentaire, de plus; **no e. charge** sans supplément de prix; **e. time** *(in sporting contest)* prolongation *f* (**b**) *(spare)* de réserve, de rechange
   3 *adv* (**a**) *(more than usual)* extrêmement; **to be e. careful** faire particulièrement attention; **e. large** *(clothing)* grand patron; **e. special** très spécial(e) (**b**) *(charge, pay)* en plus, en sus

extract1 *n* ['ekstrækt] (**a**) *(concentrate)* extrait *m*, concentré *m* (**b**) *(from book, film)* extrait *m*
   2 *vt* [ɪks'trækt] *(tooth, raw material)* extraire (**from** de); *(confession, information)* soutirer (**from** à)

extraction [ɪks'trækʃən] *n* (**a**) *(removal)* extraction *f* (**b**) *(origin) (social)* extraction *f; (geographical)* origine *f;* **she is of Danish e.** elle est d'origine danoise

extractor fan [ɪks'træktəfæn] *n* aérateur *m*

extracurricular ['ekstrəkə'rɪkjʊlə(r)] *adj Sch* extrascolaire

extradite ['ekstrədaɪt] *vt* extrader

extradition [ekstrə'dɪʃən] *n* extradition *f*

extrajudicial ['ekstrədʒuː'dɪʃəl] *adj* extrajudiciaire

extramarital ['ekstrə'mærɪtəl] *adj* extraconjugal(e)

extramural ['ekstrə'mjʊərəl] *adj Univ* de formation continue

extraneous [ɪks'treɪnɪəs] *adj Formal (details)* sans rapport; *(considerations)* en dehors de la question

extraordinarily [ɪks'trɔːdənərɪlɪ] *adv* extra-ordinairement

extraordinary [ɪks'trɔːdənrɪ] *adj* extraordinaire; **e. powers** pouvoirs *mpl* extraordinaires; **e. general meeting** assemblée *f* générale extraordinaire

extrapolate [ɪk'stræpəleɪt] *vt & vi* extrapoler (**from** à partir de)

extrapolation [ɪkstræpə'leɪʃən] *n* extrapolation *f*

extrasensory perception ['ekstrə'sensərɪpə'sepʃən] *n* perception *f* extrasensorielle

extraterrestrial ['ekstrətɪ'restrɪəl] *n & adj* extra-terrestre *mf*

extravagance [ɪks'trævəgəns] *n* (**a**) *(excessive spending)* gaspillage *m* (**b**) *(extravagant purchase)* folie *f*

extravagant [ɪks'trævəgənt] *adj (person)* dépensier(-ère); *(tastes)* dispendieux(euse); *(object)* hors de prix

extravaganza [ekstrævə'gænzə] *n (lavish production)* grand spectacle *m*

extreme [ɪks'triːm] **1** *n* extrême *m;* **in the e.** à l'extrême; **to go from one e. to the other** passer d'un extrême à l'autre; **to go to extremes** pousser les choses à l'extrême
   2 *adj* extrême; *Pol* **the e. left** l'extrême gauche *f*

extremely [ɪks'triːmlɪ] *adv* extrêmement

extremism [ɪks'triːmɪzəm] *n* extrémisme *m*

extremist [ɪks'triːmɪst] *n & adj* extrémiste *mf*

extremity [ɪks'tremɪtɪ] *(pl* **extremities***) n* (**a**) *(end)* extrémité *f* (**b**) **extremities** *(of body)* extrémités *fpl* (**c**) *(extreme situation)* situation *f* extrême; *(extreme measure)* mesure *f* extrême

extricate ['ekstrɪkeɪt] *vt* dégager, tirer; **to e. oneself from** *(danger, difficulties)* se tirer de

extrovert ['ekstrəvɜːt] *n & adj* extraverti(e) *m,f*

exuberance [ɪg'zjuːbərəns] *n* exubérance *f*

exuberant [ɪg'zjuːbərənt] *adj* exubérant(e)

exude [ɪg'zjuːd] *vt (sweat, odour)* exsuder; *(health, confidence)* déborder de

exult [ɪg'zʌlt] *vi* exulter, se réjouir (**in** de)

exultant [ɪg'zʌltənt] *adj (mood)* joyeux(euse); *(cry)* de triomphe

eye [aɪ] **1** *n* (**a**) *(of person, storm)* œil *m; (of needle)* chas *m;* **to open/close one's eyes** ouvrir/fermer les yeux; **to look sb straight in the e.** regarder qn droit dans les yeux; **as far as the e. can see** à perte de vue; **to make e. contact with sb** regarder qn (droit) dans les yeux; **e. drops** *(medicine)* gouttes *fpl* pour les yeux; **at e. level** à la hauteur des yeux; **e. shadow** ombre *f* à paupières; **e. test** examen *m* de la vue
   (**b**) *(idioms)* **in the eye(s) of the law** aux yeux de la loi; **to be in the public e.** occuper une position en vue; **to have an e. for a bargain** savoir reconnaître une bonne affaire; **to have an e. for detail/colour** avoir l'œil pour les détails/les couleurs; **to look at sth with a critical e.** regarder qch d'un œil critique; **to see e. to e. with sb** voir les choses du même œil que qn; **for your eyes only** confidentiel(elle); **to keep one's eyes and ears open** rester en éveil; **to keep one's eyes peeled** *or* **skinned** ouvrir l'œil; **open sb's eyes to sth** ouvrir *ou* dessiller les yeux à qn sur qch; **to shut** *or* **close one's eyes to sth** fermer les yeux sur qch; **to do sth with one's eyes open** faire qch en connaissance de cause; **to catch sb's e.** attirer l'attention de qn; **to have eyes in** *or* **at the back of one's head** avoir des yeux derrière la tête; **he only has eyes for her** il n'a d'yeux que pour elle; **to set** *or* **lay eyes on sth** poser les yeux sur qch; **I saw it with my own eyes** je l'ai vu de mes propres yeux; **to run** *or* **cast one's e. over sth** jeter un coup d'œil sur qch; **to keep an e. on sb/sth** surveiller qn/qch; **to keep an e. out for sth** être à l'affût de qch; **to have one's e. on sb/sth** *(be watching)* avoir qn/qch à l'œil; *(have in mind)* avoir l'œil sur qn/qch; **to make eyes at sb** faire de l'œil à qn; **with an e. to...** en vue de...; **to be up to one's eyes in work** avoir du travail par-dessus la tête; **to be up to one's eyes in debt** être endetté(e) jusqu'au cou; *Fam* **that's one in the e. for him!** ça lui fera les pieds!; **an e. for an e., a tooth for a tooth** œil pour œil, dent pour dent
   2 *vt* regarder, observer

▸**eye up** *vt sep* reluquer

eyeball ['aɪbɔːl] *n* globe *m* oculaire

eyebrow ['aɪbraʊ] *n* sourcil *m; Fig* **to raise one's eyebrows** *(in surprise)* lever les sourcils

eye-catching ['aɪkætʃɪŋ] *adj* accrocheur(euse)

eyeful ['aɪfʊl] *n Fam* **to get an e. of sb/sth** *(look at)* reluquer qn/qch

eyeglass ['aɪglɑːs] *n* monocle *m*

eyeglasses ['aɪglɑːsɪz] *npl Am (spectacles)* lunettes *fpl*

eyelash ['aɪlæʃ] *n* cil *m*

eyelid ['aɪlɪd] *n* paupière *f; Fig* **she didn't bat an e.** elle n'a pas sourcillé

eyeliner ['aɪlaɪnə(r)] *n* eye-liner *m*

eye-opener ['aɪəʊpənə(r)] *n* révélation *f*; **it was an e. for him** ça lui a ouvert les yeux

eyepatch ['aɪpætʃ] *n* cache *m* (sur l'œil)

eyeshade ['aɪʃeɪd] *n* visière *f*

eyesight ['aɪsaɪt] *n* vue *f*

eyesore ['aɪsɔː(r)] *n* horreur *f*

eyestrain ['aɪstreɪn] *n* fatigue *f* oculaire

eyetooth ['aɪtuːθ] (*pl* **eyeteeth** ['aɪtiːθ]) *n* canine *f*; **I'd give my eyeteeth to go with them** je donnerais n'importe quoi pour aller avec eux

eyewash ['aɪwɒʃ] *n* (*for eye*) collyre *m*; *Fig* (*nonsense*) boniment *m*, poudre *f* aux yeux

eyewitness ['aɪwɪtnɪs] *n* témoin *m* oculaire

eyrie ['ɪərɪ] *n* aire *f*

e-zine, ezine ['iːziːn] *n* ezine *m*, e-zine *m*, magazine *m* électronique

F

F, f [ef] *n* (**a**) *(letter)* F, f *m inv*; *Br Euph* **the F word** = euphémisme désignant le mot "fuck" (**b**) *Mus* fa *m*

fa [fɑː] *n Mus* fa *m*

FA [e'feɪ] *n (abbr* **Football Association**) = fédération anglaise de football

fab [fæb] *adj Br Fam* sensass

fable ['feɪbəl] *n* fable *f*

fabled ['feɪbəld] *adj* légendaire; *Fig* fabuleux(euse)

fabric ['fæbrɪk] *n (cloth)* tissu *m*, étoffe *f*; *(of building)* structure *f*; *Fig* **the f. of society** le tissu social; **f. conditioner** (produit *m*) assouplissant *m*

fabricate ['fæbrɪkeɪt] *vt (news, story, alibi)* forger, fabriquer; *(make)* fabriquer

fabulous ['fæbjʊləs] *adj* fabuleux(euse)

fabulously ['fæbjʊləslɪ] *adv (rich)* fabuleusement

façade [fæ'sɑːd] *n also Fig* façade *f*

face [feɪs] **1** *n* (**a**) *(of person)* visage *m*, figure *f*; *very Fam* **shut your f.!** ferme-la!, la ferme!; **I know that f!** je connais cette tête-là!; **I told him to his f.** je le lui ai dit en face; **I shall never be able to look her in the f. again** je ne pourrai plus jamais la regarder en face; **to show one's f.** se montrer; **to set one's f. against sth** se braquer contre qch; **in the f. of** *(danger, threat, enemy)* devant, face à; *Fam* **in your f.** *(music, campaign)* percutant(e); **f. cloth** ≃ gant *m* de toilette; **f. cream** crème *f* pour le visage; **f. pack** masque *m*; **f. powder** poudre *f*

(**b**) *(expression)* mine *f*; **to make** *or* **pull faces** faire des grimaces; **to keep a straight f.** garder son sérieux; **to put a good f. on it** garder le sourire

(**c**) *(appearance)* **on the f. of it** à première vue; **to save f.** sauver la face; **to lose f.** perdre la face; **the changing f. of Britain** le visage changeant de la Grande-Bretagne; **to take sth at f. value** prendre qch au pied de la lettre

(**d**) *(surface) (of the earth)* surface *f*; *(of clock)* cadran *m*; *(of coin, cliff)* face *f*; *Fig* **to disappear off the f. of the earth** se volatiliser; **f. down** *(person)* sur le ventre; *(document)* face imprimée dessous; *(playing card)* à l'envers; **f. up** *(person)* sur le dos; *(document)* face imprimée dessus; *(playing card)* à l'endroit

2 *vt* (**a**) *(confront) (difficulty, danger)* affronter, faire face à; **to be faced with sth** être confronté(e) à qch; **to f. facts** regarder les choses en face; **he faces six months in prison** il risque six mois de prison; **I can't f. going to work today** je n'ai pas le courage d'aller travailler aujourd'hui; **let's f. it** soyons réalistes; *Fig* **to f. the music** *(deal with situation)* faire front; *(accept consequences)* assumer ses responsabilités

(**b**) *(look towards)* faire face à; **to f. the front** regarder devant soi

3 *vi* **to f. north/south** *(of house)* être orienté(e) au nord/sud; **to f. towards** *(of person)* se tourner vers

▸**face up to** *vt insep (person)* tenir tête à; *(reality, fears)* affronter

faceless ['feɪslɪs] *adj* anonyme

face-lift ['feɪslɪft] *n (plastic surgery)* lifting *m*; *Fig (of building)* restauration *f*; **to have a f.** se faire faire un lifting

face-saving ['feɪsseɪvɪŋ] *adj* qui permet de sauver la face

facet ['fæsɪt] *n (of gem, character)* facette *f*; *(of problem, situation)* dimension *f*

facetious [fə'siːʃəs] *adj* facétieux(euse); **don't be f.!** ne plaisante pas!

face-to-face ['feɪstə'feɪs] **1** *adj* **a f. meeting** un face à face

2 *adv (meet)* face à face

facial ['feɪʃəl] **1** *n* soin *m* du visage; **to have a f.** se faire faire un soin du visage

2 *adj* facial(e); *(expression, hair)* du visage

facile ['fæsaɪl] *adj Pej* facile

facilitate [fə'sɪlɪteɪt] *vt* faciliter

facility [fə'sɪlɪtɪ] *(pl* **facilities**) *n* (**a**) *(ease)* facilité *f* (**b**) *(skill)* **to have a f. for sth** avoir un don pour qch (**c**) **facilities** *(equipment)* équipement *m*; *(place, building)* installations *fpl*; **shopping facilities** magasins *mpl*; **transport facilities** moyens *mpl* de transport (**d**) *(building)* **a detention f.** un établissement pénitentiaire (**e**) *(feature) (of computer, stereo)* fonction *f*

facsimile [fæk'sɪmɪlɪ] *n (copy)* fac-similé *m*; *(fax)* télécopie *f*

fact [fækt] *n* fait *m*; **in f.** en fait; **to distinguish f. from fiction** discerner la fiction de la réalité; **the f. is (that)...** le fait est que...; **it's a f. that...** c'est un fait que...; **to know for a f. (that)...** savoir pertinemment que...; **it's a f. of life** c'est une réalité; **to tell sb the facts of life** expliquer à qn comment on fait les enfants

fact-finding ['fæktfaɪndɪŋ] *adj* d'enquête; **f. mission** mission *f* d'information

faction ['fækʃən] *n* faction *f*

factor ['fæktə(r)] *n (aspect, in maths)* facteur *m*

factory ['fæktərɪ] *(pl* **factories**) *n* usine *f*; *(small)* fabrique *f*; **f. farming** élevage *m* industriel

factual ['fæktʃʊəl] *adj* basé(e) sur les faits

faculty ['fækəltɪ] *(pl* **faculties**) *n (of mind, in university)* faculté *f*; *Am* **the f.** *(teaching staff)* le personnel enseignant

fad [fæd] *n* mode *f* (**for** de)

fade [feɪd] **1** vt faner
  2 vi (of flower, material, colour) se faner; (of light) baisser; (of memory) s'éteindre; (of hope) s'amenuiser; **to f. from memory** s'effacer de la mémoire
▸**fade away** vi (of sound) s'éteindre; Fig (of person) s'éteindre peu à peu
▸**fade out 1** vt sep Cin fermer en fondu; (music) terminer par un fondu
  2 vi se terminer en fondu
faded ['feɪdɪd] adj (flower, colour) fané(e); (photograph, garment) décoloré(e)
fading ['feɪdɪŋ] adj (light) pâlissant(e)
faeces ['fiːsiːz] npl fèces fpl
▸**faff about, faff around** [fæf] vi Br Fam (waste time) glander; (potter) bricoler
fag [fæg] n (a) Br Fam (cigarette) clope m or f (b) Br Fam (unpleasant job) corvée f (c) Am very Fam (homosexual) pédé m, = terme injurieux désignant un homosexuel
faggot ['fægət] n (a) (firewood) fagot m (b) Br (meatball) boulette f de viande (c) Am very Fam (homosexual) pédé m, = terme injurieux désignant un homosexuel
Fahrenheit ['færənhaɪt] adj Fahrenheit inv
fail [feɪl] **1** n (a) (in exam) échec m (b) **without f.** sans faute
  2 vt (exam, test) échouer à, rater; (candidate) recaler; **to f. a drugs test** être positif(ive) au contrôle anti-dopage; **words f. me** les mots me manquent; **his nerve failed him** le courage lui a fait défaut; **I won't f. you** vous pouvez compter sur moi
  3 vi (of person, plan) échouer; (of business) faire faillite; (of engine) caler; (of memory, eyesight, light) baisser; (of brakes) lâcher; **to f. to do sth** (not succeed) ne pas arriver à faire qch; (forget) négliger de faire qch; **I f. to see what the problem is** je ne vois pas où est le problème; **if all else fails** en désespoir de cause; **to f. in one's duty** manquer à son devoir; **it never fails** (of strategy, excuse) ça marche à tous les coups
failed [feɪld] adj (artist, politician) raté(e)
failing ['feɪlɪŋ] **1** n (fault) faiblesse f, défaut m
  2 adj (sight, strength) qui baisse; **to be in f. health** avoir une santé défaillante
  3 prep à défaut de; **f. that** à défaut; **f. all else** en désespoir de cause
fail-safe ['feɪlseɪf] adj (mechanism) à sûreté intégrée
failure ['feɪljə(r)] n (a) (of plan, attempt) échec m; (of machine) panne f; (of company) faillite f; **to be a f.** (of show, film) faire un bide; **f. to keep a promise** manquement m à une promesse; **f. to pay a bill** défaut m de paiement d'une facture (b) (person) raté(e) m,f
faint [feɪnt] **1** n **to fall down in a f.** s'évanouir
  2 adj (a) (hope, light, sound) faible; (mark, writing) à peine visible; (colour) pâle; (idea) vague; **I haven't got the faintest idea** je n'en ai pas la moindre idée (b) (weak, unwell) **to feel** or **be f.** (of person) se sentir mal
  3 vi (lose consciousness) s'évanouir
faint-hearted ['feɪnt'hɑːtɪd] adj timoré(e); **not for the f.** à déconseiller aux âmes sensibles
faintly ['feɪntlɪ] adv (a) (remember, hear, see) vaguement; (shine) faiblement (b) (slightly) (uneasy, ridiculous) légèrement
fair¹ ['feə(r)] n (a) Br (funfair) fête f foraine (b) (trade fair) foire f

fair² **1** adj (a) (just) juste, équitable; (price) raisonnable; (fight) loyal(e); **it's not f.** ce n'est pas juste; **fair's f.!** ce n'est que justice!; **f. enough!** (OK) d'accord!; (rightly so) ça se comprend!; **it is f. to say (that)...** on peut dire que...; **to be f.,...** pour être honnête,...; **by f. means or foul** par tous les moyens; Prov **all's f. in love and war** tous les moyens sont bons; Fam **to give sb a f. crack of the whip** donner sa chance à qn; **to be f. game** être une proie facile; **f. play** fair-play m, Offic franc-jeu m; **to get one's f. share** recevoir son dû; **we've had our f. share of problems** nous avons eu notre lot de problèmes
  (b) (quite good) assez bon (bonne); **a f. idea** une assez bonne idée; **at a f. pace** à une allure assez rapide; **a f. amount of** pas mal de; **f. to middling** comme ci comme ça
  (c) (weather) beau (belle)
  (d) (light-coloured) (hair) blond(e); (skin) pâle
  (e) (attractive) beau (belle); Old-fashioned **the f.** or **fairer sex** le beau sexe
  2 adv (act, fight) loyalement; (play) jouer franc jeu; **you can't say fairer than that** il n'y a pas plus équitable; **to beat sb f. and square** battre qn à plates coutures
fairground ['feəgraʊnd] n parc m d'attractions
fair-haired ['feə'heəd] adj blond(e)
fairly ['feəlɪ] adv (a) (quite) assez; **it is f. certain (that)...** il est à peu près certain que... (b) (justly) équitablement; (play, fight) loyalement; (describe) objectivement (c) (for emphasis) **we f. raced home** nous sommes rentrés ventre à terre
fair-minded ['feə'maɪndɪd] adj équitable
fairness ['feənɪs] n (a) (of person, decision) impartialité f; **in all f.** en toute justice (b) (of hair) blondeur f; (of skin) pâleur f
fair-sized ['feə'saɪzd] adj assez grand(e)
fairway ['feəweɪ] n fairway m
fair-weather friend ['feəweðə'frend] n = ami qui n'est là que quand tout va bien
fairy ['feərɪ] (pl **fairies**) n (a) (magical being) fée f; **f. godmother** bonne fée f; **f. lights** guirlande f lumineuse (pour sapin de Noël) (b) very Fam (homosexual) tapette f, = terme injurieux désignant un homosexuel
fairytale ['feərɪteɪl] n conte m de fées; **a f. ending** fin digne d'un conte de fées
faith [feɪθ] n foi f; **to have f. in sb** avoir foi en qn; **to be of the Catholic/Jewish f.** être de religion catholique/juive; **to keep f. with sb** tenir ses engagements envers qn; **in good f.** en toute bonne foi; **f. healer** guérisseur(euse) m,f
faithful ['feɪθfʊl] **1** npl **the f.** les fidèles mpl
  2 adj fidèle
faithfully ['feɪθfʊlɪ] adv fidèlement; **yours f.** (in formal letter) recevez l'expression de mes/nos sentiments distingués
fake [feɪk] **1** n (object) faux m; (person) bluffeur m
  2 adj faux (fausse); **f. tan** (product) autobronzant m
  3 vt (signature) contrefaire; (result) truquer; **to f. an illness** feindre d'être malade
falcon ['fɔːlkən] n faucon m
falconry ['fɔːlkənrɪ] n fauconnerie f
Falkland ['fɔːklənd] n **the F. Islands, the Falklands** les Malouines fpl, les Falkland fpl
fall [fɔːl] **1** n (a) (of person, prices, besieged city, snow) chute f; **to have a f.** tomber, faire une chute; Fig **to be**

heading for a **f.** courir à sa perte; *Am Fam* **f. guy** *(scapegoat)* bouc *m* émissaire

(**b**) *Am (autumn)* automne *m*

(**c**) **falls** *(waterfall)* chutes *fpl*

2 *vi (pt* **fell** [fel], *pp* **fallen** ['fɔːlən]) (**a**) *(drop, fall over)* tomber; **to f. down a hole** tomber dans un trou; **to f. off a bicycle/chair** tomber d'un vélo/d'une chaise; *Fig* **to f. into a trap** tomber dans un piège; *also Fig* **to f. flat** tomber à plat; **to f. to pieces** *(of object)* tomber en morceaux; *Fig (of person)* craquer; **to f. short of doing sth** ne pas réussir à faire qch

(**b**) *(decrease) (of price, temperature, standards)* chuter, baisser

(**c**) *(of government, city, soldier)* tomber

(**d**) *(of silence, darkness, light)* tomber; **the responsibility falls on you** c'est à vous qu'en incombe la responsabilité; *Formal* **it falls to me to introduce...** j'ai l'honneur de vous présenter...

(**e**) *(become)* **to f. asleep** s'endormir; **to f. ill** tomber malade; **to f. in love (with)** tomber amoureux(euse) (de); **to f. silent** se taire; **to f. victim to an epidemic** être victime d'une épidémie; **the match fell victim to the weather** le match a dû être annulé en raison du mauvais temps

(**f**) *(be classified)* se classer; **to f. into two categories** se diviser en deux catégories; **suddenly everything fell into place** soudain tout est devenu clair

(**g**) *(occur)* **Christmas Day falls on a Thursday** Noël tombe un jeudi

▸**fall away** *vi (of ground)* descendre; *(of attendance)* diminuer

▸**fall back on** *vt insep (resort to)* se rabattre sur

▸**fall behind** *vi (in race)* se faire distancer; **to f. behind with the rent** être en retard pour payer son loyer

▸**fall down** *vi (of person)* tomber; *(of building)* s'écrouler, s'effondrer; **that's where your argument falls down** c'est par là que pèche ton raisonnement

▸**fall for** *vt insep Fam* (**a**) *(fall in love with)* tomber amoureux(euse) de (**b**) *(trick)* se laisser prendre à; **to f. for it** s'y laisser prendre

▸**fall in** *vi* (**a**) *(of roof)* s'écrouler, s'effondrer (**b**) *Mil (of troops)* former les rangs

▸**fall off** *vi* (**a**) *(of object)* tomber (**b**) *(of profits, attendance)* diminuer

▸**fall out** *vi* (**a**) *(quarrel)* se brouiller, se fâcher (**with** avec) (**b**) *Mil* rompre les rangs

fall over 1 *vi* tomber (par terre)

2 *vt insep (stumble on)* trébucher sur; *Fig* **to be falling over oneself to do sth** *(be very keen)* se mettre en quatre pour faire qch

▸**fall through** *vi (of plan, deal)* tomber à l'eau

fallacious [fə'leɪʃəs] *adj* erroné(e)

fallacy ['fæləsɪ] *(pl* **fallacies**) *n* erreur *f*

fallen ['fɔːlən] **1** *npl* **the f.** les soldats *mpl* tombés au combat

2 *adj (angel)* déchu(e); *(woman)* perdu(e)

3 *pp of* **fall**

fallible ['fælɪbəl] *adj* faillible

Fallopian tube [fə'ləʊpɪən'tjuːb] *n Anat* trompe *f* de Fallope

fallout ['fɔːlaʊt] *n (nuclear)* retombées *fpl* radioactives; *Fig (from scandal)* retombées *fpl*; **f. shelter** abri *m* antiatomique

fallow ['fæləʊ] *adj* en jachère; **to lie f.** être en jachère; *Fig* **a f. period** un passage à vide

false [fɔːls] *adj* faux (fausse); **f. alarm** fausse alerte *f*; *Fig* **f. dawn** faux espoir *m*; **f. economy** fausse économie *f*; **f. friend** *(in foreign language)* faux ami *m*; *Psy* **f. memory syndrome** syndrome *m* des faux souvenirs; **f. modesty** fausse modestie *f*; *Fig* **to strike a f. note** *(in film)* sonner faux; *(of person)* faire une gaffe; **f. pregnancy** grossesse *f* nerveuse; **under f. pretences** *(illegally)* par des moyens frauduleux; *(by lying)* sous des prétextes fallacieux; **f. start** *(in race)* faux départ *m*; **f. teeth** dentier *m*; **to bear f. witness** faire un faux témoignage

falsehood ['fɔːlshʊd] *n* mensonge *m*

falsely ['fɔːlslɪ] *adv (described)* faussement; *(accused)* à tort; *(smile)* avec fausseté

falsetto [fɔːl'setəʊ] *(pl* **falsettos**) *n Mus* voix *f* de fausset

falsify ['fɔːlsɪfaɪ] *(pt & pp* **falsified**) *vt* (**a**) *(forge) (records, document)* falsifier (**b**) *(disprove) (theory)* prouver la fausseté de

falter ['fɔːltə(r)] *vi also Fig* vaciller; *(of voice)* hésiter

fame [feɪm] *n* renom *m*, renommée *f*; **to seek f. and fortune** rechercher la gloire et la fortune

famed [feɪmd] *adj* célèbre (**for** pour)

familiar [fə'mɪlɪə(r)] *adj* (**a**) *(well-known)* familier(ère) (**to** à) (**b**) *(intimate)* familier(ère), intime; **to be on f. terms with sb** avoir des rapports amicaux avec qn; **to get too f. with sb** se permettre trop de familiarités avec qn (**c**) *(acquainted)* **to be f. with sb/sth** bien connaître qn/qch

familiarity [fəmɪlɪ'ærɪtɪ] *n* (**a**) *(intimacy)* familiarité *f*; **f. breeds contempt** avec l'habitude vient la lassitude (**b**) *(acquaintance)* connaissance *f* (**with** de)

familiarize [fə'mɪlɪəraɪz] *vt* **to f. sb with sth** familiariser qn avec qch; **to f. oneself with sth** se familiariser avec qch

family ['fæmɪlɪ] *(pl* **families**) *n* famille *f*; **it runs in the f.** c'est de famille, ça tient de famille; **to start a f.** fonder une famille; **to treat sb as one of the f.** traiter qn comme un membre de la famille; *Fam* **to be in the f. way** être enceinte; **f. allowance** allocations *fpl* familiales; **f. business** entreprise *f* familiale; **f. doctor/life** docteur *m*/vie *f* de famille; **f. man** bon père *m* de famille; **f. planning** planning *m* familial; **f. planning clinic** (centre *m* de) planning familial; **f. resemblance** air *m* de famille; **f. room** *(in hotel)* chambre *f* familiale; *Am (in house)* salle *f* de séjour; *Br (in pub)* = salle réservée aux familles; **f. tree** arbre *m* généalogique

famine ['fæmɪn] *n* famine *f*; **f. relief** aide *f* aux victimes d'une famine

famished ['fæmɪʃd] *adj* affamé(e)

famous ['feɪməs] *adj* célèbre (**for** pour)

famously ['feɪməslɪ] *adv Fam* **to get on f. (with sb)** s'entendre à merveille (avec qn)

fan[1] [fæn] **1** *n (cooling device) (hand-held)* éventail *m*; *(mechanical)* ventilateur *m*; **f. belt** *(of car)* courroie *f* de ventilateur; **f. heater** radiateur *m* soufflant

2 *vt (pt & pp* **fanned**) (**a**) *(face, person)* éventer; **to f. oneself** s'éventer (**b**) *(fire, passions)* attiser

▸**fan out** *vi* se déployer en éventail

fan[2] *n (enthusiast)* fan *mf*; *(of sports team)* supporter *m*; *Fig* **I'm not a f. of electric cookers** je n'aime pas trop les cuisinières électriques; **f. club** fan-club *m*; **f. mail** courrier *m* des admirateurs

fanatic [fə'nætɪk] *n & adj* fanatique *mf*

fanatical [fə'nætɪkəl] *adj* fanatique

fanciful ['fænsɪfʊl] *adj* (**a**) *(unrealistic) (idea, project)* chimérique; *(person)* qui se fait des idées (**b**) *(design, style)* plein(e) de fantaisie

fancy ['fænsɪ] **1** (*pl* **fancies**) *n* (**a**) *(imagination)* imagination *f*
(**b**) *(whim)* fantaisie *f*, caprice *m*
(**c**) *(liking)* **to take a f. to sb** prendre qn en affection; *(sexually)* s'enticher de qn; **to take a f. to sth** s'enticher de qch; **the house didn't take her f.** la maison ne lui a pas plu
2 *adj (jewels, gadget, hat)* fantaisie *inv*; *(party, hotel)* chic *inv*; *(food, decoration)* recherché(e); **f. dress** déguisement *m*; **f. dress party** soirée *f* déguisée
3 *vt (pt & pp* **fancied**) (**a**) *Fam (want)* **I didn't f. the idea** ça ne me tentait pas; **do you f. a drink?** ça te dit de boire un verre?
(**b**) *Br Fam (be attracted to)* **he fancies her** elle lui plaît
(**c**) *(imagine)* **to f. (that)...** croire *ou* penser que...; **I f. I've seen her before** j'ai l'impression de l'avoir déjà vue; *Fam* **f. that!** ça alors!; **f. meeting you here!** si je m'attendais à te/vous rencontrer ici!
(**d**) *(have good opinion of)* **to f. sb to win** penser que qn va gagner; *Pej* **he fancies himself** il ne se prend pas pour n'importe qui; **to f. oneself as a writer/musician** se prendre pour un écrivain/musicien; **I don't f. his chances of getting the job** je crois qu'il a peu de chances d'obtenir le poste

fanfare ['fænfeə(r)] *n* fanfare *f*

fang [fæŋ] *n (of dog)* croc *m*; *(of snake)* crochet *m*

fanny ['fænɪ] *(pl* **fannies**) *n* (**a**) *BrVulg (vagina)* chatte *f* (**b**) *Am Fam (buttocks)* derrière *m*, fesses *fpl*; **f. pack** banane *f*

fantasize ['fæntəsaɪz] *vi* fantasmer (**about** sur)

fantastic [fæn'tæstɪk] *adj* (**a**) *Fam (excellent)* formidable, fantastique (**b**) *(enormous) (price)* astronomique; *(wealth, size)* prodigieux(euse) (**c**) *(unbelievable) (claim, story)* grotesque, absurde (**d**) *(strange) (creature)* fantastique; *(design)* plein(e) de fantaisie

fantasy ['fæntəzɪ] *(pl* **fantasies**) *n* (**a**) *(unrealistic idea)* chimère *f*; *(sexual)* fantasme *m* (**b**) *(imagination)* fantaisie *f* (**c**) *(literature)* littérature *f* fantastique

FAO [efeɪ'əʊ] *n (abbr* **Food and Agriculture Organization**) FAO *f*

FAQ [efeɪ'kjuː] *n Comput (abbr* **frequently asked questions**) FAQ

far [fɑː(r)] *(comparative* **farther** ['fɑːðə(r)] *or* **further** ['fɜːðə(r)], *superlative* **farthest** ['fɑːðɪst] *or* **furthest** ['fɜːðɪst]) **1** *adj* **in the f. distance** au loin, dans le lointain; **the f. end** l'autre bout; *Pol* **the f. left/right** l'extrême gauche *f*/droite *f*; **the F. East** l'Extrême-Orient *m*; **it's a f. cry from** ça n'a rien à voir avec
2 *adv* (**a**) *(in distance)* loin; **how f. is it to Toulouse?** combien y a-t-il jusqu'à Toulouse?; **f. away (from)** loin (de); **f. below/above** loin au-dessous/au-dessus; **as f. as** jusqu'à; *also Fig* **to go f.** aller loin; *Fig* **to go so f. as to do sth** aller jusqu'à faire qch; *Fig* **to go too f.** aller trop loin; *also Fig* **f. from...** loin de...; *Fig* **f. from it** loin de là; *Fig* **f. be it from me to...** loin de moi l'idée de...; **f. and wide** partout; *Fig* **as f. as I can see** pour autant que je puisse en juger; **as f. as I know** (pour) autant que je sache; **as f. as I'm concerned** en ce qui me concerne; *Fig* **as f. as possible** autant que possible
(**b**) *(in time)* **so f.** jusqu'ici, jusqu'à présent; **so f. so good** jusqu'ici tout va bien; **for as f. back as I can**

remember d'aussi loin que je me souvienne; **to work f. into the night** travailler jusqu'à une heure avancée de la nuit
(**c**) *(much)* beaucoup; **f. better/bigger** beaucoup mieux/plus grand; **by f.** de loin; **f. and away the best** de loin le meilleur/la meilleure

faraway ['fɑːrəweɪ] *adj* lointain(e); *(look)* perdu(e) dans le vague

farce [fɑːs] *n* farce *f*; *Fig* **it's a f.!** c'est grotesque!

farcical ['fɑːsɪkəl] *adj* grotesque

fare [feə(r)] **1** *n* (**a**) *(for journey)* tarif *m*; **to pay one's f.** acheter son billet (**b**) *(taxi passenger)* client(e) *m,f* (**c**) *Formal (food)* chère *f*
2 *vi* se débrouiller

farewell [feə'wel] *n* adieu *m*; **to say** *or* **make one's farewells** faire ses adieux; **f. dinner** dîner *m* d'adieu

far-fetched ['fɑː'fetʃt] *adj (idea, plan)* tiré(e) par les cheveux

far-flung ['fɑːflʌŋ] *adj* lointain(e)

farm [fɑːm] **1** *n* ferme *f*; **f. animals** animaux *mpl* de ferme; **f. labourer** ouvrier *m* agricole
2 *vt (land)* cultiver, exploiter
3 *vi* être cultivateur(trice)

▶**farm out** *vt sep (work)* confier en sous-traitance (**to** à); *(child)* confier (**to** à)

farmer ['fɑːmə(r)] *n* fermier(ère) *m,f*, agriculteur(trice) *m,f*

farmhouse ['fɑːmhaʊs] *n (corps m de)* ferme *f*

farming ['fɑːmɪŋ] *n (business)* agriculture *f*

farmland ['fɑːmlænd] *n* terres *fpl* arables

farmyard ['fɑːmjɑːd] *n* cour *f* de ferme

Faroe ['feərəʊ] *n* the **F. Islands, the Faroes** les îles *fpl* Féroé

far-off ['fɑːrɒf] *adj (country, time)* lointain(e); *(place)* éloigné(e)

far-out ['fɑːraʊt] *adj Fam (strange)* farfelu(e); *(avantgarde)* avant-gardiste; **f.!** *(fantastic)* génial!

far-reaching ['fɑː'riːtʃɪŋ] *adj (decision, change)* de grande envergure; *(consequences)* d'une grande portée

Farsi ['fɑːsiː] *n* farsi *m*

far-sighted ['fɑː'saɪtɪd] *adj* (**a**) *(forward-looking) (person)* prévoyant(e); *(decision)* avisé(e) (**b**) *Am (longsighted)* presbyte

fart [fɑːt] *Fam* **1** *n* pet *m*
2 *vi* péter

▶**fart about** *vi Fam (waste time)* glander

farther ['fɑːðə(r)] *comparative of* **far**

farthest ['fɑːðɪst] *superlative of* **far**

farthing ['fɑːðɪŋ] *n Br Hist* quart *m* de penny; *Fam* **he hasn't got a (brass) f.** il n'a pas le sou

fascinate ['fæsɪneɪt] *vt* fasciner

fascinating ['fæsɪneɪtɪŋ] *adj* fascinant(e)

fascination [fæsɪ'neɪʃən] *n* fascination *f*

fascism ['fæʃɪzəm] *n* fascisme *m*

fascist ['fæʃɪst] *n & adj* fasciste *mf*

fashion ['fæʃən] **1** *n* (**a**) *(in clothes)* mode *f*; **in f.** à la mode; **out of f.** démodé(e), passé(e) de mode; **f. designer** styliste *mf*; *(big name)* couturier(ère) *m,f*; **f. house** maison *f* de couture; **f. plate** gravure *f* de mode; *Fig* élégant(e) *m,f*; **f. show** défilé *m* de mode; *Pej* **f. victim** esclave *mf* de la mode (**b**) *(manner)* manière *f*; **after a f.** tant bien que mal
2 *vt (form)* façonner; *(make)* confectionner

fashionable ['fæʃənəbəl] *adj* à la mode

fast¹ [fɑːst] **1** *adj* (**a**) *(rapid)* rapide; *Fam* **he pulled a f. one on me** il m'a joué un mauvais tour; **f. food** restauration *f* rapide; **f. food restaurant** fast-food *m*; **the f. lane** *(of motorway)* la voie rapide; *Fig* **to live life in the f. lane** vivre à cent à l'heure (**b**) *(clock, watch)* **my watch is (five minutes)** ma montre avance (de cinq minutes) (**c**) *(secure) (grip)* ferme, solide; *(door, lid)* bien fermé(e); *(colour)* résistant(e)

2 *adv* (**a**) *(rapidly)* vite, rapidement; **not so f.!** pas si vite!; **to play f. and loose with the facts** truquer les faits; **to play f. and loose with sb's emotions** jouer avec les sentiments de qn (**b**) *(securely)* solidement; **to hold f.** tenir bon; **f. asleep** profondément endormi(e)

fast² **1** *n (lack of food)* jeûne *m*; *Rel* **f. day** jour *m* de jeûne

2 *vi* jeûner; *Med* être à la diète

fasten ['fɑːsən] **1** *vt (door, window)* fermer; *(belt, buttons)* attacher; *Fig* **to f. one's eyes on sth** fixer son regard sur qch

2 *vi (garment)* s'attacher

fastener ['fɑːsənə(r)] *n (of garment) (hook)* agrafe *f*; *(press stud)* bouton-pression *m*; *(of bag, jewellery)* fermoir *m*

fast-forward [fɑːst'fɔːwəd] **1** *n* avance *f* rapide

2 *vt (cassette)* mettre en avance rapide

fastidious [fæ'stɪdɪəs] *adj* difficile; *(about manners, hygiene, details)* pointilleux(euse) (**about** sur)

fast-moving ['fɑːst'muːvɪŋ] *adj* rapide

fat [fæt] **1** *n* (**a**) *(flesh)* graisse *f*; *(of cooked meat)* gras *m*; *(for cooking)* matière *f* grasse; **f. content** teneur *f* en graisse *ou* en lipides (**b**) *(idioms) Fam* **the f.'s in the fire!** ça va chauffer!; **to live off the f. of the land** vivre comme un coq en pâte; **to chew the f. (with sb)** tailler le bout de gras (avec qn)

2 *adj (person)* gros (grosse); *Fam (cheque, profit, salary)* gros; **to get f.** grossir; *Fig* **to grow f. at the expense of others** *(become rich)* s'engraisser aux dépens des autres; *Fam* **a f. lot of good that'll do you!** ça te fera une belle jambe!; *Fig* **f. cat** = personne touchant un salaire extrêmement élevé de façon injustifiée; *Fam* **f. chance!** tu parles!

fatal ['feɪtəl] *adj* mortel(elle)

fatalistic [feɪtə'lɪstɪk] *adj* fataliste

fatality [fə'tælɪtɪ] *(pl* **fatalities**) *n* (**a**) *(person killed)* mort *m* (**b**) *(fate)* fatalité *f*

fatally ['feɪtəlɪ] *adv (wounded)* mortellement; **f. ill** condamné(e); **to be f. damaging to sth** causer un tort irréparable à qch

fate [feɪt] *n* destin *m*, sort *m*; **to suffer** *or* **share the same f.** avoir le même sort; **it's a f. worse than death** c'est ce qu'on peut imaginer de pire

fated ['feɪtɪd] *adj* **to be f. to do sth** être destiné(e) à faire qch

fateful ['feɪtfʊl] *adj (words, day)* fatidique

father ['fɑːðə(r)] **1** *n (parent, priest)* père *m*; **from f. to son** de père en fils; **he was like a f. to me** il était comme un père pour moi; **like f., like son** tel père, tel fils; **Our F.** *(God)* Notre Père; **F. Christmas** le Père Noël; **F.'s Day** la fête des pères; **to be a f. figure to sb** jouer le rôle du père pour qn

2 *vt (child)* engendrer

fatherhood ['fɑːðəhʊd] *n* paternité *f*

father-in-law ['fɑːðərɪnlɔː] *n* beau-père *m*

fatherly ['fɑːðəlɪ] *adj* paternel(elle)

fathom ['fæðəm] **1** *n (unit of measurement)* = 1,8 m, brasse *f*

2 *vt (understand)* comprendre

▶**fathom out** *vt sep (understand)* comprendre

fatigue [fə'tiːg] **1** *n* (**a**) *(tiredness)* fatigue *f*; **metal f.** fatigue des métaux (**b**) *Mil* **f. (duty)** corvée *f*; **fatigues** *(clothes)* treillis *m*

2 *vt (person)* fatiguer

fatso ['fætsəʊ] *(pl* **fatsos** *or* **fatsoes**) *n Fam (man)* gros lard *m*; *(woman)* grosse vache *f*

▶**fatten up** ['fætən] *vt sep* faire grossir, engraisser

fatty ['fætɪ] **1** *n (pl* **fatties**) *Fam* gros (grosse) *m,f*; **hey f.!** eh, bouboule!

2 *adj (food, meat)* gras (grasse); *(tissue)* adipeux(-euse); **f. acid** acide *m* gras

fatuous ['fætjʊəs] *adj* idiot(e)

faucet ['fɔːsɪt] *n Am* robinet *m*

fault [fɔːlt] **1** *n* (**a**) *(flaw)* défaut *m*; *(in mechanism, on phone line)* problème *m*; **to find f. with** trouver à redire à; **to be generous to a f.** être généreux(euse) à l'excès (**b**) *(guilt)* faute *f*; **to be at f.** être en faute; **whose f. is it?** à qui la faute?; **it's my f.** c'est (de) ma faute; **through no f. of mine** sans que ce soit de ma faute (**c**) *(in tennis, squash)* faute *f* (**d**) *(geological)* faille *f*

2 *vt (person)* prendre en défaut; *(logic)* trouver une faille dans; **her attitude can't be faulted** il n'y a rien à redire à sa conduite

faultless ['fɔːltlɪs] *adj* impeccable

faulty ['fɔːltɪ] *adj* défectueux(euse)

faun [fɔːn] *n* faune *m*

fauna ['fɔːnə] *n* faune *f*

favor, favorable *etc Am* = **favour, favourable** *etc*

favour, *Am* **favor** ['feɪvə(r)] **1** *n* (**a**) *(approval)* **to be in/out of f.** *(of person)* être bien/mal vu(e); *(of method)* être/ne plus être en faveur; **to look on sb/sth with f.** être bien disposé(e) envers qn/qch; **to find f. with sb** trouver grâce aux yeux de qn (**b**) *(act of kindness)* service *m*; **to do sb a f.** rendre service à qn; *Br Fam* **do me a f. and shut up!** ferme-la, tu veux?; **to ask sb a f., to ask a f. of sb** demander un service à qn (**c**) *(advantage)* **that's a point in her f.** c'est un élément en sa faveur; *Fin* **balance in your f.** solde *m* en votre faveur (**d**) **in f. of** *(in preference to)* en faveur de; **to be in f. of sth** être partisan(e) de qch/être favorable à qch

2 *vt* (**a**) *(prefer)* être pour, être partisan(e) de; **to f. sb** *(be biased towards)* favoriser qn (**b**) *(honour)* **to f. sb with sth** gratifier qn de qch

favourable, *Am* **favorable** ['feɪvərəbəl] *adj* favorable; *(terms)* avantageux(euse); **in a f. light** sous un jour favorable

favourite, *Am* **favorite** ['feɪvərɪt] **1** *n* favori(ite) *m,f*, préféré(e) *m,f*; *(in betting)* favori

2 *adj* favori(ite), préféré(e)

favouritism, *Am* **favoritism** ['feɪvərɪtɪzəm] *n* favoritisme *m*

fawn¹ [fɔːn] **1** *n* (**a**) *(deer)* faon *m* (**b**) *(colour)* fauve *m*

2 *adj (colour)* fauve

fawn² *vi* **to f. on sb** *(of person)* ramper devant qn; *(of dog)* faire fête à qn

fax [fæks] **1** *n (machine)* fax *m*, *Offic* télécopieur *m*; *(message)* fax *m*, *Offic* télécopie *f*; **f. modem** modem-fax *m*; **f. number** numéro *m* de fax

2 *vt (message, document)* faxer, envoyer par fax; *(person)* envoyer un fax à

faze [feɪz] *vt Fam* déconcerter

FBI [efbiː'aɪ] *n Am (abbr* **Federal Bureau of Investigation)** FBI *m*

fear [fɪə(r)] **1** *n* peur *f*; *(worry)* crainte *f*; **to be** *or* **go in f. of** avoir peur de, redouter; **to go in f. of one's life** craindre pour sa vie; *Fam* **to put the f. of God into sb** faire une peur bleue à qn; **he didn't tell her for f. of her reaction** il ne lui a rien dit par peur de sa réaction; **for f. of doing sth** de peur de faire qch; **I didn't tell him, for f. that he'd be angry** je ne lui ai rien dit, de peur qu'il ne se mette en colère; *Fam* **no f.!** pas de danger!

2 *vt* craindre, redouter; **I f. there's been a misunderstanding** je crains qu'il (n')y ait eu un malentendu; **I f. so/not** je crains que oui/non; **to f. the worst** craindre le pire

3 *vi* **to f. for** craindre pour; **never f.!** ne crains rien!

fearful ['fɪəfʊl] *adj* **(a)** *(pain, consequence, noise)* épouvantable **(b)** *(person)* apeuré(e); **to be f. of doing sth** avoir peur de faire qch

fearless ['fɪəlɪs] *adj* intrépide

fearlessly ['fɪəlɪslɪ] *adv* avec intrépidité

fearsome ['fɪəsəm] *adj* effrayant(e)

feasibility [fiːzə'bɪlɪtɪ] *n* possibilité *f*; *(of plan)* faisabilité *f*; **f. study** étude *f* de faisabilité

feasible ['fiːzəbəl] *adj* faisable

feast [fiːst] **1** *n* festin *m*, banquet *m*; *Rel* **f. day** (jour *m* de) fête *f*

2 *vt* **to f. one's eyes on sth** repaître ses yeux de qch

3 *vi* **to f. on** se régaler de

feat [fiːt] *n* exploit *m*; **a f. of skill** un tour de force

feather ['feðə(r)] **1** *n* plume *f*; **you could have knocked me down with a f.** je n'en revenais pas; *Fig* **that's a f. in her cap** elle peut en être fière; **f. bed** lit *m* de plumes

2 *vt Fig* **to f. one's nest** faire son beurre

featherweight ['feðəweɪt] *n (in boxing)* poids *m* plume

feathery ['feðərɪ] *adj* doux (douce) et léger(ère) comme de la plume

feature ['fiːtʃə(r)] **1** *n* **(a)** *(of face)* trait *m* **(b)** *(characteristic)* caractéristique *f* **(c)** **f. (film)** long métrage *m* **(d)** *(in newspaper)* article *m* de fond; *(on television, radio)* reportage *m*; **f. writer** éditorialiste *mf*

2 *vt (of magazine, exhibition)* présenter; **a film featuring...** un film ayant pour vedette...

3 *vi (appear)* figurer

featureless ['fiːtʃəlɪs] *adj* sans caractéristiques marquées

Feb *(abbr* **February)** février

febrile ['fiːbraɪl] *adj* fébrile

February ['febrʊərɪ] *n* février *m*; *see also* **May**

feckless ['feklɪs] *adj* **(a)** *(irresponsible)* irresponsable **(b)** *(ineffectual)* incapable

Fed [fed] *n Am* **(a)** *(abbr* **Federal Reserve Board)** banque *f* centrale (des États-Unis) **(b)** *(abbr* **Federal Reserve (System))** (système *m* de) Réserve *f* fédérale

fed [fed] *pt & pp of* **feed**

federal ['fedərəl] *adj* fédéral(e)

federalism ['fedərəlɪzəm] *n* fédéralisme *m*

federalist ['fedərəlɪst] *n & adj* fédéraliste *mf*

federation [fedə'reɪʃən] *n* fédération *f*

fed up ['fedʌp] *adj Fam* **to be f. (with)** en avoir ras le bol (de), en avoir marre (de)

fee [fiː] *n (of lawyer, doctor)* honoraires *mpl*; *(for entrance)* droit *m* d'entrée; *(for membership)* cotisation *f*; **school fees** droits *mpl* d'inscription; **a f.-paying school** une école privée

feeble ['fiːbəl] *adj* faible; *(attempt)* peu convaincant(e)

feeble-minded ['fiːbəl'maɪndɪd] *adj* faible d'esprit

feebly ['fiːblɪ] *adv* faiblement; *(protest, reprimand)* mollement

feed [fiːd] **1** *n* **(a)** *(animal food)* nourriture *f* **(b)** *(for baby) (from breast)* tétée *f*; *(from bottle)* biberon *m*

2 *vt (pt & pp* **fed** [fed]) **(a)** *(give food to)* donner à manger à; *(baby) (from breast)* donner la tétée à; *(from bottle)* donner son biberon à; *(plant)* mettre de l'engrais à; **we were well fed** nous étions bien nourris; **to f. one's family** nourrir sa famille **(b)** *(supply)* **to f. a fire** alimenter un feu; **to f. coins into a machine** mettre des pièces dans une machine; **to f. sb with information** fournir des informations à qn

3 *vi (survive)* **to f. on** se nourrir de

feedback ['fiːdbæk] *n Elec* effet *m* Larsen; *Fig (response)* écho *m*, réactions *fpl*

feel [fiːl] **1** *n* **(a)** *(sensation)* toucher *m*; **the f. of silk against her skin** le contact de la soie contre sa peau; **the film has an authentic f. to it** le film dégage une impression d'authenticité

(b) *(knack)* **to have a f. for translation/music** avoir un sens inné de la traduction/musique; **to get the f. of sth** s'habituer à qch

2 *vt (pt & pp* **felt** [felt]) **(a)** *(touch)* toucher; *(investigate)* tâter; **to f. one's way** *(in darkness)* avancer à tâtons; *Fig (in new situation)* essayer de s'habituer

(b) *(be physically aware of)* sentir; **I felt the floor tremble** *or* **trembling** j'ai senti le sol trembler

(c) *(experience) (relief, pain, despair)* ressentir, éprouver; **I f. it in my bones** *(have intuition)* je le sens

(d) *(believe)* **to f. (that)...** penser que...

3 *vi* **(a)** *(physically)* **to f. tired** se sentir fatigué(e); **to f. ill** ne pas se sentir bien; **to f. hot/cold/hungry/thirsty** avoir chaud/froid/faim/soif; **my foot feels better** j'ai moins mal au pied; **how are you feeling?** comment ça va *ou* te sens-tu?; **I don't f. myself** je ne suis pas dans mon assiette; **to f. up to doing sth** *(well enough)* se sentir assez bien pour faire qch; *(competent enough)* se sentir de taille à faire qch; **to f. (like) a new man/woman** se sentir comme neuf/neuve

(b) *(emotionally)* se sentir; **to f. strongly about sth** avoir des idées très arrêtées sur qch; **I f. bad about leaving her** cela m'ennuie de la quitter; **how would you f. if...?** comment est-ce que tu te sentirais si...?; **it feels strange** c'est étrange; **I felt as if I'd seen him before** j'avais l'impression de l'avoir déjà vu; **to f. like doing sth** avoir envie de faire qch; **I f. like a cup of tea** *(would like)* j'ai envie d'une tasse de thé

(c) *(have sympathy)* **to f. for sb** plaindre qn

(d) *(of things)* **to f. hard/hot** être dur(e)/chaud(e); **it feels like (it's going to) rain** on dirait qu'il va pleuvoir

(e) *(search)* **to f. in one's pockets for sth** chercher qch dans ses poches; **he felt on the ground for the key** il cherchait sa clé à tâtons sur le sol

feeler ['fiːlə(r)] *n (of insect)* antenne *f*; *(of snail)* corne *f*; *Fig* **to put out feelers** tâter le terrain

feelgood ['fiːlgʊd] *adj Fam* **a f. film** un film qui donne la pêche; **the f. factor** l'optimisme *m* ambiant

feeling ['fiːlɪŋ] n (**a**) (**sense of**) f. toucher m; **to have no f. in one's arm** avoir le bras mort (**b**) (sensation) (of cold, pain) sensation f (**c**) (emotion, impression) sentiment m; **a f. of joy/anger** de la joie/colère; **to speak with f.** (emotionally) parler avec émotion; (warmly) parler avec chaleur; **I know the f.!** je sais ce que c'est!; **I had a f. I might find you here** je pensais bien vous trouver ici; **to hurt sb's feelings** blesser qn; **to have no feelings** n'avoir aucun cœur; **feelings were running high** les esprits étaient très échauffés; **no hard feelings!** sans rancune! (**d**) (sensitivity) sensibilité f; **to have a f. for sth** (music, art) être sensible à qch

feet [fiːt] pl of **foot**

feign [feɪn] vt (anger, surprise) feindre; **to f. illness/sleep** feindre d'être malade/de dormir

feint [feɪnt] **1** n (in combat sports) feinte f
  2 vi (in combat sports) faire une feinte

felicitous [fɪ'lɪsɪtəs] adj heureux(euse)

feline ['fiːlaɪn] **1** n félin m
  2 adj félin(e)

fell¹ [fel] pt of **fall**

fell² vt (tree) abattre, couper; (opponent) terrasser

fell³ adj **at one f. swoop** d'un seul coup

fell⁴ n (hill) colline f

fellow ['feləʊ] n (**a**) (comrade) camarade mf; **f. citizen** concitoyen(enne) m,f; **f. countryman/countrywoman** compatriote mf; **f. passenger** compagnon m de voyage; **f. worker** collègue mf; **f. student** camarade d'études; **f. feeling** sympathie f; Fig **f. traveller** (in politics) compagnon de route (**b**) (teacher) professeur m titulaire; (student) boursier(ère) m,f; (of academy, society) membre m (**c**) Fam (man) gars m

fellowship ['feləʊʃɪp] n (**a**) (friendship) camaraderie f (**b**) (association) association f, corporation f (**c**) (at university) bourse f de recherche

felon ['felən] n Law criminel(elle) m,f

felony ['feləni] (pl felonies) n Law crime m

felt¹ [felt] n (fabric) feutre m; (thinner) feutrine f

felt² pt & pp of **feel**

felt-tip ['felttɪp] n **f. (pen)** (crayon m) feutre m

female ['fiːmeɪl] **1** n (person) femme f; (animal, plant) femelle f
  2 adj (person) féminin(e); (animal, plant) femelle

feminine ['femɪnɪn] **1** n Gram féminin m; **in the f.** au féminin
  2 adj féminin(e)

femininity [femɪ'nɪnɪtɪ] n féminité f

feminism ['femɪnɪzəm] n féminisme m

feminist ['femɪnɪst] n & adj féministe mf

femur ['fiːmə(r)] n Anat fémur m

fen [fen] n (marshy land) marais m; **the Fens** = plaines marécageuses à l'est de l'Angleterre

fence [fens] **1** n (**a**) (barrier) clôture f; (more solid) barrière f; Fig **to sit on the f.** ménager la chèvre et le chou; Fig **to get off the f.** se prononcer (**b**) Fam (receiver of stolen property) receleur(euse) m,f
  2 vi (as sport) faire de l'escrime

fence off vt sep séparer par une clôture

fencing ['fensɪŋ] n (sport) escrime f

fend [fend] vi **to f. for oneself** se débrouiller (tout(e) seul(e))

fend off vt sep (attack, blow) parer; (question) éluder

fender ['fendə(r)] n (**a**) Am (of car) aile f (**b**) (for fireplace) garde-feu m inv

fennel ['fenəl] n fenouil m

ferment 1 n ['fɜːment] (commotion) agitation f; **in a (state of) f.** en effervescence
  2 vi [fə'ment] (of alcoholic drink) fermenter

fermentation [fɜːmen'teɪʃən] n fermentation f

fern [fɜːn] n fougère f

ferocious [fə'rəʊʃəs] adj féroce

ferocity [fə'rɒsɪtɪ] n férocité f

ferret ['ferɪt] **1** n furet m
  2 vi **to f. (about) for sth** fouiller à la recherche de qch

▶**ferret out** vt sep (object, information) dénicher

ferris wheel ['ferɪs'wiːl] n grande roue f

ferrous ['ferəs] adj ferreux(euse)

ferry ['ferɪ] **1** n (pl ferries) bac m; (larger) ferry m
  2 vt (pt & pp ferried) transporter
  3 vi **to f. back and forth** faire la navette

ferryman ['ferɪmən] n passeur m

fertile ['fɜːtaɪl] adj also Fig fertile

fertility [fɜː'tɪlɪtɪ] n also Fig fertilité f; **f. treatment** traitement m de la stérilité

fertilize ['fɜːtɪlaɪz] vt (egg, plant) féconder; (soil) fertiliser

fertilizer ['fɜːtɪlaɪzə(r)] n engrais m

fervent ['fɜːvənt] adj (admirer, nationalist) fervent(e); (belief, desire) ardent(e)

fervour, Am **fervor** ['fɜːvə(r)] n ferveur f

fester ['festə(r)] vi (of wound) s'infecter; Fig (of situation) s'envenimer; (of dislike, resentment) s'aviver

festival ['festɪvəl] n festival m; (religious) fête f

festive ['festɪv] adj de fête; **in f. mood** d'humeur festive; **the f. season** (Christmas) les fêtes fpl (de fin d'année)

festivity [fes'tɪvɪtɪ] (pl festivities) n (merriness) gaieté f; **the festivities** (celebrations) les festivités fpl

festoon [fes'tuːn] vt orner (**with** de)

fetal Am = **foetal**

fetch [fetʃ] vt (**a**) (bring) aller chercher (**b**) (be sold for) rapporter

▶**fetch up** vi (end up) (of people) se retrouver

fetching ['fetʃɪŋ] adj (person, hat, smile) ravissant(e)

fête [feɪt] **1** n fête f
  2 vt fêter

Fête

En Grande-Bretagne, les "village fêtes" sont des manifestations en plein air où l'on vend des produits faits maison et où l'on organise des manifestations sportives et des jeux pour enfants; elles sont généralement destinées à réunir des fonds pour une œuvre de charité.

---

fetid ['fetɪd] adj fétide

fetish ['fetɪʃ] n (object) fétiche m; **to have a f. for sth** faire une fixation sur qch

fetter ['fetə(r)] **1** n fetters (on slave, prisoner) fers mpl; Fig (on rights, freedom) entraves fpl
  2 vt (slave, prisoner) enchaîner; Fig (union, women) entraver la liberté de

fettle ['fetəl] n **in good** or **fine f.** en condition

fetus Am = **foetus**

feud [fjuːd] **1** n querelle f
  2 vi se quereller (**with** avec)

feudal ['fjuːdəl] adj féodal(e); Fig (approach, attitude) moyenâgeux(euse)

feudalism ['fjuːdəlɪzəm] *n* le système féodal
fever ['fiːvə(r)] *n also Fig* fièvre *f*; **to have a f.** avoir de la fièvre; **excitement had risen to f.** pitch l'excitation était à son comble
feverish ['fiːvərɪʃ] *adj* fiévreux(euse); *Fig (atmosphere)* de fièvre
few [fjuː] **1** *adj* (**a**) *(not many)* peu de; **f. friends** peu d'amis; **too f. people/opportunities** trop peu de gens/d'occasions; **f. and far between** rarissime; **every f. minutes** toutes les deux ou trois minutes; **as f. as a dozen finished the race** seuls une douzaine d'entre eux ont terminé la course
  (**b**) *(some)* **a f.** quelques; **a f. friends** quelques amis; **a good f., quite a f.** pas mal de; **in the next f. days** dans les jours qui suivent/suivirent
  2 *pron* (**a**) *(not many)* peu; **there are too f. of us** nous sommes trop peu nombreux; **f. of them** peu d'entre eux; **f., if any children** aucun enfant ou presque
  (**b**) *(some)* **a f.** quelques-uns (quelques-unes) *mpl,fpl*; **a f. of the survivors** quelques-uns des survivants; **a f. of them** quelques-uns d'entre eux
  3 *n* **the f. who came** les rares personnes qui sont venues
fewer ['fjuːə(r)] *(comparative of* **few**) **1** *adj* moins de; **f. friends** moins d'amis; **no f. than thirty** pas moins de trente; **the houses became f.** les maisons devenaient plus rares; **f. and f. people** de moins en moins de gens
  2 *pron* moins; **there are f. (of them) than I thought** il y en a moins que je ne pensais
fewest ['fjuːɪst] *(superlative of* **few**) **1** *adj* le moins de
  2 *pron* le moins
fiasco [fɪˈæskəʊ] *(pl* **fiascos**) *n* fiasco *m*
fib [fɪb] *Fam* **1** *n* bobard *m*
  2 *vi (pt & pp* **fibbed**) raconter des bobards
fibber ['fɪbə(r)] *n Fam* menteur(euse) *m,f*
fibre, *Am* **fiber** ['faɪbə(r)] *n* fibre *f*; *(in diet)* fibres *fpl*; **f. optics** technologie *f* des fibres optiques
fibreglass, *Am* **fiberglass** ['faɪbəglɑːs] *n* fibre *f* de verre
fibrous ['faɪbrəs] *adj* fibreux(euse)
fickle ['fɪkəl] *adj (friend, fan)* inconstant(e); *(lover)* inconstant, volage; *(weather)* changeant(e)
fiction ['fɪkʃən] *n (genre)* fiction *f*; *(books)* livres *mpl* de fiction; *(lie)* invention *f*
fictional ['fɪkʃənəl] *adj* fictif(ive)
fictitious [fɪkˈtɪʃəs] *adj* fictif(ive)
fiddle ['fɪdəl] **1** *n* (**a**) *(violin)* violon *m* (**b**) *Br Fam (swindle)* combine *f*; **to be on the f.** traficoter
  2 *vt Br Fam (cheat)* combiner; **to f. the accounts** truquer les comptes
  3 *vi* (**a**) *(play violin)* jouer du violon (**b**) *(fidget)* **to f. (about** *or* **around) with sth** tripoter qch
fiddler ['fɪdlə(r)] *n* violoniste *mf*
fiddlesticks ['fɪdəlstɪks] *exclam Old-fashioned (nonsense)* balivernes!; *(expressing annoyance)* zut de zut!
fiddly ['fɪdlɪ] *adj Fam* minutieux(euse)
fidelity [fɪˈdelɪtɪ] *n* fidélité *f*
fidget ['fɪdʒɪt] **1** *n* **to be a f.** ne pas tenir en place
  2 *vi* gigoter; **stop fidgeting!** arrête de gigoter!
fidgety ['fɪdʒɪtɪ] *adj* agité(e)
field [fiːld] **1** *n* (**a**) *(of farm) & Comput* champ *m*; *(for sport)* terrain *m*; *(of oil, coal)* gisement *m*; **to work in the f.** *(not in office)* travailler sur le terrain; **f. of vision** champ visuel; **f. events** *(in athletics)* le saut et le lan-

cer; *Am* **f. hockey** hockey *m* sur gazon; **f. study** étude *f* sur le terrain; *Sch & Univ* **f. trip** voyage *m* d'étude; **f. work** *(scientific)* recherches *fpl* sur le terrain
  (**b**) *Mil* **in the f.** en campagne; *Fig* **to have a f. day** s'en donner à cœur joie; **f. glasses** jumelles *fpl*; **f. gun** canon *m* (de campagne); **f. hospital** antenne *f* chirurgicale; **f. marshal** ≃ maréchal *m* de France
  (**c**) *(of knowledge)* domaine *m*
  (**d**) *(in race, contest)* partants *mpl*; **to lead the f.** *Sport* mener le peloton; *Fig* occuper la première place
  2 *vt* (**a**) *(team)* composer; *(candidates)* présenter (**b**) *(question)* répondre à
fieldmouse ['fiːldmaʊs] *(pl* **fieldmice** ['fiːldmaɪs]) *n* mulot *m*
fiend [fiːnd] *n (cruel person)* monstre *m*; *(demon)* démon *m*; **sex f.** obsédé(e) *m,f* sexuel(elle); **jazz f.** fanatique *mf* de jazz
fiendish ['fiːndɪʃ] *adj (scheme, question)* diabolique; *(weather, temper)* abominable
fiendishly ['fiːndɪʃlɪ] *adv (difficult)* horriblement
fierce ['fɪəs] *adj (animal, look)* féroce; *(appearance, person)* redoutable; *(wind, storm, criticism)* violent(e); *(heat)* torride; *(contest)* acharné(e)
fiercely ['fɪəslɪ] *adv (look)* d'un œil féroce; *(fight)* avec acharnement; *(criticize)* violemment
fiery ['faɪərɪ] *adj (red)* ardent(e); *(sky)* enflammé(e); *(taste)* très épicé(e); *(person, character)* fougueux(euse)
FIFA ['fiːfə] *n (abbr* **Fédération Internationale de Football Association**) FIFA *f*
fifteen [fɪfˈtiːn] **1** *n* (**a**) *(number)* quinze *m inv* (**b**) *Sport (rugby team)* quinze *m*
  2 *adj* quinze; *see also* **eight**
fifteenth [fɪfˈtiːnθ] **1** *n* (**a**) *(fraction)* quinzième *m* (**b**) *(in series)* quinzième *mf* (**c**) *(of month)* quinze *m inv*
  2 *adj* quinzième; *see also* **eighth**
fifth [fɪfθ] **1** *n* (**a**) *(fraction)* cinquième *m* (**b**) *(in series)* cinquième *mf* (**c**) *(of month)* cinq *m inv*
  2 *adj* cinquième; *Pol* **f. column** cinquième colonne *f*; *see also* **eighth**
fiftieth ['fɪftɪəθ] **1** *n* (**a**) *(fraction)* cinquantième *m* (**b**) *(in series)* cinquantième *mf*
  2 *adj* cinquantième
fifty ['fɪftɪ] **1** *n* cinquante *m inv*
  2 *adj* cinquante; *see also* **eighty**
fig¹ [fɪg] *n (fruit)* figue *f*; *Fam* **she doesn't give** *or* **care a f.** elle s'en fiche éperdument; **f. leaf** feuille *f* de figuier; *(in paintings)* feuille de vigne; *Fig* **it's just a f. leaf** ce n'est qu'une couverture; **f. tree** figuier *m*
fig² *(abbr* **figure**) fig
fight [faɪt] **1** *n* (**a**) *(physical)* bagarre *f*; *(verbal)* dispute *f*; *(boxing match)* combat *m*; **to get into a f. with sb** *(physical)* se battre avec qn; *(verbal)* se disputer avec qn; **to start a f. (with sb)** provoquer une bagarre (avec qn); **to put up a good f.** bien se défendre (**b**) *(spirit)* **to show some f.** résister; **there was no f. left in him** il n'avait plus le cœur à se battre (**c**) *(struggle)* lutte *f* **(for/against)** pour/contre)
  2 *vt (pt & pp* **fought** [fɔːt]) *(person)* se battre contre; *(decision, enemy)* combattre; *(disease, fire, temptation)* lutter contre; *(election)* participer à; **to f. a war** être en guerre; *Law* **to f. a case** *(of lawyer)* défendre une cause; *(of defendant)* être en procès; *Fig* **I'm not going to f. your battles for you** c'est à vous de vous débrouiller; **to f. one's way through a crowd** se frayer un chemin à travers une foule

3 vi (**a**) (physically) se battre (**against** contre); (verbally) se disputer; **to f. shy of doing sth** éviter à tout prix de faire qch (**b**) (struggle) lutter (**for/against** pour/contre); **to f. for breath** suffoquer

▸**fight back 1** vt sep (tears) retenir; (anger) réprimer
2 vi (retaliate) se défendre

▸**fight off** vt sep (attacker) repousser; (illness) combattre

▸**fight out** vt sep **f. it out amongst yourselves** réglez ça entre vous

fighter ['faɪtə(r)] n (in fight) combattant(e) m,f; (for cause) lutteur(euse) m,f; **she's a real f.** (determined) c'est une battante; **f. (plane)** avion m de chasse; **f. squadron/pilot** escadron m/pilote m de chasse

fighting ['faɪtɪŋ] **1** n (scuffles) bagarres fpl; Mil combat m
2 adj **to have a f. chance** avoir encore de bonnes chances; **to be f. fit** être dans une forme éblouissante

figment ['fɪgmənt] n **it's a f. of your imagination** c'est le fruit de ton imagination

figurative ['fɪgərətɪv] adj (sense) figuré(e); (art) figuratif(ive)

figuratively ['fɪgərətɪvlɪ] adv **f. speaking** métaphoriquement parlant

figure ['fɪgə(r)] **1** n (**a**) (number) chiffre m; **to be good at figures** être bon (bonne) en calcul; **to reach double figures** (of score) atteindre la dizaine; (of inflation, unemployment) dépasser la barre des dix pour cent (**b**) (body shape) silhouette f; **to have a good f.** (of woman) avoir une jolie silhouette; **a fine f. of a man** un bel homme; **to cut a sorry f.** avoir l'air pitoyable (**c**) (person, character) personnage m; **a distinguished f.** une personnalité (**d**) (illustration, geometric shape) figure f (**e**) (expression) **f. of speech** figure f de rhétorique; **it's just a f. of speech** c'est une façon de parler
2 vt **to f. (that)...** (think) penser que...; (estimate) supposer que...
3 vi (**a**) (appear) (in list, book) figurer (**b**) Fam (make sense) **that figures!** ça se tient!

▸**figure on** vt insep **to f. on doing sth** compter faire qch

▸**figure out** vt sep (amount) calculer; (solution) trouver; (problem, person) arriver à comprendre

figurehead ['fɪgəhed] n (on ship) figure f de proue; Fig (of country, party) représentant(e) m,f nominal(e), Pej homme m de paille

Fiji ['fiːdʒiː] n les (îles fpl) Fidji fpl

Fijian [fiː'dʒiːən] **1** n Fidjien(enne) m,f
2 adj fidjien(enne)

filament ['fɪləmənt] n Elec filament m

filch [fɪltʃ] vt Fam faucher (**from sb** à qn)

file¹ [faɪl] **1** n (tool) lime f
2 vt (metal) limer; **to f. one's nails** se limer les ongles

file² **1** n (**a**) (folder) chemise f; (ring-bound) classeur m; (documents) dossier m (**on** sur); **to have sth on f.** avoir qch dans ses dossiers (**b**) Comput fichier m; **f. manager** gestionnaire m de fichiers; **f. server** serveur m de fichiers
2 vt (**a**) (documents, letters) classer (**b**) (complaint, claim, request) déposer
3 vi **to f. for divorce** demander le divorce

file³ **1** n (line) file f; **in single f.** en file indienne
2 vi **to f. past sb/sth** défiler devant qn/qch; **to f. in/out** entrer/sortir l'un(e) après l'autre

filial ['fɪlɪəl] adj filial(e)

filigree ['fɪlɪgriː] n filigrane m

Filipino [fɪlɪ'piːnəʊ] **1** n (pl Filipinos) Philippin(e) m,f
2 adj philippin(e)

fill [fɪl] **1** n **to eat one's f.** manger à sa faim; Fig **to have had one's f. of sth** en avoir assez de qch
2 vt (**a**) (container) remplir (**with** de); **to be filled with admiration/hope** être plein(e) d'admiration/d'espoir; **to have a tooth filled** se faire plomber une dent (**b**) (occupy) (time) occuper; **to f. a vacancy** (of employer) pourvoir à un poste vacant
3 vi se remplir (**with** de)

▸**fill in 1** vt sep (**a**) (hole) combler, boucher; (form) remplir; **to f. in time** occuper son temps (**b**) Fam (inform) **to f. sb in (on sth)** mettre qn au courant (de qch)
2 vi **to f. in for sb** remplacer qn

▸**fill out 1** vt sep (form, application) remplir
2 vi (get fatter) grossir

▸**fill up 1** vt sep (glass) remplir jusqu'au bord; Fam **f. her up!** (with petrol) le plein!
2 vi (**a**) (of tank, container) se remplir (**b**) (buy petrol) faire le plein

fillet ['fɪlɪt] **1** n (of fish, beef) filet m; **f. steak** filet de bœuf
2 vt (fish) découper en filets

filling ['fɪlɪŋ] **1** n (**a**) (in tooth) plombage m; (in sandwich, pie) garniture f (**b**) **f. station** station-service f
2 adj (food, meal) bourratif(ive); **it was very f.** cela m'a rassasié

filly ['fɪlɪ] (pl fillies) n (horse) pouliche f

film [fɪlm] **1** n (movie) film m; (layer, for camera) pellicule f; **a (roll of) f.** une pellicule, un rouleau de pellicule; **f. actor/actress** acteur m/actrice f de cinéma; **f. critic** critique mf de cinéma; **f. director** réalisateur(trice) m,f; **f. festival** festival m du cinéma; **the f. industry** l'industrie f cinématographique; **f. library** cinémathèque f; **f. maker** cinéaste mf; **f. script** scénario m, script m; **f. star** vedette f de cinéma, star f; **f. studio** studio m de cinéma
2 vt & vi filmer

Filofax® ['faɪləʊfæks] n Filofax® m

filter ['fɪltə(r)] **1** n filtre m; **f. coffee** café m filtre; **f. paper** papier m filtre; Aut **f. lane** = voie réservée aux véhicules qui tournent; Aut **f. signal** (on traffic light) flèche f de dégagement
2 vt filtrer
3 vi (**a**) (move slowly) **to f. in/out** entrer/sortir lentement (**b**) Aut (of traffic) **to f. to the right/left** dégager à droite/gauche pour tourner

▸**filter out** vt sep also Fig éliminer

▸**filter through 1** vt insep (of liquid, light) passer à travers
2 vi (of information) filtrer

filth [fɪlθ] n (dirt) crasse f; (in street) immondices fpl; (obscene words) obscénités fpl; **it's f.** (of book, film) c'est dégoûtant

filthy ['fɪlθɪ] **1** adj (**a**) (very dirty) dégoûtant(e) (**b**) (very bad) **in a f. temper** d'une humeur massacrante; **to give sb a f. look** regarder qn d'un sale œil; Br **f. weather** temps m de chien (**c**) (obscene) obscène
2 adv Fam **f. rich** pourri(e) de fric

fin [fɪn] n (of fish) nageoire f; (of aeroplane) empennage m; Am (of swimmer) palme f

final ['faɪnəl] **1** n (**a**) (of competition) **the f.** la finale (**b**) Univ **finals** Br examens mpl de dernière année; Am examens mpl finaux

2 *adj* (**a**) *(last)* dernier(ère); **f. demand** dernier avis *m*; **f. warning** dernier avertissement *m* (**b**) *(definitive)* final(e); **the umpire's decision is f.** la décision de l'arbitre est sans appel; **and that's f.!** un point, c'est tout!

finale [fɪ'nɑːlɪ] *n* finale *m*

finalist ['faɪnəlɪst] *n* finaliste *mf*

finalize ['faɪnəlaɪz] *vt (details, plans)* mettre au point; *(deal)* conclure

finally ['faɪnəlɪ] *adv* (**a**) *(lastly)* finalement (**b**) *(at last)* enfin; **she had f. met him** elle l'avait enfin rencontré (**c**) *(irrevocably)* définitivement; **it hasn't been f. decided yet** aucune décision définitive n'a encore été prise

finance [faɪ'næns, fɪ'næns] **1** *n* (**a**) *(subject)* finance *f*; **f. company** *or* **house** société *f* financière (**b**) **finances** *(funds)* finances *fpl*
2 *vt* financer

financial [faɪ'nænʃəl, fɪ'nænʃəl] *adj* financier(ère); **it was not a f. success** cela n'a pas rapporté beaucoup d'argent; **f. adviser** conseiller *m* financier; **f. market** marché *m* financier; **f. statement** bilan *m* financier; *Br* **f. year** exercice *m* comptable

> **Financial Year**
> Pour les impôts sur le revenu en Grande-Bretagne, l'année fiscale commence le 5 avril.

financially [faɪ'nænʃəlɪ, fɪ'nænʃəlɪ] *adv* financièrement

financier [faɪ'nænsɪə(r)] *n* financier *m*

finch [fɪntʃ] *n* fringillidé *m*

find [faɪnd] **1** *n* découverte *f*; **it's quite a f.** c'est une fameuse trouvaille
2 *vt (pt & pp* found [faʊnd]) (**a**) *(discover)* trouver; **to try to f. sth** chercher qch; **she was nowhere to be found** elle était introuvable; **I found her waiting in the hall** je l'ai trouvée qui attendait dans le vestibule; **this flower is commonly found in England** on trouve couramment cette fleur en Angleterre; **I found myself back where I'd started** je me suis retrouvé à mon point de départ; **you will f. that I'm right** tu verras que j'ai raison; **I was surprised to f. that...** j'ai découvert avec surprise que...; **he couldn't f. it in his heart to tell her** il n'avait pas le cœur à le lui dire; **to f. one's way** trouver son chemin; **to f. a way to do sth** trouver moyen de faire qch; **to f. oneself** *(spiritually)* se trouver
(**b**) *(experience)* trouver; **they will f. it easy/difficult** cela leur sera facile/difficile; **to f. it necessary to do sth** se trouver dans la nécessité de faire qch; **she found it impossible to understand him** elle avait beaucoup de mal à le comprendre; **how did you f. the meal?** le repas vous a-t-il plu?; **I found myself agreeing with her** il s'est trouvé que j'étais d'accord avec elle
(**c**) *Law* **to f. sb guilty/not guilty** déclarer qn coupable/non coupable
3 *vi Law* **to f. for/against sb** rendre un verdict en faveur de/contre qn

▸**find out 1** *vt sep* (**a**) *(discover)* découvrir (**b**) *(person)* prendre en défaut
2 *vi* **to f. out about sth** apprendre qch

finder ['faɪndə(r)] *n* **the f. of the money** la personne qui trouva/trouvera l'argent; *Fam* **finders keepers (losers weepers)** celui qui le trouve le garde

findings ['faɪndɪŋz] *npl* conclusions *fpl*; *Law (of jury, court)* verdict *m*

fine¹ [faɪn] **1** *n (penalty)* amende *f*
2 *vt* condamner à une amende; **to f. sb £10** infliger une amende de 10 livres à qn

fine² **1** *adj* (**a**) *(excellent)* excellent(e); *(foods, wine)* fin(e); *(weather)* beau; **to appeal to sb's finer feelings** faire appel aux bons sentiments de qn; **she's a f. woman** c'est une femme admirable; **f. art, the f. arts** les beaux-arts *mpl*; **she's got it down to a f. art** elle fait ça à la perfection
(**b**) *(satisfactory)* bien *inv*; **she's/everything's f.** elle/tout va bien; **that's f. by me** je n'y vois aucune objection
(**c**) *Ironic* **you're a f. one to talk!** tu peux bien parler!; **this is another f. mess you've got us into!** tu nous a encore mis dans un beau pétrin!
(**d**) *(thin) (hair, rain, line)* fin(e)
(**e**) *(subtle) (distinction)* subtil(e); **not to put too f. a point on it** pour parler carrément; **there's a f. line between eccentricity and madness** il n'y a qu'un pas de l'excentricité à la folie
2 *adv* très bien; **they get on f.** ils s'entendent (très) bien

finely ['faɪnlɪ] *adv* (**a**) *(judged)* soigneusement; *(written, painted)* admirablement; *Fig* **f. balanced** équilibré(e) (**b**) *(chopped, ground, grated)* finement

finery ['faɪnərɪ] *n* parure *f*; **she was dressed in all her f.** elle était habillée avec élégance

finesse [fɪ'nes] *n* finesse *f*

finger ['fɪŋgə(r)] **1** *n* (**a**) *(of hand, glove)* doigt *m*; **to keep one's fingers crossed** croiser les doigts; **f. bowl** rince-doigts *m inv*; **f. food** *(snacks)* amuse-gueule *mpl* (**b**) *(measure)* **a f. of brandy** un doigt de cognac (**c**) *Aviat* passerelle *f* (**d**) *(idioms)* **he's got them (wrapped) round his little f.** il fait d'eux ce qu'il veut; **to have a f. in every pie** être mêlé(e) à tout; **don't you dare lay a f. on him** je vous défends de le toucher; **she never lifts a f. to help me** elle ne lève jamais le petit doigt pour m'aider; **I can't quite put my f. on it** je n'arrive pas à mettre le doigt dessus; **to get one's fingers burnt** se brûler les doigts; *Br very Fam* **get** *or* **pull your f. out!** remue-toi!
2 *vt* (**a**) *(feel)* tâter (**b**) *very Fam (inform on)* balancer

fingernail ['fɪŋgəneɪl] *n* ongle *m*

fingerprint ['fɪŋgəprɪnt] *n* empreinte *f* digitale

fingertip ['fɪŋgətɪp] *n* bout *m* du doigt; **to have sth at one's fingertips** savoir qch sur le bout des doigts

finicky ['fɪnɪkɪ] *adj (person)* tatillon(onne); *(job, device)* compliqué(e)

finish ['fɪnɪʃ] **1** *n* (**a**) *(end) (of day, meeting)* fin *f*; *(of race)* arrivée *f* (**b**) *(surface) (of fabric, leather)* apprêt *m*; **paint with a gloss/matt f.** peinture *f* vernie/mate (**c**) *(workmanship)* finition *f*
2 *vt* (**a**) *(end)* finir, terminer; **to f. doing sth** finir *ou* terminer de faire qch (**b**) *(kill) (person)* achever; *Fam* **he's finished!** il est fini!
3 *vi* finir, se terminer; **to f. fourth** *(in race, contest)* finir *ou* terminer quatrième

▸**finish off 1** *vt sep* (**a**) *(complete, use up)* finir, terminer (**b**) *(kill)* achever; *(ruin) (chances, hopes)* anéantir
2 *vi* finir, terminer

▸**finish up 1** *vt sep (use up)* finir
2 *vi (end up)* se retrouver; **to f. up doing sth** finir par faire qch

▸**finish with** *vt insep* (**a**) *(stop using)* **to f. with sth** finir de se servir de qch (**b**) *(boyfriend, girlfriend)* laisser tomber

finished ['fɪnɪʃt] *adj* (**a**) *(completed)* fini(e); *(supplies)* épuisé(e) (**b**) *(performance)* soigné(e)

finishing ['fɪnɪʃɪŋ] *adj* **to put the f. touches to sth** mettre la dernière main à qch; **f. line** ligne *f* d'arrivée; **f. school** = école d'arts d'agrément pour les jeunes filles

finite ['faɪnaɪt] *adj* limité(e); *Gram (verb)* conjugué(e)

Finland ['fɪnlənd] *n* la Finlande

Finn [fɪn] *n (person)* Finlandais(e) *m,f*, Finnois(e) *m,f*

Finnish ['fɪnɪʃ] **1** *n (language)* finlandais *m*, finnois *m* **2** *adj* finlandais(e), finnois(e)

fir [fɜː(r)] *n* **f. (tree)** sapin *m*; **f. cone** pomme *f* de pin

fire ['faɪə(r)] **1** *n* (**a**) *(in hearth)* feu *m*; *(large, destructive)* incendie *m*; *(heater)* appareil *m* de chauffage; **electric/gas f.** radiateur *m* électrique/au gaz; **on f.** en feu; **to catch f.** prendre feu; **to set f. to sth, to set sth on f.** mettre le feu à qch; **f.!** au feu!; *Fig* **to play with f.** jouer avec le feu; *Fig* **to fight f. with f.** combattre le feu par le feu; **f. alarm** sirène *f* d'incendie; *Br* **f. brigade,** *Am* **f. department** sapeurs-pompiers *mpl*, pompiers *mpl*; **f. door** porte *f* coupe-feu; **f. drill** exercice *m* d'évacuation en cas d'incendie; **f. engine** voiture *f* de pompiers; **f. escape** escalier *m* de secours; **f. extinguisher** extincteur *m*; **f. fighter** pompier *m*; **to be a f. hazard** constituer un risque d'incendie; **f. hydrant** bouche *f* d'incendie; **f. insurance** assurance *f* contre l'incendie; **f. regulations** *(laws)* normes *fpl* de protection contre les incendies; *(instructions)* consignes *fpl* en cas d'incendie; **f. sale** = vente d'objets endommagés dans un incendie; **f. station** caserne *f* de pompiers

(**b**) *(of artillery)* tirs *mpl*; **to open f.** ouvrir le feu; **to hold one's f.** ne pas tirer; **to come under f.** être exposé(e) aux tirs; *Fig (be criticized)* être exposé(e) à de sévères critiques; **f. power** puissance *f* de tir

(**c**) *Fig (enthusiasm)* fougue *f*, ardeur *f*

2 *vt* (**a**) *(shoot) (missile, flare)* lancer; **to f. a gun (at)** tirer un coup de fusil (sur); *Fig* **to f. a question at sb** poser une question à qn à brûle-pourpoint

(**b**) *(dismiss)* virer

(**c**) **oil/gas-fired central heating** chauffage *m* central au mazout/au gaz; *Fig* **to f. sb's imagination** enflammer l'imagination de qn

(**d**) *(pottery)* cuire

3 *vi* (**a**) *(with gun)* tirer (**at** sur); *Fam Fig* **f. away!** *(to questioner)* allez-y!

(**b**) *(of engine)* tourner

firearm ['faɪərɑːm] *n* arme *f* à feu

firebrand ['faɪəbrænd] *n (torch)* tison *m*, brandon *m*; *Fig (person)* brandon de discorde

firecracker ['faɪəkrækə(r)] *n* pétard *m*

firefly ['faɪəflaɪ] *(pl* **fireflies***)* *n* luciole *f*

fireguard ['faɪəgɑːd] *n* garde-feu *m inv*

firelight ['faɪəlaɪt] *n* lumière *f* du feu

firelighter ['faɪəlaɪtə(r)] *n* allume-feu *m inv*

fireman ['faɪəmən] *n* pompier *m*

fireplace ['faɪəpleɪs] *n* cheminée *f*

fireproof ['faɪəpruːf] *adj* ignifugé(e)

fireside ['faɪəsaɪd] *n* **by the f.** au coin du feu

firewall ['faɪəwɔːl] *n* *Comput* firewall *m*, contrôle *m* d'accès

firewood ['faɪəwʊd] *n* bois *m* de chauffage

firework ['faɪəwɜːk] *n* pièce *f* d'artifice; **fireworks** *(display)* feu *m* d'artifice; *Fig* **there'll be fireworks** il va y avoir du grabuge; **f. display** feu d'artifice

firing ['faɪərɪŋ] *n* tir *m*; *Fig* **to be in the f. line** être l'objet de violentes critiques; **f. squad** peloton *m* d'exécution

firm¹ [fɜːm] *n (company)* entreprise *f*, firme *f*

firm² **1** *adj* (**a**) *(fruit, body, mattress, handshake)* ferme; *Fig (foundations, friendship)* solide; **the f. favourite** le/la grand(e) favori(ite); **it's my f. belief (that)...** j'ai la ferme conviction que... (**b**) *(strict)* ferme (**c**) *(definite) (decision)* ferme; *(date)* précis(e); *(evidence)* sérieux(euse)

2 *adv* **to stand f.** tenir bon *ou* ferme; **to hold f. to one's principles/beliefs** être fidèle à ses principes/croyances

firmly ['fɜːmlɪ] *adv* (**a**) *(securely)* solidement; **I f. believe (that)...** j'ai la ferme conviction que... (**b**) *(strictly)* fermement

first [fɜːst] **1** *n* (**a**) *(in series)* premier(ère) *m,f*; **we were the f. to arrive** nous étions les premiers arrivés; **it's the f. I've heard of it** c'est la première fois que j'en entends parler, première nouvelle; **Edward the F.** Edward Premier

(**b**) *(of month)* premier *m*; **we're leaving on the f.** nous partons le premier

(**c**) *(beginning)* **from f. to last** du début jusqu'à la fin; **from the f.** dès le début; **at f.** d'abord

(**d**) *Br Univ* **to get a f.** *(in degree)* ≃ avoir sa licence avec mention bien ou très bien

(**e**) *(first gear)* première *f*

(**f**) *(unique event)* première *f*

2 *adj* premier(ère); **for the f. time** pour la première fois; **at f. hand** de première main; **f. things f.!** commençons par le commencement!; **I don't know the f. thing about motorbikes** je ne connais absolument rien aux motos; **f. thing (in the morning)** dès le matin; **at f. light** aux premières lueurs du jour; **at f. sight** à première vue; **in the f. place** d'abord; **f. aid** *(skill)* secourisme *m*; *(treatment)* premiers soins *mpl*; **f. cousin** cousin(e) *m,f* germain(e); **f. edition** édition *f* originale; **f. gear** première *f* (vitesse *f*); *Am* **the f. lady** la première dame des États-Unis *(épouse du président)*; *Naut* **f. mate** second *m*; **f. name** prénom *m*; **f. night** *(of play)* première *f*; *Law* **f. offender** = personne qui commet un délit pour la première fois; **the F. World War** la Première Guerre mondiale

3 *adv* (**a**) *(firstly)* d'abord; **f. and foremost** avant toute chose; **f. of all** en premier lieu, d'abord

(**b**) *(for the first time)* pour la première fois; **I f. met her in London** je l'ai rencontrée pour la première fois à Londres

(**c**) *(before others)* le premier, la première; **you go f.!** *(in queue)* passez devant!; **to come f.** *(in race)* arriver premier(ère); *(in exam)* être reçu(e) premier(ère); **my family comes f.** ma famille passe avant le reste; **f. come, f. served** les premiers arrivés sont les premiers servis; **ladies f.!** les femmes d'abord!; **I won't do it, I'd resign f.** plutôt démissionner que de faire ça

first-aid [fɜːst'eɪd] *adj* **f. certificate** brevet *m* de secourisme; **f. kit** trousse *f* de secours

first-born ['fɜːstbɔːn] *n Lit* premier-né (première-née) *m,f*

first-class ['fɜːstklɑːs] **1** *adj* (**a**) *(compartment, ticket)* de première classe (**b**) **f. stamp** timbre *m* au tarif normal (**c**) *Univ* **f. honours (degree)** ≃ licence *f* avec mention bien ou très bien (**d**) *(excellent)* excellent(e)

2 *adv* (**a**) *(travel)* en première classe (**b**) *(post)* au tarif normal

first-degree ['fɜːstdɪ'griː] *adj* **(a)** *Med (burns)* au premier degré **(b)** *Am Law* **f. murder** assassinat *m*

first-hand ['fɜːsthænd] *adj & adv* de première main

firstly ['fɜːstlɪ] *adv* premièrement, en premier lieu

first-past-the-post ['fɜːstpɑːstðə'pəʊst] *adj Pol* **f. system** scrutin *m* à un tour

first-rate ['fɜːstreɪt] *adj* excellent(e)

first-time buyer ['fɜːst'taɪm'baɪə(r)] *n* = personne achetant une propriété pour la première fois

fiscal ['fɪskəl] *adj* fiscal(e); **f. policy** politique *f* budgétaire; **f. year** année *f* fiscale

---

Fiscal Year
En Grande-Bretagne, l'année fiscale commence le 1er avril pour les entreprises et le 6 avril pour les particuliers. Aux États-Unis, l'année fiscale correspond à l'année civile pour les particuliers.

---

fish [fɪʃ] **1** *n (pl* **fish** *or* **fishes) (a)** *(animal)* poisson *m*; *Br* **f. and chips** poisson frit avec des frites; **f.-and-chip shop** = magasin où l'on vend du poisson frit et des frites ainsi que d'autres produits cuits dans la friture; **f. cake** croquette *f* de poisson; **f. farm** établissement *m* piscicole; *Br* **f. fingers,** *Am* **f. sticks** bâtonnets *mpl* de poisson; **f. knife** couteau *m* à poisson; **f. slice** pelle *f* à poisson; **f. tank** aquarium *m* **(b)** *(idioms)* **there are plenty more f. in the sea** un de perdu, dix de retrouvés; **to have other f. to fry** avoir d'autres chats à fouetter; **to feel like a f. out of water** ne pas se sentir dans son élément; **to be neither f. nor fowl** n'être ni chair ni poisson

2 *vt* **(a)** *(river)* pêcher **(b)** *(remove)* **to f. sb/sth from somewhere** sortir qn/qch de quelque part

3 *vi* pêcher; *Fig* **to f. for compliments** rechercher les compliments; **she fished around in her pocket for some change** elle a fouillé dans sa poche pour trouver de la monnaie

fisherman ['fɪʃəmən] *n* pêcheur *m*

fish-hook ['fɪʃhʊk] *n* hameçon *m*

fishing ['fɪʃɪŋ] *n* pêche *f*; **to go f.** aller à la pêche; **f. boat** bateau *m* de pêche; **f. grounds** lieux *mpl* de pêche; **f. line** ligne *f*; **f. net** filet *m* de pêche; **f. port** port *m* de pêche; **f. rod** canne *f* à pêche

fishmonger ['fɪʃmʌŋɡə(r)] *n* poissonnier(ère) *m,f*; **f.'s (shop)** poissonnerie *f*

fishnet ['fɪʃnet] *adj (stockings, tights)* résille *inv*

fishy ['fɪʃɪ] *adj* **(a)** *(smell, taste)* de poisson **(b)** *Fam (suspicious)* louche

fission ['fɪʃən] *n* fission *f*

fissure ['fɪʃə(r)] *n (in mountain, rock)* fissure *f*; *Med* scissure *f*

fist [fɪst] *n* poing *m*; *Fig* **she made a good f. of it** elle s'en est plutôt bien sortie

fistful ['fɪstfʊl] *n* poignée *f*

fisticuffs ['fɪstɪkʌfs] *npl Hum* coups *mpl* de poing

fit¹ [fɪt] *n (seizure)* attaque *f*; **to have a f.** avoir une attaque; *Fam Fig* **to have** *or* **throw a f.** piquer une crise; **in a f. of temper** dans un accès de colère; **a f. of coughing** une quinte de toux; **a f. of crying** une crise de larmes; **to be in fits (of laughter)** se tordre de rire; **in fits and starts** par à-coups

fit² **1** *n* **the jacket is a good f.** cette veste me/te/*etc* va bien; **comfortable/tight f.** coupe *f* confortable/ajustée; **these trousers are a bit of a tight f.** ce pantalon est un peu juste

2 *adj* **(a)** *(appropriate)* **f. to eat** mangeable; **f. to**

drink buvable; **f. for the bin** bon (bonne) à jeter; **f. for human consumption** propre à la consommation; **a meal f. for a king** un repas digne d'un *ou* de roi; **do as you see** *or* **think f.** faites comme bon vous semblera; **to see f. to do sth** juger bon de faire qch; **that's all he's f. for** il n'est bon qu'à cela; **to be f. to do sth** *(worthy of)* être digne de faire qch; **to be f. to drop** tomber de fatigue

(b) *(healthy)* en forme; **to get f.** retrouver la forme; **to keep f.** se maintenir en forme; **to be f. to do sth** *(healthy enough)* être en état de faire qch; *Fam* **to be as f. as a fiddle** péter la forme

(c) *Br Fam (attractive)* canon *inv*

3 *vt (pt & pp* **fitted) (a)** *(match)* correspondre à; **to make the punishment f. the crime** proportionner la peine au délit

(b) *(be the right size for)* **to f. sb** aller à qn; **this key fits the lock** cette clé rentre dans la serrure

(c) *(install)* adapter **(to/on** à/sur); **to f. a carpet** poser de la moquette; **to f. sth with sth** équiper *ou* pourvoir qch de qch

(d) *(insert)* **to f. sth into/onto sth** faire rentrer qch dans/sur qch; **we can f. another two people inside** il y a encore de la place pour deux personnes

4 *vi* **(a)** *(be the right size) (of lid, key, plug)* aller; **to f. together** s'adapter; **to f. into sth** rentrer dans qch

(b) *(of clothes)* **it fits perfectly** ça me/te/*etc* va parfaitement

▸**fit in 1** *vt sep (in timetable)* caser
2 *vi* **(a)** *(go into place)* aller **(b)** *(of person) (in company, group)* s'intégrer; **you don't f. in here** tu n'es pas à ta place ici

▸**fit up** *vt sep very Fam (frame)* **to be fitted up** être victime d'un coup monté

fitful ['fɪtfʊl] *adj (sleep)* agité(e); **to make f. progress** progresser par à-coups

fitness ['fɪtnɪs] *n* **(a)** *(health)* forme *f*; *Br* **f. centre** club *m* de gym; **f. room** salle *f* de musculation **(b)** *(suitability)* aptitude *f* **(for** à)

fitted ['fɪtɪd] *adj* **(a)** *(jacket, dress)* ajusté(e); **f. carpet** moquette *f*; **f. sheet** drap-housse *m* **(b)** *(kitchen)* intégré(e); *(wardrobe)* encastré(e)

fitting ['fɪtɪŋ] **1** *n* **(a)** *(of clothes)* essayage *m*; **f. room** cabine *f* d'essayage **(b)** **fittings** *(in office)* installations *fpl*; *(in house)* accessoires *mpl*

2 *adj* approprié(e) **(to** à)

five [faɪv] **1** *n* cinq *m inv*

2 *adj* cinq; **f. o'clock shadow** barbe *f* d'un jour; *see also* **eight**

fiver ['faɪvə(r)] *n Br Fam (sum)* cinq livres *fpl*; *(note)* billet *m* de cinq livres

fix [fɪks] **1** *n* **(a)** *Fam (difficulty)* **to be in a f.** être dans le pétrin; **to get into a f.** se fourrer dans le pétrin **(b)** *Fam (of drug)* dose *f*; *Fig* **she needs her daily f. of chocolate** il lui faut sa dose quotidienne de chocolat **(c)** *Fam* **to be a f.** *(of election, contest)* être truqué(e)

2 *vt* **(a)** *(attach securely)* fixer **(to** à); **to f. sth in one's memory** graver qch dans sa mémoire; **to f. one's attention on sth** fixer son attention sur qch; **to f. one's eyes on sb/sth** fixer qn/qch **(b)** *(decide) (limit, price)* fixer **(c)** *(repair)* arranger, réparer **(d)** *(arrange) (meeting)* arranger; **to f. one's hair** se coiffer; *Fam* **I'll f. him!** je vais lui faire son affaire! **(e)** *Fam (election, contest)* truquer

▸**fix up** *vt sep* **(a)** *(arrange)* arranger **(b)** *(provide)* **to f. sb up with a job/flat** trouver un emploi/appartement à qn; **I've fixed you up with a date** je t'ai arrangé un rendez-vous galant

fixation [fik'seɪʃən] *n* fixation *f*; **to have a f. about sth** faire une fixation sur qch

fixed [fɪkst] *adj* (**a**) *(price, costs, income)* fixe; **f. assets** immobilisations *fpl* (**b**) *(definite) (ideas)* bien arrêté(e); *(plans)* précis(e) (**c**) *Fam* **how are you f. for money/time?** tu as de l'argent/le temps? (**d**) *Fam (election, contest)* truqué(e)

fixer ['fɪksə(r)] *n Fam* combinard(e) *m,f*

fixture ['fɪkstʃə(r)] *n* (**a**) **fixtures (and fittings)** *(in house, office)* installations *fpl* fixes; **bathroom fixtures** sanitaires *mpl*; *Fam* **to be a f.** *(of person)* faire partie des meubles (**b**) *Br (in sport)* rencontre *f*

fizz [fɪz] **1** *n* (**a**) *(sound)* pétillement *m*; *(bubbles)* gaz *m* (**b**) *Fam (soft drink)* boisson *f* gazeuse; *(champagne)* champ *m*
2 *vi (of champagne)* pétiller

▸**fizzle out** ['fɪzəl] *vi Fam (of plan)* tomber à l'eau; *(of enthusiasm, interest)* retomber; *(of relationship)* partir en eau de boudin

fizzy ['fɪzɪ] *adj (wine)* mousseux(euse); *(soft drink)* gazeux(euse)

fjord [fjɔːd] *n* fjord *m*

flab [flæb] *n Fam (fat)* graisse *f*

flabbergasted ['flæbəɡɑːstɪd] *adj Fam* abasourdi(e)

flabby ['flæbɪ] *adj (person, features)* bouffi(e); *(limbs)* mou (molle); *Fig (argument, reasoning)* qui manque de rigueur

flaccid ['flæsɪd] *adj* flasque

flag [flæɡ] **1** *n* drapeau *m*; *Naut* pavillon *m*; **F. Day** *(in United States)* = le 14 juin, fête commémorant l'adoption du drapeau américain; **f. day** *(for charity)* = jour où une association caritative organise une collecte en vendant des macarons, des insignes etc
2 *vt (pt & pp* **flagged**) marquer; *(mark)* signaler; **to f. (down) a taxi** héler un taxi
3 *vi (of person, conversation, interest)* faiblir; *(of strength, spirits)* baisser

---

Flag Day

Les "flag days" britanniques, durant lesquels on sollicite des dons auprès des passants, ont généralement lieu le samedi. Les donateurs reçoivent un papillon en papier qu'ils portent tout au long de la journée.

---

flagellate ['flædʒəleɪt] *vt* flageller

flagpole ['flæɡpəʊl] *n* mât *m (de drapeau)*

flagrant ['fleɪɡrənt] *adj* flagrant(e)

flagrantly ['fleɪɡrəntlɪ] *adv* de façon flagrante; **f. dishonest** d'une malhonnêteté flagrante

flagship ['flæɡʃɪp] *n (of fleet)* navire *m* amiral; *Fig (of range of products, party)* fleuron *m*

flagstone ['flæɡstəʊn] *n* dalle *f*

flail [fleɪl] **1** *n (tool)* fléau *m*
2 *vt* agiter
3 *vi (of rope, cable)* se balancer; *(of arms, legs)* s'agiter dans tous les sens

flail about, flail around *vi (of arms, legs)* s'agiter dans tous les sens; *(of person)* se débattre

flair ['fleə(r)] *n* don *m* (**for** pour); **to do sth with f.** faire qch avec style; **to have a f. for business** avoir le sens des affaires; **to have a f. for doing sth** avoir le don de faire qch

flak [flæk] *n* tir *m* antiaérien *ou* de DCA; *Fig* critiques *fpl*; **she got a lot of f. for her decision** sa décision a été très critiquée; **f. jacket** gilet *m* pare-balles

flake [fleɪk] **1** *n (of snow, cereal)* flocon *m*; *(of paint)* écaille *f*; *(of soap)* paillette *f*; **a f. of skin** un bout de peau morte
2 *vi (of paint)* s'écailler; **my skin is flaking** je pèle

▸**flake out** *vi Fam* s'effondrer de fatigue

flaky ['fleɪkɪ] *adj* (**a**) *(paint)* écaillé(e); *(pastry)* feuilleté(e) (**b**) *Am (eccentric)* loufoque

flamboyant [flæm'bɔɪənt] *adj (person, behaviour)* extravagant(e); *(gesture)* théâtral(e); *(clothes, colours)* voyant(e)

flame [fleɪm] **1** *n* flamme *f*; **to go up in flames** prendre feu; *Fig (of hopes, chances)* partir en fumée; **to burst into flames** s'enflammer; *Fam* **an old f.** *(man)* un ancien amoureux; *(woman)* une ancienne amoureuse
2 *vt Comput* descendre en flammes
3 *vi* (**a**) *(of fire)* flamber (**b**) *Comput* rédiger un message injurieux

flamenco [flə'meŋkəʊ] *n* flamenco *m*

flameproof ['fleɪmpruːf] *adj* ignifugé(e); *(dish)* qui va sur le feu

flamethrower ['fleɪmθrəʊə(r)] *n* lance-flammes *m inv*

flaming ['fleɪmɪŋ] **1** *adj* (**a**) *(burning)* enflammé(e); *Fig (sunset)* flamboyant(e); **a f. temper** une colère noire (**b**) *Br Fam (for emphasis)* sacré(e)
2 *adv Br Fam* vachement; **don't be so f. stupid!** ne sois pas si bête, merde!
3 *n Comput* envoi *m* de messages injurieux

flamingo [flə'mɪŋɡəʊ] *(pl* **flamingos**) *n* flamant *m*

flammable ['flæməbəl] *adj* inflammable

flan [flæn] *n* tarte *f*

Flanders ['flɑːndəz] *n* les Flandres *fpl*, la Flandre

flank [flæŋk] **1** *n* flanc *m*; *(of beef, mutton)* flanchet *m*
2 *vt* flanquer (**with** *or* **by** de)

flannel ['flænəl] *n* (**a**) *(fabric)* flanelle *f*; **(pair of) flannels** pantalon *m* en flanelle (**b**) *Br (face cloth)* ≃ gant *m* de toilette (**c**) *Br Fam (evasive words, flattery)* blabla *m*

flap [flæp] **1** *n* (**a**) *(of envelope, book cover, tent)* rabat *m*; *(of aeroplane)* volet *m* (**b**) *Fam (panic)* **to be in a f.** être affolé(e), paniquer
2 *vt (pt & pp* **flapped**) **to f. its wings** *(of bird)* battre des ailes; **to f. one's arms** agiter les bras
3 *vi* (**a**) *(of wings, flag)* battre (**b**) *Fam (panic)* s'affoler, paniquer

flapjack ['flæpdʒæk] *n* (**a**) *Br (biscuit)* = biscuit épais à l'avoine (**b**) *Am (pancake)* = petite crêpe épaisse

flare [fleə(r)] **1** *n* (**a**) *(signal)* signal *m* lumineux; *(rocket)* fusée *f* éclairante (**b**) **(pair of) flares** pantalon *m* (à) pattes d'éléphant
2 *vt (nostrils)* dilater
3 *vi (of fire)* flamboyer; **tempers flared at the meeting** le ton est monté à la réunion

▸**flare up** *vi (of fire)* s'embraser; *(of medical condition)* se déclencher; *(of anger, trouble)* éclater

flash [flæʃ] **1** *n* (**a**) *(of light)* éclair *m*; **f. of lightning** un éclair; **f. of wit** trait *m* d'esprit; **f. of inspiration** éclair de génie; **in a f.** *(very quickly)* en un clin d'œil; *Fig* **a f. in the pan** un feu de paille; **f. flood** crue *f* subite; **f. point** *(of situation)* point *m* de rupture; *(region)* point chaud (**b**) *(in photography)* flash *m*; **f. photography** photographie *f* au flash
2 *adj Br Fam (showy) (clothes, car, jewellery)*

tape-à-l'œil *inv*; *(person)* aux goûts tapageurs

3 *vt (smile, look)* lancer (**at** à); *(card, badge)* montrer rapidement (**at** à); **to f. one's headlights at sb** faire un appel de phares à qn

4 *vi* (**a**) *(of diamond)* briller; *(of light)* clignoter (**b**) *(move quickly)* **to f. past** passer comme un éclair; **my life flashed before me** ma vie a défilé devant mes yeux (**c**) *Fam (expose oneself)* s'exhiber (**at** devant)

flashback ['flæʃbæk] *n (in novel, film)* flash-back *m inv*, retour *m* en arrière

flasher ['flæʃə(r)] *n Br Fam* (**a**) *(man exposing himself)* exhibitionniste *m* (**b**) *(car indicator)* clignotant *m*

flashing ['flæʃɪŋ] *adj (light)* clignotant(e)

flashlight ['flæʃlaɪt] *n* torche *f* électrique

flashy ['flæʃɪ] *adj Fam (clothes, car, jewellery)* tape-à-l'œil *inv*; *(person)* aux goûts tapageurs

flask [flɑːsk] *n (for alcohol)* flasque *f*; *(in chemistry)* fiole *f*; (**Thermos®**) **f.** (bouteille *f*) Thermos® *f*

flat [flæt] **1** *n* (**a**) *Br (apartment)* appartement *m* (**b**) *Fam (flat tyre)* pneu *m* à plat; *(punctured)* pneu crevé

2 *adj* (**a**) *(surface)* plat(e); *(nose)* camus; **as f. as a pancake** plat comme une galette; *Fam (flat-chested)* plate comme une limande; **f. cap** casquette *f*; **f. racing** plat *m*; **f. rate** tarif *m* unique; *Comput & TV* **f. screen** écran *m* plat; **f. tyre** pneu *m* à plat; *(punctured)* pneu crevé

(**b**) *(refusal)* **to give a f. refusal** refuser net

(**c**) *(existence)* monotone; *(voice)* terne; *(battery)* à plat; *(drink)* éventé(e)

(**d**) *(in music) (a semitone lower)* bémol; *(out of tune)* en dessous du ton; **B f.** si *m inv* bémol

3 *adv* (**a**) *(level)* à plat; **to fall f. on one's face** tomber à plat ventre; *Fig* se casser le nez; *Fig* **to fall f.** *(of joke)* tomber à plat; **he pressed himself f. against the wall** il s'est plaqué contre le mur

(**b**) *(completely)* **to turn sb down f.** opposer un refus catégorique à qn; **in twenty seconds f.** en vingt secondes pile; **to work f. out** travailler d'arrache-pied; *Fam* **to be f. broke** être complètement fauché(e)

flat-chested ['flæt'tʃestɪd] *adj* **to be f.** avoir peu de poitrine

flatfish ['flætfɪʃ] *n* poisson *m* plat

flat-footed ['flæt'fʊtɪd] *adj* **to be f.** avoir les pieds plats

flatly ['flætlɪ] *adv (refuse, deny)* catégoriquement

flatmate ['flætmeɪt] *n Br* colocataire *mf*; **we used to be flatmates** nous partagions un appartement

flatten ['flætən] *vt* aplatir; **to f. oneself against a wall** s'aplatir contre un mur; *Fam* **to f. sb** casser la tête à qn

flatter ['flætə(r)] *vt (of person, clothes)* flatter; *Fam* **don't f. yourself!** ne te fais pas trop d'illusions!

flattering ['flætərɪŋ] *adj (words, photo)* flatteur(euse) *(clothes, colour)* qui avantage

flattery ['flætərɪ] *n* flatterie *f*

flatulence ['flætjʊləns] *n Med* flatulence *f*

flaunt [flɔːnt] *vt (knowledge, wealth)* étaler; *(jewels)* exhiber; *Fig (ignorance, bad manners)* étaler sans complexes

flavour, *Am* **flavor** ['fleɪvə(r)] **1** *n* (**a**) *(of food)* goût *m*; *(of ice cream, yoghurt)* parfum *m* (**b**) *(characteristic)* note *f*; **her stories have a Provençal f.** ses histoires fleurent bon la Provence

2 *vt (savoury food)* relever (**with** de); *(sweet food)* parfumer (**with** à); **vanilla flavoured** parfumé(e) à la vanille

flavouring, *Am* **flavoring** ['fleɪvərɪŋ] *n* parfum *m*; **artificial f.** arôme *m* artificiel

flavourless, *Am* **flavorless** ['fleɪvəlɪs] *adj Br* sans saveur, insipide

flaw [flɔː] *n* défaut *m*; *(in plan, argument)* faille *f*

flawed [flɔːd] *adj* qui a un défaut/des défauts; *(plan, argument)* bancal(e)

flawless ['flɔːlɪs] *adj* parfait(e)

flax [flæks] *n* lin *m*

flay [fleɪ] *vt (flog)* fouetter; *Fig (criticize)* éreinter

flea [fliː] *n* puce *f*; *Fam* **to send sb away with a f. in his ear** envoyer promener qn; **f. market** (marché *m* aux) puces *fpl*

fleabite ['fliːbaɪt] *n* piqûre *f* de puce

flea-bitten ['fliːbɪtən] *adj (person, animal)* plein(e) de puces; *Fam (shabby)* miteux(euse)

fleck [flek] **1** *n (of colour, light)* petite tache *f*; *(of dust)* grain *m*

2 *vt* tacheter (**with** de); **hair flecked with grey** cheveux *mpl* grisonnants

fled [fled] *pt & pp of* **flee**

fledgling ['fledʒlɪŋ] **1** *n (young bird)* oisillon *m*

2 *adj Fig (person)* novice, débutant(e); *(company, state)* naissant(e)

flee [fliː] *(pt & pp* **fled** [fled]*) vi* fuir, s'enfuir; **to f. from persecution** fuir la persécution

fleece [fliːs] **1** *n* (**a**) *(of sheep)* toison *f* (**b**) *(garment)* fourrure *f* polaire

2 *vt Fam (cheat)* estamper

fleecy ['fliːsɪ] *adj* duveteux(euse)

fleet [fliːt] *n (of ships)* flotte *f*; *(of taxis, buses)* parc *m*; *Fig (convoy)* file *f*; **F. Street** = rue de Londres, dont le nom sert à désigner les grands journaux britanniques

---

Fleet Street

Traditionnellement, cette rue de la City était celle des journaux. Aujourd'hui, beaucoup de journaux ont établi leur siège dans d'autres quartiers, notamment les Docklands. Cependant, le terme "Fleet Street" est encore employé pour désigner la presse et le monde du journalisme.

---

fleet-footed ['fliːt'fʊtɪd] *adj Lit* au pied léger

fleeting ['fliːtɪŋ] *adj (moment, happiness, glance)* fugace; *(beauty)* éphémère; *(visit)* court(e), rapide; **to catch a f. glimpse of sb/sth** entrevoir qn/qch

Flemish ['flemɪʃ] **1** *n (language)* flamand *m*

2 *adj* flamand(e)

flesh [fleʃ] *n* chair *f*; **in the f.** en chair et en os; **to make sb's f. creep** *or* **crawl** donner la chair de poule à qn; **his own f. and blood** *(children)* la chair de sa chair; *(close family)* les siens *mpl*; **f. wound** blessure *f* superficielle

▸**flesh out** *vt sep (plan, remarks)* étoffer

fleshy ['fleʃɪ] *adj* charnu(e)

flew [fluː] *pt of* **fly**

flex [fleks] **1** *n Br (cable)* cordon *m*

2 *vt (arms, knees)* fléchir; *(muscles)* faire jouer; *Fig* **they're just flexing their muscles** ce n'est qu'une démonstration d'autorité de leur part

flexible ['fleksɪbəl] *adj (material, approach, timetable)* flexible; *(person's character)* souple

flexitime ['fleksɪtaɪm] *n* horaires *mpl* flexibles *ou* à la carte

flick [flɪk] **1** n (**a**) *(with finger)* pichenette f; *(of whip, tail)* petit coup m; **at the f. of a switch** en appuyant juste sur un bouton; **f. knife** couteau m à cran d'arrêt (**b**) *Br Fam Old-fashioned* **the flicks** *(cinema)* le ciné, le cinoche
2 vt *(with finger)* donner une chiquenaude à; **he flicked the cigarette ash onto the carpet** il fit tomber la cendre de sa cigarette sur le tapis; **to f. the hair out of one's eyes** écarter les cheveux de ses yeux
►**flick through** vt insep *(book, magazine)* feuilleter; *(photographs)* passer rapidement en revue

flicker ['flɪkə(r)] **1** n *(of flame)* vacillement m; *Fig (of hope)* lueur f; *(of interest, annoyance)* pointe f; **a f. of light** une lueur vacillante
2 vi *(of flame, light)* vaciller

flier ['flaɪə(r)] n (**a**) *(passenger)* = personne qui voyage en avion (**b**) *(leaflet)* prospectus m

flight [flaɪt] n (**a**) *(act of flying, specific trip)* vol m; **it's a two hour f. from Edinburgh** c'est à deux heures de vol d'Édimbourg; *Fig* **f. of fancy** lubie f; **f. attendant** *(male)* steward m; *(female)* hôtesse f de l'air; **f. deck** *(of aircraft)* poste m ou cabine f de pilotage; **f. path** trajectoire f de vol; **f. recorder** enregistreur m de vol; **f. simulator** simulateur m de vol (**b**) *(group of birds)* vol m, volée f; *Fig* **in the top f.** parmi les tout premiers (**c**) **f. (of stairs)** escalier m; **two flights up from me** deux étages au-dessus de chez moi (**d**) *(escape)* fuite f; **to put sb to f.** mettre qn en fuite

flightless ['flaɪtlɪs] adj coureur(euse)

flighty ['flaɪtɪ] adj *(fickle)* volage

flimsy ['flɪmzɪ] adj *(structure, fence)* peu solide; *(dress, excuse, plot)* léger(ère); *(evidence)* ténu(e)

flinch [flɪntʃ] vi *(with pain)* tressaillir; *(at an idea)* frémir; **to do sth without flinching** faire qch sans broncher; **to f. from doing sth** hésiter à faire qch

fling [flɪŋ] **1** n *Fam (affair)* aventure f
2 vt *(pt & pp* **flung** [flʌŋ]*)* jeter; *(ball)* lancer; **to f. oneself into an armchair** se jeter dans un fauteuil; **to f. one's arms around sb** prendre qn dans ses bras; *Fig* **to f. oneself into a task** se lancer dans une tâche
►**fling out** vt sep *(object)* jeter; *(person)* mettre à la porte; *(proposal, case)* rejeter

flint [flɪnt] n *(stone)* silex m; *(of lighter)* pierre f (à briquet)

flip [flɪp] **1** n *Fam* **the f. side** *(of record)* la face B; *Fig (of situation)* le revers de la médaille
2 vt *(pt & pp* **flipped***)* *(record, pancake, card)* retourner; **to f. the switch** appuyer sur l'interrupteur; **to f. a coin** jouer à pile ou face; *Fam* **to f. one's lid** *(get angry)* piquer une crise; *(go mad)* perdre la boule
3 vi *Fam (get angry)* piquer une crise; *(go mad)* perdre la boule
►**flip through** vt insep *(book, magazine)* feuilleter; *(photos, samples)* jeter un coup d'œil à

flipboard ['flɪpbɔːd], **flipchart** ['flɪptʃɑːt] n tableau m à feuilles (mobiles)

flip-flops ['flɪpɒps] npl **(a pair of) f.** des tongs fpl

flippant ['flɪpənt] adj désinvolte, cavalier(ère)

flipper ['flɪpə(r)] n *(of animal)* nageoire f; *(of diver)* palme f

flirt [flɜːt] **1** n charmeur(euse) m,f
2 vi flirter (**with** avec); *Fig* **to f. with an idea** caresser une idée

flirtatious [flɜː'teɪʃəs] adj *(look, smile)* charmeur(-euse); **to be f.** aimer flirter; **to be f. with sb** flirter avec qn

flit [flɪt] **1** n *Br Fam* **to do a moonlight f.** déménager à la cloche de bois
2 vi *(pt & pp* **flitted***)* **to f. about** *(of bird)* voleter; *Fig* **to f. from one thing to another** *(of person)* s'éparpiller

float [fləʊt] **1** n (**a**) *(on fishing line)* bouchon m; *(for swimming, on net)* flotteur m (**b**) *(in procession)* char m (**c**) *(money)* fonds m de caisse
2 vt (**a**) *(ship)* mettre à flot (**b**) *(idea, proposal)* émettre; *(company)* introduire en Bourse
3 vi flotter; **to f. to the surface** remonter à la surface; **to f. on one's back** *(of swimmer)* faire la planche; **the bottle floated out to sea** la bouteille a été emportée vers le large; *Fam Fig* **he's floating around somewhere** il traîne par là

floating ['fləʊtɪŋ] adj flottant(e); *(population)* fluctuant(e); **f. voter** électeur(trice) m,f indécis(e)

flock [flɒk] **1** n *(of sheep)* troupeau m; *(of birds)* vol m, volée f; *Rel (congregation)* ouailles fpl; *Fig (of people)* foule f
2 vi *(gather)* **to f. around sb** s'attrouper autour de qn; **people are flocking to the exhibition** les gens vont en masse ou en foule voir l'exposition

flog [flɒg] *(pt & pp* **flogged***)* vt (**a**) *(beat)* fouetter; *Fam* **to be flogging a dead horse** se dépenser en pure perte; *Fam* **to f. a subject to death** s'étendre indéfiniment sur un sujet (**b**) *Br Fam (sell)* vendre

flood [flʌd] **1** n inondation f; *(of light)* flot m; **the F. (in the Bible)** le Déluge; **to be in floods (of tears)** verser des torrents de larmes
2 vt *(land, bathroom)* inonder; **to be flooded with light** être inondé(e) de lumière; **the river flooded its banks** la rivière a débordé ou est sortie de son lit; **to f. the market (with sth)** inonder le marché (de qch); **to be flooded with complaints/telephone calls** être submergé(e) de réclamations/de coups de fil
3 vi *(of river)* déborder; **the sun's rays came flooding through the window** les rayons du soleil entraient à flots par la fenêtre; **letters came flooding in** nous avons/ils ont/*etc* été submergés de lettres; **it all came flooding back** tout m'/lui/*etc* est revenu d'un coup

floodgate ['flʌdgeɪt] n *Fig* **to open the floodgates to sth** laisser la porte ouverte à qch

flooding ['flʌdɪŋ] n inondation(s) f(pl)

floodlight ['flʌdlaɪt] n projecteur m; **by f.** à la lumière des projecteurs

floodlit ['flʌdlɪt] adj *(stadium, match)* éclairé(e) aux projecteurs; *(building)* illuminé(e)

floor [flɔː(r)] **1** n (**a**) *(of room, forest)* sol m; *(of Stock Exchange)* parquet m; *(of ocean)* fond m; **f. show** spectacle m de cabaret (**b**) *(at meeting, debate)* **to give sb the f.** donner la parole à qn; **to take the f.** prendre la parole; **questions from the f.** questions fpl du public (**c**) *(storey)* étage m; **to live ten floors up** habiter au dixième étage
2 vt *(knock down)* envoyer au tapis; *Fig (of question, criticism)* désarçonner

floorboard ['flɔːbɔːd] n latte f de plancher

floozie, floozy ['fluːzɪ] *(pl* **floozies***)* n *very Fam Pej* pouffiasse f

flop [flɒp] **1** n *(failure)* fiasco m, bide m; **to be a f. (of film)** faire un bide; *(of party)* être un bide
2 vi *(pt & pp* **flopped***)* (**a**) *(fall) (into water)* tomber; *(onto seat)* s'affaler (**b**) *(fail)* échouer; *(of film)* faire un bide; *(of party)* être un bide

floppy ['flɒpɪ] **1** n (pl **floppies**) Comput disquette f
  2 adj (ears) pendant(e); (garment) flottant(e); (hat) mou (molle); Comput **f. disk** disquette f

flora ['flɔːrə] n (plant life) flore f

floral ['flɔːrəl] adj floral(e); **f. tribute** (at funeral) couronne f de fleurs

Florence ['flɒrəns] n Florence

florid ['flɒrɪd] adj (style) fleuri(e); (complexion) rubicond(e)

Florida ['flɒrɪdə] n la Floride

florist ['flɒrɪst] n fleuriste mf; **f.'s (shop)** fleuriste m

floss [flɒs] **1** n **(dental) f.** fil m dentaire
  2 vt nettoyer avec du fil dentaire

flotation [fləʊ'teɪʃən] n Com (of company) lancement m

flotsam ['flɒtsəm] n **f. (and jetsam)** débris mpl refoulés par la mer; Fig **the f. of society** les laissés-pour-compte mpl de la société

flounce [flaʊns] **1** n (in sewing) volant m
  2 vi **to f. in/out** entrer/sortir de façon théâtrale

flounder ['flaʊndə(r)] **1** n (fish) flet m
  2 vi (in water, mud) patauger; (in job, course, speech) perdre pied

flour ['flaʊə(r)] **1** n farine f
  2 vt fariner

flourish ['flʌrɪʃ] **1** n (gesture) grand geste m théâtral; (musical, in writing) fioriture f
  2 vt (brandish) brandir
  3 vi (of plant, person) prospérer; (of business, arts) être florissant(e)

flourishing ['flʌrɪʃɪŋ] adj (plant) qui prospère; (business) florissant(e)

flout [flaʊt] vt (rule, instruction) faire fi de; (person) défier l'autorité de; (authority) défier

flow [fləʊ] **1** n (of liquid) écoulement m; (of electrical current, information) circulation f; (of tide, capital) flux m; **f. of traffic** circulation; Fig **in full f.** en plein discours; Fig **to follow the f. of an argument** suivre (le fil d')un raisonnement; Fig **to go with the f.** suivre le mouvement; **f. chart** organigramme m
  2 vi (a) (of liquid) couler; (of electrical current) circuler; (of traffic) s'écouler; Fig (of writing) couler bien; (of ideas) affluer; **to f. into the sea** (of river) se jeter dans la mer (b) **to f. from** (result from) découler de

flower ['flaʊə(r)] **1** n fleur f; **to be in f.** être en fleur(s); Fig **in the first f. of youth** dans la fleur de l'âge; **f. arranging** art m floral; **f. garden** jardin m d'agrément; **f. girl** = jeune demoiselle d'honneur; **f. show** exposition f florale
  2 vi fleurir

flowerbed ['flaʊəbed] n parterre m de fleurs

flowerpot ['flaʊəpɒt] n pot m de fleurs

flowing ['fləʊɪŋ] adj (hair) flottant(e); (movement, style) fluide

flown [fləʊn] pp of **fly**

flu [fluː] n grippe f; **a dose** or **bout of (the) f.** une grippe; **to have (the) f.** avoir la grippe

fluctuate ['flʌktjʊeɪt] vi (of prices) fluctuer; (of pulse, temperature) varier

fluctuation [flʌktjʊ'eɪʃən] n (of prices) fluctuation f; (of pulse, temperature) variation f

flue [fluː] n (of heater, chimney) tuyau m

fluency ['fluːənsɪ] n aisance f (**of/in** de/en)

fluent ['fluːənt] adj (speech, style) fluide; **he is f. in French, he speaks f. French** il parle couramment français

fluently ['fluːəntlɪ] adv (express oneself) avec facilité ou aisance; (speak language) couramment

fluff [flʌf] **1** n peluche f; **a bit of f.** une peluche; Br Fam (pretty girl) nana f, gonzesse f
  2 vt (**a**) **to f. sth (up)** (pillow, duvet) remettre qch en forme (en le secouant) (**b**) Fam (botch) rater

fluffy ['flʌfɪ] adj duveteux(euse); (clouds) cotonneux(euse)

fluid ['fluːɪd] **1** n fluide m, liquide m; **bodily fluids** sécrétions fpl
  2 adj (substance) fluide, liquide; (style, movement) fluide; (situation, plans) mal défini(e); **f. ounce** = 0,03 l

fluidity [fluːˈɪdɪtɪ] n (of style, movement) fluidité f; (of situation, plans) imprécision f

fluke [fluːk] n Fam (stroke of luck) coup m de veine ou de bol; **by a f.** par hasard; **his success was a pure f.** c'est un hasard qu'il ait réussi

fluk(e)y ['fluːkɪ] adj Fam (person) veinard(e)

flummox ['flʌməks] vt Fam scier

flung [flʌŋ] pt & pp of **fling**

flunk [flʌŋk] Fam **1** vt (exam) rater; (student) recaler, coller
  2 vi (in exam) être recalé(e) ou collé(e)

flunkey ['flʌŋkɪ] (pl **flunkeys**) n Fam Pej larbin m

fluorescent [flʊəˈresənt] adj fluorescent(e)

fluoride ['flʊəraɪd] n fluorure m; **f. toothpaste** dentifrice m au fluor

flurry ['flʌrɪ] (pl **flurries**) n (of snow) bourrasque f; **a f. of activity/excitement** une soudaine activité/excitation

flush [flʌʃ] **1** n (**a**) (beginning) **in the first f. of youth** dans tout l'éclat de sa jeunesse (**b**) (in cards) flush m (**c**) (in toilet) chasse f (d'eau)
  2 adj (**a**) (even) de niveau (**with** avec) (**b**) Fam (rich) plein(e) aux as
  3 vt **to f. the toilet** tirer la chasse (d'eau)
  4 vi (**a**) (of person) rougir (**with** de) (**b**) (of toilet) **the toilet isn't flushing properly** la chasse d'eau ne fonctionne pas bien

▸**flush out** vt sep (force to emerge) déloger

flushed [flʌʃd] adj (person, face) rouge (**with** de)

fluster ['flʌstə(r)] vt démonter; **to get flustered** se démonter

flute [fluːt] n (**a**) Mus flûte f traversière (**b**) (glass) flûte f

flutter ['flʌtə(r)] **1** n (**a**) (of wings, eyelashes, heart) battement m; Fig **to be in a f.** (of excitement) être en émoi (**b**) Br Fam (bet) petit pari m; **to have a f.** parier ou jouer une petite somme (**on** sur)
  2 vt **to f. its wings** (of bird) battre des ailes; **to f. one's eyelashes at sb** regarder qn en battant des cils
  3 vi (of birds, insects) voleter; (of heart) battre; (of flag) flotter

flux [flʌks] n **to be in a state of f.** changer perpétuellement

fly¹ [flaɪ] n (**a**) **f., flies** (of trousers) braguette f (**b**) **f. sheet** (of tent) auvent m

fly² Br Fam **1** n **to do sth on the f.** (spontaneously) faire qch sur le coup
  2 adj (cunning) malin(igne)

fly³ (pl **flies**) n (insect) mouche f; **he wouldn't hurt a f.** il ne ferait pas de mal à une mouche; **they were**

dropping like flies ils tombaient comme des mouches; *Fig* a f. in the ointment un os; *Fam Fig* there are no flies on her elle est loin d'être bête; I wish I could be a f. on the wall *(at interview, meeting)* si je pouvais être une petite souris

fly⁴ *(pt* flew [fluː], *pp* flown [fləʊn])* 1 *vt* **(a)** *(plane)* piloter; *(goods)* transporter en avion; *(route)* emprunter; to f. Air India voyager avec Air India

(b) *(kite)* faire voler; to f. a flag *(of ship)* arborer un pavillon; *Fig* to f. the flag (for one's country) défendre les couleurs de son pays

(c) *(flee)* s'enfuir de; *Fig* to f. the nest *(of child)* quitter le foyer familial

2 *vi* **(a)** *(of bird, plane)* voler; *(of passenger)* voyager en avion, prendre l'avion; to f. over London survoler Londres; to f. across the Atlantic traverser l'Atlantique en avion

(b) *(of flag, hair)* flotter

(c) *(move quickly)* I must f. il faut que je file; to f. to sb's help voler au secours de qn; how time flies! comme le temps passe! the door flew open la porte s'est ouverte brusquement; to f. into a rage sortir de ses gonds; *Fam* to send sb/sth flying envoyer rouler qn/qch; to f. in the face of reason/logic défier la raison/toute logique

▸**fly away** *vi (of bird, papers)* s'envoler

▸**fly in** 1 *vt sep (troops, rescuers)* transporter en avion

2 *vi (of passenger)* arriver en avion

▸**fly out** 1 *vt sep (survivors)* transporter en avion

2 *vi (of passenger)* partir en avion

fly-by-night ['flaɪbaɪnaɪt] *adj Fam Pej (company)* véreux(euse)

flyer = flier

flying ['flaɪɪŋ] 1 *n (as pilot)* pilotage *m; (as passenger)* voyages *mpl* en avion; she loves f. *(as pilot)* elle adore piloter; *(as passenger)* elle adore prendre l'avion; f. club aéro-club *m;* f. lessons leçons *fpl* de pilotage; f. time heures *fpl* de vol

2 *adj* **(a)** *(bird, fish)* volant(e); they were hurt by f. glass ils ont été blessés par des éclats de verre; to pass with f. colours réussir haut la main; f. boat hydravion *m;* f. doctor médecin *m* volant; f. saucer soucoupe *f* volante **(b)** *(rapid)* a f. visit une visite éclair; to get off to a f. start très bien démarrer

flyleaf ['flaɪliːf] *(pl* flyleaves ['flaɪliːvz] *)* *n* page *f* de garde

Flymo® ['flaɪməʊ] *n* = tondeuse à gazon sur coussin d'air

flyover ['flaɪəʊvə(r)] *n BrAut* pont *m* routier

flypaper ['flaɪpeɪpə(r)] *n* papier *m* tue-mouches, *Can* collant *m* à mouches

fly-past ['flaɪpɑːst] *n Aviat* défilé *m* aérien

flyweight ['flaɪweɪt] *n (in boxing)* poids *m* mouche

FM [e'fem] *n (abbr* frequency modulation) FM *f*

FO [e'fəʊ] *n Br (abbr* Foreign Office) (ministère *m* des) Affaires *fpl* étrangères

foal [fəʊl] 1 *n (horse)* poulain *m; (female)* pouliche *f*

2 *vi* pouliner

foam [fəʊm] 1 *n (on sea)* écume *f; (on beer, bath)* mousse *f;* f. rubber caoutchouc *m* Mousse®

2 *vi (of sea)* écumer; *(of beer, bath)* mousser; to f. at the mouth baver; *Fig* écumer de rage

foamy ['fəʊmɪ] *adj (sea)* écumeux(euse); *(beer)* moussant(e)

fob [fɒb] *n* chaîne *f* (de montre); f. watch montre *f* de gousset

▸**fob off** *(pt & pp* fobbed) *vt sep Fam* to f. sb off with an excuse se débarrasser de qn en lui racontant des salades; to f. sth off on sb refiler *ou* fourguer qch à qn

focal ['fəʊkəl] *adj* focal(e); f. point foyer *m; Fig (of discussion)* point *m* central

focus ['fəʊkəs] 1 *n (pl* focuses *or* foci ['fəʊkaɪ]) *(of lens)* foyer *m; Fig (of discontent)* cible *f; (of interest, attention)* centre *m; Com & Pol* f. group *(of customers)* groupe *m* témoin; to be in f. être au point; to be out of f. ne pas être au point

2 *vt (lens, camera)* mettre au point; *(rays, attention, energy)* concentrer (on sur); all eyes were focused on him tous les regards étaient tournés vers lui

3 *vi* to f. on sth *(with camera)* faire la mise au point sur qch; *(with eyes)* fixer qch; *Fig (of debate, speaker)* se concentrer sur qch

fodder ['fɒdə(r)] *n* fourrage *m*

foe [fəʊ] *n* ennemi *m*

foetal, *Am* **fetal** ['fiːtəl] *adj* fœtal(e); in the f. position en position fœtale

foetus, *Am* **fetus** ['fiːtəs] *n* fœtus *m*

fog [fɒg] *n* brouillard *m; Fig* to be in a f. *(confused)* être dans le brouillard; f. lamp *or* light *(on car)* (phare *m)* antibrouillard *m*

▸**fog up** *(pt & pp* fogged) *vi (of windows, glasses)* s'embuer

fogbound ['fɒgbaʊnd] *adj (port, airport)* bloqué(e) en raison du brouillard

fogey ['fəʊgɪ] *(pl* fogeys) *n Fam* old f. vieux (vieille) schnock *m,f*

foggy ['fɒgɪ] *adj* brumeux(euse); it's f. il y a du brouillard; *Fam* I haven't (got) the foggiest (idea)! je n'en ai pas la moindre idée!

foghorn ['fɒghɔːn] *n (on ship)* corne *f* de brume; *Fam* a voice like a f. une voix de stentor

fogy *(pl* fogies) = fogey

foible ['fɔɪbəl] *n (habit)* manie *f; (weakness)* point *m* faible

foil [fɔɪl] 1 *n* **(a)** *(metal sheet)* feuille *f;* (cooking *or* kitchen) f. papier *m* alu(minium) **(b)** *(complement)* to act as a f. (to *or* for) servir de repoussoir (à) **(c)** *(sword)* fleuret *m*

2 *vt (plan, ambitions)* contrecarrer; *(attempt, coup)* faire échouer

foist [fɔɪst] *vt* refiler (on à); *(ideas)* imposer (on à)

fold¹ [fəʊld] *n (sheep)* f. parc *m* à moutons

fold² 1 *n* pli *m; (of fat)* bourrelet *m*

2 *vt* **(a)** *(bend)* plier; to f. sth in two *or* in half plier qch en deux; to f. one's arms croiser les bras **(b)** *(in cooking)* mélanger délicatement

3 *vi* **(a)** *(of chair, table)* se plier, se replier **(b)** *Fam (of business)* plier boutique

▸**fold up** 1 *vt sep* plier, replier

2 *vi (of map, chair)* se plier, se replier

foldaway ['fəʊldəweɪ] *adj (table, bed)* pliant(e)

folder ['fəʊldə(r)] *n (file, document wallet)* chemise *f; (ring binder)* classeur *m; Comput* répertoire *m*

folding ['fəʊldɪŋ] *adj (chair, table)* pliant(e); f. doors porte *f* en accordéon

foliage ['fəʊlɪdʒ] *n* feuillage *m*

folio ['fəʊlɪəʊ] *(pl* folios) *n* folio *m*

folk [fəʊk] 1 *npl Fam (people)* gens *mpl;* my/your folks *(family)* ma/ta famille

2 *adj (traditional)* folklorique; f. (music) (musique *f)*

folk *m*; **f. singer** chanteur(euse) *m,f* folk; **f. song** chanson *f* folk

folklore ['fəʊklɔː(r)] *n* folklore *m*

follow ['fɒləʊ] **1** *vt* suivre; *(act, performance)* passer après; *(career)* poursuivre; **the road follows the coast** la route longe la côte; **to f. one's nose** *(go straight ahead)* aller tout droit; *(act instinctively)* y aller à l'instinct
   2 *vi* (**a**) *(come after)* suivre; **proceed as follows** procéder comme suit (**b**) *(result)* s'ensuivre; **it follows that...** il s'ensuit que... (**c**) *(understand)* suivre

▶**follow on** *vi* (**a**) *(go after)* **you go ahead, we'll f. on** pars devant, nous te suivons (**b**) *(continue)* **to f. on from sth** découler de qch

▶**follow through 1** *vt sep (project, plan)* mener à son terme
   2 *vi* **he's full of ideas but he seldom follows through** il a beaucoup d'idées, mais il les met rarement à exécution

▶**follow up** *vt sep (advantage, success)* exploiter; *(opportunity)* saisir; *(contact)* garder; *(clue)* suivre

follower ['fɒləʊə(r)] *n (of team)* supporter *m*; *(of ideas, politician)* partisan(e) *m,f*; *(of philosopher)* disciple *m*

following ['fɒləʊɪŋ] **1** *n (supporters) (of team)* supporters *mpl*; *(of ideas, politician)* partisans *mpl*; *(of programme)* public *m*
   2 *pron* **the f.** *(things, points)* ce qui suit; *(people)* les personnes *fpl* suivantes
   3 *adj* suivant(e); **(on) the f. day** le jour suivant, le lendemain
   4 *prep* après

follow-up ['fɒləʊʌp] *n Com (of orders)* suivi *m*

folly ['fɒlɪ] *n* folie *f*; **an act of f.** une folie

foment [fə'ment] *vt Lit* fomenter

fond [fɒnd] *adj* (**a**) **to be f. of sb/sth** aimer bien qn/qch; **to become f. of sb** s'attacher à qn; **to become f. of sth** prendre goût à qch; **to be f. of doing sth** aimer bien faire qch (**b**) *(loving)* tendre, affectueux(euse); **f. memories (of)** de bons souvenirs (de) (**c**) *(hope)* naïf(ïve)

fondle ['fɒndəl] *vt* caresser

fondly ['fɒndlɪ] *adv* (**a**) *(lovingly)* tendrement, affectueusement (**b**) *(naively)* naïvement

fondness ['fɒndnɪs] *n* (**a**) *(affection)* tendresse *f*, affection *f* (**for** pour) (**b**) *(liking)* penchant *m* (**for** pour)

font [fɒnt] *n* (**a**) *Rel* fonts *mpl* baptismaux (**b**) *Typ & Comptr* police *f* de caractères, fonte *f*

food [fuːd] *n* nourriture *f*; **Chinese/Mexican f.** la cuisine chinoise/mexicaine; **to be off one's f.** ne pas avoir d'appétit; **to give sb f. for thought** donner à penser *ou* à réfléchir à qn; *Biol* **f. chain** chaîne *f* alimentaire; **f. industry** industrie *f* alimentaire; **f. poisoning** intoxication *f* alimentaire; **f. processor** robot *m* de cuisine

foodstuffs ['fuːdstʌfs] *npl* produits *mpl* alimentaires

fool [fuːl] **1** *n (stupid person)* imbécile *mf*, idiot(e) *m,f*; *(jester)* fou *m*; **you'd be a f. to buy it** tu serais bien bête de l'acheter; **any f. knows that** le premier imbécile venu sait ça; **a f. of a doctor** un imbécile de docteur; **to play** *or* **act the f.** faire l'idiot; **to make a f. of sb** *(make look ridiculous)* ridiculiser qn; *(tease)* se moquer de qn; **to make a f. of oneself** se couvrir de ridicule; **the more f. you!** tu es vraiment bête!; **I felt such a f.** je me suis senti vraiment bête; **she's no** *or* **nobody's f.** on ne la lui fait pas, elle est maligne; **to live in a f.'s paradise** se bercer d'illusions; *Fam* **there's no**

f. like an old f. il n'y a pire fou qu'un vieux fou
   2 *vt (deceive)* avoir, duper; **you can't f. me** on ne m'a pas comme ça; **to let oneself be fooled by sth** se laisser avoir par qch; **you could have fooled me!** je ne l'aurais pas cru!

▶**fool about, fool around** *vi* (**a**) *(act foolishly)* faire l'imbécile; **to f. about** *or* **around with sth** *(clumsily, for fun)* jouer avec qch (**b**) *(waste time)* perdre son temps (**c**) *(have affair(s))* avoir une aventure/des aventures

foolhardy ['fuːlhɑːdɪ] *adj* téméraire, imprudent(e)

foolish ['fuːlɪʃ] *adj (stupid)* idiot(e); *(imprudent)* insensé(e); **to make sb look f.** ridiculiser qn

foolishly ['fuːlɪʃlɪ] *adv (stupidly)* bêtement; *(imprudently)* imprudemment

foolproof ['fuːlpruːf] *adj (method, plan)* infaillible; *(device)* indétraquable

foot [fʊt] *(pl feet* [fiːt]*)* **1** *n* (**a**) *(of person, horse, chair)* pied *m*; *(of other animal)* patte *f*; **to put one's feet up** *(have a rest)* se reposer; **to set f. on** poser le pied sur; **I shall never set f. in his house again** je ne remettrai jamais les pieds chez lui; **to be on one's feet all day** être debout du matin au soir; **to be on one's feet again** *(after illness)* être de nouveau sur pied; **on f.** à pied; **under f.** sous les pieds; *Mil* **f. patrol** patrouille *f* à pied; **f. pump** pompe *f* à pied; **f. soldier** fantassin *m*, soldat *m* d'infanterie
   (**b**) *(of mountain, stairs)* pied *m*; *(of page)* bas *m*; *(of bed, table)* bout *m*
   (**c**) *(in poetry)* pied *m*
   (**d**) *(unit of measurement)* = 0,3048 m, pied *m* (anglais); **three f.** *or* **feet six (inches)** trois pieds six pouces
   (**e**) *(idioms)* **to have one's feet firmly on the ground** avoir les pieds sur terre; **to have one f. in the grave** avoir un pied dans la tombe; **to have a f. in both camps** avoir un pied dans chaque camp; **she hasn't put a f. wrong** elle n'a pas commis la moindre erreur; **to put one's f. down** *(be firm)* faire preuve de fermeté; *(refuse)* mettre le holà; *Fam* **to put one's f. in it** mettre les pieds dans le plat, faire une gaffe; **to find one's feet** s'adapter; **to get a f. in the door** avoir un pied dans la place; *Fam* **my f.!** mon œil!
   2 *vt* **to f. the bill** payer la note

footage ['fʊtɪdʒ] *n Cin* séquences *fpl*, images *fpl*

foot-and-mouth disease [fʊtən'maʊθdɪ'ziːz] *n* fièvre *f* aphteuse

football ['fʊtbɔːl] *n (soccer)* football *m*; *(American)* football américain; *(ball)* ballon *m* (de football); **f. club** club *m* de foot(ball); **f. fan** supporter *m* d'une équipe de football; **f. ground** terrain *m* de football; **f. hooligan** hooligan *m*; **f. pitch** terrain *m* de football; **f. player** footballeur(euse) *m,f*; *Br* **f. pools** ≃ loto *m* sportif; **f. supporter** supporter *m* d'une équipe de football

footballer ['fʊtbɔːlə(r)] *n* footballeur(euse) *m,f*

footbridge ['fʊtbrɪdʒ] *n* passerelle *f*

foothills ['fʊthɪlz] *npl* contreforts *mpl*

foothold ['fʊthəʊld] *n* prise *f* (pour le pied); *Fig* **to gain a f.** *(of theory, feeling)* se propager

footing ['fʊtɪŋ] *n* (**a**) *(balance)* **to lose one's f.** perdre l'équilibre (**b**) *(level)* **on an equal f.** sur un pied d'égalité; **to be on a friendly f. with sb** avoir des rapports amicaux avec qn

footlights ['fʊtlaɪts] *npl Theat* rampe *f*

footloose ['fʊtluːs] *adj* libre; **to be f. and fancy-free** être libre comme l'air

footman ['fʊtmən] *n* valet *m* de pied

footnote ['fʊtnəʊt] *n* note *f* de bas de page; *Fig* détail *m*

footpath ['fʊtpɑːθ] *n* sentier *m*

footprint ['fʊtprɪnt] *n* trace *f* de pas; *(of bare foot)* empreinte *f* de pied

footrest ['fʊtrest] *n* repose-pieds *m inv*

footsie ['fʊtsɪ] *n Fam* **to play f. with sb** faire du pied à qn

footsore ['fʊtsɔː(r)] *adj* **to be f.** avoir mal aux pieds

footstep ['fʊtstep] *n* pas *m*; *Fig* **to follow in sb's footsteps** suivre les traces de qn

footwear ['fʊtweə(r)] *n* chaussures *fpl*

footwork ['fʊtwɜːk] *n* jeu *m* de jambes; *Fig* **it required some rather fancy f.** il a fallu faire des pieds et des mains

fop [fɒp] *n* dandy *m*

foppish ['fɒpɪʃ] *adj* de dandy

for [fɔː(r), *unstressed* fə(r)] **1** *prep* (**a**) *(expressing purpose, destination)* pour; **to leave f. France** partir pour la France; **there's no time f. that** il n'y a pas de temps pour ça; **what's it f.?** c'est pour quoi faire?; **can you give me something f. the pain?** pouvez-vous me donner quelque chose contre la douleur?
(**b**) *(because of)* pour, en raison de; **she couldn't sleep f. the pain** elle ne pouvait pas dormir à cause de la douleur
(**c**) *(expressing cost, amount)* **I bought it f. £10** je l'ai acheté 10 livres; **a cheque f. £50** un chèque de 50 livres
(**d**) *(considering)* pour; **he is big f. his age** il est grand pour son âge; **f. all the good it will do** pour ce que ça changera; **f. all his wealth, he was still unhappy** en dépit de toutes ses richesses, il était toujours malheureux
(**e**) *(representing)* **A f. Anne** A comme Anne; **what's the French f. "book"?** comment dit-on "book" en français?
(**f**) *(duration)* **I was there f. a month** je suis resté là-bas (pendant) un mois; **I've been here f. a month** il y a un mois que je suis ici, je suis ici depuis un mois; **I will be here f. a month** je serai ici pendant un mois; **I haven't been there f. a month** je n'y suis pas allé depuis un mois; **I'm going away f. a fortnight** je pars pour quinze jours; **we have enough food f. two days** nous avons suffisamment à manger pour deux jours
(**g**) *(with point in time)* **f. the first/last time** pour la première/dernière fois; **I need it f. Friday** j'en ai besoin pour vendredi
(**h**) *(as compared to)* pour; **they sell ten red bikes f. every black one** ils vendent dix vélos rouges pour un noir
(**i**) *(in favour of)* **to be f. sth** être pour qch, être favorable à qch; *Fam* **I'm all f. it!** je suis tout à fait pour!
(**j**) *(introducing an infinitive clause)* **it is too early f. me to decide** il est trop tôt pour que je prenne une décision; **it will be difficult f. her to come** il lui sera difficile de venir; **it took an hour f. us to get there** il nous a fallu une heure pour arriver là-bas
(**k**) *(idioms)* **f. all I know** pour ce que j'en sais; **that's men f. you!** c'est bien les hommes!; *Fam* **he's f. it!** qu'est-ce qu'il va prendre!
2 *conj Lit (because)* car

forage ['fɒrɪdʒ] **1** *n (animal food)* fourrage *m*; *Mil* **f. cap** calot *m*
2 *vi* **to f. for sth** fouiller pour trouver qch

foray ['fɒreɪ] *n* incursion *f* (**into** dans)

forbear [fɔː'beə(r)] *(pt* **forbore** [fɔː'bɔː(r)], *pp* **forborne** [fɔː'bɔːn]) *vi Formal* **to f. to do sth** s'abstenir de faire qch

forbearance [fɔː'beərəns] *n Formal* patience *f*

forbid [fə'bɪd] *(pt* **forbade** [fə'bæd, fə'beɪd], *pp* **forbidden** [fə'bɪdən]) *vt* interdire; **to f. sb to do sth** interdire à qn de faire qch; **smoking is forbidden** il est interdit de fumer; **God f.!** Dieu m'en/nous en préserve!

forbidding [fə'bɪdɪŋ] *adj (appearance, look, landscape)* sinistre; *(task)* rébarbatif(ive)

force [fɔːs] **1** *n* (**a**) *(strength, power, influence)* force *f*; **by sheer** *or* **brute f.** par la force; **by f. of circumstance(s)** par la force des circonstances; **f. of habit** la force de l'habitude; **several forces conspired to bring about his downfall** plusieurs facteurs ont contribué à provoquer sa chute (**b**) *Mil* **the (armed) forces** les forces *fpl* armées; **to join forces (to do sth)** joindre ses efforts (pour faire qch); **they turned out in (full) f.** ils sont venus en masse (**c**) *(effect)* **to come into f.** entrer en vigueur
2 *vt* (**a**) *(compel)* **to f. sb to do sth** *or* **into doing sth** forcer *ou* obliger qn à faire qch; **to f. sth on sb** imposer qch à qn; **they forced the enemy back** ils ont repoussé l'ennemi (**b**) *(obtain by effort)* **to f. the issue** précipiter les choses; **to f. sb's hand** forcer la main à qn; **to f. one's way through a crowd** se frayer un passage à travers la foule; **to f. oneself on sb** *(sexually)* essayer d'abuser de qn physiquement

▶**force down** *vt sep* (**a**) *(aircraft)* obliger à atterrir (**b**) *(food)* se forcer à avaler

▶**force open** *vt sep (door, window, lock)* forcer

forced [fɔːst] *adj (manner, laugh)* forcé(e), artificiel(elle); **f. labour** travail *m* forcé; *Aviat* **f. landing** atterrissage *m* forcé; *Mil* **f. march** marche *f* forcée

force-feed ['fɔːsfiːd] *(pt & pp* **force-fed** ['fɔːsfed]) *vt (person)* nourrir de force; *(livestock)* gaver

forceful ['fɔːsfʊl] *adj (person, language)* énergique; *(argument)* puissant(e)

forceps ['fɔːseps] *npl* forceps *mpl*; **f. delivery** accouchement *m* aux forceps

forcible ['fɔːsɪbəl] *adj* (**a**) *Law* **f. entry** entrée *f* par effraction (**b**) *(argument)* puissant(e); *(reminder)* brutal(e)

forcibly ['fɔːsɪblɪ] *adv* (**a**) *(by force)* de force (**b**) *(argue)* vigoureusement

ford [fɔːd] **1** *n* gué *m*
2 *vt* traverser à gué

fore [fɔː(r)] **1** *n* **to come to the f.** *(of person)* commencer à être connu(e); *(of issue)* être mis(e) en évidence
2 *adj Naut* à l'avant

forearm ['fɔːrɑːm] *n* avant-bras *m inv*

forebear ['fɔːbeə(r)] *n* ancêtre *mf*

foreboding [fɔː'bəʊdɪŋ] *n* (mauvais) pressentiment *m*

forecast ['fɔːkɑːst] **1** *n* prévisions *fpl*; *(in horseracing)* pronostics *mpl* (des courses); **(weather) f.** prévisions météorologiques, météo *f*
2 *vt (pt & pp* **forecast(ed)**) prévoir; *(in horseracing)* pronostiquer

foreclose [fɔː'kləʊz] *vt Fin* **to f. a mortgage** saisir un immeuble hypothéqué

forecourt ['fɔːkɔːt] *n (of petrol station)* devant *m*

forefathers ['fɔːfɑːðəz] npl aïeux mpl
forefinger ['fɔːfɪŋgə(r)] n index m
forefront ['fɔːfrʌnt] n to be in the f. of être au premier plan de
forego [fɔːˈgəʊ] (pt forewent [fɔːˈwent], pp foregone [fɔːˈgɒn]) vt renoncer à
foregone ['fɔːgɒn] to be a f. conclusion être couru(e) d'avance
foreground ['fɔːgraʊnd] 1 n premier plan m; in the f. au premier plan
  2 vt mettre au premier plan
forehand ['fɔːhænd] n (in tennis) coup m droit; f. volley volée f de face
forehead ['fɒrɪd, 'fɔːhed] n front m
foreign ['fɒrɪn] adj étranger(ère); f. affairs les affaires fpl étrangères; f. aid aide f aux pays étrangers; (from point of view of recipient) aide de l'étranger; Med f. body corps m étranger; Journ f. correspondent correspondant(e) m,f à l'étranger; f. currency devises fpl étrangères; f. legion légion f étrangère; Pol F. Minister, Br F. Secretary ministre m des Affaires étrangères; Br Pol F. Office ministère m des Affaires étrangères; f. trade commerce m extérieur
foreigner ['fɒrɪnə(r)] n étranger(ère) m,f
foreleg ['fɔːleg] n patte f de devant; (of horse) membre m antérieur
foreman ['fɔːmən] n (of workers) contremaître m; (of jury) président m
foremost ['fɔːməʊst] adj le (la) plus important(e)
forename ['fɔːneɪm] n prénom m
forensic [fəˈrensɪk] adj Law légal(e); f. evidence résultats mpl des expertises médico-légales; f. medicine médecine f légale; f. scientist médecin m légiste
foreplay ['fɔːpleɪ] n préliminaires mpl amoureux
forerunner ['fɔːrʌnə(r)] n (a) (person) précurseur m (of de) (b) (sign) signe m précurseur (of de)
foresee [fɔːˈsiː] (pt foresaw [fɔːˈsɔː], pp foreseen [fɔːˈsiːn]) vt prévoir
foreseeable [fɔːˈsiːəbəl] adj prévisible; in the f. future dans un avenir proche; for the f. future dans l'immédiat
foreshadow [fɔːˈʃædəʊ] vt annoncer
foresight ['fɔːsaɪt] n prévoyance f
foreskin ['fɔːskɪn] n Anat prépuce m
forest ['fɒrɪst] n forêt f; f. fire incendie m de forêt; Am f. ranger garde m forestier
forestall [fɔːˈstɔːl] vt devancer
forester ['fɒrɪstə(r)] n (garde m) forestier m
forestry ['fɒrɪstrɪ] n sylviculture f; the F. Commission ≃ Les Eaux et Forêts fpl; f. worker (forester) forestier m; (lumberjack) bûcheron m
foretaste ['fɔːteɪst] n avant-goût m (of de)
foretell [fɔːˈtel] (pt & pp foretold [fɔːˈtəʊld]) vt prédire
forethought ['fɔːθɔːt] n prévoyance f
forever [fəˈrevə(r)] adv (a) (eternally) pour toujours; nothing lasts f. tout a une fin; the journey seemed to last f. il semblait que le voyage ne finirait jamais (b) (repeatedly) sans cesse; he was f. changing his mind il changeait sans cesse ou constamment d'avis (c) Fam (a long time) une éternité; to take f. (to do sth) mettre un temps infini (à faire qch)
forewarn [fɔːˈwɔːn] vt prévenir, avertir; Prov forewarned is forearmed un homme averti en vaut deux
forewent [fɔːˈwent] pt of forego
foreword ['fɔːwɜːd] n avant-propos m inv, préface f

forfeit ['fɔːfɪt] 1 n (in game) gage m; Law amende f
  2 vt (rights) être déchu(e) de; (property) se faire confisquer; (someone's respect) perdre
forgave [fəˈgeɪv] pt of forgive
forge [fɔːdʒ] 1 n forge f
  2 vt (a) (metal, alliance) forger (b) (cheque, signature, banknote) contrefaire; to f. a document/passport faire un faux document/passeport
▸**forge ahead** vi (a) (make progress) faire des progrès; (of company) aller de l'avant (b) (outstrip competitors) prendre de l'avance (on sur)
forged [fɔːdʒd] adj faux (fausse)
forgery ['fɔːdʒərɪ] (pl forgeries) n (a) (activity) contrefaçon f; (of document, banknote) falsification f (b) (thing forged) faux m
forget [fəˈget] (pt forgot [fəˈgɒt], pp forgotten [fəˈgɒtən]) 1 vt oublier; to f. to do sth oublier de faire qch; to f. how to do sth oublier comment on fait qch, ne plus savoir faire qch; to be forgotten tomber dans l'oubli; f. it! (in reply to apology, thanks) il n'y a pas de quoi!; (stop talking about it) laisse tomber!
  2 vi oublier; to f. about sb/sth oublier qn/qch; you can f. about going to London! tu peux faire une croix sur ton voyage à Londres! let's f. about it n'y pensons plus
forgetful [fəˈgetfʊl] adj to be f. avoir mauvaise mémoire
forget-me-not [fəˈgetmiːnɒt] n myosotis m
forgivable [fəˈgɪvəbəl] adj excusable, pardonnable
forgive [fəˈgɪv] (pt forgave [fəˈgeɪv], pp forgiven [fəˈgɪvən]) 1 vt pardonner; to f. sb for sth pardonner qch à qn; if you'll f. the pun pardonnez-moi ce jeu de mots; f. me for interrupting pardonnez-moi de vous interrompre
  2 vi pardonner; to f. and forget oublier sa rancune
forgiveness [fəˈgɪvnɪs] n pardon m
forgiving [fəˈgɪvɪŋ] adj indulgent(e)
forgo = forego
forgot [fəˈgɒt] pt of forget
forgotten [fəˈgɒtən] pp of forget
fork [fɔːk] 1 n (a) (for food) fourchette f (b) (for gardening) fourche f (c) (in road, path) bifurcation f
  2 vi (of road, path) bifurquer
▸**fork out** Fam 1 vt sep allonger
  2 vi casquer (for pour)
forked [fɔːkt] adj (stick, tongue) fourchu(e); f. lightning éclairs mpl
fork-lift truck ['fɔːklɪftˈtrʌk] n chariot m (élévateur) à fourche
forlorn [fəˈlɔːn] adj (person, look) triste, malheureux(euse); (hope, attempt) désespéré(e)
form [fɔːm] 1 n (a) (shape) (of object, animal) forme f; (of person) silhouette f; to take the f. of sth prendre la forme de qch (b) (type) forme f; in the f. of sous forme de; f. of address titre m de politesse (c) (politeness) as a matter of f., for f.'s sake pour la forme, par pure formalité; it's good/bad f. to... cela se fait/ne se fait pas de... (d) (for applications, orders) formulaire m (e) (condition, performance) forme f; (in horse-racing) performances fpl; to be in or on good f. être en forme; on present f. si l'on en juge par la situation actuelle (f) Br Sch (class, year) classe f
  2 vt (government, character) former; (idea) avoir; (opinion) se faire, se former; (relationship, friendship) nouer; (organization, obstacle) constituer; to f. a plan to do sth projeter de faire qch; to f. part of

sth faire partie de qch
 3 *vi* se former

formal ['fɔːməl] *adj (manner)* cérémonieux(euse); *(offer, occasion, invitation)* officiel(elle); *(language)* soutenu(e); **f. dress** tenue *f* de soirée

formality [fɔː'mælɪtɪ] *(pl* **formalities)** *n (procedure)* formalité *f*

formalize ['fɔːməlaɪz] *vt* officialiser

formally ['fɔːməlɪ] *adv (behave)* de façon cérémonieuse; *(invite, announce)* officiellement; **to dress f.** *(for evening reception)* porter une tenue de soirée

format ['fɔːmæt] **1** *n* format *m*
 2 *vt (pt & pp* **formatted)** *Comput* formater

formation [fɔː'meɪʃən] *n (act, arrangement)* formation *f*; *(of idea, plan)* élaboration *f*; **f. flying** vol *m* de groupe

formative ['fɔːmətɪv] *adj* formateur(trice); **the f. years** les années *fpl* de formation

former ['fɔːmə(r)] **1** *pron* **the f.** le premier (la première), celui-là (celle-là); *(plural)* les premiers (les premières), ceux-là (celles-là)
 2 *adj (pupil, colleague, job)* ancien(enne) *(before noun)*; **in f. times** autrefois; **in a f. life** dans une vie antérieure

formerly ['fɔːməlɪ] *adv* autrefois; **Mrs Connelly, f. Miss Paton** Mme Connelly, née Paton; **Zambia, f. Northern Rhodesia** la Zambie, ancienne Rhodésie du Nord

formidable ['fɔːmɪdəbəl] *adj (opponent, difficulty)* redoutable; *(performance, talent)* formidable

formula ['fɔːmjʊlə] *(pl* **formulas** *or* **formulae** ['fɔːmjʊliː]*) *n* **(a)** *(scheme, in maths, chemistry)* formule *f*; **the f. for success** la clé de la réussite; **a peace f.** une solution en faveur de la paix; *Aut* **F. 1** formule 1 **(b)** *Am (baby food)* lait *m* en poudre

formulate ['fɔːmjʊleɪt] *vt (plan, proposal)* élaborer; *(thought, opinion)* formuler

fornication [fɔːnɪ'keɪʃən] *n Formal* fornication *f*

forsake [fə'seɪk] *(pt* **forsook** [fə'sʊk], *pp* **forsaken** [fə'seɪkən]) *vt Lit* **(a)** *(abandon)* abandonner **(b)** *(renounce)* renoncer à

forswear [fɔː'sweə(r)] *(pt* **forswore** [fɔː'swɔː(r)], *pp* **forsworn** [fɔː'swɔːn]) *vt Lit* renoncer à

fort [fɔːt] *n* fort *m*, forteresse *f*; *Fig* **to hold the f.** monter la garde

forte ['fɔːtɪ] *n* fort *m*

forth [fɔːθ] *adv* en avant; **to go f.** avancer; **to walk back and f.** marcher de long en large, faire les cent pas; **from that day f.** à dater de ce jour; **and so f.** et cetera, et ainsi de suite

forthcoming [fɔːθ'kʌmɪŋ] *adj* **(a)** *(election)* prochain(e); *(book, film)* qui sortira bientôt **(b)** *(available)* **no money was f.** l'argent n'est pas arrivé **(c)** *(informative)* expansif(ive) **(about** sur)

forthright ['fɔːθraɪt] *adj* franc (franche)

forthwith [fɔːθ'wɪθ] *adv Formal* immédiatement, sur-le-champ

fortieth ['fɔːtɪəθ] **1** *n* **(a)** *(fraction)* quarantième *m* **(b)** *(in series)* quarantième *mf*
 2 *adj* quarantième

fortification [fɔːtɪfɪ'keɪʃən] *n* fortification *f*

fortified ['fɔːtɪfaɪd] *adj* **(a)** *(town)* fortifié(e) **(b)** **f. wine** vin *m* doux (naturel), vin de liqueur

fortify ['fɔːtɪfaɪ] *(pt & pp* **fortified)** *vt Mil* fortifier; **to f. oneself** se prémunir

fortitude ['fɔːtɪtjuːd] *n* force *f* morale

fortnight ['fɔːtnaɪt] *n Br* quinzaine *f*, quinze jours *mpl*; **a f. today** aujourd'hui en quinze; **a f.'s holiday** quinze jours *ou* deux semaines *fpl* de vacances

fortnightly ['fɔːtnaɪtlɪ] *Br* **1** *adj* bimensuel(elle)
 2 *adv* tous les quinze jours, bimensuellement

fortress ['fɔːtrɪs] *n* forteresse *f*

fortuitous [fɔː'tjuːɪtəs] *adj Formal* fortuit(e)

fortunate ['fɔːtʃənət] *adj* heureux(euse); **to be f.** avoir de la chance; **to be f. enough to do sth** avoir la chance de faire qch

fortunately ['fɔːtʃənətlɪ] *adv* heureusement, par bonheur

fortune ['fɔːtʃən] *n* **(a)** *(riches)* fortune *f*; **to make a** *or* **one's f.** faire fortune; *Fam* **to cost a (small) f.** coûter une fortune *ou* les yeux de la tête **(b)** *(luck)* chance *f*; **good f.** chance; **bad f.** malchance *f*; **to tell sb's f.** dire la bonne aventure à qn

fortune-teller ['fɔːtʃəntelə(r)] *n* diseur(euse) *m,f* de bonne aventure

forty ['fɔːtɪ] **1** *n* quarante *m inv*
 2 *adj* quarante; *Fam* **to have f. winks** piquer *ou* faire un petit somme; *see also* **eighty**

forum ['fɔːrəm] *n* forum *m*; *Comput (on Internet)* groupe *m* de discussion; **a f. for debate** un lieu de débat

forward ['fɔːwəd] **1** *n (in sport)* avant *m*
 2 *adj* **(a)** *(position)* avant *inv*; *(movement)* en avant, vers l'avant; **f. planning** planification *f*; *Fin* **f. market** marché *m* à terme **(b)** *(impudent, bold)* effronté(e), hardi(e)
 3 *adv* **(a)** *(of time)* **from this/that day f.** à partir d'aujourd'hui/de ce jour-là; **to put the clocks f.** avancer les pendules **(b)** *(of direction)* en avant; **to walk f.** avancer **(c)** *(of position)* à l'avant; **we're sitting too far f.** *(in cinema, theatre)* nous sommes assis trop près; **the seat is too far f.** le siège est trop avancé
 4 *vt* **(a)** *(letter)* faire suivre; *(complaint, query)* faire passer **(to** à) **(b)** *(one's career, interests)* favoriser

forwarding agent ['fɔːwədɪŋ'eɪdʒənt] *n Com (agent m)* transitaire *m*

forward-looking ['fɔːwədlʊkɪŋ] *adj* progressiste

forwards ['fɔːwədz] *adv* = **forward**

fossil ['fɒsəl] *n* fossile *m*; *Fam* **an old f.** *(man)* un vieux croûton; *(woman)* une vieille bique; **f. fuel** combustible *m* fossile

fossilized ['fɒsɪlaɪzd] *adj* fossilisé(e); *Fig* sclérosé(e)

foster ['fɒstə(r)] **1** *adj* **f. child** = enfant placé dans une famille d'accueil; **f. parents** famille *f* d'accueil, parents *mpl* nourriciers
 2 *vt* **(a)** *(child)* prendre en famille d'accueil **(b)** *(idea, hope)* nourrir, entretenir; *(friendship)* stimuler

fought [fɔːt] *pt & pp of* **fight**

foul [faʊl] **1** *n (in sport)* faute *f*
 2 *adj* **(a)** *(disgusting) (smell, taste)* infect(e), nauséabond(e); *(weather)* sale; *(air)* vicié(e); *(language)* ordurier(ère); **to be in a f. mood** être d'une humeur massacrante **(b)** *(illegal)* **f. play** *Sport* jeu *m* irrégulier; *Law* acte *m* criminel; **f. play is not suspected** on ne croit pas à un meurtre
 3 *adv* **(a)** **to smell f.** puer; **to taste f.** avoir un goût infect **(b)** **to fall f. of the law** avoir des démêlés avec la justice
 4 *vt* **(a)** *(pollute)* salir **(b)** *(entangle)* s'enchevêtrer autour de **(c)** *(in sport)* commettre une faute contre
▸**foul up** *vt sep Fam (ruin)* gâcher

foul-mouthed [ˈfaʊlˈmaʊðd] *adj* grossier(ère), mal embouché(e)

found¹ [faʊnd] *vt* (**a**) *(city, organization)* fonder; *(company)* créer; *(empire)* établir (**b**) *(base)* baser, fonder (on sur)

found² *pt & pp of* **find**

foundation [faʊnˈdeɪʃən] *n* (**a**) *(of city, organization)* fondation *f*; *(of company)* création *f* (**b**) *(basis)* fondement *m*, base *f*; **to be without f.** être dénué(e) de fondement (**c**) **foundations** *(of building, society)* fondations *fpl* (**d**) *(make-up)* **f. (cream)** fond *m* de teint

founder¹ [ˈfaʊndə(r)] *n* *(of hospital, school)* fondateur(trice) *m,f*; **f. member** membre *m* fondateur

founder² *vi* *(of ship)* s'échouer; *Fig* *(of project, talks)* avorter

founding father [ˈfaʊndɪŋˈfɑːðə(r)] *n* père *m* fondateur

foundling [ˈfaʊndlɪŋ] *n* *Old-fashioned* enfant *mf* trouvé(e)

foundry [ˈfaʊndrɪ] *(pl* **foundries***)* *n* fonderie *f*

fount [faʊnt] *n* *Lit & Fig* source *f*

fountain [ˈfaʊntɪn] *n* fontaine *f*; **f. pen** stylo *m* (à) plume

four [fɔː(r)] **1** *n* quatre *m inv*; **on all fours** à quatre pattes
   2 *adj* quatre; **to the f. corners of the earth** aux quatre coins du monde; *see also* **eight**

four-eyes [ˈfɔːraɪz] *n* *Fam* binoclard(e) *m,f*

four-figure [ˈfɔːˈfɪgə(r)] *adj* **a f. sum** un montant de quatre chiffres

fourfold [ˈfɔːfəʊld] **1** *adj* **a f. increase** une augmentation au quadruple
   2 *adv* **to increase f.** quadrupler

four-legged [ˈfɔːˈlegɪd] *adj* quadrupède; *Hum* **f. friend** ami *m* à quatre pattes

four-letter word [ˈfɔːletəˈwɜːd] *n* gros mot *m*

four-poster [ˈfɔːˈpəʊstə(r)] *n* **f. (bed)** lit *m* à baldaquin

foursome [ˈfɔːsəm] *n* groupe *m* de quatre personnes

fourteen [ˈfɔːtiːn] **1** *n* quatorze *m inv*
   2 *adj* quatorze; *see also* **eight**

fourteenth [fɔːˈtiːnθ] **1** *n* (**a**) *(fraction)* quatorzième *m* (**b**) *(in series)* quatorzième *mf* (**c**) *(of month)* quatorze *m inv*
   2 *adj* quatorzième; *see also* **eighth**

fourth [fɔːθ] **1** *n* (**a**) *(fraction)* quatrième *m* (**b**) *(in series)* quatrième *mf* (**c**) *(of month)* quatre *m inv*
   2 *adj* quatrième; *see also* **eighth**

fourthly [ˈfɔːθlɪ] *adv* quatrièmement

fowl [faʊl] *(pl* **fowl***)* *n* volaille *f*

fox [fɒks] **1** *n* renard *m*; *Fig* **a sly old f.** *(cunning person)* un vieux renard; **f. cub** renardeau *m*; **f. hunt** chasse *f* au renard
   2 *vt* *(perplex)* laisser perplexe; *(deceive)* duper

foxglove [ˈfɒksglʌv] *n* digitale *f* (pourprée)

fox-hunting [ˈfɒkshʌntɪŋ] *n* chasse *f* au renard

foxtrot [ˈfɒkstrɒt] *n* fox-trot *m inv*

foxy [ˈfɒksɪ] *adj* *Fam* (**a**) *(sly)* rusé(e) (**b**) *Am* *(sexy)* sexy *inv*

foyer [ˈfɔɪeɪ] *n* *(in theatre)* foyer *m*; *(in cinema, hotel)* hall *m*

fraction [ˈfrækʃən] *n* *(in maths)* fraction *f*; *Fig* *(small part)* petite partie *f*; **a f. too small/large** un tout petit peu trop petit(e)/grand(e)

fractional [ˈfrækʃənəl] *adj* *(very small)* infime

fractious [ˈfrækʃəs] *adj* *(adult)* de mauvaise humeur; *(baby)* pleurnicheur(euse); *(tone, expression)* irrité(e)

fracture [ˈfræktʃə(r)] **1** *n* fracture *f*
   2 *vt* *(bone)* fracturer; *(pipe)* fendre
   3 *vi* *(of bone)* se fracturer; *(of pipe)* se fendre

fragile [ˈfrædʒaɪl] *adj* fragile; *Fam* **I'm feeling a bit f. this morning** *(after drinking)* j'ai un peu la gueule de bois ce matin

fragility [frəˈdʒɪlɪtɪ] *n* fragilité *f*

fragment 1 *n* [ˈfrægmənt] fragment *m*; **I only heard a f. of what was said** je n'ai entendu que des bribes de la conversation
   2 *vi* [frægˈment] *(of object)* se fragmenter; *(of organization)* éclater

fragrance [ˈfreɪgrəns] *n* parfum *m*

fragrant [ˈfreɪgrənt] *adj* odorant(e), parfumé(e)

frail [freɪl] *adj* *(person)* frêle; *(object)* fragile

frailty [ˈfreɪltɪ] *n* faiblesse *f*

frame [freɪm] **1** *n* (**a**) *(of picture)* cadre *m*, encadrement *m*; *(of door, window)* encadrement (**b**) *(of person, animal)* ossature *f*; *(of building, bridge)* charpente *f*; *(of bicycle)* cadre *m*; *(of spectacles)* monture *f* (**c**) **f. of mind** état *m* d'esprit; **f. of reference** système *m* de référence
   2 *vt* (**a**) *(surround)* encadrer (**b**) *(compose) (answer)* formuler; *(law)* rédiger (**c**) *Fam (falsely incriminate)* monter un coup contre

framework [ˈfreɪmwɜːk] *n* *(structure)* cadre *m*, structure *f*; *(of building, construction)* charpente *f*; *Fig* **within the f. of** dans le cadre de

franc [fræŋk] *n* *(currency)* franc *m*; **Belgian/French/ Swiss f.** franc belge/français/suisse

France [frɑːns] *n* la France

franchise [ˈfræntʃaɪz] **1** *n* (**a**) *Com* franchise *f* (**b**) *Pol* droit *m* de vote
   2 *vt* *Com* franchiser

francophile [ˈfræŋkəʊfaɪl] *n & adj* francophile *mf*

francophone [ˈfræŋkəʊfəʊn] *n & adj* francophone *mf*

frank [fræŋk] **1** *adj* franc (franche); **to be f....** pour être franc...
   2 *vt* *(letter)* affranchir

Frankfurt [ˈfræŋkfɜːt] *n* Francfort

frankfurter [ˈfræŋkfɜːtə(r)] *n* saucisse *f* de Francfort

frankincense [ˈfræŋkɪnsens] *n* encens *m*

frankly [ˈfræŋklɪ] *adv* franchement

frantic [ˈfræntɪk] *adj* *(rush, pace)* frénétique; *(attempt, effort)* désespéré(e); **f. with worry** fou (folle) d'inquiétude

frantically [ˈfræntɪklɪ] *adv* frénétiquement; *(work, write)* avec frénésie; *(try)* désespérément

fraternal [frəˈtɜːnəl] *adj* fraternel(elle)

fraternity [frəˈtɜːnɪtɪ] *(pl* **fraternities***)* *n* (**a**) *(brotherliness)* fraternité *f* (**b**) *(group)* confrérie *f*; **the banking/ medical f.** la confrérie des banquiers/médecins (**c**) *Am Univ* = organisation d'étudiants; **f. house** = maison communautaire (d'étudiants d'une même organisation)

fraternize [ˈfrætənaɪz] *vi* fraterniser (**with** avec)

fraud [frɔːd] *n* (**a**) *(person)* imposteur *m* (**b**) *(deception)* supercherie *f*; *(crime)* fraude *f*; **the F. Squad** ≃ (le service de) la Répression des Fraudes

fraudulent [ˈfrɔːdjʊlənt] *adj* *(charge, accusation, feelings)* faux (fausse); *(claim, transaction)* frauduleux(-euse)

fraught [frɔːt] *adj (person, situation)* tendu(e); *(day)* éprouvant(e); **f. with danger** rempli(e) d'embûches; **f. with emotion** chargé(e) d'émotion

fray¹ [freɪ] *n (brawl)* bagarre *f*; **to enter the f.** entrer dans l'arène

fray² 1 *vt (material)* user
2 *vi (of material)* s'user; *(of tempers)* s'échauffer; *(of nerves)* craquer

frazzle ['fræzəl] *n* **to be burnt to a f.** *(of food)* être carbonisé(e); *Fam (of person)* être brûlé(e) par le soleil

frazzled ['fræzəld] *adj Fam (person)* lessivé(e), épuisé(e); *(nerves)* à plat

freak [friːk] 1 *n* (a) *(strange being)* monstre *m*, phénomène *m*; **f. show** exhibition *f* de monstres (b) *(strange event)* **by a f. of fortune** par un coup de chance; **f. accident** accident *m* imprévisible; **f. storm** orage *m* inattendu (c) *(enthusiast)* fana *mf*; **jazz/film f.** fana de jazz/cinéma
2 *vi* = **freak out** *vi*
▸**freak out** *Fam* 1 *vt sep (shock, scare)* faire flipper
2 *vi (panic)* paniquer; *(become angry)* piquer une crise

freckle ['frekəl] *n* tache *f* de rousseur

free [friː] 1 *adj* (a) *(unrestricted)* libre (**from** *or* **of** de); *(movement)* dégagé(e); **to be f. of sb** être débarrassé(e) de qn; **f. from worry** sans souci; **to be f. to do sth** être libre de faire qch; **to set sb f.** rendre sa liberté à qn; **f. and easy** décontracté(e); *Fam* **feel f. to borrow the car** n'hésitez pas à emprunter la voiture; **(as) f. as a bird** libre comme l'air; **to be a f. agent** être libre (de ses mouvements); *Fig* **to have a f. hand** avoir pleine liberté d'action; *Econ* **f. enterprise** libre entreprise *f*; **f. fall** *(of parachutist, economy)* chute *f* libre; **f. kick** *(in football)* coup *m* franc; *Econ* **f. market** économie *f* de marché; **f. speech** liberté *f* d'expression; **f. throw** *(in basketball)* lancer *m* franc; **f. trade** libre-échange *m*; **f. verse** vers *mpl* libres; **f. will** libre arbitre *m*; **to do sth of one's own f. will** faire qch de son plein gré
(b) *(unoccupied) (person, seat, table, time)* libre
(c) *(without charge)* gratuit(e); **f. gift** cadeau *m*
(d) *(generous)* **to be f. with one's advice** être prodigue en conseils
2 *adv (without charge)* gratuitement; **to do sth for f.** faire qch gratuitement
3 *vt (pt & pp* **freed** [friːd]*) (prisoner, time, place)* libérer (**from** de); *(something stuck)* dégager (**from** de); **to f. oneself from** *or* **of sth** se libérer de qch

freedom ['friːdəm] *n* liberté *f*; **to have the f. to do sth** être libre de faire qch; **f. of information** libre accès *m* à l'information; **f. of speech/worship** liberté d'expression/de culte; **to give sb the f. of the city** nommer qn citoyen(enne) d'honneur de la ville; **f. fighter** guérillero *m*, révolutionnaire *mf*

free-for-all ['friːfərɔːl] *n Fam* bagarre *f*

freehold ['friːhəʊld] *n Law* propriété *f* foncière perpétuelle et libre

freeholder ['friːhəʊldə(r)] *n* propriétaire *m* foncier (à perpétuité)

freelance ['friːlɑːns] 1 *n* travailleur(euse) *m,f* indépendant(e)
2 *adj* indépendant(e), free-lance *inv*
3 *adv* **to work f.** travailler en indépendant(e) *ou* en free-lance
4 *vi* travailler en indépendant(e) *ou* en free-lance

freeloader ['friːləʊdə(r)] *n Fam* pique-assiette *mf inv*, parasite *m*

freely ['friːlɪ] *adv (give)* sans compter; *(speak)* en toute liberté; *(spend)* libéralement; **f. available** *(for sale)* en vente libre; *(easy to get hold of)* qu'on peut se procurer facilement

freemason ['friːmeɪsən] *n* franc-maçon *m*

freemasonry ['friːmeɪsənrɪ] *n* franc-maçonnerie *f*

Freepost® ['friːpəʊst] *n Br* ≃ correspondance-réponse *f*

free-range ['friːreɪndʒ] *adj (chicken)* fermier(ère); **f. eggs** œufs *mpl* de poules élevées en plein air

freestyle ['friːstaɪl] *n (in swimming)* nage *f* libre

freethinker ['friːθɪŋkə(r)] *n* libre-penseur(euse) *m,f*

freeware ['friːweə(r)] *n Comput* logiciel *m* (du domaine) public, gratuiciel *m*

freeway ['friːweɪ] *n Am* autoroute *f*

freewheel ['friːwiːl] *vi (on bicycle)* être en roue libre; *(in car)* rouler au point mort

freeze [friːz] 1 *n (in weather)* gel *m*, gelée *f*; **price/wage f.** gel des prix/salaires
2 *vt (pt* **froze** [frəʊz]*, pp* **frozen** ['frəʊzən]*) (food)* congeler; *(prices, assets)* geler; **to be frozen to death** être mort(e) de froid
3 *vi* (a) *(of weather)* **it's freezing** *(below zero)* il gèle; *Fig (very cold)* on gèle (b) *(of liquid, food)* geler; **to f. to death** mourir de froid; *Fam* **I'm freezing** je suis gelé (c) *(stand still)* s'arrêter net, se figer; **f.!** ne bougez plus!
▸**freeze out** *vt sep Fam* **to f. sb out** *(of conversation, deal)* exclure qn; *Com* **to f. out the competition** évincer les concurrents
▸**freeze over** *vi (of pond, river)* geler
▸**freeze up** *vi (of pond, mechanism)* geler

freeze-dried ['friːz'draɪd] *adj (coffee, herbs)* lyophilisé(e)

freeze-frame ['friːz'freɪm] *n Cin* arrêt *m* sur image

freezer ['friːzə(r)] *n* congélateur *m*; *(ice-box)* freezer *m*

freezing ['friːzɪŋ] *adj* **f. (cold)** *(room, weather, temperature)* glacial(e); *(water)* glacé(e); **it's f. cold in here** on meurt de froid ici

freight [freɪt] *Com* 1 *n (transport)* fret *m*, transport *m* de marchandises; *(goods)* cargaison *f*; *(price)* prix *m* de transport; **f. train** train *m* de marchandises
2 *vt (goods)* transporter

freighter ['freɪtə(r)] *n (ship)* cargo *m*

French [frentʃ] 1 *n (language)* français *m*; *Hum* **pardon my F.** *(after swearing)* excusez mon langage; **F. class/teacher** classe *f*/professeur *m* de français
2 *npl* **the F.** *(people)* les Français *mpl*
3 *adj* français(e); **F. Canadian** *(person)* Canadien(enne) *m,f* français(e); **F. fries** frites *fpl*; **F. horn** cor *m* d'harmonie; **F. kiss** baiser *m* avec la langue; *Br Old-fashioned* **F. letter** capote *f* anglaise; **F. loaf** *or* **stick** baguette *f*; **F. Polynesia** la Polynésie Française; **F. window** porte-fenêtre *f*

French-Canadian ['frentʃkə'neɪdʒən] *n* canadien(enne) français(e)

Frenchman ['frentʃmən] *n* Français *m*

French-speaking ['frentʃ'spiːkɪŋ] *adj* francophone

Frenchwoman ['frentʃwʊmən] *n* Française *f*

frenetic [frə'netɪk] *adj* frénétique

frenzied ['frenzɪd] *adj (person)* affolé(e); *(attack)* déchaîné(e); *(activity)* frénétique; **f. with rage/worry** fou (folle) de rage/d'inquiétude

frenzy ['frenzɪ] *(pl* **frenzies)** *n* frénésie *f*, folie *f*; **to work oneself into a f.** se mettre dans tous ses états

frequency ['fri:kwənsɪ] *(pl* **frequencies)** *n* fréquence *f*; **f. band** bande *f* de fréquences

frequent 1 *adj* ['fri:kwənt] fréquent(e); **it's a f. occurrence** cela se produit souvent
2 *vt* [frɪ'kwent] fréquenter

frequently ['fri:kwəntlɪ] *adv* fréquemment, souvent

fresco ['freskəʊ] *(pl* **frescos** or **frescoes)** *n* fresque *f*

fresh [freʃ] **1** *adj* (**a**) *(food, news)* frais (fraîche); **to smell f.** sentir bon le frais; **to get some f. air** s'aérer; **f. water** *(not salty)* eau *f* douce; **it's still f. in my mind** c'est encore frais dans ma mémoire; **as f. as a daisy** frais et dispos *inv* (**b**) *(page, attempt, drink)* nouveau(elle) *(before noun)*; **to make a f. start** recommencer à zéro (**c**) *(original) (approach, writing)* nouveau(elle), original(e) (**d**) *Am Fam (cheeky)* insolent(e); **to get f. with sb** *(sexually)* faire des avances à qn
2 *adv* **f. from** *(school, university)* frais émoulu(e) de; **we're f. out of lemons** nous n'avons plus de citrons

freshen ['freʃən] *vi (of wind, weather)* rafraîchir
▶**freshen up** *vi (wash)* faire un brin de toilette

fresher ['freʃər] *n Br Univ* étudiant(e) *m,f* de première année; **freshers' week** = semaine d'orientation précédant la rentrée universitaire pour les nouveaux étudiants

freshly ['freʃlɪ] *adv* fraîchement; **f. baked** sortant du four; **f. made** qui vient d'être fait

freshman ['freʃmən] *n Am Univ* étudiant(e) *m,f* de première année

freshness ['freʃnɪs] *n* (**a**) *(of food)* fraîcheur *f* (**b**) *(originality)* nouveauté *f*, originalité *f*

freshwater ['freʃwɔ:tə(r)] *adj (fish)* d'eau douce

fret [fret] *(pt & pp* **fretted)** *vi (worry)* s'inquiéter, se tourmenter

fretful ['fretfʊl] *adj* inquiet(ète)

Freudian ['frɔɪdɪən] *adj* freudien(enne); **F. slip** lapsus *m*

FRG [efɑ:'dʒi:] *n (abbr* **Federal Republic of Germany)** RFA *f*

Fri *(abbr* **Friday)** vendredi

friar ['fraɪə(r)] *n* religieux *m*, moine *m*

fricassee [frɪkə'si:] *n* fricassée *f*

friction ['frɪkʃən] *n also Fig* friction *f*

Friday ['fraɪdɪ] *n* vendredi *m*; *see also* **Saturday**

fridge [frɪdʒ] *n* frigo *m*

fridge-freezer ['frɪdʒ'fri:zə(r)] *n* frigo *m* avec congélateur

fried [fraɪd] *adj* frit(e)

friend [frend] *n* ami(e) *m,f*; **to be friends with sb** être ami avec qn; **to make friends with sb** devenir ami avec qn; **that's what friends are for** c'est à ça que servent les amis; **we're just good friends** nous sommes bons amis, c'est tout; **he's no f. of mine** ce n'est pas un ami; **to have friends in high places** avoir des amis bien placés; **to be a f. of the arts** être un défenseur des beaux-arts; *Prov* **a f. in need is a f. indeed** c'est dans le besoin que l'on connaît ses amis

friendless ['frendlɪs] *adj (person)* sans amis; *(childhood)* solitaire

friendly ['frendlɪ] **1** *n Sport* match *m* amical
2 *adj* amical(e); **f. advice** conseils *mpl* d'ami; **a f. nation** un pays ami; **to be f. with sb** être ami(e) avec qn;

to be on f. terms with sb être en bons termes avec qn; *Mil* **f. fire** tirs *mpl* provenant de son propre camp

friendship ['frendʃɪp] *n* amitié *f*

fries [fraɪz] *npl* **(French) f.** frites *fpl*

frieze [fri:z] *n Art & Archit* frise *f*

frigate ['frɪgət] *n* frégate *f*

fright [fraɪt] *n* peur *f*, effroi *m*; **to take f.** prendre peur; **to get a f.** avoir peur; **to give sb a f.** faire peur à qn; *Fam* **to look a f.** être à faire peur

frighten ['fraɪtən] **1** *vt* effrayer, faire peur à; **to f. sb into doing sth** faire peur à qn jusqu'à ce qu'il fasse qch; *Fam* **to f. the life** or **the wits out of sb** rendre qn fou (folle) de peur
2 *vi* **I don't f. easily** je ne me laisse pas effrayer facilement

frightened ['fraɪtənd] *adj* apeuré(e); **to be f. (of)** avoir peur (de); **to be f. to do sth** avoir peur de faire qch

frightening ['fraɪtənɪŋ] *adj* effrayant(e)

frightful ['fraɪtfʊl] *adj* épouvantable, affreux(euse)

frightfully ['fraɪtfʊlɪ] *adv* terriblement

frigid ['frɪdʒɪd] *adj (sexually)* frigide; *(smile, atmosphere)* glacial(e)

frill [frɪl] *n* volant *m*; *Fig* **with no frills** *(ceremony)* sans chichis; *(holiday)* rudimentaire

frilly ['frɪlɪ] *adj* à volants

fringe [frɪndʒ] *n* (**a**) *(of hair, on clothes, lampshade)* frange *f* (**b**) *(edge) (of forest)* lisière *f*; *(of town)* abords *mpl*; **on the fringes of society** en marge de la société; **f. benefits** avantages *mpl* divers; *Br Theat* **F. festival** festival *m* off; *Pol* **f. group** groupuscule *m*; **f. theatre** théâtre *m* alternatif

frisk [frɪsk] **1** *vt (search)* fouiller
2 *vi* **to f. about** gambader

frisky ['frɪskɪ] *adj (person)* plein(e) d'entrain; *(horse)* nerveux(euse)

fritter ['frɪtə(r)] *n Culin* beignet *m*
▶**fritter away** *vt sep* gaspiller

frivolity [frɪ'vɒlɪtɪ] *(pl* **frivolities)** *n* frivolité *f*

frivolous ['frɪvələs] *adj* frivole; *(remark)* futile

frizzy ['frɪzɪ] *adj* crépu(e)

fro [frəʊ] *adv* **to go to and f.** aller et venir

frock [frɒk] *n (dress)* robe *f*; **f. coat** redingote *f*

frog [frɒg] *n* (**a**) *(animal)* grenouille *f*; *Fam* **to have a f. in one's throat** avoir un chat dans la gorge (**b**) *Br Fam (French person)* = terme xénophobe, souvent humoristique, désignant un Français

frogman ['frɒgmən] *n* homme-grenouille *m*

frogmarch ['frɒgmɑ:tʃ] *vt* emmener de force

frogspawn ['frɒgspɔ:n] *n* œufs *mpl* de grenouille

frolic ['frɒlɪk] *(pt & pp* **frolicked)** *vi* s'ébattre

from [frɒm, *unstressed* frəm] *prep* (**a**) *(expressing place of origin)* de; **where are you f.?, where do you come f.?** d'où êtes-vous?, d'où venez-vous?; **she's f. Portugal** elle vient du Portugal; **f. Edinburgh to Paris** d'Édimbourg à Paris; **the train f. Manchester** le train de Manchester; **10 km f. Paris** à 10 km de Paris (**b**) *(expressing time)* à partir de; **f. tomorrow** à partir de demain; **f. then (on)** depuis ce jour-là; **f. the beginning** dès le début; **f. six to seven o'clock** de six heures à sept heures; **f. morning to** or **till night** du matin au soir; **five years f. now** dans cinq ans; **blind f. birth** aveugle de naissance (**c**) *(expressing range, change)* **f.... to...** de... à...; **children f. seven to nine years** les enfants de sept à neuf ans; **wine f. £4 a bottle** du vin à partir de 4 livres la bouteille

(**d**) *(expressing source)* de; **to buy sth f. sb** acheter qch à qn; **to drink f. a cup** boire dans une tasse; **a quotation f. the Bible** une citation tirée de la Bible; **made f. rubber** en caoutchouc

(**e**) *(expressing removal)* de; **to take sth f. sb** prendre qch à qn; **he was banned f. the club** il a été exclu du club

(**f**) *(on the basis of)* **f. what I heard/saw...** d'après ce que j'ai entendu/vu...

frond [frɒnd] *n (of fern)* fronde *f; (of palm)* feuille *f*

front [frʌnt] **1** *n* (**a**) *(not back)* devant *m; (of car, plane, boat)* avant *m; (of building)* façade *f;* **on the f. of the book** sur la couverture du livre; **at the f. of the book** au début du livre; **I sat in (the) f.** *(of car)* j'étais assis devant; *Br* **the f.** *(at seaside)* le front de mer, la promenade

(**b**) *(outward appearance)* **his kindness is only a f.** sa gentillesse n'est qu'une façade; **the company is a f. for their arms dealing** l'entreprise sert de couverture à leur trafic d'armes; **f. man** *(of TV, radio programme)* présentateur *m; (of pop group, organization)* leader *m*

(**c**) *Mil, Pol & Met* front *m; Fig* **on all fronts** sur tous les fronts; *Met* **warm/cold f.** front chaud/froid

(**d**) **in f.** devant; *(in race, contest)* en tête; **in f. of** devant

(**e**) *Fam* **to pay up f.** payer d'avance; **to be up f. about sth** être franc (franche) au sujet de qch

2 *adj* de devant; *Br Pol* **f. bench** = le banc des ministres et celui du cabinet fantôme; **f. door** porte *f* d'entrée; *Mil* **f. line** front *m;* **f. cover** couverture *f;* **f. page** *(of newspaper)* première page *f;* **f. room** *(lounge)* salon *m;* **f. row** premier rang *m;* **to have a f.-row seat** *(in theatre)* être (assis(e)) au premier rang; *Fig* être aux premières loges; **f. seat** *(in car)* siège *m* avant; **f. teeth** dents *fpl* de devant; **f. view** vue *f* de face

3 *vt (organization, pop group)* être à la tête de; *(government)* diriger; *(TV programme)* présenter

4 *vi (of building)* **the house fronts onto the river** la maison donne sur le fleuve

frontage ['frʌntɪdʒ] *n (of building)* façade *f; (of shop)* devanture *f*

frontal ['frʌntəl] *adj Anat* frontal(e); *Mil (attack)* de front

frontier ['frʌntɪə(r)] *n* frontière *f;* **the frontiers** *(of knowledge, science)* les limites *fpl;* **f. guard** garde-frontière *m;* **f. town** ville *f* frontalière

frontispiece ['frʌntɪspiːs] *n* frontispice *m*

frontrunner ['frʌntrʌnə(r)] *n* favori(ite) *m,f*

frost [frɒst] *n* gel *m;* **there was a f.** il a gelé

▶**frost over, frost up** *vi (of window)* se couvrir de givre

frostbite ['frɒstbaɪt] *n* gelure *f*

frostbitten ['frɒstbɪtən] *adj* gelé(e)

frosted ['frɒstɪd] *adj (glass)* dépoli(e)

frosting ['frɒstɪŋ] *n Am (on cake)* glaçage *m*

frosty ['frɒstɪ] *adj (night, air)* glacé(e); *Fig (welcome, smile)* glacial(e)

froth [frɒθ] **1** *n (on beer, cappuccino)* mousse *f; (on waves)* écume *f*

2 *vi (of liquid)* mousser; **he was frothing at the mouth** il bavait; *(with anger)* il écumait de rage

frothy ['frɒθɪ] *adj (beer, cappuccino)* mousseux(euse)

frown [fraʊn] **1** *n* froncement *m* de sourcils

2 *vi* froncer les sourcils; **to f. at sb** regarder qn en fronçant les sourcils

▶**frown on, frown upon** *vt insep (disapprove of)* désapprouver

froze [frəʊz] *pt of* **freeze**

frozen ['frəʊzən] **1** *adj (food)* congelé(e), surgelé(e); *(lake, hands)* gelé(e)

2 *pp of* **freeze**

fructose ['frʌktəʊs] *n* fructose *m*

frugal ['fruːgəl] *adj* frugal(e)

fruit [fruːt] *n* fruit *m;* **some f.** *(several pieces)* des fruits; *(one piece)* un fruit; *Fig* **to bear f.** *(of plan, investment)* porter ses fruits; **fruits of the forest** fruits des bois; **f. bowl** coupe *f* à fruits; **f. juice** jus *m* de fruit; *Br* **f. machine** machine *f* à sous; **f. salad** salade *f* de fruits; **f. tree** arbre *m* fruitier

fruitcake ['fruːtkeɪk] *n* cake *m; Fam (mad person)* fou (folle) *m,f*

fruitful ['fruːtfʊl] *adj (discussion)* fructueux(euse)

fruition [fruː'ɪʃən] *n* **to come to f.** *(of plan, effort)* porter ses fruits

fruitless ['fruːtlɪs] *adj (attempt, search, trip)* infructueux(euse)

fruity ['fruːtɪ] *adj (taste)* fruité(e); *Fam (voice)* étoffé(e)

frump [frʌmp] *n Fam* **she's a f.** elle fait mémère

frumpish ['frʌmpɪʃ], **frumpy** ['frʌmpɪ] *adj Fam* **to be f.** faire mémère

frustrate [frʌs'treɪt] *vt (person)* décevoir, frustrer; *(plan)* contrarier

frustrated [frʌs'treɪtɪd] *adj* frustré(e)

frustrating [frʌs'treɪtɪŋ] *adj* frustrant(e)

frustration [frʌs'treɪʃən] *n* frustration *f*

fry [fraɪ] *(pt & pp* **fried**) **1** *vt* faire frire

2 *vi* frire

frying pan ['fraɪŋpæn] *n* poêle *f* (à frire); **to jump out of the f. into the fire** tomber de Charybde en Scylla

ft *(abbr* **foot** *or* **feet**) p., pd.

FTP [efti:'pi:] *n Comput (abbr* **File Transfer Protocol**) FTP

fuchsia ['fjuːʃə] *n* fuchsia *m*

fuck [fʌk] *Vulg* **1** *n (intercourse)* baise *f;* **to have a f.** baiser; **I don't give a f.** j'en ai rien à foutre; **what the f. do you think you're doing?** putain, mais qu'est-ce que tu fous?; **f. knows why he came!** mais pourquoi il est venu, bordel!; **f.!** bordel!, merde!

2 *vt* baiser; **f. it!** et merde!; **f. you!** va te faire foutre!

3 *vi* baiser

▶**fuck about, fuck around** *vi Vulg (play the fool)* déconner; *(waste time)* glander

▶**fuck off** *vi Vulg (go away)* se casser; **f. off!** va te faire foutre!

fuck-all ['fʌk'ɔːl] *n Vulg* **he's done f. this week** il a fait que dalle cette semaine; **she knows f. about it** elle en sait que dalle

fucked ['fʌkt] *adj Vulg (broken)* foutu(e)

fucking ['fʌkɪŋ] *Vulg* **1** *adj* **he's a f. idiot!** c'est un connard!; **where's the f. car?** où est cette putain de voiture?

2 *adv (cold, brilliant, stupid)* foutrement

fuddy-duddy ['fʌdɪdʌdɪ] *(pl* **fuddy-duddies**) *n* **an old f.** *(man)* un vieux schnock; *(woman)* une vieille mémère

fudge [fʌdʒ] **1** *n (sweet)* caramel *m* mou

2 *vt* **to f. the issue** éluder la question

fuel ['fjʊəl] **1** *n* combustible *m*; *(for engine)* carburant *m*; *Fig* **to add f. to the flames** jeter de l'huile sur le feu; **f. consumption** *(of car)* consommation *f* (d'essence); **f. gauge** jauge *f* de carburant; **f. injection** injection *f* de carburant; **f. pump** pompe *f* d'alimentation; **f. tank** réservoir *m*

2 *vt (pt & pp* **fuelled,** *Am* **fueled)** *Fig (hatred)* attiser; *(speculation)* nourrir

fug [fʌg] *n Br Fam* odeur *f* de renfermé; *(in smoke-filled room)* atmosphère *f* enfumée

fugitive ['fjuːdʒɪtɪv] *n* fugitif(ive) *m,f*

fugue [fjuːg] *n Mus* fugue *f*

fulcrum ['fʌlkrəm] *n* pivot *m*

fulfil, *Am* **fulfill** [fʊl'fɪl] *(pt & pp* **fulfilled)** *vt (plan, ambition)* réaliser; *(condition, duty)* remplir; *(need)* répondre à; **to feel fulfilled** *(of person)* se sentir épanoui(e)

fulfilment, *Am* **fulfillment** [fʊl'fɪlmənt] *n (of plan, condition)* réalisation *f*; *(satisfaction)* épanouissement *m*; **to find** *or* **achieve f.** s'épanouir

full [fʊl] **1** *adj* **(a)** *(container)* plein(e) (**of** de); *(hotel, bus, car park)* complet(ète); *(day)* chargé(e); **to be f. of praise for sb** ne pas tarir d'éloges sur qn; **to be f. of oneself** être imbu(e) de soi-même; **f. to the brim** plein à ras bords; **don't speak with your mouth f.!** ne parle pas la bouche pleine!; **to be f. (up)** *(of person)* être rassasié(e); **on a f. stomach** le ventre plein **(b)** *(complete)* *(amount)* intégral(e); *(explanation, recovery)* complet(ète); *(support)* total(e); **to take f. responsibility for sth** assumer l'entière responsabilité de qch; **she gave me the f. story** elle m'a raconté toute l'histoire; **the f. horror** toute l'horreur; **to lead a f. life** avoir une vie bien remplie; **I waited two f. hours** *or* **a f. two hours** j'ai attendu deux bonnes heures; **in f. flow** *(speaker)* en plein discours; **to be in f. swing** *(of party, sales)* battre son plein; **in f. view of** sous les yeux de; **f. board** pension *f* complète; *Phot* **in f. colour** en couleur; **f. fare** plein tarif *m*; **f. house** *(in theatre)* salle *f* comble; *(in cards)* main *f* pleine; **f. moon** pleine lune *f*; **f. name** nom *m* et prénom *m*; **f. price** plein tarif; **f. stop** *(punctuation)* point *m* final; **f. time** *(in sport)* fin *f* de match **(c)** *(maximum)* **at f. speed** à toute vitesse; **at f. stretch** *(work)* à plein rendement; **to get f. marks** *(in exam)* avoir tous les points **(d)** *(skirt, sleeve)* bouffant(e); **a f. figure** *(of woman)* un corps épanoui; **f. lips** lèvres *fpl* charnues *ou* pleines

2 *adv* **you know f. well that...** tu sais parfaitement que...; **it hit him f. in the face** il a reçu le coup en pleine figure

3 *n* **to pay in f.** payer intégralement; **name in f.** nom et prénoms; **to live life to the f.** vivre pleinement

fullback ['fʊlbæk] *n (in football, rugby)* arrière *m*

full-blown ['fʊl'bləʊn] *adj (row)* vrai(e); *(crisis)* de grande envergure; **to have f. AIDS** avoir le sida

full-bodied ['fʊl'bɒdɪd] *adj (wine)* corsé(e)

full-grown ['fʊl'grəʊn] *adj* adulte

full-length ['fʊl'leŋθ] *adj (portrait, mirror)* en pied; *(dress)* long (longue); **f. film** long métrage *m*

fullness ['fʊlnɪs] *n* **in the f. of time** avec le temps

full-page ['fʊl'peɪdʒ] *adj (advert, illustration)* pleine page

full-scale ['fʊl'skeɪl] *adj* **(a)** *(model)* grandeur nature *inv* **(b)** *(search)* de grande envergure; **f. war** guerre *f* généralisée

full-time ['fʊl'taɪm] *adj & adv* à temps complet, à plein temps; *Fig* **looking after the baby is a f. job** s'occuper du bébé ne laisse pas une minute de libre; **to be in f. employment** travailler à plein temps

full-timer ['fʊl'taɪmər] *n* travailleur(euse) *m,f* à temps complet *ou* à plein temps

fully ['fʊlɪ] *adv* **(a)** *(completely)* complètement, entièrement; *(understand, be aware)* parfaitement, tout à fait; **f. booked** complet(ète); **f. grown** adulte **(b)** *(at least)* **it takes f. two hours** cela prend au moins deux heures

fully-fledged ['fʊlɪ'fledʒd] *adj Br Fig* qualifié(e)

fulminate ['fʌlmɪneɪt] *vi* fulminer (**against** contre)

fulness = fullness

fulsome ['fʊlsəm] *adj* enthousiaste; **to be f. in one's praise of sb/sth** porter qn/qch aux nues

fumble ['fʌmbəl] **1** *vt (ball)* mal attraper

2 *vi* fouiller; **to f. for sth** fouiller pour trouver qch; *(in dark)* tâtonner pour trouver qch; **to f. for words** chercher ses mots; **he fumbled with the switch** il a essayé maladroitement de faire fonctionner l'interrupteur

fume [fjuːm] **1** *npl* **fumes** émanations *fpl*; *(from car exhaust)* gaz *mpl* d'échappement; **petrol fumes** vapeurs *fpl* d'essence

2 *vi* **(a)** *(give off fumes)* fumer **(b)** *(be angry)* **to be fuming** rager, être furieux(euse)

fumigate ['fjuːmɪgeɪt] *vt* désinfecter par fumigation

fun [fʌn] *n* plaisir *m*; **to have f.** s'amuser; **it's/he's great f.** c'est/il est très amusant; **there'll be f. and games** *(trouble)* il va y avoir du grabuge; **it's no f. having to stay at home** ce n'est pas drôle de devoir rester à la maison; **to make f. of** se moquer de; **to be a figure of f.** être la risée de tous; **to say sth in f.** dire qch pour rire *ou* en plaisantant; **to do sth for f.** *or* **for the f. of it** faire qch pour s'amuser; *Ironic* **what f.!** c'est drôle!; **f. fur** fourrure *f* synthétique

function ['fʌŋkʃən] **1** *n* **(a)** *(role)* & *Math* fonction *f*; *Comput* **f. key** touche *f* de fonction **(b)** *(party)* réception *f*; *(public)* cérémonie *f*

2 *vi* fonctionner; **to f. as** jouer le rôle de, faire fonction de

functional ['fʌŋkʃənəl] *adj* **(a)** *(practical)* fonctionnel(elle) **(b)** *(operational)* opérationnel(elle)

functionary ['fʌŋkʃənərɪ] *(pl* **functionaries)** *n* fonctionnaire *mf*

fund [fʌnd] **1** *n* **(a)** *(of money)* fonds *m*; **funds** fonds *mpl*, capitaux *mpl*; **to be in funds** être en fonds; *Fin* **f. manager** gestionnaire *mf* de fonds **(b)** *(of information)* mine *f*

2 *vt* financer

fundamental [fʌndə'mentəl] **1** *n* **fundamentals** principes *mpl*, fondements *mpl*

2 *adj* fondamental(e), essentiel(elle); **her f. honesty** sa profonde honnêteté

fundamentalist [fʌndə'mentəlɪst] *n & adj (religious)* intégriste *mf*, fondamentaliste *mf*

fundamentally [fʌndə'mentəlɪ] *adv* fondamentalement

funding ['fʌndɪŋ] *n* financement *m*

fund-raiser ['fʌndreɪzə(r)] *n (person)* collecteur(trice) *m,f* de fonds; *(event)* = manifestation organisée au profit d'une œuvre de bienfaisance

funeral ['fjuːnərəl] *n* enterrement *m*; *(formal)* funérailles *fpl*, obsèques *fpl*; *Fam* **that's your f.!** c'est ton problème!; **f. director** entrepreneur *m* de pompes funèbres; *Mus* **f. march** marche *f* funèbre; **f. parlour** établissement *m* de pompes funèbres; **f. procession** cortège *m* funèbre; **f. service** service *m* funèbre

funfair ['fʌn'feə(r)] *n* fête *f* foraine

fungal ['fʌŋgəl] *adj* **f. infection** mycose *f*

fungus ['fʌŋgəs] (*pl* **fungi** ['fʌŋgaɪ]) *n* (*mushroom, toadstool*) champignon *m*; (*on walls*) moisissure *f*; *Med* fongus *m*

funk [fʌŋk] *n* (**a**) *Fam Old-fashioned* (*fright*) **to be in a f.** avoir une peur bleue (**b**) (*music*) funk *m*

funky ['fʌŋkɪ] *adj very Fam* (*clothing, suggestion, music*) cool *inv*

funnel ['fʌnəl] **1** *n* (**a**) (*of locomotive, steamship*) cheminée *f* (**b**) (*for filling*) entonnoir *m*
  2 *vt* (*pt & pp* **funnelled**, *Am* **funneled**) (*direct*) (*funds*) acheminer (**to** vers); **to f. liquid into sth** verser un liquide dans qch

funnily ['fʌnɪlɪ] *adv* (*strangely*) bizarrement; **f. enough,...** bizarrement,...

funny ['fʌnɪ] *adj* (**a**) (*amusing*) drôle, amusant(e); **are you trying to be f.?** tu te crois drôle?; *Ironic* **very f.!** très drôle!; *Fam* **f. bone** petit juif *m* (**b**) (*strange*) bizarre, drôle; **I feel a bit f.** (*ill*) je me sens un peu bizarre; **to taste/smell f.** avoir un drôle de goût/une drôle d'odeur; **f., I thought I'd locked the door** c'est curieux, je croyais avoir fermé la porte à clé; **(it's) f. you should say that** c'est drôle que tu dises ça; *Fam* **he's a bit f. in the head** il est un peu bizarre; *Fam* **I don't want any f. business!** et pas de blagues!; *Fam* **f. farm** maison *f* de fous

fur [fɜː(r)] *n* (**a**) (*hair*) poils *mpl*; (*animal skin*) fourrure *f*; *Fig* **the f. was flying** ça chauffait; **f. coat** manteau *m* de fourrure; **f. trade** commerce *m* de fourrures (**b**) (*in kettle, boiler*) tartre *m*

furious ['fjʊərɪəs] *adj* (*person*) furieux(euse) (**with** contre); (*quarrel, storm*) violent(e); **to be f. with one-self** être en colère contre soi-même; **at a f. speed** à une vitesse folle

furiously ['fjʊərɪəslɪ] *adv* furieusement; (*work, write*) frénétiquement

furlong ['fɜːlɒŋ] *n* = 201 m, furlong *m*

furnace ['fɜːnɪs] *n* fourneau *m*; *Fig* **it's like a f. in here!** quelle fournaise!

furnish ['fɜːnɪʃ] *vt* (**a**) (*house, flat*) meubler (**b**) *Formal* (*provide*) fournir; **to f. sb with sth** fournir qch à qn

furnished ['fɜːnɪʃd] *adj* (*flat, room*) meublé(e); **f. accommodation** (*logement m*) meublé *m*

furnishings ['fɜːnɪʃɪŋz] *npl* ameublement *m*

furniture ['fɜːnɪtʃə(r)] *n* meubles *mpl*, mobilier *m*; **a piece of f.** un meuble; **f. polish** encaustique *f* pour les meubles; **f. remover** déménageur *m*; **f. shop** magasin *m* de meubles *ou* d'ameublement; **f. van** camion *m* de déménagement

furore [fjʊ'rɔːrɪ], *Am* **furor** ['fjʊrɔː(r)] *n* (*uproar*) scandale *m*

furrow ['fʌrəʊ] **1** *n* (*in field*) sillon *m*; (*on face*) ride *f* profonde
  2 *vt Lit* **his brow was furrowed with worry** son front était plissé par l'inquiétude

furry ['fɜːrɪ] *adj* (*animal*) à poil; **f. toy** peluche *f*; **to have a f. tongue** avoir la langue chargée

further ['fɜːðə(r)] (*comparative of* **far**) **1** *adj* (**a**) (*more distant*) plus loin (**b**) (*additional*) supplémentaire; **upon f. consideration** après plus ample réflexion; **until f. notice** jusqu'à nouvel ordre; **without f. delay** sans plus attendre; *Br* **f. education** = enseignement supérieur dispensé par un établissement autre qu'une université
  2 *adv* (**a**) (*in general*) plus loin; **this mustn't go any f.** (*don't tell anyone else*) il faut que cela reste entre nous; **I didn't question him any f.** je ne l'ai pas interrogé davantage; **that doesn't get us much f.** ça ne nous avance pas beaucoup; **f. back** (*in space*) plus loin en arrière; (*in time*) plus loin dans le temps; **f. on** (*in space*) plus loin; (*in time*) plus tard (**b**) *Formal* (*moreover*) de plus; **f. to your letter...** suite à votre lettre...
  3 *vt* (*cause, career*) faire avancer

furthermore [fɜːðə'mɔː(r)] *adv Formal* en outre, de plus

furthermost ['fɜːðəməʊst] *adj Lit* le (la) plus reculé(e)

furthest ['fɜːðɪst] (*superlative of* **far**) **1** *adj* le (la) plus éloigné(e)
  2 *adv* le plus loin

furtive ['fɜːtɪv] *adj* sournois(e)

fury ['fjʊərɪ] *n* (*of person, storm*) fureur *f*; **to be in a f.** (*of person*) être furieux(euse); *Fam* **to work like f.** travailler avec acharnement

fuse, *Am* **fuze** [fjuːz] **1** *n* (**a**) (*for plug*) fusible *m*; **f. box** boîte *f* à fusibles; **f. wire** fusible *m* (**b**) (*for dynamite*) détonateur *m*; (*in bomb*) amorce *f*; *Fam Fig* **to have a short f.** (*be short-tempered*) se mettre facilement en colère
  2 *vt* (*melt*) fondre; (*join*) fusionner
  3 *vi* (**a**) (*of metals*) fondre; **to f. together** fusionner (**b**) (*of organizations, parties*) fusionner (**c**) *Br Elec* **the lights have fused** les plombs ont sauté

fused [fjuːzd] *adj Elec* (*plug, appliance*) muni(e) d'un fusible

fuselage ['fjuːzəlɑːʒ] *n* fuselage *m*

fusillade [fjuːzɪ'leɪd] *n* (*of bullets*) fusillade *f*; *Fig* (*of criticism, questions*) avalanche *f*

fusion ['fjuːʒən] *n* fusion *f*

fuss [fʌs] **1** *n* histoires *fpl*; **what's all the f. about?** qu'est-ce que c'est que toutes ces histoires?; **I don't want any f.** pas de cérémonie; **a lot of f. about** *or* **over nothing** beaucoup d'histoires pour pas grand-chose; **I don't see what all the f. is about** je ne vois pas pourquoi on en fait un tel cas; **to kick up** *or* **make a f.** faire des histoires; **to make a f. of sb** être aux petits soins pour qn
  2 *vt Fam* **I'm not fussed** ça m'est égal
  3 *vi* faire des histoires; **to f. about** s'activer

fusspot ['fʌspɒt] *n Fam* chichiteux(euse) *m,f*

fussy ['fʌsɪ] *adj* (**a**) (*person*) difficile, exigeant(e); **I'm not f.** (*I don't mind*) ça m'est égal (**b**) (*dress, décor*) surchargé(e)

futile ['fjuːtaɪl] *adj* (*attempt, protest*) vain(e); (*remark, suggestion*) futile

futility [fjuː'tɪlɪtɪ] *n* futilité *f*

futon ['fuːtɒn] *n* futon *m*

future ['fjuːtʃə(r)] **1** *n* (**a**) (*in time*) avenir *m*; **in (the) f.** à l'avenir; **in the near/distant f.** dans un avenir proche/lointain; **she's got a job with a (good) f.** elle a une situation pleine d'avenir (**b**) *Fin* **futures** opérations *fpl* à terme (**c**) *Gram* futur *m*; **the f. perfect** le futur antérieur
  2 *adj* futur(e); **at some f. date** à une date ultérieure; **for f. reference** à titre d'information

futuristic [fjuːtʃə'rɪstɪk] *adj* futuriste

fuze *Am* = **fuse**

fuzz [fʌz] *n* (**a**) *(on fabric)* peluches *fpl*; *(on peach, skin)* duvet *m* (**b**) *Fam* **the f.** *(police)* les flics *mpl*

fuzzy ['fʌzɪ] *adj (outline, photo)* flou(e); *(idea)* vague; *(hair)* crépu(e); **f. logic** logique *f* floue

G

G, g [dʒiː] *n* (**a**) *(letter)* G, g *m inv* (**b**) *Mus* sol *m*
g *(abbr* **gramme**) gr
gab [gæb] *(pt & pp* **gabbed**) *vi Fam (talk)* papoter; *(gossip)* jaser
gabardine [ˈgæbəˈdiːn] *n* gabardine *f*
gabble [ˈgæbəl] **1** *n* **a g. of conversation** un bruit de conversation
  2 *vi (incoherently)* bredouiller; **to g. on** papoter
gable [ˈgeɪbəl] *n* pignon *m*; **g. end** *(wall)* pignon
Gabon [ˈgæbən] *n* le Gabon
Gabonese [ˈgæbəˈniːz] **1** *n* Gabonais(e) *m,f*
  2 *adj* gabonais(e)
▶**gad about** [gæd] *(pt & pp* **gadded**) *vi Fam* être en vadrouille
gadfly [ˈgædflaɪ] *(pl* **gadflies**) *n (insect)* taon *m*; *Fig (person)* casse-pieds *mf inv*
gadget [ˈgædʒɪt] *n* gadget *m*
Gaelic [ˈgeɪlɪk, *Scot* ˈgælɪk] **1** *n* gaélique *m*
  2 *adj* gaélique; **G. football** = jeu de balle irlandais à quinze où il est autorisé de taper dans le ballon avec la main
Gaels [geɪlz] *npl* **the G.** les Gaëls *mpl*
gaff [gæf] *n* (**a**) *(in fishing)* gaffe *f* (**b**) *Br Fam (home)* piaule *f* (**c**) *Fam* **to blow the g. (on)** vendre la mèche (à propos de)
gaffe [gæf] *n (blunder)* gaffe *f*
gaffer [ˈgæfə(r)] *n* (**a**) *Br Fam (boss)* chef *m* (**b**) *Fam (old man)* **an old g.** un vieux bonhomme (**c**) *Cin* chef *m* électricien, gaffer *m*
gag [gæg] **1** *n* (**a**) *(on mouth)* bâillon *m* (**b**) *Fam (joke)* blague *f*
  2 *vt (pt & pp* **gagged**) *(person)* bâillonner; *Fig (media, opposition)* museler
  3 *vi (retch)* avoir des haut-le-cœur
gaga [ˈgɑːgɑː] *adj Fam* gâteux(euse), gaga *inv*
gage *Am* = **gauge**
gaggle [ˈgægəl] *n also Fig* troupeau *m*
gaiety [ˈgeɪətɪ] *n* gaieté *f*
gaily [ˈgeɪlɪ] *adv (happily)* joyeusement; *(laugh)* de bon cœur; **g. coloured** aux couleurs gaies
gain [geɪn] **1** *n* (**a**) *(profit)* gain *m*, profit *m*; **for personal g.** par intérêt personnel (**b**) *(increase)* augmentation *f* (**in** de); *Fin (on stock market)* hausse *f*; **to make gains** *(progress)* progresser; *Fin (of shares)* augmenter
  2 *vt* (**a**) *(advantage, degree)* obtenir; *(victory, prize)* remporter; *(reputation, experience)* acquérir; *(sympathy, respect)* gagner; **to g. entrance (to)** entrer (dans); *(of burglar)* s'introduire (dans) (**b**) *(increase)* **to g. weight/speed** prendre du poids/de la vitesse; *also*

Fig **to g. ground on** gagner du terrain sur; **to g. time** gagner du temps
  3 *vi* (**a**) *(benefit)* **to g. by sth** bénéficier de qch (**b**) *(increase)* **to g. in confidence** gagner de l'assurance; **to g. in popularity** devenir populaire (**c**) *(of clock)* avancer
▶**gain on** *vt insep also Fig* gagner du terrain sur
gainful [ˈgeɪnfʊl] *adj* **g. employment** un emploi rémunéré
gainfully [ˈgeɪnfʊlɪ] *adv* **to be g. employed** avoir un emploi rémunéré
gainsay [geɪnˈseɪ] *(pt & pp* **gainsaid** [geɪnˈsed]) *vt Formal* contredire; **there's no gainsaying her ability** son talent est indéniable
gait [geɪt] *n* démarche *f*
gal [gæl] *n Fam Old-fashioned* fille *f*
gala [ˈgɑːlə] *n* gala *m*; **swimming g.** compétition *f* de natation; **g. evening/performance** soirée *f*/représentation *f* de gala
galactic [gəˈlæktɪk] *adj* galactique
Galapagos [gəˈlæpəgəs] *npl* **the G. (Islands)** les (îles *fpl*) Galapagos *fpl*
galaxy [ˈgæləksɪ] *(pl* **galaxies**) *n* galaxie *f*; *Fig* **a g. of stars** une pléiade de vedettes
gale [geɪl] *n (strong wind)* vent *m* violent; *Fig* **a g. of laughter** un éclat de rire
gall [gɔːl] **1** *n* (**a**) *Med* bile *f*; **g. bladder** vésicule *f* biliaire (**b**) *(impudence)* culot *m*
  2 *vt (annoy)* irriter, exaspérer
gallant [ˈgælənt] *adj (brave)* brave, vaillant(e); *(polite)* galant(e)
gallantry [ˈgæləntrɪ] *n (bravery)* bravoure *f*; *(politeness)* galanterie *f*
galleon [ˈgælɪən] *n* galion *m*
gallery [ˈgælərɪ] *(pl* **galleries**) *n* (**a**) **(art) g.** *(for sale)* galerie *f* (d'art); *(for exhibition)* musée *m* (**b**) *(in theatre)* galerie *f*; *Fig* **to play to the g.** *(of politician)* chercher à épater la galerie
galley [ˈgælɪ] *(pl* **galleys**) *n* (**a**) *(ship)* galère *f*; **g. slave** galérien *m* (**b**) *(ship's kitchen)* cuisine *f* (**c**) *Typ* **g. (proof)** placard *m*
Gallic [ˈgælɪk] *adj (French)* français(e); *Hist (of Gaul)* gaulois(e)
galling [ˈgɔːlɪŋ] *adj* humiliant(e)
▶**gallivant about, gallivant around** [ˈgælɪvænt] *vi* être en vadrouille
gallon [ˈgælən] *n (in UK)* = 4,54 l, gallon *m*; *(in US)* = 3,78 l, gallon

gallop ['gæləp] **1** *n* galop *m*; **at a g.** au galop
2 *vi* galoper; *Fig* **to g. through one's work** expédier son travail

gallows ['gæləʊz] *n* potence *f*, gibet *m*; **g. humour** humour *m* noir

gallstone ['gɔːlstəʊn] *n* calcul *m* biliaire

galore [gə'lɔː(r)] *adv Fam* à profusion, à gogo

galvanize ['gælvənaɪz] *vt also Fig* galvaniser; **to g. sb into action** pousser qn à agir

galvanized ['gælvənaɪzd] *adj* galvanisé(e)

Gambia ['gæmbɪə] *n* **the G.** la Gambie

Gambian ['gæmbɪən] **1** *n* Gambien(enne) *m,f*
2 *adj* gambien(enne)

gambit ['gæmbɪt] *n (in chess)* gambit *m*; *(in negotiation, diplomacy)* tactique *f*; **opening g.** *(in negotiation, diplomacy)* manœuvre *f* d'approche

gamble ['gæmbəl] **1** *n (risk)* risque *m*; **to take a g.** prendre un risque
2 *vt (money)* jouer, parier
3 *vi* jouer (de l'argent); **to g. on the horses** jouer aux courses; **she gambled on nobody noticing** elle comptait sur le fait que personne ne s'en apercevrait

gambler ['gæmblə(r)] *n* joueur(euse) *m,f*

gambling ['gæmblɪŋ] *n* jeux *mpl* d'argent; **g. debts** dettes *fpl* de jeu; **g. den** tripot *m*

gambol ['gæmbəl] *(pt & pp* **gambolled,** *Am* **gamboled)** *vi* gambader

game [geɪm] **1** *n* (**a**) *(activity, sport)* jeu *m*; *(of cards, pool, chess)* partie *f*; *(match)* match *m*; **to have a g. of tennis/football** faire une partie de tennis/foot(-ball); **g., set and match** *(in tennis)* jeu, set et match; **politics is just a g. to them** pour eux, la politique n'est qu'un jeu; **g. show** jeu *m* télévisé
(**b**) *Br* **games** *(school subject)* sports *mpl* de plein air; *(sporting event)* jeux *mpl*
(**c**) *(animals, food)* gibier *m*; **g. reserve** réserve *f* de gibier
(**d**) *(idioms)* **to play the g.** jouer le jeu; **two can play at that g.** on peut jouer à deux à ce petit jeu-là; **to beat sb at his own g.** battre qn à sa propre jeu; **to play games with sb** jouer avec qn; **to give the g. away** vendre la mèche; **what's his g.?** où veut-il en venir?; **I know what your g. is!** je sais bien où vous voulez en venir!; **the g.'s up for him** c'est fichu pour lui; **I've been in this g. a long time** ça fait longtemps que je suis de la partie; *Br Fam* **to be on the g.** *(of prostitute)* faire le trottoir
2 *adj* (**a**) *(brave)* courageux(euse); **to be g. (to do sth)** *(willing)* être partant(e) (pour faire qch)
(**b**) *Fam* **a g. leg** une patte folle

gamekeeper ['geɪmkiːpə(r)] *n* garde-chasse *m*

gamely ['geɪmlɪ] *adv* courageusement

gamer ['geɪmə(r)] *n Comput* = amateur de jeux vidéo

gamma ['gæmə] *n* gamma *m*; *Phys* **g. rays** rayons *mpl* gamma

gammon ['gæmən] *n* jambon *m*; **g. steak** = tranche épaisse de jambon (à servir grillée)

gammy ['gæmɪ] *adj Fam* **a g. leg** une patte folle

gamut ['gæmət] *n* gamme *f*; **to run the g. of** *(emotions)* passer par toute la gamme de

gamy ['geɪmɪ] *adj (flavour)* faisandé(e)

gander ['gændə(r)] *n* (**a**) *(male goose)* jars *m* (**b**) *Br very Fam* **to take a g. (at)** *(look)* jeter un coup d'œil (à)

gang [gæŋ] *n (of criminals, children, friends)* bande *f*; *(of workers)* équipe *f*

▸**gang up** *vi* **to g. up on sb** se liguer contre qn; **to g. up with sb** s'allier avec qn

gangbang ['gæŋbæŋ] *n very Fam (group rape)* viol *m* collectif

Ganges ['gændʒiːz] *n* **the G.** le Gange

gangland ['gæŋlænd] *n (underworld)* milieu *m*, pègre *f*; **g. boss/killer** caïd *m*/tueur *m* du milieu; **g. killing** règlement *m* de compte *(entre gangsters)*

gangling ['gæŋglɪŋ] *adj* dégingandé(e)

ganglion ['gæŋglɪən] *(pl* **ganglia** ['gæŋglɪə]*) n* ganglion *m*

gangplank ['gæŋplæŋk] *n* passerelle *f*

gangrene ['gæŋgriːn] *n* gangrène *f*; **to have g.** avoir la gangrène

gangrenous ['gæŋgrɪnəs] *adj* gangreneux(euse)

gangster ['gæŋstə(r)] *n* gangster *m*; **g. film** film *m* de gangsters

gangway ['gæŋweɪ] *n (in theatre)* allée *f*; *(in plane, train)* couloir *m*; *(on ship)* passerelle *f*; **g.!** dégagez, s'il vous plaît!

gannet ['gænɪt] *n (bird)* fou *m* de Bassan; *Fig (greedy person)* goinfre *mf*

gantry ['gæntrɪ] *(pl* **gantries**) *n (for crane, over railway)* portique *m*; *(for rocket)* tour *f* de lancement

gaol *Br* = **jail**

gap [gæp] *n* (**a**) *(space)* espace *m*; *(narrower)* interstice *m*; *(in wall)* brèche *f*; *(in text)* blanc *m* (**b**) *(difference)* *(in age, ability)* écart *m*; **the g. between rich and poor** le fossé entre les riches et les pauvres (**c**) *(in knowledge)* lacune *f*; **his death leaves a g. in all our lives** sa mort nous laisse un vide; *Com* **a g. in the market** un créneau (**d**) *(in time)* intervalle *m* (**e**) *(mountain pass)* col *m*

gape [geɪp] *vi* (**a**) *(stare)* rester bouche bée; **to g. at sb/sth** regarder qn/qch bouche bée (**b**) **to g. (open)** *(of door, blouse)* s'ouvrir tout(e) grand(e); *(of wound, hole)* être béant(e)

gaping ['geɪpɪŋ] *adj* béant(e)

garage ['gæraːʒ, 'gærɪdʒ] *n (for storing or repairing car)* garage *m*; *(petrol station)* station-service *f*

garb ['gɑːb] *n Lit* costume *m*

garbage ['gɑːbɪdʒ] *n* (**a**) *Am (rubbish)* ordures *fpl*; **g. can** poubelle *f*; **g. heap** tas *m* d'ordures; **g. man** éboueur *m* (**b**) *(nonsense)* âneries *fpl*; **to talk g.** dire n'importe quoi

garbled ['gɑːbəld] *adj* confus(e)

garden ['gɑːdən] **1** *n* jardin *m*; *Fig* **to lead sb up the g. path** faire marcher qn; **g. centre** jardinerie *f*; *Br* **g. flat** appartement *m* en rez-de-chaussée avec jardin; **g. furniture** meubles *mpl* de jardin; **g. party** réception *f* en plein air, garden-party *f*; **g. shed** resserre *f*
2 *vi* jardiner, faire du jardinage

gardener ['gɑːdnə(r)] *n* jardinier(ère) *m,f*

gardening ['gɑːdnɪŋ] *n* jardinage *m*; **to do the g.** s'occuper du jardin

gargantuan [gɑː'gæntjʊən] *adj* gargantuesque

gargle ['gɑːgəl] *vi* se gargariser (**with** avec)

gargoyle ['gɑːgɔɪl] *n* gargouille *f*

garish ['geərɪʃ] *adj (clothes)* voyant(e); *(taste)* vulgaire; *(colours)* criard(e); *(light)* cru(e)

garland ['gɑːlənd] **1** *n* guirlande *f*
2 *vt* enguirlander (**with** de)

garlic ['gɑːlɪk] *n* ail *m*; **g. bread** = pain chaud au beurre d'ail; **g. butter** beurre *m* d'ail; **g. sausage** saucisson *m* à l'ail

garment ['gɑːmənt] *n* vêtement *m*
garnet ['gɑːnɪt] *n* grenat *m*
garnish ['gɑːnɪʃ] **1** *n* garniture *f*
2 *vt* garnir (**with** avec)
garret ['gærət] *n* mansarde *f*
garrison ['gærɪsən] **1** *n* garnison *f*; **g. duty** service *m* de garnison; **g. town** ville *f* de garnison
2 *vt (troops)* mettre en garnison
garrotte [gə'rɒt] **1** *n* garrot *m*
2 *vt* exécuter au garrot
garrulous ['gærʊləs] *adj (person)* loquace, bavard(e); *(account, letter)* verbeux(euse)
garter ['gɑːtə(r)] *n* jarretière *f*; *Br* **the Order of the G.** l'Ordre *m* de la Jarretière; *Am* **g. belt** porte-jarretelles *m inv*; **g. snake** couleuvre *f*
gas [gæs] **1** *n* (**a**) *(substance, fuel)* gaz *m inv*; *Med* (gaz) anesthétique *m*; **g. bill** note *f* de gaz; **g. chamber** chambre *f* à gaz; **g. cooker** cuisinière *f* à gaz; **g. cylinder** bouteille *f* de gaz; **g. fire** radiateur *m* à gaz; **g. lamp** lampe *f* à gaz; **g. mask** masque *m* à gaz (**b**) *Am (gasoline)* essence *f*; *Fam* **to step on the g.** appuyer sur le champignon; **g. station** station-service *f*; **g. tank** réservoir *m* (**c**) *Am Fam (amusing situation)* **to have a g.** rigoler; **what a g.!** quelle rigolade!
2 *vt (pt & pp gassed) (person)* asphyxier; *(deliberately)* gazer; **to g. oneself** se suicider au gaz
3 *vi Fam (chat)* jacasser
gasbag ['gæsbæg] *n Fam (chatterbox)* bavard(e) *m,f*; *(boaster)* vantard(e) *m,f*
gaseous ['gæsɪəs, 'geɪsɪəs] *adj* gazeux(euse)
gash [gæʃ] **1** *n (in skin, wood)* entaille *f*, *(in metal)* fente *f*
2 *vt* entailler
gasket ['gæskɪt] *n (in engine)* joint *m* de culasse; *Fam* **to blow a g.** piquer une colère
gasoline ['gæsəliːn] *n Am* essence *f*
gasometer [gæ'sɒmɪtə(r)] *n* gazomètre *m*
gasp [gɑːsp] **1** *n (of surprise)* sursaut *m*; **to be at one's last g.** être sur le point de rendre son dernier soupir
2 *vi* avoir le souffle coupé (**with** or **in** de); **to make sb g.** couper le souffle à qn; **to g. for breath** or **for air** haleter, suffoquer; *Fam* **to be gasping for a cigarette/a drink** mourir d'envie de fumer une cigarette/de boire un verre
gassy ['gæsɪ] *adj* gazeux(euse)
gastric ['gæstrɪk] *adj* gastrique; **g. flu** grippe *f* gastro-intestinale; **g. juices** sucs *mpl* gastriques; **g. ulcer** ulcère *m* à l'estomac
gastritis [gæs'traɪtɪs] *n* gastrite *f*; **to have g.** avoir une gastrite
gastro-enteritis [gæstrəʊəntə'raɪtɪs] *n* gastro-entérite *f*; **to have g.** avoir une gastro-entérite
gastronomic [gæstrə'nɒmɪk] *adj* gastronomique
gastronomy [gæs'trɒnəmɪ] *n* gastronomie *f*
gasworks ['gæswɜːks] *n* usine *f* à gaz
gate [geɪt] *n* (**a**) *(in garden, field)* barrière *f*; *(of city, in airport)* porte *f* (**b**) *Sport (spectators)* nombre *m* de spectateurs; *(takings)* recette *f*
gâteau ['gætəʊ] *(pl gâteaux* ['gætəʊz] *) n* gros gâteau *m* à la crème
gatecrash ['geɪtkræʃ] *vt Fam* **to g. a party** aller à une fête sans y être invité(e)
gatecrasher ['geɪtkræʃə(r)] *n Fam* intrus(e) *m,f*
gatehouse ['geɪthaʊs] *n* loge *f*
gatekeeper ['geɪtkiːpə(r)] *n* gardien(enne) *m,f*

gatepost ['geɪtpəʊst] *n* montant *m* (de porte); *Fam* **between you, me and the g.** entre nous
gateway ['geɪtweɪ] *n* entrée *f*; *Fig* **the g. to the East** la porte de l'Orient; **the g. to success** la voie de la réussite
gather ['gæðə(r)] **1** *vt* (**a**) *(collect) (people, belongings)* rassembler; *(information)* recueillir; *(wood, papers)* ramasser; *(fruit, flowers)* cueillir; *(harvest)* rentrer; **to g. one's thoughts** rassembler ses idées; **to g. sb in one's arms** serrer qn dans ses bras (**b**) *(accumulate)* **to g. dirt** s'encrasser; *also Fig* **to g. dust** ramasser de la poussière; **to g. speed** prendre de la vitesse (**c**) *(conclude, understand)* **to g. that...** croire comprendre que...; **as you may already have gathered,...** comme vous avez déjà dû le deviner,...
2 *vi (of people)* se rassembler; *(of things)* s'accumuler; *(of storm)* se préparer
▸**gather round 1** *vt insep* se rassembler autour de
2 *vi* se rassembler
▸**gather together 1** *vt sep (belongings)* rassembler; *(evidence)* recueillir
2 *vi (of people)* se rassembler
▸**gather up** *vt sep* ramasser
gathering ['gæðərɪŋ] **1** *n (group)* attroupement *m*; *(meeting)* réunion *f*
2 *adj (darkness, speed)* croissant(e); *also Fig* **the g. storm** l'orage qui se prépare
GATT [gæt] *n (abbr General Agreement on Tariffs and Trade)* GATT *m*
gauche [gəʊʃ] *adj* gauche, maladroit(e)
gaudily ['gɔːdɪlɪ] *adv* de façon criarde
gaudy ['gɔːdɪ] *adj* tape-à-l'œil *inv*; *(colours)* criard(e)
gauge [geɪdʒ] **1** *n* (**a**) *(size) (of screw, wire, gun)* calibre *m*; *(of railway track)* écartement *m* (**b**) *(measuring device)* jauge *f* (**c**) *Fig (indicator)* signe *m*, indicateur *m* (**of** de)
2 *vt* évaluer
Gaul [gɔːl] *n Hist (region)* la Gaule; *(inhabitant)* Gaulois(e) *m,f*
gaunt [gɔːnt] *adj* décharné(e)
gauntlet ['gɔːntlɪt] *n (glove)* gant *m* à manchette; *Hist* gantelet *m*; *Fig* **to throw** or **fling down the g. (to sb)** jeter le gant (à qn); *Fig* **to take up the g.** relever le gant; *Fig* **to run the g. of sth** s'exposer à qch
gauze [gɔːz] *n* gaze *f*
gave [geɪv] *pt of* **give**
gavel ['gævəl] *n* marteau *m*
gawk [gɔːk] *vi Fam* rester bouche bée; **to g. at sb/sth** rester bouche bée à regarder qn/qch
gawky ['gɔːkɪ] *adj Fam* gauche, empoté(e)
gawp [gɔːp] *vi Fam* rester bouche bée; **to g. at sb/sth** rester bouche bée à regarder qn/qch
gay [geɪ] **1** *n (homosexual)* homosexuel(elle) *m,f*
2 *adj* (**a**) *(homosexual)* homosexuel(elle), gay *inv*; **g. rights** les droits *mpl* des homosexuels (**b**) *Old-fashioned (happy)* gai(e); **with g. abandon** avec insouciance
Gaza ['gɑːzə] *n* Gaza; **the G. Strip** la Bande de Gaza
gaze [geɪz] **1** *n* regard *m*; **to meet** or **return sb's g.** regarder qn dans les yeux
2 *vi* **to g. at sb/sth** regarder fixement qn/qch; **to g. into space** regarder dans le vague
gazelle [gə'zel] *n* gazelle *f*
gazette [gə'zet] *n* journal *m* officiel
gazetteer [gæzɪ'tɪə(r)] *n* index *m* géographique

gazump [gə'zʌmp] *vt Br Fam* = revenir sur une promesse de vente de maison pour accepter l'offre plus élevée d'une tierce personne

GB ['dʒi:'bi:] *n (abbr* **Great Britain**) GB

GBH [dʒi:bi:'eɪtʃ] *n Law (abbr* **grievous bodily harm**) coups *mpl* et blessures *fpl*

GCE [dʒi:si:'i:] *n Br Formerly (abbr* **General Certificate of Education**) = diplôme de fin d'études secondaires

GCHQ [dʒi:si:eɪtʃ'kju:] *n Br (abbr* **Government Communications Headquarters**) = service de renseignement et d'écoute du gouvernement britannique

GCSE [dʒi:si:es'i:] *n Br (abbr* **General Certificate of Secondary Education**) = diplôme de fin de premier cycle de l'enseignement secondaire, sanctionnant une matière déterminée

> **GCSE**
> Cet examen a remplacé les "O levels", ou le "GCE O level", et le "CSE". On le passe après cinq ans de scolarité dans l'enseignement secondaire. Chaque élève choisit les matières dans lesquelles il veut se présenter (généralement entre cinq et dix) selon un système d'unités de valeur. Le nombre d'unités et les notes obtenues déterminent le passage dans la classe supérieure. Les élèves qui sont admis au GCSE peuvent ensuite préparer les "**A levels**" (l'équivalent du baccalauréat français). En Écosse, l'examen équivalent au GCSE s'appelle le "Standard Grade".

GDP [dʒi:di:'pi:] *n Econ (abbr* **gross domestic product**) PIB *m*

GDR [dʒi:di:'ɑ:(r)] *n Formerly (abbr* **German Democratic Republic**) **the G.** la RDA

gear [gɪə(r)] *n* (**a**) *(on car, bicycle)* vitesse *f; Fig* **to put sb's plans out of g.** perturber les projets de qn; **first / second g.** première *f*/seconde *f* (vitesse); *Br* **g. lever** changement *m* de vitesse (**b**) *Fam (equipment)* attirail *m*; *(belongings)* affaires *fpl* (**c**) *Br Fam (clothes)* fringues *fpl*

▸**gear to** *vt sep* **to g. sth to sth** adapter qch à qch

▸**gear towards** *vt sep* **to be geared towards sb/sth** s'adresser à qn/qch

gearbox ['gɪəbɒks] *n* boîte *f* (de changement) de vitesses

gearstick ['gɪəstɪk] *n* changement *m* de vitesses

gee [dʒi:] *exclam* (**a**) *(to horse)* **g. up!** hue! (**b**) *Am* **g. (whizz)!** mince alors!

gee-gee ['dʒi:dʒi:] *n Fam (in children's language)* dada *m*

geese [gi:s] *pl of* **goose**

geezer ['gi:zə(r)] *n Br Fam* type *m*; **old g.** vieux bonhomme *m*

Geiger counter ['gaɪgə'kaʊntə(r)] *n* compteur *m* Geiger

gel [dʒel] **1** *n* gel *m*
2 *vi (of liquid)* se gélifier; *Fig (of ideas, plans)* prendre forme; *(of team)* se souder

gelatine ['dʒeləti:n] *n* gélatine *f*

gelatinous [dʒɪ'lætɪnəs] *adj* gélatineux(euse)

gelding ['geldɪŋ] *n* hongre *m*

gelignite ['dʒelɪgnaɪt] *n* gélignite *f*

gem [dʒem] *n (precious stone)* pierre *f* précieuse; *Fig (person)* perle *f; (film, joke, goal)* pure merveille *f*

Gemini ['dʒemɪnaɪ] *n (sign of zodiac)* les Gémeaux *mpl*; **to be (a) G.** être (des) Gémeaux

gemstone ['dʒemstəʊn] *n* pierre *f* gemme

gen [dʒen] *n Br Fam (information)* tuyaux *mpl*

gender ['dʒendə(r)] *n* (**a**) *Gram* genre *m* (**b**) *(sex)* sexe *m*

gene [dʒi:n] *n Biol* gène *m; Fig* **it's in his genes** *(of talent, characteristic)* c'est héréditaire; **g. pool** patrimoine *m* génétique; **g. therapy** thérapie *f* génétique

genealogy [dʒi:nɪ'ælədʒɪ] *n* généalogie *f*

genera ['dʒenərə] *pl of* **genus**

general ['dʒenərəl] **1** *n* (**a**) **in g.** en général (**b**) *Mil* général *m*
2 *adj* général(e); **as a g. rule** en règle générale; **in g. terms** en termes généraux; **g. anaesthetic** anesthésie *f* générale; **G. Assembly** *(of United Nations)* Assemblée *f* générale; **g. election** élections *fpl* législatives; *Mil* **G. Headquarters** (grand) quartier *m* général; **g. knowledge** culture *f* générale; **g. manager** directeur(trice) *m,f* général(e); **g. meeting** assemblée *f* générale; **g. practice** *(in medicine)* médecine *f* générale; **g. practitioner** *(doctor)* médecin *m* généraliste; **the g. public** le grand public; **g. store** bazar *m*; **g. strike** grève *f* générale

generality [dʒenə'rælɪtɪ] *(pl* **generalities**) *n* généralité *f*

generalization [dʒenərəlaɪ'zeɪʃən] *n* généralisation *f*

generalize ['dʒenərəlaɪz] **1** *vt* **to become generalized** *(of practice, belief)* se généraliser
2 *vi* généraliser

generally ['dʒenərəlɪ] *adv (taken overall)* dans l'ensemble; *(as a general rule)* généralement, en général; **g. speaking** d'une manière générale

generate ['dʒenəreɪt] *vt (electricity, heat)* produire; *(income)* créer; *(reaction, response)* provoquer; *(interest, ideas)* faire naître

generation [dʒenə'reɪʃən] *n* (**a**) *(of people, products)* génération *f*; **from g. to g.** de génération en génération; **the younger/older g.** la jeune/l'ancienne génération; **the g. gap** le fossé entre les générations (**b**) *(of electricity)* production *f*

generator ['dʒenəreɪtə(r)] *n Elec* générateur *m*

generic [dʒɪ'nerɪk] *adj* générique

generosity [dʒenə'rɒsɪtɪ] *n* générosité *f*

generous ['dʒenərəs] *adj* généreux(euse)

generously ['dʒenərəslɪ] *adv* généreusement

genesis ['dʒenɪsɪs] *n* genèse *f*; **(the Book of) G.** la Genèse

genetic [dʒɪ'netɪk] *adj* génétique; **g. code** code *m* génétique; **g. engineering** génie *m* génétique; **g. fingerprinting** empreinte *f* génétique

genetically [dʒɪ'netɪklɪ] *adv* génétiquement; **g. modified** génétiquement modifié(e)

genetics [dʒɪ'netɪks] *n* génétique *f*

Geneva [dʒɪ'ni:və] *n* Genève; **Lake G.** le Lac de Genève, le Lac Léman; **the G. Convention** la Convention de Genève

genial ['dʒi:nɪəl] *adj* cordial(e)

geniality [dʒi:nɪ'ælɪtɪ] *n* cordialité *f*

genially ['dʒi:nɪəlɪ] *adv* cordialement

genie ['dʒi:nɪ] *(pl* **genii** ['dʒi:nɪaɪ]) *n* génie *m*

genital ['dʒenɪtəl] **1** *npl* **genitals** organes *mpl* génitaux
2 *adj* génital(e)

genitive ['dʒenɪtɪv] *Gram* **1** *n* génitif *m*; **in the g.** au génitif
2 *adj* génitif(ive)

genius ['dʒiːnɪəs] *n* génie *m*; *Ironic* **to have a g. for sth/doing sth** avoir le génie de qch/de faire qch; **man/work of g.** homme *m*/œuvre *f* de génie

Genoa ['dʒenəʊə] *n* Gênes

genocide ['dʒenəsaɪd] *n* génocide *m*

genre ['ʒɒnrə] *n (of film, novel)* genre *m*

gent [dʒent] *n Br Fam* (**a**) *(well-bred man)* gentleman *m* (**b**) *(man)* homme *m*; **gents' footwear** chaussures *fpl* pour hommes; **gents** *(toilets)* toilettes *fpl* des hommes; *(sign)* messieurs

genteel [dʒen'tiːl] *adj (refined)* distingué(e); *(respectable)* comme il faut; *Pej (affected)* maniéré(e)

Gentile ['dʒentaɪl] *n* gentil *m*

gentle ['dʒentəl] *adj (person, manner)* doux (douce); *(push, breeze, rise, slope)* léger(ère); *(hint)* discret(ète); *(exercise)* modéré(e); **to be g. with sb** être doux avec qn; **to be g. with sth** faire attention à qch; *Fam* **a g. giant** un agneau sous des airs de brute

gentleman ['dʒentəlmən] *n* (**a**) *(well-bred man)* gentleman *m*; **g.'s agreement** gentleman's agreement *m* (**b**) *(man)* homme *m*; **Ladies and Gentlemen!** mesdames et messieurs!

gentlemanly ['dʒentəlmənlɪ] *adj* bien élevé(e)

gentleness ['dʒentəlnɪs] *n* douceur *f*

gently ['dʒentlɪ] *adv (speak, remind)* gentiment; *(slope)* en pente douce; **g. (does it)!** allez-y doucement!

gentrification [dʒentrɪfɪ'keɪʃən] *n Br* embourgeoisement *m*

gentry ['dʒentrɪ] *n* petite noblesse *f*

genuflect ['dʒenjʊflekt] *vi Formal* faire une génuflexion

genuine ['dʒenjʊɪn] *adj* (**a**) *(manuscript, painting)* authentique; *(gold, leather)* véritable; *(excuse)* valable; *(offer)* sérieux(euse) (**b**) *(sincere)* sincère; **it was a g. mistake** ce n'était pas intentionnel

genuinely ['dʒenjʊɪnlɪ] *adv (sincerely)* sincèrement, vraiment

genus ['dʒiːnəs] *(pl* **genera** ['dʒenərə]) *n Biol* genre *m*

geo- ['dʒiːəʊ] *pref* géo-

geographer [dʒɪ'ɒgrəfə(r)] *n* géographe *mf*

geographic(al) [dʒɪə'græfɪk(əl)] *adj* géographique

geography [dʒɪ'ɒgrəfɪ] *n* géographie *f*

geologic(al) [dʒɪə'lɒdʒɪk(əl)] *adj* géologique

geologist [dʒɪ'ɒlədʒɪst] *n* géologue *mf*

geology [dʒɪ'ɒlədʒɪ] *n* géologie *f*

geometric(al) [dʒɪə'metrɪk(əl)] *adj* géométrique

geometry [dʒɪ'ɒmɪtrɪ] *n* géométrie *f*

geophysics [dʒɪəʊ'fɪzɪks] *n* géophysique *f*

geopolitics [dʒɪəʊ'pɒlɪtɪks] *n* géopolitique *f*

Geordie ['dʒɔːdɪ] *n Br Fam* = personne née à ou habitant Tyneside

Georgia ['dʒɔːdʒə] *n (country, US state)* la Géorgie

Georgian ['dʒɔːdʒən] **1** *n* (**a**) *(person)* Géorgien(enne) *m,f* (**b**) *(language)* géorgien *m*
2 *adj* géorgien(enne)

geothermal [dʒiːəʊ'θɜːməl] *adj* géothermique

geranium [dʒə'reɪnɪəm] *n* géranium *m*

gerbil ['dʒɜːbɪl] *n* gerbille *f*

geriatric [dʒerɪ'ætrɪk] **1** *n* malade *mf* gériatrique; *Fam Pej (old person)* gâteux(euse) *m,f*

2 *adj (hospital)* gériatrique; *(care)* aux vieillards; **g. medicine** gériatrie *f*

geriatrics [dʒerɪ'ætrɪks] *n* gériatrie *f*

germ [dʒɜːm] *n* (**a**) *(causing disease)* microbe *m*; **g. warfare** guerre *f* bactériologique (**b**) *(of seed)* & *Fig (of idea)* germe *m*

German ['dʒɜːmən] **1** *n* (**a**) *(person)* Allemand(e) *m,f* (**b**) *(language)* allemand *m*; **G. class/teacher** cours *m*/professeur *m* d'allemand
2 *adj* allemand(e); **G. measles** rubéole *f*; **G. shepherd** berger *m* allemand

germane [dʒɜː'meɪn] *adj Formal* approprié(e); **to be g. to sth** avoir rapport à qch

Germanic [dʒɜː'mænɪk] *adj* germanique

Germany ['dʒɜːmənɪ] *n* l'Allemagne *f*

germinate ['dʒɜːmɪneɪt] *vi* germer

germination [dʒɜːmɪ'neɪʃən] *n* germination *f*

gerrymandering ['dʒerɪmændərɪŋ] *n Pol* charcutage *m* électoral

gerund ['dʒerənd] *n Gram* gérondif *m*

gestation [dʒes'teɪʃən] *n also Fig* gestation *f*; **g. period** période *f* de gestation

gesticulate [dʒes'tɪkjʊleɪt] *vi* gesticuler

gesture ['dʒestʃə(r)] **1** *n also Fig* geste *m*; *Fig* **as a g. of friendship** en témoignage d'amitié
2 *vi (single action)* faire un geste; *(repeatedly)* faire des gestes; **to g. to sb** faire signe à qn; **to g. towards sb/sth** désigner qn/qch d'un geste

get [get] *(pt & pp* **got** [gɒt], *Am pp* **gotten** ['gɒtən]) **1** *vt* (**a**) *(obtain)* obtenir; *(job)* trouver; **to g. sth for sb** obtenir qch pour qn; **I got the idea from a book** j'ai trouvé l'idée dans un livre; **to g. the right answer** trouver la solution; **to g. the wrong answer** se tromper
(**b**) *(buy)* acheter; **to g. sth for sb** acheter qch à qn
(**c**) *(receive)* recevoir; *(present, reply)* recevoir; *(surprise, shock)* avoir; **we can't g. Radio 4 here** on ne reçoit pas Radio 4 ici; **to g. £20,000 a year** gagner 20 000 livres par an; **we don't g. many visitors here** nous ne recevons pas beaucoup de visites ici
(**d**) *(catch) (person, disease)* attraper; *(train, bus)* prendre; *Fam* **I'll g. you for that** je t'aurai
(**e**) *(fetch)* aller chercher; **to g. sth for sb** aller chercher qch pour qn; **can I g. you anything?** je te rapporte quelque chose?
(**f**) *Fam (annoy)* énerver
(**g**) *Fam (understand)* piger; **do you g. my meaning?** tu vois ce que je veux dire?; **to g. the point** piger; **to g. a joke** saisir une blague
(**h**) *(send)* **to g. sth to sb** faire parvenir qch à qn
(**i**) *(cause to be in a certain state)* **to g. sth dry/wet** sécher/mouiller qch; **to g. sth clean/dirty** nettoyer/salir qch; **you've got him worried** tu l'as fait s'inquiéter; **to g. sb pregnant** mettre qn enceinte; **to g. the children to bed** envoyer les enfants au lit
(**j**) *(cause to be done)* **to g. sth done** faire faire qch; **to g. the house painted** faire peindre la maison; **she got her work finished** elle a terminé son travail
(**k**) *(cause to do)* **to g. sb to do sth** faire faire qch à qn; **she got me to help her** elle m'a persuadé de l'aider; **you can g. them to wrap it for you** tu peux leur demander de te l'emballer
(**l**) *(do gradually)* **to g. to know sb** apprendre à connaître qn; **you'll g. to like him** tu finiras par l'apprécier; **she soon got to thinking that...** elle se mit bientôt à penser que...

(**m**) *(have opportunity)* **to g. to do sth** avoir l'occasion de faire qch

(**n**) *(possess)* *(with have)* **she hasn't got a car** elle n'a pas de voiture; **she's got measles/AIDS** elle a la rougeole/le sida; **what's that got to do with it?** qu'est-ce que ça a à voir?

(**o**) *(must)* *(with have)* **I've got to go** il faut que j'y aille; **it's got to be done** il faut que ce soit fait

2 *vi* (**a**) *(arrive)* arriver; **to g. home** arriver chez soi; **to g. back** arriver; **how do you g. there?** comment fait-on pour y aller?; **he got as far as chapter five** il est allé jusqu'au chapitre cinq; **it got to the point where...** ça en est arrivé à un point où...

(**b**) *(move)* *also Fig* **to g. in sb's way** se mettre sur le chemin de qn; **where has he got to?** où est-il passé?; **we're getting nowhere** on n'avance pas

(**c**) *(become)* **to g. angry** se mettre en colère; **to g. better** s'améliorer; **to g. drunk** se soûler; **to g. old** vieillir

(**d**) *(with past participle)* **to g. broken** être cassé(e); **to g. stolen** être volé(e); **to g. killed** se faire tuer; **to g. dressed** s'habiller; **to g. married** se marier

(**e**) *(start)* **to g. going** *(leave)* se mettre en route; *(start working)* se mettre au travail; **to g. talking with sb** entrer en conversation avec qn

▸**get about** *vi (of person)* se déplacer; *(of news, rumour)* circuler

▸**get across** *vt sep (ideas, message)* faire passer

▸**get ahead** *vi* avancer

▸**get along** *vi* (**a**) *(leave)* s'en aller, partir (**b**) *(progress)* **how are you getting along in your new job?** comment ça va, votre nouveau travail?; **we can g. along without them** nous pouvons très bien nous passer d'eux (**c**) *(have good relationship)* s'entendre

▸**get around 1** *vt insep (problem, difficulty)* contourner; **there's no getting around it, we'll have to tell her** on n'a pas le choix, il va falloir lui dire

2 *vi* = **get about**

▸**get around to** *vt insep* **to g. around to doing sth** trouver le temps de faire qch

▸**get at** *vt insep* (**a**) *(have access to)* accéder à; *(reach)* atteindre; **to g. at the truth** découvrir la vérité (**b**) *(imply)* **what are you getting at?** où veux-tu en venir? (**c**) *Fam (criticize)* s'en prendre à

▸**get away** *vi (escape, leave)* se sauver; *(have a holiday)* s'échapper; *Fam* **g. away!** *(expressing disbelief)* sans blague!

▸**get away with** *vt insep* (**a**) *(fine, warning)* s'en tirer avec (**b**) *(crime)* **he stole the money and got away with it** il a volé l'argent et il ne s'est pas fait prendre; *Fig* **that child gets away with murder** on lui passe tout à ce gosse

▸**get back 1** *vt sep (recover)* récupérer; *(strength)* reprendre

2 *vi (return)* revenir

▸**get back at** *vt insep* **to g. back at sb (for sth)** se venger de qn (pour qch)

▸**get behind 1** *vt insep (support)* soutenir

2 *vi (become delayed)* prendre du retard (**with** *or* **in** dans)

▸**get by** *vi (manage)* se débrouiller, s'en tirer (**on/in** avec/en)

▸**get down 1** *vt sep* (**a**) *(reduce)* *(weight)* perdre; *(costs, temperature)* faire baisser (**b**) *(depress)* déprimer (**c**) *(fetch)* descendre

2 *vi (descend)* descendre (**from** de)

▸**get down to** *vt insep* se mettre à; **to g. down to the facts** en venir aux faits

▸**get in 1** *vt sep* (**a**) *(bring inside)* rentrer (**b**) *(insert)* **I couldn't g. a word in** je n'ai pas pu en placer une (**c**) *(stock up with)* faire provision de

2 *vi* (**a**) *(gain entrance)* entrer (**b**) *(arrive)* arriver (**c**) *(be elected)* être élu(e)

▸**get into** *vt insep* (**a**) *(house)* entrer dans; *(car)* monter dans; **to g. into Parliament** être élu(e) député; **to g. into trouble** s'attirer des ennuis; *Fam* **I don't know what's got into her** je ne sais pas ce qui lui prend (**b**) *(clothes, boots)* enfiler; **I can't g. into my dress any more** je n'entre plus dans ma robe (**c**) *Fam (become interested in)* *(activity)* commencer à s'intéresser à; *(book)* rentrer dans

▸**get in with** *vt insep (group of people)* se mettre bien avec

▸**get off 1** *vt sep* (**a**) **to g. sb off** *(save from punishment)* tirer qn de là (**b**) *(send)* **to g. the children off to school** envoyer les enfants à l'école

2 *vt insep (train, bus)* descendre de

3 *vi* (**a**) *(from train, bus)* descendre; *Fig* **I told him where to g. off** je l'ai envoyé promener (**b**) *(go unpunished)* s'en tirer (**c**) *(begin)* **to g. off to sleep** s'endormir; **to g. off to a good/bad start** commencer bien/mal

▸**get off on** *vt insep very Fam* **to g. off on sth** être excité(e) par qch; **to g. off on doing sth** prendre son pied à faire qch

▸**get off with** *vt insep Br Fam* lever

▸**get on 1** *vt sep (clothes)* mettre, enfiler

2 *vt insep (train, bus, plane)* monter dans

3 *vi* (**a**) *(enter train, bus)* monter (**b**) *(progress)* réussir; **to g. on in life** *or* **in the world** réussir dans la vie; **how are you getting on?** *(how are you?)* comment ça va?; **how did you g. on?** *(in exam, at meeting)* comment ça s'est passé? (**c**) *(have good relationship)* s'entendre; **to g. on well/badly with sb** s'entendre bien/mal avec qn(**d**) *(age)* **to be getting on (in years)** se faire vieux (vieille)

▸**get on for** *vt insep (approach)* **he must be getting on for fifty now** il doit approcher la cinquantaine; **it was getting on for midnight** il était presque minuit; **there were getting on for 200 people there** on approchait les 200 personnes

▸**get onto** *vt insep* (**a**) *(contact)* se mettre en rapport avec (**b**) *(move onto subject of)* en arriver à; **they eventually got onto (the subject of) money** ils en vinrent finalement à parler d'argent

▸**get out 1** *vt sep* (**a**) *(bring out)* sortir (**b**) *(remove)* *(nail, splinter)* retirer; *(stain)* faire partir

2 *vi* (**a**) *(leave)* sortir (**b**) *(of secret, news)* transpirer

▸**get out of** *vt insep (vehicle)* sortir de; **to g. out of the way** s'écarter; **g. out of here!** *(go away)* va-t-en!; *Fam (I don't believe you)* arrête de dire des bêtises!; **to g. out of doing sth** s'arranger pour ne pas faire qch

▸**get over 1** *vt sep (idea, information)* faire passer; *(facts)* expliquer

2 *vt insep* (**a**) *(road, river)* traverser, franchir; *(wall, fence)* passer par-dessus (**b**) *(illness, trauma)* se remettre de

▸**get over with** *vt sep* **to g. sth over with** en finir avec qch

▸**get round 1** *vt insep* = **get around**

2 *vi* = **get about**

▸**get round to** *vt insep* = **get around to**

▶**get through 1** *vt sep (communicate)* **to g. sth through to sb** faire comprendre qch à qn
   2 *vt insep* (**a**) *(pass through) (hole, roof)* passer à travers (**b**) *(survive) (test, interview)* survivre à; *(period of time)* tenir (**c**) *(finish)* achever (**d**) *(consume) (food, drink)* consommer; *(money)* dépenser
   3 *vi* (**a**) *(arrive) (of news)* parvenir; *(of messenger)* arriver (**b**) **to g. through to sb** *(on telephone)* obtenir la communication avec qn; *Fig (make understand)* se faire comprendre par qn

▶**get together 1** *vt sep (money)* réunir; *(belongings, ideas)* rassembler
   2 *vi (of people)* se réunir

▶**get up 1** *vt sep* (**a**) *(out of bed)* faire lever (**b**) *(dress up)* **he got himself up in his best clothes** il a mis ses plus beaux vêtements (**c**) *very Fam (achieve erection)* **he couldn't g. it up** il n'a pas réussi à bander
   2 *vt insep Fig* **to g. up sb's nose** taper sur les nerfs à qn
   3 *vi (rise)* se lever

▶**get up to** *vt insep (do)* **what have you been getting up to recently?** qu'est-ce que tu as fait ces derniers temps?; **to g. up to mischief** faire des bêtises; **he's been getting up to his old tricks** il a encore fait des siennes

getaway ['getəweɪ] *n* fuite *f*; **to make one's g.** prendre la fuite; **g. car** = voiture utilisée pour prendre la fuite

get-rich-quick ['get'rɪtʃ'kwɪk] *adj Fam* **a g. scheme** un moyen de devenir riche rapidement

get-together ['getəgeðə(r)] *n Fam* réunion *f* (entre amis)

get-up ['getʌp] *n Fam (clothes)* accoutrement *m*; *(fancy dress)* déguisement *m*

get-up-and-go ['getʌpənd'gəʊ] *n Fam* énergie *f*

get-well card ['get'wel'kɑːd] *n* carte *f* de prompt rétablissement

geyser ['giːzə(r)] *n* (**a**) *(spring)* geyser *m* (**b**) *Br (water heater)* chauffe-eau *m inv*

Ghana ['gɑːnə] *n* le Ghana

Ghanaian [gɑːˈneɪən] **1** *n* Ghanéen(enne) *m,f*
   2 *adj* ghanéen(enne)

ghastly ['gɑːstlɪ] *adj (terrible)* horrible, épouvantable; *(mistake)* monstrueux(euse)

Ghent [gent] *n* Gand

gherkin ['gɜːkɪn] *n* cornichon *m*

ghetto ['getəʊ] *(pl* **ghettoes** *or* **ghettos)** *n* ghetto *m*; *Fam* **g. blaster** grand radiocassette *m* portatif

ghost [gəʊst] **1** *n* fantôme *m*; **you look as though you've seen a g.** on dirait que tu as vu un revenant; **not the g. of a chance** pas la moindre chance; **to give up the g.** *(of person, machine)* rendre l'âme; **g. story** histoire *f* de fantôme; **g. town** ville *f* fantôme
   2 *vt* **to g. a book** servir de nègre pour un livre

ghostly ['gəʊstlɪ] *adj* spectral(e)

ghostwrite ['gəʊstraɪt] *vt* **to g. a book** servir de nègre pour un livre

ghostwriter ['gəʊstraɪtə(r)] *n* nègre *m*

ghoul [guːl] *n (evil spirit)* goule *f*; *Fig (morbid person)* personne *f* morbide

ghoulish ['guːlɪʃ] *adj (humour, remark)* morbide; *(scene)* macabre

GHQ [dʒiːeɪtʃˈkjuː] *n Mil (abbr* **General Headquarters)** QG *m inv*

GI [dʒiːˈaɪ] *n Am Fam* GI *m inv*

giant ['dʒaɪənt] **1** *n* géant(e) *m,f*; **g. killer** *(in sport)* vainqueur *m* surprise
   2 *adj* géant(e)

gibber ['dʒɪbə(r)] *vi* baragouiner

gibbering ['dʒɪbərɪŋ] *adj* au discours incohérent; *Fam* **a g. idiot** un(e) pauvre idiot(e)

gibberish ['dʒɪbərɪʃ] *n* charabia *m*; **to talk g.** dire n'importe quoi

gibbet ['dʒɪbɪt] *n* gibet *m*, potence *f*

gibbon ['gɪbən] *n* gibbon *m*

gibe [dʒaɪb] **1** *n* moquerie *f*
   2 *vi* **to g. at sb** se moquer de qn

giblets ['dʒɪblɪts] *npl* abats *mpl*

Gibraltar [dʒɪˈbrɔːltə(r)] *n* Gibraltar

giddiness ['gɪdɪnɪs] *n* étourdissement *m*, vertige *m*

giddy ['gɪdɪ] *adj* **to be** *or* **feel g.** avoir le vertige; **it makes me (feel) g.** ça me donne le vertige; *Fig* **the g. heights** les hautes sphères *fpl*

GIF [dʒɪf] *n Comput (abbr* **Graphic Information Format)** GIF *m*

gift [gɪft] *n* (**a**) *(present)* cadeau *m*; *Prov* **never look a g. horse in the mouth** à cheval donné on ne regarde pas la bouche; **g. shop** boutique *f* de cadeaux; **g. token** chèque-cadeau *m* (**b**) *(talent)* don *m*; **to have a g. for sth** être doué(e) pour qch; **to have the g. of the gab** *(be talkative)* avoir la langue bien pendue; *(speak persuasively)* avoir du bagout

gifted ['gɪftɪd] *adj* doué(e); *(artist, musician)* de talent

gift-wrapped ['gɪftræpt] *adj* sous paquet-cadeau

gig [gɪg] *n* (**a**) *(carriage)* cabriolet *m* (**b**) *Fam (pop concert)* concert *m*

gigabyte ['dʒɪgəbaɪt] *n Comput* gigaoctet *m*

gigantic [dʒaɪˈgæntɪk] *adj* colossal(e), gigantesque

giggle ['gɪgəl] **1** *n* (**a**) *(laugh)* petit rire *m* idiot; **to have (a fit of) the giggles** avoir le fou rire (**b**) *Fam (amusement)* **what a g.!** quelle rigolade!; **to do sth for a g.** faire qch pour rigoler
   2 *vi* rire (nerveusement)

giggly ['gɪgəlɪ] *adj* **to be g.** pouffer de rire

gigolo ['dʒɪgələʊ] *(pl* **gigolos)** *n* gigolo *m*

gild [gɪld] *(pt & pp* **gilded** *or* **gilt** [gɪlt]) *vt* dorer; *Fig* **to g. the lily** surcharger

gill [dʒɪl] *n (liquid measure)* = 0,142 l, quart *m* de pinte

gills [gɪlz] *npl (of fish)* ouïes *fpl*, branchies *fpl*; *Fig* **to be green about the g.** avoir le teint verdâtre

gilt [gɪlt] **1** *n* dorure *f*; *Fin* **gilts** titres *mpl ou* fonds *mpl* d'État
   2 *adj* doré(e)
   3 *pt & pp of* **gild**

gilt-edged ['gɪltedʒd] *adj Fin* **g. securities** *or* **stocks** titres *mpl ou* fonds *mpl* d'État

gimlet ['gɪmlɪt] *n (tool)* vrille *f*; *Fig* **g. eyes** yeux *mpl* perçants

gimme ['gɪmiː] *very Fam =* **give me**

gimmick ['gɪmɪk] *n* truc *m*, astuce *f*

gimmicky ['gɪmɪkɪ] *adj* artificiel(elle), qui relève du procédé

gin [dʒɪn] *n* gin *m*; **a g. and tonic** un gin tonic

ginger ['dʒɪndʒə(r)] **1** *n* gingembre *m*; **g. ale** = boisson gazeuse au gingembre pouvant servir à couper un alcool; **g. beer** limonade *f* au gingembre
   2 *adj (hair)* roux (rousse)

▶**ginger up** *vt sep Fam (person, group)* stimuler; *(film, story)* donner du punch à

gingerbread ['dʒɪndʒəbred] *n* pain *m* d'épice; **g. man** = bonhomme en biscuit parfumé au gingembre

gingerly ['dʒɪndʒəlɪ] *adv* avec précaution

gingham ['gɪŋəm] *n* vichy *m*

gingivitis [dʒɪndʒɪ'vaɪtɪs] *n Med* gingivite *f*

ginormous [dʒaɪ'nɔːməs] *adj Fam* gigantesque, énorme

ginseng ['dʒɪnseŋ] *n* ginseng *m*

gipsy ['dʒɪpsɪ] (*pl* **gipsies**) *n* (*Eastern European*) tzigane *mf*; (*Spanish*) gitan(e) *m,f*; **g. caravan** roulotte *f*

giraffe [dʒɪ'rɑːf] *n* girafe *f*

gird [gɜːd] (*pt* & *pp* **girded** *or* **girt** [gɜːt]) *vt Lit* **to g. one's loins** se ceindre les reins

girder ['gɜːdə(r)] *n* poutre *f* (métallique)

girdle ['gɜːdəl] **1** *n* (*corset*) gaine *f*
2 *vt Lit* (*surround*) ceindre, entourer

girl [gɜːl] *n* fille *f*; **a French g.** une (jeune) Française; *Br* **G. Guide** éclaireuse *f*

girlfriend ['gɜːlfrend] *n* (*lover*) petite amie *f*; (*friend*) amie *f*

girlhood ['gɜːlhʊd] *n* enfance *f*, jeunesse *f*

girlie ['gɜːlɪ] *n Fam* **g. mag** magazine *m* érotique

girlish ['gɜːlɪʃ] *adj* (*of girl*) de fille; (*of woman, effeminate man*) de jeune fille; **g. laughter** rire *m* de jeune fille

giro ['dʒaɪrəʊ] (*pl* **giros**) *n Br* (**a**) *Fin* **g. account** compte *m* chèque postal, CCP *m* (**b**) *Fam* (*unemployment cheque*) allocation *f* (de) chômage

Girobank ['dʒaɪrəʊbæŋk] *n* = service bancaire de la Poste britannique, ≃ service *m* de chèques postaux

girt [gɜːt] *pt* & *pp of* **gird**

girth [gɜːθ] *n* (*of tree*) circonférence *f*; (*of person*) corpulence *f*

gist [dʒɪst] *n* essentiel *m*; **to get the g.** saisir l'essentiel

git [gɪt] *n Br very Fam* con (conne) *m,f*

give [gɪv] **1** *vt* (*pt* **gave** [geɪv], *pp* **given** ['gɪvən]) (**a**) (*in general*) donner; (*as present*) offrir; **to g. sth to sb, to g. sb sth** donner qch à qn; (*as present*) offrir qch à qn; **to g. sb a dirty look** lancer un regard noir à qn; **he was given ten years/a fine** il a été condamné à dix ans de prison/à une amende; **g. her my love** embrasse-la pour moi; **she gave her age as twenty** elle a déclaré qu'elle avait vingt ans; **she gave me to understand that...** elle m'a fait comprendre que...; **g. or take a few minutes/pence** à quelques minutes/pence près
(**b**) (*with noun to form verbal expressions*) **to g. a laugh** partir d'un éclat de rire; **to g. a sigh** pousser un soupir; **to g. sb a smile** sourire à qn; **to g. sb a fright** faire peur à qn; **to g. sb a kiss** embrasser qn; **he gave his face a wash** il s'est lavé le visage; **she gave the soup a stir** elle a remué la soupe
2 *vi* (**a**) (*donate*) donner; **please g. generously** soyez généreux, s'il vous plaît; **to g. of one's time** donner de son temps
(**b**) (*yield, break*) (*of cloth, shoes*) se faire; (*of rope*) lâcher; (*of support, door*) céder
(**c**) *Am Fam* **what gives?** quoi de neuf?
3 *n* (*of fabric*) élasticité *f*
▸**give away** *vt sep* (**a**) (*give for nothing*) donner (**b**) (*prize*) distribuer; **to g. the bride away** conduire la mariée à l'autel (**c**) (*reveal*) trahir
▸**give back** *vt sep* rendre
▸**give in** **1** *vt sep* (*hand over*) remettre
2 *vi* (*surrender*) céder (**to** à); (*admit defeat*) abandonner

▸**give off** *vt sep* (*smell, heat*) dégager
▸**give onto** *vt insep* **the house gives directly onto the street** la maison donne directement sur la rue
▸**give out** **1** *vt sep* (**a**) (*money, food*) distribuer; (*information*) donner (**b**) (*noise*) émettre; (*heat*) répandre
2 *vi* (*of supplies, patience*) s'épuiser; (*of luck*) tourner
▸**give over** **1** *vt sep* (*money, objects*) remettre; (*devote*) consacrer (**to** à)
2 *vi Fam* (*stop*) **g. over, will you?** arrête, d'accord?
▸**give up** **1** *vt sep* (*possessions*) renoncer à; (*activity, hope*) abandonner; **to g. up smoking** arrêter de fumer; **to g. up one's job** quitter son emploi; **to g. sb up for dead** considérer qn comme mort(e)
2 *vi* abandonner; **to g. up on sb** perdre tout espoir en qn; (*of doctors*) perdre tout espoir en ce qui concerne qn; **to g. up on sth** laisser tomber qch
▸**give way** *vi* (**a**) (*collapse*) (*of support*) céder; (*of floor, ceiling*) s'effondrer; (*of rope, legs*) lâcher; (*of ground*) se dérober (**b**) (*yield*) (*in argument*) céder (**to** à); (*in car*) céder le passage (**to** à); **her tears gave way to laughter** ses larmes ont cédé la place au rire

give-and-take ['gɪvən'teɪk] *n* concessions *fpl* (mutuelles); **there has to be some g.** il faut que chacun y mette du sien

giveaway ['gɪvəweɪ] *n Fam* (**a**) (*revelation*) **what she said about the night before was the g.** ce qu'elle a dit sur la soirée précédente l'a trahie; **it was a dead g.** cela en disait long (**b**) (*free gift*) cadeau *m*; **g. price** prix *m* imbattable

given ['gɪvən] **1** *adj* (**a**) (*specific*) (*time, place*) donné(e); **at a g. point** à un moment donné; **g. name** prénom *m* (**b**) (*apt, likely*) **to be g. to doing sth** avoir tendance à faire qch
2 *conj* (**a**) (*considering*) étant donné; **g. that...** étant donné que...; **g. the nature of the case** étant donné la nature de l'affaire (**b**) **g. the chance again** si l'occasion se représentait
3 *pp of* **give**

gizmo ['gɪzməʊ] (*pl* **gizmos**) *n Fam* truc *m*, machin *m*

gizzard ['gɪzəd] *n* gésier *m*

glacé cherry ['glæseɪ'tʃerɪ] *n* cerise *f* confite

glacial ['gleɪsɪəl] *adj* glaciaire; *Fig* glacial(e)

glacier ['glæsɪə(r)] *n* glacier *m*

glad [glæd] *adj* heureux(euse), content(e) (**about** de); **I would be g. to assist you** je serais ravi de pouvoir vous aider; **to be g. of sth** (*grateful for*) être heureux d'avoir qch; *Fig* **to give sb the g. eye** faire de l'œil à qn; *Fam* **to put on one's g. rags** se mettre sur son trente et un

gladden ['glædən] *vt* réjouir

glade [gleɪd] *n Lit* clairière *f*

gladiator ['glædɪeɪtə(r)] *n* gladiateur *m*

gladiolus [glædɪ'əʊləs] (*pl* **gladioli** [glædɪ'əʊlaɪ]) *n* glaïeul *m*

gladly ['glædlɪ] *adv* avec plaisir, volontiers

glamorize ['glæməraɪz] *vt* (*lifestyle*) rendre séduisant(e); (*violence*) esthétiser; (*person*) idéaliser

glamorous ['glæmərəs] *adj* (*person*) élégant(e); (*job, image, lifestyle*) prestigieux(euse); (*place*) chic *inv*, élégant; (*dress*) magnifique

glamour, *Am* **glamor** ['glæmə(r)] *n* (*of person*) élégance *f*; (*of job, image, lifestyle*) prestige *m*; (*of place*) chic *m inv*, élégance; *Fam* **g. girl** belle fille *f*, pin-up *f*

glance [glɑːns] **1** *n* coup *m* d'œil; **to have a g. at sth** jeter un coup d'œil à qch; **at a g.** d'un coup d'œil; **at first g.** au premier coup d'œil

2 *vi* **to g. at** regarder brièvement, jeter un coup d'œil à; **to g. through sth** parcourir qch rapidement

▸**glance off** *vt insep (of blow, missile)* ricocher sur

glancing ['glɑːnsɪŋ] *adj (blow)* oblique

gland [glænd] *n* glande *f*

glandular ['glændjʊlə(r)] *adj* glandulaire; **g. fever** mononucléose *f* infectieuse

glare [gleə(r)] **1** *n* (**a**) *(angry stare)* regard *m* furieux (**b**) *(bright light)* éclat *m*, lumière *f* éblouissante; *Fig* **in the full g. of publicity** sous les feux de médias
2 *vi (stare angrily)* **to g. at sb/sth** fixer qn/qch d'un air furieux

glaringly ['gleərɪŋlɪ] *adv* **it's g. obvious** ça saute aux yeux

Glasgow ['glɑːzgəʊ] *n* Glasgow

glass [glɑːs] *n* verre *m*; *(glassware)* verrerie *f*; **a g. of wine** un verre de vin; **g. bottle** bouteille *f* en verre; **g. case** vitrine *f*; **g. door** porte *f* vitrée; **g. eye** œil *m* de verre; **g. wool** laine *f* de verre

glass-blowing ['glɑːsbləʊɪŋ] *n* soufflage *m* du verre

glasses ['glɑːsɪz] *npl (spectacles)* lunettes *fpl*

glassful ['glɑːsfʊl] *n* verre *m*

glasshouse ['glɑːshaʊs] *n Br* serre *f*; *Prov* **people who live in glasshouses shouldn't throw stones** il faut être sans défauts pour critiquer autrui

glasspaper ['glɑːspeɪpə(r)] *n* papier *m* de verre

glassware ['glɑːsweə(r)] *n* verrerie *f*

glassworks ['glɑːswɜːks] *n* verrerie *f*; *(for crystal)* crystallerie *f*

glassy ['glɑːsɪ] *adj (eyes, look)* vitreux(euse); *(water)* immobile

Glaswegian [glæz'wiːdʒən] **1** *n* = personne née à ou habitant Glasgow
2 *adj* de Glasgow

glaucoma [glɔː'kəʊmə] *n* glaucome *m*; **to have g.** avoir un glaucome

glaze [gleɪz] **1** *n (on pottery)* vernis *m*; *(on pastry)* glaçage *m*
2 *vt* (**a**) *(window)* vitrer (**b**) *(pottery)* vernisser; *(pastry)* glacer

▸**glaze over** *vi (of eyes)* devenir vitreux(euse)

glazed [gleɪzd] *adj* (**a**) *(roof, door)* vitré(e) (**b**) *(pottery)* vernissé(e) (**c**) *(eyes, look)* vitreux(euse), terne

glazier ['gleɪzɪə(r)] *n* vitrier *m*

gleam [gliːm] **1** *n (of light)* rayon *m*; *Fig* **a g. of hope** une lueur d'espoir
2 *vi* luire, briller; *(of water)* miroiter

gleaming ['gliːmɪŋ] *adj* étincelant(e)

glean [gliːn] *vt* glaner

glee [gliː] *n (delight)* joie *f*; *(malicious pleasure)* jubilation *f*

gleeful ['gliːfʊl] *adj (happy)* joyeux(euse); **to be g.** *(maliciously happy)* jubiler

glen [glen] *n Ir & Scot* vallée *f*

glib [glɪb] *adj (person, excuse)* désinvolte; *(reply)* spécieux(euse)

glibly ['glɪblɪ] *adv (reply)* de façon désinvolte; *(speak)* avec aisance

glide [glaɪd] *vi (move smoothly)* glisser; *(of aircraft, bird)* planer

glider ['glaɪdə(r)] *n (aircraft)* planeur *m*

gliding ['glaɪdɪŋ] *n (sport)* vol *m* à voile

glimmer ['glɪmə(r)] **1** *n* faible lueur *f*; *(of water)* reflet *m*; *Fig* **a g. of hope** une lueur d'espoir

2 *vi (of light)* luire; *(of water)* miroiter; *(of metal)* étinceler

glimpse [glɪmps] **1** *n* **to catch a g. of** entrevoir; **a g. of the future** un aperçu de (ce que sera) l'avenir
2 *vt* entrevoir

glint [glɪnt] **1** *n (of light) (flash)* éclat *m*; *(continuous)* scintillement *m*; *(of water)* reflet *m*; **with a g. in her eye** avec une lueur dans le regard
2 *vi (of light, eye)* briller; *(of water, metal)* scintiller

glisten ['glɪsən] *vi (of water, metal)* scintiller; **his forehead glistened with sweat** la sueur perlait sur son front

glitter ['glɪtə(r)] **1** *n (sparkle)* scintillement *m*; *Fig (of occasion)* éclat *m*, faste *m*
2 *vi* scintiller; *Prov* **all that glitters is not gold** tout ce qui brille n'est pas d'or

glittering ['glɪtərɪŋ] *adj (jewels)* scintillant(e); *Fig (occasion, career)* brillant(e)

glitz [glɪts] *n* clinquant *m*, tape-à-l'œil *m*

glitzy ['glɪtsɪ] *adj Fam* tape-à-l'œil *inv*

gloat [gləʊt] *vi (at one's own success)* jubiler (**at** à l'idée de); *(about somebody else's misfortune)* se réjouir (**about** or **over** de); **I don't like to g., but...** ce n'est pas que ça me réjouisse, mais...

global ['gləʊbəl] *adj (comprehensive)* global(e); *(worldwide)* mondial(e); **g. village** village *m* planétaire; **g. warming** réchauffement *m* de la planète

globalization ['gləʊbəlaɪ'zeɪʃən] *n Econ* mondialisation *f*

globally ['gləʊbəlɪ] *adv (comprehensively)* globalement; *(worldwide)* mondialement

globe [gləʊb] *n (sphere)* globe *m*; *(with map)* globe terrestre; **the g.** *(the earth)* le globe terrestre; **to travel the g.** voyager dans le monde entier

globetrotter ['gləʊbtrɒtə(r)] *n Fam* globe-trotter *mf*

globule ['glɒbjuːl] *n* gouttelette *f*

gloom [gluːm] *n* (**a**) *(darkness)* obscurité *f* (**b**) *(sadness)* morosité *f*

gloomily ['gluːmɪlɪ] *adv (sadly)* sombrement

gloomy ['gluːmɪ] *adj* (**a**) *(dark)* sombre; *(weather)* morose (**b**) *(sad)* triste (**c**) *(pessimistic)* pessimiste; **g. thoughts** idées *fpl* noires

glorified ['glɔːrɪfaɪd] *adj* **she's just a g. secretary** elle n'est rien de plus qu'une secrétaire; **it's just a g. motor scooter** ce n'est pas qu'un scooter amélioré

glorify ['glɔːrɪfaɪ] *(pt & pp* **glorified)** *vt* (**a**) *(extol)* célébrer; *Rel* **to g. God** rendre gloire à Dieu (**b**) *(war, violence)* glorifier

glorious ['glɔːrɪəs] *adj* (**a**) *(reign, victory)* glorieux(euse) (**b**) *(view, sunshine)* magnifique

gloriously ['glɔːrɪəslɪ] *adv* (**a**) *(die, reign)* avec gloire (**b**) *(beautifully)* superbement; **it was g. sunny** il faisait un soleil splendide

glory ['glɔːrɪ] *n* (**a**) *(honour)* gloire *f* (**b**) *(splendour)* splendeur *f*

▸**glory in** *vt insep* se glorifier de

gloss¹ [glɒs] *n (in text)* glose *f*

gloss² *n (shine)* lustre *m*; *Fig* vernis *m*; *Fig* **to take the g. off sth** gâcher qch; **g. paint** peinture *f* brillante

▸**gloss over** *vt insep* passer sur

glossary ['glɒsərɪ] *(pl* **glossaries)** *n* glossaire *m*

glossy ['glɒsɪ] *adj (hair)* brillant(e); *(fur, leather)* luisant(e), lustré(e); *(surface)* brillant, poli(e); **g. brochure** brochure *f* luxueuse; **g. magazine** magazine *m* de luxe; **g. paper** papier *m* glacé

glottal stop ['glɒtəl'stɒp] *n Ling* coup *m* de glotte

glove [glʌv] *n* gant *m*; *Fig* **the gloves are off** tous les coups sont permis; **g. compartment** *(in car)* boîte *f* à gants; **g. puppet** marionnette *f* à gaine

glow [gləʊ] **1** *n (light)* lueur *f*; *(on cheeks)* couleurs *fpl*; **the g. of the setting sun** l'embrasement du couchant; *Fig* **a g. of pride/satisfaction** un vif sentiment de fierté/satisfaction

2 *vi (of light, fire)* rougeoyer; *Fig* **to be glowing with health** être resplendissant(e) de santé; *Fig* **to g. with pride/pleasure** rayonner de fierté/plaisir

glower ['glaʊə(r)] *vi* **to g. at sb** lancer des regards noirs à qn

glowing ['gləʊɪŋ] *adj (cigarette, coal)* incandescent(e); *(metal)* chauffé(e) au rouge; *Fig (praise, words)* chaleureux(euse); *(description, report)* enthousiaste; *Fig* **to paint sth in g. colours** présenter qch sous un jour très favorable

glow-worm ['gləʊwɜːm] *n* ver *m* luisant

glucose ['gluːkəʊs] *n* glucose *m*

glue [gluː] **1** *n* colle *f*

2 *vt* coller (**to** à); *Fig* **to be glued to the television** être cloué(e) devant la télévision

glue-sniffing ['gluːsnɪfɪŋ] *n* inhalation *f* de colle

glum [glʌm] *adj* triste, morose

glut [glʌt] **1** *n (of goods)* encombrement *m*

2 *vt (pt & pp* **glutted**) (**a**) *(market, economy)* encombrer, inonder (**b**) **to g. oneself (on)** se gaver (de)

glutinous ['gluːtɪnəs] *adj* gluant(e)

glutton ['glʌtən] *n (greedy person)* goinfre *mf*, glouton(onne) *m,f*; *Fig* **to be a g. for punishment** être masochiste

gluttony ['glʌtənɪ] *n* goinfrerie *f*, gloutonnerie *f*

glycerin ['glɪsərɪn], **glycerine** ['glɪsəriːn], **glycerol** ['glɪsərɒl] *n* glycérine *f*

GM [dʒiː'em] *adj* (**a**) *(abbr* **genetically modified**) génétiquement modifié(e) (**b**) *(abbr* **grant maintained**) subventionné(e) *(par l'État)*

GMO [dʒiːem'əʊ] *n (abbr* **genetically modified organism**) OGM *m*

GMT [dʒiːem'tiː] *n (abbr* **Greenwich Mean Time**) GMT *m*

gnarled [nɑːld] *adj* noueux(euse)

gnash [næʃ] *vt* **to g. one's teeth** grincer des dents

gnat [næt] *n* moucheron *m*

gnaw [nɔː] **1** *vt (of rodent)* ronger

2 *vi* (**a**) *(of rodent)* **to g. through sth** ronger qch (**b**) *Fig (of doubt, guilt)* **to g. away at sb** ronger qn

gnome [nəʊm] *n* gnome *m*

GNP [dʒiːen'piː] *n Econ (abbr* **Gross National Product**) PNB *m*

gnu [nuː] *n* gnou *m*

go [gəʊ] **1** *vi (3rd person singular* **goes** [gəʊz], *pt* **went** [went], *pp* **gone** [gɒn]) (**a**) *(move)* aller; **to go to France** aller en France; **to go to the doctor** aller chez le docteur; **to go home** rentrer chez soi; **to go swimming/skiing** (aller) nager/skier; **the proceeds will go to charity** l'argent recueilli sera versé à des œuvres de charité; *Fig* **where do we go from here?** et maintenant, qu'est-ce qu'on fait?

(**b**) *(leave)* partir, s'en aller; **I've got to go** il faut que j'y aille; **let's go!** allons-y!

(**c**) *(function)* marcher; *(of bell)* sonner; **to keep the conversation going** entretenir la conversation

(**d**) *(progress)* aller; **to go well/badly** bien/mal se passer; *Fam* **how's it going?** comment ça va?; **how**

does the tune/story go? c'est quoi, l'air/l'histoire, déjà?

(**e**) *(of time)* passer; **the time went quickly/slowly** le temps a passé vite/lentement; **it has just gone eight** il est huit heures à peine passées; **there are only five minutes to go** il ne reste que cinq minutes

(**f**) *(disappear, deteriorate)* disparaître; *(of light bulb)* griller; *(of fuse)* sauter; *(of batteries)* s'user; **her sight/voice is going** elle est en train de perdre la vue/la voix; **most of my money goes on food** l'essentiel de mon argent passe dans la nourriture

(**g**) *(forming future)* **to be going to do sth** aller faire qch; **I was going to walk** j'allais y aller à pied; **it's going to rain** il va pleuvoir

(**h**) *(match)* aller (**with** avec); **these colours go/don't go** ces couleurs vont bien/ne vont pas ensemble

(**i**) *(be available)* **there's a job going at the factory** il y a une place à l'usine; **is there any wine going?** est-ce qu'il y a du vin?; **it went for £12** on l'a vendu 12 livres

(**j**) *(fit)* entrer; **the piano won't go through the door** le piano ne passera pas par la porte; **four into three won't go** trois n'est pas divisible par quatre

(**k**) *(belong)* aller; **the cups go on that shelf** les tasses vont sur cette étagère

(**l**) *(become)* devenir; **to go crazy** devenir fou (folle); **to go red** rougir; **to go cold** refroidir

(**m**) *(be the rule)* **what she says goes** c'est elle qui commande

(**n**) *Fam (urinate)* aller aux toilettes

(**o**) *Am* **two burgers to go** *(to take away)* deux hamburgers à emporter

2 *vt* (**a**) *(make sound) & Fam (say)* faire; **cows go moo** la vache fait meuh; **to go bang/plop** faire paf/plouf

(**b**) *(idioms)* **to go it alone** se lancer en solo; **to go one better than sb** faire mieux que qn, surenchérir sur qn; *Fam* **I could really go a beer!** je me ferais bien une bière!

3 *n (pl* **goes**) (**a**) *(expressing activity)* **to be on the go** ne pas arrêter; **she had three boyfriends on the go at the same time** elle avait trois copains en même temps; **it's all go** ça n'arrête pas; **from the word go** dès le début

(**b**) *(energy)* **to be full of go** être très dynamique

(**c**) *(success)* **to make a go of sth** réussir qch

(**d**) *(turn)* tour *m*; **(it's) your go!** *(in game)* c'est ton tour!, c'est à toi!; **to have a go at doing sth** essayer de faire qch; *Fam* **let's have a go!** allons-y!; *(let us try)* laisse-moi essayer!; **at one go** d'un coup; **£1 a go** *(at fair)* 1 livre le tour

(**e**) *(idioms)* **to have a go at sb** incendier qn

▸**go about 1** *vi (circulate) (of person)* se promener; *(of rumour)* circuler; **you can't go about saying things like that!** il ne faut pas raconter des choses pareilles!; **there's a bug going about** il y a un microbe qui se promène

2 *vt insep* (**a**) *(travel) (country)* parcourir (**b**) *(tackle) (task)* vaquer à; **to go about doing sth** s'y prendre pour faire qch; **how do I go about getting a licence?** que dois-je faire pour obtenir un permis?

▸**go across** *vt insep & vi* traverser

▸**go after** *vt insep (pursue)* **to go after sb** courir après qn; **to go after sth** essayer d'obtenir qch

▸**go against** *vt insep* (**a**) *(contradict) (principles, instincts)* aller à l'encontre de (**b**) *(be unfavourable to)*

the decision went against him la décision lui a été défavorable

▶**go ahead** *vi* (**a**) *(take place)* avoir lieu; **to go ahead with sth** commencer *ou* entreprendre qch; **may I say something? – go ahead** puis-je dire quelque chose? – allez-y (**b**) *(go in front)* passer devant; **to go ahead of sb** devancer qn

▶**go along** *vi (proceed)* se dérouler; **as we go along** en chemin; **to do sth as one goes along** faire qch au fur et à mesure

▶**go along with** *vt insep (suggestion, plan)* approuver, être d'accord avec

▶**go at** *vt insep (person, task)* s'attaquer à

▶**go away** *vi (leave)* partir; *(disappear)* disparaître; **go away!** allez-vous-en!; **to go away on business/for the weekend** partir en voyage d'affaires/en weekend

▶**go back** *vi* (**a**) *(return)* revenir; **to go back to doing sth** se remettre à faire qch; **to go back to sleep** se rendormir; **to go back to one's old ways** reprendre ses anciennes habitudes (**b**) *(in time)* **to go back to** remonter à; *Fam* **we go back a long way** ça fait long-temps qu'on se connaît

▶**go back on** *vt insep (promise)* revenir sur

▶**go before 1** *vi (precede)* précéder

2 *vt insep* **to go before the court** *(of defendant, case)* passer au tribunal

▶**go by 1** *vi* (**a**) *(pass)* passer; **to watch the world go by** regarder passer les gens (**b**) *(of time)* s'écouler

2 *vt insep* (**a**) *(be guided by)* **to go by appearances** juger d'après les apparences; **to go by the rules** respecter les règles (**b**) *(be known by)* **to go by the name of** être connu(e) sous le nom de

▶**go down 1** *vt insep (descend)* descendre

2 *vi* (**a**) *(descend)* descendre; *(of sun)* se coucher; *(of ship)* sombrer; **to go down on one's knees** s'age-nouiller; *Fig* se mettre à genoux; **to go down with an illness** tomber malade (**b**) *(be defeated)* être vain-cu(e); **I'm not going to go down without a fight** je me battrai jusqu'au bout (**c**) *(of level, temperature, prices)* baisser; *(of tyre, balloon)* se dégonfler (**d**) *(be received)* **to go down well/badly** être bien/mal re-çu(e); **he has gone down in history as a tyrant** l'his-toire a retenu de lui l'image d'un tyran

▶**go for** *vt insep* (**a**) *(attack)* attaquer; **if you really want the job, go for it!** si tu veux vraiment le poste, bats-toi!; *Fam* **go for it!** vas-y! (**b**) *(like)* avoir un faible pour (**c**) *(choose)* prendre (**d**) **he has got a lot going for him** il a bien des atouts (**e**) *(apply to)* s'ap-pliquer à; **the same goes for you** ça vaut aussi pour toi

▶**go in** *vi (enter)* entrer; *(fit)* rentrer; *(of sun)* se cacher

▶**go in for** *vt insep* (**a**) *(competition)* s'inscrire à (**b**) *(like)* **she doesn't go in for cooking/sports** elle n'est pas très portée sur la cuisine/les sports

▶**go into** *vt insep* (**a**) *(enter)* entrer dans (**b**) *(examine)* examiner

▶**go off** *vi* (**a**) *(leave)* partir (**with** avec) (**b**) *(of meat, fish)* s'avarier; *(of milk)* tourner (**c**) *(of bomb)* exploser; *(of alarm)* se déclencher; **the gun went off** le coup est parti (**d**) *(of event)* **to go off well** *or* **smoothly** se dérouler bien (**e**) *(stop working)* **the power went off** l'électricité a été coupée; **the light went off** la lumi-ère s'est éteinte

2 *vt insep (lose liking for)* ne plus aimer, se lasser de; **I've gone off the idea** l'idée ne me séduit plus

▶**go on 1** *vi* (**a**) *(continue)* continuer; **to go on doing sth** continuer à faire qch; **as time went on** avec le temps (**b**) *(proceed)* **to go on to sth** passer à qch; **to go on to do sth** poursuivre en faisant qch (**c**) *(talk excessively)* **don't go on about it!** arrête de parler de ça!; **he does go on a bit** il est un peu soûlant; **to go on at sb** s'en prendre à qn (**d**) *(happen)* se passer; **what's going on here?** qu'est-ce qui se passe ici? (**e**) *(of electricity, light, heating)* s'allumer

2 *vt insep* (**a**) *(be guided by)* se fonder sur; **the police have nothing to go on** la police n'a rien sur quoi se fonder (**b**) *(approach)* **she's two going on three** elle va sur ses trois ans; *Hum* **he's nine going on nineteen** il a neuf ans mais il est déjà très mûr

▶**go out** *vi* (**a**) *(leave)* sortir; **to go out for a meal** aller au restaurant; **to go out on strike** se mettre en grève (**b**) *(date)* sortir ensemble; **to go out with sb** sortir avec qn (**c**) *(of fire, light)* s'éteindre (**d**) *(become un-fashionable)* passer de mode (**e**) *(be eliminated)* être éliminé(e) (**f**) *(of TV, radio programme)* être diffusé(e)

▶**go over 1** *vi* (**a**) *(cross)* **to go over to sb** aller vers qn (**b**) *(switch)* **to go over to sth** passer à qch (**c**) *(of sug-gestion, joke)* **to go over well/badly** être bien/mal reçu(e)

2 *vt insep* (**a**) *(bridge)* passer; *(road)* traverser; **the ball went over the wall** la balle est passée par-des-sus le mur (**b**) *(examine)* passer en revue; *(figures, ac-counts)* vérifier; **to go over sth in one's mind** repasser qch dans son esprit

▶**go round 1** *vt insep* **to go round town** faire un tour en ville; **to go round the shops** faire les magasins

2 *vi* (**a**) *(visit)* **I said I'd go round (and see her)** j'ai dit que j'irai la voir; **she's gone round to a friend's** elle est allée voir un ami (**b**) *(circulate)* *(of rumour)* circu-ler; *(of cold, flu)* se promener (**c**) *(be enough)* **there was enough food/drink to go round** il y avait assez à manger/boire pour tout le monde

▶**go through 1** *vt insep* (**a**) *(penetrate)* traverser (**b**) *(suffer)* subir (**c**) *(complete)* *(formalities)* accomplir (**d**) *(examine)* passer en revue; *(one's notes, speech)* revoir; *(suitcase, house)* fouiller; **to go through sb's pockets** fouiller les poches de qn (**e**) *(use up)* *(money)* dépenser; *(food)* consommer; **we've gone through six bottles of milk** nous avons bu six bouteilles de lait

2 *vi (be completed)* *(of deal)* être conclu(e); *(of bill)* passer; *(of divorce)* être prononcé(e)

▶**go through with** *vt insep* aller jusqu'au bout de; **I can't go through with the wedding** finalement, je ne me marie pas; **I can't go through with it** je ne peux pas le faire

▶**go under** *vi (of ship)* couler; *Fig (of firm)* faire faillite

▶**go up 1** *vt insep* monter

2 *vi* (**a**) *(climb, rise)* monter; *(of theatre curtain)* se le-ver; **to go up to bed** monter se coucher; **a shout went up from the crowd** un cri s'éleva de la foule; *Fig* **to go up in the world** *(socially)* faire son chemin (**b**) *(of prices, temperature)* monter, grimper; **to go up in sb's estimation** monter dans l'estime de qn (**c**) *(ex-plode)* sauter

▶**go up to** *vt insep* (**a**) *(approach)* se diriger vers (**b**) *(reach)* aller jusqu'à

▶**go with** *vt insep* (**a**) *(accompany)* aller (de pair) avec; **a company car goes with the job** le poste donne droit à une voiture de fonction (**b**) *(harmonize with)* aller avec

▶**go without 1** *vi* se priver; **I'd rather go without** je préfère m'en passer
2 *vt insep* se passer de
goad [gəʊd] **1** *n Fig (remark, criticism)* aiguillon *m*
2 *vt Fig (person)* provoquer; **to g. sb into doing sth** harceler qn jusqu'à ce qu'il fasse qch
▶**goad on** *vt sep* aiguillonner
go-ahead ['gəʊəhed] **1** *n* **to give sb/sth the g.** donner le feu vert à qn/qch
2 *adj (enterprising)* entreprenant(e), dynamique
goal [gəʊl] *n* (**a**) *(aim)* but *m*, objectif *m* (**b**) *(in football, hockey)* but *m*; **g. kick** coup *m* de pied de but; **g. line** ligne *f* de but; **g. scorer** buteur(euse) *m,f*
goalkeeper ['gəʊlkiːpə(r)], *Fam* **goalie** ['gəʊlɪ] *n* gardien *m* de but, goal *m*
goalless ['gəʊllɪs] *adj* **g. draw** match *m* nul
goalmouth ['gəʊlmaʊθ] *n (in football)* (entrée *f* du) but *m*
goalpost ['gəʊlpəʊst] *n* poteau *m* de but; **the goalposts** les buts *mpl; Fig* **to move** *or* **shift the goalposts** changer les règles du jeu
goat [gəʊt] *n* chèvre *f*; **g.'s milk** lait *m* de chèvre; *Fam* **it really gets my g.!** ça me tape vraiment sur les nerfs!; *Fam* **to act** *or* **play the g.** faire l'idiot(e)
goatherd ['gəʊthɜːd] *n* chevrier(ère) *m,f*
goatskin ['gəʊtskɪn] *n* peau *f* de chèvre
gob [gɒb] *Br very Fam* **1** *n (mouth)* gueule *f*; **shut your g.!** *(ferme)* ta gueule!
2 *vi (pt & pp* **gobbed***) (spit)* mollarder
gobble ['gɒbəl] **1** *vt (eat)* engloutir
2 *vi (of turkey)* glouglouter
▶**gobble up** *vt sep also Fig* engloutir
gobbledygook ['gɒbəldɪɡuːk] *n Fam* charabia *m*
go-between ['gəʊbɪtwiːn] *n* intermédiaire *mf*
goblet ['gɒblɪt] *n* verre *m* à pied; *(in medieval times)* coupe *f*
goblin ['gɒblɪn] *n* lutin *m*
gobsmacked ['gɒbsmækt] *adj Br Fam* **to be g.** en rester estomaqué(e)
go-cart = **go-kart**
god [gɒd] *n* (**a**) *(divine being)* dieu *m*; **G.** Dieu *m*; **G. forbid!** Dieu m'en garde!; **G. willing** si Dieu le veut; **I wish to G. I hadn't told him** si seulement je ne lui avais rien dit; **in G.'s name** au nom du Ciel; *Fam* **(oh) my G.!** mon Dieu!; *Fam* **for G.'s sake!** pour l'amour du ciel!; *Fam* **G. knows** Dieu seul le sait; *Fam* **he thinks he's G.'s gift to women** il s'imagine que toutes les femmes sont folles de lui (**b**) *Fam* **the gods** *(in theatre)* le poulailler
godchild ['gɒdtʃaɪld] *n* filleul(e) *m,f*
goddam(n) ['gɒdæm] *Am very Fam* **1** *adj* sacré(e), fichu(e); **that g. dog!** ce sacré chien!
2 *adv* vachement
3 *exclam* nom de Dieu!
goddaughter ['gɒddɔːtə(r)] *n* filleule *f*
goddess ['gɒdɪs] *n* déesse *f*
godfather ['gɒdfɑːðə(r)] *n* parrain *m*
god-fearing ['gɒdfɪːrɪŋ] *adj* pieux(euse)
godforsaken ['gɒdfəseɪkən] *adj* perdu(e)
godless ['gɒdlɪs] *adj* impie
godmother ['gɒdmʌðə(r)] *n* marraine *f*
godparent ['gɒdpeərənt] *n (godfather)* parrain *m; (godmother)* marraine *f*; **my godparents** mon parrain et ma marraine
godsend ['gɒdsend] *n* aubaine *f*

godson ['gɒdsʌn] *n* filleul *m*
go-getter ['gəʊgetə(r)] *n Fam* battant(e) *m,f*
goggle ['gɒgəl] *vi* ouvrir des yeux ronds; **to g. at sb/sth** regarder qn/qch avec des yeux ronds
goggle-eyed ['gɒgəlaɪd] *adv Fam* avec des yeux ronds
goggles ['gɒgəlz] *npl (for swimming)* lunettes *fpl* de plongée; *(for skiing)* lunettes de ski; *(for worker)* lunettes protectrices
go-go dancer ['gəʊgəʊ'dɑːnsə(r)] *n* danseuse *f* de boîte de nuit
going ['gəʊɪŋ] **1** *n* (**a**) *(progress)* **that's very good g.!** voilà qui n'est pas mal du tout!; **it's slow g.** *(at work)* ça n'avance pas vite (**b**) *(condition of ground)* terrain *m*; *Fig* **the book/film was pretty heavy g.** le livre/film était plutôt indigeste; *Fig* **to get out while the g. is good** se retirer tant que la chance nous/leur/*etc* est favorable
2 *adj* (**a**) *(successful)* **a g. concern** une affaire qui tourne (**b**) *(current) (price, rate)* courant(e), actuel(elle)
going-away ['gəʊɪŋə'weɪ] *adj* **g. outfit** = tenue de voyage de noces; **g. party/present** fête *f*/cadeau *m* d'adieu
going-over ['gəʊɪŋ'əʊvə(r)] *n Fam* **to give sb a g.** *(beating)* tabasser qn; *(criticism)* sonner les cloches à qn
goings-on ['gəʊɪŋzɒn] *npl Fam (activities)* activités *fpl*; *(events)* événements *mpl*
goitre, *Am* **goiter** ['gɔɪtə(r)] *n* goitre *m*
go-kart ['gəʊkɑːt] *n (child's toy)* petit chariot *m; (with engine)* kart *m*; **g. racing** karting *m*
gold [gəʊld] **1** *n* or *m*; **g. bullion** or en barre; **g. dust** poussière *f* d'or; **tickets are like g. dust** les billets valent de l'or; **g. leaf** *or* **foil** feuille *f* d'or; **g. medal** médaille *f* d'or; *also Fig* **g. mine** mine *f* d'or; **g. plate** orfèvrerie *f*; *Fin* **g. reserves** réserves *fpl* d'or; *Am Hist* **the G. Rush** la ruée vers l'or
2 *adj (made of gold)* en or; *(gold-coloured)* doré(e)
gold-digger ['gəʊld'dɪgə(r)] *n Fam Pej (woman)* croqueuse *f* de diamants
golden ['gəʊldən] *adj (made of gold)* en or; *(gold-coloured)* doré(e); **a g. opportunity** une occasion en or; **the g. age** l'âge *m* d'or; **g. boy** enfant *m* chéri; **g. eagle** aigle *m* royal; **g. girl** enfant *f* chérie; **g. handshake** *(retirement bonus)* indemnité *f* de départ; **g. jubilee** jubilé *m*; **g. rule** règle *f* d'or; *Fin* **g. share** action *f* privilégiée; **g. wedding** noces *fpl* d'or
goldfinch ['gəʊldfɪntʃ] *n* chardonneret *m*
goldfish ['gəʊldfɪʃ] *n (pl* **goldfish***)* poisson *m* rouge; **g. bowl** bocal *m* à poissons rouges; **it's like living in a g. bowl** c'est comme vivre en vitrine
gold-plated [gəʊld'pleɪtɪd] *adj* plaqué(e) or
goldsmith ['gəʊldsmɪθ] *n* orfèvre *m*
golf [gɒlf] *n* golf *m*; **g. ball** balle *f* de golf; **g. club** *(stick, association)* club *m* de golf; **g. course** terrain *m* de golf
golfer ['gɒlfə(r)] *n* joueur(euse) *m,f* de golf
golfing ['gɒlfɪŋ] *n* golf *m*; **g. umbrella** grand parapluie *m* (de golf)
golly ['gɒlɪ] *exclam Fam Old-fashioned* fichtre!
gondola ['gɒndələ] *n* (**a**) *(boat)* gondole *f* (**b**) *(cable car)* cabine *f* de téléphérique
gondolier [gɒndə'lɪə(r)] *n* gondolier *m*
gone [gɒn] **1** *adj* (**a**) *(past)* **it's g. nine o'clock** il est neuf heures passées (**b**) *Fam* **to be six months g.** *(pregnant)* être enceinte de six mois; *Fam* **to be pretty far g.** *(drunk)* être complètement bourré(e);

Fam **to be g. on sb** *(infatuated)* avoir le béguin pour qn

2 *pp of* **go**

goner ['gɒnə(r)] *n Fam* **I thought she was a g.** *(would die)* j'ai cru qu'elle allait y passer; **I'm a g. if she finds out** si elle l'apprend, je suis mort

gong [gɒŋ] *n* gong *m*; *Br Fam (medal)* breloque *f*

gonna ['gɒnə] *Fam* = **going to**

gonorrhoea, *Am* **gonorrhea** [gɒnə'rɪə] *n* blennorragie *f*; **to have g.** avoir une blennorragie

goo [gu:] *n Fam* (**a**) *(sticky substance)* substance *f* visqueuse (**b**) *(sentimentality)* guimauve *f*

good [gʊd] **1** *n* (**a**) bien *m*; **to do g.** faire le bien; **he's up to no g.** il prépare un mauvais coup; **to see the g. in sb/sth** voir les bons côtés de qn/qch

(**b**) *(benefit)* **I did it for your own g.** je l'ai fait pour ton bien; **it was all to the g.** c'était tout bénéfice; **we were £100 to the g.** nous avons fait 100 livres de bénéfice; **for the g. of one's health** pour sa santé; **for the common g.** dans l'intérêt général; **it will do you g.** cela te fera du bien; **it won't do any g.** cela ne servira à rien; **what's the g. of that?** à quoi bon?; **it's no g.** ça ne sert à rien; **it's no g. complaining** cela ne sert à rien de se plaindre; **he's no g.** *(incompetent)* il est nul; *(morally bad)* il ne vaut pas grand-chose

(**c**) **for g.** *(permanently)* pour toujours; **she is gone for g.** elle est partie pour de bon

2 *adj (comparative* **better** ['betə(r)], *superlative* **best** [best]) (**a**) *(in quality)* bon (bonne); *(weather, handwriting)* beau (belle); **she looks g. in that hat** ce chapeau lui va bien, elle est bien avec ce chapeau; **to taste g.** avoir bon goût; **(that) sounds g.!** bonne idée!; **g. to eat** comestible; **it's g. to see you** ça fait plaisir de vous voir; *Fam* **that's a g. one!** *(of story, joke)* elle est bien bonne!; **he thinks he's too g. for us** il se croit trop bien pour nous; **to earn g. money** bien gagner sa vie; **you've got a g. chance** tu as tes chances; **to be on to a g. thing** être sur un bon filon; **to have a g. time** s'amuser; **to show sb a g. time** faire passer un bon moment à qn; **all in g. time** chaque chose en son temps; **too g. to be true** trop beau pour être vrai; **as g. as new** comme neuf (neuve); **he as g. as called me a liar** pour un peu, il m'aurait traité de menteur; **the g. old days** le bon vieux temps; **g. afternoon!** bonjour!; **the G. Book** la sainte Bible; **he's a g. friend** c'est un ami; **G. Friday** le Vendredi Saint; *Fam* **g. grief!** fichtre!; **the g. life** la belle vie; *Fam* **g. Lord!, g. heavens!, g. gracious!** bon sang!; **g. morning!** bonjour!; **g. night!** bonne nuit!; **the G. Samaritan** le bon Samaritain

(**b**) *(advantageous)* **a g. opportunity** une bonne occasion; **to be in a g. position to do sth** être bien placé(e) pour faire qch; **it's looking g.** ça se présente bien

(**c**) *(beneficial)* bon (bonne); **he doesn't know what's g. for him** il n'a pas un sou de bon sens; **to be g. for business** être bon pour les affaires; **it's a g. thing we were here** heureusement que nous étions là; **g. riddance!** bon débarras!

(**d**) *(skilful)* bon (bonne) (**at** en); **to be g. with one's hands** être habile de ses mains; **to be g. with children** savoir y faire avec les enfants; **to be g. in bed** bien faire l'amour

(**e**) *(well-behaved)* sage; **be g.!** *(to child)* sois sage!; **to be as g. as gold** être sage comme une image; **to lead a g. life** mener une vie respectable; **g. conduct** *or* **behaviour** bonne conduite *f*

(**f**) *(kind)* gentil(ille); **that's very g. of you** c'est bien aimable *ou* très gentil de votre part; **he was very g. about it** il s'est montré très compréhensif; **to do sb a g. turn** rendre un service à qn

(**g**) *(valid)* **a g. reason** une bonne raison, une raison valable; **he's g. for £25,000** *(has in credit)* il dispose de 25 000 livres

(**h**) *(for emphasis)* bon (bonne); **a g. two hours** deux bonnes heures; **a g. deal of, a g. many** beaucoup de; **to have a g. look at sb/sth** bien regarder qn/qch; **to have a g. cry** pleurer un bon coup; **a g. long time** un bien long moment

(**i**) **to make g.** *(of person)* faire son chemin; **to make g. one's losses** compenser ses pertes; **to make g. one's promise** tenir sa promesse; **he made g. his escape** il a réussi son évasion

3 *adv* (**a**) **I'll do it when I'm g. and ready** je le ferai quand ça me chantera

(**b**) *(as comment, answer)* bien; **I feel better today – g.** je me sens mieux aujourd'hui – tant mieux

> **Good Friday**
>
> En Grande-Bretagne, il est traditionnel, le jour du vendredi saint, de manger des "hot cross buns" (petits pains ronds aux fruits secs, marqués d'une croix).

goodbye [gʊd'baɪ] *n* au revoir *m*; **g.!** au revoir!; **to say g. to sb** dire au revoir à qn; **he can say g. to his hopes of winning** il peut dire adieu à ses espoirs de victoire

good-for-nothing ['gʊdfənʌθɪŋ] *n* bon (bonne) *m,f* à rien

good-humoured, *Am* **good-humored** [gʊd'hju:məd] *adj (debate, meeting)* détendu(e); **to be g.** *(of person)* avoir un caractère enjoué

good-looking ['gʊdlʊkɪŋ] *adj* beau (belle)

good-natured [gʊd'neɪtʃəd] *adj (person)* d'un caractère agréable; *(remarks, laugh)* bon enfant *inv*

goodness ['gʊdnɪs] *n* (**a**) *(of person)* bonté *f* (**b**) *(of food)* qualités *fpl* nutritives (**c**) *(in exclamations)* **g. (me)!** mon Dieu!; **thank g.!** Dieu merci!; **for g. sake!** pour l'amour de Dieu!

goods [gʊdz] *npl* (**a**) *Law* biens *mpl* (**b**) *(articles)* articles *mpl*, marchandises *fpl*; *Fig* **to deliver the g.** remplir ses engagements; *Fig* **to come up with the g.** faire le nécessaire; **g. train/depot** train *m*/dépôt *m* de marchandises

good-tempered [gʊd'tempəd] *adj (person)* d'un caractère facile; *(discussion)* aimable

goodwill [gʊd'wɪl] *n* (**a**) *(benevolence)* bienveillance *f*; *(willingness)* bonne volonté *f* (**b**) *Com* fonds *m* de commerce

goody ['gʊdɪ] *Fam* **1** *n (pl* **goodies)** (**a**) *(person)* bon *m*; **the goodies and the baddies** les bons *mpl* et les méchants *mpl* (**b**) **goodies** *(nice food)* bonnes choses *fpl*; *(nice things)* petits cadeaux *mpl*

2 *exclam* chouette!

goody-goody ['gʊdɪgʊdɪ] *Fam Pej* **1** *n (pl* **goody-goodies)** fayot *m*

2 *adj* fayot

gooey ['gu:ɪ] *adj Fam* (**a**) *(sticky)* gluant(e) (**b**) *(sentimental)* à la guimauve

goof [gu:f] *Am Fam* **1** *n* (**a**) *(blunder)* gaffe *f*, bourde *f* (**b**) *(idiot)* cave *m*

2 *vi* faire une gaffe *ou* une bourde

▸**goof about, goof around** *vi Am Fam* faire l'idiot(e)

▶**goof off** *Am Fam* **1** *vt insep* **to g. off work** ne pas aller bosser
2 *vi* flemmarder, glandouiller

▶**goof up** *Fam* **1** *vt sep* bousiller, saloper
2 *vi* merder

goofy ['gu:fɪ] *adj Fam* (**a**) *(stupid)* loufoque (**b**) *Br (buck-toothed)* qui a les dents en avant

goolies ['gu:lɪz] *npl Br very Fam (testicles)* couilles *fpl*

goon [gu:n] *n Fam* (**a**) *Br (stupid person)* imbécile *mf* (**b**) *Am (thug)* gorille *m*

goose [gu:s] *(pl* **geese** [gi:s]) *n* oie *f; Fig* **his g. is cooked** il est fichu; **to kill the g. that lays the golden egg** tuer la poule aux œufs d'or; *Br* **g. pimples,** *Am* **g. bumps** chair *f* de poule

gooseberry ['gʊzbərɪ] *(pl* **gooseberries**) *n* groseille *f* à maquereau; *Br Fam* **to play g.** tenir la chandelle; **g. bush** groseillier *m*

gooseflesh ['gu:sfleʃ] *n* chair *f* de poule

goose-step ['gu:sstep] **1** *n* pas *m* de l'oie
2 *vi (pt & pp* **goose-stepped**) marcher au pas de l'oie

gopher ['gəʊfə(r)] *n (animal)* spermophile *m*

gore [gɔ:(r)] **1** *n (blood)* sang *m* (versé)
2 *vt (of bull)* encorner; **to be gored to death** être tué(e) à coups de corne

gorge [gɔ:dʒ] **1** *n (valley)* gorge *f,* défilé *m*
2 *vt* **to g. oneself** se gorger, se gaver (**on** de)
3 *vi* se gorger, se gaver (**on** de)

gorgeous ['gɔ:dʒəs] *adj* magnifique; *(meal, food)* excellent(e)

gorilla [gə'rɪlə] *n* gorille *m*

gormless ['gɔ:mlɪs] *adj Br Fam* balourd(e)

gorse [gɔ:s] *n* ajoncs *mpl*

gory ['gɔ:rɪ] *adj (film, crime, war)* sanglant(e); *(covered in blood)* ensanglanté(e); *Fig & Hum* **in g. detail** avec tous les détails

gosh [gɒʃ] *exclam Fam* ça alors!

goshawk ['gɒshɔ:k] *n* autour *m*

gosling ['gɒzlɪŋ] *n* oison *m*

go-slow [gəʊ'sləʊ] *n Br* grève *f* du zèle

gospel ['gɒspəl] *n* évangile *m;* **to take sth as g.** accepter qch comme parole d'évangile; **g. (music)** gospel *m;* **g. singer** chanteur(euse) *m,f* de gospel

gossamer ['gɒsəmə(r)] *n* (**a**) *(spider's web)* fils *mpl* de la Vierge (**b**) *(fabric)* gaze *f* légère

gossip ['gɒsɪp] **1** *n* (**a**) *(person)* bavard(e) *m,f; (ill-natured)* commère *f* (**b**) *(talk)* bavardages *mpl; (ill-natured)* commérage(s) *m(pl);* **have you heard the latest g.?** tu sais la nouvelle?; **to have a g. (about)** bavarder (à propos de); **g. column** *(in newspaper)* chronique *f* mondaine
2 *vi* bavarder; *(ill-naturedly)* colporter des commérages

gossipy ['gɒsɪpɪ] *adj (person)* bavard(e); *(ill-natured)* cancanier(ère); *(letter, conversation)* plein(e) de petits potins

got [gɒt] *pt & pp of* **get**

Gothic ['gɒθɪk] **1** *n (artistic style, language)* gothique *m*
2 *adj* gothique

gotta ['gɒtə] *very Fam* = **got to**

gotten ['gɒtən] *Am pp of* **get**

▶**gouge out** [gaʊdʒ] *vt sep (hole, path)* creuser; **to g. sb's eye out** arracher l'œil à qn

goulash ['gu:læʃ] *n* goulasch *m*

gourd [gʊəd] *n* gourde *f*

gourmet ['gʊəmeɪ] *n* gourmet *m,* gastronome *mf;* **g. restaurant** restaurant *m* gastronomique

gout [gaʊt] *n (disease)* goutte *f*

Gov (**a**) *(abbr* **government**) gouvernement *m* (**b**) *(abbr* **governor**) gouverneur *m*

govern ['gʌvən] *vt* (**a**) *(state, country)* gouverner (**b**) *(of scientific law)* régir (**c**) *(emotions)* maîtriser, contenir

governess ['gʌvənɪs] *n* gouvernante *f*

governing ['gʌvənɪŋ] *adj (party, coalition)* au pouvoir; *(concept, principle)* directeur(trice); **g. body** conseil *m* d'administration

government ['gʌvənmənt] *n* gouvernement *m;* **g. intervention** intervention *f* du gouvernement

governmental [gʌvən'mentəl] *adj* gouvernemental(e)

governor ['gʌvənə(r)] *n (of colony, bank, US state)* gouverneur *m; (of prison)* directeur *m; (of school)* = fonctionnaire gestionnaire d'une école; *Br Fam* **the g.** *(boss)* le patron; **g. general** gouverneur *m* général

governorship ['gʌvənəʃɪp] *n (post)* poste *m* de gouverneur; *(function)* fonctions *fpl* de gouverneur

Govt *(abbr* **government**) gouvernement *m*

gown [gaʊn] *n (of woman)* robe *f; (of magistrate, academic)* robe, toge *f; (of surgeon)* blouse *f*

GP [dʒi:'pi:] *n Br (abbr* **general practitioner**) *(médecin m)* généraliste *mf*

GPO [dʒi:pi:'əʊ] *n Br Formerly (abbr* **General Post Office**) ≃ PTT *fpl*

gr *(abbr* **gramme(s)**) g

grab [græb] **1** *n* **to make a g. at** *or* **for sth** essayer d'attraper qch; *Fam* **to be up for grabs** être à qui veut le prendre; *(be for sale)* être à qui veut l'acheter
2 *vt (pt & pp* **grabbed**) (**a**) *(seize)* **to g. (hold of) sb/ sth** saisir qn/qch; *(more tightly)* empoigner qn/qch; **I'll g. a sandwich later** j'avalerai un sandwich plus tard (**b**) *Fam (attract)* **the idea doesn't g. me** ça ne me dit rien; **how does that g. you?** ça te dit?
3 *vi* **to g. at sb** essayer de s'agripper à qn; **to g. at sth** essayer d'attraper qch

grace [greɪs] **1** *n* (**a**) *(of movement, dancer, manners)* grâce *f;* **to do sth with (a) good/bad g.** faire qch de bonne/mauvaise grâce; **to have the (good) g. to do sth** avoir la grâce de faire qch (**b**) *(favour)* **to be in sb's good graces** être dans les bonnes grâces de qn (**c**) *Rel* **in a state of g.** en état de grâce; **to fall from g.** perdre la grâce; *Fig* tomber en disgrâce; **there, but for the g. of God, go I** je remercie le ciel de m'avoir épargné (**d**) *(for payment of a bill)* **seven days' g.** sept jours de délai *ou* de grâce (**e**) *(prayer before meal)* bénédicité *m* (**f**) *(form of address)* **Your G.** *(to bishop)* Monseigneur; *(to duke)* Monsieur le duc; *(to duchess)* Madame la duchesse
2 *vt* (**a**) *(honour)* honorer (**with** de) (**b**) *(decorate)* embellir, enjoliver

graceful ['greɪsfʊl] *adj (person, movement)* gracieux(euse); *(speech, style)* élégant(e)

gracefully ['greɪsfʊlɪ] *adv* avec grâce, gracieusement

graceless ['greɪslɪs] *adj* (**a**) *(inelegant)* disgracieux(-euse) (**b**) *(rude)* effronté(e)

gracious ['greɪʃəs] **1** *adj* (**a**) *(kind, polite)* poli(e), affable; *(in victory)* courtois(e) (**b**) *(elegant)* pleine(e) de raffinement
2 *exclam* **g. (me)!, goodness g.!** mon Dieu!

graciously ['greɪʃəslɪ] *adv* avec grâce; *(accept, invite)* de bonne grâce

gradation [grə'deɪʃən] *n (of colours)* gradation *f; (on thermometer)* degré *m; (of meaning)* nuance *f*

grade [greɪd] **1** *n* (**a**) *(rank)* grade *m*, rang *m; (in profession)* échelon *m* (**b**) *(quality)* qualité *f; (of vegetable, fruit)* calibre *m; Fig* **to make the g.** se montrer à la hauteur (**c**) *Am Sch (mark)* note *f* (**d**) *Am (year at school)* classe *f;* **g. school** ≃ école *f* primaire

    2 *vt* (**a**) *(classify)* classer; *(fruit, vegetables)* calibrer (**b**) *Am (essay, exercise)* noter

gradient ['greɪdɪənt] *n* (**a**) *(of slope)* dénivellation *f* (**b**) *(of temperature)* gradient *m*

gradual ['grædjʊəl] *adj* progressif(ive), graduel(elle)

gradualism ['grædjʊəlɪzm] *n* gradualisme *m*

gradually ['grædjʊəlɪ] *adv* progressivement, peu à peu

graduate 1 *n* ['grædjʊət] *Br (from university)* ≃ licencié(e) *m,f; Am (from high school)* bachelier(ère) *m,f*

    2 *adj* ['grædjʊət] *Am (postgraduate)* **g. studies** études *fpl* de troisième cycle

    3 *vi* ['grædjʊeɪt] (**a**) *Br (from university)* obtenir sa licence; *Am (from high school)* avoir son bac (**b**) *(progress)* **to g. from sth to sth** passer de qch à qch

graduated ['grædjʊeɪtɪd] *adj (thermometer)* gradué(e); *(pay rise)* progressif(ive)

graduation [grædjʊ'eɪʃən] *n (from school, university)* remise *f* des diplômes; **g. ceremony** cérémonie *f* de remise des diplômes

---

Graduation

Dans les pays anglo-saxons, la "graduation" est la cérémonie officielle au cours de laquelle les étudiants reçoivent leur diplôme des mains du président de l'université. La cérémonie de remise des diplômes est une occasion solennelle; dans certaines universités elle se fait en latin et les étudiants doivent porter la toge traditionnelle avec capuchon et mortier. Le diplôme ainsi que la photo prise le jour de la cérémonie sont ensuite gardés précieusement par la famille. Aux États-Unis, le terme "graduation" désigne également la cérémonie organisée en l'honneur des élèves qui achèvent leurs études secondaires.

---

graffiti [græ'fiːtiː] *n* graffiti *mpl;* **a piece of g.** un graffiti

graft¹ [grɑːft] **1** *n (technique)* greffe *f; (thing grafted)* greffon *m*

    2 *vt* greffer (**onto** sur)

graft² *Fam* **1** *n* (**a**) *Am (bribe)* pot-de-vin *m* (**b**) *Br (work)* **(hard) g.** boulot *m*

    2 *vi Br (work hard)* bosser dur

grafter ['grɑːftə(r)] *n Br Fam* bosseur(euse) *m,f*

grain [greɪn] *n* (**a**) *(of wheat, salt, sand)* grain *m;* **a g. of truth** une once de vérité (**b**) *(in photo, wood)* grain *m; (in meat, material)* fil *m; Fig* **it goes against the g. for me to do it** ce n'est pas dans ma nature de le faire (**c**) *(cereals)* céréales *fpl*

grainy ['greɪnɪ] *adj* granuleux(euse)

gram [græm] *n* gramme *m*

grammar ['græmə(r)] *n* grammaire *f;* **g. (book)** (livre *m* de) grammaire; *Br* **g. school** ≃ lycée *m*

Grammar School

En Grande-Bretagne, ce terme désigne une école secondaire recevant une aide de l'État mais pouvant être privée, réputée dispenser un enseignement de qualité de type traditionnel et préparant aux études supérieures. L'admission se fait sur concours ("eleven-plus") ou sur dossier. Moins de cinq pour cent des élèves britanniques fréquentent ce type d'école, qui existe en Angleterre, au pays de Galles et en Irlande du Nord.

---

grammarian [grə'meərɪən] *n* grammairien(enne) *m,f*

grammatical [grə'mætɪkəl] *adj* grammatical(e)

grammatically [grə'mætɪklɪ] *adv* grammaticalement

gramme [græm] *n* gramme *m*

gramophone ['græməfəʊn] *n Br Old-fashioned* gramophone *m*

gran [græn] *n Br Fam (grandmother)* grand-mère *f; (term of address)* mamie *f*, mémé *f*

granary ['grænərɪ] *(pl* **granaries***) n* grenier *m; Br* **g. bread** = sorte de pain complet

grand [grænd] **1** *adj* (**a**) *(imposing)* grandiose, imposant(e);* **to do things on a g. scale** faire les choses en grand; *Mus & Fig* **g. finale** apothéose *f; Am* **g. jury** = jury qui décide si une affaire doit être portée ou non devant les tribunaux;* **g. master** *(in chess)* grand maître *m;* **the G. National** = steeple-chase le plus célèbre d'Angleterre;* **g. piano** piano *m* à queue;* **g. slam** grand chelem *m;* **g. total** somme *f* totale (**b**) *Fam (excellent)* excellent(e)

    2 *n (pl* **grand***) Fam (thousand pounds)* mille livres *fpl; (thousand dollars)* mille dollars *mpl*

grandchild ['græntʃaɪld] *(pl* **grandchildren** ['græntʃɪldrən] *) n (boy)* petit-fils *m; (girl)* petite fille *f;* **grandchildren** petits-enfants *mpl*

grandad ['grændæd] *n Fam* (**a**) *(grandfather)* grandpère *m; (term of address)* papy *m*, pépé *m* (**b**) *Pej (old man)* pépé *m*

grand-dad ['grændæd], **grandaddy** ['grændædɪ] *(pl* **grandaddies***) n Fam* grand-père *m; (term of address)* papy *m*, pépé *m*

granddaughter ['grændɔːtə(r)] *n* petite fille *f*

grandeur ['grændjə(r)] *n (of person)* grandeur *f*, noblesse *f; (of building, surroundings)* splendeur *f*, magnificence *f*

grandfather ['grænfɑːðə(r)] *n* grand-père *m;* **g. clock** horloge *f* (de parquet)

grandiloquent [græn'dɪləkwənt] *adj* grandiloquent(e)

grandiose ['grændɪəʊs] *adj (building)* monumental(e); *(term, title)* pompeux(euse); *(idea, scheme)* démesuré(e)

grandly ['grændlɪ] *adv (impressively)* de façon grandiose; *(pompously)* de façon pompeuse

grandma ['grænmɑː] *n Fam* grand-mère *f; (term of address)* mamie *f*, mémé *f*

grandmother ['grænmʌðə(r)] *n* grand-mère *f*

grandpa ['grænpɑː] *n Fam* grand-père *m; (term of address)* papy *m*, pépé *m*

grandparent ['grænpeərənt] *n* grand-parent *m*

grandson ['grænsʌn] *n* petit-fils *m*

grandstand ['grænstænd] *n* tribune *f* d'honneur; *Fig* **to have a g. view of sth** être bien placé(e) pour voir qch

granite ['grænɪt] *n* granit *m*

granny ['grænɪ] *(pl* **grannies***) n Fam* grand-mère *f; (term of address)* mamie *f*, mémé *f;* **g. flat** = partie d'une maison aménagée indépendamment pour héberger un parent âgé;* **g. knot** double nœud *m*

grant [grɑːnt] **1** n *(financial aid)* subvention f; *(for student)* bourse f (d'études)

2 vt (**a**) *(allow) (permission)* donner; *(interview, request)* accorder; **to take sth for granted** considérer qch comme allant de soi ou comme étant dû; **to take sb for granted** croire que qn sera toujours là (**b**) *(award) (money, subsidy)* accorder, allouer (**c**) *(admit)* admettre; **I g. that he's talented** je reconnais qu'il a du talent

granular ['grænjʊlə(r)] adj granuleux(euse)

granulated sugar ['grænjʊleɪtɪd'ʃʊgə(r)] n sucre m semoule

granule ['grænjʊl] n *(of salt, sand)* grain m; *(of coffee)* granule m

grape [greɪp] n grain m de raisin; **some grapes** du raisin; **g. harvest** vendange(s) f(pl); **g. juice** jus m de raisin; **g. picker** vendangeur(euse) m,f

grapefruit ['greɪpfruːt] n pamplemousse m; **g. juice** jus m de pamplemousse

grapevine ['greɪpvaɪn] n vigne f; *(climbing)* treille f; Fam **I heard on the g. that...** j'ai entendu par le téléphone arabe que...

graph [grɑːf] n graphique m, diagramme m; **g. paper** papier m millimétré

graphic ['græfɪk] adj (**a**) *(vivid)* très détaillé(e); *(language)* cru(e); **in g. detail** de façon très détaillée (**b**) **g. artist** graphiste mf; **g. arts** arts mpl graphiques; **g. design** conception f graphique; **g. designer** graphiste; **g. equalizer** égalisateur m graphique; **g. novel** bande f dessinée (pour adultes)

graphically ['græfɪklɪ] adv *(describe)* de façon très détaillée

graphics ['græfɪks] **1** n *(art)* arts mpl graphiques

2 npl Comput graphismes mpl, graphiques mpl

graphite ['græfaɪt] n graphite m, mine f de plomb

graphology [græ'fɒlədʒɪ] n graphologie f

grapnel ['græpnəl] n Naut grappin m

grapple ['græpəl] vi *(fight)* lutter corps à corps (**with** avec); Fig *(with problem)* se débattre (**with** avec)

grappling hook ['græplɪŋ'hʊk], **grappling iron** ['græplɪŋ'aɪən] n Naut grappin m

grasp [grɑːsp] **1** n (**a**) *(hold)* prise f; Fig **to have sth within one's g.** avoir qch à sa portée (**b**) *(understanding)* compréhension f (**of** de)

2 vt (**a**) *(hold firmly)* saisir; *(more tightly)* empoigner; **to g. sb's arm** saisir qn par le bras; Fig **to g. the opportunity** saisir l'occasion (**b**) *(understand)* saisir, comprendre

grasping ['grɑːspɪŋ] adj *(mean)* avide, cupide

grass [grɑːs] **1** n (**a**) *(plant)* herbe f; Fig **she doesn't let the g. grow under her feet** elle ne perd pas de temps; **the g. is always greener (on the other side of the fence)** c'est toujours mieux ailleurs; Fig **g. roots** *(of organization)* base f; **g. roots support/opposition** soutien m/opposition f de la base; **g. snake** couleuvre f (à collier); **g. widow** = femme dont le mari est souvent en déplacement (**b**) *(lawn)* pelouse f, gazon m; **keep off the g.** *(sign)* pelouse interdite; **g. court** *(in tennis)* court m en gazon (**c**) *(pasture)* herbage m; Fig **to put sb out to g.** mettre qn à la retraite (**d**) Fam *(marijuana)* herbe f (**e**) Br Fam *(informer)* balance f, indic m

2 vi Br Fam *(inform)* moucharder; **to g. on sb** balancer qn

grass-green ['grɑːs'griːn] adj vert gazon inv

grasshopper ['grɑːshɒpə(r)] n sauterelle f

grassland ['grɑːslænd] n prairie f, pré m

grassy ['grɑːsɪ] adj herbu(e), herbeux(euse)

grate¹ [greɪt] n *(of hearth)* grille f; *(fireplace)* foyer m

grate² **1** vt *(cheese, nutmeg)* râper

2 vi *(of machinery)* grincer; **to g. on the ear** *(of voice)* écorcher les oreilles; *(of sound)* faire mal aux oreilles; **it really grates on me** or **on my nerves** ça me tape vraiment sur les nerfs

grateful ['greɪtfʊl] adj reconnaissant(e) (**for** de); **I would be g. if you could let me know** je vous serais reconnaissant de m'en informer

gratefully ['greɪtfʊlɪ] adv avec reconnaissance

grater ['greɪtə(r)] n râpe f

gratification [grætɪfɪ'keɪʃən] n satisfaction f

gratified ['grætɪfaɪd] adj satisfait(e), content(e)

gratify ['grætɪfaɪ] *(pt & pp gratified)* vt *(person)* faire plaisir à; *(wish, desire)* satisfaire

gratifying ['grætɪfaɪɪŋ] adj satisfaisant(e)

grating¹ ['greɪtɪŋ] adj *(noise)* grinçant(e); *(voice)* éraillé(e)

grating² n *(grille)* grille f

gratis ['grɑːtɪs] adv gratis

gratitude ['grætɪtjuːd] n gratitude f, reconnaissance f

gratuitous [grə'tjuːɪtəs] adj gratuit(e)

gratuitously [grə'tjuːɪtəslɪ] adv gratuitement, sans raison

gratuity [grə'tjuːɪtɪ] *(pl gratuities)* n Formal *(tip)* pourboire m

grave [greɪv] **1** n tombe f; Fig **it would make him turn in his g.** ça le ferait se retourner dans sa tombe; **to have one foot in the g.** avoir un pied dans la tombe

2 adj *(manner, voice)* solennel(elle); *(situation)* grave; **to make a g. mistake** se tromper lourdement

gravedigger ['greɪvdɪgə(r)] n fossoyeur m

gravel ['grævəl] n gravier m; **g. path** allée f de gravier; **g. pit** carrière f de gravier

gravelly ['grævəlɪ] adj *(sand, soil)* graveleux(euse); *(voice)* râpeux(euse)

gravely ['greɪvlɪ] adv gravement

graven ['greɪvən] adj **g. image** idole f

graveside ['greɪvsaɪd] n **at the g.** près de la tombe

gravestone ['greɪvstəʊn] n pierre f tombale

graveyard ['greɪvjɑːd] n cimetière m

gravitate ['grævɪteɪt] vi **to g. towards sth** *(of person)* être attiré(e) par qch; **most of the guests had gravitated towards the bar** la plupart des invités s'étaient rapprochés du bar

gravitational [grævɪ'teɪʃənəl] adj gravitationnel(elle); **g. pull** gravitation f

gravity ['grævɪtɪ] n (**a**) *(physical force)* gravité f, pesanteur f (**b**) *(seriousness)* gravité f

gravy ['greɪvɪ] n = sauce à base de jus de viande; **g. boat** saucière f; Fam **g. train** assiette f au beurre; **to get on the g. train** trouver un filon

gray Am = **grey**

graze¹ [greɪz] **1** vt *(of farmer) (cattle)* faire paître

2 vi *(of cattle)* paître

graze² **1** n écorchure f; *(less serious)* égratignure f

2 vt écorcher; *(less seriously)* égratigner

grease [griːs] **1** n graisse f; **g. gun** pistolet m graisseur

2 vt *(machine)* graisser, lubrifier; *(cake tin)* beurrer; **to g. back one's hair** se gominer les cheveux; Fam Fig **to g. sb's palm** graisser la patte à qn; Fam **like greased lightning** en quatrième vitesse

greasepaint ['gri:speɪnt] *n* maquillage *m* de théâtre
greaseproof paper ['gri:spru:f'peɪpə(r)] *n* papier *m* sulfurisé
greasy ['gri:sɪ] *adj* (**a**) *(covered in grease)* graisseux(-euse); *(hair, skin, food)* gras (grasse) (**b**) *Fam Pej (manner)* mielleux(euse)
great [greɪt] **1** *n* grand nom *m*
  2 *adj* (**a**) *(large, important)* grand(e); **a g. many people** beaucoup de monde; **to reach a g. age** parvenir à un âge avancé; **to take g. care (of)** prendre grand soin (de); **they are g. friends** ce sont de grands amis (**b**) *(in proper names)* **G. Britain** la Grande-Bretagne; **G. Dane** danois *m*; **the G. Lakes** les Grands Lacs *mpl*; **Greater London** Londres et son agglomération; *Hist* **the G. War** la Grande Guerre
  (**c**) *Fam (very good)* formidable, génial(e); **to have a g. time** bien s'amuser
  (**d**) *(enthusiastic)* **to be a g. knitter/reader** adorer tricoter/la lecture; **to be a g. believer in doing sth** être partisan(e) de faire qch; *Fam* **she's a g. one for having everything planned in advance** avec elle, on peut être sûr que tout sera préparé à l'avance
  3 *adv Fam* (**a**) *(well)* très bien; **to feel g.** se sentir en super forme
  (**b**) *(for emphasis)* **a g. big dog** un chien énorme; **you g. fat slob!** espèce de gros tas!
great-aunt ['greɪta:nt] *n* grand-tante *f*
greatcoat ['greɪtkəʊt] *n* pardessus *m*
great-grandchild ['greɪt'grænt∫aɪld] (*pl* **great-grandchildren** ['greɪt'grænt∫ɪldrən]) *n (boy)* arrière-petit-fils *m*; *(girl)* arrière-petite-fille *f*; **great-grandchildren** arrière-petits-enfants *mpl*
great-granddaughter ['greɪt'grændɔ:tə(r)] *n* arrière-petite-fille *f*
great-grandfather ['greɪt'grænfɑ:ðə(r)] *n* arrière-grand-père *m*
great-grandmother ['greɪt'grænmʌðə(r)] *n* arrière-grand-mère *f*
great-grandparents ['greɪt'grænpeərənts] *npl* arrière-grands-parents *mpl*
great-grandson ['greɪt'grænsʌn] *n* arrière-petit-fils *m*
greatly ['greɪtlɪ] *adv* très
greatness ['greɪtnɪs] *n* (**a**) *(of person, action)* grandeur *f*; **to achieve g.** rejoindre les plus grands (**b**) *(of thing, problem)* importance *f*
great-uncle ['greɪtʌŋkəl] *n* grand-oncle *m*
grebe [gri:b] *n* grèbe *m*
Grecian ['gri:∫ən] *adj* grec (grecque)
Greece [gri:s] *n* la Grèce
greed [gri:d] *n (for food)* gourmandise *f*; *(for money)* avidité *f*, cupidité *f*; *(for fame, power)* recherche *f* avide (**for** de)
greedily ['gri:dɪlɪ] *adv (eat)* goulûment; *(look, say)* avec gourmandise
greediness ['gri:dɪnɪs] = **greed**
greedy ['gri:dɪ] *adj (for food)* gourmand(e); *(for money, fame, power)* avide; *Fam* **g. guts** goinfre *mf*
Greek [gri:k] **1** *n* (**a**) *(person)* Grec (Grecque) *m,f* (**b**) *(language)* grec *m*; **modern G.** le grec moderne; *Fam* **it's all G. to me** c'est de l'hébreu pour moi
  2 *adj* grec (grecque)
green [gri:n] **1** *n* (**a**) *(colour)* vert *m* (**b**) **greens** *(vegetables)* légumes *mpl* verts (**c**) *(grassy area)* pelouse *f*, gazon *m*; *(in golf)* green *m* (**d**) *(environmentalist)* écologiste *mf*

  2 *adj* (**a**) *(colour)* vert(e); **to go** *or* **turn g.** *(of traffic lights)* passer au vert; *(of person, fields)* verdir; **to be g. with envy** être vert de jalousie; *Fig* **to give sb the g. light (to do sth)** donner le feu vert à qn (pour faire qch); **to have** *Br* **g. fingers** *or Am* **a g. thumb** avoir la main verte; **g. beans** haricots *mpl* verts; **g. belt** zone *f* verte; *Am* **g. card** ≃ permis *m* de travail; **g. salad** salade *f* verte (**b**) *(young, inexperienced)* jeune, inexpérimenté(e); *(naive)* naïf (naïve) (**c**) *(environmentalist)* écologiste; **the G. Party** le parti écologiste, les Verts *mpl*
greenback ['gri:nbæk] *n Am Fam* billet *m* vert
greenery ['gri:nərɪ] *n* verdure *f*
green-eyed ['gri:naɪd] *adj* aux yeux verts; **the g. monster** la jalousie
greenfield ['gri:nfi:ld] *n* **g. site** terrain *m* non-bâti *(à l'extérieur d'une ville)*
greenfly ['gri:nflaɪ] (*pl* **greenflies**) *n* puceron *m*
greengage ['gri:ngeɪdʒ] *n* reine-claude *f*
greengrocer ['gri:ngrəʊsə(r)] *n Br* marchand(e) *m,f* de fruits et légumes; **g.'s (shop)** magasin *m* de fruits et légumes
greenhouse ['gri:nhaʊs] *n* serre *f*; **g. effect** effet *m* de serre
Greenland ['gri:nlənd] *n* le Groenland
Greenlander ['gri:nləndə(r)] *n* Groenlandais(e) *m,f*
Greenwich Mean Time ['grenɪt∫'mi:ntaɪm] *n* temps *m* universel
greet [gri:t] *vt (say hello to)* saluer; *(welcome) (person, idea)* accueillir
greeting ['gri:tɪŋ] *n* salut *m*; *(more formal)* salutation *f*; **New Year greetings** vœux *mpl* de bonne année; **greetings card** carte *f* de vœux
gregarious [grɪ'geərɪəs] *adj* sociable
gremlin ['gremlɪn] *n Fam* diablotin *m*
Grenada [grə'neɪdə] *n* la Grenade
grenade [grə'neɪd] *n* grenade *f*
grenadier [grenə'dɪə(r)] *n* grenadier *m*
grenadine ['grenədi:n] *n* grenadine *f*
grew [gru:] *pt of* **grow**
grey, *Am* **gray** [greɪ] **1** *n (colour)* gris *m*
  2 *adj* gris(e); *Fig (dull)* morne; **to go g.** *(grey-haired)* grisonner; *Fig* **a g. area** une zone d'ombre; **g. matter** *(brain)* matière *f* grise
  3 *vi (of hair)* grisonner
grey-haired ['greɪheəd] *adj* aux cheveux gris
greyhound ['greɪhaʊnd] *n* lévrier *m*; **g. racing** courses *fpl* de lévriers; **g. stadium** cynodrome *m*
greying ['greɪɪŋ] *adj (hair)* grisonnant(e)
grid [grɪd] *n* (**a**) *(bars)* grille *f*, grillage *m* (**b**) *(on map)* quadrillage *m*; **g. layout** *(of town)* quadrillage, damier *m*; **g. reference** coordonnées *fpl* (**c**) *Br (for electricity)* réseau *m* électrique
griddle ['grɪdəl] *n (for cooking)* tôle *f*
gridiron ['grɪdaɪən] *n* (**a**) *(for cooking)* gril *m* (**b**) *Am (American football)* football *m* américain; *(playing field)* terrain *m* de football
gridlock ['grɪdlɒk] *n* embouteillage *m* monstre
gridlocked ['grɪdlɒkt] *adj (road, negotiations)* bloqué(e)
grief [gri:f] *n* (**a**) *(pain)* chagrin *m*; **to come to g.** échouer; *Fam* **good g.!** mon Dieu! (**b**) *Fam (hassle)* **to give sb g.** embêter qn
grief-stricken ['gri:fstrɪkən] *adj* accablé(e) de douleur *ou* de chagrin

grievance ['gri:vəns] n (**a**) *(resentment)* grief m (**b**) *(complaint)* doléance f; **to air one's grievances** exprimer ses doléances; *Ind* **g. procedure** procédure f pour porter plainte

grieve [gri:v] **1** vt chagriner, affliger
2 vi **to g. for sb/over sth** pleurer qn/qch

grieving ['gri:vɪŋ] adj éploré(e)

grievous ['gri:vəs] adj *Formal* grave; *Law* **g. bodily harm** coups mpl et blessures fpl

grievously ['gri:vəslɪ] adv *(seriously)* gravement; **you are g. mistaken** vous commettez une grave erreur

griffin ['grɪfɪn] n griffon m

grill [grɪl] **1** n *Br (for cooking)* gril m; *(food)* grillade f; **a mixed g.** un assortiment de grillades
2 vt (**a**) *Br (cook)* griller (**b**) *Fam (interrogate)* cuisiner

grille [grɪl] n *(bars)* grille f; **(radiator) g.** *(on car)* calandre f

grilling ['grɪlɪŋ] n *Fam (interrogation)* **to give sb a g.** cuisiner qn

grim [grɪm] adj (**a**) *(stern)* sévère; *(gloomy) (place)* sinistre; *(news, report)* sombre; **to hang on like g. death** se cramponner; **to look g.** *(of person) (serious)* avoir l'air sombre; *(ill)* avoir très mauvaise mine (**b**) *Fam (bad)* lamentable; **how do you feel? – pretty g.!** comment te sens-tu? – pas terrible!

grimace ['grɪməs] **1** n grimace f
2 vi grimacer, faire la grimace

grime [graɪm] n saleté f

grimly ['grɪmlɪ] adv *(fight, hold on)* avec acharnement

grimy ['graɪmɪ] adj encrassé(e)

grin [grɪn] **1** n grand sourire m
2 vi *(pt & pp grinned)* faire un grand sourire (**at** à); *Fig* **to g. and bear it** tâcher de garder le sourire

grind [graɪnd] **1** n *Fam (work)* corvée f; **the daily g.** le train-train quotidien
2 vt *(pt & pp ground* [graʊnd]*)* (**a**) *(grain, coffee)* moudre; **to g. one's teeth** grincer des dents (**b**) *(glass, gems)* dépolir
3 vi *(of wheels, gears)* grisser; **to g. to a halt** *(of car, machine)* s'immobiliser; *(of project, economy)* s'arrêter

▸**grind down** vt sep *Fig* venir à bout de

▸**grind on** vi *(proceed relentlessly)* ne pas en finir

▸**grind out** vt sep *(article, novel)* pondre

grinder ['graɪndə(r)] n *(for coffee, pepper)* moulin m; *(for polishing)* polissoire f; *(for sharpening)* meule f

grinding ['graɪndɪŋ] adj *(poverty)* extrême; **to come to a g. halt** *(of car, machine)* s'immobiliser; *(of project, economy)* s'arrêter

grindstone ['graɪndstəʊn] n meule f; *Fig* **to keep one's nose to the g.** travailler dur

gringo ['grɪŋgəʊ] *(pl gringos)* n *Am Fam* gringo m

grip [grɪp] **1** n (**a**) *(hold, grasp)* prise f; **to have a strong g.** avoir une bonne poigne; **to get a g. on sth** avoir prise sur qch; *Fig* **to get to grips with sth** s'attaquer à qch; *Fig* **to get a g. on oneself** se ressaisir; *Fig* **get a g.!** reprends-toi!, ressaisis-toi!; *Fig* **to have a firm g. on a situation** avoir la situation bien en main; **to lose one's g.** lâcher prise; **to lose one's g. on sth** lâcher qch; *Fig* **to lose one's g. on reality** perdre pied avec la réalité; *Fig* **to be in the g. of a disease/a crisis** être en proie à une maladie/une crise (**b**) *(handle)* poignée f (**c**) **(hair) g.** pince f (à cheveux) (**d**) *Am (bag)* mallette f
2 vt *(pt & pp gripped)* *(seize)* saisir, prendre; *(hold)* empoigner, agripper; *(of tyres)* adhérer à; *Fig* **to be**

gripped by panic être pris(e) de panique; *Fig* **the audience was gripped by the play** la pièce a captivé les spectateurs
3 vi *(of tyre)* adhérer

gripe [graɪp] **1** n (**a**) *Fam (complaint)* **to have a g. about sth** avoir à se plaindre de qch; **what's your g.?** de quoi te plains-tu? (**b**) *(pain)* **gripes** coliques fpl; **g. water** = médicament pour coliques infantiles
2 vi *Fam (complain)* ronchonner, râler (**about** à propos de)

gripping ['grɪpɪŋ] adj passionnant(e), palpitant(e)

grisly ['grɪzlɪ] adj macabre, sinistre

grist [grɪst] n **it's all g. to the mill** cela apporte de l'eau à mon/ton/*etc* moulin

gristle ['grɪsəl] n nerfs mpl

gristly ['grɪslɪ] adj nerveux(euse)

grit [grɪt] **1** n (**a**) *(gravel)* gravillons mpl; *(in eye)* poussière f; *(for icy roads)* sable m (**b**) *(courage, determination)* cran m
2 vt *(pt & pp gritted)* (**a**) *(road)* sabler (**b**) *(clench)* **to g. one's teeth** grincer des dents; *Fig* serrer les dents

gritter ['grɪtə(r)] n *Br* camion m de sablage

gritty ['grɪtɪ] adj (**a**) *(soil, road)* plein(e) de gravillons (**b**) *(determined)* qui a du cran, résolu(e) (**c**) **g. realism** réalisme m cru

grizzle ['grɪzəl] vi *(complain)* ronchonner, râler (**about** à propos de)

grizzled ['grɪzəld] adj *(hair, person)* grisonnant(e)

grizzly ['grɪzlɪ] **1** n *(pl grizzlies)* **g. (bear)** grizzly m
2 adj *(hair, person)* grisonnant(e)

groan [grəʊn] **1** n *(of pain)* gémissement m; *(of disappointment, dismay)* grognement m; *(of chair, floor)* grincement m
2 vi *(in pain)* gémir, pousser un gémissement; *(in disappointment, dismay)* grogner, pousser un grognement; **to g. under the weight of sth** *(of shelf, chair)* se creuser sous le poids de qch

grocer ['grəʊsə(r)] n épicier(ère) m,f; **g.'s (shop)** épicerie f

groceries ['grəʊsəriz] npl *(provisions)* provisions fpl

grocery ['grəʊsəri] *(pl groceries)* n *(shop)* épicerie f

grog [grɒg] n *Fam* grog m

groggy ['grɒgi] adj *Fam* groggy inv

groin [grɔɪn] n aine f

groom [gru:m] **1** n (**a**) *(of horse)* palefrenier m (**b**) *(at wedding)* marié m
2 vt *(horse)* panser; *(dog)* toiletter; *Fig (candidate)* préparer

groomed [gru:md] adj soigné(e); **to be well-g.** *(of person)* être soigné(e) de sa personne; *(of horse)* être bien entretenu(e)

groove [gru:v] n *(in wood, metal)* rainure f; *(in record)* sillon m; *Fig* **to get stuck in a g.** s'encroûter

groovy ['gru:vi] adj *Fam* chouette

grope [grəʊp] **1** vt (**a**) **to g. one's way forward** avancer à tâtons (**b**) *Fam (sexually)* peloter, tripoter
2 vi **to g. (about) for sth** chercher qch à tâtons

gross [grəʊs] **1** n *(pl gross)* *(quantity)* grosse f, douze douzaines fpl
2 adj (**a**) *(fat)* obèse (**b**) *(blatant) (error)* grossier(ère); *(ignorance)* crasse; *(abuse)* choquant(e); *(injustice)* flagrant(e); *Law* **g. negligence** négligence f coupable (**c**) *(vulgar)* grossier(ère) (**d**) *(profit, income, weight)* brut(e); *Econ* **g. domestic product** produit m intérieur brut; **g. national product** produit

national brut (**e**) *Fam (disgusting)* répugnant(e)
3 *vt (profit)* gagner brut; **to g. £40,000 a year** gagner brut 40 000 livres par an

▸**gross out** *vt sep Am Fam* dégoûter, débecter

grossly [ˈɡrəʊslɪ] *adv (exaggerated)* grossièrement; *(negligent)* extrêmement; *(unfair)* vraiment; **g. overweight** obèse

grotesque [ɡrəʊˈtesk] *adj* grotesque

grotto [ˈɡrɒtəʊ] *(pl* grottoes *or* grottos*) n* grotte *f*

grotty [ˈɡrɒtɪ] *adj Br Fam* minable; **to feel g.** se sentir vaseux(euse)

grouch [ɡraʊtʃ] *Fam* **1** *n* (**a**) *(person)* râleur(euse) *m,f* (**b**) *(complaint)* plainte *f*
2 *vi* râler, ronchonner (**about** à propos de)

grouchy [ˈɡraʊtʃɪ] *adj Fam* râleur(euse), ronchon(onne)

ground [ɡraʊnd] **1** *n* (**a**) *(earth)* sol *m*, terre *f*; **to sit on the g.** s'asseoir par terre; **above g.** en surface; **below g.** sous terre; **burnt to the g.** entièrement brûlé(e); *Fig* **to get off the g.** *(of project)* démarrer; *Fig* **to work oneself into the g.** se tuer au travail; **to go to g.** se cacher; **to run sb to g.** traquer qn; **g. control** contrôle *m* au sol; **g. crew** personnel *m* au sol; **floor** rez-de chaussée *m*; *Mil* **g. forces** forces *fpl* au sol; **g. frost** gelée *f* blanche; **at g. level** au rez-de-chaussée; **g. rules** règles *fpl* de base; **g. staff** = personnel responsable de l'entretien d'un terrain de sport (**b**) *(land)* terrain *m*; *Fig* **to find common g. for negotiations** trouver un terrain d'entente en vue de négociations; **to be sure of one's g.** être sûr(e) de son fait; *Fig* **to be on shaky g.** être en terrain miné; *Fig* **to change** *or* **shift one's g.** changer de tactique; *Fig* **to break new g.** faire œuvre de pionnier; *Fig* **to cover a lot of g.** *(of book, lecture)* couvrir de très nombreux domaines; *Fig* **to gain g. on sb** gagner du terrain sur qn; *Fig* **to lose g. to sb** perdre du terrain sur qn; *Fig* **to stand** *or* **hold one's g.** tenir bon
(**c**) **grounds** *(of school, hospital, country house)* parc *m*
(**d**) **grounds** *(reasons)* raisons *fpl*, motifs *mpl*; **to have (good) grounds for doing sth** avoir de bonnes raisons de faire qch; **on grounds of ill-health** pour raisons de santé; *Law* **grounds for divorce** motif *m* de divorce
2 *adj (coffee, pepper)* moulu(e); *Am* **g. meat** viande *f* hachée
3 *vt* (**a**) *(base)* baser, appuyer (**on** sur)
(**b**) *(educate)* **to g. sb in sth** former qn à qch
(**c**) *Am (electrical current)* mettre à la masse
(**d**) *(aeroplane)* interdire de vol
(**e**) *(prevent from going out)* priver de sortie
4 *pt & pp of* **grind**

ground-breaking [ˈɡraʊndbreɪkɪŋ] *adv* révolutionnaire

groundhog [ˈɡraʊndhɒɡ] *n* marmotte *f* d'Amérique

grounding [ˈɡraʊndɪŋ] *n* (**a**) *(basis)* fondement *m* (**b**) *(basic knowledge)* bases *fpl* (**in** de *ou* en)

groundless [ˈɡraʊndlɪs] *adj* sans fondement

groundnut [ˈɡraʊndnʌt] *n Br* arachide *f*; **g. oil** huile *f* d'arachide

groundsheet [ˈɡraʊndʃiːt] *n* tapis *m* de sol

groundsman [ˈɡraʊndzmən] *n* = responsable de l'entretien d'un terrain de sport

groundswell [ˈɡraʊndswel] *n* **a g. of support** un raz-de-marée

groundwork [ˈɡraʊndwɜːk] *n* travail *m* préparatoire; **to do** *or* **lay the g. (for sth)** préparer le terrain (pour qch)

group [ɡruːp] **1** *n* groupe *m*; **g. booking** réservation *f* de groupe; **g. decision** décision *f* collective; **g. dynamics** dynamique *f* de groupe; **g. photograph** photographie *f* de groupe; **g. therapy** thérapie *f* de groupe
2 *vt* grouper
3 *vi* se grouper

groupie [ˈɡruːpɪ] *n Fam* groupie *f*

grouping [ˈɡruːpɪŋ] *n (of people)* groupe *m*

grouse¹ [ɡraʊs] *(pl* grouse*) n (bird)* tétras *m*, grouse *f*

grouse² *Fam* **1** *n (complaint)* **to have a g. (about sth)** avoir des raisons de se plaindre (de qch)
2 *vi* ronchonner, grogner (**about** au sujet de)

grout [ɡraʊt] *n* mastic *m*

grove [ɡrəʊv] *n* bosquet *m*

grovel [ˈɡrɒvəl] *(pt & pp* grovelled*, Am* groveled*) vi (on ground)* être à quatre pattes; **to g. to sb** ramper *ou* s'aplatir devant qn

grovelling, *Am* **groveling** [ˈɡrɒvəlɪŋ] *adj* obséquieux(euse)

grow [ɡrəʊ] *(pt* grew [ɡruː]*, pp* grown [ɡrəʊn]*)* **1** *vt* (**a**) *(vegetables)* cultiver; *(flowers)* faire pousser; **to g. a beard** se laisser pousser la barbe; **to g. one's hair** se laisser pousser les cheveux (**b**) *Com (company)* développer
2 *vi* (**a**) *(increase in size) (plant)* pousser; *(person, animal)* grandir; *(problem)* s'aggraver; *(economy, feeling)* croître; *Fam* **it'll g. on you** *(of music, book)* tu finiras par t'y intéresser (**b**) *(become)* devenir; **to g. old** vieillir; **to g. angry** se fâcher (**c**) *(come eventually)* **to g. to like sth** finir par aimer qch

▸**grow apart** *vi (of people)* s'éloigner

▸**grow out of** *vt insep* (**a**) *(become too big for)* **he's grown out of his shoes** ses chaussures sont maintenant trop petites pour lui (**b**) *(become too old for)* **she grew out of her dolls** elle a passé l'âge de jouer à la poupée; **most children g. out of such behaviour** la plupart des enfants cessent de se conduire ainsi en grandissant

▸**grow up** *vi (become adult)* grandir; **when I g. up** quand je serai grand; **when I was growing up** quand j'étais petit; *Fam* **g. up!** ne fais pas l'enfant!

grower [ˈɡrəʊə(r)] *n (person)* cultivateur(trice) *m,f*; *(of trees, flowers)* horticulteur(trice) *m,f*

growing [ˈɡrəʊɪŋ] *adj (child)* en pleine croissance; *(town, population)* en pleine expansion; *(debt)* qui augmente, qui va croissant; *(discontent)* croissant(e); **there was a g. fear that...** on craignait de plus en plus que...; **g. pains** *(of child)* douleurs *fpl* de croissance; *Fig (of firm, country)* difficultés *fpl* de croissance

growl [ɡraʊl] **1** *n (of dog)* grondement *m*
2 *vi (of dog)* gronder; *(of person)* grogner, grommeler (**at** contre)

growling [ˈɡraʊlɪŋ] *n (of dog)* grondement *m*

grown [ɡrəʊn] **1** *adj* grand(e); **a g. woman** une adulte; **to be fully g.** avoir atteint sa taille adulte
2 *pp of* **grow**

grown-up **1** *n* [ˈɡrəʊnʌp] grand(e) *m,f*, grande personne *f*; **the grown-ups** les grands, les grandes personnes
2 *adj* [ɡrəʊnˈʌp] *(person, topic)* adulte; **he was very g. about it** il a fait preuve de beaucoup de maturité

growth [grəʊθ] *n* (**a**) *(of person, plant, economy)* croissance *f*; *(of population, demand)* augmentation *f*; **a week's g. of beard** une barbe d'une semaine; **g. area** secteur *m* en expansion; **g. industry** industrie *f* en expansion (**b**) *(tumour)* grosseur *f*

grub [grʌb] *n* (**a**) *(larva)* larve *f* (**b**) *Fam (food)* bouffe *f*; **g.'s up!** à la bouffe!

▸**grub about, grub around** *(pt & pp* **grubbed***) vi Fam* farfouiller (**for sth** pour trouver qch)

grubby ['grʌbɪ] *adj* crasseux(euse)

grudge [grʌdʒ] **1** *n* rancune *f*; **to bear sb a g.** en vouloir à qn
  2 *vt* (**a**) *(give unwillingly)* **to g. sb sth** donner qch à qn à contrecœur (**b**) *(resent)* **to g. doing sth** faire qch à contrecœur; **she grudges him his success** elle lui en veut parce qu'il a réussi

grudging ['grʌdʒɪŋ] *adj* accordé(e) à contrecœur; **to be g. in one's praise** être avare de compliments

grudgingly ['grʌdʒɪŋlɪ] *adv* à contrecœur

gruel ['gruːəl] *n* gruau *m*

gruelling, *Am* **grueling** ['gruːəlɪŋ] *adj (journey, experience)* épuisant(e)

gruesome ['gruːsəm] *adj* abominable, horrible; **to relate sth in g. detail** raconter qch jusqu'aux détails les plus horribles

gruesomely ['gruːsəmlɪ] *adv* abominablement

gruff [grʌf] *adj (tone, manner)* bourru(e); *(voice)* gros (grosse)

gruffly ['grʌflɪ] *adv* d'un ton bourru

grumble ['grʌmbəl] **1** *n* grommellement *m*, grognement *m*; **she obeyed without so much as a g.** elle a obéi sans la moindre protestation
  2 *vi (of person)* grommeler; *(of stomach)* gargouiller; **to g. about sth** rouspéter contre qch; **(I) mustn't g.** il ne faut pas se plaindre

grumbler ['grʌmblə(r)] *n* grincheux(euse) *m,f*

grumbling ['grʌmblɪŋ] **1** *n* ronchonnements *mpl*
  2 *adj* grognon(onne); **g. appendix** appendicite *f* chronique

grump [grʌmp] *n Fam* grincheux(euse) *m,f*

grumpily ['grʌmpɪlɪ] *adv* en ronchonnant

grumpy ['grʌmpɪ] *adj* grognon(onne)

grunge [grʌndʒ] *n (music, fashion)* grunge *m*

grunt [grʌnt] **1** *n (of pig, person)* grognement *m*; **to give a g.** pousser un grognement
  2 *vi (of pig, person)* grogner

Guadeloupe [gwɑːdə'luːp] *n* la Guadeloupe

guarantee [gærən'tiː] **1** *n (spoken, written)* garantie *f*; **she gave me her g. that it wouldn't happen again** elle m'a assuré que cela ne se reproduirait plus; **there's no g. that she'll come** ce n'est pas sûr qu'elle vienne; *Com* **under g.** sous garantie
  2 *vt* garantir; **I can't g. that she'll come** je ne garantis pas qu'elle viendra; **the watch is guaranteed for two years** cette montre est garantie deux ans; *Fin* **to g. sb against loss** garantir qn contre les pertes

guaranteed [gærən'tiːd] *adj* garanti(e)

guarantor [gærən'tɔː(r)] *n* garant(e) *m,f*

guard [gɑːd] **1** *n* (**a**) *(defences)* **to be on one's g.** être sur ses gardes; **to put sb on his g.** mettre qn en garde; **to put sb off his g.** déjouer la vigilance de qn; **to catch sb off his g.** prendre qn au dépourvu; **his g. was down** il ne se méfiait pas (**b**) *(supervision)* garde *f*; **to keep sb under g.** garder qn sous surveillance; **to be on g. duty** être de garde; **g. dog** chien *m* de garde (**c**) *(sentry)* garde *m*; *(on train)* chef *m* de train; *Am (in*

prison) gardien *m*; *Mil (group of sentries)* garde *f*; **g. of honour** garde *f* d'honneur; *Br* **g.'s van** *(on train)* fourgon *m* du chef de train (**d**) *(device) (on machine)* protection *f* (**e**) *(in basketball)* défenseur *m*
  2 *vt* garder; **to g. sb from danger** protéger qn d'un danger

▸**guard against** *vt insep* se prémunir contre; **he was keen to g. against any further mistakes** il prenait garde de ne pas commettre de nouvelles erreurs

guarded ['gɑːdɪd] *adj* circonspect(e), prudent(e)

guardedly ['gɑːdɪdlɪ] *adv* avec circonspection, avec prudence

guardhouse ['gɑːdhaʊs] *n Mil* poste *m* de garde; *(prison)* prison *f*

guardian ['gɑːdɪən] *n (of standards)* gardien(enne) *m,f*; *Law (of minor)* tuteur(trice) *m,f*; **g. angel** ange *m* gardien

guardianship ['gɑːdɪənʃɪp] *n Law (of minor)* tutelle *f*

guardrail ['gɑːdreɪl] *n* garde-fou *m*, parapet *m*; *(on ship)* bastingage *m*

guardroom ['gɑːdruːm] *n* corps *m* de garde

guardsman ['gɑːdzmən] *n* garde *m* *(de la garde royale)*

Guatemala [gwætɪ'mɑːlə] *n* le Guatemala

Guatemalan [gwætɪ'mɑːlən] **1** *n* Guatémaltèque *mf*
  2 *adj* guatémaltèque

guava ['gwɑːvə] *n* goyave *f*; **g. tree** goyavier *m*

guerrilla [gə'rɪlə] *n* guérillero *m*; **g. warfare** guérilla *f*

guess [ges] **1** *n* estimation *f*; **to have** *or* **make a g.** deviner; *Ironic* **I'll give you three guesses!** devine!; **at a g., (I'd say) three hundred** je dirais environ trois cents; **your g. is as good as mine** j'en ai pas la moindre idée; **it's anybody's g.** qui sait?
  2 *vt* (**a**) *(attempt to answer)* deviner; **g. who I saw!** devine qui j'ai vu!; **g. what!** tu sais quoi?; **you've guessed it!** tu as deviné! (**b**) *(suppose)* supposer, croire; **I g. you're right** tu dois avoir raison
  3 *vi* deviner; **to g. right** deviner juste; **to g. wrong** se tromper; **to keep sb guessing** laisser qn dans l'ignorance; **to g. at sth** essayer de deviner qch

guessing game ['gesɪŋ'geɪm] *n* jeu *m* de devinettes; *Fig* **it's a bit of a g.** on ne peut que spéculer

guesstimate ['gestɪmɪt] *n Fam* calcul *m* au pif

guesswork ['gesw3ːk] *n* conjecture *f*; **it's pure** *or* **sheer g.** c'est de la pure conjecture

guest [gest] *n (at home, party, on TV programme)* invité(e) *m,f*; *(at hotel)* client(e) *m,f*; **be my g.!** je t'en prie!; **to make a g. appearance** *(on TV programme)* passer en invité vedette; *(in film)* participer à titre exceptionnel; **g. artist** invité vedette; **g. room** chambre *f* d'amis; **g. speaker** conférencier(ère) *m,f (invité par une organisation ou une association)*; **g. star** invité(e) *m,f* vedette; **g. worker** travailleur(euse) *m,f* immigré(e)

guesthouse ['gesthaʊs] *n* pension *f* de famille

guff [gʌf] *n Fam* âneries *fpl*

guffaw [gʌ'fɔː] **1** *n* gros rire *m*
  2 *vi* s'esclaffer

GUI ['guːɪ] *n Comput (abbr* **Graphical User Interface)** interface *f* utilisateur graphique

Guiana [gaɪ'ɑːnə] *n* la Guyane

guidance ['gaɪdəns] *n* direction *f*; **under the g. of** sous la direction de; **for your g.** à titre d'information; *Am* **g. counselor** conseiller(ère) *m,f* d'orientation

guide [gaɪd] **1** *n* (**a**) *(person)* guide *m*; **(Girl) G.** éclaireuse *f*; **g. dog** chien *m* d'aveugle (**b**) *(book)* guide *m* (**to** de) (**c**) *(indication)* indication *f* (**to** sur); **as a g.** à titre indicatif
   2 *vt* guider; **to be guided by sth** suivre qch

guidebook ['gaɪdbʊk] *n* guide *m*

guided ['gaɪdɪd] *adj* **g. missile** missile *m* guidé; **g. tour** visite *f* guidée

guideline ['gaɪdlaɪn] *n* *(indication)* indication *f*; **guidelines** directives *fpl*; **as a general g.** en règle générale

guiding ['gaɪdɪŋ] *adj* *(principle, concept)* directeur(-trice)

guild [gɪld] *n* *(association)* association *f*

guilder ['gɪldə] *n* florin *m*

guile [gaɪl] *n* ruse *f*

guileless ['gaɪllɪs] *adj* candide

guillemot ['gɪlɪmɒt] *n* guillemot *m*

guillotine ['gɪləti:n] **1** *n* *(for execution)* guillotine *f*; *(for cutting paper)* massicot *m*; *Br Pol* **to put a g. on a bill** = imposer une limite de temps aux débats précédant un vote
   2 *vt* *(execute)* guillotiner

guilt [gɪlt] *n* culpabilité *f*; **to feel g.** se sentir coupable; **g. complex** complexe *m* de culpabilité; **to be on a g. trip** culpabiliser

guiltily ['gɪltɪlɪ] *adv* d'un air coupable

guiltless ['gɪltlɪs] *adj* innocent(e)

guilty ['gɪltɪ] *adj* coupable; **to find sb g./not g.** déclarer qn coupable/non coupable; **to feel g.** se sentir coupable; **to have a g. conscience** avoir mauvaise conscience; **g. secret** secret *m* inavouable

Guinea ['gɪnɪ] *n* la Guinée

guinea ['gɪnɪ] *n* (**a**) *Br (coin)* guinée *f* (**b**) **g. fowl** pintade *f*; **g. pig** cobaye *m*, cochon *m* d'Inde; *Fig* **to be a g. pig** servir de cobaye

Guinea-Bissau ['gɪnɪbɪ'saʊ] *n* la Guinée-Bissau

Guinean [gɪ'neɪən] **1** *n* Guinéen(enne) *m,f*
   2 *adj* guinéen(enne)

guise [gaɪz] *n* apparence *f*; **in** *or* **under the g. of** sous l'apparence de; **in a different g.** sous une autre forme

guitar [gɪ'tɑ:(r)] *n* guitare *f*

guitarist [gɪ'tɑ:rɪst] *n* guitariste *mf*

gulch [gʌltʃ] *n* *Am* ravin *m*

gulf [gʌlf] *n* (**a**) *(bay)* golfe *m*; **the (Persian) G.** le golfe Persique; **the G. of Mexico** le golfe du Mexique; **the G. Stream** le Gulf Stream; **the G. War** la guerre du Golfe; **G. War syndrome** syndrome *m* de la guerre du Golfe (**b**) *(between people, ideas)* abîme *m*, gouffre *m* (**between** entre)

gull [gʌl] *n* mouette *f*, goéland *m*

gullet ['gʌlɪt] *n* gosier *m*

gullibility [gʌlɪ'bɪlɪtɪ] *n* crédulité *f*

gullible ['gʌlɪbəl] *adj* crédule

gully ['gʌlɪ] *(pl* **gullies***)* *n* petit ravin *m*

gulp [gʌlp] **1** *n* (**a**) *(of food)* bouchée *f*; *(of drink)* gorgée *f*; **in** *or* **at one g.** d'un coup (**b**) *(of surprise)* serrement *m* de gorge
   2 *vt (food, drink)* engloutir
   3 *vi (with surprise)* avoir un serrement de gorge

gulp down *vt sep (food, drink)* engloutir

gum [gʌm] **1** *n* (**a**) *(in mouth)* gencive *f*; **g. disease** gingivite *f* (**b**) *(adhesive)* colle *f* (**c**) **(chewing) g.** chewing gum *m* (**d**) *(resin)* **g. arabic** gomme *f* arabique; **g. tree** gommier *m*; *Fam Fig* **to be up a g. tree** être dans le pétrin
   2 *vt (pt & pp* **gummed***)* *(stick)* coller

▸**gum up** *vt sep (mechanism)* enrayer; *(eyes)* coller

gumboot ['gʌmbu:t] *n* botte *f* de caoutchouc

gummed [gʌmd] *adj* gommé(e)

gummy ['gʌmɪ] *adj* collant(e)

gumption ['gʌmʃən] *n Fam (common sense)* jugeote *f*; *(courage)* cran *m*

gumshield ['gʌmʃi:ld] *n* protège-dents *m inv*

gun [gʌn] **1** *n* (**a**) *(pistol)* pistolet *m*; *(rifle)* fusil *m*; *(artillery piece)* canon *m*; **g. carriage** affût *m* de canon; **g. dog** chien *m* d'arrêt; **g. laws** législation *f* sur les armes à feu; **g. licence** permis *m* de port d'armes (**b**) *(idioms)* *Fam* **big g.** huile *f*; *Fam* **to be going great guns** marcher très fort; **to stick to one's guns** tenir bon; **to jump the g.** s'emballer
   2 *vt (pt & pp* **gunned***)* *(engine)* accélérer

▸**gun down** *vt sep* abattre

▸**gun for** *vt insep* **to be gunning for sb** en avoir après qn; **she's gunning for his job** elle fait tout ce qu'elle peut pour lui prendre son poste

gunboat ['gʌnbəʊt] *n* cannonière *f*; **g. diplomacy** politique *f* de la cannonière

gunfight ['gʌnfaɪt] *n* fusillade *f*

gunfire ['gʌnfaɪə(r)] *n* *(of artillery)* tirs *mpl* d'artillerie; *(of smaller guns)* coups *mpl* de feu

gunge [gʌndʒ] *n Fam* matière *f* gluante

gung-ho [gʌŋ'həʊ] *adj* (**a**) *(overly enthusiastic)* d'un enthousiasme irritant (**b**) *(keen for war)* va-t-en-guerre *inv*

gunk [gʌŋk] *n Fam* matière *f* gluante

gunman ['gʌnmən] *n* homme *m* armé

gunner ['gʌnə(r)] *n* artilleur *m*

gunpoint ['gʌnpɔɪnt] *n* **at g.** sous la menace d'une arme à feu

gunpowder ['gʌnpaʊdə(r)] *n* poudre *f* (à canon)

gunrunner ['gʌnrʌnə(r)] *n* trafiquant(e) *m,f* d'armes

gunrunning ['gʌnrʌnɪŋ] *n* trafic *m* d'armes

gunship ['gʌnʃɪp] *n* **(helicopter) g.** hélicoptère *m* de combat

gunshot ['gʌnʃɒt] *n* coup *m* de feu; **g. wound** blessure *f* par balle

gunsmith ['gʌnsmɪθ] *n* armurier *m*

gunwale ['gʌnəl] *n Naut* plat-bord *m*

gurgle ['gɜ:gəl] **1** *n* *(of liquid)* gargouillement *m*; *(of baby)* gazouillis *m*
   2 *vi (of liquid)* gargouiller; *(of baby)* gazouiller

guru ['gʊru:] *n* gourou *m*

gush [gʌʃ] **1** *n* *(of water)* jaillissement *m*; *Fig (of words)* flot *m*
   2 *vi* (**a**) *(of water)* jaillir; **tears gushed from her eyes** elle pleurait à chaudes larmes (**b**) *Pej (talk effusively)* s'extasier *(* **over** *or* **about** devant)

gushing ['gʌʃɪŋ] *adj Pej (person, praise)* exubérant(-e)

gusset ['gʌsɪt] *n* soufflet *m*

gust [gʌst] **1** *n* *(of wind)* rafale *f*; *(of hot air)* bouffée *f*
   2 *vi (of wind)* souffler par rafales

gusto ['gʌstəʊ] *n* enthousiasme *m*; **with (great) g.** avec (beaucoup d')enthousiasme

gusty ['gʌstɪ] *adj (wind)* qui souffle par rafales; *(day, weather)* de grand vent

gut [gʌt] **1** *n* (**a**) *(intestine)* intestin *m*; *Fam* **guts** *(of person, machine)* entrailles *fpl*; *Fam* **to sweat** *or* **work one's guts out** se tuer à la tâche; *Fam* **to hate sb's guts** ne pas pouvoir sentir qn; *Fam* **I'll have his guts for garters** je vais le massacrer; **a g. feeling** une intuition; **g. reaction** réaction *f* viscérale (**b**) *Fam (stomach)* bide *m* (**c**) *Fam* **guts** *(courage)* cran *m*; **I didn't have the guts to tell them** je n'ai pas eu le courage de le leur dire
2 *vt (pt & pp* **gutted**) (**a**) *(fish)* vider (**b**) *(building) (of fire)* ravager; *(of builder)* vider entièrement

gutless ['gʌtlɪs] *adj Fam* lâche

gutsy ['gʌtsɪ] *adj Fam* courageux(euse), qui a du cran

gutted ['gʌtɪd] *adj Br Fam (disappointed)* effondré(e)

gutter ['gʌtə(r)] **1** *n (in street)* caniveau *m*; *(on roof)* gouttière *f*; *Fig* **to end up in the g.** finir sous les ponts; *Fig* **to drag oneself out of the g.** se sortir de la misère; *Fam Pej* **g. press** presse *f* à scandales
2 *vi (of candle)* vasciller

guttural ['gʌtərəl] *adj* guttural(e)

guy¹ [gaɪ] *n Fam* (**a**) *(man)* type *m*, mec *m*; **a tough g.** un dur (**b**) *(person)* **hi guys!** salut la compagnie!

guy² *n* **g. (rope)** *(for tent)* tendeur *m*

Guyana [gaɪ'ænə] *n* le Guyana

Guyanese [gaɪə'niːz] **1** *n* Guyanais(e) *m,f*
2 *adj* guyanais(e)

Guy Fawkes Night ['gaɪ'fɔːks'naɪt] *n Br* = soirée du 5 novembre, célébration de la tentative de Guy Fawkes de faire sauter le Parlement en 1605

Guy Fawkes Night

Cette fête se déroule en plein air autour d'un grand feu de joie sur lequel on est censé brûler une effigie ("the Guy") de Guy Fawkes, l'instigateur de la conspiration des poudres. Des feux d'artifice sont également organisés.

---

guzzle ['gʌzəl] *vt Fam (food)* engloutir; *(drink)* siffler

gym [dʒɪm] *n (gymnasium)* gymnase *m*; *(gymnastics)* gym *f*; **g. shoes** chaussures *fpl* de gym

gymkhana [dʒɪm'kɑːnə] *n* concours *m* hippique

gymnasium [dʒɪm'neɪzɪəm] *n* gymnase *m*

gymnast ['dʒɪmnæst] *n* gymnaste *mf*

gymnastic [dʒɪm'næstɪk] *adj* gymnastique

gymnastics [dʒɪm'næstɪks] **1** *n* gymnastique *f*
2 *npl Fig* **mental/verbal g.** gymnastique *f* intellectuelle/verbale

gynaecological, *Am* **gynecological** [gaɪnɪkə-'lɒdʒɪkəl] *adj* gynécologique

gynaecologist, *Am* **gynecologist** [gaɪnɪ'kɒlədʒɪst] *n* gynécologue *mf*

gynaecology, *Am* **gynecology** [gaɪnɪ'kɒlədʒɪ] *n* gynécologie *f*

gyp [dʒɪp] *n Br Fam* **to give sb g.** faire souffrir qn

gypsum ['dʒɪpsəm] *n* gypse *m*

gypsy = gipsy

gyrate [dʒaɪ'reɪt] *vi (of planet, sphere)* tourner; *(of dancer)* tournoyer

gyration [dʒaɪ'reɪʃən] *n* giration *f*

gyroscope ['dʒaɪrəskəʊp] *n* gyroscope *m*

H

H, h [eɪtʃ] *n (letter)* H, h *m inv*; **H bomb** bombe *f* H

haberdashery ['hæbədæʃərɪ] *(pl* **haberdasheries)** *n*
(**a**) *Br (sewing items, shop)* mercerie *f* (**b**) *Am (men's
clothes, shop)* chemiserie *f*

habit ['hæbɪt] *n* (**a**) *(custom, practice)* habitude *f*; **to be
in the h. of doing sth** avoir l'habitude de faire qch; **to
get into the h. of doing sth** prendre l'habitude de
faire qch; **to get out of the h. of doing sth** perdre
l'habitude de faire qch; **don't make a h. of it!** que
cela ne devienne pas une habitude!; **from force of
h.** par habitude (**b**) *Fam (addiction to drugs)* accoutumance *f*; **to kick the h.** décrocher (**c**) *(of monk, nun)*
habit *m*

habitable ['hæbɪtəbəl] *adj* habitable

habitat ['hæbɪtæt] *n* habitat *m*

habitation [hæbɪ'teɪʃən] *n* habitation *f*; **there were
no signs of h.** l'endroit semblait inhabité; **fit for h.**
habitable; **unfit for h.** inhabitable

habitual [hə'bɪtjʊəl] *adj (generosity, rudeness)* habi-
tuel(elle); *(liar, drunk)* invétéré(e)

habitually [hə'bɪtjʊəlɪ] *adv* habituellement

habituate [hə'bɪtjʊeɪt] *vt Formal* habituer (**to** à); **to
become habituated to sth** s'habituer à qch

hacienda [hæsɪ'endə] *n* ranch *m*, hacienda *f*

hack¹ [hæk] **1** *vt* (**a**) *(cut)* tailler, taillader; **to h. sb/sth
to pieces** tailler qn/qch en pièces; **to h. one's way
through the jungle** se frayer un chemin dans la jungle à la machette (**b**) *very Fam (cope with)* **he can't h.
it** il ne s'en sort pas
   2 *vi* (**a**) *(cut)* **to h. at sth** taillader qch (**b**) *(cough)*
tousser d'une toux sèche (**c**) *Comput* **to h. into sth**
entrer dans qch par effraction

▶**hack down** *vt sep* abattre

▶**hack off** *vt sep* (**a**) *(branch, limb)* couper (**b**) *Fam* **to
be hacked off (with sb/sth)** en avoir marre (de qn/
qch)

hack² *n* (**a**) *Fam Pej (journalist)* journaliste *mf* beso-
gneux(euse); *(political activist)* militant(e) *m,f* (**b**)
(horseride) **to go for a h.** aller faire une promenade
à cheval (**c**) *Am Fam (taxi)* taxi *m*

hacker ['hækə(r)] *n Comput* pirate *m* informatique

hacking jacket ['hækɪŋ'dʒækɪt] *n* veste *f* d'équitation

hackles ['hækəlz] *npl (of dog)* poils *mpl* du cou; *(of
bird)* plumes *fpl* du cou; *Fig* **to make sb's h. rise** hérisser qn

hackney cab ['hæknɪkæb], **hackney carriage**
['hæknɪ'kærɪdʒ] *n Formal (taxi)* fiacre *m*

hackneyed ['hæknɪd] *adj (argument)* rebattu(e); *(language)* banal(e); **h. expression** lieu *m* commun

hacksaw ['hæksɔ:] *n* scie *f* à métaux

had [hæd] *pt & pp of* **have**

haddock ['hædək] *(pl* **haddock** *or* **haddocks)** *n* églefin *m*

hadn't ['hædənt] = **had not**

haemoglobin, *Am* **hemoglobin** [hi:məʊ'gləʊbɪn] *n*
hémoglobine *f*

haemophilia, *Am* **hemophilia** [hi:məʊ'fɪlɪə] *n* hémophilie *f*

haemophiliac, *Am* **hemophiliac** [hi:məʊ'fɪlɪæk] *n*
hémophile *mf*

haemorrhage, *Am* **hemorrhage** ['hemərɪdʒ] **1** *n
also Fig* hémorragie *f*
   2 *vi Med* faire une hémorragie; *Fig (of support, funds)*
diminuer

haemorrhoids, *Am* **hemorrhoids** ['hemərɔɪdz] *npl
Med* hémorroïdes *fpl*

hag [hæg] *n Pej* vieille taupe *f*

haggard ['hægəd] *adj* hâve

haggis ['hægɪs] *n* = panse de brebis farcie *(plat national écossais)*

haggle ['hægəl] *vi* marchander (**with sb** avec qn); **to
h. over sth** marchander qch; **to h. about** *or* **over the
price of sth** chicaner sur le prix de qch

hagiography [hægɪ'ɒgrəfɪ] *n* hagiographie *f*

Hague [heɪg] *n* **the H.** La Haye

hail¹ [heɪl] **1** *n* grêle *f*; *Fig* **a h. of bullets/insults** une
pluie de balles/d'injures; **a h. of blows** une volée de
coups
   2 *vi* **it's hailing** il grêle

hail² *vt* (**a**) *(attract attention of)* héler (**b**) *(acclaim)* saluer (**as** comme)

▶**hail from** *vt insep* être originaire de

hailstone ['heɪlstəʊn] *n* grêlon *m*

hailstorm ['heɪlstɔ:m] *n* averse *f* de grêle

hair [heə(r)] *n (on head)* cheveux *mpl*; *(on body, animal)* poils *mpl*; *(single hair) (on head)* cheveu *m*; *(on
body, animal)* poil *m*; **to have fair/long h.** avoir les
cheveux clairs/longs; **to do one's h.** se coiffer; **to
comb one's h.** se peigner; **to brush one's h.** se brosser les cheveux; **to have** *or* **get one's h. cut** se faire
couper les cheveux; **if you harm** *or* **touch a h. on
that child's head...** si tu touches à un cheveu de la
tête de cet enfant...; **to make sb's h. stand on end**
faire dresser les cheveux sur la tête à qn; *Fam* **keep
your h. on!** calmez-vous!; *Fam* **to get in sb's h.** enquiquiner qn; *Fig* **to let one's h. down** se laisser aller;
Fam Hum **that'll put hairs on your chest!** ça va te
donner du poil de la bête!; *Fam* **h. of the dog** *(for
hangover)* = verre d'alcool pris pour calmer la gueule

de bois; **h. gel** gel *m* pour les cheveux; *Br* **h. slide** barrette *f*

hairband ['heəbænd] *n* bandeau *m*

hairbrush ['heəbrʌʃ] *n* brosse *f* à cheveux

haircut ['heəkʌt] *n* coupe *f* de cheveux; **to have a h.** se faire couper les cheveux

hairdo ['heəduː] (*pl* **hairdos**) *n Fam* coiffure *f*

hairdresser ['heədresə(r)] *n* coiffeur(euse) *m,f*; **to go to the h.'s** aller chez le coiffeur

hairdressing ['heədresɪŋ] *n* coiffure *f*; **h. salon** salon *m* de coiffure

hairdryer ['heədraɪə(r)] *n* sèche-cheveux *m inv*

hairgrip ['heəgrɪp] *n* pince *f* à cheveux

hairless ['heəlɪs] *adj* (*face*) glabre; (*puppy*) sans poils

hairline ['heəlaɪn] *n* (**a**) (*of person*) naissance *f* des cheveux; **to have a receding h.** avoir le front qui se dégarnit (**b**) **h. crack** (*in pipe, wall*) légère fêlure *f*; **h. fracture** (*of bone*) fêlure

hairnet ['heənet] *n* résille *f*, filet *m* à cheveux

hairpiece ['heəpiːs] *n* postiche *m*

hairpin ['heəpɪn] *n* épingle *f* à cheveux; **h. bend** (*on road*) virage *m* en épingle à cheveux

hair-raising ['heəreɪzɪŋ] *adj* à faire dresser les cheveux sur la tête

hair's-breadth ['heəzbredθ] *n* **by a h.** (*win, lose*) de justesse; **the car missed him by a h.** la voiture l'a frôlé; **to be within a h. of** être à deux doigts de

hairspray ['heəspreɪ] *n* laque *f*

hairstyle ['heəstaɪl] *n* coiffure *f*

hairy ['heərɪ] *adj* (**a**) (*covered in hair*) velu(e), poilu(e) (**b**) *Fam* (*scary*) effrayant(e)

Haiti ['heɪtɪ] *n* Haïti

Haitian ['heɪʃən] **1** *n* Haïtien(enne) *m,f*
   2 *adj* haïtien(enne)

hake [heɪk] (*pl* **hake** or **hakes**) *n* merlu *m*, colin *m*

halcyon days ['hælsɪən'deɪz] *npl Lit* jours *mpl* heureux

hale [heɪl] *adj* vigoureux(euse); **to be h. and hearty** être en pleine forme

half [hɑːf] **1** *n* (*pl* **halves** [hɑːvz]) (**a**) (*in general*) moitié *f*; **h. an hour** une demi-heure; **h. past ten** dix heures et demie; **it's h. past** il est la demie; **to fold/cut sth in h.** plier/couper qch en deux; **h. a dozen** une demi-douzaine; **h. of them** la moitié d'entre eux; **to have h. a mind to do sth** avoir bien envie de faire qch; *Hum* **my better** or **other h.** ma moitié; *Br* **she is too clever by h.** elle est beaucoup trop maligne; **she doesn't do things by halves** elle ne fait pas les choses à moitié; **to go halves with sb** partager avec qn; *Fam* **you don't know the h. of it!** tu ne sais pas tout!
   (**b**) (*fraction*) demie *f*, moitié *f*; **three and a h.** trois et demi
   (**c**) **first/second h.** (*in match*) première/deuxième mi-temps *f*
   (**d**) (*ticket*) billet *m* demi-tarif
   (**e**) *Br* (*half pint*) demi *m*
   2 *adj* demi(e); **h. board** demi-pension *f*; **h. day** demi-journée *f*; **h. hour** demi-heure *f*; **every h. hour** toutes les demi-heures; **h. price** demi-tarif *m*; **at h. price** à moitié prix
   3 *adv* à moitié; **to h. do sth** faire qch à moitié; **h. full/empty** à moitié plein(e)/vide; **you're h. right** tu n'as pas tout à fait tort; *Br Fam* **not h.!** plutôt!; *Br Fam* **it isn't h. cold!** il fait rudement froid!

half- [hɑːf] *pref* **h.-asleep** à moitié endormi(e); **h.-dead** à moitié mort(e); **h.-naked** à moitié nu(e)

half-baked [hɑːf'beɪkt] *adj Fam* bancal(e)

halfbreed ['hɑːfbriːd] *n* métis(isse) *m,f*

half-brother ['hɑːfbrʌðə(r)] *n* demi-frère *m*

half-caste ['hɑːfkɑːst] *n* métis(isse) *m,f*

half-cock ['hɑːfkɒk] *n Fam Fig* **to go off at h.** (*of plan, event*) avorter, échouer

half-hearted ['hɑːf'hɑːtɪd] *adj* (*effort, performance*) timide, hésitant(e); (*belief, support*) peu enthousiaste

half-heartedly ['hɑːf'hɑːtɪdlɪ] *adv* sans grand enthousiasme, sans conviction

half-hourly [hɑːf'aʊəlɪ] *adv* toutes les demi-heures

half-life ['hɑːflaɪf] *n Phys* demi-vie *f*

half-mast ['hɑːf'mɑːst] *n Br* **at h.** (*flag*) en berne; *Fam* (*socks*) en accordéon

half-sister ['hɑːf'sɪstə(r)] *n* demi-sœur *f*

half-size ['hɑːf'saɪz] *n* (*in shoes*) demi-pointure *f*

half-term ['hɑːf'tɜːm] *n Br* **h. (holiday)** = congé de milieu de trimestre

half-timbered [hɑːf'tɪmbəd] *adj Archit & Constr* à colombages

half time ['hɑːf'taɪm] *n* (*in match*) mi-temps *f*

half-truth ['hɑːf'truːθ] *n* demi-vérité *f*

halfway [hɑːf'weɪ] **1** *adj* **at the h. point** (*in space*) à mi-chemin; (*in time*) à la moitié; **h. house** (*for rehabilitation*) centre *m* de réadaptation (*pour anciens détenus, malades mentaux, drogués etc*); *Fig* compromis *m*; **h. line** (*on sports pitch*) ligne *f* médiane
   2 *adv* à mi-chemin; *Fig* **to meet sb h.** faire un compromis avec qn

halfwit ['hɑːfwɪt] *n* simple *mf* d'esprit

halfwitted [hɑːf'wɪtɪd] *adj* stupide

half-yearly ['hɑːf'jɪəlɪ] *adj* semestriel(elle)

halibut ['hælɪbət] (*pl* **halibut** or **halibuts**) *n* flétan *m*

halitosis [hælɪ'təʊsɪs] *n* mauvaise haleine *f*

hall [hɔːl] *n* (**a**) (*entrance room*) entrée *f*; (*corridor*) couloir *m* (**b**) (*for concerts, meetings*) salle *f* (**c**) *Br Univ* **h. of residence** résidence *f* universitaire

hallmark ['hɔːlmɑːk] *n* (*on metal*) poinçon *m*; *Fig* (*typical quality*) signe *m*

hallo = **hello**

hallowed ['hæləʊd] *adj* saint(e), béni(e)

Hallowe'en [hæləʊ'iːn] *n* = veille de la Toussaint

Hallowe'en

Il s'agit d'une fête d'origine païenne célébrée dans les pays anglo-saxons la veille de la Toussaint, à l'époque de l'année où les morts étaient censés rendre visite aux vivants. Aujourd'hui la tradition demeure: on évide des citrouilles pour les transformer en lanternes en forme de crâne, et les enfants vont de maison en maison déguisés en sorcières ou en fantômes. De nos jours, la coutume britannique a adopté la tradition américaine de "trick or treat", consistant pour les enfants à demander un petit cadeau aux habitants des maisons visitées et à les menacer d'un mauvais tour s'ils refusent.

---

hallucinate [hə'luːsɪneɪt] *vi* avoir des hallucinations

hallucination [həluːsɪ'neɪʃən] *n* hallucination *f*

hallucinatory [hə'luːsɪnətərɪ] *adj* hallucinatoire

hallucinogenic [həluːsɪnəʊ'dʒenɪk] *adj* hallucinogène

hallway ['hɔːlweɪ] *n (entrance room)* entrée *f*; *(corridor)* couloir *m*

halo ['heɪləʊ] *(pl* **haloes** *or* **halos**) *n* auréole *f*

halt [hɒlt] **1** *n* halte *f*, arrêt *m*; **to come to a h.** s'arrêter; **to bring sth to a h.** interrompre *ou* faire cesser qch; **to call a h. to sth** mettre fin à qch
2 *vt* interrompre
3 *vi* s'arrêter

halter ['hɔːltə(r)] *n (for horse)* licou *m*

halterneck ['hɔːltənek] *adj (dress, top)* dos-nu *inv*

halting ['hɔːltɪŋ] *adj (voice, progress)* hésitant(e)

halve [hɑːv] *vt* (**a**) *(divide in two)* diviser en deux; *(cake, fruit)* couper en deux (**b**) *(reduce by half)* réduire de moitié

halves [hɑːvz] *pl of* **half**

ham [hæm] **1** *n* (**a**) *(meat)* jambon *m* (**b**) *Fam (actor)* cabotin(e) *m,f*; **h. acting** cabotinage *m*
2 *vt (pt & pp* **hammed**) *Fam (of actor)* **to h. it up** en faire trop

Hamburg ['hæmbɜːg] *n* Hambourg

hamburger ['hæmbɜːgə(r)] *n* hamburger *m*

ham-fisted ['hæm'fɪstɪd] *adj Fam* maladroit(e)

hamlet ['hæmlɪt] *n* hameau *m*

hammer ['hæmə(r)] **1** *n* marteau *m*; **to come under the h.** *(be auctioned)* être mis(e) aux enchères; *Fam* **to go at it h. and tongs** mettre le paquet; **the h. and sickle** la faucille et le marteau
2 *vt* (**a**) *(hit with hammer) (nail)* enfoncer (**into** dans); *(wall)* taper à coups de marteau; *Fig* **to h. one's point home** insister lourdement (**b**) *(hit with fist) (object)* frapper du poing; *(person)* frapper à coups de poing (**c**) *Fam (defeat)* écraser

▸**hammer away at** *vt insep Fig (problem)* travailler avec acharnement sur

▸**hammer out** *vt sep Fig (plan, compromise)* mettre au point

hammering ['hæmərɪŋ] *n* (**a**) *(noise)* martèlement *m* (**b**) *Fam (defeat)* raclée *f*; **they gave us a real h.** ils nous ont mis une vraie raclée

hammock ['hæmək] *n* hamac *m*

hamper ['hæmpə(r)] **1** *n (for food)* panier *m*; **(Christmas) h.** = panier garni de gourmandises offert à Noël
2 *vt (hinder)* gêner, entraver

hamster ['hæmstə(r)] *n* hamster *m*

hamstring ['hæmstrɪŋ] **1** *n* tendon *m* du jarret
2 *vt (pt & pp* **hamstrung** ['hæmstrʌŋ]) *(incapacitate)* paralyser

hand [hænd] **1** *n* (**a**) *(part of body)* main *f*; *(of clock, watch)* aiguille *f*; **to hold hands** se tenir par la main; **h. in h.** la main dans la main; **to hold sth in one's h.** tenir qch à la main; **to take sb by the h.** prendre qn par la main; **on one's hands and knees** à quatre pattes; **by h.** *(make, wash)* à la main; *(on envelope)* en ville, E.V.; **hands off!** pas touche!; **hands up!** haut les mains!; **h. basin** lavabo *m*; **h. cream** crème *f* pour les mains; **h. grenade** grenade *f*; **h. luggage** bagages *mpl* à main
(**b**) *(worker)* ouvrier(ère) *m,f*; *(sailor)* matelot *m*; **to be an old h. at sth** avoir une expérience considérable de qch
(**c**) *(handwriting)* **in his own h.** de sa main
(**d**) *(in cards)* main *f*, jeu *m*; *Fig* **to show one's h.** dévoiler son jeu
(**e**) *(idioms)* **at** *or* **on h.** disponible; **to have sth to h.** avoir qch sous la main; **to ask for sb's h. (in marriage)** demander la main de qn; **to be in good hands**

être en de bonnes mains; **to fall into the wrong hands** tomber en de mauvaises mains; **it's out of my hands** ça ne dépend plus de moi; **to change hands** *(of money, car)* changer de mains; **to have a h. in sth** être impliqué(e) dans qch; **to go h. in h. with sth** aller de pair avec qch; **to try one's h. at sth** s'essayer à qch; **to turn one's h. to sth** s'essayer à qch; **to give** *or* **lend sb a h.** donner un coup de main à qn; **to give sb a big h.** *(applaud)* applaudir qn bien fort; **to suffer at sb's hands** souffrir aux mains de qn; **on (the) one h.** d'une part; **on the other h.** d'autre part; **to have time on one's hands** avoir du temps à soi; **to have a situation in h.** maîtriser une situation; **to take sb in h.** prendre qn en main; **to get out of h.** devenir incontrôlable; **to dismiss a suggestion out of h.** rejeter une proposition sur-le-champ; **to have one's hands full** être débordé(e); **to have one's hands tied** avoir les mains liées; **to be h. in glove with sb** être de mèche avec qn; **to live from h. to mouth** mener une existence précaire; **to lose money h. over fist** perdre des sommes considérables; **to make money h. over fist** gagner une fortune; **to win hands down** gagner haut la main
2 *vt* donner, passer; **he handed her the letter to read** il lui a passé la lettre pour qu'elle la lise; *Fig* **to h. sth to sb on a plate** apporter qch à qn sur un plateau; *Fig* **you've got to h. it to him** c'est une qualité qu'il faut lui reconnaître

▸**hand back** *vt sep* rendre, repasser

▸**hand down** *vt sep* (**a**) *(jewellery, tradition, skill)* transmettre (**b**) *(give)* passer

▸**hand in** *vt sep* remettre; **to h. in one's resignation** donner sa démission

▸**hand on** *vt sep* transmettre

▸**hand out** *vt sep* distribuer

▸**hand over** *vt sep* donner

▸**hand round** *vt sep* faire circuler

handbag ['hændbæg] *n* sac *m* à main

handball ['hændbɔːl] *n* (**a**) *(game)* handball *m* (**b**) *(offence)* main *f*

handbook ['hændbʊk] *n* guide *m*, manuel *m*

handbrake ['hændbreɪk] *n* frein *m* à main

handclap ['hændklæp] *n* **to give sb the slow h.** = applaudir quelqu'un très lentement pour signifier son dédain

handcuff ['hændkʌf] *vt* passer les menottes à

handcuffs ['hændkʌfs] *npl* menottes *fpl*

handful ['hændfʊl] *n (of sand, rice, people)* poignée *f*; *Fig* **that child is a real h.** cet enfant n'est pas facile

handgun ['hændgʌn] *n* revolver *m*, pistolet *m*

handicap ['hændɪkæp] **1** *n* handicap *m*
2 *vt (pt & pp* **handicapped**) handicaper

handicapped ['hændɪkæpt] **1** *npl* **the h.** les handicapés *mpl*
2 *adj* handicapé(e)

handicraft ['hændɪkrɑːft] *n (skill)* artisanat *m*; *(object)* objet *m* artisanal

handiwork ['hændɪwɜːk] *n* travail *m* manuel; *Hum* **this looks like Jane's h.!** ça, c'est signé Jane!

handkerchief ['hæŋkətʃɪf] *n* mouchoir *m*

handle ['hændəl] **1** *n (of broom, knife, saucepan)* manche *m*; *(of suitcase, door)* poignée *f*; *(of cup)* anse *f*; *Fig* **to fly off the h.** piquer une colère; *Fig* **to get a h. on sth** piger qch
2 *vt* (**a**) *(touch, hold)* manipuler, toucher à; **h. with care** *(on parcel)* ≃ fragile; **to h. the ball** *(in football)*

toucher le ballon avec la main (**b**) *Fam (cope with) (situation, crisis)* faire face à (**c**) *Com (business, contract, client)* s'occuper de
3 *vi (of car, boat)* **to h. well** être maniable
handlebars ['hændəlbɑːz] *npl* guidon *m*
handmade ['hænd'meɪd] *adj* fait(e) à la main
hand-me-downs ['hændmɪdaʊnz] *npl Fam* **I wear my brother's h.** je mets les vieilles frusques de mon frère
handout ['hændaʊt] *n* (**a**) *(donation)* don *m* (**b**) *(leaflet)* prospectus *m*
hand-picked ['hænd'pɪkd] *adj (person, team)* trié(e) sur le volet
handrail ['hændreɪl] *n* rampe *f*
handset ['hændset] *n (of telephone)* combiné *m*
handshake ['hændʃeɪk] *n* poignée *f* de main
hands-off ['hæn'zɒf] *adj (approach, style)* non-interventionniste
handsome ['hænsəm] *adj* (**a**) *(physically attractive)* beau (belle) (**b**) *(praise)* sincère; *(price, profit)* considérable; *(reward)* beau (belle)
handsomely ['hænsəmlɪ] *adv* (**a**) *(dressed, furnished)* élégamment (**b**) *(rewarded, paid)* généreusement
hands-on ['hæn'zɒn] *adj* **the director has a h. style of management** le directeur n'a pas peur de mettre la main à la pâte; **h. training** formation *f* pratique
handstand ['hændstænd] *n* **to do a h.** faire un équilibre sur les mains
hand-to-hand ['hæntə'hænd] *adj (combat)* au corps à corps
hand-to-mouth ['hæntə'maʊθ] **1** *adj (existence)* précaire
2 *adv* **to live h.** tirer le diable par la queue
handwriting ['hændraɪtɪŋ] *n* écriture *f*
handwritten ['hændrɪtən] *adj* manuscrit(e)
handy ['hændɪ] *adj* (**a**) *(useful)* pratique; **to come in h.** être utile (**b**) *(convenient)* commode; **the flat is very h. for the shops** l'appartement est tout près des commerces (**c**) *(within reach)* à portée de la main; **have you got a pen h.?** est-ce que tu as un stylo à portée de la main? (**d**) *(skilful)* bricoleur(euse); **he's very h. in the kitchen** il est bon cuisinier
handyman ['hændɪmæn] *n* homme *m* à tout faire
hang [hæŋ] **1** *n Fam* **to get the h. of sth** piger qch
2 *vt (pt & pp hung* [hʌŋ]) (**a**) *(suspend) (from ceiling)* pendre, suspendre; *(on wall)* accrocher (**b**) **to h. one's head** baisser la tête; **he hung his head in shame** il baissa la tête sous l'effet de la honte (**c**) *(pt & pp* **hanged**) *(criminal)* pendre
3 *vi* (**a**) *(be suspended) (from ceiling)* être suspendu(e); *(on wall)* être accroché(e); *Fig* **she hung on his every word** elle était pendue à ses lèvres (**b**) *(be executed)* être pendu(e) (**c**) *(of clothes)* tomber
▸**hang about, hang around** *vi Fam (wait)* poireauter; **to keep sb hanging about** *or* **around** faire poireauter qn
▸**hang back** *vi* hésiter
▸**hang in** *vi Fam* **h. in there!** accroche-toi!, tiens bon!
▸**hang on 1** *vi* (**a**) *Fam (wait)* patienter, attendre (**b**) *(survive)* tenir le coup
2 *vt insep (depend on)* dépendre de
▸**hang on to** *vt insep* garder
▸**hang out 1** *vt sep (washing)* étendre
2 *vi* (**a**) *(from pocket, box)* dépasser (**b**) *Fam (spend time)* traîner

▸**hang together** *vi (of argument, statements)* se tenir
▸**hang up 1** *vt sep (hat, picture)* accrocher
2 *vi (on telephone)* raccrocher; **to h. up on sb** raccrocher au nez de qn
hangar ['hæŋə(r)] *n* hangar *m*
hangdog ['hæŋdɒg] *adj (look, expression)* de chien battu
hanger ['hæŋə(r)] *n (for clothes)* cintre *m*
hanger-on [hæŋə'rɒn] *(pl* **hangers-on**) *n* parasite *m*, pique-assiette *m inv*
hang-glider ['hæŋglaɪdə(r)] *n* deltaplane *m*
hang-gliding ['hæŋglaɪdɪŋ] *n* deltaplane *m*; **to go h.** faire du deltaplane
hanging ['hæŋɪŋ] *n (execution)* pendaison *f*
hangman ['hæŋmən] *n* bourreau *m*
hangnail ['hæŋneɪl] *n* envie *f*
hang-out ['hæŋaʊt] *n Fam* repaire *m*
hangover ['hæŋəʊvə(r)] *n* (**a**) *(from drinking)* gueule *f* de bois (**b**) *(practice, belief)* reste *m*, vestige *m*
hang-up ['hæŋʌp] *n Fam* complexe *m*; **to have a h. about sth** être complexé(e) à propos de qch
hanker ['hæŋkə(r)] *vi* **to h. after** *or* **for sth** avoir très envie de qch
hankering ['hæŋkərɪŋ] *n* **to have a h. for sth** avoir très envie de qch
hankie, hanky ['hæŋkɪ] *(pl* **hankies**) *n Fam* mouchoir *m*
hanky-panky ['hæŋkɪ'pæŋkɪ] *n Fam* (**a**) *(sexual activity)* galipettes *fpl* (**b**) *(underhand behaviour)* entourloupettes *fpl*
Hanover ['hænəʊvə(r)] *n* Hanovre *m*
haphazard [hæp'hæzəd] *adj (choice, decision)* pris(e) au hasard; *(attempt)* mal organisé(e)
haphazardly [hæp'hæzədlɪ] *adv* n'importe comment
hapless ['hæplɪs] *adj Formal* infortuné(e)
happen ['hæpən] *vi* arriver, se produire; **it happened ten years ago** c'est arrivé il y a dix ans; **what happened?** que s'est-il passé?; **to h. again** se reproduire; **it so happens (that)...** il se trouve justement que...; **as if nothing had happened** comme si de rien n'était; **as it happens,...** justement...; **what has happened to him?** que lui est-il arrivé?; **to h. to meet sb** rencontrer qn par hasard; **I h. to know (that)...** il se trouve que je sais que...; **do you h. to know whether...?** savez-vous par hasard si...?
▸**happen on, happen upon** *vt insep* tomber sur
happening ['hæpənɪŋ] **1** *n* événement *m*
2 *adj Fam (town) (lively)* dynamique; *(trendy)* branché(e), dans le coup
happily ['hæpɪlɪ] *adv* (**a**) *(play)* gentiment; *(chat)* tranquillement; **a h. married couple** un ménage heureux; **they lived h. ever after** ≃ ils vécurent heureux et eurent beaucoup d'enfants (**b**) *(fortunately)* heureusement, par bonheur (**c**) *(willingly)* volontiers
happiness ['hæpɪnɪs] *n* bonheur *m*
happy ['hæpɪ] *adj* (**a**) *(content, cheerful)* heureux(-euse); **to be h. with sth** être satisfait(e) de qch; **to make sb h.** rendre qn heureux; **to keep sb h.** satisfaire qn; **a story with a h. ending** une histoire qui finit bien; **a h. medium** le juste milieu; **h. birthday/ Christmas!** joyeux anniversaire/Noël!; **h. New Year!** bonne année! (**b**) *(fortunate) (choice, phrase)* heureux(euse) (**c**) *(willing)* **to be h. to do sth** être heureux(euse) de faire qch

happy-clappy ['hæpɪ'klæpɪ] *adj Br Fam Pej* agaçant(e) de par sa joie exubérante *(appliqué aux chrétiens évangéliques)*

happy-go-lucky ['hæpɪgəʊ'lʌkɪ] *adj* insouciant(e)

harangue [hə'ræŋ] **1** *n* harangue *f*
2 *vt* haranguer (**about** au sujet de)

harass [hə'ræs, 'hærəs] *vt* harceler

harassed [hə'ræst, 'hærəst] *adj* stressé(e)

harassment ['hærəsmənt, hə'ræsmənt] *n* harcèlement *m*; **police h.** harcèlement policier

harbour, *Am* **harbor** ['hɑːbə(r)] **1** *n* port *m*
2 *vt (fugitive)* cacher; *(hope, suspicion)* nourrir; **to h. a grudge against sb** garder rancune à qn

hard [hɑːd] **1** *adj* (**a**) *(substance)* dur(e); *(fact, evidence)* tangible; *Fig* **to be as h. as nails** être un(e) dur(e) à cuire; **in h. cash** en liquide; *Comput* **h. copy** copie *f* sur papier; **h. core** *(of group)* noyau *m* dur; **h. court** *(for tennis)* court *m* en dur; *Comput* **h. disk** disque *m* dur; **h. drugs** drogues *fpl* dures; *Pol* **h. left/right** extrême gauche *f*/droite *f*; *Comput* **h. return** retour *m* chariot obligatoire; *Br* **h. shoulder** *(on motorway)* bande *f* d'arrêt d'urgence
(**b**) *(difficult)* difficile; *(strenuous)* pénible; **it was h. work persuading him to come** ça n'a pas été facile de le convaincre de venir; **it's h. to say...** il est difficile de dire...; **to be h. to please** être difficile (à satisfaire); **to learn sth the h. way** apprendre qch à ses dépens; **to do things the h. way** se compliquer la vie; **h. of hearing** dur(e) d'oreille
(**c**) *(harsh) (person, conditions, life)* dur(e); **to be h. on sb** être dur avec qn; **to have a h. time (of it)** en baver; **to give sb a h. time** mener la vie dure à qn; **a h. winter** un hiver rigoureux; **no h. feelings?** sans rancune?; **to take a h. line on sth** prendre une position très ferme sur qch; **h. luck!,** *Fam* **h. cheese!** pas de chance!
(**d**) *(intense)* **to be a h. worker** travailler dur; *Law* **h. labour** travaux *mpl* forcés; *Com* **to give sb the h. sell** essayer de convaincre qn d'acheter à toute force
(**e**) *(water)* calcaire
2 *adv* (**a**) *(work)* dur; *(push, hit)* fort; **to try h.** faire de son mieux; **to look h. at sb/sth** regarder qn/qch fixement; **to think h.** bien réfléchir; **to be h. at work** être en plein travail; **it's raining h.** il pleut à verse; **to feel h. done by** se sentir brimé(e); *Fam* **h. up** *(short of money)* fauché(e)
(**b**) *(near)* **h. by** tout près de; **to follow h. upon sb/sth** suivre qn/qch de près

hard-and-fast ['hɑːdən'fɑːst] *adj (rule)* absolu(e)

hardback ['hɑːdbæk] *n* livre *m* relié

hard-bitten ['hɑːd'bɪtən] *adj* endurci(e)

hardboard ['hɑːdbɔːd] *n* aggloméré *m*

hard-boiled [hɑːd'bɔɪld] *adj (egg)* dur(e); *Fig (person)* dur à cuire

hard-core ['hɑːdkɔː(r)] *adj (supporter)* inconditionnel(elle); *(pornography)* hard *inv*; *(punk)* hard-core *inv*

hard-earned [hɑːd'ɜːnd] *adj* durement gagné(e)

harden ['hɑːdən] **1** *vt* endurcir; **to h. oneself to sth** s'endurcir à qch
2 *vi (of substance, attitude)* durcir

hardened ['hɑːdənd] *adj (steel)* trempé(e); *(drinker)* invétéré(e); *(criminal)* endurci(e)

hard-fought ['hɑːd'fɔːt] *adj (election, contest)* âprement disputé(e)

hard-headed ['hɑːd'hedɪd] *adj (attitude, person)* réaliste

hard-hearted ['hɑːd'hɑːtɪd] *adj* dur(e)

hard-hitting [hɑːd'hɪtɪŋ] *adj (criticism, report)* sans indulgence

hardliner [hɑːd'laɪnə(r)] *n (politician, activist)* jusqu'au-boutiste *mf*

hardly ['hɑːdlɪ] *adv (scarcely)* à peine; **h. had I arrived when...** j'étais à peine arrivé que...; **you can h. expect me to do that** vous ne vous attendez tout de même pas à ce que je fasse ça; **I can h. believe it** j'ai du mal à y croire; *also Ironic* **I can h. wait** j'ai hâte d'y être; **h. ever** presque jamais; **h. anyone/anything** presque personne/rien

hardness ['hɑːdnɪs] *n* (**a**) *(of substance)* dureté *f* (**b**) *(of problem)* difficulté *f*

hard-on ['hɑːdɒn] *n Vulg* **to have/get a h.** bander

hard-pressed [hɑːd'prest], **hard-pushed** [hɑːd'pʊʃt] *adj* en difficulté; **to be h. for time/money** manquer de temps/d'argent; **to be h. to do sth** avoir du mal à faire qch

hardship ['hɑːdʃɪp] *n* épreuve *f*; **to live in h.** vivre dans la misère

hardware ['hɑːdweə(r)] *n* (**a**) *(tools)* matériel *m*; **(military) h.** *(weapons)* matériel militaire, armement *m*; **h. store** quincaillerie *f* (**b**) *Comput* matériel *m*, hardware *m*

hard-wearing [hɑːd'weərɪŋ] *adj* résistant(e)

hard-won [hɑːd'wʌn] *adj* durement acquis(e)

hard-working ['hɑːd'wɜːkɪŋ] *adj* travailleur(euse)

hardy ['hɑːdɪ] *adj* résistant(e), robuste

hare [heə(r)] *n* lièvre *m*; **to run with the hares and hunt with the hounds** manger à tous les râteliers

▶**hare off** *vi Br Fam* partir en trombe

harebrained ['heəbreɪnd] *adj* écervelé(e)

harelip ['heəlɪp] *n* bec-de-lièvre *m*

harem ['hɑːriːm] *n* harem *m*

haricot ['hærɪkəʊ] *n* **h. (bean)** haricot *m* blanc

hark [hɑːk] *exclam Lit* écoutez!; *Fam* **h. at him!** comme il y va!

▶**hark back** *vi* **to h. back to sth** évoquer qch; **he's always harking back to that mistake I made** il revient toujours sur l'erreur que j'ai faite

harlot ['hɑːlət] *n Lit* prostituée *f*

harm [hɑːm] **1** *n* mal *m*; *(to reputation)* tort *m*; **to do sb h.** faire du mal à qn; **to do oneself h.** se faire du tort; **it will do more h. than good** cela va faire plus de mal que de bien; **I can't see any h. in it** je ne vois pas de mal à ça; **there's no h. in trying** ça ne coûte rien d'essayer; **you will come to no h.** il ne t'arrivera rien (de mal); **out of h.'s way** en sûreté, en lieu sûr
2 *vt (physically)* faire du mal à; *(health, reputation, cause)* nuire à; *(skin, fabric)* abîmer

harmful ['hɑːmfʊl] *adj (influence, activity)* néfaste; *(substance, ray)* nocif(ive)

harmless ['hɑːmlɪs] *adj (person, animal)* inoffensif(ive); *(joke)* innocent(e); **it's just a bit of h. fun** ça ne fait de mal à personne

harmonica [hɑː'mɒnɪkə] *n* harmonica *m*

harmonious [hɑː'məʊnɪəs] *adj* harmonieux(euse)

harmonization [hɑːmənaɪ'zeɪʃən] *n* harmonisation *f*

harmonize ['hɑːmənaɪz] **1** *vt* harmoniser
2 *vi* s'harmoniser (**with** avec)

harmony ['hɑːmənɪ] *(pl* harmonies*) n also Fig* harmonie *f*; **in h. with** en harmonie *ou* en accord avec; **to live in h. (with)** vivre en harmonie (avec)

harness ['hɑːnɪs] **1** n (**a**) (for horse, baby, of parachute) harnais m; (for climber) baudrier m (**b**) (idioms) **to work in h. (with)** travailler en équipe (avec); **to die in h.** mourir à la tâche
2 vt (horse) harnacher; (to a cart) atteler; (resources) exploiter

harp [hɑːp] n harpe f
▶**harp on** vi **to h. on about sth** revenir sans arrêt sur qch

harpist ['hɑːpɪst] n harpiste mf

harpoon [hɑː'puːn] **1** n harpon m
2 vt harponner

harpsichord ['hɑːpsɪkɔːd] n clavecin m

harpy ['hɑːpɪ] (pl **harpies**) n harpie f

harrow ['hærəʊ] n herse f

harrowing ['hærəʊɪŋ] adj (experience, sight) pénible; (account, image) déchirant(e)

harry ['hærɪ] (pt & pp **harried**) vt harceler

harsh [hɑːʃ] adj (voice, sound) strident(e); (climate) rude; (treatment, person) dur(e)

harshly ['hɑːʃlɪ] adv (answer, speak, treat) durement

harvest ['hɑːvɪst] **1** n (of fruit) récolte f; (of crops) moisson f; (of grapes) vendange f; **h. festival** = fête religieuse pour célébrer la fin de la moisson
2 vt (fruit) récolter; (crops) moissonner; (grapes) vendanger; Fig (information) récolter

has [hæz] 3rd pers singular of **have**

has-been ['hæzbiːn] n Fam Pej has been mf inv

hash [hæʃ] n (**a**) (stew) hachis m; Am **h. browns** = pommes de terre rapées et sautées (présentees parfois sous forme de galette) (**b**) very Fam (hashish) hasch m (**c**) (symbol) **h. mark, h. sign** dièse m (**d**) (idioms) Fam **to make a h. of sth** faire un beau gâchis de qch

hashish ['hæʃiːʃ] n haschich m

hasn't ['hæznt] = has not

hassle ['hæsəl] Fam **1** n embêtements mpl; **it's too much h.** c'est trop de tintouin; **it's a real h. buying a house** l'achat d'une maison est un vrai casse-tête; **to give sb h.** faire des histoires à qn
2 vt embêter, harceler; **don't h. me!** arrête de m'embêter!

haste [heɪst] n hâte f; **in h.** en hâte, à la hâte; **to make h.** se dépêcher, se hâter; Prov **more h. less speed** hâtez-vous lentement

hasten ['heɪsən] **1** vt (accelerate) précipiter; **to h. sb's departure** avancer ou hâter le départ de qn
2 vi se presser; **I h. to add...** je m'empresse d'ajouter...

hastily ['heɪstɪlɪ] adv (write, prepare) hâtivement; (say, eat) précipitamment; **too h.** trop vite

hasty ['heɪstɪ] adj (departure, removal) précipité(e); (meal) rapide; (reply, decision) irréfléchi(e); **to jump to a h. conclusion** conclure à la légère

hat [hæt] n chapeau m; also Fig **to take one's h. off to sb** tirer son chapeau à qn; Fig **to pass the h. round** (collect money) faire la quête; Fig **to throw one's h. in the ring** (enter contest) se porter candidat(e); Fam Fig **to keep sth under one's h.** garder qch pour soi; Fig **I'm speaking with my lawyer's h. on** je parle en ma qualité de juriste; **h. stand** portemanteau m; **h. trick** (of goals) = trois buts marqués par le même joueur; (of victories) triplé m

hatch¹ [hætʃ] n (of ship) écoutille f; Fam **down the h.!** cul sec!; (serving) **h.** passe-plat m

hatch² **1** vt (egg) faire éclore; Fig (scheme, plot) tramer
2 vi (of egg) éclore

hatchback ['hætʃbæk] n (car) (three-door) voiture f à trois portes, trois-portes f inv; (five-door) voiture f à cinq portes, cinq-portes f inv

hatchet ['hætʃɪt] n hachette f; Fam **to do a h. job on sb/sth** (of critic, reviewer) démolir qn/qch; Fam **h. man** homme m de main

hate [heɪt] **1** n haine f; **h. mail** lettres fpl d'injures
2 vt détester, haïr; **to h. doing sth** détester faire qch, avoir horreur de faire qch; **she hates to be contradicted** elle a horreur qu'on la contredise; Fam **I h. to tell you, but I think you've missed your train** ça m'ennuie de te le dire, mais je pense que tu as raté ton train

hateful ['heɪtfʊl] adj odieux(euse)

hatpin ['hætpɪn] n épingle f à chapeau

hatred ['heɪtrɪd] n haine f (**of/for** de/pour)

haughty ['hɔːtɪ] adj hautain(e)

haul [hɔːl] **1** n (**a**) (fish caught) prise f; (loot) butin m; (of drugs, stolen goods) saisie f (**b**) Fam (journey) parcours m, trajet m; **it's a long h.** la route est longue; Fig c'est un travail de longue haleine
2 vt (**a**) (pull) tirer; (tow) remorquer; Fam **he was hauled in for questioning** on l'a emmené pour l'interroger; Fam Fig **to h. sb over the coals** (reprimand) passer un savon à qn; **she was hauled up before the headmaster** elle a été convoquée chez le proviseur (**b**) (transport) transporter par camion

haulage ['hɔːlɪdʒ] n (transportation) transport m (routier); (costs) (frais mpl de) transport; **h. firm** entreprise f de transports routiers

haulier ['hɔːlɪə(r)], Am **hauler** ['hɔːlə(r)] n (company) entreprise f de transports routiers

haunch [hɔːntʃ] n (of person) hanche f; (of venison) cuissot m; **to sit** or **squat on one's haunches** être accroupi(e)

haunt [hɔːnt] **1** n (of criminals) repaire m; (of group of people) (lieu m de) rendez-vous m; **it's one of his favourite haunts** (favourite places) c'est un des endroits qu'il fréquente habituellement
2 vt also Fig hanter

haunted ['hɔːntɪd] adj (castle, room) hanté(e); Fig **he has a h. look** il a l'air égaré

haunting ['hɔːntɪŋ] adj obsédant(e)

Havana [hə'vænə] n la Havane; **H. (cigar)** havane m

have [hæv]

> Les formes négatives, **haven't** et **hasn't**, s'écrivent **have not** et **has not** dans un style plus soutenu.

1 vt (pt & pp **had**) (**a**) (own) avoir; **they've (got) a big house** ils ont une grande maison; **she doesn't h.** or **hasn't got a car** elle n'a pas de voiture; **I've (got) things to do** j'ai des choses à faire; **you can h. it back tomorrow** je te le rendrai demain; **to h. sb in one's power** tenir qn à sa merci; **to h. it on good authority that...** tenir de source sûre que...
(**b**) (with noun to denote activity) **to h. a swim** se baigner; **to h. a shave** se raser; **to h. a bath** prendre un bain; **to h. lunch** déjeuner; **to h. a cigarette** fumer une cigarette; **to h. a drink** prendre un verre; **to h. a good/bad time** passer un bon/mauvais moment
(**c**) (with illnesses) **to h. a cold** être enrhumé(e); **to h. flu/cancer** avoir la grippe/un cancer
(**d**) (cause to do, to be done) **to h. sb do sth** faire faire qch à qn; **to h. sth done** faire faire qch; **to h. one's**

hair cut se faire couper les cheveux; **h. him call me** dis-lui de m'appeler; **I'll h. you know that...!** je vous signale que...!

(**e**) *(in passive constructions)* **I had my watch stolen** on m'a volé ma montre; **three houses had their windows broken** il y a des fenêtres brisées dans trois maisons

(**f**) *(allow)* **I won't h. it!** je n'accepte pas ça!; **I won't h. you causing trouble!** pas question que tu fasses des histoires!

(**g**) *(be compelled)* **to h. (got) to do sth** devoir faire qch; **I h.** *or* **I've got to go** je dois y aller; **you don't h. to come with me** tu n'es pas obligé de venir avec moi; **do you h.** *or* **h. you got to work?** est-ce qu'il faut vraiment que tu travailles?; **it has** *or* **it's got to be done** il faut que ce soit fait

(**h**) *Fam (idioms)* **to be had** *(cheated)* se faire avoir; **to h. had it** être fichu(e); **to h. had it with sb/sth** en avoir marre de qn/qch; **he had it coming** ça lui pendait au nez

2 *v aux* avoir/être

> Most French verbs will conjugate with **avoir** to form the perfect tense. However, all reflexive verbs and many intransitive verbs – mainly of motion – will conjugate with **être**.

to h. seen avoir vu; **to h. left** être parti(e); **to h. hurt oneself** s'être blessé(e); **I've worked here for three years** je travaille ici depuis trois ans; **we've seen this film before – no we haven't!** nous avons déjà vu ce film – mais non!; **you haven't done the dishes – yes, I h.!** tu n'as pas fait la vaisselle – si, je l'ai faite!; **you h. told him, haven't you?** tu le lui as dit, n'est-ce pas *ou* non?; **you haven't forgotten, h. you?** tu n'as pas oublié, n'est-ce pas *ou* hein?

3 *n* **the haves and the have-nots** les riches *mpl* et les pauvres

▶**have in** *vt sep Fam* **to h. it in for sb** en avoir après qn

▶**have off** *vt sep Br very Fam* **to h. it off (with sb)** *(have sexual intercourse)* s'envoyer en l'air (avec qn)

▶**have on** *vt sep* (**a**) *(be wearing)* porter; **to h. nothing on** être nu(e) (**b**) *Fam (fool)* **to h. sb on** faire marcher qn (**c**) *(have arranged)* **to h. a lot on** avoir beaucoup à faire; **to h. nothing on** n'avoir rien de prévu (**d**) **to h. sth on sb** disposer d'informations compromettantes pour qn

▶**have out** *vt sep* (**a**) *(have removed)* **to h. a tooth out** se faire arracher une dent; **to h. one's appendix out** se faire opérer de l'appendicite (**b**) *(resolve)* **to h. it out with sb** s'expliquer avec qn

▶**have up** *vt sep* **to be had up (for sth)** être jugé(e) (pour qch)

haven ['heɪvən] *n* refuge *m*

haven't ['hævənt] = have not

haversack ['hævəsæk] *n* sac *m* à dos

havoc ['hævək] *n* (**a**) *(damage)* ravages *mpl*, dégâts *mpl*; **to cause** *or* **wreak h.** faire des ravages (**b**) *(confusion)* pagaille *f*; **to play h. with sth** *(plans)* chambouler qch

Hawaii [hə'waɪɪ] *n* Hawaii

Hawaiian [hə'waɪən] **1** *n* Hawaiien(enne) *m,f*
2 *adj* hawaiien(enne)

hawk¹ [hɔːk] *n also Pol* faucon *m*; **to watch sb/sth like a h.** ne pas quitter qn/qch du regard

hawk² *vt* **to h. one's wares** *(in market, street)* vendre ses marchandises à la criée; *(from door to door)* faire du porte-à-porte

hawk-eyed ['hɔːkaɪd] *adj* **to be h.** avoir des yeux de lynx

hawkish ['hɔːkɪʃ] *adj Pol* belliciste

hawser ['hɔːzə(r)] *n* aussière *f*

hawthorn ['hɔːθɔːn] *n* aubépine *f*

hay [heɪ] *n* foin *m*; **to make h.** faire les foins; *Fig* **to make h. while the sun shines** en profiter tant que ça dure

hayfever ['heɪfiːvə(r)] *n* rhume *m* des foins

hayloft ['heɪlɒft] *n* fenil *m*

haystack ['heɪstæk] *n* meule *f* de foin

haywire ['heɪwaɪə(r)] *adv Fam* **to go h.** *(of plan)* mal tourner; *(of mechanism)* se détraquer

hazard ['hæzəd] **1** *n* *(danger)* danger *m*, risque *m*; **a fire h.** un risque d'incendie; **a health h.** un danger pour la santé; **h. lights** feux *mpl* de détresse
2 *vt* *(one's life, fortune)* risquer; *(opinion)* hasarder; **to h. a guess** essayer de deviner

hazardous ['hæzədəs] *adj* dangereux(euse); *(financial venture)* hasardeux(euse)

haze [heɪz] *n* *(mist)* brume *f*; *(of doubt, confusion)* atmosphère *f*; **my mind was in a h.** j'avais l'esprit embrouillé

hazel ['heɪzəl] **1** *n* *(colour)* (couleur *f*) noisette *f*; **h. (tree)** noisetier *m*
2 *adj* *(colour)* noisette *inv*; **h. eyes** yeux *mpl* (couleur) noisette

hazelnut ['heɪzəlnʌt] *n* noisette *f*

hazily ['heɪzɪlɪ] *adv* vaguement

hazy ['heɪzɪ] *adj* *(weather)* brumeux(euse); *(image, memory)* flou(e), vague; **to be h. about sth** *(remember vaguely)* n'avoir qu'un vague souvenir de qch

he [hiː] **1** *pron* il; **he's Scottish** il est écossais; **HE hasn't got it!** ce n'est pas lui qui l'a!
2 *n* **it's a he** *(of animal)* c'est un mâle

head [hed] **1** *n* (**a**) *(part of body)* tête *f*; **a fine h. of hair** une belle chevelure; **from h. to foot** *or* **toe** de la tête aux pieds; **to stand on one's h.** faire le poirier; *Fig* **to stand sth on its h.** retourner qch; **to win by a h.** *(of horse)* gagner d'une tête; *Fig* **she's h. and shoulders above the other candidates** les autres candidats ne lui arrivent pas à la cheville; **h. cold** rhume *m* de cerveau; **h. start** *(advantage)* avantage *m*; *(in race)* avance *f*

(**b**) *(intellect, mind)* tête *f*; **to do sums in one's h.** calculer de tête; **to have a good h. on one's shoulders** avoir la tête sur les épaules; **to have a good h. for business** avoir le sens des affaires; **to have a good h. for figures** être à l'aise avec les chiffres; **to have a (good) h. for heights** ne pas avoir le vertige; **to take it into one's h. to do sth** se mettre en tête de faire qch; **to take it into one's h. that...** se mettre dans la tête que...; **it never entered my h. that...** il ne m'est jamais venu à l'esprit que...; **to put ideas into sb's h.** donner des idées à qn; *Fam* **he's not right in the h.** il a un grain

(**c**) *(of pin, hammer, list, bed)* tête *f*; *(of arrow)* pointe *f*; *(of page, stairs)* haut *m*; *(of table)* bout *m*; *(on beer)* mousse *f*; *(on tape recorder)* tête; **a h. of lettuce/cabbage** un pied de laitue/chou; **heads or tails?** *(when tossing coin)* pile ou face?; **to build up a h. of steam** *(of campaign)* s'intensifier; *(of person)* progresser rapidement; **to come to a h.** *(of conflict, crisis)* atteindre un paroxysme (**d**) *(person in charge) (of family, the Church, business)* chef *m*; **h. of state** chef d'État; *Br Sch* **h. (teacher)** directeur(trice) *m,f*; *Br Sch* **h. boy/girl** = élève choisi parmi les grands pour maintenir la discipline et représenter son école; **h. office** siège *m* (social); **h. waiter** maître *m* d'hôtel

(**e**) *(unit)* **£10 per h.** *or* **a h.** 10 livres par personne; **six h. of cattle** six têtes de bétail

(**f**) *(idioms)* **we put our heads together** nous nous y sommes tous mis; **they'll have your h. (on a plate) for this** cela te coûtera ta tête; **to bury** *or* **have one's h. in the sand** pratiquer la politique de l'autruche; **to give sb his h.** lâcher la bride à qn; **on your own h. be it** à tes risques et périls; **to go over sb's h.** *(appeal to higher authority)* ne pas consulter qn *(en suivant la voie hiérarchique)*; *Fam* **to shout one's h. off** crier à tue-tête; **the wine/praise went to his h.** le vin/compliment lui est monté à la tête; *Prov* **two heads are better than one** deux avis valent mieux qu'un; **off the top of one's h.** au hasard; **it was** *or* **went over my h.** ça m'a dépassé; **I can't make h. nor tail of this** ça n'a ni queue ni tête; *Fam* **to lose one's h.** *(panic)* perdre la tête; *(get angry)* perdre son calme; *Fam* **to keep one's h.** garder son calme; *Fam* **to be off one's h.** avoir perdu la boule; **to fall h. over heels in love with sb** tomber éperdument amoureux de qn

2 *vt* (**a**) *(lead) (organization, campaign)* diriger; *(list)* venir en tête de

(**b**) *(steer)* diriger; **one of the locals headed me in the right direction** un des habitants m'a indiqué la bonne direction

(**c**) *(put a title on) (page, chapter)* intituler

(**d**) *(in football)* **to h. the ball** faire une tête

3 *vi (move)* se diriger; **they were heading out of town** ils sortaient de la ville

▸**head for** *vt insep* se diriger vers; **you're heading for disaster** tu vas droit au désastre; **you're heading for trouble** tu vas avoir des ennuis

▸**head off 1** *vt sep (divert)* éviter

2 *vi (depart)* partir

headache ['hedeɪk] *n* mal *m* de tête; *Fig (problem)* casse-tête *m inv*; **to have a h.** avoir mal à la tête

headband ['hedbænd] *n* bandeau *m*

headboard ['hedbɔːd] *n* tête *f* de lit

headbutt ['hedbʌt] *vt* donner un coup de tête à

headcase ['hedkeɪs] *n Fam* cinglé(e) *m,f*

headdress ['heddres] *n* coiffure *f*

headed ['hedɪd] *adj* **h. (note)paper** papier *m* à en-tête

header ['hedə(r)] *n* (**a**) *Typ* en-tête *m* (**b**) *(in football)* (coup *m* de) tête *f*

headfirst ['hedˈfɜːst] *adv* la tête la première

headgear ['hedgɪə(r)] *n* couvre-chef *m*

head-hunt ['hedˈhʌnt] *vt Com* **to be head-hunted** être recruté(e) par un chasseur de têtes

head-hunter ['hedhʌntə(r)] *n Com* chasseur *m* de têtes

heading ['hedɪŋ] *n (of chapter, article)* titre *m*; *(of letter)* en-tête *m*; **it comes** *or* **falls under the h. of...** c'est à mettre sous la rubrique de...

headlamp ['hedlæmp] *n (on car)* phare *m*

headland ['hedlənd] *n* cap *m*, pointe *f*

headlight ['hedlaɪt] *n (on car)* phare *m*

headline ['hedlaɪn] **1** *n (of TV news)* titre *m*; *(of newspaper)* (gros) titre; **to hit the headlines** faire la une des journaux; **to be h. news** faire la une des journaux

2 *vt (article, story)* intituler

headlong ['hedlɒŋ] **1** *adj* **there was a h. rush for the bar** tout le monde s'est rué vers le bar

2 *adv (fall)* la tête la première; *(rush)* tête baissée

headmaster [hedˈmɑːstə(r)] *n Br Sch* directeur *m*

headmistress [hedˈmɪstrɪs] *n Br Sch* directrice *f*

head-on ['heˈdɒn] *adj & adv* de front; **to meet sb h.** aborder qn de front; **a h. collision** une collision frontale

headphones ['hedfəʊnz] *npl* écouteurs *mpl*

headquarters [hedˈkwɔːtəz] *npl (of organization)* siège *m* (social); *Mil* quartier *m* général

headrest ['hedrest] *n* appui-tête *m inv*

headroom ['hedruːm] *n (under bridge, inside car)* hauteur *f*

headscarf ['hedskɑːf] *(pl* **headscarves** ['hedskɑːvz]) *n* foulard *m*

headset ['hedset] *n* écouteurs *mpl*

headstone ['hedstəʊn] *n (on grave)* pierre *f* tombale

headstrong ['hedstrɒŋ] *adj* têtu(e), entêté(e)

headway ['hedweɪ] *n* **to make h.** avancer, faire des progrès

headwind ['hedwɪnd] *n* vent *m* contraire; *Naut* vent debout

heady ['hedɪ] *adj (atmosphere)* enivrant(e); *(wine, perfume)* capiteux(euse); *(heights, days)* grisant(e)

heal [hiːl] **1** *vt (wound, person)* guérir; *(disagreement)* régler; *Fig* **wounds which only time would h.** des blessures que seul le temps cicatriserait

2 *vi (of wound)* **to h. (up** *or* **over)** cicatriser

health [helθ] *n* santé *f*; **to be in good/poor h.** être en bonne/mauvaise santé; *Fig* **the economy is in good h.** l'économie se porte bien; **the Department of H.** ≃ le ministère de la Santé; **to drink (to) sb's h.** boire à la santé de qn; **h. care** soins *mpl* médicaux; *Br* **h. centre** dispensaire *m*; **h. club** club *m* de remise en forme; **h. cover** *(insurance)* assurance *f* médicale; **h. farm** centre *m* de remise en forme; **h. food** produits *mpl* biologiques; **h. hazard** *or* **risk** risque *m* pour la santé; **h. insurance** assurance maladie; **h. resort** station *f* climatique; *(by sea)* station balnéaire; **the H. Service** ≃ la Sécurité *f* sociale; **h. visitor** = infirmière effectuant des visites de contrôle à domicile

healthy ['helθɪ] *adj (person)* en bonne santé; *(climate)* salubre; *(food, habit, economy)* sain(e); **a h. appetite** un bon appétit; **it is a h. sign that...** c'est bon signe que...; **he has a h. respect for his opponents** il apprécie ses adversaires à leur juste valeur

heap [hiːp] **1** *n* tas *m*; *Fig* **people at the top/bottom of the h.** ceux qui sont en haut/bas de l'échelle sociale; *Fam* **she's got heaps of money** elle a plein d'argent; *Fam* **we've got heaps of time** on a largement le temps

2 *vt* entasser; **his plate was heaped with food** son assiette était remplie de nourriture; **to h. sth with** remplir qch de; **a heaped spoonful** *(in recipe)* une cuillerée bien pleine; **to h. riches/praise on sb** couvrir qn de richesses/d'éloges; **to h. insults on sb** abreuver qn d'injures

hear [hɪə(r)] *(pt & pp* **heard** [hɜːd]) **1** *vt* (**a**) *(perceive)* entendre; **to h. sb speak** entendre qn parler; **I can hardly h. myself think!** on ne s'entend plus ici!; **to make oneself heard** se faire entendre; **let's h. it for...** applaudissons bien fort...; **have you heard the one about...?** est-ce que tu connais celle de...? (**b**) *(listen to)* écouter; **h., h.!** *(at meeting)* bravo!; *Law* **to h. a case** juger une affaire (**c**) *(find out)* entendre (dire), apprendre; **have you heard the news?** tu connais la nouvelle?; **I h. you're getting married** j'ai entendu dire que tu te mariais

2 *vi* entendre; **I can't h. properly** je n'entends pas bien; **to h. from sb** avoir des nouvelles de qn; **you'll be hearing from my lawyer!** vous allez entendre parler de mon avocat!; **to h. of** *or* **about sth** entendre parler de qch; **I won't h. of it!** je ne veux pas en entendre parler!

▸**hear out** *vt sep* **to h. sb out** écouter qn jusqu'au bout

hearing ['hɪərɪŋ] *n* (**a**) *(sense)* ouïe *f*, audition *f*; **h. aid** audiophone *m* (**b**) *(earshot)* **to be within/out of h.** être à portée/hors de portée de voix (**c**) *(chance to explain)* **to give sb a fair h.** laisser parler qn, laisser qn s'expliquer (**d**) *Law (inquiry)* audition *f*

hearsay ['hɪəseɪ] *n* ouï-dire *m inv*, on-dit *m inv*; *Law* **h. evidence** déposition *f* sur la foi d'autrui

hearse [hɜːs] *n* corbillard *m*

heart [hɑːt] *n* (**a**) *(organ)* cœur *m*; **to have h. trouble,** **to have a weak** *or* **bad h.** être cardiaque; **h. attack** crise *f* cardiaque; **h. disease** maladie *f* cardiaque; **h. failure** arrêt *m* cardiaque; **h. surgeon** chirurgien(-enne) *m,f* cardiologique; **h. surgery** chirurgie *f* cardiaque; **h. transplant** transplantation *f* cardiaque

(**b**) *(seat of the emotions)* cœur *m*; **to have a big h.** avoir bon cœur; **a h. of gold** un cœur d'or; **a h. of stone** un cœur de pierre; **have a h.!** ayez un peu de cœur!; **her h.'s in the right place** elle a bon cœur; **with a heavy h.** le cœur gros; **my h. sank** j'ai été très déçu; **to have one's h. in one's mouth** être terrorisé(e); **to break sb's h.** briser le cœur à qn; **to wear one's h. on one's sleeve** ne pas cacher ses sentiments; **affairs** *or* **matters of the h.** affaires *fpl* de cœur; *Ironic* **my h. bleeds for you** ça me fait de la peine pour toi; **in my h. of hearts** au fond de mon cœur; **from the bottom of one's h.** du fond du cœur; **he loved her with all his h.** il l'aimait de toute son âme; **at h.** au fond; **to have sb's welfare/interests at h.** avoir le bien-être/les intérêts de qn à cœur; **to take sth to h.** prendre qch à cœur; **to set one's h. on sth** vouloir qch à tout prix; **he's a man after my own h.** il est comme moi; **to one's h.'s content** tout son soûl

(**c**) *(enthusiasm, courage)* **to take h.** reprendre courage; **to lose h.** se décourager; **he tried to convince them but his h. wasn't in it** il a essayé de les convaincre mais le cœur n'y était pas; **I didn't have the h. to tell him** je n'ai pas eu le cœur de lui dire

(**d**) **by h.** *(know, learn)* par cœur

(**e**) *(centre) (of city, forest)* cœur *m*; **the h. of the matter** le fond du problème

(**f**) *(in cards)* **hearts** cœur *m*

heartache ['hɑːteɪk] *n* chagrin *m*, peine *f*

heartbeat ['hɑːtbiːt] *n* *(rhythm)* pouls *m*; *(single beat)* battement *m* de cœur

heartbreaking ['hɑːtbreɪkɪŋ] *adj* déchirant(e), navrant(e)

heartbroken ['hɑːtbrəʊkən] *adj* **to be h.** avoir le cœur brisé

heartburn ['hɑːtbɜːn] *n* *(indigestion)* brûlures *fpl* d'estomac

hearten ['hɑːtən] *vt* encourager

heartening ['hɑːtənɪŋ] *adj* encourageant(e)

heartfelt ['hɑːtfelt] *adj* sincère, qui vient du cœur

hearth [hɑːθ] *n* *(fireplace, home)* foyer *m*

hearthrug ['hɑːθrʌg] *n* devant *m* de foyer

heartily ['hɑːtɪlɪ] *adv (welcome, applaud)* chaleureusement; *(agree)* de tout cœur; *(eat)* avec appétit; **to be h. sick of sth** être profondément dégoûté(e) de qch

heartlands ['hɑːtlændz] *npl* centre *m*, cœur *m*

heartless ['hɑːtlɪs] *adj* sans cœur, cruel(elle)

heartrending ['hɑːtrendɪŋ] *adj* déchirant(e), navrant(e)

heart-searching ['hɑːtsɜːtʃɪŋ] *n* **after much h.** après avoir longuement réfléchi

heartstrings ['hɑːtstrɪŋz] *npl* **to tug at sb's h.** jouer sur la corde sensible de qn

heart-throb ['hɑːtθrɒb] *n* *Fam* idole *f*

heart-to-heart ['hɑːtə'hɑːt] *n* **to have a h. with sb** avoir une conversation à cœur ouvert avec qn

heart-warming ['hɑːtwɔːmɪŋ] *adj* réconfortant(e), qui réchauffe le cœur

hearty ['hɑːtɪ] *adj* (**a**) *(person, laugh)* jovial(e); *(approval, welcome)* chaleureux(euse); **to have a h. dislike of sth** avoir une sainte horreur de qch; **my heartiest congratulations** mes plus sincères félicitations (**b**) *(substantial) (meal, appetite)* solide

heat [hiːt] **1** *n* (**a**) *(high temperature)* chaleur *f*; **to give out h.** dégager de la chaleur; **to cook at a moderate/low h.** faire cuire à feu moyen/doux; **h. exhaustion** coup *m* de chaleur; **h. haze** brume *f* de chaleur; **h. loss** déperdition *f* de chaleur; **h. rash** boutons *mpl* de chaleur; *Med* **h. treatment** thermothérapie *f* (**b**) *(passion)* feu *m*; **in the h. of the moment/argument** dans le feu de l'action/de la discussion (**c**) *Fam (pressure)* **to turn up the h.** mettre la pression; **the h. is on** la tension est à son comble (**d**) *(of female animal)* **in** *or* **on h.** en chaleur (**e**) *(in sport)* éliminatoire *f*

2 *vt (food, water)* faire chauffer; *(room, building)* chauffer

▸**heat up 1** *vt sep* réchauffer

2 *vi (of water)* chauffer; *(of room)* se réchauffer; *Fig (of argument, contest)* s'animer

heated ['hiːtɪd] *adj* (**a**) *(room, building, swimming pool)* chauffé(e) (**b**) *(argument)* animé(e); **to become h.** *(of person)* s'échauffer

heater ['hiːtə(r)] *n* radiateur *m*

heath [hiːθ] *n* *(land)* lande *f*

heathen ['hiːðən] *n Rel* païen(enne) *m,f*; *Hum* barbare *mf*

heather ['heðə(r)] *n* bruyère *f*

heating ['hiːtɪŋ] *n* chauffage *m*

heatproof ['hiːtpruːf] *adj* résistant(e) à la chaleur; *(clothing)* isolant(e)

heatstroke ['hiːtstrəʊk] *n* coup *m* de chaleur

heatwave ['hiːtweɪv] *n* vague *f* de chaleur

heave [hiːv] **1** *n* effort *m*

2 *vt* (**a**) *(pull)* tirer fort; *(push)* pousser fortement; *(lift)* soulever avec effort; **she heaved herself out of her chair** elle s'extirpa de sa chaise; **to h. a sigh of relief** pousser un soupir de soulagement (**b**) *Fam (throw)* balancer

3 *vi* (**a**) *(pull)* **they heaved on the rope** ils tirèrent sur la corde fortement (**b**) *(of deck, ground)* tanguer, se soulever; *(of bosom)* se soulever (**c**) *(retch)* avoir des haut-le-cœur; *(vomit)* vomir (**d**) *(pt & pp* **hove** [həʊv]) *also Fig* **to h. into view** paraître à l'horizon

▸**heave to** *(pt & pp* **hove** [həʊv] *) vi Naut* se mettre en panne

heaven ['hevən] *n* paradis *m*, ciel *m*; **in h.** au paradis, au ciel; *Fig (overjoyed)* aux anges; **this is h.!** c'est le paradis!; **to move h. and earth to do sth** remuer ciel et terre pour faire qch; **the heavens opened** il s'est mis à pleuvoir à torrents; *Fam* **it stinks to high h.** ça pue; **(good) heavens!, heavens above!** juste ciel!, mon Dieu!; **thank h. (for that)!** Dieu merci!; **h. knows why...** Dieu seul sait pourquoi...; **for h.'s sake!** pour l'amour du ciel!; **h. forbid!** que le ciel nous en préserve!

heavenly ['hevənlɪ] *adj* (**a**) **h. body** corps *m* céleste (**b**) *Fam (weather, food)* divin(e)

heaven-sent ['hevənsent] *adj* providentiel(elle)

heavily ['hevɪlɪ] *adv (fall, walk, tax)* lourdement; *(sleep)* profondément; *(breathe)* bruyamment; **to drink/smoke h.** boire/fumer beaucoup; **it was raining h.** il pleuvait à torrents; **to rely** *or* **depend h. on** dépendre beaucoup de; **h. built** solidement charpenté(e); **to be h. defeated** subir une lourde défaite

heaving ['hiːvɪŋ] *adj Br Fam (very busy)* hyper animé(e)

heavy ['hevɪ] **1** *n (pl* **heavies***) Fam (tough guy)* dur *m*
2 *adj* (**a**) *(in weight, food)* lourd(e); **how h. is it?** combien est-ce que ça pèse?; **a h. blow** un coup violent; *Fig* un coup rude; **h. goods vehicle** poids *m* lourd; **h. industry** industrie *f* lourde; **h. metal** *Chem* métal *m* lourd; *(music)* heavy metal *m*
(**b**) *(large, thick) (coat, shoes)* gros (grosse); **h. losses** lourdes pertes *fpl*
(**c**) *(intense) (fighting)* violent(e); *(rain, showers)* fort(e); *(drinker, smoker)* gros (grosse); **a h. cold** un gros rhume; **there was h. traffic** il y avait beaucoup de circulation; **to be a h. sleeper** avoir le sommeil lourd; **to come under h. fire** essuyer un feu nourri
(**d**) *(oppressive) (smell)* fort(e); *(sky, fine, sentence)* lourd(e); **h. responsibility** lourde responsabilité *f*
(**e**) *(hard) (work, day, breathing)* pénible; **it was h. going** c'était difficile *ou* ardu; **h. seas** grosse mer *f*
(**f**) *Fam (threatening) (situation)* difficile, pénible; **to get h. with sb** être agressif(ive) avec qn
(**g**) *Fam (serious) (book, article)* intello

heavy-duty [hevɪ'djuːtɪ] *adj (machine)* à usage industriel; *(clothing, boots)* résistant(e)

heavy-handed [hevɪ'hændɪd] *adj (clumsy)* maladroit(e); *(government, policy)* autoritaire; **the police responded in a h. way** la police est intervenue de façon très agressive

heavyweight ['hevɪweɪt] *n (in boxing)* poids *m* lourd; *Fig* **a political h.** un grand ponte de la politique; **an intellectual h.** un grand intellectuel

Hebrew ['hiːbruː] **1** *n (language)* hébreu *m*
2 *adj* hébraïque

Hebrides ['hebrɪdiːz] *npl* **the H.** les (îles *fpl*) Hébrides *fpl*

heck [hek] *n Fam* **h.!** zut!; **what the h. are you doing here?** qu'est-ce que tu fiches là?; **what the h.!** et puis flûte!; **a h. of a lot** des masses

heckle ['hekəl] **1** *vt* interpeller, interrompre
2 *vi* chahuter

heckler ['heklə(r)] *n* chahuteur(euse) *m,f*

heckling ['heklɪŋ] *n* chahut *m*

hectare ['hektɑː(r)] *n* hectare *m*

hectic ['hektɪk] *adj (busy)* agité(e); *(eventful)* mouvementé(e); **a h. life** une vie trépidante

hector ['hektə(r)] *vt* rudoyer

hectoring ['hektərɪŋ] *adj* autoritaire

he'd [hiːd] = he had, he would

hedge [hedʒ] **1** *n* (**a**) *(in field, garden)* haie *f* (**b**) *(barrier)* **a h. against inflation** une protection contre l'inflation
2 *vt* (**a**) *(field)* entourer d'une haie (**b**) **to h. one's bets** se couvrir
3 *vi (in discussion)* ne pas se mouiller

hedgehog ['hedʒhɒg] *n* hérisson *m*

hedgerow ['hedʒrəʊ] *n* haie *f*

hedonism ['hedənɪzəm, 'hiːdənɪzəm] *n* hédonisme *m*

hedonist ['hedənɪst, 'hiːdənɪst] *n & adj* hédoniste *mf*

heed [hiːd] **1** *n* **to pay (no) h. to, to take (no) h. of** (ne pas) tenir compte de
2 *vt (warning, advice)* tenir compte de

heedless ['hiːdlɪs] *adj* **to be h. of** ne pas tenir compte de

heel [hiːl] **1** *n (of foot, shoe, sock)* talon *m*; **high heels** talons hauts; **he had the police at his heels** il avait la police sur les talons *ou* à ses trousses; **to take to one's heels** prendre ses jambes à son cou; **to turn on one's h.** tourner les talons; *Fam* **to cool** *or* **kick one's heels** *(wait)* poireauter; *Fig* **to bring sb to h.** *(bring under control)* mettre qn au pas
2 *vt (shoe)* réparer le talon de

hefty ['heftɪ] *adj Fam (person)* costaud(e); *(suitcase, box)* lourd(e); *(blow)* puissant(e); *(bill, fine)* gros (grosse)

heifer ['hefə(r)] *n* génisse *f*

height [haɪt] *n (of building, tree)* hauteur *f*; *(of mountain)* altitude *f*; *(of person)* taille *f*; **what h. are you?** combien mesurez-vous?; **to gain/lose h.** *(of plane)* prendre/perdre de l'altitude; **to be afraid of heights** avoir le vertige; **she's at the h. of her powers** elle est au maximum de ses capacités; **she's at the h. of her career** elle est à l'apogée de sa carrière; **the h. of fashion** la dernière mode; **it's the h. of madness!** c'est de la folie pure!; **at the h. of the storm** au plus fort de l'orage; **the season is at its h.** la saison bat son plein

heighten ['haɪtən] *vt (sensation)* intensifier; *(tension)* augmenter; **to h. public awareness** sensibiliser l'opinion

heinous ['heɪnəs] *adj Formal (crime)* abominable, atroce

heir [eə(r)] *n* héritier(ère) *m,f*; **to be h. to sth** être l'héritier de qch; **h. apparent** héritier présomptif

heiress ['eərɪs] *n* héritière *f*

heirloom ['eəluːm] *n* **a family h.** un objet de famille

held [held] *pt & pp of* hold

helicopter ['helɪkɒptə(r)] *n* hélicoptère *m*

heliport ['helɪpɔːt] *n* héliport *m*

helium ['hiːlɪəm] *n* hélium *m*

hell [hel] *n* (**a**) *Rel* enfer *m*; *Fam* **h.!** zut alors!
(**b**) *Fam (for emphasis)* **a h. of a price** un prix salé; **what the h. do you think you're doing?** qu'est-ce que tu fous?; **who the h. are you?** qui diable êtes-vous?; **she put up a h. of a fight** elle s'est bien défendue; **to have a h. of a time** *(good)* s'éclater; *(bad)* en baver; **a h. of a lot of...** énormément de...; **he's one** *or* **a h. of a guy** c'est un brave type
(**c**) *Fam (idioms)* **it was h.** c'était l'enfer; **to feel like h.** se sentir horriblement mal; **to make sb's life h.** faire de la vie de qn un enfer; **these shoes are giving me h.** ces chaussures me font un mal de chien; **all h. was let** *or* **broke loose** ce fut le chaos; **there'll be h. to pay if...** ça va barder si...; **go to h.!** va te faire voir!; **to run like h.** courir comme un dératé; **like h. (I will)!**

certainement pas!; **until h. freezes over** jusqu'à la saint-glinglin; **come h. or high water** quoi qu'il arrive; **to run h. for leather** courir ventre à terre; **to do sth for the h. of it** faire qch sans raison particulière

he'll [hi:l] = he will, he shall

hellbent ['helbent] *adj Fam* **to be h. on doing sth** vouloir à tout prix faire qch

hellhole ['helhəʊl] *n Fam (bar, club)* bouge *m*; *(prison)* enfer *m*

hellish ['helɪʃ] *adj Fam* infernal(e)

hello [he'ləʊ] *exclam* bonjour!; *(on phone)* allô!; **to say h. to sb** dire bonjour à qn; **h., what's this?** *(indicating surprise)* tiens, qu'est-ce que c'est que ça?

hell-raiser ['helreɪzə(r)] *n Fam* perturbateur(trice) *m,f*

helm [helm] *n (of ship)* barre *f*; *also Fig* **to be at the h.** être à la barre

helmet ['helmɪt] *n* casque *m*

helmsman ['helmzmən] *n* timonier *m*

help [help] **1** *n* **(a)** *(aid)* aide *f*; **to shout for h.** crier à l'aide; **h.!** à l'aide!, au secours!; **to be of h. to sb** aider qn; **thank you, you've been a great h.** merci beaucoup de votre aide; **there was no h. for it** il n'y avait rien à faire; **with the h. of sb** avec l'aide de qn; **with the h. of sth** *(implement)* à l'aide de qch **(b)** *(cleaning woman)* femme *f* de ménage

  2 *vt* **(a)** *(aid)* aider; **to h. sb (to) do sth** aider qn à faire qch; **to h. sb to their feet** aider qn à se mettre debout; **to h. sb on/off with his coat** aider qn à mettre/enlever son manteau; **to h. one another** s'entraider; **to h. oneself to sth** se servir en *ou* de qch; **h. yourself!** servez-vous! **(b)** *(prevent)* **I can't h. it** je ne peux pas m'en empêcher; **it can't be helped** on n'y peut rien; **I couldn't h. laughing/overhearing** je ne pouvais pas m'empêcher de rire/d'écouter; **he can't h. being bald** ce n'est pas de sa faute s'il est chauve; **not if I can h. it!** pas si je peux l'éviter!

  3 *vi* aider; **can I h.?** puis-je vous aider?; **that doesn't h. very much** cela ne nous avance pas beaucoup

▶**help out** *vt sep & vi* aider

helper ['helpə(r)] *n* aide *mf*, assistant(e) *m,f*

helpful ['helpfʊl] *adj (person)* serviable; *(advice, device, book)* utile; **to be h.** *(of person)* se rendre utile, aider

helpfully ['helpfʊlɪ] *adv* obligeamment

helping ['helpɪŋ] **1** *n (portion)* part *f*, portion *f*; **I had a second h. of spaghetti** je me suis resservi des spaghettis

  2 *adj* **to lend a h. hand** donner un coup de main

helpless ['helplɪs] *adj (powerless)* impuissant(e); *(invalid)* impotent(e); **we were h. to prevent it** nous n'avons pas pu l'empêcher; **to be h. with laughter** être plié(e) de rire

helplessly ['helplɪslɪ] *adv (watch)* sans pouvoir agir; *(struggle)* en vain

helpline ['helplaɪn] *n* service *m* d'assistance téléphonique

Helsinki [hel'sɪŋkɪ] *n* Helsinki

helter-skelter ['heltə'skeltə(r)] **1** *n (at fairground)* toboggan *m*

  2 *adv* **to run h.** courir comme un fou (une folle); **to fall h.** faire une chute spectaculaire

hem [hem] **1** *n* ourlet *m*

  2 *vt (pt & pp* **hemmed**) ourler

▶**hem in** *vt sep (surround)* cerner

he-man ['hi:mæn] *n Fam* homme *m* viril

hemisphere ['hemɪsfɪə(r)] *n* hémisphère *m*

hemline ['hemlaɪn] *n* ourlet *m*

hemlock ['hemlɒk] *n* ciguë *f*

hemoglobin, hemophilia *etc Am* = **haemoglobin, haemophilia** *etc*

hemorrhage, hemorrhoids *Am* = **haemorrhage, haemorrhoids**

hemp [hemp] *n* chanvre *m*

hen [hen] *n* poule *f*; *Br Fam* **h. night, h. party** = soirée organisée entre amies avant le mariage de l'une d'entre elles; **she's having her h. night** elle enterre sa vie de célibataire

hence [hens] *adv* **(a)** *(thus)* d'où; **h. his anger** d'où sa colère **(b)** *(from now)* d'ici; **five years h.** d'ici cinq ans

henceforth [hens'fɔːθ] *adv Formal* dès lors, désormais

henchman ['henʃmən] *n Pej* acolyte *m*

hencoop ['henkuːp] *n* cage *f* à poules

henhouse ['henhaʊs] *n* poulailler *m*

henna ['henə] *n* henné *m*

henpecked ['henpekt] *adj* mené(e) par le bout du nez

hepatitis [hepə'taɪtɪs] *n* hépatite *f*

her [*unstressed* hə(r), *stressed* hɜː(r)] **1** *pron* **(a)** *(direct object)* la; **I hate h.** je la déteste; **I love h.** je l'aime; **I can understand her son but not HER** je comprends son fils, mais elle, je ne la comprends pas **(b)** *(indirect object)* lui; **I gave h. the book** je lui ai donné le livre; **I gave it to h.** je le lui ai donné **(c)** *(after preposition)* elle; **I'm thinking of h.** je pense à elle **(d)** *(as complement of verb* **to be**) elle; **it's h.!** c'est elle!; **it was h. who did it** c'est elle qui l'a fait

  2 *possessive adj* **(a)** *(singular)* son (sa); *(plural)* ses; **h. husband** son mari; **h. family** sa famille; **h. parents** ses parents; **it wasn't HER idea!** ce n'est pas elle qui en a eu l'idée! **(b)** *(for parts of body)* **she hit h. head** elle s'est cogné la tête

herald ['herəld] **1** *n (messenger)* héraut *m*; *Fig (sign)* signe *m* avant-coureur

  2 *vt* annoncer

heraldry ['herəldrɪ] *n* héraldique *f*

herb [hɜːb] *n* herbe *f* aromatique

herbal ['hɜːbəl] *adj* à base de plantes; **h. tea** tisane *f*

herbalist ['hɜːbəlɪst] *n* herboriste *mf*

herbicide ['hɜːbɪsaɪd] *n* herbicide *m*

herbivorous [hɜː'bɪvərəs] *adj* herbivore

herd [hɜːd] **1** *n (of cattle, sheep, elephants)* troupeau *m*; *(of horses)* troupe *f*; *(of people)* groupe *m*; *Pej* troupeau *m*; **the h. instinct** l'instinct grégaire

  2 *vt (cattle, people)* rassembler

herdsman ['hɜːdzmən] *n* gardien *m* de troupeau

here [hɪə(r)] **1** *adv* ici; **over h.** par ici; **h. it/he is** le voilà; **h.!** *(at roll call)* présent!; **come h.!** viens ici!; **h., come and look at this!** eh! viens voir ça!; **she's not h.** elle n'est pas là; **h. she comes** la voilà; **h. and now** immédiatement; **h. and there** çà et là; *Fig* **that's neither h. nor there** ça n'a aucun rapport; **what have we h.?** qu'est-ce que c'est que ça?; **h.'s what you have to do** voilà ce que tu as à faire; **h. goes!** allons-y!; **h.'s to the future!** à l'avenir!

  2 *n* **the h. and now** le présent

hereafter [hɪər'ɑːftə(r)] **1** *n Lit* **the h.** l'au-delà *m*

  2 *adv Formal (below)* ci-après; *(in the future)* dorénavant

hereby [hɪə'baɪ] *adv Formal (in writing)* par la présente; *(in speech)* solennellement

hereditary [hɪ'redɪtərɪ] *adj* héréditaire
heredity [hɪ'redɪtɪ] *n* hérédité *f*
heresy ['herəsɪ] (*pl* **heresies**) *n* hérésie *f*
heretic ['herətɪk] *n* hérétique *mf*
heretical [hɪ'retɪkəl] *adj* hérétique
heritage ['herɪtɪdʒ] *n* patrimoine *m*
hermaphrodite [hɜ:'mæfrədaɪt] *n & adj* hermaphrodite *mf*
hermetic [hɜ:'metɪk] *adj* hermétique
hermetically [hɜ:'metɪklɪ] *adv* hermétiquement
hermit ['hɜ:mɪt] *n* ermite *m*; **h. crab** bernard-l'ermite *m inv*
hernia ['hɜ:nɪə] *n* hernie *f*
hero ['hɪərəʊ] (*pl* **heroes**) *n* héros *m*; **h. worship** adulation *f*, idolâtrie *f*
heroic [hɪ'rəʊɪk] *adj* héroïque
heroically [hɪ'rəʊɪklɪ] *adv* héroïquement
heroics [hɪ'rəʊɪks] *npl* coup *m* d'éclat
heroin ['herəʊɪn] *n* (*drug*) héroïne *f*; **h. addict** héroïnomane *mf*
heroine ['herəʊɪn] *n* (*female hero*) héroïne *f*
heroism ['herəʊɪzəm] *n* héroïsme *m*
heron ['herən] *n* héron *m*
hero-worship ['hɪərəʊwɜ:ʃɪp] (*pt & pp* **hero-worshipped**) *vt* idolâtrer
herpes ['hɜ:pi:z] *n* herpès *m*
herring ['herɪŋ] (*pl* **herring** or **herrings**) *n* hareng *m*
hers [hɜ:z] *possessive pron* (**a**) (*singular*) le sien (la sienne) *m,f*, (*plural*) les siens (les siennes) *mpl, fpl*; **my house is big, but h. is bigger** j'ai une grande maison, mais la sienne est plus grande encore (**b**) (*used attributively*) **this book is h.** ce livre est à elle; **a friend of h.** un de ses amis; **where's that brother of h.?** où son frère a-t-il bien pu passer?
herself [hɜ:'self] *pron* (**a**) (*reflexive*) **she spoils h.** elle se gâte; **she hurt h.** elle s'est blessée (**b**) (*emphatic*) elle-même; **she h. has never...** elle-même n'a jamais...; **she told me h.** elle me l'a dit elle-même; **she's not h. today** elle n'est pas dans son état normal aujourd'hui (**c**) (*after preposition*) **she lives by h.** elle vit seule; **she bought it for h.** elle se l'est acheté; **she talks to h.** elle parle toute seule
he's [hi:z] = **he is, he has**
hesitancy ['hezɪtənsɪ] *n* hésitation *f*
hesitant ['hezɪtənt] *adj* hésitant(e); **to be h. about doing sth** hésiter à faire qch
hesitate ['hezɪteɪt] *vi* hésiter
hesitation [hezɪ'teɪʃən] *n* hésitation *f*; **without h.** sans hésitation, sans hésiter
heterogeneous [hetərə'dʒi:nɪəs] *adj* hétérogène
heterosexual [hetərəʊ'seksjʊəl] *n & adj* hétérosexuel(elle) *m,f*
heterosexuality [hetərəʊseksjʊ'ælɪtɪ] *n* hétérosexualité
het up ['hetʌp] *adj Br Fam* énervé(e); **to get h. (about sth)** se mettre dans tous ses états (pour qch)
heuristics [hjʊ'rɪstɪks] *npl* heuristique *f*
hew [hju:] (*pp* **hewn** [hju:n] or **hewed**) *vt* (*wood*) couper; (*rock*) tailler
hexagon ['heksəgən] *n* hexagone *m*
hexagonal [hek'sægənəl] *adj* hexagonal(e)
hey [heɪ] *exclam* eh!; **h. presto!** le tour est joué!
heyday ['heɪdeɪ] *n* apogée *m*; **in its h.** à son apogée; **in his h.** au sommet de sa gloire

HGV [eɪtʃdʒi:'vi:] *n Br* (*abbr* **heavy goods vehicle**) PL *m*; **H. licence** permis *m* PL
hi [haɪ] *exclam Fam* salut!
hiatus [haɪ'eɪtəs] *n* (*interruption*) interruption *f*; (*in conversation*) silence *m*; (*in manuscript, records*) lacune *f*
hibernate ['haɪbəneɪt] *vi* hiberner
hibernation [haɪbə'neɪʃən] *n* hibernation *f*; **to go into h.** entrer en hibernation
hiccup ['hɪkʌp] **1** *n* hoquet *m*; *Fig* (*in plan*) accroc *m*; **to have (the) hiccups** avoir le hoquet
   2 *vi* avoir le hoquet; (*once*) avoir un hoquet
hick [hɪk] *n Am Fam* péquenaud(e) *m,f*
hickory ['hɪkərɪ] (*pl* **hickories**) *n* (*tree, wood*) hickory *m*, noyer *m* blanc d'Amérique
hid [hɪd] *pt of* **hide**
hidden ['hɪdən] **1** *adj* caché(e); **h. agenda** programme *m* secret
   2 *pp of* **hide**
hide¹ [haɪd] **1** *n* (*for birdwatching*) affût *m*
   2 *vt* (*pt* **hid** [hɪd], *pp* **hidden** ['hɪdən]) cacher (**from** à); **to have nothing to h.** n'avoir rien à cacher; **to be hidden from sight** être caché(e); **to h. oneself** se cacher
   3 *vi* se cacher (**from** de)
hide² *n* (*skin*) peau *f*; *Fig* **to save one's h.** sauver sa peau; **I haven't seen h. nor hair of her** je ne l'ai pas vue du tout
hide-and-seek [haɪdən'si:k] *n* cache-cache *m*; **to play h.** jouer à cache-cache
hidebound ['haɪdbaʊnd] *adj* rigide, borné(e)
hideous ['hɪdɪəs] *adj* (*ugly*) hideux(euse); (*horrific*) horrible
hideously ['hɪdɪəslɪ] *adv* horriblement, affreusement
hide-out ['haɪdaʊt] *n* cachette *f*
hiding¹ ['haɪdɪŋ] *n* (*concealment*) **to be in h.** se cacher; **to go into h.** se cacher; **to come out of h.** sortir de sa cachette; (*after war*) sortir de la clandestinité; **h. place** cachette *f*
hiding² *n Fam* (*beating*) raclée *f*; **to give sb a h.** donner une raclée à qn; *Fig* **to be on a h. to nothing** n'avoir aucune chance
hierarchical [haɪə'rɑ:kɪkəl] *adj* hiérarchique
hierarchy ['haɪərɑ:kɪ] (*pl* **hierarchies**) *n* hiérarchie *f*
hieroglyphics [haɪərə'glɪfɪks] *npl* hiéroglyphes *mpl*
hi-fi ['haɪfaɪ] *n* hi-fi *f inv*; (*stereo system*) chaîne *f* (hi-fi)
higgledy-piggledy ['hɪgəldɪ'pɪgəldɪ] *Fam* **1** *adj* en désordre
   2 *adv* pêle-mêle
high [haɪ] **1** *n* (**a**) (*peak*) (*in career, performance*) sommet *m*; (*in quantity, degree*) maximum *m*; **unemployment has reached a new h.** le chômage a atteint un nouveau record; **to be on a h.** (*from drugs*) planer; (*from success*) être sur un petit nuage; **the highs and lows** les hauts *mpl* et les bas *mpl*
   (**b**) (*weather front*) anticyclone *m*
   2 *adj* (**a**) (*mountain, building*) haut(e), élevé(e); **to be 2 metres h.** faire 2 mètres de haut; *Fam* **to be left h. and dry** être laissé(e) en plan; **h. jump** saut *m* en hauteur; *Fam Fig* **you'll be for the h. jump** tu vas te faire engueuler; **h. jumper** sauteur(euse) *m,f* en hauteur; **h. tide** marée *f* haute; **h. wire** corde *f* raide
   (**b**) (*price, speed, standards*) élevé(e); (*quality*) premier(ère); **to have a h. opinion of sb** avoir une haute opinion de qn; **h. explosive** explosif *m* puissant; **h. point** point *m* culminant; **in h. spirits** plein(e) d'entrain; *Law* **h. treason** haute trahison *f*; **h. winds** vents *mpl* forts

(**c**) *(rank, position)* haut(e); **to act all h. and mighty** agir avec beaucoup d'arrogance; *Mil* **h. command** haut commandement *m*; **H. Commission** haut-commissariat *m*; **H. Court** ≃ tribunal *m* de grande instance; **H. Mass** grand-messe *f*; **h. school** = école secondaire qui accueille les élèves de 11 à 18 ans; **h. society** haute société *f*

(**d**) *(in tone, pitch)* aigu(ë); *Fig* **h. note** *(of career, performance)* point *m* culminant

(**e**) *(with time)* **it's h. time you got yourself a job** il est grand temps que tu trouves un travail; **h. noon** plein midi; **h. summer** plein été; *Br* **h. tea** = dîner pris assez tôt dans la soirée

(**f**) *(meat)* avancé(e)

(**g**) *Fam* **to be h.** *(on drugs)* planer; *Fig (on success, excitement)* être euphorique

3 *adv (aim, jump)* haut; **to hunt h. and low for sth** remuer ciel et terre pour trouver qch; **feelings were running h.** la tension montait

highbrow ['haɪbraʊ] *adj* intellectuel(elle)

highchair ['haɪtʃeə(r)] *n* chaise *f* haute

Higher ['haɪər] *n Scot* = diplôme de fin d'études secondaires sanctionnant une matière déterminée

higher education ['haɪəredjʊ'keɪʃən] *n* enseignement *m* supérieur

high-flier, high-flyer ['haɪ'flaɪə(r)] *n (person)* battant(e) *m,f*; *(company)* société *f* qui va de l'avant

high-flying ['haɪ'flaɪɪŋ] *adj* ambitieux(euse)

high-frequency [haɪ'friːkwənsɪ] *adj* (à) haute fréquence *inv*

high-handed [haɪ'hændɪd] *adj* autoritaire, despotique

high-heeled ['haɪ'hiːld] *adj* à talons hauts

Highland ['haɪlənd] *adj (from Scottish Highlands)* des Highlands; **H. cattle** vaches *fpl* des Highlands; **H. games** jeux *mpl* écossais

---

Highland Games

En Écosse, il s'agit d'une sorte de kermesse locale en plein air où se déroulent simultanément toutes sortes de concours (danse, cornemuse) et d'épreuves sportives (courses, lancer du marteau, mais aussi "tossing the caber", "tug o' war" etc).

Highlander ['haɪləndə(r)] *n (of Scotland)* habitant(e) *m,f* des Highlands

Highlands ['haɪləndz] *npl* **the H.** *(of Scotland)* les Highlands *fpl*

high-level ['haɪlevəl] *adj (talks)* à haut niveau; *(delegation)* de haut niveau

highlight ['haɪlaɪt] **1** *n* (**a**) *(of performance, career)* point *m* culminant; **highlights** *(of match, event)* moments *mpl* forts (**b**) **highlights** *(in hair) (artificial)* mèches *fpl*; *(natural)* reflets *mpl*

2 *vt* (**a**) *(problem, difference)* mettre en évidence, souligner (**b**) *(with highlighter)* surligner; *Comput (block of text)* sélectionner

highlighter ['haɪlaɪtə(r)] *n (pen)* surligneur *m*

highly ['haɪlɪ] *adv* (**a**) *(very)* très, extrêmement; **h. paid** très bien payé(e); **h. seasoned** fortement assaisonné(e); **h. strung** hypersensible (**b**) *(favourably)* **to think h. of sb** avoir une haute opinion de qn; **to speak h. of sb** parler de qn en termes élogieux

high-minded ['haɪ'maɪndɪd] *adj (sentiments, behaviour)* noble; *(person)* qui a des principes

Highness ['haɪnɪs] *n* **His/Her Royal H.** Son Altesse *f*

high-pitched ['haɪpɪtʃt] *adj* aigu(ë)

high-powered ['haɪ'paʊəd] *adj (engine, car, telescope)* très puissant(e); *(job)* à hautes responsabilités; *(person)* qui occupe un poste à hautes responsabilités

high-pressure ['haɪ'preʃə(r)] *adj* (**a**) *(cylinder, gas, machine)* à haute pression (**b**) *(salesman)* agressif(-ive)

high-profile ['haɪ'prəʊfaɪl] *adj (person)* très en vue; *(campaign)* de grande envergure

high-resolution ['haɪrezə'luːʃən] *adj Comput (screen, graphics)* à haute résolution

high-rise ['haɪ'raɪz] **1** *n (block of flats)* tour *f* **2** *adj* **h. building** tour *f*

high-risk ['haɪrɪsk] *adj (strategy, investment)* à haut risque

highroad ['haɪrəʊd] *n Old-fashioned* grand-route *f*; *Fig* **the h. to success** la voie du succès

high-speed ['haɪ'spiːd] *adj* ultrarapide; *(train)* à grande vitesse

high-spirited [haɪ'spɪrɪtɪd] *adj* plein(e) d'entrain

high-tech ['haɪ'tek] *adj (appliance)* perfectionné(e); *(industry)* de pointe; *(approach, solution)* qui a recours à une technologie de pointe

high-up ['haɪʌp] *adj Fam (important)* haut placé(e)

highway ['haɪweɪ] *n (main road)* (route *f*) nationale *f*; *(motorway)* autoroute *f*; **H. Code** code *m* de la route

highwayman ['haɪweɪmən] *n* bandit *m* de grand chemin

hijack ['haɪdʒæk] *vt (plane)* détourner; *(car, lorry)* s'emparer de force de; *(idea)* s'approprier

hijacker ['haɪdʒækə(r)] *n (of plane)* pirate *m* de l'air

hike [haɪk] **1** *n* (**a**) *(walk)* randonnée *f*; **to go on** *or* **for a h.** faire une randonnée; *Fam Fig* **go take a h.!** lâche-moi les baskets! (**b**) *(in prices)* hausse *f*

2 *vt (prices)* augmenter

3 *vi (walk)* faire de la randonnée

hiker ['haɪkə(r)] *n* randonneur(euse) *m,f*

hiking ['haɪkɪŋ] *n* randonnée *f*; **to go h.** faire de la randonnée; **h. boots** chaussures *fpl* de marche

hilarious [hɪ'leərɪəs] *adj* hilarant(e)

hilariously [hɪ'leərɪəslɪ] *adv* **h. funny** à se tordre de rire; **to laugh h.** se tordre de rire

hilarity [hɪ'lærɪtɪ] *n* hilarité *f*; **his suggestion was greeted with much h.** sa suggestion déclencha l'hilarité générale

hill [hɪl] *n* (**a**) *(small mountain)* colline *f*; *Fig* **to be over the h.** commencer à se faire vieux (vieille) (**b**) *(slope)* côte *f*, pente *f*; **to go down/up the h.** descendre/monter la côte

hillbilly ['hɪlbɪlɪ] *(pl* **hillbillies)** *n Am* péquenaud(e) *m,f*

hillock ['hɪlək] *n* butte *f*

hillside ['hɪlsaɪd] *n* coteau *m*

hilltop ['hɪltɒp] *n* sommet *m* de la colline

hillwalker ['hɪlwɔːkə(r)] *n* randonneur(euse) *m,f*

hillwalking ['hɪlwɔːkɪŋ] *n* randonnée *f* en basse montagne

hilly ['hɪlɪ] *adj* vallonné(e)

hilt [hɪlt] *n (of sword)* poignée *f*; *(of knife, dagger)* manche *m*; *Fig* **to back sb to the h.** soutenir qn sans réserve

him [hɪm] *pron* (**a**) *(direct object)* le; **I hate h.** je le déteste; **I love h.** je l'aime; **I can understand his son but not HIM** je comprends son fils, mais lui, je ne le comprends pas (**b**) *(indirect object)* lui; **I gave h. the book**

je lui ai donné le livre; **I gave it to h.** je le lui ai donné (**c**) *(after preposition)* lui; **I'm thinking of h.** je pense à lui (**d**) *(as complement of verb to be)* lui; **it's h.!** c'est lui!; **it was h. who did it** c'est lui qui l'a fait

Himalayan [hɪmə'leɪən] *adj* himalayen(enne)

Himalayas [hɪmə'leɪəz] *npl* l'Himalaya *m*

himself [hɪm'self] *pron* (**a**) *(reflexive)* **he spoils h.** il se gâte; **he hurt h.** il s'est blessé (**b**) *(emphatic)* lui-même; **he h. has never...** lui-même n'a jamais...; **he told me h.** il me l'a dit lui-même; **he's not h. today** il n'est pas dans son état normal aujourd'hui (**c**) *(after preposition)* **he lives by h.** il vit seul; **he bought it for h.** il se l'est acheté; **he talks to h.** il parle tout seul

hind¹ [haɪnd] *adj (back)* de derrière; **h. legs** pattes *fpl* de derrière

hind² *n (female deer)* daim *m* femelle

hinder ['hɪndə(r)] *vt (impede)* gêner; *(delay)* retarder; **to h. sb from doing sth** empêcher qn de faire qch

Hindi ['hɪndɪ] *n (language)* hindi *m*

hindquarters ['haɪndkwɔːtəz] *npl* arrière-train *m*

hindrance ['hɪndrəns] *n* entrave *f*, obstacle *m*

hindsight ['haɪndsaɪt] *n* recul *m*; **with (the benefit of) h.** avec le recul

Hindu ['hɪnduː] **1** *n* Hindou(e) *m,f*
2 *adj* hindou(e)

Hinduism ['hɪnduːɪzəm] *n* hindouisme *m*

hinge [hɪndʒ] *n* charnière *f*, gond *m*; **to come off its hinges** sortir de ses gonds

▸**hinge on, hinge upon** *vt insep (depend on)* dépendre de

hint [hɪnt] **1** *n* (**a**) *(allusion)* allusion *f*; *(clue)* indice *m*; **to drop sb a h.** faire une allusion à l'intention de qn; **to take the h.** comprendre l'allusion; **he can't take a h.** il faut lui mettre les points sur les i (**b**) *(sign)* signe *m* (**c**) *(small amount)* soupçon *m* (**d**) *(piece of advice)* truc *m*, conseil *m*
2 *vt* **to h. that...** insinuer *ou* laisser entendre que...

▸**hint at** *vt insep* faire allusion à

hinterland ['hɪntəlænd] *n* arrière-pays *m inv*

hip¹ [hɪp] *n (part of body)* hanche *f*; **to break one's h.** se casser le col du fémur; **h. flask** flasque *f*; **h. joint** articulation *f* de la hanche; **h. pocket** poche *f* revolver

hip² *adj Fam (fashionable)* branché(e)

hippo ['hɪpəʊ] *(pl* **hippos**) *n Fam* hippopotame *m*

hippopotamus [hɪpə'pɒtəməs] *(pl* **hippopotami** [hɪpə'pɒtəmaɪ]) *n* hippopotame *m*

hippy ['hɪpɪ] *(pl* **hippies**) *n* hippie *mf*

hire [haɪə(r)] **1** *n Br (of car, equipment)* location *f*; **for h.** à louer; *(taxi)* libre; **h. car** voiture *f* de location; *Com* **h. purchase** achat *m* à crédit; **h. purchase agreement** contrat *m* de vente à tempérament
2 *vt* (**a**) *(car, equipment)* louer (**b**) *(lawyer, worker)* engager

▸**hire out** *vt sep Br (boat, bicycle)* louer; *(one's services)* offrir

hired ['haɪəd] *adj (car, suit)* de location; **h. hand** *(on farm)* ouvrier(ère) *m,f* agricole

hirsute ['hɜːsjuːt] *adj Lit* velu(e)

his [hɪz] **1** *possessive adj* (**a**) *(singular)* son (sa); *(plural)* ses; **h. job** son travail; **h. wife** sa femme; **h. parents** ses parents; **it wasn't HIS idea!** ce n'est pas lui qui en a eu l'idée! (**b**) *(for parts of body)* **he hit h. head** il s'est cogné la tête

2 *possessive pron* (**a**) *(singular)* le sien (la sienne) *m,f*; *(plural)* les siens (les siennes) *mpl, fpl*; **my house is big, but h. is bigger** j'ai une grande maison, mais la sienne est plus grande encore (**b**) *(used attributively)* **this book is h.** ce livre est à lui; **a friend of h.** un de ses amis; **where's that brother of h.?** où son frère a-t-il bien pu passer?

Hispanic [hɪs'pænɪk] **1** *n Am* Latino-Américain(e) *m,f*
2 *adj* hispanique

hiss [hɪs] **1** *n (sound)* sifflement *m*; *(to express disapproval)* sifflet *m*
2 *vt & vi* siffler

histogram ['hɪstəgræm] *n* histogramme *m*

historian [hɪs'tɔːrɪən] *n* historien(enne) *m,f*

historic [hɪs'tɒrɪk] *adj* historique

historical [hɪs'tɒrɪkəl] *adj* historique

historically [hɪs'tɒrɪklɪ] *adv* historiquement

history ['hɪstərɪ] *(pl* **histories**) *n* (**a**) *(the past)* histoire *f*; **to go down in h., to make h.** *(of event)* faire date; *(of person)* entrer dans l'histoire; *Fig* **that's (ancient) h.** c'est de l'histoire ancienne; **h. book/teacher** livre *m*/professeur *m* d'histoire (**b**) *(medical record)* antécédents *mpl*; **there is a h. of diabetes in his family** il y a des cas de diabète dans sa famille

histrionic [hɪstrɪ'ɒnɪk] *adj Pej* théâtral(e)

histrionics [hɪstrɪ'ɒnɪks] *npl Pej* comédie *f*, cinéma *m*; **to have h.** faire une scène *ou* du cinéma

hit [hɪt] **1** *n* (**a**) *(blow)* coup *m*; *(in shooting)* tir *m* réussi; **to score a direct h.** taper dans le mille; **h. list** *(of targets)* liste *f* noire; **h. man** tueur *m* à gages (**b**) *(success)* succès *m*; **to be a h. with sb** avoir beaucoup de succès auprès de qn; **h. (record)** hit *m* (**c**) *Comput (visit to Web site)* hit *m*, accès *m*; **this Web site counted 5,000 hits last week** ce site Web a été consulté 5 000 fois la semaine dernière
2 *adj (film, play)* à succès
3 *vt (pt & pp* **hit**) (**a**) *(of person)* frapper; *(of bullet)* atteindre; *(of car)* percuter; *Comput (key)* frapper, appuyer sur; **to h. one's head (on sth)** se cogner la tête (contre qch); *Fig* **it suddenly hit me that...** j'ai réalisé tout d'un coup que...; *Fig* **he didn't know what had hit him** il n'a pas eu le temps de se rendre compte de ce qui lui arrivait
(**b**) *(reach) (barrier, difficulty)* se heurter à; **to h. a note** atteindre une note; **to h. 90 (miles an hour)** ≃ faire du 140 (à l'heure); **to h. an all-time low** *(of investment, relationship)* être au plus bas; **the circus hits town tomorrow** le cirque arrive en ville demain; **it hits the shops next week** c'est en vente la semaine prochaine; *Fam* **to h. the road** *(leave)* se mettre en route
(**c**) *(affect)* toucher; **to be hard hit by sth** être durement touché(e) par qch
4 *vi* frapper

▸**hit back 1** *vt sep* **to h. sb back** rendre un coup à qn
2 *vi Fig* riposter (**at** à)

▸**hit off** *vt sep Fam* **to h. it off** accrocher

▸**hit on** *vt insep (idea, solution)* trouver

▸**hit out** *vi* **to h. out at sb** *(physically)* frapper qn; *(verbally)* s'en prendre à qn

▸**hit upon** = hit on

hit-and-run ['hɪtən'rʌn] *adj* **h. accident** ≃ accident à la suite duquel l'automobiliste prend la fuite

hitch [hɪtʃ] **1** *n* (**a**) *(difficulty)* problème *m*; **without a h.** sans anicroche (**b**) *(knot)* nœud *m*
2 *vt* (**a**) *(attach)* attacher (**to** à); *Fam Fig* **to get**

hitched *(married)* passer devant Monsieur le Maire (**b**) *Fam* **to h. a lift** faire du stop

3 *vi Fam* faire du stop; **to h. to Paris** aller à Paris en stop

▶ **hitch up** *vt sep (trousers, skirt)* remonter

hitchhike ['hɪtʃhaɪk] *vi* faire de l'auto-stop; **to h. to Paris** aller à Paris en auto-stop

hitchhiker ['hɪtʃhaɪkə(r)] *n* auto-stoppeur(euse) *m,f*

hi-tech = **high-tech**

hither ['hɪðə(r)] *adv Lit* ici; **h. and thither** çà et là

hitherto ['hɪðə'tuː] *adv* jusqu'ici, jusqu'à présent

hit-or-miss ['hɪtɔː'mɪs] *adj* aléatoire, approximatif(ive)

HIV [eɪtʃaɪ'viː] *n (abbr* **human immunodeficiency virus)** VIH *m*; **to be H. positive/negative** être séropositif(ive)/séronégatif(ive)

hive [haɪv] *n* ruche *f*; *Fig* **a h. of activity** une véritable ruche

▶ **hive off** *vt sep (money, profits)* séparer

HMG [eɪtʃem'dʒiː] *n Br (abbr* **Her/His Majesty's Government)** = le gouvernement de sa majesté *(expression utilisée sur les documents officiels)*

HMI [eɪtʃem'aɪ] *n Br* (**a**) *(abbr* **Her/His Majesty's Inspectorate)** ≃ Inspection *f* académique (**b**) *(abbr* **Her/His Majesty's Inspector)** ≃ inspecteur(trice) *m,f* de l'éducation nationale

HMS [eɪtʃem'es] *n (abbr* **Her/His Majesty's Ship)** = abréviation précédant le nom des navires de la marine britannique

HMSO [eɪtʃemes'əʊ] *n (abbr* **Her/His Majesty's Stationery Office)** ≃ Imprimerie *f* nationale

HNC [eɪtʃen'siː] *n Br (abbr* **Higher National Certificate)** = brevet de technicien en Grande-Bretagne, ≃ BTS *m*

HND [eɪtʃen'diː] *n Br (abbr* **Higher National Diploma)** = brevet de technicien supérieur en Grande-Bretagne, ≃ DUT *m*

hoard [hɔːd] **1** *n (of food)* réserve *f*, provisions *fpl*; *(of money)* trésor *m*

2 *vt (food)* amasser, stocker; *(money)* amasser, thésauriser

hoarder ['hɔːdə(r)] *n* personne *f* qui fait des réserves; **she's a real h.** elle ne jette rien

hoarding ['hɔːdɪŋ] *n* (**a**) *(of food)* stockage *m* (**b**) *(for poster)* panneau *m* d'affichage

hoarfrost ['hɔːfrɒst] *n* givre *m*, gelée *f* blanche

hoarse [hɔːs] *adj* enroué(e); **to shout oneself h.** s'enrouer à force de crier

hoary ['hɔːrɪ] *adj (story)* vieux (vieille); *(joke)* éculé(e)

hoax [həʊks] **1** *n* canular *m*; **to play a h. on sb** faire un canular à qn; (**bomb**) **h.** fausse alerte *f* à la bombe; **h. caller** auteur *m* de canular(s) téléphonique(s)

2 *vt* faire un canular à

hob [hɒb] *n (on electric cooker)* table *f* de cuisson; *(on hearth)* plaque *f*

hobble ['hɒbəl] *vi* boitiller

hobby ['hɒbɪ] *(pl* **hobbies)** *n* passe-temps *m inv*, hobby *m*

hobbyhorse ['hɒbɪhɔːs] *n (toy)* cheval *m* de bois *(tête emmanchée sur un bâton)*; *Fig (favourite subject)* dada *m*

hobnail boot ['hɒbneɪl'buːt] *n* chaussure *f* ferrée

hobnob ['hɒbnɒb] *(pt & pp* **hobnobbed)** *vi Fam* **to h. with sb** frayer avec qn

hock¹ [hɒk] *n (wine)* vin *m* du Rhin

hock² *Fam* **1** *n* **to be in h.** *(of object)* être au clou; *(of person)* être endetté(e)

2 *vt* mettre au clou

hockey ['hɒkɪ] *n Br (on grass)* hockey *m* (sur gazon); *Am (on ice)* hockey (sur glace); **h. stick** crosse *f* de hockey

hocus-pocus ['həʊkəs'pəʊkəs] *n (trickery)* tromperie *f*, supercherie *f*; *(talk)* paroles *fpl* trompeuses

hoe [həʊ] **1** *n* houe *f*, binette *f*

2 *vt (pt & pp* **hoed)** biner, sarcler

hog [hɒg] **1** *n* (**a**) *(pig)* porc *m* châtré; *Fam* **to go the whole h.** aller jusqu'au bout (**b**) *(glutton)* glouton(onne) *m,f*, goinfre *mf*

2 *vt (pt & pp* **hogged)** *Fam (monopolize)* monopoliser; **to h. the limelight** monopoliser l'attention

Hogmanay [hɒgmə'neɪ] *n Scot* la Saint-Sylvestre

Hogmanay

Ce mot désigne les fêtes de la veille du nouvel an célébrées en Écosse. Traditionnellement, les Écossais préféraient célébrer la nouvelle année plutôt que Noël et jusqu'au XVIIIème siècle, la tradition était d'offrir des cadeaux le jour de l'an. Les coutumes écossaises sont aussi anciennes que diverses: des coups de canon sont tirés à minuit; à ce moment les gens vont rendre visite à leurs voisins avec un morceau de charbon en guise de cadeau, et tout le monde boit une petite goutte de whisky pour fêter la nouvelle année.

---

hogwash ['hɒgwɒʃ] *n Fam* âneries *fpl*

hoist [hɔɪst] **1** *n (device)* appareil *m* de levage

2 *vt* hisser; **he hoisted himself on to the wall** il s'est hissé sur le mur; *Fig* **to be hoist with one's own petard** se faire prendre à son propre piège

hoity-toity ['hɔɪtɪ'tɔɪtɪ] *adj* **to be h.** se donner de grands airs

hold [həʊld] **1** *n* (**a**) *(grip)* prise *f*; **to have h. of sb/sth** tenir qn/qch; **to catch** *or* **take h. of sth** saisir qch; *Fig* **to get h. of sb** *(find)* trouver qn; *(on phone)* joindre qn; *Fig* **to get h. of sth** se procurer qch; **to let go one's h.** relâcher son étreinte, lâcher prise; **to lose one's h. on reality** perdre le sens des réalités; *Fig* **to have a h. on** *or* **over sb** avoir de l'emprise sur qn

(**b**) *(in wrestling)* prise *f*; *Fig* **no holds barred** tous les coups sont permis

(**c**) **to be on h.** *(of project)* être en suspens; *(of telephone caller)* être en attente; **to put sth on h.** mettre qch en suspens; **to put sb on h.** *(on telephone)* mettre qn en attente

(**d**) *(of ship)* cale *f*; *(of plane)* soute *f*

2 *vt (pt & pp* **held)** (**a**) *(grip)* tenir; **to h. sb/sth tight** tenir qn/qch serré(e), serrer qn/qch; **to h. hands** se tenir (par) la main; **to h. sth in position** maintenir qch en place; **to h. sb prisoner** retenir qn prisonnier(ère); **the police are holding him for questioning** il a été placé en garde à vue; **to h. sb's interest/attention** retenir l'intérêt/l'attention de qn; **to h. sb to his promise** obliger qn à tenir sa promesse; **to h. one's breath** retenir sa respiration *ou* son souffle; *Fig* **don't h. your breath!** ce n'est pas pour demain! **there's no holding her** il n'y a pas moyen de l'arrêter; **h. your tongue!** tais-toi!; *Fam* **h. it!, h. your horses!** attendez!, minute!; **to h. a note** *(of singer)* tenir une note; **h. the line!** *(on telephone)* ne quittez pas!

(**b**) *(keep) (town, position)* tenir; *(ticket, room)* réserver; **to h. one's ground** tenir bon; **to h. one's own** se défendre

(**c**) *(carry)* **to h. one's head high** garder la tête haute; **to h. oneself well** se tenir bien (**d**) *(contain)* contenir; *Fig* **to h. water** *(of theory, story)* tenir la route; **nobody knows what the future holds** personne ne sait ce que l'avenir nous réserve; **it holds no interest for me** ça ne présente aucun intérêt pour moi

(**e**) *(conduct) (negotiations)* mener; *(meeting)* organiser; *(conversation)* avoir

(**f**) *(possess) (title, rank, opinion)* avoir; *(job, position)* occuper; *(record)* détenir; **to h. office** être en fonction

(**g**) *(consider)* **to h. sb responsible** tenir qn pour responsable; **to h. sb in respect** respecter qn; **to h. that...** soutenir que...

3 *vi* (**a**) *(of rope)* tenir; **h. tight!** tiens bon!

(**b**) *(of agreement, weather)* durer; *(of luck)* persister; **the same holds (true) for you** cela vaut aussi pour toi

▸**hold against** *vt sep* **to h. sth against sb** reprocher qch à qn

▸**hold back 1** *vt sep* (**a**) *(restrain) (person, emotion)* retenir; *(progress, project)* ralentir, freiner (**b**) *(conceal)* cacher

2 *vi* *(refrain)* se retenir (**from doing** de faire)

▸**hold down** *vt sep* (**a**) *(restrain) (person)* immobiliser; *(taxes, prices)* bloquer (**b**) *(job) (occupy)* avoir; *(keep)* garder

▸**hold forth** *vi* disserter, pérorer (**about** or **on** sur)

▸**hold off 1** *vt sep* (**a**) *(keep at bay)* tenir à distance (**b**) *(delay)* remettre à plus tard, repousser; **to h. off making a decision** remettre une décision à plus tard

2 *vi* *(delay)* attendre

▸**hold on** *vi* (**a**) *(last)* tenir (**b**) *(wait)* patienter; **h. on!** attendez!; *(on telephone)* ne quittez pas! (**c**) *(not let go)* s'accrocher

▸**hold on to** *vt insep* (**a**) *(rope, handle)* s'agripper à; *Fig (idea, hope)* s'accrocher à (**b**) *(keep)* garder

▸**hold out 1** *vt sep* *(one's hand)* tendre; *(hope, opportunity)* offrir

2 *vi* (**a**) *(resist)* tenir (le coup) (**b**) *(wait)* **to h. out for a better offer** attendre une meilleure offre (**c**) *(last)* durer

▸**hold over** *vt sep* remettre, reporter

▸**hold together 1** *vt sep* **to h. sth together** faire tenir qch; **to be held together with sth** tenir avec qch

2 *vi* *(of party, group of people)* rester uni(e); *(of marriage, relationship)* tenir

▸**hold up 1** *vt sep* (**a**) *(support)* soutenir (**b**) *(raise)* lever; *Fig* **to h. sb/sth up as an example** montrer *ou* citer qn/qch en exemple; *Fig* **to h. sb/sth up to ridicule** tourner qn/qch en ridicule (**c**) *(delay)* retarder (**d**) *(rob)* attaquer

2 *vi* *(of theory, alibi)* (se) tenir; *(of good weather)* se maintenir; **she's holding up well under the pressure** elle tient bien le coup

▸**hold with** *vt insep* *(agree with)* être d'accord avec; *(approve of)* approuver

holdall ['həʊldɔːl] *n* fourre-tout *m inv*

holder ['həʊldə(r)] *n* (**a**) *(of licence, ticket, record, trophy)* détenteur(trice) *m,f*; *(of passport, degree)* titulaire *mf*; *(of belief, opinion)* tenant *m* (**b**) *(device)* support *m*

holding ['həʊldɪŋ] *n* (**a**) *(property)* propriété *f* (**b**) *(of shares)* participation *f*; *Com* **h. company** holding *m* (**c**) *Fig* **h. operation** opération *f* destinée à gagner du temps

hold-up ['həʊldʌp] *n* (**a**) *(delay) (in plan)* retard *m*; *(of traffic)* ralentissement *m* (**b**) *(armed robbery)* hold-up

m inv, attaque *f* à main armée (**c**) **hold-ups** *(stockings)* bas *mpl* jarretière

hole [həʊl] **1** *n* (**a**) *(opening)* trou *m*; *(of rabbit, fox)* terrier *m*; *also Fig* **to make a h. in sth** faire un trou dans qch; *Fig* **to pick holes in sth** relever les failles de qch; *Fig* **a h. in the law** un vide juridique; **to get a h. in one** *(in golf)* faire un trou en un; *Fam Fig* **to be in a h.** *(in difficulty)* être dans le pétrin (**b**) *Fam Pej (room, house)* taudis *m*; *(town)* trou *m*

2 *vt* *(ship)* faire une brèche dans; *(in golf)* **to h. a putt** faire le trou

▸**hole up** *vi Fam (hide)* se terrer

holiday ['hɒlɪdeɪ] **1** *n* (**a**) *Br (vacation)* vacances *fpl*; **a month's h.** un mois de vacances; **to be on h.** être en vacances; **to go on h.** aller *ou* partir en vacances; **h. camp** camp *m* de vacances; *Fig* **it was no h. camp** ce n'était pas une partie de plaisir; **h. home** résidence *f* secondaire; **h. season** saison *f* touristique (**b**) *(day off)* (jour *m* de) congé *m* (**c**) *(public)* jour *m* férié

2 *vi Br* passer les vacances; *(in summer)* passer les vacances d'été

holidaymaker ['hɒlɪdeɪˌmeɪkə(r)] *n Br* vacancier(ère) *m,f*; *(in summer)* estivant(e) *m,f*

holiness ['həʊlɪnɪs] *n* sainteté *f*; **Your H.** Votre Sainteté

holistic [həʊ'lɪstɪk] *adj* holistique

Holland ['hɒlənd] *n* la Hollande

holler ['hɒlə(r)] *vi Fam* brailler

hollow ['hɒləʊ] **1** *n* creux *m*

2 *adj* (**a**) *(container, cheeks)* creux(euse); *(eyes)* cave (**b**) *(sound)* creux(euse); *(voice)* blanc (blanche); *(laugh)* forcé(e) (**c**) *(promise, guarantee)* vain(e); *(victory)* sans signification

3 *adv* (**a**) **to sound h.** sonner creux (**b**) *Fam* **to beat sb h.** battre qn à plate(s) couture(s)

▸**hollow out** *vt sep* évider

holly ['hɒlɪ] *n* houx *m*

hollyhock ['hɒlɪhɒk] *n* rose *f* trémière

holocaust ['hɒləkɔːst] *n* holocauste *m*

hologram ['hɒləgræm] *n* hologramme *m*

holster ['həʊlstə(r)] *n* étui *m* de revolver

holy ['həʊlɪ] *adj* saint(e); *Fam* **h. cow** or **smoke** or **mackerel!** ça alors!; **the H. Bible** la Sainte Bible; **H. Communion** communion *f*; **the H. Father** le saint-père; **the H. Ghost** or **Spirit** le Saint-Esprit; *Fam Pej* **H. Joe** grenouille *f* de bénitier; **the H. Land** la Terre Sainte; **h. orders** ordres *mpl*; **h. war** guerre *f* sainte; **h. water** eau *f* bénite; **H. Week** la semaine sainte

homage ['hɒmɪdʒ] *n* hommage *m*; **to pay h. to sb** rendre hommage à qn

home [həʊm] **1** *n* (**a**) *(house)* maison *f*; *(of animal, plant)* habitat *m*; **at h.** à la maison, chez soi; **to feel at h.** se sentir chez soi; **make yourself at h.** faites comme chez vous; **to leave h.** *(in the morning)* partir de chez soi; *(one's parents' home)* partir de chez ses parents; **to be away from h.** être en déplacement; **to work at** or **from h.** travailler à domicile; **to be a h. from h.** être un second chez-soi; **to make one's h. in France** s'établir en France; **old people's h.** maison *f* de retraite; **children's h.** foyer *m* pour enfants; **h. address** adresse *f* personnelle, domicile *m*; **h. banking** banque *f* à domicile; **h. brew** bière *f* maison; **h. cooking** cuisine *f* familiale; *Br* **the H. Counties** = les comtés limitrophes de Londres; **h. economics** *(school subject)* arts *mpl* ménagers; **h. help** aide *f* ménagère; **h. life** vie *f* de famille; *Fin* **h. loan** prêt *m* immobilier; **h. movie** film *m* amateur; **h. owner** propriétaire *mf*; *Am*

Sch **h. room** = salle où l'on fait l'appel; **h. run** *(in baseball)* tour *m* complet; **the h. straight** *(in athletics)* la dernière ligne droite; **h. town** ville *f* natale; **to tell sb a few h. truths** dire ses quatre vérités à qn

(**b**) *(country, region)* patrie *f*; **at h. and abroad** dans notre pays et à l'étranger; **an example nearer h.** un exemple qui nous concerne plus; **Milan, the h. of fashion** Milan, capitale de la mode; **h. front** arrière *m*; **h. news** nouvelles *fpl* nationales; *Br Pol* **H. Office** ≃ ministère *m* de l'Intérieur; *Pol* **h. rule** régime *m* d'autonomie politique; *Br Pol* **the H. Secretary** ≃ le ministre de l'Intérieur

2 *adv* (**a**) *(to or at one's house)* à la maison, chez soi; *Fig* **to bring sth h. to sb** faire comprendre qch à qn; **to send sb h.** *(to house)* renvoyer qn chez soi; *(to home country)* rapatrier qn

(**b**) *(all the way)* **he hammered the nail h.** il enfonça complètement le clou; **the bolt slid h.** le verrou se ferma

▶**home in on** *vt insep (target)* se diriger vers; *(mistake, evidence)* relever

homecoming ['həʊmkʌmɪŋ] *n (to one's house)* retour *m* (au foyer); *(to one's country)* retour au pays

home-grown ['həʊm'grəʊn] *adj (vegetables)* du jardin; *Fig (not imported)* national(e)

homeland ['həʊmlænd] *n* patrie *f*, pays *m* (d'origine)

homeless ['həʊmlɪs] **1** *npl* **the h.** les sans-abri *mpl*

2 *adj* sans abri

homely ['həʊmlɪ] *adj* (**a**) *Br (person, atmosphere, decor)* agréable et sans prétention (**b**) *Am (plain)* sans charme

home-made ['həʊm'meɪd] *adj* fait(e) maison

homeopath ['həʊmɪəʊpæθ] *n* homéopathe *mf*

homeopathic [həʊmɪəʊ'pæθɪk] *adj* homéopathique

homeopathy [həʊmɪ'ɒpəθɪ] *n* homéopathie *f*

homesick ['həʊmsɪk] *adj* **to be** *or* **feel h.** avoir le mal du pays; *(of child)* s'ennuyer de ses parents; **to be h. for sth** avoir la nostalgie de qch

homesickness ['həʊmsɪknɪs] *n* mal *m* du pays

homespun ['həʊmspʌn] *adj Fig (wisdom, advice)* simple

homestead ['həʊmsted] *n* propriété *f*; *(farm)* ferme *f*

homeward ['həʊmwəd] **1** *adj* de retour

2 *adv (to one's house)* vers sa maison; *(to one's country)* vers son pays; **to be h.-bound** être sur le chemin du retour

homewards ['həʊmwədz] *adv* = **homeward**

homework ['həʊmwɜːk] *n Sch* devoirs *mpl*; **to do one's h.** faire ses devoirs; *Fig* faire des recherches

homicidal [hɒmɪ'saɪdəl] *adj* meurtrier(ère)

homicide ['hɒmɪsaɪd] *n* homicide *m*

homily ['hɒmɪlɪ] *(pl* **homilies**) *n* homélie *f*, sermon *m*

homing ['həʊmɪŋ] *adj* **h. device** mécanisme *m* d'auto-guidage; **h. pigeon** pigeon *m* voyageur

homogeneous [hɒmə'dʒiːnɪəs, hə'mɒdʒɪnəs] *adj* homogène

homogenize [hɒ'mɒdʒənaɪz] *vt* homogénéiser

homonym ['hɒmənɪm] *n* homonyme *m*

homophobia [hɒmə'fəʊbɪə] *n* homophobie *f*

homosexual [hɒmə'seksjʊəl] *n & adj* homosexuel(elle) *m,f*

homosexuality [hɒməseksjʊ'ælɪtɪ] *n* homosexualité *f*

Hon *adj Br Parl (abbr* **Honourable**) **the H. member for** Monsieur/Madame le député de

honcho ['hɒntʃəʊ] *(pl* **honchos**) *n Fam* **the head h.** le boss

Honduras [hɒn'djʊərəs] *n* le Honduras

hone [həʊn] *vt (skill)* peaufiner

honest ['ɒnɪst] *adj* honnête (**with** avec); **she has an h. face** elle a un visage franc; **the h. truth** la vérité vraie; **to be h., I don't know** honnêtement *ou* à dire vrai, je ne sais pas; **to earn an h. living** gagner honnêtement sa vie; *Hum* **to make an h. woman of sb** *(marry)* faire de qn une honnête femme

honestly ['ɒnɪstlɪ] *adv* (**a**) *(legitimately, sincerely)* honnêtement; **to obtain sth h.** obtenir qch par des moyens honnêtes; **I can h. say that...** honnêtement, je peux dire que... (**b**) *(expressing indignation)* **well h.!** franchement!; **h.! some people!** il y a des gens, je te jure!

honesty ['ɒnɪstɪ] *n* honnêteté *f*; **in all h.** en toute honnêteté; *Prov* **h. is the best policy** l'honnêteté est toujours récompensée

honey ['hʌnɪ] *n* (**a**) *(food)* miel *m* (**b**) *Fam (term of endearment)* chéri(e) *m,f*

honeycomb ['hʌnɪkəʊm] **1** *n* rayon *m* de miel

2 *vt* **the mountain is honeycombed with tunnels** la montagne est truffée de tunnels

honeymoon ['hʌnɪmuːn] **1** *n* voyage *m* de noces; *Fig* **the h. is over** l'état de grâce est terminé

2 *vi* partir en voyage de noces

honeysuckle ['hʌnɪsʌkəl] *n* chèvrefeuille *m*

Hong Kong ['hɒŋ'kɒŋ] *n* Hongkong

honk [hɒŋk] **1** *n (of goose)* cri *m*; *(of car horn)* coup *m* de Klaxon®

2 *vi (of goose)* cacarder; *(of car driver)* klaxonner

honky ['hɒŋkɪ] *(pl* **honkies**) *n Am very Fam* sale Blanc (Blanche) *m,f*, = terme injurieux désignant un Blanc

honor, honorable *etc Am* = **honour, honourable** *etc*

honorary ['ɒnərərɪ] *adj (member)* honoraire; *(title)* honorifique; *Univ* **h. degree** grade *m* honoris causa

honour, *Am* **honor** ['ɒnə(r)] **1** *n* (**a**) *(respect)* honneur *m*; **in h. of** en l'honneur de; **in h. of the occasion** pour l'occasion; **to have the h. of doing sth** avoir l'honneur de faire qch; *Hum* **to what do I owe this h.?** qu'est-ce qui me vaut cet honneur?; **Your H.** *(judge)* Votre Honneur

(**b**) *(good name)* honneur *m*; **to feel h. bound to do sth** se sentir tenu(e) par l'honneur de faire qch; **on my (word of) h.!** parole d'honneur!; *Prov* **(there is) h. among thieves** les loups ne se mangent pas entre eux

(**c**) *(award, distinction)* **honours list** = liste de distinctions honorifiques accordées par le souverain britannique; **honours degree** = diplôme universitaire obtenu avec mention; **he was buried with full military honours** il a été enterré avec tous les honneurs militaires; *Hum* **to do the honours** *(serve food or drink)* faire les honneurs; *(make introductions)* faire les présentations

2 *vt* honorer; **I felt honoured that they had invited me** je me suis senti honoré par leur invitation

honourable, *Am* **honorable** ['ɒnərəbəl] *adj* honorable; *Br Parl* **the H. member for** Monsieur/Madame le député de; **h. mention** mention *f* spéciale

honourably, *Am* **honorably** ['ɒnərəblɪ] *adv* honorablement

hooch [huːtʃ] *n Am Fam (liquor)* gnôle *f*

hood [hʊd] *n* (**a**) *(of coat, cloak)* capuche *f*; *(with eyeholes)* cagoule *f*; *Br (of car, pram)* capote *f*; *Am (car bonnet)* capot *m*; *(over cooker, fireplace)* hotte *f* (**b**) *Am Fam (gangster)* truand *m*

hoodlum ['huːdləm] *n Fam* voyou *m*

hoodwink ['hʊdwɪŋk] *vt Fam* embobiner; **to h. sb into doing sth** embobiner qn pour qu'il fasse qch

hoof [huːf] **1** *n* (*pl* **hooves** [huːvz]) sabot *m* **2** *vt Fam* **to h. it** aller à pinces

hoo-ha ['huːhɑː] *n Fam (fuss)* tintouin *m*

hook [hʊk] **1** *n* (**a**) *(for hanging) (in general)* crochet *m*; *(for coats)* patère *f*; *(for meat)* croc *m*; *(on clothes)* agrafe *f*; *(for fishing)* hameçon *m*; **to leave the phone off the h.** *(on purpose)* laisser le téléphone décroché; *(accidentally)* mal raccrocher son téléphone; *Fam Fig* **to get** *or* **let sb off the h.** tirer qn d'affaire; *Fam* **he swallowed it h., line and sinker** *(believed it)* il a tout gobé; *Fam* **by h. or by crook** coûte que coûte (**b**) *(in boxing)* crochet *m* **2** *vt* accrocher; **to h. a fish** attraper un poisson

▸**hook up 1** *vt sep Comput* connecter (**to** à) **2** *vi* (**a**) *(of dress)* s'agrafer (**b**) *Comput* se connecter; *TV* **to h. up with** faire une émission en duplex avec

hooked [hʊkt] *adj* (**a**) **h. nose** nez *m* crochu (**b**) *Fam (addicted)* **to be h. (on)** être accro (à); *(on cinema, jazz)* être mordu(e) (de)

hooker [hʊkər] *n* (**a**) *Br (in rugby)* talonneur *m* (**b**) *Am Fam (prostitute)* pute *f*

hook(e)y ['hʊkɪ] *n Am Fam* **to play h.** sécher les cours

hooligan ['huːlɪgən] *n* hooligan *m*, vandale *m*

hooliganism ['huːlɪgənɪzəm] *n* hooliganisme *m*, vandalisme *m*

hoop [huːp] *n* cerceau *m*; *(in croquet)* arceau *m*; *Fig* **to put sb through the hoops** mettre qn à l'épreuve

hooray [hʊ'reɪ] *exclam* hourra!

hoot [huːt] *n* (**a**) *(of owl)* hululement *m*; *(of horn)* coup *m* de Klaxon®; *(of ship, factory whistle)* mugissement *m*; **hoots of laughter** éclats *mpl* de rire; *Fam Fig* **I don't give a h.** *or* **two hoots** je m'en fiche comme de l'an quarante (**b**) *Fam* **she's a h.!** elle est tordante!; **it was a h.!** c'était tordant! **2** *vt (person)* huer; **he was hooted off the stage** il a quitté la scène sous les huées **3** *vi (of owl)* hululer; *(of train)* siffler; *(of car)* klaxonner; **to h. with laughter** hurler de rire

hooter ['huːtə(r)] *n Br* (**a**) *(of ship, factory)* sirène *f*; *(of car)* Klaxon® *m* (**b**) *Fam (nose)* pif *m*

hoover® ['huːvə(r)] **1** *n* aspirateur *m* **2** *vt (room)* passer l'aspirateur dans; *(carpet)* passer l'aspirateur sur

hooves [huːvz] *pl of* **hoof**

hop [hɒp] **1** *n (jump)* saut *m*; *Fam (dance)* bal *m*; **a short h.** *(journey)* un petit voyage; *Fam Fig* **to catch sb on the h.** prendre qn de court *ou* au dépourvu **2** *vt (pt & pp* **hopped***) Fam* **h. it!** fiche le camp! **3** *vi (jump)* sautiller; *(on one leg)* sauter à cloche-pied; *Fam* **h. in!** *(to car)* allez, grimpe!; **he hopped onto the first train** il a sauté dans le premier train

▸**hop off** *vi Fam* ficher le camp

hope [həʊp] **1** *n* espoir *m*; **in the h. of doing sth** dans l'espoir de faire qch; **in the h. that...** dans l'espoir que...; **to have little h. of doing sth** avoir peu de chances de faire qch; **to have hopes of doing sth** avoir l'espoir de faire qch; **don't get your hopes up** n'espère pas trop; **to raise hopes of sth** faire naître l'espoir de qch; **she hasn't got a h. of winning** elle n'a aucun espoir de gagner; *Ironic* **some h.!** tu peux toujours rêver!; *Fam* **we live in h.!** l'espoir fait vivre! **2** *vt* **to h. to do sth** espérer faire qch; **to h. (that)...** espérer que...; **I h. you're right** j'espère que tu as raison; **I h. and pray that...** je prie le ciel que...; **I h. so**

j'espère (bien); **I h. not** j'espère que non **3** *vi* espérer; **to h. for sth** espérer qch; **don't h. for too much** n'en attends pas trop; **we'll just have to h. for the best** espérons que tout se passe bien; **to h. against h.** espérer malgré tout

hopeful ['həʊpfʊl] **1** *n Fam* **a young h.** un jeune espoir **2** *adj (situation)* encourageant(e); *(person)* optimiste; **to be h. that...** avoir bon espoir que...

hopefully ['həʊpfʊlɪ] *adv* (**a**) *(with luck)* avec un peu de chance; **h. not** espérons que non (**b**) *(in a hopeful manner)* **to do sth h.** faire qch plein(e) d'espoir

hopeless ['həʊplɪs] *adj* (**a**) *(without hope) (person, cause, situation)* désespéré(e); **it's h.!** ça ne sert à rien! (**b**) *Fam (very bad)* nul (nulle) (**at** en)

hopelessly ['həʊplɪslɪ] *adv* (**a**) *(inconsolably)* avec désespoir (**b**) *(completely)* complètement; **he was h. in love with her** il était éperdument amoureux d'elle

hopping ['hɒpɪŋ] *adv Fam* **to be h. mad** être fou (folle) de rage

hops [hɒps] *npl (for making beer)* houblon *m*

hopscotch ['hɒpskɒtʃ] *n* marelle *f*

horde [hɔːd] *n* horde *f*

horizon [hə'raɪzən] *n* horizon *m*; **on the h.** à l'horizon; *Fig* en vue

horizontal [hɒrɪ'zɒntəl] **1** *n* horizontale *f* **2** *adj* horizontal(e)

horizontally [hɒrɪ'zɒntəlɪ] *adv* horizontalement

hormonal [hɔː'məʊnəl] *adj* hormonal(e)

hormone ['hɔːməʊn] *n* hormone *f*; **h. replacement therapy** hormonothérapie *f* de substitution

horn [hɔːn] *n* (**a**) *(of animal)* corne *f*; *(of insect)* antenne *f* (**b**) *(musical instrument)* cor *m*; *(on car)* Klaxon® *m*; **to sound one's h.** klaxonner (**c**) *(idioms)* **to be on the horns of a dilemma** être en proie à un dilemme

horned [hɔːnd] *adj* à cornes

hornet ['hɔːnɪt] *n* frelon *m*; *Fig* **to stir up a h.'s nest** mettre le feu aux poudres

hornpipe ['hɔːnpaɪp] *n* matelote *f*

horn-rimmed ['hɔːnrɪmd] *adj* **h. spectacles** *or* **glasses** lunettes *fpl* à monture d'écaille

horny ['hɔːnɪ] *adj* (**a**) *(hands)* calleux(euse) (**b**) *very Fam (sexually aroused)* excité(e); *(sexually attractive)* bandant(e)

horoscope ['hɒrəskəʊp] *n* horoscope *m*

horrendous [hɒ'rendəs] *adj* horrible, affreux(euse)

horrendously [hɒ'rendəslɪ] *adv* horriblement, affreusement

horrible ['hɒrəbəl] *adj* (**a**) *(unpleasant)* horrible, affreux(euse); **how h.!** quelle horreur! (**b**) *(unkind)* méchant(e) (**to** avec)

horribly ['hɒrɪblɪ] *adv* horriblement; **to behave h.** se conduire horriblement mal

horrid ['hɒrɪd] *adj* (**a**) *(unpleasant)* affreux(euse) (**b**) *(unkind)* méchant(e) (**to** avec)

horrific [hɒ'rɪfɪk] *adj* horrible

horrify ['hɒrɪfaɪ] *(pt & pp* **horrified***) vt* horrifier

horrifying ['hɒrɪfaɪɪŋ] *adj* horrifiant(e)

horror ['hɒrə(r)] *n* horreur *f*; **to my h.,...** à ma grande horreur,...; **to have a h. of sth** avoir horreur de qch; **it gives me the horrors** ça me donne le frisson; *Fam* **that child's a little h.** cet enfant est un petit monstre; **h. film** film *m* d'horreur; *Fig* **h. story** histoire *f* épouvantable

horror-stricken ['hɒrəstrɪkən], **horror-struck** ['hɒrə-strʌk] *adj* frappé(e) d'horreur

horse [hɔːs] *n* (**a**) *(animal)* cheval *m*; **h. chestnut** *(tree)* marronnier *m*; *(fruit)* marron *m*; **h. racing** courses *fpl* de chevaux; **h. riding** équitation *f*; **h. show** concours *m* hippique *(in negotiation)* maquignonnage *m* (**b**) *(in gymnastics)* cheval *m* d'arçons (**c**) *(idioms)* **to get on one's high h.** monter sur ses grands chevaux; *Fam* **I could eat a h!** j'ai un faim de loup!; **to eat like a h.** manger comme quatre; **to hear sth straight from the h.'s mouth** entendre qch de la bouche de l'intéressé

▶**horse about, horse around** *vi* chahuter

horseback ['hɔːsbæk] *n* **on h.** à cheval

horsebox ['hɔːsbɒks] *n* van *m*

horse-drawn ['hɔːsdrɔːn] *adj* tiré(e) par des chevaux

horsefly ['hɔːsflaɪ] *(pl* **horseflies)** *n* taon *m*

horsehair ['hɔːsheə(r)] *n* crin *m* (de cheval)

horseman ['hɔːsmən] *n* cavalier *m*

horsemanship ['hɔːsmənʃɪp] *n (skill)* talent *m* de cavalier

horseplay ['hɔːspleɪ] *n* chahut *m*

horsepower ['hɔːspaʊə(r)] *n* puissance *f* (en chevaux); *(unit)* cheval-vapeur *m*

horseradish ['hɔːsrædɪʃ] *n* raifort *m*

horseshoe ['hɔːsʃuː] *n* fer *m* à cheval

horsewhip ['hɔːswɪp] **1** *n* cravache *f*
2 *vt (pt & pp* **horsewhipped)** cravacher

horsewoman ['hɔːswʊmən] *n* cavalière *f*

hors(e)y ['hɔːsɪ] *adj* (**a**) *(horse-like)* chevalin(e) (**b**) *(keen on horses)* passionné(e) de chevaux (**c**) *Br Fam (upper-class)* = typique de la noblesse de campagne britannique, élégant et féru d'équitation

horticultural [hɔːtɪˈkʌltʃərəl] *adj* horticole

horticulture ['hɔːtɪkʌltʃə(r)] *n* horticulture *f*

hose [həʊz] **1** *n (pipe)* tuyau *m*
2 *vt* arroser (au jet d'eau)

▶**hose down** *vt sep* laver au jet

hosepipe ['həʊzpaɪp] *n* tuyau *m* d'arrosage

hosiery ['həʊzɪərɪ] *n* bonneterie *f*

hospice ['hɒspɪs] *n (hospital)* = établissement pour malades en phase terminale

hospitable [hɒsˈpɪtəbəl] *adj* hospitalier(ère)

hospitably [hɒsˈpɪtəblɪ] *adv* avec hospitalité

hospital ['hɒspɪtəl] *n* hôpital *m*; **in h.** à l'hôpital; **h. bed/food** lit *m*/nourriture *f* d'hôpital; **h. care** soins *mpl* hospitaliers

hospitality [hɒspɪˈtælɪtɪ] *n* hospitalité *f*

hospitalize ['hɒspɪtəlaɪz] *vt* **to be hospitalized** être hospitalisé(e)

host¹ [həʊst] **1** *n* (**a**) *(at home, party)* hôte *m*; *(on TV, radio)* animateur(trice) *m,f*; **h. city/country** ville *f*/ pays *m* d'accueil (**b**) *Biol (of parasite)* hôte *m*
2 *vt* (**a**) *(party)* donner, organiser; *(TV, radio show)* animer (**b**) *Comput (Web site)* héberger

host² *n (great number)* **a (whole) h. of** (toute) une foule de

host³ *n Rel* hostie *f*

hostage ['hɒstɪdʒ] *n* otage *m*; **to take/hold sb h.** prendre/garder qn en otage; **to offer a h. to fortune** hypothéquer l'avenir

hostel ['hɒstəl] *n (for homeless people, students)* foyer *m*; *(youth hostel)* auberge *f* de jeunesse

hostess ['həʊstɪs] *n (at home, party)* hôtesse *f*; *(on TV, radio)* animatrice *f*; *(on plane)* hôtesse (de l'air); **h. trolley** desserte *f*

hostile ['hɒstaɪl, *Am* 'hɒstəl] *adj* hostile (**to** à); *Com* **h. takeover bid** OPA *f* hostile

hostility [hɒsˈtɪlɪtɪ] *(pl* **hostilities)** *n* hostilité *f* (**towards** envers); **hostilities** *(fighting)* hostilités

hot [hɒt] *adj* (**a**) *(having high temperature)* chaud(e); **to get h.** *(of person)* commencer à avoir chaud; **to be h.** *(of person)* avoir chaud; *(of thing)* être chaud; **it's h.** *(of weather)* il fait chaud; *Med* **h. flushes** bouffées *fpl* de chaleur; *Am* **h. tub** = sorte de Jacuzzi® que l'on installe dehors

(**b**) *(spicy) (food)* épicé(e); *(pepper, mustard)* fort(e)

(**c**) *(close)* **you're getting h.** *(in guessing game)* tu brûles; **to be h. on sb's trail** être aux trousses de qn

(**d**) *Fam (good)* **to be h. on sth** *(be knowledgeable about)* être calé(e) en qch; *(attach importance to)* être très à cheval sur qch; **it wasn't such a h. idea** l'idée n'était pas si géniale; **how are you? – not so h.** comment ça va? – pas terrible; **to be h. stuff (at)** être un as (en)

(**e**) *Fam (sexy)* sexy *inv*

(**f**) *Fam (stolen)* chouré(e)

(**g**) *(idioms)* **h. off the press** *(of news)* de dernière minute; *(of book)* qui vient juste de paraître; **too h. to handle** *(issue)* brûlant(e); **to have a h. temper** s'emporter facilement; **to get h. under the collar** se mettre en colère; **a h. favourite** *(in race)* un grand favori; *Fam* **it's all just h. air** tout ça, c'est du vent; **they're selling like h. cakes** ils se vendent comme des petits pains; **h. desking** = pratique qui consiste à ne pas assigner de bureaux individuels aux employés, ces derniers étant libres de s'installer à n'importe quel poste de travail inoccupé; **the h. gossip** les derniers potins *mpl*; **h. line** *(telephone number)* permanence *f* téléphonique; **h. news** les toutes dernières nouvelles; *Fam* **h. potato** *(controversial issue)* sujet *m* brûlant; **to be in the h. seat** *(of politician, manager)* avoir toutes les responsabilités; **h. spot** *(trouble spot)* point *m* chaud; *Fam* **to get into h. water** *(in difficult situation)* s'attirer des ennuis

▶**hot up** *(pt & pp* **hotted)** *vi Fam (of situation, conflict)* s'envenimer; *(of race, debate, contest)* s'animer

hot-air balloon ['hɒteəbə'luːn] *n* montgolfière *f*

hotbed ['hɒtbed] *n* **a h. of rebellion/intrigue** un foyer de rébellion/d'intrigue

hot-blooded ['hɒt'blʌdɪd] *adj* au sang chaud, passionné(e)

hotchpotch ['hɒtʃpɒtʃ] *n Fam* mélange *m*

hotdog ['hɒtdɒg] *n* hot dog *m*

hotel [həʊ'tel] *n* hôtel *m*; **h. room/manager** chambre *f*/gérant(e) *m,f* d'hôtel; **the h. trade** l'industrie *f* hôtelière

hotelier [həʊ'telɪeɪ] *n* hôtelier(ère) *m,f*

hotfoot ['hɒt'fʊt] *Fam* **1** *adv* en vitesse
2 *vt* **to h. it** aller à toute vitesse

hothead ['hɒthed] *n* tête *f* brûlée

hotheaded ['hɒt'hedɪd] *adj* exalté(e)

hothouse ['hɒthaʊs] *n* serre *f* (chaude)

hotly ['hɒtlɪ] *adv (reply, protest)* vivement; **h. contested** âprement disputé(e)

hotplate ['hɒtpleɪt] *n (on cooker)* plaque *f* (chauffante); *(for keeping food warm)* chauffe-plat *m*

hotpot ['hɒtpɒt] *n (stew)* ragoût *m*

hots ['hɒts] *npl very Fam* **to have the h. for sb** craquer pour qn

hotshot ['hɒtʃɒt] *n Fam (expert)* as *m*, crack *m*

hot-tempered ['hɒt'tempəd] *adj* colérique, coléreux(euse)

hot-water [hɒt'wɔːtə(r)] *adj* d'eau chaude; **h. bottle** bouillotte *f*

hound [haʊnd] **1** *n (dog)* chien *m* de chasse
2 *vt (persecute)* traquer, pourchasser

hour ['aʊə(r)] *n* heure *f*; **an h. and a half** une heure et demie; **half an h.** une demi-heure; **to pay sb by the h.** payer qn à l'heure; **to take hours over sth** mettre des heures à faire qch; **we've been waiting for hours** ça fait des heures que nous attendons; **to work long hours** faire de longues journées (de travail); **to keep late hours** *(of person)* se coucher tard; **till all hours** jusqu'à très tard; **where were you in my h. of need?** où étais-tu quand j'avais besoin de toi?; **h. hand** *(of watch, clock)* petite aiguille *f*

hourglass ['aʊəglɑːs] *n* sablier *m*; **an h. figure** une taille de guêpe

hourly ['aʊəlɪ] **1** *adj* **at h. intervals** toutes les heures; **h. rate** taux *m* horaire
2 *adv (every hour)* toutes les heures; *(at any time)* d'un moment à l'autre

house 1 *n* [haʊs] **(a)** *(dwelling)* maison *f*; **to stay at sb's h.** loger chez qn; **from h. to h.** de porte à porte; **they keep open h.** leur maison est toujours ouverte; *Fig* **to put one's h. in order** balayer devant sa porte; **to get on like a h. on fire** *(very well)* s'entendre comme larrons en foire; **the H. of Commons/Lords** la Chambre des communes/lords; **the Houses of Parliament** le Parlement; **the H. of Representatives** la Chambre des représentants; *Law* **to be under h. arrest** être assigné(e) à résidence; **h. guest** invité(e) *m,f*; **h. martin** hirondelle *f* de fenêtre; **h. painter** peintre *m* en bâtiment; **h. party** partie *f* de campagne; **h. plant** plante *f* d'intérieur *ou* d'appartement; **h. spider** araignée *f* commune
(b) *Com (company)* maison *f*; **h. style** style *m* maison
(c) *(restaurant)* **on the h.** aux frais de la maison; **h. wine** vin *m* de la maison
(d) *Theat* **an empty/good h.** une salle vide/pleine
(e) **h. (music)** house music *f*
(f) *Br Sch* = groupe d'élèves d'une école secondaire qui disputent ensemble des compétitions sportives etc
2 *vt* [haʊz] *(person)* loger; *(collection, mechanism)* contenir, recevoir

---

House of Commons
La Chambre des communes britannique est composée de 659 députés ("MPs") élus pour cinq ans et qui siègent environ 175 jours par an. Les députés du parti majoritaire s'assoient d'un côté de la Chambre (les "government benches"), tandis que les députés de l'opposition s'assoient de l'autre côté (sur les "opposition benches"). Si un projet de loi n'obtient pas l'approbation de la majorité des députés dans la Chambre des communes, il est renvoyé à la Chambre des lords, et doit par ailleurs obtenir l'assentiment du souverain avant de devenir loi.

House of Lords
La Chambre des lords est composée de pairs et d'hommes d'Église. Il s'agit de la plus haute cour au Royaume-Uni (en excluant l'Écosse). Elle a le pouvoir d'amender certains projets de loi qui ont été votés par la Chambre des communes. Le gouvernement travailliste de Tony Blair, élu en 1997, a entrepris des réformes visant à réduire les pouvoirs de la Chambre des lords de façon radicale.

House of Representatives
La Chambre des représentants constitue, avec le Sénat, l'organe législatif américain; ses membres sont élus par le peuple, en proportion de la population de chaque État.

---

houseboat ['haʊsbəʊt] *n* péniche *f* aménagée

housebound ['haʊsbaʊnd] *adj* confiné(e) chez soi

housebreaker ['haʊsbreɪkə(r)] *n* cambrioleur(euse) *m,f*

housebreaking ['haʊsbreɪkɪŋ] *n* cambriolage *m*

housecoat ['haʊskəʊt] *n* robe *f* d'intérieur

housefly ['haʊsflaɪ] *(pl* **houseflies)** *n* mouche *f* domestique

household ['haʊshəʊld] *n* ménage *m*; **h. appliance** appareil *m* électroménager; **h. chores** tâches *fpl* ménagères; **he's a h. name** tout le monde connaît son nom

householder ['haʊshəʊldə(r)] *n (owner)* propriétaire *mf*; *(tenant)* locataire *mf*

househusband ['haʊsˌhʌzbənd] *n* homme *m* au foyer

housekeeper ['haʊskiːpə(r)] *n (private)* gouvernante *f*; *(in institution)* intendante *f*

housekeeping ['haʊskiːpɪŋ] *n* **h. (money)** argent *m* du ménage

housemaid ['haʊsmeɪd] *n* bonne *f*, femme *f* de chambre; **h.'s knee** *(inflammation)* inflammation *f* du genou

houseman ['haʊsmən] *n Br Med* interne *mf*

housemaster ['haʊsmɑːstə(r)] *n Br Sch* = dans une école secondaire, professeur chargé d'un "house"

housemistress ['haʊsmɪstrɪs] *n Br Sch* = dans une école secondaire, professeur chargée d'un "house"

houseproud ['haʊspraʊd] *adj* **she's very h.** elle prend grand soin de son intérieur

houseroom ['haʊsruːm] *n* **I wouldn't give it h.** *(theory, suggestion)* je ne perdrais pas mon temps avec ça; **I wouldn't give that table h.!** je ne voudrais pas de cette table chez moi!

house-sitter ['haʊsˌsɪtə(r)] *n* = personne qui garde la maison en l'absence de ses occupants

house-to-house ['haʊstə'haʊs] *adj* **to make a h. search** fouiller chaque maison

house-trained ['haʊstreɪnd] *adj (dog)* propre; *Hum (husband, partner)* bien dressé(e)

housewarming ['haʊswɔːmɪŋ] *n* **h. (party)** pendaison *f* de crémaillère; **to have a h. party** pendre la crémaillère

housewife ['haʊswaɪf] *(pl* **housewives** ['haʊswaɪvz] *) n* femme *f* au foyer

housework ['haʊswɜːk] *n* ménage *m*

housing ['haʊzɪŋ] *n* logement *m*; *Br* **h. association** = organisme *m* d'aide au logement; *Br* **h. benefit** ≃ allocation *f* logement; *Br* **h. estate** *(council-owned)* cité *f*

HLM; *(private)* lotissement *m*; **the h. market** le marché de l'immobilier; *Am* **h. project** cité *f* HLM

hove [həʊv] *pt & pp of* **heave**

hovel ['hɒvəl] *n* taudis *m*

hover ['hɒvə(r)] *vi* (**a**) *(of bird)* planer; *(of helicopter)* effectuer un vol stationnaire (**b**) *(of person)* **to h. near sb** être derrière le dos de qn

hovercraft ['hɒvəkrɑːft] *n* hovercraft *m*, aéroglisseur *m*

how [haʊ] *adv* (**a**) *(in what way, by what means)* comment; **h. did they find out?** comment l'ont-ils appris?; **h. do you spell this word?** comment s'écrit ce mot?; *Fam* **h. come?** comment ça se fait?; *Fam* **and h.!** et comment!
   (**b**) *(to what extent)* **h. much money?** combien d'argent?; **h. many people?** combien de gens?; **h. old are you?** quel âge as-tu?; **h. big is it?** c'est grand comment?; **h. long have you been here?** depuis combien de temps êtes-vous ici?; **h. often do you see him?** tu le vois tous les combien?; **you know h. difficult it is** tu sais à quel point c'est difficile; **h. useful will it be?** est-ce que ce sera très utile?
   (**c**) *(greetings, enquiries after health)* **h. are you?** comment vas-tu?; *Fam* **h. are things?** ça va?; **h.'s business?** comment vont les affaires?
   (**d**) *(in exclamations)* que, comme; **h. pretty she is!** qu'elle est jolie!, comme elle est jolie!; **h. disgusting!** c'est vraiment dégoûtant!; **h. true!** c'est bien vrai!; **h. she's changed!** comme elle a changé!
   (**e**) *(in suggestions)* **h. about a game of cards?** et si on faisait une partie de cartes?; **h. about going out for a meal?** et si on allait manger quelque part?; **h. about it?** ça te dirait?; **h. about you?** et toi?

however [haʊ'evə(r)] **1** *adv* (**a**) *(in whatever degree)* si... que + *subjunctive*; **h. clever she is** si intelligente qu'elle soit; **h. hard she tried, she couldn't do it** elle avait beau essayer, elle n'y arrivait pas (**b**) *(in whatever way)* **h. you look at it...** de quelque façon qu'on envisage la chose... (**c**) *(in what way)* comment; **h. did she find out?** comment a-t-elle bien pu l'apprendre?
   2 *conj* pourtant, cependant; **h., this does not explain why she...** ceci n'explique pourtant pas pourquoi elle...

howl [haʊl] **1** *n (of animal, person)* hurlement *m*; **howls of derision** des huées *fpl*
   2 *vi (of animal, person)* hurler; **to h. with laughter** hurler de rire

▸**howl down** *vt sep* huer

howler ['haʊlə(r)] *n Fam (mistake)* bourde *f*

howling ['haʊlɪŋ] **1** *n (of wind, wolf)* hurlement *m*; *(of baby)* hurlements
   2 *adj (wolf)* qui hurle; *(gale, wind)* furieux(euse); *Fam* **it wasn't exactly a h. success** ça n'a pas vraiment eu un succès fou

HP, hp [eɪtʃ'piː] *n* (**a**) *(abbr* **horsepower***)* CV *m* (**b**) *(abbr* **hire purchase***)* achat *m* à crédit

HQ [eɪtʃ'kjuː] *n (abbr* **headquarters***)* QG *m*

hr *(abbr* **hour***)* h

HRH [eɪtʃɑː'reɪtʃ] *n Br (abbr* **Her/His Royal Highness***)* SAR

HRM [eɪtʃɑː'rem] *n (abbr* **human resource management***)* GRH *f*

HRT [eɪtʃɑː'tiː] *n Med (abbr* **hormone replacement therapy***)* hormonothérapie *f* de substitution

HTML [eɪtʃtiːem'el] *n Comput (abbr* **HyperText Markup Language***)* HTML

HTTP [eɪtʃtiːtiː'piː] *n Comput (abbr* **HyperText Transfer Protocol***)* HTTP

hub [hʌb] *n* (**a**) *(of wheel)* moyeu *m* (**b**) *(of community)* centre *m*

hubbub ['hʌbʌb] *n* brouhaha *m*

hubby ['hʌbɪ] *(pl* **hubbies***)* *n Fam* petit mari *m*

hubcap ['hʌbkæp] *n (of wheel)* enjoliveur *m*

huddle ['hʌdəl] **1** *n (of people)* petit groupe *m*; *(of things)* tas *m*
   2 *vi* se blottir

▸**huddle together** *vi* se blottir les uns contre les autres

▸**huddle up** *vi* se blottir

Hudson Bay [hʌdsən'beɪ] *n* la baie d'Hudson

hue¹ [hjuː] *n (colour)* teinte *f*

hue² *n* **h. and cry** tollé *m*; **to raise a h. and cry about sth** crier haro sur qch

huff [hʌf] **1** *n Fam* **to be in a h.** faire la tête
   2 *vi* **to h. and puff** *(blow)* souffler; *Fig (show annoyance)* maugréer

huffy ['hʌfɪ] *adj Fam (sulky)* susceptible

hug [hʌg] **1** *n* étreinte *f*; **to give sb a h.** serrer qn (dans ses bras)
   2 *vt (pt & pp* **hugged***)* (**a**) *(embrace)* serrer (dans ses bras) (**b**) *Fig (shore, kerb)* serrer; *(ground)* raser

huge [hjuːdʒ] *adj (very big)* énorme; *(very tall, long)* immense

hugely ['hjuːdʒlɪ] *adv* énormément, extrêmement

hulk [hʌlk] *n* (**a**) *(of ship)* épave *f* (**b**) *(person)* mastodonte *m*

hulking ['hʌlkɪŋ] *adj Fam* **a h. great man** une armoire à glace

hull [hʌl] **1** *n* (**a**) *(of ship)* coque *f* (**b**) *(of pea)* cosse *f*
   2 *vt (peas)* écosser

hullabaloo [hʌləbə'luː] *(pl* **hullabaloos***)* *n Fam* raffut *m*

hullo = **hello**

hum [hʌm] **1** *n* bourdonnement *m*
   2 *vt (pt & pp* **hummed***)* *(tune)* fredonner
   3 *vi* (**a**) *(of person)* fredonner; *(of insect, computer)* bourdonner; *(of engine, fridge)* ronronner; **to h. and haw** hésiter; **to h. with activity** bourdonner d'activité (**b**) *Fam (smell)* chlinguer

human ['hjuːmən] **1** *n* (être *m*) humain *m*
   2 *adj* humain(e); **h. being** être *m* humain; **h. cloning** clonage *m* humain; **h. error** erreur *f* humaine; **h. nature** la nature humaine; **h. resources** ressources *fpl* humaines; **h. rights** droits *mpl* de l'homme; **h. shield** bouclier *m* humain

humane [hjʊ'meɪn] *adj* humain(e)

humanely [hjʊ'meɪnlɪ] *adv* humainement

humanism ['hjuːmənɪzəm] *n* humanisme *m*

humanistic [hjʊmə'nɪstɪk] *adj* humaniste

humanitarian [hjʊmænɪ'teərɪən] **1** *n* philanthrope *mf*
   2 *adj* humanitaire

humanity [hjʊ'mænɪtɪ] *n* humanité *f*; *Univ* **humanities** lettres *fpl*

humanize ['hjuːmənaɪz] *vt* humaniser

humankind [hjʊmən'kaɪnd] *n* humanité *f*

humanly ['hjuːmənlɪ] *adv* **to do everything h. possible** faire tout ce qui est humainement possible

humble ['hʌmbəl] **1** *adj (meek)* humble; *(unpretentious)* modeste; **in my h. opinion** à mon humble avis;

Fig **to eat h. pie** reconnaître qu'on a tort
  2 *vt* humilier
humbling ['hʌmbəlɪŋ] *adj* humiliant(e)
humbly ['hʌmbəlɪ] *adv (meekly)* humblement; *(modestly)* modestement
humbug ['hʌmbʌg] *n* **(a)** *(nonsense)* balivernes *fpl* **(b)** *(hypocrite)* charlatan *m* **(c)** *Br (sweet)* berlingot *m*
humdinger ['hʌmdɪŋə(r)] *n Fam* **a h. of a film/book** un film/livre extra
humdrum ['hʌmdrʌm] *adj* monotone
humerus ['hju:mərəs] *(pl* **humeri** ['hju:mərai]) *n Anat* humérus *m*
humid ['hju:mɪd] *adj* humide
humidifier [hjʊ'mɪdɪfaɪə(r)] *n* humidificateur *m*
humidity [hjʊ'mɪdɪtɪ] *n* humidité *f*
humiliate [hjʊ'mɪlɪeɪt] *vt* humilier
humiliating [hjʊ'mɪlɪeɪtɪŋ] *adj* humiliant(e)
humiliation [hjʊmɪlɪ'eɪʃən] *n* humiliation *f*
humility [hjʊ'mɪlɪtɪ] *n* humilité *f*
hummingbird ['hʌmɪŋbɜ:d] *n* colibri *m*
hummus ['hʊmʊs, 'hʌməs] *n* houmous *m*
humor, humorless *Am* = **humour, humourless**
humorous ['hju:mərəs] *adj (situation)* drôle, comique; *(writer, drawing, remark)* humoristique
humorously ['hju:mərəslɪ] *adv* avec humour
humour, *Am* **humor** ['hju:mə(r)] **1** *n* **(a)** *(fun)* humour *m* **(b)** *Formal (mood)* humeur *f*
  2 *vt (indulge)* faire plaisir à
humourless, *Am* **humorless** ['hju:məlɪs] *adj* dépourvu(e) d'humour
hump [hʌmp] **1** *n (on back, road)* bosse *f*
  2 *vt* **(a)** *Fam (carry)* trimbaler **(b)** *Vulg (have sex with)* sauter
humpback ['hʌmpbæk] *n* **h. bridge** pont *m* en dos d'âne; **h. whale** baleine *f* à bosse
humus ['hju:məs] *n* humus *m*
hunch [hʌntʃ] **1** *n (intuition)* intuition *f*; **to have a h. that...** avoir l'intuition que...
  2 *vt* **to h. one's shoulders** rentrer les épaules
hunchback ['hʌntʃbæk] *n* bossu(e) *m,f*
hundred ['hʌndrəd] **1** *n* cent *m*; **one** *or* **a h.** cent; **a h. and twenty-five pages** cent vingt-cinq pages; **two h. pages** deux cents pages; **I've told you hundreds of times** je te l'ai dit des centaines de fois; **to live to be a h.** vivre jusqu'à cent ans
  2 *adj* cent; **a h. kilometres an hour** cent kilomètres à l'heure; **one** *or* **a h. per cent** cent pour cent; **to be a h. per cent certain** être sûr(e) à cent pour cent; **I'm not feeling a h. per cent** je ne me sens pas au mieux de ma forme; **the h. metres** *(in athletics)* le cent mètres
hundredfold ['hʌndrədfəʊld] *adv* **to increase a h.** centupler
hundredth ['hʌndrədθ] **1** *n* **(a)** *(fraction)* centième *m* **(b)** *(in series)* centième *mf*
  2 *adj* centième; *Fam* **for the h. time, no!** pour la centième fois, non!; *see also* **eighth**
hundredweight ['hʌndrədweɪt] *n Br* = 50,8 kg, (poids *m* de) 112 livres *fpl*; *Am* = 45,36 kg, (poids de) 100 livres
hung [hʌŋ] **1** *adj* **h. jury/parliament** jury *m*/parlement *m* sans majorité
  2 *pt & pp of* **hang**

Hungarian [hʌŋ'geərɪən] **1** *n* **(a)** *(person)* Hongrois(e) *m,f* **(b)** *(language)* hongrois *m*
  2 *adj* hongrois(e)
Hungary ['hʌŋgərɪ] *n* la Hongrie
hunger ['hʌŋgə(r)] *n* faim *f*; *Fig (for power)* soif *f* **(for** de); **h. strike** grève *f* de la faim
▸**hunger after, hunger for** *vt insep Fig* avoir soif de
hungrily ['hʌŋgrɪlɪ] *adv also Fig* avidement
hungry ['hʌŋgrɪ] *adj* **to be h.** avoir faim; **to be h. for knowledge** être avide de connaissances
hunk [hʌŋk] *n* **(a)** *(of bread, meat)* gros morceau *m* **(b)** *Fam (attractive man)* beau mec *m*
hunky ['hʌŋkɪ] *adj Fam (man)* bien foutu
hunt [hʌnt] **1** *n* **(a)** *(for animals)* chasse *f*; *(for person, work)* recherche *f*
  2 *vt (animal)* chasser; *(criminal)* pourchasser
  3 *vi* **(a)** *(search)* **to h. for** rechercher **(b)** *(kill animals)* chasser
▸**hunt down** *vt sep (animal, person)* traquer; *(information)* dénicher
▸**hunt out** *vt sep (find) (person)* retrouver; *(thing)* dénicher
hunted ['hʌntɪd] *adj (look)* hagard(e)
hunter ['hʌntə(r)] *n* chasseur *m*
hunting ['hʌntɪŋ] *n* chasse *f*; **to go h.** aller à la chasse; **h. ground** terrain *m* de chasse; **h. lodge** pavillon *m* de chasse

---

Hunting

Depuis plusieurs années, la chasse à courre au renard constitue pour le gouvernement britannique un dossier controversé. En effet, une partie de plus en plus importante de la population s'oppose à ce type de chasse, considéré comme barbare; mais il existe également en face un groupe de pression pro-chasse très actif qui s'oppose à toute réforme et qui met l'accent sur les conséquences néfastes qu'une interdiction de la chasse au renard aurait sur le mode de vie rural et sur l'emploi dans les campagnes.

---

huntsman ['hʌntsmən] *n* chasseur *m*
hurdle ['hɜ:dəl] **1** *n (in race)* haie *f*; *Fig (obstacle)* obstacle *m*
  2 *vt (jump over)* sauter, franchir
hurdler ['hɜ:dlə(r)] *n Sport* coureur(euse) *m,f* de haies
hurdling ['hɜ:dəlɪŋ] *n Sport* course *f* de haies
hurl [hɜ:l] **1** *vt* jeter, lancer (**at** sur); *(insults)* lancer (**at** à); **to h. oneself at sb** se jeter *ou* se ruer sur qn
  2 *vi Fam (vomit)* dégobiller
hurling ['hɜ:lɪŋ] *n* = jeu irlandais voisin du hockey sur gazon qui oppose deux équipes de quinze joueurs
hurly-burly ['hɜ:lɪ'bɜ:lɪ] *n Fam* tohu-bohu *m inv*
hurrah [hʊ'rɑ:], **hurray** [hʊ'reɪ] *exclam* hourra!
hurricane ['hʌrɪkən, *Am* 'hʌrɪkeɪn] *n* ouragan *m*; **h. lamp** lampe *f* tempête
hurried ['hʌrɪd] *adj (gesture, conversation, meal)* rapide; *(departure)* précipité(e); *(work)* fait(e) à la hâte; *(decision, choice)* pris(e) à la hâte
hurriedly ['hʌrɪdlɪ] *adv* précipitamment
hurry ['hʌrɪ] **1** *n* hâte *f*; **to be in a h. (to do sth)** être pressé(e) (de faire qch); **to do sth in a h.** faire qch à la hâte; **to leave in a h.** partir à la hâte; **I won't do that again in a h.** je ne suis pas prêt de recommencer; **there's no h.** rien ne presse; **what's the h.?** qu'est-ce qui presse?

2 vt (pt & pp **hurried**) (person) presser; (work) hâter; **he was hurried to hospital** on l'a transporté d'urgence à l'hôpital

3 vi se dépêcher, se presser; **to h. to do sth** se dépêcher ou se presser de faire qch; **to h. into/out of a room** se précipiter dans une/hors d'une pièce

▶**hurry along 1** vt sep (person) faire se dépêcher; (work) accélérer

2 vi se presser

▶**hurry back** vi se dépêcher de revenir

▶**hurry on 1** vt sep (person) faire circuler; (work) faire accélérer

2 vi (leave) partir en hâte

▶**hurry up 1** vt sep faire accélérer

2 vi se dépêcher; **h. up!** vite!, dépêche-toi!

hurt [hɜːt] **1** n (emotional) blessure f

2 adj blessé(e)

3 vt (pt & pp **hurt**) (**a**) (physically) faire mal à; (reputation, chances) nuire à; **to h. oneself** se faire mal; **to h. one's foot** se faire mal au pied; **to get h.** se blesser; Fig **it won't h. him to have to wait** ça ne lui fera pas de mal d'attendre un peu (**b**) (emotionally) faire du mal ou de la peine à; **to h. sb's feelings** blesser qn

4 vi (**a**) (cause pain) faire mal; **where does it h.?** où est-ce que ça fait mal?; **my foot hurts** j'ai mal au pied, mon pied me fait mal (**b**) (emotionally) faire mal

hurtful ['hɜːtfʊl] adj blessant(e)

hurtle ['hɜːtəl] vi **to h. along** avancer à toute vitesse; **to h. down the street** dévaler la rue; **to h. towards** foncer sur

husband ['hʌzbənd] **1** n mari m

2 vt Formal (one's resources) ménager

husbandry ['hʌzbəndrɪ] n agriculture f; **animal h.** élevage m

hush [hʌʃ] **1** n (quiet) silence m; **h.!** chut!

2 vt calmer

▶**hush up** vt sep (scandal) étouffer

hushed [hʌʃt] adj (conversation) étouffé(e); (silence) profond(e); **to talk in h. tones** parler à voix basse

hush-hush ['hʌʃhʌʃ] adj Fam top secret inv

husk [hʌsk] **1** n (of seed) enveloppe f; (of pea) cosse f; (of nut) brou m

2 vt (grain) décortiquer

husky¹ ['hʌskɪ] adj (voice) rauque

husky² (pl **huskies**) n (dog) husky m

hussar [hʊˈzɑː(r)] n Mil hussard m

hussy ['hʌsɪ] (pl **hussies**) n Old-fashioned or Hum gourgandine f

hustings ['hʌstɪŋz] npl **on the h.** en campagne

hustle ['hʌsəl] **1** n **h. (and bustle)** effervescence f

2 vt (shove, push) **to h. sb away** emmener qn de force; **I was hustled into a small room** on m'a poussé dans une petite pièce

hustler ['hʌslə(r)] n Am Fam (swindler) arnaqueur(-euse) m,f; (prostitute) prostitué(e) m,f

hut [hʌt] n (shed) cabane f; (dwelling) hutte f

hutch [hʌtʃ] n (for rabbit) clapier m

hyacinth ['haɪəsɪnθ] n jacinthe f

hybrid ['haɪbrɪd] **1** n hybride m

2 adj hybride

hydrangea [haɪˈdreɪndʒə] n hortensia m

hydrant ['haɪdrənt] n prise f d'eau; **fire h.** bouche f d'incendie

hydraulic [haɪˈdrɔːlɪk] adj hydraulique; **h. engineering** hydraulique f

hydraulics [haɪˈdrɔːlɪks] n hydraulique f

hydrocarbon [haɪdrəʊˈkɑːbən] n hydrocarbure m

hydrochloric acid [haɪdrəʊˈklɒrɪkˈæsɪd] n acide m chlorhydrique

hydroelectric [haɪdrəʊɪˈlektrɪk] adj hydroélectrique

hydroelectricity [haɪdrəʊɪlekˈtrɪsɪtɪ] n hydroélectricité f

hydrofoil ['haɪdrəfɔɪl] n hydrofoil m, hydroptère m

hydrogen ['haɪdrədʒən] n hydrogène m; **h. bomb** bombe f à hydrogène

hydrolysis [haɪˈdrɒlɪsɪs] n hydrolyse f

hydrophobia [haɪdrəˈfəʊbɪə] n Med (rabies) rage f

hydroplane ['haɪdrəpleɪn] n (boat) hydroglisseur m; (seaplane) hydravion m

hydroxide [haɪˈdrɒksaɪd] n hydroxyde m

hyena [haɪˈiːnə] n hyène f

hygiene ['haɪdʒiːn] n hygiène f

hygienic [haɪˈdʒiːnɪk] adj hygiénique

hymen ['haɪmen] n hymen m

hymn [hɪm] n cantique m; **h. book** livre m de cantiques

hymnal ['hɪmnəl] n livre m de cantiques

hype [haɪp] Fam **1** n (publicity) battage m publicitaire

2 vt (publicize) faire du battage publicitaire pour

hype up vt sep Fam (**a**) (publicize) faire du battage publicitaire pour (**b**) **to be hyped up** (excited) être surexcité(e)

hyper ['haɪpə(r)] adj Fam (overexcited) surexcité(e); **she's very h.** elle est très speed

hyperactive [haɪpəˈræktɪv] adj hyperactif(ive)

hyperbola [haɪˈpɜːbələ] n Math hyperbole f

hyperbole [haɪˈpɜːbəlɪ] n hyperbole f

hypercritical [haɪpəˈkrɪtɪkəl] adj hypercritique

hyperinflation [haɪpərɪnˈfleɪʃən] n Econ hyperinflation f

hyperlink ['haɪpəlɪŋk] n Comput hyperlien m

hypermarket ['haɪpəmɑːkɪt] n hypermarché m

hypersensitive [haɪpəˈsensɪtɪv] adj hypersensible

hypertension [haɪpəˈtenʃən] n Med hypertension f

hypertext ['haɪpətekst] n Comput hypertexte m; **h. link** lien m hypertexte

hyphen ['haɪfən] n trait m d'union

hyphenate ['haɪfəneɪt] vt (word) mettre un trait d'union à; **a hyphenated word** un mot à trait d'union

hypnosis [hɪpˈnəʊsɪs] n hypnose f

hypnotic [hɪpˈnɒtɪk] adj hypnotique

hypnotism ['hɪpnətɪzəm] n hypnotisme m

hypnotist ['hɪpnətɪst] n hypnotiseur(euse) m,f

hypnotize ['hɪpnətaɪz] vt hypnotiser

hypoallergenic [haɪpəʊæləˈdʒenɪk] adj hypoallergénique

hypochondria [haɪpəˈkɒndrɪə] n hypocondrie f

hypochondriac [haɪpəˈkɒndrɪæk] n hypocondriaque mf

hypocrisy [hɪˈpɒkrɪsɪ] n hypocrisie f

hypocrite ['hɪpəkrɪt] n hypocrite mf

hypocritical [hɪpəˈkrɪtɪkəl] adj hypocrite

hypodermic [haɪpəˈdɜːmɪk] **1** n seringue f hypodermique

2 adj hypodermique

hypotenuse [haɪˈpɒtənjuːz] n Math hypoténuse f

hypothermia [haɪpəʊˈθɜːmɪə] n hypothermie f; **to have h.** faire de l'hypothermie

hypothesis [haɪˈpɒθəsɪs] (pl **hypotheses** [haɪˈpɒθəsiːz]) n hypothèse f

hypothesize [haɪ'pɒθəsaɪz] **1** *vt* **to h. that...** émettre l'hypothèse que...
    2 *vi* faire des hypothèses
hypothetical [haɪpə'θetɪkəl] *adj* hypothétique
hysterectomy [hɪstə'rektəmɪ] (*pl* **hysterectomies**) *n* hystérectomie *f*; **to have a h.** subir une hystérectomie
hysteria [hɪs'tɪərɪə] *n* (**a**) *(panic)* hystérie *f* (**b**) *(laughter)* fou rire *m*

hysterical [hɪs'terɪkəl] *adj* (**a**) *(uncontrolled)* hystérique; **to be h.** faire une crise de nerfs; **h. laughter** fou rire *m* (**b**) *(very funny)* tordant(e)
hysterically [hɪs'terɪklɪ] *adv* (**a**) *(uncontrolledly)* sans pouvoir se contrôler; **to laugh h.** avoir le fou rire (**b**) **h. funny** tordant(e)
hysterics [hɪs'terɪks] *npl* (**a**) *(panic)* crise *f* de nerfs; **to go into** *or* **have h.** avoir une crise de nerfs (**b**) *(laughter)* fou rire *m*; **to be in h.** avoir le fou rire

I¹, i [aɪ] *n (letter)* I, i *m inv*

I² *pron* je; **I'm Scottish** je suis écossais; **I haven't got it!** ce n'est pas moi qui l'ai!

IAEA [aɪeɪiː'eɪ] *n (abbr* **International Atomic Energy Agency)** AIEA *f*

IAP [aɪeɪ'piː] *n Comput (abbr* **Internet Access Provider)** fournisseur *m* d'accès à l'Internet

IBA [aɪbiː'eɪ] *n (abbr* **Independent Broadcasting Authority)** ≃ CSA *m (organisme qui contrôle les chaînes de télévision et de stations de radio privées britanniques)*

Iberian [aɪ'bɪːrɪən] *adj* ibérique; **the I. Peninsula** la péninsule Ibérique

ibex ['aɪbeks] *n* bouquetin *m*

ibid ['ɪbɪd] *adv (abbr* **ibidem)** ibid

IBM [aɪbiː'em] *n (abbr* **intercontinental ballistic missile)** MBI *m*

IBRD [aɪbiːɑː'diː] *n (abbr* **International Bank for Reconstruction and Development)** BIRD *f*

IBS [aɪbiː'es] *n (abbr* **irritable bowel syndrome)** colopathie *f* fonctionnelle

ice [aɪs] **1** *n* **(a)** *(frozen water, ice-cream)* glace *f*; *(on road)* verglas *m*; **i. age** période *f* glaciaire; **i. bucket** seau *m* à glace; **i. cube** glaçon *m*; **i. floe** banquise *f*; **i. hockey** hockey *m* sur glace; **i. lolly** glace *f* à l'eau; **i. pack** sachet *m* de glace; **i. pick** pic *m* à glace; **i. rink** patinoire *f* **(b)** *(idioms)* **to put a project on i.** geler un projet; **to break the i.** rompre la glace; **to be skating on thin i.** avancer sur un terrain glissant; **that cuts no i. with me** ça ne marche pas avec moi
2 *vt (cake)* glacer

ice over *vi* geler

ice up *vi* se givrer

iceberg ['aɪsbɜːg] *n* iceberg *m*; *Fig* **that's just the tip of the i.** ce n'est que la partie visible de l'iceberg; **i. lettuce** = variété croquante de laitue de serre

icebound ['aɪsbaʊnd] *adj* bloqué(e) par les glaces

icebox ['aɪsbɒks] *n Br (in fridge)* freezer *m*; *Am (fridge)* réfrigérateur *m*

icebreaker ['aɪs'breɪkə(r)] *n (ship)* brise-glace *m inv*; *Fig (at party, in conversation)* **it's a good i.** c'est un bon moyen de briser la glace

icecap ['aɪskæp] *n* calotte *f* glaciaire

ice-cold ['aɪs'kəʊld] *adj* glacé(e); *(wind)* glacial(e)

ice-cream [aɪs'kriːm] *n* glace *f*; **i. cone** cornet *m* de glace; **i. van** camionnette *f* de vendeur de glaces

iced [aɪst] *adj* **(a)** *(water)* avec des glaçons **(b)** *(cake)* glacé(e)

Iceland ['aɪslənd] *n* l'Islande *f*

Icelander ['aɪsləndə(r)] *n* Islandais(e) *m,f*

Icelandic [aɪs'lændɪk] **1** *n (language)* islandais *m*
2 *adj* islandais(e)

ice-skate ['aɪs'skeɪt] **1** *n* patin *m* à glace
2 *vi* faire du patin à glace

ice-skating ['aɪs'skeɪtɪŋ] *n* patinage *m* (sur glace)

icicle ['aɪsɪkəl] *n* glaçon *m (qui pend d'une gouttière etc)*

icing ['aɪsɪŋ] *n (on cake)* glaçage *m*; *Fig* **the i. on the cake** la cerise sur le gâteau; **i. sugar** sucre *m* glace

icon ['aɪkɒn] *n Rel & Comput* icône *f*; *Fig* **gay i.** idole *f* gay

iconoclastic [aɪkɒnəʊ'klæstɪk] *adj* iconoclaste

icy ['aɪsɪ] *adj* **(a)** *(road)* verglacé(e); *(ground)* gelé(e); *(water, hands)* glacé(e); *(wind)* glacial(e) **(b)** *Fig (expression, reply)* glacial(e)

ID ['aɪ'diː] *n (abbr* **identification)** papiers *mpl* (d'identité); **ID card** carte *f* d'identité

I'd [aɪd] = **I had, I would**

idea [aɪ'dɪə] *n* **(a)** *(individual notion)* idée *f*; **to put an i. into sb's head** mettre une idée dans la tête de qn; **the very i.!** quelle idée!; *Fam* **what's the big i.?** qu'est-ce qui te prend? **(b)** *(concept)* conception *f*; **to have an i. that...** avoir l'impression que...; **that's not my i. of fun** ce n'est pas vraiment comme ça que je m'amuserais; **it's her i. of a joke** elle trouve ça drôle; **I have no i.** je n'ai aucune idée; **I had no i. that...** je ne savais pas que...; **I thought the i. was for them to come here** je croyais qu'il était prévu qu'ils viennent ici; **the general i. is to...** l'idée est de...

ideal [aɪ'dɪəl] **1** *n* idéal *m*
2 *adj* idéal(e) (**for** pour)

idealism [aɪ'dɪəlɪzəm] *n* idéalisme *m*

idealist [aɪ'dɪəlɪst] *n* idéaliste *mf*

idealistic [aɪdɪə'lɪstɪk] *adj* idéaliste

idealize [aɪ'dɪəlaɪz] *vt* idéaliser

ideally [aɪ'dɪəlɪ] *adv* **(a)** *(extremely well)* idéalement; **they're i. matched** ils vont parfaitement bien ensemble **(b)** *(in an ideal situation)* dans l'idéal

identical [aɪ'dentɪkəl] *adj* identique; **i. twins** *(boys)* vrais jumeaux *mpl*; *(girls)* vraies jumelles *fpl*

identification [aɪdentɪfɪ'keɪʃən] *n* **(a)** *(of body, criminal)* identification *f* **(b)** *(documents)* papiers *mpl* (d'identité)

identify [aɪ'dentɪfaɪ] *(pt & pp* **identified) 1** *vt* **(a)** *(recognize)* identifier **(b)** *(associate)* **to i. sth with sth** identifier qch à qch
2 *vi* s'identifier (**with sb** à qn); **I can't i. with his problems** j'ai du mal à comprendre ses problèmes

identifying mark [aɪ'dentɪfaɪŋ'mɑːk] *n* signe *m* particulier

Identikit® [aɪ'dentɪkɪt] *n* **I. (picture)** portrait-robot *m*

identity [aɪ'dentɪtɪ] *(pl* **identities)** *n* identité *f*; **it was a case of mistaken i.** il y a eu erreur sur la personne; **i. card** carte *f* d'identité; **i. crisis** crise *f* d'identité; **i. parade** séance *f* d'identification

ideological [aɪdɪə'lɒdʒɪkəl] *adj* idéologique
ideology [aɪdɪ'ɒlədʒi] *(pl* **ideologies**) *n* idéologie *f*
idiocy ['ɪdɪəsɪ] *n* idiotie *f*
idiom ['ɪdɪəm] *n (expression)* expression *f*, locution *f*; *(dialect)* idiome *m*
idiomatic [ɪdɪə'mætɪk] *adj* idiomatique
idiosyncrasy [ɪdɪəʊ'sɪŋkrəsɪ] *(pl* **ideosyncracies**) *n* particularité *f*; *(foible)* petite manie *f*
idiosyncratic [ɪdɪəʊsɪŋ'krætɪk] *adj* particulier(ère)
idiot ['ɪdɪət] *n* idiot(e) *m,f*
idiotic [ɪdɪ'ɒtɪk] *adj* idiot(e)
idle ['aɪdəl] **1** *adj* **(a)** *(unoccupied) (factory, machine)* arrêté(e); *(person)* désœuvré(e); **an i. moment** un moment libre **(b)** *(lazy)* oisif(ive) **(c)** *(futile) (threat, boast)* vain(e); *(gossip, rumour)* pour passer le temps; *(curiosity)* simple
   2 *vi (of engine)* tourner au ralenti
▶**idle away** *vt sep (time)* passer à ne rien faire; **we idled the afternoon away chatting** nous avons passé l'après-midi à bavarder
idleness ['aɪdəlnɪs] *n* **(a)** *(inaction)* inactivité *f* **(b)** *(laziness)* oisiveté *f*
idler ['aɪdlə(r)] *n (lazy person)* paresseux(euse) *m,f*
idly ['aɪdlɪ] *adv* **(a)** *(inactively)* sans rien faire **(b)** *(casually)* négligemment
idol ['aɪdəl] *n* idole *f*
idolatry [aɪ'dɒlətrɪ] *n* idolâtrie *f*
idolize ['aɪdəlaɪz] *vt* idolâtrer
idyll ['ɪdɪl] *n (situation)* situation *f* idyllique; *(place)* endroit *m* idyllique
idyllic [ɪ'dɪlɪk] *adj* idyllique
ie ['aɪ'iː] *(abbr* **id est)** c.-à-d.
if [ɪf] **1** *conj* **(a)** *(conditional)* si; **if I were rich...** si j'étais riche...; **if I were you...** si j'étais toi..., à ta place...
   (b) *(conceding)* **the film was good, if rather long** le film était un peu long, mais bien; **if anything it's better** c'est presque mieux
   (c) *(whether)* si; **I asked if it was true** j'ai demandé si c'était vrai
   (d) *(in phrases)* **if not** sinon; **there were hundreds, if not thousands, of people** il y avait des centaines de gens, voire des milliers; **if so** si c'est le cas; **if only I had more money...** si seulement j'avais plus d'argent...; **if and when they arrive...** quand ils arriveront, s'ils arrivent...; **she sees them rarely, if at all** *or* **if ever** elle ne les voit jamais, ou alors très rarement
   2 *n* **ifs and buts** restrictions *fpl*; **it's a big if** c'est un grand point d'interrogation
IFA [aɪef'eɪ] *n Fin (abbr* **independent financial adviser)** conseiller(ère) *m,f* financier(ère) indépendant(e)
iffy ['ɪfɪ] *adj Fam (doubtful)* incertain(e); *(suspect)* louche
igloo ['ɪgluː] *(pl* **igloos)** *n* igloo *m*
ignite [ɪg'naɪt] **1** *vt (fire)* allumer; *(paper)* enflammer; *Fig (conflict)* déclencher
   2 *vi (of fire)* prendre; *(of paper)* s'enflammer; *Fig (of conflict)* se déclencher
ignition [ɪg'nɪʃən] *n (of car)* allumage *m*; **to switch on/off the i.** mettre/couper le contact; **i. key** clé *f* de contact
ignoble [ɪg'nəʊbəl] *adj* ignoble
ignominious [ɪgnə'mɪnɪəs] *adj* ignominieux(euse)
ignoramus [ɪgnə'reɪməs] *n* ignorant(e) *m,f*, ignare *mf*

ignorance ['ɪgnərəns] *n* **(a)** *(lack of knowledge)* ignorance *f*; **out of** *or* **through i.** par ignorance **(b)** *(ill manners)* manque *m* d'éducation
ignorant ['ɪgnərənt] *adj* **(a)** *(lacking knowledge) (person)* ignorant(e); *(remark)* d'ignorant; **to be i. of sth** ignorer qch **(b)** *(ill-mannered)* mal élevé(e)
ignore [ɪg'nɔː(r)] *vt* ignorer; **just i. him!** ne fais pas attention à lui!
iguana [ɪg'waːnə] *n* iguane *m*
ilk [ɪlk] *n* **of that i.** de ce genre
ill¹ [ɪl] **1** *npl* **ills** maux *mpl*
   2 *adj* **(a)** *(unwell)* malade; **to feel i.** ne pas se sentir bien; **to fall** *or* **be taken i.** tomber malade **(b)** *(bad, poor)* **i. effects** effets *mpl* néfastes; **i. feeling** animosité *f*; **i. fortune** malchance *f*; **to be in i. health** être en mauvaise santé; **i. at ease** mal à l'aise; **of i. repute** mal famé(e); **i. will** malveillance *f*
   3 *adv* mal; **I can i. afford it** je peux difficilement me le permettre; **to speak/think i. of sb** dire/penser du mal de qn
ill² *(abbr* **illustration)** ill
I'll [aɪl] = **I will, I shall**
ill-advised ['ɪləd'vaɪzd] *adj (person)* malavisé(e); *(decision, comment)* peu judicieux(euse); **to be i. to do sth** être malavisé de faire qch
ill-bred ['ɪl'bred] *adj* mal élevé(e)
ill-concealed ['ɪlkən'siːld] *adj* mal dissimulé(e)
ill-considered ['ɪlkən'sɪdəd] *adj* irréfléchi(e)
ill-disposed ['ɪldɪs'pəʊzd] *adj* **to be i. towards sb/sth** être mal disposé(e) envers qn/qch
illegal [ɪ'liːgəl] *adj* illégal(e); *(immigrant)* clandestin(e)
illegality [ɪlɪ'gælɪtɪ] *n* illégalité *f*
illegible [ɪ'ledʒɪbəl] *adj* illisible
illegitimate [ɪlɪ'dʒɪtɪmət] *adj* illégitime
ill-equipped ['ɪlɪ'kwɪpd] *adj* mal équipé(e); *Fig* **to be i. to do sth** ne pas être apte à faire qch
ill-fated ['ɪl'feɪtɪd] *adj (day, occasion)* fatal(e); *(person, enterprise)* malheureux(euse)
ill-founded ['ɪl'faʊndɪd] *adj* sans fondement
ill-gotten gains ['ɪlgɒtən'gaɪnz] *npl* biens *mpl* mal acquis
illiberal [ɪ'lɪbərəl] *adj (person)* intolérant(e); *(measure)* restrictif(ive)
illicit [ɪ'lɪsɪt] *adj* illicite
ill-informed [ɪlɪn'fɔːmd] *adj* mal informé(e); *(idea)* inexact(e)
ill-intentioned ['ɪlɪn'tenʃənd] *adj* malintentionné(e)
illiteracy [ɪ'lɪtərəsɪ] *n* analphabétisme *m*
illiterate [ɪ'lɪtərət] **1** *n* analphabète *mf*
   2 *adj* analphabète
ill-mannered ['ɪl'mænəd] *adj* grossier(ère)
ill-natured ['ɪl'neɪtʃəd] *adj* désagréable
illness ['ɪlnɪs] *n* maladie *f*
illogical [ɪ'lɒdʒɪkəl] *adj* illogique
ill-suited ['ɪl'suːtɪd] *adj* inapproprié(e) **(to** à); *(person)* inapte **(to** à)
ill-tempered ['ɪl'tempəd] *adj (person)* qui a mauvais caractère; *(remark)* désagréable
ill-timed ['ɪl'taɪmd] *adj* inopportun(e)
ill-treat ['ɪl'triːt] *vt* maltraiter
illuminate [ɪ'luːmɪneɪt] *vt* **(a)** *(light up) (room)* éclairer; *(building)* illuminer **(b)** *(clarify)* éclairer
illuminating [ɪ'luːmɪneɪtɪŋ] *adj* éclairant(e)

illumination [ɪluːmɪ'neɪʃən] n (**a**) *(lighting)* éclairage m; **illuminations** *(decorative lights)* illuminations fpl (**b**) *(clarification)* éclaircissements mpl

ill-use 1 n ['ɪl'juːs] mauvais traitement m
 2 vt ['ɪl'juːz] maltraiter

illusion [ɪ'luːʒən] n illusion f; **to be under the i. that...** s'imaginer que...; **to be under** or **have no illusions about sb/sth** ne se faire aucune illusion sur qn/qch

illusory [ɪ'luːsərɪ] adj illusoire

illustrate ['ɪləstreɪt] vt illustrer

illustration [ɪləs'treɪʃən] n illustration f

illustrator ['ɪləstreɪtə(r)] n illustrateur(trice) m,f

illustrious [ɪ'lʌstrɪəs] adj illustre

ILO [aɪe'ləʊ] n (abbr **International Labour Organization**) OIT f

I'm [aɪm] = **I am**

image ['ɪmɪdʒ] n image f; **to be the i. of sb** être le portrait de qn

imagery ['ɪmɪdʒərɪ] n imagerie f, images fpl

imaginary [ɪ'mædʒɪnərɪ] adj imaginaire

imagination [ɪmædʒɪ'neɪʃən] n imagination f; **it's (all in) your i.** tu te fais des idées; **use your i!** fais preuve d'un peu d'imagination!

imaginative [ɪ'mædʒɪnətɪv] adj *(person)* imaginatif(-ive); *(excuse, solution)* original(e)

imagine [ɪ'mædʒɪn] vt imaginer; **to i. doing sth** s'imaginer faire qch; **to i. sb doing sth** imaginer qn faisant qch; **I can't i. why...** je n'arrive pas à comprendre pourquoi...; **you're imagining things** tu te fais des idées; **you must have imagined it** tu as dû rêver

imbalance [ɪm'bæləns] n déséquilibre m

imbecile ['ɪmbɪsiːl] n imbécile mf

imbibe [ɪm'baɪb] vt Formal *(drink)* absorber; Fig *(knowledge, ideas)* absorber, assimiler

imbue [ɪm'bjuː] vt Formal **to i. sb with sth** imprégner qn de qch; **to be imbued with scorn/fervour** *(of speech, book)* être empreint(e) de mépris/ferveur

IMF [aɪe'mef] n (abbr **International Monetary Fund**) FMI m

imitate ['ɪmɪteɪt] vt imiter

imitation [ɪmɪ'teɪʃən] n *(action, copy)* imitation f; **in i. of** à l'imitation de; **i. jewellery** faux bijoux mpl; **i. leather** similicuir m, imitation cuir

imitative ['ɪmɪtətɪv] adj imitatif(ive)

imitator ['ɪmɪteɪtə(r)] n imitateur(trice) m,f

immaculate [ɪ'mækjʊlət] adj impeccable; Rel **the I. Conception** l'Immaculée Conception f

immaterial [ɪmə'tɪərɪəl] adj sans importance

immature [ɪmə'tjʊə(r)] adj immature

immaturity [ɪmə'tjʊərɪtɪ] n immaturité f

immeasurable [ɪ'meʒərəbəl] adj incommensurable

immediacy [ɪ'miːdɪəsɪ] n immédiateté f; *(of danger, disaster)* imminence f

immediate [ɪ'miːdɪət] adj (**a**) *(instant)* immédiat(e); *(danger)* imminent(e) (**b**) *(nearest)* *(vicinity)* proche; *(future)* immédiat(e); **the i. family** les proches parents mpl

immediately [ɪ'miːdɪətlɪ] **1** adv immédiatement, tout de suite
 2 conj dès que

immemorial [ɪmɪ'mɔːrɪəl] adj **from time i.** depuis des temps immémoriaux

immense [ɪ'mens] adj immense

immensely [ɪ'menslɪ] adv *(interesting, painful)* extrêmement; *(rich)* immensément; *(enjoy oneself)* énormément

immensity [ɪ'mensɪtɪ] n immensité f; *(of problem, task)* énormité f

immerse [ɪ'mɜːs] vt also Fig plonger (**in** dans); **to i. oneself in sth** se plonger dans qch

immigrant ['ɪmɪɡrənt] n & adj immigré(e) m,f

immigrate ['ɪmɪɡreɪt] vi immigrer

immigration [ɪmɪ'ɡreɪʃən] n immigration f; **to go through i.** passer (à) l'immigration; **i. control** services mpl de l'immigration; **i. officer** agent m des services de l'immigration

imminent ['ɪmɪnənt] adj imminent(e)

immobile [ɪ'məʊbaɪl] adj immobile

immobilize [ɪ'məʊbɪlaɪz] vt immobiliser

immoderate [ɪ'mɒdərət] adj immodéré(e)

immodest [ɪ'mɒdɪst] adj *(vain)* présomptueux(euse); *(indecent)* impudique

immoral [ɪ'mɒrəl] adj immoral(e); **i. earnings** gains mpl du proxénétisme

immorality [ɪmə'rælɪtɪ] n immoralité f

immortal [ɪ'mɔːtəl] **1** n immortel(elle) m,f
 2 adj immortel(elle); *(memory)* impérissable

immortality [ɪmɔː'tælɪtɪ] n immortalité f

immovable [ɪ'muːvəbəl] adj *(object)* fixe; Fig *(person, opposition)* inébranlable

immune [ɪ'mjuːn] adj *(to disease)* immunisé(e) (**to** contre); Fig *(to criticism)* imperméable (**to** à); **i. from taxation** exonéré(e) d'impôts; Med **i. deficiency** immunodéficience f; Med **i. system** système m immunitaire

immunity [ɪ'mjuːnɪtɪ] n *(to disease)* immunité f; *(from taxation)* exonération f; Law **i. (from prosecution)** immunité

immunization [ɪmjʊnaɪ'zeɪʃən] n immunisation f

immunize ['ɪmjʊnaɪz] vt immuniser (**against** contre)

immunosuppression ['ɪmjuːnəʊsə'preʃən] n Med immunosuppression f

immutable [ɪ'mjuːtəbəl] adj immuable

imp [ɪmp] n *(sprite)* lutin m; Fig *(mischievous child)* garnement m

impact 1 n ['ɪmpækt] impact m; **to make an i. on sb/ sth** avoir un impact sur qn/qch; **on i.** au moment de l'impact
 2 vt [ɪm'pækt] *(collide with)* heurter; *(influence)* avoir un impact sur

impacted [ɪm'pæktɪd] adj *(tooth)* inclus(e)

impair [ɪm'peə(r)] vt *(sight, hearing)* affaiblir; *(relations, chances)* compromettre

impale [ɪm'peɪl] vt empaler (**on** sur)

impart [ɪm'pɑːt] vt Formal *(heat, light, quality)* donner; *(knowledge, news)* transmettre

impartial [ɪm'pɑːʃəl] adj impartial(e)

impartiality [ɪmpɑːʃɪ'ælɪtɪ] n impartialité f

impassable [ɪm'pɑːsəbəl] adj *(river, barrier)* infranchissable; *(road)* impraticable

impasse ['æmpɑːs] n impasse f; **to have reached an i.** être dans une impasse

impassioned [ɪm'pæʃənd] adj passionné(e)

impassive [ɪm'pæsɪv] adj impassible

impassively [ɪm'pæsɪvlɪ] adv impassiblement

impatience [ɪm'peɪʃəns] n impatience f

impatient [ɪm'peɪʃənt] adj impatient(e); **to be i. to do sth** être impatient de faire qch; **to be i. for sth** avoir soif de qch; **to get i. (with sb)** s'impatienter (contre qn)

impatiently [ɪmˈpeɪʃəntlɪ] *adv* avec impatience

impeach [ɪmˈpiːtʃ] *vt Am Law* mettre en accusation *(selon la procédure qui vise les hauts fonctionnaires américains)*

impeccable [ɪmˈpekəbəl] *adj* impeccable

impede [ɪmˈpiːd] *vt* gêner

impediment [ɪmˈpedɪmənt] *n* (**a**) *(obstacle)* obstacle *m* (**b**) *(disability)* handicap *m*

impel [ɪmˈpel] *(pt & pp* impelled*)* *vt* (**a**) *(oblige)* obliger; *(incite)* pousser (**b**) *(push)* propulser

impending [ɪmˈpendɪŋ] *adj* imminent(e)

impenetrable [ɪmˈpenɪtrəbəl] *adj (defences, mystery)* impénétrable; *(jargon)* incompréhensible

imperative [ɪmˈperətɪv] **1** *n Gram* impératif *m*; **in the i.** à l'impératif
2 *adj* impératif(ive); **it is i. that he should come** il faut impérativement qu'il vienne

imperceptible [ɪmpəˈseptɪbəl] *adj* imperceptible

imperfect [ɪmˈpɜːfɪkt] **1** *n Gram* **the i.** l'imparfait *m*; **in the i.** à l'imparfait
2 *adj (not perfect)* imparfait(e); *Gram* de l'imparfait; **i. tense** imparfait *m*

imperfection [ɪmpəˈfekʃən] *n* imperfection *f*

imperial [ɪmˈpɪərɪəl] *adj* (**a**) *(of empire)* impérial(e) (**b**) *(weights and measures)* = relatif au système de mesure anglo-saxon utilisant les miles, les pints etc

imperialism [ɪmˈpɪərɪəlɪzəm] *n* impérialisme *m*

imperialist [ɪmˈpɪərɪəlɪst] *n & adj* impérialiste *mf*

imperil [ɪmˈperɪl] *(pt & pp* imperilled, *Am* imperiled*)* *vt* mettre en péril

imperious [ɪmˈpɪərɪəs] *adj* impérieux(euse)

impermanent [ɪmˈpɜːmənənt] *adj* temporaire

impersonal [ɪmˈpɜːsənəl] *adj* impersonnel(elle)

impersonate [ɪmˈpɜːsəneɪt] *vt (pretend to be)* se faire passer pour; *(imitate)* imiter

impersonation [ɪmpɜːsəˈneɪʃən] *n (pretence of being)* usurpation *f* d'identité; *(imitation)* imitation *f*

impersonator [ɪmˈpɜːsəneɪtə(r)] *n (impostor)* imposteur *m*; *(mimic)* imitateur(trice) *m,f*

impertinence [ɪmˈpɜːtɪnəns] *n* impertinence *f*

impertinent [ɪmˈpɜːtɪnənt] *adj* impertinent(e)

imperturbable [ɪmpəˈtɜːbəbəl] *adj* imperturbable

impervious [ɪmˈpɜːvɪəs] *adj also Fig* imperméable (**to** à)

impetuous [ɪmˈpetjʊəs] *adj* impétueux(euse)

impetus [ˈɪmpɪtəs] *n* élan *m*

▸**impinge on** [ɪmˈpɪndʒ] *vt insep* affecter, avoir un effet sur

impious [ˈɪmpɪəs] *adj* impie

impish [ˈɪmpɪʃ] *adj* espiègle

implacable [ɪmˈplækəbəl] *adj* implacable

implant 1 *n* [ˈɪmplɑːnt] *Med* implant *m*
2 *vt* [ɪmˈplɑːnt] (**a**) *Med* implanter (**b**) *(opinion, belief)* inculquer

implausible [ɪmˈplɔːzɪbəl] *adj* peu plausible, invraisemblable

implement 1 *n* [ˈɪmplɪmənt] instrument *m*; *(for cooking)* ustensile *m*; *(for gardening, DIY)* outil *m*
2 *vt* [ˈɪmplɪment] *(plan, agreement)* mettre en application

implementation [ɪmplɪmenˈteɪʃən] *n (of plan, agreement)* mise *f* en œuvre, application *f*

implicate [ˈɪmplɪkeɪt] *vt* impliquer

implication [ɪmplɪˈkeɪʃən] *n* implication *f*; **by i.** implicitement

implicit [ɪmˈplɪsɪt] *adj* (**a**) *(implied)* implicite; **it was i. in her remarks** c'était impliqué dans ses remarques (**b**) *(absolute)* absolu(e); **i. faith** confiance *f* aveugle

implied [ɪmˈplaɪd] *adj* implicite

implore [ɪmˈplɔː(r)] *vt* implorer; **to i. sb to do sth** implorer qn de faire qch

imploring [ɪmˈplɔːrɪŋ] *adj* implorant(e)

imply [ɪmˈplaɪ] *(pt & pp* implied*)* *vt* (**a**) *(insinuate)* insinuer, sous-entendre (**b**) *(involve)* impliquer; *(presuppose)* supposer

impolite [ɪmpəˈlaɪt] *adj* impoli(e)

impoliteness [ɪmpəˈlaɪtnɪs] *n* impolitesse *f*

imponderable [ɪmˈpɒndərəbəl] **1** *n* impondérable *m*
2 *adj* impondérable

import 1 *n* [ˈɪmpɔːt] (**a**) *(item, activity)* importation *f*; **i. duty** droit *m* de douane à l'importation (**b**) *Formal (importance)* importance *f*
2 *vt* [ɪmˈpɔːt] *also Comput* importer

importance [ɪmˈpɔːtəns] *n* importance *f*; **of the utmost i.** de la plus haute importance; **it is of no great i.** ça n'a pas grande importance; **to attach i. to sth** attacher de l'importance à qch; **to be full of one's own i.** être imbu(e) de sa personne

important [ɪmˈpɔːtənt] *adj* important(e); **to be i. to sb** être important pour qn; **to become more i.** prendre de l'importance; **it's not i.** c'est sans importance

importantly [ɪmˈpɔːtəntlɪ] *adv (speak)* d'un air important; **but, more i....** mais, plus important...

importation [ɪmpɔːˈteɪʃən] *n* importation *f*

importer [ɪmˈpɔːtə(r)] *n* importateur(trice) *m,f*

import-export [ˈɪmpɔːtˈekspɔːt] *n* **i. (trade)** import-export *m*

importune [ɪmˈpɔːtjuːn] *vt Formal* importuner

impose [ɪmˈpəʊz] **1** *vt (silence, one's will, restrictions)* imposer (**on** à); **to i. a tax on sth** taxer qch; **to i. a fine on sb** condamner qn à (payer) une amende
2 *vi (take advantage)* s'imposer

▸**impose on, impose upon** *vt insep (take advantage of)* abuser de; **to i. on** *or* **upon sb** abuser de la gentillesse de qn

imposing [ɪmˈpəʊzɪŋ] *adj* imposant(e)

imposition [ɪmpəˈzɪʃən] *n* (**a**) *(of tax, fine)* imposition *f* (**b**) *(unfair demand)* **it was a bit of an i.** il y avait de l'abus

impossibility [ɪmpɒsɪˈbɪlɪtɪ] *(pl* impossibilities*)* *n* impossibilité *f*; **it's a physical i.** c'est matériellement impossible

impossible [ɪmˈpɒsɪbəl] **1** **the i.** l'impossible *m*; **to do/achieve the i.** faire/réussir l'impossible
2 *adj* impossible; **to make it i. for sb to do sth** mettre qn dans l'impossibilité de faire qch

impossibly [ɪmˈpɒsɪblɪ] *adv (extremely)* incroyablement

impostor [ɪmˈpɒstə(r)] *n* imposteur *m*

impotence [ˈɪmpətəns] *n* impuissance *f*

impotent [ˈɪmpətənt] *adj* impuissant(e)

impound [ɪmˈpaʊnd] *vt Law* saisir; *(car)* mettre à la fourrière

impoverish [ɪmˈpɒvərɪʃ] *vt* appauvrir

impoverished [ɪmˈpɒvərɪʃd] *adj* appauvri(e)

impracticable [ɪmˈpræktɪkəbəl] *adj* impraticable, irréalisable

impractical [ɪm'præktɪkəl] *adj (suggestion)* irréaliste; *(person)* qui manque de sens pratique
imprecise [ɪmprɪ'saɪs] *adj* imprécis(e)
imprecision [ɪmprɪ'sɪʒən] *n* imprécision *f*
impregnable [ɪm'pregnəbəl] *adj (fortress)* imprenable; *Fig (argument)* irréfutable, inattaquable
impregnate ['ɪmpregneɪt] *vt* (**a**) *(fertilize)* féconder (**b**) *(soak)* imprégner (**with** de)
impresario [ɪmpre'saːrɪəʊ] *(pl* impresarios *or* impresari* [ɪmpre'saːriː]) *n* imprésario *m*
impress [ɪm'pres] *vt* (**a**) *(make an impression on)* impressionner; **to be impressed with** *or* **by sb/sth** être impressionné(e) par qn/qch; **to i. sb favourably/unfavourably** faire une impression favorable/défavorable à qn (**b**) *(emphasize)* **to i. sth on sb** faire comprendre qch à qn (**c**) *(imprint)* **to i. sth on sth** imprimer qch sur qch
impression [ɪm'preʃən] *n* (**a**) *(effect)* impression *f*; **to make an i. on sb** marquer qn; **to make an i. on sth** avoir un impact sur qch; **to make a good/bad i. (on sb)** faire bonne/mauvaise impression (à qn); **to create a false i.** donner une fausse impression; **to be under the i. that...** avoir l'impression que...; **to give the i. that...** donner l'impression que...
(**b**) *(imprint) (in wax, snow)* empreinte *f*
(**c**) *(of book)* réimpression *f*
(**d**) *(imitation)* imitation *f*; **to do impressions** faire des imitations; **to do an i. of sb** imiter qn
impressionable [ɪm'preʃənəbəl] *adj* impressionnable
impressionism [ɪm'preʃənɪzəm] *n Art* impressionnisme *m*
impressionist [ɪm'preʃənɪst] **1** *n* (**a**) *Art* impressionniste *mf* (**b**) *(mimic)* imitateur(trice) *m,f*
2 *adj Art* impressionniste
impressionistic [ɪmpreʃə'nɪstɪk] *adj* vague
impressive [ɪm'presɪv] *adj* impressionnant(e)
imprint 1 *n* ['ɪmprɪnt] empreinte *f*
2 *vt* [ɪm'prɪnt] imprimer (**on** sur); **her words are imprinted on my memory** ses mots restent gravés dans ma mémoire
imprison [ɪm'prɪzən] *vt* emprisonner
imprisonment [ɪm'prɪzənmənt] *n* emprisonnement *m*
improbability [ɪmprɒbə'bɪlɪtɪ] *(pl* improbabilities) *n* improbabilité *f*
improbable [ɪm'prɒbəbəl] *adj (unlikely)* improbable; *(unbelievable)* invraisemblable
impromptu [ɪm'prɒmptjuː] **1** *adj (speech, party)* improvisé(e)
2 *adv (unexpectedly)* à l'improviste; *(ad lib)* au pied levé
improper [ɪm'prɒpə(r)] *adj* (**a**) *(use, purpose)* mauvais(e); *(behaviour)* déplacé(e); *Law* **i. practices** pratiques *fpl* malhonnêtes (**b**) *(lewd)* indécent(e)
impropriety [ɪmprə'praɪətɪ] *n* inconvenance *f*; *(of language)* impropriété *f*
improve [ɪm'pruːv] **1** *vt* améliorer; *(invention, technique)* perfectionner; **to i. one's mind** se cultiver
2 *vi* s'améliorer; *(of business)* reprendre
improve on, improve upon *vt insep* améliorer; **to i. on a bid** surenchérir
improved [ɪm'pruːvd] *adj (system, design)* perfectionné(e)
improvement [ɪm'pruːvmənt] *n* amélioration *f* (**in** de); *(of invention, technique)* perfectionnement *m*;

to be an i. on être meilleur(e) que; **there's room for i.** on peut faire mieux; **to make improvements (to a house)** faire des travaux d'aménagement (dans une maison)
improvident [ɪm'prɒvɪdənt] *adj Formal (person)* imprévoyant(e)
improvisation [ɪmprəvaɪ'zeɪʃən] *n* improvisation *f*
improvise ['ɪmprəvaɪz] *vt & vi* improviser
imprudent [ɪm'pruːdənt] *adj* imprudent(e)
impudence ['ɪmpjʊdəns] *n* impudence *f*, insolence *f*
impudent ['ɪmpjʊdənt] *adj* impudent(e), insolent(e)
impugn [ɪm'pjuːn] *vt Formal* mettre en doute
impulse ['ɪmpʌls] *n* impulsion *f*; **to feel an i. to do sth** avoir une soudaine envie de faire qch; **on i.** sur un coup de tête; **i. buying** achat *m* d'impulsion
impulsive [ɪm'pʌlsɪv] *adj* impulsif(ive)
impunity [ɪm'pjuːnɪtɪ] *n* impunité *f*; **with i.** en toute impunité
impure [ɪm'pjʊə(r)] *adj* impur(e)
impurity [ɪm'pjʊərətɪ] *(pl* impurities) *n* impureté *f*
impute [ɪm'pjuːt] *vt Formal* **to i. sth to sb** imputer *ou* attribuer qch à qn
in [ɪn] **1** *prep* (**a**) *(with place)* dans; **in the garden** dans le jardin; **in France** en France; **in Japan** au Japon; **in the USA** aux États-Unis; **in Paris** à Paris; **in hospital** à l'hôpital; **in town** en ville; **in bed** au lit; **in here** ici; **in there** là
(**b**) *(with expressions of time)* **in 1927/April** en 1927/avril; **in (the) spring** au printemps; **in (the) summer** en été; **in the afternoon** l'après-midi; **in the 70s** dans les années 70
(**c**) *(expressing manner)* **in French** en français; **to write in pen** écrire au stylo; **in a loud voice** d'une voix forte; **in this way** ainsi, de cette façon
(**d**) *(within, during)* **she did it in three hours** elle l'a fait en trois heures; **he'll be here in three hours** il sera ici dans trois heures; **I haven't seen him in years** ça fait des années que je ne l'ai pas vu
(**e**) *(with situation, arrangement)* **in the rain** sous la pluie; **in the sun** au soleil; **dressed in white** habillé(e) en blanc; **in danger** en danger; **in twos** deux par deux; **in a circle/line** en rond/rang
(**f**) *(with numbers, quantities, ratios)* **one in ten** un sur dix; **in small/large quantities** en petite/grande quantité; **2 metres in length/height/width** 2 mètres de long/de haut/de large; **she's in her sixties** elle a la soixantaine; **the temperature was in the nineties** ≃ il faisait dans les trente degrés
(**g**) *(with gerund)* **to have no difficulty in doing sth** ne pas avoir de mal à faire qch; **in saying this...** en disant cela...
(**h**) *(with field of activity)* **to be in insurance/publishing** être dans les assurances/l'édition
(**i**) *(idioms)* **I didn't think she had it in her to...** je ne l'aurais pas crue capable de...
2 *adv* (**a**) *(inside)* dedans; **to go in** entrer, rentrer
(**b**) *(not out)* là; **is your mother in?** est-ce que ta mère est là?; **to stay in** *(at home)* rester à la maison
(**c**) **to be in** *(of plane, train)* être arrivé(e)
(**d**) *(fashionable)* à la mode
(**e**) **in that...** puisque..., vu que...
(**f**) *(idioms)* **to have it in for sb** en vouloir à qn; **she's in for a shock/surprise** elle va avoir un choc/une surprise; **to be in on a plan/secret** être dans le coup; **he's in for it** ça va être sa fête
3 *adj* **the in crowd** les branchés *mpl*

4 *n* **the ins and outs** *(of question)* les tenants *mpl* et les aboutissants; *(of plot)* les subtilités *fpl*

inability [ɪnəˈbɪlɪtɪ] *n* incapacité *f* (**to do sth** à faire qch)

inaccessibility [ɪnæksesɪˈbɪlɪtɪ] *n* inaccessibilité *f*

inaccessible [ɪnækˈsesɪbəl] *adj* inaccessible (**to** à)

inaccuracy [ɪnˈækjʊrəsɪ] *(pl* **inaccuracies)** *n (of estimate, translation, report)* inexactitude *f*; *(of rifle, instrument)* manque *m* de précision

inaccurate [ɪnˈækjʊrət] *adj (estimate, translation, report)* inexact(e); *(rifle, instrument)* qui manque de précision

inaction [ɪnˈækʃən] *n* inaction *f*

inactive [ɪnˈæktɪv] *adj* inactif(ive)

inactivity [ɪnækˈtɪvɪtɪ] *n* inactivité *f*

inadequacy [ɪnˈædɪkwəsɪ] *(pl* **inadequacies)** *n* insuffisance *f*; **a feeling of i.** un complexe d'infériorité

inadequate [ɪnˈædɪkwət] *adj* insuffisant(e); **to feel i.** ne pas se sentir à la hauteur

inadmissible [ɪnədˈmɪsɪbəl] *adj Law (evidence)* irrecevable

inadvertent [ɪnədˈvɜːtənt] *adj* involontaire

inadvertently [ɪnədˈvɜːtəntlɪ] *adv* par inadvertance

inadvisable [ɪnədˈvaɪzəbəl] *adj* déconseillé(e)

inalienable [ɪnˈeɪlɪənəbəl] *adj Formal* inaliénable

inane [ɪˈneɪn] *adj* idiot(e), stupide

inanimate [ɪnˈænɪmət] *adj* inanimé(e)

inanity [ɪˈnænɪtɪ] *n* ineptie *f*

inapplicable [ɪnˈæplɪkəbəl] *adj* inapplicable (**to** à); **delete where i.** *(sign)* rayer la mention inutile

inappropriate [ɪnəˈprəʊprɪət] *adj (behaviour, remark)* déplacé(e); *(dress)* peu approprié(e) (**to** à); *(time)* inopportun(e)

inapt [ɪnˈæpt] *adj* peu approprié(e)

inarticulate [ɪnɑːˈtɪkjʊlɪt] *adj (sound)* inarticulé(e); **to be i.** *(of person)* avoir du mal à s'exprimer; **to be i. with rage** bégayer de rage

inasmuch as [ɪnəzˈmʌtʃəz] *conj Formal* dans la mesure où

inattention [ɪnəˈtenʃən] *n* inattention *f*

inattentive [ɪnəˈtentɪv] *adj* inattentif(ive) (**to** à)

inaudible [ɪnˈɔːdɪbəl] *adj* inaudible

inaugural [ɪˈnɔːgjʊrəl] *adj* inaugural(e)

inaugurate [ɪˈnɔːgjʊreɪt] *vt (building, exhibition)* inaugurer; *(president)* investir

inauguration [ɪnɔːgjʊˈreɪʃən] *n (of building, exhibition)* inauguration *f*; *(of president)* cérémonie *f* de prise de fonctions

inauspicious [ɪnɔːsˈpɪʃəs] *adj* peu propice; **to get off to an i. start** mal commencer

inauthentic [ɪnɔːˈθentɪk] *adj* inauthentique

in-between [ɪnbɪˈtwiːn] *adj* intermédiaire

inborn [ˈɪnbɔːn] *adj* inné(e)

inbound [ˈɪnbaʊnd] *adj (flight, passenger)* à l'arrivée

inbred [ˈɪnbred] *adj (person)* de parents consanguins; *(distrust, confidence)* inné(e)

in-built [ˈɪnbɪlt] *adj (trait)* inhérent(e); **his height gives him an i. advantage** sa taille lui donne un avantage dès le départ

Inc [ɪŋk] *adj (abbr* **Incorporated**) ≃ SARL

Inca [ˈɪŋkə] **1** *n* Inca *mf*
2 *adj* inca

incalculable [ɪnˈkælkjʊləbəl] *adj (consequences, damage)* incalculable; *(help, value)* inestimable

incandescent [ɪnkænˈdesənt] *adj* incandescent(e); *Fig* **i. with rage** fou (folle) de rage

incantation [ɪnkænˈteɪʃən] *n* incantation *f*

incapable [ɪnˈkeɪpəbəl] *adj* incapable (**of** de); *(through illness)* impotent(e); *(through drink)* ivre mort(e); **to be i. of doing sth** être incapable de faire qch

incapacitate [ɪnkəˈpæsɪteɪt] *vt* rendre impotent(e); **to be incapacitated for work** être inapte au travail

incapacity [ɪnkəˈpæsɪtɪ] *n* incapacité *f*; **i. to do sth** incapacité à faire qch

incarcerate [ɪnˈkɑːsəreɪt] *vt Formal* incarcérer

incarceration [ɪnkɑːsəˈreɪʃən] *n Formal* incarcération *f*

incarnate [ɪnˈkɑːneɪt] *adj* incarné(e)

incarnation [ɪnkɑːˈneɪʃən] *n* incarnation *f*; **in a previous i.** dans une vie antérieure

incautious [ɪnˈkɔːʃəs] *adj* imprudent(e)

incendiary [ɪnˈsendɪərɪ] **1** *n (pl* **incendiaries)** *(arsonist)* incendiaire *mf*; *(bomb)* bombe *f* incendiaire
2 *adj also Fig* incendiaire

incense¹ [ˈɪnsens] *n* encens *m*

incense² [ɪnˈsens] *vt (anger)* rendre furieux(euse)

incentive [ɪnˈsentɪv] *n (stimulus)* motivation *f*; *(payment)* prime *f*; **there is no i. for students to work hard** il n'y a rien qui encourage les étudiants à travailler dur; **i. bonus** *or* **payment** prime *f* de rendement; **i. scheme** *(for workers)* système *m* de primes

inception [ɪnˈsepʃən] *n* début *m*

incessant [ɪnˈsesənt] *adj* incessant(e)

incest [ˈɪnsest] *n* inceste *m*

incestuous [ɪnˈsestjʊəs] *adj* incestueux(euse); *Fig (environment, group)* très fermé(e)

inch [ɪntʃ] *n* (**a**) *(unit of measurement)* = 2,54 cm, pouce *m*; **i. by i.** petit à petit, peu à peu (**b**) *(idioms)* **I know every i. of this town** je connais cette ville comme ma poche; **he's every i. the gentleman** c'est le parfait gentleman; **to miss sth by inches** manquer qch d'un cheveu; **to be within an i. of doing sth** être à deux doigts de faire qch; **she won't give an i.** elle ne cédera pas d'un pouce; **give her an i. and she'll take a mile** tu lui en donnes jusqu'au coude, elle en demande long comme le bras

▸**inch along, inch forward** *vi* avancer tout doucement

incidence [ˈɪnsɪdəns] *n (frequency)* taux *m*; *(of disease)* incidence *f*

incident [ˈɪnsɪdənt] *n* incident *m*; *(in book, film)* scène *f*; **full of i.** riche en incidents; *Br* **i. room** *(in police station)* salle *f* des opérations

incidental [ɪnsɪˈdentəl] *adj (minor)* accessoire (**to** par rapport à); **i. expenses** faux frais *mpl*; **i. music** *(in film)* musique *f*

incidentally [ɪnsɪˈdentəlɪ] *adv (by the way)* au fait

incinerate [ɪnˈsɪnəreɪt] *vt* incinérer; *Fig* carboniser

incineration [ɪnsɪnəˈreɪʃən] *n* incinération *f*

incinerator [ɪnˈsɪnəreɪtə(r)] *n* incinérateur *m*

incipient [ɪnˈsɪpɪənt] *adj Formal* naissant(e)

incision [ɪnˈsɪʒən] *n* incision *f*

incisive [ɪnˈsaɪsɪv] *adj* incisif(ive)

incisor [ɪnˈsaɪzə(r)] *n* incisive *f*

incite [ɪnˈsaɪt] *vt (violence, unrest)* inciter à; **to i. sb to do sth** inciter qn à faire qch

incitement [ɪnˈsaɪtmənt] *n* incitation *f* (**to** à)

incivility [ɪnsɪˈvɪlɪtɪ] *(pl* **incivilities)** *n Formal* incivilité *f*

inclement [ɪn'klemənt] *adj Formal (weather)* inclément(e)

inclination [ɪnklɪ'neɪʃən] *n* (**a**) *(liking)* inclination *f*, penchant *m* (**for** pour); *(desire)* envie *f*; **to have an i. to do sth** avoir envie de faire qch (**b**) *(tendency)* tendance *f* (**towards** à); **to have an i. to do sth** avoir tendance à faire qch; **by i.** de *ou* par nature (**c**) *(angle)* inclinaison *f*

incline 1 *n* ['ɪnklaɪn] *(slope)* pente *f*
2 *vt* [ɪn'klaɪn] (**a**) *(cause)* **to i. sb to do sth** inciter qn à faire qch (**b**) *(lean)* incliner; **to i. one's head** incliner la tête (**c**) **to be inclined to do sth** *(tend)* avoir tendance à faire qch; **I'm inclined to agree** j'aurais tendance à être d'accord
3 *vi* [ɪn'klaɪn] *(lean)* s'incliner; *(tend)* **to i. to** *or* **towards** pencher pour; **to i. to the belief that...** être porté(e) à croire que...

include [ɪn'kluːd] *vt* inclure, comprendre; *(in letter)* joindre; **the price does not i. accommodation** le logement n'est pas compris dans le prix

including [ɪn'kluːdɪŋ] *prep* y compris; **seven not i. the children** sept sans compter les enfants; **up to and i. page 40** jusqu'à la page 40 incluse

inclusion [ɪn'kluːʒən] *n* inclusion *f*

inclusive [ɪn'kluːsɪv] *adj (price, sum)* net (nette); **to be i. of** comprendre; **i. of VAT** TVA comprise; **from 4 to 12 February i.** du 4 au 12 février inclus

incognito [ɪnkɒg'niːtəʊ] *adv* incognito

incoherence [ɪnkəʊ'hɪərəns] *n* incohérence *f*

incoherent [ɪnkəʊ'hɪərənt] *adj* incohérent(e)

income ['ɪnkəm] *n* revenu *m*; *Br* **i. support** ≃ RMI *m*; **i. tax** impôt *m* sur le revenu

incoming ['ɪnkʌmɪŋ] *adj (government, president)* nouveau(elle); *(plane, train)* à l'arrivée; *(phone call)* de l'extérieur; *(tide)* montant(e) **i. mail** courrier *m* (du jour)

incommensurate [ɪnkə'menʃərɪt] *adj* **to be i. with** ne pas être proportionné(e) à

incommunicado [ɪnkəmjuːnɪ'kaːdəʊ] *adj (uncontactable)* injoignable

in-company ['ɪnkʌmpənɪ] *adj* **i. training** formation *f* sur le lieu de travail

incomparable [ɪn'kɒmpərəbəl] *adj* incomparable

incompatible [ɪnkəm'pætɪbəl] *adj* incompatible (**with** avec)

incompetence [ɪn'kɒmpɪtəns] *n* incompétence *f*

incompetent [ɪn'kɒmpɪtənt] *adj* incompétent(e)

incomplete [ɪnkəm'pliːt] *adj* (**a**) *(not whole)* incomplet(ète) (**b**) *(not finished)* inachevé(e)

incomprehensible [ɪnkɒmprɪ'hensɪbəl] *adj* incompréhensible

incomprehension [ɪnkɒmprɪ'henʃən] *n* incompréhension *f*

inconceivable [ɪnkən'siːvəbəl] *adj* inconcevable

inconclusive [ɪnkən'kluːsɪv] *adj (evidence, results)* peu concluant(e); **the meeting/investigation was i.** la réunion/l'enquête n'a abouti à rien

incongruity [ɪnkɒn'gruːɪtɪ] *(pl* **incongruities**) *n* incongruité *f*

incongruous [ɪn'kɒŋgrʊəs] *adj* incongru(e)

inconsequential [ɪnkɒnsɪ'kwenʃəl] *adj* insignifiant(e), sans importance

inconsiderate [ɪnkən'sɪdərɪt] *adj (person)* sans égards pour les autres; *(remark)* déplacé(e); **it was i.**

of you not to invite her ce n'est pas gentil de ta part de ne pas l'avoir invitée

inconsistency [ɪnkən'sɪstənsɪ] *(pl* **inconsistencies**) *n (in argument)* incohérence *f*; *(between reports, descriptions)* contradiction *f*; *(uneven quality)* irrégularité *f*

inconsistent [ɪnkən'sɪstənt] *adj (person)* incohérent(e); *(uneven)* irrégulier(ère); **to be i. with** ne pas concorder *ou* cadrer avec

inconsolable [ɪnkən'səʊləbəl] *adj* inconsolable

inconspicuous [ɪnkən'spɪkjʊəs] *adj* qui passe inaperçu(e)

incontestable [ɪnkən'testəbəl] *adj* incontestable

incontinence [ɪn'kɒntɪnəns] *n* incontinence *f*

incontinent [ɪn'kɒntɪnənt] *adj* incontinent(e)

incontrovertible [ɪnkɒntrə'vɜːtɪbəl] *adj Formal* incontestable

inconvenience [ɪnkən'viːnjəns] **1** *n* désagrément *m*; **to be an i. to sb** déranger qn
2 *vt* déranger

inconvenient [ɪnkən'viːnjənt] *adj (time)* mauvais(e); *(place, arrangement)* peu commode; **if it's not i.** si cela ne vous dérange pas; **it's a bit i. just now** ça ne tombe pas très bien en ce moment

incorporate [ɪn'kɔːpəreɪt] *vt* incorporer; *(have as quality)* comprendre

incorrect [ɪnkə'rekt] *adj* incorrect(e)

incorrigible [ɪn'kɒrɪdʒɪbəl] *adj* incorrigible

incorruptible [ɪnkə'rʌptɪbəl] *adj* incorruptible

increase 1 *n* ['ɪnkriːs] *(in price, rate, sales)* augmentation *f*, hausse *f* (**in** de); *(in salary)* augmentation (de salaire); *(in pain, population)* accroissement *m* (**in** de); **to be on the i.** être en hausse
2 *vt* [ɪn'kriːs] augmenter; **to i. one's efforts** redoubler d'efforts; **to i. one's speed** accélérer
3 *vi* [ɪn'kriːs] augmenter; **to i. in price** augmenter; **to i. in value** prendre de la valeur

increasing [ɪn'kriːsɪŋ] *adj* croissant(e)

increasingly [ɪn'kriːsɪŋlɪ] *adv* de plus en plus

incredible [ɪn'kredɪbəl] *adj* (**a**) *(unbelievable)* incroyable (**b**) *Fam (excellent)* génial(e)

incredibly [ɪn'kredɪblɪ] *adv* (**a**) *(extremely)* incroyablement; *Fam* **i. good** génial(e) (**b**) *(unbelievably)* **i., no one was hurt** aussi incroyable que cela puisse paraître, personne n'a été blessé

incredulous [ɪn'kredjʊləs] *adj* incrédule

increment ['ɪnkrɪmənt] *n* augmentation *f*

incremental [ɪnkrɪ'mentəl] *adj (increasing)* croissant(e); **i. increases** augmentations *fpl* régulières

incriminate [ɪn'krɪmɪneɪt] *vt* incriminer, mettre en cause

incriminating [ɪn'krɪmɪneɪtɪŋ] *adj* compromettant(e)

incubate ['ɪnkjʊbeɪt] *vt (of bird)* couver; *(baby)* mettre en couveuse

incubation [ɪnkjʊ'beɪʃən] *n* incubation *f*; *Med* **i. period** *(of infection)* durée *f* d'incubation

incubator ['ɪnkjʊbeɪtə(r)] *n (for babies)* couveuse *f*; *(for eggs)* incubateur *m*

inculcate ['ɪnkʌlkeɪt] *vt Formal* **to i. sth in sb, to i. sb with sth** inculquer qch à qn

incumbent [ɪn'kʌmbənt] *Formal* **1** *n* **the present i. (of the presidency)** le président en exercice
2 *adj* **it is i. on sb to do sth** il incombe *ou* appartient à qn de faire qch

incur [ɪnˈkɜː(r)] (pt & pp **incurred**) vt (blame, expense) encourir; (loss) subir; (risk) courir; (person's anger) s'attirer; (debt) contracter

incurable [ɪnˈkjʊərəbəl] adj also Fig incurable

incurious [ɪnˈkjʊərɪəs] adj peu curieux(euse)

incursion [ɪnˈkɜːʃən] n Formal incursion f

indebted [ɪnˈdetɪd] adj (financially) endetté(e); (for help, advice) redevable (**to** à); **I am i. to my family for all their support** je suis reconnaissant à ma famille pour son soutien

indebtedness [ɪnˈdetɪdnɪs] n (financial) endettement m; (for help, advice) dette f (**to** envers)

indecency [ɪnˈdiːsənsɪ] n indécence f; Law attentat m à la pudeur

indecent [ɪnˈdiːsənt] adj indécent(e); **to do sth with i. haste** mettre un empressement déplacé à faire qch; Law **i. assault** attentat m à la pudeur; Law **i. exposure** outrage m public à la pudeur

indecipherable [ɪndɪˈsaɪfərəbəl] adj indéchiffrable

indecision [ɪndɪˈsɪʒən] n indécision f

indecisive [ɪndɪˈsaɪsɪv] adj (person) indécis(e); (battle, election) à l'issue peu claire

indecorous [ɪnˈdekərəs] adj Formal peu digne

indeed [ɪnˈdiːd] adv (a) (used with 'very') vraiment; **very big i.** vraiment très grand; **thank you very much i.** merci mille fois

(b) (in confirmation) en effet, effectivement; (certainly) certainement

(c) (what's more) en fait, et même; **I think so, i. I'm sure of it** je pense que oui, en fait j'en suis sûr

(d) (expressing ironic surprise) **have you i.?** vraiment?

indefatigable [ɪndɪˈfætɪɡəbəl] adj Formal infatigable

indefensible [ɪndɪˈfensɪbəl] adj (behaviour, attitude) injustifiable, impardonnable; (theory) indéfendable

indefinable [ɪndɪˈfaɪnəbəl] adj indéfinissable

indefinite [ɪnˈdefɪnɪt] adj (**a**) (period of time, number) indéterminé(e) (**b**) (idea, plan) mal défini(e) (**c**) Gram indéfini(e)

indefinitely [ɪnˈdefɪnɪtlɪ] adv indéfiniment

indelible [ɪnˈdelɪbəl] adj also Fig indélébile

indelicate [ɪnˈdelɪkət] adj indélicat(e)

indemnify [ɪnˈdemnɪfaɪ] (pt & pp **indemnified**) vt **to i. sb for sth** (compensate) indemniser ou dédommager qn de qch; **to i. sb against sth** (give security) assurer qn contre qch

indemnity [ɪnˈdemnɪtɪ] (pl **indemnities**) n (guarantee) garantie f, assurance f; (money) indemnité f, dédommagement m

indent Typ **1** n [ˈɪndent] alinéa m

2 vt [ɪnˈdent] mettre en retrait

indentation [ɪndenˈteɪʃən] n (mark) trace f, empreinte f; (in coastline) découpure f; Typ alinéa m

independence [ɪndɪˈpendəns] n indépendance f (**from** par rapport à)

independent [ɪndɪˈpendənt] adj indépendant(e) (**of** de); Fin **i. financial adviser** conseiller(ère) m,f financier(ère) indépendant(e); Br **i. school** école f privée

independently [ɪndɪˈpendəntlɪ] adv indépendamment; **i. of** indépendamment de; **to live i.** être indépendant(e)

in-depth [ˈɪndepθ] adj approfondi(e), en profondeur

indescribable [ɪndɪsˈkraɪbəbəl] adj indescriptible

indestructible [ɪndɪsˈtrʌktəbəl] adj indestructible

indeterminate [ɪndɪˈtɜːmɪnət] adj indéterminé(e)

index [ˈɪndeks] **1** n (of book) index m; (in library) fichier m; **i. finger** index m; Fin **i. fund** fonds m indiciel

2 vt (**a**) (book) dresser l'index de (**b**) Fin (wages) indexer (**to** sur)

index-linked [ˈɪndeksˈlɪŋkt] adj Fin indexé(e)

India [ˈɪndɪə] n l'Inde f

Indian [ˈɪndɪən] **1** n Indien(enne) m,f

2 adj indien(enne); **I. elephant** éléphant m d'Asie; **in I. file** en file indienne; **the I. Ocean** l'océan m Indien; **I. summer** été m indien

indicate [ˈɪndɪkeɪt] **1** vt (**a**) (point to, show) indiquer (**b**) (intention, opposition, willingness) signaler

2 vi (of car driver) mettre son clignotant

indication [ɪndɪˈkeɪʃən] n (sign) signe m; (information) indication f; **she gave no i. of her feelings** elle n'a rien laissé voir de ses sentiments; **there is every i. that…, all the indications are that…** tout porte à croire que…

indicative [ɪnˈdɪkətɪv] **1** n Gram indicatif m; **in the i.** à l'indicatif

2 adj **to be i. of** être symptomatique de

indicator [ˈɪndɪkeɪtə(r)] n (**a**) (sign) indice m; **economic indicators** indicateurs mpl économiques (**b**) Br (of car) clignotant m, Belg clignoteur m, Suisse signofil(e) m

indict [ɪnˈdaɪt] vt Law inculper (**for** de)

indictable [ɪnˈdaɪtəbəl] adj Law **i. offence** délit m

indictment [ɪnˈdaɪtmənt] n Law inculpation f; Fig **it is an i. of our society** c'est une preuve accablante de l'état de notre société

indie [ˈɪndɪ] adj Br (music, band) indépendant(e)

indifference [ɪnˈdɪfərəns] n indifférence f (**to** pour); **it's a matter of complete i. to me** cela m'est complètement indifférent

indifferent [ɪnˈdɪfərənt] adj (**a**) (not interested) indifférent(e) (**to** à); **I am** or **feel i. about him** il m'est indifférent (**b**) (mediocre) médiocre

indigenous [ɪnˈdɪdʒɪnəs] adj indigène

indigestible [ɪndɪˈdʒestɪbəl] adj also Fig indigeste

indigestion [ɪndɪˈdʒestʃən] n troubles mpl digestifs; **to have an attack of i.** avoir des troubles digestifs

indignant [ɪnˈdɪɡnənt] adj indigné(e); **to get i. about sth** s'indigner de qch

indignation [ɪndɪɡˈneɪʃən] n indignation f

indignity [ɪnˈdɪɡnɪtɪ] n indignité f

indigo [ˈɪndɪɡəʊ] **1** n indigo m

2 adj indigo inv

indirect [ɪndɪˈrekt] adj indirect(e); (person) pas direct(e); Com **i. costs** frais mpl indirects; Gram **i. object** complément m d'objet indirect; Gram **i. speech** discours m indirect

indirectly [ɪndɪˈrektlɪ] adv indirectement

indiscernible [ɪndɪˈsɜːnɪbəl] adj (reason) obscur(e); (difference) imperceptible

indiscipline [ɪnˈdɪsɪplɪn] n indiscipline f

indiscreet [ɪndɪsˈkriːt] adj indiscret(ète)

indiscretion [ɪndɪsˈkreʃən] n indiscrétion f

indiscriminate [ɪndɪsˈkrɪmɪnɪt] adj **i. killing** tuerie f générale; **to be i. in one's praise** distribuer les compliments à tort et à travers

indispensable [ɪndɪsˈpensəbəl] adj indispensable

indisposed [ɪndɪsˈpəʊzd] adj Formal (ill) indisposé(e)

indisputable [ɪndɪsˈpjuːtəbəl] adj (evidence, argument) incontestable; (leader) incontesté(e)

indissoluble [ɪndɪˈsɒljʊbəl] adj Formal indissoluble

indistinct [ɪndɪs'tɪŋkt] *adj* indistinct(e)
indistinguishable [ɪndɪs'tɪŋgwɪʃəbəl] *adj* impossible à distinguer (**from** de)
individual [ɪndɪ'vɪdjʊəl] **1** *n (person)* individu *m*; **a private i.** un particulier
  2 *adj* (**a**) *(of or for one person)* individuel(elle); *(bathroom)* privé(e); **i. tuition** cours *mpl* particuliers (**b**) *(characteristic)* personnel(elle)
individualist [ɪndɪ'vɪdjʊəlɪst] *n* individualiste *mf*
individuality [ɪndɪvɪdjʊ'ælɪtɪ] *n* individualité *f*
individually [ɪndɪ'vɪdjʊəlɪ] *adv* individuellement
indivisible [ɪndɪ'vɪzɪbəl] *adj* indivisible
Indochina [ɪndəʊ'tʃaɪnə] *n* l'Indochine *f*
indoctrinate [ɪn'dɒktrɪneɪt] *vt* endoctriner; **to i. sb with an idea** inculquer une idée à qn
indoctrination [ɪndɒktrɪ'neɪʃən] *n* endoctrinement *m*
indolent ['ɪndələnt] *adj Formal* paresseux(euse)
indomitable [ɪn'dɒmɪtəbəl] *adj* indomptable
Indonesia [ɪndəʊ'niːʒə] *n* l'Indonésie *f*
Indonesian [ɪndəʊ'niːʒən] **1** *n* (**a**) *(person)* Indonésien(enne) *m,f* (**b**) *(language)* indonésien *m*
  2 *adj* indonésien(enne)
indoor ['ɪndɔː(r)] *adj (swimming pool, tennis court)* couvert(e); *(plant)* d'appartement; *(photography)* d'intérieur; **i. athletics** athlétisme *m* en salle
indoors [ɪn'dɔːz] *adv* à l'intérieur; **to go i.** rentrer; **I've been i. all day** je suis resté enfermé toute la journée
induce [ɪn'djuːs] *vt* (**a**) *(persuade)* **to i. sb to do sth** persuader qn de faire qch (**b**) *(cause)* provoquer (**c**) *Med* **to i. labour** provoquer l'accouchement; **she's had to be induced** il a fallu provoquer l'accouchement
inducement [ɪn'djuːsmənt] *n (incentive)* incitation *f*; *(financial)* avantage *m* financier
induction [ɪn'dʌkʃən] *n* (**a**) *(into job)* période *f* d'introduction; **i. course** stage *m* de formation (**b**) *Med (of labour)* déclenchement *m* (**c**) *Elec* induction *f*
inductive [ɪn'dʌktɪv] *adj (reasoning)* inductif(ive)
indulge [ɪn'dʌldʒ] **1** *vt (child)* gâter; *(passion)* donner libre cours à; **they indulged his every whim** ils lui passaient tous ses caprices; **to i. oneself** se faire plaisir; **go on, i. me!** allez, fais-moi plaisir!
  2 *vi* **to i. in sth** *(as a habit)* se livrer à qch; *(as a treat)* s'offrir qch
indulgence [ɪn'dʌldʒəns] *n* (**a**) *(leniency)* indulgence *f* (**b**) *(treat)* gâterie *f*
indulgent [ɪn'dʌldʒənt] *adj* indulgent(e) (**to** avec)
industrial [ɪn'dʌstrɪəl] *adj* industriel(elle); **i. action** grève *f*; **to take i. action** faire grève; **i. disease** maladie *f* professionnelle; **i. dispute** conflit *m* entre la direction et les travailleurs; **i. espionage** espionnage *m* industriel; *Br* **i. estate** zone *f* industrielle; **i. injury** accident *m* du travail; **i. park** zone *f* industrielle; **i. relations** relations *fpl* entre les travailleurs et le patronat; **the I. Revolution** la révolution industrielle; **i. tribunal** ≃ conseil *m* de prud'hommes; **i. unrest** conflits *mpl* sociaux; **i. waste** déchets *mpl* industriels
industrialist [ɪn'dʌstrɪəlɪst] *n* industriel *m*
industrialize [ɪn'dʌstrɪəlaɪz] *vt* industrialiser
industrious [ɪn'dʌstrɪəs] *adj* travailleur(euse)
industry ['ɪndʌstrɪ] *(pl* **industries)** *n* (**a**) *(economic sector)* industrie *f*; **heavy/light i.** l'industrie lourde/légère; **the aircraft/mining i.** l'industrie aéronautique/minière; **the tourist/entertainment i.** l'indus-

trie du tourisme/du spectacle (**b**) *(hard work)* assiduité *f*
inebriated [ɪn'iːbrɪeɪtɪd] *adj Formal or Hum* ivre
inedible [ɪn'edɪbəl] *adj (plant, mushroom)* non comestible; *(food)* immangeable
ineffable [ɪn'efəbəl] *adj Formal* ineffable
ineffective [ɪnɪ'fektɪv] *adj* inefficace
ineffectual [ɪnɪ'fektjʊəl] *adj* inefficace
inefficiency [ɪnɪ'fɪʃənsɪ] *n* inefficacité *f*, manque *m* d'efficacité
inefficient [ɪnɪ'fɪʃənt] *adj* inefficace
inelegant [ɪn'elɪgənt] *adj* inélégant(e)
ineligible [ɪn'elɪdʒɪbəl] *adj* **to be i. for sth** ne pas avoir droit à qch; **to be i. to do sth** ne pas avoir le droit de faire qch
inept [ɪn'ept] *adj (person)* incompétent(e); *(remark)* inepte
ineptitude [ɪn'eptɪtjuːd] *n* incompétence *f*
inequality [ɪnɪ'kwɒlɪtɪ] *(pl* **inequalities)** *n* inégalité *f*
inequitable [ɪn'ekwɪtəbəl] *adj Formal* inéquitable
inert [ɪ'nɜːt] *adj* inerte
inertia [ɪ'nɜːʃə] *n* inertie *f*
inescapable [ɪnɪ'skeɪpəbəl] *adj (conclusion)* incontournable; *(resemblance)* indéniable; **it's an i. fact that...** il est indéniable que...
inessential [ɪnɪ'senʃəl] *adj* non essentiel(elle)
inestimable [ɪn'estɪməbəl] *adj* inestimable
inevitability [ɪnevɪtə'bɪlɪtɪ] *n* caractère *m* inévitable
inevitable [ɪn'evɪtəbəl] **1** *n* **the i.** l'inévitable *m*
  2 *adj* inévitable; *(conclusion)* incontournable
inevitably [ɪn'evɪtəblɪ] *adv* inévitablement
inexact [ɪnɪg'zækt] *adj (memory, estimate)* imprécis(e)
inexcusable [ɪnɪks'kjuːzəbəl] *adj* inexcusable
inexhaustible [ɪnɪg'zɔːstɪbəl] *adj* inépuisable
inexorable [ɪn'eksərəbəl] *adj* inexorable
inexpensive [ɪnɪks'pensɪv] *adj* pas cher (chère), bon marché *inv*
inexperience [ɪnɪks'pɪərɪəns] *n* inexpérience *f*
inexperienced [ɪnɪks'pɪərɪənst] *adj* (**a**) *(person)* inexpérimenté(e); **to be i. in doing sth** ne pas avoir l'habitude de faire qch (**b**) *(ear, eye)* inexercé(e)
inexplicable [ɪnɪks'plɪkəbəl] *adj* inexplicable
inexpressible [ɪnɪks'presɪbəl] *adj* inexprimable
inexpressive [ɪnɪks'presɪv] *adj* inexpressif(ive)
inextricably [ɪneks'trɪkəblɪ] *adv* inextricablement
infallibility [ɪnfælɪ'bɪlɪtɪ] *n* infaillibilité *f*
infallible [ɪn'fælɪbəl] *adj* infaillible
infamous ['ɪnfəməs] *adj (well-known)* tristement célèbre; *(crime, rumour)* infâme
infamy ['ɪnfəmɪ] *n Formal* infamie *f*
infancy ['ɪnfənsɪ] *n (childhood)* petite enfance *f*; *Fig* **when medicine was still in its i.** alors que la médecine en était encore à ses balbutiements
infant ['ɪnfənt] *n* bébé *m*; **i. mortality** mortalité *f* infantile; **i. school** = école primaire pour enfants de 5 à 7 ans
infanticide [ɪn'fæntɪsaɪd] *n* infanticide *m*
infantile ['ɪnfəntaɪl] *adj Pej* infantile, puéril(e)
infantry ['ɪnfəntrɪ] *n* infanterie *f*
infantryman ['ɪnfəntrɪmən] *n* soldat *m* d'infanterie, fantassin *m*
infatuated [ɪn'fætjʊeɪtɪd] *adj* **to be i. with sb** être entiché(e) de qn

infatuation [ɪnfætjʊ'eɪʃən] *n (with person)* tocade *f*, passade *f* (**with** pour)

infect [ɪn'fekt] *vt (water, food)* contaminer; *(with prejudice)* corrompre; **to become infected** *(of wound)* s'infecter; **to i. sb with sth** transmettre qch à qn; **her enthusiasm infected us all** elle nous a communiqué son enthousiasme

infection [ɪn'fekʃən] *n* infection *f*

infectious [ɪn'fekʃəs] *adj* (**a**) *(disease)* infectieux(-euse); *(person)* contagieux(euse) (**b**) *(laughter, enthusiasm)* communicatif(ive)

infer [ɪn'fɜː(r)] *(pt & pp* **inferred**) *vt* déduire (**from** de)

inference ['ɪnfərəns] *n* conclusion *f*; **by i.** par déduction

inferior [ɪn'fɪərɪə(r)] **1** *n* inférieur(e) *m,f*; **to be sb's i.** être inférieur à qn
2 *adj* inférieur(e) (**to** à)

inferiority [ɪnfɪərɪ'ɒrɪtɪ] *n* infériorité *f*; **i. complex** complexe *m* d'infériorité

infernal [ɪn'fɜːnəl] *adj* (**a**) *(diabolical)* infernal(e), diabolique (**b**) *Fam (for emphasis)* **it's an i. nuisance** c'est diablement imbêtant; **that i. idiot!** cette espèce d'idiot!

inferno [ɪn'fɜːnəʊ] *(pl* **infernos**) *n (hell)* enfer *m*; *(blaze)* brasier *m*

infertile [ɪn'fɜːtaɪl] *adj* stérile

infertility [ɪnfɜː'tɪlɪtɪ] *n* stérilité *f*

infest [ɪn'fest] *vt* **to be infested with** *or* **by sth** être infesté(e) de qch

infidelity [ɪnfɪ'delɪtɪ] *n* infidélité *f*

infighting ['ɪnfaɪtɪŋ] *n* querelles *fpl* intestines

infiltrate ['ɪnfɪltreɪt] **1** *vt* infiltrer
2 *vi* s'infiltrer

infiltration [ɪnfɪl'treɪʃən] *n* infiltration *f*

infinite ['ɪnfɪnɪt] **1** *n* **the i.** l'infini *m*
2 *adj* infini(e); *Rel & Hum* **in her i. wisdom** dans son infinie sagesse

infinitely ['ɪnfɪnɪtlɪ] *adv* infiniment

infinitesimal [ɪnfɪnɪ'tesɪməl] *adj* infinitésimal(e)

infinitive [ɪn'fɪnɪtɪv] *n Gram* infinitif *m*; **in the i.** à l'infinitif

infinity [ɪn'fɪnɪtɪ] *n* infinité *f*; *Math* infini *m*

infirm [ɪn'fɜːm] *adj* infirme

infirmary [ɪn'fɜːmərɪ] *(pl* **infirmaries**) *n (hospital)* hôpital *m*; *(in school, prison)* infirmerie *f*

infirmity [ɪn'fɜːmɪtɪ] *(pl* **infirmities**) *n (weakness)* infirmité *f*

inflame [ɪn'fleɪm] *vt* (**a**) *(desire)* allumer; *(curiosity)* attiser; *(crowd)* enflammer (**b**) **to become inflamed** *(of wound)* s'enflammer

inflammable [ɪn'flæməbəl] *adj (substance)* inflammable; *Fig (situation)* explosif(ive)

inflammation [ɪnflə'meɪʃən] *n* inflammation *f*

inflammatory [ɪn'flæmətrɪ] *adj* incendiaire

inflatable [ɪn'fleɪtəbəl] **1** *n (rubber dinghy)* canot *m* pneumatique
2 *adj* gonflable

inflate [ɪn'fleɪt] **1** *vt* (**a**) *(tyre, lifejacket)* gonfler (**b**) *(prices)* faire monter
2 *vi* se gonfler

inflated [ɪn'fleɪtɪd] *adj (tyre, lifejacket)* gonflé(e); **to have an i. opinion of oneself** avoir une opinion trop flatteuse de soi-même

inflation [ɪn'fleɪʃən] *n Econ* inflation *f*

inflationary [ɪn'fleɪʃənrɪ] *adj Econ* inflationniste

inflect [ɪn'flekt] **1** *vt* (**a**) *(voice)* moduler (**b**) *Gram* ajouter la désinence de
2 *vi Gram* prendre une désinence

inflexibility [ɪnfleksɪ'bɪlɪtɪ] *n* rigidité *f*

inflexible [ɪn'fleksɪbəl] *adj* rigide

inflict [ɪn'flɪkt] *vt (suffering, punishment, defeat)* infliger (**on** à); *(damage)* causer (**on** à); **to i. oneself on sb** infliger sa présence à qn

in-flight ['ɪnflaɪt] *adj* **i. entertainment** distractions *fpl* en vol; **i. meal** repas *m* servi pendant le vol

influence ['ɪnflʊəns] **1** *n* influence *f* (**on** sur); **to be a good/bad i. (on sb)** avoir une bonne/mauvaise influence (sur qn); **to have i. over sb** avoir de l'influence sur qn; **under the i. of drink** sous l'empire de la boisson
2 *vt* influencer; **to be easily influenced** être influençable

influential [ɪnflʊ'enʃəl] *adj* influent(e)

influenza [ɪnflʊ'enzə] *n* grippe *f*

influx ['ɪnflʌks] *n* afflux *m*

info ['ɪnfəʊ] *n Fam* renseignements *mpl*

infomercial [ɪnfəʊ'mɜːʃəl] *n* infomercial *m*

inform [ɪn'fɔːm] **1** *vt* informer (**of** *or* **about** de); **to keep sb informed of sth** tenir qn au courant de qch
2 *vi* **to i. on sb** dénoncer qn

informal [ɪn'fɔːməl] *adj* (**a**) *(unaffected)* simple (**b**) *(casual)* décontracté(e); *(word, language)* familier(-ère) (**c**) *(unofficial) (meeting, talks)* officieux(euse)

informality [ɪnfɔː'mælɪtɪ] *n* (**a**) *(unaffectedness)* simplicité *f* (**b**) *(casualness)* décontraction *f* (**c**) *(of talks)* caractère *m* officieux

informally [ɪn'fɔːmәlɪ] *adv* (**a**) *(unaffectedly)* avec simplicité (**b**) *(casually)* avec décontraction (**c**) *(hold talks)* officieusement

informant [ɪn'fɔːmənt] *n* informateur(trice) *m,f*

information [ɪnfə'meɪʃən] *n* (**a**) *(news, facts)* renseignements *mpl*; **a piece of i.** un renseignement; **for further i.** pour de plus amples renseignements; **i. bureau** bureau *m* des renseignements; **i. officer** *(press officer)* responsable *mf* de la communication; *(archivist)* documentaliste *mf*; **i. pack** dossier *m* d'information (**b**) *Comput* **i. processing** traitement *m* de l'information; **i. retrieval** recherche *f* documentaire; **i. science** informatique *f*; **the i. superhighway** l'autoroute *f* de l'information, *Can* l'inforoute *f*; **i. technology** informatique

informative [ɪn'fɔːmətɪv] *adj* instructif(ive); **she was very i.** elle nous a appris beaucoup de choses

informed [ɪn'fɔːmd] *adj (person)* bien renseigné(e), bien informé(e); **my i. guess is that...** en me basant sur ce que je sais, je dirais que...; **an i. decision** une décision prise en connaissance de cause

informer [ɪn'fɔːmə(r)] *n* indicateur *m*

infra dig ['ɪnfrə'dɪg] *adj Fam* rabaissant(e), dégradant(e)

infrared [ɪnfrə'red] *adj* infrarouge

infrastructure ['ɪnfrəstrʌktʃə(r)] *n* infrastructure *f*

infrequent [ɪn'friːkwənt] *adj* rare, peu fréquent(e)

infringe [ɪn'frɪndʒ] *vt (rule, law)* enfreindre; *(right)* empiéter sur
▸**infringe on** *vt insep* empiéter sur

infringement [ɪn'frɪndʒmənt] *n (of rule, law)* infraction *f* (**of** à); *(of right)* atteinte *f* (**of** à)

infuriate [ɪn'fjʊːrɪeɪt] *vt* exaspérer

infuriating [ɪn'fjʊːrɪeɪtɪŋ] *adj* exaspérant(e)

infuse [ɪn'fjuːz] **1** vt (**a**) *(energy, hope)* insuffler (**into** à) (**b**) *(tea)* faire infuser
  2 vi *(of tea)* infuser
infusion [ɪn'fjuːʒən] n *(drink)* infusion f
ingenious [ɪn'dʒiːnɪəs] *adj* ingénieux(euse)
ingenuity [ɪndʒɪ'njuːɪtɪ] n ingéniosité f
ingenuous [ɪn'dʒenʊəs] *adj (naive)* ingénu(e); *(frank)* franc (franche)
inglorious [ɪn'ɡlɔːrɪəs] *adj* déshonorant(e), honteux(-euse)
ingot ['ɪŋɡət] n lingot m
ingrained [ɪn'ɡreɪnd] *adj (prejudice, habit)* enraciné(e); **i. dirt** crasse f
ingratiate [ɪn'ɡreɪʃɪeɪt] vt **to i. oneself (with sb)** se faire bien voir (de *ou* par qn)
ingratiating [ɪn'ɡreɪʃɪeɪtɪŋ] *adj* doucereux(euse)
ingratitude [ɪn'ɡrætɪtjuːd] n ingratitude f
ingredient [ɪn'ɡriːdɪənt] n *also Fig* ingrédient m; *Fig* **the missing i.** l'élément m manquant
ingrowing ['ɪnɡrəʊɪŋ], **ingrown** ['ɪnɡrəʊn] *adj* **i. toenail** ongle m incarné
inhabit [ɪn'hæbɪt] vt habiter
inhabitable [ɪn'hæbɪtəbəl] *adj* habitable
inhabitant [ɪn'hæbɪtənt] n habitant(e) m,f
inhabited [ɪn'hæbɪtɪd] *adj* habité(e) (**by** par)
inhale [ɪn'heɪl] **1** vt *(gas, fumes)* inhaler; *(cigarette smoke)* avaler
  2 vi inspirer; *(in smoking)* avaler la fumée
inhaler [ɪn'heɪlə(r)] n *(for asthmatics)* inhalateur m
inherent [ɪn'herənt] *adj* inhérent(e) (**in** à)
inherit [ɪn'herɪt] vt hériter (**from** de)
inheritance [ɪn'herɪtəns] n héritage m; **i. tax** droits mpl de succession
inhibit [ɪn'hɪbɪt] vt *(progress, growth)* entraver; *(person)* inhiber
inhibited [ɪn'hɪbɪtɪd] *adj (person)* inhibé(e)
inhibition [ɪnɪ'bɪʃən] n inhibition f; **to have no inhibitions about doing sth** n'avoir aucune honte à faire qch
inhospitable [ɪnhɒ'spɪtəbəl] *adj* inhospitalier(ère)
in-house ['ɪnhaʊs] **1** *adj (training)* interne; *(staff)* qui travaille sur place
  2 *adv* sur place
inhuman [ɪn'hjuːmən] *adj* inhumain(e)
inhumane [ɪnhjuː'meɪn] *adj* inhumain(e)
inhumanity [ɪnhjuː'mænɪtɪ] n inhumanité f, cruauté f
inimical [ɪ'nɪmɪkəl] *adj Formal (people)* ennemi(e), hostile; *(conditions)* contraire (**to** à)
inimitable [ɪ'nɪmɪtəbəl] *adj* inimitable
iniquitous [ɪ'nɪkwɪtəs] *adj* inique
iniquity [ɪ'nɪkwɪtɪ] *(pl* **iniquities**) n iniquité f
initial [ɪ'nɪʃəl] **1** n initiale f; **initials** *(signature)* paraphe m
  2 *adj* initial(e), premier(ère); **in the i. stages of sth** au stade initial de qch
  3 vt *(pt & pp* **initialled**, *Am* **initialed**) parapher
initially [ɪ'nɪʃəlɪ] *adv* au début
initiate [ɪ'nɪʃɪeɪt] vt (**a**) *(negotiations)* amorcer; *(rumour, project)* lancer; *Law* **to i. proceedings (against sb)** entamer des poursuites (contre qn) (**b**) **to i. sb into a secret society/gang** faire subir à qn les épreuves initiatiques d'une société secrète/d'un gang

initiation [ɪnɪʃɪ'eɪʃən] n (**a**) *(beginning)* commencement m, début(s) m(pl) (**b**) *(induction)* initiation f; **i. ceremony** rite m d'initiation
initiative [ɪ'nɪʃətɪv] n initiative f; **to take the i. (in doing sth)** prendre l'initiative (de faire qch); **to use one's i.** faire preuve d'initiative; **on one's own i.** de sa propre initiative
inject [ɪn'dʒekt] vt *(drug, money)* injecter; *(enthusiasm)* communiquer; **to i. new life into sth** donner un nouvel essor à qch
injection [ɪn'dʒekʃən] n injection f, piqûre f; *Fig* injection; **polio i.** vaccin m contre la polio; **to give sb an i.** faire une piqûre à qn
injudicious [ɪndʒuː'dɪʃəs] *adj* peu judicieux(euse), malavisé(e)
injunction [ɪn'dʒʌŋkʃən] n *Law* arrêt m, jugement m; **to take out an i. against sb** mettre qn en demeure
injure ['ɪndʒə(r)] vt *(person)* blesser; *(reputation, interests)* nuire à; **to i. oneself** se blesser; **to i. one's leg** se blesser à la jambe; **her pride is injured** elle est blessée dans son orgueil
injured ['ɪndʒəd] **1** n **the i.** les blessés mpl
  2 *adj* blessé(e); *(look, voice)* offensé(e); *Law* **the i. party** la partie lésée
injurious [ɪn'dʒʊərɪəs] *adj* nuisible, préjudiciable (**to** à)
injury ['ɪndʒərɪ] *(pl* **injuries**) n *(physical)* blessure f; **to do oneself an i.** se blesser; **i. time** *(in football match)* arrêts mpl de jeu
injustice [ɪn'dʒʌstɪs] n injustice f; **to do sb an i.** être injuste envers qn
ink [ɪŋk] n encre f; **i. pad** tampon m (encreur)
ink-jet ['ɪŋkdʒet] *adj Comput* **i. (printer)** imprimante f à jet d'encre
inkling ['ɪŋklɪŋ] n soupçon m; **to have an i. of sth** se douter de qch
inkwell ['ɪŋkwel] n encrier m *(de pupitre)*
inky ['ɪŋkɪ] *adj* (**a**) *(stained with ink)* taché(e) d'encre (**b**) **i. (black)** noir(e) comme (de) l'encre
inlaid [ɪn'leɪd] *adj (with wood)* marqueté(e), *(with jewels)* incrusté(e) (**with** de)
inland **1** *adj* ['ɪnlənd] intérieur(e); **the I. Revenue** ~ le fisc
  2 *adv* [ɪn'lænd] *(travel)* vers l'intérieur; *(live)* dans les terres
in-laws ['ɪnlɔːz] npl *(spouse's parents)* beaux-parents mpl; *(spouse's family)* belle-famille f
inlet ['ɪnlet] n (**a**) *(of sea)* petit bras m de mer (**b**) *(of pipe, machine)* (orifice m d')entrée f
inmate ['ɪnmeɪt] n *(in prison)* détenu(e) m,f; *(in mental hospital)* interné(e) m,f
inn [ɪn] n auberge f
innards ['ɪnədz] npl entrailles fpl
innate [ɪ'neɪt] *adj* inné(e)
inner ['ɪnə(r)] *adj* (**a**) *(chamber, lining)* intérieur(e); **i. circle** *(of party, association)* initiés mpl; **i. city** quartiers mpl déshérités du centre-ville; **i. ear** oreille f interne; **i. tube** chambre f à air (**b**) *(thought, feeling)* intime; *(peace)* intérieur(e)
innermost ['ɪnəməʊst] *adj (part)* le (la) plus profond(e); *(thoughts, feelings)* le (la) plus secret(ète)
innings ['ɪnɪŋz] n *(in cricket)* tournée f, tour m de batte; *Fig* **she had a good i.** elle a bien profité de la vie
innkeeper ['ɪnkiːpə(r)] n aubergiste mf
innocence ['ɪnəsəns] n innocence f

innocent ['ɪnəsənt] **1** n innocent(e) m,f; **to act the i.** faire l'innocent
2 adj innocent(e)

innocuous [ɪ'nɒkjʊəs] adj inoffensif(ive); (remark) anodin(e)

innovate ['ɪnəveɪt] vi innover

innovation [ɪnə'veɪʃən] n innovation f

innovative ['ɪnəveɪtɪv] adj (in)novateur(trice)

innovator ['ɪnəveɪtə(r)] n (in)novateur(trice) m,f

innuendo [ɪnjʊ'endəʊ] (pl **innuendos** or **innuendoes**) n (insinuation) insinuation f; (in jokes) allusion f grivoise

innumerable [ɪ'njuːmərəbəl] adj innombrable

inoculate [ɪ'nɒkjʊleɪt] vt vacciner; **to i. sb with sth** inoculer qch à qn; **to i. sb against sth** vacciner qn contre qch

inoculation [ɪnɒkjʊ'leɪʃən] n inoculation f

inoffensive [ɪnə'fensɪv] adj (animal, person) inoffensif(ive); (remark, humour) qui n'a rien d'offensant; (odour) qui n'a rien de désagréable

inoperable [ɪn'ɒpərəbəl] adj inopérable

inoperative [ɪn'ɒpərətɪv] adj (rule) inopérant(e); (machine) arrêté(e)

inopportune [ɪn'ɒpətjuːn] adj inopportun(e)

inordinate [ɪn'ɔːdɪnət] adj démesuré(e)

inorganic [ɪnɔː'gænɪk] adj inorganique

in-patient ['ɪnpeɪʃənt] n patient(e) m,f hospitalisé(e)

input ['ɪnpʊt] **1** n (**a**) Elec puissance f d'alimentation; (terminal) entrée f; Comput entrée, introduction f (**b**) (contribution) contribution f
2 vt (pt & pp **input**) Comput (data) entrer

inquest ['ɪnkwest] n Law enquête f; Fig (in politics, business) analyse f; **to hold an i.** Law (of coroner) mener une enquête (**into** sur); (in politics, business) faire une analyse (**into** de)

inquire [ɪn'kwaɪə(r)] **1** vt demander
2 vi se renseigner (**about** sur); **i. within** (sign) s'adresser ici

▸**inquire after** vt insep demander des nouvelles de
▸**inquire into** vt insep faire des recherches sur

inquiring [ɪn'kwaɪrɪŋ] adj (mind) curieux(euse); (look, voice) interrogateur(trice)

inquiry [ɪn'kwaɪrɪ] (pl **inquiries**) n (**a**) (official investigation) enquête f; **to hold an i. (into sth)** faire une enquête (sur qch) (**b**) (request for information) demande f de renseignements; **to make inquiries (about sth)** se renseigner (sur qch); **i. desk** bureau m de(s) renseignements

Inquisition [ɪnkwɪ'zɪʃən] n **the I.** l'Inquisition f

inquisitive [ɪn'kwɪzɪtɪv] adj (person, mind) curieux(euse); (look) interrogateur(trice)

inroads ['ɪnrəʊdz] npl **to make i. into** (capital, savings) entamer; (market) pénétrer

insane [ɪn'seɪn] adj (person) dément(e); Fam (desire, scheme) fou (folle); **to go i.** devenir fou, perdre la raison; **to be i. with grief/jealousy** être fou de douleur/jalousie

insanely [ɪn'seɪnlɪ] adv comme un fou (une folle); **i. jealous** d'une jalousie maladive

insanitary [ɪn'sænɪtrɪ] adj insalubre, malsain(e)

insanity [ɪn'sænɪtɪ] n (of person) démence f; Fam (of desire, scheme) folie f

insatiable [ɪn'seɪʃəbəl] adj insatiable

inscribe [ɪn'skraɪb] vt (write) écrire; (engrave) inscrire, graver

inscription [ɪn'skrɪpʃən] n (on stone, coin) inscription f; (in book) dédicace f

inscrutable [ɪn'skruːtəbəl] adj (look, face) impénétrable; (remark) énigmatique

insect ['ɪnsekt] n insecte m; **i. bite** piqûre f d'insecte; **i. repellent** anti-moustiques m inv

insecticide [ɪn'sektɪsaɪd] n insecticide m

insecure [ɪnsɪ'kjʊə(r)] adj (**a**) (person) (generally) pas sûr(e) de soi, qui manque d'assurance; (temporarily) angoissé(e) (**b**) (government) fragile; (job, future) précaire; **to be financially i.** être dans une situation financière précaire

insecurity [ɪnsɪ'kjʊərɪtɪ] n (**a**) (of person) (lack of confidence) manque m d'assurance; (anxiety) angoisse f (**b**) (of job, future) précarité f

insemination [ɪnsemɪ'neɪʃən] n insémination f

insensible [ɪn'sensɪbəl] adj Formal (unaware, unconscious) inconscient(e) (**to** de)

insensitive [ɪn'sensɪtɪv] adj (person) insensible (**to** à); (remark) indélicat(e)

insensitivity [ɪnsensɪ'tɪvɪtɪ] n insensibilité f

inseparable [ɪn'sepərəbəl] adj inséparable

insert 1 n ['ɪnsɜːt] (in magazine) encart m
2 vt [ɪn'sɜːt] (key, finger) introduire (**into** dans); (clause) insérer (**in** dans); (advertisement) mettre (**in** dans)

insertion [ɪn'sɜːʃən] n insertion f

inset ['ɪnset] n (in map, picture) médaillon m

inshore [ɪn'ʃɔː(r)] **1** adj (navigation, fishing) côtier(ère)
2 adv (be situated) sur la côte; (travel) vers la côte, vers les terres

inside 1 n ['ɪnsaɪd] (**a**) (of house) intérieur m; **on/from the i.** à/de l'intérieur; **to overtake on the i.** (in Britain) doubler par la gauche; (in Europe, USA) doubler par la droite (**b**) Fam **insides** (internal organs) entrailles fpl (**c**) (in phrases) **i. out** (clothes) à l'envers; Fig **to know sth i. out** connaître qch comme sa poche
2 adj ['ɪnsaɪd] intérieur(e); **to have i. information** avoir des informations de première main; Fam **it's an i. job** c'est quelqu'un de la maison qui a fait ça; **i. lane** (in Britain) voie f de gauche; (in Europe, USA) voie de droite; **i. left** (in football) intérieur m gauche; **to know the i. story** connaître les dessous de l'affaire
3 adv [ɪn'saɪd] (**a**) (indoors) à l'intérieur; **come i.!** entrez! (**b**) (within oneself) en son for intérieur (**c**) Fam (in prison) en taule
4 prep [ɪn'saɪd] (**a**) (place) à l'intérieur de, dans (**b**) (with time) **i. (of) a week/an hour** en moins d'une semaine/heure

insider [ɪn'saɪdə(r)] n initié(e) m,f; Fin **i. dealing, i. trading** délit m d'initié

insidious [ɪn'sɪdɪəs] adj insidieux(euse)

insight ['ɪnsaɪt] n (**a**) (perspicacity) perspicacité f (**b**) (understanding) aperçu m; **to get an i. into sth** avoir un aperçu de qch

insignia [ɪn'sɪgnɪə] n insigne m

insignificance [ɪnsɪg'nɪfɪkəns] n insignifiance f; **to pale into i. (beside sth)** sembler totalement insignifiant(e) (à côté de qch)

insignificant [ɪnsɪg'nɪfɪkənt] adj insignifiant(e)

insincere [ɪnsɪn'sɪə(r)] adj peu sincère, faux (fausse)

insincerity [ɪnsɪn'serɪtɪ] n manque m de sincérité, fausseté f

insinuate [ɪnˈsɪnjʊeɪt] *vt* insinuer; **to i. oneself into sb's favour** s'insinuer dans les bonnes grâces de qn

insinuation [ɪnsɪnjʊˈeɪʃən] *n* insinuation *f*

insipid [ɪnˈsɪpɪd] *adj* insipide

insist [ɪnˈsɪst] **1** *vt* (**a**) *(maintain)* **to i. that...** soutenir *ou* maintenir que... (**b**) *(demand)* **to i. (that) sb does sth** insister pour que qn fasse qch
2 *vi* insister; **to i. on sth** exiger qch; **to i. on doing sth** tenir à faire qch

insistence [ɪnˈsɪstəns] *n* insistance *f* (**on** à); **I stayed at her i.** elle insista, et je restai

insistent [ɪnˈsɪstənt] *adj (person, demand)* pressant(e); **to be i.** se montrer pressant; **to be i. about sth** insister sur qch

insofar as [ˈɪnsəʊˈfɑːrəz] *adv* dans la mesure où

insole [ˈɪnsəʊl] *n* semelle *f* intérieure

insolence [ˈɪnsələns] *n* insolence *f* (**to** envers)

insolent [ˈɪnsələnt] *adj* insolent(e) (**to** envers)

insoluble [ɪnˈsɒljʊbəl] *adj* insoluble

insolvency [ɪnˈsɒlvənsɪ] *n Fin (of person)* insolvabilité *f*; *(of company)* faillite *f*

insolvent [ɪnˈsɒlvənt] *adj Fin (person)* insolvable; *(company)* en faillite

insomnia [ɪnˈsɒmnɪə] *n* insomnie *f*

insomniac [ɪnˈsɒmnɪæk] *n* insomniaque *mf*

inspect [ɪnˈspekt] *vt (passport, luggage, picture)* examiner; *(school, factory)* inspecter; *(troops)* passer en revue

inspection [ɪnˈspekʃən] *n (of passport, luggage, picture)* examen *m*; *(of school, factory)* (visite *f* d')inspection *f*; *(of troops)* revue *f*; **on closer i.** en y regardant de plus près

inspector [ɪnˈspektə(r)] *n (of schools, factories)* inspecteur(trice) *m,f*; *Br (on train, bus)* contrôleur(euse) *m,f*; *Br* (**police**) **i.** inspecteur *m* de police

inspiration [ɪnspɪˈreɪʃən] *n* inspiration *f*; **to be an i. to sb** inspirer qn

inspire [ɪnˈspaɪə(r)] *vt* inspirer; **to i. sb to do sth** pousser qn à faire qch; **to i. sth in sb, to i. sb with sth** inspirer qch à qn

inspired [ɪnˈspaɪəd] *adj* inspiré(e)

inspiring [ɪnˈspaɪərɪŋ] *adj (music, speech)* exaltant(e); *(leader)* enthousiasmant(e); **the menu wasn't very i.** le menu n'avait rien de bien tentant

instability [ɪnstəˈbɪlɪtɪ] *n* instabilité *f*

install, *Am* **instal** [ɪnˈstɔːl] *vt* installer; **to i. sb in a post** mettre qn à un poste; **to i. oneself in an armchair** s'installer dans un fauteuil

installation [ɪnstəˈleɪʃən] *n* installation *f*

instalment, *Am* **installment** [ɪnˈstɔːlmənt] *n* (**a**) *(part payment)* versement *m*; **to pay by instalments** payer par versements échelonnés (**b**) *(of radio, TV programme)* épisode *m*

instance [ˈɪnstəns] *n (example)* cas *m*; **for i.** par exemple; **in the first i.** en (tout) premier lieu

instant [ˈɪnstənt] **1** *n (moment)* instant *m*, moment *m*; **this i.** immédiatement; **not an i. too soon** juste à temps; **the i. I saw her** dès que je l'ai vue
2 *adj* (**a**) *(reply, success, dislike)* immédiat(e); *(solution)* instantané(e); *TV* **i. replay** reprise *f* de l'action (**b**) *(coffee, soup)* instantané(e)

instant-access [ɪnstəntˈækses] *adj (bank account)* à accès immédiat

instantaneous [ɪnstənˈteɪnɪəs] *adj* instantané(e)

instantly [ˈɪnstəntlɪ] *adv* instantanément

instead [ɪnˈsted] *adv (in place of something)* à la place; *(in place of somebody)* à ma/sa/*etc* place; **i. of** *(thing)* au lieu de; *(person)* à la place de; **i. of doing sth** au lieu de faire qch

instep [ˈɪnstep] *n (of foot)* cou-de-pied *m*; *(of shoe)* cambrure *f*

instigate [ˈɪnstɪgeɪt] *vt* être à l'origine de

instigation [ɪnstɪˈgeɪʃən] *n* instigation *f*; **at sb's i.** à l'instigation de qn

instigator [ˈɪnstɪgeɪtə(r)] *n* instigateur(trice) *m,f*

instil, *Am* **instill** [ɪnˈstɪl] *(pt & pp* **instilled)** *vt (courage, pride)* inspirer (**in** à); *(doubt, jealousy)* instiller (**in** à); *(idea)* inculquer (**into** à)

instinct [ˈɪnstɪŋkt] *n* instinct *m*; **he has an i. for the game** ce jeu, chez lui, c'est instinctif

instinctive [ɪnˈstɪŋktɪv] *adj* instinctif(ive)

institute [ˈɪnstɪtjuːt] **1** *n* institut *m*
2 *vt (system, procedure)* établir, instituer; *(search)* lancer; *Law (enquiry)* ordonner; **to i. proceedings (against sb)** entamer *ou* engager des poursuites (contre qn)

institution [ɪnstɪˈtjuːʃən] *n (organization)* institution *f*; *(public, financial)* établissement *m*; *(for old people)* hospice *m*; *(for mental patients)* asile *m*; *Fig* **to become a national i.** *(of event, TV programme)* devenir une institution nationale

institutional [ɪnstɪˈtjuːʃənəl] *adj* institutionnel(elle)

institutionalize [ɪnstɪˈtjuːʃənəlaɪz] *vt* (**a**) *(put in a home)* placer dans un établissement spécialisé; **to become institutionalized** *(of prisoner, patient)* devenir complètement dépendant(e) (**b**) *(turn into an institution)* institutionnaliser

instruct [ɪnˈstrʌkt] *vt* (**a**) *(teach)* enseigner; **to i. sb in sth** enseigner qch à qn (**b**) *(command)* ordonner; **to i. sb to do sth** ordonner à qn de faire qch

instruction [ɪnˈstrʌkʃən] *n* (**a**) *(training)* instruction *f*, enseignement *m* (**b**) **instructions** *(orders)* instructions *fpl*, directives *fpl* (**c**) **instructions (for use)** notice *f* (d'emploi); **i. manual** manuel *m* d'entretien

instructive [ɪnˈstrʌktɪv] *adj* instructif(ive)

instructor [ɪnˈstrʌktə(r)] *n* (**a**) *(of sporting activity, driving)* moniteur(trice) *m,f* (**b**) *Am (university lecturer)* professeur *m*

instrument [ˈɪnstrʊmənt] *n* instrument *m*; **i. board** *or* **panel** *(in plane, car)* tableau *m* de bord

instrumental [ɪnstrʊˈmentəl] **1** *n (music without words)* instrumental *m*
2 *adj* (**a**) *(contributory)* **to be i. in sth** jouer un rôle décisif dans qch (**b**) *(in music)* instrumental(e)

instrumentalist [ɪnstrʊˈmentəlɪst] *n* instrumentiste *mf*

instrumentation [ɪnstrʊmenˈteɪʃən] *n* instrumentation *f*

insubordinate [ɪnsəˈbɔːdɪnət] *adj* insubordonné(e)

insubordination [ɪnsəbɔːdɪˈneɪʃən] *n* insubordination *f*

insubstantial [ɪnsəbˈstænʃəl] *adj (structure, argument)* peu solide; *(meal)* frugal(e); *(book)* creux(euse), qui manque de substance

insufferable [ɪnˈsʌfrəbəl] *adj* insupportable, intolérable

insufficient [ɪnsəˈfɪʃənt] *adj* insuffisant(e)

insular [ˈɪnsjʊlə(r)] *adj* borné(e); *(climate)* insulaire

insulate [ˈɪnsjʊleɪt] *vt* isoler; *Fig* **to be insulated from sth** être protégé(e) de qch

insulating tape [ɪnsjʊleɪtɪŋ'teɪp] n chatterton m
insulation [ɪnsjʊ'leɪʃən] n isolation f
insulin ['ɪnsjʊlɪn] n insuline f
insult 1 n ['ɪnsʌlt] (words, action) insulte f; **to add i. to injury** aggraver les choses
    2 vt [ɪn'sʌlt] insulter
insulting [ɪn'sʌltɪŋ] adj insultant(e)
insuperable [ɪn'suːpərəbəl] adj insurmontable
insurance [ɪn'ʃʊərəns] n assurance f; Fig (protection) garantie f; **to take out i.** prendre une assurance; **i. broker** courtier m en assurances; **i. claim** demande f d'indemnité; (for more serious damage) déclaration f de sinistre; **i. company** companie f d'assurances; **i. policy** police f d'assurance; **i. premium** prime f d'assurance
insure [ɪn'ʃʊə(r)] vt assurer (**against** contre); **to i. one's life** s'assurer sur la vie
insured [ɪn'ʃʊəd] adj assuré(e) (**against** contre); **i. value** valeur f assurée
insurer [ɪn'ʃʊərə(r)] n assureur m
insurgent [ɪn'sɜːdʒənt] n insurgé(e) m,f
insurmountable [ɪnsə'maʊntəbəl] adj insurmontable
insurrection [ɪnsə'rekʃən] n insurrection f
intact [ɪn'tækt] adj intact(e)
intake ['ɪnteɪk] n (**a**) (of alcohol, food) consommation f; (of calories) absorption f (**b**) (pupils) élèves mpl; (recruits) contingent m (**c**) Tech admission f
intangible [ɪn'tændʒɪbəl] adj impalpable
integer ['ɪntɪdʒə(r)] n Math nombre m entier
integral ['ɪntɪgrəl] adj (essential) indispensable; **to be an i. part of sth** faire partie intégrante de qch; Math **i. calculus** calcul m intégral
integrate ['ɪntɪgreɪt] **1** vt intégrer (**into** à)
    2 vi s'intégrer (**into** à)
integrated ['ɪntɪgreɪtɪd] adj intégré(e); (school) qui pratique la déségrégation raciale
integration [ɪntɪ'greɪʃən] n intégration f
integrity [ɪn'tegrɪtɪ] n intégrité f
intellect ['ɪntɪlekt] n intellect m, intelligence f
intellectual [ɪntɪ'lektjʊəl] **1** n intellectuel(elle) m,f
    2 adj intellectuel(elle)
intelligence [ɪn'telɪdʒəns] n (**a**) (faculty) intelligence f; Psy **i. quotient** quotient m intellectuel; **i. test** test m d'intelligence (**b**) (secret service) services mpl secrets; **i. officer** agent m de renseignements; **i. service** services secrets
intelligent [ɪn'telɪdʒənt] adj intelligent(e)
intelligentsia [ɪntelɪ'dʒensɪə] n intelligentsia f
intelligible [ɪn'telɪdʒɪbəl] adj intelligible
intemperate [ɪn'tempərət] adj Formal (climate) rude; (person, behaviour) intempérant(e)
intend [ɪn'tend] vt **to i. to do sth** avoir l'intention de faire qch; **to i. sth for sb** destiner qch à qn; **was that intended?** était-ce intentionnel?; **it was intended as a compliment/a joke** c'était un compliment/pour plaisanter; **I didn't i. her to see it yet** il n'était pas dans mes intentions qu'elle le voie si tôt
intended [ɪn'tendɪd] **1** n Old-fashioned or Hum (future spouse) futur(e) m,f
    2 adj (consequence, outcome) prévu(e); (effect) escompté(e); (insult, mistake) voulu(e)
intense [ɪn'tens] adj intense; (interest, anger) vif (vive); (person) passionné(e)

intensely [ɪn'tenslɪ] adv (**a**) (amusing, boring) extrêmement (**b**) (look at, speak) intensément, avec intensité
intensify [ɪn'tensɪfaɪ] (pt & pp intensified) **1** vt (search, effort) intensifier; (pressure) augmenter
    2 vi s'intensifier
intensity [ɪn'tensɪtɪ] n intensité f
intensive [ɪn'tensɪv] adj intensif(ive); Med **i. care** soins mpl intensifs; Med **i. care unit** unité f de soins intensifs
intent [ɪn'tent] **1** n intention f; **to all intents and purposes** quasiment
    2 adj (look) intense; **to be i. on doing sth** être résolu(e) ou déterminé(e) à faire qch
intention [ɪn'tenʃən] n intention f; **to have every i. of doing sth** avoir la ferme intention de faire qch; **to have no i. of doing sth** n'avoir nullement l'intention de faire qch
intentional [ɪn'tenʃənəl] adj intentionnel(elle), voulu(e)
intentionally [ɪn'tenʃənəlɪ] adv intentionnellement; **I didn't do it i.** je ne l'ai pas fait exprès
intently [ɪn'tentlɪ] adv (listen, look at) attentivement
inter [ɪn'tɜː(r)] (pt & pp interred) vt inhumer, enterrer
interact [ɪntə'rækt] vi (**a**) (of person) communiquer (**with** avec); (of two or more people) communiquer entre eux (elles) (**b**) (of chemical) réagir (**with** avec); (of two or more chemicals) réagir entre eux (elles)
interaction [ɪntə'rækʃən] n interaction f
interactive [ɪntə'ræktɪv] adj interactif(ive)
intercede [ɪntə'siːd] vi intercéder (**with/for** auprès de/en faveur de)
intercept [ɪntə'sept] vt intercepter
interception [ɪntə'sepʃən] n interception f
intercession [ɪntə'seʃən] n intercession f
interchange 1 n ['ɪntətʃeɪndʒ] (exchange) échange m; (on motorway) échangeur m
    2 vt [ɪntə'tʃeɪndʒ] (exchange) échanger; (transpose) intervertir
interchangeable [ɪntə'tʃeɪndʒəbəl] adj interchangeable
intercom ['ɪntəkɒm] n Interphone® m
interconnect [ɪntəkə'nekt] vt interconnecter
intercontinental [ɪntəkɒntɪ'nentəl] adj intercontinental(e); **i. ballistic missile** missile m balistique intercontinental
intercourse ['ɪntəkɔːs] n (**a**) (**sexual**) **i.** rapports mpl (sexuels) (**b**) Formal (dealings) commerce m, relations fpl
interdependent ['ɪntədɪ'pendənt] adj interdépendant(e)
interest ['ɪntrest] **1** n (**a**) (curiosity) intérêt m; (hobby) centre m d'intérêt; **of i.** intéressant(e); **of historical i.** intéressant du point de vue historique; **to be of i. to sb** intéresser qn; **to take an i. in sth** s'intéresser à qch; **to lose i. (in sth)** se désintéresser (de qch)
    (**b**) (stake) intérêt m; **to have a financial i. in sth** avoir investi financièrement dans qch
    (**c**) (benefit) intérêt m; **to act in sb's interests** agir dans l'intérêt de qn; **the public i.** l'intérêt public; **it's in my i. to do it** j'ai tout intérêt à le faire; **in the interests of...** dans l'intérêt de...
    (**d**) (on loan, investment) intérêt(s) m(pl)
    2 vt intéresser; **to i. sb in sth** intéresser qn à qch; **can I i. you in a drink?** je peux vous offrir un verre?

interested ['ɪntrestɪd] *adj* intéressé(e); **to be interested in sth** s'intéresser à qch; **he seemed i. in the proposal** il a semblé intéressé par cette proposition
interest-free ['ɪntrest'friː] *adj (loan)* sans intérêt; *(credit)* gratuit(e)
interesting ['ɪntrestɪŋ] *adj* intéressant(e)
interface ['ɪntəfeɪs] *n Comput* interface *f*
interfere [ɪntə'fɪə(r)] *vi* (**a**) *(meddle)* se mêler (**in** de); **he's always interfering** il est toujours à se mêler de ce qui ne le regarde pas; **don't i. with my papers** ne touche pas à mes papiers; *Euph* **to i. with sb** *(sexually)* abuser de qn (**b**) **to i. with sth** *(hinder)* gêner qch
interference [ɪntə'fɪərəns] *n* (**a**) *(meddling)* ingérence *f* (**b**) *Rad & TV* interférences *fpl*
interfering [ɪntə'fɪərɪŋ] *adj* importun(e)
interim ['ɪntərɪm] **1** *n* **in the i.** entre-temps **2** *adj (agreement, report)* provisoire
interior [ɪn'tɪərɪə(r)] **1** *n* intérieur *m* **2** *adj* intérieur(e); **i. decorator** décorateur(trice) *m,f* (d'intérieurs); **i. designer** architecte *mf* d'intérieur
interject [ɪntə'dʒekt] *vt (remark)* lancer; *(protest)* émettre
interjection [ɪntə'dʒekʃən] *n* interjection *f*
interlocking [ɪntə'lɒkɪŋ] *adj (parts)* emboîtable; *(gears)* qui s'enclenchent
interlocutor [ɪntə'lɒkjuːtə(r)] *n Formal* interlocuteur (trice) *m,f*
interloper ['ɪntələʊpə(r)] *n* intrus(e) *m,f*
interlude ['ɪntəluːd] *n also Fig* intermède *m*
intermarriage [ɪntə'mærɪdʒ] *n (within a family)* mariage *m* consanguin; *(with member of another group)* mariage
intermarry [ɪntə'mærɪ] *(pt & pp* **intermarried)** *vi* se marier *(au sein de la même famille)*
intermediary [ɪntə'miːdɪərɪ] *(pl* **intermediaries)** *n* intermédiaire *mf*
intermediate [ɪntə'miːdɪət] *adj* intermédiaire; *(student)* de niveau moyen
interminable [ɪn'tɜːmɪnəbəl] *adj* interminable
intermingle [ɪntə'mɪŋgəl] **1** *vt* mélanger (**with** avec) **2** *vi* se mêler (**with** à), se mélanger (**with** avec)
intermission [ɪntə'mɪʃən] *n* entracte *m*
intermittent [ɪntə'mɪtənt] *adj* intermittent(e)
intern 1 *n* ['ɪntɜːn] *Am Med* interne *mf* **2** *vt* [ɪn'tɜːn] interner
internal [ɪn'tɜːnəl] *adj* interne; *(flight)* intérieur(e); **i. combustion engine** moteur *m* à combustion interne
internalize [ɪn'tɜːnəlaɪz] *vt* intérioriser
internally [ɪn'tɜːnəlɪ] *adv* intérieurement; **not to be taken i.** *(on medicine container)* à usage externe
international [ɪntə'næʃənəl] **1** *n (in sport) (player)* international(e) *m,f*; *(match)* match *m* international **2** *adj* international(e); **i. reply coupon** coupon-réponse *m* international; **I. Date Line** ligne *f* de changement de date; *Fin* **I. Monetary Fund** Fonds *m* monétaire international
internee [ɪntɜː'niː] *n* interné(e) *m,f*
Internet ['ɪntənet] *n Comput* **the I.** l'Internet *m*; **I. access** accès *m* (à l')Internet; **I. protocol** protocole *m* Internet; **I. relay chat** service *m* de bavardage; **I. service provider** fournisseur *m* d'accès à l'Internet
internment [ɪn'tɜːnmənt] *n* internement *m*
interpersonal [ɪntə'pɜːsənəl] *adj* interpersonnel(elle)

interplay ['ɪntəpleɪ] *n* interaction *f* (**of** *or* **between** entre)
Interpol ['ɪntəpɒl] *n* Interpol
interpolate [ɪn'tɜːpəleɪt] *vt Formal (remark, question)* glisser; *(word, passage)* intercaler
interpose [ɪntə'pəʊz] *vt* interposer (**between** entre)
interpret [ɪn'tɜːprɪt] **1** *vt* interpréter **2** *vi* faire l'interprète
interpretation [ɪntɜːprɪ'teɪʃən] *n* interprétation *f*
interpreter [ɪn'tɜːprɪtə(r)] *n* interprète *mf*
interracial [ɪntə'reɪʃəl] *adj* interracial(e)
interrelated [ɪntərɪ'leɪtɪd] *adj* lié(e)
interrogate [ɪn'terəgeɪt] *vt* interroger
interrogation [ɪntərə'geɪʃən] *n* interrogatoire *m*
interrogative [ɪntə'rɒgətɪv] **1** *n Gram* interrogatif *m*; *(question mark)* point *m* d'interrogation **2** *adj (look, tone)* interrogateur(trice); *Gram* interrogatif(ive)
interrogator [ɪn'terəgeɪtə(r)] *n* interrogateur(trice) *m,f*
interrupt [ɪntə'rʌpt] **1** *vt* interrompre **2** *vi* **it's rude to i.** ce n'est pas poli d'interrompre les gens; **I'm sorry to i.** je suis désolé de vous interrompre
interruption [ɪntə'rʌpʃən] *n* interruption *f*
intersect [ɪntə'sekt] **1** *vt* couper **2** *vi* se couper
intersection [ɪntə'sekʃən] *n* (**a**) *(of roads)* carrefour *m* (**b**) *Math* intersection *f*
intersperse [ɪntə'spɜːs] *vt* **to be interspersed with sth** être parsemé(e) de qch; **sunshine interspersed with showers** temps ensoleillé entrecoupé d'averses
intertwine [ɪntə'twaɪn] **1** *vt* entremêler (**with** de); **to be intertwined** *(of two things)* être entrelacés(ées) **2** *vi* s'entrelacer
interval ['ɪntəvəl] *n* intervalle *m*; *(at theatre)* entracte *m*; **at regular intervals** à intervalles réguliers; **at weekly intervals** toutes les semaines; **sunny intervals** éclaircies *fpl*
intervene [ɪntə'viːn] *vi (of person)* intervenir (**in** dans); *(of event)* survenir
intervening [ɪntə'viːnɪŋ] *adj* intermédiaire; **in the i. period** entre-temps, dans l'intervalle
intervention [ɪntə'venʃən] *n* intervention *f*
interview ['ɪntəvjuː] **1** *n (for job)* entretien *m*; *TV & Journ* interview *f* **2** *vt (for job)* faire passer un entretien à; *TV & Journ* interviewer
interviewee [ɪntəvjuː'iː] *n (for job)* candidat(e) *m,f (à qui l'on fait passer un entretien)*; *TV & Journ* personne *f* interviewée
interviewer ['ɪntəvjuːə(r)] *n (for job)* = personne qui fait passer un entretien; *TV & Journ* intervieweur(-euse) *m,f*
intestate [ɪn'testeɪt] *adj Law* **to die i.** mourir intestat
intestinal [ɪntes'taɪnəl] *adj* intestinal(e)
intestine [ɪn'testɪn] *n* intestin *m*; **large i.** gros intestin; **small i.** intestin grêle
intimacy ['ɪntɪməsɪ] *n (of relationship, atmosphere)* intimité *f*; *Euph (sexual)* relations *fpl* intimes
intimate 1 *n* ['ɪntɪmət] intime *mf* **2** *adj* ['ɪntɪmət] *(friend, restaurant)* intime; *(knowledge)* approfondi(e); *Euph* **to be i. with sb** *(sexually)* avoir des relations intimes avec qn

3 *vt* ['ɪntɪmeɪt] *Formal (hint at)* faire comprendre; *(make known)* signifier

intimately ['ɪntɪmətlɪ] *adv* intimement

intimidate [ɪn'tɪmɪdeɪt] *vt* intimider; **to i. sb into doing sth** forcer qn à faire qch en usant d'intimidation

intimidation [ɪntɪmɪ'deɪʃən] *n* intimidation *f*

into ['ɪntʊ] *prep* (**a**) *(with motion, direction)* dans; **to go i. a house** entrer dans une maison; **to get i. bed** se mettre au lit; **to crash i. sth** rentrer dans qch
 (**b**) *(expressing change)* en; **to change i. sth** se changer en qch; **to translate sth i. English** traduire qch en anglais; **to break sth i. pieces** mettre qch en morceaux
 (**c**) *(in division)* **three i. six goes twice** six divisé par trois donne deux
 (**d**) *Fam (keen on)* **to be i. jazz** être branché(e) jazz; **he's really i. my sister** il en pince vraiment pour ma sœur

intolerable [ɪn'tɒlərəbəl] *adj* intolérable

intolerance [ɪn'tɒlərəns] *n* intolérance *f*

intolerant [ɪn'tɒlərənt] *adj* **to be i. of sb** être intolérant(e) à l'égard de qn; **to be i. of sth** ne pas tolérer qch

intonation [ɪntə'neɪʃən] *n* intonation *f*

intone [ɪn'təʊn] *vt (speak)* débiter; *(of preacher)* psalmodier

intoxicated [ɪn'tɒksɪkeɪtɪd] *adj (drunk)* ivre; *Fig* **i. with power/fame** ivre de puissance/gloire

intoxication [ɪntɒksɪ'keɪʃən] *n also Fig* ivresse *f*

intractable [ɪn'træktəbəl] *adj (person)* intraitable; *(problem)* très délicat(e)

Intranet ['ɪntrənet] *n Comput* Intranet *m*

intransigence [ɪn'trænzɪdʒəns] *n Formal* intransigeance *f* (**over** sur)

intransigent [ɪn'trænzɪdʒənt] *adj Formal* intransigeant(e) (**over** sur)

intransitive [ɪn'trænzɪtɪv] *adj Gram* intransitif(ive)

intrauterine device ['ɪntrə'juːtəraɪndɪ'vaɪs] *n Med* stérilet *m*

intravenous ['ɪntrə'viːnəs] *adj Med (drip)* veineux(-euse); **i. injection** intraveineuse *f*

intravenously ['ɪntrə'viːnəslɪ] *adv Med* par voie intraveineuse

in-tray ['ɪntreɪ] *n* bac *m* du courrier à traiter

intrepid [ɪn'trepɪd] *adj* intrépide

intricacy ['ɪntrɪkəsɪ] *(pl* **intricacies**) *n* complexité *f*; **the intricacies of the law** les subtilités du droit

intricate ['ɪntrɪkət] *adj* compliqué(e)

intrigue 1 *n* ['ɪntriːg] intrigue *f*
 2 *vt* [ɪn'triːg] *(interest)* intriguer

intrinsic [ɪn'trɪnsɪk] *adj* intrinsèque

introduce [ɪntrə'djuːs] *vt* (**a**) *(person)* présenter (**to** à); **to i. oneself** se présenter; **to i. sb to sth** initier qn à qch (**b**) *(reform, practice)* introduire

introduction [ɪntrə'dʌkʃən] *n* (**a**) *(of person)* présentation *f*; **to make the introductions** faire les présentations (**b**) *(to book)* avant-propos *m inv*, introduction *f* (**c**) *(of reform, practice)* introduction *f* (**d**) *(first experience)* initiation *f* (**to** à)

introductory [ɪntrə'dʌktərɪ] *adj* d'introduction; *(price, offer)* de lancement

introspection [ɪntrə'spekʃən] *n* introspection *f*

introspective [ɪntrə'spektɪv] *adj (person)* introverti(e); *(mood)* introspectif(ive)

introvert ['ɪntrəvɜːt] *n* introverti(e) *m,f*

introverted [ɪntrə'vɜːtɪd] *adj* introverti(e)

intrude [ɪn'truːd] *vi* (**a**) *(impose oneself)* déranger (**b**) *(interfere)* **her work intrudes on her family life** son travail empiète sur sa vie de famille; **to i. on sb's privacy** s'immiscer dans la vie privée de qn

intruder [ɪn'truːdə(r)] *n* intrus(e) *m,f*

intrusion [ɪn'truːʒən] *n* intrusion *f*

intrusive [ɪn'truːsɪv] *adj* importun(e)

intuition [ɪntjuː'ɪʃən] *n* intuition *f*

intuitive [ɪn'tjuːɪtɪv] *adj* intuitif(ive)

Inuit ['ɪnʊɪt] **1** *n* Inuit *mf*
 2 *adj* inuit

inundate ['ɪnʌndeɪt] *vt* inonder (**with** de); *Fig (with phone calls, letters)* submerger (**with** de)

invade [ɪn'veɪd] *vt* envahir; **to i. sb's privacy** s'immiscer dans la vie privée de qn

invader [ɪn'veɪdə(r)] *n* envahisseur(euse) *m,f*

invalid¹ [ɪn'vælɪd] *adj (document, argument)* non valable; *(marriage)* non valide

invalid² ['ɪnvəlɪd] *n (disabled person)* invalide *mf*, infirme *mf*; *(ill person)* malade *mf*

invalidate [ɪn'vælɪdeɪt] *vt (theory)* infirmer; *(document, contract)* invalider

invaluable [ɪn'væljʊəbəl] *adj* précieux(euse)

invariable [ɪn'veərɪəbəl] *adj* invariable

invariably [ɪn'veərɪəblɪ] *adv* invariablement

invasion [ɪn'veɪʒən] *n* invasion *f*

invective [ɪn'vektɪv] *n* invectives *fpl*

inveigh [ɪn'veɪ] *vi Formal* **to i. against** invectiver contre

inveigle [ɪn'veɪgəl] *vt* **to i. sb into doing sth** entortiller qn pour qu'il fasse qch

invent [ɪn'vent] *vt* inventer

invention [ɪn'venʃən] *n* (**a**) *(action, thing invented)* invention *f* (**b**) *(creativity)* inventivité *f*

inventive [ɪn'ventɪv] *adj* inventif(ive)

inventiveness [ɪn'ventɪvnəs] *n* inventivité *f*

inventor [ɪn'ventə(r)] *n* inventeur(trice) *m,f*

inventory ['ɪnvəntərɪ] *n (pl* **inventories**) *n (list)* inventaire *m*; *(stock)* stock(s) *m(pl)*

inverse ['ɪnvɜːs] *adj* inverse

invert [ɪn'vɜːt] *vt (turn upside down)* renverser; *(reverse)* inverser, intervertir

invertebrate [ɪn'vɜːtɪbrɪt] **1** *n* invertébré *m*
 2 *adj* invertébré(e)

inverted [ɪn'vɜːtɪd] *adj (upside down)* renversé(e); *(reversed)* inversé(e); **(in) i. commas** (entre) guillemets *mpl*; **to be an i. snob** faire du snobisme à l'envers

invest [ɪn'vest] **1** *vt* (**a**) *(money, time)* investir (**in** dans) (**b**) *(right, power)* investir (**with** de)
 2 *vi* investir (**in** dans)

investigate [ɪn'vestɪgeɪt] *vt (crime)* enquêter sur; *(question)* examiner

investigation [ɪnvestɪ'geɪʃən] *n* enquête *f*

investigative [ɪn'vestɪgətɪv] *adj (journalism)* d'investigation

investigator [ɪn'vestɪgeɪtə(r)] *n* enquêteur(euse) *m,f*

investment [ɪn'vestmənt] *n* investissement *m*; **i. account** compte *m* d'investissement; **i. analyst** analyste *mf* en placements; **i. bank** banque *f* d'affaires; **i. fund** fonds *m* commun de placement, fonds d'investissement; **i. income** revenu *m* provenant d'investissements; **i. trust** société *f* de placement

investor [ɪn'vestə(r)] *n* investisseur *m*

inveterate [ɪn'vetərɪt] *adj (gambler, drunkard, liar)* invétéré(e); *(critic)* acharné(e)

invidious [ɪn'vɪdɪəs] *adj (choice, comparison)* inéquitable; *(position, task)* peu enviable

invigilate [ɪn'vɪdʒɪleɪt] *Br* **1** *vt (exam)* surveiller
2 *vi* surveiller les candidats *(à un examen)*

invigilator [ɪn'vɪdʒɪleɪtə(r)] *n Br (in exam)* surveillant(e) *m,f (des candidats à un examen)*

invigorating [ɪn'vɪgəreɪt] *adj* vivifiant(e)

invincible [ɪn'vɪnsɪbəl] *adj* invincible

inviolable [ɪn'vaɪələbəl] *adj Formal* inviolable

inviolate [ɪn'vaɪələt] *adj Formal* inviolé(e)

invisible [ɪn'vɪzɪbəl] *adj* invisible (**to** à); **i. earnings** invisibles *mpl*; **i. ink** encre *f* sympathique

invitation [ɪnvɪ'teɪʃən] *n* invitation *f*

invite 1 *n* ['ɪnvaɪt] *Fam* invit' *f*
2 *vt* [ɪn'vaɪt] (**a**) *(guest)* inviter; **to i. sb in/up** inviter qn à entrer/monter; **to i. sb to do sth** inviter qn à faire qch; **applications are invited for the post of…** ≃ nous recrutons un… (**b**) *(trouble, criticism) (of person)* aller au-devant de

inviting [ɪn'vaɪtɪŋ] *adj* attrayant(e); *(food)* appétissant(e)

in vitro fertilization [ɪn'viːtrəʊfertɪlaɪ'zeɪʃən] *n* fécondation *f* in vitro

invoice ['ɪnvɔɪs] *Com* **1** *n* facture *f*; **to make out an i.** établir une facture
2 *vt (goods)* facturer; *(person, company)* envoyer la facture à

invoke [ɪn'vəʊk] *vt Formal (God, law)* invoquer; *(spirit, feeling)* évoquer; **to i. sb's aid** appeler qn à son secours

involuntary [ɪn'vɒlʌntərɪ] *adj* involontaire

involve [ɪn'vɒlv] *vt* (**a**) *(implicate)* **to i. sb in sth** impliquer qn dans qch; **this doesn't i. you** ça ne te concerne pas (**b**) *(entail) (work, expense)* impliquer, entraîner; **my job involves a lot of travel** je suis amené à voyager pour mon travail

involved [ɪn'vɒlvd] *adj* (**a**) *(implicated)* **to be/get i. in sth** *(crime, affair)* être impliqué(e) dans qch; **to be i. in an accident** avoir un accident; **to be i. in teaching/banking** être dans l'enseignement/la banque; **50 people are i. in the project** 50 personnes ont pris part au projet; **the police became i.** la police est intervenue; **don't get i.!** ne te mêle pas de ça!; **how much money is i.?** de combien d'argent s'agit-il?
(**b**) *(emotionally)* **to be/get i. with sb** sortir avec qn; **I don't want to get i.** je ne veux pas m'engager
(**c**) *(engrossed)* **to get i. in a book/film** s'absorber dans un livre/film; **I'm getting really i. in this job** je commence à trouver ce travail vraiment intéressant
(**d**) *(complicated)* compliqué(e)

involvement [ɪn'vɒlvmənt] *n* (**a**) *(participation)* participation *f* (**in** à) (**b**) *(commitment)* engagement *m* (**in** dans)

invulnerable [ɪn'vʌlnərəbəl] *adj* invulnérable (**to** à)

inward ['ɪnwəd] *adj* (**a**) *(thoughts, feelings)* intime (**b**) *(movement)* vers l'intérieur; *Econ* **i. investment** investissements *mpl* étrangers

inward-looking ['ɪnwəd'lʊkɪŋ] *adj* replié(e) sur soi-même

inwards ['ɪnwədz] *adv* vers l'intérieur

in-your-face ['ɪnjɔː'feɪs] *adj Fam (film, advertisement)* cru(e); *(attitude, personality)* agressif(ive)

iodine ['aɪədiːn] *n Chem* iode *m*; *(antiseptic)* teinture *f* d'iode

ion ['aɪən] *n* ion *m*

Ionian [aɪ'əʊnɪən] *n* **the I. (Sea)** la mer Ionienne

ionize ['aɪənaɪz] *vt* ioniser

iota [aɪ'əʊtə] *n* iota *m*; **she hadn't changed one i.** elle n'avait pas du tout changé; **not an i. of truth** pas une once de vérité

IOU [aɪəʊ'juː] *n (= I owe you)* reconnaissance *f* de dette

IP [aɪ'piː] *n Comput (abbr* **Internet Protocol**) **IP address** adresse *f* IP

IPA [aɪpiː'eɪ] *n (abbr* **International Phonetic Alphabet**) API *m*

IQ [aɪ'kjuː] *n (abbr* **intelligence quotient**) QI *m*

IRA [aɪɑː'reɪ] *n (abbr* **Irish Republican Army**) IRA *f*

IRA

L'IRA est une organisation qui lutte pour la réunification de l'Irlande. En 1969, elle s'est scindée en deux factions: la "Provisional IRA", qui a recours à la violence, et la "Official IRA", qui privilégiait un réglement politique du conflit en Irlande du Nord. En 1995, au début du processus de paix qui a abouti à l'accord de 1998 (le "Good Friday Agreement") la "Provisional IRA" a déclaré un cessez-le-feu. Cependant, quelques groupes dissidents, notamment la "Continuity IRA" et la "Real IRA", ont poursuivi les actes terroristes.

Iran [ɪ'rɑːn] *n* l'Iran *m*

Iranian [ɪ'reɪnɪən] **1** *n* (**a**) *(person)* Iranien(enne) *m,f* (**b**) *(language)* iranien *m*
2 *adj* iranien(enne)

Iraq [ɪ'rɑːk] *n* l'Irak *m*

Iraqi [ɪ'rɑːkɪ] **1** *n* Irakien(enne) *m,f,* Iraquien(enne) *m,f*
2 *adj* irakien(enne), iraquien(enne)

irascible [ɪ'ræsɪbəl] *adj (person)* irascible; *(temperament)* colérique

irate [aɪ'reɪt] *adj* furieux(euse)

IRC [aɪɑː'siː] *n Comput (abbr* **Internet Relay Chat**) IRC, service *m* de bavardage Internet

ire ['aɪə(r)] *n Lit* courroux *m*

Ireland ['aɪələnd] *n* l'Irlande *f*

iris ['aɪrɪs] *n* iris *m*

Irish ['aɪrɪʃ] **1** *npl (people)* **the I.** les Irlandais *mpl*
2 *n (language)* irlandais *m*
3 *adj* irlandais(e); **I. coffee** Irish coffee *m*; **the I. Sea** la mer d'Irlande; **I. stew** = ragoût de mouton, aux pommes de terre et aux oignons

Irishman ['aɪrɪʃmən] *n* Irlandais *m*

Irishwoman ['aɪrɪʃwʊmən] *n* Irlandaise *f*

irk [ɜːk] *vt* agacer

irksome ['ɜːksəm] *adj* agaçant(e)

iron ['aɪən] **1** *n* (**a**) *(metal, golf club)* fer *m*; **made of i.** en fer; **to have an i. constitution** avoir une santé de fer; **an i. will** une volonté de fer; **i. discipline** discipline *f* de fer; **the I. Age** l'âge *m* de fer; **the I. Curtain** le rideau de fer; **i. lung** poumon *m* d'acier; **i. ore** minerai *m* de fer (**b**) *(for clothes)* fer *m* (à repasser); *Fig* **to have several irons in the fire** avoir plusieurs fers au feu
2 *vt & vi (clothes)* repasser

▸**iron out** *vt sep (difficulty)* aplanir; *(problem)* résoudre

ironic(al) [aɪ'rɒnɪk(əl)] *adj* ironique

ironing ['aɪənɪŋ] *n* repassage *m*; **to do the i.** repasser, faire le repassage; **i. board** planche *f ou* table *f* à repasser

ironmonger ['aɪənmʌŋgə(r)] *n Br* quincaillier(ère) *m,f*; **i.'s (shop)** quincaillerie *f*

irony ['aɪrənɪ] (*pl* **ironies**) *n* ironie *f*; **the i. is that...** ce qu'il y a d'ironique, c'est que...

irrational [ɪ'ræʃənəl] *adj* irrationnel(elle)

irreconcilable [ɪrekən'saɪləbəl] *adj (enemy)* irréconciliable; *(hatred)* implacable; *(belief, idea)* incompatible, inconciliable

irredeemable [ɪrɪ'diːməbəl] *adj (fault)* irréparable; *(situation)* irrémédiable

irrefutable [ɪrɪ'fjuːtəbəl] *adj* irréfutable

irregular [ɪ'regjʊlə(r)] *adj* irrégulier(ère)

irregularity [ɪregjʊ'lærɪtɪ] (*pl* **irregularities**) *n* irrégularité *f*

irrelevance [ɪ'reləvəns], **irrelevancy** [ɪ'reləvənsɪ] *n (of remark, advice)* manque *m* d'à-propos

irrelevant [ɪ'reləvənt] *adj (remark, advice)* hors de propos; **that's i.** cela n'a rien à voir (avec la question)

irreligious [ɪrɪ'lɪdʒəs] *adj* irréligieux(euse)

irremediable [ɪrɪ'miːdɪəbəl] *adj Formal (situation, loss)* irrémédiable; *(mistake)* irréparable

irreparable [ɪ'repərəbəl] *adj* irréparable

irreplaceable [ɪrɪ'pleɪsəbəl] *adj* irremplaçable

irrepressible [ɪrɪ'presɪbəl] *adj (urge)* irrépressible; *(good humour)* à toute épreuve; **he's i.** rien n'entame sa bonne humeur

irreproachable [ɪrɪ'prəʊtʃəbəl] *adj* irréprochable

irresistible [ɪrɪ'zɪstɪbəl] *adj* irrésistible

irresolute [ɪ'rezəluːt] *adj* irrésolu(e), indécis(e)

irrespective of [ɪrɪ'spektɪvəv] *prep* indépendamment de, sans tenir compte de

irresponsible [ɪrɪ'spɒnsɪbəl] *adj* irresponsable

irretrievable [ɪrɪ'triːvəbəl] *adj (loss)* irrémédiable; *(money)* irrécupérable; *(mistake, situation)* irréparable

irreverent [ɪ'revərənt] *adj* irrévérencieux(euse)

irreversible [ɪrɪ'vɜːsɪbəl] *adj (decision, process)* irréversible

irrevocable [ɪ'revəkəbəl] *adj* irrévocable

irrigate ['ɪrɪgeɪt] *vt* irriguer

irrigation [ɪrɪ'geɪʃən] *n* irrigation *f*; **i. canal** *or* **ditch** canal *m* d'irrigation

irritable ['ɪrɪtəbəl] *adj* irritable; **i. bowel syndrome** colopathie *f* fonctionnelle

irritant ['ɪrɪtənt] *n (to eyes, skin)* irritant *m*; *(to person, government)* empêcheur(euse) *m,f* de tourner en rond

irritate ['ɪrɪteɪt] *vt (annoy)* agacer, irriter; *Med* irriter

irritating ['ɪrɪteɪtɪŋ] *adj* agaçant(e), irritant(e)

irritation [ɪrɪ'teɪʃən] *n* agacement *m*, irritation *f*; *Med* irritation *f*

IRS [aɪɑː'res] *n Am (abbr* **Internal Revenue Service**) **the I.** le fisc

IS [aɪ'es] *n (abbr* **information system**) système *m* informatique

is [ɪz] *3rd pers singular of* **be**

ISA ['aɪsə] *n Br Fin (abbr* **individual savings account**) ≃ PEA *m*, plan *m* d'épargne en actions

ISBN [aɪesbiː'en] *n (abbr* **International Standard Book Number**) ISBN *m*

Islam ['ɪzlɑːm] *n* l'Islam *m*

Islamic [ɪz'læmɪk] *adj* islamique

island ['aɪlənd] *n* île *f*; *(small)* îlot *m*; *(in road)* refuge *m*

islander ['aɪləndə(r)] *n (in general)* insulaire *mf*; *(of specific island)* habitant(e) *m,f* de l'île

isle [aɪl] *n* île *f*; **the I. of Man** l'île de Man; **the I. of Wight** l'île de Wight

isn't ['ɪzənt] = **is not**

ISO [aɪes'əʊ] *n (abbr* **International Standards Organization**) ISO *f*

isobar ['aɪsəʊbɑː(r)] *n* isobare *f*

isolate ['aɪsəleɪt] *vt* isoler (**from** de)

isolated ['aɪsəleɪtɪd] *adj* isolé(e)

isolation [aɪsə'leɪʃən] *n* isolement *m*; **in i. (from)** isolément (de); **i. ward** salle *f* des contagieux

isotope ['aɪsəʊtəʊp] *n Phys* isotope *m*

ISP [aɪes'piː] *n Comput (abbr* **Internet Service Provider**) fournisseur *m* d'accès à l'Internet

Israel ['ɪzreɪəl] *n* Israël *m*

Israeli [ɪz'reɪlɪ] **1** *n* Israélien(enne) *m,f*
2 *adj* israélien(enne)

Israelite ['ɪzrəlaɪt] *n Hist* Israélite *mf*

issue ['ɪsjuː, 'ɪʃuː] **1** *n* (**a**) *(topic)* problème *m*, question *f*; **the issues of the day** les questions du jour; **that's not the i.** ce n'est pas (là) le problème; **to avoid the i.** esquiver le problème; **to confuse the i.** compliquer les choses; **to make an i. of sth** faire toute une affaire de qch; **at i.** en cause; **to take i. with sb** exprimer son désaccord avec qn (**b**) *(of banknotes, stamps)* émission *f* (**c**) *(of magazine)* numéro *m*
2 *vt (banknote, stamp)* émettre; *(order)* donner; **to i. sb with sth** délivrer qch à qn; **to i. a statement** faire une déclaration; *Law* **to i. a summons** notifier une citation
3 *vi Formal (of blood, smoke, water)* s'échapper (**from** de); *(of noise)* provenir (**from** de)

Istanbul [ɪstæn'bʊl] *n* Istanbul

isthmus ['ɪsməs] *n* isthme *m*

IT [aɪ'tiː] *n Comput (abbr* **information technology**) l'informatique *f*

it [ɪt] *pron* (**a**) *(subject)* il (elle) *m,f*; **where's the book? – it's on the shelf** où est le livre? – il est sur l'étagère; **put the TV on – it's not working** allume la télé – elle est en panne; **it's a big house** c'est une grande maison; **it's the best film I've ever seen** c'est le meilleur film que j'aie jamais vu
(**b**) *(direct object)* le (la) *m,f*; **I can do it** je peux le/la faire; **I saw it** je l'ai vu
(**c**) *(indirect object)* lui; **give it something to eat** donne-lui à manger
(**d**) *(prepositional object)* **on it** dessus; **under it** dessous; **beside it** à côté; **I forgot about it** j'ai oublié
(**e**) *(as impersonal subject)* **it's raining** il pleut; **it's ten o'clock** il est dix heures; **it's cold today** il fait froid aujourd'hui; **it's impossible to work in this heat** il est impossible de travailler avec cette chaleur; **it's me** c'est moi
(**f**) *(as complement of verb* **to be**) **that's it** *(that's all)* c'est tout

Italian [ɪ'tælɪən] **1** *n* (**a**) *(person)* Italien(enne) *m,f* (**b**) *(language)* italien *m*; **I. class/teacher** classe *f*/professeur *m* d'italien
2 *adj* italien(enne)

italic [ɪ'tælɪk] *Typ* **1** *n* **italic(s)** italique *m*
2 *adj* italique

Italy ['ɪtəlɪ] *n* l'Italie *f*

itch [ɪtʃ] **1** *n* démangeaison *f*; *Fig* **to have an i. to do sth** brûler d'envie de faire qch
2 *vi (of person)* éprouver des démangeaisons; **my hand itches** j'ai la main qui me démange; *Fig* **to be itching to do sth** brûler d'envie de faire qch

itchy ['ɪtʃɪ] *adj* **I've got an i. hand, my hand's i.** j'ai la main qui me démange; *Fig* **to have i. feet** avoir la bougeotte

it'd ['ɪtəd] = **it would, it had**

item ['aɪtəm] *n (in collection, list)* article *m; (in news)* entrefilet *m; (longer)* article *m;* **an i. of clothing** un vêtement; **personal items** objets *mpl* personnels; *Fam* **they're an i.** ils sortent ensemble

itemize ['aɪtəmaɪz] *vt* détailler

iterative ['ɪtərətɪv] *adj Comput* itératif(ive)

itinerant [ɪ'tɪnərənt] *adj (preacher)* itinérant(e); *(salesman, musician)* ambulant(e)

itinerary [aɪ'tɪnərərɪ] *(pl* **itineraries***) n* itinéraire *m*

it'll ['ɪtəl] = **it will**

ITN [aɪtiː'en] *n Br (abbr* **Independent Television News**) = service produisant le journal télévisé d'ITV

its [ɪts] *possessive adj* **(a)** *(singular)* son (sa); *(plural)* ses; **i. bone** son os; **i. litter** sa litière; **i. kittens** ses châtons **(b)** *(for parts of body)* **the bear hurt i. paw** l'ours s'est blessé à la patte

it's [ɪts] = **it is, it has**

itself [ɪt'self] *pron* **(a)** *(reflexive)* **the dog hurt i.** le chien s'est blessé **(b)** *(emphatic)* **this method is simplicity i.** cette méthode est la simplicité même; **the town i. isn't very interesting** la ville (elle-)même n'est pas d'un grand intérêt **(c)** *(after preposition)* **by i.** tout(e) seul(e); **in i.** en soi

ITV [aɪti:'vi:] *n Br (abbr* **Independent Television**) = chaîne de télévision privée britannique

IUD [aɪju:'di:] *n Med (abbr* **intra-uterine device**) stérilet *m*

I've [aɪv] = **I have**

IVF [aɪvi:'ef] *n Med (abbr* **in vitro fertilization**) FIV *f*

ivory ['aɪvərɪ] *n* ivoire *m;* **the I. Coast** la Côte d'Ivoire; *Fig* **i. tower** tour *f* d'ivoire

ivy ['aɪvɪ] *n (plant)* lierre *m; Am* **I. League** = ensemble des huit universités les plus prestigieuses du nord-est des États-Unis

---

Ivy League

On désigne ainsi un groupe de huit universités du nord-est des États-Unis: Brown, Columbia, Cornell, Dartmouth, Harvard, l'Université de Pennsylvanie, Princeton et Yale. Ces universités se caractérisent par une forte proportion d'étudiants de troisième cycle, des moyens financiers importants et la réputation d'excellence de leurs universitaires. Si à l'origine, "Ivy League" servait à promouvoir les rencontres sportives entre les universités qui la composaient, elle est depuis devenue synonyme d'un enseignement prestigieux très compétitif, réservé à l'élite.

J

J, j [dʒeɪ] *n (letter)* J, j *m inv*

jab [dʒæb] **1** *n* (**a**) *(with elbow, finger)* coup *m*; *(in boxing)* direct *m* (**b**) *Br Fam (injection)* piqûre *f*

2 *vt (pt & pp* **jabbed***)* **he jabbed her in the leg with a pencil** il lui a enfoncé un crayon dans la jambe; **to j. a finger at sb** agiter son doigt sous le nez de qn

jabber ['dʒæbə(r)] *vi Fam (talk unclearly)* marmonner; *(chatter)* jacasser

Jack [dʒæk] *n* **J. Frost** le Bonhomme Hiver; *Br Fam* **I'm all right, J.** moi, ça va, merci; *Br Fam* **before you could say J. Robinson** avant d'avoir pu dire "ouf"

jack [dʒæk] *n* (**a**) *(person)* **every man j. of them** absolument tout le monde; **j. of all trades** touche-à-tout *mf* (**b**) *(for car)* cric *m* (**c**) *(in cards)* valet *m* (**d**) *(electric plug)* prise *f ou* fiche *f* mâle

▸**jack in** *vt sep Br Fam* plaquer

▸**jack off** *vi Vulg* se branler

▸**jack up** *vt sep Fam (price, salaries)* augmenter

jackal ['dʒækəl] *n* chacal *m*

jackass ['dʒækæs] *n also Fig* âne *m*

jackboot ['dʒækbuːt] *n* botte *f* de cavalier; *Fig* **under the j. of** sous la botte de

jackdaw ['dʒækdɔː] *n* choucas *m*

jacket ['dʒækɪt] *n (coat)* veste *f*; *(of boiler)* chemise *f*, enveloppe *f*; **j. potatoes** pommes de terre *fpl* en robe des champs *ou* en robe de chambre

jackhammer ['dʒækhæmə(r)] *n* marteau-piqueur *m*

jack-in-the-box ['dʒækɪnðəbɒks] *n* diable *m* à ressort

jackknife ['dʒæknaɪf] **1** *n (pl* **jackknives***)* couteau *m* de poche

2 *vi (of articulated lorry)* **the lorry jackknifed** la remorque du camion s'est soudain mise en travers de la route

jack-o'-lantern ['dʒækəˈlæntən] *n Am* = lanterne faite dans une citrouille sur laquelle on a creusé un visage

jackpot ['dʒækpɒt] *n (in lottery)* gros lot *m*; **to hit** *or* **win the j.** gagner le gros lot

jack rabbit *n* = gros lièvre commun en Amérique du Nord

Jacobean [dʒækəˈbɪən] *adj* = de l'époque de Jacques 1ᵉʳ (1603–1625)

Jacobite ['dʒækəbaɪt] *n & adj* Jacobite *mf*

Jacuzzi® [dʒəˈkuːzɪ] *n* Jacuzzi® *m*

jade [dʒeɪd] **1** *n (stone, colour)* jade *m*

2 *adj (colour)* **j.(-green)** vert jade *inv*

jaded ['dʒeɪdɪd] *adj (tired)* las (lasse); *(bored)* blasé(e); **to be j. with sth** être las de qch; **to have a j. palate** avoir le palais blasé

Jag [dʒæg] *n Fam (car)* Jaguar *m*

jag [dʒæg] *n Fam* (**a**) **to go on a (drinking) j.** prendre une cuite; **to have a crying j.** avoir une crise de larmes (**b**) *Scot (injection)* piqûre *f*

jagged ['dʒægɪd] *adj (coastline, mountain top)* déchiqueté(e), découpé(e); *(blade)* ébréché(e)

jaguar ['dʒægjʊə(r), *Am* 'dʒægwɑː(r)] *n Zool* jaguar *m*

jail [dʒeɪl] **1** *n* prison *f*; **to be in j.** être en prison; **to go to j.** aller en prison

2 *vt* emprisonner, mettre en prison

jailbird ['dʒeɪlbɜːd] *n Fam (in prison)* taulard(e) *m,f*; *(recidivist)* cheval *m* de retour

jailbreak ['dʒeɪlbreɪk] *n* évasion *f*

jailer ['dʒeɪlə(r)] *n* geôlier(ère) *m,f*

jailhouse ['dʒeɪlhaʊs] *n Am* prison *f*

jailor = jailer

Jakarta [dʒəˈkɑːtə] *n* Djakarta

jalop(p)y [dʒəˈlɒpɪ] *(pl* **jalop(p)ies***)* *n Fam* vieille guimbarde *f*, vieux tacot *m*

jam¹ [dʒæm] **1** *n* (**a**) *(crowd) (of people)* foule *f*; *(of traffic)* encombrement *m* (**b**) *Fam (difficult situation)* **to be in/get into a (bit of a) j.** être/se fourrer dans le pétrin (**c**) *(improvised performance)* **j. (session)** jam-session *f*, bœuf *m*

2 *vt (pt & pp* **jammed***)* (**a**) *(pack tightly) (objects)* entasser (**into** dans); *(container)* bourrer (**with** de); **people/cars jammed the street** la rue était noire de monde/embouteillée (**b**) *(immobilize) (drawer, mechanism)* coincer, bloquer; *(radio broadcast, station)* brouiller; *(switchboard)* saturer

3 *vi* (**a**) *(of drawer, mechanism)* se coincer, se bloquer (**b**) *(of crowd)* s'entasser (**into** dans) (**c**) *(of musicians)* improviser

▸**jam on** *vt sep* **to j. on the brakes** écraser la pédale de frein

jam² *n (fruit preserve)* confiture *f*; **j. tart** tarte *f* à la confiture

Jamaica [dʒəˈmeɪkə] *n* la Jamaïque

Jamaican [dʒəˈmeɪkən] **1** *n* Jamaïcain(e) *m,f*

2 *adj* jamaïcain(e)

jamb [dʒæm] *n* montant *m*

jamboree [dʒæmbəˈriː] *n (scouts' meeting)* jamboree *m*; *Fam (celebration)* fête *f*

jamming ['dʒæmɪŋ] *n (of radio broadcast, station)* brouillage *m*

jammy ['dʒæmɪ] *adj* (**a**) *(covered with jam)* plein(e) de confiture (**b**) *Br Fam (lucky)* verni(e)

jam-packed ['dʒæmˈpækd] *adj* plein(e) à craquer; *(street)* noir(e) de monde, bondé(e)

Jan *(abbr* **January***)* janvier

jangle ['dʒæŋgəl] **1** n cliquetis m
  2 vt faire cliqueter
  3 vi cliqueter; Fig **her voice made his nerves j.** sa voix lui mettait les nerfs en pelote

janitor ['dʒænɪtə(r)] n Am & Scot (caretaker) concierge mf

January ['dʒænjʊərɪ] n janvier m; see also **May**

Jap [dʒæp] n very Fam Jap mf, = terme raciste désignant un Japonais

Japan [dʒə'pæn] n le Japon

Japanese [dʒæpə'niːz] **1** npl (people) **the J.** les Japonais mpl
  2 n (**a**) (person) Japonais(e) m,f (**b**) (language) japonais m; **J. class/teacher** classe f/professeur m de japonais
  3 adj japonais(e)

jape [dʒeɪp] n blague f

jar¹ [dʒɑː(r)] **1** n (jolt) choc m, secousse f
  2 vt (pt & pp **jarred**) also Fig secouer; **someone jarred my elbow** quelqu'un m'a cogné le coude
  3 vi (**a**) (make unpleasant sound) rendre un son discordant; **to j. on the ears** écorcher les oreilles; **to j. on the nerves** taper sur les nerfs (**b**) (of colours) jurer; (of ideas) être en contradiction

jar² n (container) pot m; (earthenware) jarre f; Br Fam **to have a j.** prendre un pot

jargon ['dʒɑːgən] n Pej jargon m

jarring ['dʒɑːrɪŋ] adj (noise, voice) discordant(e); (blow) qui ébranle tout le corps

jasmine ['dʒæzmɪn] n jasmin m

jaundice ['dʒɔːndɪs] n jaunisse f

jaundiced ['dʒɔːndɪst] adj Fig (attitude, view) aigu(ë), amer(ère); **to take a j. view of sth** voir qch d'un mauvais œil

jaunt [dʒɔːnt] n excursion f, sortie f

jauntiness ['dʒɔːntɪnɪs] n (cheerfulness) enjouement m; (carefreeness) insouciance f

jaunty ['dʒɔːntɪ] adj (cheerful) enjoué(e); (carefree) insouciant(e)

Java¹ ['dʒɑːvə] n Geog Java

Java²® ['dʒɑːvə] n Comput Java® m; **J. script** (langage m) Javascript® m

javelin ['dʒævlɪn] n javelot m

jaw [dʒɔː] **1** n mâchoire f; **jaws** (of animal) gueule f; **the jaws of death** les griffes fpl de la mort
  2 vi Fam (chat) papoter

jawbone ['dʒɔːbəʊn] n maxillaire m

jawbreaker ['dʒɔːbreɪkə(r)] n Fam (word) mot m imprononçable; (name) nom m à coucher dehors

jay [dʒeɪ] n geai m

jaywalker ['dʒeɪwɔːkə(r)] n = piéton qui traverse en dehors des passages cloutés

jaywalking ['dʒeɪwɔːkɪŋ] n = fait de traverser en dehors des passages cloutés

jazz [dʒæz] n jazz m; Fam **and all that j.** et tout le tremblement ou le bazar

▶**jazz up** vt sep Fam (enliven) (clothes, room, style) égayer; (party) animer; (taste) relever

jazzy ['dʒæzɪ] adj (tune) jazzy inv; (clothes, pattern) aux couleurs vives

jealous ['dʒeləs] adj jaloux(ouse); **to be j. of sb** être jaloux de qn

jealously ['dʒeləslɪ] adv jalousement; **to guard sth j.** veiller jalousement sur qch

jealousy ['dʒeləsɪ] n jalousie f

jeans [dʒiːnz] npl jeans m

Jeep® [dʒiːp] n Jeep® f

jeer [dʒɪə(r)] **1** n (mocking) moquerie f; **the jeers of the crowd** (booing) les huées fpl de la foule
  2 vt (boo) huer; (mock) se moquer de
  3 vi **to j. at sb/sth** (boo) huer qn/qch; (mock) se moquer de qn/qch

jeering ['dʒɪərɪŋ] **1** n (booing) huées fpl; (mocking) moqueries fpl
  2 adj railleur(euse), moqueur(euse)

jeez [dʒiːz] exclam Fam mince alors!

Jehovah [dʒɪ'həʊvə] n Jéhovah; **J.'s Witness** témoin m de Jéhovah

jell [dʒel] vi (of liquid) se gélifier; Fig (of ideas, plans) prendre forme; Fig (of team) se souder

jelly ['dʒelɪ] (pl **jellies**) n (dessert, jam) gelée f; Br **j. baby** = bonbon à base de gelatine, en forme de petit bonhomme

jellybean ['dʒelɪbiːn] n = bonbon couvert de sucre, en forme de haricot

jellyfish ['dʒelɪfɪʃ] n méduse f

jemmy ['dʒemɪ] (pl **jemmies**) n Br pince-monseigneur f

jeopardize ['dʒepədaɪz] vt compromettre; (life) mettre en danger

jeopardy ['dʒepədɪ] n **in j.** en danger, en péril; **to put sb/sth in j.** mettre qn/qch en danger ou en péril

jerk¹ [dʒɜːk] **1** n (sudden pull) secousse f, coup m sec; **to give sth a j.** tirer sur qch d'un coup sec
  2 vt (pull) tirer brusquement; (in order to move) déplacer par à-coups
  3 vi **to j. forward** (of car) faire un bond en avant; (of head) partir en avant; **to j. to a halt** s'arrêter avec des soubresauts

jerk² n Fam (person) abruti(e) m,f

▶**jerk off** vi Vulg (masturbate) se branler

jerkily ['dʒɜːkɪlɪ] adv de manière saccadée

jerky ['dʒɜːkɪ] adj (movement) saccadé(e); (style) haché(e)

jerrican ['dʒerɪkæn] n jerrican m

jerry-built ['dʒerɪbɪlt] adj construit(e) à la va-vite

Jersey ['dʒɜːzɪ] n (island) Jersey; **J. (cow)** jersiaise f

jersey ['dʒɜːzɪ] (pl **jerseys**) n (garment) pull(-over) m, tricot m

Jerusalem [dʒə'ruːsələm] n Jérusalem; **J. artichoke** topinambour m

jest [dʒest] **1** n plaisanterie f; **in j.** pour plaisanter
  2 vi plaisanter

jester ['dʒestə(r)] n farceur(euse) m,f; Hist (court) **j.** fou m (du roi)

jesting ['dʒestɪŋ] adj (remark) pour rire; (tone) de la plaisanterie

Jesuit ['dʒezjʊɪt] n jésuite m

Jesuitical [dʒezjʊ'ɪtɪkəl] adj Pej (argument, reasoning) de jésuite

Jesus ['dʒiːzəs] **1** n Jésus m; **J. Christ** Jésus-Christ
  2 exclam Fam **J. (Christ)!** nom de Dieu!

jet¹ [dʒet] **1** n (**a**) (plane) jet m, avion m à réaction; **j. engine** réacteur m, moteur m à réaction; **j. fighter** chasseur m à réaction; **j. lag** fatigue f due au décalage horaire; **j. propulsion** propulsion f par réaction; **the j. set** la jet-set; **j. ski** scooter m des mers, jet-ski m (**b**) (nozzle, of liquid) jet m
  2 vi (pt & pp **jetted**) Fam (travel by plane) **to j. in** venir

en avion; **to j. off** s'envoler; **to j. around the world** passer son temps dans les avions

jet² **1** *n (stone)* jais *m*
2 *adj* **j. (black)** de jais

jet-lagged ['dʒetlægd] *adj* fatigué(e) par le décalage horaire

jet-powered [dʒet'paʊəd], **jet-propelled** [dʒetprə-'peld] *adj* à réaction

jettison ['dʒetɪsən] *vt (cargo)* jeter à la mer *ou* par-dessus bord; *(plan, tradition)* abandonner

jetty ['dʒetɪ] *(pl* **jetties)** *n* jetée *f*; *(for landing)* embarcadère *m*

Jew [dʒuː] *n* Juif (Juive) *m,f*

jewel ['dʒuːəl] *n (gem, piece of jewellery)* bijou *m*; *Fig (person)* perle *f*

jeweller, *Am* **jeweler** ['dʒuːələ(r)] *n* bijoutier(ère) *m,f*; **j.'s (shop)** bijouterie *f*

jewellery, *Am* **jewelry** ['dʒuːəlrɪ] *n* bijoux *mpl*; **a piece of j.** un bijou

Jewess ['dʒuːɪs] *n Old-fashioned* Juive *f*

Jewish ['dʒuːɪʃ] *adj* juif (juive)

Jewry ['dʒuːərɪ] *n* communauté *f* juive

jib¹ [dʒɪb] *n* **(a)** *(sail)* foc *m* **(b)** *(of crane)* flèche *f* **(b)** *(idioms)* **I don't like the cut of his j.** je n'aime pas son allure

jib² *(pt & pp* **jibbed)** *vi* **to j. at sth/at doing sth** rechigner à qch/à faire qch

jibe [dʒaɪb] **1** *n* moquerie *f*
2 *vi* **to j. at sb** se moquer de qn

jiffy ['dʒɪfɪ] *n Fam* **in a j.** dans un instant, tout de suite

Jiffy bag® ['dʒɪfɪbæg] *n Br* enveloppe *f* matelassée

jig [dʒɪg] **1** *n (dance, music)* gigue *f*
2 *vi (pt & pp* **jigged)** *(dance)* danser la gigue

jigger ['dʒɪgə(r)] *vt Fam (TV, microwave)* bousiller; **to j. one's back/knee** s'esquinter le dos/genou

jiggered ['dʒɪgəd] *adj Fam (TV, microwave)* bousillé(e); *(back, knee)* esquinté(e)

jiggery-pokery ['dʒɪgərɪ'pəʊkərɪ] *n Br Fam* micmac *m*

jiggle ['dʒɪgəl] **1** *vt* secouer rapidement
2 *vi* remuer dans tous les sens

▸**jiggle about, jiggle around** *vt sep & vi* = **jiggle**

jigsaw ['dʒɪgsɔː] *n* **(a)** *(saw)* scie *f* sauteuse **(b)** *(game)* **j. (puzzle)** puzzle *m*

jihad [dʒɪ'hæd] *n* djihad *m*

jilt [dʒɪlt] *vt (lover)* plaquer

jingle ['dʒɪŋgəl] **1** *n* **(a)** *(of bells, coins)* tintement *m*; *(of keys)* cliquetis *m* **(b)** *(catchy tune)* jingle *m*; *Rad & TV (in advertisement)* jingle *m, Offic* signal *m*
2 *vt (bells, coins)* faire tinter; *(keys)* faire cliqueter
3 *vi (of bells, coins)* tinter; *(of keys)* cliqueter

jingoism ['dʒɪŋgəʊɪzəm] *n Pej* chauvinisme *m*

jingoistic ['dʒɪŋgəʊ'ɪstɪk] *adj Pej* chauvin(e)

jinx [dʒɪŋks] *Fam* **1** *n (spell, curse)* (mauvais) sort *m*; **to put a j. on sb/sth** jeter un sort à qn/qch
2 *vt* **to be jinxed** avoir la poisse

JIT [dʒɪt] *adj Com (abbr* **just in time)** juste à temps

jitters ['dʒɪtəz] *npl Fam* **to have** *or* **get the j.** être à cran

jittery ['dʒɪtərɪ] *adj Fam* à cran

jive [dʒaɪv] **1** *n (music, dance)* swing *m*
2 *vi (dance)* danser le swing

Jnr *(abbr* **Junior) Thomas Smith, J.** Thomas Smith fils

job [dʒɒb] *n* **(a)** *(employment, post)* travail *m*, emploi *m*; **to be out of a j.** être sans travail *ou* emploi; *Br*

Fam **it's jobs for the boys** on place d'abord les petits copains; **j. creation** création *f* d'emplois; **j. description** description *f* de poste; **to go j. hunting** chercher du travail; **j. losses** suppressions *fpl* d'emplois; **j. offer** offre *f* d'emploi; **j. opportunities** débouchés *mpl*; **j. satisfaction** satisfaction *f* dans le travail; **j. security** sécurité *f* de l'emploi; **j. sharing** partage *m* de poste; **j. title** fonction *f*

(b) *(piece of work, task)* tâche *f*; **to do a good j.** faire du beau travail; *Fig* **to do the j.** *(serve purpose)* convenir, faire l'affaire; **it was quite a j. getting her to come** la convaincre de venir n'a pas été une mince affaire; *Com* **j. lot** lot *m*

(c) *(responsibility, duty)* travail *m*; **to have the j. of doing sth** être chargé(e) de faire qch

(d) *Fam (crime)* coup *m*

(e) *(idioms) Br* **it's a good j. (that)...!** heureusement que...!; **that's just the j.!** c'est juste ce qu'il faut!

jobbing ['dʒɒbɪŋ] *adj Br (carpenter, electrician)* à la tâche *ou* pièce

Jobcentre ['dʒɒbsentə(r)] *n Br* ≃ agence *f* nationale pour l'emploi, ANPE *f*

jobless ['dʒɒblɪs] **1** *npl* **the j.** les sans-emploi *mpl*
2 *adj* sans emploi

job-share ['dʒɒbʃeə(r)] **1** *n* poste *m* partagé
2 *vi* partager un poste

jockey ['dʒɒkɪ] **1** *n (pl* **jockeys)** jockey *m*
2 *vi* **to j. for position** jouer des coudes

jockstrap ['dʒɒkstræp] *n* slip *m* à coquille

jocular ['dʒɒkjʊlə(r)] *adj* enjoué(e)

jodhpurs ['dʒɒdpəz] *npl* jodhpurs *mpl*

Joe [dʒəʊ] *n Am Fam* **he's an ordinary J.** c'est un mec ordinaire; *Br* **J. Bloggs, J. Public** Monsieur Tout-le-monde

jog [dʒɒg] **1** *n* **(a)** *(push)* secousse *f*; *(with elbow)* coup *m* de coude; **to give sb's memory a j.** rafraîchir la mémoire de qn **(b)** *(run)* course *f* (à petites foulées); **to break into a j.** se mettre à courir (à petites foulées); **to go for a j.** aller faire un jogging
2 *vt (pt & pp* **jogged)** *(push)* pousser; **to j. sb's elbow** donner un coup de coude à qn; **to j. sb's memory** rafraîchir la mémoire à qn
3 *vi (run)* faire du jogging; **to go jogging** aller faire un jogging

▸**jog along** *vi (run)* courir à petites foulées; *Fig (in job, life)* aller son petit bonhomme de chemin

jogger ['dʒɒgə(r)] *n* joggeur(euse) *m,f*

jogging ['dʒɒgɪŋ] *n* jogging *m*; **j. bottoms** pantalon *m* de jogging; **j. suit** tenue *f* de jogging

joggle ['dʒɒgəl] *vt* secouer légèrement

Johannesburg [dʒəʊ'hænɪzbɜːg] *n* Johannesburg *m*

john [dʒɒn] *n Am Fam (lavatory)* petit coin *m*

John Bull ['dʒɒn'bʊl] *n (Englishman)* l'Anglais *m* moyen; *(England)* l'Angleterre *f*

join [dʒɔɪn] **1** *n* raccord *m*; *(in fabric)* couture *f*
2 *vt* **(a)** *(unite, connect)* relier; *(planks)* joindre; **to j. two things together** relier une chose à une autre; **to j. battle** engager le combat; **to j. forces (with sb)** s'unir (à qn)

(b) *(club, political party)* adhérer à; *(army)* s'engager dans; *(discussion, game)* se joindre à; **to j. a union** se syndiquer; **to j. the queue** se mettre dans la queue; *Fam Fig* **j. the queue!** tu n'es pas le seul (la seule)!

(c) *(meet with)* rejoindre; **may I j. you?** *(to somebody at table)* puis-je me joindre à vous?

(d) *(of river, road)* rejoindre; **where the river joins**

the sea où le fleuve se jette dans la mer
3 *vi* (**a**) *(of pipes, roads, rivers)* se rejoindre
(**b**) *(in club, political party)* adhérer; *(in union)* devenir membre

▸**join in 1** *vt insep* participer à, prendre part à
2 *vi* participer

▸**join up** *vi Mil* s'engager

joiner ['dʒɔɪnə(r)] *n Br (carpenter)* menuisier *m*

joint [dʒɔɪnt] **1** *n* (**a**) *(in body)* articulation *f*; **out of j.**
déboîté(e); *Br Fig* **to put sb's nose out of j.** dépiter qn
(**b**) *(in woodwork)* assemblage *m*; *(in metalwork)*
joint *m*
(**c**) *(of beef)* rôti *m*; *(of lamb)* gigot *m*
(**d**) *Fam (nightclub)* boîte *f*; *(restaurant)* resto *m*
(**e**) *Fam (cannabis cigarette)* joint *m*
2 *adj* commun(e); *(effort)* conjugué(e); **j. account**
compte *m* joint; **j. custody** garde *f* conjointe; **j. ownership** copropriété *f*; **j. stock company** société *f* par
actions; **j. venture** *(undertaking)* entreprise *f* commune; *(company)* société *f* commune *ou* en participation
3 *vt (chicken)* découper

jointly ['dʒɔɪntlɪ] *adv* conjointement

joist [dʒɔɪst] *n* solive *f*

joke [dʒəʊk] **1** *n* (**a**) *(remark)* plaisanterie *f*, blague *f*;
(prank, trick) tour *m*, farce *f*; **to tell** *or* **crack a j. (about
sth)** raconter une blague (sur qch); **to make a j.
(about sth)** faire une plaisanterie (sur qch); **to make
a j. of sth** rire de qch; **to say/do sth for a j.** dire/faire
qch pour rire; **the j. was on him** la plaisanterie s'est
retournée contre lui; **she can't take a j.** elle n'aime
pas la plaisanterie; **it's no j.!** ce n'est pas une mince
affaire!; **it's no j. waiting for hours** ce n'est pas drôle
d'attendre pendant des heures; **it's getting beyond a
j.** ça n'est plus drôle, la plaisanterie a assez duré; **to
play a j. on sb** jouer un tour à qn (**b**) *Fam* **to be a j.**
(ridiculous) être lamentable
2 *vi* plaisanter; **to j. about sth** plaisanter sur qch; **I
was only joking** je plaisantais; **you're joking!, you
must be joking!** tu plaisantes!, tu veux rire!; **joking
apart...** blague à part...

joker ['dʒəʊkə(r)] *n* (**a**) *(clown)* farceur(euse) *m,f*; *(incompetent person)* plaisantin *m* (**b**) *(in cards)* joker *m*;
Fig **the j. in the pack** la grande inconnue

jokily ['dʒəʊkɪlɪ] *adv* en plaisantant

jokingly ['dʒəʊkɪŋlɪ] *adv* en plaisantant

joky ['dʒəʊkɪ] *adj (person)* blagueur(euse); *(mood,
conversation)* jovial(e); *(remark, comment)* moqueur(euse)

jolly ['dʒɒlɪ] **1** *adj (cheerful)* joyeux(euse), gai(e); **the
J. Roger** le pavillon noir
2 *adv Br Fam (very)* rudement, drôlement; **j. good!**
super!; **it serves him j. well right!** c'est vraiment bien
fait pour lui!
3 *vt (pt & pp jollied)* **to j. sb into doing sth** amadouer qn pour qu'il fasse qch; **to j. sb along** amadouer qn

jolt [dʒəʊlt] **1** *n* (**a**) *(shake)* secousse *f* (**b**) *(shock, surprise)* choc *m*, coup *m*; **to give sb a j.** faire un choc *ou*
un coup à qn
2 *vt (shake)* secouer; *(shock, surprise)* ébranler; **to j.
sb into action** secouer les puces à qn; **to j. sb out of a
depression** faire sortir qn de son état dépressif
3 *vi (shake)* secouer; **to j. along** *(of vehicle)* cahoter;
to j. to a stop *(of vehicle)* s'arrêter avec des à-coups;

his head jolted forward/back sa tête est partie en
avant/en arrière

Jordan ['dʒɔːdən] *n (country)* la Jordanie; **the (River) J.**
le Jourdain

Jordanian [dʒɔː'deɪnɪən] **1** *n* Jordanien(enne) *m,f*
2 *adj* jordanien(enne)

josh [dʒɒʃ] *vt Fam* mettre en boîte

joss stick ['dʒɒsstɪk] *n* bâton *m* d'encens

jostle ['dʒɒsəl] **1** *vt* bousculer; **to j. sb out of the way**
écarter qn en jouant des coudes
2 *vi (push)* se bousculer; **to j. for position** *(in contest, job)* jouer des coudes

jot [dʒɒt] *n* **he doesn't care a j.** il s'en fiche complètement; **there isn't a j. of truth in what you say** il n'y a
pas une once de vérité dans ce que vous dites; **it
doesn't make a j. of difference** ça ne fait pas la
moindre différence

▸**jot down** *(pt & pp jotted)* *vt sep* noter

jotter ['dʒɒtə(r)] *n* cahier *m*

jottings ['dʒɒtɪŋz] *npl* notes *fpl*

joule [dʒuːl] *n Phys* joule *m*

journal ['dʒɜːnəl] *n (publication)* revue *f*; *(diary)* journal *m*; **to keep a j.** tenir un journal

journalese [dʒɜːnə'liːz] *n Fam Pej* jargon *m* journalistique

journalism ['dʒɜːnəlɪzəm] *n* journalisme *m*

journalist ['dʒɜːnəlɪst] *n* journaliste *mf*

journalistic [dʒɜːnə'lɪstɪk] *adj* journalistique

journey ['dʒɜːnɪ] **1** *n (pl* **journeys***)* voyage *m*; *(short)*
trajet *m*; **a train j.** un voyage en train; **to make a j.**
faire un voyage; **to go (away) on a j.** partir en voyage; **to get to** *or* **reach the end of one's j.** arriver à
destination; **j. time** durée *f* du voyage; *(shorter distance)* durée du trajet
2 *vi* voyager

joust [dʒaʊst] *vi Hist* jouter; *Fig (compete)* se chamailler

jovial ['dʒəʊvɪəl] *adj* jovial(e), enjoué(e)

jovially ['dʒəʊvɪəlɪ] *adv* jovialement

jowl [dʒaʊl] *n (jaw)* mâchoire *f*; *(cheek)* bajoue *f*

joy [dʒɔɪ] *n* (**a**) *(happiness)* joie *f* (**b**) *(pleasure)* plaisir
m; **she's a j. to be with** c'est un plaisir d'être avec elle
(**c**) *Br Fam (success)* **(did you have** *or* **get) any j.?** ça a
marché?

joyful ['dʒɔɪfʊl] *adj (occasion, news)* heureux(euse);
(person, party) joyeux(euse)

joyfully ['dʒɔɪfəlɪ] *adv* joyeusement

joyless ['dʒɔɪlɪs] *adj* triste

joyous ['dʒɔɪəs] *adj (occasion, news)* heureux(euse);
(person, party) joyeux(euse)

joyride ['dʒɔɪraɪd] *n (in stolen car)* = virée dans une
voiture volée; **to go for a j.** = faire une virée dans
une voiture volée

joyrider ['dʒɔɪraɪdə(r)] *n* = chauffard qui conduit une
voiture volée

joystick ['dʒɔɪstɪk] *n (in aircraft)* manche *m* à balai;
(for computer) manette *f*

JP [dʒeɪ'piː] *n Law (abbr* **Justice of the Peace***)* juge *m* de
paix

Jr *(abbr* **Junior***)* **Thomas Smith, Jr** Thomas Smith fils

jubilant ['dʒuːbɪlənt] *adj (shouts)* de joie; *(expression)*
réjoui(e); *(person)* exultant(e); *(celebration)* joyeux(euse); **to be j. (at** *or* **about sth)** être transporté(e) de
joie (par qch)

jubilation [dʒuːbɪ'leɪʃən] *n (grande)* joie *f*, jubilation *f*

jubilee ['dʒuːbɪliː] *n* (**golden**) **j.** cinquantième anniversaire *m*, jubilé *m*; **silver/diamond j.** vingt-cinquième/soixantième anniversaire

Judaic [dʒuː'deɪk] *adj* judaïque

Judaism ['dʒuːdeɪɪzəm] *n* judaïsme *m*

Judas ['dʒuːdəs] *n (traitor)* Judas *m*

judder ['dʒʌdə(r)] *vi Br* être agité(e) de secousses; **to j. to a halt** s'arrêter avec des secousses

judge [dʒʌdʒ] **1** *n* (**a**) *(in law, sport)* juge *m*; *(in competition)* membre *m* du jury (**b**) *(expert)* **to be a good/poor j. of sth** s'y connaître/ne pas s'y connaître en qch; **I will be the j. of that** c'est moi qui (en) jugerai **2** *vt* (**a**) *(in law, sport)* juger (**b**) *(assess critically)* juger; **to j. sb by** *ou* **on sth** juger qn *ou* d'après qch; **to j. sb/sth a success/failure** considérer que qn/qch a réussi/échoué; **to j. it necessary to do sth** estimer *ou* juger nécessaire de faire qch; **don't j. a book by its cover** l'habit ne fait pas le moine (**c**) *(estimate)* estimer, évaluer **3** *vi* juger; **to j. by appearances** juger d'après les apparences; **to j. for oneself** juger par soi-même; **judging by...** à en juger par...

judg(e)ment, *Am* **judgment** ['dʒʌdʒmənt] *n* (**a**) *(decision)* jugement *m*; **to sit in j.** *(of judge, court)* siéger; **to pass j.** *(of judge, court)* rendre un jugement; *Fig* **to sit in** *or* **pass j. on sb** porter des jugements sur qn, juger qn; *Rel* **J. Day** le (jour du) Jugement dernier (**b**) *(opinion)* avis *m*, opinion *f*; **to form a j.** se faire un avis *ou* une opinion (**c**) *(discernment)* jugement *m*; **to have good j.** faire preuve de jugement; **to have poor j.** manquer de jugement; **to trust sb's j.** s'en remettre au jugement de qn; **in my j.** à mon sens; **against my better j.** en sachant que c'est/c'était une erreur

judg(e)mental, *Am* **judgmental** [dʒʌdʒ'mentəl] *adj* critique

judicial [dʒuː'dɪʃəl] *adj* judiciaire

judiciary [dʒuː'dɪʃərɪ] *n (judges)* magistrature *f*; *(branch of government)* pouvoir *m* judiciaire

judicious [dʒuː'dɪʃəs] *adj* judicieux(euse)

judiciously [dʒuː'dɪʃəslɪ] *adv* judicieusement

judiciousness [dʒuː'dɪʃəsnɪs] *n* bon sens *m*

judo ['dʒuːdəʊ] *n* judo *m*

jug [dʒʌg] *n* (**a**) *(for wine, water)* pichet *m*; *(for cream, milk)* pot *m* (**b**) *very Fam (prison)* **in the j.** en taule

juggernaut ['dʒʌgənɔːt] *n Br* poids *m* lourd

juggle ['dʒʌgəl] **1** *vt also Fig* jongler avec **2** *vi also Fig* jongler (**with** avec)

juggler ['dʒʌglə(r)] *n* jongleur(euse) *m,f*

jugular ['dʒʌgjʊlə(r)] **1** *n* jugulaire *f*; *Fig* **to go for the j.** frapper au point sensible **2** *adj* jugulaire

juice [dʒuːs] *n* (**a**) *(of fruit, meat)* jus *m*; *(of plant)* suc *m* (**b**) *Fam (petrol)* jus *m*

juicy ['dʒuːsɪ] *adj* (**a**) *(fruit)* juteux(euse); *(meat)* qui rend du jus (**b**) *Fig (contract, deal)* juteux(euse); *(story)* croustillant(e)

jukebox ['dʒuːkbɒks] *n* juke-box *m*

Jul *(abbr* **July**) juillet

July [dʒuː'laɪ] *n* juillet *m*; *see also* **May**

jumble ['dʒʌmbəl] **1** *n (of things)* tas *m*; *(of ideas, words)* fatras *m*; **in a j.** *(things)* en désordre, en pagaïe; *(ideas, words)* embrouillé(e); *Br* **j. sale** vente *f* de charité **2** *vt (things)* mélanger; *(ideas, words)* embrouiller

jumbo ['dʒʌmbəʊ] *adj* **j.** (**sized**) énorme, géant(e); **j. jet** jumbo jet *m*, gros-porteur *m*

jump [dʒʌmp] **1** *n* (**a**) *(leap)* saut *m*; *Fig* **go take a j.!** va te faire voir ailleurs!; *Fig* **to be one j. ahead** avoir une longueur d'avance; **j. jet** ADAV *m*; *Br* **j. leads** câbles *mpl* de démarrage; **j. suit** combinaison *f* (**b**) *(rise)* hausse *f* soudaine (**in** de) (**c**) *(on racecourse)* obstacle *m* **2** *vt (hedge, ditch)* sauter; *Fam* **to j. sb** attaquer qn; **to j. bail** se dérober à la justice *(alors qu'on est en liberté provisoire)*; **to j. the gun** *(in race)* faire un faux départ; *Fig* anticiper, agir prématurément; **to j. the lights** *(in car)* brûler un feu rouge; *Br* **to j. the queue** passer avant son tour; **to j. ship** déserter le navire **3** *vi* (**a**) *(leap)* sauter; **to j. to one's feet** se lever d'un bond; **to j. for joy** sauter de joie; **to j. onto a train** sauter dans un train; **to j. out of the window** sauter par la fenêtre; **to j. to conclusions** tirer des conclusions hâtives; *Fig* **let's wait and see which way she jumps** attendons de voir ce qu'elle va faire; *Fam* **to j. down sb's throat** rabrouer qn; *Fig* **to j. out at sb** *(of mistake, surprising detail)* sauter aux yeux de qn (**b**) *(go directly)* **to j. from one subject to another** *or* **to the next** sauter d'un sujet à l'autre; **the film then jumps to the present** le film passe d'un seul coup au présent (**c**) *(of unemployment, inflation)* faire un bond (**d**) *(make a sudden movement) (of person)* sursauter; *(of heart)* faire un bond; *(of record player needle)* sauter; **we nearly jumped out of our skins** ça nous a fichu un coup

▸**jump at** *vt insep (offer, chance)* sauter sur

▸**jump on** *vt insep Fam (reprimand)* sauter sur (**for doing** d'avoir fait)

jumped-up [dʒʌmp'tʌp] *adj Br Fam Pej* prétentieux(-euse)

jumper ['dʒʌmpə(r)] *n Br (sweater)* pull(-over) *m*; *Am (sleeveless dress)* robe-chasuble *f*

jumping-off place ['dʒʌmpɪŋ'ɒf'pleɪs], **jumping-off point** ['dʒʌmpɪŋ'ɒf'pɔɪnt] *n* point *m* de départ; *Fig* tremplin *m*

jump-start ['dʒʌmpstaːt] *vt* faire démarrer avec des câbles de démarrage

jumpy ['dʒʌmpɪ] *adj* nerveux(euse)

Jun *(abbr* **June**) juin

junction ['dʒʌŋkʃən] *n (of roads, railway lines)* embranchement *m*; *Elec* **j. box** boîte *f* de dérivation

juncture ['dʒʌŋktʃə(r)] *n Formal* **at this j.** à ce moment(-là)

June [dʒuːn] *n* juin *m*; *see also* **May**

jungle ['dʒʌŋgəl] *n also Fig* jungle *f*

junior ['dʒuːnjə(r)] **1** *n* (**a**) *(in age)* **to be sb's j.** être plus jeune que qn; **he's three years my j.** il a trois ans de moins que moi (**b**) *(in rank)* subalterne *mf* **2** *adj* (**a**) *(in age)* **to be j. to sb** être plus jeune que qn; **Thomas Smith, J.** Thomas Smith fils; *Am* **j. high (school)** *(between 11 and 15)* ≃ collège *m* d'enseignement secondaire; *Br* **j. school** *(between 7 and 11)* = classes primaires du cours élémentaire au cours moyen (**b**) *(in rank)* subalterne; **to be j. to sb** être au-dessous de qn; **j. teacher/executive** jeune professeur *m*/cadre *m*; *Br Univ* **j. common room** salle *f* des étudiants de premier cycle et de licence; **j. doctor** interne *mf*; *Br Parl* **j. minister** secrétaire *mf* d'État

juniper ['dʒuːnɪpə(r)] *n* **j.** (**tree**) genévrier *m*, genièvre *m*; **j. berry** baie *f* de genièvre

junk¹ [dʒʌŋk] **1** *n (unwanted objects)* bric-à-brac *m*; *(inferior goods)* camelote *f*; *Fin* **j. bond** obligation *f*; **j.**

food cochonneries *fpl*; **j. mail** prospectus *mpl*; **j. shop** brocante *f*
  2 *vt Fam (discard) (objects)* bazarder; *(plan)* laisser tomber

junk² *n (boat)* jonque *f*

junket ['dʒʌŋkɪt] *n* (**a**) *(food)* lait *m* caillé (**b**) *Pej (trip by public official)* voyage *m* aux frais du contribuable

junkie, junky ['dʒʌŋkɪ] *(pl* **junkies***) n Fam (drug addict)* drogué(e) *m,f*; **a fast-food/game-show j.** un accro des fast-food/jeux télévisés

junkyard ['dʒʌŋkjɑːd] *n (for metal)* férraille *f*

junta ['dʒʌntə] *n* junte *f*

Jupiter ['dʒuːpɪtə(r)] *n (planet)* Jupiter

jurisdiction [dʒʊərɪs'dɪkʃən] *n* juridiction *f*; **to have j. over sb** avoir autorité sur qn; **to come within** *or* **under the j. of...** être sous la juridiction de...

jurisprudence [dʒʊərɪs'pruːdəns] *n* jurisprudence *f*

jurist ['dʒʊərɪst] *n (legal expert)* juriste *mf*

juror ['dʒʊərə(r)] *n Law* juré(e) *m,f*

jury ['dʒʊərɪ] *(pl* **juries***) n Law* jury *m*; **to be** *or* **serve on the j.** être membre *ou* faire partie du jury; **to be on j. duty** *or* **service** être convoqué(e) pour faire partie d'un jury; *Fig* **the j. is still out on that one** ça reste à voir; **j. box** banc *m* des jurés

just [dʒʌst] **1** *adj (fair)* juste; **it's only j. that...** c'est normal que... + *subjunctive*; **to get one's j. deserts** n'avoir que ce que l'on mérite
  2 *adv* (**a**) *(exactly)* exactement; **that's j. what I told her** c'est exactement ce que je lui ai dit; **j. how many are there?** combien y en a-t-il au juste?; **that's j. the point!** justement!, précisément!; **j. my luck!** c'est bien ma chance!; **it's j. as good/difficult as...** c'est tout aussi bon/difficile que...; **j. then** juste à ce moment-là; **j. now** en ce moment; **j. as I was leaving...** juste au moment où je partais...; **I can j. see her as a doctor** je la vois très bien médecin
  (**b**) *(only)* juste; **she's j. a baby** ce n'est qu'un bébé; **it costs j. $10** ça coûte juste 10 dollars
  (**c**) *(barely)* juste; **j. before/after** juste avant/après; **j. over/under £50** à peine plus/moins de 50 livres; **j. in time** juste à temps; **it's only j. big enough** c'est tout juste assez grand; **they j. caught the train** ils ont eu le train de justesse; **they j. missed the train** ils ont raté le train d'un cheveu
  (**d**) *(recently)* **to have j. done sth** venir de faire qch; **j.**

yesterday/last year pas plus tard qu'hier/que l'année dernière
  (**e**) *(simply)* **it was j. wonderful/dreadful!** c'était tout simplement merveilleux/affreux!; **he j. refuses to listen!** il refuse carrément d'écouter!; **j. ask if you need money** si tu as besoin d'argent, tu n'as qu'à demander
  (**f**) *(in threats, exhortations)* **j. (you) try/wait!** essaie/attends un peu pour voir!; **(that's) j. as well!** heureusement!
  (**g**) **j. about** *(almost)* à peu près; **they're j. about the same** ils se valent; **I can j. about manage** j'y arrive tout juste; **to be j. about to do sth** être sur le point de faire qch

justice ['dʒʌstɪs] *n* (**a**) *(power of law)* justice *f*; **to bring sb to j.** traduire qn en justice (**b**) *(fairness)* légitimité *f*; **this photograph doesn't do him j.** cette photo ne le met pas en valeur; **to do j. to a meal** faire honneur à un repas; **to do oneself j.** se montrer sous son meilleur jour (**c**) *(judge)* juge *m*; *Br* **J. of the Peace** juge de paix

justifiable ['dʒʌstɪfaɪəbəl] *adj* justifié(e), légitime; **j. homicide** légitime défense *f*

justifiably ['dʒʌstɪfaɪəblɪ] *adv* à juste titre

justification [dʒʌstɪfɪ'keɪʃən] *n* justification *f*; **in j. of sth** pour justifier qch

justify ['dʒʌstɪfaɪ] *(pt & pp* **justified***) vt* (**a**) *(act, behaviour)* justifier; **to be justified in doing sth** avoir de bonnes raisons de faire qch (**b**) *Comput & Typ (text)* justifier

justly ['dʒʌstlɪ] *adv (fairly)* avec justice; *(deservedly)* à juste titre

▶**jut out** [dʒʌt] *(pt & pp* **jutted***)* **1** *vt sep (chin)* avancer
  2 *vi (of balcony, rock)* faire saillie; **to j. out over sth** surplomber qch; **to j. out into the sea** s'avancer dans la mer

jute [dʒuːt] *n* jute *m*

juvenile ['dʒuːvɪnaɪl, *Am* 'dʒuːvɪnəl] **1** *n Law* mineur(e) *m,f*
  2 *adj* (**a**) *Law (crime, delinquency)* juvénile; **j. court** tribunal *m* pour enfants; **j. delinquent** jeune délinquant(e) *m,f* (**b**) *Pej (childish)* puéril(e)

juxtapose [dʒʌkstə'pəʊz] *vt* mettre en juxtaposition (**with** avec)

juxtaposition [dʒʌkstəpə'zɪʃən] *n* juxtaposition *f*

K

K, k [keɪ] *n* (**a**) *(letter)* K, k *m inv* (**b**) *(abbr* **thousand, thousand pounds**) **he earns 30K** il gagne 30 000 livres sterling (**c**) *Comput (abbr* **kilobyte**) KO

Kabul [ˈkɑːbʊl] *n* Kaboul

Kaffir [ˈkæfə(r)] *n very Fam* nègre (négresse) *m,f*, = terme raciste désignant un Noir d'Afrique du Sud

kaftan [ˈkæftæn] *n* caf(e)tan *m*

kalashnikov [kəˈlæʃnɪkɒv] *n* kalachnikov *m ou f*

kale [keɪl] *n* chou *m* frisé

kaleidoscope [kəˈlaɪdəskəʊp] *n* kaléidoscope *m*

kamikaze [kæmɪˈkɑːzɪ] **1** *n also Fig* kamikaze *m*
2 *adj* kamikaze

Kampuchea [kæmpʊˈtʃɪə] *n Formerly* le Kampuchéa

kangaroo [kæŋgəˈruː] *n* kangourou *m*; **k. court** tribunal *m* irrégulier

kaput [kəˈpʊt] *adj Fam* kaput *inv*

karate [kəˈrɑːtɪ] *n* karaté *m*; **k. chop** coup *m* de karaté

Kashmir [kæʃˈmɪə(r)] *n* Cachemire

Kashmiri [kæʃˈmɪərɪ] **1** *n* (**a**) *(person)* Cachemirien (enne) *m,f* (**b**) *(language)* cachemirien *m*
2 *adj* cachemirien(enne)

Katmandu [kætmænˈduː] *n* Katmandou

kayak [ˈkaɪæk] *n* kayak *m*

Kazak(h)stan [kæzækˈstɑːn] *n* Kazakhstan *m*

KB [keɪˈbiː] *n Comput (abbr* **kilobyte**) Ko *m*

kebab [kəˈbæb] *n* brochette *f*; **shish k.** chiche-kébab *m*; **doner k.** sandwich *m* grec

kedgeree [kedʒəˈriː] *n* = riz pilaf au poisson fumé et aux œufs durs

keel [kiːl] *n (of ship)* quille *f*; *Fig* **to be on an even k.** être stable

▶**keel over** *vi (of boat)* chavirer; *Fam (of person)* s'écrouler

keen [kiːn] *adj* (**a**) *(enthusiastic)* enthousiaste; *(student)* assidu(e); **to be k. on sb** avoir un faible pour qn; **to be k. on doing sth** *(habitually)* adorer faire qch; *(want to do)* avoir très envie de faire qch; **to be k. to do sth** avoir très envie de faire qch; **to be k. for sth to happen** tenir beaucoup à ce que qch arrive; *Fam* **to be as k. as mustard** déborder d'enthousiasme; **to take a k. interest in sth** s'intéresser de très près à qch
(**b**) *(eye, mind, look)* vif (vive); *(price)* compétitif(-ive); **to have a k. eye for detail** remarquer jusqu'au moindre détail
(**c**) *(intense)* vif (vive); *(remorse)* cuisant(e); *(competition)* intense

keenly [ˈkiːnlɪ] *adv* (**a**) *(enthusiastically)* avec enthousiasme (**b**) *(intensely)* profondément; **to be k. aware of sth** avoir une conscience aiguë de qch; **k. contested** âprement disputé(e)

keep [kiːp] **1** *n* (**a**) **to pay for one's k.** payer sa pension; **to earn one's k.** *(make a living)* gagner sa vie; *(pay one's way)* payer sa pension
(**b**) *(of castle)* donjon *m*
(**c**) *Fam* **for keeps** pour de bon
2 *vt (pt & pp* **kept** [kept]) (**a**) *(retain)* garder; *(store)* ranger; **to k. sth from sb** dissimuler qch à qn; **to k. its shape/colour** *(of garment)* ne pas se déformer/déteindre; **to k. sb's attention** retenir l'attention de qn; **k. the change** gardez la monnaie
(**b**) *(maintain)* **to k. a diary** tenir un journal; **to k. order** maintenir l'ordre; **to k. a record of sth** garder une trace écrite de qch; **to k. a secret** garder un secret
(**c**) *(maintain in a certain condition)* **to k. sth secret** garder qch secret; **to k. sb awake** empêcher qn de (s'en)dormir; **to k. sb waiting** faire attendre qn; **she keeps her flat clean** son appartement est toujours bien tenu
(**d**) *(look after)* *(poultry, cows)* élever; *(shop)* tenir; *(family, mistress)* entretenir; **a kept woman** une femme entretenue
(**e**) *(detain)* retenir; **what kept you?** pourquoi ce retard?
(**f**) *(observe)* respecter; *(promise)* tenir; **to k. late hours** se coucher tard; **to k. one's word** tenir parole
3 *vi* (**a**) *(remain)* rester; **to k. well** rester en bonne santé; **to k. quiet** se tenir tranquille; **how are you keeping?** comment allez-vous?
(**b**) *(continue)* **to k. straight on** continuer tout droit; **k. (to the) left/right** serrez à gauche/à droite; **to k. doing sth** ne pas arrêter de faire qch; **to k. smiling** garder le sourire; **to k. going** tenir le coup
(**c**) *(of food)* se conserver; *Fig* **it will k.** *(of problem)* ça peut attendre

▶**keep away 1** *vt sep* **to k. sb away (from sb/sth)** empêcher qn de s'approcher (de qn/qch)
2 *vi* **to k. away from sb/sth** ne pas s'approcher de qn/qch

▶**keep back 1** *vt sep* (**a**) *(crowd, tears)* retenir; **to k. back from sb** cacher qch à qn (**b**) *(delay)* retarder
2 *vi (not approach)* ne pas s'approcher

▶**keep down 1** *vt sep* (**a**) *(head)* baisser; **to k. one's voice down** parler moins fort; **to k. the noise down** faire moins de bruit; *Fig* **to k. one's head down** ne pas se faire remarquer; **I can't k. my food down** je vomis tout ce que je mange (**b**) *(repress) (people)* opprimer; *(prices)* empêcher d'augmenter
2 *vi (not stand up)* se tapir

▶**keep from** *vt sep* to k. sb from doing sth empêcher qn de faire qch; **to k. sb from his work** empêcher qn de travailler

▶**keep in** *vt sep (pupil)* garder en retenue; **to k. sb in overnight** *(in hospital)* garder qn pour la nuit

▶**keep in with** *vt insep Fam* **to k. in with sb** rester en bons termes avec qn

▶**keep off 1** *vt sep* to k. one's hands off sb/sth ne pas toucher à qn/qch
  2 *vt insep* **k. off the grass** *(sign)* Pelouse interdite
  3 *vi (stay away)* ne pas intervenir

▶**keep on 1** *vt sep (clothing, employee)* garder; *(lights, TV)* laisser allumé(e); *Fam* **k. your hair on!** on se calme!
  2 *vi* continuer; **to k. on doing sth** continuer de faire qch; **to k. on about sth** insister constamment sur qch

▶**keep on at** *vt insep Fam* **to k. on at sb (to do sth)** être toujours sur le dos de qn (pour qu'il fasse qch)

▶**keep out 1** *vt sep (not allow to enter)* empêcher d'entrer
  2 *vi (stay away from)* **to k. out of sth** éviter qch; **to k. out of sb's way** éviter qn; **to k. out of danger** rester à l'abri du danger; **to k. out of trouble** ne pas s'attirer d'ennuis; **to k. out of an argument** rester en dehors d'une dispute; **k. out** *(sign)* défense d'entrer

▶**keep to 1** *vt sep* **(a)** *(hold)* **to k. sb to a promise** faire tenir une promesse à qn; **to k. sth to a minimum** minimiser qch **(b)** *(not reveal)* **to k. sth to oneself** garder qch pour soi; **to k. oneself to oneself** rester à l'écart
  2 *vt insep (promise)* tenir; *(contract, agreement)* respecter; *(subject)* s'en tenir à; **to k. to one's bed** garder le lit

▶**keep up 1** *vt sep* **(a)** *(custom)* conserver; **to k. up the payments** continuer à payer; **to k. it up** *(continue to do well)* continuer comme ça; **k. up the good work!** continuez à bien travailler!; **to k. up appearances** sauver les apparences **(b)** *(keep awake)* empêcher de dormir
  2 *vi* **(a)** *(of rain, snow)* continuer **(b)** *(remain level)* tenir le rythme; **to k. up with sb** aller à la même allure que qn; **to k. up with the Joneses** rivaliser de standing avec ses voisins; **to k. up with events** se tenir informé(e) de l'actualité; **to k. up with the times** être à la page

keeper ['ki:pə(r)] *n (in zoo, park, museum)* gardien(-enne) *m,f*; *(gamekeeper)* garde-chasse *m*; *Fam (goalkeeper)* goal *m*

keep-fit ['ki:p'fɪt] *n* gymnastique *f*; **to do k.** faire de la gymnastique; **k. class** cours *m* de gymnastique

keeping ['ki:pɪŋ] *n* **(a)** *(care)* garde *f*; **to have sb/sth in one's k.** avoir qn/qch sous sa garde **(b)** *(conformity)* **in k. with** conformément à; **out of k. with** en désaccord avec

keepsake ['ki:pseɪk] *n* souvenir *m*

keg [keg] *n* baril *m*

ken [ken] *n* **to be beyond sb's k.** être en dehors des compétences de qn

kennel ['kenəl] *n (for guard dog)* niche *f*; *(for hunting dogs)* chenil *m*; **to put a dog into kennels** mettre un chien en pension

Kenya ['kenjə, 'ki:njə] *n* Kenya *m*

Kenyan ['kenjən] **1** *n* Kenyan(e) *m,f*
  2 *adj* kenyan(e)

kept [kept] *pt & pp of* **keep**

kerb [kɜːb] *n Br* bordure *f* de trottoir

kerbcrawler ['kɜːbkrɔːlə(r)] *n* = personne au volant qui accoste les prostituées

kerbcrawling ['kɜːbkrɔːlɪŋ] *n* = fait d'accoster des prostituées tout en restant dans sa voiture

kerbstone ['kɜːbstəʊn] *n Br* bordure *f* de trottoir

kerfuffle [kə'fʌfəl] *n Fam (fuss)* histoires *fpl*; *(noise, excitement)* remue-ménage *m*

kernel ['kɜːnəl] *n (of nut)* amande *f*; *(of grain)* grain *m*; *Fig (of problem)* fond *m*, essentiel *m*

kerosene ['kerəsi:n] *n* **(a)** *Am* pétrole *m* (lampant); **k. lamp** lampe *f* à pétrole **(b)** *(aircraft fuel)* kérosène *m*

kestrel ['kestrəl] *n* faucon *m* crécerelle

ketchup ['ketʃəp] *n* **(tomato) k.** ketchup *m*

kettle ['ketəl] *n* bouilloire *f*; **to put the k. on** mettre l'eau à chauffer; *Fam* **that's a different k. of fish** c'est une autre paire de manches

kettledrum ['ketəldrʌm] *n* timbale *f*

key [ki:] **1** *n* **(a)** *(of door, clock, toy)* clé *f*; *(of piano, type-writer)* touche *f*; *Fig* **the k. to happiness/success** la clé du bonheur/de la réussite **(b)** *(to map)* légende *f*; *(to exercise)* solutions *fpl* **(c)** *(in music)* ton *m*; **in the k. of C** en ut; **to be off k.** *(of singer)* chanter faux; *(of musician)* jouer faux
  2 *adj (role, factor, figure)* clé; *(influence, consideration)* capital(e); **k. person** pivot *m*; *Br Sch* **k. stage** étape *f* clé de la scolarité

▶**key in** *vt sep (data)* saisir

keyboard ['ki:bɔːd] *n (of piano, computer)* clavier *m*

keyboarder ['ki:bɔːdə(r)] *n* claviste *mf*, opérateur(-trice) *m,f* de saisie

keycard ['ki:kɑːd] *n* carte *f* magnétique *(servant à ouvrir la porte d'une chambre d'hôtel)*

keyhole ['ki:həʊl] *n* trou *m* de serrure; **k. surgery** chirurgie *f* à incision minimale

keynote ['ki:nəʊt] **1** *n* tonique *f*; *Fig (of speech, approach)* point *m* essentiel
  2 *adj (speech)* programme; *(speaker)* principal(e)

keypad ['ki:pæd] *n Comput* pavé *m*

keyring ['ki:rɪŋ] *n* porte-clés *m inv*

keystone ['ki:stəʊn] *n also Fig* clef *f* de voûte

keystroke ['ki:strəʊk] *n Comput* touche *f*

kg *(abbr* **kilogram)** kg

KGB [keɪdʒiː'biː] *n Formerly* KGB *m*

khaki ['kɑːkɪ] **1** *n* kaki *m*
  2 *adj* kaki *inv*

Khartoum [kɑː'tuːm] *n* Khartoum

kHz *(abbr* **kilohertz)** kHz

kibbutz [kɪ'bʊts] *(pl* **kibbutzim** [kɪbʊt'siːm] *) n* kibboutz *m*

kibosh ['kaɪbɒʃ] *n Fam* **to put the k. on sth** faire tomber qch à l'eau

kick [kɪk] **1** *n* **(a)** *(with foot)* coup *m* de pied; *(of horse)* ruade *f*; *(of gun)* recul *m*; **to give sb/sth a k.** donner un coup de pied à qn/dans qch; *Fam Fig* **she needs a k. up the backside** elle a besoin d'un bon coup de pied au derrière; *Fig* **that was a k. in the teeth for him** ça lui a fait un sacré coup; **that drink has a real k. to it!** cette boisson est vraiment traître!
  (b) *Fam (thrill)* **to get a k. out of doing sth** prendre son pied à faire qch; **to do sth for kicks** faire qch pour s'amuser
  2 *vt* donner un coup/des coups de pied à; *(football)* taper dans; **to get kicked** recevoir un coup/des coups de pied; *Fam Fig* **to k. the bucket** casser sa pipe; *Fig* **to k. a man when he's down** s'acharner

sur qn qui a perdu ses moyens; **I could have kicked myself** je me serais donné des gifles; **to k. the habit** *(stop taking drugs)* arrêter (la drogue); *Br Fam* **to k. sb upstairs** *(promote)* promouvoir qn pour se débarrasser de lui

3 *vi* donner un coup/des coups de pied; *(of horse)* ruer; *(of gun)* reculer; *Fam Fig* **to k. against sth** regimber contre qch

▸**kick about, kick around 1** *vt sep (ball)* taper dans; *Fam (idea)* tester; **don't let them k. you around** tu ne devrais pas les laisser te traiter comme ça

2 *vi Fam (hang around)* traîner; **there are plenty of people like that kicking around** des gens comme ça, ce n'est pas ce qui manque

▸**kick in 1** *vt sep (door)* enfoncer à coups de pied; *Fam* **to k. sb's head in** casser la tête à qn

2 *vi Fam* entrer en action; **the painkillers haven't kicked in yet** les analgésiques n'ont pas encore fait effet

▸**kick off** *vi (in football)* donner le coup d'envoi; *Fam Fig (in meeting, debate)* démarrer

▸**kick out** *vt sep Fam* mettre à la porte

▸**kick up** *vt sep Fam* **to k. up a fuss** faire tout un plat *ou* toute une histoire; **to k. up a row** *or* **a racket** faire du boucan

kickback ['kɪkbæk] *n Fam (payment)* pot-de-vin *m*

kickoff ['kɪkɒf] *n (in football)* coup *m* d'envoi; *Fam Fig* **for a k.** *(to start with)* pour commencer

kick-start ['kɪkstɑːt] **1** *n (on motorbike)* kick *m*

2 *vt (motorbike)* démarrer au kick; *Fig (economy)* donner un sérieux coup de pouce à

kid [kɪd] **1** *n* (**a**) *Fam (child)* gamin(e) *m,f*, gosse *mf*; **my k. brother** mon petit frère; **it's k.'s stuff** *(easy)* c'est un jeu d'enfant; *(childish)* c'est bon pour les gosses (**b**) *(young goat)* chevreau *m*; *(female)* chevrette *f*; *(skin)* chevreau; **k. gloves** gants *mpl* en chevreau; *Fig* **to handle sb with k. gloves** prendre des gants avec qn

2 *vt (pt & pp kidded) Fam (fool)* faire marcher; **to k. oneself** se faire des illusions; **who do you think you're kidding?** tu te fous de moi?

3 *vi* **to be kidding** plaisanter; **no kidding!** sans blague!

kidnap ['kɪdnæp] *(pt & pp kidnapped, Am kidnaped) vt* kidnapper, enlever

kidnapper ['kɪdnæpə(r)] *n* ravisseur(euse) *m,f*, kidnappeur(euse) *m,f*

kidnapping ['kɪdnæpɪŋ] *n* enlèvement *m*, kidnapping *m*

kidney ['kɪdnɪ] *(pl kidneys) n (of person)* rein *m*; *(offal)* rognon *m*; **k. bean** haricot *m* rouge; **k. donor** donneur(euse) *m,f* de rein; **k. machine** rein artificiel

kill [kɪl] **1** *n (in hunting) (action)* mise *f* à mort; *(animals killed)* tableau *m* de chasse; **to be in at the k.** assister à la mise à mort; *Fig* assister au dénouement

2 *vt* (**a**) *(person, animal)* tuer; **to k. oneself** se tuer; *Fam* **to k. oneself laughing** mourir de rire; *Ironic* **don't k. yourself!** surtout, ne te surmène pas!; *Fam* **this one'll k. you** *(of joke)* ça va te faire mourir de rire; **to k. two birds with one stone** faire d'une pierre deux coups; *Fam* **my feet/these shoes are killing me** mes pieds/ces chaussures me font un mal de chien (**b**) *Fig (friendship)* détruire; *(sound)* amortir; *(pain)* calmer; *(chances)* anéantir; *Journ* **to k. a story** retirer une information; **to k. time** tuer le temps

3 *vi* tuer; **to shoot to k.** tirer dans l'intention de tuer; *Rel* **thou shalt not k.** tu ne tueras point

▸**kill off** *vt sep (people)* tuer; *(character in film, novel)* faire mourir; *Fig (hope)* anéantir

killer ['kɪlə(r)] *n* tueur(euse) *m,f*; **he knew his k.** il connaissait son meurtrier; *Fam Fig* **those steps were a k.!** ces escaliers m'ont tué!; *Fam Fig* **this one's a k.** *(joke)* celle-ci est à mourir de rire; **k. (disease)** maladie *f* meurtrière; *Fig* **to have the k. instinct** être impitoyable; **k. whale** épaulard *m*

killing ['kɪlɪŋ] **1** *n (of person)* meurtre *m*; *(of animals)* destruction *f*; *Fam* **to make a k.** faire un bénéfice énorme

2 *adj Fam (exhausting)* tuant(e); *(very amusing)* tordant(e)

killjoy ['kɪldʒɔɪ] *n* rabat-joie *m inv*

kiln [kɪln] *n* four *m*

kilo ['kiːləʊ] *(pl kilos) n* kilo *m*

kilobyte ['kɪləbaɪt] *n Comput* kilo-octet *m*

kilogram(me) ['kɪləgræm] *n* kilogramme *m*

kilohertz ['kɪləʊhɜːts] *(pl kilohertz) n* kilohertz *m*

kilometre, *Am* **kilometer** ['kɪləmiːtə(r), kɪ'lɒmɪtə(r)] *n* kilomètre *m*

kilowatt ['kɪləwɒt] *n* kilowatt *m*; **k.-hour** kilowattheure *m*

kilt [kɪlt] *n* kilt *m*

kilter ['kɪltə(r)] *n Fam* **out of k.** *(of machine part)* déréglé(e) (**with** par rapport à); *(of budget)* déséquilibré(e)

kimono [kɪ'məʊnəʊ] *(pl kimonos) n* kimono *m*

kin [kɪn] *n Formal* parents *mpl*

kind¹ [kaɪnd] *n* (**a**) *(sort)* genre *m*, espèce *f*; **all kinds of...** toutes sortes de...; **something of the k.** quelque chose comme ça, quelque chose de ce genre; **I said nothing of the k.!** je n'ai jamais dit ça!; **she's really boring – she's nothing of the k.!** elle est vraiment ennuyeuse – mais pas du tout!; **in a k. of way** d'une certaine manière; **well, it's coffee of a k. I suppose** je suppose qu'on peut appeler ça du café; **we're two of a k.** nous sommes pareils; **it's the only one of its k.** c'est le seul de ce genre; **he's that k. of person** il est comme ça; **this is my k. of party!** voilà le genre de soirée que j'aime!; **this k. of thing** ce genre de chose (**b**) **in k.** *(payment)* en nature

(**c**) *Fam* **you look k. of tired** tu as l'air un peu fatigué; **I k. of expected this** je m'y attendais un peu; **do you like it? – k. of** ça te plaît? – oui, plus ou moins; **it was a k. of saucer-shaped thing** c'était quelque chose qui ressemblait à une soucoupe

kind² *adj* gentil(ille); **to be k. to sb** être gentil avec qn; *Formal* **would you be k. enough to** *or* **so k. as to...?** auriez-vous la bonté de...?; **you are really too k.** vous êtes vraiment trop aimable; **k. to the skin** *(of detergent, soap)* qui n'irrite pas la peau; **by k. permission of...** avec l'aimable autorisation de...

kinda ['kaɪndə] *Fam* = **kind of**

kindergarten ['kɪndəgɑːtən] *n* jardin *m* d'enfants

kind-hearted ['kaɪnd'hɑːtɪd] *adj (person)* qui a bon cœur; *(action)* généreux(euse)

kindle ['kɪndəl] *vt (flame)* allumer; *Fig (emotions)* éveiller

kindling ['kɪndlɪŋ] *n* petit bois *m*

kindly ['kaɪndlɪ] **1** *adv* gentiment; **to speak k. of sb** dire du bien de qn; *Formal* **(would you) k. be quiet!** voudriez-vous avoir la bonté de vous taire!; **she didn't take k. to being criticized** elle n'a pas apprécié qu'on la critique

2 *adj* *(person)* gentil(ille); *(tone, advice)* bienveillant(e)

kindness [ˈkaɪndnɪs] *n* gentillesse *f*; **to do sth out of the k. of one's heart** faire qch par bonté d'âme; **to do sb a k.** rendre service à qn

kindred [ˈkɪndrɪd] *adj* du même genre, de la même nature; **we are k. spirits** c'est mon alter ego

kinetic [kɪˈnetɪk] *adj* cinétique

king [kɪŋ] *n* roi *m*; **K. Charles the First** le roi Charles Iᵉʳ; **the three kings** *(in the Bible)* les Rois mages; **the k. of the beasts** le roi des animaux; *Fig* **to live like a k.** vivre en grand seigneur

kingdom [ˈkɪŋdəm] *n* royaume *m*; **the k. of heaven** le royaume des cieux; **the animal/plant k.** le règne animal/végétal; *Fam* **until** *or* **till k. come** jusqu'à la saint-glinglin; *Fam* **to send sb to k. come** envoyer qn ad patres

kingfisher [ˈkɪŋfɪʃə(r)] *n* martin-pêcheur *m*

kingpin [ˈkɪŋpɪn] *n* *Fig (of organization, company)* cheville *f* ouvrière

king-size(d) [ˈkɪŋsaɪz(d)] *adj* **(a)** *(cigarette)* long (longue); **a k. bed** = un lit d'1 m 95 de large **(b)** *Fam (headache, problem)* sacré(e)

kink [kɪŋk] *n (in wire, rope)* boucle *f*; *(in hair)* frisette *f*; *(in character)* bizarrerie *f*

kinky [ˈkɪŋkɪ] *adj* **(a)** *(hair)* frisotté(e) **(b)** *Fam (person) (sexually)* qui a des goûts sexuels bizarres; *(eccentric)* extravagant(e); *(garment)* sexy *inv*; *(behaviour, practice)* pervers(e)

kinship [ˈkɪnʃɪp] *n* parenté *f*

kinsman [ˈkɪnzmən] *n Lit* parent *m*

kinswoman [ˈkɪnzwʊmən] *n Lit* parente *f*

kiosk [ˈkiːɒsk] *n* kiosque *m*

kip [kɪp] *Br Fam* **1** *n (sleep)* **to have a k.** piquer un roupillon; **to get some k.** roupiller
2 *vi (pt & pp* **kipped***) (sleep)* roupiller

kipper [ˈkɪpə(r)] *n* hareng *m* salé et fumé

Kirg(h)izia [kɜːˈgiːzɪə], **Kirg(h)izstan** [kɜːgɪzˈstæn] *n* le Kirghizistan

kirk [kɜːk] *n Scot* église *f*; **the K.** l'Église (presbytérienne) d'Écosse

kiss [kɪs] **1** *n* baiser *m*; **to give sb a k.** donner un baiser à qn; **to give sb the k. of life** faire du bouche-à-bouche à qn; *Fig* **to be the k. of death for sth** porter un coup fatal à qch; *Br* **k. curl** accroche-cœur *m*
2 *vt* embrasser; **to k. sb goodbye** dire au revoir à qn en l'embrassant; **he kissed her on the mouth/hand** il l'a embrassée sur la bouche/lui a baisé la main; *Fig* **you can k. your promotion goodbye** tu peux dire adieu à ta promotion
3 *vi* s'embrasser; **to k. and make up** se réconcilier; **to k. and tell** dévoiler à la presse ses secrets d'alcôve *(impliquant généralement une personne célèbre)*

kissogram [ˈkɪsəgræm] *n* = service permettant de faire délivrer un message, un poème, une chanson etc, souvent grivois, accompagnés d'un baiser, pour une occasion particulière

kit [kɪt] *n* **(a)** *(equipment)* équipement *m*, matériel *m* **(b)** *(clothes)* tenue *f*; *Fam* **to get one's k. off** se mettre à poil **(c)** *(for assembly)* **(model) k.** maquette *f*; **to make sth from a k.** faire qch à partir de pièces détachées; **in k. form** en kit

▸**kit out** *(pt & pp* **kitted***) vt sep* équiper **(with** de**)**

kitbag [ˈkɪtbæg] *n* sac *m* de marin; *Mil* sac à paquetage

kitchen [ˈkɪtʃɪn] *n* cuisine *f*; **k. knife** couteau *m* de cuisine; *Br* **k. paper, k. roll** essuie-tout *m inv*, Sopalin® *m*; **k. sink** évier *m*; *Fam* **to take everything but the k. sink** emporter des tonnes de choses; *(of thief)* ne laisser que les murs; **k. unit** élément *m* de cuisine

kitchenette [kɪtʃɪˈnet] *n* coin-cuisine *m*, kitchenette *f*, *Offic* cuisinette *f*

kitchenware [ˈkɪtʃɪnweə(r)] *n* vaisselle *f* et ustensiles *mpl* de cuisine

kite [kaɪt] *n* **(a)** *(toy)* cerf-volant *m*; **to fly a k.** faire voler un cerf-volant; *Fig* lancer un ballon d'essai; *Fam* **go fly a k.!** va voir là-bas si j'y suis!; *Fam* **as high as a k.** excité(e) comme une puce **(b)** *(bird)* milan *m*

kith [kɪθ] *n Lit* **k. and kin** parents *mpl* et amis *mpl*

kitsch [kɪtʃ] *n* kitsch *m*

kitten [ˈkɪtən] *n* chaton *m*; *Fig* **to have kittens** être dans tous ses états

kitty [ˈkɪtɪ] *(pl* **kitties***) n* **(a)** *Fam (cat)* minou *m* **(b)** *(for bills, in cards)* cagnotte *f*

kiwi [ˈkiːwiː] *n* **(a)** *(bird)* kiwi *m*; **k. fruit** kiwi **(b)** *Fam* **K.** *(New Zealander)* Néo-Zélandais(e) *m,f*

kleptomania [kleptəˈmeɪnɪə] *n* kleptomanie *f*

kleptomaniac [kleptəˈmeɪnɪæk] *n* kleptomane *mf*

km *(abbr* **kilometre***)* km

kmph *(abbr* **kilometres per hour***)* km/h

knack [næk] *n* talent *m*; *(for manual activity)* tour *m* de main; **to have the k. of** *or* **a k. for doing sth** avoir un don pour faire qch; *Ironic* avoir le don de faire qch; **to get the k. (of doing sth)** attraper le tour de main (pour faire qch)

knacker [ˈnækə(r)] *n* équarrisseur *m*; **k.'s yard** chantier *m* d'équarrissage

knackered [ˈnækəd] *adj Br very Fam (tired)* crevé(e); *(broken, damaged)* foutu(e)

knapsack [ˈnæpsæk] *n* sac *m* à dos

knave [neɪv] *n* **(a)** *(in cards)* valet *m* **(b)** *Lit (scoundrel)* coquin *m*, fripon *m*

knead [niːd] *vt (dough)* pétrir; *(muscles)* masser

knee [niː] **1** *n* genou *m*; **to go down on one's knees** s'agenouiller; *Fig* **to bring sb to his knees** obliger qn à capituler
2 *vt (hit with knee)* donner un coup de genou à

kneecap [ˈniːkæp] **1** *n* rotule *f*
2 *vt (pt & pp* **kneecapped***)* tirer dans les rotules à

knee-deep [ˈniːˈdiːp] *adj* **to be k. in sth** *(in water, snow)* être enfoncé(e) jusqu'aux genoux dans qch; *Fig (in problems)* avoir qch jusqu'au cou; *(in work)* être débordé(e) de qch

knee-high [ˈniːˈhaɪ] *adj* **to be k.** *(of water, snow)* arriver à hauteur du genou; *Fam* **when I was k. to a grasshopper** quand j'étais haut comme trois pommes

kneejerk [ˈniːdʒɜːk] *adj (reaction, response)* instinctif(ive)

kneel [niːl] *(pt & pp* **knelt** [nelt] *) vi* s'agenouiller, se mettre à genoux **(before/to** devant**)**

knee-length [ˈniːleŋθ] *adj (skirt)* qui descend jusqu'aux genoux; *(boots, socks)* qui monte jusqu'aux genoux

knees-up [ˈniːzʌp] *n Br Fam* **to have a k.** faire la fête

knell [nel] *n Lit* glas *m*; **to toll the k. for sb** signer l'arrêt de mort de qn; **to toll the k. for sth** sonner le glas de qch

knelt [nelt] *pt & pp of* **kneel**

knew [njuː] *pt of* **know**

knickerbocker glory ['nɪkəbɒkə'glɔːrɪ] *n* = coupe de glace avec fruits et crème Chantilly

knickerbockers ['nɪkəbɒkəz] *npl* knickers *mpl*

knickers ['nɪkəz] *npl* (**a**) *(underwear)* culotte *f*, slip *m*; *Br Fam* **to get one's k. in a twist** perdre les pédales (**b**) *Am (breeches)* knickers *mpl*

knick-knack ['nɪknæk] *n Fam* babiole *f*

knife [naɪf] **1** *n (pl* **knives** [naɪvz]) couteau *m*; **k. and fork** couvert *m*; *Fig* **to get** *or* **have one's k. into sb** en vouloir à qn; *Fig* **the knives are out** ils sont/nous sommes/*etc* à couteaux tirés *ou* en guerre ouverte; **k. sharpener** aiguisoir *m*
2 *vt (stab)* donner un coup de couteau à, poignarder

knife-edge ['naɪfedʒ] *n Fig* **to be on a k.** *(of person)* être sur les nerfs; **to be balanced on a k.** *(of situation, game)* ne tenir qu'à un fil

knife-point ['naɪfpɔɪnt] *n* **at k.** sous la menace d'un couteau

knifing ['naɪfɪŋ] *n* agression *f* au couteau

knight [naɪt] **1** *n* chevalier *m*; *(in chess)* cavalier *m*
2 *vt* faire chevalier

knighthood ['naɪthʊd] *n (title)* **to be given a k.** être fait chevalier

knit [nɪt] *(pt & pp* **knitted** *or* **knit**) **1** *vt (sweater)* tricoter; **to k. one's brows** froncer les sourcils
2 *vi* tricoter, faire du tricot

▶**knit together** *vi (of broken bones)* se ressouder

knitted ['nɪtəd] *adj* tricoté(e)

knitting ['nɪtɪŋ] *n (item produced)* tricot *m*; **to do some k.** tricoter; **k. machine** machine *f* à tricoter; **k. needle** aiguille *f* à tricoter

knitwear ['nɪtweə(r)] *n* lainages *mpl*

knives [naɪvz] *pl of* **knife**

knob [nɒb] *n (on cane)* pommeau *m*; *(on banisters)* pomme *f*; *(on drawer, door)* poignée *f*; *(on radio)* bouton *m*; **a k. of butter** une noix de beurre

knobbly ['nɒblɪ] *adj* couvert(e) de bosses; *(tree)* noueux(euse); **k. knees** genoux *mpl* cagneux

knock [nɒk] **1** *n (blow)* coup *m*; **there was a k. at the door** on frappa à la porte
2 *vt* (**a**) *(hit)* frapper, heurter; **to k. sb to the ground** faire tomber qn en le frappant; **to k. sb unconscious** assommer qn; **to k. one's head against sth** se cogner la tête contre qch; **to k. a hole in sth** faire un trou dans qch; **to k. holes in an argument** démolir un argument; **to k. some sense into sb** apprendre à vivre à qn; *Fig* **to k. sb into shape** mettre qn au pas (**b**) *Fam (criticize)* débiner; **don't k. it until you've tried it** il faut essayer avant de critiquer
3 *vi* (**a**) *(hit)* frapper; **to k. at the door** frapper à la porte; **to k. against sth** heurter qch; **his knees were knocking** ses genoux s'entrechoquaient (**b**) *(of engine)* cogner

▶**knock about, knock around 1** *vt sep* (**a**) *(mistreat)* malmener; *(beat up)* battre (**b**) *Fam (idea, suggestion)* discuter de
2 *vi Fam (hang around)* traîner; **to k. about with sb** fréquenter qn
3 *vt insep Fam (spend time in)* **to k. about the world** rouler sa bosse; **she's been knocking about Glasgow for years** elle traîne à Glasgow depuis des lustres

▶**knock back** *vt sep Fam* (**a**) *(drink)* s'envoyer (**b**) *(reject)* envoyer bouler

▶**knock down** *vt sep* (**a**) *(pedestrian)* renverser (**b**) *(building)* abattre (**c**) *(price)* baisser

▶**knock off 1** *vt sep* (**a**) *(cause to fall off)* faire tomber; **he was knocked off his bike by a car** une voiture a heurté son vélo et il est tombé; *Fam* **to k. sb's head** *or* **block off** casser la figure à qn; *Fam* **to k. sth off the price** baisser un peu le prix (**b**) *Br very Fam (steal)* piquer, faucher (**c**) *Fam (kill)* zigouiller (**d**) *Fam* **k. it off!** *(stop it)* ça suffit!, arrête! (**e**) *Fam (produce quickly)* expédier
2 *vi Fam (finish work)* cesser le travail, finir

▶**knock out** *vt sep* (**a**) *(make unconscious)* mettre K.-O.; *Fam* **to k. sb's brains** *or* **teeth out** arranger le portrait à qn (**b**) *(eliminate from competition)* éliminer

▶**knock over** *vt sep* faire tomber

▶**knock up** *vt sep* (**a**) *(make hastily)* construire en vitesse; *(meal)* préparer en vitesse (**b**) *very Fam (make pregnant)* mettre en cloque

knockdown price ['nɒkdaʊn'praɪs] *n Fam* **at a k.** à très bas prix

knocker ['nɒkə(r)] *n* (**a**) *(on door)* heurtoir *m* (**b**) *very Fam* **knockers** *(breasts)* nichons *mpl*

knocking ['nɒkɪŋ] *n (at door)* coups *mpl*; *(of engine)* cognement *m*

knock-kneed ['nɒk'niːd] *adj* **to be k.** avoir les genoux en dedans

knock-on effect ['nɒkɒnɪ'fekt] *n* répercussions *fpl* en chaîne

knockout ['nɒkaʊt] **1** *n* (**a**) *(in boxing)* knock-out *m inv*; *Fig* **k.** coup *m* de grâce (**b**) *Fam* **he's/she's a k.** *(attractive)* il/elle est canon
2 *adj* (**a**) **k. blow** *(in boxing)* coup *m* qui provoque un K.-O.; *Fig* coup de grâce; *Fig* **to deliver the k. blow** donner le coup de grâce (**b**) **k. competition** compétition *f* avec épreuves éliminatoires

knot [nɒt] **1** *n* (**a**) *(in general)* nœud *m*; **to tie/untie a k.** faire/défaire un nœud; *Fam Fig* **to tie the k.** *(get married)* se marier (**b**) *Naut (unit of speed)* nœud *m*; *Fam Fig* **at a rate of knots** à toute allure (**c**) *(group of people)* petit groupe *m*
2 *vt (pt & pp* **knotted**) *(rope, string)* nouer; *very Fam* **get knotted!** va te faire voir!

knotty ['nɒtɪ] *adj (problem)* épineux(euse)

know [nəʊ] **1** *n Fam* **to be in the k.** être au courant
2 *vt (pt* **knew** [njuː], *pp* **known** [nəʊn]) (**a**) *(be acquainted with)* connaître; **to get to k. sb** apprendre à connaître qn; **when I first knew her** quand j'ai fait sa connaissance; **I've never known anything like it** je n'ai jamais rien vu de tel; **I k. her to say hello to** nous nous saluons, c'est tout; **knowing him...** le connaissant...
(**b**) *(have knowledge of)* savoir; **she thinks she knows all the answers** elle croit avoir réponse à tout; **to k. Spanish** connaître l'espagnol; **to k. a lot/a little about sth** bien s'y connaître/s'y connaître un peu en qch; **she knows what she is talking about** elle sait de quoi elle parle; *Fam* **to k. how to do sth** savoir faire qch; *Fam* **to k. a thing or two** être malin(igne); **to k. one's own mind** savoir ce que l'on veut; **heaven** *or* **God knows!** Dieu seul le sait!
(**c**) *(recognize)* reconnaître (**by** à); *(distinguish)* distinguer (**from** de); **to k. right from wrong** savoir faire la distinction entre le bien et le mal
3 *vi* savoir; **to k. about sth** être au courant de qch; **to get to k. of sth** apprendre qch; **as far as I k.** *(pour)* autant que je sache; **how should I k.?** comment le saurais-je?; **you never k.** on ne sait jamais; **not that**

I k. of pas que je sache; **to k. better than to do sth**
savoir qu'il ne faut pas faire qch; **you k....** tu sais...
know-all ['nəʊɔːl] *n Fam* monsieur *m*/madame *f* je-
sais-tout
know-how ['nəʊhaʊ] *n Fam* savoir-faire *m*; *(technical)*
know-how *m*
knowing ['nəʊɪŋ] **1** *n* **there's no k.** c'est impossible à
savoir
2 *adj (look, smile)* entendu(e), complice
knowledge ['nɒlɪdʒ] *n* (**a**) *(of fact)* connaissance *f*;
(not) to my k. (pas) à ma connaissance; **to have no
k. of sth** ignorer qch; **to have full k. of sth** avoir
pleine connaissance de qch; **it is common k. that...**
c'est un fait notoire que...; *Formal* **it has recently
come to our k. that...** il a été récemment porté à notre connaissance que... (**b**) *(learning)* savoir *m*, connaissances *fpl*; *Prov* **k. is power** savoir c'est pouvoir;
Comput **k.-based system** système *m* basé sur les connaissances
knowledgeable ['nɒlɪdʒəbəl] *adj* savant(e); **to be k.
about sth** bien s'y connaître en qch
known [nəʊn] **1** *adj* connu(e); *(notorious)* notoire
2 *pp of* **know**
knuckle ['nʌkəl] *n* articulation *f ou* jointure *f* (du doigt)
▸**knuckle down** *vi Fam* se mettre au boulot; **to k.
down to sth** se mettre à qch
▸**knuckle under** *vi Fam* mettre les pouces
knuckle-duster ['nʌkəldʌstə(r)] *n* coup-de-poing *m*
américain
KO ['keɪ'əʊ] *Fam* **1** *n (pl* **KO's** ['keɪ'əʊz]) *(in boxing)*
K.-O. *m*
2 *vt (pt & pp* **KO'd** ['keɪ'əʊd]) *(in boxing)* mettre K.-O.
koala [kəʊ'ɑːlə] *n* **k. (bear)** koala *m*

kopeck ['kəʊpek] *n* kopeck *m*
Koran [kə'rɑːn] *n* **the K.** le Coran
Koranic [kə'rænɪk] *adj* coranique
Korea [kə'rɪə] *n* la Corée; **North/South K.** la Corée du
Nord/du Sud
Korean [kə'rɪən] **1** *n* (**a**) *(person)* Coréen(enne) *m,f* (**b**)
(language) coréen *m*
2 *adj* coréen(enne); **the K. War** la guerre de Corée
kosher ['kəʊʃə(r)] *adj* (**a**) *(in Judaism)* casher *inv*,
kasher *inv* (**b**) *Fam (legitimate)* réglo *inv*
Kosovan ['kɒsəvən] **1** *n* Kosovar *mf*
2 *adj* kosovar(e)
Kosovo ['kɒsəvəʊ] *n* le Kosovo
kowtow ['kaʊ'taʊ] *vi* **to k. to sb** faire des courbettes
devant qn
Kraut [kraʊt] *n very Fam* Boche *mf*, = terme injurieux
désignant un Allemand
Kremlin ['kremlɪn] *n* **the K.** le Kremlin
krona ['krəʊnə] *(pl* **kronor** ['krəʊnɔː(r)]) *n* couronne *f*
krone ['krəʊnə] *(pl* **kroner** ['krəʊnə(r)]) *n* couronne *f*
kudos ['kjuːdɒs] *n (prestige)* prestige *m*; *(fame)* célébrité *f*
Kurd [kɜːd] **1** *n* Kurde *mf*
2 *adj* kurde
Kurdish ['kɜːdɪʃ] **1** *n (language)* kurde *m*
2 *adj* kurde
Kurdistan [kɜːdɪ'stæn] *n* le Kurdistan
Kuwait [kʊ'weɪt] *n* le Koweït
Kuwaiti [kʊ'weɪtɪ] **1** *n* Koweïtien(enne) *m,f*
2 *adj* koweïtien(enne)
kW *(abbr* **kilowatt**) kW

L

L, l [el] *n* (**a**) *(letter)* L, l *m inv* (**b**) *Br* **L-driver** = personne qui apprend à conduire; **L-plate** = plaque apposée sur une voiture pour signaler que le conducteur est en conduite accompagnée

---

L-driver
En Grande-Bretagne, la lettre "L" apposée sur l'arrière d'un véhicule indique que le conducteur n'a pas encore son permis mais qu'il est en conduite accompagnée.

LA [el'eɪ] *n (abbr* **Los Angeles**) Los Angeles

Lab *Br Pol (abbr* **Labour**) les travaillistes *mpl*

lab [læb] *n Fam (abbr* **laboratory**) labo *m*

label ['leɪbəl] **1** *n* (**a**) *also Fig* étiquette *f* (**b**) *(of record company)* label *m*
2 *vt (pt & pp* **labelled,** *Am* **labeled**) *also Fig* étiqueter; *Fig* **to l. sb a liar** qualifier qn de menteur(euse)

labor, labored *etc Am* = **labour, laboured** *etc*

laboratory [lə'bɒrətrɪ] *(pl* **laboratories**) *n* laboratoire *m*; **l. assistant** laborantin(e) *m,f*

laborious [lə'bɔːrɪəs] *adj (work)* pénible, fatigant(e); *(explanation)* laborieux(euse)

laboriously [lə'bɔːrɪəslɪ] *adv* laborieusement

labour, *Am* **labor** ['leɪbə(r)] **1** *n* (**a**) *(work)* labeur *m*; **l. camp** camp *m* de travail
(**b**) *(workers)* main-d'œuvre *f*; **l. costs** coût *m* de la main-d'œuvre; *Am* **L. Day** fête *f* du travail *(aux États-Unis, célébrée le premiere lundi de septembre)*; **l. dispute** conflit *m* du travail; *Br Formerly* **L. Exchange** bureau *m* de placement; **l. force** effectifs *mpl*; **l. market** marché *m* du travail; **l. shortage** pénurie *f* de main-d'œuvre
(**c**) *Br Pol* **L., the L. Party** le parti travailliste, les travaillistes *mpl*
(**d**) *(task)* effort *m*; **to do sth as a l. of love** faire qch pour le plaisir
(**e**) *(childbirth)* travail *m*; **to be in l.** être en travail; **l. pains** douleurs *fpl* de l'accouchement
2 *vt* **to l. a point** s'étendre sur un sujet
3 *vi* (**a**) *(of person)* peiner (**over** sur); **to l. in vain** s'échiner en vain; **to be labouring under a misapprehension** être dans l'erreur
(**b**) *(of engine)* peiner

laboured, *Am* **labored** ['leɪbəd] *adj* laborieux(euse); *(breathing)* pénible, difficile

labourer, *Am* **laborer** ['leɪbərə(r)] *n* manœuvre *m*; *(on farm)* ouvrier(ère) *m,f* agricole

labouring, *Am* **laboring** ['leɪbərɪŋ] *adj* **a l. job** du travail *m* de manœuvre

labour-intensive, *Am* **labor-intensive** [leɪbərɪn-'tensɪv] *adj* qui demande une main-d'œuvre importante

labour-saving, *Am* **labor-saving** ['leɪbəseɪvɪŋ] *adj* qui simplifie la tâche

labrador ['læbrədɔː(r)] *n* labrador *m*

laburnum [lə'bɜːnəm] *n* cytise *m*

labyrinth ['læbərɪnθ] *n* labyrinthe *m*

labyrinthine [læbɪ'rɪnθaɪn] *adj Archit* en labyrinthe; *Fig* labyrinthique

lace [leɪs] **1** *n* (**a**) *(cloth)* dentelle *f*; **l. curtain** rideau *m* en *ou* de dentelle (**b**) *(of shoe)* lacet *m*
2 *vt* (**a**) *(shoes)* **to l. (up)** lacer (**b**) *(drink)* ajouter de l'alcool à; *Fig (story)* entremêler (**with** de); **to l. a drink with sth** ajouter qch dans une boisson

lacerate ['læsəreɪt] *vt* lacérer

laceration [læsə'reɪʃən] *n* lacération *f*

lace-up ['leɪsʌp] **1** *n (shoe)* chaussure *f* à lacets
2 *adj (shoe)* à lacets

lachrymose ['lækrɪməʊs] *adj Lit* larmoyant(e)

lack [læk] **1** *n* manque *m* (**of** de); **for l. of...** faute de...; **there's no l. of volunteers** ce ne sont pas les volontaires qui manquent
2 *vt* manquer de
3 *vi* **to be lacking in sth** manquer de qch

lackadaisical [lækə'deɪzɪkəl] *adj* désinvolte

lackey ['lækɪ] *(pl* **lackeys**) *n Pej* larbin *m*

lacklustre, *Am* **lackluster** ['læklʌstə(r)] *adj* terne

laconic [lə'kɒnɪk] *adj* laconique

lacquer ['lækə(r)] **1** *n* laque *f*
2 *vt* laquer

lacrosse [lə'krɒs] *n Sport* crosse *f*

lacuna [lə'kjuːnə] *(pl* **lacunae** [lə'kjuːniː] *or* **lacunas**) *n* lacune *f*

lad [læd] *n Fam* (**a**) *(young man)* jeune gars *m*; *(boy)* garçon *m*; **he's a big l.** c'est un grand gaillard; **he's a bit of a l.** *or* **quite a l.** c'est un sacré fêtard (**b**) **lads** *(friends)* copains *mpl*, potes *mpl*; **he's gone out with the lads** il est sorti avec les copains; **come on, lads!** allez les mecs!

ladder ['lædə(r)] **1** *n (for climbing, in tights)* échelle *f*; **the social l.** l'échelle sociale; *Fig* **to get one's foot on the l.** mettre un pied à l'étrier; *Fig* **to reach the top of the l.** atteindre le sommet de l'échelle
2 *vt (tights)* filer
3 *vi (of tights)* filer

laden ['leɪdən] *adj* chargé(e) (**with** de)

ladle ['leɪdəl] **1** *n* louche *f*
2 *vt (soup)* servir (à la louche)

►**ladle out** *vt sep (soup)* servir (à la louche); *Fig* **to l. out advice/praise** distribuer les conseils/les compliments

lady ['leɪdɪ] (*pl* **ladies**) *n* (**a**) *(woman)* dame *f*; **a young l.** *(unmarried)* une jeune fille; *(married)* une jeune dame; **the l. of the house** la maîtresse de maison; **she's no l.** elle n'a aucune classe; **ladies and gentlemen!** mesdames et messieurs!; **ladies' man** homme *m* à femmes; **ladies' (room)** toilettes *fpl* (des dames); **l. friend** amie *f* (**b**) **Our L.** Notre-Dame *f* (**c**) *(title)* **L. Browne** lady Browne *(titre de noblesse féminin)*; **l. of the manor** châtelaine *f*; **my L.** Madame la Marquise/la Baronne/*etc*; **L. Luck** la chance; *Fam* **to act like L. Muck** jouer à la grande dame

ladybird ['leɪdɪbɜːd] *n* coccinelle *f*

lady-in-waiting ['leɪdɪm'weɪtɪŋ] (*pl* **ladies-in-waiting**) *n* dame *f* d'honneur

lady-killer ['leɪdɪkɪlə(r)] *n Fam* bourreau *m* des cœurs

ladylike ['leɪdɪlaɪk] *adj (woman)* comme il faut; *(air, behaviour)* distingué(e)

ladyship ['leɪdɪʃɪp] *n also Ironic* **Her/Your L.** madame *f*

lag [læg] **1** *n* (**a**) *(gap)* décalage *m* (**b**) *very Fam (prisoner)* **old l.** repris *m* de justice
2 *vt (pt & pp* **lagged**) *(pipes, boiler)* isoler
3 *vi (of person, economy)* **to l. behind** être à la traîne; **to l. behind sb/sth** etre à la traîne derrière qn/qch

lager ['lɑːgə(r)] *n* bière *f* blonde; *Fam* **l. lout** = voyou imbibé de bière

laggard ['lægəd] *n* traînard(e) *m,f*

lagoon [lə'guːn] *n* lagune *f*; *(of atoll)* lagon *m*

laid [leɪd] *pt & pp of* **lay**

laid-back [leɪd'bæk] *adj Fam* cool *inv*, relax *inv*

lain [leɪn] *pp of* **lie²**

lair [leə(r)] *n* repaire *m*

laird [leəd] *n Scot* propriétaire *m* foncier

laisser-faire [leseɪ'feə(r)] **1** *n* laisser-faire *m*
2 *adj* de laisser-faire

laity ['leɪtɪ] *n* **the l.** les laïques *mpl*

lake [leɪk] *n* lac *m*; **L. Geneva** le lac de Genève, le lac Léman; **the L. District, the Lakes** la région des lacs *(dans le nord-ouest de l'Angleterre)*

lamb [læm] *n* agneau *m*; **poor l.!** pauvre biquet!; **like lambs to the slaughter** comme des veaux que l'on mène à l'abattoir; **l. chop** côtelette *f* d'agneau

lambast [læm'bæst] *vt* fustiger

lambing ['læmɪŋ] *n* agnelage *m*

lambskin ['læmskɪn] *n* peau *f* d'agneau

lambswool ['læmswʊl] **1** *n* lambswool *m*
2 *adj* en lambswool

lame [leɪm] **1** *adj (person, horse)* boiteux(euse); *Fig (excuse)* bancal(e); *(plot, argument)* boiteux; **to be l.** boiter; **to go l.** se mettre à boiter; *Fig* **l. duck** canard *m* boiteux
2 *vt* rendre boiteux(euse)

lamé ['lɑːmeɪ] *n* lamé *m*; **a l. dress** une robe en lamé

lamely ['leɪmlɪ] *adv* maladroitement

lament [lə'ment] **1** *n* lamentation *f*; *Mus* complainte *f*
2 *vt* se lamenter sur; **the late lamented Mr Jones** le regretté M. Jones
3 *vi* se lamenter (**over** sur)

lamentable ['læməntəbəl] *adj* lamentable; *(decision, loss)* déplorable

lamentably ['læməntəblɪ] *adv* lamentablement

lamentation [læmən'teɪʃən] *n* lamentation *f*

laminate ['læmɪneɪt] *n* stratifié *m*

laminated ['læmɪneɪtəd] *adj* (**a**) *(glass)* feuilleté(e); *(wood, plastic)* stratifié(e) (**b**) *(paper, identity card)* plastifié(e)

lamp [læmp] *n* lampe *f*

lamplight ['læmplaɪt] *n* **by l.** à la lumière d'une lampe

lampoon [læm'puːn] **1** *n* pamphlet *m*
2 *vt* brocarder

lamppost ['læmppəʊst] *n* réverbère *m*

lamprey ['læmprɪ] (*pl* **lampreys**) *n* lamproie *f*

lampshade ['læmpʃeɪd] *n* abat-jour *m inv*

lampstand ['læmpstænd] *n* pied *m* de lampe

LAN [eleɪ'en] *n Comput (abbr* **local area network**) réseau *m* local

lance [lɑːns] **1** *n (weapon)* lance *f*
2 *vt (abscess)* percer, inciser

lance corporal ['lɑːns'kɔːpərəl] *n* ≃ caporal *m*

lancer ['lɑːnsə(r)] *n (soldier)* lancier *m*

lancet ['lɑːnsɪt] *n* lancette *f*

land [lænd] **1** *n* (**a**) *(ground, earth)* terre *f*; **on l.** sur terre; **to live off the l.** vivre du produit de la terre; **to be in the l. of the living** être toujours de ce monde; *Mil* **l. forces** armée *f* de terre; **l. reclamation** mise *f* en valeur des sols; **l. reform** réforme *f* agraire
(**b**) *(property)* terres *fpl*; **a piece of l.** *(for farming)* un lopin de terre; *(for building)* un terrain (à bâtir)
(**c**) *Lit or Formal (nation)* pays *m*; **distant lands** pays lointains
2 *vt* (**a**) *(passengers, cargo)* débarquer
(**b**) *(plane)* poser
(**c**) *(fish)* sortir de l'eau
(**d**) *Fam (job, prize)* décrocher
(**e**) *Fam (put)* **to l. sb in prison/court** mener qn en prison/au tribunal; **to l. sb in trouble** attirer des ennuis à qn
(**f**) *Fam* **to be landed with sth** rester avec qch sur les bras; **I got landed with doing the dishes** c'est moi qui ai dû me taper la vaisselle
(**g**) *Fam (hit)* **to l. sb one** en coller une à qn
3 *vi (of plane)* atterrir; *(of gymnast)* se réceptionner; *Fig* **to l. on one's feet** retomber sur ses pieds

►**land up** *vi* atterrir

landed ['lændəd] *adj* **l. gentry** noblesse *f* terrienne; **l. proprietor** propriétaire *mf* terrien(enne)

landfall ['lændfɔːl] *n Naut* **to make l.** arriver en vue des côtes

landfill site ['lændfɪl'saɪt] *n* décharge *f* publique

landing ['lændɪŋ] *n* (**a**) *(of cargo, troops)* débarquement *m*; **l. card** carte *f* de débarquement; **l. craft** navire *m* de débarquement; **l. stage** débarcadère *m* (**b**) *(of aircraft)* atterrissage *m*; **l. gear** train *m* d'atterrissage; **l. lights** phares *mpl* d'atterrissage; **l. strip** piste *f* d'atterrissage (**c**) *(of staircase)* palier *m*

landlady ['lændleɪdɪ] (*pl* **landladies**) *n* (**a**) *(of rented accommodation)* propriétaire *f* (**b**) *(of small hotel)* logeuse *f*; *(of pub)* patronne *f*

landlocked ['lændlɒkt] *adj* sans accès à la mer

landlord ['lændlɔːd] *n* (**a**) *(of rented accommodation)* propriétaire *m* (**b**) *(of pub)* patron *m*

landmark ['lændmɑːk] *n (distinctive feature)* point *m* de repère; *Fig (important event)* événement *m* marquant

landmass ['lændmæs] *n* masse *f* continentale

landmine ['lændmaɪn] *n* mine *f* terrestre

landowner ['lændəʊnə(r)] *n* propriétaire *mf* foncier(-ère)

landowning ['lændəʊnɪŋ] adj **the l. classes** la propriété foncière

landscape ['lændskeɪp] **1** n paysage m; **l. design** aménagement m d'espaces verts; **l. gardener** jardinier(ère) m,f paysagiste; Comput **l. (orientation)** format m paysage; **l. painter** paysagiste mf
2 vt aménager en espaces verts

landslide ['lændslaɪd] n (**a**) (of earth, rocks) glissement m de terrain (**b**) (election victory) raz m inv de marée électoral; **to win by a l.** gagner avec une majorité écrasante

landslip ['lændslɪp] n glissement m de terrain

landward ['lændwəd] **1** adj (wind) marin(e); **on the l. side** du côté des terres
2 adv vers la terre

lane [leɪn] n (**a**) (in country) chemin m; (in town) ruelle f, passage m (**b**) (on road) voie f, file f; **get in l.** (sign) = panneau indiquant aux automobilistes de se placer dans la file appropriée (**c**) (for runner, swimmer) couloir m

language ['læŋgwɪdʒ] n (**a**) (of a people) langue f; Fam Fig **we don't talk the same l.** nous ne parlons pas la même langue; **l. laboratory** laboratoire m de langues; **l. learning/teaching** apprentissage m/enseignement m des langues (**b**) (style of speech or writing) langage m

languid ['læŋgwɪd] adj alangui(e)

languidly ['læŋgwɪdlɪ] adv paresseusement

languish ['læŋgwɪʃ] vi languir (**for** après); **to l. in prison** moisir en prison

languor ['læŋgə(r)] n langueur f

languorous ['læŋgərəs] adj alangui(e)

lank [læŋk] adj (hair) terne

lanky ['læŋkɪ] adj dégingandé(e)

lanolin(e) ['lænəlɪn] n lanoline f

lantern ['læntən] n lanterne f

Laos [laʊs] n le Laos

Laotian ['laʊʃɪən] **1** n Laotien(enne) m,f
2 adj laotien(enne)

lap¹ [læp] n (**a**) (part of body) genoux mpl; **to sit on sb's l.** s'asseoir sur les genoux de qn; **l. dancer** entraîneuse qui danse nue pour un client (**b**) (idioms) **it's in the l. of the gods** on ne peut que s'en remettre au sort; **she expects everything to fall into her l.** elle s'attend à ce que tout lui tombe tout cuit dans le bec; **to live in the l. of luxury** vivre dans le luxe

lap² **1** n (in race) tour m; **l. of honour** tour d'honneur
2 vt (pt & pp **lapped**) (overtake) prendre un tour d'avance sur

lap³ (pt & pp **lapped**) vi (of animal) laper; **to l. against sth** (of waves) clapoter contre qch

▶**lap up** vt sep (drink) laper; Fam Fig (enjoy indiscriminately) se délecter de; (believe) gober, avaler

laparotomy [læpə'rɒtəmɪ] (pl **laparotomies**) n Med laparotomie f

lapdog ['læpdɒg] n chien m d'appartement; Fig toutou m

lapel [lə'pel] n revers m

Lapland ['læplænd] n la Laponie

Laplander ['læplændə(r)] n Lapon(one) m,f

Lapp [læp] **1** n (**a**) (person) Lapon(one) m,f (**b**) (language) lapon m
2 adj lapon(one)

lapse [læps] **1** n (**a**) (of time) laps m de temps (**b**) (in standards, concentration) baisse f (**in** de); (in behaviour) écart m (**in** de)

2 vi (**a**) (of concentration, standards) baisser; (of person) retomber dans un travers; **to l. into silence** se taire (**b**) (of permit, membership) expirer

lapsed [læpst] adj (Catholic) qui ne pratique plus

laptop ['læptɒp] n Comput portable m

lapwing ['læpwɪŋ] n vanneau m

larceny ['lɑːsənɪ] n Law vol m

larch [lɑːtʃ] n mélèze m

lard [lɑːd] **1** n (fat) saindoux m
2 vt Fam Fig **to l. one's writings with quotations** truffer ses écrits de citations

larder ['lɑːdə(r)] n garde-manger m inv

large [lɑːdʒ] **1** n **to be at l.** être en liberté; **people at l., the public at l.** le grand public
2 adj (**a**) (big) grand(e); (fat, bulky) gros (grosse); (audience) nombreux(euse); **to grow** or **get larger** s'agrandir; (of person) grossir; **to make sth larger** agrandir qch; **as l. as life** en chair et en os; **larger than life** haut(e) en couleur (**b**) (extensive, significant) **to a l. extent** en grande partie; **a l. part of** une grande partie de
3 adv **by and l.** dans l'ensemble

largely ['lɑːdʒlɪ] adv en grande partie

large-scale ['lɑːdʒ'skeɪl] adj (map) à grande échelle; (undertaking) ambitieux(euse); (disaster) immense

largesse [lɑː'ʒes] n largesse f

lark¹ [lɑːk] n (bird) alouette f; **to rise with the l.** se lever au chant du coq

lark² n (joke) rigolade f; **to do sth for a l.** faire qch pour rire; **I don't like this fancy dress l.** je n'aime pas du tout cette histoire de bal masqué

▶**lark about, lark around** vi faire le fou (la folle)

larva ['lɑːvə] (pl **larvae** ['lɑːviː]) n larve f

laryngitis [lærɪn'dʒaɪtɪs] n laryngite f; **to have l.** avoir une laryngite

larynx ['lærɪŋks] n larynx m

lasagne [lə'sænjə] n lasagnes fpl

lascivious [lə'sɪvɪəs] adj lascif(ive)

laser ['leɪzə(r)] n laser m; **l. beam** rayon m laser; **l. disc** disque m laser; **l. printer** imprimante f laser; **l. surgery** chirurgie f au laser

lash [læʃ] **1** n (**a**) (eyelash) cil m (**b**) (of whip) coup m de fouet
2 vt (**a**) (with whip) cingler; (of rain, waves) fouetter (**b**) (tie) lier, attacher
3 vi **the rain** or **it was lashing down** il pleuvait dru

▶**lash out** vi (**a**) (attack) **to l. out at sb** (physically) donner un coup/des coups à qn; (verbally) s'en prendre violemment à qn (**b**) Fam (spend extravagantly) claquer un fric fou (**on** pour)

lashings ['læʃɪŋz] npl Fam (lots) des tas; **l. of cream/jam** une tonne de crème/confiture

lass [læs] n jeune fille f

lassitude ['læsɪtjuːd] n (weariness) lassitude f; (laziness) paresse f

lasso [læ'suː] **1** n (pl **lassoes** or **lassos**) lasso m
2 vt (pt & pp **lassoed**) attraper au lasso

last¹ [lɑːst] **1** n **the l.** le dernier (la dernière) m,f; **the l. but one** l'avant-dernier(ère) m,f; **we'll never hear the l. of it** on n'a pas fini d'en entendre parler; **I don't think we've heard the l. of him** je crois que nous n'en sommes pas encore débarrassés; **that's the l. I saw of her** je ne l'ai pas revue depuis; **that's the l. of the wine** on a fini le vin; **to** or **till the l.** jusqu'à la fin; **at (long) l.** enfin

2 *adj* (**a**) *(final)* dernier(ère); **you are my l. hope** vous êtes mon dernier espoir; **to have the l. word** avoir le dernier mot; **the l. word in comfort/style** le summum du confort/de l'élégance; **at the l. moment** *or* **minute** au dernier moment, à la dernière minute; **l. thing at night** avant de se coucher; **to be on one's l. legs** être au bout du rouleau; **he's the l. person l'd ask to help me** c'est (bien) la dernière personne à qui je demanderais de m'aider; **that's the l. thing l'd do** c'est (bien) la dernière chose que je ferais; **as a l. resort** en dernier recours; **the L. Judgement** le Jugement dernier; **l. name** nom *m* de famille; **l. rites** derniers sacrements *mpl*; *Fig* **the l. straw** la goutte d'eau qui a fait déborder le vase

(**b**) *(most recent)* dernier(ère); **the l. time I saw him** la dernière fois que je l'ai vu; **l. January** en janvier (dernier); **l. night** *(during the night)* la nuit dernière; *(in the evening)* hier (au) soir; **l. Tuesday** mardi dernier; **l. week** la semaine dernière

3 *adv* **to arrive/finish l.** arriver/finir dernier; **when I l. saw him** la dernière fois que je l'ai vu; **l. but not least** enfin

last² *n (for shoe)* forme *f* (à chaussure)

last³ 1 *vt* **that watch will l. you a lifetime** vous pourrez garder cette montre toute votre vie; **it has lasted him well** ça lui a fait de l'usage; **have we got enough to l. us until tomorrow?** en avons-nous assez pour tenir jusqu'à demain?

2 *vi* durer; **it's too good to l.** c'est trop beau pour durer; **the supplies won't l. two months** les provisions ne seront pas suffisantes pour deux mois; **he won't l. long in that job** il ne tiendra pas très long temps à ce poste; **she won't l. the night** elle ne passera pas la nuit

▸**last out 1** *vt sep* **to l. the year out** *(of person)* survivre jusqu'à la fin de l'année; *(of supplies)* suffire pour l'année

2 *vi (of person)* tenir le coup; *(of supplies)* suffire

last-ditch [lɑːst'dɪtʃ] *adj* ultime; **a l. attempt** un ultime effort

lasting ['lɑːstɪŋ] *adj* durable

lastly ['lɑːstlɪ] *adv* pour finir, en dernier lieu

last-minute [lɑːst'mɪnɪt] *adj* de dernière minute

latch [lætʃ] *n* loquet *m*

▸**latch onto** *vt insep Fam* (**a**) *(attach oneself to)* **to l. onto sb/sth** s'accrocher à qn/qch (**b**) *(understand)* **to l. onto sth** piger qch

latchkey ['lætʃkiː] *(pl* **latchkeys***) n* clef *f* de la porte d'entrée; **l. child** = enfant dont les parents travaillent et qui doit rentrer seul après l'école

late [leɪt] **1** *adj* (**a**) *(not on time)* en retard; **to be l. (for sth)** être en retard (pour qch); **to be ten minutes l.** avoir dix minutes de retard

(**b**) *(far on in time)* tard; **it's getting l.** il se fait tard; **to keep l. hours** se coucher tard; **in the l. afternoon** en fin d'après-midi; **in l. summer** vers la fin de l'été; **to be in one's l. thirties** approcher de la quarantaine; **in the l. eighties** vers la fin des années 80; *Fig* **it's a bit l. in the day to...** il est un peu tard pour...; **l. booking** réservation *f* de dernière minute

(**c**) *(dead)* feu(e); **my l. husband** feu mon mari

2 *adv* (**a**) *(in general)* tard; **to work l.** travailler tard; **l. into the night** jusqu'à une heure avancée de la nuit; **l. in the year** vers la fin de l'année; **l. in life** sur le tard; *Prov* **better l. than never** mieux vaut tard que jamais

(**b**) *(recently)* **as l. as last week** pas plus tard que la semaine dernière; **of l.** récemment

latecomer ['leɪtkʌmə(r)] *n* retardataire *mf*

lately ['leɪtlɪ] *adv* dernièrement, récemment; **until l.** jusqu'à ces derniers temps

lateness ['leɪtnɪs] *n (of person, train)* retard *m*; **the l. of the hour** l'heure *f* tardive

latent ['leɪtənt] *adj (disease, tendency)* latent(e); *(period)* de latence

later ['leɪtə(r)] **1** *adj* ultérieur(e); **I caught a l. train** j'ai pris un train qui partait plus tard; **l. events proved that...** la suite des événements a prouvé que...; **her l. novels** ses derniers romans; **in l. life** avec l'âge

2 *adv* **l. (on)** plus tard; **a few days l.** quelques jours plus tard; **no l. than tomorrow** demain au plus tard; **as we shall see l.** comme nous le verrons par la suite; *Fam* **see you l.!** à plus tard!

lateral ['lætərəl] *adj* latéral(e); **l. thinking** approche *f* originale

latest ['leɪtɪst] **1** *n* **at the l.** au plus tard; **the l. I can stay is four o'clock** je peux rester jusqu'à quatre heures au plus tard; **have you heard the l.?** vous savez la dernière?

2 *adj (most recent)* dernier(ère)

latex ['leɪteks] *n* latex *m*

lathe [leɪð] *n* tour *m*

lather ['læðə(r)] **1** *n* mousse *f*; *Fam* **to work oneself** *or* **get into a l. (about sth)** se mettre dans tous ses états (à propos de qch)

2 *vt* savonner

Latin ['lætɪn] **1** *n* (**a**) *(person) (European)* Latin(e) *m,f*; *(Latin American)* Latino-Américain(e) *m,f* (**b**) *(language)* latin *m*

2 *adj* latin(e); **L. America** l'Amérique *f* latine; **L. American** latino-américain(e)

latitude ['lætɪtjuːd] *n also Fig* latitude *f*

latrine [lə'triːn] *n* latrines *fpl*

latte ['læteɪ] *n* café *m* au lait

latter ['lætə(r)] **1** *n (of two)* **the l.** le second (la seconde)

2 *adj* (**a**) *(of two)* second(e) (**b**) *(last)* dernier(ère); **the l. half** *or* **part of June** la deuxième moitié de juin

latter-day ['lætə'deɪ] *adj* moderne; *Rel* **the L. Saints** les mormons *mpl*

latterly ['lætəlɪ] *adv (recently)* dernièrement, récemment; *(towards the end of a period)* vers la fin

lattice ['lætɪs] *n* treillis *m*; **l. window** fenêtre *f* à croisillons de plomb

latticework ['lætɪswɜːk] *n* treillis *m*

Latvia ['lætvɪə] *n* la Lettonie

Latvian ['lætvɪən] **1** *n* (**a**) *(person)* Letton(onne) *m,f* (**b**) *(language)* letton *m*

2 *adj* letton(onne)

laudable ['lɔːdəbəl] *adj* louable, digne de louanges

laudanum ['lɔːdənəm] *n* laudanum *m*

laugh [lɑːf] **1** *n* rire *m*; *Fam* **to have a good l.** bien se marrer; *Fam* **to do sth for a l.** faire qch pour rire; *Ironic* **that's a l.!** la bonne blague!; *Fam* **he's a good l.** on se marre avec lui; **to have the last l.** être bien vengé(e)

2 *vi* rire (**at** de); *Fam* **don't make me l.!** laisse-moi rire!; *Fam* **to l. one's head off** être mort(e) de rire; *Fam* **if you get that job, you'll be laughing** si tu obtiens le poste, ça sera super; **he'll be laughing on the other side of his face when...** il rira jaune quand...; *Fam* **to l. all the way to the bank** s'en mettre plein les poches; *Prov* **he who laughs last laughs longest** rira bien qui rira le dernier

3 *vt* **to l. oneself silly** se tordre de rire; **you'll be laughed out of court** vous vous couvrirez de ridicule

▶**laugh off** *vt sep* tourner en plaisanterie

laughable ['lɑ:fəbəl] *adj* ridicule

laughing ['lɑ:fɪŋ] **1** *n* rires *mpl*

2 *adj* rieur(euse); **it's no l. matter** ce n'est pas à prendre à la légère; **she was in no l. mood** elle n'était pas d'humeur à rire; **l. gas** gaz *m* hilarant; **l. stock** risée *f*; **to make sb a l. stock** faire de qn un sujet de plaisanterie

laughter ['lɑ:ftə(r)] *n* rires *mpl*

launch [lɔ:ntʃ] **1** *n* (**a**) *(boat)* chaloupe *f*; **(motor) l.** vedette *f* (**b**) *(of ship, rocket, product)* lancement *m*; **l. pad** plate-forme *f* de lancement

2 *vt* *(ship, rocket, product)* lancer; *(enquiry)* ouvrir; **to l. sb on a career** *(of event)* marquer le début de la carrière de qn

▶**launch into** *vt insep* *(attack, story, complaint)* se lancer dans

launching ['lɔ:ntʃɪŋ] *n* *(of ship, rocket, product)* lancement *m*; *(of enquiry)* ouverture *f*; **l. pad** plate-forme *f* de lancement

launder ['lɔ:ndə(r)] *vt also Fig* blanchir

laundrette [lɔ:n'dret] *n Br* laverie *f* automatique

laundry ['lɔ:ndrɪ] *n* linge *m*; **to do the l.** faire la lessive; **l. basket** panier *m* à linge

laurel ['lɒrəl] *n* laurier *m*; *Fig* **to rest on one's laurels** se reposer sur ses lauriers; **l. wreath** couronne *f* de lauriers

lava ['lɑ:və] *n* lave *f*

lavatory ['lævətrɪ] *(pl* **lavatories**) *n* toilettes *fpl*; **to go to the l.** aller aux toilettes; **l. paper** papier *m* hygiénique

lavender ['lævɪndə(r)] **1** *n* *(shrub)* lavande *f*; **l. water** (eau *f* de Cologne à la) lavande

2 *adj* *(colour)* bleu lavande *inv*

lavish ['lævɪʃ] **1** *adj* (**a**) *(person)* prodigue (**with/in** de) (**b**) *(gift, meal, décor)* somptueux(euse); *(spending)* extravagant(e); *(portion)* généreux(euse)

2 *vt* **to l. sth on sb** couvrir qn de qch

lavishly ['lævɪʃlɪ] *adv* somptueusement; **to spend l.** dépenser sans compter; **to praise sb l.** couvrir qn d'éloges

law [lɔ:] *n* (**a**) *(rule)* loi *f*; **there's no l. against it** aucune loi ne l'interdit; **the laws of gravity** les lois de la pesanteur; **to be a l. unto oneself** n'en faire qu'à sa tête (**b**) *(set of rules)* loi *f*; **to be against the l.** être illégal(e); **to break the l.** enfreindre la loi; **to be above the l.** être au-dessus des lois; **to take the l. into one's own hands** se faire justice soi-même; **l. and order** l'ordre *m* public; **l. enforcement** le respect de la loi; **l. firm** cabinet *m* d'avocats (**c**) *(system of justice, subject)* droit *m*; **to practise l.** exercer une profession juridique; **l. school** faculté *f* de droit (**d**) *Br Fam* **the l.** *(police)* les flics *mpl*

law-abiding ['lɔ:əbaɪdɪŋ] *adj* respectueux(euse) des lois

lawbreaker ['lɔ:breɪkə(r)] *n* personne *f* qui transgresse la loi

lawcourt ['lɔ:kɔ:t] *n* cour *f* de justice

lawful ['lɔ:fəl] *adj* *(legal)* légal(e); *(rightful)* légitime

lawless ['lɔ:lɪs] *adj* *(country, society)* livré(e) à l'anarchie; *(mob)* sans foi ni loi

lawlessness ['lɔ:lɪsnɪs] *n* anarchie *f*

lawmaker ['lɔ:meɪkə(r)] *n* législateur(trice) *m,f*

lawn [lɔ:n] *n* pelouse *f*, gazon *m*; **l. tennis** tennis *m*

lawnmower ['lɔ:nməʊə(r)] *n* tondeuse *f* (à gazon)

lawsuit ['lɔ:su:t] *n* action *f* en justice; **to bring a l. against sb** intenter une action en justice contre qn

lawyer ['lɔ:jə(r)] *n* avocat(e) *m,f*; *(for wills, conveyancing)* notaire *m*; *(in company)* conseiller(ère) *m,f* juridique

lax [læks] *adj* *(discipline, principles, conduct)* relâché(e); *(person)* laxiste

laxative ['læksətɪv] **1** *n* laxatif *m*

2 *adj* laxatif(ive)

laxity ['læksɪtɪ], **laxness** ['læksnɪs] *n* *(of discipline, principles, conduct)* relâchement *m*; *(of person)* laxisme *m*

lay¹ [leɪ] *adj Rel* laïque; **l. preacher** prédicateur *m* laïque

lay² *(pt & pp* **laid** [leɪd] *)* **1** *vt* (**a**) *(place)* mettre, poser; **to l. sb flat** coucher *ou* étendre qn; **to l. sth flat** poser *ou* coucher qch à plat; **to l. sb to rest** inhumer qn; **to l. one's hands on sth** mettre la main sur qch; **she reads everything she can l. her hands on** elle lit tout ce qui lui tombe sous la main; **if you l. a finger on her...** si tu touches à un seul cheveu de sa tête...; **to have nowhere to l. one's head** n'avoir nulle part où dormir; **to l. eyes on sb/sth** poser les yeux sur qn/qch; **to l. emphasis on sth** insister sur qch; **to l. the facts before sb** exposer les faits à qn; **to l. claim to sth** prétendre à qch; **to l. the blame on sb** faire porter la responsabilité à qn; **to l. sth bare** mettre qch à nu; **to l. oneself open to criticism** s'exposer à la critique; **to l. sb's fears to rest** apaiser les craintes de qn (**b**) *(foundations, carpet, trap, cable)* poser; *Br* **to l. the table** mettre la table (**c**) *(egg)* pondre (**d**) **to l. a bet (on)** parier (sur) (**e**) *very Fam* **to get laid** s'envoyer en l'air

2 *vi* *(of bird)* pondre

3 *pt of* **lie²**

▶**lay aside** *vt sep* (**a**) *(money)* mettre de côté (**b**) *(prejudices, doubt)* oublier

▶**lay by** *vt sep* *(money)* mettre de côté

▶**lay down** *vt sep* (**a**) **to l. down one's arms** rendre *ou* déposer les armes; **to l. down one's life** sacrifier sa vie (**b**) *(principle, rule)* établir, poser; **to l. down the law** dicter sa loi

▶**lay in** *vt sep* *(supplies, food)* stocker

▶**lay into** *vt insep Fam (physically)* rosser; *(verbally)* voler dans les plumes à

▶**lay off** **1** *vt sep* *(make redundant)* licencier; *(temporarily)* mettre en chômage technique

2 *vt insep Fam* (**a**) *(abstain from)* arrêter; **to l. off drink** arrêter de boire (**b**) *(leave alone)* ficher la paix à

3 *vi Fam (desist)* arrêter

▶**lay on** *vt sep* *(food, drink)* fournir; *(party, entertainment)* organiser

▶**lay out** *vt sep* (**a**) *(arrange, display)* arranger, disposer; *(dead body)* faire la toilette de (**b**) *(house, town)* concevoir

layabout ['leɪəbaʊt] *n Fam* bon (bonne) *m,f* à rien

lay-by ['leɪbaɪ] *(pl* **lay-bys**) *n* aire *f* de stationnement

layer ['leɪə(r)] **1** *n* couche *f*

2 *vt* *(hair)* dégrader; **to have one's hair layered** se faire faire un dégradé

layman ['leɪmən] *n Rel* laïque *mf*; *(non-specialist)* profane *mf*, non-initié(e) *m,f*

lay-off ['leɪɒf] *n* licenciement *m*; *(temporary)* mise *f* en chômage technique

layout ['leɪaʊt] *n (of town)* plan *m*; *(of building)* agencement *m*; *(of text)* mise *f* en page

laywoman ['leɪwʊmən] *n Rel* laïque *f*; *(non-specialist)* profane *f*, non-initiée *f*

laze [leɪz] *vi* **to l. (about** *or* **around)** paresser, fainéanter

laziness ['leɪzɪnɪs] *n* paresse *f*, fainéantise *f*

lazy ['leɪzɪ] *adj (person)* paresseux(euse), fainéant(e); *(afternoon)* passé(e) à ne rien faire

lazybones ['leɪzɪbəʊnz] *(pl* **lazybones)** *n Fam* flemmard(e) *m,f*

lb *(abbr* **pound)** livre *f*

LCD [elsiː'diː] *n (abbr* **liquid crystal display)** affichage *m* à cristaux liquides

LDC [eldiː'siː] *n Econ (abbr* **less developed country)** PVD *m*

LEA [eliː'eɪ] *n (abbr* **local education authority)** = organisme chargé de l'enseignement au niveau régional

lead¹ [led] *n* (**a**) *(metal)* plomb *m*; **l. poisoning** saturnisme *m* (**b**) *(for pencil)* mine *f* (**c**) *(idioms)* **to go down like a l. balloon** tomber à plat; *Fam* **to fill sb full of l.** truffer qn de plomb; *Fam* **to swing the l.** tirer au flanc

lead² [liːd] **1** *n* (**a**) *(advantage)* avance *f*; **to be in the l.** être en tête; **to take** *or* **go into the l.** *(in race)* prendre la tête; *(in match)* mener; **to have a 10-point l.** avoir 10 points d'avance; *Ind* **l. time** *(for production)* délai *m* de production; *(for delivery)* délai de livraison

  (**b**) *(example)* exemple *m*; **to give sb the l.** donner l'exemple à qn; **to follow sb's l.** suivre l'exemple de qn
  (**c**) *(clue)* indice *m*
  (**d**) *(in card game)* **it's your l.** à vous de jouer
  (**e**) *(in film, play)* premier rôle *m*, rôle principal
  (**f**) *(for dog)* laisse *f*
  (**g**) *(cable)* câble *m ou* fil *m* (électrique)

  2 *vt (pt & pp* **led** [led]) (**a**) *(guide)* mener, conduire; **you l. the way** montre-nous le chemin; **to l. the conversation away from a subject** détourner la conversation; **to be easily led** être très influençable; **that leads me to believe that...** cela m'amène à penser que...

  (**b**) **to l. a happy/sad life** mener une vie heureuse/triste
  (**c**) *(be leader of)* mener
  (**d**) *(be ahead of)* **to l. the field** mener; *Fig* **to l. the field in sth** être en tête dans le domaine de qch; **to l. sb by 8 points** avoir une avance de 8 points sur qn

  3 *vi* (**a**) *(of road)* mener, conduire (**to** à)
  (**b**) **to l. to sth** *(cause)* mener à qch
  (**c**) *(in competition, race)* mener; *(in card game)* jouer le premier; **you l. and I'll follow** vas-y, je te suis

lead away *vt sep* emmener

lead off *vi* (**a**) *(road, corridor)* partir (**from** de) (**b**) *(in discussion)* commencer

lead on *vt sep (deceive)* tromper, duper

lead up to *vt insep (of person)* en venir à; *(of event)* précéder; **what are you leading up to?** où veux-tu en venir?

leaded ['ledɪd] *adj* **l. window** fenêtre *f* à croisillons de plomb; **l. petrol** essence *f* au plomb

leaden ['ledən] *adj (heavy)* lourd(e)

leader ['liːdə(r)] *n* (**a**) *(of group)* chef *m*; *Pol* chef, leader *m*, dirigeant(e) *m,f*; *(of riot)* meneur(euse) *m,f*; *(in race)* premier(ère) *m,f*; **to be a born l.** être fait(e) pour commander (**b**) *(in newspaper)* éditorial *m*

leadership ['liːdəʃɪp] *n (people in charge)* dirigeants *mpl*; *(position)* direction *f*; *(quality)* qualités *fpl* d'encadrement

lead-free [led'friː] *adj (petrol, paint)* sans plomb

lead-in ['liːdɪn] *n TV & Rad* introduction *f*

leading ['liːdɪŋ] *adj* (**a**) *(best, most important)* principal(e); **l. article** *(in newspaper)* éditorial *m*; **l. lady** *(in film, play)* premier rôle *m* féminin; *Fig* **l. light** personnalité *f* de premier plan; **l. man** *(in film, play)* premier rôle masculin; **l. role** *(in film, play)* premier rôle (**b**) *(team, runner)* de tête (**c**) **l. question** question *f* tendancieuse

leaf [liːf] *(pl* **leaves** [liːvz]) *n* (**a**) *(of plant)* feuille *f*; *(of book)* feuillet *m*; *Fig* **to turn over a new l.** s'acheter une conduite; *Fig* **to take a l. out of sb's book** prendre exemple sur qn (**b**) *(of table) (inserted)* rallonge *f*; *(hinged)* battant *m*

▸**leaf through** *vt insep (book, magazine)* feuilleter

leaflet ['liːflɪt] **1** *n* prospectus *m*; *(political)* tract *m*; *(folded)* dépliant *m*
  2 *vt (area)* distribuer des prospectus dans

leafy ['liːfɪ] *adj (tree)* feuillu(e); *(street)* ombragé(e); **a l. suburb** une banlieue verte

league [liːg] *n* ligue *f*; *(in sport)* championnat *m*; **to be in l. with sb** être de mèche avec qn; *Fig* **to be in a different l.** être hors classe; *Fig* **they're not in the same l.** ils ne sont pas du même niveau; **l. champions** vainqueurs *mpl* du championnat

leak [liːk] **1** *n also Fig* fuite *f*; *(in boat)* voie *f* d'eau; *Fam* **to take** *or* **have a l.** pisser un coup
  2 *vt (information)* divulguer (**to** à); **the pipe was leaking gas/water** du gaz/de l'eau fuyait du tuyau
  3 *vi* fuir; *(of shoe)* prendre l'eau; *(of boat)* faire eau; **the roof is leaking** il y a une fuite dans le toit

leakage ['liːkɪdʒ] *n* fuite *f*

leaky ['liːkɪ] *adj (bucket, pipe, tap)* qui fuit; *(roof)* qui a une fuite; *(shoe)* qui prend l'eau; *(boat)* qui fait eau

lean¹ [liːn] *adj* (**a**) *(person, face)* mince; *(meat)* maigre (**b**) *(harvest)* maigre; *(year)* de vaches maigres

lean² *(pt & pp* **leant** [lent] *or* **leaned)** **1** *vt* **to l. sth on/against sth** appuyer qch sur/contre qch
  2 *vi (of building)* pencher; **to l. on/against sth** s'appuyer sur/contre qch; *Fig* **to l. on sb** *(rely on)* s'appuyer sur qn; *(pressurize)* faire pression sur qn; **the Leaning Tower of Pisa** la tour de Pise; **to l. out of the window** se pencher à la fenêtre

▸**lean back** *vi* se pencher en arrière

▸**lean over 1** *vt insep* **to l. over sb/sth** se pencher par-dessus qn/qch
  2 *vi* se pencher

leaning ['liːnɪŋ] *n (tendency)* inclination *f*, penchant *m* (**towards** pour); **to have artistic leanings** avoir des dispositions artistiques

leant [lent] *pt & pp of* **lean**

lean-to ['liːntuː] *(pl* **lean-tos)** *n* appentis *m*

leap [liːp] **1** *n* saut *m*, bond *m*; *Fig* **to take a l. in the dark** faire un saut dans l'inconnu; *Fig* **to advance by leaps and bounds** avancer à pas de géant; **l. year** année *f* bissextile
  2 *vt (pt & pp* **leapt** [lept] *or* **leaped)** franchir d'un bond *ou* d'un saut
  3 *vi* sauter, bondir; **to l. to one's feet** se lever d'un

bond; **to l. at the chance** sauter sur l'occasion; **to l. for joy** sauter de joie

leapfrog ['liːpfrɒg] **1** *n* saute-mouton *m*; **to play l.** jouer à saute-mouton

2 *vt* (*pt & pp* **leapfrogged**) *Fig* passer avant

leapt [lept] *pt & pp of* **leap**

learn [lɜːn] (*pt & pp* **learnt** [lɜːnt] *or* **learned**) **1** *vt* apprendre

2 *vi* apprendre; **to l. of** *or* **about sth** apprendre qch; **to l. from one's mistakes** tirer un enseignement de ses erreurs

learned ['lɜːnɪd] *adj* savant(e), érudit(e); *Br Law* **my l. friend** mon éminent confrère

learner ['lɜːnə(r)] *n* (*beginner*) débutant(e) *m,f*; (*student*) étudiant(e) *m,f*; **to be a quick/slow l.** apprendre vite/lentement; **l. (driver)** apprenti(e) *m,f* conducteur(trice)

learning ['lɜːnɪŋ] *n* (*act of learning*) apprentissage *m*; (*knowledge*) savoir *m*, connaissances *fpl*; **l. curve** courbe *f* d'assimilation; **it was a steep l. curve** l'apprentissage a été difficile

learnt [lɜːnt] *pt & pp of* **learn**

lease [liːs] **1** *n* bail *m*; *Fig* **to give sb a new l. of life** redonner à qn goût à la vie; **to take on a new l. of life** (*of person*) renaître à la vie; (*of industry, town*) retrouver un nouveau souffle

2 *vt* louer (**from/to** à)

leasehold ['liːshəʊld] *n* (*contract*) bail *m*; (*property*) location *f* à bail

leaseholder ['liːshəʊldə(r)] *n* locataire *mf*

leash [liːʃ] *n* (*for dog*) laisse *f*; *Fig* **to keep sb on a tight l.** tenir la bride haute à qn

leasing ['liːsɪŋ] *n Com* location-vente *f*

least [liːst] **1** *n* **the l.** le moins qu'on puisse dire, c'est que...; **it's the l. I can do** c'est la moindre des choses; **that's the l. of my worries** c'est le cadet de mes soucis; **at l.** au moins; **he's leaving, at l. that's what I've heard** il part, du moins c'est ce que j'ai entendu dire; **at l. as old as...** au moins aussi vieux que...; **at the very l. they should pay your expenses** ce serait vraiment la moindre des choses qu'ils te remboursent tes frais; **not in the l.** pas du tout; **it doesn't matter in the l.** cela n'a pas la moindre importance

2 *adj* (*superlative of* **little**) (*smallest*) moindre; **the l. thing annoys her** un rien l'agace

3 *adv* **the l. difficult** le (la) moins difficile; **l. of all her** elle encore moins que les autres; **when I was l. expecting it** au moment où je m'y attendais le moins

leather ['leðə(r)] **1** *n* cuir *m*

2 *vt Fam* (*beat*) tanner le cuir à

leather-bound ['leðəbaʊnd] *adj* (*book*) relié(e) en cuir

leathery ['leðərɪ] *adj* (*face, skin*) tanné(e); (*meat*) coriace

leave [liːv] **1** *n* (**a**) (*permission*) permission *f*, autorisation *f*; **to ask l. to do sth** demander la permission *ou* l'autorisation de faire qch; **to grant** *or* **give sb l. to do sth** accorder *ou* donner à qn l'autorisation de faire qch

(**b**) (*holiday*) congé *m*; **to be on l.** (*from work*) être en congé; (*from army*) être en permission; **l. of absence** (*from work*) congé exceptionnel; (*from army*) permission *f* exceptionnelle

(**c**) (*farewell*) **to take one's l. (of sb)** prendre congé (de qn); **to take l. of one's senses** perdre l'esprit

2 *vt* (*pt & pp* **left** [left]) (**a**) (*depart from*) quitter; **to l. the table** se lever de table; **the car left the road** la voiture a quitté la route

(**b**) (*put, deposit*) **to l. sth somewhere** (*on purpose*) laisser qch quelque part; (*accidentally*) oublier qch quelque part; **take it or l. it** (*of offer*) c'est à prendre ou à laisser; **to l. a message for sb** laisser un message pour qn

(**c**) (*allow to remain*) laisser; **to l. the door open** laisser la porte ouverte; **to l. oneself open to criticism** laisser la porte ouverte aux critiques; **to l. sth unfinished** laisser qch inachevé(e); **to l. sb to do sth** laisser qn faire qch; **l. it to me** laisse-moi faire; **to l. much** *or* **a lot to be desired** laisser beaucoup à désirer; **let's l. it at that** restons-en là; **to l. well alone** ne pas s'en mêler; **l. me alone!** fiche-moi la paix!

(**d**) (*bequeath*) laisser (**to** à); **he leaves a wife and three children** (*after dying*) il laisse une femme et trois enfants

(**e**) **to be left** (*remain*) rester; **there are a few chocolates left** il reste quelques chocolats; **three from seven leaves four** sept moins trois égale quatre

3 *vi* (*depart*) partir

▸**leave behind** *vt sep* **to l. sth behind** (*on purpose*) laisser qch; (*accidentally*) oublier qch; **to l. sb behind** partir sans qn

▸**leave off 1** *vt insep Fam* **to l. off doing sth** arrêter de faire qch; **to l. off work** cesser le travail

2 *vi* s'arrêter

▸**leave on** *vt sep* (*light, TV*) laisser allumé(e)

▸**leave out** *vt sep* (**a**) (*omit*) omettre (**b**) (*not involve*) **to l. sb out of sth** laisser qn en dehors de qch; **to feel left out** se sentir exclu(e) (**c**) (*leave ready, available*) **I'll l. your dinner out on the table for you** je laisserai ton dîner sur la table; **l. the disks out where I can see them** laisse les disquettes en évidence (**d**) (*leave outside*) laisser dehors; **who left the milk out?** qui a oublié de mettre le lait au frigo? (**e**) *Br Fam* **l. it out!** (*stop it*) arrête!

▸**leave over** *vt sep* **to be left over** (*of food, money*) rester; **there's some lasagne left over** il reste des lasagnes

leaven ['levən] *n* levain *m*

leaves [liːvz] *pl of* **leaf**

leave-taking ['liːveɪkɪŋ] *n* adieux *mpl*

Lebanese [lebə'niːz] **1** *npl* (*people*) **the L.** les Libanais *mpl*

2 *n* (*pl* **Lebanese**) (*person*) Libanais(e) *m,f*

3 *adj* libanais(e)

Lebanon ['lebənən] *n* le Liban

lecher ['letʃə(r)] *n* obsédé *m*

lecherous ['letʃərəs] *adj* lubrique

lechery ['letʃərɪ] *n* lubricité *f*

lectern ['lektən] *n* lutrin *m*

lecture ['lektʃə(r)] **1** *n* (**a**) (*talk*) conférence *f*; (*at university*) cours *m* magistral; **l. theatre** amphithéâtre *m* (**b**) *Fam* (*reprimand*) sermon *m*; **to give sb a l.** faire la morale à qn

2 *vt Fam* (*reprimand*) faire la morale à

3 *vi* (*give public lectures*) donner une conférence/des conférences; (*at university*) donner un cours magistral/des cours magistraux

lecturer ['lektʃərə(r)] *n Univ* enseignant(e) *m,f* (*d'université*)

LED [eliː'diː] *n Elec* (*abbr* **light-emitting diode**) LED *f*

led [led] *pt & pp of* **lead**

ledge [ledʒ] *n (on cliff)* corniche *f; (of window, on building)* rebord *m*

ledger ['ledʒə(r)] *n* grand livre *m*

leech [liːtʃ] *n also Fig* sangsue *f;* **to cling to sb like a l.** se cramponner à qn comme une sangsue

leek [liːk] *n* poireau *m*

leer ['lɪə(r)] **1** *n (lustful)* regard *m* lubrique; *(cruel)* regard sadique
  2 *vi* **to l. at sb** *(lustfully)* regarder qn d'un air lubrique; *(cruelly)* regarder qn d'un air sadique

lees [liːz] *npl (of wine)* lie *f*

leeward ['liːwəd] **1** *n* côté *m* sous le vent
  2 *adj* sous le vent; **the L. Islands** les îles *fpl* Sous-le-Vent

leeway ['liːweɪ] *n* marge *f* de manœuvre

left¹ [left] **1** *n* gauche *f;* **on** *or* **to the l.** à gauche; **on my l.** à ma gauche
  2 *adj* gauche; **the l. wing** *(of party)* l'aile *f* gauche
  3 *adv* à gauche

left² *pt & pp of* **leave**

left-field ['left'fiːld] *adj Am Fam (bizarre)* bizarroïde

left-hand ['left'hænd] *adj* de gauche; *(corner, side)* gauche; **l. drive** conduite *f* à gauche; **on the l. side** à gauche

left-handed [left'hændɪd] **1** *adj* gaucher(ère)
  2 *adv* de la main gauche

left-hander [left'hændə(r)] *n (person)* gaucher(ère) *m,f*

left luggage (office) ['left'lʌgɪdʒ('ɒfɪs)] *n* consigne *f*

leftover ['leftəʊvə(r)] **1** *adj* **l. food/paint** un reste de nourriture/de peinture
  2 *n* **leftovers** restes *mpl*

left-wing ['leftwɪŋ] *adj* de gauche

left-winger ['left'wɪŋə(r)] *n* homme (femme) *m,f* de gauche

leg [leg] **1** *n* (**a**) *(of person, trousers)* jambe *f; (of animal)* patte *f; (of table, chair)* pied *m* (**b**) *Culin (of lamb)* gigot *m; (of chicken)* cuisse *f; (of pork)* rôti *m* (**c**) *(of journey, race)* étape *f* (**d**) *(idioms)* **to pull sb's l.** faire marcher qn; **to show a l.** se lever; **to shake a l.** se remuer; **you don't have a l. to stand on** tu n'as rien sur quoi t'appuyer; **to give sb a l. up** donner un coup de pouce à qn; *very Fam* **to get one's l. over** s'envoyer en l'air
  2 *vt (pt & pp* **legged)** *Fam* **to l. it** jouer des gambettes

legacy ['legəsɪ] *(pl* **legacies)** *n also Fig* legs *m;* **to come into a l.** faire un héritage

legal ['liːgəl] *adj* légal(e); **to take l. action (against sb)** intenter une action (contre qn); **to take l. advice** consulter un avocat; **l. aid** aide *f* juridique; *Am* **l. holiday** jour *m* férié; **the l. profession** les professions *fpl* juridiques; **to be l. tender** avoir cours (légal)

legality [lɪ'gælɪtɪ] *n* légalité *f*

legalization [liːgəlaɪ'zeɪʃən] *n* légalisation *f*

legalize ['liːgəlaɪz] *vt* légaliser

legally ['liːgəlɪ] *adv* légalement

legate ['legɪt] *n Rel* légat *m*

legation [lɪ'geɪʃən] *n* légation *f*

legend ['ledʒənd] *n* légende *f;* **to be a l. in one's own lifetime** être une légende vivante

legendary ['ledʒəndərɪ] *adj* légendaire

leggings ['legɪŋz] *npl (of woman)* caleçon *m; (of cowboy)* jambières *fpl*

leggy ['legɪ] *adj (person)* tout en jambes

legible ['ledʒɪbəl] *adj* lisible

legion ['liːdʒən] *n* légion *f*

legionary ['liːdʒənərɪ] *(pl* **legionaries)** *n* légionnaire *m*

legionnaire [liːdʒə'neə(r)] *n* légionnaire *m;* **l.'s disease** maladie *f* du légionnaire

legislate ['ledʒɪsleɪt] *vi* légiférer (**against** contre)

legislation [ledʒɪs'leɪʃən] *n (laws)* législation *f; (action)* élaboration *f* des lois

legislative ['ledʒɪslətɪv] *adj* législatif(ive)

legislator ['ledʒɪsleɪtə(r)] *n* législateur(trice) *m,f*

legislature ['ledʒɪslətjə(r)] *n* corps *m* législatif

legitimacy [lɪ'dʒɪtɪməsɪ] *n* légitimité *f*

legitimate 1 *adj* [lɪ'dʒɪtɪmət] légitime
  2 *vt* [lɪ'dʒɪtɪmeɪt] légitimer

legitimately [lɪ'dʒɪtɪmətlɪ] *adv* légitimement

legless ['leglɪs] *adj Br Fam (drunk)* complètement bourré(e)

legroom ['legrʊm] *n* place *f* pour les jambes

legume ['legjuːm] *n Bot* légumineuse *f*

legwarmers ['legwɔːməz] *npl* jambières *fpl*

leisure ['leʒə(r), *Am* 'liːʒər] *n* loisirs *mpl;* **to do sth at one's l.** faire qch à son rythme; **a life of l.** une vie de loisirs; **l. activities** activités *fpl* de loisirs; **l. centre** centre *m* de loisirs; **l. club** club *m* de loisirs; **l. industry** industrie *f* des loisirs; **l. time** temps *m* libre

leisurely ['leʒəlɪ, *Am* 'liːʒərlɪ] *adj (weekend)* relax *inv;* **at a l. pace** sans se presser; **to make l. progress** avancer à son rythme; **to go for a l. stroll** se promener tranquillement

lemming ['lemɪŋ] *n* lemming *m;* **to follow sb like lemmings** suivre qn comme des moutons

lemon ['lemən] **1** *n (fruit, colour)* citron *m; Fam* **I felt like a real l.** j'ai vraiment eu l'air malin; **l. curd** = pâte à tartiner au citron; **l. sole** limande-sole *f;* **l. squeezer** presse-citron *m;* **l. tea** thé *m* au citron; **l. tree** citronnier *m*
  2 *adj* **l. (coloured)** jaune citron *inv*

lemonade [lemə'neɪd] *n (carbonated)* limonade *f; (freshly squeezed)* citronnade *f*

lemur ['liːmə(r)] *n* maki *m*

lend [lend] *(pt & pp* **lent** [lent]) *vt (money, book, pen)* prêter; *(support)* apporter (**to** à); **to l. credibility to sth** rendre qch crédible; **to l. sb a (helping) hand** donner un coup de main à qn; **to l. an ear** *or* **one's ear to...** prêter l'oreille à...; **her work doesn't l. itself to dramatization** son œuvre ne se prête pas à une adaptation théâtrale

lender ['lendə(r)] *n* prêteur(euse) *m,f*

lending ['lendɪŋ] *n* prêt *m;* **l. library** bibliothèque *f* de prêt; **l. rate** taux *m* (d'un prêt)

length [leŋθ] *n* (**a**) *(in space)* longueur *f;* **it's 4.50 m in l.** ça fait 4,50 m de long; **the l. and breadth of the country** dans tout le pays
  (**b**) *(in time)* durée *f;* **at (great) l.** longuement; **a great l. of time** longtemps; **l. of service** ancienneté *f*
  (**c**) **to go to the l. of doing sth** aller jusqu'à faire qch; **to go to great lengths to do sth** se donner beaucoup de mal pour faire qch; **he would go to any lengths (to do sth)** il ne reculerait devant rien (pour faire qch)
  (**d**) *(of wood, string)* morceau *m*

lengthen ['leŋθən] **1** *vt* allonger, rallonger
  2 *vi (of days)* allonger, rallonger; *(of shadows)* s'allonger

lengthily ['leŋθɪlɪ] *adv* longuement

lengthways ['leŋθweɪz], **lengthwise** ['leŋθwaɪz] *adv* dans le sens de la longueur

lengthy ['leŋθɪ] *adj* long (longue)

lenient ['liːnɪənt] *adj* indulgent(e)

Leningrad ['lenɪŋgræd] *n Formerly* Leningrad

lens [lenz] (*pl* **lenses**) *n (of spectacles)* verre *m*; *(of camera)* objectif *m*; *(of eye)* cristallin *m*; **(contact) l.** lentille *f* (de contact); **l. cap** capuchon *m* d'objectif

Lent [lent] *n Rel* carême *m*; **to keep L.** faire carême

lent [lent] *pt & pp of* **lend**

lentil ['lentɪl] *n* lentille *f*

Leo ['liːəʊ] (*pl* **Leos**) *n (sign of zodiac)* le Lion; **to be (a) L.** être (du) Lion

leopard ['lepəd] *n* léopard *m*

leotard ['liːətɑːd] *n* justaucorps *m*

leper ['lepə(r)] *n* lépreux(euse) *m,f*; **l. colony** léproserie *f*

leprechaun ['leprəkɔːn] *n* lutin *m*, farfadet *m*

leprosy ['leprəsɪ] *n* lèpre *f*; **to have l.** avoir la lèpre

lesbian ['lezbɪən] **1** *n* lesbienne *f*
2 *adj* lesbien(enne)

lesion ['liːʒən] *n* lésion *f*

Lesotho [lɪˈsuːtuː] *n* le Lesotho

less [les] **1** *adj (comparative of* **little***)* moins de; **it's l. than a week's work** cela représente moins d'une semaine de travail; **the distance is l. than I thought** c'est moins loin que je ne pensais
2 *prep* moins; **a year l. two days** un an moins deux jours; **I've got £50, l. what I spent on the train ticket** j'ai 50 livres, moins ce que j'ai dépensé pour le billet de train
3 *pron* moins; **I don't think any (the) l. of you** tu n'as pas baissé dans mon estime; **I see l. of her nowadays** je la vois moins ces temps-ci; **in l. than an hour** en moins d'une heure; **the l. said about it the better** moins on en parle mieux c'est; *Fam* **l. of that!** ça suffit!
4 *adv* moins; **l. and l.** de moins en moins; **no more, no l.** ni plus ni moins; **still l., even l.** encore moins; **nothing l. than total obedience** rien moins qu'une obéissance totale; **she was driving a Rolls, no l.!** elle conduisait une Rolls, rien que ça!; **I expected no l. from you** je n'en attendais pas moins de vous; **they haven't got a fridge, much l. a freezer** ils n'ont pas de réfrigérateur et encore moins de congélateur

lessen ['lesən] **1** *vt (importance, cost)* diminuer, réduire; *(noise)* atténuer; *(enthusiasm, pain)* calmer
2 *vi (of pain, anger)* se calmer; *(of noise)* s'atténuer

lesser ['lesə(r)] *adj (in size)* plus petit(e); *(in importance)* moindre; **the l. of two evils** un moindre mal; **to a l. extent** *or* **degree** dans une moindre mesure

lesson ['lesən] *n* leçon *f*; **to give English lessons** donner des cours d'anglais; *Fig* **he has learnt his l.** ça lui a servi de leçon; *Fig* **to teach sb a l.** *(of person)* donner une bonne leçon à qn; *(of event, experience)* servir de leçon à qn

lest [lest] *conj Formal* de peur *ou* de crainte que + *subjunctive*; **l. we forget** *(on war memorial)* pour ne pas oublier

let¹ [let] *n (in tennis)* let *m*

let² **1** *n (of property)* location *f*; **short/long l.** location *f* de courte/longue durée
2 *vt (pt & pp* **let***) (rent out)* louer; **(house) to l.** (maison) à louer

let³ (*pt & pp* **let***) vt* **(a)** *(allow)* **to l. sb do sth** laisser qn faire qch, permettre à qn de faire qch; **l. me see**

voyons un peu; *(show me)* fais(-moi) voir; **to l. sb know sth** faire savoir qch à qn; **to l. sth pass** laisser passer qch; **to l. sth go** lâcher qch; **to l. oneself go** se laisser aller; **to l. sb go** laisser partir qn; *(make redundant)* se séparer de qn; **don't l. it get you down/get to you** ne te laisse pas abattre/affecter par ça; **don't l. me see you here again!** que je ne vous retrouve plus ici!; **can you l. me have it back tomorrow?** pouvez-vous me le rendre demain?; *Math* **l. AB be equal to CD** soit AB égal à CD
(b) *(with suggestions)* **l.'s go!** allons-y!; **l.'s hurry!** dépêchons-nous!; **l.'s not have an argument about it!** on ne va pas se disputer pour ça!; **now, don't l.'s have any nonsense!** allons, pas de bêtises!

▶**let by** *vt sep (allow to pass)* laisser passer

▶**let down** *vt sep* **(a)** *(hem)* rallonger; *(tyre)* dégonfler; *Fig* **to l. one's hair down** se défouler **(b)** *Fam (disappoint, fail)* décevoir; **the car l. us down again** la voiture nous a encore lâchés

▶**let in** *vt sep* **(a)** *(allow to enter)* laisser entrer; **to l. oneself in** *(to house)* entrer; **to l. in the light** laisser entrer *ou* passer la lumière; **to l. in water** *(of shoes)* prendre l'eau **(b)** **to l. sb in on a plan** mettre qn au courant d'un projet; **to l. sb in on a secret** mettre qn dans le secret **(c)** *Fam* **to l. oneself in for a hard time** aller au-devant de grandes difficultés; **what are you letting yourself in for?** est-ce que tu sais à quoi tu t'exposes?

▶**let into** *vt sep* **to l. sb into the house** faire entrer qn; **to l. sb into a secret** mettre qn dans le secret

▶**let off** *vt sep* **(a)** *(bomb)* lâcher; *(firework)* tirer; *Fig* **to l. off steam** se défouler **(b)** *(excuse)* ne pas sanctionner; **I'll l. you off this time** ça va pour cette fois; **they l. him off with a fine** il s'en est tiré avec une amende

▶**let on** *vt sep Fam (tell)* dire; **don't l. on that I was there** n'allez pas dire que j'y étais **(b)** *(claim)* prétendre; **he wasn't as ill as he l. on** il n'était pas aussi malade qu'il le prétendait

▶**let out** *vt sep* **(a)** *(release) (person)* laisser sortir; *(prisoner)* libérer; *(air, yell)* laisser échapper; *(secret)* divulguer **(b)** *(jacket, trousers)* élargir **(c)** *(rent out)* louer

▶**let up** *vi (lessen)* diminuer; *(stop)* cesser; **once he's started, he never lets up** une fois lancé, il ne s'arrête plus

let-down ['letdaʊn] *n Fam* déception *f*

lethal ['liːθəl] *adj* mortel(elle); *Fam* **that vodka's l.!** elle est mortelle, cette vodka!; **l. dose** dose *f* létale *ou* mortelle; **l. weapon** arme *f* meurtrière

lethargic [lɪˈθɑːdʒɪk] *adj* mou (molle)

lethargy ['leθədʒɪ] *n* mollesse *f*

let-out ['letaʊt] *n Fam (from obligation)* excuse *f*, prétexte *m*

letter ['letə(r)] *n* lettre *f*; **the l. of the law** la lettre de la loi; **to do sth to the l.** faire qch à la lettre; **to publish a writer's letters** publier la correspondance d'un écrivain; *Com* **l. of credit/exchange** lettre de crédit/de change; **l. of acknowledgement** accusé *m* de réception; **l. bomb** lettre piégée; **l. box** boîte *f* aux lettres; **l. opener** coupe-papier *m inv*

letterhead ['letəhed] *n* en-tête *m*; *(paper)* papier *m* à en-tête

lettuce ['letɪs] *n* salade *f* (verte)

let-up ['letʌp] *n Fam (in conflict)* trêve *f*; *(in weather)* accalmie *f*; *(in pressure)* relâchement *m*; **to work**

fifteen hours without a l. travailler quinze heures sans répit

leukaemia, *Am* **leukemia** [luː'kiːmɪə] *n* leucémie *f*

level ['levəl] **1** *n* niveau *m*; **at eye l.** à (la) hauteur des yeux; **to be on a l. with sb** être sur un pied d'égalité avec qn; *Fam* **on the l.** régulier(ère); **to come down to sb's l.** se mettre à la portée de qn; **to sink to sb's l.** tomber au niveau de qn; **at ministerial/international l.** à l'échelon ministériel/international

2 *adj* (**a**) *(not sloping)* plat(e); *Fig* **a l. playing field** une situation qui ne défavorise personne

(**b**) **to be l. with sb/sth** *(physically)* être au niveau de qn/qch; *(in race, ability, progress)* être au même niveau que qn/qch; **to draw l. with** *(in race, match)* rattraper; **to do one's l. best** faire tout son possible; **l. crossing** passage *m* à niveau; **l. pegging** à égalité; **l. spoonful** cuillerée *f* rase

(**c**) *(voice, tone)* égal(e); **to keep a l. head** garder son sang-froid

3 *vt* (*pt & pp* **levelled,** *Am* **leveled**) (**a**) *(make level)* niveler, égaliser; *(building)* raser

(**b**) *(aim) (blow)* porter (**at** à); *(criticism)* adresser (**at** à); *(accusation)* porter (**at** contre)

4 *vi Fam* **to l. with sb** parler franchement à qn

▶**level off, level out** *vi (of ground)* s'aplanir; *(of prices, demand)* se stabiliser; *(of aircraft)* se redresser

level-headed ['levəl'hedɪd] *adj* pondéré(e)

lever ['liːvə(r), *Am* 'levə(r)] **1** *n also Fig* levier *m*

2 *vt* **to l. sth open** ouvrir qch au moyen d'un levier

leverage ['liːvərɪdʒ] *n (power)* effet *m* de levier; *Fig (influence)* pression *f*

leveraged buyout ['liːvərɪdʒd'baɪaʊt] *n Fin* OPA *f* à crédit

levitate ['levɪteɪt] *vi* léviter

levitation [levɪ'teɪʃən] *n* lévitation *f*

levity ['levɪtɪ] *n* légèreté *f*

levy ['levɪ] **1** *n* (*pl* **levies**) taxe *f* (**on** sur)

2 *vt* (*pt & pp* **levied**) lever, percevoir (**on** sur)

lewd [luːd] *adj* obscène

lexical ['leksɪkəl] *adj* lexical(e)

lexicographer [leksɪ'kɒgrəfə(r)] *n* lexicographe *mf*

liability [laɪə'bɪlɪtɪ] *n* (*pl* **liabilities**) (**a**) *Law (responsibility)* responsabilité *f* (**for** de); *Fin* **liabilities** passif *m* (**b**) *(disadvantage)* handicap *m* (**to** pour)

liable ['laɪəbəl] *adj* (**a**) *Law (responsible)* responsable (**for** de) (**b**) *(to tax)* assujetti(e) (**to** à); *(to fine)* passible (**to** de) (**c**) *(likely)* **to be l. to do sth** risquer de faire qch

liaise [liː'eɪz] *vi* **to l. with sb** *(be in contact with)* assurer la liaison avec qn; *(work together with)* collaborer avec qn

liaison [lɪ'eɪzɒn] *n* (**a**) *(contact)* liaison *f*; *(co-operation)* collaboration *f*; *Mil* **l. officer** officier *m* de liaison (**b**) *(love affair)* liaison *f*

liar ['laɪə(r)] *n* menteur(euse) *m,f*

Lib Dem [lɪb'dem] *Br Pol* **1** *n* = membre du parti libéral démocrate

2 *adj* libéral(e) démocrate(e)

libel ['laɪbəl] *Law* **1** *n* diffamation *f*; **l. action** procès *m* en diffamation; **l. laws** lois *fpl* contre la diffamation

2 *vt* (*pt & pp* **libelled,** *Am* **libeled**) diffamer (par écrit)

libellous, *Am* **libelous** ['laɪbələs] *adj* diffamatoire

liberal ['lɪbərəl] **1** *n Pol* **L.** libéral(e) *m,f*

2 *adj* (**a**) *(tolerant)* libéral(e) (**b**) *(generous, abundant)* généreux(euse); **to be l. with one's praise/advice** ne pas être avare de compliments/de conseils

(**c**) *Pol* **L.** libéral(e); *Br* **the L. Democrats** parti *m* libéral démocrate *(parti politique britannique de tendance centriste)*

liberalism ['lɪbərəlɪzəm] *n* libéralisme *m*

liberalize ['lɪbərəlaɪz] *vt* libéraliser; *(law)* assouplir

liberally ['lɪbərəlɪ] *adv* libéralement, généreusement

liberate ['lɪbəreɪt] *vt* libérer

liberated ['lɪbəreɪtɪd] *adj (person)* libéré(e); *(views, ideas)* progressiste

liberating ['lɪbəreɪtɪŋ] *adj* libérateur(trice)

liberation [lɪbə'reɪʃən] *n* libération *f*; **l. movement** mouvement *m* de libération

liberator ['lɪbəreɪtə(r)] *n* libérateur(trice) *m,f*

Liberia [laɪ'bɪərɪə] *n* le Liberia

Liberian [laɪ'bɪərɪən] **1** *n* Libérien(enne) *m,f*

2 *adj* libérien(enne)

libertarian [lɪbə'teərɪən] *n & adj* libertaire *mf*

liberty ['lɪbətɪ] (*pl* **liberties**) *n* liberté *f*; **at l.** en liberté; **to be at l. to do sth** être libre de faire qch; **to take the l. of doing sth** prendre la liberté de faire qch; **to take liberties with sb/sth** prendre des libertés avec qn/qch; *Fam* **what a l.!** quel culot!

libido [lɪ'biːdəʊ] *n* libido *f*

Libra ['liːbrə] *n (sign of zodiac)* la Balance; **to be (a) L.** etre (de la) Balance

librarian [laɪ'breərɪən] *n* bibliothécaire *mf*

library ['laɪbrərɪ] (*pl* **libraries**) *n* bibliothèque *f*; **l. book** livre *m* de bibliothèque; **l. card** carte *f* de bibliothèque

libretto [lɪ'bretəʊ] (*pl* **librettos** *or* **libretti** [lɪ'bretiː]) *n Mus* livret *m*

Libya ['lɪbɪə] *n* la Libye

Libyan ['lɪbɪən] **1** *n* Libyen(enne) *m,f*

2 *adj* libyen(enne)

lice [laɪs] *pl of* **louse**

licence, *Am* **license**[1] ['laɪsəns] *n* (**a**) *(permit)* permis *m*; *(for trade, bar)* licence *f*; *Com* **under l.** sous licence; *(driving)* **l.** permis de conduire; *(TV)* **l.** redevance *f* (télé); *Br* **l. fee** redevance *f* télévisuelle; **l. number** *(of car)* numéro *m* d'immatriculation; **l. plate** plaque *f* d'immatriculation (**b**) *(freedom)* liberté *f*; *(excessive freedom)* licence *f*

license[2] *vt Com* accorder une licence à; **to be licensed to carry a gun** avoir un permis de port d'armes

licensed ['laɪsənst] *adj* **l. premises** débit *m* de boissons; **l. restaurant** = restaurant possédant une licence de débit de boissons

licensing ['laɪsənsɪŋ] *n* **l. hours** *(of pub)* heures *fpl* d'ouverture; **l. laws** lois *fpl* relatives aux débits de boissons

Licensing Hours

Traditionnellement, les heures d'ouverture des pubs répondent à une réglementation très stricte (liée à la législation sur la vente des boissons alcoolisées), mais celle-ci a été assouplie en 1988. Au lieu d'ouvrir uniquement de 11h30 à 14h30 et de 18h à 22h30, les pubs en Angleterre peuvent désormais rester ouverts de 11h à 23h. En Écosse, en revanche, la réglementation est moins stricte et les pubs qui en font la demande peuvent ouvrir plus tard certains soirs. Dans l'avenir, la réglementation en vigueur en Angleterre et au pays de Galles, qui fait actuellement l'objet de débats au Parlement, va probablement être assouplie sur le modèle écossais.

licentious [laɪˈsenʃəs] *adj* licencieux(euse)

lichen [ˈlaɪkən] *n* lichen *m*

lick [lɪk] **1** *n* (**a**) *(with tongue)* coup *m* de langue; *Fam* **a l. of paint** un petit coup de peinture (**b**) *Fam* **at a great l., at full l.** à toute allure

2 *vt* (**a**) *(with tongue)* lécher; **to l. one's lips** se lécher les lèvres; *Fig* **to l. one's (pour)lécher les babines**; *Fig* **to l. one's wounds** panser ses blessures; *Fam Fig* **to l. sb's boots** lécher les bottes à qn; *Vulg* **to l. sb's arse** faire du lèche-cul à qn; *Fam* **to l. sb into shape** dresser qn (**b**) *Fam (defeat)* mettre une raclée à

licorice = **liquorice**

lid [lɪd] *n* (**a**) *(of pot, jar)* couvercle *m* (**b**) *(idioms)* **to take the l. off sth** exposer qch au grand jour; **to keep the l. on sth** étouffer qch

lie¹ [laɪ] **1** *n* mensonge *m*; **to tell a l.** dire un mensonge; **to give the l. to sth** démentir qch; **l. detector** détecteur *m* de mensonges

2 *vi* mentir; **to l. through one's teeth** mentir effrontément

lie² **1** *n* **to find out the l. of the land** *(in politics, business)* tâter le terrain

2 *vi* (*pt* **lay** [leɪ], *pp* **lain** [leɪn]) (**a**) *(of person, animal) (be in a lying position)* être couché(e) *ou* allongé(e); *(get down)* se coucher, s'allonger; **here lies...** *(on gravestone)* ci-gît...; **to l. in bed** rester au lit; **I lay awake all night** je n'ai pas dormi de la nuit; *Fig* **to l. low** garder un profil bas; *Fig* **to l. in wait for sb** guetter l'arrivée de qn

(**b**) *(of object)* être, se trouver; **snow lay on the hills** il y avait de la neige sur les collines; **to l. in ruins** *(of building)* être en ruines; *(of career, hopes)* être détruit(e)

(**c**) *(of abstract thing)* **the responsibility lies with the author** la responsabilité incombe à l'auteur; **to know where one's interests l.** savoir où se trouve son intérêt; **the difference lies in that...** la différence réside dans le fait que...; **a brilliant future lies before her** un brillant avenir s'ouvre devant elle; **what lies behind this uncharacteristic generosity?** que cache cette générosité inhabituelle?

▸**lie about** *vi* traîner

▸**lie back** *vi* s'allonger

▸**lie down** *vi* se coucher, s'étendre; *Fig* **to take criticism/an insult lying down** se laisser critiquer/insulter sans réagir; **I'm not going to take this lying down** je ne vais pas me laisser faire

▸**lie in** *vi* faire la grasse matinée

Liechtenstein [ˈlɪktenstaɪn] *n* le Liechtenstein

lie-down [ˈlaɪˈdaʊn] *n* **to have a l.** faire une sieste

lie-in [ˈlaɪˈɪn] *n* **to have a l.** faire la grasse matinée

lieu [ljuː, luː] *n* **in l.** à la place; **in l. of** au lieu de

lieutenant [lefˈtenənt, *Am* luːˈtenənt] *n Mil* lieutenant *m*; *Naut* lieutenant de vaisseau; *Am (police officer)* inspecteur *m* de police; *Fig (helper)* lieutenant; **l. colonel** lieutenant-colonel *m*

life [laɪf] (*pl* **lives** [laɪvz]) *n* (**a**) *(existence)* vie *f*; **to take sb's l.** tuer qn; **to take one's own l.** se suicider; **to bring sb back to l.** ramener qn à la vie; **a matter of l. and death** une question de vie ou de mort; **l. after death** la vie après la mort; **to risk one's l., to risk l. and limb** risquer sa vie *ou* sa peau; **to escape with one's l.** avoir la vie sauve; **to lose one's l.** perdre la vie; **no lives were lost** on ne déplore aucune victime; **he held on to the rope for dear l.** il s'accrochait au cordage avec l'énergie du désespoir; **run for your lives!** sauve qui peut!; *Fam* **not on your l.!** jamais de la vie!; *Fam* **I couldn't for the l. of me remember** je n'arrivais absolument pas à me rappeler; **from l.** *(to draw, paint)* d'après nature; **bird l.** oiseaux *mpl*; **plant l.** végétaux *mpl*; **l. belt** ceinture *f* de sauvetage; **l. cycle** cycle *m* de vie; **l. drawing** dessin *m* d'après modèle; **l. force** force *f* vitale; **l. form** forme *f* de vie; **l. jacket** gilet *m* de sauvetage; **l. sciences** sciences *fpl* de la vie

(**b**) *(period of existence)* vie *f*; **she had worked all her l.** elle avait travaillé toute sa vie; **never in (all) my l.** jamais de ma vie; **a l. of Tolstoy** une biographie de Tolstoï; *Fam* **to get l.** en prendre pour perpète; **l. annuity** rente *f* viagère; **l. expectancy** espérance *f* de vie; **l. imprisonment** emprisonnement *m* à vie; **l. insurance** assurance-vie *f*; **l. member** membre *m* à vie; *Br* **l. peer** pair *m* à vie; **l. pension** pension *f* à vie; **l. sentence** condamnation *f* à perpétuité; **l. span** *(of person, animal)* espérance *f* de vie; *(of machine)* durée *f* de vie; **to write one's l. story** écrire son autobiographie

(**c**) *(mode of existence)* vie *f*; *Fam* **to live** *or* **lead the l. of Riley** se la couler douce; **to make a new l. for oneself** refaire sa vie; **way of l.** style *m* de vie; **he makes her l. a misery** il lui rend la vie insupportable; **to make l. worth living** donner un sens à l'existence; *Fam* **how's l.?** comment ça va?; **what a l.!** quelle vie!; **such is** *or* **that's l.!** c'est la vie!; **this is the l.!** voilà ce que j'appelle vivre!; *Fam* **get a l.!** t'es vraiment nul!

(**d**) *(liveliness)* **to come to l.** s'animer; **to bring sb to l.** *(of book, author)* donner vie à qn; **the l. and soul of the party** le boute-en-train de la soirée; **there's l. in the old dog yet** il n'a pas encore dit son dernier mot, le vieux

lifeblood [ˈlaɪfblʌd] *n (of person)* souffle *m* vital; *Fig (of economy, society)* moteur *m*

lifeboat [ˈlaɪfbəʊt] *n* canot *m* de sauvetage

life-giving [ˈlaɪfgɪvɪŋ] *adj (sun, water)* nourricier(-ère); *(aid)* vital(e)

lifeguard [ˈlaɪfgɑːd] *n (at the seaside)* surveillant(e) *m,f* de baignade; *(at swimming pool)* maître *m* nageur

lifeless [ˈlaɪflɪs] *adj* sans vie; *(performance, style)* qui manque de vie

lifelessly [ˈlaɪflɪslɪ] *adv* sans vie

lifelike [ˈlaɪflaɪk] *adj (portrait)* très ressemblant(e)

lifeline [ˈlaɪflaɪn] *n Fig* planche *f* (de salut); **to throw sb a l.** offrir *ou* tendre à qn une planche (de salut)

lifelong [ˈlaɪflɒŋ] *adj* de toujours

lifer [ˈlaɪfə(r)] *n Fam (prisoner)* condamné(e) *m,f* à perpète

life-saver [ˈlaɪfseɪvə(r)] *n Fam* **seatbelts can be life-savers** le port de la ceinture de sécurité peut sauver des vies; *Fig* **you're a l.!** tu me sauves la vie!

life-saving [ˈlaɪfseɪvɪŋ] *adj* salvateur(trice); *(equipment)* de réanimation; **she needed a l. operation** elle devait se faire opérer, c'était une question de vie ou de mort

life-size(d) [ˈlaɪfsaɪz(d)] *adj* grandeur nature *inv*

lifestyle [ˈlaɪfstaɪl] *n* style *m ou* mode *m* de vie

life-support [ˈlaɪfsəpɔːt] *adj* **l. system** *or* **machine** respirateur *m* artificiel

life-threatening [ˈlaɪfθretnɪŋ] *adj (disease)* potentiellement mortel(elle); **to be in a l. situation** être en danger de mort

lifetime [ˈlaɪftaɪm] *n (of person)* vie *f*; **in my l.** de mon vivant; **it's the chance of a l.** une telle chance ne se présente qu'une fois dans la vie; **the holiday of a l.** des vacances exceptionnelles

lift [lɪft] **1** n (**a**) *(elevator)* ascenseur m; **(goods) l.** monte-charge m inv; **l. attendant** garçon m d'ascenseur; **l. shaft** cage f d'ascenseur

(**b**) *(car ride)* **to give sb a l.** prendre ou emmener qn en voiture; **could you give me a l. to the station?** est-ce que tu peux m'emmener à la gare?

(**c**) *Fam* **to give sb a l.** *(cheer up)* remonter le moral à qn

2 vt (**a**) *(one's head, eyes, arm)* lever; **he won't l. a finger to help** il ne lèvera pas le petit doigt; **to l. sb (up)** *(after fall)* aider qn à se relever; **to l. a child up** prendre un enfant dans ses bras

(**b**) *Fam (take, steal)* piquer; *(arrest)* choper

(**c**) *(restrictions, siege)* lever

3 vi *(of mist, fog)* se lever, se dissiper

▸**lift off** vi *(of rocket)* décoller

liftoff ['lɪftɒf] n *(of rocket)* décollage m

ligament ['lɪgəmənt] n ligament m

light¹ [laɪt] **1** n (**a**) *(illumination)* lumière f; **by the l. of the moon** à la clarté de la lune; **things will look different in the cold l. of day** demain vous verrez les choses sous un autre jour; **to be in sb's l.** faire de l'ombre à qn; *Comput* **l. pen** crayon m optique; **l. year** année-lumière f

(**b**) *(lamp)* lumière f; *Fam* **to go out like a l.** s'endormir aussitôt couché(e); **(traffic) lights** feux mpl de circulation; **l. bulb** ampoule f

(**c**) *(fire)* **to set l. to sth** mettre le feu à qch; **have you got a l.?** vous avez du feu?

(**d**) *(idioms)* **the l. at the end of the tunnel** le bout du tunnel; **to throw** or **cast l. on sth** faire la lumière sur qch; **to bring sth to l.** mettre qch en lumière; **to come to l.** être découvert(e); **to see sb/sth in a new/ different l.** voir qn/qch sous un jour nouveau/différent; **in (the) l. of...** *(considering)* à la lumière de...

2 adj *(not dark)* clair(e); **it will soon be l.** il fera bientôt jour

3 vt *(pt & pp* lit [lɪt]) (**a**) *(fire, cigarette)* allumer (**b**) *(room, street)* éclairer, illuminer

light² **1** adj (**a**) *(not heavy)* léger(ère); **to be l. on one's feet** avoir le pas léger; **to be a l. sleeper** avoir le sommeil léger; **to have a l. touch** avoir la main légère; **l. aircraft** avion m petit porteur; **l. artillery** artillerie f légère; **l. industry** industrie f légère; **l. infantry** infanterie f légère

(**b**) *(not severe) (job, exercise)* facile, peu fatigant(e); *(rain)* fin(e); *(prison sentence)* léger(ère)

(**c**) *(not serious)* léger(ère); **to make l. of sth** prendre qch à la légère; **l. entertainment** variétés fpl; **l. reading** lectures fpl récréatives; **l. verse** poésie f facile

2 adv **to travel l.** voyager léger

▸**light on** *(pt & pp* lighted) vt insep tomber sur

▸**light up** **1** vt sep *(house, room)* éclairer; *(cigarette)* allumer

2 vi s'éclairer; *Fam (of smoker)* allumer une cigarette

lighten¹ ['laɪtən] **1** vt *(make less dark)* éclaircir

2 vi *(of sky)* s'éclaircir

lighten² vt *(make less heavy)* alléger; *Fig* **to l. sb's load** soulager qn

▸**lighten up** vi *Fam* se détendre

lighter ['laɪtə(r)] n briquet m; **l. fluid** or **fuel** essence f à briquet

light-fingered [laɪt'fɪŋgəd] adj *Fam* **to be l.** être chapardeur(euse)

light-headed [laɪt'hedɪd] adj étourdi(e)

light-hearted [laɪt'hɑːtɪd] adj *(person, discussion)* enjoué(e); *(remark)* badin(e); **to take a l. look at sth** poser un regard amusé sur qch

lighthouse ['laɪthaʊs] n phare m; **l. keeper** gardien m de phare

lighting ['laɪtɪŋ] n *(act, system)* éclairage m

lighting-up time ['laɪtɪŋ'ʌptaɪm] n = heure à laquelle les automobilistes sont tenus d'allumer leurs phares

lightly ['laɪtlɪ] adv légèrement; **to sleep l.** avoir le sommeil léger; **to get off l.** s'en tirer à bon compte; **to speak l. of sth** parler de qch à la légère; **to speak l. of sb** parler de qn sur un ton léger; **to take a decision l.** prendre une décision à la légère

lightness ['laɪtnɪs] n (**a**) *(brightness)* clarté f (**b**) *(in weight)* légèreté f

lightning ['laɪtnɪŋ] n (**a**) *(bolt)* éclairs mpl, foudre f; **l. conductor** paratonnerre m (**b**) *(idioms)* **as quick as l., with l. speed** rapide comme l'éclair; **l. attack** attaque f éclair; **l. strike** grève f surprise; **l. visit** visite f éclair

lightweight ['laɪtweɪt] **1** n *(in boxing)* poids m léger; *Fig & Pej (in character, intellect)* personne f qui manque d'envergure

2 adj *(garment, fabric)* léger(ère)

lignite ['lɪgnaɪt] n lignite m

like¹ [laɪk] **1** n **he and his l.** lui et ses semblables; **it's not for the likes of me** ce n'est pas pour des gens comme moi; **music, painting and the l.** la musique, la peinture et autres choses du même genre; **I've never seen the l. of it** je n'ai jamais vu une chose pareille

2 adj semblable, pareil(eille); **they are as l. as two peas (in a pod)** ils se ressemblent comme deux gouttes d'eau

3 prep (**a**) *(similar to)* **to be l. sb/sth** être semblable à qn/qch, ressembler à qn/qch; **to taste l. sth** avoir le même goût que qch; **to look l. sb/sth** ressembler à qn/qch; **what's the weather l.?** comment est le temps?; **people l. you** des gens comme vous; **you know what she's l.** tu sais comment elle est; **it costs something l. £10** cela coûte dans les 10 livres; **that's more l. it** voilà qui est mieux; **we don't have anything l. as many as that** on est loin d'en avoir autant; **there's nothing l. it!** il n'y a rien de tel!; **she's nothing l. as intelligent as you** elle est loin d'être aussi intelligente que vous; **that's not l. her** cela ne lui ressemble pas; **that's just l. him!** c'est bien de lui!; *Prov* **l. father, l. son** tel père, tel fils

(**b**) *(in the manner of)* comme; **just l. anybody else** comme tout le monde; *Fam* **don't be l. that!** ne fais pas l'idiot!

(**c**) *(such as)* tel (telle) que; **take more exercise, l. jogging** fais plus d'exercice, du jogging par exemple

4 adv *Fam* **as l. as not** à coup sûr

5 conj *Fam* **do it l. I said** fais comme je t'ai dit; **he looked l. he'd seen a ghost** on aurait dit qu'il avait vu un fantôme; **it's not l. he's ill or anything** ce n'est pas comme s'il était malade ou quoi que ce soit

like² **1** n **likes** goûts mpl, préférences fpl; **likes and dislikes** préférences

2 vt (**a**) *(person)* bien aimer; **she is well liked** elle est très appréciée

(**b**) *(enjoy)* aimer; **whether she likes it or not,...** que ça lui plaise ou non,...; **I l. to think my father would have agreed** j'aime à penser que mon père aurait approuvé; *Fam Ironic* **well, I l. that!** elle est bien bonne, celle-là!

(**c**) *(want)* **would you l. a cigarette?** est-ce que tu aimerais une cigarette?; **I would very much l. to go** j'aimerais beaucoup y aller; **I would l. nothing better than...** rien ne me ferait plus plaisir que...; **he doesn't l. people to talk about it** il n'aime pas que l'on en parle; **he thinks he can do anything he likes** il se croit tout permis; **if/when you l.** si/quand vous voulez; **as much as you l.** tant que vous voulez; **as often as you l.** aussi souvent que vous voulez; **I didn't l. to mention it** j'ai préféré ne pas le mentionner

likeable ['laɪkəbəl] *adj* sympathique

likelihood ['laɪklɪhʊd] *n* probabilité *f*; **in all l.** selon toute vraisemblance *ou* probabilité; **there is little l. of finding it** il y a peu de chance pour qu'on le trouve; **the l. is that...** il est probable que... + *subjunctive*

likely ['laɪklɪ] **1** *adj* (**a**) *(probable)* probable; **it's more than l.** c'est plus que probable; **it's l. to rain** il est probable qu'il pleuve, il pleuvra probablement; *Ironic* **a l. story!** à d'autres! (**b**) *(suitable)* approprié(e)
2 *adv* **very l.** très probablement; **as l. as not** sûrement; *Fam* **not l.!** tu plaisantes?

like-minded [laɪk'maɪndɪd] *adj* du même avis; *(having same tastes)* qui ont les mêmes goûts

liken ['laɪkən] *vt* comparer (**to** à)

likeness ['laɪknɪs] *n* (**a**) *(similarity)* ressemblance *f*; **family l.** air *m* de famille (**b**) *(portrait)* portrait *m*

likewise ['laɪkwaɪz] *adv* (*similarly*) de même, aussi; **to do l.** en faire autant

liking ['laɪkɪŋ] *n* goût *m*, penchant *m*; **is it to your l.?** cela est-il à votre goût?; **to have a l. for sth** avoir du goût pour qch, aimer qch; **to take a l. to sth** prendre goût à qch; **to take a l. to sb** se prendre d'amitié pour qn

lilac ['laɪlək] **1** *n* lilas *m*
2 *adj* lilas *inv*

Lilo® ['laɪləʊ] *(pl* **Lilos)** *n* matelas *m* pneumatique

lilt [lɪlt] *n (of voice)* inflexions *fpl*

lilting ['lɪltɪŋ] *adj* chantant(e)

lily ['lɪlɪ] *(pl* **lilies)** *n* lis *m*; **l. of the valley** muguet *m*

lily-livered ['lɪlɪlɪvəd] *adj Fam* froussard(e)

lima bean ['liːmə'biːn] *n* haricot *m* de Lima

limb [lɪm] *n* (**a**) *(of body)* membre *m*; **to tear sb l. from l.** déchiqueter qn, mettre qn en pièces (**b**) *(of tree)* grosse branche *f*; *Fig* **to be out on a l.** *(be in dangerous position)* être dans une situation délicate; *(be alone)* être en plan; **to go out on a l.** prendre des risques

limber ['lɪmbə(r)] *adj* souple

▶**limber up** *vi* s'échauffer

limbo ['lɪmbəʊ] *(pl* **limbos)** *n* (**a**) *Rel* les limbes *mpl*; *Fig* **to be in l.** être dans les limbes (**b**) *(dance)* limbo *m*

lime¹ [laɪm] *n (fruit)* citron *m* vert; *(citrus tree)* limettier *m*; *(linden tree)* tilleul *m*; **l. green** vert *m* jaune; **l. juice** jus *m* de citron vert

lime² *n Chem* chaux *f*

limelight ['laɪmlaɪt] *n* **to be in the l.** être sous les projecteurs; **to steal the l.** voler la vedette

limerick ['lɪmərɪk] *n* = poème burlesque en cinq vers

limestone ['laɪmstəʊn] *n* calcaire *m*

limey ['laɪmɪ] *(pl* **limeys)** *n Am Fam (British person)* Rosbif *m*

limit ['lɪmɪt] **1** *n* limite *f*; **within limits** jusqu'à un certain point; **off limits (to)** inaccessible (à); *(forbidden)*

interdit(e) (à); **to know no limits** être sans limites; **that's the l.!** ce n'est plus possible!; **he's the l.!** il est impossible!
2 *vt* limiter; **to l. oneself to sth/to doing sth** se limiter à qch/à faire qch

limitation [lɪmɪ'teɪʃən] *n* limitation *f*; **to know one's limitations** connaître ses limites

limited ['lɪmɪtəd] *adj* limité(e); **l. company** société *f* à responsabilité limitée; **l. edition** édition *f* à tirage limité; *Law* **l. liability** responsabilité *f* limitée

limitless ['lɪmɪtlɪs] *adj (wealth, amount, supply)* illimité(e); *(generosity)* sans bornes

limo ['lɪməʊ] *(pl* **limos)** *n Fam* limousine *f*

limousine [lɪmə'ziːn] *n* limousine *f*

limp¹ [lɪmp] **1** *n* boitement *m*; **to have a l.** boiter
2 *vi* boiter

limp² *adj* mou (molle); **to go l.** s'affaisser

limpet ['lɪmpɪt] *n* bernique *f*, patelle *f*; *Fig* **to stick to sb like a l.** ne pas lâcher qn; *Mil* **l. mine** mine *f* magnétique

limpid ['lɪmpɪd] *adj* limpide

limply ['lɪmplɪ] *adv* mollement

linchpin ['lɪntʃpɪn] *n Fig (person)* cheville *f* ouvrière; *(thing)* clé *f* de voûte

linctus ['lɪŋktəs] *n* sirop *m*

linden ['lɪndən] *n* **l. (tree)** tilleul *m*

line¹ [laɪn] **1** *n* (**a**) *(mark)* ligne *f*; *(drawn)* trait *m*; *(on face)* ride *f*; *Fig* **to draw the l. at doing sth** se refuser à faire qch; **l. drawing** dessin *m* au trait
(**b**) *(row)* ligne *f*, rangée *f*, *(one behind the other)* file *f*; *Am (queue)* queue *f*; **to stand in a l.** être en rang; *(one behind the other)* être en file; *Am* **to stand in l.** *(queue)* faire la queue; *Fig* **to be out of l.** dépasser les bornes; **to be in l. with sth** être conforme à qch; *Fig* **to be in l. for promotion** être sur la liste des promotions; *Fig* **to be on the l.** *(of one's job, reputation)* être en jeu; **l. dancing** = danse de style country effectuée en rangs; *Com & Ind* **l. manager** chef *m* d'équipe
(**c**) *(rope)* ligne *f*; *(for clothes)* fil *m* à linge
(**d**) *(railway track)* voie *f*; *(railway route)* ligne *f*
(**e**) *(direction)* **l. of argument** raisonnement *m*; **l. of attack** plan *m* d'attaque; **to be in the l. of fire** être dans la ligne de tir; *Fig* être en butte aux critiques; **to be on the right/wrong lines** être sur la bonne/mauvaise voie; **something along the lines of...** quelque chose dans le genre de...
(**f**) *(policy)* ligne *f*; **the party l.** la ligne du parti; **to take a firm l. with sb** se montrer ferme avec qn
(**g**) *(of text)* ligne *f*; *(of poem)* vers *m*; **to drop sb a l.** écrire un mot à qn; **to learn one's lines** apprendre son rôle; *Fig* **to read between the lines** lire entre les lignes
(**h**) *(family)* lignée *f*; **in a direct l.** en ligne directe
(**i**) *(telephone connection)* ligne *f*
(**j**) *Fam (job)* **what l. (of business) are you in?** vous travaillez dans quelle branche?
(**k**) *Com (of goods)* ligne *f*
2 *vt (road, river)* border; **the crowd lined the street** la foule s'alignait le long du trottoir

▶**line up 1** *vt sep* (**a**) *(form into a line)* mettre en ligne, aligner (**b**) *(prepare)* **to have sb lined up for sth** avoir qn en vue pour qch; **have you got anything lined up for this evening?** avez-vous quelque chose de prévu pour ce soir?
2 *vi (form a line)* se mettre en rang

line² vt (coat, curtain) doubler (**with** de); (box, drawer) tapisser (**with** de); Fig **to l. one's pockets** se remplir les poches

lineage ['lɪnɪdʒ] n lignée f

linear ['lɪnɪə(r)] adj linéaire; Math **l. equation** équation f linéaire; Comput **l. programming** programmation f linéaire

lined¹ [laɪnd] adj (paper) réglé(e); (face) ridé(e)

lined² adj (coat, curtain) doublé(e) (**with** de)

linen ['lɪnɪn] n (a) (fabric) lin m; **a l. dress** une robe en lin (**b**) (clothes) linge m; (sheets, tablecloths etc) linge (de maison); Fig **don't wash your dirty l. in public** il faut laver son linge sale en famille; **l. basket** panier m à linge

liner ['laɪnə(r)] n (ship) (paquebot m) transatlantique m

linesman ['laɪnzmən] n (in tennis) juge m de ligne; (in football) juge m de touche

line-up ['laɪnʌp] n (a) (of team) composition f; (on TV show) plateau m (**b**) Am (identity parade) séance f d'identification

linger ['lɪŋɡə(r)] vi (of person) s'attarder; (of smell, custom) subsister, persister; **to l. behind** rester en arrière; **to l. over doing sth** prendre son temps pour faire qch

lingerie ['lɔːnʒərɪ] n lingerie f

lingering ['lɪŋɡrɪŋ] adj (look) long (longue); (doubt) persistant(e); (death) lent(e)

lingo ['lɪŋɡəʊ] (pl **lingoes**) n Fam (language) langue f; (jargon) charabia m

lingua franca ['lɪŋɡwə'fræŋkə] n langue f véhiculaire

linguist ['lɪŋɡwɪst] n (a) (specialist in linguistics) linguiste mf (**b**) (polyglot) **to be a l.** être doué(e) pour les langues

linguistic [lɪŋ'ɡwɪstɪk] adj linguistique

linguistics [lɪŋ'ɡwɪstɪks] n linguistique f

lining ['laɪnɪŋ] n (of coat, curtain) doublure f; (of brakes) garniture f; (of stomach) paroi f

link [lɪŋk] **1** n (a) (of chain) chaînon m, maillon m; Fig **the weak l.** (in an argument) le point faible; (in team) l'élément m faible (**b**) (connection) lien m (**between** entre) (**c**) Comput lien m (**to** avec)
2 vt (physically) relier; (by association) lier; **to l. hands** se donner la main

▸**link up 1** vt relier
2 vi (of roads, travellers) se rejoindre

lino ['laɪnəʊ] n Fam lino m

linoleum [lɪ'nəʊlɪəm] n linoléum m

linseed ['lɪnsiːd] n graine f de lin; **l. oil** huile f de lin

lintel ['lɪntəl] n linteau m

lion ['laɪən] n lion m; Fig **the l.'s share** la part du lion; **l. cub** lionceau m; **l. tamer** dresseur m de lions

lioness ['laɪənes] n lionne f

lion-hearted ['laɪən'hɑːtɪd] adj courageux(euse) comme un lion

lip [lɪp] n (a) (of person) lèvre f; (of animal) babine f; **to read sb's lips** lire sur les lèvres de qn; **to pay l. service to sth** faire semblant de s'intéresser à qch (**b**) (of jug) bec m (**c**) Fam (impudence) insolence f; **less of your l.!** sois un peu moins insolent(e)!

liposuction ['lɪpəʊsʌkʃən] n lipposuccion f

lip-read ['lɪpriːd] (pt & pp **lip-read** ['lɪpred]) **1** vt lire sur les lèvres de
2 vi lire sur les lèvres

lipstick ['lɪpstɪk] n rouge m à lèvres

liquefy ['lɪkwɪfaɪ] (pt & pp **liquefied**) **1** vt liquéfier
2 vi se liquéfier

liqueur [lɪ'kjʊə(r)] n liqueur f

liquid ['lɪkwɪd] **1** n liquide m
2 adj liquide; Fin **l. assets** liquidités fpl; **l. crystal display** affichage m à cristaux liquides

liquidate ['lɪkwɪdeɪt] vt (a) Fin (company, debt) liquider; (capital) mobiliser (**b**) Fam (kill) liquider

liquidation [lɪkwɪ'deɪʃən] n Fin (of company, debt) liquidation f; (of capital) mobilisation f; **to go into l.** entrer en liquidation

liquidity [lɪ'kwɪdɪtɪ] n Fin liquidité f; **l. ratio** ratio m de liquidité

liquidize ['lɪkwɪdaɪz] vt (a) (gas, solid) liquéfier (**b**) (food) passer au mixeur

liquidizer ['lɪkwɪdaɪzə(r)] n mixeur m

liquor ['lɪkə(r)] n Am alcool m; **l. store** magasin m de vins et spiritueux

liquorice ['lɪkərɪs] n réglisse f

lira ['lɪərə] (pl **lire** ['lɪərə]) n lire f

Lisbon ['lɪzbən] n Lisbonne

lisp [lɪsp] **1** n zézaiement m; **to have a l.** avoir un cheveu sur la langue
2 vi avoir un cheveu sur la langue, zézayer

list¹ [lɪst] **1** n liste f
2 vt (enter in list) faire une liste de; **her phone number isn't listed in the directory** son numéro de téléphone ne figure pas dans l'annuaire; **to be listed on the Stock Exchange** être coté(e) en Bourse; **listed building** immeuble m classé

list² **1** n (of ship) bande f, gîte f
2 vi (of ship) donner de la bande ou de la gîte

listen ['lɪsən] vi écouter; **to l. to sb/sth** écouter qn/qch; **to l. for sth** tendre l'oreille afin d'entendre qch; **to l. (out) for the phone** guetter la sonnerie du téléphone; **to l. to reason** entendre raison; **he wouldn't l.** il n'a rien voulu savoir

▸**listen in** vi **to l. in (on sth)** écouter (qch)

listener ['lɪsnə(r)] n (a) **to be a good l.** savoir écouter (**b**) (to radio programme) auditeur(trice) m,f

listing ['lɪstɪŋ] n (list) liste f; **listings** (in newspaper) rubrique f des spectacles; **listings magazine** programme m de spectacles

listless ['lɪstlɪs] adj apathique

lit [lɪt] pt & pp of **light**

litany ['lɪtənɪ] (pl **litanies**) n litanie f

liter Am = **litre**

literacy ['lɪtərəsɪ] n alphabétisation f; **l. rate** taux m d'alphabétisation

literal ['lɪtərəl] adj littéral(e)

literally ['lɪtərəlɪ] adv littéralement, **to take sth l.** prendre qch au pied de la lettre

literary ['lɪtərərɪ] adj littéraire

literate ['lɪtərɪt] adj **to be l.** (able to read and write) savoir lire et écrire; (educated) être cultivé(e)

literature ['lɪtərɪtʃə(r)] n (a) (fiction, poetry) littérature f (**b**) (information) documentation f

lithe [laɪð] adj agile

lithium ['lɪθɪəm] n lithium m

lithograph ['lɪθəɡræf] n lithographie f

Lithuania [lɪθjʊ'eɪnɪə] n la Lituanie

Lithuanian [lɪθjʊ'eɪnɪən] **1** n (a) (person) Lituanien(enne) m,f (**b**) (language) lituanien m
2 adj lituanien(enne)

litigant ['lɪtɪɡənt] n Law partie f

litigate ['lɪtɪgeɪt] *vi Law* intenter une action en justice

litigation [lɪtɪ'geɪʃən] *n Law* action *f* en justice

litmus ['lɪtməs] *n* **l. paper** papier *m* (de) tournesol; *Fig* **l. test** test *m* décisif

litre, *Am* **liter** ['li:tə(r)] *n* litre *m*

litter ['lɪtə(r)] **1** *n* (**a**) *(rubbish)* détritus *mpl*, ordures *fpl*; **l. bin** poubelle *f*; **l. lout** = personne qui jette des détritus n'importe où (**b**) *(of animal)* portée *f* (**c**) *(for cat)* litière *f*; **l. tray** caisse *f* (pour litière) (**d**) *Hist (conveyance)* litière *f*
  2 *vt* **to be littered with** être couvert(e) *ou* jonché(e) de

litterbug ['lɪtəbʌg] *n Fam* = personne qui jette des détritus n'importe où

little ['lɪtəl] **1** *n* peu *m*; **to eat l. or nothing** manger peu ou pas du tout; **he knows very l.** il ne sait pas grand-chose; **a l. more** un peu plus; **a l. hot/slow** un peu chaud(e)/lent(e); **every l. helps** les petits ruisseaux font les grandes rivières
  2 *adj* (**a**) *(small)* petit(e); **a l. while** un petit moment; **l. finger** petit doigt *m* (**b**) *(comparative* **less,** *superlative* **least)** *(not much)* peu de; **l. money** peu d'argent; **a l. money** un peu d'argent; **it makes l. sense** ça n'a pas beaucoup de sens
  3 *adv (comparative* **less,** *superlative* **least)** peu; **l. by l.** peu à peu; **l. more than an hour ago** il y a à peine une heure; **that's l. short of bribery** ça frise la corruption; **l. did I think that...** j'étais loin de penser que...

littoral ['lɪtərəl] **1** *n* littoral *m*
  2 *adj* littoral(e)

liturgy ['lɪtədʒɪ] *(pl* **liturgies)** *n* liturgie *f*

live¹ [laɪv] **1** *adj* (**a**) *(person, animal)* vivant(e), en vie; *Fam* **a real l. film star** une vedette de cinéma en chair et en os; **a l. issue** un sujet brûlant (**b**) *(performance, broadcast)* en direct (**c**) *(bomb)* non explosé(e); **l. ammunition** balles *fpl* réelles; **l. wire** fil *m* sous tension; *Fig* **to be a l. wire** déborder de vie (**d**) *(volcano)* actif(-ive)
  2 *adv (broadcast)* en direct; **to perform l.** *(of comedian, dancer)* être sur scène; *(of band)* jouer en concert

live² [lɪv] **1** *vt* vivre; **to l. a long life** vivre longtemps; **to l. a happy life** mener une vie heureuse; **to l. a lie** vivre dans le mensonge; **it makes life worth living** cela donne un sens à la vie
  2 *vi* vivre; *(reside)* habiter, vivre; **to l. with sb** vivre avec qn; **as long as I l.** tant que je vivrai; **to l. a little** profiter un peu de la vie; **l. and let l.!** un peu de tolérance!; **you l. and learn** on en apprend tous les jours

▶**live down** *vt sep (mistake, one's past)* faire oublier; **I'll never l. it down!** je n'ai pas fini d'en entendre parler!

▶**live off** *vt insep* **to l. off sth** vivre de qch; **to l. off sb** vivre aux crochets de qn

▶**live on** **1** *vt insep (food)* se nourrir de; *(capital)* vivre sur; **it's not enough to l. on** ce n'est pas suffisant pour vivre
  2 *vi (of person)* continuer à vivre; *(of memory)* survivre

▶**live out** *vt sep* **to l. out one's life** *or* **days** passer ses jours; **to l. out a fantasy** réaliser un fantasme

▶**live through** *vt insep* connaître, vivre

▶**live together** *vi* vivre ensemble

▶**live up** *vt sep Fam* **to l. it up** faire la fête

▶**live up to** *vt insep* **to l. up to sb's expectations** répondre aux attentes de qn; **to fail to l. up to expecta-**

tions ne pas tenir ses promesses; **to l. up to one's reputation** être à la hauteur de sa réputation

live-in ['lɪvɪn] *adj (chauffeur, nanny)* logé(e) et nourri(e); **l. lover** compagnon (compagne) *m,f*

livelihood ['laɪvlɪhʊd] *n* gagne-pain *m inv*; **to earn one's l.** gagner sa vie

liveliness ['laɪvlɪnɪs] *n* vivacité *f*

lively ['laɪvlɪ] *adj (person)* plein(e) de vie; *(place, party, conversation)* animé(e); *(music)* entraînant(e); *(imagination)* fertile; **to take a l. interest in sth** s'intéresser vivement à qch; *Br Fam* **look l.!** grouillez-vous!

▶**liven up** ['laɪvən] **1** *vt sep (person)* égayer; *(place, party, conversation)* animer; *(proceedings)* activer
  2 *vi (of person)* s'égayer; *(of place, party, conversation)* s'animer

liver ['lɪvə(r)] *n* foie *m*; **l. spot** tache *f* de vieillesse

Liverpool ['lɪvəpu:l] *n* Liverpool

Liverpudlian [lɪvə'pʌdlɪən] **1** *n* = personne née ou habitant à Liverpool
  2 *adj* de Liverpool

livery ['lɪvərɪ] *n* livrée *f*

lives [laɪvz] *pl of* **life**

livestock ['laɪvstɒk] *n* bétail *m*

livid ['lɪvɪd] *adj* (**a**) *(angry)* furieux(euse) (**b**) *(bluish-grey)* livide, blême

living ['lɪvɪŋ] **1** *n* vie *f*; **to earn one's l.** gagner sa vie; **what does she do for a l.?** qu'est-ce qu'elle fait dans la vie?; **l. conditions** conditions *fpl* de vie; **l. expenses** faux frais *mpl*; **l. room** (salle *f* de) séjour *m*, salon *m*; **l. standards** niveau *m* de vie
  2 *adj* vivant(e); **there is not a l. soul to be seen** il n'y a pas âme qui vive; **within l. memory** de mémoire d'homme

lizard ['lɪzəd] *n* lézard *m*

llama ['lɑ:mə] *n* lama *m*

lo [ləʊ] *exclam Lit or Hum* **lo and behold...** ô surprise...

load [ləʊd] **1** *n* (**a**) *(burden)* fardeau *m*, charge *f*; **to share** *or* **spread the l.** répartir le travail; **that's a l. off my mind!** cela m'enlève un poids! (**b**) *Fam (lot)* **a l. of, loads of** plein de; **it's just a l. of rubbish!** c'est n'importe quoi!; **we've got loads of time** on a largement le temps
  2 *vt (lorry, gun, camera)* charger; *(software)* installer; *(washing machine)* remplir
  3 *vi (of lorry)* prendre un chargement

▶**load up 1** *vt sep* charger
  2 *vi* prendre un chargement

loaded ['ləʊdɪd] *adj* (**a**) *(lorry, gun, camera)* chargé(e) (**b**) *(dice)* pipé(e); *(question)* insidieux(euse) (**c**) *Fam (rich)* plein(e) aux as

loading ['ləʊdɪŋ] *n* chargement *m*; **l. bay** aire *f* de chargement

loaf [ləʊf] *(pl* **loaves** [ləʊvz] *)* *n* **a l. (of bread)** un pain; *Fig* **to use one's l.** faire marcher son ciboulot

▶**loaf about, loaf around** *vi* traîner

loafer ['ləʊfə(r)] *n* (**a**) *(person)* fainéant(e) *m,f* (**b**) *(shoe)* mocassin *m*

loam [ləʊm] *n* terreau *m*

loan [ləʊn] **1** *n (from lender's point of view)* prêt *m*; *(from borrower's point of view)* emprunt *m*; **to give sb a l. of sth** prêter qch à qn; **to take out a l.** faire un emprunt; *Fam* **l. shark** usurier(ère) *m,f*
  2 *vt (money)* prêter

loath [ləʊθ] *adj* **to be l. to do sth** répugner à faire qch

loathe [ləʊð] *vt* détester; **to l. doing sth** détester faire qch

loathing ['ləʊðɪŋ] *n* dégoût *m*, répugnance *f*

loathsome ['ləʊðsəm] *adj* répugnant(e)

loaves [ləʊvz] *pl of* **loaf**

lob [lɒb] **1** *n* (*in tennis*) lob *m*
  2 *vt* (*pt & pp* **lobbed**) (**a**) (*in tennis*) lober (**b**) *Fam* (*throw*) balancer

lobby ['lɒbɪ] **1** *n* (*pl* **lobbies**) (**a**) (*of hotel*) hall *m*; (*of theatre*) foyer *m* (**b**) (*pressure group*) groupe *m* de pression, lobby *m*
  2 *vt* (*pt & pp* **lobbied**) faire pression sur
  3 *vi* **to l. for/against sth** faire pression en faveur de/contre qch

lobbyist ['lɒbɪɪst] *n* membre *m* d'un groupe de pression

lobe [ləʊb] *n* lobe *m*

lobotomy [lə'bɒtəmɪ] (*pl* **lobotomies**) *n* lobotomie *f*

lobster ['lɒbstə(r)] *n* homard *m*; **as red as a l.** (*sunburnt*) rouge comme une écrevisse; **l. pot** casier *m* à homards

local ['ləʊkəl] **1** *n* (**a**) (*person*) **the locals** les gens *mpl* du coin (**b**) *Fam* (*pub*) = pub du voisinage
  2 *adj* local(e); **l. anaesthetic** anesthésie *f* locale; **l. colour** couleur *f* locale; **l. government** ≃ administration *f* municipale; **l. time** heure *f* locale

locale [ləʊ'kɑːl] *n* (*of events*) lieu *m*; (*for a film*) lieu de tournage

locality [ləʊ'kælɪtɪ] (*pl* **localities**) *n* voisinage *m*, environs *mpl*

locally ['ləʊkəlɪ] *adv* (*in neighbourhood*) dans le quartier; (*in region*) dans la région

locate [ləʊ'keɪt] **1** *vt* (*find*) localiser; (*situate*) situer
  2 *vi* (*of company*) s'installer

location [ləʊ'keɪʃən] *n* (**a**) (*place*) emplacement *m*; *Cin* **on l.** en extérieur; *Cin* **l. shot** plan *m* en extérieur (**b**) (*act of finding*) localisation *f*

loch [lɒx] *n Scot* (*lake*) loch *m*, lac *m*

lock¹ [lɒk] **1** *n* (**a**) (*on door*) serrure *f*; **under l. and key** (*object*) sous clef; (*person*) sous les verrous; *Fig* **l., stock and barrel** en entier (**b**) (*in wrestling*) clef *f* (**c**) (*on canal*) écluse *f*
  2 *vt* (*door, padlock*) fermer à clef; **to be locked in each other's arms** être étroitement enlacés(ées); *Fig* **to l. horns with sb** livrer bataille à qn
  3 *vi* (*of door*) se fermer; (*of car wheels*) se bloquer

▶**lock in** *vt sep* enfermer à clef

▶**lock out** *vt sep* enfermer dehors; **I locked myself out of my flat** je me suis enfermé dehors

▶**lock up 1** *vt sep* (*person, valuables*) enfermer; (*house*) fermer à clef
  2 *vi* fermer

lock² *n* (*of hair*) mèche *f*

locker ['lɒkə(r)] *n* casier *m*; *Am* **l. room** vestiaire *m*

locket ['lɒkɪt] *n* médaillon *m*

lockjaw ['lɒkdʒɔː] *n Old-fashioned* tétanos *m*

lock-out ['lɒkaʊt] *n* lock-out *m inv*

locksmith ['lɒksmɪθ] *n* serrurier *m*

lockup ['lɒkʌp] *n* (**a**) *Br* (*for storage*) garage *m* (**b**) *Fam* (*police cells*) violon *m*, bloc *m*

locomotion [ləʊkə'məʊʃən] *n* locomotion *f*

locomotive [ləʊkə'məʊtɪv] **1** *n* (*train*) locomotive *f*
  2 *adj* locomotif(ive)

locum ['ləʊkəm] *n Br* remplaçant(e) *m,f*

locust ['ləʊkəst] *n* sauterelle *f*

locution [ləʊ'kjuːʃən] *n* locution *f*

lodge [lɒdʒ] **1** *n* (*of porter, caretaker, masons*) loge *f*; (*small house*) pavillon *m*
  2 *vt* (**a**) (*accommodate*) loger, héberger (**b**) *Law* **to l. an appeal** faire appel; **to l. a complaint** porter plainte
  3 *vi* (**a**) (*live*) loger (**b**) (*become fixed*) se loger; **to be lodged in sb's memory** être gravé(e) dans la mémoire de qn

lodger ['lɒdʒə(r)] *n* locataire *mf* (en meublé); (*who has meals provided*) pensionnaire *mf*

lodging ['lɒdʒɪŋ] *n* logement *m*; **lodgings** chambre *f* meublée; *Old-fashioned* **l. house** (hôtel *m*) garni *m*

loft [lɒft] *n* grenier *m*

lofty ['lɒftɪ] *adj* (*aim, desire*) noble (**b**) *Lit* (*high*) haut(e)

log [lɒg] **1** *n* (**a**) (*of wood*) bûche *f*; **to sleep like a l.** dormir comme une souche; **l. cabin** hutte *f* en rondins; **l. fire** feu *m* de bois (**b**) (*record*) registre *m*; (*of ship, traveller*) journal *m* de bord; (*of plane*) carnet *m* de vol
  2 *vt* (*pt & pp* **logged**) (*record*) enregistrer; (*in ship's, traveller's log*) noter dans le journal de bord; (*in plane's log*) noter dans le carnet de vol

▶**log in** *vi Comput* entrer

▶**log off** *vi Comput* sortir

▶**log on** *vi Comput* entrer

▶**log out** *vi Comput* sortir

logarithm ['lɒgərɪθəm] *n* logarithme *m*

logbook ['lɒgbʊk] *n* (**a**) (*of ship, traveller*) journal *m* de bord; (*of plane*) carnet *m* de vol (**b**) *Br* (*for car*) ≃ carte *f* grise

loggerheads ['lɒgəhedz] *n Fam* **to be at l. with sb** être en conflit avec qn

logic ['lɒdʒɪk] *n* logique *f*

logical ['lɒdʒɪkəl] *adj* logique

logically ['lɒdʒɪklɪ] *adv* logiquement

logistic(al) [lə'dʒɪstɪk(əl)] *adj* logistique

logistics [lə'dʒɪstɪks] *npl* logistique *f*; **the l. of the situation** les données logistiques de la situation

logjam ['lɒgdʒæm] *n* impasse *f*

logo ['ləʊgəʊ] (*pl* **logos**) *n* sigle *m*, logo *m*

loin [lɔɪn] *n* (**a**) (*of beef*) aloyau *m*; (*of mutton, pork*) filet *m*; (*of veal*) longe *f*; **l. chop** côtes *fpl* premières (**b**) **loins** (*of person*) reins *mpl*

loincloth ['lɔɪnklɒθ] *n* pagne *m*

loiter ['lɔɪtə(r)] *vi* traîner; (*suspiciously*) rôder; *Law* **to l. with intent** = rôder d'une manière suspecte

loll [lɒl] *vi* (*of person*) se prélasser; (*of head*) tomber en avant; (*of tongue*) pendre

lollipop ['lɒlɪpɒp] *n* sucette *f*; *Br Fam* **l. man/lady** = contractuel qui aide les écoliers à traverser la rue

lollop ['lɒləp] *vi Fam* **to l. along** courir lourdement

lolly ['lɒlɪ] (*pl* **lollies**) *n Fam* (**a**) (*ice*) **l.** glace *f* à l'eau (**b**) (*lollipop*) sucette *f* (**c**) *Br* (*money*) fric *m*, flouze *m*

London ['lʌndən] *n* Londres

Londoner ['lʌndənə(r)] *n* Londonien(enne) *m,f*

lone [ləʊn] *adj* (*single, solitary*) solitaire; *Fig* **a l. wolf** un(e) solitaire

loneliness ['ləʊnlɪnɪs] *n* (*feeling*) solitude *f*; (*of place*) isolement *m*

lonely ['ləʊnlɪ] *adj* (*person*) seul(e); (*life, job*) solitaire; (*place*) isolé(e); **to feel l.** se sentir seul; **l. hearts club** club *m* de rencontres; **l. hearts column** rubrique *f* rencontres

loner ['ləʊnə(r)] *n* solitaire *mf*

lonesome ['ləʊnsəm] **1** *n Fam* **to be on one's l.** être abandonné(e) à son triste sort
2 *adj Am* solitaire, seul(e)

long¹ [lɒŋ] **1** *n* **the l. and the short of it is that...** bref,...
2 *adj* (**a**) *(in size)* long (longue); **how l. is the table?** quelle est la longueur de la table?; **to be 4 metres l.** faire 4 mètres de long; **to go the l. way (round)** prendre le chemin le plus long; *Fig* **the best by a l. way** de loin le meilleur (la meilleure); *Fig* **she'll go a l. way** elle ira loin; *Fig* **to go a l. way towards doing sth** beaucoup contribuer à faire qch; *Fam* **to be l. on charm/good ideas** être plein(e) de charme/de bonnes idées; **the l. arm of the law** (le bras de) la justice; *Fig* **to have a l. face** faire une tête de six pieds de long; **it's a l. shot** ça n'a pas beaucoup de chances de réussir; **not by a l. shot** *or* **chalk** loin s'en faut; **l. johns** caleçon *m* long; *Sport* **l. jump** saut *m* en longueur; *Rad* **l. wave** grandes ondes *fpl*
(**b**) *(in time)* long (longue); **a l. time ago** il y a longtemps; **it's been a l. day** ça a été une longue journée; **the days are getting longer** les jours rallongent; **to take a l. look at sth** regarder longuement qch; **in the l. term** *or* **run** à long terme, à longue échéance; **to have a l. memory** avoir bonne mémoire; **to take the l. view** envisager les choses à long terme; **l. weekend** long week-end *m*, week-end prolongé
3 *adv* (**a**) *(for a long period)* longtemps; **l. live the King/Queen!** vive le roi/la reine!; **as l. as** *(providing)* du moment que, tant que; *(while)* tant que; **to think l. and hard (about sth)** réfléchir longuement (à qch); **she won't be l.** elle ne tardera pas; *(will soon have finished)* elle n'en a pas pour longtemps; **I have l. been convinced of it** j'en suis convaincu depuis longtemps; **how l. have you known her?** depuis combien de temps la connais-tu?; *Fam* **so l.!** au revoir!, à bientôt!; **l. before/after** longtemps avant/après; **l. ago** il y a longtemps
(**b**) *(for the duration of)* **all day l.** toute la journée
(**c**) **I could no longer hear him** je ne l'entendais plus; **I couldn't wait any longer** je ne pouvais plus attendre; **five minutes longer** cinq minutes de plus

long² *vi* **to l. to do sth** rêver de faire qch; **to l. for sth** rêver de qch; *(look forward to)* attendre qch avec impatience; **we're longing for them to leave** il nous tarde qu'ils partent; **a longed-for holiday** des vacances *fpl* très attendues

long³ *(abbr* **longitude)** long

longboat ['lɒŋbəʊt] *n* chaloupe *f*

longbow ['lɒŋbəʊ] *n* arc *m*

long-distance ['lɒŋ'dɪstəns] **1** *adj (runner, race)* de fond; *(telephone call)* longue distance; *Br* **l. lorry driver** conducteur(trice) *m,f* de poids lourd
2 *adv* **to telephone l.** faire un appel longue distance

longevity [lɒn'dʒevɪtɪ] *n* longévité *f*

long-forgotten ['lɒŋfə'gɒtən] *adj* depuis longtemps oublié(e)

longhaired ['lɒŋ'heəd] *adj (cat, dog)* à poil(s) long(s); *(person)* aux cheveux longs

long-haul ['lɒŋ'hɔːl] *adj* long-courrier

longing ['lɒŋɪŋ] *n* profond désir *m*, grande envie *f* (**for** de)

longingly ['lɒŋɪŋlɪ] *adv* avec envie

longitude ['lɒndʒɪtjuːd] *n* longitude *f*

longitudinal [lɒndʒɪ'tjuːdɪnəl] *adj* longitudinal(e)

long-lasting ['lɒŋ'lɑːstɪŋ] *adj* durable, qui dure longtemps

long-life ['lɒŋ'laɪf] *adj (juice, milk)* longue conservation *inv*; *(battery)* longue durée *inv*

long-lost ['lɒŋ'lɒst] *adj* perdu(e) depuis longtemps; *(relative)* perdu de vue depuis longtemps

long-range ['lɒŋ'reɪndʒ] *adj (missile)* longue portée; *(forecast)* à long terme; *(plane)* à long rayon d'action

longshoreman [lɒŋ'ʃɔːmən] *n Am* docker *m*

long-sighted [lɒŋ'saɪtɪd] *adj (from birth)* hyper-métrope; *(from adulthood)* presbyte

long-sleeved [lɒŋ'sliːvd] *adj* à manches longues

long-standing [lɒŋ'stændɪŋ] *adj (arrangement, friendship)* de longue date

long-suffering [lɒŋ'sʌfərɪŋ] *adj* patient(e)

long-term ['lɒŋtɜːm] *adj (prisoner)* condamné(e) à une longue peine; *(loan, planning)* à long terme; **the l. unemployed** les chômeurs *mpl* de longue durée

long-winded [lɒŋ'wɪndɪd] *adj* verbeux(euse)

loo [luː] *(pl* **loos)** *n Br Fam* cabinets *mpl*; **l. paper** papier *m* toilette

loofah ['luːfə] *n* loofa *m*, luffa *m*

look [lʊk] **1** *n* (**a**) *(act of looking)* **to have** *or* **take a l. at sth** regarder qch; *(quickly)* jeter un coup d'œil à *ou* sur qch; **to have a l. for sth** chercher qch; **let me have a l.** fais(-moi) voir; **to have a l. round the town** faire un tour dans la ville; **to have a l. through some magazines** jeter un coup d'œil à des magazines
(**b**) *(glance)* regard *m*; **to give sb. a dirty l.** jeter un regard noir à qn; **if looks could kill** il y a des regards qui tuent
(**c**) *(appearance)* air *m*; **I don't like the l. of this** cela ne me dit rien qui vaille; **I don't like the l. of him** sa tête ne me revient pas; **by the l. of it,...** on dirait bien que...
(**d**) (**good**) **looks** beauté *f*; **to have lost one's looks** être moins beau (belle); **looks don't matter** le physique n'a pas d'importance
2 *vt* **to l. sb in the face** regarder qn en face *ou* dans les yeux; **to l. sb up and down** toiser qn; **l. what you've done!** regarde ce que tu as fait!; **l. where you're going!** vous ne pouvez pas faire attention, non?
3 *vi* (**a**) *(in general)* regarder; **to l. at sb/sth** regarder qn/qch; **he's not much to l. at** il n'est pas très beau; *Fig* **to l. the other way** fermer les yeux; **I'm just looking, thank you** *(in shop)* je ne fais que regarder, merci; **to l. on the bright side** voir les choses du bon côté; **l. here!** dites donc!; **I don't l. at it that way** je ne vois pas les choses comme ça; *Prov* **l. before you leap** il faut réfléchir avant d'agir
(**b**) *(search)* **to l. for sb/sth** chercher qn/qch; **we've looked everywhere** nous avons cherché partout
(**c**) *(seem, appear)* avoir l'air, paraître; **to l. old** avoir l'air vieux (vieille); **things are looking bad** les choses prennent une mauvaise tournure; **things are looking good** ça a l'air de bien se passer; **to l. one's age** faire son âge; **to l. the part** avoir l'allure qui convient; **what does she l. like?** comment est-elle?; **to l. like sb** ressembler à qn; **it looks like** *or* **as if...** on dirait que...; **it looks like rain** on dirait qu'il va pleuvoir; **you l. as if you've slept badly** vous avez l'air d'avoir mal dormi

▶**look after** *vt insep (take care of)* s'occuper de; **to l. after oneself** se débrouiller tout(e) seul(e); **to l. after sb's house/bag** surveiller la maison/le sac de qn; **can** you I. **after the children tomorrow?** tu peux garder les enfants demain?

▶**look around 1** vt insep (town, shops) faire un tour dans
2 vi (in town) faire un tour; (in shop) jeter un coup d'œil; **to I. around for sth** essayer de trouver qch

▶**look back** vi (**a**) (in space) regarder en arrière ou derrière soi (**b**) (in time) **to I. back on sth** revenir sur qch; **she has never looked back since that day** depuis ce jour sa situation n'a cessé de s'améliorer

▶**look down** vi (from above) regarder en bas ou vers le bas; (lower one's eyes) baisser les yeux; Fig **to I. down on sb** regarder qn de haut

▶**look forward to** vt insep **to I. forward to sth** attendre qch avec impatience; **I'm looking forward to seeing her again** il me tarde de la revoir; **I I. forward to hearing from you** (in letter) dans l'attente de vous lire

▶**look in** vi **to I. in (on sb)** passer (voir qn)

▶**look into** vt insep examiner

▶**look on 1** vt insep (consider) **to I. on sb/sth as** considérer qn/qch comme
2 vi (watch) regarder

▶**look out 1** vt sep (find) trouver, dénicher
2 vi (**a**) (from indoors) regarder dehors; **to I. out of the window** regarder par la fenêtre (**b**) (be careful) faire attention; **I. out!** attention!

▶**look out for** vt insep (**a**) (look for) (person) guetter; (thing) chercher (**b**) (be on guard for) faire attention à

▶**look over** vt insep jeter un coup d'œil sur

▶**look round** – look around

▶**look through** vt insep (**a**) (inspect) (written material) parcourir; (clothes, CDs) passer en revue (**b**) (not see) **to I. straight through sb** regarder qn sans le voir; (deliberately) ignorer qn

▶**look to** vt insep (**a**) (rely on) **to I. to sb (for sth)** compter sur qn (pour qch) (**b**) **to I. to the future** se tourner vers l'avenir

▶**look up 1** vt sep (word, address) chercher; (person) passer voir
2 vi (from below) regarder vers le haut; (raise one's eyes) lever les yeux; Fig **things are looking up** la situation s'améliore

▶**look upon** vt insep (consider) **to I. upon sb/sth as** considérer qn/qch comme

▶**look up to** vt insep respecter, estimer

lookalike ['lʊkəlaɪk] n sosie m

look-in ['lʊkɪn] n Fam (chance) **he won't have** or **get a I.** il n'a pas la moindre chance; (in conversation) il ne pourra pas en placer une

looking-glass ['lʊkɪŋglɑːs] n Old-fashioned miroir m

lookout ['lʊkaʊt] n (person) guetteur m; (on ship) vigie f; **to keep a I. for sb/sth** guetter qn/qch; **to be on the I. for sb/sth** être à la recherche de qn/qch; Fam **that's your I.!** ça c'est ton affaire!; **I. post/tower** poste m/ tour f de guet

loom¹ [luːm] n (for making cloth) métier m à tisser

loom² vi (of person, building) se dresser; (of danger, event) être imminent(e); **to I. large** être très présent(e)

loony ['luːnɪ] Fam **1** n (pl **loonies**) dingue mf; **I. bin** maison f de fous
2 adj dingue

loop [luːp] **1** n boucle f
2 vt faire une boucle/des boucles à; **to I. sth around**

sth enrouler qch autour de qch; **to I. the loop** (in plane) faire un looping

loophole ['luːphəʊl] n (in law, regulations etc) point m faible; **to find a I.** trouver une échappatoire; **legal I.** vide m juridique

loopy ['luːpɪ] adj Fam barjo(t)

loose [luːs] **1** n **to be on the I.** (of prisoner) être en cavale; (of animal) être en liberté
2 adj (animal) qui s'est échappé(e); (tooth, plank) qui bouge; (piece of clothing) large, ample; (skin) flasque; (alliance, network) peu structuré(e); (translation) approximatif(ive); (morals, lifestyle) dissolu(e); **to come I.** (of knot) se défaire; (of screw) se desserrer; **to let sb I.** relâcher qn; **to let sb I. on sth** laisser qn toucher à qch; **don't let him I. in the kitchen!** ne le laisse pas faire la cuisine tout seul!; **to let I. a torrent of abuse** lâcher des torrents d'injures; **to buy sth I.** acheter qch en vrac; **I. change** petite ou menue monnaie f; **I. connection** (in appliance) faux contact m; **to be at a I. end** ne pas savoir quoi faire; Fig **to tie up the I. ends** régler les derniers détails; **I. talk** propos mpl irréfléchis; **to have a I. tongue** ne pas savoir tenir sa langue; **a I. woman** une femme de mauvaise vie
3 vt Lit (arrow) décocher; (bullet) tirer

▶**loose off** vt sep (arrow) décocher; (bullet) tirer

loose-fitting ['luːsfɪtɪŋ] adj ample, large

loose-leaf ['luːsliːf] adj à feuilles mobiles; **I. binder** classeur m

loose-limbed ['luːs'lɪmd] adj souple

loosely ['luːslɪ] adv (**a**) (attached) de façon lâche; **I. packed** (snow) poudreux(euse) (**b**) (roughly) de façon approximative; **to be I. connected** avoir un lointain rapport; **I. speaking** en gros; **I. translated** traduit librement

loosen ['luːsən] **1** vt (screw, knot, belt) desserrer; (restrictions) assouplir; **to I. one's grip** relâcher son étreinte; **to I. sb's tongue** délier la langue à qn
2 vi se desserrer

▶**loosen up** vi (relax) se détendre

loot [luːt] **1** n (booty) butin m; Fam (money) oseille f
2 vt piller

looter ['luːtə(r)] n pillard(e) m,f

looting ['luːtɪŋ] n pillage m

lopsided [lɒp'saɪdɪd] adj (face) asymétrique; (picture) de guingois, de travers; (grin) en coin

loquacious [lɒ'kweɪʃəs] adj Formal loquace

lord [lɔːd] **1** n (**a**) (aristocrat) noble m; (feudal) seigneur m; **L. Browne** lord Browne (titre de noblesse masculin); **I. of the manor** châtelain m; Br **the (House of) Lords** la Chambre des Lords; **the L. Mayor** le lord-maire; **my L.** (to noble) Monsieur le Marquis/le Baron/ etc; (to judge) Monsieur le juge (**b**) Rel **the L.** le Seigneur; **the L.'s Prayer** le Notre Père; Fam **good L.!** mon Dieu!; Fam **L. knows** Dieu seul le sait
2 vt **to I. it over sb** traiter qn de haut

lordly ['lɔːdlɪ] adj (noble) altier(ère); Pej (arrogant) hautain(e)

lordship ['lɔːdʃɪp] n autorité f; also Ironic **His/Your L.** monsieur; (to judge) son/votre Honneur

lore [lɔː(r)] n tradition f orale

lorry ['lɒrɪ] (pl **lorries**) n Br camion m; Fam Euph **it fell off the back of a I.** (was stolen) c'est de la marchandise volée; **I. driver** chauffeur m de poids lourd

Los Angeles [lɒs'ændʒəliːz] n Los Angeles

lose [luːz] (pt & pp **lost** [lɒst]) **1** vt perdre; **to have nothing to I.** n'avoir rien à perdre; **he had lost**

interest in his work son travail ne l'intéressait plus; **it loses something in translation** ça perd à la traduction; **to be lost at sea** périr en mer; **the joke was lost on him** il n'a pas saisi la plaisanterie; **that clock loses five minutes a day** cette pendule retarde de cinq minutes par jour; **that mistake lost her the match** cette erreur lui a coûté le match; **to l. one's way, to get lost** se perdre; *Fam* **get lost!** va te faire voir!; **to l. one's balance** perdre l'équilibre; **to l. sight of sb/sth** perdre qn/qch de vue; *Fam Fig* **you've lost me!** je ne vous sus plus!; **to l. weight** perdre du poids; **we lost him in the crowd** nous avons été séparés dans la cohue; **to l. oneself in a book/one's work** se plonger dans un livre/son travail

  2 *vi* *(in contest)* perdre

▶**lose out** *vi* être perdant(e) (**to sb** par rapport à qn); **to l. out on a deal** être perdant(e) dans une affaire

loser ['luːzə(r)] *n* (**a**) *(in contest)* perdant(e) *m,f*; **to be a bad l.** être mauvais(e) perdant(e) (**b**) *Fam (unsuccessful person)* raté(e) *m,f*, minable *mf*; **a born l.** un(e) vrai(e) raté(e)

losing ['luːzɪŋ] *adj* **to fight a l. battle** être battu(e) d'avance; **the l. side** *(in war)* les vaincus *mpl*; *(in contest)* l'équipe *f* perdante

loss [lɒs] *n* (**a**) *(in contest, war)* perte *f*; **there was a great l. of life** il y a eu de grosses pertes en vies humaines; **to suffer heavy losses** subir de grosses pertes; **it's no great l.** ce n'est pas une grosse perte; *Fam* **it's your l.!** tu ne sais pas ce que tu perds!; **without l. of face** sans perdre la face; **to be at a l. to do sth** être incapable de faire qch; **she's never at a l. for an answer** elle a toujours réponse à tout (**b**) *(financial)* **to make a l.** perdre de l'argent, être déficitaire; **to sell at a l.** vendre à perte; *Fig* **to cut one's losses** sauver les meubles; **l. leader** article *m* ou produit *m* d'appel

loss-making ['lɒsmeɪkɪŋ] *adj* déficitaire

lost [lɒst] **1** *adj* perdu(e); **to give sb/sth up for l.** abandonner tout espoir de retrouver qn/qch; **l. cause** cause *f* perdue; **l. property (office)** (bureau *m* des) objets *mpl* trouvés; **l. soul** âme *f* en peine

  2 *pt & pp of* **lose**

lot [lɒt] **1** *n* (**a**) *(large quantity)* **a l., lots** beaucoup; **the l.** tout; **I bought the l.** j'ai tout acheté; **a l. of** *or* **lots of people** beaucoup de monde; **I see quite a l. of her** je la vois assez souvent; **we had a l. of** *or* **lots of fun** nous nous sommes bien amusés; *Fam* **listen, you l.!** écoutez, vous tous!; *Fam* **that l. next door** la bande d'à côté; *Fam* **he's a bad l.** c'est un bon à rien
    (**b**) *(destiny)* sort *m*, destin *m*; **to draw** *or* **cast lots for sth** tirer qch au sort; **to throw in one's l. with sb** partager le sort de qn
    (**c**) *(piece of land)* (lot *m* de) terrain *m*; *(at auction)* lot *m*

  2 *adv* **a l.** beaucoup; **a l. bigger** beaucoup *ou* bien plus grand(e); **thanks a l.** merci beaucoup

lotion ['ləʊʃən] *n* lotion *f*

lottery ['lɒtərɪ] *(pl* **lotteries**) *n also Fig* loterie *f*

lotto ['lɒtəʊ] *n* loto *m*

lotus ['ləʊtəs] *n* lotus *m*; **l. position** (position *f* du) lotus *m*

loud [laʊd] **1** *adj* (**a**) *(noise)* bruyant(e); *(voice, music)* fort(e); *Pej (person)* fort(e) en gueule; **to be l. in one's praise/condemnation of sth** louer/condamner qch avec force (**b**) *(colour, clothes)* voyant(e)

  2 *adv* fort; **to think out l.** penser tout haut; **l. and clear** parfaitement

loudhailer [laʊd'heɪlə(r)] *n* porte-voix *m inv*

loudly ['laʊdlɪ] *adv* fort; *(complain)* bruyamment

loudmouth ['laʊdmaʊθ] *n Fam* **to be a l.** être *ou* avoir une grande gueule

loudmouthed ['laʊdmaʊðd] *adj Fam* fort(e) en gueule

loudness ['laʊdnɪs] *n (of noise, voice)* volume *m*

loudspeaker [laʊd'spiːkə(r)] *n* haut-parleur *m*

Louisiana [luːɪzɪ'ænə] *n* la Louisiane

lounge [laʊndʒ] **1** *n (in house, hotel)* salon *m*; **l. bar** = dans un pub, salle plus confortable où les prix sont légèrement plus élevés; **l. suit** costume *m* de ville; *(on invitation)* tenue *f* de ville
    2 *vi* fainéanter

▶**lounge about, lounge around** *vi* traîner

louse [laʊs] *n* (**a**) *(pl* **lice** [laɪs]) *(insect)* pou *m* (**b**) *Fam (pl* **louses**) *(person)* salaud *m*

lousy ['laʊzɪ] *adj Fam* nul (nulle); *(weather)* dégueulasse; *(trick)* sale; **to feel l.** se sentir vraiment mal; **we had a l. time on holiday** nous avons passé des vacances nulles

lout [laʊt] *n* voyou *m*

loutish ['laʊtɪʃ] *adj* de voyou

louvre door ['luːvə'dɔː(r)] *adj* porte *f* à persiennes

lovable ['lʌvəbəl] *adj* attachant(e)

love [lʌv] **1** *n* (**a**) *(for family, country)* amour *m* (**of** *or* **for** de *ou* pour); **give my l. to your parents** embrasse tes parents pour moi; **with l. from...** *(at end of letter)* affectueusement,...; **Bill sends (you) his l.** Bill t'embrasse; **there's no l. lost between them** ils ne peuvent pas se sentir; **I wouldn't do it for l. or money** je ne le ferais pour rien au monde; **to do sth for the l. of it** faire qch pour le plaisir
    (**b**) *(between lovers)* amour *m*; **to be/fall in l. with sb** être/tomber amoureux(euse) de qn; **to make l. with** *or* **to sb** faire l'amour avec qn; **the l. of my life** l'homme (la femme) de ma vie; **it was l. at first sight** ce fut le coup de foudre; **(my) l.** *(term of endearment)* mon amour; **a l.-hate relationship** une relation faite à la fois d'amour et de haine; **l. affair** liaison *f* (amoureuse); *Fig* passion *f*; **his l. affair with Paris** sa passion pour Paris; *Euph* **l. child** enfant *mf* de l'amour; **l. letter** lettre *f* d'amour; **l. life** vie *f* amoureuse; **l. match** mariage *m* d'amour; **l. nest** nid *m* d'amour; **l. triangle** ménage *m* à trois
    (**c**) *(in tennis)* **15 l.** 15 à rien; **l. game** jeu *m* blanc
    2 *vt (person)* aimer; *(thing)* adorer; **I l. Chinese food** j'adore manger chinois; **to l. to do** *or* **doing sth** adorer faire qch; **I'd l. to come** j'aimerais beaucoup venir

lovebird ['lʌvbɜːd] *n Fam Fig* **a pair of lovebirds** un couple de tourtereaux

lovebite ['lʌvbaɪt] *n* suçon *m*

loveless ['lʌvlɪs] *adj* sans amour

lovely ['lʌvlɪ] *adj (idea, smell)* très bon (bonne); *(weather)* beau (belle); *(person)* charmant(e); **to have a l. time** passer un bon moment; *Fam* **it's l. and warm** il fait bon

lovemaking ['lʌvmeɪkɪŋ] *n (sexual intercourse)* ébats *mpl* amoureux

lover ['lʌvə(r)] *n (of person) (man)* amant *m*; *(woman)* maîtresse *f*; *(of nature, good food)* amoureux(euse) *m,f*

lovesick ['lʌvsɪk] *adj* qui languit d'amour

lovey-dovey ['lʌvɪ'dʌvɪ] *adj Fam (talk)* mièvre, à la guimauve; *(person)* roucoulant(e)

loving ['lʌvɪŋ] *adj* affectueux(euse), tendre
low¹ [ləʊ] **1** *n* (**a**) **to reach a new** *or* **an all-time l.** atteindre son niveau le plus bas
(**b**) *(weather front)* zone *f* de basse pression
2 *adj* (**a**) *(not high, not loud)* bas (basse); *(neckline)* profond(e); **fuel is getting l.** on n'a plus beaucoup d'essence; **to cook sth over a l. heat** cuire qch à feu doux; **of l. birth** de basse extraction; **the lower classes** les classes les moins aisées; **lower ranks** *(in army)* rangs *mpl* inférieurs; **to have a l. opinion of sb** avoir une mauvaise opinion de qn; *Fig* **a l. blow** un coup bas; **the L. Countries** les Pays-Bas *mpl*; **l. tide** marée *f* basse
(**b**) *(depressed)* déprimé(e)
(**c**) *(ignoble)* **the lowest of the l.** le dernier des derniers (la dernière des dernières); **that's a l. trick!** c'est vraiment un coup vache!
3 *adv* bas; **the l. paid** les petits salaires *mpl*; **turn the music/the lights down l.** baisse la musique/la lumière; **to be running l. on sth** être presque à court de qch
low² *vi (of cattle)* meugler
lowbrow ['ləʊbraʊ] *adj Pej (tastes, interests)* peu intellectuel(elle)
low-budget [ləʊ'bʌdʒɪt] *adj (film)* à petit budget; *(holiday)* bon marché *inv*
low-calorie [ləʊ'kælərɪ] *adj* basses calories, hypocalorique
low-cost [ləʊ'kɒst] *adj* économique; *(housing)* à loyer modéré
low-cut [ləʊ'kʌt] *adj* décolleté(e)
low-down ['ləʊdaʊn] *n Fam* **to give sb the l. on sth** tuyauter qn sur qch; **what's the l. on Peter's resignation?** tu as des tuyaux sur la démission de Peter?
lower¹ ['ləʊə(r)] *vt* (**a**) *(eyes, blind, head, window)* baisser; *(sail)* amener; *also Fig* **to l. one's guard** baisser sa garde; **to l. one's voice** baisser la voix; **to l. oneself into/onto sth** se laisser glisser dans/sur qch (**b**) *(morally)* **to l. oneself (to do sth)** s'abaisser (à faire qch)
lower² ['laʊə(r)] *vi (of sky)* se couvrir; **to l. at sb** *(of person)* lancer des regards noirs à qn
low-flying ['ləʊ'flaɪŋ] *adj* volant à basse altitude
low-grade ['ləʊ'greɪd] *adj* de qualité inférieure
low-key [ləʊ'kiː] *adj (approach, debate)* modéré(e); *(film, style)* sobre, dépouillé(e); *(person)* réservé(e)
lowlands ['ləʊləndz] *npl* basses terres *fpl*; **the L.** *(of Scotland)* les Basses Terres de l'Écosse
low-level ['ləʊ'levəl] *adj* (**a**) *(discussion)* à bas niveau (**b**) *(radiation)* de faible intensité
lowly ['ləʊlɪ] *adj* humble, modeste
low-lying ['ləʊ'laɪŋ] *adj* de basse altitude
low-spirited ['ləʊ'spɪrɪtɪd] *adj* abattu(e)
low-tech ['ləʊtek] *adj* rudimentaire
loyal ['lɔɪəl] *adj (friend)* loyal(e), dévoué(e); **to be l. to sb/sth** être fidèle à qn/qch
loyalist ['lɔɪəlɪst] *n & adj* loyaliste *mf*

> **Loyalist**
> Dans le contexte britannique, le mot "Loyalist" désigne un protestant d'Irlande du Nord souhaitant rester au sein du Royaume-Uni.

loyally ['lɔɪəlɪ] *adv* loyalement
loyalty ['lɔɪəltɪ] *(pl* **loyalties)** *n* loyauté *f*; **you'll have to decide where your loyalties lie** il faudra que vous

décidiez de quel côté vous êtes; **to have divided loyalties** être partagé(e); *Com* **l. card** carte *f* de fidélité
lozenge ['lɒzɪndʒ] *n (shape)* losange *m*; *(cough sweet)* pastille *f*
LP [el'piː] *n (abbr* **long player)** 33 tours *m*
LSD [eles'diː] *n (abbr* **lysergic acid diethylamide)** LSD *m*
Lt *(abbr* **Lieutenant)** lt
Ltd *Br (abbr* **limited)** ≃ SARL, *Can* limité
lubricant ['luːbrɪkənt] *n* lubrifiant *m*
lubricate ['luːbrɪkeɪt] *vt* lubrifier
lubrication [luːbrɪ'keɪʃən] *n* lubrification *f*
lucid ['luːsɪd] *adj* lucide; *(explanation)* clair(e)
luck [lʌk] *n* chance *f*; **(good) l.** bonheur *m*, chance; **good l.!** bonne chance!; **bad l.** malchance *f*; **bad l.!** pas de chance!; **to wish sb l.** souhaiter bonne chance à qn; **to be in l.** avoir de la chance; **to be out of l.** ne pas avoir de chance; **to be down on one's l.** être sur la paille; **to try one's l.** tenter sa chance; **don't push your l.!** ne pousse pas le bouchon trop loin!; **some people have all the l.** il y a vraiment des gens qui ont de la veine; **just my l.!** c'est bien ma chance!; **no such l.!** je n'ai pas (eu) cette chance!; **with any l.** avec un peu de chance
luckily ['lʌkɪlɪ] *adv* par bonheur, heureusement
lucky ['lʌkɪ] *adj (person)* **to be l.** avoir de la chance; **to make a l. guess** tomber juste; **to have a l. escape** l'échapper belle; *Fam* **l. devil, l. beggar** sacré(e) veinard(e) *m,f*; *Ironic* **you'll be l.!** tu peux toujours courir!; **it's l. you came when you did** c'est une chance que tu sois arrivé à ce moment-là; **she's l. to be alive** elle a de la chance d'être encore en vie; **my l. number** mon chiffre porte-bonheur; **it's not my l. day** ce n'est pas mon jour de chance; **that was l.** ça a été un coup de chance; **to strike it l.** décrocher le gros lot; **l. charm** porte-bonheur *m inv*; *Br* **l. dip** = baquet rempli de sciure etc où l'on plonge la main pour en retirer une surprise; **you can thank your l. stars she didn't see you!** tu peux t'estimer heureux qu'elle ne t'ait pas vu!
lucrative ['luːkrətɪv] *adj* lucratif(ive)
lucre ['luːkə(r)] *n Pej or Hum* lucre *m*
ludicrous ['luːdɪkrəs] *adj* risible, ridicule
lug [lʌg] *(pt & pp* **lugged)** *vt Fam* trimbaler
luggage ['lʌgɪdʒ] *n* bagages *mpl*; **l. label** étiquette *f* à bagages; **l. locker** consigne *f* automatique; **l. rack** *(in train)* porte-bagages *m inv*; *(on car)* galerie *f*; *Br* **l. van** *(on train)* fourgon *m*
lughole ['lʌghəʊl] *n Br Fam* esgourde *f*
lugubrious [luː'guːbrɪəs] *adj* lugubre
lukewarm ['luːkwɔːm] *adj also Fig* tiède; **she was rather l. about my suggestion** ma suggestion ne l'a pas enthousiasmée
lull [lʌl] **1** *n (in fighting)* accalmie *f*; *(in conversation)* pause *f*; *Fig* **the l. before the storm** le calme avant la tempête
2 *vt* **to l. sb to sleep** endormir qn en le berçant; **they were lulled into a false sense of security** ils se sont laissés aller à un sentiment de sécurité illusoire
lullaby ['lʌləbaɪ] *(pl* **lullabies)** *n* berceuse *f*
lumbago [lʌm'beɪgəʊ] *n* lumbago *m*
lumbar ['lʌmbə(r)] *adj Anat* lombaire
lumber ['lʌmbə(r)] **1** *n* (**a**) *Br (junk)* bric-à-brac *m*; **l. room** débarras *m* (**b**) *Am (wood)* bois *m* de charpente *ou* de construction

2 *vt* **to get lumbered with sth** se taper *ou* se coltiner qch; **I got lumbered with a huge bill** je me suis retrouvé avec une facture gratinée

3 *vi* to **l. about** *or* **around** avancer d'un pas lourd

lumbering ['lʌmbərɪŋ] *adj (walk)* lourd(e), pesant(e)

lumberjack ['lʌmbədʒæk] *n* bûcheron *m*

luminary ['luːmɪnərɪ] *(pl* **luminaries)** *n Lit* sommité *f*

luminescent [luːmɪ'nesənt] *adj* luminescent(e)

luminous ['luːmɪnəs] *adj (paint, road sign, colour)* fluorescent(e)

lump [lʌmp] **1** *n* **(a)** *(of earth)* motte *f; (of stone, coal)* morceau *m; (in sauce)* grumeau *m; (on body)* grosseur *f;* **a l. of sugar** un sucre; *Fig* **it brought a l. to my throat** *(made me sad)* ma gorge se serra; *Fin* **l. sum** somme *f* forfaitaire; **to pay in a l. sum** payer en une seule fois **(b)** *Fam Pej (person)* empoté(e) *m,f*

2 *vt* **(a)** *(group)* **to l. (together)** regrouper; *Pej* mettre dans le même sac **(b)** *Fam (endure)* **you'll just have to (like it or) l. it!** il faudra que tu fasses avec!

lumpy ['lʌmpɪ] *adj (sauce)* grumeleux(euse); *(mattress)* bosselé(e)

lunacy ['luːnəsɪ] *n* folie *f*

lunar ['luːnə(r)] *adj* lunaire; **l. eclipse** éclipse *f* de lune; **l. landing** alunissage *m*

lunatic ['luːnətɪk] **1** *n* fou (folle) *m,f;* **l. asylum** asile *m* d'aliénés

2 *adj (idea, behaviour)* dément(e); **l. fringe** extrémistes *mpl* fanatiques

lunch [lʌntʃ] **1** *n* déjeuner *m, Can* dîner *m;* **to have l.** prendre son déjeuner, déjeuner; *Fam Fig* **to be out to l.** *(be crazy)* débloquer; **l. hour** heure *f* du déjeuner

2 *vi* déjeuner, *Can* dîner **(on** de)

luncheon ['lʌntʃən] *n* **(a)** *Formal* déjeuner *m* **(b)** **l. meat** = viande à base de porc présentée en tranches; **l. voucher** chèque-restaurant *m*

lunchtime ['lʌntʃtaɪm] *n* heure *f* du déjeuner

lung [lʌŋ] *n* poumon *m;* **l. cancer** cancer *m* des poumons

lunge [lʌndʒ] **1** *n* mouvement *m* brusque en avant; **to make a l. for** se ruer vers

2 *vi* se ruer **(at** vers)

lupin ['luːpɪn] *n* lupin *m*

lupus ['luːpəs] *n Med* lupus *m*

lurch [lɜːtʃ] **1** *n (of ship, car)* embardée *f;* **a l. to the left/right** *(of politician, party)* un virage à gauche/droite; *Fam* **to leave sb in the l.** laisser qn dans le pétrin

2 *vi (of ship, car)* faire une embardée; *(of person)* tituber; **to l. to the left/right** *(of politician, party)* virer à gauche/droite

lure ['lʊə(r)] **1** *n (attraction)* attrait *m*

2 *vt (into trap, ambush)* attirer; **nothing could l. her away from her computer** rien ne pouvait l'éloigner de son ordinateur

lurid ['lʊərɪd] *adj* **(a)** *(story, description)* cru(e); *(headline)* sensationnel(elle); **she described it in l. detail** elle en a fait une description qui ne laissait rien à l'imagination **(b)** *(gaudy)* criard(e)

lurk [lɜːk] *vi* être tapi(e); *(of doubt, fear)* subsister

luscious ['lʌʃəs] *adj (woman)* appétissant(e); *(lips)* pulpeux(euse); *(fruit)* succulent(e)

lush [lʌʃ] *adj (plant, vegetation)* luxuriant(e); *Fig (surroundings)* luxueux(euse)

lust [lʌst] *n (sexual)* désir *m* (charnel); *Fig (for power, knowledge)* soif *f* **(for** de)

▸**lust after** *vt insep* convoiter

luster *Am* = lustre

lustful ['lʌstfʊl] *adj* lubrique

lustre, *Am* **luster** ['lʌstə(r)] *n* lustre *m*, éclat *m*

lustrous ['lʌstrəs] *adj* brillant(e)

lusty ['lʌstɪ] *adj (person)* vigoureux(euse); *(cry, blow)* puissant(e)

lute [luːt] *n* luth *m*

Luxemb(o)urg ['lʌksəmbɜːg] *n* le Luxembourg

Luxemburger ['lʌksəmbɜːgə(r)] *n* Luxembourgeois(e) *m,f*

luxuriant [lʌg'zjʊərɪənt] *adj* luxuriant(e)

luxuriate [lʌg'zjʊərɪeɪt] *vi* se prélasser **(in** dans)

luxurious [lʌg'zjʊərɪəs] *adj* somptueux(euse)

luxury ['lʌkʃərɪ] **1** *n (pl* **luxuries)** luxe *m;* **to lead a life of l.** vivre dans le luxe

2 *adj* de luxe

lychee [laɪ'tʃiː] *n* litchi *m*

lying ['laɪɪŋ] **1** *n* mensonges *mpl*

2 *adj (person)* menteur(euse)

lymph [lɪmf] *n Anat* lymphe *f;* **l. node** ganglion *m* lymphatique

lymphatic [lɪm'fætɪk] *adj* lymphatique

lymphoma [lɪm'fəʊmə] *n Med* lymphone *m*

lynch [lɪntʃ] *vt* lyncher

lynching ['lɪntʃɪŋ] *n* lynchage *m*

lynx [lɪŋks] *n* lynx *m*

Lyons ['liːɒn] *n* Lyon

lyre ['laɪə(r)] *n* lyre *f*

lyric ['lɪrɪk] *adj* lyrique

lyrical ['lɪrɪkəl] *adj* lyrique

lyricism ['lɪrɪsɪzəm] *n* lyrisme *m*

lyricist ['lɪrɪsɪst] *n* parolier(ère) *m,f*

lyrics ['lɪrɪks] *npl (of song)* paroles *fpl*

M

M¹, m¹ [em] *n (letter)* M, m *m inv*
M² *Br Aut (abbr* **motorway**) autoroute *f*
m² (**a**) *(abbr* **metre(s)**) m (**b**) *(abbr* **mile(s)**) mile(s)
MA [em'eɪ] *n Univ (abbr* **Master of Arts**) **to have an MA in linguistics** ≃ avoir une maîtrise de linguistique; **John Smith MA** John Smith, titulaire d'une maîtrise de lettres/droit/*etc*
ma [mɑː] *n Fam* maman *f*
ma'am [mɑːm] *n Old-fashioned* madame *f*
mac [mæk] *n Br Fam (raincoat)* imper *m*
macabre [mə'kɑːbə(r)] *adj* macabre
macaque [mə'kɑːk] *n Zool* macaque *m*
macaroni [mækə'rəʊnɪ] *n* macaronis *mpl*; **m. cheese** gratin *m* de macaronis
macaroon [mækə'ruːn] *n* macaron *m*
macaw [mə'kɔː] *n* ara *m*
Mace® [meɪs] *n (spray)* gaz *m* lacrymogène
mace¹ [meɪs] *n (weapon, symbol of office)* masse *f*
mace² *n (spice)* macis *m*
Macedonia [mæsə'dəʊnɪə] *n* la Macédoine
Macedonian [mæsə'dəʊnɪən] **1** *n* (**a**) *(person)* Macédonien(enne) *m,f* (**b**) *(language)* macédonien *m* **2** *adj* macédonien(enne)
Mach [mæk] *n Phys* **M. (number)** (nombre *m* de) Mach
machete [mə'ʃetɪ] *n* machette *f*
Machiavellian [mækɪə'velɪən] *adj* machiavélique
machinations [mæʃɪ'neɪʃənz] *npl* machinations *fpl*, manœuvres *fpl*
machine [mə'ʃiːn] **1** *n* machine *f*; *Fig (person)* robot *m*; **party/propaganda m.** appareil *m* du parti/de la propagande; *Comput* **m. code** code *m* machine; **m. gun** mitrailleuse *f*; *Comput* **m. language** langage *m* machine; **m. shop** atelier *m* d'usinage; **m. tool** machine-outil *f*; **m. translation** traduction *f* assistée par ordinateur
2 *vt* (**a**) *Ind* usiner (**b**) *(with sewing machine)* coudre *ou* piquer à la machine
machine-gun [mə'ʃiːngʌn] *vt* mitrailler
machine-readable [mə'ʃiːn'riːdəbəl] *adj Comput* lisible par ordinateur
machinery [mə'ʃiːnərɪ] *n (machines)* machines *fpl*, machinerie *f*; *Fig (of organization)* rouages *mpl*
machinist [mə'ʃiːnɪst] *n (on sewing machine)* mécanicienne *f*; *(on machine tool)* ouvrier(ère) *m,f*
machismo [mæ'tʃɪzməʊ] *n* machisme *m*
macho [mætʃəʊ] *adj* macho *inv*
macintosh = **mackintosh**
mackerel [mækrəl] *n* maquereau *m*
mackintosh [mækɪntɒʃ] *n* imperméable *m*

macro [mækrəʊ] *(pl* **macros**) *n Comput* macro *f*, macrocommande *f*
macrobiotics [mækrəʊbaɪ'ɒtɪks] *n* macrobiotique *f*
macrocosm [mækrəʊkɒzəm] *n* macrocosme *m*
macroeconomics [mækrəʊiːkə'nɒmɪks] *n* macroéconomie *f*
mad [mæd] *adj* (**a**) *(insane) (person)* fou (folle); *(idea, plan)* insensé(e); *(dog)* enragé(e); **to go m.** devenir fou; **as m. as a hatter** fou à lier; **m. with fear** mort(e) de peur; **there was a m. rush for the door** les gens se ruèrent vers la porte; *Fam* **to run/work like m.** courir/travailler comme un fou (une folle); *Fam* **m. cow disease** maladie *f* de la vache folle (**b**) *Fam (enthusiastic)* **to be m. about sth** être fou (folle) de qch; **the crowd went m.** ce fut le délire parmi les spectateurs (**c**) *Fam (angry)* furieux(euse) (**with** *or* **at** contre); **to go m.** piquer une colère
Madagascan [mædə'gæskən] **1** *n* Malgache *mf* **2** *adj* malgache
Madagascar [mædə'gæskə(r)] *n* Madagascar
madam [mædəm] *n (as form of address)* madame *f*; *Br Fam* **she's a proper little m.** *(of child)* c'est une vraie petite pimbêche
madcap [mædkæp] *adj* insensé(e)
madden [mædən] *vt* exaspérer
maddening [mædənɪŋ] *adj* exaspérant(e)
made [meɪd] *pt & pp of* **make**
Madeira [mə'dɪərə] *n (island)* Madère *f*; *(wine)* madère *m*
made-up [meɪd'ʌp] *adj* (**a**) *(story, excuse)* inventé(e) de toutes pièces (**b**) *(wearing make-up)* maquillé(e)
madhouse [mædhaʊs] *n Fam* maison *f* de fous
madly [mædlɪ] *adv* (**a**) *(insanely, desperately)* comme un fou (une folle) (**b**) *Fam (exciting, interested, jealous)* follement; **m. in love** follement *ou* éperdument amoureux(euse)
madman [mædmən] *n* fou *m*, dément *m*
madness [mædnɪs] *n* folie *f*, démence *f*; **it's sheer m.!** c'est de la folie pure!
madonna [mə'dɒnə] *n* madone *f*
Madrid [mə'drɪd] *n* Madrid
madwoman [mædwʊmən] *n* folle *f*, démente *f*
maelstrom [meɪlstrəm] *n (confusion)* tourbillon *m*
maestro [maɪstrəʊ] *(pl* **maestros**) *n* maestro *m*
Mafia [mæfɪə] *n* **the M.** la Mafia
mag [mæg] *n Fam* magazine *m*, revue *f*
magazine [mægə'ziːn] *n* (**a**) *(publication)* magazine *m*, revue *f* (**b**) *(on radio, TV)* **m. (show)** magazine *m* (**c**) *(for gun)* magasin *m*; *(ammunition store)* dépôt *m* de munitions

magenta [mə'dʒentə] **1** *n* magenta *m*
   2 *adj* magenta *inv*
maggot ['mægət] *n* asticot *m*
Maghreb [mæ'greb] *n* **the M.** le Maghreb
Magi ['meɪdʒaɪ] *npl* **the M.** les Rois *mpl* mages
magic ['mædʒɪk] **1** *n* magie *f*; **as if by m.** comme par
   enchantement; **black/white m.** magie noire/blanche
   2 *adj* (**a**) *(supernatural)* magique; **m. carpet** tapis *m*
   volant; *Fam* **m. mushrooms** champignons *mpl* (hallu-
   cinogènes); **m. wand** baguette *f* magique (**b**) *Br Fam*
   (excellent) génial(e)
▸**magic away** *(pt & pp* **magicked**) *vt sep* faire disparaître comme par enchantement
magical ['mædʒɪkəl] *adj* magique
magician [mə'dʒɪʃən] *n* magicien(enne) *m,f*
magisterial [mædʒɪs'tɪərɪəl] *adj* magistral(e); *Law* de
   magistrat
magistrate ['mædʒɪstreɪt] *n Law* magistrat *m*; **magistrates' court** ≃ tribunal *m* d'instance
magnanimity [mægnə'nɪmɪtɪ] *n* magnanimité *f*
magnanimous [mæg'nænɪməs] *adj* magnanime
magnate ['mægneɪt] *n* magnat *m*
magnesium [mæg'niːzɪəm] *n Chem* magnésium *m*
magnet ['mægnɪt] *n* aimant *m*; *Fig (for tourists, investors)* pôle *m* d'attraction
magnetic [mæg'netɪk] *adj also Fig* magnétique; **m.
   card** carte *f* magnétique; **m. compass** boussole *f*; **m.
   tape** bande *f* magnétique
magnetism ['mægnɪtɪzəm] *n also Fig* magnétisme *m*
magnification [mægnɪfɪ'keɪʃən] *n* grossissement *m*;
   (of sound) amplification *f*
magnificence [mæg'nɪfɪsəns] *n* magnificence *f*
magnificent [mæg'nɪfɪsənt] *adj* magnifique; *(meal,
   wine)* excellent(e)
magnify ['mægnɪfaɪ] *(pt & pp* **magnified**) *vt (image)*
   grossir, agrandir; *(sound)* amplifier; *Fig (importance,
   problem)* exagérer
magnifying glass ['mægnɪfaɪɪŋ'glɑːs] *n* loupe *f*
magnitude ['mægnɪtjuːd] *n* ampleur *f*; **a problem of
   the first m.** un problème majeur
magnolia [mæg'nəʊlɪə] **1** *n (tree)* magnolia *m*
   2 *adj* couleur magnolia *(inv)*, blanc rosé *(inv)*
magnum ['mægnəm] *n (of champagne)* magnum *m*
magpie ['mægpaɪ] *n* pie *f*; *Fig* **he's a bit of a m.** il a
   quelque chose du collectionneur fou
mahogany [mə'hɒgənɪ] **1** *n (wood, colour)* acajou *m*
   2 *adj* en acajou
maid [meɪd] *n (servant)* bonne *f*, domestique *f*; **m. of
   honour** *(to queen)* demoiselle *f* d'honneur; *Am (at
   wedding)* première demoiselle d'honneur
maiden ['meɪdən] **1** *n Lit (girl)* jeune fille *f*
   2 *adj (flight, voyage)* inaugural(e); **m. aunt** tante *f*
   célibataire; **m. name** nom *m* de jeune fille; *Parl* **m.
   speech** premier discours *m*
mail¹ [meɪl] **1** *n* (**a**) *(letters, parcels)* courrier *m*; **it came
   in the m.** c'est arrivé au courrier
   (**b**) *(system)* poste *f*; **by m.** par la poste; *Comput* **m.
   merge** publipostage *m*; *Com* **m. order catalogue/
   company** catalogue *m*/entreprise *f* de vente par correspondance; **by m. order** par correspondance; **m.
   train** train *m* postal
   (**c**) *Comput* courrier *m* électronique, mél *m*, *Can*
   courriel *m*
   2 *vt* (**a**) *(letter)* poster; *(parcel)* envoyer *ou* expédier
   par la poste

(**b**) *Comput (message, document)* envoyer par courrier électronique; *(person)* envoyer un courrier électronique à
mail² *n (armour)* mailles *fpl*
mailbag ['meɪlbæg] *n* sac *m* postal; **she gets a huge
   m.** *(of celebrity, politician)* elle reçoit énormément de
   courrier
mailbox ['meɪlbɒks] *n Am & Comput* boîte *f* aux lettres
mailing ['meɪlɪŋ] *n (mailshot)* publipostage *m*, mailing
   m; **m. list** fichier *m* d'adresses
mailshot ['meɪlʃɒt] *n* publipostage *m*, mailing *m*
maim [meɪm] *vt* mutiler, estropier
main [meɪn] **1** *n* (**a**) *(pipe)* conduite *f* (principale); **the
   mains** *(electricity)* le secteur; **to turn the water off at
   the mains** couper l'arrivée d'eau; **gas from the mains**
   gaz de ville (**b**) **in the m.** *(generally)* en général, en
   gros
   2 *adj* principal(e); **the m. thing is to...** l'essentiel est
   de...; *Gram* **m. clause** proposition *f* principale; **m.
   course** plat *m* de résistance; **m. entrance** entrée *f*
   principale; *Rail* **m. line** grande ligne *f*; **m. road** grande
   route *f*; *Fam* **m. squeeze** petit(e) ami(e) *m,f*; **m. street**
   rue *f* principale
mainframe ['meɪnfreɪm] *n Comput* ordinateur *m* central
mainland ['meɪnlænd] *n* continent *m*; **m. Europe**
   l'Europe continentale
mainline ['meɪnlaɪn] *vi Fam (inject drugs)* se piquer
mainly ['meɪnlɪ] *adv* principalement; **the passengers
   were m. Spanish** la plupart des passagers étaient
   espagnols
mainspring ['meɪnsprɪŋ] *n Fig (of change, revolution)*
   moteur *m*
mainstay ['meɪnsteɪ] *n (of economy, philosophy)* pilier
   m, base *f*
mainstream ['meɪnstriːm] **1** *n* courant *m* principal
   2 *adj* ordinaire
maintain [meɪn'teɪn] *vt* (**a**) *(preserve) (order, reputation)* maintenir; *(silence, attitude)* garder; **to m. one's
   enthusiasm** rester enthousiaste (**b**) *(building, machine, road)* entretenir (**c**) *(family)* subvenir aux besoins de (**d**) *(state)* **to m. that...** soutenir que...
maintenance ['meɪntɪnəns] *n* (**a**) *(of car, building,
   roads)* entretien *m*; **m. costs** frais *mpl* d'entretien (**b**)
   Law (alimony) pension *f* alimentaire
maisonette [meɪzə'net] *n (appartement m)* duplex *m*
maize [meɪz] *n* maïs *m*
Maj (**a**) *Mil (abbr* **Major**) Cdt (**b**) *Mus (abbr* **Major**) M
majestic [mə'dʒestɪk] *adj* majestueux(euse)
majesty ['mædʒəstɪ] *n* majesté *f*; **His/Her M.** Sa Majesté le Roi/la Reine
major ['meɪdʒə(r)] **1** *n* (**a**) *Mil (in air force)* ≃ commandant *m*, *Can & Belg* ≃ major *m*; *(in infantry)* chef *m* de
   bataillon; *(in cavalry)* chef *m* d'escadron; **m. general**
   général *m* de division (**b**) *Am Univ (subject)* matière *f*
   principale
   2 *adj* (**a**) *(important)* majeur(e); *(most important)*
   principal(e); *(accident, illness)* très grave; **of m. importance** de la plus haute importance (**b**) *Mus* ma-
   jeur(e)
   3 *vi Am Univ* **to m. in sth** se spécialiser en qch
Majorca [mə'jɔːkə] *n* Majorque *f*
Majorcan [mə'jɔːkən] **1** *n* Majorquin(e) *m,f*
   2 *adj* majorquin(e)
majority [mə'dʒɒrɪtɪ] *(pl* **majorities**) *n* (**a**) *(in vote)*
   majorité *f*; **to be in a** *or* **the m.** être majoritaire; **m.**

decision décision *f* prise à la majorité; *Pol* **m. rule** système *m* majoritaire; *Law* **m. verdict** verdict *m* de la majorité; *Pol* **there was a m. vote in favour of...** on a voté à la majorité pour... (**b**) *Law (age)* majorité *f*

make [meɪk] **1** *vt (pt & pp* **made** [meɪd]) (**a**) *(produce, perform)* faire; *(payment)* effectuer; *(decision)* prendre; **made in Spain** fabriqué(e) en Espagne; **made from** *or* **of stone/wood** en pierre/bois; **I'll show them what I'm made of!** je vais leur montrer de quel bois je me chauffe!; **I'm not made of money!** je ne suis pas millionnaire!; **to m. something of oneself** faire quelque chose de sa vie; **two and two m. four** deux et deux font quatre; **to m. a choice** prendre une décision; **it doesn't m. any difference** cela ne change rien; **to m. a noise** faire du bruit

(**b**) *(earn)* gagner; **to m. a living** gagner sa vie; **to m. a name for oneself** se faire un nom

(**c**) *(make successful)* **this is the book that made her** ce livre l'a rendue célèbre; *Fam* **to m. it** *(be successful)* réussir; **you've got it made** tu as la belle vie; **it's m. or break** ça passe ou ça casse; **it made my day** il m'a fait très plaisir

(**d**) *(cause to be)* **to m. sb happy/sad** rendre qn heureux(euse)/triste; **to m. sb hungry** donner faim à qn; **to m. sb tired** fatiguer qn

(**e**) *(compel)* **to m. sb do sth** faire faire qch à qn; **don't m. me laugh!** tu me fais rire!

(**f**) *(estimate, calculate)* **what time do you m. it?** quelle heure avez-vous?; **I m. it £50 in total** j'arrive à 50 livres en tout

(**g**) *(reach)* **to m. it** *(arrive in time)* arriver à temps; *(finish in time)* finir à temps; **to m. the final** *(of team, competitor)* arriver en finale; **to m. the first team** être sélectionné(e) pour jouer dans la première équipe

(**h**) *(become, be)* **she'll m. a good doctor/singer** elle fera un bon médecin/une bonne chanteuse; **the report makes interesting reading** le rapport est intéressant à lire

(**i**) *(manage to attend) (show, meeting)* assister à; **I can m. two o'clock** je peux être là à deux heures

2 *vi* (**a**) **to m. as if** *or* **as though to do sth** *(get ready to)* s'apprêter à faire qch; *(pretend)* faire semblant de faire qch

(**b**) **to m. do** *(cope)* se débrouiller; **to m. do with** se contenter de; **to m. believe (that)...** imaginer que...

(**c**) **to m. sure** *or* **certain of** s'assurer de

3 *n* (**a**) *(brand)* marque *f*

(**b**) *Fam* **to be on the m.** *(financially)* chercher à s'en mettre plein les poches; *(sexually)* draguer

▸**make after** *vt insep (chase)* se lancer à la poursuite de

▸**make for** *vt insep* (**a**) *(head towards)* se diriger vers (**b**) *(contribute to)* contribuer à

▸**make of** *vt sep* **what do you m. of the new manager?** que pensez-vous du nouveau directeur?; **I don't know what to m. of that remark** je ne sais pas comment interpréter cette remarque

▸**make off** *vi Fam (leave)* filer, décamper

▸**make off with** *vt insep Fam (steal)* filer avec

▸**make out 1** *vt sep* (**a**) *(understand, decipher)* comprendre; *(see, hear)* distinguer; *(handwriting)* déchiffrer (**b**) *(write) (list, cheque)* faire (**c**) *Fam (claim)* **to m. out (that)...** prétendre que...

2 *vi Am Fam (sexually)* se peloter

▸**make over** *vt sep (transfer)* céder (**to** à)

▸**make up 1** *vt sep* (**a**) *(story, excuses)* inventer (**b**) *(deficit, loss)* combler; **I'll m. it up to you later, I promise**

je te le revaudrai, je te le promets (**c**) *(complete) (team, amount)* compléter (**d**) *(form)* constituer, composer; **to m. up one's mind** se décider (**e**) *(put together) (list)* faire; *(parcel, bed)* faire; **to m. up a prescription** préparer les médicaments prescrits sur une ordonnance (**f**) *(apply make-up to)* maquiller; **to m. oneself up** se maquiller

2 *vi (end quarrel)* se réconcilier

▸**make up for** *vt insep* compenser; *(lost time)* rattraper

make-believe ['meɪkbɪliːv] **1** *n* fantaisie *f*; **to live in a land of m.** ne pas avoir le sens des réalités

2 *adj* imaginaire

makeover ['meɪkəʊvə(r)] *n (of appearance)* séance *f* de maquillage; *Fig* transformation *f*

maker ['meɪkə(r)] *n* (**a**) *(manufacturer)* fabricant *m*; *(of planes, cars)* constructeur *m* (**b**) **to meet one's M.** monter au ciel

makeshift ['meɪkʃɪft] *adj* de fortune

make-up ['meɪkʌp] *n* (**a**) *(cosmetics)* maquillage *m*; **m. artist** maquilleur(euse) *m,f*; **m. bag** trousse *f* à maquillage; **m. remover** démaquillant *m* (**b**) *(composition) (of team, group)* composition *f*; *(of person)* caractéére *m*

making ['meɪkɪŋ] *n (of goods)* fabrication *f*; **the film was three years in the m.** le tournage du film a duré trois ans; **history in the m.** l'histoire en train de se faire; **a poet in the m.** un poète en herbe; **the problem is of her own m.** c'est un problème qu'elle s'est elle-même créé; **he has the makings of an actor** il a tout ce qu'il faut pour devenir acteur

maladjusted [mælə'dʒʌstɪd] *adj* inadapté(e)

maladroit [mælə'drɔɪt] *adj* maladroit(e)

malady ['mælədɪ] *(pl* **maladies**) *n Fig* mal *m*

Malagasy ['mæləgæsɪ] **1** *n (language)* malgache *m*

2 *adj* malgache

malaise [mæ'leɪz] *n* malaise *m*

malaria [mə'leərɪə] *n* malaria *f*, paludisme *m*

Malawi [mə'lɑːwɪ] *n* le Malawi

Malawian [mə'lɑːwɪən] **1** *n* Malawien(enne) *m,f*

2 *adj* malawien(enne)

Malay [mə'leɪ] **1** *n* (**a**) *(person)* Malais(e) *m,f* (**b**) *(language)* malais *m*

2 *adj* malais(e)

Malaysia [mə'leɪzɪə] *n* la Malaisie

Malaysian [mə'leɪən] **1** *n* Malais(e) *m,f*

2 *adj* malais(e)

Maldives ['mɔːldiːvz] *npl* **the M.** les (îles *fpl*) Maldives *fpl*

male [meɪl] **1** *n (person)* homme *m*; *(animal)* mâle *m*

2 *adj* mâle; *(sex, attitude, public)* masculin(e); **m. chauvinist pig** phallocrate *m*; **m. nurse** infirmier *m*

malefactor ['mælɪfæktə(r)] *n Lit* malfaiteur(trice) *m, f*

malevolence [mə'levələns] *n* malveillance *f*

malevolent [mə'levələnt] *adj* malveillant(e)

malformed [mæl'fɔːmd] *adj* difforme

malfunction [mæl'fʌŋkʃən] **1** *n* mauvais fonctionnement *m*

2 *vi* mal fonctionner

Mali ['mɑːlɪ] *n* le Mali

malice ['mælɪs] *n* méchanceté *f*; *Law* **with m. aforethought** avec préméditation

malicious [mə'lɪʃəs] *adj* méchant(e), malveillant(e)

maliciously [mə'lɪʃəslɪ] *adv* méchamment, avec malveillance

malign [mə'laɪn] **1** *adj* pernicieux(euse) **2** *vt* calomnier, diffamer

malignant [mə'lɪgnənt] *adj (person)* malveillant(e), méchant(e); *(tumour)* malin(igne)

malinger [mə'lɪŋgə(r)] *vi* faire semblant d'être malade

malingerer [mə'lɪŋgərə(r)] *n* simulateur(trice) *m,f*

mall [mɔːl] *n Am* **(shopping) m.** centre *m* commercial

mallard ['mælɑːd] *n* colvert *m*

malleable ['mælɪəbəl] *adj also Fig* malléable

mallet ['mælɪt] *n* maillet *m*

malnutrition [mælnjuː'trɪʃən] *n* malnutrition *f*

malpractice [mæl'præktɪs] *n* faute *f* professionnelle

malt [mɔːlt] *n* malt *m*; **m. vinegar** vinaigre *m* de malt; **m. whisky** whisky *m* de malt

Malta ['mɔːltə] *n* Malte *f*

Maltese [mɔːl'tiːz] **1** *n* (**a**) *(person)* Maltais(e) *m,f*; **the M.** les Maltais *mpl* (**b**) *(language)* maltais *m* **2** *adj* maltais(e); **the M. cross** la croix de Malte

maltreat [mæl'triːt] *vt* maltraiter

maltreatment [mæl'triːtmənt] *n* mauvais traitements *mpl*

mammal ['mæməl] *n* mammifère *m*

mammary ['mæmərɪ] *adj Anat* mammaire; **m. glands** glandes *fpl* mammaires

mammography [mæ'mɒgrəfɪ] *n Med* mammographie *f*

mammoth ['mæməθ] **1** *n (animal)* mammouth *m* **2** *adj (huge)* gigantesque

mammy ['mæmɪ] *(pl* **mammies)** *n Fam* maman *f*

man [mæn] **1** *n (pl* **men** [men]) (**a**) *(adult male)* homme *m*; *Fam* **hey, m.!** eh toi!; *Fam* **how are you doing, m.?** comment ça va, vieux?; **a m.'s jacket/bicycle** une veste/bicyclette d'homme; **the army will make a m. of him** l'armée en fera un homme; **he took it like a m.** il a pris ça courageusement; **this will separate the men from the boys** c'est là qu'on verra les vrais hommes; **to be m. enough to do sth** être assez courageux pour faire qch; **to talk to sb m. to m.** parler à qn d'homme à homme; **he's just the m. for the job** c'est l'homme qu'il nous faut; **to be one's own m.** être son (propre) maître; **he's a m.'s m.** il aime bien être avec ses copains; **the m. in the street** l'homme de la rue; **a m. of God** un homme d'église; **a m. of the world** un homme d'expérience (**b**) *(individual, person)* homme *m*; **any m.** n'importe qui; **few men** peu d'hommes; **to reply as one m.** répondre d'une seule voix; **they were patriots to a m.** ils étaient tous patriotes (**c**) *(husband, partner)* **my m.** mon homme (**d**) *(humanity)* l'homme *m* (**e**) *(employee) (in factory)* homme *m*, ouvrier *m*; *(servant)* valet *m*, domestique *m*; *(soldier)* homme, soldat *m*; **our m. in Rome** *(diplomat)* notre envoyé à Rome; *(spy)* notre agent à Rome; *(reporter)* notre correspondant à Rome (**f**) *(in chess)* pièce *f*; *(in draughts)* pion *m* **2** *vt (pt & pp* **manned)** *(machine)* assurer le fonctionnement de; *(plane, boat)* être membre de l'équipage de; **to m. the phone** répondre au téléphone; **a manned flight** un vol habité

manacles ['mænəkəlz] *npl* menottes *fpl*

manage ['mænɪdʒ] **1** *vt* (**a**) *(company, project)* diriger; *(shop, hotel)* être le gérant de; *(economy, resources, money, time)* gérer (**b**) *(deal with) (situation)* gérer; **to know how to m. sb** savoir (comment) prendre qn; **to m. to do sth** *(succeed)* réussir *ou* arriver à faire qch; **I can't m. three suitcases** je ne peux pas porter trois valises; **£100 is the most that I can m.** *(to pay)* je ne peux pas aller au-delà de 100 livres; **can you m. dinner on Thursday?** est-ce que vous pouvez venir dîner jeudi? **2** *vi (cope)* se débrouiller (**with** avec); **to m. without sb/sth** pouvoir se passer de qn/qch; **he'll never m. on his own** il n'y arrivera pas tout seul

manageable ['mænɪdʒəbəl] *adj (object, size, vehicle)* maniable; *(hair)* facile à coiffer

management ['mænɪdʒmənt] *n* (**a**) *(activity) (of company, project)* gestion *f*, direction *f*; *(of economy, resources, shop, hotel)* gestion; **m. consultant** conseiller(ère) *m,f* en gestion; **m. studies** études *fpl* de gestion (**b**) *(managers, employers)* direction *f*; **under new m.** *(sign)* changement de propriétaire; **m. buyout** = rachat d'une société par la direction; **m. team** équipe *f* dirigeante

manager ['mænɪdʒə(r)] *n (of bank, company)* directeur(trice) *m,f*; *(of shop, hotel, bar)* gérant(e) *m,f*; *(of boxer, singer, football team)* manager *m*

manageress [mænɪdʒə'res] *n (of bank, company)* directrice *f*; *(of shop, hotel, bar)* gérante *f*

managerial [mænɪ'dʒɪərɪəl] *adj* directorial(e); **m. staff** cadres *mpl*; **m. skills** qualités *fpl* de gestionnaire

managing director ['mænɪdʒɪŋdaɪ'rektə(r)] *n* directeur(trice) *m,f* général(e)

Manchester ['mæntʃestə(r)] *n* Manchester

Mancunian [mæŋ'kjuːnɪən] **1** *n* = personne née à ou habitant Manchester **2** *adj* de Manchester

Mandarin ['mændərɪn] *n (language)* mandarin *m*

mandarin ['mændərɪn] *n* (**a**) *(fruit)* mandarine *f* (**b**) *(official)* mandarin *m*

mandate ['mændeɪt] *n* mandat *m*

mandatory ['mændətərɪ] *adj* obligatoire

mandible ['mændɪbəl] *n (of insect)* mandibule *f*; *(of vertebrate)* mâchoire *f* inférieure

mandolin ['mændəlɪn] *n* mandoline *f*

mane [meɪn] *n* crinière *f*

man-eater ['mæniːtə(r)] *n* (**a**) *(animal)* mangeur *m* d'hommes (**b**) *Hum (woman)* mangeuse *f* d'hommes

man-eating ['mæniːtɪŋ] *adj* mangeur(euse) d'hommes

maneuver *Am* = manoeuvre

manfully ['mænfʊlɪ] *adv* courageusement, vaillamment

manganese [mæŋgə'niːz] *n Chem* manganèse *m*

mange [meɪndʒ] *n* gale *f*

manger ['meɪndʒə(r)] *n* mangeoire *f*

mangle ['mæŋgəl] **1** *n (for clothes)* essoreuse *f* (à rouleaux) **2** *vt (body)* mutiler; *(car)* broyer; *(text)* massacrer

mango ['mæŋgəʊ] *(pl* **mangoes)** *n* mangue *f*

mangrove ['mæŋgrəʊv] *n* palétuvier *m*; **m. swamp** mangrove *f*

mangy ['meɪndʒɪ] *adj (animal)* galeux(euse); *(carpet, coat)* minable, miteux(euse)

manhandle ['mænhændəl] *vt (person)* malmener; *(large object)* transporter à la force des bras

manhole ['mænhəʊl] *n (in road)* bouche *f* d'égout; **m. cover** plaque *f* d'égout

manhood ['mænhʊd] n (**a**) (maturity) âge m d'homme; **to reach m.** devenir un homme (**b**) (masculinity) virilité f (**c**) (men collectively) Scottish **m.** les hommes écossais

man-hour ['mænaʊə(r)] n Econ heure f de travail

manhunt ['mænhʌnt] n chasse f à l'homme

mania ['meɪnɪə] n (liking) passion f (**for** pour); (psychological) manie f; **to have a m. for doing sth** avoir la manie de faire qch

maniac ['meɪnɪæk] n fou (folle) m,f; **to drive like a m.** conduire comme un fou

manic ['mænɪk] adj Fig (person) stressé(e); (activity) frénétique

manic-depressive ['mænɪkdɪ'presɪv] n & adj Psy maniaco-dépressif(ive) m,f

manicure ['mænɪkjʊə(r)] **1** n manucure f; **to have a m.** se faire faire les ongles
  2 vt **to m. one's nails** se faire les ongles

manifest ['mænɪfest] **1** n (of ship, aircraft) manifeste m
  2 adj manifeste, évident(e)
  3 vt manifester

manifestation [mænɪfes'teɪʃən] n manifestation f

manifestly ['mænɪfestlɪ] adv manifestement

manifesto [mænɪ'festəʊ] (pl **manifestos**) n Pol manifeste m

manifold ['mænɪfəʊld] **1** n Aut collecteur m
  2 adj Lit (numerous) multiple, nombreux(euse)

Manila [mə'nɪlə] n Manille f

mani(l)la envelope [mə'nɪlə'envələʊp] n enveloppe f en papier kraft

manipulate [mə'nɪpjʊleɪt] vt also Fig manipuler

manipulation [mənɪpjʊ'leɪʃən] n also Fig manipulation f

manipulative [mə'nɪpjʊlətɪv] adj Pej manipulateur (trice)

mankind [mæn'kaɪnd] n l'humanité f

manky ['mæŋkɪ] adj Br Fam (dirty) miteux(euse); (worthless) nul (nulle)

manliness ['mænlɪnɪs] n virilité f

manly ['mænlɪ] adj viril(e)

man-made ['mænmeɪd] adj (fabric, product) synthétique; (lake, beach) artificiel(elle); **a m. disaster** un désastre provoqué par l'homme

mannequin ['mænɪkɪn] n (person) mannequin m

manner ['mænə(r)] n (**a**) (way, method, style) manière f, façon f; **the m. in which...** la manière ou façon dont...; **in a m. of speaking** pour ainsi dire, en quelque sorte (**b**) **manners** (etiquette) manières fpl; **it's bad manners to stare** il est mal élevé de dévisager les gens; **he's got no manners** il ne sait pas se tenir (**c**) (type) **all m. of people/things** toutes sortes de gens/choses; **by no m. of means, not by any m. of means** absolument pas (**d**) (attitude, behaviour) **I don't like his m.** je n'aime pas sa façon d'être; **she's got a very abrasive m.** elle est très acerbe (**e**) **manners** (social usages) mœurs fpl

mannered ['mænəd] adj maniéré(e)

mannerism ['mænərɪzəm] n manie f, tic m

manoeuvrable, Am **maneuverable** [mə'nu:vrəbəl] adj maniable

manoeuvre, Am **maneuver** [mə'nu:və(r)] **1** n also Fig manœuvre f; Fig **there wasn't much room for m.** la marge de manœuvre était assez limitée; **to be on manoeuvres** (of soldiers) être en manœuvre(s)
  2 vt manœuvrer; **she manoeuvred the car into the** space elle a garé la voiture dans l'emplacement
  3 vi manœuvrer

manor ['mænə(r)] n **m. (house)** manoir m

manpower ['mænpaʊə(r)] n main-d'œuvre f

mansion ['mænʃən] n (in country) château m; (in town) hôtel m particulier

manslaughter ['mænslɔ:tə(r)] n Law homicide m involontaire

mantelpiece ['mæntəlpi:s] n dessus m de cheminée; **on the m.** sur la cheminée

mantis ['mæntɪs] n Am mante f religieuse

mantle ['mæntəl] n (**a**) Lit (of snow) manteau m; Fig **to take on the m. of office** assumer les responsabilités qui incombent au poste (**b**) (of gas lamp) manchon m (**c**) Geol manteau m

man-to-man [mæntʊ'mæn] adj & adv d'homme à homme

manual ['mænjʊəl] **1** n (handbook) manuel m
  2 adj (work, worker) manuel(elle); **m. dexterity** dextérité f

manually ['mænjʊəlɪ] adv manuellement

manufacture [mænjʊ'fæktʃə(r)] **1** n fabrication f; (of vehicles) construction f
  2 vt fabriquer; (vehicles) construire; (clothes) confectionner; Fig (evidence) fabriquer (de toutes pièces)

manufacturer [mænjʊ'fæktʃərə(r)] n Ind fabricant m; (of vehicles) constructeur m

manufacturing [mænjʊ'fæktʃərɪŋ] Ind **1** n l'industrie f (manufacturière)
  2 adj (centre, sector) industriel(elle); **m. capacity** capacité f de production; **m. industries** industries fpl manufacturières

manure [mə'njʊə(r)] **1** n fumier m; **liquid m.** purin m
  2 vt engraisser

manuscript ['mænjʊskrɪpt] n manuscrit m

many ['menɪ] (comparative **more** [mɔ:(r)], superlative **most** [məʊst]) **1** pron beaucoup; **m. of us/them** beaucoup d'entre nous/eux; **not m.** pas beaucoup; **too m.** trop; **as m. as you like** autant que vous voulez; **there were as m. as 100 people there** il y avait bien jusqu'à 100 personnes; Fam **to have had one too m.** avoir bu un coup de trop
  2 adj beaucoup de; **m. people** beaucoup de gens; **m. times** souvent, bien des fois; **not m.** pas beaucoup de; **in m. ways** de bien des façons; **not in so m. words** pas aussi explicitement; **there were so m. people that...** il y avait tant de gens que...; **a good m. people** un bon nombre de gens; **too m.** trop de; **as m.... as** autant de... que; **m.'s the time I've done that** j'ai fait ça bien des fois; Prov **m. hands make light work** à plusieurs, l'ouvrage avance vite

many-coloured ['menɪ'kʌləd] adj multicolore

Maori ['maʊrɪ] **1** n Maori(e) m,f
  2 adj maori(e)

map [mæp] **1** n carte f; (of underground, town) plan m; Fig **this will put Stonybridge on the m.** cela va faire parler de Stonybridge; **m. reference** coordonnées fpl
  2 vt (pt & pp **mapped**) (region) dresser une carte de

▸**map out** vt sep (route) tracer; (plan, programme) élaborer; **she had her career all mapped out** sa carrière était toute tracée

maple ['meɪpəl] n érable m; **m. leaf** feuille f d'érable; **m. syrup** sirop m d'érable

mar [mɑ:(r)] (pt & pp **marred**) vt gâcher

Mar (abbr **March**) mars

maracas [mə'rækəz] npl Mus maracas fpl

marathon ['mærəθən] *n also Fig* marathon *m*; **a m. speech** un discours-marathon; **m. runner** marathonien(enne) *m,f*

marauder [mə'rɔːdə(r)] *n* maraudeur(euse) *m,f*

marauding [mə'rɔːdɪŋ] *adj* en maraude

marble ['mɑːbəl] *n* (**a**) *(stone)* marbre *m* (**b**) *(glass ball)* bille *f*; **to play marbles** jouer aux billes; *Fam Fig* **to lose one's marbles** *(go mad)* perdre la boule

marbled ['mɑːbəld] *adj* marbré(e)

March [mɑːtʃ] *n* mars *m*; *see also* **May**

march [mɑːtʃ] **1** *n* marche *f*; *Fig* **the m. of time** la marche du temps; **on the m.** en marche; **m. past** défilé *m*

 2 *vt (soldiers)* faire défiler; **he was marched off to prison** il a été emmené en prison

 3 *vi (of soldiers)* marcher au pas; *(of soldiers on parade, demonstrators)* défiler; **to m. off** partir; **to m. by** *or* **past (sb/sth)** défiler (devant qn/qch)

marcher ['mɑːtʃə(r)] *n (demonstrator)* manifestant(e) *m,f*

marching orders ['mɑːtʃɪŋ'ɔːdəz] *npl Fam* **to give sb his m.** mettre qn à la porte

mare [meə(r)] *n* jument *f*

margarine [mɑːdʒə'riːn], *Fam* **marge** [mɑːdʒ] *n* margarine *f*

margin ['mɑːdʒɪn] *n* (**a**) *(on page)* marge *f*; **in the m.** dans la marge (**b**) *(edge) (of forest)* orée *f*; **on the margin(s) of society** en marge de la société (**c**) *(gap)* **to win by a narrow m.** gagner de justesse; **to win by an enormous m.** gagner haut la main; **a m. of error** une marge d'erreur (**d**) *Com* marge *f* bénéficiaire

marginal ['mɑːdʒɪnəl] **1** *n Br Pol* siège *m* à majorité précaire

 2 *adj* (**a**) *(improvement, increase)* léger(ère) (**b**) *(note)* en marge (**c**) *Br Pol (seat)* à majorité précaire

marginalize ['mɑːdʒɪnəlaɪz] *vt* marginaliser

marginally ['mɑːdʒɪnəlɪ] *adv* légèrement

marigold ['mærɪɡəʊld] *n* souci *m*

marihuana, marijuana [mærɪ'wɑːnə] *n* marijuana *f*

marina [mə'riːnə] *n* port *m* de plaisance

marinade ['mærɪneɪd] *Culin* **1** *n* marinade *f*

 2 *vt* (faire) mariner

marinate ['mærɪneɪt] *vt Culin* (faire) mariner

marine [mə'riːn] **1** *n (soldier)* fusilier *m* marin; *Am Fam* **(go) tell it to the marines!** (allez dire ça) à d'autres!

 2 *adj (life, biology)* marin(e); **m. engineering** génie *m* maritime

mariner ['mærɪnə(r)] *n Lit* marin *m*

marionette [mærɪə'net] *n* marionnette *f* à fils

marital ['mærɪtəl] *adj* conjugal(e); **m. status** situation *f* de famille

maritime ['mærɪtaɪm] *adj* maritime

marjoram ['mɑːdʒərəm] *n* marjolaine *f*

mark¹ [mɑːk] *n (German currency)* mark *m*

mark² **1** *n* (**a**) *(scratch, stain)* tache *f*, marque *f*

 (**b**) *(symbol)* marque *f*

 (**c**) *(sign, proof)* signe *m*; **as a m. of respect** en signe de respect; **years of imprisonment had left their m. on him** ses années de captivité l'avaient marqué; **to make one's m.** *(succeed)* faire ses preuves

 (**d**) *(target)* **his comments hit the m.** ses remarques ont touché en plein dans le mille; **unemployment has passed the three million m.** le nombre des chômeurs a dépassé la barre des trois millions; **her accusation was wide of the m.** son accusation était

complètement à côté de la plaque; **he's not up to the m.** il n'est pas à la hauteur

 (**e**) *(in test,exam)* note *f*; **full marks** la note maximale

 (**f**) *(in race)* **on your marks! get set! go!** à vos marques! prêts! partez!; **to be quick off the m.** démarrer vite; *Fig* avoir l'esprit vif; **to be slow off the m.** prendre un mauvais départ; *Fig* être long à la détente

 (**g**) *(model, of machine)* **m. II/III** série II/III

 (**h**) *(on cooker)* **(gas) m. 4** thermostat *m* 4

 2 *vt* (**a**) *(put mark on)* marquer

 (**b**) *(homework, exam)* noter; **to m. sth right/wrong** compter qch comme juste/faux

 (**c**) *(indicate)* indiquer; *(anniversary, end, occasion)* marquer; **this decision marks a change in policy** cette décision est le signe d'un changement de politique; *Fig* **to m. time** *(wait)* piétiner

 (**d**) *(characterize)* caractériser; **his comments were marked by their sarcasm** ses commentaires étaient empreints de sarcasme

 (**e**) *(in sport) (opponent)* marquer

 (**f**) *(pay attention to)* **m. my words** notez bien ce que je vais dire

▸**mark down** *vt sep* (**a**) *(make note of)* noter; **they had him marked down as a troublemaker** ils l'avaient étiqueté comme fauteur de troubles (**b**) *Com (price)* baisser; *(goods)* démarquer

▸**mark off** *vt sep* (**a**) *(area)* délimiter (**b**) *(tick off)* cocher

▸**mark out** *vt sep* **to m. sb out** distinguer qn

▸**mark up** *vt sep (price)* augmenter, majorer; **to be marked up** *(of goods)* avoir augmenté

marked [mɑːkt] *adj* (**a**) *(difference, improvement)* marqué(e), sensible (**b**) *(bearing a mark)* **m. cards** cartes truquées *ou* marquées; **to be a m. man** être surveillé

markedly ['mɑːkɪdlɪ] *adv* nettement

marker ['mɑːkə(r)] *n* (**a**) *(of essay, exam)* correcteur(-trice) *m,f*; **he's a hard m.** il note sévèrement (**b**) **m. (pen)** marqueur *m* (**c**) *(flag, post)* balise *f*; **m. buoy** bouée *f* de balisage

market ['mɑːkɪt] **1** *n* marché *m*; **to put sth on the m.** mettre qch en vente; *Fin* **m. analyst** analyste *mf* du marché; **m. day** jour *m* de marché; *Econ* **m. (free) m. economy** économie *f* de marché; *Econ* **m. forces** tendances *fpl* du marché; *Br* **m. garden** jardin *m* maraîcher; *Com* **m. leader** leader *m* du marché; *Econ* **m. price** prix *m* du marché; *Com* **m. research** étude *f* de marché; *Com* **m. share** part *f* de marché; *Com* **m. survey** étude *f* de marché; **m. town** ville *f* de marché

 2 *vt* commercialiser

marketable ['mɑːkɪtəbəl] *adj* commercialisable

marketing ['mɑːkɪtɪŋ] *n Com (study, theory)* marketing *m*, mercatique *f*; *(of product)* commercialisation *f*; **m. campaign** campagne *f* de marketing; **m. department** service *m* de marketing; **m. manager** responsable *mf* ou directeur(trice) *m,f* du marketing; **m. strategy** stratégie *f* marketing

marketplace ['mɑːkɪtpleɪs] *n* (**a**) *(in village, town)* place *f* du marché (**b**) *Econ* marché *m*; **in the m.** sur le marché

marking ['mɑːkɪŋ] *n* (**a**) **markings** *(on animal) (spots)* taches *fpl*; *(stripes)* rayures *fpl*; *(on plane)* insignes *mpl* (**b**) *(of essay, exam)* correction *f*; **I've got a lot of m. to do** j'ai beaucoup de copies à corriger

markka ['mɑːkə] *n* mark *m* finlandais

marksman ['mɑːksmən] *n* tireur *m* d'élite

mark-up ['mɑːkʌp] *n (on price)* majoration *f*

marmalade ['mɑːmǝleɪd] n confiture f d'oranges

maroon¹ [mǝ'ruːn] n (**a**) (colour) bordeaux m (**b**) (firework) fusée f de détresse

maroon² vt abandonner; **we were marooned by the floods** nous étions isolés à cause des inondations

marquee [mɑː'kiː] n grande tente f; (at circus) chapiteau m

marquis ['mɑːkwɪs] n marquis m

Marrakesh ['mærǝkeʃ] n Marrakech

marriage ['mærɪdʒ] n also Fig mariage m; **a happy m.** un ménage heureux; **she's my aunt by m.** c'est ma tante par alliance; **m. of convenience** mariage de convenance; Fig **it was a m. of minds** c'était la rencontre de deux esprits; **m. certificate** certificat m de mariage; **m. guidance counsellor** conseiller(ère) m,f conjugal(e); **m. vows** vœux mpl du mariage

marriageable ['mærɪdʒǝbǝl] adj **a girl of m. age** une fille en âge de se marier

married ['mærɪd] adj marié(e); **to get m. (to)** se marier (avec); **m. life** la vie maritale; **m. name** nom m de femme mariée; Mil **m. quarters** logements mpl pour familles

marrow ['mærǝʊ] n (**a**) (of bone) moelle f (**b**) (vegetable) courge f

marrowbone ['mærǝʊbǝʊn] n os m à moelle

marrowfat pea ['mærǝʊfæt'piː] n pois m carré

marry ['mærɪ] (pt & pp **married**) **1** vt (**a**) (get married to) épouser, se marier avec; (of priest, parent) marier; **will you m. me?** veux-tu m'épouser?; Fig **he's married to his job** il n'y a que son travail qui compte (**b**) (combine) marier
2 vi se marier

▸**marry off** vt sep marier

Mars [mɑːz] n (planet) Mars f

Marseilles [mɑː'seɪ] n Marseille

marsh [mɑːʃ] n marais m, marécage m

marshal ['mɑːʃǝl] **1** n (**a**) (army officer) maréchal m (**b**) (at race, demonstration) membre m du service d'ordre
2 vt (pt & pp **marshalled**, Am **marshaled**) (vehicles, troops) rassembler; (crowd) canaliser; (arguments, thoughts) mettre en ordre

marshland ['mɑːʃlænd] n région f marécageuse

marshmallow [mɑːʃ'mælǝʊ] n guimauve f

marshy ['mɑːʃɪ] adj marécageux(euse)

marsupial [mɑː'suːpɪǝl] n marsupial m

martial ['mɑːʃǝl] adj martial(e); **m. arts** arts mpl martiaux; **to declare m. law** proclamer la loi martiale

Martian ['mɑːʃǝn] n Martien(enne) m,f

martyr ['mɑːtǝ(r)] **1** n martyr(e) m,f; Fig **to be a m. to rheumatism** souffrir le martyre à cause de rhumatismes
2 vt martyriser

martyrdom ['mɑːtǝdǝm] n martyre m

marvel ['mɑːvǝl] **1** n merveille f; **to work marvels** faire des merveilles; **it's a m. they survived** c'est un miracle qu'ils soient encore vivants; Fam **you're a m.!** tu es un as!
2 vi (pt & pp **marvelled**, Am **marveled**) s'émerveiller (**at** de)

marvellous, Am **marvelous** ['mɑːvǝlǝs] adj merveilleux(euse); Ironic (**isn't it) m.!** ça, c'est le bouquet ou le comble!

Marxism ['mɑːksɪzǝm] n marxisme m

Marxist ['mɑːksɪst] n & adj marxiste mf

marzipan ['mɑːzɪpæn] n pâte f d'amandes

mascara [mæs'kɑːrǝ] n mascara m

mascot ['mæskǝt] n mascotte f

masculine ['mæskjʊlɪn] **1** n Gram masculin m; **in the m.** au masculin
2 adj masculin(e)

masculinity [mæskjʊ'lɪnɪtɪ] n masculinité f

mash [mæʃ] **1** n (**a**) Fam (mashed potato) purée f (**b**) (for pigs, poultry) pâtée f
2 vt **to m. (up)** broyer; (vegetables) écraser

mashed potato [mæʃtpǝ'teɪtǝʊ] n purée f de pommes de terre

mask [mɑːsk] **1** n masque m; (for eyes only) loup m
2 vt (conceal) dissimuler

masked [mɑːskt] adj masqué(e)

masking tape ['mɑːskɪŋteɪp] n ruban m de papier adhésif

masochism ['mæsǝkɪzǝm] n masochisme m

masochist ['mæsǝkɪst] n masochiste mf

masochistic [mæsǝ'kɪstɪk] adj masochiste

mason ['meɪsǝn] n (builder) maçon m; (freemason) franc-maçon m

masonry ['meɪsǝnrɪ] n (stonework) maçonnerie f

masquerade [mæskǝ'reɪd] **1** n (**a**) Fig (disguise) mascarade f (**b**) (dance) bal m masqué
2 vi **to m. as sb** se faire passer pour qn

mass¹ [mæs] **1** n (**a**) (large number) foule f, multitude f; Fam **I've got masses (of things) to do** j'ai des tas de choses à faire; Fam **there's masses of room** il y a plein de place; **m. culture** culture f de masse; **m. demonstration** grande manifestation f; **m. grave** charnier m; **m. hysteria** hystérie f collective; **m. media** médias mpl; **m. meeting** grand rassemblement m; **m. murderer** tueur m fou; **m. production** fabrication f en série; **m. protest** protestation f en masse; **m. unemployment** chômage m sur une grande échelle (**b**) (shapeless substance) masse f (**c**) Pol **the masses** le peuple m (**d**) Phys masse f
2 vi (of troops, people, clouds) se masser

mass² n Rel messe f; **to go to m.** aller à la messe

massacre ['mæsǝkǝ(r)] **1** n massacre m; Fam Fig **it was a m.** (in sport, election) ça a été le massacre
2 vt also Fig massacrer

massage ['mæsɑːʒ] **1** n massage m; **m. parlour** salon m de massage
2 vt (body) masser; Fig **to m. the figures** manipuler les chiffres

masseur [mæ'sɜː(r)] n masseur m

masseuse [mæ'sɜːz] n masseuse f

massive ['mæsɪv] adj (increase, scale, dose) massif(ive); (amount, building, obstacle) énorme; (room) immense; (heart attack, stroke) foudroyant(e)

mass-produce [mæsprǝ'djuːs] vt fabriquer en série

mast [mɑːst] n (of ship) mât m; (of radio, TV transmitter) pylône m

mastectomy [mæs'tektǝmɪ] (pl **mastectomies**) n Med mastectomie f

master ['mɑːstǝ(r)] **1** n (**a**) (man in charge) maître m; (of ship) capitaine m; **the m. of the house** le maître de maison; **to be one's own m.** être son propre maître; **to be m. of the situation** être maître de la situation; **m. of ceremonies** maître des cérémonies; (for TV programme) présentateur m; **m. bedroom** chambre f principale; **m. copy** original m; **m. key** passepartout m; **m. plan** plan m d'ensemble; **m. race** race f supérieure
(**b**) (skilled person) maître m, expert(e) m,f; Univ **M.**

of Arts *(qualification)* ≃ maîtrise *f* ès lettres; *(person)* ≃ maître ès lettres; *Univ* **M. of Science** *(qualification)* ≃ maîtrise *f* ès sciences; *(person)* ≃ maître ès sciences; **m. mason/builder** maître maçon/d'œuvre; *Mus* **m. class** cours *m* de maître; *Univ* **m.'s (degree)** ≃ maîtrise *f* (**in** de)

(**c**) *(teacher)* professeur *m*; **fencing/dancing m.** maître d'escrime/de ballet

(**d**) *(young boy)* **M. David Thomas** Monsieur David Thomas

(**e**) *Art* **an old m.** une œuvre de maître

2 *vt* maîtriser; *(situation)* dominer

masterful ['mɑːstəfʊl] *adj* autoritaire

masterly ['mɑːstəlɪ] *adj* magistral(e)

mastermind ['mɑːstəmaɪnd] **1** *n* cerveau *m*

2 *vt* *(project)* diriger, organiser; *(plot, crime)* échafauder

masterpiece ['mɑːstəpiːs] *n* chef-d'œuvre *m*

masterstroke ['mɑːstəstrəʊk] *n* coup *m* de maître

mastery ['mɑːstərɪ] *n* maîtrise *f*

mastiff ['mæstɪf] *n* mastiff *m*

mastitis [mæs'taɪtəs] *n Med* mastite *f*

masturbate ['mæstəbeɪt] *vi* se masturber

masturbation [mæstə'beɪʃən] *n* masturbation *f*

mat [mæt] *n* *(on floor)* tapis *m*; *(of straw)* natte *f*; *(at door)* paillasson *m*; **(table) m.** *(for plates)* set *m* de table; *(for dishes)* dessous-de-plat *m inv*

match¹ [mætʃ] *n* *(for lighting fire, cigarette)* allumette *f*

match² **1** *n* (**a**) *(in sport)* match *m*; **m. point** *(in tennis)* balle *f* de match (**b**) **they're a good m.** *(of clothes)* ils vont bien ensemble; **to meet one's m.** trouver son maître; **to be no m. for sb** ne pas être à l'hauteur par rapport à qn

2 *vt* (**a**) *(equal)* égaler (**b**) *(of colours, clothes)* être assorti(e) à; *(of description, account)* concorder avec (**c**) *(marriage)* **to make a good m.** faire un bon mariage; **we can't m. their prices** nous ne pouvons pas rivaliser avec leurs prix; **to m. sb against sb** opposer qn à qn; **to be well matched** *(of teams, players)* être de même niveau; **a well-matched couple** un couple bien assorti

3 *vi* *(of colours, clothes)* être assortis(ties); *(of descriptions, accounts)* concorder

▸**match up 1** *vt sep* *(colours, clothes)* assortir

2 *vi* *(of clothes, colours)* être assortis(ties); *(of explanations)* concorder; **to m. up to sb's expectations** répondre à l'attente de qn

matchbox ['mætʃbɒks] *n* boîte *f* d'allumettes

matching ['mætʃɪŋ] *adj* assorti(e)

matchless ['mætʃlɪs] *adj* sans pareil

matchmaker ['mætʃmeɪkə(r)] *n* marieur(euse) *m,f*

matchstick ['mætʃstɪk] *n* allumette *f*; **m. man** *or* **figure** bonhomme *m* dessiné de simples traits

mate¹ [meɪt] **1** *n* (**a**) *(sexual partner)* *(male animal)* mâle *m*; *(female animal)* femelle *f*; *(person)* partenaire *mf* (**b**) *Br Fam* *(friend)* copain (copine) *m,f*, **thanks, m.** merci mon vieux (**c**) *(assistant)* assistant(e) *m,f* (**d**) *(on ship)* officier *m*; **(first) m.** second *m*

2 *vt* *(animals)* accoupler

3 *vi* *(of animals)* s'accoupler

mate² *(in chess)* **1** *n* mat *m*

2 *vt* mettre mat

material [mə'tɪərɪəl] **1** *n* (**a**) *(substance)* matériau *m*, matière *f*; *Fig* **he isn't officer m.** il n'a pas l'étoffe d'un officier (**b**) *(for book, article)* matériaux *mpl*; **reading m.** de quoi lire; **she writes all her own m.** *(of singer)* elle écrit ses chansons elle-même (**c**) *(cloth)* tissu *m* (**d**) **materials** *(equipment)* matériel *m*

2 *adj* (**a**) *(needs, possessions)* matériel(elle) (**b**) *(important, relevant)* essentiel(elle); *(fact)* pertinent(e); **the point is m. to my argument** c'est un point essentiel de mon argumentation

materialism [mə'tɪərɪəlɪzəm] *n* matérialisme *m*

materialistic [mətɪərɪə'lɪstɪk] *adj* matérialiste

materialize [mə'tɪərɪəlaɪz] *vi* *(of hope, threat)* se réaliser; *(of event)* avoir lieu; *(of spirit)* apparaître

materially [mə'tɪərɪəlɪ] *adv* (**a**) *(in money, goods)* matériellement (**b**) *(appreciably)* sensiblement

maternal [mə'tɜːnəl] *adj* maternel(elle)

maternity [mə'tɜːnɪtɪ] *n* maternité *f*; **m. dress** robe *f* de grossesse; **m. hospital** maternité; **m. leave** congé *m* de maternité; **m. ward** maternité

matey ['meɪtɪ] *Br Fam* **1** *n* listen, **m.** écoute, mon pote

2 *adj* pote (**with** avec)

math [mæθ] *n Am* maths *fpl*

mathematical [mæθə'mætɪkəl] *adj* mathématique

mathematician [mæθəmə'tɪʃən] *n* mathématici-en(-enne) *m,f*

mathematics [mæθə'mætɪks] *n* *(subject)* mathématiques *fpl*; *(calculations)* calculs *mpl*

maths [mæθs] *n Br* maths *fpl*

matinée ['mætɪneɪ] *n* *(of play, film)* matinée *f*

mating ['meɪtɪŋ] *n* accouplement *m*; **m. call** appel *m* du mâle; **m. ritual** parade *f* nuptiale; **m. season** saison *f* des amours

matriarch ['meɪtrɪɑːk] *n* = femme ayant le statut de chef de famille

matriarchal ['meɪtrɪɑːkəl] *adj* matriarcal(e)

matriculate [mə'trɪkjʊleɪt] *vi* s'inscrire

matriculation [mətrɪkjʊ'leɪʃən] *n* inscription *f*

matrimonial [mætrɪ'məʊnɪəl] *adj* matrimonial(e)

matrimony ['mætrɪmənɪ] *n* mariage *m*

matrix ['meɪtrɪks] *(pl* **matrixes** ['meɪtrɪksɪz] *or* **matrices** ['meɪtrɪsiːz] *) n Math & Tech* matrice *f*

matron ['meɪtrən] *n* (**a**) *Br* *(in hospital)* infirmière *f* en chef; *(in school)* = intendante et infirmière (**b**) *(older woman)* matrone *f* (**c**) **m. of honour** *(at wedding)* première demoiselle *f* d'honneur

matt [mæt] *adj* mat(e)

matted ['mætɪd] *adj* *(hair)* emmêlé(e)

matter ['mætə(r)] **1** *n* (**a**) *(affair, issue)* question *f*, problème *m*; **that's a m. of opinion/taste** c'est une question d'opinion/de goût; **it's no easy m.** ce n'est pas simple; **that's quite another m.** ce n'est pas du tout la même chose; **within a m. of hours** en quelques heures; **for that m.** d'ailleurs; **as a m. of course** bien évidemment; **as a m. of fact** en fait; **as matters stand** au point où en sont les choses; **and to make matters worse...** et pour aggraver les choses...; **military matters** questions *fpl* militaires; **business matters** affaires *fpl*

(**b**) *(problem)* **what's the m.?** qu'est-ce qu'il y a?; **what's the m. with you?** qu'est-ce que tu as?; **there's something the m. with the car/my foot** j'ai un problème avec la voiture/mon pied

(**c**) *(substance)* matière *f*

(**d**) *(with no)* **no m.!** peu importe!; **no m. who/where** qui/où que ce soit; **no m. how hard I try...** j'ai beau essayer...; **no m. what I do** quoi que je fasse

2 *vi* avoir de l'importance (**to** pour); **it doesn't m.** cela n'a pas d'importance, ça ne fait rien; **nothing**

else matters le reste est sans importance; **it doesn't m. to me** ça m'est égal

Matterhorn ['mætəhɔːn] *n* **the M.** le mont Cervin

matter-of-fact ['mætərə'fækt] *adj (person, statement)* terre à terre; *(tone, voice)* neutre; **he was very m. about it** il avait l'air très détaché

matting ['mætɪŋ] *n* tapis *m* de sol tressé

mattress ['mætrɪs] *n* matelas *m*

mature [mə'tjʊə(r)] **1** *adj (person, fruit)* mûr(e); *(hard cheese)* fort(e); **m. garden** jardin *m* planté depuis plusieurs années; *Br Univ* **m. student** = adulte qui reprend des études
2 *vt (wine)* faire vieillir
3 *vi (of person, fruit)* mûrir; *(of wine)* vieillir; *Fin (of investment)* arriver à échéance

maturity [mə'tjʊərɪtɪ] *n* maturité *f*; *Fin* **on m.** à l'échéance

maudlin ['mɔːdlɪn] *adj* larmoyant(e)

maul [mɔːl] *vt (of lion, tiger)* mutiler; *Fig (criticize)* tailler en pièces

Mauritania [mɒrɪ'teɪnɪə] *n* la Mauritanie

Mauritanian [mɒrɪ'teɪnɪən] **1** *n* Mauritanien(enne) *m,f*
2 *adj* mauritanien(enne)

Mauritian [mə'rɪʃən] **1** *n* Mauricien(enne) *m,f*
2 *adj* mauricien(enne)

Mauritius [mə'rɪʃəs] *n* l'île *f* Maurice

mausoleum [mɔːsə'liːəm] *n* mausolée *m*

mauve [məʊv] **1** *n* mauve *m*
2 *adj* mauve

maverick ['mævərɪk] *n* franc-tireur *m*, non-conformiste *mf*

mawkish ['mɔːkɪʃ] *adj Pej* mièvre

max [mæks] *(abbr* **maximum)** **1** *n* max
2 *adv Fam* maximum; **it'll take three days m.** ça prendra trois jours maximum

maxim ['mæksɪm] *n* maxime *f*

maximize ['mæksɪmaɪz] *vt* maximaliser

maximum ['mæksɪməm] **1** *n (pl* **maximums** *or* **maxima** ['mæksɪmə]) maximum *m*; **to the m.** au maximum
2 *adj* maximum *inv*, maximal(e)

May [meɪ] *n* mai *m*; **in M.** en mai, au mois de mai; **at the beginning/end of M.** début/fin mai; **during M.** en mai; **each** *or* **every M.** chaque année en mai; **in the middle of M.** mi-mai; **last/next M.** en mai dernier/prochain; **on the sixteenth of M.** le seize mai; **she was born on 22 M. 1953** elle est née le 22 mai 1953; **M. Day** le Premier Mai

may [meɪ] *v aux (3rd person singular* **may**, *pt* **might** [maɪt])

> **may** et **might** peuvent s'utiliser indifféremment ou presque dans les expressions de la catégorie (**a**).

(**a**) *(expressing possibility)* **he m. return at any moment** il pourrait rentrer à tout moment; **he m. have lost it** il se peut *ou* se pourrait qu'il l'ait perdu; **it m. be that...** il se peut *ou* se pourrait que... + *subjunctive*; **you m. be wondering why...** vous vous demandez peut-être pourquoi...; **you m. well ask!** bonne question!; **we m. as well go** autant y aller; **you m. as well tell them the truth** autant que tu leur dises la vérité
(**b**) *Formal (asking for or giving permission)* **m. I come in?** puis-je entrer?; **if I m. say so** si je peux me permettre; **m. I?** *(when borrowing)* vous permettez?
(**c**) *Formal (expressing wish, purpose)* **m. she rest in peace!** paix à son âme!; **m. the best man win!** que le meilleur gagne!
(**d**) *(with concessions)* **he m. be very talented but I still don't like him** il est peut-être très doué, mais il me déplaît quand même; **be that as it m., that's as m. be** quoi qu'il en soit

Mayan ['maɪən] **1** *n* Maya *mf*
2 *adj* maya

maybe ['meɪbiː] *adv* peut-être; **m. she won't accept** elle n'acceptera peut-être pas

Mayday ['meɪdeɪ] *n (distress signal)* signal *m* de détresse, SOS *m*; **M.!** mayday!

mayhem ['meɪhem] *n* **it was m.** c'était la pagaille

mayonnaise [meɪə'neɪz] *n* mayonnaise *f*

mayor ['meə(r)] *n* maire *m*

mayoress ['meəres] *n* mairesse *f*; *(mayor's wife)* femme *f* du maire

maypole ['meɪpəʊl] *n* = mât autour duquel les gens dansent pour célébrer le Premier Mai

maze [meɪz] *n* labyrinthe *m*; *Fig* dédale *m*

MBA [embiː'eɪ] *n Univ (abbr* **Master of Business Administration**) MBA *m*

MBE [embiː'iː] *n Br (abbr* **Member of the Order of the British Empire**) = titre honorifique britannique

MBO [embiː'əʊ] *n Com (abbr* **management buyout**) = rachat d'une entreprise par ses cadres

MC [em'siː] *n (abbr* **Master of Ceremonies**) maître *m* des cérémonies; *(for TV programme)* présentateur *m*

MD [em'diː] *n* (**a**) *Med (abbr* **Doctor of Medicine**) docteur *m* en médecine (**b**) *Com (abbr* **Managing Director**) directeur(trice) *m,f* général(e)

ME [e'miː] *n Med (abbr* **myalgic encephalomyelitis**) encéphalomyélite *f* myalgique

me¹ [*unstressed* mɪ, *stressed* miː] *pron* (**a**) *(direct object)* me; **she hates me** elle me déteste; **she loves me** elle m'aime; **she can understand my son but not ME** elle comprend mon fils, mais moi, elle ne me comprend pas
(**b**) *(indirect object)* **she gave me the book** elle m'a donné le livre; **she gave it to me** elle me l'a donné
(**c**) *(after preposition)* moi; **she's thinking of me** elle pense à moi
(**d**) *(as complement of verb* **to be**) moi; **it's me!** c'est moi!; **it was me who did it** c'est moi qui l'ai fait
(**e**) *(with interjections)* **silly me!** que je suis bête!; **poor me!** pauvre de moi!

me² [miː] *n Mus* mi *m*

meadow ['medəʊ] *n* prairie *f*, pré *m*

meagre, *Am* **meager** ['miːgə(r)] *adj* maigre

meal¹ [miːl] *n* repas *m*; *Fig* **to make a m. of sth** faire tout un plat de qch

meal² *n (flour)* farine *f*

mealtime ['miːltaɪm] *n* heure *f* du repas

mealy ['miːlɪ] *adj* farineux(euse)

mealy-mouthed [miːlɪ'maʊðd] *adj Pej* mielleux(euse)

mean¹ [miːn] **1** *n (average)* moyenne *f*
2 *adj (average)* moyen(enne)

mean² *adj* (**a**) *(miserly)* mesquin(e), avare (**b**) *(nasty)* méchant(e); **she has a m. streak** elle peut être méchante quand elle veut; **that was a m. thing to do/ say** ce n'est pas chic d'avoir dit ça/fait ça (**c**) *(poor)* **she's no m. photographer** c'est une sacrée photographe; **it was no m. feat** ce n'est pas un mince exploit (**d**) *Fam (good)* **he plays a m. game of pool** c'est un as du billard

mean³ *(pt & pp* **meant** [ment]) *vt* (**a**) *(signify) (of word, event)* signifier; *(of person)* vouloir dire; **what does the word "tacky" m.?** que signifie le mot "tacky"?; **this is Tim, I m. Tom** je vous présente Tim, je veux dire Tom; **I know what you m.** je comprends; **what do you m.?** qu'est-ce que tu veux dire?; **it doesn't m. anything** ça ne veut rien dire (**b**) *(be serious about)* **do you think he meant what he said?** pensez-vous qu'il l'ait dit sérieusement?; **I didn't m. that** ce n'est pas ce que je voulais dire; **I m. it** je parle sérieusement; **you don't m. it!** tu plaisantes! (**c**) *(be of importance)* **the price means nothing to him** le prix importe peu pour lui; **it means a lot to me** c'est très important pour moi (**d**) *(intend)* **to m. to do sth** avoir l'intention de faire qch; **I didn't m. to do it** je ne l'ai pas fait exprès; **I m. him no harm** je ne lui veux pas de mal; **she means well** ses intentions sont bonnes; **I m. to succeed** je veux réussir; **she meant you to have this ring** elle voulait que tu aies cette bague; **it was meant as a joke/compliment** c'était une blague/un compliment; **this portrait is meant to be of the duke** ce portrait est censé représenter le duc; **you were meant to be here at eight** vous étiez censé arriver à huit heures; **it's meant to be a good film** il paraît que c'est un bon film; **they were meant for each other** ils sont faits l'un pour l'autre

meander [mɪˈændə(r)] **1** *n* méandre *m*
2 *vi (of river, road)* serpenter; *(of person)* flâner

meaning [ˈmiːnɪŋ] *n* sens *m*, signification *f*; *Fam* **if you get my m.** si tu vois ce que je veux dire; **what's the m. of this?** *(expressing indignation)* qu'est-ce que ça signifie?; **the m. of life** le sens de la vie

meaningful [ˈmiːnɪŋfʊl] *adj* significatif(ive); *(relationship)* sérieux(euse)

meaningless [ˈmiːnɪŋlɪs] *adj* vide de sens, sans signification

meanness [ˈmiːnnɪs] *n* (**a**) *(miserliness)* avarice *f* (**b**) *(nastiness)* mesquinerie *f*

means [miːnz] **1** *n (pl* **means**) *(method)* moyen *m*; **by m. of...** au moyen de..., à l'aide de...; **there is no m. of escape** il n'y a aucun moyen de s'échapper; **by some m. or other** d'une manière ou d'une autre; **a m. to an end** un moyen (d'arriver à ses fins); **by all m.** *(certainly)* je vous en prie; **by no m.** pas du tout, nullement; **she is by no m. stupid** elle est loin d'être bête; **m. of communication** moyen de communication; **m. of production** moyens de production; **m. of transport** moyen de transport
2 *npl (income, wealth)* moyens *mpl*, ressources *fpl*; **a man of m.** un homme fortuné; **to live beyond/within one's m.** vivre au-dessus de/selon ses moyens; **m. test** *(for state benefit)* enquête *f* sur les revenus

meant [ment] *pt & pp of* **mean**

meantime [ˈmiːntaɪm], **meanwhile** [ˈmiːnwaɪl] **1** *n* **in the m.** *(at the same time)* pendant ce temps; *(between two events)* entre-temps
2 *adv (at the same time)* pendant ce temps; *(between two events)* entre-temps

measles [ˈmiːzəlz] *n* rougeole *f*; **to have (the) m.** avoir la rougeole

measly [ˈmiːzlɪ] *adj Fam* minable

measurable [ˈmeʒərəbəl] *adj* mesurable; *Fig (difference, improvement)* notable, sensible

measure [ˈmeʒə(r)] **1** *n* (**a**) *(measurement, quantity)* mesure *f*; **this was a m. of how serious the situation was** cela montrait à quel point la situation était sérieuse; **they allowed her a m. of freedom** on lui accordait une certaine liberté; **to get the m. of sb** jauger qn; **then he called me a liar for good m.** par-dessus le marché, il m'a traité de menteur (**b**) *(degree)* **in some m.** dans une certaine mesure (**c**) *(action, step)* mesure *f*; **to take measures to do sth** prendre des mesures pour faire qch
2 *vt & vi* mesurer

▸**measure up** *vi* être à la hauteur (**to** de)

measured [ˈmeʒəd] *adj* mesuré(e)

measurement [ˈmeʒəmənt] *n* mesure *f*

measuring [ˈmeʒərɪŋ] *n* **m. jug** verre *m* gradué; **m. spoon** cuillère-mesure *f*; **m. tape** mètre *m* ruban

meat [miːt] *n* (**a**) *(food)* viande *f*; *Fig* **to be m. and drink to sb** être une aubaine pour qn; **m. loaf** pain *m* de viande; *Br Fam Pej* **m. market** = boîte réputée pour être un lieu de drague (**b**) *Fig (substantial content)* substance *f*

meatball [ˈmiːtbɔːl] *n* boulette *f* de viande

meaty [ˈmiːtɪ] *adj (taste, smell)* de viande; *Fig (book, film)* riche

Mecca [ˈmekə] *n* La Mecque; *Fig* paradis *m*

mechanic [mɪˈkænɪk] *n* mécanicien(enne) *m,f*

mechanical [mɪˈkænɪkəl] *adj also Fig* mécanique; **m. engineer** ingénieur *m* mécanicien; **m. engineering** construction *f* mécanique

mechanics [mɪˈkænɪks] **1** *n* (**a**) *(science)* mécanique *f* (**b**) *(working parts)* mécanisme *m*
2 *npl Fig (processes)* mécanisme *m*

mechanism [ˈmekənɪzəm] *n* mécanisme *m*

mechanize [ˈmekənaɪz] *vt* mécaniser

mechanized [ˈmekənaɪzd] *adj* **m. industry** industrie *f* mécanisée; **m. troops** troupes *fpl* motorisées

MEd [eˈmed] *n Univ (abbr* **Master of Education**) maîtrise *f* en sciences de l'éducation

medal [ˈmedəl] *n* médaille *f*

medalist *Am =* **medallist**

medallion [mɪˈdæljən] *n* médaillon *m*

medallist, *Am* **medalist** [ˈmedəlɪst] *n* médaillé(e) *m,f*

meddle [ˈmedəl] *vi (interfere)* se mêler (**in** de); *(tamper)* toucher (**with** à)

meddler [ˈmedlə(r)] *n* indiscret(ète) *m,f*

meddlesome [ˈmedəlsəm] *adj* indiscret(ète)

media [ˈmiːdɪə] *n* (**a**) *(TV, press)* médias *mpl*; **m. circus** cirque *m* médiatique; **m. coverage** couverture *f* médiatique; **m. studies** études *fpl* de communication (**b**) *pl of* **medium**

mediaeval *=* **medieval**

median [ˈmiːdɪən] *Math* **1** *n* médiane *f*
2 *adj* médian(e)

mediate [ˈmiːdɪeɪt] *vi* servir de médiateur (**for/between** pour/entre)

mediation [miːdɪˈeɪʃən] *n* médiation *f*; **to go to m.** recourir à une médiation

mediator [ˈmiːdɪeɪtə(r)] *n* médiateur(trice) *m,f*

medic [ˈmedɪk] *n Fam (student)* étudiant(e) *m,f* en médecine; *(doctor)* médecin *m*

medical [ˈmedɪkəl] **1** *adj (record, treatment, profession)* médical(e); *(book)* de médecine; *(student)* en médecine; **to seek m. advice** consulter un médecin; **m. board** commission *f* médicale; **m. care** soins *mpl* médicaux; **m. certificate** certificat *m* médical; **m. examination** visite *f* médicale; **m. insurance** assurance *f* maladie; **m. practitioner** (médecin *m*) généraliste *mf*; **m. records** dossier *m* médical

2 *n* *(physical examination)* visite *f* médicale; **to pass/fail a m.** être déclaré(e) apte/inapte à la visite médicale

medicated ['medɪkeɪtɪd] *adj* *(soap)* médical(e); *(shampoo)* traitant(e)

medication [medɪ'keɪʃən] *n* médicaments *mpl*; **to be on m.** être sous traitement

medicinal [me'dɪsɪnəl] *adj* médicinal(e)

medicine ['medsɪn] *n* **(a)** *(science)* médecine *f*; **to practise m.** exercer la médecine; **to study m.** faire des études de médecine **(b)** *(drugs)* médicament *m*; *Fig* **to give sb a taste of his own m.** rendre à qn la monnaie de sa pièce; **m. chest** *or* **cabinet** (armoire *f* à) pharmacie *f*; **m. man** *(traditional healer)* sorcier *m*, guérisseur *m*

medieval [medɪ'iːvəl] *adj* médiéval(e)

mediocre [miːdɪ'əʊkə(r)] *adj* médiocre

mediocrity [miːdɪ'ɒkrɪtɪ] *n* médiocrité *f*

meditate ['medɪteɪt] *vi* méditer (**on** sur)

meditation [medɪ'teɪʃən] *n* méditation *f*

Mediterranean [medɪtə'reɪnɪən] **1** *n* **the M.** la (mer) Méditerranée

2 *adj* méditerranéen(enne); **the M. Sea** la mer Méditerranée

medium ['miːdɪəm] **1** *n* **(a)** *(pl* **media** ['miːdɪə] *or* **mediums**) *(means of communication)* moyen *m* de communication; *(means of expression)* moyen d'expression; **through the m. of the press** par voie de presse **(b)** *(in spiritualism)* médium *mf*

2 *adj* moyen(enne); **of m. height** de taille moyenne; **in the m. term** à moyen terme; **m. dry** demi-sec; **m. rare** à point; **m. wave** ondes *fpl* moyennes

medley ['medlɪ] *(pl* **medleys**) *n* *(mixture)* mélange *m*; *(in music)* pot-pourri *m*; **the 400 metres m.** *(in swimming)* le 400 mètres quatre nages

meek [miːk] *adj* docile; **m. and mild** doux (douce) comme un agneau

meekly [miːklɪ] *adv* docilement

meet [miːt] *(pt & pp* **met** [met]) **1** *vt* **(a)** *(encounter) (by accident)* rencontrer; *(by arrangement)* rejoindre, retrouver; *(collect)* attendre, aller chercher; **his eyes met mine** nos regards se sont croisés; **a remarkable sight met our eyes** un spectacle extraordinaire s'offrait à nos yeux; **there's more to this than meets the eye** on ne connaît pas les dessous de cette affaire; **there's more to her than meets the eye** elle cache bien son jeu

(b) *(become acquainted with)* rencontrer, faire la connaissance de; **have you met my husband?** connaissez-vous mon mari?; **m. Mr Ford** je vous présente M. Ford

(c) *(join with) (river)* se jeter dans; *(road)* rejoindre

(d) *(satisfy) (demand, order)* satisfaire; *(condition, requirement)* satisfaire à; *(objection, criticism)* répondre à; *(cost, expense)* prendre en charge, payer

(e) *(danger)* affronter; *(difficulties)* rencontrer; **to m. one's death** trouver la mort; **to m. one's match** trouver son maître

2 *vi* **(a)** *(encounter) (by accident)* se rencontrer; *(by arrangement)* se retrouver; **our eyes met** nos regards

se sont croisés

(b) *(become acquainted)* se rencontrer

(c) *(of society, assembly)* se réunir

(d) *(join)* se rencontrer; *(of rivers, roads)* se rejoindre

▸**meet up** *vi* *(by accident)* se rencontrer; *(by arrangement)* se retrouver; **to m. up with sb** *(by accident)* rencontrer qn; *(by arrangement)* retrouver qn

▸**meet with** *vt insep* *(difficulty, refusal)* se heurter à; *(danger)* affronter; **to m. with disaster** se solder par un désastre; **to m. with failure** échouer; **to m. with an accident** avoir un accident; **to m. with sb's approval** recevoir l'accord de qn

meeting ['miːtɪŋ] *n* **(a)** *(encounter) (by accident)* rencontre *f*; *(by arrangement)* rendez-vous *m*; **m. place** (lieu *m* de) rendez-vous **(b)** *(for business, discussion)* réunion *f*; *(of shareholders)* assemblée *f*; **to be in a m.** être en réunion; **to hold a m.** se réunir

megabyte ['megəbaɪt] *n Comput* mégaoctet *m*

megahertz ['megəhɜːts] *(pl* **megahertz**) *n Elec* mégahertz *m*

megalomania [megələʊ'meɪnɪə] *n* mégalomanie *f*

megalomaniac [megələʊ'meɪnɪæk] *n* mégalomane *mf*

megaphone ['megəfəʊn] *n* mégaphone *m*, porte-voix *m inv*

megaton ['megətʌn] *n* mégatonne *f*

megawatt ['megəwɒt] *n Elec* mégawatt *m*

melancholy ['melənkəlɪ] **1** *n* mélancolie *f*

2 *adj* *(person)* mélancolique; *(atmosphere, news)* triste

melanin ['melənɪn] *n* mélanine *f*

melanoma [melə'nəʊmə] *n Med* mélanome *m*

melee ['meleɪ] *n* mêlée *f*

mellifluous [mə'lɪflʊəs] *adj* mélodieux(euse)

mellow ['meləʊ] **1** *adj* *(flavour)* suave; *(voice, colour)* chaud(e); *(wine)* moelleux(euse); *(light)* doux (douce); *(person)* détendu(e), serein(e)

2 *vi* s'adoucir

melodic [mɪ'lɒdɪk] *adj* mélodique

melodious [mɪ'ləʊdɪəs] *adj* mélodieux(euse)

melodrama ['melədrɑːmə] *n* mélodrame *m*

melodramatic [melədrə'mætɪk] *adj* mélodramatique

melody ['melədɪ] *(pl* **melodies**) *n* mélodie *f*

melon ['melən] *n* melon *m*

melt [melt] **1** *vt also Fig* faire fondre

2 *vi* fondre; **to m. into thin air** s'évaporer, disparaître; **to m. into the crowd** se fondre dans la foule

▸**melt away** *vi* *(of snow)* fondre; *(of clouds, vapour)* se dissiper; *(of crowd)* se disperser; *(of objections, opposition)* s'évanouir

▸**melt down** *vt sep* *(metal)* fondre

meltdown ['meltdaʊn] *n Phys* fusion *f*

melting ['meltɪŋ] *n* **m. point** point *m* de fusion; *Fig* **m. pot** melting-pot *m*

member ['membə(r)] **1** *n* membre *m*; *Br & Can Pol* **M. of Parliament** député(e) *m,f*

2 *adj* **m. country/state** pays *m*/État *m* membre

membership ['membəʃɪp] *n* **(a)** *(state)* adhésion *f*; **m. card** carte *f* de membre *ou* d'adhérent; **m. fee** cotisation *f* **(b)** *(members)* membres *mpl*, adhérents *mpl*; **a large/small m.** une forte/faible adhésion

membrane ['membreɪn] *n* membrane *f*

memento [mɪ'mentəʊ] *(pl* **mementos** *or* **mementoes**) *n* souvenir *m*

memo ['meməʊ] (*pl* **memos**) *n* note *f* de service; **m. pad** bloc-notes *m*

memoir ['memwɑː(r)] *n* (*essay*) mémoire *m*; (*biography*) biographie *f*; **memoirs** (*autobiography*) mémoires

memorable ['memərəbəl] *adj* mémorable

memorandum [memə'rændəm] (*pl* **memoranda** [memə'rændə] *or* **memorandums**) *n* note *f* de service

memorial [mɪ'mɔːrɪəl] **1** *n* (*monument*) mémorial *m*
  2 *adj* commémoratif(ive)

memorize ['meməraɪz] *vt* mémoriser

memory ['memərɪ] (*pl* **memories**) *n* (**a**) (*faculty*) & *Comput* mémoire *f*; **to have a good/bad m.** avoir (une) bonne/mauvaise mémoire; **if my m. serves me right** si ma mémoire est bonne; **from m.** de mémoire; **to lose one's m.** perdre la mémoire; **to commit sth to m.** apprendre qch par cœur; **within living m.** de mémoire d'homme (**b**) (*thing remembered*) souvenir *m*; **in m. of...** en souvenir de..., à la mémoire de...; **to take a trip down m. lane** se remémorer le passé

men [men] *pl of* **man**

menace ['menɪs] **1** *n* (*threat*) menace *f*; (*danger*) danger *m*; *Fam Fig* (*pest*) plaie *f*
  2 *vt* menacer

menacing ['menəsɪŋ] *adj* menaçant(e)

menagerie [mɪ'nædʒərɪ] *n* ménagerie *f*

mend [mend] **1** *vt* (*repair*) réparer; (*clothing*) raccommoder; **to m. one's ways** s'amender
  2 *vi* (*of broken bone*) se ressouder
  3 *n Fam* **to be on the m.** aller mieux

menfolk ['menfəʊk] *npl* **the m.** les hommes *mpl*

menial ['miːnɪəl] **1** *n Pej* laquais *m*
  2 *adj* (*job*) subalterne; **m. tasks** corvées *fpl*

meningitis [menɪn'dʒaɪtɪs] *n* méningite *f*; **to have m.** avoir la méningite

menopause ['menəpɔːz] *n* ménopause *f*

menstrual ['menstrʊəl] *adj* menstruel(elle)

menstruate ['menstrʊeɪt] *vi* avoir ses règles

menstruation [menstrʊ'eɪʃən] *n* menstruation *f*

menswear ['menzweə(r)] *n* vêtements *mpl* pour hommes

mental ['mentəl] *adj* (**a**) (*state, age*) mental(e); **to make a m. note of sth/to do sth** essayer de se souvenir de qch/de faire qch; **to have a m. block about sth** faire un blocage sur qch; **m. arithmetic** calcul *m* mental; **m. breakdown** dépression *f* (nerveuse); **m. health** santé *f* mentale; **m. hospital** hôpital *m* psychiatrique; **m. illness** maladie *f* mentale; **m. patient** malade *mf* mental(e) (**b**) *very Fam* (*mad*) malade, dingue; **to go m.** (*lose one's temper*) devenir dingue

mentality [men'tælɪtɪ] (*pl* **mentalities**) *n* mentalité *f*

mentally ['mentəlɪ] *adv* mentalement; **to be m. handicapped** être handicapé(e) mental(e); **to be m. ill** avoir une maladie mentale

menthol ['menθɒl] *n* menthol *m*; **m. cigarettes** cigarettes *fpl* mentholées

mention ['menʃən] **1** *n* mention *f*; **he gets a brief m. in her autobiography** elle le mentionne brièvement dans son autobiographie; **to make no m. of sth** ne pas faire référence à qch
  2 *vt* parler de; (*allude to*) mentionner; **to m. that...** dire que...; **to m. sb in one's will** coucher qn sur son testament; **to be mentioned in dispatches** être cité(e) à l'ordre du jour; **not to m....** sans parler de...; **now (that) you m. it** maintenant que tu le dis; **don't m. it!** il n'y a pas de quoi!

menu ['menjuː] *n* (**a**) (*in restaurant*) (*set*) menu *m*; (*à la carte*) carte *f* (**b**) *Comput* menu *m*

MEP [emiː'piː] *n Br Pol* (*abbr* **Member of the European Parliament**) député *m* au Parlement européen

mercantile ['mɜːkəntaɪl] *adj* commercial(e)

mercenary ['mɜːsɪnərɪ] **1** *n* (*pl* **mercenaries**) mercenaire *m*
  2 *adj Pej* intéressé(e)

merchandise ['mɜːtʃəndaɪz] **1** *n* marchandises *fpl*
  2 *vt* marchandiser

merchandising ['mɜːtʃəndaɪzɪŋ] *n* merchandising *m*, marchandisage *m*

merchant ['mɜːtʃənt] *n* (*retail*) marchand(e) *m,f*; (*wholesale*) négociant(e) *m,f*; **m. bank** banque *f* d'affaires; **m. navy** marine *f* marchande; **m. seaman** marin *m* de la marine marchande; **m. ship** navire *m* marchand

merchantman ['mɜːtʃəntmən] *n* (*ship*) navire *m* marchand

merciful ['mɜːsɪfʊl] *adj* (*person*) clément(e); (*act*) charitable

mercifully ['mɜːsɪfʊlɪ] *adv* (**a**) (*showing mercy*) avec clémence (**b**) (*fortunately*) heureusement

merciless ['mɜːsɪlɪs] *adj* sans pitié, impitoyable

mercurial [mɜː'kjʊərɪəl] *adj* (*lively*) vif (vive); (*changeable*) changeant(e), lunatique

Mercury ['mɜːkjʊrɪ] *n* (*planet*) Mercure *f*

mercury ['mɜːkjʊrɪ] *n* (*metal*) mercure *m*

mercy ['mɜːsɪ] (*pl* **mercies**) *n* (**a**) (*clemency*) pitié *f*, clémence *f*; **to have m. on sb** avoir pitié de qn; **to beg for m.** demander grâce; **at the m. of** à la merci de; **m. killing** acte *m* d'euthanasie (**b**) (*blessing*) bonheur *m*, chance *f*; **it's a m. that...** c'est une chance que...; **to be thankful** *or* **grateful for small mercies** apprécier ce dont on dispose

mere [mɪə(r)] *adj* simple; **he's a m. child** ce n'est qu'un enfant

merely ['mɪəlɪ] *adv* simplement, seulement

merge [mɜːdʒ] **1** *vt* (*companies*) & *Comput* fusionner
  2 *vi* (*of colours, sounds*) se fondre, se confondre; (*of companies*) fusionner; **to m. into the background** se fondre dans le décor

merger ['mɜːdʒə(r)] *n* fusion *f*

meridian [mə'rɪdɪən] *n* méridien *m*

meringue [mə'ræŋ] *n* meringue *f*

merit ['merɪt] **1** *n* (*advantage, worth*) mérite *m*; **of little/great m.** de peu de/grande valeur; **to judge sth on its merits** juger qch pour ce qu'il vaut; **in order of m.** par ordre de mérite
  2 *vt* mériter

meritocracy [merɪ'tɒkrəsɪ] (*pl* **meritocracies**) *n* méritocratie *f*

meritorious [merɪ'tɔːrɪəs] *adj Formal* méritoire, louable

mermaid ['mɜːmeɪd] *n* sirène *f*

merrily ['merɪlɪ] *adv* joyeusement, gaiement

merriment ['merɪmənt] *n* gaieté *f*

merry ['merɪ] *adj* (**a**) (*happy*) joyeux(euse), gai(e); **to make m.** s'amuser; **M. Christmas!** Joyeux Noël!; **the more the merrier** plus on est de fous, plus on rit (**b**) (*slightly drunk*) gai(e)

merry-go-round ['merɪgəʊraʊnd] *n* manège *m*, *Can, Belg & Suisse* carrousel *m*

mesh [meʃ] **1** *n* (*of net, sieve*) mailles *fpl*
  2 *vi* (*of gears*) s'engrener

mesmerize ['mezmǝraɪz] *vt* hypnotiser

mess [mes] **1** *n* (**a**) *(disorder)* désordre *m*; **you look a m.!** tu es dans un triste état!; **to be (in) a m.** *(of room)* être en désordre; *Fig (of person)* être dans le pétrin; *(of one's life)* être un désastre; **he's a m.** il est dans un triste état; *Fig* **to make a m. of sth** *(essay, job)* saloper qch (**b**) *(dirt)* saletés *fpl*; **to make a m. of sth** salir qch; **the dog's done a m. on the carpet** le chien a fait ses besoins sur le tapis (**c**) *Mil (for officers)* mess *m*; *(for soldiers)* réfectoire *m*; **m. tin** gamelle *f*
2 *vi Fam (of dog, cat)* faire ses besoins

▶**mess about, mess around 1** *vt sep (treat badly)* se moquer de
2 *vi* (**a**) *(fool about)* faire l'imbécile; *(waste time)* traîner (**b**) *(tinker)* **to m. about** *or* **around with sth** tripoter qch

▶**mess up** *vt sep (hair, room, papers)* mettre en désordre; *(plans)* ficher en l'air

message ['mesɪdʒ] *n* message *m*; **to leave a m. for sb** laisser un message pour qn; *Fam Fig* **to get the m.** piger

messenger ['mesɪndʒǝ(r)] *n* messager(ère) *m,f*; **m. boy** garçon *m* de courses, coursier *m*

Messiah [mɪ'saɪǝ] *n Rel* Messie *m*

messianic [mesɪ'ænɪk] *adj* messianique

messily ['mesɪlɪ] *adv* salement; *Fig* **to end m.** *(of relationship)* mal terminer

Messrs ['mesǝz] *(abbr* **Messieurs)** MM

messy ['mesɪ] *adj* (**a**) *(dirty)* sale; *(job)* salissant(e); **to be a m. eater** manger salement (**b**) *(untidy) (room, hair)* en désordre; *(handwriting)* peu soigné(e); *(appearance)* négligé(e) (**c**) *(unpleasantly complex) (affair, situation)* embrouillé(e); *(private life)* troublé(e)

met [met] *pt & pp of* **meet**

metabolic [metǝ'bɒlɪk] *adj* métabolique

metabolism [mɪ'tæbǝlɪzǝm] *n* métabolisme *m*

metal ['metǝl] **1** *n* métal *m*; **m. detector** détecteur *m* de métaux
2 *adj* en métal

metalled road ['metǝld'rǝʊd] *n* route *f* empierrée

metallic [mɪ'tælɪk] *adj (sound, voice)* métallique; *(paint)* métallisé(e); *(taste)* de métal

metallurgy [me'tælǝdʒɪ] *n* métallurgie *f*

metalwork ['metǝlwɜːk] *n* ferronnerie *f*

metamorphosis [metǝ'mɔːfǝsɪs] *n (pl* **metamorphoses** [metǝ'mɔːfǝsiːz]*)* *n* métamorphose *f*

metaphor ['metǝfǝ(r)] *n* métaphore *f*

metaphoric(al) [metǝ'fɒrɪk(ǝl)] *adj* métaphorique

metaphysical [metǝ'fɪzɪkǝl] *adj* métaphysique

metaphysics [metǝ'fɪzɪks] *n* métaphysique *f*

mete out [miːt] *vt sep (punishment)* infliger (**to** à); *(justice)* rendre

meteor ['miːtɪǝ(r)] *n* météore *m*

meteoric [miːtɪ'ɒrɪk] *adj* météorique; *Fig* **a m. rise** une ascension fulgurante

meteorite ['miːtɪǝraɪt] *n* météorite *f*

meteorological [miːtɪǝrǝ'lɒdʒɪkǝl] *adj* météorologique

meteorology [miːtɪǝ'rɒlǝdʒɪ] *n* météorologie *f*

meter¹ ['miːtǝ(r)] *n* compteur *m*; **to read the m.** relever le compteur; **(parking) m.** parcmètre *m*

meter² *Am* = **metre**

methane ['miːθeɪn] *n* méthane *m*

method ['meθǝd] *n* méthode *f*; **there's m. in his madness** il n'est pas aussi fou qu'il en a l'air; **m. acting** méthode de Stanislavski

methodical [mɪ'θɒdɪkǝl] *adj* méthodique

Methodism ['meθǝdɪzǝm] *n Rel* méthodisme *m*

Methodist ['meθǝdɪst] *n Rel* méthodiste *mf*

methodology [meθǝ'dɒlǝdʒɪ] *n* méthodologie *f*

meths [meθs] *n Br Fam (methylated spirits)* alcool *m* à brûler

methylated spirits ['meθɪleɪtɪd'spɪrɪts] *n Br* alcool *m* à brûler

meticulous [mɪ'tɪkjʊlǝs] *adj* méticuleux(euse)

metre¹, *Am* **meter** ['miːtǝ(r)] *n (measurement)* mètre *m*

metre², *Am* **meter** *n (of poetry)* mètre *m*

metric ['metrɪk] *adj* métrique

metronome ['metrǝnǝʊm] *n* métronome *m*

metropolis [mɪ'trɒpǝlɪs] *n* métropole *f*

metropolitan [metrǝ'pɒlɪtǝn] *adj* urbain(e); **M. France** la France métropolitaine; **the M. Police** la police de Londres

mettle ['metǝl] *n (courage)* courage *m*; **to be on one's m.** être fin prêt(e); **to show one's m.** montrer de quoi on est capable

mew [mjuː] **1** *n* miaulement *m*
2 *vi* miauler

mews [mjuːz] *(pl* **mews)** *n Br* ruelle *f*; **m. cottage** = maison luxueuse aménagée dans une ancienne écurie

Mexican ['meksɪkǝn] **1** *n* Mexicain(e) *m,f*
2 *adj* mexicain(e); **M. wave** *(at match)* ola *f*

Mexico ['meksɪkǝʊ] *n* le Mexique; **M. City** Mexico

mezzanine ['metsǝniːn] *n* **m. (floor)** mezzanine *f*

mg [em'dʒiː] *n (abbr* **milligram(s))** mg

Mgr *(abbr* **Monsignor)** Mgr

MHz *(abbr* **megahertz)** MHz

mi [miː] *n Mus* mi *m*

MI5 [emaɪ'faɪv] *n Br (abbr* **Military Intelligence Section 5)** ≃ DST *f*

MI6 [emaɪ'sɪks] *n Br (abbr* **Military Intelligence Section 6)** ≃ DGSE *f*

miaow [mɪ'aʊ] **1** *n* miaulement *m*; **m.!** miaou!
2 *vi* miauler

mica ['maɪkǝ] *n* mica *m*

mice [maɪs] *pl of* **mouse**

Michelangelo [maɪkǝl'ændʒǝlǝʊ] *n* Michel-Ange

mickey ['mɪkɪ] *n Br Fam* **to take the m. (out of sb)** se moquer (de qn)

Mickey Mouse ['mɪkɪ'maʊs] *adj Fam Pej (job, qualification)* à la noix

micro ['maɪkrǝʊ] *(pl* **micros)** *n* micro *m*

microbe ['maɪkrǝʊb] *n* microbe *m*

microbiology [maɪkrǝʊbaɪ'ɒlǝdʒɪ] *n* microbiologie *f*

microchip ['maɪkrǝʊtʃɪp] *n* microprocesseur *m*

microcomputer ['maɪkrǝʊkǝm'pjuːtǝ(r)] *n* micro-ordinateur *m*

microcomputing ['maɪkrǝʊkǝm'pjuːtɪŋ] *n* micro-informatique *f*

microcosm ['maɪkrǝʊkɒzǝm] *n* microcosme *m*

microfiche ['maɪkrǝʊfiːʃ] *n* microfiche *f*

microfilm ['maɪkrǝʊfɪlm] **1** *n* microfilm *m*
2 *vt* microfilmer

micrometer [maɪ'krɒmɪtǝ(r)] *n* micromètre *m*

microphone ['maɪkrǝfǝʊn] *n* microphone *m*

microprocessor ['maɪkrəʊ'prəʊsesə(r)] *n* micro-processeur *m*

microscope ['maɪkrəskəʊp] *n* microscope *m*

microscopic [maɪkrə'skɒpɪk] *adj* microscopique

microsurgery [maɪkrəʊ'sɜːdʒərɪ] *n* microchirurgie *f*

microwave ['maɪkrəʊweɪv] **1** *n Phys* micro-onde *f*; **m. (oven)** (four *m* à) micro-ondes *m inv*
2 *vt* faire cuire au micro-ondes

mid [mɪd] *adj* **in m. ocean** au milieu de l'océan; **m. June** mi-juin; **he stopped in m. sentence** il s'est arrêté au milieu d'une phrase

midair [mɪd'eə(r)] **1** *n* **in m.** en plein ciel
2 *adj (collision)* en plein ciel

mid-Atlantic accent [mɪdət'læntɪk'æksent] *n* accent *m* mi-américain mi-britannique

midday ['mɪd'deɪ] *n* midi *m*; **m. meal** déjeuner *m*

middle ['mɪdəl] **1** *n* **(a)** *(centre)* milieu *m*; **to be in the m. of doing sth** être en train de faire qch; **in the m. of the night** en pleine nuit; **in the m. of nowhere** dans un coin perdu; *Fig* **to split sth down the m.** partager qch en deux **(b)** *(waist)* taille *f*
2 *adj* du milieu; **m. age** l'âge *m* mûr; *Hist* **the M. Ages** le Moyen Âge; *Mus* **m. C** do *m* du milieu du clavier; **the m. class(es)** les classes *mpl* moyennes; *Fig* **to steer a m. course** adopter une solution intermédiaire; **in the m. distance** au second plan; **the M. East** le Moyen-Orient; **M. Eastern** du Moyen-Orient; *Pol* **the m. ground** le centre; **m. management** cadres *mpl* moyens; **m. name** deuxième prénom *m*; *Fam* **"generosity" isn't exactly his m. name!** on ne peut pas dire qu'il soit particulièrement généreux!

middle-aged [mɪdəl'eɪdʒd] *adj* d'âge mûr; **he was already m. when...** il avait déjà un certain âge quand...

middlebrow ['mɪdəlbraʊ] *adj* moyen(enne); **a m. novelist** un romancier sans prétentions

middle-class [mɪdəl'klɑːs] *adj* bourgeois(e)

middleman ['mɪdəlmæn] *n* intermédiaire *mf*

middle-of-the-road ['mɪdləvðə'rəʊd] *adj (policy)* modéré(e); *(music)* grand public *inv*

middle-sized ['mɪdəl'saɪzd] *adj* de taille moyenne

middleweight ['mɪdəlweɪt] *n (in boxing)* poids *m* moyen

middling ['mɪdlɪŋ] *adj (fairly good)* moyen(enne); *(mediocre)* médiocre

midfield [mɪd'fiːld] *n (in football)* milieu *m* de terrain; **m. player** milieu de terrain

midfielder [mɪd'fiːldə(r)] *n (in football)* milieu *m* de terrain

midge [mɪdʒ] *n* moucheron *m*

midget ['mɪdʒɪt] **1** *n (small person)* nain(e) *m,f*
2 *adj (miniature)* miniature

midi system ['mɪdɪsɪstəm] *n (stereo)* chaîne *f* midi

Midlands ['mɪdləndz] *npl* **the M.** les Midlands *fpl*

midlife crisis ['mɪdlaɪf'kraɪsɪs] *n* crise *f* aux alentours de la cinquantaine

midmorning [mɪd'mɔːnɪŋ] *n* milieu *m* de matinée

midnight ['mɪdnaɪt] *n* minuit *m*; **to burn the m. oil** travailler tard dans la nuit

midriff ['mɪdrɪf] *n* ventre *m*

midshipman ['mɪdʃɪpmən] *n* aspirant *m* de marine

midst [mɪdst] *n* milieu *m*, cœur *m*; **in the m. of** au milieu de; **in our/their m.** parmi nous/eux

midstream [mɪd'striːm] *n* **in m.** au milieu du courant; *Fig (when speaking)* en plein milieu d'une phrase

midsummer ['mɪdsʌmə(r)] *n* milieu *m* de l'été; **M.'s Day** la Saint-Jean

midterm ['mɪd'tɜːm] *n* **(a)** *Pol Br* **m. by-election** = élection législative en milieu de mandat; *Am* **m. elections** = élections qui ont lieu au milieu du mandat présidentiel **(b)** *Sch & Univ* milieu *m* du trimestre; **m. break** vacances *fpl* de milieu de trimestre

midway ['mɪdweɪ] **1** *adj* **at the m. point** *(in space)* à la mi-chemin; *(in time)* à la moitié
2 *adv* à mi-chemin

midweek [mɪd'wiːk] *adv* en milieu de semaine

Mid-West ['mɪd'west] *n* Midwest *m*

Mid-Western [mɪd'westən] *adj* du Midwest

midwife ['mɪdwaɪf] *(pl* **midwives** [mɪdwaɪvz] *) n* sage-femme *f*

midwifery [mɪd'wɪfərɪ] *n* profession *f* de sage-femme

midwinter ['mɪd'wɪntə(r)] *n* milieu *m* de l'hiver

might¹ [maɪt] *n (strength)* force *f*; **with all one's m.** de toutes ses forces; *Prov* **m. is right** la raison du plus fort est toujours la meilleure

might² *v aux*

> La forme négative **mightn't** s'écrit **might not** dans un style plus soutenu. **Might** et **may** peuvent s'utiliser indifféremment ou presque dans les expressions de la catégorie **(a)**.

(a) *(expressing possibility)* **it m. be difficult** il se peut *ou* se pourrait que ce soit difficile; **it m. be better to phone first** il vaudrait peut-être mieux téléphoner d'abord; **it m. be that...** il se peut *ou* se pourrait que... + *subjunctive*; **you m. want to...** tu pourrais peut-être...; **we m. as well go home** autant rentrer; **you m. as well stay here** autant que vous restiez ici; **I m. as well be talking to myself!** autant parler à un mur!

(b) *(as past form of* **may***)* **I knew he m. be angry** je me doutais qu'il pourrait se fâcher; **he said he m. be late** il a dit qu'il se pourrait qu'il soit en retard

(c) *Formal (asking for permission)* **m. I have a word with you?** pourrais-je vous parler un instant?

(d) *(with concessions)* **it might not be the fastest car in the world, but...** ce n'est peut-être pas la voiture la plus rapide du monde, mais...

mightily ['maɪtɪlɪ] *adv* **(a)** *(powerfully)* avec force, vigoureusement **(b)** *Am Fam (for emphasis)* drôlement

mightn't ['maɪtənt] = **might not**

might've ['maɪtəv] = **might have**

mighty ['maɪtɪ] **1** *adj* **(a)** *(powerful) (nation, army)* puissant(e); *(blow)* grand(e) **(b)** *(large, imposing)* majestueux(euse)
2 *adv Am Fam (for emphasis)* drôlement

migraine ['miːgreɪn] *n* migraine *f*; **to have a m.** avoir la migraine

migrant ['maɪgrənt] **1** *n (person)* migrant(e) *m,f*; *(bird)* (oiseau *m*) migrateur *m*
2 *adj (bird)* migrateur(trice); **m. worker** travailleur(-euse) *m,f* immigré(e)

migrate [maɪ'greɪt] *vi (of bird)* migrer; *(of person)* émigrer

migration [maɪ'greɪʃən] *n (of birds)* migration *f*; *(of people)* émigration *f*

migratory ['maɪgrətrɪ] *adj* migratoire; *(bird)* migrateur(trice)

mike [maɪk] *n Fam (microphone)* micro *m*

mild [maɪld] **1** *adj (person, climate, soap, cheese)* doux (douce); *(curry)* peu épicé(e); *(punishment, annoyance,*

amusement, criticism) léger(ère); *(illness)* bénin(igne)
2 *n Br (beer)* = bière brune à faible teneur en houblon
mildew ['mɪldjuː] *n* moisissure *f*
mildly ['maɪldlɪ] *adv* (**a**) *(say)* doucement; **... to put it m.** ... pour ne pas dire plus (**b**) *(moderately)* légèrement
mildness ['maɪldnɪs] *n (of person, weather, punishment)* douceur *f*; *(of criticism)* modération *f*
mile [maɪl] *n (distance)* = 1609 m, mile *m*; **a 200-m. journey** ≃ un voyage de 320 km; **to see for miles** voir à des kilomètres; **it's miles from anywhere** c'est loin de tout; **miles per hour** ≃ kilomètres à l'heure; **he lives miles away** il habite très loin d'ici; *Fam Fig* **to be miles away** être dans la lune; *Fam* **miles better** cent fois mieux; *Fam* **it sticks** *or* **stands out a m.** ça crève les yeux
mileage ['maɪlɪdʒ] *n* (**a**) *(distance travelled)* ≃ kilométrage *m*; **m. allowance** ≃ indemnité *f* kilométrique (**b**) *(rate of fuel consumption)* consommation *f*; *Fig* **to get a lot of m. out of sth** tirer le maximum de qch
milestone ['maɪlstəʊn] *n (on road)* ≃ borne *f* kilométrique; *Fig (in career, history)* étape *f* importante
milieu ['miːljɜː] *n* milieu *m*
militant ['mɪlɪtənt] *adj & n* militant(e) *m,f*
militarism ['mɪlɪtərɪzəm] *n* militarisme *m*
military ['mɪlɪtərɪ] **1** *adj* militaire; **m. academy** école *f* militaire; **m. man** militaire *m*; **m. police** police *f* militaire; **m. service** service *m* militaire
2 *npl* **the m.** les militaires *mpl*, l'armée *f*
militate ['mɪlɪteɪt] *vi* **to m. against sth** compromettre qch
militia [mɪ'lɪʃə] *n* milice *f*
milk [mɪlk] **1** *n* lait *m*; **m. of magnesia** lait *m* de magnésie; **m. bottle** bouteille *f* de lait; **m. chocolate** chocolat *m* au lait; **m. churn** bidon *m* à lait; **m. float** camionnette *f* de laitier; **m. jug** pot *m* à lait; **m. round** tournée *f* du laitier; **m. shake** milk-shake *m*; **m. tooth** dent *f* de lait; **m. train** premier train *m* (du matin)
2 *vt (cow)* traire; *Fam Fig* **to m. sb dry** dépouiller qn; *Fig* **they milked the story for all it was worth** ils ont tiré tout ce qu'ils ont pu de l'histoire
milking ['mɪlkɪŋ] *n* traite *f*; **m. machine** trayeuse *f*; **m. parlour** salle *f* de traite
milkman ['mɪlkmən] *n* = homme qui livre le lait à domicile
milky ['mɪlkɪ] *adj (drink)* avec du lait; *(taste)* de lait; *(colour)* laiteux(euse); **the M. Way** la Voie lactée
mill [mɪl] **1** *n* (**a**) *(grinder)* moulin *m*; *Fam* **to put sb through the m.** en faire baver à qn (**b**) *(textile factory)* filature *f*
2 *vt (grain)* moudre
mill about, mill around *vi (of crowd)* grouiller; *(of thoughts, ideas)* se bousculer
millennium [mɪ'lenɪəm] *n* millénaire *m*; *Comput* **m. bug** bogue *m* de l'an deux mille; **M. Dome** = centre d'expositions en forme de dôme construit à Londres à l'occasion de l'an 2000
miller ['mɪlə(r)] *n* meunier(ère) *m,f*
millet ['mɪlɪt] *n* millet *m*
milligram(me) ['mɪlɪgræm] *n* milligramme *m*
millilitre, *Am* **milliliter** ['mɪlɪliːtə(r)] *n* millilitre *m*
millimetre, *Am* **millimeter** ['mɪlɪmiːtə(r)] *n* millimètre *m*
milliner ['mɪlɪnə(r)] *n* modiste *mf*

million ['mɪljən] *n* million *m*; **two m. men** deux millions d'hommes; *Fam* **I've told him a m. times** je le lui ai dit mille fois; *Fam* **thanks a m.!** merci mille fois!; *Fam* **she's one in a m.** elle est unique
millionaire [mɪljə'neə(r)] *n* millionnaire *m*
millionairess [mɪljə'neərɪs] *n* millionnaire *f*
millionth ['mɪljənθ] **1** *n* (**a**) *(fraction)* millionième *m* (**b**) *(in series)* millionième *mf*
2 *adj* millionième; *see also* **eighth**
millipede ['mɪlɪpiːd] *n* mille-pattes *m inv*
millpond ['mɪlpɒnd] *n* **as calm as a m.** *(of sea)* d'huile
millstone ['mɪlstəʊn] *n* meule *f*; *Fig* **it's a m. round my neck** c'est un boulet que je traîne
milometer [maɪ'lɒmɪtə(r)] *n (in car)* ≃ compteur *m* (kilométrique)
mime [maɪm] **1** *n* mime *m*; **m. (artist)** mime *mf*
2 *vt* mimer
3 *vi* mimer; *(of singer)* chanter en play-back
mimic ['mɪmɪk] **1** *n* imitateur(trice) *m,f*
2 *vt (pt & pp* **mimicked***)* imiter
mimicry ['mɪmɪkrɪ] *n* imitation *f*
Min *Mus (abbr* **Minor***)* m
min (**a**) *(abbr* **minute(s)***)* min (**b**) *(abbr* **minimum***)* min
minaret [mɪnə'ret] *n* minaret *m*
mince [mɪns] **1** *n Br* viande *f* hachée; **m. pie** *(containing meat)* tourte *f* à la viande hachée; *(containing fruit)* = tartelette fourrée aux fruits secs et aux épices
2 *vt (chop up)* hacher; *Fig* **she doesn't m. her words** elle ne mâche pas ses mots
3 *vi (walk)* marcher à petits pas
mincemeat ['mɪnsmiːt] *n* = mélange de fruits secs et d'épices utilisé en pâtisserie; *Fam Fig* **to make m. of sb** faire de la chair à pâté de qn
mincer ['mɪnsə(r)] *n* hachoir *m*
mincing ['mɪnsɪŋ] *adj (walk, voice)* affecté(e)
mind [maɪnd] **1** *n* (**a**) *(thoughts)* esprit *m*; **in one's m.'s eye** en imagination; **to put** *or* **set sb's m. at rest** rassurer qn; **to bear** *or* **keep sth in m.** garder qch à l'esprit *ou* en tête; **it went completely** *or* **clean out of my m.** ça m'est complètement sorti de l'esprit *ou* de la tête; **to have sth on one's m.** être préoccupé(e) par qch; **to take sb's m. off sth** distraire qn de qch; **I couldn't get it off my m.** je ne pouvais pas m'empêcher d'y penser; **it puts me in m. of sb/sth** ça me rappelle qn/qch
(**b**) *(opinion)* **to my m.** à mon avis; **to speak one's m.** dire ce qu'on pense; **to change one's m. (about sth)** changer d'avis (au sujet de qch); *Fam* **to give sb a piece of one's m.** dire à qn sa façon de penser; **to be of one m., to be of the same m.** être du même avis
(**c**) *(will)* **to know one's own m.** savoir ce qu'on veut; **to have a m. of one's own** savoir penser par soi-même; **to make up one's m.** se décider; **to be in two minds (about sth/about doing sth)** hésiter (sur qch/ à faire qch); **to have a good m./half a m. to do sth** avoir bien envie/presque envie de faire qch; **this shopping trolley has a m. of its own** ce caddie n'en fait qu'à sa tête; **to have sb in m.** avoir qn en vue; **to have sth in m.** avoir qch en tête
(**d**) *(attention)* **to keep one's m. on sth** se concentrer sur qch; **my m. isn't on the job** je n'ai pas la tête à ce que je fais; **if you put your m. to it you could do it** si tu t'y mettais, tu pourrais le faire
(**e**) *(reason)* raison *f*; **her m. is going** elle perd la raison; *Fam* **to be out of one's m.** avoir perdu la tête; **to**

be bored out of one's m. s'ennuyer à mourir; **to be out of one's m. with worry** être fou (folle) d'inquiétude; **no one in his right m. would do that** aucune personne saine d'esprit ne ferait ça

(**f**) *(person)* esprit *m*; *Prov* **great minds think alike** les grands esprits se rencontrent

2 *vt* (**a**) *(pay attention to)* faire attention à; **m. you don't fall** fais attention à ne pas tomber; **m. you're not late!** fais en sorte de ne pas être en retard!; **m. the step!** attention à la marche!; **to m. one's language/manners** surveiller son langage/ses manières

(**b**) *(concern oneself with)* **never m. the car/money** ne t'inquiéète pas pour la voiture/l'argent; **m. you,...** remarque,...

(**c**) *(object to)* **what I m. is...** ce qui me gêne, c'est...; **I don't m. the cold** le froid ne me gêne pas; **I don't m. trying** je veux bien essayer; **if you don't m. my asking,...** si je peux me permettre,...; **would you m. not doing that?** pourrais-tu arrêter ça?; **I wouldn't m. a cup of tea** je prendrais bien une tasse de thé

(**d**) *(look after)* s'occuper de, garder

3 *vi* (**a**) *(object)* **I don't m.** ça m'est égal; **do you m.!** dites donc!; **do you m. if I smoke?** ça vous dérange si je fume?; **I don't m. if I do!** *(accepting offer)* ce n'est pas de refus!

(**b**) *(concern oneself)* **never m.!** ça ne fait rien!; **never m. about that now** ne t'inquiète pas de ça maintenant; *Fam* **never you m.!** occupe-toi de tes oignons!

▸**mind out** *vi Br* m. out! attention!

mind-boggling ['maɪndbɒɡlɪŋ], **mind-blowing** ['maɪndbləʊɪŋ] *adj Fam* époustouflant(e)

minded ['maɪndɪd] *adj* **to be m. to do sth** vouloir faire qch; **to be mechanically m.** avoir le sens de la mécanique; **to be scientifically m.** avoir l'esprit scientifique

minder ['maɪndə(r)] *n Fam (bodyguard)* gorille *m*

mindful ['maɪndfʊl] *adj* **to be m. of sth** être soucieux(euse) de qch

mindless ['maɪndlɪs] *adj (destruction, violence)* gratuit(e); *(task, job)* abrutissant(e)

mind-numbing ['maɪndnʌmɪŋ] *adj* abêtissant(e)

mind-reader ['maɪndriːdə(r)] *n Fam Hum* **I'm not a m.!** je ne suis pas devin!

mine¹ [maɪn] **1** *n* (**a**) *(for coal, tin, diamonds)* mine *f*; *Fig* **a m. of information** une mine d'informations; **m. shaft** puits *m* de mine (**b**) *(bomb)* **(land) m.** mine *f*; **m. detector** détecteur *m* de mines

2 *vt* (**a**) *(coal, gold)* extraire; *(seam)* exploiter (**b**) *(place mines in)* miner

3 *vi* **to m. for coal/gold** extraire du charbon/de l'or

mine² *possessive pron* (**a**) *(singular)* le mien (la mienne) *m,f*; *(plural)* les miens (les miennes) *mpl,fpl*; **her house is big but m. is bigger** elle a une grande maison, mais la mienne est plus grande encore (**b**) *(used attributively)* **this book is m.** c'est livre est à moi; **a friend of m.** un de mes amis; **where's that brother of m.?** où mon frère a-t-il bien pu passer?

minefield ['maɪnfiːld] *n* champ *m* de mines; *Fig* terrain *m* miné

miner ['maɪnə(r)] *n* mineur *m*

mineral ['mɪnərəl] *n* minéral *m*; *(extracted)* minerai *m*; **m. water** eau *m* minérale

minesweeper ['maɪnswiːpə(r)] *n* dragueur *m* de mines

mingle ['mɪŋɡəl] **1** *vt* mélanger, mêler

2 *vi (of things)* se mélanger, se mêler; *(of person)* parler un peu à tout le monde; **to m. with the crowd** se mêler à la foule

mini ['mɪnɪ] *n (miniskirt)* minijupe *f*

miniature ['mɪnɪtʃə(r)] **1** *n* miniature *f*

2 *adj* miniature

miniaturize ['mɪnɪtʃəraɪz] *vt* miniaturiser

minibus ['mɪnɪbʌs] *n* minibus *m*

minicab ['mɪnɪkæb] *n* radio-taxi *m*

MiniDisc® ['mɪnɪdɪsk] *n* MiniDisc® *m*

minidisk ['mɪnɪdɪsk] *n* mini-disquette *f*

minigolf ['mɪnɪɡɒlf] *n* minigolf *m*

minim ['mɪnɪm] *n Mus* blanche *f*

minimal ['mɪnɪməl] *adj* minime

minimize ['mɪnɪmaɪz] *vt (importance)* minimiser; *(noise, risk)* réduire au minimum

minimum ['mɪnɪməm] **1** *n* minimum *m*; **to keep sth to a m.** réduire qch au minimum

2 *adj* minimum *inv*, minimal(e); *Fin* **m. lending rate** taux *m* de base; **m. wage** salaire *m* minimum

mining ['maɪnɪŋ] *n* exploitation *f* minière; **m. engineer** ingénieur *m* des mines; **m. industry** industrie *f* minière

minion ['mɪnjən] *n* esclave *mf*

miniskirt ['mɪnɪskɜːt] *n* minijupe *f*

minister ['mɪnɪstə(r)] **1** *n* (**a**) *Pol* ministre *m*; *Br* **M. of Defence/Health** ministre de la Défense/de la Santé (**b**) *Rel* pasteur *m*

2 *vi* **to m. to sb** s'occuper de qn; **to m. to sb's needs** pourvoir aux besoins de qn

ministerial [mɪnɪ'stɪərɪəl] *adj Pol* ministériel(elle)

ministry ['mɪnɪstrɪ] *(pl* **ministries***)* *n* (**a**) *Pol* ministère *m*; *Br* **the M. of Defence/Transport** le ministère de la Défense/des Transports (**b**) *Rel* **the m.** le sacerdoce

mink [mɪŋk] *n* vison *m*; **m. (coat)** (manteau *m* de) vison

minnow ['mɪnəʊ] *n (fish)* vairon *m*; *Fig* (menu) fretin *m*

minor ['maɪnə(r)] **1** *adj* (**a**) *(unimportant)* mineur(e); *(operation)* bénin(igne); *(road)* secondaire (**b**) *Mus* mineur(e)

2 *n Law* mineur(e) *m,f*

Minorca [mɪ'nɔːkə] *n* Minorque

Minorcan [mɪ'nɔːkən] **1** *n* Minorquin(e) *m,f*

2 *adj* minorquin(e)

minority [maɪ'nɒrɪtɪ] *(pl* **minorities***)* *n* minorité *f*; **to be in a** *or* **the m.** être en minorité; **m. party/government** parti *m*/gouvernement *m* minoritaire

minstrel ['mɪnstrəl] *n* ménestrel *m*

mint¹ [mɪnt] *n (plant)* menthe *f*; *(sweet)* bonbon *m* à la menthe; **m. sauce** sauce *f* à la menthe; **m. tea** infusion *f* de menthe

mint² **1** *n* **the (Royal) M.** ≃ (l'hôtel *m* de) la Monnaie; *Fam* **to make a m.** gagner une fortune; **in m. condition** à l'état neuf

2 *vt (coins)* frapper

minuet [mɪnjʊ'et] *n Mus* menuet *m*

minus ['maɪnəs] **1** *n (sign)* moins *m*; *(negative aspect)* inconvénient *m*

2 *adj (quantity, number)* négatif(ive); **B m.** *(grade)* B moins; **on the m. side** quant aux inconvénients; **m. sign** signe *m* moins

3 *prep* moins; **ten m. eight leaves two** dix moins huit égale deux; **it's m. 12 (degrees)** il fait moins 12;

he managed to escape, but m. his luggage il a réussi à s'enfuir, mais sans ses bagages

minuscule ['mɪnəskjuːl] *adj* minuscule

minute¹ ['mɪnɪt] **1** *n* (**a**) *(of time)* minute *f*; **ten minutes past/to three** trois heures dix/moins dix; **wait a m.!** attendez une minute!; **go downstairs this m.!** descends immédiatement!; **just a m.** une minute; **the m. my back was turned** dès que j'ai eu le dos tourné; **any m.** d'une minute à l'autre; **in a m.** dans une minute; **at the last m.** à la dernière minute; **m. hand** *(of watch)* grande aiguille *f*; **m. steak** steak *m* minute (**b**) *(note)* note *f*; **minutes** *(of meeting)* compte rendu *m*
   2 *vt (make note of)* inscrire au procès-verbal

minute² [maɪ'njuːt] *adj* (**a**) *(small)* infime, minuscule (**b**) *(detailed)* minutieux(euse)

minutely [maɪ'njuːtlɪ] *adv* minutieusement

mips *Comput (abbr* **million instructions per second**) MIPS *m*

miracle ['mɪrəkəl] *n also Fig* miracle *m*; **to perform** *or* **work miracles** faire des miracles; **by a** *or* **some m.** par miracle; **m. worker** faiseur(euse) *m,f* de miracles

miraculous [mɪ'rækjʊləs] *adj also Fig* miraculeux(euse)

mirage [mɪ'rɑːʒ] *n* mirage *m*

MIRAS ['maɪræs] *n (abbr* **Mortgage Interest Relief at Source**) = système par lequel les intérêts dus à une société de crédit immobilier sont déductibles des impôts

mire [maɪə(r)] *n (mud)* boue *f*; *Fig* bourbier *m*

mirror ['mɪrə(r)] **1** *n* miroir *m*, glace *f*; *Fig* **to hold a m. to sth** refléter qch; **m. image** *(reversed image)* image *f* inversée; *(exact copy)* copie *f* conforme
   2 *vt also Fig* refléter

mirth [mɜːθ] *n* gaieté *f*, joie *f*

misadventure [mɪsəd'ventʃə(r)] *n* mésaventure *f*; *Law* **death by m.** mort *f* accidentelle

misanthropic [mɪsən'θrɒpɪk] *adj* misanthrope

misanthropist [mɪ'sænθrəpɪst] *n* misanthrope *mf*

misapprehension [mɪsæprɪ'henʃən] *n* malentendu *m*; **to be (labouring) under a m.** se méprendre

misappropriation ['mɪsəprəʊprɪ'eɪʃən] *n* détournement *m*

misbehave [mɪsbɪ'heɪv] *vi* se conduire mal

misbehaviour, *Am* **misbehavior** [mɪsbɪ'heɪvjə(r)] *n* mauvaise conduite *f*

misc *(abbr* **miscellaneous**) divers

miscalculate [mɪs'kælkjʊleɪt] **1** *vt* mal calculer; *Fig* mal évaluer
   2 *vi* faire une erreur de calcul; *Fig* faire un mauvais calcul

miscalculation [mɪskælkjʊ'leɪʃən] *n* erreur *f* de calcul; *Fig* mauvais calcul *m*

miscarriage [mɪs'kærɪdʒ] *n* (**a**) *Med* fausse couche *f*; **to have a m.** faire une fausse couche (**b**) *Law* **m. of justice** erreur *f* judiciaire

miscarry [mɪs'kærɪ] *(pt & pp* **miscarried**) *vi* (**a**) *(of woman)* faire une fausse couche (**b**) *Fig (of plan)* avorter

miscast [mɪs'kɑːst] *(pt & pp* **miscast**) *vt* **to m. an actor** = donner à un acteur un rôle qui ne lui convient pas

miscellaneous [mɪsə'leɪnɪəs] *adj* divers(es)

miscellany [mɪ'selənɪ] *(pl* **miscellanies**) *n* mélange *m*

mischief ['mɪstʃɪf] *n* (**a**) *(naughtiness)* espièglerie *f*; **to get up to m.** faire des bêtises; *Hum* **to keep sb out of**

m. occuper qn (**b**) *(trouble)* problèmes *mpl*; **to make m. (for sb)** créer des problèmes (à qn) (**c**) *Fam (injury)* **to do oneself a m.** se faire mal

mischievous ['mɪstʃɪvəs] *adj (naughty)* espiègle; *(malicious)* malveillant(e)

misconception [mɪskən'sepʃən] *n* idée *f* fausse

misconduct [mɪs'kɒndʌkt] *n* inconduite *f*

misconstrue [mɪskən'struː] *vt* mal interpréter

misdemeanour, *Am* **misdemeanor** [mɪsdɪ'miːnə(r)] *n Law* délit *m*

misdiagnose [mɪsdaɪəg'nəʊz] *vt* mal diagnostiquer

misdirect [mɪsdɪ'rekt] *vt* (**a**) *(person)* mal orienter (**b**) *(letter)* mal adresser

miser ['maɪzə(r)] *n* avare *mf*

miserable ['mɪzərəbəl] *adj* (**a**) *(unhappy)* malheureux(euse), triste; **to make sb's life m.** faire de la vie de qn un enfer (**b**) *(unpleasant)* déplorable; *(weather)* épouvantable (**c**) *(wretched)* misérable; **I only got a m. £70** je n'ai eu que 70 malheureuses livres

miserably ['mɪzərəblɪ] *adv* (**a**) *(unhappily)* tristement (**b**) *(wretchedly)* misérablement (**c**) *(very badly)* lamentablement

miserly ['maɪzəlɪ] *adj* avare

misery ['mɪzərɪ] *(pt* **miseries**) *n* (**a**) *(unhappiness)* détresse *f*; *(suffering)* malheur *m*; **to make sb's life a m.** faire de la vie de qn un enfer; **to put an animal out of its m.** achever un animal; *Hum* **to put sb out of his m.** *(tell secret)* mettre fin au supplice de qn (**b**) *Br Fam (person)* grincheux(euse) *m,f*

misery-guts ['mɪzərɪgʌts] *n Fam* grincheux(euse) *m,f*

misfire [mɪs'faɪə(r)] *vi (of gun)* faire long feu; *Fig (of plan)* rater

misfit ['mɪsfɪt] *n* inadapté(e) *m,f*

misfortune [mɪs'fɔːtʃən] *n* malheur *m*, malchance *f*

misgiving [mɪs'gɪvɪŋ] *n* doute *m*; **to have misgivings (about sth)** avoir des doutes (sur qch)

misgovern [mɪs'gʌvən] *vt* mal gouverner

misguided [mɪs'gaɪdɪd] *adj (person, decision)* mal inspiré(e); *(attempt)* malencontreux(euse); *(energy, idealism)* mal placé(e)

mishandle [mɪs'hændəl] *vt (device)* mal utiliser; *(situation)* mal gérer; *(person)* malmener

mishap ['mɪshæp] *n* incident *m*; **without m.** sans encombre

mishear [mɪs'hɪə(r)] *(pt & pp* **misheard** [mɪs'hɜːd] *) vt & vi* mal comprendre

mishmash ['mɪʃmæʃ] *n Fam* méli-mélo *m*

misinterpret [mɪsɪn'tɜːprɪt] *vt (words)* mal interpréter; *(person)* mal interpréter les paroles de

misjudge [mɪs'dʒʌdʒ] *vt (person)* mal juger; *(distance, situation)* mal évaluer

misjudg(e)ment [mɪs'dʒʌdʒmənt] *n* erreur *f* de jugement

mislay [mɪs'leɪ] *(pt & pp* **mislaid** [mɪs'leɪd] *) vt* égarer

mislead [mɪs'liːd] *(pt & pp* **misled** [mɪs'led] *) vt* induire en erreur, tromper

misleading [mɪs'liːdɪŋ] *adj* trompeur(euse)

mismanage [mɪs'mænɪdʒ] *vt* mal gérer

mismanagement [mɪs'mænɪdʒmənt] *n* mauvaise gestion *f*

misnomer [mɪs'nəʊmə(r)] *n* terme *m* mal approprié

misogynist [mɪ'sɒdʒɪnɪst] *n* misogyne *mf*

misplace [mɪs'pleɪs] *vt* (**a**) *(mislay)* égarer (**b**) *(trust, confidence)* mal placer

misprint ['mɪsprɪnt] *n* faute *f* d'impression, coquille *f*

mispronounce [mɪsprə'naʊns] *vt* mal prononcer
mispronunciation [mɪsprənʌnsɪ'eɪʃən] *n* mauvaise prononciation *f*
misquote [mɪs'kwəʊt] *vt* citer incorrectement
misread [mɪs'riːd] (*pt & pp* **misread** [mɪs'red]) *vt* (**a**) (*notice, timetable*) mal lire (**b**) (*misinterpret*) mal interpréter
misrepresent [mɪsreprɪ'zent] *vt* (*facts, theory*) dénaturer, déformer; (*person*) présenter sous un faux jour
misrepresentation [mɪsreprɪzen'teɪʃən] *n* déformation *f*
misrule [mɪs'ruːl] *n* mauvais gouvernement *m*
Miss [mɪs] *n* Mademoiselle *f*; **M. World** Miss Monde
miss [mɪs] **1** *n* coup *m* manqué; *Fam* **to give sth a m.** (*event*) s'abstenir d'aller à
2 *vt* (**a**) (*target, bus, chance*) manquer, rater; *Fig* **to m. the boat** louper le coche; **you're missing the point** ce n'est pas le problème; **you've just missed him** tu l'as loupé de peu
(**b**) (*not hear*) ne pas entendre; **she doesn't m. a thing** rien ne lui échappe
(**c**) (*feel lack of*) **I m. you** tu me manques; **do you m. me?** est-ce que je te manque?
(**d**) (*avoid*) **the car just missed me** la voiture m'a évité de peu; **she just missed being killed** elle a failli *ou* manqué être tuée
(**e**) (*word, line*) sauter
(**f**) (*lack*) **the table is missing one of its legs** il manque un pied à la table
3 *vi* (*miss target*) rater *ou* manquer son coup
▸**miss out 1** *vt sep* (*accidentally*) oublier; (*intentionally*) omettre
2 *vi* (*not benefit*) **to m. out on sth** rater qch; **you missed out there** tu as raté quelque chose
missal ['mɪsəl] *n Rel* missel *m*
misshapen [mɪs'ʃeɪpən] *adj* difforme
missile ['mɪsaɪl, *Am* 'mɪsəl] *n* (*rocket*) missile *m*; (*object thrown*) projectile *m*; **m. launcher** lance-missiles *m inv*
missing ['mɪsɪŋ] *adj* (*person*) (*lost*) disparu(e); (*absent*) absent(e); (*object*) manquant(e); **nothing is m.** il ne manque rien; **m. link** chaînon *m* manquant; **m. person** personne *f* disparue
mission ['mɪʃən] *n* mission *f*
missionary ['mɪʃənərɪ] (*pl* **missionaries**) *n Rel* missionnaire *mf*; **the m. position** la position du missionnaire
missive ['mɪsɪv] *n Formal* missive *f*
misspell ['mɪs'spel] (*pt & pp* **misspelt** ['mɪs'spelt]) *vt* mal écrire
misspent ['mɪs'spent] *adj* (*time, money*) gaspillé(e); **m. youth** jeunesse *f* dissipée
missus ['mɪsɪz] *n Br Fam* (*wife*) **the m.** la patronne
mist [mɪst] *n* (*fog*) brume *f*; (*condensation*) buée *f*
▸**mist over, mist up** *vi* (*of mirror, glasses*) s'embuer
mistakable [mɪs'teɪkəbəl] *adj* facile à confondre (**for** avec)
mistake [mɪs'teɪk] **1** *n* erreur *f*; (*in grammar, spelling*) faute *f*; **to make a m.** faire *ou* commettre une erreur; **by m.** par erreur; *Fam* **this is hard work and no m.!** pas de doute, c'est vraiment très dur!
2 *vt* (*pt* **mistook** [mɪs'tʊk], *pp* **mistaken** [mɪs'teɪkən]) (**a**) (*misunderstand*) se tromper sur (**b**) (*confuse*) **to m. sb for** prendre qn pour; **there's no mistaking a voice like that!** avec une voix pareille, on ne peut pas se tromper!

mistakeable = mistakable
mistaken [mɪs'teɪkən] *adj* (*belief, impression*) erroné(e), faux (fausse); **to be m.** se tromper
Mister ['mɪstə(r)] *n* Monsieur *m*
mistime [mɪs'taɪm] *vt* mal calculer
mistletoe ['mɪsəltəʊ] *n* gui *m*
mistranslation [mɪstræns'leɪʃən] *n* erreur *f* de traduction
mistreat [mɪs'triːt] *vt* maltraiter
mistress ['mɪstrɪs] *n* maîtresse *f*; (*in secondary school*) professeur *m*
mistrial [mɪs'traɪəl] *n Law Br* jugement *m* entaché d'un vice de procédure; *Am* = procès dans lequel le jury ne parvient pas à prendre de décision
mistrust [mɪs'trʌst] **1** *n* méfiance *f* (**of** à l'égard de)
2 *vt* se méfier de, ne pas avoir confiance en
mistrustful [mɪs'trʌstfʊl] *adj* méfiant(e); **to be m. of** se méfier de
misty ['mɪstɪ] *adj* (*place, weather*) brumeux(euse); (*outline, shape*) flou(e)
misunderstand [mɪsʌndə'stænd] (*pt & pp* **misunderstood** [mɪsʌndə'stʊd]) *vt & vi* mal comprendre
misunderstanding [mɪsʌndə'stændɪŋ] *n* (**a**) (*misconception*) malentendu *m* (**about** sur) (**b**) (*disagreement*) mésentente *f*
misuse 1 *n* [mɪs'juːs] (*of equipment, resources*) mauvais emploi *m*; (*of authority*) abus *m*; (*of funds*) détournement *m*
2 *vt* [mɪs'juːz] (*equipment, resources*) mal employer; (*authority*) abuser de; (*funds*) détourner
mite [maɪt] *n* (**a**) (*bug*) acarien *m* (**b**) *Fam* (*child*) **poor little m.!** pauvre petit! (**c**) *Fam* (*little bit*) **a m. expensive/tired** un tantinet cher (chère)/fatigué(e)
miter *Am* = mitre
mitigate ['mɪtɪgeɪt] *vt* atténuer; *Law* **mitigating circumstances** circonstances *fpl* atténuantes
mitigation [mɪtɪ'geɪʃən] *n* atténuation *f*; *Law* **to say sth in m.** dire qch pour sa défense
mitre, *Am* **miter** ['maɪtə(r)] *n Rel* mitre *f*
mitt [mɪt] *n* (**a**) (*mitten*) moufle *f*; *Am* **baseball m.** gant *m* de baseball (**b**) *Fam* (*hand*) patte *f*
mitten ['mɪtən] *n* (*glove*) moufle *f*
mix [mɪks] **1** *vt* mélanger; (*drink*) préparer; **to m. business with pleasure** mélanger les affaires et le plaisir
2 *vi* (**a**) (*blend*) se mélanger (**with** avec) (**b**) (*socially*) **to m. with** fréquenter
3 *n* mélange *m*; (*in music*) remix *m*
▸**mix up** *vt sep* (**a**) (*ingredients, papers*) mélanger (**b**) (*people, dates*) confondre (**c**) *Fam* **to be mixed up in sth** (*involved*) être mêlé(e) à qch, être impliqué(e) dans qch; **to get mixed up with sb** se mettre à fréquenter qn
mixed ['mɪkst] *adj* mélangé(e); *Fam* **it was a m. bag** il y avait de tout; **to have m. feelings (about sth)** avoir des sentiments mitigés (envers qch); **m. doubles** (*in tennis*) double *m* mixte; **m. grill** assortiment *m* de grillades; **m. marriage** mariage *m* mixte; **m. school** école *f* mixte
mixed-up [mɪks'tʌp] *adj Fam* (*person*) déboussolé(e)
mixer ['mɪksə(r)] *n* (**a**) (*for cooking*) mixe(u)r *m*; *Br* **m. tap** (robinet *m*) mélangeur *m* (**b**) (*socially*) **to be a good m.** être très sociable (**c**) (*drink*) = boisson servant à allonger un alcool
mixing bowl ['mɪksɪŋ'bəʊl] *n* saladier *m*
mixture ['mɪkstʃə(r)] *n* mélange *m*

mix-up ['mɪksʌp] *n* confusion *f* (**over** *or* **with** dans)
mktg *Com* (*abbr* **marketing**) marketing
ml (*abbr* **millilitre(s)**) ml
MLR [emel'ɑ:(r)] *n* Fin (*abbr* **minimum lending rate**) taux *m* de base
mm (*abbr* **millimetre(s)**) mm
mnemonic [nɪ'mɒnɪk] *n* moyen *m* mnémotechnique
moan [məʊn] **1** *n* (**a**) (*sound*) gémissement *m* (**b**) (*complaint*) plainte *f*
2 *vi* (**a**) (*make sound*) gémir (**b**) (*complain*) ronchonner; **to m. about sth** se plaindre de qch
moat [məʊt] *n* douve *f*
mob [mɒb] **1** *n* (*crowd*) foule *f*; *Fam* **the M.** la Mafia; **m. rule** loi *f* de la rue
2 *vt* (*pt & pp* **mobbed**) prendre d'assaut
mobile ['məʊbaɪl] **1** *adj* mobile; **m. home** mobile home *m*; **m. phone** téléphone *m* portable *ou* mobile, *Can* cellulaire *m*
2 *n* (**a**) (*hanging ornament*) mobile *m* (**b**) *Fam* (*mobile phone*) (téléphone *m*) portable *m* ou mobile *m*, *Can* cellulaire *m*
mobility [məʊ'bɪlɪtɪ] *n* mobilité *f*
mobilize ['məʊbɪlaɪz] *vt* mobiliser
mobster ['mɒbstə(r)] *n Am Fam* gangster *m*
moccasin ['mɒkəsɪn] *n* mocassin *m*
mock [mɒk] **1** *adj* faux (fausse), factice; *Br Sch* **m. exam** examen *m* blanc
2 *vt* (*ridicule*) se moquer de
mockery ['mɒkərɪ] *n* (**a**) (*ridicule*) moqueries *fpl* (**b**) (*travesty*) parodie *f*; **to make a m. of sb** ridiculiser qn; **to make a m. of sth** faire perdre toute crédibilité à qch
mockingbird ['mɒkɪŋbɜːd] *n* moqueur *m*
mock-up ['mɒkʌp] *n* maquette *f*
MOD [eməʊ'diː] *n Br Pol* (*abbr* **Ministry of Defence**) ministère *m* de la Défense
mod cons ['mɒd'kɒnz] *npl Fam* **with all m.** (*house*) tout confort; (*car*) avec toutes les options
mode [məʊd] *n* mode *m*
model ['mɒdəl] **1** *n* (**a**) (*small version*) maquette *f*, modèle *m* réduit; **m. aircraft** maquette d'avion (**b**) (*example, paragon*) modèle *m*; **m. pupil** élève *mf* modèle (**c**) (*fashion model*) mannequin *m*; (*for artist*) modèle *m*
2 *vt* (*pt & pp* **modelled**, *Am* **modeled**) (**a**) **to m. oneself on sb** prendre exemple sur qn (**b**) **to m. clothes** être mannequin (**c**) *Comput* modéliser
3 *vi* (*on catwalk, for photographer*) travailler comme mannequin; (*for artist*) poser
modem ['məʊdem] *n Comput* modem *m*
moderate 1 *n* ['mɒdərɪt] *Pol* modéré(e) *m,f*
2 *adj* ['mɒdərɪt] modéré(e)
3 *vt* ['mɒdəreɪt] modérer
4 *vi* ['mɒdəreɪt] *Formal* présider
moderately ['mɒdərɪtlɪ] *adv* (**a**) (*in moderation*) modérément (**b**) (*quite*) assez
moderation [mɒdə'reɪʃən] *n* modération *f*; **in m.** avec modération
modern ['mɒdən] *adj* moderne; **m. art** art *m* moderne; **m. languages** langues *fpl* vivantes
modernism ['mɒdənɪzəm] *n* modernisme *m*
modernization [mɒdənaɪ'zeɪʃən] *n* modernisation *f*
modernize ['mɒdənaɪz] **1** *vt* moderniser
2 *vi* se moderniser

modest ['mɒdɪst] *adj* (**a**) (*unassuming, moderate*) modeste (**b**) (*chaste*) pudique
modestly ['mɒdɪstlɪ] *adv* (**a**) (*unassumingly*) modestement (**b**) (*moderately*) assez, moyennement
modesty ['mɒdɪstɪ] *n* modestie *f*
modicum ['mɒdɪkəm] *n* **a m. of** un minimum de
modification [mɒdɪfɪ'keɪʃən] *n* modification *f*; **to make modifications to sth** apporter des modifications à qch
modify ['mɒdɪfaɪ] (*pt & pp* **modified**) *vt* modifier
modular ['mɒdjʊlə(r)] *adj* modulaire
modulate ['mɒdjʊleɪt] *vt* moduler
modulation [mɒdjʊ'leɪʃən] *n* modulation *f*
module ['mɒdjuːl] *n* module *m*
mogul ['məʊgəl] *n Fig* magnat *m*
mohair ['məʊheə(r)] *n* mohair *m*; **m. sweater** pull *m* en mohair
Mohammed [məʊ'hæmɪd] *n* Mahomet
moist [mɔɪst] *adj* humide; (*skin, hand*) moite; (*cake*) moelleux(euse)
moisten ['mɔɪsən] *vt* humecter
moisture ['mɔɪstʃə(r)] *n* humidité *f*
moisturize ['mɔɪstʃəraɪz] *vt* hydrater
moisturizer ['mɔɪstʃəraɪzə(r)] *n* crème *f* hydratante
molar ['məʊlə(r)] *n* molaire *f*
molasses [mə'læsɪz] *n* mélasse *f*
mold, molder *etc Am* = **mould, moulder** *etc*
Moldavia [mɒl'deɪvɪə], **Moldova** [mɒl'dəʊvə] *n* la Moldavie
Moldavian [mɒl'deɪvɪən], **Moldovan** [mɒl'dəʊvən] **1** *n* Moldave *mf*
2 *adj* moldave
mole¹ [məʊl] *n* (*birthmark*) grain *m* de beauté
mole² *n* (*animal, spy*) taupe *f*
molecular [mə'lekjʊlə(r)] *adj* moléculaire
molecule ['mɒlɪkjuːl] *n* molécule *f*
molehill ['məʊlhɪl] *n* taupinière *f*
molest [mə'lest] *vt* (*pester*) importuner; (*sexually*) agresser (sexuellement)
mollify ['mɒlɪfaɪ] (*pt & pp* **mollified**) *vt* calmer, apaiser
mollusc, *Am* **mollusk** ['mɒləsk] *n* mollusque *m*
mollycoddle ['mɒlɪkɒdəl] *vt Fam* dorloter
molten ['məʊltən] *adj* en fusion
mom [mɒm] *n Am Fam* maman *f*
moment ['məʊmənt] *n* moment *m*, instant *m*; **at the m.** en ce moment; **at the last m.** au dernier moment; **for the m.** pour le moment *ou* l'instant; **in a m.** dans un instant; **any m.** d'un instant à l'autre; **wait a m.!, one m.!** un moment!, un instant!; **the m. he arrives** dès qu'il arrive; **without a m.'s hesitation** sans une seconde d'hésitation; **to live for the m.** profiter du moment présent; **the man of the m.** l'homme du moment; **the m. of truth** le moment de vérité; **he's not a genius, but he has his moments** ce n'est pas un génie, mais il a parfois des moments d'inspiration
momentary ['məʊməntərɪ] *adj* momentané(e)
momentous [məʊ'mentəs] *adj* capital(e)
momentum [məʊ'mentəm] *n Phys* moment *m*; **to gather m.** (*of campaign*) prendre de l'ampleur; **to lose m.** (*of campaign*) s'essouffler
Mon (*abbr* **Monday**) lundi
Monaco ['mɒnəkəʊ] *n* Monaco
monarch ['mɒnək] *n* monarque *m*
monarchist ['mɒnəkɪst] *n* monarchiste *mf*

monarchy ['mɒnəkɪ] (*pl* **monarchies**) *n* monarchie *f*
monastery ['mɒnəstrɪ] (*pl* **monastries**) *n* monastère *m*
monastic [mə'næstɪk] *adj* monastique, monacal(e)
Monday ['mʌndɪ] *n* lundi *m*; *see also* **Saturday**
monetarism ['mʌnɪtərɪzm] *n* monétarisme *m*
monetarist ['mʌnɪtərɪst] *n & adj* monétariste *mf*
monetary ['mʌnɪtərɪ] *adj* monétaire
money ['mʌnɪ] *n* argent *m*; **to do sth for the m.** faire qch pour l'argent; **to make m.** *(of person)* gagner de l'argent; *(of business)* rapporter de l'argent; **to be worth a lot of m.** *(of thing)* valoir cher; *(of person)* être très riche; **there's no m. in it** ça ne paie pas; *Fam* **to be in the m.** être plein(e) aux as; **to get one's m.'s worth** en avoir pour son argent; *Fam* **it was m. for old rope** c'était de l'argent facilement gagné; **to put one's m. where one's mouth is** joindre le geste à la parole; *Fam* **to spend m. like water** dépenser sans compter; *Fam* **m. doesn't grow on trees!** l'argent ne se trouve pas sous le sabot d'un cheval!; **for my m.,...** à mon avis,...; **m. laundering** blanchiment *m* d'argent; *Fin* **m. market** marché *m* monétaire; *Econ* **m. supply** masse *f* monétaire
moneybags ['mʌnɪbægz] *n Fam (person)* richard(e) *m,f*
moneybox ['mʌnɪbɒks] *n* tirelire *f*
moneyed ['mʌnɪd] *adj* fortuné(e)
moneylender ['mʌnɪlendə(r)] *n* prêteur(euse) *m,f*; *(usurer)* usurier(ère) *m,f*
moneymaker ['mʌnɪmeɪkə(r)] *n* **to be a m.** *(of shop, business, product)* rapporter
moneymaking ['mʌnɪmeɪkɪŋ] *adj* qui rapporte
Mongol ['mɒŋgəl] *Hist* **1** *n* Mongol(e) *m,f*
  2 *adj* mongol(e)
mongol ['mɒŋgəl] *n Old-fashioned* mongolien(enne) *m,f*, = terme injurieux désignant un trisomique
Mongolia [mɒŋ'gəʊlɪə] *n* la Mongolie
Mongolian [mɒŋ'gəʊlɪən] **1** *n* Mongol(e) *m,f*
  2 *adj* mongol(e)
mongoose ['mɒŋguːs] *n* mangouste *f*
mongrel ['mʌŋgrəl] *n* bâtard *m*
monitor ['mɒnɪtə(r)] **1** *n* (**a**) *(supervisor)* superviseur *m* (**b**) *TV & Comput (screen)* moniteur *m*
  2 *vt (broadcast, conversation)* écouter; *(patient's condition, operation, results)* surveiller; *(performance)* suivre
monk [mʌŋk] *n* moine *m*
monkey ['mʌŋkɪ] (*pl* **monkeys**) *n (animal)* singe *m*; *Fam Fig (naughty child)* petit(e) diable(esse) *m,f*; *Fam* **to make a m. out of sb** se payer la tête de qn; *very Fam* **I don't give a m.'s** je m'en fous complètement; *Fam* **m. business** *(dishonest behaviour)* magouilles *fpl*; *(mischief)* bêtises *fpl*; **m. nut** cacah(o)uète *f*; **m. puzzle (tree)** désespoir *m* des singes; **m. wrench** clef *f* anglaise *ou* à molette
▸**monkey about, monkey around** *vi Fam (fool around)* faire l'imbécile
monkfish ['mʌŋkfɪʃ] *n* lotte *f*
mono ['mɒnəʊ] *n* mono *f*
monochrome ['mɒnəkrəʊm] *adj* monochrome; *(photo)* en noir et blanc
monocle ['mɒnəkəl] *n* monocle *m*
monogamous [mɒ'nɒgəməs] *adj* monogame
monogamy [mɒ'nɒgəmɪ] *n* monogamie *f*
monogram ['mɒnəgræm] *n* monogramme *m*

monograph ['mɒnəgræf] *n* monographie *f*
monolingual [mɒnəʊ'lɪŋgwəl] *adj* monolingue
monolithic [mɒnə'lɪθɪk] *adj* monolithique
monologue ['mɒnəlɒg] *n* monologue *m*
monopolize [mə'nɒpəlaɪz] *vt also Fig* monopoliser
monopoly [mə'nɒpəlɪ] (*pl* **monopolies**) *n also Fig* monopole *m*; **to have a m. on sth** avoir le monopole de qch
monorail ['mɒnəʊreɪl] *n* monorail *m*
monoski ['mɒnəʊskiː] *n* monoski *m*
monosyllabic [mɒnəʊsɪ'læbɪk] *adj (word)* monosyllabique; *(reply)* laconique
monosyllable [mɒnəʊ'sɪləbəl] *n* monosyllabe *m*
monotone ['mɒnətəʊn] *n* ton *m* monotone; **to speak in a m.** parler d'une voix monotone
monotonous [mə'nɒtənəs] *adj* monotone
monotony [mə'nɒtənɪ] *n* monotonie *f*
Monsignor [mɒn'siːnjə(r)] *n* Monseigneur
monsoon [mɒn'suːn] *n* mousson *f*
monster ['mɒnstə(r)] **1** *n* monstre *m*
  2 *adj Fam (enormous)* monstre, colossal(e)
monstrosity [mɒn'strɒsɪtɪ] (*pl* **monstrosities**) *n* monstruosité *f*
monstrous ['mɒnstrəs] *adj* monstrueux(euse)
montage ['mɒntɑːʒ] *n* montage *m*
month [mʌnθ] *n* mois *m*; **in the m. of August** au mois d'août; *Fam* **never in a m. of Sundays** jamais de la vie
monthly ['mʌnθlɪ] **1** *n* (*pl* **monthlies**) *(magazine)* mensuel *m*
  2 *adj* mensuel(elle); **m. payment** *or* **instalment** mensualité *f*
  3 *adv* tous les mois
monument ['mɒnjʊmənt] *n also Fig* monument *m* (**to** à)
monumental [mɒnjʊ'mentəl] *adj* monumental(e); *(importance)* capital(e)
moo [muː] **1** *n* (*pl* **moos**) meuglement *m*, beuglement *m*; **m.!** meuh!
  2 *vi* (*pt & pp* **mooed**) meugler, beugler
▸**mooch about, mooch around** [muːtʃ] *vi Fam* traîner
mood [muːd] *n* (**a**) *(state of mind)* humeur *f*; **to be in a good/bad m.** être de bonne/mauvaise humeur; **she's in one of her moods** elle est de mauvaise humeur; **to be in the m. for sth** avoir envie de qch; **to be in the m. for doing sth** être d'humeur à faire qch (**b**) *Gram* mode *m*
moodily ['muːdɪlɪ] *adv (answer, speak)* d'un ton maussade
moody ['muːdɪ] *adj* (**a**) *(sulky)* maussade (**b**) *(changeable)* lunatique
moon [muːn] **1** *n* lune *f*; **the M.** la Lune; *Fam* **to ask for the m.** demander la lune; *Fam* **to promise sb the m.** promettre la lune à qn; *Fam* **to be over the m.** être aux anges; **m. landing** alunissage *m*
  2 *vi Fam (expose one's buttocks)* montrer ses fesses
▸**moon about, moon around** *vi* musarder, flâner
moonbeam ['muːnbiːm] *n* rayon *m* de lune
moonlight ['muːnlaɪt] **1** *n* clair *m* de lune; **in the m.**, **by m.** au clair de lune; *Fam* **to do a m. flit** partir à la cloche de bois
  2 *vi Fam (work illegally)* travailler au noir
moonlighting ['muːnlaɪtɪŋ] *n Fam* travail *m* au noir
moonlit ['muːnlɪt] *adj* éclairé(e) par la lune

moonshine ['muːnʃaɪn] n Fam (a) (nonsense) balivernes fpl, bêtises fpl (b) Am (illegal alcohol) alcool m de contrebande
Moor [mʊə(r)] n Maure mf
moor¹ [mʊə(r)] n (heath) lande f
moor² vt (ship) amarrer
mooring ['mʊərɪŋ] n (a) (place) mouillage m (b) **moorings** (chains, ropes) amarres fpl
Moorish ['mʊərɪʃ] adj maure, mauresque
moorland ['mʊələnd] n lande f
moose [muːs] (pl moose) n orignal m
moot [muːt] 1 adj it's a m. point c'est difficile à dire
2 vt (suggest) suggérer
mop [mɒp] 1 n (for floor) balai m à franges; (with sponge) balai-éponge m; Fam **m. (of hair)** tignasse f
2 vt (pt & pp mopped) **to m. the floor** laver par terre; **to m. one's brow** s'éponger le front
▶**mop up** vt sep (liquid) éponger; Fig (enemy forces) liquider
▶**mope about, mope around** [məʊp] vi broyer du noir
moped ['məʊped] n (motorbike) Mobylette® f
moral ['mɒrəl] 1 n (a) (of story) morale f (b) **morals** (principles) moralité f
2 adj moral(e); **m. fibre** force f de caractère; **the m. majority** les néo-conservateurs mpl (surtout aux États-Unis); **m. support** soutien m moral; **m. victory** victoire f morale
morale [mɒ'rɑːl] n moral m; **to be good/bad for m.** être bon (bonne)/mauvais(e) pour le moral
moralistic [mɒrə'lɪstɪk] adj moraliste
morality [mə'rælɪtɪ] n moralité f
moralize ['mɒrəlaɪz] vi faire la morale, moraliser
morally ['mɒrəlɪ] adv moralement; **m. right** moralement correct(e); **m. wrong** contraire à la morale
morass [mə'ræs] n (marsh) marais m; Fig (of detail, despair) bourbier m
moratorium [mɒrə'tɔːrɪəm] (pl moratoria [mɒrə'tɔːrɪə] or moratoriums) n moratoire m (on sur)
morbid ['mɔːbɪd] adj morbide
morbidly ['mɔːbɪdlɪ] adv de façon morbide
mordant ['mɔːdənt] adj Formal (sarcasm, wit) mordant(e)
more [mɔː(r)] (comparative of many, much) 1 pron plus; **there are m. of us** nous sommes plus nombreux; **have (some) m.** reprenez-en; **there's no m.** il n'y en a plus; **let's say no m. about it** n'en parlons plus; **she knows m. than you** elle en sait plus long que toi; **we should see m. of each other** nous devrions nous voir plus souvent; **it's just m. of the same** c'est encore et toujours la même chose; **the m. I see her, the m. I like her** plus je la vois, plus elle me plaît; **what's m.,...** qui plus est,...; **what m. can I say?** que puis-je dire de plus?
2 adj (a) (larger quantity or number of) plus de; **m. water/children** plus d'eau/d'enfants; **m. than a hundred people were there** il y avait plus de cent personnes; **he has m. patience than I have** il a plus de patience que moi; **there are m. and m. accidents every year** chaque année, il y a de plus en plus d'accidents
(b) (additional quantity or number of) one **m. month** un mois de plus; **is there any m. bread?** est-ce qu'il y a encore du pain?; **I've no m. money** je n'ai plus d'argent; **I need m. time** il me faut plus de temps
3 adv (a) (to form comparative of adjectives and adverbs) plus (than que); **m. interesting** plus intéressant(e); **m. easily** plus facilement; **things are getting m. and m. difficult** les choses deviennent de plus en plus difficiles
(b) (to a greater extent) plus; **you should eat m.** tu devrais manger plus; **I'm m. than satisfied** je suis plus que satisfait; **he was m. surprised than annoyed** il était plus surpris que fâché; **I like her m. than I used to** je l'aime plus qu'avant; **that's m. like it!** voilà qui est mieux!; **m. or less** plus ou moins
(c) (with time) **once/twice m.** une/deux fois de plus; **he doesn't drink any m.** il ne boit plus; **I can't see you any m.** nous ne pouvons plus nous voir
moreover [mɔː'rəʊvə(r)] adv de plus
mores ['mɔːreɪz] npl Formal mœurs fpl
morgue [mɔːg] n morgue f; Fig **this place is like a m.** c'est complètement mort ici
moribund ['mɒrɪbʌnd] adj moribond(e)
Mormon ['mɔːmən] n Rel mormon(e) m,f
morning ['mɔːnɪŋ] n matin m; (referring to duration) matinée f; **tomorrow m.** demain matin; **yesterday m.** hier matin; **the next m., the m. after** le lendemain matin; **the m. before** la veille au matin; Fam **it's the m. after (the night before)** c'est un lendemain de cuite; **m., noon and night** du matin au soir; **in the m.** le matin; **on Wednesday m.** mercredi matin; **good m.!, Fam m.!** bonjour!; **m. sickness** nausées fpl matinales; **m. star** étoile f du matin
morning-after pill ['mɔːnɪŋ'ɑːftəpɪl] n pilule f du lendemain
Moroccan [mə'rɒkən] 1 n Marocain(e) m,f
2 adj marocain(e)
Morocco [mə'rɒkəʊ] n le Maroc
moron ['mɔːrɒn] n crétin(e) m,f
moronic [mə'rɒnɪk] adj débile
morose [mə'rəʊs] adj morose
morphing ['mɔːfɪŋ] n Comput morphing m
Morse [mɔːs] n **M. (code)** morse m
morsel ['mɔːsəl] n morceau m
mortal ['mɔːtəl] 1 n mortel(elle) m,f; Fig & Ironic **mere mortals** de simples mortels
2 adj mortel(elle); **m. enemy** ennemi m mortel; **m. remains** dépouille f mortelle; **m. sin** péché m mortel; **m. wound** blessure f mortelle
mortality [mɔː'tælɪtɪ] n mortalité f
mortally ['mɔːtəlɪ] adv mortellement
mortar ['mɔːtə(r)] n mortier m
mortgage ['mɔːgɪdʒ] 1 n (from lender's point of view) prêt m immobilier; (from borrower's point of view) emprunt m immobilier; **m. broker** courtier m en prêts hypothécaires; **m. (re)payments** remboursements mpl d'emprunt; **m. rate** taux m de crédit immobilier
2 vt (property, one's future) hypothéquer
mortician [mɔː'tɪʃən] n Am (undertaker) entrepreneur m de pompes funèbres
mortification [mɔːtɪfɪ'keɪʃən] n Rel mortification f; Fig (embarrassment) honte f
mortify ['mɔːtɪfaɪ] (pt & pp mortified) vt Rel mortifier; Fig **to be mortified** être mort(e) de honte
mortise ['mɔːtɪs] n mortaise f; **m. lock** serrure f encastrée
mortuary ['mɔːtjʊərɪ] (pl mortuaries) n morgue f
mosaic [məʊ'zeɪɪk] n also Fig mosaïque f
Moscow ['mɒskəʊ] n Moscou
Moses ['məʊzɪz] n Moïse

Moslem ['mɒzləm] *n & adj* musulman(e) *m,f*

mosque [mɒsk] *n* mosquée *f*

mosquito [məs'ki:təʊ] *(pl* **mosquitos** *or* **mosquitoes)** *n* moustique *m*; **m. bite** piqûre *f* de moustique; **m. net** moustiquaire *f*

moss [mɒs] *n* mousse *f*

most [məʊst] *(superlative of* **many, much) 1** *pron* (**a**) *(the majority)* la plupart; **m. of the people/time** la plupart des gens/du temps; **m. of us/them** la plupart d'entre nous/eux; **he is more interesting than m.** il est plus intéressant que la plupart des gens
(**b**) *(greatest amount)* **the m.** le plus; **he earns the m.** c'est lui qui gagne le plus; **at the (very) m.** au maximum; **to make the m. of sth** *(situation, talents)* tirer le meilleur parti de qch; *(time, holiday)* profiter au maximum de qch
2 *adj* (**a**) *(the majority of)* la plupart de; **m. women** la plupart des femmes
(**b**) *(greatest amount of)* **the m.** le plus de; **he has the m. money** c'est lui qui a le plus d'argent; **for the m. part** dans l'ensemble
3 *adv* (**a**) *(to form superlative of adjectives and adverbs)* plus; **the m. interesting book** le livre le plus intéressant; **the m. beautiful woman** la plus belle femme; **these are the m. expensive** ce sont les plus chers; **those who answered m. honestly** ceux qui ont répondu le plus franchement
(**b**) *(to the greatest extent)* le plus; **the one who works (the) m. is...** celui qui travaille le plus est...; **that's what worries me (the) m.** c'est ce qui m'inquiète le plus; **who do you like m.?** qui préfères-tu?; **what I want m.** ce que je veux par-dessus tout
(**c**) *(very)* extrêmement; **m. unhappy** extrêmement malheureux(euse)

mostly ['məʊstlɪ] *adv* (**a**) *(in the main)* principalement, surtout (**b**) *(most often)* le plus souvent, la plupart du temps

MOT [eməʊ'ti:] *n Br* ≃ contrôle *m* technique des véhicules

motel [məʊ'tel] *n* motel *m*

moth [mɒθ] *n* papillon *m* de nuit; *(in clothes)* mite *f*

mothball ['mɒθbɔːl] *n* boule *f* de naphtaline; *Fig* **to put a project in mothballs** mettre un projet au placard

moth-eaten ['mɒθi:tən] *adj* mité(e); *Fam (in poor condition)* miteux(euse)

mother ['mʌðə(r)] **1** *n* mère *f*; **M.'s Day** la fête des Mères; **m. country** patrie *f*; **M. Nature** Dame Nature *f*; *Rel* **M. Superior** Mère supérieure; **m. tongue** langue *f* maternelle
2 *vt* materner

motherboard ['mʌðəbɔːd] *n Comput* carte *f* mère

motherhood ['mʌðəhʊd] *n* maternité *f*

mother-in-law ['mʌðərɪnlɔː] *(pl* **mothers-in-law)** *n* belle-mère *f*

motherland ['mʌðəlænd] *n* patrie *f*

mother-of-pearl ['mʌðərəv'pɜːl] *n* nacre *f*

mother-to-be ['mʌðətə'bi:] *(pl* **mothers-to-be)** *n* future mère *f*

motif [məʊ'ti:f] *n* motif *m*

motion ['məʊʃən] **1** *n* (**a**) *(movement)* mouvement *m*; **to set sth in m.** *(machine)* mettre qch en marche; *(process)* déclencher qch; *Fig* **to go through the motions** agir machinalement; *Am* **m. picture** film *m* (**b**) *(in meeting, debate)* motion *f*; **to propose/second a m.** présenter/appuyer une motion (**c**) *(faeces)* selles *fpl*

2 *vt* **to m. sb to do sth** faire signe à qn de faire qch
3 *vi* **to m. to sb to do sth** faire signe à qn de faire qch

motionless ['məʊʃənlɪs] *adj* immobile

motivate ['məʊtɪveɪt] *vt* motiver

motivation [məʊtɪ'veɪʃən] *n* motivation *f*

motive ['məʊtɪv] **1** *n* *(reason)* motif *m*; *Law (for crime)* mobile *m*
2 *adj* **m. force** *or* **power** force *f* motrice

motley ['mɒtlɪ] *adj* hétéroclite; **m. crew** groupe *m* hétéroclite

motor ['məʊtə(r)] **1** *n* *(engine)* moteur *m*; *Br Fam (car)* bagnole *f*; **m. industry** industrie *f* automobile; **m. insurance** assurance *f* automobile; *Med* **m. neurone disease** maladie *f* de Charcot; **m. racing** courses *fpl* automobiles; **m. show** salon *m* de l'automobile; **m. vehicle** véhicule *m* automobile
2 *vi* voyager en voiture

motorbike ['məʊtəbaɪk] *n* moto *f*

motorboat ['məʊtəbəʊt] *n* canot *m* à moteur

motorcade ['məʊtəkeɪd] *n* cortège *m* de voitures

motorcar ['məʊtəkɑː(r)] *n Br* voiture *f*

motorcycle ['məʊtəsaɪkəl] *n* moto *f*, motocyclette *f*

motorcyclist ['məʊtəsaɪklɪst] *n* motocycliste *mf*

motoring ['məʊtərɪŋ] *n* conduite *f*; **school of m.** auto-école *f*; **m. offence** infraction *f* au Code de la route

motorist ['məʊtərɪst] *n* automobiliste *mf*

motorize ['məʊtəraɪz] *vt* motoriser

motorized ['məʊtəraɪzd] *adj* motorisé(e)

motorway ['məʊtəweɪ] *n Br* autoroute *f*; **m. services** services *mpl* autoroutiers

mottled ['mɒtəld] *adj (skin)* marbré(e); *(coat, surface)* tacheté(e), moucheté(e)

motto ['mɒtəʊ] *(pl* **mottoes)** *n* devise *f*

mould¹, *Am* **mold** [məʊld] *n (fungus)* moisissure *f*

mould², *Am* **mold 1** *n (in art, cooking)* moule *m*; *Fig* **cast in the same m.** fait(e) dans le même moule; *Fig* **a star in the John Wayne m.** une star dans le style John Wayne; *Fig* **to break the m.** rompre avec la tradition
2 *vt (plastic, person's character)* modeler, façonner

moulder, *Am* **molder** ['məʊldə(r)] *vi (of food)* moisir; *(of building)* se délabrer

moulding, *Am* **molding** ['məʊldɪŋ] *n Archit* moulure *f*

mouldy, *Am* **moldy** ['məʊldɪ] *adj* moisi(e)

moult [məʊlt] *vi (of bird)* muer; *(of cat, dog)* perdre ses poils

mound [maʊnd] *n (hill)* butte *f*; *(of earth, sand)* tas *m*

mount¹ [maʊnt] *n (mountain)* mont *m*; **M. Vesuvius** le Vésuve

mount² **1** *n* (**a**) *(for painting)* carton *m* de montage; *(for slide)* cadre *m* (**b**) *(horse)* monture *f*
2 *vt* (**a**) *(bicycle, horse)* monter sur, enfourcher; *(stairs)* monter; *(ladder)* monter à (**b**) *(photograph, exhibition)* monter; *(machine gun)* installer; *(offensive)* lancer; **to m. guard** monter la garde
3 *vi* (**a**) *(get onto horse)* se mettre en selle (**b**) *(increase)* monter, augmenter

▸**mount up** *vi (of cost, debts)* monter, augmenter

mountain ['maʊntɪn] *n also Fig* montagne *f*; **to make a m. out of a molehill** faire une montagne d'un rien; **m. bike** vélo *m* tout terrain; **m. climbing** alpinisme *m*; **m. lion** puma *m*; **m. range** chaîne *f* de montagnes; **m. rescue team** équipe *f* de secours en montagne; *Am* **M. Standard Time** heure *f* des montagnes Rocheuses

mountaineer [maʊntɪ'nɪə(r)] *n* alpiniste *mf*

mountaineering [maʊntɪ'nɪərɪŋ] n alpinisme m
mountainous ['maʊntɪnəs] adj montagneux(euse)
mounted ['maʊntɪd] adj monté(e), à cheval; **the m. police** la police montée
mounting ['maʊntɪŋ] **1** n (for engine, gun) support m **2** adj (increasing) croissant(e)
mourn [mɔːn] **1** vt pleurer
  2 vi **to m. for sb/sth** pleurer qn/qch
mourner ['mɔːnə(r)] n = personne assistant aux obsèques
mournful ['mɔːnfʊl] adj triste
mourning ['mɔːnɪŋ] n deuil m; **to be in m. (for sb)** être en deuil (de qn); **to go into m.** prendre le deuil
mouse [maʊs] (pl **mice** [maɪs]) n also Comput souris f; **m. mat, m. pad** tapis m de souris
mousetrap ['maʊstræp] n tapette f, souricieère f
mousse [muːs] n mousse f; **chocolate m.** mousse au chocolat
moustache [mə'stɑːʃ], Am **mustache** ['mʌstæʃ] n moustache f
mousy ['maʊsɪ] adj (a) (hair) châtain terne inv (b) (person, manner) timide, effacé(e)
mouth 1 n [maʊθ] (of person, horse) bouche f; (of other animal) gueule f; (of tunnel) entrée f; (of river) embouchure f; **we have seven mouths to feed** nous avons sept bouches à nourrir; Fam **keep your m. shut about this** garde ça pour toi; Fam Fig **to have a big m.** avoir une grande gueule; Fam **he's all m.** c'est une grande gueule; **don't put words into my m.** ne me fais pas dire ce que je n'ai pas dit; **m. organ** harmonica m
  2 vt [maʊð] (insincerely) débiter; (silently) articuler silencieusement
mouthful ['maʊθfʊl] n (of food) bouchée f; (of drink) gorgée f; Fam Fig (long word) = mot long et difficile à prononcer; (long name) nom m à coucher dehors; Fam **to give sb a m.** enguirlander qn
mouthpiece ['maʊθpiːs] n (a) (of musical instrument) embouchure f; (of telephone) microphone m (b) (of government, political party) porte-parole m inv
mouth-to-mouth resuscitation ['maʊθtə-'maʊθrɪsʌsɪ'teɪʃən] n bouche-à-bouche m inv
mouthwash ['maʊθwɒʃ] n bain m de bouche
mouthwatering ['maʊθwɔːtərɪŋ] adj (smell) appétissant(e); (prospect) alléchant(e)
movable ['muːvəbəl] adj mobile; Rel **m. feast** fête f mobile
move [muːv] **1** n (a) (motion) mouvement m; **to make a m.** (leave) partir; **to make a m. towards sb/sth** se diriger vers qn/qch; **on the m.** en mouvement; Fam **to get a m. on** se grouiller, se magner
  (b) (action, step) pas m, démarche f; **to make the first m.** faire le premier pas
  (c) (from home) déménagement m; (from job) changement m de poste
  (d) (in games) coup m; **(it's) your m.** (c'est) à toi de jouer
  2 vt (a) (change position of) déplacer; (set in motion) remuer; (employee) muter; **to m. house/premises** déménager; **to m. jobs** (within company, sector) changer de poste; Fam **to m. oneself** se remuer
  (b) Fig (sway) faire changer d'avis; **to feel moved to do sth** se sentir obligé(e) de faire qch
  (c) (affect emotionally) émouvoir; **to m. sb to anger** provoquer la colère de qn; **to m. sb to tears** émouvoir qn jusqu'aux larmes

  (d) (in debate) proposer
  3 vi (a) (change position) se déplacer; (stir) bouger; (progress, advance) avancer; (leave) partir; **to get things moving** faire avancer les choses; **could you m., please?** pourriez-vous vous pousser, s'il vous plaît?; Fam **come on, m.!** allez, remue-toi!
  (b) (act) agir
  (c) (to new home, office) emménager; **to m. to another job** changer de travail; **to m. to the country** s'installer à la campagne
  (d) Fig (be swayed) céder
  (e) (in games) (of player) jouer; (of piece) avancer
▶**move about, move around 1** vt sep (furniture) déplacer; (employee) muter, transférer
  2 vi (change position) se déplacer; (stir) bouger; **he moves around a lot** (in job) il est souvent en déplacement
▶**move along** = move on
▶**move away 1** vt sep éloigner, écarter (**from** de)
  2 vi (from window, person) s'éloigner, s'écarter (**from** de); (move house) déménager
▶**move back 1** vt sep (further away) reculer; (to former position) remettre en place
  2 vi (retreat) s'écarter, (se) reculer; (to former position) retourner (**to** à)
▶**move forward 1** vt sep (object, date, meeting) avancer; (troops) faire avancer
  2 vi (of person, car) (s')avancer
▶**move in** vi (take up residence) emménager
▶**move off** vi (go away) partir, s'éloigner; (start journey) se mettre en marche; (of car) démarrer
▶**move on 1** vt sep (crowd) faire circuler
  2 vi (a) time's moving on il se fait tard; **it's time we were moving on** il est temps de partir (b) (change subject) passer à autre chose; **to m. on to sth** passer à qch (c) (progress, develop) changer
▶**move out** vi (leave home) déménager
▶**move over** vi (make room) se pousser
▶**move up** vi (a) (make room) se pousser (b) (be promoted) avoir de l'avancement
moveable = movable
movement ['muːvmənt] n mouvement m; **to watch sb's movements** surveiller les faits et gestes de qn; **(bowel) m.** selles fpl
mover ['muːvə(r)] n (in debate) auteur m d'une motion; **the movers and shakers** les grands pontes mpl
movie ['muːvɪ] n Am film m; **to go to the movies** aller au cinéma; **to be in the movies** faire du cinéma; **m. actor/actress** acteur m/actrice f de cinéma; **m. camera** caméra f; **m. industry** industrie f cinématographique; **m. star** vedette f de cinéma; **m. theater** cinéma m
moviegoer ['muːvɪɡəʊə(r)] n Am spectateur(trice) m,f de cinéma
moving ['muːvɪŋ] adj (a) (in motion) en mouvement; (train, vehicle) en marche; (parts) mobile; **m. staircase** escalier m mécanique (b) (touching) émouvant(e)
mow [məʊ] (pp **mown** [məʊn]) vt (lawn) tondre; (hay) faucher
▶**mow down** vt sep (slaughter) faucher
Mozambican [məʊzæm'biːkən] **1** n Mozambicain(e) m,f
  2 adj mozambicain(e)
Mozambique [məʊzæm'biːk] n le Mozambique

MP [em'piː] n (**a**) Br & Can Pol (abbr **Member of Parliament**) député(e) m,f (**b**) Mil (abbr **Military Police**) police f militaire

mpg [empiː'dʒiː] n (abbr **miles per gallon**) ≃ litre m aux cent (kilomètres)

mph [empiː'eɪtʃ] n (abbr **miles per hour**) ≃ km/h

Mr ['mɪstə(r)] (abbr **Mister**) **Mr McLean** M. McLean; **Mr Right** (ideal husband) l'homme m idéal

Mrs ['mɪsɪz] (abbr **Mistress**) **Mrs Sole** Mme Sole

Ms [mɪz] ≃ Mme (ne donne pas d'indications sur le statut de famille)

MS n (**a**) (abbr **multiple sclerosis**) sclérose f en plaques (**b**) (abbr **manuscript**) manuscrit m

ms (abbr **millisecond**) millième m de seconde

MSc [emes'siː] n Univ (abbr **Master of Science**) **to have an M. in chemistry** ≃ avoir une maîtrise de chimie; **John Smith M.** John Smith, titulaire d'une maîtrise de sciences

MSG [emes'dʒiː] n Culin (abbr **monosodium glutamate**) glutamate m de sodium

MSP [emes'piː] n (abbr **Member of the Scottish Parliament**) député(e) m,f du parlement écossais

MST [emes'tiː] n Am (abbr **Mountain Standard Time**) heure f d'hiver des montagnes Rocheuses

Mt (abbr **Mount**) Mt.

much [mʌtʃ] (comparative **more** [mɔː(r)], superlative **most** [məʊst]) **1** pron beaucoup; **there isn't m. left** il n'en reste pas beaucoup; **it's not worth m.** ça ne vaut pas grand-chose; Formal **m. has happened since you left** il s'est passé beaucoup de choses depuis ton départ; **I'll say this m. for him, he's very polite** je dois reconnaître une chose, c'est qu'il est très poli; **I don't think m. of him** je n'ai pas grande estime pour lui; **it didn't come as m. of a surprise** ça n'a pas été une grande surprise; **she isn't m. of a singer** comme chanteuse, elle n'est pas très bonne; **twice as m.** deux fois plus; **I thought as m.** c'est ce que je pensais; **as m. as possible** autant que possible; **it was as m. as we could do to stay upright** nous avions déjà assez de mal à rester debout; **he left without so m. as saying goodbye** il est parti sans même dire au revoir; **he has drunk so m. that...** il a tellement bu que...; **so m. the better** tant mieux; **so m. so that...** à tel point que...; **so m. for her promises of help!** c'était bien la peine de promettre qu'elle m'/nous/etc aiderait!; Fam **that's a bit m.!** c'est un peu fort!

2 adj

> Hormis dans la langue soutenue et dans certaines expressions, ne s'utilise que dans des structures négatives ou interrogatives.

how m. money? combien d'argent?; **there isn't m. traffic** il n'y a pas de circulation; **too m. work** trop de travail; **so m. time** tant de temps; **as m. food as** autant de nourriture que; Formal **m. work still needs to be done** il reste encore beaucoup de travail à faire

3 adv beaucoup; **I don't like it m.** ça ne me plaît pas beaucoup; **m. better** bien meilleur(e); **m. more difficult** beaucoup plus difficile; **m. the best** de loin le meilleur (la meilleure); **m. the most interesting** de loin le (la) plus intéressant(e); **thank you very m.** merci beaucoup; **m. the same** presque pareil(eille); **m. to my astonishment** à mon grand étonnement; **m. as I like him, I don't really trust him** j'ai beau l'apprécier, je ne lui fais pas vraiment confiance; **the result**

was m. as I expected** le résultat correspondait assez à mes attentes; **so m.** autant; **I love him so m.** je l'aime tellement; **too m.** trop; **£10 too m.** 10 livres de trop; **this is (really) too m.!** trop c'est trop!

muchness ['mʌtʃnɪs] n Fam **they're much of a m.** ils se valent

muck [mʌk] n Fam (dirt) saleté f; (manure) fumier m; (bad food) cochonneries fpl; (bad quality book, TV programme) idioties fpl

▸**muck about, muck around** Br Fam **1** vt sep (treat badly) se moquer de
2 vi (**a**) (fool about) faire l'imbécile; (waste time) traîner (**b**) (tinker) **to m. about or around with sth** tripoter qch

▸**muck in** vi Br Fam (help) s'y mettre

▸**muck out** vt sep (stables) nettoyer

▸**muck up** vt sep Fam (**a**) (make dirty) cochonner (**b**) (task) bâcler; (plans) chambouler; (interview, exam) rater

muckraking ['mʌkreɪkɪŋ] n Fam (in journalism) = pratique consistant à révéler et exploiter à fond des scandales

mucky ['mʌkɪ] adj Br Fam sale

mucous ['mjuːkəs] adj muqueux(euse)

mucus ['mjuːkəs] n mucus m, mucosités fpl

mud [mʌd] n boue f; Fig **to throw m. at sb** couvrir qn de boue; Fam **his name is m.** il n'a pas la cote; **m. hut** hutte f en terre; **m. wrestling** catch m dans la boue

mudbank ['mʌdbæŋk] n banc m de vase

mudflat ['mʌdflæt] n banc m de vase

muddle ['mʌdəl] **1** n confusion f; **to be in a m.** (of things) être en désordre; (of person) ne plus s'y retrouver; **to get into a m.** (of things) se mélanger; (of person) s'embrouiller
2 vt (**a**) (put in disorder) mélanger (**b**) (bewilder) embrouiller; **to get muddled** s'embrouiller

▸**muddle along** vi se débrouiller tant bien que mal

▸**muddle through** vi se débrouiller

▸**muddle up** vt sep (**a**) (put in disorder) mélanger (**b**) (confuse) embrouiller; **to get muddled up** s'embrouiller

muddleheaded [mʌdəl'hedɪd] adj (person) brouillon(onne); (thinking) confus(e)

muddy ['mʌdɪ] **1** adj (path, water) boueux(euse); (clothing, hands) couvert(e) de boue; (complexion) terreux(euse); (colour) sale
2 vt (pt & pp **muddied**) salir; Fig **to m. the waters** brouiller les pistes

mudguard ['mʌdgɑːd] n garde-boue m inv

mudpack ['mʌdpæk] n masque m à l'argile

mudslinging ['mʌdslɪŋɪŋ] n Fam = fait de dénigrer systématiquement ses adversaires

muesli ['mjuːzlɪ] n muesli m

muff¹ [mʌf] vt Br Fam (bungle) rater, louper

muff² n (for hands) manchon m

muffin ['mʌfɪn] n muffin m

muffle ['mʌfəl] vt (**a**) (sound) assourdir, étouffer (**b**) **to m. oneself up** s'emmitoufler

muffled ['mʌfəld] adj (sound, footstep) assourdi(e), étouffé(e)

muffler ['mʌflə(r)] n (**a**) (scarf) cache-nez m inv (**b**) Am (of car) silencieux m

mufti ['mʌftɪ] n Fam **in m.** (soldier) en civil

mug [mʌg] **1** n (**a**) (cup) grande tasse f (**b**) Fam (face) gueule f; **m. shot** photo f d'identité judiciaire (**c**) Br

Fam (gullible person) poire *f*; **it's a m.'s game** on est toujours perdant à ce jeu-là
  2 *vt (pt & pp mugged) (attack)* agresser
▸**mug up** *vi Br Fam (study)* bûcher; **to m. up on sth** potasser qch
mugger ['mʌɡə(r)] *n* agresseur *m*
mugging ['mʌɡɪŋ] *n* agression *f*
muggins ['mʌɡɪnz] *n Br Fam* mézigue
muggy ['mʌɡɪ] *adj* lourd(e), étouffant(e)
mulatto [mjuː'lætəʊ] *(pl mulattos or mulattoes) n* mulâtre *mf*
mulberry ['mʌlbərɪ] *(pl mulberries) n (fruit)* mûre *f*; *(tree)* mûrier *m*
mule [mjuːl] *n* mulet *m*; *(female)* mule *f*
▸**mull over** [mʌl] *vt sep (consider)* **to m. sth over** retourner qch dans sa tête
mulled wine ['mʌld'waɪn] *n* vin *m* chaud épicé
mullet ['mʌlɪt] *n* **grey m.** mulet *m* gris; **red m.** rouget *m*
multi-access ['mʌltɪ'ækses] *adj Comput* à accès multiple
multicoloured ['mʌltɪkʌləd] *adj* multicolore
multicultural [mʌltɪ'kʌltʃərəl] *adj* multiculturel(elle)
multidisciplinary ['mʌltɪdɪsɪ'plɪnərɪ] *adj Br* pluridisciplinaire
multifarious [mʌltɪ'feərɪəs] *adj* varié(e), divers(e)
multi-functional [mʌltɪ'fʌŋkʃənəl] *adj* multifonctions *inv*
multilateral [mʌltɪ'lætərəl] *adj* multilatéral(e)
multimedia [mʌltɪ'miːdɪə] *adj* multimédia
multimillionaire [mʌltɪmɪlɪə'neə(r)] *n* multimillionnaire *mf*
multinational [mʌltɪ'næʃənəl] **1** *n* multinationale *f*
  2 *adj* multinational(e)
multiparty [mʌltɪ'pɑːtɪ] *adj* **m. system** pluripartisme *m*
multiple ['mʌltɪpəl] **1** *n* (a) *Math* multiple *m* (b) *Com (chain store)* chaîne *f* de magasins
  2 *adj* multiple; **m. sclerosis** sclérose *f* en plaques
multiple-choice ['mʌltɪpl'tʃɔɪs] *adj* à choix multiples
multiplex ['mʌltɪpleks] *n Cin* multiplexe *m*, complexe *m* multisalles
multiplication [mʌltɪplɪ'keɪʃən] *n* multiplication *f*; **m. table** table *f* de multiplication
multiplicity [mʌltɪ'plɪsɪtɪ] *n* multiplicité *f*
multiply ['mʌltɪplaɪ] *(pt & pp multiplied)* **1** *vt* multiplier (**by** par)
  2 *vi (reproduce)* se multiplier
multipurpose [mʌltɪ'pɜːpəs] *adj* polyvalent(e)
multiracial [mʌltɪ'reɪʃəl] *adj* multiracial(e)
multistorey, *Am* **multistory** [mʌltɪ'stɔːrɪ] *adj* à étages; **m. (car park)** parking *m* à plusieurs niveaux
multitude ['mʌltɪtjuːd] *n* multitude *f*
multivitamin [mʌltɪ'vɪtəmɪn, *Am* mʌltɪ'vaɪtəmɪn] *n* multivitamine *f*
mum [mʌm] *Fam* **1** *n Br (mother)* maman *f*; **m.'s the word!** motus et bouche cousue!
  2 *adj* **to keep m. (about sth)** ne pas souffler mot (de qch)
mumble ['mʌmbəl] **1** *n* marmonnement *m*
  2 *vt & vi* marmonner
mumbo jumbo ['mʌmbəʊ'dʒʌmbəʊ] *n (nonsense)* âneries *fpl*; *(jargon)* charabia *m*
mummify ['mʌmɪfaɪ] *(pt & pp mummified) vt* momifier

mummy¹ ['mʌmɪ] *(pl mummies) n (embalmed body)* momie *f*
mummy² *n Br Fam (mother)* maman *f*; **a m.'s boy** un petit garçon à sa maman
mumps [mʌmps] *n (illness)* oreillons *mpl*; **to have m.** avoir les oreillons
munch [mʌntʃ] *vt* mâcher
munchies ['mʌntʃɪz] *npl Fam* (a) *(snacks)* amuse-gueule *mpl* (b) *(desire to eat)* **to have the m.** avoir la fringale
mundane [mʌn'deɪn] *adj* banal(e), ordinaire
municipal [mjuː'nɪsɪpəl] *adj* municipal(e)
municipality [mjuːnɪsɪ'pælɪtɪ] *(pl municipalities) n* municipalité *f*
munitions [mjuː'nɪʃənz] *npl* munitions *fpl*
mural ['mjʊərəl] *n* peinture *f* murale
murder ['mɜːdə(r)] **1** *n* (a) *(killing)* meurtre *m*; *Fig* **she gets away with m.** elle peut tout se permettre; **m. case** affaire *f* de meurtre; **m. inquiry** enquête *f* sur une affaire de meurtre (b) *Fam Fig (difficult task)* cauchemar *m*, enfer *m*; **finding a parking place on a Saturday is m.** c'est l'enfer pour trouver à se garer le samedi
  2 *vt* (a) *(kill)* assassiner; *Fam Fig* **I'll m. you!** je vais te tuer!; *Fam* **I could m. a beer/pizza** je me taperais bien une bière/une pizza (b) *Fig (song, tune)* massacrer
murderer ['mɜːdərə(r)] *n* meurtrier(ère) *m,f*, assassin *m*
murky ['mɜːkɪ] *adj (weather, sky)* sombre; *(details, past)* trouble
murmur ['mɜːmə(r)] **1** *n* murmure *m*; **to do sth without a m.** faire qch sans broncher
  2 *vi also Fig* murmurer
muscle ['mʌsəl] *n* muscle *m*; *Fig (power)* poids *m*; **not to move a m.** rester immobile
▸**muscle in** *vi* intervenir (**on** dans)
muscleman ['mʌsəlmæn] *n* Monsieur *m* muscle
Muscovite ['mʌskəvaɪt] **1** *n* Moscovite *mf*
  2 *adj* moscovite
muscular ['mʌskjʊlə(r)] *adj (tissue, pain)* musculaire; *(person)* musclé(e); **m. dystrophy** myopathie *f*
Muse [mjuːz] *n (in mythology)* Muse *f*; *(of poet)* muse *f*
muse [mjuːz] *vi* rêvasser, songer (**on** or **about** à)
museum [mjuː'zɪəm] *n* musée *m*
mush [mʌʃ] *n* (a) *(pulp)* bouillie *f* (b) *Fig (sentimentality)* mièvrerie *f*
mushroom ['mʌʃrʊm] **1** *n* champignon *m*; **m. cloud** champignon atomique
  2 *vi (of costs, prices)* grimper (en flèche); *(of town)* se développer; *(of houses, factories)* pousser comme des champignons
mushy ['mʌʃɪ] *adj* (a) *(food)* en bouillie; *(ground)* détrempé(e) (b) *Fam Fig Pej (sentimental)* à l'eau de rose, mièvre
music ['mjuːzɪk] *n* musique *f*; *Fig* **those words were m. to her ears** elle était ravie d'entendre ces mots; **m. box** boîte *f* à musique; **m. hall** music-hall *m*; **m. stand** pupitre *m* (à musique); **m. teacher** professeur *m* de musique
musical ['mjuːzɪkəl] **1** *n (show, film)* comédie *f* musicale
  2 *adj (tuneful)* musical(e); *(musically gifted)* musicien(enne); **m. box** boîte *f* à musique; **m. chairs** (jeu *m* des) chaises *fpl* musicales; *also Fig* **to play m. chairs** jouer aux chaises musicales; **m. comedy**

comédie f musicale; **m. instrument** instrument m de musique

musician [mju:'zɪʃən] n musicien(enne) m,f

musicologist [mju:zɪ'kɒlədʒɪst] n musicologue mf

musings ['mju:zɪŋz] npl rêverie(s) f(pl)

musk [mʌsk] n musc m

musket ['mʌskɪt] n mousquet m

musketeer [mʌskə'tɪə(r)] n mousquetaire m

muskrat ['mʌskræt] n rat m musqué

Muslim ['mʊzlɪm] n & adj musulman(e) m,f

muslin ['mʌzlɪn] n mousseline f

mussel ['mʌsəl] n moule f; **m. bed** parc m à moules

must [mʌst] **1** modal aux v (**a**) (expressing obligation) devoir; **you m. do it** tu dois le faire, il faut que tu le fasses; **they mustn't find out** il ne faut pas qu'ils l'apprennent; **you mustn't tell anyone** surtout, n'en parle à personne; **this plant m. be watered daily** cette plante doit être arrosée chaque jour; **I m. say I thought it was rather good** je dois avouer que j'ai trouvé ça plutôt bon; **will you come with me? – if I m.** tu viens avec moi? – s'il le faut; **take it if you m.** prends-le, si tu le veux vraiment; **m. you be so silly?** tu te sens obligé d'être aussi bête?

(**b**) (suggesting, inviting) **you m. come and visit us** il faut vraiment que vous nous rendiez visite; **we m. go out for a drink sometime** il faudrait que nous allions prendre un verre, un de ces jours

(**c**) (expressing probability) devoir; **you m. be hungry** vous devez avoir faim; **I m. have made a mistake** j'ai dû faire une erreur; **you m. be joking!** tu veux rire!

2 n Fam (**a**) (necessity) **to be a m.** être une nécessité; **sunglasses/hiking boots are a m.** il faut absolument emporter des lunettes de soleil/des chaussures de marche

(**b**) (thing not to be missed) **this film's a m.** ce film est un must

mustache ['mʌstæʃ] Am = moustache

mustard ['mʌstəd] n moutarde f; Am Fam Fig **he couldn't cut the m.** il n'a pas été à la hauteur; **m. bath** bain m sinapisé; **m. gas** gaz m moutarde

muster ['mʌstə(r)] **1** n Fig **to pass m.** être acceptable
2 vt (gather) rassembler; **to m. one's strength/courage** rassembler ses forces/son courage

musty ['mʌstɪ] adj (smell) de moisi; **to have a m. smell** (of room) sentir le renfermé

mutant ['mju:tənt] n & adj mutant(e) m,f

mutate [mju:'teɪt] vi muter

mutation [mju:'teɪʃən] n mutation f

mute [mju:t] **1** n (**a**) (dumb person) muet(ette) m,f (**b**) Mus sourdine f
2 adj muet(ette)

muted ['mju:tɪd] adj (sound) assourdi(e); (applause) faible; (protest, criticism) voilé(e); (colour) sourd(e)

mutilate ['mju:tɪleɪt] vt also Fig mutiler

mutilation [mju:tɪ'leɪʃən] n mutilation f

mutineer [mju:tɪ'nɪə(r)] n mutiné(e) m,f

mutinous ['mju:tɪnəs] adj rebelle

mutiny ['mju:tɪnɪ] **1** n (pl **mutinies**) (on ship) mutinerie f; (of workers) révolte f

2 vi (pt & pp **mutinied**) (of crew, soldiers) se mutiner; (of workers) se révolter

mutt [mʌt] n Fam (dog) clébard m

mutter ['mʌtə(r)] **1** n murmure m
2 vt & vi marmonner

mutton ['mʌtən] n mouton m; Fam **to look like m. dressed as lamb** être habillé(e) trop jeune pour son âge

mutual ['mju:tʃʊəl] adj (reciprocal) mutuel(elle), réciproque; (shared) commun(e); **the feeling is m.** c'est réciproque

mutually ['mju:tʃʊəlɪ] adv mutuellement, réciproquement; **to be m. exclusive** s'exclure mutuellement

Muzak® ['mju:zæk] n musique f de fond, fond m sonore

muzzle ['mʌzəl] **1** n (**a**) (dog's nose) museau m; (guard) muselière f (**b**) (of gun) canon m
2 vt also Fig museler

MW (**a**) (abbr **Medium Wave**) OM (**b**) Elec (abbr **Megawatts**) MW

my [maɪ] **1** possessive adj (**a**) (singular) mon (ma); (plural) mes; **my job** mon travail; **my wife** ma femme; **my parents** mes parents; **it wasn't MY idea!** ce n'est pas moi qui en ai eu l'idée! (**b**) (with parts of body) **I hit my head** je me suis cogné la tête
2 exclam oh là là!

Myanmar [maɪæn'mɑ:(r)] n le Myanmar

mynah ['maɪnə] n **m. (bird)** mainate m

myopia [maɪ'əʊpɪə] n myopie f; Fig manque m de perspicacité

myopic [maɪ'ɒpɪk] adj myope; Fig à courte vue

myriad ['mɪrɪəd] adj Lit innombrable

myrrh [mɜ:(r)] n myrrhe f

myrtle ['mɜ:təl] n myrte m

myself [maɪ'self] pron (**a**) (reflexive) **I hurt m.** je me suis blessé (**b**) (emphatic) moi-même; **I m. have never...** moi-même n'ai jamais...; **I told her m.** je lui ai dit moi-même; **I'm not m. today** je ne suis pas dans mon état normal aujourd'hui (**c**) (after preposition) moi; **I live by m.** je vis seul; **I bought it for m.** je me le suis acheté; **I talk to m.** je parle tout seul

mysterious [mɪs'tɪərɪəs] adj mystérieux(euse)

mysteriously [mɪs'tɪərɪəslɪ] adv mystérieusement

mystery ['mɪstərɪ] **1** n (pl **mysteries**) mystère m; **m. tour** voyage m surprise
2 adj (guest, prize) surprise inv; (benefactor, witness) mystérieux(euse)

mystic ['mɪstɪk] n & adj mystique mf

mystical ['mɪstɪkəl] adj (person) mystique; (power, ceremony) occulte

mysticism ['mɪstɪsɪzəm] n mysticisme m

mystify ['mɪstɪfaɪ] (pt & pp **mystified**) vt déconcerter

mystique [mɪs'ti:k] n mystère m

myth [mɪθ] n mythe m

mythical ['mɪθɪkəl] adj mythique

mythological [mɪθə'lɒdʒɪkəl] adj mythologique

mythology [mɪ'θɒlədʒɪ] (pl **mystologies**) n mythologie f

myxomatosis [mɪksəmə'təʊsɪs] n myxomatose f

N

N, n [en] *n* (**a**) *(letter)* N, n *m inv* (**b**) *(abbr* **north**) N

NAACP [eneɪeɪsiː'piː] *n Am Pol (abbr* **National Association for the Advancement of Colored People**) = association pour la défense des droits des personnes de couleur

naan [nɑːn] *n* **n. (bread)** = sorte de pain indien servi comme accompagnement

nab [næb] *(pt & pp* **nabbed**) *vt Fam* (**a**) *(catch, arrest)* choper (**b**) *(steal)* piquer, faucher

nadir ['neɪdɪə(r)] *n Astron* nadir *m*; *Fig* **to reach a n.** atteindre son niveau le plus bas

naff [næf] *adj Br Fam (of poor quality)* nul (nulle); *(of poor taste)* ringard(e)

▶**naff off** *vi Br Fam* **n. off!** dégage!

NAFTA ['næftə] *n (abbr* **North American Free Trade Agreement**) ALENA *m*

nag¹ [næg] *n Fam (horse)* carne *f*

nag² **1** *n (person)* enquiquineur(euse) *m,f*
  2 *vt (pt & pp* **nagged**) *(of person)* être sur le dos de; *(of doubt, conscience)* tourmenter; **to n. sb into doing sth** harceler qn pour qu'il fasse qch
  3 *vi* **he's always nagging** il est tout le temps sur mon dos

nagging ['nægɪŋ] **1** *n* harcèlement *m*; **I've had enough of your n.** arrête de me harceler
  2 *adj (pain, doubt, worry)* tenace

nail [neɪl] **1** *n* (**a**) *(in carpentry)* clou *m*; *Fig* **it was another n. in his coffin** c'était un pas de plus vers la fin; *Fig* **the final n. in the coffin** la goutte d'eau qui fait déborder la vase; *Fig* **to hit the n. on the head** mettre le doigt dessus (**b**) *(of person)* ongle *m*; **n. file** lime *f* à ongles; **n. scissors** ciseaux *mpl* à ongles; **n. varnish** *or* **polish** vernis *m* à ongles; **n. varnish** *or* **polish remover** dissolvant *m*
  2 *vt* (**a**) *(fasten)* clouer; **to n. sth shut** clouer qch; *Fig* **to stand nailed to the spot** rester cloué(e) sur place (**b**) *(idioms) Fam* **to n. sb** *(for crime)* coincer qn; *Fam* **to n. a lie** dénoncer un mensonge

▶**nail down** *vt sep (fasten)* clouer, fixer avec des clous; *Fam Fig* **to n. sb down to a date/price** obtenir de qn qu'il fixe une date/un prix

nail-biting ['neɪlbaɪtɪŋ] *adj Fam (contest, finish)* palpitant(e); *(wait)* angoissant(e)

nailbrush ['neɪlbrʌʃ] *n* brosse *f* à ongles

naive [naɪ'iːv] *adj* naïf(ïve)

naively [naɪ'iːvlɪ] *adv* naïvement

naivety [naɪ'iːvətɪ] *n* naïveté *f*

naked ['neɪkɪd] *adj (body, flame)* nu(e); *Fig (aggression, exploitation)* délibéré(e); **visible to the n. eye** visible à l'œil nu

namby-pamby ['næmbɪ'pæmbɪ] *Pej* **1** *n (pl* **namby-pambies**) mollasson(onne) *m,f*
  2 *adj* gnangnan *inv*

name [neɪm] **1** *n* (**a**) *(in general)* nom *m*; **my n. is...** je m'appelle...; **what's your n.?** comment t'appelles-tu?; **to mention sb by n.** désigner nommément qn; **a big n. in the theatre** un grand nom du théâtre; **to put one's n. down (for sth)** s'inscrire (pour qch); **to go by** *or* **under the n. of...** être connu(e) sous le nom de...; **in the n. of...** au nom de...; **in the n. of God** *or* **Heaven!** au nom du Ciel!; **he was President in all but n.** c'était lui le président, même s'il n'en avait pas le titre; **to call sb names** insulter qn; **he hasn't got a penny to his n.** il n'a pas un sou
  (**b**) *(reputation)* réputation *f*; **to have a good/bad n.** avoir (une) bonne/mauvaise réputation; **to have a n. for** être réputé(e) pour; **to make a n. for oneself** se faire un nom
  2 *vt* (**a**) *(give name to, appoint)* nommer; **to n. sb** *Br* **after** *or Am* **for sb** donner à qn le nom de qn
  (**b**) *(designate, identify)* citer; **to n. names** donner des noms; **n. your price** dites votre prix

name-calling ['neɪmkɔːlɪŋ] *n* insultes *fpl*

name-dropper ['neɪmdrɒpə(r)] *n Fam* = personne qui se vante de connaître des gens célèbres

name-dropping ['neɪmdrɒpɪŋ] *n Fam* = fait de se vanter de connaître des gens célèbres

nameless ['neɪmlɪs] *adj (person)* anonyme; **someone who shall remain n.** quelqu'un que je ne nommerai pas

namely ['neɪmlɪ] *adv* c'est-à-dire, à savoir

nameplate ['neɪmpleɪt] *n* plaque *f*

namesake ['neɪmseɪk] *n* homonyme *mf*

Namibia [nə'mɪbɪə] *n* la Namibie

Namibian [nə'mɪbɪən] **1** *n* Namibien(enne) *m,f*
  2 *adj* namibien(enne)

nancy ['nænsɪ] *(pl* **nancies**) *n very Fam* **n. (boy)** *(homosexual)* tapette *f*, pédale *f*; *(effeminate man)* chochotte *f*

nanny ['nænɪ] *(pl* **nannies**) *n* (**a**) *(for children)* jeune fille *f* au pair (**b**) **n. goat** chèvre *f*

nanosecond ['nænəʊsekənd] *n Phys* nanoseconde *f*

nanotechnology ['nænəʊtek'nɒlədʒɪ] *n* nanotechnologie *f*

nap¹ [næp] **1** *n (sleep)* (petit) somme *m*; **to take** *or* **have a n.** faire un (petit) somme
  2 *vi (pt & pp* **napped**) faire un (petit) somme; *Fig* **to be caught napping** être pris(e) au dépourvu

nap² *n (of cloth)* poil *m*

napalm ['neɪpɑːm] *n* napalm *m*

nape [neɪp] *n* **n. (of the neck)** nuque *f*
naphthalene ['næfθəliːn] *n* naphtaline *f*
napkin ['næpkɪn] *n* (**a**) **(table) n.** serviette *f* (de table); **n. ring** rond *m* de serviette (**b**) *Am (sanitary towel)* serviette *f* hygiénique
Naples ['neɪpəlz] *n* Naples
Napoleonic [nəpəʊlɪ'ɒnɪk] *adj* napoléonien(enne)
nappy ['næpɪ] *(pl* **nappies***) n Br* couche *f*; **n. rash** érythème *m* fessier
narc [nɑːk] *n Am Fam* agent *m* de la brigade des stups
narcissus [nɑː'sɪsəs] *(pl* **narcissi** [nɑː'sɪsaɪ] *) n* narcisse *m*
narcosis [nɑː'kəʊsɪs] *n* narcose *f*
narcotic [nɑː'kɒtɪk] **1** *n (medicine)* narcotique *m*; *(illegal drug)* stupéfiant *m*; *Am* **narcotics agent** agent *m* de la brigade des stupéfiants
   2 *adj* narcotique
nark [nɑːk] *n Br Fam* (**a**) *(informer)* indic *m* (**b**) *(irritable person)* râleur(euse) *m,f*
narky ['nɑːkɪ] *adj Br Fam* grognon
narrate [nə'reɪt] *vt* raconter
narrative ['nærətɪv] **1** *n* récit *m*
   2 *adj* narratif(ive)
narrator [nə'reɪtə(r)] *n* narrateur(trice) *m,f*
narrow ['nærəʊ] **1** *adj* étroit(e); *(majority)* faible; **to grow** *or* **become n.** se rétrécir; **to have a n. mind** avoir l'esprit étroit; **to have a n. escape** l'échapper belle; **to win/lose by a n. margin** gagner/perdre de justesse; **to take a n. view of sth** adopter un point de vue étroit sur qch
   2 *vt* **to n. one's eyes** *(in suspicion, anger)* froncer les sourcils
   3 *vi (of road)* se rétrécir, se resserrer
▸**narrow down** *vt sep* limiter, réduire
narrowly ['nærəʊlɪ] *adv (only just)* de peu; **she n. missed being run over** elle a failli se faire écraser
narrow-minded [nærəʊ'maɪndɪd] *adj* étroit(e) d'esprit, borné(e)
NASA ['næsə] *n (abbr* **National Aeronautics and Space Administration***)* NASA *f*
nasal ['neɪzəl] *adj* nasal(e); **to have a n. voice** parler du nez
nastily ['nɑːstɪlɪ] *adv* méchamment
nastiness ['nɑːstɪnɪs] *n (of person, remark)* méchanceté *f*
nasturtium [nə'stɜːʃəm] *n* capucine *f*
nasty ['nɑːstɪ] *adj* mauvais(e); *(crime)* ignoble; *(shock, business)* sale; *(accident)* grave; **to be n. to sb** être méchant(e) avec qn; **to have a n. mind** penser toujours à mal; **to turn n.** *(of situation, weather)* se dégrader, se gâter; **that was a really n. thing to do** c'était vraiment ignoble de sa/ta/*etc* part; *Fig* **it left a n. taste in my mouth** ça m'a laissé un arrière-goût désagréable; **a n. piece of work** *(man)* un sale type; *(woman)* une vraie peste
nation ['neɪʃən] *n* nation *f*
national ['næʃənəl] **1** *n* (**a**) *(person)* ressortissant(e) *m,f* (**b**) *(newspaper)* journal *m* national
   2 *adj* national(e); **n. anthem** hymne *m* national; *Br* **n. curriculum** programme *m* scolaire; **n. debt** dette *f* publique; **N. Front** = parti britannique d'extrême droite; **n. grid** réseau *m* national (d'électricité); *Br* **N. Health Service** = système de santé britannique; **N. Heritage** = organisme ayant pour mission la conservation du patrimoine; *Br* **N. Insurance** contributions

fpl sociales; **n. park** parc *m* national; **n. service** service *m* militaire; **N. Trust** = organisme britannique de conservation du patrimoine historique et naturel

---

National Health Service

Le National Health Service ou NHS fut créé par le gouvernement travailliste en 1948, donnant accès à chacun aux soins médicaux gratuits. Cependant, suite notamment aux coupes budgétaires réalisées dans les années 80, le système de santé britannique est aujourd'hui en crise. Au cours des dernières années, la polémique autour du National Health Service s'est intensifiée et est devenu un enjeu majeur lors des élections en Grande-Bretagne.

---

nationalism ['næʃənəlɪzəm] *n* nationalisme *m*
nationalist ['næʃənəlɪst] *n & adj* nationaliste *mf*
nationalistic [næʃənə'lɪstɪk] *adj* nationaliste
nationality [næʃə'nælɪtɪ] *(pl* **nationalities***) n* nationalité *f*
nationalization [næʃənəlaɪ'zeɪʃən] *n* nationalisation *f*
nationalize ['næʃənəlaɪz] *vt* nationaliser
nationally ['næʃənəlɪ] *adv* nationalement
nationwide ['neɪʃənwaɪd] **1** *adj* national(e)
   2 *adv* dans tout le pays
native ['neɪtɪv] **1** *n (person)* natif(ive) *m,f*; *(plant)* plante *f* indigène; *(animal)* animal *m* indigène; **to be a n. of** être originaire de; **she speaks English like a n.** elle parle anglais comme si c'était sa langue maternelle
   2 *adj* natal(e); **he returned to his n. London** il est retourné à Londres, sa ville natale; **n. American** Indien(enne) *m,f* d'Amérique; **n. land** pays *m* natal; **n. language** langue *f* maternelle; **I'm not a n. speaker of Spanish** ma langue maternelle n'est pas l'espagnol
Nativity [nə'tɪvɪtɪ] *n Rel* **the N.** la Nativité *f*; **N. play** mystère *m* de la Nativité
NATO ['neɪtəʊ] *n Mil (abbr* **North Atlantic Treaty Organization***)* l'OTAN *f*
natter ['nætə(r)] *Br Fam* **1** *n* **to have a n.** bavarder, papoter (**about** sur)
   2 *vi* bavarder, papoter (**about** sur)
natty ['nætɪ] *adj Fam* chic *inv*
natural ['nætʃərəl] **1** *adj* (**a**) *(colour, taste)* naturel(elle); *(gift, talent)* inné(e); **to die from n. causes** mourir de mort naturelle; **n. childbirth** accouchement *m* naturel; **n. disaster** catastrophe *f* naturelle; **n. gas** gaz *m* naturel; **n. history** histoire *f* naturelle; **n. mother** mère *f* naturelle; **n. resources** ressources *fpl* naturelles; **n. sciences** sciences *fpl* naturelles; **n. yoghurt** yaourt *m* nature (**b**) *(normal)* naturel(elle); **it's only n.** c'est tout à fait naturel; *Ind* **n. wastage** = réduction des effectifs due aux départs d'employés non remplacés (**c**) *(unaffected)* naturel(elle)
   2 *n* **he's a n. as an actor** c'est un acteur né
naturalism ['nætʃərəlɪzəm] *n* naturalisme *m*
naturalist ['nætʃərəlɪst] *n* naturaliste *mf*
naturalistic ['nætʃərəlɪstɪk] *adj* naturaliste
naturalization [nætʃərəlaɪ'zeɪʃən] *n* naturalisation *f*
naturalize ['nætʃərəlaɪz] *vt* naturaliser
naturally ['nætʃərəlɪ] *adv* (**a**) *(unaffectedly)* naturellement; *(by nature)* de nature; **to come n. to sb** être un don chez qn (**b**) *(of course)* naturellement

nature ['neɪtʃə(r)] n (**a**) *(the natural world)* nature f; **to let n. take its course** laisser faire la nature; **n. reserve** réserve f naturelle; *Sch* **n. study** sciences fpl naturelles; **n. trail** = sentier aménagé doté d'explications concernant la faune et la flore (**b**) *(character)* nature f; **to have a jealous n.** être d'une nature jalouse; **it's not in her n.** ça n'est pas dans sa nature; **to be shy by n.** être timide de nature (**c**) *(sort)* nature f, genre m; **problems of this n.** des problèmes de cette nature; *Formal* **what is the n. of your complaint?** quelle est la nature de votre réclamation?

naturist ['neɪtʃərɪst] n & adj naturiste mf

naught [nɔːt] n (**a**) *Lit (nothing)* néant m; **to come to n.** se réduire à néant (**b**) *Am* = **nought**

naughtily ['nɔːtɪlɪ] adv **to behave n.** être vilain(e)

naughty ['nɔːtɪ] adj *(child)* méchant(e), vilain(e); *(book, picture)* coquin(e)

nausea ['nɔːzɪə] n nausée f

nauseate ['nɔːzɪeɪt] vt donner la nausée à; *Fig* écœurer

nauseating ['nɔːzɪeɪtɪŋ] adj *also Fig* écœurant(e)

nauseous ['nɔːzɪəs] adj *(disgusting)* écœurant(e); **to feel n.** avoir envie de vomir

nautical ['nɔːtɪkəl] adj nautique; **n. mile** mille m marin *ou* nautique

naval ['neɪvəl] adj naval(e); **n. battle** bataille f navale; **the N. College** ≃ l'École f navale; **n. officer** officier m de marine

nave [neɪv] n *(of church)* nef f

navel ['neɪvəl] n nombril m

navel-gazing ['neɪvəlɡeɪzɪŋ] n nombrilisme m

navigable ['nævɪɡəbəl] adj navigable

navigate ['nævɪɡeɪt] **1** vt (**a**) *(seas)* naviguer sur; *(ship, plane)* piloter (**b**) *Comput (Web site)* naviguer sur **2** vi *(in ship, plane)* naviguer; *(in car)* faire le pilote

navigation [nævɪ'ɡeɪʃən] n navigation f

navigational [nævɪ'ɡeɪʃənəl] adj de navigation

navigator ['nævɪɡeɪtə(r)] n *(in ship, plane)* navigateur(trice) m,f; *(in car)* copilote mf

navvy ['nævɪ] (pl **navvies**) n Br terrassier m

navy ['neɪvɪ] (pl **navies**) n marine f; **n. (blue)** bleu marine m inv

Nazi ['nɑːtsɪ] **1** n Nazi(e) m,f **2** adj nazi(e)

Nazism ['nɑːtsɪzəm] n nazisme m

NB [en'biː] *(abbr* **nota bene**) NB

NBA [enbiː'eɪ] n *Am (abbr* **National Basketball Association**) fédération américaine de basket-ball

NCO [ensiː'əʊ] n *Mil (abbr* **non-commissioned officer**) sous-officier m

NE *(abbr* **northeast**) N-E

Neanderthal [nɪ'ændətɑːl] **1** n (**a**) *(during Stone Age)* homme m de Neandertal (**b**) *Fig (uncivilized man)* homme m des cavernes **2** adj (**a**) *(during Stone Age)* **N. man** homme m de Neandertal (**b**) *Fig (attitude, behaviour)* d'homme des cavernes

Neapolitan [nɪə'pɒlɪtən] **1** n Napolitain(e) m,f **2** adj napolitain(e)

near [nɪə(r)] **1** adj proche; **to the nearest metre** au mètre près; **in the n. future** dans un avenir proche; **it was a n. thing** il s'en est fallu de peu; **the N. East** le Proche-Orient **2** adv près; **to be n. to sth** *(in space)* être près de qch; *(in time)* être proche de qch; **n. at hand** *(of thing)* tout près; *(of event)* tout proche; **to be n. to doing sth** être sur le point de faire qch; **n. to tears/despair** au bord des larmes/du désespoir; **she's nowhere n. finished** elle est loin d'avoir fini; **a n. total failure** un échec presque total **3** prep près de; **he came n. to being run over** il a failli se faire écraser; **nobody comes anywhere n. her** *(in skill, performance)* il n'y a personne à son niveau **4** n *Fam* **my nearest and dearest** mes plus proches parents **5** vt (s')approcher de; **to be nearing completion** être presque terminé(e)

nearby 1 adj ['nɪəbaɪ] proche **2** adv [nɪə'baɪ] tout près

nearly ['nɪəlɪ] adv presque; **we're n. there** *(finished)* nous y sommes presque; *(at destination)* nous sommes presque arrivés; **he n. died** il a failli mourir; **not n. enough money/time** vraiment pas assez d'argent/de temps; **not n. so beautiful** bien moins beau (belle)

nearly-new ['nɪəlɪ'njuː] adj = d'occasion mais en parfait état

nearside ['nɪəsaɪd] **1** n *(on right)* côté m droit; *(on left)* côté m gauche **2** adj *(on right)* droit(e); *(on left)* gauche

near-sighted [nɪə'saɪtɪd] adj Am myope

neat [niːt] adj (**a**) *(in habits)* ordonné(e); *(in appearance)* soigné(e); *(work, handwriting)* soigné; *(room, house)* bien rangé(e); **to make a n. job of doing sth** faire qch très bien (**b**) *(undiluted)* pur(e) (**c**) *Am Fam (good)* super inv

▶**neaten up** ['niːtən] vt sep *(hair, garden)* arranger; *(piece of work)* peaufiner

neatly ['niːtlɪ] adv (**a**) *(carefully)* soigneusement (**b**) *(skilfully)* habilement, adroitement

neatness ['niːtnɪs] n *(of appearance)* aspect m soigné; *(of work)* soin m; *(of handwriting)* netteté f; *(of room, house)* ordre m

nebula ['nebjʊlə] (pl **nebulas** or **nebulae** ['nebjʊlaɪ]) n *Astron* nébuleuse f

nebulous ['nebjʊləs] adj *(vague)* nébuleux(euse)

necessarily [nesɪ'serəlɪ] adv nécessairement, forcément

necessary ['nesɪsərɪ] **1** adj nécessaire; **it is n. to remind them** il faut le leur rappeler; **to do what is n.** faire le nécessaire; **when(ever) n.** si nécessaire, si besoin est; **a n. evil** un mal nécessaire **2** n *Fam* **the n.** *(thing, action)* le nécessaire; *(money)* l'argent

necessitate [nɪ'sesɪteɪt] vt *Formal* nécessiter, rendre nécessaire

necessity [nɪ'sesɪtɪ] (pl **necessities**) n nécessité f; **out of n.** par nécessité; **the necessities** *(things needed)* le nécessaire; *Prov* **n. is the mother of invention** en cas de besoin, on trouve toujours une solution

neck [nek] **1** n (**a**) *(of person, animal)* cou m; *(of dress)* encolure f, col m; *(of bottle)* goulot m; *(of guitar, violin)* manche m; *(of land)* langue f; *(of lamb, beef)* collier m (**b**) *(idioms)* *Fam* **to risk one's n.** risquer sa peau; *Fam* **he got it in the n.** il s'est pris un savon; *Fam* **he's in it up to his n.** il est impliqué là-dedans jusqu'au cou; **to finish n. and n.** finir au coude à coude; *Fam* **to stick one's n. out** se lancer; *Fam* **in this n. of the woods** dans le coin **2** vi *Fam (of couple)* se peloter

necklace ['neklɪs] *n* collier *m*

neckline ['neklaɪn] *n* encolure *f*

necromancy ['nekrəʊmænsɪ] *n Formal* nécromancie *f*

nectar ['nektə(r)] *n* nectar *m*

nectarine ['nektəriːn] *n* nectarine *f*, brugnon *m*

née [neɪ] *adj* née; **Mrs Richardson, n. Johnston** Mme Richardson, née Johnston

need [niːd] **1** *n* besoin *m* (**for** de); **there is no n. to shout/worry** inutile de crier/de t'inquiéter; **if n. be** en cas de besoin; **to be in n.** *(poor)* être dans le besoin; **to be in n. of sth** avoir besoin de qch; **in time of n.** dans les moments difficiles; **their n. is greater than mine** ils en ont plus besoin que moi

2 *vt* **to n. sth/to do sth** avoir besoin de qch/de faire qch; **I n. more time** il me faut plus de temps; **you'll n. to take more money** il te faudra prendre plus d'argent, il faudra que tu prennes plus d'argent; **I didn't n. to be reminded of it** je n'avais pas besoin qu'on me le rappelle, il était inutile de me le rappeler; **his hair needs cutting** il a besoin d'une coupe de cheveux; **the torch needs a new battery** la lampe a besoin d'une nouvelle pile; **this work needs a lot of patience** ce travail demande beaucoup de patience; *Ironic* **that's all I n.!** il ne (me) manquait plus que ça!

3 *modal aux v*

La forme modale de **need** est la même à toutes les personnes, et s'utilise sans **do/does** (**he need only worry about himself**; **need she go?**; **it needn't matter**).

you needn't worry inutile de t'inquiéter; **you needn't wait** tu n'as pas besoin d'attendre; **n. I say more?** ai-je besoin d'en dire plus?

needful ['niːdfʊl] *n Fam* **to do the n.** faire le nécessaire

needle ['niːdəl] **1** *n* aiguille *f*; **it's like looking for a n. in a haystack** c'est comme chercher une aiguille dans une botte de foin; *Fam Fig* **to give sb the n.** taper sur les nerfs de qn; *Fam* **n. match** *(in football)* match *m* acharné

2 *vt Fam* asticoter

needlecraft ['niːdəlkraːft] *n* travaux *mpl* d'aiguille

needless ['niːdlɪs] *adj (waste, suffering, worry)* inutile; *(remark)* déplacé(e); **n. to say...** il va de soi que...

needlessly ['niːdlɪslɪ] *adv* inutilement

needlework ['niːdəlwɜːk] *n (sewing)* couture *f*; *(embroidery)* broderie *f*

need-to-know [niːdtə'nəʊ] *adj* **information is given on a n. basis** les renseignements ne sont donnés qu'aux personnes concernées

needy ['niːdɪ] **1** *npl* **the n.** les nécessiteux *mpl*

2 *adj (person)* nécessiteux(euse), dans le besoin

nefarious [nɪ'feərɪəs] *adj* infâme, ignoble

negate [nɪ'geɪt] *vt (effect)* annuler; *(work, efforts)* anéantir

negation [nɪ'geɪʃən] *n (of work, efforts)* anéantissement *m*

negative ['negətɪv] **1** *n* **(a)** *Gram* **the n.** la forme négative; **to answer in the n.** répondre par la négative **(b)** *(of photo)* négatif *m*

2 *adj* négatif(ive); **don't be so n.** ne sois pas si négatif; *Fin* **n. equity** plus-value *f* immobilière négative, = situation où l'acquéreur d'un bien immobilier reste redevable de l'emprunt contracté alors que son

logement enregistre une moins-value; **n. feedback** réaction *f* négative

negatively ['negətɪvlɪ] *adv* négativement

negativity [negə'tɪvɪtɪ] *n* négativité *f*

neglect [nɪ'glekt] **1** *n (of person)* négligence *f*; *(of machine, garden)* manque *m* d'entretien; *(of duties, responsibilities)* manquement *m*; **from** *or* **through n.** par négligence

2 *vt* **(a)** *(not care for)* négliger; **to n. oneself** se négliger **(b)** *(ignore) (duties, responsibilities)* manquer à; *(post)* abandonner; **to n. to do sth** négliger de faire qch

neglectful [nɪ'glektfʊl] *adj* négligent(e); **to be n. of sb/sth** négliger qn/qch

negligée ['neglɪʒeɪ] *n* négligé *m*, déshabillé *m*

negligence ['neglɪdʒəns] *n* négligence *f*; *(of duties, responsibilities)* manquement *m* (**of** à)

negligent ['neglɪdʒənt] *adj* négligent(e)

negligently ['neglɪdʒəntlɪ] *adv* négligemment

negligible ['neglɪdʒɪbəl] *adj* négligeable

negotiable [nɪ'gəʊʃəbəl] *adj (demand, salary)* négociable; *(price)* à débattre; *(obstacle)* franchissable; *(road)* praticable

negotiate [nɪ'gəʊʃɪeɪt] **1** *vt* **(a)** *(price, treaty, salary, contract)* négocier **(b)** *(obstacle)* franchir; *(difficulty)* surmonter; *(bend)* négocier

2 *vi* négocier

negotiation [nɪgəʊʃɪ'eɪʃən] *n* négociation *f*; **under n.** en négociation

negotiator [nɪ'gəʊʃɪeɪtə(r)] *n* négociateur(trice) *m,f*

Negress ['niːgrɪs] *n Old-fashioned* négresse *f*

Negro ['niːgrəʊ] *Old-fashioned* **1** *n (pl* **Negroes)** nègre *m*

2 *adj* nègre; **N. spiritual** *(song)* Negro spiritual *m*

neigh [neɪ] **1** *n* hennissement *m*

2 *vi* hennir

neighbor, neighborhood *etc Am* = **neighbour, neighbourhood** *etc*

neighbour, *Am* **neighbor** ['neɪbə(r)] *n* voisin(e) *m,f*; **to be a good n.** être bon voisin

neighbourhood, *Am* **neighborhood** ['neɪbəhʊd] *n* **(a)** *(district)* quartier *m*; *(people)* voisinage *m*; *Br* **n. watch** = système de surveillance mis en œuvre par les habitants d'un quartier **(b)** *(vicinity)* voisinage *m*, environs *mpl*; **in the n.** dans les environs; **a figure in the n. of £2,000** un chiffre avoisinant les 2000 livres

neighbouring, *Am* **neighboring** ['neɪbərɪŋ] *adj* voisin(e)

neighbourliness, *Am* **neighborliness** ['neɪbəlɪnɪs] *n (relations fpl de)* bon voisinage *m*

neighbourly, *Am* **neighborly** ['neɪbəlɪ] *adj* **they're very n.** ce sont de très bons voisins

neither ['naɪðə(r), 'niːðə(r)] **1** *conj* **n.... nor...** ni... ni...; **n. you nor your brother** ni toi ni ton frère; **he n. drinks nor smokes** il ne boit pas et ne fume pas non plus; *Fig* **that's n. here nor there** là n'est pas la question

2 *adv* **n. do I** moi non plus; **if you don't go n. shall I** si tu n'y vas pas, moi non plus; **the workers aren't happy and n. is the management** les ouvriers ne sont pas contents et la direction non plus

3 *adj* **n. driver was injured** aucun des deux conducteurs n'a été blessé

4 *pron* **n. (of them) will do** aucun (des deux) ne fera l'affaire; **n. of my two brothers can come** aucun de mes deux frères ne peut venir

neo- ['niːəʊ] *pref* néo-

neoclassical [niːəʊ'klæsɪkəl] *adj* néoclassique

neofascist [niːəʊ'fæʃɪst] *n & adj* néofasciste *mf*

neolithic [niːəʊ'lɪθɪk] *adj* néolithique

neon ['niːɒn] *n* néon *m*; **n. light** lumière *f* au néon; **n. sign** enseigne *f* au néon

Nepal [nɪ'pɔːl] *n* le Népal

Nepalese [nepə'liːz], **Nepali** [ne'pɔːlɪ] **1** *n* (*pl* **Nepalese** *or* **Nepalis**) (**a**) *(person)* Népalais(e) *m,f* (**b**) *(language)* népalais *m*
  2 *adj* népalais(e)

nephew ['nefjuː] *n* neveu *m*

nepotism ['nepətɪzəm] *n* népotisme *m*

Neptune ['neptjuːn] *n (planet)* Neptune *f*

nerd [nɜːd] *n Fam Pej (stupid person)* crétin(e) *m,f*; *(unfashionable person)* ringard(e) *m,f*

nerdy ['nɜːdɪ] *adj Fam Pej* ringard(e)

nerve [nɜːv] **1** *n* (**a**) *(in body)* nerf *m*; *Fam* **to get on sb's nerves** taper sur les nerfs à qn; **her nerves were in a terrible state** elle était à bout de nerfs; *Anat* **n. cell** cellule *f* nerveuse; *Fig* **n. centre** *(of organization)* centre *m* nerveux; **n. gas** gaz *m* neurotoxique (**b**) *(courage)* courage *m*; **to have nerves of steel** avoir des nerfs d'acier; **to keep/lose one's n.** garder/perdre son sang-froid (**c**) *Fam (cheek)* culot *m*; **to have the n. to do sth** avoir le culot de faire qch
  2 *vt* **to n. oneself to do sth** s'armer de courage pour faire qch

nerve-(w)racking ['nɜːvrækɪŋ] *adj* éprouvant(e)

nervous ['nɜːvəs] *adj* (**a**) *(apprehensive)* nerveux(-euse), anxieux(euse); **to be n. about sth/doing sth** être nerveux *ou* anxieux à l'idée de qch/de faire qch (**b**) *(energy, exhaustion)* nerveux(euse); **n. breakdown** dépression *f* nerveuse; **n. system** système *m* nerveux

nervously ['nɜːvəslɪ] *adv* nerveusement

nervousness ['nɜːvəsnɪs] *n* nervosité *f*

nervy ['nɜːvɪ] *adj Fam (tense)* nerveux(euse)

nest [nest] **1** *n* (*of bird, insects*) nid *m*; *Fig (of criminals)* repaire *m*; *Fig* **to fly the n.** quitter le nid; **n. of tables** tables *fpl* gigognes; *Fig* **n. egg** pécule *m*
  2 *vi (of bird)* faire son nid

nestle ['nesəl] *vi* se pelotonner, se blottir; **to n. up to sb** se blottir contre qn

nestling ['neslɪŋ] *n* oisillon *m*

Net [net] *n Fam Comput* **the N.** le Net

net¹ [net] **1** *n* filet *m*; *Fig* **to slip through the n.** passer à travers les mailles du filet; **n. curtain** voilage *m*
  2 *vt (pt & pp* **netted**) *(animals, fish)* prendre au filet; *Fig (drugs, criminals)* mettre la main sur; *(donations, contracts)* récolter

net² **1** *adj (weight, price, profit)* net (nette)
  2 *vt (earn)* **to n. £2,000** gagner 2000 livres net

netball ['netbɔːl] *n* = sport féminin proche du basketball

nethead ['nethed] *n Fam Comput* accro *mf* de l'Internet

Netherlands ['neðələndz] *npl* **the N.** les Pays-Bas *mpl*

netiquette ['netɪket] *n Fam Comput* netiquette *f*

netsurfer ['netsɜːfə(r)] *n Comput* internaute *mf*

netting ['netɪŋ] *n* filet *m*

nettle ['netəl] **1** *n (plant)* ortie *f*
  2 *vt (irritate)* irriter, énerver

network ['netwɜːk] **1** *n* réseau *m*
  2 *vi (make contacts)* établir un réseau de contacts

networking ['netwɜːkɪŋ] *n (making contacts)* établissement *m* d'un réseau de contacts

neural ['njʊərəl] *adj Anat* neural(e)

neuralgia [njʊ'rældʒə] *n* névralgie *f*

neurologist [njʊə'rɒlədʒɪst] *n* neurologue *mf*

neurology [njʊə'rɒlədʒɪ] *n* neurologie *f*

neuron ['njʊərɒn] *n Anat* neurone *m*

neurosis [njʊ'rəʊsɪs] *(pl* **neuroses** [njʊ'rəʊsiːz] *) n* névrose *f*

neurosurgery ['njʊərəʊˌsɜːdʒərɪ] *n* neurochirurgie *f*

neurotic [njʊ'rɒtɪk] **1** *n* névrosé(e) *m,f*
  2 *adj* névrosé(e); **to be n. about sth** être obsédé(e) par qch

neuter ['njuːtə(r)] **1** *n Gram* neutre *m*
  2 *adj Gram* neutre
  3 *vt (animal)* castrer, châtrer

neutral ['njuːtrəl] **1** *n* (**a**) *(country)* pays *m* neutre; *(person)* personne *f* neutre (**b**) *(of car)* point *m* mort; **in n.** au point mort
  2 *adj (country, colour)* neutre

neutrality [njuː'trælɪtɪ] *n* neutralité *f*

neutralize ['njuːtrəlaɪz] *vt* neutraliser

neutrino [njʊ'triːnəʊ] *(pl* **neutrinos**) *n Phys* neutrino *m*

neutron ['njuːtrɒn] *n Phys* neutron *m*; **n. bomb** bombe *f* à neutrons

never ['nevə(r)] *adv* (**a**) *(not once)* jamais; **I've n. met him** je ne l'ai jamais rencontré; **n. again!** plus jamais!; **he's n. yet been beaten** il n'a encore jamais été battu; **I've n. yet understood why** je n'ai jamais compris pourquoi (**b**) *(emphatic negative)* **she n. said a word** elle n'a pas dit un mot; **I n. expected this** je ne m'attendais vraiment pas à ça; **he n. even congratulated me** il ne m'a même pas félicité; *Br Fam* **well I n.!** ça alors!

never-ending [nevər'endɪŋ] *adj* interminable

never-never ['nevə'nevə(r)] *n Br Fam* **to buy sth on the n.** acheter qch à crédit

nevertheless [nevəðə'les] *adv* néanmoins, cependant

new [njuː] *adj* nouveau(elle); *(not used)* neuf (neuve); **what's n.?** quoi de neuf?; **that's nothing n.!** ça n'est pas nouveau!; **she's n. to this work** elle débute dans ce travail; **to be n. to a town** être nouveau dans une ville; **N. Age** *(music, thinking)* new age *inv*; **N. Brunswick** le Nouveau-Brunswick; **N. Caledonia** la Nouvelle-Calédonie; **N. Delhi** New Delhi; **N. England** la Nouvelle-Angleterre; **N. Guinea** la Nouvelle-Guinée; *Br Pol* **N. Labour** = nouveau nom donné au parti travailliste vers le milieu des années 90 dans le souci d'en moderniser l'image; **N. Man** homme *m* de la nouvelle génération *(qui participe équitablement à l'éducation des enfants et aux tâches ménagères)*; **N. Mexico** le Nouveau-Mexique; **n. moon** nouvelle lune *f*; **N. Orleans** la Nouvelle-Orléans; **N. South Wales** la Nouvelle-Galles du Sud; **the N. Testament** le Nouveau Testament; **n. town** ville *f* nouvelle; **n. wave** *(trend)* Nouvelle Vague *f*; **the N. World** le Nouveau Monde; **N. Year** Nouvel An *m*; **N. Year's Day** le jour de l'an; **N. Year's Eve** la Saint-Sylvestre; **N. Year's resolution** résolution *f* du jour de l'an; **N. York** New York; **N. Yorker** New-Yorkais(e) *m,f*

newbie ['njuːbɪ] *n Fam* (**a**) *Am (new recruit)* bleu(e) *m,f* (**b**) *Comput (Internet user)* internaute *mf* novice

newborn ['njuːbɔːn] *adj* nouveau-né(e); **n. baby** nouveau-né(e) *m,f*

newcomer ['njuːkʌmə(r)] *n* nouveau(elle) venu(e) *m,f* (**to** dans)

newfangled [njuː'fæŋgəld] *adj Pej (idea)* nouveau(elle); *(gadget)* dernier cri *inv*

Newfoundland ['njuːfəndlænd] *n* Terre-Neuve

newly ['njuːlɪ] *adv* nouvellement, récemment

newlyweds ['njuːlɪwedz] *npl* jeunes mariés *mpl*

newness ['njuːnɪs] *n (of design)* nouveauté *f*; *(of clothing)* état *m* neuf

news [njuːz] *n* nouvelles *fpl*; *(on TV, radio)* informations *fpl*; **a piece of n.** une nouvelle; **in the n.** sous les feux de l'actualité; *Fam* **he's bad n.** il n'est pas fréquentable; *Fam* **that's n. to me!** première nouvelle!; *Prov* **no n. is good n.** pas de nouvelles, bonnes nouvelles; **n. agency** agence *f* de presse; **n. bulletin** bulletin *m* d'informations; **n. conference** conférence *f* de presse; **n. item** information *f*, nouvelle *f*; **n. summary** rappel *m* des titres

newsagent ['njuːzeɪdʒənt] *n Br* marchand(e) *m,f* de journaux; **n.'s (shop)** marchand *m* de journaux

newscaster ['njuːzkɑːstə(r)] *n* présentateur(trice) *m,f* du journal

newsdealer ['njuːzdiːlə(r)] *n Am* marchand(e) *m,f* de journaux

newsflash ['njuːzflæʃ] *n* flash *m* d'informations

newsgroup ['njuːzgruːp] *n Comput* newsgroup *m*, forum *m* de discussion

newsletter ['njuːzletə(r)] *n* bulletin *m*

newspaper ['njuːzpeɪpə(r)] *n* journal *m*; **n. report** reportage *m*

newspaperman ['njuːzpeɪpəmæn] *n (reporter)* journaliste *m*; *(proprietor)* propriétaire *m* d'un journal

newsprint ['njuːzprɪnt] *n* papier *m* journal

newsreader ['njuːzriːdə(r)] *n* présentateur(trice) *m,f* du journal

newsreel ['njuːzriːl] *n* actualités *fpl*

newsroom ['njuːzruːm] *n* (salle *f* de) rédaction *f*

newsstand ['njuːzstænd] *n* kiosque *m* à journaux

newsworthy ['njuːzwɜːðɪ] *adj* d'un intérêt médiatique

newt [njuːt] *n* triton *m*

New Zealand [njuː'ziːlənd] *n* la Nouvelle-Zélande

New Zealander [njuː'ziːləndə(r)] *n* Néo-Zélandais(e) *m,f*

next [nekst] **1** *adj* (**a**) *(in space)* d'à côté; **n. door** à côté (**b**) *(in time, order)* prochain(e); *(subsequent)* suivant(e), d'après; **n. week** la semaine prochaine; **the n. week** la semaine suivante *ou* d'après; **the year after n.** dans deux ans; **the n. time** la prochaine fois; **your name is n. on the list** votre nom est le suivant sur la liste; **the n. but one** pas le prochain, mais celui d'après; **(the) n. to arrive was Carmen** Carmen est arrivée ensuite; **who's n.?** c'est à qui?; **n. please!** au suivant!; **the n. size up/down** la taille au-dessus/au-dessous

2 *adv* (**a**) *(in space)* **n. to** à côté de (**b**) *(in time, order)* ensuite, après; *Fam* **what will they think of n.?** qu'est-ce qu'ils vont encore inventer?; **n. to Paris I like Madrid best** après Paris, la ville que je préfère, c'est Madrid; **when shall we meet n.?** quand nous reverrons-nous?; **the n. best thing would be to...** à défaut, le mieux serait de...; **the n. fastest after the Ferrari was...** la voiture la plus rapide après la Ferrari était...; **who is the n. oldest/youngest after Mark?**

qui est le plus âgé/le plus jeune après Mark?; **n. to nothing** quasiment rien; **there is n. to no evidence** il n'y a pratiquement aucune preuve; **in n. to no time** en un rien de temps

next-door ['neks'dɔː(r)] *adj* d'à côté; **n. neighbour** voisin(e) *m,f* d'à côté

next-of-kin [nekstəv'kɪn] *n* plus proche parent *m*

NFL [enef'el] *n Am (abbr* **National Football League**) = fédération nationale de football américain

NGO [endʒiː'əʊ] *n (abbr* **non-governmental organization**) ONG *f*

NHS [eneɪtʃ'es] *n Br (abbr* **National Health Service**) = système de santé britannique

NI [en'aɪ] *n Br (abbr* **National Insurance**) contributions *fpl* sociales

nib [nɪb] *n* plume *f*

nibble ['nɪbəl] **1** *n* **to have a n. at sth** grignoter qch; **nibbles** *(snacks)* amuse-gueule *mpl*
   2 *vt* grignoter

Nicaragua [nɪkə'rægjʊə] *n* le Nicaragua

Nicaraguan [nɪkə'rægjʊən] **1** *n* Nicaraguayen(enne) *m,f*
   2 *adj* nicaraguayen(enne)

nice [naɪs] *adj* (**a**) *(pleasant)* agréable; *(physically attractive)* beau (belle); *(tasty)* bon (bonne); **a n. idea** une bonne idée; **to be n. to sb** se montrer aimable avec qn; **to have a n. time** bien s'amuser; **have a n. day!** bonne journée!; **it was n. of her to...** c'était gentil de sa part de...; *Ironic* **that's a n. way to behave!** en voilà des manières! (**b**) *(intensive)* **n. and easy** très facile; **n. and handy** bien commode; **a n. warm bath** un bain bien chaud

nice-looking ['naɪslʊkɪŋ] *adj* beau (belle)

nicely ['naɪslɪ] *adv (ask)* gentiment; *(behave, sit)* bien; **to be doing n.** aller bien; **to do n. for oneself** bien se débrouiller

niceties ['naɪsɪtɪz] *npl* subtilités *fpl*

niche [niːʃ] *n (in wall)* niche *f*; *(in market)* créneau *m*; **to find one's n. (in life)** trouver sa voie

nick [nɪk] **1** *n* (**a**) *(in wood, on face)* entaille *f* (**b**) **in the n. of time** juste à temps (**c**) *Fam (condition)* **in good/bad n.** en bon/mauvais état (**d**) *Br Fam (prison)* taule *f*; *(police station)* poste *m*
   2 *vt* (**a**) *(cut)* entailler (**b**) *Br Fam (arrest)* pincer, épingler
   (**c**) *Br Fam (steal)* piquer, faucher

nickel ['nɪkəl] *n* (**a**) *(metal)* nickel *m* (**b**) *Am (coin)* pièece *f* de cinq cents

nickname ['nɪkneɪm] **1** *n* surnom *m*
   2 *vt* surnommer

nicotine ['nɪkətiːn] *n* nicotine *f*; **n. patch** timbre *m ou* patch *m* anti-tabac

niece [niːs] *n* nièce *f*

niff [nɪf] *Br Fam* **1** *n (bad smell)* puanteur *f*
   2 *vi (smell bad)* puer

nifty ['nɪftɪ] *adj Fam* (**a**) *(idea, device)* génial(e) (**b**) *(agile)* vif (vive)

Niger ['naɪdʒə(r)] *n* le Niger

Nigeria [naɪ'dʒɪərɪə] *n* le Nigéria

Nigerian [naɪ'dʒɪərɪən] **1** *n* Nigérien(e) *m,f*
   2 *adj* nigérian(e)

niggardly ['nɪgədlɪ] *adj (person)* avare, pingre; *(sum, portion)* maigre

nigger ['nɪgə(r)] *n* nègre (négresse) *m,f*, = terme raciste désignant un Noir

niggle ['nɪg(ə)l] **1** vt (worry) tracasser
  2 vi (be overfussy) couper les cheveux en quatre; **to n. (away) at sb** (worry) tracasser qn; (hassle) enquiquiner qn

niggling ['nɪgəlɪŋ] adj (detail) insignifiant(e); (pain, doubt) persistant(e); **I have a n. feeling that...** je ne peux pas m'empêcher de penser que...

nigh [naɪ] adv (**a**) Lit (near) près, proche; **the end is n.!** la fin est proche! (**b**) **well n.** (almost) presque

night [naɪt] n nuit f; (evening) soir m; **at n.** la nuit; (in the evening) le soir; **late at n.** tard dans la nuit; **all n.** toute la nuit; **last n.** la nuit dernière; (evening) hier soir; **tomorrow n.** demain soir; **on Thursday n.** jeudi soir; **good n.!** (when going to bed) bonne nuit!, bonsoir!; (when leaving) bonsoir!; **to work nights** travailler la nuit; **to have a n. out** sortir; **let's make a n. of it** et si on continuait la soirée?; **n. flight** vol m de nuit; **n. owl** oiseau m de nuit; **n. school** cours m du soir; Am **n. table** table f de chevet; **n. watchman** veilleur m de nuit

nightcap ['naɪtkæp] n (**a**) (hat) bonnet m de nuit (**b**) (drink) petit verre m (avant d'aller se coucher)

nightclub ['naɪtklʌb] n boîte f de nuit, Can club m de nuit

nightdress ['naɪtdres] n chemise f de nuit

nightfall ['naɪtfɔ:l] n tombée f de la nuit; **at n.** à la nuit tombante

nightgown ['naɪtgaʊn] n chemise f de nuit

nightie ['naɪtɪ] n Fam chemise f de nuit

nightingale ['naɪtɪŋgeɪl] n rossignol m

nightjar ['naɪtdʒɑ:(r)] n engoulevent m (d'Europe)

nightlife ['naɪtlaɪf] n vie f nocturne; **there's not much n.** il n'y a pas grand-chose à faire le soir

nightlong ['naɪtlɒŋ] adj qui dure toute la nuit

nightly ['naɪtlɪ] **1** adj de toutes les nuits; (in the evening) du soir
  2 adv toutes les nuits; (in the evening) tous les soirs

nightmare ['naɪtmeə(r)] n also Fig cauchemar m

nightmarish ['naɪtmeərɪʃ] adj cauchemardesque

nightshirt ['naɪtʃɜ:t] n chemise f de nuit

night-time ['naɪttaɪm] **1** n nuit f; **at n.** la nuit
  2 adj nocturne

nihilistic [naɪ(h)ɪ'lɪstɪk] adj nihiliste

nil [nɪl] n néant m; (in sport) zéro m; **two n.** deux à zéro

Nile [naɪl] n **the N.** le Nil

nimble ['nɪmbəl] adj (person) souple; (leap, movement) leste; (fingers) preste; (mind) vif (vive)

nimbly ['nɪmblɪ] adv avec souplesse

nincompoop ['nɪŋkəmpu:p] n Fam nigaud(e) m,f

nine [naɪn] **1** n neuf m inv; Fam **dressed up to the nines** sur son trente et un
  2 adj neuf; **n. times out of ten** neuf fois sur dix; **a n.-to-five job** un travail de bureau; **to have n. lives** (of person) avoir l'âme chevillée au corps; see also **eight**

nineteen [naɪn'ti:n] **1** n dix-neuf m inv; Br Fam **to talk n. to the dozen** bavarder comme une pie
  2 adj dix-neuf; see also **eight**

nineteenth [naɪn'ti:nθ] **1** n (**a**) (fraction) dix-neuvième m (**b**) (in series) dix-neuvième mf (**c**) (of month) dix-neuf m inv
  2 adj dix-neuvième; Fam Hum **the n. hole** (of golf course) le bar du golf; see also **eighth**

ninetieth ['naɪntɪθ] **1** n (**a**) (fraction) quatre-vingt-dixième m (**b**) (in series) quatre-vingt-dixième mf
  2 adj quatre-vingt-dix; see also **eighth**

ninety ['naɪntɪ] **1** n quatre-vingt-dix m inv
  2 adj quatre-vingt-dix; **n. nine times out of a hundred** quatre-vingt-dix-neuf fois sur cent; see also **eighty**

ninth [naɪnθ] **1** n (**a**) (fraction) neuvième m (**b**) (in series) neuvième mf (**c**) (of month) neuf m inv
  2 adj neuvième; see also **eighth**

nip [nɪp] **1** n (**a**) (pinch) pincement m; (bite) morsure f légère (**b**) (of cold, frost) **there's a n. in the air** il fait frisquet (**c**) Fam (of drink) petit verre m
  2 (pt & pp **nipped**) vt (**a**) (pinch) pincer; (bite) mordre légèrement; Fam Fig **to n. sth in the bud** étouffer qch dans l'œuf (**b**) (of cold, frost) pincer, piquer
  3 vi (sting) piquer

▸**nip out** vi Br Fam sortir quelques instants; **to n. out to the supermarket/pub** faire un saut au supermarché/au pub

nipper ['nɪpə(r)] n Br Fam (child) gamin(e) m,f

nipple ['nɪp(ə)l] n mamelon m; (on baby's bottle) tétine f

nippy ['nɪpɪ] adj Fam (**a**) (person, car) rapide (**b**) (cold) vif (vive); **it's a bit n. today** il fait plutôt frisquet aujourd'hui

nit [nɪt] n (**a**) (in hair) lente f; **to have nits** avoir des poux (**b**) Br Fam (person) nigaud(e) m,f

nit-picker ['nɪtpɪkə(r)] n Fam chipoteur(euse) m,f

nit-picking ['nɪtpɪkɪŋ] Fam **1** n chipotage m
  2 adj chipoteur(euse)

nitrate ['naɪtreɪt] n nitrate m

nitric ['naɪtrɪk] adj nitrique

nitrogen ['naɪtrədʒən] n azote m

nitroglycerine ['naɪtrəʊ'glɪsəri:n] n nitroglycérine f

nitrous ['naɪtrəs] adj nitreux(euse)

nitty-gritty ['nɪtɪ'grɪtɪ] n Fam **to get down to the n.** entrer dans le vif du sujet

nitwit ['nɪtwɪt] n Fam crétin(e) m,f

NNE (abbr **north-northeast**) NNE

NNW (abbr **north-northwest**) NNO

No, no (abbr **number**) no

no [nəʊ] **1** n (pl **noes** or **nos**) non m; **she won't take no for an answer** elle n'accepte pas qu'on lui dise non
  2 adj (**a**) (not any) pas de; **there's no bread** il n'y a pas de pain; **of no importance** sans importance; **I am in no way surprised** je ne suis pas du tout surpris; **he's no friend of mine** je ne le compte certainement pas au nombre de mes amis; Fam **no way!** pas question!
  (**b**) (with gerund) **there's no denying it** on ne peut pas le nier; **there's no pleasing him** il n'est jamais satisfait; **no smoking** (sign) interdiction de fumer
  3 adv (**a**) (interjection) non
  (**b**) (not any) **no richer/poorer** pas plus riche/pauvre; **no more/less than £100** pas plus/moins de 100 livres; **he no longer lives there** il n'habite plus là

Noah ['nəʊə] n Noé; **N.'s ark** l'arche f de Noé

nobble ['nɒbəl] vt Br Fam (**a**) (bribe) payer (**b**) (waylay) coincer

Nobel Prize [nəʊ'bel'praɪz] n prix m Nobel

nobility [nəʊ'bɪlɪtɪ] n noblesse f

noble ['nəʊbəl] **1** n noble mf
  2 adj noble; Fig (building) majestueux(euse)

nobleman ['nəʊbəlmən] n noble m

nobleminded [nəʊbəl'maɪndɪd] adj (person) au cœur noble, magnanime; (sentiment, action) noble

noblewoman ['nəʊbəlwʊmən] *n* noble *f*

nobly ['nəʊbəlɪ] *adv* avec noblesse

nobody ['nəʊbədɪ] **1** *pron* personne; **n. spoke to me** personne ne m'a parlé; **n. else** personne d'autre; **she's n.'s fool** elle n'est pas née de la dernière pluie; **if you don't have money, you're n.** si on n'a pas d'argent on est un moins que rien
   2 *n* (*pl* **nobodies**) **a n.** un(e) moins que rien

no-claims bonus ['nəʊ'kleɪmz'bəʊnəs] *n* bonus *m*

nocturnal [nɒk'tɜːnəl] *adj* nocturne

nod [nɒd] **1** *n* (*in greeting, as signal*) signe *m* de tête; (*in agreement*) signe de tête affirmatif; *Fig* **to give sb/sth the n.** donner le feu vert à qn/qch;
   2 *vt* (*pt & pp* **nodded**) **to n. one's head** (*in greeting, as signal*) faire un signe de tête; (*in agreement*) faire oui de la tête; **to n. one's agreement/approval** consentir/approuver d'un signe de tête
   3 *vi* **to n. in agreement/approval** consentir/approuver d'un signe de tête

▸**nod off** *vi Fam* s'assoupir

node [nəʊd] *n* (*of curve, plant*) nœud *m*; *Med* ganglion *m*; *Comput* noyau *m*

nodule ['nɒdjuːl] *n* nodule *m*

no-fly zone [nəʊ'flaɪzəʊn] *n Mil* zone *f* d'exclusion aérienne

no-frills [nəʊ'frɪlz] *adj* (*wedding*) tout(e) simple; (*airline, travel*) sans prestation de services; (*car, bicycle*) sans gadgets

no-go area [nəʊ'gəʊeərɪə] *adj* zone *f* interdite

no-good ['nəʊgʊd] *adj Fam* **a n. idiot** un imbécile propre à rien; **that n. husband of hers** son bon à rien de mari

no-hoper [nəʊ'həʊpə(r)] *n* tocard(e) *m,f*

noise [nɔɪz] *n* bruit *m*; *Fig* **to make noises about doing sth** parler de faire qch; *Fig* **a big n.** une huile

noiselessly ['nɔɪzlɪslɪ] *adv* sans bruit, silencieusement

noisily ['nɔɪzɪlɪ] *adv* bruyamment

noisy ['nɔɪzɪ] *adj* bruyant(e)

nomad ['nəʊmæd] *n & adj* nomade *mf*

nomadic [nəʊ'mædɪk] *adj* nomade

no man's land ['nəʊmænz'lænd] *n Fig* no man's land *m*

nomenclature [nəʊ'menklətʃə(r)] *n* nomenclature *f*

nominal ['nɒmɪnəl] *adj* nominal(e); (*damages*) symbolique; (*rent*) insignifiant(e)

nominally ['nɒmɪnəlɪ] *adv* nominalement

nominate ['nɒmɪneɪt] *vt* (*propose*) proposer (**for/as** pour/comme); (*appoint*) nommer (**to/as** à/comme)

nomination [nɒmɪ'neɪʃən] *n* (**a**) (*proposal*) candidature *f*; (*for film, TV awards*) nomination *f* (**b**) (*appointment*) nomination *f*

nominee [nɒmɪ'niː] *n* (*proposed*) candidat(e) *m,f*; (*appointed*) personne *f* nommée

non- [nɒn] *pref* non(-)

non-aggression pact [nɒnə'greʃən'pækt] *n Pol* pacte *m* de non-agression

nonalcoholic [nɒnælkə'hɒlɪk] *adj* sans alcool

nonaligned [nɒnə'laɪnd] *adj Pol* non-aligné(e)

nonattendance [nɒnə'tendəns] *n* absence *f*

nonchalance ['nɒnʃələns] *n* désinvolture *f*

nonchalant ['nɒnʃələnt] *adj* désinvolte

nonchalantly [nɒnʃə'læntlɪ] *adv* avec désinvolture

noncombatant [nɒn'kɒmbətənt] *n & adj Mil* noncombattant(e) *m,f*

noncommissioned officer ['nɒnkə'mɪʃənd-'ɒfɪsə(r)] *n Mil* sous-officier *m*

noncommittal [nɒnkə'mɪtəl] *adj* (*answer*) de Normand; **to be n.** ne pas s'engager

nonconformist [nɒnkən'fɔːmɪst] *n & adj* nonconformiste *mf*

non-denominational [nɒndɪ'nɒmɪ'neɪʃənəl] *adj* (*school, education*) non confessionel(elle)

nondescript ['nɒndɪskrɪpt] *adj* banal(e); (*colour*) fade

none [nʌn] **1** *pron* aucun(e) *m,f*; **n. of you/us** aucun d'entre vous/nous; **n. of my friends** aucun de mes amis; **n. of this concerns me** rien de tout cela ne me concerne; **it was n. other than the President** c'était le Président, rien de moins; **there was/were n. left** il n'en restait plus; *Fam* **we'll have n. of that!** pas de ça!
   2 *adv* **his answer left me n. the wiser** sa réponse ne m'a pas avancé; **n. too happy** pas très satisfait(e); **n. too soon** pas trop tôt

nonentity [nɒ'nentɪtɪ] (*pl* **nonentities**) *n* personne *f* sans intérêt

nonessential [nɒnɪ'senʃəl] *adj* qui n'est pas essentiel(elle)

nonetheless [nʌnðə'les] *adv* néanmoins, cependant

nonevent [nɒnɪ'vent] *n* **to be a n.** être décevant(e)

nonexecutive director [nɒnɪg'zekjʊtɪvdaɪ'rektə(r)] *n* = administrateur à titre consultatif

nonexistent [nɒnɪg'zɪstənt] *adj* inexistant(e)

non-fiction [nɒn'fɪkʃən] *n* ouvrages *mpl* généraux

nonflammable [nɒn'flæməbəl] *adj* ininflammable

non-linear [nɒn'lɪnɪə(r)] *adj Comput* non linéaire

non-negotiable [nɒnnɪ'gəʊʃɪəbəl] *adj* non négociable

non-nuclear [nɒn'njuːklɪə(r)] *adj* (*country*) non nucléarisé(e); (*war, defence*) non nucléaire

no-no ['nəʊnəʊ] (*pl* **no-nos** *or* **no-noes**) *n Fam* **that's a n.** c'est à ne pas faire

no-nonsense [nəʊ'nɒnsəns] *adj* direct(e)

non-partisan [nɒn'pɑːtɪzæn] *adj* impartial(e)

non-payment [nɒn'peɪmənt] *n* non-paiement *m*

non-person ['nɒn'pɜːsən] *n* proscrit(e) *m,f*

nonplussed [nɒn'plʌst] *adj* interloqué(e)

non-profit-making [nɒn'prɒfɪtmeɪkɪŋ] *adj* à but non lucratif

non-racist [nɒn'reɪsɪst] *adj* non raciste

nonresident [nɒn'rezɪdənt] *n* (*of country*) non-résident(e) *m,f*; (*of hotel*) client(e) *m,f*

nonreturnable [nɒnrɪ'tɜːnəbəl] *adj* (*bottle*) non signé(e); (*deposit*) non remboursable

nonsense ['nɒnsəns] *n* bêtises *fpl*, idioties *fpl*; **n.!** n'importe quoi!; **to talk (a lot of) n.** dire des bêtises; **to make a n. of sth** ôter tout sens à qch

nonsensical [nɒn'sensɪkəl] *adj* absurde, qui n'a pas de sens

non sequitur [nɒn'sekwɪtə(r)] *n* absurdité *f*

non-sexist [nɒn'seksɪst] *adj* non sexiste

non-smoker [nɒn'sməʊkə(r)] *n* non-fumeur(euse) *m,f*; (*train compartment*) compartiment *m* non-fumeurs

non-specialist [nɒn'speʃəlɪst] **1** *n* non-spécialiste *mf*
   2 *adj* non spécialisé(e)

nonstarter [nɒn'stɑːtə(r)] *n* **to be a n.** (*of plan*) être fichu(e) d'avance

nonstick ['nɒn'stɪk] *adj* (*surface*) anti-adhésif(ive); (*frying pan*) qui n'attache pas

non-stop ['nɒn'stɒp] **1** *adj (journey)* sans arrêt; *(flight)* sans escale
  2 *adv* sans arrêt; *(fly)* sans escale
non-tariff barrier ['nɒn'tærɪf'bærɪə(r)] *n Econ* barrière *f* non tarifaire
nontransferable ['nɒntræns'fɜːrəbəl] *adj (ticket, membership)* nominatif(ive); *(property, right)* incessible
nonverbal [nɒn'vɜːbəl] *adj* non-verbal(e)
nonviolent [nɒn'vaɪələnt] *adj* non-violent(e)
noodles ['nuːdəlz] *npl* nouilles *fpl*
nook [nʊk] *n (corner)* recoin *m*; *(retreat)* coin *m*; **every n. and cranny** le moindre recoin
nookie, nooky ['nʊkɪ] *n Fam* crac-crac *m*; **to have a bit of n.** faire une partie de jambes en l'air
noon [nuːn] *n* midi *m*; **at n.** à midi
noonday ['nuːndeɪ] *n Lit* midi *m*; **the n. sun** le soleil de midi
no-one ['nəʊwʌn] = **nobody**
noose [nuːs] *n* nœud *m* coulant; *Fig* **to put one's head in a n.** signer son arrêt de mort
nope [nəʊp] *adv Fam* non
nor [nɔː(r)] **1** *conj* **neither you n. your brother** ni toi ni ton frère; **neither... n.** ni... ni; **he neither drinks n. smokes** il ne boit pas et ne fume pas non plus
  2 *adv* **n. do I** moi non plus; **if you don't go n. shall I** si tu n'y vas pas, moi non plus
Nordic ['nɔːdɪk] *adj* nordique
norm [nɔːm] *n* norme *f*
normal ['nɔːməl] **1** *n* **above/below n.** *(temperature, rate)* au-dessus/au-dessous de la normale; **to get back to n.** redevenir normal(e)
  2 *adj* normal(e)
normality [nɔː'mælɪtɪ], *Am* **normalcy** ['nɔːməlsɪ] *n* normalité *f*; **a return to n.** un retour à la normale
normalization [nɔːməlaɪ'zeɪʃən] *n* normalisation *f*
normalize ['nɔːməlaɪz] **1** *vt* normaliser
  2 *vi* redevenir normal(e)
normally ['nɔːməlɪ] *adv* normalement
Norman ['nɔːmən] **1** *n* Normand(e) *m,f*
  2 *adj* normand(e)
Normandy ['nɔːməndɪ] *n* la Normandie
north [nɔːθ] **1** *n* nord *m*; **to the n. (of)** au nord (de)
  2 *adj (coast, side)* nord; *(wind)* du nord; **N. Africa** Afrique *f* du Nord; **N. African** nord-africain(e); *(person)* Nord-Africain(e) *m,f*; **N. America** Amérique *f* du Nord; **N. American** nord-américain(e); *(person)* Nord-Américain(e) *m,f*; **N. Carolina** la Caroline du Nord; **N. Dakota** le Dakota du Nord; **N. Korea** Corée *f* du Nord; **N. Korean** nord-coréen(enne); *(person)* Nord-Coréen(enne) *m,f*; **the N. Pole** le Pôle Nord; **the N. Sea** la mer du Nord
  3 *adv* au nord; *(travel)* vers le nord; **to face n.** *(of house)* être exposé(e) au nord
northbound ['nɔːθbaʊnd] *adj (train, traffic)* en direction du nord; **n. carriageway** voie *f* nord
northeast [nɔːθ'iːst] **1** *n* nord-est *m*
  2 *adj (side)* nord-est; *(wind)* du nord-est
  3 *adv* au nord-est; *(travel)* vers le nord-est
northeasterly [nɔːθ'iːstəlɪ] **1** *n (wind)* vent *m* du nord-est
  2 *adj (direction)* vers le nord-est; *(wind)* du nord-est
northeastern [nɔːθ'iːstən] *adj (region)* (du) nord-est
northerly ['nɔːðəlɪ] **1** *n (pl* **northerlies)** *(wind)* vent *m* du nord

2 *adj (direction)* vers le nord; *(wind)* du nord; **the most n. point** le point le plus au nord
northern ['nɔːðən] *adj (region, accent)* du nord; **n. France** le nord de la France; **n. hemisphere** hémisphère *m* nord; **N. Ireland** l'Irlande *f* du Nord; **N. Irish** de l'Irlande du Nord; **the N. Irish** les Irlandais *mpl* du Nord; **N. Lights** aurore *f* boréale

> ### Northern Ireland
> L'Irlande du Nord désigne la partie de l'Irlande à majorité protestante restée rattachée à la Grande-Bretagne lors de la partition du pays, en 1921. Les émeutes sanglantes qui ont éclaté en 1969 à la suite de manifestations revendiquant l'égalité des droits pour la minorité catholique ont marqué le début de trente ans de conflit entre catholiques et protestants. Ce conflit vit s'affronter les nationalistes de l'IRA, favorables à un rattachement avec la République d'Irlande, différents groupes paramilitaires protestants anti-catholiques, et l'armée et la police, sous contrôle britannique. Le processus de paix, amorcé en 1994 et qui aboutit au "Good Friday Agreement" de 1998 marqua une nouvelle étape dans l'histoire de l'Irlande du Nord.

northerner ['nɔːðənə(r)] *n* habitant(e) *m,f* du Nord *(de l'Angleterre)*
north-facing ['nɔːθ'feɪsɪŋ] *adj* exposé(e) au nord
north-northeast [nɔːθnɔːθ'iːst] *adv* au nord-nord-est; *(travel)* vers le nord-nord-est
north-northwest [nɔːθnɔːθ'west] *adv* au nord-nord-ouest; *(travel)* vers le nord-nord-ouest
northward ['nɔːθwəd] **1** *adj* au nord
  2 *adv* vers le nord
northwards ['nɔːθwədz] *adv* vers le nord
northwest [nɔːθ'west] **1** *n* nord-ouest *m*
  2 *adj (side)* nord-ouest; *(wind)* du nord-ouest
  3 *adv* au nord-ouest; *(travel)* vers le nord-ouest
northwesterly [nɔːθ'westəlɪ] **1** *n (pl* **north-westerlies)** *(wind)* vent *m* du nord-ouest
  2 *adj (direction)* vers le nord-ouest; *(wind)* du nord-ouest
northwestern [nɔːθ'westən] *adj (region)* (du) nord-ouest
North-West Territories ['nɔːθ'west'terɪtriːz] *npl* les Territoires *mpl* du Nord-Ouest
Norway ['nɔːweɪ] *n* la Norvège
Norwegian [nɔː'wiːdʒən] **1** *n* **(a)** *(person)* Norvégien(enne) *m,f* **(b)** *(language)* norvégien *m*
  2 *adj* norvégien(enne)
nose [nəʊz] *n* **(a)** *(of person, animal, aeroplane)* nez *m*; **her n. is bleeding** elle saigne du nez; **to blow one's n.** se moucher (le nez); **to hold one's n.** se boucher le nez; *Fam* **to have a n. job** se faire refaire le nez; **the traffic was n. to tail** les voitures se suivaient pare-chocs contre pare-chocs **(b)** *(idioms)* **it's under your n.** vous l'avez sous le nez; **to turn one's n. up at sth** dédaigner qch; **she walked by with her n. in the air** elle passa, l'air dédaigneux; **to look down one's n. at sb** prendre qn de haut; **to pay through the n. for sth** payer qch une fortune; **to get up sb's n.** taper sur les nerfs à qn; **to lead sb by the n.** mener qn par le bout du nez; **to keep one's n. clean** se tenir à carreau; **to have a n. for sth** savoir flairer qch; **to poke one's n. into other people's business** fourrer son nez dans les affaires des autres

▶**nose about, nose around** *vi Fam* fouiner

nosebleed ['nəʊzbliːd] *n* **to have a n.** saigner du nez

nose-dive ['nəʊzdaɪv] **1** *n (of plane)* (vol *m* en) piqué *m*; *Fig (of prices)* chute *f* rapide

2 *vi (of plane)* piquer du nez; *Fig (of prices)* chuter fortement

nosey ['nəʊzɪ] *adj Fam* fouineur(euse); *(questions)* indiscret(ète); *Br* **n. parker** fouineur(euse) *m,f*

nosh [nɒʃ] *Fam* **1** *n (food)* bouffe *f*

2 *vi (eat)* bouffer

no-show [nəʊ'ʃəʊ] *n* défection *f*

nosiness ['nəʊzɪnəs] *n* curiosité *f*

no-smoking [nəʊ'sməʊkɪŋ] *adj (carriage, area)* non-fumeurs; *(seat)* non-fumeur

nostalgia [nɒs'tældʒɪə] *n* nostalgie *f*

nostalgic [nɒs'tældʒɪk] *adj* nostalgique

nostalgically [nɒs'tældʒɪklɪ] *adv* avec nostalgie

nostril ['nɒstrɪl] *n* narine *f*

nosy = nosey

not [nɒt] *adv*

À l'oral, et à l'écrit dans un style familier, on utilise généralement **not** à la forme contractée lorsqu'il suit un modal ou un auxiliaire (**don't go!**; **she wasn't there**; **he couldn't see me**).

n. me/him pas moi/lui; **I don't know** je ne sais pas; **don't move!** ne bouge pas!; **whether she likes it or n.** que ça lui plaise ou non; **I think/hope n.** je pense/j'espère que non; **she asked me n. to tell him** elle m'a demandé de ne pas le lui dire; **n. wishing to cause an argument, he said nothing** ne voulant pas provoquer de dispute, il s'est tu; **you understand, don't you?** tu comprends, n'est-ce pas?; **n. at all** pas du tout; *(you're welcome)* je vous en prie; **n. any more** plus maintenant; **n. even** pas même, même pas; **n. only..., but also...** non seulement..., mais encore...; **n. yet** pas encore; **n. that I minded** non pas que ça me dérangeait; **n. that it matters** non pas que ça ait de l'importance; **n. that I know of** pas que je sache

notable ['nəʊtəbəl] *adj (person, thing)* notable; *(achievement, success)* remarquable; **with a few n. exceptions** à quelques exceptions près, et non des moindres

notably ['nəʊtəblɪ] *adv* notamment

notary ['nəʊtərɪ] *(pl* **notaries)** *n Law* **n. (public)** notaire *m*

notation [nəʊ'teɪʃən] *n* notation *f*

notch [nɒtʃ] **1** *n* **(a)** *(in stick)* encoche *f*; *(in belt)* cran *m* **(b)** *(grade, level)* cran *m*

2 *vt* encocher

▶**notch up** *vt sep (victory, sale)* remporter; *(points)* marquer

note [nəʊt] **1** *n* **(a)** *(information, reminder)* note *f*; *(short letter)* mot *m*; **(lecture) notes** notes (de cours); **to take** *or* **make a n. of sth** prendre note de qch; **to take n. of sb/sth** remarquer qn/qch **(b)** *(musical)* note *f*; *Fig (of impatience, anger)* pointe *f*; **on a lighter/more serious n.** pour en venir à un sujet moins/plus sérieux **(c)** *(banknote)* billet *m* **(d)** *(significance)* **of n.** *(event)* remarquable; *(person)* éminent(e)

2 *vt* noter, remarquer; *(error)* relever; *(fact)* constater

▶**note down** *vt sep* prendre note de, noter

notebook ['nəʊtbʊk] *n* carnet *m*; *(larger)* cahier *m*; *Comput* agenda *m*

noted ['nəʊtɪd] *adj* éminent(e); **to be n. for sth** être réputé(e) pour qch

notepad ['nəʊtpæd] *n* bloc-notes *m*

notepaper ['nəʊtpeɪpə(r)] *n* papier *m* à lettres

noteworthy ['nəʊtwɜːðɪ] *adj* remarquable

nothing ['nʌθɪŋ] **1** *pron* rien; **n. happened** il ne s'est rien passé; **I have n. to do** je n'ai rien à faire; **to have n. to do with sb/sth** *(be unconnected to)* n'avoir rien à voir avec qn/qch; *(not get involved with)* n'avoir rien à faire avec qn/qch; **to say n. of...** sans parler de...; **she was n. if not discreet** elle a été très discrète; **n. new/remarkable** rien de nouveau/d'exceptionnel; **n. but** rien que; **n. else** rien d'autre; **n. much** pas grand-chose; **there is n. more to be said** il n'y a plus rien à dire; **there's n. like a nice steak!** rien de tel qu'un bon steak!; **as a pianist, he has n. on his brother** en tant que pianiste, son frère n'a rien à lui envier; **there's n. in it** *(it's untrue)* il n'y a rien de vrai dans tout ça; **to think n. of doing sth** trouver normal de faire qch; *Fam* **there's n. to it** ce n'est pas sorcier; **£1,000 is n. to her** 1000 livres, ce n'est rien pour elle; **to get angry/worried for** *or* **about n.** se fâcher/s'inquiéter pour un rien; **to do sth for n.** *(in vain, free of charge)* faire qch pour rien

2 *n* **to come to n.** être anéanti(e); **a hundred pounds? – a mere n.!** cent livres? – une bagatelle!

3 *adv* **she looks n. like her sister** elle ne ressemble pas du tout à sa sœur; **it was n. like as difficult as they said** c'était loin d'être aussi difficile qu'on le disait

notice ['nəʊtɪs] **1** *n* **(a)** *(warning)* avertissement *m*; *(of resignation, redundancy)* préavis *m*; **to give sb n. (of sth)** avertir qn (de qch); *(of resignation, redundancy)* donner un préavis à qn (pour qch); **until further n.** jusqu'à nouvel ordre; **at short n.** au pied levé; **at a moment's n.** sur-le-champ; **to give in one's n.** *(resign)* donner sa démission, démissionner; **to give sb n.** *(of employer)* licencier qn **(b)** *(attention)* **to take n. of sb/sth** faire *ou* prêter attention à qn/qch; **to take no n. of sb/sth** ne pas prêter la moindre attention à qn/qch; **the fact escaped everyone's n.** ce fait a échappé à tout le monde; **it has come to my n. that...** *(I was told)* on m'a signalé que...; *(I read it)* je me suis rendu compte que... **(c)** *(sign)* écriteau *m*, pancarte *f*; *(poster)* affiche *f* **(d)** *(criticism of play, film)* critique *f*

2 *vt* remarquer, s'apercevoir de; **to be noticed, to get oneself noticed** se faire remarquer

3 *vi* remarquer

noticeable ['nəʊtɪsəbəl] *adj (change, difference)* sensible, perceptible; **it was n. that...** il était évident que...

noticeably ['nəʊtɪsəblɪ] *adv* sensiblement

noticeboard ['nəʊtɪsbɔːd] *n* panneau *m* d'affichage

notification [nəʊtɪfɪ'keɪʃən] *n* avis *m*, notification *f*; **to give sb n. of sth** avertir qn de qch

notify ['nəʊtɪfaɪ] *(pt & pp* **notified)** *vt* annoncer, notifier; **to n. sb of sth** avertir qn de qch

notion ['nəʊʃən] *n* notion *f*; **to have a n. that...** avoir dans l'idée que...; **to have a n. to do sth** avoir envie de faire qch

notoriety [nəʊtə'raɪətɪ] *n* notoriété *f*; **to achieve** *or* **gain n.** se rendre célèbre

notorious [nəʊ'tɔːrɪəs] *adj* tristement célèbre; *(criminal)* notoire; *(place)* mal famé(e); *(liar)* fieffé(e)

notoriously [nəʊ'tɔːrɪəslɪ] *adv* **to be n. tactless/rude** être bien connu(e) pour son manque de tact/son impolitesse; **Scottish weather is n. unpredictable** il est bien connu qu'en Écosse, le temps est très changeant

notwithstanding [nɒtwɪθ'stændɪŋ] *Formal* **1** *prep* en dépit de, malgré

2 *adv* néanmoins; **difficulties n.,...** ces difficultés mises à part,...

nougat ['nuːgɑː] *n* nougat *m*

nought [nɔːt] *n* zéro *m*; **noughts and crosses** ≃ morpion *m (jeu)*

noun [naʊn] *n* nom *m*

nourish ['nʌrɪʃ] *vt* nourrir

nourishing ['nʌrɪʃɪŋ] *adj* nourrissant(e)

nourishment ['nʌrɪʃmənt] *n* nourriture *f; (nourishing quality)* richesse *f* nutritive

nous [naʊs] *n Br Fam (common sense)* sens *m* commun, bon sens

Nov *(abbr* **November)** novembre

Nova Scotia ['nəʊvə'skəʊʃə] *n* la Nouvelle-Écosse

novel ['nɒvəl] **1** *n* roman *m*

2 *adj (original)* nouveau(elle), original(e)

novelist ['nɒvəlɪst] *n* romancier(ère) *m,f*

novelty ['nɒvəltɪ] *(pl* **novelties)** *n (newness)* nouveauté *f; (cheap object)* bricole *f;* **the n. will soon wear off** l'attrait de la nouveauté ne tardera pas à s'estomper; **n. value** attrait *m* de la nouveauté

November [nəʊ'vembə(r)] *n* novembre *m; see also* **May**

novice ['nɒvɪs] *n (beginner)* débutant(e) *m,f* (**at** en); *Rel* novice *mf*

now [naʊ] **1** *adv* (**a**) *(at this moment, these days)* maintenant; **it's n. or never** c'est maintenant ou jamais; **that'll do for n.** ça suffit pour le moment; **it's two years n. since his mother died** ça fait maintenant deux ans que sa mère est morte; **she won't be long n.** elle ne va plus tarder; **any minute/day n.** d'une minute/d'un jour à l'autre; **n. is the time to...** c'est le moment de...; **right n.** *(immediately)* tout de suite; *(at the moment)* pour le moment; **(every) n. and then, (every) n. and again** de temps en temps, de temps à autre; **up to** *or* **until n.** jusqu'à présent *ou* maintenant; **from n. on** dorénavant; **in three days from n.** dans trois jours; **she ought to be here by n.** elle devrait déjà être ici; **and n. for some music** et maintenant, un peu de musique (**b**) *(before statement, argument)* bon; **n., there are two ways of interpreting this** bon, il y a deux interprétations possibles; **come n.!** allons!; **n., n.! stop quarrelling!** allons, allons! arrêtez de vous disputer!

2 *conj* **n. (that)...** maintenant que...; **n. (that) you mention it,...** maintenant que tu le dis,...

nowadays ['naʊədeɪz] *adv* de nos jours

nowhere ['nəʊweə(r)] **1** *adv* nulle part; **n. else** nulle part ailleurs; **she was n. to be found** elle était introuvable; **qualifications alone will get you n.** les diplômes seuls ne servent à rien; **to be n. near as nice/stupid (as)** être loin d'être aussi agréable/stupide (que); **it's n. near the shopping centre** c'est à des kilomètres du centre commercial; **to finish n.** *(in contest)* finir loin derrière les autres; *Fam* **we're getting n. fast** on perd notre temps

2 *n* **in the middle of n.** dans un coin paumé; **he came from n. to win the race** il a gagné la course après une remontée spectaculaire

noxious ['nɒkʃəs] *adj* nocif(ive)

nozzle ['nɒzəl] *n (of petrol pump)* pistolet *m; (of vacuum cleaner)* suceur *m; (of pipe)* jet *m; (for icing)* douille *f*

nr *(abbr* **near)** près de

NRA [enɑː'reɪ] *n Am (abbr* **National Rifle Association)** = association américaine favorable à la généralisation des armes à feu

NSPCC [enespiːsiː'siː] *n Br (abbr* **National Society for the Prevention of Cruelty to Children)** = comité britannique pour la protection des enfants maltraités

nth [enθ] *adj Fam* énième

nuance ['njuːɒns] *n* nuance *f*

nub [nʌb] *n (of question, argument)* cœur *m*

nubile ['njuːbaɪl] *adj* désirable

nuclear ['njuːklɪə(r)] *adj* nucléaire; **n. bomb** bombe *f* atomique; **n. disarmament** désarmement *m* nucléaire; **n. energy** énergie *f* nucléaire *ou* atomique; **n. family** famille *f* nucléaire; **n. physics** physique *f* nucléaire; **n. power** énergie *f* nucléaire; **n. power station** centrale *f* atomique *ou* nucléaire; **n. reactor** réacteur *m* nucléaire; **n. war** guerre *f* atomique *ou* nucléaire; **n. waste** déchets *mpl* nucléaires; **n. weapon** arme *f* atomique *ou* nucléaire; **n. winter** hiver *m* nucléaire

nuclear-free zone ['njuːklɪə'friː'zəʊn] *n* zone *f* dénucléarisée

nucleus ['njuːklɪəs] *(pl* **nuclei** ['njuːklaɪ] *) n also Fig* noyau *m*

nude [njuːd] **1** *n* nu *m;* **in the n.** tout(e) nu(e)

2 *adj* nu(e)

nudge [nʌdʒ] **1** *n* coup *m* de coude

2 *vt* donner un coup de coude à

nudist ['njuːdɪst] *n* nudiste *mf;* **n. camp** *or* **colony** camp *m* de nudistes

nudity ['njuːdɪtɪ] *n* nudité *f*

nugatory ['njuːgətɒrɪ] *adj* sans valeur

nugget ['nʌgɪt] *n (of gold)* pépite *f; Fig* **a n. of information** un renseignement précieux

nuisance ['njuːsəns] *n* **to be a n.** *(of person, situation)* être embêtant(e); **to make a n. of oneself** embêter le monde; **n. call** *(on telephone)* appel *m* anonyme

nuke [njuːk] *vt Fam* lâcher la bombe sur

null [nʌl] *adj* nul (nulle); **n. and void** nul et non avenu

nullify ['nʌlɪfaɪ] *(pt & pp* **nullified)** *vt* annuler; *(decree)* invalider

NUM [enjuː'em] *n Br (abbr* **National Union of Mineworkers)** = syndicat britannique de mineurs

numb [nʌm] **1** *adj* engourdi(e); **to go n.** s'engourdir; **n. with cold** engourdi par le froid; **n. with fear** paralysé(e) par la peur

2 *vt (of cold)* engourdir; *(of fear)* paralyser

number ['nʌmbə(r)] **1** *n* (**a**) *(numeral)* nombre *m; (when written)* chiffre *m; Comput* **n. crunching** calculs *mpl* (rapides)

(**b**) *(of house, page, telephone)* numéro *m;* **I live at n. 40** j'habite au (numéro) 40; **(telephone) n.** numéro de téléphone; *Fam* **to look after n. one** s'occuper de sa petite personne; *Br* **N. Ten** le dix Downing Street *(résidence du premier ministre britannique)*

(**c**) *(quantity)* nombre *m;* **a large n. of** un grand nombre de; **in small/great numbers** en petit/grand nombre

(**d**) *(song)* chanson *f*

(**e**) *(idioms)* **he's my n. two** *(subordinate)* c'est mon adjoint; *Fam* **I've got your n.!** je sais ce que tu as en tête!; *Fam* **his n.'s up** son compte est bon; *Fam* **that**

car/dress is a nice little n. c'est une jolie petite voiture/robe; *Fam* **she's got a nice little n. there** *(situation)* elle s'est dégoté un bon plan
   2 *vt* (**a**) *(assign number to)* numéroter
   (**b**) *(count)* compter; **his days are numbered** ses jours sont comptés; **to n. sb among one's friends** compter qn parmi *ou* au nombre de ses amis

numberplate ['nʌmbəpleɪt] *n Br* plaque *f* d'immatriculation *ou* minéralogique

numbly ['nʌmlɪ] *adv (say, react)* mollement; *(stare)* d'un air hébété

numbness ['nʌmnɪs] *n (in body)* engourdissement *m*; *(of emotions)* torpeur *f*

numbskull ['nʌmskʌl] *n Fam* bêta(asse) *m,f*

numeracy ['njuːmərəsɪ] *n* degré *m* d'aptitude en calcul

numeral ['njuːmərəl] *n* chiffre *m*

numerate ['njuːmərət] *adj* **to be n.** savoir compter

numerator ['njuːməreɪtə(r)] *n Math* numérateur *m*

numerical [njuːˈmerɪkəl] *adj* numérique

numerically [njuːˈmerɪklɪ] *adv* numériquement

numerous ['njuːmərəs] *adj* nombreux(euse); **on n. occasions** en de nombreuses occasions

nun [nʌn] *n* religieuse *f*, nonne *f*; **to become a n.** prendre la voile

nunnery ['nʌnərɪ] *(pl* **nunneries***) n* couvent *m*

nuptial ['nʌpʃəl] **1** *npl Hum or Lit* **nuptials** noces *fpl*
   2 *adj Lit* nuptial(e)

nurse [nɜːs] **1** *n* (**a**) *(medical)* infirmière *f*; **(male) n.** infirmier *m* (**b**) *(looking after children)* nurse *f*
   2 *vt (look after)* soigner; *(suckle)* allaiter; *Fig (feeling, hope)* nourrir; *(grievance)* entretenir; **to n. sb back to health** faire recouvrer la santé à qn

nursery ['nɜːsərɪ] *(pl* **nurseries***) n* (**a**) *(for children) (establishment)* garderie *f*; *(room in house)* chambre *f* d'enfants; **n. education** enseignement *m* en maternelle; **n. rhyme** comptine *f*; **n. (school)** maternelle *f*; **n. slopes** *(in skiing)* pistes *fpl* pour débutants (**b**) *(for plants)* pépinière *f*

nursing ['nɜːsɪŋ] *n (profession)* profession *f* d'infirmière; *(care)* soins *mpl*; **n. home** *(for old people)* maison *f* de retraite; *(for convalescents)* maison *f* de repos; **n. mother** mère *f* qui allaite; **n. staff** personnel *m* soignant

nurture ['nɜːtʃə(r)] *vt* (**a**) *(feed) (children, plants)* nourrir; *(plan, idea)* élaborer (**b**) *(bring up)* faire l'éducation de

NUS [enjuːˈes] *n Br (abbr* **National Union of Students**) = syndicat britannique d'étudiants

NUT [enjuːˈtiː] *n Br (abbr* **National Union of Teachers**) = syndicat britannique d'enseignants

nut [nʌt] *n* (**a**) *(food)* = noix, noisette, cacahuète, pistache ou autre fruit sec de cette nature; *Fig* **he's a hard** *or* **tough n.** c'est un dur; *Fig* **a tough** *or* **hard n. to crack** *(problem)* un problème difficile à résoudre (**b**) *Fam (head)* caboche *f*; **to do one's n.** piquer une crise (**c**) *Fam (mad person)* dingue *mf*; **a tennis n.** un dingue de tennis (**d**) *(for fastening bolt)* écrou *m*; *Fig* **the nuts and bolts** les notions de base (**e**) *very Fam* **nuts** *(testicles)* couilles *fpl*

nutcase ['nʌtkeɪs] *n Fam* cinglé(e) *m,f*

nutcrackers ['nʌtkrækəz] *npl* **(pair of) n.** casse-noisettes *m inv*, casse-noix *m inv*

nuthouse ['nʌthaʊs] *n Fam* maison *f* de fous

nutmeg ['nʌtmeg] *n* (noix *f* de) muscade *f*

nutrient ['njuːtrɪənt] **1** *n* élément *m* nutritif
   2 *adj* nutritif(ive)

nutrition [njuːˈtrɪʃən] *n* nutrition *f*

nutritional [njuːˈtrɪʃənəl] *adj* nutritionnel(elle); *(value)* nutritif(ive)

nutritious [njuːˈtrɪʃəs] *adj* nutritif(ive)

nuts [nʌts] *adj Fam (mad)* dingue; **to be n. about sb/sth** être dingue de qn/qch

nutshell ['nʌtʃel] *n* coquille *f* de noix/noisette/*etc*; *Fig* **in a n.,...** bref,...

nutter ['nʌtə(r)] *n Br Fam (mad person)* dingue *mf*

nutty ['nʌtɪ] *adj* (**a**) *(in taste)* au goût de noisette/noix/*etc*; *(containing nuts)* aux noisettes/noix/*etc* (**b**) *Fam (mad)* dingue

nuzzle ['nʌzəl] **1** *vt* renifler
   2 *vi* **to n. against sb** renifler qn

NVQ [enviːˈkjuː] *n Br (abbr* **National Vocational Qualification**) = diplôme professionnel destiné notamment aux personnes travaillant déjà

NW *(abbr* **northwest**) N-O

NY [enˈwaɪ] *n Am (abbr* **New York**) New York

nylon ['naɪlɒn] *n* Nylon® *m*; **nylons** *(stockings)* bas *mpl* Nylon®

nymph [nɪmf] *n* nymphe *f*

nymphomania [nɪmfəʊˈmeɪnɪə] *n* nymphomanie *f*

nymphomaniac [nɪmfəʊˈmeɪnɪæk] *n* nymphomane *f*

NZ *(abbr* **New Zealand**) la Nouvelle-Zélande

O

O, o [əʊ] *n* (**a**) *(letter)* O, o *m inv*; *Br Formerly Sch* **O-level** = diplôme de fin de premier cycle de l'enseignement secondaire, sanctionnant une matière déterminée; *Br Formerly Sch* **O-levels** ≃ brevet *m* des collèges (**b**) *(zero)* zéro *m*

oaf [əʊf] *n* lourdaud *m*

oak [əʊk] *n* chêne *m*; **o. apple** noix *f* de galle

OAP [əʊeɪ'piː] *n Br* (*abbr* **old age pensioner**) retraité(e) *m,f*

oar [ɔː(r)] *n* aviron *m*, rame *f*; *Fig* **to put** *or* **stick one's o. in** mettre son grain de sel

oarsman ['ɔːzmən] *n* rameur *m*

oarswoman ['ɔːzwʊmən] *n* rameuse *f*

OAS [əʊeɪ'es] *n* (*abbr* **Organization of American States**) OEA *f*

oasis [əʊ'eɪsɪs] (*pl* **oases** [əʊ'eɪsiːz]) *n also Fig* oasis *f*

oatcake ['əʊtkeɪk] *n* galette *f* d'avoine

oath [əʊθ] *n* (**a**) *(pledge)* serment *m*; **o. of allegiance** serment d'allégeance; **to take** *or* **swear an o.** prêter serment; **on** *or* **under o.** sous serment (**b**) *(swear word)* juron *m*

oatmeal ['əʊtmiːl] *n* farine *f* d'avoine; *(colour)* beige *m*

oats [əʊts] *npl (plant)* avoine *f*; **(porridge) o.** *(food)* flocons *mpl* d'avoine; *Br very Fam* **to get one's o.** s'envoyer en l'air

OAU [əʊeɪ'juː] *n* (*abbr* **Organization of African Unity**) OUA *f*

obdurate ['ɒbdjʊrɪt] *adj* obstiné(e)

OBE [əʊbiː'iː] *n Br* (*abbr* **Officer of the Order of the British Empire**) = titre honorifique britannique

obedience [ə'biːdɪəns] *n* obéissance *f*

obedient [ə'biːdɪənt] *adj* obéissant(e)

obelisk ['ɒbəlɪsk] *n* obélisque *m*

obese [əʊ'biːs] *adj* obèse

obesity [əʊ'biːsɪtɪ] *n* obésité *f*

obey [ə'beɪ] **1** *vt* obéir à
　　2 *vi* obéir

obfuscation [ɒbfʌ'skeɪʃən] *n* obscurcissement *m*

obituary [ə'bɪtjʊərɪ] (*pl* **obituaries**) *n* nécrologie *f*; **o. column** rubrique *f* nécrologique; **o. notice** nécrologie *f*

object1 *n* ['ɒbdʒɪkt] (**a**) *(thing, recipient)* objet *m*; **an o. of contempt/desire** un objet de mépris/de désir; **an o. lesson** un parfait exemple de (**b**) *(aim)* objet *m*, but *m*; **the o. of the exercise is to...** cet exercice a pour objet *ou* but de... (**c**) *(obstacle)* **money/distance is no o.** le prix/la distance importe peu (**d**) *Gram* complément *m* d'objet
　　2 *vi* [ə'bdʒekt] émettre une objection; **to o. to sth/to doing sth** ne pas être d'accord avec qch/pour faire qch

objectify [əb'dʒektɪfaɪ] *vt* objectiver

objection [əb'dʒekʃən] *n* (**a**) *(protest)* objection *f*; **to have no o. to sth** ne voir aucune objection à qch; **I have no o. to going** ça ne me dérange pas d'y aller (**b**) *(reason for objecting)* inconvénient *m* (**to** de)

objectionable [əb'dʒekʃənəbəl] *adj (unpleasant)* déplaisant(e)

objective [əb'dʒektɪv] **1** *n (aim, goal)* objectif *m*
　　2 *adj (impartial)* objectif(ive)

objectively [əb'dʒektɪvlɪ] *adv* objectivement

objectivity [ɒbdʒek'tɪvɪtɪ] *n* objectivité *f*

obligation [ɒblɪ'geɪʃən] *n* obligation *f*; **to be under an o. to sb** avoir une dette envers qn; **to be under an o. to do sth** être dans l'obligation de faire qch

obligatory [ɒ'blɪgətərɪ] *adj* obligatoire

oblige [ə'blaɪdʒ] *vt* (**a**) *(compel)* obliger; **to be obliged to do sth** être obligé(e) de faire qch (**b**) *(do a favour for)* rendre service à (**c**) *(be grateful)* **to be obliged to sb** être reconnaissant(e) à qn; **I'd be obliged if you'd...** ça me rendrait service si vous pouviez...; **much obliged** merci infiniment

obliging [ə'blaɪdʒɪŋ] *adj* serviable; **it was very o. of her** c'était très aimable de sa part

oblique [ə'bliːk] *adj (line, angle)* oblique; *(reference, hint)* indirect(e)

obliterate [ə'blɪtəreɪt] *vt* (**a**) *also Fig (erase)* effacer (**b**) *(destroy)* détruire; *(town)* rayer de la carte

oblivion [ə'blɪvɪən] *n* oubli *m*; **to sink into o.** sombrer dans l'oubli

oblivious [ə'blɪvɪəs] *adj* **to be o. to sth** ne pas avoir conscience de qch

oblong ['ɒblɒŋ] **1** *n* rectangle *m*
　　2 *adj* rectangulaire

obnoxious [əb'nɒkʃəs] *adj (person, action)* odieux(euse); *(smell)* repoussant(e)

oboe ['əʊbəʊ] *n* hautbois *m*

oboist ['əʊbəʊɪst] *n* hautboïste *mf*

obscene [əb'siːn] *adj* obscène; *Fig (profits, prices)* scandaleux(euse)

obscenely [əb'siːnlɪ] *adv* d'une manière obscène; *Fig (rich)* scandaleusement

obscenity [əb'senɪtɪ] (*pl* **obscenities**) *n* obscénité *f*

obscure [əb'skjʊə(r)] **1** *adj* obscur(e)
　　2 *vt* (**a**) *(hide from view)* cacher (**b**) *(make unclear)* obscurcir

obscurity [əb'skjʊərɪtɪ] *n* obscurité *f*; **to fall into o.** tomber dans l'oubli

obsequious [əb'siːkwɪəs] *adj Formal* obséquieux(euse)

observable [əb'zɜːvəbəl] *adj* observable; *(change, difference)* perceptible

observance [əb'zɜːvəns] *n (of law, custom)* observation *f*

observant [əb'zɜːvənt] *adj* observateur(trice)

observation [ɒbzə'veɪʃən] *n* observation *f*; *(by police)* surveillance *f*; **to keep sb under o.** surveiller qn; *(in hospital)* garder qn en observation; **to escape o.** passer inaperçu(e); **to make an o.** faire une observation; *Mil* **o. post** poste *m* d'observation

observatory [əb'zɜːvətərɪ] *(pl* **observatories***) n* observatoire *m*

observe [əb'zɜːv] *vt* observer

observer [əb'zɜːvə(r)] *n* observateur(trice) *m,f*

obsess [əb'ses] *vt* obséder; **to be obsessed with** *or* **by sb** faire une fixation sur qn; **to be obsessed with** *or* **by sth** être obsédé(e) par qch

obsession [əb'seʃən] *n* obsession *f*; **to become an o.** tourner à l'obsession

obsessive [əb'sesɪv] *adj (person)* à tendances obsessionnelles; *(fear, hatred, behaviour)* obsessionnel(elle)

obsolescence [ɒbsə'lesəns] *n* obsolescence *f*

obsolete ['ɒbsəliːt] *adj* obsolète; *(design, model)* dépassé(e), démodé(e)

obstacle ['ɒbstəkəl] *n* obstacle *m*; **to put obstacles in sb's way** mettre des bâtons dans les roues à qn; *also Fig* **o. course** course *f* d'obstacles

obstetrician [ɒbste'trɪʃən] *n* obstétricien(enne) *m,f*

obstetrics [ɒb'stetrɪks] *n* obstétrique *f*

obstinacy ['ɒbstɪnəsɪ] *n* obstination *f*

obstinate ['ɒbstɪnɪt] *adj* obstiné(e); **to be o. about doing sth** s'obstiner à vouloir faire qch

obstreperous [əb'strepərəs] *adj Formal* tapageur(euse); **to get o. (about sth)** faire un scandale (à propos de qch)

obstruct [əb'strʌkt] *vt* (**a**) *(block) (road, pipe)* obstruer; *(view)* boucher, cacher (**b**) *(hinder)* gêner; *(in sport)* faire obstruction à; *Pol* **to o. a bill** faire de l'obstruction; *Law* **to o. the course of justice** entraver le cours de la justice

obstruction [əb'strʌkʃən] *n* (**a**) *(action) (of street, in sport)* obstruction *f* (**b**) *(blockage) (in road)* encombrement *m*; *(in pipe)* engorgement *m*; *Med* obstruction *f*; **to cause an o.** *(on road)* entraver la circulation

obstructive [əb'strʌktɪv] *adj* **to be o.** faire de l'obstruction

obtain [əb'teɪn] **1** *vt* obtenir
   2 *vi Formal (of practice)* avoir cours; *(of rule)* être en vigueur

obtainable [əb'teɪnəbəl] *adj* que l'on peut se procurer; **easily o.** facile à obtenir

obtrusive [əb'truːsɪv] *adj (person, behaviour)* importun(e); *(smell)* pénétrant(e)

obtuse [əb'tjuːs] *adj* obtus(e)

obverse ['ɒbvɜːs] **1** *n* (**a**) *(of medal)* avers *m* (**b**) *(opposite)* contraire *m*
   2 *adj* **o. side** *(of medal)* avers *m*

obviate ['ɒbvɪeɪt] *vt Formal (difficulty, danger)* parer à

obvious ['ɒbvɪəs] **1** *n* **to state the o.** enfoncer une porte ouverte
   2 *adj* évident(e)

obviously ['ɒbvɪəslɪ] *adv* (**a**) *(in an obvious way)* manifestement (**b**) *(of course)* évidemment; **o. not** certainement pas

occasion [ə'keɪʒən] **1** *n* (**a**) *(time)* occasion *f*; **on one o.** une fois; **on several occasions** plusieurs fois, à plusieurs reprises; **on o.** parfois, de temps en temps (**b**) *(event)* occasion *f*, événement *m*; **on the o. of...** à l'occasion de...; **to have a sense of o.** savoir marquer le coup (**c**) *(opportunity)* occasion *f*; **I'd like to take this o. to...** j'aimerais profiter de cette occasion pour... (**d**) *Formal (cause)* sujet *m*, cause *f*; **to have o. for complaint** avoir des raisons de se plaindre; **to have o. to do sth** avoir lieu de faire qch
   2 *vt Formal (cause)* occasionner, causer

occasional [ə'keɪʒənəl] *adj* occasionnel(elle); *(showers)* intermittent(e); **I have the o. cigar** il m'arrive de fumer un cigare de temps en temps; **o. table** table *f* d'appoint

occasionally [ə'keɪʒənəlɪ] *adv* occasionnellement, de temps en temps

occidental [ɒksɪ'dentəl] *adj* occidental(e)

occult [ɒ'kʌlt] **1** *n* **the o.** l'occulte *m*
   2 *adj* occulte

occupant ['ɒkjʊpənt] *n (of house, car)* occupant(e) *m,f*; *(of bus, plane)* passager(ère) *m,f*

occupation [ɒkjʊ'peɪʃən] *n* (**a**) *(profession)* métier *m*, profession *f*; *(pastime)* occupation *f* (**b**) *(of house, land)* occupation *f*

occupational [ɒkjʊ'peɪʃənəl] *adj* **o. disease** maladie *f* professionnelle; **o. hazard** risque *m* du métier; **o. therapist** ergothérapeute *mf*; **o. therapy** ergothérapie *f*

occupied ['ɒkjʊpaɪd] *adj* occupé(e); **to be o. with sth** être occupé à qch; **to keep sb o.** occuper qn

occupier ['ɒkjʊpaɪə(r)] *n (of house)* occupant(e) *m,f*

occupy ['ɒkjʊpaɪ] *(pt & pp* **occupied***) vt (house, attention)* occuper; **to o. one's time (in doing sth)** occuper son temps (à faire qch)

occur [ə'kɜː(r)] *(pt & pp* **occurred***) vi* (**a**) *(happen) (of event)* avoir lieu; *(of opportunity)* se présenter; *(of problem)* surgir (**b**) *(be present)* apparaître (**c**) *(of idea)* **to o. to sb** venir à l'esprit de qn

occurrence [ə'kʌrəns] *n* (**a**) *(event)* événement *m* (**b**) *(of disease)* incidence *f*; **to be a regular o.** se produire régulièrement

ocean ['əʊʃən] *n* océan *m*; *Am* **the o.** *(the sea)* la mer; *Fam* **oceans of** plein de; **o. liner** paquebot *m*

ocean-going ['əʊʃəngəʊɪŋ] *adj* de haute mer

Oceania [əʊʃɪ'eɪnɪə] *n* l'Océanie *f*

oceanic [əʊʃɪ'ænɪk] *adj* océanique

ocelot ['ɒsəlɒt] *n* ocelot *m*

ochre, *Am* **ocher** ['əʊkə(r)] **1** *n* ocre *m*
   2 *adj* ocre *inv*

o'clock [ə'klɒk] *adv* **(it's) one o.** (il est) une heure; **two o.** deux heures

OCR [əʊsiː'ɑː(r)] *n Comput* (**a**) *(abbr* **optical character reader***)* lecteur *m* optique (**b**) *(abbr* **optical character recognition***)* ROC *f*

Oct *(abbr* **October***)* octobre

octagon ['ɒktəgən] *n* octogone *m*

octagonal [ɒk'tægənəl] *adj* octogonal(e)

octane ['ɒkteɪn] *n Chem* octane *m*; **o. number** indice *m* d'octane

octave ['ɒktɪv] *n* octave *f*

October [ɒk'təʊbə(r)] *n* octobre *m*; *see also* **May**

octogenarian [ɒktədʒɪ'neərɪən] *n & adj* octogénaire *mf*

octopus ['ɒktəpəs] *n* pieuvre *f*, poulpe *m*

OD [əʊ'diː] (pt & pp **OD'd**, **OD'ed**) vi Fam (abbr **overdose**) faire une overdose (**on** de); Fig **I think I've rather OD'd on pizzas** je crois que j'y suis allé un peu fort sur les pizzas

odd [ɒd] **1** adj (**a**) (strange) bizarre, curieux(euse) (**b**) (number) impair(e); **to be the o. man out** être à part; **I felt the o. one out** je ne me suis pas senti à ma place (**c**) (one of a pair) dépareillé(e) (**d**) (occasional) **I smoke the o. cigarette** il m'arrive de fumer une cigarette de temps en temps; **you've made the o. mistake** tu as fait deux ou trois fautes; **o. jobs** petits travaux mpl
2 adv **a hundred o. sheep** cent et quelques moutons; **she must be thirty o.** elle doit avoir trente ans ou plus

oddball ['ɒdbɔːl] n & adj Fam excentrique mf

oddity ['ɒdɪtɪ] (pl **oddities**) n (**a**) (strangeness) bizarrerie f (**b**) (person) (strange) excentrique mf; (exceptional) cas m à part; (thing) curiosité f

oddly ['ɒdlɪ] adv bizarrement, curieusement; **o. enough,...** chose curieuse,...

oddness ['ɒdnɪs] n bizarrerie f

odds [ɒdz] npl (**a**) (probability) chances fpl; (in betting) cote f; **the o. are that...** il y a de grandes chances pour que... + subjunctive; **the o. are against her/in her favour** il y a peu de chance(s)/de grosses chances qu'elle réussisse; **against the o.** contre toute attente; **to pay over the o. (for sth)** payer (qch) plus cher que le tarif normal; Fam **it makes no o.** ça n'a pas d'importance (**b**) **to be at o. (with sb)** (of person) être en désaccord (avec qn); **to be at o. with sth** (of thing) contredire qch (**c**) Fam **o. and ends, o. and sods** bricoles fpl

odds-on [ɒd'zɒn] adj (horse) **o. favourite** grand favori m; Fam **it's o. that...** il y a gros à parier que...

ode [əʊd] n ode f

odious ['əʊdɪəs] adj odieux(euse)

odour, Am **odor** ['əʊdə(r)] n odeur f

odourless, Am **odorless** ['əʊdəlɪs] adj inodore

odyssey ['ɒdɪsɪ] (pl **odysseys**) n odyssée f

OECD [əʊiːsiː'diː] n (abbr **Organization for Economic Co-operation and Development**) OCDE f

Oedipal ['iːdɪpəl] adj oedipien(enne)

oesophagus, Am **esophagus** [iːˈsɒfəgəs] (pl **oesophagi** [iːˈsɒfəgaɪ]) n œsophage m

oestrogen, Am **estrogen** ['iːstrədʒən] n œstrogène m

of [ɒv, unstressed əv] prep (**a**) (belonging to) de; **a friend of mine** un de mes amis; **a car of her own** une voiture à elle; **the University of Manchester** l'université de Manchester (**b**) (with amount, quantity) **a litre of milk** un litre de lait; **a bottle of wine** une bouteille de vin; **a year of her life** un an de sa vie; **many of us** beaucoup d'entre nous; **there are six of us** nous sommes six; **hundreds of people** des centaines de gens; **a girl of ten** une fille de dix ans; **you of all people should know that** si quelqu'un doit le savoir, c'est bien toi (**c**) (indicating agency) **it was nice/clever of you to...** c'était gentil/intelligent de ta part de... (**d**) (with material) **made of wood/glass** en bois/verre (**e**) (with dates, time) **the 4th of October** le 4 octobre; Am **a quarter of one** une heure moins le quart

off [ɒf] **1** adj (**a**) (not functioning) (light, TV) éteint(e); (water, electricity) coupé(e); **the rain is o.** il ne pleut plus; **o. and on, on and o.** (intermittently) par intermittence (**b**) (cancelled) annulé(e); **the deal is o.** l'affaire ne se fera pas (**c**) (absent from work, school) absent(e) (**d**) (food) abîmé(e); (milk) tourné(e) (**e**) (unsuccessful) **I'm having an o. day** c'est un jour sans; **the o. season** (in tourism) la morte-saison (**f**) **to be well/badly o.** être aisé(e)/pauvre; **you'd be better o. staying where you are** tu ferais mieux de rester où tu es
2 adv (**a**) (away) **two weeks o.** dans deux semaines; **5 miles o.** ≃ à 8 kilomètres; **to be o.** (leave) s'en aller; **I'm o. to London** je pars pour Londres; **o. you go!** allez, file maintenant! (**b**) (indicating removal) **to take o. one's coat** enlever son manteau; **the handle has come o.** la poignée est partie (**c**) (with prices) **20 percent/£5 o.** 20 pour cent/5 livres de réduction (**d**) (away from work, school) **to have a day/week o.** avoir un jour/une semaine de congé; **to take some time o.** prendre des vacances
3 prep (**a**) (away from) **o. the coast** au large de la côte; **o. the main road** qui donne dans la rue principale; **o. the record** officieusement (**b**) (indicating removal from) **to fall/jump o. sth** tomber/sauter de qch; **the handle has come o. the saucepan** la poignée s'est détachée de la casserole (**c**) (with prices) **20 percent/£5 o. the price** 20 pour cent/5 livres de réduction sur le prix (**d**) (absent from) **to be o. work/school** être absent(e) de son travail/de l'école (**e**) (not liking) **to be o. one's food** ne pas avoir d'appétit; **to go o. sb/sth** ne plus aimer qn/qch (**f**) Fam (from) **to buy/borrow sth o. sb** acheter/emprunter qch à qn; **to get a cold o. sb** attraper le rhume de qn

offal ['ɒfəl] n abats mpl

offbeat ['ɒfbiːt] adj Fam original(e)

off-chance ['ɒftʃɑːns] n **on the o.** à tout hasard; **on the o. that...** en espérant que...

off-colour, Am **off-color** [ɒf'kʌlə(r)] adj (**a**) Br (unwell) **to be o.** ne pas se sentir dans son assiette (**b**) (joke) d'un goût douteux

offcut ['ɒfkʌt] n chute f

off-duty ['ɒf'djuːtɪ] adj qui n'est pas de service

offence, Am **offense** [ə'fens] n (**a**) Law infraction f; (more serious) délit m (**b**) (displeasure) **to cause sb o.** (of person, remark) vexer qn; (of film, book) choquer qn; **to take o.** se vexer; **to take o. at sth** mal prendre qch; **no o., but...** ne le prends pas mal, mais...

offend [ə'fend] **1** vt (of person, remark) vexer; (of book, film) choquer; **to be offended at or by sth** mal prendre qch
2 vi Law commettre une infraction; (more serious) commettre un délit; **to o. against good taste** être une insulte au bon goût

offended [ə'fendɪd] adj vexé(e)

offender [ə'fendə(r)] n Law délinquant(e) m,f

offending [ə'fendɪŋ] adj fautif(ive)

offense Am = offence

offensive [ə'fensɪv] **1** n also Fig offensive f; **to be on/to take the o.** être passé(e)/passer à l'attaque
2 adj choquant(e); (smell) repoussant(e); **to be o. to**

sb se montrer blessant(e) envers qn; **o. weapon** arme *f* offensive

offer ['ɒfə(r)] **1** *n* offre *f*, proposition *f*; **to make sb an o.** faire une offre *ou* une proposition à qn; **on special o.** en promotion; **o. of marriage** demande *f* en mariage

2 *vt* offrir; *(explanation)* donner; *(apologies)* présenter; **to o. sb sth, to o. sth to sb** offrir qch à qn; **to o. to do sth** offrir *ou* proposer de faire qch

▸**offer up** *vt sep* offrir

offering ['ɒfərɪŋ] *n* offre *f*; *(in church)* offrande *f*

offhand [ɒf'hænd] **1** *adj (nonchalant)* désinvolte; *(abrupt)* brusque, abrupt(e)

2 *adv (immediately)* au pied levé; *(at a rough guess)* à première vue

office ['ɒfɪs] *n* (**a**) *(place)* bureau *m*; **o. boy** garçon *m* de bureau; **o. building** immeuble *m* de bureaux; **o. hours** heures *fpl* de bureau; **o. junior** = employé de bureau chargé de tâches mineures; **o. worker** employé(e) *m,f* de bureau (**b**) *(position)* charge *f*, fonctions *fpl*; **to hold o.** être au pouvoir; **to be out of o.** ne plus être au pouvoir; **to run for** *or* **to seek o.** se présenter aux élections

officeholder ['ɒfɪshəʊldə(r)] *n* responsable *mf*

officer ['ɒfɪsə(r)] *n (in army)* officier *m*; *(in police)* agent *m* de police; *(in local government)* fonctionnaire *mf* municipal(e)

official [ə'fɪʃəl] **1** *n (in public sector)* fonctionnaire *mf*; *(of political party)* responsable *mf*

2 *adj* officiel(elle); *Br* **O. Secrets Act** = document relatif au secret-défense, signé par tous les fonctionnaires

officialdom [ə'fɪʃəldəm] *n Pej* bureaucratie *f*

officialese [əfɪʃə'liːz] *n Pej* jargon *m* administratif

officially [ə'fɪʃəlɪ] *adv* officiellement

officiate [ə'fɪʃɪeɪt] *vi Rel* officier

officious [ə'fɪʃəs] *adj* trop zélé(e)

officiously [ə'fɪʃəslɪ] *adv* avec trop de zèle

offie ['ɒfɪ] *n Br Fam (abbr* **off-licence**) ≃ magasin *m* de vins et spiritueux

offing ['ɒfɪŋ] *n* **in the o.** en perspective, en vue

off-key ['ɒf'kiː] **1** *adj* faux (fausse); *Fig (remark)* déplacé(e)

2 *adv* faux

off-licence ['ɒflaɪsəns] *n Br* ≃ magasin *m* de vins et spiritueux

off-line, offline ['ɒflaɪn] *adj Comput (processing)* en différé; *(printer)* déconnecté(e)

off-load [ɒf'ləʊd] *vt (surplus goods)* écouler; **to o. sth onto sb** *(task)* se décharger de qch sur qn; *(blame, responsibility)* rejeter qch sur qn; **to o. sb on sb** refiler qn à qn

off-peak ['ɒf'piːk] *adj (electricity)* consommé(e) pendant les heures creuses; *(holidays)* en basse saison; *(telephone call, travel)* en dehors des heures de pointe

offprint ['ɒfprɪnt] *n Typ* tirage *m* à part

off-putting ['ɒfpʊtɪŋ] *adj* peu engageant(e)

off-sales ['ɒfseɪlz] *n Br* = vente de boissons alcoolisées à emporter

off-season ['ɒfsiːzən] *adj* hors saison, en basse saison

offset ['ɒfset] **1** *n Typ* offset *m*

2 *vt (pt & pp* **offset**) compenser

offshoot ['ɒfʃuːt] *n (of tree)* rejeton *m*; *(of family)* branche *f*; *(of political party, artistic movement)* ramification *f*

offshore 1 *adj* ['ɒfʃɔː(r)] *(island)* proche de la côte; *(oil rig)* off shore *inv*; *Fin* **o. investment** placement *m* off-shore

2 *adv* [ɒf'ʃɔː(r)] au large, en mer

offside 1 *n* ['ɒfsaɪd] côté *m* du conducteur

2 *adj* (**a**) ['ɒfsaɪd] *(of car)* côté conducteur (**b**) [ɒf'saɪd] *(in sport)* hors jeu

offspring ['ɒfsprɪŋ] *n* progéniture *f*

offstage [ɒf'steɪdʒ] *adj & adv* dans les coulisses

off-the-cuff [ɒfðə'kʌf] **1** *adj* impromptu(e)

2 *adv* au pied levé

off-the-record [ɒfðə'rekɔːd] *adj* officieux(euse)

off-the-wall [ɒfðə'wɔːl] *adj Fam* loufoque

off-white ['ɒf'waɪt] **1** *n* blanc *m* cassé

2 *adj* blanc cassé *inv*

OFGAS ['ɒfgæs] *n Br (abbr* **Office of Gas Supply**) = organisme chargé de contrôler les activités des sociétés de distribution de gaz en Grande-Bretagne

OFLOT ['ɒflɒt] *n Br (abbr* **Office of the National Lottery**) = organisme chargé de contrôler la gestion de la loterie nationale britannique

OFSTED ['ɒfsted] *n Br (abbr* **Office for Standards in Education**) = organisme chargé de veiller au maintien du niveau des élèves dans l'enseignement public en Grande-Bretagne

OFTEL ['ɒftel] *n Br (abbr* **Office of Telecommunications**) = organisme chargé de contrôler les activités des sociétés de télécommunications en Grande-Bretagne

often ['ɒfən, 'ɒftən] *adv* souvent; **how o.?** *(how many times?)* combien de fois?; *(how frequently?)* tous les combien?; **as o. as not** très souvent; **more o. than not** le plus souvent; **every so o.** de temps en temps, de temps à autre

OFWAT ['ɒfwɒt] *n Br (abbr* **Office of Water Services**) = organisme chargé de contrôler les activités des sociétés de distribution d'eau en Grande-Bretagne

ogle ['əʊgəl] *vt* lorgner, reluquer

ogre ['əʊgə(r)] *n* ogre *m*

ogress ['əʊgrɪs] *n* ogresse *f*

oh [əʊ] *exclam* oh!

ohm [əʊm] *n* ohm *m*

OHMS [əʊeɪtʃem'es] *Br (abbr* **On Her/His Majesty's Service**) = formule apposée sur le courrier émis par les services gouvernementaux

oho [əʊ'həʊ] *exclam* ah ah!

OHP [əʊeɪtʃ'piː] *n (abbr* **overhead projector**) rétroprojecteur *m*

oil [ɔɪl] **1** *n (for cooking, lubricating)* huile *f*; *(petroleum)* pétrole *m*; *(for heating)* mazout *m*; *Fig* **to pour o. on troubled waters** apaiser les esprits; **o. company** compagnie *f* pétrolière; **o. crisis** choc *m* pétrolier; **o. drum** bidon *m* à pétrole; **o. lamp** lampe *f* à pétrole; **o. painting** peinture *f* à l'huile; *Fig Hum* **she's no o. painting** ce n'est pas une beauté; **o. refinery** raffinerie *f* de pétrole; **o. rig** *(on land)* derrick *m*; *(offshore)* plate-forme *f* pétrolière *ou* de forage; **o. slick** *(on sea)* nappe *f* de pétrole; *(on shore)* marée *f* noire; **o. tanker** pétrolier *m*; **o. well** puits *m* de pétrole

2 *vt* huiler, lubrifier; *Fig* **to o. the wheels** faciliter les choses

oilcan ['ɔɪlkæn] *n (for applying oil)* burette *f*; *(large container)* bidon *m* à huile

oilfield ['ɔɪlfiːld] *n* gisement *m* de pétrole

oil-fired ['ɔɪlfaɪəd] *adj (heating)* au mazout

oilskin ['ɔɪlskɪn] *n (fabric)* toile *f* cirée; **oilskins** *(garment)* ciré *m*

oily ['ɔɪlɪ] *adj* (**a**) *(hands, rag)* graisseux(euse); *(skin, hair)* gras (grasse); *(food)* huileux(euse) (**b**) *Pej (manner)* onctueux(euse)

oink [ɔɪŋk] *vi* grogner

ointment ['ɔɪntmənt] *n* pommade *f*

OK, okay ['əʊ'keɪ] *Fam* **1** *adj (in order)* correct(e), exact(e); *(acceptable)* pas mal; **that's OK by** *or* **with me** ça me va; **is it OK to wear jeans?** ça va si on vient en jean?; **no, it is NOT OK** (il n'en est) pas question; **she was OK about it** elle n'a pas fait d'histoires; **he's an OK sort of guy** c'est un type plutôt bien; **are we OK for time?** est-ce qu'on a assez de temps?
2 *exclam* OK!; **OK, OK! I'll do it now** OK, ça va, je vais le faire
3 *n* **to give (sb) the OK** donner le feu vert (à qn)
4 *vt (pt & pp* **OK'd** *or* **okayed)** donner le feu vert à

okra ['ɒkrə] *n* gombo *m*, okra *m*

old [əʊld] **1** *adj* (**a**) *(aged) (person)* vieux (vieille), âgé(e); *(car)* vieux; **to grow** *or* **get older** vieillir; **o. people** personnes *fpl* âgées; **o. people's home** maison *f* de retraite; **o. age** vieillesse *f*; **o. age pension** (pension *f* de) retraite *f*; **o. age pensioner** retraité(e) *m,f*; **to go over o. ground** revenir sur des choses qui ont déjà été dites; **to be an o. hand at sth** être rompu(e) à qch; **o. maid** vieille fille *f*; **to be o. hat** être démodé(e); *Fig* **to be one of the o. school** être de la vieille école; **the O. Testament** l'AncienTestament *m*; **o. wives' tale** conte *m* de bonne femme
(**b**) *(with specific age)* **how o. are you?** quel âge avez-vous?; **to be five years o.** avoir cinq ans; **when you're older** *(to child)* quand tu seras plus grand; **at six years o.** à (l'âge de) six ans; **a two-year-o. (child)** un enfant (âgé) de deux ans; **you're o. enough to do that yourself** tu es assez grand pour le faire toi-même
(**c**) *(former)* ancien(enne); **in the o. days** autrefois; *Br* **o. boy/girl** *(of school)* ancien(enne) élève *mf*; *Br* **the o. boy network** = la franc-maçonnerie des écoles privées et des universités; **an o. flame** un(e) ancien(enne) amoureux(euse)
(**d**) *(longstanding)* **an o. friend** un(e) vieil (vieille) ami(e); **o. habits die hard** il n'est pas facile de se défaire de ses habitudes
(**e**) *Fam (intensifier)* **any o. how** n'importe comment; **any o. thing** n'importe quoi
(**f**) *Fam (affectionate)* **o. Fred** ce vieux Fred; **the poor o. thing** le (la) pauvre vieux (vieille); **my** *or* **the o. man** *(father)* le pater, *(husband)* mon homme; **my** *or* **the o. woman** *(mother)* la mater, *(wife)* la bourgeoise
2 *npl* **the o.** les personnes *fpl* âgées

old-fashioned [əʊld'fæʃənd] *adj* (**a**) *(outdated)* démodé(e); *(person)* vieux jeu *inv* (**b**) *(traditional)* à l'ancienne

old-timer [əʊld'taɪmə(r)] *n Fam* (**a**) *(experienced person)* ancien(enne) *m,f* (**b**) *Am (form of address)* vieux *m*

old-world ['əʊld'wɜːld] *adj (atmosphere, elegance)* suranné(e); *(furnishings)* à l'ancienne

oleander [əʊlɪ'ændə(r)] *n* laurier-rose *m*

olfactory [ɒl'fæktərɪ] *adj* olfactif(ive)

oligarchy ['ɒlɪgɑːkɪ] *(pl* **oligarchies)** *n* oligarchie *f*

olive ['ɒlɪv] **1** *n* olive *f*; *Fig* **to hold out the o. branch** proposer la paix; **o. grove** oliveraie *f*; **o. oil** huile *f* d'olive; **o. tree** olivier *m*
2 *adj (skin)* olivâtre; **o. (green)** (vert) olive *inv*

Olympic [ə'lɪmpɪk] **1** *n* **the Olympics** les Jeux *mpl* olympiques
2 *adj* olympique; **the O. Games** les Jeux *mpl* olympiques

Oman [əʊ'mæn] *n* Oman

Omani [əʊ'mænɪ] **1** *n* Omanais(e) *m,f*
2 *adj* omanais(e)

ombudsman ['ɒmbʊdzmən] *n* ≃ médiateur *m* de la République

omelette, *Am* **omelet** ['ɒmlɪt] *n* omelette *f*; **ham o.** omelette au jambon

omen ['əʊmən] *n* présage *m*, augure *m*

ominous ['ɒmɪnəs] *adj* inquiétant(e); *(event)* de mauvais augure; **an o.-looking sky** un ciel menaçant; **an emergency meeting? – that sounds o.** une réunion d'urgence? – ça ne présage rien de bon

ominously ['ɒmɪnəslɪ] *adv* **she spoke o.** ce qu'elle a dit ne présage rien de bon; **it was o. quiet** il régnait un silence inquiétant

omission [əʊ'mɪʃən] *n* omission *f*

omit [əʊ'mɪt] *(pt & pp* **omitted)** *vt* omettre; **to o. to do sth** omettre de faire qch

omnibus ['ɒmnɪbəs] **1** *n* (**a**) *(book)* recueil *m* (**b**) *Old-fashioned (bus)* omnibus *m*
2 *adj* **o. edition** *(of stories, poems)* recueil *m*; *(on TV, radio)* rediffusion *f* de plusieurs épisodes en continu

omnipotence [ɒm'nɪpətəns] *n* omnipotence *f*, toute-puissance *f*

omnipotent [ɒm'nɪpətənt] *adj* omnipotent(e), tout-puissant (toute-puissante)

omnipresent [ɒmnɪ'prezənt] *adj* omniprésent(e)

omniscient [ɒm'nɪsɪənt] *adj* omniscient(e)

omnivorous [ɒm'nɪvərəs] *adj* omnivore; *Fig (reader)* qui lit de tout

on [ɒn] **1** *adv* (**a**) *(in operation) (light, television)* allumé(e); *(engine)* en marche; **the "on" position** la position marche
(**b**) *(taking place)* **what's on?** *(on TV)* qu'est-ce qu'il y a à la télé?; *(at cinema)* qu'est-ce qui passe au cinéma?; **is the meeting still on?** la réunion doit-elle toujours avoir lieu?; **I've got a lot on** j'ai beaucoup de choses à faire; **on and off, off and on** *(intermittently)* par intermittence
(**c**) *(on duty) (in hospital, surgery)* de garde; *(in shop)* de service
(**d**) *(with clothing)* **to have sth on** porter qch; **to put sth on** mettre qch; **to have nothing on** être nu(e)
(**e**) *(in time)* **earlier on** plus tôt; **later on** plus tard; **from that day on** à dater *ou* à partir de ce jour
(**f**) *(expressing continuation)* **to read/talk/work on** continuer à lire/bavarder/travailler; **he went on and on about it** il n'en finissait pas
(**g**) *(in phrases) Fam* **it's not on!** c'est inadmissible!
2 *prep* (**a**) *(expressing position)* sur; **on the table** sur la table; **on the second floor** au deuxième étage; **on the wall** sur le mur; *(hanging)* au mur; **on page 4** à la page 4; **on the right/left** à droite/gauche; **on foot** à pied; **on horseback** à cheval; **on (the) television** à la télévision; **to be on a committee** faire partie d'un comité; **I haven't got any money on me** je n'ai pas d'argent sur moi
(**b**) *(with time)* **on the 15th** le 15; **on Sunday**

dimanche; **on the hour** à l'heure pile; **on that occasion** à cette occasion

(**c**) *(about)* sur; **a book on France** un livre sur la France

(**d**) *(introducing a gerund)* **on completing the test, you should...** une fois l'examen terminé, les candidats devront...; **on discovering the corpse, she screamed** elle hurla lorsqu'elle découvrit le corps

(**e**) *(expressing use, support)* **to live on £200 a week** vivre avec 200 livres par semaine; **the drinks are on me** c'est ma tournée; **to be on antibiotics** prendre des antibiotiques; **to be on drugs** se droguer

once [wʌns] **1** *adv* (**a**) *(on one occasion)* une fois; **not o.** jamais; **o. a week** une fois par semaine; **o. or twice** une ou deux fois, une fois ou deux; **o. in a while** une fois de temps en temps; **o. more, o. again** encore une fois; **o. too often** une fois de trop; **o. and for all** une fois pour toutes; **a o.-in-a-lifetime opportunity** une occasion qui ne se présente qu'une fois (**b**) *(formerly)* autrefois; **o. upon a time there was a princess** il était une fois une princesse (**c**) **at o.** *(immediately)* immédiatement, tout de suite; *(at the same time)* à la fois, en même temps

2 *conj* **o. he reached home, he collapsed** une fois arrivé chez lui, il s'effondra; **o. he finishes, we can leave** une fois qu'il aura terminé, nous pourrons partir

once-over [wʌnsəʊvə(r)] *n Fam* **to give sb/sth the o.** jeter un coup d'œil à qn/qch

oncoming [ˈɒnkʌmɪŋ] *adj (traffic)* venant en sens inverse

one [wʌn] **1** *n (number)* un (une) *m,f*; **in ones and twos** par petits groupes; *Fam* **to get o. up on sb** prendre l'avantage sur qn

2 *pron* (**a**) *(identifying)* **this o.** celui-ci (celle-ci); **that o.** celui-là (celle-là); **these ones** ceux-ci (celles-ci); **those ones** ceux-là (celles-là); **which o. do you want?** lequel veux-tu?; **the o. I told you about** celui dont je t'ai parlé; **the big o.** le (la) grand(e); **the ones with the long sleeves** ceux qui ont les manches longues; **that's a difficult o.!** *(question)* c'est une question difficile!

(**b**) *(indefinite)* un (une); **have you got o.?** tu en as un?; **any o. of us** n'importe lequel d'entre nous; **o. of my friends** un de mes amis; **she's o. of the family** elle fait partie de la famille; **o. of these days** un de ces jours; **it was just o. of those things** on n'y peut rien; **o. after the other** l'un après l'autre; **o. at a time** un à la fois; **o. by o.** un par un; **to have had o. too many** *(drinks)* avoir bu un coup de trop

(**c**) *(particular person)* **to act like o. possessed** se conduire comme un (une) possédé(e); **I, for o., do not believe it** quant à moi, je n'y crois pas; **I'm not o. to complain** je ne suis pas du genre à me plaindre; **she's not a great o. for parties** les soirées, ce n'est pas son fort

(**d**) *(people in general) (subject)* on; *(object)* vous; **o. never knows** on ne sait jamais; **it can make o. unhappy** cela peut vous rendre malheureux; **to do o.'s best** faire de son mieux

3 *adj* (**a**) *(number)* un (une); **page/number o.** page/numéro un; **o. o'clock** une heure; **to be o. (year old)** avoir un an; **o. day/evening** un jour/soir; **o. or two people** une ou deux personnes; **for o. thing...** d'abord...; **o. American in two thinks that...** un Américain sur deux pense que...

(**b**) *(single)* un (une) seul(e); **I have just o. thing to**

say je n'ai qu'une seule chose à dire; **my o. regret** mon seul regret; **the o. person who...** la seule personne qui...; **my o. and only suit** mon seul et unique costume

(**c**) *(same)* le même (la même); **they all live in the o. house** ils habitent dans la même maison; **they are o. and the same thing/person** ils ne font qu'un; *Fam* **it's all o. to me** ça m'est égal

one-armed [ˈwʌnɑːmd] *adj (person)* manchot(e); *Br Fam* **o. bandit** machine *f* à sous

one-eyed [ˈwʌnaɪd] *adj* borgne

one-horse town [ˈwʌnhɔːsˈtaʊn] *n Fam* trou *m* perdu

one-legged [wʌnˈlegɪd] *adj* unijambiste

one-liner [wʌnˈlaɪnə(r)] *n Fam* bon mot *m*

one-man [ˈwʌnmæn] *adj (job)* pour un seul homme; **o. band** homme-orchestre *m*; **o. show** *(by performer)* spectacle *m* solo, one-man-show *m inv*; *(by artist)* exposition *f* individuelle

one-night stand [ˈwʌnnaɪtˈstænd] *n Fam (sexual encounter)* rencontre *f* sans lendemain *ou* d'un soir; *(of performer)* représentation *f* unique; *(of musician)* concert *m* unique

one-off [ˈwʌnɒf] *Br Fam* **1** *n (object)* objet *m* unique; *(event)* événement *m* unique; **it was a o.** *(mistake, success)* ça ne se reproduira pas

2 *adj* unique

one-parent family [ˈwʌnpeərəntˈfæmɪlɪ] *n* famille *f* monoparentale

one-party [ˈwʌnˈpɑːtɪ] *adj* à parti unique

one-piece swimsuit [ˈwʌnˈpiːsˈswɪmsuːt] *n* maillot *m* de bain une pièce

onerous [ˈəʊnərəs] *adj Formal* lourd(e)

oneself [wʌnˈself] *pron* (**a**) *(reflexive)* se; **to look after o.** *(when ill)* se soigner; *(generally)* s'occuper de soi; **to feel o. again** se sentir complètement rétabli(e) (**b**) *(emphatic)* soi-même; **to do sth all by o.** faire qch tout(e) seul(e); **to see for o.** regarder soi-même

one-sided [wʌnˈsaɪdɪd] *adj* (**a**) *(unequal) (contest)* inégal(e); *(relationship)* à sens unique (**b**) *(biased)* partial(e)

one-time [ˈwʌntaɪm] *adj* ancien(enne)

one-to-one [ˈwʌntəˈwʌn] *adj (talk, meeting)* seul à seul, en tête-à-tête; **o. tuition** cours *mpl* particuliers

one-track [ˈwʌntræk] *adj* **to have a o. mind** *(be obsessed with one thing)* avoir une idée fixe; *(be obsessed with sex)* être obsédé(e), ne penser qu'à ça

one-upmanship [wʌnˈʌpmənʃɪp] *n Fam* = tendance à s'affirmer supérieur aux autres

one-way [ˈwʌnweɪ] *adj (street, traffic)* à sens unique; **o. ticket** aller *m* simple

ongoing [ˈɒngəʊɪŋ] *adj* en cours; *(situation, problem)* qui dure

onion [ˈʌnjən] *n* oignon *m*; *Br Fam* **to know one's onions** connaître son affaire

on-line, online [ɒnˈlaɪn] *adj & adv Comput* en ligne

onlooker [ˈɒnlʊkə(r)] *n* spectateur(trice) *m,f*; *(at accident)* badaud *m*

only [ˈəʊnlɪ] **1** *adj* seul(e), unique; **o. child** *(boy)* fils *m* unique; *(girl)* fille *f* unique; **you're not the o. one** tu n'es pas le seul

2 *adv* seulement, ne... que; **I was o. joking** c'était (uniquement) pour rire; **permit holders o.** *(sign)* stationnement réservé; **o. an expert could advise us** seul un expert pourrait nous conseiller; **I o. touched it** je n'ai fait que le toucher; **I shall be o. too pleased to come** je serais ravi de venir; **if o. they knew!**, **if o.**, they o. knew! s'ils savaient!; **not o....,** **but also...** non seulement..., mais encore...; **I saw her o. yesterday** je l'ai vue pas plus tard qu'hier; **o. just** de justesse; **it's o. me** ce n'est que moi

3 *conj* mais

ono [əʊen'əʊ] *adv* Com (*abbr* **or nearest offer**) à débattre

on-off switch ['ɒn'ɒfswɪtʃ] *n* interrupteur *m* marche-arrêt

onomatopoeic [ɒnəmætə'piːɪk] *adj* onomatopéique

onrush ['ɒnrʌʃ] *n* (*of emotions*) vague *f*; (*of people*) ruée *f*

onset ['ɒnset] *n* début *m*, commencement *m*

on-site ['ɒnsaɪt] *adj & adv* sur place

onslaught ['ɒnslɔːt] *n* assaut *m*, attaque *f* (**on** contre)

onto ['ɒntʊ, *unstressed* 'ɒntə] *prep* (**a**) (*with direction*) sur (**b**) (*idioms*) **to be o. sb** être sur la piste de qn; **to get o. sb** contacter qn; **to be o. a good thing** avoir tiré le gros lot

onus ['əʊnəs] *n* responsabilité *f*, obligation *f*; **the o. is on the government to resolve the problem** il incombe au gouvernement de résoudre ce problème; *Law* **o. of proof** charge *f* de la preuve

onward ['ɒnwəd] **1** *adj* en avant
2 *adv* = **onwards**

onwards ['ɒnwədz] *adv* **from tomorrow o.** à partir de demain; **from now o.** désormais, dorénavant; **from then o.** à partir de ce moment-là

onyx ['ɒnɪks] *n* onyx *m*

oodles ['uːdəlz] *npl Fam* **o. of** des tonnes de; **to have o. of time** avoir largement le temps

oomph [ʊmf] *n Fam* (*energy*) punch *m*; **to have plenty of o.** avoir du punch

oops [uːps] *exclam* houp là!

ooze [uːz] **1** *n* (**a**) (*mud*) vase *f* (**b**) (*flow*) suintement *m*
2 *vt* (*liquid*) laisser suinter; *Fig* (*confidence*) déborder de; **to o. charm** avoir un charme fou
3 *vi* (*of liquid*) suinter (**from** de); *Fig* **to o. with confidence** déborder d'assurance

op [ɒp] *n Fam* (*medical operation*) opération *f*

opal ['əʊpəl] *n* opale *f*

opaque [əʊ'peɪk] *adj* opaque; *Fig* (*difficult to understand*) obscur(e)

op cit [ɒp'sɪt] *n* (*abbr* **opere citato**) op. cit.

OPEC ['əʊpek] *n* (*abbr* **Organization of Petroleum-Exporting Countries**) OPEP *f*

open ['əʊpən] **1** *n* (**a**) **in the o.** (*outside*) dehors; (*not hidden*) sur la place publique; **to bring sth out into the o.** étaler qch au grand jour; **to come out into the o. about sth** révéler qch (**b**) (*sporting competition*) open *m*
2 *adj* (**a**) (*not shut*) ouvert(e); **o. to the public** ouvert au public; **o. late** ouvert en nocturne; **to be o. to sb/sth** (*accessible to*) être ouvert à qn/qch; **to be o. to doubt** être sujet(ette) à caution; **to be o. to ridicule** s'exposer à être ridiculisé(e); **to be o. to suggestions** être ouvert à toute suggestion; **in the o. air** au grand air; **to welcome sb with o. arms** accueillir qn à bras ouverts; **o. country** rase campagne *f*; *Law* **in o. court** en audience publique; *Br* **o. day,** *Am* **o. house** journée *f* portes ouvertes; **o. invitation** invitation *f* permanente; *Fig* (*to thieves*) invitation; *Econ* **o. market** marché *m* libre; **to keep an o. mind (on sth)** réserver son jugement (sur qch); **o. prison** prison *f* ouverte; **o. sandwich** canapé *m*; **the o. sea** le large, la haute mer; **o. season** (*for hunting*) saison *f* de la chasse; *Fig* **to**

declare **o. season on sb/sth** partir en guerre contre qn/qch; **o. spaces** (*parks*) espaces *mpl* verts; **o. ticket** billet *m* open; *Br* **O. University** = organisme d'enseignement universitaire par correspondance doublé d'émissions de télévision et de radio; *Law* **o. verdict** verdict *m* de décès sans cause déterminée; **o. wound** plaie *f* béante
(**b**) (*person, manner*) ouvert(e), franc (franche); (*conflict*) ouvert; **to be o. with sb** être franc avec qn; **to be o. about sth** être franc sur qch; **o. letter** (*in newspaper*) lettre *f* ouverte; **o. secret** secret *m* de Polichinelle
3 *adv* **to cut/break sth o.** couper/casser qch; **the door flew o.** la porte s'ouvrit brusquement
4 *vt* ouvrir; (*legs, arms*) écarter; (*negotiations, conversation*) entamer; **to o. fire (on sb)** ouvrir le feu (sur qn); **to o. one's heart to sb** ouvrir son cœur à qn, s'ouvrir à qn
5 *vi* (*of door, window, flower*) s'ouvrir; (*of shop, bank*) ouvrir; (*of film*) sortir; (*of meeting, negotiations*) commencer; **to o. late** (*of shop*) ouvrir en nocturne; **to o. onto sth** donner sur qch; **the play opens with a death scene** la pièce s'ouvre sur une scène de mort

▶**open out 1** *vt sep* (*paper, map*) ouvrir, déplier
2 *vi* (*of flower*) s'ouvrir; (*of wings*) se déployer; (*of view*) s'étendre; (*of road, valley*) s'élargir

▶**open up 1** *vt sep* (*shop, business, area*) ouvrir (**to** à); (*possibility, opportunity*) offrir
2 *vi* (*of shopkeeper, new shop*) ouvrir; (*of flower*) s'ouvrir; *Fig* (*of person*) s'ouvrir, s'épancher

open-air [əʊpə'neə(r)] *adj* (*restaurant, market*) en plein air; (*swimming pool*) découvert(e)

open-and-shut case [əʊpənən'ʃʌt'keɪs] *n* **to be an o.** ne pas faire l'ombre d'un doute

opencast ['əʊpənkɑːst] *adj* à ciel ouvert

open-door policy ['əʊpən'dɔːpɒlɪsɪ] *n* (*for immigrants*) politique *f* d'ouverture des frontières; (*for university*) politique non sélective

open-ended ['əʊpən'endɪd] *adj* (*contract*) à durée indéterminée; (*question*) ouvert(e); (*discussion*) sans cadre strict

open-heart surgery ['əʊpən'hɑːt'sɜːdʒərɪ] *n* opération *f* à cœur ouvert

opening ['əʊpənɪŋ] **1** *n* (**a**) (*of play, new era*) commencement *m*; (*of negotiations, Parliament*) ouverture *f* (**b**) (*gap*) ouverture *f*, trou *m* (**c**) (*of cave, tunnel*) entrée *f* (**d**) (*opportunity*) occasion *f* favorable; (*job*) débouché *m*
2 *adj* **o. address** or **speech** (*in court case*) déclaration *f* préliminaire; (*in cricket*) premier batteur *m*; **o. ceremony** cérémonie *f* d'ouverture, inauguration *f*; **o. gambit** (*in chess*) gambit *m*; (*in conversation, negotiation*) manœuvre *f* d'approche; **o. hours** heures *fpl* d'ouverture; *Theat* **o. night** première *f*; *Br* **o. time** (*of pub*) heure d'ouverture

openly ['əʊpənlɪ] *adv* ouvertement; **she wept o.** elle a pleuré sans retenue

open-minded [əʊpən'maɪndɪd] *adj* **to be o.** avoir l'esprit ouvert

open-mouthed [əʊpən'maʊðd] *adj & adv* bouche bée *inv*

openness ['əʊpənnɪs] *n* franchise *f*

open-plan ['əʊpənplæn] *adj* (*office*) paysager(ère); (*house*) sans cloisons; **o. kitchen** coin-cuisine *m*

opera ['ɒpərə] *n* opéra *m*; **o. glasses** jumelles *fpl* de théâtre; **o. house** opéra; **o. singer** chanteur(euse) *m,f* d'opéra

operable ['ɒpərəbəl] *adj* opérable

operate ['ɒpəreɪt] **1** *vt* (*machine*) faire fonctionner; (*bus service*) assurer; **to be operated by electricity** fonctionner à l'électricité

2 *vi* (**a**) (*of machine*) fonctionner; (*of company*) opérer, travailler (**b**) (*of surgeon*) opérer; **to o. on sb (for)** opérer qn (de); **to be operated on** se faire opérer

operatic [ɒpə'rætɪk] *adj* d'opéra

operating ['ɒpəreɪtɪŋ] *adj* **o. costs** coûts *mpl ou* frais *mpl* d'exploitation; *Comput* **o. system** système *m* d'exploitation; **o. table** table *f* d'opération; *Br* **o. theatre,** *Am* **o. room** salle *f* d'opération

operation [ɒpə'reɪʃən] *n* (**a**) (*of machine*) fonctionnement *m*; **to be in o.** (*of machine*) être en service; (*of law*) être en vigueur; **to come into o.** (*of law*) entrer en vigueur (**b**) (*process*) opération *f* (**c**) (*of company*) activité *f* (**d**) (*military, surgical*) opération *f*; **to have an o. (for sth)** se faire opérer (de qch); *Mil* **operations room** salle *f* d'opérations (*d'un état-major*)

operational [ɒpə'reɪʃənəl] *adj* (*system, factory*) opérationnel(elle)

operative ['ɒpərətɪv] **1** *n* (*manual worker*) ouvrier(ère) *m,f*; (*of machine*) opérateur(trice) *m,f*; *Am* (*spy*) agent *m*

2 *adj* (*law, rule*) en vigueur; **to become o.** entrer en vigueur; **the o. word** le mot-clé

operator ['ɒpəreɪtə(r)] *n* (**a**) (*of machine*) opérateur(trice) *m,f* (**b**) *Tel* opérateur(trice) *m,f*; (**switchboard**) **o.** standardiste *mf* (**c**) *Fam* **a smooth o.** un petit finaud

operetta [ɒpə'retə] *n* opérette *f*

ophthalmology [ɒfθæl'mɒlədʒɪ] *n* ophtalmologie *f*

opinion [ə'pɪnjən] *n* opinion *f*; **in my o.** à mon avis; **to be of the o. that...** être d'avis *ou* estimer que...; **to ask sb's o.** demander l'avis *ou* l'opinion de qn; **to form an o. of sb/sth** se faire une opinion sur qn/qch; **to have a high/low o. of sb** avoir une haute/mauvaise opinion de qn; **o. poll** sondage *m* (d'opinion)

opinionated [ə'pɪnjəneɪtɪd] *adj* dogmatique

opium ['əʊpɪəm] *n* opium *m*; **o. addict** opiomane *mf*; **o. den** fumerie *f* d'opium

opossum [ɒ'pɒsəm] *n* opossum *m*

opp (*abbr* **opposite**) ci-contre

opponent [ə'pəʊnənt] *n* adversaire *mf*; (*of government*) opposant(e) *m,f* (**of** à)

opportune ['ɒpətjuːn] *adj* opportun(e)

opportunism [ɒpə'tjuːnɪzəm] *n* opportunisme *m*

opportunist [ɒpə'tjuːnɪst] *n & adj* opportuniste *mf*

opportunity [ɒpə'tjuːnɪtɪ] (*pl* **opportunities**) *n* occasion *f*; **to have the o. of doing** *or* **to do sth** avoir l'occasion de faire qch; **at every o.** à la moindre occasion; **at the first** *or* **earliest o.** à la première occasion; **if you get an o.** si tu en as l'occasion; **the o. of a lifetime** la chance de sa/ta/*etc* vie; **a job with opportunities** un emploi qui offre des perspectives

oppose [ə'pəʊz] *vt* s'opposer à; **to be opposed to sth** être opposé(e) à qch; **as opposed to...** par opposition à...

opposing [ə'pəʊzɪŋ] *adj* (*characters, viewpoints*) oppo-sé(e); (*armies*) ennemi(e); (*team*) adverse

opposite ['ɒpəzɪt] **1** *n* **the o.** le contraire

2 *adj* (**a**) (*side, shore*) opposé(e); (*page*) d'en face; **on the o. side of the street** de l'autre côté de la rue (**b**) (*opinion*) contraire; **in the o. direction** en sens inverse, dans le sens opposé; **the o. sex** l'autre sexe

3 *adv* en face; **the house o.** la maison d'en face

4 *prep* en face de

opposition [ɒpə'zɪʃən] *n* (**a**) (*resistance*) opposition *f* (**to** à); **to meet with o.** (*of idea, plan*) être contesté(e) (**b**) (*contrast*) **in o. to** contre (**c**) (*opponents*) **the o.** le camp adverse; *Br Pol* **the O.** l'opposition *f*; *Br Pol* **to be in o.** être dans l'opposition

oppress [ə'pres] *vt* opprimer

oppressed [ə'prest] **1** *npl* **the o.** les opprimés *mpl*

2 *adj* opprimé(e)

oppression [ə'preʃən] *n* oppression *f*

oppressive [ə'presɪv] *adj* (**a**) (*law, regime*) oppressif(-ive) (**b**) (*atmosphere, heat*) oppressant(e), étouffant(e)

opt [ɒpt] **1** *vt* **to o. to do sth** choisir de faire qch

2 *vi* **to o. for sth** opter pour qch

▶**opt out** *vi* (*of local authority control*) devenir autonome; (*of project, responsibilities*) se désengager

optic ['ɒptɪk] *adj* optique; **o. nerve** nerf *m* optique

optical ['ɒptɪkəl] *adj* optique; (*instrument*) d'optique; *Comput* **o. character reader** lecteur *m* optique de caractères; *Comput* **o. character recognition** reconnaissance *f* optique de caractères; *Comput* **o. disk** disque *m* optique; **o. fibre** fibre *f* optique; **o. illusion** illusion *f* d'optique

optician [ɒp'tɪʃən] *n* (*prescribing*) ophtalmologue *mf*; (*dispensing*) opticien(enne) *m,f*

optics ['ɒptɪks] *n* optique *f*

optimism ['ɒptɪmɪzəm] *n* optimisme *m*

optimist ['ɒptɪmɪst] *n* optimiste *mf*

optimistic [ɒptɪ'mɪstɪk] *adj* optimiste (**about** quant à)

optimize ['ɒptɪmaɪz] *vt* optimiser

optimum ['ɒptɪməm] **1** *n* optimum *m*

2 *adj* optimum *inv*, optimal(e)

option ['ɒpʃən] *n* (**a**) (*choice*) option *f*, choix *m*; **to have the o. of doing sth** avoir la possibilité de faire qch; **to have no o. (but to do sth)** ne pas pouvoir faire autrement (que de faire qch); **a soft** *or* **easy o.** une solution de facilité; **to leave** *or* **keep one's options open** ne pas prendre de décision tout de suite (**b**) *Fin* option *f* (**c**) (*school or university subject*) option *f*

optional ['ɒpʃənəl] *adj* facultatif(ive); **o. extra** (accessoire *m* en) option *f*; **o. subject** (*at school, university*) matière *f* à option

opt-out ['ɒptaʊt] **1** *n* désengagement *m*

2 *adj* de désengagement

opulent ['ɒpjʊlənt] *adj* opulent(e)

OR [ɜːr'ɑː(r)] *n* *Am* (*abbr* **operating room**) salle *f* d'opération

or [ɔː(r), *unstressed* ə(r)] *conj* (**a**) (*in general*) ou; **an hour or so** une heure environ; **in a day or two** dans un jour ou deux; **did she do it or not?** est-ce qu'elle l'a fait ou pas?; **snow or no snow, I'm going!** qu'il neige ou pas, j'y vais! (**b**) (*otherwise*) sinon; **stop it or I'll tell mum!** arrête, sinon je vais le dire à maman! (**c**) (*with negative*) ni; **she didn't write or phone** elle n'a ni écrit ni téléphoné

oracle ['ɒrəkəl] *n* oracle *m*

oral ['ɔːrəl] **1** *n* (*exam*) oral *m*

2 *adj* (*tradition, contraception*) oral(e); (*medication*) par voie orale; (*hygiene*) buccal(e); **o. examination** (examen *m*) oral *m*; **o. sex** rapports *mpl* bucco-génitaux

orally ['ɔːrəlɪ] *adv* oralement, de vive voix; *(take medicine)* par voie orale

Orange ['ɒrɪndʒ] *adj (in Northern Ireland)* orangiste *(protestant)*; **O. march, O. parade** défilé *m* des Orangistes; **O. Order** Ordre *m* des Orangistes

> ## Orange marches
>
> Depuis des siècles, les Orangistes défilent dans les villes d'Irlande du Nord pour commémorer les dates clés de l'histoire du protestantisme en Irlande. L'événement le plus important fut la bataille de la Boyne en 1690 où le protestant Guillaume d'Orange l'emporta sur Jacques II, roi catholique déposé. Les Orangistes sont farouchement attachés à la Couronne britannique et s'opposent à tout rapprochement avec la République d'Irlande. Leurs défilés annuels donnent souvent lieu à de violents affrontements, notamment quand ils traversent les quartiers catholiques.

orange ['ɒrɪndʒ] **1** *n (fruit)* orange *f; (colour)* orange *m;* **o. blossom** fleurs *fpl* d'oranger; **o. grove** orangeraie *f;* **o. juice** jus *m* d'orange; **o. peel** peau *f ou* écorce *f* d'orange; **o. squash** ≃ orangeade *f;* **o. tree** oranger *m*
> **2** *adj (colour)* orange *inv*

orang-outan(g) [ɔːˈræŋuːtæŋ] *n* orang-outan(g) *m*

oration [ɔːˈreɪʃən] *n* allocution *f*

orator ['ɒrətə(r)] *n* orateur(trice) *m,f*

oratory ['ɒrətərɪ] *(pl* **oratories)** *n* **(a)** *(art of speaking)* art *m* oratoire, éloquence *f* **(b)** *Rel (chapel)* oratoire *m*

orb [ɔːb] *n (of regalia)* globe *m; Lit (sphere)* orbe *m*

orbit ['ɔːbɪt] **1** *n* **(a)** *(of planet)* orbite *f;* **in o.** en orbite; **to go into o.** se mettre en orbite **(b)** *(scope)* domaine *m*
> **2** *vt* être en orbite *ou* décrire une orbite autour de
> **3** *vi* être en orbite, décrire une orbite

orchard ['ɔːtʃəd] *n* verger *m*

orchestra ['ɔːkɪstrə] *n* orchestre *m;* **o. pit** fosse *f* d'orchestre

orchestral [ɔːˈkestrəl] *adj* orchestral(e)

orchestrate ['ɔːkɪstreɪt] *vt also Fig* orchestrer

orchid ['ɔːkɪd] *n* orchidée *f*

ordain [ɔːˈdeɪn] *vt* **(a)** *Formal (decree)* ordonner; *(measure)* décréter; *Fig* **fate ordained that we should meet** il était écrit que nous devions nous rencontrer **(b)** *(priest)* ordonner

ordeal [ɔːˈdiːl] *n* épreuve *f;* **it was a bit of an o.** ça a été éprouvant

order ['ɔːdə(r)] **1** *n* **(a)** *(instruction)* ordre *m;* **to give sb an o.** donner un ordre à qn; **to be under orders (to do sth)** avoir reçu des ordres (pour faire qch); **to take orders from sb** recevoir des ordres de qn; *Fin* **pay to the o. of S. Fraser** payer à l'ordre de S. Fraser
> **(b)** *Com* commande *f;* **to place an o. (with sb)** passer (une) commande (à qn); **to make sth to o.** faire qch sur commande; **o. book** carnet *m* de commandes; **o. form** bon *m* de commande
> **(c)** *(peace, tidiness)* ordre *m; Fig* **to put one's own house in o.** faire le ménage chez soi
> **(d)** *(condition)* **out of o.** *(lift, toilets, machine)* hors service; *(telephone)* en dérangement; **in (good) working** *or* **running o.** en (bon) état de fonctionnement
> **(e)** *(in meeting)* **o. of the day** ordre *m* du jour; **to call sb to o.** rappeler qn à l'ordre; *Fig* **I think a celebration is in o.** je pense que ça mérite d'être fêté; *Fam* **that's out of o.!** ça ne se fait vraiment pas!; *Rel* **o. of service** office *m; Pol* **o. paper** (copie *f* de l')ordre du jour
> **(f)** *(system)* ordre *m;* **the new world o.** le nouvel ordre mondial
> **(g)** *(sequence)* ordre *m;* **in the right/wrong o.** dans le bon ordre/le désordre; **in o.** en ordre; **out of o.** en désordre; **in o. of age/size** par ordre d'âge/de taille
> **(h)** *(degree)* ordre *m;* **of the highest o.** de premier ordre; **the higher/lower orders** *(social classes)* les classes *fpl* supérieures/inférieures
> **(i)** *Rel* ordre *m;* **to take holy orders** entrer dans les ordres
> **(j)** **in o. to do sth** afin de *ou* pour faire qch; **in o. that...** afin *ou* pour que... + *subjunctive*
> **2** *vt* **(a)** *(instruct)* **to o. sb to do sth** ordonner à qn de faire qch; **to be ordered to do sth** recevoir l'ordre de faire qch; *Law* **to be ordered to pay costs** être condamné(e) aux dépens
> **(b)** *Com & (in restaurant)* commander
> **(c)** *(arrange) (papers, books)* classer, ranger; *(one's thoughts)* mettre de l'ordre dans; **to o. sth according to size** classer *ou* ranger qch par taille
> **3** *vi (in restaurant)* commander; **are you ready to o.?** vous avez choisi?

▸**order about, order around** *vt sep (person)* commander

▸**order in** *vt sep (supplies)* commander; *(troops)* faire venir

ordered ['ɔːdəd] *adj (organized)* ordonné(e); *(life)* régulier(ère)

orderly ['ɔːdəlɪ] **1** *n (pl* **orderlies)** *(in army)* planton *m; (in hospital)* aide-soignant(e) *m,f*
> **2** *adj* **(a)** *(tidy)* méthodique; *(life, room)* rangé(e) **(b)** *(well-behaved)* discipliné(e); **in an o. fashion** avec calme

ordinal ['ɔːdɪnəl] **1** *n (nombre m)* ordinal *m*
> **2** *adj* ordinal(e)

ordinance ['ɔːdɪnəns] *n Formal (decree)* ordonnance *f*

ordinarily ['ɔːdɪnərɪlɪ] *adv* normalement

ordinary ['ɔːdɪnərɪ] **1** *n* **out of the o.** qui sort de l'ordinaire, exceptionnel(elle)
> **2** *adj* ordinaire; **she was just an o. tourist** c'était une touriste comme une autre; *Br Naut* **o. seaman** ≃ matelot *m; Br Fin* **o. share** action *f* ordinaire

ordination [ɔːdɪˈneɪʃən] *n Rel* ordination *f*

ordnance ['ɔːdnəns] *n Mil (supplies)* matériel *m; (guns)* artillerie *f;* **o. factory** manufacture *f* d'artillerie; *Br* **O. Survey** ≃ Institut *m* Géographique National

ore [ɔː(r)] *n* minerai *m*

oregano [ɒrɪˈgɑːnəʊ] *n* origan *m*

organ ['ɔːgən] *n* **(a)** *(part of body, newspaper)* organe *m;* **o. donor** donneur(euse) *m,f* d'organe; **o. transplant** greffe *f* d'organe **(b)** *(musical instrument)* orgue *m*

organ-grinder ['ɔːgəngraɪndə(r)] *n* joueur(euse) *m,f* d'orgue de Barbarie

organic [ɔːˈgænɪk] *adj (disease, chemistry)* organique; *(food, farming)* biologique; **an o. whole** un tout

organism ['ɔːgənɪzəm] *n* organisme *m*

organist ['ɔːgənɪst] *n* organiste *mf*

organization [ɔːgənaɪˈzeɪʃən] *n* organisation *f*

organize ['ɔːgənaɪz] **1** *vt* **(a)** *(put into order)* organiser; **to o. one's time** s'organiser **(b)** *(take care of)* s'occuper de
> **2** *vi (of workers)* se syndiquer

organized [ˈɔːgənaɪzd] *adj (trip)* organisé(e); **o. crime** le crime organisé, le grand banditisme; **o. labour** main-d'œuvre *f* syndiquée

organizer [ˈɔːgənaɪzə(r)] *n (person)* organisateur(-trice) *m,f; (diary)* agenda *m*

orgasm [ˈɔːgæzəm] *n* orgasme *m*; **to have an o.** avoir un orgasme

orgy [ˈɔːdʒɪ] *(pl* **orgies)** *n* orgie *f; Fig* **an o. of violence** un déchaînement de violence

orient [ˈɔːrɪənt] **1** *n* **the O.** l'Orient *m*
  2 *vt* = **orientate**

oriental [ɔːrɪˈentəl] **1** *n Old-fashioned* **O.** Oriental(e) *m,f*
  2 *adj* oriental(e)

orientate [ˈɔːrɪənteɪt] *vt* orienter (**to** *or* **towards** vers); **to o. oneself** s'orienter; **to be orientated towards sb/sth** *(aimed at)* être destiné(e) à qn/qch

orientation [ɔːrɪənˈteɪʃən] *n* orientation *f*; **o. course** stage *m* d'initiation

orienteering [ɔːrɪənˈtɪərɪŋ] *n* course *f* d'orientation

orifice [ˈɒrɪfɪs] *n* orifice *m*

origin [ˈɒrɪdʒɪn] *n* origine *f*; **country of o.** pays *m* d'origine; **of Greek o.** d'origine grecque

original [əˈrɪdʒɪnəl] **1** *n (painting, document)* original *m*
  2 *adj* **(a)** *(not copied, innovative)* original(e) **(b)** *(first)* d'origine; *Rel* **o. sin** péché *m* originel

originality [ərɪdʒɪˈnælɪtɪ] *n* originalité *f*

originally [əˈrɪdʒɪnəlɪ] *adv* **(a)** *(initially)* à l'origine, au départ; **where do you come from o.?** d'où êtes-vous originaire? **(b)** *(in an innovative way)* d'une façon originale

originate [əˈrɪdʒɪneɪt] **1** *vt* être à l'origine de
  2 *vi (of fire)* prendre naissance; **to o. from** *(of person)* être originaire de; **to o. in** *(of custom)* être originaire de

Orkney [ˈɔːknɪ] *n* **the O. Islands, the Orkneys** les Orcades *fpl*

ornament 1 *n* [ˈɔːnəmənt] ornement *m*
  2 *vt* [ˈɔːnəment] orner

ornamental [ɔːnəˈmentəl] *adj* ornemental(e), décoratif(ive); **o. lake** pièce *f* d'eau

ornate [ɔːˈneɪt] *adj (building, surroundings)* orné(e), ornementé(e); *(style)* fleuri(e)

ornithology [ɔːnɪˈθɒlədʒɪ] *n* ornithologie *f*

orphan [ˈɔːfən] **1** *n* orphelin(e) *m,f*; **to be left an o.** devenir orphelin
  2 *adj* **an o. child** un (une) orphelin(e)
  3 *vt* **to be orphaned** devenir orphelin(e)

orphanage [ˈɔːfənɪdʒ] *n* orphelinat *m*

orthodontist [ɔːθəʊˈdɒntɪst] *n* orthodontiste *mf*

orthodox [ˈɔːθədɒks] *adj* orthodoxe

orthodoxy [ˈɔːθədɒksɪ] *n* orthodoxie *f*

orthopaedic, *Am* **orthopedic** [ɔːθəˈpiːdɪk] *adj* orthopédique; **o. surgeon** (chirurgien *m*) orthopédiste *mf*

orthopaedics, *Am* **orthopedics** [ɔːθəˈpiːdɪks] *n* orthopédie *f*

oscillate [ˈɒsɪleɪt] *vi* osciller

osmosis [ɒzˈməʊsɪs] *n also Fig* osmose *f*

osprey [ˈɒspreɪ] *(pl* **ospreys)** *n* balbuzard *m, Can* aigle *m* pêcheur

ossify [ˈɒsɪfaɪ] *(pt & pp* **ossified)** *vi Anat* s'ossifier; *Fig (of person)* se fossiliser; *(of system, organization)* se scléroser

ostensible [ɒsˈtensɪbəl] *adj* soi-disant *inv*

ostensibly [ɒsˈtensɪblɪ] *adv* soi-disant

ostentation [ɒstenˈteɪʃən] *n* ostentation *f*

ostentatious [ɒstenˈteɪʃəs] *adj (person)* m'as-tu-vu *inv; (thing)* prétentieux(euse)

osteoarthritis [ɒstɪəʊɑːˈθraɪtɪs] *n* ostéoarthrite *f*

osteopath [ˈɒstɪəpæθ] *n* ostéopathe *mf*

osteoplasty [ˈɒstɪəʊplæstɪ] *n Med* ostéoplastie *f*

osteoporosis [ɒstɪəʊpəˈrəʊsɪs] *n Med* ostéoporose *f*

ostracism [ˈɒstrəsɪzəm] *n* ostracisme *m*

ostracize [ˈɒstrəsaɪz] *vt* mettre en quarantaine

ostrich [ˈɒstrɪtʃ] *n* autruche *f*

OTC [əʊtiːˈsiː] *n Br Mil (abbr* **Officers' Training Corps)** = centre de formation pour ceux qui envisagent de devenir officier dans l'armée

other [ˈʌðə(r)] **1** *adj* autre; **the o. one** l'autre; **every o. day/week** un jour/une semaine sur deux; **the o. day/week** l'autre jour/semaine; **the o. four** les quatre autres; **o. people seem to like it** d'autres ont l'air de bien aimer ça; **any o. book** n'importe quel autre livre; **somebody o. than me** quelqu'un d'autre que moi
  2 *pron* autre; **others** d'autres; **the others** les autres; **one after the o.** l'un(e) après l'autre; **one or o. of us** l'un d'entre nous; **somewhere or o.** quelque part; **somebody or o.** quelqu'un; **some woman or o.** une femme
  3 *adv* **the colour's odd, but o. than that, it's perfect** la couleur est bizarre mais à part cela, il est très bien; **she never speaks of him o. than admiringly** elle ne parle jamais de lui autrement qu'avec admiration

otherwise [ˈʌðəwaɪz] **1** *adv* autrement; **to be o. engaged** avoir d'autres engagements; **except where o. stated** sauf indication contraire
  2 *conj* autrement, sinon

other-worldly [ʌðəˈwɜːldlɪ] *adj (person)* détaché(e) de ce monde

OTT [əʊtiːˈtiː] *adj Br Fam (abbr* **over the top)** trop *inv*; **that's a bit O.!** c'est un peu exagéré!

Ottawa [ˈɒtəwə] *n* Ottawa

otter [ˈɒtə(r)] *n* loutre *f*

Ottoman [ˈɒtəmən] *Hist* **1** *n* Ottoman(e) *m,f*
  2 *adj* ottoman(e)

ottoman [ˈɒtəmən] *n (furniture)* ottomane *f*

OU [əʊˈjuː] *n Br (abbr* **Open University)** = organisme d'enseignement universitaire par correspondance doublé d'émissions de télévision et de radio

ouch [aʊtʃ] *exclam (expressing pain)* aïe!, ouïe!

ought [ɔːt] *v aux*

> La forme négative **ought not** s'écrit **oughtn't** en forme contractée.

(a) *(expressing obligation, desirability)* **I o. to be going** je devrais m'en aller; **you oughtn't to worry so much** vous ne devriez pas vous inquiéter autant; **he had drunk more than he o. to** il n'aurait pas dû boire autant; **this o. to have been done before** on aurait dû le faire avant; **they o. not to have waited** ils n'auraient pas dû attendre **(b)** *(expressing probability)* **they o. to be in Paris by now** ils ont dû arriver à Paris maintenant; **you o. to be able to get £150 for the painting** vous devriez pouvoir tirer 150 livres de ce tableau

oughtn't [ˈɔːtənt] = **ought not**

ounce [aʊns] *n (unit of weight)* = 28,35 g, once *f; Fig* **an o. of** une once de

our [ˈaʊə(r)] *possessive adj* (**a**) *(singular)* notre; *(plural)* nos; **o. job** notre travail; **o. wives** nos femmes; **it wasn't** OUR **idea!** ce n'est pas nous qui en avons eu l'idée! (**b**) *(for parts of body)* **we hit o. heads** nous nous sommes cogné la tête

ours [ˈaʊəz] *possessive pron* (**a**) *(singular)* le nôtre (la nôtre) *m,f; (plural)* les nôtres; **their house is big but o. is bigger** leur maison est grande, mais la nôtre est plus grande encore (**b**) *(used attributively)* **this book is o.** ce livre est à nous; **a friend of o.** un de nos amis; **where's that brother of o.?** où notre frère a-t-il bien pu passer?

ourselves [aʊəˈselvz] *pron* (**a**) *(reflexive)* **we hurt o.** nous nous sommes blessés (**b**) *(emphatic)* nous-mêmes; **we o. have never...** nous-mêmes n'avons jamais...; **we told you o.** nous vous l'avons dit nous-mêmes; **we're not o. today** nous ne sommes pas dans notre état normal aujourd'hui (**c**) *(after preposition)* **we live by o.** nous vivons seuls; **we bought it for o.** nous nous le sommes acheté; **we talk to o.** nous parlons tout seuls

oust [aʊst] *vt* évincer (**from** de)

out [aʊt] **1** *adv* (**a**) *(outside)* dehors; **to go o.** sortir; **o. here** ici; **o. there** dehors; **o.!** *(in tennis)* faute!
(**b**) *(not at home, not in)* **to be o.** être sorti(e); **to stay o. late** rentrer tard
(**c**) *(not concealed)* **the secret is o.** on a révélé le secret; **he's o.** *(openly gay)* il a révélé son homosexualité; **the sun is o.** il y a du soleil; **the moon is o.** la lune est levée
(**d**) *(published)* sorti(e)
(**e**) *(not in fashion)* passé(e) de mode
(**f**) *(indicating aim)* **to be o. to do sth** chercher à faire qch; **to be o. for money** vouloir à tout prix de l'argent; *Fam* **to be o. to get sb** chercher la perte de qn
(**g**) *(unconscious, asleep)* **to be o. cold** *or* **for the count** être K-O; *Fam* **to go o. like a light** s'endormir comme une masse
(**h**) *(extinguished)* éteint(e)
(**i**) **to be o.** **(on strike)** faire grève
(**j**) *(inaccurate)* faux (fausse); **I was £25 o.** *(over)* j'avais 25 livres de trop; *(under)* il me manquait 25 livres
(**k**) *(indicating completion)* **before the week is o.** avant la fin de la semaine
(**l**) *(in phrases with of)* **o. of** *(outside)* hors de; **to go o. of the office** sortir du bureau; **to look o. of the window** regarder par la fenêtre; **to be o. of the country** être en voyage à l'étranger; **o. of reach/danger** hors de portée/danger; **to be o. of cash/ideas** ne plus avoir de liquide/d'idées; **to do sth o. of friendship/curiosity** faire qch par amitié/curiosité; **she paid for it o. of her own money** elle l'a payé de ses propres deniers; **20 o. of 20** 20 sur 20; **three days o. of four** trois jours sur quatre; *Fam* **to feel o. of it** ne pas se sentir dans le coup
2 *prep (through)* **to look o. the window** regarder par la fenêtre

out-and-out [aʊtəˈnaʊt] *adj (villain, liar)* fieffé(e); *(failure)* total(e); *(disgrace, scandal)* véritable

outback [ˈaʊtbæk] *n* **the o.** l'intérieur *m*

outbid [aʊtˈbɪd] *(pt & pp* **outbid**) *vt* enchérir avec succès sur

outboard [ˈaʊtbɔːd] **1** *n (motor)* moteur *m* hors-bord
2 *adj* **o. motor** moteur *m* hors-bord

outbreak [ˈaʊtbreɪk] *n (of hostilities, war)* déclenchement *m; (of rioting, violence)* flambée *f; (of disease)* épidémie *f*

outbuilding [ˈaʊtbɪldɪŋ] *n* dépendance *f*

outburst [ˈaʊtbɜːst] *n* éclat *m; (of activity, temper)* accès *m; (of hatred, violence)* explosion *f; (of enthusiasm)* élan *m*

outcast [ˈaʊtkɑːst] *n* paria *m*

outclass [aʊtˈklɑːs] *vt* surclasser

outcome [ˈaʊtkʌm] *n* résultat *m*, issue *f*

outcrop [ˈaʊtkrɒp] *n* affleurement *m*

outcry [ˈaʊtkraɪ] *(pl* **outcries**) *n (protest)* tollé *m*; **public o.** tollé général

outdated [aʊtˈdeɪtɪd] *adj* démodé(e)

outdid [aʊtˈdɪd] *pt of* **outdo**

outdistance [aʊtˈdɪstəns] *vt* distancer, dépasser

outdo [aʊtˈduː] *(pt* **outdid** [aʊtˈdɪd], *pp* **outdone** [aʊtˈdʌn]) *vt* surpasser; **not to be outdone,...** pour ne pas être en reste,...

outdoor [ˈaʊtdɔː(r)] *adj (life)* au grand air; *(activities, games)* de plein air; *(swimming pool)* découvert(e); **she's an o. person** elle aime le grand air

outdoors [aʊtˈdɔːz] **1** *n* **the great o.** les grands espaces *mpl*
2 *adv* dehors

outer [ˈaʊtə(r)] *adj* extérieur(e); **O. London** la grande banlieue de Londres; **o. space** espace *m* intersidéral

outermost [ˈaʊtəməʊst] *adj (nearest the outside)* le (la) plus à l'extérieur; *(most remote)* le (la) plus reculé(e)

outfit [ˈaʊtfɪt] *n* (**a**) *(clothes)* ensemble *m*, tenue *f* (**b**) *Fam (organization)* boîte *f*

outflank [aʊtˈflæŋk] *vt Mil* déborder; *Fig* prendre par surprise

outflow [ˈaʊtfləʊ] *n (of liquid)* écoulement *m; (of capital)* fuite *f*

outgoing [ˈaʊtgəʊɪŋ] *adj* (**a**) *(departing)* sortant(e) (**b**) *(sociable)* extraverti(e)

outgoings [ˈaʊtgəʊɪŋz] *npl* dépenses *fpl*

outgrow [aʊtˈgrəʊ] *(pt* **outgrew** [aʊtˈgruː], *pp* **outgrown** [aʊtˈgrəʊn]) *vt (habit, behaviour, toys)* passer l'âge de; **she's outgrown her jacket** son blouson est devenu trop petit pour elle

outhouse [ˈaʊthaʊs] *n* dépendance *f*

outing [ˈaʊtɪŋ] *n* (**a**) *(excursion)* excursion *f*, sortie *f* (**b**) *(of homosexual)* = fait, principalement pour une organisation militante, de rendre publique l'homosexualité d'une personne connue

outlandish [aʊtˈlændɪʃ] *adj* incongru(e), bizarre

outlast [aʊtˈlɑːst] *vt (object)* durer plus longtemps que; *(person)* survivre à

outlaw [ˈaʊtlɔː] **1** *n* hors-la-loi *m inv*
2 *vt (practice)* rendre illégal(e); *(person)* mettre hors la loi

outlay [ˈaʊtleɪ] *n (expense)* frais *mpl*, dépenses *fpl*

outlet [ˈaʊtlet] *n* (**a**) *(for water, steam)* orifice *m* de sortie; *(for emotions, energy)* exutoire *m* (**b**) *(shop)* point *m* de vente

outline [ˈaʊtlaɪn] **1** *n* (**a**) *(shape)* silhouette *f; (drawing)* tracé *m* (**b**) *(summary) (of play, novel)* résumé *m; (of plan, policy)* grandes lignes *fpl*; **in o.** en gros, dans les grandes lignes
2 *vt* (**a**) *(shape)* repasser les contours de; **her figure was outlined against the sky** sa silhouette se

découpait sur le ciel (**b**) *(plot of novel)* résumer; *(plan, policy)* donner les grandes lignes de

outlive [aʊt'lɪv] *vt* survivre à; **she will o. us all** elle nous enterrera tous; **to have outlived its usefulness** *(of machine, theory)* ne plus servir (à rien)

outlook ['aʊtlʊk] *n* (**a**) *(prospect)* perspectives *fpl*; *(of weather)* prévisions *fpl* (**b**) *(attitude)* façon *f* de voir les choses; **o. on life** conception *f* de la vie (**c**) *(view)* vue *f* (**over** sur)

outlying ['aʊtlaɪɪŋ] *adj* éloigné(e), isolé(e)

outmanoeuvre, *Am* **outmaneuver** [aʊtmə-'nuːvə(r)] *vt Mil* l'emporter tactiquement sur; *(in politics, sport)* déjouer les tactiques de

outmoded [aʊt'məʊdɪd] *adj* démodé(e)

outnumber [aʊt'nʌmbə(r)] *vt* l'emporter en nombre sur; **we were outnumbered** ils étaient plus nombreux (que nous)

out-of-date [aʊtəv'deɪt] *adj (idea, attitude, clothes)* démodé(e); *(passport)* périmé(e)

out-of-doors [aʊtəv'dɔːz] *adv* = **outdoors**

out-of-pocket expenses [aʊtəv'pɒkɪt'ɪk'spensɪz] *npl* menues dépenses *fpl*

out-of-the-way [aʊtəvðə'weɪ] *adj (remote)* écarté(e), loin de tout; *(unusual)* insolite, qui sort de l'ordinaire

outpatient ['aʊtpeɪʃənt] *n* malade *mf* en consultation externe; **outpatients' (department)** service *m* des consultations externes

outplacement ['aʊtpleɪsmənt] *n* = aide à la recherche d'un nouvel emploi, fournie par l'employeur lors d'un licenciement

outpost ['aʊtpəʊst] *n Mil* poste *m* avancé; *Fig* bastion *m*

output ['aʊtpʊt] **1** *n (of goods)* production *f*; *(of data, information)* sortie *f*; *(of generator, machine)* débit *m*
2 *vt (pt & pp* **output)** produire; *(data, information)* sortir

outrage ['aʊtreɪdʒ] **1** *n* (**a**) *(act)* atrocité *f*; **it's an o.!** c'est un scandale! (**b**) *(indignation)* indignation *f* (**at** face à)
2 *vt (make indignant)* scandaliser, outrer

outrageous [aʊt'reɪdʒəs] *adj (shocking)* scandaleux(euse); *(clothes, haircut)* extravagant(e)

outrageously [aʊt'reɪdʒəslɪ] *adv (expensive)* scandaleusement; *(behave)* de façon scandaleuse; *(dressed)* de façon extravagante

outreach worker ['aʊtriːtʃwɜːkə(r)] *n* = employé d'une association travaillant sur le terrain

outrider ['aʊtraɪdə(r)] *n Br (motorcyclist)* motard *m* (d'escorte)

outright 1 *adv* [aʊt'raɪt] (**a**) *(completely)* **to buy sth o.** acheter qch au comptant; **he was killed o.** il fut tué sur le coup (**b**) *(ask, tell)* franchement; *(refuse)* catégoriquement
2 *adj* ['aʊtraɪt] *(refusal)* catégorique; *(failure)* total(e); *(winner)* incontesté(e)

outrun [aʊt'rʌn] *(pt* **outran** [aʊt'ræn], *pp* **outrun)** *vt* courir plus vite que

outsell [aʊt'sel] *(pt & pp* **outsold** [aʊt'səʊld] *) vt* se vendre mieux que

outset ['aʊtset] *n* **at the o.** au départ; **from the o.** dès le départ

outshine [aʊt'ʃaɪn] *(pt & pp* **outshone** [aʊt'ʃɒn] *) vt (surpass)* éclipser

outside ['aʊtsaɪd, aʊt'saɪd] **1** *n* extérieur *m*, dehors *m*; **on the o.** à l'extérieur; *Fig* extérieurement; **from the o.** du dehors, de l'extérieur; **at the o.** *(of estimate)* tout au plus

2 *adj (influence)* extérieur(e); *Rad & TV* **o.** broadcast reportage *m*; **o. lane** *(when driving on left)* file *f* de droite; *(when driving on right)* file de gauche; **the o. world** le monde extérieur; **an o. chance** une petite chance

3 *adv* dehors, à l'extérieur; **to go o.** sortir

4 *prep* (**a**) *(physically)* en dehors de, à l'extérieur de; *(in front of)* devant; **o. office hours** en dehors des heures de bureau (**b**) *(apart from)* en dehors de; **o. (of) a few friends** en dehors de quelques amis

outsider [aʊt'saɪdə(r)] *n* (**a**) *(socially)* étranger(ère) *m,f* (**b**) *(in race, election)* outsider *m*

outsize ['aʊtsaɪz] *adj (clothes)* très grande taille; *(appetite, ego)* démesuré(e)

outskirts ['aʊtskɜːts] *npl* **the o.** la banlieue

outsmart [aʊt'smaːt] *vt* se montrer plus fin(e) que

outsource ['aʊtsɔːs] *vt Com* externaliser

outsourcing ['aʊtsɔːsɪŋ] *n Com* externalisation *f*

outspoken [aʊt'spəʊkən] *adj* franc (franche)

outstanding [aʊt'stændɪŋ] *adj* (**a**) *(remarkable)* exceptionnel(elle) (**b**) *(unresolved) (business)* en suspens (**c**) *(unpaid) (amount, debt)* impayé(e); *(payment)* en retard; *(interest)* échu(e)

outstay [aʊt'steɪ] *vt* **I hope I haven't outstayed my welcome** j'espère ne pas avoir abusé de votre hospitalité

outstretched ['aʊtstretʃt] *adj (leg, arm)* tendu(e)

outstrip [aʊt'strɪp] *(pt & pp* **outstripped)** *vt* dépasser

out-tray ['aʊtreɪ] *n* courrier *m* à expédier

outward ['aʊtwəd] **1** *adj* (**a**) *(external)* extérieur(e) (**b**) **o. voyage** *or* **journey** voyage *m* aller
2 *adv* = **outwards**

outwardly ['aʊtwədlɪ] *adv* en apparence

outwards ['aʊtwədz] *adv* vers l'extérieur

outweigh [aʊt'weɪ] *vt (be more important than)* l'emporter sur

outwit [aʊt'wɪt] *(pt & pp* **outwitted)** *vt* se montrer plus malin(igne) que

outworker ['aʊtwɜːkə(r)] *n* travailleur(euse) *m,f* à domicile

outworn [aʊt'wɔːn] *adj (theory, idea)* périmé(e)

ova ['əʊvə] *pl of* **ovum**

oval ['əʊvəl] **1** *n* ovale *m*
2 *adj* ovale

ovarian [əʊ'veərɪən] *adj Anat* ovarien(enne)

ovary ['əʊvərɪ] *(pl* **ovaries)** *n Anat* ovaire *m*

ovation [əʊ'veɪʃən] *n* ovation *f*; **to give sb a standing o.** se lever pour applaudir qn

oven ['ʌvən] *n* four *m*; **o. glove** gant *m* isolant

oven-proof ['ʌvənpruːf] *adj* qui va au four

oven-ready ['ʌvənredɪ] *adj* prêt(e) à rôtir

ovenware ['ʌvənweə(r)] *n* vaisselle *f* allant au four

over ['əʊvə(r)] **1** *prep* (**a**) *(above)* au-dessus de; **the plane flew o. our heads** l'avion est passé au-dessus de nos têtes; **I couldn't hear her o. the noise** impossible de l'entendre avec tout ce bruit; *Fig* **her talk was way o. my head** son exposé m'est passé complètement au-dessus de la tête

(**b**) *(on top of)* sur; **to put a blanket o. sb** mettre une couverture sur qn

(**c**) *(from one side to the other of)* par-dessus; **to throw sth o. the wall** jeter qch par-dessus le mur; **to read o. sb's shoulder** lire par-dessus l'épaule de qn

(**d**) *(across)* **to go o. the road** traverser la rue; **to live o. the road** habiter en face; **o. the border** de l'autre côté de la frontière; **the bridge o. the river** le pont qui traverse la rivière

(**e**) *(about)* **to laugh o. sth** rire de qch; **to fight o. sth** se battre pour qch

(**f**) *(more than)* plus de; **he's o. fifty** il a plus de cinquante ans; **children o. five** les enfants de plus de cinq ans; **o. and above** en plus de

(**g**) *(during)* pendant; **o. the last three years** les trois dernières années; **o. lunch** en déjeunant

(**h**) *(recovered from)* **to be o. sth** *(illness, disappointment)* s'être remis(e) de qch

2 *adv* (**a**) *(across)* **o. here** ici; **o. there** là-bas; **to cross o.** *(the street)* traverser; **to ask** or **invite sb o. (to one's house)** inviter qn (chez soi)

(**b**) *(down)* **to fall o.** tomber; **to bend o.** se pencher; **to push sb/sth o.** faire tomber qn/qch

(**c**) *(everywhere)* **famous the world o.** célèbre dans le monde entier

(**d**) *(expressing repetition)* **three times o.** trois fois de suite; **o. and o. again** encore et encore; **to do sth all o. again** refaire qch

(**e**) *(in excess)* **children of five and o.** les enfants de cinq ans et plus; **there was £5 left o.** il restait 5 livres

(**f**) *(on radio)* **o.!** à vous!; **o. and out!** terminé!

3 *adj* **to be (all) o.** être fini(e); **to get sth o. (and done) with** en finir avec qch

4 *n (in cricket)* = série de six balles

overabundant [əʊvərə'bʌndənt] *adj* surabondant(e)

overactive [əʊvər'æktɪv] *adj (imagination)* débridé(e)

overall ['əʊvərɔːl] **1** *adj* global(e); *(size, area)* total(e); **she has o. responsibility for sales** elle est responsable de l'ensemble du service des ventes

2 *adv* dans l'ensemble; **£10 o.** 10 livres en tout; **third o.** troisième au classement général

overalls ['əʊvərɔːlz] *npl* (**a**) *(work garment)* bleu *m* de travail (**b**) *Am (dungarees)* salopette *f*

overanxious [əʊvər'æŋkʃəs] *adj* trop inquiet(ète)

overawe [əʊvə'rɔː] *vt* **to be overawed by sb/sth** se laisser impressionner par qn/qch

overbalance [əʊvə'bæləns] *vi (of person)* perdre l'équi-libre; *(of pile, load)* se renverser

overbearing [əʊvə'beərɪŋ] *adj* autoritaire

overblown [əʊvə'bləʊn] *adj (style)* ampoulé(e)

overboard ['əʊvəbɔːd] *adv* par-dessus bord; **man o.!** un homme à la mer!; *Fig* **to go o. (about)** s'emballer (pour)

overbook ['əʊvəbʊk] *vt* faire du surbooking sur

overcapacity ['əʊvəkə'pæsɪti] *n Ind* surcapacité *f*

overcast ['əʊvəkɑːst] *adj (sky, day)* nuageux(euse)

overcautious [əʊvə'kɔːʃəs] *adj* trop prudent(e)

overcharge [əʊvə'tʃɑːdʒ] *vt* **to o. sb for sth** faire payer qch trop cher à qn; **he overcharged me by a pound** il m'a fait payer une livre en trop

overcoat ['əʊvəkəʊt] *n* pardessus *m*

overcome [əʊvə'kʌm] *(pt* **overcame** [əʊvə'keɪm], *pp* **overcome)** *vt (opponent, one's fears)* vaincre; *(problem, obstacle)* surmonter; **to be overcome with** or **by grief** être accablé(e) de chagrin; **I was quite overcome** j'ai été bouleversé

overcompensate [əʊvə'kɒmpenseɪt] *vi* **to o. for sth** surcompenser qch

overconfident [əʊvə'kɒnfɪdənt] *adj* trop confiant(e)

overcook [əʊvə'kʊk] *vt (faire)* trop cuire

overcrowded [əʊvə'kraʊdəd] *adj* bondé(e)

overcrowding [əʊvə'kraʊdɪŋ] *n* surpeuplement *m*

overdeveloped [əʊvədɪ'veləpt] *adj* trop développé(e)

overdo [əʊvə'duː] *(pt* **overdid** [əʊvə'dɪd], *pp* **overdone** [əʊvə'dʌn]) *vt* exagérer; **to o. it** *(work too hard)* se surmener; **to o. the salt/make-up** forcer sur le sel/le maquillage

overdone ['əʊvədʌn] *adj (food)* trop cuit(e)

overdose [əʊvə'dəʊs] **1** *n* overdose *f*

2 *vi* faire une overdose (**on** de); *Fig* **to o. on chocolate** exagérer avec le chocolat

overdraft ['əʊvədrɑːft] *n Fin* découvert *m*

overdrawn [əʊvə'drɔːn] *adj* à découvert

overdressed [əʊvə'drest] *adj* trop habillé(e)

overdrive ['əʊvədraɪv] *n Fig* **to go into o.** passer à la vitesse supérieure

overdue [əʊvə'djuː] *adj (person, train)* en retard; *(bill)* impayé(e); *(library book)* qui n'a pas été rendu(e); **this measure is long o.** cette mesure aurait dû être prise il y a longtemps

overeat [əʊvə'riːt] *(pt* **overate** [əʊvə'ret], *pp* **overeaten** [əʊvə'riːtən]) *vi* trop manger

overemphasize [əʊvər'emfəsaɪz] *vt* trop mettre l'accent sur

overenthusiastic ['əʊvərɪnθjuːzɪ'æstɪk] *adj* trop enthousiaste

overestimate [əʊvə'restɪmeɪt] *vt* surestimer; *(danger)* exagérer

overexcited [əʊvərɪk'saɪtɪd] *adj* surexcité(e)

overexpose [əʊvərɪks'pəʊz] *vt Phot* surexposer

overextended [əʊvərɪk'stendɪd] *adj Fin* incapable de faire face à ses engagements

overfishing [əʊvə'fɪʃɪŋ] *n* surpêche *f*

overflow 1 *n* ['əʊvəfləʊ] *(liquid)* trop-plein *m*; **o. (pipe)** trop-plein

2 *vi* [əʊvə'fləʊ] déborder; **his desk was overflowing with papers** son bureau disparaissait sous la paperasse

overgrown [əʊvə'grəʊn] *adj (garden)* envahi(e) par les mauvaises herbes; **he's like an o. schoolboy** il se conduit comme un collégien

overhang 1 *n* ['əʊvəhæŋ] *(of roof, cliff)* surplomb *m*

2 *vt* [əʊvə'hæŋ] *(pt & pp* **overhung** [əʊvə'hʌŋ]) surplomber

overhaul 1 *n* ['əʊvəhɔːl] *also Fig* révision *f*

2 *vt* [əʊvə'hɔːl] (**a**) *(machine, policy)* réviser (**b**) *(overtake)* dépasser

overhead 1 *n* ['əʊvəhed] *Am Com* = **overheads**

2 *adj* ['əʊvəhed] *(cable)* aérien(enne); **o. projector** rétroprojecteur *m*

3 *adv* [əʊvə'hed] au-dessus; **a plane flew o.** un avion passa au-dessus de nos têtes

overheads ['əʊvəhedz] *npl Br Com* frais *mpl* généraux

overhear [əʊvə'hɪə(r)] *(pt & pp* **overheard** [əʊvə'hɜːd]) *vt (person)* entendre (par hasard); *(words)* surprendre

overheat [əʊvə'hiːt] *vi (of engine)* chauffer; *(of economy)* être en surchauffe

overindulge [əʊvərɪn'dʌldʒ] **1** *vt (child)* trop gâter; **to o. oneself** *(drink, eat to excess)* faire des excès

2 *vi* faire des excès

overjoyed [əʊvə'dʒɔɪd] *adj* absolument ravi(e) (**at** de)

overkill ['əʊvəkɪl] *n* **it's o.** c'est exagéré, c'est trop; **media o.** matraquage *m*

overland ['əʊvəlænd] *adv & adj* par voie de terre

overlap 1 n ['əʊvəlæp] (between planks, tiles) chevauchement m

2 vi [əʊvə'læp] (pt & pp **overlapped**) (of planks, tiles, periods) se chevaucher; (of theories) avoir des points communs (**with** avec); **to o. with** (in time) empiéter sur

overleaf [əʊvə'liːf] adv au verso; **see o.** voir au verso

overload 1 n ['əʊvələʊd] Elec surcharge f

2 vt [əʊvə'ləʊd] also Fig surcharger (**with** de)

overlong [əʊvə'lɒŋ] adj trop long (longue)

overlook [əʊvə'lʊk] vt (**a**) (of building, window) donner sur; **the town is overlooked by the castle** le château surplombe la ville (**b**) (fail to notice) oublier (**c**) (disregard) fermer les yeux sur

overly ['əʊvəlɪ] adv excessivement, trop

overmanning [əʊvə'mænɪŋ] n sureffectifs mpl

overmuch [əʊvə'mʌtʃ] adv outre mesure, trop

overnight 1 adv [əʊvə'naɪt] (**a**) (during the night) (pendant) la nuit; **to stay o.** passer la nuit; **leave to soak o.** laisser tremper toute la nuit (**b**) (suddenly) du jour au lendemain

2 adj ['əʊvənaɪt] (**a**) (for one night) **o. train/flight** train m/vol m de nuit; **o. bag** petit sac m de voyage; **o. stay** séjour m d'une nuit; (in hotel) nuit f (**b**) (sudden) soudain(e)

overoptimistic [əʊvərɒptɪ'mɪstɪk] adj trop optimiste (**about** quant à)

overpaid [əʊvə'peɪd] adj trop payé(e)

overpass ['əʊvəpɑːs] n (road) pont m; (for pedestrians) passerelle f

overpayment [əʊvə'peɪmənt] n (of taxes) trop-perçu m; (of employee) rémunération f excessive

overpopulation [əʊvəpɒpjʊ'leɪʃən] n surpopulation f, surpeuplement m

overpower [əʊvə'paʊə(r)] vt maîtriser

overpowering [əʊvə'paʊərɪŋ] adj (heat, smell) suffocant(e); (taste) qui prend à la gorge; (desire) irrépressible

overpriced [əʊvə'praɪst] adj trop cher(ère)

overproduction [əʊvəprə'dʌkʃən] n Econ sur-production f

overrated [əʊvə'reɪtɪd] adj surfait(e)

overreach [əʊvə'riːtʃ] vt **to o. oneself** trop présumer de ses forces

overreact [əʊvərɪ'ækt] vi réagir de façon excessive

override [əʊvə'raɪd] vt (pt **overrode** [əʊvə'rəʊd], pp **overridden** [əʊvə'rɪdən]) (**a**) (objections, wishes, regulations) passer outre à; (decision) annuler (**b**) (take precedence over) avoir la priorité sur; Tech (device) annuler

overriding [əʊvə'raɪdɪŋ] adj (importance) capital(e); (factor) prépondérant(e)

overrule [əʊvə'ruːl] vt (opinion) rejeter; (decision) annuler; **she was overruled by her boss** son patron a rejeté sa proposition

overrun 1 vt [əʊvə'rʌn] (pt **overran** [əʊvə'ræn], pp **overrun**) (**a**) (country) envahir; **the house was overrun with mice** la maison était infestée de souris (**b**) (allotted time) dépasser

2 vi [əʊvə'rʌn] (of TV, radio programme) déborder sur l'horaire

3 n ['əʊvərʌn] Com (cost) **o.** dépassement m du budget

overseas 1 adj ['əʊvəsiːz] d'outre-mer; (trade, debt) extérieur(e)

2 adv [əʊvə'siːz] à l'étranger

oversee [əʊvə'siː] (pt **oversaw** [əʊvə'sɔː], pp **overseen** [əʊvə'siːn]) vt superviser

overseer ['əʊvəsɪə(r)] n Old-fashioned contremaître m

oversensitive [əʊvə'sensɪtɪv] adj hypersensible

oversexed [əʊvə'sekst] adj qui a une libido démesurée

overshadow [əʊvə'ʃædəʊ] vt Fig (of atmosphere, threat) planer sur; (of person) éclipser

overshoe ['əʊvəʃuː] n Am caoutchouc m

overshoot [əʊvə'ʃuːt] (pt & pp **overshot** [əʊvə'ʃɒt]) vt dépasser

oversight ['əʊvəsaɪt] n oubli m, omission f

oversimplify [əʊvə'sɪmplɪfaɪ] (pt & pp **oversimplified**) vt simplifier à outrance

oversized ['əʊvəsaɪzd] adj (very big) énorme; (clothes) trop grand(e)

oversleep [əʊvə'sliːp] (pt & pp **overslept** [əʊvə'slept]) vi ne pas se réveiller à temps

overspend [əʊvə'spend] (pt & pp **overspent** [əʊvə'spent]) **1** vt **to o. one's budget** dépasser son budget

2 vi trop dépenser

overspill ['əʊvəspɪl] n (of population) excédent m; (from meeting, party) trop-plein m

overstaffing [əʊvə'stɑːfɪŋ] n sureffectifs mpl

overstate [əʊvə'steɪt] vt exagérer

overstay [əʊvə'steɪ] = **outstay**

overstep [əʊvə'step] (pt & pp **overstepped**) vt outrepasser; Fig **to o. the mark** dépasser les bornes

oversubscribed [əʊvəsəb'skraɪbd] adj Fin sursouscrit(e)

overt [əʊ'vɜːt] adj manifeste

overtake [əʊvə'teɪk] (pt **overtook** [əʊvə'tʊk], pp **overtaken** [əʊvə'teɪkən]) vt & vi dépasser, doubler; **to be overtaken by events** être dépassé(e) par les événements

over-the-top [əʊvəðɪ'tɒp] adj Br Fam excessif(ive); **that's a bit o.!** c'est un peu exagéré!

overthrow 1 n ['əʊvəθrəʊ] renversement m

2 vt [əʊvə'θrəʊ] (pt **overthrew** [əʊvə'θruː], pp **overthrown** [əʊvə'θrəʊn]) renverser

overtime ['əʊvətaɪm] **1** n heures fpl supplémentaires

2 adv **to work o.** faire des heures supplémentaires; Fig (of imagination) s'emballer

overtly [əʊ'vɜːtlɪ] adv ouvertement

overtone ['əʊvətəʊn] n (of sadness, bitterness) pointe f; (of violence, racism) relent m; **his speech was full of racist overtones** son discours était truffé de sous-entendus racistes

overture ['əʊvətjʊə(r)] n Mus ouverture f; Fig **to make overtures to sb** (sexually) faire des avances à qn; (in business, politics) faire des démarches auprès de qn

overturn [əʊvə'tɜːn] **1** vt (table, government) renverser; (boat) faire chavirer; (decision) annuler

2 vi se renverser; (of boat) chavirer

overuse 1 n [əʊvə'juːs] emploi m excessif

2 vt [əʊvə'juːz] abuser de

overvalue [əʊvə'væljuː] vt (currency) surévaluer; (ability) surestimer

overview ['əʊvəvjuː] n vue f d'ensemble

overweight [əʊvə'weɪt] adj trop gros (grosse); **to be 10 kilos o.** avoir 10 kilos de trop

overwhelm [əʊvə'welm] vt (enemy, opponent) écraser; **overwhelmed with joy** au comble de la joie; **overwhelmed by grief/with work** accablé(e) de chagrin/de travail

overwhelming [əʊvə'welmɪŋ] *adj (need, desire)* irré-pressible; *(pressure, defeat, majority)* écrasant(e)
overwhelmingly [əʊvə'welmɪŋlɪ] *adv* massivement
overwork 1 *n* ['əʊvəwɜːk] surmenage *m*
  2 *vt* [əʊvə'wɜːk] *(person)* surcharger de travail
  3 *vi* [əʊvə'wɜːk] se surmener
overwrite [əʊvə'raɪt] *(pt* **overwrote** [əʊvə'rəʊt], *pp*
  overwritten [əʊvə'rɪtən]) *vt Comput (file)* écraser
overwrought [əʊvə'rɔːt] *adj* à bout; **to get o. (about sth)** se mettre dans tous ses états (à propos de qch)
ovulate ['ɒvjʊleɪt] *vi Biol* ovuler
ovulation [ɒvjʊ'leɪʃən] *n Biol* ovulation *f*
ovum ['əʊvəm] *(pl* **ova** ['əʊvə]) *n Biol* ovule *m*
ow [aʊ] *exclam* aïe!, ouïe!
owe [əʊ] *vt also Fig* devoir; **to o. sb sth, to o. sth to sb** devoir qch à qn; **to o. sb an apology** devoir des ex-cuses à qn; **to o. it to oneself to do sth** se devoir de faire qch
owing ['əʊɪŋ] *adj* (**a**) **the money o. to me** l'argent qui m'est dû (**b**) **o. to** *(because of)* en raison de, à cause de
owl [aʊl] *n* hibou *m*, chouette *f*
own [əʊn] **1** *adj* propre; **her o. money** son propre ar-gent; **I saw it with my o. eyes** je l'ai vu de mes propres yeux; **I do my o. accounts** je fais mes comptes moi-même; **she's famous in her o. right** elle est célèbre elle aussi; **o. goal** *(in football)* = but marqué contre son propre camp; *Fig* **to score an o. goal** apporter de l'eau au moulin de l'adversaire
  2 *pron* (**a**) **my o.** le mien (la mienne); **the house is my o.** la maison est à moi; **I have money of my o.** j'ai de l'argent à moi; **to make sth one's o.** s'approprier qch; **for reasons of her o.** pour des raisons qui ne regardent qu'elle
  (**b**) **to do sth on one's o.** *(without company)* faire qch tout(e) seul(e); **I am (all) on my o.** je suis seul; **you're on your o.!** *(I won't support you)* débrouille-toi tout seul!
  (**c**) *(idioms)* **to come into one's o.** montrer ce dont on est capable; **to get one's o. back (on sb)** se venger (de qn); **to hold one's o.** se maintenir
  3 *vt* (**a**) *(property)* posséder, être propriétaire de; **who owns this jumper?** à qui est ce pull?; **he be-haves as if he owns the place** il se conduit comme en pays conquis
  (**b**) *Old-fashioned (admit)* avouer
▸**own up** *vi (confess)* avouer; **to o. up to sth** avouer qch
own-brand ['əʊnbrænd] *adj Com* vendu(e) sous la marque du distributeur

owner ['əʊnə(r)] *n* propriétaire *mf*
owner-occupier ['əʊnər'ɒkjʊpaɪə(r)] *n* propriétaire *mf* occupant(e)
ownership ['əʊnəʃɪp] *n* propriété *f*; **under new o.** *(sign)* changement de propriétaire; **to be in private/ public o.** appartenir au secteur privé/public
ox [ɒks] *(pl* **oxen** ['ɒksən]) *n* bœuf *m*
Oxbridge ['ɒksbrɪdʒ] *n* les universités *fpl* d'Oxford et de Cambridge

---

Oxbridge

Oxbridge désigne conjointement les universités d'Oxford et de Cambridge, les plus anciennes et les plus prestigieuses d'Angleterre. Oxford et Cambridge se distinguent des autres établissements d'enseignement supérieur, notamment par leur structure collégiale et leurs conditions d'admission très rigoureuses.
  De nos jours, Oxbridge est toujours synonyme d'élitisme en dépit des efforts entrepris pour élargir le recrutement des deux universités. Jusqu'à une époque très récente, un diplôme d'Oxbridge était considéré comme indispensable pour accéder à des postes importants dans le monde de la politique ou de la diplomatie.

---

oxide ['ɒksaɪd] *n Chem* oxyde *m*
oxidize ['ɒksɪdaɪz] *Chem* **1** *vt* oxyder
  2 *vi* s'oxyder
oxtail ['ɒksteɪl] *n* queue *f* de bœuf
oxyacetylene [ɒksɪə'setɪliːn] *n Chem* **o. torch** chalu-meau *m* oxyacétylénique
oxygen ['ɒksɪdʒən] *n* oxygène *m*; **o. bottle** *or* **cylinder** bouteille *f* d'oxygène; **o. mask** masque *m* à oxygène
oxymoron [ɒksɪ'mɔːrɒn] *(pl* **oxymora**) *n* oxymore *m*, oxymoron *m*
oyster ['ɔɪstə(r)] *n* huître *f*; *Fig* **the world's your o.** le monde t'appartient; **o. bed** parc *m* à huîtres; **o. farm-ing** ostréiculture *f*
oystercatcher ['ɔɪstəkætʃə(r)] *n* huîtrier *m*
Oz [ɒz] *n Fam* l'Australie *f*
oz *(abbr* **ounce(s)**) once *f*
ozone ['əʊzəʊn] *n Chem* ozone *m*; **o. depletion** di-minution *f* de la couche d'ozone; **the o. layer** la couche d'ozone
ozone-friendly ['əʊzəʊn'frendlɪ] *adj* qui préserve la couche d'ozone

P

P, p¹ [piː] *n (letter)* P, p *m inv; Fam* **to mind one's P's and Q's** bien se tenir; *Br* **P45** = document administratif donné à tout employé lorsqu'il quitte un emploi et devant être présenté à tout nouvel employeur, où figurent le total de ses rémunérations, cotisations et impôts; **to be handed one's P45** se faire licencier

p² [piː] *Br (abbr* **penny)** penny *m; (abbr* **pence)** pence *mpl*

PA ['piː'eɪ] *n* (**a**) *(abbr* **public address)** PA (**system**) (système *m* de) sonorisation *f* (**b**) *Com (abbr* **personal assistant)** secrétaire *mf* de direction

pa [pɑː] *n Am Fam (dad)* papa *m*

p.a. *(abbr* **per annum)** par an

pace [peɪs] **1** *n* (**a**) *(step)* pas *m; Fig* **to put sb through his paces** mettre qn à l'épreuve (**b**) *(speed)* vitesse *f,* allure *f;* **at a slow/fast p.** à petite/vive allure; **to set the p.** donner l'allure; *Fig* montrer la voie; **to keep p. with sb** suivre qn; *Fig (in activity)* suivre le rythme de qn; **the slower p. of country life** le rythme plus paisible de la vie à la campagne

2 *vt (room, street)* arpenter; **to p. oneself** *(in race, work)* trouver son rythme

3 *vi* **to p. up and down** faire les cent pas

pacemaker ['peɪsmeɪkə(r)] *n* (**a**) *(in race)* meneur(euse) *m,f* de train (**b**) *(for heart)* stimulateur *m* cardiaque

Pacific [pə'sɪfɪk] *adj* **the P. (Ocean)** le Pacifique, l'océan *m* Pacifique; **the P. Rim** les pays *mpl* de l'Asie-Pacifique; *Am* **P. Standard Time** heure *f* de la côte ouest de l'Amérique du Nord

pacifier ['pæsɪfaɪə(r)] *n Am* tétine *f*

pacifism ['pæsɪfɪzəm] *n* pacifisme *m*

pacifist ['pæsɪfɪst] *n & adj* pacifiste *mf*

pacify ['pæsɪfaɪ] *(pt & pp* **pacified)** *vt (country)* pacifier; *(person)* apaiser, calmer

pack [pæk] **1** *n* (**a**) *(rucksack)* sac *m* à dos (**b**) *(of cigarettes, washing powder)* paquet *m; (of beer)* pack *m; (of playing cards)* jeu *m* (**c**) *(of thieves, photographers)* bande *f; (of runners, cyclists)* peloton *m; (in rugby)* pack *m; (of wolves)* meute *f;* **a p. of lies** un tissu de mensonges; **p. animal** animal *m* de bât; **p. ice** banquise *f*

2 *vt* (**a**) *(in box, suitcase)* mettre (dans sa valise/son sac/sa malle, *etc)* (**b**) *(cram) (earth into hole)* tasser; *(passengers into bus, train)* entasser (**c**) *(fill) (hole, box)* bourrer (**with** de); *also Fig* **to p. one's bags** faire ses valises (**d**) **to p. a punch** *(of fighter)* cogner dur; *(of drink)* être costaud

3 *vi* (**a**) *(prepare luggage)* faire ses valises *ou* bagages; *Fam Fig* **to send sb packing** envoyer

promener qn (**b**) *(cram)* **to p. into a room/bus** s'entasser dans une pièce/un bus

▸**pack in** *Fam* **1** *vt (job, course)* laisser tomber; **p. it in!** arrête!, ça suffit!

2 *vi (of car, machine)* tomber en rade

▸**pack off** *vt sep Fam (send away)* expédier

▸**pack up 1** *vt sep (tidy away)* ranger

2 *vi Fam* (**a**) *(of car, machine)* tomber en rade (**b**) *(finish work)* arrêter

package ['pækɪdʒ] **1** *n (parcel)* paquet *m,* colis *m; (of measures, laws)* ensemble *m; (contract)* contrat *m* global; **p. deal** *or* **holiday** forfait *m (comprenant au moins transport et logement)*

2 *vt* emballer, conditionner; *Fig* **to p. sb** *(pop star, politician)* créer l'image de marque de qn

packaging ['pækɪdʒɪŋ] *n* emballage *m*

packed [pækt] *adj* (**a**) *(crowded)* bondé(e) (**b**) **p. lunch** = déjeuner qu'on emporte à l'école ou au bureau

packer ['pækə(r)] *n (person)* emballeur(euse) *m,f*

packet ['pækɪt] *n* (**a**) *(of food, washing powder, cigarettes)* paquet *m;* **p. soup** soupe *f* en sachet (**b**) *Fam (lot of money)* **to make** *or* **earn a p.** se faire un fric fou; **that'll cost a p.** ça va coûter bonbon

packhorse ['pækhɔːs] *n* cheval *m* de bât

packing ['pækɪŋ] *n (packing material)* emballage *m;* **p. case** caisse *f* d'emballage (**b**) *(for trip)* **to do one's p.** faire ses valises *ou* bagages

pact [pækt] *n* pacte *m*

pad [pæd] **1** *n* (**a**) *(for protection)* protection *f; (of dog's, cat's paw)* coussinet *m; (of cotton wool)* tampon *m; (for helicopters)* aire *f* d'atterrissage; **(writing) p.** bloc *m* (**b**) *Fam (home)* piaule *f*

2 *vt (pt & pp* **padded)** *(furniture)* capitonner (**with** avec)

3 *vi* **to p. about** aller et venir à pas feutrés

▸**pad out** *vt sep (speech, essay)* étoffer

padded ['pædɪd] *adj (furniture, wall, cell)* capitonné(e); *(jacket)* matelassé(e); **p. shoulders** épaulettes *fpl*

padding ['pædɪŋ] *n (for clothes)* ouate *f; Fig (in speech, essay)* remplissage *m*

paddle ['pædəl] **1** *n* (**a**) *(for canoe)* pagaie *f; (of paddle boat)* aube *f;* **p. boat** bateau *m* à aubes (**b**) *(walk in water)* **to have a p.** patauger

2 *vt* **to p. a canoe** pagayer

3 *vi* (**a**) *(in canoe)* pagayer; *(of duck)* nager (**b**) *(walk in water)* patauger

paddling pool ['pædlɪŋ'puːl] *n Br* pataugeoire *f, Can* barboteuse *f*

paddock ['pædək] *n* paddock *m*
Paddy ['pædɪ] (*pl* **Paddies**) *n Br Fam (Irish man)* = terme injurieux désignant un Irlandais
paddy ['pædɪ] (*pl* **paddies**) *n* **p. (field)** rizière *f*
padlock ['pædlɒk] **1** *n* cadenas *m*
    2 *vt* cadenasser
padre ['pɑːdreɪ] *n* aumônier *m* (militaire)
paediatric, *Am* **pediatric** [piːdɪ'ætrɪk] *adj Med (ward)* de pédiatrie; *(specialist, nurse)* en pédiatrie
paediatrician, *Am* **pediatrician** [piːdɪə'trɪʃən] *n Med* pédiatre *mf*
paediatrics, *Am* **pediatrics** [piːdɪ'ætrɪks] *n Med* pédiatrie *f*
paedophile, *Am* **pedophile** ['piːdəʊfaɪl] *n* pédophile *mf*
pagan ['peɪgən] *n & adj* païen(enne) *m,f*
paganism ['peɪgənɪzəm] *n* paganisme *m*
page¹ [peɪdʒ] *n (of book, on Internet)* page *f*; **on p. 6** (à la) page 6
page² **1** *n (servant, at wedding)* page *m*
    2 *vt (call) (by loudspeaker)* appeler par haut-parleur; *(by electronic device)* biper
pageant ['pædʒənt] *n (procession)* spectacle *m* grandiose; *(historical)* spectacle *m* historique
pageantry ['pædʒəntrɪ] *n* pompe *f*, apparat *m*
pageboy ['peɪdʒbɔɪ] *n* page *m*; **p. (haircut)** coiffure *f* à la Jeanne d'Arc
pager ['peɪdʒə(r)] *n* récepteur *m* d'appel
pagination [pædʒɪ'neɪʃən] *n Typ* pagination *f*
pagoda [pə'gəʊdə] *n* pagode *f*
paid [peɪd] **1** *adj* (**a**) *(person, work)* rémunéré(e), payé(e) (**b**) **to put p. to sb's chances/hopes** réduire les chances/espoirs de qn à néant
    2 *pt & pp of* **pay**
paid-up ['peɪdʌp] *adj (member)* qui a payé sa cotisation
pail [peɪl] *n* seau *m*
pain [peɪn] **1** *n* (**a**) *(physical)* douleur *f*; *(emotional)* peine *f*; **to cause sb p.** *(physical)* faire souffrir qn; *(emotional)* faire de la peine à qn; **to be in p.** souffrir; **I have a p. in my leg** j'ai une douleur à la jambe (**b**) *(trouble)* **to take pains** *or* **be at great pains to do sth** se donner du mal pour faire qch; **for my pains** pour ma peine (**c**) *Formal* **under p. of death** sous peine de mort (**d**) *(idioms) Fam* **he's a p. (in the neck)** il est casse-pieds; *Vulg* **it's a p. in the arse** c'est chiant; *Fam* **cooking is such a p.!** c'est tellement casse-pieds de faire la cuisine!
    2 *vt* peiner
pained [peɪnd] *adj (look, expression)* peiné(e), affligé(e)
painful ['peɪnfʊl] *adj (physically)* douloureux(euse); *(emotionally)* pénible; **it's p. to watch** c'est un spectacle pénible
painfully ['peɪnfʊlɪ] *adv (walk)* avec difficulté; **she fell p.** elle s'est fait mal en tombant; *Fig* **p. shy** d'une timidité maladive
painkiller ['peɪnkɪlə(r)] *n* analgésique *m*
painless ['peɪnlɪs] *adj (not painful)* indolore; *Fig (easy)* facile
painstaking ['peɪnzteɪkɪŋ] *adj* minutieux(euse)
paint [peɪnt] **1** *n* peinture *f*; **wet p.** *(sign)* peinture fraîche; **p. gun** pistolet *m* à peinture; **p. remover** décapant *m*
    2 *vt* peindre; *Fam* **to p. one's face** *(put on make-up)*

se maquiller; **to p. one's nails** se faire les ongles; *Fig* **to p. a favourable picture of a situation** brosser un tableau favorable d'une situation; *Fig* **to p. the town red** faire la noce
    3 *vi* peindre
paintball ['peɪntbɔːl] *n (game)* paintball *m*
paintbox ['peɪntbɒks] *n* boîte *f* de couleurs
paintbrush ['peɪntbrʌʃ] *n* pinceau *m*
painter ['peɪntə(r)] *n* peintre *m*; **p. and decorator** peintre-tapissier *m*
painting ['peɪntɪŋ] *n (picture)* tableau *m*, peinture *f*; *(activity)* la peinture
paintwork ['peɪntwɜːk] *n* peinture *f*
pair [peə(r)] **1** *n* paire *f*; **in pairs** deux par deux; **a p. of glasses** une paire de lunettes; **a p. of scissors** une paire de ciseaux; **a p. of trousers** un pantalon
    2 *vt* **to p. sb with sb** mettre qn avec qn
►**pair off 1** *vt sep (people)* mettre deux par deux
    2 *vi (of people)* se mettre deux par deux
►**pair up** *vi* se mettre ensemble
pajamas *Am* = **pyjamas**
Pakistan [pɑːkɪ'stɑːn] *n* le Pakistan
Pakistani [pɑːkɪ'stɑːnɪ] **1** *n* Pakistanais(e) *m,f*
    2 *adj* pakistanais(e)
PAL [pæl] *n TV (abbr* **phase alternation line)** PAL
pal [pæl] *n Fam* copain (copine) *m,f*; **listen, p.!** fais gaffe, mon vieux!
palace ['pælɪs] *n* palais *m*
palatable ['pælətəbəl] *adj (food)* agréable au palais; *Fig (suggestion)* acceptable
palate ['pælɪt] *n (in mouth)* palais *m*
palatial [pə'leɪʃəl] *adj (impressive)* grandiose; *(luxurious)* luxueux(euse)
palaver [pə'lɑːvə(r)] *n Fam (fuss)* histoire *f*
pale¹ [peɪl] **1** *adj* pâle; **to turn p.** pâlir; **p. with fright** blanc de peur; *Br* **p. ale** = bière brune de couleur claire
    2 *vi (of person)* pâlir; **to p. into insignificance** être insignifiant(e)
pale² *n* **beyond the p.** *(behaviour)* inacceptable; *(person)* infréquentable
paleness ['peɪlnɪs] *n* pâleur *f*
Palestine ['pælɪstaɪn] *n* la Palestine
Palestinian [pælɪ'stɪnɪən] **1** *n* Palestinien(enne) *m,f*
    2 *adj* palestinien(enne)
palette ['pælɪt] *n Art* palette *f*; **p. knife** couteau *m* à palette
palings ['peɪlɪŋz] *npl (fence)* palissade *f*
palisade [pælɪ'seɪd] *n* palissade *f*
pall¹ [pɔːl] *n (of smoke)* voile *m*
pall² *vi (become uninteresting)* perdre son attrait
pallbearer ['pɔːlbeərə(r)] *n* porteur *m* (du cercueil)
pallet ['pælɪt] *n* palette *f*
palliative ['pælɪətɪv] *n* palliatif *m*
pallid ['pælɪd] *adj* blême, blafard(e)
pally ['pælɪ] *adj Br Fam* **to be p. with sb** être copain (copine) avec qn
palm¹ [pɑːm] *n* **p. (tree)** palmier *m*; **p. (leaf)** palme *f*; **P. Sunday** Dimanche *m* des Rameaux
palm² *n (of hand)* paume *f*; *Fig* **to have sb in the p. of one's hand** avoir qn dans sa poche
►**palm off** *vt sep* **to p. sth off on sb** refiler qch à qn
palmistry ['pɑːmɪstrɪ] *n* chiromancie *f*
palmtop ['pɑːmtɒp] *n Comput* **p. (computer)** ordinateur *m* de poche

palomino [pælə'miːnəʊ] (pl **palominos**) n (horse) palomino m

palpable ['pælpəbəl] adj (atmosphere) palpable; (lie) manifeste; (difference) sensible

palpate ['pælpeɪt] vt Med palper

palpitate ['pælpɪteɪt] vi also Fig palpiter

palpitations [pælpɪ'teɪʃənz] npl palpitations fpl

paltry ['pɔːltrɪ] adj (amount, sum) dérisoire; (excuse) piètre

pamper ['pæmpə(r)] vt (person) dorloter; **to p. oneself** se faire plaisir

pamphlet ['pæmflɪt] n (informative) brochure f; (political) pamphlet m

pan¹ [pæn] **1** n (saucepan) casserole f; (frying pan) poêle f; (of scales) plateau m; (of lavatory) cuvette f; Fam Fig **to go down the p.** s'en aller en fumée
2 vi (pt & pp **panned**) **to p. for gold** faire de l'orpaillage

pan² (pt & pp **panned**) vt Fam (criticize) descendre en flammes

▸**pan out** vi Fam (turn out) marcher, se dérouler; **it depends how things p. out** ça dépend de comment les choses vont s'arranger

panacea [pænə'sɪə] n panacée f

panache [pə'næʃ] n panache m

Pan-African [pæn'æfrɪkən] adj panafricain(e)

Panama ['pænəmɑː] n le Panama; **the P. Canal** le canal de Panama; **P. (hat)** panama m

Panamanian [pænə'meɪnɪən] **1** n Panaméen(enne) m,f
2 adj panaméen(enne)

Pan-American [pænə'merɪkən] adj panaméricain(e)

pancake ['pænkeɪk] n crêpe f; **P. Day** or **Tuesday** mardi m gras

pancreas ['pæŋkrɪəs] n Anat pancréas m

panda ['pændə] n panda m; Br **p. car** voiture f de police

pandemonium [pændɪ'məʊnɪəm] n (confusion) chaos m; (uproar) vacarme m assourdissant

pander ['pændə(r)] vi **to p. to sb/sth** flatter qn/qch

p & p [piːən'piː] n Br (abbr **postage and packing**) frais mpl de port et d'emballage

pane [peɪn] n **p. (of glass)** vitre f

panel ['pænəl] n (**a**) (of wood, metal) panneau m (**b**) (of switches, lights) tableau m de bord; **p. beater** carrossier m (**c**) (of experts) comité m; **p. discussion** table f ronde; (on radio, TV programme) invités mpl

panelling, Am **paneling** ['pænəlɪŋ] n lambris m

panellist, Am **panelist** ['pænəlɪst] n (on radio, TV programme) invité(e) m,f

pang [pæŋ] n (of guilt, jealousy) accès m; **pangs of hunger** tiraillements mpl d'estomac

panhandle ['pænhændəl] Am **1** n langue f de terre
2 vt Fam **to p. money from sb** taper qn
3 vi Fam faire la manche

panic ['pænɪk] **1** n panique f, affolement m; **in a p.** paniqué(e), affolé(e); **to get into a p.** paniquer, s'affoler; **p. attack** crise f d'angoisse; **p. button** bouton m déclencheur du signal d'alarme; Fin **p. buying/selling** achat m/vente f sous le coup de la panique; Fam **it was p. stations** c'était l'affolement général
2 vt (pt & pp **panicked**) affoler
3 vi paniquer, s'affoler

panicky ['pænɪkɪ] adj Fam **to be/get p.** paniquer, s'affoler

panic-stricken ['pænɪkstrɪkən] adj pris(e) de panique, affolé(e)

pannier ['pænɪə(r)] n (on bicycle) sacoche f; (on animal) panier m de bât

panoply ['pænəplɪ] n panoplie f

panorama [pænə'rɑːmə] n panorama m

panoramic [pænə'ræmɪk] adj panoramique

panpipes ['pænpaɪps] npl Mus flûte f de Pan

pansy ['pænzɪ] (pl **pansies**) n (**a**) (flower) pensée f (**b**) Fam (effeminate man) tante f

pant [pænt] vi haleter; **to p. for breath** chercher son souffle

panther ['pænθə(r)] n panthère f

pantihose = **pantyhose**

panties ['pæntɪz] npl (petite) culotte f, slip m

pantomime ['pæntəmaɪm] n (**a**) Br (show) = spectacle de Noël inspiré d'un conte de fée (**b**) (mime) mime m

Pantomime

Le genre typiquement britannique de la "pantomime" est très conventionnel; certains personnages-types ("pantomime dame", "principal boy") et certaines rengaines ("Behind you!", "Oh yes he is! Oh no he isn't!") apparaissent dans toutes les pièces. Ces pièces, qui se jouent au moment des fêtes de fin d'année, sont généralement inspirées d'un conte de fées.

pantry ['pæntrɪ] (pl **pantries**) n garde-manger m inv

pants [pænts] npl (**a**) Br (underwear) slip m (**b**) Am (trousers) pantalon m; Fam **to scare the p. off sb** flanquer la trouille à qn

pantyhose ['pæntɪhəʊz] n Am collant m

pap [pæp] n Fam Pej (nonsense) idioties fpl

papa [pə'pɑː] n Old-fashioned papa m

papacy ['peɪpəsɪ] n papauté f

papal ['peɪpəl] adj papal(e)

paper ['peɪpə(r)] **1** n (**a**) (material) papier m; **a piece of p.** un bout ou un morceau de papier; Fig **on p.** (in theory) sur le papier; **p. aeroplane** avion m en papier; **p. bag** sac m en papier; **p. cup** gobelet m en carton; Comput **p. feed** alimentation f en papier; **p. mill** papeterie f; **p. money** papier-monnaie m; **p. plate** assiette f en carton; **p. towel** essuie-tout m inv; Comput **p. tray** chariot m d'alimentation en papier (**b**) **papers** (documents) papiers mpl (**c**) (examination) épreuve f écrite (**d**) (scholarly study, report) article m; **to read** or **give a p.** faire un exposé (**e**) (newspaper) journal m; **p. boy/girl** livreur m/livreuse f de journaux; **p. round** tournée f de distribution des journaux; **p. shop** marchand m de journaux
2 vt (wall, room) tapisser

▸**paper over** vt sep Fig **to p. over the cracks** masquer les problèmes

paperback ['peɪpəbæk] n livre m de poche

paperclip ['peɪpəklɪp] n trombone m

paperknife ['peɪpənaɪf] (pl **paperknives**) n coupe-papier m

paperweight ['peɪpəweɪt] n presse-papiers m inv

paperwork ['peɪpəwɜːk] n travail m administratif, paperasserie f; (documentation) documents mpl

papery ['peɪpərɪ] adj (skin) parcheminé(e)

papier-mâché ['pæpjeɪ'mæʃeɪ] n papier m mâché

paprika ['pæprɪkə] n paprika m

Papuan ['pæpjʊən] **1** *n* Papou(e) *m,f*
  2 *adj* papou(e)
Papua New Guinea ['pæpjʊənjuː'gɪniː] *n* Papouasie-Nouvelle-Guinée *f*
papyrus [pə'paɪrəs] *n* papyrus *m*
par [pɑː(r)] *n* (**a**) *(equality)* égalité *f*, pair *m*; **to be on a p. with sb/sth** être au même niveau que qn/qch (**b**) *(in golf)* par *m*; **a p.-three (hole)** un par trois; *Fig* **to be p. for the course** n'avoir rien de surprenant (**c**) *Fin (of bills, shares)* pair *m*; **above/below p.** au-dessus/au-dessous du pair; *Fig* **to feel below p.** ne pas être dans son assiette
parable ['pærəbəl] *n* parabole *f*
parabolic [pærə'bɒlɪk] *adj* parabolique
paracetamol [pærə'siːtəmɒl] *n* paracétamol *m*
parachute ['pærəʃuːt] **1** *n* parachute *m*; **p. jump** saut *m* en parachute; **to make a p. jump** sauter en parachute
  2 *vt* parachuter
  3 *vi* sauter en parachute
parachuting ['pærəʃuːtɪŋ] *n* parachutisme *m*; **to go p.** faire du parachutisme
parachutist ['pærəʃuːtɪst] *n* parachutiste *mf*
parade [pə'reɪd] **1** *n* *(procession)* défilé *m*; **on p.** *(troops)* à l'exercice; **a p. of shops** une rangée de magasins; **p. ground** terrain *m* de manœuvres
  2 *vt (troops)* faire défiler; *Fig (wealth, knowledge)* faire étalage de
  3 *vi (of troops)* défiler; **to p. about** *or* **around** *(of person)* se pavaner
paradigm ['pærədaɪm] *n* paradigme *m*
paradise ['pærədaɪs] *n* paradis *m*
paradox ['pærədɒks] *n* paradoxe *m*
paradoxical [pærə'dɒksɪkəl] *adj* paradoxal(e)
paraffin ['pærəfɪn] *n* paraffine *f*; **p. heater** chauffage *m* à pétrole; **p. lamp** lampe *f* à pétrole; **p. wax** paraffine
paragliding ['pærəglaɪdɪŋ] *n* parapente *m*; **to go p.** faire du parapente
paragon ['pærəgən] *n* modèle *m*; **a p. of virtue** un modèle de vertu
paragraph ['pærəgræf] *n* paragraphe *m*
Paraguay ['pærəgwaɪ] *n* le Paraguay *m*
Paraguayan [pærə'gwaɪən] **1** *n* Paraguayen(enne) *m,f*
  2 *adj* paraguayen(enne)
parakeet ['pærəkiːt] *n* perruche *f*
parallel ['pærəlel] **1** *n* *Math* parallèle *f*; *Fig (analogy)* parallèle *m*; **to draw a p. between two things** établir un parallèle entre deux choses; **without p.** sans égal, sans pareil
  2 *adj Math* parallèle; *Fig (analogous)* pareil(eille), sem-blable; **to be** *or* **run p. to sth** être parallèle à qch; **p. bars** barres *fpl* parallèles; **p. lines** lignes *fpl* parallèles; *Comput* **p. processing** traitement *m* en simultanéité
  3 *vt (be similar to)* être analogue à; *(be equal to)* égaler
parallelogram [pærə'leləgræm] *n* parallélogramme *m*
paralyse, *Am* **paralyze** ['pærəlaɪz] *vt also Fig* paralyser
paralysis [pə'ræləsɪs] *(pl* **paralyses)** *n* paralysie *f*
paralytic [pærə'lɪtɪk] **1** *n* paralytique *mf*
  2 *adj* paralytique; *Br Fam (very drunk)* complètement bourré(e)

paralyze *Am* = **paralyse**
paramedic [pærə'medɪk] *n* auxiliaire *mf* médical(e)
parameter [pə'ræmɪtə(r)] *n* paramètre *m*
paramilitary [pærə'mɪlɪtrɪ] *adj* paramilitaire
paramount ['pærəmaʊnt] *adj* primordial(e); **of p. importance** d'une importance capitale
paranoia [pærə'nɔɪə] *n* paranoïa *f*
paranoid ['pærənɔɪd] *adj* paranoïaque; **to be p. about sth** être obsédé(e) par qch
paranormal [pærə'nɔːməl] **1** *n* **the p.** le paranormal
  2 *adj* paranormal(e)
parapet ['pærəpet] *n* parapet *m*
paraphernalia [pærəfə'neɪlɪə] *n (equipment)* attirail *m*; *(things)* affaires *fpl*; *(clutter)* bazar *m*
paraphrase ['pærəfreɪz] **1** *n* paraphrase *f*
  2 *vt* paraphraser
paraplegic [pærə'pliːdʒɪk] *n & adj* paraplégique *mf*
parascending ['pærəsendɪŋ] *n* parachute *m* ascensionnel
parasite ['pærəsaɪt] *n also Fig* parasite *m*
parasitic [pærə'sɪtɪk] *adj also Fig* parasite; *(existence)* de parasite
parasol ['pærəsɒl] *n* ombrelle *f*
paratrooper ['pærətruːpə(r)] *n* parachutiste *m*
parboil ['pɑːbɔɪl] *vt* faire cuire à demi
parcel ['pɑːsəl] *n* (**a**) *(package)* colis *m*, paquet *m*; **p. bomb** colis piégé; **p. post** service *m* de colis postaux (**b**) *(of land)* parcelle *f*
▸**parcel out** *(pt & pp* **parcelled,** *Am* **parceled)** *vt sep* répartir
▸**parcel up** *vt sep* empaqueter, emballer
parchment ['pɑːtʃmənt] *n* parchemin *m*; **p. paper** papier *m* parchemin
pardon ['pɑːdən] **1** *n (forgiveness)* pardon *m*; *Law* grâce *f*; **(I beg your) p.?** *(what did you say?)* pardon?, comment?; **I beg your p.!** *(in apology)* je vous demande pardon!
  2 *vt (action, person)* pardonner; *Law* gracier; **to p. sb for sth** pardonner qch à qn; **p. me?** *(what did you say?)* (je vous demande) pardon?; **p. me!** *(in apology)* pardonnez-moi!
pardonable ['pɑːdənəbəl] *adj* pardonnable, excusable
pare [peə(r)] *vt (vegetable)* éplucher; *(apple)* peler; *(nails)* rogner; *(expenses)* réduire
▸**pare down** *vt sep (expenses)* réduire
parent ['peərənt] *n (father)* père *m*; *(mother)* mère *f*; **parents** parents *mpl*; **p. company** société *f ou* maison *f* mère; **p.-teacher association** = association des parents d'élèves et des professeurs
parentage ['peərəntɪdʒ] *n* origine *f*
parental [pə'rentəl] *adj* parental(e)
parenthesis [pə'renθəsɪs] *(pl* **parentheses** [pə'renθəsiːz]) *n* parenthèse *f*; **in parentheses** entre parenthèses
parenthood ['peərənthʊd] *n (fatherhood)* paternité *f*; *(motherhood)* maternité *f*; **the joys of p.** le bonheur d'être parent
parenting ['peərəntɪŋ] *n* art *m* d'être parent; **p. skills** capacité *f* à élever des enfants
pariah [pə'raɪə] *n* paria *m*
Paris ['pærɪs] *n* Paris
parish ['pærɪʃ] *n* paroisse *f*; **p. church** église *f* paroissiale; **p. council** conseil *m* municipal; **p. priest** *(Catholic)* curé *m*; *(Protestant)* pasteur *m*

parishioner [pəˈrɪʃənə(r)] *n* paroissien(enne) *m,f*
Parisian [pəˈrɪzɪən] **1** *n* Parisien(enne) *m,f*
 2 *adj* parisien(enne)
parity [ˈpærɪtɪ] *n* égalité *f*; **to achieve p.** *(of pay)* obtenir l'égalité
park [pɑːk] **1** *n* jardin *m* public, parc *m*; **p. keeper** gardien(enne) *m,f* de parc
 2 *vt (car)* garer; *Fam* **to p. oneself in a chair/in front of the TV** s'installer dans un fauteuil/devant la télé
parka [ˈpɑːkə] *n* parka *f*
parking [ˈpɑːkɪŋ] *n* stationnement *m*; **no p.** *(sign)* défense de stationner; **p. attendant** gardien(enne) *m,f* de parking; **p. bay** place *f* de stationnement; **p. lights** *(on car)* feux *mpl* de position; *Am* **p. lot** parking *m*; **p. meter** parcmètre *m*, *Can* compteur *m* de stationnement; **p. space** place *f* (de parking); **p. ticket** contravention *f*
Parkinson's disease [ˈpɑːkɪnsənzdɪˈziːz] *n* la maladie de Parkinson
parkland [ˈpɑːklænd] *n* espace(s) *m(pl)* vert(s)
parkway [ˈpɑːkweɪ] *n Am* route *f* bordée d'arbres et de verdure
parlance [ˈpɑːləns] *n* langage *m*; **in legal/political p.** en termes juridiques/politiques; **in common p.** en langage ordinaire
parley [ˈpɑːlɪ] *vi* parlementer (**with** avec); *(more officially)* être en pourparlers (**with** avec)
parliament [ˈpɑːləmənt] *n* parlement *m*
parliamentarian [pɑːləmənˈteərɪən] *n* parlementaire *mf*
parliamentary [pɑːləˈmentərɪ] *adj* parlementaire; **p. privilege** immunité *f* parlementaire
parlour, *Am* **parlor** [ˈpɑːlə(r)] *n* salon *m*
Parmesan [pɑːmɪˈzæn] *n* **P. (cheese)** parmesan *m*
parochial [pəˈrəʊkɪəl] *adj Rel* paroissial(e); *Fig Pej* de clocher; **to be p.** *(of person)* avoir l'esprit de clocher
parody [ˈpærədɪ] **1** *n (pl* **parodies)** parodie *f* (**of** de)
 2 *vt (pt & pp* **parodied)** parodier
parole [pəˈrəʊl] **1** *n* liberté *f* conditionnelle; **to be (out) on p.** être en liberté conditionnelle; **p. officer** contrôleur *m* judiciaire
 2 *vt* mettre en liberté conditionnelle
paroxysm [ˈpærəksɪzəm] *n (of anger, guilt, jealousy)* crise *f*; **to be in paroxysms of laughter** avoir le fou rire
parquet [ˈpɑːkeɪ] *n* **p. (floor)** parquet *m*
parrot [ˈpærət] **1** *n also Fig* perroquet *m*
 2 *vt* répéter comme un perroquet
parrot-fashion [ˈpærətfæʃən] *adv* comme un perroquet
parry [ˈpærɪ] *(pt & pp* **parried)** *vt (blow)* parer; *(question)* éluder
parsimonious [pɑːsɪˈməʊnɪəs] *adj* parcimonieux(euse)
parsley [ˈpɑːslɪ] *n* persil *m*
parsnip [ˈpɑːsnɪp] *n* panais *m*
parson [ˈpɑːsən] *n* pasteur *m*
parsonage [ˈpɑːsənɪdʒ] *n* presbytère *m*
part [pɑːt] **1** *n* **(a)** *(portion, component)* partie *f*; **p. of the body** partie du corps; **p. of speech** partie du discours; **(spare) parts** pièces *fpl* détachées; **p. two** *(of TV series, story)* deuxième partie; **in that p. of the world** dans cette région du monde; **in these parts** dans ces régions; **good in parts** bon (bonne) en partie; **the best/worst p. was when...** le meilleur/le pire

ça a été quand...; **the difficult p. is remembering** ce qui est difficile, c'est de se souvenir; **for the best or greater p. of five years** pendant presque cinq ans; **the greater p. of the population** la plus grande partie de la population; **to be p. of sth** faire partie de qch; **it's all p. of growing up** c'est ce qui arrive quand on grandit; **it is p. and parcel of...** c'est partie intégrante de...; **in p.** en partie; **for the most p.** pour la plupart; **p. exchange** reprise *f* (en compte); **p. owner** copropriétaire *mf*
 (b) *(role)* rôle *m*; **to take p. (in sth)** prendre part (à qch); **to have** *or* **play a p. in sth** jouer un rôle dans qch; **I want no p. in it** je ne veux rien avoir à faire là-dedans
 (c) *(side)* **to take sb's p.** prendre le parti de qn; **on the p. of...** de la part de...; **for my p.** pour ma part
 (d) *Am (in hair)* raie *f*
 2 *adv* **she's p. French** elle est en partie française; **p. silk, p. cotton** soie et coton
 3 *vt (fighters, lovers)* séparer; **to p. one's hair** se faire une raie; **to p. company** se séparer
 4 *vi* **(a)** *(leave one another)* se quitter; *(split up)* se rompre; **to p. (as) friends** se séparer (en) bons amis; **to p. with sth** se défaire de qch
 (b) *(of curtains, lips)* s'entrouvrir; *(of crowd)* s'ouvrir
partake [pɑːˈteɪk] *(pt* **partook** [pɑːˈtʊk], *pp* **partaken** [pɑːˈteɪkən]) *vi Formal* **(a) to p. of** *(eat, drink)* prendre **(b)** *(have quality)* **to p. of** relever de
partial [ˈpɑːʃəl] *adj* **(a)** *(incomplete)* partiel(elle) **(b)** *(biased)* partial(e) **(c)** *(fond)* **to be p. to sb/sth** avoir un faible pour qn/qch
partially [ˈpɑːʃəlɪ] *adv* **(a)** *(in part)* en partie, partiellement **(b)** *(with bias)* avec partialité
participant [pɑːˈtɪsɪpənt] *n* participant(e) *m,f*
participate [pɑːˈtɪsɪpeɪt] *vi* participer (**in** à)
participation [pɑːtɪsɪˈpeɪʃən] *n* participation (**in** à)
participle [ˈpɑːtɪsɪpəl] *n Gram* participe *m*
particle [ˈpɑːtɪkəl] *n (of matter)* particule *f*; *(of dust, sand)* grain *m*; *Fig (of truth)* once *f*
particular [pəˈtɪkjʊlə(r)] **1** *n* détail *m*; **in p.** en particulier; **I didn't see anything in p.** je n'ai rien vu de particulier; **to go into particulars** entrer dans les détails; **to take down sb's particulars** noter les coordonnées de qn
 2 *adj* **(a)** *(specific)* particulier(ère); *(reason, case, example)* précis(e); **which p. thing/person did you have in mind?** à quoi/à qui pensiez-vous en particulier?; **on that p. day** ce jour-là
 (b) *(special)* particulier(ère); **a p. favourite of mine** un (une) de mes favoris (favorites); **she is a p. friend of mine** c'est une de mes meilleures amies; **to take p. care over sth** mettre un soin particulier à qch
 (c) *(exacting)* méticuleux(euse); **to be p. about sth** être exigeant(e) pour qch; **I'm not p.** ça m'est égal
particularly [pəˈtɪkjʊləlɪ] *adv (especially)* particulièrement, spécialement
parting [ˈpɑːtɪŋ] *n* **(a)** *(separation)* séparation *f*; **the p. of the ways** la croisée des chemins; **p. shot** pique *f* *(lancée en partant)*; **p. words** mots *mpl* d'adieu **(b)** *Br (in hair)* raie *f*
partisan [pɑːtɪˈzæn] *n & adj* partisan(e) *m,f*
partition [pɑːˈtɪʃən] **1** *n (in room)* cloison *f*
 2 *vt (country)* partager
▸**partition off** *vt sep (room)* cloisonner
partly [ˈpɑːtlɪ] *adv* partiellement, en partie

partner ['pɑːtnə(r)] **1** *n (in games)* partenaire *mf*; *(in business)* associé(e) *m,f*; *(in dancing)* cavalier(ère) *m,f*; *(in relationship)* compagnon (compagne) *m,f*; **p. in crime** complice *mf*
  2 *vt (in games)* faire équipe avec; *(in dancing)* être le (la) cavalier(ère) de
partnership ['pɑːtnəʃɪp] *n* association *f*; **to enter** *or* **go into p. (with sb)** s'associer (avec qn)
partridge ['pɑːtrɪdʒ] *n* perdrix *f*
part-time [pɑːt'taɪm] *adj & adv* à temps partiel
part-timer [pɑːt'taɪmə(r)] *n* travailleur(euse) *m,f* à temps partiel
partway ['pɑːtweɪ] *adv* **to be p. through sth** ne pas avoir complètement terminé qch; **this will go p. towards covering the costs** cela couvrira en partie les dépenses
party ['pɑːtɪ] **1** *n (pl* **parties)** **(a)** *(political)* parti *m*; **to follow** *or* **toe the p. line** suivre la ligne du parti; **p. member** membre *m* du parti; **p. political broadcast** émission *f* réservée à un parti politique; **p. politics** politique *f* de parti; *Pej* politique politicienne
  (b) *(celebration)* fête *f*; **to have** *or* **give** *or* **throw a p.** organiser *ou* faire une fête; *Fig* **the p.'s over** la fête est finie; *Fam* **p. animal** fêtard(e) *m,f*; *Hum* **p. piece** numéro *m* favori
  (c) *(group)* groupe *m*; *(of workers)* équipe *f*; *Tel* **p. line** ligne *f* commune (à plusieurs abonnés); **p. wall** mur *m* mitoyen
  (d) *Law (participant)* partie *f*; **to be (a) p. to sth** se faire complice de qch
  2 *vi (pt & pp* **partied)** *Fam (celebrate)* faire la fête
pass¹ [pɑːs] *n (over mountains)* col *m*
pass² **1** *n* **(a)** *(permit)* laissez-passer *m inv*; *Mil* sauf-conduit *m*; *(for travel)* carte *f* d'abonnement
  (b) *(in examination)* **to get a p.** avoir la moyenne; **p. mark** moyenne *f*
  (c) *(in sport)* passe *f*
  (d) *Fam* **to make a p. at sb** faire des avances à qn
  2 *vt* **(a)** *(go past)* *(person)* croiser; *(destination)* dépasser; *(frontier)* traverser; *(car, runner)* dépasser, doubler
  (b) *(exam, test)* réussir
  (c) *(bill, resolution)* voter
  (d) *(give)* passer; **p. (me) the salt, please** passe-moi le sel, s'il te plaît
  (e) **to p. the time** *(of person)* passer le temps; **it passes the time** ça fait passer le temps
  (f) *Law* **to p. sentence** prononcer le verdict; **to p. judgement on sb** porter un jugement sur qn
  (g) **to p. water** uriner; **to p. wind** avoir des vents
  3 *vi* **(a)** *(go past)* passer; *(overtake)* dépasser, doubler; **to p. unobserved** passer inaperçu(e); **to let sth p.** laisser tomber qch; *also Fig* **p.!** je passe!; **I think I'll p. on the onions** je crois que je ne prendrai pas d'oignons
  (b) *(of time)* s'écouler, (se) passer; **the weekend passed uneventfully** le week-end s'est passé sans surprises
  (c) *(go away)* passer
  (d) *(in exam)* avoir la moyenne
  (e) *Lit (take place)* **it came to p. that...** c'est alors qu'il arriva que...
▶**pass away** *vi Euph* décéder
▶**pass down** *vt sep (knowledge, tradition)* transmettre
▶**pass for** *vt insep* passer pour; **she'd p. for 25** on pourrait lui donner 25 ans

▶**pass off 1** *vt sep* **to p. oneself off as sb** se faire passer pour qn; **to p. sth off as sth** faire passer qch pour qch; **she passed it off as a joke** elle a prétendu que c'était une plaisanterie
  2 *vi (take place)* se passer
▶**pass on 1** *vt sep (object)* faire passer; *(news, information)* faire circuler; *(disease)* passer
  2 *vi Euph* décéder
▶**pass out** *vi* **(a)** *(faint)* perdre connaissance **(b)** *(of military cadet)* sortir avec ses diplômes
▶**pass over** *vt sep* **to p. sb over (for promotion)** ignorer qn au moment d'une promotion
▶**pass through 1** *vt insep* traverser
  2 *vi* passer
▶**pass up** *vt sep (opportunity)* laisser passer
passable ['pɑːsəbəl] *adj* **(a)** *(of acceptable quality)* passable **(b)** *(road, bridge)* praticable; *(river)* franchissable
passage ['pæsɪdʒ] *n* **(a)** *(journey)* passage *m*; **with the p. of time** avec le temps; **to work one's p.** *(on ship)* travailler pour payer sa traversée **(b)** *(corridor)* couloir *m*, corridor *m*; *(alley)* passage *m* **(c)** *(extract)* passage *m*
passageway ['pæsɪdʒweɪ] *n (corridor)* couloir *m*, corridor *m*; *(alley)* passage *m*
passé [pæ'seɪ] *adj* dépassé(e)
passenger ['pæsəndʒə(r)] *n* passager(ère) *m,f*; **p. seat** place *f* du passager
passer-by ['pɑːsə'baɪ] *(pl* **passers-by)** *n* passant(e) *m,f*
passing ['pɑːsɪŋ] **1** *n* **(a)** *(going past)* passage *m*; **to say sth in p.** dire qch en passant; **p. place** *(on road)* aire *f* de croisement **(b)** *(of time)* écoulement *m* **(c)** *(death)* décès *m*
  2 *adj (car, motorist)* qui passe; *(remark)* en passant; *(whim, attraction)* passager(ère)
passion ['pæʃən] *n (desire)* passion *f*; *(anger, vehemence)* emportement *m*, colère *f*; **to have a p. for sth** adorer qch; **in a fit of p.** sous le coup de la passion; **she hates him with a p.** elle le hait de toute son âme; **crime of p.** crime *m* passionnel; *Rel* **the P. (of Christ)** la Passion (du Christ); **p. fruit** fruit *m* de la passion
passionate ['pæʃənɪt] *adj (lover, embrace)* passionné(e); *(plea, speech)* véhément(e); *(believer, defender)* fervent(e); **to make p. love** faire l'amour avec passion
passive ['pæsɪv] **1** *n Gram* **the p.** le passif; **in the p.** au passif
  2 *adj* passif(ive); **p. resistance** résistance *f* passive; **p. smoking** tabagisme *m* passif
passively ['pæsɪvlɪ] *adv* passivement, avec passivité
passkey ['pɑːskiː] *(pl* **passkeys)** *n* passe-partout *m*
Passover ['pɑːsəʊvə(r)] *n Rel* la Pâque (Juive)
passport ['pɑːspɔːt] *n* passeport *m*; **p. photo** photo *f* d'identité
password ['pɑːswɜːd] *n* mot *m* de passe
past [pɑːst] **1** *n* passé *m*; **in the p.** autrefois; **a thing of the p.** une chose qui appartient au passé; **to live in the p.** vivre dans le passé
  2 *adj* passé(e); **those days are p.** ces jours sont révolus; **in times p.** autrefois; **to be a p. master at sth** être passé(e) maître dans l'art de qch; **the p. week** la semaine dernière; **the p. few days** ces derniers jours; *Gram* **p. participle** participe *m* passé; **in the p. tense** au passé
  3 *prep (beyond)* au-delà de; **to walk p. the house** passer devant la maison; **it's p. four (o'clock)** il est quatre heures passées; **ten p. four** quatre heures

dix; **I'm p. caring** je n'en ai plus rien à faire; *Fam* **to be p. it** avoir fait son temps; *Fam* **I wouldn't put it p. her** elle en est bien capable

4 *adv* **to walk** *or* **go p.** passer; **to run p.** passer en courant

pasta ['pæstə] *n* pâtes *fpl*

paste [peɪst] **1** *n* (**a**) *(substance)* pâte *f* (**b**) *(pâté)* mousse *f* (**c**) *(glue)* colle *f*
2 *vt (glue)* coller

pastel ['pæstəl] **1** *n* pastel *m*
2 *adj* pastel *inv*; **p. shades** tons *mpl* pastel

pasteurize ['pæstjʊraɪz] *vt* pasteuriser; **pasteurized milk** lait *m* pasteurisé

pastiche [pæ'stiːʃ] *n* pastiche *m*

pastille ['pæstɪl] *n* pastille *f*

pastime ['pɑːstaɪm] *n* passe-temps *m inv*

pasting ['peɪstɪŋ] *n Fam (beating)* raclée *f*; **to give sb a p.** flanquer une raclée à qn

pastor ['pɑːstə(r)] *n Rel* pasteur *m*

pastoral ['pɑːstərəl] *adj* (**a**) *(rural)* pastoral(e) (**b**) *(work, activities)* de conseiller(ère)

pastry ['peɪstrɪ] (*pl* **pastries**) *n (dough)* pâte *f*; *(cake)* pâtisserie *f*; **p. chef** pâtissier(ère) *m,f*

pasture ['pɑːstʃə(r)] *n* pâture *f*, pré *m*; **to be put out to p.** *(of animals)* être mis(e) au pré; *Fig (of person)* être mis au vert; *Fig* **to move on to pastures new** aller vers de nouveaux horizons

pasty¹ ['pæstɪ] (*pl* **pasties**) *n (savoury)* ≃ feuilleté *m*

pasty² ['peɪstɪ] *adj (face, complexion)* terreux(euse); **p.-faced** au teint terreux

pat [pæt] **1** *n* (**a**) *(tap)* petite tape *f*; *(on animal)* caresse *f*; *Fig* **to give sb a p. on the back** féliciter qn (**b**) *(of butter)* médaillon *m*
2 *adj (answer, explanation)* tout(e) prêt(e)
3 *adv* **to know** *or* **have sth off p.** savoir qch par cœur
4 *vt (pt & pp* **patted***) (tap)* tapoter; *(animal)* caresser; **to p. sb on the head/shoulder** donner une tape sur la tête/l'épaule de qn; *Fig* **to p. sb on the back** féliciter qn

Patagonia [pætə'gəʊnɪə] *n* la Patagonie

patch [pætʃ] **1** *n* (**a**) *(of cloth)* pièce *f*; **(eye) p.** bandeau *m*; *Fam* **his last novel isn't a p. on the others** son dernier roman est loin de valoir les autres (**b**) *(of colour, light)* tache *f*; *(of fog, mist)* nappe *f*; *(of ice)* plaque *f*; **a p. of blue sky** un coin de ciel bleu; *Fam Fig* **to be going through a bad p.** traverser une mauvaise passe (**c**) *(of land)* lopin *m*; *(of prostitute, salesperson)* secteur *m*; *Fam* **keep off my p.!** hors de mon territoire!
2 *vt (hole, garment)* rapiécer

▸**patch up** *vt sep Fam (wounded person)* donner les premiers soins à; *(marriage, friendship)* raccommoder; **to p. things up** *(after argument)* se raccommoder

patchwork ['pætʃwɜːk] *n also Fig* patchwork *m*; **p. quilt** couvre-lit *m* en patchwork

patchy ['pætʃɪ] *adj* inégal(e)

pâté ['pæteɪ] *n* pâté *m*

patent ['peɪtənt] **1** *n (licence)* brevet *m* d'invention; **to take out a p. on sth** faire breveter qch; *Com* **p. applied for, p. pending** demande de brevet déposée
2 *adj* (**a**) *(patented)* breveté(e); **p. medicine** spécialité *f* pharmaceutique (**b**) *(evident)* manifeste (**c**) **p. leather** cuir *m* verni
3 *vt (of authorities)* breveter; *(of inventor)* faire breveter

patently ['peɪtəntlɪ] *adv* manifestement

paternal [pə'tɜːnəl] *adj (feelings)* paternel(elle); *(duty, responsibilities)* de père

paternally [pə'tɜːnəlɪ] *adv* paternellement

paternity [pə'tɜːnɪtɪ] *n* paternité *f*; **p. leave** congé *m* de paternité; *Law* **p. suit** action *f* en recherche de paternité

path [pɑːθ] *n* (**a**) *(track)* chemin *m*; *(narrow)* sentier *m*; *(in garden)* allée *f*; **their paths had crossed before** leurs chemins s'étaient croisés auparavant (**b**) *(of rocket, planet)* trajectoire *f*; *(of inquiry, to success)* voie *f*; **the storm destroyed everything in its p.** la tempête a tout détruit sur son passage (**c**) *Comput* chemin *m*

pathetic [pə'θetɪk] *adj (useless)* lamentable; *(touching)* attendrissant(e)

pathetically [pə'θetɪklɪ] *adv (uselessly)* lamentablement; *(touchingly)* de manière attendrissante

pathological [pæθə'lɒdʒɪkəl] *adj* pathologique

pathologist [pə'θɒlədʒɪst] *n* pathologiste *mf*

pathology [pə'θɒlədʒɪ] *n* pathologie *f*

pathos ['peɪθɒs] *n* pathétique *m*

pathway ['pɑːθweɪ] *n* sentier *m*

patience ['peɪʃəns] *n* (**a**) *(quality)* patience *f*; **to try** *or* **tax sb's p.** mettre la patience de qn à l'épreuve; **to exhaust sb's p.** abuser de la patience de qn; **to lose one's p. (with sb)** perdre patience (avec qn); **I've no p. with him** il m'énerve (**b**) *(card game)* réussite *f*; **to play p.** faire une réussite

patient ['peɪʃənt] **1** *n* patient(e) *m,f*
2 *adj* patient(e)

patiently ['peɪʃəntlɪ] *adv* patiemment

patio ['pætɪəʊ] (*pl* **patios**) *n* patio *m*

patriarch ['peɪtrɪɑːk] *n* patriarche *m*

patriarchal [peɪtrɪ'ɑːkəl] *adj* patriarcal(e)

patriarchy ['peɪtrɪɑːkɪ] (*pl* **patriarchies**) *n* patriarcat *m*

patrimony ['pætrɪmənɪ] *n* patrimoine *m*, héritage *m*

patriot ['pætrɪət, 'peɪtrɪət] *n* patriote *mf*

patriotic [pætrɪ'ɒtɪk, peɪtrɪ'ɒtɪk] *adj* patriotique

patriotism ['pætrɪətɪzəm, 'peɪtrɪətɪzəm] *n* patriotisme *m*

patrol [pə'trəʊl] **1** *n* patrouille *f*; **to be on p.** être de patrouille; **p. car** voiture *f* de police
2 *vt (pt & pp* **patrolled***)* patrouiller dans
3 *vi* patrouiller; **to p. up and down** faire les cent pas

patrolman [pə'trəʊlmæn] *n Am* agent *m* de police

patron ['peɪtrən] *n* (**a**) *(of arts)* protecteur(trice) *m,f*, mécène *m*; *(of charity)* patron(onne) *m,f*; **p. saint** (saint(e)) patron(onne) *m,f* (**b**) *(of shop)* client(e) *m,f*

patronage ['pætrənɪdʒ] *n* (**a**) *(of arts, charity)* patronage *m*; **under the p. of** sous le patronage de (**b**) *Pej (in politics)* copinage *m*

patronize ['pætrənaɪz] *vt* (**a**) *(arts)* protéger; *(shop, restaurant)* fréquenter (**b**) *(treat condescendingly)* traiter avec condescendance

patronizing ['pætrənaɪzɪŋ] *adj* condescendant(e)

patter¹ ['pætə(r)] **1** *n (of footsteps)* petit bruit *m*; *(of rain)* crépitement *m*
2 *vi (of rain)* crépiter; **she pattered along the corridor** elle trottinait le long du couloir

patter² *n Br Fam (talk)* boniment *m*, baratin *m*

pattern ['pætən] **1** *n* (**a**) *(design)* dessin *m*, motif *m*; **p. book** catalogue *m* d'échantillons (**b**) **p. of behaviour** comportement *m* type; **a normal p. of events** une suite typique d'événements; **the evening followed**

the usual p. la soirée s'est déroulée comme d'habitude; **some clear patterns emerge from the statistics** des tendances nettes ressortent des statistiques (**c**) *(in sewing)* patron *m*; *(in knitting)* modèle *m* (**d**) *(norm)* modèle *m*; **to set a p.** créer un modèle
  2 *vt (model)* **to p. sth on sth** modeler qch sur qch
patterned ['pætənd] *adj* à motifs
paunch [pɔːntʃ] *n* ventre *m*; **to have a p.** avoir du ventre
pauper ['pɔːpə(r)] *n* indigent(e) *m,f*; **p.'s grave** fosse *f* commune
pause [pɔːz] **1** *n (in conversation)* silence *m*; *(rest)* pause *f*; *(in music)* point *m* d'orgue
  2 *vi* faire une pause; **to p. for breath** reprendre son souffle
pave [peɪv] *vt (road)* paver (**with** de); *Fig* **to p. the way for sth** ouvrir la voie à qch
pavement ['peɪvmənt] *n Br (beside road)* trottoir *m*; *Am (roadway)* chaussée *f*; **p. artist** artiste *mf* qui dessine sur les trottoirs; **p. café** café *m* avec terrasse
pavilion [pə'vɪlɪən] *n* pavillon *m*
paving ['peɪvɪŋ] *n (with tiles)* carrelage *m*; *(with slabs)* dallage *m*; **p. stone** pavé *m*
paw [pɔː] **1** *n* patte *f*; *Fam* **paws off!** bas les pattes!
  2 *vt (of animal)* donner un coup/des coups de patte à; **to p. the ground** frapper le sol du sabot
pawn¹ [pɔːn] *vt* mettre au mont-de-piété *ou* en gage
pawn² *n (in chess) & Fig* pion *m*
pawnbroker ['pɔːnbrəʊkə(r)] *n* prêteur(euse) *m,f* sur gage
pawnshop ['pɔːnʃɒp] *n* mont-de-piété *m*, bureau *m* de prêt sur gage
pay [peɪ] **1** *n* paie *f*, salaire *m*; **the p.'s good/bad** ça paie bien/mal; **to be in sb's p.** être à la solde de qn; **p. cheque** chèque *m* de paie; **p. packet** enveloppe *f* de paie; **p. rise** augmentation *f* de salaire; **p. slip** bulletin *m* de salaire; **p. talks** négociations *fpl* salariales
  2 *vt (pt & pp paid)* (**a**) *(person, money, bill)* payer; **I paid £5 for it** je l'ai payé 5 livres; **to be well/badly paid** être bien/mal payé(e); **I wouldn't do it if you paid me** je ne le ferais pas même si on me payait; **to p. one's way** payer son écot; **to p. cash** payer (argent) comptant; **to p. money into sb's account** verser de l'argent sur le compte de qn
  (**b**) *(give)* **to p. sb a compliment** faire un compliment à qn; **to p. sb a visit** rendre visite à qn; **to p. tribute to sb** rendre hommage à qn; **to p. one's respects to sb** présenter ses respects à qn
  (**c**) *(profit)* **it will p. you to do it** c'est dans votre intérêt de le faire
  3 *vi* (**a**) *(give payment)* payer; **to p. through the nose** payer le prix fort; **to p. by cheque** payer par chèque
  (**b**) *(be profitable)* être rentable; **crime doesn't p.** le crime ne paie pas; **it pays to be honest** l'honnêteté est toujours récompensée
▸**pay back** *vt sep (loan, person)* rembourser; *Fig* **I'll p. you back for this!** tu me le paieras!
▸**pay in** *vt sep (cheque, money)* verser sur un compte
▸**pay off 1** *vt sep* (**a**) *(debt)* régler; *(mortgage)* purger; *Fam* **to p. sb off** *(bribe)* soudoyer qn (**b**) *(make redundant)* licencier
  2 *vi (of work, efforts)* porter ses fruits
▸**pay out 1** *vt sep* (**a**) *(money)* débourser, dépenser (**b**) *(pt payed) (rope)* laisser filer
  2 *vi* payer

▸**pay up** *vi* payer
payable ['peɪəbəl] *adj* payable; **to make a cheque p. to sb** libeller un chèque à l'ordre de qn
pay-as-you-earn [peɪæzjuː'ɜːn] *n Br* prélèvement *m* de l'impôt à la source
payday ['peɪdeɪ] *n* jour *m* de paie
PAYE [piːeɪwaɪ'iː] *n Br (abbr* **pay-as-you-earn***)* prélèvement *m* de l'impôt à la source
payee [peɪ'iː] *n* bénéficiaire *mf*
paying ['peɪɪŋ] *adj* payant(e); **p. guest** hôte *m* payant
payload ['peɪləʊd] *n* charge *f* utile
paymaster ['peɪmɑːstə(r)] *n* caissier *m*
payment ['peɪmənt] *n* paiement *m*; **to make a p.** effectuer un versement; **to stop p. (on a cheque)** faire opposition sur un chèque; **on p. of £100** contre paiement de 100 livres; **p. by instalments** paiement par acomptes; **p. in full** paiement intégral
payoff ['peɪɒf] *n Fam* (**a**) *(bribe)* pot-de-vin *m* (**b**) *(reward)* récompense *f*
pay-per-view [peɪpə'vjuː] **1** *n* = système de télévision à la carte
  2 *adj* à la carte
payphone ['peɪfəʊn] *n* téléphone *m* public
payroll ['peɪrəʊl] *n Com* liste *f* du personnel; **to be on the p.** faire partie du personnel
PC ['piː'siː] **1** *n* (**a**) *Br (abbr* **Police Constable***)* = agent de police (**b**) *(abbr* **personal computer***)* PC *m*
  2 *adj (abbr* **politically correct***)* politiquement correct(e)
pc *(abbr* **postcard***)* carte *f* postale
PDQ *adv Fam (abbr* **pretty damn quick***)* illico
PE ['piː'iː] *n (abbr* **physical education***)* EPS *f*
pea [piː] *n* pois *m*; **like two peas in a pod** comme deux gouttes d'eau
peace [piːs] *n* paix *f*; **at p.** en paix; **to make (one's) p. with sb** faire la paix avec qn; **p. of mind** tranquillité *f* d'esprit; *Law* **to disturb the p.** troubler l'ordre public; **p. campaigner** militant(e) *m,f* pour la paix; **P. Corps** = organisation américaine d'aide aux pays du tiers-monde, composée de bénévoles intervenant sur le terrain; **p. movement** mouvement *m* pour la paix; **p. offering** cadeau *m* de réconciliation; **p. process** processus *m* de paix; **p. talks** pourparlers *mpl* de paix; **p. treaty** traité *m* de paix
peaceable ['piːsəbəl] *adj* pacifique
peaceful ['piːsfʊl] *adj (calm)* paisible; *(non-violent)* pacifique
peacekeeping ['piːskiːpɪŋ] *n* maintien *m* de la paix; **p. force** force *f* de maintien de la paix
peace-loving ['piːslʌvɪŋ] *adj* pacifique
peacetime ['piːstaɪm] *n* temps *m* de paix
peach [piːtʃ] *n (fruit)* pêche *f*; *Fam* **she's a p.** elle est canon; *Fam* **a p. of a goal** un but de toute beauté; **p. Melba** pêche Melba; **p. tree** pêcher *m*
peacock ['piːkɒk] *n* paon *m*
peak [piːk] **1** *n* (**a**) *(summit of mountain)* sommet *m*; *(mountain)* pic *m*; *Fig (of success, career)* apogée *m* (**b**) *(of price, inflation, fitness)* maximum *m*; **in p. condition** dans une forme excellente; **p. period** *(for traffic)* heures *fpl* de pointe; *(in shop)* heures d'affluence; **p. season** haute saison *f*; *Br TV* **p. time** heures *fpl* de grande écoute, prime time *m* (**c**) *(of cap)* visière *f*
  2 *vi* culminer (**at** à)
peaky ['piːkɪ] *adj Fam* patraque

peal [piːl] *n (of bells)* sonnerie *f*; *(of thunder)* coup *m*; **peals of laughter** éclats *mpl* de rire

▸**peal out** *vi (of bells)* sonner à toute volée

peanut ['piːnʌt] *n* cacah(o)uète *f*; *Fam Fig* **peanuts** *(small sum of money)* clopinettes *fpl*; **p. butter** beurre *m* de cacah(o)uètes; **p. oil** huile *f* d'arachide

pear [peə(r)] *n* poire *f*; **p. tree** poirier *m*

pearl [pɜːl] *n* (**a**) *(jewel)* perle *f*; **p. diver** pêcheur(-euse) *m,f* de perles; **p. necklace** collier *m* de perles (**b**) *(idioms)* **pearls of wisdom** paroles *fpl* pleines de sagesse; **to cast pearls before swine** jeter des perles aux cochons

pearly ['pɜːlɪ] *adj* nacré(e); **the P. Gates** les portes *fpl* du paradis

pear-shaped ['peəʃeɪpt] *adj* en forme de poire; *(female figure)* plus fort(e) au niveau des hanches; *Br Fam Fig* **to go p.** partir en eau de boudin

peasant ['pezənt] *n* paysan(anne) *m,f*; *Pej (ignorant person)* péquenaud(e) *m,f*

peashooter ['piːʃuːtə(r)] *n* petite sarbacane *f*

peat [piːt] *n* tourbe *f*; **p. bog** tourbière *f*

pebble ['pebəl] *n* caillou *m*; *(on beach)* galet *m*; **p. beach** plage *f* de galets

pebbledash ['pebəldæʃ] *n* crépi *m*

pebbly ['peblɪ] *adj* caillouteux(euse); *(beach)* de galets

pecan ['piːkən] *n* **p. (nut)** noix *f* de pecan

peccary ['pekərɪ] *(pl* **peccaries**) *n* pécari *m*

peck [pek] **1** *n* (**a**) *(of bird)* coup *m* de bec (**b**) *(kiss)* bise *f*; **to give sb a p. on the cheek** faire une bise à qn
2 *vt* (**a**) *(of bird) (grain)* picorer; *(person)* donner un coup/des coups de bec à (**b**) *(kiss)* **to p. sb on the cheek** faire une bise à qn

peckish ['pekɪʃ] *adj Fam* **to be p.** avoir un creux

pecs [peks] *npl Fam (pectoral muscles)* pectoraux *mpl*

pectin ['pektɪn] *n Chem* pectine *f*

pectoral ['pektərəl] **1** *n* **pectorals** pectoraux *mpl*
2 *adj* pectoral(e)

peculiar [pɪ'kjuːlɪə(r)] *adj* (**a**) *(strange)* curieux(euse), bizarre (**b**) *(particular)* **p. to** particulier(ère) à, propre à; **this species is p. to France** cette espèce n'existe qu'en France

peculiarity [pɪkjuːlɪ'ærɪtɪ] *(pl* **peculiarities**) *n (strangeness)* singularité *f*, bizarrerie *f*; *(unusual characteristic)* particularité *f*

peculiarly [pɪ'kjuːlɪəlɪ] *adv* (**a**) *(strangely)* singulièrement (**b**) *(especially)* particulièrement

pecuniary [pɪ'kjuːnɪərɪ] *adj Formal* pécuniaire

pedagogic(al) [pedə'gɒdʒɪk(əl)] *adj* pédagogique

pedagogy ['pedəgɒdʒɪ] *n* pédagogie *f*

pedal ['pedəl] **1** *n* pédale *f*; **p. bin** poubelle *f* à pédale
2 *vt (pt & pp* **pedalled**, *Am* **pedaled**) **to p. a bicycle** être à bicyclette
3 *vi* pédaler

pedalo ['pedələʊ] *(pl* **pedaloes** *or* **pedalos**) *n* Pédalo® *m*

pedant ['pedənt] *n* pédant(e) *m,f*

pedantic [pɪ'dæntɪk] *adj* pédant(e)

pedantry ['pedəntrɪ] *n* pédantisme *m*, pédanterie *f*

peddle ['pedəl] *vt (goods, ideas, theories)* colporter; *(drugs)* faire du trafic de

peddler ['pedlə(r)] *n (of goods, ideas, theories)* colporteur(euse) *m,f*; *(of drugs)* trafiquant(e) *m,f*

pederast ['pedəræst] *n Formal* pédéraste *m*

pedestal ['pedɪstəl] *n* piédestal *m*; *Fig* **to put sb on a p.** mettre qn sur un piédestal; **p. lamp** lampe *f* sur piédestal

pedestrian [pɪ'destrɪən] **1** *n* piéton(onne) *m,f*; **p. crossing** passage *m* pour piétons, passage clouté; **p. precinct** zone *f* piétonnière
2 *adj (unimaginative)* banal(e)

pedestrianize [pɪ'destrɪənaɪz] *vt* transformer en zone piétonnière

pediatric, pediatrician *Am* = paediatric, paediatrician

pedicure ['pedɪkjʊə(r)] *n* **to have a p.** se faire soigner les pieds

pedigree ['pedɪgriː] **1** *n* (**a**) *(of animal)* pedigree *m* (**b**) *(of person)* ascendance *f*, généalogie *f*; *Fig (background)* passé *m*, antécédents *mpl*
2 *adj (animal)* de race

pedlar ['pedlə(r)] *n* colporteur(euse) *m,f*

pedophile *Am* = paedophile

pee [piː] *Fam* **1** *n* pipi *m*; **to have a p.** faire pipi
2 *vi* faire pipi

peek [piːk] **1** *n* coup *m* d'œil furtif; **to take** *or* **have a p. (at)** jeter un coup d'œil furtif (à)
2 *vi* jeter un coup d'œil furtif (**at** à)

peel [piːl] **1** *n (of apple, vegetable)* peau *f*; *(of orange, lemon)* écorce *f*
2 *vt (fruit)* peler; *(vegetable)* éplucher; *Fam* **to keep one's eyes peeled** ouvrir l'œil
3 *vi (of paint)* s'écailler; *(of skin, person)* peler

▸**peel off 1** *vt sep* enlever
2 *vi (of paint)* s'écailler; *(of skin)* peler; *(of label)* s'enlever

peelings ['piːlɪŋz] *npl (of potato, carrot)* épluchures *fpl*

peep¹ [piːp] **1** *n (furtive glance)* coup *m* d'œil furtif; **to have** *or* **take a p. (at)** jeter un coup d'œil furtif (à)
2 *vi* **to p. at sb/sth** jeter un coup d'œil furtif à qn/qch; **to p. through the keyhole** regarder par le trou de la serrure

peep² *n (sound) (of bird)* pépiement *m*; *(of mouse)* cri *m*; *Fam* **I don't want to hear another p. out of you** je ne veux plus entendre un mot

peephole ['piːphəʊl] *n* judas *m*

Peeping Tom ['piːpɪŋ'tɒm] *n Fam* voyeur *m*

peer¹ [pɪə(r)] *n* (**a**) *(equal)* pair *m*; **p. group** pairs *mpl*; **p. pressure** influence *f* du groupe (**b**) *Br (nobleman)* pair *m*

peer² *vi* **to p. at sb/sth** scruter qn/qch du regard; **to p. over sth** jeter un coup d'œil par-dessus qch

peerage ['pɪərɪdʒ] *n Br (rank)* pairie *f*; **the p.** les pairs *mpl*

peeress [pɪə'res] *n Br* pairesse *f*

peerless ['pɪəlɪs] *adj* sans pareil(eille), hors pair

peeve [piːv] *vt Fam* mettre en rogne; **to be peeved (at)** être en rogne (à cause de)

peevish ['piːvɪʃ] *adj* irritable, maussade

peewit ['piːwɪt] *n* vanneau *m* (huppé)

peg [peg] **1** *n (wooden)* cheville *f*; *(metal)* fiche *f*; *(for coat, hat)* patère *f*; **(clothes) p.** pince *f* à linge; **(tent) p.** piquet *m* de tente; **to buy clothes off the p.** acheter du prêt-à-porter; *Fig* **to take sb down a p. (or two)** remettre qn à sa place
2 *vt (pt & pp* **pegged**) (**a**) **to p. sth in place** fixer qch avec des piquets; **to p. the washing on the line** étendre le linge *(en utilisant des pinces à linge)* (**b**) *(set) (prices)* fixer; *(tie) (currency)* indexer; **to p. sth**

to the rate of inflation indexer qch sur le taux de l'inflation

▸**peg out** *vi Fam (die)* casser sa pipe

pejorative [pɪ'dʒɒrətɪv] *adj* péjoratif(ive)

Pekinese [pi:kɪ'ni:z] *n (dog)* pékinois *m*

Peking [pi:'kɪŋ] *n* Pékin

pelican ['pelɪkən] *n* pélican *m*; *Br* **p. crossing** feux *mpl* (à commande manuelle)

pellet ['pelɪt] *n (of paper, bread, clay)* boulette *f*; *(for gun)* plomb *m*

pell-mell ['pel'mel] *adv (run)* de façon désordonnée

pelmet ['pelmɪt] *n* cantonnière *f*

pelt¹ [pelt] *n (animal skin)* peau *f*, fourrure *f*

pelt² 1 *vt* bombarder (**with** de)
  2 *vi Fam* (**a**) *(rain)* **it was pelting down** il pleuvait à verse (**b**) *(go fast)* aller à toute allure; **to p. upstairs** grimper l'escalier quatre à quatre; **she came pelting along the corridor** elle a déboulé du fond du couloir

pelvic ['pelvɪk] *adj* pelvien(enne)

pelvis ['pelvɪs] *n* pelvis *m*

pen¹ [pen] **1** *n (for writing)* stylo *m*; **to put p. to paper** prendre la plume; **p. friend** *or* **pal** correspondant(e) *m,f*; **p. name** nom *m* de plume
  2 *vt (pt & pp* **penned**) écrire, rédiger

pen² *n (for sheep, cattle)* enclos *m*

pen³ *n Am Fam (prison)* taule *f*

▸**pen in** *vt sep (animals, people)* parquer

penal ['pi:nəl] *adj* pénal(e); **p. code** code *m* pénal; **p. colony** colonie *f* pénitentiaire; **p. servitude** travaux *mpl* forcés

penalize ['pi:nəlaɪz] *vt* pénaliser

penalty ['penltɪ] *(pl* **penalties**) *n* (**a**) *(punishment)* peine *f*; **to impose a p. (on sb)** prendre une sanction (contre qn); **on** *or* **under p. of death** sous peine de mort; *Fig* **to pay the p. for sth** subir les conséquences de qch; *Com* **p. clause** clause *f* pénale (**b**) *(in football)* penalty *m*; *(in rugby)* pénalité *f*; **p. area** surface *f* de réparation; **p. kick** penalty

penance ['penəns] *n also Fig* pénitence *f*; **to do p. (for sth)** faire pénitence (pour qch)

pence [pens] *pl of* **penny**

pencil ['pensəl] **1** *n* crayon *m*; **p. case** trousse *f*; **p. drawing** dessin *m* au crayon; **p. sharpener** taille-crayon *m*
  2 *vt (pt & pp* **pencilled**, *Am* **penciled**) *(draw)* dessiner au crayon; *(write)* écrire au crayon

▸**pencil in** *vt sep (date)* fixer provisoirement; **to p. sb in** fixer provisoirement un rendez-vous à qn

pendant ['pendənt] *n* pendentif *m*

pending ['pendɪŋ] **1** *adj (trial)* en instance; *(negotiations)* en cours; *(documents)* en souffrance, en attente
  2 *prep* en attendant

pendulum ['pendjʊləm] *n* pendule *m*

penetrate ['penɪtreɪt] *vt & vi* pénétrer

penetrating ['penɪtreɪtɪŋ] *adj (sound, wind, cold)* pénétrant(e); *(voice, scream, stare)* perçant(e)

penetration [penɪ'treɪʃən] *n* pénétration *f*

penguin ['peŋgwɪn] *n* manchot *m*

penicillin [penɪ'sɪlɪn] *n* pénicilline *f*

peninsula [pɪ'nɪnsjʊlə] *n* péninsule *f*; *(smaller)* presqu'île *f*

peninsular [pɪ'nɪnsjʊlə(r)] *adj* péninsulaire

penis ['pi:nɪs] *n* pénis *m*

penitence ['penɪtəns] *n* pénitence *f*, repentir *m*

penitent ['penɪtənt] *n & adj* pénitent(e) *m,f*

penitentiary [penɪ'tenʃərɪ] *(pl* **penitentiaries**) *n Am* pénitencier *m*

penknife ['pennaɪf] *(pl* **penknives** ['pennaɪvz]) *n* canif *m*

pennant ['penənt] *n* flamme *f*

penniless ['penlɪs] *adj* sans le sou

Pennsylvania [pensɪl'veɪnɪə] *n* la Pennsylvanie

penny ['penɪ] *n* (**a**) *Br (coin) (pl* **pence** [pens]) penny *m*; **a 10/50 pence piece** une pièce de 10/50 pence; **it was worth every p.** ça valait le coup; **it didn't cost them a p.** cela ne leur a pas coûté un sou; **p. farthing** vélocipède *m*; **p. pinching** économies *fpl* de bouts de chandelle; **p. whistle** flûtiau *m*
  (**b**) *Am (cent)* cent *m*
  (**c**) *(idioms)* **they haven't a p. to their name** il n'ont pas un sou vaillant; **the p.'s dropped** ça a fait tilt; **they're ten a p.** il y en a à la pelle; **a p. for your thoughts** à quoi penses-tu?; **a bad p.** un(e) bon (bonne) à rien

penny-pinching ['penɪpɪntʃɪŋ] *adj (person)* pingre; *(ways, habits)* de radin

pension ['penʃən] *n* pension *f*; *(after retirement)* (pension de) retraite *f*; **to be on a p.** recevoir une pension; *(after retirement)* recevoir une retraite; **p. fund** caisse *f* de retraite; **p. scheme** plan *m* de retraite

▸**pension off** *vt sep* mettre à la retraite

pensionable ['penʃənəbəl] *adj* **p. age** âge *m* de départ en retraite

pensioner ['penʃənə(r)] *n* **(old-age) p.** retraité(e) *m,f*

pensive ['pensɪv] *adj* pensif(ive), songeur(euse)

pensively ['pensɪvlɪ] *adv* pensivement

pentagon ['pentəgən] *n* pentagone *m*; **the P.** *(building)* le Pentagone

pentathlon [pen'tæθlən] *n* pentathlon *m*

Pentecost ['pentɪkɒst] *n* la Pentecôte

penthouse ['penthaʊs] *n* = appartement de standing au dernier étage d'un immeuble

pent-up [pen'tʌp] *adj (desire)* refoulé(e); *(rage, energy)* contenu(e)

penultimate [pe'nʌltɪmɪt] *adj* pénultième, avant-dernier(ère)

penury ['penjʊrɪ] *n* indigence *f*

peony ['pi:ənɪ] *(pl* **peonies**) *n* pivoine *f*

people ['pi:pəl] **1** *npl* (**a**) *(as group)* gens *mpl*; *(as individuals)* personnes *fpl*; **most p.** la plupart des gens; **old p.** les personnes âgées; **he's one of those p. who think (that)...** c'est le genre de type qui pense que...; **p. say (that)...** les gens disent que...; *Aut* **p. carrier**, **p. mover** monospace *m*; **p. power** pouvoir *m* populaire (**b**) *(citizens)* peuple *m*; **the common p.** le peuple; **a man of the p.** un homme du peuple; **p. power** pouvoir *m* populaire; **P.'s Republic** République *f* populaire (**c**) *Fam (family)* **my/his p.** ma/sa famille
  2 *n (nation)* peuple *m*; **the Scottish p.** les Écossais *mpl*
  3 *vt* peupler

PEP [pep] *n Formerly Fin (abbr* **personal equity plan**) ≃ PEA *m*

pep [pep] *n Fam* entrain *m*, allant *m*; **p. pill** excitant *m*; **p. talk** petit discours *m* d'encouragement

▸**pep up** *(pt & pp* **pepped**) *vt sep Fam (person)* ragaillardir, revigorer; *(event)* animer; *(dish)* relever

pepper ['pepə(r)] **1** *n (spice)* poivre *m*; *(vegetable)* poivron *m*; **p. mill** moulin *m* à poivre; **p. pot** poivrière *f*
  2 *vt* (**a**) *(in cooking)* poivrer (**b**) *Fig (speech, essay)*

parsemer (**with** de); **to p. sb with bullets** cribler qn de balles

peppercorn ['pepəkɔːn] *n* grain *m* de poivre

peppermint ['pepəmɪnt] *n (plant)* menthe *f* poivrée; *(sweet)* bonbon *m* à la menthe; **p. tea** thé *m* à la menthe

peppery ['pepərɪ] *adj* (**a**) *(dish)* poivré(e) (**b**) *(irritable)* irascible, colérique

peptic ulcer ['peptɪk'ʌlsə(r)] *n* ulcère *m* gastro-duodénal

per [pɜː(r)] *prep* par; **p. day** par jour; **100 km p. hour** 100 km à l'heure; *Formal* **as p. your instructions** conformément à vos instructions; **as p. usual** comme d'habitude; **p. annum** par an; **p. capita** par habitant; **p. se** en soi

perceive [pə'siːv] *vt* percevoir

percent [pə'sent] **1** *n* pourcentage *m*
2 *adv* pour cent

percentage [pə'sentɪdʒ] *n* pourcentage *m*

perceptible [pə'septɪbəl] *adj* perceptible

perceptibly [pə'septɪblɪ] *adv* sensiblement

perception [pə'sepʃən] *n* perception *f*

perceptive [pə'septɪv] *adj (person, remark)* perspicace; *(analysis, article)* pertinent(e)

perch¹ [pɜːtʃ] **1** *n (for bird) & Fig* perchoir *m*; *Fam Fig* **to knock sb off his p.** détrôner qn
2 *vi* se percher

perch² *n (fish)* perche *f*

percolate ['pɜːkəleɪt] **1** *vt (coffee)* passer; **percolated coffee** = café préparé dans une cafetière à pression
2 *vi (of liquid)* passer; *Fig (of information)* filtrer

percolator ['pɜːkəleɪtə(r)] *n* cafetière *f* à pression

percussion [pə'kʌʃən] *n* percussion *f*; **p. instrument** instrument *m* à percussion

percussionist [pə'kʌʃənɪst] *n* percussionniste *mf*

peregrine falcon ['perɪɡrɪn'fɔːlkən] *n* faucon *m* pèlerin

peremptory [pə'remptərɪ] *adj* péremptoire; *(refusal)* absolu(e)

perennial [pə'renɪəl] **1** *n (plant)* plante *f* vivace
2 *adj (plant)* vivace; *(problem, beauty)* éternel(elle); *(worry)* perpétuel(elle)

perfect 1 *adj* ['pɜːfɪkt] (**a**) *(ideal)* parfait(e); **nobody's p.** personne n'est parfait; **Tuesday would be p.** mardi me conviendrait parfaitement; **to have p. pitch** avoir l'oreille absolue (**b**) *(complete)* **it makes p. sense** c'est parfaitement logique; **she's a p. stranger** je ne la connais pas du tout; **he's a p. gentleman/fool** c'est un parfait homme du monde/imbécile (**c**) *Gram* **the p. (tense)** le passé composé
2 *vt* [pə'fekt] parfaire

perfection [pə'fekʃən] *n* perfection *f*

perfectionist [pə'fekʃənɪst] *n* perfectionniste *mf*

perfectly ['pɜːfɪktlɪ] *adv (faultlessly)* à la perfection; *(completely)* parfaitement

perfidious [pə'fɪdɪəs] *adj Lit* perfide

perforate ['pɜːfəreɪt] *vt* perforer

perforated ['pɜːfəreɪtɪd] *adj* perforé(e); **p. ulcer** perforation *f* ulcéreuse

perforation [pɜːfə'reɪʃən] *n (hole)* perforation *f*; *(on stamp)* dentelure *f*

perform [pə'fɔːm] **1** *vt (play, role, piece of music)* jouer; *(miracle)* faire; *(one's duty)* remplir; **to p. an operation on sb** opérer qn

2 *vi (of machine, car)* marcher; *(of actor)* jouer; *(of singer)* chanter

performance [pə'fɔːməns] *n* (**a**) *(of task, duty)* accomplissement *m*; **p. appraisal** appréciation *f*, évaluation *f* (**b**) *(of sportsperson)* performance *f*; *(of actor)* interprétation *f*; *(of pupil, economy)* résultats *mpl*, performance; *(of machine, car)* performances *fpl* (**c**) *(of play)* représentation *f*; *Fig* **to make a p.** faire toute une histoire; **p. art** performance *f*, action *f*; **p. artist** = artiste spécialisé dans la performance

performance-related [pə'fɔːmənsrɪ'leɪtɪd] *adj* en fonction du mérite *ou* résultat; **p. pay** salaire *m* au mérite

performer [pə'fɔːmə(r)] *n* artiste *mf (des arts du spectacle)*

performing [pə'fɔːmɪŋ] *adj (dog, seal)* savant(e); **p. arts** arts *mpl* du spectacle

perfume 1 *n* ['pɜːfjuːm] parfum *m*; **p. counter** rayon *m* parfumerie
2 *vt* [pə'fjuːm] parfumer

perfumed ['pɜːfjuːmd] *adj* parfumé(e)

perfunctory [pə'fʌŋktərɪ] *adj (examination, glance)* rapide; *(smile)* mécanique; *(letter, instructions)* sommaire

perhaps [pə'hæps] *adv* peut-être; **p. so/not** peut-être que oui/non; **p. she'll come** elle viendra peut-être, peut-être qu'elle viendra

peril ['perəl] *n* péril *m*, danger *m*; **at one's p.** à ses risques et périls

perilous ['perɪləs] *adj* dangereux(euse)

perilously ['perɪləslɪ] *adv* dangereusement

perimeter [pə'rɪmɪtə(r)] *n* périmètre *m*; **p. fence** clôture *f*

period ['pɪərɪəd] *n* (**a**) *(stretch of time)* période *f*; **within the agreed p.** dans les délais convenus; **sunny periods** intervalles *mpl* ensoleillés
(**b**) *(in school)* heure *f* de cours; **a French/maths p.** un cours de français/maths
(**c**) *(menstruation)* règles *fpl*; **to have one's p.** avoir ses règles; **p. pains** règles douloureuses
(**d**) *(historical age)* époque *f*; **p. drama** *(on TV)* drame *m* historique; **p. dress** costume(s) *m(pl)* d'époque; **p. furniture** meubles *mpl* d'époque
(**e**) *Am (full stop)* point *m*

periodic [pɪərɪ'ɒdɪk] *adj* périodique; *Chem* **p. table** classification *f* périodique

periodical [pɪərɪ'ɒdɪkəl] *n* périodique *m*

periodically [pɪərɪ'ɒdɪklɪ] *adv* périodiquement

peripheral [pə'rɪfərəl] **1** *n Comput* périphérique *m*
2 *adj (area, vision)* périphérique; *(issue, importance)* accessoire

periphery [pə'rɪfərɪ] *(pl* **peripheries***) n* périphérie *f*

periscope ['perɪskəʊp] *n* périscope *m*

perish ['perɪʃ] *vi* (**a**) *(of person)* périr; **p. the thought!** loin de moi cette pensée! (**b**) *(of rubber, leather)* se détériorer; *(of food)* s'avarier

perishable ['perɪʃəbəl] **1** *n* **perishables** denrées *fpl* périssables
2 *adj* périssable

perishing ['perɪʃɪŋ] *adj Fam (very cold)* **it's p.** il fait un froid de canard

peritonitis [perɪtə'naɪtɪs] *n* péritonite *f*

perjure ['pɜːdʒə(r)] *vt Law* **to p. oneself** faire un faux témoignage

perjury ['pɜːdʒərɪ] *n Law* faux témoignage *m*; **to commit p.** faire un faux témoignage

perk [pɜːk] *n Br Fam* avantage *m*, à-côté *m*
▸**perk up** *Fam* **1** *vt sep (revive)* requinquer, ragaillardir; *(cheer up)* remonter le moral à
 2 *vi (revive)* se requinquer, se ragaillardir; *(cheer up)* retrouver sa bonne humeur

perky ['pɜːkɪ] *adj Fam (lively)* plein(e) d'entrain; *(cheerful)* guilleret(ette)

perm [pɜːm] **1** *n* permanente *f*; **to have a p.** se faire faire une permanente
 2 *vt* **to have one's hair permed** se faire faire une permanente

permanence ['pɜːmənəns] *n* permanence *f*

permanent ['pɜːmənənt] *adj* permanent(e); *(ink, stain)* indélébile; *(residence, address)* fixe; **p. wave** permanente *f*

permeate ['pɜːmɪeɪt] **1** *vt* **to be permeated with sth** *(liquid)* être saturé(e) de qch; *(smell)* être rempli(e) de qch; *Fig (feeling)* être imprégné(e) de qch
 2 *vi* **to p. through sth** *(of liquid)* passer à travers qch; *(of smell)* se répandre dans qch; *Fig (of feeling)* imprégner qch

permissible [pə'mɪsɪbəl] *adj* admissible, acceptable

permission [pə'mɪʃən] *n* permission *f*, autorisation *f*; **to ask for p. to do sth** demander la permission de faire qch; **to give sb p. to do sth** donner à qn la permission de faire qch, autoriser qn à faire qch

permissive [pə'mɪsɪv] *adj* permissif(ive)

permit 1 *n* ['pɜːmɪt] permis *m*; **p. holders only** *(sign)* réservé aux personnes autorisées
 2 *vt* [pə'mɪt] *(pt & pp* **permitted**) permettre; **to p. sb to do sth** permettre à qn de faire qch, autoriser qn à faire qch
 3 *vi* [pə'mɪt] **weather permitting** si le temps le permet

permutation [pɜːmjʊ'teɪʃən] *n* permutation *f*

pernicious [pə'nɪʃəs] *adj* pernicieux(euse)

pernickety [pə'nɪkɪtɪ] *adj Fam (person)* tatillon(-onne), pointilleux(euse); *(task)* délicat(e), minutieux(euse)

peroxide [pə'rɒksaɪd] *n Chem* peroxyde *m*; **p. blonde** blonde *f* décolorée

perpendicular [pɜːpən'dɪkjʊlə(r)] **1** *n* perpendiculaire *f*
 2 *adj* perpendiculaire

perpetrate ['pɜːpɪtreɪt] *vt (crime)* perpétrer; *(fraud, error)* commettre

perpetrator ['pɜːpɪtreɪtə(r)] *n* auteur *m*

perpetual [pə'petjʊəl] *adj (eternal)* perpétuel(elle), éternel(elle); *(constant)* incessant(e), continuel(elle); *Phys* **p. motion** mouvement *m* perpétuel

perpetually [pə'petjʊəlɪ] *adv* perpétuellement

perpetuate [pə'petjʊeɪt] *vt* perpétuer

perpetuity [pɜːpɪ'tjuːɪtɪ] *n Formal* perpétuité *f*; **in p.** à perpétuité

perplex [pə'pleks] *vt* rendre *ou* laisser perplexe

perplexing [pə'pleksɪŋ] *adj* difficile; *(person)* déconcertant(e)

perplexity [pə'pleksɪtɪ] *n* perplexité *f*

persecute ['pɜːsɪkjuːt] *vt* persécuter

persecution [pɜːsɪ'kjuːʃən] *n* persécution *f*; *Psy* **p. complex** délire *m* de persécution

persecutor ['pɜːsɪkjuːtə(r)] *n* persécuteur(trice) *m,f*

perseverance [pɜːsɪ'vɪərəns] *n* persévérance *f*

persevere [pɜːsɪ'vɪə(r)] *vi* persévérer (**with** dans); **to p. in doing sth** persister à faire qch

Persia ['pɜːʒə] *n Hist* la Perse

Persian ['pɜːʒən] **1** *n* (**a**) *(person) Hist* Perse *mf*; *(after 7th century)* Persan(e) *m,f* (**b**) *(language)* persan *m*
 2 *adj Hist* perse; *(after 7th century)* persan(e); **P. carpet** tapis *m* persan; **P. cat** chat *m* persan; **the P. Gulf** le golfe Persique

persimmon [pɜː'sɪmən] *n (arbre)* plaqueminier *m*; *(fruit)* kaki *m*

persist [pə'sɪst] *vi* persister; **to p. in doing sth** s'obstiner à faire qch; **to p. in one's belief that...** persister à croire que...

persistence [pə'sɪstəns] *n (of person)* ténacité *f*, obstination *f*; *(of fog, belief)* persistance *f*

persistent [pə'sɪstənt] *adj (person)* tenace; *(problems, pain)* incessant(e), continuel(elle); *(rumours)* persistant(e); **p. offender** récidiviste *mf*; *Med* **p. vegetative state** état *m* végétatif chronique

persistently [pə'sɪstəntlɪ] *adv* continuellement

person ['pɜːsən] *(pl* **people** ['piːpəl], *Formal* **persons**) *n* personne *f*; **in p.** en personne; **on one's p.** sur soi; *Gram* **in the first/second/third p.** à la première/deuxième/troisième personne; *Law* **by a p. or persons unknown** par un ou plusieurs inconnus

personable ['pɜːsənəbəl] *adj* charmant(e)

personage ['pɜːsənɪdʒ] *n* personnage *m*

personal ['pɜːsənəl] *adj* personnel(elle); **to make a p. appearance** venir *ou* apparaître en personne; **for p. reasons** pour des raisons personnelles; **don't be p.** ne parle pas des choses aussi personnelles; **it's nothing p., but...** ça n'a rien de personnel, mais...; **p. friend** ami(e) *m,f* personnel(elle); **p. ad** petite annonce *f*; **p. assistant** secrétaire *mf* de direction; **p. best** *(in sport)* record *m* personnel; **p. column** petites annonces; **p. computer** ordinateur *m* individuel; **p. effects** effets *mpl* personnels; **p. growth** développement *m* personnel; **p. hygiene** hygiène *f*; **p. loan** prêt *m* personnel; **p. organizer** *(book)* agenda *m*; *(electronic)* agenda électronique; *Gram* **p. pronoun** pronom *m* personnel; **p. stereo** baladeur *m*

personality [pɜːsə'nælɪtɪ] *(pl* **personalities**) *n* personnalité *f*; **p. cult** culte *m* de la personnalité; *Psy* **p. disorder** trouble *m* de la personnalité

personally ['pɜːsənəlɪ] *adv* personnellement; **don't take it p.** n'en faites pas une affaire personnelle

personification [pɜːsɒnɪfɪ'keɪʃən] *n* incarnation *f*; **to be the p. of meanness** être l'avarice incarnée

personify [pɜː'sɒnɪfaɪ] *(pt & pp* **personified**) *vt* personnifier

personnel [pɜːsə'nel] *n* personnel *m*; **p. department** service *m* du personnel; **p. manager** directeur(trice) *m,f* du personnel

perspective [pə'spektɪv] *n* perspective *f*; **to see things in p.** relativiser les choses; **to put sth in(to) p.** relativiser qch

perspicacious [pɜːspɪ'keɪʃəs] *adj Formal* perspicace

perspiration [pɜːspə'reɪʃən] *n* transpiration *f*

perspire [pə'spaɪə(r)] *vi* transpirer

persuade [pə'sweɪd] *vt* persuader, convaincre; **to p. sb to do sth** persuader *ou* convaincre qn de faire qch; **to p. sb not to do sth** dissuader qn de faire qch

persuasion [pə'sweɪʒən] *n* (**a**) *(act, ability)* persuasion *f*; **powers of p.** pouvoir *m* de persuasion (**b**) *(beliefs)* **political p.** opinions *fpl* politiques; **religious p.** religion *f*, confession *f*

persuasive [pə'sweɪsɪv] *adj (person)* persuasif(ive); *(argument)* convaincant(e)

persuasively [pə'sweɪzɪvlɪ] *adv (say)* d'un ton persuasif; *(argue)* de façon convaincante

pert [pɜːt] *adj* (**a**) *(cheeky)* espiègle; *(reply)* direct(e) (**b**) *(nose, breasts)* pointu(e); *(bottom)* petit(e) et ferme

pertain [pə'teɪn] *vi Formal* **to p. to** *(belong to)* appartenir à; *(be relevant to)* se rapporter à

pertinent ['pɜːtɪnənt] *adj* pertinent(e); **to be p. to** avoir rapport à

perturb [pə'tɜːb] *vt* inquiéter, troubler

Peru [pə'ruː] *n* le Pérou

perusal [pə'ruːzəl] *n Formal* lecture *f*

peruse [pə'ruːz] *vt Formal (read carefully)* lire attentivement; *(read quickly)* feuilleter; *(article)* survoler

Peruvian [pə'ruːvɪən] **1** *n* Péruvien(enne) *m,f*
2 *adj* péruvien(enne)

pervade [pɜː'veɪd] *vt* imprégner

pervasive [pɜː'veɪsɪv] *adj (feeling)* général(e); *(smell)* envahissant(e)

perverse [pə'vɜːs] *adj* (**a**) *(contrary)* contrariant(e); **he's just being p.** il fait ça pour contrarier; **to take a p. pleasure in doing sth** prendre un malin plaisir à faire qch (**b**) *(sexually deviant)* pervers(e)

perversely [pə'vɜːslɪ] *adv (contrarily)* par pur esprit de contradiction

perversion [pə'vɜːʃən] *n (sexual)* perversion *f*; *(of truth, justice)* travestissement *m*

pervert1 *n* ['pɜːvɜːt] *(sexual deviant)* pervers(e) *m,f*
2 *vt* [pə'vɜːt] *(corrupt)* pervertir; *(distort)* altérer, dénaturer; *Law* **to p. the course of justice** entraver le bon fonctionnement de la justice

peseta [pə'seɪtə] *n* peseta *f*

pesky ['peskɪ] *adj Am Fam* embêtant(e), empoisonnant(e)

peso ['peɪsəʊ] *(pl* **pesos**) *n* peso *m*

pessary ['pesərɪ] *(pl* **pessaries**) *n* ovule *m*

pessimism ['pesɪmɪzəm] *n* pessimisme *m*

pessimist ['pesɪmɪst] *n* pessimiste *mf*

pessimistic [pesɪ'mɪstɪk] *adj* pessimiste

pest [pest] *n* (**a**) *(animal)* animal *m* nuisible; *(insect)* insecte *m* nuisible; **p. control** *(of rats)* dératisation *f*; *(of insects)* déinsectisation *f* (**b**) *Fam (nuisance)* poison *m*, plaie *f*

pester ['pestə(r)] *vt* tourmenter, importuner; **to p. sb to do sth** harceler qn pour qu'il fasse qch; **to p. sb into doing sth** harceler qn jusqu'à ce qu'il fasse qch

pesticide ['pestɪsaɪd] *n* pesticide *m*

pestilence ['pestɪləns] *n Lit* peste *f*

pestle ['pesəl] *n* pilon *m*; **p. and mortar** pilon et mortier

pet [pet] **1** *n* (**a**) *(animal)* animal *m* familier *ou* domestique; **p. food** nourriture *f* pour animaux familiers; **p. shop** animalerie *f* (**b**) *(favourite)* **the teacher's p.** le chouchou du professeur; **p. hate** bête *f* noire; **p. name** surnom *m*; **p. subject** dada *m* (**c**) *(term of address)* mon petit chou
2 *vt (pt & pp* **petted**) *(person, dog)* caresser, câliner
3 *vi Fam (sexually)* se peloter

petal ['petəl] *n* pétale *m*

▸**peter out** ['piːtə(r)] *vi (of conversation, enthusiasm)* tarir; *(of scheme)* n'aboutir à rien; *(of path, stream)* disparaître

petite [pə'tiːt] *adj* menu(e)

petition [pɪ'tɪʃən] **1** *n* pétition *f*
2 *vt (court, sovereign)* adresser *ou* présenter une pétition à

3 *vi* **to p. for sth** faire une pétition pour qch; *Law* **to p. for divorce** faire une demande de divorce

petitioner [pɪ'tɪʃənə(r)] *n Law (for divorce)* pétitionnaire *mf*, requérant(e) *m,f*

petrify ['petrɪfaɪ] *(pt & pp* **petrified**) *vt* pétrifier

petrochemical [petrəʊ'kemɪkəl] **1** *n* produit *m* pétrochimique
2 *adj* pétrochimique

petrol ['petrəl] *n Br* essence *f*; **p. bomb** cocktail *m* Molotov; **p. can** bidon *m* d'essence; **p. pump** pompe *f* à essence; **p. station** station *f* d'essence, station-service *f*; **p. tank** réservoir *m* d'essence

petroleum [pə'trəʊlɪəm] *n* pétrole *m*; **p. jelly** vaseline *f*

petticoat ['petɪkəʊt] *n (from waist)* jupon *m*; *(full-length)* combinaison *f*

petty ['petɪ] *adj* (**a**) *(insignificant)* insignifiant(e); **p. cash** petite caisse *f*; **p. crime** petite délinquance *f*; *Naut* **p. officer** second maître *m* (**b**) *(small-minded)* mesquin(e)

petulance ['petjʊləns] *n* irascibilité *f*

petulant ['petjʊlənt] *adj* irascible

petunia [pɪ'tjuːnɪə] *n* pétunia *m*

pew [pjuː] *n* banc *m* d'église; *Fam* **take a p.!** assieds-toi!

pewter ['pjuːtə(r)] *n* étain *m*

PG [piː'dʒiː] *adj Br Cin (abbr* **Parental Guidance**) = qui exige une autorisation parentale

pH [piː'eɪtʃ] *n Chem* pH *m*

phalanx ['fælæŋks] *n Mil Hist* phalange *f*; *Fig (of officials, journalists)* armée *f*

phallic ['fælɪk] *adj* phallique; **p. symbol** symbole *m* phallique

phallus ['fæləs] *n* phallus *m*

phantom ['fæntəm] *n* fantôme *m*, spectre *m*; **p. pregnancy** grossesse *f* nerveuse

Pharaoh ['feərəʊ] *n* pharaon *m*

pharmaceutical [fɑːmə'sjuːtɪkəl] **1** *n* **pharmaceuticals** produits *mpl* pharmaceutiques
2 *adj* pharmaceutique

pharmacist ['fɑːməsɪst] *n* pharmacien(enne) *m,f*

pharmacology [fɑːmə'kɒlədʒɪ] *n* pharmacologie *f*

pharmacy ['fɑːməsɪ] *(pl* **pharmacies**) *n* pharmacie *f*

phase [feɪz] *n* phase *f*; **it's just a p. (he's going through)** ça lui passera; *Fig* **out of p.** déphasé(e)

▸**phase in** *vt sep* mettre en place progressivement

▸**phase out** *vt sep* éliminer progressivement

phased [feɪzd] *adj* progressif(ive)

PhD [piːeɪtʃ'diː] *n Univ (abbr* **Doctor of Philosophy**) *(person)* docteur *m*; *(degree)* doctorat *m* (**in** de)

pheasant ['fezənt] *n* faisan *m*

phenomenal [fɪ'nɒmɪnəl] *adj* phénoménal(e)

phenomenally [fɪ'nɒmɪnəlɪ] *adv* prodigieusement

phenomenon [fɪ'nɒmɪnən] *(pl* **phenomena** [fɪ'nɒmɪnə]) *n* phénomène *m*

phew [fjuː] *exclam (when hot)* pfff!; *(in relief)* ouf!

phial ['faɪəl] *n* fiole *f*

Philadelphia [fɪlə'delfɪə] *n* Philadelphie

philanderer [fɪ'lændərə(r)] *n Pej* coureur *m* de jupons

philanthropic [fɪlən'θrɒpɪk] *adj* philanthropique; *(person)* philanthrope

philanthropist [fɪ'lænθrəpɪst] *n* philanthrope *mf*

philanthropy [fɪ'lænθrəpɪ] *n* philanthropie *f*

philately [fɪ'lætəlɪ] *n* philatélie *f*

philharmonic [filə'mɒnɪk] *Mus* **1** *n* (orchestre *m*) philharmonique *m*
2 *adj* philharmonique
Philippines ['fɪlɪpiːnz] *npl* **the P.** les Philippines *fpl*
philology [fɪ'lɒlədʒɪ] *n* philologie *f*
philosopher [fɪ'lɒsəfə(r)] *n* philosophe *mf*
philosophic(al) [fɪlə'sɒfɪk(əl)] *adj* philosophique; *(person, attitude)* philosophe
philosophize [fɪ'lɒsəfaɪz] *vi* philosopher
philosophy [fɪ'lɒsəfɪ] *(pl* **philosophies**) *n* philosophie *f*
phlegm [flem] *n* flegme *m*
phlegmatic [fleg'mætɪk] *adj* flegmatique
phobia ['fəʊbɪə] *n* phobie *f*; **to have a p. about sth** avoir la phobie de qch
phoenix ['fiːnɪks] *n* phénix *m*; **to rise like a p.** renaître tel un phénix
phone [fəʊn] **1** *n* téléphone *m*; **to be on the p.** *(talking)* être au téléphone; *(have a telephone)* avoir le téléphone; **to give sb a p.** donner un coup de téléphone à qn; **p. bill** facture *f* de téléphone; **p. book** annuaire *m* (du téléphone); **p. box/booth** cabine *f* téléphonique; **p. call** coup *m* de téléphone; **p. number** numéro *m* de téléphone
2 *vt* téléphoner à
3 *vi* téléphoner
phonecard ['fəʊnkɑːd] *n* carte *f* de téléphone
phone-in ['fəʊnɪn] *n* **p. (programme)** = émission au cours de laquelle les téléspectateurs ou les auditeurs peuvent intervenir par téléphone
phoneme ['fəʊniːm] *n* phonème *m*
phonetic [fə'netɪk] *adj* phonétique
phonetics [fə'netɪks] **1** *n (science)* phonétique *f*
2 *npl (symbols)* symboles *mpl* phonétiques
phoney, *Am* **phony** ['fəʊnɪ] *(pl* **phonies**) *Fam* **1** *n (impostor)* imposteur *m*; *(insincere person)* faux jeton *m*; *(thing)* faux *m*
2 *adj* bidon
phosphate ['fɒsfeɪt] *n* phosphate *m*
phosphorescent [fɒsfə'resənt] *adj* phosphorescent(e)
phosphorus ['fɒsfərəs] *n* phosphore *m*
photo ['fəʊtəʊ] *(pl* **photos**) *n* photo *f*; **to take sb's p.** prendre qn en photo; **p. album** album *m* (de) photos; **p. booth** Photomaton® *m*; **p. finish** photo-finish *f*; **it's just another p. opportunity** ce n'est qu'un nouveau prétexte pour se faire photographier
photocopier ['fəʊtəʊkɒpɪə(r)] *n* photocopieuse *f*
photocopy ['fəʊtəʊkɒpɪ] **1** *n (pl* **photocopies**) photocopie *f*
2 *vt (pt & pp* **photocopied**) photocopier
photoelectric [fəʊtəʊɪ'lektrɪk] *adj* photoélectrique; **p. cell** cellule *f* photoélectrique
photogenic [fəʊtə'dʒenɪk] *adj* photogénique
photograph ['fəʊtəgræf] **1** *n* photographie *f*; **to take sb's p.** prendre qn en photo; **p. album** album *m* de photographies
2 *vt* photographier, prendre en photo
photographer [fə'tɒgrəfə(r)] *n* photographe *mf*
photographic [fəʊtə'græfɪk] *adj* photographique; **to have a p. memory** avoir une mémoire photographique
photography [fə'tɒgrəfɪ] *n* photographie *f*
photosensitive [fəʊtəʊ'sensɪtɪv] *adj* photosensible
Photostat® ['fəʊtəʊstæt] *n* photostat *m*

photosynthesis [fəʊtəʊ'sɪnθɪsɪs] *n Bot* photosynthèse *f*
photosynthesize [fəʊtəʊ'sɪnθɪsaɪz] *vt Bot* fabriquer par photosynthèse
phrasal verb ['freɪzəl'vɜːb] *n Gram* verbe *m* à particule
phrase [freɪz] **1** *n* phrase *f*; **p. book** manuel *m ou* guide *m* de conversation
2 *vt* (**a**) *(verbally)* exprimer; *(in writing)* tourner (**b**) *Mus* phraser
phraseology [freɪzɪ'ɒlədʒɪ] *n* phraséologie *f*
physical ['fɪzɪkəl] **1** *n (examination)* visite *f* médicale
2 *adj* physique; **p. education** éducation *f* physique; **p. exercise** *or* **training** (exercices *mpl* de) gymnastique *f*; **p. fitness** forme *f* physique; **p. geography** géographie *f* physique; **p. impossibility** impossibilité *f* physique *ou* matérielle; **p. sciences** sciences *fpl* physiques
physically ['fɪzɪklɪ] *adv* physiquement; **p. fit** en bonne forme physique; **p. handicapped** handicapé(e) physique
physician [fɪ'zɪʃən] *n* médecin *m*
physicist ['fɪzɪsɪst] *n* physicien(enne) *m,f*
physics ['fɪzɪks] *n* physique *f*
physiognomy [fɪzɪ'ɒnəmɪ] *n Formal* physionomie *f*
physiological [fɪzɪə'lɒdʒɪkəl] *adj* physiologique
physiology [fɪzɪ'ɒlədʒɪ] *n* physiologie *f*
physiotherapist [fɪzɪəʊ'θerəpɪst] *n* kinésithérapeute *mf*
physiotherapy [fɪzɪəʊ'θerəpɪ] *n* kinésithérapie *f*
physique [fɪ'ziːk] *n* physique *m*
pianist ['pɪənɪst] *n* pianiste *mf*
piano [pɪ'ænəʊ] *(pl* **pianos**) *n* piano *m*; **p. concerto** concerto *m* pour piano; **p. stool** tabouret *m* de piano; **p. tuner** accordeur *m* de pianos
piccolo ['pɪkələʊ] *(pl* **piccolos**) *n* piccolo *m*
piccy ['pɪkɪ] *(pl* **piccies**) *n Br Fam (photograph)* photo *f*
pick [pɪk] **1** *n* (**a**) *(tool)* pic *m*, pioche *f*
(**b**) *(choice)* **to take one's p.** choisir; **the p. of the bunch** le (la) meilleur(e) du lot
2 *vt* (**a**) *(choose)* choisir; **to p. a fight (with sb)** chercher la bagarre (avec qn)
(**b**) *(flowers, fruit)* cueillir
(**c**) *(other uses)* **to p. a lock** crocheter une serrure; **to p. a guitar** pincer la guitare; **to p. one's nose** mettre les doigts dans le nez; **to p. one's teeth** se curer les dents; **to p. a spot** tripoter un bouton; **to p. sb's pocket** voler dans les poches de qn; **to p. a hole in sth** faire un trou à qch en tirant dessus; *Fig* **to p. holes in sth** trouver des failles dans qch; **to p. sb's brains** soumettre quelque chose à la sagacité de qn
3 *vi* **to p. and choose** se permettre de choisir
▶**pick off** *vt sep (remove)* enlever, ôter; *(of gunman, sniper)* éliminer
▶**pick on** *vt insep* utiliser comme souffre-douleur
▶**pick out** *vt sep* (**a**) *(remove)* retirer (**b**) *(select)* choisir (**c**) *(recognize)* repérer
▶**pick up 1** *vt sep* (**a**) *(lift up)* ramasser; *(to upright position)* relever; **to p. up the phone** décrocher (le téléphone); *Fig* **to p. oneself up** se remettre, se reprendre; *Fig* **to p. up the pieces** ramasser les morceaux; *Fig* **to p. up the bill** payer l'addition
(**b**) *(collect)* prendre; *(arrest)* arrêter; **to p. up survivors** recueillir des survivants
(**c**) *Fam (sexually)* ramasser
(**d**) *(learn)* apprendre; *(acquire)* acquérir; **to p. up**

speed prendre de la vitesse (**e**) *(radio station, message)* capter (**f**) *(notice)* relever (**g**) *(discussion)* reprendre (**h**) *(make better)* remonter **2** *vi* (**a**) *(improve)* s'améliorer; *(after illness)* se remettre; *(of match, party)* s'animer; **business is picking up** les affaires reprennent (**b**) *(continue)* **let's p. up where we left off** reprenons (là où nous en étions restés)

pickaxe ['pɪkæks] *n* pioche *f*, pic *m*

picket ['pɪkɪt] **1** *n* (**a**) *(in strike)* piquet *m* de grève; **p. line** piquet de grève (**b**) *(stake)* piquet *m*, pieu *m*; **p. fence** palissade *f* **2** *vt (during strike)* former un piquet de grève aux portes de

pickings ['pɪkɪŋz] *npl* bénéfices *mpl*; **rich p.** gros bénéfices

pickle ['pɪkəl] **1** *n* = condiment à base de légumes conservés dans du vinaigre; **pickles** conserves *fpl* au vinaigre; *Fam Fig* **to be in a p.** être dans le pétrin **2** *vt* conserver dans du vinaigre; **pickled cabbage/onions** chou *m* rouge/oignons *mpl* au vinaigre

pick-me-up ['pɪkmɪʌp] *n Fam* remontant *m*

pickpocket ['pɪkpɒkɪt] *n* pickpocket *m*, voleur(euse) *m,f* à la tire

pick-up ['pɪkʌp] *n* (**a**) **p. (arm)** *(on record player)* lecteur *m* (phonographique); **p. (truck)** pick-up *m inv (petite camionnette à plateau)*; **p. point** *(for goods, passengers)* point *m* de ramassage (**b**) *Fam (improvement)* amélioration *f*; *(of business)* reprise *f*

picky ['pɪkɪ] *adj Fam* difficile (**about** sur)

picnic ['pɪknɪk] **1** *n* pique-nique *m*; **to go on a p.** aller faire un pique-nique, aller pique-niquer; *Fam Fig* **it was no p.** ça n'a pas été une partie de plaisir; **p. basket** *or* **hamper** panier *m* à pique-nique **2** *vi (pt & pp* **picnicked***)* pique-niquer, faire un pique-nique

picnicker ['pɪknɪkə(r)] *n* pique-niqueur(euse) *m,f*

Pict [pɪkt] *n Hist* Picte *mf*

pictorial [pɪk'tɔːrɪəl] *adj (magazine)* illustré(e); *(representation)* en images

picture ['pɪktʃə(r)] **1** *n* (**a**) *(painting)* tableau *m*; *(drawing)* dessin *m*; *(in book, on TV)* image *f*; *(photograph)* photo *f*; *Fig (situation)* situation *f*; **to be the p. of health** respirer la santé; **her face was a p.** elle a fait une de ces têtes; *Fig* **to put sb in the p.** mettre qn au courant; *Fam Fig* **I get the p.** je pige; **p. book** livre *m* d'images; **p. frame** cadre *m*; **p. gallery** galerie *f* de peintures; **p. library** banque *f* d'images; **p. postcard** carte *f* postale illustrée; **p. window** baie *f* vitrée (**b**) *Br Fam (film)* **the pictures** le cinéma **2** *vt* (**a**) *(imagine)* **to p. sth (to oneself)** s'imaginer qch; **to p. sb/sth as sth** s'imaginer qn/qch en qch; **to p. sb doing sth** s'imaginer qn en train de faire qch (**b**) *(in photo, painting)* représenter; *Fig (in words)* dépeindre, décrire

picturesque [pɪktʃə'resk] *adj* pittoresque

pidgin ['pɪdʒɪn] *n* pidgin *m*; **p. English/French** ≃ petit nègre *m*

pie [paɪ] *n* tourte *f*; *Fam* **p. in the sky** des châteaux en Espagne; **p. chart** camembert *m*

piece [piːs] *n* (**a**) *(in general)* morceau *m*; *(smaller)* bout *m*; *(of cake)* part *f*; *(newspaper article)* article *m*; **p. of land** *(parcelle f de)* terrain *m*; **a p. of furniture** un meuble; **a p. of luggage** *(suitcase)* une valise;

(bag) un sac; **a p. of advice** un conseil; **a p. of luck** un coup de chance; **a p. of news** une nouvelle; **p. rate** *(pay)* salaire *m* à la pièce (**b**) *(in chess, of jigsaw puzzle)* pièce *f*; *(in dominoes)* domino *m*; *(in draughts)* pion *m* (**c**) *(coin)* pièce *f* (**d**) *(of music)* morceau *m* (**e**) *(of artillery)* pièce *f*; *(firearm)* arme *f* (**f**) *(idioms)* **to be still in one p.** être encore entier(ère); **to give sb a p. of one's mind** dire ses quatre vérités à qn; **to say one's p.** dire ce qu'on a à dire; **p. by p.** par morceaux; *Fig* **to go to pieces** s'effondrer (complètement); **to fall to pieces** tomber en morceaux; *(of house)* se délabrer, crouler; *(of garment)* partir en morceaux; **to take sth to pieces** démonter qch; **to be a p. of cake** être facile comme tout; *Br Fam* **he's a nasty p. of work** c'est un sale type

▸**piece together** *vt sep (parts)* assembler les morceaux de; *(something broken)* recoller les morceaux de; *(facts)* reconstituer

piecemeal ['piːsmiːl] **1** *adj* fragmentaire, parcellaire; *(work)* fait(e) petit à petit **2** *adv* petit à petit

piecework ['piːswɜːk] *n* travail *m* à la tâche *ou* à la pièce

Piedmont ['piːdmɒnt] *n* le Piémont

pier [pɪə(r)] *n (landing stage)* embarcadère *m*; *(at seaside resort)* jetée *f*; *(of bridge)* pilier *m*

pierce [pɪəs] *vt* percer, transpercer; **to have pierced ears** avoir les oreilles percées

piercing ['pɪəsɪŋ] *adj (cry, look)* perçant(e); *(cold)* vif (vive)

piety ['paɪətɪ] *n* piété *f*

pig [pɪg] **1** *n* (**a**) *(animal)* cochon *m*, porc *m* (**b**) *Fam (greedy person)* goinfre *m*, glouton(onne) *m,f*; *(unpleasant man)* salaud *m*; *(unpleasant woman)* salope *f* (**c**) *Fam (policeman)* poulet *m* (**d**) *Fam (idioms)* **to buy a p. in a poke** acheter chat en poche; **pigs might fly!** on peut toujours rêver!; **to make a p.'s ear of sth** bousiller qch; saloper qch; **to make a p. of oneself** s'en mettre plein la lampe **2** *vt (pt & pp* **pigged***) Fam* **to p. oneself** s'en mettre plein la lampe

pig out *vi Fam* s'en mettre plein la lampe

pigeon ['pɪdʒɪn] *n* pigeon *m*

pigeonhole ['pɪdʒɪnhəʊl] **1** *n* casier *m* **2** *vt (person)* étiqueter, mettre une étiquette à

piggy ['pɪgɪ] *Fam* **1** *n (pl* **piggies***)* petit cochon *m*; **p. bank** tirelire *f*, *Can* cochon *m* **2** *adj (eyes)* de cochon

piggyback ['pɪgɪbæk] *n* **to give sb a p.** porter qn sur son dos

pig-headed [pɪg'hedɪd] *adj* entêté(e), têtu(e)

piglet ['pɪglɪt] *n* porcelet *m*

pigment ['pɪgmənt] *n* pigment *m*

pigmentation [pɪgmən'teɪʃən] *n* pigmentation *f*

pigmy ['pɪgmɪ] *(pl* **pigmies***) n* Pigmée *mf*

pigsty ['pɪgstaɪ] *(pl* **pigsties***) n also Fig* porcherie *f*

pigtail ['pɪgteɪl] *n* natte *f*

pike¹ [paɪk] *n (weapon)* pique *f*

pike² *n (fish)* brochet *m*

pilchard ['pɪltʃəd] *n* pilchard *m*

pile [paɪl] **1** *n* (**a**) *(heap)* tas *m*; *(stack)* pile *f*; **to put things in(to) a p.** *(heap)* mettre des choses en tas; *(stack)* empiler des choses; *Fam* **to make one's p.** faire fortune; *Fam* **to have piles of** *or* **a p. of things/work**

to do avoir un tas de choses/des tonnes de travail à faire; *Fam Fig* **to be at the top/bottom of the p.** être favorisé(e)/défavorisé(e)
　(**b**) *(of carpet)* poils *mpl*
　(**c**) *Phys* (**atomic**) **p.** pile *f* atomique
　(**d**) *(building)* édifice *m; (column, pillar)* pieu *m*
　2 *vt* entasser; *(stack)* empiler; **to p. food onto one's plate** bien remplir son assiette
　3 *vi Fam* **to p. into a car** s'entasser dans une voiture
▸**pile in** *vi* s'entasser
▸**pile on** *vt sep* **to p. on the pressure** faire monter la pression; **to p. on the agony** dramatiser; *Fam* **to p. it on** en rajouter
▸**pile out** *vi* sortir en masse
▸**pile up** *vi* s'accumuler
pile-driver ['paɪldraɪvə(r)] *n* sonnette *f*
piles [paɪlz] *npl (haemorrhoids)* hémorroïdes *fpl;* **to have p.** avoir des hémorroïdes
pile-up ['paɪlʌp] *n Fam* carambolage *m*
pilfer ['pɪlfə(r)] *vt & vi* chaparder
pilgrim ['pɪlgrɪm] *n* pèlerin(e) *m,f*
pilgrimage ['pɪlgrɪmɪdʒ] *n* pèlerinage *m;* **to go on** *or* **make a p.** aller en pèlerinage, faire un pèlerinage
pill [pɪl] *n* pilule *f;* **the p.** *(contraceptive)* la pilule; **to be on the p.** prendre la pilule
pillage ['pɪlɪdʒ] 1 *n* pillage *m*
　2 *vt & vi* piller
pillar ['pɪlə(r)] *n also Fig* pilier *m;* **to go from p. to post** courir à droite et à gauche; **a p. of society** un pilier de la société; **to be a p. of strength** être d'un grand soutien; **p. box** boîte *f* aux lettres
pillion ['pɪljən] 1 *n* **p.** (**seat**) siège *m* arrière
　2 *adv* **to ride p.** monter derrière
pillory ['pɪlərɪ] 1 *n (pl* **pillories**) pilori *m*
　2 *vt (pt & pp* **pilloried**) mettre au pilori
pillow ['pɪləʊ] *n* oreiller *m*
pillowcase ['pɪləʊkeɪs], **pillowslip** ['pɪləʊslɪp] *n* taie *f* d'oreiller
pilot ['paɪlət] 1 *n (of plane, ship)* pilote *m;* **p.** (**programme**) *(on TV)* émission *f* pilote; **p. light** veilleuse *f;* **p. scheme** projet-pilote *m;* **p. study** étude-pilote *f*
　2 *vt (plane, ship)* piloter
pimp [pɪmp] *n* souteneur *m,* proxénète *m*
pimple ['pɪmpəl] *n* bouton *m*
pimply ['pɪmplɪ] *adj* boutonneux(euse)
PIN [pɪn] *n (abbr* **personal identification number**) code *m* confidentiel
pin [pɪn] 1 *n (for sewing)* épingle *f; (for surgery)* broche *f; (in grenade)* goupille *f;* **three-p. plug** prise *f* à trois broches; (**firing**) **p.** percuteur *m;* (**safety**) **p.** épingle à nourrice; *Fam* **to have pins and needles** avoir des fourmis; **you could have heard a p. drop** on aurait entendu une mouche voler; **p. money** argent *m* de poche
　2 *vt (pt & pp* **pinned**) *(fasten with pin)* épingler; *(with drawing pin, safety pin)* attacher; **to p. sb against** *or* **to a wall** plaquer qn contre un mur; **to p. the blame on sb** rejeter la responsabilité sur qn; **to p. one's hopes on sb/sth** mettre tous ses espoirs en qn/qch
▸**pin down** *vt sep* (**a**) *(trap)* coincer (**b**) *(identify)* mettre le doigt sur (**c**) *(force to be definite)* **to p. sb down** obliger qn à s'engager; **to p. sb down to a date** obliger qn à donner une date
▸**pin up** *vt sep (notice)* fixer *ou* accrocher au mur; *(hair)* relever; *(hem)* rabattre avec des épingles

pinafore ['pɪnəfɔː(r)] *n (apron)* tablier *m;* **p.** (**dress**) robe *f* chasuble
pinball ['pɪnbɔːl] *n* flipper *m*
pincer ['pɪnsə(r)] *n (of crab, insect)* pince *f; Mil* **p. movement** mouvement *m* en tenailles
pincers ['pɪnsəz] *npl (tool)* tenailles *fpl,* pince *f*
pinch [pɪntʃ] 1 *n* (**a**) *(action)* pincement *m;* **to give sb a p.** pincer qn; *Fam Fig* **to feel the p.** être gêné(e); **at a p.** à la rigueur (**b**) *(of salt, herbs)* pincée *f; Fig* **to take sth with a p. of salt** ne pas prendre qch pour argent comptant
　2 *vt* (**a**) *(nip)* pincer; **these shoes p. my feet** ces chaussures me serrent (**b**) *Fam (steal)* piquer, faucher
　3 *vi (of shoes)* serrer
pincushion ['pɪnkʊʃən] *n* pelote *f* à épingles
pine¹ [paɪn] *n (tree, wood)* pin *m;* **p. cone** pomme *f* de pin, *Can* cocotte *f;* **p. forest** pinède *f;* **p. needle** aiguille *f* de pin; **p. nut** pignon *m*
pine² *vi* **to p. for sb/sth** se languir de qn/qch
▸**pine away** *vi* languir
pineapple ['paɪnæpəl] *n* ananas *m*
ping [pɪŋ] 1 *n* tintement *m*
　2 *vi* tinter
ping-pong ['pɪŋpɒŋ] *n* ping-pong *m*
pinion ['pɪnjən] 1 *n* pignon *m*
　2 *vt (restrain)* **to p. sb** (**to/against**) clouer *ou* plaquer qn (à/contre)
pink [pɪŋk] 1 *n* (**a**) *(colour)* rose *m; Fam* **to be in the p.** être en parfaite santé (**b**) *(flower)* œillet *m*
　2 *adj* rose; **to turn p.** rosir; **p. gin** = cocktail à base de gin et d'angusture; *Br* **p. pound** = le pouvoir d'achat des homosexuels; *Am Fam* **p. slip** lettre *f ou* avis *m* de licenciement
pinkeye ['pɪŋkaɪ] *n Am* conjonctivite *f* infectieuse
pinkie ['pɪŋkɪ] *n Am, Can & Scot* petit doigt *m*
pinnacle ['pɪnəkəl] *n* sommet *m; Fig (of fame, career)* apogée *m*
pinpoint ['pɪnpɔɪnt] *vt* déterminer, identifier; *(place)* localiser exactement
pinprick ['pɪnprɪk] *n* piqûre *f* d'aiguille
pinstripe ['pɪnstraɪp] *n* rayures *fpl* fines; **p. suit** costume *m* rayé
pint [paɪnt] *n (unit of measurement) Br* = 0,568 l, pinte *f; Am* = 0,473 l, pinte; *Br* **a p.** *(of beer)* ≃ un demi-litre de bière; **I'm going for a p.** je vais prendre une bière
pinto bean ['pɪntəʊ'biːn] *n* haricot *m* pinto
pint-size(d) ['paɪntsaɪz(d)] *adj Fam* minuscule
pin-up ['pɪnʌp] *n Fam* pin-up *f inv*
pioneer [paɪə'nɪə(r)] 1 *n also Fig* pionnier(ère) *m,f*
　2 *vt* **to p. sth** être le (la) premier(ère) à mettre au point qch
pioneering [paɪə'nɪərɪŋ] *adj (work)* innovateur(trice); *(person)* qui fait œuvre de pionnier
pious ['paɪəs] *adj* pieux(euse)
piously ['paɪəslɪ] *adv* pieusement, avec piété
pip [pɪp] 1 *n* (**a**) *(of fruit)* pépin *m* (**b**) *(on card, die)* point *m* (**c**) *(sound)* **the pips** *(on radio)* les bips *mpl* sonores; *(on public telephone)* = la tonalité indiquant que le crédit est épuisé
　2 *vt (pt & pp* **pipped**) *Br Fam* **to be pipped at the post** être coiffé(e) sur le poteau
pipe [paɪp] 1 *n* (**a**) *(tube)* tuyau *m,* canalisation *f; (musical instrument)* chalumeau *m;* **the pipes** la cornemuse; **p. band** orchestre *m* de cornemuses (**b**) *(for*

smoking) pipe *f*; **to smoke a p.** fumer la pipe; *Fam Fig* **put that in your p. and smoke it!** mettez ça dans votre poche et votre mouchoir par-dessus!; **p. cleaner** cure-pipe *m*; **p. dream** chimère *f*

2 *vt (water, oil)* canaliser; *Fam* **piped music** musiquette *f*

▸**pipe down** *vi Fam (make less noise)* faire moins de bruit; *(not talk so much)* se taire

▸**pipe up** *vi (of person)* risquer un commentaire; *(of voice)* se faire entendre

pipeline ['paɪplaɪn] *n (for oil)* pipeline *m*, oléoduc *m*; *(for gas)* gazoduc *m*; *Fig* **to be in the p.** être en préparation

piper ['paɪpə(r)] *n (bagpipe player)* joueur(euse) *m,f* de cornemuse; *Prov* **he who pays the p. calls the tune** il est normal que celui qui paie ait le droit de choisir

pipette [pɪ'pet] *n* pipette *f*

piping ['paɪpɪŋ] **1** *n* (**a**) *(pipes)* tuyauterie *f*, canalisations *fpl* (**b**) *(sound of bagpipes)* son *m* de la cornemuse (**c**) *(on uniform)* passepoil *m*

2 *adj (sound, voice)* flûté(e)

3 *adv* **p. hot** tout(e) chaud(e)

pipsqueak ['pɪpskwiːk] *n Fam* minus *m*

piquant ['piːkənt] *adj* piquant(e)

pique [piːk] **1** *n* dépit *m*; **in a fit of p.** dans un accès de dépit

2 *vt* piquer

piracy ['paɪrəsɪ] *n* (**a**) *(of ships)* piraterie *f* (**b**) *(of videos, software)* piratage *m*

piranha [pɪ'rɑːnə] *n* piranha *m*

pirate ['paɪrət] *n* pirate *m*; **p. edition** édition *f* pirate; **p. radio** radio *f* pirate

pirouette [pɪrʊ'et] **1** *n* pirouette *f*

2 *vi* pirouetter

Pisa ['piːzə] *n* Pise

Pisces ['paɪsiːz] *n* les Poissons *mpl*; **to be (a) P.** être Poissons

piss [pɪs] *very Fam* **1** *n (urine)* pisse *f*; **to have a p.** pisser; *Br Fig* **to take the p. out of sb/sth** se foutre de qn/qch; *Br* **p. artist** soûlard(e) *m,f*

2 *vt* **to p. oneself, to p. one's pants** pisser dans son froc

3 *vi* pisser

▸**piss about, piss around** *vi Br very Fam (behave foolishly)* déconner; *(waste time)* glandouiller

▸**piss off** *very Fam* **1** *vt sep (annoy)* faire chier; **to be pissed off** en avoir plein le cul

2 *vi (go away)* foutre le camp

pissed [pɪst] *adj very Fam* (**a**) *Br (drunk)* bourré(e); **to get p.** se soûler la gueule (**b**) *Am (angry)* en rogne

piss-up ['pɪsʌp] *n Br very Fam* beuverie *f*

pistachio [pɪ'stɑːʃɪəʊ] *(pl* **pistachios**) *n (nut)* pistache *f*; *(tree)* pistachier *m*

pistol ['pɪstəl] *n* pistolet *m*; **p. shot** coup *m* de pistolet

piston ['pɪstən] *n* piston *m*

pit¹ [pɪt] *n* (**a**) *(hole in ground)* fosse *f*; *(coal mine)* mine *f*; **in the p. of one's stomach** au creux de l'estomac; *Fam* **to be the pits** être nul (nulle) (**b**) *(in theatre)* parterre *m*; **the pits** *(in motor racing)* les stands *mpl* de ravitaillement (**c**) *(on metal, glass)* piqûre *f*; *(on skin)* marque *f*, cicatrice *f*

pit² *n (of cherry, olive)* noyau *m*

pit³ *(pt & pp* **pitted**) *vt* **to p. sb against sb** mettre qn aux prises avec qn, opposer qn à qn; **to p. oneself against sb** se mesurer à qn; **to p. one's wits against sb** se mesurer intellectuellement à qn

pit-a-pat ['pɪtə'pæt] **1** *n (of rain)* crépitement *m*; *(of feet)* trottinement *m*; *(of heart)* battement *m*

2 *adv* **to go p.** *(of rain)* crépiter; *(of feet)* trottiner; *(of heart)* palpiter

pitch¹ [pɪtʃ] **1** *n* (**a**) *Br (for market stall)* place *f*, emplacement *m* (**b**) *(for sport)* terrain *m* (**c**) *(in music)* hauteur *f*; *Fig* **to reach such a p. that...** atteindre un tel point que... (**d**) *(talk)* **(sales) p.** baratin *m* publicitaire (**e**) *(slope)* inclinaison *f*

2 *vt* (**a**) *(throw)* lancer (**b**) *(aim)* adapter (**at** à) (**c**) *(tent)* monter, dresser

3 *vi (of ship, plane)* tanguer

▸**pitch in** *vi* mettre du sien

pitch² *n (tar)* poix *f*

pitch-black [pɪtʃ'blæk] *adj* noir(e) comme dans un four; **it's p. outside** il fait nuit noire

pitched [pɪtʃt] *adj* (**a**) *(sloping)* en pente (**b**) **p. battle** bataille *f* rangée

pitcher¹ ['pɪtʃə(r)] *n Am (jug)* cruche *f*, pichet *m*

pitcher² *n Am (in baseball)* lanceur *m*

pitchfork ['pɪtʃfɔːk] *n* fourche *f*

piteous ['pɪtɪəs] *adj* pitoyable

pitfall ['pɪtfɔːl] *n* piège *m*

pith [pɪθ] *n (of orange)* peau *f* blanche; *(of argument, idea)* essence *f*; **p. helmet** casque *m* colonial (en sola)

pithy ['pɪθɪ] *adj* concis(e)

pitiable ['pɪtɪəbəl] *adj* pitoyable

pitiful ['pɪtɪfʊl] *adj* pitoyable

pitifully ['pɪtɪfʊlɪ] *adv* pitoyablement

pitiless ['pɪtɪlɪs] *adj* impitoyable

pitta bread ['pɪtəbred] *n* pita *m*

pittance ['pɪtəns] *n* salaire *m* de misère

pituitary gland [pɪ'tjuːɪtərɪ'glænd] *n* hypophyse *f*

pity ['pɪtɪ] **1** *n* (**a**) *(compassion)* pitié *f*; **to take** *or* **have p. on sb** prendre qn en pitié; **for p.'s sake!** par pitié! (**b**) *(misfortune)* **it's a p. (that...)** c'est dommage *(que... + subjunctive)*; **what a p.!** quel dommage!; **more's the p.** c'est bien dommage

2 *vt (pt & pp* **pitied**) plaindre, avoir pitié de

pitying ['pɪtɪɪŋ] *adj* compatissant(e)

pivot ['pɪvət] **1** *n also Fig* pivot *m*

2 *vi* pivoter (**on** sur); *Fig (of plan)* reposer (**on** *or* **around** sur)

pivotal ['pɪvətəl] *adj (position)* clef; *(importance)* capital(e)

pixel ['pɪksəl] *n Comput* pixel *m*

pixelize ['pɪksəlaɪz] *vt TV (to hide identity)* mosaïquer

pixie ['pɪksɪ] *n* lutin *m*

pizza ['piːtsə] *n* pizza *f*; **p. parlour** pizzeria *f*

Pk *abbr* **Park**

pkt *(abbr* **packet**) paquet

Pl *abbr* **Place**

placard ['plækɑːd] *n* pancarte *f*

placate [plə'keɪt] *vt* apaiser, calmer

place [pleɪs] **1** *n* (**a**) *(location)* endroit *m*, lieu *m*; *(in street names)* rue *f*; **to live/eat** un logement/un restaurant; **I can't be in two places at once** je ne peux pas être à deux endroits à la fois; *Fam* **all over the p.** *(everywhere)* un peu partout; **my hair was all over the p.** j'étais coiffé n'importe comment; **at the interview he was all over the p.** à l'entretien, il a raconté n'importe quoi; *Fam Fig* **to go places** réussir (dans la vie); **p. of birth/death/business** lieu de

naissance/décès/travail; **p. of residence** domicile *m*; **p. of worship** lieu *m* de culte; **p. name** nom *m* de lieu
(**b**) *(assigned to person, thing)* place *f*; **to find a p. for sb** *(job)* trouver une place pour qn; **to get a p. at university** être admis(e) à l'université; **there's a time and a p. for everything** il y a un temps pour tout; **to hold sth in p.** tenir qch en place; **to lose one's p.** *(in a book)* perdre sa page; **to take p.** avoir lieu; **to take sb's p.** remplacer qn; *(oust)* prendre la place de qn; *Fig* **out of p.** *(remark)* déplacé(e); **to feel out of p.** ne pas se sentir à sa place
(**c**) *Fam (residence)* chez soi; **my parents' p.** chez mes parents; **your p. or mine?** on va chez toi ou chez moi?
(**d**) *(seat, position in queue)* place *f*; **to set** *or* **lay an extra p. at the table** mettre un couvert de plus; **to change places with sb** changer de place avec qn; *Fig* être à la place de qn; *Fig* **put yourself in my p.** mettez-vous à ma place; **p. mat** set *m* de table
(**e**) *(in competition, society)* place *f*, rang *m*; **in first/second p.** à la première/seconde place; **in the first p...., in the second p....** *(parts of an argument)* en premier lieu..., en second lieu...; **you shouldn't have said it in the first p.** d'abord, tu n'aurais pas dû le dire; **to know one's p.** savoir où est sa place; **to put sb in his p.** remettre qn à sa place
(**f**) *Math* **to three decimal places** à trois décimales
2 *vt* (**a**) *(put)* placer, mettre; **the house is well placed** la maison est bien située; **to be well placed to do sth** être bien placé(e) pour faire qch; **I know her face but I can't p. her** je l'ai déjà vue mais je ne sais pas où
(**b**) *Com & Fin (order)* passer (**with** à); *(contract)* adjuger (**with** à); **to p. a bet (on sth)** parier (sur qch)
(**c**) *(find a job for)* placer
(**d**) *(classify)* classer; **to be placed third** se classer troisième
placebo [pləˈsiːbəʊ] *(pl* **placebos)** *n also Fig* placebo *m*; **p. effect** effet *m* placebo
placement [ˈpleɪsmənt] *n* stage *m*
placenta [pləˈsentə] *n* placenta *m*
placid [ˈplæsɪd] *adj* placide, calme
plagiarism [ˈpleɪdʒərɪzəm] *n* plagiat *m*
plagiarize [ˈpleɪdʒəraɪz] *vt* plagier
plague [pleɪg] **1** *n (disease)* peste *f*; *(of insects, frogs)* invasion *f*; **to avoid sb/sth like the p.** éviter qn/qch comme la peste
2 *vt (of person)* harceler; *(of problem)* tourmenter; **to p. sb with questions** harceler qn de questions
plaice [pleɪs] *n* carrelet *m*
plaid [plæd] *n (fabric)* tissu *m* écossais; *(garment)* plaid *m*
plain [pleɪn] **1** *n* plaine *f*
2 *adj* (**a**) *(clear, unambiguous)* clair(e), évident(e); **to make sth p. to sb** faire comprendre qch à qn; **I'll be quite p. with you** je vais être franc avec vous; *Fam* **it's as p. as the nose on your face** ça se voit comme le nez au milieu de la figure; **in p. English** clairement; *Fig* **to be p. sailing** aller tout seul; **p. speaking** franc-parler *m*
(**b**) *(simple)* simple; *Fam* **that's just p. foolishness/ignorance** c'est de la pure bêtise/ignorance; **one p., one purl** *(in knitting)* une maille à l'endroit, une maille à l'envers; **p. chocolate** chocolat *m* noir; **a p. clothes policeman** un agent en civil; **p. flour** farine *f* *(sans levure)*

(**c**) *(not beautiful)* quelconque; **a p. Jane** une jeune fille plutôt quelconque
plainly [ˈpleɪnlɪ] *adv* (**a**) *(clearly)* clairement, nettement; **to speak p.** parler franchement *ou* sans détours (**b**) *(simply)* simplement
plain-spoken [pleɪnˈspəʊkən] *adj* franc (franche)
plaintiff [ˈpleɪntɪf] *n Law* plaignant(e) *m,f*
plaintive [ˈpleɪntɪv] *adj* plaintif(ive)
plaintively [ˈpleɪntɪvlɪ] *adv* d'un ton plaintif
plait [plæt] **1** *n* natte *f*, tresse *f*
2 *vt* natter, tresser
plan [plæn] **1** *n* (**a**) *(proposal, intention)* projet *m*; **to go according to p.** marcher comme prévu; **the best p. would be to...** le mieux serait de... (**b**) *(of building, town, essay)* plan *m*
2 *vt (pt & pp* **planned)** (**a**) *(arrange)* projeter; *(crime)* comploter, tramer; **to p. to do sth** projeter de faire qch; **to go as planned** marcher comme prévu (**b**) *(building, town)* faire le plan de; *(economy)* planifier
3 *vi* faire des projets; **to p. for the future** faire des projets d'avenir
▶**plan out** *vt sep* prévoir (en détail)
plane¹ [pleɪn] *n (surface)* plan *m*
plane² *n (aeroplane)* avion *m*; **by p.** en avion; **p. ticket** billet *m* d'avion
plane³ **1** *n (tool)* rabot *m*
2 *vt* raboter, aplanir
plane⁴ *n* **p. (tree)** platane *m*
planet [ˈplænɪt] *n* planète *f*
planetarium [plænɪˈteərɪəm] *(pl* **planetariums** *or* **planetaria** [plænɪˈteərɪə] *) n* planétarium *m*
planetary [ˈplænɪtərɪ] *adj* planétaire
plank [plæŋk] *n (of wood)* planche *f*; *Fig (policy)* point *m*
plankton [ˈplæŋktən] *n* plancton *m*
planner [ˈplænə(r)] *n* planificateur(trice) *m,f*; *(for towns)* urbaniste *mf*
planning [ˈplænɪŋ] *n* conception *f*, élaboration *f*; **it's still at the p. stage** c'est encore à l'état de projet; **p. permission** permis *m* de construire
plant [plɑːnt] **1** *n* (**a**) *(living thing)* plante *f*; **p. life** flore *f* (**b**) *Ind (equipment)* matériel *m*; *(factory)* usine *f*; **p. hire** location *f* de matériel industriel; **p. maintenance** entretien *m* du matériel
2 *vt (tree, flower)* planter; *(crops, field)* semer; *(bomb)* poser; **to p. an idea in sb's mind** mettre une idée dans l'esprit de qn; *Fam* **to p. sth on sb** cacher qch dans les affaires de qn *(pour le/la compromettre en cas de découverte)*
plantain [ˈplæntɪn] *n* (**a**) *(wild plant)* plantain *m* (**b**) *(fruit)* banane *f* des Antilles, *(tree)* bananier *m* du paradis
plantation [plænˈteɪʃən] *n* plantation *f*
planter [ˈplɑːntə(r)] *n (person)* planteur(euse) *m,f*; *(machine)* planteuse
plaque [plɑːk] *n* (**a**) *(sign)* plaque *f* (commémorative) (**b**) *(on teeth)* plaque *f* dentaire
plasma [ˈplæzmə] *n* plasma *m*
plaster [ˈplɑːstə(r)] **1** *n* (**a**) *(on wall)* plâtre *m*; **p. of Paris** plâtre de Paris; **to put sb's leg in p.** mettre la jambe de qn dans le plâtre; **p. cast** *(for broken bone)* plâtre; *(in art)* moulage *m* en plâtre (**b**) *Br* **(sticking) p.** pansement *m* adhésif
2 *vt* (**a**) *(wall)* plâtrer (**b**) *(cover)* tapisser (**with** de); **plastered with mud** couvert(e) de boue; **her name**

was plastered over the front pages son nom s'étalait en première page (**c**) *(make stick)* coller; **the rain had plastered his shirt to his back** la pluie lui avait plaqué la chemise sur le dos

plasterboard ['plɑːstəbɔːd] *n* placoplâtre® *m*

plastered ['plɑːstəd] *adj Fam (drunk)* beurré(e)

plasterer ['plɑːstərə(r)] *n* plâtrier *m*

plastic ['plæstɪk] **1** *n* (**a**) *(material)* plastique *m* (**b**) *Fam (credit cards)* cartes *fpl* de crédit; **do they take p.?** est-ce qu'ils acceptent les cartes de crédit? **2** *adj (cup, bag)* en plastique; *(bullet)* de plastique; **p. explosive** plastic *m*; **p. surgeon** chirurgien(enne) *m,f* esthétique; **p. surgery** *(cosmetic)* chirurgie *f* esthétique; *(after accident)* chirurgie réparatrice

plate [pleɪt] **1** *n* (**a**) *(for food)* assiette *f*; *(for church offering)* plateau *m* de quête; *Fam Fig* **to have a lot on one's p.** avoir du pain sur la planche; *Fam Fig* **to hand sth to sb on a p.** apporter qch à qn sur un plateau; **p. rack** égouttoir *m* (**b**) *(sheet of glass, plastic)* lamelle *f*; *(sheet of metal)* plaque *f*; **p. glass** vitrage *m* très épais **2** *vt (with gold)* plaquer en or; *(with silver)* plaquer en argent

plateau ['plætəʊ] (*pl* **plateaux** ['plætəʊz] *or* **plateaus**) *n Geog* plateau *m*; *Fig* **to reach a p.** *(of career, economy)* atteindre un palier

platform ['plætfɔːm] *n* (**a**) *(raised flat surface)* plateforme *f*; *(in train station) (where passengers stand)* quai *m*; *(where train stops)* voie *f*; **p. 4** *(in train station)* quai n° 4; **p. shoes** chaussures *fpl* à semelles compensées *(à la façon des années 70)* (**b**) *(at meeting)* estrade *f*, tribune *f*; *(political programme)* programme *m* (**c**) *Comput* plate-forme *f*

platform-independent ['plætfɔːmɪndɪ'pendənt] *adj Comput* indépendant(e) de la plate-forme

platinum ['plætɪnəm] *n Chem* platine *m*; **p. blond hair** cheveux blond platine

platitude ['plætɪtjuːd] *n* platitude *f*

platonic [plə'tɒnɪk] *adj* platonique

platoon [plə'tuːn] *n Mil* section *f*, peloton *m*

platter ['plætə(r)] *n (serving plate)* plat *m*

platypus ['plætɪpəs] *n* ornithorynque *m*

plausible ['plɔːzəbəl] *adj (excuse, argument)* plausible; *(person)* convaincant(e)

play [pleɪ] **1** *n* (**a**) *(drama)* pièce *f* (de théâtre) (**b**) *(of children)* **at p.** en train de jouer; **to make great p. of sth** beaucoup insister sur qch; **p. on words** jeu *m* de mots (**c**) *(in sport)* jeu *m*; **in p.** en jeu; **out of p.** hors jeu; *Fig* **to come into p.** entrer en jeu; *Fig* **to make a p. for sth** tenter sa chance à qch (**d**) *Tech* jeu *m* **2** *vt* (**a**) *(game, sport)* jouer à; *(opponent)* affronter; *(shot, card, position)* jouer; **to p. football/chess** jouer au football/aux échecs; *Fig* **stop playing games!** arrête de te moquer de moi!; *Fig* **to p. ball** *(co-operate)* coopérer; *Fig* **to p. the Stock Exchange** jouer à la Bourse; **to p. a joke** *or* **a trick on sb** jouer un tour à qn (**b**) *(in play, film)* jouer; **to p. Macbeth** jouer le rôle de Macbeth; *Fig* **to p. an important part in sth** jouer un rôle important dans qch; *Fig* **to p. no part in sth** ne pas intervenir dans qch; *Fig* **to p. the fool** faire l'idiot (**c**) *(musical instrument)* jouer de; *(piece, tune)* jouer; *(CD, tape, record)* mettre; **to p. the piano/the flute** jouer du piano/de la flûte **3** *vi* (**a**) *(of children)* jouer; *(of animals)* folâtrer; **to p.**

with sth *(pen, hair)* tripoter qch; *Fig* **to p. with fire** jouer avec le feu; *Fam Fig* **what's she playing at?** à quoi elle joue? (**b**) *(of sportsperson)* jouer; **to p. fair/dirty** jouer franc jeu/en traître; *Fig* **to p. for time** essayer de gagner du temps; *Fig* **to p. into sb's hands** faire le jeu de qn; *Fig* **to p. safe** ne pas prendre de risques (**c**) *(of musician)* jouer (**d**) *(of actor)* jouer; *(of film, play)* être à l'affiche

▸**play about, play around** *vi* jouer, s'amuser

▸**play along** *vi* coopérer

▸**play back** *vt sep (tape, recording) (for first time)* écouter; *(replay)* réécouter

▸**play down** *vt sep* minimiser

▸**play off** *vt sep* **to p. sb off against sb** monter qn contre qn

▸**play on 1** *vt insep (feelings, fears)* jouer sur **2** *vi (of musician, sportsperson)* continuer à jouer

▸**play out** *vt sep* **the drama being played out before them** le drame qui se déroule sous leurs yeux

▸**play up** *vi Br Fam (of car, child, injury)* faire des siennes

play-acting ['pleɪæktɪŋ] *n* comédie *f*

playboy ['pleɪbɔɪ] *n* play-boy *m*

player ['pleɪə(r)] *n (of game, instrument)* joueur(euse) *m,f*; *(actor)* acteur(trice) *m,f*; *Fig* **the key players** les acteurs principaux

playful ['pleɪfʊl] *adj (person, animal)* joueur(euse); *(mood, tone)* enjoué(e); *(remark)* espiègle

playground ['pleɪgraʊnd] *n (at school)* cour *f* de récréation; *(in park)* aire *f* de jeu

playgroup ['pleɪgruːp] *n* garderie *f*

playhouse ['pleɪhaʊs] *n* (**a**) *(theatre)* théâtre *m* (**b**) *(children's)* maison *f* de poupée

playing ['pleɪɪŋ] *n* **p. card** carte *f* à jouer; **p. field** terrain *m* de jeu

playmate ['pleɪmeɪt] *n* camarade *mf* de jeu

play-off ['pleɪɒf] *n Sport* match *m* de barrage

playpen ['pleɪpen] *n* parc *m (pour bébé)*

playroom ['pleɪruːm] *n* salle *f* de jeu

playschool ['pleɪskuːl] *n* garderie *f*

plaything ['pleɪθɪŋ] *n* jouet *m*

playtime ['pleɪtaɪm] *n (at school)* récréation *f*

playwright ['pleɪraɪt] *n* auteur *m* dramatique

plaza ['plɑːzə] *n Am (shopping centre)* centre *m* commercial

PLC, plc [piːel'siː] *n Br Com (abbr* **public limited company)** ≃ SA *f*

plea [pliː] *n* (**a**) *(appeal)* appel *m* (**for** à) (**b**) *(excuse)* excuse *f* (**c**) *Law* **to enter a p. of guilty/not guilty** plaider coupable/non coupable; *Am* **p. bargaining** = possibilité donnée à l'accusé de voir ses charges réduites s'il plaide coupable

plead [pliːd] **1** *vt Law* **to p. sb's case** *(of lawyer)* plaider la cause de qn; *Law* **to p. insanity** plaider la démence; **to p. ignorance** faire l'ignorant(e) **2** *vi* **to p. with sb (to do sth)** supplier qn (de faire qch); *Law* **to p. guilty/not guilty** plaider coupable/non coupable

pleasant ['plezənt] *adj* agréable

pleasantly ['plezəntlɪ] *adv (smile, behave)* aimablement; *(surprised)* agréablement

pleasantry ['plezəntrɪ] (*pl* **pleasantries**) *n (joke)* plaisanterie *f*; **to exchange pleasantries** *(polite remarks)* échanger des politesses

please [pli:z] **1** *adv* s'il vous/te plaît; **come in, p. en-trez**, je vous prie; **p. don't cry** s'il te plaît, ne pleure pas; **p. tell me the truth** dis-moi la vérité(, je t'en prie); **may I? – p. do** puis-je? – je vous en prie; **p. sit down** asseyez-vous, je vous en prie; **yes, p.** oui, s'il te plaît

2 *vt* faire plaisir à; **you can't p. everybody** on ne peut pas contenter tout le monde; **p. yourself!** fais comme tu voudras!; **to be easy/hard to p.** être facile/difficile à contenter; **p. God!** plaise à Dieu!

3 *vi* (**a**) *(like)* **to do as one pleases** faire ce que l'on veut; **this way, if you p.** par ici, s'il vous plaît; **and then, if you p., he blamed me for it!** et le comble, c'est qu'il a dit que c'était de ma faute! (**b**) *(give pleasure)* **to be eager to p.** vouloir plaire

pleased [pli:zd] *adj* content(e) (**with** de); **to be p. to do sth** faire qch avec plaisir; **to be p. for sb** être content pour qn; **to be as p. as Punch** être content comme tout; **he's very p. with himself** il est très content de lui; **p. to meet you!** enchanté!; **I'm p. to say that...** je suis heureux de vous dire que...

pleasurable ['pleʒərəbəl] *adj* agréable

pleasure ['pleʒə(r)] *n* (**a**) *(contentment, enjoyment)* plaisir *m*; **to take p. in doing sth** prendre plaisir à faire qch; **with p.** avec plaisir; **my p.!** je t'en prie!; *Formal* **I have p. in informing you that...** j'ai le plaisir de vous informer que...; **p. boat** bateau *m* de plaisance; **p. trip** excursion *f* (**b**) *(will)* **at your p.** à votre gré; *Law* **to be detained at** *or* **during Her Majesty's p.** être emprisonné(e)

pleat [pli:t] *n* pli *m*

pleated ['pli:tɪd] *adj* plissé(e)

plebeian [plə'bi:ən] *n & adj* plébéien(enne) *m,f*

plebiscite ['plebɪsɪt] *n* plébiscite *m*

plectrum ['plektrəm] *n Mus* médiator *m*

pledge [pledʒ] **1** *n* (**a**) *(promise)* promesse *f* (**b**) *(object)* gage *m*

2 *vt (promise)* **to p. to do sth** s'engager à faire qch; **to p. one's loyalty/support** accorder sa loyauté/son soutien; **to p. money** *(in radio, television appeal)* faire une promesse de don

plenary ['pli:nərɪ] *adj* plénier(ère); **p. session** séance *f* plénière

plentiful ['plentɪfʊl] *adj* abondant(e)

plenty ['plentɪ] **1** *n* abondance *f*; **a land of p.** un pays d'abondance

2 *pron* **p. of** beaucoup de; **you've got p. of time** tu as largement le temps; **that's p.** *(of food)* merci, j'en ai assez

3 *adv Fam* **it's p. big enough** c'est bien assez grand

plethora ['pleθərə] *n* pléthore *f*

pleurisy ['plʊərɪsɪ] *n* pleurésie *f*

pliable ['plaɪəbəl] *adj (wood, plastic)* souple; *(person)* malléable

pliers ['plaɪəz] *npl* pince *f*, tenaille *f*; **a pair of p.** une pince, une tenaille

plight [plaɪt] *n* situation *f* critique; *(of refugees)* détresse *f*

plimsolls ['plɪmsəlz] *npl* tennis *mpl*

plinth [plɪnθ] *n* socle *m*

PLO [pi:e'ləʊ] *n (abbr* **Palestine Liberation Organization**) OLP *f*

plod [plɒd] *(pt & pp* **plodded**) *vi* (**a**) *(walk)* marcher péniblement (**b**) *(work)* **to p. (away)** trimer

plonk¹ [plɒŋk] **1** *n (sound)* bruit *m* sourd

2 *vt Fam* **just p. it down there** tu n'as qu'à le poser là;

to p. oneself down in an armchair s'affaler dans un fauteuil

plonk² *n Br Fam (wine)* vin *m* ordinaire

plop [plɒp] **1** *n* plouf *m*

2 *vi (pt & pp* **plopped**) faire plouf

plot [plɒt] **1** *n* (**a**) *(conspiracy)* complot *m* (**b**) *(of play, novel)* intrigue *f*; *Fig* **the p. thickens** l'affaire se corse (**c**) *(land)* parcelle *f*; **(vegetable) p.** potager *m*

2 *vt (pt & pp* **plotted**) (**a**) *(plan)* comploter; **to p. to do sth** comploter de faire qch (**b**) *(position, course)* déterminer; *(progress, development)* suivre de près (**c**) *Math* tracer

plotter ['plɒtə(r)] *n (conspirator)* conspirateur(trice) *m,f*

plough, *Am* **plow** [plaʊ] **1** *n* charrue *f*; **the P.** *(constellation)* le Grand Chariot

2 *vt (field)* labourer; *Fig (profits)* réinvestir

3 *vi* labourer; *Fig* **to p. through sth** *(work, reading)* avancer péniblement dans qch; *Fig* **to p. into sth** *(of vehicle)* rentrer dans qch

▸ **plough on with** *vt insep* poursuivre laborieusement

▸ **plough up** *vt sep (field)* labourer

ploughman ['plaʊmən] *n* laboureur *m*; **p.'s lunch** = assiette de fromage ou jambon avec de la salade et des condiments

plover ['plʌvə(r)] *n* pluvier *m*

plow *Am* = **plough**

ploy [plɔɪ] *n* stratagème *m*, ruse *f*

pluck [plʌk] **1** *n (courage)* courage *m*

2 *vt (hair, feathers)* arracher; *(flower)* cueillir; *(chicken, turkey)* plumer; *(string of guitar)* pincer; **to p. one's eyebrows** s'épiler les sourcils; **they were plucked from danger by a helicopter** un hélicoptère les a sauvés du danger

3 *vi* **to p. at sb's sleeve** tirer qn par la manche

▸ **pluck up** *vt sep* **to p. up the courage to do sth** trouver le courage de faire qch

plucky ['plʌkɪ] *adj* courageux(euse)

plug [plʌg] **1** *n* (**a**) *(for sink)* bonde *f* (**b**) *(electrical) (on device)* fiche *f*; *(socket)* prise *f* (de courant); *Fam Fig* **to pull the p. on sth** *(put a stop to)* mettre le holà à qch; *(stop funding)* arrêter de financer qch (**c**) *Aut* **(spark) p.** bougie *f* (**d**) *Fam (publicity)* pub *f*

2 *vt (pt & pp* **plugged**) (**a**) *(gap, hole)* boucher; *(leak)* colmater (**b**) *Fam (promote)* faire de la pub pour

▸ **plug away** *vi Fam* s'acharner (**at** sur)

▸ **plug in** *vt sep* brancher

plughole ['plʌghəʊl] *n* trou *m* d'écoulement; *Fam Fig* **that's £300 down the p.!** c'est 300 livres foutues en l'air!

plug-in ['plʌgɪn] *n Comput* module *m* externe, *Can* plugiciel *m*

plum [plʌm] **1** *n (fruit)* prune *f*; **p. pudding** plum-pudding *m*; **p. tomato** olivette *f*; **p. tree** prunier *m*

2 *adj* (**a**) *(colour)* prune *inv* (**b**) *Fam (very good)* **a p. job** un boulot en or

plumage ['plu:mɪdʒ] *n* plumage *m*

plumb [plʌm] **1** *n* **p. (line)** fil *m* à plomb; **to be out of p.** ne pas être d'aplomb

2 *adv (exactly)* **p. in the centre** en plein centre

3 *vt Fig* **to p. the depths** toucher le fond; **that's really plumbing the depths!** c'est vraiment le comble du mauvais goût!

▸ **plumb in** *vt sep (washing machine)* brancher

plumber ['plʌmə(r)] *n* plombier *m*

plumbing ['plʌmɪŋ] *n (job, system)* plomberie *f*

plume [pluːm] *n (feather)* plume *f; (on hat)* aigrette *f; Fig (of smoke)* volute *f*

plummet ['plʌmɪt] *vi (of morale, standards)* chuter; *(of prices)* s'effondrer; **the plane plummeted to the ground** l'avion a piqué et s'est écrasé au sol

plummy ['plʌmɪ] *adj Fam (voice, accent)* snob *inv*

plump [plʌmp] *adj* dodu(e); *(cheeks, face)* rond(e)

▸**plump down** *vt sep Fam* laisser tomber lourdement

▸**plump for** *vt insep Fam (choose)* se décider pour

plunder ['plʌndə(r)] **1** *n (action)* pillage *m; (loot)* butin *m*
 2 *vt* piller

plunge [plʌndʒ] **1** *n (dive)* plongeon *m; Fig (decrease)* chute *f; Fam Fig* **to take the p.** se jeter à l'eau
 2 *vt* plonger (**into** dans)
 3 *vi (fall)* plonger; *Fig (decrease)* chuter; **she plunged to her death** elle a fait une chute mortelle

plunger ['plʌndʒə(r)] *n (of cafetière, syringe)* piston *m; (for clearing sink)* ventouse *f*

plunging ['plʌndʒɪŋ] *adj (prices)* en chute libre; **p. neckline** décolleté *m* plongeant

pluperfect ['pluːˈpɜːfɪkt] *n Gram* **the p.** le plus-que-parfait

plural ['plʊərəl] *Gram* **1** *adj* pluriel(elle)
 2 *n* pluriel *m*

pluralism ['plʊərəlɪzəm] *n* pluralisme *m*

plurality [plʊəˈrælɪtɪ] *n* pluralité *f*

plus [plʌs] **1** *n (pl* **plusses** ['plʌsɪz]) *(a)* **p. (sign)** *(signe m)* plus *m* **(b)** *(advantage)* plus *m*
 2 *adj* **but on the p. side...** mais d'un autre côté...; **fifteen p.** plus de quinze
 3 *prep* plus; **seven p. nine** sept plus neuf

plush [plʌʃ] **1** *n Tex* peluche *f*
 2 *adj Fam* luxueux(euse)

Pluto ['pluːtəʊ] *n (planet)* Pluton *f*

plutonium [pluːˈtəʊnɪəm] *n Chem* plutonium *m*

ply¹ [plaɪ] *n* **three-p.** *(wood, paper handkerchief)* triple épaisseur; *(wool)* à trois fils

ply² *(pt & pp* **plied**) **1** *vt (trade)* exercer; **to p. sb with questions** assaillir qn de questions; **to p. sb with drink** ne pas arrêter de verser à boire à qn
 2 *vi (of ship, bus)* **to p. between** faire la navette entre

plywood ['plaɪwʊd] *n* contreplaqué *m*

PM [piːˈem] *n (abbr* **Prime Minister**) Premier ministre *m*

p.m. ['piːem] *adv (abbr* **post meridiem**) **6 p.m.** 18 h

PMT [piːemˈtiː] *n (abbr* **premenstrual tension**) syndrome *m* prémenstruel

pneumatic [njuːˈmætɪk] *adj* pneumatique; **p. drill** marteau *m* piqueur

pneumonia [njuːˈməʊnɪə] *n* pneumonie *f*

PO [piːˈəʊ] *n (a) (abbr* **Post Office**) poste *f;* **PO Box** BP **(b)** *(abbr* **postal order**) mandat *m* postal

poach¹ [pəʊtʃ] *vt Culin (eggs, fish)* pocher

poach² *vt (a) (catch illegally) (fish)* pêcher sans permis; *(game)* chasser sans permis **(b)** *(employee)* débaucher

poacher ['pəʊtʃə(r)] *n (of fish, game)* braconnier *m*

pocket ['pɒkɪt] **1** *n (a) (of clothes, bag)* poche *f;* **to go through sb's pockets** faire les poches à qn; **prices to suit every p.** des prix pour toutes les bourses; **to be out of p.** en être de sa poche; **how much are you out of p.?** tu en as eu pour combien?; **to pay for sth out of one's own p.** payer qch de sa poche; *Fig* **to line one's pockets** se remplir les poches; *Fig* **to have sb**

in one's p. avoir qn dans sa poche; **p. calculator** calculette *f;* **p. money** argent *m* de poche **(b)** *(in snooker, pool)* poche *f,* blouse *f* **(c)** *(of gas, air, resistance)* poche *f*
 2 *vt (put in pocket)* empocher; *Fam (steal)* rafler

pocketbook ['pɒkɪtbʊk] *n Am (wallet)* portefeuille *m; (handbag)* sac *m* à main

pocketknife ['pɒkɪtnaɪf] *(pl* **pocketknives** ['pɒkɪtnaɪvz]) *n* couteau *m* de poche

pockmarked ['pɒkmɑːkt] *adj* grêlé(e)

pod [pɒd] *n (of plant)* gousse *f*

podgy ['pɒdʒɪ] *adj* grassouillet(ette)

podiatrist [pəˈdaɪətrɪst] *n* pédicure *mf*

podium ['pəʊdɪəm] *n (for speaker, conductor)* estrade *f; (for winner)* podium *m*

poem ['pəʊɪm] *n* poème *m*

poet ['pəʊɪt] *n* poète *m*

poetic [pəʊˈetɪk] *adj* poétique; **it's p. justice that...** ça n'est que justice que...; **p. licence** licence *f* poétique

poetical [pəʊˈetɪkəl] *adj* poétique

poetry ['pəʊɪtrɪ] *n* poésie *f;* **p. in motion** un véritable plaisir; **p. reading** lecture *f* de textes poétiques

poignancy ['pɔɪnjənsɪ] *n* caractère *m* poignant

poignant ['pɔɪnjənt] *adj* poignant(e)

point [pɔɪnt] **1** *n (a) (location)* endroit *m;* **the highest p.** le point le plus haut; **p. of sale** point *m* de vente; **p. of view** point *m* de vue
 (b) *(in time)* moment *m;* **at this p. in time** actuellement; **at this p. the phone rang** à ce moment le téléphone a sonné; **to be on the p. of doing sth** être sur le point de faire qch; **to reach the p. of no return** arriver au point de non-retour; **outspoken to the p. of rudeness** d'une franchise qui frise l'impolitesse
 (c) *(of argument, discussion)* point *m;* **the p. is that...** le fait est que...; **I take your p.** je vois ce que tu veux dire; **she has a p.** elle a raison; **to make a p.** faire une remarque; **to get to the p.** en arriver au fait; **that's beside the p.** ça n'a rien à voir; **that's not the p.** il ne s'agit pas de cela; **what's the p.?** à quoi bon?; **to make a p. of doing sth** mettre un point d'honneur à faire qch; **there is no p. in waiting any longer** cela ne sert à rien d'attendre plus longtemps; **in p. of fact** en fait; **to the p.** *(relevant)* pertinent(e); **it has its good points** ça a ses avantages; **up to a p.** jusqu'à un certain point; **not to put too fine a p. on it...** pour parler franchement...; **p. of grammar/of law** question *f* de grammaire/de droit; **p. of order** question *f* de procédure
 (d) *(punctuation mark)* point *m; Math* **(decimal) p.** virgule *f* (décimale); **three p. five** trois virgule cinq
 (e) *(in game, exam, on scale)* point *m;* **to win on points** gagner aux points
 (f) *(on compass)* point *m*
 (g) *(of needle, pencil, sword)* pointe *f;* **to end in a p.** avoir un bout pointu
 (h) *(plug socket)* prise *f* (de courant)
 (i) *(of land)* pointe *f*
 (j) *Rail* **points** aiguillage *m*
 2 *vt (camera, gun)* braquer (**at** sur); *Fig* **to p. the finger at sb** montrer qn du doigt; **can you p. me in the right direction?** pouvez-vous me dire quelle direction je dois prendre?; **to p. the way (to)** montrer le chemin (à); *Fig* montrer la voie (à)
 3 *vi* **to point at** *or* **to sb/sth** *(with finger)* montrer qn/qch du doigt; **to p. north** *(of arrow, compass needle)* indiquer le nord; **to be pointing towards sth** *(of car,*

chair) être face à qch; **this points to the fact that...** ceci montre *ou* indique que...; **all the evidence points to suicide** tout laisse penser à un suicide

▸**point out** *vt sep (with finger)* montrer; *(error, fact)* signaler

▸**point up** *vt sep (highlight)* mettre en évidence

point-blank ['pɔɪnt'blæŋk] **1** *adj (refusal, denial)* catégorique; **at p. range** à bout portant
2 *adv (fire)* à bout portant; *(ask)* de but en blanc; *(refuse, deny)* catégoriquement

pointed ['pɔɪntɪd] *adj* (**a**) *(sharp)* pointu(e) (**b**) *(remark)* mordant(e)

pointedly ['pɔɪntɪdlɪ] *adv* ostensiblement

pointer ['pɔɪntə(r)] *n* (**a**) *(indicator)* aiguille *f; (stick)* baguette *f* (**b**) *Fam (advice)* tuyau *m* (**c**) *(dog)* pointer *m*

pointless ['pɔɪntlɪs] *adj* inutile; *(life)* absurde; **it would be p.** ça ne servirait à rien

poise [pɔɪz] *n (composure)* assurance *f; (balance)* équilibre *m*

poised [pɔɪzd] *adj* (**a**) *(composed)* posé(e) (**b**) *(ready)* **to be p. to do sth** être prêt(e) à faire qch (**c**) *(suspended)* suspendu(e)

poison ['pɔɪzən] **1** *n* poison *m; Fam* **what's your p.?** qu'est-ce que tu veux boire?; **p. gas** gaz *m* toxique; **p. ivy** sumac *m* vénéneux; **p. pen letter** lettre *f* anonyme malfaisante
2 *vt* (**a**) *(person, food)* empoisonner; **to p. sb's mind against sb** monter qn contre qn (**b**) *(pollute)* contaminer

poisoning ['pɔɪzənɪŋ] *n* (**a**) *(of person, food)* empoisonnement *m;* **to die of p.** mourir empoisonné(e) (**b**) *(pollution)* contamination *f*

poisonous ['pɔɪzənəs] *adj (snake, remark)* venimeux(euse); *(chemical, fumes)* toxique; *(plant, mushroom)* vénéneux(euse); *Fig (rumour, doctrine)* pernicieux(euse)

poke [pəʊk] **1** *n* coup *m* léger
2 *vt (person)* donner un coup à; *(object)* tâter; *(fire)* attiser; **to p. sb in the eye** mettre le doigt dans l'œil à qn; **to p. sb in the ribs** *(with elbow)* donner un coup de coude à qn; **to p. a hole in sth** faire un trou dans qch; **to p. one's nose into other people's business** mettre son nez dans les affaires des autres; **to p. one's head out of the window** passer la tête par la fenêtre; **to p. fun at** se moquer de
3 *vi* **to p. at sth (with one's finger/a stick)** tâter qch (du doigt/avec le bout d'un bâton)

▸**poke about, poke around** *vi (search) (of person)* fouiller; *(be nosy)* fourrer son nez partout

▸**poke out 1** *vt sep* **you nearly poked my eye out!** un peu plus et tu me crevais l'œil!
2 *vi (protrude)* sortir, dépasser

poker¹ ['pəʊkə(r)] *n (for fire)* tisonnier *m*

poker² *n (card game)* poker *m*

poker-faced ['pəʊkəfeɪst] *adj* au visage impassible

poky ['pəʊkɪ] *adj* **a p. little flat** un appartement exigu

Poland ['pəʊlənd] *n* la Pologne

polar ['pəʊlə(r)] *adj* polaire; **p. bear** ours *m* polaire *ou* blanc

polarity [pəʊ'lærɪtɪ] *n* polarité *f*

polarization [pəʊləraɪ'zeɪʃən] *n (of opinion, country)* division *f*

polarize ['pəʊləraɪz] *vt (opinion, country)* diviser

Polaroid® ['pəʊlərɔɪd] *n (camera, photo)* polaroid® *m*

Pole [pəʊl] *n* Polonais(e) *m,f*

pole¹ [pəʊl] *n (post, stick)* perche *f; (for flag)* hampe *f;* **the p. vault** le saut à la perche

pole² *n Elec & Geog* pôle *m; Fig* **to be poles apart** être diamétralement opposés; **the P. Star** l'étoile *f* polaire

poleaxe, *Am* **poleax** ['pəʊlæks] *vt (physically)* assommer; *(emotionally)* abasourdir

polecat ['pəʊlkæt] *n* putois *m*

polemic [pə'lemɪk] *n* polémique *f*

polemical [pə'lemɪkəl] *adj* polémique

police [pə'liːs] **1** *npl* **the p.** la police; **two hundred p.** deux cents policiers; **p. car** voiture *f* de police; **p. constable** agent *m* de police; *Am* **p. department** service *m* de police; **p. dog** chien *m* policier; **p. force** police; **p. officer** policier *m;* **p. record** casier *m* judiciaire; **p. state** État *m* policier; **p. station** poste *m* de police
2 *vt (area, city)* maintenir l'ordre dans; *Fig* réglementer

policeman [pə'liːsmən] *n* agent *m* de police

policewoman [pə'liːswʊmən] *n* femme *f* agent de police

policy ['pɒlɪsɪ] *(pl* **policies**) *n* (**a**) *(of government, personal)* politique *f;* **it's a matter of p.** c'est une question de principe; **a good/bad p.** une bonne/mauvaise idée (**b**) *Fin* **(insurance) p.** police *f* (d'assurance); *Fin* **p. holder** assuré(e) *m,f*

polio ['pəʊlɪəʊ] *n* polio *f*

Polish ['pəʊlɪʃ] **1** *n (language)* polonais *m*
2 *adj* polonais(e)

polish ['pɒlɪʃ] **1** *n* (**a**) *(for shoes)* cirage *m; (for furniture, floors)* cire *f; (for metal)* pâte *f* à polir; *(for nails)* vernis *m* à ongles (**b**) *(finish, shine)* éclat *m,* brillant *m;* **to give sth a p.** faire briller qch (**c**) *(refinement)* raffinement *m*
2 *vt (silver, brass)* astiquer; *(shoes, furniture, floor)* cirer; *(stone, metal)* polir

▸**polish off** *vt sep Fam (food)* avaler; *(drink)* descendre; *(work)* expédier; *(opponent)* liquider

▸**polish up** *vt sep (improve)* perfectionner

polished ['pɒlɪʃt] *adj (shoes, furniture, floor)* ciré(e); *(metal, stone, glass)* poli(e); *Fig (manners, style)* raffiné(e)

polite [pə'laɪt] *adj* poli(e) **(to** avec); **in p. society** chez les gens bien

politely [pə'laɪtlɪ] *adv* poliment

politeness [pə'laɪtnɪs] *n* politesse *f*

politic ['pɒlɪtɪk] *adj Formal* sage; **it would not be p. to refuse** ce ne serait pas prudent de refuser

political [pə'lɪtɪkəl] *adj* politique; **she isn't very p.** elle ne s'intéresse pas beaucoup à la politique; **p. asylum** asile *m* politique; **p. correctness** le politiquement correct; **p. prisoner** prisonnier(ère) *m,f* politique; **p. science** sciences *fpl* politiques

---

Political correctness
Apparu dans les campus américains dans les années 80, le politiquement correct (ou "political correctness" en anglais) est un mouvement qui se consacre à l'élimination des termes susceptibles d'être perçus comme racistes, sexistes ou injurieux par différentes minorités.

---

politically [pə'lɪtɪklɪ] *adv* politiquement; **p. correct** politiquement correct(e)

politician [pɒlɪ'tɪʃən] *n* homme *m*/femme *f* politique

politicize [pə'lɪtɪsaɪz] *vt* politiser

politics ['pɒlɪtɪks] **1** n politique f
2 npl (**a**) (views) opinions fpl politiques (**b**) **office p.**
intrigues fpl de bureau
polka ['pɒlkə] n polka f; **a p. dot tie** une cravate à pois
poll [pəʊl] **1** n (votes cast) scrutin m; (opinion) p. (survey) sondage m; **to go to the polls** aller aux urnes;
Formerly **the p. tax** = en Grande-Bretagne, anciens
impôts locaux à payer à titre individuel
2 vt (votes) obtenir; (people) sonder
pollen ['pɒlən] n pollen m; **p. count** taux m de pollen
dans l'atmosphère
pollinate ['pɒlɪneɪt] vt polliniser
polling ['pəʊlɪŋ] n élections fpl, scrutin m; **p. booth**
isoloir m; **p. day** jour m du scrutin; **p. station** bureau
m de vote
pollutant [pə'luːtənt] n polluant m
pollute [pə'luːt] vt polluer
polluter [pə'luːtə(r)] n pollueur(euse) m,f
pollution [pə'luːʃən] n pollution f
polo ['pəʊləʊ] n (**a**) Sport polo m (**b**) Br **p. neck**
(**sweater**) (pull m à) col m roulé
poltergeist ['pɒltəgaɪst] n esprit m frappeur
poly ['pɒlɪ] (pl **polys**) n Br Fam Formerly (polytechnic)
établissement m d'enseignement supérieur
poly bag ['pɒlɪˈbæg] n Fam sac m en plastique
polyester [pɒlɪ'estə(r)] n polyester m
polygamy [pə'lɪgəmɪ] n polygamie f
polyglot ['pɒlɪglɒt] n & adj polyglotte mf
polygon ['pɒlɪgən] n polygone m
polymer ['pɒlɪmə(r)] n Chem polymère m
Polynesia [pɒlɪ'niːzɪə] n la Polynésie
Polynesian [pɒlɪ'niːzɪən] **1** n Polynésien(enne) m,f
2 adj polynésien(enne)
polyp ['pɒlɪp] n Med polype m
polyphonic [pɒlɪ'fɒnɪk] adj Mus polyphonique
polystyrene [pɒlɪ'staɪriːn] n polystyrène m
polytechnic [pɒlɪ'teknɪk] n Br Formerly établissement
m d'enseignement supérieur
polythene ['pɒlɪθiːn] n polyéthylène m; **p. bag** sac m
en plastique
polyunsaturated [pɒlɪʌn'sætjʊreɪtɪd] adj poly-insa-
turé(e)
polyurethane [pɒlɪ'jʊərɪθeɪn] n polyuréthane m
pom [pɒm] = pommie
pomegranate ['pɒmɪgrænɪt] n (fruit) grenade f; **p.**
(**tree**) grenadier m
pommie, pommy ['pɒmɪ] (pl **pommies**) n Fam An-
glais(e) m,f
pomp [pɒmp] n pompe f; **p. and circumstance** grand
apparat m
pompom ['pɒmpɒm] n pompon m
pomposity [pɒm'pɒsɪtɪ] n suffisance f
pompous ['pɒmpəs] adj pompeux(euse)
ponce [pɒns] n very Fam (**a**) (effeminate man) tapette f
(**b**) (pimp) maquereau m
▸**ponce about, ponce around** vi Fam (**a**) (waste
time) traîner (**b**) (of effeminate man) se pavaner
poncho ['pɒntʃəʊ] (pl **ponchos**) n poncho m
pond [pɒnd] n étang m; (smaller) mare f
ponder ['pɒndə(r)] **1** vt réfléchir à, considérer
2 vi réfléchir (**on** or **over** à)
ponderous ['pɒndərəs] adj (movement, person)
lourd(e); (progress, piece of writing) laborieux(euse)
pong [pɒŋ] Br Fam **1** n (smell) puanteur f
2 vi puer

pontiff ['pɒntɪf] n pontife m
pontificate [pɒn'tɪfɪkeɪt] vi pontifier (**about** sur)
pontoon¹ [pɒn'tuːn] n (float) ponton m; **p. bridge**
pont m flottant
pontoon² n (card game) vingt-et-un m
pony ['pəʊnɪ] (pl **ponies**) n poney m; **p. trekking** randonnée f à dos de poney
ponytail ['pəʊnɪteɪl] n queue f de cheval
poo [puː] n Fam caca m; **to do** or **have a p.** faire caca
poodle ['puːdəl] n caniche m
poof [pʊf], **poofter** ['pʊftə(r)] n very Fam pédé m, =
terme injurieux désignant un homosexuel
pooh¹ [puː] exclam bah!
pooh² = poo
pooh-pooh ['puː'puː] vt rejeter
pool¹ [puːl] n (pond, of blood) mare f; (puddle) flaque f;
(**swimming**) **p.** piscine f
pool² **1** n (**a**) (of money, helpers) réserve f; (of knowledge) mine f; **car p.** parc m de voitures (**b**) **the (football) pools** = concours de pronostics des matchs de
football
2 vt (ideas, resources) mettre en commun, grouper
pool³ n (game) billard m américain; **p. table** (table f
de) billard
pooped [puːpt] adj Fam vanné(e)
poor [pʊə(r)] **1** adj (**a**) (not rich) pauvre; **the p. man's**
champagne le champagne du pauvre (**b**) (bad) mau-
vais(e); (chances) faible; (harvest, reward) maigre; **to**
be in p. health ne pas bien se porter; **to have a p.**
memory ne pas avoir une bonne mémoire; **to be p.**
at maths être faible en maths; **p. loser** mauvais(e)
perdant(e) m,f; **in p. taste** de mauvais goût (**c**) (expressing sympathy) **you p. thing!** pauvre petit(e)!; **p.**
(**old**) **Simon** le pauvre Simon
2 npl **the p.** les pauvres mpl
poorly ['pʊəlɪ] **1** adv mal; (dressed) pauvrement; **to**
be p. off être pauvre
2 adj Br malade, souffrant(e)
pop¹ [pɒp] **1** n (music) pop f
2 adj **p. art** pop art m; **p. group** groupe m de pop; **p.**
music musique f pop; **p. singer** chanteur(euse) m,f
pop; **p. song** chanson f pop
pop² n Am (father) papa m
pop³ **1** n (**a**) (sound) bruit m sec (**b**) Fam (fizzy drink)
soda m
2 vt (pt & pp **popped**) (**a**) (burst) faire éclater (**b**) Fam
(put quickly) mettre; **to p. one's head out of the window** passer la tête par la fenêtre; Fam **to p. the question** faire sa demande en mariage; **to p. pills** se
bourrer de comprimés
3 vi (**a**) (burst) éclater; (of cork) sauter; (of ears) se
déboucher (**b**) Fam (go quickly) **I'm just popping**
next door je fais juste un saut chez les voisins; **we**
popped over to France for the weekend nous avons
fait un saut en France pour le week-end
▸**pop in** vi Fam passer
▸**pop off** vi very Fam (die) claquer
▸**pop out** vi Fam (go out) sortir
pop. (abbr population) population f
popcorn ['pɒpkɔːn] n pop-corn m
pope [pəʊp] n pape m
popgun ['pɒpgʌn] n pistolet m à bouchon
poplar ['pɒplə(r)] n peuplier m
poplin ['pɒplɪn] n popeline f

popper ['pɒpə(r)] *n Br Fam (fastener)* bouton-pression *m*

poppet ['pɒpɪt] *n Fam Old-fashioned* **she's a p.** elle est charmante; **my p.l** ma puce!

poppy ['pɒpɪ] *(pl* **poppies**) *n* coquelicot *m*; **p. seed** graine *f* de pavot

poppycock ['pɒpɪkɒk] *n Fam (nonsense)* bêtises *fpl*

populace ['pɒpjʊləs] *n Formal* **the p.** la population

popular ['pɒpjʊlə(r)] *adj* populaire; *(fashionable)* à la mode; *(restaurant, film)* qui a beaucoup de succès; **to make oneself p.** se faire bien voir; **she is p. with her colleagues** elle est appréciée par ses collègues; **by p. demand** à la demande générale; **contrary to p. belief** contrairement à ce que les gens croient

popularity [pɒpjʊ'lærɪtɪ] *n* popularité *f*; **p. rating** cote *f* de popularité

popularize ['pɒpjʊləraɪz] *vt* populariser

popularly ['pɒpjʊləlɪ] *adv* communément; **it is p. believed that...** les gens croient généralement que...

populate ['pɒpjʊleɪt] *vt* peupler

population [pɒpjʊ'leɪʃən] *n* population *f*; **p. explosion** explosion *f* démographique

populous ['pɒpjʊləs] *adj* populeux(euse)

porcelain ['pɔːslɪn] *n* porcelaine *f*; **p. ware** porcelaine

porch [pɔːtʃ] *n Br (entrance)* porche *m*; *Am (veranda)* véranda *f*

porcupine ['pɔːkjʊpaɪn] *n* porc-épic *m*

pore [pɔːr] *n* pore *m*

▶**pore over** *vt insep (examine closely)* étudier soigneuse-ment

pork [pɔːk] *n* porc *m*; **p. chop** côte *f* de porc; **p. pie** ≃ pâté *m* en croûte

porn [pɔːn] *n & adj Fam* porno *m*

pornographic [pɔːnə'græfɪk] *adj* pornographique

pornography [pɔː'nɒgrəfɪ] *n* pornographie *f*

porous ['pɔːrəs] *adj* poreux(euse)

porpoise ['pɔːpəs] *n* marsouin *m*

porridge ['pɒrɪdʒ] *n* porridge *m*; **p. oats** flocons *mpl* d'avoine

port¹ [pɔːt] *n* (**a**) *(harbour, town)* port *m*; **in p.** au port; *also Fig* **p. of call** escale *f*; *Prov* **any p. in a storm** nécessité fait loi (**b**) *Comput* port *m*

port² *n Naut (left-hand side)* bâbord *m*

port³ *n (drink)* porto *m*

portable ['pɔːtəbəl] *adj* portable

portal ['pɔːtəl] *n Archit & Comput* portail *m*

Port-au-Prince [pɔːtəʊ'prɛs] *n* Port-au-Prince

portcullis [pɔːt'kʌlɪs] *n* sarrasine *f*

portend [pɔː'tend] *vt Formal* présager

portent ['pɔːtent] *n Formal* présage *m*

portentous [pɔː'tentəs] *adj Formal* majeur(e)

porter ['pɔːtə(r)] *n (for carrying luggage)* porteur *m*; *(door attendant)* chasseur *m*; *(in hospital)* brancardier *m*

portfolio [pɔːt'fəʊlɪəʊ] *(pl* **portfolios**) *n (for documents)* porte-documents *m*; *(for drawings)* carton *m*; *(of shares, government minister)* portefeuille *m*; *(of model, artist)* portfolio *m*

porthole ['pɔːthəʊl] *n* hublot *m*

portion ['pɔːʃən] *n* part *f*, partie *f*; *(of food)* portion *f*

▶**portion out** *vt sep* partager

portly ['pɔːtlɪ] *adj* corpulent(e)

portrait ['pɔːtreɪt] *n also Fig* portrait *m*; **to have one's p. painted** faire faire son portrait; **p. gallery** galerie *f*

de portraits; *Comput* **p. (orientation)** (orientation *f*) portrait; **p. painter** portraitiste *mf*

portray [pɔː'treɪ] *vt (describe)* dépeindre; *(of actor)* interpréter

portrayal [pɔː'treɪəl] *n (description)* tableau *m*; *(by actor)* interprétation *f*

Portugal ['pɔːtjʊgəl] *n* le Portugal

Portuguese [pɔːtjʊ'giːz] **1** *npl* **the P.** *(people)* les Portugais *mpl*

2 *n* (**a**) *(person)* Portugais(e) *m,f* (**b**) *(language)* portugais *m*

3 *adj* portugais(e)

POS [piːəʊ'es] *n Com (abbr* **point of sale**) PDV *m*

pose [pəʊz] **1** *n* (**a**) *(position)* pose *f* (**b**) *Pej (affectation)* **it's just a p.** c'est pour épater la galerie

2 *vt (problem, question)* poser; *(danger, threat)* représenter

3 *vi also Pej* poser; **to p. as** *(pretend to be)* se faire passer pour

poser ['pəʊzə(r)] *n Fam* (**a**) *Pej (affected person)* poseur(euse) *m,f* (**b**) *(difficult question)* colle *f*

posh [pɒʃ] *Br* **1** *adj (person)* huppé(e); *(accent)* snob *inv*; *(restaurant, area, clothes)* chic *inv*

2 *adv* **to talk p.** parler d'une manière snob

position [pə'zɪʃən] **1** *n* (**a**) *(of person) (posture, opinion)* position *f* (**b**) *(of object)* emplacement *m*; *(of enemy, plane, in team sport)* position *f*; **in the on/off p.** *(of switch, lever)* en position marche/arrêt; **in p.** en place; **out of p.** déplacé(e) (**c**) *(situation)* situation *f*; **to be in a strong p.** être dans une position forte; **put yourself in my p.** mets-toi à ma place; **to be in a p. to do sth** être en mesure de faire qch; **to be in no p. to do sth** être mal placé(e) pour faire qch (**d**) *(job)* poste *m*; **a p. of responsibility** un poste à responsabilité

2 *vt (object)* placer; *(town)* situer; *(troops)* poster; **to p. oneself** se placer; **to be well/poorly positioned to do sth** être bien/mal placé(e) pour faire qch

positioning [pə'zɪʃənɪŋ] *n Com* positionnement *m*

positive ['pɒzɪtɪv] *adj* (**a**) *(person, answer, test)* positif(ive); *(evidence, proof)* formel(elle); **to be p. about sth** être optimiste à propos de qch; **on the p. side,...** le bon côté des choses, c'est que...; **p. discrimination** = mesures antidiscriminatoires favorisant les groupes minoritaires (**b**) *(certain)* certain(e), sûr(e) (**about** de) (**c**) *Fam (for emphasis)* véritable (**d**) *Math & Elec* positif(ive)

positively ['pɒzɪtɪvlɪ] *adv* (**a**) *(identify)* formellement (**b**) *(think, react)* de façon positive (**c**) *(for emphasis)* absolument

posse ['pɒsɪ] *n (to catch criminal)* = dans le Far West, groupe d'hommes commandé par un shérif, lancé à la poursuite d'un criminel; *(of reporters)* troupe *f*; *Fam (of friends)* bande *f*

possess [pə'zes] *vt* (**a**) *(property)* posséder; *(quality, faculty)* avoir (**b**) *(of evil spirit)* posséder; **possessed by fear** pris(e) de terreur; **what possessed you to do that?** qu'est-ce qui t'a pris de faire ça?

possession [pə'zeʃən] *n (ownership)* possession *f*; *(thing possessed)* bien *m*; **to be in p. of sth** être en possession de qch; **in full p. of one's faculties** en pleine possession de ses facultés

possessive [pə'zesɪv] **1** *n Gram* **the p.** le possessif

2 *adj* possessif(ive); **she's very p. about** *or* **of her children** c'est une mère possessive

possessor [pə'zesə(r)] *n* possesseur *m*

possibility [pɒsɪ'bɪlɪtɪ] (pl **possibilities**) n possibilité f; **to be within/outside the bounds of p.** être dans la limite du possible/au delà des limites du possible; **it's a distinct p.** c'est bien possible

possible ['pɒsɪbəl] **1** adj possible; **it's p. that...** il est possible que... + subjunctive; **as soon as p.** dès que possible; **as much as p.** autant que possible; **anything's p.** tout est possible

2 n (person) candidat(e) possible m,f; (thing) option f

possibly ['pɒsɪblɪ] adv (a) (perhaps) peut-être; **p. not** peut-être pas (b) (for emphasis) **I can't p. accept it** je ne peux vraiment pas l'accepter; **I'll do all I p. can** je ferai tout mon possible

post¹ [pəʊst] **1** n (a) (wooden stake) piquet m; (of goal) poteau m (b) (job, military position) poste m

2 vt (assign) affecter

post² vt (affix) afficher; **p. no bills** (sign) défense d'afficher

post³ Br **1** n (mail) courrier m; **the first p.** la première distribution; **to miss the p.** manquer la levée; **it's in the p.** c'est parti au courrier; **p. office** (bureau m de) poste f; **the P. Office** (government department) ≃ la Poste

2 vt (letter) poster; Fam Fig **to keep sb posted** tenir qn au courant

postage ['pəʊstɪdʒ] n affranchissement m; **p. and packing** frais mpl de port et d'emballage; **p. paid** port m payé; **p. stamp** timbre-poste m

postal ['pəʊstəl] adj postal(e); **p. order** mandat m postal; **p. vote** vote m par correspondance

postbag ['pəʊstbæg] n Br sac m postal

postbox ['pəʊstbɒks] n Br boîte f aux lettres

postcard ['pəʊstkɑːd] n carte f postale

postcode ['pəʊstkəʊd] n Br code m postal

postdate [pəʊst'deɪt] vt postdater

poster ['pəʊstə(r)] n (for advertising) affiche f; (for decoration) poster m; **p. advertising** publicité f par affichage; **p. paint** gouache f

posterior [pɒs'tɪərɪə(r)] n Hum (buttocks) postérieur m

posterity [pɒs'terɪtɪ] n postérité f

postgraduate [pəʊst'grædjʊɪt] **1** n étudiant(e) m,f de troisième cycle

2 adj de troisième cycle

posthaste ['pəʊst'heɪst] adv en toute hâte

posthumous ['pɒstjʊməs] adj posthume

posthumously ['pɒstjʊməslɪ] adv à titre posthume

posting ['pəʊstɪŋ] n (assignment) affectation f

postman ['pəʊstmən] n Br facteur m

postmark ['pəʊstmɑːk] n cachet m de la poste

postmaster ['pəʊstmɑːstə(r)] n (a) (in post office) receveur m des postes (b) Comput (for e-mail) maître m de poste

postmistress ['pəʊstmɪstrɪs] n receveuse f des postes

postmortem [pəʊst'mɔːtəm] n autopsie f

postnatal [pəʊst'neɪtəl] adj postnatal(e)

postoperative [pəʊst'ɒpərətɪv] adj postopératoire

postpone [pəʊst'pəʊn] vt reporter

postponement [pəʊst'pəʊnmənt] n report m

postscript ['pəʊsskrɪpt] n post-scriptum m

postulate ['pɒstjʊleɪt] vt poser comme hypothèse

posture ['pɒstʃə(r)] **1** n (a) (physical) posture f; **to have good/bad p.** se tenir bien/mal (b) Fig (attitude) position f

2 vi prendre des poses

postwar ['pəʊst'wɔː(r)] adj d'après-guerre; **the p. period** l'après-guerre m

posy ['pəʊzɪ] (pl **posies**) n petit bouquet m

pot [pɒt] **1** n (a) (container) pot m; (saucepan) casserole f; (for tea) théière f; (for coffee) cafetière f; **pots and pans** casseroles fpl; **a p. of tea** un thé; Fam **to have pots of money** avoir plein de fric; Fam **to go to p.** aller à la ruine; **to take a p. shot at sth** tirer à vue sur qch; Br Prov **it's a case of the p. calling the kettle black** c'est l'hôpital qui se moque de la charité; **p. plant** plante f en pot (b) Fam (marijuana) hasch m

2 vt (pt & pp **potted**) (a) (butter, meat) mettre en pot; (plant) empoter (b) (in snooker, pool) blouser

potash ['pɒtæʃ] n potasse f

potassium [pə'tæsɪəm] n potassium m

potato [pə'teɪtəʊ] (pl **potatoes**) n pomme f de terre; Br **p. crisps**, Am **p. chips** chips mpl; **p. peeler** épluche-légumes m; **p. salad** salade f de pommes de terre

potbellied [pɒt'belɪd] adj (from over-eating) bedonnant(e); (from malnourishment) au ventre ballonné; **p. stove** poêle m

potency ['pəʊtənsɪ] n puissance f; (virility) virilité f

potent ['pəʊtənt] adj puissant(e); (drink) fort(e)

potentate ['pəʊtənteɪt] n potentat m

potential [pə'tenʃəl] **1** n potentiel m; **to have p.** avoir du potentiel; **to fulfil one's p.** aller au maximum de ses capacités

2 adj potentiel(elle)

potentially [pə'tenʃəlɪ] adv potentiellement

pothole ['pɒthəʊl] n (cave) marmite f torrentielle; (in road) nid m de poule

potholer ['pɒthəʊlə(r)] n spéléologue mf

potholing ['pɒthəʊlɪŋ] n spéléologie f; **to go p.** faire de la spéléologie

potion ['pəʊʃən] n potion f

potluck ['pɒt'lʌk] n Fam **to take p.** prendre ce que l'on trouve

potpourri [pəʊ'pʊərɪ] n (of flowers, music) pot-pourri m

potted ['pɒtɪd] adj (a) (food) en terrine (b) (description, history) condensé(e)

potter ['pɒtə(r)] n potier(ère) m,f; **p.'s wheel** tour m de potier

▶**potter about, potter around** vi Br (do odd jobs) bricoler; (spend time leisurely) traîner

pottery ['pɒtərɪ] (pl **potteries**) n poterie f

potty¹ ['pɒtɪ] (pl **potties**) n pot m; **p. training** apprentissage m de la propreté

potty² adj Br Fam (crazy) dingue (**about** de)

potty-trained ['pɒtɪtreɪnd] adj propre

pouch [paʊtʃ] n (a) (for money) bourse f; (for tobacco) blague f; (for ammunition) étui m (b) (of marsupial) poche f

pouf(fe) [puːf] n pouf m

poulterer ['pəʊltərə(r)] n volailler(ère) m,f

poultice ['pəʊltɪs] n cataplasme m

poultry ['pəʊltrɪ] n volaille f; **p. farm** élevage m de volaille; **p. farmer** éleveur(euse) m,f de volaille

pounce [paʊns] vi **to p. on** (of animal) bondir sur; (of person) se précipiter sur

pound¹ [paʊnd] n (**a**) (unit of weight) = 453,6 g, livre f (**b**) (British currency) livre f; **p. sign** symbole m de la livre sterling; **p. sterling** livre sterling

pound² n (for dogs, cars) fourrière f

pound³ 1 vt (crush) (spices, garlic) piler; (meat) attendrir; (with artillery) pilonner; **to p. sth to pieces** réduire qch en miettes

2 vi (of heart) battre à tout rompre; **to p. on the door** cogner à la porte; **my head is pounding** j'ai des élancements dans la tête

pour [pɔː(r)] 1 vt verser (**into/down** dans); **to p. sb a drink** verser à boire à qn; **to p. money into sth** investir beaucoup d'argent dans qch

2 vi couler; **it's pouring (with rain)** il pleut à verse; **sweat was pouring off him** il ruisselait de sueur; **tourists were pouring into the palace** les touristes entraient en masse dans le palais

▸**pour in** 1 vt sep (liquid) verser

2 vi (of liquid) couler; Fig (of people, letters) affluer

▸**pour out** 1 vt sep (tea, coffee) verser; Fig (anger, grief) déverser; (emotions) déballer

2 vi (of liquid) se déverser; Fig (of people) sortir en masse

pouring ['pɔːrɪŋ] adj (rain) torrentiel(elle)

pout [paʊt] 1 n moue f

2 vi faire la moue

poverty ['pɒvətɪ] n pauvreté f; Fig (of ideas, resources) pénurie f; **to live in p.** vivre dans la misère; **p. line** seuil m de pauvreté

poverty-stricken ['pɒvətɪstrɪkən] adj très pauvre

POW [piːəʊ'dʌbəljuː] n (abbr prisoner of war) prisonnier(ère) m,f de guerre

powder ['paʊdə(r)] 1 n poudre f; **p. blue** bleu m pastel; Fig **p. keg** poudrière f; **p. puff** houppe f; **p. room** toilettes fpl pour dames

2 vt saupoudrer (**with** de); **to p. one's face** se poudrer le visage; Euph **to p. one's nose** aller se laver les mains

powdered ['paʊdəd] adj (milk, eggs) en poudre

powdery ['paʊdərɪ] adj poudreux(euse)

power ['paʊə(r)] 1 n (**a**) (authority, capacity) pouvoir m; **to come to/be in p.** arriver/être au pouvoir; **to have sb in one's p.** tenir qn à sa merci; **to have the p. to do sth** avoir le pouvoir de faire qch; **to do everything in one's (to do sth)** faire tout ce qui est en son pouvoir (pour faire qch); **to be at the height** or **peak of one's powers** être au sommet de ses capacités; **it is beyond my p. to help you** je ne peux pas t'aider, cela dépasse mes capacités; Fam **to do sb a p. of good** faire énormément de bien à qn; **powers of concentration/persuasion** force f de concentration/persuasion; **p. of speech** usage m de la parole; **p. base** base f politique; **p. struggle** lutte f pour le pouvoir

(**b**) (physical strength) force f, puissance f; **p. steering** (in car) direction f assistée

(**c**) (powerful person, group, nation) puissance f; Fig **the p. behind the throne** l'éminence f grise; **the powers that be** les autorités fpl

(**d**) Law pouvoir m; **p. of attorney** procuration f

(**e**) (electricity) courant m; **p. cut** coupure f de courant; **p. pack** bloc m d'alimentation; **p. plant** centrale f électrique; **p. point** prise f de courant; **p. shower** douche f à jet puissant; **p. station** centrale f électrique

(**f**) Math puissance f; **three to the p. of ten** trois (à

la) puissance dix

2 vt (provide with power) actionner; **powered by two engines** propulsé(e) par deux moteurs

power-assisted steering ['paʊərəsɪstɪd'stɪərɪŋ] n Aut direction f assistée

powerful ['paʊəfʊl] adj (muscles, engine, voice, country) puissant(e); (politician) influent(e); (drug, smell) fort(e); (speech, image) impressionnant(e)

powerhouse ['paʊəhaʊs] n Fam (person) moteur m

powerless ['paʊəlɪs] adj impuissant(e); **to be p. to do sth** être impuissant(e) à faire qch

PR [piː'ɑ(r)] n (**a**) (abbr **public relations**) RP (**b**) Pol (abbr **proportional representation**) représentation f proportionnelle

practicable ['præktɪkəbəl] adj réalisable

practical ['præktɪkəl] 1 n (lesson) travaux mpl pratiques; (exam) épreuve f pratique

2 adj (**a**) (mind, solution) pratique; **she's very p.** elle a l'esprit pratique; **for all p. purposes** dans la pratique; **p. joke** farce f (**b**) (virtual) **it's a p. certainty** c'est pratiquement certain

practicality [præktɪ'kælɪtɪ] (pl **practicalities**) n (of suggestion, plan) aspect m pratique; **practicalities** détails mpl pratiques

practically ['præktɪklɪ] adv (**a**) (in a practical manner) de façon pratique (**b**) (almost) pratiquement, presque

practice ['præktɪs] 1 n (**a**) (action, exercise) pratique f; (in sport) entraînement m; **in p.** dans la ou en pratique; **to put sth into p.** mettre qch en pratique; **to be out of p.** avoir perdu l'habitude; Prov **p. makes perfect** c'est en forgeant qu'on devient forgeron; **p. match** (in football, rugby) match m d'entraînement (**b**) (of medicine, law) exercice m (**c**) (surgery) centre m médical; (lawyer's office) cabinet m d'avocat (**d**) (custom) pratique f; **to make a p. of doing sth** se faire une règle de faire qch; **to be good/bad p.** être conseillé(e)/déconseillé(e)

2 vt & vi Am = practise

practiced, practicing Am = practised, practising

practise, Am **practice** ['præktɪs] 1 vt (**a**) (musical instrument) travailler; (language, sport) pratiquer; (**b**) (medicine, law) exercer (**c**) (religion, custom) pratiquer; **to p. what one preaches** mettre en pratique ce que l'on prêche

2 vi (**a**) (of musician) s'exercer; (of sportsperson) s'entraîner (**b**) (of doctor, lawyer) exercer

practised, Am **practiced** ['præktɪst] adj (teacher, nurse, speaker) expérimenté(e); (liar) professionnel(elle); (eye, ear) exercé(e); (charm) étudié(e)

practising, Am **practicing** ['præktɪsɪŋ] adj (doctor, lawyer) en exercice; (Christian) pratiquant(e)

pragmatic [præg'mætɪk] adj pragmatique

pragmatism ['prægmətɪzəm] n pragmatisme m

pragmatist ['prægmətɪst] n pragmatiste mf

Prague [prɑːg] n Prague

prairie ['preərɪ] n prairie f; **p. dog** chien m de prairie; Am **p. schooner** chariot m bâché

praise [preɪz] 1 n éloges mpl; **to sing the praises of** faire l'éloge de

2 vt faire l'éloge de; (God) louer; **to p. sb to the skies** porter qn aux nues

praiseworthy ['preɪzwɜːðɪ] adj digne d'éloges

pram [præm] n Br landau m

prance [prɑːns] vi (of horse) caracoler; (of person) sautiller; **to p. in/out** entrer/sortir en sautillant

prank [præŋk] n farce f; **to play a p. on sb** faire une farce à qn

prat [præt] n Br Fam andouille f

prattle ['prætəl] **1** n papotage m
2 vi papoter (**about** de)

prawn [prɔːn] n crevette f rose; **p. cocktail** crevettes à la mayonnaise; **p. cracker** beignet m de crevette

pray [preɪ] vi prier (**for** pour); **to p. to God** prier Dieu; Fig **to p. for good weather/rain** prier pour qu'il fasse beau/qu'il pleuve

prayer [preə(r)] n prière f; **to say one's prayers** dire ses prières; Fam Fig **he doesn't have a p.** il n'a aucune chance; **p. beads** chapelet m; **p. book** livre m de prières; **p. mat** tapis m de prière; **p. meeting** réunion f de prière

preach [priːtʃ] **1** vt prêcher
2 vi prêcher; Fig (moralize) faire la morale; Fig **to p. to the converted** prêcher un converti

preacher ['priːtʃə(r)] n prédicateur(trice) m,f

preamble ['priːæmbəl] n Formal préambule m

prearranged [priːə'reɪndʒd] adj convenu(e)

precarious [prɪ'keərɪəs] adj précaire

precariously [prɪ'keərɪəslɪ] adv de façon précaire; **p. balanced** en équilibre précaire

precaution [prɪ'kɔːʃən] n précaution f; **to take precautions** prendre des précautions; **as a p.** par précaution

precautionary [prɪ'kɔːʃənərɪ] adj préventif(ive)

precede [prɪ'siːd] vt précéder

precedence ['presɪdəns] n priorité f; **in order of p.** par ordre de préséance; **to take p. over sb** avoir la préséance sur qn; **to take p. over sth** passer avant qch

precedent ['presɪdənt] n précédent m

preceding [prɪ'siːdɪŋ] adj précédent(e)

precept ['priːsept] n précepte m

precinct ['priːsɪŋkt] n (**a**) Br (area) (shopping) **p.** quartier m commerçant piétonnier; **within the precincts of** dans l'enceinte de (**b**) Am (administrative district) circonscription f; (police division) quartier m

precious ['preʃəs] **1** n (term of endearment) **my p.** mon trésor
2 adj also Pej précieux(euse); **that photo is very p. to me** cette photo m'est très chère; Ironic **you and your p. books!** toi et tes sacrés bouquins!
3 adv Fam (for emphasis) **p. little** très peu; **p. little money** très peu d'argent

precipice ['presɪpɪs] n précipice m

precipitate 1 n [prɪ'sɪpɪtɪt] Chem précipité m
2 adj [prɪ'sɪpɪtət] Formal précipité(e)
3 vt [prɪ'sɪpɪteɪt] Formal précipiter

precipitately [prɪ'sɪpɪtətlɪ] adv précipitamment

precipitation [prɪsɪpɪ'teɪʃən] n précipitation f; **annual p.** précipitations annuelles

precipitous [prɪ'sɪpɪtəs] adj (descent) à pic; (steps) raide

précis ['preɪsiː] (pl **précis** ['preɪsiːz]) n résumé m

precise [prɪ'saɪs] adj (**a**) (exact) précis(e); **..., to be p. ...,** pour être précis (**b**) (meticulous) méticuleux(-euse)

precisely [prɪ'saɪslɪ] adv exactement, précisément; **at six (o'clock) p.** à six heures précises; **p.!** exactement!

precision [prɪ'sɪʒən] n précision f; Mil **p. bombing** bombardement m de précision; **p. instrument** instrument m de précision

preclude [prɪ'kluːd] vt Formal empêcher; **to p. sb from doing sth** empêcher qn de faire qch

precocious [prɪ'kəʊʃəs] adj précoce

precociousness [prɪ'kəʊʃəsnɪs], **precocity** [prɪ-'kɒsɪtɪ] n précocité f

preconceived [priːkən'siːvd] adj préconçu(e)

preconception [priːkən'sepʃən] n idée f préconçue; (prejudice) préjugé m

precondition [priːkən'dɪʃən] n condition f préalable

precooked [priː'kʊkt] adj précuit(e)

precursor [prɪ'kɜːsə(r)] n précurseur m

predate [priː'deɪt] vt (**a**) (precede) précéder (**b**) (put earlier date on) antidater

predator ['predətə(r)] n prédateur m

predatory ['predətərɪ] adj prédateur(trice), Fig avide

predecessor ['priːdɪsesə(r)] n (person) prédécesseur m; (object) précédent(e) m,f

predestination [priːdestɪ'neɪʃən] n prédestination f

predestine [priː'destɪn] vt **to be predestined to do sth** être prédestiné(e) à faire qch

predetermine [priːdɪ'tɜːmɪn] vt prédéterminer

predicament [prɪ'dɪkəmənt] n situation f difficile; **to be in a p.** être dans le pétrin

predicate 1 n ['predɪkət] Gram prédicat m
2 vt ['predɪkeɪt] **to be predicated on sth** être fondé(e) sur qch

predict [prɪ'dɪkt] vt (from instinct) prédire; (from information) prévoir

predictable [prɪ'dɪktəbəl] adj prévisible; Fam **you're so p.!** j'aurais pu le deviner!

predictably [prɪ'dɪktəblɪ] adv de manière prévisible; **p., he arrived an hour late** comme on pouvait s'y attendre, il est arrivé une heure en retard

prediction [prɪ'dɪkʃən] n (from instinct) prédiction f; (from information) prévision f

predispose [priːdɪs'pəʊz] vt prédisposer; **to be predisposed to do sth** être prédisposé(e) à faire qch

predisposition [priːdɪspə'zɪʃən] n prédisposition f (**to** or **towards** envers)

predominance [prɪ'dɒmɪnəns] n prédominance f

predominant [prɪ'dɒmɪnənt] adj prédominant(e)

predominantly [prɪ'dɒmɪnəntlɪ] adv en majorité, principalement

predominate [prɪ'dɒmɪneɪt] vi prédominer

pre-eminence [prɪ'emɪnəns] n prééminence f

pre-eminent [prɪ'emɪnənt] adj prééminent(e)

pre-empt [prɪ'empt] vt devancer

pre-emptive [prɪ'emptɪv] adj préventif(ive)

preen [priːn] vt **to p. itself** (of bird) se lisser les plumes; **to p. oneself** (of person) se faire beau (belle), se pomponner; Fig **to p. oneself on one's success** s'enorgueillir de son succès

pre-established [priːɪs'tæblɪʃt] adj préétabli(e)

prefab ['priːfæb] n Fam (house) préfabriqué m

prefabricated [priː'fæbrɪkeɪtɪd] adj préfabriqué(e)

preface ['prefɪs] **1** n (of book) préface f; (to speech) préambule m
2 vt commencer (**with** par)

prefect ['priːfekt] n Sch = élève des grandes classes chargé de la surveillance

prefer [prɪ'fɜː(r)] (pt & pp **preferred**) vt (**a**) (favour) préférer (**to** à); **to p. to do sth** préférer faire qch (**b**) Law **to p. charges** porter plainte

preferable ['prefərəbəl] adj préférable

preferably ['prefərəblɪ] adv de préférence

preference ['prefərəns] *n* préférence *f*; **to give sth p., to give p. to sth** donner la préférence à qch; **in p. to** plutôt que; **in order of p.** par ordre de préférence
preferential [prefə'renʃəl] *adj (treatment)* de faveur; *(tariff)* préférentiel(elle)
preferred [prɪ'fɜːd] *adj* préféré(e)
prefigure [priː'fɪgə(r)] *vt* préfigurer
prefix ['priːfɪks] *n* préfixe *m*
pregnancy ['pregnənsɪ] *(pl* **pregnancies**) *n* grossesse *f*; **p. test** test *m* de grossesse
pregnant ['pregnənt] *adj* (**a**) *(woman)* enceinte; *(animal)* pleine; **to be three months p.** être enceinte de trois mois (**b**) *Fig (pause, silence)* éloquent(e)
preheat [priː'hiːt] *vt* préchauffer
prehensile [prɪ'hensaɪl] *adj* préhensile
prehistoric [priːhɪs'tɒrɪk] *adj* préhistorique
prehistory [priː'hɪstərɪ] *n* préhistoire *f*
prejudge [priː'dʒʌdʒ] *vt (actions, motives)* préjuger de; *(person)* juger sans connaître
prejudice ['predʒʊdɪs] **1** *n* (**a**) *(bias)* préjugé *m* (**against/in favour of** contre/en faveur de) (**b**) *Law* **without p. to** sans préjudice de
2 *vt* (**a**) *(bias)* prévenir (**against/in favour of** contre/en faveur de) (**b**) *(harm)* nuire à, faire du tort à
prejudiced ['predʒʊdɪst] *adj* **to be p.** avoir des préjugés (**against/in favour of** contre/en faveur de)
prejudicial [predʒʊ'dɪʃəl] *adj* préjudiciable (**to** à)
preliminary [prɪ'lɪmɪnərɪ] **1** *(pl* **preliminaries**) *n* préliminaire *m*; **preliminaries** *(to investigation, meeting)* préliminaires
2 *adj* préliminaire
prelude ['preljuːd] *n* prélude *m*
premarital [priː'mærɪtəl] *adj* avant le mariage
premature ['premətjʊə(r)] *adj (baby, action, comment)* prématuré(e); *(baldness, senility, ejaculation)* précoce; *Fam* **you're being a bit p.!** tu vas un peu vite!
prematurely ['premətjʊəlɪ] *adv* prématurément
premeditated [priː'medɪteɪtɪd] *adj* prémédité(e)
premenstrual [priː'menstrəəl] *adj* prémenstruel(elle); **p.** *Br* **tension** *or Am* **syndrome** syndrome *m* prémenstruel
premier ['premɪə(r)] **1** *n (prime minister)* Premier ministre *m*
2 *adj* premier(ère)
premiere ['premɪeə(r)] *n (of play, film)* première *f*
premise ['premɪs] **1** *n (of argument, theory)* prémisse *f*
2 *vt* **to be premised on sth** être fondé(e) sur qch
premises ['premɪsɪz] *npl* locaux *mpl*; **business p.** locaux commerciaux; **on the p.** sur place; **off the p.** en dehors de l'établissement; **to see sb off the p.** accompagner qn jusqu'au dehors
premium ['priːmɪəm] *n* (**a**) *Fin (for insurance)* prime *f*; *(additional sum)* supplément *m*; **at a p.** au prix fort; *Br* **p. bonds** ≃ obligations *fpl* à lots (**b**) *(idioms)* **to be at a p.** être très recherché(e); **to put a p. on sth** accorder de l'importance à qch
premonition [priːmə'nɪʃən] *n* prémonition *f*; **to have a p. that...** avoir le préssentiment que...
prenatal [priː'neɪtəl] *adj* prénatal(e)
preoccupation [priːɒkjʊ'peɪʃən] *n* préoccupation *f* (**with** pour); **to have a p. with sth** être préoccupé(e) par qch
preoccupied [priː'ɒkjʊpaɪd] *adj* préoccupé(e) (**with** par)

preoccupy [priː'ɒkjʊpaɪ] *(pt & pp* **preoccupied**) *vt* préoccuper au plus haut point
prep [prep] *n Br Fam (homework)* devoirs *mpl*; **p. school** école *f* primaire privée
prepaid [priː'peɪd] *adj* prépayé(e)
preparation [prepə'reɪʃən] *n* préparation *f*; **preparations** *(for ceremony, party)* préparatifs *mpl*
preparatory [prɪ'pærətərɪ] *adj* préparatoire; **p. school** *Br* école *f* primaire privée; *Am* école préparatoire
prepare [prɪ'peə(r)] **1** *vt* préparer
2 *vi* se préparer (**for** à); **to p. to do sth** se préparer à faire qch
prepared [prɪ'peəd] *adj* (**a**) *(willing)* **to be p. to do sth** être prêt(e) à faire qch (**b**) *(ready)* **to be p. for sth** s'attendre à qch (**c**) *(made in advance)* préparé(e) à l'avance; *(excuse, explanation)* tout(e) prêt(e)
prepayment [priː'peɪmənt] *n* paiement *m* d'avance
preponderance [prɪ'pɒndərəns] *n* prépondérance *f*
preposition [prepə'zɪʃən] *n* préposition *f*
prepositional [prepə'zɪʃənəl] *adj* prépositif(ive)
prepossessing [priːpə'zesɪŋ] *adj* avenant(e), engageant(e)
preposterous [prɪ'pɒstərəs] *adj* ridicule
preppy ['prepɪ] *adj Am Fam* ≃ BCBG *inv*
preprogrammed [priː'prəʊgræmd] *adj Comput* préprogrammé(e)
prerecorded [priːrɪ'kɔːdɪd] *adj* préenregistré(e)
prerequisite [priː'rekwɪzɪt] *n* (condition *f*) préalable *m*
prerogative [prɪ'rɒgətɪv] *n* prérogative *f*
presage ['presɪdʒ] *Lit* **1** *n* présage *m*
2 *vt* présager
Presbyterian [prezbɪ'tɪərɪən] *n & adj* presbyté-rien(-enne) *m,f*
preschool [priː'skuːl] **1** *n Am* école *f* maternelle
2 *adj* préscolaire
prescribe [prɪ'skraɪb] *vt (medicine, punishment)* prescrire; *(solution)* préconiser; *(task, rule)* exiger
prescription [prɪ'skrɪpʃən] *n* ordonnance *f*; **available only on p.** délivré(e) seulement sur ordonnance; **p. charge** = prix fixe payé sur chaque médicament prescrit sur ordonnance
presence ['prezəns] *n* présence *f*; **in the p. of** en présence de; **to have p.** avoir de la présence; **to make one's p. felt** ne pas passer inaperçu(e); **p. of mind** présence d'esprit
present¹ ['prezənt] **1** *n* **the p.** le présent; **at p.** en ce moment; **for the p.** pour l'instant
2 *adj* (**a**) *(in attendance)* présent(e) (**at** à) (**b**) *(current)* actuel(elle); **at the p. time** *or* **moment** actuellement; *Gram* **the p. tense** le présent; **p. participle** participe *m* présent
present² **1** *n* ['prezənt] *(gift)* cadeau *m*; **to give sb a p.** offrir un cadeau à qn
2 *vt* [prɪ'zent] (**a**) *(introduce, put forward)* présenter; **if the opportunity presents itself** si l'occasion se présente (**b**) *(give) (gift)* donner; *(award, certificate)* remettre; **to p. sth to sb, to p. sb with sth** *(gift)* donner qch à qn; *(award, certificate)* remettre qch à qn (**c**) *Mil* **p. arms!** présentez armes!
presentable [prɪ'zentəbəl] *adj* présentable; **to make oneself p.** s'arranger
presentation [prezən'teɪʃən] *n* (**a**) *(of person)* présentation *f* (**b**) *(of gift, award)* remise *f*; **to make a p. to sb** *(give present)* offrir un cadeau à qn; *(give award)*

remettre un prix à qn (**c**) *(formal talk)* présentation *f*; *(by student)* exposé *m* (**d**) **on p. of** *(passport, coupon)* sur présentation de

present-day [prezənt'deɪ] *adj* actuel(elle)

presenter [prɪ'zentə(r)] *n (on radio, TV)* présentateur(trice) *m,f*

presentiment [prɪ'zentɪmənt] *n* pressentiment *m*

presently ['prezəntlɪ] *adv* (**a**) *(soon)* bientôt; *(soon afterwards)* peu de temps après (**b**) *Am (now)* actuellement

preservation [prezə'veɪʃən] *n* (**a**) *(maintenance)* maintien *m* (**b**) *(protection) (of species)* protection *f*; *(of building)* conservation *f*; **to put a p. order on a building** classer un bâtiment monument historique

preservative [prɪ'zɜːvətɪv] *n* conservateur *m*

preserve [prɪ'zɜːv] **1** *n* (**a**) *(jam)* confiture *f* (**b**) *(in hunting)* réserve *f* (**c**) *(area of dominance)* domaine *m*; **engineering is no longer a male p.** le métier d'ingénieur n'est plus réservé aux hommes

2 *vt* (**a**) *(custom, belief)* préserver; *(calm, sense of humour)* garder; *(dignity, self-respect)* conserver (**b**) *(leather, wood)* entretenir (**c**) *(fruit)* mettre en conserve (**d**) *(protect)* préserver (**from** de); **saints p. us!** le ciel nous préserve!

preshrunk [priː'ʃrʌŋk] *adj* lavé(e)

preside [prɪ'zaɪd] *vi* présider; **to p. over a meeting** présider une réunion

presidency ['prezɪdənsɪ] *(pl* **presidencies**) *n* présidence *f*

president ['prezɪdənt] *n (of country)* président *m*; *Am (of company)* P-DG *m*

presidential [prezɪ'denʃəl] *adj* présidentiel(elle)

press [pres] **1** *n* (**a**) *(act of pushing)* pression *f*; **at the p. of a button** en appuyant sur le bouton; **p. stud** bouton-pression *m*

(**b**) *(newspapers)* **the p.** la presse; **to get a good/ bad p.** avoir bonne/mauvaise presse; **p. agency** agence *f* de presse; **p. box** tribune *f* de la presse; **p. conference** conférence *f* de presse; **p. cutting** coupure *f* de presse; **p. photographer** photographe *mf* de presse; **p. release** communiqué *m* de presse

(**c**) *(machine)* **(printing) p.** presse *f* (typographique); **to go to p.** *(of newspaper)* partir à l'impression

2 *vt* (**a**) *(button, switch)* appuyer sur; *(into clay, cement)* **she pressed the note into my hand** elle m'a glissé le billet dans la main

(**b**) *(squeeze)* serrer

(**c**) *(grapes, olives, flowers)* presser

(**d**) *(iron)* repasser

(**e**) *(pressurize)* faire pression sur; **to p. sb to do sth** presser qn de faire qch; **to be pressed for time/ money** être pressé(e) par le temps/l'argent

(**f**) *(force)* **to p. sth on sb** forcer qn à accepter qch; **to p. home one's advantage** profiter de son avantage; **to p. one's attentions on sb** faire des avances à qn

(**g**) *(insist on) Law* **to p. charges (against sb)** porter plainte (contre qn); **I didn't p. the point** je n'ai pas insisté

3 *vi (push)* appuyer; *(of crowd)* se presser

▸**press ahead** = press on

▸**press for** *vt insep (demand)* exiger

▸**press on** *vi* continuer; **to p. on with one's work** continuer de travailler

press-gang ['presgæŋ] *vt* **to p. sb into doing sth** forcer qn à faire qch

pressing ['presɪŋ] *adj (urgent)* pressant(e)

pressman ['presmən] *n Br* journaliste *m*

press-up ['presʌp] *n (exercise)* pompe *f*

pressure ['preʃə(r)] **1** *n* pression *f*; **to put p. on sb (to do sth)** faire pression sur qn (pour qu'il fasse qch); **to be under p.** être stressé(e); **p. of work** stress *m* lié au travail; **p. cooker** Cocotte-Minute® *f*, autocuiseur *m*; **p. gauge** manomètre *m*; **p. group** groupe *m* de pression; *Med* **p. point** point *m* de compression

2 *vt* **to p. sb to do sth** *or* **into doing sth** faire pression sur qn pour qu'il/elle fasse qch

pressurize ['preʃəraɪz] *vt* (**a**) *Tech (container)* pressuriser (**b**) *(person)* **p. sb (into doing sth)** faire pression sur qn (pour qu'il fasse qch)

prestige [pres'tiːʒ] *n* prestige *m*

prestigious [pres'tɪdʒəs] *adj* prestigieux(euse)

presumably [prɪ'zjuːməblɪ] *adv* sans doute; **p. she'll come** je suppose qu'elle viendra

presume [prɪ'zjuːm] **1** *vt* présumer, supposer; **to p. to do sth** se permettre de faire qch; **I p. so** je suppose que oui

2 *vi* abuser; **I don't want to p. on you** je ne voudrais pas abuser

presumption [prɪ'zʌmpʃən] *n* présomption *f*

presumptuous [prɪ'zʌmptjʊəs] *adj* présomptueux(euse)

presuppose [priːsə'pəʊz] *vt* présupposer, supposer

presupposition [priːsʌpə'zɪʃən] *n* présupposition *f*

pretence [prɪ'tens] *n* simulation *f*; **he says he doesn't mind, but it's all a p.** il dit que ça lui est égal, mais il fait semblant; **to make a p. of doing sth** faire semblant de faire qch

pretend [prɪ'tend] **1** *vt* (**a**) *(feign)* feindre, simuler; **to p. to do sth** faire semblant de faire qch; **they pretended that nothing had happened** ils ont fait comme si de rien n'était (**b**) *(claim)* prétendre

2 *vi (put on an act)* faire semblant

3 *adj Fam* **p. money** de l'argent pour faire semblant; **a. p. slap** une gifle pour rire

pretension [prɪ'tenʃən] *n* prétention *f*

pretentious [prɪ'tenʃəs] *adj* prétentieux(euse)

pretentiousness [prɪ'tenʃəsnəs] *n* prétention *f*

preterite ['pretərɪt] *n Gram* **the p.** le prétérit

pretext ['priːtekst] *n* prétexte *m*; **under** *or* **on the p. of doing sth** sous prétexte de faire qch

Pretoria [prɪ'tɔːrɪə] *n* Prétoria

pretty ['prɪtɪ] **1** *adj* joli(e); **it's not a p. sight** ce n'est pas beau à voir; **to cost a p. penny** coûter la peau des fesses

2 *adv* (**a**) *(fairly)* plutôt; **p. certain** pratiquement sûr(e); **they're p. much the same** ils sont pratiquement pareils (**b**) *Fam* **to be sitting p.** ne pas avoir à s'en faire

pretzel ['pretzəl] *n* bretzel *m*

prevail [prɪ'veɪl] *vi* (**a**) *(be successful)* l'emporter (**over** sur) (**b**) *(persuade)* **to p. (up)on sb to do sth** amener qn à faire qch (**c**) *(predominate)* prédominer

prevailing [prɪ'veɪlɪŋ] *adj* prédominant(e); *(wind)* dominant(e)

prevalent ['prevələnt] *adj* très répandu(e)

prevaricate [prɪ'værɪkeɪt] *vi* tergiverser

prevarication [prɪværɪ'keɪʃən] *n* tergiversation *f*

prevent [prɪ'vent] *vt* empêcher, éviter; **to p. sb from doing sth** empêcher qn de faire qch; **to p. sth from happening** empêcher que qch n'arrive

preventable [prɪ'ventəbəl] *adj* évitable
preventative [prɪ'ventətɪv] = **preventive**
prevention [prɪ'venʃən] *n* prévention *f*; *Prov* **p. is better than cure** mieux vaut prévenir que guérir
preventive [prɪ'ventɪv] *adj* préventif(ive)
preview ['pri:vju:] **1** *n* (*of play, film*) avant-première *f*; (*of new product*) aperçu *m*
  2 *vt* **to be previewed** (*of film*) sortir en avant-première
previous ['pri:vɪəs] **1** *adj* précédent(e); **to have a p. engagement** être déjà pris(e); *Law* **p. conviction** condamnation *f* antérieure
  2 *adv* **p. to** avant
previously ['pri:vɪəslɪ] *adv* auparavant
prewar ['pri:'wɔ:(r)] *adj* d'avant-guerre
prey [preɪ] *n* proie *f*; *Fig* **to be a p. to** être la proie de; **to fall p. to** devenir la proie de
▸**prey on, prey upon** *vt insep* (*person*) prendre pour cible; (*fears, doubts*) exploiter; **to p. on sb's mind** tourmenter qn
price [praɪs] **1** *n* prix *m*; **to rise** *or* **increase in p.** augmenter; **at any p.** à tout prix; **not at any p.** à aucun prix; *Fig* **to pay the p. (for sth)** faire les frais (de qch); *Fig* **it's too high a p. (to pay)** c'est trop cher payé; **to put** *or* **set a p. on sb's head** mettre la tête de qn à prix; *Fig* **everyone has his p.** il n'y a pas d'homme qu'on ne puisse acheter; *Fam* **what p. patriotism now?** que vaut le patriotisme maintenant?; **p. cut** baisse *f* des prix; **p. freeze** gel *m* des prix; **p. increase** hausse *f* des prix; **p. index** indice *m* des prix; **p. list** liste *f* de prix; **p. range** gamme *f* de prix; (*budget*) budget *m*; **p. tag** étiquette *f* de prix; **p. war** guerre *f* des prix
  2 *vt* (*decide cost of*) fixer le prix de; (*indicate cost of*) mettre le prix sur; **the toy is priced at £10** le prix du jouet est 10 livres; **to p. oneself out of the market** perdre ses clients en pratiquant des prix trop élevés
price-cutting ['praɪs'kʌtɪŋ] *n Com* baisse *f* des prix
price-fixing ['praɪs'fɪksɪŋ] *n Com* alignement *m* des prix
priceless ['praɪslɪs] *adj* (**a**) (*invaluable*) qui n'a pas de prix (**b**) *Fam* (*funny*) impayable
pricey ['praɪsɪ] *adj Fam* cher(ère)
prick [prɪk] **1** *n* (**a**) (*of needle*) piqûre *f*; *Fig* (*of conscience*) remords *m* (**b**) *Vulg* (*penis*) bite *f*; (*man*) con *m*
  2 *vt* (*sausage, potato*) piquer; (*balloon*) percer; **to p. one's finger** se piquer le doigt; **to p. a hole in sth** percer qch
▸**prick up** *vt sep* **to p. up one's ears** (*of animal*) dresser les oreilles; (*of person*) tendre l'oreille
prickle ['prɪkəl] **1** *n* (**a**) (*of hedgehog*) piquant *m*; (*of plant*) épine *f* (**b**) (*sensation*) picotement *m*
  2 *vi* (*of skin*) picoter
prickly ['prɪklɪ] *adj* (**a**) (*animal*) couvert(e) de piquants; (*plant*) à épines; *Fig* (*person*) susceptible; **p. pear** (*tree*) figuier *m* de Barbarie; (*fruit*) figue *f* de Barbarie (**b**) (*sensation*) de picotement; **p. heat** miliaire *f*
pride [praɪd] **1** *n* (**a**) (*satisfaction*) fierté *f*; (*self-esteem*) amour-propre *m*; *Pej* (*vanity*) orgueil *m*; **to take p. in sth** mettre sa fierté dans qch (**b**) (*person, thing*) **she is the p. of the family** elle fait la fierté de la famille; **the p. of my collection** le clou de ma collection; **she's his p. and joy** elle fait son bonheur; **to have p. of place** trôner (**c**) (*of lions*) troupe *f*
  2 *vt* **to p. oneself on sth** être fier(ère) de qch
priest [pri:st] *n* prêtre *m*
priestess ['pri:stɪs] *n* prêtresse *f*

priesthood ['pri:sthʊd] *n* prêtrise *f*; **to enter the p.** entrer dans les ordres
prig [prɪg] *n* prêcheur(euse) *m,f*
priggish ['prɪgɪʃ] *adj* prêcheur(euse)
prim [prɪm] *adj* **p. (and proper)** (*person, expression*) collet monté *inv*; (*manner*) guindé(e)
primacy ['praɪməsɪ] *n* primauté *f*
prima facie ['praɪmə'feɪʃɪ] **1** *adj Law* **p. case** = affaire qui, au premier abord, paraît légitime
  2 *adv* de prime abord
primarily [praɪ'merɪlɪ] *adv* principalement
primary ['praɪmərɪ] **1** *n* (*pl* **primaries**) (*election*) primaire *f*
  2 *adj* (**a**) (*main*) principal(e); **p. colours** couleurs *fpl* fondamentales (**b**) (*initial*) primaire; **p. education** enseignement *m* primaire; **p. school** école *f* primaire

> **Primaries**
> Les élections primaires américaines (directes ou indirectes selon les États) aboutissent à la sélection des candidats qui seront en lice pour représenter les deux grands partis nationaux à l'élection présidentielle.

primate ['praɪmeɪt] *n* (**a**) (*animal*) primate *m* (**b**) *Rel* primat *m*
prime [praɪm] **1** *n* (*best time*) **the p. of life** la fleur de l'âge; **to be in one's p.** être à la fleur de l'âge; **to be past one's p.** ne plus être de première jeunesse
  2 *adj* (**a**) (*principal*) principal(e); (*importance*) capital(e); **p. minister** premier ministre *m*; *Math* **p. number** nombre *m* premier; **p. time** (*on TV*) prime time *m* (**b**) (*excellent*) excellent(e); **a p. example (of)** un exemple typique (de); **p. quality** de premier choix
  3 *vt* (**a**) (*engine, pump*) amorcer; (*surface*) apprêter (**b**) (*provide with information*) **to p. sb for an interview/an exam** préparer qn à un entretien/un examen
primer¹ ['praɪmə(r)] *n* (*paint*) apprêt *m*
primer² *n* (*textbook*) manuel *m* élémentaire
primeval [praɪ'mi:vəl] *adj* primitif(ive)
primitive ['prɪmɪtɪv] *adj* (*original*) primitif(ive); (*basic*) primitif, rudimentaire
primly ['prɪmlɪ] *adv* d'une manière guindée
primordial [praɪ'mɔ:dɪəl] *adj* primordial(e); **p. soup** soupe *f* primitive
primrose ['prɪmrəʊz] *n* (*plant*) primevère *f*; **p. yellow** jaune pâle *inv*
primula ['prɪmjʊlə] *n* primula *f*
primus (stove)® ['praɪməs('stəʊv)] *n* réchaud *m* portatif
prince [prɪns] *n* prince *m*; **the P. of Wales** le prince de Galles; **P. Charming** le prince charmant
princely ['prɪnslɪ] *adj also Fig* princier(ère)
princess [prɪn'ses] *n* princesse *f*; **the P. Royal** la princesse royale (*fille aînée du souverain*)
principal ['prɪnsɪpəl] **1** *n* (**a**) *Am & Ir* (*of school*) directeur(trice) *m,f* (**b**) (*of university*) ≃ président *m*
  2 *adj* principal(e)
principality [prɪnsɪ'pælɪtɪ] (*pl* **principalities**) *n* principauté *f*
principle ['prɪnsɪpəl] *n* principe *m*; **in p.** en principe; **on p.** par principe
principled ['prɪnsɪpəld] *adj* (*person*) de principes; (*behaviour*) dicté(e) par des principes; **to be p.** avoir des principes

print [prɪnt] **1** *n* (**a**) *(of fingers)* empreinte *f* (**b**) *(printed matter)* texte *m*; **in p.** disponible en librairie; **out of p.** épuisé(e); **to appear in p.** être publié(e) (**c**) *(characters)* caractères *mpl*; *Fig* **to read the small p.** *(in contract)* lire ce qu'il y a d'écrit en petits caractères (**d**) *(engraving)* estampe *f*; *(photograph)* épreuve *f*; *(textile)* imprimé *m*
2 *vt* (**a**) *(book, newspaper)* imprimer (**b**) *(write clearly)* écrire en script (**c**) *(in photography)* **to p. a negative** tirer une épreuve d'un négatif
3 *vi (write clearly)* écrire en script
▸**print out** *vt sep Comput* imprimer
printed ['prɪntɪd] *adj* imprimé(e); **p. circuit** circuit *m* imprimé; **p. matter** imprimés *mpl*
printer ['prɪntə(r)] *n (person)* imprimeur *m*; *(machine)* imprimante *f*
printing ['prɪntɪŋ] *n (process, industry)* imprimerie *f*; *(action)* tirage *m*; **p. error** faute *f* d'impression; **p. press** presse *f*
printout ['prɪntaʊt] *n Comput* sortie *f* papier
prior[1] ['praɪə(r)] **1** *adj* antérieur(e); **to have p. knowledge (of sth)** avoir une connaissance préalable (de qch)
2 *adv* **p. to** avant
prior[2] *n Rel* prieur *m*
prioritize [praɪ'ɒrɪtaɪz] **1** *vt* donner la priorité à
2 *vi* établir ses priorités
priority [praɪ'ɒrɪtɪ] *(pl* **priorities)** *n* priorité *f*; **to have** *or* **take p. over sb/sth** avoir la priorité sur qn/qch; **to get one's priorities right/wrong** savoir/ne pas savoir ce qui est important
priory ['praɪərɪ] *(pl* **priories)** *n Rel* prieuré *m*
prise [praɪz] *vt* **to p. sth off/open** retirer/ouvrir qch en forçant; *Fig* **to p. sth out of sb** *(secret, truth)* soutirer qch à qn
prism ['prɪzəm] *n* prisme *m*
prison ['prɪzən] *n* prison *f*; **p. camp** camp *m* de prisonniers; **p. officer** gardien(enne) *m,f* de prison
prisoner ['prɪzənə(r)] *n* prisonnier(ère) *m,f*; **to take/hold sb p.** faire/retenir qn prisonnier; *Fig* **to take no prisoners** être impitoyable; **p. of war** prisonnier de guerre
prissy ['prɪsɪ] *adj Fam* collet monté *inv*
pristine ['prɪstiːn] *adj* impeccable
privacy ['prɪvəsɪ, 'praɪvəsɪ] *n* intimité *f*; **in the p. of one's own home** dans l'intimité de son foyer
private ['praɪvɪt] **1** *adj* (**a**) *(personal)* personnel(elle); **can we go somewhere p.?** est-ce qu'on peut se voir en privé?; **p. life** vie *f* privée; *Parl* **p. member** simple député *m*; *Fam* **p. parts** parties *fpl* (génitales) (**b**) *(secret)* confidentiel(elle); **p. and confidential** *(on letter)* confidentiel (**c**) *(for personal use)* privé(e); **p. house** maison *f* particulière; **p. lessons** leçons *fpl* particulières; **p. line** ligne *f* privée; **p. office** bureau *m* personnel; **p. secretary** secrétaire *mf* particulier(ère) (**d**) *(not state-run)* privé(e); **p. detective** *or* **investigator** détective *m* privé; **p. education** enseignement *m* privé; **p. enterprise** entreprise *f* privée; **p. health insurance** assurance *f* maladie privée; **p. school** école *f* privée; **p. sector** secteur *m* privé (**e**) *(not for the public)* privé(e); **p. party** soirée *f* privée; **p. property** propriété *f* privée; **p. road** voie *f* privée
2 *n* (**a**) **in p.** en privé
(**b**) *(soldier)* simple soldat *m*

privately ['praɪvɪtlɪ] *adv (in private)* en privé; **to be p. educated** faire sa scolarité dans le privé; **p. owned** *(company)* privé(e); *(hotel)* familial(e)
privation [praɪ'veɪʃən] *n* privation *f*
privatization [praɪvɪtaɪ'zeɪʃən] *n* privatisation *f*
privatize ['praɪvɪtaɪz] *vt* privatiser
privet ['prɪvɪt] *n* troène *m*
privilege ['prɪvɪlɪdʒ] **1** *n* privilège *m*; **to have the p. of doing sth** avoir le privilège de faire qch
2 *vt* **to be privileged to do sth** avoir le privilège de faire qch
privy ['prɪvɪ] **1** *n (pl* **privies)** *Old-fashioned (toilet)* cabinets *mpl*
2 *adj* (**a**) *Formal* **to be p. to sth** avoir connaissance de qch (**b**) *Br Pol* **the P. Council** le Conseil privé du souverain
prize[1] [praɪz] **1** *n (award)* prix *m*; **to win a p.** remporter un prix; *Fig* **no prizes for guessing** ce n'est pas difficile de deviner; **p. day** jour *m* de distribution des prix; **p. draw** tombola *f*; **p. money** argent *m* du prix
2 *vt (value)* attacher de la valeur à
prize[2] = **prise**
prizefight ['praɪzfaɪt] *n* combat *m* professionnel
prizefighter ['praɪzfaɪtə(r)] *n* boxeur *m* professionnel
prizegiving ['praɪzgɪvɪŋ] *n* distribution *f* des prix
prizewinner ['praɪzwɪnə(r)] *n* gagnant(e) *m,f*
pro[1] [prəʊ] *(pl* **pros)** *n Fam (professional)* pro *mf*
pro[2] **1** *n (advantage)* **the pros and cons** le pour et le contre
2 *prep (in favour of)* pour
proactive [prəʊ'æktɪv] *adj* qui fait preuve d'initiative
pro-am ['prəʊ'æm] *n Sport* tournoi *m* professionnel-amateur
probability [prɒbə'bɪlɪtɪ] *(pl* **probabilities)** *n* probabilité *f*; **in all p....** il y a de fortes chances que...
probable ['prɒbəbəl] *adj* probable
probably ['prɒbəblɪ] *adv* probablement
probation [prə'beɪʃən] *n (in job)* période *f* d'essai; *Law* mise *f* en liberté surveillée; **on p.** *(in job)* à l'essai; *Law* en liberté surveillée; **p. officer** agent *m* de probation
probationary [prə'beɪʃənərɪ] *adj* d'essai
probationer [prə'beɪʃənə(r)] *n (in job)* personne *f* à l'essai
probe [prəʊb] **1** *n* (**a**) *(instrument)* sonde *f*; **(space) p.** sonde spatiale (**b**) *Fam (enquiry)* enquête *f*
2 *vt* (**a**) *(prod)* sonder (**b**) *(enquire into)* enquêter sur
3 *vi* **to p. into sth** *(past, private life)* fouiller dans qch
probity ['prəʊbɪtɪ] *n Formal* probité *f*
problem ['prɒbləm] *n* problème *m*; *Fam* **no p.!** pas de problème!; **p. area** *(in town)* quartier *m* à problèmes; *(in project)* source *f* de problèmes; **p. child** enfant *mf* à problèmes; **p. page** courrier *m* du cœur
problematic(al) [prɒblɪ'mætɪk(əl)] *adj* problématique
procedure [prə'siːdʒə(r)] *n* procédure *f*
proceed [prə'siːd] **1** *vt* **to p. to do sth** se mettre à faire qch
2 *vi* (**a**) *(go on)* se poursuivre; **to p. to sth** passer à qch; **to p. with sth** poursuivre qch; **how shall we p.?** comment allons-nous procéder? (**b**) *(result)* **to p. from** provenir de
proceedings [prə'siːdɪŋz] *npl* (**a**) *(events)* opérations *fpl* (**b**) *Law* poursuites *fpl*; **to take p. (against sb)** engager des poursuites (contre qn)

proceeds ['prəʊsiːdz] *npl* recette *f*

process ['prəʊses] **1** *n* processus *m*; **by a p. of elimination** en procédant par élimination; **she fell down the stairs, breaking her leg in the p.** elle est tombée dans les escaliers, et s'est cassée la jambe; **to be in the p. of doing sth** être en train de faire qch
  2 *vt (raw material, information, application)* traiter; *(film)* développer; **processed food** aliments *mpl* conditionnés

processing ['prəʊsesɪŋ] *n (of raw material, information)* traitement *m*; *(of photographs)* développement *m*; *Comput* **p. language** langage *m* de traitement; *Comput* **p. speed** vitesse *f* de traitement

procession [prə'seʃən] *n* défilé *m*; **in p.** en cortège

processor ['prəʊsesə(r)] *n Comput* processeur *m*

pro-choice ['prəʊtʃɔɪs] *adj* partisan(e) de l'avortement

proclaim [prə'kleɪm] *vt* proclamer

proclamation [prɒklə'meɪʃən] *n* proclamation *f*

proclivity [prə'klɪvɪtɪ] *(pl* **proclivities***) n Formal* tendance *f* **(for** à**)**

procrastinate [prəʊ'kræstɪneɪt] *vi* atermoyer

procrastination [prəʊkræstɪ'neɪʃən] *n* atermoiements *mpl*

procreate ['prəʊkrɪeɪt] *vi* procréer

procreation [prəʊkrɪ'eɪʃən] *n* procréation *f*

procure [prə'kjʊə(r)] *vt* procurer **(for sb** à qn**); to p. sth (for oneself)** se procurer qch

procurement [prə'kjʊəmənt] *n* acquisition *f*

prod [prɒd] **1** *n* **to give sb a p.** donner un petit coup à qn; *Fig* pousser qn; **to give sth a p.** donner un petit coup à qch
  2 *vt (pt & pp* **prodded***) (poke)* donner un petit coup dans; *Fig* **to p. sb (into doing sth)** pousser qn (à faire qch)

prodigal ['prɒdɪgəl] *adj* prodigue

prodigious [prə'dɪdʒəs] *adj* prodigieux(euse)

prodigy ['prɒdɪdʒɪ] *(pl* **prodigies***) n* prodige *m*

produce 1 *n* ['prɒdjuːs] *(products)* produits *mpl*
  2 *vt* [prə'djuːs] **(a)** *(create)* produire; *(machine, car)* fabriquer; *(reaction, feeling)* entraîner **(b)** *(present) (ticket, passport)* présenter; *(documents, alibi)* fournir; *(from pocket, bag)* sortir **(c)** *(film, play, radio, TV programme)* produire

producer [prə'djuːsə(r)] *n* **(a)** *(of crops, goods)* producteur(trice) *m,f* **(b)** *(of film, play, radio, TV programme)* producteur(trice) *m,f*

product ['prɒdʌkt] *n* produit *m*; *Com* **p. development** mise *f* au point de produit

production [prə'dʌkʃən] *n* **(a)** *(manufacture)* production *f*, fabrication *f*; **to go into/out of p.** être/ne plus être fabriqué(e); **p. costs** coûts *mpl* de production; **p. line** chaîne *f* de fabrication; **p. manager** directeur(trice) *m,f* de production; **p. process** procédé *m* de fabrication; **p. target** cible *f* de production **(b)** *(of document, ticket)* présentation *f*; **on p. of** sur présentation de **(c)** *(play)* mise *f* en scène; *(film, radio, TV programme)* production *f*

productive [prə'dʌktɪv] *adj* productif(ive)

productivity [prɒdʌk'tɪvɪtɪ] *n Ind* productivité *f*; **p. agreement** accord *m* de productivité; **p. bonus** prime *f* de rendement

Prof *(abbr* **Professor***)* **(a)** *(title)* Professeur **(b)** *Fam* prof *mf*

profane [prə'feɪn] **1** *adj* **(a)** *(language)* grossier(ère) **(b)** *Rel (secular)* profane
  2 *vt* profaner

profanity [prə'fænɪtɪ] *(pl* **profanities***) n* grossièreté *f*

profess [prə'fes] *vt* **(a)** *(declare)* professer **(b)** *(claim)* prétendre

professed [prə'fest] *adj* **(a)** *(self-declared)* avoué(e) **(b)** *(pretended)* prétendu(e)

profession [prə'feʃən] *n* **(a)** *(occupation)* profession *f*; **the medical/teaching p.** le corps médical/enseignant; **by p.** de profession **(b)** *(declaration)* déclaration *f*

professional [prə'feʃənəl] **1** *n* professionnel(elle) *m,f*
  2 *adj (paid, competent)* professionnel(elle); *(soldier)* de carrière; *(army)* de métier; **he made a very p. job of it** il a fait du bon travail; **to turn** *or* **go p.** *(of sportsperson)* passer en catégorie professionnelle; **to take p. advice on sth** demander l'avis d'un professionnel sur qch; **p. misconduct** faute *f* professionnelle; **p. training** formation *f* professionnelle

professionalism [prə'feʃənəlɪzəm] *n* professionnalisme *m*

professor [prə'fesə(r)] *n Univ Br* ≃ professeur *m*; *Am* enseignant(e) *m,f* d'université

proffer ['prɒfə(r)] *vt Formal (advice)* offrir; *(opinion)* avancer; *(thanks)* présenter; *(hand, object)* tendre

proficiency [prə'fɪʃənsɪ] *n* compétence *f* **(in** *or* **at** en *ou* dans**);** *(in language)* maîtrise *f* **(in** en**)**

proficient [prə'fɪʃənt] *adj* compétent(e) **(in** *or* **at** en *ou* dans**)**

profile ['prəʊfaɪl] **1** *n* **(a)** *(side view, outline)* profil *m*; **to keep a low p.** garder un profil bas **(b)** *(description)* por-trait *m*
  2 *vt (describe)* faire le portrait de

profiling ['prəʊfaɪlɪŋ] *n Psy* profilage *m*

profit ['prɒfɪt] **1** *n* **(a)** *(of company, on deal)* bénéfice *m*, profit *m*; **at a p.** à profit; **to make a p.** réaliser un bénéfice; **p. and loss account** compte *m* de pertes et profits; **p. margin** marge *f* bénéficiaire **(b)** *(advantage)* avantage *m*
  2 *vi* **to p. by** *or* **from** tirer profit de

profitability [prɒfɪtə'bɪlɪtɪ] *n* rentabilité *f*

profitable ['prɒfɪtəbəl] *adj (company, deal)* rentable; *(experience)* profitable

profitably ['prɒfɪtəblɪ] *adv (trade, operate)* à profit; *(use one's time)* profitablement

profiteer [prɒfɪ'tɪə(r)] *Pej* **1** *n* profiteur(euse) *m,f*
  2 *vi* profiter d'une situation pour faire des bénéfices

profit-making ['prɒfɪtmeɪkɪŋ] *adj* rentable

profit-sharing ['prɒfɪtʃeərɪŋ] *n Com* intéressement *m*

profligate ['prɒflɪgət] *adj Formal* prodigue

profound [prə'faʊnd] *adj* profond(e)

profundity [prə'fʌndɪtɪ] *(pl* **profundities***) n* profondeur *f*

profuse [prə'fjuːs] *adj* abondant(e)

profusely [prə'fjuːslɪ] *adv (sweat, bleed)* abondamment; **to apologize p.** se confondre en excuses; **to thank sb p.** remercier qn avec effusion

profusion [prə'fjuːʒən] *n* profusion *f*

progeny ['prɒdʒɪnɪ] *(pl* **progenies***) n Formal* progéniture *f*

prognosis [prɒg'nəʊsɪs] *(pl* **prognoses** [prɒg'nəʊsiːz]*) n Med* pronostic *m*; *Fig* pronostics

program¹ ['prəʊgræm] *Comput* **1** *n* programme *m*
  2 *vt & vi* programmer

program² *Am* = programme
programmable [prəʊ'græməbəl] *adj* programmable
programme, *Am* **program** ['prəʊgræm] **1** *n (for play, of political party)* programme *m*; *(on TV, radio)* émission *f*; **p. seller** vendeur(euse) *m,f* de programmes
 2 *vt (machine)* programmer; **to p. sth to do sth** programmer qch pour faire qch
programmed ['prəʊgræmd] *adj Educ* **p. instruction** *or* **learning** enseignement *m* programmé
programmer ['prəʊgræmə(r)] *n Comput* programmeur(euse) *m,f*
progress1 *n* ['prəʊgres] (**a**) *(improvement)* progrès *m*; **to make p.** faire des progrès (**b**) *(movement)* marche *f*; **in p.** en cours; **to make p. (in sth)** progresser (dans qch); **p. report** rapport *m*
 2 *vi* [prə'gres] (**a**) *(improve)* progresser (**b**) *(advance)* avancer; *(of meeting)* progresser
progression [prə'greʃən] *n* progression *f*
progressive [prə'gresɪv] **1** *adj* (**a**) *(increasing)* progressif(ive); **p. disease** maladie *f* évolutive (**b**) *(radical) (person, idea)* progressiste
 2 *n (radical)* progressiste *mf*
progressively [prə'gresɪvlɪ] *adv* progressivement
prohibit [prə'hɪbɪt] *vt* interdire; **to p. sb from doing sth** interdire à qn de faire qch
prohibition [prəʊɪ'bɪʃən] *n* interdiction *f*; *Am Hist* la Prohibition
prohibitive [prə'hɪbɪtɪv] *adj* prohibitif(ive)
prohibitively [prə'hɪbɪtɪvlɪ] *adv* **p. expensive** à un prix prohibitif
project1 *n* ['prɒdʒekt] *(undertaking, plan)* projet *m*; *(at school)* dossier *m*; *(at university)* mémoire *m*; *Com* **p. manager** directeur(trice) *m,f* de projet
 2 *vt* [prə'dʒekt] (**a**) *(plan)* prévoir (**b**) *(propel)* projeter; **to p. one's voice** projeter sa voix
 3 *vi* [prə'dʒekt] *(protrude)* dépasser
projectile [prə'dʒektaɪl] *n* projectile *m*
projection [prə'dʒekʃən] *n* (**a**) *(in general)* projection *f*; **p. room** *(in cinema)* salle *f* de projection (**b**) *(protruding part)* saillie *f*
projectionist [prə'dʒekʃənɪst] *n* projectionniste *mf*
projector [prə'dʒektə(r)] *n* projecteur *m*
prolapse ['prəʊlæps] *n Med* prolapsus *m*
proletarian [prəʊlɪ'teərɪən] **1** *n* prolétaire *mf*
 2 *adj* prolétarien(enne)
proletariat [prəʊlɪ'teərɪət] *n* prolétariat *m*
pro-life ['prəʊlaɪf] *adj* contre l'avortement
proliferate [prə'lɪfəreɪt] *vi* proliférer
proliferation [prəlɪfə'reɪʃən] *n* prolifération *f*
prolific [prə'lɪfɪk] *adj* prolifique
prolix ['prəʊlɪks] *adj Formal* prolixe
prologue ['prəʊlɒg] *n* prologue *m*
prolong [prə'lɒŋ] *vt* prolonger
prom [prɒm] *n* (**a**) *Br Fam (at seaside)* front *m* de mer (**b**) *Br Fam (concert)* concert *m* (**c**) *Am (school dance)* soirée *f* dansante
promenade ['prɒmənɑːd] **1** *n Br (at seaside)* front *m* de mer; **p. deck** *(on ship)* pont *m* promenade
 2 *vi* se promener
prominence ['prɒmɪnəns] *n* (**a**) *(of land)* saillie *f*; *(of physical feature)* proéminence *f* (**b**) *(importance)* importance *f*; **to give sth p.** donner de l'importance à qch; **to come to p.** devenir célèbre

prominent ['prɒmɪnənt] *adj* (**a**) *(peak, landscape)* en saillie; *(physical feature)* proéminent(e); **to be in a p. position** être en évidence (**b**) *(important)* important(e)
prominently ['prɒmɪnəntlɪ] *adv* bien en vue; **to figure p. in sth** figurer en bonne place dans qch
promiscuity [prɒmɪs'kjuːɪtɪ] *n* promiscuité *f* sexuelle
promiscuous [prə'mɪskjʊəs] *adj* qui a des partenaires multiples
promise ['prɒmɪs] **1** *n* (**a**) *(pledge)* promesse *f*; **to make a p.** faire une promesse; **to keep/break one's p.** tenir/ne pas tenir sa promesse (**b**) *(potential)* **to show p.** promettre; **she never fulfilled her early p.** *(as a writer, musician)* elle n'a jamais eu le succès qu'elle promettait d'avoir
 2 *vt* promettre (**to do** de faire); **to p. sth to sb, to p. sb sth** promettre qch à qn; **it promises to be hot** le temps promet d'être chaud
promising ['prɒmɪsɪŋ] *adj* prometteur(euse)
promontory ['prɒməntərɪ] *(pl* **promontories**) *n* promontoire *m*
promote [prə'məʊt] *vt* (**a**) *(raise in rank, encourage)* promouvoir; **to be promoted** *(of officer, employee)* être promu(e); *(of football team)* passer dans la division supérieure; **to p. sb's interests** servir les intérêts de qn (**b**) *Com* faire la publicité de
promoter [prə'məʊtə(r)] *n (of theory, cause)* défenseur(euse) *m,f*; *(of boxing match)* organisateur(trice) *m,f*; *(of show)* imprésario *m*
promotion [prə'məʊʃən] *n* promotion *f*
promotional [prə'məʊʃənəl] *adj* promotionnel(elle)
prompt [prɒmpt] **1** *adj* (**a**) *(swift)* rapide; **p. payment** paiement *m* dans les plus brefs délais (**b**) *(punctual)* ponctuel(elle)
 2 *adv* **at three o'clock p.** à trois heures précises
 3 *vt* (**a**) *(cause)* provoquer; **to p. sb to do sth** pousser qn à faire qch (**b**) **to p. sb** *(encourage to speak)* = aider quelqu'un à répondre en lui suggérant quelque chose; **"was he tall?" the policeman prompted** "est-ce qu'il était grand?" suggéra le policier (**c**) *(in theatre)* souffler à
 4 *n* (**a**) **to give an actor a p.** souffler sa réplique à un acteur (**b**) *Comput* invite *f*
prompter ['prɒmptə(r)] *n Theat* souffleur(euse) *m,f*
promptly ['prɒmptlɪ] *adv (rapidly, punctually)* rapidement; *(immediately)* immédiatement
prone [prəʊn] *adj* (**a**) *(inclined)* **to be p. to sth** être sujet(ette) à qch; **to be p. to do sth** avoir tendance à faire qch (**b**) *Formal (lying face down)* couché(e) sur le ventre
prong [prɒŋ] *n (of fork)* dent *f*
pronoun ['prəʊnaʊn] *n Gram* pronom *m*
pronounce [prə'naʊns] **1** *vt* (**a**) *(word)* prononcer (**b**) *(declare) (opinion)* émettre; **to p. that...** déclarer que...; **to p. oneself for/against sth** se prononcer en faveur de/contre qch; **he was pronounced dead/ innocent** il a été déclaré mort/innocent; *Law* **to p. sentence** rendre le verdict
 2 *vi* **to p. on** se prononcer sur
pronounced [prə'naʊnst] *adj* prononcé(e)
pronouncement [prə'naʊnsmənt] *n Formal* déclaration *f*
pronto ['prɒntəʊ] *adv Fam* illico
pronunciation [prənʌnsɪ'eɪʃən] *n* prononciation *f*
proof [pruːf] **1** *n* (**a**) *(evidence)* preuve *f*; **to give p. of sth** prouver qch; **p. of identity** pièce *f* d'identité; **p. of**

purchase preuve *f* d'achat; **to put sth to the p.** mettre qch à l'épreuve; *Prov* **the p. of the pudding is in the eating** il faut juger les choses à l'usage (**b**) *Typ* épreuve *f* (**c**) *(of alcohol)* teneur *f* en alcool; **to be 40 percent p.** faire 40 degrés

 2 *adj (resistant)* **to be p. against sth** être résistant(e) à qch

proofread ['pruːfriːd] *(pt & pp* **proofread** ['pruːfred] *) vt Typ* relire, corriger

proofreader ['pruːfriːdə(r)] *n Typ* correcteur(trice) *m,f*

prop [prɒp] **1** *n* (**a**) *(physical support)* support *m*; *(emotional support)* soutien *m* (**b**) *(in theatre)* accessoire *m*

 2 *vt (pt & pp* **propped**) **to p. sth against sth** appuyer qch contre qch

▸**prop up** *vt sep (building, tunnel)* étayer; *Fig (economy, regime)* soutenir; **to p. sth up against sth** appuyer qch contre qch

propaganda [prɒpə'gændə] *n* propagande *f*

propagate ['prɒpəgeɪt] **1** *vt* propager

 2 *vi* se propager

propagation [prɒpə'geɪʃən] *n* propagation *f*

propane ['prəʊpeɪn] *n Chem* propane *m*

propel [prə'pel] *(pt & pp* **propelled**) *vt* propulser; *Fig* pousser

propellant, propellent [prə'pelənt] *n (for rocket)* propergol *m*; *(for aerosol)* gaz *m* propulseur

propeller [prə'pelə(r)] *n* hélice *f*

propelling pencil [prə'pelɪŋ'pensəl] *n* porte-mine *m inv*

propensity [prə'pensɪtɪ] *(pl* **propensities**) *n* propension *f* (**for** à)

proper ['prɒpə(r)] *adj* (**a**) *(correct, real)* vrai(e); *(word)* correct(e); *Gram* **p. noun** nom *m* propre (**b**) *(appropriate)* bon (bonne); *(equipment, clothing)* adéquat(e); *(behaviour)* convenable (**c**) *(characteristic)* **p. to** propre à (**d**) *Br Fam (for emphasis)* **it was a p. disaster** c'était une véritable catastrophe; **we're in a p. mess** nous voilà propres; **he's a p. fool** c'est vraiment un imbécile

properly ['prɒpəlɪ] *adv* (**a**) *(correctly)* correctement (**b**) *(suitably)* convenablement

property ['prɒpətɪ] *(pl* **properties**) *n* (**a**) *(possessions)* biens *mpl*; *(land, house)* propriété *f*; **p. developer** promoteur(trice) *m,f* (immobilier(ère)); **p. market** marché *m* immobilier; **p. tax** impôt *m* foncier (**b**) *(quality)* propriété *f*

prophecy ['prɒfɪsɪ] *(pl* **prophecies**) *n* prophétie *f*

prophesy ['prɒfɪsaɪ] *(pt & pp* **prophesied**) *vt* prédire

prophet ['prɒfɪt] *n* prophète *m*

prophetic [prə'fetɪk] *adj* prophétique

prophylactic [prɒfɪ'læktɪk] *Med* **1** *n* prophylactique *m*; *(condom)* préservatif *m*

 2 *adj* prophylactique

propitiate [prə'pɪʃɪeɪt] *vt Formal* gagner les faveurs de

propitious [prə'pɪʃəs] *adj Formal* favorable

proportion [prə'pɔːʃən] **1** *n* (**a**) *(relationship)* proportion *f*; **in p.** proportionné(e); **out of p.** disproportionné(e); **the payment is out of all p. to the work involved** la rétribution n'est pas du tout proportionnelle au travail requis (**b**) *(part, amount)* proportion *f*; **to get sth out of p.** exagérer qch; **try to keep things in p.** essaie de ne pas dramatiser (**c**) **proportions** *(dimensions)* proportions *fpl*

 2 *vt* proportionner

proportional [prə'pɔːʃənəl] *adj* proportionnel(elle) (**to** à); *Pol* **p. representation** (représentation *f*) proportionnelle *f*

proportionate [prə'pɔːʃənɪt] *adj* proportionnel(elle) (**to** à)

proposal [prə'pəʊzəl] *n (offer)* proposition *f*; *(plan)* projet *m*; **p. (of marriage)** demande *f* en mariage

propose [prə'pəʊz] **1** *vt* proposer; **to p. a toast** porter un toast; **to p. to do sth, to p. doing sth** *(suggest)* suggérer de faire qch; *(intend)* avoir l'intention de faire qch

 2 *vi* **to p. to sb** demander qn en mariage

proposition [prɒpə'zɪʃən] **1** *n* proposition *f*

 2 *vt* faire des avances à

propound [prə'paʊnd] *vt Formal* exposer

proprietary [prə'praɪətərɪ] *adj (air, attitude)* possessif(ive); *Com* **p. brand** marque *f* déposée

proprietor [prə'praɪətə(r)] *n* propriétaire *mf*

propriety [prə'praɪətɪ] *n* bienséance *f*

propulsion [prə'pʌlʃən] *n* propulsion *f*

pro rata ['prəʊ'rɑːtə] *adj & adv* au prorata

prosaic [prəʊ'zeɪk] *adj* prosaïque

proscribe [prəʊ'skraɪb] *vt* proscrire

prose [prəʊz] *n* prose *f*; *(translation in exam)* thème *m*

prosecute ['prɒsɪkjuːt] *Law* **1** *vt* poursuivre en justice

 2 *vi (of lawyer)* représenter le ministère public

prosecution [prɒsɪ'kjuːʃən] *n Law (proceedings)* poursuites *fpl* judiciaires; **the p.** *(in trial)* les plaignants *mpl*; *(in crown case)* ≃ le ministère public

prosecutor ['prɒsɪkjuːtə(r)] *n Law* procureur *m*

prospect 1 *n* ['prɒspekt] (**a**) *(expectation, thought)* perspective *f* (**b**) *(chance, likelihood)* perspectives *fpl*; **there is no p. of success** il n'y a aucune chance de réussite; **future prospects** perspectives d'avenir; **a job with prospects** un travail qui offre des perspectives d'avenir (**c**) *(view)* vue *f*

 2 *vi* [prə'spekt] **to p. for gold** chercher de l'or

prospective [prə'spektɪv] *adj (future)* futur(e); *(potential)* potentiel(elle)

prospector [prə'spektə(r)] *n* prospecteur(trice) *m,f*; *(for gold)* chercheur(euse) *m,f*

prospectus [prə'spektəs] *n* prospectus *m*

prosper ['prɒspə(r)] *vi* prospérer

prosperity [prɒs'perɪtɪ] *n* prospérité *f*

prosperous ['prɒspərəs] *adj* prospère

prostate ['prɒsteɪt] *n Anat* **p. (gland)** prostate *f*

prosthesis [prɒs'θiːsɪs] *(pl* **prostheses** [prɒs'θiːsiːz] *) n* prothèse *f*

prostitute ['prɒstɪtjuːt] **1** *n* prostituée *f*; **male p.** prostitué *m*

 2 *vt also Fig* **to p. oneself** se prostituer

prostitution [prɒstɪ'tjuːʃən] *n* prostitution *f*

prostrate 1 *adj* ['prɒstreɪt] *(lying down)* couché(e); *Fig* **p. with grief** terrassé(e) par le chagrin

 2 *vt* [prə'streɪt] **to p. oneself** se prosterner

protagonist [prə'tægənɪst] *n* protagoniste *mf*; *(of idea, theory)* partisan(e) *m,f*

protease ['prəʊteɪz] *n* protéase *f*; **p. inhibitor** antiprotéase *f*, inhibiteur *m* de protéase

protect [prə'tekt] *vt* protéger (**from** *or* **against** de)

protection [prə'tekʃən] *n* protection *f*; **p. money** = argent versé à un racketteur; **p. racket** racket *m*

protectionism [prə'tekʃənɪzəm] *n Econ* protectionnisme *m*

protective [prə'tektɪv] *adj* protecteur(trice); **to put sb in p. custody** mettre qn en lieu sûr

protector [prə'tektə(r)] *n (device)* protecteur *m*; *(person)* protecteur(trice) *m,f*

protégé ['prɒtəʒeɪ] *n* protégé(e) *m,f*

protein ['prəʊtiːn] *n* protéine *f*

protest 1 *n* ['prəʊtest] protestation *f*; **to do sth under p.** faire qch contre son gré; **to do sth in p.** faire qch en signe de protestation; **p. song** chanson *f* engagée; **p. vote** vote *m* de protestation

  2 *vt* [prə'test] (**a**) *(protest against)* protester contre (**b**) *(one's innocence, love)* protester de; **to p. that...** protester en disant que...

  3 *vi* [prə'test] protester (**about/against** à propos de/contre)

Protestant ['prɒtɪstənt] *n & adj* protestant(e) *m,f*

Protestantism ['prɒtɪstəntɪzəm] *n* protestantisme *m*

protestation [prɒtes'teɪʃən] *n* protestation *f*

protester [prə'testə(r)] *n* protestataire *mf*

protocol ['prəʊtəkɒl] *n* protocole *m*

proton ['prəʊtɒn] *n Phys* proton *m*

prototype ['prəʊtətaɪp] *n* prototype *m*

protracted [prə'træktɪd] *adj* prolongé(e)

protractor [prə'træktə(r)] *n* rapporteur *m*

protrude [prə'truːd] *vi* dépasser (**from** de); *(of jaw, teeth)* avancer

protruding [prə'truːdɪŋ] *adj* en saillie; *(jaw, teeth)* qui avance

protuberance [prə'tjuːbərəns] *n* protubérance *f*

proud [praʊd] **1** *adj (person)* fier(ère) (**of** de); *(moment)* grand(e); **as p. as a peacock** fier comme un paon

  2 *adv* **to do sb p.** faire honneur à qn; **to do oneself p.** se distinguer

proudly ['praʊdlɪ] *adv* fièrement

prove [pruːv] *(pp* **proven** ['pruːvən, 'prəʊvən] *or* **proved**) **1** *vt (demonstrate)* prouver; **to p. sb wrong/ guilty** prouver que qn a tort/est coupable; **to p. oneself** se prouver quelque chose

  2 *vi* **to p. (to be) correct** se révéler correct(e)

proverb ['prɒvɜːb] *n* proverbe *m*

proverbial [prə'vɜːbɪəl] *adj* proverbial(e)

provide [prə'vaɪd] *vt* (**a**) *(supply)* fournir; *(service, support)* offrir; **to p. sb with sth** fournir qch à qn (**b**) *(stipulate)* stipuler

▸**provide against** *vt insep (danger, possibility)* parer à

▸**provide for** *vt insep* (**a**) *(support)* pourvoir aux besoins de; **he left his family well provided for** il a laissé sa famille à l'abri du besoin (**b**) *Formal (allow for)* parer à

provided [prə'vaɪdɪd] *conj* **p. (that)** à condition que + *subjunctive*

providence ['prɒvɪdəns] *n* providence *f*

providential [prɒvɪ'denʃəl] *adj* providentiel(elle)

provider [prə'vaɪdə(r)] *n* pourvoyeur(euse) *m,f*

providing [prə'vaɪdɪŋ] *conj* **p. (that)** à condition que + *subjunctive*

province ['prɒvɪns] *n* (**a**) *(of country)* province *f*; **in the provinces** en province (**b**) *Fig (domain)* domaine *m*

provincial [prə'vɪnʃəl] *adj* de province; *Pej (parochial)* provincial(e)

provision [prə'vɪʒən] *n* (**a**) **provisions** *(supplies)* provisions *fpl* (**b**) *(supplying)* approvisionnement *m* (**of** en); *(of services)* prestation *f* (**of** de) (**c**) *(allowance)* to

make p. for sth prévoir qch (**d**) *(in treaty)* disposition *f*; *(in contract)* clause *f*

provisional [prə'vɪʒənəl] *adj* provisoire

provisionally [prə'vɪʒənəlɪ] *adv* provisoirement

proviso [prə'vaɪzəʊ] *(pl* **provisos** *or* **provisoes**) *n* condition *f*; **with the p. that** à condition que + *subjunctive*

provocation [prɒvə'keɪʃən] *n* provocation *f*; **at the slightest p.** pour un rien

provocative [prə'vɒkətɪv] *adj* provocateur(trice)

provoke [prə'vəʊk] *vt* provoquer; **to p. sb into doing sth** pousser qn à faire qch

provoking [prə'vəʊkɪŋ] *adj (irritating)* agaçant(e)

provost ['prɒvəst] *n* (**a**) *Br Univ (head of college)* doyen *m* (**b**) *Scot (mayor)* maire *m*

prow [praʊ] *n (of ship)* proue *f*

prowess ['praʊɪs] *n (skill)* prouesses *fpl*

prowl [praʊl] **1** *n* **to be on the p.** *(of person, animal)* être en chasse; **to be on the p. for sth** être à l'affût de qch

  2 *vt (streets, area)* rôder dans

  3 *vi* rôder

prowler ['praʊlə(r)] *n* rôdeur(euse) *m,f*

proximity [prɒk'sɪmɪtɪ] *n* proximité *f*; **in p. to** à proximité de

proxy ['prɒksɪ] *(pl* **proxies**) *n (power)* procuration *f*; *(person)* mandataire *mf*; **by p.** par procuration; *Comput* **p. server** serveur *m* proxy; *Pol* **p. vote** vote *m* par procuration

Prozac® ['prəʊzæk] *n* Prozac *m*

prude [pruːd] *n* prude *f*

prudence ['pruːdəns] *n* prudence *f*

prudent ['pruːdənt] *adj* prudent(e)

prudish ['pruːdɪʃ] *adj* pudibond(e)

prune¹ [pruːn] *n (fruit)* pruneau *m*

prune² *vt (bush, tree)* tailler; *Fig (article)* élaguer

prurient ['prʊərɪənt] *adj* malsain(e)

Prussia ['prʌʃə] *n* la Prusse

Prussian ['prʌʃən] **1** *n* Prussien(enne) *m,f*

  2 *adj* prussien(enne)

pry [praɪ] *(pt & pp* **pried**) *vi* être indiscret(ète); **to p. into sth** mettre son nez dans qch

prying ['praɪɪŋ] *adj* indiscret(ète)

PS ['piː'es] *n (abbr* **postscript**) PS *m*

psalm [sɑːm] *n* psaume *m*

pseud [sjuːd] *n Fam* prétentieux(euse) *m,f*

pseudo- ['sjuːdəʊ] *pref Fam* pseudo-

pseudonym ['sjuːdənɪm] *n* pseudonyme *m*

PST [piːes'tiː] *n Am (abbr* **Pacific Standard Time**) PST *m*

psyche ['saɪkɪ] *n* psychisme *m*

▸**psyche out** [saɪk] *vt sep Fam (unnerve)* déstabiliser

▸**psyche up** [saɪk] *vt sep Fam* **to p. sb up (for sth)** préparer qn psychologiquement (à qch); **to p. oneself up (for sth)** se préparer psychologiquement (à qch)

psychedelic [saɪkə'delɪk] *adj* psychédélique

psychiatric [saɪkɪ'ætrɪk] *adj* psychiatrique

psychiatrist [saɪ'kaɪətrɪst] *n* psychiatre *mf*

psychiatry [saɪ'kaɪətrɪ] *n* psychiatrie *f*

psychic ['saɪkɪk] **1** *n* médium *m*

  2 *adj* (**a**) *(paranormal)* paranormal(e) (**b**) *(clairvoyant)* **to be p., to have p. powers** être médium; *Fam* **I'm not p.!** je ne suis pas médium!

psycho ['saɪkəʊ] *(pl* **psychos**) *n Fam* dingue *mf*

psychoanalysis [saɪkəʊə'nælɪsɪs] *n* psychanalyse *f*

psychoanalyst [saɪkəʊ'ænəlɪst] *n* psychanalyste *mf*
psychoanalyze [saɪkəʊ'ænəlaɪz] *vt* psychanalyser
psychological [saɪkə'lɒdʒɪkəl] *adj* psychologique; **p. warfare** guerre *f* psychologique
psychologist [saɪ'kɒlədʒɪst] *n* psychologue *mf*
psychology [saɪ'kɒlədʒɪ] *n* psychologie *f*
psychometric [saɪkə'metrɪk] *adj* psychométrique
psychopath ['saɪkəʊpæθ] *n* psychopathe *mf*
psychosis [saɪ'kəʊsɪs] (*pl* **psychoses** [saɪ'kəʊsiːz]) *n* psychose *f*
psychosomatic [saɪkəʊsə'mætɪk] *adj* psychosomatique
psychotherapist [saɪkəʊ'θerəpɪst] *n* psychothérapeute *mf*
psychotherapy [saɪkəʊ'θerəpɪ] *n* psychothérapie *f*
psychotic [saɪ'kɒtɪk] *n & adj* psychotique *mf*
PT [piː'tiː] *n* (*abbr* **physical training**) EPS *f*
PTA [piːtiː'eɪ] *n Sch* (*abbr* **Parent-Teacher Association**) ≃ APE *f*
ptarmigan ['tɑːmɪɡən] *n* lagopède *m*
Pte *Mil* (*abbr* **private**) **p. Robbie McLean** = Soldat Robbie McLean
PTO [piːtiː'əʊ] (*abbr* **please turn over**) TSVP
pub [pʌb] *n Br* pub *m*

Pubs
Dans l'ensemble des îles Britanniques, le pub est un des grands foyers de la vie locale, mais son rôle varie selon les régions et selon qu'il se trouve en ville ou dans un village. Ces établissements interdits aux personnes de moins de seize ans étaient soumis à des horaires sévèrement réglementés, qui se sont beaucoup assouplis récemment. De même, le pub a cessé d'être un simple débit de boissons pour devenir de plus en plus une sorte de brasserie-restaurant, servant des repas légers.

---

pub-crawl ['pʌbkrɔːl] *n Br Fam* **to go on a p.** faire la tournée des bars
puberty ['pjuːbətɪ] *n* puberté *f*
pubic ['pjuːbɪk] *adj* pubien(enne), du pubis
public ['pʌblɪk] **1** *n* **the (general) p.** le grand public; **in p.** en public
2 *adj* public(ique); (*library, swimming pool*) municipal(e); **to go p. with sth** (*reveal information*) révéler qch (*à la presse*); **the company's going p.** la compagnie va être cotée en Bourse; **to make sth p.** rendre qch public; **to make a p. appearance** faire une apparition en public; **to be in the p. domain** être dans le domaine public; **at p. expense** aux frais du contribuable; **to be in the p. eye** être très en vue; **a p. figure** une personnalité en vue; **in the p. interest** dans l'intérêt du public; **p. address system** sonorisation *f*; **p. call box** cabine *f* téléphonique; **p. convenience** toilettes *fpl* publiques; *Com* **p. enterprise** entreprise *f* publique; **p. holiday** jour *m* férié; **p. house** pub *m*; *Am* **p. housing** logements *mpl* sociaux; ≃ HLM *f inv*; **p. library** bibliothèque *f* municipale; **p. limited company** ≃ société *f* anonyme; **p. opinion** l'opinion *f* publique; **p. ownership** nationalisation *f*, étatisation *f*; **to be under p. ownership** appartenir à l'état; *Law* **p. prosecutor** procureur *m*; **p. relations** relations *fpl* publiques; **p. school** *Br* école *f* privée, *Am* école publique; **p. sector** secteur *m* public; **p. spending**

dépenses *fpl* publiques; **p. transport** transports *mpl* en commun; *Com* **p. utility** service *m* public

---

Public schools
En Angleterre et au pays de Galles, le terme "public school" désigne une école privée de type traditionnel. Certaines de ces écoles (Eton et Harrow, par exemple) sont très prestigieuses et élitistes. Les "public schools" sont censées former l'élite de la nation. Aux États-Unis et parfois en Écosse, le terme désigne une école publique.

---

publican ['pʌblɪkən] *n* patron(onne) *m,f* d'un pub
publication [pʌblɪ'keɪʃən] *n* publication *f*
publicity [pʌb'lɪsɪtɪ] *n* publicité *f*; **p. campaign** campagne *f* publicitaire; **p. stunt** coup *m* de pub
publicize ['pʌblɪsaɪz] *vt* faire connaître au public
publicly ['pʌblɪklɪ] *adv* publiquement; **p. owned** à capitaux publics
public-spirited ['pʌblɪkspɪrɪtɪd] *adj* (*person*) qui a le sens civique; (*gesture, response*) dicté(e) par le sens civique
publish ['pʌblɪʃ] *vt* publier
publisher ['pʌblɪʃə(r)] *n* (*person*) éditeur(trice) *m,f*; (*company*) maison *f* d'édition
publishing ['pʌblɪʃɪŋ] *n* édition *f*; **p. house** maison *f* d'édition
pucker ['pʌkə(r)] **1** *vt* (*brow*) froncer; (*lips*) pincer
2 *vi* (*of face*) se rider; (*lips*) se plisser
pudding ['pʊdɪŋ] *n* (**a**) (*dessert*) dessert *m* (**b**) (*dish*) pudding *m*; **p. basin** *or* **bowl** jatte *f*
puddle ['pʌdəl] *n* flaque *f*
pudgy ['pʌdʒɪ] *adj* rondelet(ette)
puerile ['pjʊəraɪl] *adj Pej* puéril(e)
Puerto Rican [pweətəʊ'riːkən] **1** *n* Portoricain(e) *m,f*
2 *adj* portoricain(e)
Puerto Rico [pweətəʊ'riːkəʊ] *n* Porto Rico
puff [pʌf] **1** *n* (*of breath, air*) souffle *m*; (*of smoke, cigarette*) bouffée *f*; *Fam* **to be out of p.** être essoufflé(e); **p. pastry** pâte *f* feuilletée
2 *vt* **to p. smoke into sb's face** envoyer de la fumée à la figure de qn
3 *vi* (*of person*) souffler; (*of steam engine*) lancer des bouffées de vapeur; **to p. on a cigarette** fumer une cigarette
▸**puff out** *vt sep* (*cheeks, chest*) gonfler
▸**puff up** *vt sep* (*cheeks*) gonfler; **to be puffed up with pride** être gonflé(e) d'orgueil
puffin ['pʌfɪn] *n* macareux *m*
puffy ['pʌfɪ] *adj* gonflé(e)
pug [pʌg] *n* (*dog*) carlin *m*; **p.-nosed** au nez camus
pugnacious [pʌg'neɪʃəs] *adj* pugnace
puke [pjuːk] *Fam* **1** *n* dégueulis *m*
2 *vt & vi* dégueuler
pull [pʊl] **1** *n* (**a**) (*act of pulling*) traction *f*; (*of water current*) force *f*; **to give sth a p.** tirer qch; **to take a p. at a bottle** boire une gorgée d'une bouteille (**b**) *Fam* (*influence*) influence *f*; **to have a lot of p.** avoir le bras long
2 *vt* (**a**) (*tug*) tirer; **to p. sth open/shut** ouvrir/fermer qch; **to p. a muscle** se froisser un muscle; **to p. a pint** servir une bière; **to p. the trigger** appuyer sur la gâchette; *Fig* **to p. sth to pieces** démolir qch; *Fam Fig* **to p. sb's leg** faire marcher qn; *Fam Fig* **p. the other one! (it's got bells on)** à d'autres!

(**b**) *(attract)* attirer
 (**c**) *(extract) (cork)* retirer, enlever; *(tooth)* arracher; **to p. a gun on sb** braquer un pistolet sur qn; *Fam Fig* **it's like pulling teeth** il faut t'/lui/*etc* arracher les vers du nez
 (**d**) *Fam (sexually)* **to p. sb** lever qn, emballer qn
 (**e**) *(idioms)* **to p. a face** faire la grimace; *Fam* **to p. a bank job** se faire une banque; *Fam* **to p. a fast one on sb** rouler qn
 3 *vi* tirer (**on** sur); **to p. clear of sth** s'éloigner de qch
▸**pull about** *vt sep (handle roughly)* malmener
▸**pull ahead** *vi (in race, election)* prendre la tête (**of** de)
▸**pull apart** *vt sep (break up)* séparer; *Fig (criticize)* massacrer
▸**pull away** *vi (of car, train)* partir; *(from embrace)* s'écarter
▸**pull back 1** *vt sep (curtains)* ouvrir
 2 *vi (of person)* se retirer
▸**pull down** *vt sep (demolish)* démolir
▸**pull in 1** *vt sep* (**a**) *(rope, fishing line)* ramener (**b**) *(money)* gagner; *(of deal)* rapporter; **to p. sb in for questioning** arrêter qn pour l'interroger (**c**) *(attract)* attirer
 2 *vi (of car)* s'arrêter; *(of train, bus)* arriver
▸**pull off** *vt sep* (**a**) *(clothes)* retirer (**b**) *(task, deal)* réaliser; *(bank raid, burglary)* réussir; **to p. it off** réussir
▸**pull on** *vt sep (clothes)* enfiler, mettre
▸**pull out 1** *vt sep (tooth)* arracher; *Fam Fig* **to p. out all the stops** faire tout son possible
 2 *vi* (**a**) *(of car)* déboîter; *(of train)* partir (**b**) *(from race, agreement, deal)* se retirer (**of** de)
▸**pull over** *vi (of driver)* s'arrêter
▸**pull through** *vi (recover)* s'en sortir
▸**pull together 1** *vt sep* **to p. oneself together** se ressaisir
 2 *vi* s'entendre
▸**pull up 1** *vt sep Fig* **to p. one's socks up** se ressaisir; **to p. sb up (short)** couper qn dans son élan
 2 *vi (of car)* s'arreûter
pull-down menu ['pʊldaʊn'menju:] *n Comput* menu *m* déroulant
pullet ['pʊlɪt] *n* poulette *f*
pulley ['pʊlɪ] *(pl* **pulleys***) n* poulie *f*
pull-out ['pʊlaʊt] *n (in newspaper, magazine)* supplément *m* détachable
pullover ['pʊləʊvə(r)] *n* pull-over *m*
pulmonary ['pʌlmənərɪ] *adj* pulmonaire
pulp [pʌlp] **1** *n (of fruit)* pulpe *f*; **to reduce sth to (a) p.** écraser qch; *Fam* **to beat sb to a p.** mettre qn en bouillie; **p. fiction** romans *mpl* de gare
 2 *vt* écraser
pulpit ['pʊlpɪt] *n* chaire *f*
pulsate [pʌl'seɪt] *vi (of vein)* palpiter; *(of room, music)* vibrer; *(of heart)* battre
pulse[1] [pʌls] *n (of blood)* pouls *m*; *(of light, sound)* vibration *f*; **to feel** *or* **take sb's p.** prendre le pouls de qn
pulse[2] *n (seed)* légumineuse *f*
pulverize ['pʌlvəraɪz] *vt* pulvériser; *Fam Fig (beat up)* démolir; *(defeat heavily)* pulvériser
puma ['pju:mə] *n* puma *m*
pumice ['pʌmɪs] *n* **p. (stone)** pierre *f* ponce
pummel ['pʌməl] *(pt & pp* **pummelled**, *Am* **pummeled***) vt* marteler
pump[1] [pʌmp] *n (flat shoe)* escarpin *m*; *(ballet shoe)* ballerine *f*; *(plimsoll)* tennis *m ou f*

pump[2] **1** *n (machine)* pompe *f*
 2 *vt* pomper; **to p. sb's stomach** faire un lavage d'estomac à qn; *Fig* **to p. money into sth** injecter des capitaux dans qch; *Fam* **to p. sb for information** tirer les vers du nez à qn; **to p. sb's hand** *(shake vigorously)* donner une poignée de main vigoureuse à qn; *Fam* **to p. iron** *(do weightlifting)* faire de la gonflette
 3 *vi (of heart)* battre; *(of machine)* pomper
▸**pump out** *vt sep* pomper
▸**pump up** *vt sep* gonfler
pumpkin ['pʌmpkɪn] *n* potiron *m*, citrouille *f*
pun [pʌn] *n* jeu *m* de mots
punch[1] [pʌntʃ] **1** *n (tool)* poinçon *m*; *(for tickets)* poinçonneuse *f*
 2 *vt (metal)* percer; *(ticket)* poinçonner
punch[2] **1** *n* (**a**) *(blow)* coup *m* (de poing); *Fig* **she didn't pull her punches** elle n'y est pas allée de main morte (**b**) *(energy)* punch *m*; **p. line** *(of joke, story)* chute *f*
 2 *vt (hit)* donner un coup de poing à; **to p. sb in the face/on the nose** donner un coup de poing à qn dans la figure/dans le nez
punch[3] *n (drink)* punch *m*
Punch and Judy show ['pʌntʃən'dʒu:dɪ'ʃəʊ] *n* ≃ spectacle *m* de Guignol

---

Punch and Judy
En Grande-Bretagne, le "Punch and Judy show" est un spectacle pour enfants semblable aux Guignols en France. Il est souvent présenté dans un jardin public ou sur une plage. On y retrouve Punch le bossu, sa femme Judy avec laquelle il se querelle constamment, et leur chien Toby.

---

punchbag ['pʌntʃbæg] *n* sac *m* de sable
punchball ['pʌntʃbɔ:l] *n* punching-ball *m*
punch-drunk ['pʌntʃdrʌŋk] *adj* assommé(e)
punch-up ['pʌntʃʌp] *n Fam* bagarre *f*
punchy ['pʌntʃɪ] *adj Fam* plein(e) de punch
punctilious [pʌŋk'tɪlɪəs] *adj* pointilleux(euse)
punctual ['pʌŋktjʊəl] *adj* ponctuel(elle)
punctuality [pʌŋktjʊ'ælɪtɪ] *n* ponctualité *f*
punctually ['pʌŋktjʊəlɪ] *adv* à l'heure
punctuate ['pʌŋktjʊeɪt] *vt* ponctuer (**with** de)
punctuation [pʌŋktjʊ'eɪʃən] *n* ponctuation *f*; **p. mark** signe *m* de ponctuation
puncture ['pʌŋktʃə(r)] **1** *n (in tyre)* crevaison *f*; *(in skin, metal)* perforation *f*; **to have a p.** *(of cyclist, driver)* crever; *(of bicycle, car)* avoir un pneu crevé
 2 *vt (tyre)* crever; *(metal, lung)* perforer; *(blister, abscess)* percer
pundit ['pʌndɪt] *n* expert(e) *m,f*
pungent ['pʌndʒənt] *adj (smell, taste)* âcre; *(style, wit)* mordant(e)
punish ['pʌnɪʃ] *vt* punir; **to p. sb for doing sth** punir qn pour avoir fait qch
punishment ['pʌnɪʃmənt] *n* punition *f*; *Law* peine *f*; **to make the p. fit the crime** adapter la punition à la faute; **to take a lot of p.** être mis(e) à rude épreuve
punitive ['pju:nɪtɪv] *adj* punitif(ive)
punk [pʌŋk] *n* punk *mf*; **p. (rock)** punk *m*
punnet ['pʌnɪt] *n* barquette *f*
punt[1] [pʌnt] **1** *n (boat)* barque *f* à fond plat
 2 *vi* **to go punting** faire de la barque
punt[2] [pʊnt] *n (Irish currency)* livre *f* irlandaise

punter ['pʌntə(r)] *n (gambler)* parieur(euse) *m,f*; *Fam (customer)* client(e) *m,f*

puny ['pjuːnɪ] *adj* chétif(ive)

pup [pʌp] *n* (**a**) *(of dog)* chiot *m*; *(of seal)* bébé-phoque *m* (**b**) *Fam Pej (youth)* freluquet *m*

pupil¹ ['pjuːpəl] *n (student)* élève *mf*

pupil² *n (of eye)* pupille *f*

puppet ['pʌpɪt] *n also Fig* marionnette *f*; *Fig* **p. government** gouvernement *m* fantoche; **p. show** (spectacle *m* de) marionnettes *fpl*

puppy ['pʌpɪ] *(pl* **puppies)** *n* chiot *m*; **p. fat** rondeurs *fpl* préadolescentes; **p. love** amour *m* d'adolescence

purchase ['pɜːtʃɪs] **1** *n* (**a**) *(action, thing bought)* achat *m*; **p. price** prix *m* d'achat (**b**) *(grip)* prise *f*; **to get a p. on sth** trouver une prise sur qch
 2 *vt* acheter

purchaser ['pɜːtʃəsə(r)] *n* acheteur(euse) *m,f*

purchasing ['pɜːtʃəsɪŋ] *n* **p. manager** directeur(trice) *m,f* des achats; **p. power** pouvoir *m* d'achat

pure [pjʊə(r)] *adj* pur(e); **by p. chance** par pur hasard; **p. mathematics** mathématiques *fpl* pures

purebred ['pjʊəbred] *adj (dog)* de race pure; *(horse)* pur-sang *inv*

purée ['pjʊəreɪ] **1** *n* purée *f*
 2 *vt* réduire en purée

purely ['pjʊəlɪ] *adv* purement; **p. and simply** purement et simplement

purgatory ['pɜːgətərɪ] *n Rel* purgatoire *m*; *Fig* enfer *m*

purge [pɜːdʒ] **1** *n* purge *f*
 2 *vt* purger

purification [pjʊərɪfɪ'keɪʃən] *n* purification *f*

purify ['pjʊərɪfaɪ] *(pt & pp* **purified**) *vt* purifier

purist ['pjʊərɪst] *n* puriste *mf*

puritan ['pjʊərɪtən] *n* puritain(e) *m,f*

puritanical [pjʊərɪ'tænɪkəl] *adj* puritain(e)

purity ['pjʊərɪtɪ] *n* pureté *f*

purl [pɜːl] **1** *n* maille *f* à l'envers
 2 *vt* tricoter à l'envers

purloin [pɜː'lɔɪn] *vt Formal or Hum* dérober

purple ['pɜːpəl] **1** *n* violet *m*
 2 *adj* violet(ette); **to turn** *or* **go p.** *(of person)* devenir cramoisi(e); **pages of p. prose** des pages d'un style ampoulé

purport *Formal* **1** *n* ['pɜːpɔːt] teneur *f*
 2 *vt* [pɜː'pɔːt] **to p. to be sth** prétendre être qch

purpose ['pɜːpəs] *n* (**a**) *(object, aim)* but *m*, objectif *m*; **on p.** exprès; **what is the p. of your visit?** quel est l'objet de votre visite?; **to have a sense of p.** savoir ce que l'on veut; **to be to no p.** ne servir à rien (**b**) *(use)* utilité *f*; **to serve a p.** servir à quelque chose; **to serve no p.** ne servir à rien; **to serve sb's purpose(s)** faire l'affaire de qn; **for all practical purposes** à toutes fins utiles; **for the purposes of** pour les besoins de

purpose-built ['pɜːpəs'bɪlt] *adj* spécialement construit(e)

purposeful ['pɜːpəsfʊl] *adj* résolu(e)

purposely ['pɜːpəslɪ] *adv* délibérément; **to be p. rude** faire exprès d'être grossier(ère)

purr [pɜː(r)] **1** *n* ronron *m*, ronronnement *m*
 2 *vi* ronronner

purse [pɜːs] **1** *n Br (wallet)* porte-monnaie *m inv*; *Am (handbag)* sac *m* à main; **the public p.** le Trésor public; *Fig* **to hold the p. strings** tenir les cordons de la bourse
 2 *vt* **to p. one's lips** pincer les lèvres

pursue [pə'sjuː] *vt* poursuivre; *(pleasure, happiness)* rechercher; *(profession)* exercer

pursuer [pə'sjuːə(r)] *n* poursuivant(e) *m,f*

pursuit [pə'sjuːt] *n* (**a**) *(of person, animal)* poursuite *f*; *(of pleasure, knowledge, happiness)* quête *f*; **to be in p. of** être à la poursuite de; **in hot p.** à ses trousses (**b**) *(activity)* activité *f*

purveyor [pə'veɪə(r)] *n Formal* fournisseur(euse) *m,f*

pus [pʌs] *n* pus *m*

push [pʊʃ] **1** *n* (**a**) *(act of pushing)* poussée *f*; **to give sb/sth a p.** pousser qn/qch; *Fam* **to give sb the p.** *(of employer)* virer qn; *(of lover)* plaquer qn; **at a p.** à la rigueur; **when p. comes to shove, if it comes to the p.** dans le pire des cas
 (**b**) *Mil (attack)* poussée *f*; **sales p.** campagne *f* de vente; **to make a p. for sth** lutter pour qch
 2 *vt* (**a**) *(in general)* pousser; *(button)* appuyer sur; **to p. the door shut/open** fermer/ouvrir la porte; **p.** *(sign)* poussez; **to p. sb out of the way** écarter qn; **to p. one's way through the crowd** se frayer un chemin à travers la foule; *Fig* **don't p. yourself too hard** ne force pas trop; *Fig* **to p. sb into doing sth** pousser qn à faire qch; **to p. one's luck** y aller un peu fort; **to be pushed for time** être très pressé(e)
 (**b**) *(promote)* faire la promotion de; *(theory)* promouvoir
 (**c**) *Fam (drugs)* vendre
 (**d**) *Fam* **to be pushing sixty** approcher de la soixantaine
 3 *vi (in general)* pousser; *(move forward)* avancer; **to p. past sb** passer devant qn en le bousculant; **to p. forward** pousser en avant

▶**push about, push around** *vt sep Fam Fig (bully)* **to p. sb about** faire de qn ce que l'on veut

▶**push ahead** *vi* continuer; **to p. ahead with sth** continuer qch

▶**push aside** *vt sep also Fig* écarter

▶**push in** *vi (in queue)* resquiller

▶**push off** *vi Fam* ficher le camp

▶**push on** *vi (continue)* continuer; **to p. on with sth** continuer qch

▶**push over** *vt sep* faire tomber

▶**push through** *vt sep (reform, law)* faire passer

push-bike ['pʊʃbaɪk] *n Fam* vélo *m*

push-button ['pʊʃ'bʌtən] *adj* à touches

pushchair ['pʊʃtʃeə(r)] *n (for baby)* poussette *f*

pusher ['pʊʃə(r)] *n Fam* **(drug) p. dealer** *m*

pushover ['pʊʃəʊvə(r)] *n Fam* **it's a p.** c'est un jeu d'enfant; **she's no p.** elle ne se laisse pas avoir facilement

push-up ['pʊʃʌp] *n* pompe *f*

pushy ['pʊʃɪ] *adj Fam* batailleur(euse)

puss [pʊs] *n Fam (cat)* minou *m*

pussy ['pʊsɪ] *(pl* **pussies)** *n Fam* **p. (cat)** minou *m*; **p. willow** saule *m* blanc

pussyfoot ['pʊsɪfʊt] *vi Fam* **to p. (around** *or* **about)** *(when speaking)* tourner autour du pot; *(in one's actions)* toujours remettre les choses à plus tard

pustule ['pʌstjuːl] *n* pustule *f*

put [pʊt] *(pt & pp* **put)** **1** *vt* (**a**) *(place)* mettre; *(on flat surface)* poser; **to p. one's arms around sb** prendre qn dans ses bras; **to p. a man on the moon** envoyer un homme sur la lune; **to p. a limit on sth** mettre une limite à qch; *Fam* **p. it there!** *(shake hands)* tope là!; *Fig* **to p. oneself in sb's hands** s'en remettre à qn; *Fig* **to p. sb in his place** remettre qn à sa place; *Fig* **p. yourself in my position** mets-toi à ma place; **to p. a**

matter right mettre les choses au point; **to p. money on a horse** parier sur un cheval; **to p. a lot of work into sth** beaucoup travailler à qch; **to p. a stop to sth** mettre fin à qch; **to p. a child to bed** mettre un enfant au lit; **to p. sb to the test** mettre qn à l'épreuve; *Fam Fig* **I didn't know where to p. myself** je ne savais pas où me mettre
(**b**) *(present)* **to p. a question to sb** poser une question à qn; **to p. a proposal to sb** soumettre une proposition à qn; **I p. it to you that...** *(in court)* n'est-il pas vrai que...?
(**c**) *(express)* **to p. sth well** bien tourner qch; **I couldn't have put it better myself** je n'aurais pas mieux dit; **to p. it bluntly** pour parler franchement; **how shall I p. it...?** comment dire...?
(**d**) *(estimate)* estimer (**at** à); **I would p. her age at forty** je dirais qu'elle a quarante ans
2 *vi* **to p. to sea** prendre la mer
▸**put about** *vt sep (rumour)* faire courir; **to p. it about that...** faire courir le bruit que...
▸**put across** *vt sep (message, idea)* faire comprendre (**to** à); **to p. oneself across well/badly** *(at interview)* se mettre/ne pas se mettre en valeur
▸**put aside** *vt sep* (**a**) *(goods, money)* mettre de côté (**b**) *(problem, fact)* laisser de côté
▸**put away** *vt sep* (**a**) *(tidy away)* ranger (**b**) *Fam (prisoner)* enfermer (**c**) *Fam (eat, drink)* s'enfiler, ingurgiter
▸**put back** *vt sep* (**a**) *(replace)* remettre (**b**) *(postpone)* reporter; *(clock, schedule)* retarder; *Fig* **that puts the clock back ten years** cela nous ramène dix ans en arrière
▸**put by** *vt sep (save)* mettre de côté
▸**put down** *vt sep* (**a**) *(set down)* poser; **I couldn't put it down** *(book)* je ne pouvais pas m'arrêter de (le) lire (**b**) *(revolt, opposition)* réprimer (**c**) *(write)* écrire, mettre par écrit; **to p. sth down in writing** mettre qch par écrit; **to p. one's name down for sth** s'inscrire à qch (**d**) *(attribute)* **to p. sth down to sb/sth** attribuer qch à qn/qch (**e**) *(animal)* piquer; **to have a cat/dog put down** faire piquer un chat/un chien (**f**) *(criticize)* rabaisser; **to p. oneself down** se rabaisser
▸**put forward** *vt sep* (**a**) *(plan, theory, candidate)* proposer; *(proposal)* faire (**b**) *(clock, time of meeting)* avancer
▸**put in** 1 *vt sep* (**a**) *(install)* installer (**b**) *(claim, application)* soumettre; **to p. in a (good) word for sb** dire un mot en faveur de qn (**c**) *(time)* passer; **they've p. in a lot of work** ils ont énormément travaillé
2 *vi (of ship)* faire escale
▸**put off** *vt sep* (**a**) *(postpone)* remettre à plus tard; **to p. off doing sth** retarder le moment de faire qch (**b**) *(cause to dislike)* **to p. sb off sth** dégoûter qn de qch (**c**) *(disturb)* gêner (**d**) *(discourage)* **to p. sb off doing sth** enlever à qn l'envie de faire qch (**e**) *(make wait)* faire patienter
▸**put on** *vt sep* (**a**) *(clothes)* mettre; **to p. on one's make-up** se maquiller; **to p. on an act** jouer la comédie; **to p. on an accent** prendre un accent; *Fam* **she's just putting it on!** elle fait semblant!; **to p. on weight** grossir, prendre du poids (**b**) *(light, TV, heating)* allumer; *(music, video)* mettre; **to p. the kettle on** mettre l'eau à chauffer (**c**) *(play, show)* monter
▸**put out** *vt sep* (**a**) *(fire, light)* éteindre (**b**) *(place outside)* mettre dehors (**c**) *(extend)* **to p. out one's hand** tendre la main (**d**) *(arrange for use)* sortir (**e**) *(report,*

statement) publier (**f**) *(annoy)* **to be put out** être contrarié(e) (**g**) *(inconvenience)* déranger; **to p. oneself out (for sb)** se donner du mal (pour qn) (**h**) *(dislocate)* **to p. one's shoulder/knee out** se démettre l'épaule/le genou
▸**put through** *vt sep* (**a**) *(on phone)* **to p. sb through to sb** passer qn à qn (**b**) *(subject to)* **to p. sb through sth** faire subir qch à qn; **to p. sb through hell** faire souffrir le martyre à qn
▸**put together** *vt sep (assemble)* assembler; *(file, report)* préparer; *(meal, team)* composer; **she's more intelligent than the rest of them put together** elle est cent fois plus intelligente qu'eux; *Fig* **to p. two and two together** tirer ses conclusions
▸**put up** *vt sep* (**a**) *(tent, fence)* monter; *(ladder)* dresser; *(building)* construire; *(statue)* ériger; *(notice)* afficher; *(painting)* accrocher; *(umbrella)* ouvrir; **to p. up one's hand** lever la main; **to p. one's hair up** relever ses cheveux (**b**) *(increase) (price, fee, rent)* augmenter (**c**) *(provide accommodation for)* loger, héberger (**d**) *(provide) (money)* verser, fournir; *(candidate)* présenter; **to p. sth up for sale** mettre qch en vente; **to p. up a fight** *or* **a struggle** se défendre
▸**put upon** *vt insep* **to feel put upon** se sentir exploité(e)
▸**put up to** *vt sep* **to p. sb up to doing sth** pousser qn à faire qch; **he put me up to it** c'est lui qui m'a poussé à le faire
▸**put up with** *vt insep* supporter
putative ['pju:tǝtɪv] *adj Formal* putatif(ive)
put-down ['pʊtdaʊn] *n Fam* remarque *f* humiliante
putrefy ['pju:trɪfaɪ] *(pt & pp* **putrefied**) *vi* se putréfier
putrid ['pju:trɪd] *adj* putride
putsch [pʊtʃ] *n* putsch *m*
putt [pʌt] **1** *n (in golf)* putt *m*
2 *vi (in golf)* putter
putter ['pʌtǝ(r)] *n (golf club)* putter *m*
putty ['pʌtɪ] *n* mastic *m*; *Fig* **he's p. in her hands** elle en fait ce qu'elle veut
put-up job ['pʊtʌp'dʒɒb] *n Fam* coup *m* monté
puzzle ['pʌzl] **1** *n* (**a**) *(game)* casse-tête *m*; *(mental)* devinette *f*; *(jigsaw)* puzzle *m*; **p. book** livre *m* de devinettes et de jeux (**b**) *(mystery)* énigme *f*
2 *vt (person)* rendre perplexe
▸**puzzle out** *vt sep (solution, meaning)* trouver; *(action, motive)* essayer de comprendre
▸**puzzle over** *vt insep* essayer de comprendre
puzzled ['pʌzld] *adj* perplexe
puzzling ['pʌzlɪŋ] *adj* bizarre
PVC [pi:vi:'si:] *n (abbr* **polyvinyl chloride)** PVC *m*
pygmy ['pɪgmɪ] *(pl* **pygmies)** *n* pygmée *m*
pyjamas, *Am* **pajamas** [pǝ'dʒɑ:mǝz] *npl* pyjama *m*; **a pair of p.** un pyjama
pylon ['paɪlǝn] *n* pylône *m*
pyramid ['pɪrǝmɪd] *n* pyramide *f*; *Com* **p. scheme** plan *m* commercial en cascade
pyre ['paɪǝ(r)] *n* bûcher *m* (funéraire)
Pyrenean [pɪrǝ'nɪǝn] *adj* pyrénéen(enne)
Pyrenees [pɪrǝ'ni:z] *npl* **the P.** les Pyrénées *fpl*
Pyrex® ['paɪreks] *n* pyrex® *m*; **P. dish** plat *m* en pyrex®
pyromaniac [paɪrǝʊ'meɪnɪæk] *n* pyromane *mf*
pyrotechnics [paɪrǝʊ'teknɪks] **1** *n (science)* pyrotechnie *f*
2 *npl (fireworks display)* feu *m* d'artifice; *Fig (in speech, writing)* prouesses *fpl*
python ['paɪθǝn] *n* python *m*

Q, q [kju:] *n (letter)* Q, q *m inv*

Qatar [kæ'tɑ:(r)] *n* le Qatar

Qatari [kæ'tɑ:rɪ] **1** *n* habitant(e) *m,f* du Qatar
2 *adj* du Qatar

QC [kju:'si:] *n Br Law (abbr* **Queen's Counsel**) = membre haut placé du barreau

QED [kju:i:'di:] *(abbr* **quod erat demonstrandum**) CQFD

Q-tip® ['kju:tɪp] *n Am* coton-tige® *m*

qty *Com (abbr* **quantity**) qté

quack¹ [kwæk] **1** *n (of duck)* coin-coin *m*
2 *vi (of duck)* faire coin-coin

quack² *n (doctor) Pej* charlatan *m*; *Hum* toubib *m*

quad [kwɒd] *n Fam (of school, college)* cour *f*

quadrangle ['kwɒdræŋgəl] *n* (**a**) *(shape)* quadrilatère *m* (**b**) *(of school, college)* cour *f*

quadrant ['kwɒdrənt] *n* quart *m* de cercle

quadraphonic [kwɒdrə'fɒnɪk] *adj* quadriphonique

quadratic equation [kwɒ'drætɪkɪ'kweɪʒən] *n Math* équation *f* du second degré

quadrilateral [kwɒdrɪ'lætərəl] **1** *n* quadrilatère *m*
2 *adj* quadrilatéral(e)

quadriplegic [kwɒdrɪ'pli:dʒɪk] *n & adj* tétraplégique *mf*

quadruped ['kwɒdrʊped] *n* quadrupède *m*

quadruple [kwɒ'drʊpəl] **1** *adj* quadruple
2 *vt & vi* quadrupler

quadruplet ['kwɒdrʊplet] *n* quadruplé(e) *m,f*

quaff [kwɒf] *vt Lit* boire

quagmire ['kwægmaɪə(r)] *n also Fig* bourbier *m*

quail¹ [kweɪl] *(pl* **quail**) *n (bird)* caille *f*

quail² *vi (of person)* avoir un mouvement de recul

quaint [kweɪnt] *adj (picturesque)* pittoresque; *(old-fashioned)* vieillot(otte)

quake [kweɪk] **1** *n Fam (earthquake)* tremblement *m* de terre
2 *vi* trembler; **to q. in one's boots** trembler de peur

Quaker ['kweɪkə(r)] *n Rel* quaker(eresse) *m,f*

qualification [kwɒlɪfɪ'keɪʃən] *n* (**a**) *(diploma)* diplôme *m*; *(skill)* compétence *f* (**b**) *(completion of studies)* **on/after q.** une fois le diplôme obtenu (**c**) *(modification)* précision *f* (**d**) *(for competition)* qualification *f*

qualified ['kwɒlɪfaɪd] *adj* (**a**) *(having diploma)* diplômé(e); *(competent)* compétent(e); **to be q. to do sth** *(have diploma)* avoir les diplômes requis pour faire qch; *(be competent)* avoir les compétences requises pour faire qch (**b**) *(modified)* mitigé(e); **a q. success** un demi-succès

qualifier ['kwɒlɪfaɪə(r)] *n* (**a**) *(person, team)* qualifié(e) *m,f*, *(match)* match *m* de qualification (**b**) *Gram* qualificatif *m*

qualify ['kwɒlɪfaɪ] *(pt & pp* **qualified**) **1** *vt* (**a**) *(make competent)* **to q. sb to do sth** donner les compétences nécessaires à qn pour faire qch (**b**) *(modify)* nuancer
2 *vi* (**a**) *(in competition)* se qualifier; **to q. as a doctor/teacher** obtenir son diplôme de médecin/professeur (**b**) *(be eligible)* **to q. for sth** avoir droit à qch

qualifying ['kwɒlɪfaɪɪŋ] *adj* (**a**) *(round, match)* éliminatoire (**b**) *(exam)* d'entrée

qualitative ['kwɒlɪtətɪv] *adj* qualitatif(ive)

quality ['kwɒlɪtɪ] *(pl* **qualities**) *n* qualité *f*; **of good/poor q.** de bonne/mauvaise qualité; **q. of life** qualité de la vie; **q. circle** cercle *m* de qualité; **q. control** contrôle *m* (de) qualité; **q. goods** marchandises *fpl* de qualité; *Br* **q. newspaper** journal *m* sérieux; **she wants to spend more q. time with her children** elle veut passer davantage de temps avec ses enfants

qualm [kwɑ:m] *n* doute *m*; **to have no qualms about doing sth** *(doubts)* ne pas hésiter une seconde avant de faire qch; *(scruples)* n'avoir aucun scrupule à faire qch

quandary ['kwɒndərɪ] *(pl* **quandaries**) *n* dilemme *m*; **to be in a q. (about sth)** être face à un dilemme (à propos de qch)

quango ['kwæŋgəʊ] *(pl* **quangoes**) *n Br Pol (abbr* **quasi-autonomous non-governmental organization**) = organisme créé par le gouvernement et doté de pouvoirs quasi autonomes

> ### Quango
> En Grande-Bretagne, un "quango" est un organisme semi-public principalement financé par l'État mais disposant d'une certaine autonomie. Certains de ces organismes ont un rôle purement consultatif. D'autres sont habilités à prendre des décisions, notamment au niveau local, et c'est pourquoi au cours de ces dernières années les "quangos" ont fait l'objet de critiques, car leurs membres sont nommés par le gouvernement et non pas élus.

quantifier ['kwɒntɪfaɪə(r)] *n Math* quantificateur *m*

quantify ['kwɒntɪfaɪ] *(pt & pp* **quantified**) *vt* évaluer

quantitative ['kwɒntɪtətɪv] *adj* quantitatif(ive)

quantity ['kwɒntɪtɪ] *(pl* **quantities**) *n* quantité *f*; **q. surveyor** métreur vérificateur *m*

quantum ['kwɒntəm] *n Phys* quantum *m*; *Fig* **q. leap** bond *m* en avant; **q. mechanics** mécanique *f* quantique; **q. theory** théorie *f* des quanta

quarantine ['kwɒrəntiːn] **1** *n* quarantaine *f*; **to be in q.** être en quarantaine
2 *vt* mettre en quarantaine

quark [kwɑːk] *n Phys* quark *m*

quarrel ['kwɒrəl] **1** *n* (**a**) *(argument)* dispute *f*, querelle *f*; **to have a q.** se disputer; **to pick a q. with sb** chercher querelle à qn (**b**) *(disagreement)* désaccord *m*; **to have no q. with sb** n'avoir rien à reprocher à qn
2 *vi* *(pt & pp* quarrelled, *Am* quarreled) (**a**) *(argue)* se disputer (**with** avec) (**b**) *(disagree)* **to q. with sth** ne pas être d'accord avec qch

quarrelling, *Am* **quarreling** ['kwɒrəlɪŋ] *n* disputes *fpl*

quarrelsome ['kwɒrəlsəm] *adj* querelleur(euse)

quarry¹ ['kwɒrɪ] *(pl* quarries) *n (prey) & Fig* proie *f*

quarry² **1** *(pl* quarries) *n (for stone)* carrière *f*
2 *vt* *(pt & pp* quarried) *(hill)* exploiter; *(stone)* extraire

quart [kwɔːt] *n (liquid measurement) Br* = 1,136 l; *Am* = 0,946 l

quarter ['kwɔːtə(r)] **1** *n* (**a**) *(fraction)* quart *m*; *(of orange, moon)* quartier *m*; **a q. of a century** un quart de siècle; **a q. of an hour** un quart d'heure; **a q. (of a pound)** = 113,4 g, un quart de livre; **three quarters** trois quarts; **three and a q.** trois un quart; **three and a q. litres** trois litres un quart; **a q. full** au quart plein(e)
(**b**) *(in telling time) Br* **a q. to six,** *Am* **a q. of six** six heures moins le quart; **it's a q. to** il est moins le quart; *Br* **a q. past six,** *Am* **a q. after six** six heures un *ou* et quart; **it's a q. past** il est le quart
(**c**) *(three-month period)* trimestre *m*
(**d**) *(area)* quartier *m*
(**e**) *(group)* milieu *m*; **help came from an unexpected q.** nous avons reçu une aide inespérée
(**f**) *Mil* **quarters** *(lodgings)* quartiers *mpl*
(**g**) *Am (coin)* pièce *f* de 25 cents
2 *vt* (**a**) *(divide into four)* partager en quatre
(**b**) *Mil (troops)* loger

quarterback ['kwɔːtəbæk] *n* quarterback *m*, *Can* quart-arrière *m*

quarterdeck ['kwɔːtədek] *n (of ship)* plage *f* arrière

quarterfinal [kwɔːtə'faɪnəl] *n* quart *m* de finale

quarterly ['kwɔːtəlɪ] **1** *n (pl* quarterlies) publication *f* trimestrielle
2 *adj* trimestriel(elle)
3 *adv* tous les trimestres

quartermaster ['kwɔːtəmɑːstə(r)] *n Mil* intendant *m*

quarter-pounder [kwɔːtə'paʊndə(r)] *n* gros hamburger *m*

quartet [kwɔː'tet] *n* quatuor *m*

quarto ['kwɔːtəʊ] *(pl* quartos) *n* in-quarto *m*

quartz [kwɔːts] *n* quartz *m*; **q. watch** montre *f* à quartz

quasar ['kweɪzɑː(r)] *n Astron* quasar *m*

quash [kwɒʃ] *vt (objection, plan)* rejeter; *(revolt, feeling)* réprimer; *Law (sentence)* annuler

quaver ['kweɪvə(r)] **1** *n* (**a**) *Mus* croche *f* (**b**) *(in voice)* tremblement *m*
2 *vi (of voice)* trembler

quay [kiː] *n* quai *m*

quayside ['kiːsaɪd] *n* quai *m*

queasy ['kwiːzɪ] *adj* **to feel q.** avoir mal au cœur

Quebec [kwɪ'bek] *n* le Québec; **Q. City** Québec

queen [kwiːn] **1** *n* (**a**) *(of country, in cards, chess)* reine *f*; *Fam Fig* **she's the q. bee around here** c'est elle la patronne ici; *Br* **Q.'s Counsel** = membre haut placé du barreau; **the Q.'s English** l'anglais *m* correct; **the Q. Mother** la reine mère (**b**) *very Fam (homosexual)* tante *f*, folle *f*, = terme injurieux désignant un homosexuel
2 *vt Br Fam* **to q. it** prendre des airs de (grande) marquise

queer ['kwɪə(r)] **1** *adj* (**a**) *(strange)* bizarre (**b**) *very Fam (homosexual)* homo, pédé
2 *n very Fam (male homosexual)* homo *m*, pédé *m*, = terme injurieux désignant un homosexuel
3 *vt Fam* **to q. the pitch for sb, to q. sb's pitch** bouleverser les plans de qn

quell [kwel] *vt (revolt)* réprimer; *(doubt, worry)* dissiper

quench [kwentʃ] *vt (thirst)* étancher

querulous ['kwerʊləs] *adj (person)* grincheux(euse); *(tone)* maussade, plaintif(ive)

query ['kwɪərɪ] **1** *n* *(pl* queries) question *f*
2 *vt* *(pt & pp* queried) mettre en question; **to q. if** *or* **whether...** mettre en question le fait que...

quest [kwest] *Lit* **1** *n* quête *f*, poursuite *f* (**for** de); **to go** *or* **be in q. of sth** être en quête *ou* à la poursuite de qch
2 *vi* **to q. after** *or* **for sth** être en quête *ou* à la poursuite de qch

question ['kwestʃən] **1** *n* (**a**) *(query)* question *f*; **to ask (sb) a q.** poser une question (à qn); **q. mark** point *m* d'interrogation; *Fig* **a q. mark hangs over the future of the project** l'avenir du projet reste en suspens; *Br Pol* **q. time** ≃ session *f* des questions orales *(à l'Assemblée nationale)*
(**b**) *(doubt)* doute *m*; **to call sth into q.** mettre qch en doute; **beyond q.** indiscutable; **it's open to q. whether...** reste à savoir si...; **without q.** indiscutablement
(**c**) *(matter)* question *f*, problème *m*; **it is a q. of...** il s'agit de...; **there is no q. of our agreeing to that** il n'est pas question que nous acceptions cela; **to be out of the q.** être hors de question; **it's only a q. of time** ce n'est qu'une question de temps; **the matter/person in q.** l'affaire/la personne en question
2 *vt* (**a**) *(put questions to)* interroger (**on** sur)
(**b**) *(cast doubt on)* mettre en doute

questionable ['kwestʃənəbəl] *adj* discutable

questioning ['kwestʃənɪŋ] **1** *n (interrogation)* interrogation *f*; **to be held for q.** *(by police)* être interrogé(e)
2 *adj (look)* interrogateur(trice); *(mind)* curieux(euse)

questionnaire [kwestʃə'neə(r)] *n* questionnaire *m*

queue [kjuː] **1** *n* queue *f*, file *f* (d'attente); **to jump the q.** resquiller
2 *vi* faire la queue

queue-jump ['kjuːdʒʌmp] *vi* resquiller

quibble ['kwɪbəl] **1** *n* petite question *f*
2 *vi* chipoter (**about** *or* **over** à propos de)

quiche [kiːʃ] *n* quiche *f*

quick [kwɪk] **1** *adj* (**a**) *(rapid)* rapide; **to have a q. bath/drink** prendre un bain/un verre en vitesse; **to be q.** *(hurry)* faire vite; **that was q.!** tu as fait vite!; **q. as a flash** *or* **a wink** rapide comme l'éclair; **to be q. to do sth** faire qch vite *ou* rapidement; **to be q. off the mark** *(to act)* réagir vite; *(to understand)* avoir l'esprit vif; **to have a q. temper** s'emporter facilement (**b**) *(clever)* vif (vive)

2 *adv Fam (run, take, think)* vite

3 *n* **to bite one's nails to the q.** se ronger les ongles jusqu'au sang; *Fig* **to cut sb to the q.** piquer qn au vif

quicken ['kwɪkən] **1** *vt* (**a**) *(make faster)* accélérer; **to q. one's pace** presser le pas (**b**) *(imagination)* stimuler; *(interest)* éveiller, exciter

2 *vi (of pace, pulse)* s'accélérer

quickfire ['kwɪkfaɪə(r)] *adj* rapide

quickie ['kwɪkɪ] *Fam* **1** *n* **to have a q.** *(drink)* prendre un verre en vitesse; *(sex)* faire l'amour en vitesse

2 *adj* **q. divorce** divorce *m* rapide

quicklime ['kwɪklaɪm] *n* chaux *f* vive

quickly ['kwɪklɪ] *adv* vite, rapidement

quickness ['kwɪknɪs] *n (speed)* rapidité *f*; *(of mind)* vivacité *f*

quicksand ['kwɪksænd] *n* sables *mpl* mouvants

quicksilver ['kwɪksɪlvə(r)] *n Old-fashioned (mercury)* vif-argent *m*

quick-tempered ['kwɪk'tempəd] *adj* emporté(e)

quick-witted ['kwɪk'wɪtɪd] *adj* vif (vive)

quid [kwɪd] *(pl* **quid**) *n Br Fam (pound)* livre *f*

quiescent [kwar'esənt] *adj Formal* passif(ive)

quiet ['kwaɪət] **1** *n* silence *m*; *Fam* **to do sth on the q.** faire qch en douce

2 *adj* (**a**) *(not loud)* silencieux(euse); *(voice)* petit(e); *(music)* doux (douce); **to keep sb q.** faire tenir qn tranquille; **to keep q.** *(make no noise)* ne pas faire de bruit; *(say nothing)* se taire; **to keep q. about sth** ne rien dire au sujet de qch; **to keep sth q.** cacher qch; **be q.!** tais-toi!; **as q. as a mouse** *(person)* silencieux

(**b**) *(discreet)* discret(ète); **to have a q. laugh at sb/sth** se moquer discrètement de qn/qch

(**c**) *(peaceful)* tranquille; **a q. wedding** un mariage célébré dans l'intimité

(**d**) *(business, market)* calme

▸**quiet down** = **quieten down**

quieten ['kwaɪətən] *vt* calmer

▸**quieten down 1** *vt sep* calmer

2 *vi* se calmer

quietly ['kwaɪətlɪ] *adv* (**a**) *(silently)* tranquillement, silencieusement (**b**) *(discreetly)* discrètement; **to be q. confident** être optimiste sans excès

quietness ['kwaɪətnɪs] *n (of person, place)* tranquillité *f*; *(of manner)* douceur *f*

quiff [kwɪf] *n (of hair)* toupet *m*

quill [kwɪl] *n (feather)* penne *f*; *(pen)* plume *f* d'oie; *(of porcupine)* piquant *m*

quilt [kwɪlt] **1** *n* édredon *m*; *(duvet)* couette *f*

2 *vt (garment)* matelasser; **quilted jacket** blouson *m* matelassé

quince [kwɪns] *n* coing *m*; **q. jelly** gelée *f* de coing

quinine [kwɪ'ni:n] *n* quinine *f*

quintessential [kwɪntɪ'senʃəl] *adj Formal* quintessentiel(elle)

quintessentially [kwɪntɪ'senʃəlɪ] *adv Formal* fondamentalement

quintet [kwɪn'tet] *n* quintette *m*

quintuplet [kwɪn'tʊplɪt] *n* quintuplé(e) *m,f*

quip [kwɪp] **1** *n* boutade *f*

2 *vi (pt & pp* **quipped**) plaisanter

quirk [kwɜ:k] *n* (**a**) *(of character)* particularité *f* (**b**) *(of fate, nature)* caprice *m*; **by a q. of fate** par un caprice du destin

quirky ['kwɜ:kɪ] *adj* bizarre, insolite

quisling ['kwɪzlɪŋ] *n* collaborateur(trice) *m,f*

quit [kwɪt] **1** *vt (pt & pp* **quit**) *(person, place)* quitter; *Comput (programme)* sortir de; **to q. one's job** démissionner; **to q. doing sth** arreûter de faire qch

2 *vi (give up)* abandonner; *(resign)* démissionner; *Comput* sortir

3 *adj* **to be q. of** être débarrassé(e) de

quite [kwaɪt] *adv* (**a**) *(entirely)* tout à fait; **q. enough** bien assez; **that's q. enough of that!** ça suffit comme ça!; **q. apart from the fact that...** mis à part le fait que...; **q.!** tout à fait!; **that's q. all right** *(it doesn't matter)* ça n'a pas d'importance du tout; *(you're welcome)* mais pas du tout!; **you know q. well what I mean!** vous savez parfaitement ce que je veux dire!; **I q. understand** je comprends parfaitement

(**b**) *(fairly)* assez, plutôt; **I q. like him** il me plaît bien; **q. a lot of people** pas mal de monde

(**c**) *(for emphasis)* **it was q. a surprise** ça a été une véritable surprise; **it's been q. a day!** quelle journée!; **that film is q. something** ce film, c'est vraiment quelque chose!

quits [kwɪts] *adj* **to be q. (with sb)** être quitte (envers qn); **let's call it q.** restons-en là

quiver¹ ['kwɪvə(r)] *n (for arrows)* carquois *m*

quiver² **1** *n (tremble)* tremblement *m*

2 *vi (tremble)* trembler (**with** de); *(of flame)* vaciller

quivering ['kwɪvərɪŋ] *adj* tremblant(e)

quixotic [kwɪk'sɒtɪk] *adj* chimérique

quiz [kwɪz] **1** *n (pl* **quizzes**) *(on radio)* jeu *m* radiophonique; *(on TV)* jeu télévisé; *(in magazine)* questionnaire *m*

2 *vt (pt & pp* **quizzed**) interroger

quizzical ['kwɪzɪkəl] *adj (look, air)* interrogateur(trice)

Quorn® [kwɔ:n] *n* = aliment aux protéines végétales servant de substitut à la viande

quorum ['kwɔ:rəm] *n* quorum *m*

quota ['kwəʊtə] *n (share)* quota *m*

quotation [kwəʊ'teɪʃən] *n* (**a**) *(from author)* citation *f*; **q. marks** guillemets *mpl*; **in q. marks** entre guillemets (**b**) *Com (for work)* devis *m*

quote [kwəʊt] **1** *n Fam* (**a**) *(from author)* citation *f*; **in quotes** *(in quotation marks)* entre guillemets (**b**) *Com (for work)* devis *m*

2 *vt* (**a**) *(author, passage)* citer; **she was quoted as saying that...** elle aurait dit que... (**b**) *Com (price)* indiquer; *Fin* **quoted company** société *f* cotée en Bourse

quotient ['kwəʊʃənt] *n Math* quotient *m*

R

R¹, r [ɑː(r)] *n (letter)* R, r *m inv*; *Fam* **the three R's** = la lecture, l'écriture et l'arithmétique, fondements de l'enseignement primaire

R² *Am Pol (abbr* **Republican***)* républicain(e)

RA [ɑːˈreɪ] *n Br (abbr* **Royal Academy***)* = académie royale des beaux-arts

rabbi [ˈræbaɪ] *n* rabbin *m*

rabbit [ˈræbɪt] *n* lapin *m*; **r. hole** terrier *m*; **r. hutch** clapier *m*

▸**rabbit on** *vi Fam* ne pas cesser de parler

rabble [ˈræbəl] *n* foule *f* bruyante; **r. rouser** agitateur(-trice) *m,f*

rabid [ˈræbɪd] *adj (animal)* & *Fig (person)* enragé(e); *(prejudice)* profondément enraciné(e)

rabies [ˈreɪbiːz] *n* rage *f*

RAC [ɑːreɪˈsiː] *n Aut (abbr* **Royal Automobile Club***)* = club automobile britannique offrant notamment des services de dépannage

raccoon [rəˈkuːn] *n* raton *m* laveur

race¹ [reɪs] **1** *n (contest)* course *f*; *Fig* **a r. against time** une course contre la montre; **the races** *(horseraces)* les courses; **a r. meeting** *(for horseraces)* des courses de chevaux
   2 *vt* **(a)** *(person)* faire la course avec; **I'll r. you home!** on fait la course jusqu'à la maison! **(b)** *(horse)* faire courir
   3 *vi* **(a)** *(of athlete, horse)* courir **(b)** *(move quickly)* aller à toute vitesse; **to r. in/out** entrer/sortir à toute vitesse; **to r. down the street** dévaler la rue à toute vitesse; **to r. by** *(of time)* passer vite, filer **(c)** *(of engine)* s'emballer; *(of pulse, heart)* battre la chamade

race² *n (of people, animals)* race *f*; **the human r.** le genre humain; **r. relations** relations *fpl* interraciales

racecourse [ˈreɪskɔːs] *n* champ *m* de courses

racehorse [ˈreɪshɔːs] *n* cheval *m* de course

racer [ˈreɪsə(r)] *n (person)* coureur(euse) *m,f*, *(bicycle)* vélo *m* de course

racetrack [ˈreɪstræk] *n (for athletes, cars)* piste *f*; *Am (for horses)* champ *m* de courses

racial [ˈreɪʃəl] *adj* racial(e); **r. discrimination** discrimination *f* raciale

racing [ˈreɪsɪŋ] **1** *n* les courses *fpl*
   2 *adj* **r. bicycle/car** vélo *m*/voiture *f* de course

racism [ˈreɪsɪzəm] *n* racisme *m*

racist [ˈreɪsɪst] *n & adj* raciste *mf*

rack [ræk] **1** *n* **(a)** *(for bottles)* casier *m*; *(for plates)* égouttoir *m*; *(for goods in shop)* présentoir *m*; *(for luggage)* porte-bagages *m inv*; **r. and pinion** crémaillère *f* **(b)** *(for torture)* chevalet *m*; *Fig* **to be on the r.** avoir des ennuis **(c)** *(idioms)* **to go to r. and ruin** aller de

mal en pis
   2 *vt (torment)* tourmenter; **to be racked with guilt** être rongé(e) par le remords; **to be racked with pain** être tenaillé(e) par la douleur; **to r. one's brains** se creuser la tête

racket¹ [ˈrækɪt] *n (for tennis)* raquette *f*

racket² *n Fam* **(a)** *(noise)* vacarme *m*, tapage *m*; **to make a r.** faire du vacarme *ou* tapage **(b)** *(criminal activity)* racket *m*

racketeer [rækɪˈtɪə(r)] *n* racketteur *m*

racketeering [rækɪˈtɪərɪŋ] *n* racket *m*

racquet [ˈrækɪt] *n (for tennis)* raquette *f*

racy [ˈreɪsɪ] *adj (risqué)* osé(e); *(lively)* savoureux(-euse), piquant(e)

RADA [ˈrɑːdə] *n Br (abbr* **Royal Academy of Dramatic Art***)* ≃ le Conservatoire national d'art dramatique

radar [ˈreɪdɑː(r)] *n* radar *m*; **r. operator** radariste *mf*; **r. screen** écran *m* radar

radial [ˈreɪdɪəl] **1** *n (tyre)* pneu *m* radial
   2 *adj* radial(e)

radiance [ˈreɪdɪəns] *n* éclat *m*, rayonnement *m*

radiant [ˈreɪdɪənt] *adj (light)* éclatant(e); *(person)* resplendissant(e)

radiate [ˈreɪdɪeɪt] **1** *vt (heat, light)* émettre; *Fig (happiness, health)* être rayonnant(e) de; *Fig (optimism, enthusiasm)* être débordant(e) de
   2 *vi* rayonner (**from** à partir de)

radiation [reɪdɪˈeɪʃən] *n* radiation *f*

radiator [ˈreɪdɪeɪtə(r)] *n (heater)* radiateur *m*

radical [ˈrædɪkəl] *n & adj* radical(e) *m,f*

radicalism [ˈrædɪkəlɪzəm] *n* radicalisme *m*

radio [ˈreɪdɪəʊ] **1** *n (pl* **radios***)* radio *f*; **r. alarm (clock)** radio-réveil *m*; **r. cassette (recorder** *or* **player)** radio-cassette *m*; **r. station** station *f* de radio
   2 *vt (pt & pp* **radioed***) (information)* communiquer par radio; *(person)* contacter par radio
   3 *vi* **to r. for help** demander de l'aide par radio

Radio

Les principales stations de radio de la BBC sont: Radio 1 (bulletins d'information, musique pop et rock); Radio 2 (variétés); Radio 3 (musique classique); Radio 4 (actualités, reportages, théâtre, programmes éducatifs); Radio 5 Live (sports, programmes éducatifs, musique pop et rock). La BBC comprend également trente-neuf stations locales. Il existe d'autre part plus de cent stations indépendantes.

---

radioactive [reɪdɪəʊˈæktɪv] *adj* radioactif(ive); **r. waste** déchets *mpl* radioactifs

radioactivity [reɪdɪəʊæk'tɪvɪtɪ] n radioactivité f
radio-controlled [reɪdɪəʊkən'trəʊld] adj télécommandé(e)
radiographer [reɪdɪ'ɒgrəfə(r)] n radiologue mf
radiography [reɪdɪ'ɒgrəfɪ] n radiographie f
radiologist [reɪdɪ'ɒlədʒɪst] n radiologue mf
radiology [reɪdɪ'ɒlədʒɪ] n radiologie f
radiotherapy [reɪdɪəʊ'θerəpɪ] n radiothérapie f
radish ['rædɪʃ] n radis m
radium ['reɪdɪəm] n Chem radium m
radius ['reɪdɪəs] (pl **radii** ['reɪdɪaɪ]) n rayon m; **within a r. of** dans un rayon de
radon ['reɪdɒn] n Chem radon m
RAF [ɑːreɪ'ef] n Mil (abbr **Royal Air Force**) = armée de l'air britannique
raffia ['ræfɪə] n raphia m
raffish ['ræfɪʃ] adj canaille
raffle ['ræfəl] **1** n tombola f; **r. ticket** billet m de tombola
2 vt donner comme lot à une tombola
raft [rɑːft] n radeau m
rafter ['rɑːftə(r)] n chevron m
rag¹ [ræg] n (**a**) (piece of cloth) chiffon m; **rags** (clothes) haillons mpl, guenilles fpl; **to go from rags to riches** passer de la misère à la richesse; **hers is a rags to riches story** elle est partie de rien; Br Fam **to lose one's r.** piquer une crise; **r. doll** poupée f de chiffon; Fam **the r. trade** la confection (**b**) Fam Pej (newspaper) torchon m
rag² **1** n Old-fashioned (prank) farce f, canular m; Univ **r. week** = semaine de divertissements organisés par les étudiants au profit d'œuvres de charité
2 vt (pt & pp **ragged**) Old-fashioned (tease) taquiner
ragamuffin ['rægəmʌfɪn] n polisson(onne) m,f
rag-and-bone man [rægən'bəʊnmæn] n chiffonnier m
ragbag ['rægbæg] n ramassis m
rage [reɪdʒ] **1** n (**a**) (fury) rage f, fureur f; **to be in a r.** être furieux(euse) (**b**) Fam (fashion) **to be all the r.** faire fureur
2 vi (**a**) (of person) être furieux(euse) (**against** or **at** contre) (**b**) (of sea) être démonté(e); (of epidemic, war) faire rage
ragga ['rægə] n Mus ragga m
ragged ['rægɪd] adj (clothes) en haillons, en lambeaux; (edge) irrégulier(ère); (person) en haillons; Fam **to run oneself r.** s'épuiser
raging ['reɪdʒɪŋ] adj (**a**) (person) furieux(euse); **to be in a r. temper** être furieux (**b**) (sea) démonté(e); (fever, headache) violent(e); (thirst) terrible
ragwort ['rægwɜːt] n Bot séneçon m
raid [reɪd] **1** n (on bank) hold-up m inv; (by army) raid m; (by police) descente f
2 vt (of robbers) attaquer; (of army) faire un raid sur; (of police) faire une descente dans; Fig & Hum **to r. the fridge** faire la razzia dans le frigo
raider ['reɪdə(r)] n (criminal) voleur(euse) m,f
rail¹ [reɪl] n (**a**) (of stairway) rampe f; (of balcony) balustrade f (**b**) (train system) chemin m de fer; (track) rail m; **by r.** par le ou en chemin de fer; Fig **to go off the rails** (of person) s'écarter du droit chemin; **r. network** réseau m ferroviaire; **r. strike** grève f des chemins de fer ou des cheminots
rail² vi **to r. at** or **against sth** s'insurger contre qch
railcar ['reɪlkɑː(r)] n Am wagon m

railcard ['reɪlkɑːd] n carte f d'abonnement de train; Br **young person's r.** ≃ carte Jeunes
railings ['reɪlɪŋz] npl grille f
railroad ['reɪlrəʊd] **1** n Am (system) chemin m de fer; (track) voie f ferrée
2 vt Fam **to r. sb into doing sth** forcer qn à faire qch
railway ['reɪlweɪ] n Br (system) chemin m de fer; (track) voie f ferrée; **r. carriage** voiture f; **r. line** ligne f de chemin de fer; **r. station** gare f
railwayman ['reɪlweɪmən] n Br & Can cheminot m
rain [reɪn] **1** n pluie f; **in the r.** sous la pluie; **it looks like r.** on dirait qu'il va pleuvoir; **the rains** la saison des pluies; **come r. or shine** (whatever the weather) qu'il pleuve ou qu'il vente; (whatever the circumstances) quoi qu'il arrive; Fam Fig **I'll take a r. check on that** ça sera pour une autre fois; **r. cloud** nuage m de pluie; **r. dance** danse f de la pluie
2 vt **to r. gifts on sb** couvrir qn de cadeaux; **to r. blows on sb** rouer qn de coups
3 vi pleuvoir; **it's raining** il pleut; Br Fam **it's raining cats and dogs** il pleut des cordes; Prov **it never rains but it pours** un malheur n'arrive jamais seul
rainbow ['reɪnbəʊ] n arc-en-ciel m; **r. coalition** coalition f des minorités; **r. trout** truite f arc-en-ciel
raincoat ['reɪnkəʊt] n imperméable m
raindrop ['reɪndrɒp] n goutte f de pluie
rainfall ['reɪnfɔːl] n précipitations fpl
rainforest ['reɪnfɒrɪst] n forêt f tropicale humide
rainproof ['reɪnpruːf] adj imperméable
rainslicker ['reɪnslɪkə(r)] n Am ciré m
rainstorm ['reɪnstɔːm] n pluie f torrentielle
rainwater ['reɪnwɔːtə(r)] n eau f de pluie
rainy ['reɪnɪ] adj pluvieux(euse); (day) de pluie; Fig **to save sth for a r. day** mettre qch de côté; **the r. season** la saison des pluies
raise [reɪz] **1** vt (**a**) (lift) lever; **to r. one's voice** élever la voix; **to r. one's glass to one's lips** porter son verre à ses lèvres; Fig **to r. one's hat to sb** tirer son chapeau à qn; Fam Fig **to r. the roof** faire du raffut (**b**) (price, salary) augmenter; (standard) élever; Fig **to r. the stakes** faire monter la mise (**c**) (problem, subject) soulever (**d**) (fears, doubts) faire naître; **to r. a smile/laugh** faire sourire/rire; **to r. sb's hopes** donner trop d'espoir à qn; **to r. the alarm** donner l'alarme; Fam **to r. hell** or **Cain** faire un foin d'enfer (**e**) (money) rassembler; (for charity) collecter (**f**) (children, cattle) élever; (crops) cultiver (**g**) (statue) dresser
2 n Am (pay increase) augmentation f (de salaire)
raisin ['reɪzən] n raisin m sec
rake [reɪk] **1** n (**a**) (garden tool) râteau m; **to be as thin as a r.** être maigre comme un clou (**b**) (dissolute man) libertin m
2 vt (leaves, soil) ratisser; **to r. one's memory** fouiller dans sa mémoire
▸**rake about, rake around** vi (search) fouiller (**for** pour trouver)
▸**rake in** vt sep Fam (money) rapporter; **she's raking it in!** elle s'en met plein les poches!
▸**rake off** vt sep Fam (money) empocher
▸**rake over** vt sep (subject, the past) ressasser
rakish ['reɪkɪʃ] adj (dissolute) libertin(e); (jaunty) désinvolte
rally ['rælɪ] **1** n (pl **rallies**) (**a**) (protest gathering) manifestation f (**b**) (in tennis) échange m (**c**) (car race) rallye m; **r. driver** pilote mf de rallye
2 vt (pt & pp **rallied**) (troops) rallier; **to r. support for**

sb/sth gagner des appuis à la cause de qn/qch; **to r. sb's spirits** redonner courage à qn; **rallying cry** cri *m* de ralliement

3 *vi (of prices)* se redresser; *(of patient)* aller mieux; **to r. to sb's defence** se porter au secours de qn

▸**rally round 1** *vt insep* soutenir

2 *vi* apporter son soutien

RAM [ræm] *n Comput (abbr* **random access memory)** mémoire *f* vive

ram [ræm] **1** *n* (**a**) *(animal)* bélier *m* (**b**) *(implement)* (**battering) r.** bélier *m*

2 *vt (pt & pp* **rammed)** (**a**) *(crash into)* percuter; *(of ship)* aborder (**b**) *(force into place)* tasser; *Fam* **to r. one's views down sb's throat** bassiner qn avec ses opinions

Ramadan [ræmə'dɑːn] *n Rel* le ramadan

ramble ['ræmbəl] **1** *n (walk)* randonnée *f* (pédestre)

2 *vi* (**a**) *(walk)* faire une randonnée (**b**) *(digress)* divaguer

▸**ramble on** *vi* divaguer; **to r. on about sth** radoter à propos de qch

rambler ['ræmblə(r)] *n (walker)* randonneur(euse) *m,f*

rambling ['ræmblɪŋ] **1** *n* (**a**) *(walking)* **to go r.** aller en randonnée (**b**) **ramblings** *(words)* divagations *fpl*

2 *adj* (**a**) *(letter, speech)* décousu(e) (**b**) *(house)* plein(e) de coins et de recoins; **r. rose** rosier *m* grimpant

ramification [ræmɪfɪ'keɪʃən] *n (consequence)* conséquence *f*

ramp [ræmp] *n* rampe *f*; *(to plane)* passerelle *f*; *(on road)* petit dos *m* d'âne

rampage 1 *n* ['ræmpeɪdʒ] **to go on the r.** *(lose control)* se déchaîner; *(cause damage)* tout saccager

2 *vi* [ræm'peɪdʒ] **to r. about** se déchaîner

rampant ['ræmpənt] *adj* endémique; **corruption is r.** la corruption sévit

rampart ['ræmpɑːt] *n* rempart *m*

ramrod ['ræmrɒd] *n (for rifle)* écouvillon *m*; *Fig* **r. straight** raide comme un piquet

ramshackle ['ræmʃækəl] *adj (building)* délabré(e); *(economy, organization)* qui s'effondre

ran [ræn] *pt of* **run**

ranch [rɑːntʃ] *n* ranch *m*

rancher ['rɑːntʃə(r)] *n* propriétaire *mf* de ranch

rancid ['rænsɪd] *adj* rance; **to go r.** rancir

rancour ['ræŋkə(r)] *n* rancœur *f*

rand [rænd] *n* rand *m*

random ['rændəm] **1** *n* **at r.** au hasard

2 *adj (choice, sample)* (fait(e)) au hasard; *Comput* **r. access memory** mémoire *f* vive; **r. sampling** prélèvement *m* d'échantillons au hasard

randy ['rændɪ] *adj Br Fam* excité(e)

rang [ræŋ] *pt of* **ring²**

range [reɪndʒ] **1** *n* (**a**) *(of weapon, telescope)* portée *f*; **within r.** *(of fire)* à portée de tir; *(of hearing)* à portée de la voix; **out of r.** hors de portée (**b**) *(of prices, colours, products)* gamme *f*; *(of instrument, voice)* registre *m*; *(of knowledge, research)* étendue *f* (**c**) *(of hills, mountains)* chaîne *f* (**d**) *(practice area)* **(shooting) r.** champ *m* de tir (**e**) *(cooker)* fourneau *m*

2 *vt* (**a**) *(arrange in row)* ranger; **to r. oneself with sb** se ranger du côté de qn; **to r. oneself against sb** s'opposer à qn (**b**) *(travel)* parcourir

3 *vi* (**a**) *(extend)* **to r. from... to** aller de... à (**b**) **to r. over** *(include)* porter sur

rangefinder ['reɪndʒfaɪndə(r)] *n* télémètre *m*

ranger ['reɪndʒə(r)] *n (in forest)* garde *m* forestier; *Am Mil* commando *m*

rangy ['reɪndʒɪ] *adj* élancé(e)

rank¹ [ræŋk] **1** *n* (**a**) *(status)* grade *m*; *Fig* **to pull r.** abuser de son rang (**b**) *(row)* rangée *f*; *Mil* **the ranks** les hommes *mpl* du rang; *Fig* **to rise from the ranks** sortir du rang; *Fig* **the ranks of the unemployed** les rangs des chômeurs; *Fig* **to break ranks (with)** se désolidariser (de); *Fig* **to close ranks** se montrer solidaire; **(taxi) r.** station *f* de taxis

2 *vt* placer (**among** parmi); **to r. sb/sth as** considérer qn/qch comme

3 *vi* compter (**among** parmi); **to r. as** être considéré(e) comme; **to r. above/below sb** être supérieur(e)/inférieur(e) à qn; **this ranks as a major disaster** on peut qualifier ceci de catastrophe majeure

rank² *adj* (**a**) *(foul-smelling)* fétide (**b**) *(absolute)* total(e); **she's a r. outsider** elle n'est vraiment pas dans la course

rank-and-file [ræŋkən'faɪl] *n* **the r.** *(in army)* les hommes *mpl* du rang; *(of political party)* la base

ranking ['ræŋkɪŋ] *n (classification)* classement *m*

rankle ['ræŋkəl] *vi* **it still rankles with me** cela m'est resté sur l'estomac

ransack ['rænsæk] *vt (house, desk)* mettre sens dessus dessous; *(shop, town)* piller

ransom ['rænsəm] **1** *n* rançon *f*; **to hold sb to r.** rançonner qn; *Fig* retenir qn en otage

2 *vt* rançonner

rant [rænt] *vi Fam* déblatérer (**about/at** au sujet de/contre); **to r. and rave** tempêter (**about/at** au sujet de/contre)

rap [ræp] **1** *n* (**a**) *(sharp blow)* coup *m* sec; *Fig* **to take the r. for sth** écoper *ou* trinquer pour qch (**b**) *(music)* rap *m*

2 *vt (pt & pp* **rapped)** *(window, door)* frapper à; *(table)* frapper sur; *Fig* **to r. sb's knuckles, to r. sb over the knuckles** taper sur les doigts de qn

3 *vi* (**a**) *(hit)* frapper (**on** à) (**b**) *(sing)* rapper

rapacious [rə'peɪʃəs] *adj* rapace

rape¹ [reɪp] **1** *n (crime)* viol *m*; *Fig (of countryside, environment)* destruction *f*

2 *vt* violer

rape² *n (crop)* colza *m*

rapid ['ræpɪd] *adj* rapide; **r. reaction force** force *f* d'intervention rapide

rapidity [rə'pɪdɪtɪ] *n* rapidité *f*

rapidly ['ræpɪdlɪ] *adv* rapidement

rapids ['ræpɪdz] *npl (in river)* rapides *mpl*

rapier ['reɪpɪə(r)] *n* rapière *f*

rapist ['reɪpɪst] *n* violeur *m*

rapper ['ræpə(r)] *n (singer)* rappeur(euse) *m,f*

rapport [ræ'pɔː(r)] *n* **to have a good r. (with sb)** avoir de bons rapports (avec qn)

rapt [ræpt] *adj (attention)* profond(e); *(look)* absorbé(e); *(smile)* d'extase

rapture ['ræptʃə(r)] *n* extase *f*; **to be in raptures** être ravi(e); **to go into raptures over sb/sth** s'extasier devant qn/sur qch

rapturous ['ræptʃərəs] *adj (cries)* d'extase; *(applause)* frénétique; *(reception, welcome)* enthousiaste

rare [reə(r)] *adj* (**a**) *(animal, stamp)* rare; **to have a r. gift (for sth)** être exceptionnellement doué(e) (pour qch) (**b**) *(steak)* saignant(e)

rarefied ['reərɪfaɪd] *adj (air, gas)* raréfié(e); *Fig (atmosphere, ideas)* fermé(e)

rarely ['reəlɪ] *adv* rarement

raring ['reərɪŋ] *adj* **to be r. to do sth** être impatient(e) de faire qch; **to be r. to go** piaffer d'impatience

rarity ['reərɪtɪ] (*pl* **rarities**) *n* rareté *f*; **to be/become a r. value** rareté

rascal ['rɑːskəl] *n (child)* coquin(e) *m,f*; *Old-fashioned or Hum (scoundrel)* vaurien(enne) *m,f*

rash¹ [ræʃ] *n* (**a**) *(on skin) (spots)* éruption *f*; *(red area)* rougeurs *fpl* (**b**) *(series)* série *f*

rash² *adj (imprudent)* irréfléchi(e)

rasher ['ræʃə(r)] *n Br (of bacon)* tranche *f*

rashly ['ræʃlɪ] *adv* sans réfléchir

rasp [rɑːsp] **1** *n* (**a**) *(tool)* râpe *f* (**b**) *(sound)* grincement *m*
2 *vt (say hoarsely)* grogner

raspberry ['rɑːzbərɪ] (*pl* **raspberries**) *n (fruit)* framboise *f*; *(plant)* framboisier *m*; *Fam Fig* **to blow a r.** souffler en signe de dérision; **r. jam** confiture *f* de framboises

rat [ræt] **1** *n* (**a**) *(animal)* rat *m*; **r. poison** mort-aux-rats *f inv*; **r. trap** piège *m* à rats, ratière *f* (**b**) *Fam (scoundrel)* dégueulasse *mf* (**c**) *(idioms)* **to smell a r.** flairer quelque chose de louche; **r. race** foire *f* d'empoigne
2 *vi (pt & pp* **ratted**) *Fam (inform)* **to r. on sb** dénoncer qn

ratchet ['rætʃɪt] *n* rochet *m*; **r. (wheel)** roue *f* à rochet

rate [reɪt] **1** *n* (**a**) *(of inflation, interest)* taux *m*; *Fin* **r. of return** taux de rendement (**b**) *(speed)* rythme *m*; **at this r.** à ce rythme (**c**) **at any r.** en tout cas (**d**) *(price, charge)* tarif *m* (**e**) *Br Formerly* **rates** *(local tax)* impôts *mpl* locaux
2 *vt* (**a**) *(classify)* placer (**among** parmi); **to r. sb/sth as** considérer qn/qch comme; **to r. sb/sth highly** tenir qn/qch en haute estime (**b**) *(deserve)* mériter; **to r. a mention** mériter d'être mentionné(e)
3 *vi* **to r. as** être considéré(e) comme

rateable value ['reɪtəbəl'vælju:] *n Br Formerly* valeur *f* locative nette

ratepayer ['reɪtpeɪə(r)] *n Br Formerly* contribuable *mf* *(pour les impôts locaux)*

rather ['rɑːðə(r)] *adv* (**a**) *(preferably)* **I'd r. stay** j'aimerais mieux rester; **I'd r. not go** j'aimerais mieux ne pas y aller; **I'd r. not** je n'y tiens pas; **r. you than me!** je n'aimerais pas être à ta place (**b**) *(more exactly)* plutôt; **he sounded surprised or, r., annoyed** il semblait surpris, ou plutôt, fâché (**c**) *(fairly)* assez; **I r. liked it** j'ai bien aimé (**d**) **r. than him** plutôt que lui; **r. than staying** plutôt que de rester

ratification ['rætɪfɪkeɪʃən] *n* ratification *f*

ratify ['rætɪfaɪ] (*pt & pp* **ratified**) *vt* ratifier

rating ['reɪtɪŋ] *n (of popularity)* classement *m*; **the ratings** *(for TV, radio)* l'indice *m* d'écoute, l'Audimat® *m*

ratio ['reɪʃɪəʊ] (*pl* **ratios**) *n* rapport *m*

ration ['ræʃən, *Am* 'reɪʃən] **1** *n* ration *f*; *Fig (dose)* dose *f*; **rations** *(supplies)* provisions *fpl*; **r. book** carte *f* de rationnement
2 *vt* rationner

rational ['ræʃənəl] *adj (sensible)* raisonnable, sensé(e); *(sane)* rationnel(elle)

rationalism ['ræʃənəlɪzəm] *n* rationalisme *m*

rationalist ['ræʃənəlɪst] *n* rationaliste *mf*

rationalization [ræʃənəlaɪ'zeɪʃən] *n (of company)* rationalisation *f*

rationalize ['ræʃənəlaɪz] *vt* (**a**) *(action, dislike)* justifier (**b**) *(company)* rationaliser

rationally ['ræʃənəlɪ] *adv (sensibly)* raisonnablement; *(sanely)* rationnellement

rationing [ræʃənɪŋ] *n* rationnement *m*

rattle ['rætəl] **1** *n* (**a**) *(for baby)* hochet *m* (**b**) *(noise) (of train, chains, keys)* cliquetis *m*; *(of gunfire)* crépitement *m*; *(of door, window)* frottement *m*
2 *vt* (**a**) *(chains, keys)* faire cliqueter; *(door, window)* faire vibrer (**b**) *Fam (make nervous)* démonter
3 *vi (of chains, keys)* cliqueter; *(of door, window)* vibrer

▸**rattle off** *vt sep Fam (list, facts)* débiter

▸**rattle on** *vi Fam* parler sans cesse

▸**rattle through** *vt insep Fam (work, book)* expédier

rattlesnake ['rætəlsneɪk] *n* serpent *m* à sonnette

ratty ['rætɪ] *adj Br Fam (annoyed)* irrité(e); *(irritable)* irritable

raucous ['rɔːkəs] *adj (hoarse)* rauque; *(rowdy)* bruyant(e)

raunchy ['rɔːntʃɪ] *adj Fam (film, scene, lyrics)* osé(e); *(dress)* provocant(e)

ravage [rævɪdʒ] **1** *npl* **ravages** ravages *mpl*
2 *vt* ravager

rave [reɪv] **1** *n* rave *f*
2 *adj (review)* dithyrambique
3 *vi (deliriously)* délirer; **to r. about sb/sth** *(enthusiastically)* être dithyrambique à propos de qn/qch

raven ['reɪvən] **1** *n (bird)* grand corbeau *m*
2 *adj (colour)* noir de jais *inv*

ravenous ['rævənəs] *adj (animal)* vorace; *(person)* affamé(e)

raver ['reɪvə(r)] *n Br Fam (socially active person)* noceur(euse) *m,f*; *(who goes to raves)* raver *mf*

rave-up ['reɪvʌp] *n Br Fam* fiesta *f*, nouba *f*

ravine [rə'viːn] *n* ravin *m*

raving ['reɪvɪŋ] *adj* (**a**) *(delirious)* **r. mad** complètement fou (folle); **a r. lunatic** un fou furieux (une folle furieuse) (**b**) *(success)* éclatant(e)

ravish ['rævɪʃ] *vt* (**a**) *Lit (delight)* enchanter, ravir (**b**) *Old-fashioned (rape)* violenter

ravishing ['rævɪʃɪŋ] *adj* magnifique

raw [rɔː] *adj* (**a**) *(food)* cru(e); *(silk, sugar, statistics)* brut(e); **r. materials** matières *fpl* premières; **r. recruit** bleu *m* (**b**) *(skin)* écorché(e); *Fig* **to get a r. deal** être mal traité(e); *Fig* **to touch a r. nerve** toucher un point sensible (**c**) *(weather, wind)* glacial(e)

ray¹ [reɪ] *n (of light, sun)* rayon *m*; *Fig (of hope)* lueur *f*

ray² *n (fish)* raie *f*

rayon ['reɪɒn] *n (fabric)* rayonne *f*

raze [reɪz] *vt* **to r. sth to the ground** raser qch

razor ['reɪzə(r)] *n* rasoir *m*; **r. blade** lame *f* de rasoir

razor-sharp ['reɪzəʃɑːp] *adj (knife)* effilé(e); *Fig (intelligence, wit)* vif (vive)

razor-shell ['reɪzəʃel] *n* couteau *m*

razzmatazz ['ræzmətæz] *n Fam* tape-à-l'œil *m inv*

RC [ɑː'siː] *n & adj (abbr* **Roman Catholic**) catholique *mf*

R & D [ɑːrən'diː] *n Com (abbr* **research and development**) recherche et développement

Rd *(abbr* **Road**) rue

RDA [ɑːdiː'eɪ] *n* (*abbr* **recommended daily allowance**) recommandation *f* quotidienne officielle (*en vitamines, sels minéraux etc*)

RE [ɑː'riː] *n* (*abbr* **Religious Education**) instruction *f* religieuse

re¹ [riː] *prep* concernant; **re your letter** suite à votre lettre; **re: 1997 sales figures** Réf: les ventes de 1997

re² [reɪ] *n Mus* ré *m*

reach [riːtʃ] **1** *n* (**a**) (*accessibility*) portée *f*; **within r.** (*thing*) à portée de main; (*location*) tout(e) proche; **out of r.** hors de portée (**b**) (*of river*) **the upper reaches** l'amont *m*

2 *vt* (**a**) (*destination, conclusion*) atteindre, arriver à; (*agreement*) aboutir à; (*decision*) prendre; **the news didn't r. her** les nouvelles ne lui sont pas parvenues (**b**) (*contact*) joindre; **to r. a wider audience** toucher un public plus important (**c**) (*stretch as far as*) (*one's shoulder, waist*) atteindre, arriver jusqu'à

3 *vi* (*extend*) (*of forest, property*) s'étendre (**to** jusqu'à); (*of noise, voice*) porter (**to** jusqu'à); **to r. for sth** tendre le bras pour prendre qch; *Fig* **to r. for the sky** *or* **the stars** viser très haut

▸**reach out** *vi* tendre le bras

reachable ['riːtʃəbəl] *adj* accessible

react [rɪ'ækt] *vi* réagir (**against/to** contre/à)

reaction [rɪ'ækʃən] *n* réaction *f*

reactionary [rɪ'ækʃənərɪ] (*pl* **reactionaries**) *n & adj* réactionnaire *mf*

reactivate [rɪ'æktɪveɪt] *vt* réactiver

reactor [rɪ'æktə(r)] *n* réacteur *m*

read [riːd] **1** *n* to have a r. lire; **her books are a good r.** ses livres se lisent bien

2 *vt* (*pt & pp* **read** [red]) (**a**) (*book, newspaper, letter*) lire; **do you r. me?** (*on radio*) est-ce que vous me recevez?; *Fig* **to take it as read that...** considérer comme acquis que... (**b**) (*interpret*) interpréter; **to r. sb's mind** lire dans les pensées de qn; **to r. the future** prédire l'avenir (**c**) *Br Univ* (*study*) étudier (**d**) (*of dial, thermometer*) indiquer; (*of inscription*) être; **the sign read...** sur l'écriteau, on pouvait lire...

3 *vi* (**a**) (*of person*) lire; **to r. aloud** lire à haute voix; **I'd read about it in the newspapers** je l'avais lu dans les journaux; *Fig* **to r. between the lines** lire entre les lignes (**b**) (*of text*) **to r. well/badly** se lire facilement/difficilement

▸**read out** *vt sep* lire (à haute voix)

▸**read up on** *vt sep* étudier

readable ['riːdəbəl] *adj* (*book*) facile à lire; (*handwriting*) lisible

reader ['riːdə(r)] *n* (**a**) (*of book, newspaper etc*) lecteur(trice) *m,f* (**b**) (*reading book*) livre *m* de lecture (**c**) (*device*) lecteur *m* (**d**) *Am Univ* ≃ assistant(e) *m,f*; *Can Univ* ≃ chargé(e) *m,f* de cours

readily ['redɪlɪ] *adv* (*willingly*) volontiers; (*easily*) facilement

reading ['riːdɪŋ] *n* (**a**) (*action, interpretation, pastime*) lecture *f*; **r. glasses** lunettes *fpl* de lecture (**b**) (*measurement*) relevé *m*

readjust [riːə'dʒʌst] **1** *vt* (*figures, salaries*) réajuster; (*instrument*) remettre au point; (*clothing*) rajuster

2 *vi* se réadapter (**to** à)

readjustment [riːə'dʒʌstmənt] *n* (*of figures, salaries*) réajustement *m*; (*of person*) réadaptation *f*

readmit [riːəd'mɪt] (*pt & pp* **readmitted**) *vt* (*to club, party*) réintégrer (**to** à); **to r. sb (to hospital)** réhospitaliser qn

read-only ['riːd'əʊnlɪ] *adj Comput* (*file*) à lecture seule; **r. memory** mémoire *f* morte

readvertise [riː'ædvətaɪz] *vt* repasser une annonce pour

ready ['redɪ] **1** *adj* (**a**) (*prepared*) prêt(e) (**for** pour); **to be r. to do sth** être prêt à faire qch; **to get r.** se préparer; **to get sth r.** préparer qch; **to be r. for bed** être prêt à se coucher; **r.!, steady!, go!** à vos marques, prêts, partez!; **r. cash** argent *m* liquide (**b**) (*willing*) **to be r. to do sth** être prêt(e) *ou* disposé(e) à faire qch (**c**) (*quick*) **to have a r. wit** avoir l'esprit vif

2 *vt* (*pt & pp* **readied**) (*prepare*) préparer

3 *n* (**a**) **at the r.** prêt(e) (**b**) *Fam* **readies** (*cash*) ronds *mpl*

ready-made [redɪ'meɪd] *adj* (*food*) tout(e) préparé(e); (*excuse, phrase*) tout(e) fait(e)

reaffirm [riːə'fɜːm] *vt* réaffirmer

reafforestation [riːəfɒrɪ'steɪʃən] *n* reboisement *m*

real [rɪəl] **1** *adj* (**a**) (*authentic*) vrai(e); (*gold, leather*) véritable; (*danger, fear, effort*) réel(elle); **r. ale** = bière brune de fabrication traditionnelle (**b**) (*actual*) réel(elle); **the r. world** la réalité; **what does that mean in r. terms?** qu'est-ce que cela signifie en clair?; *Com* **r. estate** (*property*) biens *mpl* immobiliers; (*profession*) l'immobilier *m* (**c**) (*for emphasis*) **a r. idiot** un véritable idiot

2 *adv Am Fam* (*very*) très

realism ['rɪəlɪzəm] *n* réalisme *m*

realist ['rɪəlɪst] *n* réaliste *mf*

realistic [rɪə'lɪstɪk] *adj* réaliste

reality [rɪ'ælɪtɪ] (*pl* **realities**) *n* réalité *f*; **in r.** en réalité; *Fam* **it was a r. check for him** ça l'a ramené à la réalité; *TV* **r. show** reality show *m*

realize ['rɪəlaɪz] *vt* (**a**) (*become aware of*) se rendre compte de; **I r. he's busy, but...** j'ai bien conscience qu'il est occupé mais... (**b**) (*ambition, dream*) réaliser

really ['rɪəlɪ] *adv* vraiment; (*in actual fact*) en réalité

realm [relm] *n* (**a**) (*kingdom*) royaume *m* (**b**) (*field*) domaine *m*

realtor ['rɪəltə(r)] *n Am* agent *m* immobilier

ream [riːm] *n* (*of paper*) rame *f*; *Fig* **reams of** des quantités de

reanimate [riː'ænɪmeɪt] *vt* r(é)animer

reap [riːp] *vt* moissonner; **to r. the benefits (of)** récolter les bénéfices (de)

reaper ['riːpə(r)] *n* (*machine*) moissonneuse *f*; *Lit* **the Grim R.** la Faucheuse

reappear [riːə'pɪə(r)] *vi* réapparaître

reappearance [riːə'pɪərəns] *n* réapparition *f*

reapply [riːə'plaɪ] (*pt & pp* **reapplied**) *vi* (*for job*) poser à nouveau sa candidature (**for** à)

reappraise [riːə'preɪz] *vt* réévaluer; (*policy*) réexaminer

rear¹ [rɪə(r)] *n* (**a**) (*back part*) arrière *m*; **at the r. of** (*inside*) à l'arrière de; (*behind*) derrière; **in the r.** à l'arrière; **to bring up the r.** être en queue; **r. admiral** contre-amiral *m*; **r. entrance** entrée *f* de derrière; **r. legs** pattes *fpl* de derrière; **r. lights** feux *mpl* arrière; **r. window** vitre *f* arrière (**b**) *Fam* (*buttocks*) derrière *m*

rear² *vt* (**a**) (*child, livestock*) élever (**b**) (*one's head*) relever; *Fig* **to r. its ugly head** faire son apparition

▸**rear up** *vi* (*of horse*) se cabrer

rearguard ['rɪəɡɑːd] *n Mil* arrière-garde *f*; *also Fig* **r. action** combat *m* d'arrière-garde

rearm [riː'ɑːm] *vt & vi* réarmer

rearmament [riː'ɑːməmənt] *n* réarmement *m*

rearrange [riːə'reɪndʒ] *vt (books, furniture)* changer la disposition de; *(appointment)* changer

reason ['riːzən] **1** *n* (**a**) *(cause, motive)* raison *f* (**for** de); **for no particular r.** sans raison précise; **I don't know the r. why** je ne sais pas pourquoi; *Ironic* **for reasons best known to himself** pour une raison connue de lui seul; **give me one good r. why I should!** donne-moi une raison valable de le faire! (**b**) *(sanity, common sense)* raison *f*; **to listen to** *or* **see r.** entendre raison; **it stands to r.** il va de soi *ou* sans dire; **within r.** dans des limites raisonnables
2 *vt* **to r. that** estimer que
3 *vi* raisonner (**about/with** sur/avec)

reasonable ['riːzənəbəl] *adj* (**a**) *(fair)* raisonnable; *(excuse)* valable (**b**) *(quite good)* passable

reasonably ['riːzənəblɪ] *adv* (**a**) *(behave, act)* raisonnablement (**b**) *(quite)* plutôt

reasoning ['riːzənɪŋ] *n (thinking)* raisonnement *m*

reassemble [riːə'sembəl] **1** *vt (people)* rassembler; *(machine)* remonter
2 *vi (of people)* se rassembler

reassess [riːə'ses] *vt* (**a**) *(policy, situation)* reconsidérer (**b**) *Fin (tax, property)* réévaluer

reassurance [riːə'ʃʊərəns] *n (comfort)* réconfort *m*; *(guarantee)* assurance *f*

reassure [riːə'ʃʊə(r)] *vt* rassurer

reassuring [riːə'ʃʊərɪŋ] *adj* rassurant(e)

reawaken [riːə'weɪkən] **1** *vt (interest, feeling)* faire renaître
2 *vi (of person)* se réveiller à nouveau

rebate ['riːbeɪt] *n (refund)* remboursement *m*; *(discount)* rabais *m*

rebel 1 *n* ['rebəl] rebelle *mf*
2 *vi* [rɪ'bel] *(pt & pp* **rebelled***)* se rebeller (**against** contre)

rebellion [rɪ'beljən] *n* rébellion *f*

rebellious [rɪ'beljəs] *adj* rebelle

rebirth [riː'bɜːθ] *n* renaissance *f*

reborn [riː'bɔːn] *adj* **to be r.** renaître

rebound 1 *n* ['riːbaʊnd] *(of ball)* rebond *m*; *Fig* **she married him on the r.** elle l'a épousé à la suite d'une déception sentimentale
2 *vi* [rɪ'baʊnd] *(of ball)* rebondir; *Fig (of joke, lie)* se retourner (**on** contre)

rebuff [rɪ'bʌf] **1** *n (of person)* rebuffade *f*; *(of suggestion)* refus *m*; **to meet with a r.** *(of person)* essuyer une rebuffade; *(of suggestion)* être repoussé(e)
2 *vt* repousser

rebuild [riː'bɪld] *(pt & pp* **rebuilt** [riː'bɪlt]) *vt* reconstruire

rebuke [rɪ'bjuːk] **1** *n* réprimande *f*
2 *vt* réprimander

rebut [rɪ'bʌt] *(pt & pp* **rebutted***) vt* réfuter

rebuttal [rɪ'bʌtəl] *n* réfutation *f*

recalcitrant [rɪ'kælsɪtrənt] *adj* récalcitrant(e)

recall 1 *n* ['riːkɔːl] *(memory)* mémoire *f*; **lost beyond r.** irrévocablement perdu(e)
2 *vt* [rɪ'kɔːl] (**a**) *(remember)* se souvenir de, se rappeler; **to r. doing sth** se souvenir d'avoir fait qch, se rappeler avoir fait qch (**b**) *(defective goods)* rappeler; *(library book)* demander le retour de; *Br Pol* **to r. Parliament** rappeler le Parlement en session extraordinaire

recant [rɪ'kænt] **1** *vt (opinion)* rétracter
2 *vi* se rétracter

recap ['riːkæp] **1** *n (summary)* récapitulation *f*
2 *vi (pt & pp* **recapped***)* récapituler

recapitulate [riːkə'pɪtjʊleɪt] *vt & vi* récapituler

recapture [riː'kæptʃə(r)] **1** *n (of criminal)* capture *f*; *(of town, territory)* reprise *f*
2 *vt* (**a**) *(criminal)* capturer; *(town, territory)* reprendre (**b**) *Fig (memory, atmosphere)* faire revivre; *(one's youth)* retrouver

recede [rɪ'siːd] *vi (of tide)* se retirer; *(of coastline)* reculer; **to have a receding chin** avoir le menton fuyant; **to have a receding hairline** avoir le front qui se dégarnit

receipt [rɪ'siːt] *n* (**a**) *(act of receiving)* réception *f*; **to be in r. of sth** avoir reçu qch (**b**) *(proof of payment)* reçu *m*; **receipts** *(at box office)* recette *f*, entrées *fpl*

receive [rɪ'siːv] *vt* recevoir; *(stolen goods)* receler; **to be well/badly received** *(of film, proposal)* être bien/mal reçu(e); **to r. sb into the Church** admettre qn au sein de l'Église

received [rɪ'siːvd] *adj (idea)* reçu(e); *(opinion)* admis(e); **r. pronunciation** la prononciation standard de l'anglais *(celle du sud-est de l'Angleterre)*

receiver [rɪ'siːvə(r)] *n* (**a**) *(of stolen goods)* receleur(-euse) *m,f* (**b**) *(of telephone, radio set)* récepteur *m*; **to pick up the r.** décrocher; **to replace the r.** raccrocher (**c**) *Fin* administrateur *m* judiciaire

receivership [rɪ'siːvəʃɪp] *n Fin* **to go into r.** être placé(e) sous règlement judiciaire

receiving [rɪ'siːvɪŋ] **1** *n (of stolen goods)* recel *m*
2 *adj Fam* **to be on the r. end (of sth)** faire les frais (de qch)

recent ['riːsənt] *adj* récent(e); *(acquaintance)* nouveau(elle); *(development)* dernier(ère); **in r. months** au cours des derniers mois; **in r. times** récemment

recently ['riːsəntlɪ] *adv* récemment; **as r. as yesterday** pas plus tard qu'hier; **until quite r.** jusqu'à ces derniers temps

receptacle [rɪ'septəkəl] *n* récipient *m*

reception [rɪ'sepʃən] *n* (**a**) *(of guests, announcement, book)* accueil *m*; **to get a warm r.** être accueilli(e) chaleureusement; **r. centre** *(for refugees)* centre *m* d'accueil; **r. room** *(in house)* salon *m* (**b**) *(party)* réception *f*; **(wedding) r.** réception (**c**) *(in hotel)* **r. (desk)** réception *f* (**d**) *(of radio, TV programme)* réception *f*

receptionist [rɪ'sepʃənɪst] *n* réceptionniste *mf*

receptive [rɪ'septɪv] *adj* réceptif(ive)

recess ['riːses] *n* (**a**) *(of law courts, Parliament)* vacances *fpl* (**b**) *(in wall)* renfoncement *m*; *(smaller)* niche *f*; *(of mind, past)* recoins *mpl* (**c**) *Am Sch (between classes)* récréation *f*

recession [rɪ'seʃən] *n* récession *f*

recharge [riː'tʃɑːdʒ] *vt (battery)* recharger; *Fig* **to r. one's batteries** recharger ses batteries

rechargeable [riː'tʃɑːdʒəbəl] *adj* rechargeable

recidivism [rɪ'sɪdɪvɪzəm] *n Law* récidivisme *m*

recipe ['resɪpɪ] *n also Fig* recette *f*; **a r. for success** le secret de la réussite; **to be a r. for disaster** mener à la catastrophe; **r. book** livre *m* de recettes

recipient [rɪ'sɪpɪənt] *n (of gift, letter)* destinataire *mf*; *(of cheque, money)* bénéficiaire *mf*; *(of award, honour)* lauréat(e) *m,f*

reciprocal [rɪ'sɪprəkəl] *adj* réciproque

reciprocate [rɪ'sɪprəkeɪt] **1** *vt* retourner
2 *vi* rendre la pareille
recital [rɪ'saɪtəl] *n (of poetry, music)* récital *m*
recitation [resɪ'teɪʃən] *n (of poem)* récitation *f*
recite [rɪ'saɪt] **1** *vt (poem)* réciter; *(complaints, details)* énumérer
2 *vi* réciter
reckless ['reklɪs] *adj* imprudent(e); **r. driver** chauffard *m*
reckon ['rekən] **1** *vt* (**a**) *(consider)* considérer; **she is reckoned to be...** on la considère comme... (**b**) *(calculate)* calculer (**c**) *Fam (think)* penser
2 *vi* compter, calculer
▸**reckon on** *vt insep* compter sur
▸**reckon up** *vt sep* calculer
▸**reckon with** *vt insep* compter avec
reckoning ['rekənɪŋ] *n* estimation *f*; **by my r.** d'après mes calculs; **day of r.** moment *m* de vérité
reclaim [rɪ'kleɪm] *vt (lost property, waste materials)* récupérer; *(expenses)* se faire rembourser; **to r. land from the sea/the desert** gagner du terrain sur la mer/le désert
reclamation [reklə'meɪʃən] *n (of waste materials)* récupération *f*
recline [rɪ'klaɪn] *vi* s'allonger
reclining [rɪ'klaɪnɪŋ] *adj* **in a r. position** *(person)* en position allongée; **r. seat** siège *m* à dossier inclinable
recluse [rɪ'kluːs] *n* reclus(e) *m,f*
recognition [rekəg'nɪʃən] *n* reconnaissance *f*; **to have changed beyond** *or* **out of all r.** être devenu(e) méconnaissable; **in r. of** en reconnaissance de
recognizable [rekəg'naɪzəbəl] *adj* reconnaissable
recognize ['rekəgnaɪz] *vt* reconnaître
recognized ['rekəgnaɪzd] *adj* reconnu(e); **to be a r. authority (on sth)** faire autorité (en matière de qch)
recoil 1 *n* ['riːkɔɪl] *(of gun)* recul *m*
2 *vi* [rɪ'kɔɪl] *(of gun)* reculer; *(of person)* avoir un mouvement de recul
recollect [rekə'lekt] *vt* se souvenir de
recollection [rekə'lekʃən] *n* souvenir *m*; **to the best of my r.** autant que je m'en souvienne
recommend [rekə'mend] *vt* (**a**) *(praise)* recommander; **to r. sth to sb** recommander qch à qn; **the proposal has a lot to r. it** cette proposition présente de nombreux avantages (**b**) *(advise)* recommander, conseiller; **to r. sb to do sth** conseiller à qn de faire qch; *Com* **recommended retail price** prix *m* conseillé
recommendation [rekəmen'deɪʃən] *n* recommandation *f*
recompense ['rekəmpens] **1** *n* dédommagement *m*; **in r. for** en dédommagement de
2 *vt* dédommager
reconcile ['rekənsaɪl] *vt* (**a**) *(person)* réconcilier; **to be reconciled with sb** s'être réconcilié(e) avec qn; **to be reconciled to sth** se résigner à qch (**b**) *(facts, differences, opinions)* concilier
reconciliation [rekənsɪlɪ'eɪʃən] *n* réconciliation *f*
reconditioned [riːkən'dɪʃənd] *adj (TV, washing machine)* remis(e) à neuf
reconnaissance [rɪ'kɒnɪsəns] *n Mil* reconnaissance *f*; **r. flight/mission** vol *m*/mission *f* de reconnaissance
reconquer [riː'kɒŋkə(r)] *vt* reconquérir
reconquest [riː'kɒŋkwest] *n* reconquête *f*
reconsider [riːkən'sɪdə(r)] **1** *vt* réexaminer
2 *vi* réconsidérer la question

reconstitute [riː'kɒnstɪtjuːt] *vt* reconstituer
reconstruct [riːkən'strʌkt] *vt* reconstruire; *(crime, event)* reconstituer
reconstruction [riːkən'strʌkʃən] *n* reconstruction *f*; *(of crime, event)* reconstitution *f*
record 1 *n* ['rekɔːd] (**a**) *(account)* rapport *m*; *(file)* dossier *m*; **we have no r. of this** nous n'en avons aucune trace; **to keep a r. of sth** garder une trace écrite de qch; **the coldest winter on r.** l'hiver le plus froid qu'on ait jamais enregistré; **she's on r. as saying that...** elle a déclaré officiellement que...; **(just) for the r.** au passage; **to put** *or* **set the r. straight** mettre les choses au point; **r. office** archives *fpl*
(**b**) *(personal history)* passé *m*; *(achievements)* résultats *mpl*; *(of criminal)* casier *m* judiciaire; **to have a good/bad safety r.** avoir bonne/mauvaise réputation en matière de sécurité
(**c**) *(musical)* disque *m*; **r. company** maison *f* de disques; **r. player** tourne-disques *m inv*
(**d**) *(best performance)* record *m*; **to set/break a r.** établir/battre un record
(**e**) *Comput* enregistrement *m*
2 *adj* ['rekɔːd] record *inv*; **in r. time** en un temps record; **unemployment is at a r. high/low** le chômage a atteint son taux le plus haut/bas
3 *vt* [rɪ'kɔːd] (**a**) *(on video, cassette)* enregistrer
(**b**) *(write down)* noter; **to send sth recorded delivery** envoyer qch en recommandé
record-breaking ['rekɔːdbreɪkɪŋ] *adj* record *inv*
recorder [rɪ'kɔːdə(r)] *n (musical instrument)* flûte *f* à bec
record-holder ['rekɔːdhəʊldə(r)] *n* détenteur(trice) *m,f* du record
recording [rɪ'kɔːdɪŋ] *n (on tape)* enregistrement *m*; **r. studio** studio *m* d'enregistrement
recount [rɪ'kaʊnt] *vt (relate)* raconter
re-count ['riːkaʊnt] *n (in election)* deuxième décompte *m*
recoup [rɪ'kuːp] *vt* récupérer
recourse [rɪ'kɔːs] *n* recours *m*; **to have r. to** avoir recours à
recover [rɪ'kʌvə(r)] **1** *vt (territory, customers)* & *Comput* récupérer; *(one's appetite, balance)* retrouver
2 *vi (from illness, setback)* se remettre; *(after running, travelling)* récupérer; *Fig (of economy)* se redresser; *(of sales)* reprendre
recoverable [rɪ'kʌvərəbəl] *adj (money)* recouvrable
recovery [rɪ'kʌvərɪ] *(pl* **recoveries)** *n* (**a**) *(of lost or stolen item)* récupération *f*; **r. vehicle** dépanneuse *f* (**b**) *(from illness)* rétablissement *m*; *Fig (of economy)* redressement *m*; *(of sales)* reprise *f*; **to make a r.** se rétablir
re-create [riːkrɪ'eɪt] *vt* recréer
recreation [rekrɪ'eɪʃən] *n (leisure)* divertissement *m*; *Sch (break)* récréation *f*; **r. area** aire *f* de jeux; **r. ground** terrain *m* de jeux; **r. room** salle *f* de jeux
recreational [rekrɪ'eɪʃənəl] *adj* de loisirs; **r. drug** = drogue prise occasionnellement, dans un but récréatif
recrimination [rɪkrɪmɪ'neɪʃən] *n* récrimination *f*
recruit [rɪ'kruːt] *also Mil* **1** *n* recrue *f*
2 *vt* recruter
recruitment [rɪ'kruːtmənt] *n also Mil* recrutement *m*
rectangle ['rektæŋgəl] *n* rectangle *m*
rectangular [rek'tæŋgjʊlə(r)] *adj* rectangulaire
rectify ['rektɪfaɪ] *(pt & pp* **rectified)** *vt* rectifier

rectitude ['rektɪtjuːd] *n Formal* rectitude *f*

rector ['rektə(r)] *n* (**a**) *Rel* pasteur *m* anglican (**b**) *Scot Univ* = personnalité élue par les étudiants pour les représenter; *Scot Sch* ≃ proviseur *m*

rectory ['rektərɪ] (*pl* **rectories**) *n Rel* presbytère *m*

rectum ['rektəm] *n* rectum *m*

recumbent [rɪ'kʌmbənt] *adj Formal* allongé(e)

recuperate [rɪ'kuːpəreɪt] *vi (from illness)* se rétablir

recuperation [rɪkuːpə'reɪʃən] *n (from illness)* rétablissement *m*

recur [rɪ'kɜː(r)] (*pt & pp* **recurred**) *vi (of event, problem)* se reproduire; *(of theme, illness)* revenir, réapparaître

recurrence [rɪ'kʌrəns] *n* récurrence *f*

recurring [rɪ'kɜːrɪŋ] *adj (problem)* récurrent(e); *(nightmare)* qui revient souvent; **six point six r.** six virgule six à l'infini

recycle [riː'saɪkəl] *vt* recycler

recycling [riː'saɪklɪŋ] *n* recyclage *m*; **r. plant** usine *f* de recyclage

red [red] **1** *n (colour)* rouge *m*; *Fam Fig* **to see r.** *(get angry)* voir rouge; **to be in the r.** *(in debt)* être à découvert *ou* dans le rouge
2 *adj* rouge; *(hair)* roux (rousse); **to turn** *or* **go r.** rougir; **to be as r. as a beetroot** être rouge comme une pivoine; **r. alert** alerte *f* rouge; **the R. Army** l'Armée *f* rouge; **r. blood cell** globule *m* rouge, hématie *f*; **r. card** *(in football)* carton *m* rouge; *Fig* **to roll out the r. carpet** dérouler le tapis rouge; **the R. Cross** la Croix-Rouge; *Fig* **r. herring** diversion *f*; *(in film, book)* fausse piste *f*; *Old-fashioned* **R. Indian** Peau-Rouge *mf*; **r. light** feu *m* rouge; **r. light district** quartier *m* chaud; **r. meat** viande *f* rouge; **r. pepper** poivron *m* rouge; **mentioning her name to him is like a r. rag to a bull** le simple fait d'entendre son nom le met dans une colère noire; **(Little) R. Riding Hood** le Petit Chaperon rouge; **the R. Sea** la mer Rouge; **r. squirrel** écureuil *m* roux; **r. tape** paperasserie *f*; **r. wine** vin *m* rouge

red-blooded [red'blʌdɪd] *adj* **a r. male** un homme viril

redbrick ['redbrɪk] *adj (building)* en brique rouge; *Br* **r. university** = université construite à la fin du XIXᵉ siècle

redcurrant ['redkʌrənt] *n* groseille *f*

redden ['redən] **1** *vt* rougir
2 *vi (of sky)* rougeoyer; *(of person)* rougir

reddish ['redɪʃ] *adj (light, colour)* rougeâtre; *(hair)* légèrement roux (rousse)

redecorate [riː'dekəreɪt] *vt (repaint)* refaire la peinture de; *(re-wallpaper)* retapisser

redeem [rɪ'diːm] *vt* (**a**) *(pawned item)* racheter; *(promise)* tenir; *(gift token, coupon)* échanger; *(mortgage, loan)* rembourser (**b**) *(rescue)* racheter; **to r. oneself** se racheter

Redeemer [rɪ'diːmə(r)] *n Rel* **the R.** le Rédempteur

redeeming [rɪ'diːmɪŋ] *adj* **he has no r. features** il n'a rien pour le racheter; **his one r. feature is...** la seule chose qui le rachète, c'est...

redemption [rɪ'dem(p)ʃən] *n Rel* rédemption *f*; *also Fig* **to be beyond** *or* **past r.** être irrécupérable

redeploy [riːdɪ'plɔɪ] *vt (troops)* redéployer; *(staff)* réaffecter

redeployment [riːdɪ'plɔɪmənt] *n (of troops)* redéploiement *m*; *(of staff)* réaffectation *f*

redevelop [riːdɪ'veləp] *vt* réaménager

red-faced ['red'feɪst] *adj (naturally)* rougeaud(e); *(with anger, embarrassment)* rouge

red-handed ['red'hændɪd] *adj* **to be caught r.** être pris(e) la main dans le sac

redhead ['redhed] *n* roux (rousse) *m,f*

red-hot [red'hɒt] *adj* (**a**) *(very hot)* brûlant(e) (**b**) *Fam (very good)* super bon (bonne); **r. news** des nouvelles de dernière minute

redial [riː'daɪəl] **1** *n* **r. button** *(on phone)* touche *f* bis
2 *vt (pt & pp* **redialled**, *Am* **redialed**) *(phone number)* recomposer

redirect [riːdɪ'rekt, riːdaɪ'rekt] *vt (letter)* faire suivre; *(plane, traffic)* dévier; *(energy)* canaliser

rediscover [riːdɪs'kʌvə(r)] *vt* redécouvrir

redistribute [riːdɪs'trɪbjuːt] *vt* redistribuer

red-letter day ['red'letədeɪ] *n* journée *f* mémorable

redo [riː'duː] *(pt* **redid** [riː'dɪd], *pp* **redone** [riː'dʌn] *) vt* refaire

redolent ['redələnt] *adj* **to be r. of** *(smell of)* sentir; *(suggest)* avoir un parfum de

redraft [riː'drɑːft] *vt* rédiger de nouveau

redress [rɪ'dres] **1** *n (of injustice, grievance)* réparation *f*
2 *vt (injustice, grievance)* réparer; **to r. the balance** rétablir l'équilibre

redskin ['redskɪn] *n Old-fashioned* Peau-Rouge *mf*

reduce [rɪ'djuːs] *vt* (**a**) *(cost, amount, tax)* réduire; *(importance)* minimiser; *(price)* baisser; *(number of people)* faire baisser; *(sauce)* faire réduire; **to r. speed** ralentir (**b**) *(bring to a certain state)* **to r. sth to ashes/ dust** réduire qch en cendres/poussière; **to r. sb to silence** réduire qn au silence; **to r. sb to tears** faire fondre qn en larmes; **to be reduced to doing sth** être réduit(e) à faire qch

reduced [rɪ'djuːst] *adj* réduit(e); **to live in r. circumstances** vivre dans la gêne

reduction [rɪ'dʌkʃən] *n (of price, temperature)* baisse *f* (**in** de); *(of spending, on item)* réduction *f* (**in/on** de/ sur)

redundancy [rɪ'dʌndənsɪ] (*pl* **redundancies**) *n (dismissal)* licenciement *m*; **r. notice** avis *m* de licenciement; **r. pay** prime *f* de licenciement

redundant [rɪ'dʌndənt] *adj* (**a**) *(worker)* **to make sb r.** licencier qn; **to be made r.** être licencié(e) (**b**) *(superfluous)* inutile

reed [riːd] *n* (**a**) *(plant)* roseau *m* (**b**) *(of musical instrument)* anche *f*

reef [riːf] *n* récif *m*

reek [riːk] **1** *n* relent *m*
2 *vi also Fig* **to r. (of sth)** puer (qch)

reel [riːl] **1** *n* (**a**) *Br (for film, thread)* bobine *f*; *(for fishing line)* moulinet *m* (**b**) *(dance, music)* quadrille *m*
2 *vi (sway)* chanceler; *Fig* **my head is reeling** la tête me tourne

▸**reel off** *vt sep (names, statistics)* débiter

re-elect [riːɪ'lekt] *vt* réélire

re-election [riːɪ'lekʃən] *n* réélection *f*

re-enact [riːɪ'nækt] *vt* reconstituer

re-enter [riː'entə(r)] **1** entrer à nouveau dans
2 *vi* rentrer

re-establish [riːɪ'stæblɪʃ] *vt* rétablir

re-examine [riːɪg'zæmɪn] *vt* réexaminer

ref [ref] *n* (**a**) *(abbr* **reference)** réf (**b**) *Fam (abbr* **referee)** arbitre *m*

refectory [rɪ'fektərɪ] (*pl* **refectories**) *n* réfectoire *m*

refer [rɪ'fɜː(r)] (pt & pp **referred**) vt soumettre (**to** à); **to r. a patient to a specialist** envoyer un patient chez un spécialiste

▸**refer to** vt insep (a) (mention) parler de; **she never refers to it** elle n'en parle jamais (b) (allude to) faire allusion à; **referred to as...** appelé(e)... (c) (consult) consulter (d) (apply to) s'appliquer à

referee [refə'riː] **1** n (a) (in sport) arbitre m (b) (for job) **please give the names of two referees** veuillez fournir deux références
2 vt & vi arbitrer

reference ['refərəns] n (a) (consultation, source) référence f; **for future r.** à titre d'information; **I can't do it without r. to Head Office** je ne peux pas le faire sans en référer au bureau central; **r. book** ouvrage m de référence; **r. number** (numéro m de) référence; **r. point, point of r.** point m de repère (b) (allusion) allusion f; **with r. to** (in letter) suite à (c) (from employer) lettre f de référence

referendum [refə'rendəm] n référendum m

refill 1 n ['riːfɪl] (for notebook) feuillets fpl de rechange; (for pen) cartouche f; (for lighter) recharge f; **would you like a r.?** (of drink) je te ressers?
2 vt [riː'fɪl] (glass) remplir à nouveau; (lighter, pen) recharger

refine [rɪ'faɪn] vt (a) (sugar, petroleum) raffiner (b) (improve) perfectionner

refined [rɪ'faɪnd] adj also Fig raffiné(e)

refinement [rɪ'faɪnmənt] n (a) (of manners, taste, person) raffinement m (b) (improvement) perfectionnement m; **to make refinements to sth** perfectionner qch

refinery [rɪ'faɪnərɪ] (pl refineries) n raffinerie f

refit 1 n ['riːfɪt] (of ship) remise f en état
2 vt [riː'fɪt] (pt & pp refitted) (ship) remettre en état

reflate [riː'fleɪt] vt Econ relancer

reflation [riː'fleɪʃən] n Econ relance f

reflect [rɪ'flekt] **1** vt (a) (image, light) réfléchir, refléter; **to be reflected (in)** se réfléchir ou se refléter (dans) (b) Fig (portray) refléter (c) (think) **to r. that...** se dire que...
2 vi (a) (think) réfléchir (**on** à) (b) **to r. well/badly on sb/sth** faire honneur/du tort à qn/qch

reflection [rɪ'flekʃən] n (a) (image, indication) reflet m; Fig **it is no r. on your own capabilities** cela ne remet pas en cause vos compétences (b) (thought) réflexion f; **on r.** après réflexion

reflective [rɪ'flektɪv] adj (a) (surface) réfléchissant(e) (b) (person) réfléchi(e)

reflector [rɪ'flektə(r)] n (on bicycle, vehicle) catadioptre m

reflex ['riːfleks] **1** n réflexe m
2 adj réflexe; **r. action** réflexe m; **r. camera** réflex m

reflexive [rɪ'fleksɪv] adj Gram **r. pronoun** pronom m réfléchi; **r. verb** verbe m pronominal réfléchi

reflexology [riːflek'sɒlədʒɪ] n réflexologie f

reforestation [riːfɒrɪ'steɪʃən] n reboisement m

reform [rɪ'fɔːm] **1** n réforme f
2 vt réformer
3 vi se réformer

re-form ['riː'fɔːm] vi (of organization, pop group) se reformer

re-format ['riː'fɔːmæt] (pt & pp re-formatted) vt Comput (disk) reformater

reformation [refə'meɪʃən] n réforme f; Hist **the R.** la Réforme

reformatory [rɪ'fɔːmətərɪ] (pl reformatories) n Br ≃ maison f de redressement; Am ≃ centre m d'éducation surveillée

reformed [rɪ'fɔːmd] adj (alcoholic, drug addict) ancien(enne); **he's a r. character** il s'est assagi

reformer [rɪ'fɔːmə(r)] n réformateur(trice) m,f

reformist [rɪ'fɔːmɪst] n & adj réformiste mf

refract [rɪ'frækt] vt réfracter

refrain [rɪ'freɪn] **1** n also Fig refrain m
2 vi **to r. from sth/doing sth** s'abstenir de qch/de faire qch

re-freeze [riː'friːz] (pt re-froze [riː'frəʊz], pp re-frozen [riː'frəʊzən]) vt recongeler

refresh [rɪ'freʃ] vt (of drink) rafraîchir; (of nap, holiday) reposer; (bath) revigorer; Comput actualiser; **to r. one's memory** se rafraîchir la mémoire; **to r. sb's glass** (top up) resservir à boire à qn

refreshing [rɪ'freʃɪŋ] adj (breeze, drink) rafraîchissant(e); (nap, holiday) reposant(e); (bath) revigorant(e); Fig (honesty) qui fait l'effet d'une bouffée d'air frais

refreshments [rɪ'freʃmənts] npl rafraîchissements mpl

refrigerate [rɪ'frɪdʒəreɪt] vt réfrigérer; **r. after opening** (on packet) à conserver au frais après ouverture

refrigeration [rɪfrɪdʒə'reɪʃən] n réfrigération f

refrigerator [rɪ'frɪdʒəreɪtə(r)] n (domestic) réfrigérateur m, frigidaire® m; (industrial) chambre f froide

refuel [riː'fjʊəl] (pt & pp refuelled, Am refueled) **1** vt (ship, aircraft) ravitailler en carburant
2 vi (of ship, aircraft) se ravitailler en carburant

refuge ['refjuːdʒ] n (from danger, weather) refuge m; (for battered women) foyer m; **to seek r.** chercher refuge; **to take r.** se réfugier

refugee [refjʊ'dʒiː] n réfugié(e) m,f; **r. camp** camp m de réfugiés; **r. status** statut m de réfugié

refund 1 n ['riːfʌnd] remboursement m
2 vt [riː'fʌnd] rembourser

refurbish [riː'fɜːbɪʃ] vt rénover

refusal [rɪ'fjuːzəl] n refus m; **to give a flat r.** refuser catégoriquement; **to have first r. (on sth)** avoir la priorité (pour qch)

refuse¹ ['refjuːs] n (rubbish) ordures fpl; **r. collection** ramassage m des ordures (ménagères); **r. disposal** traitement m des ordures; **r. dump** dépôt m d'ordures

refuse² [rɪ'fjuːz] **1** vt (invitation, offer) refuser; (request) rejeter; **to r. to do sth** refuser de faire qch; **to r. sb sth** refuser qch à qn
2 vi (of person) refuser; (of horse) refuser l'obstacle

refute [rɪ'fjuːt] vt (argument, theory) réfuter; (allegation) nier

regain [rɪ'geɪn] vt (a) (get back) retrouver; (power, political seat) reconquérir; **to r. possession of sth** rentrer en possession de qch; **to r. consciousness** revenir à soi; **to r. the lead** (in contest) reprendre l'avantage (b) (reach again) regagner

regal ['riːgəl] adj royal(e)

regale [rɪ'geɪl] vt **to r. sb with sth** gratifier qn de qch

regalia [rɪ'geɪlɪə] npl insignes mpl

regard [rɪ'gɑːd] **1** n (a) (admiration) respect m, estime f; **to hold sb in high r.** tenir qn en haute estime (b) (consideration) égard m; **out of r. for** par égard pour; **without r. to** sans tenir compte de (c) (connection) **in this r.** à cet égard; **in all regards** à tous égards; **with r. to** en ce qui concerne (d) **regards** (good wishes)

amitiés *fpl*; **give her my regards** transmets-lui mes amitiés
2 *vt* (**a**) *(admire, respect)* estimer (**b**) *(consider)* **to r. sb/sth as** considérer qn/qch comme; **to r. sb/sth with suspicion** être soupçonneux(euse) à l'égard de qn/qch (**c**) *(concern)* concerner; **as regards...** en ce qui concerne..., concernant...

regarding [rɪ'gɑːdɪŋ] *prep* en ce qui concerne, concernant

regardless [rɪ'gɑːdlɪs] *adv* (**a**) *(despite everything)* quand même (**b**) **r. of** *(without considering)* sans tenir compte de; **r. of the expense** sans regarder à la dépense

regatta [rɪ'gætə] *n* régate *f*

regency ['riːdʒənsɪ] *(pl* **regencies**) *n* régence *f*

regenerate [rɪ'dʒenəreɪt] **1** *vt (sector, city)* régénérer; *(interest, enthusiasm)* raviver
2 *vi* se régénérer

regeneration [rɪdʒenə'reɪʃən] *n* régénération *f*

regent ['riːdʒənt] *n & adj* régent(e) *m,f*

reggae ['regeɪ] *n* reggae *m*

regime [reɪ'ʒiːm] *n* régime *m*

regiment ['redʒɪmənt] **1** *n* régiment *m*
2 *vt* enrégimenter

regimental [redʒɪ'mentəl] *adj* du régiment

regimentation [redʒɪmen'teɪʃən] *n* discipline *f* draconienne

regimented ['redʒɪmentɪd] *adj* très strict(e)

region ['riːdʒən] *n* région *f*; *Fig* **in the r. of** environ

regional ['riːdʒənəl] *adj* régional(e)

regionalism ['riːdʒənəlɪzəm] *n* régionalisme *m*

register ['redʒɪstə(r)] **1** *n* registre *m*; *(at school)* cahier *m* d'appel; *(of voters)* liste *f* électorale; **to take the r.** *(at school)* faire l'appel; **r. of births, marriages and deaths** registre de l'état civil; **(cash) r.** caisse *f* (enregistreuse); *Br* **r. office** bureau *m* de l'état civil
2 *vt* (**a**) *(member, student)* inscrire; *(birth, marriage, death)* déclarer; *(complaint)* déposer, **to r. a protest** protester (**b**) *(temperature, speed)* enregistrer; *(astonishment, displeasure)* manifester (**c**) *(realize)* se rendre compte de (**d**) *(achieve)* *(victory, progress)* enregistrer
3 *vi* (**a**) *(for course)* s'inscrire; *(at hotel)* signer le registre; *(of voter)* s'inscrire sur les listes électorales (**b**) *Fam (of fact)* **I told him but it didn't r.** je lui ai dit mais il n'a pas enregistré

registered ['redʒɪstəd] *adj (charity)* reconnu(e) par l'État; *(childminder)* agréé(e); *(letter)* recommandé(e); **r. trademark** marque *f* déposée

registrar ['redʒɪstrɑː(r)] *n* (**a**) *(record keeper)* officier *m* de l'état civil (**b**) *(in university)* responsable *mf* des inscriptions (**c**) *(in hospital)* chef *m* de clinique

registration [redʒɪs'treɪʃən] *n (of student)* inscription *f*; *(of voter)* inscription sur les listes électorales; *(of birth, death, marriage)* déclaration *f*; **r. number** *(of car)* numéro *m* d'immatriculation

registry office ['redʒɪstrɪ'ɒfɪs] *n* bureau *m* de l'état civil; **to get married at a r.** se marier civilement, ≃ se marier à la mairie

regress [rɪ'gres] *vi* régresser

regression [rɪ'greʃən] *n* régression *f*

regressive [rɪ'gresɪv] *adj* régressif(ive)

regret [rɪ'gret] **1** *n* regret *m*; **to send one's regrets** *(apologies)* envoyer ses excuses; *(condolences)* envoyer ses condoléances
2 *vt* (*pt & pp* **regretted**) regretter; **to r. doing** *or*

having done sth regretter d'avoir fait qch; **I r. to (have to) inform you that...** j'ai le regret de vous annoncer que...

regretful [rɪ'gretfʊl] *adj (voice, smile)* plein(e) de regret; *(person)* qui a des regrets

regrettable [rɪ'gretəbəl] *adj* regrettable

regroup [riː'gruːp] **1** *vt* regrouper
2 *vi* se regrouper

regular ['regjʊlə(r)] **1** *n (in bar, restaurant)* habitué(e) *m,f*
2 *adj* (**a**) *(features, pulse, verb)* régulier(ère); **on a r. basis** régulièrement; **he comes twice a week, as r. as clockwork** il vient deux fois par semaine, c'est réglé comme du papier à musique (**b**) *(normal, habitual)* habituel(elle); *(in size)* moyen(enne); *(listener, viewer)* fidèle; *(customer)* régulier(ère); **she was a r. visitor to the house** elle venait régulièrement à la maison (**c**) *(army, soldier)* régulier(ère) (**d**) *Fam (for emphasis)* vrai(e)

regularity [regjʊ'lærɪtɪ] *n* régularité *f*

regulate ['regjʊleɪt] *vt* (**a**) *(adjust)* régler (**b**) *(control)* réglementer

regulation [regjʊ'leɪʃən] **1** *n* (**a**) *(action)* réglementation *f* (**b**) *(rule)* règlement *m*
2 *adj (statutory)* réglementaire

regulator ['regjʊleɪtə(r)] *n* régulateur *m*

regulatory [regjʊ'leɪtərɪ] *adj* de contrôle

regurgitate [rɪ'gɜːdʒɪteɪt] *vt* régurgiter; *Fig* recracher

rehabilitate [riːhə'bɪlɪteɪt] *vt* réhabiliter

rehabilitation [riːhəbɪlɪ'teɪʃən] *n* réhabilitation *f*

rehash *Fam* **1** *n* ['riːhæʃ] resucée *f*
2 *vt* [riː'hæʃ] *(ideas, proposal)* reprendre; *(film, book)* remanier

rehearsal [rɪ'hɜːsəl] *n* répétition *f*

rehearse [rɪ'hɜːs] *vt & vi* répéter

rehouse [riː'haʊz] *vt* reloger

reign [reɪn] **1** *n* règne *m*
2 *vi also Fig* régner

reigning ['reɪnɪŋ] *adj (monarch)* régnant(e); *(champion)* en titre

reimburse [riːɪm'bɜːs] *vt* rembourser

rein [reɪn] *n also Fig* rêne *f*; *Fig* **to give sb free r. to do sth** donner carte blanche à qn pour qu'il/elle fasse qch; *Fig* **to give free r. to one's imagination** donner libre cours à son imagination; *Fig* **to keep a tight r. on sb** tenir la bride haute à qn

reincarnate [riːɪn'kɑːneɪt] *vt* **to be reincarnated** être réincarné(e)

reincarnation [riːɪnkɑː'neɪʃən] *n* réincarnation *f*

reindeer ['reɪndɪə(r)] *n* renne *m*

reinforce [riːɪn'fɔːs] *vt also Fig* renforcer; **reinforced concrete** béton *m* armé

reinforcement [riːɪn'fɔːsmənt] *n* renforcement *m*; *also Fig* **reinforcements** renforts *mpl*

reinsert [riːɪn'sɜːt] *vt* réinsérer

reinstate [riːɪn'steɪt] *vt* réintégrer

reinsurance [riːɪn'ʃʊərəns] *n* réassurance *f*

reinsure [riːɪn'ʃʊə(r)] *vt* réassurer

reinvent [riːɪn'vent] *vt Fig* **to r. oneself** changer d'image; **to r. the wheel** refaire ce qui a déjà été fait

reinvest [riːɪn'vest] *vt* réinvestir

reissue [riː'ɪʃuː] **1** *n (of book, record)* réédition *f*
2 *vt (book, record)* rééditer

reiterate [riː'ɪtəreɪt] *vt* réitérer

reiteration [riːɪtə'reɪʃən] *n* réitération *f*

reject 1 n ['riːdʒekt] (object) rebut m; Fam (person) inadapté(e) m,f

2 vt [rɪ'dʒekt] rejeter; (offer, goods) refuser

rejection [rɪ'dʒekʃən] n rejet m; (of offer, goods) refus m; **to meet with r.** être rejeté(e)

rejoice [rɪ'dʒɔɪs] vi se réjouir

rejoicing [rɪ'dʒɔɪsɪŋ] n réjouissance f

rejoin¹ [riː'dʒɔɪn] vt (**a**) (group, motorway) rejoindre; (race) reprendre (**b**) (join again) réintégrer

rejoin² [rɪ'dʒɔɪn] vt & vi (retort) répliquer, rétorquer

rejoinder [rɪ'dʒɔɪndə(r)] n réplique f

rejuvenate [rɪ'dʒuːvɪneɪt] vt rajeunir

rekindle [riː'kɪndəl] vt raviver

relapse 1 n ['riːlæps] rechute f

2 vi [rɪ'læps] rechuter; **to r. into** retomber dans

relate [rɪ'leɪt] **1** vt (**a**) (narrate) raconter (**b**) (connect) mettre en rapport (**to** avec)

2 vi (**a**) (be relevant) **to r. to** avoir rapport à (**b**) **to r. to** (understand) (person) avoir des affinités avec; (music) apprécier; (idea) comprendre

related [rɪ'leɪtɪd] adj (people, animals, languages) apparenté(e); (ideas, events, activities) lié(e)

relation [rɪ'leɪʃən] n (**a**) (relative) parent(e) m,f (**b**) (connection) rapport m; **to bear no r. to** n'avoir aucun rapport avec

relationship [rɪ'leɪʃənʃɪp] n (**a**) (between people) relation f; (romantic, sexual) relation amoureuse; (between countries) relations fpl; (within family) lien m de parenté; **to have a good/bad r. with sb** s'entendre/ne pas bien s'entendre avec qn (**b**) (connection) rapport m

relative ['relətɪv] **1** n (person) parent(e) m,f

2 adj (comparative) relatif(ive); **r. to** en rapport avec; Gram **r. clause** proposition f relative

relatively ['relətɪvlɪ] adv relativement

relativity [relə'tɪvɪtɪ] n Phys relativité f

relax [rɪ'læks] **1** vt (person) détendre; (muscles, discipline) relâcher; (law, control) assouplir; **to r. one's grip (on)** relâcher son étreinte (sur); Fig relâcher son emprise (sur)

2 vi (of person) se détendre; (of muscles) se relâcher; **r.!** (calm down) du calme!

relaxation [riːlæk'seɪʃən] n (**a**) (of person) détente f; (of discipline) relâchement m; (of control) assouplissement m (**b**) (as therapy) relaxation f; **r. exercises/classes** exercices mpl/cours mpl de relaxation

relaxed [rɪ'lækst] adj détendu(e)

relaxing [rɪ'læksɪŋ] adj relaxant(e)

relay 1 n ['riːleɪ] (of workers) équipe f de relais; **to work in relays** se relayer; **r. (race)** (course f de) relais m; Rad & TV **r. station** relais m

2 vt [rɪ'leɪ] retransmettre; (information) transmettre

release [rɪ'liːs] **1** n (**a**) (of prisoner) libération f; (of gas) émission f; (emotional) soulagement m (**b**) (of record, film) sortie f; **to be on general r.** (of film) être sorti(e) dans toutes les grandes salles de cinéma

2 vt (**a**) (prisoner) libérer; (gas, fumes) émettre; (balloon, bomb) lâcher; (funds) dégager; (brake) desserrer; **to r. sb from an obligation** dégager qn d'une obligation; **to r. sb's hand** lâcher la main de qn (**b**) (record, film) sortir; (news, information) communiquer

relegate ['relɪgeɪt] vt reléguer (**to** à); **to be relegated** (of team) descendre en division inférieure

relegation [relɪ'geɪʃən] n (of person) relégation f (**to** à); (of team) descente f en division inférieure

relent [rɪ'lent] vi (of storm, wind) se calmer; (of person) céder

relentless [rɪ'lentlɪs] adj (person, attitude) implacable; (rain, criticism) incessant(e)

relevance ['reləvəns] n pertinence f; **to have r. to sth** avoir un rapport avec qch

relevant ['reləvənt] adj (**a**) (apt) pertinent(e); **to be r. (to sth)** avoir un rapport (avec qch) (**b**) (appropriate) (chapter) correspondant(e); (authorities) compétent(e); (experience, qualifications) requis(e) (**c**) (topical) d'actualité

reliability [rɪlaɪə'bɪlɪtɪ] n (of person, information) sérieux m; (of machine) sûreté f, fiabilité f

reliable [rɪ'laɪəbəl] adj (person, machine) fiable; (information) sûr(e); **from a r. source** de source sûre

reliably [rɪ'laɪəblɪ] adv **to be r. informed that...** savoir de source sûre que...

reliance [rɪ'laɪəns] n (**a**) (dependence) dépendance f (**on** vis-à-vis de) (**b**) (trust) confiance f; **to place r. on sb/sth** faire confiance à qn/qch

reliant [rɪ'laɪənt] adj **to be r. on** être dépendant(e) de

relic ['relɪk] n Rel relique f; Fig vestige m

relief [rɪ'liːf] n (**a**) (comfort) soulagement m; **to bring r. to sb** soulager qn (**b**) (help) secours m, aide f; **r. fund** fonds m d'aide (**c**) (replacement) remplaçant(e) m,f (**d**) (of besieged city, troops) libération f (**e**) (in art) relief m; **in r.** en relief; Fig **to throw sth into r.** mettre qch en relief; **r. map** carte f en relief

relieve [rɪ'liːv] vt (**a**) (alleviate) soulager; (boredom) tromper; (pressure) réduire; Euph **to r. oneself** se soulager (**b**) (replace) remplacer (**c**) (liberate) libérer; **to r. sb of his duties** relever qn de ses fonctions; Hum **to r. sb of his wallet** soulager qn de son portefeuille

religion [rɪ'lɪdʒən] n religion f; **what is your r.?** quelle est votre religion?; (on form) à quelle confession appartenez-vous?

religious [rɪ'lɪdʒəs] adj also Fig religieux(euse); **r. education, r. instruction** instruction f religieuse

religiously [rɪ'lɪdʒəslɪ] adv also Fig religieusement

relinquish [rɪ'lɪŋkwɪʃ] vt (hope, habit, thought) abandonner; (claim, share) renoncer à; Fig **to r. one's hold on sb/sth** relâcher son emprise sur qn/qch

relish ['relɪʃ] **1** n (**a**) (pleasure) goût m (**for** pour); **to do sth with r.** faire qch avec délectation (**b**) (pickle) condiments mpl

2 vt savourer; **I didn't r. the idea** l'idée ne m'enthousiasmait guère

relive [riː'lɪv] vt revivre

relocate [riːləʊ'keɪt] **1** vt (company) transférer; (person) muter

2 vi (of company) être transféré(e); (of person) se déplacer

relocation [riːləʊ'keɪʃən] n déménagement m

reluctance [rɪ'lʌktəns] n réticence f; **to do sth with r.** faire qch à contrecœur

reluctant [rɪ'lʌktənt] adj (smile, promise) accordé(e) à contrecœur; **to be r. to do sth** être réticent(e) à faire qch

▶**rely on, rely upon** [rɪ'laɪ] (pt & pp relied) vt insep (**a**) **to r. on sb (to do sth)** compter sur qn (pour faire qch) (**b**) (be dependent on) dépendre de

REM [aːriː'em] n (abbr rapid eye movement) mouvements mpl oculaires rapides

remain [rɪ'meɪn] vi (**a**) (stay behind, continue to be) rester (**b**) (be left) subsister; **it remains to be seen** cela reste à voir

remainder [rɪ'meɪndə(r)] *n* reste *m*

remaindered [rɪ'meɪndɜːd] *adj (book)* soldé(e)

remaining [rɪ'meɪnɪŋ] *adj* restant(e)

remains [rɪ'meɪnz] *npl (of meal, fortune)* restes *mpl; (of civilization, building)* vestiges *mpl;* **(human) r.** restes humains

remake 1 *n* ['riːmeɪk] *(of film)* remake *m*
 2 *vt* [riː'meɪk] *(pt & pp* **remade** [riː'meɪd] *) (film)* faire un remake de

remand [rɪ'mɑːnd] *Law* **1** *n* **on r.** en détention préventive; **r. home** maison *f* de détention préventive
 2 *vt* **to r. sb (in custody)** placer qn en détention préventive

remark [rɪ'mɑːk] **1** *n* remarque *f;* **to make** *or* **pass a r.** faire une remarque
 2 *vt* faire remarquer

remarkable [rɪ'mɑːkəbəl] *adj* remarquable

remarkably [rɪ'mɑːkəblɪ] *adv* remarquablement

remarry [riː'mærɪ] *(pt & pp* **remarried**) *vi* se remarier

remedial [rɪ'miːdɪəl] *adj* **(a)** *(class)* de rattrapage; **r. education** rattrapage *m* scolaire **(b)** *(corrective)* **to take r. measures** prendre des mesures

remedy ['remɪdɪ] **1** *n (pl* **remedies**) *also Fig* remède *m*
 2 *vt (pt & pp* **remedied**) remédier à

remember [rɪ'membə(r)] **1** *vt* **(a)** *(recall)* se souvenir de, se rappeler; **to r. doing sth** se souvenir d'avoir fait qch; **to r. to do sth** penser à faire qch; **a night to r.** une nuit mémorable **(b)** *(commemorate)* commémorer; **to r. the dead** rendre hommage aux disparus **(c)** *(speak of)* **to r. sb to sb** rappeler qn au bon souvenir de qn
 2 *vi* se souvenir, se rappeler; **as far as I r.** pour autant que je me souvienne

remembrance [rɪ'membrəns] *n Formal (memory)* souvenir *m;* **in r. of** en souvenir de; **R. Day** *or* **Sunday** = commémoration de la fin des deux guerres mondiales, ≃ le 11 novembre

remind [rɪ'maɪnd] *vt* **to r. sb of sth** rappeler qch à qn; **to r. sb to do sth** rappeler à qn de faire qch; **that reminds me...** à propos...

reminder [rɪ'maɪndə(r)] *n* rappel *m*

reminisce [remɪ'nɪs] *vi* évoquer des souvenirs; **to r. about sth** évoquer qch

reminiscence [remɪ'nɪsəns] *n* souvenir *m*

reminiscent [remɪ'nɪsənt] *adj* **to be r. of** rappeler

remiss [rɪ'mɪs] *adj* négligent(e); **it was very r. of him not to phone** c'était très négligent de sa part de ne pas téléphoner

remission [rɪ'mɪʃən] *n* **(a)** *Law* remise *f* de peine **(b)** *(of disease)* **to be in r.** être en phase de rémission

remit 1 *n* ['riːmɪt] *(area of authority)* attributions *fpl*
 2 *vt* [rɪ'mɪt] *(pt & pp* **remitted**) *(payment)* remettre

remittance [rɪ'mɪtəns] *n* versement *m*

remnant ['remnənt] *n* reste *m; (of civilization, building)* vestige *m; (of cloth)* coupon *m*

remonstrate ['remənstreɪt] *vi* protester; **to r. with sb** faire des remontrances à qn

remorse [rɪ'mɔːs] *n* remords *m;* **to feel r.** avoir du *ou* des remords

remorseful [rɪ'mɔːsfʊl] *adj* plein(e) de remords

remorseless [rɪ'mɔːslɪs] *adj* impitoyable

remortgage [riː'mɔːgɪdʒ] *vt (house, property)* hypothéquer de nouveau, prendre une nouvelle hypothèque sur

remote [rɪ'məʊt] *adj* **(a)** *(far-off) (in space)* éloigné(e) **(from** de); *(in time)* lointain(e) **(from** de); **r. control** télécommande *f* **(b)** *(aloof)* distant(e) **(c)** *(chance, possibility)* vague; **the remotest chance/idea** la moindre chance/idée

remote-controlled [rɪ'məʊtkən'trəʊld] *adj* télécommandé(e)

remotely [rɪ'məʊtlɪ] *adv* **(a)** *(distantly)* **r. situated** isolé(e) **(b)** *(slightly)* vaguement; **not r.** pas du tout

remould ['riːməʊld] *n (tyre)* pneu *m* rechapé

removal [rɪ'muːvəl] *n* **(a)** *(of politician, official)* renvoi *m; (of control, doubt, threat)* suppression *f; (of stain)* nettoyage *m* **(b)** *(moving house)* déménagement *m;* **r. man** déménageur *m;* **r. van** camion *m* de déménagement

remove [rɪ'muːv] *vt* **(a)** *(take away) (thing)* enlever; *(doubt)* dissiper; *(stain)* faire partir; *(politician, official)* renvoyer; **to r. one's child from a school** retirer son enfant d'une école **(b)** *(take off) (coat, hat)* enlever, retirer; *(tyre)* démonter

remover [rɪ'muːvə(r)] *n* **(a)** *(for paint)* décapant *m; (for nail varnish)* dissolvant *m* **(b)** **(furniture) removers** déménageurs *mpl*

remunerate [rɪ'mjuːnəreɪt] *vt Formal* rémunérer

remuneration [rɪmjuːnə'reɪʃən] *n Formal* rémunération *f*

remunerative [rɪ'mjuːnərətɪv] *adj Formal* rémunérateur(trice)

renaissance [rɪ'neɪsəns] *n* renouveau *m;* **the R.** la Renaissance

renal ['riːnəl] *adj* rénal(e)

rename [riː'neɪm] *vt* rebaptiser

rend [rend] *(pt & pp* **rent** [rent] *) vt Lit (tear)* déchirer

render ['rendə(r)] *vt Formal* rendre; **to r. homage to sb** rendre hommage à qn; **to r. sth into French** rendre qch en français; **for services rendered** pour services rendus; **the news rendered her speechless** la nouvelle l'a laissée sans voix

rendezvous ['rɒndɪvuː] **1** *n (pl* **rendezvous** ['rɒndɪvuːz] *)* rendez-vous *m inv*
 2 *vi (pt & pp* **rendezvoused** ['rɒndɪvuːd] *)* se retrouver

rendition [ren'dɪʃən] *n* interprétation *f*

renegade ['renɪgeɪd] *n* renégat(e) *m,f*

renege [rɪ'neɪg] *vi* **to r. on sth** revenir sur qch

renew [rɪ'njuː] *vt (passport, membership)* renouveler; *(activity, negotiations, library book)* reprendre; *(optimism, strength, interest)* raviver; *(speculation)* relancer

renewable [rɪ'njuːəbəl] *adj* renouvelable

renewal [rɪ'njuːəl] *n (of passport, membership)* renouvellement *m, (of activity, negotiations)* reprise *f; (of library book)* renouvellement de prêt; *(of optimism, interest)* regain *m*

rennet ['renɪt] *n* présure *f*

renounce [rɪ'naʊns] *vt* renoncer à; *(treaty)* dénoncer; *(friends, faith, principles)* renier

renovate ['renəveɪt] *vt* rénover

renovation [renə'veɪʃən] *n* rénovation *f*

renown [rɪ'naʊn] *n* renommée *f*

renowned [rɪ'naʊnd] *adj* renommé(e) **(for** pour)

rent¹ [rent] **1** *n (on flat, house)* loyer *m;* **for r.** à louer; *Br Fam* **r. boy** jeune prostitué *m*
 2 *vt* louer

rent² *pt & pp of* **rend**

rental ['rentəl] n (a) (hire) location f (b) (money) (for house) loyer m; (for car, equipment, TV) location f; (for telephone) abonnement m

rent-free [rent'friː] 1 adj exempt(e) de loyer
2 adv sans payer de loyer

reopen [riː'əʊpən] 1 vt rouvrir; (talks) reprendre; Fig to r. old wounds rouvrir une plaie
2 vi (of talks) reprendre; (of shop, theatre) rouvrir; school reopens on the 21st of August la rentrée des classes aura lieu le 21 août

reorder [riː'ɔːdə(r)] vt passer une nouvelle commande de

reorganization [riːɔːgənaɪ'zeɪʃən] n réorganisation f

reorganize [riː'ɔːgənaɪz] vt réorganiser

rep [rep] n Fam (abbr representative) VRP m

repaint [riː'peɪnt] vt repeindre

repair [rɪ'peə(r)] 1 n réparation f; to be beyond r. être irréparable; to be in good/bad r. être en bon/mauvais état; to be under r. être en réparation; r. shop atelier m de réparations
2 vt réparer

repairman [rɪ'peəmæn] n réparateur m

reparation [repə'reɪʃən] n (a) Formal (compensation) réparation f; to make r. for sth réparer qch (b) (after war) reparations réparations fpl

repartee [repɑː'tiː] n repartie f

repast [rɪ'pɑːst] n Lit repas m

repatriate [riː'pætrɪeɪt] vt rapatrier (to vers)

repatriation [riːpætrɪ'eɪʃən] n rapatriement m

repay [riː'peɪ] (pt & pp repaid [riː'peɪd]) vt (a) (reimburse) (person, money) rembourser (b) (reward) (person) remercier (for de); (kindness) payer de retour; (loyalty) récompenser

repayable [riː'peɪəbəl] adj remboursable

repayment [riː'peɪmənt] n remboursement m; r. plan calendrier m des paiements

repeal [rɪ'piːl] vt abroger

repeat [rɪ'piːt] 1 n (of event) répétition f; (of TV or radio programme) rediffusion f; r. prescription ≃ ordonnance f renouvelable
2 vt répéter; (attempt) renouveler; (TV programme) rediffuser; to r. oneself se répéter

repeated [rɪ'piːtɪd] adj répété(e)

repeatedly [rɪ'piːtɪdlɪ] adv à maintes reprises

repel [rɪ'pel] (pt & pp repelled) vt also Fig repousser

repellent [rɪ'pelənt] 1 n (for insects) anti-moustiques m inv
2 adj (disgusting) repoussant(e)

repent [rɪ'pent] 1 vt se repentir de
2 vi se repentir (of de)

repentance [rɪ'pentəns] n repentir m

repentant [rɪ'pentənt] adj repentant(e) (of de)

repercussion [riːpə'kʌʃən] n répercussion f

repertoire ['repətwɑː(r)] n répertoire m

repertory ['repətərɪ] (pl repertories) n Theat répertoire m; r. company troupe f de répertoire

repetition [repɪ'tɪʃən] n répétition f; (of attempt) renouvellement m

repetitive [rɪ'petɪtɪv] adj répétitif(ive); r. strain injury = douleurs dans les bras et les mains dues à la répétition de certains mouvements

rephrase [riː'freɪz] vt reformuler

replace [rɪ'pleɪs] vt (a) (put back) to r. sth remettre qch à sa place; to r. the receiver (on telephone) raccrocher (b) (substitute for) remplacer

replacement [rɪ'pleɪsmənt] n (a) (putting back) remise f en place; (substituting) remplacement m; Fin r. cost coût m de remplacement; r. parts pièces fpl de remplacement; r. value valeur f de remplacement (b) (person) remplaçant(e) m,f

replay 1 n ['riːpleɪ] (of match) nouvelle rencontre f; (action) r. (on TV) = répétition d'une séquence précédente; (at slow speed) ralenti m
2 vt [riː'pleɪ] (match) rejouer

replenish [rɪ'plenɪʃ] vt (cup, tank) remplir à nouveau (with de); to r. one's supplies se réapprovisionner

replete [rɪ'pliːt] adj Formal rassasié(e) (with de)

replica ['replɪkə] n réplique f, Fig (of person) portrait m

replicate ['replɪkeɪt] vt reproduire

reply [rɪ'plaɪ] 1 n (pl replies) réponse f; in r. to your letter en réponse à votre lettre; to say sth in r. (to sth) répondre qch (à qch); there was no r. (on telephone) ça ne répondait pas
2 vt & vi (pt & pp replied) répondre (to à)

report [rɪ'pɔːt] 1 n (a) (account) compte rendu m; (analysis) rapport m; (in newspaper, on radio, television) reportage m; Br Sch bulletin m (scolaire); there are reports that... il paraîtrait que...; r. card (for primary school) carnet m de notes; (for secondary school) bulletin m scolaire (b) (sound) détonation f
2 vt (information) rapporter; (accident, theft) signaler; to r. sb missing signaler la disparition de qn; to r. sb to the police/the authorities dénoncer qn à la police/aux autorités; to r. one's findings (to sb) faire un rapport (à qn); nothing to r. rien à signaler
3 vi (a) (present oneself) se présenter (to à); to r. for duty prendre son service (b) (give account) faire un rapport (to à); (of journalist) faire un reportage (on sur) (c) (be accountable) to r. to sb rendre compte à qn

▸**report back** vi (a) (return) rentrer, être de retour; (of soldier) regagner ses quartiers (b) (present report) présenter son rapport (to à)

reportedly [rɪ'pɔːtɪdlɪ] adv he r. said that... il aurait dit que...; he is r. resident in Paris il résiderait à Paris

reporter [rɪ'pɔːtə(r)] n (for newspaper) journaliste mf; (on television, radio) reporter m

repose [rɪ'pəʊz] Formal 1 n repos m
2 vi reposer

repository [rɪ'pɒzɪtərɪ] (pl repositories) n (for books, furniture) dépôt m

repossess [riːpə'zes] vt saisir

reprehensible [reprɪ'hensɪbəl] adj répréhensible

represent [reprɪ'zent] vt représenter; (describe) présenter

representation [reprɪzen'teɪʃən] n (in Parliament) représentation f; (of facts) exposé m; Formal to make representations (to sb) faire des démarches (auprès de qn)

representative [reprɪ'zentətɪv] 1 n représentant(e) m,f
2 adj représentatif(ive)

repress [rɪ'pres] vt réprimer; (memories, feelings) refouler; to be repressed (of person) être un(e) refoulé(e)

repression [rɪ'preʃən] n répression f; (of memories, feelings) refoulement m

repressive [rɪ'presɪv] adj répressif(ive)

reprieve [rɪ'priːv] 1 n Law (cancellation) commutation f de la peine capitale; (postponement) sursis m; Fig to win a r. (of project, company) bénéficier d'un sursis

2 *vt Law* **to r. sb** *(cancel punishment of)* commuer la peine capitale de qn en réclusion à perpétuité; *(postpone punishment of)* accorder un sursis à qn

reprimand [ˈreprɪmɑːnd] **1** *n (to child)* réprimande *f*; *(to employee)* avertissement *m*
2 *vt (child)* réprimander; *(employee)* avertir

reprint 1 *n* [ˈriːprɪnt] réimpression *f*
2 *vt* [riːˈprɪnt] réimprimer

reprisal [rɪˈpraɪzəl] *n* représailles *fpl*; **to take reprisals** exercer des représailles; **in r. for** en représailles à

reproach [rɪˈprəʊtʃ] **1** *n* reproche *m*; **a look of r.** un regard plein de reproche; **beyond** *or* **above r.** irréprochable
2 *vt* faire des reproches à; **to r. sb for** *or* **with sth** reprocher qch à qn; **to r. oneself for sth** se reprocher qch

reproachful [rɪˈprəʊtʃfʊl] *adj (tone)* de reproche; *(look)* plein(e) de reproche

reprobate [ˈreprəbeɪt] *n* réprouvé(e) *m,f*; *Hum* dépravé(e) *m,f*

reproduce [riːprəˈdjuːs] **1** *vt* reproduire
2 *vi* se reproduire

reproduction [riːprəˈdʌkʃən] *n* reproduction *f*; **r. furniture** copies *fpl* (de meubles anciens)

reproductive [riːprəˈdʌktɪv] *adj* reproducteur(trice); **r. organs** organes *mpl* reproducteurs

reproof [rɪˈpruːf] *n Formal* réprobation *f*

reprove [rɪˈpruːv] *vt Formal (person)* réprimander; *(action)* condamner

reproving [rɪˈpruːvɪŋ] *adj Formal* réprobateur(trice)

reptile [ˈreptaɪl] *n* reptile *m*

reptilian [repˈtɪlɪən] *adj* reptilien(enne); *Fig (manner, looks)* de reptile

republic [rɪˈpʌblɪk] *n* république *f*

Republican [rəˈpʌblɪkən] *n & adj (in US, Ireland)* républicain(e) *m,f*

> ### Republican
> Aux États-Unis, un "Republican" est un partisan du parti républicain.
> En Irlande, le terme "Republican" désigne une personne qui souhaite le rattachement de l'Irlande du Nord à la république d'Irlande.
> Au Royaume-Uni et en Australie, le terme désigne les personnes favorables à l'abolition de la monarchie et à l'établissement d'une république.

republican [rəˈpʌblɪkən] *n & adj* républicain(e) *m,f*

repudiate [rɪˈpjuːdɪeɪt] *vt Formal (offer)* rejeter; *(person, belief)* renier; *(wife)* répudier; *(rumour)* démentir

repudiation [rɪpjuːdɪˈeɪʃən] *n Formal (of offer)* rejet *m*; *(of person, belief)* reniement *m*; *(of wife)* répudiation *f*; *(of rumour)* démenti *m*

repugnant [rɪˈpʌgnənt] *adj* répugnant(e)

repulse [rɪˈpʌls] *vt* repousser

repulsive [rɪˈpʌlsɪv] *adj* repoussant(e)

reputable [ˈrepjʊtəbəl] *adj* de bonne réputation

reputation [repjuːˈteɪʃən] *n* réputation *f*; **to have a good/bad r.** avoir (une) bonne/mauvaise réputation; **to have a r. for doing sth** avoir la réputation de faire qch; **to have a r. for frankness** avoir la réputation d'être franc (franche); **to live up to one's r.** être à la hauteur de sa réputation

repute [rɪˈpjuːt] **1** *n Formal* réputation *f*; **to be held in high r.** être estimé(e); **of r.** réputé(e)

2 *vt* **she is reputed to be wealthy/a genius** on la dit riche/géniale

reputedly [rɪˈpjuːtɪdlɪ] *adv* à ce qu'on dit

request [rɪˈkwest] **1** *n* demande *f* (**for** de); **available on r.** qui peut être obtenu(e) sur simple demande; **to make a r. (for)** faire une demande (de); **at sb's r.** à la demande de qn; **by popular r.** à la demande générale; **r. stop** *(for bus)* arrêt *m* facultatif
2 *vt* demander; **to r. sb to do sth** prier qn de faire qch

requiem [ˈrekwɪəm] *n* requiem *m*; **r. (mass)** messe *f* de requiem

require [rɪˈkwaɪə(r)] *vt (of task, problem, situation)* requérir; *(of person)* avoir besoin de; **to be required to do sth** être tenu(e) de faire qch; **if required** si besoin est/était; **when required** quand il le faut/fallait/faudra

requirement [rɪˈkwaɪəmənt] *n (need)* exigence *f*; *(condition)* condition *f* (requise); **to meet** *or* **satisfy sb's requirements** *(needs)* correspondre aux besoins de qn; *(demands)* satisfaire aux exigences de qn

requisite [ˈrekwɪzɪt] **1** *n* élément *m* essentiel
2 *adj* requis(e)

requisition [rekwɪˈzɪʃən] *vt* réquisitionner

rerun 1 *n* [ˈriːrʌn] *(on TV)* rediffusion *f*; *Fig (of situation, conflict)* répétition *f*
2 *vt* [riːˈrʌn] *(pt* **reran** [riːˈræn]*, pp* **rerun)** **(a)** *(TV programme)* rediffuser **(b)** *(race)* courir de nouveau

resale [riːˈseɪl] *n* revente *f*

reschedule [riːˈʃedjuːl] *vt* **(a)** *(meeting, flight) (change time of)* changer l'heure de; *(change date of)* changer la date de **(b)** *(debt)* rééchelonner

rescind [rɪˈsɪnd] *vt (law)* abroger; *(contract)* résilier

rescue [ˈreskjuː] **1** *n* secours *m*; *(from drowning)* sauvetage *m*; **to come to sb's r.** venir au secours de qn; **r. attempt, r. operation** opération *f* de sauvetage; **r. services** secours *mpl*
2 *vt (from death)* sauver; *(from difficulty)* secourir

rescuer [ˈreskjuə(r)] *n* sauveteur *m*

research [rɪˈsɜːtʃ] **1** *n* recherche *f*; **to do r.** faire de la recherche; **to do r. into sth** faire des recherches sur qch; **r. and development** recherche et développement *m*; **r. assistant/laboratory** assistant(e) *m,f*/laboratoire *m* de recherche
2 *vt* faire des recherches sur
3 *vi* faire des recherches (**into** sur)

researcher [rɪˈsɜːtʃə(r)] *n* chercheur(euse) *m,f*

resemblance [rɪˈzembləns] *n* ressemblance *f* (**to** avec); **to bear a r. to** ressembler à

resemble [rɪˈzembəl] *vt* ressembler à

resent [rɪˈzent] *vt (person)* en vouloir à; *(remark, criticism)* ne pas apprécier du tout

resentful [rɪˈzentfʊl] *adj* plein(e) de ressentiment; **to be** *or* **feel r.** éprouver du ressentiment

resentment [rɪˈzentmənt] *n* ressentiment *m*; **to feel r. towards sb** éprouver du ressentiment à l'égard de qn

reservation [rezəˈveɪʃən] *n* **(a)** *(booking)* réservation *f*; **to make a r.** faire une réservation; **r. desk** bureau *m* des réservations **(b)** *(doubt)* réserve *f*; **to have reservations about** avoir des doutes sur **(c)** *(for Native Americans)* réserve *f* (indienne)

reserve [rɪˈzɜːv] **1** *n* **(a)** *(supply)* réserve *f*; **to draw on one's reserves** puiser dans ses réserves; **to keep sth in r.** garder qch en réserve **(b)** *(in sport)* remplaçant(e) *m,f*; *Mil* **the reserves** les réservistes *mpl* **(c)** *(for birds, game)* réserve *f* **(d)** *(reticence)* réserve *f*

2 vt (book, keep) réserver; **to r. the right to do sth** se réserver le droit de faire qch; **to r. one's strength** ménager ses forces; **to r. judgement (on sth)** réserver son jugement (sur qch)

reserved [rɪ'zɜːvd] adj réservé(e)

reservist [rɪ'zɜːvɪst] n Mil réserviste m

reservoir ['rezəvwɑː(r)] n (lake) réservoir m; Fig (of strength, courage) réserve f

reset [riː'set] (pt & pp reset) vt (**a**) (clock, watch) mettre à l'heure; (counter) remettre à zéro; **r. button** bouton m de remise à zéro (**b**) (fracture) réduire

reshape [riː'ʃeɪp] vt réorganiser

reshuffle ['riːʃʌfəl] n réorganisation f; Br Pol (Cabinet) **r.** remaniement m (ministériel)

reside [rɪ'zaɪd] vi résider (**at/in** à/dans/en)

residence ['rezɪdəns] n (**a**) (stay) séjour m; **to take up r.** s'installer; **place of r.** lieu m de résidence; **r. permit** permis m de séjour (**b**) Formal (home) demeure f (**c**) Br Univ (hall of) **r.** résidence f universitaire

resident ['rezɪdənt] **1** n (of country, street) habitant(e) m,f; (of hotel) pensionnaire mf; **residents only** (sign) (in street) interdit sauf aux riverains; (in hotel) réservé a la clientèle de l'hôtel; **residents' association** = association de propriétaires ou de locataires d'un immeuble ou d'un quartier **2** adj **to be r. in Manchester** résider à Manchester

residential [rezɪ'denʃəl] adj (**a**) (neighbourhood) résidentiel(elle) (**b**) (staff) à demeure; **r. course** = stage qui nécessite un déplacement de plusieurs jours

residual [rɪ'zɪdjʊəl] adj résiduel(elle); Fig (doubt, worry) qui persiste; (income) net (nette)

residue ['rezɪdjuː] n (**a**) (remainder) reste m (**b**) Chem résidu m

resign [rɪ'zaɪn] **1** vt (**a**) (job, position) démissionner de (**b**) **to r. oneself to sth/to doing sth** se résigner à qch/à faire qch **2** vi démissionner

resignation [rezɪg'neɪʃən] n (**a**) (from job) démission f; **to hand in one's r.** donner sa démission (**b**) (attitude) résignation f

resilience [rɪ'zɪlɪəns] n (of material, metal) élasticité f; (of person, economy) résistance f

resilient [rɪ'zɪlɪənt] adj (material, metal) élastique; (person) résistant(e)

resin ['rezɪn] n résine f

resist [rɪ'zɪst] **1** vt résister à; Law **to r. arrest** refuser d'obtempérer (lors d'une arrestation); **to r. doing sth** s'empêcher de faire qch **2** vi résister

resistance [rɪ'zɪstəns] n résistance f (**to** à); **to put up** or **offer r.** offrir une résistance; **to meet with r.** rencontrer une résistance; **to take the line of least r.** adopter la solution de facilité; Hist **the (French) R.** la Résistance (française); **r. fighter** résistant(e) m,f

resistant [rɪ'zɪstənt] adj **to be r. to sth** résister à qch

resistor [rɪ'zɪstə(r)] n Elec résistance f

resit [riː'sɪt](pt & pp resat [riː'sæt]) vt (exam, driving test) repasser

resolute ['rezəluːt] adj résolu(e); (refusal, opposition) clair(e)

resolution [rezə'luːʃən] n (**a**) (decision, solution) résolution f; **to pass** or **carry a r.** adopter une résolution (**b**) (firmness) fermeté f

resolve [rɪ'zɒlv] **1** n résolution f **2** vt (**a**) (decide) **to r. to do sth** (of individual) se résoudre à faire qch; (of committee) décider de faire qch

(**b**) (solve) résoudre **3** vi **to r. on/against doing sth** se résoudre à faire/ ne pas faire qch

resonance ['rezənəns] n résonance f

resonant ['rezənənt] adj qui résonne

resonate ['rezəneɪt] vi résonner

resort [rɪ'zɔːt] **1** n (**a**) (recourse) recours m; **without r. to** sans avoir recours à; **as a last r.** en dernier recours (**b**) (holiday place) lieu m de villégiature **2** vi **to r. to sth** recourir à qch; **to r. to doing sth** finir par faire qch

resound [rɪ'zaʊnd] vi résonner (**with** de)

resounding [rɪ'zaʊndɪŋ] adj (crash, applause, failure) retentissant(e); (success) éclatant(e)

resource [rɪ'zɔːs] **1** n ressource f; **to be left to one's own resources** être livré(e) à soi-même; **r. management** gestion f des ressources **2** vt financer

resourceful [rɪ'zɔːsfʊl] adj ingénieux(euse)

respect [rɪ'spekt] **1** n (**a**) (admiration, consideration) respect m; **to have r. for** avoir du respect pour; **treat mountains with r.** soyez prudent en montagne; **with all due r.** sauf le respect que je vous dois; **to pay one's last respects to sb** rendre les derniers hommages à qn (**b**) (aspect) égard m; **in many respects** à bien des égards; **in some** or **certain respects** à certains égards; **in all respects** or **every r.** à tous les égards; **with r. to, in r. of** concernant **2** vt respecter

respectability [rɪspektə'bɪlɪtɪ] n respectabilité f

respectable [rɪ'spektəbəl] adj (decent, fairly large) respectable; (fairly good) honorable

respectably [rɪ'spektəblɪ] adv (**a**) (honourably, decently) de manière respectable; (dressed) convenablement (**b**) (fairly well) honorablement

respecter [rɪ'spektə(r)] n **to be no r. of** n'avoir aucun respect pour

respectful [rɪ'spektfʊl] adj respectueux(euse)

respective [rɪ'spektɪv] adj respectif(ive)

respectively [rɪ'spektɪvlɪ] adv respectivement

respiration [respɪ'reɪʃən] n respiration f

respirator ['respɪreɪtə(r)] n respirateur m; **to be on a r.** être branché(e) sur un respirateur

respiratory [rɪ'spɪrɪtərɪ] adj respiratoire

respite ['respaɪt] n (rest) répit m; (delay) sursis m

resplendent [rɪ'splendənt] adj resplendissant(e)

respond [rɪ'spɒnd] vi (answer) répondre (**to** à); (react) réagir (**to** à); **to r. (to treatment)** (of patient) bien réagir (au traitement)

respondent [rɪ'spɒndənt] n (**a**) Law défendeur/eresse) m,f (**b**) (to questionnaire) sondé(e) m,f

response [rɪ'spɒns] n (answer) réponse f; (reaction) réaction f; **in r. to** en réponse à; **the appeal met with a generous r.** le public a répondu généreusement à l'appel; **r. time** temps m de réponse

responsibility [rɪspɒnsɪ'bɪlɪtɪ] (pl responsibilities) n responsabilité f (**for** de); **to take** or **accept r. for sth** accepter la responsabilité de qch

responsible [rɪ'spɒnsɪbəl] adj responsable (**for** de); (job) à responsabilité; **to hold sb r.** tenir qn pour responsable

responsive [rɪ'spɒnsɪv] adj (to kindness, praise) sensible (**to** à); (to idea, suggestion) réceptif(ive) (**to** à)

rest¹ [rest] **1** n (**a**) (repose) repos m; **to have** or **take a r.** se reposer; Euph **to be at r.** reposer en paix; **to put** or set sb's mind at r. rassurer qn; *Fam* give it a r.! tu veux bien arrêter cinq minutes!; to come to r. *(of ball, car)* s'arrêter

(**b**) *(support)* support *m*

(**c**) *Mus (pause)* silence *m*

2 *vt* (**a**) *(cause to repose)* to r. one's eyes/legs se reposer les yeux/les jambes; God r. his soul! que Dieu ait son âme!

(**b**) *(lean)* poser (**on** sur)

(**c**) *(argument, hopes, confidence)* fonder (**on** sur); *Fig* I r. my case! sans commentaire!

3 *vi* (**a**) *(repose)* se reposer, prendre du repos; I won't r. until she has been caught je n'aurai de cesse qu'elle ne soit prise; r. in peace *(on gravestone)* qu'il/elle repose en paix

(**b**) *(lean)* être posé(e) (**on** sur)

(**c**) *(remain)* to r. with sb *(of decision, responsibility)* incomber à qn; there the matter rests l'affaire n'en est là; I won't let it r. at that je n'en resterai pas là; r. assured... soyez assuré que...

(**d**) *(of argument, theory)* to r. on reposer sur

rest² *n* the r. *(remainder)* le reste; *(others)* les autres *mfpl*; the r. of the time/the men le reste du temps/des hommes; the r. of them will stay here les autres resteront ici

restaurant ['restrɒnt] *n* restaurant *m*; r. car *(in train)* wagon-restaurant *m*

restful ['restfʊl] *adj* reposant(e)

restive ['restɪv] *adj* agité(e)

restless ['restlɪs] *adj* agité(e); to have a r. night passer une nuit agitée

restoration [restə'reɪʃən] *n (of furniture, monarchy)* restauration *f*; *(of communications, law and order)* rétablissement *m*; *(of property)* restitution *f*

restore [rɪ'stɔː(r)] *vt (furniture, monarchy, faith, calm)* restaurer; *(communications, law and order, confidence)* rétablir; *(property)* restituer (**to** à); to r. sb to health/strength redonner la santé/des forces à qn

restrain [rɪ'streɪn] *vt (person, dog)* maîtriser; *(passions)* refréner; *(anger, crowd)* contenir; to r. sb from doing sth retenir qn pour qu'il/elle ne fasse pas qch; to r. oneself (from doing sth) se retenir (de faire qch)

restrained [rɪ'streɪnd] *adj (person, manner)* réservé(e); *(tone, terms)* mesuré(e); *(style)* sobre

restraint [rɪ'streɪnt] *n* (**a**) *(moderation)* mesure *f*, modération *f*; to show *or* exercise great r. faire preuve d'une grande modération (**b**) *(restriction)* restriction *f*; without r. sans retenue

restrict [rɪ'strɪkt] *vt (person, freedom)* restreindre; to r. oneself to sth/to doing sth se limiter à qch/à faire qch

restricted [rɪ'strɪktɪd] *adj* restreint(e), limité(e); *(document)* secret(ète); r. area *Mil* zone *f* interdite; *(for parking)* zone bleue

restriction [rɪ'strɪkʃən] *n* restriction *f*; *(of speed)* limitation *f*; to place restrictions on sth apporter des restrictions à qch

restrictive [rɪ'strɪktɪv] *adj* restrictif(ive); *Ind* r. practices pratiques *fpl* restrictives

restroom ['restruːm] *n Am* toilettes *fpl*

restructure [riː'strʌktʃə(r)] *vt* restructurer

restructuring [riː'strʌktʃərɪŋ] *n* restructuration *f*

result [rɪ'zʌlt] 1 *n* résultat *m*; as a r. en conséquence; as a r. of à la suite de; the r. is that... il en résulte que...; to yield *or* show results donner des résultats

2 *vi* to r. from résulter de; to r. in entraîner

resultant [rɪ'zʌltənt] *adj* résultant(e)

resume [rɪ'zjuːm] 1 *vt* reprendre; *(relations)* renouer; *(attempt)* renouveler; *(interest)* retrouver

2 *vi* reprendre

résumé ['rezjʊmeɪ] *n (summary)* résumé *m*; *Am (curriculum vitae)* curriculum vitae *m inv*

resumption [rɪ'zʌmpʃən] *n* reprise *f*

resurface [riː'sɜːfɪs] 1 *vt (road)* refaire le revêtement de

2 *vi also Fig* refaire surface

resurgent [rɪ'sɜːdʒənt] *adj* renaissant(e); *(economy)* qui connaît une reprise

resurrect [rezə'rekt] *vt Rel* ressusciter; *Fig (fashion)* remettre au goût du jour; *(argument)* ressortir; *(tradition)* faire renaître

resurrection [rezə'rekʃən] *n Fig* réapparition *f*; *Rel* the R. la Résurrection (du Christ)

resuscitate [rɪ'sʌsɪteɪt] *vt (person)* ranimer; *Fig (career)* redonner un nouvel élan à; *(scheme)* ressortir

retail ['riːteɪl] 1 *n Com* (vente *f* au) détail *m*; r. outlet magasin *m* de détail; r. price prix *m* de détail; *Econ* r. price index indice *m* des prix de détail; r. trade commerce *m* de détail; *Hum* I did a bit of r. therapy this weekend j'ai fait un peu de shopping pour me remonter le moral ce week-end

2 *vt (goods)* vendre au détail

3 *vi* se vendre (**at** à)

retailer ['riːteɪlə(r)] *n* détaillant(e) *m,f*

retain [rɪ'teɪn] *vt* (**a**) *(keep)* conserver, garder (**b**) *(hold in place)* maintenir; retaining wall mur *m* de soutènement (**c**) *(remember)* retenir

retainer [rɪ'teɪnə(r)] *n* (**a**) *(fee)* appointements *mpl* (**b**) *Old-fashioned (servant)* serviteur *m*, servante *f*

retaliate [rɪ'tælɪeɪt] *vi* riposter

retaliation [rɪtælɪ'eɪʃən] *n* représailles *fpl*; in r. (for sth) en représailles (à qch)

retard [rɪ'tɑːd] *vt* retarder

retarded [rɪ'tɑːdɪd] *adj* (**mentally**) r. arriéré(e)

retch [retʃ] *vi* avoir des haut-le-cœur

retention [rɪ'tenʃən] *n (of custom, practice)* maintien *m*; *(of fact, impression)* mémorisation *f*

retentive [rɪ'tentɪv] *adj (memory)* fidèle; *(person)* qui a (une) bonne mémoire

rethink 1 *n* ['riːθɪŋk] to have a r. (about sth) réfléchir à nouveau (à qch)

2 *vt* [riː'θɪŋk] *(pt & pp* rethought [riː'θɔːt] *)* repenser

reticent ['retɪsənt] *adj* réservé(e), réticent(e); to be r. about sth parler peu de qch

retina ['retɪnə] *n* rétine *f*

retinue ['retɪnjuː] *n* suite *f*, cortège *m*

retire [rɪ'taɪə(r)] 1 *vt* mettre à la retraite

2 *vi* (**a**) *(of employee)* prendre sa retraite (**b**) *(withdraw)* se retirer; *(go to bed)* (aller) se coucher

retired [rɪ'taɪəd] *adj* retraité(e), à la retraite

retirement [rɪ'taɪəmənt] *n (from work, army)* retraite *f*; to take early r. partir en retraite anticipée; to come out of r. reprendre sa carrière; r. age l'âge *m* de la retraite; r. pension (pension *f* de) retraite

retiring [rɪ'taɪərɪŋ] *adj* (**a**) *(reserved)* réservé(e) (**b**) *(chairman, MP)* sortant(e); *(employee)* qui prend sa retraite; r. age l'âge *m* de la retraite

retort [rɪ'tɔːt] 1 *n (answer)* réplique *f*

2 *vt & vi* répliquer

retrace [rɪ'treɪs] *vt* to r. one's steps revenir sur ses pas

retract [rɪˈtrækt] **1** *vt* (**a**) *(statement, offer)* revenir sur (**b**) *(claws, aircraft undercarriage)* rentrer **2** *vi* (**a**) *(of person)* se rétracter (**b**) *(of claws, aircraft undercarriage)* rentrer

retractable [rɪˈtræktəbəl] *adj* rétractable; *(antenna, aircraft undercarriage)* escamotable

retrain [riːˈtreɪn] **1** *vt* recycler **2** *vi* se recycler

retraining [riːˈtreɪnɪŋ] *n* recyclage *m*

retread [ˈriːtred] *n* pneu *m* rechapé

retreat [rɪˈtriːt] **1** *n* (**a**) *(withdrawal)* retraite *f*; *also Fig* **to beat a (hasty) r.** battre en retraite (**b**) *(place)* retraite *f* **2** *vi* battre en retraite; *Fig* se réfugier

retrial [riːˈtraɪəl] *n Law* nouveau procès *m*

retribution [retrɪˈbjuːʃən] *n* châtiment *m*

retrieve [rɪˈtriːv] *vt* récupérer; *Comput (file)* ouvrir

retriever [rɪˈtriːvə(r)] *n (dog)* retriever *m*

retroactive [retrəʊˈæktɪv] *adj Formal* rétroactif(ive)

retrograde [ˈretrəgreɪd] *adj* rétrograde

retrospect [ˈretrəspekt] *n* **in r.** après coup, rétrospectivement

retrospective [retrəˈspektɪv] **1** *n (exhibition)* rétrospective *f* **2** *adj* rétrospectif(ive); *(measure, decision)* à effet rétroactif

return [rɪˈtɜːn] **1** *n* (**a**) *(of person, peace, season, tennis service)* retour *m*; *(of goods)* renvoi *m*; **on my r.** à mon retour; **by r. of post** par retour du courrier; **in r. (for)** en échange (de); **to do sth in r.** faire qch en retour; **many happy returns (of the day)!** bon anniversaire!; **r. journey** (voyage *m* de) retour; **r. match** match *m* retour; **r. ticket** (billet *m*) aller et retour *m* (**b**) *Fin (profit)* rapport *m*; **to bring a good r.** rapporter un bon bénéfice; **r. on investment** retour *m* sur investissement **2** *vt* (**a**) *(give or send back)* rendre; **to r. a favour** rendre la pareille; **r. to sender** *(on letter)* retour à l'envoyeur; **to r. service** *(in tennis)* renvoyer le service; **to r. sb's call** *(on phone)* rappeler qn; *Law* **to r. a verdict of guilty/not guilty** déclarer l'accusé(e) coupable/non coupable (**b**) *Fin (profit)* rapporter **3** *vi (come back)* revenir; *(go back)* retourner; **to r. to work** reprendre son travail

returnable [rɪˈtɜːnəbəl] *adj (bottle)* consigné(e)

reunification [riːjuːnɪfɪˈkeɪʃən] *n* réunification *f*

reunify [riːˈjuːnɪfaɪ] *(pt & pp* **reunified**) *vt* réunifier

reunion [riːˈjuːnɪən] *n* réunion *f*

reunite [riːjuːˈnaɪt] *vt* réconcilier; **to be reunited with sb** retrouver qn

reusable [riːˈjuːzəbəl] *adj* réutilisable

reuse [riːˈjuːz] *vt* réutiliser

Rev *Rel (abbr* **Reverend**) **R. Gray** le révérend Gray

rev [rev] *Fam* **1** *n (abbr* **revolution**) tour *m*; **r. counter** compte-tours *m inv* **2** *vt (pt & pp* **revved**) **to r. the engine** faire monter le régime (du moteur)

revalue [riːˈvæljuː] *vt Fin* réévaluer

revamp [riːˈvæmp] *vt Fam (image)* rajeunir; *(company)* restructurer; *(house)* retaper

reveal [rɪˈviːl] *vt* révéler

revealing [rɪˈviːlɪŋ] *adj (sign, comment)* révélateur(-trice); *(clothing)* qui ne cache pas grand-chose

revel [ˈrevəl] *(pt & pp* **revelled**, *Am* **reveled**) *vi* faire la fête; **to r. in sth** savourer qch

revelation [revəˈleɪʃən] *n* révélation *f*; **(the Book of) Revelations** l'Apocalypse *f*

reveller, *Am* **reveler** [ˈrevələ(r)] *n* fêtard(e) *m,f*

revenge [rɪˈvendʒ] **1** *n (punishment)* vengeance *f*; *(getting one's own back)* revanche *f*; **to take r. (on sb)** se venger (de qn); *Prov* **r. is sweet** ça fait du bien de se venger! **2** *vt* venger

revenue [ˈrevənjuː] *n* revenu *m*; *(from sales)* recettes *fpl*

reverberate [rɪˈvɜːbəreɪt] *vi* (**a**) *(of sound)* résonner (**b**) *(of news, rumour)* se propager

reverberation [rɪvɜːbəˈreɪʃən] *n* (**a**) *(sound)* réverbération *f* (**b**) *(of news, rumour)* répercussion *f*

revere [rɪˈvɪə(r)] *vt* révérer

reverence [ˈrevərəns] *n* révérence *f*

Reverend [ˈrevərənd] *adj Rel* révérend; **Right R.** très révérend

reverential [revəˈrenʃəl] *adj* révérencieux(euse)

reverie [ˈrevərɪ] *n* rêverie *f*

reversal [rɪˈvɜːsəl] *n (of opinion, policy)* revirement *m*; *(of roles)* renversement *m*; *(of fortune)* revers *m*; *Law (of decision)* annulation *f*

reverse [rɪˈvɜːs] **1** *n* (**a**) *(opposite)* contraire *m*; **quite the r.!** bien au contraire! (**b**) *(of coin)* revers *m*; *(of fabric)* envers *m* (**c**) *(defeat)* échec *m*; *(misfortune)* revers *m*; **to suffer a r.** *(defeat)* subir un échec; *(misfortune)* subir un revers (**d**) *(gear)* marche *f* arrière; **to put the car into r.** passer la marche arrière **2** *adj* inverse; **in r. order** en ordre inverse; **the r. side** *(of coin)* le revers; *(of fabric)* l'envers *m*; *Br* **r.-charge call** communication *f* en PCV, *Can* appel *m* à frais virés; **r. gear** marche *f* arrière **3** *vt* (**a**) *(order, policy, roles)* inverser; *(decision)* revenir sur; *(situation, trend)* renverser; *Br* **to r. the charges** appeler en PCV (**b**) *(vehicle)* **to r. the car** faire marche arrière

reversible [rɪˈvɜːsəbəl] *adj* (**a**) *(jacket)* réversible (**b**) *(decree)* révocable; *(surgery)* réversible; **not r.** *(decision)* irrévocable; *(surgery)* irréversible

revert to [rɪˈvɜːt] *vt insep* revenir à; **to r. to type** reprendre ses vielles habitudes

review [rɪˈvjuː] **1** *n* (**a**) *(of policy, salary)* révision *f*; *(of situation)* examen *m*; **to be under r.** faire l'objet d'une révision (**b**) *(of book, play, film)* critique *f* (**c**) *Mil* revue *f* **2** *vt* (**a**) *(policy, salary)* réviser; *(situation)* faire le point sur (**b**) *(book, play, film)* faire la critique de (**c**) *Mil (troops)* passer en revue

reviewer [rɪˈvjuːə(r)] *n (of book, play, film)* critique *mf*

revile [rɪˈvaɪl] *vt Formal* vilipender

revise [rɪˈvaɪz] **1** *vt* (**a**) *(text, law)* réviser; *(decision)* réexaminer; **to r. one's opinion (of)** changer d'opinion (à l'égard de) (**b**) *Br (for exam) (subject, notes)* réviser **2** *vi Br (for exam)* réviser, faire des révisions

revision [rɪˈvɪʒən] *n* (**a**) *(of text, law)* révision *f* (**b**) *Br (for exam)* révisions *fpl*

revisionism [rɪˈvɪʒənɪzəm] *n Pol* révisionnisme *m*

revisit [rɪˈvɪzɪt] *vt (place)* revisiter; *(person)* retourner voir

revitalize [rɪˈvaɪtəlaɪz] *vt (person)* revigorer; *(arts, industry)* donner un nouvel essor à

revival [rɪ'vaɪvəl] *n (of person)* réanimation *f; (of hopes)* renaissance *f; (of industry, custom, fashion)* renouveau *m; (of play)* reprise *f*

revive [rɪ'vaɪv] **1** *vt (person)* ranimer; *(industry, hopes, custom)* faire renaître; *(fashion)* relancer
2 *vi (of person)* reprendre connaissance; *(of industry)* connaître un renouveau; *(of hopes)* renaître

revoke [rɪ'vəʊk] *vt (law)* abroger; *(decision)* revenir sur; *(privilege)* abolir; **to r. sb's licence** retirer son permis à qn

revolt [rɪ'vəʊlt] **1** *n* révolte *f;* **to be in r.** être en révolte
2 *vt (disgust)* dégoûter
3 *vi (rebel)* se révolter (**against** contre)

revolting [rɪ'vəʊltɪŋ] *adj (disgusting)* dégoûtant(e)

revolution [revə'luːʃən] *n* (**a**) *(radical change)* révolution *f* (**b**) *(turn)* tour *m*, révolution *f*

revolutionary [revə'luːʃənərɪ] *(pl* **revolutionaries**) *n & adj* révolutionnaire *mf*

revolutionize [revə'luːʃənaɪz] *vt* révolutionner

revolve [rɪ'vɒlv] *vi* tourner (**around** autour de); *Fig* **to r. around sth** s'articuler autour de qch

revolver [rɪ'vɒlvə(r)] *n* revolver *m*

revolving [rɪ'vɒlvɪŋ] *adj (chair)* pivotant(e); *(platform)* tournant(e); *Fin (credit)* revolving *inv;* **r. door** porte *f* à tambour

revue [rɪ'vjuː] *n Theat* revue *f*

revulsion [rɪ'vʌlʃən] *n* dégoût *m*

reward [rɪ'wɔːd] **1** *n* récompense *f;* **as a r. for** en récompense de
2 *vt* récompenser (**for** de *ou* pour)

rewarding [rɪ'wɔːdɪŋ] *adj (experience)* enrichissant(e), intéressant(e); *(job)* gratifiant(e)

rewind [riː'waɪnd] *(pt & pp* **rewound** [riː'waʊnd]) *vt (tape, film)* rembobiner

rewire [riː'waɪə(r)] *vt* refaire l'installation électrique de

reword [riː'wɜːd] *vt* reformuler

rework [iː'wɜːk] *vt* retravailler

rewrite [riː'raɪt] *(pt* **rewrote** [riː'rəʊt], *pp* **rewritten** [riː'rɪtən]) *vt* réécrire

Reykjavik ['rekjəvɪk] *n* Reykjavik

RFU [ɑːref'juː] *n Br Sport (abbr* **Rugby Football Union**) = fédération britannique de rugby

rhapsodic(al) [ræp'sɒdɪk(əl)] *adj (prose, description)* dithyrambique; *(person)* enthousiaste

rhapsodize ['ræpsədaɪz] *vi* s'extasier (**over** *or* **about** sur)

rhapsody ['ræpsədɪ] *(pl* **rhapsodies**) *n Mus* rhapsodie *f;* **to go into rhapsodies over sth** s'extasier sur qch

rhesus ['riːsəs] *n* **r. factor** facteur *m* rhésus; **r. positive/negative** rhésus *m* positif/négatif; **r. monkey** rhésus *m*

rhetoric ['retərɪk] *n* rhétorique *f;* **the speech was nothing but empty r.** le discours ne consistait qu'en de belles phrases creuses

rhetorical [rɪ'tɒrɪkəl] *adj (style, question)* rhétorique; *(term)* de rhétorique

rheumatic [ruː'mætɪk] *adj (pain)* rhumatismal(e); *(joint)* atteint(e) de rhumatisme; **r. fever** rhumatisme *m* articulaire aigu

rheumatism ['ruːmətɪzəm] *n* rhumatisme *m*

rheumatoid arthritis ['ruːmətɔɪdɑːˈθraɪtɪs] *n* polyarthrite *f* rhumatoïde

Rhine [raɪn] *n* **the R.** le Rhin

rhinestone ['raɪnstəʊn] *n* faux diamant *m*

rhino ['raɪnəʊ] *(pl* **rhinos**) *n Fam* rhinocéros *m*

rhinoceros [raɪ'nɒsərəs] *n* rhinocéros *m*

Rhodes [rəʊdz] *n* Rhodes

rhododendron [rəʊdə'dendrən] *n* rhododendron *m*

rhomboid ['rɒmbɔɪd] *n* rhomboïde *m*

rhombus ['rɒmbəs] *(pl* **rhombuses** *or* **rhombi** ['rɒmbaɪ]) *n* losange *m*

Rhone [rəʊn] *n* **the R.** le Rhône

rhubarb ['ruːbɑːb] *n* rhubarbe *f;* **r. jam/tart** confiture *f*/tarte *f* à la rhubarbe

rhyme [raɪm] **1** *n (sound)* rime *f; (poem)* vers *mpl;* **without r. or reason** sans rime ni raison
2 *vi* rimer (**with** avec)

rhyming slang ['raɪmɪŋslæŋ] *n* = argot cockney où les mots sont remplacés par des locutions choisies pour la rime

---

Rhyming slang

Il s'agit d'un procédé complexe consistant à remplacer un mot par une expression dont le dernier terme rime avec le mot en question; bien souvent n'est prononcé que le premier terme de l'expression, à savoir celui qui ne rime pas avec le mot remplacé. Exemple: kids = dustbin lids = dustbins; head = loaf of bread = loaf. À l'origine ce type d'argot était pratiqué par les Cockneys (habitants de l'est de Londres) mais certains termes sont maintenant passés dans la langue courante et sont connus de la plupart des Britanniques.

---

rhythm ['rɪðəm] *n* rythme *m;* **r. method** *(of contraception)* méthode *f* du calendrier

rhythmic(al) ['rɪðmɪk(əl)] *adj* rythmé(e), cadencé(e)

rib [rɪb] **1** *n* (**a**) *(of person, animal)* côte *f* (**b**) *(of umbrella)* baleine *f*
2 *vt (pt & pp* **ribbed**) *Fam (tease)* taquiner (**about** à propos de)

ribald ['rɪbəld, 'raɪbəld] *adj* grivois(e), paillard(e)

ribbed [rɪbd] *adj (fabric, jumper)* à côtes

ribbon ['rɪbən] *n (for hair, typewriter)* ruban *m; (of land)* bande *f* étroite; **to tear sth to ribbons** déchiqueter qch; *Fig (criticize)* éreinter qch

ribcage ['rɪbkeɪdʒ] *n* cage *f* thoracique

Ribena® [raɪ'biːnə] *n* sirop *m* de cassis

riboflavin(e) [raɪbəʊ'fleɪvɪn] *n Chem* riboflavine *f*

rice [raɪs] *n* riz *m;* **r. field** *or* **paddy** rizière *f;* **r. pudding** riz au lait

rich [rɪtʃ] **1** *npl* **the r.** les riches *mpl;* **riches** *(wealth)* richesses *fpl*
2 *adj* riche; *(harvest, supply)* abondant(e); *(colour)* intense; *(voice)* chaud(e); **to be r. in sth** être riche en qch; *Fam* **that's r.!** c'est un peu fort!

richly ['rɪtʃlɪ] *adv* richement; **r. deserved** bien mérité(e)

Richter Scale ['rɪktə'skeɪl] *n* échelle *f* de Richter

rick¹ [rɪk] *n (of hay, straw)* meule *f*

rick² *vt* **to r. one's neck** attraper un torticolis; **to r. one's back** se donner un tour de reins

rickets ['rɪkɪts] *npl* rachitisme *m;* **to have r.** être rachitique

rickety ['rɪkɪtɪ] *adj Fam (furniture, staircase)* branlant(e); *(alliance, ulibi)* boiteux(euse)

ricochet ['rɪkəʃeɪ] **1** *n* ricochet *m*
2 *vi (pt & pp* **ricochetted** ['rɪkəʃeɪd]) ricocher (**off** sur)

rid [rɪd] (*pt* **rid**, *pp* **rid** *or* **ridden** ['rɪdən]) *vt* **to r. sb of sth** débarrasser qn de qch; **to get r. of sth** se débarrasser de qch

riddance ['rɪdəns] *n Fam* **good r.!** bon débarras!

ridden ['rɪdən] *pp of* **rid, ride**

riddle ['rɪdəl] **1** *n* (*puzzle*) devinette *f*; (*mystery*) énigme *f*
2 *vt* **to r. sb/sth with bullets** cribler qn/qch de balles; **riddled with mistakes** truffé(e) de fautes

ride [raɪd] **1** *n* (**a**) (*on bicycle, in car*) tour *m*; (*on horse*) promenade *f*; **to go for a r.** aller faire un tour; **to give sb a r.** (*in car*) conduire qn en voiture; **It's only a short r. away** ce n'est pas très loin; *Fig* **she was given a rough r.** on lui en a fait voir de toutes les couleurs; *Fig* **to take sb for a r.** mener qn en bateau (**b**) (*at funfair*) attraction *f*
2 *vt* (*pt* **rode** [rəʊd], *pp* **ridden** ['rɪdən]) (*horse, bicycle*) monter à; (*bus, train*) prendre
3 *vi* (*on horse*) faire du cheval; (*on bicycle*) faire de la bicyclette; *Fig* **to be riding high** connaître une période de succès; *Fam Fig* **to let it r.** laisser courir
▸**ride out** *vt sep* (*problem, crisis*) survivre à; *Fig* **to r. out the storm** surmonter la crise

rider ['raɪdə(r)] *n* (**a**) (*on horse*) cavalier(ère) *m,f*; (*on bicycle*) cycliste *mf*; (*on motorbike*) motocycliste *mf* (**b**) *Law* (*to document, treaty*) annexe *f*; (*to bill*) clause *f* additionnelle

ridge [rɪdʒ] *n* (*of mountain*) crête *f*; (*of roof*) faîte *m*; (*on surface*) strie *f*; *Met* **r. of high pressure** dorsale *f* barométrique

ridicule ['rɪdɪkjuːl] **1** *n* ridicule *m*; **to hold sb/sth up to r.** tourner qn/qch en ridicule
2 *vt* ridiculiser, tourner en ridicule

ridiculous [rɪ'dɪkjʊləs] *adj* ridicule; **to make sb/sth look r.** rendre qn/qch ridicule; **to make oneself look r.** se rendre ridicule, se ridiculiser

riding ['raɪdɪŋ] *n* équitation *f*; **to go r.** faire du cheval; **r. boots** bottes *fpl* de cheval; **r. crop** *or* **whip** cravache *f*; **r. school** école *f* d'équitation

rife [raɪf] *adj* **to be r.** être très répandu(e); (*of rumours*) aller bon train

riffraff ['rɪfræf] *n* racaille *f*

rifle[1] ['raɪfəl] *n* fusil *m*; **r. range** champ *m* de tir; (*at funfair*) stand *m* de tir; **r. shot** coup *m* de fusil

rifle[2] *vt* (*house, office*) mettre sens dessus dessous; (*pockets, drawer*) fouiller dans

rifleman ['raɪfəlmən] *n Mil* fusilier *m*

rift [rɪft] *n* (*in earth, rock*) fissure *f*; (*in relationship*) rupture *f*; (*difference of opinion*) désaccord *m*

rig [rɪg] **1** *n* (**a**) (*of ship*) gréement *m* (**b**) (oil) **r.** derrick *m*; (*at sea*) plate-forme *f* pétrolière
2 *vt* (*pt & pp* **rigged**) (**a**) (*ship*) gréer (**b**) *Fam* (*election, contest*) truquer
▸**rig out** *vt sep Fam* **to be rigged out in** être attifé(e) de
▸**rig up** *vt sep* monter, installer

Riga ['riːgə] *n* Riga

rigging ['rɪgɪŋ] *n* (*of ship*) gréement *m*

right [raɪt] **1** *n* (**a**) (*morality*) bien *m*; **to be in the r.** avoir raison; **to set things to rights** arranger les choses
(**b**) (*entitlement*) droit *m*; **to have the r. to do sth** avoir le droit de faire qch; **to be within one's rights** être dans son droit; **by rights** en principe; **by r.** de droit; **to be famous in one's own r.** être soi-même une célébrité; *Br* **r. to roam** = droit d'emprunter des sentiers sur des terres appartenant à de grands

propriétaires terriens; **the r. to vote** le droit de vote; **r. of way** (*on land*) droit de passage; (*on road*) priorité *f*
(**c**) (*right-hand side*) droite *f*, côté *m* droit; **on** *or* **to the r.** à droite; **on my r.** à *ou* sur ma droite; **the r.** (*in politics*) la droite
2 *adj* (**a**) (*correct*) exact(e), bon (bonne); (*word*) juste; **to be r.** (*of person*) avoir raison; **to keep on the r. side of sb** veiller à ne pas se mettre qn à dos; **to be on the r. lines** être sur la bonne voie
(**b**) (*morally good*) bien *inv*; **to do the r. thing** faire ce qu'il faut
(**c**) (*appropriate*) bon (bonne); **the r. thing to do** la meilleure chose à faire; **to know the r. people** connaître les gens qu'il faut; **to be in the r. place at the r. time** se trouver là au bon moment
(**d**) (*mentally, physically well*) **I'm not feeling quite r.** je ne me sens pas très bien; **to be as r. as rain** être en parfaite santé; **no one in his r. mind would do that** aucune personne sensée ne ferait cela; **he's not quite r. in the head** il n'a pas toute sa tête
(**e**) *Fam* (*for emphasis*) véritable; **I felt a r. fool** je me suis vraiment senti stupide; **my hair was in a r. mess** mes cheveux étaient complètement en bataille
(**f**) (*right-hand*) droit(e); **on the r. side** à *ou* sur la droite; *Pol* **the r. wing** l'aile *f* droite
(**g**) *Math* **r. angle** angle *m* droit
3 *adv* (**a**) (*straight*) (tout) droit; **to put things r.** arranger les choses; **to put sb r.** détromper qn
(**b**) **r. away** (*immediately*) sur-le-champ, immédiatement; **I'll be r. back** je reviens tout de suite; **r. now** (*immediately*) tout de suite; (*at the moment*) en ce moment
(**c**) (*completely*) **to go r. through sth** traverser qch de part en part; **to go r. up to sb** se diriger (tout) droit vers qn; **to turn r. round** se retourner; **r. at the top/back** tout en haut/à l'arrière
(**d**) (*exactly*) **r. here/there** juste ici/là; **r. in the middle** en plein milieu; **r. behind** juste derrière; *Fig* **to be r. behind sb** soutenir qn à fond
(**e**) (*answer*) correctement; (*guess*) juste; **to understand/remember r.** bien comprendre/se souvenir
(**f**) (*well*) **I'm sure it'll all come r. for you** je suis sûr que tout s'arrangera pour vous; *Fam* **to see sb r.** veiller à ce que qn ne soit pas à court d'argent; **it was a mistake, r. enough** c'était bien une erreur
(**g**) (*look, turn*) à droite; *Fig* **r., left and centre** de tous les côtés
4 *vt* (**a**) (*put upright*) redresser
(**b**) (*redress*) **to r. a wrong** réparer un tort

right-angled ['raɪtæŋgəld] *adj* à angle droit; (*triangle*) rectangle

righteous ['raɪtʃəs] *adj* (*person*) droit(e), vertueux(-euse); (*indignation*) vertueux(euse)

rightful ['raɪtfəl] *adj* (*heir, owner*) légitime; (*share*) auquel (à laquelle) on a droit

right-hand ['raɪthænd] *adj* de droite; (*corner, side*) droit(e); **r. bend** virage *m* à droite; **r. drive** conduite *f* à droite; **on the r. side** à droite; **to be sb's r. man** être le bras droit de qn

right-handed [raɪt'hændɪd] **1** *adj* droitier(ère)
2 *adv* de la main droite

right-hander [raɪt'hændə(r)] *n* (*person*) droitier(ére) *m,f*

rightly ['raɪtlɪ] *adv* (*correctly*) bien; (*justifiably*) à juste titre; **I don't r. know why...** je ne sais pas exactement pourquoi...; **r. or wrongly** à tort ou à raison; **... and r. so** ... et non sans raison

right-minded [raɪt'maɪndɪd], **right-thinking** [raɪt-'θɪŋkɪŋ] *adj* sensé(e)

right-wing [raɪt'wɪŋ] *adj Pol* de droite

right-winger [raɪt'wɪŋə(r)] *n Pol (man)* homme *m* de droite; *(woman)* femme *f* de droite

rigid ['rɪdʒɪd] *adj* rigide; *Fig (person, ideas)* inflexible; *Br Fam* **to be bored r.** s'ennuyer ferme

rigidity [rɪ'dʒɪdɪtɪ] *n* rigidité *f*

rigmarole ['rɪgmərəʊl] *n Fam (process)* procédure *f* compliquée; *(speech)* long discours *m*

rigor mortis ['rɪgə'mɔːtɪs] *n* rigidité *f* cadavérique

rigorous ['rɪgərəs] *adj* rigoureux(euse)

rigour ['rɪgə(r)] *n* rigueur *f*

rigout ['rɪgaʊt] *n Fam (outfit)* tenue *f*

rile [raɪl] *vt Fam* agacer

rim [rɪm] *n (of cup, bowl)* bord *m*; *(of wheel)* jante *f*; *(of spectacles)* monture *f*

rind [raɪnd] *n (of fruit)* écorce *f*; *(of cheese)* croûte *f*; *(of bacon)* couenne *f*

ring¹ [rɪŋ] **1** *n* (**a**) *(for finger) (with stone)* bague *f*; *(without stone)* anneau *m*; *(for keys)* porte-clés *m inv*; **the rings** *(in gymnastics)* les anneaux; **r. binder** classeur *m* à anneaux; **r. finger** annulaire *m* (**b**) *(of people, chairs)* cercle *m*; *(on stove)* brûleur *m*; *(stain)* marque *f*; **to have rings under one's eyes** avoir des cernes sous les yeux; *Fig* **to run rings round sb** éclipser qn; **r. road** périphérique *m* (**c**) *(for boxing, wrestling)* ring *m* (**d**) *(of criminals)* bande *f*; *(of spies)* réseau *m*
2 *vt (surround)* encercler

ring² **1** *n (sound) (of doorbell, telephone)* sonnerie *f*; *(of small bell, coins)* tintement *m*; **there was a r. at the door** on sonna à la porte; *Fam* **to give sb a r.** passer un coup de fil à qn; **to have a r. of truth** avoir l'air vrai(e); **the name has a familiar r. to it** ce nom me dit quelque chose
2 *vt (pt* **rang** [ræŋ]*, pp* **rung** [rʌŋ] *) (bell)* sonner; *(alarm)* déclencher; *(on phone)* appeler; **to r. the doorbell** sonner à la porte; *Fig* **that rings a bell** cela me dit quelque chose; *Fig* **to r. the changes** introduire des changements
3 *vi* (**a**) *(of bell, telephone)* sonner; **to r. at the door** sonner à la porte; *Fig* **to r. true** avoir l'air vrai(e); **to r. false** sonner faux (**b**) *(resonate) (of ears)* bourdonner; **to r. with** *(of street, room)* retentir de (**c**) *(make a phone call)* appeler

▶**ring back** *vt sep (on phone)* rappeler
▶**ring off** *vi (on phone)* raccrocher
▶**ring out** *vi (of voice, shout)* retentir
▶**ring up** *vt sep* (**a**) *(on phone)* téléphoner à, appeler (**b**) *(on cash register)* enregistrer; **to r. up a profit** enregistrer un bénéfice

ringleader ['rɪŋliːdə(r)] *n (of strike)* meneur(euse) *m,f*; *(of gang)* chef *m* de bande

ringlet ['rɪŋlɪt] *n* anglaise *f*

ringmaster ['rɪŋmɑːstə(r)] *n* ≃ Monsieur *m* Loyal

ring-pull ['rɪŋpʊl] *n* bague *f* (d'ouverture)

ringside ['rɪŋsaɪd] *n* **at the r.** près du ring; **to have a r. seat** avoir une place au premier rang; *Fig* être aux premières loges

ringworm ['rɪŋwɜːm] *n Med* teigne *f*

rink [rɪŋk] *n (for roller skating)* piste *f*; *(for ice skating)* patinoire *f*

rinse [rɪns] **1** *n* **to give sth a r.** rincer qch
2 *vt (clothes, dishes)* rincer; **to r. one's hands/hair** se rincer les mains/les cheveux
▶**rinse out** *vt sep* rincer

Rio (de Janeiro) ['riːəʊ(dɪdʒə'neərəʊ)] *n* Rio (de Janeiro)

riot ['raɪət] **1** *n (uprising)* émeute *f*; *Fig* **a r. of colour** une explosion de couleurs; **to run r.** se déchaîner; **her imagination was running r.** elle s'imaginait toutes sortes de choses; **to read sb the r. act** passer un savon à qn; **r. police** police *f* anti-émeute, ≃ CRS *mpl*
2 *vi* faire une émeute; *(of prisoners)* se mutiner

rioter ['raɪətə(r)] *n* émeutier(ère) *m,f*

rioting ['raɪətɪŋ] *n* émeutes *fpl*

riotous ['raɪətəs] *adj (party, behaviour, event)* tapageur(euse); **r. living** vie *f* déréglée

RIP [ɑːraɪ'piː] *(abbr* **Rest In Peace)** qu'il/elle repose en paix

rip [rɪp] **1** *n* déchirure *f*
2 *vt (pt & pp* **ripped)** déchirer; **to r. sth to pieces** *(cloth)* mettre qch en lambeaux; *(paper)* déchirer qch en mille morceaux; *Fig (criticize)* mettre qch en pièces
3 *vi* (**a**) *(of cloth, paper)* se déchirer (**b**) *Fam* **to let r.** *(in performance)* se déchaîner; **to let r. at sb** s'en prendre violemment à qn

▶**rip off** *vt sep* (**a**) *(tear)* arracher (**b**) *Fam (swindle)* arna-quer; *(steal)* piquer
▶**rip open** *vt sep* **to r. open a letter** ouvrir une lettre en déchirant l'enveloppe; **to r. open a parcel** ouvrir un paquet en le déchirant
▶**rip up** *vt sep* (**a**) *(letter)* déchirer (**b**) *(floorboards)* arracher; *(pavement)* creuser des trous dans

ripe [raɪp] *adj (fruit)* mûr(e); *(cheese)* fait(e) à point; **to live to a r. old age** vivre jusqu'à un âge avancé; **the time is r. (to do sth)** le temps est venu (de faire qch)

ripen ['raɪpən] *vi* mûrir; *(of cheese)* se faire

rip-off ['rɪpɒf] *n Fam* arnaque *f*

riposte [rɪ'pɒst] *n* riposte *f*, réplique *f*

ripple ['rɪpəl] **1** *n (on water)* ride *f*; *(of applause)* vague *f*; *(of excitement)* frémissement *m*
2 *vi (of water)* se rider; **laughter rippled through the audience** des vagues de rires ont parcouru le public

rise [raɪz] **1** *n* (**a**) *(in price, temperature, pressure)* hausse *f*; **(pay) r.** augmentation *f* (de salaire); **to be on the r.** *(of prices)* être en hausse; *(of crime, inflation)* être en augmentation; **the r. and fall of** la grandeur et la décadence de
(**b**) *(of leader, party)* ascension *f*; **r. to power** accession *f* au pouvoir
(**c**) *(in road, ground)* éminence *f*
(**d**) *(idioms)* **to give r. to sth** donner lieu à qch; *Fam* **to take a r. out of sb** faire enrager qn
2 *vi (pt* **rose** [rəʊz]*, pp* **risen** ['rɪzən] *)* (**a**) *(get up)* se lever; *(after falling)* se relever; *Fam* **r. and shine!** debout là-dedans!
(**b**) *(of smoke, balloon, ground)* monter; *(of sun, moon)* se lever; *(in career)* monter; **a murmur rose from the crowd** un murmure s'éleva de la foule; **to r. to the occasion** se montrer à la hauteur de la situation; **to r. to the position of managing director** accéder au poste de P-DG; **to r. to power** accéder au pouvoir; **to r. in sb's esteem** monter dans l'estime de qn

(c) *(of temperature)* s'élever, monter; *(of price)* augmenter; *(of hope)* grandir; *(of dough)* lever; **my spirits rose** je repris courage; **her voice rose in anger** elle a élevé la voix sous l'effet de la colère

(d) *(revolt)* se soulever; **to r. in arms** prendre les armes; **to r. in protest (against sth)** se soulever (contre qch)

▸**rise above** *vt insep (problem, criticism)* surmonter

▸**rise up** *vi (revolt)* se soulever; **to r. up in arms** prendre les armes; **to r. up in protest (against sth)** se soulever (contre qch)

risible ['rɪzɪbəl] *adj Formal* risible

rising ['raɪzɪŋ] **1** *n (revolt)* soulèvement *m*
   2 *adj (sun)* levant; *(temperature)* en hausse; *(prices, inflation)* en augmentation; *(artist, politician)* qui monte; *Fig* **r. star** étoile *f* montante

risk [rɪsk] **1** *n* risque *m*; **to take a r.** prendre un risque; **at r.** *(life, person)* en danger; *(job)* menacé(e); **to put one's health at r.** risquer de s'abîmer la santé; **at the r. of doing sth** au risque de faire qch; **to run the r. of doing sth** courir le risque de faire qch; **at one's own r.** à ses risques et périls; **r. assessment** évaluation *f* des risques; **r. capital** capital *m* à risque; **r. management** gestion *f* des risques
   2 *vt* **(a)** *(life, reputation)* risquer; **to r. one's neck** risquer sa peau **(b)** *(take the chance of)* **to r. failure** risquer d'échouer; **to r. death** risquer sa vie; **I can't r. going** je ne peux pas prendre le risque d'y aller; **they r. losing all their money** ils risquent de perdre tout leur argent; **we can't r. it** nous ne pouvons pas courir ce risque

risky ['rɪskɪ] *adj* risqué(e)

risotto [rɪ'zɒtəʊ] *(pl* **risottos**) *n* risotto *m*

risqué ['rɪskeɪ] *adj* osé(e)

rissole ['rɪsəʊl] *n* croquette *f*

rite [raɪt] *n* rite *m*

ritual ['rɪtjʊəl] **1** *n* rituel *m*
   2 *adj* rituel(elle)

ritzy ['rɪtsɪ] *adj Fam* chic *inv*

rival ['raɪvəl] **1** *n & adj* rival(e) *m,f*
   2 *vt (pt & pp* **rivalled**, *Am* **rivaled**) *(compete with)* rivaliser avec; *(equal)* égaler

rivalry ['raɪvəlrɪ] *n* rivalité *f*

river ['rɪvə(r)] *n* rivière *f*; *(flowing into sea)* fleuve *m*; *Fig (of blood)* flot *m*

riverbed ['rɪvəbed] *n* lit *m* de la rivière

riverside ['rɪvəsaɪd] *n* bord *m* de l'eau; **r. villa** villa *f* au bord de l'eau

rivet ['rɪvɪt] **1** *n* rivet *m*
   2 *vt* river; **to be riveted (by)** être fasciné(e) (par); *Fig* **to be riveted to the spot** *(with fear, surprise)* être cloué(e) sur place

riveting ['rɪvɪtɪŋ] *adj Fig* fascinant(e)

Riviera [rɪvɪ'eərə] *n* **the (French) R.** la Côte d'Azur

RN [ɑː'ren] *Br (abbr* **Royal Navy**) ≃ Marine *f* Nationale

RNA [ɑːren'eɪ] *n (abbr* **ribonucleic acid**) ARN *m*

RNLI [ɑːrenel'aɪ] *n Br (abbr* **Royal National Lifeboat Institution**) ≃ Société *f* nationale de sauvetage en mer

roach [rəʊtʃ] *n* **(a)** *(fish)* gardon *m* **(b)** *Am Fam (cockroach)* cafard *m*

road [rəʊd] *n* route *f*; *(in town)* rue *f*; **they live across** or **over the r.** ils habitent en face; **by r.** par la route; **to be off the r.** *(of car)* être en panne; **down/up the r.** un peu plus loin dans la rue; *Fam* **one for the r.** *(final drink)* un petit dernier pour la route; **to be on the r.** *(of salesman)* être sur la route; *(of pop group)* être en

tournée; **after three hours on the r.** après trois heures de route; **to be on the r. to recovery** être en voie de guérison; *Fig* **to be on the right r.** être sur la bonne voie; *Fam* **let's get this show on the r.!** allez, c'est parti, on y va!; **a few years down the r.** dans quelques années; *Fig* **to come to the end of the r.** *(of relationship)* toucher à sa fin; **r. accident** accident *m* de la route; **r. conditions** états *mpl* des routes; *Fam* **r. hog** chauffard *m*; **r. map** carte *f* routière; **r. rage** agressivité *f* au volant; **r. safety** sécurité *f* routière; **r. sign** panneau *m* de signalisation; **r. tax** ≃ vignette *f* (automobile); **r. works** or **repairs** travaux *mpl* de voirie

roadblock ['rəʊdblɒk] *n* barrage *m* routier

roadside ['rəʊdsaɪd] *n* bord *m* de la route; **r. bar/hotel** bar *m*/hôtel *m* situé en bord de route

road-test ['rəʊdtest] *vt (car)* essayer sur route

roadway ['rəʊdweɪ] *n* chaussée *f*

roadworthy ['rəʊdwɜːðɪ] *adj* en état de rouler

roam [rəʊm] **1** *vt (streets, world)* parcourir; *(seas)* sillonner
   2 *vi* **to r. (about)** errer; **to r. about the streets** traîner dans les rues

roaming ['rəʊmɪŋ] **1** *n* **(a)** *(wandering)* vagabondage *m* **(b)** *Tel (of mobile phone)* roaming *m*, itinérance *f*; *Comput (on Internet)* roaming
   2 *adj* vagabond(e), errant(e)

roar [rɔː(r)] **1** *n (of person, crowd)* hurlement *m*; *(of animal, engine)* rugissement *m*; *(of sea, wind)* mugissement *m*; *(of cars)* vacarme *m*
   2 *vi (of person, crowd)* hurler; *(of animal, engine)* rugir; *(of sea, wind)* mugir; *(of cars)* vrombir; **to r. with laughter** hurler de rire

roaring ['rɔːrɪŋ] *adj* **r. drunk** ivre mort(e); **a r. fire** une belle flambée; **a r. success** un succès fou; **to do a r. trade** faire des affaires en or

roast [rəʊst] **1** *n (piece of meat)* rôti *m*
   2 *adj* rôti(e)
   3 *vt* **(a)** *(meat, potatoes)* faire rôtir; *(nuts, coffee)* faire griller **(b)** *Fam (criticize)* éreinter

roasting ['rəʊstɪŋ] *Fam* **1** *n* **to give sb a r.** *(reprimand)* passer un savon à qn; *(criticize)* descendre qn en flammes
   2 *adj* **r.(-hot)** brûlant(e); **it's r. in here** il fait une chaleur à crever ici

rob [rɒb] *(pt & pp* **robbed**) *vt (bank)* dévaliser; *(person)* voler; *(house)* cambrioler; **to r. sb of sth** *(money, jewellery)* voler qch à qn; *Fig (youth, opportunity)* priver qn de qch

robber ['rɒbə(r)] *n* voleur(euse) *m,f*

robbery ['rɒbərɪ] *(pl* **robberies**) *n* vol *m*

robe [rəʊb] *n (of priest, judge)* robe *f*; *Am (dressing gown)* robe de chambre

robin ['rɒbɪn] *n* rouge-gorge *m*

robot ['rəʊbɒt] *n* robot *m*

robotics [rəʊ'bɒtɪks] *n* robotique *f*

robust [rəʊ'bʌst] *adj (person)* robuste; *(material, suitcase)* solide; *(defence, speech)* musclé(e)

rock [rɒk] **1** *n* **(a)** *(substance)* roche *f*; *(large stone)* rocher *m*; *Fig* **to be on the rocks** *(of marriage, company)* être en pleine débâcle; **on the rocks** *(drink)* avec des glaçons, *Can* sur glace; **the R. of Gibraltar** le Rocher de Gibraltar; **to reach** or **hit r. bottom** toucher le fond; **r. climbing** varappe *f*; **r. face** paroi *f* rocheuse; **r. garden** rocaille *f*; **r. pool** = flaque d'eau dans les rochers à marée basse; **r. salt** sel *m* gemme; **r. solid**

solide comme le roc

(**b**) *Br (sweet)* = sucrerie en forme de bâton parfumée à la menthe

(**c**) *(rocking motion)* **to give the cradle a r.** balancer un peu le berceau

(**d**) *(music)* rock *m*; **r. and roll** rock-and-roll *m*; **r. concert** concert *m* de rock; **r. group** groupe *m* de rock; **r. singer** chanteur(euse) *m,f* de rock

2 *vt (boat, chair)* balancer; *(building)* secouer; **to r. a baby to sleep** bercer un enfant pour qu'il s'endorme; *Fig* **to r. the boat** faire des histoires; *Fig* **the country has been rocked by these revelations** le pays a été secoué par ces révélations

3 *vi (sway)* se balancer; *(of building)* trembler; **to r. with laughter** être secoué(e) par un fou rire

rock-bottom ['rɒkbɒtəm] *adj* **r. prices** prix *mpl* incroyables

rocker ['rɒkə(r)] *n* (**a**) *(chair)* fauteuil *m* à bascule, *Can* berçante *f*; *Fam* **to be off one's r.** être givré(e) (**b**) *(musician, fan)* rocker(euse) *m,f*

rockery ['rɒkərɪ] *(pl* **rockeries)** *n* rocaille *f*

rocket ['rɒkɪt] **1** *n* (**a**) *Aviat & Astron* fusée *f*; **r. launcher** lance-fusées *m inv* (**b**) *Br Fam Fig (telling-off)* engueulade *f*; **to give sb a r.** engueuler qn

2 *vi (of prices, inflation, unemployment)* monter en flèche

rockfall ['rɒkfɔːl] *n* éboulement *m*

rock-hard [rɒk'hɑːd] *adj* dur(e) comme (de la) pierre

Rockies ['rɒkɪz] *npl* **the R.** les Rocheuses *fpl*

rocking chair ['rɒkɪŋtʃeə(r)] *n* fauteuil *m* à bascule, *Can* berçante *f*

rocky ['rɒkɪ] *adj* (**a**) *(path, soil)* rocailleux(euse); **the R. Mountains** les Montagnes *fpl* Rocheuses (**b**) *Fig (economy, relationship)* instable

rod [rɒd] *n (wooden)* baguette *f*; *(metal)* tige *f*; *(for curtain)* tringle *f*; *(for fishing)* canne *f* à pêche; *Fig* **to rule with a r. of iron** gouverner d'une main de fer; *Fig* **to make a r. for one's own back** se préparer des ennuis

rode [rəʊd] *pt of* **ride**

rodent ['rəʊdənt] *n* rongeur *m*

rodeo ['rəʊdɪəʊ] *(pl* **rodeos)** *n* rodéo *m*

roe¹ [rəʊ] *n* **r. (deer)** chevreuil *m*

roe² *n (of fish)* œufs *mpl* de poisson

roger¹ ['rɒdʒə(r)] *exclam (in radio message)* bien reçu!

roger² *vt Br very Fam (have sex with)* baiser

rogue [rəʊg] *n (dishonest)* filou *m*; *(mischievous)* coquin(e) *m,f*; **r. elephant** éléphant *m* solitaire

roguish ['rəʊgɪʃ] *adj* canaille

role [rəʊl] *n* rôle *m*; *Fig* **to play an important/a leading r. (in sth)** jouer un rôle important/prépondérant (dans qch); **r. model** modèle *m*

role-playing ['rəʊlpleɪŋ] *n* jeu *m* de rôle

roll [rəʊl] **1** *n* (**a**) *(of paper)* rouleau *m*; *(of fat)* bourrelet *m*; *(of banknotes)* liasse *f*; **a r. of film** une pellicule (photo); **r. neck** col *m* roulé

(**b**) *(bread)* petit pain *m*; **cheese r.** ≃ sandwich *m* au fromage

(**c**) *(of drum, thunder)* roulement *m*

(**d**) *(movement)* roulis *m*; *Fam* **to be on a r.** avoir la chance de son côté

(**e**) *(list)* liste *f*; **r. call** appel *m*; *Mil* **r. of honour** liste de ceux qui sont morts pour la patrie

2 *vt* (**a**) *(ball)* faire rouler; **to r. sth along the ground** faire rouler qch sur le sol; **to r. one's eyes** lever les yeux au ciel; **to r. one's r's** rouler les r; **the animal rolled itself into a ball** l'animal se mit en boule

(**b**) *(lawn)* passer au rouleau; *(road)* cylindrer; *(metal)* laminer

(**c**) *(cigarette)* rouler

3 *vi* (**a**) *(of ball, ship)* rouler; *(of camera)* tourner; *Fig* **heads will r.** il y a des têtes qui vont tomber; *Fam* **to be rolling in money, to be rolling in it** rouler sur l'or; *Fig* **to start the ball rolling** mettre les choses en route

(**b**) *(of thunder)* gronder

▸**roll down 1** *vt sep (sleeves)* redescendre; *(blind, car window)* descendre

2 *vi (of tears, sweat)* couler

▸**roll on** *vi Fam* **r. on Friday/Christmas!** vivement vendredi/Noël!

▸**roll over** *vi (of person) (once)* se retourner; *(several times)* se rouler; *(of car) (once)* capoter; *(several times)* faire des tonneaux

▸**roll up 1** *vt sep (newspaper)* rouler; *(sleeves)* retrousser; *(blind, car window)* remonter; **to r. sth up in paper** envelopper qch dans du papier

2 *vi Fam (arrive)* rappliquer; **r. up!, r. up!** venez nombreux!

rolled-up [rəʊl'dʌp] *adj (sleeves, trousers)* retroussé(e); *(umbrella)* replié(e); *(newspaper)* roulé(e)

roller ['rəʊlə(r)] *n (for paint, garden)* rouleau *m*; *(for hair)* bigoudi *m*; **r. blind** store *m (à cylindre)*; **r. coaster** montagnes *fpl* russes; **r. skates** patins *mpl* à roulettes

rollerblades ['rəʊləbleɪdz] *npl* patins *mpl* en ligne

rollerblading ['rəʊləbleɪdɪŋ] *n* **to go r.** faire du patin à roulettes *(avec des patins en ligne)*

roller-skate ['rəʊləskeɪt] *vi* faire du patin à roulettes

roller-skating ['rəʊləskeɪtɪŋ] *n* **to go r.** faire du patin à roulettes

rolling ['rəʊlɪŋ] *adj (hills, fields)* ondulant(e); *(sea, waves)* gros (grosse); *(thunder)* qui gronde; **r. mill** *(for steel)* laminoir *m*; **r. pin** rouleau *m* à pâtisserie, *Rail* **r. stock** matériel *m* roulant

rollneck ['rəʊlnek] *adj (sweater)* à col roulé

roll-on ['rəʊlɒn] *adj* (**a**) **r. (deodorant)** déodorant *m* à bille (**b**) *Naut* **r.-roll-off ferry** ferry *m* de type roll-on-roll-off

rollover ['rəʊləʊvə(r)] *n (in lottery)* = à la loterie nationale, situation où, personne n'ayant gagné le gros lot, celui-ci est ajouté à l'enjeu du tirage suivant

Rolls [rəʊlz] *n Br Fam (Rolls-Royce)* Rolls Royce *f*

roll-top desk ['rəʊltɒp'desk] *n* bureau *m* à cylindre

roll-up ['rəʊlʌp] *n Fam (cigarette)* cigarette *f* roulée

roly-poly ['rəʊlɪ'pəʊlɪ] *adj Fam (plump)* grassouillet(-ette)

ROM [rɒm] *n Comput (abbr* **read only memory)** mémoire *f* morte

Roman ['rəʊmən] **1** *n* Romain(e) *m,f*

2 *adj* romain(e); **R. Catholic** catholique; **R. nose** nez *m* aquilin; **R. numerals** chiffres *mpl* romains

roman ['rəʊmən] *Typ* **1** *n* romain *m*

2 *adj* romain(e)

romance ['rəʊmæns, rə'mæns] *n* (**a**) *(book)* roman *m* d'amour; *(film)* histoire *f* d'amour (**b**) *(love affair)* aventure *f* (**c**) *(charm)* charme *m*

Romania [rə'meɪnɪə] *n* la Roumanie

Romanian [rə'meɪnɪən] **1** *n* (**a**) *(person)* Roumain(e) *m,f* (**b**) *(language)* roumain *m*

2 *adj* roumain(e)

romantic [rəʊ'mæntɪk, rə'mæntɪk] **1** *n* romantique *mf*

2 *adj* romantique; *(scheme, notion)* romanesque

romanticism [rəʊ'mæntɪsɪzəm] *n* romantisme *m*
romanticize [rəʊ'mæntɪsaɪz] *vt (incident)* romancer; *(idea, war)* présenter sous un jour romantique
Romany ['rɒməni] **1** *n (pl* **Romanies**) (**a**) *(person)* Tzigane *mf* (**b**) *(language)* tzigane *m*
2 *adj* tzigane
Rome [rəʊm] *n* Rome; **R. wasn't built in a day** Paris ne s'est pas fait en un jour; **when in R.(, do as the Romans do)** il faut adopter les usages de l'endroit où l'on se trouve
romp [rɒmp] **1** *n* **to have a r.** chahuter
2 *vi* **to r. (about** *or* **around)** s'ébattre; **to r. through an exam** réussir un examen les doigts dans le nez
romper ['rɒmpə(r)] *n* **r. suit, rompers** barboteuse *f*
roof [ruːf] **1** *n (of building, car)* toit *m; (of tunnel, cave)* plafond *m;* **to have a r. over one's head** avoir un endroit où vivre; **to live under one** *or* **the same r.** vivre sous le même toit; *Fam* **to hit the r.** sortir de ses gonds; *Fam* **to go through the r.** connaître une flambée; **r. of the mouth** voûte *f* du palais; **r. garden** jardin *m* aménagé sur le toit; **r. rack** galerie *f*
2 *vt* couvrir
roofing ['ruːfɪŋ] *n* toiture *f;* **r. material** matériaux *mpl* de couverture
rooftop ['ruːftɒp] *n* toit *m; Fig* **to shout sth from the rooftops** crier qch sur les toits
rook [rʊk] *n (bird)* freux *m; (in chess)* tour *f*
rookery ['rʊkəri] *(pl* **rookeries**) *n* colonie *f* de freux
rookie ['rʊki] *n Am Fam* bleu *m*
room [ruːm] **1** *n* (**a**) *(in house)* pièce *f; (bedroom, in hotel)* chambre *f; (large, public)* salle *f;* **r. and board** chambre et pension; **r. service** service *m* dans les chambres; **r. temperature** température *f* ambiante (**b**) *(space)* place *f;* **there's no r. to move** il n'y a pas de place; **to make r. (for sb)** faire de la place (pour qn); **there's no r. for doubt** cela ne fait aucun doute; **there is r. for improvement** ça pourrait être mieux
2 *vi Am* **to r. with sb** partager une chambre avec qn
roommate ['ruːmmeɪt] *n (in boarding school)* camarade *mf* de chambre; *Am (in apartment)* colocataire *mf*
roomy ['ruːmi] *adj* spacieux(euse); *(clothes)* ample
roost [ruːst] **1** *n* perchoir *m;* **to rule the r.** faire la loi
2 *vi* se percher; *Fig* **her actions have come home to r.** ses actions se sont retournées contre elle
rooster ['ruːstə(r)] *n* coq *m*
root [ruːt] **1** *n* (**a**) *(of plant, tooth, word, hair)* racine *f;* **to pull up by the roots** *(plant)* déraciner; *also Fig* **to take r.** prendre racine; **they destroyed the party r. and branch** ils ont entièrement détruit le parti; *Fig* **to put down roots** s'intégrer; *Fig* **to get back to one's roots** retrouver ses racines; *Am* **r. beer** = boisson gazeuse aux extraits de plantes; **r. crops** racines comestibles; **r. vegetables** légumes *mpl* à racine comestible (**b**) *(origin)* origine *f; Prov* **money is the r. of all evil** l'argent est la source de tous les maux
2 *vt* **to be rooted to the spot** être figé(e) sur place
3 *vi* (**a**) **to r. about** *or* **around (for sth)** fouiller (pour trouver qch) (**b**) *Am* **to r. for sb** appuyer qn
▶**root for** *vt insep (support)* être pour
▶**root out** *vt sep* supprimer
rope [rəʊp] **1** *n* (**a**) *(cord)* corde *f; (of pearls)* sautoir *m; (of onions)* chapelet *m;* **r. ladder** échelle *f* de corde (**b**) *(idioms)* **to be on the ropes** *(of company)* battre de l'aile; **to learn the ropes** apprendre les ficelles; **to show sb the ropes** former qn; **to give sb plenty of**

r. donner du mou à qn
2 *vt (fasten)* lier (avec une corde) (**to** à); **they roped themselves together** *(for climbing)* ils se sont encordés
▶**rope in** *vt sep Fam (recruit)* recruter; **to get roped in to do sth** se laisser convaincre de faire qch
▶**rope off** *vt sep* **to r. sth off** interdire l'accès de qch avec une corde
rop(e)y ['rəʊpi] *adj Br Fam (unreliable)* pas terrible; *(ill)* patraque
rosary ['rəʊzəri] *(pl* **rosaries**) *n Rel* chapelet *m;* **to say one's r.** dire son chapelet
rose¹ [rəʊz] **1** *n* (**a**) *(flower)* rose *f; (on watering can)* pomme *f;* **r. bed** parterre *m* de rosiers; **r. bush** rosier *m;* **r. garden** roseraie *f;* **r. grower** rosiériste *mf;* **r. window** rosace *f* (**b**) *(idioms)* **life isn't a bed of roses** tout n'est pas rose dans la vie; **to come up roses** se passer à merveille
2 *adj (colour)* rose
rose² *pt of* **rise**
rosé ['rəʊzeɪ] *n* rosé *m*
rosebud ['rəʊzbʌd] *n* bouton *m* de rose
rose-coloured ['rəʊzkʌləd], **rose-tinted** ['rəʊztɪntɪd] *adj* **to see things through r. glasses** *or* **spectacles** voir la vie en rose
rosehip ['rəʊzhɪp] *n* gratte-cul *m*
rosemary ['rəʊzməri] *n* romarin *m*
rosette [rəʊ'zet] *n* rosette *f*
rosewater ['rəʊzwɔːtə(r)] *n* eau *f* de rose
rosewood ['rəʊzwʊd] *n* bois *m* de rose
roster ['rɒstə(r)] *n* liste *f* de service
rostrum ['rɒstrəm] *(pl* **rostrums** *or* **rostra** ['rɒstrə]) *n (for speaker)* estrade *f; (for prizewinner)* podium *m*
rosy ['rəʊzi] *adj (pink)* rose; *(complexion)* de rose; *Fig (future)* prometteur(euse)
rot [rɒt] **1** *n* (**a**) *(in house, wood)* pourriture *f; Fig* **the r. has set in** ça se gâte; *Fig* **to stop the r.** empêcher la situation de se dégrader (**b**) *Fam (nonsense)* bêtises *fpl*
2 *vt (pt & pp* **rotted**) (faire) pourrir
3 *vi* pourrir; **to r. in prison** moisir en prison
rota ['rəʊtə] *n* roulement *m*
rotary ['rəʊtəri] **1** *n (pl* **rotaries**) *Am (roundabout)* rond-point *m*
2 *adj* rotatif(ive)
rotate [rəʊ'teɪt] **1** *vt* (**a**) *(turn)* faire tourner (**b**) *(alternate)* *(duties)* remplir à tour de rôle; *(crops)* alterner
2 *vi* (**a**) *(turn)* tourner (**b**) *(in job)* remplir des fonctions à tour de rôle
rotation [rəʊ'teɪʃən] *n* (**a**) *(of planet)* rotation *f* (**b**) *(in job)* roulement *m; (of crops)* alternance *f;* **by** *or* **in r.** à tour de rôle
rote [rəʊt] *n* **by r.** par cœur; **r. learning** apprentissage *m* par cœur
rotor ['rəʊtə(r)] *n* rotor *m*
rotten ['rɒtən] *adj* (**a**) *(wood, egg, fruit)* pourri(e) (**b**) *Fam (bad)* nul (nulle); *(weather)* pourri(e); **to feel r.** *(ill)* ne pas se sentir dans son assiette; *(guilty)* ne pas être fier(ère) (**about** de); **to have r. luck** avoir la guigne (**c**) *(unpleasant)* dégueulasse; **a r. trick** un tour de cochon
rotter ['rɒtə(r)] *n Br Fam Old-fashioned* peau *f* de vache
rottweiler ['rɒtvaɪlə(r)] *n* rottweiler *m*
rotund [rəʊ'tʌnd] *adj* rond(e)

rouble ['ruːbəl] *n* rouble *m*

rouge [ruːʒ] *n Old-fashioned* rouge *m* (à joues)

rough [rʌf] **1** *n* (**a**) *(in golf)* rough *m*
(**b**) *Fam Old-fashioned (hooligan)* voyou *m*
(**c**) *(difficulty)* **you have to take the r. with the smooth** on ne peut pas tout avoir dans la vie
2 *adj* (**a**) *(surface, skin)* rugueux(euse); *(terrain)* accidenté(e)
(**b**) *(unrefined) (manners)* fruste; *Fig* **a r. diamond** un cœur d'or sous des dehors frustes; **r. draft** brouillon *m*; **r. sketch** ébauche *f*
(**c**) *Fam (ill)* **to feel/look r.** se sentir/avoir l'air patraque
(**d**) *(violent)* brutal(e); *(crossing, sea)* agité(e)
(**e**) *(harsh) (voice)* rude; *(wine, spirits)* âpre; *Fam* **it was r. on her** c'était dur pour elle; **r. justice** justice *f* sommaire
(**f**) *(approximate)* approximatif(ive); **at a r. guess** à vue de nez; **I've got a r. idea of what he wants** j'ai une petite idée de ce qu'il veut
3 *adv* **to play r.** jouer avec brutalité; *Fig* ne pas faire de cadeaux; *Fam* **to sleep r.** coucher à la dure
4 *vt Fam* **to r. it** vivre à la dure

▸**rough up** *vt sep Fam (beat up)* tabasser

roughage ['rʌfɪdʒ] *n* fibres *fpl* (alimentaires)

rough-and-ready [rʌfən'redɪ] *adj (meal, accommodation)* sommaire; *(person)* rustre

rough-and-tumble [rʌfən'tʌmbəl] *n* bousculade *f*; *Fig* **the r. of politics** le monde sans pitié de la politique

roughly ['rʌflɪ] *adv* (**a**) *(violently)* brutalement; **to treat sb r.** rudoyer qn (**b**) *(crudely)* grossièrement
(**c**) *(approximately)* à peu près; **r. (speaking)** en gros

roughness ['rʌfnɪs] *n* (**a**) *(of surface, skin)* rugosité *f*
(**b**) *(of behaviour)* rudesse *f*

roughshod ['rʌfʃɒd] *adv* **to ride r. over sth** ne faire aucun cas de qch

rough-spoken [rʌf'spəʊkən] *adj* au langage grossier

roulette [ruːˈlet] *n* roulette *f*; **r. table** table *f* de roulette; **r. wheel** roulette

round [raʊnd] **1** *n* (**a**) *(slice) (of bread)* tranche *f*; **a r. of sandwiches** = un sandwich au pain de mie coupé en deux ou en quatre
(**b**) *(stage of match)* manche *f*; *(stage of tournament)* tour *m*; *(in boxing)* round *m*; *(of golf)* partie *f*; **to get/be through to the next r.** se qualifier/s'être qualifié(e) pour le tour suivant
(**c**) *(of talks, visits)* série *f*; *(of drinks)* tournée *f*; **r. of applause** applaudissements *mpl*; **to give sb a r. of applause** applaudir qn
(**d**) **to do one's rounds** *(of doctor)* faire ses visites; **to do the rounds** *(of rumour, illness)* circuler; **the daily r.** *(of tasks)* le train-train quotidien
(**e**) *Mil (bullet)* balle *f*
(**f**) *Mus* canon *m*
2 *adj* rond(e); **to have r. shoulders** avoir le dos rond; **a r. dozen** une douzaine exactement; **in r. figures** en arrondissant; **r. table (conference)** table *f* ronde; **r. trip** aller (et) retour *m*
3 *adv* autour; **all (the) year r.** toute l'année; **all r.** *(on the whole)* dans l'ensemble; **the wrong way r.** à l'envers; **the right way r.** *(not back to front)* à l'endroit; *(in the correct order)* dans le bon ordre; **the other way r.** *(in the other direction)* dans l'autre sens; **do it the other way r.** fais l'inverse; **to go r. (to sb's house)** passer (chez qn); **to invite sb r.** inviter qn
4 *prep* (**a**) *(position)* autour de; **r. here** dans le coin
(**b**) *(motion)* **to look r. a room** parcourir une pièce du regard; **to travel r. the world** parcourir le monde; **to go r. an obstacle** contourner un obstacle; **to go r. the corner** *(of person)* tourner le coin; *(of vehicle)* prendre le virage; **it's just r. the corner** c'est juste au coin (de la rue); *Fig* **to drive** *or* **send sb r. the bend** rendre qn maboul(e)
(**c**) *(approximately)* **r. about** environ; **r. about midday** vers midi
5 *vt* (**a**) *(make round)* arrondir
(**b**) *(obstacle)* contourner; *(corner)* tourner

▸**round down** *vt sep (figure)* arrondir au chiffre inférieur

▸**round off** *vt sep (conclude)* conclure

▸**round up** *vt sep* (**a**) *(cattle)* rassembler; *(criminals, suspects)* ramasser (**b**) *(figure)* arrondir au chiffre supérieur

roundabout ['raʊndəbaʊt] **1** *n* (**a**) *(at fairground)* manège *m* (**b**) *(for cars)* rond-point *m*
2 *adj (approach, route)* détourné(e); **to lead up to a question in a r. way** aborder une question de biais

rounders ['raʊndəz] *n Br* = jeu similaire au base-ball

roundly ['raʊndlɪ] *adv (praise, condemn)* vivement; *(beat)* sévèrement

round-trip ['raʊndtrɪp] *adj Am (ticket)* aller (et) retour

roundup ['raʊndʌp] *n (of criminals)* rafle *f*; *(of events, news)* résumé *m*

rouse [raʊz] *vt* réveiller; **to r. oneself (to do sth)** se secouer (et faire qch); **to r. sb to action** pousser qn à agir; **to r. sb to anger** susciter la colère de qn

rousing ['raʊzɪŋ] *adj (music, speech)* exaltant(e); *(welcome, cheers)* enthousiaste

rout [raʊt] **1** *n* déroute *f*
2 *vt* mettre en déroute

▸**rout out** *vt sep (get rid of)* se débarrasser de

route [ruːt] **1** *n (of traveller)* itinéraire *m*; *(of plane, ship)* route *f*; *(of bus, parade)* parcours *m*; *Fig (to success)* voie *f* (**to** de)
2 *vt (parcel, goods)* acheminer; *(bus, train, flight)* faire passer

router ['ruːtə(r)] *n Comput* routeur *m*

routine [ruːˈtiːn] **1** *n* (**a**) *(habit)* routine *f*; **the daily r.** le train-train quotidien (**b**) *(of performer, comedian)* numéro *m*; *Fam Fig* **don't give me that r.** arrête ton numéro (**c**) *Comput* sous-programme *m*
2 *adj* (**a**) *(normal)* de routine (**b**) *(dull)* routinier(ère)

routinely [ruːˈtiːnlɪ] *adv* systématiquement

rove [rəʊv] **1** *vt* parcourir
2 *vi* rôder, vagabonder; **her eyes roved around the room** son regard parcourait la pièce

row¹ [rəʊ] *n (line)* rangée *f*; **in a r.** en rang; **two Sundays in a r.** deux dimanches d'affilée; **in the front r.** *(of seats)* au premier rang

row² **1** *n (in boat)* promenade *f* en canot; **to go for a r.** canoter
2 *vt (boat)* faire aller à la rame; *(person)* transporter en canot
3 *vi (in boat)* ramer

row³ [raʊ] **1** *n* (**a**) *(noise)* vacarme *m*; *(protest)* tollé *m*
(**b**) *(quarrel)* dispute *f*; **to have a r. (with sb)** se disputer (avec qn)
2 *vi (quarrel)* se disputer (**about** à propos de)

rowan ['rəʊən] *n* sorbier *m*

rowboat ['rəʊbəʊt] *n Am* bateau *m* à rames

rowdy ['raʊdɪ] **1** n (pl **rowdies**) chahuteur(euse) m,f
2 adj (person) chahuteur(euse); (event, party) bruyant(e); **to be r.** chahuter

rower ['raʊə(r)] n rameur(euse) m,f

rowing ['raʊɪŋ] n canotage m; (as sport) aviron m; **r. boat** bateau m à rames; **r. machine** rameur m

royal ['rɔɪəl] **1** adj royal(e); Fig (splendid) princier(-ère); **His/Her R. Highness** Son Altesse Royale; **r. blue** bleu roi m inv; **the R. Family** la famille royale; **r. flush** (in cards) quinte f royale; **r. jelly** gelée f royale; **R. Mail** = la Poste britannique; **the R. Navy** = la marine nationale britannique
2 n Fam membre m de la famille royale; **the Royals** la famille royale

royalist ['rɔɪəlɪst] n & adj royaliste mf

royally ['rɔɪəlɪ] adv (entertain, welcome) royalement

royalty ['rɔɪəltɪ] n (a) (rank, position) royauté f; **to be r.** faire partie de la famille royale; **to be treated like r.** être traité(e) royalement (b) **royalties** (for author, singer) droits mpl d'auteur

RP [ɑː'piː] n Ling (abbr **received pronunciation**) = prononciation de l'anglais considérée comme la norme

RPI [ɑːpiː'aɪ] n Econ (abbr **retail price index**) indice m des prix de détail

rpm [ɑːpiː'em] n Aut (abbr **revolutions per minute**) tr/min

R & R [ɑːrən'ɑː(r)] n Mil (abbr **rest and recreation**) permission f

RRP [ɑːrɑː'piː] n Com (abbr **recommended retail price**) prix m conseillé

RS [ɑː'res] n Br (abbr **Royal Society**) ≃ Académie f des Sciences

RSA [ɑːres'eɪ] n (abbr **Republic of South Africa**) Afrique f du Sud

RSI [ɑːres'aɪ] n (abbr **repetitive strain injury**) = douleurs dans les bras et les mains dues à la répétition de certains mouvements

RSPB [ɑːrespiː'biː] n Br (abbr **Royal Society for the Protection of Birds**) = ligue pour la protection des oiseaux

RSPCA [ɑːrespiːsiː'eɪ] n Br (abbr **Royal Society for the Prevention of Cruelty to Animals**) ≃ SPA f

RSPCC [ɑːrespiːsiː'siː] n Br (abbr **Royal Society for the Prevention of Cruelty to Children**) ≃ fondation f pour l'enfance

RSVP [ɑːresviː'piː] (abbr **répondez s'il vous plaît**) (on invitation) RSVP

Rt Hon Br Parl (abbr **Right Honourable**) = formule accolée au nom des ministres et anciens ministres

rub [rʌb] **1** n to give sth a r. frotter qch; Fig **there's the r.!** voilà le hic!
2 vt (pt & pp **rubbed**) frotter; **to r. one's hands together** se frotter les mains; Fig **to r. shoulders with sb** côtoyer qn; Fam **to r. sb up the wrong way** prendre qn à rebrousse-poil
3 vi (of straps, shoes) frotter (**against** contre)

▸**rub along** vi Fam (a) (manage) se débrouiller (b) (get on) s'entendre (**with** avec)

▸**rub in** vt sep (lotion, ointment) faire pénétrer; Fam **to r. it in** retourner le couteau dans la plaie

▸**rub off 1** vt sep (dirt, stain) enlever en frottant; (writing) effacer
2 vi partir, s'enlever; Fig **to r. off on sb** (of manners, enthusiasm) déteindre sur qn

▸**rub out** vt sep (a) (erase) effacer (b) Fam (murder) buter

rubber ['rʌbə(r)] n (a) (substance) caoutchouc m; **r. ball/gloves** balle f/gants mpl en caoutchouc; **r. band** élastique m; **r. dinghy** canot m pneumatique; **r. plant** caoutchouc m; **r. ring** bouée f; **r. stamp** tampon m (b) (eraser) gomme f; (for blackboards) brosse f (c) Am Fam (condom) capote f

rubber-stamp [rʌbə'stæmp] vt Fig (approve) approuver sans discussion

rubbery ['rʌbərɪ] adj caoutchouteux(euse)

rubbish ['rʌbɪʃ] Br **1** n (a) (refuse) détritus mpl; (from house) ordures fpl; (junk) cochonneries fpl; **r. bag** sac m poubelle; **r. bin** poubelle f; **r. collection** ramassage m des ordures; **r. dump** dépotoir m; Fig **to throw sb/sth on the r. heap** mettre qn/qch au rancart (b) Fam (nonsense) idioties fpl; **that book/film is a load of r.** ce livre/film est nul; **r.!** n'importe quoi!
2 vt Fam (book, plan) descendre en flammes

rubble ['rʌbəl] n décombres mpl

rubella [ruː'belə] n rubéole f

rubric ['ruːbrɪk] n instructions fpl

ruby ['ruːbɪ] **1** n (pl **rubies**) rubis m
2 adj (colour) rubis

RUC [ɑːjuː'siː] n (abbr **Royal Ulster Constabulary**) = forces de l'ordre d'Irlande du Nord

ruck¹ [rʌk] n (a) (in rugby) mêlée f ouverte (b) (fight) bagarre f

ruck² **1** n (in cloth) faux pli m
2 vi **to r. up** (of sheet) se froisser

rucksack ['rʌksæk] n sac m à dos

ructions ['rʌkʃənz] npl Fam grabuge m

rudder ['rʌdə(r)] n gouvernail m

ruddy ['rʌdɪ] adj (a) (complexion) rose (b) Br Fam Euph fichu(e); **the r. fool!** quel espèce d'imbécile!

rude [ruːd] adj (a) (impolite) impoli(e) (b) (vulgar) grossier(ère); (gesture) obscène (c) (primitive) rudimentaire (d) (shock, surprise) **to receive a r. awakening** être brutalement rappelé(e) à la réalité (e) (vigorous) **to be in r. health** jouir d'une santé robuste

rudeness ['ruːdnɪs] n (a) (impoliteness) impolitesse f (b) (vulgarity) grossièreté f

rudimentary [ruːdɪ'mentərɪ] adj rudimentaire

rudiments ['ruːdɪmənts] npl rudiments mpl

rue [ruː] vt Lit regretter amèrement; **I r. the day I met her** je maudis le jour où je l'ai rencontrée

rueful ['ruːfʊl] adj (voice, smile) de regret; (person) qui a des regrets

ruff [rʌf] n (on costume) fraise f

ruffian ['rʌfɪən] n Old-fashioned voyou m

ruffle ['rʌfəl] vt (water) troubler; (hair) ébouriffer; **to r. sb's feathers** froisser qn; **to r. sb's composure** faire perdre contenance à qn

rug [rʌg] n (a) (carpet) tapis m; Fig **to pull the r. from under sb's feet** couper l'herbe sous le pied à qn (b) (blanket) couverture f

rugby ['rʌgbɪ] n rugby m; **r. ball** ballon m de rugby; **r. league** rugby à treize; **r. player** rugbyman m; **r. union** rugby à quinze

rugby-tackle ['rʌgbɪ'tækəl] vt **to r. sb** plaquer qn au sol

rugged ['rʌgɪd] adj (ground, country) accidenté(e); (features, manner) rude; **r. good looks** beauté f un peu rude

rugger ['rʌgə(r)] n Br Fam (rugby) rugby m

rugrat ['rʌgræt] n Fam môme mf

ruin ['ruːɪn] **1** *n* ruine *f*; **to fall into ruin(s)** tomber en ruine(s); **it will be the r. of him** ça le perdra

2 *vt (suit, shoes)* abîmer; *(person)* ruiner; *(meal, evening, holiday)* gâcher; **to r. one's health** se ruiner la santé; **to r. one's eyesight** s'user la vue; **tourism has ruined the town** le tourisme a défiguré la ville; **a ruined castle** un château en ruine(s)

ruinous ['ruːɪnəs] *adj (expensive)* ruineux(euse)

rule [ruːl] **1** *n* (**a**) *(principle)* règle *f*; *(regulation)* règlement *m*; **rules** *(of club, school)* règlement; **as a r.** en règle générale; **to make it a r. to do sth** se faire un principe de faire qch; **rules and regulations** règles; *Ind* **to work to r.** faire la grève du zèle; **it's against the rules** c'est contraire au règlement; **as a r. of thumb** pour avoir une idée approximative; **r. book** règlement (**b**) *(government)* autorité *f* (**c**) *(for measuring)* règle *f*

2 *vt* (**a**) *(country, people)* gouverner; **to let sth r. one's life** laisser qch dominer toute sa vie; *Fig* **to r. the roost** commander (**b**) *(decide, decree)* décider; **to be ruled illegal** être décrété(e) illégal(e) (**c**) *(paper)* régler

3 *vi* (**a**) *(of monarch)* régner (**b**) *(of judge)* statuer (**on** sur); **to r. in favour of/against sb** décider en faveur de/contre qn

▸**rule out** *vt sep* exclure

ruler ['ruːlə(r)] *n* (**a**) *(of country)* dirigeant(e) *m,f* (**b**) *(for measuring)* règle *f*

ruling ['ruːlɪŋ] **1** *n (of judge, umpire)* décision *f*

2 *adj* (**a**) *(party)* au pouvoir; *(class)* dirigeant(e) (**b**) *(passion)* dominant(e); *(consideration)* premier(ère)

rum¹ [rʌm] *n (drink)* rhum *m*

rum² *adj Fam (strange)* bizarre; *(suspect)* louche

Rumania = Romania

Rumanian = Romanian

rumble ['rʌmbəl] **1** *n (of thunder, gunfire, traffic)* grondement *m*; *(of voices)* bourdonnement *m*; *(of stomach)* gargouillement *m*; **rumbles of discontent** murmures *mpl* de protestation

2 *vt Fam (find out) (person)* deviner le jeu de; *(plot)* découvrir

3 *vi (of thunder, traffic)* gronder; *(of stomach)* gargouiller

rumbustious [rʌm'bʌstjəs] *adj* exubérant(e)

ruminant ['ruːmɪnənt] *n Zool* ruminant *m*

ruminate ['ruːmɪneɪt] *vi Formal* **to r. (about** *or* **on sth)** ruminer (qch)

rummage ['rʌmɪdʒ] **1** *vi* **to r. about** *or* **around (for sth)** farfouiller (à la recherche de qch); **to r. through sth** fouiller qch

2 *n Am* **r. sale** vente *f* de charité

rumour ['ruːmə(r)] **1** *n* rumeur *f*, bruit *m*; **r. has it...** on raconte que...; **there's a r. going round that...** le bruit court que...

2 *vt* **it is rumoured that...** le bruit court que...; **he is rumoured to be very rich/in hiding** le bruit court qu'il est très riche/qu'il se cache

rump [rʌmp] *n* (**a**) *(of animal)* croupe *f*; *Fam (of person)* postérieur *m*; **r. steak** romsteck *m* (**b**) *(of political party, assembly)* restant *m*; **r. state** état *m* croupion

rumple ['rʌmpəl] *vt (clothes, sheets)* friper, froisser; *(hair)* ébouriffer

rumpus ['rʌmpəs] *n Fam (noise)* chahut *m*; **to kick up** *or* **cause a r. (about sth)** faire un scandale (à propos de qch)

run [rʌn] **1** *n* (**a**) *(act of running)* course *f*; **at a r.** en courant; **to go for a r.** aller courir; **to be on the r.** être en fuite; *Fig* **we've got them on the r.** nous les avons mis en déroute; **to give sb the r. of the house** mettre sa maison à la disposition de qn; *Fam* **to make a r. for it** *(escape)* se tirer; *(to catch train)* se grouiller; *Fam* **to give sb a r. for his money** donner du fil à retordre à qn; *Fam* **to have the runs** avoir la courante

(**b**) *(trip)* trajet *m*; *(for pleasure)* balade *f*; **to go for a r.** *(in car)* aller se balader en voiture

(**c**) *Com (of book)* tirage *m*; *(of product)* série *f*

(**d**) *(sequence, series)* série *f*; *(in cards)* suite *f*; **a r. of good luck** une période faste; **a r. of bad luck** une série de malheurs; **in the short/long r.** à court/long terme

(**e**) *Fin (on currency, stock exchange)* ruée *f* (**on** sur); *(on bank)* retrait *m* massif

(**f**) *(in stocking)* échelle *f*

(**g**) *(in cricket, baseball)* point *m*

(**h**) *(for skier)* piste *f*

(**i**) *(for chickens, rabbits)* enclos *m*

(**j**) *Mus* roulade *f*

2 *vt (pt* **ran** [ræn], *pp* **run**) (**a**) *(distance, race)* courir; **to r. an errand** faire une course; **to allow things to r. their course** laisser les choses se faire; **to r. sb close** talonner qn; *Fam* **to be run off one's feet** être débordé(e)

(**b**) *(drive)* **to r. sb to the airport** conduire qn à l'aéroport

(**c**) *(drugs, arms)* faire le trafic de

(**d**) *(machine)* faire fonctionner; *(tests)* effectuer; *Comput (program)* exécuter

(**e**) *(business)* diriger; *(hotel)* tenir; *(car)* avoir; **to r. sb's life for them** dire à qn comment vivre sa vie

(**f**) *(cables, pipes)* faire passer; **to r. one's fingers over/through sth** passer la main sur/dans qch; **to r. one's eye over sth** parcourir qch du regard

(**g**) *(water, bath)* faire couler

(**h**) **to r. a temperature** avoir de la température

(**i**) **to r. a deficit** enregistrer un déficit

(**j**) **to r. an article** publier un article

3 *vi* (**a**) *(of person)* courir; **to r. up/down the street** monter/descendre la rue en courant; **to r. about** courir çà et là; **I'll just r. across/round to the shop** je fais un saut à l'épicerie; **to r. after sb** courir après qn; **to r. for help** courir chercher de l'aide; **to r. in/out** entrer/sortir en courant

(**b**) *(flee)* s'enfuir, se sauver; **r. for it!** sauve qui peut!

(**c**) *(compete in race)* courir; **to r. for Parliament** se présenter aux législatives

(**d**) *(flow)* couler; **the river runs into a lake** la rivière se jette dans un lac; **my nose is running** j'ai le nez qui coule; **my blood ran cold** mon sang se glaça

(**e**) **to r. aground** *(of ship)* s'échouer; *Fig (of project, economy)* échouer

(**f**) *(of contract, lease)* courir; *(of play)* être à l'affiche; **it runs in the family** c'est de famille; **the total ran to £2,000** le montant total s'élevait à 2000 livres

(**g**) *(of bus, train)* circuler; **to be running late** *(of bus, train)* avoir du retard; *(of person)* être en retard

(**h**) *(operate) (of machine)* marcher, fonctionner; *(of engine)* tourner; **to r. on gas/electricity** marcher *ou* fonctionner au gaz/à l'électricité; **to r. off the mains** marcher *ou* fonctionner sur secteur; **the car runs on unleaded petrol** la voiture roule à l'essence sans plomb; **things are running smoothly** tout marche comme sur des roulettes (**i**) *(of road, railway)* passer; **the line runs along the coast** la ligne suit *ou* longe la côte

(**j**) **feelings** *or* **tempers are running high** les esprits sont échauffés; **to be running low** *(of funds, supplies)* s'épuiser; **to r. dry** *(of river)* s'assécher

(**k**) *(of colour, dye)* déteindre

▸**run away** *vi (of person)* s'enfuir, se sauver (**from** de); **to r. away from home** faire une fugue; *Fig* **to r. away from the facts** refuser l'évidence; *Fig* **don't r. away with the idea that...** ne va pas t'imaginer que...

▸**run down 1** *vt sep* (**a**) *(in car)* renverser (**b**) *(find)* dénicher (**c**) *(criticize)* dénigrer (**d**) *(reduce)* *(production, stocks)* diminuer, réduire; *(industry, factory)* fermer progressivement

2 *vi (of battery)* se décharger

▸**run in** *vt sep* (**a**) *Fam (arrest)* pincer (**b**) *(engine)* roder

▸**run into** *vt insep* (**a**) *(collide with)* rentrer dans; *Fig (difficulties)* rencontrer; **to r. into trouble** s'attirer des ennuis (**b**) *(meet by chance)* tomber sur

▸**run off 1** *vt sep (print)* imprimer; *(photocopy)* photocopier; **to r. off a copy of sth** faire une copie de qch

2 *vi (of person)* s'enfuir, se sauver (**with** avec)

▸**run on** *vi* (**a**) *(of meeting)* durer (**b**) *Fam (talk a lot)* parler sans arrêt

▸**run out** *vi (of lease, contract)* expirer; *(of money, supplies)* s'épuiser; **to have run out of sth** ne plus avoir de qch; **time is running out** il ne reste plus beaucoup de temps; *Fig* **to r. out of steam** *(of person, project)* s'essouffler

▸**run over 1** *vt sep (in car)* renverser, écraser

2 *vt insep (speech, lines)* revoir

3 *vi (of speech, TV programme)* déborder

▸**run to** *vt insep (amount to)* s'élever à; **we can't r. to a new car** *(afford)* nous ne pouvons pas nous permettre d'acheter une nouvelle voiture

▸**run up** *vt sep* (**a**) *(debts)* accumuler (**b**) *(flag)* hisser (**c**) *(clothes)* confectionner à la hâte

run-around ['rʌnəraʊnd] *n Fam* **to give sb the r.** faire tourner qn en bourrique

runaway ['rʌnəweɪ] **1** *n* fugitif(ive) *m,f*; *(child)* fugueur(euse) *m,f*

2 *adj (prisoner, slave)* en fuite; *(train, lorry)* fou (folle); *(inflation)* galopant(e); *(victory)* remporté(e) haut la main; *(success)* fou (folle)

rundown ['rʌndaʊn] *n (summary)* résumé *m*; **to give sb a r. (on sth)** mettre qn au courant (de qch)

run-down [rʌn'daʊn] *adj (building)* délabré(e); *(person)* fatigué(e)

rung¹ [rʌŋ]*n (of ladder)* échelon *m*; *Fig* **on the bottom/top r.** tout en bas/en haut de l'échelle

rung² *pp of* **ring²**

run-in ['rʌnɪn] *n Fam* **to have a r. with sb** avoir un accrochage avec qn

runner ['rʌnə(r)] *n* (**a**) *(athlete)* coureur(euse) *m,f*; *(messenger)* coursier(ère) *m,f*; *(for drugs, guns)* passeur(euse) *m,f* (**b**) **r. bean** haricot *m* d'Espagne (**c**) *(on sleigh)* patin *m*; *(on drawer)* glissière *f* (**d**) *Fam* **to do a r.** se tirer

runner-up [rʌnə'rʌp] *(pl* **runners-up**) *n* suivant(e) *m,f*; *(in second place)* second(e) *m,f*

running ['rʌnɪŋ] **1** *n* (**a**) *(activity)* course *f*; **to go r.** courir; *Fig* **to be out of the r.** *(in competition, race)* n'avoir aucune chance; **to be in the r. for sth** être sur les rangs *ou* dans la course pour qch; **to make all the r.** *(in relationship)* prendre toutes les initiatives; *Am Pol* **r. mate** = candidat à la vice-présidence

accompagnant dans sa campagne le candidat à la présidence des États-Unis; **r. shoe** chaussure *f* de course; **r. track** piste *f* (**b**) *(of machine, car)* **r. costs** frais *mpl* d'entretien (**c**) *(management)* gestion *f*

2 *adj (battle, feud)* incessant(e); *Fam* **go take a r. jump!** va voir ailleurs si j'y suis!; **r. board** *(on car)* marchepied *m*; **r. commentary** commentaire *m* en direct; **r. repairs** petites réparations *fpl*; **r. sore** plaie *f* qui suppure; **to keep a r. total (of sth)** comptabiliser (qch) au fur et à mesure; **r. water** eau *f* courante

runny ['rʌnɪ] *adj (liquid)* liquide; **to have a r. nose** avoir le nez qui coule

run-off ['rʌnɒf] *n* (**a**) *(election)* deuxième tour *m*; *(contest)* manche *f* pour départager deux candidats (**b**) *(from fields)* eaux *fpl* de ruissellement

run-of-the-mill [rʌnəvðə'mɪl] *adj* ordinaire

runt [rʌnt] *n* (**a**) *(of litter)* **the r.** le (la) plus faible de la portée (**b**) *(weak person)* avorton *m*

run-up ['rʌnʌp] *n (before jump)* course *f* d'élan; **the r. to the wedding/the election** la période précédant le mariage/les élections

runway ['rʌnweɪ] *n* piste *f*

rupee [ru:'pi:] *n* roupie *f*

rupture ['rʌptʃə(r)] **1** *n* rupture *f*

2 *vt (relations)* rompre; *(container)* faire éclater

3 *vi also Med* éclater

rural ['rʊərəl] *adj* rural(e)

ruse [ru:z] *n* ruse *f*

rush¹ [rʌʃ] *n (plant)* jonc *m*; **r. matting** natte *f* (de jonc)

rush² **1** *n* (**a**) *(hurry)* **what's the r.?** pourquoi tant de hâte?; **to be in a r.** être pressé(e); **to do sth in a r.** faire qch à toute vitesse; **there's no r.** il n'y a rien qui presse; **to make a r. for sth** se précipiter vers qch; **r. hour** heures *fpl* de pointe; **a r. job** *(urgent)* un travail urgent; *(hurried)* un travail bâclé

(**b**) *(surge) (of air)* bouffée *f*; *(of water)* flot *m* soudain; *(of requests)* flot *m*

(**c**) *(demand)* ruée *f*; **there's been a r. on tickets** les gens se sont rués sur les billets

(**d**) *Cin* **rushes** rush(e)s *mpl*

2 *vt* (**a**) *(hurry) (task)* faire à la hâte; *(person)* bousculer; **to r. sb into doing sth** bousculer qn pour qu'elle fasse qch; **to be rushed off one's feet** être débordé(e)

(**b**) *(transport quickly)* transporter d'urgence

(**c**) *(attack)* prendre d'assaut

3 *vi (move quickly)* se ruer (**at/towards** sur/vers); *(act quickly)* se dépêcher; **the blood rushed to her cheeks** le sang afflua à ses joues; **to r. to do sth** s'empresser de faire qch; **to r. into doing sth** faire qch sans réfléchir; **to r. into marriage** se marier sans réfléchir

▸**rush about, rush around** *vi* courir à droite et à gauche

▸**rush in** *vi (enter)* entrer précipitamment

▸**rush off** *vi* partir précipitamment

▸**rush out 1** *vt sep (book)* publier à la hâte

2 *vi (exit)* sortir précipitamment

▸**rush through 1** *vt sep (bill)* faire passer à la hâte; *(decision)* prendre à la hâte

2 *vt insep (book)* lire à toute vitesse; *(meal, work)* expédier

rusk [rʌsk] *n* gros biscuit *m (pour bébés)*

russet ['rʌsɪt] **1** *n (colour)* brun *m* roux

2 *adj* brun roux *inv*

Russia ['rʌʃə] *n* la Russie

Russian ['rʌʃən] **1** *n* (**a**) *(person)* Russe *mf* (**b**) *(language)* russe *m*
  2 *adj* russe; **the R. Federation** la Fédération de Russie; **R. roulette** roulette *f* russe
rust [rʌst] **1** *n* rouille *f*
  2 *adj (colour)* rouille *inv*
  3 *vi* rouiller
rustic ['rʌstɪk] *adj* rustique
rustle¹ ['rʌsəl] **1** *n (of leaves, paper)* bruissement *m*
  2 *vt (leaves, paper)* faire bruire
  3 *vi (of leaves, paper)* bruire
rustle² *vt (cattle)* voler
▶**rustle up** *vt sep Fam (meal, snack)* improviser; **to r. up support** rassembler des partisans
rustler ['rʌslə(r)] *n (cattle thief)* voleur(euse) *m,f* de bétail

rustproof ['rʌstpruːf] *adj (paint)* antirouille *inv*; *(metal)* inoxydable
rusty ['rʌstɪ] *adj also Fig* rouillé(e); *(colour)* rouille *inv*
rut¹ [rʌt] *n (groove)* ornière *f*; *Fig* **to be in a r.** être prisonnier(ère) de la routine
rut² **1** *n (of stag)* rut *m*
  2 *vi (pt & pp* **rutted***)(of stag)* être en rut
rutabaga ['ruːtəbeɪgə] *n Am* rutabaga *m*
ruthless ['ruːθlɪs] *adj* impitoyable
RV [ɑːˈviː] *n Am (abbr* **recreational vehicle***)* mobile home *m*
Rwanda [rəˈwændə] *n* le Rwanda
Rwandan [rəˈwændən] **1** *n* Rwandais(e) *m,f*
  2 *adj* rwandais(e)
rye [raɪ] *n* seigle *m*; **r. bread** pain *m* de seigle

S

S, s [es] n (**a**) (letter) S, s m inv (**b**) (abbr **south**) S
Sabbath ['sæbəθ] n (Jewish) (jour m du) sabbat m;
(Christian) jour du seigneur
sabbatical [sə'bætɪkəl] Univ **1** n congé m sabbatique;
to be on s. être en congé sabbatique
  2 adj (term, year) sabbatique
sable ['seɪbəl] **1** n (animal) zibeline f; **s. coat** manteau
m de ou en zibeline
  2 adj Lit (black) noir(e)
sabotage ['sæbətɑːʒ] **1** n sabotage m
  2 vt saboter
saboteur [sæbə'tɜː(r)] n saboteur(euse) m,f
sabre ['seɪbə(r)] n sabre m
sac [sæk] n Biol sac m
saccharin ['sækərɪn] n saccharine f
saccharine ['sækərɪn] adj Pej (smile, words) miel-
leux(euse); (film) à l'eau de rose
sachet ['sæʃeɪ] n sachet m
sack¹ [sæk] **1** n (**a**) (bag) sac m; Fam **to hit the s.** se
pieuter (**b**) Fam (dismissal) renvoi m; **to give sb the
s.** virer qn; **to get the s.** se faire virer
  2 vt Fam (dismiss) virer
sack² **1** n (plundering) sac m
  2 vt (plunder) mettre à sac
sacking ['sækɪŋ] n (**a**) (textile) grosse toile f (**b**) Fam
(dismissal) renvoi m
sacrament ['sækrəmənt] n Rel sacrement m; **to take
or receive the sacraments** communier
sacred ['seɪkrɪd] adj sacré(e); Fig **s. cow** (belief, institution) véritable institution f
sacrifice ['sækrɪfaɪs] **1** n sacrifice m; **to make sacrifices** faire des sacrifices
  2 vt sacrifier (**to** à); **to s. oneself** se sacrifier
sacrificial [sækrɪ'fɪʃəl] adj sacrificiel(elle); Fig **s. lamb
or victim** bouc m émissaire
sacrilege ['sækrɪlɪdʒ] n also Fig sacrilège m
sacrilegious [sækrɪ'lɪdʒəs] adj also Fig sacrilège
sacristan ['sækrɪstən] n Rel sacristain m
sacrosanct ['sækrəʊsæŋkt] adj sacro-saint(e)
SAD [sæd] n Med (abbr **Seasonal Affective Disorder**) =
dépression due au manque de soleil en hiver
sad [sæd] adj (**a**) (unhappy, depressing) triste; **to make
sb s.** attrister qn (**b**) Fam (pathetic) pitoyable
sadden ['sædən] vt attrister
saddle ['sædəl] **1** n (on horse, bicycle) selle f; **to be in
the s.** être en selle; Fig être aux commandes
  2 vt (horse) seller; Fam Fig **to s. sb with sb/sth** refiler
qn/qch à qn; **to get saddled with sb/sth** se retrouver
avec qn/qch sur les bras
saddlebag ['sædəlbæg] n sacoche f
sadism ['seɪdɪzəm] n sadisme m
sadist ['seɪdɪst] n sadique mf

sadistic [sə'dɪstɪk] adj sadique
sadly ['sædlɪ] adv (**a**) (unhappily) tristement (**b**) (unfortunately) malheureusement (**c**) (greatly) **to be s.
mistaken** se tromper lourdement; **he is s. missed** il
nous/leur/etc manque beaucoup
sadness ['sædnɪs] n tristesse f
sadomasochism [seɪdəʊ'mæsəkɪzəm] n sadomasochisme m
sadomasochist [seɪdəʊ'mæsəkɪst] n sadomasochiste
mf
SAE [eseɪ'iː] n (abbr **stamped addressed envelope**)
enveloppe f timbrée
safari [sə'fɑːrɪ] n safari m; **to go on s.** faire un safari; **s.
jacket** saharienne f; **s. park** réserve f d'animaux sauvages
safe [seɪf] **1** adj (**a**) (not in danger) en sécurité; (house,
activity) sûr(e); (topic of conversation) sans danger; **s.
from sth** à l'abri de qch; **s. and sound** sain et sauf
(saine et sauve); **as s. as houses** qui ne présente aucun risque; Prov **better s. than sorry** deux précautions valent mieux qu'une; **s. seat** (in parliament) =
siège parlementaire en principe acquis à un parti
donné
  (**b**) (not dangerous) **it is s. to say that...** on peut dire
sans risque de se tromper que...; **it's a s. bet that...** il
y a fort à parier que...; **at a s. distance** à distance respectueuse; **in s. hands** entre de bonnes mains; **to
wish sb a s. journey** souhaiter bon voyage à qn;
...to be on the s. side ...pour plus de sûreté; **s. house**
(for spies) cachette f sûre; **s. sex** rapports mpl sexuels
protégés
  2 n (for money) coffre-fort m
  3 adv **to play (it) s.** ne pas prendre de risques
safe-conduct [seɪf'kɒndʌkt] n sauf-conduit m
safeguard ['seɪfgɑːd] **1** n garantie f
  2 vt sauvegarder
  3 vi **to s. against sth** se protéger contre qch
safe-keeping [seɪf'kiːpɪŋ] n **in s.** en lieu sûr; **to give
sth to sb for s.** confier qch à la garde de qn
safely ['seɪflɪ] adv (**a**) (without risk) en toute sécurité;
(drive) prudemment; **to arrive s.** (of person) bien arriver; (of goods) arriver sans dommage (**b**) (with certainty) avec certitude
safety ['seɪftɪ] n sûreté f; **for s.'s sake** pour plus de sûreté; **to be s. conscious** se préoccuper beaucoup de
la sécurité; Prov **(there's) s. in numbers** plus on est
nombreux, moins on court de risques; **s. belt** ceinture f de sécurité; **s. catch** cran m de sûreté; **s. glass**
verre m de sécurité; **s. matches** allumettes fpl de sûreté; **s. measures** mesures fpl de sûreté; **s. net** filet m;
Fig mesure f de sécurité; **s. pin** épingle f de sûreté;
also Fig **s. valve** soupape f de sûreté

saffron ['sæfrən] **1** n safran m
 2 adj safran inv
sag [sæg] (pt & pp **sagged**) vi (of roof, bridge) s'affaisser; (of flesh) être flasque; (of rope) pendre; (of breasts) être tombant(e); (of prices, support) baisser
saga ['sɑːɡə] n also Fig (story) saga f
sagacious [sə'ɡeɪʃəs] adj Formal sagace
sagacity [sə'ɡæsɪtɪ] n Formal sagacité f
sage¹ [seɪdʒ] **1** n (wise man) sage m
 2 adj (person, conduct) sage
sage² n (herb) sauge f
Sagittarius [sædʒɪ'teərɪəs] n (sign of zodiac) le Sagittaire; **to be (a) S.** être (du) Sagittaire
Sahara [sə'hɑːrə] n **the S. (Desert)** le Sahara
said [sed] pt & pp of **say**
sail [seɪl] **1** n (on boat) voile f; (of windmill) aile f; **to set s.** prendre la mer; **to go for a s.** faire un tour en voilier
 2 vi (of ship, person) naviguer; (start voyage) prendre la mer; Fig **the clouds sailed by** les nuages passaient dans le ciel; Fig **his book sailed out of the window** son livre vola par la fenêtre; Fig **to s. close to the wind** jouer avec le feu; Fam **to s. through an examination** réussir un examen les doigts dans le nez
sailing ['seɪlɪŋ] n (activity) voile f; (departure) appareillage m; **to go s.** faire de la voile; Br **s. boat/ship** voilier m
sailor ['seɪlə(r)] n marin m; **to be a good/bad s.** avoir/ne pas avoir le pied marin; **s. suit** costume m marin (d'enfant)
saint [seɪnt] n saint(e) m,f; **All Saints' (Day)** la Toussaint; **S. Bernard** (dog) saint-bernard m inv; **S. Patrick's Day** la Saint Patrick

Saint Patrick's Day
Patrick, le saint patron de l'Irlande, est célébré le 17 mars, qui est le jour de sa mort, en l'an 461. Saint Patrick convertit les Irlandais au christianisme et établit monastères, églises et écoles dans tout le pays. Selon la légende, il aurait également réussi à chasser tous les serpents d'Irlande. Chômée en Irlande, la St Patrick est également fêtée dans certaines villes américaines comptant une forte proportion de personnes d'origine irlandaise.

saintly ['seɪntlɪ] adj (life, behaviour) de saint; (smile) d'ange
sake [seɪk] n **for the s. of sb, for sb's s.** (for the good of) pour le bien de qn; (out of respect for) par égard de qn; **for God's** or **heaven's s.!** mais bon sang!; **for the s. of peace** pour avoir la paix; **for old times' s.** en souvenir du passé; **this is just talking for talking's s.** c'est parler pour parler; **let's say, for the s. of argument...** admettons que...
salacious [sə'leɪʃəs] adj salace
salad ['sæləd] n salade f; **s. bowl** saladier m; Br **s. cream** = sorte de mayonnaise liquide; Fig **s. days** années fpl de jeunesse; **s. dressing** = vinaigrette ou sauce pour salade; **s. spinner** essoreuse f à salade
salamander ['sæləmændə(r)] n salamandre f
salami [sə'lɑːmɪ] n salami m
salaried ['sælərɪd] adj salarié(e)
salary ['sælərɪ] (pl **salaries**) n salaire m; **s. earner** salarié(e) m,f; **s. grade** échelon m de salaire; **s. scale** échelle f des salaires
sale [seɪl] n (a) (action, event) vente f; **for s.** à vendre; **to put sth up for s.** mettre qch en vente; **on s.** en

vente; Br **sales assistant** vendeur(euse) m,f; **sales department** service m commercial; **sales drive** campagne f de vente; **sales force** force f de vente; **sales forecast** prévision f des ventes; **sales manager** directeur(trice) m,f commercial(e); **sales pitch** arguments mpl de vente; **sales target** objectif m de vente; **s. price** prix m de vente; **s. of work** vente f de charité (**b**) (at reduced prices) soldes mpl; **the sales** les soldes; **in the sales** en solde
saleable ['seɪləbəl] adj vendable
saleroom ['seɪlruːm] n salle f des ventes
salesclerk ['seɪlzklɑːk] n Am vendeur(euse) m,f
salesgirl ['seɪlzɡɜːl] n vendeuse f
salesman ['seɪlzmən] n (for company) représentant m; (in shop) vendeur m
salesmanship ['seɪlzmənʃɪp] n technique f de vente
salesperson ['seɪlzpɜːsən] (pl **salespeople**) n (for company) représentant(e) m,f; (in shop) vendeur(-euse) m,f
saleswoman ['seɪlzwʊmən] n (for company) représentante f; (in shop) vendeuse f
salient ['seɪlɪənt] adj Formal (feature) marquant(e); (point) essentiel(elle)
saline ['seɪlaɪn] adj salin(e); **s. drip** perfusion f de solution saline; **s. solution** solution f saline
saliva [sə'laɪvə] n salive f
salivate ['sælɪveɪt] vi also Fig saliver
sallow ['sæləʊ] adj jaunâtre
►**sally forth** ['sælɪ] (pt & pp **sallied**) vi Lit partir
salmon ['sæmən] (pl **salmon**) n saumon m; **s. (pink)** (rose m) saumon; **s. trout** truite f saumonée
salmonella [sælmə'nelə] n salmonelle f
salon ['sælɒn] n **(beauty) s.** institut m de beauté; **(hairdressing) s.** salon m de coiffure
saloon [sə'luːn] n (**a**) (room) salle f; Am (bar) bar m (**b**) Br **s. (car)** berline f
SALT [sɔːlt] n (abbr **Strategic Arms Limitation Talks**) SALT m
salt [sɔːlt] **1** n (**a**) (substance) sel m; **s. flat** marais m salant; **s. mine** mine f de sel (**b**) (idioms) **to be worth one's s.** être à la hauteur; **to rub s. in sb's wounds** remuer le couteau dans la plaie; Fig **that woman is the s. of the earth!** cette femme est la bonté incarnée! (**c**) Fam **an old s.** (sailor) un vieux loup de mer
 2 adj **s. beef** bœuf m salé; **s. cod** morue f salée; **s. water** eau f salée
 3 vt (food) saler; (roads) sabler
►**salt away** vt sep (money) mettre de côté
saltcellar ['sɔːltselə(r)] n salière f
salt-free ['sɔːltfriː] adj sans sel
saltpetre [sɒlt'piːtə(r)] n salpêtre m
saltwater ['sɔːltwɔːtə(r)] adj (lake) salé(e); (fish) de mer
salty ['sɔːltɪ] adj salé(e)
salubrious [sə'luːbrɪəs] adj Formal salubre
salutary ['sæljʊtərɪ] adj salutaire
salute [sə'luːt] **1** n salut m; **to take the s.** passer les troupes en revue
 2 vt also Fig saluer
 3 vi faire un salut
salvage ['sælvɪdʒ] **1** n (of ship) sauvetage m; (of waste material) récupération f; **s. vessel** bateau m de sauvetage
 2 vt also Fig sauver

salvation [sæl'veɪʃən] n salut m; **S. Army** Armée f du Salut

salve [sælv] vt **to s. one's conscience** se donner bonne conscience

salver ['sælvə(r)] n (tray) plateau m (de présentation)

salvo ['sælvəʊ] (pl **salvos** or **salvoes**) n also Fig salve f; (of questions) flot m; (of insults) torrent m

Samaritan [sə'mærɪtən] n also Fig **the Good S.** le bon Samaritain; **the Samaritans** ≃ S.O.S. Amitié

same [seɪm] **1** adj **the s. man** le même homme; **the s. woman** la même femme; **the s. children** les mêmes enfants; **in the s. way** de la même façon; Fig **to go the s. way** prendre le même chemin; **the s. day** le même jour; **the** or **that (very) s. day** (for emphasis) le jour même; **it all comes to the s. thing** cela revient au même; **at the s. time** (regularly) au même moment; (simultaneously) en même temps, à la fois

2 pron **the s.** le même, la même; (plural) les mêmes; **I would have done the s.** j'aurais fait la même chose ou pareil; **if it's all the s. to you** si cela vous est égal; Fam **(the) s. again?** (in pub) la même chose?; Fam **s. here!** (so do I) moi aussi!; (neither do I) moi non plus!; (I did the same thing) pareil!; **the house isn't the s. without her** la maison n'est plus la même sans elle

3 adv **to think/feel the s.** penser/ressentir la même chose; **to look the s.** (of two things) sembler pareils; **to taste the s.** avoir le même goût; **all the s.** (nevertheless) tout de même

sameness ['seɪmnɪs] n monotonie f

Samoa [sə'məʊə] n Samoa m

Samoan [sə'məʊən] **1** n **(a)** (person) Samoan(e) m,f **(b)** (language) samoan m **2** adj samoan(e)

samosa [səm'əʊsə] n samosa m

sample ['sɑːmpəl] **1** n échantillon m; (of blood, urine) prélèvement m; **to take a blood s.** faire une prise de sang; Comput **s. prices** prix mpl données à titre d'exemple

2 vt **(a)** (food, experience) goûter **(b)** (public opinion) sonder **(c)** (piece of music) sampler

sanatorium [sænə'tɔːrɪəm] (pl **sanatoria** [sænə'tɔːrɪə]) n sanatorium m

sanctify ['sæŋ(k)tɪfaɪ] vt sanctifier; Fig consacrer

sanctimonious [sæŋ(k)tɪ'məʊnɪəs] adj moralisateur(trice)

sanction ['sæŋ(k)ʃən] **1** n **(a)** (penalty) sanction f; **to impose sanctions on a country** imposer des sanctions à un pays **(b)** Formal (consent) consentement m, accord m

2 vt Formal (consent to) sanctionner

sanctity ['sæŋ(k)tɪtɪ] n sainteté f; Fig (of life, marriage) caractère m sacré

sanctuary ['sæŋ(k)tjʊ)ərɪ] n Rel sanctuaire m; (for fugitive, refugee) refuge m, asile m; (for birds, wildlife) réserve f; **to seek/find s.** chercher/trouver refuge

sand [sænd] **1** n sable m; **s. castle** château m de sable; **s. dune** dune f

2 vt **(a)** (smooth with sandpaper) poncer **(b)** (cover with sand) sabler

sandal ['sændəl] n sandale f

sandbag ['sændbæg] n sac m de sable

sandbank ['sændbæŋk] n banc m de sable

sandblast ['sændblæst] vt décaper à la sableuse

S&M [esən'dem] n Fam (abbr **sadomasochism**) sadomasochisme m

sandpaper ['sændpeɪpə(r)] **1** n papier m de verre **2** vt poncer, passer au papier de verre

sandpit ['sændpɪt] n bac m à sable

sandstone ['sændstəʊn] n grès m

sandstorm ['sændstɔːm] n tempête f de sable

sandwich ['sændwɪtʃ] **1** n sandwich m; **ham s.** sandwich au jambon; Br **s. course** stage m de formation (professionnelle) en alternance; **s. loaf** ≃ pain m de mie

2 vt **to be sandwiched between** (of layer) être intercalé(e) entre; (of person, building) être coincé(e) entre

sandy ['sændɪ] adj **(a)** (earth) sablonneux(euse); (beach) de sable **(b)** (hair) blond roux inv

sane [seɪn] adj (person) sain(e) d'esprit; (action, remark) sensé(e)

San Franciscan ['sænfrən'sɪskən] **1** n habitant(e) m,f de San Francisco **2** adj de San Francisco

San Francisco ['sænfrən'sɪskəʊ] n San Francisco

sang [sæŋ] pt of **sing**

sanguine ['sæŋgwɪn] adj optimiste

sanitary ['sænɪtərɪ] adj **(a)** (clean) hygiénique **(b)** (relating to hygiene) sanitaire; Br **s. towel** serviette f hygiénique

sanitation [sænɪ'teɪʃən] n installations fpl sanitaires

sanitize ['sænɪtaɪz] vt expurger

sanity ['sænɪtɪ] n santé f mentale

sank [sæŋk] pt of **sink²**

San Marino [sænmə'riːnəʊ] n Saint-Marin

Santa (Claus) ['sæntə('klɔːz)] n le père Noël

sap¹ [sæp] n (of plant) sève f

sap² n Fam (gullible person) andouille f

sap³ (pt & pp **sapped**) vt (weaken) saper

sapling ['sæplɪŋ] n jeune arbre m

sapper ['sæpə(r)] n Br Mil soldat m du génie

sapphire ['sæfaɪə(r)] n saphir m

Sarajevo [særə'jeɪvəʊ] n Sarajevo

sarcasm ['sɑːkæzəm] n sarcasme m

sarcastic [sɑː'kæstɪk] adj sarcastique

sarcastically [sɑː'kæstɪklɪ] adv de manière sarcastique; (speak) d'un ton sarcastique

sarcophagus [sɑː'kɒfəgəs] (pl **sarcophagi** [sɑː-'kɒfəgaɪ]) n sarcophage m

sardine [sɑː'diːn] n sardine f; Fam Fig **to be packed like sardines** être serrés(es) comme des sardines

Sardinia [sɑː'dɪnɪə] n la Sardaigne

Sardinian [sɑː'dɪnɪən] **1** n Sarde mf **2** adj sarde

sardonic [sɑː'dɒnɪk] adj sardonique

sari ['sɑːrɪ] n sari m

sarong [sə'rɒŋ] n paréo m

sartorial [sɑː'tɔːrɪəl] adj Formal vestimentaire

SAS [eseɪ'es] n Br (abbr **Special Air Service**) = service d'intervention spécial de l'Armée britannique

SASE [eseɪi:] n Am (abbr **self-addressed stamped envelope**) enveloppe f timbrée (portant l'adresse à laquelle elle doit être renvoyée)

sash [sæʃ] n (around waist) large ceinture f de tissu; (around shoulder) écharpe f; **s. cord** corde f (actionnant une fenêtre à guillotine); **s. window** fenêtre f à guillotine

Sassenach ['sæsənæx] n Scot Pej Anglais(e) m,f

Sat (abbr **Saturday**) samedi

sat [sæt] pt & pp of **sit**

Satan ['seɪtən] *n* Satan
satanic [sə'tænɪk] *adj* satanique, diabolique
satchel ['sætʃəl] *n* cartable *m*
sate [seɪt] *vt Formal* assouvir
satellite ['sætəlaɪt] *n* satellite *m*; **s. dish** antenne *f* parabolique; **s. (state)** (État *m*) satellite; **s. television** télévision *f* par satellite; **s. town** ville *f* satellite
satiate ['seɪʃɪeɪt] *vt Formal* assouvir
satin ['sætɪn] *n* satin *m*
satire ['sætaɪə(r)] *n* satire *f*
satirical [sə'tɪrɪkəl] *adj* satirique
satirist ['sætɪrɪst] *n* écrivain *m* satirique
satirize ['sætɪraɪz] *vt* faire la satire de
satisfaction [sætɪs'fækʃən] *n* satisfaction *f*; **to have the s. of doing sth** avoir la satisfaction de faire qch
satisfactory [sætɪs'fæktərɪ] *adj* satisfaisant(e)
satisfied ['sætɪsfaɪd] *adj* satisfait(e)
satisfy ['sætɪsfaɪ] (*pt & pp* **satisfied**) *vt* (**a**) *(meet needs of)* *(person, curiosity)* satisfaire; *(condition)* remplir (**b**) *(convince)* convaincre, persuader
saturate ['sætʃəreɪt] *vt* saturer; **to s. the market** saturer le marché; **saturated fats** graisses *fpl* saturées
saturation [sætʃə'reɪʃən] *n* saturation *f*; **to reach s. point** arriver à saturation; *Mil* **s. bombing** bombardement *m* intensif
Saturday ['sætədɪ] *n* samedi *m*; **this S.** samedi prochain *ou* qui vient; **on S.** samedi; **on S. morning/afternoon/evening** samedi matin/après-midi/soir; **on Saturdays** le samedi; **every S.** tous les samedis; **every other S.** un samedi sur deux; **last S.** samedi dernier; **the S. before last** pas samedi dernier mais celui d'avant; **next S.** samedi prochain; **the S. after next, a week on S., S. week** le samedi d'après, samedi en huit; **the following S.** le samedi suivant; **S.'s paper** le journal de samedi; **S. job** petit boulot *m* (*du samedi*)
Saturn ['sætɜːn] *n (planet)* Saturne *f*
sauce [sɔːs] *n* (**a**) *(for food)* sauce *f*; **tomato/cheese s.** sauce tomate/au fromage; **s. boat** saucière *f* (**b**) *Fam (impudence)* culot *m*
sauced [sɔːst] *adj Fam (drunk)* bourré(e), pété(e)
saucepan ['sɔːspən] *n* casserole *f*
saucer ['sɔːsə(r)] *n* soucoupe *f*, *Belg & Suisse* sous-tasse *f*
saucy ['sɔːsɪ] *adj Fam (impertinent)* insolent(e); *(risqué)* coquin(e)
Saudi ['saʊdɪ] **1** *n (person)* Saoudien(enne) *m,f*, *Fam (country)* l'Arabie *f* Saoudite
   2 *adj* saoudien(enne)
Saudi Arabia ['saʊdɪə'reɪbɪə] *n* l'Arabie *f* Saoudite
Saudi Arabian ['saʊdɪə'reɪbɪən] **1** *n* Saoudien(enne) *m,f*
   2 *adj* saoudien(enne)
sauna ['sɔːnə] *n* sauna *m*; **to have a s.** aller au sauna
saunter ['sɔːntə(r)] **1** *n* balade *f*; **to go for a s.** partir en balade
   2 *vi* **to s. (along)** flâner
sausage ['sɒsɪdʒ] *n* saucisse *f*; *Fam* **not a s.** *(nothing)* que dalle; *Hum* **you silly s.!** patate, va!; *Fam* **s. dog** saucisson *m* à pattes; **s. meat** chair *f* à saucisse; *Br* **s. roll** feuilleté *m* à la viande
sauté ['saʊteɪ] **1** *adj* sauté(e)
   2 *vt* (*pt & pp* **sautéed**) faire sauter
savage ['sævɪdʒ] **1** *n Old-fashioned* sauvage *mf*
   2 *adj (animal, person)* féroce, brutal(e); *(attack,*

criticism) violent(e)
   3 *vt (attack physically)* attaquer; *Fig (criticize)* descendre en flammes
savagely ['sævɪdʒlɪ] *adv (beat, attack)* sauvagement; *Fig (criticize)* violemment, avec virulence
savanna(h) [sə'vænə] *n* savane *f*
save¹ [seɪv] *prep Formal (except)* hormis
save² *vt* (**a**) *(rescue)* sauver; **to s. sb's life** sauver la vie à qn; *Fam* **she can't sing to s. her life** elle chante comme un pied; *Fam* **to s. one's (own) neck** *or* **skin** sauver sa peau; **to s. sb from falling** empêcher qn de tomber; **to s. a goal** arrêter un but; **God s. the King/the Queen!** vive le Roi/la Reine!
   (**b**) *(keep for future)* garder, conserver; *(money)* mettre de côté; *Comput* sauvegarder; **to s. oneself for sth** se réserver pour qch
   (**c**) *(not waste)* *(money, space)* économiser; *(time)* gagner; **s. your breath** ne te fatigue pas
   (**d**) *(spare)* **to s. sb sth** éviter qch à qn; **to s. sb (from) doing sth** éviter à qn de faire qch
   2 *vi* faire des économies (**for/on** pour/sur)
   3 *n (of goalkeeper)* arrêt *m*; **to make a s.** arrêter un but
▸**save up** *vi* mettre de l'argent de côté (**for** pour)
saver ['seɪvə(r)] *n* épargnant(e) *m,f*
saving ['seɪvɪŋ] **1** *n* (**a**) *(economy)* économie *f* (**b**) **savings** *(money saved)* économies *fpl*; **to live off one's savings** vivre sur ses économies; **savings account** compte *m* d'épargne; **savings bank** caisse *f* d'épargne
   2 *adj* **her/its s. grace** ce qui la/le sauve
saviour ['seɪvjə(r)] *n* sauveur *m*; **the S.** le Sauveur
savour ['seɪvə(r)] **1** *n* saveur *f*
   2 *vt also Fig* savourer
   3 *vi Formal* **to s. of** sentir
savoury ['seɪvərɪ] *adj* (**a**) *(food)* salé(e) (**b**) *(conduct)* honorable
saw¹ [sɔː] *pt of* **see²**
saw² **1** *n (tool)* scie *f*
   2 *vt* (*pp* **sawn** [sɔːn] *or* **sawed**) scier
▸**saw off** *vt sep* scier
▸**saw up** *vt sep* découper à la scie
sawdust ['sɔːdʌst] *n* sciure *f*
sawmill ['sɔːmɪl] *n* scierie *f*
sawn [sɔːn] *pp of* **saw²**
sawn-off shotgun ['sɔːnɒf'ʃɒtgʌn] *n* fusil *m* à canon scié
sax [sæks] *n Fam (saxophone)* sax *m*
Saxon ['sæks(ə)n] **1** *n* (**a**) *(person)* Saxon(onne) *m,f* (**b**) *(language)* saxon *m*
   2 *adj* saxon(onne)
Saxony ['sæksənɪ] *n* Saxe *f*
saxophone ['sæksəfəʊn] *n* saxophone *m*
saxophonist [sæk'sɒfənɪst] *n* saxophoniste *mf*
say [seɪ] **1** *vt* (*pt & pp* **said** [sed]) dire; *(of clock, watch)* indiquer; **to s. sth to sb** dire qch à qn; **it says that...** *(of text, sign)* il y a écrit que...; **I wouldn't s. no to a cup of tea** je prendrais volontiers une tasse de thé; **I didn't s. a word** je n'ai pas dit un mot; **it's not for me to s.** ce n'est pas à moi de le dire; **there's no saying what might happen if...** inutile de vous dire ce qui se passerait si...; **what have you got to s. for yourself?** as-tu une excuse valable?; **there's a lot to be said for living in the country** il y a bien des avantages à vivre à la campagne; **you're honest, I'll s. that for you** tu es honnête, je te l'accorde; **it says a lot about her** ça en dit long sur sa personne; **don't s.**

you've forgotten already! ne me dis pas que tu as déjà oublié!; **you can s. that again!, you said it!** c'est le cas de le dire!, tu l'as dit!; **need I s. more?** ai-je besoin d'en dire plus?; **they s. that..., it is said that...** on dit que...; **s. we won first prize** supposons que nous gagnions le premier prix; **if I had, s., £100,000** si j'avais, mettons, 100 000 livres

2 *vi* **I'm not saying** je ne dirai rien; **as they s.** comme on dit; **I s.!** dis-donc!; **I'll s.!** absolument!, tout à fait!; *Fam* **you don't s.!** sans blagues!

3 *n* **to have one's s.** avoir son mot à dire; **to have a s./no s. in sth** avoir/ne pas avoir voix au chapitre concernant qch

saying ['seɪɪŋ] *n* maxime *f*; **as the s. goes** comme dit la maxime

say-so ['seɪsəʊ] *n Fam (permission)* permission *f*

scab [skæb] *n* (**a**) *(on skin)* croûte *f* (**b**) *Fam (strikebreaker)* jaune *mf*

scabbard ['skæbəd] *n* fourreau *m*, gaine *f*

scabies ['skeɪbiːz] *n* gale *f*

scaffold ['skæfəld] *n (outside building)* échafaudage *m*; *(for execution)* échafaud *m*

scaffolding ['skæfəldɪŋ] *n* échafaudage *m*

scalawag *Am* = **scallywag**

scald [skɔːld] **1** *n* brûlure *f*

2 *vt* ébouillanter; **to s. one's hand** s'ébouillanter la main

scalding ['skɔːldɪŋ] *adj* brûlant(e)

scale¹ [skeɪl] **1** *n (on fish, reptile)* écaille *f*; *(in pipes, kettle)* dépôt *m* calcaire

2 *vt (fish)* écailler

scale² *n* (**a**) *(of instrument)* gamme *f*; *(of salaries)* barème *m*; **on a s. of one to ten** sur une échelle allant de un à dix (**b**) *(of map, drawing)* échelle *f*; *Fig (of problem, changes)* étendue *f*; **to s.** à la bonne échelle; **s. drawing** dessin *m* à l'échelle; **s. model** modèle *m* réduit (**c**) *(of ruler, thermometer)* graduation *f*

scale³ *vt (climb)* escalader

▶**scale down** *vt sep (reduce)* revoir à la baisse

▶**scale up** *vt sep (increase)* augmenter

scales [skeɪlz] *npl* **(set of) s.** *(for kitchen)* balance *f*; *(for bathroom)* pèse-personne *m*

scallop ['skæləp, 'skɒləp] **1** *n* (**a**) *(shellfish)* coquille *f* Saint-Jacques (**b**) *(in sewing)* feston *m*

2 *vt (in sewing)* festonner

scallywag ['skælɪwæg], *Am* **scalawag** ['skæləwæg] *n Fam* coquin(e) *m,f*

scalp [skælp] **1** *n* cuir *m* chevelu; *(as war trophy)* scalp *m*

2 *vt (in war)* scalper

scalpel ['skælpəl] *n* scalpel *m*

scaly ['skeɪlɪ] *adj (fish)* écailleux(euse); *(skin)* squameux(euse)

scam [skæm] *n Fam* arnaque *f*, magouille *f*

scamp [skæmp] *n (rascal)* coquin(e) *m,f*

scamper ['skæmpə(r)] *vi* gambader, galoper

▶**scamper away, scamper off** *vi* détaler, partir en courant

scampi ['skæmpɪ] *n* scampi *mpl*

scan [skæn] **1** *vt (pt & pp* **scanned)** (**a**) *(examine closely)* scruter; *Comput* balayer; *Med* faire une scanographie de; *(with ultrasound)* faire une échographie de (**b**) *(glance at)* parcourir

2 *n Med* scanographie *f*; *(with ultrasound)* échographie *f*

scandal ['skændəl] *n* (**a**) *(outrage)* scandale *m*; **to create** *or* **cause a s.** créer *ou* provoquer un scandale (**b**) *(gossip)* ragots *mpl*

scandalize ['skændəlaɪz] *vt* scandaliser, choquer

scandalous ['skændələs] *adj* scandaleux(euse)

Scandinavia [skændɪ'neɪvɪə] *n* la Scandinavie

Scandinavian [skændɪ'neɪvɪən] **1** *n* Scandinave *mf*

2 *adj* scandinave

scanner ['skænə(r)] *n Med & Comput* scanner *m*

scant [skænt] *adj* insuffisant(e)

scantily ['skæntɪlɪ] *adv* insuffisamment, sommairement; **s. dressed** *or* **clad** légèrement vêtu(e)

scanty ['skæntɪ] *adj (dress)* léger(ère); *(amount, information)* maigre, limité(e)

scapegoat ['skeɪpgəʊt] *n* bouc *m* émissaire

scar [skɑː(r)] **1** *n also Fig* cicatrice *f*; **s. tissue** tissu *m* cicatriciel

2 *vt (pt & pp* **scarred)** marquer de cicatrices; *Fig* marquer; **to be scarred for life** garder des cicatrices toute sa vie; *Fig* être marqué(e) à vie

3 *vi (of wound)* laisser une cicatrice

scarce ['skeəs] *adj* rare; *Fam* **to make oneself s.** filer

scarcely ['skeəslɪ] *adv* à peine; **she could s. speak** elle pouvait à peine parler; **s. ever/anyone** presque jamais/personne; **it is s. likely that...** il est peu probable que...

scarcity ['skeəsɪtɪ], **scarceness** ['skeəsnɪs] *n* manque *m*, pénurie *f*

scare ['skeə(r)] **1** *n* frayeur *f*; **pollution s.** alerte *f* à la pollution; **you gave me an awful s.** tu m'as fait une belle frayeur

2 *vt* effrayer; *Fam* **to s. the life out of sb, to s. the living daylights out of sb** faire une de ces trouilles à qn

3 *vi* s'effrayer

▶**scare away, scare off** *vt sep* faire fuir

scarecrow ['skeəkrəʊ] *n* épouvantail *m*

scared [skeəd] *adj* effrayé(e); **to be s. of sb/sth** avoir peur de qn/qch; **to be s. stiff, to be s. to death** être mort(e) de peur

scaremongering ['skeəmʌŋgərɪŋ] *n* alarmisme *m*

scarf [skɑːf] *(pl* **scarves** [skɑːvz] *) n (long)* écharpe *f*; *(square)* foulard *m*

scarlet ['skɑːlɪt] **1** *n* écarlate *f*

2 *adj* écarlate; *Fig* **to go** *or* **turn s.** *(with anger, embarrassment)* devenir rouge; **s. fever** scarlatine *f*

scarper ['skɑːpə(r)] *vi Br Fam* ficher le camp, se tailler

scary ['skeərɪ] *adj Fam* effrayant(e)

scat [skæt] *exclam Fam* fiche le camp!, dégage!

scathing ['skeɪðɪŋ] *adj (remark, sarcasm)* acerbe; **to be s. about sb/sth** faire des remarques acerbes sur qn/qch

scatological [skætə'lɒdʒɪkəl] *adj* scatologique

scatter ['skætə(r)] **1** *vt (clouds, demonstrators)* disperser, éparpiller; *(corn, seed)* jeter *ou* semer à la volée; *(crumbs, papers)* laisser traîner

2 *vi (of crowd)* se disperser

scatterbrain ['skætəbreɪn] *n Fam* tête *f* de linotte

scatty ['skætɪ] *adj Br Fam* farfelu(e)

scavenge ['skævɪndʒ] **1** *vt* récupérer

2 *vi* **to s. for sth** fouiller pour trouver qch; **to s. in the dustbins** fouiller dans *ou* faire les poubelles

scavenger ['skævɪndʒə(r)] *n (animal)* charognard *m*; *Fig (person)* fouilleur(euse) *m,f* de poubelles

scenario [sɪ'nɑːrɪəʊ] *(pl* **scenarios)** *n* **(a)** *(of film)* scénario *m* **(b)** *(situation)* hypothèse *f*

scene [siːn] *n* **(a)** *(in book, film, play)* scène *f*; *also Fig* **a touching/terrifying s.** une scène touchante/terrifiante; *also Fig* **behind the scenes** dans les coulisses; *Theat* **s. shifter** machiniste *mf* **(b)** *(of event)* lieu *m*, endroit *m*; **a change of s.** un changement de décor; **to arrive** *or* **come on the s.** *(of police, ambulance)* arriver sur les lieux; *Fig* faire son apparition; **the s. of the crime/accident** le lieu du crime/de l'accident; **a s. of devastation** un spectacle de dévastation; **I can picture the s.** j'imagine la scène; *Fam* **it's not my s.** ce n'est pas mon truc **(c)** *(fuss)* scandale *m*; **to make a s.** faire un scandale

scenery ['siːnərɪ] *n* **(a)** *(in play)* décor(s) *m(pl)* **(b)** *(landscape)* paysage *m*; *Fam* **to need a change of s.** avoir besoin de changer de décor *ou* d'air

scenic ['siːnɪk] *adj* pittoresque; **s. railway** petit train *m* (touristique); **s. route** route *f* touristique

scent [sent] **1** *n* **(a)** *(smell)* odeur *f* **(b)** *(perfume)* parfum *m* **(c)** *(in hunting)* fumet *m*; **to pick up the s.** trouver la piste; **to be on the s. of sth** être sur la trace de qch; **to lose the s.** perdre la trace; **she threw her pursuers off the s.** elle sema ses poursuivants
     2 *vt* **(a)** *(smell)* flairer; *Fig* **to s. blood** sentir que sa victime est affaiblie; *Fig* **to s. danger** flairer le danger **(b)** *(perfume)* parfumer

sceptic, *Am* **skeptic** ['skeptɪk] *n* sceptique *mf*

sceptical, *Am* **skeptical** ['skeptɪkəl] *adj* sceptique

sceptically, *Am* **skeptically** ['skeptɪklɪ] *adv* avec scepticisme

scepticism, *Am* **skepticism** ['skeptɪsɪzəm] *n* scepticisme *m*

sceptre ['septə(r)] *n* sceptre *m*

schedule ['ʃedjuːl, *Am* 'skedjuːl] **1** *n* **(a)** *(plan)* *(for work, project)* planning *m*; *(for events)* programme *m*, calendrier *m*; *Am (for trains, buses)* horaire *m*; **on s.** *(train, bus)* à l'heure; *(person)* dans les temps; **to be behind/ahead of s.** être en retard/en avance sur le programme; **to go according to s.** se dérouler comme prévu; **to work to a tight s.** avoir un emploi du temps serré **(b)** *Com (list of prices)* barème *m*
     2 *vt* prévoir; **we're scheduled to arrive at 21.45** notre arrivée est prévue à 21h45; **the museum is scheduled to open in August** l'ouverture du musée est prévue pour le mois d'août

scheduled ['ʃedjuːld, *Am* 'skedjuːld] *adj* prévu(e); **s. flight** vol *m* régulier

schematic [skɪ'mætɪk] *adj* schématique

scheme [skiːm] **1** *n* *(arrangement, system)* arrangement *m*; *(plan)* plan *m*; *(plot)* machination *f*, complot *m*; **in the (great) s. of things** dans le fond; **(housing) s.** lotissement *m*
     2 *vi Pej* comploter, intriguer **(against** contre)

schilling ['ʃɪlɪŋ] *n* schilling *m*

schism ['s(k)ɪzəm] *n* schisme *m*

schizoid ['skɪtsɔɪd] *n & adj* schizoïde *mf*

schizophrenia [skɪtsəʊ'friːnɪə] *n* schizophrénie *f*

schizophrenic [skɪtsəʊ'frenɪk] *n & adj* schizophrène *mf*

schmaltzy ['ʃmɔːltsɪ] *adj Fam* à l'eau de rose, cucul *inv*

scholar ['skɒlə(r)] *n (learned person)* érudit(e) *m,f*

scholarly ['skɒləlɪ] *adj* érudit(e)

scholarship ['skɒləʃɪp] *n* **(a)** *(learning)* érudition *f*, savoir *m* **(b)** *(grant)* bourse *f* (d'études)

scholastic [skə'læstɪk] *adj Formal* scolaire

school¹ [skuːl] **1** *n* **(a)** *(for children)* école *f*; **to go to s.** aller à l'école; **s. of art, art s.** école d'art; **of s. age** d'âge scolaire; *Fig* **I went to the s. of hard knocks** j'ai été à rude école; **s. bag** cartable *m*; *Br* **s. board** conseil *m* d'administration de l'établissement; **s. book** manuel *m* *ou* livre *m* scolaire; **s. day** journée *f* d'école *ou* scolaire; **s. friend** camarade *mf* d'école; **s. leaver** = jeune qui vient de terminer ses études secondaires; **s. report** *(for primary school)* carnet *m* de notes; *(for secondary school)* bulletin *m* scolaire; **s. uniform** forme *m* scolaire; **s. year** année *f* scolaire **(b)** *Am (college, university)* faculté *f*, université *f* **(c)** *(of artists, thinkers)* école *f*; **s. of thought** école de pensée; *Fig* **he's one of the old s.** il est de la vieille école
     2 *vt (educate)* scolariser; *(train)* former, entraîner; **to s. sb in sth** former qn à qch

school² *n (of fish)* banc *m*

schoolboy ['skuːlbɔɪ] *n* écolier *m*, élève *m*

schoolchild ['skuːltʃaɪld] *n* écolier(ère) *m,f*, élève *mf*

schoolfellow ['skuːlfeləʊ] *n* camarade *mf* de classe

schoolgirl ['skuːlgɜːl] *n* écolière *f*, élève *f*

schooling ['skuːlɪŋ] *n* scolarité *f*, éducation *f*

schoolmaster ['skuːlmɑːstə(r)] *n Formal (primary)* instituteur *m*, maître *m* d'école; *(secondary)* professeur *m*

schoolmate ['skuːlmeɪt] *n* camarade *mf* de classe

schoolmistress ['skuːlmɪstrɪs] *n Formal (primary)* institutrice *f*, maîtresse *f* d'école; *(secondary)* professeur *m*

schoolroom ['skuːlruːm] *n* salle *f* de classe

schoolteacher ['skuːltiːtʃə(r)] *n (primary)* instituteur(trice) *m,f*; *(secondary)* professeur *m*

schooner ['skuːnə(r)] *n* **(a)** *(ship)* schooner *m* **(b)** *(glass)* grand verre *m* (à xérès)

sciatica [saɪ'ætɪkə] *n* sciatique *f*

science ['saɪəns] *n* science *f*; **she's good at s.** elle est bonne en sciences; **s. fiction** science-fiction *f*; **s. park** parc *m* scientifique; **s. teacher** professeur *m* de sciences

scientific [saɪən'tɪfɪk] *adj* scientifique

scientist ['saɪəntɪst] *n* scientifique *mf*

sci-fi ['saɪfaɪ] *Fam* **1** *n* SF *f*
     2 *adj* de SF

Scilly ['sɪlɪ] *n* **the S. Isles, the Scillies** les Sorlingues *fpl*

scimitar ['sɪmɪtə(r)] *n* cimeterre *m*

scintillating ['sɪntɪleɪtɪŋ] *adj* brillant(e)

scissors ['sɪzəz] *npl* ciseaux *mpl*; **a pair of s.** une paire de ciseaux

sclerosis [sklə'rəʊsɪs] *n Med* sclérose *f*

scoff [skɒf] **1** *vt Br Fam (eat)* bouffer
     2 *vi (mock)* se moquer **(at** de)

scold [skəʊld] *vt* gronder

scone [skɒn] *n* scone *m*

scoop [skuːp] **1** *n* **(a)** *(device) (for ice cream)* cuillère *f* à glace; *(for flour, sugar)* pelle *f*; *(for mashed potato)* cuillère *f* **(b)** *(portion) (of ice cream)* boule *f*; *(of mashed potato)* portion *f* *Fam (in journalism)* scoop *m*
     2 *vt* **(a)** *(with hands, spoon)* ramasser **(b)** *(story)* publier en exclusivité

▶**scoop up** *vt sep* ramasser

scoot [skuːt] *vi Fam* **to s. (off** *or* **away)** filer

scooter ['skuːtə(r)] *n (for child)* trottinette *f*; *(small motorbike)* scooter *m*

scope [skəʊp] *n (of action)* possibilité *f*; *(of enquiry)* étendue *f*, portée *f*; **to give s. for...** *(interpretation, explanation)* laisser le champ libre à...; **the book is too narrow in s.** le livre est d'une portée trop limitée; **there's plenty of s. for improvement** les possibilités d'amélioration ne manquent pas; **the job gave him little s. to demonstrate his talents** son travail lui fournissait peu d'occasions de montrer ses talents

scorch [skɔːtʃ] **1** *vt* roussir; **scorched earth policy** politique *f* de la terre brûlée
  2 *n* **s. mark** brûlure *f*

scorcher ['skɔːtʃə(r)] *n Fam (hot day)* **it's been a s.** ça a été la canicule

scorching ['skɔːtʃɪŋ] *adj (day, weather)* torride; *(sun)* brûlant(e)

score [skɔː(r)] **1** *n* **(a)** *(in sport, quiz)* score *m*; **there was still no s.** personne n'avait encore marqué; **to keep the s.** compter les points; *Fam Fig* **to know the s.** connaître le topo
  (b) *(line)* rayure *f*, entaille *f*
  (c) *(quarrel)* **to have a s. to settle with sb** avoir un compte à régler avec qn
  (d) *(reason, grounds)* **on that s.** à ce sujet, sur ce point
  (e) *(in music)* partition *f*
  (f) *Old-fashioned (twenty)* **a s.** vingt; *Fam* **scores of** *(a lot)* des tas de
  2 *vt* **(a)** *(in sport)* marquer; **to s. a hit** *(hit target)* atteindre la cible; *Fig (of person, film)* remporter un grand succès; *Fig* **to s. points off sb** avoir le dessus
  (b) *(cut line in)* entailler
  (c) *Fam (buy)* **to s. drugs** acheter de la drogue
  3 *vi* **(a)** *(score a goal)* marquer un but
  (b) *Fam (sexually)* faire une touche; *(buy drugs)* acheter de la drogue

▶**score off** *vt sep (delete)* biffer, barrer
▶**score out** *vt sep (delete)* biffer, barrer

scoreboard ['skɔːbɔːd] *n* tableau *m* d'affichage (des scores)

scorecard ['skɔːkɑːd] *n* carte *f* de score

scorer ['skɔːrə(r)] *n* marqueur(euse) *m,f*

scorn [skɔːn] **1** *n* mépris *m*; **to pour s. on sb/sth** n'avoir que du mépris pour qn/qch
  2 *vt* mépriser

scornful ['skɔːnfʊl] *adj* méprisant(e); **to be s. of sb/ sth** considérer qn/qch avec mépris

Scorpio ['skɔːpɪəʊ] *n (sign of zodiac)* Scorpion *m*; **to be (a) S.** être (du) Scorpion

scorpion ['skɔːpɪən] *n* scorpion *m*

Scot [skɒt] *n* Écossais(e) *m,f*

Scotch [skɒtʃ] **1** *n (whisky)* scotch *m*
  2 *adj* **S. broth** = potage écossais à base de légumes et d'orge perlé; **S. egg** = œuf dur enrobé de chair à saucisse et pané; *Am* **S. tape**® scotch® *m*; **S. terrier** scotch-terrier *m*; **S. whisky** scotch *m*

scotch [skɒtʃ] *vt (rumour)* étouffer

scot-free ['skɒt'friː] *adj Fam* **to get off s.** s'en tirer sans la moindre punition

Scotland ['skɒtlənd] *n* l'Écosse *f*

Scots [skɒts] **1** *n (dialect)* écossais *m*
  2 *adj* écossais(e)

Scotsman ['skɒtsmən] *n* Écossais *m*

Scotswoman ['skɒtswʊmən] *n* Écossaise *f*

Scottie dog ['skɒtɪ'dɒg] *n Fam* scotch-terrier *m*

Scottish ['skɒtɪʃ] *adj* écossais(e); **the S. Parliament** le parlement écossais; **S. terrier** scotch-terrier *m*

Scottish Parliament

Le parlement écossais fut établi dans le cadre du projet de décentralisation ("devolution") du gouvernement travailliste et fut inauguré à Édimbourg en mai 1999. Les 129 membres du parlement écossais (MSP) siègent sous la houlette du "First Minister". Le parlement est pourvu d'une grande autonomie en matière de fiscalité mais ses pouvoirs législatifs sont néanmoins limités.

---

scoundrel ['skaʊndr(ə)l] *n* crapule *f*; *Fam (child)* coquin(e) *m,f*

scour ['skaʊə(r)] *vt* **(a)** *(pot, surface)* récurer, frotter **(b)** *(area, house)* ratisser, fouiller

scourer ['skaʊərə(r)] *n* tampon *m* à récurer

scourge [skɜːdʒ] *n* fléau *m*

scout [skaʊt] **1** *n* **(a) (boy) s.** (boy-)scout *m*, éclaireur *m*; **(girl) s.** éclaireuse *f*; **(talent) s.** dénicheur(euse) *m,f* de talents **(b)** *Mil (searcher)* éclaireur *m* **(c)** *(action)* **to have a s. around (for sth)** chercher (qch)
  2 *vi* **to s. for talent** dénicher des talents

scoutmaster ['skaʊtmɑːstə(r)] *n* chef *m* scout

scowl [skaʊl] **1** *n* regard *m* noir
  2 *vi* lancer des regards noirs (**at** à)

scrabble ['skræbəl] *vi* **to s. about** *or* **around for sth** chercher qch à tâtons

scraggy ['skrægɪ] *adj* maigre, décharné(e)

scram [skræm] *(pt & pp* **scrammed)** *vi Fam* se tirer

scramble ['skræmbəl] **1** *n* **(a)** *(rush)* ruée *f*, *(struggle)* bousculade *f* (**for** pour)
  2 *vt Tel (signal)* brouiller
  3 *vi* **to s. for sth** se précipiter pour qch; **to s. up a hill** gravir une colline avec les mains

scrambled eggs ['skræmbəl'egz] *npl* œufs *mpl* brouillés

scrap¹ [skræp] **1** *n* **(a)** *(of material, paper)* bout *m*; *(of information)* bribe *f*; *(of evidence)* semblant *m*; **scraps** *(of food)* restes *mpl*; **a s. of truth** une once de vérité; **s. paper** (papier *m*) brouillon *m* **(b)** **s. (metal)** ferraille *f*; **s. merchant** *or* **dealer** ferrailleur *m*; **to sell sth for s.** vendre qch à la casse
  2 *vt (pt & pp* **scrapped)** *(car)* envoyer à la casse; *(submarine, missile)* mettre au rebut; *(project)* abandonner

scrap² *Fam* **1** *n (fight)* bagarre *f*; **to have a s., to get into a s.** se bagarrer
  2 *vi (fight)* se bagarrer

scrapbook ['skræpbʊk] *n* album *m (de coupures de presse etc)*

scrape [skreɪp] **1** *n* **(a)** *(action)* coup *m* de grattoir; *(mark)* éraflure *f*; *(sound)* raclement *m*; **to give sth a s.** donner un coup de grattoir à qch **(b)** *Fam* **to get into a s.** se mettre dans le pétrin
  2 *vt* **(a)** *(skin, side of car)* érafler; *(dirt, wallpaper, vegetables)* gratter; **to s. one's plate clean** nettoyer son assiette; *Fig* **to s. the bottom of the barrel** être tombé(e) bien bas **(b)** *(barely obtain)* **to s. a living** arriver tout juste à vivre; **to s. a pass** *(in exam)* passer de justesse
  3 *vi* **(a)** *(make sound)* gratter, grincer **(b)** *(barely manage)* **to s. home** *(in contest)* réussir de justesse; **to s. into college** passer de justesse à l'université

▶**scrape through** *vt insep* passer de justesse
▶**scrape together** *vt sep (money, resources)* parvenir à rassembler

scraper ['skreɪpə(r)] *n (tool)* grattoir *m*

scrapheap ['skræphiːp] *n* tas *m* de ferraille; *Fig* **to be on the s.** être au rebut

scrappy ['skræpɪ] *adj (performance)* décousu(e); *(knowledge)* limité(e)

scratch [skrætʃ] **1** *n* (**a**) *(on skin)* égratignure *f*; *(on record, furniture)* rayure *f*; *(by claw)* griffure *f* (**b**) *(action)* **to give one's arm a s.** se gratter le bras (**c**) *Fam (idioms)* **to start from s.** partir de rien *ou* de zéro; *(restart)* recommencer à zéro; **to come up** *or* **be up to s.** être à la hauteur; **to bring sth/sb up to s.** mettre qch/qn à niveau

2 *adj (meal, team)* improvisé(e)

3 *vt* (**a**) *(skin) (by accident)* égratigner; *(to relieve itching)* gratter; *(with claw, nail)* griffer; *(glass, record)* rayer; **to s. oneself** se gratter; **to s. one's arm** se gratter le bras; *Fig* **you s. my back and I'll s. yours** un service en vaut un autre; *Fig* **we've only scratched the surface of the problem** nous n'avons fait que survoler le problème (**b**) *(write, draw)* griffonner (**c**) *(in sport)* retirer

4 *vi (of person)* se gratter; *(of pen, new clothes)* gratter; *(of thorns)* piquer; **the dog was scratching at the door** le chien grattait à la porte

▶**scratch out** *vt sep (number, name)* rayer; *Fig* **to s. sb's eyes out** arracher les yeux à qn

scratchcard ['skrætʃkɑːd] *n* = carte de loterie à gratter

scratchy ['skrætʃɪ] *adj (garment, towel)* qui gratte; *(record)* rayé(e)

scrawl [skrɔːl] **1** *n (writing)* gribouillage *m*
2 *vt & vi* gribouiller

scrawny ['skrɔːnɪ] *adj* maigrelet(ette)

scream [skriːm] **1** *n* (**a**) *(of person)* hurlement *m*; **screams of laughter** éclats *mpl* de rire (**b**) *Fam (good fun)* **it/he was a s.** c'était/il était tordant
2 *vt* hurler; **the headlines screamed "guilty"** le mot "coupable" s'étalait en gros à la une des journaux
3 *vi* hurler; **the car screamed past** la voiture est passée en rugissant; **to s. with pain** hurler de douleur; **to s. with laughter** se tordre de rire

screamingly ['skriːmɪŋlɪ] *adv Fam* **s. funny** tordant(e)

scree [skriː] *n* éboulis *m*

screech [skriːtʃ] **1** *n (of bird, person)* cri *m* strident; *(of brakes)* crissement *m*; *(of laughter)* éclat *m*
2 *vt* hurler
3 *vi (of bird)* pousser des cris stridents; *(of person)* hurler; *(of brakes)* crisser; **the car screeched to a halt** la voiture s'est arrêtée dans un crissement de pneus

screen [skriːn] **1** *n* (**a**) *(barrier)* écran *m*; *(folding)* paravent *m*; *Am* **s. door** porte *f* avec moustiquaire (**b**) *(of TV, computer, in cinema)* écran *m*; **the big/small s.** le grand/petit écran; **s. actor/actress** acteur *m*/actrice *f* de cinéma; *Comput* **s. saver** économiseur *m* d'écran; *Cin* **s. test** bout *m* d'essai; *Aut* **s. wash** liquide *m* lave-glace
2 *vt* (**a**) *(protect)* protéger; **to s. sth from view** cacher qch aux regards (**b**) *(film)* projeter; *(TV programme)* diffuser (**c**) *(test) (for security)* effectuer une enquête sur; *(for disease)* tester

screening ['skriːnɪŋ] *n* (**a**) *Cin* projection *f* (**b**) *(for security)* enquête *f*; *(for disease)* dépistage *m*

screenplay ['skriːnpleɪ] *n Cin* scénario *m*

screenwriter ['skriːnraɪtə(r)] *n Cin* scénariste *mf*

screw [skruː] **1** *n* (**a**) *(for fixing)* vis *f*; *Fam Fig* **she's got a s. loose** elle a une case en moins; *Fam Fig* **to put the screws on sb** faire pression sur qn; **s. top** *(of bottle,*

jar) couvercle *m* qui se visse (**b**) *(propeller)* hélice *f* (**c**) *very Fam (prison officer)* maton(onne) *m,f* (**d**) *Vulg (sex)* **to have a s.** s'envoyer en l'air

2 *vt* (**a**) *(fix)* visser (**to** à); **to s. one's face into a smile** se forcer à sourire; *Fam* **to s. money out of sb** extorquer de l'argent à qn (**b**) *Vulg (have sex with)* baiser; **go and s. yourself!** va te faire foutre!

3 *vi Vulg (have sex)* baiser

▶**screw around** *vi Vulg* baiser à droite et à gauche

▶**screw on 1** *vt sep (attach)* visser; *Fam* **she's got her head screwed on** elle a la tête sur les épaules
2 *vi (of lid)* se visser

▶**screw up 1** *vt sep* (**a**) *(paper)* froisser; **to s. up one's face** faire la grimace; *Fig* **to s. up one's courage** prendre son courage à deux mains (**b**) *very Fam (spoil)* foutre en l'air
2 *vi very Fam (fail)* cafouiller

screwdriver ['skruːdraɪvə(r)] *n* tournevis *m*

scribble ['skrɪbəl] **1** *n* gribouillage *m*
2 *vt & vi* griffonner

scribe [skraɪb] *n* scribe *m*

scrimmage ['skrɪmɪdʒ] *n* (**a**) *(pushing)* bousculade *f* (**b**) *Am (in football)* mêlée *f*

scrimp [skrɪmp] *vi* **to s. (and save)** économiser sur tout

script [skrɪpt] *n* (**a**) *(for play)* texte *m*; *(for film, TV programme)* script *m*; *(in exam)* copie *f* d'examen (**b**) *(handwriting)* script *m*

Scripture ['skrɪptʃə(r)] *n* **(Holy) S., the Scriptures** les saintes Écritures *fpl*

scriptwriter ['skrɪptraɪtə(r)] *n Cin & TV* scénariste *mf*

scroll [skrəʊl] **1** *n* (**a**) *(of paper, parchment)* rouleau *m* (**b**) *Archit* volute *f*
2 *vi Comput* défiler

▶**scroll down** *vi Comput* défiler vers le bas

▶**scroll up** *vi Comput* défiler vers le haut

scrooge [skruːdʒ] *n* avare *mf*

scrotum ['skrəʊtəm] *n* scrotum *m*

scrounge [skraʊndʒ] *Fam* **1** *n* **to be on the s.** venir quémander
2 *vt* **to s. sth from** *or* **off sb** taper qch à qn
3 *vi* **to s. off sb** vivre aux crochets de qn

scrounger ['skraʊndʒə(r)] *n Fam* parasite *m*

scrub [skrʌb] **1** *n* (**a**) *(bushes)* broussailles *fpl* (**b**) *(wash)* **to give sth a (good) s.** (bien) frotter qch (**c**) *(for skin, face)* gommage *m*
2 *vt (pt & pp scrubbed)* (**a**) *(floor)* frotter; *(pots)* récurer; **to s. one's hands** bien se frotter les mains (**b**) *Fam (cancel)* annuler

▶**scrub up** *vi Med* se brosser les mains

scrubber ['skrʌbə(r)] *n* (**a**) *(for dishes)* tampon *m* à récurer (**b**) *Br very Fam Pej (woman)* pute *f*

scrubbing brush ['skrʌbɪŋ'brʌʃ] *n* brosse *f* en chiendent

scrubland ['skrʌblænd] *n* brousse *f*

scruff [skrʌf] *n* (**a**) **by the s. of the neck** par la peau du cou (**b**) *Fam (unkempt person)* **he's a bit of a s.** il n'est pas très soigné

scruffily ['skrʌfɪlɪ] *adv* **to be s. dressed** être dépenaillé(e)

scruffy ['skrʌfɪ] *adj (person)* peu soigné(e); *(clothes)* miteux(euse)

scrum [skrʌm] *n (in rugby)* mêlée *f*; *Fig* bousculade *f*; **s. half** demi *m* de mêlée

scrumptious ['skrʌm(p)ʃəs] *adj Fam* délicieux(euse)

scrunch [skrʌntʃ] **1** *vt (paper)* froisser en boule; *(can, cigarette)* écraser
  2 *vi* crisser

scrunchie ['skrʌntʃɪ] *n (for hair)* chouchou *m*

scruple ['skruːpəl] *n* scrupule *m*; **to have no scruples** n'avoir aucun scrupule

scrupulous ['skruːpjʊləs] *adj* scrupuleux(euse)

scrupulously ['skruːpjʊləslɪ] *adv* scrupuleusement

scrutineer [skruːtɪ'nɪə(r)] *n* scrutateur(trice) *m,f*

scrutinize ['skruːtɪnaɪz] *vt (document, contract)* éplucher; *(votes)* vérifier

scrutiny ['skruːtɪnɪ] *n (of document, votes)* examen *m* minutieux; **to come under s.** être examiné(e)

scuba ['skuːbə] *n* **s. diver** plongeur(euse) *m,f* sous-marin(e); **s. diving** plongée *f* sous-marine

scuff [skʌf] **1** *n* **s. mark** éraflure *f*
  2 *vt (shoe)* érafler

scuffle ['skʌfəl] **1** *n* échauffourée *f*
  2 *vi* se bagarrer

scull [skʌl] **1** *n (oar)* aviron *m*
  2 *vi* ramer

scullery ['skʌlərɪ] *n Br* arrière-cuisine *f*

sculpt [skʌlpt] *vt* sculpter

sculptor ['skʌlptə(r)] *n* sculpteur *m*

sculpture ['skʌlptʃə(r)] **1** *n* sculpture *f*
  2 *vt* sculpter

scum [skʌm] *n* (**a**) *(layer of dirt)* crasse *f*; *(froth)* écume *f* (**b**) *very Fam Pej (person)* ordure *f*; *(people)* racaille *f*; **the s. of the earth** le rebut de la société

scupper ['skʌpə(r)] *vt (ship, project)* couler

scurrilous ['skʌrɪləs] *adj* calomnieux(euse)

scurry ['skʌrɪ] *vi (dash)* courir

▸**scurry away, scurry off** *vi* se sauver

scurvy ['skɜːvɪ] *n Med* scorbut *m*

scuttle¹ ['skʌtəl] **1** *n (coal)* **s.** seau *m* à charbon
  2 *vt (ship, plan)* saborder

scuttle² *vi (run)* courir

▸**scuttle away, scuttle off** *vi* déguerpir

scuzzy ['skʌzɪ] *adj Fam* dégueulasse, cradingue

scythe [saɪð] **1** *n* faux *f*
  2 *vt* faucher

SDLP [esdiːel'piː] *n Br (abbr* **Social Democratic Labour Party**) = parti démocrate d'Irlande du Nord en faveur de la réunification de l'Irlande

SDP [esdiː'piː] *n Br Formerly (abbr* **Social Democratic Party**) parti *m* social-démocrate

SE [es'iː] *n (abbr* **southeast**) SE

SEA [esiː'eɪ] *n (abbr* **Single European Act**) AUE *m*

sea [siː] *n* mer *f*; **by the s.** au bord de la mer; **to go to s.** *(become a sailor)* devenir marin; *Fig* **a s. of people** une marée humaine; **heavy seas** mer démontée; **on the high seas, out at s.** en haute mer; **to find** *or* **get one's s. legs** s'habituer au roulis; *Fig* **to be all at s.** être complètement perdu(e); **s. air** air *m* marin; **s. anemone** anémone *f* de mer; **s. battle** bataille *f* navale; **s. breeze** brise *f* de mer; **s. change** changement *m* radical; *Fam* **(old) s. dog** (vieux) loup *m* de mer; **s. horse** hippocampe *m*; *Naut* **s. lane** couloir *m* maritime; **s. level** niveau *m* de la mer; **s. lion** otarie *f*; **s. salt** sel *m* de mer; **s. urchin** oursin *m*; **s. voyage** voyage *m* en mer

seaboard ['siːbɔːd] *n* côte *f*

seaborne ['siːbɔːn] *adj (trade)* maritime; *(invasion)* naval(e)

seafarer ['siːfeərə(r)] *n* marin *m*

seafaring ['siːfeərɪŋ] *adj (people)* de navigateurs

seafood ['siːfuːd] *n* fruits *mpl* de mer

seafront ['siːfrʌnt] *n* front *m* de mer

seagoing ['siːgəʊɪŋ] *adj (boat)* de mer

seagull ['siːgʌl] *n* mouette *f*

seal¹ [siːl] *n (animal)* phoque *m*

seal² **1** *n* (**a**) *(stamp)* sceau *m*; **to give one's s. of approval to sth** donner son approbation à qch; **to set the s. on sth** *(on alliance, friendship)* sceller qch; *(on victory, defeat)* confirmer qch (**b**) *(device)* joint *m* (d'étanchéité); *(on food container)* = fermeture garantissant la fraîcheur d'un produit
  2 *vt (document, envelope)* cacheter; *(with official seal)* sceller; *(jar)* fermer hermétiquement; *(joint)* assurer l'étanchéité de; **to s. sb's fate** décider du sort de qn; **my lips are sealed** je ne dirai rien

▸**seal in** *vt sep* enfermer

▸**seal off** *vt sep (area)* boucler; *(people)* isoler

sealing wax ['siːlɪŋ'wæks] *n* cire *f* à cacheter

sealskin ['siːlskɪn] *n* peau *f* de phoque

seam [siːm] *n* (**a**) *(of garment)* couture *f*; *(in metalwork)* soudure *f*; **to be coming apart at the seams** *(of clothing)* craquer de partout; *Fig (of plan, organization)* s'effondrer (**b**) *(of coal)* veine *f*

seaman ['siːmən] *n Naut* marin *m*

seamanship ['siːmənʃɪp] *n Naut* qualités *fpl* de navigateur

seamstress ['semstrɪs] *n* couturière *f*

seamy ['siːmɪ] *adj* sordide

seance ['seɪɒns] *n* séance *f* de spiritisme

seaplane ['siːpleɪn] *n* hydravion *m*

seaport ['siːpɔːt] *n* port *m* maritime

sear [sɪə(r)] *vt (skin)* brûler; *Fig* **the image was seared on her memory** l'image était gravée dans sa mémoire

search [sɜːtʃ] **1** *n* recherches *fpl*; *(of building, room)* fouille *f*; **to have a s. for sth** chercher qch; **in s. of** à la recherche de; **to make a s.** faire des recherches; *Comput* **to do a s.** faire une recherche; *Comput* **s. engine** moteur *m* de recherche; **s. party** équipe *f* de secours; *Law* **s. warrant** mandat *m* de perquisition
  2 *vt (person, place)* fouiller; *Comput (file, directory)* rechercher dans; *Fam* **s. me!** je n'en ai pas la moindre idée!
  3 *vi* chercher; **to s. for sth** chercher qch; *Comput* **s. and replace** rechercher et remplacer

searching ['sɜːtʃɪŋ] *adj (examination)* minutieux(-euse); *(look)* pénétrant(e)

searchlight ['sɜːtʃlaɪt] *n* projecteur *m*

searing ['sɪərɪŋ] *adj (pain, heat)* fulgurant(e); *(criticism, indictment)* virulent(e)

seascape ['siːskeɪp] *n Art* marine *f*

seashell ['siːʃel] *n* coquillage *m*

seashore ['siːʃɔː(r)] *n* rivage *m*

seasick ['siːsɪk] *adj* **to be s.** avoir le mal de mer

seasickness ['siːsɪknɪs] *n* mal *m* de mer

seaside ['siːsaɪd] *n* **the s.** le bord de la mer; **at the s.** au bord de la mer; **s. resort** station *f* balnéaire

season¹ ['siːzən] *n* saison *f*; *(of films)* cycle *m*; **S.'s Greetings** meilleurs vœux de fin d'année; **the high s.** *(for tourism)* la haute saison; **cherries are out of s.** ce n'est pas la saison des cerises; **s. ticket** abonnement *m*

season² *vt* (**a**) *(with salt, pepper)* assaisonner; *(with spice)* épicer (**b**) *(wood)* faire sécher

seasonable ['siːzənəbəl] *adj* **s. weather** un temps de saison

seasonal ['siːzənəl] *adj (work, fluctuations)* saisonnier(ère)

seasoned ['siːzənd] *adj* (**a**) *(food)* assaisonné(e); **a highly s. dish** un plat très relevé (**b**) *(wood)* sec (sèche) (**c**) *(person)* expérimenté(e); *(soldier)* aguerri(e)

seasoning ['siːzənɪŋ] *n Culin* assaisonnement *m*

seat [siːt] **1** *n* (**a**) *(chair)* chaise *f*; *(on bus, train, in theatre, cinema)* place *f*, siège *m*; *(in Parliament)* siège *m*; **to take a s.** s'asseoir; **s. belt** ceinture *f* de sécurité (**b**) *(part of chair, toilet)* siège *m*; *(of trousers)* fond *m* (**c**) *(centre) (of government)* siège *m*; **a s. of learning** un haut lieu du savoir; **country s.** *(of aristocrat)* demeure *f* familiale

2 *vt* (**a**) *(cause to sit) (child)* asseoir; *(guests)* faire asseoir; **to be/remain seated** être/rester assis(e); *Formal* **please be seated** veuillez vous asseoir (**b**) *(accommodate)* **the bus seats thirty** il y a trente places assises dans le bus; **this table seats twelve** on tient douze à cette table; **the hall seats two hundred** la salle compte deux cents places

seating ['siːtɪŋ] *n (seats)* sièges *mpl*; *(positioning)* placement *m*; **s. capacity** nombre *m* de places assises; **s. plan** plan *m* de table

SEATO ['siːtəʊ] *n (abbr* **Southeast Asia Treaty Organization)** OTASE *f*

seaway ['siːweɪ] *n* route *f* (maritime)

seaweed ['siːwiːd] *n* algues *fpl*

seaworthy ['siːwɜːðɪ] *adj* en état de naviguer

sebaceous [sɪ'beɪʃəs] *adj* sébacé(e)

sec¹ *(abbr* **second(s))** s.

sec² [sek] *n Fam (second)* **I'll be there in a s.** j'arrive tout de suite; **wait a s.!** attends une seconde!

secateurs [sekə'tɜːz] *npl* sécateur *m*

secede [sɪ'siːd] *vi* faire sécession (**from** de)

secession [sɪ'seʃən] *n* sécession *f*

secluded [sɪ'kluːdɪd] *adj (place)* reculé(e); *(life)* de reclus(e)

seclusion [sɪ'kluːʒən] *n* isolement *m*

second¹ ['sekənd] *n (of time)* seconde *f*; **I won't be a s.** j'en ai pour deux secondes; **s. hand** *(of clock)* trotteuse *f*

second² **1** *n* (**a**) *(in series)* deuxième *mf*, second(e) *m,f*; **Edward the S.** Edward II; **I was s. in the race** je suis arrivé deuxième à la course (**b**) *(of month)* deux *m*; **the s. of May** le deux mai (**c**) *Com* **seconds** articles *mpl* défectueux (**d**) *(in duel)* témoin *m*; *(in boxing)* soigneur *m* (**e**) *Br Univ* **to get a s.** *(in degree)* ≃ avoir sa licence avec mention assez bien (**f**) **s. (gear)** seconde *f* (**g**) *Fam* **anyone for seconds?** *(at meal)* quelqu'un veut du rab?

2 *adj* deuxième, second(e); **twenty-s.** vingt-deuxième; **ninety-s.** quatre-vingt-deuxième; **to be s. to none** être sans égal(e); **s. in command** *Mil* commandant *m* en second; *(in organization)* adjoint(e) *m,f*; **the s. largest city in England** la deuxième ville d'Angleterre; **a s. Picasso/Churchill** un nouveau Picasso/Churchill; **on s. thoughts** tout bien réfléchi; **to have s. thoughts (about sth)** ne plus être très sûr(e) (de qch), *Fig* **to play s. fiddle to sb** être dans l'ombre de qn; **it's s. nature to her** elle le fait automatiquement; **to get one's s. wind** trouver un second souffle; **s.**

chance deuxième chance *f*; **to be in one's s. childhood** être retombé(e) en enfance; **s. class** *(on train)* deuxième classe *f*; *Rel* **the S. Coming** le second avènement; **s. cousin** petit(e) cousin(e) *m,f*; **s. floor** *Br* deuxième étage *m*, *Am* premier étage *m*; **s. language** seconde langue *f*; **s. name** nom *m* de famille; *Law* **s. offence** récidive *f*; **s. opinion** deuxième avis *m*; *Gram* **s. person** deuxième personne *f*; **s. sight** don *m* de double vue; **s. violin** second violon *m*; **the S. World War** la Seconde Guerre mondiale

second³ *vt (motion)* appuyer

second⁴ [sɪ'kɒnd] *vt (officer, employee)* détacher (**from/to** de/à)

secondary ['sekəndərɪ] *adj* secondaire; **s. school** établissement *m* secondaire, *Can & Suisse* école *f* secondaire

second-best ['sekənd'best] **1** *n* pis-aller *m*; **to be content with s.** se contenter d'un pis-aller

2 *adv* **to come off s.** être battu(e)

second-class ['sekənd'klɑːs] **1** *adj (ticket, carriage)* de deuxième classe; **s. citizen** citoyen(enne) *m,f* de second rang; *Br Univ* **s. degree** licence *f* avec mention assez bien; **s. mail** courrier *m* au tarif lent

2 *adv* **to travel s.** voyager en seconde classe

Second-class mail

Le tarif postal réduit est utilisé en Grande-Bretagne pour les lettres et les paquets non urgents. Aux États-Unis, il est réservé aux magazines et aux journaux.

---

seconder ['sekəndə(r)] *n* = personne qui appuie une motion

second-guess ['sekənd'ges] *vt* **to s. sb** anticiper ce que qn va faire

second-hand ['sekənd'hænd] **1** *adj (car, clothes)* d'occasion; **s. shop** magasin *m* d'articles d'occasion

2 *adv (buy)* d'occasion; **to hear news s.** avoir des nouvelles de seconde main

secondly ['sekəndlɪ] *adv* deuxièmement

secondment [sɪ'kɒndmənt] *n* **to be on s.** être en détachement

second-rate ['sekəndreɪt] *adj* médiocre

secrecy ['siːkrɪsɪ] *n* secret *m*; **in s.** en secret; **to swear sb to s.** faire jurer le silence à qn

secret ['siːkrɪt] **1** *n* secret *m*; **to do sth in s.** faire qch secrètement; **I make no s. of it** je ne m'en cache pas; **it's no s.** tout le monde le sait

2 *adj* secret(ète); **to keep sth s. from sb** cacher qch à qn; **s. agent** agent *m* secret; **s. police** police *f* secrète; **the S. Service** = service de sécurité du président américain; *also Fig* **s. weapon** arme *f* secrète

secretarial [sekrə'teərɪəl] *adj (work)* administratif(-ive); *(job, college, course)* de secrétariat

secretariat [sekrə'teərɪət] *n* secrétariat *m*

secretary ['sekrətərɪ] *n* (**a**) *(in office)* secrétaire *mf* (**b**) *Br Pol* ministre *m*

secretary-general ['sekrətərɪ'dʒenərəl] *n Pol* secrétaire *m* général

secrete [sɪ'kriːt] *vt* (**a**) *(discharge)* sécréter (**b**) *(hide)* cacher

secretion [sɪ'kriːʃən] *n* sécrétion *f*

secretive ['siːkrɪtɪv] *adj* secret(ète); **to be s. about sth** faire des cachotteries à propos de qch

secretly ['siːkrɪtlɪ] *adv* secrètement

sect [sekt] *n* secte *f*

sectarian [sek'teərɪən] *adj* sectaire

sectarianism [sek'teərɪənɪzəm] *n* sectarisme *m*

section ['sekʃən] **1** *n* (**a**) *(in general)* partie *f*; *(of road, railway)* tronçon *m*; *(of machine)* élément *m*; *(of organization)* département *m*; *(in orchestra)* section *f*; *(of law, treaty)* article *m*; **all sections of society** toutes les catégories sociales (**b**) *(of soldiers)* section *f* (**c**) *(cross-section)* coupe *f*
 2 *vt (cut)* sectionner

sector ['sektə(r)] *n* secteur *m*

secular ['sekjʊlə(r)] *adj (history, art)* laïque; *(music)* profane

secure [sɪ'kjʊə(r)] **1** *adj* (**a**) *(free from anxiety)* en sécurité; **s. in the knowledge that...** ayant l'assurance que... (**b**) *(investment, place)* sûr(e); *(foothold)* ferme; *(nomination, future)* assuré(e); *(load, rope)* bien attaché(e); *(foundations, lock)* solide
 2 *vt* (**a**) *(make safe) (position, future)* assurer (**b**) *(fasten) (load)* bien amarrer; *(door, window)* bien fermer (**c**) *(obtain) (support, promise, loan)* obtenir

securely [sɪ'kjʊəlɪ] *adv* (**a**) *(stored, hidden)* en toute sécurité; *(protected)* bien (**b**) *(firmly)* solidement; **the door was s. fastened** la porte était bien fermée

security [sɪ'kjʊərɪtɪ] *n* (**a**) *(stability, safety)* sécurité *f*; **s. of tenure** sécurité de l'emploi; **the S. Council** le Conseil de sécurité; **s. forces** forces *fpl* de sécurité; **s. guard** garde *m*; **s. officer** agent *m* de sécurité; **to be a s. risk** être un danger pour la sécurité (**b**) *Fin (for loan)* garantie *f* (**c**) *Fin* **securities** titres *mpl*

sedan [sɪ'dæn] *n* (**a**) *Am (car)* berline *f* (**b**) **s. chair** chaise *f* à porteurs

sedate [sɪ'deɪt] **1** *adj* tranquille
 2 *vt* donner des calmants à

sedately [sɪ'deɪtlɪ] *adv* tranquillement

sedation [sɪ'deɪʃən] *n* **under s.** sous calmants

sedative ['sedətɪv] *n* sédatif *m*, calmant *m*

sedentary ['sedəntrɪ] *adj* sédentaire

sediment ['sedɪmənt] *n* sédiment *m*

sedition [sɪ'dɪʃən] *n* sédition *f*

seditious [sɪ'dɪʃəs] *adj* séditieux(euse)

seduce [sɪ'djuːs] *vt (sexually)* séduire; *Fig* **to s. sb into doing sth** persuader qn de faire qch

seducer [sɪ'djuːsə(r)] *n* séducteur(trice) *m,f*

seduction [sɪ'dʌkʃən] *n* séduction *f*

seductive [sɪ'dʌktɪv] *adj (look)* séducteur(trice); *(argument, offer)* séduisant(e)

see¹ [siː] *n Rel* évêché *m*

see² (*pt* **saw** [sɔː], *pp* **seen** [siːn]) **1** *vt* (**a**) *(with eyes, perceive)* voir; **now s. what you've done!** regarde ce que tu as fait!; **s. page 50** voir page 50; **to be seeing things** *(hallucinate)* avoir des visions; **it has to be seen to be believed** il faut le voir pour le croire; **to s. sb do** *or* **doing sth** voir qn faire qch; **I can't s. a way out of this problem** je ne vois pas comment on peut s'en sortir; **could you s. your way to lending me your car?** cela te serait-il possible de me prêter ta voiture?; **to s. sense** *or* **reason** entendre raison; **the city has seen many changes** la ville a connu de grands changements; **I don't know what you s. in her** je ne vois pas ce que tu lui trouves; **it remains to be seen whether...** reste à savoir si...; **I'll s. what I can do** je vais voir ce que je peux faire
 (**b**) *(understand)* voir; **I s. what you mean** je vois ce que tu veux dire; **I don't s. the point** je n'en vois pas l'intérêt

(**c**) *(envisage, imagine)* imaginer, voir; **what do you s. happening next?** à ton avis, qu'est-ce qui va se passer maintenant?; **I can't s. them arriving before six** ça m'étonnerait qu'ils arrivent avant six heures; **I can't s. you as a boxer** je ne t'imagine pas boxeur
 (**d**) *(make sure)* **I shall s. that he comes** je ferai en sorte qu'il vienne; **s. that this doesn't happen again!** fais en sorte que ça ne se reproduise pas!
 (**e**) *(meet) (person, doctor, solicitor)* voir; **I'm seeing Bill tomorrow** je vois Bill demain; **s. you (soon)!** à bientôt!
 (**f**) *(accompany)* **to s. sb home** accompagner qn chez lui; **to s. sb to the door** accompagner qn jusqu'à la porte
 2 *vi* (**a**) *(with eyes)* voir; **s. for yourself** à toi de juger; **we shall s.** nous verrons bien
 (**b**) *(understand)* comprendre; **ah, I s.!** ah, je vois!
 (**c**) *(consider)* **let me s.!**, **let's s.!** voyons!; **have you got a free room? – let me s.** avez-vous une chambre libre? – voyons voir
 (**d**) *(find out)* **I'll go and s.** je vais voir

▸**see about** *vt insep* (**a**) *(deal with)* s'occuper de (**b**) *(consider)* voir; *Fam* **we'll (soon) s. about that!** c'est ce qu'on va voir!

▸**see in** *vt sep* **to s. the New Year in** fêter le Nouvel An

▸**see off** *vt sep* (**a**) *(say goodbye to)* dire au revoir à (**b**) *(attacker)* faire fuir

▸**see out** *vt sep* accompagner jusqu'à la porte; **I'll s. myself out** inutile de me raccompagner

▸**see through 1** *vt sep (project, policy)* mener à bien
 2 *vt insep (person, lie, plan)* percer à jour

▸**see to** *vt insep (deal with)* s'occuper de; **to get sth seen to** *(machine, roof)* faire réparer qch; *(wound, injury)* faire examiner qch; **I'll s. to it that you're not disturbed** je ferai en sorte que tu ne sois pas dérangé

seed [siːd] **1** *n* (**a**) *(for sowing)* graine *f*; *(of fruit)* pépin *m*; **to go** *or* **run to s.** *(of plant)* monter en graine; **s. corn** blé *m* de semence; *Fig* capital *m* initial; **s. merchant** grainetier(ère) *m,f*; **s. potatoes** pommes *fpl* de terre de semence (**b**) *Sport (in tournament)* tête *f* de série (**c**) *Lit (semen)* semence *f*
 2 *vt* (**a**) *(remove seeds from)* épépiner (**b**) *(lawn)* ensemencer (**c**) *(in tournament)* **seeded players** joueurs *mpl* classés tête de série
 3 *vi (of plant)* monter en graine

seedless ['siːdlɪs] *adj* sans pépins

seedling ['siːdlɪŋ] *n* plant *m*

seedy ['siːdɪ] *adj* (**a**) *(shabby) (person, hotel, area)* miteux(euse) (**b**) *Fam (unwell)* mal fichu(e)

seeing ['siːɪŋ] **1** *conj* **s. (that** *or* **how)...** étant donné que...
 2 s. **is believing** voir c'est croire

seek [siːk] *(pt & pp* **sought** [sɔːt] *) vt* (**a**) *(look for) (thing lost, job)* chercher; *(someone's friendship, promotion)* essayer d'obtenir (**b**) *(request)* **to s. sth from sb** demander qch à qn; **to s. sb's advice** demander conseil à qn (**c**) *(try)* **to s. to do sth** essayer de faire qch

▸**seek after** *vt insep* **to be much sought after** être très recherché(e)

▸**seek out** *vt sep (person)* dénicher

seem [siːm] *vi* sembler; **to s. tired** avoir l'air fatigué(e); **do what seems best** fais au mieux; **it seemed like a dream** j'avais l'impression de rêver; **I s. to have heard her name somewhere** il me semble avoir entendu son nom quelque part; **I can't s. to get it right** je n'y arrive pas; **it seems (that)..., it would s. that...** il semble que...+ *subjunctive*; **it seems to me that...** il me semble que...; **it seems** *or* **would s. so** il paraît; **it seems** *or* **would s. not** il paraît que non

seeming ['si:mɪŋ] *adj* apparent(e)

seemingly ['si:mɪŋlɪ] *adv* apparemment

seemly ['si:mlɪ] *adj Formal* bienséant(e)

seen [si:n] *pp of* **see²**

seep [si:p] *vi* suinter; **to s. into sth** s'infiltrer dans qch

seepage ['si:pɪdʒ] *n (oozing)* suintement *m*; *(into surface)* infiltration *f*

seer [sɪə(r)] *n Lit* voyant(e) *m,f*

seesaw ['si:sɔ:] **1** *n* tapecul *m*
  2 *vi Fig (of prices)* être en dents de scie

seethe [si:ð] *vi (of liquid)* bouillonner; *(of street)* grouiller (**with** de); **to be seething (with anger)** bouillir (de rage)

see-through ['si:θru:] *adj* transparent(e)

segment 1 *n* ['segmənt] segment *m*; *(of orange)* quartier *m*
  2 *vt* [seg'ment] *(orange)* couper en quartiers; *(line)* segmenter

segmentation [segmen'teɪʃən] *n Econ* segmentation *f*

segregate ['segrɪgeɪt] *vt* séparer (**from** de); *(prisoner)* isoler (**from** de)

segregation [segrɪ'geɪʃən] *n* ségrégation *f*; *(of prisoner)* isolement *m*

Seine [seɪn] *n* **the S.** la Seine

seismic ['saɪzmɪk] *adj* sismique

seismograph ['saɪzməgru:f] *n* sismographe *m*

seismology [saɪz'mɒlədʒɪ] *n* sismologie *f*

seize [si:z] *vt* (**a**) *(grab) & Fig (opportunity)* saisir; **to s. hold of** saisir (**b**) *(city, territory)* s'emparer de; *(drugs, stolen goods)* saisir

►**seize on, seize upon** *vt insep* sauter sur

►**seize up** *vi (of engine, back)* se bloquer

seizure ['si:ʒə(r)] *n* (**a**) *(of land, city)* prise *f*; *Law (of property, drugs)* saisie *f* (**b**) *Med* crise *f*

seldom ['seldəm] *adv* rarement; **s. have I seen such courage** j'ai rarement vu un tel courage

select [sɪ'lekt] **1** *adj (exclusive)* sélect(e); **a s. few** quelques privilégiés(ées); *Br Parl* **s. committee** commission *f* d'enquête
  2 *vt* sélectionner

selected [sɪ'lektɪd] *adj* choisi(e)

selection [sɪ'lekʃən] *n* sélection *f*, choix *m*; **to make a s.** faire un choix; **a wide s.** un grand choix

selective [sɪ'lektɪv] *adj* sélectif(ive)

selector [sɪ'lektə(r)] *n (of team)* sélectionneur(euse) *m,f*

self [self] *(pl* **selves** [selvz] *) n* (**a**) **he's quite his old s. again** il est redevenu comme avant; **she was her usual cheerful s.** comme à son habitude, elle était gaie (**b**) *Psy* **the s.** le moi

self-addressed envelope ['selfə'drest'envələʊp] *n* enveloppe *f* libellée à ses nom et adresse

self-appointed ['selfə'pɔɪntɪd] *adj* **he's the s. spokesman** il s'est proclamé porte-parole

self-assessment ['selfə'sesmənt] *n* (**a**) *(of person)* auto-évaluation *f* (**b**) *Br (for taxes)* = système de déclaration des revenus pour le paiement des impôts, par opposition au prélèvement à la source

self-assured ['selfə'ʃʊəd] *adj* plein(e) d'assurance

self-catering ['self'keɪtərɪŋ] *adj (holiday)* en appartement meublé; *(accommodation)* meublé(e)

self-centred ['self'sentəd] *adj* égocentrique

self-confessed ['selfkən'fest] *adj* **he's a s. liar/cheat** il est menteur/tricheur de son propre aveu

self-confidence ['self'kɒnfɪdəns] *n* confiance *f* en soi

self-confident ['self'kɒnfɪdənt] *adj* plein(e) d'assurance

self-conscious ['self'kɒnʃəs] *adj* timide, gêné(e)

self-contained ['selfkən'teɪnd] *adj (person)* réservé(e); *(apartment)* indépendant(e)

self-contradictory ['selfkɒntrə'dɪktərɪ] *adj* qui contient des contradictions

self-control ['selfkən'trəʊl] *n* maîtrise *f* de soi

self-deception ['selfdɪ'sepʃən] *n* aveuglement *m*

self-defeating ['selfdɪ'fi:tɪŋ] *adj* qui va à l'encontre du but recherché

self-defence, *Am* **self-defense** ['selfdɪ'fens] *n* autodéfense *f*; *Law* légitime défense *f*; **in s.** en état de légitime défense

self-denial ['selfdɪ'naɪəl] *n* abnégation *f*

self-destruct ['selfdɪ'strʌkt] *vi* s'autodétruire

self-determination ['selfdɪtɜ:mɪ'neɪʃən] *n* autodétermination *f*

self-discipline ['self'dɪsɪplɪn] *n* autodiscipline *f*

self-doubt ['self'daʊt] *n* manque *m* de confiance en soi

self-effacing ['selfɪ'feɪsɪŋ] *adj* effacé(e)

self-employed ['selfɪm'plɔɪd] *adj* indépendant(e)

self-esteem [selfə'sti:m] *n* confiance *f* en soi

self-evident ['self'evɪdənt] *adj* évident(e)

self-explanatory ['selfɪk'splænətərɪ] *adj* **to be s.** se passer d'explications

self-expression ['selfɪk'spreʃən] *n* expression *f* individuelle

self-government ['self'gʌvənmənt] *n* autonomie *f*

self-help ['self'help] *n* **s. group** groupe *m* d'entraide

self-important ['selfɪm'pɔ:tənt] *adj* suffisant(e)

self-indulgent ['selfɪn'dʌldʒənt] *adj (person)* qui ne se refuse rien; *(book, film)* complaisant(e)

self-inflicted ['selfɪn'flɪktɪd] *adj* que l'on s'inflige à soi-même

self-interest ['self'ɪntərest] *n* intérêt *m* personnel

selfish ['selfɪʃ] *adj* égoïste

selfishness ['selfɪʃnɪs] *n* égoïsme *m*

self-knowledge ['self'nɒlɪdʒ] *n* connaissance *f* de soi

selfless ['selflɪs] *adj* désintéressé(e)

self-made man ['selfmeɪd'mæn] *n* self-made-man *m*

self-pity ['self'pɪtɪ] *n* apitoiement *m* sur son propre sort; **to be full of s.** s'apitoyer sur son sort

self-portrait ['self'pɔ:treɪt] *n* autoportrait *m*

self-possessed ['selfpə'zest] *adj* qui a une grande maîtrise de soi

self-preservation ['selfprezə'veɪʃən] *n* **instinct for s.** instinct *m* de conservation

self-raising flour ['selfreɪzɪŋ'flaʊə(r)], *Am* **self-rising flour** ['selfraɪzɪŋ'flaʊə(r)] *n* = farine contenant de la levure chimique

self-reliant ['selfrɪ'laɪənt] *adj* indépendant(e)

self-respect ['selfrɪ'spekt] *n* amour-propre *m*

self-respecting ['selfrɪ'spektɪŋ] *adj* qui se respecte

self-restraint ['selfrɪs'treɪnt] *n* retenue *f*, maîtrise *f* de soi

self-righteous ['self'raɪtʃəs] *adj* suffisant(e)

self-rising flour ['selfraɪzɪŋ'flaʊə(r)] *Am* = **self-raising flour**

selfsame ['selfseɪm] *adj* **the s. day** le même jour exactement; **the s. thing** la même chose exactement

self-satisfied ['self'sætɪsfaɪd] *adj* suffisant(e), content(e) de soi

self-service ['self'sɜːvɪs] **1** *n* self-service *m*
   2 *adj* self-service

self-starter ['self'stɑːtə(r)] *n* (*person*) personne *f* très motivée

self-styled ['selfstaɪld] *adj* prétendu(e), soi-disant *inv*

self-sufficient ['selfsə'fɪʃənt] *adj* (*person*) indépendant(e); (*country*) auto-suffisant(e)

self-taught ['self'tɔːt] *adj* autodidacte

sell [sel] (*pt & pp* **sold** [səʊld]) **1** *vt* vendre; **to s. sb sth, to s. sth to sb** vendre qch à qn; **scandal sells newspapers** le scandale fait vendre les journaux; *Fig* **to s. oneself** (*present oneself*) se vendre; *Fig* **to s. sb an idea** faire accepter une idée à qn; *Fig* **to s. sb down the river** trahir qn
   2 *vi* (*of product*) se vendre; (*of person*) vendre; **to s. like hot cakes** se vendre comme des petits pains

▸**sell off** *vt sep* (*at reduced prices*) solder; (*clear*) liquider; (*privatize*) privatiser

▸**sell out 1** *vt sep* (**a**) **to be sold out** (*of book, item*) être épuisé(e); (*of show, concert*) afficher complet; **the tickets are sold out** il n'y a plus de billets (**b**) (*betray*) trahir, vendre
   2 *vi* (**a**) **to s. out of sth** ne plus avoir de qch (**b**) (*betray beliefs*) renier ses principes

▸**sell up** *vi* (*sell home, business*) tout vendre

sell-by date ['selbaɪdeɪt] *n* date *f* limite de vente; *Fig* **to be past one's s.** avoir fait son temps

seller ['selə(r)] *n* vendeur(euse) *m,f*; *Econ* **s.'s market** marché *m* favorable au vendeur

selling ['selɪŋ] *n* vente *f*; **s. point** atout *m*; **s. price** prix *m* de vente

sell-off ['selɒf] *n* (*of state-owned company*) vente *f*

Sellotape® ['seləteɪp] *n* Scotch® *m*

sellotape ['seləteɪp] *vt* scotcher

sellout ['selaʊt] *n* (**a**) **the play was a s.** il n'y avait plus de places pour cette pièce, la pièce a joué à guichets fermés (**b**) (*betrayal*) trahison *f*

semantic [sɪ'mæntɪk] *adj* sémantique

semantics [sɪ'mæntɪks] *n* sémantique *f*

semaphore ['seməfɔː(r)] *n* signaux *mpl* à bras

semblance ['sembləns] *n* semblant *m*

semen ['siːmən] *n* sperme *m*

semester [sɪ'mestə(r)] *n* semestre *m*

semi ['semɪ] *n Br Fam* (*semi-detached house*) maison *f* jumelée

semiautomatic ['semɪɔːtə'mætɪk] *adj* semi-automatique

semicircle ['semɪsɜːkəl] *n* demi-cercle *m*

semicircular ['semɪ'sɜːkjʊlə(r)] *adj* semi-circulaire, en demi-cercle

semicolon ['semɪkəʊlən] *n* point-virgule *m*

semiconductor ['semɪkən'dʌktə(r)] *n Elec* semi-conducteur *m*

semiconscious ['semɪ'kɒnʃəs] *adj* à demi conscient(e)

semidetached ['semɪdɪ'tætʃt] **1** *n* maison *f* jumelée
   2 *adj* jumelé(e)

semifinal ['semɪ'faɪnəl] *n* demi-finale *f*

semifinalist ['semɪ'faɪnəlɪst] *n* demi-finaliste *mf*

seminal ['semɪnəl] *adj* majeur(e), de première importance

seminar ['semɪnɑː(r)] *n* séminaire *m*

semi-precious ['semɪ'preʃəs] *adj* semi-précieux(-euse)

semiquaver ['semɪkweɪvə(r)] *n Mus* double croche *f*

semi-skimmed [semɪ'skɪmd] *adj* (*milk*) demi-écrémé(e)

Semite ['semaɪt] *n* Sémite *mf*

Semitic [sɪ'mɪtɪk] *adj* (*language*) sémitique; (*people*) sémite

semitone ['semɪtəʊn] *n Mus* demi-ton *m*

semitropical ['semɪ'trɒpɪkəl] *adj* semi-tropical(e)

semolina [semə'liːnə] *n* semoule *f*

Senate ['senɪt] *n* **the S.** le Sénat

> **Senate**
>
> Le Sénat constitue, avec la Chambre des représentants, l'organe législatif américain; composé de 100 membres (deux par État), il détient l'exclusivité du droit d'impeachment.

senator ['senətə(r)] *n* sénateur *m*

send [send] (*pt & pp* **sent** [sent]) *vt* (*letter, message, person*) envoyer; **to s. sb sth, to s. sth to sb** envoyer qch à qn; **to s. sb home** renvoyer qn chez soi; **to s. sb to prison** envoyer qn en prison; **to s. sb on an errand** envoyer qn faire une course; *Fig* **to s. sb/sth flying** envoyer qn/qch valser; **to s. sb into fits of laughter** faire rire qn aux larmes

▸**send away 1** *vt sep* (*person*) renvoyer
   2 *vi* **to s. away for sth** se faire envoyer qch

▸**send back** *vt sep* renvoyer

▸**send down** *vt sep Br* (**a**) (*expel from university*) renvoyer (**b**) *Fam* (*send to prison*) mettre en taule (**for** pour)

▸**send for** *vt insep* (*help, supplies*) envoyer chercher; (*doctor*) faire venir

▸**send in** *vt sep* envoyer

▸**send off 1** *vt sep* (**a**) (*letter, order*) expédier, envoyer (**b**) (*player*) expulser
   2 *vi* **to s. off for sth** se faire envoyer qch

▸**send on** *vt sep* (*ahead*) expédier; (*later*) faire suivre

▸**send out 1** *vt sep* envoyer
   2 *vi* **to s. out for sth** envoyer chercher qch

▸**send up** *vt sep Br Fam* (*parody*) se moquer de

sender ['sendə(r)] *n* expéditeur(trice) *m,f*

send-off ['sendɒf] *n Fam* **to give sb a good s.** faire des adieux en règle à qn

send-up ['sendʌp] *n Br Fam* parodie *f*, pastiche *m*

Senegal [senɪ'gɔːl] *n* le Sénégal

Senegalese [senɪgə'liːz] **1** *n* (*person*) Sénégalais(e) *m,f*
   2 *adj* sénégalais(e)

senile ['siːnaɪl] *adj* sénile; **s. dementia** démence *f* sénile

senility [sɪ'nɪlɪtɪ] *n* sénilité *f*

senior ['siːnjə(r)] **1** *n* (**a**) (*in age*) **to be sb's s.** être l'aîné(e) de qn; **she's three years his s.** elle est son aînée de trois ans (**b**) (*in rank*) supérieur(e) *m,f*
   2 *adj* (**a**) (*in age*) aîné(e); **Thomas Smith, S.** Thomas Smith père; **he's two years s. to me** il a deux ans de plus que moi; **s. citizen** personne *f* du troisième âge (**b**) (*in rank, position*) supérieur(e); **(the) s. management** la direction; **s. officer** officier *m* supérieur; **s. partner** (*in company*) associé(e) *m,f* principal(e)

seniority [siːnɪ'ɒrɪtɪ] *n* (*in age, length of service*) ancienneté *f*; (*in rank*) supériorité *f*

sensation [sen'seɪʃən] n (**a**) *(feeling)* sensation f; **a tingling/burning s.** une sensation de picotement/brûlure (**b**) *(excitement)* **to cause a s.** faire sensation
sensational [sen'seɪʃənəl] adj sensationnel(elle)
sensationalism [sen'seɪʃənəlɪzəm] n sensationnalisme m
sense [sens] **1** n (**a**) *(faculty)* sens m; **to come to one's senses** *(recover consciousness)* revenir à soi; *(see reason)* revenir à la raison; **s. of direction** sens de l'orientation; **s. of duty** sens du devoir; **s. of hearing** ouïe f; **s. of humour** sens de l'humour
(**b**) *(rationality)* bon sens m, intelligence f; **there's no s. in staying/leaving** ça ne sert à rien de rester/partir (**c**) *(feeling)* sentiment m; **to lose all s. of time/reality** perdre toute notion du temps/de la réalité; **a s. of achievement** un sentiment de satisfaction (**d**) *(meaning)* sens m, signification f; **to make s.** être logique; **to make no s.** n'avoir aucun sens; **to make s. of sth** comprendre qch; **in a s.** dans un sens
2 vt *(perceive)* sentir, deviner; **to s. that** sentir que
senseless ['senslɪs] adj (**a**) *(unconscious)* sans connaissance (**b**) *(pointless)* absurde
sensibilities [sensɪ'bɪlɪtɪz] npl susceptibilité f
sensible ['sensɪbəl] adj (**a**) *(rational)* sensé(e) (**b**) *(practical)* pratique (**c**) *Formal (aware)* **to be s. of sth** être sensible à qch
sensibly ['sensɪblɪ] adv *(rationally)* raisonnablement
sensitive ['sensɪtɪv] adj (**a**) *(person)* sensible (**to** à) (**b**) *(subject, issue)* délicat(e); *(document, information)* confidentiel(elle)
sensor ['sensə(r)] n détecteur m
sensory ['sensərɪ] adj sensoriel(elle); **s. organs** organes mpl sensoriels
sensual ['sensjʊəl] adj sensuel(elle)
sensuality [sensjʊ'ælɪtɪ] n sensualité f
sensuous ['sensjʊəs] adj sensuel(elle)
sent [sent] pt & pp of **send**
sentence ['sentəns] **1** n (**a**) *(phrase)* phrase f (**b**) *(in prison)* peine f; **to pass s.** prononcer la sentence
2 vt *(criminal)* condamner (**to** à)
sententious [sen'tenʃəs] adj *Formal* sentencieux(-euse)
sentient ['sentɪənt] adj sensible
sentiment ['sentɪmənt] n (**a**) *(opinion)* sentiment m; **my sentiments exactly** je suis tout à fait du même avis (**b**) *(sentimentality)* sentimentalité f
sentimental [sentɪ'mentəl] adj sentimental(e); **to have s. value** avoir une valeur sentimentale
sentimentality [sentɪmen'tælɪtɪ] n sentimentalité f, sensiblerie f
sentry ['sentrɪ] n sentinelle f; **to be on s. duty** être de garde; **s. box** guérite f
Seoul [səʊl] n Séoul
Sep *(abbr* **September**) septembre
separable ['sepərəbəl] adj séparable
separate 1 adj ['sepərət] *(parts)* séparé(e), distinct(e); *(box, room, document)* à part; *(occasion, attempt, entrance)* différent(e); *(organization)* indépendant(e); **fish and meat should be kept s.** le poisson et la viande doivent être gardés séparément; **he was kept s. from the others** on le tenait à l'écart *ou* on l'isolait des autres; **to lead s. lives** avoir chacun sa vie; *also Fig* **they went their s. ways** ils sont partis chacun de leur côté; *Can* **s. school** ≃ école f libre
2 vt ['sepəreɪt] séparer (**from** de)
3 vi ['sepəreɪt] se séparer (**from** de)

separation [sepə'reɪʃən] n séparation f
separatist ['sepərətɪst] n Pol séparatiste mf
sepia ['siːpɪə] n sépia f
sepsis ['sepsɪs] n infection f
Sept *(abbr* **September**) septembre
September [sep'tembə(r)] n septembre m; *see also* **May**
septet [sep'tet] n septuor m
septic ['septɪk] adj septique; **to go s.** s'infecter; **s. tank** fosse f septique
septicaemia, *Am* **septicemia** [septɪ'siːmɪə] n septicémie f
sepulchre, *Am* **sepulcher** ['sepəlkə(r)] n *Formal* sépulcre m
sequel ['siːkwəl] n (**a**) *(book, film)* suite f (**to** de) (**b**) *(result)* conséquence f (**to** de)
sequence ['siːkwəns] n (**a**) *(order)* ordre m, suite f; **in s.** par ordre; **out of s.** dans le désordre (**b**) *(of numbers, events)* suite f, série f; *(in film)* séquence f
sequencing ['siːkwənsɪŋ] n Biol & Chem séquençage m
sequential [sɪ'kwenʃəl] adj séquentiel(elle)
sequestrate [sɪ'kwestreɪt] vt Law séquestrer
sequestration [siːkwe'streɪʃən] n Law mise f sous séquestre
sequin ['siːkwɪn] n paillette f
sequoia [se'kwɔɪə] n séquoia m
Serbia ['sɜːbɪə] n la Serbie
Serb ['sɜːb], **Serbian** ['sɜːbɪən] **1** n Serbe mf
2 adj serbe
Serbo-Croat ['sɜːbəʊ'krəʊæt] **1** n serbo-croate m
2 adj serbo-croate
serenade [serə'neɪd] **1** n sérénade f
2 vt chanter une sérénade à
serene [sɪ'riːn] adj serein(e)
serenity [sɪ'renɪtɪ] n sérénité f
serf [sɜːf] n Hist serf (serve) m,f
serfdom ['sɜːfdəm] n Hist servage m
serge [sɜːdʒ] n serge f
sergeant ['sɑːdʒənt] n *(in police)* brigadier m; *Mil* sergent m
sergeant-major ['sɑːdʒənt'meɪdʒə(r)] n sergent-major m
serial ['sɪərɪəl] **1** n *(in magazine)* roman-feuilleton m; *(on TV)* feuilleton m
2 adj d'une série, en série; **s. killer** tueur(euse) m,f en série; **s. number** numéro m de série
serialize ['sɪərɪəlaɪz] vt *(in magazine)* publier en feuilleton; *(on TV)* adapter en feuilleton
series ['sɪəriːz] *(pl* **series**) n série f
serious ['sɪərɪəs] adj *(person)* sérieux(euse); *(situation, problem, injury)* grave; **to be s. about doing sth** envisager sérieusement de faire qch; **are you s.?** tu parles sérieusement?; *Fam* **s. money** un bon paquet d'argent
seriously ['sɪərɪəslɪ] adv (**a**) *(in earnest)* sérieusement; **to take sb/sth s.** prendre qn/qch au sérieux; **to take oneself too s.** se prendre trop au sérieux; **you can't s. expect...** sérieusement, vous ne pensez pas que... (**b**) *(gravely, critically)* gravement
sermon ['sɜːmən] n *also Fig* sermon m
serotonin [serə'təʊnɪn] n sérotonine f
serpent ['sɜːpənt] n *Lit* serpent m
serpentine ['sɜːpəntaɪn] adj *Lit* qui serpente, sinueux(euse)

SERPS [sɜːps] *n Br Fin (abbr* **State Earnings Related Pension Scheme**) = retraite versée par l'État, calculée sur le salaire

serrated [se'reɪtɪd] *adj* en dents de scie

serum ['sɪərəm] *n* sérum *m*

servant ['sɜːvənt] *n* domestique *mf*

serve [sɜːv] **1** *vt* (**a**) *(country, cause)* servir; **to s. one's own interests** servir ses propres intérêts
(**b**) *(be useful to)* servir à, être utile à; **to s. a purpose** avoir une utilité; **it doesn't s. my purpose** cela ne me sert à rien; **it has served me well** ça m'a fait de l'usage; **if my memory serves me right** si ma mémoire est bonne
(**c**) *(prison sentence)* purger; *(apprenticeship)* faire
(**d**) *(meal, customer, drink)* servir; **s. chilled** *(on wine)* servir frais; **serves four** *(on packet, in recipe)* pour quatre personnes
(**e**) *Law* **to s. sb with a summons** remettre une assignation à qn
(**f**) (it) **serves her right!** bien fait pour elle!
2 *vi* servir; **to s. as** *(be used as)* servir de
3 *n (in tennis)* service *m*; **(it's) your s.!** à toi de servir!

▸**serve up** *vt sep* servir

server ['sɜːvə(r)] *n* (**a**) *(in tennis)* serveur(euse) *m,f* (**b**) *Comput* serveur *m*

service ['sɜːvɪs] **1** *n* (**a**) *(with army, firm)* service *m*; *Mil* **the services** les forces *fpl* armées; **to do sb a s.** rendre un service à qn; **to be at sb's s.** être au service de qn; **to be of s. to sb** être utile à qn; **to offer one's services** offrir ses services; *Comput* **s. provider** *(for Internet)* fournisseur *m* d'accès
(**b**) *(in shop, restaurant)* service *m*; **s. included/not included** service compris/non compris; **s. charge** service; **s. industry** industrie *f* de services; *Br* **s. lift** ascenseur *m* de service
(**c**) *(system)* **postal/air/train s.** service *m* postal/aérien/des trains
(**d**) *(maintenance) (of machine)* entretien *m*; *(of car)* révision *f*; **s. area** *(on motorway)* aire *f* de service; **s. station** *(on motorway)* station-service *f*
(**e**) *(in church)* service *m*, office *m*
(**f**) *(in tennis)* service *m*; **s. line** ligne *f* de service
(**g**) *Old-fashioned* **to be in/go into s.** *(of servant)* être/devenir domestique
2 *vt (machine)* entretenir; *(car)* réviser

serviceable ['sɜːvɪsəbəl] *adj* (**a**) *(in working order)* en état de marche (**b**) *(durable)* résistant(e)

serviceman ['sɜːvɪsmən] *n* militaire *m*

servicewoman ['sɜːvɪswʊmən] *n* femme *f* soldat

serviette [sɜːvɪ'et] *n Br* serviette *f* (de table)

servile ['sɜːvaɪl] *adj* servile, obséquieux(euse)

serving ['sɜːvɪŋ] *n (portion)* portion *f*; **s. hatch** passe-plat *m*

servitude ['sɜːvɪtjuːd] *n* servitude *f*, asservissement *m*

servo ['sɜːvəʊ] **1** *n (pl* **servos)** *Fam (servomechanism)* servomécanisme *m*
2 *adj* **s. brake** servofrein *m*

sesame ['sesəmɪ] *n* (**a**) **s. oil** huile *f* de sésame; **s. seeds** graines *fpl* de sésame (**b**) **open s.!** sésame, ouvre-toi!

session ['seʃən] *n* (**a**) *(period of activity)* séance *f*, session *f* (**b**) *(meeting)* séance *f*; **to be in s.** siéger (**c**) *(university, school term)* trimestre *m*; *(university year)* année *f* universitaire; *(school year)* année scolaire

SET [esɪ'tiː] *n Comput (abbr* **secure electronic transaction)** SET *f*

set [set] **1** *n* (**a**) *(of keys)* jeu *m*; *(of saucepans)* série *f*, assortiment *m*; *(of books)* collection *f*; *(of tyres)* train *m*; *(of problems, rules, symptoms)* ensemble *m*; **s. of teeth** dentition *f*
(**b**) *(of people)* cercle *m*
(**c**) *(TV, radio)* poste *m*
(**d**) *(in theatre)* décor *m*; *(in cinema)* plateau *m*
(**e**) *(in tennis)* set *m*; **s. point** balle *f* de set
2 *adj* (**a**) *(fixed) (look)* figé(e); *(ideas)* déterminé(e); *(price)* fixe; **to be s. in one's ways** tenir à ses habitudes; **s. menu** menu *m*; **s. phrase** expression *f* figée; **s. piece** *(in play, film)* morceau *m* de bravoure; *(in sport)* tactique *f*
(**b**) *(ready)* **to be (all) s. for sth/to do sth** être (fin) prêt(e) pour qch/à faire qch
(**c**) *(determined)* **to be (dead) s. on sth** avoir fixé son choix sur qch; **to be (dead) s. on doing sth** être fermement décidé(e) à faire qch; **to be dead s. against** être formellement opposé(e) à
3 *vt (pt & pp* **set)** (**a**) *(place)* placer, mettre; *(jewel)* sertir; **to s. the table** mettre la table; **to s. a trap (for sb)** tendre un piège (à qn); **the novel/film is set in Edinburgh** le roman/film se passe à Édimbourg
(**b**) *(fix) (date, day, limit, price)* fixer, déterminer; *(watch)* régler; *(alarm clock)* mettre; *(record)* établir; **to s. a value on sth** estimer la valeur de qch; **to s. the scene** planter le décor; **the scene was set for the arms negotiations** tout était prêt pour les négociations sur les armements
(**c**) *(cause to start)* **to s. sb thinking** faire réfléchir qn; **to s. sb free** libérer qn; **to s. sth on fire** mettre le feu à qch
(**d**) *(task)* fixer; *(essay, homework)* donner
(**e**) *(bone, fracture)* réduire
4 *vi* (**a**) *(of sun, moon)* se coucher
(**b**) *(become firm) (of jelly, concrete)* prendre; *(of broken bone)* se ressouder

▸**set about** *vt insep* (**a**) *(task, job)* se mettre à; **to s. about doing sth** se mettre à faire qch (**b**) *(attack)* attaquer

▸**set against** *vt sep* (**a**) *(cause to oppose)* **to s. sb against sb** monter qn contre qn (**b**) *(compare)* **to s. sth against sth** comparer qch à qch (**c**) *(deduct)* **to s. expenses against tax** déduire les dépenses des impôts

▸**set apart** *vt sep* distinguer (**from** de)

▸**set aside** *vt sep* (**a**) *(put down, disregard)* laisser de côté (**b**) *(save) (money)* mettre de côté; *(time)* réserver

▸**set back** *vt sep* (**a**) *(delay)* retarder (**b**) *Fam (cost)* coûter

▸**set down** *vt sep (put down)* poser, laisser; **to s. sth down in writing** coucher qch par écrit

▸**set forth** *vi Lit (depart)* partir, se mettre en route

▸**set in** *vi (of winter, mood)* s'installer; *(of fog, night)* tomber; *(of infection)* se déclarer

▸**set off 1** *vt sep* (**a**) *(bomb, explosion, alarm)* déclencher; *(argument, chain of events)* provoquer; **to s. sb off (laughing)** faire éclater qn de rire; **to s. sb off (crying)** faire éclater qn en sanglots (**b**) *(enhance)* mettre en valeur, rehausser
2 *vi (depart)* partir, se mettre en route

▸**set out 1** *vt sep (arrange)* disposer
2 *vi* (**a**) *(depart)* partir, se mettre en route; *(in job, task)* démarrer (**b**) *(intend)* **to s. out to do sth** avoir l'intention de faire qch

▸**set to** *vi* (**a**) *(start working)* s'y mettre (**b**) *Fam (start arguing)* recommencer à se disputer

▶**set up 1** *vt sep* (**a**) *(statue)* ériger; *(tent, barrier)* monter; *(roadblock)* mettre en place (**b**) *(meeting)* arranger; *(company)* créer, fonder; *(system)* mettre en place; **to s. up house** *or* **home** s'installer; **to s. sb up in business (as)** installer qn (comme) (**c**) *(trick, frame)* monter un coup contre; **to be set up** être victime d'un coup monté

2 *vi (establish oneself)* s'installer (**as** comme); **to s. up in business (as)** s'installer (comme)

▶**set upon** *vt insep (attack)* attaquer

setback ['setbæk] *n* revers *m*, échec *m*

set-square ['setskweə(r)] *n* équerre *f* (à dessin)

settee [se'ti:] *n* canapé *m*

setter ['setə(r)] *n (dog)* setter *m*

setting ['setɪŋ] **1** *n* (**a**) *(of story, film)* cadre *m* (**b**) *(of sun)* coucher *m* (**c**) *(on machine)* réglage *m* (**d**) **s. lotion** lotion *f* pour mise en plis

2 *adj (sun)* couchant(e)

settle ['setəl] **1** *vt* (**a**) *(put in place)* installer; **to s. oneself** s'installer (**b**) *(nerves)* calmer; **to s. one's stomach** calmer ses douleurs d'estomac (**c**) *(day, venue)* décider, régler (**d**) *(problem, dispute, bill)* régler; **to s. one's affairs** régler ses affaires; *Fam* **that settles it!** c'est décidé!; *Law* **to s. a matter out of court** régler une affaire à l'amiable (**e**) *(colonize)* coloniser

2 *vi* (**a**) *(of bird, insect)* se poser; *(of dust, liquid, beer)* se déposer (**b**) *(of person, family)* s'installer, s'établir; *(of crowd)* se calmer, s'apaiser; **to s. into an armchair** s'installer confortablement dans un fauteuil (**c**) *Law* **to s. out of court** régler l'affaire à l'amiable

▶**settle down 1** *vt sep* (**a**) *(make comfortable)* installer (**b**) *(make calm)* calmer

2 *vi* (**a**) *(make oneself comfortable)* s'installer confortablement; **to s. down to work** se mettre au travail (**b**) *(in new home)* s'installer; *(adopt steady lifestyle)* se ranger, s'assagir; **to s. down with sb** se mettre en couple (**c**) *(of situation, excitement)* se calmer

▶**settle for** *vt insep* accepter, se contenter de

▶**settle in** *vi (in new home)* s'installer; *(in new school, job)* s'adapter

▶**settle on** *vt insep* se décider pour, choisir

▶**settle up** *vi (pay bill)* régler

settled ['setəld] *adj (person, life)* rangé(e), établi(e); *(weather)* stable

settlement ['setəlmənt] *n* (**a**) *(of problem, dispute, bill)* règlement *m*; **to reach a s.** parvenir à un accord (**b**) *(village)* village *m*

settler ['setlə(r)] *n* colon *m*

set-to ['set'tu:] *n Fam* bagarre *f*

set-top box ['set'tɒpbɒks] *n TV* décodeur *m* numérique

setup ['setʌp] *n Fam (arrangement)* système *m*

seven ['sevən] **1** *n* sept *m inv*

2 *adj* sept; **the s. deadly sins** les sept péchés capitaux; *Lit* **to sail the s. seas** parcourir les mers; *see also* **eight**

seventeen [sevən'ti:n] **1** *n* dix-sept *m inv*

2 *adj* dix-sept; *see also* **eight**

seventeenth [sevən'ti:nθ] **1** *n* (**a**) *(fraction)* dix-septième *m* (**b**) *(in series)* dix-septième *mf* (**c**) *(of month)* dix-sept *m inv*

2 *adj* dix-septième; *see also* **eighth**

seventh ['sevənθ] **1** *n* (**a**) *(fraction)* septième *m* (**b**) *(in series)* septième *mf* (**c**) *(of month)* sept *m inv*

2 *adj* septième; **to be in s. heaven** être au septième ciel; *see also* **eighth**

seventieth ['sevəntɪθ] **1** *n* (**a**) *(fraction)* soixante-dixième *m* (**b**) *(in series)* soixante-dixième *mf*

2 *adj* soixante-dixième

seventy ['sevəntɪ] **1** *n* soixante-dix *m inv, Belg & Suisse* septante *m inv*

2 *adj* soixante-dix, *Belg & Suisse* septante; *see also* **eighty**

sever ['sevə(r)] *vt (arm, finger)* couper, trancher; *Fig (link, relationship)* rompre

several ['sevərəl] **1** *adj* plusieurs

2 *pron* plusieurs; **s. of us/them** plusieurs d'entre nous/eux

severance ['sevərəns] *n* rupture *f*; **s. pay** indemnité *f* de licenciement

severe [sɪ'vɪə(r)] *adj (person, punishment, criticism)* sévère; *(pain)* vif (vive); *(illness, injury)* grave; *(winter)* rude; *(weather)* très mauvais(e); *(style)* austère, sévère

severity [sɪ'verɪtɪ] *n (of person, punishment, criticism)* sévérité *f*; *(of pain)* intensité *f*; *(of injury, illness)* gravité *f*; *(of winter)* rigueur *f*; *(of style)* austérité *f*, sévérité

sew [səʊ] (*pp* **sewn** [səʊn]) *vt & vi* coudre

▶**sew up** *vt sep* (**a**) *(stitch)* coudre (**b**) *Fam* **it's all sewn up** *(decided, settled)* l'affaire est dans le sac

sewage ['su:ɪdʒ] *n* eaux *fpl* usées *ou* d'égout; **s. disposal** évacuation *f* des eaux usées; **s. works** champ *m* d'épandage

sewer ['su:ə(r)] *n* égout *m*; *Fam* **to have a mind like a s.** avoir l'esprit mal tourné

sewing ['səʊɪŋ] *n (activity)* couture *f*; *(work)* ouvrage *m*; **s. machine** machine *f* à coudre

sewn [səʊn] *pp of* **sew**

sex [seks] *n* sexe *m*; **to have s. with sb** faire l'amour avec qn; **s. appeal** sex-appeal *m*; **s. education** éducation *f* sexuelle; **s. life** vie *f* sexuelle; **s. maniac** obsédé(e) *m,f* sexuel(elle); **s. shop** sex-shop *m*; **s. symbol** sex-symbol *m*

sexagenarian [seksədʒɪ'neərɪən] *n* sexagénaire *mf*

sexism ['seksɪzəm] *n* sexisme *m*

sexist ['seksɪst] *n & adj* sexiste *mf*

sexologist [sek'sɒlədʒɪst] *n* sexologue *mf*

sextant ['sekstənt] *n* sextant *m*

sextet [seks'tet] *n* sextuor *m*

sexton ['sekstən] *n* sacristain *m*, bedeau *m*

sexual ['seksjʊəl] *adj* sexuel(elle); **s. assault** agression *f* sexuelle; **s. discrimination** discrimination *f* sexuelle; **s. harassment** harcèlement *m* sexuel; **s. intercourse** rapports *mpl* sexuels; **s. reproduction** reproduction *f* sexuée

sexuality [seksjʊ'ælɪtɪ] *n* sexualité *f*

sexually ['seksjʊəlɪ] *adv* sexuellement; **s. transmitted disease** maladie *f* sexuellement transmissible

sexy ['seksɪ] *adj Fam* sexy *inv*; *Fig (car, hi-fi)* branché(e)

Seychelles [seɪ'ʃelz] *npl* **the S.** les Seychelles *fpl*

Sgt *(abbr* **Sergeant)** Sgt

sh [ʃ] *exclam* chut!

shabbily ['ʃæbɪlɪ] *adv* (**a**) *(furnished, dressed)* pauvrement (**b**) *(treat, behave)* avec mesquinerie

shabbiness ['ʃæbɪnɪs] *n* (**a**) *(of person, clothes, area)* apparence *f* miteuse (**b**) *(of treatment, behaviour)* mesquinerie *f*

shabby [ˈʃæbɪ] adj (**a**) (dingy, worn out) miteux(euse) (**b**) (behaviour, treatment) minable, mesquin(e)

shack [ʃæk] n cabane f, hutte f

▸**shack up** vi Fam **to s. up with sb** se mettre à la colle avec qn

shackle [ˈʃækəl] **1** n **shackles** chaînes fpl, fers mpl **2** vt (prisoner) enchaîner

shade [ʃeɪd] **1** n (**a**) (shadow) ombre f; **in the s.** à l'ombre; Fig **to put sb in the s.** éclipser qn; **shades of 1968/the Beatles** (reminders, suggestions) ça rappelle 1968/les Beatles (**b**) (of colour, meaning, opinion) nuance f, ton m; **a s. better/longer** un tout petit mieux/plus long (**c**) Fam **shades** (sunglasses) lunettes fpl de soleil **2** vt (from sun) **to s. one's eyes** se protéger les yeux

shaded [ˈʃeɪdɪd] adj (**a**) (garden, path) à l'ombre, ombragé(e) (**b**) (area on diagram, map) hachuré(e)

shading [ˈʃeɪdɪŋ] n (on drawing) ombres fpl; (on diagram, map) hachure f

shadow [ˈʃædəʊ] **1** n ombre f; **to cast a s.** projeter une ombre; Fig **to cast a s. over sth** jeter une ombre sur qch; **to be a s. of one's former self** n'être plus que l'ombre de soi-même; **without a s. of doubt** sans l'ombre d'un doute; **the s. of death/war** le spectre de la mort/de la guerre; **to have shadows under one's eyes** avoir des cernes, avoir les yeux cernés **2** adj Br Pol **s. cabinet** cabinet m fantôme; **s. minister** = député de l'opposition chargé d'un dossier administratif tel que l'Intérieur, les Affaires étrangères etc **3** vt (follow) filer, prendre en filature

Shadow cabinet

En Grande-Bretagne, le "shadow cabinet" est composé de parlementaires de l'opposition qui deviendraient ministres si l'opposition accédait au pouvoir. Chaque ministre du gouvernement dispose de son homologue "fantôme" dans l'opposition (on parle de "shadow minister"), qui étudie les mêmes dossiers et se spécialise ainsi dans un domaine donné. Les ministres fantômes occupent les "frontbenches" de l'opposition à la Chambre des communes.

shadowy [ˈʃædəʊɪ] adj (dark) ombragé(e); (form, outline) vague

shady [ˈʃeɪdɪ] adj (**a**) (garden, lane) ombragé(e) (**b**) Fam (suspicious) louche

shaft [ʃɑːft] **1** n (**a**) (of golf club, tool) manche m; (of light) rayon m (**b**) (of mine) puits m; (for lift) cage f **2** vt very Fam (cheat) entuber

shag¹ [ʃæg] n (tobacco) tabac m

shag² Br Vulg **1** n (sexual intercourse) **to have a s.** baiser **2** vt & vi (pt & pp **shagged**) baiser

shagged [ʃægd] adj Br very Fam (exhausted) crevé(e)

shaggy [ˈʃægɪ] adj (hairy) hirsute; Fam **s. dog story** histoire f sans queue ni tête

shah [ʃɑː] n schah m

shake [ʃeɪk] **1** n (**a**) (action) secousse f; **to give sb/sth a s.** secouer qn/qch; Fig **to give oneself a s.** se secouer; Fam **to have the shakes** avoir la tremblote; Fam **in two shakes (of a lamb's tail)** en un rien de temps; Fam **to be no great shakes** ne pas casser trois pattes à un canard (**b**) (**milk**) **s.** (milk-)shake m **2** vt (pt **shook** [ʃʊk], pp **shaken** [ˈʃeɪkən]) (person, box, bottle) secouer; (building) faire trembler,

ébranler; Fig **to s. sb's faith/trust** ébranler la foi/la confiance de qn; **to s. one's head** faire non de la tête; **to s. one's fist at sb** menacer qn du poing; **to s. hands with sb** serrer la main à qn; **to s. hands on a deal** conclure un accord par une poignée de mains **3** vi (**a**) (of person, building, voice) trembler; **to s. like a leaf** trembler comme une feuille (**b**) Fam **to s. on it** (shake hands) toper; **s. on it!** tope là!

▸**shake off** vt sep (illness, depression) sortir de; (pursuer) semer

▸**shake up** vt sep (**a**) (upset) secouer (**b**) (reorganize) réorganiser de fond en comble

shaken [ˈʃeɪkən] pp of **shake**

Shakespearean [ʃeɪksˈpɪərɪən] adj shakespearien(-enne)

shake-up [ˈʃeɪkʌp] n Fam (reorganization) chambardement m

shakily [ˈʃeɪkɪlɪ] adv (walk) d'un pas vacillant; (write) d'une main tremblante; (speak) d'une voix tremblante

shaky [ˈʃeɪkɪ] adj (table, ladder) branlant(e); (handwriting) tremblé(e); (voice) tremblant(e); (health, position) précaire

shale [ʃeɪl] n schiste m argileux

shall [stressed ʃæl, unstressed ʃəl]

On trouve généralement **I/you/he/etc shall** sous leurs formes contractées **I'll/you'll/he'll/etc**. La forme négative correspondante est **shan't**, que l'on écrira **shall not** dans des contextes formels.

modal aux v (**a**) (with first person) (expressing future tense) **I s. be there** j'y serai; **where s. I sit?** où veux-tu que je m'asseye?; **I shan't say this more than once** je ne le dirai pas plus d'une fois; **as we s. see** comme nous le verrons (**b**) (making suggestions, offers) **s. I make some coffee?** veux-tu que je fasse du café?; **let's go in, s. we?** entrons, tu veux bien? (**c**) Formal (with 2nd and 3rd person) (expressing determination) **you s. pay for this!** tu me le paieras! (**d**) (indicating general truth) **all members s. be entitled to vote** tous les membres auront le droit de vote

shallot [ʃəˈlɒt] n échalote f

shallow [ˈʃæləʊ] adj (**a**) (water, dish) peu profond(e); **s. end** (of swimming pool) petit bain m (**b**) Fig (person, mind) superficiel(elle)

sham [ʃæm] **1** n (trial, election) comédie f, farce f; (person) imposteur m **2** adj feint(e); **a s. election** un simulacre d'élections **3** vt (pt & pp **shammed**) feindre, simuler **4** vi faire semblant

shamble [ˈʃæmbəl] vi **to s. along** marcher en traînant les pieds

shambles [ˈʃæmbəlz] n désordre m, pagaille f; **this place is a s.!** quel désordre!, quelle pagaille!

shambolic [ʃæmˈbɒlɪk] adj Fam bordélique

shame [ʃeɪm] **1** n (**a**) (disgrace, guilt) honte f; **to my s.** à ma grande honte; **s. on you!** tu devrais avoir honte!; **to put sb to s.** faire honte à qn (**b**) (pity) dommage m; **it's a s. (that...)** c'est dommage (que... + subjunctive); **what a s.!** quel dommage! **2** vt (**a**) (cause to feel ashamed) faire honte à; **to s. sb into doing sth** obliger qn à faire qch en lui faisant honte (**b**) (bring shame on) couvrir de honte

shamefaced [ˈʃeɪmfeɪst] adj honteux(euse), penaud(e)

shameful ['ʃeɪmfʊl] *adj* honteux(euse), scandaleux (euse)

shamefully ['ʃeɪmfəlɪ] *adv* honteusement

shameless ['ʃeɪmlɪs] *adj* impudique; **to be s. about doing sth** n'avoir aucun scrupule à faire qch

shammy ['ʃæmɪ] *n* **s. (leather)** peau *f* de chamois

shampoo [ʃæm'puː] **1** *n* shampoing *m*
2 *vt* **to s. one's hair** se faire un shampoing

shamrock ['ʃæmrɒk] *n* trèfle *m*

shandy ['ʃændɪ] *n* panaché *m*

shank [ʃæŋk] *n (of lamb, beef)* jarret *m*

shan't [ʃɑːnt] = **shall not**

shanty¹ ['ʃæntɪ] *n (hut)* baraque *f*, cabane *f*; **s. town** bidonville *m*

shanty² *n (song)* chanson *f* de marins

shape [ʃeɪp] **1** *n* **(a)** *(form)* forme *f*; **what s. is it?** quelle forme cela a-t-il?; **to be the same s. as...** avoir la même forme que...; **to take s.** *(of plan)* prendre forme; *Fig* **in any s. or form** quel (quelle) qu'il (elle) soit; *Fig* **in the s. of** sous la forme de; *(person)* en la personne de **(b)** *(condition)* **to be in good/bad s.** *(of person)* être en bonne/mauvaise forme; *(of company, economy)* bien/mal marcher; **to get into/keep in s.** *(of person)* retrouver/garder la forme
2 *vt* **(a)** *(clay)* modeler; *(wood)* façonner **(b)** *Fig (perception, events, future)* influencer; *(character)* former

▶**shape up** *vi (of person)* progresser; *(of team, plans)* prendre forme

shapeless ['ʃeɪplɪs] *adj* informe

shapely ['ʃeɪplɪ] *adj* bien fait(e)

shard [ʃɑːd] *n (of glass)* éclat *m*; *(of pottery)* tesson *m*

share [ʃeə(r)] **1** *n* **(a)** *(portion)* part *f*; **in equal shares** en parts égales; **to have a s. in sth** avoir une part dans qch; **to do one's s.** mettre la main à la pâte; *Fig* **to get one's fair s. of sth** avoir sa part de qch **(b)** *Fin* action *f*; **s. capital** capital *m* social; **s. certificate** certificat *m* ou titre *m* d'actions; **s. option** option *f* d'achat des actions
2 *vt* partager
3 *vi* partager; **to s. in sth** partager qch; **s. and s. alike!** chacun sa part!

▶**share out** *vt sep* partager, répartir

shareholder ['ʃeəhəʊldə(r)] *n Fin* actionnaire *mf*

shareholding ['ʃeəhəʊldɪŋ] *n Fin* actionnariat *m*

shareware ['ʃeəweə(r)] *n Comput* shareware *m*, partagiciel *m*

shark [ʃɑːk] *n also Fig* requin *m*

sharp [ʃɑːp] **1** *adj* **(a)** *(knife)* bien aiguisé(e); *(pencil)* bien taillé(e); *(scissors, razor)* qui coupe bien; *(point)* aigu(uë); *(claws)* acéré(e)
(b) *(features)* anguleux(euse); *(turning, rise, fall)* brusque; *(photo, outline, focus)* net (nette); *(contrast)* marqué(e); *(hearing)* fin(e); *(eyesight)* perçant(e); *Fig* **to be at the s. end** être en première ligne
(c) *(intelligent)* vif (vive)
(d) *(harsh) (voice, words)* cinglant(e); *(person)* mordant(e); **to have a s. tongue** être mordant
(e) *(taste, sauce)* acide; *(sound)* perçant(e); *(pain, wind)* vif (vive)
(f) *(in music)* **C s.** do dièse
2 *adv* **(a)** *(punctually)* pile; **at four o'clock s.** à quatre heures pile *ou* précises
(b) *(immediately)* **to turn s. left/right** tourner tout de suite à gauche/à droite
(c) *(idioms) Fam* **look s.!** grouille-toi!
3 *n (in music)* dièse *m*

sharpen ['ʃɑːpən] *vt* **(a)** *(knife, tool)* aiguiser; *(pencil)* tailler, *Can* affiler **(b)** *(pain)* accentuer; *(passion, desire)* exacerber; **to s. one's wits** faire travailler sa matière grise

sharpener ['ʃɑːpənə(r)] *n (for knife)* aiguisoir *m* (à couteaux); *(for pencil)* taille-crayon *m*

sharp-eyed ['ʃɑːpaɪd] *adj* observateur(trice)

sharply ['ʃɑːplɪ] *adv* **(a)** *(contrast)* nettement **(b)** *(rise, fall, brake)* brusquement

sharpness ['ʃɑːpnɪs] *n* **(a)** *(of knife)* tranchant *m* **(b)** *(of outline, photo)* netteté *f* **(c)** *(of mind, hearing, sight)* acuité *f* **(d)** *(of voice, words)* brusquerie *f* **(e)** *(of pain)* acuité *f*; *(of wind)* âpreté *f*

sharpshooter ['ʃɑːpʃuːtə(r)] *n* tireur *m* d'élite

sharp-sighted [ʃɑːp'saɪtɪd] *adj* observateur(trice)

sharp-tongued [ʃɑːp'tʌŋd] *adj* mordant(e)

shat [ʃæt] *pt of* **shit**

shatter ['ʃætə(r)] **1** *vt* **(a)** *(glass, bone)* briser en mille morceaux; *Fig (hopes, silence, nerves)* briser; *(health)* ruiner **(b)** *Fam* **to be shattered** *(stunned)* être accablé(e); *Br (exhausted)* être crevé(e)
2 *vi* se briser en mille morceaux

shattering ['ʃætərɪŋ] *adj* **(a)** *(defeat)* accablant(e); **it was a s. blow** ça a été un coup terrible **(b)** *Fam (stunning)* accablant(e); *Br (exhausting)* crevant(e)

shatterproof ['ʃætəpruːf] *adj (glass)* Sécurit®; *(windscreen, door)* en verre Sécurit®

shave [ʃeɪv] **1** *n* **to have a s.** se raser; *Fig* **that was a close s.** il était moins une
2 *vt* **(a)** *(face, legs)* raser; **to s. one's legs** se raser les jambes **(b)** *(wood)* raboter
3 *vi* se raser

▶**shave off** *vt sep* se raser

shaven ['ʃeɪvən] *adj* rasé(e)

shaver ['ʃeɪvə(r)] *n* rasoir *m* électrique

shaving ['ʃeɪvɪŋ] *n* **(a)** **s. brush** blaireau *m*; **s. foam** mousse *f* à raser **(b)** *(piece of wood)* copeau *m*; *(piece of metal)* rognure *f*

shawl [ʃɔːl] *n* châle *m*

she [ʃiː] **1** *pron* elle; **she's Scottish** elle est écossaise; **SHE hasn't got it!** ce n'est pas elle qui l'a!
2 *n* **it's a s.** *(of animal)* c'est une femelle

sheaf [ʃiːf] *(pl* **sheaves** [ʃiːvz] *) n (of corn)* gerbe *f*; *(of papers)* liasse *f*

shear [ʃɪə(r)] *(pp* **shorn** [ʃɔːn] *or* **sheared**) **1** *vt (sheep)* tondre; *Fig* **to be shorn of sth** être dépouillé(e) de qch
2 *vi (cut)* **to s. through sth** couper qch

shears [ʃɪəz] *npl* cisailles *fpl*

sheath [ʃiːθ] *n* **(a)** *(for sword, knife)* fourreau *m*; *(for electric cable)* gaine *f*; **s. knife** couteau *m* à gaine **(b)** *(contraceptive)* préservatif *m*

shed¹ [ʃed] *n (in garden)* abri *m*, remise *f*; *(in factory)* atelier *m*

shed² [ʃed] *(pt & pp* **shed**) *vt (leaves)* perdre; *(tears)* verser; **to s. its skin** *(of snake)* muer; **to s. light on sth** jeter de la lumière sur qch; **to s. weight** perdre du poids; **to s. its load** *(of lorry)* perdre son chargement

she'd [ʃiːd] = **she had, she would**

sheen [ʃiːn] *n (on metal, silk)* lustre *m*; *(on hair)* brillant *m*

sheep [ʃiːp] *(pl* **sheep**) *n* mouton *m*

sheepdog ['ʃiːpdɒg] *n* chien *m* de berger

sheepfold ['ʃiːpfəʊld] *n* parc *m* à moutons

sheepish ['ʃiːpɪʃ] *adj* penaud(e)

sheepskin ['ʃiːpskɪn] *n* peau *f* de mouton; **s. jacket** veste *f* en peau de mouton

sheer [ʃɪə(r)] *adj* (**a**) *(pure)* pur(e); **it's s. madness** c'est de la folie pure; **by s. chance** tout à fait par hasard (**b**) *(steep)* à pic *inv* (**c**) *(stockings, fabric)* très fin(e)

sheet [ʃiːt] *n (on bed)* drap *m*; *(of paper)* feuille *f*; *(of glass, ice, metal)* plaque *f*; *(of flame)* rideau *m*; **s. lightning** éclair *m* en nappe(s); **s. metal** tôle *f*; **s. music** partitions *fpl*

sheetfeed ['ʃiːtfiːd] *n Comput* avancement *m* du papier

sheik(h) [ʃeɪk] *n* cheikh *m*

shekel ['ʃekəl] *n* shekel *m*

shelf [ʃelf] (*pl* **shelves** [ʃelvz]) *n* (**a**) *(in cupboard, bookcase)* étagère *f*; **(set of) shelves** étagère; *Fig* **to be left on the s.** rester vieille fille; *Com* **s. life** *(of goods)* durée *f* de conservation avant vente (**b**) *(of cliff, rock face)* rebord *m*

shell [ʃel] **1** *n* (**a**) *(of snail, oyster, egg, nut)* coquille *f*; *(of lobster, tortoise)* carapace *f*; *(on beach)* coquillage *m*; *Fig* **to come out of one's s.** sortir de sa coquille; **s. suit** = survêtement en synthétique brillant (**b**) *(of building)* carcasse *f* (**c**) *(bomb)* obus *m*; **s. shock** psychose *f* traumatique *(à la suite d'une explosion)*
2 *vt* (**a**) *(nuts)* décortiquer; *(peas)* écosser; *(eggs)* écaler (**b**) *(bombard)* bombarder

▸**shell out** *Fam* **1** *vt sep (money)* casquer
2 *vi* **to s. out (for sth)** casquer (pour qch)

she'll [ʃiːl] = **she will, she shall**

shellfire ['ʃelfaɪə(r)] *n* tirs *mpl* d'obus

shellfish ['ʃelfɪʃ] *n (crustacean)* crustacé *m*; *(mollusc)* coquillage *m*; *(as food)* fruits *mpl* de mer

shelling ['ʃelɪŋ] *n* bombardement *m*

shellshocked ['ʃelʃɒkt] *adj (soldier)* commotionné(e) *(à la suite d'une explosion)*; *Fig* sous le choc

shelter ['ʃeltə(r)] **1** *n (place, protection)* abri *m*; **to take s.** se mettre à l'abri, s'abriter
2 *vt* abriter (**from** de); *(criminal, refugee)* accueillir
3 *vi* s'abriter, se mettre à l'abri (**from** de)

sheltered ['ʃeltəd] *adj (place)* abrité(e); *(life, childhood)* protégé(e); **s. housing** = logements spécialement conçus pour les personnes âgées

shelve [ʃelv] *vt (postpone)* mettre au placard

shelving ['ʃelvɪŋ] *n* étagères *fpl*

shepherd ['ʃepəd] **1** *n* berger *m*; **s.'s pie** ≃ hachis *m* Parmentier
2 *vt (sheep)* garder; *Fig (people)* guider, conduire

shepherdess [ʃepə'des] *n* bergère *f*

sherbet ['ʃɜːbət] *n Br (powder)* poudre *f* acidulée; *Am (sorbet)* sorbet *m*

sheriff ['ʃerɪf] *n* (**a**) *Br Law (in England)* = plus haut fonctionnaire du comté, dont le rôle est essentiellement protocolaire; *(in Scotland)* ≃ juge *m* au tribunal de grande instance (**b**) *Am* sherif *m*

sherry ['ʃerɪ] *n* sherry *m*, xérès *m*

she's [ʃiːz] = **she has, she is**

Shetland ['ʃetlənd] *n* **the S. Islands, the Shetlands** les (îles *fpl*) Shetland *fpl*; **S. pony** poney *m* des Shetland

shield [ʃiːld] **1** *n (of knight)* & *Fig (protection)* bouclier *m*; *(police badge)* badge *m*; *(trophy)* trophée *m* en forme d'écusson
2 *vt (protect)* protéger (**from** de); **to s. one's eyes** se protéger les yeux

shift [ʃɪft] **1** *n* (**a**) *(change of position)* changement *m*; **a s. in meaning** un glissement de sens; **a s. to the right/left** *(in politics)* un revirement à droite/

gauche; **s. key** *(on typewriter, computer)* touche *f* des majuscules (**b**) *(period)* poste *m*; *(workers)* équipe *f*; **to work (in) shifts** avoir un travail posté (**c**) **s. (dress)** robe *f* chasuble
2 *vt* (**a**) *(move)* déplacer; *(stain)* enlever, faire partir; **to s. the blame onto sb** rejeter la responsabilité sur qn (**b**) *Fam (sell)* écouler
3 *vi (move)* bouger; *(of stain)* partir; *Fam (move quickly)* foncer

shiftless ['ʃɪftlɪs] *adj* fainéant(e)

shiftwork ['ʃɪftwɜːk] *n* travail *m* posté

shifty ['ʃɪftɪ] *adj (person)* louche; *(look)* fuyant(e)

shilling ['ʃɪlɪŋ] *n* shilling *m*

shimmer ['ʃɪmə(r)] **1** *n (of light)* scintillement *m*; *(of water)* miroitement *m*; *(of silk)* chatoiement *m*
2 *vi (of light)* scintiller; *(of water)* miroiter; *(of silk)* chatoyer

shimmering ['ʃɪmərɪŋ] *adj (light)* scintillant(e); *(water)* miroitant(e); *(silk)* chatoyant(e)

shin [ʃɪn] *n* tibia *m*; **s. guard** *or* **pad** *(in sport)* jambière *f*

▸**shin up** *(pt & pp* **shinned)** *vt insep (climb)* grimper à

shinbone ['ʃɪnbəʊn] *n* tibia *m*

shindy ['ʃɪndɪ] *n Fam (din)* boucan *m*; **to kick up a s.** faire du boucan

shine [ʃaɪn] **1** *n* (**a**) brillant *m*, éclat *m* (**b**) *(idioms)* **to take the s. off sth** faire perdre son éclat à qch, ternir qch; *Fam* **to take a s. to sb** *(take a liking to)* se prendre d'amitié pour qn; *(get a crush on)* s'enticher de qn
2 *vt (pt & pp* **shone** [ʃɒn]) (**a**) *(light, torch)* braquer (**on** sur) (**b**) *(pt & pp* **shined)** *(polish)* faire briller
3 *vi* briller; *Fig* **to s. at sth** *(excel)* briller en qch; **her face shone with joy** son visage rayonna de joie

shiner ['ʃaɪnə(r)] *n Fam (black eye)* œil *m* au beurre noir

shingle ['ʃɪŋɡəl] *n* (**a**) *(wooden tile)* bardeau *m* (**b**) *(pebbles)* galets *mpl*

shingles ['ʃɪŋɡəlz] *n (disease)* zona *m*; **to have s.** avoir un zona

shining ['ʃaɪnɪŋ] *adj* brillant(e); *Fig* **a s. example (of)** un parfait exemple (de)

shiny ['ʃaɪnɪ] *adj* brillant(e)

ship [ʃɪp] **1** *n* navire *m*; *Fig* **when my s. comes in** quand je serai riche
2 *vt (pt & pp* **shipped)** *(transport)* transporter; *(send)* expédier; *(take on board)* embarquer

▸**ship off** *vt sep Fam* expédier

shipboard ['ʃɪpbɔːd] *n Naut* **on s.** à bord

shipbuilder ['ʃɪpbɪldə(r)] *n* constructeur *m* naval

shipbuilding ['ʃɪpbɪldɪŋ] *n* construction *f* navale; **the s. industry** (l'industrie *f* de) la construction navale

shipload ['ʃɪpləʊd] *n* cargaison *f*; *Fig* **by the s.** en masse

shipmate ['ʃɪpmeɪt] *n Naut* camarade *m* de bord

shipment ['ʃɪpmənt] *n* cargaison *f*

shipowner ['ʃɪpəʊnə(r)] *n* armateur *m*

shipping ['ʃɪpɪŋ] *n (ships)* navires *mpl*; **s. agent** *(person)* agent *m* maritime; *(company)* agence *f* maritime; **s. lane** voie *f* de navigation

shipshape ['ʃɪpʃeɪp] *adj* rangé(e), en ordre

shipwreck ['ʃɪprek] **1** *n (disaster)* naufrage *m*; *(ship)* épave *f*
2 *vt* **to be shipwrecked** faire naufrage

shipwrecked ['ʃɪprekt] *adj* naufragé(e)

shipwright ['ʃɪpraɪt] *n Naut (company)* constructeur *m* naval; *(worker)* ouvrier(ère) *m,f* de chantier naval

shipyard ['ʃɪpjɑːd] *n* chantier *m* naval

shire ['ʃaɪə(r)] *n Br* comté *m*; **s. horse** shire *m*

shirk [ʃɜːk] **1** *vt (task)* éviter de faire; *(obligation, responsibility)* se dérober à
2 *vi (avoid work)* tirer au flanc

shirker ['ʃɜːkə(r)] *n* tire-au-flanc *mf inv*

shirt [ʃɜːt] *n* chemise *f*; *Fam* **keep your s. on!** on se calme!

shirtmaker ['ʃɜːtmeɪkə(r)] *n* fabricant(e) *m,f* de chemises

shirtsleeves ['ʃɜːtsliːvz] *npl* **to be in s.** être en bras de chemise

shirt-tail ['ʃɜːtteɪl] *n* pan *m* de chemise

shirty ['ʃɜːtɪ] *adj Br Fam* en rogne; **to get s. (with sb)** se mettre en rogne (contre qn)

shit [ʃɪt] *Vulg* **1** *n* (**a**) *(excrement)* merde *f*; *(mess)* bordel *m*; *(nonsense)* conneries *fpl*; **to have a s.** chier (**b**) *(nasty man)* salaud *m*; *(nasty woman)* salope *f* (**c**) *(idioms)* **to talk s.** dire des conneries; **to be in the s.** être dans la merde; **he doesn't give a s.** il n'en a rien à foutre; **to beat the s. out of sb** casser la gueule à qn; **to scare the s. out of sb** foutre une de ces trouilles à qn
2 *vt (pt & pp* **shitted** *or* **shat** [ʃæt]) **to s. oneself** chier dans son froc
3 *vi* chier
4 *exclam* merde!

shitty ['ʃɪtɪ] *adj Vulg* (**a**) *(nappies, trousers)* dégueulasse (**b**) *(weather, job)* merdique; *(behaviour, remark)* dégueulasse; **to feel s.** *(ill)* avoir la tête dans le cul; *(guilty)* se sentir merdeux(euse)

shiver ['ʃɪvə(r)] **1** *n (of cold, fear)* frisson *m*; **to send shivers down sb's spine** donner le frisson à qn
2 *vi* frissonner, trembler (**with** de)

shoal [ʃəʊl] *n (of fish)* banc *m*; *Fig (of people)* foule *f*

shock¹ [ʃɒk] *n (of hair)* crinière *f*

shock² **1** *n* (**a**) *(impact)* choc *m*; *(of earthquake)* secousse *f*; **s. absorber** amortisseur *m*; **s. tactics** tactique *f* de choc; *Mil* **s. troops** troupes *fpl* de choc; *also Fig* **s. wave** onde *f* de choc (**b**) *(emotional blow)* choc *m*, coup *m*; **I got a real s. when...** cela m'a vraiment fait un choc quand...; **to be in s.** être en état de choc (**c**) *(electric)* décharge *f* (électrique); **s. therapy** (traitement *m* par) électrochocs *mpl*
2 *vt (surprise, startle)* stupéfier; *(scandalize)* choquer; **to s. sb into doing sth** pousser qn à faire qch en lui faisant peur

shocked [ʃɒkt] *adj (startled)* stupéfié(e); *(scandalized)* choqué(e)

shocking ['ʃɒkɪŋ] *adj* (**a**) *(scandalous)* choquant(e); **s. pink** rose *m* bonbon (**b**) *(very bad)* atroce

shockproof ['ʃɒkpruːf] *adj (watch)* antichoc *inv*

shoddy ['ʃɒdɪ] *adj (goods)* de mauvaise qualité; *(workmanship)* mal fait(e); *(conduct)* méprisable

shoe [ʃuː] **1** *n* chaussure *f*; *(horseshoe)* fer *m* (à cheval); *Fig* **I wouldn't like to be in her shoes** je n'aimerais pas être à sa place; *Fig* **put yourself in my shoes** mets-toi à ma place; **s. polish** cirage *m*; **s. shop** magasin *m* de chaussures
2 *vt (pt & pp* **shod** [ʃɒd] *or* **shoed**) *(horse)* ferrer

shoebrush ['ʃuːbrʌʃ] *n* brosse *f* à chaussures

shoehorn ['ʃuːhɔːn] *n* chausse-pied *m*

shoelace ['ʃuːleɪs] *n* lacet *m* (de chaussure)

shoemaker ['ʃuːmeɪkə(r)] *n (manufacturer)* bottier *m*; *(seller)* chausseur *m*

shoeshine ['ʃuːʃaɪn] *n Am (person)* cireur *m* de chaussures

shoestring ['ʃuːstrɪŋ] *n* (**a**) *Fam* **on a s.** avec trois fois rien; **s. budget** petit budget *m* (**b**) *Am* lacet *m* (de chaussure)

shone [ʃɒn] *pt & pp of* **shine**

shoo [ʃuː] *exclam* ouste!

▶**shoo away, shoo off** *vt sep* chasser

shook [ʃʊk] *pt of* **shake**

shoot [ʃuːt] **1** *vt (pt & pp* **shot** [ʃɒt]) (**a**) *(fire) (bullet)* tirer; *(arrow)* & *Fig (glance)* lancer
(**b**) **to s. sb** *(wound)* blesser qn par balle; *(kill)* tuer qn par balle; *(execute)* fusiller qn; **to be shot in the arm** recevoir une balle dans le bras; **to s. rabbits/grouse** chasser le lapin/la grouse; *Fig* **to s. oneself in the foot** compromettre ses chances; *Am Fam* **to s. the breeze** *or* **(the) bull** tailler une bavette
(**c**) *(film, TV programme)* tourner
(**d**) *(pass rapidly)* **to s. the rapids** franchir les rapides; **to s. the lights** *(in car)* brûler *ou* griller le feu rouge
(**e**) **to s. dice/pool** jouer aux dés/au billard
2 *vi* (**a**) *(with gun)* tirer (**at** sur); *(in football)* tirer, shooter
(**b**) *(move rapidly)* filer; **he shot into/out of the house** il se précipita dans/hors de la maison; **the pain shot up her left side** elle ressentit soudain une vive douleur au côté gauche
3 *n* (**a**) *(of plant)* pousse *f*
(**b**) *(hunting party)* chasse *f*

▶**shoot down** *vt sep (person)* descendre; *(plane)* abattre

▶**shoot off** *vi (leave quickly)* filer

▶**shoot out** *vi (emerge quickly)* jaillir

▶**shoot up** *vi* (**a**) *(of plant)* pousser vite; *(of child)* monter en graine; *(of buildings)* pousser comme des champignons (**b**) *(of rocket)* s'élever; *(of prices)* monter *ou* grimper en flèche (**c**) *Fam (with drugs)* se shooter

shooting ['ʃuːtɪŋ] **1** *n* (**a**) *(gunfire)* coups *mpl* de feu; *(incident)* fusillade *f*; **s. stick** canne-siège *f* (**b**) *(of film, TV programme)* tournage *m*
2 *adj* **s. star** étoile *f* filante

shoot-out ['ʃuːtaʊt] *n* fusillade *f*

shop [ʃɒp] **1** *n* (**a**) *(for goods)* magasin *m*; **s. assistant** vendeur(euse) *m,f*; **s. window** vitrine *f* (**b**) *Fam* **to do a s.** *(go shopping)* faire ses courses (**c**) *(workshop)* atelier *m*; *Fig* **the s. floor** les ouvriers *mpl* (**d**) *(idioms) Fam* **to talk s.** parler boutique; *Fam Fig* **all over the s.** *(everywhere)* un peu partout; *Fig* **his explanation was all over the s.** son explication ne tenait pas debout; **my hair was all over the s.** j'étais coiffé n'importe comment; **at the interview he was all over the s.** à l'entretien, il a raconté n'importe quoi
2 *vt (pt & pp* **shopped**) *Br Fam (betray)* balancer
3 *vi* faire ses courses; **to go shopping** faire des courses; *(for food)* faire ses courses; **to s. around** comparer les prix

shopaholic [ʃɒpə'hɒlɪk] *n* **he's a real s.** il adore faire les magasins

shopgirl ['ʃɒpgɜːl] *n* vendeuse *f*

shopkeeper ['ʃɒpkiːpə(r)] *n* commerçant(e) *m,f*

shoplifter ['ʃɒplɪftə(r)] *n* voleur(euse) *m,f* à l'étalage

shoplifting ['ʃɒplɪftɪŋ] *n* vol *m* à l'étalage

shopper ['ʃɒpə(r)] *n* personne *f* qui fait ses courses; *(customer)* client(e) *m,f*

shopping ['ʃɒpɪŋ] *n* courses *fpl*; **to do the s.** faire les courses; **to do one's s.** faire ses courses; **s. bag** sac *m* à provisions, cabas *m*; **s. basket** panier *m* (à provisions); *Econ* panier de la ménagère; **s. centre** *or* **precinct** centre *m* commercial; **s. list** liste *f* des courses; **s. trolley** chariot *m*

shopsoiled ['ʃɒpsɔɪld] *adj Br* défraîchi(e)

shore [ʃɔː(r)] *n* (*of sea*) rivage *m*; (*of lake*) bord *m*; **on s.** à terre; **to go on s.** (*from ship*) débarquer; **s. leave** permission *f* à terre

▶**shore up** *vt sep* (*house, wall*) étayer; *Fig* (*reputation*) consolider

shoreline ['ʃɔːlaɪn] *n* littoral *m*

shorn [ʃɔːn] *pp of* **shear**

short [ʃɔːt] **1** *adj* (**a**) (*physically*) court(e); (*person*) petit(e); **Bill is s. for William** Bill est le diminutif de William; **the s. answer is no** en deux mots la réponse est non; **to have a s. temper** *or* **fuse** être soupe au lait; **s. story** nouvelle *f*
  (**b**) (*in time*) court(e), bref (brève); **in s.** en bref; **to make s. work of sb/sth** expédier qn/qch; **s. and sweet** bref (brève)
  (**c**) (*abrupt*) brusque, sec (sèche) (**with** avec)
  (**d**) (*insufficient, lacking*) insuffisant(e); **to be in s. supply** manquer; **to be s. of sth** être à court *ou* manquer de qch; **I'm 50 pence s.** il me manque 50 pence; **little** *or* **not far s. of** (*almost*) pas loin de; **he's not far s. of forty** il n'est pas loin de la quarantaine; **it was nothing s. of miraculous that she survived** c'est vraiment un miracle qu'elle ait survécu
  2 *adv* (**a**) (*suddenly*) **to stop s.** s'arrêter net; **to bring sb up s.** arrêter net qn
  (**b**) (*in length, duration*) **to stop s. of doing sth** se retenir tout juste de faire qch; **to cut sb s.** couper la parole à qn, interrompre qn; **to cut sth s.** abréger qch
  (**c**) (*without*) **to go s. (of sth)** se priver (de qch)
  (**d**) (*insufficiency*) **to be running s. of sth** n'avoir presque plus de qch; **to fall s. of sth** (*target*) ne pas atteindre qch; (*expectations*) ne pas répondre à qch; *Fig* **to sell sb s.** rouler qn; **to be taken** *or* **caught s.** être pris(e) d'un besoin pressant
  3 *n Fam* (**a**) (*short film*) court-métrage *m*
  (**b**) (*drink*) alcool *m* fort
  (**c**) (*short circuit*) court-circuit *m*

shortage ['ʃɔːtɪdʒ] *n* pénurie *f*; **petrol/food s.** pénurie d'essence/de nourriture; **housing s.** crise *f* du logement; **to have no s. of sth** ne pas manquer de qch

shortbread ['ʃɔːtbred], **shortcake** ['ʃɔːtkeɪk] *n* sablés *mpl* au beurre

short-change [ʃɔːt'(t)ʃeɪndʒ] *vt* (*in shop*) ne pas rendre assez de monnaie à; *Fig* (*cheat*) escroquer

short-circuit [ʃɔːt'sɜːkɪt] **1** *n* court-circuit *m*
  2 *vt also Fig* court-circuiter
  3 *vi* se mettre en court-circuit

shortcomings ['ʃɔːtkʌmɪŋz] *npl* défauts *mpl*

shorten ['ʃɔːtən] *vt* (*skirt, text*) raccourcir; (*visit, task*) abréger

shortfall ['ʃɔːtfɔːl] *n* manque *m*, insuffisance *f*

shorthaired ['ʃɔːtheəd] *adj* (*cat, dog*) à poil(s) court(s); (*person*) aux cheveux courts

shorthand ['ʃɔːthænd] *n* sténographie *f*, sténo *f*; **s. typist** sténodactylo *mf*

short-haul ['ʃɔːthɔːl] *adj* moyen-courrier *m*

shortlist ['ʃɔːtlɪst] **1** *n* = liste de candidats après une première sélection

2 *vt* **to be shortlisted (for sth)** être parmi les candidats retenus (à qch)

short-lived [ʃɔːt'lɪvd] *adj* de courte durée

shortly ['ʃɔːtlɪ] *adv* (**a**) (*soon*) bientôt; **s. after(wards)** peu (de temps) après (**b**) (*abruptly*) sèchement

short-range ['ʃɔːtreɪndʒ] *adj* (*missile*) de courte portée

shorts [ʃɔːts] *npl* (*short trousers*) short *m*

short-sighted [ʃɔːt'saɪtɪd] *adj* myope; *Fig* peu clairvoyant(e)

short-sleeved [ʃɔːt'sliːvd] *adj* à manches courtes

shortstop ['ʃɔːtstɒp] *n Am Sport* bloqueur *m*

short-tempered [ʃɔːt'tempəd] *adj* coléreux(euse)

short-term ['ʃɔːttɜːm] *adj* à court terme

shot [ʃɒt] **1** *n* (**a**) (*act of firing, sound*) coup *m* (de feu); **to fire a s.** tirer; *Fig* **like a s.** sans hésiter; *Fig* **to take a s. in the dark** tenter le coup; *Fig* **to call the shots** faire la loi; **s. put** lancer *m* du poids
  (**b**) (*marksman*) tireur *m*
  (**c**) (*in football, rugby*) coup *m* de pied; (*in basketball*) lancer *m*; **good s.!** bien joué!
  (**d**) (*photograph*) photo *f*; (*of film, TV programme*) prise *f* de vue, plan *m*
  (**e**) *Fam* (*injection*) piqûre *f*
  (**f**) (*attempt*) tentative *f*, essai *m*; **to have a s. at sth/ at doing sth** essayer qch/de faire qch
  (**g**) (*drink*) petit verre *m*
  2 *pt & pp of* **shoot**

shotgun ['ʃɒtɡʌn] *n* fusil *m* de chasse; *Fam* **s. wedding** mariage *m* en catastrophe

should [ʃʊd]

La forme négative **should not** s'écrit **shouldn't** en forme contractée.

modal aux v (**a**) (*expressing obligation, desirability*) **you s. do it at once** vous devriez le faire tout de suite; **you s. have come earlier** vous auriez dû venir plus tôt; **she shouldn't have told them** elle n'aurait pas dû leur dire
  (**b**) (*expressing probability*) **the weather s. improve from now on** le temps devrait s'améliorer à partir de maintenant; **she s. have arrived by this time** elle devrait être arrivée à l'heure qu'il est
  (**c**) (*in exclamations, rhetorical questions*) **why s. you suspect me?** pourquoi me soupçonnez-vous?; **who s. I meet but Martin!** et qui a-t-il fallu que je rencontre? Martin!; **he apologized – I s. think so, too!** il s'est excusé – j'espère bien!
  (**d**) (*in subordinate clauses*) **he ordered that they s. be released** il a ordonné leur libération; **she insisted that he s. meet her parents** elle a insisté pour qu'il rencontre ses parents
  (**e**) (*in conditional clauses*) **if he s. come** *or Formal* **s. he come, let me know** s'il vient, fais-le-moi savoir
  (**f**) (*expressing opinions, preferences*) **I s. like a drink** je prendrais bien un verre; **I s. imagine he was rather angry** j'imagine qu'il était plutôt en colère; **I shouldn't be surprised if...** cela ne m'étonnerait pas si...

shoulder ['ʃəʊldə(r)] **1** *n* (*of person, meat*) épaule *f*; **to stand s. to s.** (*of two people*) se tenir l'un(e) contre l'autre; *Fig* **to rub shoulders with sb** côtoyer qn; *Fig* **to be looking over one's s.** être constamment sur ses gardes; *Fig* **to cry on sb's s.** pleurer sur l'épaule de qn; **s. bag** (sac *m*) besace *f*; **s. blade** omoplate *f*; **s. pad** épaulette *f*; **s. strap** (*of bag*) bandoulière *f*; (*of garment*) bretelle *f*

2 *vt* (**a**) *(push)* **to s. one's way through a crowd** se frayer un passage à travers la foule à coups d'épaule; **to s. sb aside** écarter qn d'un coup d'épaule (**b**) *(put on shoulder)* mettre sur son épaule; *Fig* **to s. the responsibility** endosser la responsabilité

shouldn't [ʃʊdənt] = **should not**

shout [ʃaʊt] **1** *n* cri *m*; **shouts of laughter** des éclats *mpl* de rire; **give me a s. when you're ready** appelle-moi quand tu seras prêt

2 *vt* crier; **to s. sth at sb** crier qch à qn

3 *vi* crier; **to s. at sb** crier après qn; **to s. for help** crier au secours; *Fig* **to have something to s. about** pouvoir être fier(ère) de qch

▸**shout down** *vt sep* **to s. sb down** huer qn

shouting [ʃaʊtɪŋ] *n* cris *mpl*

shove [ʃʌv] **1** *n* poussée *f*; **to give sb/sth a s.** pousser qn/qch

2 *vt & vi* pousser

▸**shove around** *vt sep Fam (bully)* chahuter

▸**shove off** *vi Fam (leave)* dégager

shovel [ʃʌvəl] **1** *n* pelle *f*

2 *vt (pt & pp shovelled)* pelleter; *Fam* **to s. food into one's mouth** enfourner de la nourriture

shovelful [ʃʌvəlfʊl] *n* pelletée *f*

show [ʃəʊ] **1** *n* (**a**) *(exhibition)* exposition *f*; **to be on s.** être exposé(e); **to put sth on s.** exposer qch; **s. house** maison *f* témoin; **s. jumper** = cavalier spécialisé dans le jumping; **s. jumping** jumping *m*; *Pej* **s. trial** procès *m* à grand spectacle

(**b**) *(concert, play)* spectacle *m*; *(on TV, radio)* émission *f*; *Fig* **to run the s.** commander; **s. business** show-business *m*, monde *m* du spectacle; **s. girl** girl *f*; *Fam* **to be a s. stopper** être le clou du spectacle

(**c**) *(act of showing)* démonstration *f*, manifestation *f*; **s. of hands** vote *m* à main levée; **it's all s.** tout ça, c'est de la comédie; **to do sth for s.** faire qch pour épater la galerie; *Fam* **good s.!** *(well done)* bravo!

2 *vt (pp shown* [ʃəʊn] *)* (**a**) *(display)* montrer; *(picture)* exposer; *(courage, talent)* faire preuve de; **to s. sb sth, to s. sth to sb** montrer qch à qn; *Fig* **to s. one's cards** *or* **one's hand** abattre ses cartes; **they had nothing to s. for all that work** ils avaient fait tout ce travail pour rien; **he won't s. his face round here again** on ne le reverra pas de sitôt; **to s. oneself** se montrer; **to s. a profit/a loss** enregistrer un bénéfice/une perte; **you're showing your age** ça ne te rajeunit pas!; **to s. oneself to be...** se révéler...

(**b**) *(indicate)* montrer, indiquer

(**c**) *(prove, demonstrate)* démontrer, prouver; **it goes to s. that...** cela montre bien que...

(**d**) *(teach)* montrer; **to s. sb how to do sth** montrer à qn comment faire qch

(**e**) *(film)* passer; *('IV programme)* diffuser

(**f**) *(escort, lead)* **to s. sb the way** montrer le chemin à qn; **to s. sb to his/her room** conduire qn à sa chambre; **to s. sb round the town** faire visiter la ville à qn

3 *vi* (**a**) *(be visible)* se voir

(**b**) *(of film)* passer

▸**show in** *vt sep (escort in)* faire entrer

▸**show off 1** *vt sep* exhiber

2 *vi* frimer

▸**show out** *vt sep (escort out)* reconduire, raccompagner

▸**show up 1** *vt sep* (**a**) *(reveal)* révéler (**b**) *(embarrass)* faire honte à

2 *vi* (**a**) *(stand out)* ressortir, se voir (**b**) *Fam (arrive)* se pointer

showbiz [ʃəʊbɪz] *n Fam* show-biz *m*, monde *m* du spectacle

showcase [ʃəʊkeɪs] *n* vitrine *f*

showdown [ʃəʊdaʊn] *n* confrontation *f*

shower [ʃaʊə(r)] **1** *n* (**a**) *(of rain)* averse *f*; *(of stones, insults)* pluie *f* (**b**) *(for washing)* douche *f*; **to have** *or* **take a s.** prendre une douche; **s. cap** bonnet *m* de douche; **s. curtain** rideau *m* de douche; **s. gel** gel *m* douche; **s. head** pomme *f* de douche (**c**) *Br Fam (group)* **what a s.!** quelle bande de crétins!

2 *vt* **to s. sb with sth, to s. sth on sb** couvrir qn de qch

3 *vi (take a shower)* se doucher

showery [ʃaʊərɪ] *adj* pluvieux(euse)

showing [ʃəʊɪŋ] *n (exhibition)* exposition *f*; *(of film)* séance *f*

showman [ʃəʊmən] *n (at circus)* forain *m*; *Fig* cabotin *m*

showmanship [ʃəʊmənʃɪp] *n* sens *m* du spectacle

shown [ʃəʊn] *pp of* **show**

show-off [ʃəʊɒf] *n Fam* frimeur(euse) *m,f*

showpiece [ʃəʊpiːs] *n* joyau *m*

showroom [ʃəʊruːm] *n* magasin *m*

showstopping [ʃəʊstɒpɪŋ] *adj* sensationnel(elle)

showy [ʃəʊɪ] *adj* voyant(e)

shrank [ʃræŋk] *pt of* **shrink**

shrapnel [ʃræpnəl] *n* éclats *mpl* d'obus

shred [ʃred] **1** *n* lambeau *m*; **in shreds** en lambeaux; **to tear sth to shreds** mettre qch en lambeaux; *Fig (criticize)* mettre qch en pièces; *Fig* **there isn't a s. of evidence** il n'y a pas l'ombre d'une preuve

2 *vt (pt & pp shredded) (documents)* déchiqueter; *(food)* couper grossièrement

shredder [ʃredə(r)] *n (for paper)* déchiqueteuse *f*

shrew [ʃruː] *n* (**a**) *(animal)* musaraigne *f* (**b**) *(nagging woman)* mégère *f*

shrewd [ʃruːd] *adj (person)* perspicace; *(decision)* judicieux(euse)

shrewdly [ʃruːdlɪ] *adv* judicieusement

shriek [ʃriːk] **1** *n* cri *m* strident; **shrieks of laughter** hurlements *mpl* de rire; **to give a s.** pousser un cri strident

2 *vt* hurler

3 *vi* pousser un cri strident; **to s. with laughter** hurler de rire

shrift [ʃrɪft] *n* **to give sb short s.** envoyer qn promener

shrill [ʃrɪl] *adj* strident(e), aigu(uë)

shrimp [ʃrɪmp] *n* crevette *f*

shrimping net [ʃrɪmpɪŋ'net] *n* crevettier *m (filet)*

shrine [ʃraɪn] *n (tomb)* tombeau *m*; *(place)* lieu *m* de pèlerinage; *Fig* haut lieu *m*

shrink [ʃrɪŋk] **1** *vt (pt shrank* [ʃræŋk]*, pp shrunk* [ʃrʌŋk] *)* faire rétrécir

2 *vi* (**a**) *(of material)* rétrécir; *(of income, budget)* diminuer, se réduire (**b**) *(move back)* **to s. from sth** se dérober devant qch; **to s. from doing sth** répugner à faire qch

3 *n Fam (psychiatrist)* psy *mf*

shrinkage [ʃrɪŋkɪdʒ] *n (of material)* rétrécissement *m*; *Fig (in sales, profit)* diminution *f*

shrink-wrapped [ʃrɪŋk'ræpt] *adj* emballé(e) sous film plastique

shrivel [ʃrɪvəl] *(pt & pp shrivelled, Am shriveled)* **1** *vt* dessécher

2 *vi* se dessécher

▶**shrivel up** *vi* se dessécher

shroud [ʃraʊd] **1** *n* linceul *m*; *Fig (of mystery, darkness)* voile *m*

  2 *vt Fig* **to be shrouded in sth** être enveloppé(e) de qch

Shrove Tuesday [ˈʃrəʊvˈtjuːzdɪ] *n* Mardi *m* gras

shrub [ʃrʌb] *n* arbuste *m*

shrubbery [ˈʃrʌbərɪ] *(pl* **shrubberies)** *n* jardin *m* d'arbustes

shrug [ʃrʌg] **1** *n* haussement *m* d'épaules

  2 *vt (pt & pp* **shrugged)** **to s. one's shoulders** hausser les épaules

  3 *vi* hausser les épaules

▶**shrug off** *vt sep* ignorer

shrunk [ʃrʌŋk] *pp of* **shrink**

shrunken [ˈʃrʌŋkən] *adj* rétréci(e)

shudder [ˈʃʌdə(r)] **1** *n (of person)* frisson *m*

  2 *vi (of person)* frissonner; *(of vehicle)* vibrer; **I s. to think!** j'ai des frissons quand j'y pense!

shuffle [ˈʃʌfəl] **1** *n* **(a) to walk with a s.** marcher en traînant les pieds **(b) to give the cards a s.** battre les cartes

  2 *vt (papers)* brasser; *(cards)* battre

  3 *vi (when walking)* traîner les pieds

shun [ʃʌn] *(pt & pp* **shunned)** *vt* fuir, éviter

shunt [ʃʌnt] *vt (train, carriages)* aiguiller; *Fam Fig (people)* transbahuter

shush [ʃʊʃ] **1** *vt* faire taire

  2 *exclam* chut!

shut [ʃʌt] **1** *adj* fermé(e); *Fam* **to keep one's mouth s.** se taire

  2 *vt (pt & pp* **shut)** fermer; **to s. the door on sb** fermer la porte au nez de qn; **to s. one's finger in the door** se coincer le doigt dans la porte; *Fam* **s. your mouth!** ferme-la!

  3 *vi (of door)* se fermer; *(of shop)* fermer

▶**shut down 1** *vt sep* fermer; *(production)* arrêter

  2 *vi* fermer

▶**shut in** *vt sep (confine)* enfermer

▶**shut off** *vt sep* **(a)** *(electricity, water, funds)* couper **(b)** *(road, exit)* fermer **(c)** *(isolate)* isoler **(from** de)

▶**shut out** *vt sep* **(a)** *(exclude)* exclure; *(light, view)* bloquer **(b)** *(keep outside)* empêcher d'entrer; **to s. oneself out** s'enfermer dehors

▶**shut up 1** *vt sep* **(a)** *(confine)* enfermer **(b)** *(close)* fermer **(c)** *Fam (silence)* faire taire

  2 *vi Fam (be quiet)* se taire

shutdown [ˈʃʌtdaʊn] *n (of factory)* fermeture *f*

shut-eye [ˈʃʌtaɪ] *n Fam* roupillon *m*; **to get some s.** roupiller

shutter [ˈʃʌtə(r)] *n* **(a)** *(on window)* volet *m*; *(of shop)* store *m*; **to put up the shutters** *(of shop)* fermer le magasin **(b)** *(in camera)* obturateur *m*

shuttle [ˈʃʌtəl] **1** *n* **(a)** *(in sewing, train, bus, plane)* navette *f*; **s. service** service *m* de navettes **(b)** *(in badminton)* volant *m*

  2 *vt* véhiculer

  3 *vi* faire la navette **(between** entre)

shuttlecock [ˈʃʌtəlkɒk] *n* volant *m*

shy [ʃaɪ] **1** *adj* timide; **to be s. of sb** être intimidé(e) par qn; **to be s. of doing sth** éviter de faire qch à tout prix

  2 *vi (pt &pp* **shied)** *(of horse)* s'effaroucher **(at** devant)

▶**shy away** *vi* **to s. away from sth/from doing sth** éviter qch/de faire qch

shyly [ˈʃaɪlɪ] *adv* timidement

Siamese [saɪəˈmiːz] **1** *n (pl* **Siamese)** *(cat)* siamois *m*

  2 *adj* siamois(e); **S. cat** chat *m* siamois; **S. twins** *(boys)* frères *mpl* siamois; *(girls)* sœurs *fpl* siamoises

Siberia [saɪˈbɪərɪə] *n* la Sibérie

Siberian [saɪˈbɪərɪən] **1** *n* Sibérien(enne) *m,f*

  2 *adj* sibérien(enne)

sibling [ˈsɪblɪŋ] *n (brother)* frère *m*; *(sister)* sœur *f*; **s. rivalry** rivalité *f* entre frères et sœurs

sic [sɪk] *adv* sic

Sicilian [sɪˈsɪlɪən] **1** *n* Sicilien(enne) *m,f*

  2 *adj* sicilien(enne)

Sicily [ˈsɪsɪlɪ] *n* la Sicile

sick [sɪk] **1** *adj* **(a)** *(ill)* malade; **to be s.** *(be ill)* être malade; *(vomit)* vomir; **to feel s.** avoir envie de vomir; *Fig* **it makes me s.!** ça me dégoûte!; *Fig* **to be worried s.** se faire un sang d'encre; **s. bay** infirmerie *f*; **s. leave** congé *m* de maladie; **s. note** *(from parents)* mot *m* d'absence; *(from doctor)* certificat *m* médical; **s. pay** indemnité *f* de maladie **(b)** *(fed up)* **to be s. of sb/sth** en avoir assez de qn/qch; **to be s. and tired** *or* **s. to death of sb/sth** en avoir ras le bol de qn/qch **(c)** *(humour, joke)* de mauvais goût; *(person)* malsain(e); **to have a s. mind** avoir l'esprit dérangé

  2 *n Fam (vomit)* vomi *m*

  3 *npl* **the s.** les malades *mpl*

▶**sick up** *vt sep Br Fam (vomit)* vomir

sicken [ˈsɪkən] **1** *vt (make ill)* rendre malade; *Fig (disgust)* écœurer

  2 *vi* **to be sickening for something** couver quelque chose

sickening [ˈsɪknɪŋ] *adj* écœurant(e)

sickle [ˈsɪkəl] *n* faucille *f*

sickly [ˈsɪklɪ] *adj* **(a)** *(person, complexion)* maladif(-ive); *(plant)* rabougri(e); *(colour, light, smile)* faible **(b)** *(taste, sentiment)* écœurant(e); **s. sweet** douceâtre

sickness [ˈsɪknɪs] *n (illness)* maladie *f*; *(nausea)* écœurement *m*; **s. benefit** indemnité *f* journalière

sickroom [ˈsɪkruːm] *n* chambre *f* de malade

side [saɪd] **1** *n* **(a)** *(of person, animal, object)* côté *m*; *(of mountain)* flanc *m*, versant *m*; **by sb's s.** aux côtés de qn; **s. by s.** côte à côte; *Fam* **to split one's sides** *(laughing)* se tordre de rire; **s. door/entrance** porte *f*/entrée *f* latérale

  (b) *(of record)* face *f*; *(paper)* côté *m*

  (c) *(adjacent area)* côté *m*; **on this/that s. (of)** de ce côté (de); **on the other s. (of)** de l'autre côté (de); **from all sides, from every s.** de toutes parts; **to move from s. to s.** osciller; **the left-/right-hand s.** le côté gauche/droit; **to lean to one s.** se pencher sur le côté; **to stand to one s.** se tenir à l'écart; **s. dish** plat *m* d'accompagnement; **s. salad** salade *f* *(pour accompagner un plat)*; **s. view** vue *f* latérale

  (d) *(aspect)* côté *m*; **to look on the bright/gloomy s. (of things)** voir le bon/mauvais côté (des choses)

  (e) *(in game)* camp *m*; *(in dispute)* côté *m*; **to be on sb's s.** être du côté de qn; **to take sides** prendre parti; **to change sides** changer de camp; **he had let the s. down** il nous/les/*etc* avait fait faux bond

  (f) *(secondary)* **s. effects** effets *mpl* secondaires; **s. issue** question *f* d'intérêt secondaire; **s. road** petite route *f*; **s. street** ruelle *f*

  (g) *(idioms)* **on his mother's s.** *(of family)* du côté de sa mère; **to put sth to one s.** mettre qch de côté; **to take sb to one s.** prendre qn à part; **to be on the**

wrong **s. of forty** avoir plus de quarante ans; **to get on the right s. of sb** se faire bien voir de qn; **to get on the wrong s. of sb** prendre qn à rebrousse-poil; **it's a bit on the expensive/long s.** c'est un peu cher/long; **to do sth on the s.** *(as extra job)* faire qch pour arrondir ses fins de mois; *Fam* **to have a bit on the s.** *(of man)* avoir une maîtresse; *(of woman)* avoir un amant
   2 *vi* **to s. with** prendre le parti de; **to s. against** prendre parti contre

sideboard ['saɪdbɔːd] *n* buffet *m*

sideboards ['saɪdbɔːdz], **sideburns** ['saɪdbɜːnz] *npl (facial hair)* pattes *fpl*

sidecar ['saɪdkɑː(r)] *n* side-car *m*

sidekick ['saɪdkɪk] *n Fam* acolyte *m*

sidelight ['saɪdlaɪt] *n* feu *m* de position

sideline ['saɪdlaɪn] **1** *n* (**a**) *(of football, rugby pitch)* ligne *f* de touche; *Fig* **to sit on the sidelines** rester sur la touche (**b**) *(business, job)* à-côté *m*; **we sell guide books as a s.** nous vendons également des guides
   2 *vt Sport & Fig* mettre sur la touche

side-saddle ['saɪdsædəl] *adv* **to ride s.** monter en amazone

sideshow ['saɪdʃəʊ] *n (at fair)* attraction *f*; *Fig* événement *m* mineur

side-splitting ['saɪdsplɪtɪŋ] *adj Fam* tordant(e)

sidestep ['saɪdstep] *(pt & pp* **sidestepped**) **1** *vt (tackle, player)* éviter; *Fig (question)* éluder
   2 *vi (in boxing)* esquiver

sideswipe ['saɪdswaɪp] *n* remarque *f* désobligeante

sidetrack ['saɪdtræk] *vt* distraire

sidewalk ['saɪdwɔːk] *n Am* trottoir *m*

sideways ['saɪdweɪz] **1** *adj (look, movement)* de côté
   2 *adv (move, walk)* latéralement; *(turn, fall, lean)* sur le côté

siding ['saɪdɪŋ] *n (on railway)* voie *f* de garage

sidle ['saɪdəl] *vi* **to s. up to sb** se glisser vers qn

siege [siːdʒ] *n* siège *m*; **to lay s. to a town** assiéger une ville; **under s.** assiégé(e); **to have a s. mentality** se sentir persécuté(e)

Sierra Leone [sɪˈerəliˈəʊn] *n* la Sierra Leone

sieve [sɪv] **1** *n* crible *m*; *(in kitchen)* passoire *f*; *Fam* **to have a memory like a s.** avoir la tête comme une passoire
   2 *vt* tamiser

sift [sɪft] **1** *vt (flour, sugar)* tamiser
   2 *vi Fig* **to s. through sth** passer qch au crible

sigh [saɪ] **1** *n* soupir *m*
   2 *vi* soupirer; *(of wind)* gémir

sight [saɪt] **1** *n* (**a**) *(faculty)* vue *f*; **to lose one's s.** perdre la vue
   (**b**) *(act of seeing)* **to catch s. of sb/sth** apercevoir qn/qch; **to lose s. of sb/sth** perdre qn/qch de vue; **I hate the s. of him** je ne peux pas le voir; **I can't stand the s. of blood** je ne supporte pas la vue du sang; **to shoot on s.** tirer à vue; **at first s.** à première vue; **it was love at first s.** ça a été le coup de foudre; **to know sb by s.** connaître qn de vue; **to buy sth s. unseen** acheter qch sans l'avoir vu
   (**c**) *(range of vision)* **to come into s.** apparaître; **in s.** en vue; **to keep sb in s.** garder un œil sur qn; **out of s.** caché(e); **to put sth out of s.** cacher qch; **to keep out of s.** se cacher; *Prov* **out of s., out of mind** loin des yeux, loin du cœur
   (**d**) *(of instrument, gun)* viseur *m*; *Fig* **to have sb/sth in one's sights** avoir qn/qch en vue; *Fig* **to have** *or* **set**

one's sights on sb/sth avoir des vues sur qn/qch
   (**e**) *(spectacle)* spectacle *m*; **you're/it's a s. for sore eyes** c'est un plaisir de te voir/de voir ça; *Fam* **to look a s.** ne pas être beau (belle) à voir; **sights** *(of city)* attractions *fpl* touristiques
   (**f**) *Fam (for emphasis)* **a damn s. easier/longer** bien plus facile/long (longue)
   2 *vt (see)* apercevoir

sighted ['saɪtɪd] **1** *npl* **the s.** les voyants *mpl*
   2 *adj (person)* voyant(e)

sighting ['saɪtɪŋ] *n* **several sightings of the fugitive have been reported** on a aperçu le fugitif à plusieurs reprises; **there have been several UFO sightings in the area** on a aperçu plusieurs ovnis dans les parages

sightless ['saɪtləs] *adj* aveugle

sight-read ['saɪtriːd] *(pt & pp* **sight-read** ['saɪtred]) *vt & vi* déchiffrer

sightseeing ['saɪtsiːɪŋ] *n* tourisme *m*; **to go s.** faire du tourisme

sightseer ['saɪtsiːə(r)] *n* touriste *mf*

sign [saɪn] **1** *n* (**a**) *(gesture, symbol, indication)* signe *m*; **to make a s. to sb** faire un signe à qn; **it's a sure s. that...** on peut être sûr que...; **a s. of the times** un signe des temps; **there's no s. of an improvement** il n'y a rien qui annonce une quelconque amélioration; **there's no s. of it/him** je ne le vois nulle part; **she gave no s. of having heard** elle n'a pas semblé avoir entendu; **all the signs are that...** tout laisse à penser que...; **the equipment showed signs of having been used** on voyait que l'équipement avait déjà été utilisé; **s. language** langage *m* des sourds-muets
   (**b**) *(notice)* panneau *m*; *(of pub, shop)* enseigne *f*; *(on road)* panneau de signalisation routière; **follow the signs for Manchester** suivre la direction de Manchester
   2 *vt* (**a**) *(write signature on)* signer
   (**b**) *(in sign language)* dire en langage des sourds-muets
   (**c**) *(in sport)* engager
   3 *vi* (**a**) *(write signature)* signer
   (**b**) *(in sport)* signer *(for* avec)

▸**sign away** *vt sep (rights)* renoncer à

▸**sign for** *vt insep (delivery, parcel)* signer un reçu pour

▸**sign in** *vi (in factory)* pointer; *(in hotel)* signer le registre en arrivant

▸**sign off** *vi* (**a**) *(of radio, TV presenter)* terminer l'émission (**b**) *(close letter)* finir la lettre

▸**sign on** *vi Fam (for unemployment benefit) (initially)* s'inscrire au chômage; *(regularly)* pointer

▸**sign out 1** *vt sep* **to s. sth out** *(book, equipment)* signer un registre pour emprunter qch
   2 *vi (from hotel)* signer le registre à son départ

▸**sign up** *vi* (**a**) *(register)* s'inscrire *(for* à) (**b**) *(of soldier)* s'engager

signal ['sɪgnəl] **1** *n* signal *m*; **radio s.** signal *m* radiophonique; *Fig* **to send the wrong signals** ne pas être clair(e); **s. box** poste *m* d'aiguillage; **s. flare** fusée *f* éclairante; **s. rocket** fusée de signalisation
   2 *vt (pt & pp* **signalled,** *Am* **signaled**) (**a**) *(make gesture to)* faire signe à; **to s. sb to do sth** faire signe à qn de faire qch (**b**) *(be sign of)* être le signe de
   3 *vi* (**a**) *(make gesture)* faire signe (**to** à) (**b**) *(in car)* clignoter

signalman ['sɪgnəlmən] *(pl* **signalmen**) *n* aiguilleur *m*

signatory ['sɪgnətərɪ] *(pl* **signatories**) *n* signataire *mf*

signature ['sɪgnətʃə(r)] *n* signature *f*; **s. tune** *(of radio, TV programme)* indicatif *m*

signboard ['saɪnbɔːd] *n* enseigne *f*

signet ring ['sɪgnɪt'rɪŋ] *n* chevalière *f*

significance [sɪg'nɪfɪkəns] *n* (**a**) *(importance)* importance *f*; **of great s.** d'une grande importance; **of no s.** sans importance (**b**) *(meaning)* signification *f*

significant [sɪg'nɪfɪkənt] *adj (important)* important(e), considérable; *(meaningful)* significatif(ive); **s. other** partenaire *mf (dans une relation affective)*; *Psy* = personne dont on se sent très proche

significantly [sɪg'nɪfɪkəntlɪ] *adv* (**a**) *(appreciably)* nettement; **to vary/change s.** varier/changer considérablement (**b**) *(meaningfully)* d'une manière significative; **s., no one mentioned it** fait révélateur, personne n'en a parlé

signify ['sɪgnɪfaɪ] *(pt & pp signified) vt* signifier

signpost ['saɪnpəʊst] **1** *n* poteau *m* indicateur; *Fig* indice *m*
2 *vt* signaliser

Sikh [siːk] *n & adj* sikh *mf*

silage ['saɪlɪdʒ] *n* ensilage *m*

silence ['saɪləns] **1** *n* silence *m*; **to listen/watch in s.** écouter/regarder en silence; *Prov* **s. is golden** le silence est d'or
2 *vt* faire taire

silencer ['saɪlənsə(r)] *n (on car, gun)* silencieux *m*

silent ['saɪlənt] *adj (person, place)* silencieux(euse); *(letter)* muet(ette); **to fall s.** se taire; **to remain** *or* **keep s.** garder le silence; **s. film** film *m* muet; **s. majority** majorité *f* silencieuse; **s. protest** manifestation *f* silencieuse

silently ['saɪləntlɪ] *adv* silencieusement

silhouette [sɪluː'et] **1** *n* silhouette *f*
2 *vt* **she was silhouetted against the light** sa silhouette se détachait à contre-jour

silica ['sɪlɪkə] *n* silice *f*

silicon ['sɪlɪkən] *n* silicium *m*; **s. chip** puce *f* électronique

silk [sɪlk] *n* soie *f*; **s. screen printing** sérigraphie *f*

silkworm ['sɪlkwɜːm] *n* ver *m* à soie

silky ['sɪlkɪ] *adj* soyeux(euse); *(voice)* suave

sill [sɪl] *n (of window)* rebord *m*

silliness ['sɪlɪnɪs] *n* stupidité *f*

silly ['sɪlɪ] **1** *adj* idiot(e), stupide; **the s. thing is that...** ce qui est idiot, c'est que...; **to look s.** avoir l'air ridicule; **to say/do something s.** dire/faire une bêtise; **to laugh/worry oneself s.** mourir de rire/d'inquiétude; **to knock sb s.** assommer qn
2 *n Fam* bêta(asse) *m,f*

silo ['saɪləʊ] *(pl silos) n* silo *m*

silt [sɪlt] *n* vase *f*
▶**silt up** *vi* s'envaser

silver ['sɪlvə(r)] **1** *n* (**a**) *(metal)* argent *m*; *Prov* **every cloud has a s. lining** à quelque chose malheur est bon; **s. haired** aux cheveux argentés; **s. (medal)** médaille *f* d'argent; **s. paper** papier *m* d'argent; **s. plate** *(coating)* plaqué *m* argent; *(articles)* argenterie *f*; **the s. screen** le grand écran; **s. wedding** noces *fpl* d'argent (**b**) *Br (coins)* pièces *fpl* en argent (**c**) *(silverware)* argenterie *f*
2 *adj* (**a**) *(made of silver)* en argent (**b**) **s.(-coloured)** argenté(e)

silver-plated [sɪlvə'pleɪtɪd] *adj* plaqué(e) argent

silversmith ['sɪlvəsmɪθ] *n* orfèvre *mf*

silverware ['sɪlvəweə(r)] *n* argenterie *f*

silverwork ['sɪlvəwɜːk] *n* orfèvrerie *f*

silvery ['sɪlvərɪ] *adj (colour)* argenté(e); *(sound)* argentin(e)

simian ['sɪmɪən] *adj* simien(enne)

similar ['sɪmɪlə(r)] *adj* semblable, similaire (**to** à); **s. in appearance/size** d'apparence/de taille semblable; **they are very s.** ils se ressemblent beaucoup

similarity [sɪmɪ'lærɪtɪ] *(pl similarities) n* ressemblance *f*

similarly ['sɪmɪləlɪ] *adv* de la même façon

simile ['sɪmɪlɪ] *n* comparaison *f*

simmer ['sɪmə(r)] **1** *n* **at a s.** à feu doux
2 *vt* mijoter
3 *vi* mijoter; *Fig (of revolt, discontent)* couver; **to s. with rage** bouillonner de rage
▶**simmer down** *vi Fam* se calmer

simper ['sɪmpə(r)] *vi* minauder

simple ['sɪmpəl] *adj* (**a**) *(easy)* simple; **in s. terms** dit simplement; **the s. truth** la vérité pure et simple (**b**) *(unintelligent)* simplet(ette)

simple-minded [sɪmpəl'maɪndɪd] *adj (person)* simple d'esprit; *(ideas, belief)* naïf(ïve)

simpleton ['sɪmpəltən] *n* simple *mf* d'esprit

simplicity [sɪm'plɪsɪtɪ] *n* simplicité *f*

simplification [sɪmplɪfɪ'keɪʃən] *n* simplification *f*

simplify ['sɪmplɪfaɪ] *(pt & pp simplified) vt* simplifier

simplistic [sɪm'plɪstɪk] *adj* simpliste

simply ['sɪmplɪ] *adv* (**a**) *(in simple manner)* simplement (**b**) *(absolutely)* absolument (**c**) *(just)* simplement; **it's s. a question of time** c'est une simple question de temps; **she s. had to snap her fingers and...** elle n'avait qu'à claquer des doigts et...

simulate ['sɪmjʊleɪt] *vt* simuler

simulated ['sɪmjʊleɪtɪd] *adj (leather, marble)* faux (fausse); *(surprise, anger)* simulé(e)

simulation [sɪmjʊ'leɪʃən] *n* simulation *f*

simultaneous [sɪməl'teɪnɪəs, *Am* saɪməl'teɪnɪəs] *adj* simultané(e); **s. broadcast** retransmission *f* simultanée; **s. translation** traduction *f* simultanée

simultaneously [sɪməl'teɪnɪəslɪ, *Am* saɪməl'teɪnɪəslɪ] *adv* simultanément

sin [sɪn] **1** *n* péché *m*; *Old-fashioned or Hum* **to be living in s.** *(of unmarried couple)* vivre dans le péché; *Fam* **it would be a s. to...** ce serait un crime de...
2 *vi (pt & pp sinned)* pécher

since [sɪns] **1** *adv* depuis; **long s.** depuis longtemps
2 *prep* depuis; **s. June/1984** depuis le mois de juin/1984; **s. then** depuis
3 *conj* (**a**) *(in time)* depuis que; **it's a long time s. I saw her** cela fait longtemps que je ne l'ai pas vue (**b**) *(because)* puisque

sincere [sɪn'sɪə(r)] *adj* sincère

sincerely [sɪn'sɪəlɪ] *adv* sincèrement; **Yours s.** *(ending letter)* Veuillez agréer, Monsieur/Madame, l'expression de mes salutations distinguées

sincerity [sɪn'serɪtɪ] *n* sincérité *f*; **in all s.** en toute sincérité

sinecure ['saɪnɪkjʊə(r)] *n* sinécure *f*

sinew ['sɪnjuː] *n* tendon *m*

sinewy ['sɪnjuːɪ] *adj* musclé(e)

sinful ['sɪnfʊl] *adj (act, life)* coupable; *(waste)* scandaleux(euse); **s. person** pécheur(eresse) *m,f*

sing [sɪŋ] *(pt sang [sæŋ], pp sung [sʌŋ])* **1** *vt (song)* chanter
2 *vi (of person, bird, kettle)* chanter

▶**sing out** *vi (sing loudly)* chanter fort

Singapore [sɪŋə'pɔ:(r)] *n* Singapour

Singaporean [sɪŋə'pɔ:rɪən] **1** *n* Singapourien(enne) *m,f*

    2 *adj* singapourien(enne)

singe [sɪndʒ] *vt* roussir

singer ['sɪŋə(r)] *n* chanteur(euse) *m,f*; **s. songwriter** auteur-compositeur-interprète *m*

singing ['sɪŋɪŋ] *n* chant *m*; **his s. is awful** il chante atrocement; **s. lessons** cours *mpl* de chant; **to have a fine s. voice** chanter admirablement

single ['sɪŋgəl] **1** *adj* (**a**) *(just one)* seul(e); **every s. day** tous les jours; **not a s. one** pas un(e); **don't say a s. word** ne dis pas un mot; **s. cream** ≃ crème *f* fraîche liquide; *Fin* **s. currency** monnaie *f* unique; *Econ* **s. European market** marché *m* unique européen (**b**) *(not double)* **in s. figures** inférieur à dix; **in s. file** en file indienne; **s. bed** lit *m* à une place; **s. room** chambre *f* pour une personne (**c**) *(not married)* célibataire; **s. mother** mère *f* célibataire; **s. parent** parent *m* isolé; **s. parent family** famille *f* monoparentale

    2 *n* (**a**) *(record)* single *m* (**b**) *(ticket)* aller *m* simple (**c**) *(hotel room)* chambre *f* pour une personne (**d**) **singles** *(in tennis)* simple *m*

▶**single out** *vt sep* distinguer; **she was singled out for praise** on n'a choisi de faire des compliments qu'à elle

single-breasted ['sɪŋgəl'brestɪd] *adj (jacket, suit)* droit(e)

single-decker ['sɪŋgəl'dekə(r)] *n* autobus *m* sans impériale

single-handedly ['sɪŋgəl'hændɪdlɪ] *adv* tout(e) seul(e)

single-income ['sɪŋgəl'ɪŋkʌm] *adj (family)* à salaire unique

single-minded ['sɪŋgəl'maɪndɪd] *adj (person)* résolu(e); *(determination, conviction)* farouche

single-sex school ['sɪŋgəl'seks'sku:l] *n* école *f* non mixte

singlet ['sɪŋglɪt] *n* maillot *m* de corps

single-track railway ['sɪŋgəl'træk'reɪlweɪ] *n* chemin *m* de fer à une seule voie

singsong ['sɪŋsɒŋ] **1** *n* (**a**) *(voice, tone)* voix *f* chantante (**b**) *Fam (singing session)* **to have a s.** chanter en chœur

    2 *adj (voice, tone)* chantant(e)

singular ['sɪŋgjʊlə(r)] **1** *n Gram* singulier *m*; **in the s.** au singulier

    2 *adj* (**a**) *Gram* singulier(ère) (**b**) *(remarkable)* remarquable

singularly ['sɪŋgjʊləlɪ] *adv* remarquablement

Sinhalese [sɪnə'li:z] **1** *n (pl* **Sinhalese**) (**a**) *(person)* Cinghalais(e) *m,f* (**b**) *(language)* cinghalais *m*

    2 *adj* cinghalais(e)

sinister ['sɪnɪstə(r)] *adj* sinistre

sink¹ [sɪŋk] *n (in kitchen)* évier *m*; *(in bathroom)* lavabo *m*; *Br* **s. estate** cité *f* dépotoir

sink² *(pt* **sank** [sæŋk], *pp* **sunk** [sʌŋk]) **1** *vt* (**a**) *(ship)* couler; **to be sunk in thought** être perdu(e) dans ses pensées; *Fam Fig* **to be sunk** être fichu(e) (**b**) *(well)* creuser; **to s. one's teeth into sth** mordre à pleines dents dans qch; **to s. money into sth** investir des capitaux dans qch; *Br Fam* **to s. a pint** s'envoyer une pinte de bière

    2 *vi (in water, mud)* couler; **her heart sank** son cœur s'est serré; **his spirits sank** il a perdu tout son courage; **to s. into sb's memory** *(of information)* se graver dans la mémoire de qn; **to s. into oblivion** tomber dans l'oubli; **to s. into a deep sleep** sombrer dans un profond sommeil; **to s. into an armchair** s'affaler dans un fauteuil; **to s. to the ground** s'effondrer par terre; **to s. in sb's estimation** baisser dans l'estime de qn; **how could you s. so low?** comment peux-tu tomber aussi bas?

▶**sink in** *vi (of liquid)* pénétrer; *(of information)* être assimilé(e); *Fig* **it hasn't sunk in yet** je n'ai/il n'a/etc pas encore digéré la nouvelle

sinking ['sɪŋkɪŋ] **1** *n* (**a**) *(of ship)* naufrage *m* (**b**) *Fin* **s. fund** fonds *m* d'amortissement

    2 *adj (feeling)* d'angoisse; **with a s. heart** avec un serrement de cœur

sinner ['sɪnə(r)] *n* pécheur(eresse) *m,f*

sinuous ['sɪnjʊəs] *adj (river, curves)* sinueux(euse); *(snake, dancer)* qui ondule; *(movement)* ondulant(e)

sinus ['saɪnəs] *n* sinus *m*

sinusitis [saɪnə'saɪtɪs] *n* sinusite *f*

sip [sɪp] **1** *n* petite gorgée *f*; **to take a s. (of sth)** boire une petite gorgée (de qch)

    2 *vt (pt & pp* **sipped**) siroter

    3 *vi* **to s. at sth** siroter qch

siphon ['saɪfən] **1** *n* siphon *m*

    2 *vt* siphonner

▶**siphon off** *vt sep (liquid)* siphonner; *Fig (money, supplies)* détourner

sir [sɜ:(r)] *n* (**a**) *(form of address)* monsieur *m*; **Dear S./ Sirs** *(in letter)* Monsieur/Messieurs (**b**) *(title)* **S. Clyde** sir Clyde *(titre de noblesse masculin)*

sire ['saɪə(r)] **1** *n* (**a**) *(father of animal)* père *m* (**b**) *Old-fashioned (address to sovereign)* sire *m*

    2 *vt* engendrer

siren ['saɪərən] *n* sirène *f*

sirloin ['sɜ:lɔɪn] *n* **s. (steak)** steak *m* d'aloyau

sissy ['sɪsɪ] *n Fam (weak male)* poule *f* mouillée; *(effeminate male)* garçon *m* efféminé

sister ['sɪstə(r)] *n* (**a**) *(sibling, nun)* sœur *f*; **s. company** société *f* sœur; **s. ship** sister-ship *m* (**b**) *(nurse)* infirmière-chef *f*

sisterhood ['sɪstəhʊd] *n* (**a**) *(community of nuns)* communauté *f* religieuse (**b**) *(solidarity)* solidarité *f* féminine

sister-in-law ['sɪstərɪn'lɔ:] *(pl* **sisters-in-law**) *n* belle-sœur *f*

sisterly ['sɪstəlɪ] *adj (advice, devotion)* de sœur

sit [sɪt] *(pt & pp* **sat** [sæt]) **1** *vt* (**a**) **to s. a child on one's knee** asseoir un enfant sur ses genoux (**b**) *Br (exam)* passer

    2 *vi* (**a**) *(of person)* s'asseoir; **to be sitting** être assis(e); **to be sitting reading** être assis en train de lire; **s.!** *(to dog)* assis!; *Fam* **to s. tight** *(not move)* ne pas bouger de sa place; *(not take action)* ne rien faire (**b**) *(of assembly, court)* siéger; **to s. on a jury** faire partie d'un jury (**c**) *(of object)* **to be sitting on the radiator/ outside** être sur le radiateur/dehors

▶**sit about, sit around** *vi* rester assis(e) à ne rien faire

▶**sit back** *vi* (**a**) *(lean back)* **to s. back in one's chair** s'installer confortablement sur sa chaise (**b**) *Fam (relax)* se détendre; *(not intervene)* ne rien faire

▶**sit down 1** *vt sep* asseoir; *Fam* **s. yourself down!** assieds-toi donc!

    2 *vi* s'asseoir; **to be sitting down** être assis(e)

▶**sit in** *vi (at meeting)* assister (**on** à)

▶**sit on** *vt insep Fam* (**a**) *(not deal with)* laisser traîner (**b**) *(repress)* rembarrer

▶**sit out 1** *vt sep (not participate in)* ne pas participer à **2** *vi (in garden)* s'asseoir dehors

▶**sit through** *vt insep* rester jusqu'au bout de

▶**sit up** *vi* (**a**) *(straighten one's back)* se redresser; *(from lying position)* s'asseoir; *Fig* **to make sb s. up (and take notice)** secouer qn (**b**) *(not go to bed)* veiller

sitar ['sɪtɑː(r)] *n* sitar *m*

sitcom ['sɪtkɒm] *n* sitcom *m*

site [saɪt] **1** *n* (**a**) *(of building)* emplacement *m*; *(archaeological)* site *m* (**b**) **(building) s.** chantier *m* (de construction) (**c**) *Comput (on Internet)* site *m* **2** *vt* situer

sit-in ['sɪtɪn] *n* occupation *f* des locaux

sitting ['sɪtɪŋ] **1** *n (of committee, for portrait)* séance *f*; *(for meal)* service *m*; **at one s.** d'un trait; **s. room** *(in house)* salon *m* **2** *adj* (**a**) *(seated)* assis(e); *Fam Fig* **s. duck** *or* **target** cible *f* facile (**b**) *(current) Pol* **s. member** député *m* en exercice; **s. tenant** locataire *mf* dans les lieux

situate ['sɪtjʊeɪt] *vt* situer

situated ['sɪtjʊeɪtɪd] *adj* situé(e)

situation [sɪtjʊ'eɪʃən] *n* (**a**) *(circumstances)* situation *f*; **s. comedy** *(on TV)* sitcom *m* (**b**) *(job)* **situations vacant/wanted** *(in advertisements)* offres *fpl*/demandes *fpl* d'emploi (**c**) *(location)* emplacement *m*

sit-up ['sɪtʌp] *n* **to do sit-ups** faire des abdominaux

six [sɪks] **1** *n* six *m inv*; *Fam* **it's s. of one and half a dozen of the other** c'est kif-kif; **at sixes and sevens** sens dessus dessous; *Fam* **to knock sb for s.** étendre qn **2** *adj* six; *see also* **eight**

six-figure ['sɪks'fɪgə(r)] *adj* **a s. sum** une somme à six chiffres

six-pack ['sɪkspæk] *n* (**a**) *(of beer)* pack *m* de six (**b**) *Fam Hum (stomach muscles)* abdos *mpl*

sixpence ['sɪkspəns] *n Br Formerly* = ancienne pièce de 6 pence

six-shooter ['sɪksʃuːtə(r)] *n* six-coups *m inv*

sixteen [sɪks'tiːn] **1** *n* seize *m inv* **2** *adj* seize; *see also* **eight**

sixteenth [sɪks'tiːnθ] **1** *n* (**a**) *(fraction)* seizième *m* (**b**) *(in series)* seizième *mf* (**c**) *(of month)* seize *m inv* **2** *adj* seizième; *see also* **eighth**

sixth [sɪksθ] **1** *n* (**a**) *(fraction)* sixième *m* (**b**) *(in series)* sixième *mf* (**c**) *(of month)* six *m inv* **2** *adj* sixième; *Br Sch* **the s. form** ≃ les classes *fpl* de première et de terminale; *Br Sch* **s. former** ≃ élève *mf* de première ou de terminale; **s. sense** sixième sens *m*; *see also* **eighth**

sixtieth ['sɪkstɪɪθ] **1** *n* (**a**) *(fraction)* soixantième *m* (**b**) *(in series)* soixantième *mf* **2** *adj* soixantième

sixty ['sɪkstɪ] **1** *n* soixante *m inv* **2** *adj* soixante; *see also* **eighty**

size [saɪz] *n (of person, clothes)* taille *f*; *(of shoe)* pointure *f*; *(of place, object)* dimensions *fpl*; *(of country)* superficie *f*; *(of problem, undertaking)* ampleur *f*; *Fam* **that's about the s. of it** c'est à peu près ça; **s. 10 shoes** ≃ des chaussures du 44; **what s. do you take?** *(of clothes)* quelle taille faites-vous?; *(of shoes)* quelle est votre pointure?, vous chaussez du combien?; **to try sth (on) for s.** essayer qch pour voir si la taille convient

▶**size up** *vt sep (person)* jauger; *(situation)* évaluer

sizeable ['saɪzəbəl] *adj* non négligeable; *(improvement)* net (nette)

sizzle ['sɪzəl] **1** *n* grésillement *m* **2** *vi* grésiller

skate¹ [skeɪt] *n (fish)* raie *f*

skate² **1** *n* patin *m*; *Fam Fig* **to get one's skates on** se dépêcher **2** *vi (on ice skates)* faire du patin à glace; *(on roller skates)* faire du roller; *Fig* **to s. round sth** tourner autour de qch

▶**skate over** *vt insep (deal with superficially)* survoler

skateboard ['skeɪtbɔːd] *n* planche *f* à roulettes

skater ['skeɪtə(r)] *n* patineur(euse) *m,f*

skating ['skeɪtɪŋ] *n* patinage *m*; **s. rink** *(for ice skating)* patinoire *f*; *(for roller skating)* piste *f*

skeletal ['skelɪtəl] *adj* squelettique

skeleton ['skelɪtən] *n (of person)* squelette *m*; *(of building)* charpente *f*; *Fig* **to have a s. in the cupboard** *or* **closet** avoir un secret honteux; **s. staff/ crew** personnel *m*/équipage *m* réduit; **s. key** passe-partout *m inv*

skeptic, skeptical *etc Am* = **sceptic, sceptical** *etc*

sketch [sketʃ] **1** *n* (**a**) *(drawing, description)* croquis *m*; **s. pad** bloc *m* à dessin (**b**) *(on stage, TV)* sketch *m* **2** *vt also Fig* esquisser

▶**sketch in** *vt sep also Fig* esquisser

▶**sketch out** *vt sep* ébaucher

sketchbook ['sketʃbʊk] *n* carnet *m* de croquis

sketchily ['sketʃɪlɪ] *adv* vaguement

sketchy ['sketʃɪ] *adj* vague (**about** à propos de)

skew [skjuː] **1** *n* **on the s.** de travers **2** *vt (distort)* fausser

skewer ['skjuːə(r)] **1** *n* brochette *f* **2** *vt* embrocher

ski [skiː] **1** *n* ski *m*; **s. boots** chaussures *fpl* de ski; **s. instructor** moniteur(trice) *m,f* de ski; **s. jump** saut *m* à skis; **s. jumper** sauteur(euse) *m,f* à ski; **s. lift** remontée *f* mécanique; **s. pants** fuseau *m*; **s. resort** station *f* de ski; **s. run** *or* **slope** piste *f* de ski; **s. stick** bâton *m* de ski **2** *vi (pt & pp* **skied**) skier, faire du ski

skid [skɪd] **1** *n* (**a**) *(of car)* dérapage *m*; **to go into a s.** faire un dérapage (**b**) *(idioms) Fam* **to put the skids under sb/sth** faire accélérer qn/qch; *Fam* **to be on the skids** battre de l'aile; *Am Fam* **to be on s. row** être à la rue **2** *vi (pt & pp* **skidded**) déraper

skier ['skiːə(r)] *n* skieur(euse) *m,f*

skiing ['skiːɪŋ] *n* ski *m*; **to go s.** aller faire du ski; **s. instructor** moniteur(trice) *m,f* de ski

skilful, *Am* **skillful** ['skɪlfʊl] *adj* habile

skilfully, *Am* **skillfully** ['skɪlfʊlɪ] *adv* habilement

skill [skɪl] *n (ability)* qualités *fpl*; *(technique)* compétence *f*, connaissances *fpl*

skilled [skɪld] *adj (person, work)* qualifié(e); **to be s. in doing sth** être habile à faire qch; **s. worker** ouvrier(ère) *m,f* qualifié(e)

skillful, skillfully *Am* = **skilful, skilfully**

skim [skɪm] *(pt & pp* **skimmed**) **1** *vt* (**a**) *(milk)* écrémer; *(soup)* écumer (**b**) *(surface)* effleurer; **to s. stones on water** faire des ricochets **2** *vi* **to s. along** *or* **over the ground** voler au ras du sol; **to s. over the water** raser la surface de l'eau

▶**skim off** *vt sep (fat, cream)* enlever; *Fig (money)* ponctionner

▶**skim through** *vt insep (novel, document)* lire en diagonale

skimmed milk ['skɪmd'mɪlk], *Am* **skim milk** ['skɪm'mɪlk] *n* lait *m* écrémé

skimp [skɪmp] **1** *vt* lésiner sur; *(work)* bâcler **2** *vi* **to s. on sth** lésiner sur qch

skimpy ['skɪmpɪ] *adj (meal)* maigre; *(clothes)* étriqué(e)

skin [skɪn] **1** *n* (**a**) *(of person, animal, fruit, on milk, sauce)* peau *f*; **to be all s. and bone** n'avoir que la peau et les os; *Fam* **to jump out of one's s.** sauter au plafond; **by the s. of one's teeth** de justesse; **to save one's (own) s.** sauver sa peau; *Fam* **to get under sb's s.** taper sur les nerfs de qn; *Fam* **it's no s. off my nose** je m'en balance; **s. cancer** cancer *m* de la peau; **s. complaint** problème *m* de peau; **s. cream** crème *f* pour la peau; **s. disease** maladie *f* de peau; **s. diving** plongée *f* sous-marine; *Am Fam* **s. flick** *(porn film)* film *m* porno; *Med* **s. graft** greffe *f* de peau; **s. patch** timbre *m* transdermique (**b**) *Fam (skinhead)* skin *mf* **2** *vt (pt & pp* **skinned)** *(animal)* écorcher; *(tomato)* peler; **to s. one's knees** s'écorcher les genoux

▶**skin up** *vi Br very Fam* rouler un pétard

skinflint ['skɪnflɪnt] *n Fam* radin(e) *m,f*

skinhead ['skɪnhed] *n* skinhead *mf*

skinny ['skɪnɪ] *adj* maigre

skint [skɪnt] *adj Br Fam* fauché(e)

skintight ['skɪntaɪt] *adj* moulant(e)

skip¹ [skɪp] **1** *n (jump)* saut *m* **2** *vt (pt & pp* **skipped)** *(meal, page, stage)* sauter **3** *vi (of lambs, children)* gambader; *(with rope)* sauter à la corde

skip² *n (for rubbish)* benne *f*

skipper ['skɪpə(r)] **1** *n (of ship, team)* capitaine *m* **2** *vt Fam* commander

skipping ['skɪpɪŋ] *n* saut *m* à la corde; **s. rope** corde *f* à sauter

skirmish ['skɜːmɪʃ] **1** *n Mil* escarmouche *f*; *Fig* accrochage *m* **2** *vi* s'engager dans une escarmouche

skirt [skɜːt] **1** *n* jupe *f* **2** *vt (village, hill)* contourner; **to s. (a)round a problem** contourner un problème

skirting board ['skɜːtɪŋbɔːd] *n Br* plinthe *f*

skit [skɪt] *n* satire *f*

skittish ['skɪtɪʃ] *adj* (**a**) *(nervous)* nerveux(euse) (**b**) *(playful)* espiègle

skittle ['skɪtəl] *n* quille *f*

skive [skaɪv] *vi Br Fam* tirer au flanc

▶**skive off** *vi Br Fam* s'esquiver

skiver ['skaɪvə(r)] *n Br Fam* tire-au-flanc *m inv*

skivvy ['skɪvɪ] *(pl* **skivvies)** *n Br Pej* bonne *f* à tout faire

skulduggery [skʌl'dʌgərɪ] *n* magouille *f*

skulk [skʌlk] *vi* rôder

skull [skʌl] *n* crâne *m*; **s. and crossbones** tête *f* de mort

skullcap ['skʌlkæp] *n* calotte *f*

skunk [skʌŋk] *n (animal)* moufette *f*, *Can* bête *f* puante; *Fam Pej (person)* mufle *m*

sky [skaɪ] *n* ciel *m*; *Fam* **the s.'s the limit** tout est possible; *Fam* **to praise sb to the skies** porter qn aux nues; **s. high** *(price, costs)* astronomique

sky-blue [skaɪ'bluː] *adj* bleu ciel *inv*

skydiver ['skaɪdaɪvə(r)] *n* parachutiste *mf (qui pratique la chute libre)*

skydiving ['skaɪdaɪvɪŋ] *n* parachutisme *m (en chute libre)*

skylark ['skaɪlɑːk] *n* alouette *f* des champs

skylight ['skaɪlaɪt] *n* lucarne *f* faîtière

skyline ['skaɪlaɪn] *n (horizon)* horizon *m*; *(of city)* silhouette *f*

skyscraper ['skaɪskreɪpə(r)] *n* gratte-ciel *m inv*

slab [slæb] *n* (**a**) *(of stone, concrete)* dalle *f*; *(of cake)* tranche *f*; *(of meat)* pavé *m*; *(of chocolate)* plaque *f* (**b**) *(in mortuary)* table *f* d'autopsie

slack [slæk] **1** *adj* (**a**) *(not tight)* mou (molle); **trade is s.** le commerce marche mal; **in s. periods** en période creuse (**b**) *(careless)* négligent(e) **2** *n* **to take up the s.** *(in rope)* tendre la corde; *Fig* prendre le relais **3** *vi Fam* se relâcher

▶**slack off** *vi (of rain)* se calmer; *(of trade, demand)* se ralentir

slacken ['slækən] **1** *vt (pace)* ralentir; *(rope)* détendre **2** *vi (of person, rope)* se relâcher; *(of speed)* se ralentir; *(of storm, wind)* se calmer; *(of energy, enthusiasm)* retomber

▶**slacken off** *vi (of rain)* se calmer; *(of trade, demand)* se ralentir

slacker ['slækə(r)] *n Fam* flemmard(e) *m,f*

slackness ['slæknɪs] *n* (**a**) *(negligence)* négligence *f*; *(laziness)* fainéantise *f* (**b**) *(of rope)* mou *m* (**c**) *(of business)* stagnation *f*

slacks [slæks] *npl Old-fashioned (trousers)* pantalon *m*

slag [slæg] *n* (**a**) *(from coalmine)* scories *fpl*; **s. heap** terril *m* (**b**) *Br very Fam Pej (woman)* salope *f*

▶**slag off** *(pt & pp* **slagged)** *vt sep Br Fam (criticize)* débiner

slain [sleɪn] **1** *npl* **the s.** les morts *mpl* **2** *pp of* **slay**

slake [sleɪk] *vt Lit* **to s. one's thirst** étancher sa soif

slalom ['slɑːləm] *n* slalom *m*

slam [slæm] **1** *vt (pt & pp* **slammed)** (**a**) *(door)* claquer; *(lid, drawer)* fermer violemment; **to s. the door in sb's face** claquer la porte au nez de qn; **to s. sth down** flanquer qch (**b**) *Fam (criticize)* éreinter **2** *vi (of door)* claquer; **to s. on the brakes** freiner à fond **3** *n (of door)* claquement *m*

slander ['slɑːndə(r)] **1** *n* calomnie *f* **2** *vt* calomnier

slanderous ['slɑːndərəs] *adj* calomnieux(euse)

slang [slæŋ] **1** *n* argot *m* **2** *vt Fam (insult)* injurier

slanging match ['slæŋɪŋ'mætʃ] *n* échange *m* d'insultes

slant [slɑːnt] **1** *n* (**a**) *(slope)* pente *f* (**b**) *(point of view)* perspective *f*; *(bias)* parti *m* pris; **to put a s. on sth** présenter qch d'une manière partiale **2** *vt* (**a**) *(set at angle)* incliner (**b**) *(bias)* présenter avec parti pris **3** *vi (slope)* être incliné(e)

slanting ['slɑːntɪŋ] *adj (roof)* en pente; *(writing)* penché(e)

slap [slæp] **1** *n (with hand)* claque *f*; *also Fig* **a s. in the face** une gifle; **to get a s. on the wrist** *(reprimand)* se faire taper sur les doigts **2** *adv Fam* **s. (bang) in the middle** en plein milieu **3** *vt (pt & pp* **slapped)** donner une claque à; **to s. sb's face, to s. sb in the face** gifler qn; **to s. sb on the back** donner une tape dans le dos à qn; *Fig* **to s. sb down**

remettre qn à sa place; **to s. some paint on sth** passer un coup de peinture sur qch

slapdash ['slæpdæʃ] adj (work) fait n'importe comment ou à la va-vite; (person) négligent(e)

slapper ['slæpə(r)] n Br Fam pouffiasse f, traînée f

slapstick ['slæpstɪk] n **s. (comedy)** comique m tarte à la crème

slap-up ['slæpʌp] adj Br Fam **s. meal** gueuleton m

slash [slæʃ] **1** n (**a**) (cut) coupure f, balafre f (**b**) Typ barre f oblique (**c**) Br very Fam **to have/go for a s.** pisser/aller pisser un coup
2 vt (cut) taillader, balafrer; (reduce) réduire considérablement; **prices slashed** (sign) prix sacrifiés

slat [slæt] n latte f

slate [sleɪt] **1** n (**a**) (stone) ardoise f; **s. grey** ardoise m inv; **s. quarry** ardoisière f (**b**) (idioms) Fam **put it on the s.** mettez-le-moi sur mon ardoise; **to wipe the s. clean** faire table rase
2 vt Fam (criticize) éreinter

slaughter ['slɔːtə(r)] **1** n (of animals) abattage m; (of people) massacre m
2 vt (animals) abattre; (people) massacrer; Fam (defeat heavily) massacrer

slaughterhouse ['slɔːtəhaʊs] n abattoir m

Slav [slɑːv] n Slave mf

slave [sleɪv] **1** n esclave mf; Fam Fig **s. driver** négrier m; **s. labour** travail m de forçat; **s. trade** commerce m des esclaves
2 vi trimer (**over** sur); **I've been slaving over a hot stove all day** j'ai passé ma journée aux fourneaux

slaver ['slævə(r)] vi baver

slavery ['sleɪvərɪ] n esclavage m

Slavic ['slɑːvɪk] adj slave

slavish ['sleɪvɪʃ] adj servile

Slavonic [slə'vɒnɪk] adj slave

slay [sleɪ] (pt **slew** [sluː], pp **slain** [sleɪn]) vt Lit (kill) tuer

sleaze [sliːz] n Fam (**a**) (immorality) côté m scabreux (**b**) (in politics) scandales mpl

sleazy ['sliːzɪ] adj Fam (affair, place) sordide; (person) louche

sledge [sledʒ], Am **sled** [sled] **1** n luge f; (for transporting) traîneau m
2 vi (Am pt & pp **sledded**) faire de la luge

sledgehammer ['sledʒhæmə(r)] n masse f; Fig **to use a s. to crack a nut** avoir recours à des moyens démesurés

sleek [sliːk] adj (hair) lisse et brillant(e); (manner) mielleux(euse)

▸**sleek down** vt sep **to s. down one's hair** se lisser les cheveux

sleep [sliːp] **1** n (**a**) (rest) sommeil m; **to go to s.** s'endormir; **to put sb to s.** (anaesthetize) endormir qn; **to put an animal to s.** (kill) faire piquer un animal; Fig **to send sb to s.** (bore) endormir qn; **I won't lose any s. over it** cela ne va pas m'empêcher de dormir; **to walk in one's s.** être somnambule; **to talk in one's s.** parler en dormant; **my foot has gone to s.** je ne sens plus mon pied (**b**) (in eye) **to have s. in one's eyes** avoir les yeux chassieux
2 vi (pt & pp **slept** [slept]) dormir; Euph **to s. with sb** coucher avec qn; **I slept through the alarm** je n'ai pas entendu le réveil; **I'll s. on it** la nuit porte conseil; **to s. rough** dormir dehors ou dans la rue
3 vt **the flat sleeps four** on peut dormir à quatre dans l'appartement; **I haven't slept a wink all night** je n'ai pas fermé l'œil de la nuit

▸**sleep around** vi Fam coucher à droite et à gauche

▸**sleep in** vi ne pas se réveiller à l'heure

▸**sleep off** vt sep **to s. off a hangover** cuver son vin

▸**sleep together** vi coucher ensemble

sleeper ['sliːpə(r)] n (**a**) (person) dormeur(euse) m,f; **to be a light/heavy s.** avoir le sommeil léger/lourd (**b**) Rail (train) train-couchettes m; Br (on track) traverse f, Can dormant m

sleepily ['sliːpɪlɪ] adv d'un air endormi

sleeping ['sliːpɪŋ] **1** n **s. arrangements** couchage m; **s. bag** sac m de couchage; **s. car** (on train) wagon-lit m; **s. pill** somnifère m
2 adj endormi(e); Prov **let s. dogs lie** ne réveillez pas le chat qui dort; **s. partner** (in company) commanditaire m; Br **s. policeman** (in road) ralentisseur m

sleepless ['sliːpləs] adj **to have a s. night** passer une nuit blanche, ne pas fermer l'œil de la nuit

sleepwalk ['sliːpwɔːk] vi être somnambule

sleepwalker ['sliːpwɔːkə(r)] n somnambule mf

sleepy ['sliːpɪ] adj somnolent(e); **to be** or **feel s.** avoir sommeil

sleet [sliːt] **1** n neige f fondue
2 vi **it's sleeting** il tombe de la neige fondue

sleeve [sliːv] n (**a**) (of shirt, jacket) manche f; Fig **he's still got something up his s.** il n'a pas encore dit son dernier mot (**b**) (of record) pochette f

sleeveless ['sliːvlɪs] adj sans manches

sleigh [sleɪ] n traîneau m

sleight [slaɪt] n **s. of hand** tour m de passe-passe

slender ['slendə(r)] adj (**a**) (person, figure) svelte; (waist) fin(e) (**b**) (hope) mince; (income) maigre; (majority) faible; **of s. means** qui a peu de moyens

slept [slept] pt & pp of **sleep**

sleuth [sluːθ] n Fam limier m

slew [sluː] pt of **slay**

slice [slaɪs] **1** n (of bread, meat, cake) tranche f; (of pizza) part f; (of cheese) lamelle f; (of salami) rondelle f; Fig **a s. of the profits** une part des bénéfices
2 vt (**a**) (bread, meat, cake) couper en tranches; (cheese) couper en lamelles; (salami) couper en rondelles; **to s. sth in two** or **in half** couper qch en deux (**b**) (in sport) slicer

▸**slice off** vt sep couper

▸**slice through** vt insep trancher

▸**slice up** vt sep couper en tranches

sliced bread ['slaɪst'bred] n pain m en tranches; Fam **it's the best thing since s.** on n'a rien fait de mieux depuis l'invention du fil à couper le beurre

slick [slɪk] adj (**a**) (campaign, event) bien mené(e) (**b**) Pej (reply, person, manner) habile (**c**) (surface, tyre) lisse
2 n (oil) **s.** marée f noire

▸**slick back** vt sep **to s. one's hair back** se lisser les cheveux

slide [slaɪd] **1** n (**a**) (fall) (in prices, popularity) chute f; Math **s. rule** règle f à calcul (**b**) (in playground) toboggan m (**c**) (for microscope) lame f; (photographic) diapositive f; **s. projector** projecteur m de diapositives; **s. show** diaporama m (**d**) Br (for hair) barrette f
2 vt (pt & pp **slid** [slɪd]) glisser; **s. the lid off** faites glisser le couvercle
3 vi (**a**) (slip) (of person) glisser; (of door, hatch) coulisser; **the door slid open** la porte coulissante s'est ouverte; Fig **to let things s.** laisser les choses se

dégrader; **to s. down a rope** glisser le long d'une corde (**b**) *(move quietly)* se glisser

sliding ['slaɪdɪŋ] *adj* coulissant(e); **s. door** porte *f* coulissante; **s. scale** échelle *f* mobile

slight [slaɪt] **1** *adj* (**a**) *(small, unimportant)* léger(ère); **not the slightest danger/interest** pas le moindre danger/intérêt; **not in the slightest** pas du tout (**b**) *(person)* menu(e)
2 *n (affront)* affront *m*
3 *vt* blesser

slightly ['slaɪtlɪ] *adv* (**a**) *(to a small degree)* légèrement (**b**) **s. built** menu(e)

slim [slɪm] **1** *adj (person)* mince, svelte; *(book, chance, hope)* mince; *(majority)* faible
2 *vi (pt & pp **slimmed**)* faire un régime

▸**slim down 1** *vt sep Fig (budget, company)* réduire
2 *vi (of person)* perdre du poids; *Fig (of company)* réduire ses effectifs

slime [slaɪm] *n (mud)* vase *f*; *(of snail, slug)* bave *f*

slimmer ['slɪmə(r)] *n* personne *f* qui fait un régime amaigrissant

slimming ['slɪmɪŋ] *n* **s. can be bad for you** les régimes amaigrissants peuvent être dangereux pour la santé; **s. diet** régime *m* amaigrissant; **s. product** produit *m* amaigrissant

slimy ['slaɪmɪ] *adj (frog, snail)* visqueux(euse); *Pej (person)* mielleux(euse)

sling [slɪŋ] **1** *n* (**a**) *(for injured arm)* écharpe *f*; **he had his arm in a s.** il avait le bras en écharpe (**b**) *(weapon)* fronde *f*
2 *vt (pt & pp **slung** [slʌŋ]) (throw)* lancer; **to s. sth over one's shoulder** mettre qch sur son épaule; *Br Fam Fig* **s. your hook!** dégage!

▸**sling out** *vt sep Fam (throw away)* balancer; *(person)* vider

▸**slingshot** ['slɪŋʃɒt] *n Am* lance-pierres *m inv*

slink [slɪŋk] *(pt & pp **slunk** [slʌŋk]) vi* **to s. off** *or* **away** s'éclipser

slinky ['slɪŋkɪ] *adj (dress)* long (longue) et sexy

slip [slɪp] **1** *n* (**a**) *(fall)* chute *f*; *(of land)* glissement *m*; *(in prices, standards)* chute
(**b**) *(error)* erreur *f*; **a s. of the pen/tongue** un lapsus
(**c**) **to give sb the s.** semer qn
(**d**) *(of paper)* bout *m* de papier; *(printed)* bordereau *m*
(**e**) *Br* **a s. of a girl** une petite jeune, une gamine; **a s. of a lad** un gamin
(**f**) *Br Aut* **s. road** bretelle *f*
(**g**) *(garment)* combinaison *f*; **(pillow) s.** taie *f* d'oreiller
2 *vt (pt & pp **slipped**)* (**a**) *(escape)* **her name has slipped my mind** son nom m'échappe; **the ship slipped its moorings** le bateau a quitté son mouillage
(**b**) *(put)* glisser; **to s. sth into the conversation** glisser qch dans la conversation; **to s. a coat on/off** enfiler/quitter un manteau
(**c**) **to s. a disc** se faire une hernie discale
3 *vi* (**a**) *(slide) (of person, foot)* glisser; *(of prices, popularity)* chuter; **to s. from sb's hands** *or* **grasp** glisser des mains de qn; *Fig* **to s. through sb's fingers** glisser entre les doigts de qn; **to let one's guard/concentration s.** relâcher sa vigilance/concentration
(**b**) *(move quickly)* **to s. into sth** *(bed, room, shoes)* se glisser dans qch; *(clothes)* enfiler qch; **to s. out of sth** *(clothes)* quitter qch

(**c**) *(make mistake)* faire une erreur; **you're slipping!** tu baisses!
(**d**) **to let sth s.** *(words, information)* lâcher qch

▸**slip away** *vi (leave)* s'éclipser

▸**slip by** *vi (of time, years)* passer vite

▸**slip out** *vi (escape)* s'échapper; **to s. out to the shop** faire un saut au magasin

▸**slip through** *vi (of mistake)* échapper à l'attention

▸**slip up** *vi (make mistake)* se planter

slip-on ['slɪpɒn] **1** *n Fam* **slip-ons** chaussures *fpl* sans lacets
2 *adj (shoes)* sans lacets

slipper ['slɪpə(r)] *n* pantoufle *f*

slippery ['slɪpərɪ] *adj* glissant(e); *(person)* fuyant(e); *Fig* **to be on a s. slope** être sur une pente savonneuse

slippy ['slɪpɪ] *adj* glissant(e)

slipshod ['slɪpʃɒd] *adj (work)* bâclé(e)

slipstream ['slɪpstriːm] *n* sillage *m*

slip-up ['slɪpʌp] *n* bourde *f*

slipway ['slɪpweɪ] *n Naut (for repairs)* cale *f* de construction; *(for launching)* cale de lancement

slit [slɪt] **1** *n* fente *f*
2 *vt (pt & pp **slit**)* fendre; **to s. sth open** ouvrir qch; **to s. sb's throat** couper la gorge à qn

slither ['slɪðə(r)] *vi* glisser

sliver ['slɪvə(r)] *n (of ham, cheese)* mince tranche *f*; *(of wood, glass)* éclat *m*

slob [slɒb] *n Fam (untidy person)* dégueulasse *mf*; *(lazy person)* flemmard(e) *m,f*

slobber ['slɒbə(r)] *vi* baver

sloe [sləʊ] *n (fruit)* prunelle *f*; **s. gin** alcool *m* de prunelles

slog [slɒg] *Fam* **1** *vi (pt & pp **slogged**) (work hard)* trimer, bosser (**at** sur)
2 *n* **it was a bit of a s.** ça a été dur; **it's a long s.** *(walk)* ça fait une trotte

slogan ['sləʊgən] *n* slogan *m*

slo-mo ['sləʊməʊ] *adj Fam (abbr **slow-motion**)* au ralenti

sloop [sluːp] *n (ship)* sloop *m*

slop [slɒp] **1** *n* (**a**) *(pig food)* pâtée *f* (**b**) *Fam Pej (sentimentality)* sensiblerie *f*
2 *vt (pt & pp **slopped**)* renverser
3 *vi* se renverser

slope [sləʊp] **1** *n* pente *f*
2 *vi* être en pente

▸**slope off** *vi Fam* se tailler

sloping ['sləʊpɪŋ] *adj (roof, ground)* en pente; *(handwriting)* penché(e); **s. shoulders** épaules *fpl* tombantes

sloppy ['slɒpɪ] *adj* (**a**) *(careless) (person)* sans soin; *(attitude)* négligé(e); *(work)* bâclé(e) (**b**) *Fam Pej (sentimental)* sentimental(e)

slosh [slɒʃ] *vi (of liquid)* clapoter; *(spill)* se renverser

sloshed [slɒʃt] *adj Fam (drunk)* bourré(e); **to get s.** prendre une cuite

slot [slɒt] **1** *n (in box, machine)* fente *f*; *(in schedule, list)* créneau *m*; **s. machine** *(for vending)* distributeur *m* automatique; *(for gambling)* machine *f* à sous
2 *vt (pt & pp **slotted**) (part)* insérer

▸**slot in 1** *vt sep (into schedule)* caser
2 *vi (of part)* rentrer; *(into team)* s'intégrer

sloth [sləʊθ] *n* (**a**) *(laziness)* paresse *f* (**b**) *(animal)* paresseux *m*

slothful ['sləʊθfʊl] *adj* paresseux(euse)

slouch [slaʊtʃ] **1** n Fam **he's no s.** il n'est pas empoté **2** vi (on chair) être avachi(e); **she slouched out of the room** elle est sortie de la pièce en traînant les pieds; **don't s.!** tiens-toi droit!

slough [slʌf] vt **to s. its skin** (of reptile) muer

Slovak ['sləʊvæk] **1** n (**a**) (person) Slovaque mf (**b**) (language) slovaque m **2** adj slovaque

Slovakia [sləʊ'vækɪə] n la Slovaquie

Slovakian [sləʊ'vækɪən] **1** n Slovaque mf **2** adj slovaque

Slovene ['sləʊviːn] **1** n (**a**) (person) Slovène mf (**b**) (language) slovène m **2** adj slovène

Slovenia [sləʊ'viːnɪə] n la Slovénie

Slovenian [sləʊ'viːnɪən] **1** n Slovène mf **2** adj slovène

slovenly ['slʌvənlɪ] adj (untidy) négligé(e); (careless) négligent(e); (unkempt) débraillé(e)

slow [sləʊ] **1** adj (not fast, stupid) lent(e); **business is s.** les affaires tournent au ralenti; **my watch is s.** ma montre a du retard; **to be s. to do sth** être lent à faire qch; **to be s. off the mark** (in race) être lent à démarrer; (to understand) être lent à la détente; Culin **in a s. oven** à four doux; **we're making s. progress** nous avançons lentement; **she's a s. worker** elle travaille lentement; Aut **s. lane** voie f lente; Cin & TV **(in) s. motion** (au) ralenti m; **s. train** (train m) omnibus m **2** adv lentement **3** vi ralentir

▶**slow down, slow up** vt sep & vi ralentir

slowcoach ['sləʊkəʊtʃ] n Br Fam lambin(e) m,f

slowly ['sləʊlɪ] adv lentement; **s. but surely** lentement mais sûrement

slowness ['sləʊnɪs] n lenteur f

slowpoke ['sləʊpəʊk] n Am Fam lambin(e) m,f

slow-witted ['sləʊ'wɪtɪd] adj à l'esprit lent

slow-worm ['sləʊwɜːm] n orvet m

SLR [esel'ɑː(r)] n Phot (abbr **single-lens reflex**) reflex m monoculaire

sludge [slʌdʒ] n vase f, boue f

slug [slʌg] **1** n (**a**) (mollusc) limace f (**b**) Fam (bullet) balle f (**c**) Fam (of drink) goutte f **2** vt (pt & pp **slugged**) Fam (hit) cogner

sluggish ['slʌgɪʃ] adj (person) (lazy) paresseux(-euse); (not energetic) léthargique; (business, market) au ralenti

sluice [sluːs] **1** n (**a**) (channel) canal m (**b**) (sluicegate) écluse f **2** vt **to s. sth down/out** laver qch à grande eau

sluicegate ['sluːsgeɪt] n écluse f

slum [slʌm] **1** n (district) quartier m délabré; (shanty-town) bidonville m; (house) taudis m **2** vt (pt & pp **slummed**) **to s. it** s'encanailler

slumber ['slʌmbə(r)] **1** n (**a**) Lit sommeil m (**b**) Am **s. party** = soirée entre fillettes, où les invitées restent dormir chez leur hôte **2** vi dormir

slump [slʌmp] **1** n (in prices, sales) effondrement m; (economic depression) crise f (économique) **2** vi (of person, economy, prices) s'effondrer

slung [slʌŋ] pt & pp of **sling**

slunk [slʌŋk] pt & pp of **slink**

slur [slɜː(r)] **1** n (**a**) (insult) insulte f; **to cast a s. on sb's reputation** entacher la réputation de qn (**b**) (in speech) **there was a s. in her voice** elle avait du mal à articuler **2** vt (pt & pp **slurred**) mal articuler

slurp [slɜːp] vt & vi (drink) boire bruyamment; (eat) manger bruyamment

slush [slʌʃ] n (**a**) (snow) neige f fondue (**b**) Pol **s. fund** caisse f noire (**c**) Fam Pej (sentimentality) sensiblerie f

slushy [slʌʃɪ] adj (**a**) (snow) fondu(e) (**b**) Fam Pej (film, book) à l'eau de rose

slut [slʌt] n (promiscuous woman) salope f

sluttish ['slʌtɪʃ] adj (slovenly) négligé(e)

sly [slaɪ] **1** adj (**a**) (cunning) rusé(e) (**b**) (dishonest) sournois(e) (**c**) (mischievous) espiègle **2** n **on the s.** en douce

smack [smæk] **1** n (**a**) (blow) claque f; (on bottom) fessée f; (sound) claquement m; **a s. in the face** une gifle (**b**) Fam (heroin) héro f **2** adv Fam **to bump s. into a tree** rentrer en plein dans un arbre **3** vt (hit) donner une claque à; (on bottom) donner une fessée à; **to s. one's lips** faire claquer ses lèvres

▶**smack of** vt insep (suggest) avoir des relents de

smacker ['smækə(r)] n Fam (**a**) (kiss) grosse bise f (**b**) **50 smackers** (pounds) 50 livres; (dollars) 50 dollars

small [smɔːl] **1** adj (**a**) (not large) petit(e); **to make sth smaller** rapetisser qch; Fig **it made me feel s.** (inconsequential) je me suis senti tout petit; **the s. hours** le petit matin; Journ **s. ads** petites annonces fpl; **s. arms** armes fpl portatives; **s. business** petite entreprise f; **s. businessman** petit entrepreneur m; **s. letters** (not capitals) minuscules fpl; **s. talk** banalités fpl; **to make s. talk** échanger des banalités (**b**) (not important) peu important(e); **it's s. wonder that...** ce n'est pas très étonnant que...; **in a s. way** à sa façon; Fam **to be s. beer** (of money) être que dalle; **s. change** petite monnaie f; **s. fry** menu fretin m **2** adv (chop) menu; (write) petit; **to think s.** voir petit **3** n (**a**) **the s. of the back** la chute des reins (**b**) Fam **smalls** (underwear) sous-vêtements mpl

smallholder ['smɔːlhəʊldə(r)] n petit(e) exploitant(e) m,f

smallholding ['smɔːlhəʊldɪŋ] n petite exploitation f

small-minded [smɔːl'maɪndɪd] adj étroit(e) d'esprit

smallness ['smɔːlnɪs] n petitesse f

smallpox ['smɔːlpɒks] n variole f

small-scale ['smɔːlskeɪl] adj (model) réduit(e); (research, project) à petite échelle

small-time ['smɔːltaɪm] adj Fam (criminal, businessman) petit(e)

smarmy ['smɑːmɪ] adj Pej mielleux(euse)

smart [smɑːt] **1** adj (**a**) (clever, sharp) (person) futé(e); (decision, move) habile; **don't get s. with me** n'essaie pas de faire le malin avec moi; Fam **s. aleck** petit malin m; **s. bomb** bombe f intelligente; **s. card** carte f à puce; **s. drug** psychotrope m (**b**) (elegant) (clothes) élégant(e); (hotel, area) chic inv; **the s. set** le beau monde; **to be a s. dresser** bien s'habiller (**c**) (quick) (pace, work) rapide; **look s. (about it)!** et que ça saute! (**d**) Fam (excellent) génial(e); (pretty) canon inv **2** vi (sting) (of wound, graze) brûler; (of eyes) piquer; Fig (of person) être piqué(e) au vif

▶**smarten up** ['smɑːtən] **1** vt sep égayer; **to s. oneself up** se faire beau **2** vi (improve) se reprendre

smarty-pants ['smɑːtɪpænts] (pl **smarty-pants**) n Fam Pej petit(e) malin(igne) m,f

smash [smæʃ] **1** *n (blow)* coup *m*; *(noise)* fracas *m*; *(collision)* collision *f*; *(in tennis)* smash *m*; **s. (hit)** *(record, film)* gros succès *m*
  2 *vt* **(a)** **to s. sth (to pieces)** fracasser qch; **to s. sth open** défoncer qch; **to s. down a door** défoncer une porte **(b)** *(ruin)* anéantir; **to s. a drugs ring** démanteler un réseau de trafiquants de drogue; **she smashed the world record** elle a pulvérisé le record du monde
  3 *vi* **(a)** *(strike)* **to s. into sth** s'écraser contre qch **(b)** **to s. (into pieces)** éclater (en morceaux)
▸**smash up** *vt sep (room, car, furniture)* saccager
smash-and-grab raid [smæʃən'græb'reɪd] *n* pillage *m* de vitrines
smashed [smæʃt] *adj Fam (drunk)* pété(e)
smasher ['smæʃə(r)] *n Br Fam* **what a s.!** *(person)* il/elle est génial(e)!
smashing ['smæʃɪŋ] *adj* **(a)** *(blow)* violent(e) **(b)** *Br Fam (excellent)* génial(e); **we had a s. time!** on s'est éclatés!
smattering ['smætərɪŋ] *n* notions *fpl*
smear [smɪə(r)] **1** *n* **(a)** *(stain)* tache *f*; *Med* **s. test** frottis *m* **(b)** *(slander)* propos *m* diffamatoire; **s. campaign** campagne *f* de diffamation
  2 *vt* **(a)** *(stain)* tacher; *(spread)* enduire, barbouiller; *(smudge) (paint)* salir **(b)** *(slander)* calomnier
smell [smel] **1** *n* **(a)** *(sense)* odorat *m* **(b)** *(odour)* odeur *f*; **there's a bad s.** ça sent mauvais; **to have a s. of sth** sentir qch
  2 *vt (pt & pp smelled or smelt* [smelt] *) also Fig* sentir; *Fig* **I s. a rat** ça sent l'embrouille
  3 *vi* sentir; *(stink)* sentir mauvais; **to s. of sth** sentir qch; **his breath smells** il a mauvaise haleine
smelly ['smelɪ] *adj* qui sent mauvais
smelt [smelt] **1** *vt (ore)* fondre
  2 *pt & pp of* **smell**
smile [smaɪl] **1** *n* sourire *m*; **to give sb a s.** sourire à qn; **she was all smiles** elle était tout sourire; **to take or wipe the s. off sb's face** passer l'envie de sourire à qn
  2 *vi* sourire (**at** à); **fortune smiled on them** la fortune leur sourit; **s.!** *(for photograph)* un petit sourire!
smiley ['smaɪlɪ] *n Comput* souriant *m*, émoticon *m*, *Can* binette *f*
smiling ['smaɪlɪŋ] *adj* souriant(e)
smirk [smɜːk] **1** *n* sourire *m* en coin
  2 *vi* sourire en coin
smite [smaɪt] *(pt* **smote** [sməʊt], *pp* **smitten** ['smɪtən] *)* *vt* **(a)** *Lit (strike)* frapper **(b)** **smitten with terror** terrorisé(e); **smitten with remorse** envahi(e) par les remords
smith [smɪθ] *n* forgeron *m*
smithereens [smɪðə'riːnz] *npl* **to smash/blow sth to s.** réduire qch en miettes
smithy ['smɪðɪ] *(pl* **smithies)** *n* forge *f*
smitten ['smɪtən] **1** *adj (in love)* très épris(e) (**with** de)
  2 *pp of* **smite**
smock [smɒk] *n* blouse *f*
smog [smɒg] *n* smog *m*
smoke [sməʊk] **1** *n* fumée *f*; **to have a s.** fumer une cigarette; *Fig* **to go up in s.** partir en fumée; *Prov* **there's no s. without fire** il n'y a pas de fumée sans feu; **s. bomb** bombe *f* fumigène; **s. detector** détecteur *m* de fumée; *also Fig* **s. screen** rideau *m* de fumée; **s. signals** signaux *mpl* de fumée
  2 *vt* **(a)** *(cigarette)* fumer; **to s. a pipe** fumer la pipe **(b)** *(meat, fish)* fumer
  3 *vi* **(a)** *(of person)* fumer **(b)** *(of chimney, oil)* fumer

▸**smoke out** *vt sep (insects)* enfumer; *Fig (rebels)* débusquer
smoked [sməʊkt] *adj* fumé(e); **s. glass** verre *m* fumé; **s. salmon** saumon *m* fumé
smokeless ['sməʊklɪs] *adj* **s. fuel** combustible *m* non polluant; **s. zone** = zone où l'usage de combustible polluant n'est pas autorisé
smoker ['sməʊkə(r)] *n* fumeur(euse) *m,f*; **to be a cigarette/pipe s.** fumer des cigarettes/la pipe; **to be a heavy s.** être un grand fumeur; **s.'s cough** toux *f* de fumeur
smoking ['sməʊkɪŋ] *n* **s. can damage your health** fumer *ou* le tabac nuit à la santé; **no s.** *(sign)* défense de fumer; **s. compartment** compartiment *m* fumeurs; *Fig* **s. gun** *(clue)* indice *m* flagrant; **s. jacket** veste *f* d'intérieur; **s. room** salle *f* fumeurs
smoky ['sməʊkɪ] *adj (atmosphere, room)* enfumé(e); *(fire)* qui dégage de la fumée; *(surface)* noirci(e) par la fumée; *(taste)* de fumée
smolder *Am* = **smoulder**
smooch [smuːtʃ] *vi Fam* se bécoter
smooth [smuːð] **1** *adj* **(a)** *(not rough)* lisse; *(sea)* calme; *(sauce)* homogène; *(skin, wine, whisky)* doux *(douce)*; *(style)* coulant(e); *(flight, crossing)* calme; **a s. shave** un rasage de près **(b)** *(person, manner)* onctueux(euse); **he's a s. talker** c'est un beau parleur; **to be a s. operator** savoir y faire **(c)** *(without problems)* sans problèmes; **to get off to a s. start** commencer sans problèmes
  2 *vt (feathers, hair)* lisser; *(pillow, sheet, clothing)* défroisser; *(surface)* égaliser; **to s. the way for sb** faciliter les choses à qn; **to s. the way for sth** faciliter qch
▸**smooth back** *vt sep* **to s. back one's hair** lisser ses cheveux en arrière
▸**smooth down** *vt sep* lisser
▸**smooth out** *vt sep (map, sheets)* défroisser; *(crease)* faire disparaître; *Fig (difficulty)* aplanir
▸**smooth over** *vt sep (difficulties)* aplanir; *(differences)* atténuer; **to s. things over** arranger les choses
smoothly ['smuːðlɪ] *adv* sans problèmes; **to go s.** se passer sans problèmes
smoothness ['smuːðnɪs] *n (of skin, wine, whisky)* douceur *f*; *(of surface)* aspect *m* lisse; *(of flight, crossing)* calme *m*; *(of sauce)* homogénéité *f*
smooth-talking ['smuːð'tɔːkɪŋ] *adj* mielleux(euse)
smote [sməʊt] *pt of* **smite**
smother ['smʌðə(r)] *vt* **(a)** *(person, fire, yawn)* étouffer; **to s. sb with kisses** couvrir qn de baisers **(b)** *(cover)* **to s. sth in sth** recouvrir qch de qch
smoulder, *Am* **smolder** ['sməʊldə(r)] *vi (of fire)* couver; *Fig* **to s. with anger/passion** se consumer de colère/passion
smudge [smʌdʒ] **1** *n* tache *f*
  2 *vt (ink, lipstick)* étaler; *(drawing)* maculer
  3 *vi (of ink, lipstick)* s'étaler
smug [smʌg] *adj* suffisant(e)
smuggle ['smʌgəl] *vt (arms, drugs)* faire de la contrebande de; **to s. sth in/out** faire entrer/sortir qch en contrebande; **to s. sb in/out** faire entrer/sortir qn clandestinement; **to s. sth through customs** passer qch en fraude à la douane
smuggler ['smʌglə(r)] *n* contrebandier(ère) *m,f*; *(of drugs)* trafiquant(e) *m,f*
smuggling ['smʌglɪŋ] *n* contrebande *f*; *(of drugs)* trafic *m*

smut [smʌt] *n* (**a**) *(soot)* tache *f* de suie (**b**) *(obscenity)* cochonneries *fpl*

smutty ['smʌtɪ] *adj* (**a**) *(dirty)* sale, noirci(e) (**b**) *(obscene)* cochon(onne)

snack [snæk] **1** *n* casse-croûte *m inv*; **to have a s.** grignoter quelque chose; **s. bar** snack-bar *m*
2 *vi* **to s. on sth** grignoter qch

snag [snæg] **1** *n (problem)* problème *m*
2 *vt (pt & pp* **snagged)** *(clothing)* faire un accroc à

snail [sneɪl] *n* escargot *m*; **at a s.'s pace** *(move)* comme un escargot; *(change, learn, progress)* très lentement; *Fam* **s. mail** = terme humoristique désignant les services postaux par opposition aux messageries électroniques

snake [sneɪk] **1** *n* serpent *m*; *Fig* **s. in the grass** traître(esse) *m,f*; **snakes and ladders** ≃ jeu *m* de l'oie; **s. charmer** charmeur(euse) *m,f* de serpent; *Am Fig* **s. pit** fosse *f* aux serpents
2 *vi (of road, river)* serpenter

snakebite ['sneɪkbaɪt] *n* (**a**) *(of snake)* morsure *f* de serpent (**b**) *(drink)* = boisson composée d'une mesure de bière et d'une mesure de cidre

snakeskin ['sneɪkskɪn] *n* peau *f* de serpent

snap [snæp] **1** *n* (**a**) *(bite)* coup *m* de dents (**b**) *(sound)* craquement *m*; **a s. of the fingers** un claquement de doigts (**c**) *(of weather)* **a cold s.** une brusque vague de froid (**d**) *Fam (photograph)* photo *f* (**e**) *(card game)* = jeu de cartes dont le but est de crier "snap" lorsque l'on pose sur la table une carte similaire à celle qui vient d'être posée; *Fam* **I'm going to Paris – s.!** je vais à Paris – tiens, moi aussi!
2 *adj (judgement, decision)* hâtif(ive); **to call a s. election** procéder à une élection surprise
3 *vt (pt & pp* **snapped)** (**a**) *(break)* casser net; **to s. sth in two** casser qch en deux (**b**) **to s. one's fingers** faire claquer ses doigts (**c**) *(say sharply)* dire sèchement (**d**) *Fam (take photograph of)* prendre en photo
4 *vi* (**a**) *(break cleanly)* casser net; *(break noisily)* casser avec un bruit sec (**b**) *(bite)* **to s. (at)** essayer de mordre; **to s. shut** *(of jaws, lid)* se refermer avec un bruit sec (**c**) *(speak abruptly)* parler sèchement (at à) (**d**) *(idioms)* **to s. out of it** *(of depression, apathy)* se secouer; *(of sulk)* arrêter de faire la tête

▸**snap off 1** *vt sep* (**a**) *(break)* casser net (**b**) *Fam* **to s. sb's head off** rembarrer qn
2 *vi* casser net

▸**snap up** *vt sep* (**a**) *(seize in jaws)* attraper (**b**) *(buy, take quickly)* rafler

snapdragon ['snæpdrægən] *n* gueule-de-loup *f*

snappy ['snæpɪ] *adj Fam (style, prose)* vif (vive); *(slogan)* accrocheur(euse); **to be a s. dresser** s'habiller toujours à la mode; **make it s.!** *(be quick)* au trot!

snapshot ['snæpʃɒt] *n Fam (photograph)* photo *f*

snare [sneə(r)] **1** *n* collet *m*; *Fig* piège *m*; **s. drum** caisse *f* claire
2 *vt* prendre au collet; *Fig* prendre au piège

snarl [snɑːl] **1** *n* grognement *m*
2 *vi* grogner (**at** après)

▸**snarl up 1** *vt sep (thread, hair)* emmêler; *Br (traffic)* bloquer; **to get snarled up** *(thread)* s'emmêler; *Br (traffic)* se bloquer, bouchonner
2 *vi (of thread, hair)* s'emmêler, *Br (of traffic)* se bloquer

snarl-up ['snɑːlʌp] *n (of traffic)* bouchon *m*; *(in system)* paralysie *f*

snatch [snætʃ] **1** *n (of conversation)* bribe *f*; **to sleep in snatches** avoir un sommeil fragmenté; **a s. of music** quelques notes de musique
2 *vt* (**a**) *(grab)* saisir; **to s. something to eat** avaler quelque chose à la hâte; **to s. some sleep** dormir un peu (**b**) *(steal, abduct) (wallet, handbag)* arracher; *(person)* enlever
3 *vi* **to s. at sth** essayer de saisir qch

▸**snatch away** *vt sep* arracher

snazzy ['snæzɪ] *adj Fam* chicos, classe

sneak [sniːk] **1** *n* (**a**) *Fam (telltale)* mouchard(e) *m,f* (**b**) **to get a s. preview of sth** voir qch en avant-première
2 *vt (pt & pp* **sneaked**, *Am* **snuck** [snʌk]) **to s. sth past sb** passer qch subrepticement devant qn; **to s. sb in/out** faire entrer/sortir qn subrepticement; **to s. a glance at sb** jeter un coup d'œil furtif à qn
3 *vi* (**a**) *(tell tales)* rapporter (**b**) *(move furtively)* se déplacer furtivement; **to s. past sb** passer furtivement devant qn; **to s. in/out** entrer/sortir furtivement

▸**sneak away, sneak off** *vi* s'esquiver

sneaker ['sniːkə(r)] *n Am (running shoe)* chaussure *f* de sport

sneaky ['sniːkɪ] *adj* sournois(e)

sneer [snɪə(r)] **1** *n (expression)* sourire *m* méprisant
2 *vt* **"you couldn't do that,"** he sneered "vous n'en seriez pas capable," dit-il d'un air méprisant
3 *vi* ricaner; **to s. at sb/sth** se moquer de qn/qch

sneering ['snɪərɪŋ] **1** *n (laughter)* ricanement *m*; *(remarks)* sarcasmes *mpl*
2 *adj* méprisant(e)

sneeze [sniːz] **1** *n* éternuement *m*
2 *vi* éternuer; *Fam Fig* **it's not to be sneezed at** il ne faut pas cracher dessus

snicker ['snɪkə(r)] *Am* **1** *n* ricanement *m*
2 *vi* ricaner

snide [snaɪd] *adj* méprisant(e)

sniff [snɪf] **1** *vt* (**a**) *(smell)* sentir; *(detect)* flairer (**b**) *(inhale) (air)* respirer; *(cocaine, glue)* sniffer
2 *vi (disdainfully)* avoir une moue de dédain; *Fam* **it's not to be sniffed at** il ne faut pas cracher dessus
3 *n* **to take a s. at sth** sentir qch; **with a s. of disgust** avec une moue de dégoût

▸**sniff out** *vt sep (of dog)* découvrir à l'odeur; *Fig (of investigator)* découvrir

sniffer dog ['snɪfədɒg] *n* chien *m* renifleur

sniffle ['snɪfəl] **1** *n (slight cold)* petit rhume *m*; *Fam* **to have the sniffles** avoir un petit rhume
2 *vi* (**a**) *(sniff repeatedly)* renifler (**b**) *(cry quietly)* pleurer (doucement)

sniffy ['snɪfɪ] *adj Fam (disdainful)* dédaigneux(euse); **to be s. about sth** éprouver du dédain pour qch

snifter ['snɪftə(r)] *n Br Fam Old-fashioned (drink)* petit verre *m*

snigger ['snɪgə(r)] **1** *n* ricanement *m* étouffé
2 *vi* ricaner

snip [snɪp] **1** *n* (**a**) *(cut)* petite entaille *f* (**b**) *(piece cut off)* bout *m* (**c**) *Br Fam (bargain)* (bonne) affaire *f*
2 *vt (pt & pp* **snipped)** couper

▸**snip off** *vt sep* couper

snipe¹ [snaɪp] *(pl* **snipe)** *n (bird)* bécassine *f*

snipe² *vi (shoot)* tirer (d'une position cachée); **to s. at sb** tirer sur qn (d'une position cachée); *Fig (criticize)* critiquer qn de façon malveillante

sniper ['snaɪpə(r)] *n* tireur(euse) *m,f* embusqué(e)

snippet ['snɪpɪt] *n (of information, conversation)* bribe *f*; **a s. of news** une nouvelle brève

snitch [snɪtʃ] *Fam* **1** *n* (**a**) *(informer)* mouchard(e) *m,f* (**b**) *(nose)* pif *m*
2 *vi* moucharder; **to s. on sb** moucharder qn

snivel ['snɪvəl] *(pt & pp* **snivelled,** *Am* **sniveled**) *vi* pleurnicher

snivelling, *Am* **sniveling** ['snɪvəlɪŋ] *adj* pleurni-cheur(euse)

snob [snɒb] *n* snob *mf*

snobbery ['snɒbərɪ] *n* snobisme *m*

snobbish ['snɒbɪʃ] *adj* snob *inv*

snog [snɒg] *Br Fam* **1** *n* **to have a s.** se bécoter
2 *vi (pt & pp* **snogged**) se bécoter

snooker ['snuːkə(r)] **1** *n (game)* snooker *(sorte de bil-lard qui se joue avec vingt-deux billes)*
2 *vt* **to s. sb** *(in game)* laisser qn dans une position difficile; *Fig* mettre qn dans l'embarras

snoop [snuːp] *Fam* **1** *n* (**a**) *(person)* fouineur(euse) *m,f* (**b**) *(look)* **to have a s. (around)** jeter un coup d'œil
2 *vi* fouiner, fureter

snooper ['snuːpə(r)] *n Fam* fouineur(euse) *m,f*

snooty ['snuːtɪ] *adj Fam* prétentieux(euse)

snooze [snuːz] *Fam* **1** *n* petit somme *m*; **to have a s.** faire un petit somme
2 *vi* faire un petit somme

snore [snɔː(r)] **1** *n* ronflement *m*
2 *vi* ronfler

snoring ['snɔːrɪŋ] *n* ronflements *mpl*

snorkel ['snɔːkəl] **1** *n* tuba *m*
2 *vi (pt & pp* **snorkelled,** *Am* **snorkeled**) nager sous l'eau avec un tuba

snort [snɔːt] **1** *n (of person)* grognement *m*; *(of horse)* ébrouement *m*
2 *vt Fam (drugs)* sniffer
3 *vi (of person)* grogner; *(of horse)* s'ébrouer

snot [snɒt] *n Fam* morve *f*

snotty ['snɒtɪ] *adj Fam* (**a**) *(nose)* qui coule (**b**) *(arro-gant)* arrogant(e)

snout [snaʊt] *n (of pig)* groin *m*; *(of other animal)* mu-seau *m*; *Fam (of person)* pif *m*

snow [snəʊ] **1** *n* neige *f*; **s. blindness** cécité *f* des neiges; *Am Fam* **s. job** baratin *m*; **s. line** limite *f* des neiges éternelles
2 *vi* neiger; **it's snowing** il neige

▸**snow in** *vt sep* **to be snowed in** être bloqué(e) par la neige

▸**snow under** *vt sep* **to be snowed under (with)** *(work)* être débordé(e) (de); *(invitations, offers)* être submergé(e) (de)

snowball ['snəʊbɔːl] **1** *n* boule *f* de neige, *Can* balle *f* de neige; **s. fight** bataille *f* de boules de neige; *Fam* **she hasn't a s.'s chance (in hell)** elle n'a pas la moindre chance
2 *vi Fig* faire boule de neige

snowbike ['snəʊbaɪk] *n* motoski *m*

snowboarding ['snəʊbɔːdɪŋ] *n* snowboard *m*; **to go s.** faire du snowboard

snowbound ['snəʊbaʊnd] *adj* bloqué(e) par la neige

snowcapped ['snəʊkæpt] *adj* couronné(e) de neige

snowdrift ['snəʊdrɪft] *n* congère *f*

snowdrop ['snəʊdrɒp] *n (flower)* perce-neige *m ou f inv*

snowfall ['snəʊfɔːl] *n* chute *f* de neige

snowflake ['snəʊfleɪk] *n* flocon *m* de neige

snowman ['snəʊmæn] *n* bonhomme *m* de neige

snowmobile ['snəʊməʊbiːl] *n (enclosed)* autoneige *f*; *(open)* motoneige *f*

snowplough, *Am* **snowplow** ['snəʊplaʊ] *n* chasse-neige *m inv*

snowshoe ['snəʊʃuː] *n* raquette *f*

snowstorm ['snəʊstɔːm] *n* tempête *f* de neige

snowsuit ['snəʊsuːt] *n* combinaison *f* de ski *(pour en-fants)*

Snow White ['snəʊ'waɪt] *n* **S. and the Seven Dwarfs** Blanche-Neige et les sept nains

snowy ['snəʊɪ] *adj (landscape, field)* enneigé(e); *(weather)* neigeux(euse); *(day)* de neige

SNP [esen'piː] *n Br Pol (abbr* **Scottish National Party**) = parti politique écossais indépendantiste

Snr *(abbr* **Senior**) **Jonathan Pye-Finch S.** Jonathan Pye-Finch père

snub [snʌb] **1** *n (refusal)* rebuffade *f*; *(insult)* affront *m*
2 *vt (pt & pp* **snubbed**) snober

snub nose ['snʌb'nəʊz] *n* nez *m* retroussé

snuck [snʌk] *Am pt & pp of* **sneak**

snuff [snʌf] **1** *n* tabac *m* à priser
2 *vt (candle)* moucher; *Br Fam* **to s. it** *(die)* casser sa pipe

▸**snuff out** *vt sep (candle)* moucher; *(life, opposition)* mettre fin à

snuffbox ['snʌfbɒks] *n* tabatière *f*

snuffle ['snʌfəl] **1** *n (sniff)* reniflement *m*
2 *vi (sniff)* renifler

snug [snʌg] *adj* (**a**) *(place)* douillet(ette); *(person)* bien au chaud (**b**) *(tight-fitting)* bien ajusté(e)

▸**snuggle up** ['snʌgəl] *vi* **to s. up to sb** se blottir contre qn

snugly ['snʌglɪ] *adv (comfortably)* confortablement; **to fit s.** être bien ajusté(e)

so [səʊ] **1** *adv* (**a**) *(to such an extent)* tellement, si (**that** que); **I was so angry (that) I almost hit him** j'étais tellement en colère que j'ai failli le frapper; **he's not so clever as she is** il n'est pas aussi intelligent qu'elle; **it isn't so very old** il n'est pas si vieux; **I'm not so sure of that** je n'en suis pas si sûr; **so much money/many people** tant *ou* autant d'argent/de gens; **it was diffi-cult, so much so that...** c'était difficile, à tel point que...
(**b**) *(for emphasis)* tellement; **I was SO disap-pointed!** j'étais tellement déçu!; **we enjoyed our-selves SO much!** nous nous sommes tellement amusés!
(**c**) *(expressing agreement)* **you're late – so I am!** tu es en retard – ah oui, tu as raison!; **that's Johnny Depp – so it is!** c'est Johnny Depp – ah oui, tu as rai-son!
(**d**) *(referring to statement already mentioned)* **I hope so** j'espère bien; **I think so** je crois; **I suppose so** je le suppose; **so I believe** c'est ce que je crois; **I told you so!** je vous l'avais bien dit!; **I'm not very organized – so I see!** je ne suis pas très bien organisé – c'est ce que je vois!; **so be it!** soit!
(**e**) *(also)* **so am I** moi aussi; **so do we** nous aussi; **so can they** eux aussi; **so is my brother** mon frère aussi
(**f**) *(in this way)* ainsi; **do it (like) so** fais-le comme ça; **and so on, and so forth** et ainsi de suite
2 *conj* (**a**) *(because of this)* donc; **she has a bad tem-per, so be careful** elle a mauvais caractère, donc fais attention
(**b**) *(introducing remark)* alors; **so you're not coming?**

alors, tu ne viens pas?; **so that's why!** alors, c'est pour ça!; **so (what)?** et alors?, et après?

(**c**) **so as to** afin de; **we hurried so as not to be late** nous nous sommes dépêchés afin de ne pas être en retard

(**d**) **so that** pour que + *subjunctive*; **she sat down so that I could see better** elle s'est assise pour que je puisse mieux voir; **we hurried so that we wouldn't be late** nous nous sommes dépêchés pour ne pas arriver en retard

soak [səʊk] **1** *vt (leave in water)* faire *ou* laisser tremper; *(make very wet)* tremper (**with** de)

2 *vi (of food, clothes)* tremper; **to leave sth to s.** faire *ou* laisser tremper qch

▸**soak in** *vi (of liquid)* pénétrer

▸**soak up** *vt sep (liquid)* absorber; *Fig* **to s. up the sun** prendre un bain de soleil

soaked [səʊkt] *adj* trempé(e); **s. to the skin** trempé(e) jusqu'aux os

so-and-so ['səʊənsəʊ] *n Fam* (**a**) *(unspecified person)* untel (unetelle) *m,f*; **Mr S.** M. Untel; **Mrs S.** Mme Unetelle (**b**) *(unpleasant person)* peau *f* de vache

soap [səʊp] **1** *n* savon *m*; **a bar of s.** un morceau de savon; **s. (opera)** feuilleton *m* populaire; **s. powder** lessive *f* (en poudre)

2 *vt* savonner

Soap opera

Le soap opera est un genre radiophonique et télévisé très populaire dans les pays anglophones. Il s'agit de feuilletons diffusés à raison de trois ou quatre épisodes par semaine sur une très longue période. Les soap operas sont ainsi nommés car les premiers d'entre eux étaient financés par des marques de détergents, aux États-Unis. Il n'est pas rare que les soap operas alimentent les conversations de tous les jours, ou soient le sujet d'articles de journaux. Les soap operas britanniques ('Eastenders' et 'Coronation Street' par exemple) ont souvent pour cadre le milieu ouvrier et diffèrent en cela de leurs équivalents américains et australiens dont le ton est beaucoup moins réaliste et dont l'action se déroule le plus souvent dans des milieux privilégiés.

soapbox ['səʊpbɒks] *n* tribune *f* improvisée à l'extérieur; **s. orator** harangueur(euse) *m,f*

soapdish ['səʊpdɪʃ] *n* porte-savon *m*

soapflakes ['səʊpfleɪks] *npl* savon *m* en paillettes

soapsuds ['səʊpsʌdz] *npl* mousse *f* de savon

soapy ['səʊpɪ] *adj (water)* savonneux(euse); *(body)* couvert(e) de savon; *(taste, smell)* de savon

soar [sɔː(r)] *vi (of bird, plane)* & *Fig (of prices)* monter en flèche; *Fig (of building)* se dresser

soaring ['sɔːrɪŋ] *adj Fig (prices)* en forte hausse; *(building)* élancé(e)

sob [sɒb] **1** *n* sanglot *m*; *Fam* **s. story** histoire *f* larmoyante

2 *vi (pt & pp* **sobbed**) sangloter

s.o.b. [esəʊ'biː] *n Am very Fam (abbr* **son of a bitch**) salaud *m*

sobbing ['sɒbɪŋ] *n* sanglots *mpl*

sober ['səʊbə(r)] *adj* (**a**) *(not drunk)* qui n'a pas bu (**b**) *(sensible)* sobre

▸**sober up** *vt sep & vi* dessoûler

sobering ['səʊbərɪŋ] *adj (news, thought)* qui donne à réfléchir

sobriety [səʊ'braɪətɪ] *n* sobriété *f*

Soc *n (abbr* **society**) club *m*, société *f*

so-called [səʊ'kɔːld] *adj* (**a**) *(supposed)* soi-disant *inv*; **his s. aunt** sa soi-disant tante (**b**) *(so named)* appelé(e) ainsi; **the s. temperate zone** la zone dite tempérée

soccer ['sɒkə(r)] *n* football *m*; **s. match** match *m* de football

sociable ['səʊʃəbəl] *adj* sociable

social ['səʊʃəl] **1** *adj* social(e); *EU* **the S. Chapter** le volet social *(du traité de Maastricht)*; **s. class** classe *f* sociale; **s. climber** arriviste *mf*; *Pol* **s. democrat** social(e)-démocrate *m,f*; **s. intercourse** relations *fpl* avec les gens; **s. life** vie *f* sociale; **he doesn't have much of a s. life** il ne sort pas beaucoup; **s. outcast** paria *m*; **s. sciences** sciences *fpl* humaines; **s. security** prestations *fpl* sociales; **the s. services** les services *mpl* sociaux; **s. work** assistance *f* sociale; **s. worker** assistant(e) social(e) *m,f*

2 *n (party)* fête *f*

socialism ['səʊʃəlɪzəm] *n* socialisme *m*

socialist ['səʊʃəlɪst] *n & adj* socialiste *mf*

socialite ['səʊʃəlaɪt] *n* mondain(e) *m,f*

socialize ['səʊʃəlaɪz] *vi* fréquenter des gens; **to s. with sb** fréquenter qn

socially ['səʊʃəlɪ] *adv* socialement; **to see sb s.** fréquenter qn

society [sə'saɪətɪ] *(pl* **societies**) *n* (**a**) *(community)* société *f*; **(high) s.** haute société, (beau) monde *m* (**b**) *(club)* club *m*, société *f*

socioeconomic [səʊsɪəʊɪkə'nɒmɪk] *adj* socio-économique

sociological [səʊsɪəʊ'lɒdʒɪkəl] *adj* sociologique

sociologist [səʊsɪ'ɒlədʒɪst] *n* sociologue *mf*

sociology [səʊsɪ'ɒlədʒɪ] *n* sociologie *f*

sock [sɒk] **1** *n* (**a**) *(garment)* chaussette *f*; *Br Fam Fig* **to pull one's socks up** se secouer (**b**) *Fam (blow)* coup *m* de poing

2 *vt Fam (hit)* donner un coup de poing à; *Fig* **to s. it to sb** montrer à qn de quoi on est capable

socket ['sɒkɪt] *n (of eye)* orbite *f*; *(for plug)* prise *f* de courant

sod¹ [sɒd] *n (of earth)* motte *f*

sod² *Br* **1** *n very Fam (man)* salaud *m*; *(woman)* salope *f*; **poor s.!** pauvre bougre!; **s. all** que dalle; **S.'s law** la loi de l'emmerdement maximum

2 *vt Vulg* **s. it!** merde!; **s. you!** va te faire voir!; **s. the party, I'm tired** tant pis pour la soirée, je suis fatigué

▸**sod off** *(pt & pp* **sodded**) *vi Br Vulg (go away)* aller se faire voir

soda ['səʊdə] *n* (**a**) **s. (water)** eau *f* de Seltz; **s. fountain** cafétéria *f* (**b**) *Am (fizzy drink)* boisson *f* gazeuse (**c**) *Chem* soude *f*

sodden ['sɒdən] *adj* trempé(e)

sodium ['səʊdɪəm] *n Chem* sodium *m*; **s. bicarbonate** bicarbonate *m* de soude; **s. chloride** chlorure *m* de sodium

sodomize ['sɒdəmaɪz] *vt* sodomiser

sodomy ['sɒdəmɪ] *n* sodomie *f*

sofa ['səʊfə] *n* canapé *m*; **s. bed** canapé-lit *m*

Sofia ['səʊfɪə] *n* Sofia

soft [sɒft] *adj* (**a**) *(in texture)* mou (molle); *(ground)* meuble; *(pillow, carpet)* moelleux(euse); *(fabric, skin)* doux (douce); **s. cheese** fromage *m* frais; *Comput* **s.**

copy visualisation *f* sur écran; **s. furnishings** tissus *mpl* d'ameublement; *Comput* **s. return** retour *m* de chariot conditionnel, changement *m* de ligne facultatif; **s. shoulder** *(on road)* accottement *m* non stabilisé; *Anat* **s. tissue** parties *fpl* charnues; **s. toy** peluche *f*

(**b**) *(voice)* doux (douce); *(rain)* léger(ère); *(colour)* doux, tendre; **s. currency** devise *f* faible; **s. drinks** boissons *fpl* non alcoolisées; **s. drugs** drogues *fpl* douces; *Phot* **in s. focus** dans le flou artistique; *Fin* **s. loan** prêt *m* offrant des conditions avantageuses; **s. porn** soft *m*; *Comput* **s. sell** méthode *f* de vente non agressive

(**c**) *(not strict)* indulgent(e), faible; **to have a s. spot for sb** avoir un faible pour qn; **to have a s. heart** avoir le cœur tendre

(**d**) *Fam (stupid)* idiot(e)

(**e**) *(easy) (job, life)* facile; *Fam* **to be a s. touch** être bonne pâte; **s. option** solution *f* de facilité

softback ['sɒftbæk] *n* livre *m* broché

softball ['sɒftbɔːl] *n Am* = sorte de base-ball joué sur un plus petit terrain avec une balle moins dure

soft-boiled ['sɒftbɔɪld] *adj (egg)* à la coque

soften ['sɒfən] **1** *vt (wax, butter)* ramollir; *(leather, fabric)* assouplir; *(skin, light)* adoucir; *Fig* **to s. the blow** amortir le choc

2 *vi (of wax, butter)* ramollir; *Fig (of person)* se radoucir; *(of opinions, resolve, stance)* devenir plus modéré(e)

►**soften up** *vt sep Fam (before attack)* affaiblir; *(before request)* amadouer

softener ['sɒfənə(r)] *n* adoucissant *m*

softhearted [sɒft'hɑːtɪd] *adj* qui se laisse facilement attendrir

softie = softy

softly ['sɒftlɪ] *adv (quietly, gently)* doucement; **to be s. lit** être légèrement éclairé(e)

softly-softly ['sɒftlɪ'sɒftlɪ] *adj Fam (approach, attitude)* en douceur

softness ['sɒftnɪs] *n (of ground)* consistance *f* meuble; *(of fabric, skin, voice)* douceur *f*

soft-pedal [sɒft'pedəl] *(pt & pp* soft-pedalled, *Am* soft-pedaled) *vi also Fig* mettre la pédale douce

soft-soap ['sɒftsəʊp] *vt Fam* amadouer

soft-spoken [sɒft'spəʊkən] *adj* qui a une voix douce

software ['sɒftweə(r)] *n Comput* logiciel *m*; **s. package** progiciel *m*

softy ['sɒftɪ] *(pl* **softies**) *n Fam (gentle person)* bonne pâte *f*; *(coward)* froussard(e) *m,f*

soggy ['sɒgɪ] *adj* trempé(e)

soh [səʊ] *n Mus* sol *m*

soil [sɔɪl] **1** *n (earth)* terre *f*; **on British s.** sur le sol britannique

2 *vt (clothes, sheet)* salir; *Fig* **to s. one's hands** se salir les mains

solace ['sɒləs] *n Lit* réconfort *m*

solar ['səʊlə(r)] *adj* solaire; **s. eclipse** éclipse *f* solaire; **s. plexus** plexus *m* solaire; **s. system** système *m* solaire

sold [səʊld] *pt & pp of* sell

solder ['səʊldə(r)] **1** *n* soudure *f*
2 *vt* souder

soldering iron ['səʊldərɪŋ'aɪən] *n* fer *m* à souder

soldier ['səʊldʒə(r)] **1** *n* soldat *m*
2 *vi* être soldat

►**soldier on** *vi* persévérer

sole¹ [səʊl] **1** *n (of foot)* plante *f*; *(of shoe)* semelle *f*
2 *vt (shoe)* ressemeler

sole² *n (fish)* sole *f*

sole³ *adj (only)* unique; *Com* **s. agent** agent *m* exclusif

solely ['səʊllɪ] *adv* uniquement

solemn ['sɒləm] *adj* solennel(elle)

solemnity [sə'lemnɪtɪ] *n* solennité *f*

sol-fa [sɒl'fɑː] *n Mus* solfège *m*

solicit [sə'lɪsɪt] **1** *vt (request)* solliciter, demander
2 *vi (of prostitute)* racoler

solicitor [sə'lɪsɪtə(r)] *n Br (for property, wills)* notaire *m*; *(in court cases)* avocat(e) *m,f*; **S. General** conseiller *m* juridique de la Couronne

solicitous [sə'lɪsɪtəs] *adj Formal* empressé(e); *(caring)* plein(e) de sollicitude; *(concerned)* soucieux(euse) (**for** de)

solid ['sɒlɪd] **1** *n* solide *m*; **solids** *(food)* aliments *mpl* solides

2 *adj* (**a**) *(not liquid)* solide; **s. food** aliments *mpl* solides; **s. fuel** combustible *m* solide (**b**) *(not hollow)* plein(e); *(gold, silver)* massif(ive); **made of s. brick** construit(e) entièrement en brique (**c**) *(worker)* sérieux(euse)

3 *adv* **ten hours s.** dix heures d'affilée

solidarity [sɒlɪ'dærɪtɪ] *n* solidarité *f*

solidify [sə'lɪdɪfaɪ] *(pt & pp* **solidified**) *vi* se solidifier

solidity [sə'lɪdɪtɪ] *n* solidité *f*

solidly ['sɒlɪdlɪ] *adv (firmly)* solidement; *(without interruption)* sans arrêt

solid-state [sɒlɪd'steɪt] *adj Elec* transistorisé(e)

soliloquy [sə'lɪləkwɪ] *(pl* **soliloquies**) *n* soliloque *m*

solitaire [sɒlɪ'teə(r)] *n (card game)* réussite *f*; *(board game, jewellery)* solitaire *m*

solitary ['sɒlɪtərɪ] *adj* (**a**) *(single)* seul(e) (**b**) *(alone)* solitaire; **s. confinement** isolement *m* cellulaire

solitude ['sɒlɪtjuːd] *n* solitude *f*

solo ['səʊləʊ] **1** *n (pl* **solos**) *(musical)* solo *m*

2 *adj (flight, crossing)* en solitaire; *(performance)* solo

3 *adv* en solitaire; **to go s.** *(of musician)* faire une carrière solo; *(of business partner)* s'établir à son compte

soloist ['səʊləʊɪst] *n* soliste *mf*

Solomon Islands ['sɒləmən'aɪləndz] *npl* **the S.** les îles *fpl* Salomon

solstice ['sɒlstɪs] *n* solstice *m*

soluble ['sɒljʊbəl] *adj* soluble

solution [sə'luːʃən] *n* solution *f*

solve [sɒlv] *vt* résoudre

solvency ['sɒlvənsɪ] *n* solvabilité *f*

solvent ['sɒlvənt] **1** *n* solvant *m*, dissolvant *m*; **s. abuse** – utilisation de solvants comme stupéfiants
2 *adj (financially)* solvable

Somali [sə'mɑːlɪ] **1** *n* (**a**) *(person)* Somalien(enne) *m,f*
(**b**) *(language)* somali *m*
2 *adj* somalien(enne)

Somalia [sə'mɑːlɪə] *n* la Somalie

sombre, *Am* **somber** ['sɒmbə(r)] *adj* sombre

some [sʌm] **1** *pron* (**a**) *(certain quantity or number)* **there is/are s. over there** il y en a là-bas; *(a few)* il y en a quelques-uns là-bas; **give me s. (of them)** donne-m'en; *(a few)* donne-m'en quelques-uns; **do you want s.?** en veux-tu?; *(a few)* en veux-tu quelques-uns?; **s. of my wine** un peu de mon vin; **s. of my sweets** quelques-uns de mes bonbons; **s. of the time** une partie du temps (**b**) *(as opposed to others)* certains *mpl*, certaines *fpl*; **s. say...** certains disent que..., il y en a qui disent que...; **s. of the guests** certains invités; **they went off, s. one way, s. another** ils sont partis, certains par là, d'autres par là-bas

2 *adj* (**a**) *(certain quantity or number of)* **s. wine** du vin; **s. ice-cream** de la glace; **s. water** de l'eau; **s. books** des livres; *(a few)* quelques livres; **in s. ways** par certains côtés; **to s. extent** jusqu'à un certain point

(**b**) *(as opposed to other)* certain(e); **s. people say...** certains disent que..., il y a des gens qui disent que...

(**c**) *(considerable quantity or number of)* **I've been waiting for s. time/hours** ça fait un moment/plusieurs heures que j'attends; **s. distance away** assez loin; **s. miles away** à plusieurs kilomètres

(**d**) *(unspecified)* **for s. reason or other** pour une raison ou pour une autre; **she'll come s. day** elle viendra un jour (ou l'autre); **at s. time in the future** plus tard; **in s. book or other** dans un livre quelconque; **s. fool left the door open** un imbécile a laissé la porte ouverte

(**e**) *Fam (for emphasis)* **that was s. storm/meal!** quel orage/repas!; *Ironic* **s. hope!** je peux/il peut/*etc* toujours y compter!; *Ironic* **s. friend you are!** quel ami tu fais!

3 *adv (approximately)* environ; **s. fifteen minutes** environ quinze minutes

somebody ['sʌmbədɪ] **1** *pron* quelqu'un; **she's s. you can trust** c'est quelqu'un en qui vous pouvez avoir confiance; **s.'s coming** on vient; **s. important/taller** quelqu'un d'important/de plus grand; **s. else** quelqu'un d'autre

2 *n* **she thinks she's s.** elle se croit importante; **I want to be s.** je veux devenir quelqu'un

somehow ['sʌmhaʊ] *adv* (**a**) *(in some way or other)* d'une façon ou d'une autre (**b**) *(for some reason or other)* pour une raison ou pour une autre

someone ['sʌmwʌn] = **somebody**

somersault ['sʌməsɔːlt] **1** *n (on the ground)* roulade *f*; *(in the air)* saut *m* périlleux

2 *vi (of person) (on the ground)* faire une roulade; *(in the air)* faire un saut périlleux; *(of car)* faire un tonneau

something ['sʌmθɪŋ] **1** *pron* quelque chose; **there's s. about him I don't like** il y a quelque chose chez lui que je n'aime pas; **s. tells me she'll be there** quelque chose me dit qu'elle sera là; **s. to drink/to eat/to read** quelque chose à boire/à manger/à lire; **s. red/ different/special** quelque chose de rouge/de différent/de spécial; **he's s. in publishing** il a un poste important dans l'édition; **in nineteen-fifty s.** dans les années cinquante; **she's eighty s.** elle a quatre-vingts ans et quelques; **what's his name? – Simon s.** comment s'appelle-t-il? – Simon quelque chose; **at least he apologized, that's s.!** au moins, il s'est excusé, c'est déjà ça!; **there's s. in what you say** il y a quelque chose d'intéressant dans ce que vous dites; **she has s. to do with what happened** elle a quelque chose à voir avec ce qui s'est passé; **that was quite s.!** ce n'était pas mal du tout!; **he's a mechanic or s. like that** il est mécanicien ou un truc comme ça; **she's got a cold or s. (like that)** elle a un rhume, je crois

2 *adv* (**a**) *(expressing degree)* **there's been s. of an improvement** il y a eu une certaine amélioration; **she's s. of a miser** elle est plutôt avare; **it's s. like a guinea pig** ça ressemble à un cobaye (**b**) *(for emphasis)*

it hurt s. awful! ça faisait mal, quelque chose de bien!

3 *n* **a little s.** un petit quelque chose

sometime ['sʌmtaɪm] *adv* **see you s.** à un de ces jours; **s. last week** la semaine dernière; **s. before Christmas** avant Noël; **you'll have to make up your mind s.** il faudra bien que tu te décides un jour; **s. soon** d'ici peu, bientôt; **s. or other** un jour ou l'autre

sometimes ['sʌmtaɪmz] *adv* quelquefois

somewhat ['sʌmwɒt] *adv* quelque peu, un peu

somewhere ['sʌmweə(r)] *adv* (**a**) *(some place)* quelque part; **s. else** ailleurs; **do you have s. to stay?** est-ce que tu as trouvé à te loger?; *Fig* **now we're getting s.!** nous voilà enfin sur la bonne route *ou* voie! (**b**) *(approximately)* environ; **she's s. around fifty** elle a environ cinquante ans; **it costs s. in the region of £500** cela coûte environ 500 livres

somnolent ['sɒmnələnt] *adj Formal* somnolent(e)

son [sʌn] *n* fils *m*; *Am very Fam* **s. of a bitch** salaud *m*

sonar ['səʊnɑː(r)] *n* sonar *m*

sonata [sə'nɑːtə] *n* sonate *f*

song [sɒŋ] *n* (**a**) *(music with words)* chanson *f*; **to burst** *or* **break into s.** se mettre à chanter; **s. book** livre *m* de chansons; **s. thrush** grive *f* musicienne (**b**) *(idioms)* **to buy sth for a s.** acheter qch pour une bouchée de pain; *Br* **to make a s. and dance (about sth)** faire toute une histoire (de qch)

songbird ['sɒŋbɜːd] *n* oiseau *m* chanteur

songwriter ['sɒŋraɪtə(r)] *n* auteur-compositeur *m*

sonic ['sɒnɪk] *adj* sonique; **s. boom** bang *m*

son-in-law ['sʌnɪnlɔː] *(pl* **sons-in-law***) n* gendre *m*

sonnet ['sɒnɪt] *n* sonnet *m*

sonny ['sʌnɪ] *n Fam* fiston *m*

sonorous ['sɒnərəs] *adj (deep)* sonore; *(impressive)* imposant(e)

soon [suːn] *adv* (**a**) *(within a short time)* bientôt; *(in past)* vite; **it will s. be Friday** c'est bientôt vendredi; **she s. changed her mind** elle a vite changé d'avis; **s. after(wards)** peu après; **s. after four** peu après quatre heures; **no sooner had she left than...** elle n'était pas plus tôt partie que...

(**b**) *(early)* tôt; **none too s.** pas trop tôt; **how s. can you get here?** quand pouvez-vous être ici au plus tôt?; **sooner or later** tôt ou tard; **the sooner the better** le plus tôt sera le mieux; **as s. as** aussitôt que, dès que; **as s. as possible** aussitôt que possible, dès que possible

(**c**) *(expressing preference)* **I would just as s. stay** j'aimerais autant rester; **I would sooner do it alone** je préférerais le faire seul

soot [sʊt] *n* suie *f*

soothe [suːð] *vt* apaiser

soothing ['suːðɪŋ] *adj* apaisant(e)

soothsayer ['suːθseɪə(r)] *n* devin (devineresse) *m,f*

sooty ['sʊtɪ] *adj (covered in soot)* couvert(e) de suie; *(black)* noir(e) comme de la suie

sop [sɒp] *n (concession)* concession *f* (**to** à)

sophist ['sɒfɪst] *n* sophiste *mf*

sophisticated [sə'fɪstɪkeɪtɪd] *adj (person, taste)* raffiné(e); *(style, humour)* recherché(e); *(machinery, technique)* sophistiqué(e)

sophistication [səfɪstɪ'keɪʃən] *n (of person, taste)* raffinement *m*; *(of style, humour)* recherche *f*; *(of machinery, technique)* sophistication *f*

sophistry ['sɒfɪstrɪ] *n (reasoning)* sophistique *f*; *(argument)* sophisme *m*

sophomore ['sɒfəmɔː(r)] *n Am* étudiant(e) *m,f* de deuxième année

soporific [sɒpə'rɪfɪk] *adj Formal* soporifique

sopping ['sɒpɪŋ] *adj* **s. (wet)** trempé(e)

soppy ['sɒpɪ] *adj Br Fam* sentimental(e)

soprano [sɒ'prɑːnəʊ] *(pl* **sopranos** *or* **soprani** [sɒ'prɑːniː]*) n (singer)* soprano *mf;* **s. voice** voix *f* de soprano

sorbet ['sɔːbeɪ] *n* sorbet *m*

sorcerer ['sɔːsərə(r)] *n* sorcier *m*

sorceress ['sɔːsərɪs] *n* sorcière *f*

sorcery ['sɔːsərɪ] *n* sorcellerie *f*

sordid ['sɔːdɪd] *adj* sordide

sore [sɔː(r)] **1** *adj* (**a**) *(painful)* douloureux(euse); **to have a s. throat/back** avoir mal à la gorge/au dos; **my feet are s.** mes pieds me font mal (**b**) *Fam (annoyed)* en colère (**about** à propos de); **it's a s. point (with him)** c'est un sujet douloureux (pour lui)
  2 *n (wound)* plaie *f*

sorely ['sɔːlɪ] *adv (greatly)* sérieusement; **she will be s. missed** elle nous/leur manquera beaucoup; **to be s. in need of sth** avoir vraiment besoin de qch; **s. tempted** sérieusement tenté(e)

sorrow ['sɒrəʊ] *n* chagrin *m;* **to my great s.** à mon grand regret

sorrowful ['sɒrəfʊl] *adj* triste

sorry ['sɒrɪ] *adj* (**a**) *(regretful, disappointed)* désolé(e); **to be s. about sth** être désolé de qch; **to be s. one did sth** regretter d'avoir fait qch; **to say s. (to sb)** s'excuser (auprès de qn); **I'm s. you didn't like it** je suis désolé que tu n'aies pas aimé; **s. to keep you waiting** désolé de vous faire attendre; **I'm s. to hear (that)...** je suis désolé d'apprendre que...; *Fam* **you'll be s.!** tu vas le regretter!; **s.?** *(pardon?)* pardon?
  (**b**) *(sympathetic)* **to feel s. for sb** plaindre qn; **to feel s. for oneself** s'apitoyer sur son propre sort; **I'm just feeling a bit s. for myself** je suis juste un peu déprimé
  (**c**) *(pathetic)* triste; **to be a s. sight** être dans un triste état; **to be in a s. state** être dans un triste état

sort [sɔːt] **1** *n* (**a**) *(kind)* sorte *f;* **all sorts of** toutes sortes de; **what s. of tree is it?** qu'est-ce que c'est comme arbre?; **that s. of thing** ce genre de chose; **she's that s. of person** elle est comme ça; **something of the s.** quelque chose de ce genre; **I did nothing of the s.** je n'ai jamais fait ça; **he's so arrogant – he's nothing of the s.!** il est vraiment arrogant – pas du tout!; **it takes all sorts** il faut de tout pour faire un monde; *Fam* **she's a good s.** c'est une brave fille; **she's not the s. to give in easily** elle n'est pas du genre à abandonner facilement; **we don't want your s. here** nous ne voulons pas de personnes de votre genre ici; **to be out of sorts** *(unwell)* ne pas être dans son assiette; *(in a bad mood)* être de mauvaise humeur; **they served us coffee of a s.** ils nous ont servi du café, si on peut appeler ça du café; **an artist of sorts** une espèce d'artiste
  (**b**) *Fam* **this is s. of embarrassing** c'est plutôt gênant; **I s. of expected it** je m'y attendais un peu; **do you like it? – s. of** ça te plaît? – oui, plus ou moins
  (**c**) *(in order to organize)* **to have a s. through sth** faire du tri dans qch
  2 *vt also Comput* trier

▶**sort out** *vt sep* (**a**) *(organize)* ranger; **to s. oneself out** résoudre ses problèmes (**b**) *(problem)* régler; *Fam* **to s. sb out** régler son compte à qn

sorted ['sɔːtɪd] *adj Br Fam* bien dans sa peau, équilibré(e)

sortie ['sɔːtiː] *n Mil* sortie *f; Fig* escapade *f*

sorting ['sɔːtɪŋ] *n* tri *m;* **s. office** bureau *m* de tri

SOS [esəʊ'es] *n* S.O.S. *m;* **to send out an S.** lancer un S.O.S.

soufflé ['suːfleɪ] *n* soufflé *m;* **cheese s.** soufflé au fromage

sought [sɔːt] *pt & pp of* **seek**

sought-after ['sɔːtɑːftə(r)] *adj* recherché(e)

soul [səʊl] *n* (**a**) *(spirit)* âme *f;* **to sell one's s.** vendre son âme au diable; *Fig* **she's the s. of discretion** c'est la discrétion même; *Fig* **it lacks s.** cela n'a pas d'âme; **All Souls' Day** le jour des Morts (**b**) *(person)* âme *f,* personne *f;* **he's a good s.** c'est une bonne personne; **there wasn't a s. in the street** il n'y avait pas âme qui vive dans la rue; **poor s.!** le/la pauvre! (**c**) *(music)* soul *f*

soul-destroying ['səʊldɪstrɔɪɪŋ] *adj* démoralisant(e)

soulful ['səʊlfʊl] *adj (look, eyes)* mélancolique; *(song)* émouvant(e)

soulless ['səʊllɪs] *adj (person)* insensible; *(place)* sans âme

soulmate ['səʊlmeɪt] *n* âme *f* sœur

soul-searching ['səʊlsɜːtʃɪŋ] *n* examen *m* de conscience

sound[1] [saʊnd] **1** *n* son *m; (noise)* bruit *m;* **not a s. could be heard** on n'entendait pas un bruit; **she likes the s. of her own voice** elle aime s'écouter parler; **to turn the s. up/down** *(on TV, radio)* monter/baisser le son; *Fig* **I don't like the s. of it** cela ne me dit rien qui vaille; **she's angry, by the s. of it** elle est en colère, on dirait; **s. barrier** mur *m* du son; **s. bite** petite phrase *f (prononcée par un homme politique à la radio ou à la télévision pour frapper les esprits); Comput* **s. card** carte *f* son; **s. effects** bruitage *m;* **s. engineer** ingénieur *m* du son; **s. wave** onde *f* sonore
  2 *vt* (**a**) *(bell)* sonner; *also Fig (alarm)* donner; **to s. one's horn** klaxonner (**b**) *(pronounce)* prononcer; **the "h" is not sounded** le "h" ne se prononce pas
  3 *vi* (**a**) *(make sound) (of trumpet, bell)* sonner (**b**) *(seem)* avoir l'air, sembler; **she sounds French** on dirait qu'elle est française; **that sounds like a good idea** ça me semble une bonne idée; **he sounds like a nice guy** ça a l'air d'être un type bien; **it sounds like Mozart** on dirait du Mozart; **that sounds like trouble!** c'est signe de problèmes!; **how does that s. to you?** *(referring to suggestion)* qu'en pensez-vous?

▶**sound off** *vi Fam* se plaindre (**about** de)

▶**sound out** *vt sep* sonder (**about** à propos de)

sound[2] **1** *adj* (**a**) *(healthy)* sain(e); *(in good condition)* en bon état; **to be of s. mind** être sain d'esprit (**b**) *(sensible, logical) (argument)* valable; *(basis)* solide; *(advice)* bon (bonne) (**c**) *(reliable) (investment)* sûr(e); *(business)* sain(e); *(person)* compétent(e)
  2 *adv* **to be s. asleep** être profondément endormi(e)

sounding board ['saʊndɪŋbɔːd] *n (on pulpit, stage)* abat-voix *m; Fig* **I use John as a s.** j'utilise John pour tester mes idées

soundings ['saʊndɪŋz] *npl* **to take s.** faire des sondages

soundly ['saʊndlɪ] *adv* (**a**) *(solidly)* solidement (**b**) *(logically)* judicieusement (**c**) *(thoroughly)* **to sleep s.** dormir profondément; **to thrash sb s.** donner une bonne correction à qn

soundproof ['saʊndpruːf] **1** *adj* insonorisé(e) **2** *vt* insonoriser

soundtrack ['saʊndtræk] *n* bande *f* sonore

soup [suːp] *n* soupe *f*; *Fig* **to be in the s.** être dans le pétrin; **s. kitchen** soupe populaire; **s. ladle** louche *f*; **s. plate** assiette *f* creuse; **s. spoon** cuillère *f* à soupe

▶**soup up** *vt sep Fam (engine)* gonfler; *(car)* gonfler le moteur de

sour ['saʊə(r)] **1** *adj (fruit, milk, taste)* aigre; *Fig (person)* aigri(e); **to turn s.** *(of milk)* tourner; *Fig (of situation, relationship)* tourner à l'aigre, mal tourner; **s. cream** crème *f* aigre; *Fig* **it was just s. grapes** c'était par dépit

2 *vt (milk)* faire tourner; *Fig (atmosphere, relationship)* empoisonner

3 *vi (of milk)* tourner; *Fig (of atmosphere, relationship)* détériorer

source [sɔːs] *n* source *f*; *(of unrest, discontent)* origine *f*; *(of infection)* foyer *m*

sourly ['saʊəlɪ] *adv* avec aigreur

souse [saʊs] *vt* tremper

south [saʊθ] **1** *n* sud *m*; **to the s. of** au sud de **2** *adj (coast, side)* sud; *(wind)* du sud; **S. Africa** Afrique *f* du Sud; **S. African** sud-africain(e); *(person)* Sud-Africain(e) *m,f*; **S. America** Amérique *f* du Sud; **S. American** sud-américain(e); *(person)* Sud-Américain(e) *m,f*; **S. Carolina** la Caroline du Sud; **S. China Sea** mer *f* de Chine du Sud; **S. Dakota** le Dakota du Sud; **S. Korea** Corée *f* du Sud; **S. Korean** sud-coréen(-enne); *(person)* Sud-Coréen(enne) *m,f*; **S. Pole** pôle *m* sud

3 *adv* au sud; *(travel)* vers le sud; **to face s.** *(of house)* être exposé(e) au sud

southbound ['saʊθbaʊnd] *adj (train, traffic)* en direction du sud; **s. carriageway** voie *f* sud

southeast [saʊθ'iːst] **1** *n* sud-est *m* **2** *adj (side)* sud-est; *(wind)* du sud-est **3** *adv* au sud-est; *(travel)* vers le sud-est

southeasterly [saʊθ'iːstəlɪ] **1** *n (wind)* vent *m* du sud-est **2** *adj (direction)* vers le sud-est; *(wind)* du sud-est

southeastern [saʊθ'iːstən] *adj (region)* (du) sud-est

southerly ['sʌðəlɪ] **1** *n (wind)* vent *m* du sud **2** *adj (direction)* vers le sud; *(wind)* du sud; **the most s. point** le point le plus au sud

southern ['sʌðən] *adj (region, accent)* du sud; **s. France** le sud de la France; **s. hemisphere** hémisphère *m* sud

southerner ['sʌðənə(r)] *n* habitant(e) *m,f* du Sud *(de l'Angleterre)*

south-facing ['saʊθfeɪsɪŋ] *adj* exposé(e) au sud

south-southeast ['saʊθsaʊθ'iːst] *adv* au sud-sud-est; *(travel)* vers le sud-sud-est

south-southwest ['saʊθsaʊθ'west] *adv* au sud-sud-ouest; *(travel)* vers le sud-sud-ouest

southward ['saʊθwəd] **1** *adj* au sud **2** *adv* vers le sud

southwards ['saʊθwədz] *adv* vers le sud

southwest [saʊθ'west] **1** *n* sud-ouest *m* **2** *adj (side)* sud-ouest; *(wind)* du sud-ouest **3** *adv* au sud-ouest; *(travel)* vers le sud-ouest

southwesterly [saʊθ'westəlɪ] **1** *n (wind)* vent *m* du sud-ouest **2** *adj (direction)* vers le sud-ouest; *(wind)* du sud-ouest

southwestern [saʊθ'westən] *adj (region)* (du) sud-ouest

souvenir [suːvə'nɪə(r)] *n* souvenir *m*

sovereign ['sɒvrɪn] *n & adj* souverain(e) *m,f*

sovereignty ['sɒvrəntɪ] *n* souveraineté *f*

Soviet ['səʊvɪət] **1** *n (person)* Soviétique *mf* **2** *adj* soviétique; *Formerly* **the S. Union** l'Union *f* soviétique

sow¹ [səʊ] *(pt* **sowed** [səʊd]*, pp* **sown** [səʊn] *or* **sowed)** *vt (seeds) & Fig (discord, doubt)* semer; *(field)* ensemencer *(with* en)

sow² [saʊ] *n (female pig)* truie *f*

sown [səʊn] *pp of* **sow¹**

soya ['sɔɪə] *n* soja *m*

soy sauce [sɔɪ'sɔːs] *n* sauce *f* de soja

sozzled ['sɒzəld] *adj Br Fam (drunk)* bourré(e); **to get s.** se cuiter

spa [spɑː] *n (place)* ville *f* d'eau; *(spring)* source *f* thermale

space [speɪs] **1** *n* **(a)** *(room)* place *f*; **to stare into s.** regarder dans le vide **(b)** *(individual place)* place *f*; *(on printed form)* espace *m*; **wide open spaces** grands espaces; **s. bar** *(on keyboard)* barre *f* d'espacement **(c)** *(period of time)* espace *m*; **in the s. of a year** en l'espace d'une année **(d)** *(outer space)* espace *m*; **the s. age** l'ère *f* spatiale; *Fam* **to be a s. cadet** planer; **s. rocket** fusée *f* spatiale; **s. shuttle** navette *f* spatiale; **s. suit** combinaison *f* spatiale; **s. travel** voyages *mpl* dans l'espace **(e)** *(gap)* espace *m*, vide *m*; *(in timetable)* trou *m*

2 *vt* espacer

▶**space out** *vt sep* espacer

space-age ['speɪseɪdʒ] *adj* futuriste

spacecraft ['speɪskrɑːft] *n* vaisseau *m* spatial

spaced out ['speɪst'aʊt] *adj Fam* **to be s.** planer complètement

spaceman ['speɪsmæn] *n* astronaute *m*

spaceship ['speɪsʃɪp] *n* vaisseau *m* spatial

spacing ['speɪsɪŋ] *n* espacement *m*; *Typ* **single/double s.** simple/double interligne *m*

spacious ['speɪʃəs] *adj* spacieux(euse)

spade [speɪd] *n* **(a)** *(tool)* bêche *f*; **to call a s. a s.** appeler un chat un chat **(b)** *(in cards)* pique *m*

spaghetti [spə'getɪ] *n* spaghetti *mpl*

Spain [speɪn] *n* l'Espagne *f*

spam [spæm] *vi Comput* envoyer des messages publicitaires en masse

spamming ['spæmɪŋ] *n Comput* envoi *m* de messages publicitaires en masse

span [spæn] **1** *n* **(a)** *(of hand)* empan *m*; *(of wing)* envergure *f* **(b)** *(of arch)* portée *f*; *(of bridge)* travée *f* **(c)** *(period of time)* période *f* **(d)** *(of knowledge, interests)* éten-due *f*

2 *vt (pt & pp* **spanned**) *(of bridge)* franchir; *Fig (of life, knowledge)* couvrir

Spaniard ['spænjəd] *n* Espagnol(e) *m,f*

spaniel ['spænjəl] *n* épagneul *m*

Spanish ['spænɪʃ] **1** *npl (people)* **the S.** les Espagnols *mpl*

2 *n (language)* espagnol *m*

3 *adj* espagnol(e); **the S. Inquisition** l'Inquisition *f* espagnole; *Culin* **S. omelette** omelette *f* à l'espagnole

spank [spæŋk] **1** *n* **to give sb a s.** donner une claque sur les fesses à qn **2** *vt* donner une claque sur les fesses à

spanking ['spæŋkɪŋ] **1** *n* fessée *f*; **to give sb a s.** donner une fessée à qn

2 *adv Fam* **s. new** flambant neuf (neuve); **they had a s. good time** ils se sont rudement bien amusés

spanner ['spænǝ(r)] *n Br* clef *f*; *Fig* **to throw a s. in the works** compliquer les choses

spar¹ [spɑː(r)] *n (on ship)* espar *m*

spar² (*pt & pp* **sparred**) *vi* **to s. with sb** *(in boxing)* s'entraîner avec qn; *(argue)* se chamailler avec qn

spare ['speǝ(r)] **1** *n (spare part)* pièce *f* de rechange; *(tyre)* pneu *m* de rechange
2 *adj* (**a**) *(available)* disponible; *(surplus)* en trop, qui reste; *(reserve)* de rechange; **do you have a s. pen?** tu as un stylo à me prêter?; **to be going s.** être en trop; **a s. moment** un moment de libre; **s. part** pièce *f* de rechange; **s. ribs** travers *mpl* de porc; **s. room** chambre *f* d'amis; **s. time** temps *m* (de) libre; **s. tyre** pneu *m* de secours *ou* de rechange; *Br Fam Fig (around waist)* bourrelet *m*; **s. wheel** roue *f* de secours
(**b**) *(frugal) (meal)* frugal(e); *(style)* dépouillé(e); *(room)* austère
(**c**) *Br Fam (angry)* **to go s.** sortir de ses gonds
3 *vt* (**a**) *(give away, go without) (person)* se passer de; **to have no time to s.** ne pas avoir le temps; **can you s. the time?** avez-vous le temps?; **with five minutes to s.** avec cinq minutes d'avance; **to have a few moments to s.** disposer de quelques minutes; **can you s. me a few moments?** pouvez-vous m'accorder quelques minutes?; **could you s. me some milk?** est-ce que tu peux me donner un peu de lait?; **to s. a thought for sb** penser à qn
(**b**) *(avoid)* **to s. no expense** ne pas regarder à la dépense
(**c**) *(save from)* **to s. sb sth** épargner qch à qn; **s. me the details!** épargnez-moi les détails!
(**d**) *(show mercy towards)* épargner; **to s. sb's life** épargner la vie de qn; **to s. sb's feelings** ménager les sentiments de qn

sparing ['speǝrɪŋ] *adj* économe (**with** avec); **to be s. with one's compliments** être avare de compliments

sparingly ['speǝrɪŋlɪ] *adv* en petite quantité

spark [spɑːk] **1** *n (electrical, from fire)* étincelle *f*; *Fig (of intelligence, interest)* lueur *f*; *Fig* **sparks will fly** cela va faire des étincelles; *Fig* **s. plug** bougie *f*
2 *vi* jeter *ou* faire des étincelles

▶**spark off** *vt sep* déclencher

sparkle ['spɑːkǝl] **1** *n also Fig* éclat *m*
2 *vi (of light, eyes)* & *Fig (of person, conversation)* briller; *(of diamond)* scintiller

sparkler ['spɑːklǝ(r)] *n* (**a**) *(firework)* cierge *m* magique (**b**) *Fam (diamond)* diam *m*

sparkling ['spɑːklɪŋ] *adj (light, eyes)* & *Fig (person, conversation)* brillant(e); *(diamond)* scintillant(e); *(wine)* pétillant(e)

sparring partner ['spɑːrɪŋ'pɑːtnǝ(r)] *n (in boxing)* partenaire *mf* d'entraînement; *Fig* adversaire *mf*

sparrow ['spærǝʊ] *n* moineau *m*

sparse [spɑːs] *adj* clairsemé(e)

sparsely ['spɑːslɪ] *adv (populated, furnished)* peu; **s. covered with trees** aux arbres clairsemés

spartan ['spɑːtǝn] *adj also Fig* spartiate

spasm ['spæzǝm] *n* spasme *m*; *Fig (of coughing)* quinte *f*; *(of jealousy)* crise *f*

spasmodic [spæz'mɒdɪk] *adj (irregular)* irrégulier(-ère)

spasmodically [spæz'mɒdɪklɪ] *adv (irregularly)* irrégulièrement

spastic ['spæstɪk] *n* (**a**) *Med* handicapé(e) *m,f* moteur (**b**) *very Fam Pej (clumsy, useless person)* empoté(e) *m,f*

spat¹ [spæt] *n Fam (quarrel)* querelle *f*

spat² *pt & pp of* **spit²**

spate [speɪt] *n (of letters, calls)* avalanche *f*; *(of crimes)* vague *f*

spatial ['speɪʃǝl] *adj* spatial(e)

spatter ['spætǝ(r)] *vt* éclabousser (**with** avec)

spatula ['spætjʊlǝ] *n* spatule *f*

spawn [spɔːn] **1** *n (of frog, fish)* œufs *mpl*
2 *vt (give rise to)* engendrer
3 *vi (of frog, fish)* frayer

speak [spiːk] (*pt* **spoke** [spǝʊk], *pp* **spoken** ['spǝʊkǝn])
1 *vt* (**a**) *(utter)* dire (**b**) *(language)* parler
2 *vi (talk, give a speech)* parler (**to/about** à/de); **they're not speaking** *(to each other)* ils ne se parlent pas; **I know her to s. to** on se parle quelquefois; **legally/morally speaking** légalement/moralement parlant; **so to s.** pour ainsi dire; **who's speaking?** *(on phone)* qui est à l'appareil?; **Mr Curry? – yes, speaking** Mr Curry? – lui-même

▶**speak for** *vt insep* **to s. for sb** *(on behalf of)* parler pour qn; **s. for yourself!** parle pour toi!; **the facts s. for themselves** les faits parlent d'eux-mêmes

▶**speak out** *vi* parler franchement; **to s. out against sth** s'élever contre qch

▶**speak up** *vi* (**a**) *(speak more loudly)* parler plus fort (**b**) *(speak in favour of)* **to s. up for sb/sth** parler en faveur de qn/qch; **to s. up for oneself** se défendre

speaker ['spiːkǝ(r)] *n* (**a**) *(at meeting)* intervenant(e) *m,f*; *(at conference)* conférencier(ère) *m,f*; **an Italian s.** une personne qui parle italien; **a Spanish/Portuguese s.** un(e) hispanophone/lusophone; **to be a slow/fast s.** parler lentement/vite; *Pol* **the S.** *Br* le Président de la Chambre des Communes; *Am* le Président du Congrès (**b**) *(loudspeaker)* enceinte *f*

speaking ['spiːkɪŋ] *adj (doll, robot)* parlant(e); **s. clock** horloge *f* parlante; **s. part** *(in play, film)* rôle *m* parlant

spear ['spɪǝ(r)] **1** *n* lance *f*
2 *vt* transpercer d'un coup de lance

spearhead ['spɪǝhed] **1** *n also Fig* fer *m* de lance
2 *vt (attack, campaign)* être le fer de lance de

spearmint ['spɪǝmɪnt] *n* menthe *f* verte

spec [spek] *n Fam* **on s.** à tout hasard

special ['speʃǝl] **1** *adj* spécial(e); *(friend)* proche; *(reason, effort, attention)* particulier(ère); **what's so s. about the 19th of November?** qu'est-ce que le 19 novembre a de si spécial?; **s. agent** agent *m* secret; *Br* **S. Branch** = service de renseignements britannique; **s. delivery** envoi *m* en exprès; **s. effects** effets *mpl* spéciaux; **s. interest group** groupe *m* d'intérêt commun; *Comput* groupe d'intérêt; **s. interest holidays** vacances *fpl* à thème; **s. needs** difficultés *fpl* d'apprentissage; **s. offer** offre *f* spéciale; *Pol* **s. powers** pouvoirs *mpl* exceptionnels
2 *n (on menu)* plat *m* du jour

specialist ['speʃǝlɪst] **1** *n* spécialiste *mf*; *Med* **heart s.** cardiologue *mf*; **lung s.** pneumologue *mf*
2 *adj (skills, equipment)* d'un spécialiste; *(shop)* spécialisé(e)

speciality [speʃɪ'ælɪtɪ] *(pl* **specialities***)* *n* spécialité *f*

specialization [speʃǝlaɪ'zeɪʃǝn] *n* spécialisation *f*

specialize ['speʃǝlaɪz] *vi* se spécialiser (**in** en)

specially ['speʃǝlɪ] *adv (expressly)* spécialement

specialty ['speʃǝltɪ] *(pl* **specialties***)* *n Am* spécialité *f*

species ['spiːʃiːz] (*pl* **species**) *n* espèce *f*

specific [spɪ'sɪfɪk] **1** *adj* précis(e) (**about** au sujet de); **to be s.,...** pour être précis,...; *Phys* **s. gravity** densité *f* **2** *npl* **specifics** détails *mpl*

specifically [spɪ'sɪfɪkəlɪ] *adv* (**a**) *(explicitly)* expressément (**b**) *(specially)* spécialement (**c**) *(precisely)* précisément

specification [spesɪfɪ'keɪʃən] *n* spécification *f*

specify ['spesɪfaɪ] (*pt & pp* **specified**) *vt* (**a**) *(state exactly)* préciser (**b**) *(stipulate)* stipuler

specimen ['spesɪmɪn] *n* (**a**) *(sample amount) (of handwriting, blood)* échantillon *m*; **s. copy** spécimen *m* (**b**) *(individual example)* spécimen *m*; *Fam* **he's an odd s.** c'est un drôle de spécimen

specious ['spiːʃəs] *adj* spécieux(euse)

speck [spek] *n (of dust)* grain *m*; *(of paint, ink)* petite tache *f*; **a s. of dirt** une poussière

speckled ['spekəld] *adj* tacheté(e) (**with** de)

specs [speks] *npl Fam (spectacles)* lunettes *fpl*

spectacle ['spektəkəl] *n* (**a**) *(show, sight)* spectacle *m*; **to make a s. of oneself** se donner en spectacle (**b**) **spectacles** *(glasses)* lunettes *fpl*

spectacular [spek'tækjʊlə(r)] **1** *n* production *f* à grand spectacle **2** *adj* spectaculaire

spectator [spek'teɪtə(r)] *n* spectateur(trice) *m,f*; **s. sport** sport *m* à grand public

spectre, *Am* **specter** ['spektə(r)] *n* spectre *m*

spectrum ['spektrəm] (*pl* **spectra** ['spektrə]) *n* spectre *m*; *Fig* éventail *m*

speculate ['spekjʊleɪt] *vi* (**a**) *(hypothesize)* faire des suppositions (**about** au sujet de) (**b**) *Fin* **to s. (on the Stock Market)** spéculer (à la Bourse)

speculation [spekjʊ'leɪʃən] *n* suppositions *fpl*

speculative ['spekjʊlətɪv] *adj* spéculatif(ive)

speculator ['spekjʊleɪtə(r)] *n Fin* spéculateur(trice) *m,f*

sped [sped] *pt & pp of* **speed**

speech [spiːtʃ] *n* (**a**) *(faculty)* parole *f*; **s. defect** *or* **impediment** défaut *m* d'élocution; **s. therapist** orthophoniste *mf, Belg & Suisse* logopède *mf*; **s. therapy** orthophonie *f* (**b**) *(address)* discours *m*; **to give** *or* **make a s.** faire un discours; *Br Sch* **s. day** remise *f* des prix (**c**) *(way of speaking)* langue *f* (**d**) *Gram* **part of s.** partie *f* du discours

---

Speech day
À la fin de l'année scolaire en Grande-Bretagne, certaines écoles invitent une personnalité à prononcer un discours et à distribuer des prix.

---

speechless ['spiːtʃlɪs] *adj* muet(ette) (**with** de); **to be left s.** rester sans voix

speechwriter ['spiːtʃraɪtə(r)] *n* personne *f* qui écrit des discours

speed [spiːd] **1** *n* (**a**) *(rapidity)* vitesse *f*; **the s. of light / sound** la vitesse de la lumière/du son; **at s.** à toute vitesse; **to gather** *or* **pick up/lose s.** prendre/perdre de la vitesse; *Fig* **to be up to s. on sth** être au courant de qch; **s. bump** ralentisseur *m*; **s. camera** radar *m*; *Am Fam* **s. cop** motard *m* (de la police); **s. limit** limitation *f* de vitesse; **s. trap** contrôle *m* de vitesse (**b**) *(gear)* vitesse *f*; **five-s. gearbox** boîte *f* à cinq vitesses (**c**) *Fam (amphetamine)* amphés *fpl*, speed *m*
2 *vi* (**a**) (*pt & pp* **sped** [sped] *or* **speeded**) *(move quickly)* **to s. along** foncer; **to s. away/out** partir/sortir

à toute vitesse (**b**) *(exceed speed limit)* faire un excès de vitesse; **to be caught speeding** être arrêté pour excès de vitesse (**c**) *Fam* **to be speeding** *(under effect of amphetamines)* être sous amphés

▶**speed off** *vi* partir à toute vitesse

▶**speed up 1** *vt sep (person)* faire aller plus vite; *(work, project, process)* accélérer
2 *vi* aller plus vite

speedboat ['spiːdbəʊt] *n* vedette *f*; *(with outboard motor)* hors-bord *m inv*

speedily ['spiːdɪlɪ] *adv* vite, rapidement

speeding ['spiːdɪŋ] *n* excès *m* de vitesse

speedometer [spiː'dɒmɪtə(r)] *n* compteur *m* de vitesse

speedway ['spiːdweɪ] *n* speedway *m*

speedy ['spiːdɪ] *adj* rapide

spell¹ [spel] *n (magic words)* formule *f* magique; **to cast a s. on sb** jeter un sort à qn; **to break the s.** rompre le charme; **to be under a s.** être envoûté(e); **to be under sb's s.** être sous le charme de qn

spell² (*pt & pp* **spelt** [spelt] *or* **spelled**) **1** *vt* (**a**) *(in writing)* écrire, orthographier; *(aloud)* épeler; **how do you s. it?** comment ça s'écrit? (**b**) *(signify)* signifier; **to s. disaster** être un désastre; **to s. trouble** être mauvais signe
2 *vi* **he can s. well** il a une bonne orthographe; **he can't s.** il a une mauvaise orthographe

▶**spell out** *vt sep (address, name)* épeler; *Fig (explain explicitly)* expliquer clairement; **do I have to s. it out for you?** est-ce qu'il faut que je te fasse un dessin?

spell³ *n (period)* période *f*; **after a s. as a teacher, he...** après avoir été professeur pendant un temps, il...; **a cold s.** une période de froid; **a good/bad s.** une bonne/mauvaise période

spellbound ['spelbaʊnd] *adj* fasciné(e)

spell-checker ['speltʃekə(r)] *n Comput* correcteur *m* d'orthographe

speller ['spelə(r)] *n Am* manuel *m* d'orthographe

spelling ['spelɪŋ] *n* orthographe *f*; **to be good/bad at s.** être bon (bonne)/mauvais(e) en orthographe; **s. mistake** faute *f* d'orthographe

spelt [spelt] *pt & pp of* **spell²**

spend [spend] (*pt & pp* **spent** [spent]) *vt* (**a**) *(money)* dépenser; **to s. money on sb** dépenser de l'argent pour qn; **to s. money on sth** *(object)* dépenser de l'argent en qch; *(holidays, education)* dépenser de l'argent pour qch (**b**) *(time)* passer; **to s. time on sth/ doing sth** passer du temps sur qch/à faire qch

spender ['spendə(r)] *n* **to be a big s.** être très dépensier(ère)

spending ['spendɪŋ] *n* dépenses *fpl*; **s. money** argent *m* de poche; **s. power** pouvoir *m* d'achat; **to go on a s. spree** faire des folies

spendthrift ['spendθrɪft] *n* dépensier(ère) *m,f*

spent [spent] **1** *adj (bullet, match)* utilisé(e); **to be a s. force** ne plus avoir d'influence
2 *pt & pp of* **spend**

sperm [spɜːm] *n (semen)* sperme *m*; **s. bank** banque *f* de sperme; **s. donor** donneur *m* de sperme; **s. whale** cachalot *m*

spermicide ['spɜːmɪsaɪd] *n* spermicide *m*

spew [spjuː] *vt & vi Br Fam (vomit)* dégobiller

sphere [sfɪə(r)] *n also Fig* sphère *f*; **that's outside my s.** ce n'est pas dans mes compétences; **s. of influence** sphère d'influence

spherical ['sferɪkəl] *adj* sphérique
sphincter ['sfɪŋktə(r)] *n Anat* sphincter *m*
sphinx [sfɪŋks] *n* sphinx *m*
spice [spaɪs] **1** *n (seasoning)* épice *f*; *Fig (excitement)* sel *m*, piquant *m*; **s. rack** présentoir *m* à épices
   2 *vt (food)* épicer; *Fig* **to s. sth (up)** *(make more exciting)* ajouter du piquant à qch
spick [spɪk] *n Am very Fam* = terme injurieux désignant une personne originaire d'Amérique latine
spick-and-span [spɪkən'spæn] *adj Fam* nickel, impeccable
spicy ['spaɪsɪ] *adj (food)* épicé(e); *Fig (story, gossip)* croustillant(e)
spider ['spaɪdə(r)] *n* araignée *f*; **s.'s web** toile *f* d'araignée; **s. plant** chlorophytum *m*
spiel [ʃpiːl] *n Fam* baratin *m*
spike [spaɪk] **1** *n* pointe *f*; **spikes** *(running shoes)* pointes *fpl*
   2 *vt* **to s. sb's guns** mettre des bâtons dans les roues de qn; **to s. sb's drink** ajouter de l'alcool dans la boisson de qn
spiky ['spaɪkɪ] *adj (plant)* couvert(e) de piquants; *(hair)* en épis
spill [spɪl] **1** *n* **to take a s.** *(fall)* faire une chute
   2 *vt (pt & pp* spilt [spɪlt] *or* spilled) renverser; *Fig* **to s. the beans** vendre la mèche
   3 *vi (of liquid)* se répandre
►**spill over** *vi (of liquid)* déborder; *Fig (of conflict)* s'étendre
spillage ['spɪlɪdʒ] *n* déversement *m*
spilt [spɪlt] *pt & pp of* spill
spin [spɪn] **1** *n (a) (turning movement)* tournoiement *m*; **to go into a s.** *(of car)* faire un tête-à-queue; *Pej Pol* **s. doctor** = spécialiste en communication chargé de présenter l'information de façon à mettre en valeur un parti politique **(b)** *Fam (in car)* **to go for a s.** aller faire un tour **(c)** *(on ball)* effet *m*; **to put s. on a ball** donner de l'effet à une balle
   2 *vt (pt & pp* spun [spʌn]) **(a)** *(wool, cotton)* filer **(b)** *(wheel, top)* faire tourner, faire tournoyer; **to s. a coin** jouer à pile ou face **(c)** *(spin-dry)* essorer
   3 *vi* tourner, tournoyer; **my head's spinning** j'ai la tête qui tourne; **the room's spinning** la pièce tourne (autour de moi)
►**spin out** *vt sep (speech, debate)* faire traîner (en longueur); *(money)* faire durer
spinach ['spɪnɪtʃ] *n* épinards *mpl*
spinal ['spaɪnəl] *adj* vertébral(e); **s. column** colonne *f* vertébrale; **s. cord** moelle *f* épinière; **s. injury** lésion *f* de la colonne vertébrale
spindly ['spɪndlɪ] *adj (person)* chétif(ive); *(arms, legs)* maigre
spin-dry ['spɪn'draɪ] *(pt & pp* spin-dried) *vt* essorer
spin-dryer ['spɪn'draɪə(r)] *n* essoreuse *f*
spine [spaɪn] *n (a) (backbone)* colonne *f* vertébrale **(b)** *(of book)* dos *m* **(c)** *(of plant, hedgehog)* piquant *m*
spine-chilling ['spaɪntʃɪlɪŋ] *adj* à vous glacer le sang
spineless ['spaɪnlɪs] *adj (weak)* mou (molle)
spinney ['spɪnɪ] *(pl* spinneys) *n* bosquet *m*
spinning ['spɪnɪŋ] *n* **s. top** toupie *f*; **s. wheel** rouet *m*
spin-off ['spɪnɒf] *n (a) (result)* retombée *f* **(b)** *(TV programme)* = feuilleton tiré d'un film ou d'un autre feuilleton
spinster ['spɪnstə(r)] *n* vieille fille *f*
spiny ['spaɪnɪ] *adj* couvert(e) de piquants; **s. lobster** langouste *f*

spiral ['spaɪərəl] **1** *n* spirale *f*; **s. staircase** escalier *m* en colimaçon
   2 *vi (pt & pp* spiralled) *(of smoke)* s'élever *ou* monter en spirale; *(of prices)* s'envoler
spire ['spaɪə(r)] *n (of church)* flèche *f*
spirit ['spɪrɪt] *n (a) (soul, being)* esprit *m*; **the Holy S.** le Saint-Esprit **(b)** *(mood, attitude)* esprit *m*; **to enter into the s. of sth** participer de bon cœur à qch; **to take sth in the right/wrong s.** bien/mal prendre qch; **to be in good/poor spirits** être de bonne humeur/déprimé(e); *Fam* **that's the s.!** à la bonne heure! **(c)** *(determination)* courage *m*; **to break sb's s.** entamer le courage de qn **(d)** **spirits** *(drinks)* spiritueux *mpl*; **s. lamp** lampe *f* à alcool; **s. level** niveau *m* (à bulle)
►**spirit away, spirit off** *vt sep* faire disparaître (comme par enchantement)
spirited ['spɪrɪtɪd] *adj (person, defence)* courageux(euse); *(reply)* énergique; *(performance)* plein de brio
spiritual ['spɪrɪtʃʊəl] **1** *adj* spirituel(elle); **France is my s. home** c'est en France que je me sens vraiment chez moi
   2 *n* **(Negro) s.** Negro spiritual *m*
spiritualism ['spɪrɪtʃʊəlɪzəm] *n* spiritisme *m*
spirituality [spɪrɪtʃʊ'ælɪtɪ] *n* spiritualité *f*
spit¹ [spɪt] *n (a) (for cooking)* broche *f* **(b)** *(of land)* pointe *f*
spit² **1** *n (saliva)* salive *f*; *(spittle)* crachat *m*; *Fam* **s. and polish** astiquage *m*
   2 *vt (pt & pp* spat [spæt]) cracher
   3 *vi (of person, cat)* cracher; *(of hot fat)* sauter; *Fig* **to be within spitting distance (of)** être à deux pas (de); **it's spitting** *(with rain)* il pleuvote
►**spit out** *vt sep* cracher; *Fam* **s. it out!** *(say what you want to)* allez, accouche!
spite [spaɪt] **1** *n (a) (malice)* dépit *m*; **out of s.** par dépit **(b)** **in s. of** malgré; **to do sth in s. of oneself** faire qch malgré soi
   2 *vt* vexer
spiteful ['spaɪtfʊl] *adj* vexant(e)
spitting image ['spɪtɪŋ'ɪmɪdʒ] *n Fam* **he's the s. of his father** c'est son père tout craché
spittle ['spɪtəl] *n* crachat *m*
spiv [spɪv] *n Br very Fam* aigrefin *m*
splash [splæʃ] **1** *n (a) (of liquid)* éclaboussure *f*; *(sound)* plouf *m*; *Fam Fig* **to make a s.** faire sensation **(b)** *(of colour, light)* tache *f*
   2 *vt* éclabousser (**with** de); **to s. one's face with water** se passer le visage à l'eau; **the photo was splashed across the front page** la photo était étalée à la une
   3 *vi (of liquid, waves)* faire des éclaboussures
►**splash about, splash around** *vi* patauger
►**splash down** *vi (of spacecraft)* amerrir
►**splash out** *vt sep Fam* claquer des ronds (**on** en achetant)
splatter ['splætə(r)] **1** *n* éclaboussure *f*; *(sound)* crépitement *m*
   2 *vt* éclabousser (**with** de)
splay [spleɪ] *vt* écarter
spleen [spliːn] *n (a) (part of body)* rate *f* **(b)** *Formal (anger)* mauvaise humeur *f*; **to vent one's s. (on sb)** passer sa mauvaise humeur (sur qn)
splendid ['splendɪd] *adj* magnifique
splendour, *Am* **splendor** ['splendə(r)] *n* splendeur *f*

splice [splaɪs] *vt (film)* coller; *(rope)* épisser; *Fam* **to get spliced** *(marry)* se caser

splint [splɪnt] *n* attelle *f*

splinter ['splɪntə(r)] **1** *n (of wood, glass)* éclat *m*; *(in finger)* écharde *f*; *(of bone)* esquille *f*; *Pol* **s. group** groupe *m* dissident
   2 *vt* briser
   3 *vi* se briser; *Fig (of political party)* se scinder

split [splɪt] **1** *n (in wood)* fente *f*; *(in group)* division *f*; *(in garment) (tear)* déchirure *f*; *(by design)* fente *f*; **to do the splits** faire le grand écart
   2 *adj* brisé(e); **s. ends** *(in hair)* fourches *fpl*; **s. peas** pois *mpl* cassés; **s. personality** dédoublement *m* de la personnalité; *Cin & Comput* **s. screen** écran *m* divisé; **in a s. second** en quelques dixièmes de seconde
   3 *vt (pt & pp split)* **(a)** *(wood)* fendre; *(cloth)* déchirer; *(seam)* faire craquer; *(group)* diviser; *(political party)* scinder; **to s. one's head open** se fendre le crâne; **to s. the vote** éparpiller les voix; *Fam* **to s. one's sides (laughing)** se tordre de rire; *Fig* **to s. hairs** couper les cheveux en quatre **(b)** *(share)* partager; **to s. the difference** partager la différence
   4 *vi* **(a)** *(of wood)* se fendre; *(of cloth)* se déchirer; *(of seam)* craquer; *(of group)* se diviser; *(of political party)* se scinder; *Fam* **my head's splitting** j'ai un mal de tête atroce **(b)** *very Fam (leave)* se casser

▸**split up 1** *vt sep (share out)* diviser, partager
   2 *vi (of couple, group)* se séparer; **to s. up with sb** rompre avec qn

split-second ['splɪtsekənd] *adj (decision)* pris(e) en un rien de temps; *(timing)* au quart de seconde

splitting ['splɪtɪŋ] *adj* **to have a s. headache** avoir un mal de tête atroce

splodge [splɒdʒ] *n Fam* tache *f*

splutter ['splʌtə(r)] *vi (of person)* bredouiller; *(of engine)* tousser; *(of flame, candle)* crépiter

spoil [spɔɪl] *(pt & pp spoilt* [spɔɪlt] *or spoiled)* **1** *vt* **(a)** *(ruin)* gâcher; **to s. sb's fun** gâcher le plaisir de qn; **to s. sb's appetite** couper l'appétit à qn; *Pol* **spoilt ballot** vote *m* nul **(b)** *(indulge)* gâter; **spoilt child** enfant gâté; **to be spoilt for choice** avoir l'embarras du choix
   2 *vi* **(a)** *(of food)* s'abîmer **(b)** **to be spoiling for a fight** chercher la bagarre

spoils [spɔɪlz] *npl (of war, crime)* butin *m*

spoilsport ['spɔɪlspɔːt] *n Fam* rabat-joie *mf inv*

spoilt [spɔɪlt] *pt & pp of* **spoil**

spoke¹ [spəʊk] *n (of wheel)* rayon *m*; *Fig* **to put a s. in sb's wheel** mettre des bâtons dans les roues à qn

spoke² *pt of* **speak**

spoken ['spəʊkən] *pp of* **speak**

spokesman ['spəʊksmən] *n* porte-parole *m*

spokesperson ['spəʊkspɜːsən] *n* porte-parole *m*

spokeswoman ['spəʊkswʊmən] *n* porte-parole *m*

sponge [spʌndʒ] **1** *n* éponge *f*; *Fig* **to throw in the s.** jeter l'éponge; **s. bag** trousse *f* de toilette; **s. cake** génoise *f*; **s. pudding** = sorte de génoise, cuite à la vapeur et servie avec une sauce au chocolat, de la confiture etc
   2 *vt* **(a)** *(wash)* nettoyer avec une éponge **(b)** *Fam (scrounge)* taper (**off** *or* **from** à)
   3 *vi Fam (scrounge)* taper les autres

▸**sponge down** *vt sep (wash)* nettoyer avec une éponge

▸**sponge off 1** *vt sep (stain)* faire partir d'un coup d'éponge
   2 *vt insep Fam (scrounge from)* taper

sponger ['spʌndʒə(r)] *n Fam* tapeur(euse) *m,f*

spongy ['spʌndʒɪ] *adj* spongieux(euse)

sponsor ['spɒnsə(r)] **1** *n* sponsor *m*; *(of student, club member)* parrain *m*
   2 *vt* sponsoriser; *(student)* financer les études de; *(club member)* parrainer; **sponsored walk** marche *f* parrainée

Sponsored event

La Grande-Bretagne compte de très nombreuses organisations caritatives ("charities"). L'un des moyens employés pour rassembler des fonds est de s'engager auprès d'autres gens (généralement des amis, voisins et collègues de travail) à accomplir une épreuve en échange d'une somme d'argent déterminée. Il peut s'agir d'épreuves physiques ("sponsored walk", "sponsored swim") ou de défis saugrenus, tels que se rendre au bureau en pyjama ou bien encore garder le silence pendant toute une journée ("sponsored silence"). Des "sponsored events" sont également organisés par des écoles et des clubs sportifs afin d'obtenir de l'argent pour acheter du matériel.

sponsorship ['spɒnsəʃɪp] *n* sponsoring *m*; *(of student, club member)* parrainage *m*; **s. deal** *(for athlete, team)* contrat *m* de sponsoring

spontaneity [spɒntə'neɪtɪ] *n* spontanéité *f*

spontaneous [spɒn'teɪnɪəs] *adj* spontané(e)

spoof [spuːf] *n Fam* **(a)** *(parody)* parodie *f* (**on** de) **(b)** *(hoax)* canular *m*

spook [spuːk] *Fam* **1** *n* fantôme *m*
   2 *vt* ficher la trouille à

spooky ['spuːkɪ] *adj Fam* qui fait froid dans le dos

spool [spuːl] *n* bobine *f*

spoon [spuːn] **1** *n* cuillère *f*
   2 *vt* **to s. sth onto sth** mettre qch sur qch avec une cuillère

spoon-feed ['spuːnfiːd] *(pt & pp spoon-fed* ['spuːnfed] *) vt* faire manger à la cuillère; *Fig* mâcher le travail de

spoonful ['spuːnfʊl] *n* cuillerée *f*

sporadic [spə'rædɪk] *adj* sporadique

spore [spɔː(r)] *n* spore *f*

sporran ['spɒrən] *n Scot* = bourse portée sur le devant du kilt

sport [spɔːt] **1** *n* **(a)** *(activity)* sport *m* **(b)** *Fam (person)* **to be a (good) s.** *(man)* être un chic type; *(woman)* être une chic fille; **to be a bad s.** être mauvais(e) joueur(euse)
   2 *vt (wear)* arborer

sporting ['spɔːtɪŋ] *adj* **(a)** *(related to sport)* sportif(ive) **(b)** *(fair)* chic *inv*; **to give sb a s. chance** donner sa chance à qn

sports [spɔːts] *adj* **s. car** voiture *f* de sport; **s. centre** complexe *m* sportif; **s. day** = competition sportive annuelle organisée à l'école; **s. ground** terrain *m* de sport; *Br* **s. jacket** veste *f* sport; **s. page** page *f* des sports; **s. shop** magasin *m* de sports

sportsman ['spɔːtsmən] *n* sportif *m*

sportsmanship ['spɔːtsmənʃɪp] *n* esprit *m* sportif

sportsperson ['spɔːtspɜːsən] *n* sportif(ive) *m,f*

sportswoman ['spɔːtswʊmən] *n* sportive *f*

sporty ['spɔːtɪ] *adj (person)* sportif(ive); *(car, clothing)* de sport

spot [spɒt] **1** *n* (**a**) *(place)* endroit *m*; **on the s.** sur place; *Fam* **to put sb on the s.** mettre qn en mauvaise posture; *Fam* **to be in a (tight) s.** être dans le pétrin; **s. check** contrôle *m* surprise
(**b**) *(stain)* tache *f*
(**c**) *(pimple)* bouton *m*
(**d**) *(forming pattern on cloth)* pois *m*; *(on leopard)* tache *f*
(**e**) *Br Fam (small amount)* goutte *f*; **to have a s. of lunch** manger un morceau; **a s. of bother** de petits problèmes *mpl*
(**f**) *(spotlight)* projecteur *m*; *(smaller)* spot *m*
(**g**) *(on TV, radio, in show)* numéro *m*
2 *vt (pt & pp* **spotted**) (**a**) *(stain, mark)* tacher
(**b**) *(notice)* remarquer; *(opportunity, opening)* repérer; **to s. sb doing sth** apercevoir qn en train de faire qch; **well spotted!** bien vu!

spotless ['spɒtlɪs] *adj* impeccable; *Fig (reputation)* irréprochable

spotlight ['spɒtlaɪt] *n* projecteur *m*; *(smaller)* spot *m*; *Fig* **to be in the s.** être sous le feu des projecteurs

spot-on ['spɒt'ɒn] *adj Fam* tout à fait exact(e)

spotter plane ['spɒtə'pleɪn] *n* avion-espion *m*

spotty ['spɒtɪ] *adj (pimply)* boutonneux(euse)

spouse [spaʊz] *n* époux (épouse) *m,f*

spout [spaʊt] **1** *n (of teapot, kettle)* bec *m*; *Fam Fig* **to be up the s.** être fichu(e); *(of economy, business)* s'être cassé la figure; *(pregnant)* être enceinte
2 *vt (water)* faire jaillir; *Fam Fig (speech, nonsense)* débiter
3 *vi (of liquid)* jaillir; *Fam Fig (of person)* faire des discours

sprain [spreɪn] **1** *n (injury)* entorse *f*
2 *vt* **to s. one's ankle/wrist** se fouler la cheville/le poignet

sprang [spræŋ] *pt of* **spring**

sprat [spræt] *n* sprat *m*

sprawl [sprɔːl] *vi (of person)* s'affaler; *(of town)* s'étendre

sprawling ['sprɔːlɪŋ] *adj (person)* affalé(e); *(town)* tentaculaire

spray¹ [spreɪ] *n (of flowers)* bouquet *m*

spray² *n* (**a**) *(of liquid)* fines gouttelettes *fpl*; *(from sea)* embruns *mpl* (**b**) *(act of spraying)* **to give sth a s.** *(flowers, crops)* pulvériser; *(room)* vaporiser (**c**) *(device)* bombe *f*; *(for perfume)* atomiseur *m*; **s. can** bombe aérosol; **s. gun** *(for paint)* pistolet *m* (à peinture)
2 *vt (flowers, crops)* pulvériser; *(room)* vaporiser; **to s. oneself with perfume** se mettre du parfum *(avec un vaporisateur)*; **to s. sb with sth** asperger qn de qch

spray-on ['spreɪɒn] *adj (product, lotion etc)* en bombe, en aérosol

spray-paint ['spreɪpeɪnt] **1** *n* peinture *f* en bombe
2 *vt (with spray can)* peindre à la bombe; *(with spray gun)* peindre au pistolet

spread [spred] **1** *n* (**a**) *(of idea, religion, language)* diffusion *f*; *(of disease)* propagation *f* (**b**) *(of products, ages)* éventail *m* (**c**) *(in newspaper)* **full-page s.** pleine page *f*; **two-page s.** double page *f* (**d**) *(paste)* **cheese/chocolate s.** fromage *m*/chocolat *m* à tartiner (**e**) *(of wings, sails)* envergure *f* (**f**) *Fam (big meal)* festin *m*
2 *vt (pt & pp* **spread**) (**a**) *(arms, legs)* écarter; *Fig* **to s. one's wings** acquérir de l'indépendance (**b**) *(sand, sawdust, terror)* répandre; *(rumour, disease, germs)*

propager; *(payments)* étaler (**c**) *(butter, ointment)* étaler; **to s. a surface with sth** étaler qch sur une surface
3 *vi* se répandre; *(of rumour, disease, fire)* se propager
▸ **spread out 1** *vt sep* (**a**) *(map, newspaper)* étaler (**b**) **to be spread out** *(of fields, city)* s'étendre
2 *vi (of person)* s'étendre; *(of search party)* se disperser

spreadsheet ['spredʃiːt] *n Comput* tableur *m*

spree [spriː] *n Fam* **to go on a s.** *(go drinking)* prendre une cuite; **to go on a shopping** *or* **spending s.** faire des folies dans les magasins

sprig [sprɪg] *n (of parsley)* brin *m*; *(of holly, mistletoe)* branche *f*

sprightly ['spraɪtlɪ] *adj* alerte

spring [sprɪŋ] **1** *n* (**a**) *(of water)* source *f* (**b**) *(season)* printemps *m*; **in (the) s.** au printemps; **s. onion** ciboule *f*; **s. roll** rouleau *m* de printemps; **s. tide** grande marée *f* (**c**) *(leap)* bond *m* (**d**) *(elasticity)* élasticité *f*; **to walk with a s. in one's step** marcher d'un pas souple (**e**) *(device)* ressort *m*
2 *vt (pt* **sprang** [spræŋ], *pp* **sprung** [sprʌŋ]) (**a**) *(reveal unexpectedly)* **to s. sth on sb** annoncer qch à qn de but en blanc; **to s. a surprise on sb** faire une surprise à qn (**b**) *(develop)* **to s. a leak** commencer à fuir; *(of boat)* commencer à prendre l'eau (**c**) *Fam (prisoner)* faire évader
3 *vi* (**a**) *(jump)* bondir, sauter; **to s. to one's feet** se lever d'un bond; **to s. into action** passer rapidement à l'action; **to s. to life** *(of person, town)* s'animer; *(of machine)* se mettre en marche; **to s. to sb's defence** prendre vivement la défense de qn; **to s. open/shut** s'ouvrir/se fermer brusquement; **to s. to mind** venir à l'esprit (**b**) *(originate)* **to s. from** venir de; **to s. into existence** voir le jour; *Fam* **where did you s. from?** d'où sortez-vous?
▸ **spring up** *vi* (**a**) *(jump to one's feet)* se lever d'un bond (**b**) *(appear suddenly)* surgir; *(of wind)* se lever; *(of feeling)* prendre naissance

springboard ['sprɪŋbɔːd] *n also Fig* tremplin *m*

spring-clean [sprɪŋ'kliːn] **1** *n* grand nettoyage *m*
2 *vt* nettoyer à fond

spring-cleaning [sprɪŋ'kliːnɪŋ] *n* grand nettoyage *m*; **to do the s.** faire le grand nettoyage

springtime ['sprɪŋtaɪm] *n* printemps *m*

springy ['sprɪŋɪ] *adj* souple

sprinkle ['sprɪŋkəl] **1** *n (of salt, flour)* pincée *f*
2 *vt (with liquid)* arroser, asperger (**with** de); *(with salt, flour)* saupoudrer (**with** de); **to s. liquid on sth** arroser *ou* asperger qch de liquide; **to s. salt/flour on sth** saupoudrer qch de sel/farine

sprinkler ['sprɪŋklə(r)] *n (for lawns)* arroseur *m*; *(for fire prevention)* sprinkler *m*

sprinkling ['sprɪŋklɪŋ] *n* **a s. of** *(liquid)* quelques gouttes de; *(salt, flour)* un peu de; *Fig (people)* quelques

sprint [sprɪnt] **1** *n (fast run)* sprint *m*; *(running race)* course *f* (de vitesse); **to put on a s.** piquer un sprint
2 *vi (run fast)* piquer un sprint; **to s. off** partir en courant

sprinter ['sprɪntə(r)] *n* sprinter(euse) *m,f*

sprocket ['sprɒkɪt] *n* **s. (wheel)** pignon *m*

sprout [spraʊt] **1** *n (of plant)* pousse *f*; **(Brussels) s.** chou *m* de Bruxelles
2 *vt (leaves, shoots)* faire; *Fam (moustache, beard)* se laisser pousser
3 *vi (of leaves, hair)* pousser

▸**sprout up** *vi (of plant, child)* pousser; *(of new buildings, towns)* surgir

spruce¹ [spruːs] *n (tree)* épicéa *m*

spruce² *adj* impeccable

▸**spruce up** *vt sep (room)* bien nettoyer; **to s. oneself up** se faire beau (belle)

sprung [sprʌŋ] **1** *adj (mattress)* à ressorts
   2 *pp of* **spring**

spry [spraɪ] *adj* alerte

spud [spʌd] *n Fam (potato)* patate *f*

spun [spʌn] **1** *adj* **s. silk** schappe *f*
   2 *pt & pp of* **spin**

spunk [spʌŋk] *n* (**a**) *Fam (courage)* cran *m* (**b**) *Vulg (semen)* sperme *m*

spur [spɜː(r)] **1** *n* (**a**) *(for riding)* éperon *m*; *Fig (stimulus)* motivation *f*; *Fig* **to win one's spurs** faire ses preuves; **on the s. of the moment** sur un coup de tête (**b**) *(of land, rock)* éperon *m*
   2 *vt (pt & pp* **spurred**) *(horse)* éperonner; *Fig* **to s. sb on** stimuler qn; **to s. sb on to do sth** inciter qn à faire qch; *Fig* **to s. sb into action** inciter qn à agir

spurious ['spjʊərɪəs] *adj (argument, reasoning)* spécieux(euse); *(claim, story, charge)* sans fondement

spurn [spɜːn] *vt* repousser, rejeter

spurt [spɜːt] **1** *n (of liquid)* giclée *f*; *(of activity, energy)* regain *m*; *(increase in speed)* accélération *f*; **to do sth in spurts** faire qch par à-coups; **to put on a s.** accélérer
   2 *vt* **the wound was spurting blood** le sang giclait de la blessure; **the pen spurted ink** l'encre giclait du stylo
   3 *vi* (**a**) *(of liquid)* gicler (**b**) *(move quickly)* **to s. off** s'élancer brusquement

sputter ['spʌtə(r)] *vi (of engine)* toussoter; *(of flame, candle)* crépiter

spy [spaɪ] **1** *n* espion(onne) *m,f*; **s. plane** avion *m* espion; **s. ring** réseau *m* d'espionnage; **s. satellite** satellite *m* espion
   2 *vt (notice)* repérer
   3 *vi* espionner, faire de l'espionnage; **to s. on sb** espionner qn

▸**spy out** *vt sep Fig* **to s. out the land** tâter le terrain

Sq *(abbr* **Square**) pl

sq *(abbr* **square**) carré; **sq ft** ≃ mètres *mpl* carrés

squabble ['skwɒbəl] **1** *n* querelle *f*
   2 *vi* se quereller (**about** *or* **over** à propos de)

squabbling ['skwɒblɪŋ] *n* querelles *fpl*

squad [skwɒd] *n (of workmen)* équipe *f*; *(of athletes, footballers)* délégation *f*; *(of soldiers)* section *f*; *(of police)* brigade *f*; **s. car** voiture *f* de patrouille

squadron ['skwɒdrən] *n Mil (of planes)* escadron *m*; *(of ships)* escadrille *f*

squalid ['skwɒlɪd] *adj (dirty)* crasseux(euse); *(sordid)* sordide

squall [skwɔːl] **1** *n (of wind)* bourrasque *f*
   2 *vi (cry)* pousser des hurlements

squalor ['skwɒlə(r)] *n (dirtiness)* crasse *f*; *(poverty)* misère *f* noire

squander ['skwɒndə(r)] *vt (money, resources, talents)* gaspiller; *(time)* perdre; *(fortune, inheritance)* dilapider; *(opportunity)* laisser passer

square [skweə(r)] **1** *n* (**a**) *(shape)* carré *m*; *(on chessboard, map)* case *f*; *Fig* **to be back at s. one** être de retour à la case départ (**b**) *Math* carré *m* (**c**) *(of town, village)* place *f* (**d**) *Fam (unfashionable person)* **to be a s.** être ringard(e)

   2 *adj* (**a**) *(in shape)* carré(e) (**b**) *(right-angled)* **s. corner** angle *m* droit (**c**) *Math* carré(e); **s. root** racine *f* carrée (**d**) *Fam (unfashionable)* vieux jeu *inv*, ringard(e) (**e**) *(idioms)* **to be s. with sb** être honnête avec qn; **that's us s.** nous sommes quittes; **to feel like a s. peg in a round hole** ne pas se sentir à sa place; **s. deal** arrangement *m* équitable; **s. meal** bon repas *m*
   3 *adv* **to hit sb s. on the jaw** frapper qn en pleine mâchoire; **to look sb s. in the eye** regarder qn bien en face
   4 *vt* (**a**) *(make square)* mettre en forme de carré; *Math (number)* élever au carré; **squared paper** papier *m* quadrillé (**b**) *(settle) (account, debt)* régler (**c**) *(arrange)* **to s. sth with sb** arranger qch avec qn
   5 *vi (agree)* coller; **to s. with** correspondre à

▸**square up** *vi* (**a**) *(settle debts)* régler ses comptes (**b**) *(of fighters)* se mettre en garde; *Fig* **to s. up to a problem/an opponent** faire face à un problème/un adversaire

squarely ['skweəlɪ] *adv* (**a**) *(directly)* **to hit sb s. in the chest/face** frapper qn en pleine poitrine/figure (**b**) *(honestly)* honnêtement

squash¹ [skwɒʃ] **1** *n* (**a**) *(crush)* cohue *f*; **it was a s.** on était serrés comme des sardines (**b**) *Br (drink)* **orange/lemon s.** ≃ sirop *m* d'orange/de citron (**c**) *(sport)* squash *m*; **s. court** court *m* de squash
   2 *vt* écraser
   3 *vi* **to s. into a room/car** s'entasser dans une pièce/voiture

squash² *n Am (vegetable)* courge *f*

▸**squash up** *vi* se serrer

squat [skwɒt] **1** *n (illegally occupied dwelling)* squat *m*
   2 *adj (person, object, building)* trapu(e)
   3 *vi (pt & pp* **squatted**) (**a**) *(crouch down) (of person)* s'accroupir; *(of animal)* se tapir (**b**) *(occupy illegally)* squatter

squatter ['skwɒtə(r)] *n* squatter *m*

squaw [skwɔː] *n* squaw *f*

squawk [skwɔːk] **1** *n (of bird)* cri *m* rauque; *Fam (of person)* braillement *m*
   2 *vi (of bird)* pousser un cri rauque; *Fam (of person)* brailler

squeak [skwiːk] **1** *n (of animal, person)* cri *m* aigu; *(of door, hinges)* grincement *m*; *Fam* **I don't want to hear another s. out of you** je ne veux plus vous entendre
   2 *vi (of animal, person)* pousser un cri aigu; *(of door, hinges)* grincer; *(of shoes)* craquer

squeaky ['skwiːkɪ] *adj (voice)* aigu(uë); *(door, hinges)* qui grince; *(shoes)* qui craque; **s. clean** impeccable

squeal [skwiːl] **1** *n (of person, animal)* cri *m* perçant; *(of brakes)* crissement *m*
   2 *vt* crier
   3 *vi* (**a**) *(of person, animal)* pousser un cri perçant; *(of brakes)* crisser; *Fam* **to s. about sth** *(complain)* se lamenter au sujet de qch (**b**) *very Fam (inform)* moucharder; **to s. on sb** balancer qn

squeamish ['skwiːmɪʃ] *adj* de nature délicate; **to be s. about sth** ne pas supporter qch

squeeze [skwiːz] **1** *n* pression *f*; **to give sth a s.** presser qch; **to give sb a s.** *(hug)* serrer qn dans ses bras; **a s. of lemon** quelques gouttes de citron; *Fam* **it was a tight s.** nous étions/ils etaient/*etc* serrés comme des sardines; *Fam* **to put the s. on sb** *(pressurize)* faire pression sur qn
   2 *vt* (**a**) *(press)* presser; **to s. sb's hand** serrer la main à qn; *Fig* **to s. sb** *(pressurize)* faire pression sur qn (**b**)

(squash) **to s. sth into sth** faire rentrer qch dans qch; **I think we can just s. you in** je pense qu'on peut vous trouver une place

3 *vi* **to s. into sth** s'entasser dans qch; **to s. past sb** se glisser devant qn; **s. up a bit!** serrez-vous un peu!

▶**squeeze out** *vt sep (juice)* exprimer

squelch [skweltʃ] *vi* patauger; **to s. through the mud** avancer en pataugeant dans la boue

squib [skwɪb] *n (firework)* pétard *m*; *Fig* **to be a damp s.** être bidon *inv*

squid [skwɪd] *(pl* **squid***)* *n* calmar *m*

squiggle ['skwɪgəl] *n* gribouillis *m*

squint [skwɪnt] **1** *n* **(a)** *(eye defect)* strabisme *m*; **to have a s.** loucher **(b)** *(quick look)* coup d'œil *m*; **to have a s. at** jeter un coup d'œil à

2 *vi* **(a)** *(have eye defect)* loucher **(b)** *(narrow one's eyes)* plisser les yeux; **to s. at** plisser les yeux pour voir

squire ['skwaɪə(r)] *n (landowner)* châtelain *m*; *Hist* écuyer *m*

squirm [skwɜːm] *vi (wriggle)* se tortiller; *Fig* **to s. (with embarrassment)** être mal à l'aise

squirrel ['skwɪrəl] *n* écureuil *m*

squirt [skwɜːt] **1** *n* **(a)** *(of liquid)* giclée *f* **(b)** *Fam Pej (insignificant person)* petit(e) morveux(euse) *m,f*

2 *vt (liquid)* faire gicler; **to s. sth on sb/sth, to s. sb/sth with sth** asperger qn/qch de qch

3 *vi (of liquid)* **to s. out** gicler

Sr *(abbr* **Senior) Thomas Smith, Sr** Thomas Smith père

Sri Lanka [sriː'læŋkə] *n* le Sri Lanka

Sri Lankan [sriː'læŋkən] **1** *n* Sri Lankais(e) *m,f*

2 *adj* sri lankais(e)

SSE *(abbr* **south-southeast)** sud-sud-est

SSN [eses'en] *n Am (abbr* **social security number)** numéro *m* de sécurité sociale

SSW *(abbr* **south-southwest)** sud-sud-ouest

St (a) *(abbr* **Street)** ruc *f* **(b)** *(abbr* **Saint)** st(e); *Bot & Med* **St John's wort** millepertuis *m*; *Geog* **St Kitts and Nevis** Saint-Kitts-et-Nevis; **St Lucia** Sainte-Lucie; **St Petersburg** Saint-Petersbourg; **St Vincent and the Grenadines** Saint-Vincent-et-Grenadines; *see also* **saint**

stab [stæb] **1** *n* **(a)** *(with knife)* coup *m* de couteau; *Fig* **a s. of pain** un élancement; **a s. of envy** un pincement de jalousie; **a s. of guilt** un accès de culpabilité **(b)** *Fam (attempt)* **to have a s. at sth/at doing sth** essayer qch/de faire qch

2 *vt (pt & pp* **stabbed)** *(with knife)* poignarder; *(with other weapon)* transpercer; **to s. sb to death** tuer qn d'un coup de couteau; *Fig* **to s. sb in the back** poignarder qn dans le dos

stabbing ['stæbɪŋ] **1** *n (attack)* agression *f* au couteau

2 *adj (pain)* lancinant(e)

stability [stə'bɪlɪtɪ] *n* stabilité *f*

stabilize ['steɪbɪlaɪz] **1** *vt* stabiliser

2 *vi* se stabiliser

stabilizer ['steɪbɪlaɪzə(r)] *n (on bicycle)* stabilisateur *m*

stable¹ ['steɪbəl] **1** *n* écurie *f*; *Fig* **to lock the s. door after the horse has bolted** prendre des mesures trop tard

2 *vt* mettre à l'écurie

stable² *adj* stable

stack [stæk] **1** *n* **(a)** *(pile)* pile *f*; *Fam* **stacks of** des tas de **(b)** *(chimney)* cheminée *f*

2 *vt* empiler; **to be stacked with sth** *(full of)* être

plein(e) de qch; **the odds were stacked against them** ils n'avaient aucune chance

stadium ['steɪdɪəm] *(pl* **stadiums** *or* **stadia** ['steɪdɪə] *) n* stade *m*

staff [stɑːf] **1** *n* **(a)** *(stick)* bâton *m* **(b)** *(personnel)* personnel *m*; **teaching/nursing s.** personnel *m* enseignant/infirmier; *Br* **s. nurse** infirmier(ère) *m,f* diplômé(e); **s. room** *(in school)* salle *f* des professeurs **(c)** *(pl* **staves** [steɪvz]*) Mus* portée *f*

2 *vt* **the office is staffed by volunteers** le personnel du bureau est composé de volontaires; **the desk is staffed at all times** il y a toujours quelqu'un au bureau

stag [stæg] *n (animal)* cerf *m*; **s. beetle** cerf-volant *m*; **s. night** *or* **party** *(before wedding)* enterrement *m* de la vie de garçon

stage [steɪdʒ] **1** *n* **(a)** *(platform)* plate-forme *f*; *(in theatre)* scène *f*; **to go on the s.** faire du théâtre; *Fig* **to set the s. for sth** préparer le terrain à qch; **s. directions** indications *fpl* scéniques; **s. door** entrée *f* des artistes; **s. fright** trac *m*; **s. manager** régisseur *m*; **s. name** nom *m* de scène; **s. whisper** aparté *m* **(b)** *(phase)* stade *m*; **at this s. in...** à ce stade de...; **to do sth in stages** faire qch par étapes **(c)** **s. (coach)** diligence *f*

2 *vt (play)* monter, mettre en scène; *Fig (demonstration, invasion)* organiser

stagehand ['steɪdʒhænd] *n* machiniste *m*

stage-manage ['steɪdʒmænɪdʒ] *vt (play)* s'occuper de la régie de; *Fig (event, demonstration)* mettre en scène

stage-struck ['steɪdʒstrʌk] *adj* fou (folle) de théâtre

stagflation [stæg'fleɪʃən] *n Econ* stagflation *f*

stagger ['stægə(r)] **1** *vt* **(a)** *(astound)* stupéfier **(b)** *(tea-breaks, holidays)* échelonner

2 *vi (stumble)* tituber; **to s. along/in/out** marcher/entrer/sortir en titubant; **to s. to one's feet** se relever péniblement

stagnant ['stægnənt] *adj* stagnant(e)

stagnate [stæg'neɪt] *vi* stagner

stagnation [stæg'neɪʃən] *n* stagnation *f*

staid [steɪd] *adj* collet monté *inv*

stain [steɪn] **1** *n (mark)* tache *f*; *(dye)* teinture *f*; **s. remover** détachant *m*

2 *vt (mark)* tacher; *(dye)* teindre; *Fig (reputation)* salir

stained-glass ['steɪndglɑːs] *n* vitrail *m*; **s. window** vitrail

stainless steel ['steɪnlɪs'stiːl] *n* acier *m* inoxydable, inox® *m*

stair [steə(r)] *n (single step)* marche *f*; **stairs** *(staircase)* escalier *m*

staircase ['steəkeɪs] *n* escalier *m*

stairway ['steəweɪ] *n* escalier *m*

stairwell ['steəwel] *n* cage *f* d'escalier

stake [steɪk] **1** *n* **(a)** *(piece of wood)* pieu *m*; *(piece of metal)* piquet *m*; *(for plant)* tuteur *m*; **to be burnt at the s.** périr sur le bûcher **(b)** *(bet)* enjeu *m*; **to be at s.** être en jeu **(c)** *(share)* **to have a s. in sth** avoir des intérêts dans qch; *Fig* être concerné(e) par qch

2 *vt* **(a)** *(money)* miser (**on** sur); *Fig (one's reputation, job)* risquer (**on** sur); **I'd s. my life on it** j'en mettrais ma tête à couper **(b)** **to s. a claim (to sth)** revendiquer un droit (à qch)

stakeout ['steɪkaʊt] *n* surveillance *f*

stalactite ['stæləktaɪt] *n* stalactite *f*

stalagmite ['stæləgmaɪt] *n* stalagmite *f*

stale [steɪl] *adj* (**a**) *(bread, cake)* rassis(e); *(air)* confiné(e); *(smell)* âcre (**b**) *Fig (social life, politics)* sans intérêt; *(excuse, joke)* éculé(e); *(person)* blasé(e)

stalemate ['steɪlmeɪt] *n (in chess)* pat *m*; *(in negotiations)* impasse *f*; **to reach a s.** être dans l'impasse

stalk¹ [stɔːk] **1** *vt (suspect, wild animal)* traquer; *(obsessively)* harceler

2 *vt (of obsessive fan, infatuated person etc)* suivre en permanence *(de façon obsessionelle)*

3 *vi (walk angrily)* **to s. in/out** entrer/sortir d'un air furieux mais digne

stalk² *n (of plant, flower)* tige *f*; *(of fruit)* queue *f*

stalker ['stɔːkə(r)] *n* = admirateur obsessionnel qui harcèle une de ses connaissances ou une célébrité

stall [stɔːl] **1** *n* (**a**) *(in stable)* stalle *f*; *(for shower, toilet)* cabine *f* (**b**) *(in market)* étal *m*; *(at exhibition)* stand *m* (**c**) **the stalls** *(in theatre)* l'orchestre *m*

2 *vt (hold off)* faire patienter

3 *vi* (**a**) *(of car)* caler; *Fig (of campaign)* être interrompu(e) (**b**) *(delay)* **to s. (for time)** essayer de gagner du temps

stallion ['stæljən] *n* étalon *m*

stalwart ['stɔːlwət] **1** *n* fidèle *mf*

2 *adj* résolu(e)

stamen ['steɪmən] *n* étamine *f*

stamina ['stæmɪnə] *n* résistance *f* physique

stammer ['stæmə(r)] **1** *n* bégaiement *m*; **to have a s.** bégayer

2 *vi* bégayer

3 *vt* balbutier

▸**stammer out** *vt insep* balbutier

stamp [stæmp] **1** *n (for letter)* timbre *m*; *(mark)* cachet *m*; *(device)* tampon *m*; *Fig* **to bear the s. of sth** porter l'empreinte de qch; *Fig* **s. of approval** aval *m*, approbation *f*; **s. album** album *m* de timbres; **s. collector** philatéliste *mf*; *Fin* **s. duty** droit *m* de timbre; **s. machine** distributeur *m* de timbres-poste

2 *vt* (**a**) *(document)* tamponner; **to s. the date on sth** tamponner la date sur qch; **stamped addressed envelope** enveloppe *f* timbrée libellée à ses noms et adresse (**b**) **to s. one's foot** taper du pied

3 *vi* **to s. on sth** *(on purpose)* écraser qch avec le pied; *(accidentally)* écraser qch du pied; **to s. off/out** partir/sortir en tapant des pieds

▸**stamp out** *vt sep* (**a**) *(resistance, dissent)* anéantir; *(poverty)* éradiquer (**b**) *(fire)* éteindre en piétinant

stampede [stæmˈpiːd] **1** *n* débandade *f*; **there was a s. for the door** il y a eu une ruée vers la porte

2 *vi* se ruer

stance [stɑːns] *n also Fig* position *f*

stand [stænd] **1** *n* (**a**) *(opinion)* position *f*; **to take a s. (on sth)** prendre position (sur qch)

(**b**) *(of lamp, microphone)* pied *m*; *(for books, postcards)* présentoir *m*

(**c**) *(stall) (outside)* étalage *m*; *(at exhibition)* stand *m*

(**d**) *(at sports ground)* tribune *f*

(**e**) *(taxi rank)* station *f*

2 *vt (pt & pp* **stood** [stʊd] *)* (**a**) *(place)* poser; **to s. sth against sth** mettre qch contre qch

(**b**) *(endure)* supporter; **to s. comparison with sb/sth** soutenir la comparaison avec qn/qch; **to s. one's ground** tenir bon

(**c**) *(pay for)* **to s. sb a drink/meal** payer à boire/manger à qn

(**d**) *(have)* **to s. a chance (of doing sth)** avoir des chances (de faire qch); **she doesn't s. a chance** elle n'a aucune chance

(**e**) *Law* **to s. trial** passer en jugement

3 *vi* (**a**) *(of person) (get up)* se mettre debout; *(be upright)* être debout; *(remain upright)* rester debout; **to s. on one's head** faire le poirier; **I could hardly s.** je tenais à peine debout; **don't just s. there!** ne reste pas planté là les bras ballants!; **to s. fast** *or* **firm** tenir bon; **to s. still** *(of person)* se tenir immobile; **time seemed to s. still** le temps semblait s'être arrêté

(**b**) *(of building)* se dresser; *(of object)* être, se trouver

(**c**) *(be in situation)* **inflation/unemployment stands at...** le taux d'inflation/de chômage s'élève à...; **to s. in need of sth** avoir besoin de qch; **to s. to do sth** risquer de faire qch; **it stands to reason that...** il est clair que...

(**d**) *(idioms)* **to be standing right behind sb** être avec qn; **to s. on one's own two feet** se débrouiller tout(e) seul(e); **I don't know where I s.** je ne sais pas à quoi m'en tenir; **to know how things s.** savoir où en sont les choses; **I s. corrected** autant pour moi; **to s. for Parliament** se présenter aux élections législatives; **the offer still stands** l'offre tient toujours

▸**stand aside** *vi* s'écarter

▸**stand back** *vi (move away)* reculer (**from** de); *Fig* prendre de la distance (**from** par rapport à)

▸**stand by 1** *vt insep* (**a**) *(person, cause)* défendre, soutenir (**b**) *(promise, decision)* maintenir

2 *vi* (**a**) *(be ready)* **to s. by (for sth/to do sth)** *(of person)* se tenir prêt(e) (pour qch/à faire qch); *(of vehicle)* être prêt (pour qch/à faire qch) (**b**) *(not get involved)* rester sans rien faire

▸**stand down** *vi (retire)* se retirer

▸**stand for** *vt insep* (**a**) *(mean, represent)* vouloir dire (**b**) *(tolerate)* supporter

▸**stand out** *vi* (**a**) *(be prominent)* ressortir; **to s. out in a crowd** se détacher dans la foule; *Fam* **it stands out a mile** ça se voit comme le nez au milieu de la figure (**b**) *(oppose)* **to s. out against sth** résister à qch

▸**stand up 1** *vt sep* (**a**) *(put in upright position)* mettre à la verticale (**b**) *Fam* **to s. sb up** *(on date)* poser un lapin à qn

2 *vi* (**a**) *(get up)* se mettre debout; *(be standing)* être debout; *Fig* **to s. up for sb/sth** défendre qn/qch; *Fig* **to s. up to sb** tenir tête à qn (**b**) *(of argument, theory)* faire le poids; **to s. up to sth** résister à qch; **it'll never s. up in court** ça ne sera pas valable au tribunal

stand-alone word processor ['stændələʊn-'wɜːdprəʊsesə(r)] *n Comput* machine *f* à traitement de texte autonome

standard ['stændəd] **1** *n* (**a**) *(point of reference)* référence *f*; *(set requirement)* norme *f*; *(for weight, measurement)* étalon *m* (**b**) *(required level)* niveau *m*; **to be up to/below s.** être du/en dessous du niveau requis; **s. of living** niveau de vie; **s. of accommodation** qualité *f* du logement (**c**) **standards** *(morals)* principes *mpl* moraux; **to have high/low standards** être/ne pas être exigeant(e) (**d**) *(flag)* étendard *m*; *also Fig* **s. bearer** porte-drapeau *m*

2 *adj* (**a**) *(design, size)* standard *inv*; *Math* **s. deviation** écart *m* type; **s. lamp** lampadaire *m*; **s. measure** mesure *f* étalon; **s. time** heure *f* légale (**b**) *(usual)* habituel(elle); **S. English** anglais *m* standard; **s. practice** pratique *f* courante

standardization [stændədaɪˈzeɪʃən] *n* normalisation *f*

standardize ['stændədaɪz] *vt* normaliser

stand-by ['stændbaɪ] *n* (**a**) *(fuel, food)* réserve *f*; **to have sth as a s.** avoir qch en réserve; **to be on s.** *(of troops, emergency services)* être en état d'alerte (**b**) *(for air travel)* **to be on s.** être en stand-by; **s. passenger** passager(ère) *m,f* en stand-by; **s. ticket** billet *m* en stand-by

stand-in ['stændɪn] *n* remplaçant(e) *m,f*; *(for actor)* doublure *f*

standing ['stændɪŋ] **1** *n* (**a**) *(status)* réputation *f* (**b**) *(duration)* **of long s.** de longue date
2 *adj* (**a**) *(upright)* debout; **to give sb a s. ovation** se lever pour applaudir qn (**b**) *(permanent)* permanent(e); **I have a s. invitation** je peux y aller quand je veux; **s. army** armée *f* de métier; **s. charges** *(on bill)* frais *mpl* d'abonnement; **s. joke** plaisanterie *f* classique; *Fin* **s. order** virement *m* automatique

standoffish [stænd'ɒfɪʃ] *adj* distant(e)

standpoint ['stændpɔɪnt] *n* point *m* de vue

standstill ['stændstɪl] *n* **to be at a s.** *(of traffic)* être immobilisé(e); *(of production, economy)* être paralysé(e); **to come to a s.** *(of traffic)* s'immobiliser; *(of production)* s'arrêter; *(of economy)* être paralysé(e)

stand-up ['stændʌp] *adj* (**a**) **s. comedian** comique *mf* *(qui se produit seul en scène)*; **s. comedy** spectacle *m* comique (**b**) *(fight, argument)* en règle

stank [stæŋk] *pt of* **stink**

stanza ['stænzə] *n* strophe *f*

staple¹ ['steɪpəl] **1** *n* *(for fastening paper)* agrafe *f*; **s. gun** agrafeuse *f*
2 *vt* agrafer

staple² *n* *(basic food)* aliment *m* de base; *(basic product)* principale production *f*; *Fig* **such stories are a s. of the tabloid press** la presse à sensation se nourrit de telles histoires

stapler ['steɪplə(r)] *n* agrafeuse *f*

star [stɑː(r)] **1** *n* (**a**) *(heavenly body)* étoile *f*; **the Stars and Stripes** *(US flag)* la bannière étoilée; *Fig* **to reach for the stars** essayer d'atteindre les sommets; *Fig* **to see stars** *(after blow to head)* voir trente-six chandelles; **s. fruit** carambole *f*; **s. sign** signe *m* du zodiaque (**b**) *(famous person)* star *f*, vedette *f*; **s. player** vedette *f* (**c**) *Fam* **stars** *(horoscope)* horoscope *m*
2 *vt* *(pt & pp* **starred***)* *(of film, play)* avoir pour vedette
3 *vi* **to s. in a film/play** jouer dans un film/une pièce

starboard ['stɑːbəd] *n Naut* tribord *m*

starch [stɑːtʃ] **1** *n* *(for shirts, in food)* amidon *m*
2 *vt* *(shirt)* amidonner

starchy ['stɑːtʃɪ] *adj* (**a**) *(food)* riche en féculents (**b**) *Fam (person, manner)* guindé(e)

stardom ['stɑːdəm] *n* célébrité *f*

stare [steə(r)] **1** *n* regard *m* fixe
2 *vt* **to be staring sb in the face** *(be obvious)* crever les yeux à qn
3 *vi* **to s. at sb** dévisager qn; **to s. at sth** regarder qch fixement; **to s. into space** regarder dans le vague; **it's rude to s.** ce n'est pas poli de dévisager les gens

starfish ['stɑːfɪʃ] *n* étoile *f* de mer

stark [stɑːk] **1** *adj (contrast)* net (nette); *(light, colours)* cru(e); *(truth, facts)* brut(e); *(landscape)* nu(e)
2 *adv* **s. naked** tout(e) nu(e); *Fam* **s. staring mad** complètement dingue

starkers ['stɑːkəz] *adj Br Fam* à poil

starlet ['stɑːlɪt] *n (young actress)* starlette *f*

starlight ['stɑːlaɪt] *n* lumière *f* des étoiles

starling ['stɑːlɪŋ] *n* étourneau *m*

starlit ['stɑːlɪt] *adj* étoilé(e)

starry ['stɑːrɪ] *adj* étoilé(e)

starry-eyed [stɑːrɪ'aɪd] *adj* naïf(ïve)

start [stɑːt] **1** *n* (**a**) *(beginning)* début *m*; *(starting place, of journey, race)* départ *m*; **for a s.** pour commencer; **at the s.** au début; **from the s.** dès le départ; **from s. to finish** du début à la fin; **to make a s. on sth** commencer qch; **he lent her £50 to give her a s.** il lui a prêté 50 livres pour l'aider à démarrer; **to give sb a 60-metre s.** *(in race)* laisser 60 mètres d'avance à qn (**b**) *(sudden movement)* sursaut *m*; **to wake with a s.** se réveiller en sursaut; **to give sb a s.** faire sursauter qn
2 *vt* (**a**) *(begin)* commencer; *(conversation, talks)* entamer; *(fire)* déclencher; *(fashion, rumour)* lancer; *(business)* monter; **to s. doing sth, to s. to do sth** commencer de faire qch; **to s. crying/laughing/sneezing** se mettre à pleurer/rire/éternuer; **to get started** démarrer (**b**) *(machine, engine)* mettre en marche; *(car)* démarrer
3 *vi* (**a**) *(begin)* commencer; **to s. at the beginning** commencer par le commencement; **to s. by doing sth** commencer par faire qch; **to s. on sth** commencer qch; **she had started as a doctor** elle avait commencé sa carrière comme médecin; **to s. with** au début, d'abord; **now don't YOU s.!** tu ne vas pas t'y mettre aussi! (**b**) *(make sudden movement)* sursauter (**c**) *(begin journey)* se mettre en route (**d**) *(of car, engine)* démarrer

▶**start off 1** *vt sep (argument, debate)* commencer; **to s. sb off** *(in business)* aider qn à démarrer; *(on a subject)* lancer qn
2 *vi (begin)* commencer; *(on journey)* se mettre en route

▶**start out** *vi (begin)* débuter; *(on journey)* se mettre en route

▶**start up 1** *vt sep (car)* démarrer; *(machine)* mettre en marche; *(business)* monter
2 *vi (of engine)* démarrer; **to s. up in business** monter son entreprise

starter ['stɑːtə(r)] *n* (**a**) *(competitor)* partant(e) *m,f*; *(official)* starter *m* (**b**) **to be a late s.** *(of child)* ne pas être très précoce; **to be a slow s.** *(of person)* être lent(e) à démarrer (**c**) *(device)* starter *m* (**d**) *(in meal)* hors-d'œuvre *m inv*; *Fig* **for starters** pour commencer

starting ['stɑːtɪŋ] *n* (**a**) *(in sport)* **s. block** starting-block *m*; **s. line** ligne *f* de départ; **s. pistol** pistolet *m* de starter (**b**) *(initial)* **s. point** *or* **place** point *m* de départ; **s. price** *(in betting)* cote *f* au départ; **s. salary** salaire *m* de départ

startle ['stɑːtəl] *vt* faire sursauter

startling ['stɑːtlɪŋ] *adj (noise)* effrayant(e); *(news, event)* incroyable

start-up ['stɑːtʌp] *n Com* démarrage *m*; **s. costs** coûts *mpl* d'installation

starvation [stɑː'veɪʃən] *n* privation *f* totale de nourriture; **to die of s.** mourir de faim; **to be on a s. diet** *(not have enough to eat)* n'avoir presque rien à manger; **s. wages** salaires *mpl* de misère

starve [stɑːv] **1** *vt* priver de nourriture; **to s. sb to death** faire mourir qn de faim; *Fig* **to be starved of sth** être privé(e) de qch
2 *vi (lack food)* souffrir de la faim; **to s. (to death)** mourir de faim; *Fam* **I'm starving!** je meurs de faim!

starving ['stɑːvɪŋ] *adj* famélique

stash [stæʃ] *Fam* **1** *n* réserve *f*
   2 *vt* planquer
state [steɪt] **1** *n* (**a**) *(condition)* état *m*; *(situation)* situation *f*; **I'm not in a fit s. to travel** je ne suis pas en état de voyager; **s. of war/emergency** état de guerre/d'urgence; **s. of affaires** situation *f*; **s. of health** état de santé; **s. of mind** état d'esprit; **in a s. of terror** terrifié(e); **in a s. of shock** en état de choc; **to be in a terrible s.** être dans un état lamentable; **to lie in s.** *(of dead person)* être exposé(e) au public (**b**) *(country, administrative region)* État *m*; *Fam* **the States** *(the USA)* les États-Unis; **s. control** étatisme *m*; *Am* **S. Department** ≃ ministère *m* des Affaires étrangères; **s. occasions** cérémonie *f* officielle; **s. school** école *f* publique; **s. secret** secret *m* d'État; **s. sector** secteur *m* public; **S. Supreme Court** = la plus haute instance judiciaire dans chaque État américain; *Am Pol* **S. of the Union address** le discours sur l'état de l'Union; **s. visit** visite *f* officielle
   2 *vt* (*declare*) déclarer; *(address, age)* indiquer, préciser; **to s. the obvious** enfoncer une porte ouverte; **as stated earlier/above** comme mentionné précédemment/ci-dessus; **at the stated times** aux heures prévues

> ### State of the Union
> Ce discours radiotélévisé, dans lequel le président des États-Unis dresse le bilan de son programme et en définit les orientations, est prononcé devant le Congrès. L'allocution présidentielle a lieu tous les ans en janvier.

stateless ['steɪtlɪs] *adj* apatride
stately ['steɪtlɪ] *adj* imposant(e); **s. home** ≃ château *m*
statement ['steɪtmənt] *n* (**a**) *(of opinion)* déclaration *f*; *(of facts)* exposé *m*; **to make a s.** *(of spokesperson)* faire une déclaration; *(of witness)* faire une déposition; *Fig (of lifestyle, behaviour)* faire passer un message (**b**) *(from bank)* relevé *m* de compte
state-of-the-art [steɪtəvðɪ'ɑːt] *adj (technology, computer etc)* de pointe; **it's s.** c'est du dernier cri
state-owned ['steɪt'əʊnd] *adj (company)* d'État; *(property)* de l'État
statesman ['steɪtsmən] *n* homme *m* d'État
statesmanlike ['steɪtsmənlaɪk] *adj* digne d'un homme d'État
static ['stætɪk] **1** *adj* statique; **s. electricity** électricité *f* statique
   2 *n* électricité *f* statique
station ['steɪʃən] **1** *n* (**a**) *(for trains)* gare *f*; **s. master** chef *m* de gare; *Am* **s. wagon** *(car)* break *m* (**b**) *(post)* poste *m*; **(police) s.** poste (de police); **(radio/television) s.** station *f* de radio/télévision (**c**) *(social condition)* condition *f*; **to have ideas above one's s.** ne pas avoir les moyens de ses ambitions
   2 *vt (person)* placer; *(soldier, troops)* poster
stationary ['steɪʃənərɪ] *adj* immobile
stationer ['steɪʃənə(r)] *n* **s.'s (shop)** papeterie *f*
stationery ['steɪʃənərɪ] *n (writing materials)* papeterie *f*; *(writing paper)* papier *m* à lettres
statistic [stə'tɪstɪk] *n* chiffre *m* statistique; **statistics** statistiques *fpl*
statistical [stə'tɪstɪkəl] *adj* statistique
statistician [stætɪs'tɪʃən] *n* statisticien(enne) *m,f*
statue ['stætjuː] *n* statue *f*
statuesque [stætjʊ'esk] *adj* sculptural(e)

statuette [stætjʊ'et] *n* statuette *f*
stature ['stætjə(r)] *n (physical build)* stature *f*; *(reputation)* envergure *f*, réputation *f*
status ['steɪtəs] *n (position, prestige)* statut *m*; *Comput* **s. bar** barre *f* d'état; *Comput* **s. line** ligne *f* d'état; **s. meeting** réunion *f* de bilan; **s. report** rapport *m* de situation; **s. symbol** marque *f* de prestige
status quo ['steɪtəs'kwəʊ] *n* statu quo *m inv*
statute ['stætjuːt] *n* texte *m* de loi; **by s.** par la loi; **s. book** recueil *m* de lois
statutory ['stætjʊtərɪ] *adj* légal(e); **s. duty** obligation *f* légale; **s. holiday** jour *m* férié
staunch[1] [stɔːntʃ] *adj (resolute)* convaincu(e); *(supporter)* ardent(e)
staunch[2] *vt (blood)* étancher
staunchly ['stɔːntʃlɪ] *adv* résolument
stave [steɪv] *n* (**a**) *(of barrel)* douve *f* (**b**) *Mus* portée *f*
▸**stave in** *(pt & pp* staved *or* stove [stəʊv] *) vt sep* défoncer; *(ribs)* enfoncer
▸**stave off** *vt sep (problem, disaster)* éviter; *(hunger)* tromper
stay [steɪ] **1** *vt (endure)* **to s. the course** *or* **distance** tenir la distance
   2 *vi* (**a**) *(not move, remain)* rester; *Fam* **to s. put** rester tranquille; **to s. still** rester tranquille; **computers are here to s.** l'informatique est entrée dans les mœurs (**b**) *(reside temporarily)* séjourner; **I stayed five years in the States** j'ai passé cinq ans aux États-Unis; **to s. with sb** loger chez qn (**c**) *Scot (live)* habiter
   3 *n* (**a**) *(visit)* séjour *m* (**b**) *Law & Fig* **s. of execution** sursis *m*
▸**stay away** *vi* **to s. away from sb/sth** ne pas s'approcher de qn/qch; **to s. away from school** ne pas aller à l'école
▸**stay in** *vi (not go out)* rester chez soi
▸**stay on** *vi* rester
▸**stay out** *vi* (**a**) *(not go home)* ne pas rentrer; **to s. out all night** ne pas rentrer de la nuit; **to s. out late** rentrer tard (**b**) *(of strikers)* continuer la grève (**c**) *(not interfere)* **to s. out of sth** ne pas se mêler de qch
▸**stay up** *vi* ne pas aller se coucher
staying power ['steɪŋ'paʊə(r)] *n* endurance *f*
STD [estiː'diː] *n* (**a**) *(abbr* **subscriber trunk dialling**) indicatif *m* (**b**) *(abbr* **sexually transmitted disease**) MST *f*
stead [sted] *n* **to stand sb in good s.** être fort utile à qn; **in sb's s.** à la place de qn
steadfast ['stedfɑːst] *adj* dévoué(e); *(opponent, resistance)* constant(e)
steadily ['stedɪlɪ] *adv (change, grow)* progressivement; *(work)* assidûment; *(walk)* d'un pas régulier; *(look)* fixement; *(breathe, increase)* régulièrement
steady ['stedɪ] **1** *adj* (**a**) *(stable)* stable; **in a s. voice** d'une voix assurée (**b**) *(regular)* régulier(ère); *(progress)* constant(e); *(relationship)* durable; **to have a s. girlfriend** avoir une copine (attitrée); **to drive at a s. 50 mph** ≃ rouler à une vitesse régulière de 80 km/h
   2 *adv* **to be going s.** sortir ensemble sérieusement; *Br Fam* **s. (on)!** du calme!
   3 *vt* faire tenir; **to s. oneself** trouver son équilibre; **to s. one's nerves** se calmer; **to s. one's voice** contrôler sa voix

steak [steɪk] *n* (*beef*) steak *m*; (*of fish*) darne *f*; **s. and kidney pie** = tourte à la viande de bœuf et aux rognons

steal [stiːl] (*pt* **stole** [stəʊl], *pp* **stolen** ['stəʊlən]) **1** *vt* (**a**) (*thieve*) voler; **to s. sth from sb** voler qch à qn (**b**) (*idioms*) **to s. a glance at sb** jeter un coup d'œil à qn; **to s. the show** ravir la vedette
 2 *vi* (**a**) (*thieve*) voler (**b**) (*move quietly*) **to s. away/in/out** s'en aller/rentrer/sortir sans faire de bruit; **to s. up on sb** s'approcher de qn sans faire de bruit; *Fig* prendre qn par surprise

stealth [stelθ] *n* ruse *f*

stealthily ['stelθɪlɪ] *adv* furtivement

stealthy ['stelθɪ] *adj* furtif(ive)

steam [stiːm] **1** *n* (**a**) (*water vapour*) vapeur *f*; (*on glass*) buée *f*; **s. bath** bain *m* de vapeur; **s. engine** locomotive *f* à vapeur; **s. iron** fer *m* à vapeur; **s. shovel** pelleteuse *f* (**b**) (*idioms*) **to get up s.** prendre de l'élan; **to run out of s.** s'essouffler; **to let off s.** se défouler; **to do sth under one's own s.** faire qch tout(e) seul(e)
 2 *vt* (*food*) faire cuire à la vapeur
 3 *vi* (*give off steam*) fumer
▸**steam open** *vt sep* (*envelope*) décacheter à la vapeur
▸**steam up 1** *vt sep* **to get all steamed up (about sth)** (*of person*) se mettre dans tous ses états (à propos de qch)
 2 *vi* (*of window, glasses*) s'embuer

steamer ['stiːmə(r)] *n* (**a**) (*ship*) (bateau *m* à) vapeur *m* (**b**) (*for food*) panier *m* de cuisson à la vapeur

steamroller ['stiːmrəʊlə(r)] **1** *n* rouleau *m* compresseur
 2 *vt* **to s. sb into doing sth** forcer qn à faire qch

steamship ['stiːmʃɪp] *n* bateau *m* à vapeur

steamy ['stiːmɪ] *adj* (**a**) (*room*) plein(e) de vapeur; (*mirror*) embué(e) (**b**) *Fam* (*novel, film*) torride

steel [stiːl] **1** *n* acier *m*; **nerves of s.** nerfs *mpl* d'acier; **the s. industry** la sidérurgie; **s. band** steel band *m*; **s. mill** aciérie *f*; **s. wool** paille *f* de fer
 2 *vt* **to s. oneself to do sth** s'armer de courage pour faire qch; **to s. oneself against sth** se blinder contre qch

steelworker ['stiːlwɜːkə(r)] *n* employé(e) *m,f* de la sidérurgie

steep¹ [stiːp] *adj* (**a**) (*path, hill*) pentu(e), escarpé(e); (*climb*) raide; *Fig* (*increase*) considérable (**b**) *Fam* (*expensive*) salé(e); (*unreasonable*) raide

steep² *vt* (*soak*) faire tremper; *Fig* **steeped in history/tradition** imprégné(e) d'histoire/de tradition

steeple ['stiːpəl] *n* clocher *m*

steeplechase ['stiːpəltʃeɪs] *n* steeple-chase *m*

steeplejack ['stiːpəldʒæk] *n* réparateur *m* de clochers et de cheminées d'usines

steer¹ [stɪə(r)] **1** *vt* (*car*) conduire; (*ship*) barrer; **to s. sb out of trouble** sortir qn du pétrin
 2 *vi* (*of person*) conduire; (*of ship*) se diriger (**for** vers); **to s. clear of sb/sth** éviter qn/qch

steer² *n* (*bull*) bouvillon *m*

steering ['stɪərɪŋ] *n* (*mechanism*) direction *f*; **s. column** colonne *f* de direction; *Pol* **s. committee** comité *m* d'organisation; **s. wheel** volant *m*

stem [stem] **1** *n* (*of plant*) tige *f*; (*of glass*) pied *m*; (*of pipe*) tuyau *m*; (*of word*) radical *m*, *Biol* **s. cell** cellule *f* souche
 2 *vt* (*pt & pp* **stemmed**) (*halt*) stopper; **to s. the tide of sth** enrayer le flot de qch
 3 *vi* **to s. from** provenir de

stench [stentʃ] *n* puanteur *f*

stencil ['stensəl] **1** *n* pochoir *m*
 2 *vt* (*pt & pp* **stencilled**, *Am* **stenciled**) dessiner au pochoir

stenographer [stə'nɒɡrəfə(r)] *n* sténographe *mf*

step [step] **1** *n* (**a**) (*movement, sound*) pas *m*; **to take a s.** faire un pas; **s. by s.** pas à pas; *Fig* petit à petit; *also Fig* **to watch one's s.** faire attention où l'on met les pieds; **to keep in s.** (*in dance*) danser en mesure; *Fig* **to be out of s. (with sb)** être en décalage (par rapport à qn)
 (**b**) (*action, measure*) mesure *f*; **to take steps (to do sth)** prendre des mesures (pour faire qch); **the next s. is to...** la prochaine chose à faire, c'est de...; **a s. in the right direction** un pas dans la bonne direction
 (**c**) (*stage*) étape *f*; **at every s.** à chaque étape; **every s. of the way** sur toute la ligne
 (**d**) (*of staircase*) marche *f*; (*of stepladder*) échelon *m*; **(flight of) steps** escalier *m*; (*on outside of building*) perron *m*
 (**e**) (*exercise*) step *m*; **s. class** cours *m* de step
 2 *vi* (*pt & pp* **stepped**) (*take a step*) faire un pas; (*walk*) marcher; **to s. on sth** marcher sur qch; **s. this way** venez par ici; *Fam Fig* **to s. on it** se grouiller
▸**step back** *vi* reculer (**from** de); *Fig* prendre du recul (**from** par rapport à)
▸**step down** *vi* (*resign*) démissionner
▸**step forward** *vi* (*volunteer*) se porter volontaire
▸**step in** *vi* (*intervene*) intervenir
▸**step up** *vt sep* (*increase*) accélérer; (*pressure*) augmenter

stepbrother ['stepbrʌðə(r)] *n* = fils du conjoint d'un des parents

stepchild ['steptʃaɪld] *n* (*boy*) beau-fils *m*; (*girl*) belle-fille *f*

stepdaughter ['stepdɔːtə(r)] *n* belle-fille *f*

stepfather ['stepfɑːðə(r)] *n* beau-père *m*

stepladder ['steplædə(r)] *n* escabeau *m*

stepmother ['stepmʌðə(r)] *n* belle-mère *f*

stepparent ['steppeərənt] *n* (*father*) beau-père *m*; (*mother*) belle-mère *f*

steppe [step] *n* steppe *f*

stepsister ['stepsɪstə(r)] *n* = fille du conjoint d'un des parents

stepson ['stepsʌn] *n* beau-fils *m*

stereo ['sterɪəʊ] **1** *n* (*pl* **stereos**) (*equipment*) chaîne *f* stéréo; (*sound*) stéréo *f*; **in s.** en stéréo
 2 *adj* stéréo *inv*

stereophonic [sterɪə'fɒnɪk] *adj* stéréophonique

stereoscopic [sterɪəʊ'skɒpɪk] *adj* stéréoscopique

stereotype ['sterɪətaɪp] *n* stéréotype *m*

stereotyped ['sterɪətaɪpt] *adj* stéréotypé(e)

sterile ['steraɪl] *adj* stérile

sterility [ste'rɪlɪtɪ] *n* stérilité *f*

sterilization [sterɪlaɪ'zeɪʃən] *n* stérilisation *f*

sterilize ['sterɪlaɪz] *vt* stériliser

sterling ['stɜːlɪŋ] **1** *n* (*British currency*) livre *f* sterling
 2 *adj* (**a**) (*silver*) fin(e) (**b**) (*effort, quality*) remarquable

stern¹ [stɜːn] *adj* (*person, look*) sévère

stern² *n* (*of boat*) poupe *f*

sternum ['stɜːnəm] (*pl* **sternums** *or* **sterna** ['stɜːnə]) *n* sternum *m*

steroid ['stɪərɔɪd] *n* stéroïde *m*

stethoscope ['steθəskəʊp] *n* stéthoscope *m*

stevedore ['sti:vədɔː(r)] n docker m

stew [stju:] **1** n ragoût m; Br Fam Fig **to be in a s.** (of person) être dans le pétrin

2 vt (meat) faire cuire en ragoût; (fruit) faire de la compote de

3 vi (of meat) mijoter; Br Fam **to let sb s. (in his/her own juice)** laisser qn mariner

steward ['stjʊəd] n (on estate) régisseur m; (on ship, plane) steward m; (at sporting event) organisateur m; (at demonstration) membre m du service d'ordre

stewardess [stjʊə'des] n (on ship, plane) hôtesse f

stewed [stju:d] adj (a) Culin **s. beef** bœuf m en ragoût; **s. fruit** compote f de fruits; **this tea is s.** ce thé a trop infusé (b) Fam (drunk) bourré(e)

stick¹ [stɪk] n (a) (of wood, glue, chewing gum) bâton m; (for walking) canne f; (of celery, rhubarb) tige f; Fam Fig **to get hold of the wrong end of the s.** comprendre de travers; Fam **she lives out in the sticks** elle habite dans un trou perdu; **s. insect** phasme m (b) Fam (criticism) **to give sb s. (for sth)** taper sur les doigts de qn (à cause de qch); Br **to take a lot of s.** se faire beaucoup critiquer

stick² (pt & pp **stuck** [stʌk]) **1** vt (a) (insert) **to s. sth in(to) sth** planter qch dans qch (b) Fam (put) mettre, poser (c) (attach with glue) coller (**on/in** sur/dans) (d) Fam (endure) supporter

2 vi (a) (adhere) coller; Fig **the name stuck** ce nom lui/leur/etc est resté; Fig **to s. to one's guns** ne pas en démordre; **to s. to the facts** s'en tenir aux faits; **to s. to one's principles** rester fidèle à ses principes (b) (become jammed) se coincer; Fig **it sticks in my throat** c'est dur à avaler

▶**stick around** vi Fam attendre

▶**stick at** vt insep (persevere with) persévérer dans; **to s. at nothing** ne reculer devant rien

▶**stick by** vt insep (friend) soutenir; (promise, statement) maintenir

▶**stick out 1** vt sep (a) (cause to protrude) faire sortir; **to s. one's tongue out (at sb)** tirer la langue (à qn); Fam **to s. one's neck out (for sb)** prendre des risques (pour qn) (b) Fam (endure) **to s. it out** tenir bon

2 vi (a) (protrude) ressortir; (of ears) être décollés (ées); (of teeth) avancer (b) Fam (be noticeable) se voir; **it sticks out a mile** or **like a sore thumb** ça se voit comme le nez au milieu de la figure

▶**stick together 1** vt sep coller

2 vi (a) (with glue) être collé(e) (b) (of friends) rester ensemble

▶**stick up 1** vt sep (sign, poster) mettre; Fam **s. 'em up!** haut les mains!

2 vi (of building, hair) se dresser

▶**stick up for** vt insep (person, rights) prendre la défense de

▶**stick with** vt insep (not give up) rester avec

sticker ['stɪkə(r)] n autocollant m

stick-in-the-mud ['stɪkɪnðəmʌd] n Fam rabat-joie m inv

stickleback ['stɪkəlbæk] n épinoche f

stickler ['stɪklə(r)] n **to be a s. for sth** être à cheval sur qch

stick-on ['stɪkɒn] adj autocollant(e)

stick-up ['stɪkʌp] n Fam (robbery) braquage m

sticky ['stɪkɪ] adj (a) (substance) collant(e); (climate) humide, moite; (label) adhésif(ive); Fig **to have s. fingers** avoir une tendance pickpocket; **s. tape** ruban m adhésif (b) Fig (awkward) délicat(e); **to come to a s.**

end mal finir; Fam **to be on a s. wicket** être dans une situation délicate

stiff [stɪf] adj (a) (rigid) rigide; (paste) ferme; **as s. as a board** tout(e) raide; **to be bored s.** s'ennuyer à mourir; **to be scared s.** avoir une trouille bleue; **to be frozen s.** être frigorifié(e) (b) (joint) ankylosé(e); **to be s.** (of person) avoir des courbatures; **to have a s. neck** avoir un torticolis; **my leg is s.** j'ai la jambe ankylosée (c) (handle, hinge, drawer) dur(e) (d) (severe) (punishment, fine) sévère; (resistance) opiniâtre; (competition) rude; (exam) dur(e); (breeze) fort(e); **a s. drink** une boisson forte (e) (formal) rigide; (smile) forcé(e)

stiffen ['stɪfən] **1** vt renforcer; (paste) épaissir

2 vi se raidir

stiffly ['stɪflɪ] adv (bow) avec raideur; (answer, greet) avec froideur

stifle ['staɪfəl] vt also Fig étouffer

stifling ['staɪflɪŋ] adj étouffant(e)

stigma ['stɪgmə] (pl **stigmas**) n honte f

stigmata [stɪg'mɑːtə] npl (of saint) stigmates mpl

stigmatize ['stɪgmətaɪz] vt stigmatiser

stile [staɪl] n échalier m

stiletto [stɪ'letəʊ] (pl **stilettos**) n (dagger) stylet m; (shoe) talon m aiguille; **s. heels** talons aiguille

still¹ [stɪl] **1** adj (motionless) immobile; (calm) calme; (silent) silencieux(euse); (drink) non gazeux(euse); **to stand s.** ne pas bouger; Art **s. life** nature f morte; Prov **s. waters run deep** il faut se méfier de l'eau qui dort

2 vt calmer, apaiser

3 n (a) **in the s. of the night** dans le silence de la nuit (b) (photograph) photo f de plateau

still² adv (a) (up to given point in time) toujours, encore; **she's s. alive** elle vit toujours; **I s. think/say that...** je continue de penser/dire que...; **I s. have 500 euros** il me reste encore 500 euros (b) (nonetheless) tout de même; **s., it could have been worse** enfin, ç'aurait pu être pire (c) (even) encore; **s. more/better** encore plus/mieux

still³ n (distilling equipment) alambic m

stillbirth ['stɪlbɜːθ] n enfant mf mort-né(e)

stillborn ['stɪlbɔːn] adj mort-né(e)

stillness ['stɪlnɪs] n tranquillité f

stilt [stɪlt] n (for walking) échasse f; (for building) pilotis m

stilted ['stɪltɪd] adj guindé(e)

stimulant ['stɪmjʊlənt] n stimulant m

stimulate ['stɪmjʊleɪt] vt stimuler

stimulating ['stɪmjʊleɪtɪŋ] adj stimulant(e)

stimulation [stɪmjʊ'leɪʃən] n stimulation f

stimulus ['stɪmjʊləs] (pl **stimuli** ['stɪmjʊlaɪ]) n encouragement m; (physiological) stimulus m inv

sting [stɪŋ] **1** n (a) (of bee) dard m; (of scorpion) aiguillon m; (wound) piqûre f (b) (sensation) brûlure f (c) (idioms) **to have a s. in the tail** (of story, proposal) avoir une fin inattendue (et désagréable); **to take the s. out of sth** atténuer les effets de qch

2 vt (pt & pp **stung** [stʌŋ]) (of bee, nettle) piquer; Fig (of remark) blesser, piquer au vif; Fig **to s. sb into action** inciter qn à agir; Fam Fig **they stung him for £10** ils l'ont arnaqué de 10 livres

3 vi (of eyes, skin) piquer

stinging ['stɪŋɪŋ] adj (pain) cuisant(e); (remark, criticism) cinglant(e); **s. nettle** ortie f

stingray ['stɪŋreɪ] n pastenague f

stingy ['stɪndʒɪ] *adj (person)* pingre; *(portion)* minuscule; **to be s. with one's praise** être avare de compliments

stink ['stɪŋk] **1** *n (smell)* puanteur *f; Fam Fig* **to kick up a s. (about sth)** faire tout un scandale (à propos de qch)
2 *vi (pt* **stank** [stæŋk] *or* **stunk** [stʌŋk], *pp* **stunk**) **(a)** *(smell)* puer; **to s. of sth** puer qch; *Fam Fig* **to s. of corruption** sentir la corruption à plein nez **(b)** *Fam Fig (be of bad quality)* craindre

stinkbomb ['stɪŋkbɒm] *n* boule *f* puante

stinker ['stɪŋkə(r)] *n Fam (person)* peau *f* de vache; *(difficult task)* casse-tête *m;* **a s. of a cold** un rhume carabiné

stinking ['stɪŋkɪŋ] **1** *adj* puant(e); **a s. cold** un rhume carabiné
2 *adv Fam* **to be s. rich** être bourré(e) de fric

stint [stɪnt] **1** *n (period)* période *f; (share of work)* part *f* de travail; **to take a s. at the wheel** prendre le volant; **he had a two-year s. in the army** il a fait deux ans d'armée
2 *vt* épargner; **to s. oneself** se sacrifier
3 *vi* **to s. on sth** lésiner sur qch

stipend ['staɪpend] *n* traitement *m*

stipulate ['stɪpjʊleɪt] *vt* stipuler

stipulation [stɪpjʊ'leɪʃən] *n* stipulation *f*

stir [stɜː(r)] **1** *vt (pt & pp* **stirred**) **(a)** *(liquid, mixture)* remuer; *(leaves)* agiter **(b)** *Fig (person)* émouvoir, remuer; *(emotion)* réveiller; *(curiosity)* exciter; **to s. sb to do sth** inciter qn à faire qch; *Fam* **to s. oneself** se remuer; *Fam* **to s. it** *(make trouble)* envenimer les choses
2 *vi (move)* bouger, remuer
3 *n* **(a)** **to give sth a s.** remuer qch **(b)** *Fig* **to cause a s.** faire du bruit

▶**stir up** *vt sep* **(a)** *(dust, leaves)* remuer **(b)** *Fig (rebellion, anger, resentment)* attiser; *(workers, crowd)* inciter à la révolte; **to s. up trouble** semer la zizanie; **to s. things up** envenimer les choses

stir-fry ['stɜːfraɪ] *Culin* **1** *n* sauté *m*
2 *vt (pt & pp* **stir-fried**) faire sauter

stirrer ['stɜːrə(r)] *n Fam (trouble-maker)* semeur(euse) *m,f* de zizanie

stirring ['stɜːrɪŋ] **1** *n* **the first stirrings of** les premiers signes de
2 *adj (speech, film)* poignant(e)

stirrup ['stɪrəp] *n* étrier *m*

stitch [stɪtʃ] **1** *n* **(a)** *(in sewing)* point *m; (in knitting)* maille *f; Med* point (de suture); *Fam* **she didn't have a s. on** elle était nue comme un ver; *Prov* **a s. in time saves nine** un point à temps en vaut cent **(b)** *(sharp pain)* point *m* (de côté); **to get a s.** prendre un point **(c)** *Fam* **we were in stitches** *(laughing)* on était pliés
2 *vt (clothing)* coudre; *Med* recoudre

▶**stitch up** *vt sep Fam (falsely incriminate)* faire porter le chapeau à

stoat [stəʊt] *n* hermine *f*

stock [stɒk] **1** *n* **(a)** *(supply)* provisions *fpl; Com* stock *m; Com* **while stocks last** jusqu'à épuisement des stocks; **to have sth in s.** avoir qch en stock; **to be out of s.** être épuisé(e); *Fig* **to take s.** faire le point; *Com* **s. control** gestion *f* des stocks; *Com* **s. list** inventaire *m* des stocks **(b)** *(livestock)* bétail *m* **(c)** *Fin* valeurs *fpl,* actions *fpl; Fig* **her s. is going up/down** sa cote est en hausse/baisse; **stocks and shares** valeurs mobilières; **s. exchange** Bourse *f* (des valeurs); **s.**
market marché *m* des valeurs; **s. option** stock-option *f,* option *f* de titres **(d)** *(descent)* **of German s.** de souche allemande **(e)** *(of rifle)* fût *m* **(f)** **stocks** *(for punishment)* pilori *m* **(g)** *(in cooking)* bouillon *m;* **s. cube** bouillon cube *m*
2 *adj (argument, excuse)* classique
3 *vt* **(a)** *(goods)* vendre **(b)** *(supply) (shop)* approvisionner (**with** en)

▶**stock up** *vi* faire des provisions (**with** de)

stockade [stɒ'keɪd] *n* palissade *f*

stockbroker ['stɒkbrəʊkə(r)] *n Fin* agent *m* de change

stockholder ['stɒkhəʊldə(r)] *n Fin* actionnaire *mf*

Stockholm ['stɒkhəʊm] *n* Stockholm

stocking ['stɒkɪŋ] *n (garment)* bas *m*

stockist ['stɒkɪst] *n Com* stockiste *mf*

stockpile ['stɒkpaɪl] **1** *n* réserves *fpl*
2 *vt* faire des réserves de

stockroom ['stɒkruːm] *n* réserve *f,* magasin *m*

stock-still ['stɒk'stɪl] *adv* **to stand s.** se tenir complètement immobile

stocktaking ['stɒkteɪkɪŋ] *n Com* inventaire *m* des stocks; *Fig* **a s. exercise** un examen de situation

stocky ['stɒkɪ] *adj* trapu(e)

stodge [stɒdʒ] *n Fam (food)* aliments *mpl* bourratifs

stodgy ['stɒdʒɪ] *adj (food)* bourratif(ive); *(book)* indigeste

stoic ['stəʊɪk] *n & adj* stoïque *mf*

stoical ['stəʊɪkəl] *adj* stoïque

stoicism ['stəʊɪsɪzəm] *n* stoïcisme *m*

stoke [stəʊk] *vt (fire, boiler)* alimenter; *Fig* entretenir

STOL [stɒl] *n Aviat (abbr* **short take-off and landing)** ADAC *m*

stole¹ [stəʊl] *n (garment)* étole *f*

stole² *pt of* **steal**

stolen ['stəʊlən] **1** *adj* volé(e)
2 *pp of* **steal**

stolid ['stɒlɪd] *adj* impassible

stomach ['stʌmək] **1** *n* ventre *m; (organ)* estomac *m;* **on an empty s.** à jeun; *Fig* **it turns my s.** ça m'écœure; *Fig* **I've no s. for his vulgar jokes this evening** je n'ai aucune envie d'écouter ses plaisanteries vulgaires ce soir; **to have (a) s. ache** avoir mal au ventre; *(in organ)* avoir mal à l'estomac; *Med* **s. pump** pompe *f* stomacale
2 *vt Fig (tolerate)* supporter

stomp [stɒmp] *vi* marcher en tapant des pieds; **to s. in/out** entrer/sortir en tapant des pieds

stomping ground ['stɒmpɪŋ'graʊnd] *n* lieu *m* de prédilection; **this was one of my old stomping grounds** j'y allais tout le temps

stone [stəʊn] **1** *n* **(a)** *(material, piece of rock)* pierre *f; (smaller)* caillou *m; Fig* **to leave no s. unturned** remuer ciel et terre; *Fig* **a s.'s throw from here** à deux pas d'ici; **the S. Age** l'âge *m* de pierre; *Zool* **s. marten** fouine *f* **(b)** *(of fruit)* noyau *m* **(c)** *(unit of weight)* = 6,35kg
2 *adj* en pierre; *(jug)* en grès
3 *vt* **(a)** *(fruit)* dénoyauter **(b)** *(person)* lapider

stone-cold ['stəʊn'kəʊld] *adj* glacé(e)

stoned [stəʊnd] *adj Fam (on drugs)* défoncé(e)

stone-dead ['stəʊn'ded] *adj* raide mort(e)

stone-deaf ['stəʊn'def] *adj* sourd(e) comme un pot

stonemason ['stəʊnmeɪsən] *n* maçon *m*

stonewall ['stəʊn'wɔːl] *vi (in game)* pratiquer un jeu défensif; *(in inquiry)* refuser de répondre

stoneware ['stəʊnweə(r)] *n* poterie *f* en grès
stonework ['stəʊnwɜːk] *n* maçonnerie *f*
stonily ['stəʊnɪlɪ] *adv* froidement
stony ['stəʊnɪ] *adj (ground, beach)* caillouteux(euse); *Fig (look, silence)* glacial(e); *Fam Fig* **to be s. broke** n'avoir pas un rond
stood [stʊd] *pt & pp of* **stand**
stooge [stuːdʒ] *n (comedian's fall guy)* faire-valoir *m*; *(minion)* larbin *m*
stool [stuːl] *n* (**a**) *(seat)* tabouret *m*; *Fig* **to fall between two stools** être assis(e) entre deux chaises; *Fam* **s. pigeon** balance *f*, indic *m* (**b**) *Med (faeces)* selles *fpl*
stoop¹ [stuːp] **1** *n* **to have a s.** être voûté(e); **to walk with a s.** marcher le dos courbé
2 *vi (bend down)* se pencher; *Fig* **to s. to sth/doing sth** s'abaisser à qch/à faire qch
stoop² *n Am (of house) (with roof)* véranda *f*; *(without roof)* perron *m*
stop [stɒp] **1** *n* (**a**) *(halt)* arrêt *m*; **to put a s. to sth** mettre fin à qch; **to come to a s.** s'arrêter; *Aut* **s. sign** stop *m* (**b**) *(pause) (in work)* pause *f*; *(in journey)* halte *f*; *(of plane)* escale *f*; *(of train)* arrêt *m* (**c**) *(for bus, train)* arrêt *m* (**d**) *(full stop)* point *m*; *(in telegram)* stop *m* (**e**) *Mus (on organ)* jeu *m*; *Fig* **to pull out all the stops** remuer ciel et terre
2 *vt (pt & pp* **stopped***)* (**a**) *(halt) (person, vehicle)* arrêter; *(conversation, speaker)* interrompre; *(corruption, abuse)* mettre fin à; *Fin* **to s. a cheque** faire opposition à un chèque; **s., thief!** au voleur! (**b**) *(cease)* arrêter; **to s. doing sth** arrêter de faire qch (**c**) *(prevent)* empêcher; **to s. sb from doing sth** empêcher qn de faire qch; **I couldn't s. myself** je n'ai pas pu m'en empêcher (**d**) *(fill in) (hole, gap)* boucher
3 *vi* (**a**) *(halt) (of moving person, vehicle)* s'arrêter (**b**) *(cease) (of speaker, worker)* s'arrêter; *(of pain, bleeding)* cesser; *(of rain)* s'arrêter, cesser; **she'll s. at nothing** rien ne l'arrêtera; **to s. short** s'arrêter net (**c**) *(stay)* rester
▸**stop by** *vi (visit)* passer; **I'll s. by your place tomorrow** je passerai chez toi demain
▸**stop off** *vi* faire une halte
▸**stop over** *vi Aviat* faire escale
▸**stop up** *vt sep (hole, sink, pipe)* boucher
stopcock ['stɒpkɒk] *n* robinet *m* d'arrêt
stopgap ['stɒpgæp] *n (thing, person)* bouche-trou *m*; **s. measure** mesure *f* transitoire
stoplight ['stɒplaɪt] *n Am Aut* feux *mpl* (tricolores *ou* de signalisation)
stopover ['stɒpəʊvə(r)] *n Aviat* escale *f*
stoppage ['stɒpɪdʒ] *n* (**a**) *(of flow, traffic)* arrêt *m*; *(strike)* débrayage *m* (**b**) *Fin (deduction)* retenue *f*
stopper ['stɒpə(r)] *n* bouchon *m*
stop-press ['stɒppres] *adj Journ* de dernière minute
stopwatch ['stɒpwɒtʃ] *n* chronomètre *m*
storage ['stɔːrɪdʒ] *n* (**a**) *(action)* emmagasinage *m*; *(space available)* (espace *m* de) rangement *m*; **to put sth into s.** entreposer qch; **s. heater** radiateur *m* à accumulation; **s. space** espace *m* de rangement; **s. tank** citerne *f* (**b**) *Comput* mémoire *f*
store [stɔː(r)] **1** *n* (**a**) *(supply) (of goods, food)* provision *f*; *Fig (of knowledge)* fonds *m*; **stores** réserves *fpl* (**b**) *(warehouse)* entrepôt *m* (**c**) *Am (shop)* magasin *m*; *also Br* **s. detective** vigile *m*; **s. card** carte *f* de crédit *(d'un grand magasin)* (**d**) *(idioms)* **to hold** *or* **keep sth in s.** tenir *ou* garder qch en réserve; **I have a surprise in s. for her** je lui réserve une surprise; **to set great s.**

by sth faire grand cas de qch
2 *vt (put in storage)* entreposer; *(food)* ranger; *(electricity, heat)* emmagasiner; **s. in a cool place** conserver au frais
▸**store up** *vt sep* accumuler
storehouse ['stɔːhaʊs] *n* entrepôt *m*
storeroom ['stɔːruːm] *n (in office, factory)* réserve *f*; *(at home)* débarras *m*
storey, *Am* **story** ['stɔːrɪ] *n* étage *m*; **a four-s. building** un immeuble de quatre étages
stork [stɔːk] *n* cigogne *f*
storm [stɔːm] **1** *n* (**a**) *(bad weather)* tempête *f*; *(thunderstorm)* orage *m*; *Fig* **a s. in a teacup** une tempête dans un verre d'eau; **s. cloud** nuée *f* d'orage; **s. door** double porte *f* (**b**) *Fig (scandal, of protest)* tempête *f*; *(of abuse)* bordée *f* (**c**) *Mil* **to take sth by s.** prendre qch d'assaut; *Fig* **she/the show took London by s.** elle/le spectacle a eu un succès foudroyant à Londres; **s. troops** troupes *fpl* d'assaut
2 *vt (town, fortress)* prendre d'assaut
3 *vi (of person)* tempêter (**at sb** contre qn); **to s. in/ out** entrer/sortir comme un ouragan
stormy ['stɔːmɪ] *adj also Fig* orageux(euse)
story¹ ['stɔːrɪ] *(pl* **stories***) n* (**a**) *(account)* histoire *f*; *Fig* **to tell stories** *(lie)* raconter des histoires (**b**) *(plot) (of novel, play)* intrigue *f*, histoire *f* (**c**) *(in newspaper)* article *m* (**d**) *(idioms)* **that's quite another s.** ça c'est une autre histoire; **it's the same old s.** c'est toujours la même histoire; **or so the s. goes** c'est du moins ce que l'on raconte; *Fam* **it's the s. of my life** je suis le/la spécialiste de ce genre de choses; **it's a long s.** c'est une longue histoire; **to cut a long s. short,...** bref, pour résumer...
story² *Am* = **storey**
storybook ['stɔːrɪbʊk] *n* livre *m* d'histoires
storyteller ['stɔːrɪtelə(r)] *n* conteur(euse) *m,f*
stout [staʊt] **1** *n (beer)* stout *f*, bière *f* brune forte
2 *adj* (**a**) *(fat)* corpulent(e) (**b**) *(solid) (door, shoes)* solide (**c**) *(brave) (person, resistance)* acharné(e)
stouthearted [staʊt'hɑːtɪd] *adj Lit* vaillant(e)
stoutly ['staʊtlɪ] *adv (resist, maintain)* avec fermeté
stove [stəʊv] *n (for cooking)* cuisinière *f*; *(for heating)* poêle *m*
stow [stəʊ] *vt (put away)* ranger; *Naut* arrimer
▸**stow away** *vi (on ship)* s'embarquer clandestinement
stowaway ['stəʊəweɪ] *n* passager(ère) *m,f* clandestin(e)
straddle ['strædəl] *vt (horse)* enfourcher; *(chair)* se mettre à califourchon sur; *Fig (period of time, subject)* couvrir
strafe [streɪf] *vt Mil* mitrailler en rase-mottes
straggle ['strægəl] *vi* (**a**) *(lag behind)* être à la traîne (**b**) *(of hair)* pendouiller
straggler ['stræglə(r)] *n* retardataire *mf*
straggly ['stræglɪ] *adj (hair)* épars(e)
straight [streɪt] **1** *adj* (**a**) *(level, not curved) (line, tie, skirt, picture, back)* droit(e); *(hair)* raide; **to keep a s. face** garder son sérieux; **to put things** *or* **matters s.** arranger les choses; **to put sb s. about sth** éclairer qn sur qch
(**b**) *(consecutive)* consécutif(ive); **s. flush** *(in cards)* quinte *f* flush
(**c**) *(honest) (person)* honnête; *(answer)* clair(e); **to be s. with sb** jouer franc jeu avec qn
(**d**) *(conventional)* conformiste; *Theat* **s. man** faire-valoir *m*

(**e**) *Fam (heterosexual)* hétéro

(**f**) *(undiluted)* pur(e)

2 *adv* (**a**) *(in straight line)* droit; **sit up s.!** tiens-toi droit sur ton siège!; **to see s.** voir bien; **I can't think s.** je n'ai pas les idées claires; **to look s. ahead** regarder droit devant soi; **go s. on** allez tout droit; *Fig* **to go s.** *(of criminal)* se ranger

(**b**) *(immediately)* immédiatement; **I'll be s. back** je reviens tout de suite; **s. away** *or* **off** tout de suite

(**c**) *(directly)* directement; **to come** *or* **get s. to the point** allez droit au fait; **to come s. out with sth** dire qch tout net

3 *n* (**a**) **to keep to the s. and narrow** rester sur le droit chemin

(**b**) *(on running track, racecourse)* ligne *f* droite

straightaway ['streɪtəweɪ] *adv* tout de suite

straighten ['streɪtən] *vt (bent nail, rod)* redresser; *(picture)* remettre droit; *(tie, hat)* ajuster; **to s. one's back** se redresser

▸**straighten out** *vt sep (problem)* régler; *(one's affairs)* mettre de l'ordre dans

straight-faced ['streɪt'feɪst] *adj* à l'air sérieux

straightforward [streɪt'fɔːwəd] *adj* (**a**) *(honest)* direct(e), franc (franche) (**b**) *(simple)* simple

strain¹ [streɪn] **1** *n* (**a**) *(on rope, beam, economy, friendship)* tension *f*; *(on muscle, ankle)* foulure *f*; **to put a s. on** *(economy)* grever; *(friendship)* éprouver (**b**) *(mental stress)* stress *m*; **to be under a lot of s.** être très stressé(e)

2 *vt* (**a**) *(muscle, ankle)* se fouler; *(economy)* grever; *(friendship)* éprouver; **to s. one's back** se faire mal au dos; **to s. one's ears** tendre l'oreille (**b**) *Culin (liquid)* filtrer, passer; *(vegetables)* égoutter

3 *vi* **to s. at a rope** tirer sur une corde; *Fig* **to s. at the leash** ne plus tenir en place

strain² *n (variety) (of virus)* souche *f*; *(of plant)* variété *f*

strained [streɪnd] *adj (muscle)* froissé(e); *Fig (atmosphere, relationship)* tendu(e)

strainer ['streɪnə(r)] *n* passoire *f*

strait [streɪt] *n* détroit *m*; **the Straits of Gibraltar** le détroit de Gibraltar

straitlaced ['streɪt'leɪst] *adj* collet monté *inv*

strand¹ [strænd] *vt (ship)* échouer; **to be stranded** *(of person)* être bloqué(e)

strand² *n (of rope, cotton)* brin *m*; *(of hair)* mèche *f*; *Fig (of plot)* fil *m*

strange [streɪndʒ] *adj* (**a**) *(odd) (person, behaviour)* bizarre (**b**) *(unfamiliar)* inconnu(e)

strangely ['streɪndʒlɪ] *adv (behave, dress)* bizarrement; **s. enough,...** chose bizarre,...

strangeness ['streɪndʒnɪs] *n* (**a**) *(oddness)* bizarrerie *f* (**b**) *(unfamiliarity)* étrangeté *f*

stranger ['streɪndʒə(r)] *n (unknown person)* inconnu(e) *m,f*; *(from somewhere else)* étranger(ère) *m,f*; **I'm a s. here myself** je ne suis pas d'ici

strangle ['stræŋgəl] *vt also Fig* étrangler

stranglehold ['stræŋgəlhəʊld] *n Fig* **to have a s. on sth** avoir la mainmise sur qch

strangulation [stræŋgjʊ'leɪʃən] *n* strangulation *f*

strap [stræp] **1** *n (of leather, canvas)* sangle *f*, lanière *f*; *(on dress, bra)* bretelle *f*; *(for watch)* bracelet *m*; *(for shoe)* bride *f*

2 *vt (pt & pp strapped)* **to s. sth to sth** sangler qch à qch; *Fam* **to be strapped (for cash)** être un peu juste

▸**strap in** *vt sep* attacher; **to s. oneself in** attacher sa ceinture de sécurité

strapless ['stræplɪs] *adj (dress, bra)* sans bretelles

strapping ['stræpɪŋ] *adj* costaud(e)

Strasbourg ['stræzbɜːg] *n* Strasbourg

strategic [strə'tiːdʒɪk] *adj* stratégique

strategist ['strætədʒɪst] *n* stratège *m*

strategy ['strætɪdʒɪ] *(pl* **strategies***) n* stratégie *f*

stratification [strætɪfɪ'keɪʃən] *n* stratification *f*

stratosphere ['strætəsfɪə(r)] *n* stratosphère *f*

stratum ['strɑːtəm] *(pl* **strata** ['strɑːtə] *) n* strate *f*; *Fig* couche *f*

straw [strɔː] *n* (**a**) *(from wheat, for drinking)* paille *f*; **s. hat** chapeau *m* de paille; *Fig* **s. man** homme *m* de paille; **s. poll** sondage *m* d'opinion (**b**) *(idioms)* **to clutch** *or* **grasp at straws** se raccrocher à de faux espoirs; **that's the last s.!** ça c'est le comble!

strawberry ['strɔːbərɪ] *(pl* **strawberries***) n* fraise *f*; **s. jam** confiture *f* de fraises

---

Strawberries and cream

En Grande-Bretagne, les fraises à la crème sont traditionnellement consommées lors de certaines manifestations en plein air, notamment au tournoi de tennis de Wimbledon.

---

straw-coloured ['strɔːkʌləd] *adj* jaune paille *inv*

stray [streɪ] **1** *n (dog)* chien *m* errant; *(cat)* chat *m* égaré

2 *adj (animal)* égaré(e); *(dog)* errant(e); *(bullet)* perdu(e)

3 *vi (of person, animal)* s'égarer; **to s. from the point** s'écarter du sujet

streak [striːk] **1** *n (stripe) (of paint, dirt)* traînée *f*; *(of light)* rai *m*; *(in hair)* mèche *f*; **a s. of lightning** un éclair; **a s. of luck** une période de chance; **to be on a winning/losing s.** être dans une période de chance/poisse; **to have a mean/cruel s.** avoir un côté mesquin/cruel

2 *vt* **streaked with dirt** plein(e) de traînées sales; **streaked with tears** strié(e) de larmes; **his hair is streaked with silver** ses cheveux sont parsemés de cheveux gris; **to have one's hair streaked** se faire faire des mèches

3 *vi* (**a**) *(move quickly)* **to s. off** partir à toute vitesse; **to s. past** passer en trombe (**b**) *Fam (run naked)* courir nu(e) (en public)

streaker ['striːkə(r)] *n Fam* = personne qui court nue en public

streaky ['striːkɪ] *adj (surface, pattern)* strié(e); **s. bacon** bacon *m* entrelardé

stream [striːm] **1** *n* (**a**) *(brook)* ruisseau *m* (**b**) *(of light, blood, water)* jet *m*; *(of tears, insults)* torrent *m*; *(of people)* flot *m*; **to come on s.** *(of industrial plant)* entrer en production

2 *vt* (**a**) *(spurt)* **to s. blood** ruisseler de sang (**b**) *Br Sch* **to s. pupils** répartir des élèves par niveau

3 *vi* (**a**) *(of liquid)* ruisseler; *(of people)* affluer; *(of traffic)* s'écouler; **her eyes were streaming** ses yeux étaient ruisselants de larmes (**b**) *(of hair, banner)* flotter

streamer ['striːmə(r)] *n* banderole *f*

streamline ['striːmlaɪn] *vt (vehicle)* caréner; *Fig (system)* rationaliser; *(department)* dégraisser

streamlined ['striːmlaɪnd] *adj (vehicle)* caréné(e); *Fig (system)* rationalisé(e); *(department)* dégraissé(e)

street [striːt] *n* (**a**) *(road)* rue *f*; **on the s.** dans la rue; **to take to the streets** *(of protesters)* descendre dans la rue; **s. fighting** combats *mpl* de rue; **s. lamp** lampadaire *m*; **s. map** plan *m* (de la ville); **s. market** marché *m* de plein air; **s. sweeper** balayeur(euse) *m,f*; **s. theatre** théâtre *m* de rue; **s. value** *(of drugs)* valeur *f* à la revente (**b**) *(idioms)* **to walk the streets** *(of prostitute)* faire le tapin *ou* le trottoir; **the man in the s.** Monsieur Tout-le-Monde; *Fam* **to be streets ahead** dépasser tout le monde; **that's right up my s.** c'est tout à fait mon rayon; *Fam* **to have s. cred** être très branché(e)

streetcar ['striːtkɑː(r)] *n Am* tramway *m*

streetwalker ['striːtwɔːkə(r)] *n* racoleuse *f*

streetwise ['striːtwaɪz] *adj* dégourdi(e)

strength [streŋθ] *n* (**a**) *(of person, wind, emotion, currency)* force *f*; *(of rope, fabric)* solidité *f*; *(of light, alcohol, army)* puissance *f*; **to be at full s.** *(of department, regiment)* avoir des effectifs complets; **to be under s.** *(of department, regiment)* ne pas avoir des effectifs complets; **in s.** en force; **to go from s. to s.** aller de mieux en mieux; **on the s. of** sur la base de; **on the s. of her qualifications** grâce à ses diplômes (**b**) *(strong point)* point *m* fort

strengthen ['streŋθən] **1** *vt (wall, building)* renforcer, consolider; *(muscle)* affermir; *(friendship)* consolider; *(determination, position)* renforcer
2 *vi (of friendship)* se consolider; *(of determination)* se renforcer; *(of currency)* se raffermir; *(of wind)* souffler plus fort

strenuous ['strenjʊəs] *adj (activity, lifestyle)* fatigant(e); *(effort, opposition)* vigoureux(euse); *(denial)* énergique

strenuously ['strenjʊəslɪ] *adv (campaign, deny)* énergiquement; *(resist)* vigoureusement

stress [stres] **1** *n* (**a**) *(tension) (physical)* tension *f*; *(mental)* stress *m*; **to be under a lot of s.** être très stressé(e); **s. factor** facteur *m* de stress; *Med* **s. fracture** fracture *f* de surmenage (**b**) *(emphasis)* insistance *f*; *Ling* accentuation *f*; **to put s. on sth** insister sur qch
2 *vt (emphasize)* insister sur; *Ling* accentuer

stressful ['stresfʊl] *adj* stressant(e)

stretch [stretʃ] **1** *n* (**a**) *(of body)* **to have a s.** s'étirer; *Fig* **by no s. of the imagination** même avec beaucoup d'imagination; **s. marks** vergetures *fpl* (**b**) *(of water, land)* étendue *f*; *(of road)* tronçon *m*; *(of time, silence)* période *f*; **at one s.** d'une traite (**c**) **at full s.** *(factory)* au maximum de ses capacités
2 *vt* (**a**) *(elastic)* étirer; *(belt, arm, hand)* tendre; **to s. the truth** exagérer; **to s. one's legs** se dégourdir les jambes (**b**) *(put demands on) (person)* pousser à son maximum; *(resources)* utiliser au maximum; *(someone's patience)* abuser de; **we're fully stretched at the moment** nous sommes au maximum de notre rendement en ce moment (**c**) *(make last) (income, supplies)* faire durer
3 *vi* (**a**) *(of elastic)* s'étendre; *(of person, fabric)* s'étirer (**b**) *(of road, land, years)* s'étendre, s'étaler (**c**) *(of resources, budget)* **my budget won't s. to a new car** je n'ai pas les moyens de m'acheter une nouvelle voiture
▶**stretch out 1** *vt sep (arm, hand)* tendre
2 *vi* (**a**) *(of person)* s'étirer (**b**) *(of road, land, time)* s'étaler, s'étendre

stretcher ['stretʃə(r)] *n* brancard *m*; **s. bearer** brancardier *m*

stretchy ['stretʃɪ] *adj* extensible

strew [struː] *(pp* **strewed** *or* **strewn** [struːn] *) vt (objects)* éparpiller; **to be strewn with sth** *(of surface)* être jonché(e) de qch

stricken ['strɪkən] *adj (with grief, guilt)* accablé(e) (**with** de); *(with illness, by disaster)* frappé(e) (**with** par); **the s. city** la ville sinistrée

strict [strɪkt] *adj* (**a**) *(person, instruction, discipline)* strict(e); **s. morals** morale *f* sévère; **a s. Muslim** un musulman de stricte obédience (**b**) *(meaning, minimum)* strict(e); **in strictest confidence** en toute confidence

strictly ['strɪktlɪ] *adv* (**a**) *(severely, only)* strictement (**b**) *(exactly)* **s. speaking** à proprement parler; **not s. true** pas tout à fait vrai(e)

strictness ['strɪktnɪs] *n (of discipline, rules)* sévérité *f*

stride [straɪd] **1** *n* (**a**) *(walking)* pas *m*; *(when running)* foulée *f* (**b**) *(idioms)* **to make great strides** faire des pas de géant; **to take sth in one's s.** prendre qch calmement; **to get into one's s.** trouver son rythme
2 *vi (pt* **strode** [strəʊd], *pp* **stridden** ['strɪdən] *)* **to s. in/out** entrer/sortir à grands pas

strident ['straɪdənt] *adj* strident(e)

strife [straɪf] *n* conflits *mpl*

strike [straɪk] **1** *n* (**a**) *(refusal to work)* grève *f*; **to be on s.** être en grève; **s. fund** = caisse de prévoyance permettant d'aider les grévistes; **s. pay** indemnité *f* de grève
  (**b**) *(discovery) (of ore, oil)* découverte *f*
  (**c**) *(blow)* coup *m*; *Mil* attaque *f*, raid *m*
2 *vt (pt & pp* **struck** [strʌk] *)* (**a**) *(hit)* frapper; *(collide with)* heurter, taper contre; **to be struck by lightning** être frappé(e) par la foudre; **to s. sb in the face** frapper qn à la figure; **to s. a blow** donner un coup; *Fig* **to s. a blow for freedom** se battre pour défendre sa liberté; **the clock struck ten** l'horloge a sonné dix heures; *Fig* **to s. the right/wrong note** *(of speech, remark)* sonner juste/faux; **to s. terror into sb** frapper qn de terreur; **to be struck dumb/blind** être frappé(e) de mutisme/cécité; **a stray bullet struck him dead** il a été tué par une balle perdue
  (**b**) *(match)* craquer
  (**c**) *(coin, medal)* frapper
  (**d**) *(impress)* frapper; **she strikes me as a reasonable person** elle me paraît raisonnable; **it struck me that...** il m'a semblé que...
  (**e**) *(discover) (gold, oil)* découvrir; *Fam* **to s. it rich** faire fortune; *Fam* **to s. it lucky** avoir un coup de chance
  (**f**) *(reach) (bargain, deal)* conclure; **to s. a balance** trouver un équilibre
3 *vi* (**a**) *(attack) (of enemy)* attaquer; *(of criminal)* frapper; *(of disaster, earthquake)* se produire; *(of clock)* sonner; **to s. home** *(of criticism)* faire mouche; *Prov* **s. while the iron is hot** il faut battre le fer pendant qu'il est chaud
  (**b**) *(of workers)* faire grève
▶**strike back** *vi (retaliate)* riposter
▶**strike down** *vt sep (of disease)* terrasser; *(of bullet)* abattre
▶**strike off** *vt sep (doctor, lawyer)* radier
▶**strike out 1** *vt sep (delete)* rayer
2 *vi* (**a**) *(hit out)* **to s. out at sb** essayer de frapper qn (**b**) *(leave)* s'élancer (**for** vers); **to s. out on one's own** s'établir à son compte
▶**strike up** *vt sep (song)* entonner; *(conversation)* entamer; **to s. up a friendship (with sb)** se lier d'amitié (avec qn)

strikebreaker ['straɪkbreɪkə(r)] *n* briseur(euse) *m,f* de grève

striker ['straɪkə(r)] n (a) (striking worker) gréviste mf (b) (in football) buteur m

striking ['straɪkɪŋ] adj (a) (similarity, appearance) frappant(e), saisissant(e) (b) (worker) en grève (c) **she lives within s. distance of New York** elle habite tout près de New York

string [strɪŋ] 1 n (a) (for tying) ficelle f; (of violin, tennis racket, bow) corde f; (of puppet) fil m; Mus **the strings** (in orchestra) les cordes; Fig **to have more than one s. to one's bow** avoir plus d'une corde à son arc; Fig **with no strings attached** sans conditions; Fig **to pull strings for sb** (obtain favours) faire jouer ses relations pour qn; (get job, promotion) pistonner qn; Mus **s. quartet** quatuor m à cordes; Br **s. vest** maillot m de corps à grosses mailles (b) (of onions, islands) chapelet m; (of words, shops, defeats) série f; Comput série 2 vt (pp & pt strung [strʌŋ]) (a) (violin) monter; (tennis racket) corder; (bow) bander (b) (pearls, beads) enfiler

▸**string along** vt sep Fam mener en bateau
▸**string up** vt sep Fam (hang) (criminal) pendre

stringed [strɪŋd] adj (instrument) à cordes

stringent ['strɪndʒənt] adj rigoureux(euse)

strip¹ [strɪp] n (a) (of cloth, paper) bande f; (of metal) lame f; Fam **to tear sb off a s.** passer un savon à qn; **s. cartoon** bande f dessinée; **s. lighting** éclairage m au néon (b) (of sports team) tenue f

strip² 1 n **to do a s.** (undress) se déshabiller; (for show) faire un strip-tease; **s. club** boîte f de strip-tease; **s. poker** strip-poker m; **s. show** strip-tease m 2 vt (pt & pp **stripped**) (person) déshabiller; (bed) défaire; (paint) gratter; (wallpaper) décoller; **to s. sb of sth** dépouiller qn de qch 3 vi (undress) se déshabiller

▸**strip off** 1 vt sep (paint) gratter; (wallpaper) décoller 2 vi (undress) se déshabiller

stripe [straɪp] n (a) (on cloth, animal's coat) rayure f, raie f (b) (indicating rank) galon m

striped [straɪpt] adj à rayures, rayé(e)

stripling ['strɪplɪŋ] n tout jeune homme m

strlpper ['strɪpə(r)] n (woman) strip-teaseuse f; (male) **s.** strip-teaseur m

strip-search ['strɪpsɜːtʃ] 1 n fouille f corporelle 2 vt **to s. sb** faire subir une fouille corporelle à qn

striptease ['strɪptiːz] n strip-tease m

strive [straɪv] (pt **strove** [strəʊv], pp **striven** ['strɪvən]) vi **to s. to do sth** s'efforcer de faire qch; **to s. for** or **after sth** se battre pour obtenir qch

strobe [strəʊb] n Phys stroboscope m; **s. lighting** lumières fpl stroboscopiques

strode [strəʊd] pt of **stride**

stroke [strəʊk] 1 n (a) (blow, tennis shot) coup m; (in rowing, swimming) (style) nage f; (single movement) mouvement m; **a brush s.** un coup de pinceau (b) (of clock, bell) **on the s. of nine** à neuf heures sonnantes (c) (caress) caresse f; **to give sb/sth a s.** caresser qn/qch (d) Med attaque f (e) (idioms) **she hasn't done a s. of work** elle n'a rien fichu; **a s. of luck** un coup de chance; **a s. of genius** un coup de génie; **at a s.** d'un seul coup 2 vt (caress) caresser

stroll [strəʊl] 1 n promenade f, tour m; **to go for a s.** aller se promener ou faire un tour 2 vi se promener, flâner

strong [strɒŋ] 1 adj (a) (physically, mentally) fort(e); (candidate, team) bon (bonne); (friendship, argument)

solide; **the pound is s. against the dollar** la livre est solide face au dollar (b) (in degree) (colour, light, protest) vif (vive); (smell, drink, accent, possibility) fort(e); (resemblance) grand(e); (measures) énergique; **s. language** grossièretés fpl; **s. point** point m fort (c) (sturdy) (rope, chair, shoes) solide 2 adv **to be still going s.** (band, programme) marcher toujours très bien; (person) être toujours d'attaque 3 npl **the s.** les forts mpl

strong-arm tactics ['strɒŋɑːm'tæktɪks] npl manière f forte

strong-box ['strɒŋbɒks] n coffre-fort m

stronghold ['strɒŋhəʊld] n (fortress) forteresse f; Fig (of political party, religion) bastion m

strongly ['strɒŋlɪ] adv (oppose, endorse) vigoureusement; (believe) fermement; **s. built** solide; **a s. worded letter** une lettre bien sentie; **to feel s. about sth** être convaincu(e) de qch

strongman ['strɒŋmæn] n (in circus) hercule m (de foire); Fig (dictator) homme m fort

strong-minded [strɒŋ'maɪndɪd] adj résolu(e)

strongroom ['strɒŋruːm] n chambre f forte

strong-willed [strɒŋ'wɪld] adj résolu(e)

strontium ['strɒntɪəm] n Chem strontium m

strop [strɒp] n (a) (for razor) cuir m (à rasoir) (b) Br Fam **to be in a s.** être de mauvais poil

stroppy ['strɒpɪ] adj Br Fam hargneux(euse); **to get s.** monter sur ses grands chevaux

strove [strəʊv] pt of **strive**

struck [strʌk] pt & pp of **strike**

structural ['strʌktʃərəl] adj structurel(elle); **s. damage** dégâts mpl de structure; **s. survey** = inspection pour vérifier la solidité d'un bâtiment

structurally ['strʌktʃərəlɪ] adv structurellement

structure ['strʌktʃə(r)] 1 n (a) (of society, language, story) structure f (b) (building, monument) édifice m, construction f 2 vt structurer

struggle ['strʌgəl] 1 n lutte f (for pour); **without a s.** sans résistance; **life is a s.** la vie est un combat 2 vi lutter (for pour); **to s. to do sth** lutter pour faire qch; **to be struggling** (of person, company) avoir des difficultés ou du mal

strum [strʌm] (pt & pp **strummed**) vt (guitar) gratter

strung [strʌŋ] pt & pp of **string**

strut¹ [strʌt] n (for frame) étai m; Aviat pilier m

strut² (pt & pp **strutted**) vi se pavaner

strychnine ['strɪkniːn] n strychnine f

stub [stʌb] 1 n (of pencil) bout m; (of cigarette) mégot m; (of cheque) talon m 2 vt (pt & pp **stubbed**) **to s. one's toe** (on or against) se cogner l'orteil (contre)

▸**stub out** vt sep (cigarette) écraser

stubble ['stʌbəl] n (a) (in field) chaume m (b) (on face) barbe f de plusieurs jours

stubborn ['stʌbən] adj (person) têtu(e); (determination, resistance) farouche; (stain, infection) rebelle

stubbornness ['stʌbənnɪs] n (of person) entêtement m, obstination f; (of determination, resistance) inflexibilité f

stubby ['stʌbɪ] adj court(e) et boudiné(e)

stucco ['stʌkəʊ] n stuc m

stuck [stʌk] 1 adj bloqué(e), coincé(e); **to get s.** être coincé; (in mud, sand, with problem) s'enliser; **to be s. for sth** être à court de qch; Fam **to be s. with sb/sth**

ne pas pouvoir se débarrasser de qn/qch
  2 pt & pp of **stick²**
stuck-up ['stʌk'ʌp] adj Fam snob inv
stud¹ [stʌd] n (fastener) bouton-pression m; (on football, rugby boots) crampon m; (earring) clou m d'oreille
stud² n (**a**) (farm) haras m; (stallion) étalon m (**b**) Fam (man) étalon m
student ['stjuːdənt] n (at university) étudiant(e) m,f; (at school) élève mf; **law s.** étudiant(e) m,f en droit; **s. card** carte f d'étudiant; **s. life** vie f étudiante; **s. loan** = prêt bancaire pour étudiants; **s. nurse** élève mf infirmier(ère); **s. teacher** enseignant(e) m,f stagiaire; **students' union** (association) = association d'aide et de services aux étudiants; (place) foyer m des étudiants

> ### Students' union
> Dans les universités britanniques et américaines, on appelle "students' union" à la fois le syndicat et les locaux où il se trouve. Le syndicat est chargé de défendre les intérêts des étudiants, sert de centre d'information et de conseil en matière de logement, de santé et de financement, et organise des événements culturels et des activités.

studied ['stʌdɪd] adj (manner, attitude) calculé(e)
studio ['stjuːdɪəʊ] (pl **studios**) n studio m; (of artist) atelier m; TV **s. audience** public m (présent lors de l'enregistrement); Br **s. flat** studio
studious ['stjuːdɪəs] adj studieux(euse)
study ['stʌdɪ] **1** n (**a**) (investigation, by artist) étude f; **to make a s. of sth** faire une étude sur qch; **s. group** groupe m d'étude; **s. trip** voyage m d'études (**b**) (room) bureau m, cabinet m de travail
  2 vt (pt & pp **studied**) (facts, evidence) examiner; (behaviour, school subject) étudier; (university subject) faire des études de
  3 vi (revise) travailler; (be at university) faire des études
stuff [stʌf] **1** n (**a**) (objects, possessions) affaires fpl; **some s.** (substance) un truc; Fam **he reads all that intellectual s.** il lit tous ces trucs intellos; Fam **she writes good s.** c'est bien, ce qu'elle écrit; Fam **he knows his s.** il s'y connaît; Fam **that's the s.!** c'est bien! (**b**) (cloth) étoffe f
  2 vt (fill) (cushion) rembourrer; (chicken, tomatoes) farcir; (pocket) remplir; **to s. sth into sth** fourrer qch dans qch; Fam **to s. oneself** s'empiffrer; Br very Fam **get stuffed!** va te faire foutre!
stuffing ['stʌfɪŋ] n (for furniture) rembourrage m; (for chicken) farce f; Fam **to knock the s. out of sb** ficher un coup à qn
stuffy ['stʌfɪ] adj (**a**) (room) qui sent le renfermé (**b**) (person) vieux jeu inv
stultifying ['stʌltɪfaɪɪŋ] adj abrutissant(e)
stumble ['stʌmbəl] **1** n faux-pas m
  2 vi (when walking, speaking) trébucher
▸**stumble across** vt insep (find) tomber par hasard sur
stump [stʌmp] **1** n (**a**) (of tree) souche f; (of arm, leg) moignon m (**b**) (in cricket) piquet m (**c**) Am Fam (of politician) **to be on the s.** être en campagne électorale
  2 vt (baffle) laisser perplexe; **to be stumped for an answer** ne pas savoir quoi répondre
▸**stump up** vt insep Br Fam (pay) cracher

stumpy ['stʌmpɪ] adj court(e) et boudiné(e)
stun [stʌn] (pt & pp **stunned**) vt (make unconscious) assommer; Fig (shock) abasourdir
stung [stʌŋ] pt & pp of **sting**
stunk [stʌŋk] pt & pp of **stink**
stunner ['stʌnə(r)] n Br Fam (man, woman) canon m
stunning ['stʌnɪŋ] adj (shocking) étourdissant(e); (excellent) excellent(e); (beautiful) superbe
stunt¹ [stʌnt] vt (person) ralentir la croissance de; (growth) ralentir
stunt² n (in film) cascade f; (for publicity) coup m de pub; **s. man** cascadeur m
stunted [stʌntɪd] adj (plant, person) chétif(ive); (growth) retardé(e)
stupefy ['stjuːpɪfaɪ] (pt & pp **stupified**) vt (of alcohol, drugs) abrutir; (of news, behaviour) stupéfier
stupefying ['stjuːpɪfaɪɪŋ] adj stupéfiant(e)
stupendous [stjuːˈpendəs] adj fantastique
stupid ['stjuːpɪd] adj bête, stupide; **the s. TV keeps breaking down** cette saleté de télé est sans arrêt en panne; **what a s. thing to do!** c'est vraiment idiot d'avoir fait ça!
stupidity [stjuːˈpɪdɪtɪ] n bêtise f, stupidité f
stupidly ['stjuːpɪdlɪ] adv bêtement
stupor ['stjuːpə(r)] n état m d'abrutissement
sturdy ['stɜːdɪ] adj (person, object) robuste; (opposition, resistance) résolu(e)
sturgeon ['stɜːdʒən] n esturgeon m
stutter ['stʌtə(r)] **1** n bégaiement m
  2 vi bégayer
sty¹ [staɪ] n (for pigs) & Fig porcherie f
sty², stye [staɪ] n (in eye) orgelet m
style [staɪl] **1** n (**a**) (manner, design) style m (**b**) (sophistication) classe f; **to live in s.** mener grand train
  2 vt (design) créer; (hair) coiffer
stylish ['staɪlɪʃ] adj élégant(e), chic inv
stylist ['staɪlɪst] n (hairdresser) coiffeur(euse) m,f
stylistic [staɪˈlɪstɪk] adj stylistique
stylized ['staɪəlaɪzd] adj stylisé(e)
stylus ['staɪləs] (pl **styluses** or **styli** ['staɪlaɪ]) n (for engraving) style m; (on record player) pointe f de lecture
stymie ['staɪmɪ] vt Br Fam coincer
suave [swɑːv] adj affable; Pej mielleux(euse)
sub [sʌb] Fam **1** n (**a**) (abbr **subscription**) cotisation f (**b**) (abbr **substitute**) remplaçant(e) m,f (**c**) (abbr **submarine**) sous-marin m (**d**) Journ (abbr **subeditor**) secrétaire mf de rédaction
  2 vt (pt & pp **subbed**) Journ (abbr **subedit**) mettre au point
  3 vi (abbr **substitute**) **to s. for sb** remplacer qn
subaltern ['sʌbəltən] n Mil officier m subalterne
subcommittee ['sʌbkəmɪtɪ] n sous-comité m
subconscious [sʌbˈkɒnʃəs] **1** n **the s.** l'inconscient m
  2 adj inconscient(e)
subcontinent [sʌbˈkɒntɪnənt] n sous-continent m
subcontract 1 n [sʌbˈkɒntrækt] sous-traitance f
  2 vt [sʌbkənˈtrækt] sous-traiter
subcontractor ['sʌbkəntræktə(r)] n sous-traitant m
subculture ['sʌbkʌltʃə(r)] n phénomène m de groupe
subdivision [sʌbdɪˈvɪʒən] n subdivision f
subdue [səbˈdjuː] vt (enemy, rioter) soumettre; (emotions) maîtriser
subdued [səbˈdjuːd] adj (person, event) inhabituellement calme; (light) tamisé(e); (sound, voice) bas (basse)

subedit ['sʌb'edɪt] *vt Journ* mettre au point
subeditor [sʌb'edɪtə(r)] *n Journ* secrétaire *mf* de rédaction
subhuman [sʌb'hjuːmən] **1** *n* sous-homme *m*
 2 *adj* inférieur(e) (aux humains)
subject 1 *n* ['sʌbdʒɪkt] (**a**) *(of conversation, book, painting, photograph)* sujet *m*; *(at school, university)* matière *f*; **while we're on the s.** à ce propos; **to change the s.** parler d'autre chose; **s. matter** *(of letter)* contenu *m*; *(of book)* sujet (**b**) *Gram* sujet *m* (**c**) *(of monarch)* sujet(ette) *m,f*
 2 *adj* ['sʌbdʒɪkt] (**a**) *(prone)* **to be s. to** *(illness)* être sujet(ette) à; *(fine, taxation)* être passible de; **to be s. to jealousy/depression** avoir tendance à être jaloux(ouse)/dépressif(ive) (**b**) **s. to** *(dependent on)* sous réserve de
 3 *vt* [səb'dʒekt] *(control)* soumettre, assujettir; **to s. sb to sth** *(force to undergo)* soumettre qn à qch
subjective [səb'dʒektɪv] *adj* subjectif(ive)
subjectivity [sʌbdʒek'tɪvɪtɪ] *n* subjectivité *f*
sub judice ['sʌb'dʒuːdɪsɪ] *adj Law* en instance
subjugate ['sʌbdʒʊgeɪt] *vt* assujettir
subjunctive [səb'dʒʌŋktɪv] *Gram* **1** *n* subjonctif *m*
 2 *adj* subjonctif(ive)
sublet [sʌb'let] *(pt & pp* **sublet**) *vt* sous-louer
sublimate ['sʌblɪmeɪt] *vt* sublimer
sublime [sə'blaɪm] **1** *adj* sublime; *(utter)* suprême
 2 *n* **from the s. to the ridiculous** du sublime au ridicule
subliminal [sʌb'lɪmɪnəl] *adj* subliminal(e)
sub-machine gun [sʌbmə'ʃiːngʌn] *n* mitraillette *f*
submarine [sʌbmə'riːn] *n* sous-marin *m*
submerge [səb'mɜːdʒ] **1** *vt (immerse)* immerger; *(cover)* submerger; *Fig* **to be submerged in sth** être submergé(e) par qch
 2 *vi* plonger
submersion [səb'mɜːʃən] *n* submersion *f*
submission [səb'mɪʃən] *n* (**a**) *(to will, authority)* soumission *f*; **to starve sb into s.** réduire qn à la soumission en le/la privant de nourriture; **to beat sb into s.** battre qn jusqu'à ce qu'il/elle se soumette (**b**) *(of document)* présentation *f* (**c**) *(report)* soumission *f*
submissive [səb'mɪsɪv] *adj* soumis(e)
submit [səb'mɪt] *(pt & pp* **submitted**) **1** *vt* soumettre (**for** à)
 2 *vi (to person, authority)* se soumettre (**to** à)
subnormal [sʌb'nɔːməl] *adj* arriéré(e)
subordinate 1 *n* [sə'bɔːdɪnət] subordonné(e) *m,f*
 2 *adj* [sə'bɔːdɪnət] *(rank)* subalterne; *(role)* secondaire; **to be s. to sb** être subordonné(e) à qn; *Gram* **s. clause** proposition *f* subordonnée
 3 *vt* [sə'bɔːdɪneɪt] subordonner
subordination [səbɔːdɪ'neɪʃən] *n* subordination *f*
subplot ['sʌbplɒt] *n* intrigue *f* secondaire
subpoena [sə'piːnə] *Law* **1** *n* citation *f* ou assignation *f* à comparaître
 2 *vt* citer ou assigner à comparaître
subscribe [səb'skraɪb] *vi* (**a**) *(to newspaper, magazine)* s'abonner (**to** à); *(to charity, organization)* être membre (**to** de) (**b**) **to s. to** *(opinion, theory)* souscrire à
subscriber [səb'skraɪbə(r)] *n (to newspaper, magazine, telephone, ISP)* abonné(e) *m,f*; *(to charity, organization)* membre *m*
subscript ['sʌbskrɪpt] *n Typ* indice *m*

subscription [səb'skrɪpʃən] *n (to newspaper, magazine, telephone, ISP)* abonnement *m*; *(to charity, organization, club)* cotisation *f*
subsection ['sʌbsekʃən] *n* subdivision *f*
subsequent ['sʌbsɪkwənt] *adj* ultérieur(e)
subsequently ['sʌbsɪkwəntlɪ] *adv* par la suite, ultérieurement
subservient [səb'sɜːvɪənt] *adj* servile
subside [səb'saɪd] *vi (of ground, building)* s'affaisser; *(of water)* baisser; *(of bump)* dégonfler; *(of storm, excitement, fever)* s'apaiser; *(of noise, pain)* s'affaiblir
subsidence [səb'saɪdəns] *n (of ground, building)* affaissement *m*; *(of water)* baisse *f*
subsidiarity [sʌbsɪdɪ'ærɪtɪ] *n* subsidiarité *f*
subsidiary [səb'sɪdɪərɪ] **1** *n (pl* **subsidiaries**) *(company)* filiale *f*
 2 *adj* subsidiaire
subsidize ['sʌbsɪdaɪz] *vt* subventionner
subsidy ['sʌbsɪdɪ] *(pl* **subsidies**) *n* subvention *f*
subsist [səb'sɪst] *vi* **to s. on** vivre de
subsistence [səb'sɪstəns] *n* subsistance *f*; **s. allowance** faux frais *mpl*; **s. wage** salaire *m* à peine suffisant pour vivre
substance ['sʌbstəns] *n* (**a**) *(matter)* substance *f*, **s. abuse** usage *m* de stupéfiants (**b**) *(essential element)* fond *m* (**c**) *(solidity, worth)* fondement *m*
substandard [sʌb'stændəd] *adj* de qualité inférieure
substantial [səb'stænʃəl] *adj* (**a**) *(significant)* important(e); *(meal)* substantiel(elle); **a s. number of** un nombre important de (**b**) *(solid, robust)* solide
substantially [səb'stænʃəlɪ] *adv* (**a**) *(considerably)* considérablement (**b**) *(for the most part)* pour l'essentiel; **they are s. the same** ils sont pareils dans l'ensemble (**c**) *(solidly)* solidement
substantiate [səb'stænʃɪeɪt] *vt (statement)* corroborer; *(claim)* justifier
substantive ['sʌbstəntɪv] **1** *n Gram* substantif *m*
 2 *adj* important(e)
substitute ['sʌbstɪtjuːt] **1** *n (person)* remplaçant(e) *m,f*; *(foodstuff, drug)* succédané *m*; **to be a s./no s. for** remplacer/ne pas remplacer
 2 *vt* **to s. A for B** remplacer B par A
 3 *vi* **to s. for sb** remplacer qn
substitution [sʌbstɪ'tjuːʃən] *n* substitution *f*; *(of person, player)* remplacement *m*
subsume [sʌb'sjuːm] *vt Formal* subsumer
subterfuge ['sʌbtəfjuːdʒ] *n* subterfuge *m*
subterranean [sʌbtə'reɪnɪən] *adj* souterrain(e)
subtitle ['sʌbtaɪtəl] **1** *n* sous-titre *m*
 2 *vt* sous-titrer
subtle ['sʌtəl] *adj* subtil(e)
subtlety ['sʌtəltɪ] *(pl* **subtleties**) *n* subtilité *f*
subtly ['sʌtlɪ] *adv* subtilement
subtotal ['sʌbtəʊtəl] *n* sous-total *m*
subtract [səb'trækt] *vt* soustraire (**from** de)
subtraction [səb'trækʃən] *n* soustraction *f*
subtropical [sʌb'trɒpɪkəl] *adj* subtropical(e)
suburb ['sʌbɜːb] *n* banlieue *f*; **the suburbs** la banlieue
suburban [sə'bɜːbən] *adj* (**a**) *(of suburb)* de banlieue; *(population, development)* suburbain(e) (**b**) *Pej (narrow-minded)* étriqué(e)
suburbia [sə'bɜːbɪə] *n* la banlieue
subversion [səb'vɜːʃən] *n* subversion *f*
subversive [səb'vɜːsɪv] *n & adj* subversif(ive) *m,f*
subvert [səb'vɜːt] *vt* renverser, subvertir

subway ['sʌbweɪ] *n* (**a**) *Br (underpass)* passage *m* souterrain (**b**) *Am (underground railway)* métro *m*

sub-zero [sʌb'zɪərəʊ] *adj* au-dessous de zéro

succeed [sək'siːd] **1** *vt (follow)* succéder à

2 *vi* (**a**) *(be successful)* réussir; **to s. in doing sth** réussir à faire qch (**b**) **to s. to the throne** monter sur le trône

succeeding [sək'siːdɪŋ] *adj (following)* suivant(e)

success [sək'ses] *n* réussite *f*, succès *m*; **to be a s.** avoir du succès; **s. story** réussite *f*

successful [sək'sesfʊl] *adj (person)* brillant(e); *(project, application)* couronné(e) de succès; **to be s.** réussir; **to be s. in doing sth** réussir à faire qch

successfully [sək'sesfəlɪ] *adv* avec succès

succession [sək'seʃən] *n* succession *f*, série *f*; **two years in s.** deux années de suite

successive [sək'sesɪv] *adj* successif(ive); **on five s. Sundays** cinq dimanches consécutifs

successor [sək'sesə(r)] *n* successeur *m*

succinct [sʌk'sɪŋ(k)t] *adj* succinct(e)

succulent ['sʌkjʊlənt] **1** *adj (delicious)* succulent(e)

2 *n (plant)* plante *f* grasse

succumb [sə'kʌm] *vi* succomber (**to** à)

such [sʌtʃ] **1** *pron* tel (telle) *m,f*; **if s. were the case** si tel était le cas; **and s.** et des choses comme ça; **as s.** en tant que tel; **s. is life!** c'est la vie!

2 *adj* tel (telle), pareil(eille); **s. a question** une telle question, une question pareille; **animals s. as the lion or the tiger** des animaux tels que le lion ou le tigre; **s. books as these, books s. as these** de tels livres, des livres pareils; **here's my bedroom, s. as it is** voici ce qui me sert de chambre; **s. as?** par exemple?; **do you have s. a thing as a screwdriver?** est-ce que tu aurais un tournevis, par hasard?; **there's no s. thing as aliens** les extraterrestres n'existent pas; **I said/did no s. thing** je n'ai rien dit/fait de tel; **in s. a way that** d'une façon telle que; **on s. and s. a day** tel jour

3 *adv* (**a**) *(in comparisons)* **s. a big house** une si *ou* aussi grande maison; **I had never heard s. good music** je n'avais jamais entendu de si bonne musique (**b**) *(for emphasis)* **we had s. a good time** nous nous sommes tellement bien amusés; **it was s. a long time ago** ça fait tellement longtemps; **s. a lot of people** tant de gens

suchlike ['sʌtʃlaɪk] *pron* **...and s.** ...et autres

suck [sʌk] **1** *vt (lollipop, thumb)* sucer; *(liquid, air)* aspirer; *(mother's milk)* téter

2 *vi very Fam (be of bad quality)* être nul (nulle)

▸**suck in** *vt sep* aspirer; *Fig* **to get sucked into sth** se laisser entraîner dans qch

▸**suck up 1** *vt sep (liquid, dust)* aspirer

2 *vi Fam* **to s. up to sb** lécher les bottes a qn

sucker ['sʌkə(r)] *n* (**a**) *(of octopus)* suçoir *m*; *(of plant)* rejeton *m* (**b**) *Fam (gullible person)* niais(e) *m,f*; **to be a s. for sth** craquer pour qch

suckle ['sʌkəl] **1** *vt* allaiter

2 *vi* téter

sucrose ['suːkrəʊs] *n* saccharose *m*

suction ['sʌkʃən] *n* succion *f*

Sudan [suː'dæn] *n* le Soudan

Sudanese [suːdə'niːz] **1** *npl (people)* **the S.** les Soudanais *mpl*

2 *n* Soudanais(e) *m,f*

3 *adj* soudanais(e)

sudden ['sʌdən] *adj* soudain(e), subit(e); **all of a s.** tout à coup; *Fig* **s. death** *(in match, contest)* la mort subite

suddenly ['sʌdənlɪ] *adv* soudain, tout à coup; *(die, happen)* subitement

suddenness ['sʌdənnɪs] *n* soudaineté *f*

suds [sʌdz] *npl (of soap)* mousse *f*

sue [suː] **1** *vt* intenter un procès à (**for** en)

2 *vi* **to s. for divorce** entamer une procédure de divorce; **to s. for damages** demander des dommages-intérêts

suede [sweɪd] *n* daim *m*

suet ['suːɪt] *n* graisse *f* de rognon

Suez ['suːɪz] *n* **the S. Canal** le canal de Suez

suffer ['sʌfə(r)] **1** *vt* (**a**) *(loss, defeat, consequence)* subir; *(pain)* avoir (**b**) *(tolerate)* supporter; **she doesn't s. fools gladly** elle ne supporte pas les imbéciles

2 *vi (of person)* souffrir (**from** de); *(of health, work)* en pâtir

sufferance ['sʌf(ə)rəns] *n* **I'm just here on s.** on me tolère tout juste ici

sufferer ['sʌfərə(r)] *n* victime *f*

suffering ['sʌfərɪŋ] *n* souffrance *f*

suffice [sə'faɪs] *vi Formal* suffire

sufficient [sə'fɪʃənt] *adj* suffisant(e); **to be s.** suffire, être suffisant

sufficiently [sə'fɪʃəntlɪ] *adv* suffisamment

suffix ['sʌfɪks] *n Gram* suffixe *m*

suffocate ['sʌfəkeɪt] *also Fig* **1** *vt* étouffer

2 *vi* suffoquer

suffocating ['sʌfəkeɪtɪŋ] *adj* suffocant(e)

suffocation [sʌfə'keɪʃən] *n* suffocation *f*

suffrage ['sʌfrɪdʒ] *n* droit *m* de vote

suffragette [sʌfrə'dʒet] *n* suffragette *f*

suffuse [sə'fjuːz] *vt Lit (of light, liquid, colour)* inonder; *(of heat)* envahir

sugar ['ʃʊgə(r)] **1** *n* (**a**) *(food)* sucre *m*; **two sugars, please** deux sucres, s'il te plaît; **s. almond** dragée *f*; **s. beet** betterave *f* sucrière; **s. bowl** sucrier *m*; **s. cane** canne *f* à sucre; *Fam* **s. daddy** vieux *m* plein de fric *(qui entretient une jeune femme)*; **s. lump** morceau *m* de sucre; **s. plantation** plantation *f* de canne à sucre; **s. refinery** raffinerie *f* de sucre (**b**) *Fam (term of address)* mon trésor

2 *vt (coffee, tea)* sucrer; *Fig* **to s. the pill** dorer la pilule

sugar-coated [ʃʊgə'kəʊtɪd] *adj* recouvert(e) de sucre

sugar-free [ʃʊgə'friː] *adj* sans sucre

sugary ['ʃʊgərɪ] *adj* (**a**) *(containing sugar)* sucré(e) (**b**) *Fig (smile, tone)* mielleux(euse), doucereux(euse)

suggest [sə'dʒest] *vt* (**a**) *(propose)* suggérer (**b**) *(imply)* indiquer

suggestible [sə'dʒestɪbəl] *adj* influençable

suggestion [sə'dʒestʃən] *n* (**a**) *(proposal)* suggestion *f*; **suggestions box** boîte *f* à idées (**b**) *(insinuation, hint)* indication *f*; **there is no s. that...** rien ne dit que...; **a s. of** une pointe de

suggestive [sə'dʒestɪv] *adj* suggestif(ive); **to be s. of** évoquer

suicidal [sʊɪ'saɪdəl] *adj* suicidaire

suicide ['sʊɪsaɪd] *n* suicide *m*; **to commit s.** se suicider; **s. attempt** tentative *f* de suicide; **s. mission** mission *f* suicide; **s. note** lettre *f (laissée par un suicidé)*

suit [suːt] **1** *n* (**a**) *(clothing) (man's)* costume *m*, complet *m*; *(woman's)* tailleur *m*; **s. of armour** armure *f* complète (**b**) *(in cards)* couleur *f*; *Fig* **to follow s.** faire de même; *Fig* **politeness is not her strong s.** la politesse n'est pas son fort (**c**) *Law* procès *m*
2 *vt* (**a**) *(of clothes, colours)* aller à (**b**) *(of arrangement, time, job)* convenir à; **to be suited to** *or* **for sth** *(purpose, job)* être fait(e) pour qch; **to s. sb down to the ground** convenir parfaitement à qn; **they are well suited** ils sont vraiment faits l'un pour l'autre; *Fam* **s. yourself** fais comme tu voudras (**c**) *(adapt)* **to s. sth to sth** adapter qch à qch

suitability [suːtəˈbɪlɪtɪ] *n* *(of behaviour)* caractère *m* convenable; *(of clothing)* caractère *m* approprié; *(of person)* aptitude *f*

suitable [ˈsuːtəbəl] *adj* *(behaviour, subject)* convenable; *(clothing)* approprié(e); *(candidate, date, title)* adéquat(e); **the film is not s. for children** ce n'est pas un film pour les enfants

suitably [ˈsuːtəblɪ] *adv* *(behave, dress)* convenablement; **s. impressed/embarrassed** vraiment impressionné(e)/gêné(e)

suitcase [ˈsjuːtkeɪs] *n* valise *f*

suite [swiːt] *n* (**a**) *(of rooms)* suite *f* (**b**) *(of furniture)* **(three-piece) s.** canapé *m* avec deux fauteuils assortis (**c**) *Mus* suite *f*

suitor [ˈsuːtə(r)] *n* *Old-fashioned (admirer)* soupirant *m*

sulfate, sulfide *etc Am* = **sulphate, sulphide** *etc*

sulk [sʌlk] **1** *n* **to be in a s.** bouder
2 *vi* bouder

sulky [ˈsʌlkɪ] *adj* bondeur(euse)

sullen [ˈsʌlən] *adj* renfrogné(e)

sully [ˈsʌlɪ] *vt* *Lit (reputation)* ternir; *Fig* **to s. one's hands (with sth)** se salir les mains (en faisant qch)

sulphate, *Am* **sulfate** [ˈsʌlfeɪt] *n Chem* sulfate *m*

sulphide, *Am* **sulfide** [ˈsʌlfaɪd] *n Chem* sulfure *m*

sulphur, *Am* **sulfur** [ˈsʌlfə(r)] *n Chem* soutre *m*; **s. dioxide** anhydride *m* sulfureux

sulphuric, *Am* **sulfuric** [sʌlˈfjʊərɪk] *adj Chem* sulfurique; **s. acid** acide *m* sulfurique

sultan [ˈsʌltən] *n* sultan *m*

sultana [sʌlˈtɑːnə] *n* raisin *m* de Smyrne

sultry [ˈsʌltrɪ] *adj* *(heat)* étouffant(e); *(weather)* lourd(e); *(look, smile)* sensuel(elle)

sum [sʌm] *n (amount of money)* somme *f*; *(mathematical problem)* problème *m*; **the s. of** la somme de; **s. total** somme totale

▶**sum up** *(pt & pp summed)* **1** *vt sep* (**a**) *(summarize)* résumer (**b**) *(assess quickly)* jauger, évaluer
2 *vi (summarize)* résumer

summarily [ˈsʌmərɪlɪ] *adv* sommairement

summarize [ˈsʌməraɪz] *vt* résumer

summary [ˈsʌmərɪ] **1** *n (pl* **summaries**) résumé *m*
2 *adj (brief)* sommaire

summer [ˈsʌmə(r)] **1** *n* été *m*; **in (the) s.** en été; **s. holidays** vacances *fpl* d'été; **s. school** cours *mpl* d'été
2 *vi* passer l'été

summerhouse [ˈsʌməhaʊs] *n (in garden)* pavillon *m*

summertime [ˈsʌmətaɪm] *n* été *m*

summery [ˈsʌmərɪ] *adj* d'été

summing-up [sʌmɪŋˈʌp] *n Law* résumé *m* des débats

summit [ˈsʌmɪt] *n* sommet *m*; **to hold a s.** tenir un sommet

summon [ˈsʌmən] *vt (person, meeting)* convoquer; *(police, doctor, help)* appeler, faire venir; *Law (witness)* assigner *ou* citer à comparaître

▶**summon up** *vt sep* rassembler

summons [ˈsʌmənz] *Law* **1** *n (pl* **summonses** [ˈsʌmənzɪz]) assignation *f ou* citation *f* à comparaître
2 *vt* assigner *ou* citer à comparaître

sump [sʌmp] *n* (**a**) *(in engine)* carter *m* à huile (**b**) *(cesspool)* fosse *f* d'aisance

sumptuous [ˈsʌm(p)tjʊəs] *adj* somptueux(euse)

Sun *(abbr* **Sunday**) dimanche

sun [sʌn] **1** *n* soleil *m*; **in the s.** au soleil; **to catch the s.** prendre le soleil; **everything under the s.** tout ce qu'il est possible d'imaginer; **s. lamp** lampe *f* à bronzer; **s. lotion** lotion *f* solaire; **s. shield** *or* **visor** *(in car)* pare-soleil *m*
2 *vt (pt & pp* **sunned**) **to s. oneself** prendre le soleil

sunbathe [ˈsʌnbeɪð] *vi* se faire bronzer

sunbeam [ˈsʌnbiːm] *n* rayon *m* de soleil

sunbed [ˈsʌnbed] *n* lit *m* à ultraviolets

sunburn [ˈsʌnbɜːn] *n* coup *m* de soleil; **to have s.** avoir un coup de soleil

sunburnt [ˈsʌnbɜːnt], **sunburned** [ˈsʌnbɜːnd] *adj* **to be s.** avoir un coup de soleil

sundae [ˈsʌndeɪ] *n* coupe *f* glacée

Sunday [ˈsʌndeɪ] *n* dimanche *m*; **S. best** habits *mpl* du dimanche; **S. paper** journal *m* du dimanche; **S. school** ≃ catéchisme *m*; **S. trading** = ouverture des magasins le dimanche; *see also* **Saturday**

Sunday papers

La lecture des journaux du dimanche constitue une sorte de rituel pour de nombreux Britanniques. Les journaux du dimanche sont très volumineux; ils comprennent de nombreux suppléments sur des sujets tels que le sport, la mode, les voyages et les arts, et sont souvent accompagnés d'un magazine en couleurs. Ils coûtent plus cher que les journaux vendus en semaine. Certains journaux du dimanche sont des éditions dominicales de quotidiens paraissant en semaine (c'est le cas de 'The Sunday Times' et de 'The Independent on Sunday' par exemple) tandis que d'autres, comme 'The Observer', paraissent uniquement le dimanche.

---

sundial [ˈsʌndaɪəl] *n* cadran *m* solaire

sundown [ˈsʌndaʊn] *n* coucher *m* du soleil

sun-drenched [ˈsʌndren(t)ʃt] *adj* inondé(e) de soleil

sun-dried [ˈsʌndraɪd] *adj* séché(e) au soleil

sundry [ˈsʌndrɪ] **1** *n* (**a**) **all and s.** tout le monde (**b**) **sundries** *(items)* articles *mpl* divers; *(costs)* frais *mpl* divers
2 *adj* divers(e)

sunflower [ˈsʌnflaʊə(r)] *n* tournesol *m*; **s. oil** huile *f* de tournesol; **s. seeds** *(as snack)* graines *fpl* de tournesol

sung [ˈsʌŋ] *pp of* **sing**

sunglasses [ˈsʌnglɑːsɪz] *npl* lunettes *fpl* de soleil, *Belg* lunettes *fpl* solaires

sunhat [ˈsʌnhæt] *n* chapeau *m* de soleil

sunk [ˈsʌŋk] *pp of* **sink**[2]

sunken [ˈsʌŋkən] *adj (ship)* englouti(e); *(eyes)* enfoncé(e); *(rock)* immergé(e)

sunlight [ˈsʌnlaɪt] *n* lumière *f* du soleil; **in the s.** au soleil

sunlit ['sʌnlɪt] *adj* éclairé(e) par le soleil

sunny ['sʌnɪ] *adj* (**a**) *(day, place)* ensoleillé(e); **it's s.** il fait du soleil (**b**) *Fig (face)* radieux(euse); **to have a s. personality** être toujours content(e)

sunray lamp ['sʌnreɪ'læmp] *n* lampe *f* à bronzer

sunrise ['sʌnraɪz] *n* lever *m* de soleil; **at s.** au lever du soleil, au soleil levant; *Econ* **s. industry** industrie *f* d'avenir

sunroof ['sʌnruːf] *n* toit *m* ouvrant

sunset ['sʌnset] *n* coucher *m* de soleil; **at s.** au coucher du soleil, au soleil couchant

sunshade ['sʌnʃeɪd] *n* parasol *m*

sunshine ['sʌnʃaɪn] *n* soleil *m*

sunspot ['sʌnspɒt] *n* (**a**) *(on sun)* tache *f* solaire (**b**) *Fam (holiday resort)* destination *f* ensoleillée

sunstroke ['sʌnstrəʊk] *n* insolation *f*; **to have s.** avoir une insolation

suntan ['sʌntæn] *n* bronzage *m*; **to have a s.** être bronzé(e); **s. lotion** lotion *f* solaire

suntrap ['sʌntræp] *n* coin *m* très ensoleillé

sup [sʌp] *(pt & pp* **supped)** *vt* boire à petites gorgées

super ['suːpə(r)] **1** *adj Fam (excellent)* super *inv*
2 *n (petrol)* super *m*

superannuation [suːpərænjʊ'eɪʃən] *n Fin* retraite *f*

superb [suː'pɜːb] *adj* excellent(e)

supercharger ['suːpətʃɑːdʒə(r)] *n Aut & Aviat* compresseur *m*

supercilious [suːpə'sɪlɪəs] *adj* hautain(e)

superconductor [suːpəkən'dʌktə(r)] *n Phys* supraconducteur *m*

super-duper ['suːpə'duːpə(r)] *adj Fam* super, génial(e)

superego ['suːpəriːgəʊ] *n Psy* surmoi *m*

superficial [suːpə'fɪʃəl] *adj* superficiel(elle)

superficiality [suːpəfɪʃɪ'ælɪtɪ] *n* superficialité *f*

superficially [suːpə'fɪʃəlɪ] *adv* superficiellement

superfluous [suː'pɜːflʊəs] *adj* superflu(e)

superhuman [suːpə'hjuːmən] *adj* surhumain(e)

superimpose [suːpərɪm'pəʊz] *vt* superposer

superintend [suːpərɪn'tend] *vt (run)* diriger; *(supervise)* surveiller

superintendent [suːpərɪn'tendənt] *n (supervisor)* directeur(trice) *m,f*, *(police officer)* ≃ commissaire *m* de police

superior [suː'pɪərɪə(r)] **1** *adj* (**a**) *(better, more senior)* supérieur(e) *Pej* (**b**) *(arrogant) (person)* qui se croit supérieur(e); *(tone, air, smile)* de supériorité
2 *n (senior)* supérieur(e) *m,f*

superiority [suːpɪərɪ'ɒrɪtɪ] *n* supériorité *f*

superlative [suː'pɜːlətɪv] **1** *n Gram* superlatif *m*
2 *adj* (**a**) *(excellent)* excellent(e) (**b**) *Gram* superlatif(ive)

superman ['suːpəmæn] *n* surhomme *m*

supermarket ['suːpəmɑːkɪt] *n* supermarché *m*

supermodel ['suːpəmɒdəl] *n* top model *m*

supernatural [suːpə'nætʃərəl] **1** *n* **the s.** le surnaturel
2 *adj* surnaturel(elle)

superpower ['suːpəpaʊə(r)] *n* superpuissance *f*

supersede [suːpə'siːd] *vt* supplanter, détrôner

supersonic [suːpə'sɒnɪk] *adj* supersonique

superstar ['suːpəstɑː(r)] *n* superstar *f*

superstition [suːpə'stɪʃən] *n* superstition *f*

superstitious [suːpə'stɪʃəs] *adj* superstitieux(euse)

superstore ['suːpəstɔː(r)] *n* hypermarché *m*

superstructure ['suːpəstrʌktʃə(r)] *n* superstructure *f*

supertanker ['suːpətæŋkə(r)] *n* supertanker *m*

supervise ['suːpəvaɪz] *vt (children)* surveiller; *(staff)* superviser

supervision [suːpə'vɪʒən] *n (of children)* surveillance *f*; *(of staff)* supervision *f*

supervisor ['suːpəvaɪzə(r)] *n* (**a**) *(in office)* chef *m* de service; *(in factory)* chef d'équipe (**b**) *(for thesis)* directeur(trice) *m,f* de thèse

supervisory [suːpə'vaɪzərɪ] *adj* de supervision

supine ['suːpaɪn] **1** *adj* couché(e) sur le dos; *Fig (inactive)* mou (molle)
2 *adv* **to lie s.** être couché(e) sur le dos

supper ['sʌpə(r)] *n (evening meal)* dîner *m*; *(snack before going to bed)* = casse-croûte pris avant d'aller se coucher

supplant [sə'plɑːnt] *vt* supplanter

supple ['sʌpəl] *adj* souple

supplement ['sʌplɪmənt] **1** *n* supplément *m*
2 *vt* compléter

supplementary [sʌplɪ'mentərɪ] *adj* supplémentaire

supplication [sʌplɪ'keɪʃən] *n* supplication *f*

supplier [sə'plaɪə(r)] *n* fournisseur(euse) *m,f*

supply [sə'plaɪ] **1** *n (pl* **supplies)** *(stock)* provision *f*; *(act of supplying)* approvisionnement *m*, fourniture *f*; **a week's/month's s. of sth** une provision de qch pour une semaine/un mois; **petrol is in short s.** on manque d'essence; *Econ* **s. and demand** l'offre *f* et la demande; **s. lines** lignes *fpl* de ravitaillement; **s. ship** ravitailleur *m*; **s. teacher** remplaçant(e) *m,f*, suppléant(e) *m,f*
2 *vt (pt & pp* **supplied)** *(provide)* fournir; **to s. sb with sth** fournir qch à qn

support [sə'pɔːt] **1** *n* (**a**) *(backing)* soutien *m*; **to give sb/sth s.** appuyer qn/qch; **in s. of** *(theory, claim)* à l'appui de; *(cause)* en faveur de; **s. band** *(at concert)* première partie *f* (**b**) *(person supporting)* soutien *m*; *(thing supporting)* support *m*
2 *vt* (**a**) *(hold up)* supporter, soutenir; **I supported her with my arm** je lui ai donné le bras pour qu'elle s'appuie dessus (**b**) *(encourage, aid)* soutenir, apporter son soutien à; *(team in sport)* supporter (**c**) *(sustain)* pourvoir aux besoins de; **to s. oneself** subvenir à ses propres besoins

supporter [sə'pɔːtə(r)] *n (of opinion, party, policy)* défenseur *m*, sympathisant(e) *m,f*, *(of team)* supporter *m*

supporting [sə'pɔːtɪŋ] *adj (role)* secondaire; *(actor)* qui a un rôle secondaire; **s. film** film *m* qui passe en première partie; **s. cast** seconds rôles *mpl*

supportive [sə'pɔːtɪv] *adj* d'un grand soutien

suppose [sə'pəʊz] *vt* supposer; **I s. so/not** je suppose que oui/non; **s. or supposing he came back** supposons qu'il revienne; **I don't s. you'd consider sharing it?** je suppose que tu ne veux pas partager?; **s. we change the subject?** et si nous changions de sujet?

supposed [sə'pəʊzd] *adj* (**a**) *(meant)* **to be s. to do sth** être censé(e) faire qch; **there's s. to be a meeting today** il est censé y avoir une réunion aujourd'hui (**b**) *(reputed)* **the film's s. to be very good** il paraît que c'est un très bon film

supposition [sʌpə'zɪʃən] *n* supposition *f*; **on the s. that...** en supposant que...

suppository [sə'pɒzɪtrɪ] *(pl* **suppositories)** *n Med* suppositoire *m*

suppress [sə'pres] *vt (revolt)* réprimer; *(fact, evidence)* faire disparaître; *(emotions)* refouler; *(cough, smile)* réprimer

suppressed [sə'prest] *adj (emotion)* refoulé(e)

suppression [sə'preʃən] *n (of revolt)* répression *f*; *(of fact, evidence)* dissimulation *f*; *(of emotions)* refoulement *m*

suppurate ['sʌpjʊreɪt] *vi* suppurer

supranational [su:prə'næʃənəl] *adj* supranational(e)

supremacy [su:'preməsɪ] *n* suprématie *f*

supreme [su:'pri:m] *adj* suprême; **to make the s. sacrifice** se sacrifier; *Fig* **to reign s.** régner; *Mil* **S. Commander** commandant *m* en chef; *Am Law* **S. Court** Cour *f* suprême

supremely [su:'pri:mlɪ] *adv* suprêmement

supremo [su:'pri:məʊ] *(pl* **supremos**) *n Fam* grand chef *m*

surcharge ['sɜ:tʃɑ:dʒ] **1** *n* supplément *m*
2 *vt* faire payer un supplément à

sure [ʃʊə(r)] **1** *adj* sûr(e); **to be s. of** *or* **about sth** être sûr de qch; **to be s. to do sth** ne pas oublier de faire qch; **to be s. of oneself** être sûr de soi; **to make s. of sth** s'assurer de qch; **to make s. that...** s'assurer que...; **I don't know for s.** je ne suis pas absolument certain(e); **that's for s.** ça, c'est sûr; *Fam* **s. thing!** bien sûr!
2 *adv* **(a)** *Am Fam (really)* **it s. is cold** il fait vachement froid; **are you tired? – I s. am** tu es fatigué? – ça oui **(b)** *(yes)* bien sûr **(c)** **s. enough he was there** il était bien là

surefooted [ʃʊə'fʊtɪd] *adj* **to be s.** avoir le pied sûr

surely ['ʃʊəlɪ] *adv* **(a)** *(certainly)* sûrement; **s. you don't believe that!** tu ne crois quand même pas ça!; **s. not!** c'est pas vrai! **(b)** *(in a sure manner)* **slowly but s.** lentement mais sûrement

surety ['ʃʊərətɪ] *n Law* caution *f*; **to stand s. (for sb)** se porter caution (pour qn)

surf [sɜ:f] **1** *n* surf *m*
2 *vi (go surfing)* faire du surf
3 *vt Comput* **to s. the Net** naviguer sur l'Internet

surface ['sɜ:fɪs] **1** *n* surface *f*; *Fig* **on the s.** en apparence; *Fig* **beneath the s.** au fond; **s. mail** courrier *m* par voie de terre; **s. tension** tension *f* de surface; **s. water** eaux *fpl* de surface
2 *vt (road)* revêtir
3 *vi (from water)* & *Fam Hum (from bed)* faire surface; *Fig (of person, emotion)* réapparaître

surface-to-air missile ['sɜ:fɪstʊ'eə'mɪsaɪl] *n Mil* missile *m* sol-air

surface-to-surface missile ['sɜ:fɪstə'sɜ:fɪs'mɪsaɪl] *n Mil* missile *m* sol-sol

surfboard ['sɜ:fbɔ:d] *n (planche f de)* surf *m*

surfeit ['sɜ:fɪt] *n Formal* surabondance *f*

surfer ['sɜ:fə(r)] *n* surfer *m*

surfing ['sɜ:fɪŋ] *n* surf *m*; **to go s.** aller faire du surf

surge [sɜ:dʒ] **1** *n (of electricity)* surtension *f*; *(of enthusiasm, support, demand)* sursaut *m*; *(of profits)* hausse *f* soudaine; *(of crowd)* ruée *f*
2 *vi (of water, crowd)* déferler; *(of feeling)* monter

surgeon ['sɜ:dʒən] *n* chirurgien *m*

surgery ['sɜ:dʒərɪ] *n* **(a)** *(technique)* chirurgie *f*; *(operation)* intervention *f* chirurgicale; **to perform s. on sb** opérer qn **(b)** *Br (doctor's office)* cabinet *m* (de consultation); *(period)* heures *fpl* de consultation **(c)** *Br (of MP)* permanence *f*

surgical ['sɜ:dʒɪkəl] *adj* chirurgical(e); *Fig* **with s. precision** avec une précision mathématique; **s. instruments** instruments *mpl* de chirurgie; **s. spirit** alcool *m* à 90°; *Mil* **s. strike** frappe *f* chirurgicale

Surinam ['sʊrɪnæm] *n* le Surinam

surly ['sɜ:lɪ] *adj* revêche

surmise [sɜ:'maɪz] *vt* conjecturer

surmount [sɜ:'maʊnt] *vt* surmonter

surname ['sɜ:neɪm] *n* nom *m* de famille

surpass [sɜ:'pɑ:s] *vt (person)* surpasser; *(record)* battre; *(expectation)* dépasser; **to s. oneself** se surpasser

surplice ['sɜ:plɪs] *n Rel* surplis *m*

surplus ['sɜ:pləs] **1** *n* surplus *m*; *Econ (of trade)* excédent *m*
2 *adj (items)* en trop, en surplus; **to be s. to requirements** être en trop

surprise [sə'praɪz] **1** *n* surprise *f*; **to take sb by s.** prendre qn par surprise; **to give sb a s.** faire une surprise à qn; **it was no s.** cela n'a étonné personne
2 *adj (attack, defeat)* surprise *inv*; **s. party** soirée *f* surprise
3 *vt* surprendre, étonner; **I'm not surprised** ça ne m'étonne pas

surprising [sə'praɪzɪŋ] *adj* surprenant(e), étonnant(e)

surprisingly [sə'praɪzɪŋlɪ] *adv* étonnamment; **not s.** comme il fallait s'y attendre; **s. enough,...** chose surprenante...

surreal [sə'rɪəl] *adj (surrealist)* surréaliste; *(strange)* délirant(e)

surrealism [sə'rɪəlɪzəm] *n Art* surréalisme *m*

surrealist [sə'rɪəlɪst] *n* & *adj Art* surréaliste *mf*

surrender [sə'rendə(r)] **1** *n* **(a)** *(of army, weapons)* reddition *f*; **no s.!** nous ne nous rendrons pas! **(b)** *Fin* **s. value** valeur *f* de rachat
2 *vt (town)* livrer; *(right, possessions)* abandonner; *(advantage)* perdre; **to s. control of sth** abandonner la direction de qch
3 *vi* se rendre

surreptitious [sʌrəp'tɪʃəs] *adj* furtif(ive)

surrogate ['sʌrəgət] *n* substitut *m*; **s. mother** mère *f* porteuse

surround [sə'raʊnd] **1** *vt* entourer; *(of police)* cerner
2 *n* encadrement *m*; *Cin, TV* & *Comput* **s. sound** son *m* 3D

surrounding [sə'raʊndɪŋ] *adj* environnant(e)

surroundings [sə'raʊndɪŋz] *npl* environnement *m*

surtax ['sɜ:tæks] **1** *n* surtaxe *f*
2 *vt* surtaxer

surveillance [sə'veɪləns] *n* surveillance *f*; **under s.** sous surveillance

survey 1 *n* ['sɜ:veɪ] **(a)** *(look at)* contempler **(b)** *(of subject, situation)* étude *f*; *(of opinions)* sondage *m* **(b)** *(of house)* expertise *f*; *(of land)* relevé *m*
2 *vt* [sə'veɪ] **(a)** *(look at)* contempler **(b)** *(subject, situation)* étudier, examiner **(c)** *(house)* faire l'expertise de; *(land)* faire un relevé de

surveying [sɜ:'veɪɪŋ] *n (of house)* expertise *f*; *(of land)* relevé *m*

surveyor [sə'veɪə(r)] *n (of building)* expert *m*; *(of land)* géomètre *mf*

survival [sə'vaɪvəl] *n* **(a)** *(continued existence)* survie *f*; *also Fig* **the s. of the fittest** la survie du plus apte; **s. kit** équipement *m* de survie **(b)** *(relic)* vestige *m*

survive [sə'vaɪv] **1** *vt (of person)* survivre à; *(of object)* résister à; **he is survived by a wife and son** il laisse

une épouse et un fils
2 *vi* survivre

surviving [sə'vaɪvɪŋ] *adj (person)* survivant(e); *(remains, copy)* restant(e)

survivor [sə'vaɪvə(r)] *n* survivant(e) *m,f*

susceptible [sə'septɪbəl] *adj* sensible (**to** à)

suspect 1 *n* ['sʌspekt] suspect(e) *m,f*
2 *adj* ['sʌspekt] suspect(e)
3 *vt* [sə'spekt] (**a**) *(person)* soupçonner (**b**) *(have intuition of)* se douter de; **to s. the truth** soupçonner la vérité (**c**) *(consider likely)* croire

suspend [sə'spend] *vt* (**a**) *(hang)* suspendre (**from** à) (**b**) *(service, employee, player)* suspendre; *(pupil)* renvoyer temporairement

suspended [sə'spendɪd] *adj* suspendu(e); **in s. animation** en hibernation; *Law* **s. sentence** condamnation *f* avec sursis

suspender [sə'spendə(r)] *n* (**a**) *Br (for stocking)* jarretelle *f*; *(for sock)* fixe-chaussette *m*; **s. belt** porte-jarretelles *m inv* (**b**) *Am* **suspenders** *(braces)* bretelles *fpl*

suspense [sə'spens] *n (uncertainty)* incertitude *f*; *(in film)* suspense *m*; **to keep sb in s.** tenir qn en haleine

suspension [sə'spenʃən] *n* (**a**) *(of car)* suspension *f*; **s. bridge** pont *m* suspendu (**b**) *(of service, employee)* suspension *f*; *(of pupil)* renvoi *m*

suspicion [sə'spɪʃən] *n* (**a**) *(belief of guilt)* soupçon *m*; **to be under s.** être soupçonné(e); **to be above s.** être au-dessus de tout soupçon; **to have one's suspicions about sb/sth** avoir des doutes sur qn/qch; **to arouse s.** éveiller les soupçons (**b**) *(small amount)* soupçon *m*

suspicious [sə'spɪʃəs] *adj (arousing suspicions)* suspect(e); *(having suspicions)* méfiant(e) (**of** *or* **about** à l'égard de); **to make sb s.** éveiller les soupçons de qn

suspiciously [sə'spɪʃəslɪ] *adv (behave)* d'une manière suspecte; *(ask)* avec méfiance; *Fam* **it looks s. like...** ça ressemble étrangement à...

▸**suss out** [sʌs] *vt sep Br Fam* piger; *(person)* cerner

sustain [sə'steɪn] *vt* (**a**) *(maintain)* soutenir; *(life)* maintenir; **a proper breakfast will s. you until lunchtime** un bon petit déjeuner vous permettra de tenir jusqu'à midi; *Law* **objection sustained** objection accordée (**b**) *(loss, attack, damage)* subir; **to s. an injury** être blessé(e)

sustainable [sə'steɪnəbəl] *adj (growth, development)* durable

sustained [sə'steɪnd] *adj* soutenu(e); **s. applause** applaudissements *mpl* prolongés

sustenance ['sʌstɪnəns] *n* subsistance *f*

suture ['suːtʃə(r)] *n* suture *f*

svelte [svelt] *adj* svelte

SW *n* (**a**) *(abbr* **southwest)** SO (**b**) *Rad (abbr* **Short Wave)** OC

swab [swɒb] **1** *n (cotton wool)* tampon *m*
2 *vt (pt & pp* **swabbed)** *(wound)* nettoyer; *(floor)* laver

swag [swæg] *n very Fam (of thief)* butin *m*

swagger ['swægə(r)] **1** *n* démarche *f* balancée et crâneuse
2 *vi (strut)* se pavaner

swallow¹ ['swɒləʊ] **1** *n (of drink)* gorgée *f*; *(of food)* bouchée *f*
2 *vt* (**a**) *(food, drink)* avaler; *Fig (pride, anger)* ravaler; **to s. sth whole** avaler qch tout rond (**b**) *Fam (believe)* gober, avaler

3 *vi* avaler; **to s. hard** *(when nervous, afraid)* avaler sa salive

swallow² *n (bird)* hirondelle *f*; *Prov* **one s. doesn't make a summer** une hirondelle ne fait pas le printemps

▸**swallow up** *vt sep Fig (company, country)* engloutir

swam [swæm] *pt of* **swim**

swamp [swɒmp] **1** *n* marais *m*
2 *vt (flood)* inonder; *Fig* **to be swamped with sth** être submergé(e) de qch

swan [swɒn] **1** *n* cygne *m*; *Fig* **s. song** chant *m* du cygne
2 *vi (pt & pp* **swanned)** *Fam* **to s. in/out/off** arriver/sortir/partir tranquillement

▸**swan about, swan around** *vi Fam* musarder

swank [swæŋk] *Fam* **1** *n (ostentation)* épate *f*; *(ostentatious person)* frimeur(euse) *m,f*
2 *vi* frimer

swanky ['swæŋkɪ] *adj Fam* chic *inv*

swap [swɒp] **1** *n* échange *m*; **to do a s.** faire un échange
2 *vt (pt & pp* **swapped)** **to s. sth for sth** échanger qch contre qch; **to s. places with sb** changer de place avec qn; **to s. insults/ideas** échanger des insultes/idées
3 *vi* échanger

swarm [swɔːm] **1** *n (of bees)* essaim *m*; *(of people)* nuée *f*
2 *vi (of bees)* essaimer; *(of people)* accourir en masse; **to be swarming with** *(of place)* grouiller de

swarthy ['swɔːðɪ] *adj* basané(e)

swashbuckling ['swɒʃbʌklɪŋ] *adj* de cape et d'épée

swastika ['swɒstɪkə] *n* svastika *m*

SWAT [swɒt] *n Am (abbr* **Special Weapons and Tactics) S. team** = groupe d'intervention d'élite de la police américaine

swat [swɒt] *(pt & pp* **swatted)** *vt* écraser

swatch [swɒtʃ] *n* échantillon *m*

swathe [sweɪð] **1** *n (of grass)* andain *m*; *(of material, land)* bande *f*; *Fig* **to cut a s. through sth** *(of fire, storm)* détruire qch sur son passage
2 *vt* envelopper (**in** de)

sway [sweɪ] **1** *n* (**a**) *(movement)* balancement *m* (**b**) *(influence)* influence *f*; **to be under sb's s.** être sous l'influence de qn; **to hold s. over sb/sth** tenir qn/qch sous sa domination
2 *vt (influence)* influencer
3 *vi* se balancer; **to s. from side to side** se balancer d'un côté à l'autre

Swazi ['swɑːzɪ] **1** *n* (**a**) *(person)* Swazi(e) *m,f* (**b**) *(language)* swazi *m*
2 *adj* swazi(e)

Swaziland ['swɑːzɪlænd] *n* le Swaziland

swear [sweə(r)] *(pt* **swore** [swɔː(r)], *pp* **sworn** [swɔːn])
1 *vt (vow)* jurer; **to s. to do sth** jurer de faire qch; *Law* **to s. an oath** prêter serment
2 *vi (use swearwords)* jurer; **to s. at sb** injurier qn

▸**swear by** *vt insep (have confidence in)* se fier à

▸**swear in** *vt sep Law (jury, witness)* faire prêter serment à

swearing ['sweərɪŋ] *n* grossièretés *fpl*

swearword ['sweəwɜːd] *n* juron *m*, mot *m* grossier

sweat [swet] **1** *n* transpiration *f*, sueur *f*; *Fig* **to be in a s. about sth** avoir des sueurs froides à propos de qch; *Fam* **no s.!** pas de problèmes!; **s. gland** glande *f* sudoripare

2 *vt Fam* **to s. buckets** être en nage; *Fig* **to s. blood** suer sang et eau

3 *vi* (**a**) *(perspire)* transpirer, suer; *Fam* **to s. like a pig** suer comme un bœuf (**b**) *Fam Fig (worry)* se faire de la bile; **to make sb s.** laisser mariner qn

sweatband ['swetbænd] *n (on head)* bandeau *m*; *(on wrist)* poignet *m*

sweater ['swetə(r)] *n* pullover *m*, pull *m*

sweatshirt ['swetʃɜːt] *n* sweatshirt *m*

sweatshop ['swetʃɒp] *n* = atelier de confection où l'on exploite le personnel

sweaty ['swetɪ] *adj (person)* en sueur; *(hands)* moite; *(clothes)* imprégné(e) de sueur; *(work)* qui fait transpirer

Swede [swiːd] *n (person)* Suédois(e) *m,f*

swede [swiːd] *n Br (vegetable)* rutabaga *m*

Sweden ['swiːdən] *n* la Suède

Swedish ['swiːdɪʃ] **1** *npl (people)* **the S.** les Suédois *mpl*
   2 *n (language)* suédois *m*
   3 *adj* suédois(e)

sweep [swiːp] **1** *n* (**a**) *(action)* coup *m* de balai; **to give sth a s.** donner un coup de balai à qch; *Fig* **at one s.** d'un seul coup; *Fig* **to make a clean s.** *(win everything)* tout gagner (**b**) *(movement)* **with a s. of the arm** d'un geste large (**c**) *(of land, hills)* étendue *f*; *(of road, river)* courbe *f*
   2 *vt (pt & pp swept* [swept]) (**a**) *(floor, street)* balayer; *(chimney)* ramoner; **to be swept overboard** être emporté(e) par une vague; **the boat was swept out to sea** le bateau a été emporté vers le large (**b**) *(idioms)* **to s. sth under the carpet** tirer le rideau sur qch; **to s. the board** *(in competition)* rafler tous les prix; **the latest craze to s. the country** la dernière folie qui a envahi le pays; *Fig* **he swept her off her feet** elle est tombée follement amoureuse de lui
   3 *vi* (**a**) *(with broom)* balayer (**b**) *(move rapidly)* **to s. in/out** faire une entrée/une sortie majestueuse; **to s. to power** être propulsé(e) au pouvoir; **a wave of nationalism swept through the country** une vague de nationalisme a déferlé sur le pays

▸**sweep aside** *vt sep (opposition, criticism)* écarter

▸**sweep away** *vt sep (building)* emporter; *Fig (obstacle, difficulty)* balayer; *Fig* **to be swept away by sth** *(enthusiasm, passion)* être emporté(e) par qch

▸**sweep up** *vt sep & vi* balayer

sweeper ['swiːpə(r)] *n* (**a**) **(carpet) s.** balai *m* mécanique (**b**) *(footballer)* arrière *mf* volant(e)

sweeping ['swiːpɪŋ] *adj (gesture)* large; *(statement)* généralisateur(trice); *(change, proposal)* radical(e)

sweepstake ['swiːpsteɪk] *n* sweepstake *m*

sweet [swiːt] **1** *adj* (**a**) *(sugary)* sucré(e); *(wine)* doux (douce); **to taste s.** avoir un goût sucré; **as s. as honey** doux comme le miel; **to have a s. tooth** aimer les sucreries; **s. pea** pois *m* de senteur; **s. potato** patate *f* douce; **s. william** œillet *m* de poète (**b**) *(smell)* agréable; *(sound)* doux (douce) (**c**) *(pretty, kind)* adorable; **to whisper s. nothings to sb** dire des mots doux à qn
   2 *n Br (piece of confectionery)* bonbon *m*; *(dessert)* dessert *m*; **s. shop** confiserie *f*

sweetbreads ['swiːtbredz] *npl* ris *m* *(de veau, d'agneau)*

sweet-and-sour [swiːtən'saʊə(r)] *adj* aigre-doux (aigre-douce)

sweetcorn ['swiːtkɔːn] *n* maïs *m*

sweeten ['swiːtən] *vt (food)* sucrer; *Fig* **to s. sb up** amadouer qn

sweetener ['swiːtənə(r)] *n* (**a**) *(in food)* édulcorant *m* (**b**) *Fam (bribe)* pot-de-vin *m*

sweetheart ['swiːthɑːt] *n (term of address) (to woman)* chérie *f*; *(to man)* chéri *m*

sweetie ['swiːtɪ] *n Fam* (**a**) *Br (piece of confectionery)* bonbon *m* (**b**) *(darling)* chou *m*; **he's such a s.** il est adorable

sweetly ['swiːtlɪ] *adv (sing)* d'une voix douce; *(smile, answer)* gentiment

sweetness ['swiːtnɪs] *n* douceur *f*; **to be all s. and light** être tout sucre tout miel

sweet-talk ['swiːttɔːk] *vt Fam* **to s. sb into doing sth** baratiner qn pour qu'il fasse qch

sweet-tempered [swiːt'tempəd] *adj* doux (douce)

swell [swel] **1** *vt (pp* **swollen** ['swəʊlən] *or* **swelled**) *(numbers, crowd)* gonfler
   2 *vi (of part of body)* enfler; *(of number, crowd)* grossir; *(of sea)* se soulever; **to s. with pride** se gonfler d'orgueil
   3 *n (of sea)* houle *f*
   4 *adj Am Fam (excellent)* super *inv*

▸**swell up** *vi (part of body)* enfler

swelling ['swelɪŋ] *n* gonflement *m*, enflure *f*; **the s. had gone down** ça avait désenflé

sweltering ['sweltərɪŋ] *adj* étouffant(e)

swept [swept] *pt & pp of* **sweep**

swerve [swɜːv] **1** *n (of car)* embardée *f*; *(of player)* écart *m*
   2 *vi (of car, driver)* faire une embardée; *(of player)* faire un écart; *(of ball)* décrire une courbe

swift [swɪft] **1** *n (bird)* martinet *m*
   2 *adj* rapide

swift-footed ['swɪftfʊtɪd] *adj* rapide à la course

swiftly ['swɪftlɪ] *adv* rapidement, vite

swiftness ['swɪftnɪs] *n* rapidité *f*

swig [swɪg] *Fam* **1** *n* lampée *f*; **to take a s. from a bottle** boire un coup à une bouteille
   2 *vt (pt & pp swigged)* boire à grands traits

swill [swɪl] **1** *n (food) (for pigs)* pâtée *f*; *Pej (for people)* nourriture *f* infâme
   2 *vt Fam (drink)* écluser

▸**swill about, swill around** *vi (of liquid)* se répandre

▸**swill out** *vt sep (rinse)* rincer à grande eau

swim [swɪm] **1** *n* **to go for** *or* **have a s.** aller nager
   2 *vt (pt* **swam** [swæm], *pp* **swum** [swʌm]) nager; **to s. the breast stroke** nager la brasse; **to s. the Channel** traverser la Manche à la nage
   3 *vi* (**a**) *(in water)* nager; **to go swimming** aller nager; **to s. across sth** traverser qch à la nage; *Fig* **to s. with the tide** suivre le courant (**b**) *(be dizzy)* **my head is swimming** j'ai la tête qui tourne

swimmer ['swɪmə(r)] *n* nageur(euse) *m,f*

swimming ['swɪmɪŋ] *n* natation *f*; **s. cap** bonnet *m* de bain; *Br* **s. costume** maillot *m* de bain; **s. lesson** cours *m* de natation; **s. pool** piscine *f*; **s. trunks** slip *m* de bain

swimmingly ['swɪmɪŋlɪ] *adv Br Fam* au mieux; **things are going s.** ça baigne

swimsuit ['swɪmsuːt] *n* maillot *m* de bain

swindle ['swɪndəl] **1** *n* escroquerie *f*
   2 *vt* escroquer; **to s. sb out of sth** soutirer qch à qn

swindler ['swɪndlə(r)] *n* escroc *m*

swine [swaɪn] (*pl* **swine**) *n* (**a**) *Lit (pig)* porc *m*; **s. fever** peste *f* porcine (**b**) *Fam (man)* salaud *m*; *(woman)* garce *f*

swing [swɪŋ] **1** *n* (**a**) *(movement) (of rope, chain)* balancement *m*; *(in golf)* swing *m*; *Fam* **to take a s. at sb/sth** balancer un coup de poing à qn/qch; **to be in full s.** battre son plein; *Fam* **to go with a s.** *(of party)* swinguer; *(of business)* marcher très bien; *Fam* **to get into the s. of things** se mettre dans le bain; **s. door** porte *f* battante (**b**) *(change) (in opinion)* revirement *m* (**in** de); *(in economy)* fluctuation *f* (**in** de); *(in mood)* saute *f* (**in** de) (**c**) *(in playground)* balançoire *f*; *Fam* **it's swings and roundabouts** ce qu'on gagne d'un côté on le perd de l'autre

2 *vt* (*pt & pp* **swung** [swʌŋ]) *(arms, racquet, axe)* balancer; **to s. one's hips** balancer les hanches; **to s. sb/sth onto one's shoulder** hisser qn/qch sur ses épaules; *Fam* **to s. it so that...** arranger les choses de manière à ce que... + *subjunctive*

3 *vi* (**a**) *(move to and fro)* se balancer; **to s. open** *(of door)* s'ouvrir; **to s. into action** passer à l'action; *Fam* **he should s. for this** *(be hanged)* il mérite d'être pendu; *Fam* **the party was really swinging** la fête battait son plein (**b**) *(change direction)* virer; **to s. round** se retourner

swingeing ['swɪndʒɪŋ] *adj* énorme

swipe [swaɪp] **1** *vt* (**a**) *(through electronic reader)* passer dans un lecteur de cartes (**b**) *Fam (steal)* faucher

2 *vi (hit)* **to s. at** essayer de frapper

3 *n* (**a**) **to take a s. at** *(aim blow at)* essayer de frapper; *Fig (criticize)* s'en prendre à (**b**) *(for electronic reader)* **s. card** badge *m*

swirl [swɜːl] **1** *n (of cream)* spirale *f*; *(of smoke, leaves, dust)* tourbillon *m*

2 *vt* remuer

3 *vi* tourbillonner, tournoyer

swish [swɪʃ] **1** *n (of cane, whip)* sifflement *m*; *(of dress, silk)* froufrou *m*

2 *adj Fam (elegant)* chic *inv*

3 *vt (cane)* faire siffler; **to s. its tail** *(of animal)* remuer la queue

4 *vi (of cane, whip)* siffler; *(of dress, silk)* froufrouter

Swiss [swɪs] **1** *npl* **the S.** *(people)* les Suisses *mpl*

2 *adj* suisse; **S. army knife** couteau *m* suisse; **S. chard** bette *f*; **S. cheese plant** philodendron *m*; **s. roll** roulé *m*

Switch® [swɪtʃ] *n Br* **to pay by S.** ≃ payer par carte bleue®; **S. card** ≃ carte *f* bleue®

switch [swɪtʃ] **1** *n* (**a**) *(electrical)* interrupteur *m* (**b**) *(change)* revirement *m*; **to make a s.** effectuer un changement (**c**) *(stick)* baguette *f*

2 *vt* (**a**) *(change)* **to s. channels/jobs** changer de chaîne/d'emploi; **they switched their attention to...** leur attention s'est portée sur...; **he's been switched to another department** il a été muté dans un autre service (**b**) *(exchange)* échanger

3 *vi (change)* **to s. to** passer à; *Comput* basculer vers

▶**switch off 1** *vt sep (appliance, heating)* éteindre

2 *vi* (**a**) *(of appliance, heating)* s'éteindre (**b**) *Fam (of person)* décrocher

▶**switch on 1** *vt sep (appliance, heating)* allumer

2 *vi (of appliance, heating)* s'allumer

▶**switch over** *vi (change TV channel)* passer sur une autre chaîne; **to s. over to sth** passer à qch

switchback ['swɪtʃbæk] *n* route *f* en lacets

switchboard ['swɪtʃbɔːd] *n* standard *m*; **s. operator** standardiste *mf*

Switzerland ['swɪtsələnd] *n* la Suisse

swivel ['swɪvəl] **1** *n* pivot *m*; **s. chair** chaise *f* pivotante

2 *vi* (*pt & pp* **swivelled**) pivoter

swizz [swɪz] *n Fam* arnaque *f*

swollen ['swəʊlən] **1** *pp of* **swell**

2 *adj* enflé(e)

swoon [swuːn] **1** *n* évanouissement *m*

2 *vi* s'évanouir

swoop [swuːp] **1** *n (of bird, plane)* descente *f* en piqué; *(of police)* descente *f*

2 *vi (of bird, plane)* descendre en piqué; *(of police)* faire une descente

swop = **swap**

sword [sɔːd] *n* épée *f*; **s. dance** danse *f* du sabre

swordfish ['sɔːdfɪʃ] *n* espadon *m*

swore [swɔː(r)] *pt of* **swear**

sworn [swɔːn] **1** *adj* **s. enemy** ennemi(e) *m,f* juré(e)

2 *pp of* **swear**

swot [swɒt] *Br Fam* **1** *n (studious pupil)* bûcheur(euse) *m,f*

2 *vi* (*pt & pp* **swotted**) *(study hard)* bûcher

▶**swot up on** *vt insep Br Fam (subject)* potasser

swum [swʌm] *pp of* **swim**

swung [swʌŋ] *pt & pp of* **swing**

sycamore ['sɪkəmɔː(r)] *n* sycomore *m*

sycophant ['sɪkəfənt] *n* flagorneur(euse) *m,f*

sycophantic [sɪkə'fæntɪk] *adj* flagorneur(euse)

Sydney ['sɪdnɪ] *n* Sydney

syllable ['sɪləbəl] *n* syllabe *f*

syllabus ['sɪləbəs] *n* programme *m*

sylph-like ['sɪlflaɪk] *adj Hum* **a s. woman** une sylphide

symbiotic [sɪmb(a)ɪ'ɒtɪk] *adj* symbiotique

symbol ['sɪmbəl] *n* symbole *m*

symbolic [sɪm'bɒlɪk] *adj* symbolique

symbolism ['sɪmbəlɪzəm] *n Art* symbolisme *m*

symbolist ['sɪmbəlɪst] *n & adj Art* symboliste *mf*

symbolize ['sɪmbəlaɪz] *vt* symboliser

symmetrical [sɪ'metrɪkəl] *adj* symétrique

symmetry ['sɪmɪtrɪ] *n* symétrie *f*

sympathetic [sɪmpə'θetɪk] *adj (understanding)* compéhensif(ive); *(compassionate)* compatissant(e); **to be s. to a proposal/cause** être favorable à une proposition/cause

sympathize ['sɪmpəθaɪz] *vi* (**a**) *(show compassion)* compatir (**with** avec) (**b**) *(show understanding)* **to s. (with sb)** comprendre (qn)

sympathizer ['sɪmpəθaɪzə(r)] *n* sympathisant(e) *m,f*

sympathy ['sɪmpəθɪ] *n* (**a**) *(pity, compassion)* compassion *f*; **to have s. for sb** éprouver de la compassion pour qn; **with deepest s.** avec toutes mes/nos condoléances (**b**) *(understanding, support)* sympathie *f*; **to feel s. for sb** éprouver de la sympathie pour qn; **s. strike** grève *f* de solidarité

symphony ['sɪmfənɪ] *n* symphonie *f*; **s. orchestra** orchestre *m* symphonique

symposium [sɪm'pəʊzɪəm] (*pl* **symposia** [sɪm'pəʊzɪə]) *n* symposium *m*

symptom ['sɪm(p)təm] *n also Fig* symptôme *m*

symptomatic [sɪm(p)tə'mætɪk] *adj* symptomatique

synagogue ['sɪnəgɒg] *n* synagogue *f*

sync, synch [sɪŋk] *n Fam* synchronisation *f*; **in/out of s. (with)** synchrone/pas synchrone (avec)

synchronization [sɪŋkrənaɪ'zeɪʃən] *n* synchronisation *f*

synchronize ['sıŋkrənaız] *vt* synchroniser
syncopation [sıŋkə'peıʃən] *n Mus* syncope *f*
syndicalism ['sındıkəlızəm] *n Pol* syndicalisme *m*
syndicalist ['sındıkəlıst] *n & adj Pol* syndicaliste *mf*
syndicate 1 *n* ['sındıkət] syndicat *m*
    2 *vt* ['sındıkeıt] *Journ* publier simultanément dans plusieurs journaux; **syndicated columnist** journaliste *mf* d'agence
syndrome ['sındrəʊm] *n Fig* syndrôme *m*
synergy ['sınədʒı] *n* synergie *f*
synod ['sınəd] *n Rel* synode *m*
synonym ['sınənım] *n* synonyme *m*
synonymous [sı'nɒnıməs] *adj* synonyme (**with** de)
synopsis [sı'nɒpsıs] (*pl* **synopses** [sı'nɒpsi:z]) *n* résumé *m; (of film)* synopsis *m*
syntax ['sıntæks] *n Ling* syntaxe *f; Comput* **s. error** erreur *f* de syntaxe
synthesis ['sınθısıs] (*pl* **syntheses** ['sınθısi:z]) *n* synthèse *f*
synthesize ['sınθəsaız] *vt* synthétiser
synthesizer ['sınθəsaızə(r)] *n* synthétiseur *m*

synthetic [sın'θetık] **1** *adj* synthétique
    2 *n* **synthetics** synthétique *m*
syphilis ['sıfılıs] *n* syphilis *f*
syphon = siphon
Syria ['sırıə] *n* la Syrie
Syrian ['sırıən] **1** *n* Syrien(enne) *m,f*
    2 *adj* syrien(enne)
syringe [sı'rındʒ] **1** *n* seringue *f*
    2 *vt (ears)* déboucher
syrup ['sırəp] *n* sirop *m*
syrupy ['sırəpı] *adj (smile, music)* sirupeux(euse)
SYSOP ['sısɒp] *n Comput (abbr* **Systems Operator***)* sysop *m,* opérateur *m* système
system ['sıstəm] *n* (**a**) *(structure)* système *m;* **the S.** *(established order)* le système; *Fam* **it was a shock to the s.** ça a été un choc; *Fam* **to get sb out of one's s.** oublier qn; *Fam* **to get sth out of one's s.** se débarrasser de qch (**b**) *Comput* système *m;* **systems analyst** analyste-programmeur(euse) *m,f* (**c**) *(method)* méthode *f*
systematic [sıstə'mætık] *adj* systématique
systematize ['sıstəmətaız] *vt* systématiser

T

T, t¹ [tiː] *n* (**a**) *(letter)* T, t *m inv* (**b**) *(idioms)* **that's you to a T** c'est tout à fait toi; **to suit sb to a T** convenir parfaitement à qn

t² *(abbr* **ton(s)***)* t

TA [tiː'eɪ] *n Br (abbr* **territorial army***)* = armée de réserve, constituée de volontaires

ta [tɑː] *exclam Br Fam* merci!

tab [tæb] *n* (**a**) *(on garment)* étiquette *f*; *Fam* **to keep tabs on sb/sth** avoir qn/qch à l'œil (**b**) *(on typewriter, word processor)* tabulation *f*; **t. (key)** tabulateur *m* (**c**) *Am Fam (for meal, drinks)* addition *f*; *also Fig* **to pick up the t.** payer l'addition (**d**) *(of LSD, ecstasy)* pilule *f*

tabby ['tæbɪ] *n* **t. (cat)** chat *m* tigré

tabernacle ['tæbənækəl] *n (church)* temple *m*; *(on altar)* tabernacle *m*

table ['teɪbəl] **1** *n* (**a**) *(furniture)* table *f*; **to lay** *or* **set the t.** mettre *ou* dresser la table; **to clear the t.** débarrasser la table; **t. lamp** petite lampe *f*; **t. linen** linge *m* de table; **to have good/bad t. manners** bien/mal se tenir à table; **t. mat** set *m* de table; **t. salt** sel *m* de table; **t. tennis** tennis *m* de table; **t. wine** vin *m* de table (**b**) *(of facts, figures)* tableau *m*, table *f*; **t. of contents** table des matières; **twelve times t.** table de douze (**c**) *(idioms)* **the offer is still on the t.** l'offre tient toujours; **to turn the tables on sb** renverser les rôles
2 *vt* **to t. a motion/proposal** *Br (present)* présenter une motion/une proposition; *Am (postpone)* ajourner une motion/une proposition

tablecloth ['teɪbəlklɒθ] *n* nappe *f*

tablespoon ['teɪbəlspuːn] *n* cuillère *f* à soupe

tablet ['tæblɪt] *n* (**a**) *(pill)* cachet *m* (**b**) *(inscribed stone)* tablette *f* (**c**) *(of soap)* pain *m*

tableware ['teɪbəlweə(r)] *n* vaisselle *f*

tabloid ['tæblɔɪd] *n (newspaper)* tabloïd *m*; **the t. press** la presse populaire

---

Tabloids

Dans les pays anglo-saxons, le format tabloïde est caractéristique des journaux populaires. En Grande-Bretagne, les plus connus sont le 'Sun', le 'Daily Mirror', le 'Daily Mail' et le 'Daily Express'. Ces journaux sont très influents en Grande-Bretagne – le 'Sun' affiche ainsi les plus grands tirages de la presse britannique. Les "tabloids" privilégient tout particulièrement les histoires à scandale et à sensation, ce qui a suscité un débat sur le code de conduite de la presse et sur la législation à mettre en place pour protéger la vie privée.

---

taboo [tə'buː] **1** *n (pl* **taboos***)* tabou *m*
2 *adj* tabou(e)

tabular ['tæbjʊlə(r)] *adj* **in t. form** sous forme de tableau

tabulate ['tæbjʊleɪt] *vt* présenter sous forme de tableau

tachometer [tæk'ɒmɪtə(r)] *n* compte-tours *m*

tacit ['tæsɪt] *adj* tacite

tacitly ['tæsɪtlɪ] *adv* tacitement

taciturn ['tæsɪtɜːn] *adj* taciturne

tack [tæk] **1** *n* (**a**) *(small nail)* clou *m*; *Am (drawing pin)* punaise *f* (**b**) *Naut (course)* bordée *f*; *Fig* **to change t.** changer de tactique
2 *vt* (**a**) *(fasten)* clouer; *Am (with drawing pin)* punaiser; *Fig* **to t. sth on** *(add)* rajouter qch (**b**) *(in sewing)* faufiler
3 *vi Naut* louvoyer

tackle ['tækəl] **1** *n* (**a**) *(equipment)* matériel *m*, équipement *m* (**b**) *(in football)* tacle *m*; *(in rugby)* placage *m*
2 *vt* (**a**) *(deal with) (problem)* s'attaquer à; *(subject)* aborder; **to t. sb about sth** *(confront)* confronter qn à propos de qch (**b**) *(in football)* tacler; *(in rugby)* plaquer

tacky ['tækɪ] *adj* (**a**) *(sticky)* collant(e) (**b**) *Fam Pej (tasteless)* de mauvais goût; *(person)* vulgaire

tact [tækt] *n* tact *m*

tactful ['tæktfʊl] *adj (person)* qui a du tact; *(answer, remark)* diplomatique

tactic ['tæktɪk] *n* tactique *f*

tactical ['tæktɪkəl] *adj* tactique; *Pol* **t. voting** vote *m* utile

tactician [tæk'tɪʃən] *n* tacticien(enne) *m,f*

tactile ['tæktaɪl] *adj* tactile

tactless ['tæktlɪs] *adj* dépourvu(e) de tact

tactlessly ['tæktlɪslɪ] *adv* sans tact

tad [tæd] *n Fam* **a t.** un tantinet, un peu

tadpole ['tædpəʊl] *n* têtard *m*

Tadzhikistan [tædʒɪkɪ'stɑːn] *n* le Tadjikistan

taffeta ['tæfɪtə] *n* taffetas *m*

tag [tæg] **1** *n* (**a**) *(label)* étiquette *f*; *Gram* **t. question** tag *m* (**b**) *(game)* **to play t.** jouer à chat
2 *vt (pt & pp* **tagged***) (label)* étiqueter

▸**tag along** *vi* **she always tags along** elle me/le/*etc* suit partout; **to t. along with sb** venir avec qn

▸**tag on** *vt sep* **to t. sth on** rajouter qch

Tagus ['teɪgəs] *n* **the T.** le Tage

Tahiti [tə'hiːtɪ] *n* Tahiti *f*

Tahitian [tə'hiːʃən] **1** *n* Tahitien(enne) *m,f*
2 *adj* tahitien(enne)

tail [teɪl] **1** *n* (**a**) *(of animal, plane)* queue *f*; *(of shirt)* pan *m*; **heads or tails?** *(when tossing coin)* pile ou face?; **tails, t. coat** queue-de-pie *f*; **t. end** *(last part)* fin *f*; *Am Aut* **t. light** feu *m* arrière (**b**) *(idioms)* **with one's t. between one's legs** la queue entre les jambes; *Fam* **to put a t. on sb** prendre qn en filature; *Fam* **to turn t.** tourner les talons

2 *vt Fam (follow)* filer

▶**tail away, tail off** *vi* décliner; *(of voice)* baisser

tailback ['teɪlbæk] *n (traffic jam)* bouchon *m*

tailboard ['teɪlbɔːd], *Am* **tailgate** ['teɪlgeɪt] *n* hayon *m*

tailor ['teɪlə(r)] **1** *n* tailleur *m*; **t.'s dummy** mannequin *m*; **t.'s shop** atelier *m* de tailleur

2 *vt (suit)* faire; *Fig (speech, policy)* adapter (**to** à)

tailored ['teɪləd] *adj* ajusté(e)

tailor-made ['teɪləmeɪd] *adj also Fig* fait(e) sur mesure

tailplane ['teɪlpleɪn] *n Aviat* stabilisateur *m*

tailspin ['teɪlspɪn] *n Aviat* descente *f* en vrille; **to go into a t.** descendre en vrille; *Fig* paniquer

tailwind ['teɪlwɪnd] *n* vent *m* arrière

taint [teɪnt] **1** *n* contamination *f*; *Fig* tare *f*

2 *vt (contaminate)* contaminer; *Fig* souiller

Taiwan [taɪ'wɑːn] *n* Taiwan

Taiwanese [taɪwə'niːz] **1** *n* Taiwanais(e) *m,f*

2 *adj* taiwanais(e)

Tajikistan = **Tadzhikistan**

take [teɪk] **1** *vt (pt* took [tʊk], *pp* taken ['teɪkən]) (**a**) *(grasp)* prendre; **to t. hold of** prendre *ou* saisir; **to t. sb by the arm** prendre qn par le bras; **to t. sb in one's arms** prendre qn dans ses bras; **to t. the opportunity to do sth** profiter de l'occasion pour faire qch

(**b**) *(remove)* prendre; **to t. sth away from sb** prendre qch à qn; **to t. sth out of sth** prendre qch dans qch

(**c**) *(tolerate)* supporter; **he can't t. a joke** il prend mal la plaisanterie; **I can't t. (it) any more** je n'en peux plus

(**d**) *(lead, carry)* amener; **to t. sb home/to the station** conduire qn chez lui/à la gare; **to t. sb to court** faire un procès à qn; **to t. the dog for a walk** aller promener le chien; **her job takes her all over the world** son travail l'amène à voyager dans le monde entier; **if you can get the money we'll t. it from there** quand tu auras l'argent on verra comment on procède

(**e**) *(go by) (bus, road, turning)* prendre

(**f**) *(require)* prendre; **it takes courage (to do)** il faut du courage (pour faire); **how long does it t.?** combien de temps cela prend-il?; **it took me an hour to get here** il m'a fallu une heure pour venir; **that will t. a lot of explaining** ça ne va pas être facile de se faire pardonner

(**g**) *(adopt) (precautions, measures)* prendre; **to t. legal advice** consulter un avocat; **to t. sth as an example** prendre qch comme exemple

(**h**) *(record) (temperature, notes)* prendre

(**i**) *(capture) (power, town, chess piece)* prendre; **to t. first prize** remporter le premier prix

(**j**) *(assume)* **I t. it (that)...** je suppose que...

(**k**) *(accept) (cheque, credit card)* accepter; **my car only takes unleaded** ma voiture ne marche qu'à l'essence sans plomb; **t. it or leave it!** c'est à prendre ou à laisser!; **to t. sth well/badly** prendre bien/mal qch; **to t. sth the wrong way** mal comprendre qch; **how much** *or* **what will you t. for it?** combien est-ce que tu en veux?; **you can t. it from me that...** je peux te garantir que...

(**l**) *(contain)* avoir une capacité de

(**m**) *(subject)* faire; *(course)* suivre; *(exam)* passer; **he takes them for English** il leur enseigne l'anglais

(**n**) *(in phrases)* **to t. a bath** prendre un bain; **to t. drugs** se droguer; **to t. fright** prendre peur; **to be taken ill** tomber malade; **to t. a look at sth** jeter un coup d'œil à qch; **to t. a photograph of sb/sth** prendre qn/qch en photo; **to t. a seat** s'asseoir; **to t. a walk** se promener

2 *vi (be successful) (of fire, plant cutting, dye)* prendre

3 *n* (**a**) *(of film, music)* prise *f*

(**b**) *(money)* recette *f*; *Fam* **to be on the t.** toucher des pots-de-vin

▶**take after** *vt insep* ressembler à

▶**take apart** *vt (machine, engine)* démonter; *(argument)* démolir

▶**take away 1** *vt sep (remove)* enlever, retirer; *(deduct)* ôter; **to t. sth away from sb** enlever qch à qn; *Br* **sandwiches to t. away** sandwichs à emporter

2 *vi* **to t. away from the pleasure/value of sth** diminuer le plaisir/la valeur de qch

▶**take back** *vt sep* (**a**) *(return)* ramener, rapporter; **that takes me back to my childhood** cela me rappelle mon enfance (**b**) *(accept)* reprendre (**c**) *(withdraw)* retirer; **t. that back!** retire ce que tu viens de dire!

▶**take down** *vt sep* (**a**) *(remove) (from shelf)* prendre; *(downstairs)* descendre; *(poster, decorations)* enlever (**b**) *(lower)* baisser; *Fam* **to t. sb down a peg or two** remettre qn à sa place (**c**) *(dismantle) (tent, scaffolding)* démonter; *(wall, barricade)* démolir (**d**) *(record)* noter; *(notes)* prendre

▶**take for** *vt insep* **to t. sb for somebody else** prendre qn pour quelqu'un d'autre; **what do you t. me for?** pour qui est-ce que tu me prends?

▶**take in** *vt sep* (**a**) *(lead, carry) (person)* faire entrer; *(harvest)* rentrer (**b**) *(orphan)* recueillir; *(lodger)* prendre (**c**) *(garment)* reprendre (**d**) *(include)* inclure, comprendre (**e**) *(understand)* saisir (**f**) *(deceive)* tromper, rouler

▶**take off 1** *vt sep* (**a**) *(remove)* enlever; **to t. sth off sb's hands** retirer qch des mains de qn; **to t. years off sb** *(of clothes, diet)* rajeunir qn; **he took £10 off (the price)** il a baissé (le prix) de 10 livres; **he never took his eyes off us** il ne nous a pas quittés des yeux (**b**) *(lead) (person)* emmener; **to t. oneself off** s'en aller (**c**) *(mimic)* imiter

2 *vi* (**a**) *(of plane)* décoller (**b**) *Fam (of person)* se casser

(**c**) *Fam (succeed)* prendre

▶**take on** *vt sep* (**a**) *(task, responsibility)* assumer; *(problem)* s'occuper de; *(opponent)* défier; *(fuel, supplies)* prendre (**b**) *(employ)* embaucher (**c**) *(acquire)* prendre

▶**take out** *vt sep* (**a**) *(remove)* sortir; *Fam* **to t. it** *or* **a lot out of sb** épuiser qn; **to t. it out on sb** passer sa colère sur qn (**b**) *(person)* inviter (à sortir) (**c**) *(obtain) (licence)* obtenir; *(insurance policy)* souscrire; *(subscription)* prendre

▶**take over 1** *vt sep* (**a**) *(become responsible for) (job, business)* reprendre (**b**) *(take control of) (place)* envahir; *(company)* racheter

2 *vi* (**a**) *(assume power)* prendre le pouvoir (**b**) *(relieve)* prendre la relève (**from** de)

▶**take to** *vt insep* (**a**) *(go to)* **to t. to one's heels** prendre ses jambes à son cou; **to t. to one's bed** s'aliter; **to t. to the hills** se réfugier dans les collines (**b**) *(adopt habit)* **to t. to doing sth** se mettre à faire qch (**c**) *(like)* **to t. to sb** se prendre de sympathie pour qn; **to t. to sth** prendre goût à qch

▶**take up 1** *vt sep* (**a**) *(carry)* monter
(**b**) *(lead) (person)* faire monter
(**c**) *(lift)* enlever
(**d**) *(shorten) (skirt, hem)* raccourcir
(**e**) *(challenge)* relever; *(offer, suggestion)* accepter; **to t. sb up on an offer** accepter l'offre de qn
(**f**) *(subject, problem)* parler de (**with sb** avec qn)
(**g**) *(assume) (position, post)* prendre
(**h**) *(hobby, studies)* se mettre à; **we t. up the story just after...** nous reprenons l'histoire juste après...
(**i**) *(space, time)* prendre
2 *vi* **to t. up with sb** se lier avec qn

▶**take upon** *vt sep* **to t. it upon oneself to do sth** prendre sur soi de faire qch

takeaway ['teɪkəweɪ] *Br* **1** *n (food)* plat *m* à emporter; *(restaurant)* restaurant *m* qui fait des plats à emporter
2 *adj (food)* à emporter

take-home pay ['teɪkhəʊmpeɪ] *n* salaire *m* net

taken ['teɪkən] **1** *adj* (**a**) *(occupied)* pris(e) (**b**) *(impressed)* **I was very t. with him** il m'a fait très bonne impression
2 *pp of* take

takeoff ['teɪkɒf] *n* (**a**) *(imitation)* imitation *f*; **to do a t. of sb** imiter qn (**b**) *(of plane)* décollage *m*

takeover ['teɪkəʊvə(r)] *n* (**a**) *Com (of company)* rachat *m*; **t. bid** offre *f* publique d'achat (**b**) *(of government, country)* prise *f* de pouvoir

taker ['teɪkə(r)] *n (buyer)* acheteur(euse) *m,f*, preneur(euse) *m,f*; **there were no takers** personne n'en voulait; **any takers?** *(for food)* y a-t-il des amateurs?

taking ['teɪkɪŋ] *n* (**a**) **it's yours for the t.** tu n'as plus qu'à accepter (**b**) *Com* **takings** recette *f*

talc [tælk] *n* talc *m*

talcum powder ['tælkəmpaʊdə(r)] *n* talc *m*

tale [teɪl] *n* (**a**) *(story)* histoire *f*; *(legend)* conte *m*; **to live to tell the t.** survivre (**b**) *(lie)* histoire *f*, salades *fpl* (**c**) **to tell tales (on sb)** moucharder (qn)

talent ['tælənt] *n* (**a**) *(person, ability)* talent *m*; **t. scout** *or* **spotter** dénicheur(euse) *m,f* de talents (**b**) *Br Fam (attractive women)* belles nanas *fpl*; *(attractive men)* beaux mecs *mpl*

talented ['tæləntɪd] *adj* talentueux(euse)

talisman ['tælɪzmən] *n* talisman *m*

talk [tɔːk] **1** *n* (**a**) *(conversation)* conversation *f*; **to have a t. with sb** parler *ou* s'entretenir avec qn; *Fam* **to be all t. (and no action)** parler beaucoup (et ne pas faire grand-chose); **t. show** *(on TV, radio)* talk-show *m*
(**b**) **talks** *(negotiations)* pourparlers *mpl*
(**c**) *(gossip)* **there is some t. of him resigning** le bruit court qu'il va démissionner; **it's the t. of the town** on ne parle que de cela
(**d**) *(lecture)* intervention *f*
2 *vt (speak)* parler; **to t. nonsense** dire des bêtises; **to t. business/politics** parler business/politique; **to t. sense** tenir des propos sensés; **to t. (some) sense into sb** faire entendre raison à qn; **she can t. her way out of anything** avec son bagou elle arrive toujours à se tirer d'affaire; **to t. sb into/out of doing sth** convaincre/dissuader qn de faire qch
3 *vi* (**a**) *(speak)* parler (**to/about** à/de); **to t. to oneself** parler tout(e) seul(e); **talking of embarrassing situations,...** à propos de situations embarrassantes,...; *Fam* **now you're talking!** voilà qui est mieux!; *Fam* **YOU can t.!, look who's talking!** tu peux parler!

(**b**) *(gossip)* cancaner, jaser
(**c**) *(give lecture)* faire une intervention (**on** sur)

▶**talk back** *vi* répondre avec insolence

▶**talk down to** *vt insep* **to t. down to sb** parler à qn sur un ton de supériorité

▶**talk over** *vt sep* discuter

talkative ['tɔːkətɪv] *adj* bavard(e)

talker ['tɔːkə(r)] *n* **he was never much of a t.** il n'a jamais été très bavard

talking ['tɔːkɪŋ] *adj* **t. book** livre *m* enregistré; **t. point** sujet *m* de conversation; *Fam* **t. shop** = organisation où l'on parle beaucoup mais où l'on agit peu

talking-to ['tɔːkɪŋtuː] *n Fam* savon *m*; **to give sb a t.** passer un savon à qn

tall [tɔːl] **1** *adj (person)* grand(e); *(building)* haut(e); **how t. are you?** combien est-ce que tu mesures?; **to be 2 metres t.** *(of person)* mesurer 2 mètres; *(of object)* faire 2 mètres de haut; *Fig* **that's a t. order** c'est beaucoup demander; *Fig* **a t. story** une histoire invraisemblable
2 *adv* **to walk** *or* **stand t.** marcher la tête haute

tallboy ['tɔːlbɔɪ] *n* commode *f* haute

Tallin(n) ['tælɪn] *n* Tallinn

tallow ['tæləʊ] *n* suif *m*

tally ['tælɪ] **1** *n* compte *m*; **to keep a t. of sth** tenir le compte de qch
2 *vi (of figure, report)* concorder

talon ['tælən] *n* serre *f*

tamarind ['tæmərɪnd] *n (fruit)* tamarin *m*; *(tree)* tamarinier *m*

tambourine [tæmbə'riːn] *n* tambourin *m*

tame [teɪm] **1** *adj* (**a**) *(not timid or vicious)* familier(-ère); *(domesticated)* apprivoisé(e) (**b**) *(unadventurous)* timide; *(speech, attempt)* mou (molle); *(party, evening)* morne
2 *vt (animal)* apprivoiser; *Fig (emotion)* dominer

tamely ['teɪmlɪ] *adv (say, ask)* timidement; *(accept)* docilement

Tamil ['tæmɪl] **1** *n* (**a**) *(person)* Tamoul(e) *m,f* (**b**) *(language)* tamoul *m*
2 *adj* tamoul(e)

▶**tamper with** ['tæmpə(r)] *vt insep* toucher à; *(lock)* tripoter; *(documents, records)* trafiquer

tampon ['tæmpɒn] *n* tampon *m* (hygiénique)

tan¹ [tæn] *n Math (abbr* **tangent**) tan *f*, tg *f*

tan² **1** *n* (**a**) *(colour)* marron *m* clair (**b**) *(from sun)* bronzage *m*
2 *adj (colour)* marron clair *inv*
3 *vt (pt & pp* **tanned**) (**a**) *(of sun) (skin)* hâler (**b**) *(leather)* tanner; *Fam* **to t. sb, to t. sb's hide** tanner le cuir à qn
4 *vi (of person, skin)* bronzer

tandem ['tændəm] *n* (**a**) *(bicycle)* tandem *m* (**b**) **to do sth in t.** faire qch à deux

tang [tæŋ] *n (taste)* saveur *f* acidulée; *(smell)* odeur *f* acidulée

tangent ['tændʒənt] *n Math* tangente *f*; *Fig* **to go off at a t.** changer de sujet

tangerine [tændʒə'riːn] **1** *n (fruit, colour)* mandarine *f*
2 *adj (colour)* mandarine *inv*

tangible ['tændʒɪbəl] *adj* tangible; *Fig (real)* évident(e); *Fin* **t. assets** biens *mpl* corporels

tangibly ['tændʒɪblɪ] *adv* manifestement

Tangier [tæn'dʒɪə(r)], **Tangiers** [tæn'dʒɪəz] *n* Tanger

tangle ['tæŋgəl] **1** *n* enchevêtrement *m*; **to be in a t.** être emmêlé(e); *Fig (of person, figures, accounts)* être embrouillé(e); **to get into a t.** s'emmêler; *Fig (of person, figures, accounts)* s'embrouiller

2 *vt* **to get tangled up in sth** se prendre dans qch; *Fig* se retrouver mêlé(e) à qch

▸**tangle with** *vt insep Fam* s'en prendre à

tangled ['tæŋgəld] *adj* emmêlé(e); *Fig* embrouillé(e)

tango ['tæŋgəʊ] **1** *n (pl* **tangos)** *(dance)* tango *m*

2 *vi* danser le tango; *Fam* **it takes two to t.** chacun a sa part de responsabilité

tangy ['tæŋɪ] *adj* acidulé(e)

tank [tæŋk] *n* (**a**) *(container)* réservoir *m* (**b**) *Mil* tank *m* (**c**) **t. top** *(garment)* débardeur *m* en laine

▸**tank along** *vi Fam* foncer

▸**tank up** *vt sep Br Fam* **to be tanked up** être bourré(e); **to get tanked up** se prendre une biture

tankard ['tæŋkəd] *n* chope *f*

tanker ['tæŋkə(r)] *n (ship)* navire-citerne *m*; *(lorry)* camion-citerne *m*

tanned [tænd] *adj* bronzé(e)

tanner ['tænə(r)] *n* tanneur(euse) *m,f*

tannery ['tænərɪ] *n* tannerie *f*

tannin ['tænɪn] *n* tan(n)in *m*

tannoy® ['tænɔɪ] *n* système *m* de haut-parleurs; **over the t.** au haut-parleur

tantalize ['tæntəlaɪz] *vt* allécher (**with** avec)

tantalizing ['tæntəlaɪzɪŋ] *adj (smell)* alléchant(e); *(hint, possibility)* tentant(e)

tantamount ['tæntəmaʊnt] *adj* **t. to** équivalent(e) à

Tantric ['tæntrɪk] *adj* tantrique

tantrum ['tæntrəm] *n* caprice *m*; **to throw a t.** faire un caprice

Tanzania [tænzə'nɪə] *n* la Tanzanie

Tanzanian [tænzə'nɪən] **1** *n* Tanzanien(enne) *m,f*

2 *adj* tanzanien(enne)

tap¹ [tæp] **1** *n* (**a**) *Br (for water, gas)* robinet *m*; **to be on t.** *(of beer)* être à la pression; *Fig (of person, information)* être toujours disponible; **t. water** eau *f* du robinet (**b**) **to put a t. on a phone** mettre un téléphone sur écoute

2 *vt (pt & pp* **tapped)** (**a**) *(tree)* inciser; *(resources)* puiser dans; *Fam* **to t. sb for money** taper de l'argent à qn (**b**) *(phone)* mettre sur écoute

tap² **1** *n* (**a**) *(light blow)* petit coup *m*; *(with hand)* tape *f* (**b**) **t. dancer** danseur(euse) *m,f* de claquettes; **t. dancing** claquettes *fpl*

2 *vt (pt & pp* **tapped)** donner un petit coup à; *(with hand)* donner une tape à

3 *vi* **to t. (at** *or* **on)** frapper doucement (à)

tape [teɪp] **1** *n* (**a**) *(ribbon)* ruban *m*; *(of paper)* bande *f*; **(adhesive** *or Fam* **sticky) t.** ruban *m* adhésif, Scotch® *m*; *Sport* **(finishing) t.** ligne *f* d'arrivée; **t. (measure)** mètre *m* (**b**) *(for recording)* bande *f*; *(cassette)* cassette *f*; **t. deck** platine *f* cassette; **t. recorder** magnétophone *m*; **t. recording** enregistrement *m*

2 *vt* (**a**) *(stick with tape)* scotcher; *Fig* **to have sb taped** connaître qn comme sa poche; **to have sth taped** avoir compris qch (**b**) *(record)* enregistrer

taper ['teɪpə(r)] **1** *n (candle)* bougie *f* filée

2 *vi* s'effiler; **to t. to a point** se terminer en pointe

▸**taper off** *vi (of object)* s'effiler; *Fig (decrease)* s'amenuiser

tape-record ['teɪprɪkɔːd] *vt* enregistrer

tapestry ['tæpɪstrɪ] *n* tapisserie *f*

tapeworm ['teɪpwɜːm] *n* ver *m* solitaire

tapioca [tæpɪ'əʊkə] *n* tapioca *m*

tapping ['tæpɪŋ] *n (sound)* petits coups *mpl*

tar [tɑː(r)] **1** *n* (**a**) *(substance)* goudron *m* (**b**) *Fam Old-fashioned (sailor)* matelot *m*

2 *vt (pt & pp* **tarred)** goudronner; **to t. and feather sb** rouler qn dans le goudron et les plumes; *Fig* **we've been tarred with the same brush** on nous a mis dans le même sac

tarantula [tə'ræntjʊlə] *n* tarantule *f*

tardily ['tɑːdɪlɪ] *adv Formal (late)* tardivement; *(slowly)* lentement

tardy ['tɑːdɪ] *adj Formal (late)* tardif(ive); *(slow)* lent(e)

target ['tɑːgɪt] **1** *n* (**a**) *(of bullet, missile, joke)* cible *f*; **t. language** *(in translating)* langue *f* d'arrivée; **t. practice** exercices *mpl* de tir (**b**) *Fig (goal)* objectif *m*; **to set oneself a t.** se fixer un objectif; **to be on t. (to do sth)** être dans les temps (pour faire qch); **t. audience** type *m* d'écoute ciblé; **t. market** marché *m* ciblé

2 *vt* (**a**) *(aim)* **to t. sth at sth** *(missile)* diriger qch vers qch; *Fig (campaign, TV programme, benefits)* destiner qch à qch (**b**) *also Fig (aim at)* viser

tariff ['tærɪf] *n (tax)* tarif *m*, droit *m* de douane; *(price list)* tarif; **t. barrier** barrière *f* douanière

tarmac® ['tɑːmæk] **1** *n* macadam *m*; **the t.** *(runway)* le tarmac

2 *vt (pt & pp* **tarmacked)** goudronner

tarnish ['tɑːnɪʃ] **1** *vt also Fig* ternir

2 *vi* se ternir

tarot ['tærəʊ] *n* tarot *m*; **t. card** carte *f* de tarot

tarpaulin [tɑː'pɔːlɪn] *n* bâche *f*

tarragon ['tærəgən] *n* estragon *m*

tart [tɑːt] **1** *n* (**a**) *(cake) (large)* tarte *f*; *(small)* tartelette *f* (**b**) *Br Fam Pej (promiscuous woman, prostitute)* pute *f*

2 *adj* (**a**) *(in taste)* âpre (**b**) *(tone, remark)* aigrelet(ette)

▸**tart up** *vt sep Fam (room, pub)* retaper; **to t. oneself up** se faire une beauté

tartan ['tɑːtən] *n* tartan *m*, écossais *m*; **t. tie/jacket** cravate *f*/veste *f* écossaise

Tartar ['tɑːtə(r)] *n* Tatar(e) *m,f*

tartar ['tɑːtə(r)] *n (on teeth)* tartre *m*

tartar(e) sauce ['tɑːtə'sɔːs] *n* sauce *f* tartare

tartly ['tɑːtlɪ] *adv* avec aigreur

task [tɑːsk] *n* tâche *f*; **to take sb to t. for sth/for doing sth** reprocher qch à qn/à qn d'avoir fait qch

taskforce ['tɑːskfɔːs] *n Mil* corps *m* expéditionnaire; *Fig* commission *f*

taskmaster ['tɑːskmɑːstə(r)] *n* **to be a hard t.** être très exigeant(e)

Tasmania [tæz'meɪnɪə] *n* la Tasmanie

Tasmanian [tæz'meɪnɪən] **1** *n* Tasmanien(enne) *m,f*

2 *adj* tasmanien(enne)

Tasman Sea ['tæzmən'siː] *n* **the T.** la mer de Tasman

tassel ['tæsəl] *n* gland *m*

taste [teɪst] **1** *n* (**a**) *(flavour, sense)* goût *m*; **t. bud** papille *f* gustative (**b**) *(sample) also Fig* **to have a t. of sth** goûter à qch; **a t. of things to come** un avant-goût des choses à venir; **to give sb a t. of his own medicine** rendre la pareille à qn (**c**) *(liking)* goût *m* (**for** pour); **to acquire** *or* **develop a t. for sth** prendre goût à qch; **add sugar to t.** ajouter du sucre à volonté; **violent films are not to my t.** les films violents ne me plaisent pas (**d**) *(judgement)* goût *m*; **in good/bad** *or* **poor t.** de bon/mauvais goût

2 *vt* (**a**) *(detect flavour of)* sentir (le goût de) (**b**) *(sample)* goûter; *Fig (happiness, success)* goûter à

3 *vi* **to t. of** *or* **like sth** avoir un goût de qch; **to t. good/bad** être bon (bonne)/mauvais(e)

tasteful ['teɪstfʊl] *adj* de bon goût

tastefully ['teɪstfəlɪ] *adv* avec goût

tasteless ['teɪstlɪs] *adj* (**a**) *(food)* insipide (**b**) *(remark, clothes)* de mauvais goût

taster ['teɪstə(r)] *n* (**a**) *(person)* goûteur(euse) *m,f* (**b**) *(foretaste)* avant-goût *m*

tasty ['teɪstɪ] *adj* (**a**) *(food)* savoureux(euse) (**b**) *Fam (attractive)* bien foutu(e)

tat [tæt] *n Fam* camelote *f*

ta-ta [tæ'tɑː] *exclam Br Fam* au revoir!

tatters ['tætəz] *npl also Fig* **in t.** en lambeaux

tattered ['tætəd] *adj* déguenillé(e)

tattle ['tætəl] **1** *n* potins *mpl*, commérages *mpl*
2 *vi* commérer

tattoo¹ [tə'tuː] *n* (**a**) *(on drum)* retraite *f* du soir (**b**) *(military show)* parade *f* militaire

tattoo² **1** *n (design)* tatouage *m*
2 *vt* tatouer

tatty ['tætɪ] *adj Br Fam* minable

taught [tɔːt] *pt & pp of* **teach**

taunt [tɔːnt] **1** *n (words)* raillerie *f*
2 *vt* railler

Taurus ['tɔːrəs] *n* le Taureau; **to be (a) T.** être Taureau

taut [tɔːt] *adj* tendu(e)

tauten ['tɔːtən] **1** *vt* tendre
2 *vi* se tendre

tautness ['tɔːtnɪs] *n* tension *f*

tautological [tɔːtə'lɒdʒɪkəl] *adj* tautologique

tautology [tɔː'tɒlədʒɪ] *n* tautologie *f*

tavern ['tævən] *n* taverne *f*

tawdry ['tɔːdrɪ] *adj* (**a**) *(conduct, motive)* lâche (**b**) *(decor, jewellery)* tape-à-l'œil *inv*

tawny ['tɔːnɪ] *adj* fauve; **t. owl** chouette *f* hulotte

tax [tæks] **1** *n* impôt *m*, taxe *f*; **t. allowance** abattement *m* fiscal; **t. avoidance** = moyen (légal) pour payer moins d'impôts; **t. bracket** tranche *f* d'imposition; **t. break** allègement *m* fiscal; **t. collector** percepteur(-trice) *m,f*; **t. cut** réduction *f* d'impôt; *Br* **t. disc** ≃ vignette *f* automobile; **t. evasion** évasion *f* fiscale; **t. exile** = personne vivant à l'étranger pour échapper au fisc; **t. haven** paradis *m* fiscal; **t. incentive** incitation *f* fiscale; **t. inspector** inspecteur(trice) *m,f* des impôts; **t. relief** dégrèvement *m* fiscal; **t. return** déclaration *f* d'impôt
2 *vt* (**a**) *(subject to tax)* imposer, frapper d'un impôt (**b**) *(put under strain)* mettre à l'épreuve (**c**) *Formal (accuse)* **to t. sb with sth** taxer qn de qch

taxable ['tæksəbl] *adj* imposable

taxation [tæk'seɪʃən] *n* imposition *f*; **an increase in t.** une augmentation des impôts

tax-deductible [tæksdɪ'dʌktɪbəl] *adj* déductible des impôts

tax-free [tæks'friː] *adj* exempt(e) d'impôt

taxi ['tæksɪ] **1** *n* taxi *m*; **t. driver** chauffeur *m* de taxi; **t. rank** station *f* de taxi
2 *vi (of aircraft)* rouler

taxidermist ['tæksɪdɜːmɪst] *n* taxidermiste *mf*

taxing ['tæksɪŋ] *adj* ardu(e)

taxonomy [tæk'sɒnəmɪ] *n* taxonomie *f*

taxpayer ['tækspeɪə(r)] *n* contribuable *mf*

TB [tiː'biː] *n (abbr* **tuberculosis)** tuberculose *f*

T-bone steak [tiːbəʊn'steɪk] *n* côte *f* de bœuf à l'os

te [tiː] *n Mus* si *m*

tea [tiː] *n* (**a**) *(plant, drink)* thé *m*; *(herbal infusion)* tisane *f*; **t. break** ≃ pause-café *f*; **t. caddy** boîte *f* à thé; **t. cosy** couvre-théière *m*; **t. leaves** feuilles *fpl* de thé; **t. party** goûter *m*; **t. set** service *m* à thé; **t. strainer** passoire *f* à thé; **t. towel** torchon *m* (pour la vaisselle); **t. tray** plateau *m* (**b**) *Br (evening meal)* dîner *m*; **(afternoon) t.** thé *m*

Tea

Bien que, dans certains milieux, le thé ait été récemment supplanté par le café, le thé reste en Grande-Bretagne comme en Irlande une boisson extrêmement populaire. Si la tradition de l'"afternoon tea" a largement disparu, de même que les "tea ladies" qui servaient sur le lieu de travail le thé sur une table roulante, les britanniques et les irlandais restent de grands consommateurs de thé.

---

teabag ['tiːbæg] *n* sachet *m* de thé

teach [tiːtʃ] *(pt & pp* **taught** [tɔːt]) **1** *vt* enseigner; **to t. sb sth, to t. sth to sb** enseigner qch à qn; **to t. sb (how) to do sth** apprendre à qn à faire qch; **to t. one-self sth** apprendre qch tout seul; *Am* **to t. school** enseigner; *Fig* **to t. sb a lesson** donner une leçon à qn; *Fam* **that'll t. him!** ça lui apprendra!
2 *vi* enseigner

teacher ['tiːtʃə(r)] *n (at primary school)* instituteur(-trice) *m,f*; *(at secondary school)* professeur *m*, enseignant(e) *m,f*; **t.'s pet** chouchou(te) *m,f* du professeur; **t. training** formation *f* pédagogique; **t. training college** ≃ IUFM *m*

teaching ['tiːtʃɪŋ] *n* (**a**) *(profession, action)* enseignement *m*; **t. hospital** CHU *m*; **t. practice** stage *m* pratique d'enseignement; **t. staff** personnel *m* enseignant (**b**) *(doctrine)* doctrine *f*

teacup ['tiːkʌp] *n* tasse *f* à thé

teak [tiːk] *n* teck *m*

team [tiːm] *n* équipe *f*; **a t. effort** un travail d'équipe; **t. games** jeux *mpl* d'équipe; **t. player** joueur(euse) *m,f* qui a l'esprit d'équipe; **t. spirit** esprit *m* d'équipe

▸**team up** *vi* s'associer (**with** avec)

team-mate ['tiːmmeɪt] *n* coéquipier(ère) *m,f*

teamwork ['tiːmwɜːk] *n* travail *m* d'équipe

teamster ['tiːmstə(r)] *n Am (lorry driver)* routier *m*

teapot ['tiːpɒt] *n* théière *f*

tear¹ [tɪə(r)] *n* larme *f*; **in tears** en larmes; **t. duct** canal *m* lacrymal; **t. gas** gaz *m* lacrymogène

tear² [teə(r)] **1** *vt (pt* **tore** [tɔː(r)], *pp* **torn** [tɔːn]) *(rip)* déchirer; *(snatch)* arracher (**from** à); **to t. sth in two** *or* **in half** déchirer qch en deux; **to t. sth to pieces** déchirer qch en mille morceaux; *Fig* démolir qch; *Fig* **to t. sb to pieces** mettre qn en pièces; **to be torn between two things** se sentir tiraillé(e) entre deux choses; *Fam* **that's torn it!** il ne manquait plus que ça!
2 *vi* (**a**) *(rip)* se déchirer (**b**) **to t. at sth** déchirer qch (**c**) *(move quickly)* **to t. along/past/away** aller/passer/partir à toute vitesse
3 *n* déchirure *f*

▸**tear apart** *vt sep Fig* déchirer

▸**tear away** *vt sep Fig* **to t. oneself away from sth** s'arracher de qch

▸**tear down** *vt sep (building)* démolir; *(statue)* renverser; *(poster)* arracher

▶**tear into** *vt insep* **to t. into sb** *(physically)* se jeter sur qn; *(verbally)* passer un savon à qn

▶**tear off 1** *vt sep (remove)* arracher
2 *vi (run away)* se sauver à toute vitesse

▶**tear out** *vt sep* arracher; *Fig* **to t. one's hair out** s'arracher les cheveux

▶**tear up** *vt sep (document, photo)* déchirer; *(plant)* déraciner; *(floorboards)* enlever

tearaway ['teərəweɪ] *n* casse-cou *m inv*

teardrop ['tɪədrɒp] *n* larme *f*

tearful ['tɪəfʊl] *adj* en larmes; **in a t. voice** avec des larmes dans la voix

tearfully ['tɪəfəlɪ] *adv* en pleurant

tearjerker ['tɪədʒɜːkə(r)] *n Fam (film, book)* **it's a real t.** c'est complètement mélo

tearoom ['tiːruːm] *n* salon *m* de thé

tearstained ['tɪəsteɪnd] *adj* barbouillé(e) de larmes

tease [tiːz] **1** *vt* taquiner (**about** sur *ou* à propos de)
2 *vi* plaisanter
3 *n (person)* taquin(e) *m,f*

▶**tease out** *vt sep* clarifier

teaser ['tiːzə(r)] *n Fam (problem)* colle *f*

teashop ['tiːʃɒp] *n* salon *m* de thé

teasing ['tiːzɪŋ] *n* taquinerie *f*

teaspoon ['tiːspuːn] *n* cuillère *f* à café

teat [tiːt] *n (of animal)* trayon *m; (of feeding bottle)* tétine *f*

teatime ['tiːtaɪm] *n (in the afternoon)* l'heure *f* du thé; *(in the evening)* l'heure *f* du dîner

technical ['teknɪkəl] *adj* technique; *Br* **t. college** ≃ institut *m* universitaire; **t. drawing** *(school subject)* dessin *m* industriel; **t. hitch** incident *m* technique

technicality [teknɪ'kælɪtɪ] *n* détail *m* technique

technically ['teknɪklɪ] *adv* techniquement

technician [tek'nɪʃən] *n* technicien(enne) *m,f*

technique [tek'niːk] *n* technique *f*

techno ['teknəʊ] *n Mus* techno *f*

technological [teknə'lɒdʒɪkəl] *adj* technologique

technology [tek'nɒlədʒɪ] *n* technologie *f*

teddy ['tedɪ] *n* **t. (bear)** ours *m* en peluche

tedious ['tiːdɪəs] *adj* ennuyeux(euse); *(task)* fastidieux(euse)

tedium [tiːdɪəm] *n* ennui *m*

tee [tiː] *n (in golf)* tee *m*

▶**tee off** *vi (in golf)* jouer le départ

teem [tiːm] *vi* (**a**) *(rain)* **to t. (down)** pleuvoir à verse (**b**) **to be teeming with sth** *(insects, ideas)* grouiller de qch

teeming ['tiːmɪŋ] *adj* grouillant(e)

teenage ['tiːneɪdʒ] *adj* adolescent(e)

teenager ['tiːneɪdʒə(r)] *n* adolescent(e) *m,f*

teen ['tiːn] *adj* adolescent(e); **t. idol** idole *f* des jeunes

teens [tiːnz] *npl* adolescence *f;* **to be in one's t.** être adolescent(e)

teensy(-weensy) ['tiːnzɪ('wiːnzɪ)] *adj Fam* tout(e) petit(e)

teeny-bopper ['tiːnɪbɒpə(r)] *n Fam* petite minette *f*

teeny(-weeny) ['tiːnɪ('wiːnɪ)] *adj Fam* tout(e) petit(e)

teeshirt ['tiːʃɜːt] *n* tee-shirt *m*

teeter ['tiːtə(r)] *vi* chanceler; *Fig* **to t. on the brink of sth** être au bord de qch

teeth [tiːθ] *pl of* **tooth**

teethe [tiːð] *vi* **to be teething** faire ses dents

teething ['tiːðɪŋ] *n* poussée *f* dentaire; *Fig* **t. troubles** *(of project)* difficultés *fpl* initiales

teetotal [tiː'təʊtəl] *adj* qui ne boit jamais d'alcool

teetotaller, *Am* **teetotaler** [tiː'təʊtələ(r)] *n* = personne qui ne boit jamais d'alcool

TEFL ['tefəl] *n (abbr* **Teaching of English as a Foreign Language**) enseignement *m* de l'anglais langue étrangère

Teh(e)ran [teə'rɑːn] *n* Téhéran

tel *(abbr* **telephone**) tél

telebanking ['telɪbæŋkɪŋ] *n* monétique *f; (home banking)* banque *f* à domicile

telecommunications [telɪkəmjuːnɪ'keɪʃənz] *npl* télécommunications *fpl*

telecommuting [telɪkə'mjuːtɪŋ] *n* télétravail *m*

teleconference [telɪ'kɒnfərəns] *n* téléconférence *f*

telegenic [telɪ'dʒenɪk] *adj* télégénique

telegram ['telɪgræm] *n* télégramme *m*

telegraph ['telɪgrɑːf] **1** *n* télégraphe *m;* **t. pole/wire** poteau *m*/fil *m* télégraphique
2 *vt* télégraphier

telegraphic [telɪ'græfɪk] *adj* télégraphique

telemarketing [telɪ'mɑːkɪtɪŋ] *n* télémarketing *m*

telepathic [telɪ'pæθɪk] *adj* télépathique

telepathy [tɪ'lepəθɪ] *n* télépathie *f*

telephone ['telɪfəʊn] **1** *n* téléphone *m;* **to be on the t.** *(talking)* être au téléphone; *(have a telephone)* avoir le téléphone; *Com* **t. banking** opérations *fpl* bancaires par téléphone, banque *f* à domicile; **t. bill** facture *f* de téléphone; **t. box** cabine *f* téléphonique; **t. call** appel *m* téléphonique, coup *m* de téléphone; **t. directory** *or* **book** annuaire *m* (téléphonique); **t. exchange** central *m* téléphonique; **t. number** numéro *m* de téléphone
2 *vt* téléphoner à
3 *vi* téléphoner

telephonist [tɪ'lefənɪst] *n Br* téléphoniste *mf*

telephoto lens ['telɪfəʊtəʊlenz] *n* téléobjectif *m*

teleprinter ['telɪprɪntə(r)] *n* téléimprimeur *m*

telesales ['telɪseɪlz] *npl Com* téléventes *fpl*

telescope ['telɪskəʊp] *n* télescope *m*

telescopic [telɪs'kɒpɪk] *adj* télescopique; **t. sight** *(of rifle)* lunette *f*

teleshopping ['telɪʃɒpɪŋ] *n* téléachat *m*

teletext ['telɪtekst] *n* Télétexte® *m*

televangelist [telɪ'vændʒəlɪst] *n* = évangéliste qui prêche à la télévision

televise ['telɪvaɪz] *vt* téléviser

television [telɪ'vɪʒən] *n* télévision *f;* **on t.** à la télévision; **t. camera** caméra *f* de télévision; *Br* **t. licence** redevance *f* télévision; **t. programme** émission *f* de télévision; **t. screen** écran *m* de télévision; **t. set** téléviseur *m*, poste *m* de télévision

telex ['teleks] **1** *n* télex *m*
2 *vt (message)* télexer

tell [tel] *(pt & pp* **told** [təʊld] *)* **1** *vt* (**a**) *(say)* dire; *(story, joke)* raconter; **to t. sb sth, to t. sth to sb** dire qch à qn; **to t. the truth/a lie** dire la vérité/un mensonge; **to t. you the truth, I don't know** je t'avouerai que je ne sais pas; **can you t. me the way to the station?** est-ce que vous pouvez m'indiquer la gare?; **I told you so!** je te l'avais bien dit!; **you're telling me!** à qui le dis-tu!; **let me t. you, I was frightened** laissez-moi te dire que j'ai eu peur!; **to t. the time** *(of clock)* donner l'heure; **to t. sb the time** *(of person)* donner l'heure à qn; **he can't t. the time** il ne sait pas lire l'heure

(**b**) *(discern)* **I could t. he was lying** je savais qu'il mentait; **you can t. she's lived abroad** ça se voit qu'elle a vécu à l'étranger; **there's no telling what she'll do next** qui sait ce qu'elle va inventer maintenant

(**c**) *(distinguish)* **to t. sth from sth** distinguer qch de qch; **to t. two people/things apart** distinguer deux personnes/choses; **to t. right from wrong** discerner le bien du mal; **I can't t. the difference** je ne vois pas la différence

(**d**) *(order)* **to t. sb to do sth** dire à qn de faire qch; **do as you're told!** fais ce qu'on te dit!; **I'm not asking you, I'm telling you!** ce n'est pas une question, c'est un ordre!; **he wouldn't be told** il refusait d'écouter ce qu'on lui disait

(**e**) *Pol (votes)* compter; **all told** au total
2 *vi* (**a**) *(say)* dire; **that would be telling!** je ne veux pas cafarder!

(**b**) *(discern)* dire; **it's difficult** *or* **hard to t.** c'est difficile à dire; **it's too early to t.** il est trop tôt pour se prononcer; **you never can t.** on ne sait jamais

(**c**) *(have effect)* se faire sentir

▶**tell off** *vt sep (scold)* **to t. sb off** disputer qn

▶**tell on** *vt insep Fam (inform on)* dénoncer, balancer

teller ['telə(r)] *n* (**a**) *(of votes)* scrutateur(trice) *m,f* (**b**) *(in bank)* guichetier(ère) *m,f*

telling ['telɪŋ] **1** *n* (**a**) *(of story)* narration *f* (**b**) **t. off** réprimande *f*; **to give sb a t. off** disputer qn
2 *adj* (**a**) *(revealing)* révélateur(trice) (**b**) *(decisive)* qui porte

telltale ['telteɪl] **1** *n (person)* rapporteur(euse) *m,f*
2 *adj (revealing)* révélateur(trice)

telly ['telɪ] *n Br Fam* télé *f*; **on t.** à la télé; **t. addict** accro *mf* de la télé

temerity [tɪ'merɪtɪ] *n* témérité *f*, audace *f*; **to have the t. to do sth** avoir l'audace de faire qch

temp [temp] *Fam* **1** *n* intérimaire *mf*; **to be a t.** faire de l'intérim
2 *vi* faire de l'intérim

temper ['tempə(r)] **1** *n (character)* caractère *m*, tempérament *m*; *(mood)* humeur *f*; *(bad mood)* mauvaise humeur *f*; **to be in a good/bad t.** être de bonne/mauvaise humeur; **to have a short t.** être coléreux(euse); **to lose one's t.** se mettre en colère; **to fly into a t.** piquer une colère; *Fam* **t., t.!** on se calme!; **t. tantrum** caprice *m*
2 *vt* (**a**) *(steel)* tremper (**b**) *(action)* tempérer

temperament ['tempərəmənt] *n* tempérament *m*, caractère *m*

temperamental [tempərə'mentəl] *adj* capricieux(euse)

temperance ['tempərəns] *n* (**a**) *(moderation)* modération *f* (**b**) *(abstinence from alcohol)* tempérance *f*; *Hist* **t. movement** mouvement *m* antialcoolique

temperate ['tempərət] *adj* (**a**) *Geog (climate, zone)* tempéré(e) (**b**) *Formal (language, criticism)* mesuré(e)

temperature ['tempərətʃə(r)] *n* température *f*; **to take sb's t.** prendre la température de qn; **to have a t.** avoir de la température

tempered ['tempəd] *adj (steel)* trempé(e)

tempest ['tempɪst] *n Lit* tempête *f*

tempestuous [tem'pestjʊəs] *adj* tempétueux(euse)

temping ['tempɪŋ] *n* intérim *m*; **to do t.** faire de l'intérim

template ['templeɪt] *n* gabarit *m*; *Comput* modèle *m*

temple¹ ['tempəl] *n (place of worship)* temple *m*

temple² *n (side of head)* tempe *f*

tempo ['tempəʊ] *(pl* **tempos** *or* **tempi** ['tempiː] *) n Mus* tempo *m*

temporal ['tempərəl] *adj* temporel(elle)

temporarily [tempə'reərɪlɪ] *adv* temporairement

temporary ['tempərərɪ] *adj (accommodation, solution)* temporaire, provisoire; *(employment)* temporaire, intérimaire; *(improvement)* passager(ère)

tempt [tem(p)t] *vt* tenter; **to t. sb to do sth** inciter qn à faire qch; **to be tempted to do sth** être tenté(e) de faire qch; **to t. fate** tenter le diable

temptation [tem(p)'teɪʃən] *n* tentation *f*

tempting ['tem(p)tɪŋ] *adj* tentant(e)

temptress ['tem(p)trɪs] *n Lit* tentatrice *f*

ten [ten] **1** *n* (**a**) dix *m inv* (**b**) *(idioms)* **they're t. a penny** on en trouve à la pelle; **t. to one he'll find out** je te parie qu'il finira par le savoir
2 *adj* dix; **the T. Commandments** les dix commandements; *see also* **eight**

tenable ['tenəbəl] *adj* défendable

tenacious [te'neɪʃəs] *adj* tenace

tenacity [te'næsɪtɪ] *n* ténacité *f*

tenancy ['tenənsɪ] *n* location *f*; **t. agreement** bail *m* (de location)

tenant ['tenənt] *n* locataire *mf*

tend¹ [tend] *vt (look after)* s'occuper de

tend² *vi* pencher (**towards** vers); **to t. to do sth** avoir tendance à faire qch

▶**tend to** *vt insep (look after)* s'occuper de

tendency ['tendənsɪ] *n* tendance *f* (**towards** à); **to have a t. to do sth** avoir tendance à faire qch

tendentious [ten'denʃəs] *adj Formal* tendancieux(euse)

tender¹ ['tendə(r)] *n Naut* navette *f*; *Rail* tender *m*

tender² *adj* (**a**) *(affectionate)* tendre (**b**) *(sore)* sensible (**c**) *(meat)* tendre (**d**) *(young)* **at the t. age of...** dès l'âge de...

tender³ **1** *n Com (bid)* offre *f*, soumission *f*; **to make** *or* **put in a t.** soumissionner
2 *vt (services, money)* offrir; *(resignation)* donner; *(apology)* présenter
3 *vi Com* **to t. for a contract** soumissionner à un appel d'offres

tenderhearted [tendə'hɑːtɪd] *adj* au cœur tendre

tenderly ['tendəlɪ] *adv* tendrement

tenderness ['tendənɪs] *n* (**a**) *(affection)* tendresse *f* (**b**) *(soreness)* sensibilité *f* (**c**) *(of meat)* tendreté *f*

tendon ['tendən] *n* tendon *m*

tendril ['tendrɪl] *n* vrille *f*

tenement ['tenɪmənt] *n* immeuble *m*

tenet ['tenət] *n (principle)* dogme *m*; *(belief)* croyance *f*

tenfold ['tenfəʊld] **1** *adj* décuple
2 *adv* dix fois plus; **to increase t.** être multiplié(e) par dix

tenner ['tenə(r)] *n Br Fam (sum)* dix livres *fpl*; *(note)* billet *m* de dix livres

tennis ['tenɪs] *n* tennis *m*; **t. ball** balle *f* de tennis; **t. club** club *m* de tennis; **t. court** court *m* de tennis; **t. elbow** tennis-elbow *m*; **t. player** joueur(euse) *m,f* de tennis; **t. racquet** *or* **racket** raquette *f* de tennis; **t. shoe** (chaussure *f* de) tennis *m ou f*

tenor ['tenə(r)] *n* (**a**) *(singer)* ténor *m*; **t. saxophone** saxophone *m* ténor (**b**) *Formal (content, sense)* teneur *f*

tenpin bowling ['tenpɪn'bəʊlɪŋ] *n* bowling *m (jeu)*

tense¹ [tens] n Gram temps m

tense² 1 adj (cord, person, situation) tendu(e); (voice) étranglé(e); (muscle) contracté(e)
2 vt (cord) tendre; (muscle) contracter; **to t. oneself** se raidir
3 vi se tendre, se raidir

▶**tense up** vi se crisper

tensely ['tenslɪ] adv nerveusement

tension ['tenʃən] n tension f

tent [tent] n tente f; **t. peg** piquet m de tente; **t. pole** mât m de tente

tentacle ['tentəkəl] n tentacule m

tentative ['tentətɪv] adj (hesitant) hésitant(e), timide; (provisional) provisoire

tentatively ['tentətɪvlɪ] adv (hesitantly) timidement; (provisionally) provisoirement

tenterhooks ['tentəhʊks] npl **to be on t.** être sur des charbons ardents; **to keep sb on t.** mettre qn au supplice

tenth [tenθ] 1 n (a) (fraction) dixième m (b) (in series) dixième mf (c) (of month) dix m inv
2 adj dixième; see also **eighth**

tenuous ['tenjʊəs] adj (connection) ténu(e); (comparison) subtil(e); (argument) faible

tenure ['tenjə(r)] n (of land) fermage m; (of office) occupation f; (of university teaching job) titularisation f

tepid ['tepɪd] adj also Fig tiède

tequila [tɪ'kiːlə] n tequila f

term [tɜːm] 1 n (a) (word, expression) terme m; **I told her in no uncertain terms** je le lui ai dit carrément (b) **to be on good/bad terms (with sb)** (relations) être en bons/mauvais termes (avec qn); **to be on friendly terms with sb** avoir des relations amicales avec qn; **to be on speaking terms** (of two people) se parler; **to come to terms with sth** accepter qch; **in financial/international terms** sur le plan ou d'un point de vue financier/international; **in terms of** en ce qui concerne, du point de vue de; **I was thinking more in terms of a Jaguar** je pensais plutôt à une Jaguar (c) Com **terms** (conditions) conditions fpl; (of contract) termes mpl; **terms of reference** (of commission) attributions fpl; **terms of payment** conditions de paiement (d) (at school, university) trimestre m; **t. of office** (of politician) mandat m; **t. of imprisonment** peine f de prison; **in the long/short t.** à long/court terme; **to have reached (full) t.** (of pregnancy) arriver à terme
2 vt appeler

terminal ['tɜːmɪnəl] 1 n (a) (of battery) pôle m, borne f (b) (rail, bus) terminus m; (at airport) terminal m (c) Comput terminal m
2 adj terminal(e); (illness) en phase terminale

terminally ['tɜːmɪnəlɪ] adv **to be t. ill** être condamné(e)

terminate ['tɜːmɪneɪt] 1 vt (a) (employment, project) mettre fin à; (contract) résilier (b) (pregnancy) interrompre
2 vi (a) (of contract) prendre fin (b) (of bus, train) aller jusqu'à

termination [tɜːmɪ'neɪʃən] n (a) (of employment, project) fin f; (of contract) résiliation f (b) **t. (of pregnancy)** interruption f de grossesse

terminology [tɜːmɪ'nɒlədʒɪ] n terminologie f

terminus ['tɜːmɪnəs] (pl **terminuses** or **termini** ['tɜːmɪnaɪ]) n terminus m

termite ['tɜːmaɪt] n termite m

tern [tɜːn] n sterne f

Terr abbr Terrace

terrace ['terɪs] n (a) (beside house, on hillside) terrasse f (b) Br **the terraces** (in football ground) les gradins mpl (c) Br (of houses) = rangée de maisons attenantes

terraced ['terɪst] adj (a) (hillside) en terrasses (b) Br **t. house** = maison située dans une rangée d'habitations attenantes

terracotta ['terə'kɒtə] n terre f cuite

terrain [tə'reɪn] n terrain m

terrapin ['terəpɪn] n tortue f d'eau douce

terrestrial [tɪ'restrɪəl] adj terrestre; **t. broadcasting, t. television** diffusion f hertzienne ou terrestre

terrible ['terɪbəl] adj (shocking) terrible; (of poor quality) épouvantable

terribly ['terɪblɪ] adv (a) (badly) affreusement mal; (injured) très gravement (b) Fam (very) extrêmement

terrier ['terɪə(r)] n (dog) terrier m; Fig **he's a real t.** il n'abandonne jamais

terrific [tə'rɪfɪk] adj Fam (a) (excellent) super inv (b) (enormous) incroyable

terrifically [tə'rɪfɪklɪ] adv Fam (very) extrêmement

terrified ['terɪfaɪd] adj terrifié(e); **to be t. of** avoir une peur bleue de

terrify ['terɪfaɪ] vt terrifier

terrifying ['terɪfaɪɪŋ] adj terrifiant(e)

territorial [terɪ'tɔːrɪəl] adj territorial(e); (animal) qui défend son territoire; Br **the T. Army** = armée de réserve, constituée de volontaires; **t. waters** eaux fpl territoriales

territory ['terɪtərɪ] (pl **territories**) n territoire m; Fig (area of activity) domaine m

terror ['terə(r)] n terreur f; **reign of t.** régime m de terreur; Fam **that child is a t.** cet enfant est une vraie terreur

terrorism ['terərɪzəm] n terrorisme m

terrorist ['terərɪst] n & adj terroriste mf

terrorize ['terəraɪz] vt terroriser

terror-stricken ['terəstrɪkən] adj terrorisé(e)

terse [tɜːs] adj (person, reply) sec (sèche); (style, prose) concis(e)

terseness ['tɜːsnɪs] n (of person, reply) brusquerie f; (of style, prose) concision f

tertiary ['tɜːʃɪərɪ] adj tertiaire; **t. education** enseignement m supérieur

TESL ['tesəl] n (abbr Teaching of English as a Second Language) enseignement m de l'anglais deuxième langue

TESOL ['tiːsəl] n (abbr Teaching of English to Speakers of Other Languages) enseignement m de l'anglais langue étrangère

TESSA ['tesə] n Br Fin (abbr tax-exempt special savings account) = plan d'épargne exonéré d'impôts

test [test] 1 n (a) (trial, check) test m; **to put sb/sth to the t.** mettre qn/qch à l'épreuve; **to pass the t.** se montrer à la hauteur; **to stand the t. of time** résister à l'épreuve du temps; **t. ban** interdiction f des essais nucléaires; Law **t. case** affaire f qui fait jurisprudence; **t. drive** essai m sur route; **t. flight** vol m d'essai; **t. pilot** pilote m d'essai; **t. tube** tube m à essai, éprouvette f; **t. tube baby** bébé-éprouvette m (b) (examination) examen m; (driving) **t.** examen du permis de conduire; **French/maths t.** examen de français/maths (c) (in cricket, rugby) **t. (match)** match m international

2 *vt* (**a**) *(examine) (pupil)* interroger (**on** sur); *(sight, hearing)* examiner; **to t. sb's knowledge** tester les connaissances de qn; **to t. sb for Aids** faire subir à qn le test de dépistage du sida
(**b**) *(try out)* tester, mettre à l'épreuve
3 *vi* **to t. for Aids** faire un test de dépistage du sida; **to t. positive/negative** *(for drugs)* être positif/négatif; *(for Aids)* être séropositif(ive)/séronégatif(ive)
▸**test out** *vt sep* tester

testament ['testəmənt] *n* (**a**) *Law (will)* testament *m*
(**b**) *(tribute)* preuve *f* (**to** de)

test-bed ['testbed] *n* banc *m* d'essai

test-drive ['testdraiv] *vt* essayer

testicle ['testikəl] *n* testicule *m*

testify ['testifai] *Law* 1 *vt* **to t. that...** attester que...
2 *vi* témoigner (**for/against** en faveur de/contre); *Fig* **to t. to sth** *(be proof of)* témoigner de qch

testily ['testili] *adv* d'un ton irrité

testimonial [testi'məʊniəl] *n* (**a**) *(character reference)* références *fpl* (**b**) *(in football)* **t. (match)** = match en l'honneur d'un footballeur

testimony ['testiməni] *n Law* témoignage *m*, déposition *f*; *Fig* **to be a t. to sth** *(proof of)* témoigner de qch

testing ['testiŋ] 1 *n* essai *m*; **t. ground** terrain *m* d'essai
2 *adj* éprouvant(e)

testis ['testis] (*pl* **testes** ['testi:z]) *n* testicule *m*

testosterone [tes'tɒstərəʊn] *n* testostérone *f*

testy ['testi] *adj (person, mood)* irritable; *(tone, manner)* irrité(e)

tetanus ['tetənəs] *n* tétanos *m*

tetchy ['tetʃi] *adj Fam* irritable

tether ['teðə(r)] 1 *n* *(for tying animal)* longe *f*; *Fig* **to be at the end of one's t.** être à bout
2 *vt (animal)* attacher

Texan ['teksən] 1 *n* Texan(e) *m,f*
2 *adj* texan(e)

Texas ['teksəs] *n* le Texas

Tex-Mex [teks'meks] *adj* tex-mex *inv*

text [tekst] 1 *n* texte *f*; *Comput* **t. editor** éditeur *m* de texte; **t. message** message *m* texte, mini-message *m*
2 *vt (send text message to)* envoyer un message texte *ou* un mini-message à

textbook ['tekstbʊk] *n* manuel *m*; *Fig* **a t. example (of)** un parfait exemple (de)

textile ['tekstail] 1 *n* textile *m*
2 *adj* textile

textual ['tekstjʊəl] *adj* de texte

texture ['tekstʃə(r)] *n* texture *f*

Thai [tai] 1 *n* (**a**) *(person)* Thaïlandais(e) *m,f* (**b**) *(language)* thaï *m*
2 *adj* thaïlandais(e)

Thailand ['tailænd] *n* la Thaïlande

Thames [temz] *n* the **T.** la Tamise

than [ðæn, *unstressed* ðən] *conj* que; **he's taller t. me** il est plus grand que moi; **he was taller t. I had expected** il était plus grand que je (ne) l'imaginais; **more/less t. ten** plus/moins de dix; **more t. once** plus d'une fois

thank [θæŋk] *vt* remercier; **to t. sb for sth/for doing sth** remercier qn pour qch/d'avoir fait qch; **t. God!** Dieu merci!; **t. you** merci; **t. you very much** merci beaucoup; **no, t. you** non merci; **t. you for coming** merci d'être venu; *Ironic* **I'll t. you to mind your own business!** je te prierai de te mêler de tes affaires!; *also Ironic* **we have Mike to t. for this** c'est à Mike que nous devons cela

thankful ['θæŋkfʊl] *adj* reconnaissant(e) (**for** de); **to be t. that...** être heureux(euse) que...

thankfully ['θæŋkfəli] *adv* (**a**) *(gratefully)* avec gratitude (**b**) *(fortunately)* heureusement

thankless ['θæŋklis] *adj* ingrat(e)

thanks [θæŋks] 1 *npl* remerciements *mpl*; **t. to** *(because of)* grâce à; **no t. to you/them!** ce n'est pas grâce à toi/eux!
2 *exclam Fam* **t.!** merci!; *Fam* **no t.** non merci; **t. for coming/your letter** merci d'être venu/pour ta lettre; *Fam Ironic* **t. for nothing!** je te remercie!

thanksgiving [θæŋks'givin] *n* action *f* de grâces; *Am* **T. (Day)** = 4ème jeudi de novembre, fête commémorant la première action de grâce des colons anglais

Thanksgiving
Aux États-Unis, "Thanksgiving" commémore, le quatrième jeudi de novembre, l'installation des premiers colons en Amérique. Le dîner en famille qui a généralement lieu à cette occasion est traditionnellement composé d'une dinde servie avec une sauce aux airelles accompagnée de patates douces, et se termine par une tarte au potiron.

thank you ['θæŋkju] *n* merci *m*, remerciement *m*; **to say t. to sb** dire merci à qn, remercier qn; **t. letter** lettre *f* de remerciement

that [ðæt] 1 *demonstrative pron* (*pl* **those** [ðəʊz]) (**a**) *(subject)* ce, cela, ça *(in more informal contexts)*; *(object)* cela, ça *(in more informal contexts)*; **who's t.?** qui est-ce?; **what's t.?** qu'est-ce que c'est?; **t.'s strange** c'est bizarre; **t.'s what she told me** c'est ce qu'elle m'a dit; **is t. all the luggage you're taking?** c'est tout ce que vous prenez comme bagages?; **t.'s where he lives** c'est là qu'il habite; **can you run as fast as t.?** tu peux courir aussi vite que ça?; **t.'s it!** c'est ça!; **and t. t.!** un point, c'est tout!
(**b**) *(as opposed to this)* celui-là (celle-là) *m,f*; **in a case like t.** dans un cas comme celui-là
2 *demonstrative adj* (*pl* **those**) (**a**) *(indicating person, thing)* ce (cette); **t. book** ce livre; **t. question** cette question; **t. man** cet homme
(**b**) *(as opposed to this)* ce...-là (cette...-là); **I prefer t. film** je préfère ce film-là; **take t. cup** prends cette tasse-là; **t. one** celui-là (celle-là)
3 *adv* **t. high/big** haut(e)/grand(e) comme ça; **I tasted it but it wasn't t. good** j'y ai goûté mais ce n'était pas si bon que ça; **I've never seen one t. good** je n'en ai jamais vu d'aussi bon que ça; **he's t. stupid he...** il est tellement stupide qu'il...
4 *[unstressed* ðət*] relative pron*

On peut omettre le pronom relatif **that** sauf s'il est en position sujet.

(**a**) *(subject)* qui; *(object)* que; **the letter t. came yesterday** la lettre qui est arrivée hier; **the woman t. I saw** la femme que j'ai vue
(**b**) *(with preposition)* **the person t. I gave it to** la personne à qui je l'ai donné; **the woman t. we're talking about** la femme dont nous parlons; **the room t. he's sleeping in** la chambre où il dort
(**c**) *(when)* où; **the day t. you arrived** le jour où tu es arrivé
5 *[unstressed* ðət*] conj*

Sauf dans la langue soutenue, la conjonction **that** est souvent omise.

que; **she said t. she would come** elle a dit qu'elle viendrait

thatch [θætʃ] **1** n *(on roof)* chaume m; *Fam (of hair)* tignasse f

2 vt *(roof)* couvrir de chaume; **thatched cottage** chaumière f; **thatched roof** toit m de chaume

thaw [θɔː] **1** n *also Fig* dégel m

2 vt *(snow, ice)* faire fondre; *(food)* décongeler

3 vi *(of snow, ice)* fondre; *(of food)* se décongeler; *Fig (of person)* se dérider

▶**thaw out** vi *(of lake)* dégeler; *(of food)* se décongeler; *Fig (of person)* se dérider

the [before consonant sounds ðə, before vowel sounds ðɪ, stressed ðiː] definite art **(a)** *(singular)* le (la); *(plural)* les; **t. pen** le stylo; **t. house** la maison; **t. airport** l'aéroport; **in t. summer** *(this summer)* cet été; *(every summer)* l'été; **to have t. measles/flu** avoir la rougeole/la grippe; **at t. time** à ce moment-là; **t. Europe of today** l'Europe d'aujourd'hui; *Fam* **how's t. knee?** et ce genou?

(b) *(denoting concept, group)* **t. poor/blind** les pauvres/aveugles; **t. Wilsons** les Wilson; **t. supernatural** le surnaturel

(c) *(with titles)* **Edward t. Eighth** Édouard VIII; **Alexander t. Great** Alexandre le Grand; **Catherine t. Great** la Grande Catherine

(d) *(with proportions, rates)* **to be paid by t. hour** être payé(e) à l'heure; **15 kilometres to t. litre** 15 kilomètres au litre

(e) *(in exclamations)* **t. arrogance/stupidity of it!** quelle arrogance/stupidité!

(f) [stressed ðiː] **not THE Professor Branestorm?** pas le célèbre professeur Branestorm?; **it's THE car for the nineties** c'est LA voiture des années 90

(g) *(in comparisons)* **t. more I see him, t. more I like him** plus je le vois, plus il me plaît; **t. more I see him, t. less I like him** plus je le vois, moins je l'apprécie; **t. sooner t. better** le plus tôt sera le mieux

(h) *(with dates)* **t. sixties** les années soixante; **t. eighteen hundreds** le dix-neuvième siècle

theatre, *Am* **theater** ['θɪətə(r)] n **(a)** *(drama, building)* théâtre m; **t. company** compagnie f théâtrale, troupe f de théâtre **(b)** *Br* **(operating) t.** salle f d'opération **(c)** *(area)* **t. of war** théâtre m des hostilités

theatre-goer, *Am* **theater-goer** ['θɪətəɡəʊə(r)] n amateur(trice) m,f de théâtre

theatrical [θɪˈætrɪkəl] adj *also Fig* théâtral(e); **t. company** pany compagnie f théâtrale, troupe f de théâtre

thee [ðiː] pron *Lit or Rel* te; *(after preposition)* toi

theft [θeft] n vol m

theftproof ['θeftpruːf] adj *(lock)* antivol inv; *(vehicle)* muni(e) d'un dispositif antivol

their ['ðeə(r)] possessive adj **(a)** *(singular)* leur; *(plural)* leurs; **t. job** leur travail; **t. wives** leurs femmes; **it wasn't THEIR idea!** ce n'est pas eux qui en ont eu l'idée! **(b)** *(for parts of body)* **they hit t. heads** ils se sont cogné la tête **(c)** *(indefinite use)* **someone's left t. umbrella** quelqu'un a oublié son parapluie

theirs [ðeəz] possessive pron **(a)** *(singular)* le leur (la leur) m,f; *(plural)* les leurs; **our house is big, but t. is bigger** notre maison est grande, mais la leur est plus grande encore

(b) *(used attributively)* **this book is t.** ce livre est à eux/à elles; **a friend of t.** un de leurs amis; **where's that brother of t.?** où leur frère a-t-il bien pu passer?

(c) *(indefinite use)* **if anyone hasn't got t. they can**

use mine si quelqu'un n'a pas le sien, il pourra utiliser le mien

theism ['θiːɪzəm] n *Rel* théisme m

them [ðem, unstressed ðəm] pron **(a)** *(direct object)* les; **I hate t.** je les déteste; **I can understand their son but not THEM** je comprends leur fils, mais eux, je ne les comprends pas

(b) *(indirect object)* leur; **I gave t. the book** je leur ai donné le livre; **I gave it to t.** je le leur ai donné

(c) *(after preposition)* eux (elles) mpl,fpl; **I'm thinking of t.** je pense à eux/elles

(d) *(as complement of verb to be)* eux (elles) mpl,fpl; **it's t.!** ce sont eux/elles!; **it was t. who did it** c'est eux/elles qui l'ont fait

(e) *(indefinite use)* **if anyone comes, tell t....** si quelqu'un vient, dis-lui...

thematic [θiːˈmætɪk] adj thématique

theme [θiːm] n thème m; **t. park** parc m à thème; **t. restaurant** restaurant m à thème; **t. song** or **tune** chanson f du générique

themselves [ðəmˈselvz, stressed ðemˈselvz] pron **(a)** *(reflexive)* **they hurt t.** ils se sont blessés

(b) *(emphatic)* eux-mêmes (elles-mêmes) mpl,fpl; **they t. have never...** eux-mêmes/elles-mêmes n'ont jamais...; **they told me t.** ils me l'ont dit eux-mêmes; **they're not t. today** ils ne sont pas dans leur état normal aujourd'hui

(c) *(after preposition)* **they live by t.** ils vivent seuls; **they bought it for t.** ils se le sont acheté; **they talk to t.** ils parlent tout seuls

then [ðen] **1** adv **(a)** *(at that time)* alors, à ce moment-là; **since t.** depuis (ce moment-là), depuis (lors); **until t.** *(in future)* jusque-là; *(in past)* jusqu'à ce moment-là; **by t.** *(in future)* d'ici là; *(in past)* entre-temps; **there and t., t. and there** sur-le-champ

(b) *(next)* ensuite, puis; **what t.?** et alors, qu'est-ce qui va se passer?

(c) *(in that case)* alors; **if it rains, t. we get wet** s'il pleut, alors on va se mouiller

(d) *(therefore)* donc; **you already knew, t.?** donc, tu le savais déjà?

2 adj **the t. President** le Président de l'époque

thence [ðens] adv *Formal* de là

theologian [θiːəˈləʊdʒ(ɪ)ən] n théologien(enne) m,f

theological [θiːəˈlɒdʒɪkəl] adj théologique

theology [θiːˈɒlədʒɪ] n théologie f

theorem ['θɪərəm] n théorème m

theoretical [θiːəˈretɪkəl] adj théorique

theoretically [θiːəˈretɪklɪ] adv théoriquement

theoretician [θiːərɪˈtɪʃən] n théoricien(enne) m,f

theorist ['θɪərɪst] n théoricien(enne) m,f

theorize ['θɪəraɪz] vi théoriser (**about** sur)

theory ['θɪərɪ] n théorie f; **in t.** en théorie

therapeutic [θerəˈpjuːtɪk] adj *also Fig* thérapeutique

therapist ['θerəpɪst] n thérapeute mf

therapy ['θerəpɪ] n thérapie f

there [ðeə(r), unstressed ðə(r)] **1** pron **t. is/are** il y a; **t. was/were** il y avait; **t.'s somebody at the door** il y a quelqu'un à la porte; **t. isn't/aren't any** il n'y en a pas; **t. are** or *Fam* **t.'s two left** il (en) reste deux; **t.'s a page missing** il manque une page; **t. comes a time when...** il arrive un moment où...

2 adv **(a)** *(in that place)* là; *(over there)* là-bas; **he isn't t.** il n'est pas là; **the weather's nice t.** il fait beau là-bas; **I'm going t. tomorrow** j'y vais demain; **give me that book t.** donne-moi ce livre-là; **do we have**

time to get t. and back? avons-nous le temps d'y aller et de revenir?; **t. it is!** le voilà!; **t. you are!** *(I was looking for you)* te voilà!; *(when handing over something)* voilà!; *(expressing triumph, satisfaction)* tu vois!; **t. and then, then and t.** sur-le-champ; *Fam* **he's not all t.** il n'a pas toute sa tête

(**b**) *(at that point)* là; **t.'s the difficulty** voilà la difficulté; **we'll stop t. for today** nous nous arrêterons là pour aujourd'hui; *Fam* **you've got me t.!** alors là, vous me posez une colle!

3 *exclam* voilà!; **t., t.!** allons, allons!; **t., I told you so!** et voilà, je te l'avais bien dit!; **t. now, that wasn't so bad!** voilà, ce n'était pas si terrible!

thereabouts ['ðeərə'baʊts] *adv* (**a**) *(with place)* dans les environs; **he's from Stirling or t.** il est de Stirling, ou quelque part par là (**b**) *(with number, quantity, distance)* environ, à peu près; **it costs £500 or t.** ça coûte environ *ou* à peu près 500 livres

thereafter [ðeər'ɑːftə(r)] *adv Formal* après cela, par la suite

thereby ['ðeəbaɪ] *adv Formal* ainsi; **t. hangs a tale!** c'est une longue histoire!

therefore ['ðeəfɔː(r)] *adv* donc

thereupon [ðeərə'pɒn] *adv Formal* sur ce

thermal ['θɜːməl] **1** *n Met* ascendance *f* thermique

2 *adj* thermique; **t. energy** énergie *f* thermique; *Comput* **t. paper** papier *m* thermique; **t. springs** sources *fpl* thermales; **t. underwear** sous-vêtements *mpl* en Thermolactyl®

thermodynamics [θɜːməʊdaɪ'næmɪks] *n* thermodynamique *f*

thermoelectric [θɜːməʊ'lektrɪk] *adj* thermoélectrique

thermometer [θə'mɒmɪtə(r)] *n* thermomètre *m*

Thermos® ['θɜːməs] *n* **T. (flask)** (bouteille *f*) Thermos® *m ou f*

thermostat ['θɜːməstæt] *n* thermostat *m*

thesaurus [θɪ'sɔːrəs] *(pl* **thesauruses** *or* **thesauri** [θɪ'sɔːraɪ] *) n* dictionnaire *m* de synonymes

these [ðiːz] **1** *demonstrative pron* ceux-ci (celles-ci) *mpl,fpl*; **in cases like t.** dans des cas comme ceux-ci; **t. are the ones I want** voici ceux que je veux; **t. are my parents** *(introducing)* je te présente mes parents

2 *demonstrative adj* (**a**) *(indicating people or things)* ces; **t. children** ces enfants (**b**) *(as opposed to those)* ces...-ci; **I like t. shoes** j'aime bien ces chaussures-ci; **t. ones** ceux-ci (celles-ci) *mpl,fpl*

thesis ['θiːsɪs] *(pl* **theses** ['θiːsiːz]) *n* thèse *f*

thespian ['θespɪən] *n Lit or Hum* comédien(enne) *m,f*

they [ðeɪ] *pron* (**a**) *(subject)* ils (elles) *mpl,fpl*; **they're Scottish** *(masculine)* ils sont écossais; *(feminine)* elles sont écossaises; **They haven't got it!** ce ne sont pas eux/elles qui l'ont! (**b**) *(indefinite use)* **somebody called – what did t. want?** quelqu'un a appelé – qu'est-ce qu'il voulait?; **t. say that...** on dit que...

they'd [ðeɪd] = **they had, they would**

they'll [ðeɪl] = **they will, they shall**

they're [ðeə(r)] = **they are**

they've [ðeɪv] = **they have**

thick [θɪk] **1** *adj* (**a**) *(in general)* épais(aisse); **to be a metre t.** faire un mètre d'épaisseur; **the air was t. with smoke** l'air était empli d'une épaisse fumée; **the snow was t. on the ground** il y avait une épaisse couche de neige sur le sol; *Fig* **to be t. on the ground** *(plentiful)* être légion

(**b**) *(voice)* pâteux(euse); *(accent)* fort(e)

(**c**) *Fam (stupid)* bouché(e); **to be as t. as two short planks** *or* **as a brick** être bête comme ses pieds

(**d**) *(idioms)* **to have a t. skin** ne pas être susceptible; **to give sb a t. ear** donner une gifle à qn; *Fam* **to be as t. as thieves** s'entendre comme larrons en foire; *Fam* **that's a bit t.!** ça, c'est un peu fort!

2 *adv* (**a**) *(cut)* en tranches épaisses; *(spread)* en couche épaisse

(**b**) *(idioms)* **to come t. and fast** *(of questions, orders)* pleuvoir; *Fam* **to lay it on a bit t.** exagérer

3 *n* **in the t. of the forest** au beau milieu de la forêt; **to be in the t. of it** *or* **things** être au cœur de l'action; **through t. and thin** quoi qu'il arrive

thicken ['θɪkən] **1** *vt* épaissir

2 *vi* s'épaissir; *Hum* **the plot thickens...** les choses se compliquent...

thicket ['θɪkɪt] *n* fourré *m*

thickly ['θɪklɪ] *adv* (**a**) *(cut)* en tranches épaisses; *(spread)* en couche épaisse (**b**) *(populated)* fortement (**c**) *(speak)* d'une voix pâteuse

thickness ['θɪknɪs] *n* épaisseur *f*

thickset ['θɪk'set] *adj* trapu(e)

thick-skinned [θɪk'skɪnd] *adj Fig* peu susceptible

thief [θiːf] *(pl* **thieves** [θiːvz]) *n* voleur(euse) *m,f*

thieve [θiːv] *vi & vi* voler

thieving ['θiːvɪŋ] **1** *n* vol *m*

2 *adj* voleur(euse)

thigh [θaɪ] *n* cuisse *f*

thighbone ['θaɪbəʊn] *n* fémur *m*

thimble ['θɪmbəl] *n* dé *m* à coudre

thin [θɪn] **1** *adj* (**a**) *(person, wall)* mince; *(paper, slice, layer)* fin(e), mince; *(blanket, clothing)* léger(ère); *(book)* peu épais(aisse); **to get thinner** *(of person)* maigrir

(**b**) *(sparse)* *(hair, crowd, vegetation)* clairsemé(e); *(fog, mist)* léger(ère)

(**c**) *(soup, sauce)* liquide; *(paint)* dilué(e); *(blood)* appauvri(e)

(**d**) *(voice)* grêle

(**e**) *(idioms)* **to vanish into t. air** se volatiliser; **to have a t. time (of it)** avoir la vie dure; **to be t. on the ground** être rare; **it's just the t. end of the wedge** ce n'est qu'un début

2 *adv* *(cut)* en tranches fines *ou* minces; *Fig* **our forces/resources are spread very t.** nos forces/ressources sont très éparpillées

3 *vt (pt & pp* **thinned***) (paint)* diluer; *(sauce)* éclaircir

4 *vi (of crowd)* s'éclaircir; *(of fog, mist)* se lever; **his hair is thinning** il perd ses cheveux, il se dégarnit

thing [θɪŋ] *n* (**a**) *(action, remark, fact)* chose *f*; **the important t. is that...** l'important, c'est que...; **it's the only t. we can do** c'est tout ce que nous pouvons faire; **that's another t. altogether** c'est une autre affaire; **the t. is,...** le problème, c'est que...; **that was a silly t. to do/say** c'était stupide de faire/dire ça; **for one t.** d'abord; **what with one t. and another** avec tout ce qui s'est passé; **I don't know a t. about algebra** je n'y connais rien en algèbre; **to know a t. or two (about sth)** s'y connaître (en qch); **to take things too seriously** prendre les choses trop au sérieux; **it's just one of those things** ce sont des choses qui arrivent; **things are going well/badly** les choses vont bien/mal; *Fam* **how are things?, how's things?** comment ça va?

(**b**) *(object)* chose *f*; *Fam* **what's that t.?** qu'est-ce que c'est que ce truc?; *Fam* **where's that spanner t. I was using?** où est cette espèce de clé dont je me suis

servi tout à l'heure?; **things** *(belongings)* affaires *fpl*
(**c**) *Fam (person)* **you poor t.!** pauvre de toi!; **you
lucky t.!** sacré veinard!; **you silly t.!** espèce d'idiot!
(**d**) *(idioms)* **to have a t. about sb/sth** *(like)* avoir un
faible pour qn/qch; *(dislike)* avoir quelque chose
contre qn/qch; **to have a t. about tidiness/punctual-
ity** être très à cheval sur la propreté/la ponctualité;
it's not the done t. ça ne se fait pas; **the latest t. in
shoes** la dernière mode en matière de chaussures

thingummy ['θɪŋəmɪ], **thingumajig** ['θɪŋəmɪdʒɪg],
thingumabob ['θɪŋəmɪbɒb] *n Fam (object)* truc *m*;
(person) machin(e) *m,f*

think [θɪŋk] **1** *vt (pt & pp* **thought** [θɔːt] *)* (**a**) *(have in
mind)* **to t. that...** penser que...; **what are you thinking?** à quoi penses-tu?; **to t. evil thoughts** avoir de
mauvaises pensées; **to t. to do sth** penser à faire qch
(**b**) *(believe, have as opinion)* croire, penser; **he
thinks he knows everything** il croit tout savoir; **anyone would t. she was asleep** on jurerait qu'elle dort;
who'd have thought it! qui l'eût cru!; **what do you
t.?** qu'en penses-tu?; **I t. so** je pense (que oui); **I don't
t. so, I t. not** je ne pense pas, je pense que non; **I
thought so, I thought as much** c'est ce que je pensais; **I should t. so, too!** j'espère bien!; **that's what
you t.!** c'est ce que tu crois!; **what do you t. about
that idea?** qu'est-ce que tu penses de cette idée?
(**c**) *(imagine)* imaginer; **I can't t. why/what/
where...** je me demande bien pourquoi/ce que/
où...; **t. what we could do with all that money!** imagine ce qu'on pourrait faire avec tout cet argent!; **to t.
that he's only twenty!** et dire qu'il n'a que vingt ans
2 *vi* réfléchir, penser; **to t. ahead** voir loin; **to t.
aloud** penser tout haut; **to t. long and hard before
doing sth** bien réfléchir avant de faire qch; **to t. on
one's feet** réagir vite; **it makes you t.** ça fait réfléchir;
you can t. again! tu te fourres le doigt dans l'œil!
3 *n* **to have a t.** réfléchir; *Fam* **you've got another t.
coming!** tu te fourres le doigt dans l'œil!

▶**think about** *vt insep (have in mind, take into account)*
penser à; *(consider)* réfléchir à; **to t. about doing sth**
songer à faire qch; **it's quite cheap when you t.
about it** ça n'est pas très cher quand on y pense; **that
will give them something to t. about** voilà qui va
leur donner matière à réflexion

▶**think back to** *vt insep* repenser à

▶**think of** *vt insep* (**a**) *(have in mind, take into account)*
penser à; **to t. of doing sth** songer à faire qch; **come
to t. of it, I did see her that night** maintenant que j'y
pense, je l'ai effectivement vue ce soir-là; **what were
you thinking of, walking home alone?** qu'est-ce qui
t'a pris de rentrer à pied tout seul? (**b**) *(have opinion
about)* **what do you t. of this?** qu'est-ce que tu
penses de cela?; **to t. well/badly of sb** avoir une
bonne/mauvaise opinion de qn; **I don't t. much of
the idea** cette idée ne me dit pas grand-chose (**c**) *(recall)* se rappeler; **I can't t. of the right word** le mot
m'échappe

▶**think out** *vt sep* réfléchir à

▶**think over** *vt sep* réfléchir à

▶**think through** *vt sep* **to t. sth through** bien réfléchir
à qch

▶**think up** *vt sep* imaginer, inventer

thinker ['θɪŋkə(r)] *n* penseur *m*

thinking ['θɪŋkɪŋ] **1** *n* (**a**) *(process of thought)* réflexion *f*; **to do some t.** réfléchir (**b**) *(opinion)* avis *m*, opinion *f*; **to my (way of) t.** à mon avis

2 *adj Br Hum* **the t. man's crumpet** une jolie fille
avec quelque chose dans la tête

think-tank ['θɪŋktæŋk] *n* comité *m* d'experts

thinly ['θɪnlɪ] *adv* (**a**) *(cut)* en tranches fines *ou*
minces; *(spread)* en couche fine *ou* mince (**b**) *(populated)* faiblement

thinner ['θɪnə(r)] *n* diluant *m*

thinness ['θɪnnɪs] *n (of person, wall)* minceur *f*; *(of paper, slice, layer)* finesse *f*; *(of liquid)* fluidité *f*; *(of blanket, clothing)* légèreté *f*

third [θɜːd] **1** *n* (**a**) *(fraction)* tiers *m inv* (**b**) *(in series)*
troisième *mf* (**c**) *(of month)* trois *m inv* (**d**) *Mus* tierce *f*
(**e**) *Br Univ* **to get a t.** *(in degree)* ≃ avoir sa licence
avec mention passable

2 *adj* troisième; **t. degree burns** brûlures *fpl* au troisième degré; *Fam* **to give sb the t. degree** cuisiner
qn; *Law* **t. party** tiers *m*, tierce personne *f*; **t. party
cover** *(in insurance)* assurance *f* au tiers; **t. rate** *(mediocre)* très mauvais(e); **the T. World** le tiers-monde;
see also **eighth**

thirdly ['θɜːdlɪ] *adv* troisièmement

thirst [θɜːst] **1** *n* soif *f*; *Fig* **the t. for sth** la soif de qch
2 *vi Fig* être assoiffé(e) (**for** de)

thirsty ['θɜːstɪ] *adj also Fig* assoifé(e); **to be** *or* **feel t.**
avoir soif; *Fam* **all this talking is t. work** ça donne soif
de parler autant

thirteen [θɜːˈtiːn] **1** *n* treize *m inv*
2 *adj* treize; *see also* **eight**

thirteenth [θɜːˈtiːnθ] **1** *n* (**a**) *(fraction)* treizième *m*
(**b**) *(in series)* treizième *mf* (**c**) *(of month)* treize *m inv*
2 *adj* treizième; *see also* **eighth**

thirtieth ['θɜːtɪθ] **1** *n* (**a**) *(fraction)* trentième *m* (**b**)
(in series) trentième *mf* (**c**) *(of month)* trente *m inv*
2 *adj* trentième; *see also* **eighth**

thirty ['θɜːtɪ] **1** *n* trente *m inv*
2 *adj* trente; *see also* **eighty**

this [ðɪs] **1** *demonstrative pron (pl* **these** [ðiːz]*)* (**a**)
(subject) ce, ceci; *(object)* ceci; **who's t.?** qui est-ce?;
what's t.? qu'est-ce que c'est?; **t. is ridiculous!** c'est
ridicule!; **t. leads me to believe that...** ceci me mène
à croire que...; **I do it like t.** je le fais comme ceci; **t. is
what she told me** voici ce qu'elle m'a dit; **listen to t.**
écoute ça; **t. is Sarah Jervis** *(on telephone)* c'est Sarah
Jervis à l'appareil; *(introducing another person)* je te
présente Sarah Jervis; *Fam* **to talk about t. and that**
parler de choses et d'autres
(**b**) *(as opposed to* ***that****)* celui-ci (celle-ci) *m,f*; **in a
case like t.** dans un cas comme celui-ci

2 *demonstrative adj (pl* **these***)* (**a**) *(indicating person,
thing)* ce (cette); **t. book** ce livre; **t. question** cette
question; **t. man** cet homme
(**b**) *(as opposed to* ***that****)* ce ...-ci (cette...-ci); **I prefer
t. film** je préfère ce film-ci; **take t. cup** prends cette
tasse-ci; **t. one** celui-ci (celle-ci)

3 *adv* **t. high/big** haut(e)/grand(e) comme ça; **I
didn't think it would be t. good** je ne pensais pas
que ce serait aussi bon; **I've never seen one t. good**
je n'en ai jamais vu d'aussi bon que ça; **t. much is certain,...** une chose est sûre,...

thistle ['θɪsəl] *n* chardon *m*

thither ['ðɪðə(r)] *adv Lit* **hither and t.** çà et là

thong [θɒŋ] *n* lanière *f*

thorax ['θɔːræks] *n Anat* thorax *m*

thorn [θɔːn] *n* épine *f*; *Fig* **to be a t. in sb's flesh** *or* **side**
être une source d'irritation constante pour qn

thorny ['θɔːnɪ] *adj also Fig* épineux(euse)

thorough ['θʌrə] *adj* (**a**) *(search, cleaning, preparation)* minutieux(euse); *(knowledge, examination, revision)* approfondi(e); **to do** *or* **make a t. job of sth** faire qch très consciencieusement (**b**) *(work, worker)* consciencieux(euse) (**c**) *(complete)* intégral(e)

thoroughbred ['θʌrəbred] **1** *n* pur-sang *m inv*
2 *adj (horse)* pur-sang *inv*

thoroughfare ['θʌrəfeə(r)] *n* rue *f*; **no t.** *(sign) (no entry)* passage interdit; *(cul-de-sac)* voie sans issue

thoroughgoing ['θʌrəgəʊɪŋ] *adj (search)* minutieux(euse); *(knowledge, revision)* approfondi(e)

thoroughly ['θʌrəlɪ] *adv* (**a**) *(with thoroughness)* à fond (**b**) *(completely)* tout à fait

thoroughness ['θʌrənɪs] *n* minutie *f*

those [ðəʊz] *(plural of* **that**) **1** *demonstrative pron* ceux-là (celles-là) *mpl,fpl*; **in cases like t.** dans des cas comme ceux-là; **t. are the ones I want** voilà ceux que je veux; **t. of us who...** ceux d'entre nous qui...
2 *demonstrative adj* ces; **t. ones** ceux-là (celles-là) *mpl, fpl*

though [ðəʊ] **1** *conj* bien que + *subjunctive*; **t. I say so myself** sans fausse modestie; **strange t. it may seem** aussi étrange que cela puisse paraître; **even t.** même si; **as t.** comme si
2 *adv* pourtant

thought [θɔːt] **1** *n* (**a**) *(thinking, idea)* pensée *f*; **it's quite a t.!** *(pleasant)* le rêve!; *(unpleasant)* quelle horreur!; **what a kind t.!** quelle délicate attention!; **the very t. of it...** le simple fait d'y penser...; **I didn't give it another t.** je n'y ai plus pensé; **her thoughts were elsewhere** son esprit était ailleurs; **what are your thoughts on the matter?** quelle est votre opinion sur le sujet?
(**b**) *(reflection)* réflexion *f*; **after much t.** après mûre réflexion; **to give some/no t. to sth** réfléchir/ne pas réfléchir à qch; **to be deep** *or* **lost in t.** être perdu(e) *ou* plongé(e) dans ses pensées
(**c**) *(intention)* intention *f*; **to have no t. of doing sth** ne pas avoir l'intention de faire qch; **you must give up all t.** *or* **thoughts of seeing him** tu dois renoncer à le voir
2 *pt & pp of* **think**

thoughtful ['θɔːtfʊl] *adj* (**a**) *(pensive) (person)* pensif(ive); *(book, writer)* sérieux(euse) (**b**) *(considerate) (person)* attentionné(e); *(gesture, remark)* gentil(ille)

thoughtfully ['θɔːtfəlɪ] *adv* (**a**) *(pensively)* pensivement (**b**) *(considerately)* gentiment

thoughtless ['θɔːtlɪs] *adj* irréfléchi(e)

thought-out ['θɔːt'aʊt] *adj* **well/poorly t.** *(plan, scheme)* bien/mal étudié(e)

thought-provoking ['θɔːtprəvəʊkɪŋ] *adj* qui donne à réfléchir

thousand ['θaʊzənd] **1** *n* mille *m inv*; **one** *or* **a t.** mille; **thousands of people** des milliers de gens; **she's one in a t.** elle est unique
2 *adj* mille *inv*; **a t. years** mille ans; **two t. men** deux mille hommes; *Fam* **to have a t. and one things to do** avoir mille choses à faire

thousandth ['θaʊzənθ] **1** *n* (**a**) *(fraction)* millième *m* (**b**) *(in series)* millième *mf*
2 *adj* millième

thrash [θræʃ] *vt (beat)* battre; *Fam Fig (defeat heavily)* écraser, battre à plate(s) couture(s)

▸**thrash about, thrash around** *vt sep* **to t. one's arms and legs about** se débattre
2 *vi (move wildly)* se débattre

▸**thrash out** *vt sep* discuter *ou* débattre de

thread [θred] **1** *n* (**a**) *(for sewing)* fil *m*; *Fig* **his life hung by a t.** sa vie ne tenait qu'à un fil; **to lose the t. (of sth)** perdre le fil (de qch) (**b**) *(of screw, bolt)* filetage *m*
2 *vt* (**a**) *(needle, beads)* enfiler (**b**) *(move)* **to t. one's way between the cars** se faufiler entre les voitures; **to t. one's way through the crowd** se frayer un chemin à travers la foule

threadbare ['θredbeə(r)] *adj (clothes)* élimé(e); *Fig (argument, joke)* éculé(e)

threat [θret] *n* menace *f*

threaten ['θretən] **1** *vt* menacer; **to t. to do sth** menacer de faire qch; **to t. sb with sth** menacer qn de qch
2 *vi* menacer

threatening ['θretənɪŋ] *adj (look, gesture)* menaçant(e); *(letter)* de menaces

three [θriː] **1** *n* trois *m inv*; **come with us – no, (two's company,) t.'s a crowd** viens avec nous – non, je me sentirais de trop
2 *adj* trois *inv*; *see also* **eight**

three-cornered [θriː'kɔːnəd] *adj* triangulaire

three-course meal ['θriːkɔːs'miːl] *n* repas *m* à trois plats *(entrée, plat principal, dessert)*

three-dimensional [θriːdaɪ'menʃənəl] *adj (object)* tridimensionnel(elle), en trois dimensions; *(character)* qui semble réel; *(film, picture)* en relief

threefold ['θriːfəʊld] **1** *adj* triple
2 *adv* **to increase t.** être multiplié(e) par trois

three-legged [θriː'legɪd] *adj (stool)* à trois pieds; **t. race** = course dont les participants sont attachés deux à deux par une jambe

three-piece ['θriːpiːs] *adj* **t. suit** *(costume m)* trois-pièce *m inv*; **t. suite** canapé *m* avec deux fauteuils assortis

three-point turn ['θriːpɔɪnt'tɜːn] *n* demi-tour *m* en trois manœuvres

threescore ['θriːskɔː(r)] *adj Lit* soixante *inv*; **t. (years) and ten** soixante-dix *inv*

threesome ['θriːsəm] *n* groupe *m* de trois personnes

three-wheeler [θriː'wiːlə(r)] *n (car)* voiture *f* à trois roues; *(tricycle)* tricycle *m*

thresh [θreʃ] *vt* battre

threshold ['θreʃəʊld] *n also Fig* seuil *m*; **to cross the t.** franchir le seuil; *Fig* **to be on the t. of sth** être au seuil de qch

threw [θruː] *pt of* **throw**

thrice [θraɪs] *adv Lit* trois fois

thrift [θrɪft] *n* économie *f*, épargne *f*

thriftless ['θrɪftlɪs] *adj* dépensier(ère)

thrifty ['θrɪftɪ] *adj* économe

thrill [θrɪl] **1** *n (excitement)* sensation *f*; *(trembling)* frisson *m*; **to get a t. out of doing sth** adorer faire qch
2 *vt* exalter, donner des frissons à; **to be thrilled for sb/with sth** être ravi(e) pour qn/de qch
3 *vi Lit* tressaillir, frissonner

thriller ['θrɪlə(r)] *n* thriller *m*

thrilling ['θrɪlɪŋ] *adj (story, film, match)* palpitant(e); *(idea, proposal, situation)* exaltant(e)

thrive [θraɪv] *(pt & pp* **thrived** [θraɪvd], *pt also* **throve** [θrəʊv]) *vi (of child, plant)* se développer; *(of adult)* s'épanouir; *(of business)* prospérer; **to t. on sth** *(stress, danger)* avoir besoin de qch pour s'épanouir

thriving ['θraɪvɪŋ] *adj (plant, person, animal)* vigoureux(euse); *(business)* prospère, florissant(e)

throat [θrəʊt] *n* (**a**) *(part of body)* gorge *f*; **to clear one's t.** se racler la gorge, s'éclaircir la voix (**b**) *(idioms)* **to ram** *or* **shove sth down sb's t.** rebattre les oreilles à qn de qch; **to jump down sb's t.** sauter sur qn; **to be at each other's throats** se battre

throaty ['θrəʊtɪ] *adj* rauque

throb [θrɒb] **1** *n (of heart)* battement *m*; *(of pain)* élancement *m*; *(of engine)* vibration *f*

2 *vi (pt & pp* **throbbed***) (of heart)* battre; *(of engine)* vibrer; **my head is throbbing** j'ai une douleur lancinante dans la tête

throes [θrəʊz] *npl* **t. of death, death t.** affres *fpl* de la mort, l'agonie *f*; **to be in the t. of sth/of doing sth** être en plein qch/en train de faire qch

thrombosis [θrɒm'bəʊsɪs] *(pl* **thromboses***) n* thrombose *f*

throne [θrəʊn] *n* trône *m*

throng [θrɒŋ] **1** *n* foule *f*

2 *vt* se presser dans; **the streets were thronged with people** les rues étaient noires de monde

3 *vi* affluer, se presser; **to. t. round sb** se presser autour de qn

throttle ['θrɒtəl] **1** *n (valve)* papillon *m* des gaz; *(accelerator)* manette *f* des gaz; **at full t.** à pleins gaz

2 *vt also Fig* étrangler

through [θru:] **1** *prep* (**a**) *(with place)* par, à travers; **to go t. a tunnel** passer par un tunnel; **to look t. a hole** regarder par un trou; **to come in t. the window** entrer par la fenêtre; **we went t. Belgium** nous sommes passés par la Belgique

(**b**) *(in the course of)* **all t. his life** toute sa vie durant; **halfway t. a book/film** à la moitié d'un livre/film; **to get t. sth** *(finish)* venir à bout de qch; *Fam* **he's been t. a lot** il en a bavé

(**c**) *(by means of)* par; **to send sth t. the post** envoyer qch par la poste; **I found out t. my brother/ the newspaper** je l'ai appris par mon frère/le journal

(**d**) *(because of)* à cause de; **t. ignorance/carelessness** par ignorance/négligence

(**e**) *Am (up to)* **Tuesday t. Thursday** de mardi à jeudi

2 *adv* (**a**) *(to other side)* **to go t.** *(of bullet, nail)* traverser; **to let sb t.** laisser passer qn; **to get t. to the final** être en finale

(**b**) *(from start to finish)* **to sleep all night t.** dormir toute la nuit; **to read a book right t.** lire un livre tout entier; **he's bad t. and t.** il est vraiment méchant

(**c**) *(in contact)* **to get t. to sb** *(on phone)* joindre qn; **to put sb t. to sb** *(on phone)* passer qn à qn; *Fam* **I just can't get t. to him** *(make myself understood)* je n'arrive pas à le lui faire comprendre

3 *adj* (**a**) *(finished)* fini(e); **to be t. with sb/sth** en avoir fini avec qn/qch

(**b**) *(direct)* **t. train** train *m* direct

throughout [θru:'aʊt] **1** *prep (in every part of)* partout dans; *(during)* tout au long de; **t. the country** dans tout le pays; **t. her life** tout au long de sa vie, pendant toute sa vie

2 *adv (everywhere)* partout; *(the whole time)* tout le temps

throughput ['θru:pʊt] *n Comput* débit *m*

throve [θrəʊv] *pt of* **thrive**

throw [θrəʊ] **1** *vt (pt* **threw** [θru:]*, pp* **thrown** [θrəʊn] *)* (**a**) *(in general)* jeter, lancer; *(javelin, discus)* lancer; **to t. sth at sb/sth** lancer qch à qn/contre qch; **to t. sth in sb's face** lancer qch à la figure de qn; *Fig* jeter

qch à la figure de qn; **to t. sb forwards/backwards** projeter qn en avant/en arrière; *Fig* **to t. oneself into sth** *(after traumatic event)* se jeter dans qch; *(enthusiastically)* se lancer dans qch; **to t. oneself at sb** se jeter sur qn; **to t. sb into confusion** plonger qn dans l'embarras; **to t. a switch** appuyer sur un interrupteur; **to t. open the door** ouvrir la porte en grand; *Fam* **to t. one's weight about** *or* **around** la ramener

(**b**) *(image, shadow)* projeter (**on** sur); *Fig* **to t. light on sth** éclairer qch

(**c**) *(have)* **to t. a fit** piquer une crise; *Fam* **to t. a party** organiser une fête

(**d**) *(in wrestling)* renverser

(**e**) *(of horse)* désarçonner

(**f**) *Fam (disconcert)* désarçonner, déconcerter

2 *n* (**a**) *(in general)* jet *m*; *(of javelin, discus)* lancer *m*; *(in wrestling)* mise *f* à terre

(**b**) *(for furniture, bed)* jeté *m*

(**c**) *Fam* **£50 a t.** *(each)* 50 livres chaque

▸**throw away** *vt sep* (**a**) *(discard)* jeter (**b**) *(chance, life)* gâcher; *(money)* gaspiller

▸**throw in** *vt sep* (**a**) *(in general)* jeter; *Fig* **to t. in the sponge** *or* **the towel** jeter l'éponge; *Fig* **to t. in one's lot with sb** s'associer avec qn (**b**) *(add)* placer; *(give as extra)* ajouter, donner en plus

▸**throw out** *vt sep* (**a**) *(eject) (person)* exclure, mettre à la porte; *(thing)* jeter; *(proposal)* rejeter (**b**) *(emit) (light, heat)* émettre

▸**throw together** *vt sep (assemble or gather hurriedly)* assembler à la hâte; *(make hurriedly)* faire à la hâte; **chance had thrown us together** le hasard nous avait réunis

▸**throw up 1** *vt sep* (**a**) *(raise)* **to t. up one's hands** *(in horror, dismay)* lever les bras au ciel (**b**) *(reveal) (facts, information)* révéler (**c**) *(abandon) (career)* abandonner

2 *vi Fam (vomit)* vomir

throwaway ['θrəʊəweɪ] *adj* (**a**) *(disposable)* jetable (**b**) *(line, remark)* fait(e) sans y penser

throwback ['θrəʊbæk] *n Biol* régression *f* (**to** à); *Fig* retour *m* (**to** à)

throw-in ['θrəʊɪn] *n (in football)* remise *f* en jeu

thrown [θrəʊn] *pp of* **throw**

thru = **through**

thrush[1] [θrʌʃ] *n (bird)* grive *f*

thrush[2] *n (disease)* muguet *m*

thrust [θrʌst] **1** *n* (**a**) *(forward movement)* mouvement *m* en avant; *(of army)* attaque *f* (**b**) *(of argument)* idée *f* principale (**c**) *(force of engine)* poussée *f*

2 *vt (pt & pp* **thrust***)* **to t. sth into sth** enfoncer qch dans qch; **to t. one's way through the crowd** se frayer un chemin à travers la foule

▸**thrust aside** *vt sep* repousser, écarter

▸**thrust forward** *vt sep* pousser en avant; *Fig* **to t. oneself forward** se mettre en avant

▸**thrust on** *vt sep* **to t. sth on sb** imposer qch à qn; **he thrust himself on them** il s'est imposé

▸**thrust out** *vt sep (arm, leg)* allonger; *(chest)* bomber; *(chin)* avancer

▸**thrust upon** = **thrust on**

thrusting ['θrʌstɪŋ] *adj* entreprenant(e), dynamique

thruway ['θru:weɪ] *n Am* autoroute *f*

thud [θʌd] **1** *n* bruit *m* sourd

2 *vi* faire un bruit sourd; **to t. against sth** frapper qch avec un bruit sourd

thug [θʌg] *n* voyou *m*

thumb [θʌm] **1** *n* pouce *m*; *Fig* she's got him under her t. il est sous sa coupe; *Fam* to be all thumbs être maladroit(e); *Fam* to give sth the thumbs up/down accepter/rejeter qch
  2 *vt* to t. one's nose at sb faire un pied de nez à qn; *Fam* to t. a lift *or* ride faire de l'auto-stop; a well thumbed book/magazine un livre/magazine qui a beaucoup servi
  3 *vi* to t. through a book/magazine feuilleter un livre/magazine
thumbnail ['θʌmneɪl] *n* ongle *m* du pouce; t. sketch description *f* rapide
thumbprint ['θʌmprɪnt] *n* empreinte *f* du pouce
thumbtack ['θʌmtæk] *n Am* punaise *f*
thump [θʌmp] **1** *n* (*blow*) coup *m*; (*sound*) bruit *m* sourd
  2 *vt* (*hit*) cogner, frapper; (*put down heavily*) poser lourdement
  3 *vi* (**a**) to t. on sth (*table, door*) cogner, frapper qch (**b**) (*walk heavily*) to t. around *or* about marcher à pas lourds (**c**) (*of heart*) battre la chamade
thumping ['θʌmpɪŋ] *Fam* **1** *adj* (**a**) (*very large*) énorme (**b**) (*headache*) lancinant(e)
  2 *adv* a t. great book/salary un livre/un salaire énorme
thunder ['θʌndə(r)] **1** *n* tonnerre *m*; with a face like t. le visage déformé par la colère
  2 *vi also Fig* tonner; to t. along (*of train, lorry*) passer dans un bruit de tonnerre
thunderbolt ['θʌndəbəʊlt] *n* éclair *m* suivi d'un coup de tonnerre
thunderclap ['θʌndəklæp] *n* coup *m* de tonnerre
thundercloud ['θʌndəklaʊd] *n* nuage *m* orageux
thunderous ['θʌndərəs] *adj* (*voice*) tonitruant(e); t. applause un tonnerre d'applaudissements
thunderstorm ['θʌndəstɔːm] *n* orage *m*
thunderstruck ['θʌndəstrʌk] *adj* abasourdi(e)
Thur (*abbr* **Thursday**) jeudi
Thursday ['θɜːzdɪ] *n* jeudi *m*; *see also* **Saturday**
thus [ðʌs] *adv Formal* (**a**) (*in this way, therefore*) ainsi (**b**) t. far (*in present*) jusqu'ici; (*in past*) jusque-là
thwart [θwɔːt] *vt* contrecarrer
thyme [taɪm] *n* thym *m*
thyroid ['θaɪrɔɪd] **1** *n* thyroïde *f*
  2 *adj* thyroïde; t. gland thyroïde *f*
tiara [tɪˈɑːrə] *n* (*jewellery*) diadème *m*
Tibet [tɪˈbet] *n* le Tibet
Tibetan [tɪˈbetən] **1** *n* (**a**) (*person*) Tibétain(e) *m,f* (**b**) (*language*) tibétain *m*
  2 *adj* tibétain(e)
tibia ['tɪbɪə] *n Anat* tibia *m*
tic [tɪk] *n* tic *m*
tick¹ [tɪk] *n* (*parasite*) tique *f*
tick² *n Br Fam* (*credit*) to buy sth on t. acheter qch à crédit
tick³ **1** *n* (**a**) (*of clock*) tic-tac *m inv*; *Fam* (*moment*) instant *m* (**b**) (*mark*) coche *f*; to put a t. beside sth cocher qch
  2 *vt* (*mark*) cocher
  3 *vi* (*of clock*) faire tic-tac; the minutes were ticking by *or* away les minutes passaient; *Fam* I don't know what makes him t. je ne sais pas ce qui se passe dans sa tête
▶**tick off** *vt sep* (**a**) (*on list*) cocher (**b**) *Br Fam* (*reprimand*) passer un savon à (**c**) *Am Fam* (*irritate*) énerver

▶**tick over** *vi* (*of engine*) tourner au ralenti; (*of business*) tourner
ticket ['tɪkɪt] **1** *n* (**a**) (*for train, plane, cinema, lottery*) billet *m*; (*for underground, bus*) ticket *m*; (**parking**) t. P-V *m*; *Br* t. inspector contrôleur(euse) *m,f*, *Belg* accompagnateur(trice) *m,f* de train; t. office guichet *m*, billetterie *f*; t. tout revendeur(euse) *m,f* de billets (**b**) (*label*) (**price**) t. étiquette *f* (**c**) *Am Pol* (*list of candidates*) liste *f* électorale; she ran on an anti-corruption t. elle a fondé son programme électoral sur la lutte contre la corruption (**d**) *Fam* it was just the t.! c'était juste ce qu'il fallait!
  2 *vt* (*goods*) étiqueter
ticketless ['tɪkɪtles] *adj* t. travel = vol avec reçu de paiement tenant lieu de billet
ticking ['tɪkɪŋ] *n* (**a**) (*of clock*) tic-tac *m inv* (**b**) (*fabric*) toile *f* à matelas
ticking off *n Br Fam* (*reprimand*) savon *m*; to give sb a t. passer un savon à qn
tickle ['tɪkəl] **1** *n* chatouillement *m*; to have a t. in one's throat avoir des picotements dans la gorge
  2 *vt* chatouiller; *Fig* (*amuse*) amuser; to t. sb's fancy plaire à qn; to be tickled pink être ravi(e)
  3 *vi* chatouiller
ticklish ['tɪklɪʃ] *adj* (**a**) (*person*) chatouilleux(euse) (**b**) *Fam* (*situation, problem*) délicat(e)
tidal ['taɪdəl] *adj* régi(e) par les marées; t. energy énergie *f* marémotrice; t. wave raz de marée *m inv*
tiddler ['tɪdlə(r)] *n Br Fam* (*small fish*) petit poisson *m*; (*child*) mioche *m*
tiddly ['tɪdlɪ] *adj Br Fam* (**a**) (*small*) minuscule (**b**) (*drunk*) paf *inv*
tiddlywinks ['tɪdlɪwɪŋks] *n* jeu *m* de puce
tide [taɪd] *n* marée *f*; *Fig* (*of events*) cours *m*; high/low t. marée haute/basse; *Fig* to go against the t. aller à contre-courant; *Fig* the t. has turned le vent a tourné
▶**tide over** *vt sep* to t. sb over dépanner qn
tidemark ['taɪdmɑːk] *n* (*mark left by tide*) laisse *f* de haute mer; *Br Fam* (*in bath, around neck*) ligne *f* de crasse
tidings ['taɪdɪŋz] *npl Lit* nouvelles *fpl*
tidy ['taɪdɪ] **1** *adj* (**a**) (*room, house*) rangé(e), en ordre; (*hair*) bien coiffé(e); (*appearance, handwriting*) soigné(e); (*person*) (*in habits*) ordonné(e); (*in appearance*) soigné (**b**) *Fam* (*considerable*) joli(e)
  2 *vt* ranger; (*garden*) nettoyer; to t. one's hair se recoiffer
▶**tidy up** *vt sep & vi* ranger
tie [taɪ] **1** *n* (**a**) (*link*) lien *m* (**b**) (*garment*) cravate *f*; t. rack porte-cravates *m* (**c**) (*draw*) (*in match*) match *m* nul; there was a t. for second place (*in race, competition*) il y a eu égalité pour la deuxième place (**d**) (*match*) match *m* (**e**) *Am Rail* traverse *f*, *Can* dormant *m*
  2 *vt* (*shoelace, string*) attacher, nouer; to t. a knot faire un nœud; to t. sth to sth attacher qch à qch; *Fig* to have one's hands tied avoir les mains liées; *Fig* to be tied to one's desk être cloué(e) à son bureau
  3 *vi* (*in race, contest*) être à égalité; to t. for first/ second place être premiers(ères)/deuxièmes ex aequo
▶**tie back** *vt sep* (*hair, curtains*) relever
▶**tie down** *vt sep* (*immobilize*) attacher; *Fig* children t. you down les enfants sont une contrainte; she didn't want to feel tied down elle voulait garder sa liberté

►**tie in** *vi (of facts, story)* concorder, cadrer

►**tie on** *vt* attacher

►**tie up** *vt sep* (**a**) *(person, animal)* attacher; *(parcel)* ficeler; *(boat)* amarrer (**b**) *(deal)* conclure; *(money)* immobiliser (**c**) *Fig* **to be tied up** *(busy)* être occupé(e)

tie-break ['taɪbreɪk], **tie-breaker** ['taɪbreɪkə(r)] *n (in tennis)* tie-break *m*; *(in quiz, competition)* question *f* subsidiaire

tie-in ['taɪɪn] *n (link)* lien *m*, rapport *m* (**with** avec); **a film/TV t.** = livre, jouet etc commercialisé à la suite d'un film ou d'une série télévisée

tier [tɪə(r)] *n (of theatre, stadium)* gradin *m*; *(of wedding cake)* étage *m*; *(administrative)* échelon *m*

tiff [tɪf] *n Br Fam* querelle *f*

tiger ['taɪgə(r)] *n* tigre *m*

tight [taɪt] **1** *adj* (**a**) *(clothes, knot, screw)* serré(e); **to be a t. fit** *(of clothes)* être un peu juste; **to keep a t. hold** *or* **grip on sth** s'agripper à qch; **it was a t. squeeze** il a fallu se serrer un peu; *Fig* **to be in a t. spot** *or* **corner** être dans une mauvaise passe; *Fig* **to run a t. ship** mener son monde à la baguette
(**b**) *(competition, race, bend, schedule)* serré(e); *(restrictions)* strict(e); **a t. finish** *(in race)* une arrivée disputée; *Fam* **money's a bit t. at the moment** je suis un peu à court d'argent en ce moment
(**c**) *Fam (mean)* radin(e)
(**d**) *Fam (drunk)* bourré(e)
2 *adv (hold, squeeze)* fortement; *(seal, shut)* bien; **hold t.!** tiens bon!; **sleep t.!** dors bien!

tighten ['taɪtən] **1** *vt (screw, knot)* serrer; *(rope)* tendre; *(restrictions, security)* renforcer; *(conditions, rules)* durcir; **to t. one's grip on sth** *(rope, handle)* resserrer sa prise sur qch; *Fig (power, organization)* renforcer son emprise sur qch; *Fig* **to t. one's belt** se serrer la ceinture
2 *vi (of knot, grip)* se resserrer; *(of rope)* se tendre

►**tighten up** *vt sep (screw)* resserrer; *(restrictions, security)* renforcer

tightfisted [taɪt'fɪstɪd] *adj Fam* radin(e)

tightknit ['taɪt'nɪt] *adj (community)* uni(e)

tight-lipped ['taɪtlɪpt] *adj (silent)* peu bavard(e); *(angry)* renfrogné(e)

tightly ['taɪtlɪ] *adv (hold, squeeze)* fortement; *(seal, shut)* bien

tightness ['taɪtnɪs] *n (of link, clothing)* étroitesse *f*; *(of regulations, security)* rigueur *f*

tightrope ['taɪtrəʊp] *n* corde *f* raide; *Fig* **to walk a t.** être sur la corde raide; **t. walker** funambule *mf*

tights [taɪts] *npl Br (garment)* collant *m*

tigress ['taɪgrɪs] *n* tigresse *f*

'til [tɪl] = **until**

tile [taɪl] **1** *n (on roof)* tuile *f*; *(on floor, wall)* carreau *m*
2 *vt (roof)* couvrir de tuiles; *(floor, wall)* carreler

tiled [taɪld] *adj (roof)* de tuiles; *(floor, wall)* carrelé(e)

till¹ [tɪl] *vt (field)* labourer

till² *n (cash register)* caisse *f*; *Fig* **to be caught with one's hand** *or* **fingers in the t.** être pris(e) la main dans le sac

till³ = **until**

tiller ['tɪlə(r)] *n (on boat)* barre *f*

tilt [tɪlt] **1** *n* (**a**) *(angle)* inclinaison *f* (**b**) **at full t.** à toute vitesse
2 *vt (head, chair)* incliner, pencher; **to t. the balance of opinion in favour of** faire pencher l'opinion en faveur de
3 *vi* (**a**) *(incline)* pencher; **to t. backwards/forwards**

pencher vers l'arrière/vers l'avant (**b**) *Fig* **to t. at windmills** se battre contre des moulins à vent

►**tilt over** *vi* basculer

timber ['tɪmbə(r)] *n (wood)* bois *m*; **t. merchant** marchand *m* de bois

time [taɪm] **1** *n* (**a**) *(in general)* temps *m*; *Fig* **to have no t. for sb/sth** ne pas avoir de temps à perdre avec qn/qch; **to take t.** prendre du temps; **to take one's t. (doing sth)** prendre son temps (pour faire qch); **you took your t.!** tu as pris ton temps!; **in one's own t.** *(out of working hours)* pendant son temps libre; *(at one's own pace)* à son rythme; **in t.** *(eventually)* avec le temps; **in t. for sth/to do sth** à temps pour qch/pour faire qch; **in good t.** *(early)* à temps; *(in due course)* en temps voulu; **all in good t.** chaque chose en son temps; **she'll do it in her own good t.** elle le fera quand elle le pourra; **now my t. is my own** maintenant, je suis libre de mon temps; **in no t. at all, in next to no t.** en un rien de temps; **t.'s getting on** l'heure avance; **t.'s up!** c'est l'heure!; **t. will tell** l'avenir le dira; *Prov* **t. is money** le temps, c'est de l'argent; *Fam* **to do t.** *(go to prison)* faire de la taule; *also Fig* **t. bomb** bombe *f* à retardement; **to be in a t. warp** être hors du temps; **t. travel** voyage *m* dans le temps
(**b**) *(period)* **in a short/long t.** dans peu de temps/longtemps; **for some t.** pendant quelque temps; **in three weeks' t.** dans trois semaines; **to take a long t. over sth/to do sth** passer beaucoup de temps sur qch/à faire qch; **for the t. being** pour le moment; **to have a good t.** bien s'amuser; **to give sb a hard t.** faire passer un mauvais moment à qn
(**c**) *(age)* époque *f*; **before my t.** avant ma naissance; **to be ahead of one's t.** être en avance sur son temps; **to move with the times** vivre avec son temps; **she was a good singer in her t.** c'était une bonne chanteuse à son époque; **she's seen a few things in her t.** elle a vu pas mal de choses dans sa vie; **t. capsule** capsule *f* témoin *(qui doit servir de témoignage historique aux générations futures)*
(**d**) *(moment)* moment *m*; **at the t.** à ce moment-là; **at the present t.** en ce moment; **at one t.** à une époque; **at no t.** jamais, à aucun moment; **at the same t.** en même temps; **at times** parfois, par moments; **by the t. you get this, I'll already be in Paris** quand tu recevras cette lettre, je serai déjà à Paris; **this t. next year** l'année prochaine à la même époque; **from t. to t.** de temps en temps; **at this t. of (the) year** à cette époque de l'année; **the t. has come to...** le moment est venu de...; *Fam* **not before t.!** il était temps!; *Fam* **it's high t. (that)...** il est grand temps que... + subjunctive
(**e**) *(on clock)* heure *f*; **what's the t.?** quelle heure est-il?; **to pass the t. of day with sb** parler de la pluie et du beau temps avec qn; *Fam* **he wouldn't give you the t. of day** il n'est vraiment pas aimable; **this t. tomorrow** demain à la même heure; **on t.** à l'heure; **it's t. we left** il est temps de partir; **t. difference** décalage *m* horaire; **t. lag** décalage; **t. limit** délai *m*; *Ind* **t. sheet** fiche *f* horaire; **t. switch** minuterie *f*
(**f**) *(occasion)* fois *f*; **five times** cinq fois; **t. and t. again, t. after t.** encore et encore
(**g**) *(in multiplication)* **four times two is eight** quatre fois deux égalent huit; **three times as big/expensive as** trois fois plus grand(e)/cher (chère) que
(**h**) *(in music)* mesure *f*; **to keep t.** rester en mesure
2 *vt* (**a**) *(meeting, visit)* prévoir
(**b**) *(remark, action)* **well timed** opportun(e); **badly**

timed mal venu(e)
  (**c**) *(athlete, race)* chronométrer
time-consuming ['taɪmkənsjuːmɪŋ] *adj* qui prend beaucoup de temps
time-honoured ['taɪmɒnəd] *adj* consacré(e) (par l'usage)
timekeeper ['taɪmkiːpə(r)] *n (in competition)* chronométreur *m*
timekeeping ['taɪmkiːpɪŋ] *n* (**a**) *(in factory)* contrôle *m* de présence (**b**) *(punctuality)* ponctualité *f*
timeless ['taɪmlɪs] *adj* intemporel(elle)
timely ['taɪmlɪ] *adj* opportun(e)
time-out ['taɪmaʊt] *n (in sport)* temps *m* mort; *Fig* pause *f*; **to take t.** faire une pause
timepiece ['taɪmpiːs] *n (clock)* pendule *f*; *(watch)* montre *f*
timer ['taɪmə(r)] *n* minuteur *m*
time-saving ['taɪmseɪvɪŋ] *adj* qui permet de gagner du temps
timescale ['taɪmskeɪl] *n* période *f*
time-share ['taɪmʃeə(r)] *n (flat)* appartement *m* en multipropriété; *(house)* maison *f* en multipropriété
timespan ['taɪmspæn] *n* laps *m* de temps
timetable ['taɪmteɪbəl] **1** *n (at school, university)* emploi *m* du temps; *(for event, project)* calendrier *m*; *(for trains, buses)* horaire *m*; **to work to a t.** suivre un emploi du temps
  2 *vt (talks, meeting)* fixer une date pour; *(classes)* établir un emploi du temps pour
time-wasting ['taɪmweɪstɪŋ] *n* perte *f* de temps
timid ['tɪmɪd] *adj* timide
timidity [tɪ'mɪdɪtɪ] *n* timidité *f*
timidly ['tɪmɪdlɪ] *adv* timidement
timing ['taɪmɪŋ] *n* (**a**) *(of announcement, election)* moment *m* choisi (**of** pour) (**b**) *(of remark, action)* **good t.** à-propos *m*; **bad t.** manque *m* d'à-propos; **perfect t.!** ça tombe bien! (**c**) *(of musician)* sens *m* du rythme
timorous ['tɪmərəs] *adj* timoré(e)
tin [tɪn] *n* (**a**) *(metal)* étain *m*; **t. mine** mine *f* d'étain; **t. plate** fer-blanc *m*; **t. soldier** soldat *m* de plomb (**b**) *(mould)* moule *m* (**c**) *(container)* boîte *f*; *(for biscuits, cakes)* boîte en fer; **t. opener** ouvre-boîte *m*
tinder ['tɪndə(r)] *n* petit bois *m*
tinderbox ['tɪndəbɒks] *n Fig* poudrière *f*
tinfoil ['tɪnfɔɪl] *n* papier *m* aluminium
ting-a-ling ['tɪŋəlɪŋ] *n* dring-dring *m inv*
tinge [tɪn(d)ʒ] **1** *n (of colour, emotion)* pointe *f*
  2 *vt* **tinged with** teinté(e) de
tingle ['tɪŋɡəl] **1** *n (physical sensation)* picotement *m*; *(of fear)* frisson *m*; *(of excitement)* frémissement *m*
  2 *vi* picoter; **to t. with fear** frissonner de peur; **to t. with excitement** frémir d'excitation
tingling ['tɪŋɡlɪŋ] *n* picotement *m*
tinker ['tɪŋkə(r)] **1** *n (travelling person)* rétameur *m*
  2 *vi* **to t. with sth** bricoler qch
tinkle ['tɪŋkəl] **1** *n (of bell)* tintement *m*; *Br Fam (phone call)* **to give sb a t.** passer un coup de fil à qn
  2 *vi* tinter
tinned [tɪnd] *adj Br (food)* en boîte
tinnitus ['tɪnɪtəs] *n* acouphène *m*
tinny ['tɪnɪ] *adj (sound)* métallique
tinsel ['tɪnsəl] *n* guirlandes *fpl* de Noël
tint [tɪnt] **1** *n* teinte *f*, nuance *f*; *(in hair)* rinçage *m*
  2 *vt* teinter
tiny ['taɪnɪ] *adj* minuscule; **a t. bit** un tout petit peu

tip¹ [tɪp] **1** *n (end)* bout *m*; **on the tips of one's toes** sur la pointe des pieds; **it's on the t. of my tongue** je l'ai sur la bout de la langue; *Fig* **that's just the t. of the iceberg** ce n'est que la partie visible de l'iceberg
  2 *vt (pt & pp* **tipped)** **to be tipped with sth** avoir le bout recouvert de qch
tip² *n* (**a**) *(payment)* pourboire *m* (**b**) *(piece of advice)* truc *m*
  2 *vt (pt & pp* **tipped)** (**a**) *(give money to)* donner un pourboire à (**b**) *(predict)* **to t. a winner** *(in horse race)* pronostiquer un cheval gagnant; **to t. sb for success/promotion** prédire à qn le succès/une promotion; **the film is tipped to win an Oscar** de l'avis général il y a de fortes chances que le film remporte un Oscar
tip³ **1** *n (for rubbish) & Fig* dépotoir *m*
  2 *vt (pt & pp* **tipped)** (**a**) *(pour) (rubbish)* déverser; *(liquid)* verser; **to t. sth over sb/sth** renverser qch sur qn/qch (**b**) **to t. the scales at 95 kg** peser 95 kg; *Fig* **to t. the scales** *or* **balance (in sb's favour)** faire pencher la balance (en faveur de qn)
▸**tip off** *vt sep (warn)* avertir
▸**tip out** *vt sep (empty)* vider; *(discard)* jeter
▸**tip over 1** *vt sep* renverser
  2 *vi* se renverser
▸**tip up 1** *vt sep* renverser
  2 *vi* basculer
tip-off ['tɪpɒf] *n Fam* tuyau *m*
Tipp-Ex® ['tɪpeks] **1** *n* Tipp-Ex® *m inv*
  2 *vt* **to t. sth out** effacer qch avec du Tipp-Ex®
tipple ['tɪpəl] *n Fam* **what's your t.?** qu'est-ce que vous buvez habituellement?; **sherry's her favourite t.** ce qu'elle préfère, c'est le sherry
tipsy ['tɪpsɪ] *adj Fam* pompette
tiptoe ['tɪptəʊ] **1** *n* **on t.** sur la pointe des pieds
  2 *vi* marcher sur la pointe des pieds; **to t. in/out** entrer/sortir sur la pointe des pieds
tiptop ['tɪptɒp] *adj* excellent(e)
tirade [taɪ'reɪd] *n* diatribe *f*
tire¹ ['taɪə(r)] **1** *vt* fatiguer
  2 *vi* se fatiguer; **to t. of sth/of doing sth** se lasser de qch/de faire qch
▸**tire out** *vt sep (exhaust)* épuiser
tire² *Am* = **tyre**
tired ['taɪəd] *adj* fatigué(e); **to be t. of sth/of doing sth** en avoir assez de qch/de faire qch
tireless ['taɪəlɪs] *adj* infatigable
tiresome ['taɪəsəm] *adj* ennuyeux(euse)
tiring ['taɪərɪŋ] *adj* fatigant(e)
tissue ['tɪsjuː] *n* (**a**) *Biol* tissu *m* (**b**) *(paper handkerchief)* mouchoir *m* en papier; *Fig* **a t. of lies** un tissu de mensonges; **t. paper** papier *m* de soie
tit¹ [tɪt] *n (bird)* mésange *f*
tit² *n* **t. for tat** un prêté pour un rendu; **to give sb t. for tat** rendre à qn la monnaie de sa pièce
tit³ *n very Fam* (**a**) *(breast)* nichon *m*; *Br* **to get on sb's tits** courir sur le haricot à qn (**b**) *Br (idiot)* con (conne) *m,f*
titanic [taɪ'tænɪk] *adj (conflict, struggle)* titanesque
titanium [taɪ'teɪnɪəm] *n Chem* titane *m*
titbit ['tɪtbɪt] *n (snack)* morceau *m* de choix; *Fig* **t. of gossip** potin *m*; **t. of information** nouvelle *f*
titch [tɪtʃ] *n Br Fam (small person)* microbe *m*
titchy ['tɪtʃɪ] *adj Br Fam* minuscule
tit-for-tat [tɪtfə'tæt] *adj Fam (murder)* en représailles; **it's just t.** c'est un prêté pour un rendu

titillate ['tɪtɪleɪt] *vt* titiller

titillation [tɪtɪ'leɪʃən] *n* titillation *f*

title ['taɪtəl] **1** *n* titre *m*; **the titles** le générique; **t. deeds** titres de propriété; **t. fight** combat *m* comptant pour le titre; **t. page** page *f* de titre; **t. role** *(in play, film)* rôle-titre *m*; **t. track** *(of album)* morceau *m* qui donne son titre à l'album
2 *vt* intituler

titled ['taɪtəld] *adj (person)* titré(e)

titleholder ['taɪtəlhəʊldə(r)] *n (in sport)* tenant(e) *m,f* du titre

titter ['tɪtə(r)] **1** *n* petit rire *m*
2 *vi* rire bêtement

tittle-tattle ['tɪtəltætəl] *Fam* **1** *n* potins *mpl*, cancans *mpl*
2 *vi* cancaner

titular ['tɪtjʊlə(r)] *adj* en titre

tizzy ['tɪzɪ] *n Fam* **to be in/get into a t.** être/se mettre dans tous ses états

T-junction ['tiːdʒʌŋkʃən] *n* carrefour *m* en T

TLC [tiːel'siː] *n (abbr* **tender loving care)** affection *f*, tendresse *f*

TNT [tiːen'tiː] *n Chem (abbr* **trinitrotoluene)** TNT *m*

to [tuː, *unstressed* tə] **1** *prep* **(a)** *(towards)* à; **to go to church/school** aller à l'église/à l'école; **to go to France/Japan/the USA** aller en France/au Japon/aux États-Unis; **to go to sb's house** aller chez qn; **to the left/right** à gauche/droite
(b) *(until)* jusqu'à; **it's ten to (six)** il est (six heures) moins dix; **to count to ten** compter jusqu'à dix; **a year to the day** un an jour pour jour
(c) *(expressing indirect object)* **to give sth to sb** donner qch à qn; **to speak to sb** parler à qn
(d) *(with result)* **to my surprise/joy** à ma grande surprise/joie; **to my horror, I discovered that...** et, horreur!, je découvris que...
(e) *(expressing proportion)* **six votes to four** six voix contre quatre; **there are 8 francs to the pound** une livre vaut 8 francs
2 *particle* **(a)** *(with infinitive)* **to go** aller; **to have things to do** avoir des choses à faire; **it's too hot to go out** il fait trop chaud pour sortir; **he came to help me** il est venu m'aider; **I want him to know** je veux qu'il sache; **she told me to stay** elle m'a dit de rester
(b) *(representing verb)* **I want/ought to** je veux/devrais le faire; **I was told to** on m'a dit de le faire

toad [təʊd] *n (animal)* crapaud *m*; *Fam Pej (man)* type *m* répugnant; *Br* **t. in the hole** = saucisses cuites au four dans de la pâte à crêpes

toadstool ['təʊdstuːl] *n* champignon *m* non comestible

toady ['təʊdɪ] *Fam* **1** *n* lèche-bottes *mf inv*
2 *vi* **to t. to sb** lécher les bottes de qn

toast [təʊst] **1** *n* **(a)** *(toasted bread)* pain *m* grillé; **a slice** *or* **piece of t.** un toast; **t. rack** porte-toasts *m inv* **(b)** *(tribute)* toast *m*; **to drink a t. to sb/sth** porter un toast à qn/qch
2 *vt* **(a)** *(bread)* (faire) griller; **toasted cheese** fromage *m* fondu; **toasted sandwich** sandwich *m* grillé **(b)** *(tribute)* porter un toast à

toaster ['təʊstə(r)] *n* grille-pain *m inv*

toastie ['təʊstɪ] *n Fam (toasted sandwich)* sandwich *m* grillé

tobacco [tə'bækəʊ] *(pl* **tobaccos)** *n* tabac *m*; **t. pouch** blague *f* à tabac

tobacconist [tə'bækənɪst] *n* marchand(e) *m,f* de tabac; *Br* **t.'s (shop)** (bureau *m* de) tabac *m*

toboggan [tə'bɒgən] **1** *n* luge *f*
2 *vi* faire de la luge

today [tə'deɪ] *adv* aujourd'hui; **a week ago t.** il y a juste une semaine aujourd'hui; **a week from t.** aujourd'hui en huit; **t.'s date** la date d'aujourd'hui; **t.'s paper** le journal du jour

toddle ['tɒdəl] *vi (of infant)* commencer à marcher; *Fam* **to t. off** ficher le camp

toddler ['tɒdlə(r)] *n* tout-petit *m (qui fait ses premiers pas)*

to-die-for [tə'daɪfɔː(r)] *adj Fam* craquant(e)

to-do [tə'duː] *n Fam* remue-ménage *m inv*; **what a t.!** quelle histoire!

toe [təʊ] **1** *n* **(a)** *(of foot)* orteil *m*, doigt *m* de pied; *(of sock, shoe)* bout *m*; **big/little t.** gros/petit orteil **(b)** *(idioms)* **to be on one's toes** être en alerte; **to keep sb on his toes** ne pas laisser de répit à qn; **to tread on sb's toes** marcher sur les pieds de qn
2 *vt* **to t. the line** bien se tenir

toehold ['təʊhəʊld] *n (in climbing)* prise *f* de pied; *Fig* **to gain a t. in the market** mettre un pied sur le marché

toenail ['təʊneɪl] *n* ongle *m* de pied

toff [tɒf] *n Br Fam Old-fashioned* aristo *mf*

toffee ['tɒfɪ] *n* caramel *m* (au beurre); *Fam* **he can't sing for t.** il chante comme un pied; **t. apple** pomme *f* d'amour

tofu ['təʊfuː] *n* tofu *m*

together [tə'geðə(r)] **1** *adv* ensemble; **t. with** ainsi que, en même temps que
2 *adj Fam (person)* équilibré(e)

togetherness [tə'geðənɪs] *n* unité *f*, harmonie *f*

toggle ['tɒgəl] **1** *n (on coat)* olive *f*; *Comput & Elec* **t. switch** commande *f* à bascule
2 *vi Comput* basculer

Togo ['təʊgəʊ] *n* le Togo

Togolese [təʊgəʊ'liːz] **1** *n* Togolais(e) *m,f*
2 *adj* togolais(e)

togs [tɒgz] *npl Fam (clothes)* fringues *fpl*

toil [tɔɪl] **1** *n Lit* labeur *m*
2 *vi (work hard)* travailler dur; **to t. away at sth** peiner sur qch; **to t. up a hill** gravir péniblement une colline

toilet ['tɔɪlɪt] *n* **(a)** *(lavatory)* toilettes *fpl*; **to go to the t.** aller aux toilettes; **t. paper** papier *m* hygiénique; **t. roll** rouleau *m* de papier hygiénique; **t. seat** siège *m* des toilettes **(b)** *Old-fashioned (washing and dressing)* toilette *f*; **t. bag** trousse *f* de toilette; **t. soap** savon *m* de toilette

toiletries ['tɔɪlɪtrɪz] *npl* articles *mpl* de toilette

toilet-trained ['tɔɪlɪttreɪnd] *adj* propre

toilet-training ['tɔɪlɪttreɪnɪŋ] *n* apprentissage *m* de la propreté

token ['təʊkən] **1** *n* **(a)** *(symbol)* signe *m*, marque *f*; **as a t. of respect** en signe de respect; **by the same t.** de même, pareillement **(b)** *(for vending machine)* jeton *m*
2 *adj (resistance, effort)* symbolique; *(gesture)* symbolique, pour la forme; **I was the t. woman on the committee** j'étais la seule femme de la commission, parce qu'il en fallait une

Tokyo ['təʊkɪəʊ] *n* Tokyo

told [təʊld] *pt & pp of* **tell**

tolerable ['tɒlərəbəl] *adj* (**a**) *(bearable)* tolérable, supportable (**b**) *(reasonably good)* acceptable

tolerance ['tɒlərəns] *n* tolérance *f*; **to have a high/low t. for sth** bien/mal tolérer qch

tolerant ['tɒlərənt] *adj* tolérant(e); **to be t. of sb/sth** tolérer qn/qch

tolerate ['tɒləreɪt] *vt* tolérer

toleration [tɒlə'reɪʃən] *n* tolérance *f*

toll¹ [təʊl] *n* (**a**) *(charge)* péage *m*; **t. bridge** pont *m* à péage; **t. road** route *f* à péage (**b**) *(of dead, injured)* nombre *m* de victimes; *Fig* **to take its t.** faire des dégâts

toll² **1** *vt (bell)* sonner
    2 *vi (of bell)* sonner

toll-free [təʊl'friː] *Am* **1** *adj* **t. number** ≃ numéro *m* vert
    2 *adv (call)* gratuitement

Tom [tɒm] *n Fam* **anyT., Dick or Harry** le premier venu

tom [tɒm] *n Fam* matou *m*

tomahawk ['tɒməhɔːk] *n* tomahawk *m*

tomato [tə'mɑːtəʊ, *Am* tə'meɪtəʊ] *(pl* **tomatoes)** *n* tomate *f*; **t. juice** jus *m* de tomate; **t. ketchup** ketchup *m*; **t. purée** concentré *m* de tomates; **t. sauce** *(for pasta)* sauce *f* tomate; *(ketchup)* ketchup *m*; **t. soup** soupe *f* à la tomate

tomb [tuːm] *n* tombe *f*

tomboy ['tɒmbɔɪ] *n* garçon *m* manqué

tombstone ['tuːmstəʊn] *n* pierre *f* tombale

tomcat ['tɒmkæt] *n* matou *m*

tome [təʊm] *n Formal* gros volume *m*

tomfoolery [tɒm'fuːlərɪ] *n Fam* bêtises *fpl*

tomorrow [tə'mɒrəʊ] **1** *n* demain *m*; *Fam* **to do sth like there's no t.** faire qch frénétiquement
    2 *adv* demain; **t. morning/evening** demain matin/soir

tom-tom ['tɒmtɒm] *n* tam-tam *m*

ton [tʌn] *n* (**a**) *(weight)* tonne *f* (**b**) *(idioms) Fam* **to weigh a t.** peser une tonne; *Fam* **tons of** des tonnes de; *Fam* **to come down on sb like a t. of bricks** tomber dessus à qn

tone [təʊn] *n* (**a**) *(of voice)* ton *m*; *(quality of sound)* sonorité *f*; **don't speak to me in that t. of voice** ne me parle pas sur ce ton; **leave your name and number after the t.** *(on answering machine)* laissez votre nom et votre numéro de téléphone après le signal sonore; *Fig* **it set the t. for the evening** et le ton a été donné pour le reste de la soirée; *Fig* **to raise/lower the t. of the neighbourhood** améliorer/faire baisser le standing du quartier (**b**) *(colour)* ton *m*

▸**tone down** *vt sep (colour)* adoucir; *Fig (remarks)* modérer

▸**tone up** *vt sep (muscles)* raffermir, tonifier

tone-deaf [təʊn'def] *adj* **to be t.** ne pas avoir d'oreille

Tonga ['tɒŋgə] *n* les îles *fpl* Tonga

Tongan ['tɒŋgən] **1** *n* (**a**) *(person)* Tonguien(enne) *m,f* (**b**) *(language)* tongan *m*
    2 *adj* tonguien(enne)

tongs [tɒŋz] *npl* **(pair of) t.** pince *f*; **(curling) t.** *(for hair)* fer *m* à friser

tongue [tʌŋ] *n* (**a**) *(in mouth, of land, flame)* langue *f*; *(of shoe)* languette *f*; *(language)* langue *f*; **to stick one's t. out** tirer la langue; **t. twister** = mot ou phrase difficile à prononcer (**b**) *(idioms)* **hold your t.!** tiens ta langue!, tais-toi!; **have you lost your t.?** tu as perdu ta langue?; **to say sth t. in cheek** dire qch en plaisantant

tongue-tied ['tʌŋtaɪd] *adj* muet(ette)

tonic ['tɒnɪk] *n also Fig* tonique *m*, remontant *m*; **t. (water)** Schweppes® *m*

tonight [tə'naɪt] **1** *n (evening)* ce soir *m*; *(night)* cette nuit *f*
    2 *adv (evening)* ce soir; *(night)* cette nuit

tonnage ['tʌnɪdʒ] *n Naut (of ship)* tonnage *m*

tonne [tʌn] *n* tonne *f*

tonsil ['tɒnsəl] *n* amygdale *f*; **to have one's tonsils out** se faire opérer des amygdales

tonsillitis [tɒnsɪ'laɪtɪs] *n* amygdalite *f*; **to have t.** avoir une amygdalite

too [tuː] *adv* (**a**) *(excessively)* trop; **t. many people** trop de gens; **I know her all** *or* **only t. well** je ne la connais que trop; **you're t. kind** vous êtes trop aimable; **he's not t. well today** il ne va pas trop bien aujourd'hui; **t. bad** tant pis; *Fam* **t. right!** et comment! (**b**) *(also)* aussi; (**c**) *(moreover)* en plus

took [tʊk] *pt of* **take**

tool [tuːl] *n* (**a**) *(implement)* outil *m*; **(set of) tools** outillage *m*; **t. bag** trousse *f* à outils; *also Comput* **t. box** boîte *f* à outils; **t. kit** trousse *f* à outils; **t. shed** remise *f* (**b**) *(means, instrument)* instrument *m*

toot [tuːt] **1** *n* coup *m* de Klaxon®
    2 *vt* **to t. the horn** klaxonner; **to t. sb** klaxonner qn
    3 *vi* klaxonner

tooth [tuːθ] *(pl* **teeth** [tiːθ]*) n* (**a**) *(of person, saw, comb)* dent *f*; **to cut a t.** percer une dent; **t. decay** carie *f* (**b**) *(idioms)* **to fight t. and nail** se défendre bec et ongles; **to lie through one's teeth** mentir effrontément; **in the teeth of opposition** malgré l'opposition; **armed to the teeth** armé(e) jusqu'aux dents; *Fam* **to get one's teeth into sth** se mettre à fond dans qch; *Fam* **to be fed up to the back teeth with sb/sth** en avoir ras le bol de qn/qch; *Fam* **to be long in the t.** nêtre plus tout jeune

toothache ['tuːθeɪk] *n* mal *m* de dents; **to have t.** avoir mal aux dents

toothbrush ['tuːθbrʌʃ] *n* brosse *f* à dents

toothless ['tuːθlɪs] *adj* édenté(e), sans dents; *Fig (powerless)* sans pouvoir

toothpaste ['tuːθpeɪst] *n* dentifrice *m*

toothpick ['tuːθpɪk] *n* cure-dents *m inv*

toothy ['tuːθɪ] *adj* **t. grin** large sourire *m*

top¹ [tɒp] *n (toy)* toupie *f*

top² **1** *n* (**a**) *(highest part) (of tree, mountain, tower, head)* sommet *m*; *(of page, map)* haut *m*; **at the t. of the stairs/street** en haut des escaliers/de la rue; **to be (at the) t. of the class** être premier(ère) de la classe; **from t. to bottom** de haut en bas; *Fig* de fond en comble; **at the t. of one's voice** à tue-tête; **to go over the t.** *Mil* partir à l'assaut; *Fig* aller trop loin; *Fig* **over the t.** *(excessive)* exagéré(e); **to make it to the t.** parvenir au sommet; *Fig* réussir
    (**b**) *(lid) (of box)* couvercle *m*; *(of bottle)* bouchon *m*; *(of pen)* capuchon *m*
    (**c**) *(surface)* dessus *m*
    (**d**) *(garment)* haut *m*
    (**e**) **on t.** dessus; **on t. of** sur; *Fig* **to be on t. of sth** maîtriser qch; **you mustn't let things get on t. of you** il ne faut pas te laisser dépasser par les événements; *Fig* **to come out on t.** prendre le dessus; **to feel on t. of the world** se sentir en pleine forme
    2 *adj* (**a**) *(highest) (shelf, drawer)* du haut; *(floor)* dernier(ère); **the t. people** *(in society)* les gens *mpl* en vue; *(in an organization)* la direction *f*; *Fam* **the t.**

brass les gros bonnets *mpl*; **t. coat** *(of paint)* dernière couche *f*; **t. deck** *(of bus)* impériale *f*; *Fam Fig* **t. dog** chef *m*; **to feel on t. form** se sentir en pleine forme; *Aut* **t. gear** *(fourth)* quatrième *f* (vitesse *f*); *(fifth)* cinquième *f* (vitesse *f*); **t. hat** haut-de-forme *m*; **t. security** haute sécurité *f*; **t. speed** vitesse *f* de pointe; *Fig* **at t. speed** à toute vitesse

(**b**) *(best, major)* premier(ère); **the t. ten** les dix premiers; **to come t. in sth** arriver premier en qch

3 *vt* (**a**) *(place on top of)* couvrir (**with** de); *(cake, ice cream)* napper; **and to t. it all** et pour couronner le tout

(**b**) *(exceed)* dépasser

(**c**) *(be at the top of)* être en tête de; **to t. the bill** être la tête d'affiche

(**d**) *Br Fam* **to t. oneself** *(commit suicide)* se foutre en l'air

▶**top up** *vt sep* *(glass, tank)* remplir; *(sum of money)* compléter

top-heavy [tɒp'hevɪ] *adj* *(structure)* trop lourd(e) du haut, déséquilibré(e); *Fig* *(organization)* aux dirigeants trop nombreux

topic ['tɒpɪk] *n* sujet *m*, thème *m*

topical ['tɒpɪkəl] *adj* d'actualité

topless ['tɒplɪs] *adj* *(woman)* aux seins nus; **to go t.** faire du monokini

top-level ['tɒplevəl] *adj* au plus haut niveau

topmost ['tɒpməʊst] *adj* le (la) plus haut(e)

top-notch ['tɒpnɒtʃ] *adj Fam* de première classe

topography [tɒ'pɒgrəfɪ] *n* topographie *f*

topping ['tɒpɪŋ] *n (for pizza)* garniture *f*; *(for cake, ice-cream)* nappage *m*

topple ['tɒpəl] **1** *vt* faire tomber, renverser
2 *vi* tomber

top-quality ['tɒpkwɒlətɪ] *adj* de qualité supérieure

top-secret ['tɒpsiːkrɪt] *adj* top secret(ète)

topsoil ['tɒpsɔɪl] *n* couche *f* arable

topsy-turvy [tɒpsɪ'tɜːvɪ] *Fam* **1** *adj (untidy)* sens dessus dessous; *(confused)* tordu(e)
2 *adv (untidily)* sens dessus dessous

torch [tɔːtʃ] **1** *n* (**a**) *(burning)* torche *f*; *Fig* **to carry a t. for sb** aimer qn secrètement (**b**) *Br (electric)* lampe *f* de poche
2 *vt* incendier, mettre le feu à

torchlight ['tɔːtʃlaɪt] *n* **by t.** à la lumière d'une lampe de poche; **t. procession** retraite *f* aux flambeaux

tore [tɔː] *pt of* **tear²**

torment 1 *n* ['tɔːment] supplice *m*; **to be in t.** être au supplice
2 *vt* [tɔː'ment] tourmenter

tormentor [tɔː'mentə(r)] *n* bourreau *m*

torn [tɔːn] *pp of* **tear²**

tornado [tɔː'neɪdəʊ] *n* tornade *f*

Toronto [tə'rɒntəʊ] *n* Toronto

torpedo [tɔː'piːdəʊ] **1** *n* torpille *f*; **t. boat** torpilleur *m*, vedette *f* lance-torpilles
2 *vt also Fig* torpiller

torpid ['tɔːpɪd] *adj* engourdi(e), léthargique

torpor ['tɔːpə(r)] *n* torpeur *f*

torrent ['tɒrənt] *n* torrent *m*; *Fig (of abuse, insults)* flot *m*; **it's raining in torrents** il pleut à torrents

torrential [tɒ'renʃəl] *adj* torrentiel(elle)

torrid ['tɒrɪd] *adj also Fig* torride

torso ['tɔːsəʊ] *n* torse *m*

tortoise ['tɔːtəs] *n* tortue *f*

tortoiseshell ['tɔːtəsʃel] *n* écaille *f* (de tortue); **t. (cat)** chat *m* noir, blanc et roux

tortuous ['tɔːtjʊəs] *adj* tortueux(euse)

torture ['tɔːtʃə(r)] **1** *n* torture *f*; *Fig* **it was sheer t.!** c'était un vrai supplice!; **t. chamber** chambre *f* de torture
2 *vt also Fig* torturer

Tory ['tɔːrɪ] *n & adj* Tory *m*, conservateur(trice) *m,f*

tosh [tɒʃ] *n Br Fam* bêtises *fpl*

toss [tɒs] **1** *n* (**a**) *(of ball)* lancer *m*; *(of head)* mouvement *m* brusque; **to decide sth on the t. of a coin** décider qch à pile ou face; **to argue the t.** discuter inutilement (**b**) *Br very Fam* **not to give a t.** s'en ficher
2 *vt (throw)* lancer; *(pancake)* faire sauter; *(salad)* remuer; **to t. sth to sb** lancer qch à qn; **to t. a coin** jouer à pile ou face; **to t. one's head** rejeter la tête en arrière; **the ship was tossed by the sea** le bateau était ballotté par la mer
3 *vi* **to t. (up) for sth** jouer qch à pile ou face; **to t. and turn** *(in bed)* se tourner et se retourner *(pour trouver le sommeil)*

▶**toss about, toss around** *vt sep (ship)* ballotter; *Fig (idea)* lancer

▶**toss off** *vt sep* (**a**) *(write)* expédier (**b**) *Vulg (masturbate)* **to t. oneself off** se branler; **to t. sb off** branler qn

▶**toss out** *vt sep* jeter

▶**tosser** ['tɒsə(r)] *n Br very Fam* con (conne) *m,f*

toss-up ['tɒsʌp] *n* **to have a t.** jouer à pile ou face; *Fam* **it was a t. between the pub and the cinema** nous n'arrivions pas à nous décider entre le pub et le cinéma; **it's a t. whether or not she'll say yes** je ne sais vraiment pas si elle va dire oui

tot [tɒt] *n* (**a**) *(child)* tout-petit *m* (**b**) *(of drink)* (petite) goutte *f*

▶**tot up** *vt sep* additionner

total ['təʊtəl] **1** *n* total *m*; **in t.** au total
2 *adj* total(e); **t. eclipse** éclipse *f* totale
3 *vt* (**a**) *(sum)* se monter à (**b**) *Am Fam (wreck)* bousiller

totalitarian [təʊtælɪ'teərɪən] *adj* totalitaire

totality [təʊ'tælɪtɪ] *n* totalité *f*

totally ['təʊtəlɪ] *adv* totalement

tote¹ [təʊt] *n (in betting)* totalisateur *m*, totaliseur *m*

tote² *vt Fam (carry)* trimbal(l)er

totem pole ['təʊtəmpəʊl] *n* totem *m*

totter ['tɒtə(r)] *vi also Fig* chanceler; **to t. in/out** entrer/sortir d'un pas chancelant

totty ['tɒtɪ] *n Br Fam (attractive women)* belles nanas *fpl*, belles gonzesses *fpl*

toucan ['tuːkæn] *n* toucan *m*

touch [tʌtʃ] **1** *n* (**a**) *(act of touching)* toucher *m*, contact *m*; **I felt a t. on my arm** j'ai senti qu'on me touchait le bras; **it was t. and go whether...** il n'était pas certain que... + *subjunctive*

(**b**) *(sense)* toucher *m*; *(feel)* contact *m*; **hard/soft to the t.** dur/doux au toucher; **he's lost his t.** il a perdu la main

(**c**) *(detail)* **there were some nice touches in the film** il y avait quelques bons passages dans le film

(**d**) *(small amount)* pointe *f*; **a t. (too) strong/short** un peu trop fort(e)/court(e); **to have a t. of flu** être un peu grippé(e)

(**e**) *(communication)* **to be/get in t. with sb** être/se mettre en contact avec qn; **to stay in/lose t. with sb** rester en/perdre contact avec qn (**f**) *(in football, rugby)* **in t.** en touche; **t. judge** juge *m* de touche

2 *vt (physically, emotionally)* toucher; *(interfere with)* toucher à; **to t. bottom** *(of ship, economy)* toucher le fond; *Fam* **t. wood!** je touche du bois!; **I never t. alcohol** je ne touche jamais à l'alcool; **you haven't touched your meal** tu n'as pas touché à ton repas; **the law can't t. her** la loi ne peut rien contre elle; *Fig* **there's nothing to t. it** c'est sans égal; **there's nothing to t. her** elle est imbattable

▸**touch down** *vi (of plane)* atterrir

▸**touch on** *vt insep* aborder

▸**touch up** *vt sep* (**a**) *(picture)* retoucher (**b**) *Br Fam (molest)* peloter

touchdown ['tʌtʃdaʊn] *n* (**a**) *(of plane)* atterrissage *m* (**b**) *(in American football)* but *m*

touched [tʌtʃt] *adj* (**a**) *(moved)* touché(e), ému(e) (**b**) *Fam (mad)* toqué(e)

touching ['tʌtʃɪŋ] *adj (moving)* touchant(e), émouvant(e)

touchline ['tʌtʃlaɪn] *n* ligne *f* de touche

touch-sensitive screen ['tʌtʃ'sensɪtɪv'skriːn] *n Comput* écran *m* tactile

touchstone ['tʌtʃstəʊn] *n* pierre *f* de touche

touch-tone ['tʌtʃtəʊn] *adj (telephone)* à touches

touch-type ['tʌtʃtaɪp] *vi* taper au toucher

touchy ['tʌtʃɪ] *adj (subject)* délicat(e); *(person)* susceptible (**about** à propos de)

touchy-feely ['tʌtʃɪfiːlɪ] *adj Pej* qui affectionne les contacts physiques

tough [tʌf] **1** *adj* (**a**) *(strict, severe) (resistant)* résistant(e), solide; *Fam* **a t. guy** un dur à cuire; **to get t. (with sb)** se montrer plus sévère (avec qn) (**b**) *(difficult)* dur(e), difficile; *(unfair)* dur(e); *Fam* **t. luck!** pas de chance!; *Ironic* tant pis!

2 *adv* **to act t.** jouer au dur

3 *n* dur(e) *m,f*

toughen ['tʌfən] *vt (person, skin)* endurcir; *(penalties, conditions)* durcir; **toughened glass** verre *m* trempé

toughness ['tʌfnɪs] *n (of meat, skin, conditions)* dureté *f*; *(of task)* difficulté *f*; *(of person) (strength)* force *f*; *(hardness)* dureté *f*

toupee ['tuːpeɪ] *n* postiche *m*

tour [tʊə(r)] **1** *n (by tourist)* voyage *m*; *(of building, town)* visite *f*; *(by pop group, theatre company)* tournée *f*; **to go on a t.** *(of tourist)* faire un voyage organisé; **to go on t.** *(of pop group, theatre company)* partir en tournée; *Mil* **t. of duty** service *m*; **t. of inspection** tournée *f* d'inspection; **t. guide** *(person)* guide *mf*; **t. operator** voyagiste *m*

2 *vt (country, hospital)* visiter; *(of pop group, theatre company)* être en tournée à/en

3 *vi (of tourist)* faire du tourisme, voyager; *(of pop group, theatre company)* être en tournée

tour de force ['tʊədə'fɔːs] *n* tour *m* de force

tourism ['tʊərɪzəm] *n* tourisme *m*

tourist ['tʊərɪst] *n* touriste *mf*; **t. attraction** site *m* touristique; **t. class** classe *f* touriste; **t. (information) office** syndicat *m* d'initiative, office *m* du tourisme; *Fam* **t. trap** piège *m* à touristes

tournament ['tʊənəmənt] *n* tournoi *m*

tourniquet ['tʊənɪkeɪ] *n Med* garrot *m*

tousle ['taʊzəl] *vt* ébouriffer

tout [taʊt] **1** *n (ticket)* **t.** revendeur(euse) *m,f* de billets *(au marché noir)*

2 *vt (tickets, goods)* revendre

3 *vi* **to t. for trade** racoler des clients

tow [təʊ] **1** *n* **to give sb a t.** remorquer qn; **on t.** en remorque; *Fam* **to have someone in t.** avoir qn dans son sillage; **t. truck** dépanneuse *f*

2 *vt* remorquer; **to t. a car away** enlever une voiture

toward [tə'wɔːd] = **towards**

towards [tə'wɔːdz] *prep* (**a**) *(in space, time)* vers (**b**) *(directed at) (of feelings, behaviour)* envers (**c**) *(contributing to)* **to contribute t. the cost of sth** participer au coût de qch; **15% of the budget will go t. improving safety** 15% du budget sera destiné à l'amélioration de la sécurité

towbar ['təʊbaː(r)] *n* barre *f* de remorquage

towel ['taʊəl] **1** *n* serviette *f* (de toilette); **t. rail** porte-serviette *m*

2 *vt* **to t. oneself (dry)** se sécher, s'essuyer

towelling ['taʊəlɪŋ] *n* tissu-éponge *m*

tower ['taʊə(r)] **1** *n* tour *f*; *Fig* **a t. of strength** un roc; *Br* **t. block** tour d'habitation; *Comput* **t. system** tour

2 *vi* **to t. over sb/sth** dominer qn/qch

towering ['taʊərɪŋ] *adj* immense

town [taʊn] *n* ville *f*; **to go into t.** aller en ville; **to go out on the t.** faire la fête en ville; *Fam Fig* **to go to t. (on sth)** mettre le paquet (sur qch); **t. centre** centre-ville *m*; **t. clerk** secrétaire *mf* de mairie; **t. council** conseil *m* municipal; **t. hall** mairie *f*; **t. planner** urbaniste *mf*; **t. planning** urbanisme *m*

townsfolk ['taʊnzfəʊk] *npl* citadins *mpl*

township ['taʊnʃɪp] *n (in North America)* municipalité *f*; *(in South Africa)* township *f*

townspeople ['taʊnzpiːpəl] *npl* citadins *mpl*

towpath ['təʊpaːθ] *n* chemin *m* de halage

towrope ['təʊrəʊp] *n* câble *m* de remorque

toxic ['tɒksɪk] *adj* toxique

toxin ['tɒksɪn] *n* toxine *f*

toy [tɔɪ] **1** *n* jouet *m*; **t. soldier** petit soldat *m*; **t. shop** magasin *m* de jouets; **t. train** train *m* miniature

2 *vi* **to t. with sb** jouer avec qn; **to t. with an idea** caresser une idée; **to t. with sb's affections** jouer avec les sentiments de qn

toyboy ['tɔɪbɔɪ] *n Fam* jeune amant *m* *(d'une femme plus âgée)*

trace [treɪs] **1** *n* trace *f*; **without t.** sans laisser de traces; *Chem* **t. element** oligo-élément *m*

2 *vt* (**a**) *(diagram, picture)* tracer (**b**) *(person)* retrouver (la trace de); *(development, history)* retracer

trachea [trə'kiːə] *(pl* **tracheae** [trə'kiːiː]*) n Anat* trachée *f*

track [træk] **1** *n* (**a**) *(mark)* trace *f*; *(trail)* piste *f* (**b**) *(path)* piste *f*, chemin *m*; *(in athletics)* piste; *Sport* **t. and field events** épreuves *fpl* d'athlétisme; *Fig* **t. record** passé *m*; **t. shoes** chaussures *fpl* d'athlétisme (**c**) *(on record, CD)* morceau *m* (**d**) *(of tank, tractor)* chenille *f* (**e**) *(railway line)* voie *f* (**f**) *(idioms)* **to be on the right t.** être sur la bonne voie; **to keep t. of sth** surveiller qch; **to lose t. of sb** perdre qn de vue; **I've lost t. of how much money I've spent** je ne sais plus combien d'argent j'ai dépensé; **to stop sb in his tracks** stopper qn net; *Fam* **to make tracks** filer, mettre les voiles

2 *vt (animal)* suivre à la trace; *(missile)* suivre la trajectoire de; *(person)* traquer

▸**track down** *vt sep (locate)* trouver

tracked [trækt] *adj (vehicle)* chenillé(e)

tracker dog ['trækə'dɒg] *n* chien *m* policier

tracksuit ['trÆksuːt] *n* survêtement *m*; **t. top** veste *f* de survêtement; **t. trousers** *or* **bottoms** pantalon *m* de survêtement

tract¹ [trækt] *n* (**a**) *(of land)* étendue *f* (**b**) *Anat (respiratory, digestive)* appareil *m*

tract² *n (pamphlet)* tract *m*

tractable ['træktəbəl] *adj (person, animal)* docile

traction ['trækʃən] *n (force)* traction *f*; *Med* **to be in t.** être en extension; **t. engine** locomobile *f*

tractor ['træktə(r)] *n (vehicle)* tracteur *m*; *Comput* **t. feed** alimentation *f* par entraînement

trade [treɪd] **1** *n* (**a**) *Com (commerce)* commerce *m*; **t. association** association *f* professionnelle; **t. deficit** déficit *m* commercial; **t. discount** remise *f* professionnelle; **t. embargo** embargo *m* commercial; **t. fair** foire *f ou* exposition *f* commerciale; **t. gap** déficit commercial; **t. name** *(of product)* nom *m* de marque; *(of firm)* raison *f* commerciale; *also Fig* **t. secret** secret *m* de fabrication; *Geog* **t. winds** alizés *mpl* (**b**) *(swap)* échange *m*; **to do a t.** faire un échange (**c**) *(profession)* métier *m*; **he's a plumber by t.** il est plombier (de son métier); **t. union** syndicat *m*; **t. unionist** syndicaliste *mf*

2 *vt* **to t. sth (for sth)** échanger qch (contre qch); **to t. places with sb** changer de place avec qn; **to t. insults/blows** échanger des insultes/coups

3 *vi* commercer, faire du commerce

▸**trade in** *vt sep* faire reprendre; **I traded my car in for a new one** ils ont repris ma vieille voiture quand j'ai acheté la nouvelle

▸**trade on** *vt insep (exploit)* profiter de

trade-in ['treɪdɪn] *n* reprise *f*

trademark ['treɪdmɑːk] *n* marque *f* (de fabrique); *Fig* signe *m* distinctif

trade-off ['treɪdɒf] *n* compromis *m*

trader ['treɪdə(r)] *n* commerçant(e) *m,f*, marchand(e) *m,f*; *(on stock exchange)* opérateur(trice) *m,f*

tradesman ['treɪdzmən] *n* commerçant(e) *m,f*

trading ['treɪdɪŋ] *n* **t. partner** partenaire *m* commercial; **t. post** comptoir *m* commercial; **t. stamp** timbre-prime *m*

tradition [trə'dɪʃən] *n* tradition *f*

traditional [trə'dɪʃənəl] *adj* traditionnel(elle)

traditionalist [trə'dɪʃənəlɪst] *n & adj* traditionaliste *mf*

traffic ['træfɪk] **1** *n* (**a**) *(vehicles)* circulation *f*, trafic *m*; **t. cone** cône *m* de signalisation; *Fam* **t. cop** agent *m* de la circulation; **t. island** refuge *m*; **t. jam** embouteillage *m*; *Br* **t. lights** feux *mpl* (tricolores *ou* de signalisation); **t. police** police *f* de la route; *Br* **t. warden** contractuel(elle) *m,f* (**b**) *(trade)* trafic *m*

2 *vt* faire le trafic de

3 *vi* faire du trafic (**in** de)

trafficker ['træfɪkə(r)] *n* trafiquant(e) *m,f*

tragedy ['trædʒɪdɪ] *n* tragédie *f*

tragic ['trædʒɪk] *adj* tragique

tragically ['trædʒɪklɪ] *adv* tragiquement

trail [treɪl] **1** *n* (**a**) *(of smoke, blood)* traînée *f*; **to be on the t. of sb/sth** être sur les traces *ou* la piste de qn/qch (**b**) *(path)* sentier *m*, piste *f*; **t. bike** moto *f* de cross

2 *vt (drag)* traîner

3 *vi* (**a**) *(drag)* traîner (**b**) *(move slowly)* se traîner (**c**) *(in sport, contest)* **to be trailing (behind)** être mené(e)

▸**trail away, trail off** *vi (of voice)* se taire; *(of sound)* s'arrêter

trailblazer ['treɪlbleɪzə(r)] *n* pionnier(ère) *m,f*

trailer ['treɪlə(r)] *n* (**a**) *(vehicle)* remorque *f*; *Am (caravan)* camping-car *m*; *Am Fam Pej* **t. trash** prolos *mpl* (qui vivent dans les caravanes) (**b**) *(for film, TV programme)* bande-annonce *f*

train [treɪn] **1** *n* (**a**) *(means of transport)* train *m* (**b**) *(series)* suite *f*, enchaînement *m*; **t. of thought** enchaînement d'idées (**c**) *(retinue)* suite *f* (**d**) *(of dress)* traîne *f*

2 *vt* (**a**) *(person)* former; *(animal)* dresser; **to t. sb for sth/to do sth** former qn à qch/à faire qch (**b**) *(gun, telescope)* braquer (**on** sur)

3 *vi (of athlete, soldier)* s'entraîner; **to t. as a nurse/teacher** suivre une formation d'infirmière/de professeur

trained [treɪnd] *adj* (**a**) *(animal)* dressé(e) (**b**) *(teacher, nurse)* diplômé(e) (**c**) *(eye, ear)* exercé(e)

trainee [treɪ'niː] *n* stagiaire *mf*

traineeship [treɪ'niːʃɪp] *n* stage *m*

trainer ['treɪnə(r)] *n* (**a**) *(of athlete, team, racehorse)* entraîneur *m*; *(of animals)* dresseur(euse) *m,f* (**b**) *(shoe)* chaussure *f* de sport (**c**) **t. (aircraft)** avion-école *m*

training ['treɪnɪŋ] *n (in sport)* entraînement *m*; *(for job)* formation *f*; **to be in t. (for)** *(of athlete, team)* s'entraîner (pour); **to be out of t.** manquer d'entraînement; **t. course** stage *m* (de formation); **t. officer** officier *m* instructeur

trainload ['treɪnləʊd] *n* **a t. of** un train plein de

trainspotter ['treɪnspɒtə(r)] *n Br* = personne dont le passe-temps est de noter les numéros des trains; *Fam Pej* **he's a bit of a t.** il est vraiment ringard

traipse [treɪps] *vi Fam* traîner

trait [treɪt] *n* trait *m* (de caractère)

traitor ['treɪtə(r)] *n* traître(esse) *m,f*

trajectory [trə'dʒektərɪ] *n* trajectoire *f*

tram [træm] *n Br* tramway *m*

tramline ['træmlaɪn] *n* ligne *f* de tramway; **tramlines** *(in tennis)* lignes *fpl* de côté

tramp [træmp] **1** *n* (**a**) *(vagabond)* clochard(e) *m,f* (**b**) *very Fam (immoral woman)* traînée *f* (**c**) **t. (steamer)** tramp *m* (**d**) *(walk)* promenade *f*

2 *vt (country)* arpenter, parcourir; **to t. the streets** battre le pavé

3 *vi* marcher (d'un pas lourd)

trample ['træmpəl] **1** *vt* piétiner; **to t. sth underfoot** fouler qch aux pieds

2 *vi* **to t. on sb/sth** piétiner qn/qch

trampoline [træmpə'liːn] *n* trampoline *m*

trance [trɑːns] *n* transe *f*; **to go into a t.** entrer *ou* se mettre en transe

tranquil ['træŋkwɪl] *adj* tranquille, calme

tranquillity, *Am* **tranquility** [træŋ'kwɪlɪtɪ] *n* tranquillité *f*, calme *m*

tranquillizer, *Am* **tranquilizer** ['træŋkwɪlaɪzə(r)] *n* tranquillisant *m*, calmant *m*

transaction [træn'zækʃən] *n* transaction *f*, opération *f*

transatlantic [trænzət'læntɪk] *adj* transatlantique

transcend [træn'send] *vt (go beyond)* transcender; *(be superior to)* surpasser

transcendental [trænsen'dentəl] *adj* transcendantal(e); **t. meditation** méditation *f* transcendantale

transcontinental [trænzkɒntɪ'nentəl] *adj* transcontinental(e)

transcribe [træns'kraɪb] *vt* transcrire

transcript ['trænskrɪpt] *n* transcription *f*

transcription [træns'krɪpʃən] *n* transcription *f*

transfer 1 *n* ['trænsfɜː(r)] (**a**) *(move)* transfert *m*; *(of employee)* mutation *f*; *(of power)* passation *f*; **t. fee** *(for footballer)* prime *f* de transfert; **t. lounge** *(in airport)* salle *f* de transit; **t. passenger** passager *m* en transit; *Comput* **t. speed** vitesse *f* de transfert (**b**) *(sticker)* transfert *m*

2 *vt* [træns'fɜː(r)] transférer; *(employee)* muter; *(attention, affection)* déplacer

3 *vi* [træns'fɜː(r)] être transféré(e) (**to** dans); *(between planes, trains)* changer

transferable [træns'fɜːrəbəl] *adj* transmissible; **not t.** *(on ticket)* titre de transport nominal

transfigure [træns'fɪgə(r)] *vt* transfigurer

transfix [træns'fɪks] *vt* transpercer; *Fig* **to be transfixed with fear** être pétrifié(e) par la peur

transform [træns'fɔːm] *vt* transformer (**into** en)

transformation [trænsfə'meɪʃən] *n* transformation *f*

transformer [træns'fɔːmə(r)] *n Elec* transformateur *m*

transfusion [træns'fjuːʒən] *n* (**blood**) **t.** transfusion *f* (sanguine)

transgenic [trænz'dʒenɪk] *adj* transgénique

transgress [trænz'gres] *Formal* **1** *vt (law)* transgresser, enfreindre

2 *vi (violate law)* transgresser la loi; *(sin)* pécher

transient ['trænzɪənt] *adj* éphémère

transistor [træn'zɪstə(r)] *n Elec* transistor *m*; **t. (radio)** transistor

transit ['trænzɪt] *n* transit *m*; **in t.** en transit; **t. camp** camp *m* de transit; **t. visa** visa *m* de transit

transition [træn'zɪʃən] *n* transition *f*; **the t. from sth to sth** le passage de qch à qch

transitional [træn'zɪʃənəl] *adj* transitoire, de transition

transitive ['trænzɪtɪv] *adj Gram* transitif(ive)

transitory ['trænzɪtərɪ] *adj* transitoire

translate [trænz'leɪt] **1** *vt* traduire (**from/into** de/en); *Fig* **to t. one's ideas into action** mettre ses idées en pratique

2 *vi (of person)* faire de la traduction; *(of word, expression)* se traduire (**as** par)

translation [trænz'leɪʃən] *n (of language)* traduction *f*

translator [trænz'leɪtə(r)] *n* traducteur(trice) *m,f*

transliterate [trænz'lɪtəreɪt] *vt* transcrire

translucent [trænz'luːsənt] *adj* translucide

transmission [trænz'mɪʃən] *n (action)* transmission *f*; *(TV, radio programme)* émission *f*; **t. shaft** *(in vehicle)* arbre *m* de transmission

transmit [trænz'mɪt] *vt* transmettre; *(TV, radio programme)* diffuser

transmitter [trænz'mɪtə(r)] *n (emitter)* émetteur *m*; *(relay station)* réémetteur *m*

transparent [træns'pærənt] *adj* (**a**) *(see-through)* transparent(e) (**b**) *(obvious)* évident(e)

transpire [træns'paɪə(r)] **1** *vt (become apparent)* **it transpired that...** il s'est avéré que...; **she transpired to be...** elle s'est avérée être...

2 *vi (happen)* arriver, se passer

transplant 1 *n* ['trænsplɑːnt] *(of organ)* transplantation *f*, greffe *f*

2 *vt* [træns'plɑːnt] (**a**) *(organ)* transplanter, greffer (**b**) *(population)* transplanter

transport 1 *n* ['trænspɔːt] transport *m*; *Br* **t. café** routier *m (restaurant)*; **t. costs** frais *mpl* de transport

2 *vt* [træns'pɔːt] transporter

transportation [trænzpɔː'teɪʃən] *n* transport *m*; *Hist (as punishment)* transportation *f*

transporter [træns'pɔːtə(r)] *n (vehicle)* camion *m* pour transport d'automobiles

transpose [træns'pəʊz] *vt* transposer

transsexual [træn(z)'seksjʊəl] *n* transsexuel(elle) *m,f*

Transvaal ['trɑːnzvɑːl] *n* **the T.** le Transvaal

transverse ['trænzvɜːs] *adj* transversal(e)

transvestite [trænz'vestaɪt] *n* travesti *m*

trap [træp] **1** *n* (**a**) *(in hunting) & Fig* piège *m*; **to set a t.** tendre un piège; *Fig* **to walk** *or* **fall straight into the t.** tomber en plein dans le piège (**b**) *very Fam (mouth)* gueule *f*

2 *vt* piéger, prendre au piège; **to t. sb into saying/ doing sth** faire dire/faire faire qch à qn en usant de ruse

trapdoor [træp'dɔː(r)] *n* trappe *f*

trapeze [trə'piːz] *n* trapèze *m*; **t. artist** trapéziste *mf*

trapper ['træpə(r)] *n* trappeur *m*

trappings ['træpɪŋz] *npl* signes *mpl* extérieurs

trash [træʃ] **1** *n* (**a**) *(worthless objects)* camelote *f*; *Fam* **that book/film is a load of t.** ce livre/film est nul (**b**) *Am (refuse)* ordures *fpl*; **t. can** poubelle *f*

2 *vt Fam* (**a**) *(vandalize)* saccager (**b**) *(criticize)* descendre en flammes

trashy ['træʃɪ] *adj Fam* à la noix

trauma ['trɔːmə] *n* traumatisme *m*

traumatic [trɔː'mætɪk] *adj* traumatisant(e)

traumatize ['trɔːmətaɪz] *vt* traumatiser

travail ['træveɪl] *n Lit* labeur *m*

travel ['trævəl] **1** *n* voyage *m*; **on my travels** au cours de mes voyages; **I spend half my money on t.** *(to and from work)* la moitié de mon argent part dans les transports; **t. agency** agence *f* de voyages; **t. agent** agent *m* de voyages; **t. documents** titre *m* de transport; **t. insurance** assurance-voyage *f*; **t. writer** auteur *m* de récits de voyage

2 *vt (road, country)* parcourir

3 *vi* (**a**) *(of person)* voyager; *(vehicle, of light, sound, electricity)* se déplacer; **we travelled across France by train** nous avons traversé la France en train; **wine doesn't t. well** le vin supporte mal d'être transporté; *Fam* (**good**) **news travels fast** les nouvelles vont vite

traveller, *Am* **traveler** ['trævələ(r)] *n* voyageur(euse) *m,f*; *Br* (**new age**) **t.** voyageur new age; **t.'s cheque** chèque *m* de voyage

travelling, *Am* **traveling** ['trævəlɪŋ] **1** *n* déplacement *m*; **t. bag** sac *m* de voyage; **t. companion** compagnon *m* de voyage; **t. expenses** frais *mpl* de déplacement; *Br* **t. rug** plaid *m*

2 *adj (performer, circus)* itinérant(e); **t. salesman** voyageur *m* de commerce

traverse [trə'vɜːs] *vt Lit* traverser

travesty ['trævəstɪ] *n* travestissement *m*; **t. of justice** simulacre *m* de justice

trawl [trɔːl] **1** *n* (**a**) *(net)* chalut *m* (**b**) *Fig (search)* **to carry out** *or* **make a t. through sth** passer qch au crible

2 *vt* (**a**) *(sea)* aller à la pêche au chalut en (**b**) *Fig (search through)* passer au crible

3 *vi* (**a**) *(fish)* pêcher au chalut (**b**) *Fig* **to t. through sth** passer qch au crible

trawler ['trɔːlə(r)] *n (ship)* chalutier *m*

tray [treɪ] *n* plateau *m*; *(in office)* corbeille *f*

treacherous ['tretʃərəs] *adj* traître

treachery ['tretʃərɪ] *n* traîtrise *f*

treacle ['triːkəl] *n* mélasse *f*

tread [tred] **1** *vt* (*pt* **trod** [trɒd], *pp* **trodden** ['trɒdən]) marcher sur; **to t. sth underfoot** fouler qch aux pieds; **to t. sth into the carpet** mettre qch sur le tapis (avec ses chaussures); **to t. the boards** (*appear on stage*) monter sur les planches; **to t. grapes** fouler le raisin; **to t. water** faire du surplace; *Fig* (*of company*) se maintenir à flot

2 *vi* marcher (**on** sur); *also Fig* **to t. on sb's toes** marcher sur les pieds de qn; *Fig* **to t. carefully** *or* **warily** y aller doucement

3 *n* (**a**) (*sound of footstep*) pas *m* (**b**) (*of tyre*) chape *f*

treadmill ['tredmɪl] *n* (*in gym*) tapis *m* roulant de jogging; *Hist* (*in prison*) = roue ou manège auxquels étaient attachés les prisonniers; *Fig* (*routine*) routine *f*

treason ['triːzən] *n* trahison *f*

treasonable ['triːzənəbəl] *adj* qui constitue un acte de trahison

treasure ['treʒə(r)] **1** *n also Fig* trésor *m*; **t. hunt** chasse *f* au trésor

2 *vt* (*person, possession*) tenir beaucoup à; (*memory*) chérir

treasurer ['treʒərə(r)] *n* trésorier(ère) *m,f*

treasure-trove ['treʒətrəʊv] *n Law* trésor *m*; *Fig* mine *f*

treasury ['treʒərɪ] *n* trésorerie *f*; **the T.** (*government department*) ≃ le ministère des Finances; *Fin* **t. bond** ≃ bon *m* du Trésor

treat [triːt] **1** *n* (*pleasure*) plaisir *m*; (*gift*) cadeau *m*; **to give sb a t.** faire plaisir à qn; **it's my t.** (*I'm paying*) c'est moi qui régale; *also Ironic* **you've got a real t. in store** attends-toi à une belle surprise; *Fam* **to work a t.** marcher à merveille

2 *vt* (**a**) (*person, illness, metal*) traiter; **to t. sb well/ badly** bien/mal traiter qn; **to t. sth as a joke** prendre qch à la rigolade (**b**) (*give present to*) **to t. sb to sth** offrir qch à qn; **to t. oneself to sth** s'offrir qch; **I'll t. you** (*pay for you*) je t'invite; *Ironic* **she treated us to one of her tantrums** nous avons eu droit à une de ses colères

3 *vi Formal* (*negotiate*) **to t. with sb/sth** traiter avec qn/qch

treatise ['triːtɪs] *n* traité *m*

treatment ['triːtmənt] *n* traitement *m*; *Fam* **to give sb the t.** rosser qn

treaty ['triːtɪ] *n* (*international*) traité *m*; (*between individuals*) accord *m*, contrat *m*

treble ['trebəl] **1** *n Mus* (*person, voice*) soprano *m*

2 *adj* (*triple*) triple; *Mus* **t. clef** clef *f* de sol

3 *vt & vi* tripler

tree [triː] *n* arbre *m*; *Fig* **at the top of the t.** en haut de l'échelle; *Am Fam* **to be out of one's t.** débloquer; *Pej* **t. hugger** écologiste *mf* fanatique; **t. trunk** tronc *m* d'arbre

treetop ['triːtɒp] *n* cime *f* d'un arbre

trek [trek] **1** *n* (*long walk*) randonnée *f* (pédestre); *Fig* **it's quite a t. to the shops** ça fait loin à pied jusqu'aux magasins

2 *vi* faire de la randonnée; *Fig* **to t. to the shops/ home** se taper le chemin à pied jusqu'aux magasins/ jusqu'à chez soi

trellis ['trelɪs] *n* treillis *m*, treillage *m*

tremble ['trembəl] **1** *n* tremblement *m*

2 *vi* trembler (**with** de)

tremendous [trɪ'mendəs] *adj* (**a**) (*enormous*) énorme (**b**) *Fam* (*excellent*) formidable

tremendously [trɪ'mendəslɪ] *adv* (*very*) extrêmement

tremor ['tremə(r)] *n* tremblement *m*

tremulous ['tremjʊləs] *adj* (*voice, hand*) tremblant(e); (*person, smile*) timide

trench [trentʃ] *n* (*ditch*) fossé *m*; *Mil* tranchée *f*; **t. coat** trench-coat *m*; **t. warfare** guerre *f* de tranchées

trenchant ['tren(t)ʃənt] *adj* tranchant(e)

trend [trend] *n* (*tendency*) tendance *f*; (*fashion*) mode *f*; **to set** *or* **start a t.** lancer une mode

trendsetter ['trendsetə(r)] *n* lanceur(euse) *m,f* de mode

trendy ['trendɪ] *n & adj Br Fam* branché(e) *m,f*

trepidation [trepɪ'deɪʃən] *n Formal* inquiétude *f*

trespass ['trespəs] *vi Law* s'introduire illégalement dans une propriété privée

trespasser ['trespəsə(r)] *n Law* intrus(e) *m,f*; **trespassers will be prosecuted** (*sign*) défense d'entrer sous peine de poursuites

tresses ['tresɪz] *npl Lit* (*hair*) chevelure *f*

trestle ['tresəl] *n* tréteau *m*; **t. table** table *f* à tréteaux

trial ['traɪəl] *n* (**a**) *Law* procès *m*; **to bring sb to t.** traduire qn en justice; **to be on t. (for)** passer en jugement (pour) (**b**) (*test*) essai *m*; **on t.** à l'essai; **by t. and error** par tâtonnements, **t. period** période *f* d'essai; **t. run** essai; **t. separation** (*of couple*) séparation *f* à l'essai (**c**) (*ordeal*) épreuve *f*

triangle ['traɪæŋgəl] *n* triangle *m*

triangular [traɪ'æŋgjʊlə(r)] *adj* triangulaire

triathlon [traɪ'æθlɒn] *n* triathlon *m*

tribal ['traɪbəl] *adj* tribal(e)

tribalism ['traɪbəlɪzəm] *n* tribalisme *m*

tribe [traɪb] *n* tribu *f*

tribesman ['traɪbzmən] *n* membre *m* d'une tribu

tribulation [trɪbjʊ'leɪʃən] *n Formal* malheur *m*

tribunal [traɪ'bjuːnəl] *n Law* tribunal *m*

tributary ['trɪbjʊtərɪ] *n* (*of river*) affluent *m*

tribute ['trɪbjuːt] *n* (**a**) (*homage*) hommage *m*; **to pay t. to** rendre hommage à (**b**) (*testimony*) **our success is a t. to all your hard work** c'est grâce à vos efforts soutenus que nous avons réussi

trice [traɪs] *n* **in a t.** en un clin d'œil

triceps ['traɪseps] *n Anat* triceps *m*

trick [trɪk] **1** *n* (**a**) (*ruse*) tour *m*; (*practical joke*) farce *f*; **to play a t. on sb** jouer un tour à qn; (*practical joke*) faire une farce à qn; **t. photography** truquage *m*; **t. question** question *f* piège (**b**) (*by magician*) tour *m* (**c**) (*in card game*) pli *m* (**d**) (*idioms*) **to do the t.** marcher; **to know all the tricks** connaître toutes les astuces; **the tricks of the trade** les ficelles du métier; **she doesn't miss a t.** rien ne lui échappe; **he's been up to his old tricks again** il a encore fait des siennes; *Fam* **how's tricks?** comment va, quoi de neuf?

2 *vt* (*person*) duper; **to t. sb into doing sth** amener qn à faire qch par la ruse

trickery ['trɪkərɪ] *n* duperie *f*, ruse *f*

trickle ['trɪkəl] **1** *vt* (*liquid*) faire couler goutte à goutte

2 *vi* (*of liquid*) couler goutte à goutte; **to t. in/out** (*of people*) entrer/sortir au compte-gouttes

3 *n* (*of liquid*) filet *m*; (*of complaints, letters*) petit nombre *m*; *Econ* **t.-down theory** = théorie selon laquelle la richesse de quelques-uns finira par profiter à toute la société

tricky ['trɪkɪ] *adj* délicat(e)

tricycle ['traɪsɪkəl] *n* tricycle *m*

trident ['traɪdənt] n trident m

tried-and-tested ['traɪdən'testɪd] adj qui a fait ses preuves

trier ['traɪə(r)] n Fam **to be a t.** être persévérant(e)

trifle ['traɪfəl] n (**a**) (insignificant thing) broutille f, bagatelle f (**b**) **a t. wide/short** un tantinet trop large/court(e) (**c**) Br (dessert) = dessert où alternent une couche de génoise imbibée d'alcool et de fruits en gelée et une couche de crème anglaise, et recouvert de chantilly

▶**trifle with** vt insep plaisanter avec

trifling ['traɪflɪŋ] adj insignifiant(e)

trigger ['trɪgə(r)] **1** n (of gun) détente f; Fig (of change, decision) élément m déclencheur; Fam **to be t. happy** avoir la gâchette facile
  2 vt déclencher

▶**trigger off** vt sep déclencher

trigonometry [trɪgə'nɒmɪtrɪ] n trigonométrie f

trilby ['trɪlbɪ] n Br (chapeau m en) feutre m

trill [trɪl] **1** n trille m
  2 vi triller

trillion ['trɪljən] n trillion m; Fam **trillions of** (lots of) un milliard de

trilogy ['trɪlədʒɪ] (pl **trilogies**) n trilogie f

trim [trɪm] **1** adj (**a**) (neat) soigné(e) (**b**) (slim) svelte
  2 vt (pt & pp **trimmed**) (**a**) (cut) (hair) rafraîchir; (hedge) tailler, élaguer; (meat) parer; (budget) réduire (**b**) (decorate) orner, décorer (**with** de)
  3 n (**a**) **to give sb's hair a t.** faire une coupe d'entretien à qn; **to give the hedge a t.** tailler la haie (**b**) **to be/keep in t.** (keep fit) être en/garder la forme

▶**trim down** vt sep (text) élaguer; (company, expenditure) réduire

trimaran ['traɪməræn] n trimaran m

trimester [trɪ'mestə(r)] n trimestre m

trimming ['trɪmɪŋ] n (**a**) (on clothes) garniture f (**b**) **trimmings** (of meal) accompagnements mpl traditionnels

Trinidad and Tobago ['trɪnɪdædəntə'beɪgəʊ] n Trinité-et-Tobago

Trinity ['trɪnɪtɪ] n Rel **the T.** la Trinité

trinket ['trɪŋkɪt] n babiole f

trio ['triːəʊ] (pl **trios**) n trio m

trip [trɪp] **1** n (**a**) (journey) trajet m, voyage m; (for one day) excursion f (**b**) Fam (on drugs) trip m (**c**) (stumble) faux pas m; **t. wire** fil m de détente
  2 vt (pt & pp **tripped**) (**a**) (make stumble) faire un croche-pied à (**b**) **to t. a switch** déclencher un interrupteur (**c**) (idiom) Hum **to t. the light fantastic** danser
  3 vi (**a**) (stumble) trébucher (**b**) (step lightly) marcher d'un pas léger; **to t. off the tongue** (of word, name) être facile à prononcer (**c**) Fam (on drugs) **to be tripping** être en plein trip

▶**trip over 1** vt insep trébucher sur
  2 vi trébucher

▶**trip up 1** vt sep (cause to stumble) faire un croche-pied à; Fig (cause to make mistake) désarçonner
  2 vi (stumble) trébucher

tripe [traɪp] n (food) tripes fpl; Fam (nonsense) foutaises fpl

triple ['trɪpəl] **1** adj triple; **t. jump** triple saut m; Med **t. (combination) therapy** trithérapie f
  2 adv **t. the number/amount** trois fois le nombre/la quantité
  3 vt & vi tripler

triplet ['trɪplɪt] n (**a**) (person) triplé(e) m,f (**b**) Mus triolet m

triplicate ['trɪplɪkət] n **in t.** en trois exemplaires

tripod ['traɪpɒd] n trépied m

Tripoli ['trɪpəlɪ] n Tripoli

trite [traɪt] adj banal(e)

triumph ['traɪəmf] **1** n triomphe m; **in t.** triomphant(e)
  2 vi triompher (**over** de)

triumphant [traɪ'ʌmfənt] adj triomphant(e)

triumvirate [traɪ'ʌmvɪrɪt] n triumvirat m

trivet ['trɪvɪt] n (on open fire) trépied m; (stand) = support métallique surélevé pour plats chauds

trivia ['trɪvɪə] npl (unimportant details) détails mpl; (useless information) futilités fpl

trivial ['trɪvɪəl] adj (detail, matter) sans importance, insignifiant(e); (person) superficiel(elle)

trivialize ['trɪvɪəlaɪz] vt banaliser

trod [trɒd] pt of **tread**

trodden ['trɒdən] pp of **tread**

Trojan ['trəʊdʒən] Hist **1** n Troyen(enne) m,f
  2 adj de Troie, troyen(enne); **T. Horse** cheval m de Troie; **the T. War** la guerre de Troie

troll [trəʊl] n troll m

trolley ['trɒlɪ] (pl **trolleys**) n Br chariot m; Fam **to be off one's t.** débloquer; Am **t. car** tramway m

trollop ['trɒləp] n Old-fashioned or Hum gourgandine f, catin f

trombone [trɒm'bəʊn] n trombone m (instrument)

trombonist [trɒm'bəʊnɪst] n trombone m (musicien)

troop [truːp] **1** n (**a**) **troops** (soldiers) troupes fpl (**b**) (of people) groupe m
  2 vi **to t. in/out** entrer/sortir en groupe

trooper ['truːpə(r)] n (soldier) cavalier m; Am (mounted policeman) membre m de la police montée; Fam **to swear like a t.** jurer comme un charretier

trophy ['trəʊfɪ] n trophée m

tropic ['trɒpɪk] n tropique m; **in the tropics** sous les tropiques

tropical ['trɒpɪkəl] adj tropical(e)

trot [trɒt] **1** n trot m; **at a t.** au trot; Fam **on the t.** (consecutively) de suite; Fam **to have the trots** avoir la courante
  2 vi (pt & pp **trotted**) (of horse) aller au trot; (of person) trotter

▶**trot out** vt sep Fam débiter

Trotskyism ['trɒtskɪɪzəm] n trotskisme m

Trotskyist ['trɒtskɪɪst], **Trotskyite** ['trɒtskɪaɪt] n & adj trotskiste mf

trotter ['trɒtə(r)] n (of pig) pied m

trouble ['trʌbəl] **1** n (**a**) (problem) ennui m; **to have t. with sb/sth** avoir des problèmes avec qn/qch; **to have t. doing sth** avoir du mal à faire qch; **to be in/get into t.** avoir/s'attirer des ennuis; **to get sb into t.** attirer des ennuis à qn; **to get sb out of t.** tirer qn d'affaire; **to make t. (for sb)** créer des ennuis (à qn); **it's more t. than it's worth** le jeu n'en vaut pas la chandelle; Fam **man/woman t.** ennuis mpl de cœur
  (**b**) (inconvenience) problème m; **to go to the t. of doing sth** se donner la peine de faire qch; **it's not worth the t.** ça n'en vaut pas la peine; (**it's) no t.** (ça ne pose) aucun problème
  (**c**) (disorder, unrest) troubles mpl; **t. spot** point m chaud
  2 vt (worry) inquiéter; (inconvenience) déranger
  3 vi **to t. to do sth** se donner la peine de faire qch

troubled ['trʌbəld] *adj (person)* inquiet(ète); *(region)* agité(e) de troubles; *(period)* troublé(e)

trouble-free ['trʌbəlfriː] *adj (life)* sans soucis; *(visit, journey)* sans histoires

troublemaker ['trʌbəlmeɪkə(r)] *n* semeur(euse) *m,f* de troubles

troubleshooter ['trʌbəlʃuːtə(r)] *n (for organizational problems)* expert *m*; *(for industrial disputes)* conciliateur(trice) *m,f*; *(for machines)* dépanneur(euse) *m,f*

troublesome ['trʌbəlsəm] *adj* pénible

trough [trɒf] *n (for food)* mangeoire *f*; *(for drink)* abreuvoir *m*; *(of wave, on graph)* creux *m*; *(in weather front)* dépression *f*

trounce [traʊns] *vt* battre à plates coutures

troupe [truːp] *n* troupe *f*

trouser press ['traʊzə'pres] *n* presse-pantalon *m*

trousers ['traʊzəz] *npl* **(a)** *Br (garment)* pantalon *m* **(b)** *(idioms)* *Fam* **to wear the t.** porter la culotte; *Fam* **to be caught with one's t. down** être pris(e) en flagrant délit

trouser suit ['traʊzə'suːt] *n* tailleur-pantalon *m*

trousseau ['truːsəʊ] *n* trousseau *m (de jeune mariée)*

trout [traʊt] *(pl* **trout***) n* truite *f*

trowel ['traʊəl] *n* truelle *f*

truancy ['truːənsɪ] *n* absentéisme *m* scolaire

truant ['truːənt] *n (pupil)* élève *mf* qui fait l'école buissonnière; **to play t.** faire l'école buissonnière

truce [truːs] *n also Fig* trêve *f*; **to call a t.** demander une trêve

truck [trʌk] **1** *n* **(a)** *(lorry)* camion *m*; **t. driver** conducteur(trice) *m,f* de camion, camionneur *m*; *Am* **t. farm** exploitation *f* maraîchère; **t. stop** relais *m* routier **(b)** *(rail wagon)* wagon *m* **(c)** *Fam* **to have no t. with sb/sth** ne rien avoir à faire avec qn/qch
2 *vt (goods)* acheminer par camion
3 *vi Am (drive a truck)* être conducteur(trice) *m,f* de camion

trucker ['trʌkə(r)] *n Am (truck driver)* camionneur *m*

truculent ['trʌkjʊlənt] *adj* agressif(ive)

trudge [trʌdʒ] **1** *n* trajet *m* pénible
2 *vi* marcher péniblement, se traîner

true [truː] **1** *adj* **(a)** *(not fictional)* vrai(e); **to come t.** se réaliser; **to hold t. (for)** être vrai (de) **(b)** *(genuine)* véritable; **t. love** grand amour *m*; **t. north** le nord géographique **(c)** *(faithful)* fidèle; **to be t. to sb** être loyal(e) envers qn; **to be t. to sth** être fidèle à qch; **t. to life** fidèle à la réalité; **t. to form** *or* **type** fidèle à soi-même **(d)** *(accurate)* exact(e)
2 *n* **out of t.** hors d'aplomb

truffle ['trʌfəl] *n* truffe *f*

truism ['truːɪzəm] *n* truisme *m*

truly ['truːlɪ] *adv* vraiment; **yours t.** *(at end of letter)* = je vous prie d'agréer, Madame/Monsieur, l'expression de mes sentiments distingués; *Fam Hum (myself)* mézigue

trump [trʌmp] **1** *n* atout *m*; **spades are trumps** c'est atout pique; *Fig* **to play one's t. card** jouer son atout; *Fam Fig* **to turn up trumps** sauver la mise
2 *vt* couper à l'atout

trumped up ['trʌmptʌp] *adj* fabriqué(e)

trumpet ['trʌmpɪt] **1** *n* trompette *f*; *Fig* **to blow one's own t.** vanter ses propres mérites
2 *vt (proclaim)* claironner
3 *vi (of elephant)* barrir

trumpeter ['trʌmpɪtə(r)] *n* trompettiste *mf*

truncate [trʌŋ'keɪt] *vt* tronquer

truncheon ['trʌn(t)ʃən] *n Br* matraque *f*

trundle ['trʌndəl] **1** *vt* pousser péniblement
2 *vi* rouler péniblement

trunk [trʌŋk] *n* **(a)** *(of tree, body)* tronc *m*; *Br Old-fashioned* **t. call** appel *m* interurbain; *Br* **t. road** route *f* nationale **(b)** *(case)* malle *f* **(c)** *Am (of car)* coffre *m* **(d)** *(of elephant)* trompe *f* **(e)** **trunks** *(swimming costume)* slip *m* de bain

truss [trʌs] **1** *n* **(a)** *(for hernia)* bandage *m* herniaire **(b)** *(for roof, bridge)* ferme *f*
2 *vt (tie up)* ligoter

▶**truss up** *vt sep (person)* ligoter; *(chicken, turkey)* trousser

trust [trʌst] **1** *n* **(a)** *(faith)* confiance *f* (in en); **to put one's t. in sb/sth** se fier à qn/qch; **to take sth on t.** croire qch sur parole **(b)** *Law* **in t.** par fidéicommis; *Fin* **t. fund** fonds *m* en fidéicommis **(c)** *Com (group of companies)* trust *m*
2 *vt* **(a)** *(believe in)* faire confiance à; **to t. sb with sth** confier qch à qn; **to t. sb to do sth** laisser à qn le soin de faire qch; *Fam* **t. him to say that!** c'est bien de lui! **(b)** *Formal (hope)* **to t. (that)...** espérer que...
3 *vi* **to t. in sb/sth** faire confiance à qn/qch; **to t. to luck** s'en remettre au hasard

trusted ['trʌstɪd] *adj* de confiance; **t. third party** *(for Internet transactions)* tierce partie *f* de confiance

trustee [trʌs'tiː] *n Law (of fund, property)* fidéicommissaire *m*; *(of charity)* administrateur(trice) *m,f*

trusting ['trʌstɪŋ] *adj* qui fait confiance aux gens

trustworthy ['trʌstwɜːðɪ] *adj (person)* digne de confiance; *(thing)* fiable

trusty ['trʌstɪ] *adj* fidèle

truth [truːθ] *n* vérité *f*; **to tell the t.** dire la vérité; **to tell (you) the t., I don't care** à vrai dire, je m'en moque complètement

truthful ['truːθfʊl] *adj (person)* sincère; *(story)* véridique

try [traɪ] **1** *vt* **(a)** *(sample, attempt)* essayer; *(food, drink)* goûter (à); **to t. to do sth** essayer de faire qch; **I'll t. anything once** il faut tout essayer dans la vie **(b)** *Law (case, person)* juger **(c)** *(test)* tester; *(person)* mettre à l'épreuve; **to t. sb's patience** mettre la patience de qn à l'épreuve
2 *vi* essayer; **to t. harder** faire plus d'efforts; **just you t.!** essaie un peu pour voir!
3 *n* **(a)** *(attempt)* essai *m*; **to give sth a t.** essayer qch; **to have a t. at sth/at doing sth** essayer qch/de faire qch; **it's worth a t.** ça vaut le coup d'essayer **(b)** *(in rugby)* essai *m*

▶**try on** *vt sep* **(a)** *(clothes)* essayer **(b)** *Fam* **to t. it on (with sb)** tenter le coup (avec qn); *(sexually)* draguer (qn)

▶**try out** *vt sep* essayer; **to t. sth out on sb** expérimenter qch sur qn

trying ['traɪɪŋ] *adj* difficile

tsar [zɑː(r)] *n* tsar *m*

tsarist ['zɑːrɪst] *n & adj* tsariste *mf*

tsetse ['t(s)etsɪ] *n* **t. (fly)** *(mouche f)* tsé-tsé *f inv*

T-shirt ['tiːʃɜːt] *n* tee-shirt *m*

TTP [tiːtiː'piː] *n (abbr* **trusted third party***) (for Internet transactions)* TPC *f*

tub [tʌb] *n* **(a)** *(for washing clothes)* baquet *m*; *(bath)* baignoire *f* **(b)** *(for food, plants)* pot *m*

tuba ['tjuːbə] *n* tuba *m*

tubby ['tʌbɪ] *adj Fam* boulot(otte)

tube [tju:b] *n* (**a**) *(cylindrical container)* tube *m*; *(pipe)* tuyau *m*; *Fam* **to go down the tubes** *(of money)* être foutu en l'air; *(of work, plan)* tomber à l'eau (**b**) *Br Fam* **the t.** *(underground railway)* le métro; **t. station** station *f* de métro (**c**) *Am Fam (TV)* télé *f*

tuber ['tju:bə(r)] *n* tubercule *m*

tuberculosis [tjʊbɜ:kjʊ'ləʊsɪs] *n* tuberculose *f*

tubing ['tju:bɪŋ] *n* tuyaux *mpl*

tubular ['tju:bjʊlə(r)] *adj* tubulaire; **t. bells** carillon *m*

TUC [ti:ju:'si:] *n Br (abbr* **Trades Union Congress**) = confédération des syndicats britanniques

tuck [tʌk] **1** *n* (**a**) *(in sewing)* pli *m* (**b**) *Br Fam (food)* sucreries *fpl*; **t. shop** *(in school)* boutique *f* de friandises (**c**) *(in cosmetic surgery) (for face)* lifting *m*
　2 *vt* **to t. one's shirt into one's trousers** rentrer sa chemise dans son pantalon; **to t. sth under one's arm** mettre qch sous son bras; **to t. sb up in bed** border qn; **to t. sth into a drawer** glisser qch dans un tiroir
▸**tuck in 1** *vt sep (sheets, child)* border; *(clothes)* rentrer
　2 *vi Fam (start to eat)* attaquer
▸**tuck into** *vt insep Fam (meal)* attaquer

Tudor ['tju:də(r)] **1** *n Hist* **the Tudors** les Tudor
　2 *adj* des Tudor

Tue(s) *(abbr* **Tuesday**) mardi

Tuesday ['tju:zdɪ] *n* mardi *m*; *see also* **Saturday**

tuft [tʌft] *n* touffe *f*

tug [tʌg] **1** *vt (pt & pp* **tugged**) (**a**) *(pull)* tirer sur (**b**) *(tow)* remorquer
　2 *vi* **to t. at sth** tirer sur qch
　3 *n* (**a**) *(pull)* **to give sth a t.** tirer sur qch (**b**) *(boat)* remorqueur *m*

tug-of-love [tʌgəv'lʌv] *n Br* = conflit de parents séparés à propos de la garde d'un enfant

tug-of-war [tʌgəv'wɔ:(r)] *n (game)* lutte *f* (de traction) à la corde; *Fig* lutte acharnée

tuition [tjʊ'ɪʃən] *n* cours *mpl*, leçons *fpl*

tulip ['tju:lɪp] *n* tulipe *f*

tum [tʌm] *n Br (in children's language)* ventre *m*

tumble ['tʌmbəl] **1** *vi (of person)* faire une chute; *Fig (of prices)* chuter
　2 *n (fall)* chute *f*; **to take a t.** *(of person)* faire une chute; *Fig (of prices)* chuter
▸**tumble down** *vi* s'écrouler

tumbledown ['tʌmbəldaʊn] *adj* qui tombe en ruines

tumble-drier [tʌmbəl'draɪə(r)] *n* sèche-linge *m inv*

tumble-dry ['tʌmbəldraɪ] *vt* faire sécher au sèche-linge

tumbler ['tʌmblə(r)] *n* verre *m* droit

tummy ['tʌmɪ] *n Fam* ventre *m*; **to have (a) t. ache** avoir mal au ventre

tumour, *Am* **tumor** ['tju:mə(r)] *n* tumeur *f*

tumult ['tju:mʌlt] *n* tumulte *m*

tumultuous [tjʊ'mʌltjʊəs] *adj* tumultueux(euse)

tuna ['tju:nə] *n* thon *m*

tundra ['tʌndrə] *n* toundra *f*

tune [tju:n] **1** *n* (**a**) *(melody)* air *m*, mélodie *f*; **to be in/out of t.** *(of person)* chanter juste/faux; *(of instrument)* être accordé(e)/désaccordé(e) (**b**) *(idioms)* **to be in t. with sb/sth** être en harmonie avec qn/qch; **to call the t.** commander; **to change one's t.** changer de discours; **to be in debt to the t. of £200** avoir 200 livres de dettes
　2 *vt (musical instrument)* accorder; *(engine, TV, radio)* régler

▸**tune in** *vi* brancher son poste

tuneful ['tju:nfʊl] *adj* mélodieux(euse)

tuneless ['tju:nlɪs] *adj* discordant(e)

tuner ['tju:nə(r)] *n* (**a**) *(person)* accordeur(euse) *m,f* (**b**) *(on TV, radio)* tuner *m*

tungsten ['tʌŋstən] *n* tungstène *m*; **t. steel** acier *m* au tungstène

tunic ['tju:nɪk] *n* tunique *f*

tuning fork ['tju:nɪŋ'fɔ:k] *n* diapason *m*

Tunis ['tju:nɪs] *n* Tunis

Tunisia [tju:'nɪzɪə] *n* la Tunisie

Tunisian [tju:'nɪzɪən] **1** *n* Tunisien(enne) *m,f*
　2 *adj* tunisien(enne)

tunnel ['tʌnəl] **1** *n* tunnel *m*; **to have t. vision** souffrir d'un rétrécissement du champ visuel; *Fig* avoir des œillères
　2 *vt (pt & pp* **tunnelled**) **to t. one's way out of prison** s'échapper de prison en creusant un tunnel
　3 *vi* creuser un tunnel

turban ['tɜ:bən] *n* turban *m*

turbine ['tɜ:baɪn] *n* turbine *f*

turbo-charged ['tɜ:bəʊtʃɑ:dʒd] *adj* turbocompressé(e)

turbo-charger ['tɜ:bəʊtʃɑ:dʒə(r)] *n* turbocompresseur *m*

turbojet ['tɜ:bəʊdʒet] *n (engine)* turboréacteur *m*; *(plane)* avion *m* à turboréacteur

turboprop ['tɜ:bəʊprɒp] *n (engine)* turbopropulseur *m*; *(plane)* avion *m* à turbopropulseur

turbot ['tɜ:bət] *n* turbot *m*

turbulence ['tɜ:bjʊləns] *n* turbulence *f*

turbulent ['tɜ:bjʊlənt] *adj* agité(e)

turd [tɜ:d] *n very Fam* (**a**) *(excrement)* étron *m* (**b**) *(person)* connard (connasse) *m,f*

tureen [tjʊə'ri:n] *n* soupière *f*

turf [tɜ:f] **1** *n (grass-covered earth)* gazon *m*; *Fam (territory)* territoire *m*; *Br* **t. accountant** bookmaker *m*
　2 *vt* gazonner
▸**turf out** *vt sep Br Fam (person)* vider; *(thing)* balancer

Turk [tɜ:k] *n* Turc (Turque) *m,f*

Turkey ['tɜ:kɪ] *n* la Turquie

turkey ['tɜ:kɪ] *n (pl* **turkeys**) *n* (**a**) *(bird)* dinde *f* (**b**) *Fam (bad play, film)* navet *m*

Turkish ['tɜ:kɪʃ] **1** *n (language)* turc *m*
　2 *adj* turc (turque); **T. bath** bain *m* turc; **T. delight** loukoum *m*

Turkmenistan [tɜ:kmenɪ'stɑ:n] *n* le Turkménistan

turmeric ['tɜ:mərɪk] *n* curcuma *m*

turmoil ['tɜ:mɔɪl] *n (of person)* émoi *m*; *(of country)* agitation *f*; **to be in (a) t.** *(of person)* être dans tous ses états; *(of country)* être en ébullition; **his mind was in t.** il était très troublé

turn [tɜ:n] **1** *n* (**a**) *(of wheel, screw)* tour *m*; **the meat is done to a t.** la viande est cuite à point
　(**b**) *(change of direction)* demi-tour *m*; *(in road)* virage *m*; **no right/left t.** *(on sign)* défense de tourner à droite/gauche; *Fig* **at every t.** à tout bout de champ; **to take a t. for the better** s'améliorer; **to take a t. for the worse** se détériorer; **events took an unexpected t.** les événements ont pris une tournure inattendue; **the t. of the century** le tournant du siècle; **the t. of the tide** le changement de marée; *Fig* le renversement de tendances; *Am Aut* **t. signal** clignotant *m*, *Belg* clignoteur *m*, *Suisse* signafil(e) *m*
　(**c**) *(in game, queue)* tour *m*; **to take (it in) turns (to**

do sth) se relayer (pour faire qch); **in t.** à tour de rôle
(**d**) *Fam (fit)* crise *f*
(**e**) *Theat (performance)* numéro *m*
(**f**) *(service)* **to do sb a good t.** rendre un service à
qn; **one good t. deserves another** un service en vaut
un autre
(**g**) **t. of phrase** tournure *f* de phrase
2 *vt* (**a**) *(cause to move)* tourner; *Fam Fig* **without
turning a hair** sans broncher; *Fam Fig* **success has
turned her head** le succès lui a tourné la tête; **to t.
sb's stomach** soulever le cœur à qn
(**b**) *(direct)* **to t. the conversation to sb/sth** orienter
la conversation sur qn/qch
(**c**) *(go round)* **to t. the corner** tourner au coin de la
rue; *Fig* passer le moment critique; **she's just turned
forty** elle vient d'avoir quarante ans
(**d**) *(change)* **to t. sth into sth** transformer qch en
qch; **to t. sth green/black** verdir/noircir qch; **to t.
sb against sb** monter qn contre qn
(**e**) *(on lathe)* tourner
3 *vi* (**a**) *(rotate) (of wheel)* tourner; *(of person)* se retourner; **she turned to me** elle s'est tournée vers moi;
to t. to sb (for help/advice) se tourner vers qn (pour
obtenir de l'aide/des conseils); **to t. (to the) right/
left** tourner à droite/gauche
(**b**) *(change)* **to t. against sb** se retourner contre qn;
to t. nasty *(of person)* devenir méchant(e); *(of situation)* mal tourner; **to t. red** devenir rouge; **to t. sour**
(of milk) tourner; *Fig (of relationship)* tourner au vinaigre
▶**turn away 1** *vt sep (refuse entry, help to)* refuser
2 *vi* se détourner
▶**turn back 1** *vt sep (person)* refouler; *(sheets)* rabattre;
to t. the clocks back retarder les pendules; *Fig* revenir en arrière
2 *vi* faire demi-tour; **t. back to page 20** revenez à la
page 20
▶**turn down** *vt sep* (**a**) *(volume, heat)* baisser (**b**) *(request, application)* rejeter, refuser
▶**turn in 1** *vt sep (lost property)* rapporter à la police;
(person) livrer à la police
2 *vi Fam (go to bed)* aller se pieuter
▶**turn into** *vt insep (become)* devenir
▶**turn off 1** *vt sep* (**a**) *(water, gas)* fermer; *(light, TV, engine)* éteindre (**b**) *Fam* **to t. sb off** dégoûter qn; *(sexually)* couper l'envie à qn
2 *vt insep* **to t. off the road** quitter la route
3 *vi (leave road)* sortir
▶**turn on 1** *vt sep* (**a**) *(water, gas)* ouvrir; *(light, TV, engine)* allumer (**b**) *Fam* **to t. sb on** *(excite)* brancher qn;
(sexually) exciter qn
2 *vt insep* (**a**) *(attack)* **to t. on sb** attaquer qn (**b**) *(depend on)* dépendre de
▶**turn out 1** *vt sep* (**a**) *(light)* éteindre; *(gas)* fermer (**b**)
(eject) mettre à la porte (**c**) *(pocket, container)* vider
(**d**) *(produce)* produire, fabriquer; **to be well turned
out** *(of person)* être élégant(e)
2 *vi* (**a**) *(appear, attend)* se déplacer (**b**) *(result)* se
terminer; **to t. out to be** s'avérer (être); **it turns out
that...** il se trouve que...
▶**turn over 1** *vt sep* (**a**) *(change position of)* retourner;
to t. sth over in one's mind retourner qch dans sa
tête; *Fig* **to t. over a new leaf** tourner la page (**b**)
(hand in) **to t. sb/sth over to sb** remettre qn/qch entre les mains de qn
2 *vi* (**a**) *(of person)* se retourner; *(of car)* faire un ton-

neau, capoter (**b**) *(change TV channels)* changer de
chaîne
▶**turn round 1** *vt sep (object)* retourner; *(situation)*
renverser; *(company, economy)* remettre sur pied
2 *vi (of person)* se retourner
▶**turn up 1** *vt sep* (**a**) *(collar)* relever; *(trousers)* retrousser (**b**) *(volume, heat)* mettre plus fort
2 *vi (of person)* arriver; *(of lost object)* réapparaître;
something is sure to t. up quelque chose finira bien
par se présenter
turnabout ['tɜ:nəbaʊt] *n (in situation, opinion)* revirement *m*
turnaround ['tɜ:nəraʊnd] *n* (**a**) *(in situation, opinion)*
revirement *m* (**b**) *Comput* **t. time** temps *m* de rotation
turncoat ['tɜ:nkəʊt] *n* renégat(e) *m,f*
turning ['tɜ:nɪŋ] *n* (**a**) *(off road) (in country)* route *f*
transversale; *(in town)* rue *f* transversale; **the second
t. on the left** la deuxième rue à gauche (**b**) **t. circle**
(of car) rayon *m* de braquage; *Fig* **t. point** tournant *m*
turnip ['tɜ:nɪp] *n* navet *m*
turn-off ['tɜ:nɒf] *n* (**a**) *(on road)* sortie *f* (**b**) *Fam* **to be
a t.** être rébarbatif(ive); *(sexually)* couper l'envie
turn-on ['tɜ:nɒn] *n Fam* **to be a t.** *(sexually)* être exci-
tant(e)
turnout ['tɜ:naʊt] *n (attendance)* assistance *f*, *(at election)* taux *m* de participation
turnover ['tɜ:nəʊvə(r)] *n* (**a**) *(of company)* chiffre *m*
d'affaires (**b**) *(cake)* chausson *m*; **apple t.** chausson
m aux pommes
turnpike ['tɜ:npaɪk] *n Am (road)* autoroute *f*
turnstile ['tɜ:nstaɪl] *n* tourniquet *m*
turntable ['tɜ:nteɪbəl] *n* platine *f*
turn-up ['tɜ:nʌp] *n* (**a**) *Br (on trousers)* revers *m* (**b**)
Fam **what a t. for the books!** quel événement!
turpentine ['tɜ:pəntaɪn] *n* essence *f* de térébenthine
turquoise ['tɜ:kwɔɪz] **1** *n* (**a**) *(stone)* turquoise *f* (**b**)
(colour) turquoise *m*
2 *adj* turquoise *inv*
turret ['tʌrɪt] *n* tourelle *f*; **(gun) t.** *(on ship, tank)* tourelle *f*
turtle ['tɜ:təl] *n Br* tortue *f* de mer; *Am* tortue *f*; **to turn
t.** *(of ship)* chavirer; **t. dove** tourterelle *f*; **t. soup** potage *m* à la tortue
turtleneck ['tɜ:təlnek] *n* col *m* montant; **t. sweater**
pull *m* à col montant
Tuscan ['tʌskən] *adj* toscan(e)
Tuscany ['tʌskənɪ] *n* la Toscane
tusk [tʌsk] *n* défense *f*
tussle ['tʌsəl] **1** *n* empoignade *f*; **to have a t. (with sb)**
(physically) se battre (avec qn); *(verbally)* se disputer
(avec qn)
2 *vi (physically)* se battre; *(verbally)* se disputer
tutor ['tju:tə(r)] **1** *n (at university)* directeur(trice) *m,f*
d'études; *(for private lessons)* professeur *m* particulier
2 *vt* **to t. sb (in sth)** donner des leçons particulières
(de qch) à qn
tutorial [tju:'tɔ:rɪəl] *n Br Univ* travaux *mpl* dirigés
tux [tʌks] *n Fam* smoking *m*
tuxedo [tʌk'si:dəʊ] *n* smoking *m*
TV [ti:'vi:] *n (television)* télé *f*, TV *f*; **TV dinner** plateau *m*
télé; **TV movie** téléfilm *m*
TVP [ti:vi:'pi:] *n (abbr* **textured vegetable protein**)
protéine *f* végétale texturée
twaddle ['twɒdəl] *n Br Fam* fadaises *fpl*

twang [twæŋ] **1** *n (sound)* vibration *f*; *(nasal voice)* ton *m* nasillard
  2 *vi (of string)* vibrer

tweak [twiːk] **1** *n* **to give sth a t.** *(nose)* pincer qch; *(ear)* tirer qch; *Fam Fig (statistics, mechanism)* ajuster légèrement qch
  2 *vt (nose)* pincer; *(ear)* tirer; *Fam Fig (statistics, mechanism)* ajuster légèrement

twee [twiː] *adj Br Fam Pej* cucul (la praline) *inv*

tweed [twiːd] *n* tweed *m*; **tweeds** *(suit)* costume *m* de tweed

tweet [twiːt] **1** *n* pépiement *m*
  2 *vi* pépier

tweezers ['twiːzəz] *npl* pince *f* à épiler

twelfth [twelfθ] **1** *n* (**a**) *(fraction)* douzième *m* (**b**) *(in series)* douzième *mf* (**c**) *(of month)* douze *m inv*
  2 *adj* douzième; **T. Night** ≃ la fête des Rois; *see also* **eighth**

twelve [twelv] **1** *n* douze *m inv*; **half past t.** *(in the afternoon)* douze heures trente, midi et demi; *(at night)* zéro heures trente, minuit et demi
  2 *adj* douze; *see also* **eight**

twentieth ['twentɪθ] **1** *n* (**a**) *(fraction)* vingtième *m* (**b**) *(in series)* vingtième *mf* (**c**) *(of month)* vingt *m inv*
  2 *adj* vingtième; *see also* **eighth**

twenty ['twentɪ] **1** *n* vingt *m inv*
  2 *adj* vingt; **to have t.-t. vision** avoir dix sur dix à chaque œil; *see also* **eighty**

twenty-first ['twentɪ'fɜːst] **1** *n* (**a**) *(in series)* vingt et unième *mf* (**b**) *(of month)* vingt et un *m inv*
  2 *adj* vingt et unième

twenty one ['twentɪ'wʌn] **1** *n* vingt et un *m inv*
  2 *adj* vingt et un

twerp [twɜːp] *n Fam* crétin(e) *m,f*

twice [twaɪs] *adv* deux fois; **t. a week** deux fois par semaine; **t. as big (as)** deux fois plus grand (que); **it would cost t. as much elsewhere** ça coûterait le double ailleurs; **t. over** à deux reprises; **to think t. before doing sth** réfléchir à deux fois avant de faire qch; **he didn't have to be asked t.** il ne s'est pas fait prier

twiddle ['twɪdəl] **1** *vt* tripoter; **to t. one's thumbs** se tourner les pouces
  2 *vi* **to t. with sth** tripoter qch

twig¹ [twɪg] *n (small branch)* brindille *f*

twig² *(pt & pp* **twigged)** *vt & vi Br Fam* piger

twilight ['twaɪlaɪt] *n* crépuscule *m*; **his t. years** les dernières années de sa vie; **t. zone** zone *f* crépusculaire; *Fig* zone floue

twin [twɪn] **1** *n* jumeau(elle) *m,f*; **t. brother** frère *m* jumeau; **t. sister** sœur *f* jumelle
  2 *adj (paired)* jumeau(elle), jumelé(e); **t. beds** lits *mpl* jumeaux; **t.-engine(d) aircraft** avion *m* bimoteur
  3 *vt (pt & pp* **twinned)** *(town)* jumeler

twine [twaɪn] **1** *n (string)* ficelle *f*
  2 *vt* **to t. sth around sb/sth** enrouler qch autour de qn/qch

twinge [twɪn(d)ʒ] *n (of pain)* élancement *m*; **a t. of conscience** un léger remords

twinkle ['twɪŋkəl] **1** *vi (of star, light)* scintiller; *(of eyes)* pétiller
  2 *n (of star, light)* scintillement *m*; *(of eyes)* pétillement *m*

twirl [twɜːl] **1** *n (movement)* tournoiement *m*
  2 *vt* faire tournoyer
  3 *vi (of person)* tournoyer

twist [twɪst] **1** *n* (**a**) *(action)* tour *m*; **to give sth a t.** *(to open)* dévisser qch; *(to close)* visser qch (**b**) *(bend)* tortillement *m*; **twists and turns** *(in road)* tours *mpl* et détours; *Fig (of events)* rebondissements *mpl*; *Br Fam* **to be round the t.** être dingue; *Br Fam* **to drive sb around the t.** rendre qn dingue (**c**) *(in story, plot)* tour *m* inattendu; **by a strange t. of fate** par un hasard extraordinaire (**d**) **a t. of lemon** une rondelle de citron (**e**) *(dance)* **the t.** le twist
  2 *vt (hair, rope, thread)* tordre, tortiller; *Fig (words, meaning)* déformer; **to t. one's ankle** se fouler la cheville; **to t. sb's arm** tordre le bras à qn; *Fig* forcer la main à qn; *Fig* **to t. the knife in the wound** retourner *ou* remuer le couteau dans la plaie
  3 *vi (of smoke)* faire des volutes; *(of road)* faire des lacets; **to t. and turn** *(of road)* être en lacets

▶**twist off 1** *vt sep (lid)* dévisser
  2 *vi* se dévisser

twisted ['twɪstɪd] *adj also Fig* tordu(e)

twister ['twɪstə(r)] *n* (**a**) *Br Fam (dishonest person)* escroc *m* (**b**) *Am (tornado)* tornade *f*

twit [twɪt] *n Br Fam* andouille *f*

twitch [twɪtʃ] **1** *n (pull)* coup *m* sec; **to have a nervous t.** avoir un tic (nerveux)
  2 *vt (pull)* tirer d'un coup sec
  3 *vi (of muscle, limb, face)* se contracter nerveusement

twitter ['twɪtə(r)] **1** *vi (of bird)* gazouiller; *Fig (of person)* jacasser
  2 *n (of bird)* gazouillis *m*

two [tuː] **1** *n (pl* **twos)** deux *m*; **to break/fold sth in t.** casser/plier qch en deux; **to walk in twos** *or* **t. by t.** marcher deux par deux; *Fig* **to put t. and t. together** faire le rapprochement; *Fam* **that makes t. of us** comme ça, on est deux
  2 *adj* deux; *see also* **eight**

two-bit ['tuː'bɪt] *adj Am Fam (cheap)* de quatre sous

two-dimensional [tuːdaɪ'menʃənəl] *adj* à deux dimensions; *Fig (character, film)* simpliste

two-faced ['tuːfeɪst] *adj* hypocrite

twofold ['tuːfəʊld] *adj* double

two-legged [tuː'legɪd] *adj* bipède

twopence ['tʌpəns] *n Br* deux pence *mpl*; *Fam* **it isn't worth t.** ça ne vaut pas tripette

two-piece ['tuːpiːs] *adj (suit, swimsuit)* deux pièces

two-pin ['tuːpɪn] *adj (plug, socket)* à deux fiches

twosome ['tuːsəm] *n* couple *m*

two-time ['tuːtaɪm] *vt Fam (boyfriend, girlfriend)* tromper

two-way ['tuːweɪ] *adj* **t. mirror** miroir *m* sans tain; **t. radio** poste *m* émetteur-récepteur

tycoon [taɪ'kuːn] *n* magnat *m*

type [taɪp] **1** *n* (**a**) *(kind)* type *m*, genre *m*; *Fam* **he's not my t.** ce n'est pas mon genre de mec (**b**) *Typ* caractères *mpl*; **in bold t.** en caractères gras
  2 *vt & vi* taper (à la machine)

▶**type up** *vt sep* taper (à la machine)

typecast ['taɪpkɑːst] *(pt & pp* **typecast)** *vt* **to be typecast** être cantonné(e) dans un rôle

typeface ['taɪpfeɪs] *n* police *f* de caractères

typescript ['taɪpskrɪpt] *n* texte *m* dactylographié, tapuscrit *m*

typesetter ['taɪpsetə(r)] *n* typographe *mf*

typewriter ['taɪpraɪtə(r)] *n* machine *f* à écrire

typhoid ['taɪfɔɪd] *n* **t. (fever)** *(fièvre f)* typhoïde *f*; **to have t.** avoir la typhoïde

typhoon [taɪˈfuːn] *n* typhon *m*

typhus [ˈtaɪfəs] *n* typhus *m*

typical [ˈtɪpɪkəl] *adj* typique; **it was t. of him to offer to pay** c'était bien son genre de proposer de payer; *Pej* **that's t. (of him/her)!** ça ne m'étonne pas (de lui/d'elle)!

typically [ˈtɪpɪklɪ] *adv* typiquement

typify [ˈtɪpɪfaɪ] *(pt & pp* **typified***) vt* caractériser

typing [ˈtaɪpɪŋ] *n* dactylographie *f*, frappe *f*; **t. error** faute *f* de frappe; **t. paper** papier *m* machine; **t. pool** équipe *f* de dactylos; **t. speed** vitesse *f* de frappe

typist [ˈtaɪpɪst] *n* dactylo *mf*

typographic(al) [taɪpəˈɡræfɪk(əl)] *adj* typographique

typography [taɪˈpɒɡrəfɪ] *n* typographie *f*

tyrannical [tɪˈrænɪkəl] *adj* tyrannique

tyrannize [ˈtɪrənaɪz] *vt* tyranniser

tyranny [ˈtɪrənɪ] *n* tyrannie *f*

tyrant [ˈtaɪrənt] *n* tyran *m*

tyre, *Am* **tire** [ˈtaɪə(r)] *n* pneu *m*; **t. marks** traces *fpl* de pneu; **t. pressure** pression *f* des pneus

tzar, tzarist = tsar, tsarist

T-zone [tiːˈzəʊn] *n* zones *fpl* graisses du visage *(front, nez, menton)*

U

U, u [juː] *n (letter)* U, u *m inv*; **U bend** tuyau *m* U; **U boat** sous-marin *m* allemand; **U turn** *(in car)* demi-tour *m*; *Fig* virage *m* à 180 degrés

UAE [juːeɪˈiː] *n (abbr* **United Arab Emirates**) EAU *mpl*

UB40 [juːbiːˈfɔːtɪ] *n Br* = carte de pointage de demandeur d'emploi

ubiquitous [juːˈbɪkwɪtəs] *adj* omniprésent(e)

UCAS [ˈjuːkæs] *n Br (abbr* **Universities and Colleges Admissions Service**) = centre national d'inscriptions à l'université

UDA [juːdiːˈeɪ] *n Br Pol (abbr* **Ulster Defence Association**) = groupement paramilitaire protestant d'Irlande du Nord

udder [ˈʌdə(r)] *n* pis *m*, mamelle *f*

UDI [juːdiːˈaɪ] *n Pol (abbr* **Unilateral Declaration of Independence**) déclaration *f* unilatérale d'indépendance

UEFA [juːˈeɪfə] *n (abbr* **Union of European Football Associations**) UEFA *f*

UFO [juːefˈəʊ] *n (abbr* **unidentified flying object**) OVNI *m*

Uganda [juːˈgændə] *n* l'Ouganda *m*

Ugandan [juːˈgændən] **1** *n* Ougandais(e) *m,f*
  2 *adj* ougandais(e)

ugh [ʌχ] *exclam* berk!

ugly [ˈʌglɪ] *adj* (**a**) *(in appearance)* laid(e); *Fig* **u. duckling** vilain petit canard *m* (**b**) *(unpleasant)* désagréable, déplaisant(e)

UHF [juːeɪtʃˈef] *n (abbr* **ultra-high frequency**) UHF

UHT [juːeɪtʃˈtiː] *adj (abbr* **ultra-heat-treated**) UHT

UK [juːˈkeɪ] *n (abbr* **United Kingdom**) *(written)* RU; *(spoken)* Royaume-Uni *m*

Ukraine [juːˈkreɪn] *n* the U. l'Ukraine *f*

Ukrainian [juːˈkreɪnɪən] **1** *n* (**a**) *(person)* Ukrainien(enne) *m,f* (**b**) *(language)* ukrainien *m*
  2 *adj* ukrainien(enne)

ukulele [juːkəˈleɪlɪ] *n* ukulélé *m*

ulcer [ˈʌlsə(r)] *n* ulcère *m*; *(in mouth)* aphte *m*

ulcerate [ˈʌlsəreɪt] **1** *vt* ulcérer
  2 *vi* s'ulcérer

ulna [ˈʌlnə] *n* cubitus *m*

Ulster [ˈʌlstə(r)] *n* l'Ulster *m*

ulterior [ʌlˈtɪərɪə(r)] *adj* ultérieur(e); **u. motive** arrière-pensée *f*

ultimate [ˈʌltɪmət] **1** *adj* (**a**) *(last)* final(e) (**b**) *(supreme, best)* absolu(e); **the u. holiday** les vacances idéales
  2 *n Fam* **the u. (in)** le summum (de)

ultimately [ˈʌltɪmɪtlɪ] *adv* (**a**) *(finally)* finalement (**b**) *(basically)* en fin de compte

ultimatum [ʌltɪˈmeɪtəm] *n* ultimatum *m*; **to deliver an u. to sb** adresser un ultimatum à qn

ultra- [ˈʌltrə] *pref* ultra-

ultramarine [ʌltrəməˈriːn] *n* bleu *m* outremer

ultramodern [ʌltrəˈmɒdən] *adj* ultramoderne

ultrasound [ˈʌltrəsaʊnd] *n* ultrasons *mpl*

ultraviolet [ʌltrəˈvaɪələt] *adj* ultraviolet(ette)

Ulysses [ˈjuːlɪsiːz] *n* Ulysse

umbilical cord [ʌmˈbɪlɪkəlkɔːd] *n* cordon *m* ombilical

umbrage [ˈʌmbrɪdʒ] *n* **to take u. (at sth)** prendre ombrage (de qch)

umbrella [ʌmˈbrelə] *n* parapluie *m*; *Fig* **under the u. of** sous les auspices de; **u. organization** organisme *m* de tutelle; **u. stand** porte-parapluie *m*

umpire [ˈʌmpaɪə(r)] **1** *n* arbitre *mf*
  2 *vt* arbitrer

umpteen [ʌmpˈtiːn] *adj Fam* je ne sais combien de

umpteenth [ʌmpˈtiːnθ] *adj Fam* énième

UN [juːˈen] *n (abbr* **United Nations**) ONU *f*

unabashed [ʌnəˈbæʃt] *adj* nullement décontenancé(e)

unable [ʌnˈeɪbəl] *adj* **to be u. to do sth** être incapable de faire qch

unabridged [ʌnəˈbrɪdʒd] *adj* intégral(e)

unacceptable [ʌnəkˈseptəbəl] *adj* inacceptable

unaccompanied [ʌnəˈkʌmpənɪd] **1** *adj (person)* non accompagné(e); *(violin, singer)* sans accompagnement
  2 *adv (travel)* seul(e); *(play, sing)* sans accompagnement

unaccomplished [ʌnəˈkʌmplɪʃt] *adj* médiocre

unaccountable [ʌnəˈkaʊntəbəl] *adj* (**a**) *(not answerable)* **to be u. (to sb)** ne pas avoir de comptes à rendre (à qn) (**b**) *(puzzling)* inexplicable

unaccounted [ʌnəˈkaʊntɪd] *adj* **to be u. for** *(of person)* ne pas être retrouvé(e)

unaccustomed [ʌnəˈkʌstəmd] *adj* (**a**) *(not used)* **to be u. to sth/to doing sth** ne pas être habitué(e) à qch/à faire qch (**b**) *(not usual)* inhabituel(elle)

unacknowledged [ʌnəkˈnɒlɪdʒd] **1** *adj* non reconnu(e)
  2 *adv* **to go u.** *(of talent, achievement)* ne pas être reconnu(e)

unacquainted [ʌnəˈkweɪntɪd] *adj* **to be u. with sb/sth** ne pas connaître qn/qch

unadulterated [ʌnəˈdʌltəreɪtɪd] *adj* (**a**) *(food)* naturel(elle) (**b**) *(total, sheer)* pur(e)

unadventurous [ʌnədˈventʃərəs] *adj* peu audacieux(euse)

unaffected [ˌʌnəˈfektɪd] *adj* (**a**) *(sincere)* simple (**b**) *(not touched)* **to be u. (by sth)** ne pas être affecté(e) (par qch)

unaffiliated [ˌʌnəˈfɪlieɪtɪd] *adj* non affilié(e)

unafraid [ˌʌnəˈfreɪd] *adj* **to be u.** ne pas avoir peur

unaided [ʌnˈeɪdɪd] *adv* sans aide

unaltered [ʌnˈɔːltəd] *adj* inchangé(e)

unambiguous [ˌʌnæmˈbɪɡjʊəs] *adj* sans équivoque

unambitious [ˌʌnæmˈbɪʃəs] *adj* sans ambition

unanimity [ˌjuːnəˈnɪmɪtɪ] *n* unanimité *f*

unanimous [juːˈnænɪməs] *adj* unanime

unanimously [juːˈnænɪməslɪ] *adv* à l'unanimité

unannounced [ˌʌnəˈnaʊnst] **1** *adj* non annoncé(e) **2** *adv* sans prévenir

unanswerable [ʌnˈɑːnsərəbəl] *adj* irréfutable

unanswered [ʌnˈɑːnsəd] **1** *adj* sans réponse **2** *adv* **to go u.** *(of question, letter)* rester sans réponse

unappealing [ˌʌnəˈpiːlɪŋ] *adj* peu attrayant(e)

unappetizing [ʌnˈæpɪtaɪzɪŋ] *adj* peu appétissant(e)

unappreciated [ˌʌnəˈpriːʃieɪtɪd] *adj* non reconnu(e)

unapproachable [ˌʌnəˈprəʊtʃəbəl] *adj* inaccessible

unarmed [ʌnˈɑːmd] *adj* non armé(e); **u. combat** combat *m* à mains nues

unashamed [ˌʌnəˈʃeɪmd] *adj* *(joy, greed)* non dissimulé(e); **he's u. about his background** il n'a absolument pas honte de ses origines

unassailable [ˌʌnəˈseɪləbəl] *adj* *(castle, position)* imprenable; *(argument, theory)* inattaquable

unassuming [ˌʌnəˈsjuːmɪŋ] *adj* sans prétention

unattached [ˌʌnəˈtætʃt] *adj* (**a**) *(not connected)* détaché(e) (**b**) *(without partner)* sans attaches

unattainable [ˌʌnəˈteɪnəbəl] *adj* inaccessible

unattractive [ˌʌnəˈtræktɪv] *adj* *(place, habit, prospect)* peu attrayant(e); *(person, appearance)* sans charme

unauthorized [ʌnˈɔːθəraɪzd] *adj* non autorisé(e)

unavailable [ˌʌnəˈveɪləbəl] *adj* non disponible; **to be u.** ne pas être disponible

unavailing [ˌʌnəˈveɪlɪŋ] *adj* vain(e)

unavoidable [ˌʌnəˈvɔɪdəbəl] *adj* inévitable

unaware [ˌʌnəˈweə(r)] *adj* ignorant(e); **to be u. of sth** ignorer qch

unawares [ˌʌnəˈweəz] *adv* **to catch sb u.** prendre qn au dépourvu

unbalanced [ʌnˈbælənst] *adj* (**a**) *(person)* instable (**b**) *(biased)* partial(e)

unbearable [ʌnˈbeərəbəl] *adj* insupportable

unbeatable [ʌnˈbiːtəbəl] *adj* imbattable

unbecoming [ˌʌnbɪˈkʌmɪŋ] *adj* *(behaviour)* inconvenant(e); *(dress)* peu seyant(e)

unbeknown(st) [ˌʌnbɪˈnəʊn(st)] *adv* **u. to me/him** à mon/son insu

unbelievable [ˌʌnbɪˈliːvəbəl] *adj* incroyable

unbending [ʌnˈbendɪŋ] *adj* inflexible

unbias(s)ed [ʌnˈbaɪəst] *adj* impartial(e)

unblock [ʌnˈblɒk] *vt* *(sink, pipe)* déboucher; *(road)* dégager

unborn [ˈʌnbɔːn] *adj* *(child)* à naître

unbounded [ʌnˈbaʊndɪd] *adj* sans bornes

unbreakable [ʌnˈbreɪkəbəl] *adj* (**a**) *(glass, toy)* incassable (**b**) *(promise, rule)* sacré(e)

unbridled [ʌnˈbraɪdəld] *adj* débridé(e)

unbroken [ʌnˈbrəʊkən] *adj* (**a**) *(intact)* intact(e) (**b**) *(uninterrupted)* ininterrompu(e)

unburden [ʌnˈbɜːdən] *vt* **to u. oneself to sb** se confier à qn

unbusinesslike [ʌnˈbɪznɪslaɪk] *adj* peu professionnel(elle)

unbutton [ʌnˈbʌtən] *vt* déboutonner

uncalled-for [ʌnˈkɔːldfɔː(r)] *adj* *(of behaviour, remark)* déplacé(e); *(insult)* gratuit(e)

uncanny [ʌnˈkænɪ] *adj* étrange, troublant(e)

uncaring [ʌnˈkeərɪŋ] *adj* indifférent(e)

unceasing [ʌnˈsiːsɪŋ] *adj* incessant(e)

uncertain [ʌnˈsɜːtən] *adj* incertain(e); **to be u. about sth** ne pas être certain(e) de qch; **it is u. if...** on ne sait pas si...; **in no u. terms** en termes on ne peut plus clairs

uncertainty [ʌnˈsɜːtəntɪ] *(pl* **uncertainties***)* *n* incertitude *f*

unchallenged [ʌnˈtʃælɪndʒd] *adj* incontesté(e)

unchanged [ʌnˈtʃeɪndʒd] *adj* inchangé(e)

unchanging [ʌnˈtʃeɪndʒɪŋ] *adj* immuable

uncharacteristic [ˌʌnkærəktəˈrɪstɪk] *adj* inhabituel(elle)

uncharitable [ʌnˈtʃærɪtəbəl] *adj* peu charitable

uncharted [ʌnˈtʃɑːtɪd] *adj* inexploré(e)

unchecked [ʌnˈtʃekt] **1** *adj* (**a**) *(not restrained)* incontrôlé(e) (**b**) *(not verified)* non vérifié(e) **2** *adv* **to go u.** rester incontrôlé(e)

uncivil [ʌnˈsɪvɪl] *adj* impoli(e)

uncivilized [ʌnˈsɪvɪlaɪzd] *adj* non civilisé(e)

unclaimed [ʌnˈkleɪmd] *adj* non réclamé(e); **to go u.** ne pas être réclamé(e)

uncle [ˈʌŋkəl] *n* oncle *m*; *Am* **U. Sam** l'oncle Sam

unclean [ʌnˈkliːn] *adj* sale, souillé(e)

unclear [ʌnˈklɪə(r)] *adj* vague

unclothed [ʌnˈkləʊðd] *adj* nu(e)

uncoil [ʌnˈkɔɪl] *vt* dérouler

uncombed [ʌnˈkəʊmd] *adj* pas peigné(e)

uncomfortable [ʌnˈkʌmfətəbəl] *adj* inconfortable; *(silence)* gêné(e); **to feel u.** *(physically)* ne pas être à l'aise; *(ill at ease)* être mal à l'aise

uncommitted [ˌʌnkəˈmɪtɪd] *adj* indécis(e)

uncommon [ʌnˈkɒmən] *adj* peu commun(e)

uncommunicative [ˌʌnkəˈmjuːnɪkətɪv] *adj* peu communicatif(ive)

uncomplicated [ʌnˈkɒmplɪkeɪtɪd] *adj* simple, non compliqué(e)

uncomplimentary [ˌʌnkɒmplɪˈmentərɪ] *adj* peu flatteur(euse)

uncomprehending [ˌʌnkɒmprɪˈhendɪŋ] *adj* **to be u. of sth** ne pas comprendre qch; **with an u. look** l'air perplexe

uncompromising [ʌnˈkɒmprəmaɪzɪŋ] *adj* *(person, opposition)* intransigeant(e)

unconcealed [ˌʌnkənˈsiːld] *adj* non dissimulé(e)

unconcerned [ˌʌnkənˈsɜːnd] **1** *adj* indifférent(e); **to be u. about sth** ne pas s'inquiéter de qch **2** *adv* avec indifférence

unconditional [ˌʌnkənˈdɪʃənəl] *adj* sans condition

unconfirmed [ˌʌnkənˈfɜːmd] *adj* non confirmé(e)

unconnected [ˌʌnkəˈnektɪd] *adj* sans lien

unconscious [ʌnˈkɒnʃəs] **1** *adj* (**a**) *(having fainted)* sans connaissance; *(asleep)* profondément endormi(e) (**b**) *(unaware)* inconscient(e); **to be u. of sth** ne pas avoir conscience de qch **2** *n* **the u.** l'inconscient *m*

unconsciously [ʌnˈkɒnʃəslɪ] *adv* inconsciemment

unconstitutional [ʌnkɒnstɪˈtjuːʃənəl] *adj* inconstitutionnel(elle)

uncontaminated [ʌnkənˈtæmɪneɪtɪd] *adj* non contaminé(e)

uncontested [ʌnkənˈtestɪd] *adj* incontesté(e)

uncontrollable [ʌnkənˈtrəʊləbəl] *adj* incontrôlable

uncontroversial [ʌnkɒntrəˈvɜːʃəl] *adj* anodin(e)

unconventional [ʌnkənˈvenʃənəl] *adj* non-conformiste

unconvinced [ʌnkənˈvɪnst] *adj* sceptique

unconvincing [ʌnkənˈvɪnsɪŋ] *adj* peu convaincant(e)

uncooked [ʌnˈkʊkt] *adj* cru(e)

uncool [ʌnˈkuːl] *adj Fam* ringard(e)

uncooperative [ʌnkəʊˈɒpərətɪv] *adj* peu coopératif(-ive)

uncoordinated [ʌnkəʊˈɔːdɪneɪtɪd] *adj* qui manque de coordination

uncork [ʌnˈkɔːk] *vt* déboucher

uncorroborated [ʌnkəˈrɒbəreɪtɪd] *adj* non corroboré(e)

uncountable [ʌnˈkaʊntəbəl] *adj* indénombrable

uncouth [ʌnˈkuːθ] *adj* fruste

uncover [ʌnˈkʌvə(r)] *vt also Fig* découvrir

uncritical [ʌnˈkrɪtɪkəl] *adj* peu critique; **to be u. of sb/sth** ne pas être critique envers qn/qch

UNCTAD [ˈʌŋktæd] *n Econ* (*abbr* **United Nations Conference on Trade and Development**) CNUCED *f*

unction [ˈʌŋkʃən] *n Rel* onction *f*

unctuous [ˈʌŋktjʊəs] *adj Pej* onctueux(euse)

uncultivated [ʌnˈkʌltɪveɪtɪd] *adj* inculte

uncultured [ʌnˈkʌltʃəd] *adj* inculte

uncut [ʌnˈkʌt] *adj* (*gem*) brut(e); (*text, film*) intégral(e)

undamaged [ʌnˈdæmɪdʒd] *adj* intact(e)

undated [ʌnˈdeɪtɪd] *adj* non daté(e)

undaunted [ʌnˈdɔːntɪd] *adj* qui n'est pas impressionné(e); **to be u. by sth** ne pas se laisser impressionner par qch

undecided [ʌndɪˈsaɪdɪd] *adj* (**a**) (*question, problem*) sans réponse; **that's still u.** aucune décision n'a encore été prise (**b**) (*person*) indécis(e) (**about** à propos de)

undefeated [ʌndɪˈfiːtɪd] *adj* invaincu(e)

undefended [ʌndɪˈfendɪd] *adj* sans défense

undemanding [ʌndɪˈmɑːndɪŋ] *adj* (*job*) peu prenant(e); (*person*) peu exigeant(e)

undemocratic [ʌndeməˈkrætɪk] *adj* antidémocratique

undemonstrative [ʌndɪˈmɒnstrətɪv] *adj* peu démonstratif(ive)

undeniable [ʌndɪˈnaɪəbəl] *adj* indéniable

undeniably [ʌndɪˈnaɪəblɪ] *adv* indéniablement

under [ˈʌndə(r)] **1** *prep* (**a**) (*beneath*) sous; **u. the table/the stairs** sous la table/l'escalier; *Fam* **to be u. the weather** ne pas être dans son assiette

(**b**) (*less than*) moins de; **he's u. thirty** il a moins de trente ans; **children u. five** les enfants de moins de cinq ans

(**c**) (*under the control of*) sous; **he had a hundred men u. him** il avait cent hommes sous ses ordres; **Spain u. Franco** l'Espagne de Franco

(**d**) (*subject to*) **to be u. orders to do sth** avoir pour ordre de faire qch; **u. the terms of the agreement** d'après les termes de l'accord; **u. these conditions** dans ces conditions; **u. the circumstances** dans ces circonstances

(**e**) (*in the process of*) **u. repair/observation** en réparation/observation; **to be u. investigation** faire l'objet d'une enquête; **to get u. way** (*of meeting, campaign*) commencer

2 *adv* (**a**) (*underneath*) dessous; (*underwater*) sous l'eau; **to go u.** (*of company*) faire faillite

(**b**) (*less*) au-dessous; **children of five and u.** les enfants de cinq ans et au-dessous

underachiever [ʌndərəˈtʃiːvə(r)] *n* = personne qui ne tire pas profit de ses capacités intellectuelles

under-age [ʌndərˈeɪdʒ] *adj* mineur(e); **u. drinking** consommation *f* d'alcool par les mineurs; **u. sex** relations *fpl* sexuelles entre personnes mineures

undercarriage [ˈʌndəkærɪdʒ] *n* train *m* d'atterrissage

undercharge [ʌndəˈtʃɑːdʒ] *vt* se tromper dans l'addition de (*à l'avantage du client*); **he undercharged me by £5** il aurait dû me faire payer 5 livres de plus

underclass [ˈʌndəklɑːs] *n* sous-prolétariat *m*

underclothes [ˈʌndəkləʊðz] *npl* sous-vêtements *mpl*

underclothing [ˈʌndəkləʊðɪŋ] *n* sous-vêtements *mpl*

undercoat [ˈʌndəkəʊt] *n* sous-couche *f*

undercook [ʌndəˈkʊk] *vt* ne pas faire cuire assez longtemps

undercover [ˈʌndəkʌvə(r)] **1** *adj* secret(ète)

2 *adv* clandestinement

undercurrent [ˈʌndəkʌrənt] *n* (*in sea*) courant *m* sous-marin; *Fig* (*of emotion, unrest*) courant sous-jacent

undercut [ʌndəˈkʌt] (*pt & pp* **undercut**) *vt* vendre moins cher que

underdeveloped [ʌndədɪˈveləpt] *adj* sous-développé(e)

underdog [ˈʌndədɒg] *n* (**a**) (*in contest*) celui *m*/celle *f* qui risque de perdre (**b**) (*in society*) **the u.** les opprimés *mpl*

underestimate 1 *n* [ʌndərˈestɪmɪt] sous-estimation *f*

2 *vt* [ʌndərˈestɪmeɪt] sous-estimer

underexposed [ˈʌndərɪksˈpəʊzd] *adj* sous-exposé(e)

underfed [ʌndəˈfed] *adj* sous-alimenté(e)

underfoot [ʌndəˈfʊt] *adv* sous les pieds; **it's wet u.** le sol est mouillé; **to trample sth u.** piétiner qch

underfunding [ʌndəˈfʌndɪŋ] *n* insuffisance *f* de financement

undergarment [ˈʌndəgɑːmənt] *n* sous-vêtement *m*

undergo [ʌndəˈgəʊ] (*pt* **underwent** [ʌndəˈwent], *pp* **undergone** [ʌndəˈgɒn]) *vt* (*change*) connaître; (*test*) subir; **to u. surgery** être opéré(e); **to u. treatment** (*of patient*) suivre un traitement

undergraduate [ʌndəˈgrædjʊɪt] *n* étudiant(e) *m,f* prépare une licence

underground 1 *adj* [ˈʌndəgraʊnd] (**a**) (*below ground*) souterrain(e) (**b**) (*clandestine*) clandestin(e)

2 *adv* [ʌndəˈgraʊnd] (**a**) (*below ground*) sous terre (**b**) **to go u.** (*into hiding*) passer dans la clandestinité

3 *n* [ˈʌndəgraʊnd] (**a**) *Br* (*railway system*) métro *m* (**b**) (*resistance movement*) mouvement *m* de résistance

undergrowth [ˈʌndəgrəʊθ] *n* broussailles *fpl*

underhand [ˈʌndəhænd] *adj* sournois(e)

underlain [ʌndəˈleɪn] *pp of* **underlie**

underlay [ˈʌndəleɪ] *n* (*for carpet*) thibaude *f*

underlie [ʌndəˈlaɪ] (*pt* **underlay** [ʌndəˈleɪ], *pp* **underlain** [ʌndəˈleɪn]) *vt* sous-tendre

underline [ʌndəˈlaɪn] *vt also Fig* souligner

underlying [ʌndəˈlaɪɪŋ] *adj* sous-jacent(e)

undermanning [ʌndə'mænɪŋ] *n* manque *m* de main-d'œuvre

undermentioned ['ʌndəmenʃənd] *adj Formal* ci-dessous

undermine [ʌndə'maɪn] *vt (weaken) (cliff, person, authority)* saper; *(confidence)* ébranler; *(democracy)* fragiliser

underneath [ʌndə'niːθ] **1** *prep* sous
   2 *adv* dessous
   3 *n* **the u.** le dessous

undernourished [ʌndə'nʌrɪʃt] *adj* sous-alimenté(e)

underpaid [ʌndə'peɪd] *adj* sous-payé(e)

underpants ['ʌndəpænts] *npl* slip *m*

underpass ['ʌndəpɑːs] *n* passage *m* souterrain

underperform [ʌndəpə'fɔːm] *vi Fin (of shares, investment)* ne pas être performant(e)

underpin [ʌndə'pɪn] *(pt & pp* **underpinned***) vt* étayer

underpopulated [ʌndə'pɒpjʊleɪtɪd] *adj* sous-peuplé(e)

underprivileged [ʌndə'prɪvɪlɪdʒd] *adj* défavorisé(e)

underqualified [ʌndə'kwɒlɪfaɪd] *adj* sous-qualifié(e)

underrate [ʌndə'reɪt] *vt* sous-estimer

underside ['ʌndəsaɪd] *n* dessous *m*

undersized [ʌndə'saɪzd] *adj* trop petit(e)

underskirt ['ʌndəskɜːt] *n* jupon *m*; *(full-length)* combinaison *f*

understaffed [ʌndə'stɑːft] *adj* **to be u.** manquer de personnel

understand [ʌndə'stænd] *(pt & pp* **understood** [ʌndə'stʊd] *)* **1** *vt* (**a**) *(comprehend)* comprendre; **to make oneself understood** se faire comprendre; **they u. each other** ils se comprennent (**b**) *(believe, assume)* **to u. that** croire que; **I u. that you're coming to work here** j'ai appris que vous venez travailler ici; **to give sb to u. that** laisser entendre à qn que; **are we to u. that...?** devons-nous en conclure que...?
   2 *vi* comprendre

understandable [ʌndə'stændəbəl] *adj* compréhensible

understandably [ʌndə'stændəblɪ] *adv* naturellement

understanding [ʌndə'stændɪŋ] **1** *n* (**a**) *(comprehension, sympathy)* compréhension *f* (**b**) *(agreement)* accord *m*; **to come to** *or* **to reach an u.** parvenir à un accord; **on the u. that** à condition que + *subjunctive*
   2 *adj* compréhensif(ive)

understatement [ʌndə'steɪtmənt] *n* euphémisme *m*; *(in literature)* litote *f*; **that's an u.!** c'est peu dire!

understood [ʌndə'stʊd] *pt & pp of* **understand**

understudy ['ʌndəstʌdɪ] *n* doublure *f*

undertake [ʌndə'teɪk] *(pt* **undertook** [ʌndə'tʊk]*, pp* **undertaken** [ʌndə'teɪkən] *) vt* entreprendre; **to u. to do sth** entreprendre de faire qch

undertaker ['ʌndəteɪkə(r)] *n Br* entrepreneur *m* de pompes funèbres; **the undertakers** les pompes *fpl* funèbres

undertaking [ʌndə'teɪkɪŋ] *n* (**a**) *(enterprise)* entreprise *f* (**b**) *(promise)* engagement *m*, promesse *f*

undertone ['ʌndətəʊn] *n (low voice)* voix *f* basse; *Fig (hint, suggestion)* fond *m*

undertook [ʌndə'tʊk] *pt of* **undertake**

undertow ['ʌndətəʊ] *n* ressac *m*

undervalue [ʌndə'væljuː] *vt (property)* sous-évaluer; *Fig (person, ability)* sous-estimer

underwater **1** *adj* ['ʌndəwɔːtə(r)] de plongée
   2 *adv* [ʌndə'wɔːtə(r)] sous l'eau

underwear ['ʌndəweə(r)] *n* sous-vêtements *mpl*

underweight [ʌndə'weɪt] *adj* trop maigre

underwent [ʌndə'went] *pt of* **undergo**

underworld ['ʌndəwɜːld] *n* (**a**) *(in mythology)* **the U.** les Enfers *mpl* (**b**) *(of criminals)* pègre *f*

underwrite ['ʌndəraɪt] *(pt* **underwrote** [ʌndə'rəʊt]*, pp* **underwritten** [ʌndə'rɪtən] *) vt* souscrire

underwriter ['ʌndəraɪtə(r)] *n (in insurance)* souscripteur *m*

underwritten [ʌndə'rɪtən] *pp of* **underwrite**

underwrote [ʌndə'rəʊt] *pt of* **underwrite**

undeserved [ʌndɪ'zɜːvd] *adj* immérité(e)

undeserving [ʌndɪ'zɜːvɪŋ] *adj* peu méritant(e); **to be u. of sth** ne pas mériter qch

undesirable [ʌndɪ'zaɪərəbəl] *n & adj* indésirable *mf*

undetected [ʌndɪ'tektɪd] **1** *adj* non détecté(e)
   2 *adv* **to go u.** passer inaperçu(e)

undetermined [ʌndɪ'tɜːmɪnd] *adj* indéterminé(e)

undeterred [ʌndɪ'tɜːd] **1** *adj* **to be u. (by sth)** ne pas se laisser décourager (par qch)
   2 *adv* sans se laisser décourager

undeveloped [ʌndɪ'veləpt] *adj* non développé(e); *(land)* inexploité(e)

undid [ʌn'dɪd] *pt of* **undo**

undies ['ʌndɪz] *npl Fam* sous-vêtements *mpl*

undigested [ʌndaɪ'dʒestɪd] *adj also Fig* non digéré(e)

undignified [ʌn'dɪgnɪfaɪd] *adj* indigne

undiluted [ʌndaɪ'luːtɪd] *adj (liquid)* non dilué(e); *Fig (emotion)* pur(e)

undiminished [ʌndɪ'mɪnɪʃt] *adj* intact(e)

undiplomatic [ʌndɪplə'mætɪk] *adj* peu diplomate

undisciplined [ʌn'dɪsɪplɪnd] *adj* indiscipliné(e)

undisclosed [ʌndɪs'kləʊzd] *adj* non révélé(e)

undiscovered [ʌndɪs'kʌvəd] *adj* inconnu(e); **to go/ continue u.** rester ignoré(e)

undiscriminating [ʌndɪs'krɪmɪneɪtɪŋ] *adj* **to be u.** manquer de discernement

undisputed [ʌndɪs'pjuːtɪd] *adj* incontesté(e)

undistinguished [ʌndɪs'tɪŋgwɪʃt] *adj* médiocre

undisturbed [ʌndɪs'tɜːbd] *adj (sleep)* paisible; **to leave sth u.** ne pas toucher à qch

undo [ʌn'duː] *(pt* **undid** [ʌn'dɪd]*, pp* **undone** [ʌn'dʌn] *) vt* (**a**) *(mistake, damage)* réparer; *Comput (command)* annuler (**b**) *(knot, button, shoelaces)* défaire; *(parcel, zip)* ouvrir; *(bra, dress)* dégrafer

undoing [ʌn'duːɪŋ] *n* ruine *f*; **her pride was her u.** c'est sa fierté qui l'a perdue

undone [ʌn'dʌn] *pp of* **undo**

undoubted [ʌn'daʊtɪd] *adj* indubitable

undoubtedly [ʌn'daʊtɪdlɪ] *adv* indubitablement

undreamed-of [ʌn'driːmdɒv],   **undreamt-of** [ʌn'dremtɒv] *adj* inimaginable

undress [ʌn'dres] **1** *vt* déshabiller; **to get undressed** se déshabiller
   2 *vi* se déshabiller
   3 *n* **in a state of u.** *(naked)* nu(e); *(nearly naked)* en petite tenue

undue [ʌn'djuː] *adj* excessif(ive)

undulate ['ʌndjʊleɪt] *vi* onduler

undulation [ʌndjʊ'leɪʃən] *n* ondulation *f*

unduly [ʌn'djuːlɪ] *adv* trop

unearned [ʌn'ɜːnd] *adj (reward, punishment)* immérité(e); *Fin* **u. income** rentes *fpl*

unearth [ʌn'ɜːθ] vt (buried object) déterrer; Fig (information, secret) mettre à jour

unearthly [ʌn'ɜːθlɪ] adj (**a**) (supernatural) mystérieux(euse) (**b**) Fam **at an u. hour** à une heure impossible; **an u. din** or **racket** un vacarme de tous les diables; **for some u. reason** pour une raison étrange

unease [ʌn'iːz] n malaise m

uneasily [ʌn'iːzɪlɪ] adv d'un air gêné

uneasy [ʌn'iːzɪ] adj (person) mal à l'aise; (sleep) agité(e); (silence) gêné(e)

uneconomical [ʌniːkə'nɒmɪkəl] adj peu économique

uneducated [ʌn'edjʊkeɪtɪd] adj sans instruction; **to be u.** ne pas avoir d'instruction

unemotional [ʌnɪ'məʊʃənəl] adj impassible

unemployable [ʌnɪm'plɔɪəbəl] adj inemployable

unemployed [ʌnɪm'plɔɪd] **1** npl **the u.** les sans-emploi mpl, les chômeurs mpl
   2 adj sans emploi, au chômage

unemployment [ʌnɪm'plɔɪmənt] n chômage m; Br **u. benefit** allocation f chômage

unending [ʌn'endɪŋ] adj interminable

unendurable [ʌnɪn'djʊərəbəl] adj insupportable

unenlightened [ʌnɪn'laɪtənd] adj (person) peu éclairé(e)

unenlightening [ʌnɪn'laɪtnɪŋ] adj obscur(e)

unenterprising [ʌn'entəpraɪzɪŋ] adj qui manque d'initiative

unenthusiastic [ʌnɪnθjuːzɪ'æstɪk] adj peu enthousiaste

unenviable [ʌn'envɪəbəl] adj peu enviable

unequal [ʌn'iːkwəl] adj inégal(e)

unequivocal [ʌnɪ'kwɪvəkəl] adj sans équivoque

unerring [ʌn'ɜːrɪŋ] adj infaillible

UNESCO [juː'neskəʊ] n (abbr **United Nations Educational, Scientific and Cultural Organization**) UNESCO f

unethical [ʌn'eθɪkəl] adj contraire à l'éthique

uneven [ʌn'iːvən] adj inégal(e)

uneventful [ʌnɪ'ventfʊl] adj sans histoires

unexceptionable [ʌnɪk'sepʃənəbəl] adj tout à fait convenable

unexceptional [ʌnɪk'sepʃənəl] adj qui n'a rien d'exceptionnel

unexciting [ʌnɪk'saɪtɪŋ] adj peu intéressant(e)

unexpected [ʌnɪks'pektɪd] adj inattendu(e), imprévu(e)

unexplained [ʌnɪks'pleɪnd] adj inexpliqué(e)

unexplored [ʌnɪks'plɔːd] adj inexploré(e)

unfailing [ʌn'feɪlɪŋ] adj à toute épreuve

unfair [ʌn'feə(r)] adj injuste; **to be u. to sb** être injuste envers qn; **to have an u. advantage (over sb)** être injustement favorisé(e) (par rapport à qn); Com **u. competition** concurrence f déloyale; Law **u. dismissal** licenciement m abusif

unfairly [ʌn'feəlɪ] adv (act, treat) injustement; (share, distribute) inéquitablement; (dismiss) abusivement

unfairness [ʌn'feənɪs] n injustice f

unfaithful [ʌn'feɪθfʊl] adj infidèle

unfamiliar [ʌnfə'mɪlɪə(r)] adj (**a**) (unknown) inconnu(e) (**b**) (unacquainted) **to be u. with** ne pas connaître

unfashionable [ʌn'fæʃənəbəl] adj démodé(e)

unfasten [ʌn'fɑːsən] **1** vt défaire
   2 vi se défaire

unfathomable [ʌn'fæðəməbəl] adj insondable

unfavourable, Am **unfavorable** [ʌn'feɪvərəbəl] adj défavorable; (moment) peu propice

unfazed [ʌn'feɪzd] adj Fam **to be u. by sth** n'être pas du tout impressionné(e) par qch

unfeeling [ʌn'fiːlɪŋ] adj insensible

unfinished [ʌn'fɪnɪʃt] adj inachevé(e); **to have (some) u. business (with sb)** avoir des affaires à régler (avec qn)

unfit [ʌn'fɪt] adj (**a**) (unsuitable) inapte; **to be u. to do sth** être incapable de faire qch; **he's u. for the job** il est incapable d'assumer ce travail; **u. for human consumption** impropre à la consommation; **u. mother** mère f indigne (**b**) (physically) qui n'est pas en forme; **to be u.** ne pas être en forme

unflagging [ʌn'flægɪŋ] adj (optimism, courage, enthusiasm) inépuisable; (attention, interest) sans faille

unflappable [ʌn'flæpəbəl] adj imperturbable

unflattering [ʌn'flætərɪŋ] adj peu flatteur(euse)

unflinching [ʌn'flɪnʃɪŋ] adj (courage) inépuisable; (resolve, loyalty, support) à toute épreuve

unfold [ʌn'fəʊld] **1** vt (**a**) (newspaper, map) déplier (**b**) (intentions, proposal) dévoiler
   2 vi (of story, events) se développer, se dérouler

unforced [ʌn'fɔːst] adj naturel(elle)

unforeseeable [ʌnfɔː'siːəbəl] adj imprévisible

unforeseen [ʌnfɔː'siːn] adj imprévu(e)

unforgettable [ʌnfə'getəbəl] adj inoubliable

unforgivable [ʌnfə'gɪvəbəl] adj impardonnable

unforgiving [ʌnfə'gɪvɪŋ] adj implacable, impitoyable

unformatted [ʌn'fɔːmætɪd] adj Comput (disk) non formaté(e); (text) non mis(e) en forme

unforthcoming [ʌnfɔːθ'kʌmɪŋ] adj réticent(e)

unfortunate [ʌn'fɔːtjənɪt] adj (person) malchanceux(euse); (accident, event) fâcheux(euse), regrettable; **it is u. that...** il est fâcheux ou regrettable que... + subjunctive

unfortunately [ʌn'fɔːtjənɪtlɪ] adv malheureusement

unfounded [ʌn'faʊndɪd] adj infondé(e), sans fondement

unfriendly [ʌn'frendlɪ] adj (person) peu sympathique; (reception, tone, look) froid(e)

unfulfilled [ʌnfʊl'fɪld] adj (promise) non tenu(e); (desire, ambition) insatisfait(e); (potential) non réalisé(e); **to feel u.** se sentir insatisfait

unfunny [ʌn'fʌnɪ] adj qui n'a rien de drôle

unfurl [ʌn'fɜːl] **1** vt déployer
   2 vi se déployer

unfurnished [ʌn'fɜːnɪʃt] adj non meublé(e)

ungainly [ʌn'geɪnlɪ] adj disgrâcieux(euse)

ungenerous [ʌn'dʒenərəs] adj (person) qui manque de générosité; (remark) pas gentil(ille)

ungodly [ʌn'gɒdlɪ] adj impie; Fam **at an u. hour** à une heure impossible

ungovernable [ʌn'gʌvənəbəl] adj (people, country) ingouvernable; (feelings) irrépressible

ungracious [ʌn'greɪʃəs] adj peu aimable

ungrateful [ʌn'greɪtfʊl] adj ingrat(e)

ungrudging [ʌn'grʌdʒɪŋ] adj accordé(e) de bon cœur; **to be u. in one's praise** être généreux(euse) avec ses compliments

unguarded [ʌn'gɑːdɪd] adj (**a**) (place) sans surveillance (**b**) (remark) irréfléchi(e); **in an u. moment** dans un moment d'inattention

unhampered [ʌn'hæmpəd] adj non entravé(e) (**by** par)

unhappily [ʌnˈhæpɪlɪ] *adv* (**a**) *(unfortunately)* malheureusement (**b**) *(sadly)* sans joie, sans bonheur

unhappiness [ʌnˈhæpɪnɪs] *n* tristesse *f*

unhappy [ʌnˈhæpɪ] *adj* (**a**) *(sad)* triste, malheureux(-euse) (**b**) *(worried)* **to be u. about doing sth** ne pas vouloir faire qch (**c**) *(not pleased)* mécontent(e) (**with** de) (**d**) *(unfortunate)* malheureux(euse), regrettable

unharmed [ʌnˈhɑːmd] *adj* indemne

UNHCR [juːeneɪtʃˈsiːˈɑː(r)] *n* (*abbr* **United Nations High Commission for Refugees**) HCR *m*

unhealthy [ʌnˈhelθɪ] *adj* (**a**) *(person)* maladif(ive); *(environment, climate)* malsain(e) (**b**) *(unwholesome)* malsain(e)

unheard-of [ʌnˈhɜːdɒv] *adj* (**a**) *(unknown)* inconnu(e) (**b**) *(unprecedented)* inouï(e); **it was u. in my youth!** c'était inconcevable dans ma jeunesse!

unheeded [ʌnˈhiːdɪd] *adj* ignoré(e); **to go u.** rester ignoré

unhelpful [ʌnˈhelpfʊl] *adj* *(person)* peu serviable; *(criticism, advice)* de peu d'utilité

unhesitating [ʌnˈhezɪteɪtɪŋ] *adj* *(support)* résolu(e), ferme; *(reply, reaction)* immédiat(e)

unhindered [ʌnˈhɪndəd] **1** *adj* *(progress)* sans encombres; **to be u. by sth** *(doubts, worry)* ne pas être gêné(e) par qch
2 *adv* sans encombres

unhinged [ʌnˈhɪndʒd] *adj* *(mad)* déséquilibré(e)

unhip [ʌnˈhɪp] *adj Fam (unfashionable)* ringard(e)

unholy [ʌnˈhəʊlɪ] *adj* impie; *Fam* **an u. mess/noise** une pagaille/un bruit invraisemblable; **u. alliance** alliance *f* contre nature

unhurt [ʌnˈhɜːt] *adj* indemne

unhygienic [ʌnhaɪˈdʒiːnɪk] *adj* contraire à l'hygiène; *(person)* qui manque d'hygiène

UNICEF [ˈjuːnɪsef] *n* (*abbr* **United Nations International Children's Emergency Fund**) UNICEF *m*

unicorn [ˈjuːnɪkɔːn] *n* licorne *f*

unidentified [ʌnaɪˈdentɪfaɪd] *adj* non identifié(e); **u. flying object** objet *m* volant non identifié

unification [juːnɪfɪˈkeɪʃən] *n* unification *f*

uniform [ˈjuːnɪfɔːm] **1** *n* uniforme *m*
2 *adj* *(colour, size)* uniforme; *(temperature)* constant(e)

uniformity [juːnɪˈfɔːmɪtɪ] *n* uniformité *f*

uniformly [ˈjuːnɪfɔːmlɪ] *adv* uniformément

unify [ˈjuːnɪfaɪ] (*pt & pp* **unified**) **1** *vt* unifier
2 *vi* s'unifier

unilateral [juːnɪˈlætərəl] *adj* unilatéral(e)

unimaginable [ʌnɪˈmædʒɪnəbəl] *adj* inimaginable

unimaginative [ʌnɪˈmædʒɪnətɪv] *adj* qui manque d'imagination, peu imaginatif(ive)

unimpaired [ʌnɪmˈpeəd] *adj* intact(e)

unimportant [ʌnɪmˈpɔːtənt] *adj* sans importance

unimpressed [ʌnɪmˈprest] *adj* qui n'est pas impressionné(e); *(unconvinced)* qui n'est pas convaincu(e)

uninformed [ʌnɪnˈfɔːmd] *adj* mal informé(e) (**about** sur)

uninhabitable [ʌnɪnˈhæbɪtəbəl] *adj* inhabitable

uninhabited [ʌnɪnˈhæbɪtɪd] *adj* inhabité(e)

uninhibited [ʌnɪnˈhɪbɪtɪd] *adj* *(person)* sans complexes; *(feeling)* non refréné(e)

uninitiated [ʌnɪˈnɪʃɪeɪtɪd] *adj* non initié(e)

uninspiring [ʌnɪnˈspaɪrɪŋ] *adj* peu stimulant(e)

unintelligible [ʌnɪnˈtelɪdʒɪbəl] *adj* inintelligible

unintended [ʌnɪnˈtendɪd] *adj* involontaire

unintentional [ʌnɪnˈtenʃənəl] *adj* involontaire

uninterested [ʌnˈɪntərestɪd] *adj* indifférent(e)

uninteresting [ʌnˈɪntərestɪŋ] *adj* inintéressant(e)

uninterrupted [ʌnɪntəˈrʌptɪd] *adj* ininterrompu(e)

uninvited [ʌnɪnˈvaɪtɪd] **1** *adj* *(comment, advice)* non désiré(e); **u. guest** invité(e)-surprise *m,f*
2 *adv* sans invitation

uninviting [ʌnɪnˈvaɪtɪŋ] *adj* peu attrayant(e); *(food)* peu appétissant(e)

union [ˈjuːnjən] *n* (**a**) *(between countries, people)* union *f*; **the U. Jack** l'Union Jack *m* *(drapeau du Royaume-Uni)* (**b**) *(trade union)* syndicat *m*

unionist [ˈjuːnjənɪst] *n* (**a**) *(supporter of trade union)* syndicaliste *mf* (**b**) *(in Northern Ireland)* unioniste *mf*

unionize [ˈjuːnjənaɪz] *vt* syndiquer

unique [juːˈniːk] *adj* unique; **to be u. to** être propre à

unisex [ˈjuːnɪseks] *adj* unisexe

UNISON [ˈjuːnɪsən] *n Br* = principal syndicat de la fonction publique

unison [ˈjuːnɪsən] *n* **in u.** *(sing, play)* à l'unisson; *(speak, reply)* en même temps

unit [ˈjuːnɪt] *n* (**a**) *(in general)* unité *f*; **u. of measurement** unité de mesure; *Com* **u. price** prix *m* à l'unité; *Fin* **u. trust** fonds *m* commun de placement, SICAV *f* (**b**) *(part of system, machine)* bloc *m*, élément *m* (**c**) *(in hospital)* service *m*, département *m*; *(in army)* unité *f* (**d**) *(of furniture)* élément *m*

unitary [ˈjuːnɪtərɪ] *adj* unitaire

unite [juːˈnaɪt] **1** *vt* unir, rassembler
2 *vi* s'unir; **to u. in doing sth** s'unir pour faire qch

united [juːˈnaɪtɪd] *adj* uni(e); **the U. Arab Emirates** les Émirats *mpl* arabes unis; **the U. Kingdom** le Royaume-Uni; **the U. Nations** les Nations *fpl* unies; **the U. States (of America)** les États-Unis *mpl* (d'Amérique)

unity [ˈjuːnɪtɪ] *n* unité *f*

univ (*abbr* **university**) univ

universal [juːnɪˈvɜːsəl] *adj* universel(elle); **u. suffrage** suffrage *m* universel

universally [juːnɪˈvɜːsəlɪ] *adv* universellement

universe [ˈjuːnɪvɜːs] *n* univers *m*

university [juːnɪˈvɜːsɪtɪ] *n* université *f*; **u. fees** frais *mpl* d'inscription à l'université; **u. student** étudiant(e) *m,f* à l'université, *Belg & Suisse* universitaire *mf*; **u. town** ville *f* universitaire

UNIX [ˈjuːnɪks] *n Comput* (*abbr* **Uniplexed Information and Computing System**) UNIX *m*

unjust [ʌnˈdʒʌst] *adj* injuste

unjustifiable [ʌndʒʌstɪˈfaɪəbəl] *adj* injustifiable

unjustified [ʌnˈdʒʌstɪfaɪd] *adj* injustifié(e)

unkempt [ʌnˈkem(p)t] *adj* négligé(e)

unkind [ʌnˈkaɪnd] *adj* pas gentil(ille); **to be u. to sb** ne pas être gentil avec qn

unkindly [ʌnˈkaɪndlɪ] *adv* méchamment; **to take u. to sth** mal accepter qch

unknowingly [ʌnˈnəʊɪŋlɪ] *adv* inconsciemment

unknown [ʌnˈnəʊn] **1** *adj* inconnu(e); *Fig* **to be an u. quantity** rester une inconnue; **the U. Soldier** le Soldat inconnu
2 *adv* **u. to me/us** à mon/notre insu
3 *n (person)* inconnu(e) *m,f*; **the u.** l'inconnu *m*

unlace [ʌnˈleɪs] *vt* délacer, défaire

unladylike [ʌn'leɪdɪlaɪk] *adj (person)* qui ne se conduit pas comme une jeune fille; *(behaviour)* qui n'est pas digne d'une jeune fille

unlawful [ʌn'lɔːfʊl] *adj* illégal(e), illicite

unleaded [ʌn'ledɪd] **1** *adj* sans plomb
   2 *n* sans plomb *m*

unleash [ʌn'liːʃ] *vt (dog)* détacher, lâcher; *Fig (emotion, criticism)* susciter

unleavened [ʌn'levənd] *adj* sans levain

unless [ʌn'les] *conj* à moins que + *subjunctive*; **u. I hear to the contrary** sauf avis contraire

unlike [ʌn'laɪk] *prep* **to be u. sb/sth** ne pas être comme qn/qch; **he's not u. his sister** il ressemble assez à sa sœur; **he, u. his father,...** lui, à la différence de son père...; **it's u. her to do such a thing** cela ne lui ressemble pas de faire une chose pareille

unlikely [ʌn'laɪklɪ] *adj* improbable; *(story, explanation)* invraisemblable; **it's u. to happen** il est peu probable que cela se produise; **she's u. to do it** il est peu probable qu'elle le fasse; **in the u. event of an accident** dans le cas fort peu probable d'un accident

unlimited [ʌn'lɪmɪtɪd] *adj* illimité(e), sans limites; *Com* **u. liability** responsabilité *f* illimitée; **u. mileage** *(of hired car)* ≃ kilométrage *m* illimité

unlisted [ʌn'lɪstɪd] *adj* (**a**) *Fin* non inscrit(e) à la cote (**b**) *Am Tel (phone number)* qui est sur liste rouge

unlit [ʌn'lɪt] *adj (fire, cigarette)* non allumé(e); *(place)* non éclairé(e)

unload [ʌn'ləʊd] **1** *vt (boat, gun, goods)* décharger; *Fig* **to u. one's problems onto sb** se soulager de ses problèmes en en parlant à qn
   2 *vi (of lorry, ship)* décharger

unlock [ʌn'lɒk] *vt (door)* ouvrir; *Fig (mystery)* dévoiler, révéler

unlovable [ʌn'lʌvəbəl] *adj* peu attachant(e)

unloved [ʌn'lʌvd] *adj* mal aimé(e)

unlovely [ʌn'lʌvlɪ] *adj* déplaisant(e)

unluckily [ʌn'lʌkɪlɪ] *adv* malheureusement

unlucky [ʌn'lʌkɪ] *adj (coincidence, decision)* malheureux(euse); *(day)* de malchance; **to be u.** *(of person)* être malchanceux(euse); *(of thing)* porter malheur

unmanageable [ʌn'mænɪdʒəbəl] *adj (person, situation)* difficile; *(hair)* impossible à coiffer

unmanly [ʌn'mænlɪ] *adj (effeminate)* efféminé(e), peu viril(e); *(cowardly)* lâche

unmanned [ʌn'mænd] *adj (spaceship)* inhabité(e)

unmarked [ʌn'mɑːkt] *adj* (**a**) *(grave)* sans inscription; **u. (police) car** voiture *f* (de police) banalisée (**b**) *(uncorrected)* non corrigé(e)

unmarried [ʌn'mærɪd] *adj* non marié(e)

unmask [ʌn'mɑːsk] *vt* démasquer

unmentionable [ʌn'menʃənəbəl] *adj* à ne pas mentionner

unmistakable [ʌnmɪs'teɪkəbəl] *adj* caractéristique

unmitigated [ʌn'mɪtɪgeɪtɪd] *adj* total(e), absolu(e)

unmoved [ʌn'muːvd] **1** *adj* **to be u. by sth** rester insensible à qch; **he was u. by her** elle le laissait complètement indifférent
   2 *adv* sans broncher

unnamed [ʌn'neɪmd] *adj (person)* anonyme; *(thing)* sans nom

unnatural [ʌn'nætjərəl] *adj* (**a**) *(abnormal)* anormal(e) (**b**) *(affected)* affecté(e)

unnecessary [ʌn'nesɪsərɪ] *adj* inutile, superflu(e)

unnerve [ʌn'nɜːv] *vt* troubler

unnerving [ʌn'nɜːvɪŋ] *adj* troublant(e)

unnoticed [ʌn'nəʊtɪst] **1** *adj* inaperçu(e)
   2 *adv* **to pass** *or* **go u.** passer inaperçu(e)

UNO [juːen'əʊ] *n (abbr* **United Nations Organization)** ONU *f*

unobservant [ʌnəb'zɜːvənt] *adj* peu observateur(-trice)

unobserved [ʌnəb'zɜːvd] **1** *adj* inaperçu(e)
   2 *adv* **to do sth u.** faire qch sans être vu(e)

unobstructed [ʌnəb'strʌktɪd] *adj* dégagé(e); *(pipe)* non obstrué(e)

unobtainable [ʌnəb'teɪnəbəl] *adj* impossible à obtenir

unobtrusive [ʌnəb'truːsɪv] *adj* discret(ète)

unoccupied [ʌn'ɒkjʊpaɪd] *adj (person)* qui n'est pas occupé(e); *(seat)* libre; *(house)* inhabité(e), inoccupé(e)

unofficial [ʌnə'fɪʃəl] *adj* officieux(euse), non officiel(elle); *Ind* **u. strike** grève *f* sauvage

unopened [ʌn'əʊpənd] *adj* non ouvert(e)

unopposed [ʌnə'pəʊzd] **1** *adj* sans opposition; **to be u.** ne pas rencontrer d'opposition
   2 *adv* **to go u.** ne pas rencontrer d'opposition

unorthodox [ʌn'ɔːθədɒks] *adj* peu orthodoxe

unpack [ʌn'pæk] **1** *vt (suitcase)* défaire; *(contents)* déballer; *(box)* ouvrir
   2 *vi* défaire ses bagages

unpaid [ʌn'peɪd] *adj* (**a**) *(work, volunteer)* non rémunéré(e) (**b**) *(bill, debt)* impayé(e)

unpalatable [ʌn'pælətəbəl] *adj (food)* qui n'est pas très bon (bonne); *Fig (truth)* désagréable à entendre

unparalleled [ʌn'pærəleld] *adj* incomparable, sans pareil(eille)

unpardonable [ʌn'pɑːdənəbəl] *adj* impardonnable

unpatriotic [ʌnpætrɪ'ɒtɪk, ʌnpeɪtrɪ'ɒtɪk] *adj (person)* peu patriote; *(song, remark)* antipatriotique

unperturbed [ʌnpə'tɜːbd] **1** *adj* **to be u. by sth** ne pas se laisser perturber par qch
   2 *adv* imperturbablement

unplanned [ʌn'plænd] *adj* imprévu(e); *(pregnancy)* accidentel(elle)

unpleasant [ʌn'plezənt] *adj* désagréable, déplaisant(e)

unpleasantness [ʌn'plezəntnɪs] *n* (**a**) *(unpleasant nature)* côté *m* désagréable (**b**) *(ill-feeling)* désagréments *mpl*

unplug [ʌn'plʌg] *(pt & pp* **unplugged)** *vt* débrancher

unpolished [ʌn'pɒlɪʃt] *adj (shoes, surface)* non ciré(e); *Fig (performance, style)* imparfait(e)

unpolluted [ʌnpə'luːtɪd] *adj* non pollué(e)

unpopular [ʌn'pɒpjʊlə(r)] *adj* impopulaire; **she's very u. with the boss at the moment** elle n'est pas dans les bonnes grâces du patron en ce moment

unpopularity [ʌnpɒpjʊ'lærɪtɪ] *n* impopularité *f*

unpredictability [ʌnprɪdɪktə'bɪlətɪ] *n* imprévisibilité *f*

unpredictable [ʌnprɪ'dɪktəbəl] *adj* imprévisible

unprejudiced [ʌn'predʒʊdɪst] *adj (view, person)* impartial(e)

unprepared [ʌnprɪ'peəd] *adj (speech)* improvisé(e); **to be u. for sth** être mal préparé(e) à qch; *(not expect)* ne pas s'attendre à qch

unprepossessing [ʌnpriːpə'zesɪŋ] *adj* peu avenant(e)

unpresentable [ˌʌnprɪˈzentəbəl] *adj* qui n'est pas présentable

unpretentious [ˌʌnprɪˈtenʃəs] *adj* sans prétention(s)

unprincipled [ʌnˈprɪnsɪpəld] *adj* sans scrupules

unprintable [ʌnˈprɪntəbəl] *adj* licencieux(euse)

unproductive [ˌʌnprəˈdʌktɪv] *adj* improductif(ive)

unprofessional [ˌʌnprəˈfeʃənəl] *adj* qui n'est pas professionnel(elle)

unprofitable [ʌnˈprɒfɪtəbəl] *adj* peu rentable

Unprofor [ʌnˈprɒfɔː(r)] *n* (*abbr* United Nations Protection Force) FORPRONU *f*

unpromising [ʌnˈprɒmɪsɪŋ] *adj* peu prometteur(-euse)

unpronounceable [ˌʌnprəˈnaʊnsəbəl] *adj* imprononçable

unprotected [ˌʌnprəˈtektɪd] *adj* sans protection; *(sex)* non protégé(e)

unprovoked [ˌʌnprəˈvəʊkt] *adj* gratuit(e)

unpublished [ʌnˈpʌblɪʃt] *adj* inédit(e)

unpunished [ʌnˈpʌnɪʃt] **1** *adj* impuni(e)
   2 *adv* **to go u.** rester impuni(e)

unqualified [ʌnˈkwɒlɪfaɪd] *adj* (**a**) *(doctor, teacher)* non qualifié(e); **to be u. to do sth** ne pas être qualifié pour faire qch (**b**) *(support)* inconditionnel(elle), sans réserve; *(disaster, success)* total(e), complet(ète)

unquestionable [ʌnˈkwestʃənəbəl] *adj* indubitable, incontestable

unquestioning [ʌnˈkwestʃənɪŋ] *adj* *(trust, obedience)* absolu(e), aveugle

unravel [ʌnˈrævəl] (*pt & pp* unravelled) **1** *vt* *(wool, knitting)* défaire; *(threads)* démêler; *Fig (plot)* dénouer; *(mystery)* éclaircir
   2 *vi* *(of wool, knitting)* se défaire; *Fig (of plan)* péricliter; *(of mystery)* s'éclaircir

unreadable [ʌnˈriːdəbəl] *adj* illisible

unreal [ʌnˈrɪəl] *adj* irréel(elle)

unrealistic [ˌʌnrɪəˈlɪstɪk] *adj* irréaliste

unreasonable [ʌnˈriːzənəbəl] *adj* déraisonnable

unrecognizable [ˌʌnrekəɡˈnaɪzəbəl] *adj* méconnaissable

unrecognized [ʌnˈrekəɡnaɪzd] **1** *adj* méconnu(e)
   2 *adv* **to go u.** rester méconnu(e)

unrecorded [ˌʌnrɪˈkɔːdɪd] *adj* non enregistré(e)

unrefined [ˌʌnrɪˈfaɪnd] *adj* (**a**) *(sugar, petrol)* non raffiné(e) (**b**) *(person, taste)* qui manque de raffinement

unregistered [ʌnˈredʒɪstəd] *adj* *(birth)* non déclaré(e)

unrelated [ˌʌnrɪˈleɪtɪd] *adj* **to be u.** *(of events)* ne pas avoir de rapport; *(of people)* n'avoir aucun lien de parenté

unrelenting [ˌʌnrɪˈlentɪŋ] *adj* incessant(e); *(person)* tenace

unreliable [ˌʌnrɪˈlaɪəbəl] *adj* peu fiable

unrelieved [ˌʌnrɪˈliːvd] *adj* *(pain)* constant(e)

unremarkable [ˌʌnrɪˈmɑːkəbəl] *adj* quelconque

unremitting [ˌʌnrɪˈmɪtɪŋ] *adj* inlassable, infatigable

unrepentant [ˌʌnrɪˈpentənt] *adj* impénitent(e)

unreported [ˌʌnrɪˈpɔːtɪd] **1** *adj* non signalé(e)
   2 *adv* **to go u.** ne pas être signalé(e)

unrepresentative [ˌʌnreprɪˈzentətɪv] *adj* non représentatif(ive)

unrepresented [ˌʌnreprɪˈzentɪd] *adj* non représenté(e)

unrequited love [ˈʌnrɪkwaɪtɪdˈlʌv] *n* amour *m* non partagé

unreserved [ˌʌnrɪˈzɜːvd] *adj* (**a**) *(praise, support)* sans réserve (**b**) *(seat, table)* non réservé(e)

unresponsive [ˌʌnrɪˈspɒnsɪv] *adj* sans réaction; **to be u. to sth** être insensible à qch

unrest [ʌnˈrest] *n* agitation *f*, troubles *mpl*

unrestricted [ˌʌnrɪˈstrɪktɪd] *adj* illimité(e); *(access)* libre

unrewarding [ˌʌnrɪˈwɔːdɪŋ] *adj* *(financially)* qui ne rapporte pas; *(intellectually)* ingrat(e)

unripe [ʌnˈraɪp] *adj* qui n'est pas mûr(e)

unrivalled [ʌnˈraɪvəld] *adj* sans pareil(eille), incomparable

unromantic [ˌʌnrəˈmæntɪk] *adj* peu romantique

unruffled [ʌnˈrʌfəld] *adj* imperturbable

unruly [ʌnˈruːlɪ] *adj* *(child, hair)* indiscipliné(e); *(crowd)* incontrôlé(e)

unsaddle [ʌnˈsædəl] *vt (horse)* desseller

unsafe [ʌnˈseɪf] *adj* (**a**) *(in danger)* en danger (**b**) *(dangerous)* dangereux(euse)

unsaid [ʌnˈsed] *adj* **to leave sth u.** passer qch sous silence; **it's better left u.** il vaut mieux garder le silence là-dessus

unsalted [ʌnˈsɔːltɪd] *adj* sans sel; **u. butter** beurre *m* doux

unsatisfactory [ˌʌnsætɪsˈfæktərɪ] *adj* peu satisfaisant(e)

unsatisfying [ʌnˈsætɪsfaɪɪŋ] *adj* peu satisfaisant(e)

unsavoury [ʌnˈseɪvərɪ] *adj* *(person, place)* peu recommandable; *(reputation)* sale

unscathed [ʌnˈskeɪðd] *adj* indemne

unscheduled [ʌnˈʃedjuːld] *adj* imprévu(e)

unscientific [ˌʌnsaɪənˈtɪfɪk] *adj* non scientifique

unscramble [ʌnˈskræmbəl] *vt* décoder

unscrew [ʌnˈskruː] **1** *vt* dévisser
   2 *vi* se dévisser

unscrupulous [ʌnˈskruːpjʊləs] *adj* *(person)* sans scrupules; *(action)* malhonnête

unseat [ʌnˈsiːt] *vt (rider)* désarçonner; *Br Fig (MP)* faire perdre son siège à; *(leader)* faire tomber

unseemly [ʌnˈsiːmlɪ] *adj* inconvenant(e), indécent(e)

unseen [ʌnˈsiːn] **1** *adj* invisible; **u. translation** traduction *f* à vue
   2 *adv* **to do sth u.** faire qch sans qu'on vous voie

unselfconscious [ˌʌnselfˈkɒnʃəs] *adj* naturel(elle); **he's quite u. about it** il n'en est pas du tout complexé

unselfish [ʌnˈselfɪʃ] *adj* généreux(euse)

unsentimental [ˌʌnsentɪˈmentəl] *adj* *(person)* peu sentimental(e); *(book, film)* dénué(e) de tout sentimentalisme

unsettle [ʌnˈsetəl] *vt* troubler, perturber

unshakeable [ʌnˈʃeɪkəbəl] *adj* inébranlable

unshaven [ʌnˈʃeɪvən] *adj* pas rasé(e)

unsightly [ʌnˈsaɪtlɪ] *adj* laid(e)

unsigned [ʌnˈsaɪnd] *adj* non signé(e)

unskilful [ʌnˈskɪlfʊl] *adj* maladroit(e), malhabile

unskilled [ʌnˈskɪld] *adj* non qualifié(e)

unsociable [ʌnˈsəʊʃəbəl] *adj* *(by nature)* sauvage; **she's feeling rather u. at the moment** elle n'a pas envie de voir du monde en ce moment

unsold [ʌnˈsəʊld] *adj* invendu(e)

unsolicited [ˌʌnsəˈlɪsɪtɪd] *adj* non sollicité(e)

unsolved [ʌnˈsɒlvd] *adj* non résolu(e)

unsophisticated [ˌʌnsəˈfɪstɪkeɪtɪd] *adj* simple

unsound [ʌnˈsaʊnd] *adj* (**a**) *(health)* précaire; *Law* **to be of u. mind** ne pas jouir de toutes ses facultés mentales (**b**) *(decision, advice)* peu judicieux(euse); *(investment)* hasardeux(euse); **he's ideologically u.** son idéologie est suspecte

unsparing [ʌn'speərɪŋ] *adj* **to be u. of one's time/ with one's advice** ne pas être avare de son temps/ de ses conseils

unspeakable [ʌn'spiːkəbəl] *adj* indescriptible

unspecified [ʌn'spesɪfaɪd] *adj* non spécifié(e)

unspoilt [ʌn'spɔɪlt] *adj (beach, landscape)* préservé(e)

unspoken [ʌn'spəʊkən] *adj (fear, threat)* inexprimé(e); *(agreement)* tacite

unsporting [ʌn'spɔːtɪŋ], **unsportsmanlike** [ʌn'spɔːtsmənlaɪk] *adj* qui n'est pas fair-play

unstable [ʌn'steɪbəl] *adj* instable

unsteady [ʌn'stedɪ] *adj (table, chair)* bancal(e); *(hand, voice)* mal assuré(e); **to be u. on one's feet** ne pas être très solide sur ses jambes

unstinting [ʌn'stɪntɪŋ] *adj (praise, effort)* sans réserve

unstressed [ʌn'strest] *adj Ling* inaccentué(e)

unstuck [ʌn'stʌk] *adj Fam* **to come u.** *(of person)* se casser la figure; *(of plan)* tomber à l'eau

unsubstantiated [ʌnsəb'stænʃɪeɪtɪd] *adj (accusation)* sans fondement

unsuccessful [ʌnsək'sesfʊl] *adj* **to be u.** *(of person, project)* ne pas réussir

unsuccessfully [ʌnsək'sesfəlɪ] *adv* en vain, sans succès

unsuitable [ʌn'suːtəbəl] *adj (candidate)* inadéquat(e); *(friend)* pas convenable; *(time)* inopportun(e); *(choice)* inapproprié(e); **to be u. for sth** ne pas convenir à qch; **this film is u. for children** ce n'est pas un film pour les enfants

unsuited [ʌn'suːtɪd] *adj* **to be u. to sth** ne pas être fait(e) pour qch; **to be u.** *(of couple)* être mal assorti(e)

unsupervised [ʌn'suːpəvaɪzd] *adj (child)* non surveillé(e)

unsupported [ʌnsə'pɔːtɪd] *adj* (**a**) *(statement, charges)* sans fondement (**b**) *(structure)* non soutenu(e)

unsure [ʌn'ʃʊə(r)] *adj* incertain(e), peu sûr(e); **to be u. of** *or* **about sth** ne pas être sûr de qch

unsurpassed [ʌnsə'pɑːst] *adj* inégalé(e)

unsuspected [ʌnsəs'pektɪd] *adj* insoupçonné(e)

unsuspecting [ʌnsəs'pektɪŋ] *adj* qui ne se doute de rien

unsustainable [ʌnsə'steɪnəbəl] *adj* non viable

unsweetened [ʌn'swiːtənd] *adj* non sucré(e), sans sucre ajouté

unswerving [ʌn'swɜːvɪŋ] *adj* à toute épreuve

unsympathetic [ʌnsɪmpə'θetɪk] *adj* peu compatissant(e) (**to** à); *(to cause, request)* insensible (**to** à)

unsystematic [ʌnsɪstə'mætɪk] *adj* non systématique

untainted [ʌn'teɪntɪd] *adj (food)* qui n'a pas été contaminé(e); *(reputation)* qui n'a pas été entaché(e)

untalented [ʌn'tæləntɪd] *adj* peu doué(e)

untamed [ʌn'teɪmd] *adj (animal)* sauvage

untangle [ʌn'tæŋgəl] *vt* démêler; *Fig (plot)* dénouer

untapped [ʌn'tæpt] *adj* inexploité(e)

untenable [ʌn'tenəbəl] *adj (position)* intenable; *(theory)* indéfendable

untested [ʌn'testɪd] *adj (drug, product)* non testé(e); *(method, system)* qui n'a pas été mis(e) à l'épreuve

unthinkable [ʌn'θɪŋkəbəl] *adj* impensable, inconcevable

untidiness [ʌn'taɪdɪnɪs] *n* désordre *m*

untidy [ʌn'taɪdɪ] *adj (person)* désordonné(e); *(place)* en désordre

untie [ʌn'taɪ] *vt (knot, shoelaces)* défaire; *(string)* dénouer; *(person, animal)* détacher

until [ʌn'tɪl] **1** *prep* jusqu'à; **u. April** jusqu'en avril; **u. now** jusqu'à présent; **not u. tomorrow** pas avant demain; **I didn't see her u. Sunday** c'est seulement dimanche que je l'ai vue

2 *conj* jusqu'à ce que + *subjunctive*; **u. she gets back** jusqu'à ce qu'elle revienne; **don't move u. I tell you** ne bouge pas avant que je (ne) te le dise

untimely [ʌn'taɪmlɪ] *adj (death)* prématuré(e); *(remark)* inopportun(e); *(moment)* mauvais(e)

untiring [ʌn'taɪərɪŋ] *adj* infatigable, inlassable

untold [ʌn'təʊld] *adj (wealth, beauty)* immense

untouchable [ʌn'tʌtʃəbəl] **1** *n* intouchable *mf*; *Fig* paria *m*

2 *adj* intouchable

untouched [ʌn'tʌtʃt] *adj* qui n'a pas été touché(e); **to leave sth u.** ne pas toucher à qch

untoward [ʌntə'wɔːd] *adj Formal* fâcheux(euse), malencontreux(euse)

untrained [ʌn'treɪnd] *adj (animal)* non dressé(e); *(person)* sans formation

untranslatable [ʌntræns'leɪtəbəl] *adj* intraduisible

untried [ʌn'traɪd] *adj* (**a**) *(person, system)* qui n'a pas encore fait ses preuves (**b**) *Law (person, case)* non jugé(e)

untroubled [ʌn'trʌbəld] *adj* tranquille, calme; **to be u. by sth** ne pas être perturbé(e) par qch

untrue [ʌn'truː] *adj* (**a**) *(false)* faux (fausse) (**b**) *(unfaithful)* infidèle (**to** à)

untrustworthy [ʌn'trʌstwɜːðɪ] *adj (person)* qui n'est pas digne de confiance; *(information)* qui n'est pas fiable

untruth [ʌn'truːθ] *n* mensonge *m*

untruthful [ʌn'truːθfʊl] *adj (person)* menteur(euse); *(story, reply)* mensonger(ère)

unusable [ʌn'juːzəbəl] *adj* inutilisable

unused *adj* (**a**) [ʌn'juːzd] *(not in use)* inutilisé(e) (**b**) [ʌn'juːzd] *(never yet used)* neuf (neuve) (**c**) [ʌn'juːst] *(unaccustomed)* **to be u. to sth/to doing sth** ne pas avoir l'habitude de qch/de faire qch

unusual [ʌn'juːʒʊəl] *adj (not common)* inhabituel(-elle); *(strange)* bizarre, étrange; **it's u. of her not to notice** c'est rare qu'elle ne s'en rende pas compte

unusually [ʌn'juːʒʊəlɪ] *adv* exceptionnellement

unvaried [ʌn'veərɪd] *adj* monotone

unvarnished [ʌn'vɑːnɪʃt] *adj* non verni(e); *Fig* **the u. truth** la vérité pure et simple

unveil [ʌn'veɪl] *vt also Fig* dévoiler

unverifiable [ʌn'verɪfaɪəbəl] *adj* invérifiable

unvoiced [ʌn'vɔɪst] *adj* (**a**) *Ling* non voisé(e) (**b**) *(unspoken)* inexprimé(e)

unwaged [ʌn'weɪdʒd] **1** *npl* **the u.** ceux qui n'ont pas d'activité rémunérée

2 *adj* qui n'a pas d'activité rémunérée

unwanted [ʌn'wɒntɪd] *adj* non désiré(e); **to feel u.** se sentir de trop

unwarranted [ʌn'wɒrəntɪd] *adj* injustifié(e)

unwary [ʌn'weərɪ] *adj* sans méfiance

unwavering [ʌn'weɪvərɪŋ] *adj (devotion)* inébranlable; *(loyalty, support)* à toute épreuve; *(gaze)* fixe

unwelcome [ʌn'welkəm] *adj (visit, visitor)* importun(e); *(news)* fâcheux(euse); **to make sb feel u.** faire sentir à qn qu'il n'est pas le bienvenu

unwell [ʌn'wel] *adj* souffrant(e)

unwholesome [ʌn'həʊlsəm] *adj* malsain(e)

unwieldy [ʌn'wiːldɪ] *adj (object)* difficile à manier; *Fig (system, method)* lourd(e)

unwilling [ʌn'wɪlɪŋ] *adj* réticent(e); **to be u. to do sth** être réticent à faire qch

unwillingness [ʌn'wɪlɪŋnɪs] *n* réticence *f*

unwind [ʌn'waɪnd] *(pt & pp* **unwound** [ʌn'waʊnd] *)* **1** *vt (string, wool)* dérouler

2 *vi* **(a)** *(of string, wool)* se dérouler **(b)** *Fam (relax)* se détendre, se relaxer

unwise [ʌn'waɪz] *adj (person)* imprudent(e); *(decision, action)* peu judicieux(euse)

unwitting [ʌn'wɪtɪŋ] *adj* involontaire

unworkable [ʌn'wɜːkəbəl] *adj* impraticable

unworthy [ʌn'wɜːðɪ] *adj* indigne (**of** de)

unwrap [ʌn'ræp] *(pt & pp* **unwrapped**) *vt* déballer

unwritten [ʌn'rɪtən] *adj (language)* non écrit(e); *(agreement)* verbal(e); **it's an u. rule that...** il est entendu que...

unyielding [ʌn'jiːldɪŋ] *adj* inflexible

unzip [ʌn'zɪp] *(pt & pp* **unzipped**) *vt* **(a)** *(garment, bag etc)* ouvrir (la fermeture Éclair® de) **(b)** *Comput (file)* décompresser, dézipper

up [ʌp] **1** *adv* **(a)** *(with motion)* **to come/go up** monter; **to go up to sb** s'approcher de qn; **to go up north** aller au nord; **to put one's hand up** lever la main; **to put a poster up** accrocher un poster; **petrol has gone up in price** l'essence a augmenté

(b) *(with position)* en haut; **up here** ici; **up there** là-haut; **up above** au-dessus; **further up** plus haut; **petrol is up in price** l'essence a augmenté

(c) *(ahead)* **to be one goal/five points up** avoir un but/cinq points d'avance

(d) *(in phrases with* **to**) **up to now/the age of seven** jusqu'à maintenant/l'âge de sept ans; **what are the children up to?** que fabriquent les enfants?; **she's up to something** elle manigance quelque chose; **what have you been up to?** qu'est-ce que tu deviens?; **it's up to you to do it** c'est à vous de le faire; **it's up to you** *(you decide)* c'est à vous de décider; **he's not up to the job** il n'est pas à la hauteur de la tâche; **I don't feel up to it** je ne m'en sens pas capable; **it's not up to much** *(not very good)* ce n'est pas extraordinaire

2 *prep* **(a)** *(with motion)* **to go up the stairs/the street** monter les escaliers/la rue; **to run up the stairs/the street** monter les escaliers/la rue en courant; **to climb up a hill** monter à une colline; *Vulg* **up yours!** va te faire foutre!

(b) *(with position)* **to be up a tree/ladder** être dans un arbre/sur une échelle; **to live up the street (from sb)** habiter plus haut dans la rue (que qn); *Fig* **to be up against sth** avoir affaire à qch

3 *adj* **(a)** *(out of bed)* levé(e); **I was up at seven** j'étais levé à sept heures; **she was up late last night** elle a veillé tard hier soir; **we were up all night** nous sommes restés debout toute la nuit; **to be up and about** être debout; *(after illness)* être sur pied

(b) *(finished)* **the two weeks were up** les deux semaines étaient terminées; **(your) time's up** c'est terminé

(c) *Fam (wrong)* **something's up** quelque chose ne va pas; **what's up?** qu'est-ce qu'il y a?; **what's up with her?** qu'est-ce qu'elle a?

(d) *(idiom)* **to be up and running** *(of machine, system)* être opérationnel(elle)

4 *n* **ups and downs** des hauts et des bas

5 *vt Fam (price, offer)* augmenter

6 *vi Fam* **to up and go** *or* **leave** filer

up-and-coming ['ʌpənd'kʌmɪŋ] *adj* qui monte

upbeat [ʌp'biːt] *adj* optimiste

upbraid [ʌp'breɪd] *vt Formal* réprimander; **to u. sb for sth** reprocher qch à qn; **to u. sb for doing sth** reprocher à qn d'avoir fait qch

upbringing ['ʌpbrɪŋɪŋ] *n* éducation *f*

update 1 *n* ['ʌpdeɪt] mise *f* à jour, actualisation *f*

2 *vt* [ʌp'deɪt] mettre à jour, actualiser; **to u. sb on sth** mettre qn au courant de qch

upend [ʌp'end] *vt* renverser

upfront [ʌp'frʌnt] **1** *adj Fam (frank)* franc (franche), direct(e)

2 *adv (in advance)* d'avance

upgradable [ʌp'greɪdəbəl] *adj Comput (hardware, system)* évolutif(ive); *(memory)* extensible

upgrade 1 *n* ['ʌpgreɪd] *Comput (of hardware)* augmentation *f* de puissance; *(of software)* nouvelle version *f*

2 *vt* [ʌp'greɪd] **(a)** *(improve)* améliorer; *(promote)* promouvoir **(b)** *Comput (hardware)* augmenter la puissance de; *(software)* acquérir la dernière version de

upheaval [ʌp'hiːvəl] *n* bouleversement *m*

uphill ['ʌphɪl] **1** *adj* qui monte; *Fig (struggle)* ardu(e), pénible

2 *adv* **to go u.** monter

uphold [ʌp'həʊld] *(pt & pp* **upheld** [ʌp'held] *)* *vt (opinion, principle)* soutenir; *(decision)* maintenir; **to u. the law** faire respecter la loi

upholstered [ʌp'həʊlstəd] *adj* tapissé(e)

upholstery [ʌp'həʊlstərɪ] *n* tapisserie *f*; *(in car)* sièges *mpl*

upkeep ['ʌpkiːp] *n* entretien *m*

uplift 1 *n* ['ʌplɪft] élévation *f* morale *ou* spirituelle

2 *vt* [ʌp'lɪft] élever

uplifting [ʌp'lɪftɪŋ] *adj* édifiant(e)

upmarket ['ʌpmɑːkɪt] *adj (product)* haut de gamme *inv*; *(area, place)* chic *inv*

upon [ə'pɒn] *prep* sur; **u. my word!** ma parole!

upper ['ʌpə(r)] **1** *adj* supérieur(e); **the u. class** l'aristocratie *f*; **to get/have the u. hand** prendre/avoir le dessus; *Br Pol* **the U. House** la Chambre des Lords

2 *n (of shoe)* empeigne *f*; *Fam* **to be on one's uppers** manger de la vache enragée

upper-class ['ʌpəklɑːs] *adj* aristocratique

upper-crust ['ʌpəkrʌst] *adj Fam* aristo

uppermost ['ʌpəməʊst] *adj* le (la) plus haut(e); *Fig* **it was u. in my mind** c'était la première de mes préoccupations

uppity ['ʌpɪtɪ] *adj Fam* crâneur(euse); **to get u.** crâner

upright ['ʌpraɪt] **1** *adj* **(a)** *(vertical)* droit(e); **u. piano** piano *m* droit; **u. vacuum cleaner** aspirateur *m* balai **(b)** *(honest)* droit(e)

2 *adv* droit; **to set** *or* **stand sth u.** mettre qch debout *ou* d'aplomb

3 *n (beam)* montant *m*

uprising ['ʌpraɪzɪŋ] *n* soulèvement *m*, révolte *f*

uproar ['ʌprɔ:(r)] *n (noise, protest)* tumulte *m*; **the house was in an u.** ce fut le tumulte dans la maison

uproarious [ʌp'rɔ:rɪəs] *adj (noisy)* tonitruant(e); *(funny)* hilarant(e)

uproot [ʌp'ru:t] *vt* déraciner

upset 1 *vt* [ʌp'set] *(pt & pp upset)* (**a**) *(liquid, container)* renverser (**b**) *(person, plans, schedule)* bouleverser

   2 *n* ['ʌpset] *(disturbance)* bouleversement *m*; *(surprise)* défaite *f*; **to have a stomach u.** avoir l'estomac dérangé

   3 *adj* [ʌp'set] *(unhappy)* bouleversé(e) (**about** par); **to have an u. stomach** avoir l'estomac dérangé

upsetting [ʌp'setɪŋ] *adj* bouleversant(e)

upshot ['ʌpʃɒt] *n* conséquence *f*, résultat *m*

upside down ['ʌpsaɪd'daʊn] **1** *adj* à l'envers

   2 *adv* à l'envers; **to turn sth u.** retourner qch; *Fig* mettre qch sens dessus dessous

upstage [ʌp'steɪdʒ] **1** *adv Theat (move)* vers le fond de la scène; **u. of sb/sth** à l'arrière-plan par rapport à qn/qch

   2 *vt Theat & Fig* éclipser, voler la vedette à

upstairs 1 *n* [ʌp'steəz] étage *m*

   2 *adj* ['ʌpsteəz] de l'étage du dessus; **u. neighbours** les voisins du dessus; **the u. bathroom** la salle de bains du haut

   3 *adv* [ʌp'steəz] en haut; **to come/go u.** monter; **he lives u.** il habite à l'étage au-dessus

upstanding [ʌp'stændɪŋ] *adj* droit(e)

upstart ['ʌpstɑ:t] *n* parvenu(e) *m,f*

upstream [ʌp'stri:m] *adv* en amont; *(with movement)* vers l'amont

upsurge ['ʌpsɜ:dʒ] *n (of anger, enthusiasm)* vague *f*; *(of interest)* recrudescence *f*

upswing ['ʌpswɪŋ] *n* amélioration *f* (**in** de); *(in economy)* redressement *m* (**in** de)

uptake ['ʌpteɪk] *n Fam* **to be quick on the u.** piger vite; **to be slow on the u.** être lent(e) à la détente

uptight [ʌp'taɪt] *adj Fam (nervous)* tendu(e), crispé(e); *(inhibited)* coincé(e)

up-to-date [ʌptə'deɪt] *adj* (**a**) *(most recent)* à jour; *(news)* récent(e); **to bring sb u. (on sth)** mettre qn au courant (de qch) (**b**) *(modern)* à la mode

up-to-the-minute [ʌptəðə'mɪnɪt] *adj (news, information)* de dernière minute; *(style, fashion)* dernier cri *inv*

upturn ['ʌptɜ:n] *n* amélioration *f* (**in** de); *(in economy)* redressement *m* (**in** de)

upturned ['ʌptɜ:nd] *adj (bucket, box)* retourné(e); *(nose)* retroussé(e)

upward ['ʌpwəd] **1** *adj* vers le haut; **u. mobility** ascension *f* sociale; **an u. trend** une tendance à la hausse

   2 *adv* = **upwards**

upwardly mobile ['ʌpwədlɪ'məʊbaɪl] *adj* qui connaît une ascension sociale rapide

upwards ['ʌpwədz] *adv* vers le haut; **from £100 u.** à partir de 100 livres; **u. of** plus de

Urals ['jʊərəlz] *npl* **the U.** l'Oural *m*

uranium [jʊ'reɪnɪəm] *n* uranium *m*

Uranus [jʊ'reɪnəs] *n (planet)* Uranus *f*

urban ['ɜ:bən] *adj* urbain(e); **u. legend** *or* **myth** = anecdote souvent inventée mais qui passe pour vraie; **u. renewal** rénovations *fpl* urbaines; **u. sprawl** étalement *m* urbain

urbane [ɜ:'beɪn] *adj* urbain(e), courtois(e)

urbanization [ɜ:bənaɪ'zeɪʃən] *n (process)* urbanisation *f*

urchin ['ɜ:tʃɪn] *n* galopin(e) *m,f*

Urdu ['ʊədu:] *n* ourdou *m*

urethra [jʊ'ri:θrə] *n* urètre *m*

urge [ɜ:dʒ] **1** *n* terrible envie *f*; **to have an u. to do sth** avoir très envie de faire qch

   2 *vt* (**a**) *(encourage)* **to u. sb to do sth** presser qn de faire qch (**b**) *(recommend)* conseiller; **to u. that sth be done** insister pour que qch soit fait

▶**urge on** *vt sep* encourager; **to u. sb on to do sth** encourager qn à faire qch

urgency ['ɜ:dʒənsɪ] *n* urgence *f*; **it's a matter of u.** il y a urgence

urgent ['ɜ:dʒənt] *adj* urgent(e); **to be in u. need of sth** avoir un besoin urgent de qch

urgently ['ɜ:dʒəntlɪ] *adv* d'urgence

urinal [jə'raɪnəl] *n* urinoir *m*

urinary ['jʊərɪnərɪ] *adj* urinaire

urinate ['jʊərɪneɪt] *vi* uriner

urine ['jʊərɪn] *n* urine *f*

URL [ju:ɑ:'rel] *n Comput (abbr* **uniform resource locator**) *(adresse f)* URL *m*

urn [ɜ:n] *n* urne *f*; **(tea) u.** fontaine *f* (à thé)

urology [jʊ'rɒlədʒɪ] *n Med* urologie *f*

Uruguay ['jʊərəgwaɪ] *n* l'Uruguay *m*

Uruguayan [jʊərə'gwaɪən] **1** *n* Uruguayen(enne) *m,f*

   2 *adj* uruguayen(enne)

us [*stressed* ʌs, *unstressed* əs] *pron* (**a**) *(direct object)* nous; **she hates us** elle nous déteste; **she can understand our son but not US** elle comprend notre fils, mais nous, elle ne nous comprend pas (**b**) *(indirect object)* nous; **she gave us the book** elle nous a donné le livre; **she gave it to us** elle nous l'a donné (**c**) *(after preposition)* nous; **she's thinking of us** elle pense à nous (**d**) *(as complement of verb* **to be**) nous; **it's us!** c'est nous!; **it was us who did it** c'est nous qui l'avons fait

US [ju:'es] **1** *n (abbr* **United States**) **the US** les USA *mpl*

   2 *adj (forces, officials)* américain(e), des États-Unis

USA [ju:es'eɪ] *n* (**a**) *(abbr* **United States of America**) **the U.** les USA *mpl* (**b**) *Am (abbr* **United States Army**) armée *f* de terre des États-Unis

usable ['ju:zəbəl] *adj* utilisable

USAF [ju:es'ef] *n Am (abbr* **United States Air Force**) armée *f* de l'air des États-Unis

usage ['ju:sɪdʒ] *n* usage *m*

use 1 *n* [ju:s] (**a**) *(utilization)* utilisation *f*, emploi *m*; **to make (good) u. of sth** faire (bon) usage de qch; **to be in u.** être utilisé(e); **not in u., out of u.** hors d'usage

   (**b**) *(ability, permission to use)* usage *m*; **to have the u. of sth** pouvoir utiliser qch; **she has full u. of her faculties** elle jouit de toutes ses facultés

   (**c**) *(usefulness)* **to be of u.** être utile; **can I be of any u. to you?** puis-je vous être d'une quelconque utilité?; **it's not much u.** cela ne sert pas à grand-chose; **to have no u. for sth** ne pas avoir l'usage de qch; *Fam* **he's no u.** il n'est bon à rien; **it's no u.** cela ne sert à rien; **it's no u. crying** cela ne sert à rien de pleurer; **what's the u. of worrying?** à quoi bon s'inquiéter?

   2 *vt* [ju:z] (**a**) *(utilize)* utiliser, se servir de; *(force, diplomacy)* avoir recours à; *Fam* **u. your head!** réfléchis un peu!; *Fam* **I could u. some sleep** un peu de sommeil ne me ferait pas de mal (**b**) *(exploit)* utiliser, se servir de (**c**) *(consume) (petrol, electricity)* consommer; **who's**

used all the milk? qui a pris tout le lait?

3 *v aux* **used to** ['ju:stə] *(translated by imperfect of main verb)* **we used to live abroad** (autrefois,) nous vivions à l'étranger; **I didn't u. to like him** avant, je ne l'aimais pas; **do you travel much? – I used to** tu voyages beaucoup? – autrefois, oui

►**use up** *vt sep (food, fuel)* finir; *(ideas)* épuiser; *(money)* dépenser

use-by date ['ju:zbaɪdeɪt] *n* date *f* limite de consommation

used *adj* (**a**) [ju:zd] *(second-hand)* d'occasion (**b**) [ju:st] *(accustomed)* **to be u. to sth/to doing sth** être habitué(e) à qch/à faire qch; **to get u. to sb/sth** s'habituer à qn/qch

useful ['ju:sfʊl] *adj* utile; **to make oneself u.** se rendre utile

usefully ['ju:sfəlɪ] *adv* utilement

usefulness ['ju:sfʊlnɪs] *n* utilité *f*

useless ['ju:slɪs] *adj* (**a**) *(not useful)* inutile; **to be worse than u.** ne servir strictement à rien (**b**) *(incompetent)* nul (nulle) (**at** en)

user ['ju:zə(r)] *n (of road, dictionary)* utilisateur(trice) *m,f*; *(of telephone)* usager *m*; *(of drugs)* consommateur(trice) *m,f*; *Comput* **u. name** nom *m* de l'utilisateur

user-friendly [ju:zə'frendlɪ] *adj* convivial(e)

usher ['ʌʃə(r)] **1** *n (in court)* huissier *m*; *(in theatre, cinema)* ouvreur *m*; *(at wedding)* placeur *m*

2 *vt* **to u. sb in/out** faire entrer/sortir qn

usherette [ʌʃə'ret] *n* ouvreuse *f*

USIA [ju:esaɪ'eɪ] *n Am (abbr* **United States Information Agency)** renseignements *mpl* généraux américains

USN [ju:es'en] *n Am (abbr* **United States Navy)** marine *f* de guerre des États-Unis

USP [ju:es'pi:] *n Com (abbr* **unique selling point** *or* **proposition)** avantage *m* unique

USS [ju:es'es] *n Am (abbr* **United States Ship)** **U. Lexington** le Lexington *(bâtiment de la marine américaine)*

USSR [ju:eses'ɑ:(r)] *n Formerly (abbr* **Union of Soviet Socialist Republics)** URSS *f*

usual ['ju:ʒʊəl] **1** *adj* habituel(elle); **you're not your u. cheery self today** tu n'es pas aussi gai que d'habitude aujourd'hui; **earlier/later than u.** plus tôt/tard que

d'habitude; **as u.** comme d'habitude

2 *n Fam (drink)* **the u., sir?** comme d'habitude, monsieur?

usually ['ju:ʒʊəlɪ] *adv* habituellement, d'habitude; **he was more than u. polite** il était plus poli que d'habitude

usurer ['ju:ʒərə(r)] *n* usurier(ère) *m,f*

usurp [ju:'zɜ:p] *vt* usurper

usurper [jʊ'zɜ:pə(r)] *n* usurpateur(trice) *m,f*

usury ['ju:ʒʊrɪ] *n* usure *f*

utensil [ju:'tensəl] *n* ustensile *m*

uterus ['ju:tərəs] *(pl* **uteri** ['ju:təraɪ] *) n* utérus *m*

utilitarian [ju:tɪlɪ'teərɪən] **1** *adj (approach, design)* utilitaire; *(in philosophy)* utilitariste

2 *n (in philosophy)* utilitariste *mf*

utility [ju:'tɪlɪtɪ] *n* (**a**) *(usefulness)* utilité *f*; *Comput* **u. program** (programme *m*) utilitaire *m*; **u. room** pièce *f* de rangement (**b**) **(public) utilities** services *mpl* (publics) (**c**) *Am* **utilities** *(service charges)* charges *fpl*

utilize ['ju:tɪlaɪz] *vt* utiliser, se servir de

utmost ['ʌtməʊst] **1** *n* **to the u.** au plus haut point; **to do one's u. (to do sth)** faire de son mieux (pour faire qch)

2 *adj* (**a**) *(greatest)* **the u.** le (la) plus grand(e); **it is of the u. importance that...** il est de la plus haute importance que... + *subjunctive* (**b**) *(furthest)* **to the u. ends of the earth** au bout du monde

utopia [ju:'təʊpɪə] *n* utopie *f*

utopian [ju:'təʊpɪən] **1** *n* utopiste *mf*

2 *adj* utopique

utter¹ ['ʌtə(r)] *adj* total(e); **it's u. madness** c'est de la folie pure; **it's u. rubbish** c'est complètement absurde

utter² *vt (cry)* pousser; *(word)* prononcer

utterance ['ʌtərəns] *n (act)* énonciation *f*; *(words spoken)* paroles *fpl*, déclaration *f*

utterly ['ʌtəlɪ] *adv* complètement, tout à fait

uttermost ['ʌtəməʊst] *adj* = **utmost**

UV [ju:'vi:] *adj Phys (abbr* **ultra-violet)** UV *inv*; **UV rays** UV *mpl*

uvula ['ju:vjələ] *n* luette *f*

Uzbekistan [ʊzbekɪ'stɑ:n] *n* l'Ouzbékistan *m*

V

V¹, v [viː] *n* (**a**) *(letter)* V, v *m inv*; **V. sign** *(for victory)* signe *m* de la victoire; *(as insult)* cornes *fpl* (**b**) *(abbr* **very**) t (**c**) *(abbr* **versus**) contre (**d**) *(abbr* **verse**) *(pl* vv) V

V² *(abbr* **volt**) V

VA [viː'eɪ] *n Am (abbr* **Veterans Administration**) ≃ ministère *m* des Anciens Combattants

vacancy ['veɪkənsɪ] *n* (**a**) *(position, job)* poste *m* vacant (**b**) *(at hotel)* chambre *f* libre *ou* à louer; **no vacancies** *(sign)* complet

vacant ['veɪkənt] *adj* (**a**) *(seat, space)* libre, inoccupé(e); *Am* **v. lot** terrain *m* vague (**b**) *(expression, look)* absent(e)

vacantly ['veɪkəntlɪ] *adv* d'un air absent

vacate [və'keɪt] *vt (seat, flat)* libérer, quitter; *(one's post)* démissionner de

vacation [və'keɪʃən] *n Br Univ & Am* vacances *fpl*; *Am* **to take a v.** prendre des vacances; *Am* **on v.** en vacances

vaccinate ['væksɪneɪt] *vt* vacciner

vaccination [væksɪ'neɪʃən] *n* vaccination *f*

vaccine ['væksiːn] *n* vaccin *m*

vacillate ['væsɪleɪt] *vi* hésiter (**between** entre)

vacuous ['vækjʊəs] *adj (person, look)* vide, sans expression; *(book, remark)* dénué(e) de sens

vacuum ['vækjʊm] **1** *n Phys* vacuum *m*; *Fig* vide *m*; **v. cleaner** aspirateur *m*; **v. flask** thermos® *f*

  2 *vt (room)* passer l'aspirateur dans

  3 *vi* passer l'aspirateur

vacuum-packed [vækjʊm'pækt] *adj* (emballé(e)) sous vide

vagabond ['vægəbɒnd] *n* vagabond(e) *m,f*

vagary ['veɪgərɪ] *n* caprice *m*

vagina [və'dʒaɪnə] *n* vagin *m*

vagrancy ['veɪgrənsɪ] *n* vagabondage *m*

vagrant ['veɪgrənt] *n* vagabond(e) *m,f*

vague [veɪg] *adj (idea, feeling)* vague; *(shape, outline)* flou(e), indistinct(e); **I haven't the vaguest idea** je n'en ai pas la moindre idée

vaguely ['veɪglɪ] *adv* vaguement

vagueness ['veɪgnɪs] *n* imprécision *f*, flou *m*

vain [veɪn] **1** *adj* (**a**) *(conceited)* vaniteux(euse) (**b**) *(hopeless)* vain(e)

  2 *n* **in v.** en vain

vale [veɪl] *n Lit* val *m*, vallée *f*; *Fig* **v. of tears** vallée de larmes

valency ['veɪlənsɪ] *n Chem* valence *f*

valentine ['væləntaɪn] *n* **v. (card)** carte *f* de la Saint-Valentin; **V.'s Day** la Saint-Valentin

valet ['væleɪ] *n* valet *m* de chambre

valiant ['væljənt] *adj Lit* vaillant(e)

valiantly ['væljəntlɪ] *adv* vaillamment

valid ['vælɪd] *adj* valable; **v. for six months** valable six mois; **no longer v.** périmé(e)

validate ['vælɪdeɪt] *vt (document)* valider; *(theory)* confirmer

validation [vælɪ'deɪʃən] *n (of document)* validation *f*; *(of theory)* confirmation *f*

validity [və'lɪdɪtɪ] *n* validité *f*

valise [væ'liːz] *n Am* mallette *f*

valley ['vælɪ] *n* vallée *f*

valour, *Am* **valor** ['vælə(r)] *n* bravoure *f*

valuable ['væljʊəbəl] **1** *adj (object)* de valeur; *(advice, time, contribution)* précieux(euse) (**to** à)

  2 *n* **valuables** objets *mpl* de valeur

valuation [væljʊ'eɪʃən] *n* (**a**) *(act)* estimation *f* (**b**) *(price)* évaluation *f*

value ['væljuː] **1** *n* (**a**) *(worth)* valeur *f*; **to be of v.** avoir de la valeur; **to be good/poor v. (for money)** être d'un bon/mauvais rapport qualité-prix; **to set a v. upon sth** estimer la valeur de qch; **to the v. of** pour une valeur de; **to make a v. judgment** faire un jugement de valeur (**b**) **values** *(principles)* valeurs *fpl*

  2 *vt* (**a**) *(evaluate)* estimer (**b**) *(appreciate)* apprécier

value-added tax ['væljuːædɪd'tæks] *n* taxe *f* sur la valeur ajoutée; *Can* taxe *f* sur les ventes

valued ['væljuːd] *adj* précieux(euse)

valueless ['væljʊlɪs] *adj* sans valeur

valve [vælv] *n* (**a**) *Anat* valve *f* (**b**) *Tech (in pipe, tube, air chamber)* valve *f*; *(in machine)* soupape *f*

vampire ['væmpaɪə(r)] *n* vampire *m*; **v. bat** vampire *m*

van¹ [væn] *n* (**a**) *(vehicle)* camionnette *f*, fourgonnette *f*; **v. driver** chauffeur *m* de camionnette (**b**) *Br Rail* fourgon *m*

van² = **vanguard**

Vancouver [væn'kuːvə(r)] *n* Vancouver

vandal ['vændəl] *n* vandale *mf*

vandalism ['vændəlɪzəm] *n* vandalisme *m*

vandalize ['vændəlaɪz] *vt* saccager

vane [veɪn] *n* girouette *f*

vanguard ['vængɑːd] *n* avant-garde *f*; **to be in the v. of** être à l'avant-garde de

vanilla [və'nɪlə] *n* vanille *f*; **v. essence** extrait *m* de vanille; **v. ice cream** glace *f* à la vanille

vanish ['vænɪʃ] *vi* disparaître

vanishing ['vænɪʃɪŋ] *adj* **to do a v. act** disparaître dans la nature; **v. point** point *m* de fuite

vanity ['vænɪtɪ] *n* vanité *f*; **v. case** vanity-case *m*, mallette *f* de toilette; **v. plate** plaque *f* d'immatriculation personnalisée

vanquish ['væŋkwɪʃ] *vt Lit* vaincre

vantage point ['vɑːntɪdʒ'pɔɪnt] *n* point *m* de vue; *Fig* position *f* objective

Vanuatu [vænuː'ætuː] *n* Vanuatu *m*

vapid ['væpɪd] *adj* insipide

vapor *Am* = **vapour**

vaporize ['veɪpəraɪz] **1** *vt* vaporiser
2 *vi* se vaporiser

vapour, *Am* **vapor** ['veɪpə(r)] *n* vapeur *f*; **v. trail** traînée *f* de condensation

variable ['veərɪəbəl] **1** *n* variable *f*
2 *adj* variable

variance ['veərɪəns] *n* désaccord *m*; **to be at v. with sb** être en désaccord avec qn; **to be at v. with sth** ne pas concorder avec qch

variant ['veərɪənt] **1** *n* variante *f*
2 *adj* différent(e)

variation [veərɪ'eɪʃən] *n* variation *f*

varicose vein ['værɪkəʊs'veɪn] *n* varice *f*

varied ['veəriːd] *adj* varié(e)

variegated ['veərɪgeɪtɪd] *adj* panaché(e)

variety [və'raɪətɪ] *n* (**a**) *(diversity)* variété *f*; **a v. of** toutes sortes de; *Prov* **v. is the spice of life** la diversité est le sel de la vie (**b**) *(of plant)* variété *f* (**c**) *(in theatre, on TV)* variétés *fpl*; **v. show** spectacle *m* de variétés

various ['veərɪəs] *adj (different)* divers(e); *(several)* plusieurs

variously ['veərɪəslɪ] *adv* **v. described as a hero or a rogue** parfois décrit comme un héros, d'autres fois comme un escroc

varnish ['vɑːnɪʃ] **1** *n* vernis *m*
2 *vt* vernir

▶**varnish over** *vt sep Fig* maquiller, dissimuler

vary ['veərɪ] **1** *vt* varier
2 *vi* varier (**in/with** en/selon)

varying ['veərɪŋ] *adj* qui varie, variable

vase [vɑːz, *Am* veɪz] *n* vase *m*

vasectomy [və'sektəmɪ] *n* vasectomie *f*; **to have a v.** subir une vasectomie

Vaseline® ['væsəliːn] *n* vaseline *f*

vast [vɑːst] *adj* immense

vastly ['vɑːstlɪ] *adv* à l'extrême; *(superior)* infiniment

VAT [viːerˈtiː] *n (abbr* **value added tax)** TVA *f*

vat [væt] *n (container)* cuve *f*, bac *m*

Vatican ['vætɪkən] *n* **the V.** le Vatican; **V. City** la cité du Vatican, le Vatican

vaudeville ['vɔːdəvɪl] *n* music-hall *m*

vault¹ [vɔːlt] *n* (**a**) *(roof)* voûte *f* (**b**) *(cellar)* cave *f*; *(for burial)* caveau *m*; *(of bank)* chambre *f* forte, salle *f* des coffres

vault² *vt & vi* sauter

vaulted ['vɔːltɪd] *adj (ceiling)* voûté(e)

vaulting horse ['vɔːltɪŋ'hɔːs] *n* cheval *m* d'arçons

vaunt [vɔːnt] *vt* vanter; **his much vaunted reputation as...** sa réputation tant vantée de...

VC [viːˈsiː] *n* (**a**) *(abbr* **Vice-Chairman)** vice-président *m* (**b**) *(abbr* **Victoria Cross)** = la plus haute distinction militaire britannique

vCJD [viːsiːdʒeɪˈdiː] *n Med (abbr* **new-variant Creutzfeldt-Jakob disease)** vMCJ *m*

VCR [viːsiːˈɑː(r)] *n (abbr* **video cassette recorder)** magnétoscope *m*

VD [viːˈdiː] *n (abbr* **venereal disease)** maladie *f* vénérienne

VDU [viːdiːˈjuː] *n Comput (abbr* **visual display unit)** moniteur *m*

veal [viːl] *n* veau *m*

vector ['vektə(r)] *n* vecteur *m*

veer ['vɪə(r)] *vi* virer; **to v. to the left/right** virer à gauche/droit

▶**veer round** *vi* tourner, changer de direction; *Fig* **she has veered round to our point of view** elle s'est ralliée à notre point de vue

veg [vedʒ] *npl Br Fam (abbr* **vegetables)** légumes *mpl*

vegan ['viːgən] *n* végétalien(enne) *m,f*

vegetable ['vedʒtəbəl] *n* (**a**) *(food)* légume *m*; **v. garden** potager *m* (**b**) *(brain-damaged person)* légume *m*

vegetarian [vedʒɪ'teərɪən] *n & adj* végétarien(enne) *m,f*

vegetarianism [vedʒɪ'teərɪənɪzəm] *n* végétarisme *m*

Vegetarianism

Que ce soit pour des raisons éthiques, religieuses ou diététiques, le végétarisme s'est considérablement répandu au cours des dernières années en Grande-Bretagne – sensiblement plus que dans les autres pays européens ou aux États-Unis. Aujourd'hui, la majorité des restaurants proposent un menu avec un ou plusieurs plats sans viande, et lorsque l'on invite des gens à dîner, il est d'usage de s'enquérir s'ils sont végétariens ou non.

---

vegetate ['vedʒɪteɪt] *vi* végéter

vegetation [vedʒɪ'teɪʃən] *n* végétation *f*

veggie ['vedʒɪ] *n & adj Br Fam (abbr* **vegetarian)** végétarien(enne) *m,f*

vehemence ['viːɪməns] *n* véhémence *f*

vehement ['viːɪmənt] *adj* véhément(e)

vehicle ['viːɪkəl] *n also Fig* véhicule *m*

vehicular [vɪ'hɪkjʊlə(r)] *adj* de véhicules; **v. traffic** circulation *f* automobile

veil [veɪl] **1** *n also Fig* voile *m*; *Fig* **to draw a v. over sth** jeter un voile sur qch; *Fig* **under a v. of secrecy** sous le voile du secret
2 *vt* voiler; *Fig* **veiled in secrecy** secret(ète)

veiled [veɪld] *adj also Fig* voilé(e)

vein [veɪn] *n* (**a**) *(in body, wood, marble)* veine *f*; *(in leaf)* nervure *f*; *(in rock)* filon *m* (**b**) *(idioms)* **and now, in a lighter v....** et maintenant, dans un registre plus léger...; **in (a) similar v.** de la même veine

Velcro® ['velkrəʊ] *n (bande f)* Velcro® *m*

vellum ['veləm] *n* vélin *m*; **v. (paper)** papier *m* vélin

velocity [vɪ'lɒsɪtɪ] *n* vélocité *f*

velvet ['velvɪt] *n* velours *m*; **v. jacket** veste *f* en velours *Fig* **an iron fist** *or* **hand in a v. glove** une main de fer dans un gant de velours

velveteen [velvɪ'tiːn] *n* velvantine *f*

velvety ['velvɪtɪ] *adj* velouté(e)

venal ['viːnəl] *adj* vénal(e)

vendetta [ven'detə] *n* vendetta *f*; **to carry on a v. against sb** mener une vendetta contre qn

vending machine ['vendɪŋmə'ʃiːn] *n* distributeur *m* automatique

vendor ['vendɔː(r)] *n* vendeur(euse) *m,f*

veneer [və'nɪə(r)] *n* placage *m*; *Fig* vernis *m*, apparence *f*

venerable ['venərəbəl] *adj* vénérable

venerate ['venəreɪt] *vt* vénérer

veneration [venə'reɪʃən] *n* vénération *f*

venereal [vɪ'nɪərɪəl] *adj* vénérien(enne); **v. disease** maladie *f* vénérienne

Venetian [vɪ'niːʃən] **1** *n* Vénitien(enne) *m,f*
2 *adj* vénitien(enne); **V. blind** store *m* vénitien

Venezuela [vene'zweɪlə] *n* le Vénézuela

Venezuelan [veneˈzweɪlən] **1** n Vénézuélien(enne) m,f

   2 adj vénézuélien(enne)

vengeance [ˈvendʒəns] n vengeance f; **to take v. on sb** se venger de qn; Fig **it started to rain with a v.** il s'est mis à pleuvoir de plus belle; **she's back with a v.** elle fait un retour en force

vengeful [ˈvendʒfʊl] adj vengeur(eresse)

venial [ˈviːnɪəl] adj véniel(elle)

Venice [ˈvenɪs] n Venise

venison [ˈvenɪsən] n viande f de chevreuil

venom [ˈvenəm] n also Fig venin m

venomous [ˈvenəməs] adj also Fig venimeux(euse)

vent [vent] **1** n conduit m; Fig **to give v. to sth** donner ou laisser libre cours à qch

   2 vt **to v. one's anger (on)** décharger sa colère (sur)

ventilate [ˈventɪleɪt] vt ventiler, aérer

ventilation [ventɪˈleɪʃən] n ventilation f, aération f

ventilator [ˈventɪleɪtə(r)] n **(a)** Tech ventilateur m **(b)** Med respirateur m; **to be on a v.** être branché(e) sur respirateur

ventriloquism [venˈtrɪləkwɪzəm] n ventriloquie f

ventriloquist [venˈtrɪləkwɪst] n ventriloque mf; **v.'s dummy** marionnette f de ventriloque

venture [ˈventʃə(r)] **1** n entreprise f hasardeuse; (in business) entreprise; Fin **v. capital** capital-risque m

   2 vt (fortune, life) risquer; (opinion, suggestion) hasarder; **to v. to do sth** se risquer à faire qch; Prov **nothing ventured, nothing gained** qui ne risque rien n'a rien

   3 vi s'aventurer

▸**venture on, venture upon** vt insep s'aventurer dans

venue [ˈvenjuː] n (for meeting, concert) salle f; (for football match) stade m

Venus [ˈviːnəs] n (planet) Vénus f

veracity [vəˈræsɪtɪ] n Formal véracité f

veranda(h) [vəˈrændə] n véranda f

verb [vɜːb] n verbe m

verbal [ˈvɜːbəl] adj verbal(e); **v. abuse** insultes fpl verbales

verbalize [ˈvɜːbəlaɪz] vt verbaliser

verbally [ˈvɜːbəlɪ] adv verbalement

verbatim [vɜːˈbeɪtɪm] **1** adj textuel(elle)

   2 adv mot pour mot

verbiage [ˈvɜːbɪɪdʒ] n verbiage m

verbose [vɜːˈbəʊs] adj verbeux(euse)

verbosity [vɜːˈbɒsɪtɪ] n verbosité f

verdict [ˈvɜːdɪkt] n also Fig verdict m; **to return a v. of guilty/not guilty** rendre un verdict de culpabilité/non-culpabilité; **to give one's v. on sth** se prononcer sur qch

verge [vɜːdʒ] n (of road) bord m; Fig **on the v. of sth** au bord de qch; (victory, defeat) à deux doigts de qch; Fig **to be on the v. of doing sth** être sur le point de faire qch

▸**verge on** vt insep friser

verger [ˈvɜːdʒə(r)] n (in Church of England) bedeau m

verifiable [verɪˈfaɪəbəl] adj vérifiable

verification [verɪfɪˈkeɪʃən] n vérification f

verify [ˈverɪfaɪ] (pt & pp **verified**) vt vérifier

verisimilitude [verɪsɪˈmɪlɪtjuːd] n Formal vraisemblance f

veritable [ˈverɪtəbəl] adj Formal véritable

vermilion [vəˈmɪljən] **1** n vermillon m

   2 adj vermillon inv

vermin [ˈvɜːmɪn] npl also Fig vermine f

vermouth [ˈvɜːməθ] n vermouth m

vernacular [vəˈnækjʊlə(r)] **1** n langue f vernaculaire

   2 adj vernaculaire

verruca [veˈruːkə] n verrue f plantaire

versatile [ˈvɜːsətaɪl] adj (person) aux talents variés; (tool) polyvalent(e)

versatility [vɜːsəˈtɪlɪtɪ] n (of person) variété f de talents; (of tool) polyvalence f

verse [vɜːs] n **(a)** (poetry) vers mpl **(b)** (stanza) strophe f **(c)** (of Bible) verset m

versed [vɜːst] adj **to be (well) v. in sth** être versé(e) dans qch

version [ˈvɜːʃən] n version f

versus [ˈvɜːsəs] prep **(a)** (in law, sport) contre **(b)** (compared to) comparé(e) à

vertebra [ˈvɜːtɪbrə] (pl **vertebrae** [ˈvɜːtɪbriː]) n vertèbre f

vertebral column [ˈvɜːtɪbrəlˈkɒləm] n colonne f vertébrale

vertebrate [ˈvɜːtɪbrɪt] **1** n vertébré m

   2 adj vertébré(e)

vertex [ˈvɜːteks] (pl **vertices** [ˈvɜːtɪsiːz]) n sommet m

vertical [ˈvɜːtɪkəl] **1** n verticale f

   2 adj vertical(e)

vertically [ˈvɜːtɪklɪ] adv à la verticale

vertigo [ˈvɜːtɪgəʊ] n vertige m

verve [vɜːv] n verve f

very [ˈverɪ] **1** adv **(a)** (extremely) très; **v. little** très peu; **v. much** beaucoup; **are you hungry? – yes, v.** as-tu faim? – oui, très; Rad **v. high frequency** hyperfréquences fpl **(b)** (emphatic use) **the v. first/last** le (la) tout(e) premier(ère)/dernier(ère); **the v. best** tout ce qu'il y a de mieux; **at the v. most/least** tout au plus/moins; **at the v. earliest/latest** au plus tôt/tard; **the v. same** exactement le même; **I v. nearly died** j'ai bien failli mourir; **the v. next day** le lendemain même

   2 adj (emphatic use) **this v. house** cette maison même; **this v. day** aujourd'hui même; **those were her v. words** c'est ce qu'elle a dit mot pour mot; **at the v. beginning** au tout début; **the v. thought of it!** rien que d'y penser!

vessel [ˈvesəl] n **(a)** (ship) vaisseau m **(b)** (container) récipient m

vest [vest] n Br (undershirt) maillot m de corps; Am (waistcoat) gilet m

vested [ˈvestɪd] adj **to have a v. interest in sth/in doing sth** avoir un intérêt personnel dans qch/à faire qch

vestibule [ˈvestɪbjuːl] n hall m

vestige [ˈvestɪdʒ] n vestige m

vestments [ˈvestmənts] npl Rel habits mpl sacerdotaux

vestry [ˈvestrɪ] n Rel sacristie f

vet¹ [vet] n (veterinary surgeon) vétérinaire mf

vet² (pt & pp **vetted**) vt (person) effectuer une enquête sur; (application) examiner minutieusement; (figures) vérifier soigneusement

vet³ n Am Fam Mil (veteran) ancien combattant m

veteran [ˈvetərən] **1** n Mil ancien combattant m; Fig vétéran m

   2 adj de longue date

veterinarian [vetərɪˈneərɪən] n Am vétérinaire mf

veterinary ['vetərɪnərɪ] *adj* vétérinaire; **v. medicine** médecine *f* vétérinaire; *Formal* **v. surgeon** vétérinaire *mf*

veto ['viːtəʊ] **1** *n* (*pl* **vetoes**) veto *m*; **right** *or* **power of v.** droit *m* de veto; **to impose a v. on sth** mettre son veto à qch
2 *vt* mettre son veto à

vetting ['vetɪŋ] *n* (*of person*) enquête *f* (**of** sur); (*of things*) contrôle *m* (**of** de)

vex [veks] *vt* contrarier

vexation [vek'seɪʃən] *n* (*annoyance*) contrariété *f*

vexed [vekst] *adj* (**a**) (*annoyed*) très contrarié(e) (**b**) **v. question** question *f* controversée

VHF [viːeɪtʃ'ef] *n* (*abbr* **very high frequency**) VHF *f*

VHS [viːeɪtʃ'es] *n* (*abbr* **video home system**)VHS *m*

via ['vaɪə] *prep* par, via

viability [vaɪə'bɪlɪtɪ] *n* viabilité *f*

viable ['vaɪəbəl] *adj* viable

viaduct ['vaɪədʌkt] *n* viaduc *m*

Viagra® [vaɪ'ægrə] *n*Viagra® *m*

vibes [vaɪbz] *npl Fam* ambiance *f*; **I got good/bad v. from her** je la sentais/je ne la sentais pas bien

vibrant ['vaɪbrənt] *adj* très actif(ive)

vibrate [vaɪ'breɪt] *vi* vibrer

vibration [vaɪ'breɪʃən] *n* vibration *f*

vibrator [vaɪ'breɪtə(r)] *n* vibromasseur *m*

vicar ['vɪkə(r)] *n* (*in Church of England*) pasteur *m*

vicarage ['vɪkərɪdʒ] *n* presbytère *m*

vicarious [vɪ'keərɪəs] *adj* indirect(e), **to lead a v. existence** vivre par procuration

vice¹ [vaɪs] *n* (*immorality, immoral activity*) vice *m*; **the V. Squad** ≃ la brigade des mœurs

vice² *n* (*tool*) étau *m*

vice-chairman [vaɪs'tʃeəmən] *n* vice-président(e) *m,f*

vice-president [vaɪs'prezɪdənt] *n* vice-président(e) *m,f*

viceroy ['vaɪsrɔɪ] *n* vice-roi *m*

vice versa [vaɪs'vɜːsə] *adv* vice versa

vicinity [vɪ'sɪnɪtɪ] *n* (*surrounding area*) environs *mpl*; (*proximity*) proximité *f*; **in the v. (of)** dans les alentours (de); **a sum in the v. of £25,000** un chiffre aux alentours de 25 000 livres

vicious ['vɪʃəs] *adj* (*violent*) violent(e); (*malicious, cruel*) malveillant(e); **v. circle** cercle *m* vicieux

vicissitudes [vɪ'sɪsɪtjuːdz] *npl Formal* vicissitudes *fpl*

victim ['vɪktɪm] *n* victime *f*; **to be the v. of sth** être victime de qch

victimization [vɪktɪmaɪ'zeɪʃən] *n* brimades *fpl*

victimize ['vɪktɪmaɪz] *vt* (*bully*) prendre comme tête deTurc; (*penalize*) pénaliser

victor ['vɪktə(r)] *n* vainqueur *m*

Victorian [vɪk'tɔːrɪən] **1** *n*Victorien(enne) *m,f*
2 *adj* victorien(enne)

victorious [vɪk'tɔːrɪəs] *adj* victorieux(euse); **to be v. over sb** vaincre qn

victory ['vɪktərɪ] *n* victoire *f*; **v. celebrations** = fêtes pour célébrer une victoire

victuals ['vɪtəlz] *npl Old-fashioned* (*food*) victuailles *fpl*

video ['vɪdɪəʊ] **1** *n* (*pl* **videos**) (*medium*) vidéo *f*; (*cassette*) (cassette *f*) vidéo; (*recorder*) magnétoscope *m*; **v. camera** caméra *f* vidéo; **v. cassette** *or* **tape** cassette *f* vidéo; **v. (cassette) recorder** magnétoscope; **v. game** jeu *m* vidéo; **v. installation** installation *f* vidéo; **v. library** vidéothèque *f*; **v. nasty** = film vidéo à contenu très violent ou pornographique; **v. shop** magasin *m* vidéo
2 *vt* (**a**) (*on video recorder*) enregistrer (**b**) (*on camcorder*) filmer en vidéo

vie [vaɪ] (*pt & pp* **vied** [vaɪd]) *vi* **to v. with sb (for sth/ to do sth)** rivaliser avec qn (pour qch/pour faire qch)

Vienna [vɪ'enə] *n*Vienne

Viennese [vɪə'niːz] **1** *n*Viennois(e) *m,f*
2 *adj* viennois(e)

Vietnam [vɪet'næm] *n* le Viêt Nam; **the V. War** la guerre duViêt Nam

Vietnamese [vɪetnə'miːz] **1** *npl* (*people*) **the V.** les Vietnamiens *mpl*
2 *n* (**a**) (*person*) Vietnamien(enne) *m,f* (**b**) (*language*) vietnamien *m*
3 *adj* vietnamien(enne)

view [vjuː] **1** *n* (**a**) (*sight, scene, prospect*) vue *f*; **a room with a v.** une chambre avec vue; **to have a good v. of sth** avoir une belle vue de qch; **in full v. of** sous les yeux de; *Fig* **in v. of** (*considering*) compte tenu de, étant donné (**b**) (*opinion*) opinion *f*; **in my v.** à mon avis (**c**) (*intention*) intention *f*; **with this in v.** dans cette intention; **with a v. to doing sth** dans l'intention de faire qch
2 *vt* (**a**) (*look at*) voir; (*prospective property, exhibition*) visiter (**b**) (*consider*) voir, considérer; **to v. sth with horror/delight** envisager qch avec horreur/ravissement

viewer ['vjuːə(r)] *n* (**a**) (*of TV*) téléspectateur(trice) *m,f* (**b**) (*for slides*) visionneuse *f*

viewfinder ['vjuːfaɪndə(r)] *n* viseur *m*

viewpoint ['vjuːpɔɪnt] *n* point *m* de vue

vigil ['vɪdʒɪl] *n* veillée *f*; **to keep v.** veiller

vigilance ['vɪdʒɪləns] *n* vigilance *f*

vigilant ['vɪdʒɪlənt] *adj* vigilant(e)

vigilante [vɪdʒɪ'læntɪ] *n* = membre d'une milice privée

vignette [vɪn'jet] *n* (*photo, picture*) buste *m* sur un fond dégradé; (*short essay*) court portrait *m*

vigor *Am* = vigour

vigorous ['vɪgərəs] *adj* vigoureux(euse)

vigour, *Am* **vigor** ['vɪgə(r)] *n* vigueur *f*

Viking ['vaɪkɪŋ] **1** *n*Viking *mf*
2 *adj* viking *inv*

vile [vaɪl] *adj* (*weather, person, thought*) abominable; (*food, drink*) infecte; (*temper*) exécrable

vilification [vɪlɪfɪ'keɪʃən] *n* calomnie *f*

vilify ['vɪlɪfaɪ] (*pt & pp* **vilified**) *vt* calomnier

villa ['vɪlə] *n* villa *f*

village ['vɪlɪdʒ] *n* village *m*; **v. hall** salle *f* des fêtes; **v. idiot** idiot *m* du village

villager ['vɪlɪdʒə(r)] *n* villageois(e) *m,f*

villain ['vɪlən] *n* (*scoundrel*) scélérat *m*; *Hum* **the v. of the piece** le/la coupable

villainous ['vɪlənəs] *adj* diabolique

villainy ['vɪlənɪ] *n* infamie *f*

Vilnius ['vɪlnɪʊs] *n*Vilnius

vindicate ['vɪndɪkeɪt] *vt* (*decision, action*) donner raison à; (*right, claim*) justifier

vindication [vɪndɪ'keɪʃən] *n* (*of decision, action*) bien-fondé *m*; (*of right, claim*) justification *f*

vindictive [vɪn'dɪktɪv] *adj* vindicatif(ive)

vine [vaɪn] *n* vigne *f*; **v. leaf** feuille *f* de vigne

vinegar ['vɪnɪgə(r)] *n* vinaigre *m*

vineyard ['vɪnjəd] *n* vigne *f*

vintage ['vɪntɪdʒ] *n (year)* année *f; (wine)* cru *m; Fig* **a v. year (for)** une grande année (pour); *Fig* **it was v. Agatha Christie** c'était de l'Agatha Christie du meilleur style; **v. car** = voiture construite entre 1919 et 1930; **v. wine** vin *m* de cru

vinyl ['vaɪnɪl] *n* vinyle *m*

viola [vɪ'əʊlə] *n* alto *m*

violate ['vaɪəleɪt] *vt (agreement)* violer; *(rule, law)* enfreindre

violation [vaɪə'leɪʃən] *n* violation *f*

violence ['vaɪələns] *n* violence *f*

violent ['vaɪələnt] *adj* violent(e); **to die a v. death** mourir de mort violente; **to take a v. dislike to sb/sth** se prendre d'une aversion violente pour qn/qch

violently ['vaɪələntlɪ] *adv* violemment; *(die)* de mort violente; **to be v. sick** être pris(e) de violents vomissements

violet ['vaɪələt] **1** *n* (**a**) *(flower)* violette *f* (**b**) *(colour)* violet *m*
2 *adj* **v.(-coloured)** violet(ette)

violin [vaɪə'lɪn] *n* violon *m*

violinist [vaɪə'lɪnɪst] *n* violoniste *mf*

VIP [viːaɪ'piː] *n (abbr* **very important person)** VIP *mf;* **V. lounge** salon *m* de luxe; **to get V. treatment** recevoir un accueil princier

viper ['vaɪpə(r)] *n* vipère *f*

viral ['vaɪrəl] *adj* viral(e)

virgin ['vɜːdʒɪn] **1** *n* vierge *mf;* **the (Blessed) V.** la Sainte Vierge; **the V. Islands** les îles *fpl* Vierges
2 *adj* vierge

Virginia [vɜː'dʒɪnjə] *n* la Virginie

virginity [və'dʒɪnɪtɪ] *n* virginité *f*

Virgo ['vɜːgəʊ] *n (sign of zodiac)* la Vierge; **to be (a) V.** être Vierge

virile ['vɪraɪl] *adj* viril(e)

virility [vɪ'rɪlɪtɪ] *n* virilité *f*

virology [vaɪ'rɒlədʒɪ] *n* virologie *f*

virtual ['vɜːtjʊəl] *adj* (**a**) *(near)* quasi; **it's a v. impossibility** c'est quasiment impossible (**b**) *Comput* virtuel(elle); **v. reality** réalité *f* virtuelle

virtually ['vɜːtjʊəlɪ] *adv* quasiment, pratiquement

virtue ['vɜːtjuː] *n* (**a**) *(goodness)* vertu *f;* **by v. of** en vertu de; **to make a v. of necessity** faire de nécessité vertu (**b**) *(advantage)* avantage *m*

virtuoso [vɜːtjʊ'əʊzəʊ] *(pl* **virtuosos** *or* **virtuosi** [vɜːtjʊ'əʊziː]) *n* virtuose *mf*

virtuous ['vɜːtjʊəs] *adj* vertueux(euse)

virulent ['vɪr(j)ʊlənt] *adj* virulent(e)

virus ['vaɪrəs] *n Med & Comput* virus *m*

visa ['viːzə] *n* visa *m*

vis-à-vis ['viːzɑːviː] *prep* par rapport à, vis-à-vis de

visceral ['vɪsərəl] *adj* viscéral(e)

viscount ['vaɪkaʊnt] *n* vicomte *m*

viscous ['vɪskəs] *adj* visqueux(euse)

visibility [vɪzɪ'bɪlɪtɪ] *n* visibilité *f*

visible ['vɪzɪbəl] *adj* visible

visibly ['vɪzɪblɪ] *adv* visiblement

vision ['vɪʒən] *n* (**a**) *(eyesight)* vue *f;* **to have good/poor v.** avoir une bonne/mauvaise vue (**b**) *(foresight, imagination)* clairvoyance *f;* **a man of v.** un visionnaire (**c**) *(apparition)* vision *f;* **I had visions of being left homeless** je me suis vu devenir sans-abri

visionary ['vɪʒənərɪ] *(pl* **visionaries)** *n & adj* visionnaire *mf*

visit ['vɪzɪt] **1** *n* visite *f;* **to pay sb a v.** rendre visite à qn; **to be on a v.** être en visite
2 *vt (person)* rendre visite à; *(museum, monument)* visiter
3 *vi* **to be visiting** être de passage

visiting ['vɪzɪtɪŋ] *adj (circus)* de passage; *(lecturer)* invité(e); **v. card** carte *f* de visite; **v. hours** heures *fpl* de visite; **v. professor** professeur *m* invité; **v. rights** *(of divorced parent)* droits *mpl* de visite

visitor ['vɪzɪtə(r)] *n* visiteur(euse) *m,f;* **visitors' book** livre *m* d'or

visor ['vaɪzə(r)] *n* visière *f*

vista ['vɪstə] *n* vue *f; Fig* perspective *f*

visual ['vɪʒʊəl] *adj* visuel(elle); **v. aid** support *m* visuel; **v. arts** arts *mpl* plastiques; *Comput* **v. display unit** console *f* de visualisation

visualize ['vɪʒʊəlaɪz] *vt (imagine)* visualiser, se représenter; *(foresee)* envisager

visually ['vɪʒʊəlɪ] *adv* visuellement; **v. handicapped** malvoyant(e)

vital ['vaɪtəl] *adj* (**a**) *(essential)* vital(e); **v. organ** organe *m* vital; *Hum* **v. statistics** *(of woman)* mensurations *fpl* (**b**) *(vigorous)* vigoureux(euse)

vitality [vaɪ'tælɪtɪ] *n* vitalité *f*

vitally ['vaɪtəlɪ] *adv* **supplies are v. needed** on a un besoin vital de vivres; **v. important** d'une importance vitale *ou* capitale

vitamin ['vɪtəmɪn, *Am* 'vaɪtəmɪn] *n* vitamine *f;* **v. C/E** vitamine C/E; **with added vitamins** vitaminé(e)

vitreous ['vɪtrɪəs] *adj* **v. enamel** émail *m* vitrifié; **v. humour** humeur *f* vitrée

vitriol ['vɪtrɪəl] *n also Fig* vitriol *m*

vitriolic [vɪtrɪ'ɒlɪk] *adj Chem* de vitriol; *Fig* au vitriol

vituperative [vɪ'tjuːpərətɪv] *adj Formal* injurieux(euse)

viva ['vaɪvə] *n Br Univ* **v. (voce)** *(oral exam)* oral *m; (for thesis)* soutenance *f* de thèse

vivacious [vɪ'veɪʃəs] *adj* enjoué(e)

vivacity [vɪ'væsɪtɪ] *n* vivacité *f*

vivid ['vɪvɪd] *adj* vif (vive); *(memory)* clair(e)

vividly ['vɪvɪdlɪ] *adv* vivement; *(remember)* clairement; *(describe)* de manière vivante

vivisection [vɪvɪ'sekʃən] *n* vivisection *f*

vixen ['vɪksən] *n* renarde *f*

viz [vɪz] *adv (abbr* **videlicet)** à savoir

VOA [viːəʊ'eɪ] *n Am (abbr* **Voice of America)** = station de radio américaine de diffusion mondiale

vocabulary [və'kæbjʊlərɪ] *n* vocabulaire *m*

vocal ['vəʊkəl] **1** *adj* (**a**) *(relating to the voice)* vocal(e); **v. cords** cordes *fpl* vocales (**b**) *(outspoken)* franc (franche); **to be v. about sth** se faire entendre à propos de qch
2 *npl* **vocals** chant *m;* **on vocals** au chant

vocalist ['vəʊkəlɪst] *n* chanteur(euse) *m,f*

vocation [vəʊ'keɪʃən] *n* vocation *f;* **to have a v. (for sth)** avoir une vocation (pour qch)

vocational [vəʊ'keɪʃənəl] *adj* professionnel(elle)

vocative ['vɒkətɪv] *n* vocatif

vociferous [və'sɪfərəs] *adj* bruyant(e)

vociferously [və'sɪfərəslɪ] *adv* bruyamment

vodka ['vɒdkə] *n* vodka *f*

vogue [vəʊg] *n* vogue *f;* **to be in v.** être en vogue

voice [vɔɪs] **1** *n* (**a**) *(of person)* voix *f;* **to raise/lower one's v.** élever/baisser la voix; **at the top of one's v.** à tue-tête; **I've lost my v.** je n'ai plus de voix; **v. box**

larynx *m*; *Comput* **v. mail** messagerie *f* vocale; *Comput* **v. recognition** reconnaissance *f* de la parole; *Mus* **v. training** cours *mpl* de chant (**b**) *Gram* **active/passive v.** voix *f* active/passive (**c**) *(idioms)* **the v. of reason** la voix de la raison; **with one v.** d'une seule voix; **to make one's v. heard** se faire entendre; **these reforms would give small parties a v.** ces réformes donneraient voix au chapitre aux petits partis
   2 *vt* (**a**) *(opinion, feelings)* exprimer (**b**) *(consonant)* sonoriser

voiced ['vɔɪst] *adj (consonant)* sonore

voiceless ['vɔɪslɪs] *adj (consonant)* sans voix

voice-over ['vɔɪsəʊvə(r)] *n* voix *f* off

void [vɔɪd] **1** *n* vide *m*; **to fill the v.** combler le vide
   2 *adj* (**a**) *(devoid)* **v. of** dépourvu(e) de (**b**) *Law (deed, contract)* **(null and) v.** nul (nulle) et non avenu(e)

volatile ['vɒlətaɪl] *adj* (**a**) *(person) (fickle)* inconstant(e); *(temperamental)* lunatique; *(situation)* explosif(ive); *(economy, market)* instable (**b**) *Chem* volatil(e)

volcanic [vɒl'kænɪk] *adj* volcanique

volcano [vɒl'keɪnəʊ] *(pl* **volcanoes***) n* volcan *m*

vole [vəʊl] *n* campagnol *m*

volition [və'lɪʃən] *n Formal* **of one's own v.** de son propre gré

volley ['vɒlɪ] *n* (**a**) *(of gunfire, blows, stones)* volée *f*; *Fig (of insults)* bordée *f* (**b**) *(in tennis)* volée *f*

volleyball ['vɒlɪbɔːl] *n* volley(-ball *m*) *m*

volt [vəʊlt] *n* volt *m*

voltage ['vəʊltɪdʒ] *n* voltage *m*; **high/low v.** haute/basse tension *f*

volte-face ['vɒltfɑːs] *n* volte-face *f inv*

voluble ['vɒljʊbəl] *adj* volubile

volubly ['vɒljʊblɪ] *adv* avec volubilité

volume ['vɒljuːm] *n* (**a**) *(book)* volume *m*, tome *m*; *Fig* **to speak volumes (about)** *(of action, expression)* en dire long (sur) (**b**) *(amount, space occupied)* volume *m*; *(of work)* quantité *f* (**c**) *(loudness)* volume *m*; **to turn the v. up/down** *(on TV, radio)* monter/baisser le volume; **v. control** bouton *m* de réglage du volume (**d**) *(of hair)* volume *m*

voluminous [və'ljuːmɪnəs] *adj (garment)* ample; *(container)* volumineux(euse)

voluntarily [vɒlən'teərɪlɪ] *adv* de plein gré

voluntary ['vɒləntərɪ] *adj* volontaire; **v. redundancy** départ *m* volontaire; **v. work** travail *m* bénévole

volunteer [vɒlən'tɪə(r)] **1** *n* volontaire *mf*; *(for charity)* bénévole *mf*
   2 *vt (information)* donner spontanément; *(advice)* offrir; **to v. to do sth** se porter volontaire pour faire qch
   3 *vi* (**a**) *(for military service)* s'engager (**b**) *(to help, for charity)* se porter volontaire (**for** pour)

voluptuous [və'lʌptjʊəs] *adj* voluptueux(euse)

vomit ['vɒmɪt] **1** *n* vomi *m*
   2 *vt & vi* vomir

voodoo ['vuːduː] *n* vaudou *m*

voracious [və'reɪʃəs] *adj* vorace

vortex ['vɔːteks] *(pl* **vortices** ['vɔːtɪsiːz] *) n* vortex *m*; *Fig* tourbillon *m*

vote [vəʊt] **1** *n (choice)* vote *m*; *(election)* scrutin *m*; *(paper)* voix *f*; **to put sth to the v.** soumettre qch au vote; **to take a v. on sth** voter sur qch; **to have the v.** avoir le droit de vote; **they got 52% of the v.** ils ont remporté 52% des voix; **the party has increased its share of the v.** le parti a amélioré ses résultats aux élections; **v. of confidence** vote de confiance; **v. of no confidence** motion *f* de censure; **to propose a v. of thanks** faire un discours de remerciement
   2 *vt* **to v. Communist** voter communiste; **to v. to do sth** voter pour faire qch; **to v. sth down** voter contre qch; **to v. sb in** élire qn; **to v. sb out** ne pas réélire qn; **I v. (that) we go** je propose qu'on y aille
   3 *vi* voter (**for/against** pour/contre); **to v. on sth** voter sur qch; *Fig* **to v. with one's feet** manifester son mécontentement en partant

voter ['vəʊtə(r)] *n* électeur(trice) *m,f*

voting ['vəʊtɪŋ] **1** *n* scrutin *m*; **v. booth** isoloir *m*
   2 *adj (member)* votant(e)

votive ['vəʊtɪv] *adj Rel* votif(ive)

►**vouch for** [vaʊtʃ] *vt insep (person)* se porter garant(e) de; *(quality, truth)* attester de

voucher ['vaʊtʃə(r)] *n* coupon ·*m*, bon *m*; **(gift) v.** chèque-cadeau *m*

vow [vaʊ] **1** *n* vœu *m*; **to make a v.** faire un vœu; **to take a v. of poverty/silence** faire vœu de pauvreté/silence
   2 *vt* jurer; **to v. to do sth** jurer de faire qch; **to v. that** jurer que

vowel ['vaʊəl] *n* voyelle *f*; **v. sound** son *m* vocalique

voyage ['vɔɪdʒ] *n* voyage *m*

voyager ['vɔɪdʒə(r)] *n* voyageur(euse) *m,f*

voyeur [vwɑː'jɜː(r)] *n* voyeur(euse) *m,f*

voyeuristic [vwɑːjɜː'rɪstɪk] *adj* voyeuriste

vs *(abbr* **versus***)* contre

VSO [viːes'əʊ] *n Br (abbr* **Voluntary Service Overseas***)* ≃ service *m* de la coopération

VTOL [viːtiːəʊ'el] *n (abbr* **vertical take-off and landing***)* ADAV *m*

VTR [viːtiː'ɑː(r)] *n (abbr* **video tape recorder***)* magnétoscope *m*

vulgar ['vʌlgə(r)] *adj* vulgaire; *Math* **v. fraction** fraction *f* ordinaire

vulgarity [vʌl'gærɪtɪ] *n* vulgarité *f*

vulnerability [vʌlnərə'bɪlɪtɪ] *n* vulnérabilité *f*

vulnerable ['vʌlnərəbəl] *adj* vulnérable

vulture ['vʌltʃə(r)] *n also Fig* vautour *m*

vulva ['vʌlvə] *(pl* **vulvas** *or* **vulvae** ['vʌlviː] *) n* vulve *f*

W

W¹, w [ˈdʌbəljuː] *n* (**a**) *(letter)* W, w *m inv* (**b**) *(abbr west)* O

W² *n (abbr* **watt(s)***)* W

WAAF [wæf] *n (abbr* **Women's Auxiliary Air Force***)* = groupe de femmes, auxiliaires de l'armée de l'air britannique durant la Seconde Guerre mondiale

wacky [ˈwækɪ] *adj Fam* farfelu(e)

wad [wɒd] *n (of cotton wool)* morceau *m*; *(of paper, bank notes)* liasse *f*

wadding [ˈwɒdɪŋ] *n* ouate *f*

waddle [ˈwɒdəl] *vi* se dandiner

wade [weɪd] *vi (in water)* marcher dans l'eau; **to w. across a stream** traverser une rivière à gué; *Fam Fig* **to w. in** intervenir; *Fig* **it took me a month to w. through that book** il m'a fallu un mois pour venir à bout de ce livre

▶**wade into** *vt insep Fam Fig (task)* s'attaquer à; *(person)* tomber sur

wader [ˈweɪdə(r)] *n* (**a**) *(bird)* échassier *m* (**b**) **waders** *(boots)* bottes *fpl* de pêcheur

wafer [ˈweɪfə(r)] *n* (**a**) *(biscuit)* gaufrette *f*, *Belg* galette *f* (**b**) *Rel (for communion)* hostie *f*

wafer-thin [weɪfəˈθɪn] *adj* ultramince

waffle¹ [ˈwɒfəl] *n (food)* gaufre *f*

waffle² *Br Fam* **1** *n (spoken)* baratin *m*; *(written)* remplissage *m*
2 *vi (in speaking)* baratiner; *(in writing)* faire du remplissage

waft [wɒft] **1** *vt (smell, sound)* porter
2 *vi (of smell, sound)* parvenir

wag¹ [wæg] **1** *vt (pt & pp* **wagged***)* agiter, remuer; **to w. one's finger at sb** menacer qn du doigt; **to w. its tail** *(of dog)* remuer la queue
2 *vi* frétiller, remuer; **its tail was wagging** *(of dog)* il remuait la queue; *Fam* **tongues will w.** les langues vont aller bon train
3 *n (action)* frétillement *m*; **with a w. of its tail** la queue frétillante

wag² *n Fam (joker)* farceur(euse) *m,f*

wage [weɪdʒ] **1** *n (pay)* **wage(s)** salaire *m*, paie *f*; **w. claim** revendication *f* salariale; **w. cut** diminution *f* de salaire; *Br* **w. differential** écart *m* salarial; **w. earner** salarié(e) *m,f*; **w. freeze** gel *m* des salaires; **w. packet** *(envelope)* enveloppe *f* de paie; *(money)* paie *f*
2 *vt* **to w. war (on)** faire la guerre (à); **to w. a campaign against smoking** mener une campagne anti-tabac

wager [ˈweɪdʒə(r)] **1** *n* pari *m*
2 *vt* parier

waggle [ˈwægəl] *vt & vi* remuer

wag(g)on [ˈwægən] *n (horse-drawn)* charrette *f*; *Br (for railway freight)* wagon *m* (découvert); *Fam Fig* **to be on the w.** être au régime sec

waif [weɪf] *n (abandoned child)* enfant *mf* abandonné(e); *(very thin girl)* fille *f* excessivement maigre; **waifs and strays** *(children)* enfants *mpl* abandonnés; *(animals)* animaux *mpl* abandonnés

wail [weɪl] **1** *n (of person)* gémissement *m*; *(of siren)* hurlement *m*
2 *vi (of person)* gémir, pousser des gémissements; *(of siren)* hurler

waist [weɪst] *n* taille *f*; **w. measurement** tour *m* de taille

waistband [ˈweɪstbænd] *n* ceinture *f*

waistcoat [ˈweɪskəʊt] *n Br* gilet *m*

waistline [ˈweɪstlaɪn] *n* taille *f*; **to watch one's w.** surveiller sa ligne

wait [weɪt] **1** *n* attente *f*; **to have a long w.** attendre longtemps; **to lie in w. for sb** guetter qn
2 *vt* attendre; **to w. one's turn** attendre son tour
3 *vi* (**a**) *(remain in expectation)* attendre; **to w. for sb/sth** attendre qn/qch; **to keep sb waiting** faire attendre qn; **I can't w. to see her** j'ai vraiment hâte de la voir; **repairs while you w.** *(sign)* réparations minute; **we must w. and see** on verra bien (**b**) **to w. at table** *(serve)* faire le service

▶**wait about, wait around** *vi* attendre

▶**wait on** *vt insep (serve)* servir; **to w. on sb hand and foot** être aux petits soins pour qn

▶**wait up** *vi* **to w. up for sb** attendre qn pour aller se coucher

waiter [ˈweɪtə(r)] *n* serveur *m*

waiting [ˈweɪtɪŋ] *n* attente *f*; **to play the w. game** faire de l'attentisme; **w. list** liste *f* d'attente; **w. room** salle *f* d'attente

waitress [ˈweɪtrɪs] *n* serveuse *f*

waive [weɪv] *vt (rights, claim)* renoncer à; *(rule)* ignorer

wake¹ [weɪk] *n (of ship)* sillage *m*; *Fig* **in the w. of sth** à la suite de qch; *Fig* **to follow in sb's w.** suivre l'exemple de qn

wake² *n (on night before funeral)* veillée *f* de corps

wake³ *(pt* **woke** [wəʊk] *or* **waked**, *pp* **woken** [ˈwəʊkən] *or* **waked)** **1** *vt* réveiller
2 *vi* se réveiller

▶**wake up 1** *vt sep* réveiller
2 *vi* se réveiller; *Fig* **to w. up to sth** prendre conscience de qch

wakeful [ˈweɪkfʊl] *adj* (**a**) *(sleepless)* éveillé(e); **to have a w. night** ne pas fermer l'œil de la nuit (**b**) *(vigilant)* vigilant(e)

waken [ˈweɪkən] *vt* réveiller

wakey ['weɪkɪ] *exclam Br Fam* **w., w.!** réveille-toi!

Wales [weɪlz] *n* le pays de Galles

walk [wɔːk] **1** *n* (**a**) *(short)* promenade *f*; *(long)* marche *f*; **it's a long w.** c'est loin à pied; **it's a ten-minute w.** c'est à dix minutes à pied; **to go for a w.** aller se promener (**b**) *(gait)* démarche *f*; **I know her by her w.** je la reconnais à sa démarche (**c**) *(speed)* **at a w.** au pas (**d**) *(path)* avenue *f* (**e**) *(profession, situation)* **people from all walks of life** des gens de tous les milieux

2 *vt* **to w. the dog** promener le chien; **to w. sb home** raccompagner qn; **to w. the streets** battre le pavé; *Euph (of prostitute)* faire le trottoir

3 *vi (move on foot)* marcher; *(as opposed to riding, driving)* aller à pied; *(for exercise, pleasure)* se promener (à pied); **to w. home** rentrer à pied

▸**walk away** *vi* s'en aller; *Fig* **to w. away from trouble** éviter les ennuis; *Fig* **to w. away with a prize** remporter un prix

▸**walk in** *vi* entrer

▸**walk into** *vt insep* (**a**) *(enter)* entrer dans (**b**) *(collide with)* rentrer dans

▸**walk off** *vi* s'en aller; **to w. off with sth** *(steal)* partir avec qch; *(win easily)* remporter qch

▸**walk out** *vi* (**a**) *(leave)* sortir; **to w. out on sb** quitter qn (**b**) *(go on strike)* se mettre en grève

▸**walk over** *vt insep Fam* **to w. all over sb** marcher sur les pieds de qn

walkabout ['wɔːkəbaʊt] *n (of politician)* bain *m* de foule

walker ['wɔːkə(r)] *n* marcheur(euse) *m, f*

walkie-talkie [wɔːkɪ'tɔːkɪ] *n* talkie-walkie *m*

walk-in cupboard ['wɔːkɪn'kʌbəd] *n (for clothes)* débarras *m*; *(for food)* cellier *m*

walking ['wɔːkɪŋ] **1** *n* marche *f*; **w. frame** déambulateur *m*; **w. shoes** chaussures *fpl* de marche; **w. stick** canne *f*

2 *adj* **at a w. pace** au pas; *Fam* **she's a w. encyclopedia** c'est une encyclopédie ambulante; **the w. wounded** les blessés *mpl* en état de marcher

Walkman® ['wɔːkmən] *n* baladeur *m*

walk-on part ['wɔːkɒn'pɑːt] *n (in film, play)* rôle *m* de figurant(e)

walkout ['wɔːkaʊt] *n (strike)* débrayage *m*; *(from meeting)* départ *m* en signe de protestation

walkover ['wɔːkəʊvə(r)] *n Fam* **it was a w.!** c'était du gâteau!

walkway ['wɔːkweɪ] *n* passage *m* (couvert)

wall [wɔːl] *n* (**a**) *(of building, room)* mur *m*; **the Great W. of China** la grande muraille de Chine; **w. cupboard** placard *m* mural; **w. hanging** tenture *f* murale (**b**) *(idioms)* **a w. of silence** un mur de silence; **to go to the w.** faire faillite; *Fam* **to drive sb up the w.** rendre qn dingue; *Fam* **I might as well talk to the w.!** c'est comme parler à un mur

▸**wall in** *vt sep* entourer

▸**wall off** *vt sep* séparer

▸**wall up** *vt sep* murer

wallaby ['wɒləbɪ] *n* wallaby *m*

wallet ['wɒlɪt] *n* portefeuille *m*

wallflower ['wɔːlflaʊə(r)] *n (plant)* giroflée *f*; *Fig* **to be a w.** *(of person)* faire tapisserie

Walloon [wɒ'luːn] **1** *n* (**a**) *(person)* Wallon(onne) *m, f* (**b**) *(language)* wallon *m*

2 *adj* wallon(onne)

wallop ['wɒləp] *Fam* **1** *n* beigne *f*, grand coup *m*

2 *vt* filer un grand coup à

walloping ['wɒləpɪŋ] *Fam* **1** *n* raclée *f*

2 *adv (for emphasis)* super; **a w. great lie** un mensonge gros comme ça

wallow ['wɒləʊ] *vi* se vautrer; **to w. in self-pity** s'apitoyer sur son propre sort

wallpaper ['wɔːlpeɪpə(r)] **1** *n* papier *m* peint

2 *vt* tapisser

wall-to-wall ['wɔːltəwɔːl] *adj* **w. carpeting** moquette *f*; *Fig* **w. coverage** couverture *f* complète

wally ['wɒlɪ] *n Br Fam (idiot)* andouille *f*

walnut ['wɔːlnʌt] *n (fruit)* noix *f*; *(tree, wood)* noyer *m*

walrus ['wɔːlrəs] *(pl* **walruses**) *n* morse *m*

waltz [wɔːls] **1** *n* valse *f*

2 *vi* (**a**) *(dance)* valser (**b**) *Fam (move confidently)* **to w. in/out** entrer/sortir avec désinvolture; *Fam* **to w. off with sth** partir avec qch

WAN ['dʌbəljuːeɪ'en] *n Comput (abbr* **wide area network)** grand réseau *m*

wan [wɒn] *adj* blême

wand [wɒnd] *n* baguette *f*

wander ['wɒndə(r)] **1** *vt (streets)* traîner dans; *(world)* courir

2 *vi* (**a**) *(roam)* errer; **to w. around the town** se promener dans la ville; **she had wandered from the path** elle s'était éloignée du chemin (**b**) *(verbally)* radoter; *(mentally)* dérailler; **to w. from the subject** s'écarter du sujet

3 *n* balade *f*; **to go for a w.** aller faire un tour

wanderer ['wɒndərə(r)] *n* vagabond(e) *m, f*

wandering ['wɒndərɪŋ] *adj (person, life)* errant(e); *(tribe)* nomade

wanderlust ['wɒndəlʌst] *n* soif *f* de voyages

wane [weɪn] **1** *vi (of moon)* décroître; *(of popularity, enthusiasm, power)* décliner

2 *n* **to be on the w.** *(of moon)* décroître; *(of popularity, enthusiasm, power)* être en déclin

wangle ['wæŋgəl] *vt Fam* se débrouiller pour avoir; **to w. sb sth, to w. sth for sb** se débrouiller pour avoir qch à qn; **to w. it so that** se débrouiller pour que + *subjunctive*

wank [wæŋk] *Br Vulg* **1** *vi* se branler

2 *n* branlette *f*; **to have a w.** se branler

wanker ['wæŋkə(r)] *n Br Vulg* connard *m*

wanna ['wɒnə] (**a**) = **want to** (**b**) = **want a**

want [wɒnt] **1** *vt* (**a**) *(wish, desire)* vouloir; **to w. to do sth** vouloir faire qch; **to w. sb to do sth** vouloir que qn fasse qch; **that's the last thing we w.** nous ne voulons surtout pas cela; **I know when I'm not wanted** je sais quand je suis de trop; **what does she w. with me?** qu'est-ce qu'elle me veut?

(**b**) *Fam (need)* avoir besoin de; **the lawn wants cutting** la pelouse a besoin d'être tondue; **you w. to be careful with him** il faut que tu fasses attention avec lui

(**c**) *(seek)* **to be wanted by the police** être recherché(e) par la police; **you're wanted on the phone** on te demande au téléphone; **accommodation wanted** *(in advertisement)* cherche appartement

2 *vi* **to w. for nothing** ne manquer de rien

3 *n* (**a**) *(need)* besoin *m*

(**b**) *(lack)* manque *m* (**of** de); **for w. of sth/of doing sth** faute de qch/de faire qch; **for w. of anything better** faute de mieux

wanting ['wɒntɪŋ] *adj* **to be w. in sth** manquer de qch; **to be found w.** *(of person)* se révéler incapable; *(of thing)* laisser à désirer

wanton ['wɒntən] *adj* (**a**) *(unjustified)* gratuit(e) (**b**) *(unrestrained)* dévergondé(e); *(sexually)* licencieux(-euse)

war [wɔː(r)] *n* guerre *f*; **to be at w. (with)** être en guerre (avec); **to go to w. (with/over)** entrer en guerre (contre/à propos de); *Fig* **w. of words** altercation *f*; *Fam Fig* **you look as if you've been through the wars** tu es dans un bel état!; **w. cabinet** cabinet *m* de guerre; **w. correspondent** correspondant(e) *mf* de guerre; **w. crime** crime *m* de guerre; **w. criminal** criminel *m* de guerre; **w. cry** cri *m* de guerre; **w. games** *Mil* manœuvres *fpl*; *(with model soldiers)* wargame *m*; **w. memorial** monument *m* aux morts

warble ['wɔːbəl] **1** *n* gazouillement *m*
2 *vi* gazouiller

warbler ['wɔːblə(r)] *n* fauvette *f*

ward [wɔːd] *n* (**a**) *(in hospital)* salle *f* (**b**) *(electoral division)* circonscription *f* (**c**) *Law* **w. of court** pupille *mf* sous tutelle judiciaire

▸**ward off** *vt sep (blow)* éviter; *(danger)* chasser

warden ['wɔːdən] *n (of institution, hostel)* directeur(-trice) *m,f*; *(of park)* gardien(enne) *mf*

warder ['wɔːdə(r)] *n Br (of prison)* gardien(enne) *m,f*

wardrobe ['wɔːdrəʊb] *n* (**a**) *(cupboard)* armoire *f* (**b**) *(clothes)* garde-robe *f*; **to have a large w.** avoir une garde-robe importante (**c**) *(theatrical costumes)* costumes *mpl*; **w. mistress** habilleuse *f*

warehouse ['weəhaʊs] *n* entrepôt *m*

wares [weə(r)z] *npl* articles *mpl*

warfare ['wɔːfeə(r)] *n* guerre *f*; **class w.** lutte *f* des classes

warhead ['wɔːhed] *n* ogive *f*

warhorse ['wɔːhɔːs] *n Fig* **an old w.** un vétéran

warily ['weərɪlɪ] *adv* avec une prudence circonspecte

wariness ['weərɪnɪs] *n* prudence *f* circonspecte

warlike ['wɔːlaɪk] *adj* guerrier(ère)

warm [wɔːm] **1** *adj* (**a**) *(in temperature)* chaud(e); **to be w.** *(of person)* avoir chaud; *(of object, water, clothing)* être chaud; **it's w.** *(of weather)* il fait chaud; **you're getting warmer** *(in guessing game)* tu chauffes (**b**) *(kind, friendly)* chaleureux(euse)
2 *vt* chauffer; **to w. oneself by the fire** se chauffer près du feu
3 *vi* **to w. to sb** se prendre de sympathie pour qn; **to w. to sth** se laisser séduire par qch

▸**warm up 1** *vt sep (food)* réchauffer
2 *vi* (**a**) *(of person, room)* se réchauffer (**b**) *(of dancer, athlete)* s'échauffer (**c**) *(of engine)* chauffer

warm-blooded [wɔːm'blʌdɪd] *adj* à sang chaud

warm-hearted [wɔːm'hɑːtɪd] *adj* chaleureux(euse)

warmly ['wɔːmlɪ] *adv* (**a**) *(dress)* chaudement (**b**) *(applaud, thank)* chaleureusement

warmonger ['wɔːmʌŋgə(r)] *n* belliciste *mf*

warmth [wɔːmθ] *n* chaleur *f*

warm-up ['wɔːmʌp] *n (of dancer, athlete)* échauffement *m*

warn [wɔːn] *vt* avertir, prévenir; **to w. sb about sb/sth** mettre qn en garde contre qn/qch; **to w. sb about doing sth** dire à qn de ne pas faire qch; **to w. sb not to do sth** déconseiller à qn de faire qch; **you have been warned!** te voilà prévenu!

warning ['wɔːnɪŋ] *n* (**a**) *(caution)* avertissement *m*; *(against danger)* mise *f* en garde; **to give sb a w.** donner un avertissement à qn; *(against danger)* mettre qn en garde; *Fig* **w. sign** signe *m* (**b**) *(advance notice)* avis *m*; **without w.** sans prévenir

warp [wɔːp] **1** *vt* (**a**) *(wood, metal)* gauchir (**b**) *(person, mind)* pervertir
2 *vi (of wood, metal)* gauchir

warpath ['wɔːpɑːθ] *n Fam* **to be on the w.** en vouloir à tout le monde

warped [wɔːpt] *adj* (**a**) *(wood, metal)* gauchi(e) (**b**) *(person)* perverti(e); *(mind)* tordu

warrant ['wɒrənt] **1** *n Law* mandat *m*; *Mil* **w. officer** adjudant *m*
2 *vt* (**a**) *(justify)* justifier (**b**) *(guarantee)* garantir

warranty ['wɒrəntɪ] *(pl* **warranties**) *n* garantie *f*; **under w.** sous garantie

warren ['wɒrən] *n (of rabbit)* garenne *f*; *Fig (of streets)* labyrinthe *m*

warring ['wɔːrɪŋ] *adj* en guerre

warrior ['wɒrɪə(r)] *n* guerrier(ère) *m,f*

Warsaw ['wɔːsɔː] *n* Varsovie; *Formerly* **the W. Pact** le pacte de Varsovie

warship ['wɔːʃɪp] *n* navire *m* de guerre

wart [wɔːt] *n* verrue *f*; **warts and all** *(biography, portrait)* sans complaisance

warthog ['wɔːthɒg] *n* phacochère *m*

wartime ['wɔːtaɪm] *n* temps *m* de guerre; **in w.** en temps de guerre

wary ['weərɪ] *adj* méfiant(e); **to be w. of sb/sth** se méfier de qn/qch

was [wɒz] *pt of* **be**

wash [wɒʃ] **1** *n* (**a**) *(action)* lavage *m*; **to have a w.** se laver; **to give sth a w.** laver qch; **your jeans are in the w.** ton jean est au lavage; *Fig* **it will all come out in the w.** tout va s'arranger (**b**) *(of ship)* remous *m*
2 *vt* (**a**) *(clean)* laver; **to w. oneself** se laver; **to w. one's face/one's hands** se laver la figure/les mains; *Fig* **to w. one's hands of sth** se laver les mains de qch; **to wash one's hands of sb** ne plus se préoccuper de qn (**b**) *(carry)* **to w. sb/sth ashore** rejeter qn/qch sur le rivage; **he was washed overboard** une vague l'a emporté par-dessus bord
3 *vi (wash oneself)* se laver; *Br Fam* **that won't w.!** ça ne marche pas!; *Br Fam* **his story just doesn't w. with me!** il ne me fera pas avaler cette histoire!

▸**wash away** *vt sep* emporter

▸**wash down** *vt sep* (**a**) *(walls, car)* laver à grande eau (**b**) *(pill)* faire descendre (**with** avec); **to w. down one's dinner with a bottle of wine** arroser son dîner d'une bouteille de vin

▸**wash off 1** *vt sep* enlever
2 *vi* partir

▸**wash out 1** *vt sep* (**a**) *(cup, bottle)* rincer (**b**) *(stain, dirt)* faire partir; **to be completely washed out** *(exhausted)* être complètement lessivé(e)
2 *vi (of stain, dirt)* partir

▸**wash over** *vt insep (of waves)* balayer; *Fig (have no effect on)* ne faire aucun effet à

▸**wash up 1** *vt sep* (**a**) *Br (clean)* laver (**b**) *(carry ashore)* rejeter sur le rivage
2 *vi* (**a**) *Br (do dishes)* faire la vaisselle (**b**) *Am (have a wash)* se débarbouiller

washbasin ['wɒʃbeɪsən] *n (cuvette f de)* lavabo *m*

washboard ['wɒʃbɔːd] *n* planche *f* à laver

washbowl ['wɒʃbəʊl] *n (small)* cuvette *f*; *(large)* bassine *f*

washcloth ['wɒʃklɒθ] *n Am (face cloth)* lingette *f*

washer ['wɒʃə(r)] n (**a**) Fam (for clothes) machine f à laver (**b**) (for screw) rondelle f; (made of rubber) joint m

washer-dryer [wɒʃə'draɪə(r)] n machine f à laver qui fait sèche-linge

wash(-)hand basin ['wɒʃhænd'beɪsən] n lavabo m

washing ['wɒʃɪŋ] n (**a**) (action) lavage m; **to do the w.** faire la lessive; **w. machine** machine f à laver; **w. powder** poudre f à laver, lessive f (en poudre) (**b**) (dirty clothes) linge m sale; (clean clothes) linge (propre)

Washington ['wɒʃɪŋtən] n Washington; **W. (State)** l'État m de Washington; **W. DC** Washington

washing-up [wɒʃɪŋ'ʌp] n Br vaisselle f; **to do the w.** faire la vaisselle; **w. bowl** cuvette f; **w. liquid** liquide f vaisselle

washout ['wɒʃaʊt] n Fam bide m

washroom ['wɒʃruːm] n Am toilettes fpl

wasn't [wɒzənt] = **was not**

Wasp, WASP [wɒsp] n Am (abbr **White Anglo-Saxon Protestant**) = Blanc d'origine anglo-saxonne et protestante, appartenant aux classes aisées et influentes

wasp [wɒsp] n guêpe f; **w.'s nest** guêpier m

waspish ['wɒspɪʃ] adj hargneux(euse)

wastage ['weɪstɪdʒ] n gaspillage m

waste [weɪst] **1** n (**a**) (of food, effort) gaspillage m; (of time, money) perte f; **to go to w.** être gaspillé(e) (**b**) (rubbish) déchets mpl; **w. disposal unit** broyeur m d'ordures (**c**) **wastes** (desert) étendues fpl désertiques
  2 adj (heat, fuel) gaspillé(e); (water) usé(e)
  3 vt (money) gaspiller; (time) perdre; (opportunity) gâcher; **to w. no time doing sth** ne pas perdre de temps pour faire qch; Prov **w. not, want not** = il ne faut pas gaspiller

▶**waste away** vi dépérir

wasted ['weɪstɪd] adj (**a**) (effort) gaspillé(e); (opportunity) gaché(e) (**b**) Fam (drunk) bourré(e), pété(e)

wasteful ['weɪstfʊl] adj **to be w.** (of process, practice) ne pas être rentable; (of person) être gaspilleur(euse)

wasteland ['weɪstlænd] n (disused) terrain m vague; (of desert, snow) désert m

wastepaper [weɪst'peɪpə(r)] n vieux papiers mpl; **w. basket** or **bin** corbeille f à papier

waster ['weɪstə(r)] n Br Fam (idle person) bon (bonne) m,f à rien

wasting disease ['weɪstɪŋdɪ'ziːz] n maladie f dégénérative

watch [wɒtʃ] **1** n (**a**) (timepiece) montre f (**b**) (period of guard duty) garde f; (guard) sentinelle f; **to be on w.** monter la garde; **to keep a close w. on sb/sth** surveiller qn/qch de près
  2 vt (**a**) (observe) regarder; **to w. television** regarder la télévision; **to w. sb doing sth** regarder qn faire qch (**b**) (keep an eye on) surveiller (**c**) (be careful of) faire attention à; **w. your language!** surveille ton langage!; Fam **w. it!** attention!
  3 vi regarder

▶**watch out** vi faire attention; **w. out!** attention!

▶**watch out for** vt insep (**a**) (look for) (person) guetter; (thing) chercher (**b**) (be on guard for) faire attention à

▶**watch over** vt insep veiller sur

watchdog ['wɒtʃdɒg] n chien m de garde; Fig (organization) organisme m de contrôle

watchful ['wɒtʃfʊl] adj vigilant(e)

watchmaker ['wɒtʃmeɪkə(r)] n horloger(ère) m,f

watchman ['wɒtʃmən] n gardien m

watchstrap ['wɒtʃstræp] n bracelet m de montre

watchtower ['wɒtʃtaʊə(r)] n tour f de guet

watchword ['wɒtʃwɜːd] n mot m d'ordre

water ['wɔːtə(r)] **1** n (**a**) (substance) eau f; **to pass w.** (urinate) uriner; **w. bed** matelas m d'eau; **w. biscuit** = biscuit sec non salé; **w. bottle** gourde f; **w. chestnut** macre f; Old-fashioned **w. closet** waters mpl; **w. cooler** distributeur m d'eau fraîche; **w. heater** chauffe-eau m; **w. level** niveau m d'eau; **w. lily** nénuphar m; **w. meter** compteur m d'eau; **w. pistol** pistolet m à eau; **w. polo** water-polo m; **w. rat** rat m d'eau; **w. skiing** ski m nautique; **w. tank** réservoir m d'eau; **w. tower** château m d'eau; **w. wings** brassards mpl de natation (**b**) (idioms) **to spend money like w.** jeter l'argent par les fenêtres; **the argument doesn't hold w.** cet argument ne tient pas debout; **to keep one's head above w.** garder la tête hors de l'eau; **that's all w. under the bridge now** c'est de l'histoire ancienne; **a lot of w. has passed under the bridge since then** il a coulé beaucoup d'eau sous les ponts depuis
  2 vt (**a**) (fields, plants) arroser (**b**) (horse) donner à boire à
  3 vi (of eyes) pleurer; **it makes my mouth w.** ça me met l'eau à la bouche; **my mouth is watering** j'en ai l'eau à la bouche

▶**water down** vt sep (liquid, chemical) diluer; Fig (criticism, legislation) atténuer

waterborne ['wɔːtəbɔːn] adj (goods) transporté(e) par voie d'eau; (disease) d'origine hydrique

watercourse ['wɔːtəkɔːs] n cours m d'eau

watercolour ['wɔːtəkʌlə(r)] n aquarelle f

watercress ['wɔːtəkres] n cresson m (de fontaine)

waterfall ['wɔːtəfɔːl] n cascade f

waterfowl ['wɔːtəfaʊl] (pl **waterfowl**) n gibier m d'eau

waterfront ['wɔːtəfrʌnt] n (by river) bord m de l'eau; (by sea) front m de mer

watering ['wɔːtərɪŋ] n (of garden, plant) arrosage m; **w. can** arrosoir m; **w. hole** (for animals) point m d'eau; Fam (bar) bar m

waterlogged ['wɔːtəlɒgd] adj (shoes, clothes) trempé(e); (land) détrempé(e)

watermark ['wɔːtəmɑːk] n filigrane m

watermelon ['wɔːtəmelən] n pastèque f

waterproof ['wɔːtəpruːf] **1** adj imperméable; (watch, joint, seal) étanche; (make-up) waterproof inv; (sun lotion) résistant(e) à l'eau
  2 n (raincoat) imperméable m
  3 vt imperméabiliser

water-resistant ['wɔːtərɪzɪstənt] adj (watch) étanche; (fabric) qui résiste à l'eau

watershed ['wɔːtəʃed] n Geog ligne f de partage des eaux; Fig (turning point) tournant m; Br **the (nine o'clock) w.** (on television) = heure après laquelle sont diffusés des programmes ne convenant pas aux enfants

waterside ['wɔːtəsaɪd] n bord m de l'eau

water-ski ['wɔːtəskiː] vi faire du ski nautique

watertight ['wɔːtətaɪt] adj (seal) hermétique; (compartment) étanche; Fig (argument, alibi) inattaquable

waterway ['wɔːtəweɪ] n voie f navigable

waterworks ['wɔːtəwɜːks] n station f hydraulique; Br Euph (urinary system) voies fpl urinaires; Fam **to turn**

on the w. *(cry)* se mettre à pleurer comme une madeleine

watery ['wɔːtərɪ] *adj (soup)* trop liquide; *(beer, tea, coffee)* insipide, fade; *(eyes)* qui pleure; *(colour)* délavé(e)

watt [wɒt] *n* watt *m*

wattage ['wɒtɪdʒ] *n* puissance *f* en watts

wave [weɪv] **1** *n* (**a**) *(of water, dislike, crime)* vague *f*; *Fig* **to make waves** faire des vagues (**b**) *(gesture)* signe *m* (de la main); **to give sb a w.** faire signe à qn (**c**) *(in hair)* ondulation *f* (**d**) *(in physics)* onde *f*
2 *vt (arm, flag)* agiter; *(stick)* brandir; **to w. one's arms about** agiter les bras; **to w. goodbye to sb** faire au revoir de la main à qn
3 *vi* (**a**) *(of person)* faire signe; **to w. to sb** faire signe à qn (**b**) *(of flag)* flotter au vent

▶**wave aside** *vt insep Fig (objection, criticism)* écarter

waveband ['weɪvbænd] *n* bande *f* de fréquences

wavelength ['weɪvleŋθ] *n* longueur *f* d'ondes; *Fig* **to be on the same w.** être sur la même longueur d'ondes

waver ['weɪvə(r)] *vi (of person)* vaciller; *(of voice)* trembler; *(of courage)* faiblir

waverer ['weɪvərə(r)] *n* indécis(e) *m,f*

wavy ['weɪvɪ] *adj* ondulé(e)

wax¹ [wæks] **1** *n (for candles, polishing)* cire *f*; *(in ear)* cérumen *m*
2 *vt (polish)* cirer

wax² *vi* (**a**) *(of moon)* croître (**b**) *(become)* **to w. lyrical (about sth)** devenir lyrique (à propos de qch)

waxed [wækst] *adj* ciré(e)

waxen ['wæksən] *adj (complexion)* de cire

waxwork ['wækswɜːk] *n* **w. (dummy)** mannequin *m* de cire; **waxworks** musée *m* de cire

way [weɪ] **1** *n* (**a**) *(route)* & *Fig* chemin *m*; **the w. in** l'entrée *f*; **the w. out** la sortie; **the w. to the station** le chemin pour aller à la gare; **to ask sb the w.** demander son chemin à qn; **to show sb the w.** montrer le chemin à qn; **to lose one's w.** se perdre; **to know one's w. about** savoir se débrouiller; **on the w.** en chemin, en route; *Fam* **they've got a baby on the w.** ils ont un bébé en route; **I must be on my w.** je dois partir; **out of the w.** isolé(e); *Fig* **to go out of one's w. to help sb** se mettre en quatre pour aider qn; *Fig* **to find a w. out of a problem** trouver une issue à un problème; *Fig* **she is well on the w. to success** elle est bien partie pour réussir; **to make one's w. to a place** se diriger vers un endroit; **to make one's w. through the crowd** se frayer un chemin à travers la foule; *Fig* **to make w. for sb** laisser la place à qn; *Fig* **to make one's w. in the world** réussir dans la vie; *also Fig* **to stand in sb's w.** barrer le passage à qn; *also Fig* **to be/get in the w.** gêner; *also Fig* **to get out of the w.** s'écarter; *also Fig* **to keep out of the w.** se tenir à l'écart
(**b**) *(manner)* manière *f*, façon *f*; **in this w.** de cette manière; **to do things in one's own w.** faire les choses à sa manière; **I don't like the w. things are going** je n'aime pas la façon dont les choses tournent; **one w. or another** d'une manière ou d'une autre; **to find a w. of doing sth** trouver un moyen de faire qch; **to get into the w. of doing sth** s'habituer à faire qch; **to have a w. with children/animals** savoir s'y prendre avec les enfants/animaux; **to get one's (own) w.** arriver à ses fins; **he's used to getting his own w.** il n'a pas l'habitude qu'on le contrarie; **to**

get used to sb's ways se faire aux habitudes de qn
(**c**) *(distance)* **to go a part of the w.** faire un bout de chemin; **to go all the w.** aller jusqu'au bout; *Fig* **I'm with you all the w.** je suis tout à fait d'accord avec toi; **San Francisco is a long w. from New York** San Francisco est loin de New York; **we've still got a long w. to go** nous avons encore du chemin à faire; **to be a little/long w. off** être proche/loin
(**d**) *(direction)* direction *f*, sens *m*; **which w. ...?** dans quel sens...?; **this/that w.** par ici/là; *Fig* **to look the other w.** se boucher les yeux; *Fam* **down our w.** chez nous; *Fig* **it works both ways** cela marche dans les deux sens; **to split sth three ways** partager qch en trois
(**e**) *(street)* rue *f*
(**f**) *(respect)* égard *m*; **in a w.** d'une certaine manière; **in every w.** en tous points; **in no w.** en aucune façon
(**g**) *(state, condition)* **to be in a good w.** bien aller; **to be in a bad w.** être mal en point
2 *adv Fam* **w. back in the 1920s** dans les années vingt; **Lucy and I go w. back** Lucy et moi sommes des amis de longue date; **w. ahead** devant tout le monde; **w. down south** tout au sud; **your guess was w. out** tu étais loin de la vérité

wayfarer ['weɪfeərə(r)] *n* voyageur(euse) *m,f*

waylay [weɪ'leɪ] *(pt & pp* **waylaid** [weɪ'leɪd] *) vt (attack)* agresser; *Fig (stop)* arrêter au passage

way-out [weɪ'aʊt] *adj Fam (person)* excentrique; *(ideas, beliefs)* bizarre, curieux(euse)

wayside ['weɪsaɪd] *n* bord *m* de la route; *Fig* **to fall by the w.** se retrouver à la traîne

wayward ['weɪwəd] *adj* difficile

WBA [dʌbəljuːbiːˈeɪ] *n (abbr* **World Boxing Association**) WBA, = association mondiale de boxe

WC [dʌbəljuːˈsiː] *n (abbr* **water closet**) WC *mpl*

we [wiː] *pron* nous; **we're Scottish** nous sommes écossais; **WE haven't got it!** ce n'est pas nous qui l'avons!; **as we say in England** comme on dit en Angleterre; **we French are...** nous autres Français, nous sommes...

WEA [dʌbəljuːiːˈeɪ] *n Br (abbr* **Workers' Educational Association**) = association d'enseignement des travailleurs

weak [wiːk] *adj (person, currency, character)* faible; *(heart)* fragile; *(argument, excuse)* peu convaincant(e); *(tea, coffee)* peu fort(e); **to grow w.** s'affaiblir; **to be w. at sth** *(school subject)* être faible en qch; *Fig* **to go w. at the knees** avoir les jambes en coton; *Fig* **w. spot** point *m* faible

weaken ['wiːkən] **1** *vt* affaiblir
2 *vi* s'affaiblir

weak-kneed [wiːkˈniːd] *adj Fig* mou (molle)

weakling ['wiːklɪŋ] *n* mauviette *f*, faible *mf*

weakly ['wiːklɪ] *adv* faiblement

weakness ['wiːknɪs] *n* faiblesse *f*; **to have a w. for sb/sth** avoir un faible pour qn/qch

weak-willed [wiːkˈwɪld] *adj* sans volonté

weal [wiːl] *n (mark)* trace *f* de coup

wealth [welθ] *n* richesse *f*; *Fig* **a w. of sth** une abondance de qch

wealthy ['welθɪ] **1** *npl* **the w.** les riches
2 *adj* riche

wean [wiːn] *vt (baby)* sevrer; *Fig* **to w. sb off sth** *(bad habit)* faire passer qch à qn; *(alcohol, drugs)* sevrer qn de qch

weapon ['wepən] *n* arme *f*; **weapons of mass destruction** armes de destruction massive

wear [weə(r)] **1** *vt* (*pt* **wore** [wɔː(r)], *pp* **worn** [wɔːn]) (**a**) *(garment, glasses)* porter; **to w. black** porter du noir; **to w. one's hair up** avoir les cheveux relevés (**b**) *(erode)* user; **to w. a hole in sth** faire un trou dans qch (**c**) *Fam (believe, accept)* avaler

2 *vi (of clothing)* s'user; **to w. thin** s'user; *Fig* **that excuse is wearing thin** cette excuse ne prend plus; **my patience is wearing thin** je suis à bout de patience; **to w. smooth** devenir lisse; **to w. well** *(of clothing, person, film)* bien vieillir

3 *n* (**a**) *(clothing)* vêtements *mpl*; **evening w.** habits *mpl* de soirée; **children's w.** vêtements pour enfants (**b**) *(use)* usure *f*; **to get a lot of w. out of sth** porter qch longtemps; *Fam* **to be the worse for w.** être bien éméché(e); **w. and tear** usure *f* naturelle

▸**wear away 1** *vt sep* user
  2 *vi* s'user

▸**wear down 1** *vt sep* user; *Fig* **to w. sb down** avoir qn à l'usure
  2 *vi* s'user

▸**wear off** *vi (of pain)* disparaître; *(of effect)* cesser; *(of anaesthetic)* cesser de faire effet; **the novelty soon wore off** l'attrait de la nouveauté n'a pas duré

▸**wear on** *vi (of time)* s'écouler

▸**wear out** *vt sep* user; **to w. sb out** épuiser qn; **to w. oneself out** s'épuiser

wearily ['wɪərɪlɪ] *adv* avec lassitude

weariness ['wɪərɪnɪs] *n* lassitude *f*

wearing ['weərɪŋ] *adj* lassant(e)

wearisome ['wɪərɪsəm] *adj* fatigant(e)

weary ['wɪərɪ] **1** *adj* las (lasse); **to be w. of sth/of doing sth** être las de qch/de faire qch; **to grow w. of sth** se lasser de qch
  2 *vt* fatiguer, lasser
  3 *vi* se lasser (**of** de)

weasel ['wiːzəl] *n* belette *f*

weather ['weðə(r)] **1** *n* (**a**) *(atmospheric conditions)* temps *m*; **what's the w. like?** quel temps fait-il?; **the w. is good/bad** il fait beau/mauvais; **in this w.** par un temps pareil; **w. permitting** si le temps le permet; **w. forecast** prévisions *fpl* météorologiques; **w. map** *or* **chart** carte *f* météorologique (**b**) *(idioms)* **to make heavy w. of sth** faire tout un plat de qch; **to be under the w.** se sentir patraque
  2 *vt* (**a**) *(rock)* éroder (**b**) *(problem, situation)* surmonter; *Fig* **to w. the storm** tenir le coup
  3 *vi (of rock)* s'éroder

weatherbeaten ['weðəbiːtən] *adj (person, face)* hâlé(e); *(cliff, rock)* battu(e) par les vents

weathercock ['weðəkɒk] *n* girouette *f*

weathergirl ['weðəgɜːl] *n* présentatrice *f* de la météo

weatherman ['weðəmæn] *n* présentateur *m* de la météo

weatherproof ['weðəpruːf] *adj* résistant(e) aux intempéries

weave [wiːv] **1** *vt* (*pt* **wove** [wəʊv] or **weaved**, *pp* **woven** ['wəʊvən]) tisser; *Fig* **a skilfully woven plot** une intrigue bien ficelée
  2 *vi* tisser; *Fig* **to w. through the traffic** se faufiler parmi les voitures
  3 *n (pattern)* tissage *m*

weaver ['wiːvə(r)] *n* tisserand(e) *m,f*

weaving ['wiːvɪŋ] *n* tissage *m*

web [web] *n* (**a**) *(of spider)* toile *f*; *Fig (of lies)* tissu *m*; *(of intrigue)* nid *m* (**b**) *(of duck, frog)* palmure *f* (**c**) *Comput* **the W.** le Web; **W. cam** caméra *f* Internet; **W. designer** concepteur(trice) *m,f* de sites Web; **W. master** Webmestre *m*, Webmaster *m*; **W. page** page *f* Web; **W. site** site *m* Web

webbed [webd] *adj (foot)* palmé(e)

webbing ['webɪŋ] *n (on chair, bed)* sangles *fpl*

web-footed [web'fʊtɪd] *adj* palmipède

webzine ['webziːn] *n Comput* webzine *m*

we'd [wiːd] = **we had, we would**

Wed (*abbr* **Wednesday**) mercredi

wed [wed] (*pt & pp* **wedded**) **1** *vt* épouser; *Fig* **to be wedded to sth** être totalement dévoué(e) à qch
  2 *vi* se marier

wedding ['wedɪŋ] *n* mariage *m*; **w. anniversary** anniversaire *m* de mariage; **w. breakfast** repas *m* de noces; **w. cake** gâteau *m* de mariage; **w. day** jour *m* du mariage; **w. dress** robe *f* de mariée; **w. night** nuit *f* de noces; **w. ring** alliance *f*

wedge [wedʒ] **1** *n (for door, wheel)* cale *f*; *(of cake)* part *f*; *(of cheese)* morceau *m*; *Fig* **it has driven a w. between them** ça les a éloignés l'un de l'autre
  2 *vt* coincer; **to w. a door open** maintenir une porte ouverte avec une cale

wedlock ['wedlɒk] *n Law* mariage *m*; **to be born out of w.** naître de parents non mariés

Wednesday ['wenzdɪ] *n* mercredi *m*; *see also* **Saturday**

wee¹ [wiː] *adj Scot (small)* petit(e); **a w. bit** un petit peu

wee² *Br Fam* **1** *n* pipi *m*; **to do a w.** faire pipi
  2 *vi* faire pipi

weed [wiːd] **1** *n* (**a**) *(plant)* mauvaise herbe *f* (**b**) *Pej (weak person) (physically)* gringalet *m*; *(in character)* mauviette *f*
  2 *vt* désherber

▸**weed out** *vt sep Fig* éliminer

weedkiller ['wiːdkɪlə(r)] *n* désherbant *m*

weeds [wiːdz] *npl (mourning clothes)* vêtements *mpl* de deuil; **in widow's w.** en deuil

weedy ['wiːdɪ] *adj Pej (person)* malingre

week [wiːk] *n* semaine *f*; **next/last w.** la semaine prochaine/dernière; **once/twice a w.** une fois/deux fois par semaine; **in a w., in a w.'s time** dans huit jours; **within a w.** sous huitaine; **w. in w. out** chaque semaine; **tomorrow/Tuesday w.** demain/mardi en huit

weekday ['wiːkdeɪ] *n* jour *m* de semaine

weekend [wiːk'end] *n* week-end *m*; *Br* **at** *or Am* **on the w.** ce week-end; *(every weekend)* le week-end; **w. break** week-end

weekly ['wiːklɪ] **1** *n (magazine)* hebdomadaire *m*
  2 *adj* hebdomadaire
  3 *adv* chaque semaine; **twice w.** deux fois par semaine

weeknight ['wiːknaɪt] *n* soir *m* de semaine

weep [wiːp] **1** *n* **to have a w.** pleurer un coup
  2 *vt & vi* (*pt & pp* **wept** [wept]) pleurer

weeping ['wiːpɪŋ] **1** *n* pleurs *mpl*
  2 *adj* qui pleure; **w. willow** saule *m* pleureur

weepy ['wiːpɪ] *adj Fam (book, film)* mélo; **to be w.** *(of person)* avoir envie de pleurer

wee(-)wee ['wiːwiː] *n Br Fam* pipi *m*; **to do a w.** faire pipi

weft [weft] *n* trame *f*

weigh [weɪ] **1** *vt* (**a**) *(measure)* peser; **to w. oneself** se peser (**b**) *(consider)* mesurer; **to w. sth against sth** mettre qch en balance avec qch (**c**) *Naut* **to w. anchor** lever l'ancre

2 *vi* *(of person, parcel)* peser; **how much do you w.?** combien tu pèses?; **it's weighing on my conscience** ça me pèse sur la conscience; **her experience weighed in her favour** son expérience a fait pencher la balance en sa faveur

▶**weigh down** *vt sep* lester; *Fig* **to be weighed down with sth** *(grief, responsibilities)* être accablé(e) de qch

▶**weigh in** *vi* *(of boxer, jockey)* être pesé(e); **to w. in at 75 kilos** peser 75 kilos

▶**weigh out** *vt sep* peser

▶**weigh up** *vt sep* *(consider)* mesurer; **to w. up the pros and cons** peser la pour et le contre

weighbridge ['weɪbrɪdʒ] *n* pont-bascule *m*

weight [weɪt] **1** *n* (**a**) *(of person, thing)* poids *m*; **they're the same w.** ils font le même poids; **to lose/put on w.** perdre/prendre du poids; **to have a w. problem** avoir un problème de poids; **weights and measures** poids et mesures; **w. training** entraînement *m* aux haltères (**b**) *(idioms)* **to throw one's w. about** affirmer son autorité; **to pull one's w.** faire sa part de travail; **that's a w. off my mind** ça m'ôte un poids; **to carry w.** avoir du poids

2 *vt Fig* **to be weighted in favour of sb/sth** favoriser/ne pas favoriser qn/qch

▶**weight down** *vt sep* *(to keep in place)* maintenir avec un poids; *(to make sink)* lester

weighting ['weɪtɪŋ] *n Fin* pondération *f*; **London w.** *(in salary)* indemnité *f* de résidence à Londres

weightless ['weɪtlɪs] *adj* *(astronaut)* en apesanteur; *(conditions)* d'apesanteur

weightlifter ['weɪtlɪftə(r)] *n* haltérophile *mf*

weightlifting ['weɪtlɪftɪŋ] *n* haltérophilie *f*

weighty ['weɪtɪ] *adj* *(heavy)* lourd(e); *Fig* *(serious, important)* grave

weir [wɪə(r)] *n* barrage *m*

weird [wɪəd] *adj* bizarre

weirdo ['wɪədəʊ] *(pl* **weirdos)** *n Fam* type *m* bizarre

welcome ['welkəm] **1** *adj* *(person, news, change)* bienvenu(e); **to make sb w.** faire un bon accueil à qn; **to feel w.** se sentir le (la) bienvenu(e); **she's always w.** elle est toujours la bienvenue; **w. home!** ça fait plaisir de te revoir!; **w. to Scotland!** bienvenue en Écosse!; **you're w.!** *(acknowledgement of thanks)* je vous en prie!, *Suisse* service!; **you're w. to borrow it** n'hésite pas à l'emprunter si tu veux

2 *vt* *(person)* souhaiter la bienvenue à; *(news, change)* accueillir favorablement; *(opportunity)* profiter de

3 *n* accueil *m*; **to give sb a warm w.** faire un accueil chaleureux à qn

welcoming ['welkəmɪŋ] *adj* accueillant(e)

weld [weld] **1** *n* soudure *f*

2 *vt* souder

welder ['weldə(r)] *n* soudeur(euse) *m,f*

welding ['weldɪŋ] *n* soudure *f*

welfare ['welfeə(r)] *n* (**a**) *(wellbeing)* bien-être *m*; *Br* **the W. State** l'État *m* providence; **w. work** assistance *f* sociale (**b**) *Am (social security)* **to be on w.** recevoir l'aide sociale

we'll [wiːl] = **we will, we shall**

well¹ [wel] *n (for water, oil)* puits *m*; *(for lift, stairwell)* cage *f*

▶**well up** *vi (of tears)* monter

well² *(comparative* **better** ['betə(r)], *superlative* **best** [best]) **1** *adj* bien; **to be w.** aller bien; **to get w.** se remettre; **it's just as w....** heureusement que...; **that's all very w., but...** tout ça, c'est très bien, mais...; **it's all very w. for you to say that** c'est facile pour toi de dire ça

2 *adv* (**a**) *(satisfactorily)* bien; **to speak w. of sb** dire du bien de qn; **I did as w. as I could** j'ai fait de mon mieux; **w. done!** bravo!; **you would do w. to keep quiet about it** vous feriez bien de vous taire à ce sujet; **he apologized, as w. he might** il s'est excusé, et c'était bien la moindre des choses; **very w.!** *(OK)* très bien!

(**b**) *(for emphasis)* **to be w. able to do sth** être parfaitement capable de faire qch; **to be w. aware of sth** avoir parfaitement conscience de qch; **to leave w. alone** ne pas s'en mêler; *Fam* **to be w. in with sb** être dans les petits papiers de qn; **it is w. known that...** il est bien connu que...; **it's w. worth the effort** ça vaut vraiment la peine; **I can w. believe it** je n'ai aucun mal à le croire; **w. before/after** bien avant/après

(**c**) **as w.** *(also)* aussi, également; **she has a flat in town as w. as a house in the country** elle a un appartement en ville ainsi qu'une maison à la campagne

3 *exclam (expressing surprise, enquiry)* eh bien!; *(expressing resignation, qualifying previous remark)* enfin; **w., who would have believed it!** eh bien, qui l'eût cru!; **w., who was it?** eh bien, qui était-ce?; **w., if you must!** enfin, si tu es vraiment obligé!; **he's nice, w. sometimes** il est gentil, enfin quelquefois

well-adjusted [welə'dʒʌstɪd] *adj* équilibré(e)

well-advised [weləd'vaɪzd] *adj* sage; **you'd be w. to stay indoors today** tu ferais bien de ne pas sortir aujourd'hui

well-appointed [welə'pɔɪntɪd] *adj* bien équipé(e)

well-argued [wel'ɑːgjuːd] *adj* bien argumenté(e)

well-balanced [wel'bælənst] *adj* équilibré(e)

well-behaved [welbɪ'heɪvd] *adj* sage

wellbeing ['welbiːɪŋ] *n* bien-être *m*

well-built [wel'bɪlt] *adj (building)* solide; *(person)* bien bâti(e)

well-chosen [wel'tʃəʊzən] *adj* bien choisi(e)

well-disposed [weldɪs'pəʊzd] *adj* **to be w. towards sb** être bien disposé(e) envers qn; **to be w. towards sth** être favorable à qch

well-dressed [wel'drest] *adj* bien habillé(e)

well-earned [wel'ɜːnd] *adj* bien mérité(e)

well-fed [wel'fed] *adj* bien nourri(e)

well-founded [wel'faʊndɪd] *adj* fondé(e)

well-heeled [wel'hiːld] *adj Fam* cossu(e)

well-informed [welɪn'fɔːmd] *adj* bien informé(e)

wellington ['welɪŋtən] *n Br* **wellingtons, w. boots** bottes *fpl* en caoutchouc

well-intentioned [welɪn'tenʃənd] *adj* bien intentionné(e)

well-kept [wel'kept] *adj (garden)* bien entretenu(e); *(secret)* bien gardé(e)

well-known [wel'nəʊn] *adj* connu(e)

well-loved [wel'lʌvd] *adj* très aimé(e)

well-made [wel'meɪd] *adj* bien fait(e)

well-meaning [wel'miːnɪŋ] *adj* bien intentionné(e)

well-nigh ['welnaɪ] *adv* pratiquement

well-off [wel'ɒf] *adj Br (wealthy)* riche; *Fig* **you don't know when you're w.** tu ne connais pas ton bonheur

well-paid [wel'peɪd] *adj* bien payé(e)

well-read [wel'red] *adj* cultivé(e)
well-spoken [wel'spəʊkən] *adj* qui s'exprime bien
well-timed [wel'taɪmd] *adj* opportun(e)
well-to-do [weltə'du:] *adj* aisé(e)
wellwisher ['welwɪʃə(r)] *n* sympathisant(e) *m,f*
well-worn [wel'wɔːn] *adj (garment)* très usé(e); *(argument)* éculé(e)
well-written [wel'rɪtən] *adj* bien écrit(e)
Welsh [welʃ] **1** *npl (people)* **the W.** les Gallois *mpl*
  2 *n (language)* gallois *m*
  3 *adj* gallois(e); **the W. Assembly** l'Assemblée *f* galloise *ou* du pays de Galles; **W. dresser** vaisselier *m*

> **Welsh Assembly**
> L'assemblée nationale du pays de Galles fut établie dans le cadre de la décentralisation engagée par le gouvernement travailliste et fut inaugurée à Cardiff en mai 1999. Les soixante membres de l'assemblée forment le "Welsh Cabinet" et siègent sous la houlette du "First Secretary" qui représente les intérêts gallois au parlement de Westminster. L'assemblée nationale du pays de Galles, la première depuis six siècles, a toutefois moins de pouvoirs que le parlement écossais mis en place en même temps.

Welshman ['welʃmən] *n* Gallois *m*
Welshwoman ['welʃwʊmən] *n* Galloise *f*
welt [welt] *n* trace *f* de coup
welter ['weltə(r)] *n (of forms, details)* masse *f*; *(of ideas, activities)* multitude *f*
welterweight ['weltəweɪt] *n Sport* poids *m* welter
wench [wentʃ] *n Old-fashioned or Hum* jeune fille *f*, jeune femme *f*
wend [wend] *vt Lit* **to w. one's way homewards** prendre le chemin du retour
went [went] *pt of* **go**
wept [wept] *pt & pp of* **weep**
we're [wɪə(r)] = **we are**
were [wɜː(r)] *pt of* **be**
weren't [wɜːnt] = **were not**
werewolf ['wɪəwʊlf] *(pl* **werewolves** ['wɪəwʊlvz] *) n* loup-garou *m*
west [west] **1** *n* ouest *m*; **to the w. (of)** à l'ouest (de); **the W.** l'Occident *m*, l'Ouest *m*
  2 *adj (coast, side)* ouest *inv*; *(wind)* d'ouest; **W. Africa** l'Afrique *f* de l'Ouest; **the W. Bank** la Cisjordanie; **the W. Country** le sud-ouest de l'Angleterre; **the W. End** = quartier chic de Londres et Glasgow où l'on trouve théâtres et restaurants; *Formerly* **W. Germany** l'Allemagne *f* de l'Ouest; **W. Indian** antillais(e); *(person)* Antillais(e) *m,f*; **the W. Indies** les Antilles *fpl*; **the W. Side** = les quartiers ouest de NewYork; **W. Virginia** la Virginie occidentale
  3 *adv* à l'ouest; *(travel)* vers l'ouest; *Fam Fig* **to go w.** *(of TV, car)* rendre l'âme
westbound ['westbaʊnd] *adj (train, traffic)* en direction de l'ouest
westerly ['westəlɪ] **1** *n (wind)* vent *m* d'ouest
  2 *adj (point)* à l'ouest; *(wind)* d'ouest, qui vient de l'ouest; **in a w. direction** vers l'ouest
western ['westən] **1** *n (film)* western *m*; *(novel)* roman-western *m*
  2 *adj (region)* de l'ouest; *(in politics, sociology)* occidental(e); **w. France** l'ouest *m* de la France; **W. Europe** l'Europe *f* de l'Ouest; **the W. Isles** *(of Scotland)* les

Hébrides *fpl*; **W. Samoa** les Samoa *fpl* occidentales; **W. Samoan** samoan(e); *(person)* Samoan(e) *m,f*
westernized ['westənaɪzd] *adj* occidentalisé(e)
Westminster ['westmɪnstə(r)] *n* Westminster *m*

> **Westminster**
> C'est dans ce quartier que se trouvent le Parlement et le palais de Buckingham. Le nom de "Westminster" est également employé pour désigner le Parlement lui-même.

westward ['westwəd] **1** *adj (in the west)* à l'ouest, dans l'ouest
  2 *adv* = **westwards**
westwards ['westwədz] *adv (face, point)* à l'ouest; *(go, travel)* vers l'ouest
wet [wet] **1** *adj* **(a)** *(not dry)* mouillé(e); *(weather)* pluvieux(euse); **to get w.** se mouiller; **the ink/paint was still w.** l'encre/la peinture n'était pas sèche; *Fam Fig* **to be still w. behind the ears** manquer d'expérience; *Fig* **w. blanket** rabat-joie *mf*; **w. dream** pollution *f* nocturne; **w. paint** *(sign)* peinture fraîche; **w. suit** combinaison *f* de plongée **(b)** *Br Fam (feeble)* minable
  2 *vt (pt & pp* **wet** *or* **wetted**) mouiller; **to w. the bed** faire pipi au lit; **to w. oneself** mouiller sa culotte
  3 *n* **(a)** *(dampness)* humidité *f*; *(rain)* pluie *f* **(b)** *Br Pol* modéré(e) *m,f*
WEU [dʌbəljuːiˈuː] *n (abbr* **Western European Union)** UEO *f*
we've [wiːv] = **we have**
whack [wæk] *Fam* **1** *n* **(a)** *(blow)* grand coup *m*; **to give sb/sth a w.** donner un grand coup à qn/qch **(b)** *(share)* part *f*
  2 *vt* **(a)** *(hit)* donner un grand coup à; **to w. sb on** *or* **over the head** donner un grand coup sur la tête de qn **(b)** *Am very Fam (murder)* liquider
whacked [wækt] *adj Fam (exhausted)* nase, vanné(e)
whacking ['wækɪŋ] *adv Fam* **a w. great increase/fine** une vache d'augmentation/d'amende
whale [weɪl] *n* baleine *f*; *Fam* **to have a w. of a time** s'éclater
whaler ['weɪlə(r)] *n* baleinier *m*
whaling ['weɪlɪŋ] *n* pêche *f* ou chasse *f* à la baleine
wharf [wɔːf] *(pl* **wharves** [wɔːvz] *) n* quai *m*
what [wɒt] **1** *pron* **(a)** *(in questions) (subject)* qu'est-ce qui; *(object)* qu'est-ce que, que; *(after preposition)* quoi; **w.'s happening?** qu'est-ce qui se passe?; **w. do you want?** qu'est-ce que tu veux?, que veux-tu?; **w. are you thinking about?** à quoi penses-tu?; **w.'s that?** qu'est-ce que c'est?; **w.'s that to you?** qu'est-ce que ça peut vous faire?; **w. for?** *(for what purpose?)* pourquoi faire?; *(why)* pourquoi?; **w.'s a modem for?** à quoi ça sert, un modem?; **w. did he do that for?** pourquoi est-ce qu'il a fait ça?; **w.'s French for "dog?"** comment dit-on "dog" en français?; **w.'s he like?** comment est-il?; **w. about the money I lent you?** et l'argent que je vous ai prêté?; **w. about a game of tennis?** et si on faisait une partie de tennis?; **w. about me?** et moi?; **if that doesn't work, w. then?** si ça ne marche pas, qu'est-ce qui reste?; *Fam* **w. of it?** et alors?; *Fam* **are you coming or w.?** tu viens ou quoi?
  (b) *(in relative constructions) (subject)* ce qui; *(object)* ce que; **I don't know w. has happened** je ne sais pas ce qui s'est passé; **I can't remember w. you told me** je ne me souviens plus de ce que tu m'as dit; **w. is**

surprising is that... ce qu'il y a de surprenant, c'est que...; **w. I like is...** ce que j'aime, c'est...; *Fam* he knows w.'s w. il sait ce qu'il en est; *Fam* **to give sb w. for** passer un savon à qn

2 *adj* (**a**) *(in questions)* quel (quelle); *(plural)* quels (quelles); **w. time is it?** quelle heure est-il?; **tell me w. time it is** dis-moi l'heure qu'il est; **show me w. books you want** montre-moi quels livres tu veux

(**b**) *(in relative constructions)* **I'll give you w. money I have** je vais vous donner l'argent que j'ai; **he took w. little food was left** il a pris le peu de nourriture qui restait

(**c**) *(in exclamations)* **w. an idea!** quelle idée!; **w. a fool he is!** qu'il est bête!; **w. a lot of people!** quel monde!

3 *exclam* quoi?; **w. next!** et quoi encore!

what-d'ye-call-her ['wɒtjəkɔːlə(r)] *n Fam (person)* Machine *f*

what-d'ye-call-him ['wɒtjəkɔːlɪm] *n Fam (person)* Machin *m*

what-d'ye-call-it ['wɒtjəkɔːlɪt] *n Fam (thing)* machin *m*, truc *m*

whatever [wɒt'evə(r)] **1** *pron* (**a**) *(no matter what)* quoi que + *subjunctive*; **w. it is, w. it may be** quoi que ce soit; **w. happens** quoi qu'il arrive (**b**) *(anything)* ce que; **do w. you like** fais ce que tu veux; **give him w. he wants** donne-lui tout ce qu'il veut; **w. you say** comme tu voudras (**c**) *(in questions)* **w. does that mean?** qu'est-ce que ça peut bien vouloir dire?

2 *adj* (**a**) *(no matter what)* **take w. food you want** prends toute la nourriture que tu veux; **pay w. price they ask** donne-leur le prix qu'ils en demandent, quel qu'il soit (**b**) *(emphatic)* **for no reason w.** sans aucune raison; **nothing w.** absolument rien

what's-her-name ['wɒtsəneɪm], **what's-his-name** ['wɒtsɪzneɪm], **what's-its-name** ['wɒtsɪtsneɪm] = **what-d'ye-call-her/him/it**

whatsit ['wɒtsɪt] *n Fam* machin *m*, truc *m*

whatsoever [wɒtsəʊ'evə(r)] *adj* **for no reason w.** sans aucune raison; **none w.** aucun(e); **nothing w.** absolument rien

wheat [wiːt] *n* blé *m*; **w. germ** germe *m* de blé

wheaten ['wiːtən] *adj (loaf, roll)* de blé *ou* froment

wheatfield ['wiːtfiːld] *n* champ *m* de blé

wheedle ['wiːdəl] *vt* **to w. sth out of sb** soutirer qch à qn par des cajoleries; **to w. sb into doing sth** amadouer qn pour qu'il/elle fasse qch

wheel [wiːl] **1** *n* (**a**) *(on car, bike, pram)* roue *f*; *(on trolley, suitcase)* roulette *f* (**b**) *(steering wheel)* volant *m*; **to be at the w.** être au volant

2 *vt (push)* pousser

3 *vi (turn)* **to w. (about** *or* **around)** *(of person)* se retourner brusquement; *(of plane)* tourner; *(of bird)* tournoyer

wheelbarrow ['wiːlbærəʊ] *n* brouette *f*

wheelbase ['wiːlbeɪs] *n* empattement *m*

wheelchair ['wiːltʃeə(r)] *n* fauteuil *m* roulant

-wheeled [wiːld] *suff* **two/three/four-w.** à deux/trois/quatre roues

wheelie bin ['wiːlɪ'bɪn] *n Br* poubelle *f (avec des roues)*

wheeling and dealing ['wiːlɪŋəndiːlɪŋ] *n* tractations *fpl*

wheeze [wiːz] **1** *n* (**a**) *(noise)* respiration *f* sifflante (**b**) *Fam (trick)* astuce *f*, combine *f*

2 *vi (breathe heavily)* respirer péniblement

whelk [welk] *n* bulot *m*

whelp [welp] *n* petit *m*

when [wen] **1** *adv (in questions)* quand; **w. will you come?** quand viendras-tu?; **tell me w. it happened** dis-moi quand cela s'est produit; *Fam* **say w.!** *(when pouring drink)* tu me dis stop!

2 *conj* (**a**) *(with time)* quand, lorsque; **w. I came into the room** quand *ou* lorsque je suis entré dans la pièce; **tell me w. you've finished** dis-moi quand tu auras terminé; **what's the good of talking w. you never listen?** à quoi sert de parler puisque tu n'écoutes jamais? (**b**) *(whereas)* alors que

whence [wens] *adv Lit* d'où

whenever [wen'evə(r)] **1** *conj* (**a**) *(every time that)* chaque fois que; **I go w. I can** j'y vais aussi souvent que je peux (**b**) *(no matter when)* n'importe quand; **come w. you like** viens quand tu veux

2 *adv* (**a**) *(referring to unspecified time)* n'importe quand; **Sunday, Monday or w.** dimanche, lundi ou n'importe quel autre jour (**b**) *(in questions)* **w. did you do that?** quand est-ce que tu as fait ça?

where [weə(r)] **1** *adv (in questions)* où; **w. are you going?** où vas-tu?; **w. does he come from?** d'où vient-il?; **tell me w. she is** dis-moi où elle est; **w. would we be if...?** que serions-nous devenus si...?

2 *conj* où; **I'll stay w. I am** je reste (là) où je suis; **that's w. he lives** c'est là qu'il habite; **that is w. you are mistaken** c'est là que vous vous trompez; **they went to Paris, w. they stayed a week** ils sont allés à Paris, où ils ont séjourné une semaine

whereabouts 1 *npl* ['weərəbaʊts] **nobody knows her w., her w. are unknown** personne ne sait où elle est

2 *adv* [weərə'baʊts] *(where)* où

whereas [weə'ræz] *conj* alors que, tandis que

whereby [weə'baɪ] *adv Formal* par lequel (laquelle)

whereupon [weərə'pɒn] *conj Lit* sur quoi

wherever [weə'revə(r)] **1** *conj* (**a**) *(everywhere that)* où que; **I see him w. I go** où que j'aille, je le vois; **w. possible** partout où cela est possible (**b**) *(no matter where)* n'importe où; **we'll go w. you want** nous irons où tu voudras

2 *adv* (**a**) *(referring to unknown or unspecified place)* **at home, in the office or w.** chez soi, au bureau ou n'importe où; **it's in Coatbridge, w. that is** c'est à Coatbridge, mais je ne sais pas où se trouve Coatbridge (**b**) *(in questions)* **w. can he be?** où peut-elle bien être?

wherewithal ['weərwɪðɔːl] *n* **to have the w. (to do sth)** avoir les moyens (de faire qch)

whet [wet] *(pt & pp* **whetted)** *vt (tool, blade, appetite)* aiguiser

whether ['weðə(r)] *conj* (**a**) *(with indirect questions)* si; **I don't know w. it's true** je ne sais pas si c'est vrai (**b**) *(conditional)* **w. she comes or not we shall leave** qu'elle vienne ou non, nous partirons

whew [hjuː] *exclam (of relief)* ouf!; *(of fatigue)* pff!; *(of astonishment)* dis donc!

whey [weɪ] *n* petit-lait *m*

which [wɪtʃ] **1** *pron* (**a**) *(in questions)* lequel (laquelle) *m,f*, *(plural)* lesquels (lesquelles) *mpl,fpl*; **w. (one) is better?** lequel est le meilleur?; **w. of you is going?** qui d'entre vous y va?; **I can never remember w. is w.** je ne me rappelle jamais la différence

(**b**) *(relative)* *(subject)* qui; *(object)* que; **the house w. is for sale** la maison qui est à vendre; **the film w. I saw last week** le film que j'ai vu la semaine dernière (**c**) *(referring back to whole clause) (subject)* ce qui; *(object)* ce que; **he's getting married, w. surprises me** il va se marier, ce qui m'étonne; **she was back in London, w. I didn't know** elle était de retour à Londres, ce que je ne savais pas

(**d**) *(with prepositions)* **behind/in front of w.** derrière/devant lequel (laquelle); **beside/above w.** à côté/au-dessus duquel (de laquelle); **the countries w. we are going to** les pays où nous allons; **the town w. we live in** la ville où nous habitons; **after w. he went out** après quoi, il est sorti

2 *adj* (**a**) *(in questions)* quel (quelle); *(plural)* quels (quelles); **w. colour do you like best?** quelle couleur préférez-vous?; **w. way do we go?** de quel côté allons-nous?; **w. one?** lequel (laquelle)?; **w. ones?** lesquels (lesquelles)?

(**b**) *(in relative constructions)* **I was there for a week, during w. time...** j'y suis resté une semaine, période pendant laquelle...; **she came at noon, by w. time I had left** elle est arrivée à midi, heure à laquelle j'étais déjà parti

whichever [wɪtʃ'evə(r)] **1** *pron* (**a**) *(no matter which)* quel (quelle) que soit celui (celle) qui; **w. you choose, I'm sure she'll like it** quel que soit celui que tu choisisses, je suis sûr que ça lui plaira (**b**) *(any)* **take w. you want** prends celui (celle) que tu voudras (**c**) *(according to which)* **come on Saturday or Sunday, w. suits you** viens samedi ou dimanche, suivant ce qui t'arrange

2 *adj (no matter which)* **take w. book you like best** choisis le livre que tu préfères

whiff [wɪf] *n* odeur *f*; **to catch a w. of sth** sentir qch; *Fig* **a w. of scandal** un parfum de scandale

while [waɪl] **1** *n* (**a**) *(time)* **a w.** un moment; **after/in a w.** après/dans un moment; **a short** *or* **little w. ago** il y a un petit moment; **a good w., quite a w.** un bon moment; **a long w.** longtemps; **once in a w.** de temps en temps

(**b**) **it's not worth my w.** ça n'en vaut pas la peine; **it's not worth my w. going** ça ne vaut pas la peine que j'y aille; **I'll make it worth your w.** vous serez récompensé de votre peine

2 *conj* (**a**) *(during the time that)* pendant que; **w. reading I fell asleep** je me suis endormi en lisant (**b**) *(as long as)* tant que; **it won't happen w. I'm in charge!** ça ne se produira pas tant que ce sera moi le responsable!

(**c**) *(although)* bien que + *subjunctive*; **w. I admit it's difficult,...** bien que j'admette que ce soit difficile...

(**d**) *(whereas)* alors que; **one wore white, w. the other was in black** l'un portait du blanc, alors que l'autre était en noir

▶**while away** *vt sep* **to w. away the time** passer le temps

whilst [waɪlst] *conj Br* = **while²**

whim [wɪm] *n* lubie *f*, fantaisie *f*; **to do sth on a w.** faire qch sur un coup de tête

whimper ['wɪmpə(r)] **1** *n* gémissement *m*, geignement *m*; *Fig* **without a w.** sans broncher
2 *vi* gémir, geindre

whimsical ['wɪmzɪkəl] *adj (person, behaviour)* fantasque; *(remark, story)* saugrenu(e)

whine [waɪn] **1** *n (of person, animal)* gémissement *m*; *(of machine)* grincement *m*
2 *vi also Fig* gémir (**about** à propos de)

whinge [wɪndʒ] *vi Br & Austr Fam* pleurnicher

whinger ['wɪndʒə(r)] *n Br & Austr Fam* râleur(euse) *m,f*

whinny ['wɪnɪ] **1** *n* hennissement *m*
2 *vi* hennir

whip [wɪp] **1** *n* (**a**) *(for punishment)* fouet *m* (**b**) *Pol* chef *m* de file *(chargé de la discipline de son parti)*

2 *vt (pt & pp* **whipped)** (**a**) *(beat with whip)* fouetter; **whipped cream** crème *f* fouettée; *Fig* **she whipped the crowd into a frenzy** son discours rendit la foule frénétique (**b**) *(defeat)* battre à plates coutures (**c**) *Fam (steal)* faucher

▶**whip off** *vt sep Fam (clothes)* ôter rapidement
▶**whip out** *vt sep Fam* sortir soudainement
▶**whip round** *vi Fam (turn quickly)* se retourner brusquement
▶**whip up** *vt sep* (**a**) *(support, enthusiasm)* susciter; *(audience)* galvaniser (**b**) *(prepare quickly) (dish, meal)* préparer vite fait

whiplash ['wɪplæʃ] *n* lésion *f* des cervicales
whippersnapper ['wɪpəsnæpə(r)] *n Fam* garnement *m*
whippet ['wɪpɪt] *n* whippet *m*
whipround ['wɪpraʊnd] *n Br Fam* **to have a w. (for sb)** organiser une collecte (pour qn)
whirl [wɜːl] **1** *n also Fig* tourbillon *m*; **the social w.** le tourbillon de la vie mondaine; *Fam* **let's give it a w.** on va tenter le coup
2 *vt* **to w. sb/sth around** faire tournoyer qn/qch
3 *vi* tourbillonner; **my head's whirling** j'ai la tête qui tourne

▶**whirl along** *vi (of car, train)* filer à toute vitesse
▶**whirl round** *vi* se retourner brusquement

whirlpool ['wɜːlpuːl] *n* tourbillon *m*; **w. bath** bain *m* à remous
whirlwind ['wɜːlwɪnd] *n* tourbillon *m*; **w. romance** passion *f* enivrante; **w. tour** visite *f* éclair
whirr [wɜː(r)] **1** *n* ronflement *m*
2 *vi* ronfler
whisk [wɪsk] **1** *n* batteur *m*, fouet *m*
2 *vt* (**a**) *(eggs)* battre (**b**) *(move quickly)* **to w. sb into hospital** transporter qn d'urgence à l'hôpital
3 *vi (move quickly)* **she whisked past me** elle est passée devant moi comme un éclair

▶**whisk away, whisk off** *vt sep (person)* emmener rapidement; *(object)* enlever rapidement

whisker ['wɪskə(r)] *n* **whiskers** *(of cat, mouse)* moustaches *fpl*; *(of man)* favoris *mpl*; *Fam* **to win by a w.** gagner de justesse
whisky, *Am & Ir* **whiskey** ['wɪskɪ] *n* whisky *m*
whisper ['wɪspə(r)] **1** *n* chuchotement *m*; **to speak in a w.** chuchoter
2 *vt* chuchoter; **to w. sth to sb** chuchoter qch à qn; **it's being whispered that...** le bruit court que...
3 *vi* chuchoter; **to w. to sb** chuchoter à l'oreille de qn
whist [wɪst] *n* whist *m*
whistle ['wɪsəl] **1** *n* (**a**) *(noise)* sifflement *m* (**b**) *(musical instrument)* flageolet *m*; *(of referee, policeman)* sifflet *m*
2 *vt (tune)* siffler
3 *vi* siffler; *Fam* **he can w. for his money** s'il compte récupérer son argent, il peut toujours courir
whistle-stop tour ['wɪsəlstɒp'tʊə(r)] *n* tournée *f* rapide
Whit [wɪt] *n* Pentecôte *f*; **W. Sunday** la Pentecôte

whit [wɪt] *n* **it doesn't matter a w.** ça n'a aucune importance; **it won't make a w. of difference** ça ne changera absolument rien

white [waɪt] **1** *n* (**a**) *(colour, of egg, eye)* blanc *m*; **w. doesn't suit her** le blanc ne lui va pas (**b**) *(person)* Blanc (Blanche) *m,f*

2 *adj* blanc (blanche); **a w. man** un Blanc; **a w. woman** une Blanche; **to turn** *or* **go w.** *(person)* devenir blême; *(object, hair)* blanchir; **w. with fear** vert(e) de peur; **w. as a ghost/sheet** pâle comme la mort/un linge; *Biol* **w. blood cell** globule *m* blanc; **w. chocolate** chocolat *m* blanc; **w. coffee** café *m* au lait; *Fig* **w. elephant** = chose coûteuse et peu rentable; **w. fish** poisson *m* à chair blanche; **w. flag** drapeau *m* blanc; **w. flour** farine *f* blanche; **the W. House** la Maison-Blanche; **w. lie** pieux mensonge *m*; **w. meat** viande *f* blanche; *Am* **W. Out**® correcteur *m* liquide; *Pol* **w. paper** livre *m* blanc; **w. sauce** sauce *f* blanche; **w. spirit** white-spirit *m*; **w. stick** canne *f* blanche; **w. supremacist** partisan(e) *m,f* de la suprématie blanche; **w. tie** *(formal dress)* tenue *f* de soirée; *Am Pej* **w. trash** pauvres blancs *mpl*; **w. wedding** mariage *m* en blanc

whitebait ['waɪtbeɪt] *n* friture *f*

white-collar worker ['waɪt'kɒlə'wɜːkə(r)] *n* col *m* blanc

white-haired ['waɪt'heəd] *adj* aux cheveux blancs

Whitehall ['waɪthɔːl] *n* = rue de Londres où se trouvent les ministères

> **Whitehall**
> De nombreux services gouvernementaux ont leurs bureaux dans cette rue londonienne dont le nom est souvent employé pour désigner le gouvernement lui-même.

white-hot ['waɪt'hɒt] *adj* chauffé(e) à blanc

whiteness ['waɪtnɪs] *n* blancheur *f*

whitewash ['waɪtwɒʃ] **1** *n* *(paint)* badigeon *m* à la chaux; *Fig (cover-up)* blanchiment *m*

2 *vt* *(paint)* badigeonner à la chaux; *Fig (cover up)* blanchir

whitewater rafting ['waɪtwɔːtə'rɑːftɪŋ] *n* descente *f* en eau vive, rafting *m*

whither ['wɪðə(r)] *adv Lit* **w. Britain/education?** où va la Grande-Bretagne/l'enseignement?

whiting ['waɪtɪŋ] *n (fish)* merlan *m*

whitish ['waɪtɪʃ] *adj* blanchâtre

Whitsun ['wɪtsən] *n* Pentecôte *f*

whittle ['wɪtəl] *vt* tailler (au couteau); *Fig* **to w. sth down** réduire qch

▸**whittle away** *vt sep Fig* **to w. sth away** réduire qch à presque rien

whizz [wɪz] **1** *n Fam (expert)* crack *m*; **w. kid** jeune prodige *m*

2 *vi (of bullet)* siffler; *(of person, car)* passer à toute vitesse; **to w. through a book/meal** lire un livre/manger à toute vitesse

WHO [dʌbəljuːeɪtʃ'əʊ] *n (abbr* **World Health Organization)** OMS *f*

who [huː] *pron* (**a**) *(in questions)* qui; **w. is it?** qui est-ce?; **w. with?** avec qui?; **do you know w. she is?** sais-tu qui elle est?; **w.'s speaking?** *(on phone)* qui est à l'appareil?; **w. did you say was there?** qui était là, déjà?; **w. does he think he is?** pour qui se prend-il?

(**b**) *(relative)* qui; **the people w. came yesterday** les gens qui sont venus hier; **those w. have already paid can leave** ceux qui ont déjà payé peuvent s'en aller; **Louise's father, w. is a doctor, was there** le père de Louise, qui est médecin, était là

whodun(n)it [huː'dʌnɪt] *n Fam* polar *m*

whoever [huː'evə(r)] *pron* (**a**) *(no matter who)* qui que + *subjunctive*; **w. you are** qui que vous soyez; **w. wrote that letter** la personne qui a écrit cette lettre; *Fam* **ask Simon or Cris or w.** demande à Simon ou à Cris ou à n'importe qui d'autre (**b**) *(anyone that)* celui (celle) qui; **w. finds it may keep it** celui qui le trouvera pourra le garder (**c**) *(in questions)* **w. can that be?** qui cela peut-il être?

whole [həʊl] **1** *adj* (**a**) *(entire, intact)* entier(ère); **the w. truth** toute la vérité; **the w. world** le monde entier; **a w. week** toute une semaine, une semaine entière; **to swallow sth w.** avaler qch sans le mâcher; *Fig* avaler qch; **w. milk** lait *m* entier (**b**) *Fam (for emphasis)* **a w. lot of** tout un tas de; **the w. lot of you** vous tous

2 *n* totalité *f*, ensemble *m*; **the w. of the village/the money** tout le village/l'argent; **as a w.** dans sa totalité; **on the w.** dans l'ensemble

wholefood ['həʊlfuːd] *n Br* aliments *mpl* complets; **w. restaurant** restaurant *m* bio

wholehearted [həʊl'hɑːtɪd] *adj* sans réserve, total(e)

wholemeal ['həʊlmiːl] *adj Br* **w. bread** pain *m* complet; **w. flour** farine *f* complète

wholesale ['həʊlseɪl] **1** *adj* de gros; *Fig (large-scale)* à grande échelle

2 *adv* en gros; *Fig (on a large scale)* à grande échelle

3 *n* (vente *f* en) gros *m*

wholesaler ['həʊlseɪlə(r)] *n* grossiste *mf*

wholesome ['həʊlsəm] *adj (food, entertainment)* sain(e); *(air, climate)* salubre; *(person)* comme il faut

wholly ['həʊllɪ] *adv* entièrement

whom [huːm] *pron Formal* (**a**) *(in questions)* qui; **w. did you see?** qui avez-vous vu?; **for/to/of w.?** pour/à/de qui? (**b**) *(relative)* que; **the woman w. you saw** la femme que vous avez vue; **the man w. you gave the money to** l'homme à qui vous avez donné l'argent; **the person of w. we were speaking** la personne dont nous parlions; **the men, both of w. were quite young,...** les hommes, tous deux assez jeunes...

whoop [wuːp] **1** *n* cri *m* de joie

2 *vi* crier de joie

whoopee 1 *n* ['wʊpiː] *Fam* **to make w.** *(have fun)* faire la bombe; *(have sex)* faire crac-crac

2 *exclam* [wʊ'piː] youpi!

whooping cough ['huːpɪŋ'kɒf] *n* coqueluche *f*

whoops [wʊps] *exclam* houp-là!

whopper ['wɒpə(r)] *n Fam* (**a**) *(huge thing)* truc *m* énorme (**b**) *(lie)* gros bobard *m*

whopping ['wɒpɪŋ] *adj Fam* **w. (great)** énorme

whore [hɔː(r)] *n very Fam* putain *f*

whorehouse ['hɔːhaʊs] *n* bordel *m*

whose [huːz] **1** *possessive pron (in questions)* à qui; **w. are these gloves?** à qui sont ces gants?; **w. is this?** à qui est-ce?; **tell me w. they are** dis-moi à qui ils sont

2 *possessive adj* (**a**) *(in questions)* à qui; **w. gloves are these?** à qui sont ces gants?; **w. daughter are you?** de qui es-tu la fille? (**b**) *(relative)* dont; **the pupil w. work I showed you** l'élève dont je t'ai montré le travail; **the man to w. wife I gave the money** l'homme à la femme de qui j'ai donné l'argent

why [waɪ] **1** *adv* (**a**) *(in questions)* pourquoi; **w. didn't you say so?** pourquoi ne l'as-tu pas dit?; **w. get**

angry? pourquoi se mettre en colère?; **w. not?** pourquoi pas? (**b**) *(in suggestions)* **w. don't you phone him?** pourquoi ne lui téléphones-tu pas?; **w. don't I come with you?** pourquoi est-ce que je ne viendrais pas avec toi?; **w. not sell the car?** pourquoi ne pas vendre la voiture?

2 *conj* pourquoi; **I'll tell you w. I don't like her** je vais vous dire pourquoi je ne l'aime pas; **that's w....** voilà pourquoi...; **the reason w....** la raison pour laquelle...

3 *n* **the whys and wherefores (of sth)** le pourquoi et le comment (de qch)

4 *exclam* **w., it's David!** mais voilà David!

WI [dʌblju:'aɪ] *n Br (abbr* **Women's Institute)** = association de femmes en milieu rural qui organise diverses activités

wick [wɪk] *n* (**a**) *(of lamp, candle)* mèche *f* (**b**) *Br Fam* **to get on sb's w.** taper sur les nerfs à qn

wicked ['wɪkɪd] *adj* (**a**) *(evil)* méchant(e); *Fig (dreadful)* affreux(euse) (**b**) *Fam (excellent)* génial(e)

wickedness ['wɪkɪdnɪs] *n* méchanceté *f*

wicker ['wɪkə(r)] *n* osier *m*

wickerwork ['wɪkəwɜːk] *n* vannerie *f*

wicket ['wɪkɪt] *n (in cricket)* guichet *m*

wicketkeeper ['wɪkɪtkiːpə(r)] *n (in cricket)* gardien *m* de guichet

wide [waɪd] **1** *adj* (**a**) *(broad)* large; **to be 100 metres w.** faire 100 mètres de large; **in the whole w. world** dans le monde entier; *Br Fam Pej* **w. boy** escroc *m*; *Cin* **w. screen** écran *m* panoramique (**b**) *(extensive)* vaste

2 *adv* **w. open** *(eyes, mouth, door)* grand ouvert(e); **to be w. open to criticism** prêter le flanc à la critique; **w. apart** très espacé(e); *(legs)* très écarté(e); **w. awake** complètement réveillé(e); **the shot went w.** la balle est passée à côté; *Fig* **w. of the mark** loin de la vérité

wide-angle ['waɪdæŋɡəl] *adj* grand angle *inv*

wide-eyed ['waɪdaɪd] *adj* aux yeux écarquillés

widely ['waɪdlɪ] *adv* (**a**) *(extensively)* largement; **it is w. believed that...** beaucoup de gens pensent que...; **w. known** connu(e) de tout le monde (**b**) *(at a distance)* **w. spaced** très espacé(e)

widen ['waɪdən] **1** *vt* agrandir; *(garment)* élargir; *Fig (influence, scope)* étendre; **to w. one's horizons** élargir son horizon

2 *vi* s'élargir; *(of gap, eyes)* s'agrandir

▸**widen out** *vi* s'élargir

widespread ['waɪdspred] *adj* répandu(e)

widow ['wɪdəʊ] **1** *n* veuve *f*; **w.'s pension** allocation *f* veuvage

2 *vt* **to be widowed** devenir veuf (veuve)

widowed ['wɪdəʊd] *adj* veuf (veuve)

widower ['wɪdəʊə(r)] *n* veuf *m*

width [wɪdθ] *n* largeur *f*

wield [wiːld] *vt* (**a**) *(sword, pen)* manier (**b**) *(power, influence)* exercer

wife [waɪf] *(pl* **wives** [waɪvz] *) n* femme *f*, épouse *f*

wifely ['waɪflɪ] *adj* de bonne épouse

wig [wɪɡ] *n* perruque *f*

wiggle ['wɪɡəl] **1** *n* trémoussement *m*

2 *vt* remuer

3 *vi* se trémousser

wiggly ['wɪɡlɪ] *adj Fam (line)* ondulé(e)

wigwam ['wɪɡwæm] *n* wigwam *m*

wild [waɪld] **1** *adj* (**a**) *(not domesticated) (animal, flower, countryside)* sauvage; *Fig* **it was a w. goose chase** ça n'a rien donné; *Fam* **w. horses wouldn't drag it**

out of me rien au monde ne me le ferait dire; *Fig* **to sow one's w. oats** jeter sa gourme; **the W. West** le Far West

(**b**) *(unrestrained) (wind)* violent(e); *(weather)* très mauvais(e); *(hair)* en bataille; *(child)* turbulent(e); *(enthusiasm)* délirant(e); *(promise, rumour)* insensé(e); **w. eyes** regard *m* fou; **to be w.** *(person)* mener une vie agitée; **to drive sb w.** rendre qn fou (folle)

(**c**) *(random)* **it was just a w. guess** j'ai dit ça au hasard; *Comput & Fig* **w. card** joker *m*

(**d**) *Fam (enthusiastic)* **to be w. about sb/sth** être dingue de qn/qch

(**e**) *Fam (excellent)* génial(e)

2 *adv* **to grow w.** *(of plant)* pousser à l'état sauvage; **to run w.** être livré(e) à soi-même; **the audience went w.** le public s'est déchaîné

3 *n* **in the w.** à l'état sauvage; **in the wilds** en pleine brousse

wildcat ['waɪldkæt] *n* chat *m* sauvage; *Ind* **w. strike** grève *f* sauvage

wilderness ['wɪldənɪs] *n* région *f* sauvage; *Fig (overgrown garden)* jungle *f*; *Fig* **to be in the w.** être en pleine traversée du désert

wildfire ['waɪldfaɪə(r)] *n* **to spread like w.** se répandre comme une traînée de poudre

wildfowl ['waɪldfaʊl] *(pl* **wildfowl)** *n* gibier *m* d'eau

wildlife ['waɪldlaɪf] *n* nature *f*; **w. programme** *(on TV)* émission *f* sur les animaux

wildly ['waɪldlɪ] *adv* (**a**) *(cheer, applaud)* frénétiquement; **to rush about w.** courir dans tous les sens (**b**) *(guess)* au hasard (**c**) *(for emphasis)* extrêmement; *(inaccurate, exaggerated)* complètement

wildness ['waɪldnɪs] *n (of countryside, animal)* état *m* sauvage; *(of wind, waves)* fureur *f*; *(of applause)* frénésie *f*; *(of ideas, words)* extravagance *f*

wilful ['wɪlfʊl] *adj* (**a**) *(stubborn)* têtu(e) (**b**) *(deliberate)* délibéré(e); *Law* **w. murder** homicide *m* volontaire

wilfully ['wɪlfəlɪ] *adv* (**a**) *(stubbornly)* avec entêtement (**b**) *(deliberately)* délibérément

will¹ [wɪl] **1** *n* (**a**) *(resolve, determination)* volonté *f* (**to do** de faire); **at w.** à volonté; *(cry)* à la demande; *(fire)* au hasard; *Mil* **fire at w.!** feu à volonté; **to show good w.** faire preuve de bonne volonté; **with the best w. in the world** avec la meilleure volonté du monde; *Prov* **where there's a w. there's a way** vouloir, c'est pouvoir (**b**) *(document)* testament *m*; **the last w. and testament of...** les dernières volontés de...; **to make one's w.** faire son testament

2 *vt* (**a**) **to w. sb to do sth** souhaiter ardemment que qn fasse qch; **to w. oneself to do sth** faire un effort de volonté pour faire qch (**b**) *(leave in one's will)* **to w. sth to sb** léguer qch à qn par testament

will²

On trouve généralement **I/you/he/***etc* **will** sous leurs formes contractées **I'll/you'll/he'll/***etc.* La forme négative correspondante est **won't**, que l'on écrira **will not** dans des contextes formels.

modal aux v (**a**) *(expressing future tense)* **I'll do it tomorrow** je le ferai demain; **it won't take long** ça ne prendra pas longtemps; **when w. he be coming?** quand viendra-t-il?; **I'll have finished by five** j'aurai fini avant cinq heures; **w. you be there? – yes I w./ no I won't** tu seras là? – oui/non; **you'll write to me, won't you?** tu m'écriras, n'est-ce pas?

(**b**) *(expressing wish, determination)* **I won't allow**

it! je ne le permettrai pas!; **w. you help me?** tu veux bien m'aider?; **she won't let me see him** elle refuse que je le voie; **won't you sit down?** vous ne voulez pas vous asseoir?; **be quiet, w. you!** tais-toi, s'il te plaît!; **if she WILL insist on doing everything herself...** si elle continue à tout vouloir faire ellemême...; **WILL you go away!** va-t'en, je te dis!; **it won't open** ça ne s'ouvre pas

  (**c**) *(expressing general truth)* **these things w. happen** ça arrive parfois; **the restaurant w. seat a hundred people** le restaurant peut accueillir cent personnes

  (**d**) *(expressing conjecture)* **you'll be tired** vous devez être fatigué; **they'll be home by now** ils ont dû arriver chez eux maintenant

William ['wɪlɪəm] *n* **W. the Conqueror** Guillaume le Conquérant

willie ['wɪlɪ] *n Br Fam (penis)* zizi *m*

willies ['wɪlɪz] *npl Fam* **to have the w.** avoir la trouille; **to give sb the w.** flanquer la trouille à qn

willing ['wɪlɪŋ] *adj (assistant, participant)* plein(e) de bonne volonté; **he was a w. accomplice** c'est de son plein gré qu'il est devenu complice; **to be w. to do sth** bien vouloir faire qch; **to show w.** faire preuve de bonne volonté

willingly ['wɪlɪŋlɪ] *adv (voluntarily)* de son plein gré; *(with pleasure)* volontiers

willingness ['wɪlɪŋnɪs] *n* bonne volonté *f*

will-o'-the-wisp [wɪləðə'wɪsp] *n also Fig* feu *m* follet

willow ['wɪləʊ] *n* **w. (tree)** saule *m*

willowy ['wɪləʊɪ] *adj (person, figure)* élancé(e)

willpower ['wɪlpaʊə(r)] *n* volonté *f*

willy ['wɪlɪ] *n Br Fam (penis)* zizi *m*

willy-nilly ['wɪlɪ'nɪlɪ] *adv* bon gré, mal gré

wilt [wɪlt] *vi (of plant)* se flétrir; *Fig (of person)* fatiguer

wily ['waɪlɪ] *adj* rusé(e)

wimp [wɪmp] *n Fam* mauviette *f*

wimpish ['wɪmpɪʃ] *adj Fam* mauviette

win [wɪn] **1** *n* victoire *f*

  2 *vt (pt & pp won* [wʌn]*)* (**a**) *(battle, race, prize)* gagner; **to w. an argument** avoir le dernier mot; *Fam* **you can't w. them all, you w. some you lose some** on ne peut pas toujours être gagnant (**b**) *(popularity, recognition)* acquérir; *(confidence, love)* gagner (**c**) *(parliamentary seat, election)* remporter

  3 *vi* gagner; *Fam* **you can't w.** j'aurai/tu auras/*etc* toujours tort; **OK, you w.!** bon, d'accord!

▸**win back** *vt sep* reconquérir

▸**win out** *vi* triompher

▸**win over, win round** *vt sep* persuader

▸**win through** *vi* réussir

wince [wɪns] **1** *n* grimace *f*

  2 *vi* **to w. (with pain/embarrassment)** grimacer de douleur/d'embarras

winch [wɪntʃ] **1** *n* treuil *m*

  2 *vt* hisser

wind¹ [wɪnd] **1** *n* (**a**) *(air current)* vent *m*; **to sail into** *or* **against the w.** naviguer vent debout; *Fig* **to sail close to the w.** *(take risks)* jouer avec le feu; *(be risqué)* friser l'indécence; **w. energy** *or* **power** énergie *f* éolienne; **w. instrument** instrument *m* à vent; **w. pump, w. turbine** aéolienne *f*; **w. tunnel** soufflerie *f*

  (**b**) *(breath)* souffle *m*; **let me get my w. back** laissemoi reprendre mon souffle

  (**c**) *(abdominal)* gaz *m*, vent *m*; **to have w.** avoir des gaz; **to break w.** lâcher un vent

  (**d**) *(idioms) Fam* **to put the w. up sb** faire une peur bleue à qn; **to take the w. out of sb's sails** couper l'herbe sous le pied à qn; **to get w. of sth** avoir vent de qch; **to be scattered to the four winds** être éparpillés aux quatre vents

  2 *vt* **to w. sb** *(with punch)* couper la respiration à qn

wind² [waɪnd] *(pt & pp* **wound** [waʊnd]*)* **1** *vt* (**a**) *(thread, string)* enrouler (**round** autour de) (**b**) *(handle)* tourner; *(clock, watch)* remonter; **to w. a cassette on/back** faire avancer/rembobiner une cassette

  2 *vi (of path, river)* serpenter

▸**wind down 1** *vt sep* (**a**) *(car window)* baisser (**b**) *(reduce) (production)* réduire progressivement; *(company)* fermer progressivement

  2 *vi (of party)* se calmer; *(of meeting)* tirer à sa fin; *Fam (of person)* se détendre, décompresser

▸**wind up 1** *vt sep* (**a**) *(car window)* remonter (**b**) *(finish) (speech, meeting)* terminer (**c**) *Fam (tease)* faire marcher; *(annoy)* mettre en boîte

  2 *vi* (**a**) *(end speech, meeting)* terminer (**b**) *Fam (end up)* finir; **to w. up doing sth** finir par faire qch; **she'll w. up in prison** elle va finir en prison

windbag ['wɪndbæg] *n Fam Pej* moulin *m* à paroles

windbreak ['wɪndbreɪk] *n* brise-vent *m inv*

windcheater ['wɪndtʃiːtə(r)] *n (jacket)* coupe-vent *m inv*

windchill factor ['wɪndtʃɪlfæktə(r)] *n* = abaissement de la température dû au vent

winder ['waɪndə(r)] *n (on watch)* remontoir *m*; *(on car door)* lève-glace *m inv*

windfall ['wɪndfɔːl] *n (fruit)* fruit *m* abattu par le vent; *Fig (money)* aubaine *f*; *Fin* **w. profits** *(of company)* bénéfices *mpl* exceptionnels; **w. tax** impôt *m* sur les bénéfices exceptionnels

winding ['waɪndɪŋ] *adj (path, stream)* sinueux(euse); *(staircase)* en colimaçon

windmill ['wɪndmɪl] *n* moulin *m* à vent

window ['wɪndəʊ] *n* (**a**) *(of house)* & *Comput* fenêtre *f*; *(of vehicle)* vitre *f*, glace *f*; *(of shop)* vitrine *f*; **w. box** jardinière *f*; **w. cleaner** laveur(euse) *m,f* de carreaux; **w. display** étalage *m*; **w. frame** châssis *m*; **w. ledge** rebord *m* de fenêtre; **w. seat** *(in vehicle, plane)* place *f* côté fenêtre (**b**) *(idioms)* **to provide a w. on sth** procurer une ouverture sur qch; **w. of opportunity** ouverture *f*; *Fam* **that's my holiday out of the w.** voilà mes vacances fichues en l'air

window-dressing ['wɪndəʊdresɪŋ] *n (in shop)* présentation de l'étalage; *Fig* façade *f*

windowpane ['wɪndəʊpeɪn] *n* vitre *f*, carreau *m*

window-shopping ['wɪndəʊʃɒpɪŋ] *n* **to go w.** faire du lèche-vitrines

windowsill ['wɪndəʊsɪl] *n* rebord *m* de fenêtre

windpipe ['wɪndpaɪp] *n* trachée *f*

windscreen ['wɪndskriːn], *Am* **windshield** ['wɪndʃiːld] *n* pare-brise *m inv*; **w. wiper** essuie-glace *m inv*

windsock ['wɪndsɒk] *n Aviat* manche *f* à air

windsurf ['wɪndsɜːf] *vi* faire de la planche à voile

windsurfing ['wɪndsɜːfɪŋ] *n* planche *f* à voile; **to go w.** faire de la planche à voile

windswept ['wɪndswept] *adj (hillside, scene)* balayé(e) par le vent; *(hair)* décoiffé(e) par le vent; *(person)* échevelé(e)

wind-up ['waɪndʌp] *n Fam* plaisanterie *f*

windward ['wɪndwəd] *adj* au vent; **the W. Islands** les îles *fpl* du Vent

windy¹ ['wɪndɪ] *adj (day)* venteux(euse); *(place)* venté(e);* I hate w. weather* je déteste le vent

windy² ['waɪndɪ] *adj (road)* sinueux(euse)

wine [waɪn] **1** *n* vin *m*; **w. bar** bar *m* à vin; **w. bottle** bouteille *f* de vin; **w. box** cubitainer *m* de vin; **w. cellar** cave *f* à vin; **w. gum** bonbon *m* à la gomme; **w. list** carte *f* des vins; **w. tasting** dégustation *f* (de vins); **w. vinegar** vinaigre *m* de vin
2 *vt* **to w. and dine sb** inviter qn dans de bons restaurants

wineglass ['waɪnɡlɑːs] *n* verre *m* à vin

wing [wɪŋ] **1** *n* (**a**) *(of bird, plane)* aile *f*; *Fig* **to take sb under one's w.** prendre qn sous son aile; *Fig* **to spread** *or* **stretch one's wings** élargir son horizon; *Tech* **w. nut** papillon *m*
(**b**) *(of car)* aile *f*; **w. mirror** rétroviseur *m* extérieur
(**c**) *(of building, hospital)* aile *f*
(**d**) *(in football, rugby) (player)* ailier *m*; *(area)* aile *f*
(**e**) **the wings** *(in theatre)* les coulisses *fpl*; *Fig* **to be waiting in the wings** attendre son heure
(**f**) *Pol* **the left/right w.** l'aile *f* gauche/droite
2 *vt* (**a**) *(injure) (bird)* blesser à l'aile; *(person)* blesser au bras
(**b**) *Fam (improvise)* **to w. it** improviser
(**c**) *(fly)* **to w. its way towards sth** *(of bird)* voler vers qch; *Fig* **my report should be winging its way towards you** j'ai posté mon rapport, tu devrais l'avoir bientôt

winger ['wɪŋə(r)] *n (in football, rugby)* ailier *m*

wingspan ['wɪŋspæn] *n* envergure *f*

wink [wɪŋk] **1** *n* clin *m* d'œil; **to give sb a w.** faire un clin d'œil à qn; *Fam* **to tip sb the w.** refiler un tuyau à qn; *Fam* **I didn't sleep a w.** je n'ai pas fermé l'œil
2 *vi* cligner de l'œil; *(of star, light)* clignoter

▸**wink at** *vt insep (person)* faire un clin d'œil à; *Fig (offence, illegal practice)* fermer les yeux sur

winkle ['wɪŋkəl] *n (mollusc)* bigorneau *m*

▸**winkle out** *vt sep Fam* **to w. sth out of sb** soutirer qch à qn

winner ['wɪnə(r)] *n* gagnant(e) *m,f*; **this book will be a w.** ce livre est assuré d'avoir du succès

winning ['wɪnɪŋ] **1** *npl* **winnings** gains *mpl*
2 *adj* (**a**) *(victorious)* gagnant(e); **w. post** poteau *m* d'arrivée (**b**) *(attractive)* charmant(e)

winnow ['wɪnəʊ] *vt* vanner

wino ['waɪnəʊ] *(pl* **winos***) n Fam (alcoholic)* poivrot(e)

winsome ['wɪnsəm] *adj* charmant(e)

winter ['wɪntə(r)] **1** *n* hiver *m*; **in (the) w.** en hiver; **w. break** vacances *fpl* d'hiver; **w. clothing** vêtements *mpl* d'hiver; **w. sports** sports *mpl* d'hiver
2 *vi* passer l'hiver

wintertime ['wɪntətaɪm] *n* hiver *m*

wint(e)ry ['wɪnt(ə)rɪ] *adj (weather)* d'hiver; *Fig (hostile)* glacial(e)

wipe [waɪp] **1** *n* (**a**) *(action)* **to give sth a w.** essuyer qch (**b**) *(moist tissue)* lingette *f*
2 *vt* (**a**) *(table, plate)* essuyer; **to w. one's nose** s'essuyer le nez; **to w. one's hands (on)** s'essuyer les mains (avec); **to w. one's shoes (on)** s'essuyer les pieds (sur); *Fam Fig* **to w. the floor with sb** ne faire qu'une bouchée de qn (**b**) *(recording, tape)* effacer

▸**wipe away** *vt sep (tears)* essuyer; *(mark)* enlever

▸**wipe off 1** *vt sep* effacer; *Fam* **that'll w. the smile off his face!** ça lui fera passer l'envie de rire!
2 *vi (of stain)* partir

▸**wipe out** *vt sep* (**a**) *(erase)* effacer; *(debt)* liquider (**b**) *(destroy)* décimer

▸**wipe up** *vt sep* essuyer

wiper ['waɪpə(r)] *n* essuie-glace *m inv*

wire ['waɪə(r)] **1** *n* (**a**) *(of metal)* fil *m* de fer; *(electrical)* fil (électrique); **w. brush** brosse *f* métallique; **w. fence** clôture *f* en fil de fer; **w. mesh** toile *f* métallique; **w. wool** paille *f* de fer
(**b**) *Am (telegram)* télégramme *m*
(**c**) *(idioms) Fam* **to get one's wires crossed** s'emmêler les pinceaux; **the tournament went right down to the w.** l'issue du tournoi a été incertaine jusqu'au bout
2 *vt* (**a**) *(house)* faire l'installation électrique de; **to w. sth to sth** *(connect electrically)* relier qch à qch; *(attach with wire)* attacher qch à qch avec du fil de fer
(**b**) *(send telegram to)* télégraphier à

▸**wire up** *vt sep* (**a**) *(attach with wire)* attacher avec du fil à fer (**b**) *Am Fam (make nervous)* énerver

wirecutters ['waɪəkʌtəz] *npl* **(pair of) w.** pince *f* coupante

wireless ['waɪəlɪs] *n Br Old-fashioned* **w. (set)** *(poste m de)* TSF *f*

wiretapping ['waɪətæpɪŋ] *n* mise *f* sur écoute d'une ligne téléphonique

wiring ['waɪərɪŋ] *n* installation *f* électrique

wiry ['waɪərɪ] *adj (hair)* crépu(e); *(person)* petit(e) et musclé(e)

wisdom ['wɪzdəm] *n* sagesse *f*; **w. tooth** dent *f* de sagesse

wise [waɪz] *adj (knowledgeable)* sage; *(advisable)* prudent(e); *Fam Pej* **a w. guy** un gros malin; **theThree W. Men** les Rois *mpl* mages; **it's easy to be w. after the event** c'est facile de savoir ce qui est bien ou pas bien après coup; **to be none the wiser** ne pas être plus avancé(e); **to get w. to sth** se rendre compte de qch; *Fam* **to get w. to sb** percer qn à jour

▸**wise up** *vi Fam* **to w. up to sb** voir qn sous son vrai jour; **to w. up to sth** se rendre compte de qch; **w. up!** ouvre les yeux!

-wise [waɪz] *suff Fam (as regards)* **health-/salary-/etc w.** du point de vue de la santé/du salaire *etc*

wisecrack ['waɪzkræk] *Fam* **1** *n* vanne *f*, blague *f*
2 *vi* sortir des vannes

wisely ['waɪzlɪ] *adv* sagement

wish [wɪʃ] **1** *n* (**a**) *(desire)* désir *m*; *(thing desired)* vœu *m*; **to make a w.** faire un vœu; **to do sth against sb's wishes** faire qch contre le souhait de qn; **w. list** liste *f* de vœux
(**b**) *(greeting)* **best wishes** meilleurs vœux; *(in letter)* amicalement
2 *vt* (**a**) *(want)* désirer; **to w. to do sth** désirer faire qch; **to w. sb well** souhaiter à qn que tout se passe bien; **to w. sb luck/a pleasant journey** souhaiter bonne chance/bon voyage à qn; **to w. sth on sb** souhaiter qch à qn
(**b**) *(want something impossible, unlikely)* **I w. she could come** j'aurais bien aimé qu'elle vienne; **I w. I had seen it!** j'aurais bien voulu voir ça!; **I w. I hadn't left so early** je regrette d'être parti aussi tôt; **I w. she wouldn't say things like that** je préférerais qu'elle s'abstienne de dire des choses pareilles; **w. you were here!** *(on postcard)* je pense/nous pensons bien à toi
3 *vi* **to w. for sth** souhaiter qch; **what more could you w. for?** que souhaiter de plus?; **as you w.** comme tu voudras

wishbone ['wɪʃbəʊn] *n* bréchet *m*

wishful ['wɪʃfʊl] *adj* that's w. thinking tu te fais/il se fait/*etc* des illusions

wishy-washy ['wɪʃɪwɒʃɪ] *adj Fam* mou (molle); *(couleur)* délavé(e)

wisp [wɪsp] *n (of straw, wool)* brin *m*; *(of hair)* mèche *f*; *(of smoke, cloud)* traînée *f*

wistful ['wɪstfʊl] *adj* nostalgique

wit [wɪt] *n* (**a**) *(intelligence, presence of mind)* esprit *m*; **to have the w. to do sth** être assez intelligent(e) pour faire qch; **to have quick wits** avoir l'esprit vif; **to have lost one's wits** avoir perdu l'esprit; **to have/ keep one's wits about one** être/rester très vigilant(e); **to be at one's wits' end** ne plus savoir que faire; **to live by one's wits** vivre d'expédients; **to scare sb out of their wits** faire une peur bleue à qn (**b**) *(humour)* esprit *m* (**c**) *(witty person) (man)* homme *m* d'esprit; *(woman)* femme *f* d'esprit

witch [wɪtʃ] *n* sorcière *f*; **w. doctor** sorcier *m*

witchcraft ['wɪtʃkrɑːft] *n* sorcellerie *f*

witch-hunt ['wɪtʃhʌnt] *n Pol* chasse *f* aux sorcières

with [wɪð] *prep* (**a**) *(expressing accompaniment)* avec; **w. me/him** avec moi/lui; **to live w. one's parents** vivre chez ses parents; **I was left w. nobody to talk to** je me suis retrouvé sans personne à qui parler (**b**) *(having)* **the girl w. glasses/blue eyes** la fille aux lunettes/aux yeux bleus; **w. one's hands in one's pockets** les mains dans les poches (**c**) *(expressing association)* **to be pleased w. sb** être content(e) de qn; **to be angry w. sb** être en colère contre qn; **to fight/compete w. sb** se battre/être en concurrence avec qn; **to be in love w. sb** être amoureux(euse) de qn; **covered w. mud** couvert(e) de boue (**d**) *(expressing manner)* **w. pleasure/difficulty** avec plaisir/difficulté; **to say sth w. a smile** dire qch avec un sourire (**e**) *(expressing instrument, agent)* **to hit sb w. sth** frapper qn avec qch; **to cut sth w. a knife** couper qch avec un couteau; **it's pouring w. rain** il pleut à verse (**f**) *(because of)* **to tremble w. rage** trembler de rage; **to cry w. laughter** pleurer de rire; **w. her money, she can surely afford it** avec l'argent qu'elle a, elle peut bien se permettre ça (**g**) *(expressing simultaneity)* **to improve w. age** s'améliorer avec l'âge; **w. those words, he left** sur ces mots, il partit; **w. Christmas coming,...** puisque c'est bientôt Noël,... (**h**) *(idioms)* **to be w. it** être dans le vent; **get w. it!** *(wake up)* réveille-toi!; *(face reality)* ouvre les yeux!; **I'm w. you** *(I support you)* je suis avec vous; **I'm not w. you** *(I don't understand)* je ne vous suis pas

withdraw [wɪð'drɔː] *(pt* **withdrew** [wɪð'druː], *pp* **withdrawn** [wɪð'drɔːn]) **1** *vt* retirer (**from** de) **2** *vi* se retirer (**from** de); **to w. in favour of sb** se désister en faveur de qn; **to w. into oneself** se replier sur soi-même

withdrawal [wɪð'drɔːəl] *n* retrait *m*; **to make a w.** *(from bank)* faire un retrait; **w. symptoms** symptômes *mpl* de manque; **to have w. symptoms** être en (état de) manque

withdrawn [wɪð'drɔːn] *adj* replié(e) sur soi-même

wither ['wɪðə(r)] *vi (of plant)* se flétrir; *(of limb)* s'atrophier

withered ['wɪðəd] *adj (plant)* flétri(e); *(limb)* atrophié(e)

withering ['wɪðərɪŋ] *adj (look)* foudroyant(e); *(tone)* cinglant(e)

withhold [wɪð'həʊld] *(pt & pp* **withheld** [wɪð'held] *) vt (consent, help)* refuser; *(money)* retenir; *(truth)* cacher; *(information)* faire de la rétention de

within [wɪð'ɪn] **1** *prep* (**a**) *(inside)* à l'intérieur de; **problems w. the company** des problèmes au sein de l'entreprise (**b**) *(not beyond)* **w. 10 miles of the town** ≃ à moins de 16 km de la ville; **w. a radius of** dans un rayon de; **w. limits** jusqu'à un certain point; **w. reason** dans des limites raisonnables; **to stay w. budget** rester dans les limites du budget; **to come w. an inch of doing sth** bien faillir faire qch (**c**) *(with expressions of time)* **w. an hour/a week** en moins d'une heure/d'une semaine; **w. minutes** en quelques minutes; **w. the next five years** *(in the space of) (in future)* au cours des cinq années à venir; *(in past)* au cours des cinq années suivantes; *(before the end of) (in future)* avant cinq ans; *(in past)* en moins de cinq ans; **they died w. a few days of each other** ils sont morts à quelques jours d'intervalle **2** *adv* à l'intérieur; **from w.** de l'intérieur

without [wɪð'aʊt] **1** *prep* sans; **w. any money/difficulty** sans argent/difficulté; **w. doing sth** sans faire qch; **do it w. him knowing** fais-le sans qu'il le sache; **it goes w. saying that...** il va sans dire que...; **to do** *or* **go w. sth** se passer de qch **2** *adv* **to do** *or* **go w.** se priver

withstand [wɪð'stænd] *(pt & pp* **withstood** [wɪð'stʊd] *) vt* supporter

witless ['wɪtlɪs] *adj (person, remark)* stupide; **to scare sb w.** faire une peur bleue à qn

witness ['wɪtnɪs] **1** *n* (**a**) *(person)* témoin *m*; **to call sb as w.** citer qn comme témoin; **w. for the defence/ prosecution** témoin à décharge/charge; **w. box** barre *f* des témoins (**b**) *(testimony)* **to bear w. (to sth)** témoigner (de qch) **2** *vt* être témoin de; **I witnessed the whole thing** j'ai assisté à tout ce qui s'est passé; *Fig* **this town has witnessed many battles** cette ville a été le théâtre de nombreuses batailles **3** *vi Law* **to w. to sth** témoigner de qch

witter ['wɪtə(r)] *vi Br Fam* **to w. (on)** bavasser

witticism ['wɪtɪsɪzəm] *n* mot *m* d'esprit

wittily ['wɪtɪlɪ] *adv* avec esprit

wittingly ['wɪtɪŋlɪ] *adv* sciemment

witty ['wɪtɪ] *adj* spirituel(elle), plein(e) d'esprit

wives [waɪvz] *pl of* **wife**

wizard ['wɪzəd] *n* magicien *m*, *Fig* as *m*

wizened ['wɪzənd] *adj* ratatiné(e)

wk *(abbr* **week**) semaine

wobble ['wɒbəl] *vi (of chair, table)* branler; *(of building, jelly)* trembler; *(of person)* être chancelant(e)

wobbly ['wɒblɪ] **1** *n Br Fam* **to throw a w.** piquer une crise **2** *adj (chair, table)* bancal(e); *(shelf, ladder)* branlant(e); *(person)* chancelant(e)

woe [wəʊ] *n Lit* malheur *m*; *Hum* **w. betide you if you're late** malheur à toi si tu es en retard

woebegone ['wəʊbɪgɒn] *adj* abattu(e)

woeful ['wəʊfʊl] *adj* (**a**) *(sad)* affligé(e) (**b**) *(very bad)* déplorable

wog [wɒg] *n Br very Fam* = terme injurieux désignant une personne qui n'est pas blanche

wok [wɒk] *n* poêle *f* chinoise

woke [wəʊk] *pt of* **wake³**

woken ['wəʊkən] *pp of* **wake³**

wolf [wʊlf] (*pl* **wolves** [wʊlvz]) *n* (**a**) loup *m*; **w. cub** louveteau *m*; **w. whistle** = sifflement admiratif au passage de quelqu'un (**b**) (*idioms*) **I don't earn much but it keeps the w. from the door** je ne gagne pas beaucoup mais ça me met à l'abri du besoin; **to throw sb to the wolves** abandonner qn à son sort; **a w. in sheep's clothing** un loup déguisé en brebis; **to cry w.** crier au loup

▸**wolf down** *vt sep* engloutir

woman ['wʊmən] (*pl* **women** ['wɪmɪn]) *n* femme *f*; **women's magazine** magazine *m* féminin; **women's movement** mouvement *m* de libération de la femme; **women's page** page *f* des lectrices; **women's refuge, women's shelter** centre *m* d'accueil pour les femmes; **w. doctor** femme médecin *f*; **w. driver** conductrice *f*

womanizer ['wʊmənaɪzə(r)] *n* coureur *m* (de jupons)

womanly ['wʊmənlɪ] *adj* féminin(e)

womb [wu:m] *n* utérus *m*

women ['wɪmɪn] *pl of* **woman**

womenfolk ['wɪmɪnfəʊk] *n* femmes *fpl*

won [wʌn] *pt & pp of* **win**

wonder ['wʌndə(r)] **1** *n* (**a**) (*miracle*) miracle *m*, merveille *f*; **to work** *or* **do wonders** faire des miracles; **it's a w. (that)...** c'est un miracle que... + *subjunctive*; **(it's) no w....** ce n'est pas étonnant que... + *subjunctive*; **w. drug** remède *m* miracle (**b**) (*astonishment*) émerveillement *m*; **in w.** avec émerveillement
2 *vt* se demander; **one wonders whether...** c'est à se demander si...; **I was wondering if you were free tonight** je voulais savoir si tu étais libre ce soir
3 *vi* (**a**) (*be curious*) se demander; *Fam* **I w. about her sometimes!** je me pose parfois des questions à son sujet! (**b**) *Lit* (*be amazed*) s'étonner (**at** de)

wonderful ['wʌndəfʊl] *adj* merveilleux(euse), formidable

wonky ['wɒŋkɪ] *adj Br Fam* déglingué(e)

won't [wəʊnt] = **will not**

wont [wəʊnt] *Formal* **1** *n* habitude *f*; **as is her w.** comme à son habitude
2 *adj* **to be w. to do sth** avoir l'habitude de faire qch

woo [wu:] (*pt & pp* **wooed**) *vt* (**a**) *Lit* (*woman*) courtiser (**b**) *Fig* (*supporters, investors*) attirer

wood [wʊd] *n* (**a**) (*forest, material*) bois *m*; **w. carving** sculpture *f* sur bois (**b**) (*idioms*) **she can't see the w. for the trees** elle se perd dans les détails; **we're not out of the woods yet** nous ne sommes pas encore tirés d'affaire; *Br* **touch w.!**, *Am* **knock on w.!** je touche du bois!

woodbine ['wʊdbaɪn] *n* (*plant*) vigne *f* vierge

woodcock ['wʊdkɒk] *n* bécasse *f*

woodcut ['wʊdkʌt] *n* gravure *f* sur bois

woodcutter ['wʊdkʌtə(r)] *n* bûcheron *m*

wooded ['wʊdɪd] *adj* boisé(e)

wooden ['wʊdən] *adj* (*made of wood*) en bois; *Fig* (*unexpressive*) impassible; **w. spoon** cuillère *f* de bois; *Fig* **to get the w. spoon** (*in contest*) arriver dernier au classement

woodland ['wʊdlənd] *n* (*woods*) bois *mpl*; (*wooded area*) région *f* boisée

woodlouse ['wʊdlaʊs] (*pl* **woodlice** ['wʊdlaɪs]) *n* cloporte *m*

woodpecker ['wʊdpekə(r)] *n* pic *m*

woodpile ['wʊdpaɪl] *n* tas *m* de bois

woodshed ['wʊdʃed] *n* remise *f* à bois

woodwind ['wʊdwɪnd] *n Mus* **the w.** (*instruments*) les bois *mpl*; **w. instrument** bois *m*

woodwork ['wʊdwɜːk] *n* (*craft*) travail *m* du bois; (*in house*) boiserie *f*; *Fig* **to come** *or* **crawl out of the w.** faire soudain surface

woodworm ['wʊdwɜːm] *n* ver *m* à bois

woof [wʊf] **1** *n* aboiement *m*
2 *exclam* ouah!

wool [wʊl] *n* laine *f*; *Fam* **to pull the w. over sb's eyes** embobiner qn

woollen, *Am* **woolen** ['wʊlən] **1** *n* **woollens** lainages *mpl*
2 *adj* (*garment*) en laine

woolly, *Am* **wooly** ['wʊlɪ] **1** *n Br Fam* (*garment*) **woollies** lainages *mpl*
2 *adj* (*garment*) en laine; *Fig* (*idea, theory*) nébuleux(euse)

woozy ['wu:zɪ] *adj Fam* dans les vapes

wop [wɒp] *n very Fam* rital(e) *m,f,* = terme raciste désignant un Italien

word [wɜːd] **1** *n* (**a**) (*in general*) mot *m*; **w. for w.** mot pour mot; **in a w.** en un mot; **in other words** autrement dit; **not in so many words** pas en ces termes-là; **not a w.** pas un mot; **in one's own words** à sa façon; **I can't put it into words** je n'arrive pas à trouver les mots; **he's a man of few words** c'est un homme qui parle peu; **I couldn't get a w. in (edgeways)** je n'ai pas pu placer un mot; **the w. of God** la parole de Dieu; **I'll take your w. for it** je te crois sur parole; **to take sb at his/her w.** prendre qn au mot; **it was too ridiculous for words** c'était d'un ridicule sans nom; **my w.!** ma parole!; *Comput* **w. count** nombre *m* des mots; **w. processor** machine *f* à traitement de texte
(**b**) (*remarks, conversation*) **to have a w. with sb** parler à qn; **to have words with sb** avoir des mots avec qn; **just say the w.** tu n'as qu'à me faire signe; **you're putting words into my mouth** tu me fais dire des choses que je n'ai pas voulu dire; **you took the words right out of my mouth** c'est justement ce que j'allais dire; **to put in a good w. for sb** glisser un mot en faveur de qn; **he never has a good w. for anyone** il ne peut pas s'empêcher de dire du mal des gens; **a w. of warning** une mise en garde; **a w. of advice** un petit conseil
(**c**) (*news*) **to receive w. from sb** avoir des nouvelles de qn; **to send sb w. of sth** faire part à qn de qch; **the w. is that...** on raconte que...; **by w. of mouth** de bouche à oreille
(**d**) (*promise*) parole *f*; **w. of honour** parole d'honneur; **to give sb one's w.** donner sa parole à qn; **to keep one's w.** tenir sa promesse; **to go back on one's w.** manquer à sa parole
(**e**) **words** (*lyrics*) paroles *fpl*
2 *vt* (*express in words*) formuler

wording ['wɜːdɪŋ] *n* formulation *f*

word-processing [wɜːd'prəʊsesɪŋ] *n Comput* traitement *m* de texte

wordy ['wɜːdɪ] *adj* prolixe

wore [wɔː(r)] *pt of* **wear**

work [wɜːk] **1** *n* (**a**) (*labour*) travail *m*; **to be at w. on sth** travailler à *ou* sur qch; **to get to w.** se mettre au travail; **w. in progress** (*sign*) travaux; *Comput* **w. station** poste *m* de travail (**b**) *(task)* travail *m*; **to put a lot of w. into sth** beaucoup travailler à qch; **to have one's w. cut out (to do sth)** avoir du mal (à faire qch); **to make quick** *or* **short w. of sth** venir rapidement à bout de qch; **good w.!** c'est du bon travail!

(**c**) *(literary, artistic)* œuvre *f*; **a w. of art** une œuvre d'art

(**d**) *(employment)* travail *m*; **to be out of w.** être sans travail; **w. experience** stage *m* (en entreprise); **w. permit** permis *m* de travail

(**e**) *Ind* **works council** comité *m* d'entreprise; **works outing** sortie *f* organisée par le comité d'entreprise

(**f**) **works** *(construction)* travaux *mpl*; **road works ahead** *(sign)* attention travaux

(**g**) **works** *(mechanism)* mécanisme *m*

(**h**) *Fam* **the works** *(everything)* le grand jeu; **to give sb the works** *(beating)* passer qn à tabac; *(luxury treatment)* jouer le grand jeu à qn

2 *vt* (**a**) *(person)* **to w. sb hard** exiger beaucoup de qn; **to w. oneself to death** se tuer à la tâche

(**b**) *(operate) (machine)* faire fonctionner

(**c**) *(bring about) (miracle, cure, change)* opérer; **to w. it** *or* **things so that** faire en sorte que

(**d**) *(move)* **to w. one's hands free** se libérer les mains; **to w. one's way through a book/list** avancer progressivement dans la lecture d'un livre/dans une liste

(**e**) *(exploit) (mine, quarry)* exploiter; *(land)* travailler

3 *vi* (**a**) *(of person)* travailler; **to w. against sb/in sb's favour** jouer en la défaveur/la faveur de qn

(**b**) *(function) (of machine, system)* marcher, fonctionner

(**c**) *(have effect) (of medicine)* faire effet; *(of plan, method)* marcher

▶**work in** *vt sep (include)* introduire, glisser

▶**work off** *vt sep (anger)* évacuer; **he worked off 5 kilos** il a perdu 5 kilos en faisant de l'exercice

▶**work on 1** *vt insep* **to w. on sth** travailler à *ou* sur qch

2 *vi (continue to work)* continuer à travailler

▶**work out 1** *vt sep (cost, total)* calculer; *(answer)* trouver; **to w. out how to do sth** trouver comment faire qch; **I'm sure we can w. this thing out** je suis sûr qu'on peut arranger ça

2 *vi* (**a**) *(turn out)* **to w. out well/badly (for sb)** bien/mal se passer (pour qn); **it all worked out in the end** finalement, tout s'est arrangé (**b**) *(total)* **to w. out at** revenir à (**c**) *(exercise)* s'entraîner

▶**work up** *vt sep* (**a**) *(develop)* **to w. up enthusiasm/ interest for sth** s'enthousiasmer pour/s'intéresser à qch; **I worked up an appetite** ça m'a ouvert l'appétit (**b**) *(excite)* **to get worked up (about sth)** se mettre dans tous ses états (à propos de qch)

▶**work up to** *vt insep* se préparer à

workable ['wɜːkəbəl] *adj* possible

workaday ['wɜːkədeɪ] *adj* de tous les jours

workaholic [wɜːkə'hɒlɪk] *n Fam* bourreau *m* de travail

workbench ['wɜːkbentʃ] *n* établi *m*

workday ['wɜːkdeɪ] *n Am* jour *m* ouvrable

worker ['wɜːkə(r)] *n* travailleur(euse) *m,f*; *(in industry)* ouvrier(ère) *m,f*; **to be a fast/slow w.** travailler vite/lentement; **w. bee** ouvrière *f*; **w. participation** participation *f* des travailleurs à la gestion

workfare ['wɜːkfeə(r)] *n Pol* = principe selon lequel les bénéficiaires de l'allocation de chômage doivent fournir un travail en échange

workforce ['wɜːkfɔːs] *n* main-d'œuvre *f*

workhouse ['wɜːkhaʊs] *n Hist* asile *m* des pauvres

working ['wɜːkɪŋ] **1** *n* (**a**) *(operation) (of machine)* fonctionnement *m* (**b**) **workings** *(mechanism)* mécanisme *m*

2 *adj (person)* qui travaille; **to have a w. knowledge of sth** avoir de bonnes bases en qch; **in w. order** en état de marche; **the w. class(es)** la classe ouvrière; **w. clothes** vêtements *mpl* de travail; **w. hours** heures *fpl* de travail; **w. lunch** déjeuner *m* d'affaires; **w. majority** majorité *f* suffisante; **w. model** maquette *f* animée; **w. party** groupe *m* de travail

working-class ['wɜːkɪŋ'klɑːs] *adj* ouvrier(ère); *(accent)* prolétaire

workload ['wɜːkləʊd] *n* charge *f* de travail

workman ['wɜːkmən] *n* ouvrier *m*

workmanlike ['wɜːkmənlaɪk] *adj* de professionnel

workmanship ['wɜːkmənʃɪp] *n* travail *m*; **a fine piece of w.** du beau travail

workout ['wɜːkaʊt] *n* séance *f* d'entraînement

workplace ['wɜːkpleɪs] *n* lieu *m* de travail

workshop ['wɜːkʃɒp] *n* atelier *m*

workshy ['wɜːkʃaɪ] *adj* fainéant(e)

worktop ['wɜːktɒp] *n (in kitchen)* plan *m* de travail, *Can* comptoir *m* de cuisine

work-to-rule [wɜːktə'ruːl] *n Ind* grève *f* du zèle

world [wɜːld] *n* (**a**) *(the earth)* monde *m*; **the best/biggest in the w.** le (la) meilleur(e)/plus grand(e) du monde; **the w. over, all over the w.** dans le monde entier; **the W. Bank** la Banque mondiale; **w. champion** champion(onne) *m,f* du monde; **the W. Cup** la Coupe du monde; **w. map** mappemonde *f*; **w. music** world music *f*; **w. record** record *m* du monde; **W. Series** = championnat national américain de base-ball; **W. War One/Two** la Première/Seconde *ou* Deuxième Guerre mondiale

(**b**) *(sphere of activity)* **the literary/political/business w.** le monde littéraire/politique/des affaires

(**c**) *(society)* **man of the w.** homme *m* d'expérience; **to go up in the w.** faire du chemin; **to come down in the w.** déchoir; **to have the w. at one's feet** avoir le monde à ses pieds

(**d**) *(for emphasis)* **to do sb the w. of good** faire le plus grand bien à qn; **a w. of difference** une différence énorme; **to think the w. of sb** admirer énormément qn; **they carried on for all the w. as if nothing had happened** ils ont continué comme si de rien n'était

(**e**) *(idioms)* **she's not long for this w.** elle n'en a plus pour longtemps; **to bring a child into the w.** mettre un enfant au monde; **to have the best of both worlds** avoir tous les avantages et aucun des inconvénients; **she lives in a w. of her own** elle vit dans un monde à elle; *Fam* **it's out of this w.** c'est extraordinaire; **not for (anything in) the w.** pour rien au monde; **it's a small w.!** le monde est petit!; **what is the w. coming to?** où va-t-on?

world-beater ['wɜːldbiːtə(r)] *n* leader *m* mondial

world-famous ['wɜːld'feɪməs] *adj* célèbre dans le monde entier

worldly ['wɜːldlɪ] *adj (pleasure, goods)* matériel(elle)

worldly-wise ['wɜːldlɪ'waɪz] *adj* qui a de l'expérience

world-weary ['wɜːldwɪərɪ] *adj* désabusé(e)

worldwide ['wɜːldwaɪd] **1** *adj* mondial(e); *Comput* **the W. Web** le Worldwide Web

2 *adv* dans le monde entier

worm [wɜːm] **1** *n* ver *m*; *(maggot)* asticot *m*; **to have worms** *(of person, animal)* avoir des vers; *Fig* **the w. has turned** il/elle/*etc* a fini par se rebiffer

2 *vt* (**a**) *(animal)* traiter contre les vers (**b**) **to w. one's way out of a situation** réussir à se tirer d'une situation; **to w. oneself into sb's favour/confidence** s'insinuer dans les bonnes grâces/la confiance de qn; **to w. a secret out of sb** arracher un secret à qn

wormeaten ['wɜːmiːtən] *adj* *(wood)* vermoulu(e); *(fruit)* véreux(euse)

worn [wɔːn] *pp of* **wear**

worried ['wʌrɪd] *adj* inquiet(ète); **to be w. about sb** être inquiet pour qn; **I'm w. about his safety** je m'inquiète pour sa sécurité; **he's w. about losing his job** il a peur de perdre son emploi

worrier ['wʌrɪə(r)] *n* anxieux(euse) *m,f*

worry ['wʌrɪ] **1** *n* souci *m*; **that's the least of my worries** c'est le cadet de mes soucis

2 *vt* (*pt & pp* **worried**) *(cause anxiety to)* inquiéter; **to w. oneself sick (about sth)** se faire un sang d'encre (à propos de qch)

3 *vi* s'inquiéter, se faire du souci; **to w. about sb** s'inquiéter pour qn; **to w. about the future** s'inquiéter pour l'avenir; **to w. about doing sth** avoir peur de faire qch; **not to w.!** ce n'est pas grave!; **there's/it's nothing to w. about** il n'y a pas de quoi s'inquiéter

worrying ['wʌrɪɪŋ] *adj* inquiétant(e)

worse [wɜːs] **1** *adj* *(comparative of* **bad***)* pire (**than** que); **there's nothing w. than...** il n'y a rien de pire que...; **to get w.** aller en empirant; **things could be w.** les choses pourraient aller plus mal; **and to make matters w.** et, pour tout arranger...; **to go from bad to w.,...** aller de mal en pis; **I'm none the w. for it** je ne m'en porte pas plus mal; **to be the w. for drink** être éméché(e); *Fam* **to be the w. for wear** *(of car, book)* être en mauvais état; *(of drunk person)* être dans un sale état; **w. luck!** quelle poisse!

2 *adv* *(comparative of* **badly***)* plus mal; **you could do w.** tu aurais pu tomber plus mal; **I don't think any w. of her for it** elle n'a pas pour autant baissé dans mon estime; **he is w. off than before** sa situation a empiré

3 *n* **there was w. to come** le pire restait à venir; **I've seen w.** j'ai vu pire; **a change for the w.** une détérioration

worsen ['wɜːsən] **1** *vt* aggraver

2 *vi* empirer

Worship ['wɜːʃɪp] *n* *(title)* **His/Her W.** *(referring to mayor)* monsieur/madame le maire; *(referring to magistrate)* monsieur/madame le juge

worship ['wɜːʃɪp] **1** *n* *(of deity)* vénération *f*, culte *m*; *(of person)* adoration *f*; **place of w.** lieu *m* de culte

2 *vt* (*pt & pp* **worshipped**) *(deity)* vénérer; *(person)* adorer

worst [wɜːst] **1** *adj* *(superlative of* **bad***)* **the w.** le (la) pire; **the w. book I've ever read** le plus mauvais livre que j'aie jamais lu; **her w. mistake** sa plus grave erreur; **the w. thing was...** le pire, c'était que...

2 *adv* *(superlative of* **badly***)* le plus mal; **the elderly are the w. off** ce sont les personnes âgées qui sont le plus mal loties

3 *n* **the w.** le pire; **the w. that could happen** le pire qui puisse arriver; **the w. of it is that...** le pire dans tout ça, c'est que...; **if the w. comes to the w.** au pire; *Fam* **do your w.!** essaie un peu pour voir!; **the w. is over** on a passé le plus dur

worst-case scenario ['wɜːstkeɪsɪ'nɑːrɪəʊ] (*pl* **worst-case scenarios**) *n* le pire qui puisse se produire

worsted ['wʊstɪd] *n* peigné *m*

worth [wɜːθ] **1** *prep* (**a**) *(having a value of)* **to be w. sth** valoir qch; **how much is it w.?** combien est-ce que cela vaut?; **that's my opinion, for what it's w.** c'est mon opinion, elle vaut ce qu'elle vaut; **he's w. millions** il est millionnaire; **he was pulling for all he was w.** il tirait de toutes ses forces (**b**) *(meriting)* **the museum is w. a visit** le musée vaut le détour; **this book is not w. buying** ce livre ne vaut pas la peine d'être acheté; **it's w./it isn't w. it** ça en vaut/ça n'en vaut pas la peine; **it's w. thinking about** ça vaut le coup d'y réfléchir

2 *n* valeur *f*; **give me £20 w. of petrol** donnez-moi pour 20 livres d'essence; **to get one's money's w.** en avoir pour son argent

worthless ['wɜːθlɪs] *adj* **to be w.** *(of object)* ne rien valoir; *(of person)* être un(e) bon (bonne) à rien

worthwhile [wɜːθ'waɪl] *adj* **to be w.** valoir la peine *ou* le coup

worthy ['wɜːðɪ] **1** *adj* *(person, life)* digne; **to be w. of sth** être digne de qch

2 *n* notable *m*

would [wʊd]

> On trouve généralement **I/you/he**/*etc* **would** sous leurs formes contractées **I'd/you'd/he'd**/*etc.* La forme négative correspondante est **wouldn't**, que l'on écrira **would not** dans des contextes formels.

modal aux v (**a**) *(expressing conditional tense)* **she w. come if you invited her** elle viendrait si vous l'invitiez; **if he had let go, he w. have fallen** s'il avait lâché prise, il serait tombé; **if she had asked me, I w. have refused** si elle m'avait demandé, j'aurais refusé; **w. you do it? – yes I w./no I wouldn't** tu le ferais? – oui/non; **you wouldn't do it, w. you?** tu ne le ferais pas, dis?

(**b**) *(expressing wish, determination)* **w. you pass the salt, please?** pourrais-tu passer le sel, s'il te plaît?; **w. you like a drink?** tu veux boire quelque chose?; **she wouldn't let me speak to him** elle m'empêchait de lui parler; **be quiet, w. you!** tais-toi, s'il te plaît!; **the car wouldn't start** la voiture ne démarrait pas

(**c**) *(for emphasis)* **you WOULD insist on going!** il fallait que tu insistes pour y aller!; **I forgot – you w.!** j'ai oublié – c'est bien (de) toi!

(**d**) *(expressing past habit)* **she w. often return home exhausted** il lui arrivait souvent de rentrer épuisée; **there w. always be some left over** il en restait toujours

(**e**) *(in reported speech)* **she told me she w. be there** elle m'a dit qu'elle serait là; **I said I w. do it** j'ai dit que je le ferais

(**f**) *(expressing conjecture)* **w. that be my pen you're using?** est-ce que, par hasard, ce serait mon stylo que vous utilisez?; **they w. have been tired after their journey** ils devaient être fatigués après leur voyage; **I wouldn't know** je n'en ai aucune idée

would-be ['wʊdbiː] *adj* (**a**) *(aspiring)* **a w. writer** une personne qui veut être écrivain (**b**) *Pej (so-called)* prétendu(e), soi-distant *inv*

wouldn't ['wʊdənt] = **would not**

wound¹ [wuːnd] **1** *n* blessure *f*

2 *vt also Fig* blesser; **to w. sb's feelings** blesser qn, heurter la sensibilité de qn

wound² [waʊnd] *pt & pp of* **wind²**

wounded ['wuːndɪd] **1** *adj* blessé(e)
  2 *npl* **the w.** les blessés *mpl*
wounding ['wuːndɪŋ] *adj* blessant(e)
wove [wəʊv] *pt of* **weave**
woven ['wəʊvən] *pp of* **weave**
wow [waʊ] *Fam* **1** *vt* séduire, emballer
  2 *exclam* la vache!
WP [dʌbəljuːˈpiː] *n Comput* (**a**) (*ubbr* **word processor**) (*machine*) machine *f* à traitement de texte; (*software*) logiciel *m* de traitement de texte (**b**) (*abbr* **word-processing**) (*skill*) traitement *m* de texte
WPC [dʌbəljuːpiːˈsiː] *n* (*abbr* **woman police constable**) = femme agent de police
wpm [dʌbəljuːpiːˈem] (*abbr* **words per minute**) mots par minute
WRAC [ræk] *n Br Mil* (*abbr* **Women's Royal Army Corps**) = section féminine de l'armée britannique
wrangle ['ræŋgəl] **1** *n* dispute *f*
  2 *vi* se disputer (**about** *or* **over** à propos de)
wrap [ræp] **1** *n* (**a**) (*shawl*) châle *m*; *Fig* **to keep sth under wraps** garder qch secret (**b**) *Culin* (*sandwich*) = tortilla fourrée
  2 *vt* (*pt & pp* **wrapped**) envelopper, emballer (**in** dans); **to w. sth around sth** enrouler qch autour de qch; *Fig* **wrapped in mystery** enveloppé(e) de mystère
▸**wrap up 1** *vt sep* (**a**) (*parcel, present*) envelopper; *Fig* **to be wrapped up in sth** être absorbé(e) par qch (**b**) *Fam* (*bring to an end*) conclure
  2 *vi* (*dress warmly*) s'emmitoufler
wraparound sunglasses ['ræpəraʊnd'sʌŋglɑːsɪz] *npl* lunettes *fpl* de soleil panoramiques
wrapper ['ræpə(r)] *n* (*of sweet*) papier *m*
wrapping ['ræpɪŋ] *n* emballage *m*; **w. paper** papier *m* d'emballage
wrath [rɒθ] *n Lit* courroux *m*
wreak [riːk] *vt* **to w. havoc** faire des ravages; **to w. vengeance on sb** assouvir sa vengeance sur qn
wreath [riːθ] *n* couronne *f*
wreathe [riːð] *vt Lit* couronner
wreck [rek] **1** *n* (*ship, car, train, plane*) épave *f*; *Fig* **to be a physical/nervous w.** être physiquement/nerveusement au bout du rouleau
  2 *vt* (*ship*) faire faire naufrage à; (*car*) démolir; (*room, house*) saccager; *Fig* (*plans, hopes, happiness*) ruiner, anéantir; (*marriage, career*) ruiner; **to w. one's health** se ruiner la santé
wreckage ['rekɪdʒ] *n* (*debris*) (*of plane, car, ship*) débris *mpl*; (*of building*) décombres *mpl*
wrecked [rekt] *adj* (**a**) (*ship*) naufragé(e); (*car, plane*) complètement détruit(e) (**b**) *Fam* (*drunk*) bourré(e), pété(e) (**c**) *Fam* (*exhausted*) crevé(e)
wrecker ['rekə(r)] *n Am* (*salvage vehicle*) dépanneuse *f*
wren [ren] *n* roitelet *m*
wrench [rentʃ] **1** *n* (**a**) (*pull*) (*to ankle, shoulder*) faux mouvement *m*; *Fig* (*emotional*) déchirement *m* (**b**) (*tool*) clef *f*
  2 *vt* **to w. one's ankle/shoulder** se fouler la cheville/l'épaule; **to w. sth out of sb's hands** arracher qch des mains de qn
wrest [rest] *vt* **to w. sth from sb** arracher qch à qn
wrestle ['resəl] *vi* (*with person*) lutter (**with** contre); *Fig* **to w. with sth** se débattre avec qch
wrestler ['reslə(r)] *n* lutteur(euse) *m,f*

wrestling ['reslɪŋ] *n* lutte *f*, catch *m*; **w. match** match *m* de catch
wretch [retʃ] *n* malheureux(euse) *m,f*
wretched ['retʃɪd] *adj* (**a**) (*very bad*) atroce (**b**) (*unhappy*) démoralisé(e) (**c**) *Fam* (*for emphasis*) **I can't find the w. umbrella!** je ne trouve pas ce maudit parapluie!
wriggle ['rɪgəl] **1** *vt* **to w. one's way out of a situation** se sortir d'une situation
  2 *vi* **to w. (about)** gigoter, se tortiller; **to w. out of sth** couper à qch; **he managed to w. out of paying me back** il s'est débrouillé pour ne pas me rembourser
wring [rɪŋ] *vt* (*pt & pp* **wrung** [rʌŋ]) (*clothes*) essorer; **to w. one's hands** se tordre les mains; **to w. sb's neck** tordre le cou à qn; *Fam* **I'd like to w. his neck** j'ai envie de lui tordre le cou; *Fig* **to w. sth from sb** réussir à arracher qch à qn
▸**wring out** *vt sep* (*clothes*) essorer
wringer ['rɪŋə(r)] *n* essoreuse *f*; *Fam Fig* **to put sb through the w.** faire passer un mauvais quart d'heure à qn
wringing ['rɪŋɪŋ] *adj* **w. (wet)** trempé(e)
wrinkle ['rɪŋkəl] **1** *n* (*on skin, paper*) ride *f*, (*in cloth*) faux pli *m*
  2 *vi* se froisser
wrinkled ['rɪŋkəld] *adj* (*skin*) ridé(e); (*clothes, fabric*) froissé(e)
wrinkly ['rɪŋklɪ] *adj* fripé(e)
wrist [rɪst] *n* poignet *m*; *Comput* **w. rest** repose-poignets *m*
wristwatch ['rɪstwɒtʃ] *n* montre-bracelet *f*
writ [rɪt] *n Law* ordre *m*, assignation *f*; **to serve a w. on sb** assigner qn en justice
write [raɪt] (*pt* **wrote** [rəʊt], *pp* **written** ['rɪtən]) **1** *vt* (*answer, name*) écrire; (*cheque*) faire; *Am* **to w. sb** écrire à qn; **she had guilt written all over her face** la culpabilité se lisait sur son visage
  2 *vi* écrire; *Br* **to w. to sb** écrire à qn; *Fam* **it's nothing to w. home about** ça n'a rien d'extraordinaire
▸**write away for** *vt insep* **to w. away for sth** écrire pour recevoir qch
▸**write back** *vi* répondre
▸**write down** *vt sep* noter
▸**write in 1** *vt sep* (*insert*) inscrire
  2 *vi* (*send letter*) écrire
▸**write off 1** *vt sep* (**a**) (*debt*) annuler (**b**) *Br Fam* (*car*) bousiller (**c**) *Fam* (*person*) enterrer; **to w. sb off as a has-been** considérer qn comme un(e) ringard(e)
  2 *vi* **to w. off for sth** écrire pour recevoir qch
▸**write out** *vt sep* (*instructions, recipe*) noter; (*cheque*) faire
▸**write up** *vt sep* (*notes, thesis*) rédiger; (*diary, journal*) tenir
write-off ['raɪtɒf] *n* (**a**) *Br Fam* (*car*) **to be a w.** être bon (bonne) pour la casse (**b**) (*of debt*) annulation *f*
write-protected ['raɪtprəˈtektɪd] *adj Comput* protégé(e) en écriture
writer ['raɪtə(r)] *n* (*by profession*) écrivain *m*, auteur *m*; (*of article, book*) auteur *m*; **w.'s block** angoisse *f* de la page blanche
write-up ['raɪtʌp] *n* (*of play*) critique *f*
writhe [raɪð] *vi* se tordre (**in** de)
writing ['raɪtɪŋ] *n* (**a**) (*action, profession*) écriture *f*; **w. desk** bureau *m*, secrétaire *m*; **w. pad** bloc-notes *m*; **w. paper** papier *m* à lettres (**b**) (*handwriting*) écriture *f*;

in w. par écrit (**c**) *(thing written)* écrit *m*; *Fig* **the w. is on the wall** la fin est proche

written ['rɪtən] **1** *adj* écrit(e); **w. consent** consentement *m* par écrit; **w. examination** écrit *m*, épreuve *f* écrite

2 *pp of* **write**

WRNS [renz] *n Br Mil (abbr* **Women's Royal Naval Service**) = section féminine de la marine britannique

wrong [rɒŋ] **1** *n (immoral action)* mal *m*; **to know right from w.** distinguer le bien du mal; *Ironic* **he can do no w.** il est parfait; **to do sb w.** faire du tort à qn; *Prov* **two wrongs don't make a right** on ne répare pas le mal par le mal; **to be in the w.** être dans son tort

2 *adj* (**a**) *(morally bad)* mauvais(e); **stealing is w.** c'est mal de voler; **it was w. of you not to tell me** ce n'est pas bien de ta part de ne pas me l'avoir dit

(**b**) *(incorrect, mistaken)* mauvais(e); **to be w.** *(of person)* avoir tort; **my watch is w.** ma montre n'est pas à l'heure; **don't get the w. idea** ne te fais pas de fausses idées; **I did/said the w. thing** j'ai fait/dit ce qu'il ne fallait pas; *Fig* **to go the w. way about doing sth** mal s'y prendre pour faire qch; *Fig* **to get on the w. side of sb** se faire mal voir de qn; **you've got the w. number** *(on phone)* vous vous êtes trompé de numéro

(**c**) *(amiss)* **what's w.?** qu'est-ce qui ne va pas?; **what's w. with you?** qu'est-ce que tu as?; **is anything w.?** quelque chose ne va pas?; **there's something w. with the car** il y a quelque chose qui ne va pas dans cette voiture; *Fam* **he's w. in the head** il ne tourne pas rond

3 *adv* (**a**) *(morally)* mal; **to do w.** mal agir

(**b**) *(incorrectly)* mal; **to go w.** se gâter; **where did I go w.?** qu'est-ce que j'ai fait qui n'allait pas?; **don't get me w., I like her** je n'ai pas dit que je ne l'aimais pas

4 *vt* faire du tort à, léser

wrongdoer ['rɒŋduːə(r)] *n* auteur *m* d'un tort

wrongdoing ['rɒŋduːɪŋ] *n (immoral action)* méfait *m*; *(crime)* infraction *f*

wrongful ['rɒŋfʊl] *adj* arbitraire; **w. dismissal** licenciement *m* abusif

wrong-headed [rɒŋ'hedɪd] *adj* buté(e), borné(e)

wrongly ['rɒŋlɪ] *adv* (**a**) *(unjustly)* à tort (**b**) *(incorrectly)* incorrectement

wrote [rəʊt] *pt of* **write**

wrought-iron ['rɔːt'aɪən] *adj* en fer forgé

wrought-up ['rɔːt'ʌp] *adj* **to be w.** être dans tous ses états

wrung [rʌŋ] *pt & pp of* **wring**

wry [raɪ] *adj* ironique

wt *(abbr* **weight**) p.

WW *(abbr* **World War**) **WWI/II** la Première/Deuxième *ou* Seconde Guerre mondiale

WWF [dʌbəljuːdʌbəljuːˈef] *n (abbr* **World Wildlife Fund, Worldwide Fund for Nature**) WWF *m*

WWW ['dʌbəljuːˈdʌbəljuːˈdʌbəljuː] *n Comput (abbr* **worldwide web**) WWW, W3

WYSIWYG ['wɪzɪwɪg] *n Comput (abbr* **what you see is what you get**) WYSIWYG *m*

X, x [eks] *n (letter)* X, x *m inv*; **for x number of years** pendant x années; *Formerly* **X (certificate) film** film *m* classé X

xenon ['zenɒn] *n Chem* xénon *m*

xenophobia [zenə'fəʊbɪə] *n* xénophobie *f*

xenophobic [zenə'fəʊbɪk] *adj* xénophobe

Xerox® ['zɪərɒks] **1** *n (machine)* photocopieur *m*; *(copy)* photocopie *f*

2 *vt* photocopier

XL ['eks'el] *(abbr* **extra large)** XL

Xmas ['eksməs] *n (abbr* **Christmas)** Noël *m*

X-ray ['eksreɪ] **1** *n (radiation)* rayon *m* X; *(picture)* radio *f*; **to have an X.** passer une radio

2 *vt* radiographier

xylophone ['zaɪləfəʊn] *n* xylophone *m*

Y, y [waɪ] *n (letter)* Y, y *m inv*; **Y-fronts** slip *m* ouvert

yacht [jɒt] *n (sailing boat)* voilier *m*; *(large private boat)* yacht *m*; **y. club** club *m* de voile; **y. race** régate *f*

yachting ['jɒtɪŋ] *n* voile *f*; **to go y.** faire de la voile

yachtsman ['jɒtsmən] *n* navigateur *m*

yachtswoman ['jɒtswʊmən] *n* navigatrice *f*

yack [jæk] *Fam* **1** *n* papotage *m*

2 *vi* papoter

yak [jæk] *n* **(a)** *Zool* yack *m* **(b)** = **yack**

yam [jæm] *n Br* igname *f*; *Am* patate *f* douce

Yank [jæŋk], **Yankee** ['jæŋkɪ] *n Br Fam (person from the USA)* Ricain(e) *m,f*; *Am Fam (person from north-eastern states of the USA)* habitant(e) *m,f* des États du Nord

yank [jæŋk] *Fam* **1** *n* **to give sth a y.** tirer qch d'un coup sec

2 *vt* tirer d'un coup sec; **to y. sth open/out** ouvrir/ arracher qch d'un coup sec

yap [jæp] *(pt & pp* **yapped)** *vi (of dog)* japper; *Fam (of person)* jacasser

yard¹ [jɑːd] *n (unit of measurement)* = 0,914 m, yard *m*

yard² *n* **(a)** *(of house, school, farm)* cour *f*; *Am (garden)* jardin *m*; *Am* **y. sale** vide-grenier *m* **(b)** *(for working)* chantier *m*; **(builder's) y.** chantier de construction **(c)** *(for storage)* dépôt *m* de marchandises

Yardie ['jɑːdɪ] *n* = membre d'un gang d'origine jamaï- caine

yardstick ['jɑːdstɪk] *n (standard)* point *m* de référence

yarn [jɑːn] *n* **(a)** *(thread, wool)* fil *m* (à tricoter) **(b)** *Fam (story)* histoire *f* à dormir debout; **to spin a y.** raconter une histoire

yawn [jɔːn] **1** *n* bâillement *m*; *Fam (boring thing)* plaie *f*

2 *vi* **(a)** *(of person)* bâiller **(b)** *(of chasm)* béer

yd *(abbr* **yard(s))** yard *m*

ye [jiː] **1** *pron Lit* = **you**

2 *definite art Lit or Hum* = **the**

yea [jeɪ] **1** *n* **yeas and nays** voix *fpl* pour et voix contre

2 *adv Lit* = **yes**

yeah [jeə] *adv Fam* ouais

year [jɪə(r)] *n (twelve-month period)* an *m*; *(referring to duration)* année *f*; **in the y. 1931** en 1931; **this y.** cette année; **last/next y.** l'année dernière/prochaine; **every y.** chaque année, tous les ans; **twice a y.** deux fois par an; **to earn £20,000 a y.** gagner 20 000 livres par an; **to be ten years old** avoir dix ans; **he got five years** *(prison sentence)* il en a pris pour cinq ans; **for many years** pendant des années; **y. in y. out** chaque année; **over the years** au fil des ans, avec les années; **years ago** il y a des années; **it's years since I saw him, I haven't seen him for** *or* **in years** ça fait des années que je ne l'ai pas vu; **from her earliest years** dès son plus jeune âge; **to be getting on in years** prendre de l'âge

yearbook ['jɪəbʊk] *n* almanach *m*

yearlong ['jɪəlɒŋ] *adj* d'un an

yearly ['jɪəlɪ] **1** *adj* annuel(elle)

2 *adv* annuellement; **twice y.** deux fois par an

yearn [jɜːn] *vi* **to y. for sth** désirer qch ardemment; **to y. to do sth** brûler de faire qch

yearning ['jɜːnɪŋ] *n* désir *m* ardent

yeast [jiːst] *n* levure *f*

yell [jel] **1** *n* hurlement *m*; **to give a y.** pousser un hurlement
   2 *vt & vi* hurler
yellow ['jeləʊ] **1** *n* jaune *m*
   2 *adj* (**a**) *(in colour)* jaune; **to turn** *or* **go y.** jaunir; **y. card** *(in football)* carton *m* jaune, *Belg* carte *f* jaune; **y. fever** fièvre *f* jaune; **y. line** bande *f* jaune; **to park on a y. line** ≃ se mettre en stationnement irrégulier; **double y. line(s)** double ligne *f* jaune; **the Y. Pages**® les Pages *fpl* Jaunes; **the Y. River** le fleuve Jaune (**b**) *Fam (cowardly)* trouillard(e)
   3 *vi* jaunir

> **Yellow lines**
> En Grande-Bretagne, une ligne jaune parallèle au trottoir signifie "arrêt autorisé réglementé"; une double ligne jaune signifie "stationnement interdit".

yelp [jelp] **1** *n* jappement *m*
   2 *vi* japper
Yemen ['jemən] *n* le Yémen
Yemeni ['jemənɪ] **1** *n* Yéménite *mf*
   2 *adj* yéménite
yen¹ [jen] *n (Japanese currency)* yen *m*
yen² *n Fam* **to have a y. for sth/to do sth** avoir envie de qch/de faire qch
Yerevan [jerə'væn] *n* Erevan
yes [jes] **1** *adv* oui; *(after negative question)* si; **haven't you seen the film? – y.(, I have)** tu n'as pas vu ce film?– mais si
   2 *n* oui *m inv*
yes-man ['jesmæn] *n Fam* béni-oui-oui *m inv*
yesterday ['jestədeɪ] **1** *n* hier *m*
   2 *adv* hier; **y. morning/evening** hier matin/soir
yet [jet] **1** *adv* (**a**) *(still)* encore; **I haven't finished y.** je n'ai pas encore fini; **don't go y.** ne pars pas tout de suite; **I'll catch her y.!** je finirai bien par l'attraper!; **as y.** jusqu'à présent; **not y.** pas encore; **y. again** encore une fois; **y. more** encore plus; **y. another mistake** encore une erreur (**b**) *(in questions)* **have they decided y.?** est-ce qu'ils ont décidé?
   2 *conj* cependant; **small y. strong** petit(e) mais fort(e); **and y. I like her** et pourtant, je l'aime bien
yeti ['jetɪ] *n* yéti *m*
yew [ju:] *n* if *m*
YHA *n (abbr* **Youth Hostels Association**) = association des auberges de jeunesse
Yiddish ['jɪdɪʃ] **1** *n* yiddish *m*
   2 *adj* yiddish *inv*
yield [ji:ld] **1** *n (of field, shares)* rendement *m*; *(of mine)* production *f*
   2 *vt* (**a**) *(interest)* rapporter; *(results)* donner; **to y. a profit** rapporter (**b**) *(territory, right)* céder
   3 *vi (surrender)* se rendre; **to y. to force** céder devant la force; **to y. to reason** se rendre à la raison; **to y. to temptation** céder à la tentation
yippee [jɪ'pi:] *exclam* youpi!
YMCA [waɪemsiː'eɪ] *n (abbr* **Young Men's Christian Association**) = association chrétienne proposant hébergement et activités sportives
yob [jɒb], **yobbo** ['jɒbəʊ] *(pl* **yobbos** *or* **yobboes**) *n Fam* loubard *m*
yodel ['jəʊdəl] *(pt & pp* **yodelled**) *vi* iodler
yoga ['jəʊgə] *n* yoga *m*
yoghurt, yogurt ['jɒgət] *n* yaourt *m*

yoke [jəʊk] **1** *n* (**a**) *(for oxen) & Fig* joug *m* (**b**) *(for carrying)* palanche *f*
   2 *vt (oxen)* atteler; *Fig* **to be yoked to sth** être lié(e) à qch
yokel ['jəʊkəl] *n Pej or Hum* péquenaud(e) *m,f*
yolk [jəʊk] *n* jaune *m* (d'œuf)
yonder ['jɒndə(r)] *adv* **(over) y.** là-bas
yonks [jɒŋks] *npl Br Fam* une éternité; **it was y. ago** ça fait une paye
Yorkshire pudding ['jɔːkʃɪə'pʊdɪŋ] *n* = croquette de pâte à frire servie avec le rosbif
you [ju:] *pron* (**a**) *(subject) (familiar)* tu; *(formal, familiar plural)* vous; **you're late** tu es/vous êtes en retard; **have YOU got it?** c'est toi qui l'as/vous qui l'avez?
   (**b**) *(direct object) (familiar)* te; *(formal, familiar plural)* vous; **I hate y.** je te/vous déteste; **I love y.** je t'aime/je vous aime; **I can understand your son but not YOU** je comprends ton fils, mais toi, je ne te comprends pas
   (**c**) *(indirect object) (familiar)* te; *(formal, familiar plural)* vous; **I gave y. the book** je t'ai/vous ai donné le livre; **I gave it to y.** je te/vous l'ai donné
   (**d**) *(after preposition) (familiar)* toi; *(formal, familiar plural)* vous; **I'm thinking of y.** je pense à toi/vous
   (**e**) *(as complement of verb* **to be***) (familiar)* toi; *(formal, familiar plural)* vous; **it's y.** c'est toi/vous; **it was y. who did it** c'est toi qui l'as fait/vous qui l'avez fait
   (**f**) *(impersonal)* on; **y. never know** on ne sait jamais; **y. have to be careful with her** il faut faire attention avec elle; **smoking is bad for y.** fumer est mauvais pour la santé
   (**g**) *(in apposition)* **y. men/French** vous les hommes/les Français; **y. idiot!** espèce d'idiot!
   (**h**) *(with imperative)* **y. sit down here** toi, tu t'assois ici; **don't y. dare!** je t'interdis de le faire!
   (**i**) *(with interjections)* **silly y.!** que tu es bête!; **poor y.!** pauvre de toi!
you'd [ju:d] = **you had, you would**
you-know-who [ju:nəʊ'hu:] *n* qui-tu-sais
you'll [ju:l] = **you will, you shall**
young [jʌŋ] **1** *adj* jeune; **she's younger than me** elle est plus jeune que moi; **she's two years younger than me** elle a deux ans de moins que moi; **you're only y. once** on n'a qu'une jeunesse; **when I was a y. man/woman** quand j'étais jeune; **in his younger days** dans sa jeunesse; **the night is y.!** la soirée ne fait que commencer!; **y. people** les jeunes *mpl*; **she's y. for her age** elle fait plus jeune que son âge; **y. in spirit** *or* **at heart** jeune d'esprit
   2 *npl* (**a**) *(people)* **the y.** les jeunes *mpl* (**b**) *(animals)* petits *mpl*
youngster ['jʌŋstə(r)] *n* jeune *mf*
your [jɔː(r)] *possessive adj* (**a**) *(with singular possession) (familiar)* ton (ta); *(formal, familiar plural)* votre; *(with plural possession) (familiar)* tes; *(formal, familiar plural)* vos; **y. job** ton/votre travail; **y. wife** ta/votre femme; **y. parents** tes/vos parents; **it wasn't YOUR idea!** ce n'est pas toi qui en as eu l'idée!
   (**b**) *(for parts of body)* **did you hit y. head?** vous vous êtes cogné la tête?
   (**c**) *(impersonal)* **you should buy y. ticket first** on doit acheter son billet d'abord; **smoking is bad for y. health** fumer est mauvais pour la santé; *Fam* **y. average Frenchman** le Français moyen
you're [jɔː(r)] = **you are**
yours [jɔːz] *possessive pron* (**a**) *(replacing singular possession) (familiar)* le tien (la tienne) *m,f*; *(formal,*

familiar plural) le vôtre (la vôtre) *m,f; (replacing plural possession) (familiar)* les tiens (les tiennes) *mpl,fpl; (formal, familiar plural)* les vôtres *mfpl;* **my house is big, but y. is bigger** ma maison est grande, mais la tienne est plus grande encore

    (**b**) *(used attributively)* **this book is y.** ce livre est à toi/à vous; **a friend of y.** un de tes/vos amis; **where's that brother of y.?** où ton frère a-t-il bien pu passer?

yourself [jɔː'self] *pron* (**a**) *(reflexive)* **did you hurt y.?** *(familiar)* tu t'es blessé?; *(formal)* vous vous êtes blessé?

    (**b**) *(emphatic) (familiar)* toi-même; *(formal)* vous-même; **you y. have never...** vous-même n'avez jamais...; **you told me y.** vous me l'avez dit vous-même; **you're not y. today** tu n'es pas dans ton état normal aujourd'hui

    (**c**) *(after preposition)* **do you live by y.?** vous vivez seul(e)?; **did you buy it for y.?** vous l'avez acheté pour vous-même?; **are you talking to y.?** tu parles tout(e) seul(e)?

yourselves [jɔː'selvz] *pron* (**a**) *(reflexive)* **have you hurt y.?** vous vous êtes blessés(ées)?

    (**b**) *(emphatic)* vous-mêmes; **you y. have never...** vous-mêmes n'avez jamais...; **you told me y.** vous me l'avez dit vous-mêmes; **you're not y. today** vous n'êtes pas dans votre état normal aujourd'hui

    (**c**) *(after preposition)* **do you live by y.?** vous vivez seuls(es)?; **did you buy it for y.?** vous l'avez acheté pour vous-mêmes?; **do you talk to y.?** vous parlez tout(es) seuls(es)?

youth [juːθ] *n* (**a**) *(period)* jeunesse *f* (**b**) *(young man)* adolescent *m*, jeune *m* (**c**) *(young people)* jeunes *mpl;* **y. club** centre *m* de loisir pour les jeunes; **y. hostel** auberge *f* de jeunesse; **y. worker** éducateur(trice) *m,f*

youthful ['juːθfʊl] *adj (person, looks)* jeune; *(enthusiasm)* juvénile

you've [juːv] = **you have**

yowl [jaʊl] **1** *n* hurlement *m*
    2 *vi* hurler

yo-yo® ['jəʊjəʊ] *(pl* **yo-yos**) *n* yo-yo® *m*

yr *(abbr* **year**) année *f*

yuan [juːæn] *n* yuan *m*

yucca ['jʌkə] *n* yucca *m*

yuck [jʌk] *exclam Fam* berk!

yucky ['jʌkɪ] *adj Fam* dégoûtant(e)

Yugoslav ['juːgəslɑːv] **1** *n* Yougoslave *mf*
    2 *adj* yougoslave

Yugoslavia [juːgəʊ'slɑːvɪə] *n* la Yougoslavie

Yugoslavian [juːgəʊ'slɑːvɪən] *adj* yougoslave

yuletide ['juːltaɪd] *n* Noël *m*

yummy ['jʌmɪ] *adj Fam* délicieux(euse)

yuppie ['jʌpɪ] *n* yuppie *mf;* **y. area** quartier *m* riche et branché; *Fam* **y. flu** syndrome *m* de la fatigue chronique

YWCA [waɪdʌbəljuːsiː'eɪ] *n (abbr* **Young Women's Christian Association**) = association chrétienne proposant hébergement et activités sportives

Z

Z, z [zed, *Am* ziː] *n (letter)* Z, z *m inv*

Zaire [zɑː'ɪə(r)] *n Formerly* le Zaïre

Zairean [zɑː'ɪərɪən] **1** *n* Zaïrois(oise) *m,f*
    2 *adj* zaïrois(oise)

Zambia ['zæmbɪə] *n* la Zambie

Zambian ['zæmbɪən] **1** *n* Zambien(enne) *m,f*
    2 *adj* zambien(enne)

zany ['zeɪnɪ] *adj* loufoque

zap [zæp] *(pt & pp* **zapped**) *Fam* **1** *vt* (**a**) *(destroy, disable)* éliminer (**b**) *Comput (delete)* effacer
    2 *vi* (**a**) *(change TV channel)* zapper (**b**) *(move quickly)* **to z. in/out/off** entrer/sortir/partir à toute pompe

zapper ['zæpə(r)] *n Fam (TV remote control)* télécommande *f*

zeal [ziːl] *n* zèle *m*

zealot ['zelət] *n* fanatique *mf*

zealous ['zeləs] *adj* zélé(e); *(campaigner, supporter)* fervent(e)

zebra [*Br* 'zebrə, *Am* 'ziːbrə] *n* zèbre *m; Br* **z. crossing** passage *m* pour piétons

zeds [zedz] *npl Fam (sleep)* **to catch some z.** piquer un roupillon

zenith ['zenɪθ] *n also Fig* zénith *m;* **at the z. of her powers/influence** au sommet de son pouvoir/influence

zephyr ['zefə(r)] *n* zéphyr *m*

zero ['zɪərəʊ] **1** *n (pl* **zeros**) zéro *m;* **22 degrees below z.** 22 degrés en dessous de zéro
    2 *adj Fam* aucun(e); **to have z. charm** n'avoir aucun charme; **z. tolerance** = politique d'intransigeance à l'égard de toute infraction à la loi ou au règlement
    3 *vi* **to z. in on sb** foncer sur qn; **to z. in on sth** se concentrer sur qch

zero-rated ['zɪərəʊreɪtɪd] *adj Fin (for VAT)* exonéré(e) de TVA

zest [zest] *n* (**a**) *(enjoyment)* enthousiasme *m* (**b**) *(of orange, lemon)* zeste *m*

zigzag ['zɪgzæg] **1** *n* zigzag *m*
    2 *vi (pt & pp* **zigzagged**) zigzaguer

zilch [zɪltʃ] *n Fam* que dalle

Zimbabwe [zɪm'bɑːbweɪ] *n* le Zimbabwe

Zimbabwean [zɪm'bɑːbweɪən] **1** *n* Zimbabwéen(enne) *m,f*
    2 *adj* zimbabwéen(enne)

zinc [zɪŋk] *n* zinc *m*

Zionism ['zaɪənɪzəm] *n* sionisme *m*

Zionist ['zaɪənɪst] *n & adj* sioniste *mf*

zip [zɪp] **1** *n* (**a**) *Br* **z. (fastener)** fermeture *f* Éclair® (**b**) *Fam (vigour)* punch *m* (**c**) *Am* **z. code** code *m* postal
    2 *vt Comput* zipper, compresser
    3 *vi (pt & pp* **zipped**) **to z. past** *(of car)* passer en trombe; *(of bullet)* passer en sifflant

▸**zip through** *vt insep Fam* **I zipped through the book** j'ai lu le livre à toute vitesse; **we zipped through the work** nous avons fait le travail à toute vitesse

▸**zip up 1** *vt sep (clothes)* remonter la fermeture Éclair® de
    2 *vi* se fermer par une fermeture Éclair®

Zip® disk ['zɪp'dɪsk] *n Comput* cartouche *f* Zip®

Zip® drive ['zɪp'draɪv] *n Comput* lecteur *m* Zip®

zipper ['zɪpə(r)] *n Am* fermeture *f* Éclair®

zippy ['zɪpɪ] *adj Fam* plein(e) de punch

zit [zɪt] *n Fam* bouton *m*

zither ['zɪðə(r)] *n* cithare *f*

zodiac ['zəʊdɪæk] *n* zodiaque *m*

zombie ['zɒmbɪ] *n* zombi *m*

zone [zəʊn] **1** *n* zone *f*
    2 *vt* diviser en zones

zonked (out) [zɒŋkt('aʊt)] *adj Fam (exhausted)* cassé(e); *(drugged)* défoncé(e); *(drunk)* pété(e)

zoo [zuː] *n* zoo *m*

zoological [zəʊə'lɒdʒɪkəl] *adj* zoologique; **z. garden(s)** jardin *m* zoologique

zoologist [zəʊ'ɒlədʒɪst] *n* zoologiste *mf*

zoology [zəʊ'ɒlədʒɪ] *n* zoologie *f*

zoom [zuːm] **1** *n* (**a**) *(noise)* vrombissement *m* (**b**) **z. lens** zoom *m*
    2 *vi Fam* (**a**) *(move quickly)* **to z. in/out/past** entrer/sortir/passer comme une flèche (**b**) *(increase quickly)* monter en flèche

▸**zoom in** *vi (of camera)* faire un zoom avant (**on** sur)

zucchini [zuː'kiːnɪ] *(pl* **zucchini** *or* **zucchinis**) *n Am* courgette *f*

Zulu ['zuːluː] **1** *n* Zoulou *mf*
    2 *adj* zoulou(e)

Supplement
Supplément

Verbes Anglais Irréguliers
English Irregular Verbs

Infinitif	Prétérit	Participe passé
arise	arose	arisen
awake	awoke	awoken
awaken	awoke, awakened	awakened, awoken
be	were/was	been
bear	bore	borne
beat	beat	beaten
become	became	become
begin	began	begun
bend	bent	bent
beseech	besought, beseeched	besought, beseeched
bet	bet, betted	bet, betted
bid	bade, bid	bidden, bid
bind	bound	bound
bite	bIt	bitten
bleed	bled	bled
blow	blew	blown
break	broke	broken
breed	bred	bred
bring	brought	brought
build	built	built
burn	burnt, burned	burnt, burned
burst	burst	burst
bust	bust, busted	bust, busted
buy	bought	bought
cast	cast	cast
catch	caught	caught
chide	chided, chid	chided, chidden
choose	chose	chosen
cleave	cleaved, cleft, clove	cleaved, cleft, cloven
cling	clung	clung
clothe	clad, clothed	clad, clothed
come	came	come
cost	cost	cost
creep	crept	crept
crow	crowed, crew	crowed
cut	cut	cut
deal	dealt	dealt
dig	dug	dug
dive	dived, *Am* dove	dived
do	did	done
draw	drew	drawn
dream	dreamt, dreamed	dreamt, dreamed
drink	drank	drunk
drive	drove	driven
dwell	dwelt	dwelt
eat	ate	eaten
fall	fell	fallen
feed	fed	fed
feel	felt	felt

Infinitif	Prétérit	Participe passé
fight	fought	fought
find	found	found
flee	fled	fled
fling	flung	flung
fly	flew	flown
forget	forgot	forgotten
forgive	forgave	forgiven
forsake	forsook	forsaken
freeze	froze	frozen
get	got	got, *Am* gotten
gild	gilded, gilt	gilded, gilt
gird	girded, girt	girded, girt
give	gave	given
go	went	gone
grind	ground	ground
grow	grew	grown
hang	hung/hanged	hung/hanged
have	had	had
hear	heard	heard
hew	hewed	hewn, hewed
hide	hid	hidden
hit	hit	hit
hold	held	held
hurt	hurt	hurt
keep	kept	kept
kneel	knelt	knelt
knit	knitted, knit	knitted, knit
know	knew	known
lay	laid	laid
lead	led	led
lean	leant, leaned	leant, leaned
leap	leapt, leaped	leapt, leaped
learn	learnt, learned	learnt, learned
leave	left	left
lend	lent	lent
let	let	let
lie	lay	lain
light	lit	lit
lose	lost	lost
make	made	made
mean	meant	meant
meet	met	met
mow	mowed	mown
pay	paid	paid
plead	pleaded, *Am* pled	pleaded, *Am* pled
prove	proved	proved, proven
put	put	put
quit	quit	quit
read	read	read
rend	rent	rent
rid	rid	rid
ride	rode	ridden
ring	rang	rung
rise	rose	risen
run	ran	run
saw	sawed	sawn, sawed
say	said	said

Infinitif	Prétérit	Participe passé
see	saw	seen
seek	sought	sought
sell	sold	sold
send	sent	sent
set	set	set
sew	sewed	sewn
shake	shook	shaken
shear	sheared	shorn, sheared
shed	shed	shed
shine	shone	shone
shit	shitted, shat	shitted, shat
shoe	shod	shod
shoot	shot	shot
show	showed	shown
shrink	shrank	shrunk
shut	shut	shut
sing	sang	sung
sink	sank	sunk
sit	sat	sat
slay	slew	slain
sleep	slept	slept
slide	slid	slid
sling	slung	slung
slink	slunk	slunk
slit	slit	slit
smell	smelled, smelt	smelled, smelt
smite	smote	smitten
sow	sowed	sown, sowed
speak	spoke	spoken
speed	sped	sped
spell	spelt, spelled	spelt, spelled
spend	spent	spent
spill	spilt, spilled	spilt, spilled
spin	span	spun
spit	spat, *Am* spit	spat, *Am* spit
split	split	split
spoil	spoilt, spoiled	spoilt, spoiled
spread	spread	spread
spring	sprang	sprung
stand	stood	stood
stave in	staved in, stove in	staved in, stove in
steal	stole	stolen
stick	stuck	stuck
sting	stung	stung
stink	stank, stunk	stunk
strew	strewed	strewed, strewn
stride	strode	stridden
strike	struck	struck
string	strung	strung
strive	strove	striven
swear	swore	sworn
sweep	swept	swept
swell	swelled	swollen, swelled
swim	swam	swum
swing	swung	swung
take	took	taken
teach	taught	taught

Infinitif	Prétérit	Participe passé
tear	tore	torn
tell	told	told
think	thought	thought
thrive	thrived, throve	thrived
throw	threw	thrown
thrust	thrust	thrust
tread	trod	trodden
wake	woke	woken
wear	wore	worn
weave	wove, weaved	woven, weaved
weep	wept	wept
wet	wet, wetted	wet, wetted
win	won	won
wind	wound	wound
wring	wrung	wrung
write	wrote	written

French Conjugation Tables
Conjugaisons Françaises

Full listings of the conjugations of French regular -er, -ir and -re verbs are given on pages (8) and (9). On the following pages you will find a list of model irregular verbs. Numbers after verbs in the French-English side of the dictionary, eg [20], refer you to these tables where you will find their irregular forms.

The more common verbs such as **aller, avoir, être** and **faire** are shown in full for all persons and all tenses. In other cases, where complete forms have not been shown they follow the pattern indicated by the first person singular and/or plural.

As the perfect tense is always formed simply by **avoir** or être plus the past participle, this has not been shown apart from the verbs mentioned above. Similarly, the conditional tense can always be formed in the same way as the future tense but with the endings **-ais, -ais, -ait, -ions, -iez** and **-aient**. When not shown, the imperative has the same form as the present tense ("tu", "nous" and "vous" forms).

Toutes les formes des verbes réguliers en **-er, -ir** et **-re** sont données pages (8) et (9), suivies d'une liste de conjugaisons irrégulières types. Les nombres apparaissant après les verbes dans la partie français-anglais du dictionnaire, par exemple [20], renvoient à cette liste.

Toutes les personnes et tous les temps sont donnés systématiquement pour les verbes d'usage fréquent tels qu'**aller, avoir, être** et **faire**. Dans tous les autres cas, seules les formes particulières, c'est-à-dire celles qui ne suivent pas le modèle déterminé par la première personne du singulier et/ou du pluriel, sont indiquées.

Le passé composé étant toujours formé sur le modèle **avoir/être** + participe passé, il n'a pas été inclus dans nos listes, sauf pour les verbes mentionnés ci-dessus. De même, le conditionnel se construira à partir du futur.

INDICATIVE

Present	Imperfect	Perfect	Past Historic	Future
REGULAR -er verb aimer				
j'aime	j'aimais	j'ai aimé	j'aimai	j'aimerai
tu aimes	tu aimais	tu as aimé	tu aimas	tu aimeras
il aime	il aimait	il a aimé	il aima	il aimera
nous aimons	nous aimions	nous avons aimé	nous aimâmes	nous aimerons
vous aimez	vous aimiez	vous avez aimé	vous aimâtes	vous aimerez
ils aiment	ils aimaient	ils ont aimé	ils aimèrent	ils aimeront
REGULAR -ir verb choisir				
je choisis	je choisissais	j'ai choisi	je choisis	je choisirai
tu choisis	tu choisissais	tu as choisi	tu choisis	tu choisiras
il choisit	il choisissait	il a choisi	il choisit	il choisira
nous choisissons	nous choisissions	nous avons choisi	nous choisîmes	nous choisirons
vous choisissez	vous choisissiez	vous avez choisi	vous choisîtes	vous choisirez
ils choisissent	ils choisissaient	ils ont choisi	ils choisirent	ils choisiront
REGULAR -re verb attendre				
j'attends	j'attendais	j'ai attendu	j'attendis	j'attendrai
tu attends	tu attendais	tu as attendu	tu attendis	tu attendras
il attend	il attendait	il a attendu	il attendit	il attendra
nous attendons	nous attendions	nous avons attendu	nous attendîmes	nous attendrons
vous attendez	vous attendiez	vous avez attendu	vous attendîtes	vous attendrez
ils attendent	ils attendaient	ils ont attendu	ils attendirent	ils attendront

CONDITIONAL Present	SUBJUNCTIVE Present	Imperfect	IMPERATIVE	PARTICIPLE Present	Past
j'aimerais	j'aime	j'aimasse		aimant	aimé
tu aimerais	tu aimes	tu aimasses	aime		
il aimerait	il aime	il aimât			
nous aimerions	nous aimions	nous aimassions	aimons		
vous aimeriez	vous aimiez	vous aimassiez	aimez		
ils aimeraient	ils aiment	ils aimassent			
je choisirais	je choisisse	je choisisse		choisissant	choisi
tu choisirais	tu choisisses	tu choisisses	choisis		
il choisirait	il choisisse	il choisît			
nous choisirions	nous choisissions	nous choisissions	choisissons		
vous choisiriez	vous choisissiez	vous choisissiez	choisissez		
ils choisiraient	ils choisissent	ils choisissent			
j'attendrais	j'attende	j'attendisse		attendant	attendu
tu attendrais	tu attendes	tu attendisses	attends		
il attendrait	il attende	il attendît			
nous attendrions	nous attendions	nous attendissions	attendons		
vous attendriez	vous attendiez	vous attendissiez	attendez		
ils attendraient	ils attendent	ils attendissent			

INDICATIVE

Present	Imperfect	Perfect	Past Historic	Future

1. avoir

j'ai	j'avais	j'ai eu	j'eus	j'aurai
tu as	tu avais	tu as eu	tu eus	tu auras
il a	il avait	il a eu	il eut	il aura
nous avons	nous avions	nous avons eu	nous eûmes	nous aurons
vous avez	vous aviez	vous avez eu	vous eûtes	vous aurez
ils ont	ils avaient	ils ont eu	ils eurent	ils auront

2. être

je suis	j'étais	j'ai été	je fus	je serai
tu es	tu étais	tu as été	tu fus	tu seras
il est	il était	il a été	il fut	il sera
nous sommes	nous étions	nous avons été	nous fûmes	nous serons
vous êtes	vous étiez	vous avez été	vous fûtes	vous serez
ils sont	ils étaient	ils ont été	ils furent	ils seront

3a. absoudre

j'absous	j'absolvais		j'absolus	j'absoudrai
il absout				
nous absolvons				

3b. résoudre *follows the above pattern except for the following*

			je résolus	

4a. accroître

j'accrois	j'accroissais		j'accrus	j'accroîtrai
il accroît				
nous accroissons				

4b. croître *follows the above pattern except for the following*

je crois			je crûs	

5. accueillir

j'accueille	j'accueillais		j'accueillis	j'accueillerai
nous accueillons				

6. acheter

j'achète	j'achetais		j'achetai	j'achèterai
nous achetons				
ils achètent				

7. acquérir

j'acquiers	j'acquérais		j'acquis	j'acquerrai
il acquiert				
nous acquérons				
ils acquièrent				

8. aller

je vais	j'allais	je suis allé	j'allai	j'irai
tu vas	tu allais	tu es allé	tu allas	tu iras
il va	il allait	il est allé	il alla	il ira
nous allons	nous allions	nous sommes allés	nous allâmes	nous irons
vous allez	vous alliez	vous êtes allés	vous allâtes	vous irez
ils vont	ils allaient	ils sont allés	ils allèrent	ils iront

CONDITIONAL Present	SUBJUNCTIVE Present	Imperfect	IMPERATIVE	PARTICIPLE Present	Past
j'aurais	j'aie	j'eusse		ayant	eu
tu aurais	tu aies	tu eusses	aie		
il aurait	il ait	il eût			
nous aurions	nous ayons	nous eussions	ayons		
vous auriez	vous ayez	vous eussiez	ayez		
ils auraient	ils aient	ils eussent			
je serais	je sois	je fusse		étant	été
tu serais	tu sois	tu fusses	sois		
il serait	il soit	il fût			
nous serions	nous soyons	nous fussions	soyons		
vous seriez	vous soyez	vous fussiez	soyez		
ils seraient	ils soient	ils fussent			
	j'absolve	*not used*		absolvant	absous (oute)
	nous absolvions				
					résolu
	j'accroisse	j'accrusse		accroissant	accru
	nous accroissions	nous accrussions			
		je crûsse			crû
	j'accueille	j'accueillisse		accueillant	accueilli
	nous accueillions	nous accueillissions	accueille		
			accueillons		
			accueillez		
	j'achète	j'achetasse		achetant	acheté
	nous achetions	nous achetassions			
	j'acquière	j'acquisse		acquérant	acquis
	nous acquérions	nous acquissions			
j'irais	j'aille	j'allasse		allant	allé
tu irais	tu ailles	tu allasses	va		
il irait	il aille	il allât			
nous irions	nous allions	nous allassions	allons		
vous iriez	vous alliez	vous allassiez	allez		
ils iraient	ils aillent	ils allassent			

INDICATIVE

Present	Imperfect	Perfect	Past Historic	Future
9. appeler				
j'appelle nous appelons ils appellent	j'appelais		j'appelai	j'appellerai
10a. s'asseoir				
je m'assieds/ assois il s'assied/assoit nous nous asseyons/ assoyons	je m'asseyais/ assoyais		je m'assis	je m'assiérai/assoirai
10b. surseoir *follows pattern of oi forms of* s'asseoir				
				je surseoirai
11. battre				
je bats il bat nous battons	je battais		je battis	je battrai
12. boire				
je bois il boit nous buvons ils boivent	je buvais		je bus	je boirai
13. bouillir				
je bous il bout nous bouillons	je bouillais		je bouillis	je bouillirai
14. choir				
je chois il chut ils choient			il chût	
15. clore				
je clos il clôt ils closent				je clorai
16. commencer				
je commence nous commençons vous commencez ils commencent	je commençais		je commençai	je commencerai
17. conclure				
je conclus il conclut nous concluons	je concluais		je conclus	je conclurai

CONDITIONAL Present	SUBJUNCTIVE Present	Imperfect	IMPERATIVE	PARTICIPLE Present	Past
	j'appelle	j'appelasse		appelant	appelé
	nous appelions	nous appelassions			
	je m'asseye/	je m'assisse		asseyant/	assis
	assoie			assoyant	
	nous nous	nous nous			
	asseyions/	assissions			
	assoyions				
je surseoirais					
	je batte	je battisse		battant	battu
	nous battions	nous battissions			
	je boive	je busse		buvant	bu
	nous buvions	nous bussions			
	je bouille	je bouillisse		bouillant	bouilli
	nous bouillions	nous bouillissions			
					chu
	je close				clos
	nous closions				
	je commence	je commençasse		commençant	commencé
	nous commencions	nous commençassions			
	je conclue	je conclusse		concluant	conclu
	nous concluions	nous conclussions			

INDICATIVE

Present	Imperfect	Perfect	Past Historic	Future

18. conduire

je conduis	je conduisais		je conduisis	je conduirai
il conduit				
nous conduisons				

19a. confire

je confis	je confisais		je confis	je confira
il confit				
nous confisons				

19b. suffire PAST PARTICIPLE suffi (invariable)

20. connaître

je connais	je connaissais		je connus	je connaîtrai
il connaît				
nous connaissons				

21. coudre

je couds	je cousais		je cousis	je coudrai
il coud				
nous cousons				

22. courir

je cours	je courais		je courus	je courrai
il court				
nous courons				

23. craindre

je crains	je craignais		je craignis	je craindrai
il craint				
nous craignons				

24. créer

je crée	je créais		je créai	je créerai
nous créons				

25. croire

je crois	je croyais		je crus	je croirai
il croit				
nous croyons				
ils croient				

26. devoir

je dois	je devais		je dus	je devrai
il doit				
nous devons				
ils doivent				

27a. dire

je dis	je disais		je dis	je dirai
il dit				
nous disons				
vous dites				

| CONDITIONAL | SUBJUNCTIVE | | IMPERATIVE | PARTICIPLE | |
Present	Present	Imperfect		Present	Past
	je conduise	je conduisisse		conduisant	conduit
	nous conduisions	nous conduisissions			
	je confise	je confisse		confisant	confit
	nous confisions	nous confissions			
	je connaisse	je connusse		connaissant	connu
	nous connaissions	nous connussions			
	je couse	je cousisse		cousant	cousu
	nous cousions	nous cousissions			
	je coure	je courusse		courant	couru
	nous courions	nous courussions			
	je craigne	je craignisse		craignant	craint
	nous craignions	nous craignissions			
	je crée	je créasse		créant	créé
	nous créions	nous créassions			
	je croie	je crusse		croyant	cru
	nous croyions	nous crussions			
	je doive	je dusse		devant	dû (due), dus (dues)
	nous devions	nous dussions			
	je dise	je disse		disant	dit
	nous disions	nous dissions			

INDICATIVE

Present	Imperfect	Perfect	Past Historic	Future

27b. contredire, interdire etc PRESENT vous contredisez, interdisez

28. distraire

je distrais	je distrayais			je distrairai
il distrait				
nous distrayons				
ils distraient				

29. dormir

je dors	je dormais		je dormis	je dormirai
il dort				
nous dormons				

30. écrire

j'écris	j'écrivais		j'écrivis	j'écrirai
il écrit				
nous écrivons				

31a. émouvoir

j'émeus	j'émouvais		j'émus	j'émouvrai
il émeut				
nous émouvons				
ils émeuvent				

31b. mouvoir PAST PARTICIPLE mû (mue), mus (mues)

32. employer

j'emploie	j'employais		j'employai	j'emploierai
nous employons				
ils emploient				

33. envoyer

j'envoie	j'envoyais		j'envoyai	j'enverrai
nous envoyons				
ils envoient				

34. espérer

j'espère	j'espérais		j'espérai	j'espérerai
nous espérons				
ils espèrent				

35. faillir

je faillis				je faillirai

36. faire

je fais	je faisais	j'ai fait	je fis	je ferai
tu fais	tu faisais	tu as fait	tu fis	tu feras
il fait	il faisait	il a fait	il fit	il fera
nous faisons	nous faisions	nous avons fait	nous fîmes	nous ferons
vous faites	vous faisiez	vous avez fait	vous fîtes	vous ferez
ils font	ils faisaient	ils ont fait	ils firent	ils feront

37. falloir

il faut	il fallait		il fallut	il faudra

| CONDITIONAL | SUBJUNCTIVE | | IMPERATIVE | PARTICIPLE | |
Present	Present	Imperfect		Present	Past
	je distraie			distrayant	distrait
	nous distrayions				
	je dorme	je dormisse		dormant	dormi
	nous dormions	nous dormissions			
	j'écrive	j'écrivisse		écrivant	écrit
	nous écrivions	nous écrivissions			
	j'émeuve	j'émusse		émouvant	ému
	nous émouvions	nous émussions			
	j'emploie	j'employasse		employant	employé
	nous employions	nous employassions			
	j'envoie	j'envoyasse		envoyant	envoyé
	nous envoyions	nous envoyassions			
	j'espère	j'espérasse		espérant	espéré
	nous espérions	nous espérassions			
				faillant	failli
je ferais	je fasse	je fisse		faisant	fait
tu ferais	tu fasses	tu fisses	fais		
il ferait	il fasse	il fît			
nous ferions	nous fassions	nous fissions	faisons		
vous feriez	vous fassiez	vous fissiez	faites		
ils feraient	ils fassent	ils fissent			
					fallu
	il faille	il fallût			

INDICATIVE

Present	Imperfect	Perfect	Past Historic	Future
38. fuir				
je fuis	je fuyais		je fuis	je fuirai
il fuit				
nous fuyons				
ils fuient				
39. geler				
je gèle	je gelais		je gelai	je gèlerai
nous gelons	nous gelions			
ils gèlent				
40. gésir				
je gis	je gisais			
il gît				
nous gisons				
41. haïr				
je hais	je haïssais		je haïs	je haïrai
il hait				
nous haïssons				
42. jeter				
je jette	je jetais		je jetai	je jetterai
nous jetons				
ils jettent				
43. joindre				
je joins	je joignais		je joignis	je joindrai
nous joignons				
44. lire				
je lis	je lisais		je lus	je lirai
nous lisons				
45. manger				
je mange	je mangeais		je mangeai	je mangerai
nous mangeons				
46. mener				
je mène	je menais		je menai	je mènerai
nous menons				
ils mènent				
47. mettre				
je mets	je mettais		je mis	je mettrai
il met				
nous mettons				
48. moudre				
je mouds	je moulais		je moulus	je moudrai
il moud				
nous moulons				

CONDITIONAL	SUBJUNCTIVE		IMPERATIVE	PARTICIPLE	
Present	Present	Imperfect		Present	Past
	je fuie	je fuisse		fuyant	fui
	nous fuyions	nous fuissions			
	je gèle	je gelasse		gelant	gelé
		nous gelassions			
				gisant	
	je haïsse	je haïsse		haïssant	haï
	nous haïssions	nous haïssions			
	je jette	je jetasse		jetant	jeté
	nous jetions	nous jetassions			
	je joigne	je joignisse		joignant	joint
	nous joignions	nous joignissions			
	je lise	je lusse		lisant	lu
	nous lisions	nous lussions			
	je mange	je mangeasse		mangeant	mangé
	nous mangions	nous mangeassions			
	je mène	je menasse		menant	mené
	nous menions	nous menassions			
	je mette	je misse		mettant	mis
	nous mettions	nous missions			
	je moule	je moulusse		moulant	moulu
	nous moulions	nous moulussions			

INDICATIVE

Present	Imperfect	Perfect	Past Historic	Future
49. mourir				
je meurs il meurt nous mourons ils meurent	je mourais		je mourus	je mourrai
50a. naître				
je nais il naît nous naissons	je naissais		je naquis	je naîtrai
50b. paître no PAST HISTORIC; PAST PARTICIPLE pu (invariable; rare)				
50c. repaître as paître but PAST HISTORIC je repus				
51. ouïr				
j'ois il oit nous oyons ils oient	j'oyais		j'ouïs	j'ouïrai
52. ouvrir				
j'ouvre nous ouvrons	j'ouvrais		j'ouvris	j'ouvrirai
53. payer				
je paie/paye nous payons ils paient/payent	je payais		je payai	je paierai/payerai
54. peindre				
je peins il peint nous peignons	je peignais		je peignis	je peindrai
55a. plaire				
je plais il plaît	je plaisais nous plaisions		je plus	je plairai
55b. taire PRESENT il tait				
56. pleuvoir				
il pleut	il pleuvait		il plut	il pleuvra
57. pouvoir				
je peux/puis il peut nous pouvons	je pouvais		je pus	je pourrai
58. prendre				
je prends il prend nous prenons ils prennent	je prenais		je pris	je prendrai

CONDITIONAL Present	SUBJUNCTIVE Present	Imperfect	IMPERATIVE	PARTICIPLE Present	Past
	je meure	je mourusse		mourant	mort
	nous mourions	nous mourussions			
	je naisse	je naquisse		naissant	né
	nous naissions	nous naquissions			
	j'oie	j'ouïsse		oyant	ouï
	nous oyions				
	j'ouvre		ouvre	ouvrant	ouvert
	nous ouvrions		ouvrons ouvrez		
	je paie/paye	je payasse		payant	payé
	nous payions	nous payassions			
	je peigne	je peignisse		peignant	peint
	nous peignions	nous peignissions			
	je plaise	je plusse		plaisant	plu
	nous plaisions	nous plussions			
	il pleuve	il plût		pleuvant	plu
	je puisse	je pusse		pouvant	pu
	nous puissions	nous pussions			
	je prenne	je prisse		prenant	pris
	nous prenions	nous prissions			

INDICATIVE

Present	Imperfect	Perfect	Past Historic	Future
59. protéger				
je protège	je protégeais		je protégeai	je protégerai
nous protégeons				
ils protègent				
60. recevoir				
je reçois	je recevais		je reçus	je recevrai
il reçoit				
nous recevons				
ils reçoivent				
61. rire				
je ris	je riais		je ris	je rirai
il rit				
nous rions				
62. savoir				
je sais	je savais		je sus	je saurai
il sait				
nous savons				
63. servir				
je sers	je servais		je servis	je servirai
il sert				
nous servons				
64a. sortir				
je sors	je sortais		je sortis	je sortirai
il sort				
nous sortons				
64b. mentir PAST PARTICIPLE is invariable				
65. suivre				
je suis	je suivais		je suivis	je suivrai
il suit				
nous suivons				
66. supplier				
je supplie	je suppliais		je suppliai	je supplierai
nous supplions				
67. tressaillir				
je tressaille	je tressaillais		je tressaillis	je tressaillirai
nous tressaillons				
68. vaincre				
je vaincs	je vainquais		je vainquis	je vaincrai
il vainc				
nous vainquons				
69. valoir				
je vaux	je valais		je valus	je vaudrai
il vaut				
nous valons				

CONDITIONAL	SUBJUNCTIVE		IMPERATIVE	PARTICIPLE	
Present	Present	Imperfect		Present	Past
	je protège	je protégeasse		protégeant	protégé
	nous protégions	nous protégeassions			
	je reçoive	je reçusse		recevant	reçu
	nous recevions	nous reçussions			
	je rie	je risse		riant	ri
	nous riions	nous rissions			
	je sache	je susse		sachant	su
	nous sachions	nous sussions	sache sachons sachez		
	je serve	je servisse		servant	servi
	nous servions	nous servissions			
	je sorte	je sortisse		sortant	sorti
	nous sortions	nous sortissions			
	je suive	je suivisse		suivant	suivi
	nous suivions	nous suivissions			
	je supplie	je suppliasse		suppliant	supplié
	nous suppliions	nous suppliassions			
	je tressaille	je tressaillisse		tressaillant	tressailli
	nous tressaillions	nous tressaillissions			
	je vainque	je vainquisse		vainquant	vaincu
	nous vainquions	nous vainquissions			
	je vaille	je valusse		valant	valu
	nous valions	nous valussions			

INDICATIVE

Present	Imperfect	Perfect	Past Historic	Future

70. venir

je viens il vient nous venons ils viennent	je venais		je vins	je viendrai

71. vêtir

je vêts il vêt nous vêtons	je vêtais		je vêtis	je vêtirai

72. vivre

je vis il vit nous vivons	je vivais		je vécus	je vivrai

73a. voir

je vois il voit nous voyons ils voient	je voyais		je vis	je verrai

73b. pourvoir *follows the above pattern except for the following*

			je pourvus	je pourvoirai

73c. prévoir *follows the above pattern except for the following*

			je prévus	je prévoirai

74. vouloir

je veux il veut nous voulons ils veulent	je voulais		je voulus	je voudrai

CONDITIONAL Present	SUBJUNCTIVE Present	Imperfect	IMPERATIVE	PARTICIPLE Present	Past
	je vienne	je vinsse		venant	venu
	nous venions	nous vinssions			
	je vête	je vêtisse		vêtant	vêtu
	nous vêtions	nous vêtissions			
	je vive	je vécusse		vivant	vécu
	nous vivions	nous vécussions			
	je voie	je visse		voyant	vu
	nous voyions	nous vissions			
je pourvoirais					
je prévoirais					
	je veuille	je voulusse		voulant	voulu
	nous voulions	nous voulussions	veuille veuillons		
			veuillez		

Guide de communication en anglais

La correspondance

Ce guide a pour objectif de vous aider à rédiger un courrier en anglais : vous y trouverez des conseils sur la mise en page, les formules d'appel et de politesse, la rédaction de l'adresse ainsi que de nombreux modèles de lettres et suggestions de tournures à employer dans la correspondance privée ou commerciale, le courrier électronique et les documents transmis par télécopie.

Formules d'appel et formules de politesse

La formule de politesse varie en fonction de la formule d'appel utilisée.

▪ formule d'appel	▪ formule de politesse
Lorsqu'on ne connaît pas le nom de la personne à qui l'on s'adresse :	
Dear Sir **Dear Madam** Lorsqu'on ne sait pas s'il s'agit d'un homme ou d'une femme : **Dear Sir or Madam** ou **Dear Sir/Madam** Lorsqu'on s'adresse à une société ou à un organisme sans préciser le nom du destinataire: **Dear Sirs** (Br) **Gentlemen** (Am)	**Yours faithfully** (Br) En anglais américain, la formule de politesse est toujours inversée : **Faithfully yours** (Am)
Lorsqu'on connaît le nom de la personne à qui l'on s'adresse :	
Dear Mr Jameson **Dear Mrs Lucas** **Dear Miss Crookshaw** **Dear Ms Greening** (L'abréviation Ms est de plus en plus employée lorsqu'on s'adresse à une femme car elle permet de ne pas préciser s'il s'agit d'une femme mariée (Mrs) ou non (Miss).) **Dear Dr Illingworth** Aux États-Unis, l'abréviation est généralement suivie d'un point : Mr., Mrs., Ms., Dr. Lorsqu'on s'adresse au rédacteur en chef d'un journal : **Sir** à un député: **Dear Mr/Mrs Brown** à un représentant ou membre du Congrès: **Sir/Madam** **Dear Congressman/Congresswoman Fox**	**Yours sincerely** (Br) **Sincerely yours** (Am) **Sincerely** (Am) Ton plus amical : **Yours very sincerely** (Br) Style moins soutenu : **With best wishes** **With kind regards** **Kindest regards** Plus rare : **Yours respectfully** (Br) **Respectfully yours** (Am) **Respectfully** (Am)

Lorsqu'on s'adresse à de la famille ou à des amis :

- **En début de lettre**

  Dear Bill
  Dear Helen
  Dear Tom and Barbara
  Dear all
  Dear Mum and Dad
  Dear Uncle Ralph/Auntie Ann
  My dear Alex
  Dearest/My dearest Kate

- **En fin de lettre**

  With love
  Love
  Love from
  Love and best wishes

  Plus affectueux :
  With all my/our love
  Much love

  Plus familier :
  Lots of love

  Plus soutenu :
  Yours
  All the best (Br)
  Best wishes
  Regards

Présentation d'une lettre dactylographiée

Les paragraphes sont alignés à gauche, sans retrait, et séparés par une ligne de blanc.

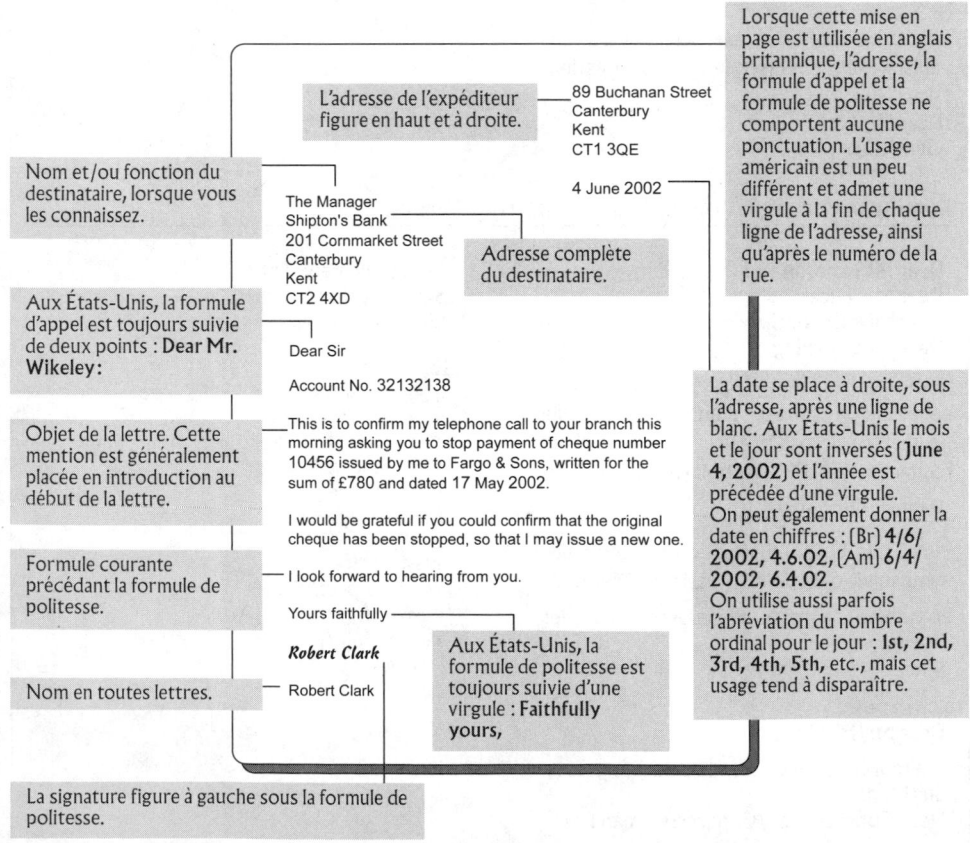

Lorsque cette mise en page est utilisée en anglais britannique, l'adresse, la formule d'appel et la formule de politesse ne comportent aucune ponctuation. L'usage américain est un peu différent et admet une virgule à la fin de chaque ligne de l'adresse, ainsi qu'après le numéro de la rue.

L'adresse de l'expéditeur figure en haut et à droite.

89 Buchanan Street
Canterbury
Kent
CT1 3QE

4 June 2002

Nom et/ou fonction du destinataire, lorsque vous les connaissez.

The Manager
Shipton's Bank
201 Cornmarket Street
Canterbury
Kent
CT2 4XD

Adresse complète du destinataire.

Aux États-Unis, la formule d'appel est toujours suivie de deux points : **Dear Mr. Wikeley:**

Dear Sir

Account No. 32132138

Objet de la lettre. Cette mention est généralement placée en introduction au début de la lettre.

This is to confirm my telephone call to your branch this morning asking you to stop payment of cheque number 10456 issued by me to Fargo & Sons, written for the sum of £780 and dated 17 May 2002.

I would be grateful if you could confirm that the original cheque has been stopped, so that I may issue a new one.

Formule courante précédant la formule de politesse.

I look forward to hearing from you.

Yours faithfully

Nom en toutes lettres.

Robert Clark

Robert Clark

Aux États-Unis, la formule de politesse est toujours suivie d'une virgule : **Faithfully yours,**

La date se place à droite, sous l'adresse, après une ligne de blanc. Aux États-Unis le mois et le jour sont inversés (**June 4, 2002**) et l'année est précédée d'une virgule.
On peut également donner la date en chiffres : (Br) **4/6/2002, 4.6.02,** (Am) **6/4/2002, 6.4.02.**
On utilise aussi parfois l'abréviation du nombre ordinal pour le jour : **1st, 2nd, 3rd, 4th, 5th,** etc., mais cet usage tend à disparaître.

La signature figure à gauche sous la formule de politesse.

Présentation d'une lettre manuscrite à un ami

Chaque paragraphe commence par un alinéa.

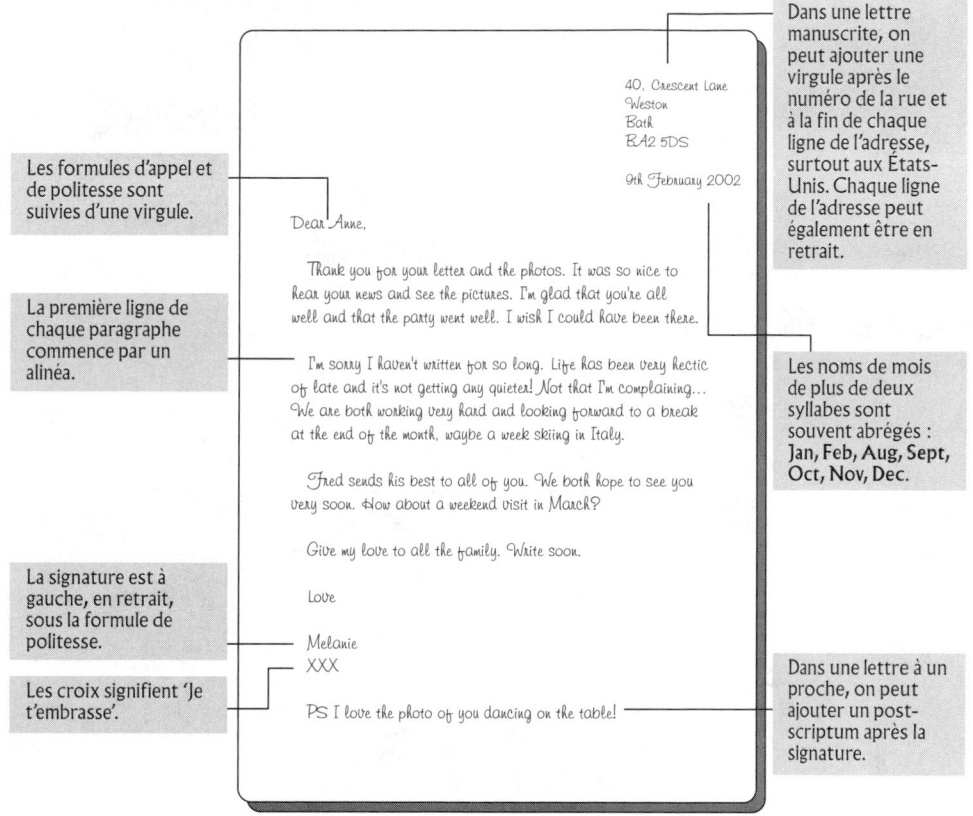

Dans une lettre manuscrite, on peut ajouter une virgule après le numéro de la rue et à la fin de chaque ligne de l'adresse, surtout aux États-Unis. Chaque ligne de l'adresse peut également être en retrait.

Les formules d'appel et de politesse sont suivies d'une virgule.

La première ligne de chaque paragraphe commence par un alinéa.

Les noms de mois de plus de deux syllabes sont souvent abrégés : Jan, Feb, Aug, Sept, Oct, Nov, Dec.

La signature est à gauche, en retrait, sous la formule de politesse.

Les croix signifient 'Je t'embrasse'.

Dans une lettre à un proche, on peut ajouter un post-scriptum après la signature.

Contenu de la lettre :

40, Crescent Lane
Weston
Bath
BA2 5DS

9th February 2002

Dear Anne,

Thank you for your letter and the photos. It was so nice to hear your news and see the pictures. I'm glad that you're all well and that the party went well. I wish I could have been there.

I'm sorry I haven't written for so long. Life has been very hectic of late and it's not getting any quieter! Not that I'm complaining... We are both working very hard and looking forward to a break at the end of the month, maybe a week skiing in Italy.

Fred sends his best to all of you. We both hope to see you very soon. How about a weekend visit in March?

Give my love to all the family. Write soon.

Love

Melanie
XXX

PS I love the photo of you dancing on the table!

Enveloppes et adresses

L'adresse doit être aussi précise que possible. Les sites Web des services postaux des différents pays peuvent être utiles pour trouver l'adresse complète d'un particulier, d'un organisme ou d'une entreprise, y compris le code postal précis.

Royaume-Uni : www.royalmail.com
Canada : www.canadapost.ca
Irlande : www.anpost.ie
États-Unis : www.usps.gov
Australie : www.auspost.com.au
Nouvelle-Zélande : www.nzpost.co.nz

Il est recommandé de n'inclure aucun signe de ponctuation et, surtout aux États-Unis et au Canada, de rédiger l'adresse en majuscules (voir les modèles ci-dessous).

- ## Au Royaume-Uni :

L'adresse doit figurer au centre de l'enveloppe, légèrement décalée vers la gauche.

On peut aussi utiliser l'abréviation **Rd**. Voir ci-dessous la liste des abréviations utilisées dans les adresses.

L'adresse de l'expéditeur peut être précisée au verso. Cet usage est beaucoup moins répandu qu'en France.

Mr Richard Hunt
26 Ashley Road
Worksop
NOTTS
S81 7JD

Pour les grandes villes, telles que **LONDON** ou **LIVERPOOL**, il suffit de donner le code postal et le nom de la ville en majuscules.

Le code postal (**postcode**) s'écrit en majuscules.

Le comté s'écrit de préférence en majuscules et peut être abrégé. Voir ci-contre la liste des abréviations des comtés du Royaume-Uni.

- ## Aux États-Unis :

L'adresse de l'expéditeur se place en haut et à gauche.

Les abréviations et les initiales sont suivies d'un point : **Mr., Mrs., Ms., Dr.**

Ms. S. Gulliver
3448 Kabel Dr
New Orleans
LA70131

Ms. WENDY ROBINSON
11867 CRESTA VERDE DRIVE
ST LOUIS, MO 63145

La municipalité, l'État et le code postal figurent sur la même ligne.

Le code postal (**ZIP code**) à cinq chiffres identifie un secteur de livraison. Depuis 1983, les services postaux le font suivre d'un code à quatre chiffres appelé **ZIP+4**. Ce code facultatif correspond à une adresse ou à une boîte postale, par exemple : **Washington DC 20260-0123**.

MO = Missouri. Voir ci-contre la liste des abréviations des États américains.

- ## Abréviations utilisées dans les adresses

Les abréviations suivantes s'emploient couramment dans les adresses. Elles peuvent figurer aussi bien dans l'en-tête de la lettre que sur l'enveloppe.

Apt	Apartment	**Mtn**	Mountain
Av ou **Ave**	Avenue	**Pde**	Parade
Blvd	Boulevard	**Pk**	Park
Cl	Close	**Pl**	Place
Cres	Crescent	**Plz**	Plaza
Ct	Court	**Rdg**	Ridge
Dr	Drive	**Rd**	Road
Est	Estate	**Rm**	Room
Gdns	Gardens	**Sq**	Square
Gr	Grove	**St**	Street
Hts	Heights	**Ter**	Terrace
La	Lane		

▪ Abréviations des comtés au Royaume-Uni

En règle générale, pour les noms des comtés se terminant en **-shire,** on ne garde que la première syllabe à laquelle on ajoute un **'s'** : Beds = Bedfordshire, Berks = Berkshire, Bucks = Buckinghamshire, Cambs = Cambridgeshire, Gloucs = Gloucester, Herts = Hertfordshire, Lancs = Lancashire, Lincs = Lincolnshire, Notts = Nottinghamshire, Staffs = Staffordshire, Wilts = Wiltshire.

Exceptions :
Northants = Northamptonshire, Oxon = Oxfordshire

Les comtés suivants ne s'abrègent pas : **Avon, Cleveland, Greater Manchester, Humberside, Kent, Merseyside, Tyne and Wear.**

▪ Abréviations des États américains

AL	Alabama	MT	Montana
AK	Alaska	NE	Nebraska
AZ	Arizona	NV	Nevada
AR	Arkansas	NH	New Hampshire
CA	California	NJ	New Jersey
CO	Colorado	NM	New Mexico
CT	Connecticut	NY	New York
DE	Delaware	NC	North Carolina
DC	District of Columbia	ND	North Dakota
FL	Florida	OH	Ohio
GA	Georgia	OK	Oklahoma
HI	Hawaii	OR	Oregon
ID	Idaho	PA	Pennsylvania
IL	Illinois	RI	Rhode Island
IN	Indiana	SC	South Carolina
IA	Iowa	SD	South Dakota
KS	Kansas	TN	Tennessee
KY	Kentucky	TX	Texas
LA	Louisiana	UT	Utah
ME	Maine	VT	Vermont
MD	Maryland	VA	Virginia
MA	Massachusetts	WA	Washington
MI	Michigan	WV	West Virginia
MN	Minnesota	WI	Wisconsin
MS	Mississippi	WY	Wyoming
MO	Missouri		

Modèles de lettres

Lettre à un ami

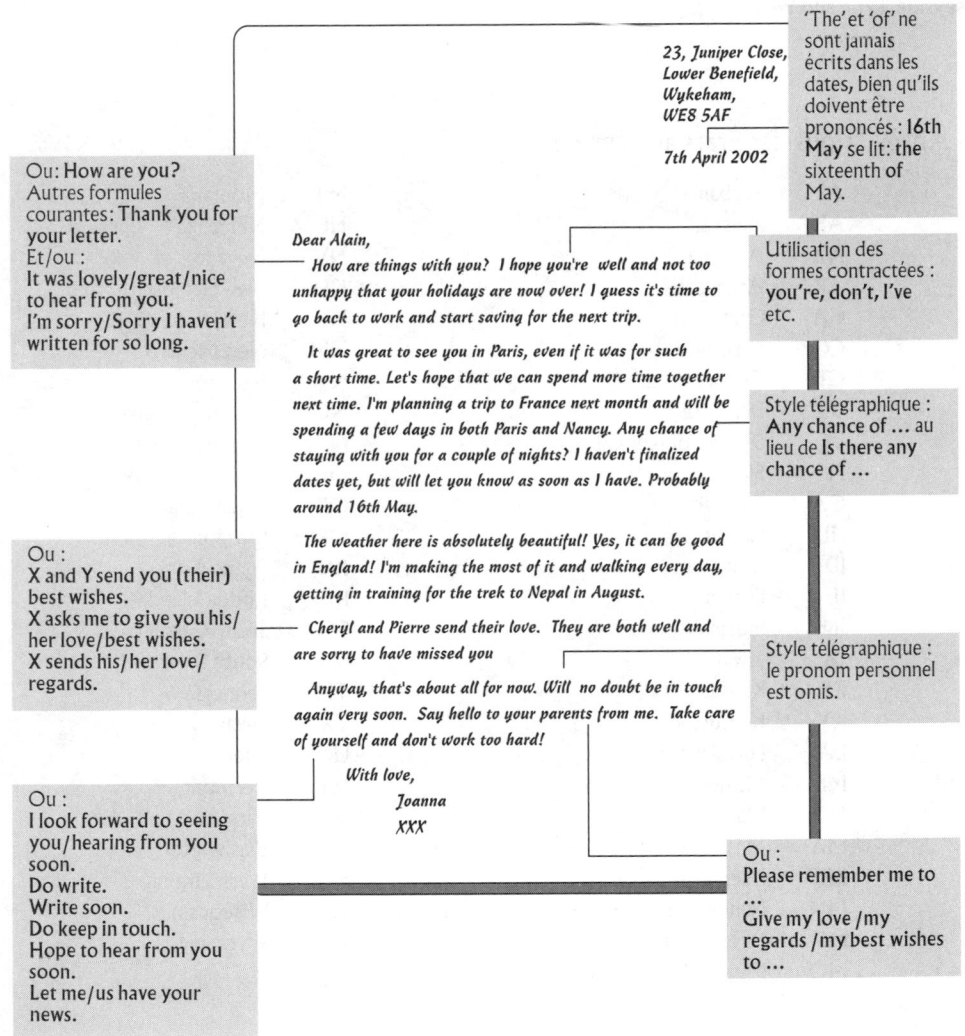

'The' et 'of' ne sont jamais écrits dans les dates, bien qu'ils doivent être prononcés : **16th May** se lit: the sixteenth of May.

23, Juniper Close,
Lower Benefield,
Wykeham,
WE8 5AF

7th April 2002

Ou: How are you?
Autres formules courantes: Thank you for your letter.
Et/ou :
It was lovely/great/nice to hear from you.
I'm sorry/Sorry I haven't written for so long.

Dear Alain,

How are things with you? I hope you're well and not too unhappy that your holidays are now over! I guess it's time to go back to work and start saving for the next trip.

It was great to see you in Paris, even if it was for such a short time. Let's hope that we can spend more time together next time. I'm planning a trip to France next month and will be spending a few days in both Paris and Nancy. Any chance of staying with you for a couple of nights? I haven't finalized dates yet, but will let you know as soon as I have. Probably around 16th May.

The weather here is absolutely beautiful! Yes, it can be good in England! I'm making the most of it and walking every day, getting in training for the trek to Nepal in August.

Cheryl and Pierre send their love. They are both well and are sorry to have missed you

Anyway, that's about all for now. Will no doubt be in touch again very soon. Say hello to your parents from me. Take care of yourself and don't work too hard!

With love,
Joanna
XXX

Utilisation des formes contractées : you're, don't, I've etc.

Style télégraphique : **Any chance of ...** au lieu de **Is there any chance of ...**

Ou :
X and Y send you (their) best wishes.
X asks me to give you his/ her love/best wishes.
X sends his/her love/ regards.

Style télégraphique : le pronom personnel est omis.

Ou :
I look forward to seeing you/hearing from you soon.
Do write.
Write soon.
Do keep in touch.
Hope to hear from you soon.
Let me/us have your news.

Ou :
Please remember me to ...
Give my love /my regards /my best wishes to ...

Cartes de vœux

Dans les pays anglo-saxons, les cartes de vœux s'envoient au mois de décembre, avant Noël, et non en janvier comme en France.

Haydn and Ann,

Merry Christmas and
a Happy New Year!

Best wishes,

Harry and Dinah

Ou :
Wishing you a Happy Christmas
Merry Christmas to you both and
health and happiness in the New
Year/in 2002
With Season's Greetings and very
best wishes for the New Year/from
...
With all our best wishes for 2002.

▪ Pour souhaiter un anniversaire

Dear Paul,

Happy Birthday!

Have a great day and enjoy
the party. Hope you like
your present!

With all our love,

Mum and Dad
XXX

Ou : Many Happy Returns (en
anglais britannique). Vous pouvez
aussi préciser l'âge de la personne :
Happy 21st Birthday!; Happy 60th!

Tournures utiles : Happy
Retirement; Happy Anniversary ;
Happy Easter; Happy Mother's/
Father's Day; Wishing you happiness
in your new home.

▪ Pour souhaiter bonne chance

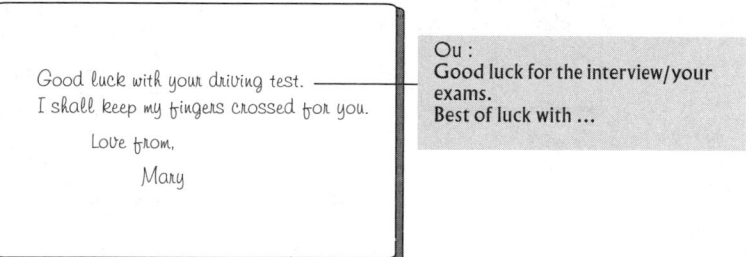

Good luck with your driving test.
I shall keep my fingers crossed for you.

Love from,

Mary

Ou :
Good luck for the interview/your
exams.
Best of luck with ...

▪ Pour féliciter

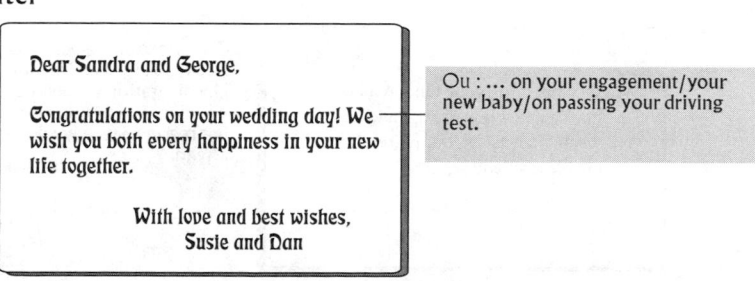

Dear Sandra and George,

Congratulations on your wedding day! We
wish you both every happiness in your new
life together.

With love and best wishes,
Susie and Dan

Ou : ... on your engagement/your
new baby/on passing your driving
test.

Invitations et réponses

▪ Carton d'invitation à un mariage

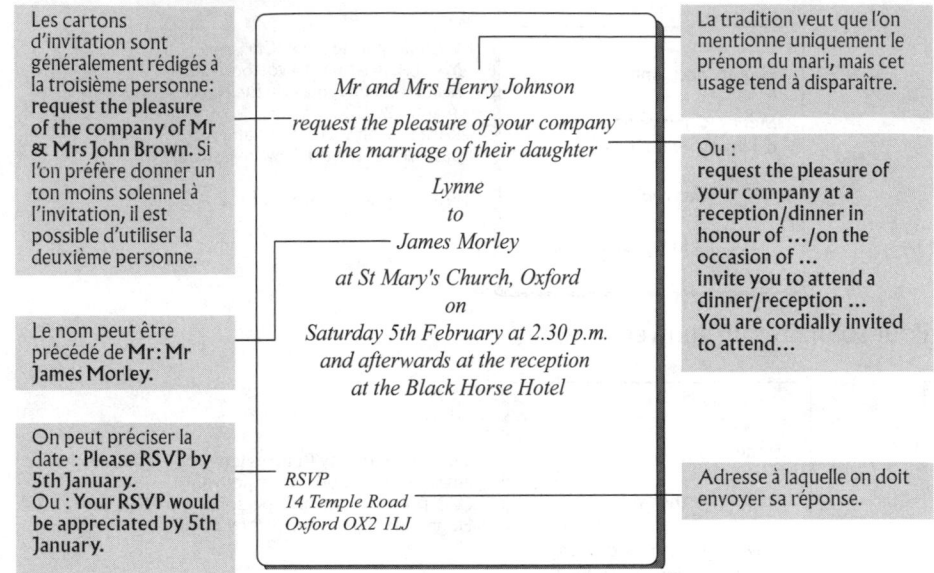

Les cartons d'invitation sont généralement rédigés à la troisième personne: **request the pleasure of the company of Mr & Mrs John Brown.** Si l'on préfère donner un ton moins solennel à l'invitation, il est possible d'utiliser la deuxième personne.

La tradition veut que l'on mentionne uniquement le prénom du mari, mais cet usage tend à disparaître.

Ou :
request the pleasure of your company at a reception/dinner in honour of …/on the occasion of … invite you to attend a dinner/reception … You are cordially invited to attend…

Le nom peut être précédé de **Mr**: **Mr James Morley.**

On peut préciser la date : **Please RSVP by 5th January.** Ou : **Your RSVP would be appreciated by 5th January.**

Adresse à laquelle on doit envoyer sa réponse.

Mr and Mrs Henry Johnson
request the pleasure of your company
at the marriage of their daughter
Lynne
to
James Morley
at St Mary's Church, Oxford
on
Saturday 5th February at 2.30 p.m.
and afterwards at the reception
at the Black Horse Hotel

RSVP
14 Temple Road
Oxford OX2 1LJ

▪ Pour accepter une invitation officielle

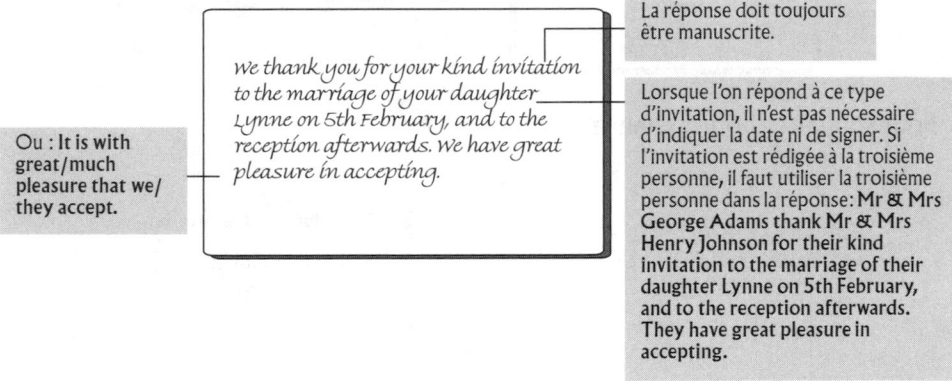

We thank you for your kind invitation to the marriage of your daughter Lynne on 5th February, and to the reception afterwards. We have great pleasure in accepting.

La réponse doit toujours être manuscrite.

Ou : **It is with great/much pleasure that we/they accept.**

Lorsque l'on répond à ce type d'invitation, il n'est pas nécessaire d'indiquer la date ni de signer. Si l'invitation est rédigée à la troisième personne, il faut utiliser la troisième personne dans la réponse: **Mr & Mrs George Adams thank Mr & Mrs Henry Johnson for their kind invitation to the marriage of their daughter Lynne on 5th February, and to the reception afterwards. They have great pleasure in accepting.**

▪ Pour refuser une invitation officielle

We thank you for your kind invitation to your daughter's wedding, and to the reception afterwards, but regret that we are unable to attend.

Ou, à la troisième personne : **Mr and Mrs Hall thank Mr and Mrs Johnson for their kind invitation to their daughter's wedding, and to the reception afterwards, but regret that they will be unable to attend.**

■ Carton d'invitation : soirée entre amis

James and Fiona

INVITE YOU TO
a house-warming party

ON: Friday 13th September
AT: 45 Rowan Crescent
FROM: 8pm onwards

Please bring a bottle   RSVP

Ou :
We're giving a dinner party/
cocktail party/birthday party
next Friday and hope you will be
able to come.

We are celebrating our
engagement by holding a dinner
dance at the ... on ..., and would
be delighted if you could join us.

I'm having/planning a party -
come along, and bring a friend.

■ Réponse à une invitation : soirée entre amis

46 Hatton Street
Bath
BA5 2GA

23 August 2002

Dear James and Fiona,

Thank you so much for the invitation to your house-warming party. I'd love to come. It will be great to see you and, of course, your new home.

If you need any help with food, I'd be only too glad to bring something along, as well as a bottle, of course!

Thanks once again for the kind invitation. I look forward to seeing you.

Love,

Emily

Ou :
I'd love to come to your
party. It was good of
you to invite me.

Thank you for your
invitation to dinner/
for the weekend - I look
forward to it very
much.

Thank you so much for
your invitation, but I'm
afraid I/we won't be
able to come.

I was/We were
delighted to get your
invitation but
unfortunately I/we
can't come.

Remerciements

167 Ecclesall Road
South Sheffield
S11 9PN

31st May 2002

Dear Ann and Ralph

Thank you so much for the beautiful crystal decanter and wine glasses you sent us as a wedding present. They will look wonderful on our dinner table and I intend to make good use of them.

I was so glad that you could come to the wedding. I hope you enjoyed it as much as we did. It was quite a hectic day really, but of course a wonderful one! Give my thanks to Tracey for the catering. everyone said how delicious the food was.

We had a lovely honeymoon and are now busy settling in to our new home. You must come very soon for a meal to try out the glasses.

Many thanks once again!

With much love.

Katie

XXX

Ou :
bought us

Ou :
We were both delighted
you could come...;
It was really nice to see
you at the wedding.

Ou :
I can't thank you
enough for...
Thank you very much
for ...

Ou :
Say thank you to ...

Réservations

Les réservations de billets ou de chambres d'hôtel se font de plus en plus par Internet et par courrier électronique. Pour toute réservation faite par téléphone, il est recommandé de confirmer par écrit.

▪ Lettre de réservation

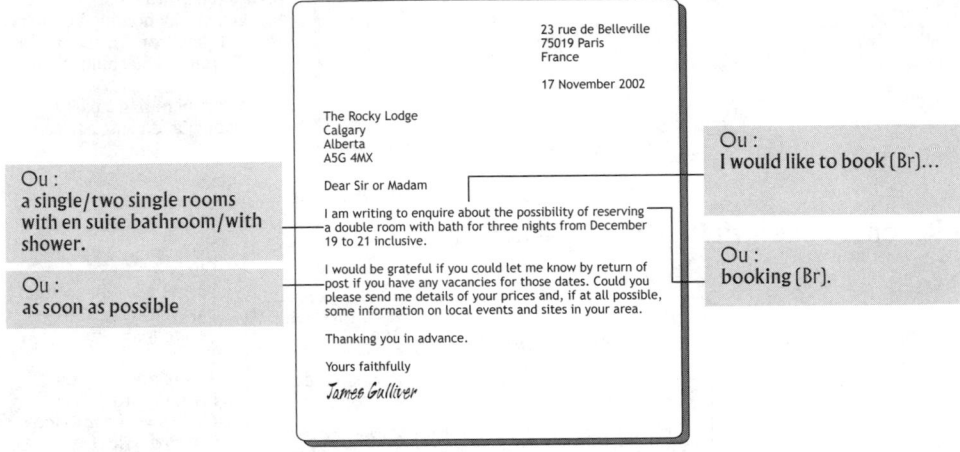

Ou :
I would like to book (Br)...

Ou :
a single/two single rooms with en suite bathroom/with shower.

Ou :
as soon as possible

Ou :
booking (Br).

▪ Pour confirmer une réservation

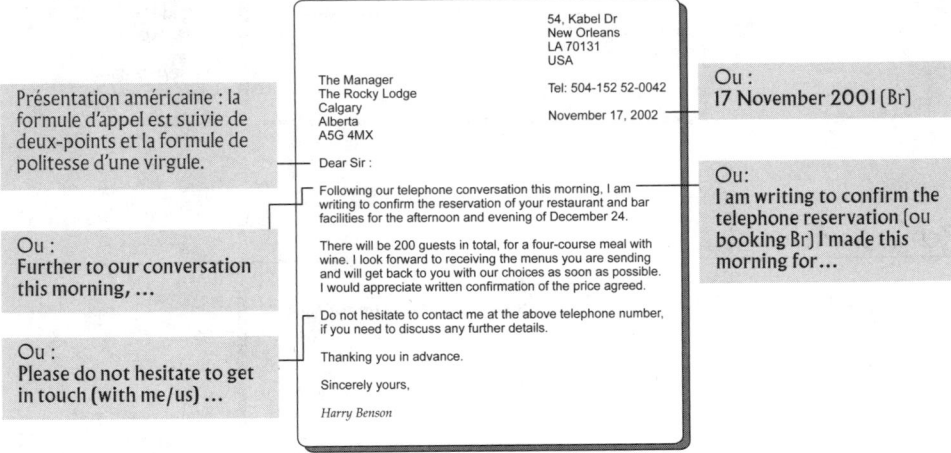

Présentation américaine : la formule d'appel est suivie de deux-points et la formule de politesse d'une virgule.

Ou :
17 November 2001 (Br)

Ou:
I am writing to confirm the telephone reservation (ou booking Br) I made this morning for...

Ou :
Further to our conversation this morning, ...

Ou :
Please do not hesitate to get in touch (with me/us) ...

▪ Pour annuler une réservation

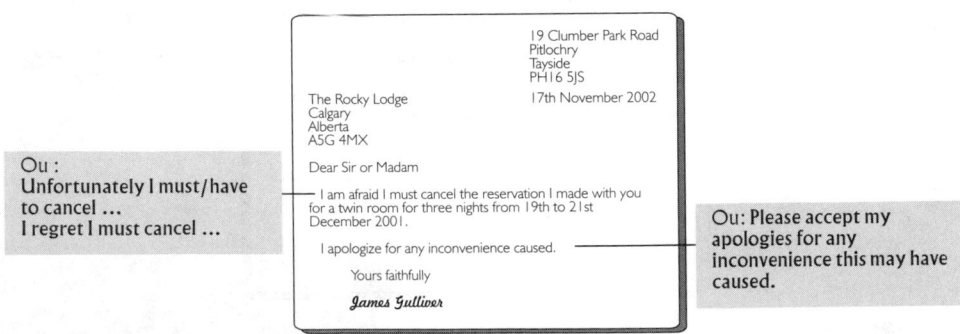

Ou :
Unfortunately I must/have to cancel ...
I regret I must cancel ...

Ou: Please accept my apologies for any inconvenience this may have caused.

Demande de renseignements

Réclamations

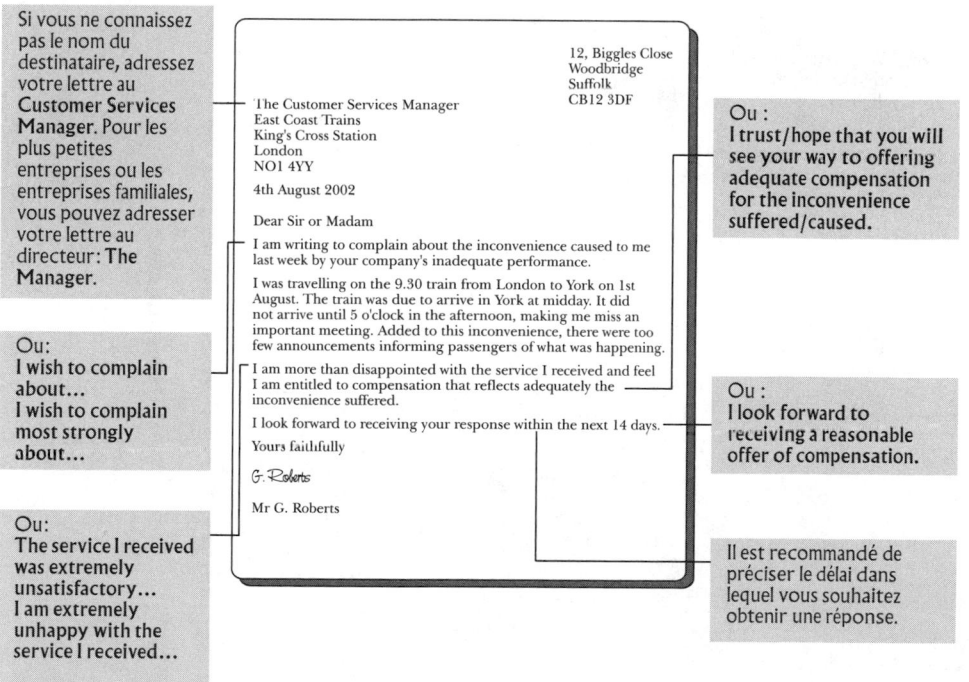

La correspondance commerciale

Pour prendre rendez-vous

Références. Ou :
Our reference:
... Your
reference: ...

Ou :
September 29,
2002 (Am)

Ou :
Mr. Patrick
Meers (Am)

Ou :
Dear Mr Meers:
(Am)

Ou :
Could you please
confirm the dates
at your earliest
convenience/as
soon as
possible...
I would
appreciate
confirmation (of
the dates) ...

Ou :
Sincerely
(yours), (Am)

LOOK NOW
14-16 avenue de Belleville
75020 Paris
E-mail: looknow@mode.fr
Tel: (00 33) (0)1 49 00 4900
Fax: (00 33) (0)1 49 00 4901

Our Ref: S901R3
Your Ref: s/02P

29 September 2002

Mr Patrick Meers
Distribution Manager
Meers Ltd
16 Roehampton Road
London
SW15 5LU

Dear Mr Meers

Thank you for your letter dated 12 September. I was extremely interested
to read your proposals and would like to arrange a meeting with you to
discuss them further.

I would be available to come to London during the last week of February,
if that is convenient for you. I would be accompanied by my personal
assistant, Martine Barry, and can arrange to bring samples of both our
winter and spring lines.

I would be grateful if you could confirm the dates as soon as possible .
If you require any further details, please do not hesitate to contact me.

I look forward to meeting you.

Yours sincerely

Suzanne Valat

Suzanne Valat
Managing Director

En-tête centré ou à
gauche.

Ou :
I refer to your letter of
12 September
enclosing/proposing
...
Further to our
telephone
conversation
yesterday, ...

Ou :
I am very
interested in
your
proposals/
products/
programme...
I confirm my
interest in your
company's
products/in
meeting with
you

Ou :
I look forward to
seeing you at the
end of the month/to
doing business with
you.
Looking forward to
hearing from you, I
remain, (suivi de la
formule de politesse)

Ou :
If you have any
questions/queries,
please ...
Should you have any
questions/Should you
require any further
information, ...
Please do not hesitate to
get in touch, if you
have/require...

Réponse à une demande de renseignements

Ou :
I am enclosing our catalogue for your review.

Ou :
If you require/ Should you require any further information, please contact me. I look forward to hearing from you soon.

After you have reviewed our material, we would appreciate your comments, and we will look forward to answering any questions you have about our product.

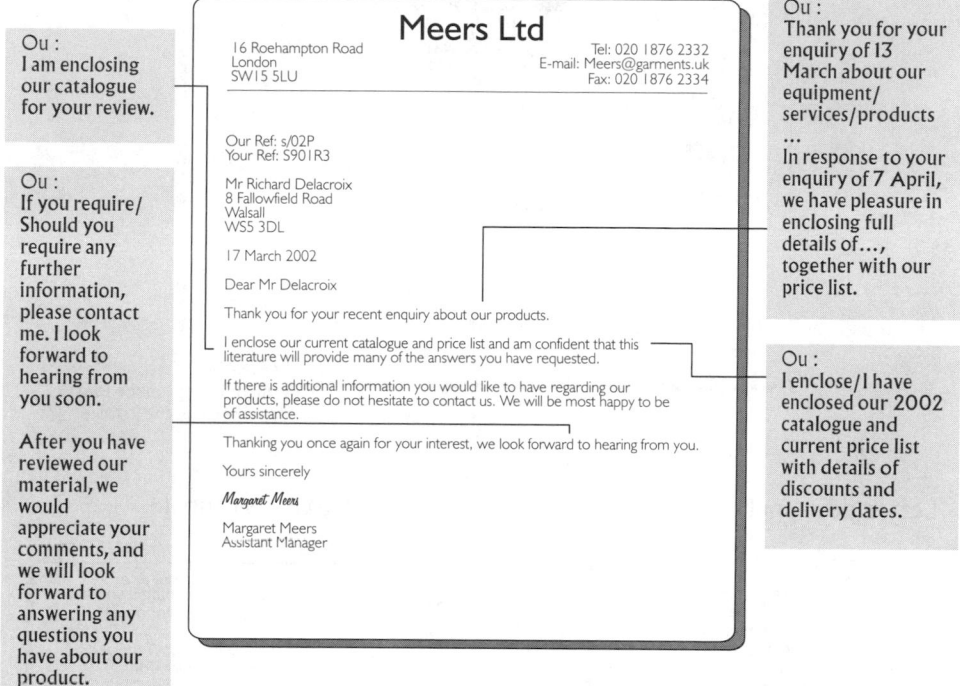

Meers Ltd

16 Roehampton Road
London
SW15 5LU

Tel: 020 1876 2332
E-mail: Meers@garments.uk
Fax: 020 1876 2334

Our Ref: s/02P
Your Ref: S901R3

Mr Richard Delacroix
8 Fallowfield Road
Walsall
WS5 3DL

17 March 2002

Dear Mr Delacroix

Thank you for your recent enquiry about our products.

I enclose our current catalogue and price list and am confident that this literature will provide many of the answers you have requested.

If there is additional information you would like to have regarding our products, please do not hesitate to contact us. We will be most happy to be of assistance.

Thanking you once again for your interest, we look forward to hearing from you.

Yours sincerely

Margaret Meers

Margaret Meers
Assistant Manager

Ou :
Thank you for your enquiry of 13 March about our equipment/ services/products ...

In response to your enquiry of 7 April, we have pleasure in enclosing full details of..., together with our price list.

Ou :
I enclose/I have enclosed our 2002 catalogue and current price list with details of discounts and delivery dates.

Commande

Ou :
Gentlemen: (Am). To whom it may concern: Cette dernière formule s'utilise en anglais britannique dans la correspondance administrative lorsqu'on ne connaît pas le nom du destinataire.

Ou :
The enclosed order is based on your current price list, assuming our usual discount of ... on bulk orders.

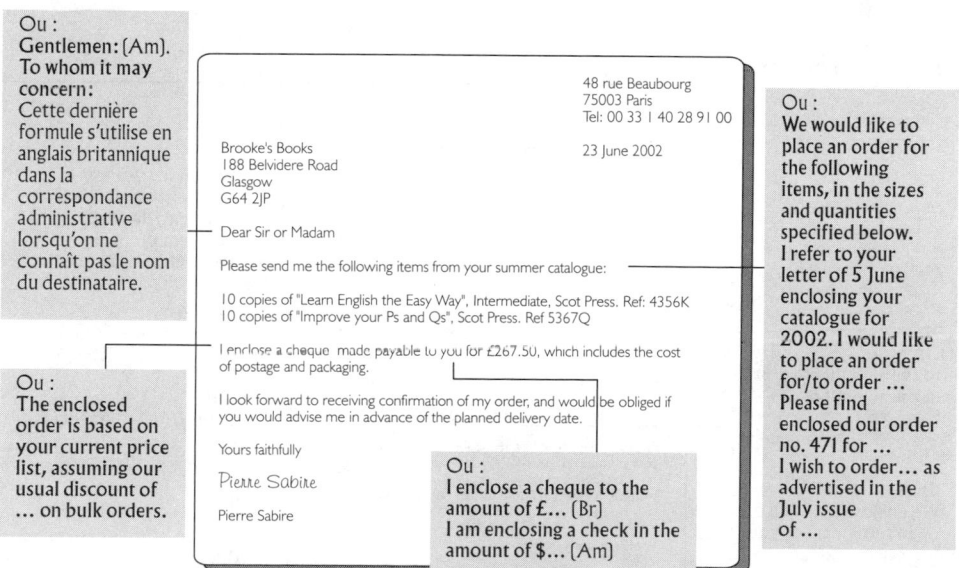

48 rue Beaubourg
75003 Paris
Tel: 00 33 1 40 28 91 00

Brooke's Books
188 Belvidere Road
Glasgow
G64 2JP

23 June 2002

Dear Sir or Madam

Please send me the following items from your summer catalogue:

10 copies of "Learn English the Easy Way", Intermediate, Scot Press. Ref: 4356K
10 copies of "Improve your Ps and Qs", Scot Press. Ref 5367Q

I enclose a cheque made payable to you for £267.50, which includes the cost of postage and packaging.

I look forward to receiving confirmation of my order, and would be obliged if you would advise me in advance of the planned delivery date.

Yours faithfully

Pierre Sabire

Pierre Sabire

Ou :
I enclose a cheque to the amount of £... (Br)
I am enclosing a check in the amount of $... (Am)

Ou :
We would like to place an order for the following items, in the sizes and quantities specified below.
I refer to your letter of 5 June enclosing your catalogue for 2002. I would like to place an order for/to order ...
Please find enclosed our order no. 471 for ...
I wish to order... as advertised in the July issue of ...

Facture

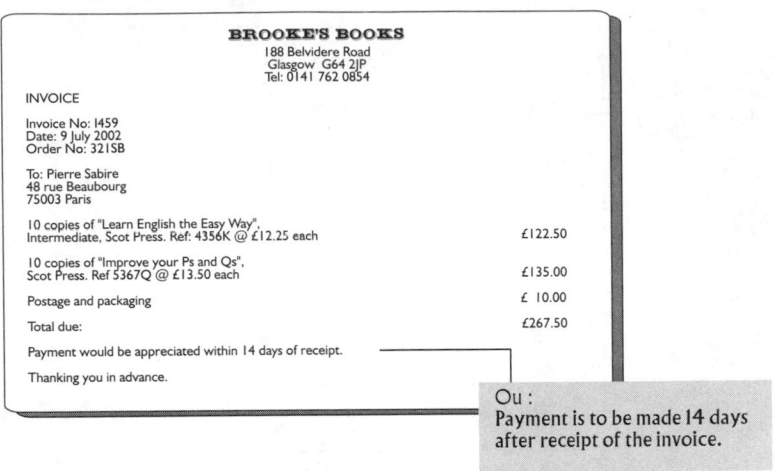

BROOKE'S BOOKS
188 Belvidere Road
Glasgow G64 2JP
Tel: 0141 762 0854

INVOICE

Invoice No: 1459
Date: 9 July 2002
Order No: 321SB

To: Pierre Sabire
48 rue Beaubourg
75003 Paris

10 copies of "Learn English the Easy Way", Intermediate, Scot Press. Ref: 4356K @ £12.25 each	£122.50
10 copies of "Improve your Ps and Qs", Scot Press. Ref 5367Q @ £13.50 each	£135.00
Postage and packaging	£ 10.00
Total due:	£267.50

Payment would be appreciated within 14 days of receipt.

Thanking you in advance.

Ou :
Payment is to be made 14 days after receipt of the invoice.

▪ Lettre de rappel

Our records indicate that payment on your account is overdue to the amount of £ ... If the amount has already been paid, please disregard this notice. If you have not yet posted your payment, please use the enclosed envelope to send payment in full.

Thank you in advance for your anticipated co-operation in this matter.

Ou :
in the amount of ... [Am]

Ou :
mailed [Am]

▪ Deuxième rappel

On 12 July 2002 we notified you of your overdue account for order no. ...

To date we still have not received payment for the above order.

Please give this matter your most urgent attention. Payment must be made within the next ten days.

Envoi du règlement

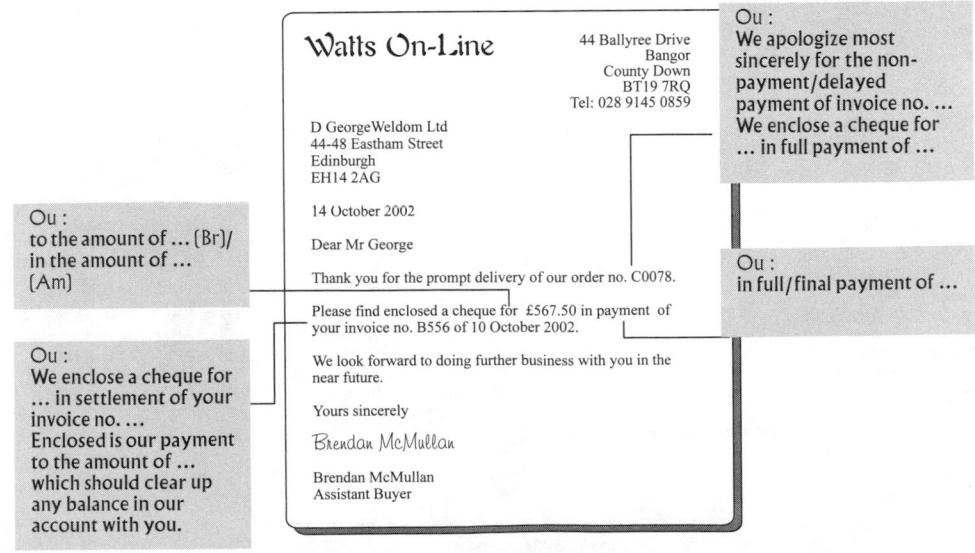

Watts On-Line

44 Ballyree Drive
Bangor
County Down
BT19 7RQ
Tel: 028 9145 0859

D GeorgeWeldom Ltd
44-48 Eastham Street
Edinburgh
EH14 2AG

14 October 2002

Dear Mr George

Thank you for the prompt delivery of our order no. C0078.

Please find enclosed a cheque for £567.50 in payment of your invoice no. B556 of 10 October 2002.

We look forward to doing further business with you in the near future.

Yours sincerely

Brendan McMullan

Brendan McMullan
Assistant Buyer

Ou :
We apologize most sincerely for the non-payment/delayed payment of invoice no. ... We enclose a cheque for ... in full payment of ...

Ou :
to the amount of ... [Br]/ in the amount of ... [Am]

Ou :
in full/final payment of ...

Ou :
We enclose a cheque for ... in settlement of your invoice no. ... Enclosed is our payment to the amount of ... which should clear up any balance in our account with you.

Recherche d'emploi

Lettre de motivation

Dans les pays anglo-saxons, la lettre de candidature doit toujours être dactylographiée, sauf si l'annonce spécifie qu'il faut envoyer une lettre manuscrite.

▪ Demande de stage

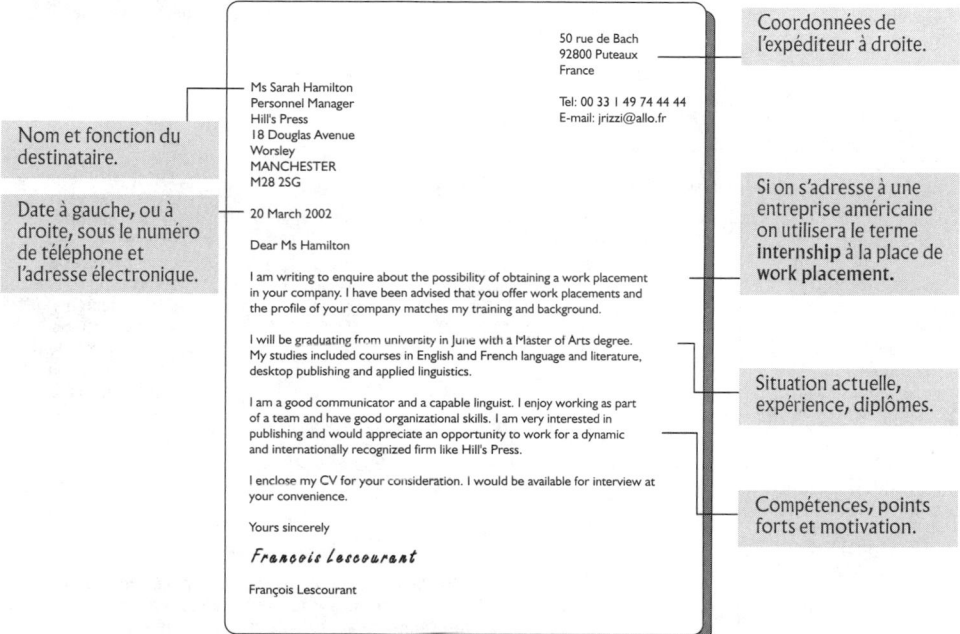

Coordonnées de l'expéditeur à droite.

Nom et fonction du destinataire.

Date à gauche, ou à droite, sous le numéro de téléphone et l'adresse électronique.

Si on s'adresse à une entreprise américaine on utilisera le terme **internship** à la place de **work placement.**

Situation actuelle, expérience, diplômes.

Compétences, points forts et motivation.

▪ Candidature spontanée

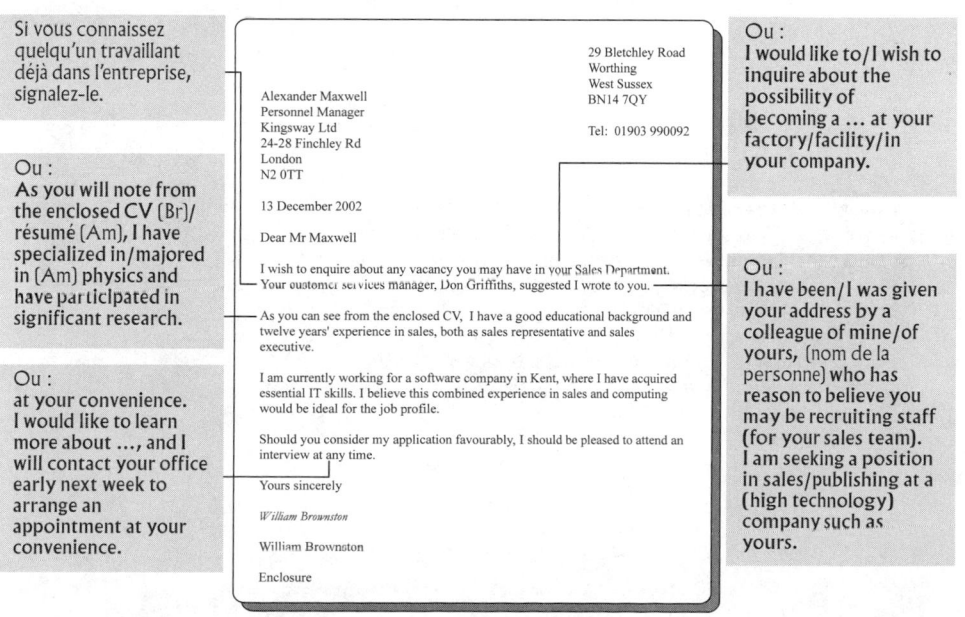

Si vous connaissez quelqu'un travaillant déjà dans l'entreprise, signalez-le.

Ou :
As you will note from the enclosed CV (Br)/ **résumé** (Am), **I have specialized in/majored in** (Am) **physics and have participated in significant research.**

Ou :
at your convenience. I would like to learn more about ..., and I will contact your office early next week to arrange an appointment at your convenience.

Ou :
I would like to/I wish to inquire about the possibility of becoming a ... at your factory/facility/in your company.

Ou :
I have been/I was given your address by a colleague of mine/of yours, (nom de la personne) **who has reason to believe you may be recruiting staff (for your sales team). I am seeking a position in sales/publishing at a (high technology) company such as yours.**

Réponse à une annonce

Ou :
I should like to apply for the above post as recently advertised in the July issue of…/ which was advertised in today's Daily Post. I am writing to apply for the above post/ for the post of … (as) advertised in …
I am writing in response to your advertisement in … for …
I would like to be considered for the above post which your company advertised in …

Ou :
and (I) enclose my (current) CV (Br)/ résumé (Am) for your consideration.

8 rue de Renac
44200 Nantes
France

Tel: 00 33 2 47 89 22 22

Mr D Smithwick
Chief Analyst
Dunworkin Investments
Threadneedle Street
London
E3 6PG
UK

19 May 2002

Objet de la lettre : fonction ou poste.

Dear Mr Smithwick

Financial Analyst

Ou :
I am confident that I can perform the job effectively and am excited about the idea of working for a dynamic firm.
My degree in … and my internship experiences have taught me how to …

I would like to apply for the above post as advertised in "Le Monde" of 14 May, and I enclose my CV for your attention.

I am an experienced financial analyst and consultant, having worked extensively in this sector in Nantes and Paris, and as a lecturer at Nantes university. I am currently looking for a position that will allow me to develop my skills and experience in a small, dynamic commercial team such as Dunworkin Investments.

I believe that my financial and academic background would be of benefit to your company. Should you consider me suitable for the post, I can provide the names of three referees.

I thank you for your consideration and remain at your disposal for any further information. I look forward to meeting you in the near future.

Ou :
The position seems to fit very well with my education, experience, and career interests. According to the advertisement, your position requires excellent communication skills and an MA degree in …

Ou :
I look forward to talking with you/to discussing matters with you (at a future interview).

Yours sincerely

Jacques Kahn

Jacques Kahn
Financial Investment Analyst

Enc.

Ou :
Thank you for considering my application/for your consideration. If you would like to schedule an interview, please call me at … I will be available at your convenience.
I would appreciate the chance to meet with you. You may reach me at the above telephone number or e-mail address.

Tournures utiles :

I know how to/I can operate a cash register/a computer/power equipment
I am computer literate/a good communicator/a good organizer
I am a capable linguist/can speak fluent English and German
I have good computer/IT/language/editing/communication/organizational skills
I can learn new tasks and enjoy/can accept a challenge
I enjoy working/can work with a variety of people
I work well in a team, and can also work under pressure
I perform well under stress/am good with difficult customers
I can handle multiple tasks simultaneously

Curriculum vitae

▪ Diplômé anglais ayant une première expérience

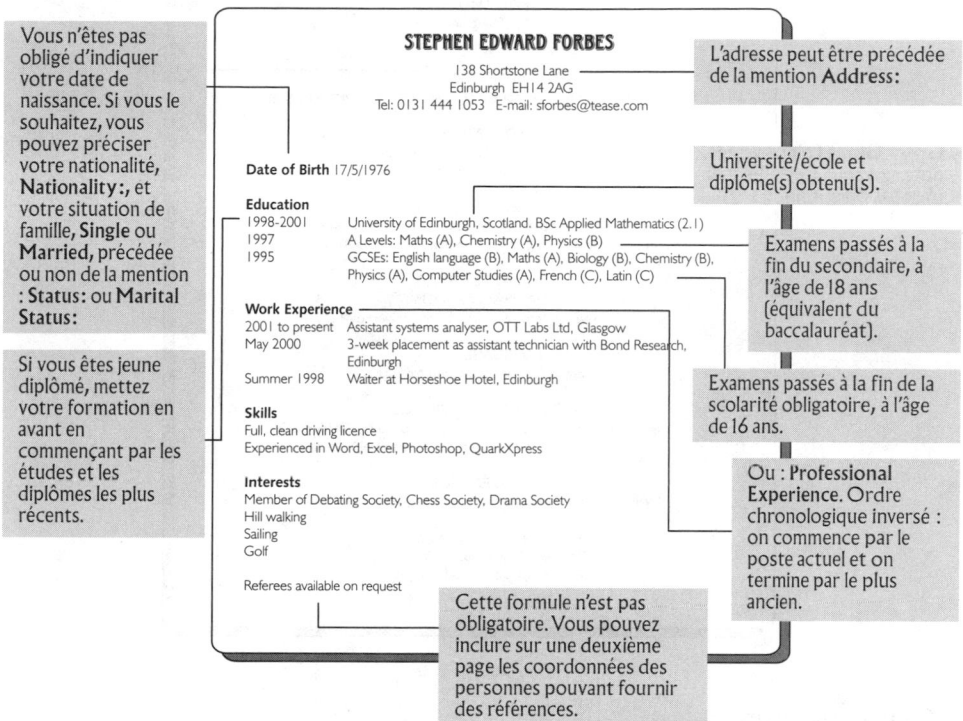

Vous n'êtes pas obligé d'indiquer votre date de naissance. Si vous le souhaitez, vous pouvez préciser votre nationalité, **Nationality:**, et votre situation de famille, **Single** ou **Married**, précédée ou non de la mention : **Status:** ou **Marital Status:**

Si vous êtes jeune diplômé, mettez votre formation en avant en commençant par les études et les diplômes les plus récents.

STEPHEN EDWARD FORBES
138 Shortstone Lane
Edinburgh EH14 2AG
Tel: 0131 444 1053   E-mail: sforbes@tease.com

Date of Birth 17/5/1976

Education
1998-2001   University of Edinburgh, Scotland. BSc Applied Mathematics (2.1)
1997   A Levels: Maths (A), Chemistry (A), Physics (B)
1995   GCSEs: English language (B), Maths (A), Biology (B), Chemistry (B), Physics (A), Computer Studies (A), French (C), Latin (C)

Work Experience
2001 to present   Assistant systems analyser, OTT Labs Ltd, Glasgow
May 2000   3-week placement as assistant technician with Bond Research, Edinburgh
Summer 1998   Waiter at Horseshoe Hotel, Edinburgh

Skills
Full, clean driving licence
Experienced in Word, Excel, Photoshop, QuarkXpress

Interests
Member of Debating Society, Chess Society, Drama Society
Hill walking
Sailing
Golf

Referees available on request

L'adresse peut être précédée de la mention **Address:**

Université/école et diplôme(s) obtenu(s).

Examens passés à la fin du secondaire, à l'âge de 18 ans (équivalent du baccalauréat).

Examens passés à la fin de la scolarité obligatoire, à l'âge de 16 ans.

Ou : **Professional Experience.** Ordre chronologique inversé : on commence par le poste actuel et on termine par le plus ancien.

Cette formule n'est pas obligatoire. Vous pouvez inclure sur une deuxième page les coordonnées des personnes pouvant fournir des références.

▪ Cadre anglais

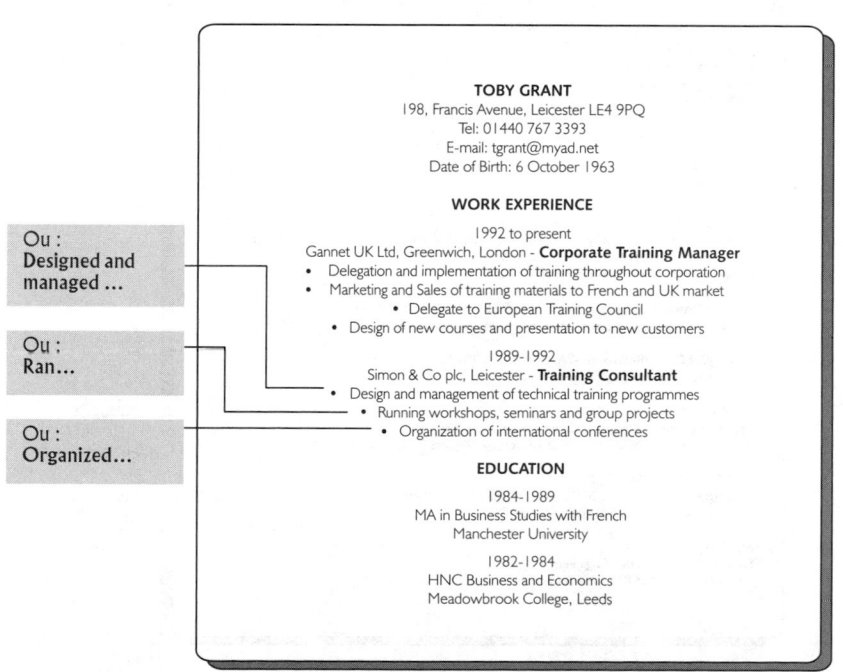

Ou : **Designed and managed ...**

Ou : **Ran...**

Ou : **Organized...**

TOBY GRANT
198, Francis Avenue, Leicester LE4 9PQ
Tel: 01440 767 3393
E-mail: tgrant@myad.net
Date of Birth: 6 October 1963

WORK EXPERIENCE

1992 to present
Gannet UK Ltd, Greenwich, London - **Corporate Training Manager**
• Delegation and implementation of training throughout corporation
• Marketing and Sales of training materials to French and UK market
• Delegate to European Training Council
• Design of new courses and presentation to new customers

1989-1992
Simon & Co plc, Leicester - **Training Consultant**
• Design and management of technical training programmes
• Running workshops, seminars and group projects
• Organization of international conferences

EDUCATION

1984-1989
MA in Business Studies with French
Manchester University

1982-1984
HNC Business and Economics
Meadowbrook College, Leeds

▪ Diplômé américain ayant une première expérience

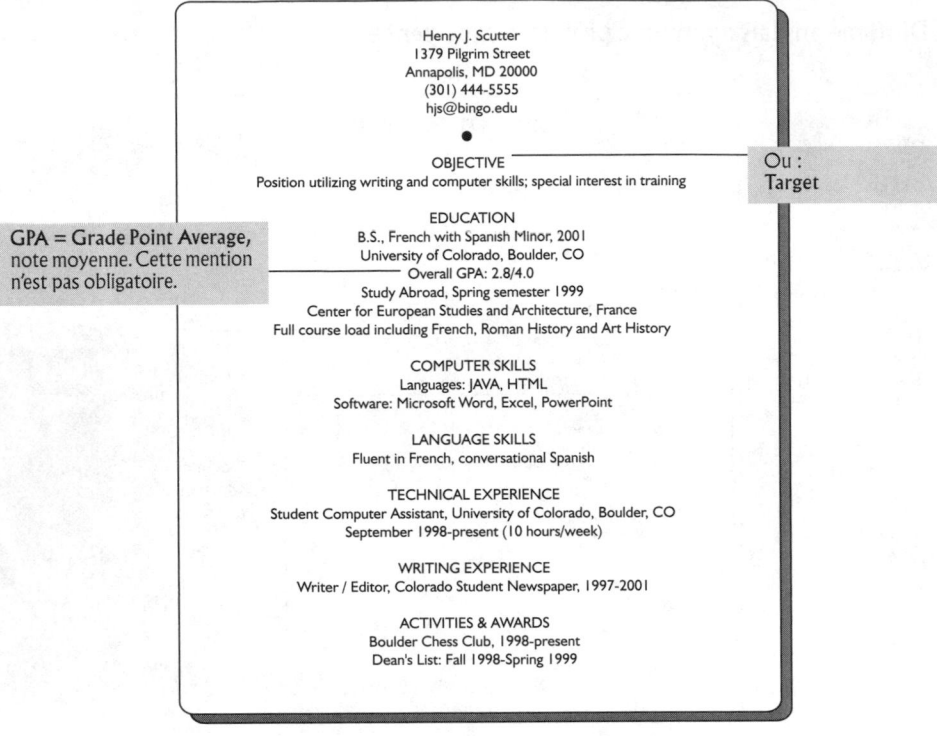

Henry J. Scutter
1379 Pilgrim Street
Annapolis, MD 20000
(301) 444-5555
hjs@bingo.edu

●

OBJECTIVE
Position utilizing writing and computer skills; special interest in training

Ou :
Target

EDUCATION
B.S., French with Spanish Minor, 2001
University of Colorado, Boulder, CO
Overall GPA: 2.8/4.0
Study Abroad, Spring semester 1999
Center for European Studies and Architecture, France
Full course load including French, Roman History and Art History

GPA = Grade Point Average, note moyenne. Cette mention n'est pas obligatoire.

COMPUTER SKILLS
Languages: JAVA, HTML
Software: Microsoft Word, Excel, PowerPoint

LANGUAGE SKILLS
Fluent in French, conversational Spanish

TECHNICAL EXPERIENCE
Student Computer Assistant, University of Colorado, Boulder, CO
September 1998-present (10 hours/week)

WRITING EXPERIENCE
Writer / Editor, Colorado Student Newspaper, 1997-2001

ACTIVITIES & AWARDS
Boulder Chess Club, 1998-present
Dean's List: Fall 1998-Spring 1999

▪ Cadre américain

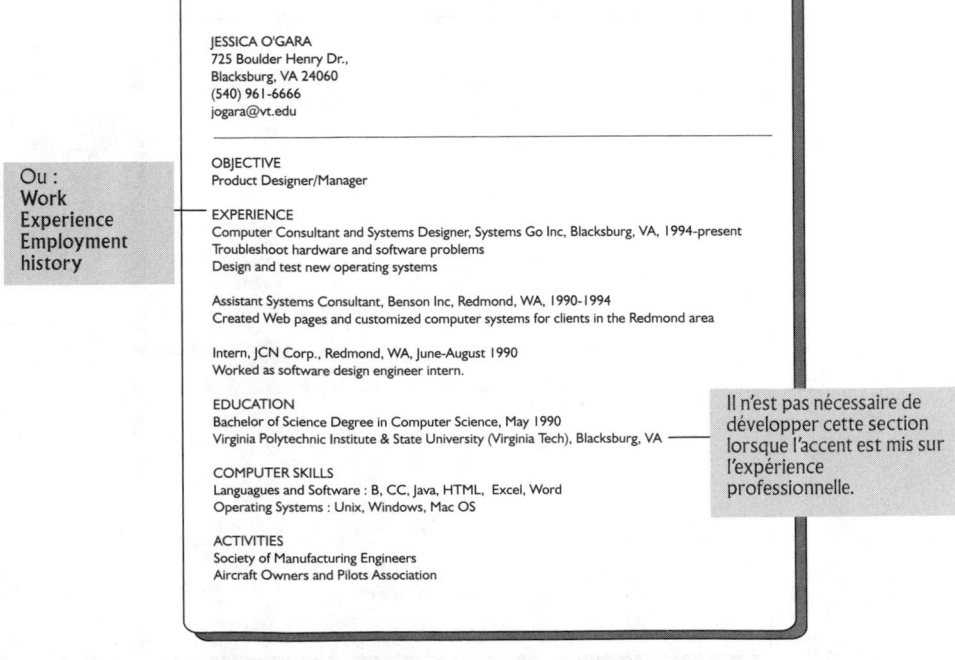

JESSICA O'GARA
725 Boulder Henry Dr.,
Blacksburg, VA 24060
(540) 961-6666
jogara@vt.edu

OBJECTIVE
Product Designer/Manager

Ou :
Work
Experience
Employment
history

EXPERIENCE
Computer Consultant and Systems Designer, Systems Go Inc, Blacksburg, VA, 1994-present
Troubleshoot hardware and software problems
Design and test new operating systems

Assistant Systems Consultant, Benson Inc, Redmond, WA, 1990-1994
Created Web pages and customized computer systems for clients in the Redmond area

Intern, JCN Corp., Redmond, WA, June-August 1990
Worked as software design engineer intern.

EDUCATION
Bachelor of Science Degree in Computer Science, May 1990
Virginia Polytechnic Institute & State University (Virginia Tech), Blacksburg, VA

Il n'est pas nécessaire de développer cette section lorsque l'accent est mis sur l'expérience professionnelle.

COMPUTER SKILLS
Languages and Software : B, CC, Java, HTML, Excel, Word
Operating Systems : Unix, Windows, Mac OS

ACTIVITIES
Society of Manufacturing Engineers
Aircraft Owners and Pilots Association

▪ Diplômé français ayant une première expérience

Isabelle Murat
40, impasse de la Colline
75003 Paris
Tel: (00 33) (0)1 40 30 40 40
E-mail: imurat@ubet.fr

Vous n'êtes pas obligé de préciser votre nationalité ou votre âge. Ces informations, tout comme la situation de famille, sont souvent omises.

Nationality	French
Date of Birth	13/2/1980

Professional Experience

April/May 2000	Three-month placement at Cabinet Desmoulin, Paris
	Customer Services
Summer 1999	Organiser in school summer camp, Port-de-Bouc

Education

1998-2000	Ecole Technique Supérieure, Bordeaux
	Three-year diploma course in Civil Engineering
1997-1998	Baccalauréat S (equivalent A Levels) in: Maths, Physics, Chemistry,
	Biology, French, English, Geography, History

Languages	French, English (fluent)
	German, Greek (basic)

Interests	Horse-riding, mountaineering
	Opera singing

▪ Cadre français

Laurent Marie
25, rue des Arquebusiers   Tel: 02 24 24 45 73
76000 Rouen   E-mail: mariel@battisto.com.fr

Human Resources Consultant

Work Experience

1991 - present	Human Resources Consultant, Cabinet Battisto-Langlade, Rouen
	Advising companies on accounting, recruitment strategies
1987 - 1990	Personnel Manager, Conseil général, Le Havre
	Recruiting, planning of training programmes, staff follow-up
1985 - 1986	Assistant to Personnel Manager, Société Pierre et Fils, Le Havre

Education

1983	Master of Business Administration, Boston University
1981 - 1982	DEA 'Langage et Médias' - Paris X
1980	Master's Degree in History - Paris IV
1976	Baccalauréat (equivalent A Levels), specialising in Maths,
	Académie de Paris.

Other Experience
Year spent in Africa (1984/5) as part of a mission with the voluntary medical aid organisation, "Médecins sans frontières"
Member of a voluntary association promoting adult literacy

Languages	Fluent English and Spanish
Computer Skills	Mac OS, Word, Excel

La télécopie

Dans une entreprise

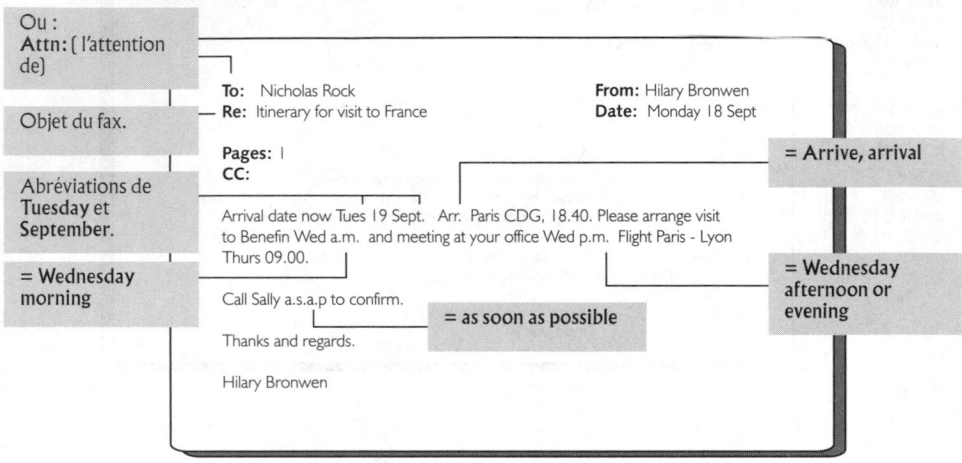

Ou :
Attn: (l'attention de)

Objet du fax.

Abréviations de **Tuesday** et **September.**

= **Wednesday morning**

To: Nicholas Rock
Re: Itinerary for visit to France

From: Hilary Bronwen
Date: Monday 18 Sept

Pages: 1
CC:

= **Arrive, arrival**

Arrival date now Tues 19 Sept. Arr. Paris CDG, 18.40. Please arrange visit to Benefin Wed a.m. and meeting at your office Wed p.m. Flight Paris - Lyon Thurs 09.00.

Call Sally a.s.a.p to confirm.

= **as soon as possible**

= **Wednesday afternoon or evening**

Thanks and regards.

Hilary Bronwen

Pour confirmer une réservation

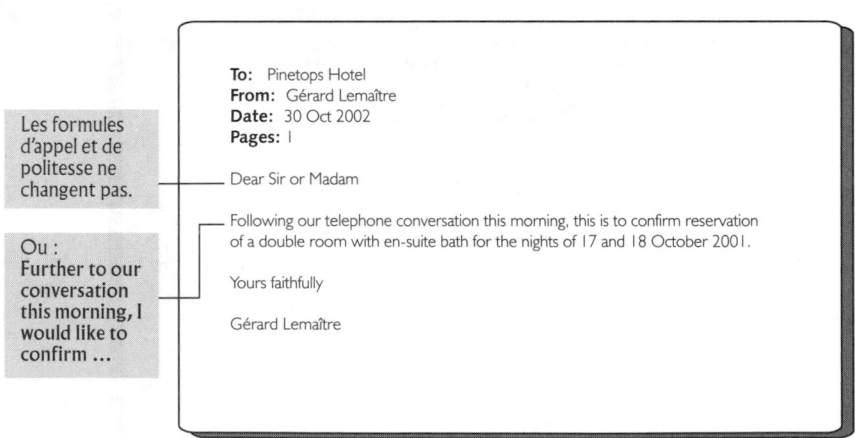

Les formules d'appel et de politesse ne changent pas.

Ou :
Further to our conversation this morning, I would like to confirm ...

To: Pinetops Hotel
From: Gérard Lemaître
Date: 30 Oct 2002
Pages: 1

Dear Sir or Madam

Following our telephone conversation this morning, this is to confirm reservation of a double room with en-suite bath for the nights of 17 and 18 October 2001.

Yours faithfully

Gérard Lemaître

Le courrier électronique

Le courrier électronique étant un moyen de communication rapide, le style des messages est souvent familier et télégraphique et l'emploi des abréviations et des acronymes est très courant. Selon la netiquette, ou code de conduite sur le réseau, il est déconseillé d'écrire un message tout en majuscules car cela pourrait être interprété comme un signe de mauvaise humeur.

Les formules d'appel traditionnelles (**Dear ...**) sont généralement omises. Si vous connaissez bien votre correspondant, vous pouvez commencer par une formule familière telle que **Hello** ou **Hi,** suivie du prénom de la personne.

Abréviations utilisées dans le courrier électronique et les forums

Les abréviations et acronymes qui suivent sont couramment employés dans le courrier électronique et les forums de discussion. Il est cependant conseillé de ne les utiliser que lorsque l'on est sûr que le destinataire connaît leur signification. Les abréviations suivies de la mention *Fam* appartiennent à un registre plus familier et doivent être réservées à une correspondance plus relâchée.

Adv	advice (conseil)
AFAICT *Fam*	as far as I can tell (pour autant que je sache)
AFAIK *Fam*	as far as I know (pour autant que je sache)
AFK	away from keyboard (indique que l'on va quitter son poste)
AIUI *Fam*	as far as I understand (si j'ai bien compris)
B4 *Fam*	before (avant)
BAK	back at keyboard (de retour devant l'écran)
BBL *Fam*	be back later (je reviens)
BTW *Fam*	by the way (à propos)
cld	could
Doc	document
EOF	end of file (fin de fichier)
F2F *Fam*	face to face (en face, face à face)
FAQ	frequently asked questions (foire aux questions)
FOC	free of charge (gratuit, gratuitement)
Foll	following, to follow (suivant, à suivre)
FYI	for your information (pour ton information)
HTH *Fam*	hope this helps (j'espère que cela te sera utile)
IIRC *Fam*	if I recall correctly (si mes souvenirs sont bons)

IMO, IMHO *Fam*	in my (humble) opinion (à mon (humble) avis)
IOW *Fam*	In other words (autrement dit)
ISTM *Fam*	it seems to me (il me semble que)
ITRO *Fam*	in the region of (environ)
NRN *Fam*	no reply necessasry (réponse facultative)
NW! *Fam*	no way! (sûrement pas!)
OTOH *Fam*	on the other hand (d'un autre côté)
OTT *Fam*	over the top (excessif)
PD	public domain (domaine public)
POV	point of view (point de vue)
prhps	perhaps (peut-être)
RTFM *très Fam*	read the f***ing manual (regarde dans le manuel, nom de Dieu!)
RUOK *Fam*	are you OK? (ça va?)
TIA *Fam*	thanks in advance (merci d'avance)
TNX *Fam*	thanks (merci)
TVM *Fam*	thanks very much (merci beaucoup)
VR	virtual reality (réalité virtuelle)
WRT *Fam*	with regard to (en ce qui concerne)
urgt	urgent

Message interne

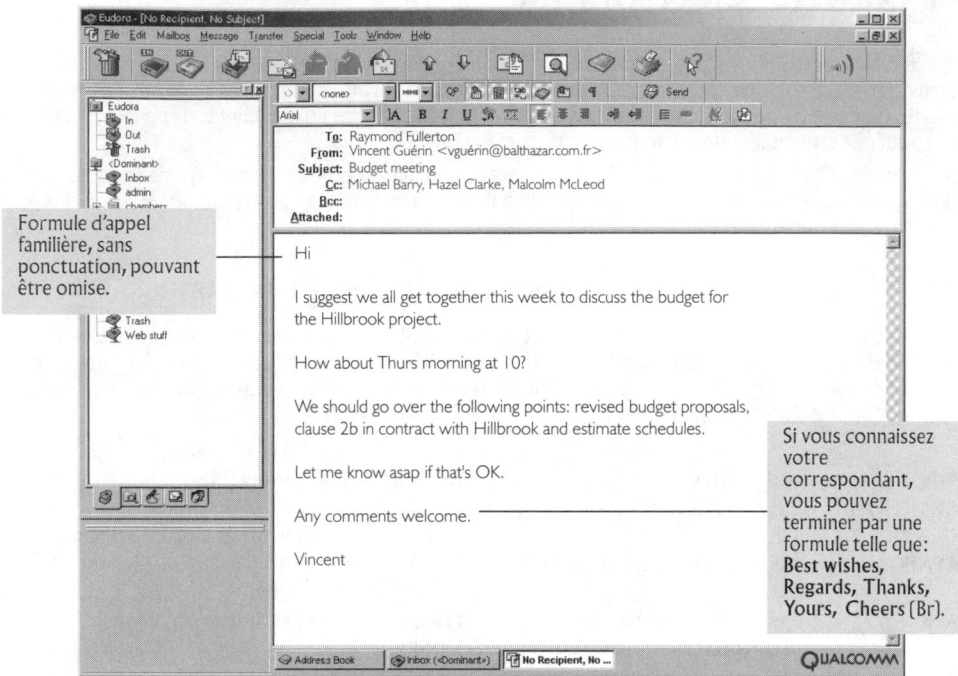

Formule d'appel familière, sans ponctuation, pouvant être omise.

Si vous connaissez votre correspondant, vous pouvez terminer par une formule telle que: Best wishes, Regards, Thanks, Yours, Cheers (Br).

Message d'une entreprise à une autre

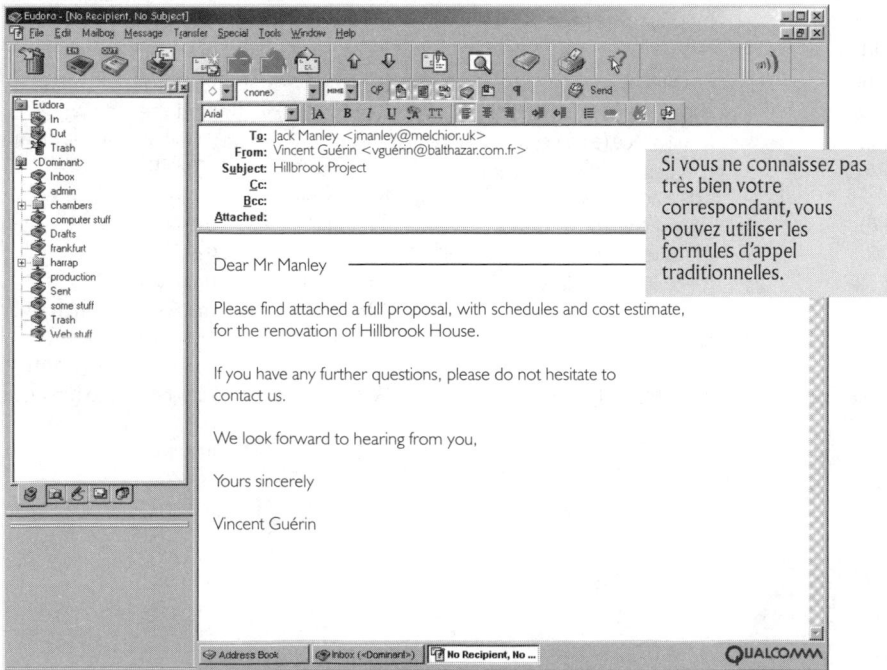

Si vous ne connaissez pas très bien votre correspondant, vous pouvez utiliser les formules d'appel traditionnelles.

Les petites annonces

Emploi

= Northeast

= August to December

French student seeks au pair work, NE London, Aug-Dec 01. References. Contact Marie Pierrefeu, tel. 0207 405 405, a.m. only.

= Morning

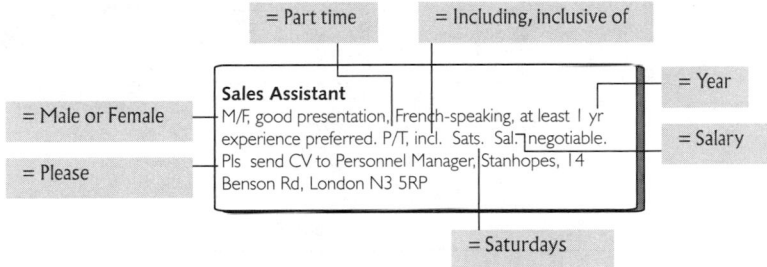

= Part time

= Including, inclusive of

= Year

= Male or Female

Sales Assistant
M/F, good presentation, French-speaking, at least 1 yr experience preferred. P/T, incl. Sats. Sal. negotiable. Pls send CV to Personnel Manager, Stanhopes, 14 Benson Rd, London N3 5RP

= Salary

= Please

= Saturdays

Vente

DRYER: Kenmore electric. Good condition, $95. Call 364-9999, between 6-8pm

= inch

DVD PLAYER, VCR, and TV 14" screen. As new. £380 ono. 530 7949 leave msg.

= or nearest offer

= Message

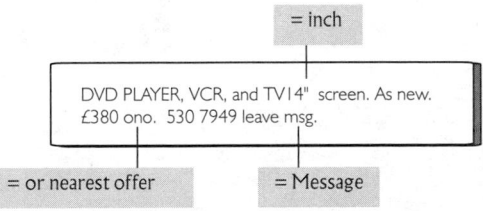

Olympus, super VHS camera, high resolution, digital effects, auto/manual focusing, etc., orig. $2500, asking $995. 4383 Powell St. 0121 445 443

= Original price, originally

Immobilier

= Large

= Room

= Week

= Southeast

= Non smoking

= Required

Lg. rm to rent in shared house, SE London, £80 per wk., plus bills. Deposit reqd. Suit NS student.
Tel: 0206 555655

= Apartment

= Kitchen

= With

= All modern conveniences

2-rm. apt. to rent in city centre. All mod cons. TV, fitted kit., bathroom w/ shower. £555 per month.
Tel: 0786 554321

Rencontres

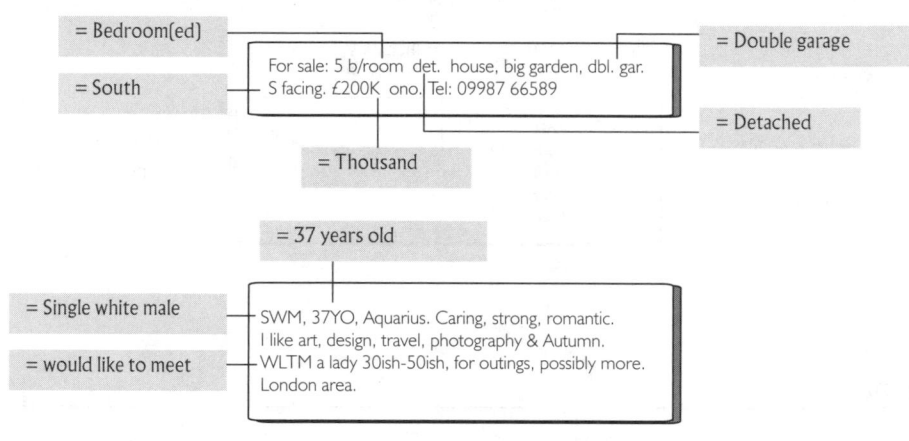

= Bedroom(ed)

= South

= Double garage

= Detached

= Thousand

For sale: 5 b/room det. house, big garden, dbl. gar. S facing. £200K ono. Tel: 09987 66589

= 37 years old

= Single white male

= would like to meet

SWM, 37YO, Aquarius. Caring, strong, romantic.
I like art, design, travel, photography & Autumn.
WLTM a lady 30ish-50ish, for outings, possibly more.
London area.

Abréviations utilisées dans les petites annonces:

AC	air conditioning	gar.	garage
adj.	adjoining	GCH	gas central heating
appt.	appointment	H/CW	hot/cold water
apt.	apartment	hr.	hour
avail.	available	kit.	kitchen
bedrm., BR	bedroom	m.	month
bsmt.	basement	nr.	near
bldg.	building	obo	or best offer
bus.	business	ono	or nearest offer
c/h	central heating	opt.	optional
cond.	condition	pkg.	parking
del.	deliver; delivery	ref.	reference
det.	detached	rm.	room
din.	dining	sal.	salary
dbl.	double	sgl.	single
ea.	each	unfurn.	unfurnished
elec.	electric	vac.	vacancy
exch.	exchange	wk.	week
ft.	foot, feet	wpm	words per minute
furn.	furniture, furnished	yr	year

Le téléphone

Prononciation des numéros de téléphone

20995   Two oh double nine five (Br)
                                          Two zero double nine five (Am)

Pour obtenir un renseignement

- Can I have directory enquiries (Br) *or* directory assistance (Am) please?
- I'm trying to get through to a London number.
- What is the (country) code for Canada?
- How do I get an outside line?

Pour demander un interlocuteur

Hello,
- could I speak to ...?
- can I speak to ...?
- I'd like to speak to ...
- (could I have) extension 593 please?

Pour répondre à un appel

- Robert McQueen speaking, can I help you?
- Hello, this is ...
- Yes, speaking (pour confirmer que l'on est bien la personne demandée)
- Hold on/hold please, I'll (just) get him/her.
- I'm sorry, he's/she's not here. Can I take a message?
- I'm afraid he's away on business/out of the office/off sick/on holiday/on vacation (Am)

Pour laisser un message

Sur un répondeur :
- I'm returning your call.
- I'll be in London next week, perhaps we can ...
- I'd like to talk to you about ...
- Could you call me back, so we can discuss ...?

une autre personne :
- Could you ask him/her to call me on ...?
- Could you tell him/her I won't be able to ...?
- I'll call back later.
- I need to speak to him/her urgently.
- Please ask him/her to confirm. Thank you.

Pour demander une confirmation

- Could you spell that please?
- Could you speak a bit more slowly please?
- I'm sorry I didn't catch that. Could you repeat that please?
- Let me check, 11 a.m. Wednesday 10th. Yes, that's fine.

Pour conclure un appel

- Thank you, I look forward to seeing you on Wednesday. Goodbye.
- Thank you for your help.

Message de répondeur téléphonique

- We are unable to take your call at the moment / I am not here at the moment. Please leave a message after the tone.

French Communication Guide

Letters

When sending a letter or other written communication, particular attention should be paid to the grammar and spelling as these are sensitive topics. Spelling mistakes and grammatical errors in a letter are considered very bad form, even in private correspondence.

The style should be simple and clear. It is a good idea to keep sentences short and to use active rather than passive verbs. Each paragraph should deal with one idea only. The idea is presented in the first sentence of the paragraph and is then developed. A new idea is expressed in a new paragraph.

Layout

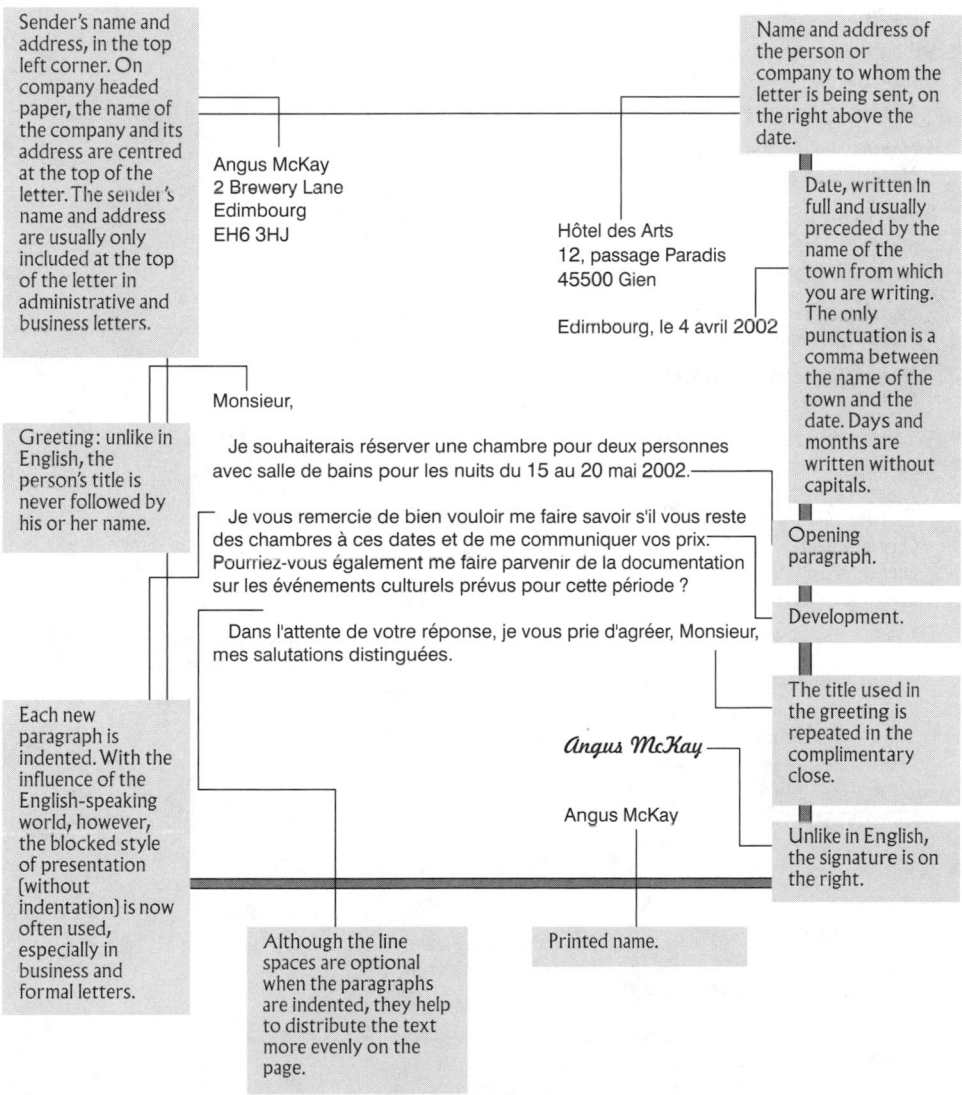

Sender's name and address, in the top left corner. On company headed paper, the name of the company and its address are centred at the top of the letter. The sender's name and address are usually only included at the top of the letter in administrative and business letters.

Name and address of the person or company to whom the letter is being sent, on the right above the date.

Angus McKay
2 Brewery Lane
Edimbourg
EH6 3HJ

Hôtel des Arts
12, passage Paradis
45500 Gien

Edimbourg, le 4 avril 2002

Date, written In full and usually preceded by the name of the town from which you are writing. The only punctuation is a comma between the name of the town and the date. Days and months are written without capitals.

Monsieur,

Greeting: unlike in English, the person's title is never followed by his or her name.

Je souhaiterais réserver une chambre pour deux personnes avec salle de bains pour les nuits du 15 au 20 mai 2002.

Je vous remercie de bien vouloir me faire savoir s'il vous reste des chambres à ces dates et de me communiquer vos prix. Pourriez-vous également me faire parvenir de la documentation sur les événements culturels prévus pour cette période ?

Opening paragraph.

Dans l'attente de votre réponse, je vous prie d'agréer, Monsieur, mes salutations distinguées.

Development.

Each new paragraph is indented. With the influence of the English-speaking world, however, the blocked style of presentation (without indentation) is now often used, especially in business and formal letters.

Angus McKay

The title used in the greeting is repeated in the complimentary close.

Angus McKay

Unlike in English, the signature is on the right.

Although the line spaces are optional when the paragraphs are indented, they help to distribute the text more evenly on the page.

Printed name.

Beginnings

The opening greetings and endings used in letters written in French follow certain well-established rules:

- If you do not know the person you are writing to, whether you know their name or not, or if you know them only slightly:

Monsieur
Madame

> The greetings *Monsieur* and *Madame* are equivalent of *Dear Sir* and *Dear Madam* in English.

Mademoiselle

> *Mademoiselle* is used for an unmarried young woman. If in doubt, use *Madame.*

- When you are unsure whether the recipient of the letter is male or female:

Madame, Monsieur

- When the letter is addressed to a company rather than to an individual:

Messieurs

- When writing to the head of a company or institution:

Monsieur le Directeur
Madame la Directrice

Monsieur le Président
Madame la Présidente

- When writing to a minister, to the Prime Minister or the President:

Monsieur le Ministre
Madame le Ministre

> The form *Madame la Ministre* is equally acceptable now.

Monsieur le Premier Ministre
Madame le Premier Ministre

Monsieur le Président de la République
Madame la Présidente de la République

- When writing to a lawyer or solicitor:

Cher Maître

> This form is used irrespective of whether one is addressing a man or woman in this context.

- When you know the person you are writing to and want to sound less formal:

Cher Monsieur
Chère Madame
Chère Mademoiselle (for an unmarried young woman)

> These greetings are never followed by the name of the person. The equivalent of *Dear Mr Allen* is *Monsieur* if you don't know him very well, or *Cher Monsieur* if you know him better and want to sound less formal. Always write the title in full and avoid abbreviations like M., Mme and Mlle.

> If you are writing to more than one person, you need to repeat *Cher* before each title:
> *Cher Monsieur, Chère Madame,*

- When you are writing to a colleague you do not know or know only slightly:

Cher collègue
Chère collègue

Cher confrère
Chère consœur

> The titles *Cher confrère* and *Chère consœur* are used between professionals such as doctors and lawyers.

Cher ami
Chère amie

> The titles *Cher ami* and *Chère amie* are still slightly formal and are not used between friends but between colleagues or acquaintances.

- When you are writing to a relative, to a friend or to a colleague with whom you are on first name terms:

  Cher Olivier
  Chère Sandrine

- When writing to a relative or close friend, especially if they are younger than you, you can also use:

  Mon cher Olivier
  Ma chère Sandrine

Endings

The complimentary close should correspond in form and tone to the opening greeting. The title used at the beginning (Monsieur, Cher Monsieur, etc.) is always repeated in the ending of the letter:

- The most neutral endings are:

  Veuillez agréer, Monsieur (Madame), mes salutations distinguées.
  Veuillez recevoir, Monsieur (Madame), mes salutations distinguées.
  Veuillez agréer, Monsieur (Madame), l'expression de mes sentiments distingués.
  Je vous prie d'agréer, Monsieur le Directeur (Madame la Directrice), mes salutations distinguées.
  Je vous prie d'agréer, cher Maître, mes salutations distinguées.
  Je vous remercie d'avance et vous prie d'agréer, Monsieur (Madame), mes salutations distinguées.
  Dans l'attente d'une réponse de votre part, veuillez agréer, Messieurs, nos salutations distinguées.

  > This form is used when addressing a lawyer or solicitor specifically.

- If you want to end on a more respectful note, such as when writing to a superior:

  Veuillez agréer, Monsieur (Madame), l'expression de ma considération distinguée.
  Je vous prie d'agréer, Monsieur (Madame), l'expression de mon profond respect.
  Veuillez agréer, je vous prie, Monsieur le Président (Madame la Présidente), l'expression de ma respectueuse con-sidération.

- If you want to show your gratitude:

  Veuillez agréer, Monsieur (Madame), l'expression de ma profonde gratitude.
  Veuillez agréer, Monsieur (Madame), l'expression de ma respectueuse reconnaissance.
  Croyez, Monsieur (Madame), à toute ma reconnaissance.
  Croyez, Monsieur (Madame), à ma sincère gratitude.

- Although still formal, the following endings are more friendly:

  Veuillez agréer, cher Monsieur (chère Madame), l'expression de mes senti-ments les plus cordiaux.
  Veuillez croire, cher Monsieur (chère Madame), à mon meilleur souvenir.
  Veuillez recevoir, cher ami (chère amie), mes plus cordiales salutations.
  Croyez, cher Olivier (chère Sandrine), à mon amical souvenir.

  > As noted above, the expression *cher ami*, although more friendly, is still formal and should not be used for a friend.

- Simplified and more informal endings are becoming more common. The following endings can be found more and more in everyday business letters, e-mails and faxes:

  Salutations distinguées.
  Cordialement. (more friendly)
  Bien à vous. (even more friendly)

- The following endings are used when writing to friends or relatives:

Polite:	Friendly:	Informal:
Amitiés.	*Je t'embrasse.*	*Grosses bises.*
Amicalement.	*À bientôt.*	*Bisous.*
Bien amicalement.	*Embrasse Pierre de ma part.*	
Bien affectueusement.		
Bien à toi.		

Addresses and postcodes

■ You might often see "bis" and "ter" after the street number in a French address. For example:

> 3 bis, rue des Lilas
> 11 ter, avenue de Bernay

They indicate that there is more than one residence, whether in the form of a self-contained apartment or an annexe to the main house or premises, at the address in question. "Bis" is used to indicate that there is a second residential (or business) unit, "ter" a third, the equivalent of 3b or 11c in English.

■ The first two numbers of a French postcode correspond to the administrative code number of the relevant "département". All postcodes for Paris begin with 75. This system also applies to vehicle licence plates. For example:

> 20, boulevard Arago
> 75013 Paris

In the example above, the first two numbers indicate the city of Paris while the last two figures indicate that the address is located in the thirteenth "arrondissement" (district) of the city.

■ The abbreviation "Cedex" is often found in French business addresses. For example:

> Société Delacour
> 77170 Fontainebleau Cedex

This is a special postcode ensuring rapid delivery of mail to businesses and certain institutions. In these cases, the first two figures, as in other postcodes, denote geographical location but the following three figures denote an individual code assigned to the company in question.

■ In Belgium addresses are often written with the street number coming after the street name, and the postcode before the town. For an apartment or a house where there are more than three letterboxes it is usual to add the letterbox number (not the apartment number) after the street number. For example:

> Monsieur Luc Dujardin
> rue du Clocher 143, bte 12   The abbreviation for boîte.
> 1040 Bruxelles

■ Swiss addresses are also usually written with the street number appearing after the street name, and the postcode before the town. If writing from outside Switzerland one may include the abbreviation CH (for "Confederatio Helvetica" or the Swiss Confederation). For example:

> Monsieur André Roux
> Avenue du Peyrou 4
> CH - 2000 Neuchâtel

■ In Canada, it is usual to write the name of the town or municipality, followed by the abbreviation corresponding to the province in which it is located, followed by the postcode, all on the same line. For example:

> Madame Chantal Lemoine   The name of the province is usually given in brackets
> 3567 rue Drummond   after the name of the town or municipality.
> Montréal (Québec) H3G 1M8   Alternatively an abbreviation can be used to designate
>   the province: for example QC for Québec. If the
>   abbreviated form is used then there is no need for
>   brackets.

The websites of the various postal services in French-speaking countries are a useful source of information regarding addresses and postcodes in particular.

France: www.laposte.fr
Belgium: www.post.be
Luxembourg: www.pt.lu
Switzerland: www.poste.ch
Canada: www.canadapost.ca

Envelopes

The top left corner can be used by the sender to add any special comment, such as **personnel** or **faire suivre.**

In administrative letters, the surname usually precedes the forename: **Madame Guimard Annie.**

The recipient's name and address are written towards the right hand side of the lower half of the envelope.

Madame Annie Guimard
325 rue Consolat
13100 AIX EN PROVENCE

The French postal services recommend that no punctuation be used on the envelope (no commas at the end of lines, no comma after the street number etc) and that the name of the town should be written in capital letters, without any accents or hyphens.

Note that **rue** is never written with a capital **R**, unlike Street or the abbreviated form St in English.

It is standard practice to write a return address on the back of the envelope at the top, in case the letter gets lost.

Model letters

Chatty letter to a friend/relative

When writing to friends and relatives, as in English, a more informal style is perfectly acceptable.

In letters to friends and relatives, the sender does not usually put his or her name and address at the top of the letter.

Note that unlike in English, months do not start with a capital letter.

Rennes, le 15 juin 2002

Chère Élodie,

The greeting is always followed by a comma.

Je suis désolée d'avoir mis si longtemps à te répondre, mais c'est que je suis très occupée en ce moment. Comme tu le sais déjà, je viens de déménager et je n'ai pas encore fini de défaire mes cartons.

Mon nouvel appart me plaît beaucoup, il est très spacieux, ça me change du studio. Le quartier est également très sympa. J'ai bien l'intention de pendre la crémaillère dès que j'aurai fini de m'installer. J'espère que tu pourras venir !

The style is colloquial: note the use of abbreviated forms.

Pour l'instant, je pense surtout aux vacances et j'attends avec impatience mon départ pour l'Écosse au mois de juillet. Tu te souviens de Fiona, mon amie écossaise ? Nous allons camper dans les Highlands avec quelques amis. J'espère qu'il fera aussi beau que l'année dernière, j'étais rentrée bronzée ! Donne-moi vite de tes nouvelles. Au fait, que fais-tu cet été ?

Je t'embrasse.

Marie-Claire

The ending is always followed by a full stop, unlike in English.

Greeting cards

▪ Season's greetings

The use of greeting cards is not as widespread in France as in English-speaking countries. Greeting cards are usually sent for New Year rather than Christmas. You can send a New Year's card at any time from before Christmas until the end of January, although usually before the middle of January. They are mostly sent to friends and relatives who live far away and business acquaintances. They are always posted and are never handed to the recipient.

*Bonne et heureuse année
2002 à tous les trois.*

À très bientôt, j'espère.

     Laurence

*Cher Simon, chère Odile,
 Tous nos vœux de bonheur pour
l'année 2002 !*

Bien à vous.

     Vincent et Sylvie

Chère Mathilde,
 Que cette nouvelle année t'apporte joie
et bonheur et soit l'occasion de nous voir
souvent !
    Irène

*Cher Jérôme, chère Nicole,
 Nous vous remercions de vos vœux
et nous vous souhaitons à notre tour
une nouvelle année pleine de joie et
de bonheur.*

Affectueusement

    Pascale et Jean-Pierre

▪ Birthdays

Birthday cards are not as popular in France as in English-speaking countries. As with other types of greeting cards, they are mostly sent to friends and relatives who live far away rather than to people who one sees regularly. Birthday cards are not usually handed directly to the recipient and presents are not systematically accompanied by a card.

Cher Thomas,

*Bon anniversaire !
Dommage que nous ne
puissions pas célébrer
ensemble tes 30 ans.
Je penserai à toi dimanche
en buvant un verre à ta
santé !*

Je t'embrasse.

    Julie

Useful phrases:

Joyeux anniversaire !
Pierre se joint à moi pour te souhaiter un très bon anniversaire.

■ Congratulations

Written congratulations are usually sent after the announcement of a birth, engagement, wedding or promotion.

> *Grenoble, le 2 juillet 2002*
>
> *Bravo ! Tes parents m'ont appris que tu as été reçu à tes examens. Quel soulagement, tu vas enfin pouvoir profiter de vacances bien méritées. Toutes mes félicitations et bon courage pour la suite de tes études !*
>
> *Je t'embrasse.*
>
> *Marie*

Useful phrases:

■ For an engagement/a wedding:
C'est avec grand plaisir que j'ai appris tes fiançailles avec Pierre.
Tous nos vœux de bonheur à tous les deux. [less formal]

■ For a birth:
C'est avec joie que nous avons appris la naissance de Matthieu.
Félicitations à tous les deux et tous nos vœux de bonheur pour votre bébé.

■ For a promotion/success:
C'est avec grand plaisir que j'ai appris votre promotion/nomination au poste de...
Je vous adresse mes sincères félicitations, ainsi que celles de mes collègues. [formal]

Letter of complaint

For serious complaints, or if a first letter has been ignored, it is standard practice to send this type of letter by recorded delivery ("lettre recommandée avec accusé de réception").

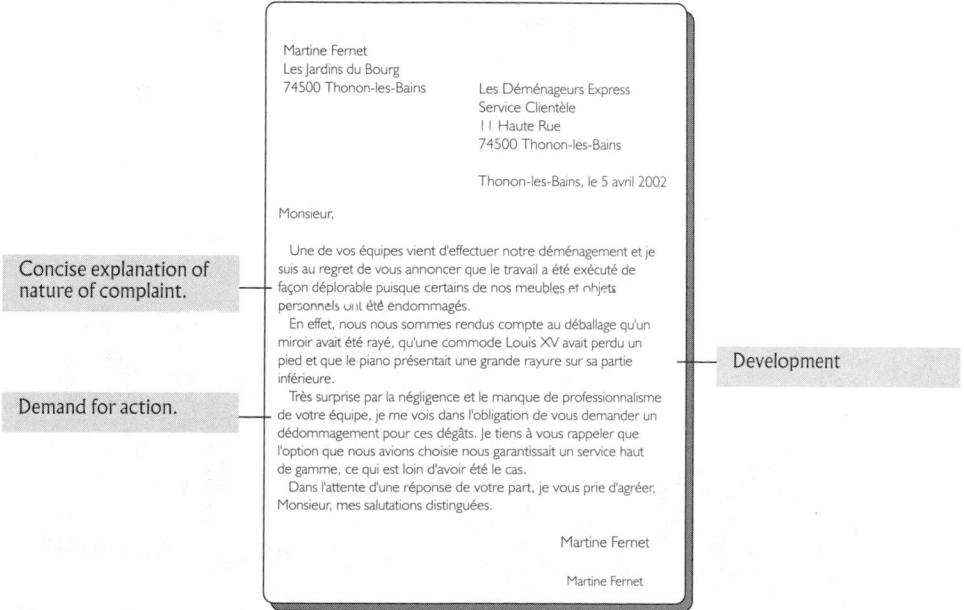

Martine Fernet
Les Jardins du Bourg
74500 Thonon-les-Bains

Les Déménageurs Express
Service Clientèle
11 Haute Rue
74500 Thonon-les-Bains

Thonon-les-Bains, le 5 avril 2002

Monsieur,

Une de vos équipes vient d'effectuer notre déménagement et je suis au regret de vous annoncer que le travail a été exécuté de façon déplorable puisque certains de nos meubles et objets personnels ont été endommagés.

En effet, nous nous sommes rendus compte au déballage qu'un miroir avait été rayé, qu'une commode Louis XV avait perdu un pied et que le piano présentait une grande rayure sur sa partie inférieure.

Très surprise par la négligence et le manque de professionnalisme de votre équipe, je me vois dans l'obligation de vous demander un dédommagement pour ces dégâts. Je tiens à vous rappeler que l'option que nous avions choisie nous garantissait un service haut de gamme, ce qui est loin d'avoir été le cas.

Dans l'attente d'une réponse de votre part, je vous prie d'agréer, Monsieur, mes salutations distinguées.

Martine Fernet

Martine Fernet

Concise explanation of nature of complaint.

Demand for action.

Development

Useful phrases:

Je vous ai commandé le 20 décembre dernier une armoire que vous deviez me livrer dans les quinze jours. Or je n'ai toujours rien reçu trois semaines plus tard.
Je suis surpris de constater que... / Je m'étonne de...
Je suis vivement surpris de... (stronger)
J'ai le regret de vous signaler que...
Nous regrettons de devoir vous signaler une erreur dans...
Nous vous demandons donc de bien vouloir...
Je vous prie de bien vouloir faire le nécessaire/d'annuler ma commande et de me rembourser la somme de...

Apologizing

Even if you have already apologized by telephone, in some situations, for example if you have missed a formal appointment, a letter of apology is expected.

Apologize and recall briefly what happened.

Ann Thorne
10, rue des Acacias
75017 Paris

TECHNO-MEDIA
À l'attention de Madame Dubreuil
14, rue du Vieux Marché
78100 Saint-Germain-en-Laye

Paris, le 3 septembre 2002

Madame,

Je suis vraiment navrée de n'avoir pas pu me présenter à l'entretien que vous m'aviez fixé le lundi 3 septembre 2002, à 14 heures. En effet, ainsi que je vous l'ai expliqué lors de mon appel hier matin, aucun train ne circulait en direction de Saint-Germain-en-Laye, en raison d'une grève surprise du personnel de la SNCF.

Je ne peux que vous renouveler mes excuses pour ce fâcheux incident indépendant de ma volonté. Vous serait-il possible de me proposer un nouveau rendez-vous, au jour et à l'heure qui vous conviendraient ?

Je vous remercie à l'avance de votre compréhension et je vous prie d'agréer, Madame, l'expression de ma considération distinguée.

Ann Thorne

Ann Thorne

Give the specific reason for the mishap.

End on a hopeful note: you hope the person you are apologizing to will excuse you.

Useful phrases:

Veuillez accepter toutes nos excuses pour ce malencontreux incident. (formal)
Nous tenons à vous présenter nos excuses pour... (formal)
Je suis vraiment navré de ce malentendu.
J'espère que vous ne me tiendrez pas rigueur de cet oubli.
Excuse-moi de ne pas t'avoir prévenu plus tôt/de t'avoir fait faux bond hier soir. (informal)

Making a reservation

Specify all your requirements

Angus McKay
2 Brewery Lane
Edimbourg EH6 3HJ

Hôtel des Arts
12, passage Paradis
45500 Gien

Edimbourg, le 3 mai 2002

Monsieur,

Suite à notre conversation téléphonique de ce matin, je vous confirme ma réservation d'une chambre à deux lits avec douche pour les nuits du 15 au 20 mai 2001.
Veuillez trouver ci-dessous comme convenu mes références de carte bancaire en garantie :

Carte ...... n° : ..... expirant le .....

Je vous serais reconnaissant de bien vouloir me faire parvenir par retour du courrier votre confirmation de réservation.
Je vous remercie d'avance et vous prie d'agréer, Monsieur, mes salutations distinguées.

Angus McKay

Mention that you expect a written response.

Useful phrases:

Je vous confirme ma réservation de votre appartement... pour la période du...
Je vous remercie de bien vouloir me faire savoir s'il vous reste des chambres à ces dates et de me communiquer vos prix.
Veuillez trouver ci-joint comme convenu un chèque de... francs à titre d'arrhes.

Letter of thanks to a friend/relative

Be specific: recall the circumstances.

Crest, le 3 juin 2001

Chère Marion, cher Yves,

Ces trois jours passés chez vous ont été formidables. Votre maison est un havre de paix, vraiment agréable à vivre. Tout était parfait. Les balades que nous avons faites en montagne m'ont beaucoup plu et m'ont fait prendre conscience que je n'étais pas en grande forme : j'ai donc pris la décision de me remettre au sport !
Encore un grand merci pour ce charmant séjour.

Grosses bises à tous les deux, je file à la poste !

A très bientôt.

Paul

Thank the person explicitly.

Useful phrases:

Merci pour ton cadeau si généreux/pour ton aide si précieuse.
Merci pour cette magnifique écharpe qui m'a fait très plaisir.
Nous tenons à vous remercier pour la belle lampe que vous nous avez offerte.

Invitations and replies

- Letter of invitation

Paris, le 25 mai 2002

Cher Andrew,

Que dirais-tu de venir passer quelques jours à la campagne ? Nous louons une maison en Normandie avec des amis du 7 au 15 juillet. Thomas nous a promis d'être des nôtres. Cela nous ferait très plaisir que tu te joignes à nous.

Tu trouveras ci-joint un plan détaillé de la région.

Donne-nous vite ta réponse !

À bientôt.

Pierre

Useful phrases:

À l'occasion du week-end du 1er mai, nous invitons quelques amis dans notre maison de campagne.
Pour fêter l'anniversaire de Simon, nous organisons une soirée le..., à partir de...
Nous comptons sur votre présence.

- Invitation card

These are usually made by a printer, who can suggest standard formulas.

M. et Mme Tessier
seront heureux de vous recevoir à
l'occasion du baptême
de leur fils

Nicolas

le samedi 16 juin
à partir de 15 heures

4, villa du Puits - 26500 Crest   R.S.V.P.

Abbreviation of "Répondez s'il vous plaît".

Useful phrases:

Sophie Tessier recevra ses amis le... à partir de...
Jacques Tessier vous invite à venir assister à sa soutenance de thèse le... à partir de...
Nous organisons une soirée le... à l'occasion de... Nous serions très heureux si vous pouviez vous joindre à nous.

▪ Wedding invitation

> Monsieur et Madame Tessier   Monsieur et Madame Legrand
>
> *ont le plaisir de vous faire part*
> *du mariage de leurs enfants*
>
> **Nathalie et Sylvain**
>
> *et vous prient d'assister à la bénédiction nuptiale qui*
> *leur sera donnée*
> *le samedi 16 juin 2002 à 16 heures en l'église*
> *Saint-Christophe à Crest*
> *ainsi qu'au dîner organisé à partir de 20 heures*
> *au restaurant Les Tilleuls de Crest.*
>
> *Réponse souhaitée avant le 10 mai*
>
> 4, villa du Puits   6, rue des Bains
> 26500 Crest   25000 Besançon

For traditional weddings, the invitation is made by the parents of the couple.

Useful phrases:

Monsieur et Madame X vous prient d'assister à la messe de mariage qui sera célébrée le... en l'église...
Monsieur et Madame X recevront à l'hôtel Les Tilleuls à l'issue de la cérémonie religieuse.
Nathalie Tessier et Sylvain Legrand sont heureux de vous annoncer leur mariage qui sera célébré le... à... à la mairie de Crest.
Un vin d'honneur sera servi à l'issue de la cérémonie à la salle des fêtes de Crest.

▪ Declining an invitation

> *Valence, le 15 juillet 2002*
>
> *Chère Aude,*
>
> *Je viens de recevoir ta lettre, et je suis très touché que tu aies pensé à m'inviter pour ton anniversaire, mais, malheureusement, je dois partir à Londres dès la semaine prochaine pour raisons professionnelles et je ne pourrai pas me joindre à vous.*
> *J'espère bien sûr que tes 30 ans seront dignement célébrés, et dans la bonne humeur ; je penserai à toi ce jour-là, en buvant un verre à ta santé !*
> *Comme cadeau d'anniversaire, je serai ravi de t'accueillir à Londres. On met à ma disposition un grand appartement et un week-end serait suffisant pour te dépayser.*
> *J'attends donc ta réponse et je te souhaite un très bon anniversaire.*
>
> *Je t'embrasse.*
>
> **Simon**

Useful phrases:

Je suis vraiment déçu de ne pouvoir accepter mais je ne pourrai pas me libérer car des obligations professionnelles me retiennent à Paris à cette date.

Nous regrettons de ne pouvoir nous libérer et nous espérons avoir très prochainement l'occasion de nous réunir.

Nous vous remercions de votre aimable invitation que nous avons le regret de ne pouvoir accepter, étant déjà retenus ce jour-là. (formal)

- **Accepting an invitation**

Express your pleasure at being invited.

Thank the sender for the invitation.

Nantes, le 14 janvier 2002

Cher Vincent,

Je viens de recevoir ta lettre et je suis ravi ! C'est vraiment gentil d'avoir pensé à moi. Ça faisait très longtemps que je rêvais de vacances et l'idée de faire du ski à Serre-Chevalier dans moins d'un mois me rend fou de joie !

J'irai à Briançon en train, et de là, je prendrai un taxi ou un bus, selon mon heure d'arrivée, pour rejoindre le chalet. Espérons qu'il continuera à neiger d'ici là !

Tout va bien ici. Mon nouveau travail me plaît énormément et l'équipe est jeune et sympa. Et toi ? Dois-tu repartir aux États-Unis avant les vacances de février ?

Je te téléphonerai bientôt pour préciser mon jour d'arrivée.

Je te remercie encore et je t'embrasse.

Michel

Useful phrases:

C'est avec grand plaisir que j'accepte votre invitation pour le.../que je me joindrais à vous le...

Je me réjouis à l'idée de vous revoir.

Nous vous remercions de votre invitation au mariage de Sylvain, que nous acceptons avec joie/auquel nous viendrons avec grand plaisir.

Letter to authorities: official statement

This type of statement follows a set formula in French.

The adjective **soussigné** varies according to the gender: Je soussignée Madame X..., Nous soussignés...

It is important that the date is included.

The standard procedure is to give your name, occupation, date and place of birth, nationality and address.

A precise statement of the facts should be given.

Je soussigné Andrew Dixon, informaticien, né le 31/03/1962 à Glasgow, en Écosse, de nationalité britannique, demeurant 6 rue des Lilas à Paris (75019), certifie avoir été témoin de l'accident survenu à M. Charmier, le 20 novembre 2002 à 23 h 15, rue Léon Jouhaux à Paris.

Alors que je venais de garer ma voiture à la hauteur du 2 rue Léon Jouhaux, j'ai vu une 406 Peugeot blanche arriver à grande vitesse de la rue Beaurepaire et renverser M. Charmier qui traversait la rue Léon Jouhaux alors que le feu tricolore indiquait la priorité aux piétons.

Fait à Paris, le 2 décembre 2002.

(signature)

Asking for a brochure/information

Angus McKay
2 Brewery Lane
Edimbourg EH6 3HJ

Office du tourisme
11 place du Général de Gaulle
06600 Antibes

Edimbourg, le 4 avril 2002

Madame, Monsieur,

Souhaitant passer mes vacances (du 1er au 16 juillet) dans la région d'Antibes, je vous serais reconnaissant de bien vouloir me faire parvenir une liste des hôtels et des chambresd'hôte, à Antibes même ou dans les environs.
Pourriez-vous également me faire parvenir de la documentation sur les événements culturels prévus pour cette période ?
Je vous remercie d'avance et je vous prie d'agréer, Madame, Monsieur, mes salutations distinguées.

Angus McKay

Angus McKay

Business correspondence

Business to business (general)

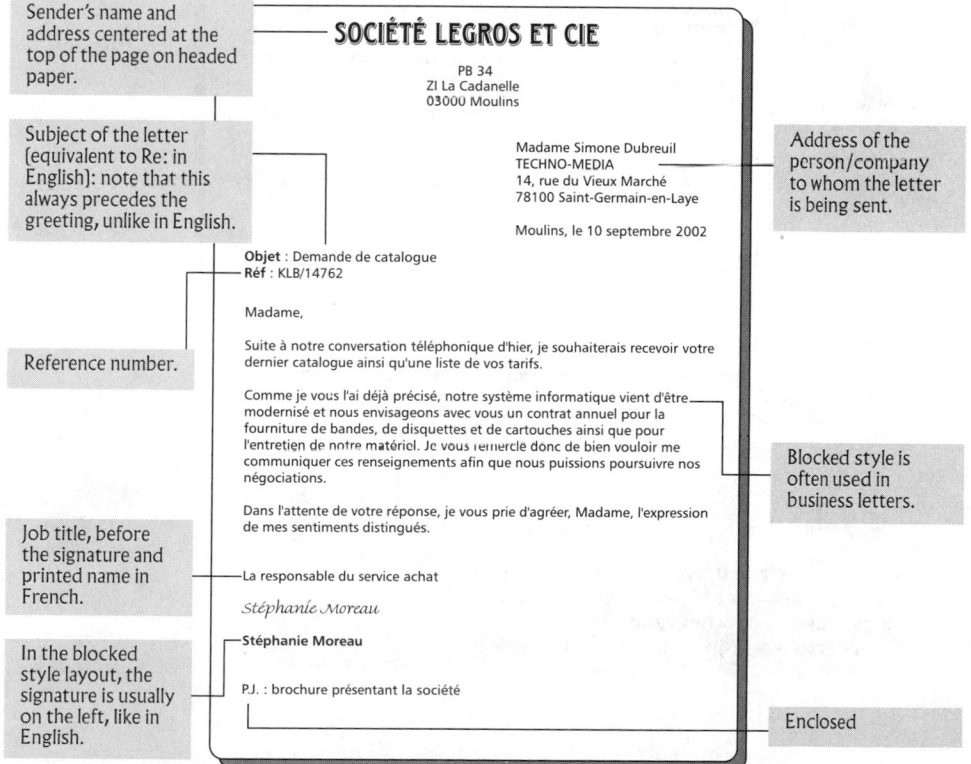

Sender's name and address centered at the top of the page on headed paper.

SOCIÉTÉ LEGROS ET CIE

PB 34
ZI La Cadanelle
03000 Moulins

Subject of the letter (equivalent to Re: in English): note that this always precedes the greeting, unlike in English.

Madame Simone Dubreuil
TECHNO-MEDIA
14, rue du Vieux Marché
78100 Saint-Germain-en-Laye

Moulins, le 10 septembre 2002

Address of the person/company to whom the letter is being sent.

Objet : Demande de catalogue
Réf : KLB/14762

Reference number.

Madame,

Suite à notre conversation téléphonique d'hier, je souhaiterais recevoir votre dernier catalogue ainsi qu'une liste de vos tarifs.

Comme je vous l'ai déjà précisé, notre système informatique vient d'être modernisé et nous envisageons avec vous un contrat annuel pour la fourniture de bandes, de disquettes et de cartouches ainsi que pour l'entretien de notre matériel. Je vous remercie donc de bien vouloir me communiquer ces renseignements afin que nous puissions poursuivre nos négociations.

Dans l'attente de votre réponse, je vous prie d'agréer, Madame, l'expression de mes sentiments distingués.

Blocked style is often used in business letters.

Job title, before the signature and printed name in French.

La responsable du service achat

Stéphanie Moreau

Stéphanie Moreau

In the blocked style layout, the signature is usually on the left, like in English.

P.J. : brochure présentant la société

Enclosed

Useful phrases:

En réponse à votre lettre du...,
Nous avons bien reçu votre lettre du... et nous vous en remercions.
Nous sommes tout particulièrement intéressés par...
Nous vous remercions de l'intérêt que vous portez à notre société et nous restons à votre disposition pour toutes informations complémentaires.

Placing an order

A letter placing an order needs to specify the items required, as well as the conditions of delivery and payment.

SOCIÉTÉ LEGROS ET CIE

PB 34
ZI La Cadanelle
03000 Moulins

Madame Simone Dubreuil
TECHNO-MEDIA
14, rue du Vieux Marché
78100 Saint-Germain-en-Laye

Moulins, le 10 septembre 2002

Objet : N/commande n°12035

Madame,

Suite à notre entretien téléphonique du 7 septembre dernier, nous vous confirmons notre commande des articles suivants :

10 lots de 20 disquettes DD/HD, réf. 12345, 119 F H.T. le lot — **List of items ordered.**
2 cartouches IBM, réf. 12698, 239 F H.T. l'une

Terms of delivery. — Nous vous serions reconnaissants de bien vouloir nous faire parvenir ces articles sous quinzaine.

Payment terms. — Nous vous réglerons en totalité à réception de la facture. Nous vous remercions de bien vouloir nous faire bénéficier de votre remise de 5 % pour un paiement comptant.

Nous vous prions d'agréer, Madame, l'expression de nos sentiments distingués.

Le directeur des achats

Jacques Dupont

Jacques Dupont

Useful phrases:

Veuillez nous faire parvenir les articles suivants...
Nous vous prions de bien vouloir nous expédier...
Nous vous passons commande de...
Veuillez trouver ci-joint notre bon de commande n°...

Informing a customer

TECHNO-MEDIA
14, rue du Vieux Marché
78100 Saint-Germain-en-Laye
http:\\www.technomedia.fr

Saint-Germain-en-Laye, le 10 septembre 2002

Monsieur,

Nous avons le plaisir de vous informer que vous pouvez désormais consulter notre catalogue et passer vos commandes sur notre site Web.

Notre site est entièrement sécurisé. Si vous souhaitez bénéficier de nos services en ligne, il suffit de vous enregistrer en vous connectant à :
http:\\www.technomedia.fr

Dans l'espoir que ce nouveau service vous donnera entière satisfaction, nous vous prions d'agréer, Monsieur, nos meilleures salutations.

La responsable du site Web

Sylvie Legrand

Sylvie Legrand

Useful phrases:

Nous vous informons que...
Nous tenons à vous signaler que...
Nous restons à votre entière disposition pour tous renseignements complémentaires.
Veuillez noter notre nouvelle adresse à partir du...

Dealing with a customer complaint

Strasbourg, le 31 octobre 2002

Monsieur,

Dans votre lettre du 29 octobre dernier, vous nous signalez un défaut de quantité dans notre livraison n° 2983. Or, notre agent à Cherbourg qui a personnellement supervisé le chargement à bord du navire nous certifie que la quantité a bien été embarquée.

Reference to letter of complaint.

Nous considérons donc que nous ne pouvons être tenus pour responsables et qu'il s'agit probablement d'un vol qui a pu se produire en cours de transport ou lors du stockage au débarquement et nous vous conseillons de prendre contact avec votre assureur.

Explanation of cause of problem.

Nous vous prions d'agréer, Monsieur, nos salutations distinguées.

La directrice des ventes

Isabelle Durand

Isabelle Durand

Useful phrases:

Nous vous prions de bien vouloir nous excuser pour cette regrettable erreur.
Veuillez accepter nos excuses pour le dérangement que nous avons pu vous causer.
Nous avons pris des mesures pour que cela ne se reproduise plus.

Invoice

Company name, registered office, telephone and fax numbers, telex number, e-mail address and company registration number.

Date of invoice.

Reference number of listed items.

Precise description of products or services.

Total including VAT.

Name and address of client.

Client reference number and order number

Unit price not including VAT.

Quantity

VAT rate.

Total price not including VAT.

TECHNO-MEDIA
14, rue du Vieux Marché
78100 Saint-Germain-en-Laye
http:\\www.technomedia.fr

SOCIÉTÉ LEGROS ET CIE
PB 34
ZI La Cadanelle
03000 Moulins

Facture n° 500298
du 15/09/2002

Invoice number.

N° client: 272
N° commande: 12035

Réf.	Désignation	Qt	Prix unitaire HT	Total HT	Tx TVA
12345	lot de 20 disquettes DD/HD	10	119,00	2380,00	19,60
12698	cartouche IBM	2	239,00	478,00	19,60

Total HT.........................258, 00F
TVA 19,6%......................... 56,16F
Total TTC 3418,16F

Net à payer
en francs........................3418,16F
en euros...........................521,10 €

Reply to invoice

Briefly explain the mistake.

Acknowledge receipt of the invoice, quoting the invoice number and date.

Ask for a new invoice.

Moulins, le 1er octobre 2002

Messieurs,

Nous avons bien reçu votre facture n°... du...
Lors de sa vérification, nous avons constaté une erreur : 20 lots de disquettes ont été facturés, alors que seuls 10 lots ont été commandés et livrés.

Nous vous demandons donc de bien vouloir corriger cette erreur et de nous adresser une nouvelle facture. Vous trouverez ci-joint une copie du bordereau de livraison.

Veuillez agréer, Messieurs, nos salutations distinguées.

Le directeur des achats

Jacques Dupont

Useful phrases:

Nous accusons réception de votre facture n°...
Les prix ne sont pas ceux qui ont été convenus lors de la commande, à savoir : ...
En vérifiant la facture que vous venez de nous faire parvenir, nous constatons que le montant ne correspond pas à notre commande.
Nous avons décelé l'erreur suivante : ...

Employment

Cover letter

When applying for a job in France, it is customary to write the cover letter ("lettre de motivation") by hand. Apart from adding a more personal touch, it is not unusual for French companies to use the services of a graphologist who analyses the applicants' handwriting. A letter of application is quite formal in its presentation. It should be concise, properly structured in paragraphs and have the standard opening and closing formulas. You should cover the following points:

- Emphasize what you consider important in your CV
- Add information about your objectives
- Explain why you are interested in the company
- Convince the reader that you are the right person for the job

Marielle Gondrand
Villa La Tourelle
37000 Tours

Centre culturel La Vague
3, place de la Mairie
37000 Tours

Tours, le 1er octobre 2002

Monsieur,

Votre annonce parue dans Les Nouvelles de Tours du 28 septembre 2002 pour un poste de secrétaire a retenu toute mon attention.

Introductory paragraph mentioning where you saw the vacancy advertised.

Je viens de terminer mon BTS de secrétariat et je suis à la recherche d'un emploi. Au cours de mes études, j'ai eu l'occasion de faire deux stages : l'un à la Banque Moreau et l'autre à la Maison des Jeunes de Tours. Par ailleurs, je m'occupe bénévolement du secrétariat d'une association à but non lucratif de mon quartier.

Outline of your current employment situation, qualifications and previous experience.

Je suis très attirée par les métiers de la culture, et ceci, ainsi que le rayonnement de votre société au niveau régional, m'incite à vouloir rejoindre votre équipe.

Why you are interested in the company.

Je me tiens à votre disposition pour un entretien éventuel.

Indicate that you are available for interview.

Je vous prie d'agréer, Monsieur, mes salutations distinguées.

Standard complimentary close.

Marielle Gondrand

Useful phrases:

En réponse à votre annonce parue dans Les Nouvelles de Tours du..., je me permets de vous adresser mon curriculum vitae pour le poste de secrétaire.
Je dispose de plusieurs années d'expérience dans différentes entreprises.
Au cours de mes cinq années d'expérience auprès de la société X, j'ai acquis une bonne maîtrise de...
En espérant que ma candidature retiendra votre attention, je vous prie d'agréer, Madame, Monsieur, l'expression de mes sentiments distingués.

Asking for a work placement

Work placements are very popular in France and are a compulsory part of many courses. It is therefore advisable to send your request well in advance.

This type of letter is always handwritten in French (see Cover letter on previous page).

Mention your course.

Explain what is expected from the placement.

Explain your reasons for choosing the company.

Specify the length of the placement and the dates.

Katherine Dixon
28 Fallowfield Road
Colchester
Essex CM16 3JF

Cabinet d'urbanisme Alphacité
22 boulevard des Dames
33000 Bordeaux

Colchester, le 17 octobre 2002

Monsieur,

Étudiante en licence d'urbanisme à l'Université de Colchester, je dois effectuer dans le cadre de mes études un stage en entreprise d'une durée de six semaines minimum, entre le mois de janvier et le mois d'avril 2002. Ce stage est destiné à enrichir l'enseignement reçu à l'université, d'une part en permettant à l'étudiant de se perfectionner dans une langue étrangère, d'autre part en le mettant en situation réelle.
Très intéressée par la signalétique urbaine, et attirée par la réputation de votre cabinet, je souhaite mettre mes compétences et mon savoir-faire au bénéfice de votre entreprise.
Dans l'espoir que ma candidature retiendra votre attention, je vous prie d'agréer, Monsieur, mes salutations distinguées.

Katherine Dixon

Useful phrases:

Vous trouverez ci-joint mon curriculum vitae.
Je vous remercie de l'attention que vous porterez à ma demande et reste à votre disposition pour un entretien.
Je reste à votre disposition pour vous rencontrer et vous fournir tout autre renseignement.
En vous remerciant à l'avance de bien vouloir examiner ma demande, je vous prie d'agréer...

Curriculum vitae

The presentation of a CV in French is in many ways similar to an English or American CV. The following differences should be respected.

■ The title "Curriculum Vitae" should never be included in a French CV.

■ Only mention hobbies if they add something personal to your profile or if they are particularly relevant to the job.

■ Do not include referees on your CV: references are not commonly used in France apart from certain jobs where personal recommendation would be expected such as catering, cleaning, child care, etc.

■ Even if you do not complete your degree, you can mention the fact that you studied for it by using the word "niveau", i.e. "niveau licence".

▪ Experienced (French)

Laure Battisto
25, rue des Arquebusiers
76000 Rouen
Tél : 02 24 24 45 73   42 ans
Télécopie : 02 24 21 13 39   divorcée
E-mail : lbattisto@battisto.com.fr   un enfant (11 ans)

Consultante en Ressources humaines
14 ans d'expérience

Expérience professionnelle

1991 - 2000   Consultante en Ressources humaines, Cabinet Battisto-Langlade,
              Rouen : conseil auprès d'entreprises, audit, recrutement

1987 - 1990   Directrice des Ressources humaines, Conseil général, Le Havre :
              recrutement, planification des formations, suivi du personnel

1985 - 1986   Assistante du Directeur des Ressources humaines, Société Pierre et
              Fils, Le Havre

Formation

1983   Master of Business Administration, Boston University

1981 - 1982   DEA 'Langage et Médias' - Paris X

1980   Maîtrise d'Histoire - Paris IV

1976   Baccalauréat Mathématiques - Académie de Paris

Autres expériences

1984 - 1985   Voyage en Afrique dans le cadre d'une mission Médecins sans
              frontières

Langues
Bilingue anglais
Espagnol : lu, écrit, parlé

Divers
Bonne maîtrise du traitement de texte sur PC et sur Mac
Responsable d'une association bénévole luttant contre l'analphabétisme

▪ Experienced (American)

John Farmer
18 rue de Turenne
75004 Paris   Né le 17 juin 1962
Tél: 01 42 22 37 89   Marié, 2 enfants (11 et 14 ans)
E-mail: jfarmer@nxl.fr   Nationalité américaine

Directeur des ventes : 6 ans d'expérience
14 ans d'expérience dans la fonction commerciale
Connaissance approfondie du marché informatique

Depuis 1996   Softlux France, Paris
                       Directeur des ventes Europe
                       · Encadrement d'une équipe de 20 commerciaux
                       · Diversification et développement des marchés existants
                       · Augmentation du chiffre d'affaires (+ 53 %)

1988 - 1996   ICN Europe, Amsterdam
                       Directeur commercial
                       · Responsable de la politique commerciale et du marketing
                       · Recrutement et encadrement d'une équipe de 7 commerciaux
                       · Dépassement des objectifs fixés: 1994:118 %, 1993: 110%

1983 - 1987   Société ADB, Paris
                       Ingénieur commercial grands comptes
                       · Responsable du développement des ventes pour le secteur de
                       la grande distribution sur la région parisienne
                       · Ouverture de nouveaux comptes

Formation
1988   MBA, Harvard Business School
1984   MS (équivalent de la maîtrise) en Économie et Gestion,
                       Université de Boston
1980   High school diploma (équivalent du baccalauréat)

Langues
Anglais : langue maternelle
Français : bilingue

▪ Experienced (British)

Mary Grant
198 Francis Avenue
Leicester LE4 9PQ
Grande-Bretagne
Tél : 00 44 1493 767 33 36   33 ans, célibataire
E-mail: mgrant@USA.net   Nationalité britannique

EXPÉRIENCE PROFESSIONNELLE
Depuis septembre 1994   Directrice des exportations, Gannett UK Ltd, Leicester
                            (Fabrication et distribution de produits cosmétiques)
                            » mise en place d'un réseau commercial (40 représentants et 10 agents)
                            » négociations avec les points de vente
                            » études de marchés

1990 - 1994   Responsable des exportations Europe, Simon & Co plc, Leicester
                            (prêt-à-porter enfants)
                            » prospection
                            » contrôle des ventes
                            » ouverture de deux nouveaux marchés (Espagne et Italie)

FORMATION
1989 - 1993   MA (équivalent de la Maîtrise) en Gestion, Université d'Édimbourg

1989   A Levels (équivalent du baccalauréat) : économie, mathématiques,
                            histoire et français (Lycée Harfield Comprehensive, Leicester)

1988   GCSE (premier examen de fin de scolarité) : anglais, mathématiques,
                            français, économie, informatique et histoire (Lycée Harfield
                            Comprehensive, Leicester)

AUTRES ACTIVITÉS
1993 - 1994   Séjour d'une année à Paris : enseignement de l'anglais commercial à la
                            Chambre de commerce et d'industrie franco-britannique

LANGUES
Anglais : langue maternelle
Bilingue français (mère française)
Espagnol : lu, écrit, parlé

DIVERS
Bonne maîtrise de l'outil informatique sur PC et sur Mac
Chant choral

▪ Recent graduate (French)

Isabelle Murat
30, impasse de la Colline
75004 Paris   25 ans
Tél : 01 40 22 57 93   Célibataire

Formation
septembre 99 - juin 2001   École Technique Supérieure, Bordeaux : Section
                            Statistiques et Prévisions

septembre 98 - juin 99   Mathématiques spéciales (Lycée Louis Leduc, Paris)

septembre 97 - juin 98   Mathématiques supérieures (Lycée Louis Leduc, Paris)

juin 1997   Baccalauréat C (mention bien)

Expérience professionnelle
avril - mai 2000   Stage de 3 mois au Cabinet Desmoulin-Marketing et
                            Communication, 44, rue des Francs-Bourgeois, 75004
                            Paris : relance et suivi de la clientèle

juillet - septembre 1997   Animatrice dans un camp d'adolescents à Port-de-Bouc
                            (13)

Langues
Bilingue allemand
Anglais courant

Divers
juillet 1999   Séjour de deux mois en Allemagne, à Dortmund
juin 1997   Obtention du diplôme du BAFA (Brevet d'aptitude aux
                            fonctions d'animateur)
juillet 91 - juin 92   Séjour d'un an à Munich

Loisirs
Course à pied, vélo, aérobic
Théâtre dans une troupe d'amateurs

■ Recent graduate (American)

Martha Jacobs
493 Huntington Avenue
Boston
MA 02575
États-Unis
Tél : (617) 267-1680   23 ans, célibataire
E-mail: mjacobs@totem.com   Nationalité américaine

Traductrice anglais/français/espagnol
Début de spécialisation en informatique

FORMATION

1999 - 2001	Diplôme de traducteur technique Université McGill, Montréal
1995 - 1999	BA (équivalent de la licence) en français et espagnol, mention très bien Université de Boston
1994	High school diploma (équivalent du baccalauréat)

EXPÉRIENCE PROFESSIONNELLE

2000 - 2001	Éditions Dulis, Montréal Travaux de traduction en free-lance
juin 1999 - septembre 2000	Société AX Networks, Boston Stage de 3 mois dans le service de traduction : adaptation de logiciels pour le marché européen
1994 - 1995	Lycée Dupuis, Grenoble Assistante de français

LANGUES
Anglais : langue maternelle
Français : bilingue (2 ans à Montréal, 1 an à Grenoble)
Espagnol : courant

CONNAISSANCES INFORMATIQUES
Word, Excel et Access (sur PC et Mac)

LOISIRS
Escrime, violoncelle

■ Recent graduate (British)

Stephen Forbes
81 Lincoln Walk
Stevenage
Herts SE19 2DN
Tél: 00 44 1283 456789   23 ans, célibataire
E-mail: sforbes@teaser.org.uk   Nationalité britannique

Formation

1996 - 2000	BSc (équivalent de la licence) en Biologie, Université de York
1996	A Levels (équivalent du baccalauréat) : Mathématiques, Chimie, Biologie et Français, Lycée Whitton Comprehensive, Bristol.
1995	GCSE (premier examen de fin de scolarité) : Anglais, Mathématiques, Chimie, Biologie, Français, Histoire et Informatique, Lycée Whitton Comprehensive, Bristol.

Expérience professionnelle

| juillet - septembre 2000 | Stage de 3 mois auprès du service d'hématologie de l'hôpital Frenchay de Bristol : analyse de prélèvements sanguins. |
| octobre 2000 - novembre 2001 | Enseignement de l'anglais langue étrangère, École de langues Babel, Osaka, Japon. |

Langues
Anglais : langue maternelle
Français courant
Japonais : notions

Divers
Bonnes connaissances informatiques : animateur du club d'informatique d'une maison des jeunes et de la culture (Bristol)

Titulaire du brevet de secourisme

Faxes

Faxes, which are by definition a form of rapid communication, can generally be drafted in a more casual and concise way than letters. The endings are usually short and simplified.

Business

It is not necessary to use an opening greeting when you know the person well.

À l'attention de : Nicolas Roche
Téléphone :　05 40 92 90 32
Télécopie :　05 40 92 97 35

De la part de : Pierre Lenoir
Téléphone :　01 40 36 08 60
Télécopie :　01 40 36 10 30

Date : 10/10/2002
Nombre de pages (y compris celle-ci) : 1

Objet :　La réunion a été reportée au mardi 16 octobre. Nous nous chargeons de la réservation de votre billet d'avion ainsi que de votre chambre d'hôtel.

Short ending.

Cordialement.
P. Lenoir

Booking a hotel room

The greeting should be used if you don't know the person or if you know them only slightly.

À l'attention de : Hôtel Le Richelieu
Téléphone :　01 42 36 16 22
Télécopie :　01 42 36 16 24

De la part de : Pierre Lenoir
Téléphone :　01 40 36 08 60
Télécopie :　01 40 36 10 30

Date : 01/10/2002
Nombre de pages (y compris celle-ci) : 1

Monsieur,

Suite à notre conversation téléphonique de ce jour, je vous confirme ma réservation d'une chambre pour une personne avec salle de bains pour les nuits du 15 et 16 octobre 2002.

M. Roche arrivera en fin d'après-midi le lundi 15 octobre.

Nous vous réglerons comme convenu à réception de la facture.

Short ending.

Cordialement.

P. Lenoir

- Alternative endings:
   Salutations.
   Salutations distinguées.
   Bien à vous. (more friendly)

E-mail

- E-mail addresses are made up of two parts, the first being the user's name and the second being the domain name. The two parts are separated by the symbol @ (pronounced "arrobas" or "arobase" in French).

- Because of the nature of the medium, e-mails are not subject to the formal code of letter-writing that is prevalent in French.

- E-mail is becoming more and more widely used in the French working environment, although it is probably not yet as well established a method of business correspondence as it is in the English-speaking world.

- E-mails in French are often written in slightly less telegraphic style than tends to be the case in English, this being mainly due to the fact that French contains fewer of the abbreviated forms that characterize so much of this type of communication in English. Endings are usually rather informal.

Within a company

Business to business

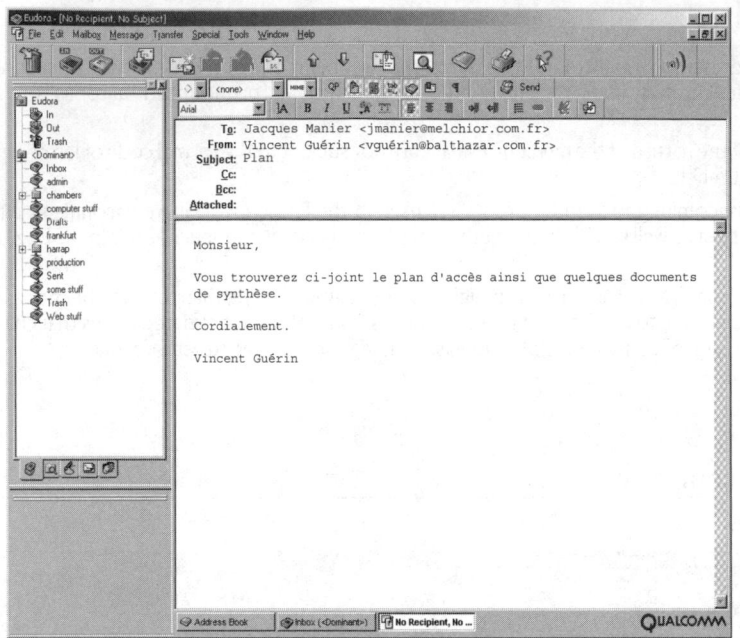

Abbreviations and acronyms

Below is a list of French abbreviations that are used in e-mail correspondence, in newsgroups and chat-rooms. These abbreviations should only be used when you are sure that the person to whom you are sending the message understands what they mean. Some are familiar in register (labelled *Fam*) and therefore should only be used in casual correspondence with friends or very close colleagues.

Note that because English is the main language of the Internet, English abbreviations are much more well established than French ones.

A+ *Fam*	à plus tard	impr.	impression/imprimer/ imprimante
actu *Fam*	actualités		
alld	allemand	info *Fam*	information
alp *Fam*	à la prochaine	K7 *Fam*	cassette
ama *Fam*	à mon avis	ltr	lettre
amha *Fam*	à mon humble avis	m	même
angl	anglais	mdr *Fam*	mort de rire
bcp *Fam*	beaucoup	MMS *Fam*	mes meilleurs souvenirs
BAL	boîte à lettres	nvx	nouveaux
B.D.	base de données	p	pour
cad	c'est-à-dire	pb, pbm	problème
dc	donc	pr	pour
doc.	documents	quoi 2/9 *Fam*	quoi de neuf ?
doss	dossier	RAS *Fam*	rien à signaler
ds	dans	stp	s'il te plaît
envoy.	envoyer	suiv.	suivant
err	erreur	svp	s'il vous plaît
esp	espagnol	svt	souvent
ex.	exemple	urgt	urgent
fr	français	we	week-end

Advertisements

Job advertisement

sérieuse   excellente présentation

jeune fille/jeune femme

écrire au journal

J.F. sér. excel. présent. ch. empl. vente ou accueil.
Écr. journ. Réf: G\650

cherche   emploi

famille   enfants   recherche

urgent

banlieue

Urgt. Fam. anglaise, 2 enf. 3 et 6 ans, rech. J. F.
au pair, banl. Londres, juil.-sept. 2001, sér. réf.
exig. Écr. Mme Dixon, 7 Stanhope Gardens London
N6 5SP

jeune fille

sérieuses références
exigées

écrire   juillet   septembre

Offering goods for sale

vends

pour cause de double
emploi

Vds cause dble empl. canapé 2 pl. t. b.ét.,
182 x 84 x 80, velours bleu. Tél: 03 20 34 28 75.

places

très bon état

vendre

pour cause de
déménagement

téléviseur

À vdre cse dém. télé. coul. écr. 55 cm, px à déb.
Tél : 01 40 62 18 24.

couleur

écran

prix à débattre

Accommodation to rent

Personal advertisement

Common abbreviations:

à déb.	à débattre	park.	parking
appt.	appartement	pces.	pièces
balc.	balcon	px	prix
c.c.	charges comprises/chauffage central	rdc.	rez-de-chaussée
ch.	chambre/cherche	sdb.	salle de bains
compr.	comprenant	séj.	séjour
cuis.	cuisine	sér.	sérieux
env.	envoyer	tbe	très bon état
équip.	équipé	tt.conf.	tout confort
gar.	garage	se prés.	se présenter
gren.	grenier	Sté.	société

Telephone calls
Pronunciation of telephone numbers

When giving their phone numbers, French people say them two by two: 01 45 67 44 32: zéro un, quarante-cinq, soixante-sept, quarante-quatre, trente-deux.

This can be a little disconcerting for the English speaker and you may have to ask them to repeat giving one number at a time.

Typical Phrases

■ Asking for information from the operator or switchboard

Est-ce que vous pouvez me passer les renseignements, s'il vous plaît ?

J'essaie d'obtenir un numéro à Marseille.

Quel est l'indicatif pour le Maroc, s'il vous plaît ?

Comment fait-on pour appeler à l'extérieur ?

■ Answering the telephone

Informally:

Allô?

To which the caller replies:

Allô, (c'est) Georges? or Salut, Georges, c'est Christophe etc

More formally:

Allô, Hélène Chapsal à l'appareil (, je vous écoute).

In a company or institution:

Éditions Paoli, bonjour.

■ Asking to speak to someone

Je voudrais parler à Monsieur Dupont.

Pouvez-vous me passer le service du/des ..., s'il vous plaît ?

Pouvez-vous me passer le poste 321, s'il vous plaît ? (pronounced trois cent vingt-et-un)

■ Phrases used by a receptionist or secretary taking a call

Qui dois-je annoncer ?

C'est de la part de qui ?

When putting a caller through:

Je vous le passe.

Ne quittez pas, je vous le passe.

When the caller cannot be connected immediately:

C'est occupé.

Il est en communication, voulez-vous patienter ?

Asking the caller if he or she wishes to leave a message:

Voulez-vous lui laisser un message ?

To which the caller may reply:

Pouvez-vous lui demander de me rappeler ?

■ Recorded messages

If you are put through to an answering machine, the usual recorded message while waiting is :

Nous vous demandons de bien vouloir patienter quelques instants. Nous allons donner suite à votre appel.

If you have to leave a message, you will hear the following standard set of sentences:

Vous êtes bien en communication avec ... Nous ne pouvons répondre à votre appel. Veuillez nous laisser votre nom et numéro de téléphone après le signal sonore et nous vous rappellerons dès que possible. Merci.

Français-Anglais
French-English

A

A¹, a¹ [ɑ] *nm inv* A, a; **connaître un sujet de A à Z** to know a subject inside out; **prouver qch par A plus B** to prove sth in a logical *or* scientific fashion

A² [ɑ] *nf (abrév* **autoroute) A1** *Br* ≃ M1, *Am* ≃ I1

a² *voir* **avoir**

à [a] *prép*

> à + le contracts to form **au** [o], à + les contracts to form **aux** [o].

(**a**) *(indique la direction)* to; **aller/venir à Paris** to go/come to Paris; **aller à la pêche** to go fishing; **partir au Venezuela** to leave for Venezuela; **rentrer à la maison** to go/come home; **au lit!** off to bed!

(**b**) *(indique la position)* at; **être à la maison/à la campagne/à Marseille** to be at home/in the country-side/in Marseilles; **j'habite au 3, place des Cardeurs** I live at number 3, place des Cardeurs; **à la page deux** on page two; **à 2 kilomètres/dix minutes d'ici** 2 kilo-metres/ten minutes from here; **à la télévision** on (the) television; **un livre à la main** with a book in his/her hand

(**c**) *(dans l'expression du temps)* **à huit heures** at eight (o'clock); **au vingtième siècle** in the twentieth century; **à la tombée de la nuit** at nightfall; **au prin-temps** in the spring; **à mon arrivée** when I arrive/ar-rived; **le 2 au soir** on the evening of the 2nd; **à lundi!/ ce soir!** see you Monday!/tonight!

(**d**) *(avec de)* to; **de Paris à Lyon** from Paris to Lyons; **du lundi au vendredi** from Monday to Friday, *Am* Monday to *or* thru Friday; **de 2 à 4** *(heure)* from 2 till *or* to 4; **de 10 à 15%** *(environ)* between 10 and 15%

(**e**) *(introduit le complément d'objet indirect)* to; **don-ner/prêter qch à qn** to give/lend sth to sb, to give/lend sb sth; **penser à qn/qch** to think of *or* about sb/sth

(**f**) *(indique l'appartenance)* **c'est à lui/à Paul** it's his/Paul's; *Fam* **un ami à moi** a friend of mine; **c'est à vous de...** *(il vous incombe de)* it's up to you to...; *(c'est votre tour de)* it's your turn to...; **à toi!** your turn!

(**g**) *(indique le moyen, la manière)* **à bicyclette** by bi-cycle; **à pied/cheval** on foot/horseback; **au crayon** in pencil; **à la française** in the French style; **fonctionner à l'électricité** to run on electricity; **jouer un air au vio-lon** to play a tune on the violin

(**h**) *(distributif)* **faire qch à deux/trois** to do sth in twos/threes; **se mettre à plusieurs pour faire qch** to team up to do sth; **100 km à l'heure** 100 km an *or* per hour; **être payé à l'heure** to be paid by the hour

(**i**) *(indique la caractéristique)* **l'homme à la barbe/ aux lunettes noires** the man with a beard/with the dark glasses; **un timbre à 3 F** a 3-franc stamp

(**j**) *(indique le but)* **maison à vendre** house for sale; **à**

louer *(sur panneau) Br* to let, *Am* to rent; **j'ai une lettre à écrire/des courses à faire** I've got a letter to write/some errands to run

(**k**) *(indique la conséquence)* **c'était à mourir de rire** it was hilarious; **laid à faire peur** hideously ugly; **c'est à se demander si...** you begin to wonder if...

abaisser [abese] **1** *vt* (**a**) *(levier, manette, pont-levis)* to lower; *(store)* to pull down (**b**) *(prix, coût, pression)* to reduce (**c**) *Litt (humilier)* to humble, to abase (**d**) *Cu-lin (pâte)* to roll out
2 s'abaisser *vpr* (**a**) *(descendre)* to slope down (**b**) **s'a. à faire qch** to lower oneself to do sth

abandon [abɑ̃dɔ̃] *nm* (**a**) *(d'un enfant, d'un projet)* abandonment; **exiger l'a. des hostilités** to call for an end to hostilities; *Jur* **a. du domicile conjugal** des-ertion; *Mil* **a. de poste** desertion of one's post (**b**) *(en sport)* **gagner par a.** to win by default; **être contraint à l'a.** to be forced to withdraw (**c**) *(d'un lieu)* neglect; **être à l'a.** to be neglected; **laisser qch à l'a.** to neglect sth (**d**) *(nonchalance)* abandon (**e**) *Ordinat* abort

abandonner [abɑ̃dɔne] **1** *vt* (**a**) *(personne, village)* to desert, to abandon; *(voiture)* to abandon; **a. le navire** to abandon ship; **a. le domicile conjugal** to desert the marital home; **mes forces m'abandonnent** my strength is failing me (**b**) *(privilège, pouvoir, combat)* to give up; *(projet)* to abandon; *(course)* to withdraw from; **a. ses études** to drop out (of school/university); **a. ses études de médecine** to give up medicine; *aussi Fig* **a. la partie** to throw in one's hand; **j'abandonne** I give up (**c**) *(céder)* to give (**à** to) (**d**) *Ordinat* to abort
2 s'abandonner *vpr (se laisser aller)* to let oneself go; **s'a. au sommeil** to drift off to sleep

abasourdi, -e [abazurdi] *adj* stunned

abat-jour [abaʒur] *nm inv* lampshade

abats [aba] *nmpl Br* offal, *Am* variety meat; *(de vo-laille)* giblets

abattage [abataʒ] *nm* (**a**) *(d'animal)* slaughter, slaughtering (**b**) **avoir de l'a.** *(acteur, politicien)* to be full of go

abattant [abatɑ̃] *nm (d'une table)* flap; *(des toilettes)* lid

abattement [abatmɑ̃] *nm* (**a**) *(physique)* exhaustion (**b**) *(moral)* dejection, depression (**c**) *Fin* **a. (fiscal)** tax allowance

abattis [abati] *nmpl* (**a**) *(de volaille)* giblets (**b**) *Fam* **numéroter ses a.** to start saying one's prayers

abattoir [abatwar] *nm* slaughterhouse, abattoir; *Fig* **envoyer qn à l'a.** to send sb to the slaughter

abattre [11] [abatr] **1** *vt* (**a**) *(faire tomber) (mur, cloison)* to knock down, to pull down; *(arbre)* to fell, to cut down; *(avion)* to bring down; *(sujet: vent) (arbre)* to blow down; **a. de la besogne** to get through a lot of work

  (**b**) *(tuer) (personne)* to kill; *(animal de boucherie)* to slaughter; *(animal malade ou dangereux)* to destroy; *Fig* **c'est l'homme à a.** he needs to be removed

  (**c**) *Fig (fatiguer) (sujet: maladie)* to lay low; **la chaleur nous a complètement abattus** the heat drained us of all energy

  (**d**) *Fig (démoraliser)* to dishearten, to depress; **ne vous laissez pas a.!** keep your chin up!

  (**e**) *aussi Fig* **a. ses cartes** *ou* **son jeu** to lay one's cards on the table

  2 s'abattre *vpr (arbre, mur)* to crash down (**sur** on); *(pluie)* to pour down (**sur** on); *(oiseau)* to swoop down (**sur** on)

abattu, -e [abaty] *adj* dejected, depressed

abbaye [abei] *nf* abbey

abbé [abe] *nm* (**a**) *(d'une abbaye)* abbot (**b**) *(prêtre)* priest; **j'en parlerai à Monsieur l'a.** I'll mention it to the priest; **l'a. Martin** Father Martin

abc [abese] *nm inv (rudiments)* basics

abcès [apsɛ] *nm* abscess; *Fig* **crever** *ou* **vider l'a.** to resolve the situation

abdiquer [abdike] *vt (trône)* to abdicate; *(droits)* to renounce, to surrender; **être contraint d'a.** to be forced to abdicate

abdomen [abdɔmɛn] *nm* abdomen

abdominal, -e, -aux, -ales [abdɔminal, -o] **1** *adj* abdominal

  2 *nmpl* **abdominaux** *(muscles)* stomach muscles; **faire des abdominaux** to do exercises for the stomach muscles

abdos [abdo] *nmpl Fam (muscles)* stomach muscles; **faire des a.** to do exercises for the stomach muscles

abécédaire [abesedɛr] *nm* ABC, alphabet book

abeille [abɛj] *nf* bee

aberrant, -e [abɛrɑ̃, -ɑ̃t] *adj* (**a**) *(insensé)* absurd (**b**) *Biol* aberrant

aberration [abɛrasjɔ̃] *nf* aberration; **c'est une a.!** it's absurd!

abêtir [abetir] **1** *vt* **a. qn** to dull sb's mind

  2 s'abêtir *vpr* to become stupid

abêtissant, -e [abetisɑ̃, -ɑ̃t] *adj* mind-numbing

abhorrer [abɔre] *vt Litt* to abhor

Abidjan [abidʒɑ̃] *n* Abidjan

abîme [abim] *nm (de l'océan)* abyss, depths; *Fig (entre deux personnes)* gulf; *Fig* **être au bord de l'a.** to be on the brink of disaster

abîmer [abime] **1** *vt (objet)* to spoil, to damage; *(vêtement, chaussures)* to ruin

  2 s'abîmer *vpr* (**a**) *(fruit)* to go bad; *(objet)* to get damaged; *(vêtement, chaussures)* to get ruined (**b**) **s'a. les yeux** to ruin one's eyesight (**c**) *Litt* **s'a. en mer** to be engulfed by the sea

abject, -e [abʒɛkt] *adj Péj* contemptible, despicable

abjurer [abʒyre] *vt (religion)* to abjure

ablation [ablasjɔ̃] *nf* removal

ablette [ablɛt] *nf* bleak *(fish)*

ablutions [ablysjɔ̃] *nfpl Litt ou Hum* **faire ses a.** to perform one's ablutions

abnégation [abnegasjɔ̃] *nf* abnegation, self-sacrifice

aboiement [abwamɑ̃] *nm* bark; **des aboiements** barking

abois [abwa] *nmpl* **être aux a.** *(cerf)* to be at bay; *Fig* **il est aux a.** *(personne)* the net's closing in on him

abolir [abɔlir] *vt* to abolish

abolition [abɔlisjɔ̃] *nf* abolition

abominable [abɔminabl] *adj (temps)* appalling, abominable; *(crime)* heinous; *(odeur)* foul; **l'a. homme des neiges** the abominable snowman

abominablement [abɔminabləmɑ̃] *adv* abominably; *(laid)* hideously

abomination [abɔminasjɔ̃] *nf* abomination; *Litt* **avoir qn/qch en a.** to loathe sb/sth

abondamment [abɔ̃damɑ̃] *adv (parler, critiquer)* at length; *(pleuvoir)* heavily; *(manger, illustrer)* copiously; **se servir a.** to help oneself to large amounts of food

abondance [abɔ̃dɑ̃s] *nf* abundance; *(d'informations, de détails)* wealth; **il y avait des fruits en a.** there was plenty of fruit; **vivre dans l'a.** to live a life of ease

abondant, -e [abɔ̃dɑ̃, -ɑ̃t] *adj* abundant, plentiful; *(repas)* hearty; *(pluie)* heavy; *(saignement)* profuse; **une chevelure abondante** a thick head of hair; **peu a.** *(récolte, chevelure)* poor; *(pluie)* light; *(repas)* frugal

abonder [abɔ̃de] *vi* (**a**) *(foisonner)* to be plentiful; **a. en qch** to abound in sth (**b**) **a. dans le sens de qn** to agree entirely with sb

abonné, -e [abɔne] **1** *nm,f (d'une revue)* subscriber; *(du gaz, de l'électricité)* consumer; *(de la SNCF, d'un théâtre)* season-ticket holder; **il n'y a pas d'a. au numéro que vous avez demandé** ≃ the number you have dialled has not been recognized

  2 *adj* **être a. à qch** *(revue)* to have a subscription to sth; *(SNCF, théâtre)* to have a season ticket to sth; *Fam (être sujet à)* to be prone to sth

abonnement [abɔnmɑ̃] *nm (à une revue)* subscription (**à** to); *(de train, de théâtre)* season ticket; *(au téléphone)* line rental; **prendre un a.** *(à une revue)* to take out a subscription; *(pour le train, pour le théâtre)* to buy a season ticket

abonner [abɔne] **1** *vt* **a. qn à une revue** to take out a subscription to a magazine for sb

  2 s'abonner *vpr (à une revue)* to take out a subscription (**à** to); *(au théâtre)* to buy a season ticket (**à** for)

abord [abɔr] *nm* (**a**) *(d'un lieu)* **l'île est d'un a. difficile** the island is not easily accessible (**b**) **abords** *(d'un bâtiment)* surroundings; *(d'une ville)* outskirts (**c**) *(d'une personne)* **être d'un a. facile/difficile** to be approachable/unapproachable; **au premier a., de prime a.** at first sight (**d**) **d'a., tout d'a.** *(pour commencer)* at first, to begin with; *(premièrement)* first (and foremost), in the first place; *Fam* **toi, d'a., je ne te parle plus!** I'm not talking to you, so there!

abordable [abɔrdabl] *adj* (**a**) *(lieu)* accessible (**b**) *(prix)* affordable (**c**) *(personne)* approachable

abordage [abɔrdaʒ] *nm (pour attaquer)* boarding; *(pour s'amarrer)* coming alongside; **monter à l'a.** to board a ship

aborder [abɔrde] **1** *vt* (**a**) *(personne)* to approach; **faire a.** to be approached (**b**) *(question)* to deal with; *(virage)* to approach (**c**) *(navire) (attaquer)* to board; *(se mettre le long de)* to come alongside

  2 *vi* to land

aborigène [abɔriʒɛn] **1** *nmf (d'un pays)* native; **les aborigènes d'Australie** the (Australian) Aborigines

  2 *adj (indigène)* native, indigenous (**de** to); *(des peuplades australiennes)* Aboriginal

abortif, -ive [abɔrtif, -iv] *adj voir* **pilule**

abouler [abule] *Fam* **1** *vt* to hand over
2 s'abouler *vpr* to turn up, to show up; **alors, tu t'aboules?** well, are you coming or not?
aboutir [abutir] *vi* (**a**) *(réussir)* to be successful; **ne pas a.** to fall through (**b**) *(dans l'espace)* **a. à/dans** *(sujet: personne)* to end up at/in; **a. à** *(sujet: chemin, escalier)* to lead to; *Fig (sujet: efforts, recherches)* to result in; **n'a. à rien** *(personne)* to get nowhere; *(efforts, recherches)* to come to nothing
aboutissants [abutisã] *nmpl voir* **tenant**
aboutissement [abutismã] *nm* result, outcome
aboyer [32] [abwaje] *vi* to bark
abracadabrant, -e [abrakadabrã, -ãt] *adj Fam (histoire)* cock-and-bull
abrasif, -ive [abrazif, -iv] *adj & nm* abrasive
abrégé [abreʒe] *nm* (**a**) *(livre)* **un a. d'histoire de France** a short history of France; **un a. de philosophie** a short guide to philosophy (**b**) **écrire en a.** to write in abbreviated form
abréger [59] [abreʒe] *vt (article, exposé)* to shorten, to cut down; *(visite)* to cut short; *(mot)* to abbreviate; *Fam* **allez, abrège!** come on, get to the point!
abreuver [abrœve] **1** *vt (chevaux, bétail)* to water; *Fig* **a. qn d'injures** to shower sb with insults
2 s'abreuver *vpr (cheval, bétail)* to drink
abreuvoir [abrœvwar] *nm (dans une rivière)* watering place; *(baquet)* drinking trough
abréviation [abrevjasjɔ̃] *nf* abbreviation
abri [abri] *nm* shelter; **mettre qn/qch à l'a.** to shelter sb/sth; **se mettre à l'a.** to (take) shelter; **être à l'a. (de qch)** to be sheltered (from sth); **être à l'a. du besoin** to have no financial worries; **personne n'est à l'a. d'une erreur** anybody can make a mistake; **a. antiatomique** fallout shelter; **a. à vélos** bike shed
abribus® [abribys] *nm* bus shelter
abricot [abriko] **1** *nm* apricot
2 *adj inv* apricot-coloured
abricotier [abrikɔtje] *nm* apricot tree
abrier [abrije] *Can* **1** *vt* to wrap up (well)
2 s'abrier *vpr* to wrap oneself up (well)
abriter [abrite] **1** *vt* (**a**) *(protéger)* to shelter (**de** from) (**b**) *(loger) (personnes)* to house, to accommodate; *(société, machine)* to house
2 s'abriter *vpr* **s'a. (de la pluie)** to (take) shelter (from the rain); **s'a. (du soleil)** to shade oneself (from the sun)
abrogation [abrɔgasjɔ̃] *nf (d'une loi)* repeal
abroger [45] [abrɔʒe] *vt (loi)* to repeal
abrupt, -e [abrypt] *adj (rocher, pente)* steep; *Fig (manière)* abrupt, blunt; **d'un ton a.** abruptly
abruti, -e [abryti] **1** *nm,f Fam* idiot, fool
2 *adj* (**a**) *(hébété)* stupefied, dazed; **a. par l'alcool** stupefied with drink (**b**) *Fam (bête)* stupid, idiotic
abrutir [abrytir] **1** *vt* (**a**) *(hébéter)* to daze; **a. qn de travail** to work sb to the point of exhaustion (**b**) *(abêtir)* to stultify
2 s'abrutir *vpr* **s'a. de travail** to work oneself to the point of exhaustion; **on s'abrutit à trop regarder la télévision** too much television numbs the brain
abrutissant, -e [abrytisã, -ãt] *adj (travail)* stultifying, mind-numbing; *(bruit)* wearing
ABS [abeɛs] *nm Aut* **(système)** A. ABS
abscisse [apsis] *nf Math* x-axis
abscons, -e [apskɔ̃, -ɔ̃s] *adj Litt* abstruse

absence [apsɑ̃s] *nf* (**a**) *(d'une personne)* absence; **en** *ou* **pendant mon a.** in *or* during my absence, while I am/was/*etc* away (**b**) *(manque)* lack (**c**) **avoir des absences** to be prone to absent-mindedness; **dans un moment d'a.** in a moment of absent-mindedness
absent, -e [apsɑ̃, -ɑ̃t] **1** *adj* (**a**) *(qui n'est pas présent)* absent (**de** from) (**b**) *(inexistant)* missing (**c**) *(distrait)* **avoir un air a.** to be miles away
2 *nm,f* absentee; **les absents ont toujours tort** it's always those who aren't there who get the blame
absentéisme [apsɑ̃teism] *nm* absenteeism
absenter [apsɑ̃te] **s'absenter** *vpr (sortir)* to go away (**de** from); **elle a dû s'a. quelques minutes** she had to go out for a few minutes
absinthe [apsɛ̃t] *nf* absinthe
absolu, -e [apsɔly] **1** *nm* **l'a.** the absolute; **dans l'a.,...** in principle,...
2 *adj* absolute; *(règle)* hard-and-fast; **être dans l'impossibilité absolue de faire qch** to be quite unable to do sth
absolument [apsɔlymɑ̃] *adv* (**a**) *(complètement)* absolutely; **a. pas!** absolutely not! (**b**) *(sans faute)* **vous devez a. y aller!** you simply MUST go!
absolution [apsɔlysjɔ̃] *nf Rel* absolution
absolvais *etc voir* **absoudre**
absorbant, -e [apsɔrbɑ̃, -ɑ̃t] *adj* (**a**) *(matériau)* absorbent (**b**) *(livre, tâche)* absorbing
absorber [apsɔrbe] *vt* (**a**) *(liquide)* to absorb, to soak up (**b**) *(nourriture)* to eat; *(boisson)* to drink; *(médicament)* to take (**c**) *(entreprise)* to take over (**d**) *(sujet: lecture)* to absorb, to engross; **son travail l'absorbe** she is absorbed *or* engrossed in her work; **être absorbé dans ses pensées** to be lost in thought
absorption [apsɔrpsjɔ̃] *nf* (**a**) *(de liquide)* absorption (**b**) *(de nourriture)* eating; *(d'une boisson)* drinking; *(d'un médicament)* taking (**c**) *(d'une entreprise)* takeover
absoudre [3a] [apsudr] *vt Litt ou Rel* **a. qn de qch** to forgive sb sth
abstenir [70] [apstənir] **s'abstenir** *vpr (ne pas voter)* to abstain (from voting); **s'a. de faire qch** to refrain from doing sth; **dans le doute, abstiens-toi** when in doubt, don't; **pas sérieux s'a.** *(dans une petite annonce)* no timewasters
abstention [apstɑ̃sjɔ̃] *nf* abstention
abstentionniste [apstɑ̃sjɔnist] *nmf* abstainer
abstinence [apstinɑ̃s] *nf* abstinence
abstraction [apstraksjɔ̃] *nf* (**a**) **faire a. de qch** to disregard sth; **a. faite de cette dépense** leaving aside this expense (**b**) *(idée abstraite)* abstract idea, abstraction
abstrait, -e [apstrɛ, -ɛt] **1** *adj* abstract
2 *nm* **dans l'a.** in the abstract
absurde [apsyrd] **1** *adj* absurd
2 *nm* **l'a.** *(d'une situation, d'une remarque)* absurdity; **démonstration par l'a.** reductio ad absurdum
absurdité [apsyrdite] *nf* (**a**) *(caractère absurde)* absurdity (**b**) *(chose absurde)* absurdity, piece of nonsense; **dire des absurdités** to talk nonsense
abus [aby] *nm* (**a**) *(excès)* overindulgence (**de** in); **l'a. d'alcool** alcohol abuse; **l'a. de médicaments est dangereux** taking too much medication is dangerous (**b**) *(pratique)* abuse; *Fam* **il y a de l'a.!** that's going too far! (**c**) *Jur* **a. de biens sociaux** misappropriation of funds; **a. de confiance** breach of trust; **a. de pouvoir** abuse of power

abuser [abyze] **1** *vt Litt* to deceive
2 abuser de *vt ind (exploiter, violer)* to take advantage of; **a. du tabac** to smoke too much; **a. de ses forces** to overexert oneself; **il ne faut pas a. des bonnes choses** good things should be enjoyed in moderation; **je ne voudrais pas a.** I don't want to cause you any inconvenience; **alors là, vous abusez!** this is a bit much!
3 s'abuser *vpr* **si je ne m'abuse** if I'm not mistaken

abusif, -ive [abyzif, -iv] *adj* (**a**) *(emploi d'un mot)* incorrect (**b**) *(excessif)* excessive; *(mère)* possessive

abysse [abis] *nm* abyssal zone

acabit [akabi] *nm Péj* **du même a.** of that type

acacia [akasja] *nm* acacia

académicien, -enne [akademisjɛ̃, -ɛn] *nm,f* = member of the "Académie française"

académie [akademi] *nf* (**a**) *(des lettres, des sciences, d'art)* academy; **l'A. française** = learned society responsible for promoting the French language and imposing standards (**b**) *(école)* school, academy; **a. de musique/dessin** music/art school (**c**) *(dans l'Éducation nationale) Br* ≃ local education authority, *Am* ≃ school district

---

Académie française

This was originally a group of men of letters who were encouraged by Cardinal Richelieu in 1635 to become an official body. Consisting of forty distinguished writers ("les Quarante" or "les Immortels"), the Académie's chief task was, and is, to produce a definitive dictionary and to be the ultimate authority in matters concerning the French language.

---

académique [akademik] *adj* (**a**) *Scol* = relating to a local education authority (**b**) *Péj (style)* conventional (**c**) *Belg, Suisse & Can* **l'année a.** the academic year

acajou [akaʒu] **1** *nm* mahogany
2 *adj inv* reddish-brown

a cap(p)ella [akapela] *adv* a cappella

acariâtre [akarjatr] *adj* cantankerous

acarien [akarjɛ̃] *nm* dust mite

accablant, -e [akablɑ̃, -ɑ̃t] *adj* (**a**) *(responsabilités)* overwhelming; *(chaleur)* oppressive (**b**) *(témoignage)* damning

accablement [akabləmɑ̃] *nm* dejection, depression

accabler [akable] *vt* (**a**) *(sujet: chaleur, malheur)* to overwhelm; **a. qn de travail** to overload sb with work; **a. qn de reproches** to heap criticism on sb (**b**) *(sujet: témoignage)* to damn

accalmie [akalmi] *nf* lull

accaparer [akapare] *vt (personne, conversation)* to monopolize; *(places, morceaux de choix)* to grab

accéder [34] [aksede] **accéder à** *vt ind* (**a**) *(atteindre)* to reach, to get to (**b**) *Fig (responsabilités, rang)* to gain; **a. au trône** to accede to the throne (**c**) *(requête)* to comply with (**d**) *Ordinat (programme)* to access

accélérateur [akseleratœr] *nm (de voiture, d'ordinateur)* accelerator; **appuyer sur l'a.** to step on the accelerator; *Ordinat* **a. graphique** graphic(s) accelerator; *Phys* **a. de particules** particle accelerator

accélération [akselerasjɔ̃] *nf* acceleration

accéléré, -e [akselere] **1** *nm Cin* **en a.** in accelerated motion

2 *adj* quick, fast; *(mouvement)* accelerated; **cours a.** crash course

accélérer [34] [akselere] **1** *vt* to speed up; *Fig* **a. le mouvement** to get a move on
2 *vi (en voiture)* to accelerate
3 s'accélérer *vpr* to accelerate, to speed up

accent [aksɑ̃] *nm* (**a**) *(sur une lettre)* accent; **a. aigu/grave/circonflexe** acute/grave/circumflex (accent); **e a. circonflexe** e circumflex (**b**) *(en phonétique)* stress; **a. tonique** (primary) stress (**c**) *(prononciation)* accent; **elle parle anglais sans a.** she speaks English without an accent (**d**) *Fig (inflexion)* **avoir des accents de vérité** to have a ring of truth; **mettre l'a. sur qch** to stress *or* emphasize sth

accentuation [aksɑ̃tɥasjɔ̃] *nf* (**a**) *(en phonétique)* stress (**b**) *(à l'écrit)* accentuation (**c**) *(d'un phénomène)* intensification

accentué, -e [aksɑ̃tɥe] *adj* (**a**) *(syllabe)* stressed (**b**) *(lettre)* accented (**c**) *Fig (net)* pronounced, marked

accentuer [aksɑ̃tɥe] **1** *vt* (**a**) *(syllabe)* to stress (**b**) *(lettre)* to put an accent on (**c**) *Fig (renforcer)* to emphasize; *(avance)* to increase
2 s'accentuer *vpr* to become more pronounced *or* marked

acceptable [akssptabl] *adj* (**a**) *(recevable)* acceptable (**b**) *(passable)* satisfactory

acceptation [akssptasjɔ̃] *nf* acceptance

accepter [aksspte] *vt* to accept; **a. de faire qch** to agree to do sth; **il est hors de question que j'accepte** I can't possibly accept; **allez, accepte!** go on, say yes!

acception [aksspsjɔ̃] *nf Formel* (**a**) *(d'un mot)* meaning, sense (**b**) **sans a. de race/de sexe** irrespective of race/sex

accès [aksɛ] *nm* (**a**) *(approche)* access, approach (**à** to); **être facile/difficile d'a.** to be easy/hard to reach; **avoir a. à qch** to have access to sth; **donner a. à qch** *(sujet: porte, chemin)* to lead to sth; *(sujet: ticket)* to allow entry to sth; **a. aux quais** *(sur panneau)* to the trains
(**b**) *(d'une personne)* **être d'un a. facile/difficile** to be approachable/unapproachable
(**c**) *(poussée)* fit, attack; **a. de colère** fit of anger; **a. de fièvre** bout of fever; **a. de toux** coughing fit
(**d**) *Ordinat* access; *(sur Internet)* hit; **avoir a. à** to be able to access

accessible [aksesibl] *adj* (**a**) *(lieu, livre)* accessible; *(prix)* affordable (**b**) *(personne)* approachable

accession [aksesjɔ̃] *nf* **a. au pouvoir/au trône** accession (to power)/to the throne; **l'a. à la propriété** home ownership

accessoire [akseswar] **1** *nm (d'appareil ménager, de mode)* accessory; *Can* **a. électrique** domestic electrical appliance; *Théât* **accessoires** props
2 *adj* minor; **c'est a.** it's a minor detail

accessoirement [akseswarmɑ̃] *adv* if necessary, if need be; *(en plus)* also

accessoiriste [akseswarist] *nmf Théât* prop man, *f* prop woman

accident [aksidɑ̃] *nm* (**a**) *(collision, malheur)* accident; **a. d'avion** plane *or* air crash; **a. de chemin de fer** train crash; **a. de la circulation** traffic accident; **a. de la route** road accident; **a. du travail** industrial accident; **a. de voiture** car accident *or* crash (**b**) *(événement inattendu)* mishap; **par a.** by accident, by chance; **a. de parcours** hitch (**c**) **a. de terrain** *(bosse)* bump; *(trou)* hole

accidenté, -e [aksidɑ̃te] **1** *nm,f* accident victim; **accidentés de la route** road accident victims
2 *adj* (**a**) *(terrain)* uneven (**b**) *(voiture)* damaged
accidentel, -elle [aksidɑ̃tɛl] *adj* accidental
accidentellement [aksidɑ̃tɛlmɑ̃] *adv (par hasard)* accidentally, by chance; *(mourir)* in an accident
acclamation [aklamasjɔ̃] *nf* cheer; **sous les acclamations de la foule** to the cheers of the crowd
acclamer [aklame] *vt* to cheer
acclimatation [aklimatasjɔ̃] *nf* acclimatization, *Am* acclimation (**à** to)
acclimater [aklimate] **1** *vt* to acclimatize, *Am* to acclimate (**à** to)
2 s'acclimater *vpr* to become *or* get acclimatized *or Am* acclimated (**à** to)
accointances [akwɛ̃tɑ̃s] *nfpl* contacts
accolade [akɔlad] *nf* (**a**) *(embrassade)* (formal) embrace; **donner l'a. à qn** to embrace sb (**b**) *(signe typographique)* curly bracket, brace
accoler [akɔle] *vt (mettre côte à côte)* to put side by side
accommodant, -e [akɔmɔdɑ̃, -ɑ̃t] *adj* accommodating
accommoder [akɔmɔde] **1** *vt (nourriture)* to prepare; *(restes)* to use up
2 *vi (œil)* to focus
3 s'accommoder *vpr* **s'a. de qch** to put up with sth
accompagnateur, -trice [akɔ̃paɲatœr, -tris] *nm,f* (**a**) *(pianiste)* accompanist (**b**) *(d'un voyage organisé)* courier, tour guide; *(d'une sortie scolaire)* accompanying adult (**c**) *Belg* **a. de train** ticket inspector
accompagnement [akɔ̃paɲmɑ̃] *nm* (**a**) *(de morceau de musique)* accompaniment; **chanter sans a.** to sing unaccompanied (**b**) *(légumes)* accompaniment
accompagner [akɔ̃paɲe] **1** *vt* (**a**) *(venir avec)* to come with, to accompany; *(aller avec)* to go with, to accompany; **il est venu accompagné d'une amie** he came with a friend
(**b**) *(conduire)* **a. qn à la gare** to take sb to the station (**c**) *(chanteur)* to accompany (**à** on)
(**d**) *(ajouter à)* **il a accompagné ses mots d'un sourire** he said it with a smile; **elle a accompagné son exposé de diapositives** she complemented her talk with a slide show; **un rôti accompagné de légumes** a roast served with vegetables
2 s'accompagner *vpr* (**a**) **s'a. au piano** to accompany oneself on the piano (**b**) *(se produire simultanément)* **s'a. de qch** to be accompanied by sth
accompli, -e [akɔ̃pli] *adj (excellent)* accomplished
accomplir [akɔ̃plir] **1** *vt* (**a**) *(tâche)* to carry out; *(bonne action)* to do; *(exploit)* to accomplish; *(souhait, promesse)* to fulfil (**b**) *(terminer)* to complete, to finish
2 s'accomplir *vpr (souhait)* to come true
accord [akɔr] *nm* (**a**) *(traité)* agreement; *(non formel)* understanding; *(pour résoudre un conflit)* settlement; **arriver** *ou* **parvenir à un a.** to come to *or* reach an agreement
(**b**) *(entente)* agreement (**sur** on); **être d'a. avec qn** to agree with sb; **se mettre d'a.** *ou* **tomber d'a. avec qn** to come to an agreement with sb; **(c'est) d'a.!** all right!, OK!; **d'un commun a.** by common consent, by mutual agreement; **faire qch en a. avec qn** to do sth in agreement with sb
(**c**) *(autorisation)* consent
(**d**) *Gram* agreement (**avec** with)
(**e**) *(en musique)* chord; **a. parfait** common chord

accord-cadre *(pl* **accords-cadres)** [akɔrkadr] *nm* outline agreement
accordéon [akɔrdeɔ̃] *nm* accordion; *Fig* **en a.** *(chaussettes)* at half-mast
accordéoniste [akɔrdeɔnist] *nmf* accordionist, accordion player
accorder [akɔrde] **1** *vt* (**a**) **a. qch à qn** *(faveur)* to grant sb sth; *(augmentation, dommages-intérêts)* to award sb sth; *(prêt, découvert bancaire)* to authorize sth to sb; **a. son pardon à qn** to pardon sb; **a. la plus grande importance à qch** to attach the utmost importance to sth; **pouvez-vous m'a. quelques minutes?** can you spare me a few minutes?; *Formel* **je ne l'aime pas, je vous l'accorde** I don't like him, I must admit (**b**) *Gram* **a. qch avec qch** to make sth agree with sth (**c**) *(instrument de musique)* to tune; *Fig* **il faudrait a. nos violons** we'd better get our story straight (**d**) *(harmoniser) (couleurs)* to co-ordinate
2 s'accorder *vpr* (**a**) *(se mettre d'accord)* to agree, to come to an agreement (**avec/sur** with/on); **on s'accorde à penser que...** there is a general belief *or* it is generally believed that... (**b**) *(couleurs)* to go together (**c**) *Gram* to agree (**avec** with) (**d**) *(à soi-même)* **s'a. qch** to allow *or* give oneself sth
accordeur [akɔrdœr] *nm* (piano) tuner
accoster [akɔste] **1** *vt (personne)* to approach
2 *vi Naut* to dock
accotement [akɔtmɑ̃] *nm* (**a**) *(d'une route)* verge; **accotements non stabilisés** *(sur panneau)* soft verges (**b**) *(de voie ferrée)* shoulder
accouchement [akuʃmɑ̃] *nm* childbirth, delivery; **avoir un a. difficile** to have a difficult birth; **a. sans douleur** = childbirth made less painful by the use of relaxation techniques
accoucher [akuʃe] **1** *vt* **a. qn** to deliver sb's baby
2 *vi* (**a**) *(avoir un bébé)* to have a baby, to give birth; **elle doit a. dans un mois** her baby's due in a month (**b**) *Fam* **accouche!** come on, spit it out!
3 accoucher de *vt ind* (**a**) *(enfant)* to give birth to (**b**) *Fam (produire)* to come up with, to produce; **il a accouché de deux minables paragraphes** he produced two measly paragraphs
accoucheur [akuʃœr] *nm* **(médecin) a.** obstetrician
accoucheuse [akuʃøz] *nf* midwife
accouder [akude] **s'accouder** *vpr* **s'a. à** *ou* **sur qch** to lean one's elbow(s) on sth
accoudoir [akudwar] *nm* armrest
accouplement [akupləmɑ̃] *nm (d'animaux)* pairing, mating
accoupler [akuple] **s'accoupler** *vpr (animaux)* to mate
accourir [22] [akurir] *vi* to run up, to rush up
accoutrement [akutrəmɑ̃] *nm* rig-out, get-up
accoutrer [akutre] **1** *vt* to rig out (**de** in)
2 s'accoutrer *vpr* to rig oneself out (**de** in)
accoutumance [akutymɑ̃s] *nf (adaptation)* familiarization (**à** with); *(à l'alcool, à la drogue)* addiction; **créer une a.** to be addictive
accoutumé, -e [akutyme] *adj* usual; **comme à l'accoutumée** as usual
accoutumer [akutyme] **1** *vt* **a. qn à qch** to accustom sb to sth, to get sb used to sth
2 s'accoutumer *vpr* **s'a. à** to get used *or* accustomed to
accréditer [akredite] *vt* (**a**) *(ambassadeur, journaliste)* to accredit (**b**) *(rendre plausible)* to substantiate

accro [akro] *adj Fam (drogué)* & *Fig* addicted (**à** to), hooked (**à** on)

accroc [akro] *nm* (**a**) *(à un tissu)* tear, catch (**b**) *Fig* hitch, snag; **sans a.** without a hitch

accrochage [akrɔʃaʒ] *nm* (**a**) *(accident)* minor accident (**b**) *(dispute)* row; *Mil* skirmish

accroche [akrɔʃ] *nf* slogan

accroche-cœur (*pl* **accroche-cœurs**) [akrɔʃkœr] *nm* kiss curl

accrocher [akrɔʃe] **1** *vt* (**a**) *(suspendre)* to hang up (**à** on); *(wagon)* to hitch on, to couple; *Fig* **une robe qui accroche le regard** an eye-catching dress; **avoir le cœur bien accroché** to have strong nerves *or* a strong stomach (**b**) *(abîmer) (vêtement)* to catch (**à** on); *(pare-chocs)* to clip
2 *vi (achopper)* to hit a stumbling block; **un titre qui accroche** an eye-catching title; *Fam* **ça n'a pas du tout accroché entre eux** they didn't hit it off at all; *Fam* **je n'accroche pas du tout en maths** I just can't get into maths at all
3 **s'accrocher** *vpr* (**a**) *aussi Fig (s'agripper)* **s'a. à qn/ qch** to cling to sb/sth; *Fam* **accroche-toi, tu n'as pas tout entendu!** brace yourself, you haven't heard everything yet! (**b**) *Fam (persévérer)* to stick at it (**c**) *(voitures)* to crash into each other (**d**) *Fam (se disputer)* to have a row (**avec** with) (**e**) *(se fixer)* to fasten

accrocheur, -euse [akrɔʃœr, -øz] *adj* (**a**) *(tenace)* tenacious, stubborn (**b**) *(titre, slogan)* catchy

accroissement [akrwasmɑ̃] *nm* increase (**de** in)

accroître [akrwatr] [4a] **1** *vt* to increase, to enlarge
2 **s'accroître** *vpr* to increase, to grow

accroupir [akrupir] **s'accroupir** *vpr* to squat (down), to crouch (down); **être accroupi** to be squatting *or* crouching

accu [aky] *nm* battery

accueil [akœj] *nm (façon d'accueillir)* reception, welcome; *(lieu)* reception; **faire bon a. à qn** to welcome sb; **faire mauvais a. à qn** to give sb a cool reception

accueillant, -e [akœjɑ̃, -ɑ̃t] *adj* welcoming

accueillir [5] [akœjir] *vt* (**a**) *(personne, proposition)* to greet; **bien a. qn** to give sb a warm welcome; **nous avons été mal accueillis** we weren't given a very warm welcome; **le film a été mal accueilli par le public** the film was badly received by the public (**b**) *(loger) (sujet: ami)* to put up; *(sujet: hôtel)* to accommodate

acculer [akyle] *vt* to drive back (**contre** against); *Fig* **a. qn à faire qch** to give sb no choice but to do sth; *Fig* **être acculé à la faillite** to be forced into bankruptcy

accumulateur [akymylatœr] *nm Élec* battery

accumulation [akymylasjɔ̃] *nf* accumulation; *(d'énergie)* storage; **chauffage par a.** storage heating

accumuler [akymyle] **1** *vt* to accumulate, to amass; *(énergie)* to store; **a. les erreurs** to make a series of mistakes
2 **s'accumuler** *vpr* to accumulate; *(nuages)* to gather, to build up; *Fin (intérêts)* to accrue; **les preuves s'accumulent contre elle** the evidence against her is growing

accusateur, -trice [akyzatœr, -tris] **1** *adj (regard, doigt)* accusing
2 *nm,f* accuser

accusation [akyzasjɔ̃] *nf* accusation; **lancer** *ou* **porter une a. contre qn** to make an accusation against sb; *Jur* **mettre qn en a.** to commit sb for trial

accusé, -e [akyze] **1** *adj (trait)* prominent, pronounced
2 *nm,f (d'un crime)* accused; *(au tribunal)* defendant
3 *nm* **a. de réception** *(pour une lettre)* acknowledgement (of receipt); *Ordinat* acknowledge, acknowledgement

accuser [akyze] **1** *vt* (**a**) *(incriminer)* to accuse; **a. qn de qch/de faire qch** to accuse sb of sth/of doing sth (**b**) *(tendance, baisse)* to show; **a. le coup** to be obviously shaken (**c**) **a. réception de qch** to acknowledge (receipt of) sth
2 **s'accuser** *vpr* (**a**) *(se déclarer coupable)* to confess (**de** to) (**b**) *(se renforcer)* to become more pronounced *or* marked

acerbe [asɛrb] *adj* acerbic; **d'un ton a.** sharply

acéré, -e [asere] *adj (lame)* sharp; *Fig (remarque)* cutting

acériculteur [aserikyltœr] *nm Can* maple syrup and sugar producer

acériculture [aserikyltyr] *nf Can* production of maple syrup and sugar

acétone [asetɔn] *nf* acetone

ACF [aseɛf] *nm (abrév* **Automobile Club de France)** = French motoring organization

achalandé, -e [aʃalɑ̃de] *adj* **magasin bien/mal a.** well/poorly stocked shop

achaler [aʃale] *vt Can* to annoy, to bother

acharné, -e [aʃarne] *adj (lutte, concurrence)* fierce; *(travail)* relentless; *(joueur)* inveterate

acharnement [aʃarnəmɑ̃] *nm* relentlessness; **avec a.** relentlessly; **se battre avec a.** to fight tooth and nail

acharner [aʃarne] **s'acharner** *vpr* **s'a. après** *ou* **contre** *ou* **sur qn** *(persécuter)* to be always after sb; **s'a. sur qn** *(sujet: meurtrier)* to savage sb; *(sujet: examinateur)* to give sb a hard time; **s'a. sur qch** to work away at sth; **s'a. à faire qch** to try very hard to do sth

achat [aʃa] *nm* (**a**) *(action)* purchase, buying; **faire un a.** to make a purchase, to buy something; **faire l'a. de qch** to buy sth (**b**) *(ce qu'on a acheté)* purchase; **achats** *(provisions, paquets)* shopping; **aller faire ses achats** to go shopping

acheminement [aʃminmɑ̃] *nm (de troupes)* transportation (**sur** *ou* **vers** to); *(de marchandises)* shipping (**sur** *ou* **vers** to); **a. du courrier** mail handling

acheminer [aʃmine] **1** *vt (troupes)* to transport (**sur** *ou* **vers** to); *(marchandises)* to ship (**sur** *ou* **vers** to); *(courrier)* to handle
2 **s'acheminer** *vpr* **s'a. vers** *(endroit)* to make one's way towards; *Fig (accord, solution)* to move towards; *(victoire)* to head towards

acheter [6] [aʃte] **1** *vt* (**a**) *(acquérir)* to buy, to purchase; **a. qch à qn** *(faire une transaction)* to buy sth from sb; *(en cadeau)* to buy sb sth; **je vais lui a. un livre** I'm going to buy him/her a book; **j'ai acheté ce livre 8 euros** I bought this book for 8 euros (**b**) *Fam (corrompre)* to buy off
2 **s'acheter** *vpr (pour soi-même)* **je vais m'a. une glace** I'm going to buy (myself) an ice cream (**b**) *(être acheté)* **ça s'achète en pharmacie** you can buy it/ them in any pharmacy; **l'amour, ça ne s'achète pas** love can't be bought and sold

acheteur, -euse [aʃtœr, -øz] *nm,f* buyer, purchaser; **je suis a.!** I'm interested!

achevé, -e [aʃve] *adj (artiste, style)* accomplished; *(travail)* perfect; **c'est d'un ridicule a.!** it's utterly ridiculous!

achèvement [aʃɛvmã] *nm* completion
achever [46] [aʃəve] **1** *vt* (**a**) *(finir) (discours)* to end, to conclude; *(travail)* to complete (**b**) *(tuer) (personne, proie)* to finish off; *(animal malade ou blessé)* to put out of its misery; *Fam* **ça m'a achevé!** that really finished me (off)!
 2 s'achever *vpr (finir)* to end
achigan [aʃigã] *nm Can* (black) bass
achoppement [aʃɔpmã] *nm voir* **pierre**
acide [asid] **1** *adj* acid(ic); *(au goût)* sour; *Fig (propos)* acid, caustic
 2 *nm* acid
acidité [asidite] *nf* acidity; *(au goût)* sourness; *Fig (de propos)* acidity
acidulé, -e [asidyle] *adj* slightly acid; **bonbons acidulés** acid drops
acier [asje] *nm* steel; **a. inoxydable** stainless steel
aciérie [asjeri] *nf* steelworks *(singulier)*
acné [akne] *nf* acne; **a. juvénile** acne
acolyte [akɔlit] *nm Péj* accomplice
acompte [akɔ̃t] *nm* deposit, down payment; **recevoir un a.** to receive something on account; **verser un a.** to make a down payment
acoquiner [akɔkine] **s'acoquiner** *vpr* **s'a. avec qn** to team up with sb
Açores [asɔr] *nfpl* **les A.** the Azores
à-côté *(pl* **à-côtés)** [akote] *nm* (**a**) *(élément secondaire)* side issue (**b**) *(financier)* extra
à-coup *(pl* **à-coups)** [aku] *nm* jolt; **travailler par à-coups** to work in fits and starts; **le moteur a des à-coups** the engine judders
acoustique [akustik] **1** *adj* acoustic
 2 *nf (discipline)* acoustics *(singulier); (qualité)* acoustics *(pluriel)*
acquéreur [akerœr] *nm* purchaser, buyer; **notre voiture n'a pas trouvé a.** we couldn't find a buyer for our car
acquérir [7] [akerir] *vt* (**a**) *(obtenir, prendre)* to acquire; **nous avons acquis la certitude de son innocence** we have established beyond doubt that he/she is innocent; **a. de la valeur** to increase in value (**b**) *(acheter)* to purchase, to buy
acquière, acquiers *etc voir* **acquérir**
acquiescer [16] [akjese] *vi* to acquiesce (**à** to); **a. d'un signe de tête** to nod in agreement
acquis, -e [aki, -iz] **1** *pp voir* **acquérir**
 2 *adj (savoir, caractères)* acquired; **tenir qch pour a.** to take sth for granted; **son aide nous est acquise** we can take it for granted that he will help us; **cela est a.** that's been established
 3 *nm (connaissances)* knowledge; **il ne fonctionne que sur ses acquis** he gets by on what he knows already; **les a. sociaux** social benefits
acquisition [akizisjɔ̃] *nf* (**a**) *(action)* acquisition; **faire l'a. de qch** *(acheter)* to purchase sth (**b**) *(bien acheté)* purchase
acquit [aki] *nm Com* receipt; **pour a.** received (with thanks), paid; **par a. de conscience** to ease one's conscience
acquittement [akitmã] *nm* (**a**) *Jur* acquittal (**b**) *(d'une dette)* payment
acquitter [akite] **1** *vt* (**a**) *(accusé)* to acquit (**b**) *(dette, facture)* to pay
 2 s'acquitter *vpr* **s'a. d'une obligation/d'un devoir** to fulfil an obligation/a duty; **s'a. envers qn** to repay sb

acre [akr] *nm ou nf Can* acre
âcre [akr] *adj (goût)* bitter; *(odeur)* acrid
acrobate [akrɔbat] *nmf* acrobat
acrobatie [akrɔbasi] *nf (art)* acrobatics *(singulier);* **faire des acrobaties** to perform acrobatics; **a. aérienne** aerobatics *(singulier)*
acrobatique [akrɔbatik] *adj* acrobatic
acronyme [akrɔnim] *nm* acronym
Acropole [akrɔpɔl] *nf* **l'A.** the Acropolis
acrylique [akrilik] *adj & nm* acrylic
acte [akt] *nm* (**a**) *(action)* act; **faire a. d'autorité** to exercise one's authority; **faire a. de candidature à un emploi** to apply for a job; **faire a. de présence** to put in an appearance; **passer aux actes** to take action; **c'était peut-être un a. manqué** maybe subconsciously I/he/*etc* did it deliberately; **a. de terrorisme** terrorist act
 (**b**) *Jur* deed, title; **dont a.** duly noted *or* acknowledged; **prendre a. de qch** to take note of sth; *Formel* **nous prenons a. de votre candidature** we acknowledge your application; **a. d'accusation** bill of indictment, charges; **a. de propriété** title deed; **a. unique européen** Single European Act; **a. de vente** bill of sale
 (**c**) *(certificat)* record; **a. de décès** death certificate; **a. d'état civil** = certificate of birth, marriage or death; **a. de mariage** marriage certificate; **a. de naissance** birth certificate
 (**d**) **actes** *(d'un procès, d'un colloque)* proceedings; *(d'un organisme scientifique)* transactions
 (**e**) *Théât* act
acter [akte] *vt Belg (noter)* to take a note of, to note; *Jur* to record
acteur [aktœr] *nm* (**a**) *(artiste)* actor; **a. de cinéma/de théâtre** film/stage actor (**b**) *(d'un événement)* **les différents acteurs de la négociation** the different participants in *or* parties involved in the negotiations; **a. économique** economic player; **les acteurs sociaux** = employers, workers and trade unions
actif, -ive [aktif, -iv] **1** *adj* (**a**) *(défenseur, participation, substance)* active; **femme active** working woman (**b**) *(énergique) (personne)* active (**c**) *Gram* active
 2 *nm* (**a**) *Com* assets; *Fig* **avoir qch à son a.** to have sth to one's name; **il faut mettre sa patience à son a.** you have to give him credit for patience (**b**) *Gram* **verbe à l'a.** verb in the active voice
action [aksjɔ̃] *nf* (**a**) *(acte)* action, act; **bonne/mauvaise a.** good/bad deed
 (**b**) *(influence, effet) (d'une substance)* action, effect (**sur** on)
 (**c**) *(activité)* **entrer en a.** *(loi)* to come into force; **mettre qch en a.** to put sth into operation; **passer à l'a.** to take action, to act; **homme d'a.** man of action
 (**d**) *(histoire)* action; *TV & Cin* **a.!** action!
 (**e**) *Fin* share
 (**f**) *Jur* action; **intenter une a. judiciaire** *ou* **en justice contre** to take legal action against
 (**g**) *Mil* action
 (**h**) *Suisse (vente promotionnelle)* sale, special offer
actionnaire [aksjɔnɛr] *nmf Fin* shareholder
actionner [aksjɔne] *vt (mettre en marche)* to start up, to turn on; *(faire fonctionner)* to operate, to drive
activement [aktivmã] *adv* actively
activer [aktive] **1** *vt* (**a**) *(accélérer)* to speed up; *(feu)* to stoke (**b**) *Ordinat* to activate; **a. une option** to select an option

2 *vi Fam* to get a move on
3 s'activer *vpr* to be busy
activiste [aktivist] *adj & nmf* activist
activité [aktivite] *nf* activity; **en a.** *(volcan)* active; *(usine)* in production; *(personne)* working
actrice [aktris] *nf* actress
actualisation [aktyalizasjɔ̃] *nf (d'un texte, d'une méthode de travail)* updating
actualiser [aktyalize] *vt (texte, méthode de travail)* to update
actualité [aktyalite] *nf* **l'a.** the news, current affairs; **l'a. politique française** the current French political scene; **cette question est toujours d'a.** this is still a topical question; **les actualités** *(à la télé, à la radio)* the news; **les actualités télévisées** the television news
actuel, -elle [aktyɛl] *adj* (**a**) *(présent)* present, current; **dans la situation actuelle** as things are *or* stand at the moment (**b**) *(d'actualité)* topical
actuellement [aktyɛlmɑ̃] *adv* at present, at the present time
acuité [akyite] *nf (de la douleur)* acuteness; *(d'un argument)* pointedness; *(d'un son)* shrillness; **a. visuelle/auditive** keenness of vision/hearing
acuponcture, acupuncture [akypɔ̃ktyr] *nf* acupuncture
adage [adaʒ] *nm* adage, (common) saying; **selon l'a.** as the saying goes
adaptateur, -trice [adaptatœr, -tris] **1** *nm (dispositif)* adapter
2 *nm,f (d'une œuvre)* adapter
adaptation [adaptasjɔ̃] *nf* (**a**) *(à une situation)* adaptation (**à** to); **faire un effort d'a.** to try to adapt; **faculté d'a.** adaptability (**b**) *(d'une œuvre)* adaptation; **a. théâtrale** stage adaptation
adapter [adapte] **1** *vt* (**a**) *(ajuster)* to adapt (**à** to); **est-ce vraiment adapté à la situation?** is it really suitable for the situation? (**b**) *(œuvre)* to adapt
2 s'adapter *vpr* (**a**) *(s'acclimater)* to adapt (**à** to); **savoir s'a.** to be very adaptable *or* flexible (**b**) *(être compatible)* **la prise s'adapte à toutes les télévisions** the plug fits all types of television
Addis-Abeba [adisabeba] *n* Addis Ababa
additif [aditif] *nm* (**a**) *(ajout)* addition (**b**) *(substance)* additive; **sans additifs** additive-free
addition [adisjɔ̃] *nf* (**a**) *(fait d'ajouter)* addition, adding (**à** to); *(pour faire un total)* adding up; **faire une a.** to do a sum (**b**) *(extension)* addition, extension (**c**) *(au restaurant)* Br bill, Am check
additionnel, -elle [adisjɔnɛl] *adj* additional, extra; *Ordinat* add-on
additionner [adisjɔne] **1** *vt* to add (up); **lait additionné d'eau** watered-down milk; **café additionné d'eau-de-vie** coffee laced with brandy
2 s'additionner *vpr* to add up; **aux longues heures de travail s'additionnent celles passées dans le métro** along with the long working hours, there are those spent on the underground
adduction [adyksjɔ̃] *nf Tech* admission, intake; *Constr* **a. d'eau** canalization
adepte [adɛpt] *nmf (d'une doctrine, d'une personnalité)* follower; *(d'une activité)* enthusiast; **faire des adeptes** to attract a following
adéquat, -e [adekwa, -at] *adj (personne, lieu, expression, méthode)* appropriate, suitable; *(montant, quantité)* adequate

adéquation [adekwasjɔ̃] *nf* appropriateness, suitability
adhérence [aderɑ̃s] *nf* adhesion, adherence; *(de pneus)* grip
adhérent, -e [aderɑ̃, -ɑ̃t] **1** *adj (substance, propriétés)* adhesive
2 *nm,f* member
adhérer [34] [adere] *vi* (**a**) *(coller)* to adhere, to stick (**à** to); **a. à la route** *(pneus)* to grip the road (**b**) **a. à** *(opinion, doctrine)* to subscribe to (**c**) *(s'inscrire)* **a. à un parti** to join a party
adhésif, -ive [adezif, -iv] *adj* adhesive, sticky
adhésion [adezjɔ̃] *nf* (**a**) *(accord)* support (**à** for) (**b**) *(inscription)* joining (**à** of)
ad hoc [adɔk] *adj & adv* ad hoc
adieu, -x [adjø] **1** *exclam* goodbye!, farewell!; **dire a. à qn** to say goodbye to sb; *Fam Fig* **dire a. à qch** to kiss *or* say goodbye to sth
2 *nm* farewell; **faire ses adieux** to say one's goodbyes; **faire ses adieux à qn** to say goodbye to sb
adipeux, -euse [adipø, -øz] *adj (tissu)* adipose; *(visage)* fat
adjacent, -e [adʒasɑ̃, ɑ̃t] *adj* adjacent (**à** to)
adjectif [adʒɛktif] *nm* adjective
adjoint, -e [adʒwɛ̃, -ɛ̃t] **1** *adj* assistant, deputy
2 *nm,f* assistant; **a. au maire** deputy mayor
adjonction [adʒɔ̃ksjɔ̃] *nf* addition; **produit sans a. de sucre** product with no added sugar
adjudant [adʒydɑ̃] *nm Br* warrant officer class II, *Am* warrant officer (junior grade); **a.-chef** *Br* warrant officer class I, *Am* chief warrant officer
adjudication [adʒydikasjɔ̃] *nf* sale by auction
adjuger [45] [adʒyʒe] **1** *vt* **a. qch à qn** *(prix, contrat)* to award sth to sb; *(aux enchères)* to knock sth down to sb; **une fois, deux fois, trois fois, adjugé, vendu!** going, going, gone!
2 s'adjuger *vpr* **s'a. qch** to appropriate sth
admettre [47] [admɛtr] *vt* (**a**) *(accueillir)* **a. qn** to admit sb, to let sb in; **les chiens ne sont pas admis** *(sur la porte d'un magasin)* no dogs allowed; **être admis à l'université** to win a place at university; **être admis à un concours** to pass an examination (**b**) *(accepter)* to allow; **je n'admets pas qu'on me mente** I won't tolerate being lied to; **cette règle n'admet aucune exception** there can be no exceptions to this rule (**c**) *(reconnaître)* to admit, to accept; **admettons que ce soit possible** assuming it's possible; **admettons que j'ai tort** *(pour clore une discussion)* I stand corrected
administrateur, -trice [administratœr, -tris] *nm,f (d'une société, d'une banque)* director (**b**) *(de fondation)* trustee
administratif, -ive [administratif, -iv] *adj* administrative
administration [administrasjɔ̃] *nf* (**a**) *(d'affaires)* administration, management; *(d'un pays)* governing (**b**) *(ensemble des directeurs)* board of directors; *(d'une institution)* governing body (**c**) **l'A.** *(service public)* ≃ the Civil Service; *(fonctionnaires)* civil servants
administré, -e [administre] *nm,f* citizen
administrer [administre] *vt* (**a**) *(propriété)* to administer, to manage; *(pays)* to govern (**b**) *(justice)* to dispense; *Rel (sacrements)* to administer; *(remède)* to administer; **je vais lui a. une bonne correction** I'm going to give him/her a good hiding

admirable [admirabl] *adj* admirable; *(très compétent)* wonderful; **elle a été a. de courage** she showed admirable courage

admirablement [admirabləmã] *adv* admirably; *(très bien)* wonderfully; **a. bien** wonderfully

admirateur, -trice [admiratœr, -tris] *nm,f* admirer

admiratif, -ive [admiratif, -iv] *adj* admiring

admiration [admirasjɔ̃] *nf* admiration; **avoir de l'a. pour qn** to admire sb; **être en a. devant qch** to be filled with admiration for sth; **tomber en a. devant qch** to be stopped in one's tracks by the beauty of sth; **faire l'a. de tous** to be universally admired

admirer [admire] *vt* to admire

admis, -e [admi, -iz] **1** *adj* (**a**) *(autorisé à entrer)* admitted, allowed (in) (**b**) *(accepté)* allowed, accepted
2 *nm,f (à un examen)* successful candidate

admissible [admisibl] *adj (excuse, preuve, conduite)* admissible, allowable; **(candidats) admissibles** candidates who have qualified for the oral examination

admission [admisjɔ̃] *nf* (**a**) *(entrée)* admission (**à/dans** to) (**b**) *Tech* intake; *Aut* induction

ADN [adeɛn] *nm (abrév* **acide désoxyribonucléique)** DNA

ado [ado] *nmf Fam* teenager

adolescence [adɔlesɑ̃s] *nf* adolescence; **pendant mon a.** when I was a teenager

adolescent, -e [adɔlesɑ̃, -ɑ̃t] **1** *nm,f* adolescent, teenager
2 *adj* adolescent, teenage

adon [adɔ̃] *nm Can Fam* coincidence

adonner [adɔne] **s'adonner** *vpr* **s'a. à qch** to devote oneself to sth; **s'a. à la boisson** to be an alcoholic

adopter [adɔpte] *vt* (**a**) *(enfant)* to adopt (**b**) *(accepter)* to accept (**c**) *(choisir)* to adopt (**d**) *(projet de loi, résolution)* to adopt, to pass

adoptif, -ive [adɔptif, -iv] *adj (enfant)* adopted; *(parent)* adoptive

adoption [adɔpsjɔ̃] *nf* (**a**) *(d'un enfant)* adoption (**b**) *(d'une idée, d'une mode)* adoption; **mon pays d'a.** my adopted country (**c**) *(d'un projet de loi)* adoption, passing

adorable [adɔrabl] *adj* adorable, charming

adoration [adɔrasjɔ̃] *nf aussi Fig* adoration; **être en a. devant qn** to worship sb

adorer [adɔre] **1** *vt aussi Fig* to adore; **j'adore monter à cheval** I love *or* adore riding
2 **s'adorer** *vpr* to adore each other

adosser [adose] **1** *vt* **a. qch à** *ou* **contre qch** to lean sth (with its back) against sth
2 **s'adosser** *vpr* **s'a. à** *ou* **contre qch** to lean (back) against sth; **le village est adossé à la colline** the village stands at the foot of the hill

adoucir [adusir] **1** *vt* (**a**) *(voix, eau, linge, peau)* to soften; *(contraste, couleur)* to tone down; **sa nouvelle coiffure adoucit son visage** her new haircut softens her face (**b**) *(douleur, chagrin)* to ease; *Prov* **la musique adoucit les mœurs** music hath charms to soothe the savage breast
2 **s'adoucir** *vpr* (**a**) *(voix, ton)* to soften (**b**) *(personne, caractère)* to mellow

adoucissant, -e [adusisɑ̃, ɑ̃t] **1** *adj* softening
2 *nm (pour le linge)* fabric softener

adoucisseur [adusisœr] *nm* (water) softener

adr. *(abrév* **adresse)** address

adrénaline [adrenalin] *nf* adrenalin(e)

adresse [adrɛs] *nf* (**a**) *(coordonnées)* address; **changer d'a.** to change one's address; *Fig* **tu te trompes d'a.** you've come to the wrong person; **il connaît de bonnes adresses** *(de restaurants, de magasins)* he knows all the good places to go to; **je l'ai dit à l'a. de ceux qui...** I said it for the benefit of those who...; **a. électronique,** *Can* **a. de courriel** e-mail address (**b**) *(habileté)* skill; *(savoir-faire)* diplomacy; **avec a.** skilfully (**c**) *Ordinat* address; **a. virtuelle** virtual address

adresser [adrese] **1** *vt* (**a**) *(lettre)* to address; **a. qch à qn** to send sth to sb (**b**) *(personne)* **on m'a adressé à vous** I have been referred to you (**c**) **a. qch à qn** *(compliments, remerciements)* to present sth to sb; **cette remarque était adressée à Martin** that remark was aimed at *or* meant for Martin; **a. un sourire à qn** to smile at sb; **a. la parole à qn** to speak to sb
2 **s'adresser** *vpr* **s'a. à qn** *(sujet: personne)* to speak to sb; *(pour un renseignement)* to ask sb; *(sujet: remarque, recommandation)* to apply to sb; **s'a. ici** *(sur écriteau)* enquire within

Adriatique [adrijatik] *nf* **l'A.** the Adriatic

adroit, -e [adrwa, -at] *adj* (**a**) *(habile)* skilful; **être a. de ses mains** to be clever with one's hands (**b**) *(réponse, diplomate)* shrewd, clever

adroitement [adrwatmɑ̃] *adv* (**a**) *(avec des gestes habiles)* skilfully (**b**) *(astucieusement)* cleverly

aduler [adyle] *vt* to worship

adulte [adylt] **1** *adj (personne)* adult, grown-up; *(plante, animal)* fully-grown
2 *nmf* adult, grown-up

adultère [adyltɛr] *nm* adultery

advenir [70] [advənir] *v impersonnel (aux* **être)** to happen; **or, il advint que...** it so happened that...; **quoi qu'il advienne** no matter what happens; **advienne que pourra** come what may; **qu'est-il advenu de lui?** whatever became of him?

adverbe [advɛrb] *nm* adverb

adverbial, -e, -aux, -ales [advɛrbjal, -o] *adj* adverbial

adversaire [advɛrsɛr] *nmf* opponent; *(dans un conflit, dans une guerre)* enemy

adverse [advɛrs] *adj (équipe)* opposing; *Jur* **la partie a.** the other side

AELE [aəɛlə] *nf (abrév* **Association européenne de libre-échange) l'A.** EFTA

aérateur [aeratœr] *nm* ventilator

aération [aerasjɔ̃] *nf (d'une pièce)* ventilation

aéré, -e [aere] *adj* (**a**) *(chambre)* airy, well-ventilated (**b**) *(présentation, texte)* well-spaced

aérer [34] [aere] **1** *vt* (**a**) *(pièce, linge)* to air (**b**) *(texte, exposé)* to lighten
2 **s'aérer** *vpr* to get some fresh air

aérien, -enne [aerjɛ̃, -ɛn] *adj* (**a**) *(défense, attaque, transport)* air (**b**) *(texture)* (light and) airy; *(grâce, allure)* ethereal (**c**) *(câble)* overhead; *(voie ferrée)* elevated

aérobic [aerɔbik] *nm* aerobics *(singulier)*

aérodrome [aerɔdrom] *nm* aerodrome, airfield

aérodynamique [aerɔdinamik] *adj (forme, voiture)* streamlined

aérogare [aerɔgar] *nf* (air) terminal

aéroglisseur [aerɔglisœr] *nm* hovercraft

aérogramme [aerɔgram] *nm* aerogramme, airmail letter

aéromodélisme [aerɔmɔdelism] *nm* making model aircraft

aéronautique [aerɔnotik] **1** *adj* aeronautic(al) **2** *nf* aeronautics *(singulier)*

aéronaval, -e, -als, -ales [aerɔnaval] **1** *adj (forces)* air and sea **2** *nf* l'**Aéronavale** *Br* ≃ the Fleet Air Arm, *Am* ≃ the Naval Air Service

aéronef [aerɔnɛf] *nm* aircraft

aérophagie [aerɔfaʒi] *nf* flatulence; **avoir** *ou* **faire de l'a.** to suffer from flatulence

aéroport [aerɔpɔr] *nm* airport

aéroporté, -e [aerɔpɔrte] *adj* airborne

aérosol [aerɔsɔl] *nm* aerosol; **vendu en a.** sold in spray form

aérospatial, -e, -aux, -ales [aerɔspasjal, -o] *adj* aerospace

aérostat [aerɔsta] *nm (montgolfière)* hot-air balloon; *(dirigeable)* airship

affabilité [afabilite] *nf* affability

affable [afabl] *adj* affable

affabulation [afabylasjɔ̃] *nf* fabrication

affabuler [afabyle] *vi* to make things up

affaiblir [afeblir] **1** *vt* (**a**) *(sujet: maladie)* to weaken (**b**) *(réduire)* to lessen, to reduce **2 s'affaiblir** *vpr (personne)* to get weaker; *(vue, ouïe)* to get worse, to deteriorate; *(sentiment)* to wane; *(son)* to grow fainter; **le sens du mot s'est affaibli** the word has lost much of its meaning

affaiblissement [afeblismã] *nm (d'une personne, d'un gouvernement, de l'économie)* weakening; *(d'un sentiment)* waning; *(d'une lumière, d'un son)* fading

affaire [afer] *nf* (**a**) *(occupation)* business, concern; **ce n'est pas votre a.** it's none of your business; **j'en fais mon a.** I'll handle it; **c'est une a. de goût** it's a matter *or* question of taste; **c'est l'a. d'une minute** it won't take a minute; **ça, c'est une autre a.** that's another matter; **avoir a. à qn** *(s'adresser à quelqu'un)* to be dealt with by sb; **s'il continue à mentir, il aura a. à moi!** if he carries on lying, he'll have me to deal with! (**b**) *(usage)* **cela fera parfaitement l'a.** that will do nicely; *Fam* **faire son a. à qn** to do sb in (**c**) *(histoire, problème)* affair, business; **une a. de pots-de-vin** a bribery scandal; **a. de cœur** love affair; **ça n'a pas été une mince a.** it wasn't easy; **c'est toute une a.** it's quite a business; **la belle a.!** big deal!; **ça ne change rien à l'a.** that doesn't change anything; **tirer qn d'a.** to get sb out of trouble; **ce n'est pas une a. d'État!** it's no big deal! (**d**) *(transaction)* deal; *(achat à bon marché)* bargain; **il a fait une a. en achetant cette voiture** he got a bargain when he bought that car; **faire a. avec qn** to make a deal with sb; **une a. en or** the bargain of the century (**e**) *(entreprise)* firm, business (**f**) **affaires** *(effets personnels)* things, belongings (**g**) **les affaires** *(activités commerciales)* business *(singulier)*; **comment vont les affaires?** how's business?; **il est dur en affaires** he's a hard-headed businessman; **les affaires sont les affaires** business is business (**h**) **les Affaires étrangères** *Br* ≃ the Foreign (and Commonwealth) Office, *Am* ≃ the State Department

affairé, -e [afere] *adj* busy

affairer [afere] **s'affairer** *vpr* to busy oneself; **s'a. autour de qn** to fuss (a)round sb

affairiste [aferist] *nmf* wheeler-dealer

affaissement [afesmã] *nm (de terrain)* subsidence; *(du plancher, d'une poutre)* sagging

affaisser [afese] **s'affaisser** *vpr* (**a**) *(s'enfoncer) (terrain)* to subside; *(poutre, fauteuil)* to sag (**b**) *(tomber, s'écrouler)* to collapse

affalé, -e [afale] *adj* **être a. dans un fauteuil** to be slumped in an armchair

affaler [afale] **s'affaler** *vpr* to collapse

affamé, -e [afame] *adj* starving

affectation [afektasjɔ̃] *nf* (**a**) *Péj (pose)* affectation, affectedness; *(simulacre)* pretence, affectation; **avec a.** affectedly; **sans a.** unaffectedly (**b**) *(de fonds, de crédits, de locaux)* assignment, allocation (**à** to) (**c**) *(à un poste)* appointment (**à** to); *(d'un soldat)* posting (**à** to) (**d**) *Ordinat (de touche)* assignment; **a. de mémoire** memory allocation

affecté, -e [afekte] *adj Péj (personne, manière)* affected

affecter [afekte] *vt* (**a**) *(fonds, crédits, locaux)* to assign (**à** to), to allocate (**à** to) (**b**) *(employé)* to appoint (**à** to); *(soldat)* to post (**à** to) (**c**) *(feindre)* to affect; **a. de faire qch** to pretend to do sth (**d**) *(émouvoir)* to affect, to move (**e**) *(frapper) (carrière, santé)* to affect, to have an effect on; **la grève a affecté plusieurs usines** the strike has affected *or* hit several factories

affectif, -ive [afektif, -iv] *adj* emotional, *Spéc* affective

affection [afeksjɔ̃] *nf* (**a**) *(attachement)* affection (**pour** for); **prendre qn en a.** to become fond of sb; **avoir de l'a. pour qn** to be fond of sb (**b**) *Litt (maladie)* ailment

affectionner [afeksjɔne] *vt* to be fond of; **votre cousin affectionné** *(dans une lettre)* your affectionate cousin

affectivité [afektivite] *nf* feelings

affectueusement [afektɥøzmã] *adv* affectionately; *(dans une lettre)* love (from)

affectueux, -euse [afektɥø, -øz] *adj* affectionate

afférent, -e [aferã, -ãt] *adj* **a. à** *(concernant)* relating to

affermir [afermir] **1** *vt* (**a**) *(muscles, chairs)* to tone (up) (**b**) *(pouvoir, position, autorité)* to strengthen, to consolidate **2 s'affermir** *vpr (chairs, muscles)* to tone up; *(pouvoir, position, autorité)* to be strengthened

affichage [afiʃaʒ] *nm* (**a**) *(pose d'affiches)* billsticking, billposting; **a. interdit** *(sur panneau)* stick no bills (**b**) *Ordinat* display; **montre à a. digital** *ou* **numérique** digital watch; **a. à cristaux liquides** liquid crystal display

affiche [afiʃ] *nf* notice; *(de publicité)* poster; **être à l'a.** *(spectacle)* to be on; **être en tête d'a.** to be top of the bill; **a. électorale** election poster

afficher [afiʃe] **1** *vt* (**a**) *(annonce, poster)* to put up; *(prix, horaires, résultats)* to display; **défense d'a.** *(sur panneau)* stick no bills; **a. complet** *(spectacle)* to be sold out (**b**) *(mépris, indifférence)* to show, to display; *(savoir)* to flaunt; *(déficit, excédent)* to show (**c**) *Ordinat (message)* to display **2 s'afficher** *vpr* (**a**) *(personne)* to flaunt oneself (**b**) *(sur un écran)* to be displayed

affichette [afiʃet] *nf* small notice; *(publicitaire)* poster

afficheur [afiʃœr] *nm (personne)* billsticker, billposter; *(société)* publicity company

affilée [afile] **d'affilée** *adv* in a row; **cinq heures d'a.** five hours solid *or* at a stretch

affiler [afile] *vt* to sharpen

affiliation [afiljasjɔ̃] *nf* joining (**à** of)

affilier [66] [afilje] **s'affilier** *vpr* to join; **s'a. à un parti** to join a party

affiner [afine] **1** *vt* (**a**) *(métal)* to refine; *(fromage)* to mature (**b**) *(esprit)* to sharpen; *(goût)* to refine
2 s'affiner *vpr (goût)* to become more refined; *(visage)* to get thinner; *(traits)* to become better defined; *(esprit)* to become sharper

affinité [afinite] *nf* affinity (**entre** between)

affirmatif, -ive [afirmatif, -iv] **1** *adj* (**a**) *(réponse)* affirmative, positive; **faire un signe a. de la tête** to nod in agreement (**b**) *(personne)* positive
2 *nf* **dans l'affirmative** if so, if the answer is yes; **répondre par l'affirmative** to answer yes
3 *exclam* affirmative!

affirmation [afirmasjɔ̃] *nf* assertion

affirmer [afirme] **1** *vt* (**a**) *(soutenir)* to maintain; **il affirme vous connaître** he maintains that he knows you (**b**) *(manifester)* to assert; **a. sa volonté de faire qch** to declare one's willingness to do sth
2 s'affirmer *vpr (personnalité)* to assert itself; *(tendance, talent)* to be confirmed

affleurer [aflœre] *vi (récif)* to be near the surface; *Géol (filon)* to outcrop; *Fig (mépris, racisme)* to come to the surface

affliction [afliksjɔ̃] *nf* affliction

affligé, -e [afliʒe] *adj* (**a**) **être a. de** *(atteint)* to be afflicted with (**b**) *(peiné)* distressed

affligeant, -e [afliʒɑ̃, -ɑ̃t] *adj (nouvelle, vision)* distressing; *(bêtise, ignorance, résultats)* appalling

affliger [45] [afliʒe] **1** *vt* (**a**) *(atteindre)* to afflict; **région affligée par le choléra** area afflicted with cholera; **la nature l'a affligé d'un grand nez** nature has cursed him with a big nose (**b**) *(peiner) (sujet: nouvelle, événement)* to distress
2 s'affliger *vpr* to be distressed (**de** about)

affluence [aflyɑ̃s] *nf (de personnes)* crowd; *(de marchandises)* abundance

affluent [aflyɑ̃] *nm* tributary

affluer [aflye] *vi (liquide)* to flow (**vers/dans** to/into); *(sang)* to rush (**à** to); *(foule)* to flock (**vers** to)

afflux [afly] *nm (de sang)* rush; *(de visiteurs)* flood; *(de capitaux)* influx

affolant, -e [afɔlɑ̃, -ɑ̃t] *adj (spectacle, nouvelle)* distressing; *Fam* **c'est a.!** it's incredible!

affolé, -e [afɔle] *adj (personne)* panic-stricken

affolement [afɔlmɑ̃] *nm* panic; **pas d'a.!** don't panic!

affoler [afɔle] **1** *vt* to throw into a panic
2 s'affoler *vpr* (**a**) *(paniquer)* to panic (**b**) *(aiguille de boussole)* to spin (**c**) *(machine)* to race

affranchir [afrɑ̃ʃir] **1** *vt* (**a**) *(lettre, colis)* to put a stamp/stamps on; *(avec une machine)* to frank (**b**) *(esclave)* to free
2 s'affranchir *vpr* (**a**) *(peuple, personne)* to free oneself (**de** from) (**b**) *Belg (prendre de l'assurance)* to become (more) self-confident

affranchissement [afrɑ̃ʃismɑ̃] *nm* (**a**) *(montant payé) (de lettre, paquet)* postage (**b**) *(d'un esclave)* freeing

affres [afr] *nfpl Litt (du doute, de la jalousie, de la faim)* pangs; **les a. de la mort** death throes

affréter [34] [afrete] *vt* to charter

affreusement [afrøzmɑ̃] *adv* horribly; **a. laid** hideously ugly; **il parle a. mal l'anglais** his English is awful

affreux, -euse [afrø, -øz] *adj* (**a**) *(laid)* hideous (**b**) *(atroce) (nouvelle, pauvreté, crime)* dreadful (**c**) *Fam (épouvantable) (temps, migraine)* awful, dreadful; **qu'est-ce que ça a augmenté, c'est a.!** it's dreadful *or* shocking how the price has gone up!; **un a. jojo** a little horror

affriolant, -e [afrijɔlɑ̃, -ɑ̃t] *adj* alluring

affront [afrɔ̃] *nm* affront, insult; **faire un a. à qn** to affront *or* insult sb

affrontement [afrɔ̃tmɑ̃] *nm* clash, confrontation

affronter [afrɔ̃te] **1** *vt (adversaire, danger, mort)* to face, to confront; **a. la colère de qn** to brave the wrath of sb
2 s'affronter *vpr (ennemis)* to clash; *(équipes, joueurs)* to clash; **deux thèses s'affrontent** there are two conflicting theories

affubler [afyble] **1** *vt* **a. qn de qch** to attire sb in sth
2 s'affubler *vpr* **s'a. de qch** to get oneself up in sth

affût [afy] **à l'affût** *adv* **être à l'a.** *(à la chasse)* to lie in wait; *Fig* **être à l'a. de qch** to be on the lookout for sth

affûter [afyte] *vt* to sharpen

afghan, -e [afgɑ̃, -an] **1** *adj* Afghan
2 *nm,f* **A.** Afghan
3 *nm (langue)* Afghan

Afghanistan [afganistɑ̃] *nm* **l'A.** Afghanistan

afin [afɛ̃] *adv* **a. de faire qch** (in order) to do sth, so as to do sth; **a. que** + *subjunctive* so that; **a. que les autres puissent le voir** so that the others may see it

AFNOR [afnɔr] *nf (abrév* **Association française de normalisation***)* = French industrial standards authority, *Br* ≃ BSI, *Am* ≃ ANSI

a fortiori [afɔrsjɔri] *adv* all the more so

AF-P [æfpe] *nf (abrév* **Agence France-Presse***)* = French international news agency

africain, -e [afrikɛ̃, -ɛn] **1** *adj* African
2 *nm,f* **A.** African

Afrique [afrik] *nf* **l'A.** Africa; **l'A. noire** Black Africa; **l'A. du Nord** North Africa; **l'A. du Sud** South Africa

afro-américain, -e *(mpl* **afro-américains,** *fpl* **afro-américaines***)* [afroamerikɛ̃, -ɛn] **1** *adj* Afro-American, African American
2 *nm,f* **A.** Afro-American, African American

after-shave [aftœrʃɛv] **1** *nm inv* aftershave
2 *adj* **lotion a.** aftershave (lotion)

A.G. [aʒe] *nf (abrév* **assemblée générale***)* AGM

agaçant, -e [agasɑ̃, -ɑ̃t] *adj* annoying, irritating

agacer [16] [agase] *vt* (**a**) *(énerver)* to annoy, to irritate; **il m'agace avec ses questions** he's getting on my nerves, asking all those questions (**b**) *(dents, nerfs)* to set on edge

agapes [agap] *nfpl Litt* feast; *Hum* **nous allons faire des a. chez Jeannot** we're going to have a real slap-up meal at Jeannot's

agate [agat] *nf (pierre)* agate; *(bille)* marble

âge [ɑʒ] *nm* (**a**) *(d'une personne)* age; **quel â. avez-vous?** how old are you?; **à ton â., je travaillais** when I was your age, I was working; **à l'â. de six ans** at the age of six; **on ne lui donne pas son â.** he doesn't look his age; **faire son â.** to look one's age; **un homme d'un grand â.** a very old man; **entre deux âges** middle-aged; **être en â. de faire qch, être d'â. à faire qch** to be old enough to do sth; **ce n'est plus de mon â.** I'm too old for that type of thing; **un whisky de quinze ans d'â.** a fifteen-year-old whisky; **l'â. adulte** adulthood; **l'â. bête** *ou* **ingrat** the awkward *or* difficult age; **â. mental** mental age; **une femme d'â. mur** a mature woman; **avoir l'â. de raison** to have reached the age of reason (**b**) *(époque)* age; **l'â. de (la) pierre** the Stone Age; **l'â. d'or du cinéma muet** the golden age of silent movies

âgé, -e [ɑʒe] *adj* (**a**) *(qui a tel âge)* **être â. de dix ans** to be ten years old; **un enfant â. de deux ans** a two-year-old child (**b**) *(vieux)* old; **être plus/moins â. que qn** to be older/younger than sb

agence [aʒɑ̃s] *nf* agency; *(de banque)* branch; **a. immobilière** *Br* estate agent's *or* agency, *Am* real estate agency; **a. matrimoniale** marriage bureau; **A. nationale pour l'emploi** = French national employment bureau, *Br* ≃ job centre; **a. de presse** press *or* news agency; **a. de voyages** travel agent's *or* agency

agencé, -e [aʒɑ̃se] *adj Suisse (cuisine)* fitted

agencement [aʒɑ̃smɑ̃] *nm (d'éléments)* arrangement; *(d'une maison, d'une pièce)* layout

agencer [16] [aʒɑ̃se] **1** *vt (éléments)* to arrange; *(maison, pièce)* to lay out, to design

2 s'agencer *vpr* **les parties du discours s'agencent bien/mal** the different parts of the speech hang/don't hang together well

agenda [aʒɛ̃da] *nm* diary; **a. électronique** personal organizer

agenouiller [aʒnuje] **s'agenouiller** *vpr* to kneel (down) (**devant** in front of)

agent [aʒɑ̃] *nm* (**a**) *(employé, espion)* agent; **a. (de police)** police officer; **pardon, Monsieur l'a.** excuse me, officer; **a. d'assurance(s)** insurance broker; **a. de change** stockbroker; **a. de la circulation** traffic policeman; **a. double** double agent; *Belg* **a. du quartier** community policeman; **a. immobilier** *Br* estate agent, *Am* realtor; **a. secret** secret agent (**b**) *(facteur)* factor (**c**) *Gram* agent

agglomération [aglɔmerasjɔ̃] *nf (ville)* town, built-up area; **l'a. lyonnaise/parisienne** Lyons/Paris and its suburbs

aggloméré [aglɔmere] *nm* chipboard

agglomérer [34] [aglɔmere] **1** *vt* to bind together

2 s'agglomérer *vpr* to bind together

agglutiner [aglytine] **s'agglutiner** *vpr (personnes)* to congregate, to gather

aggravant, -e [agravɑ̃, -ɑ̃t] *adj* aggravating

aggravation [agravasjɔ̃] *nf (d'une maladie)* aggravation; *(du temps, d'un conflit)* worsening

aggraver [agrave] **1** *vt (situation, état de santé)* to make worse; *(difficultés)* to increase; **pour a. les choses** to make matters worse

2 s'aggraver *vpr (situation)* to get worse; *(état de santé)* to deteriorate; *(difficultés)* to increase

agile [aʒil] *adj* agile, nimble

agilement [aʒilmɑ̃] *adv* agilely, nimbly

agilité [aʒilite] *nf* agility

agios [aʒjo] *nmpl* bank charges

agir [aʒir] **1** *vi* (**a**) *(faire quelque chose)* to act; **bien/mal a. envers qn** to behave well/badly towards sb; **je n'aime pas sa façon** *ou* **manière d'a.** I don't like his behaviour (**b**) *(produire un effet) (médicament, substance)* to act (**sur** on); **a. sur le moral** to have a demoralizing effect (**c**) *Jur* **a. au nom de qn** to act on behalf of sb

2 s'agir de *v impersonnel* (**a**) *(être question de)* **de**

quoi s'agit-il? what's it about?; **l'affaire dont il s'agit** the matter in hand; **il ne s'agit pas d'argent** it's not a question of money; **quand il s'agit d'aider, il est toujours occupé!** when it comes to helping, he always seems to be busy! (**b**) *(falloir)* **il s'agit de prendre une décision** we have to take a decision; **il s'agirait de savoir si…** the question is whether…; **il s'agirait de se dépêcher** we've got to hurry

agissements [aʒismɑ̃] *nmpl* dealings

agitateur, -trice [aʒitatœr, -tris] *nm,f Pol* agitator

agitation [aʒitasjɔ̃] *nf (inquiétude)* agitation; *(bougeotte)* restlessness; *(troubles)* unrest

agité, -e [aʒite] *adj (mer)* rough; *(patient, nuit)* restless; *(sommeil)* troubled; *(enfant)* fidgety; *(époque)* unsettled; *(vie)* hectic

agiter [aʒite] **1** *vt* (**a**) *(mouchoir, drapeau, bras)* to wave; *(bouteille)* to shake; *(sujet: vent) (arbre, branches)* to sway; **a. la queue** *(chien)* to wag its tail; *(cheval)* to flick its tail (**b**) *(inquiéter)* to trouble; *(malade)* to excite

2 s'agiter *vpr* (**a**) *(bouger)* to fidget; *(s'affairer)* to bustle around; **s'a. dans son sommeil** to toss and turn in one's sleep (**b**) *(s'énerver)* to get excited

agneau, -x [aɲo] *nm* lamb; **(peau d')a.** lambskin

agnelle [aɲɛl] *nf* ewe lamb

agnostique [agnɔstik] *adj & nmf* agnostic

agonie [agɔni] *nf aussi Fig* death throes; **être à l'a.** to be at death's door; *Fig (régime)* to be in its death throes

agonisant, -e [agɔnizɑ̃, -ɑ̃t] **1** *adj* dying

2 *nm,f* dying person

agoniser [agɔnize] *vi* to be dying; *Fig (régime)* to be in its death throes

agoraphobie [agɔrafɔbi] *nf Méd* agoraphobia; **souffrir d'a.** to be agoraphobic

agrafe [agraf] *nf* (**a**) *(de bureau)* staple; *(de robe)* hook; *Méd* clip (**b**) *Constr* cramp (iron)

agrafer [agrafe] *vt* (**a**) *(avec une agrafeuse)* to staple; *(robe)* to fasten (**b**) *Fam (arrêter)* to nick; **se faire a.** to get nicked

agrafeuse [agraføz] *nf* stapler

agraire [agrɛr] *adj (économie, société)* agrarian

agrandir [agrɑ̃dir] **1** *vt* (**a**) *(rendre plus grand)* to enlarge; *(maison, influence)* to extend; *(cercle de relations)* to widen (**b**) *(sujet: loupe, microscope)* to magnify; **ce papier peint agrandit la pièce** this wallpaper makes the room look bigger

2 s'agrandir *vpr (ville)* to grow, to get bigger; *(nombre, influence)* to increase; *(entreprise)* to expand

agrandissement [agrɑ̃dismɑ̃] *nm* (**a**) *(d'une maison)* extension; *(d'une ville)* growth; *(d'une entreprise)* expansion (**b**) *(cliché)* enlargement

agréable [agreabl] *adj (personne, endroit, journée)* nice, pleasant; *(apparence)* pleasing; **a. au goût** tasty; **a. à regarder** nice to look at

agréablement [agreabləmɑ̃] *adv* pleasantly

agréer [24] [agree] *vt (fournisseur, équipement)* to approve; **veuillez a. l'expression de mes sentiments distingués** *(à une personne dont on connaît le nom)* yours sincerely; *(à une personne dont on ne connaît pas le nom)* yours faithfully

agrégation [agregasjɔ̃] *nf* **(le concours de) l'a.** = competitive examination for posts on the teaching staff of lycées and universities

---

> **Agrégation**
> This is a prestigious professional qualification for teachers in France. Those who pass the challenging competitive exam for the "agrég" become teachers in secondary education or universities and are entitled to higher pay and a less onerous timetable than those who have passed the **CAPES** (*see box at this entry*).

agrégé, -e [agreʒe] **1** *adj* = who has passed the agrégation examination
  2 *nm,f* = graduate who has passed the agrégation examination

agrément [agremã] *nm* (**a**) *(plaisir)* **voyage d'a.** pleasure trip (**b**) *(charme)* **une ville sans a.** an unattractive town (**c**) *(accord)* approval, consent

agrémenter [agremãte] *vt* **a. qch de** *(décorer)* to adorn sth with; **texte agrémenté de citations** text spiced with quotations

agrès [agrɛ] *nmpl* (**a**) *Sport* (gymnastics) apparatus; **faire des a.** to do apparatus work (**b**) *Naut* tackle

agresser [agrese] *vt* to attack, to assault; *(en paroles)* to attack; *(tympans)* to assault; *(yeux)* to hurt; *(peau)* to damage; **se faire a.** to be attacked; *(pour son argent)* to be mugged

agresseur [agresœr] *nm* attacker

agressif, -ive [agresif, -iv] *adj* aggressive

agression [agresjɔ̃] *nf* *(d'une personne)* attack, assault; *(pour son argent)* mugging; *(d'un pays)* act of aggression; **être victime d'une a.** to be attacked; *(pour son argent)* to be mugged; **les agressions de la vie moderne** the stresses of modern life

agressivement [agresivmã] *adv* aggressively

agressivité [agresivite] *nf* aggressiveness

agricole [agrikɔl] *adj* agricultural; *(population)* farming; *(produits)* farm

agriculteur, -trice [agrikyltœr, -tris] *nm,f* farmer

agriculture [agrikyltyr] *nf* farming, agriculture

agripper [agripe] **1** *vt* to clutch
  2 s'agripper *vpr* to cling on (**à** to)

agroalimentaire [agrɔalimãtɛr] **1** *adj* *(industrie, secteur)* food
  2 *nm* **l'a.** the food-processing industry

agronome [agrɔnɔm] *nmf* agronomist

agronomie [agrɔnɔmi] *nf* agronomy

agrume [agrym] *nm* citrus fruit

aguets [agɛ] **aux aguets** *adv* on the lookout; **être ou se tenir aux a.** to be on the lookout

aguichant, -e [agiʃã, -ãt] *adj* seductive

aguicher [agiʃe] *vt* to seduce

ahuri, -e [ayri] **1** *adj* astounded
  2 *nm,f* numbskull

ahurissant, -e [ayrisã, -ãt] *adj* astounding

aide [ɛd] **1** *nf* help, assistance; **demander de l'a. à qn** to ask sb for help; **venir en a. à qn** to help sb; **appeler à l'a.** to call for help; **à l'a.!** help!; **à l'a. de qch** with the aid of sth; *Ordinat* **a. à la césure** hyphenation help; **a. de l'État** government aid; **a. humanitaire** aid; **a. judiciaire** legal aid; *Ordinat* **a. en ligne** on-line help; **a. sociale** *Br* social security, *Am* welfare
  2 *nmf* assistant; **un a. de camp** an aide-de-camp; **une a. familiale** a home help; **une a. ménagère** a home help

aide-mémoire [ɛdmemwar] *nm inv* aide-mémoire

aider [ede] **1** *vt* to help; *(sujet: gouvernement)* to aid; **que puis-je faire pour vous a.?** how may I help you?; **je me suis fait a. par un ami** I got a friend to help me; **a. qn à faire qch** to help sb to do sth; **a. qn à monter/sortir** to help sb up/out; *Ironique* **tu veux que je t'aide?** stop that!; **elle n'aide jamais** she never helps (out)
  2 aider à *vt ind* to contribute towards; **a. à faire qch** to help to do sth
  3 s'aider *vpr* (**a**) *(soi-même)* **s'a. de qch** to use sth; **marcher en s'aidant d'une canne/de béquilles** to walk with the aid of a stick/crutches; *Prov* **aide-toi et le ciel t'aidera** God helps those who help themselves (**b**) *(l'un l'autre)* to help each other

aide-soignant, -e *(mpl* **aides-soignants**, *fpl* **aides-soignantes)** [ɛdswaɲã, -ãt] *nm,f* nursing auxiliary

aïe [aj] *exclam* *(cri de douleur)* ow!, ouch!; *Fig* **a., j'ai fait une gaffe!** oh no, I've put my foot in it!

aïeul, -e [ajœl] *nm,f Vieilli* grandfather, *f* grandmother; **aïeuls** grandparents

aïeux [ajø] *nmpl Litt* ancestors

aigle [ɛgl] *nm* eagle; *Fig* **ce n'est pas un a.** he's no genius; **avoir un œil d'a.** to be eagle-eyed

aiglefin [ɛgləfɛ̃] *nm* haddock

aigre [ɛgr] *adj* *(goût, lait)* sour; *Fig (propos)* cutting; **d'un ton a.** sharply

aigre-doux, -douce *(mpl* **aigres-doux**, *fpl* **aigres-douces)** [ɛgrədu, -dus] *adj* *(sauce)* sweet-and-sour; *Fig (remarque)* snide

aigrelet, -ette [ɛgrəlɛ, -ɛt] *adj* *(vin, goût)* (rather) sour; *(son, voix)* shrill

aigrette [ɛgrɛt] *nf* (**a**) *(d'un oiseau)* crest (**b**) *(panache)* plume

aigreur [ɛgrœr] *nf* (**a**) *(d'un goût)* sourness; *(d'une remarque)* sharpness, bitterness (**b**) *Méd* **aigreurs (d'estomac)** heartburn

aigri, -e [ɛgri] *adj* embittered

aigu, -uë [egy] *adj* (**a**) *(douleur)* acute, sharp; *(regard)* penetrating; *(esprit)* keen; **avoir un sens a. de qch** to have a keen sense of sth (**b**) *(instrument)* sharp; *(angle)* acute (**c**) *(son)* high-pitched (**d**) *Méd* acute

aigue-marine *(pl* **aigues-marines)** [ɛgmarin] *nf* aquamarine

aiguillage [egɥijaʒ] *nm* (**a**) *(manœuvre) Br* shunting, *Am* switching; *(appareil) Br* points, *Am* switches (**b**) *Fig* **faire une erreur d'a.** to take the wrong course

aiguille [egɥij] *nf* (**a**) *(instrument, objet pointu)* needle; *Fig* **chercher une a. dans une botte de foin** to look for a needle in a haystack; **a. à coudre/repriser/tricoter** sewing/darning/knitting needle; *Méd* **a. hypodermique** hypodermic needle; **a. de pin** pine needle (**b**) *(de boussole, de compteur de vitesse)* needle; *(de montre, d'horloge)* hand; **petite a.** hour hand; **grande a.** minute hand (**c**) *(d'une église)* spire (**d**) *(sommet)* sharp peak

aiguiller [egɥije] *vt* *(train) Br* to shunt, *Am* to switch; *Fig* **a. qn vers** *(profession)* to steer sb towards; **a. ses recherches vers** to direct one's investigations towards; **a. la police sur une fausse piste** to put the police off the scent; **il a été mal aiguillé dans ses études** he was badly advised about his studies

aiguilleur [egɥijœr] *nm* *(de trains)* signalman; **a. du ciel** air-traffic controller

aiguillon [egɥijɔ̃] *nm* (**a**) *(pique-bœuf)* goad; *Fig* spur (**b**) *(d'une guêpe)* sting

aiguiser [egize] *vt* (**a**) *(outil, couteau)* to sharpen (**b**) *Fig (curiosité, jalousie)* to arouse; *(appétit)* to whet

aïkido [ajkido] *nm* aikido; **faire de l'a.** to do aikido

ail [aj] (*pl* **ails** [aj], *Vieilli* **aulx** [o]) *nm* garlic; *Can* **a. des bois** wild garlic

aile [ɛl] *nf* (**a**) *(d'oiseau, de papillon)* wing; *Fig* **battre de l'a.** to be struggling; **la peur nous donnait des ailes** fear lent us wings; *Fam* **avoir un coup dans l'a.** to have had a bit too much to drink (**b**) *(d'une voiture) Br* wing, *Am* fender; *(d'un bâtiment)* wing; *(d'une armée)* flank (**c**) *(d'un avion)* wing; *(d'un moulin)* sail; *(d'une hélice, d'une turbine)* blade (**d**) *(au football, au rugby)* wing

ailé, -e [ele] *adj* winged

aileron [ɛlrɔ̃] *nm* (**a**) *(d'oiseau)* pinion; *(de requin)* fin (**b**) *Aviat* aileron

ailette [ɛlɛt] *nf* *(d'une turbine, d'un ventilateur)* blade; *(d'une bombe, d'un missile)* wing, fin

ailier [elje] *nm* *(au football)* winger; *(au rugby, au basket)* wing

aille *etc voir* **aller**

ailler [aje] *vt* to put garlic in

ailleurs [ajœr] *adv* (**a**) *(à un autre endroit)* elsewhere, somewhere else; *Fig* **être a., avoir l'esprit a.** to be miles away; **partout a.** everywhere else; *(n'importe où)* anywhere else; **nulle part a.** nowhere else; **vous mangerez ici comme nulle part a.** you'll eat better here than anywhere else; *Fam* **va voir a. si j'y suis!** take a hike! (**b**) **d'a.** *(de plus)* besides, anyway; *(au fait)* by the way (**c**) **par a.** *(par d'autres côtés)* in other respects; *(d'autre part)* moreover

ailloli [ajɔli] = **aïoli**

aimable [ɛmabl] *adj (gentil)* kind, nice; **vous êtes bien a., c'est très a. de votre part** it's very kind of you; **peu a.** *(personne)* not very nice; *(propos)* unkind

aimablement [ɛmabləmɑ̃] *adv* kindly

aimant¹ [ɛmɑ̃] *nm* magnet

aimant², -e [ɛmɑ̃, -ɑ̃t] *adj (personne)* loving

aimanter [ɛmɑ̃te] *vt* to magnetize

aimer [eme] **1** *vt* (**a**) *(d'amour)* to love (**b**) *(apprécier, avoir de l'affection pour)* to like; **a. beaucoup qn/qch** to like sb/sth a lot, to be very fond of sb/sth; **a. bien qn/qch** to like sb/sth; **a. faire qch** to like doing sth; **j'aurais aimé le voir** I would like to have seen him; **je n'aime pas que tu fréquentes ces gens** I don't like you mixing with those people; **j'aime(rais) autant rester ici** I would rather stay here; **j'aime autant qu'il ne m'attende pas** I would rather he didn't wait for me; **a. mieux** to prefer; **ah, j'aime mieux ça!** now that's more like it!; **j'aime mieux lui en parler moi-même** I'd rather talk to him about it myself; *Fam* **j'aime mieux pas** I'd rather not; **je vais prendre un pot – qui m'aime me suive!** I'm going for a drink – anyone want to join me?

2 aimer à *vt ind Litt* **a. à faire qch** to take pleasure in doing sth; **j'aime à croire que...** I like to think (that)...

3 s'aimer *vpr* (**a**) *(l'un l'autre)* to love each other (**b**) *(être fier de soi)* to be in love with oneself; **je ne m'aime pas dans cette veste** I don't like myself in this jacket

aine [ɛn] *nf* groin

aîné, -e [ene] **1** *adj (de deux enfants)* elder; *(de plus de deux enfants)* eldest

2 *nm,f (de deux enfants)* elder (child); *(de plus de deux enfants)* eldest (child); **nos aînés** our elders; **il est mon a.** he is older than me; **il est mon a. de deux ans** he is two years older than me

aînesse [ɛnɛs] *nf voir* **droit**

ainsi [ɛ̃si] *adv* (**a**) *(de cette façon)* like this, in this way; **c'est a. qu'il est devenu soldat** that's how he became a soldier; **et a. de suite** and so on, and so forth; **pour a. dire** so to speak, as it were; *Rel* **a. soit-il** amen (**b**) **a. (donc)** *(alors)* so; **a. vous ne venez pas?** so you're not coming? (**c**) *(par exemple)* for example, for instance (**d**) **a. que** *(et)* as well as, and

aïoli [ajɔli] *nm Culin* garlic mayonnaise

air [ɛr] *nm* (**a**) *(gaz)* air; **cela manque d'a. ici** it's stuffy in here; **faire de l'a.** to let some air in; **sortir prendre l'a.** to go out for some fresh air; **laisser qch à l'a.** to leave sth uncovered; **au grand a.** in the fresh air; **en plein a., à l'a.** libre outside; **concert en plein a.** open-air concert; **activités de plein a.** outdoor pursuits; *Fam* **allez, de l'a.!** go on, clear off!; **a. comprimé** compressed air; **avoir l'a. conditionné** to have air-conditioning

(**b**) *(ciel)* **l'a.** the air; **s'élever dans les airs** to rise into the air; **regarder en l'a.** to look up

(**c**) *(atmosphère)* **changer d'a.** to have a change of scene; **il y a de la dispute/de l'orage dans l'a.** there's an argument/a storm brewing

(**d**) *(vent)* **il y a** *ou* **il fait de l'a.** there's a breeze

(**e**) *(allure)* look; *(mine)* expression; **avoir un drôle d'a.** to look odd *or* funny; **avoir l'a. fatigué/de s'ennuyer** to look tired/bored; *Fam* **avoir l'a. fin** to look daft; **tu as l'a. de ne pas comprendre** you look as if you don't understand; **n'avoir l'a. de rien** *(travail)* to look (deceptively) easy; **il n'a l'a. de rien, mais...** he doesn't look much, but...; **sans avoir l'a. de rien** inconspicuously; **se donner** *ou* **prendre des airs** to give oneself airs; **ne prends pas tes grands airs!** don't get on your high horse!; **a. de famille** family likeness; *Can* **avoir l'a. de qn** to look like sb

(**f**) *(musique)* tune; **un a. d'opéra** an (operatic) aria

(**g**) *(locutions) Fam* **ficher qch en l'a.** to mess sth up; **mettre qch en l'a.** *(en désordre)* to make an awful mess of sth; **c'est dans l'a. du temps** it's the in-thing

air-air [ɛrɛr] *adj inv Mil* air-to-air

Airbag® [ɛrbag] *nm* (**a**) *Aut* Airbag® (**b**) *Fam* **airbags** *(seins)* tits, jugs

aire [ɛr] *nf* (**a**) *(surface plane)* area; **a. (de battage)** threshing floor; **a. d'atterrissage** *(pour avions)* landing strip; *(pour hélicoptères)* helipad; **a. de jeux** play area; **a. de lancement** *(de fusée)* launch pad; **a. de repos** *(sur l'autoroute)* rest area; **a. de stationnement** lay-by (**b**) *(d'un champ, d'un triangle, d'un bâtiment)* area; *Fig* **a. d'influence** sphere of influence (**c**) *(d'un aigle)* eyrie

airelle [ɛrɛl] *nf (rouge)* cranberry

air-sol [ɛrsɔl] *adj inv Mil* air-to-ground

aisance [ɛzɑ̃s] *nf* (**a**) *(facilité, grâce)* ease (**b**) *(financière)* **vivre dans l'a.** to live comfortably

aise [ɛz] **1** *nf* **être à l'a.** *(bien installé)* to be comfortable; *(avoir beaucoup de place)* to have plenty of room; *(financièrement)* to be comfortably off; *(dans une situation)* to feel comfortable *or* at ease; **on tient à l'a. à six dans cette voiture** this car holds six comfortably; *Fam* **à l'a.!** *(c'est facile)* easy!; **ne pas être à son a., se sentir mal à l'a.** to feel uncomfortable; **il me met mal à l'a.** he makes me feel uneasy *or* uncomfortable; **mettre qn à l'a.** to put sb at his ease; **se mettre à l'a.** to make oneself comfortable; *Ironique* **elle peut en parler à son a.!** it's easy (enough) for her to say that!; **à ton a.!** suit yourself!; **prendre ses aises** to make oneself at

home
  2 *adj Litt* **être bien** *ou* **tout a. de faire qch** to be delighted to do sth
aisé, -e [eze] *adj* (**a**) *(financièrement)* comfortably off (**b**) *(tâche, mouvements)* easy
aisément [ezemã] *adv* easily
aisselle [ɛsɛl] *nf* armpit
Aix-la-Chapelle [ɛkslaʃapɛl] *n* Aachen, Aix-la-Chapelle
AJ [aʒi] *nf (abrév* **auberge de jeunesse**) youth hostel
ajonc [aʒɔ̃] *nm* gorse
ajouré, -e [aʒure] *adj (pull)* loose-knit; *(broderie, en architecture)* openwork
ajourner [aʒurne] *vt (réunion, décision, voyage)* to postpone, to put off; *(après le début de la séance)* to adjourn; *Scol (candidat)* to refer
ajout [aʒu] *nm* addition (à to)
ajouter [aʒute] **1** *vt* to add (à to); *Ordinat (à une base de données)* to append
  2 ajouter à *vt ind* to add to
  3 s'ajouter *vpr* **s'a. à** to be added to; **à ceci viennent s'a. les frais de déplacement** on top of this there are travel expenses (to be added)
ajustable [aʒystabl] *adj* adjustable
ajustage [aʒystaʒ] *nm* fitting
ajuster [aʒyste] **1** *vt* (**a**) *(régler) (appareil, outil)* to adjust; *(chapeau, coiffure)* to adjust; **a. le tir** to aim (**b**) *(adapter)* to fit (à to); *(vêtement)* to alter; **veste ajustée** fitted jacket
  2 s'ajuster *vpr* (**a**) *(personne)* to straighten one's clothes (**b**) *(s'adapter)* **s'a. à** to fit; **s'a. sur** to fit onto
ajusteur [aʒystœr] *nm* fitter
alaise [alɛz] *nf* undersheet
alambic [alãbik] *nm* still
alambiqué, -e [alãbike] *adj* convoluted
alangui, -e [alãgi] *adj* languid
alarmant, -e [alarmã, -ãt] *adj* alarming; **son état est a.** his condition is giving serious cause for concern
alarme [alarm] *nf* alarm; **donner/sonner l'a.** to give/ sound the alarm; **une fausse a.** a false alarm; **a. antivol** car alarm; **a. incendie** fire alarm
alarmer [alarme] **1** *vt* to alarm
  2 s'alarmer *vpr* to get alarmed; **il n'y a pas lieu de s'a.** there is no cause for alarm
albanais, -e [albanɛ, -ɛz] **1** *adj* Albanian
  2 *nm,f* **A.** Albanian
  3 *nm (langue)* Albanian
Albanie [albani] *nf* **l'A.** Albania
albâtre [albɑtr] *nm* alabaster
albatros [albatros] *nm* albatross
albinos [albinos] *adj & nmf* albino
album [albɔm] *nm* album; **a. de timbres/de photos** stamp/photo album
albumen [albymɛn] *nm Biol* albumen
albumine [albymin] *nf Chim* albumin
alcalin, -e [alkalɛ̃, -in] *adj Chim* alkaline
alchimie [alʃimi] *nf* alchemy
alchimiste [alʃimist] *nm* alchemist
alcolo [alkɔlo] *Fam* **1** *nmf* drunk, alky
  2 *adj* **être a.** to be a drunk
alcool [alkɔl] *nm* (**a**) *Chim* alcohol; **a. à 90°** *Br* surgical spirit, *Am* rubbing alcohol; **a. à brûler** methylated spirits (**b**) *(digestif)* liqueur; **l'a.** *(boissons alcoolisées)* alcohol; **il ne tient pas l'a.** he can't hold his drink; **l'a. au volant** drink-driving; **a. de poire** pear brandy

alcoolémie [alkɔlemi] *nf* **taux d'a.** blood alcohol level
alcoolique [alkɔlik] **1** *nmf* alcoholic
  2 *adj* alcoholic; **être a.** to be an alcoholic
alcoolisé, -e [alkɔlize] *adj* alcoholic
alcoolisme [alkɔlism] *nm* alcoholism
Alcotest® [alkɔtɛst] *nm* breath test; **faire passer un A. à qn** to breathalyze sb
alcôve [alkov] *nf* recess *(for bed)*
aléa [alea] *nm* hazard
aléatoire [aleatwar] *adj* random; *(résultat)* uncertain
alémanique [alemanik] *adj* **la Suisse a.** German-speaking Switzerland
ALENA [alena] *nm (abrév* **Accord de libre-échange nord-américain**) **l'A.** NAFTA
alentour [alãtur] **1** *adv* around, round about; **les villages a.** the surrounding villages
  2 alentours *nmpl (voisinage)* surroundings; **aux alentours** in the vicinity; **aux alentours de la ville/ 300 euros** in the vicinity of the town/300 euros; **aux alentours de midi** *(some time)* around midday
Aléoutiennes [aleusjɛn] *adj & nfpl* **les (îles) A.** the Aleutian Islands
alerte [alɛrt] **1** *nf* (**a**) *(avertissement)* alarm; **donner/ sonner l'a.** to give/sound the alarm; **a. à la bombe** bomb scare (**b**) *(menace)* threat; *(problème de santé)* scare; **à la première a.** at the first sign of danger; **fausse a.** false alarm
  2 *adj (personne) (physiquement)* sprightly; *(mentalement)* alert; *(esprit, style)* lively; **d'un pas a.** at a brisk pace
  3 *(exclam)* look out!
alerter [alɛrte] *vt* to alert (**sur** to)
alèse [alɛz] = alaise
alevin [alvɛ̃] *nm* young fish
Alexandre [alɛksɑ̃dr] *npr* **A. le Grand** Alexander the Great
Alexandrie [alɛksɑ̃dri] *n* Alexandria
alexandrin [alɛksɑ̃drɛ̃] *nm* alexandrine
alezan, -e [alzɑ̃, -an] **1** *adj (cheval)* chestnut
  2 *nm* chestnut (horse)
algèbre [alʒɛbr] *nf* algebra
algébrique [alʒebrik] *adj* algebraic
Alger [alʒe] *n* Algiers
Algérie [alʒeri] *nf* **l'A.** Algeria
algérien, -enne [alʒerjɛ̃, -ɛn] **1** *adj* Algerian
  2 *nm,f* **A.** Algerian
algérois, -e [alʒerwa, -az] **1** *adj* of Algiers
  2 *nm,f* **A.** person from Algiers
algorithme [algɔritm] *nm Math & Ordinat* algorithm; *Ordinat* **a. de tri** sorting algorithm
algothérapie [algoterapi] *nf* = alternative medicine based on marine plant extracts
algue [alg] *nf* piece of seaweed; **algues** seaweed
alias [aljas] *adv* alias
alibi [alibi] *nm* alibi
aliénation [aljenasjɔ̃] *nf* (**a**) *(de l'esprit)* alienation; *Psy* **a. mentale** insanity (**b**) *(de liberté)* loss; *Jur (des droits, de biens)* alienation
aliéné, -e [aljene] **1** *adj* insane
  2 *nm,f* insane person
aliéner [34] [aljene] **1** *vt* (**a**) *(personne)* to alienate; **ce commentaire vous a aliéné la sympathie de l'auditoire** you lost the audience's sympathy when you made that comment (**b**) *Jur (biens, droits)* to alienate
  2 s'aliéner *vpr* **s'a. la sympathie de l'électorat** to

lose the goodwill of the electorate; **s'a. un ami** to alienate a friend

alignement [aliɲəmɑ̃] *nm* (**a**) *(opération)* alignment, aligning; *Pol (sur un pays, une politique)* alignment (**sur** with) (**b**) *(ligne)* line; **être dans l'a. de qch** to be in line with sth (**c**) *(de monolithes)* = line of standing stones

aligner [aliɲe] **1** *vt* (**a**) *(mettre en ligne)* to align, to line up; *(politique, monnaie)* to align (**sur** with) (**b**) *(mettre à la suite) (arguments)* to reel off; **je passe ma journée à a. des chiffres** I spend my day producing lists of figures

2 s'aligner *vpr (se mettre en rang)* to line up; *Pol (sur un pays, une politique)* to align oneself (**sur** with); *Fam* **tu peux toujours t'a.!** not a chance!

aliment [alimɑ̃] *nm* (**a**) *(nourriture)* food (**b**) *Jur* **aliments** alimony

alimentaire [alimɑ̃tɛr] *adj* (**a**) *(plante)* edible; **habitudes alimentaires** eating habits; **l'industrie a.** the food industry (**b**) *Fig* **ce n'est qu'un travail a.** I just do this job to keep body and soul together

alimentation [alimɑ̃tasjɔ̃] *nf* (**a**) *(régime alimentaire)* diet; **avoir une a. équilibrée** to have a balanced diet; **(magasin d')a.** grocer's; **(rayon) a.** grocery department (**b**) *(action) (de personne, de plante, d'animal)* feeding; *(d'une ville, d'un marché)* supply; **l'a. d'une ville en eau** the water supply to a town (**c**) *Tech (d'une chaudière)* feeding; *(en électricité)* power supply; **a. papier** *(d'une imprimante)* sheetfeed, paper feed

alimenter [alimɑ̃te] **1** *vt (personne, plante, animal, chaudière)* to feed; *(cours d'eau)* to flow into; *Fin (compte)* to pay money into; *Fig (conversation)* to keep going; *(sentiment)* to fuel; **a. une usine en courant** to supply a factory with power

2 s'alimenter *vpr* to eat

alinéa [alinea] *nm* (**a**) *(renfoncement)* indent (**b**) *(texte)* paragraph

aliter [alite] **s'aliter** *vpr* to take to one's bed; **être alité** *(temporairement)* to be confined to one's bed; *(grabataire)* to be bedridden

alizé [alize] *adj & nm* **les (vents) alizés** the trade winds

Allah [ala] *npr* Allah

allaitement [alɛtmɑ̃] *nm* feeding; *(d'un animal)* suckling; **a. au biberon** bottle-feeding; **a. maternel** breast-feeding

allaiter [alete] *vt (enfant)* to breast-feed; *(sujet: animal)* to suckle; **est-ce que vous allaitez?** are you breast-feeding?

allant [alɑ̃] *nm* **avoir de l'a., être plein d'a.** to be full of energy

alléchant, -e [aleʃɑ̃, -ɑ̃t] *adj (offre)* tempting; *(odeur, plat)* appetizing

allécher [34] [aleʃe] *vt* to tempt

allée [ale] *nf* (**a**) *(dans un jardin)* path; *(devant une résidence)* driveway; *(dans une ville)* avenue; *(dans un supermarché, un cinéma)* aisle (**b**) **allées et venues** coming(s) and going(s); **faire des allées et venues** to go back and forth

allégation [alegasjɔ̃] *nf* allegation

allégé, -e [aleʒe] *adj (en matières grasses)* low-fat; *(en sucre)* low-sugar

allègement [alɛʒmɑ̃] *nm* (**a**) *(d'impôts, de charges)* reduction; *(des emplois du temps scolaires)* streamlining; **a. fiscal** tax relief (**b**) *(d'un véhicule, d'un fardeau)* lightening

alléger [59] [aleʒe] *vt* (**a**) *(impôts, charges)* to reduce; *(douleur, chagrin)* to soothe (**b**) *(véhicule, fardeau)* to lighten; *(emploi du temps scolaire)* to streamline

allégorie [alegɔri] *nf* allegory

allégorique [alegɔrik] *adj* allegorical

allègre [alɛgr] *adj* lively, cheerful; **d'un ton a.** cheerfully, light-heartedly; **d'un pas a.** with a spring in one's step

allègrement [alɛgrəmɑ̃] *adv* cheerfully; *(marcher)* with a spring in one's step; **il m'a a. refilé ses enfants pour le week-end** he blithely palmed his children off on me for the weekend

allégresse [alegrɛs] *nf* joy; **a. générale** general rejoicing

alléluia [aleluja] *nm & exclam Rel* hallelujah

Allemagne [almaɲ] *nf* **l'A.** Germany; *Anciennement* **l'A. de l'Ouest/de l'Est** West/East Germany

allemand, -e [almɑ̃, -ɑ̃d] **1** *adj* German

2 *nm,f* **A.** German; *Anciennement* **A. de l'Est/de l'Ouest** East/West German

3 *nm (langue)* German

aller¹ [8] [ale] *(aux* **être***)* **1** *vi* (**a**) *(se déplacer)* to go; **a. à Toulon** to go to Toulon; **ce train va à Lille** this train goes to Lille; **a. à la pêche** to go fishing; **a. et venir** to come and go

(**b**) *(sujet: chemin, route)* **a. à** to go to

(**c**) *(arriver)* **a. jusqu'à** *(dans l'espace)* to go as far as; *(dans le temps)* to last until; **jusqu'où ira-t-il?** *(pour atteindre son but)* to what lengths will he go?; **a. jusqu'à faire qch** to go so far as to do sth

(**d**) *(fonctionner)* to go; *(bien fonctionner)* to go well; **si tu touches à mes affaires, ça va a. mal!** touch my things and there'll be trouble!; **ça va (comme ça), merci** *(à table)* that's enough, thanks; **je vous en offre 100 euros, ça va?** I'll give you 100 euros for it, OK?; *Fam* **non mais ça va pas(, la tête)!** are you crazy?

(**e**) *(se porter)* **a. bien/mal** to be well/ill; **comment allez-vous?** how are you?; **ça va? – ça va!** how's things? – OK!

(**f**) *(indique le but)* **a. faire qch** to go and do sth; **a. se coucher** to go to bed; **a. se promener** to go for a walk; **va voir!** go and see!; **n'allez pas vous imaginer que...** don't you go thinking that...; **cet imbécile est allé tout lui raconter** that fool went and told him everything

(**g**) *(convenir)* **a. à qn** to suit sb; **a. bien à qn** *(vêtement, couleur)* to look good on sb; **a. (bien) avec qch** *(vêtement, couleur)* to go (well) with sth, to match sth; *Fam* **ça lui va mal de donner des conseils** he's a fine one to be giving advice

(**h**) *(se ranger, s'adapter)* **où vont les couteaux?** where do the knives go *or* belong?; **un plat qui va au four** an ovenproof dish

(**i**) *(agir)* **il est allé un peu vite dans cette affaire** he was a bit hasty; *Fam* **vas-y doucement** take it easy; *Fam* **comme tu y vas!** that's a bit much!

(**j**) *(locutions)* **y a.** *(partir)* to go; *(commencer)* to get on with it; **allez!** *(pour encourager)* come on!; *(pour consoler)* come now!; **allons!** *(pour encourager, réprimander)* come on!; **ça passera, va** don't worry, you'll get over it; **va pour 1000 euros/mardi prochain** 1,000 euros/next Tuesday, that's fine; **a. de soi** to be obvious; **a. sur ses quarante ans** to be nearing forty

2 *v aux* (**a**) *(indique le futur proche)* **a. faire qch** to be going to do sth; **il va s'en occuper** he's going to deal with it; **j'allais m'endormir quand...** I was about

to fall asleep when...
(**b**) *(indique la progression)* **a. en empirant** to be getting worse and worse
3 *v impersonnel* **il en va de même pour moi/lui** it's the same for me/him
4 s'en aller *vpr* (**a**) *(personne)* to go (away) (**b**) *(tache)* to come out; *(couleur)* to fade; *(peinture)* to flake off

aller² *nm* (**a**) *(trajet)* outward journey; **à l'a.** on the way there (**b**) *(billet)* **a. (simple)** *Br* single (ticket), *Am* one-way ticket; **a. (et) retour** *Br* return *or Am* round-trip (ticket); *Fam Fig* **un a. et retour** *(gifle)* a slap on the face

allergie [alɛrʒi] *nf* allergy; **avoir** *ou* **faire une a. à qch** to be allergic to sth

allergique [alɛrʒik] *adj aussi Fig* allergic (**à** to)

allergologiste [alɛrgɔlɔʒist], **allergologue** [alɛrgɔlɔg] *nmf Méd* allergist

alliage [aljaʒ] *nm (métallique)* alloy

alliance [aljɑ̃s] *nf* (**a**) *(entente)* alliance; *(d'un couple)* marriage; **parent par a.** relative by marriage (**b**) *(bague)* wedding ring (**c**) *(combinaison)* *(de parfums, de couleurs)* combination (**d**) **l'A. française** = organization promoting French language and culture abroad

> **Alliance française**
>
> In many respects, the activities of the Alliance française are similar to those of the British Council, although it is a private body. It organizes classes in French language and civilization and has branches all over the world.

allié, -e [alje] **1** *nm,f (partisan)* ally; **parents et alliés** extended family; *Hist* **les Alliés** the Allies
2 *adj* (**a**) *(nation)* allied (**b**) *Hist* Allied

allier [66] [alje] **1** *vt* (**a**) *(pays)* to ally; *(familles)* to unite by marriage (**b**) *(métaux)* to alloy; *(couleurs)* to combine; **a. l'intelligence à la beauté** to combine intelligence and beauty
2 s'allier *vpr* (**a**) *(s'unir)* to become allies (**avec** with); **s'a. contre qn/qch** to unite against sb/sth (**b**) *(goûts, parfums, couleurs)* to combine

alligator [aligatɔr] *nm* alligator

allitération [aliterasjɔ̃] *nf* alliteration; **a. en s** alliteration of the letter s

allô, allo [alo] *exclam* hello!

allocation [alɔkasjɔ̃] *nf* (**a**) *(d'argent, de terres)* allocation; *(de titres financiers)* allotment (**b**) *(prestation financière)* allowance; **les allocations (familiales)** child benefit; **a. (de) chômage** unemployment benefit; **a. (de) logement** housing benefit

allocs [alɔk] *nfpl Fam* child benefit

allocution [alɔkysjɔ̃] *nf* address

allongé, -e [alɔ̃ʒe] *adj* (**a**) *(forme, silhouette)* elongated; **avoir le visage a.** to have a long face (**b**) *(couché)* **être a.** to be lying down

allongement [alɔ̃ʒmɑ̃] *nm* (**a**) *(agrandissement)* lengthening (**b**) *(dans le temps)* extension; **a. de l'espérance de vie** increase in life expectancy

allonger [45] [alɔ̃ʒe] **1** *vt* (**a**) *(rendre plus long)* to lengthen; *(vêtement)* to let down; *(sauce)* to thin (down); **cette robe allonge la silhouette** this dress makes you look taller
(**b**) *(bras)* to stretch out; *(cou)* to crane; **a. le pas** to quicken one's pace; *Sport* **a. l'allure** to increase the pace
(**c**) *(personne)* to lie down

(**d**) *(vacances, délai)* to extend
(**e**) *Fam* **a. une gifle à qn** to give sb a slap; **a. le fric/1000 euros** to hand over the money/1,000 euros
2 *vi (jours)* to get longer
3 s'allonger *vpr* (**a**) *(ombres, jours)* to get longer; *Fig (enfant)* to grow (**b**) *(se coucher)* to lie down; *Fam* **s'a. (par terre)** *(tomber)* to fall flat on the ground

allopathie [alɔpati] *nf Méd* allopathy

allouer [alwe] *vt* **a. qch à qn** *(salaire, indemnité, délai)* to grant sb sth; *(actions, ration)* to allocate sb sth

allumage [alymaʒ] *nm (d'un feu)* lighting; *(d'une lampe)* switching on; *(d'un moteur)* ignition

allume-cigare *(pl* **allume-cigares)** [alymsigar] *nm* cigar lighter

allume-gaz [alymgaz] *nm inv* gas lighter

allumer [alyme] **1** *vt* (**a**) *(cigarette, briquet, feu)* to light; *(lampe, télévision, électricité)* to switch on, to turn on; *(incendie)* to start; **a. (la lumière)** to switch *or* turn the light on; **a. le salon** to switch *or* turn the light on in the lounge; **laisser la cuisinière allumée** to leave the cooker on (**b**) *Fig (passions)* to arouse; *Fam (séduire)* to tease
2 s'allumer *vpr (lumière, lampe, téléviseur)* to come on; **où est-ce que ça s'allume?** where does it switch *or* turn on?

allumette [alymɛt] *nf* match

allumeuse [alymøz] *nf Fam* tease

allure [alyr] *nf* (**a**) *(vitesse)* speed; **à toute a.** at top speed (**b**) *(démarche)* walk, gait; *(manière de se tenir)* bearing; **avoir de l'a.** to be stylish; **avoir fière a.** to cut a fine figure; **avoir une drôle d'a.** to look funny; **avoir des allures de malfrat** to look like a crook; *Belg* **n'avoir pas d'a.** to be unsophisticated (**c**) *Can* **avoir d'a.** *(être vraisemblable)* to be likely

allusion [alyzjɔ̃] *nf* allusion (**à** to); **faire a. à** to refer to, to allude to

alluvial, -e, -aux, -ales [alyvjal, -o] *adj* alluvial

alluvions [alyvjɔ̃] *nfpl* alluvium

almanach [almana] *nm* almanac

aloès [alɔɛs] *nm* aloe

aloi [alwa] *nm* **de bon a.** *(succès)* deserved; *(plaisanterie)* in good taste; **de mauvais a.** *(succès)* undeserved; *(plaisanterie)* in bad taste

alors [alɔr] *adv* (**a**) *(à ce moment-là)* then; *(dans ce cas)* then, in that case; **jusqu'a.** (up) until then; **le ministre d'a.** the minister at the time; **et a.?** so what?; **et a., qu'est-ce qu'il a répondu?** so what did he say?; *Fam* **a., tu viens?** so are you coming?; *Fam* **non mais a., pour qui il se prend, celui-là?** really, just who does he think he is?; *Fam* **ça a.!** blimey!; **a. là, il exagère!** he's going a bit far there!
(**b**) *(donc)* so; **il n'était pas là, a. je suis revenu** he wasn't there, so I came back
(**c**) **a. que** *(au moment où)* when; *(bien que)* even though; **il a une maison, a. que moi j'habite dans un appartement** he's got a house, whereas I live in a flat

alouette [alwɛt] *nf* lark

alourdir [alurdir] **1** *vt (chose)* to make heavier; *Fig (phrase)* to make cumbersome; *(charges sociales)* to increase
2 s'alourdir *vpr* to get heavy; *(taille)* to get bigger

aloyau, -x [alwajo] *nm* sirloin

alpaga [alpaga] *nm* alpaca

alpage [alpaʒ] *nm* mountain pasture

alpaguer [alpage] *vt très Fam* to collar; **se faire a. par qn** to get collared by sb

Alpes [alp] *nfpl* **les A.** the Alps; **les A. suisses** the Swiss Alps

alphabet [alfabɛ] *nm* alphabet

alphabétique [alfabetik] *adj* alphabetical

alphabétiquement [alfabetikmɑ̃] *adv* alphabetically

alphabétisation [alfabetizasjɔ̃] *nf* teaching of literacy

alphanumérique [alfanymerik] *adj* alphanumeric

alphapage [alfapaʒ] *nm* bleeper

alpin, -e [alpɛ̃, -in] *adj* alpine

alpinisme [alpinism] *nm* mountaineering, climbing; **faire de l'a.** to go mountaineering *or* climbing

alpiniste [alpinist] *nmf* mountaineer, climber

Alsace [alzas] *nf* **l'A.** Alsace

alsacien, -enne [alzasjɛ̃, -ɛn] **1** *adj* of Alsace, Alsatian
   2 *nm,f* **A.** Alsatian

altercation [altɛrkasjɔ̃] *nf* altercation

alter ego [altɛrego] *nm inv* alter ego

altérer [34] [altere] **1** *vt* (**a**) *(détériorer) (viande, vin)* to spoil; *(santé)* to damage (**b**) *(changer)* to affect
   2 s'altérer *vpr (denrée)* to spoil, to go off; *(sentiment, amitié)* to deteriorate

alternance [altɛrnɑ̃s] *nf* alternation; *Pol* change of government; **en a.** alternately

alternateur [altɛrnatœr] *nm Élec* alternator

alternatif, -ive [altɛrnatif, -iv] **1** *adj* (**a**) *(successif)* & *Élec* alternating (**b**) *(de remplacement)* alternative
   2 *nf* alternative alternative

alternativement [altɛrnativmɑ̃] *adv* alternately, in turn

alterner [altɛrne] **1** *vt (cultures)* to rotate
   2 *vi (se succéder)* to alternate (**avec** with); *(personnes)* to take turns (**avec** with)

altesse [altɛs] *nf* **son A. royale** His/Her Royal Highness

altier, -ère [altje, -ɛr] *adj* haughty

altimètre [altimɛtr] *nm* altimeter

altitude [altityd] *nf* altitude; **à basse/haute a.** at low/high altitude; **à 100 mètres d'a.** at an altitude of 100 metres; **en a.** at altitude; **prendre de l'a.** to climb

alto [alto] *Mus* **1** *nm (instrument)* viola
   2 *nf (chanteuse)* alto

altruisme [altrɥism] *nm* altruism

altruiste [altrɥist] *adj* altruistic

aluminium [alyminjɔm] *nm* aluminium

alunir [alynir] *vi* to land on the moon

alunissage [alynisaʒ] *nm* moon landing

alvéole [alveɔl] *nf (de ruche)* cell; *(pulmonaire)* alveolus; *(de dent)* socket

amabilité [amabilite] *nf* kindness; **auriez-vous l'a. de me le faire savoir?** would you be so kind as to let me know?

amadouer [amadwe] *vt* to coax

amaigrir [amegrir] **1** *vt* to make thin; **la maladie l'a beaucoup amaigri** he's much thinner following his illness
   2 s'amaigrir *vpr* to get thinner

amaigrissant, -e [amegrisɑ̃, -ɑ̃t] *adj (régime)* slimming

amaigrissement [amegrismɑ̃] *nm (involontaire)* weight loss; *(volontaire)* slimming

amalgame [amalgam] *nm* combination

amalgamer [amalgame] *vt (confondre)* to lump together

amanché, -e [amɑ̃ʃe] *adj Can* **mal a.** badly dressed

amande [amɑ̃d] *nf (fruit)* almond; *(dans un noyau)* kernel; **des yeux en a.** almond(-shaped) eyes

amandier [amɑ̃dje] *nm* almond tree

amanite [amanit] *nf* **a. phalloïde** death cap; **a. tuemouches** fly agaric

amant [amɑ̃] *nm* lover

amarrage [amaraʒ] *nm Naut* mooring

amarre [amar] *nf Naut* (mooring) rope; **rompre ses amarres** to break its moorings

amarrer [amare] *vt Naut* to moor

amaryllis [amarilis] *nf* amaryllis

amas [ama] *nm* heap, pile

amasser [amase] **1** *vt* to amass
   2 s'amasser *vpr (preuves, foule)* to build up; *(neige)* to pile up; *(troupes)* to mass

amateur [amatœr] **1** *nm* (**a**) *(passionné)* **a. de tennis/de jardinage** tennis/gardening enthusiast; **a. d'art** art lover; **a. de bons vins** connoisseur of fine wines; *Fig* **est-ce qu'il y a des amateurs?** any takers?; **avis aux amateurs!** anyone interested? (**b**) *(non professionnel)* amateur; **faire de la photo en a.** to be an amateur photographer; *Péj* **c'est du travail d'a.** it's amateurish work
   2 *adj* amateur; **photographe a.** amateur photographer

amateurisme [amatœrism] *nm* amateurism

Amazone [amazon] *nf* **l'A.** the Amazon

amazone [amazon] *nf* (**a**) *(dans la mythologie)* **les Amazones** the Amazons (**b**) *(cavalière)* horsewoman; **monter en a.** to ride side-saddle

Amazonie [amazɔni] *nf* **l'A.** the Amazon (Basin)

amazonien, -enne [amazɔnjɛ̃, -ɛn] *adj* Amazonian; *(forêt)* Amazon

ambages [ɑ̃baʒ] **sans ambages** *adv* without beating about the bush

ambassade [ɑ̃basad] *nf* embassy; **l'a. de France au Japon** the French embassy in Japan

ambassadeur, -drice [ɑ̃basadœr, -dris] **1** *nm,f* ambassador; **l'a. de France au Japon** the French ambassador to Japan; *Fig* **être l'a. de son pays** to be an ambassador for one's country
   2 *nf* **ambassadrice** *(épouse)* ambassador's wife

ambiance [ɑ̃bjɑ̃s] *nf* atmosphere, ambience; *Fam* **mettre de l'a.** to liven things up; *Fam* **il y a de l'a. ici** there's a good atmosphere here

ambiant, -e [ɑ̃bjɑ̃, -ɑ̃t] *adj (gaieté, enthousiasme)* pervading; **température ambiante** room temperature

ambidextre [ɑ̃bidɛkstr] *adj* ambidextrous

ambigu, -uë [ɑ̃bigy] *adj* ambiguous

ambiguïté [ɑ̃bigɥite] *nf* ambiguity; **répondre sans a.** to give an unambiguous answer

ambitieux, -euse [ɑ̃bisjø, -øz] **1** *adj* ambitious
   2 *nm,f* ambitious person

ambition [ɑ̃bisjɔ̃] *nf* ambition; **avoir de l'a.** to be ambitious; **j'ai l'a. de devenir médecin** my ambition is to be a doctor

ambitionner [ɑ̃bisjɔne] *vt* (**a**) *(poste)* to aspire to; **il ambitionne de gagner le Tour de France** his ambition is to win the Tour de France (**b**) *Can (exagérer)* to overdo it

ambivalent, -e [ɑ̃bivalɑ̃, -ɑ̃t] *adj* ambivalent

ambre [ãbr] *nm (résine)* amber
ambulance [ãbylãs] *nf* ambulance
ambulancier, -ère [ãbylãsje, -ɛr] *nm,f* ambulance-man, *f* ambulancewoman
ambulant, -e [ãbylã, -ãt] *adj* itinerant, travelling; *Fam* **c'est un dictionnaire a.** he's a walking dictionary
AME [aɛmə] *nm (abrév* **accord monétaire européen)** EMA
âme [ɑm] *nf* (**a**) *Rel & Phil* soul; *Fig (animateur)* moving spirit; **être artiste dans l'â.** to have an artistic temperament; **rendre l'â.** to give up the ghost; **aller comme une â. en peine** to wander around like a lost soul; **trouver l'â. sœur** to find one's soul mate; **de toute mon â.** with all my heart; **en mon â. et conscience** to the best of my knowledge and belief (**b**) *(personne)* **une bonne â.** a kind soul; **ils ne rencontrèrent â. qui vive** they didn't meet a (living) soul; **un hameau de cinquante âmes** a hamlet of fifty inhabitants; **â. damnée** devoted servant; *Hum* partner in crime (**c**) *(d'un câble)* core
amélioration [ameljɔrasjɔ̃] *nf* improvement; **apporter des améliorations à qch** to make improvements to sth
améliorer [ameljɔre] **1** *vt* to improve
  2 s'améliorer *vpr* to improve; **ça ne s'améliore pas** it's not getting any better
amen [amɛn] *nm inv* amen; *Fig* **dire a. à qch** to go along with sth
aménagement [amenaʒmã] *nm (changement)* adjustment; *(d'une pièce)* conversion (**en** into); *(d'une ville, d'une région)* development; **a. du temps de travail** flexibility of working hours; **a. du territoire** regional development, physical planning
aménager [45] [amenaʒe] *vt (changer)* to adjust; *(pièce, maison)* to convert (**en** into)
amende [amãd] *nf* (**a**) *(contravention)* fine; **avoir 200 euros d'a.** to get a 200 euro fine (**b**) **faire a. honorable** to apologize
amendement [amãdmã] *nm Pol* amendment
amender [amãde] **1** *vt* (**a**) *(loi, texte)* to amend (**b**) *Suisse (mettre une amende à)* to fine
  2 s'amender *vpr* to turn over a new leaf
amener [46] [amne] **1** *vt* (**a**) *(apporter)* to bring; **a. l'eau à ébullition** to bring the water to the boil; **a. qn à faire qch** to get sb to do sth; *(sujet: circonstances)* to lead sb to do sth; **... ce qui nous amène à parler du chômage** ... which brings us to the issue of unemployment (**b**) *(occasionner)* to bring about (**c**) *(tirer à soi)* to pull in; *(voile)* to lower
  2 s'amener *vpr Fam (arriver)* to turn up; **amène-toi!** come here!
amenuiser [amənɥize] **1** *vt* to wear down
  2 s'amenuiser *vpr* to dwindle; *(écart)* to get smaller
amer, -ère [amɛr] *adj* bitter
amèrement [amɛrmã] *adv* bitterly
américain, -e [amerikɛ̃, -ɛn] **1** *adj* American
  2 *nm,f* **A.** American
  3 *nm (langue)* American (English)
  4 *nf* **américaine** *Culin* **homard à l'américaine** = lobster cooked in a tomato, white wine and brandy sauce
américaniser [amerikanize] **1** *vt* to Americanize
  2 s'américaniser *vpr* to become Americanized
américanisme [amerikanism] *nm Ling* Americanism
amérindien, -enne [amerɛ̃djɛ̃, -ɛn] **1** *adj* Amerindian, American Indian
  2 *nm,f* **A.** Amerindian, American Indian

Amérique [amerik] *nf* **l'A.** America; **l'A. centrale** Central America; **l'A. latine** Latin America; **l'A. du Nord/du Sud** North/South America
Amerloque [amɛrlɔk] *nmf Fam* American
amerrir [amerir] *vi* to make a landing at sea; *(vaisseau spatial)* to splash down
amerrissage [amerisaʒ] *nm* landing at sea; *(d'un vaisseau spatial)* splashdown
amertume [amɛrtym] *nf* bitterness
améthyste [ametist] *nf* amethyst
ameublement [amœbləmã] *nm* (**a**) *(action de meubler)* furnishing (**b**) *(meubles)* furniture; **magasin d'a.** furniture shop
ameuter [amøte] *vt (gens)* to bring out; **elle va a. tout le voisinage si elle continue à hurler comme ça!** she'll have the whole neighbourhood out if she carries on shouting like that!
ami, -e [ami] **1** *nm,f* friend; (**petit**) **a.** *(amant)* boyfriend; (**petite**) **amie** *(maîtresse)* girlfriend; **a. d'enfance** childhood friend; **a. intime** close friend; **les amis des bêtes** animal lovers
  2 *adj* friendly; **être a. avec qn** to be friends with sb
amiable [amjabl] *Jur* **1** *adj* amicable
  2 à l'amiable *adv* out of court
amiante [amjãt] *nm* asbestos
amical, -e, -aux, -ales [amikal, -o] **1** *adj* friendly; **peu a.** unfriendly
  2 *nf* **amicale** association
amicalement [amikalmã] *adv* in a friendly way
amidon [amidɔ̃] *nm* starch
amidonner [amidɔne] *vt* to starch
amieuter [amjøte] **s'amieuter** *vpr Can* to improve, to get better
amincir [amɛ̃sir] **1** *vt* to make thinner; **cette robe t'amincit** that dress makes you look thinner
  2 s'amincir *vpr* to get thinner
amincissant, -e [amɛ̃sisã, -ãt] *adj (produit, crème)* slimming
amincissement [amɛ̃sismã] *nm (d'une personne)* slimming
aminé, -e [amine] *adj Chim* **acide a.** amino acid
amiral, -aux [amiral, -o] *nm* admiral
amitié [amitje] *nf* (**a**) *(sentiment)* friendship; **avoir de l'a. pour qn** to like sb; **se lier d'a. avec qn** to make friends with sb; **prendre qn en a.** to befriend sb (**b**) *(dans les formules de politesse)* **faites-moi l'a. de le lui dire** would you be so kind as to tell him?; **mes amitiés à votre sœur** my best wishes to your sister; **amitiés, Luc** *(en fin de lettre)* regards *or* yours, Luc
amitieux, -euse [amitjø, -øz] *adj Belg* friendly
ammoniaque [amɔnjak] *nf* ammonia
amnésie [amnezi] *nf* amnesia; **souffrir d'a.** to have amnesia
amnésique [amnezik] **1** *adj* amnesic; **être a.** to have amnesia
  2 *nmf* amnesiac
amniocentèse [amnjosɛ̃tɛz] *nf Méd* amniocentesis
amniotique [amnjɔtik] *adj* amniotic
amnistie [amnisti] *nf* amnesty

Amnistie
Parking fines as well as some prison sentences are traditionally waived by the French president immediately after a presidential election. The latter is known as "la grâce présidentielle".

amnistier [66] [amnistje] *vt* to grant an amnesty to
amocher [amɔʃe] *Fam* **1** *vt (personne)* to beat up; *(objet)* to ruin; **se faire (sérieusement) a.** to get (badly) beaten up
  2 s'amocher *vpr* to smash oneself up
amoindrir [amwɛ̃drir] **1** *vt* to diminish
  2 s'amoindrir *vpr* to diminish
amollir [amɔlir] **1** *vt* to soften
  2 s'amollir *vpr* to soften
amonceler [11] [amɔ̃sle] **1** *vt* to pile up; *(preuves)* to accumulate
  2 s'amonceler *vpr* to pile up; *(preuves)* to accumulate
amoncellement [amɔ̃sɛlmɑ̃] *nm (pile)* heap, pile
amont [amɔ̃] *nm* upstream section; *aussi Ind* **en a. (de)** upstream (from); **la Seine en a. de Paris** the Seine above Paris
amoral, -e, -aux, -ales [amɔral, -o] *adj* amoral
amorçage [amɔrsaʒ] *nm* **(a)** *Ordinat* booting; **système d'a.** *(d'une bombe)* detonating system **(b)** *(pour pêcher)* baiting
amorce [amɔrs] *nf* **(a)** *(commencement)* beginning **(b)** *(détonateur)* detonator; *(d'une petite arme)* cap; **pistolet à amorces** cap gun **(c)** *(appât)* bait
amorcer [16] [amɔrse] **1** *vt* **(a)** *(commencer)* to begin **(b)** *Ordinat* to boot (up); **a. de nouveau** to reboot **(c)** *(bombe)* to arm **(d)** *(hameçon)* to bait
  2 s'amorcer *vpr* **(a)** *(commencer)* to begin; *(tendance)* to develop **(b)** *Ordinat* to boot (up)
amorphe [amɔrf] *adj* lifeless, apathetic
amortir [amɔrtir] *vt* **(a)** *(bruit)* to deaden; *(chute)* to break; *(choc)* to absorb; *(au football)* to trap; *(au tennis)* to kill **(b)** *Fin (dette)* to pay off **(c)** *(rentabiliser)* **il a amorti sa nouvelle voiture en six mois** he recouped the cost of his new car in six months; **le matériel a été amorti dès la première année** the equipment started to pay for itself after the first year
amortissement [amɔrtismɑ̃] *nm* **(a)** *(de matériel)* depreciation **(b)** *(d'un bruit)* deadening; *(d'une chute)* breaking; *(d'un choc)* absorption **(c)** *Fin (d'une dette)* paying off
amortisseur [amɔrtisœr] *nm (d'une voiture)* shock absorber
amour [amur] **1** *nm* **(a)** *(sentiment)* love; **avec a.** lovingly; **être fou d'a. pour qn** to be madly in love with sb; **faire qch par a. pour qn** to do sth out of love for sb; **faire l'a. (avec)** to make love (with); **pour l'a. du Ciel!** for heaven's sake!; **l'a. maternel/filial** a mother's/child's love; **l'a. du prochain** love of one's neighbour; **le grand a.** true love **(b)** *(personne)* **mon a.** my love, my darling; **tu es un a.!** you're an angel!; **quel a. d'enfant!** what an adorable child!
  2 *nfpl* **amours** *(vie amoureuse)* love life; **à tes amours!** *(en buvant)* your health!, cheers!; *(quand on éternue)* bless you!
amouracher [amuraʃe] **s'amouracher** *vpr* **s'a. de qn** to become infatuated with sb
amourette [amurɛt] *nf* fling
amoureusement [amurøzmɑ̃] *adv* lovingly
amoureux, -euse [amurø, -øz] **1** *nm,f (amateur)* **un a. de** a lover of; **un a. de la nature** a nature lover
  2 *nm,f (petit ami, petite amie)* boyfriend, *f* girlfriend; **un couple d'a.** a pair of lovers
  3 *adj (soin, regard)* loving; **vie amoureuse** love life; **tomber a. (de)** to fall in love (with); **être a. de qn** to be in love with sb

amour-propre [amurprɔpr] *nm* self-respect, pride; **elle est blessée dans son a.** her pride is hurt
amovible [amɔvibl] *adj* detachable, removable; *Ordinat (disque dur)* removable
ampère [ɑ̃pɛr] *nm Élec* ampere
amphés [ɑ̃fe] *nfpl Fam* speed
amphétamine [ɑ̃fetamin] *nf* amphetamine
amphi [ɑ̃fi] *nm Fam* lecture hall *or* theatre
amphibie [ɑ̃fibi] *adj* amphibious
amphibien [ɑ̃fibjɛ̃] *nm Zool* amphibian
amphithéâtre [ɑ̃fitetr] *nm* **(a)** *(d'université)* lecture hall **(b)** *Archit* amphitheatre; **en a.** in a semicircle
amphore [ɑ̃fɔr] *nf* urn
ample [ɑ̃pl] *adj (robe, jupe)* full; *(geste)* sweeping; *Fig* **de plus amples renseignements** more detailed information; **jusqu'à plus a. informé** until further information is available
amplement [ɑ̃pləmɑ̃] *adv* amply, fully; **nous avons a. le temps** we have plenty of time; **c'est a. suffisant** it's more than enough
ampleur [ɑ̃plœr] *nf* **(a)** *(d'un vêtement)* fullness; *(d'un geste)* expansiveness **(b)** *(importance)* scale, extent; **prendre de l'a.** to grow in size
ampli [ɑ̃pli] *nm Fam* amp
amplificateur [ɑ̃plifikatœr] *nm* amplifier
amplification [ɑ̃plifikasjɔ̃] *nf (d'un son)* amplification; *(d'une tendance, d'un phénomène)* intensification
amplifier [66] [ɑ̃plifje] **1** *vt (son)* to amplify; *(tendance, phénomène)* to intensify
  2 s'amplifier *vpr (son)* to increase; *(tendance, phénomène)* to intensify
amplitude [ɑ̃plityd] *nf* **(a)** *(d'un désastre)* magnitude, scale **(b)** *(d'un geste)* expansiveness **(c)** *(variation)* range; **a. thermique** temperature range **(d)** *(d'une oscillation)* amplitude
ampoule [ɑ̃pul] *nf* **(a)** *(d'une lampe)* (light) bulb; **a. à baïonnette/vis** bayonet/screw-in light bulb **(b)** *(sur la peau)* blister **(c)** *(fiole)* phial
ampoulé, -e [ɑ̃pule] *adj* bombastic
amputation [ɑ̃pytasjɔ̃] *nf* amputation
amputer [ɑ̃pyte] *vt* to amputate; *Fig* to slash; **il fut amputé du bras gauche** his left arm was amputated
Amsterdam [amstɛrdam] *n* Amsterdam
amulette [amylɛt] *nf* amulet
amusant, -e [amyzɑ̃, -ɑ̃t] **1** *adj* amusing, funny; *(divertissant)* entertaining; *(bizarre)* weird
  2 *nm* **le plus a., c'est que...** the funniest thing is that...
amuse-gueule [amyzgœl] *nm inv* appetizer
amusement [amyzmɑ̃] *nm* amusement
amuser [amyze] **1** *vt* to amuse; **cette histoire m'a beaucoup amusé** I found the story very amusing; **si tu crois que ça m'amuse!** do you think I enjoy it?
  2 s'amuser *vpr (se distraire)* to amuse oneself; **bien s'a.** to have a good time; **s'a. avec qn** to play with sb; **s'a. à faire qch** to amuse oneself doing sth; **faire qch pour s'a.** to do sth for the fun of it
amuseur, -euse [amyzœr, -øz] *nm,f* entertainer
amygdales [amidal] *nfpl* tonsils; **se faire opérer des a.** to have one's tonsils out
an [ɑ̃] *nm* year; **l'an passé** *ou* **dernier** last year; **l'an prochain** next year; **tous les ans** every year; **tous les trois ans** every three years; **en l'an 2000** in the year 2000; **en l'an de grâce 1172** in the year of Our

Lord 1172; **dans trois ans** in three years' time, three years from now; **par an** per year; *Fin* per annum; **avoir dix ans** to be ten (years old); **bon an, mal an** on average over the years

anabolisant [anabɔlizɑ̃] *nm* anabolic steroid

anachronique [anakrɔnik] *adj* anachronistic

anachronisme [anakrɔnism] *nm* anachronism

anagramme [anagram] *nf* anagram

anal, -e, -aux, -ales [anal, -o] *adj* anal; *Psy* **stade a.** anal stage

analgésique [analʒezik] *nm* analgesic

anallergique [analɛrʒik] *adj* hypoallergenic

analogie [analɔʒi] *nf* analogy; **par a. avec** by analogy with

analogique [analɔʒik] *adj* (**a**) *(dictionnaire)* analogical (**b**) *Élec* analogue

analogue [analɔg] *adj* similar (**à** to)

analphabète [analfabɛt] **1** *adj* illiterate
   2 *nmf* illiterate person

analyse [analiz] *nf* (**a**) *(étude)* analysis; **en dernière a.** in the final analysis; **faire l'a. de qch** to analyse sth (**b**) *Méd* test; **a. de sang/d'urine** blood/urine test; **faire une a. de sang** to have a blood test (**c**) *Psy* (psycho)analysis; **faire une a.** to undergo analysis

analyser [analize] *vt* to analyse; *Méd (sang, urine)* to test

analyseur [analizœr] *nm Ordinat* **a. logique** logic analyser; *Ordinat* **a. syntaxique** parser

analyste [analist] *nmf Ordinat* analyst; *Psy* (psycho)analyst

analyste-programmeur *(pl* **analystes-programmeurs***)* [analistprɔgramœr] *nm Ordinat* systems analyst

analytique [analitik] *adj* analytical

ananas [anana(s)] *nm* pineapple

anarchie [anarʃi] *nf aussi Fig* anarchy

anarchique [anarʃik] *adj aussi Fig* anarchic

anarchisant, -e [anarʃizɑ̃, -ɑ̃t] *adj (discours)* advocating anarchy

anarchisme [anarʃism] *nm* anarchism

anarchiste [anarʃist] *adj & nmf* anarchist

anatomie [anatɔmi] *nf* anatomy

anatomique [anatɔmik] *adj* anatomical

ancestral, -e, -aux, -ales [ɑ̃sɛstral, -o] *adj* ancestral

ancêtre [ɑ̃sɛtr] *nmf* ancestor; *Fam (vieillard)* grand-dad, *f* grandma

anche [ɑ̃ʃ] *nf Mus* reed

anchois [ɑ̃ʃwa] *nm* anchovy

ancien, -enne [ɑ̃sjɛ̃, -ɛn] **1** *adj* (**a**) *(vieux)* old; **livre a.** antiquarian book; **meubles anciens** antique furniture; **dans l'a. temps** in the old days; **je suis plus a. que vous dans la profession** I've been in the profession longer than you (**b**) *(d'autrefois) (professeur, voisin)* former, old; *(voiture, maison)* old; **c'est un a. boxeur** he used to be a boxer; **a. combattant** *Br* ex-serviceman, *Am* veteran; **a. élève** former student; *Hist* **l'A. Régime** the Ancien Régime
   2 *nm* (**a**) *Rel & Pol* elder (**b**) **l'a.** *(meubles)* antiques; *(immobilier)* old(er) buildings
   3 *nm,f (par l'expérience)* **c'est un a. de la maison** he's been with the firm a long time

anciennement [ɑ̃sjɛnmɑ̃] *adv* formerly

ancienneté [ɑ̃sjɛnte] *nf* (**a**) *(âge)* age (**b**) *(expérience)* seniority; **avoir quinze ans d'a.** to have fifteen years' service; **être promu à l'a.** to be promoted by seniority

ancrage [ɑ̃kraʒ] *nm Naut* anchoring

ancre [ɑ̃kr] *nf* anchor; **lever l'a.** to weigh anchor; **jeter l'a.** to anchor

ancrer [ɑ̃kre] **1** *vt (navire)* to anchor; **cette idée est profondément ancrée en lui** this idea is firmly rooted in his mind
   2 s'ancrer *vpr Fig (idée, concept)* to become rooted

andalou, -se [ɑ̃dalu, -uz] **1** *adj* Andalusian
   2 *nm,f* **A.** Andalusian

Andalousie [ɑ̃daluzi] *nf* **l'A.** Andalusia

Andes [ɑ̃d] *nfpl* **les A.** the Andes

andorran, -e [ɑ̃dɔrɑ̃, -an] **1** *adj* Andorran
   2 *nm,f* **A.** Andorran

Andorre [ɑ̃dɔr] *nf* Andorra; **la principauté d'A.** the Principality of Andorra

Andorre-la-Vieille [ɑ̃dɔrlavjɛj] *n* Andorra la Vella

andouille [ɑ̃duj] *nf* (**a**) *Culin* = sausage made from pigs' intestines (**b**) *Fam (imbécile)* fool, twit; **faire l'a.** to play the fool

andouillette [ɑ̃dujɛt] *nf Culin* = small sausage made from pigs' intestines

androgyne [ɑ̃drɔʒin] *adj* androgynous

âne [ɑn] *nm* (**a**) *(animal)* donkey; **à dos d'â.** by donkey (**b**) *Fam (idiot)* ass; *(ignare)* dunce

anéantir [aneɑ̃tir] *vt (ville)* to destroy; *(armée)* to crush; *(espoirs)* to shatter; **la nouvelle l'a anéantie** she was staggered by the news

anéantissement [aneɑ̃tismɑ̃] *nm* (**a**) *(d'une ville, d'un empire)* destruction; *(d'un espoir)* shattering (**b**) *(abattement)* **dans un état d'a. total** completely crushed

anecdote [anɛkdɔt] *nf* anecdote

anecdotique [anɛkdɔtik] *adj* anecdotal

anémie [anemi] *nf* anaemia; **faire de l'a.** to have anaemia

anémique [anemik] *adj* anaemic; *Fig* feeble, weak

anémone [anemɔn] *nf* anemone; **a. de mer** sea anemone

ânerie [ɑnri] *nf (paroles)* stupid remark; *(acte)* stupid act; **dire des âneries** to talk rubbish; **faire des âneries** to behave stupidly

ânesse [ɑnɛs] *nf* she-ass

anesthésie [anɛstezi] *nf* anaesthesia; **être sous a.** to be under anaesthetic; **a. générale/locale** general/local anaesthetic

anesthésier [66] [anɛstezje] *vt* to anaesthetize

anesthésiste [anɛstezist] *nmf Br* anaesthetist, *Am* anesthesiologist

aneth [anɛt] *nm* dill

ange [ɑ̃ʒ] *nm aussi Fig* angel; **un visage d'a.** an angelic face; **mon a.** my darling *or* angel; **être aux anges** to be in seventh heaven; **un a. passe** someone must have walked over my grave; **a. gardien** guardian angel

angélique [ɑ̃ʒelik] **1** *adj* angelic
   2 *nf Culin* angelica

angine [ɑ̃ʒin] *nf* sore throat; **a. de poitrine** angina (pectoris)

angiome [ɑ̃ʒjom] *nm Méd* angioma

anglais, -e [ɑ̃glɛ, -ɛz] **1** *adj* English; *(britannique)* British
   2 *nm,f* **A.** Englishman, *f* Englishwoman; *(Britannique)* British man, *f* British woman; **les A.** the English; *(Britanniques)* the British
   3 *nm (langue)* English

4 *nf* **anglaise** (**a**) *Fam* **filer à l'anglaise** to slip away (**b**) **anglaises** *(boucles)* ringlets

angle [ãgl] *nm* (**a**) *(d'une pièce, d'une rue, d'une table)* corner; **elle fait l'a. avec la rue du Bac** it intersects the rue du Bac; **la maison qui fait l'a.** the house on the corner (**b**) *(point de vue)* angle (**c**) *(en géométrie)* angle; **a. droit** right angle; **se couper à angles droits** to cross at right angles; *Aut* **a. mort** blind spot

Angleterre [ãglətɛr] *nf* **l'A.** England; *(Grande-Bretagne)* Britain

anglican, -e [ãglikã, -an] *adj & nm,f* Anglican

anglicisme [ãglisism] *nm* Anglicism

anglo-américain, -e *(mpl* **anglo-américains,** *fpl* **anglo-américaines)** [ãgloamerikɛ̃, -ɛn] *adj* Anglo-American

anglo-irlandais, -e *(mpl* **anglo-irlandais,** *fpl* **anglo-irlandaises)** [ãgloirlãdɛ, -ɛz] *adj* Anglo-Irish

anglo-normand, -e *(mpl* **anglo-normands,** *fpl* **anglo-normandes)** [ãglonɔrmã, -ãd] *adj voir* **île**

anglophone [ãglofɔn] **1** *adj* English-speaking **2** *nmf* English speaker

anglo-saxon, -onne *(mpl* **anglo-saxons,** *fpl* **anglo-saxonnes)** [ãglosaksõ, -ɔn] **1** *adj* (**a**) *Hist* Anglo-Saxon (**b**) *(culture, civilisation etc)* Anglo-American, British and American **2** *nm,f* **A.** Anglo-Saxon; **les Anglo-Saxons** *(peuples)* British and American people; *Hist* the Anglo-Saxons

> **Anglo-saxon**
> Note that the adjective "anglo-saxon" and the noun "Anglo-Saxon" are often used in French to refer to British and American people, culture, customs etc: "la musique anglo-saxonne", "la littérature anglo-saxonne".

angoissant, -e [ãgwasã, -ãt] *adj (nouvelle)* distressing; *(attente)* agonizing; *(film, livre)* frightening; *(situation)* alarming

angoisse [ãgwas] *nf* anguish, distress; *Méd* **une crise d'a.** an anxiety attack; *Fam* **c'est l'a.!** what a drag!

angoissé, -e [ãgwase] **1** *adj* anxious **2** *nm,f* anxious person

angoisser [ãgwase] **1** *vt* **a. qn** to make sb anxious **2** *vi Fam* to worry, to get worked up **3 s'angoisser** *vpr* to get anxious; **s'a. pour un rien** to get worked up over nothing

Angola [ãgɔla] *nm* **l'A.** Angola

angolais, -e [ãgɔlɛ, -ɛz] **1** *adj* Angolan **2** *nm,f* **A.** Angolan

angora [ãgɔra] **1** *nm* (**a**) *(lapin)* angora rabbit; *(chat)* Persian cat (**b**) *(laine)* angora (wool) **2** *adj* angora

anguille [ãgij] *nf* eel; *Fig* **il y a a. sous roche** there's something going on

angulaire [ãgylɛr] *adj* angular

anguleux, -euse [ãgylø, -øz] *adj (visage)* angular; *(contours)* rugged

anicroche [anikrɔʃ] *nf* hitch, snag; **sans a.** without a hitch

animal, -e, -aux, -ales [animal, -o] **1** *nm aussi Fig* animal; **animaux de boucherie** animals raised for slaughter; **a. domestique** pet; **a. sauvage** wild animal **2** *adj* animal

animalerie [animalri] *nf Can* pet shop

animalier, -ère [animalje, -ɛr] *adj* **parc a.** safari park; **peintre a.** wildlife painter

animateur, -trice [animatœr, -tris] *nm,f* (**a**) *(de télé, de radio)* presenter (**b**) *(dans un club)* leader

animation [animasjõ] *nf* (**a**) *(vie)* life; **une ville pleine d'a.** a lively town; **parler avec a.** to speak animatedly; **mettre de l'a. dans une soirée** to liven up a party (**b**) *(divertissement)* event; **faire de l'a.** *(de centre aéré)* to be an entertainment officer; *(de télé, de radio)* to be a presenter (**c**) *Cin* animation (**d**) *Météo* **a. satellite** satellite picture

animé, -e [anime] *adj (personne, discussion)* lively, animated; *(rue, quartier)* busy, bustling

animer [anime] **1** *vt* (**a**) *(sujet: désir, ambition)* to drive; **être animé des meilleures intentions** to have the best of intentions (**b**) *(conversation, quartier, soirée)* to liven up (**c**) *(débat)* to conduct; *(jeu télévisé)* to present **2 s'animer** *vpr (personne)* to come to life; *(conversation, soirée)* to get more lively; *(visage)* to light up

animisme [animism] *nm* animism

animosité [animozite] *nf* animosity (**contre** towards), hostility (**contre** towards); **dire qch sans a.** to say sth calmly

anis [ani(s)] *nm (plante)* anise; **(sirop d')a.** aniseed cordial; **(graine d')a.** *(en cuisine)* aniseed; **à l'a.** aniseed-flavoured

anisette [anizɛt] *nf* anisette

Ankara [ãkara] *n* Ankara

ankylose [ãkiloz] *nf* stiffness, *Spéc* ankylosis

ankyloser [ãkiloze] **1** *vt* **être ankylosé** to be stiff **2 s'ankyloser** *vpr* to get stiff; *Fig (dans un métier, des habitudes)* to get into a rut

annales [anal] *nfpl* annals; **les a. du bac** = past baccalauréat examination papers (with sample answers); **a. de géographie/littéraires** geographical/literary review; *Fig* **ça restera dans les a.** it will go down in history

anneau, -x [ano] *nm* (**a**) *(cercle, bague)* ring; *(de chaîne)* link; **a. nuptial** *ou* **de mariage** wedding ring; **a. de rideau** curtain ring; **les anneaux** *(en gymnastique)* the rings (**b**) *(d'un serpent)* coil (**c**) *Astron* ring

année [ane] *nf* year; **Bonne A.!** Happy New Year!; **une a. de vacances** a year's holiday; **d'a. en a.** year by year; **les années 80** the 80s; **en quelle a....?** in what year...?; **l'a. prochaine/dernière** next/last year; **elle entre dans sa trentième a.** she's just turned twenty-nine; **entrer en troisième a. de médecine** to start the third year of one's medical course; **a. civile** calendar year; **a. comptable** *Br* accounting *or* financial year, *Am* fiscal year; **a. scolaire** school year; **a. universitaire** academic year

année-lumière *(pl* **années-lumière)** [anelymjɛr] *nf* light year; **à des années-lumière** *(étoile, planète)* light years away; *Fig* **nous sommes à des années-lumière l'un de l'autre** we're light years apart

annexe [anɛks] **1** *nf* (**a**) *(bâtiment)* annexe (**b**) *(de lettre)* enclosure; *(de livre, de rapport)* appendix; *(de projet de loi)* rider; *(de loi)* schedule; **en a. veuillez trouver...** please find enclosed... **2** *adj* (**a**) *(complémentaire) (pièces)* enclosed; *(revenus)* supplementary; *(industries)* subsidiary (**b**) *(mineur)* secondary

annexer [anɛkse] **1** *vt* (**a**) *(territoire)* to annex (**b**) *(document)* to append (**à** to); **pièces annexées** *(à une lettre)* enclosures **2 s'annexer** *vpr* **s'a. qch** to get hold of sth for oneself

annexion [anɛksjõ] *nf* annexation

annihilation [aniilasjõ] *nf (d'une ville, d'une armée)* annihilation; *(d'efforts, d'espoirs)* destruction

annihiler [aniile] *vt (ville, armée)* to annihilate; *(efforts, espoirs)* to destroy

anniversaire [anivɛrsɛr] **1** *nm (d'une naissance)* birthday; *(d'une victoire, d'une mort)* anniversary; **bon** *ou* **joyeux a.!** happy birthday!; **gâteau/carte d'a.** birthday cake/card; **a. de mariage** wedding anniversary
  2 *adj* anniversary; **date a.** anniversary

annonce [anɔ̃s] *nf* (**a**) *(déclaration)* announcement; *(par écrit)* notice; *(aux cartes)* declaration, bid; *Fig* sign, indication (**de** of) (**b**) *(publicitaire, de vente)* advert, advertisement; **passer une (petite) a. dans un journal** to put an advert in a newspaper; **petites annonces** *Br* small ads, *Am* want ads; **annonces classées** classified ads

annoncer [16] [anɔ̃se] **1** *vt* (**a**) *(déclarer)* to announce; **a. la nouvelle à qn** to tell sb the news (**b**) *(dans la presse) (soldes, exposition)* to advertise (**c**) *(indiquer)* to herald; **cela n'annonce rien de bon** things aren't looking too good (**d**) **a. qn** *(visiteur)* to show sb in; *(lors d'une occasion officielle)* to announce sb; **se faire a.** to give one's name
  2 s'annoncer *vpr* (**a**) *(prévenir de sa visite)* to announce one's arrival (**b**) *(situation)* **cela s'annonce bien/mal** things aren't looking too bad/good; **les négociations s'annoncent difficiles** the negotiations look like they're going to be difficult; **l'avènement de la démocratie s'annonce dans plusieurs pays** there are signs in several countries that democracy is on the way

annonceur [anɔ̃sœr] *nm (de publicité)* advertiser

annonciateur, -trice [anɔ̃sjatœr, -tris] *adj* **signes annonciateurs de crise** signs that a crisis is on the way

Annonciation [anɔ̃sjasjɔ̃] *nf* **l'A.** the Annunciation

annoncier [anɔ̃sje] *nm Can (feuille d'annonces)* advertisements page

annotation [anɔtasjɔ̃] *nf* annotation; **faire des annotations dans un texte** to annotate a text

annoter [anɔte] *vt* to annotate

annuaire [anɥɛr] *nm (d'un organisme)* yearbook; *(liste d'adresses)* directory; **l'a. du téléphone** *ou* **téléphonique** the telephone directory; **je suis dans l'a.** I'm in the (phone) book; **a. électronique** electronic telephone directory; **a. des marées** tide table

annuel, -elle [anɥɛl] *adj* annual, yearly

annuellement [anɥɛlmɑ̃] *adv* annually, yearly

annuité [anɥite] *nf* (**a**) *(sur un emprunt)* annual repayment (**b**) *Can & Suisse (rente)* annuity

annulaire [anɥlɛr] **1** *nm* ring finger
  2 *adj* annular, ring-shaped

annulation [anylasjɔ̃] *nf* (**a**) *(d'une commande, d'un rendez-vous, de vacances)* cancellation; *(d'une dette)* writing off; *(d'un mariage, d'un contrat)* annulment; *(d'un jugement)* quashing (**b**) *Ordinat* deletion; **a. d'entrée** *(commande)* cancel entry

annuler [anyle] **1** *vt* (**a**) *(commande, rendez-vous, vacances)* to cancel; *(dette)* to write off; *(mariage, contrat)* to annul; *(jugement)* to quash (**b**) *(remplacer)* to supersede (**c**) *Sport (but, essai)* to disallow
  2 s'annuler *vpr* to cancel each other out

anoblir [anɔblir] *vt* to ennoble

anode [anɔd] *nf Élec* anode

anodin, -e [anɔdɛ̃, -in] *adj (remarque)* harmless; *(personne)* insignificant; *(blessure, changement)* slight, minor; *(infection)* mild

anomalie [anɔmali] *nf* anomaly; *Méd* abnormality

ânon [anɔ̃] *nm* little donkey

ânonner [anɔne] *vt* to stumble through; **il a lu le poème en ânonnant** he read the poem haltingly

anonymat [anɔnima] *nm* anonymity; **garder l'a.** to remain anonymous

anonyme [anɔnim] *adj* anonymous; *Fig (décor, intérieur)* impersonal

anorak [anɔrak] *nm* anorak

anorexie [anɔrɛksi] *nf* anorexia; **faire de l'a.** to suffer from anorexia; **a. mentale** anorexia nervosa

anorexique [anɔrɛksik] *adj & nmf* anorexic

anormal, -e, -aux, -ales [anɔrmal, -o] **1** *adj* (**a**) *(non conforme)* abnormal; *(mentalement)* educationally subnormal; **il fait une chaleur anormale** it's abnormally hot (**b**) *(injuste)* unfair; **il est a. que tu sois si peu payé** it's unfair that you're paid so little
  2 *nm,f (mentalement)* educationally subnormal person

anormalement [anɔrmalmɑ̃] *adv* abnormally

ANPE [aɛnpeø] *nf (abrév* **Agence nationale pour l'emploi)** = French state employment agency; **pointer à l'A.** to sign on

anse [ɑ̃s] *nf* (**a**) *(d'une cruche, d'un panier)* handle (**b**) *(crique)* cove

antagonisme [ɑ̃tagɔnism] *nm* antagonism

antagoniste [ɑ̃tagɔnist] **1** *nmf* antagonist
  2 *adj (opinions, parties)* antagonistic

antalgique [ɑ̃talʒik] *adj & nm Méd* analgesic

antan [ɑ̃tɑ̃] **d'antan** *adj Litt* of yesteryear

antarctique [ɑ̃tarktik] **1** *nm* **l'A.** the Antarctic, Antarctica
  2 *adj* Antarctic

antécédent [ɑ̃tesedɑ̃] *nm* (**a**) **antécédents** *(d'une personne)* previous history, past record; **il y a des antécédents cancéreux dans ma famille** my family has a history of cancer; **avoir de bons/mauvais antécédents** to have a good/bad record; **antécédents médicaux** medical history (**b**) *Ling* antecedent

Antéchrist [ɑ̃tekrist] *nm* Antichrist

antédiluvien, -enne [ɑ̃tedilyvjɛ̃, -ɛn] *adj Hum* **ma télévision est antédiluvienne** my television is an antique

anténatal, -e, -als, -ales [ɑ̃tenatal] *adj Méd* antenatal

antenne [ɑ̃tɛn] *nf* (**a**) *(de radio)* aerial, antenna; *(d'un satellite, d'un robot)* antenna; **être à l'a.** to be on the air; **passer à l'a.** *(émission)* to be broadcast; *(personne)* to be on the television/radio; **rendre l'a.** to hand over; **à vous l'a.** over to you; **hors a.** off the air; **a. parabolique** *(satellite)* dish (**b**) *(d'un insecte)* antenna, feeler; *Fig* **avoir des antennes** *(de l'intuition)* to have a sixth sense (**c**) *Mil* **a. chirurgicale** field hospital (**d**) *(de société)* branch

antépénultième [ɑ̃tepenyltjɛm] *adj* antepenultimate

antérieur, -e [ɑ̃terjœr] *adj* (**a**) *(période)* former; *(date)* earlier; *(année)* previous; *(engagement)* prior; **tous ces événements sont antérieurs à la révolution** all these events took place before the revolution; **dans une vie antérieure** in a previous life (**b**) *(muscle)* anterior; *(membre)* fore

anthologie [ɑ̃tɔlɔʒi] *nf* anthology

anthracite [ɑ̃trasit] **1** *nm* (**a**) *(minerai)* anthracite (**b**) *(couleur)* charcoal grey
  2 *adj inv* charcoal grey

anthropologie [ɑ̃trɔpɔlɔʒi] *nf* anthropology

anthropologiste [ãtrɔpɔlɔʒist], **anthropologue** [ãtrɔpɔlɔg] *nmf* anthropologist

anthropophage [ãtrɔpɔfaʒ] **1** *nmf* cannibal **2** *adj* cannibalistic

anti- [ãti] *préf (contre)* anti-

antiadhésif, -ive [ãtiadezif, -iv] **1** *adj (revêtement, poêle)* nonstick **2** *nm* antiadhesive

antiaérien, -enne [ãtiaerjɛ̃, -ɛn] *adj* anti-aircraft

anti-âge [ãtiaʒ] *adj inv* anti-aging

antialcoolique [ãtialkɔlik] *adj (ligue)* temperance

antiatomique [ãtiatɔmik] *adj* antinuclear

antibactérien, -enne [ãtibakterjɛ̃, -ɛn] *adj* antibacterial

antibiotique [ãtibjɔtik] **1** *nm* antibiotic; **être sous antibiotiques** to be on antibiotics **2** *adj* antibiotic

antiblocage [ãtiblɔkaʒ] *adj inv Aut* **système a. (des roues)** anti-lock brakes

antibrouillard [ãtibrujar] *adj inv & nm Aut* **(phare) a.** fog lamp

antibruit [ãtibrɥi] *adj inv (mur)* soundproof; **lutte a.** noise abatement campaign

antibuée [ãtibɥe] *adj inv & nm Aut* **(dispositif) a.** demister

anticalcaire [ãtikalkɛr] *adj inv* **produit a.** *(pour machine à laver)* water softener

anticancéreux, -euse [ãtikãserø, -øz] *adj* **centre/ sérum a.** cancer hospital/serum

anticasseurs [ãtikasœr] *adj inv* **loi a.** = law banning violent behaviour during demonstrations

antichambre [ãtiʃãbr] *nf* waiting room, antechamber; *Fig* **dans les antichambres du pouvoir** on the fringes of power

antichar [ãtiʃar] *adj Mil* anti-tank

antichoc [ãtiʃɔk] *adj inv* shock-proof

anticipation [ãtisipasjɔ̃] *nf* anticipation; **payer par a.** to pay in advance; **littérature d'a.** science fiction; **film d'a.** science-fiction film

anticipé, -e [ãtisipe] *adj (paiement)* advance; *(départ, retour)* early; **avec mes remerciements anticipés** thanking you in advance

anticiper [ãtisipe] **1** *vt (réaction, réponse)* to anticipate; *(action)* to forestall; *(tendance, résultat d'élections)* to forecast; **j'anticipais déjà le pire** I was expecting the worst **2** *vi* to anticipate, to look *or* think ahead; *(en sport, aux échecs)* to anticipate what one's opponent will do next; **n'anticipons pas** let's not look too far ahead; **a. sur qch** to anticipate sth

anticlérical, -e, -aux, -ales [ãtiklerikal, -o] *adj & nm,f* anticlerical

anticoagulant, -e [ãtikɔagylã, -ãt] *adj & nm* anticoagulant

anticolonialiste [ãtikɔlɔnjalist] *adj* anti-colonialist

anticommunisme [ãtikɔmynism] *nm* anti-communism

anticommuniste [ãtikɔmynist] *adj & nmf* anti-communist

anticonceptionnel, -elle [ãtikɔ̃sɛpsjɔnɛl] *adj (pilule)* contraceptive

anticonformiste [ãtikɔ̃fɔrmist] *adj & nmf* non-conformist

anticonstitutionnel, -elle [ãtikɔ̃stitysjɔnɛl] *adj* unconstitutional

anticorps [ãtikɔr] *nm* antibody

anticyclone [ãtisiklon] *nm Météo* anticyclone

antidater [ãtidate] *vt* to backdate, to antedate

antidémocratique [ãtidemɔkratik] *adj* undemocratic

antidépresseur [ãtidepresœr] *adj m & nm* antidepressant; **être sous antidépresseurs** to be on antidepressants

antidérapant, -e [ãtiderapã, -ãt] *adj (pneu, route)* non-skid; *(semelle, tapis)* non-slip

anti-discriminatoire [ãtidiskriminatwar] *adj (mesures, politique)* anti-discriminatory

antidopage [ãtidɔpaʒ], **antidoping** [ãtidɔpiŋ] *adj inv Sport* **contrôle a.** drug(s) test

antidote [ãtidɔt] *nm aussi Fig* antidote (**contre** for)

anti-dumping [ãtidœmpiŋ] *adj inv (loi, législation)* anti-dumping

antiémeute [ãtiemøt] *adj inv* antiriot; **brigade a.** riot squad

antiesclavagiste [ãtiɛsklavaʒist] *adj* anti-slavery

antifasciste [ãtifaʃist] *adj* anti-fascist

antifongique [ãtifɔ̃ʒik] **1** *adj* fungicidal **2** *nm* fungicide

antigel [ãtiʒɛl] *nm* antifreeze

antigrippal, -e, -aux, -ales [ãtigripal, -o] *adj* anti-flu

antihéros [ãtiero] *nm* antihero

antihistaminique [ãtiistaminik] *adj & nm Méd* antihistamine

anti-inflammatoire [ãtiɛ̃flamatwar] *adj & nm Méd* anti-inflammatory

anti-inflationniste [ãtiɛ̃flasjɔnist] *adj* anti-inflationary

antillais, -e [ãtijɛ, -ɛz] **1** *adj* West Indian **2** *nm,f* **A.** West Indian

Antilles [ãtij] *nfpl* **les A.** the West Indies

antilope [ãtilɔp] *nf* antelope

antimatière [ãtimatjer] *nf Phys* antimatter

antimilitariste [ãtimilitarist] *adj & nmf* antimilitarist

antimite [ãtimit] *adj inv (produit)* moth-repellent; **bombe a.** moth spray **2** *nm* mothkiller

antinazi, -e [ãtinazi] *adj & nm,f* anti-Nazi

antinomie [ãtinɔmi] *nf* antinomy

antinucléaire [ãtinyklɛer] *adj* anti-nuclear

Antiope® [ãtjɔp] *n* = French teletext system, providing subtitles for the deaf

antioxydant, -e [ãtiɔksidã, -ãt] *adj & nm* antioxidant

antipathie [ãtipati] *nf* antipathy; **avoir** *ou* **éprouver de l'a. pour qn** to dislike sb

antipathique [ãtipatik] *adj* unpleasant; **il m'est très a.** I don't like him at all

antipelliculaire [ãtipelikylɛr] *adj* **shampooing a.** dandruff shampoo

antiphrase [ãtifraz] *nf Ling* antiphrasis

antipodes [ãtipɔd] *nmpl Géog* antipodes; **être aux a. de** to be on the other side of the world from; *Fig* to be the exact opposite of

antipoison [ãtipwazɔ̃] *adj inv Méd* **centre a.** poisons unit

antiprotéase [ãtiprɔteaz] *nf Méd* protease inhibitor

antiquaire [ãtikɛr] *nmf* antique dealer

antique [ãtik] *adj (de l'Antiquité)* ancient; *(mobilier)* antique; *Hum (voiture, télévision)* antiquated; **la Grèce/la Rome a.** ancient Greece/Rome

antiquité [ãtikite] *nf* (**a**) *Hist* **l'a. grecque/romaine** ancient Greek/Rome (**b**) **antiquités** *(meubles et objets anciens)* antiques; **magasin d'antiquités** antique shop (**c**) **antiquités** *(dans un musée)* antiquities

antirabique [ãtirabik] *adj Méd* anti-rabies

antiracisme [ãtirasism] *nm* anti-racism

antiraciste [ãtirasist] *adj & nm,f* anti-racist

antiradar [ãtiradar] *nm* anti-radar device

antireflet [ãtirəflɛ] *adj inv* non-reflecting; *Ordinat* non-reflecting, antiglare

antirides [ãtirid] *adj inv* anti-wrinkle

antirouille [ãtiruj] **1** *adj inv* rustproofing **2** *nm* rustproofing agent

antiroulis [ãtiruli] *adj Aut* **barre a.** anti-roll bar

anti-scintillements [ãtisɛ̃tijmã] *adj inv Ordinat* flicker-free

antisèche [ãtisɛʃ] *nf Fam* crib sheet

antisémite [ãtisemit] **1** *adj* anti-Semitic **2** *nmf* anti-Semite

antisémitisme [ãtisemitism] *nm* anti-Semitism

antiseptique [ãtisɛptik] *adj & nm* antiseptic

antisocial, -e, -aux, -ales [ãtisɔsjal, -o] *adj* antisocial

antispasmodique [ãtispasmɔdik] *adj & nm Méd* antispasmodic

antitabac [ãtitaba] *adj inv* **lutte** *ou* **campagne a.** anti-smoking campaign

antiterroriste [ãtitɛrɔrist] *adj* anti-terrorist

antithèse [ãtitɛz] *nf* antithesis; *Fig* **être l'a. de** to be the opposite of

antitrust [ãtitrœst] *adj inv Br* anti-monopoly, *Am* anti-trust

antivariolique [ãtivarjɔlik] *adj Méd* **vaccin a.** smallpox vaccine

antivenimeux, -euse [ãtivənimø, -øz] *adj Méd* anti-venin

antivol [ãtivɔl] **1** *adj inv (dispositif)* anti-theft **2** *nm* anti-theft device

antre [ãtr] *nm (caverne)* cave, cavern; *(d'animaux, de brigands)* den, lair; *Fig (d'une personne)* den

anus [anys] *nm* anus

Anvers [ãvɛr(s)] *n* Antwerp

anxiété [ãksjete] *nf* anxiety; **éprouver de l'a.** to feel anxious; **avec a.** anxiously

anxieux, -euse [ãksjø, -øz] **1** *adj* anxious, worried; **a. de faire qch** anxious to do sth **2** *nm,f* worrier

anxiolytique [ãksjɔlitik] *Méd* **1** *adj* anxiety-reducing **2** *nm* tranquillizer

AOC [aose] *nf (abrév* **appellation d'origine contrôlée)** = (guarantee of) high-quality wine from an identified vineyard

aorte [aɔrt] *nf* aorta

août [u(t)] *nm* August; **le quinze a.** *(fête)* Assumption Day; *voir aussi* **janvier**

aoûtat [auta] *nm Br* harvest mite, *Am* chigger

aoûtien, -enne [ausjɛ̃, -ɛn] *nm,f* August *Br* holidaymaker *orAm* vacationer

apache [apaʃ] **1** *nm* **A.** Apache **2** *adj* Apache

apaisant, -e [apɛzã, -ãt] *adj* soothing, calming

apaisement [apɛzmã] *nm (de la douleur)* alleviation; *(calme)* calm

apaiser [apeze] **1** *vt (personne)* to calm (down); *(douleur)* to soothe; *(faim)* to satisfy; *(soif)* to quench; *(craintes)* to allay **2 s'apaiser** *vpr (personne)* to calm down; *(vent, douleur, craintes)* to subside

apanage [apanaʒ] *nm* prerogative; **elle croit avoir l'a. de la sagesse** she thinks she has a monopoly on wisdom

aparté [aparte] *nm* (**a**) *Théât* aside; **en a.** in an aside (**b**) *(entre deux personnes)* private conversation; **en a.** in private

apartheid [aparted] *nm* apartheid

apathie [apati] *nf* apathy, listlessness

apathique [apatik] *adj* apathetic, listless

apatride [apatrid] **1** *adj* stateless **2** *nmf* stateless person

APEC [apɛk] *nf (abrév* **Association pour l'emploi des cadres)** = employment agency for executives and graduates

apercevoir [60] [apɛrsəvwar] **1** *vt* to see; *(soudain, rapidement)* to catch sight of; **laisser a. qch** to let sth show **2 s'apercevoir** *vpr* **s'a. de qch** *(comprendre, réaliser)* to realize *or* notice sth; **s'a. que...** to realize *or* notice that...; **sans s'en a.** inadvertently, without realizing it

aperçu [apɛrsy] *nm (idée générale)* general idea; *Ordinat* **a. avant impression** print preview

apéritif [aperitif] *nm* aperitif; **prendre l'a.** to have a drink before the meal

---

Apéritif

In France, the "apéritif", or "apéro", is an informal social ritual. It is quite usual to invite people for before-dinner drinks without actually providing dinner, or to arrange to meet someone in a café "pour l'apéritif" before going out for a meal.

---

apéro [apero] *Fam* = **apéritif**

apesanteur [apəzãtœr] *nf* weightlessness; **en (état d')a.** in weightless conditions

à-peu-près [apøprɛ] *nm inv* vague approximation; **il y a trop d'à. dans votre exposé** there is too much vagueness in your report

apeuré, -e [apœre] *adj* frightened, scared

apeurer [apœre] *vt* to frighten, to scare

aphasie [afazi] *nf Méd* aphasia

aphasique [afazik] *adj & nmf Méd* aphasic

aphone [afɔn] *adj Méd* voiceless; **elle était a. d'avoir trop crié** she'd lost her voice because she'd been shouting too much

aphorisme [afɔrism] *nm* aphorism; *Péj* platitude

aphrodisiaque [afrɔdizjak] *adj & nm* aphrodisiac

aphte [aft] *nm* mouth ulcer

aphteux, -euse [aftø, -øz] *adj* **fièvre aphteuse** foot-and-mouth disease

à-pic [apik] *nm inv* sheer face

apiculteur, -trice [apikyltœr, -tris] *nm,f* beekeeper

apiculture [apikyltyr] *nf* beekeeping

apitoiement [apitwamã] *nm* pity; **pas d'a.!** *(ne sois pas indulgent)* don't feel sorry for him/her/ etc!; *(sois sans pitié)* show no mercy!

apitoyer [32] [apitwaje] **1** *vt* **a. qn** to move sb to pity **2 s'apitoyer** *vpr* **s'a. sur (le sort de)** qn to feel sorry for sb; **s'a. sur soi-même** *ou* **sur son sort** to feel sorry for oneself

APL [apɛl] *nf (abrév* **Aide personnalisée au logement)** housing benefit

aplanir [aplanir] **1** *vt (bois)* to plane; *(route)* to level; *Fig (difficultés)* to iron out
2 s'aplanir *vpr (sol)* to level out

aplati, -e [aplati] *adj (ballon, nez)* flat; *(figure géométrique)* oblate

aplatir [aplatir] **1** *vt (objet)* to flatten; **a. qch à coups de marteau** to hammer sth flat
2 s'aplatir *vpr (coiffure)* to go flat; *(chapeau)* to get flattened; **s'a. contre un mur** to flatten oneself against a wall; *Fig* **s'a. devant qn** to grovel to sb

aplomb [aplɔ̃] *nm* **(a)** *(ligne droite)* perpendicularity; **mettre qch d'a.** to stand sth up straight; **les étagères ne sont pas d'a.** the shelves aren't level; **je ne me sens pas d'a. aujourd'hui** I'm feeling out of sorts today; **remettre qn d'a.** to perk sb up **(b)** *(assurance)* (self-)confidence; *Péj* nerve, cheek; *Péj* **il ne manque pas d'a.** he's got a nerve *or* a cheek

apnée [apne] *nf* **plonger en a.** to dive without breathing apparatus

apocalypse [apɔkalips] *nf* apocalypse; **l'A.** *(dans la Bible)* the Book of Revelation; *Fig* **une vision d'a.** an apocalyptic vision

apocalyptique [apɔkaliptik] *adj* apocalyptic

apogée [apɔʒe] *nm Astron* apogee; *Fig* **être à l'a. de sa carrière** to be at the height of one's career

apolitique [apɔlitik] *adj* apolitical

apollon [apɔlɔ̃] *nm (bel homme)* Adonis

apologie [apɔlɔʒi] *nf (défense)* apologia (**de** for); *(éloge)* eulogy; **faire l'a. de** *(défendre)* to (seek to) justify; *(louer)* to eulogize

apoplectique [apɔplɛktik] *adj & nmf Méd* apoplectic

apoplexie [apɔplɛksi] *nf Méd* apoplexy; **attaque d'a.** apoplectic seizure, stroke

a posteriori [aposterjɔri] *adv* with hindsight

apostolat [apostɔla] *nm (métier)* vocation

apostrophe [apostrɔf] *nf* **(a)** *(signe, figure de style)* apostrophe **(b)** *(interpellation)* rude remark

apostropher [apostrɔfe] **1** *vt (pour attirer l'attention)* to shout to; *(être impoli envers)* to shout at
2 s'apostropher *vpr* to shout at one another

apothéose [apoteoz] *nf (consécration)* crowning glory; **finir en a.** to end spectacularly

apothicaire [apotikɛr] *nm Vieilli* apothecary; *Fig* **tenir des comptes d'a.** to know where every penny goes

apôtre [apotr] *nm* apostle; *Fig* **se faire l'a. de qch** to become an advocate of sth

Appalaches [apalaʃ] *nmpl* **les (monts) A.** the Appalachians

apparaître [20] [aparɛtr] *(aux être)* **1** *vi* **(a)** *(devenir visible)* to appear; **il lui est apparu en rêve** he came *or* appeared to her in a dream **(b)** *(phénomène, espèce)* to appear **(c)** *(vérité, solution)* to become apparent **(d)** *(sembler)* to seem; **il m'apparaît comme le seul capable d'y parvenir** he seems to me to be the only person capable of doing it
2 *v impersonnel* **il apparaît que...** it appears (that)...

apparat [apara] *nm* pomp, show; **tenue d'a.** ceremonial dress; **en grand a.** with great pomp and ceremony

appareil [aparɛj] *nm* **(a)** *(instrument)* apparatus; **a. (dentaire)** *(correctif)* brace; *(dentier)* dentures; **appareils ménagers** household appliances; **a. (photographique),** **a. photo** camera; **a. photo numérique** digital camera
(b) *(téléphone)* telephone; **Paul à l'a.** Paul speaking *or* here; **qui est à l'a.?** who's speaking?

(c) *(avion)* aircraft, plane
(d) *(structure, système)* apparatus; **l'a. de la justice** the legal system; *Pol* **l'a. du parti** the party machine; **a. de production** *(industriel)* production facilities
(e) *Anat* system; **a. digestif** digestive system; **a. génital** genital system; **a. respiratoire** respiratory system
(f) *Litt ou Hum* **dans le plus simple a.** in one's birthday suit

appareillage [aparɛjaʒ] *nm* **(a)** *Naut* getting under way **(b)** *(matériel)* equipment; *Ind* plant

appareiller [apareje] *vi Naut* to get under way

apparemment [aparamɑ̃] *adv* apparently

apparence [aparɑ̃s] *nf* **(a)** *(aspect extérieur)* appearance, look; **un homme à l'a. négligée/soignée** an untidy-looking/a tidy-looking man; **en dépit des apparences** in spite of appearances **(b)** *(aspect trompeur)* **il ne faut pas se fier aux apparences** appearances can be deceptive; **il a l'air gentil, mais ce n'est qu'une a.** he seems nice, but it's only a façade; **en a.** outwardly; **pour sauver les apparences** to keep up appearances

apparent, -e [aparɑ̃, -ɑ̃t] *adj* **(a)** *(visible)* visible, apparent; **peu a.** hardly noticeable; **sans raison apparente** for no apparent reason **(b)** *(prétendu)* apparent; **sous cette apparente bonté se cache un grand égoïsme** beneath that kind exterior there lies great selfishness

apparenté, -e [aparɑ̃te] *adj* **(a)** *(par le mariage)* related; *(en rapport)* related, connected **(b)** *Pol* **candidat a. à un parti** = candidate who, though not a member of a party, can count on its support in an election

apparenter [aparɑ̃te] **s'apparenter** *vpr (ressembler)* to have something in common (**à** with)

appariteur [aparitœr] *nm (d'université)* porter

apparition [aparisjɔ̃] *nf* **(a)** *(manifestation)* appearance; **faire son a.** *(personne)* to make one's appearance **(b)** *(fantôme)* apparition; **avoir des apparitions** to see things

appartement [apartəmɑ̃] *nm Br* flat, *Am* apartment; *(dans un hôtel)* suite; **vivre en a.** to live in a flat; **les grands appartements** *(d'un château)* the state apartments

appartenance [apartənɑ̃s] *nf* belonging (**à** to); *(à un parti)* membership (**à** of)

appartenir [70] [apartənir] **appartenir à 1** *vt ind* **(a)** *(être possédé par)* to belong to **(b)** *(faire partie de)* *(club, parti, espèce)* to belong to, to be a member of; **elle appartient à une famille très riche** she comes from a very wealthy family
2 *v impersonnel* **il appartient au comité de prendre la décision** it is up to the committee to decide

appât [apɑ] *nm (de pêche)* bait; *Fig (du succès)* lure; **l'a. du gain** the lure of money

appâter [apɑte] *vt* **(a)** *(animaux)* to lure; *Fig (personne)* to entice **(b)** *(hameçon)* to bait

appauvrir [apovrir] **1** *vt* to impoverish
2 s'appauvrir *vpr* to get poorer; *(sol, langue)* to become impoverished

appeau, -x [apo] *nm* birdcall *(instrument)*

appel [apɛl] *nm* **(a)** *(invitation, sollicitation)* appeal; **faire a. à qn** to appeal to sb; *(plombier, médecin)* to send for sb; **faire a. à la générosité de qn** to appeal to sb's generosity; **cette formation fait a. à des connaissances commerciales** this training course calls for some knowledge of business; **faire a. à ses souvenirs** to search one's memory; **un a. à la révolte** a call to revolt; *Com* **lancer un a. d'offres** to invite bids

(**b**) *(cri)* call; **a. au secours** call for help; **faire un a. de phares à qn** to flash one's headlights at sb; *Fig* **a. du pied** veiled hint

(**c**) *(attirance)* call; **l'a. du large/de la nature** the call of the sea/of the wild; **a. d'air** *(courant d'air)* draught

(**d**) **a. (téléphonique)** (tele)phone call; **a. gratuit** *Br* Freefone® call, *Am* toll-free call; *Can* **a. à frais virés** reverse-charge call

(**e**) *(pour vérifier)* **faire l'a.** to have a roll call; *Scol* to take the register; **manquer/répondre à l'a.** to be absent/present

(**f**) *Jur* appeal; **faire a. d'une décision** to appeal against a decision; *Fig* **être sans a.** *(décision)* to be final

(**g**) *Typ* **a. de note** reference figure

(**h**) *(pour sauter)* take-off

(**i**) *Ordinat* call; *(de commande)* selection

appelé [apəle] *nm* (**a**) *Mil* conscript (**b**) *Fig* **il y a beaucoup d'appelés, mais peu d'élus** many are called, but few are chosen

appeler [9] [apəle] **1** *vt* (**a**) *(personne, chien)* to call (to); *(taxi)* to hail; **a. (qn) au secours** to call (to sb) for help; **il arrive qu'il appelle la nuit** he sometimes calls out in the night

(**b**) **a. qn (au téléphone)** to call sb, to ring sb (up); **a. un taxi/un médecin** to call *or* ring for a taxi/a doctor; **laisse-la a. la première** wait for her to call you

(**c**) *(faire venir)* to send for; *(ascenseur)* to call; **faire a. un médecin** to send for a doctor; **a. qn à faire qch** *(inviter)* to call on sb to do sth; *aussi Hum* **le devoir t'appelle** duty calls

(**d**) *(désigner)* to call

(**e**) **être appelé à faire qch** *(être destiné à)* to be destined to do sth; *(avoir l'obligation de)* to be called upon to do sth

(**f**) *(demander, réclamer)* *(solution, mesures)* to call for; *(critique)* to invite

2 en appeler à *vt ind* to appeal to

3 s'appeler *vpr* (**a**) *(avoir pour nom)* to be called; **comment vous appelez-vous?** what's your name?; **je m'appelle David** my name's David (**b**) *(se téléphoner)* to call each other; **alors, on s'appelle, hein?** talk to you on the phone, okay?

appellation [apelasjɔ̃] *nf* name; *(de produit)* designation; **a. contrôlée** *(de vin)* guaranteed vintage; **a. d'origine** = guarantee of wine quality

appendice [apɛ̃dis] *nm* (**a**) *Anat* appendix; *Zool & Bot* appendage (**b**) *(d'un livre)* appendix

appendicite [apɛ̃disit] *nf* appendicitis; **avoir l'a.** *ou* **une crise d'a.** to have appendicitis; **se faire opérer de l'a.** to have one's appendix out

appesantir [apəzɑ̃tir] **1** *vt* *(démarche)* to slow down; **les paupières appesanties par le sommeil** eyes heavy with sleep

2 s'appesantir *vpr (démarche)* to slow down; *Fig* **s'a. sur qch** *(sujet)* to dwell at length on sth

appétissant, -e [apetisɑ̃, -ɑ̃t] *adj (nourriture)* appetizing, tempting; *Hum (personne)* attractive

appétit [apeti] *nm* (**a**) *(de nourriture)* appetite; **couper l'a. à qn** to spoil sb's appetite; **donner de l'a. à qn, mettre qn en a.** to give sb an appetite; **perdre l'a.** to lose one's appetite; **manger de bon a.** to tuck in; **avoir un a. d'oiseau** to have a poor appetite; **avoir bon** *ou* **un gros a.** to have a good appetite; **bon a.!**

enjoy your meal!; *Prov* **l'a. vient en mangeant** it's only when you start eating that you realize you're hungry (**b**) *(désir)* *(de culture, de connaissances)* appetite (**de** for)

applaudimètre [aplodimɛtr] *nm* clapometer

applaudir [aplodir] **1** *vt* to applaud

2 *vi* to applaud, to clap

3 applaudir à *vt ind (décision, changement)* to applaud

applaudissements [aplodismɑ̃] *nmpl* applause, clapping; **un tonnerre** *ou* **une tempête d'a.** thunderous applause

applicable [aplikabl] *adj* applicable (**à** to)

applicateur [aplikatœr] *nm (dispositif)* applicator

application [aplikasjɔ̃] *nf* (**a**) *(de peinture, de pommade)* application (**b**) *(d'un règlement)* application; *(de la loi, d'une peine)* enforcement; **mettre une théorie en a.** to put a theory into practice; **mettre une loi en a.** to enforce a law; **entrer en a.** to come into force (**c**) *(emploi)* application (**d**) *(assiduité)* application; **travailler avec a.** to apply oneself to one's work (**e**) *Ordinat* application

applique [aplik] *nf (lampe)* wall light

appliqué, -e [aplike] *adj* (**a**) *(personne)* hard-working, diligent; *(écriture)* careful (**b**) *(sciences)* applied

appliquer [aplike] **1** *vt* (**a**) *(mettre)* to apply (**sur** to) (**b**) *(utiliser)* to apply (**à** to); *(loi, peine)* to enforce

2 s'appliquer *vpr* (**a**) *(se concentrer)* to apply oneself (**à** to); **s'a. à faire qch** to take pains to do sth (**b**) **s'a. à** *(concerner)* to apply to (**c**) *(se placer)* to be applied; **cette crème doit s'appliquer avant le coucher** this cream should be applied at bedtime

appoint [apwɛ̃] *nm* (**a**) *(monnaie)* exact money *or* change; **faire l'a.** to give the exact money (**b**) *(revenu supplémentaire)* extra income; **d'a.** *(chauffage, éclairage)* additional

appointements [apwɛ̃tmɑ̃] *nmpl* salary

apport [apɔr] *nm (contribution)* contribution (**à** to); *Fin* **a. en capital/numéraire** capital/cash contribution; **a. calorique** *(d'un aliment)* calorie content

apporter [apɔrte] *vt* (**a**) *(porter)* to bring (**à** to); *(capitaux)* to bring in; **je t'ai apporté la cassette vidéo** I've brought you the video (**b**) *(mettre)* **a. du soin à faire qch** to exercise care in doing sth (**c**) *(bonheur, soulagement)* to bring (**à** to); *(preuve)* to provide; *(changements)* to bring about; **ce travail ne m'apporte pas grand-chose** I don't get very much out of this work

apposer [apoze] *vt (affiche)* to put up; *(signature, scellés, sceau)* to affix (**à** to)

apposition [apozisjɔ̃] *nf* (**a**) *(d'un sceau, de scellés, de signature)* affixing (**à** to) (**b**) *Gram* apposition; **en a.** in apposition

appréciable [apresjabl] *adj* (**a**) *(visible)* appreciable, noticeable (**b**) *(non négligeable)* considerable, appreciable (**c**) *(agréable)* *(qualités)* praiseworthy; *(changement)* welcome

appréciation [apresjasjɔ̃] *nf* (**a**) *(évaluation)* valuation (**b**) *(opinion)* judgement, opinion; *(sur devoir scolaire)* comment; **laisser qch à l'a. de qn** to leave sth to sb's discretion (**c**) *(augmentation de valeur)* appreciation

apprécier [66] [apresje] **1** *vt* (**a**) *(température, distance, son)* to estimate; *(différences, nuances)* to appreciate; **tu ne l'apprécies pas à sa juste valeur** you don't appreciate her true worth (**b**) *(aimer)* to like; *Fam* **elle n'a pas apprécié** she wasn't too pleased

2 s'apprécier *vpr* (**a**) *(personnes)* to like each other (**b**) *(monnaie)* to appreciate

appréhender [apreɑ̃de] *vt* (**a**) *Jur (arrêter)* to arrest, to apprehend (**b**) *(craindre)* to dread; **a. de faire qch** to dread doing sth (**c**) *(comprendre)* to grasp

appréhensif, -ive [apreɑ̃sif, -iv] *adj* apprehensive

appréhension [apreɑ̃sjɔ̃] *nf (crainte)* apprehension (**de** about); **avoir une a.** to be apprehensive

apprendre [58] [aprɑ̃dr] **1** *vt* (**a**) *(leçon, langue, instrument de musique)* to learn; **a. à faire qch** to learn how to do sth; **a. vite/lentement** to be a fast/slow learner (**b**) *(nouvelle)* to hear; *(mort, mariage)* to hear of; **a. que...** to hear that... (**c**) *(enseigner)* **a. qch à qn** to teach sb sth; **a. à qn à faire qch** to teach sb how to do sth; *Fam* **je t'apprendrai à me parler sur ce ton!** I'll teach you to speak to me like that!; *Fam* **ça vous apprendra!** that'll teach you! (**d**) *(informer de)* **a. qch à qn** to tell sb sth; **vous ne m'apprenez rien!** you're telling me! (**e**) *Belg (former)* to train

2 s'apprendre *vpr* **ça s'apprend vite** it can be learned quickly; **ça s'apprend facilement** it's easy to learn

apprenti, -e [aprɑ̃ti] *nm,f* apprentice; **a. menuisier** carpenter's apprentice; *Fig* **jouer les apprentis sorciers** to bite off more than one can chew

apprentissage [aprɑ̃tisaʒ] *nm* (**a**) *(professionnel)* training; *(chez un artisan)* apprenticeship; **être en a. chez qn** to be apprenticed to sb (**b**) *(d'une matière, d'une langue)* **l'a. de qch** learning sth; *Fig* **faire l'a. de qch** to learn about sth

apprêté, -e [aprete] *adj (style, attitude)* affected

apprêter [aprete] **1** *vt* (**a**) *(repas)* to prepare (**b**) *(tissu, cuir)* to finish

2 s'apprêter *vpr (se préparer)* to get ready; **s'a. à faire qch** to get ready to do sth

apprivoisé, -e [aprivwaze] *adj* tame

apprivoiser [aprivwaze] **1** *vt (animal)* to tame; *Fig (personne)* to win over

2 s'apprivoiser *vpr (animal)* to become tame; *Fig (personne)* to become more sociable

approbateur, -trice [aprɔbatœr, -tris] *adj* approving

approbation [aprɔbasjɔ̃] *nf* approval (**de** of); **soumettre qch à l'a. de qn** to submit sth to sb for approval; **le film a reçu l'a. du public** the film was well received by the public; **pour a.** *(sur document)* for approval

approchant [aprɔʃɑ̃] *adj m* **je n'ai jamais rien vu d'a.** I've never seen anything like it; **voilà ce qu'il a dit ou quelque chose d'a.** that's what he said, or something similar

approche [aprɔʃ] *nf* (**a**) *(dans le temps)* approach; **à l'a. de la vieillesse** as old age draws/drew near; **aux approches de la trentaine elle a voulu avoir des enfants** as she approached thirty she wanted children (**b**) *(dans l'espace)* **à son a.** as she approached; *Fig* **d'une a. difficile** *(personne)* unapproachable; *(livre)* hard to understand (**c**) *(d'une question, d'un problème)* approach (**de** to) (**d**) **approches** *(d'une ville, d'un village)* outskirts (**e**) *Aviat* approach

approcher [aprɔʃe] **1** *vt* (**a**) *(mettre plus près)* to bring up; **a. qch de qn/qch** to bring sth near (to) sb/sth (**b**) *(venir près de)* to approach, to get closer to; *(aborder)* to go up to

2 *vi* (**a**) *(dans l'espace, dans le temps)* to approach, to get closer; **l'heure** *ou* **le moment approche** it will soon be time; **la nuit approchait** it was beginning to

get dark; **approche, je vais te montrer quelque chose** come (over) here, I've got something to show you; **a. de qn/qch** to approach sb/sth; **a. du but** to be nearing one's goal; **il approche de la trentaine** he's getting on for thirty (**b**) *Fig* **a. de qch** *(être semblable à)* to be close to sth

3 s'approcher *vpr* to approach, to get closer; **s'a. de qn/qch** to approach sb/sth; *Fig* **s'a. de qch** *(être semblable à)* to be close to sth

approfondi, -e [aprɔfɔ̃di] *adj (recherche)* detailed, extensive; *(connaissances, enquête)* thorough, in-depth

approfondir [aprɔfɔ̃dir] *vt (examiner)* to go thoroughly into

approprié, -e [aprɔprije] *adj* appropriate (**à** for)

approprier [66] [aprɔprije] **1** *vt Belg (nettoyer)* to clean; *(ranger)* to tidy

2 s'approprier *vpr* **s'a. qch** to appropriate sth

approuver [apruve] *vt* (**a**) *(décision, choix)* to approve of; **a. qn (d'avoir fait qch)** to think sb is right (to have done sth) (**b**) *(facture, contrat, projet de loi)* to approve

approvisionnement [aprɔvizjɔnmɑ̃] *nm* (**a**) *(ravitaillement)* *(d'une ville, d'une armée)* supplying (**en** with); *(d'un magasin)* stocking (**en** with) (**b**) **approvisionnements** *(stocks)* supplies

approvisionner [aprɔvizjɔne] **1** *vt* (**a**) *(ville, armée, personne)* to supply (**en** with); *(magasin)* to stock (**en** with) (**b**) *(compte bancaire)* to pay money into; **son compte en banque n'est plus approvisionné** his bank account is no longer in credit

2 s'approvisionner *vpr* to get in supplies (**en** of); **s'a. chez qn** to get one's supplies from sb; *(faire ses courses)* to shop at sb's

approximatif, -ive [aprɔksimatif, -iv] *adj (calcul, estimation)* approximate; **dans un anglais a.** in broken English

approximation [aprɔksimasjɔ̃] *nf* approximation

approximativement [aprɔksimativmɑ̃] *adv* approximately

appt *(abrév* **appartement**) *Br* flat, *Am* apartment

appui [apɥi] *nm* (**a**) *(support)* support; **prendre a. sur qch** *(personne)* to lean on sth; **prendre a. sur le pied gauche** *(pour sauter)* to take off from the left foot; **a. de fenêtre** window ledge *or* sill (**b**) *(moral)* support, backing; **à l'a. de qch** in support of sth; **preuves à l'a.** with supporting evidence

appui-tête *(pl* **appuis-tête**) [apɥitɛt] *nm* headrest

appuyé, -e [apɥije] *adj (plaisanterie, ironie)* laboured; **il lui lançait des regards appuyés** he stared at him intently

appuyer [32] [apɥije] **1** *vt* (**a**) *(poser)* to lean, to rest (**contre** against) (**b**) *(appliquer)* **a. qch sur qch** to press sth on sth; **a. le pied sur la pédale de frein** to put one's foot on the brake (**c**) *Fig (demande, pétition, candidat)* to support, to back; *(proposition)* to second

2 *vi* (**a**) *(presser)* to press; **a. sur un bouton** to press a button (**b**) **a. sur** *(accentuer)* *(mot, syllabe)* to stress; *Fig (insister)* to emphasize, to stress

3 s'appuyer *vpr* (**a**) *(reposer)* **s'a. sur/contre** to lean on/against; *Fig* **s'a. sur qch** *(être basé sur)* to be based on sth; *(se servir de)* to draw on sth (**b**) *Fam* **s'a. qch** *(corvée)* to get lumbered with sth

âpre [apr] *adj* (**a**) *(aigre)* bitter; *(vin)* rough (**b**) *(vent)* raw (**c**) *(concurrence)* fierce; **être â. au gain** to be money-grabbing

âprement [ɑprəmɑ̃] *adv* fiercely

après [aprɛ] **1** *prép* (**a**) *(dans le temps, dans l'espace)* after; **jour a. jour** day after day; **a. s'être rasé** after shaving; **a. vous, Monsieur/Madame!** after you!; *Fam* **courir a. qn** to run after sb; *Fig (faire la cour à)* to chase sb; **il est toujours a. moi** he's always nagging me; *Fam* **en avoir a. qn** to have it in for sb; **a. coup** after the event; **a. tout** after all (**b**) **d'a.** *(selon)* according to; **d'a. moi** in my opinion; **d'a. l'article 12** under article 12

2 *adv* afterwards; **six semaines a.** six weeks later; **a. que** after, when; **avec lui, la famille, ça passe a.** his family takes second place; **le jour d'a.** the next *or* following day; **et a.?** *(que s'est-il passé?)* what happened next?; *Fam* **et (puis) a.?** so what?

après- [aprɛ] *préf* post-; **l'a.-68** the post-1968 period; **l'a.-Gorbatchev** the post-Gorbachev era

après-demain [aprɛdəmɛ̃] *adv* the day after tomorrow

après-guerre (*pl* **après-guerres**) [aprɛgɛr] *nm* postwar period

après-midi [aprɛmidi] *nm inv ou nf inv* afternoon; **trois heures de l'a.** three (o'clock) in the afternoon

après-rasage (*pl* **après-rasages**) [aprɛrazaʒ] *nm & adj inv* aftershave

après-ski (*pl* **après-skis**) [aprɛski] *nm* snowboot

après-soleil [apresɔlej] *adj inv voir* **lait**

après-vente [aprɛvɑ̃t] *adj inv Com* **service a.** aftersales service

âpreté [ɑprəte] *nf* (**a**) *(aigreur)* bitterness; *(du vin)* roughness (**b**) *(du vent)* rawness (**c**) *(de la concurrence)* fierceness

a priori [aprijɔri] **1** *adv* in principle

2 *nm inv* preconception; **avoir des a. (contre/en faveur de qch)** to be prejudiced (against/in favour of sth); **être sans a.** to be impartial

apr. J.-C. *(abrév* **après Jésus-Christ**) AD; **en 55 apr. J.-C.** in 55 AD

à-propos [aprɔpo] *nm (d'une remarque, d'une réaction)* appropriateness; **avoir l'esprit d'à.** to have presence of mind; **répondre avec à.** to give an appropriate reply

apte [apt] *adj* **a. à qch/à faire qch** fit for sth/for doing sth; *Mil* **a. au service** fit for military service

aptitude [aptityd] *nf (capacité)* aptitude, ability (**à** *ou* **pour** for)

Aquagym® [akwaʒim] *nf* aquarobics *(singulier)*

aquaplanage [akwaplanaʒ], **aquaplaning** [akwaplaniŋ] *nm Aut* aquaplaning

aquarelle [akwarɛl] *nf* watercolour; **peindre à l'a.** to paint in watercolours

aquarelliste [akwarelist] *n* watercolourist

aquarium [akwarjɔm] *nm* aquarium

aquatique [akwatik] *adj* aquatic

aqueduc [akədyk] *nm* aqueduct

aqueux, -euse [akø, -øz] *adj Anat & Chim* aqueous; *(soupe)* watery

aquilin, -e [akilɛ̃, -in] *adj* aquiline

Aquitaine [akiten] *nf* **l'A.** Aquitaine

arabe [arab] **1** *adj (monde, littérature, pays)* Arab, Arabic; *(chiffres, langue)* Arabic; *(cheval)* Arab; *(coutumes, civilisation)* Arabian, Arabic

2 *nmf* **A.** Arab

3 *nm (langue)* Arabic

Arabe
Note that in a French context this word usually refers to people from the former colonies of North Africa, who make up the largest ethnic minority in France.

arabesque [arabɛsk] *nf* arabesque

arabica [arabika] *nm* arabica

Arabie [arabi] *nf* **l'A.** Arabia; **l'A. saoudite** Saudi Arabia

arable [arabl] *adj* arable

arachide [araʃid] *nf (plante)* peanut, groundnut; **huile d'a.** peanut *or* groundnut oil

araignée [areɲe] *nf* spider; *Fam* **avoir une a. au plafond** to have a screw loose; **a. de mer** spider crab

Aral [aral] *n voir* **mer**

arbalète [arbalɛt] *nf* crossbow

arbitrage [arbitraʒ] *nm* (**a**) *(au tennis)* umpiring; *(au football)* refereeing (**b**) *(dans un conflit)* arbitration

arbitraire [arbitrɛr] *adj* arbitrary

arbitrairement [arbitrɛrmɑ̃] *adv* arbitrarily

arbitre [arbitr] *nm* (**a**) *(au tennis)* umpire; *(au football)* referee (**b**) *(dans un conflit)* arbitrator (**c**) *Phil* **libre a.** free will

arbitrer [arbitre] *vt* (**a**) *(match de tennis)* to umpire; *(match de football)* to referee (**b**) *(dans un conflit)* to arbitrate

arborer [arbɔre] *vt (porter, exhiber)* to wear, to sport

arborescence [arbɔresɑ̃s] *nf Math & Ordinat* tree diagram

arborescent, -e [arbɔresɑ̃, -ɑ̃t] *adj* (**a**) *Bot* arborescent (**b**) *Math & Ordinat* **structure arborescente** tree diagram

arboriculteur, -trice [arbɔrikyltœr, -tris] *nm,f* tree grower

arboriculture [arbɔrikyltyr] *nf* tree growing

arbre [arbr] *nm* (**a**) *(végétal)* tree; *Fig* **les arbres cachent la forêt** you can't see the wood for the trees; **a. fruitier** fruit tree; **a. de Noël** Christmas tree (**b**) **a. généalogique** family tree; **faire son a. généalogique** to trace one's family tree (**c**) *Tech* shaft; **a. à cames** camshaft; **a. de transmission** transmission shaft

arbrisseau, -x [arbriso] *nm* shrub

arbuste [arbyst] *nm* shrub

arc [ark] *nm* (**a**) *(arme)* bow (**b**) *Archit & Anat* arch; **a. de triomphe** triumphal arch (**c**) *(de cercle)* arc; **assis en a. de cercle** sitting in a semicircle

arcade [arkad] *nf* (**a**) *Archit* archway; **arcades** *(d'une place)* arcade (**b**) *Anat* **a. sourcilière** arch of the eyebrows

arc-bouter [arkbute] **s'arc-bouter** *vpr* to brace oneself

arceau, -x [arso] *nm* (**a**) *(d'une voûte)* arch (**b**) *(au croquet)* hoop (**c**) *Aut* **a. de sécurité** roll bar

arc-en-ciel (*pl* **arcs-en-ciel**) [arkɑ̃sjɛl] *nm* rainbow

archaïque [arkaik] *adj* archaic

archaïsme [arkaism] *nm* archaism

archange [arkɑ̃ʒ] *nm* archangel

arche¹ [arʃ] *nf* **l'a. de Noé** Noah's ark

arche² *nf (d'un pont)* arch

archéologie [arkeɔlɔʒi] *nf* archaeology

archéologique [arkeɔlɔʒik] *adj* archaeological

archéologue [arkeɔlɔg] *nmf* archaeologist

archer [arʃe] *nm* archer

archet [arʃɛ] *nm* bow *(for violin)*

archétype [arketip] *nm* archetype; **c'est l'a. du père de famille** he is the archetypal father figure
archevêque [arʃəvɛk] *nm* archbishop
archiconnu, -e [arʃikɔny] *adj Fam* very well-known
archiduc [arʃidyk] *nm* archduke
archiduchesse [arʃidyʃɛs] *nf* archduchess
archifaux, -fausse [arʃifo, -fos] *adj Fam* dead wrong
Archimède [arʃimɛd] *npr* Archimedes
archipel [arʃipɛl] *nm* archipelago
architecte [arʃitɛkt] *nm* architect; *Ordinat* **a. de réseaux** network architect
architectural, -e, -aux, -ales [arʃitɛktyral, -o] *adj* architectural
architecture [arʃitɛktyr] *nf aussi Ordinat* architecture; *Fig* structure
architecturé, -e [arʃitɛktyre] *adj Ordinat* **a. autour de** with its architecture built around
archiver [arʃive] *vt (documents officiels)* to archive; *(factures)* to file
archives [arʃiv] *nfpl* archives, records; **les a. nationales** ≃ the (Public) Record Office
archiviste [arʃivist] *nmf* archivist; *(employé de bureau)* filing clerk
arçon [arsɔ̃] *nm* saddle bow
arctique [arktik] **1** *adj* arctic
 2 *nm* **l'A.** the Arctic
ardemment [ardamɑ̃] *adv (aimer)* passionately; **désirer a. qch** to long for sth
ardent, -e [ardɑ̃, -ɑ̃t] *adj* (a) *(braises, soleil)* scorching, blazing; *(soif, fièvre)* raging (b) *(tempérament, jeunesse)* fiery; *(désir)* burning; *(lutte, défenseur)* fierce; *(admirateur)* ardent, fervent
ardeur [ardœr] *nf* (a) *(enthousiasme)* ardour, fervour; **travailler avec a.** to work enthusiastically (b) *(du soleil, du feu)* intense heat
ardoise [ardwaz] *nf* (a) *(matière, plaque, pour écrire)* slate; **toit d'ardoises** slate roof (b) *Fam (compte)* tab; **il a des ardoises dans tous les bars de la ville** he owes money in every bar in town
ardu, -e [ardy] *adj* arduous
are [ar] *nm* are, = 100 m²
aréna [arena] *nf Can* = sports centre including an ice rink
arène [arɛn] *nf (d'amphithéâtre)* arena; *(de tauromachie)* bullring; **arènes** *(antiques)* amphitheatre; *Fig* **descendre dans l'a.** to enter the fray; *Fig* **l'a. politique** the political arena
arête [arɛt] *nf* (a) *(de poisson)* bone; **sans arêtes** boneless; **enlever les arêtes d'un poisson** to fillet a fish (b) *(du nez)* bridge (c) *(d'un solide)* edge (d) *Géog* ridge
argent [arʒɑ̃] **1** *nm* (a) *(métal)* silver; **bracelet d'a. ou en a.** silver bracelet (b) *(monnaie)* money; **en avoir pour son a.** to get one's money's worth; *Fig* **prendre qch pour a. comptant** to take sth at face value; *Prov* **l'a. ne fait pas le bonheur** money can't buy you happiness; *Prov* **l'a. n'a pas d'odeur** it's all money; **a. liquide** cash; **a. de poche** pocket money; **a. électronique, a. virtuel** e-cash, electronic money (c) *(couleur)* silver
 2 *adj inv* silver
argenté, -e [arʒɑ̃te] *adj* (a) *(couleur)* silver (b) *(plaqué)* silver-plated
argenterie [arʒɑ̃tri] *nf* (silver) plate, silverware

argentin, -e [arʒɑ̃tɛ̃, -in] **1** *adj* Argentinian, Argentine
 2 *nm,f* **A.** Argentinian, Argentine
Argentine [arʒɑ̃tin] *nf* **l'A.** Argentina
argile [arʒil] *nf* clay
argileux, -euse [arʒilø, -øz] *adj* clayey
argot [argo] *nm* slang

> **Argot**
> This term can refer both to "la langue verte" (the slang of the underworld) or the jargon of particular social or professional groups (such as butchers, soldiers, students etc). Some "argot" has evolved from being part of the secret language of a select group to becoming part of everyday speech, while other terms have become obsolete, supplanted by **verlan** (*see box at this entry*), the slang used by young people in the suburbs of big cities.

argotique [argɔtik] *adj* slang, slangy
arguer [arge, argɥe] **arguer de** *vt ind Litt* **a. de qch** to give sth as a reason
argument [argymɑ̃] *nm* argument; **a. de vente** selling point
argumentaire [argymɑ̃tɛr] *nm* sales blurb
argumentation [argymɑ̃tasjɔ̃] *nf (arguments)* argument
argumenter [argymɑ̃te] *vi* to argue (**contre/en faveur de** against/for)
argus [argys] *nm* = guide to used car prices
aria [arja] *nf Mus* aria
aride [arid] *adj (pays)* arid, barren; *(œuvre, sujet)* dry
aridité [aridite] *nf* aridity, barrenness
aristocrate [aristɔkrat] *nmf* aristocrat
aristocratie [aristɔkrasi] *nf* aristocracy
aristocratique [aristɔkratik] *adj* aristocratic
Aristote [aristɔt] *npr* Aristotle
arithmétique [aritmetik] **1** *adj* arithmetical
 2 *nf (matière, calculs)* arithmetic
arlequin [arləkɛ̃] *nm Théât* Harlequin
armagnac [armaɲak] *nm* Armagnac
armateur [armatœr] *nm* shipowner
armature [armatyr] *nf* framework; *(dans le béton)* reinforcement; *(de tente, d'abat-jour)* frame; *(de soutien-gorge)* underwiring
arme [arm] *nf* (a) *(de combat)* arm, weapon; *Fig* weapon; **peuple/ville en armes** nation/town in arms; **prendre les armes** to take up arms (**contre** against); **aux armes!** to arms!; **le métier ou la carrière des armes** the military profession; **passer qn par les armes** to send sb to the firing squad; *Fam* **passer l'a. à gauche** to snuff it, to kick the bucket; **faire ses premières armes** to earn one's spurs; **à armes égales** on equal terms; **avec armes et bagages** with bag and baggage; **a. blanche** knife; **a. à feu** firearm (b) *(section de l'armée)* service (c) **armes** *(blason)* (coat of) arms
armé, -e [arme] *adj* (a) *(muni d'une arme)* armed; **a. jusqu'aux dents** armed to the teeth; *aussi Fig* **être a. de qch** to be armed with sth; *Fig* **être a. pour qch** *(préparé)* to be equipped for sth (b) *(renforcé)* fortified, strengthened
armée [arme] *nf aussi Fig* army; **être dans l'a.** to be in the army; **être à l'a.** to be doing one's military service; **l'a. de l'air** the air force; **a. de métier** professional

army; **a. régulière** *ou* **active** regular army; **a. de réserve** reserves; **l'A. du salut** the Salvation Army; **l'a. de terre** the army

armement [armɔmɑ̃] *nm* (**a**) *(action) (d'un pays, d'une région)* armament; *(d'une armée)* arming (**b**) **armements** *(armes)* armaments, weaponry (**c**) *(d'une arme à feu)* cocking; *(d'un appareil photo)* setting (**d**) *(de navire)* commissioning, fitting out

Arménie [armeni] *nf* **l'A.** Armenia

arménien, -enne [armenjɛ̃, -ɛn] **1** *adj* Armenian
  2 *nm,f* **A.** Armenian
  3 *nm (langue)* Armenian

armer [arme] **1** *vt* (**a**) *(munir d'armes)* to arm (**de** with); **je sors toujours armé** I always carry a weapon when I go out (**b**) *(navire)* to commission, to fit out (**c**) *(arme à feu)* to cock; *(appareil photo)* to set
  2 s'armer *vpr* to arm oneself; **s'a. de courage/de patience** to summon up (one's) courage/patience

armistice [armistis] *nm* armistice

armoire [armwar] *nf (placard)* Br cupboard, *Am* closet; *(pour les vêtements)* Br wardrobe, *Am* closet; **a. à glace** mirrored wardrobe; *Hum* **c'est une a. à glace** he's built like a tank; **a. de toilette** *ou* **de salle de bain** bathroom cabinet

armoiries [armwari] *nfpl* (coat of) arms

armure [armyr] *nf* armour

armurier [armyrje] *nm* (**a**) *(vendeur)* gun dealer (**b**) *(dans une caserne)* armourer

ARN [aɛrɛn] *nm (abrév* **acide ribonucléique**) RNA

arnaque [arnak] *nf Fam* rip-off; **c'est de l'a.!** what a rip-off!

arnaquer [arnake] *vt Fam* to rip off; **se faire a.** to get ripped off

arnaqueur, -euse [arnakœr, -øz] *nm,f Fam* rip-off merchant

arnica [arnika] *nm ou nf* arnica

arobase [arobaz] *nf Ordinat* at (sign)

aromate [arɔmat] *nm (herbe)* herb; *(épice)* spice

aromathérapie [arɔmaterapi] *nf* aromatherapy

aromatique [arɔmatik] *adj* aromatic

aromatisé, -e [arɔmatize] *adj* flavoured; **a. à la vanille** vanilla-flavoured

arôme [arom] *nm (parfum)* aroma; *(goût)* flavour; **crème glacée, a. vanille** vanilla ice cream

arpège [arpɛʒ] *nm Mus* arpeggio

arpent [arpɑ̃] *nm* = former land measurement approximately equivalent to one acre

arpenter [arpɑ̃te] *vt* (**a**) *(mesurer)* to survey, to measure (**b**) *(parcourir)* to pace up and down

arqué, -e [arke] *adj (sourcils)* arched; *(nez)* hooked; **jambes arquées** bow legs

arquer [arke] **s'arquer** *vpr* to bend, to curve

arrachage [araʃaʒ] *nm (de plantes)* uprooting; *(de pommes de terre)* lifting; *(d'une dent, d'un clou, de piquets)* pulling out

arraché [araʃe] *nm (en haltérophilie)* snatch; *Fig* **gagner à l'a.** to snatch victory; *Fig* **ils ont obtenu le contrat à l'a.** it was a struggle for them to get the contract

arrachement [araʃmɑ̃] *nm (peine)* wrench

arrache-pied [araʃpje] **d'arrache-pied** *adv* relentlessly

arracher [araʃe] **1** *vt* (**a**) *(arbre)* to uproot; *(légumes)* to lift; *(dent, mauvaises herbes, piquets)* to pull out; *(page)* to tear out; *(affiche)* to tear down; *(vêtement, membre, toit)* to tear off; **se faire a. une dent** to have

a tooth out; **a. qch à qn/des mains de qn** to snatch sth from sb/from sb's hands; *Fig* **je vais lui a. les yeux!** I'll scratch his eyes out!
  (**b**) *(obtenir)* **a. qch à qn** *(argent)* to get sth off sb; *(secret)* to drag sth out of sb; *(promesse, sourire)* to force sth out of sb; *Fig* **nous sommes finalement parvenus à lui a. quelques mots** we did eventually manage to get a few words out of him
  (**c**) *(séparer)* **a. un enfant à sa mère** to take a child away from its mother; **a. qn à la mort** to snatch sb from the jaws of death; **a. qn à son travail** to tear *or* drag sb away from his work
  (**d**) *Fam (sujet: alcool, piment)* **ça arrache!** it brings tears to your eyes!
  2 *vi Can* **en a.** to have a hard time (of it)
  3 s'arracher *vpr* (**a**) *(se disputer)* **s'a. qn/qch** to fight over sb/sth
  (**b**) *(se retirer)* **c'est à s'a. les cheveux!** it's enough to make you tear your hair out!; **s'a. à son travail** to tear oneself away from one's work
  (**c**) *très Fam (partir)* to hit the road

arracheur [araʃœr] *nm* **mentir comme un a. de dents** to lie through one's teeth

arraisonner [arɛzɔne] *vt* to stop and examine

arrangeant, -e [arɑ̃ʒɑ̃, -ɑ̃t] *adj* helpful

arrangement [arɑ̃ʒmɑ̃] *nm* (**a**) *(fait de disposer)* arranging; *(manière d'être disposé)* arrangement (**b**) *(accord)* agreement, settlement (**c**) *Mus* arrangement

arranger [45] [arɑ̃ʒe] **1** *vt* (**a**) *(meubles, fleurs)* to arrange; *(pièce, maison)* to put in order; *(cravate, col)* to straighten
  (**b**) *(réparer)* to repair
  (**c**) *(organiser)* to arrange, to organize; **j'ai tout arrangé** I've made all the arrangements
  (**d**) *(régler) (problème)* to settle; **cela n'arrangera rien** that won't help things; *Ironique* **pour tout a., il s'est mis à pleuvoir** just to help matters, it started to rain
  (**e**) *Fam* **a. qn** *(maltraiter)* to give sb a going over; *(critiquer)* to tear sb to pieces
  (**f**) *(convenir à)* to suit; **faire qch pour a. qn** to do sth to help sb out
  (**g**) *Mus* to arrange
  2 s'arranger *vpr* (**a**) *(s'organiser)* to manage; **arrangez-vous pour être là/finir à temps** make sure you're there/you finish on time; *Fam* **je ne sais pas comment tu t'arranges, tu es toujours en retard** I don't know how you manage it, but you're always late
  (**b**) *(s'améliorer)* to work out; **ça ne s'arrange pas!** things aren't getting any better!
  (**c**) *(rectifier son apparence)* to tidy oneself up
  (**d**) *(se mettre d'accord)* to come to an agreement (**avec** with); **ça ne me regarde pas, arrange-toi avec elle** it's got nothing to do with me, sort it out with her
  (**e**) *(se contenter)* **s'a. de qch** to make do with sth

arrestation [arɛstasjɔ̃] *nf* arrest; **en état d'a.** under arrest

arrêt [arɛ] *nm* (**a**) *(interruption) (des combats, des hostilités, de la production)* stop; **Clermont-Ferrand, dix minutes d'a.** *(en train)* this is Clermont-Ferrand, there will be a ten-minute stop; **sans a.** continuously; **tomber en a. devant qn/qch** to stop and stare at sb/sth; **marquer un temps d'a.** to pause; **a. du cœur** heart failure; *Ordinat* **a. de défilement** scroll lock; *TV &* *Cin* **a. sur image** freeze frame; **a. de jeu** stoppage; **a. de travail** sick leave; **être en a. de travail** to be on sick leave (**b**) *(de véhicule)* stop; **ne pas descendre avant l'a. complet du train** *(sur la portière)* do not get off before the train has come to a complete stop; **le train est sans a. jusqu'à Hendaye** the train is non-stop to Hendaye; **je descends au prochain a.** I'm getting off at the next stop; **a. de bus** bus stop; **a. facultatif** request stop

(**c**) *Jur* judgement; *aussi Fig* **a. de mort** death sentence

arrêté, -e [arete] **1** *adj (idées)* fixed
  2 *nm (décret)* order, decree; **a. ministériel** ministerial order; **a. municipal** bylaw; **a. préfectoral** bylaw

arrêter [arete] **1** *vt* (**a**) *(personne, animal, véhicule)* to stop; *(machine, moteur, musique)* to turn off; *(fuite)* to stem; *(études)* to give up; **là je vous arrête, je ne suis pas d'accord!** hold it right there, I don't agree!; **arrête-moi au carrefour** drop me off at the crossroads; **rien ne l'arrête** nothing will stop him; **a. de faire qch** to stop doing sth; **elle n'arrête pas de me déranger** she keeps disturbing me; **ce détail arrêta mon attention** this detail caught my attention (**b**) *(criminel)* to arrest (**c**) *(déterminer)* to decide; *(date, prix)* to fix
  2 *vi* to stop; **arrête!** stop it!
  3 s'arrêter *vpr* (**a**) *(cesser, s'immobiliser)* to stop; **s'a. de faire qch** to stop doing sth; **s'a. chez qn** to call in at sb's house (**b**) **s'.a. à qch** *(faire attention à)* to pay attention to sth

arrhes [ar] *nfpl* deposit

arrière [arjɛr] **1** *adj inv* back; **feu a.** rear light; **roue a.** rear *or* back wheel
  2 *nm* (**a**) *(d'une maison, d'un avion)* back; *(d'un bateau)* **à l'a. de la voiture** in the back of the car (**b**) *Mil* **l'a.** the rear; *Fig* **protéger ses arrières** to leave oneself a way out (**c**) *(au football, au rugby)* full back
  3 *exclam* stand back!
  4 en arrière *adv* (**a**) *(derrière)* behind; **rester en a.** to lag behind; **en a. de qn/qch** behind sb/sth (**b**) *(dans la direction inverse)* backwards; **pencher la tête en a.** to lean one's head back; **retourner en a.** to go *or* turn back (**c**) *Suisse* **il y a un siècle en a.** a century ago

arriéré, -e [arjere] **1** *adj* (**a**) *(paiement)* overdue (**b**) *(dans ses idées, son développement)* backward
  2 *nm* arrears

arrière-boutique *(pl* arrière-boutiques) [arjɛrbutik] *nf Br* back shop, *Am* back store

arrière-cour *(pl* arrière-cours) [arjɛrkur] *nf* backyard

arrière-garde *(pl* arrière-gardes) [arjɛrgard] *nf* rearguard

arrière-goût *(pl* arrière-goûts) [arjɛrgu] *nm aussi Fig* aftertaste

arrière-grand-mère *(pl* arrière-grands-mères) [arjɛrgrɑ̃mɛr] *nf* great-grandmother

arrière-grand-père *(pl* arrière-grands-pères) [arjɛrgrɑ̃pɛr] *nm* great-grandfather

arrière-grands-parents [arjɛrgrɑ̃parɑ̃] *nmpl* great-grandparents

arrière-pays [arjɛrpei] *nm inv* hinterland

arrière-pensée *(pl* arrière-pensées) [arjɛrpɑ̃se] *nf* ulterior motive

arrière-petite-fille *(pl* arrière-petites-filles) [arjɛrpətitfij] *nf* great-granddaughter

arrière-petit-fils *(pl* arrière-petits-fils) [arjɛrpətifis] *nm* great-grandson

arrière-petits-enfants [arjɛrpətizɑ̃fɑ̃] *nmpl* great-grandchildren

arrière-plan *(pl* arrière-plans) [arjɛrplɑ̃] *nm aussi Fig* background; **à l'a.** in the background

arrière-saison *(pl* arrière-saisons) [arjɛrsɛzɔ̃] *nf Br* late autumn, *Am* late fall

arrière-train *(pl* arrière-trains) [arjɛrtrɛ̃] *nm (d'un animal)* (hind)quarters; *Fam (d'une personne)* rump, rear

arrimer [arime] *vt* (**a**) *Naut (cargaison)* to stow (**b**) *(fixer)* to secure *or* fasten (**à** to)

arrivage [arivaʒ] *nm* consignment

arrivant, -e [arivɑ̃, -ɑ̃t] *nm,f* arrival; **les nouveaux arrivants** the new arrivals, the newcomers

arrivé, -e [arive] **1** *adj* **être a.** *(socialement)* to have arrived, to have made it
  2 *nm,f (personne)* **le premier/dernier a.** the first/last (person) to arrive

arrivée [arive] *nf* (**a**) *(venue)* arrival; **depuis son a. au pouvoir** since he came to power; **à mon a.** when I arrive/arrived; **arrivées** *(sur panneau)* arrivals (**b**) *Tech* inlet (**c**) *(d'une course)* winning post, finish

arriver [arive] *(aux être)* **1** *vi* (**a**) *(venir)* to arrive; **a. à Lyon/in France** to arrive in Lyons/in France; **a. le premier/dernier** *(à une soirée)* to arrive first/last; **a. premier/second** *(dans un concours, une course)* to come first/second; **j'arrive!** (I'm) coming!; **c'est à cette heure-là que tu arrives?** and what time do you call this?; **nous sommes presque arrivés** we're almost there
  (**b**) *(atteindre)* **l'eau m'arrive aux chevilles** the water comes up to my ankles; **ses cheveux lui arrivent aux épaules** her hair comes down to her shoulders *or* is shoulder-length
  (**c**) **en a. à faire qch** to get to the stage of doing sth; **c'est malheureux d'en a. là** it's a shame it's got to that stage; **elle en arrive même à ne plus le souhaiter** she's even starting to wish it won't happen; **j'en arrive à penser que.../me demander si...** I'm beginning to think.../wonder if...
  (**d**) *(socialement)* to arrive, to make it
  (**e**) *(parvenir)* **a. à un résultat** to achieve a result; **a. à faire qch** to manage to do sth; **je n'arrive pas à l'ouvrir** I can't get it open; **il n'arrivera jamais à rien** he'll never make anything of himself
  (**f**) *(se produire)* to happen (**à** to)
  2 *v impersonnel* **quoi qu'il arrive** whatever happens; **il lui est arrivé quelque chose** something's happened to him; **il m'arrive d'y penser** I sometimes think about it; **il arrive à tout le monde de se tromper** anyone can make a mistake; **qu'est-ce qu'il t'arrive?** what's wrong (with you)?

arrivisme [arivism] *nm* unscrupulous ambition

arriviste [arivist] *nmf* social climber, arriviste

arrobas [arɔbas], **arrobase** [arɔbaz] *nf Ordinat (dans une adresse électronique)* at sign

arrogance [arɔgɑ̃s] *nf* arrogance; **avec a.** arrogantly

arrogant, -e [arɔgɑ̃, -ɑ̃t] *adj* arrogant

arroger [45] [arɔʒe] **s'arroger** *upr* **s'a. un droit/un privilège** to claim a right/a privilege; **s'a. le droit de faire qch** to assume the right to do sth

arrondi, -e [arɔ̃di] **1** *adj (objet, visage)* round
  2 *nm* (**a**) *(forme)* roundness, rounded form (**b**) *(d'une jupe)* hemline

arrondir [arɔ̃dir] **1** *vt* (**a**) *(forme)* **a. qch** to make sth round; **cette coiffure lui arrondit le visage** that haircut makes her face look round; *Fig* **a. les angles** to smooth things over (**b**) *(chiffre, somme) (vers le haut)* to round up; *(vers le bas)* to round down; *Fam* **a. ses fins de mois** to supplement one's income; **a. au franc supérieur/inférieur** to round up/down to the nearest franc

2 s'arrondir *vpr (corps, visage)* to fill out

arrondissement [arɔ̃dismɑ̃] *nm* = administrative subdivision of Paris, Lyons and Marseilles

---

Arrondissement

In Paris, Lyons and Marseilles, the number of the "arrondissement" corresponds to the last two figures in a postcode: thus, you can tell from the postcode 75012 that it refers to the 12th arrondissement of Paris.

---

arrosage [arozaʒ] *nm (des plantes, du sol)* watering; *(des rues)* spraying; *(d'une pelouse)* sprinkling

arroser [aroze] **1** *vt* (**a**) *(plantes, sol)* to water; *(pelouse)* to sprinkle; *(rues)* to spray; *(rôti)* to baste; **région très peu arrosée** area with little rainfall; **a. qch d'essence** to douse sth in petrol (**b**) *(fêter)* to drink to; **un repas bien arrosé** a meal washed down with plenty of alcohol (**c**) *(sujet: rivière)* to flow through

2 s'arroser *vpr (se fêter)* **ça s'arrose!** that calls for a drink!

arroseur [arozœr] *nm (appareil)* sprinkler

arrosoir [arozwar] *nm* watering can

arsenal, -aux [arsənal, -o] *nm* (**a**) *Mil* arsenal; **a. maritime** *ou* **de la marine** naval dockyard (**b**) *Fam (attirail)* gear

arsenic [arsənik] *nm* arsenic

art [ar] *nm* (**a**) *(esthétique)* art; **c'est du grand a.!** it's a work of art!; **le septième a.** cinema; **a. dramatique** drama, dramatic art; **les arts graphiques** graphic arts; **l'a. lyrique** opera; **arts martiaux** martial arts; **arts plastiques** fine art (**b**) *(savoir-faire)* **l'a. de faire qch** the art of doing sth; **cultiver l'a. de vivre** to enjoy the finer things in life; **préparer le café, c'est tout un a.** there's quite an art to making coffee; *Fig* **avoir l'a. de faire qch** to have a knack for doing sth

Arte [arte] *n* = French-German TV channel showing cultural programmes

artère [arter] *nf* (**a**) *(vaisseau)* artery (**b**) **(grande) a.** *(route)* arterial road; *(en ville)* main thoroughfare

artériel, -elle [arterjɛl] *adj (système, maladie)* arterial

artériosclérose [arterjoskleroz] *nf* hardening of the arteries, *Spéc* arteriosclerosis

arthrite [artrit] *nf* arthritis

arthrose [artroz] *nf* osteoarthritis

Arthur [artyr] *npr Fam* **je vais me faire appeler A.!** I'm going to get a real telling-off!

artichaut [artiʃo] *nm* artichoke

article [artikl] *nm* (**a**) *Com* item; **articles de toilette** toiletries; **faire l'a.** to make a sales pitch (**b**) *Journ* article; *(de dictionnaire)* entry (**c**) *(d'un traité, d'un règlement)* article (**d**) *Gram* article; **a. défini/indéfini** definite/indefinite article (**e**) **être à l'a. de la mort** to be on the point of death (**f**) *Ordinat (dans base de données)* record; *(commande)* command

articulaire [artikyler] *adj Anat* articular, articulatory

articulation [artikylasjɔ̃] *nf* (**a**) *Anat & Tech* joint (**b**) *(prononciation)* articulation (**c**) *(organisation)* structure

articuler [artikyle] **1** *vt* (**a**) *(idées, arguments)* to link (**b**) *(mots)* to articulate; **articule!** speak clearly!

2 s'articuler *vpr (pièces, idées)* to be linked; **les différentes parties du texte s'articulent bien** the different parts of the text hang well together; **s'a. autour de qch** *(théorie)* to centre on sth

artifice [artifis] *nm* trick

artificiel, -elle [artifisjɛl] *adj* (**a**) *(non naturel)* artificial; *Fig (personne)* false; *(rire)* forced (**b**) *(arbitraire)* arbitrary

artificiellement [artifisjɛlmɑ̃] *adv* (**a**) *(de façon non naturelle)* artificially (**b**) *(arbitrairement)* arbitrarily

artificier [artifisje] *nm (fabricant)* firework manufacturer; *(dans un feu d'artifice)* master of ceremonies

artillerie [artijri] *nf* artillery; **a. légère/lourde** light/heavy artillery; **pièce d'a.** artillery cannon

artilleur [artijœr] *nm* artilleryman

artisan [artizɑ̃] *nm* craftsman, *f* craftswoman; *Fig* architect

artisanal, -e, -aux, -ales [artizanal, -o] *adj* traditionally-made; *(à la main)* hand-made; **métier a.** craft

artisanat [artizana] *nm* craft industry

artiste [artist] **1** *adj (tempérament, style)* artistic; **se donner un genre a.** to cultivate an arty image

2 *nmf* (**a**) *(personne créative)* artist (**b**) *(interprète) (musicien)* performer; *(acteur)* actor, *f* actress; *(chanteur)* singer; *(danseur)* dancer; **a. (peintre)** artist

artistique [artistik] *adj* artistic

as¹ *voir* **avoir**

as² [ɑs] *nm* (**a**) *(aux cartes)* ace; *(aux dominos, aux dés)* one; *Fam* **être ficelé** *ou* **fichu comme l'as de pique** to be dressed like a tramp; **être plein aux as** to be rolling in it; *Fam* **passer à l'as** to go out of the window (**b**) *Fam (champion)* whizz; **as du volant** crack racing driver; **un as du bricolage** a DIY expert

ascendance [asɑ̃dɑ̃s] *nf (ancêtres)* ancestry

ascendant, -e [asɑ̃dɑ̃, -ɑ̃t] **1** *adj (échelle)* rising; *(mouvement, courant)* upward

2 *nm* (**a**) *(influence)* influence; **avoir de l'a. sur qn** to have influence over sb (**b**) **ascendants** *(ancêtres)* ancestry

ascenseur [asɑ̃sœr] *nm* (**a**) *(dans un bâtiment)* *Br* lift, *Am* elevator; *Fig* **je lui renverrai l'a.** I'll return the favour (**b**) *Ordinat* scroll box

ascension [asɑ̃sjɔ̃] *nf* (**a**) *(escalade)* ascent; **faire l'a. d'une montagne** to climb a mountain (**b**) *(progression)* **a. sociale** social climbing (**c**) *Rel* **(la fête** *ou* **le jeudi de) l'A.** Ascension Day

---

Ascension

Ascension Day is on the fortieth day after Easter and is a public holiday in France. Many people take an extended weekend break during this period.

---

ascensionnel, -elle [asɑ̃sjɔnɛl] *adj (mouvement)* upward

ascète [asɛt] *nmf* ascetic

ASCII [aski] *nm (abrév* **American standard code for information interchange) (code) a.** ASCII (code)

ascorbique [askɔrbik] *adj (acide)* ascorbic

aseptique [asɛptik] *adj* aseptic

aseptiser [asɛptize] *vt (blessure)* to sterilize; *(pièce)* to disinfect; *Fig & Péj* **un univers aseptisé** a sterile environment

asexué, -e [asɛksɥe], **asexuel, -elle** [asɛksɥɛl] *adj aussi Fig* asexual

ashkénaze [aʃkenaz] *adj & nmf* Ashkenazi

asiatique [azjatik] **1** *adj* oriental
  2 *nmf* **A.** Oriental

Asiatique

This word tends to refer to Oriental people (ie from countries such as China, Japan, Laos etc), rather than Asia as a whole. Note that it does not refer to the British English sense of "Asian" meaning someone from the Indian subcontinent.

Asie [azi] *nf* l'**A.** Asia; l'**A. centrale** Central Asia; l'**A. du Sud-Est** South-east Asia

asile [azil] *nm* (**a**) *(abri)* refuge; *Vieilli* **a. (d'aliénés)** mental hospital; **a. de nuit** night shelter; **a. de vieillards** old folk's home (**b**) *(statut)* **a. politique/diplomatique** political/diplomatic asylum; **demander l'a. politique** to ask for political asylum

asocial, -e, -aux, -ales [asɔsjal, -o] **1** *adj* asocial
  2 *nm,f* asocial person

aspartam(e) [aspartam] *nm* aspartame

aspect [aspɛ] *nm* (**a**) *(air)* appearance, look; **un bar d'a. louche** a shady-looking bar (**b**) *(angle)* angle, point of view; **sous tous ses aspects** from every angle, from all points of view (**c**) *Gram* aspect

asperge [aspɛrʒ] *nf* (**a**) *(plante)* asparagus (**b**) *Fam (personne)* beanpole

asperger [45] [aspɛrʒe] **1** *vt (linge, plante)* to spray with water; **a. qn de qch** to splash sb with sth; **se faire a.** to get splashed
  2 s'asperger *vpr* (**a**) *(soi-même)* **s'a. de qch** to splash oneself with sth (**b**) *(mutuellement)* to splash *or* spray one another

aspérité [asperite] *nf* (**a**) *(d'une surface)* rough part (**b**) *(d'un caractère)* harshness

aspersion [aspɛrsjɔ̃] *nf* spraying

asphalte [asfalt] *nm* asphalt

asphyxiant, -e [asfiksjɑ̃, -ɑ̃t] *adj* asphyxiating, suffocating; *Fig* stifling, suffocating; **gaz a.** poison gas

asphyxie [asfiksi] *nf* asphyxiation

asphyxier [66] [asfiksje] **1** *vt* (**a**) *(personne, animal)* to asphyxiate (**b**) *Fig (économie, industrie)* to paralyse
  2 s'asphyxier *vpr (suffoquer)* to choke; *(se suicider)* to gas oneself

aspirateur [aspiratœr] *nm* Hoover®, vacuum cleaner; **passer l'a. dans la maison** to hoover *or* vacuum the house

aspiration [aspirasjɔ̃] *nf* (**a**) *(inhalation)* inhalation; *Tech (d'eau dans une pompe)* suction (**b**) *(désir)* yearning (**à** for); *(ambition)* aspiration (**à** for) (**c**) *Ling* aspiration

aspiré, -e [aspire] *adj Ling* aspirate(d)

aspirer [aspire] **1** *vt* (**a**) *(air, parfum)* to inhale, to breathe (in) (**b**) *(liquide)* to suck up (**c**) *Ling* to aspirate
  2 aspirer à *vt ind* to aspire to; **a. à faire qch** to aspire to do sth

aspirine [aspirin] *nf* aspirin; **un cachet d'a.** an aspirin; **blanc comme un cachet d'a.** white as a ghost

assagir [asaʒir] **1** *vt* to quieten down
  2 s'assagir *vpr* to settle down

assaillant, -e [asajɑ̃, -ɑ̃t] *nm,f* assailant, attacker

assaillir [67] [asajir] *vt* to assault, to attack; *Fig (sujet: difficultés, remords, doute)* to beset; **a. qn de questions**

to bombard sb with questions; **il a été assailli par les journalistes** he was set upon by the journalists

assainir [asenir] *vt (maison, rivière)* to clean up; *(atmosphère)* to purify; *(marais)* to drain; *(économie)* to stabilize

assainissement [asenismɑ̃] *nm (d'une maison, d'une rivière)* cleaning up; *(de l'atmosphère)* purifying; *(d'un marais)* drainage; *(de l'économie)* stabilization

assaisonnement [asɛzɔnmɑ̃] *nm (de plat)* seasoning; *(de salade)* dressing

assaisonner [asɛzɔne] *vt (plat)* to season (**de** with); *(salade)* to dress; *Fam Fig* **se faire a.** to get a good telling-off

assassin, -e [asasɛ̃, -in] **1** *nm* murderer; *(d'une personnalité politique)* assassin; **à l'a.!** murder!
  2 *adj* (**a**) *(méchant) (regard)* murderous; *(remarque)* crushing (**b**) *(provocant) (sourire, œillade)* provocative

assassinat [asasina] *nm* murder; *(d'une personnalité politique)* assassination

assassiner [asasine] *vt* to murder; *(personnalité politique)* to assassinate; *Fig (chanson, texte)* to murder; *(sujet: critique)* to crucify

assaut [aso] *nm (attaque)* assault, attack; *Mil* charge; **donner l'a. à** to storm, to launch an attack on; **monter à l'a.** to attack; **prendre qch d'a.** *Mil* to storm sth; *Fig (buffet, guichets)* to make a run for sth

assèchement [asɛʃmɑ̃] *nm (d'un terrain, d'un marécage)* drainage; *(d'un cours d'eau)* drying out

assécher [34] [aseʃe] **1** *vt (terrain, marécage)* to drain; *(cours d'eau)* to dry out
  2 s'assécher *vpr* to dry up

ASSEDIC [asedik] *nfpl (abrév* **Association pour l'emploi dans l'industrie et le commerce**) = French unemployment benefits department, *Br* ≃ Unemployment Benefit Office; **toucher les A.** to get *Br* unemployment benefit *or Am* welfare

assemblage [asɑ̃blaʒ] *nm* (**a**) *(de pièces détachées)* assembly; *(en menuiserie)* joint; *(en couture)* making up; *(de feuillets)* collating (**b**) *(structure)* assembly

assemblée [asɑ̃ble] *nf* (**a**) *(réunion)* assembly; *(plus petite)* meeting; **a. générale** annual general meeting (**b**) *Pol* l'**A. nationale** the National Assembly, *Br* ≃ the House of Commons, *Am* ≃ the House of Representatives (**c**) *(foule)* crowd

---

Assemblée nationale

The French parliament has two chambers: the National Assembly and the Senate. The members of the National Assembly (the "députés") are elected in the "élections législatives" held every five years.

---

assembler [asɑ̃ble] **1** *vt* (**a**) *(machine, meuble en kit)* to assemble, to put together; *(feuillets)* to collate (**b**) *(pièces)* to join (**c**) *Ordinat (programme)* to assemble; *(modules)* to link
  2 s'assembler *vpr (foule)* to gather

assembleur [asɑ̃blœr] *nm Ordinat* assembler

asséner [34] [asene] *vt* **a. qch à qn** *(coup)* to deliver sth to sb; *(remarque)* to hurl sth at sb

assentiment [asɑ̃timɑ̃] *nm* assent

asseoir [10a] [aswar] **1** *vt* (**a**) *(installer) (personne)* to seat, to sit; **être assis** to be sitting (**b**) *Fig (autorité, réputation)* to establish
  2 *vi* **faire a. qn** to ask sb to sit down *or* to take a seat

3 s'asseoir *vpr* to sit (down); *(depuis la position allongée)* to sit up; **s'a. sur une chaise/dans un fauteuil** to sit on a chair/in an armchair; *Fam Fig* **ses problèmes, je m'assois dessus!** I don't give a damn about his problems!

assermenté, -e [asɛrmɑ̃te] *adj* sworn (in); *(témoin)* under *or* on oath; **fonctionnaire a.** sworn official; *Hist* **(prêtre) non a.** non-juring (priest)

assertion [asɛrsjɔ̃] *nf* assertion

asservir [asɛrvir] *vt* to enslave; *Tech* **moteur asservi** servomotor

asservissement [asɛrvismɑ̃] *nm* enslavement; **a. à qn/qch** subjection to sb/sth

assesseur [asɛsœr] *nm* assessor

asseyais *etc voir* **asseoir**

assez [ase] *adv* **(a)** *(suffisamment)* enough; **a. grand/ intelligent (pour faire qch)** big/clever enough (to do sth); **a. bien** well enough; *(appréciation scolaire)* fair; **tu as a. mangé** you've eaten enough; **a.!** that's enough!; **a. parlé!** that's enough talk!; **nous sommes a. de trois** three of us is enough **(b) a. de** enough; **il y a a. de pain/de pâtes** there's enough bread/pasta; **j'en ai a.** *(suffisamment)* I've got enough; *(je suis agacé)* I've had enough **(c)** *(plutôt)* quite, rather

assidu, -e [asidy] *adj* **(a)** *(toujours présent)* regular; **être a. aux cours** to attend classes regularly **(b)** *(appliqué)* diligent; **un soin a.** painstaking care **(c)** *(attentionné)* **être a. auprès de qn** to be attentive to sb; **faire une cour assidue à qn** to pay constant court to sb

assiduité [asidɥite] *nf* **(a)** *(présence régulière)* regularity; **a. aux cours** regular attendance at classes **(b)** *(zèle)* diligence **(c) poursuivre qn de ses assiduités** to force one's attentions on sb

assidûment [asidymɑ̃] *adv* **(a)** *(régulièrement)* regularly **(b)** *(avec application)* diligently

assied *etc voir* **asseoir**

assiéger [59] [asjeʒe] *vt aussi Fig* to besiege

assiéra *etc voir* **asseoir**

assiette [asjɛt] *nf* **(a)** *(vaisselle)* plate; *(contenu)* plateful; *Culin* **a. anglaise** assorted cold meats; **a. creuse** soup plate; **a. à dessert** dessert plate; **a. plate** dinner plate **(b)** *(d'un impôt, d'un taux)* base **(c)** *(d'un cavalier)* seat **(d) ne pas être dans son a.** to be out of sorts

assiettée [asjete] *nf* plateful

assignation [asiɲasjɔ̃] *nf* **(a)** *(d'une tâche)* assignment (**à** to); *(de fonds, d'une part)* allotment (**à** to) **(b)** *Jur* summons; **a. à résidence** house arrest

assigner [asiɲe] *vt* **(a)** *(tâche)* to assign (**à** to); *(fonds, part)* to allot (**à** to) **(b)** *Jur (témoin)* to summon; **a. qn à résidence** to place sb under house arrest

assimilable [asimilabl] *adj (comparable)* comparable (**à** to)

assimilation [asimilasjɔ̃] *nf* **(a)** *(absorption)* & *Fig* assimilation **(b)** *(comparaison)* comparison (**à** with)

assimilé, -e [asimile] *adj (de même nature)* similar; **cadres et assimilés** executives and those in similar categories

assimiler [asimile] **1** *vt* **(a)** *(aliment, connaissances, immigrés)* to assimilate; **un élève qui a du mal à a.** a pupil who finds it hard to take things in **(b)** *(comparer)* to compare (**à** with)
2 s'assimiler *vpr* **(a)** *(immigré)* to assimilate **(b)** *(être comparable)* to be comparable (**à** with)

assis, -e [asi, -iz] **1** *pp voir* **asseoir**
2 *adj* sitting, seated; **je travaille a. toute la journée** I

spend the whole day at work sitting down; *Fig* **une situation/réputation bien assise** a secure job/an established reputation

assise [asiz] *nf (d'une théorie)* basis, foundation

assises [asiz] *nfpl* **(a)** *(congrès)* conference **(b)** *Jur* **les a.** the assizes

assistanat [asistana] *nm* assistantship

assistance [asistɑ̃s] *nf* **(a)** *(public)* audience **(b)** *(aide)* assistance; **prêter a. à qn** to give sb assistance **(c)** **être à l'A. (publique)** to be in care

assistant, -e [asistɑ̃, -ɑ̃t] *nm,f* assistant; *(de langue)* language assistant; **a. metteur en scène** assistant director; **assistante maternelle** child minder; **assistante sociale** social worker

assisté, -e [asiste] **1** *nm,f Péj* person living on hand-outs
2 *adj* **a. par ordinateur** computer-aided

assister [asiste] **1** *vt (personne)* to assist
2 assister à *vt ind* to be (present) at, to attend; *(accident)* to witness; **je ne peux pas vous répondre, je n'ai pas assisté à la scène** I can't give you an answer, I wasn't there

associatif, -ive [asɔsjatif, -iv] *adj* **mouvement a.** associations; **la vie associative est tres développée dans ce pays** a lot of people in this country belong to clubs and associations

association [asɔsjasjɔ̃] *nf* **(a)** *(groupe, société)* association; *Com* partnership; **a. à but non lucratif** *Br* non-profit-making *or Am* not-for-profit organization; **A. européenne de libre-échange** European Free Trade Association; **a. de parents d'élèves** parent-teacher association; **a. sportive** sports club **(b)** *(de mots, d'idées)* association; *(d'aliments, de substances, de couleurs)* combination **(c)** *Jur* **a. de malfaiteurs** criminal conspiracy

associé, -e [asɔsje] **1** *nm,f* associate; *Com* partner
2 *adj* **membre a.** associate member

associer [66] [asɔsje] **1** *vt* **(a)** *(lier)* to combine (**à** with) **(b)** *(mentalement)* to associate (**à** with)
2 s'associer *vpr* **(a) s'a. à un projet** to join in a project; **s'a. à** *ou* **avec qn** *(dans une lutte)* to join forces with sb; *Com* to enter into partnership with sb; **je m'associe à votre douleur** I share your grief **(b)** *(se mêler)* to combine (**à** with)

assoiffé, -e [aswafe] *adj* thirsty; *Fig* **a. de sang** bloodthirsty; **a. de savoir** thirsty for knowledge

assolement [asɔlmɑ̃] *nm* crop rotation

assombrir [asɔ̃brir] **1** *vt* to darken; *(avenir)* to cast a shadow over
2 s'assombrir *vpr (ciel, visage)* to darken, to cloud over; *(personne)* to become gloomy

assommant, -e [asɔmɑ̃, -ɑ̃t] *adj* very boring

assommer [asɔme] *vt* **a. qn** *(étourdir)* to knock sb senseless; *(engourdir)* to make sb lethargic; *(ennuyer)* to bore sb to death

Assomption [asɔ̃psjɔ̃] *nf* **(la fête de) l'A.** (the feast of) the Assumption

Assomption

The Feast of the Assumption, on the 15th of August, is a Catholic feast day and an important holiday in France.

assonance [asɔnɑ̃s] *nf* assonance

assorti, -e [asɔrti] *adj* **(a)** *(en harmonie)* matching; **bien a.** well-matched; **mal a.** ill-matched; **pull avec**

jupe assortie jumper with matching skirt; **le pull n'était pas a. à la jupe** the jumper didn't match the skirt (**b**) *(bonbons)* assorted, mixed (**c**) **bien a.** *(magasin)* well-stocked (**d**) *(accompagné)* **a. de** accompanied by

assortiment [asɔrtimɑ̃] *nm (de produits)* assortment

assortir [asɔrtir] *vt* (**a**) *(couleurs)* to match (**à** to) (**b**) *Com* to restock

assoupir [asupir] **s'assoupir** *vpr* to doze off

assouplir [asuplir] **1** *vt (chaussures, cuir, corps)* to make supple; *Fig (réglementation)* to relax
   2 s'assouplir *vpr (chaussures, cuir, corps)* to get supple; *(personne)* to loosen up

assouplissant [asuplisɑ̃] *nm* fabric softener

assouplissement [asuplismɑ̃] *nm (du corps)* making supple; *Fig (de la réglementation)* relaxing; **exercices d'a., assouplissements** limbering-up exercises

assourdir [asurdir] *vt* (**a**) *(personne)* to deafen (**b**) *(son)* to deaden

assourdissant, -e [asurdisɑ̃, -ɑ̃t] *adj* deafening

assouvir [asuvir] *vt (faim, désir)* to satisfy

assouvissement [asuvismɑ̃] *nm (de la faim, du désir)* satisfaction

assoyant *voir* asseoir

assujettir [asyʒetir] *vt* (**a**) *(province)* to subjugate (**b**) *(soumettre)* **a. qn à qch** to subject sb to sth; **être assujetti à l'impôt** to be liable for tax (**c**) *(objet)* to fix, to fasten (**à** to)

assujettissement [asyʒetismɑ̃] *nm* (**a**) *(dépendance)* subjection (**à** to) (**b**) *(à l'impôt)* liability (**à** for)

assumer [asyme] **1** *vt* (**a**) *(responsabilité)* to assume, to take on; *(risque)* to take (**b**) *(accepter) (conséquences)* to take; *Fam* **tu vas devoir a.** you'll have to live with it
   2 s'assumer *vpr* to come to terms with oneself

assurance [asyrɑ̃s] *nf* (**a**) *(confiance)* (self-)assurance (**b**) *(garantie)* assurance; **je vous donne l'a. que tout sera fini demain** I assure you that everything will be finished tomorrow; **demander/recevoir des assurances** to ask for/to receive assurance (**c**) *(contre le vol, les accidents)* insurance; **prendre une a.** to take out insurance; *Fam* **je vais écrire à mon a.** I'm going to write to my insurance company; **a. auto** car insurance; **a. maladie** health insurance; **a. au tiers** third-party insurance; **a. tous risques** comprehensive insurance; **a. sur la vie, a.-vie** life insurance; **a. vieillesse** retirement pension

assuré, -e [asyre] **1** *adj* (**a**) *(pas, voix)* firm; *(air, personne)* assured, confident; **d'une voix mal assurée** in an unsteady voice (**b**) *(succès, victoire)* guaranteed, certain
   2 *nm,f* **l'a.** the insured; **les assurés sociaux** ≃ people who pay *Br* national insurance *or Am* social security

assurément [asyremɑ̃] *adv Vieilli* certainly

assurer [asyre] **1** *vt* (**a**) *(garantir)* to ensure, to guarantee; **a. une rente à qn** to settle an annuity on sb; **ma retraite m'assure de quoi vivre** my pension gives me enough to live on; **a. ses arrières** to leave oneself a way out
   (**b**) *(certifier)* **a. qch à qn, a. qn de qch** to assure sb of sth; **a. qn que** to assure sb that; **c'est bien vrai, je t'assure** it's absolutely true, I assure you; **mais si, je t'assure!** yes, I swear!
   (**c**) *(se charger de)* to be in charge of; **a. les fonctions de directeur de la production** to be production manager; **un service régulier est assuré entre Paris et**

Londres there is a regular service between Paris and London; **j'assure la permanence ce matin** I'm on duty this morning; **a. la défense de qn** *(sujet: avocat)* to defend sb
   (**d**) *(immobiliser)* to steady; *(attacher)* to secure
   (**e**) *(par contrat d'assurance)* to insure (**contre** against)
   2 *vi Fam* **a. en maths** to be brilliant at maths; **à l'entretien, j'ai assuré un max** I did brilliantly at the interview
   3 s'assurer *vpr* (**a**) **s'a. de qch** *(vérifier)* to make sure of sth; **s'a. que** to make sure *or* check (that); **je vais m'en a.** I'll check
   (**b**) *(par contrat d'assurance)* to insure oneself (**contre** against); **s'a. au tiers/sur la vie** to take out third-party/life insurance
   (**c**) *(se procurer)* **s'a. la collaboration de qn** to secure sb's collaboration; **les Allemands se sont assuré la victoire** the Germans are assured of victory

assureur [asyrœr] *nm* insurer

astérisque [asterisk] *nm* asterisk

astéroïde [asterɔid] *nm* asteroid

asteure, astheure [astœr] *Can Fam* **1** *adv* now
   2 asteure que *conj* now that

asthmatique [asmatik] *adj & nmf* asthmatic

asthme [asm] *nm* asthma; **avoir de l'a.** to have asthma; **crise d'a.** asthma attack

asticot [astiko] *nm* maggot

asticoter [astikɔte] *vt Fam* to bug

astigmate [astigmat] *adj & nmf* astigmatic

astiquer [astike] *vt (faire briller)* to polish; *(récurer)* to scour; **a. sa maison** to get one's house spotlessly clean

astrakan [astrakɑ̃] *nm* astrakhan

astre [astr] *nm* star; **beau comme un a.** radiantly handsome *or* beautiful

astreignant, -e [astreɲɑ̃, -ɑ̃t] *adj* exacting, demanding

astreindre [54] [astrɛ̃dr] **1** *vt* **a. qn à faire qch** to compel *or* oblige sb to do sth
   2 s'astreindre *vpr* **s'a. à un régime sévère** to strictly follow a diet; **s'a. à faire qch** to force oneself to do sth

astreinte [astrɛ̃t] *nf* constraint

astrologie [astrɔlɔʒi] *nf* astrology

astrologique [astrɔlɔʒik] *adj* astrological

astrologue [astrɔlɔg] *nmf* astrologer

astronaute [astrɔnot] *nmf* astronaut

astronautique [astrɔnotik] *nf* astronautics *(singulier)*

astronome [astrɔnɔm] *nmf* astronomer

astronomie [astrɔnɔmi] *nf* astronomy

astronomique [astrɔnɔmik] *adj aussi Fig* astronomical

astrophysique [astrofizik] *nf* astrophysics *(singulier)*

astuce [astys] *nf* (**a**) *(finesse)* shrewdness (**b**) *(truc)* trick; *(conseil)* tip; **il doit y avoir une a.** there must be a trick to it (**c**) *(plaisanterie)* witticism; *(jeu de mots)* pun; **je ne saisis pas l'a.** I don't get it

astucieusement [astysjøzmɑ̃] *adv* shrewdly

astucieux, -euse [astysjø, -øz] *adj (personne)* shrewd; *(solution)* clever

asymétrie [asimetri] *nf* asymmetry

asymétrique [asimetrik] *adj* asymmetrical

asynchrone [asɛ̃kron] *adj Ordinat* asynchronous

ataca [ataka] *nm Can* cranberry

atavisme [atavism] *nm* atavism; **faire qch par a.** to do sth because it's in one's genes

atchoum [atʃum] *exclam* atishoo!

atelier [atəlje] *nm* (**a**) *(lieu)* workshop; *(dans une maison)* workroom; *(d'artiste)* studio; **a. de carrosserie** bodyshop; **a. de montage** assembly shop; *TV & Cin* **a. de production** production studio; **a. de réparations** repair shop (**b**) *(personnel)* workshop staff (**c**) *(groupe de travail)* work-group

atermoiements [atɛrmwamɑ̃] *nmpl* procrastination

athée [ate] **1** *adj* atheistic
  2 *nmf* atheist

athéisme [ateism] *nm* atheism

athénée [atene] *nm Belg* secondary *or* high school

Athènes [atɛn] *n* Athens

athénien, -enne [atenjɛ̃, -ɛn] **1** *adj* Athenian
  2 *nm,f* **A.** Athenian

athlète [atlɛt] *nmf* athlete

athlétique [atletik] *adj* athletic

athlétisme [atletism] *nm* athletics *(singulier)*; **épreuves d'a.** athletic events

atlantique [atlɑ̃tik] **1** *adj* Atlantic
  2 *nm* **l'A.** the Atlantic (Ocean)

atlas [atlas] *nm (livre)* atlas

atmosphère [atmosfɛr] *nf aussi Fig* atmosphere

atmosphérique [atmosferik] *adj* atmospheric

atoca [atɔka] *nm Can* cranberry

atoll [atɔl] *nm* atoll

atome [atom] *nm* atom; *Fig* **avoir des atomes crochus avec qn** to hit it off with sb; **elle n'a pas un a. de bon sens** she doesn't have a bit of common sense

atomique [atɔmik] *adj* atomic

atomiser [atɔmize] *vt* (**a**) *(pulvériser)* to atomize (**b**) *(ville, région)* to destroy with nuclear weapons

atomiseur [atɔmizœr] *nm* atomizer, spray; **parfum en a.** perfume spray

atone [atɔn] *adj* (**a**) *(inerte)* lacklustre (**b**) *(voyelle)* unstressed

atours [atur] *nmpl Litt ou Hum* finery; **parée de ses plus beaux a.** in all her finery

atout [atu] *nm (aux cartes)* trump; *Fig* asset; **a. carreau** diamonds are trumps; **a. maître** master trump; *Fig* trump card; *aussi Fig* **avoir tous les atouts dans son jeu** to hold all the winning cards

âtre [ɑtr] *nm Litt* hearth; **au coin de l'â.** by the fireplace

atriqué, -e [atrike] *adj Can* **mal a.** badly dressed

atroce [atrɔs] *adj (crime)* atrocious; *(douleur)* excruciating; *(odeur, cauchemar, repas)* dreadful, horrible; **j'avais une peur a. de le rencontrer** I dreaded meeting him

atrocement [atrɔsmɑ̃] *adv (cruellement)* atrociously; *(très mal)* dreadfully, horribly; **avoir a. mal** to be in dreadful pain; **sentir a. mauvais** to smell really horrible

atrocité [atrɔsite] *nf* atrocity

atrophie [atrɔfi] *nf* atrophy

atrophier [66] [atrɔfje] **1** *vt* to atrophy
  2 *s'atrophier vpr* to atrophy

attabler [atable] *s'attabler vpr* to sit down at the/a table

attachant, -e [ataʃɑ̃, -ɑ̃t] *adj* engaging

attache [ataʃ] *nf* (**a**) *(lien)* fastener; *Fig* **attaches** *(amis)* links; *Fig* **sans attaches** unattached; **je n'avais**

plus aucune a. dans cette ville there was nothing to keep me in the town (**b**) **avoir les attaches fines** *(chevilles et poignets)* to have delicate wrists and ankles

attaché, -e [ataʃe] **1** *adj* (**a**) *(fixé)* fastened; *(chien)* chained up (**b**) *(affectivement)* **a. à** attached to (**c**) *(dépendant)* **les avantages attachés à une fonction** the benefits attached to a post
  2 *nm,f* attaché; **a. d'ambassade** attaché; **a. culturel** cultural attaché; **a. militaire** military attaché; **a. de presse** press officer

attaché-case *(pl* **attachés-cases**) [ataʃekɛz] *nm* attaché case

attachement [ataʃmɑ̃] *nm* attachment (**à** to)

attacher [ataʃe] **1** *vt* (**a**) **a. qch à qch** *(fixer)* to fasten sth to sth; *(avec de la ficelle, avec une corde)* to tie sth to sth; *(avec une chaîne)* to chain sth to sth; **a. ses cheveux** to tie one's hair back; **a. ses lacets** *ou* **chaussures** to do one's shoelaces up (**b**) *(accorder)* **a. de l'importance/de la valeur à qch** to attach importance/great value to sth
  2 *vi (dans une poêle, une casserole)* to stick to the pan; **une casserole qui n'attache pas** a non-stick saucepan
  3 *s'attacher vpr* (**a**) *(se fixer)* to be fastened (**à** to); **cette jupe s'attache par derrière** this skirt does up at the back (**b**) *(affectivement)* **s'a. à qn/qch** to get attached to sb/sth; **je ne veux pas m'a.** I don't want to commit myself (**c**) *(se concentrer)* **s'a. aux faits** to stick to the facts; **s'a. à faire qch** to strive to do sth (**d**) *(s'assurer)* **s'a. les services de qn** to procure sb's services

attaquant, -e [atakɑ̃, -ɑ̃t] **1** *nm,f Sport* attacker
  2 *adj* attacking

attaque [atak] *nf* (**a**) *(agression, en sport)* attack; *aussi Fig* **passer à l'a.** to go on the offensive; **à l'a.!** attack!; **a. aérienne** air raid; **a. à main armée** armed robbery (**b**) *Fam* **être d'a.** to be on top form; **se sentir d'a. pour faire qch** to feel up to doing sth (**c**) *Méd (crise)* attack; **une a.** *(apoplexie)* a stroke; *(crise cardiaque)* a heart attack

attaquer [atake] **1** *vt* (**a**) *(physiquement, verbalement)* to attack; *(sujet: acide)* to attack; *Jur* **a. qn en justice** to bring an action against sb (**b**) *(repas, sujet, travail)* to tackle; *Fam* **on attaque?** *(à table)* shall we get stuck in? (**c**) *Mus (morceau)* to strike up; *(note)* to attack
  2 *s'attaquer vpr* **s'a. à** *(adversaire)* to attack; *(problème)* to tackle; **s'a. à plus fort que soi** to bite off more than one can chew

attardé, -e [atarde] **1** *nm,f* **a. (mental)** (mentally) retarded person
  2 *adj* (**a**) *(qui flâne)* **il ne restait plus que quelques passants attardés** there were only a few people still about (**b**) *(vieux)* old-fashioned (**c**) *(mentalement)* (mentally) retarded

attarder [atarde] *s'attarder vpr* to linger; **s'a. à des détails** to dwell over details; **ne nous attardons pas sur ce point** let's not dwell on this point

atteignais *etc voir* **atteindre**

atteindre [54] [atɛ̃dr] **1** *vt* to reach; *(cible)* to hit; **être atteint d'une maladie** to be suffering from a disease; **il a été atteint dans son amour-propre** his pride has been wounded; **le poumon est atteint** the lung is affected; *Fig* **rien ne l'atteint** nothing affects him; *Fam* **il est très atteint** *(fou)* he's completely cracked
  2 atteindre à *vt ind* **a. à la perfection** to be close to perfection

atteinte [atɛt] *nf (attaque)* **a. à** attack on; **porter a. à** to undermine

attelage [atəlaʒ] *nm (animaux)* team

atteler [42] [atəle] **1** *vt (chevaux)* to harness; *(bœufs)* to yoke; **a. une voiture** to hitch up horses to a carriage
2 s'atteler *vpr* **s'a. à une tâche** to buckle down to a task

attelle [atɛl] *nf* splint

attenant, -e [atənã, -ãt] *adj* adjoining; **a. à** adjoining

attendre [atãdr] **1** *vt* to wait for; **a. son tour** to wait one's turn; **a. un bébé** to be expecting (a baby); **se faire a.** *(personne)* to keep people waiting; **la réponse ne s'est pas fait a.** the reply wasn't long in coming; **je l'attends d'une minute à l'autre** I'm expecting him any minute now; **a. qch de qn/qch** to expect sth from sb/sth; **qu'est-ce que tu attends pour le lui dire?** what are you waiting for? go and tell him; **a. que qn fasse qch** to wait for sb to do sth; **attends de lui avoir parlé avant de prendre une décision** wait until you've spoken to him before you take a decision; *Fig* **a. qn au tournant** to be waiting to catch sb out
2 *vi* to wait; **a. une heure** to wait (for) an hour; **sans plus a.** without further ado; **faire a. qn** to keep sb waiting; *Fam* **on ne va pas a. cent sept ans** we're not going to wait forever; **en attendant** meanwhile; *(néanmoins)* all the same; **en attendant son arrivée** until he arrives/arrived
3 s'attendre *vpr* **s'a. à qch** to expect sth; **je m'attends à tout** I'm ready for anything; **je m'y attendais** I expected as much; **il fallait s'y a.** it was only to be expected; **je m'attendais à ce que tu le lui dises** I was expecting you to tell him

attendrir [atãdrir] **1** *vt* (**a**) *(émouvoir)* to move; *(rendre indulgent)* to soften (**b**) *(viande)* to tenderize
2 s'attendrir *vpr* to be moved (**sur** by)

attendrissant, -e [atãdrisã, -ãt] *adj* moving

attendu, -e [atãdy] **1** *adj* expected; **le jour tant a. est arrivé** the long-awaited day has arrived
2 *prép Formel* **a. les circonstances** considering the circumstances
3 attendu que *conj Formel* considering that; *Jur* whereas

attentat [atãta] *nm* attack; **a. à la bombe** bombing; **a. à la pudeur** indecent assault; **a. à la sûreté de l'État** high treason; **a. à la voiture piégée** car-bomb attack

attente [atãt] *nf* (**a**) *(fait d'attendre)* waiting; *(période)* wait; **être dans l'a. de qch** to be waiting for sth; **en a.** *(au téléphone)* on hold; *Ordinat* **liste de fichiers à imprimer en a.** print queue (**b**) *(espoir)* expectations; **contre toute a.** against all expectations; **répondre à l'a. ou aux attentes de qn** to live up to sb's expectations; **dans l'a. de votre réponse/de vous rencontrer** *(dans une lettre)* I look forward to receiving your reply/to meeting you

attenter [atãte] **attenter à** *vt ind* to make an attempt on; **a. à ses jours** to attempt suicide

attentif, -ive [atãtif, -iv] *adj* attentive; **être a. aux autres** to be attentive to others; **être a. à qch** to pay attention to sth; *(ses intérêts, sa santé)* to look after sth; **écouter d'une oreille attentive** to listen attentively

attention [atãsjõ] *nf* (**a**) *(soin)* attention; **écouter avec a.** to listen attentively; **faire a. à qch** to pay attention to sth; *(sa santé, ses intérêts)* to look after sth; **il a fait a. de ne pas la blesser** he took care not to hurt her; **ne pas prêter la moindre a. à** to take no notice of; *(faites)* **a.!** look out!; **a. si je t'attrape!** if I catch you there'll be trouble!; **a., peinture fraîche** *(sur écriteau)* wet paint; **a. à la fermeture des portières, a. au départ!** stand clear of the doors, the train is about to depart!; **à l'a. de qn** *(sur une lettre)* for the attention of sb (**b**) *(amabilité)* attention; **être plein d'attentions envers qn** to be very attentive towards sb

attentionné, -e [atãsjɔne] *adj* attentive (**auprès de** towards)

attentisme [atãtism] *nm* wait-and-see policy

attentiste [atãtist] **1** *adj* **attitude a.** wait-and-see attitude
2 *nmf* **les attentistes** those who play a waiting game

attentivement [atãtivmã] *adv* attentively

atténuation [atenɥasjõ] *nf (d'un effet, de la douleur)* reduction; *(d'une lumière)* dimming; *(d'une couleur)* toning down; *(d'une chute)* breaking

atténuer [atenɥe] **1** *vt (effet, douleur)* to reduce; *(lumière)* to dim; *(couleur)* to tone down; *(chute)* to break
2 s'atténuer *vpr (douleur)* to ease; *(lumière, couleurs, bruit)* to fade

atterrant, -e [atɛrã, -ãt] *adj* appalling

atterrer [atere] *vt* to appal

atterrir [aterir] *vi* to land; **a. en catastrophe** to make an emergency landing; *Fam* **a. dans un bar/en prison** to land up in a bar/in prison

atterrissage [aterisaʒ] *nm* landing; **a. en douceur** soft landing; **a. forcé** forced landing

attestation [atɛstasjõ] *nf* certificate

attester [atɛste] *vt (témoigner)* to testify to; **a. que** to testify that; **aucun dictionnaire n'atteste l'existence de ce mot** this word is not attested in any dictionary

attifer [atife] *Fam* **1** *vt* to dress (**de** in)
2 s'attifer *vpr* to dress; **s'a. de qch** to put sth on

attirail [atiraj] *nm* paraphernalia

attirance [atirãs] *nf* attraction; **éprouver de l'a. pour ou envers qn** to be attracted to sb

attirant, -e [atirã, -ãt] *adj* attractive

attirer [atire] **1** *vt* (**a**) *(sujet: aimant, planète)* to attract; *Fig* **a. qn dans un piège** to lure sb into a trap; **a. qn dans un coin** to take sb into a corner; **a. l'attention de qn** *(sujet: chose)* to catch sb's attention; **a. l'attention de qn sur qch** to draw sb's attention to sth; **a. les regards** to catch the eye (**b**) *(séduire)* to attract; *(sujet: matière, pays)* to appeal to
2 s'attirer *vpr* (**a**) *(mutuellement)* to be attracted to each other (**b**) *(sur soi)* **s'a. des critiques** to come in for criticism; **s'a. des ennuis** to get oneself into trouble; **s'a. la colère de qn** to incur sb's anger

attiser [atize] *vt* (**a**) *(feu)* to poke (**b**) *Fig (désir, colère, racisme)* to stir up

attitré, -e [atitre] *adj* (**a**) *(habituel)* usual (**b**) *(chargé d'une fonction)* appointed

attitude [atityd] *nf* (**a**) *(conduite, position)* attitude (**envers** *ou* **à l'égard de** towards); **tu as eu une a. déplorable** your behaviour was appalling (**b**) *(maintien)* bearing, demeanour (**c**) *(affectation)* pose

attouchement [atuʃmã] *nm* fondling; **se livrer à des attouchements sur qn** to fondle sb

attraction [atraksjõ] *nf* (**a**) *(d'un aimant)* attraction; **l'a. terrestre** the earth's gravitational pull (**b**) *aussi Fig (spectacle)* attraction

attrait [atrɛ] *nm* attraction

attrape [atrap] *nf (farce)* trick

attrape-nigaud (*pl* **attrape-nigauds**) [atrapnigo] *nm* trick

attraper [atrape] **1** *vt* (**a**) *(capturer, saisir)* to catch; **se faire a.** to be caught; *Fam* **a. qn à faire qch** to catch sb doing sth (**b**) *(maladie)* to catch; **a. froid** to catch cold; **a. mal** to catch a chill (**c**) *(tromper)* **a. qn** to take sb in; **là, tu es bien attrapé** you fell for it good and proper (**d**) *Fam (gronder)* **se faire a.** to get a good talking to
  2 s'attraper *vpr (maladie)* to be caught; *(habitude)* to be picked up

attrayant, -e [atrɛjɑ̃, -ɑ̃t] *adj* attractive; **peu a.** unattractive

attribuable [atribɥabl] *adj* attributable (**à** to)

attribuer [atribɥe] **1** *vt* (**a**) *(allouer)* to assign, to allot (**à** to); *(prix, récompense, bourse)* to award (**à** to) (**b**) *(œuvre, crime, erreur)* to attribute (**à** to); **a. de l'importance à qch** to attach importance to sth
  2 s'attribuer *vpr* **s'a. qch** to claim sth; **il s'en est attribué tout le mérite** he claimed all the credit for it

attribut [atriby] **1** *nm* attribute
  2 *adj* attributive

attribution [atribysjɔ̃] *nf* (**a**) *(allocation)* assigning, allocation (**à** to); *(d'un prix, d'une récompense, d'une bourse)* awarding (**à** to); **attributions** *(fonctions)* duties; **entrer dans les attributions de qn** to be part of sb's duties (**b**) *(d'une œuvre, d'un crime, d'une erreur)* attribution (**à** to)

attristant, -e [atristɑ̃, -ɑ̃t] *adj* depressing

attrister [atriste] **1** *vt* to sadden; **cela m'attriste** it makes me sad
  2 s'attrister *vpr* to be saddened (**de** by)

attroupement [atrupmɑ̃] *nm* crowd; **provoquer un a.** to draw a crowd

attrouper [atrupe] **s'attrouper** *vpr* to gather

atypique [atipik] *adj* atypical

au [o] *voir* **à**

aubaine [obɛn] *nf* godsend; **profiter de l'a.** to take advantage of one's good luck; *Can* **à prix d'a.** at a reduced price

aube [ob] *nf* (**a**) *(matin)* dawn; **à l'a.** at dawn; *Fig* **l'a. de la civilisation** the dawn of civilization (**b**) *Rel* alb

aubépine [obepin] *nf* hawthorn; **fleurs d'a.** may blossom

auberge [obɛrʒ] *nf* inn; *Fig* **ici, c'est l'a. espagnole** you have to bring everything yourself here; *Fam* **on n'est pas sorti de l'a.** we're not out of the wood yet; **a. de jeunesse** youth hostel

aubergine [obɛrʒin] *nf* (**a**) *(plante)* Br aubergine, *Am* eggplant (**b**) *Fam (contractuelle)* (female) traffic warden

aubergiste [obɛrʒist] *nmf* innkeeper

auburn [obœrn] *adj inv* auburn

aucun, -e [okœ̃, -yn] **1** *pron indéfini* (**a**) *(personne, rien)* none; **a. des deux** neither (of them); **a. d'entre eux** none of them; **je ne me fie à a. d'entre eux** I don't trust any of them (**b**) *Litt* **d'aucuns** some people
  2 *adj indéfini* (**a**) *(négatif)* no, not any; **je n'en ai aucune idée** I've (got) no idea; **sans aucune exception** without any exception; **sans a. doute** without a doubt (**b**) *(positif)* any; **plus rapide qu'a. autre coureur** faster than any other runner

aucunement [okynmɑ̃] *adv* not at all, not in the slightest

audace [odas] *nf* (**a**) *(courage)* boldness, daring (**b**) *(culot)* audacity, impudence (**c**) *(originalité)* boldness (**d**) *(action audacieuse)* **avoir toutes les audaces** to do the most daring things

audacieusement [odasjøzmɑ̃] *adv* (**a**) *(avec courage)* boldly, daringly (**b**) *(avec culot)* impudently

audacieux, -euse [odasjø, -øz] *adj* (**a**) *(courageux)* bold, daring (**b**) *(culotté)* impudent (**c**) *(original)* bold

au-dedans [odədɑ̃] *adv* inside; **a. de** inside

au-dehors [odəɔr] *adv* outside; **a. de** outside

au-delà [odəla] **1** *nm* **l'a.** the next world
  2 *prép* **a. de** beyond
  3 *adv* beyond; **jusqu'à une certaine somme mais pas a.** up to a certain sum but no more

au-dessous [odəsu] *adv* below, underneath; *(à l'étage inférieur)* downstairs; **on en trouve à 8 euros et même a.** you can get them for 8 euros or even less; **a. de** *(dans l'espace)* below, under; *(nombre, somme)* under; *(dans une hiérarchie)* below; **15 degrés a. de zéro** 15 degrees below zero; *Fig* **être a. de tout** to be beneath contempt

au-dessus [odəsy] *adv* above; *(à l'étage supérieur)* upstairs; **une terrasse avec une marquise a.** a terrace with an awning over it; **1000 euros et a.** 1,000 euros and upwards; **a. de** *(dans l'espace, dans une hiérarchie)* above; *(nombre, somme)* over; **a. de nos têtes** *(dans le ciel)* overhead; **c'est a. de mes forces** it's beyond me; **vivre a. de ses moyens** to live beyond one's means; *Fig* **je suis a. de ça** I'm above all that

au-devant [odəvɑ̃] **au-devant de** *prép* **aller/courir a. de qn** to go/run to meet sb; **aller a. des désirs de qn** to anticipate sb's wishes; **aller a. du danger** to court danger

audible [odibl] *adj* audible

audience [odjɑ̃s] *nf* (**a**) *(entrevue)* audience; *Jur* hearing; **l'a. est suspendue** the case is adjourned (**b**) *(intérêt)* **trouver a. auprès des jeunes** to find a following among young people (**c**) *(public)* audience

Audimat® [odimat] *nm (appareil)* = device for calculating television audience ratings; *(résultats)* audience ratings; **faire de l'A.** to increase audience ratings

audioconférence [odjokɔ̃ferɑ̃s] *nf* audioconference

audionumérique [odjonymerik] *adj* digital audio; **disque a.** compact disc

audiovisuel, -elle [odjovizɥɛl] **1** *adj* (**a**) *(méthodes)* audiovisual (**b**) *TV & Rad* television and radio
  2 *nm TV & Rad* **l'a.** television and radio

auditeur, -trice [oditœr, -tris] *nm,f* (**a**) *(d'un programme de radio)* listener (**b**) *Univ* **suivre un cours en a. libre** = to follow a course without being officially registered as a student, *Am* to audit a course

auditif, -ive [oditif, -iv] *adj (nerf)* auditory; *(troubles)* hearing

audition [odisjɔ̃] *nf* (**a**) *(faculté)* hearing (**b**) *(de chanteur, d'acteur)* audition; **passer une a.** to have an audition (**c**) *Jur* **a. des témoins** examination of the witnesses

auditionner [odisjɔne] *vt & vi* to audition

auditoire [oditwar] *nm* (**a**) *(public)* audience (**b**) *Belg & Suisse (amphithéâtre)* auditorium; *(salle de cours)* lecture hall or theatre

auditorium [oditɔrjɔm] *nm* auditorium; *Rad & TV* recording studio

AUE [ayə] *nm (abrév* **acte unique européen**) SEA

auge [oʒ] *nf (mangeoire)* trough

augmentation [ɔgmɑ̃tasjɔ̃] *nf* (**a**) *(accroissement)* increase (**de** in); **a. (de salaire)** *Br* (pay-)rise; *Am* raise; **demander une a.** to ask for a (pay-)rise; **être en a.** to be on the increase (**b**) *Ordinat* **a. de puissance** upgrade

augmenter [ɔgmãte] **1** *vt* to increase; **édition augmentée** enlarged edition; **a. qn** to raise sb's salary **2** *vi* to increase (**de** by)

augure [ogyr] *nm* (**a**) *(devin)* augur (**b**) *(présage)* omen; **de bon a.** auspicious; **de mauvais a.** ominous

augurer [ogyre] *vt* **a. bien/mal de qch** to augur well/ill for sth

auguste [ogyst] *adj* august

aujourd'hui [oʒurdɥi] *adv* (**a**) *(ce jour)* today; **le journal d'a.** today's paper; *Fam* **c'est pour a. ou pour demain?** I/we haven't got all day! (**b**) *(à l'heure actuelle)* nowadays, today; **les jeunes gens d'a.** young people today; **l'Europe d'a.** present-day Europe

aulne [on] *nm* alder

aumône [omon] *nf* alms; **demander l'a.** to ask for charity; **faire l'a. à qn** to give alms to sb

aumônier [omonje] *nm* chaplain

aune [on] *nm* alder

auparavant [oparavã] *adv* *(avant)* before(hand); *(d'abord)* first

auprès [oprɛ] **auprès de** *prép* (**a**) *(près de)* by, next to; **ambassadeur a. des Nations unies** ambassador to the United Nations (**b**) *(en comparaison de)* compared with (**c**) *(en s'adressant à)* **se renseigner a. de qn** to ask sb

auquel [okɛl] *voir* **lequel**

aura¹ *etc voir* **avoir**

aura² [ɔra] *nf* aura

auréole [ɔreɔl] *nf* (**a**) *(d'un saint, d'un astre)* halo; *Fig* **parer qn d'une a.** to idolize sb (**b**) *(trace)* ring

auréoler [ɔreɔle] *vt* **tout auréolé de gloire** crowned with glory

auriculaire [ɔrikylɛr] *nm* little finger

aurifère [ɔrifɛr] *adj* gold-bearing; **gisement a.** goldfield

Aurigny [ɔriɲi] *n* Alderney

aurore [ɔrɔr] *nf* dawn, daybreak; **à l'a.** at dawn; *Fam* **aux aurores** at the crack of dawn; **a. boréale** aurora borealis, northern lights

auscultation [ɔskyltasjɔ̃] *nf* auscultation

ausculter [ɔskylte] *vt (malade, cœur)* to listen to

auspices [ɔspis] *nmpl* **sous les a. de** *(sous l'égide de)* under the auspices of; **sous d'heureux a.** auspiciously; **sous de fâcheux a.** inauspiciously

aussi [osi] **1** *adv* (**a**) *(également)* too, as well; **lui a. il sait le faire** he, too, knows how to do it, he knows how to do it as well (**b**) *(tellement)* so; **une a. belle journée** such a nice day (**c**) *(dans les phrases comparatives)* as; **a. grand que moi** as tall as me; **pas a. gros que** not as big as, not so big as; **a. bien que moi** as well as me (**d**) *(quelque)* however; **a. bizarre que cela soit** however odd it may be **2** *conj* therefore, so

aussitôt [osito] **1** *adv* immediately, straight away; **a. avant/après** immediately before/after; **a. après son retour je suis parti** as soon as he returned I left; **a. l'argent reçu je vous paierai** as soon as I get the money I'll pay you; **a. dit, a. fait** no sooner said than done **2** *conj* **a. que** as soon as

austère [ostɛr] *adj (vie, style)* austere; *(vêtement)* severe; *(expression)* stern

austérité [osterite] *nf (de la vie, d'un style)* austerity; *(d'un vêtement)* severity; *(d'une expression)* sternness; **mesures d'a.** austerity measures

austral, -e, -als *ou* **-aux** [ostral, -o] *adj* southern

Australasie [ostralazi] *nf* **l'A.** Australasia

Australie [ostrali] *nf* **l'A.** Australia

australien, -enne [ostraljɛ̃, -ɛn] **1** *adj* Australian **2** *nm,f* **A.** Australian

autant [otã] *adv* (**a**) *(tellement)* so much; **a. de** *(quantité)* so much; *(nombre)* so many; **je n'avais jamais vu a. de neige/de bateaux** I had never seen so much snow/so many boats
(**b**) *(la même quantité, le même nombre)* **remettez-m'en encore a.** give me the same again; **il m'en veut, mais je lui en veux tout a.** he's angry with me, but I'm just as angry with him; **le coût de la vie a augmenté de 5% mais les salaires n'ont pas augmenté d'a.** the cost of living has increased by 5% but salaries have not risen by the same amount; **a. que** *(quantité)* as much as; *(nombre)* as many as; **a. que possible** as far as possible; **a. de... que** *(quantité)* as much... as; *(nombre)* as many... as; **ils ont a. de terrain/d'amis que vous** they have as much land/as many friends as you
(**c**) *(de même)* **on ne peut pas en dire a. de tout le monde** you can't say the same for everybody; **essaie un peu d'en faire a.** try to do the same
(**d**) *(locutions)* **a. elle est expansive, a. il est réservé** she's as extroverted as he is shy; **a. pour moi!** I stand corrected!; **(pour) a. que je sache** as far as I know, to the best of my knowledge; **ce sera a. de moins à payer** it will be that much less to pay; **a. rester ici** we may as well stay here; **a. dire que...** which amounts to saying that...; **j'aimerais a. aller au cinéma** I'd rather go to the cinema; **j'aime a. te dire que je n'étais pas contente!** I wasn't too happy, I can tell you!; **... d'a. (plus) que...** ..., especially since...; **d'a. plus/moins que...** all the more/less because; **cela vous sera d'a. plus facile que vous êtes jeune** it will be that much easier for you since you are young; **pour a.** *(malgré cela)* for all that

autarcie [otarsi] *nf Pol* autarky; **vivre en a.** to be self-sufficient

autel [otɛl] *nm aussi Fig* altar; **conduire sa fille à l'a.** to give one's daughter away

auteur [otœr] *nm* (**a**) *(de livre)* author, writer; *(de chanson)* composer; *(de tableau)* painter (**b**) *(responsable)* author; *(d'un crime)* perpetrator; *(d'un projet)* instigator

authenticité [otãtisite] *nf* authenticity

authentification [otãtifikasjɔ̃] *nf* authentication

authentifier [66] [otãtifje] *vt* to authenticate

authentique [otãtik] *adj* authentic, genuine; *(fait, histoire)* true

authentiquement [otãtikmã] *adv* authentically, genuinely

autisme [otism] *nm* autism

autiste [otist] **1** *adj* autistic **2** *nmf* person with autism

auto [oto] *nf* car; **autos tamponneuses** bumper cars, *Br* Dodgems®; **petite a.** *(jouet)* toy car

auto- [oto] *préf* auto-, self-

autoaccusation [otoakyzasjɔ̃] *nf* self-accusation

autobiographie [otobjografi] *nf* autobiography

autobiographique [otobjografik] *adj* autobiographical

autobronzant, -e [otobrɔ̃zɑ̃, -ɑ̃t] **1** *adj* self-tanning **2** *nm* self-tanning cream

autobus [otobys] *nm* bus; **a. à impériale** double-decker (bus)

autocar [otokar] *nm* bus, *Br* coach; **a. de luxe** luxury coach

autocassable [otokasabl] *adj* **ampoule a.** break-open phial

autocensurer [otosɑ̃syre] **s'autocensurer** *vpr* to practise self-censorship

autochtone [otɔkton] **1** *nmf aussi Hum* native **2** *adj* native

autocollant, -e [otokɔlɑ̃, -ɑ̃t] **1** *adj* self-adhesive; *(enveloppe)* self-seal **2** *nm* sticker

autocorrecteur, -trice [otokɔrɛktœr, -tris] *adj Ordinat* self-correcting

autocouchette(s) [otokuʃɛt] *adj inv voir* **train**

autocrate [otokrat] *nmf* autocrat

autocratie [otokrasi] *nf* autocracy

autocratique [otokratik] *adj* autocratic

autocritique [otokritik] *nf* self-criticism; **faire son a.** to criticize oneself

autocuiseur [otokɥizœr] *nm* pressure cooker

autodafé [otodafe] *nm I list* auto-da-fé

autodéfense [otodefɑ̃s] *nf* self-defence

autodestructeur, -trice [otodɛstryktœr, -tris] *adj* self-destructive

autodestruction [otodɛstryksjɔ̃] *nf* self-destruction

autodétermination [otodetɛrminasjɔ̃] *nf Pol* self-determination

autodidacte [otodidakt] **1** *adj* self-taught **2** *nmf* self-taught person

autodrome [otodrom] *nm* motor-racing track; *(pour les essais)* car-testing track

auto-école (*pl* **auto-écoles**) [otoekɔl] *nf* driving school

autofinancement [otofinɑ̃smɑ̃] *nm* self-financing

autofinancer [45] [otofinɑ̃se] **s'autofinancer** *vpr* to be self-financing

autofocus [otofɔkys] *adj & nm Phot* autofocus

autogéré, -e [otoʒere] *adj* self-managed

autogestion [otoʒɛstjɔ̃] *nf* self-management

autographe [otograf] *nm & adj* autograph

automate [otɔmat] *nm* (**a**) *(robot) aussi Fig* automaton (**b**) *Suisse (machine)* vending machine; *(à billets)* cash dispenser

automation [otɔmasjɔ̃] *nf* automation

automatique [otɔmatik] **1** *adj* automatic; **il est absent tous les lundis, c'est a.** he's off every Monday without fail **2** *nm* (**a**) *Tél* direct dialling (**b**) *(pistolet)* automatic

automatiquement [otɔmatikmɑ̃] *adv* automatically

automatisation [otɔmatizasjɔ̃] *nf* automation

automatiser [otɔmatize] *vt* to automate

automatisme [otɔmatism] *nm* (**a**) *(réflexe)* automatism; **agir par a.** to act automatically; **fermer la porte à double tour est devenu un a.** double-locking the door has become automatic (**b**) *(dispositif)* automatic device

automédication [otɔmedikasjɔ̃] *nf* self-medication

automitrailleuse [otomitrajøz] *nf* armoured car

automnal, -e, -aux, -ales [otɔnal, -o] *adj* autumnal

automne [otɔn] *nm* autumn, *Am* fall; **en a., à l'a.** in autumn; **une soirée d'a.** an autumn evening; *Fig* **à l'a. de sa vie** in the autumn of his life

automobile [otɔmɔbil] **1** *nf* (**a**) *(voiture)* car, *Am* automobile (**b**) *(industrie)* **l'a.** the car industry **2** *adj* (**a**) *(véhicule)* self-propelling (**b**) *(industrie, accessoires)* car, *Am* automobile

automobiliste [otɔmɔbilist] *nmf* motorist

autoneige [otonɛʒ] *nf Can* snowmobile

autonettoyant, -e [otonetwajɑ̃, -ɑ̃t] *adj* **four a.** self-cleaning oven

autonome [otɔnɔm] *adj (état, région)* autonomous, self-governing; *(appareil)* self-contained; *(personne)* self-sufficient; *Ordinat* **calculateur a.** stand-alone (computer)

autonomie [otɔnɔmi] *nf* (**a**) *Pol* autonomy, self-government (**b**) *(de personne)* self-sufficiency (**c**) *(de voiture)* range; *(de batterie)* life; *Aviat* **a. (de vol)** range

autonomiste [otɔnɔmist] *nmf Pol* separatist

autoportrait [otopɔrtrɛ] *nm* self-portrait

autopsie [otɔpsi] *nf* autopsy, post-mortem; *Fig* **faire l'a. d'une œuvre** to dissect a work

autopsier [66] [otɔpsje] *vt* to perform an autopsy *or* a post-mortem on

autopunition [otopynisjɔ̃] *nf* self-punishment

autoradio [otoradjo] *nm* car radio

autorail [otoraj] *nm* railcar

autorégulation [otoregylasjɔ̃] *nf* self-regulation

autoreverse [otorivœrs] *adj* **appareil a.** auto-reverse

autorisation [otɔrizasjɔ̃] *nf* (**a**) *(permission)* authorization, permission; **donner à qn l'a. de faire qch** to give sb permission to do sth; **demander (à qn) l'a. de faire qch** to ask (sb) permission to do sth; *Ordinat* **a. d'accès** access authorization; **a. de sortie du territoire** = parental authorization for a minor to travel abroad; *Aviat* **a. de vol** flight clearance (**b**) *(document)* authorization

autorisé, -e [otɔrize] *adj* (**a**) *(qualifié)* **tenir qch de source autorisée** to have sth from an authoritative source; **les milieux autorisés** official circles (**b**) *(permis)* permitted, allowed

autoriser [otɔrize] *vt* (**a**) *(permettre à)* **a. qn à faire qch** to authorize *or* permit sb to do sth; **je ne vous autorise pas à me parler sur ce ton** I won't have you talk to me like that (**b**) *(permettre)* **ces découvertes (nous) autorisent à penser que…** these discoveries entitle us to believe that…

autoritaire [otɔritɛr] *adj* authoritarian

autoritairement [otɔritɛrmɑ̃] *adv* in an authoritarian manner

autoritarisme [otɔritarism] *nm* authoritarianism

autorité [otɔrite] *nf* (**a**) *(domination, fermeté)* authority; **avoir de l'a. sur qn** to have authority over sb; **faire qch d'a.** to do sth on one's own authority (**b**) *(poids)* **faire a. en qch** *(personne)* to be an authority on sth; **ce livre fait a.** this book is the authoritative work (**c**) *(gouvernement)* **les représentants de l'a.** the representatives of authority; **les autorités** the authorities (**d**) *(personne respectée)* authority

autoroute [otorut] *nf* (**a**) *Aut Br* motorway, *Am* freeway; **a. à péage** *Br* toll motorway, *Am* turnpike (road) (**b**) *Ordinat* **a. de l'information** information superhighway

autoroutier, -ère [otorutje, -ɛr] *adj* **réseau a.** *Br* motorway *or Am* freeway system

autosatisfaction [otosatisfaksjɔ̃] *nf* self-satisfaction

auto-stop [otostɔp] *nm* hitch-hiking, hitching; **faire de l'a.** to hitch-hike, to hitch; **prendre qn en a.** to give sb a lift; **faire le tour de l'Europe en a.** to hitch-hike around Europe

auto-stoppeur, -euse (*mpl* auto-stoppeurs, *fpl* auto-stoppeuses) [otostɔpœr, -øz] *nm,f* hitch-hiker, hitcher

autosuggestion [otosygʒestjɔ̃] *nf* auto-suggestion

autour [otur] *adv* around; **une ville avec des murs tout a.** a town with walls all around it; **a. de** (*dans l'espace*) around, round; (*environ*) about; *Fig* **discuter qch a. d'un verre** to discuss sth over a drink

autre [otr] **1** *adj indéfini* (**a**) (*différent*) other; **l'a. côté** the other side; **un a. jour** another day; **as-tu d'autres questions?** do you have any other questions?; **les choux et autres légumes** cabbages and other vegetables; **je l'ai vu l'a. jour/soir** I saw him the other day/evening

(**b**) (*avec un pronom personnel*) **nous autres Français** we French (people); *Fam* **eh, vous autres, venez par ici!** hey, you lot, come over here!

(**c**) (*locutions*) **a. chose** something else; **avez-vous a. chose à faire?** have you got anything else to do?; *Fig* **il est assez bon musicien, mais sa femme c'est autre c.!** he's not a bad musician, but his wife's in another league!; **a. part** somewhere else

2 *pron indéfini* (**a**) **l'a.** (*personne, chose*) the other (one); *Fam* **et l'a. qui se plaint tout le temps!** and then there's him and his constant complaining!; *Fam* **comme dit l'a.** as the saying goes, as they say; **un a.** (*personne, chose*) another (one); **il n'est pas plus bête qu'un a.** he is no more stupid than anyone else; **c'était un touriste comme un a.** he was just an ordinary tourist; **c'est une raison comme une a.** it's as good a reason as any; **les autres** (*personnes, choses*) the others, the other ones; **tu devrais penser un peu aux autres** you should think of others; *Fam* **à d'autres!** who do you think you're kidding?; *Fam* **j'en ai vu d'autres** I've seen worse than that

(**b**) (*avec l'un, les uns*) **l'un et l'a.** both; **l'un dit ceci, l'a. dit cela** one says this and the other says that; **les uns disent ceci, les autres disent cela** some say this and others say that; **les uns et les autres** (*deux groupes*) both parties; **l'un ou l'a.** either; **c'est l'un ou l'autre** (*il faut choisir*) it's one or the other; **ni l'un ni l'a.** neither; **je ne les connais ni l'un ni l'a.** I don't know either of them; **ni les uns ni les autres** none of them; **je n'ai vu ni les uns ni les autres** I didn't see any of them; **l'un l'a.** each other, one another; **les uns les autres** one another; **ils dépendent l'un de l'a.** they depend on each other; *Fig* **l'un dans l'a.** on the whole

(**c**) (*avec de*) **quelque chose d'a.** something else; (*dans les questions*) anything else; **rien d'autre** nothing else; **il n'y en a pas d'a.** there aren't any others; **personne d'a.** nobody else; **quelqu'un d'a.** somebody else; (*dans les questions*) anyone else; **que pouvait-il faire d'a.?** what else could he do?; **qui d'a. sera là?** who else will be there?

autrefois [otrəfwa] *adv* in the past, once; **d'a.** of long ago

autrement [otrəmɑ̃] *adv* (**a**) (*différemment*) differently; **il ne put faire a. que d'obéir** he had no alternative but to obey; **a. dit** in other words (**b**) (*sinon*) otherwise (**c**) (*bien plus*) far more; **a. plus dangereux (que)** far more dangerous (than) (**d**) **pas a.** not particularly; **cela ne me surprend pas a.** that doesn't particularly surprise me

Autriche [otriʃ] *nf* **l'A.** Austria

autrichien, -enne [otriʃjɛ̃, -ɛn] **1** *adj* Austrian **2** *nm,f* **A.** Austrian

autruche [otryʃ] *nf* ostrich; **sac en a.** ostrich-skin handbag; *Fig* **avoir un estomac d'a.** to have a cast-iron stomach; **pratiquer la politique de l'a., faire l'a.** to bury one's head in the sand

autrui [otrɥi] *pron indéfini* others, other people; **ne fais pas à a. ce que tu ne voudrais pas qu'on te fît** do as you would be done by

auvent [ovɑ̃] *nm* (*toit*) porch roof; (*de tente*) canopy, awning

auvergnat, -e [ovɛrɲa, -at] **1** *adj* of the Auvergne **2** *nm,f* **A.** person from the Auvergne

aux [o] *voir* à

auxiliaire [ɔksiljɛr] **1** *adj* auxiliary **2** *nmf* (*aide*) assistant; (*dans les hôpitaux*) auxiliary; (*dans l'administration*) temporary worker; **a. familiale** mother's help **3** *nm Gram* auxiliary verb

auxquels, auxquelles [okɛl] *voir* lequel

av. *abrév* avenue

avachi, -e [avaʃi] *adj* (**a**) (*vêtement, bottes, canapé*) misshapen (**b**) (*personne, muscles*) flabby; **être a. dans un fauteuil** to be slumped in an armchair

avachir [avaʃir] **s'avachir** *vpr* (**a**) (*vêtement, bottes, canapé*) to lose its shape (**b**) (*personne*) (*physiquement*) to get flabby; (*moralement*) to let oneself go; **s'a. dans un fauteuil** to flop into an armchair

avais *etc voir* avoir

aval¹, -als [aval] *nm Fin* (*d'un effet de commerce*) endorsement; **a. bancaire** bank guarantee; *Fig* **donner son a. à un projet** to give a project one's backing *or* support

aval² *nm* (*d'un cours d'eau*) downstream section; *aussi Ind* **en a. (de)** downstream (from); **la Seine en a. de Paris** the Seine below Paris

avalanche [avalɑ̃ʃ] *nf* avalanche; *Fig* (*d'injures*) shower; (*de lettres, de compliments*) flood

avaler [avale] *vt* to swallow; (*goulûment*) (*nourriture*) to bolt; (*boisson*) to gulp down; *Fig* (*livre*) to devour; (*croire*) to swallow; **j'ai avalé de travers** it went down the wrong way; **je meurs de faim, je n'ai rien avalé depuis hier** I'm starving, I haven't had a thing to eat since yesterday; **on lui fait avaler n'importe quoi** he's very gullible, he believes anything you tell him; **a. la fumée** to inhale; *Fig* **a. ses mots** to mumble; **a. une carte de crédit** (*distributeur automatique*) to eat up a credit card; **a. les kilomètres** to eat up the miles; **tu as avalé ta langue?** have you lost your tongue?

avaleur [avalœr] *nm* **a. de sabres** sword-swallower

avance [avɑ̃s] *nf* (**a**) (*progression*) advance; **a. rapide** (*sur magnétophone*) fast-forwarding (**b**) (*avantage*) lead; **avoir de l'a. sur qn** to be ahead of sb; **prendre de l'a. sur qn** to take the lead over sb; **avoir 2 minutes/2 km d'a. sur qn** to have a 2-minute/2-km lead over sb; **avoir un but/point d'a. (sur qn)** to be one goal/point ahead (of sb); *Scol* **avoir un an d'a.** to be a year ahead; **arriver avec cinq minutes d'a.** to arrive five minutes early; **d'a., à l'a., par a.** in advance; **d'a. merci** (*dans une lettre*) thanking you in advance; (*dans une conversation*) thanks; **en a.** early; **être en a. d'une demi-heure** to be half an hour early; **être en a. pour son âge** to be advanced for one's age; **être en a. sur son temps** to be ahead of one's time (**c**) (*d'argent*) advance; **faire une a. à qn** to give sb an advance (**d**) **faire des avances à qn** (*chercher à séduire*) to make advances to sb

avancé, -e [avɑ̃se] *adj* (**a**) (*dans l'espace*) advanced (**b**) (*précoce*) **être a. pour son âge** to be advanced for one's age (**c**) (*idées, technologie*) advanced (**d**) (*tardif*) **à une heure avancée de la nuit** late in the night; **à un âge a.** at an advanced age (**e**) (*presque à terme*) **à un stade a.** at an advanced stage; **mon travail est bien a.** I'm making good progress with my work; *Fig* **vous voilà bien a.!** a lot of good that's done you!

avancée [avɑ̃se] *nf* (**a**) (*saillie*) projection; *Constr* **a. du toit** eaves (**b**) (*de troupes, de la recherche*) advance

avancement [avɑ̃smɑ̃] *nm* (**a**) (*d'un projet*) progress; **état d'a. des travaux** progress report (**b**) (*promotion*) promotion; **avoir** *ou* **obtenir de l'a.** to be promoted (**c**) *Ordinat* **a. automatique** automatic feed; **a. ligne par ligne** line feed; **a. du papier** paper feed; **a. par friction** friction feed

avancer [16] [avɑ̃se] **1** *vt* (**a**) (*mettre en avant*) to move forward; (*pion*) to advance; (*présenter*) (*main, verre, assiette*) to hold out; *Formel ou Hum* **l'automobile de Monsieur est avancée** Sir's carriage awaits (**b**) *Fig* (*thèse*) to advance, to put forward (**c**) (*dans le temps*) to bring forward; **a. sa montre d'une heure** to put one's watch forward one hour (**d**) (*argent*) **a. qch à qn** to advance sb sth, (*prêter*) to lend sb sth (**e**) (*faire progresser*) **à quoi cela vous avancera-t-il?** what good will that do you?; **ça ne t'avancera à rien de te mettre en colère** losing your temper won't get you anywhere; **ses réponses ne m'ont pas beaucoup avancé** his answers didn't leave me much the wiser

2 *vi* (**a**) (*aller de l'avant*) to move forward; (*armée*) to advance; **a. d'un pas** to take a step forward; **faire a. qn** to move sb along; **allez, avance! on va être en retard** come on, move! we're going to be late (**b**) (*faire des progrès*) to progress; **alors, ça avance?** so how's it coming along?; **faire a. les choses** to get things moving (**c**) (*montre*) to be fast; **ma montre avance d'une minute par jour** my watch gains a minute a day; **vous avancez de dix minutes** your watch is ten minutes fast (**d**) (*promontoire, toit*) to jut out

3 s'avancer *vpr* (**a**) (*aller devant*) to move forward; **s'a. vers qch** to head towards sth; **s'a. d'un pas** to take a step forward (**b**) (*faire son travail à l'avance*) to get ahead (**c**) *Fig* (*s'engager hâtivement*) to commit oneself

avant [avɑ̃] **1** *prép* (**a**) (*dans le temps, dans l'espace*) before; **a. une heure** by one o'clock; (*dans moins d'une heure*) within an hour; **800 a. Jésus-Christ** 800 BC; **a. impôt** before tax; **je vous reverrai a. de partir** I'll see you before I leave; **ne fais rien a. d'être tout à fait sûr** don't do anything until you're absolutely sure; **je vous reverrai a. que vous (ne) partiez** I'll see you before you leave; **je serai parti a. que vous ayez fini** I'll have left by the time you've finished; **ne partez pas a. qu'on vous le dise** don't go until you are told; *Fam* **celle-là, a. qu'elle se décide!** she takes forever to make her mind up! (**b**) (*par ordre de priorité*) before; **faire passer qch a. le reste** to put sth before everything else; **pour lui, la famille passe a. tout** for him, (the) family comes first; **a. tout** (*surtout*) above all; **a. toute chose** before anything else

2 *adv* (**a**) (*auparavant*) before; (*d'abord*) beforehand; **a. j'avais les cheveux longs** I used to have long hair; **tu ferais mieux de téléphoner a.** you'd better phone first; **le jour d'a.** the day before (**b**) (*dans l'espace*) **vous voyez l'église? sa maison est juste a.** you see the church? his house is just before you get to it (**c**) *Litt* (*loin*) far; (*tard*) late; *Fig* **poussons plus a. notre enquête** let's take our investigation(s) further (**d**) **en a.** (*devant les autres*) in front, ahead; (*se pencher, tomber*) forwards; *Mil* **en a., marche!** forward march!; **partir en a.** to go on ahead; **faire deux pas en a.** to take two steps forward; *Fig* **se mettre en a.** to push oneself forward; **en a. de** in front of

3 *adj inv* front

4 *nm* (**a**) (*d'un véhicule, d'une salle*) front; **à l'a.** (*d'un véhicule*) in the front; **aller de l'a.** to get on with it (**b**) (*en sport*) forward; **jouer a.** to be a forward

avantage [avɑ̃taʒ] *nm* (**a**) (*intérêt*) advantage; **cette solution a** *ou* **présente l'a. d'être rapide** this solution has the advantage of being quick (**b**) (*supériorité*) advantage (**sur** over); **être à son a.** (*physiquement*) to look one's best (**c**) (*profit*) advantage; **tu aurais a. à être poli** you'd do well to be polite; **être/tourner à l'a. de qn** to be/to turn to sb's advantage; **tirer a. de qch** to turn sth to one's advantage; **a. fiscal** tax benefit; **a. en nature** benefit in kind; **avantages sociaux** social security benefits (**d**) *Sport* advantage; **prendre/conserver l'a.** to gain/retain the advantage

avantager [45] [avɑ̃taʒe] *vt* (**a**) (*favoriser*) **a. qn (par rapport à)** to give sb an advantage (over); **être avantagé par rapport à qn** to have an advantage over sb (**b**) (*physiquement*) **a. qn** to show sb off to advantage; **il n'a pas été avantagé par la nature** he hasn't been favoured by nature

avantageux, -euse [avɑ̃taʒø, -øz] *adj* (**a**) (*offre*) attractive; (*conditions*) favourable; (*prix*) reasonable; (*produit*) good value (**b**) (*vaniteux*) (*ton*) superior

avant-bras [avɑ̃bra] *nm inv* forearm

avant-centre (*pl* **avants-centres**) [avɑ̃sɑ̃tr] *nm* (*au football*) centre forward

avant-coureur (*pl* **avant-coureurs**) [avɑ̃kurœr] *adj m* *voir* **signe**

avant-dernier, -ère (*mpl* **avant-derniers**, *fpl* **avant-dernières**) [avɑ̃dɛrnje, -ɛr] **1** *adj* last but one, second to last; **l'avant-dernière fois** the time before last **2** *nm,f* last but one, second to last

avant-garde (*pl* **avant-gardes**) [avɑ̃gard] *nf* (**a**) *Mil* advance guard (**b**) **l'a.** (*modernité*) the avant-garde; **d'a.** (*œuvre, théâtre*) avant-garde; **être à l'a. de la mode** to be at the cutting edge of fashion

avant-goût (*pl* **avant-goûts**) [avɑ̃gu] *nm* foretaste (**de** of)

avant-guerre (*pl* **avant-guerres**) [avɑ̃gɛr] *nm ou nf* pre-war period

avant-hier [avɑ̃tjɛr] *adv* the day before yesterday; **a. au soir** the evening before last

avant-midi [avɑ̃midi] *nm inv ou nf inv* *Belg & Can* morning

avant-plan [avɑ̃plɑ̃] *nm Belg* foreground

avant-poste (*pl* **avant-postes**) [avɑ̃pɔst] *nm Mil* outpost

avant-première (*pl* **avant-premières**) [avɑ̃prǝmjɛr] *nf* preview; (**présenté**) **en a.** *(film, pièce)* previewed

avant-propos [avɑ̃prɔpo] *nm inv* foreword, preface

avant-scène (*pl* **avant-scènes**) [avɑ̃sɛn] *nf Théât* apron

avant-toit (*pl* **avant-toits**) [avɑ̃twa] *nm* eaves

avant-veille (*pl* **avant-veilles**) [avɑ̃vɛj] *nf* **l'a. (de qch)** two days before (sth)

avare [avar] **1** *adj* mean, miserly; *Fig* **il n'est pas a. de compliments** he's generous with his compliments **2** *nmf* miser

avarice [avaris] *nf* miserliness, avarice

avarie [avari] *nf* damage; **subir une a.** to be damaged

avarié, -e [avarje] *adj (nourriture)* rotten

avarier [66] [avarje] **s'avarier** *vpr (nourriture)* to go off, to go bad

avatar [avatar] *nm* (**a**) *(incarnation)* incarnation (**b**) *(mésaventure)* mishap, misadventure

avec [avɛk] **1** *prép* (**a**) *(en compagnie de)* with; **être gentil/méchant a. qn** to be nice/nasty to sb; **être bien/mal a. qn** *(s'entendre bien/mal)* to get on well/badly with sb; **je suis a. vous** *(je vous soutiens)* I'm right behind you; *Fam* **et a. ça?** *(chez le marchand)* anything else?
(**b**) *(indique la manière)* **a. enthousiasme** enthusiastically, with enthusiasm; **a. beaucoup de gentillesse** very kindly, with great kindness; **c'est a. émotion que j'accepte** I'm thrilled to accept
(**c**) *(indique la simultanéité)* **diminuer a. l'âge** to decrease with age; **cela viendra a. le temps** it will come in time
(**d**) *(indique le moyen)* with; **ouvrir qch a. une clef** to open sth with a key; **j'ai eu un accident a. cette voiture** I had an accident in this car
(**e**) *(à cause de)* **a. tous les ennuis que j'ai en ce moment...** with all the problems I have at the moment...; **impossible de sortir a. cette pluie** it's impossible to go out in this rain
(**f**) *(en ce qui concerne)* **a. elle, on ne sait jamais** you never can tell with her
(**g**) **divorcer d'a. qn** to divorce sb
2 *adv* **je suis venu a.** *(mon parapluie, mes gants)* I came with it/them; **il faut bien faire a.** I'll/we'll just have to put up with it

avenant, -e [avnɑ̃, -ɑ̃t] **1** *adj (personne, manières)* pleasant
2 *nm* (**a**) *(de police d'assurance)* endorsement (**b**) **le bâtiment est beau et le jardin est à l'a.** the building is beautiful and the garden is in keeping with it

avènement [avɛnmɑ̃] *nm (du Christ, d'une ère)* advent; *(d'un roi)* accession

avenir [avnir] *nm* future; **assurer l'a. de qn** to make provision for sb; **dans un très proche a.** in the very near future; **avoir de l'a.** *(personne, technique)* to have a future; **un métier d'a.** a career with good prospects; **un avocat d'a.** a lawyer with a great future; **à l'a.** in future

Avent [avɑ̃] *nm* **l'A.** Advent

aventure [avɑ̃tyr] *nf* (**a**) *(histoire)* adventure; **pour trouver des fruits en hiver, c'est tout une a.** it's quite a job finding fruit in winter (**b**) *(liaison)* (love) affair (**c**) **l'a.** *(le risque)* adventure; **tenter l'a.** to seek adventure; **partir à l'a.** to set off in search of adventure; *(sans préparation)* to set out without making plans (**d**) **dire la bonne a. à qn** to tell sb's fortune

aventurer [avɑ̃tyre] **s'aventurer** *vpr* to venture (**dans** into); **je ne m'aventurerai pas à dire que...** I wouldn't go so far as to say (that)...

aventureux, -euse [avɑ̃tyrø, -øz] *adj (vie, personne)* adventurous; *(projet)* risky

aventurier, -ère [avɑ̃tyrje, -ɛr] *nm,f* adventurer, *f* adventuress

avenue [avny] *nf* avenue

avérer [34] [avere] **s'avérer** *vpr (se révéler)* to prove to be; **il s'est avéré que...** it turned out that...

averse [avɛrs] *nf* shower; *Can* **a. de neige** snow flurry

aversion [avɛrsjɔ̃] *nf* aversion (**pour** to), dislike (**pour** of); **prendre qn en a.** to take a dislike to sb

averti, -e [avɛrti] *adj (bien informé)* (well-)informed; **vous voilà a.!** don't say I didn't warn you!; *Prov* **un homme a. en vaut deux** forewarned is forearmed

avertir [avɛrtir] *vt* **a. qn de qch** *(informer)* to inform sb of sth; *(d'un danger)* to warn sb of sth; **je vais me mettre en colère, je t'avertis!** I'm going to get angry, I'm warning you!

avertissement [avɛrtismɑ̃] *nm* (**a**) *(avis préalable)* warning; **a. (au lecteur)** foreword (**b**) *(réprimande)* warning; *Sport (de l'arbitre)* warning, caution (**c**) *(signal)* warning sign

avertisseur [avɛrtisœr] *nm (dispositif)* alarm; *(Klaxon®)* horn; **a. d'incendie** fire alarm

aveu, -x [avø] *nm* confession; **passer aux aveux** to make a confession; **je dois vous faire un a...** I must confess...; **de l'a. de tout le monde...** it is commonly acknowledged that...

aveuglant, -e [avøglɑ̃, -ɑ̃t] *adj* blinding, dazzling; *Fig (preuve)* blindingly obvious

aveugle [avøgl] **1** *adj aussi Fig* blind; **a. d'un œil** blind in one eye; **avoir une confiance a. en qn** to trust sb implicitly
2 *nmf* blind man, *f* blind woman; **les aveugles** the blind

aveuglement [avøglǝmɑ̃] *nm (moral, mental)* blindness

aveuglément [avøglemɑ̃] *adv* blindly

aveugle-né, -e (*mpl* **aveugles-nés**, *fpl* **aveuglesnées**) [avøglǝne] **1** *adj* blind from birth
2 *nm,f* person blind from birth

aveugler [avøgle] *vt aussi Fig* to blind; **aveuglé par la colère** blind with rage

aveuglette [avøglɛt] **à l'aveuglette** *adv* blindly; **aller à l'a.** to grope one's way

aviateur, -trice [avjatœr, -tris] *nm,f* aviator

aviation [avjasjɔ̃] *nf* (**a**) *(activité)* flying; **faire de l'a.** to go flying (**b**) *(secteur)* aviation; **a. civile/commerciale** civil/commercial aviation; **a. de tourisme** civil aviation (**c**) *Mil* air force

aviculteur, -trice [avikyltœr, -tris] *nm,f (de volailles)* poultry farmer

aviculture [avikyltyr] *nf (de volailles)* poultry farming

avide [avid] *adj* (**a**) *(passionné)* eager (**de** for); **a. de sang** bloodthirsty (**b**) *Péj (cupide)* greedy

avidement [avidmɑ̃] *adv (voracement)* greedily; *(avec passion)* eagerly

avidité [avidite] *nf (voracité, cupidité)* greed; *(passion)* eagerness; **avec a.** *(manger)* greedily; *(écouter, regarder)* eagerly

aviez *voir* **avoir**

Avignon [aviɲɔ̃] *nf* Avignon; *Théât* **le festival d'A.** the Avignon festival

Le festival d'Avignon

Founded by Jean Vilar in 1947 and held every summer in Avignon in the South of France, this arts festival is a showcase for new theatre and dance performances: "La pièce sera donnée d'abord en Avignon". Along with the programme of official shows ("le in") performed in prestigious venues such as the Court of Honour of the "Palais des Papes", a programme comprising numerous fringe shows, referred to as "le off", has also been performed since the 1970s.

avilir [avilir] **1** *vt (dégrader)* to degrade, to demean **2 s'avilir** *vpr (personne)* to demean oneself

avilissant, -e [avilisã, -ãt] *adj* degrading

avilissement [avilismã] *nm (dégradation)* degradation

aviné, -e [avine] *adj (personne)* inebriated; *(haleine)* reeking of wine

avion [avjɔ̃] *nm* plane, *Br* aeroplane, *Am* airplane; **par a.** *(sur lettre)* airmail; **voyager en a.** to travel by plane *or* by air; **a. charter** charter plane; **a. de chasse** fighter (plane); **a. gros-porteur** jumbo jet; **a. de ligne** airliner; **a. à réaction** jet (plane); **a. supersonique** supersonic plane; **a. de tourisme** private plane

avion-cargo *(pl* **avions-cargos)** [avjɔ̃kargo] *nm* freight plane, cargo plane

avions *voir* **avoir**

aviron [avirɔ̃] *nm* (**a**) *(rame)* oar; *Can* paddle (**b**) *(sport)* **l'a.** rowing; **faire de l'a.** to row

avironner [avirɔne] *vi Can* to paddle

avis [avi] *nm* (**a**) *(opinion)* opinion; **changer d'a.** to change one's mind; **les a. sont partagés** opinion is divided; **à mon a.** in my opinion; **tu vas accepter? – à ton a.?** are you going to accept? – what do you think?; **être de l'a. de qn** to be of the same opinion as sb; **de l'a. de tous...** the general opinion is that...; **être d'a. de faire qch** to be of a mind to do sth; *Prov* **deux a. valent mieux qu'un** two heads are better than one (**b**) *(conseils)* advice; **suivre l'a. de qn** to follow sb's advice (**c**) *(avertissement)* notice; **jusqu'à nouvel a.** until further notice; **sauf a. contraire** unless I/you/*etc* hear to the contrary; **a. de livraison** delivery note; **a. de prélèvement** direct debit advice; **a. de réception** acknowledgement of receipt

avisé, -e [avize] *adj (sage)* sensible, wise; *(acheteur, consommateur)* shrewd; **tu serais bien/mal a. de...** you'd be well-/ill-advised to...

aviser [avize] **1** *vt* (**a**) *(informer)* **a. qn de qch** to inform sb of sth; **a. qn que...** to inform sb that... (**b**) *Fam (entrevoir)* to spot **2** *vi (prendre une décision)* to make up one's mind **3 s'aviser** *vpr* (**a**) *(se rendre compte)* **s'a. que** to notice that (**b**) *(oser)* **s'a. de faire qch** to get it into one's head to do sth; **et ne t'avise pas de recommencer!** don't you dare start again!

aviver [avive] *vt (couleurs)* to brighten up; *(passion, querelle, feu)* to stir up; *(appétit)* to sharpen

av. J.-C. *(abrév* **avant Jésus-Christ)** BC; **en 106 av. J.-C.** in 106 BC

avocat¹, -e [avɔka, -at] *nm,f* (**a**) *Jur* lawyer; **a. d'affaires** business lawyer; **a. général** assistant public prosecutor *(in a Court of Appeal)* (**b**) *Fig* advocate; **se faire l'a. du diable** to play devil's advocate

avocat² *nm (fruit)* avocado (pear)

avocette [avɔset] *nf* avocet

avoine [avwan] *nf* (**a**) *(céréale)* oats (**b**) *Fam (argent)* dough

avoir¹ [1] [avwar] **1** *v aux* to have; **je ne l'ai pas encore fini** I haven't finished it yet; **je te l'ai dit hier** I told you yesterday; **j'avais déjà vu ce film** I had already seen the film before; **il faut que je l'aie fini pour demain** I have to finish it by tomorrow; **est-ce que tu auras terminé ce soir?** will you get it finished tonight?; **il aurait réussi s'il avait travaillé plus** he would have passed if he had worked harder

2 *vt* (**a**) *(posséder)* to have; **il a une fille** he has *or* he's got a daughter; **a. les yeux bleus** to have blue eyes; **a. une drôle de forme** to have a funny shape; **a. un rhume** to have a cold; **a. du diabète** to be diabetic; **a. mal au cœur** to feel sick; **j'ai le nez qui pique** I've got an itchy nose; **a. de l'ambition** to be ambitious; **a. de l'humour** to have a sense of humour; **a. 20 ans** to be 20 (years old); **a. de quoi manger** to have something to eat; **elle a Guy pour voisin** Guy is her neighbour; **qui as-tu comme prof de math?** who's your maths teacher?

(**b**) *(obtenir)* to get; **a. qn au téléphone** to speak to sb on the telephone; **a. son train** to catch one's train; **je l'ai eu pour 50 euros** I bought it for 50 euros; **j'ai eu mon bac en 1995** I passed my "bac" in 1995

(**c**) *(porter) (vêtement)* to wear; *(objet)* to carry

(**d**) *(faire)* **il a eu un sourire étrange** he smiled strangely

(**e**) *(atteindre) (cible)* to hit

(**f**) *Fam (duper) (personne)* to take for a ride, to con; **tu nous a bien eus!** you really had us going!; **se faire a.** to be conned; **se faire a. de 100 euros** to be conned out of 100 euros

(**g**) *(locutions)* **a. faim/froid** to be hungry/cold; **a. quelque chose à faire** to have something to do; **j'ai à faire** I've got things to do; **j'ai à lui parler** I've got to talk to him; **tu n'as qu'à le lui dire** just tell her; **tu en as pour combien de temps?** how long will you be?; **j'en ai pour 10 minutes** I'll be 10 minutes; **je n'en ai pas pour longtemps** I won't be long; **qu'est-ce que tu as?** what's wrong?; **j'ai que je suis fatigué** I'm tired, that's all; **qu'est-ce qu'il a à se plaindre sans arrêt?** why is he complaining all the time?; **on les aura!** we'll have them!

3 il y a *v impersonnel* there is/are; **il y a un problème** there's a problem; **il y a des problèmes** there are some problems; **il y a six ans** six years ago; **il y a un mois que je suis ici** I've been here for a month; **il n'y a qu'à le faire** we'll just have to do it; **il n'y a pas que ça dans la vie** there's more to life than that; **il n'y a pas de quoi!** don't mention it!; **qu'y a-t-il?, qu'est-ce qu'il y a?** what is it?, what's wrong?; **il y a que j'en ai assez** I've had enough, that's all

avoir² *nm (d'une compagnie)* assets; *(d'un compte)* credit; *(dans un magasin)* voucher

avoisinant, -e [avwazinã, -ãt] *adj* neighbouring, nearby

avoisiner [avwazine] *vt* **une somme avoisinant les 500 euros** a sum in the region of 500 euros

avons *voir* **avoir**

avortement [avɔrtəmã] *nm* (**a**) *(chez une femme)* **a. (provoqué)** abortion; **a. spontané** miscarriage; **a. thérapeutique** termination for medical reasons (**b**) *(chez un animal)* casting (**c**) *Fig (d'un projet)* failure

avorter [avɔrte] **1** *vi* (**a**) *(subir une IVG)* to have an abortion; *(faire une fausse couche)* to miscarry (**b**)

(animal) to cast (**c**) *Fig (projet)* to fall through
  2 *vt (sujet: médecin)* to abort; **se faire a.** to have an
abortion
avorteur, -euse [avɔrtœr, -øz] *nm,f* abortionist
avorton [avɔrtɔ̃] *nm Péj* runt
avoué¹ [avwe] *nm Jur Br* ≃ solicitor, *Am* ≃ attorney
avoué², -e *adj* (**a**) *(auteur, partisan)* confessed (**b**)
(but) declared
avouer [avwe] **1** *vt (faute, crime)* to confess to, to own
up to; **il a fini par a.** he finally confessed; **a. que** to
admit that; **ceci me surprend, je l'avoue** this surprises me, I must confess; **il faut bien a. que...** it must
be admitted that...
  2 s'avouer *vpr* **s'a. coupable** to admit one's guilt; **s'a.
vaincu** to acknowledge defeat
avril [avril] *nm* April; **le premier a.** *(jour des farces)*
April Fools' Day; *Prov* **en a., ne te découvre pas d'un
fil** ne'er cast a clout till May is out; *voir aussi* **janvier**
axe [aks] *nm* (**a**) *(géométrique)* axis; **a. des abscisses /
des ordonnées** x-/y-axis; **être dans l'a. de qch** to be
in line with sth; **(grand) a.** *(routier)* main road; *Fig* **les
grands axes de sa politique** the main thrust of his
policy (**b**) *(de machine, de roue de vélo)* axle (**c**) *Hist*
l'A. (Rome-Berlin) the (Rome-Berlin) Axis

axer [akse] *vt* to centre; **être axé sur** *ou* **autour de** to
centre on
axiome [aksjom] *nm* axiom
ayant *etc voir* **avoir**
ayant droit *(pl* **ayants droit***)* [ɛjɑ̃drwa] *nm Jur* beneficiary
ayatollah [ajatɔla] *nm* ayatollah
azalée [azale] *nf* azalea
Azerbaïdjan [azɛrbajdʒɑ̃] *nm* **l'A.** Azerbaijan
azerbaïdjanais, -e [azɛrbajdʒanɛ, -ɛz] **1** *adj* Azerbaijani
  2 *nm,f* **A.** Azerbaijani
azéri, -e [azeri] **1** *adj* Azeri
  2 *nm,f* **A.** Azeri
azimuts [azimyt] *nmpl Fam* **une campagne électorale tous a.** an all-out electoral campaign
azote [azɔt] *nm* nitrogen
AZT® [azɛdte] *nm Méd (abrév* **azidothymidine***)* AZT
aztèque [aztɛk] **1** *adj* Aztec
  2 *nmf* **A.** Aztec
azur [azyr] *nm Litt* (**a**) *(couleur)* azure (**b**) **l'a.** *(ciel)* the
sky
azyme [azim] *adj m voir* **pain**

B

B, b [be] *nm inv* B, b

baba¹ [baba] *nm* **b. au rhum** rum baba; *Fam* **elle l'a dans le b.** she's had it

baba² *adj inv Fam* flabbergasted; **j'en suis resté b.** I was flabbergasted

baba cool (*pl* **babas cool**) [babakul] *nmf* hippie

Babel [babɛl] *n* **la tour de B.** the Tower of Babel

babil [babil] *nm (d'un enfant)* prattling; *(des oiseaux)* twittering; *(d'un ruisseau)* babbling

babillard [babijar] *nm Ordinat* bulletin board, BBS

babiller [babije] *vi (enfant)* to prattle; *(oiseau)* to twitter; *(ruisseau)* to babble

babines [babin] *nfpl aussi Hum* chops; **d'avance, je m'en lèche les b.** my mouth's watering in anticipation

babiole [babjɔl] *nf* (**a**) *(bibelot)* knick-knack, trinket (**b**) *(broutille)* trifle

bâbord [babɔr] *nm* port (side); **à b.** to port

babouche [babuʃ] *nf* Turkish slipper

babouin [babwɛ̃] *nm* baboon

baboune [babun] *nf Can Fam* **faire la b.** to sulk

baby-boom (*pl* **baby-booms**) [bebibum] *nm* baby boom

baby-foot [babifut] *nm inv* table football

baby-sitter (*pl* **baby-sitters**) [bebisitœr] *nmf* baby-sitter

baby-sitting [bebisitiŋ] *nm* baby-sitting; **faire du b.** to baby-sit

bac¹ [bak] *nm* (**a**) *(bateau)* ferry(-boat) (**b**) *(récipient)* tank; *(d'imprimeur, de photographe)* tray; *Ordinat* **b. d'alimentation** sheet feed; **b. à glace** ice tray; **b. à légumes** salad drawer; *Belg* **b. à ordures** *Br* dustbin, *Am* garbage can; **b. de** *ou* **à papier** *(d'imprimante)* paper tray; **b. à sable** sandpit

bac² *Fam* = **baccalauréat**

baccalauréat [bakalɔrea] *nm* = secondary school examination qualifying for entry to university, *Br* ≃ A levels, *Am* ≃ high school diploma; **b. L** *ou* **littéraire** = arts-based "baccalauréat"; **b. S** *ou* **scientifique** = science-based "baccalauréat"

Baccalauréat

The "baccalauréat", or "bac", is taken by pupils who have completed their final year at the "lycée"; successful candidates may go to university. Depending on which subjects pupils choose to study at "lycée", they prepare for a "baccalauréat général", "technologique" (vocational) or "professionnel" (vocational and including professional training). Since the last major reform, in 1995, there have been three main types of "baccalauréat général", each corresponding to a specific field: "bac L" (arts subjects), "bac ES" (economics and social studies) and "bac S" (sciences).

bacchantes [bakɑ̃t] *nfpl Hum* moustache

bâche [baʃ] *nf (toile)* tarpaulin

bachelier, -ère [baʃəlje, -ɛr] *nm,f* = student who has passed the "baccalauréat"

bâcher [baʃe] *vt* **b. qch** to cover sth with a tarpaulin

bachot [baʃo] *Fam Vieilli* = **baccalauréat**

bachotage [baʃɔtaʒ] *nm Fam Vieilli* cramming, *Br* swotting

bachoter [baʃɔte] *vi Fam Vieilli* to cram, *Br* to swot

bacille [basil] *nm Biol* bacillus

bâcler [bakle] *vt Fam* to botch

bacon [bekɔn] *nm* (**a**) *(viande)* bacon (**b**) *Can Fam* **avoir du b.** to be loaded

bactérie [bakteri] *nf* bacterium

bactériologique [bakterjɔlɔʒik] *adj* bacteriological; **guerre b.** germ warfare

badaboum [badabum] *exclam Fam* **et b., il est tombé!** he fell down, crash, bang, wallop!

badaud [bado] *nm (promeneur)* stroller; *(curieux) Br* gawper, *Am* rubberneck

badge [badʒ] *nm* (**a**) *(insigne, d'identité) Br* badge, *Am* button (**b**) *(carte magnétique)* swipe card

badigeonner [badiʒɔne] *vt* (**a**) *(surface)* to daub (**de** with); *(mur)* to whitewash; *Culin* to brush (**de** with) (**b**) *(gorge, plaie)* to paint (**de** with)

badin, -e [badɛ̃, -in] *adj* playful

badinage [badinaʒ] *nm* banter

badine [badin] *nf* switch

badiner [badine] *vi* to jest, to joke; **il ne badine pas avec la ponctualité** he's very strict about punctuality

badinerie [badinri] *nf* jest

badminton [badmintɔn] *nm* badminton

bâdrant, -e [badrɑ̃, -ɑ̃t] *adj Can* bothersome

bâdrer [badre] *vt Can* to bother

baffe [baf] *nf Fam* clout, smack; **flanquer une b. à qn** to give sb a smack in the face

baffle [bafl] *nm* baffle

bafouer [bafwe] *vt (personne)* to jeer at; *(règlement, autorité)* to flout

bafouiller [bafuje] *vt & vi* to stammer

bâfrer [bafre] *vi très Fam* to stuff oneself

bagage [bagaʒ] *nm* (**a**) *(sac, valise)* **bagages** luggage, baggage; **faire ses bagages** to pack one's bags; **b. à main** piece of hand luggage (**b**) *Fig (connaissances)* knowledge (**en** of)

bagagiste [bagaʒist] *nm* baggage handler

bagarre [bagar] *nf* fight, brawl; **chercher la b.** to look for a fight

bagarrer [bagare] **se bagarrer** *upr Fam* to fight

bagarreur, -euse [bagarœr, -øz] *Fam* **1** *adj (personne, caractère)* aggressive
  2 *nm,f* brawler

bagatelle [bagatɛl] *nf (chose sans importance)* trifle; **pour la b. de 400 euros** for a mere 400 euros

Bagdad [bagdad] *n* Baghdad

bagnard [baɲar] *nm* convict

bagne [baɲ] *nm Hist (prison)* convict prison; *(peine)* penal servitude; *Fig* **c'est le b., ici!** they work you to death in this place!

bagnole [baɲɔl] *nf Fam* car

bagou(t) [bagu] *nm* glibness; **avoir du b.** to have the gift of the gab

bague [bag] *nf* (**a**) *(bijou)* ring; *Fig* **passer la b. au doigt à qn** to marry sb; **b. de fiançailles** engagement ring (**b**) *(d'une boîte de conserve)* ring-pull; *(de cigare)* band (**c**) *(d'oiseau)* ring (**d**) *Tech* bush, ring; **b. de serrage** jubilee clip

baguenauder [bagnode] **1** *vi* to saunter around
  2 **se baguenauder** *upr* to saunter around

baguer [bage] *vt (oiseau, arbre)* to ring

baguette [bagɛt] *nf (tige)* stick; *(de chef d'orchestre)* baton; *(pain)* French stick; **baguettes** *(pour manger)* chopsticks; **mener** *ou* **faire marcher qn à la b.** to rule sb with a rod of iron; **b. magique** magic wand; **d'un coup de b. magique** with a wave of my/his/*etc* magic wand; **baguettes de tambour** drumsticks; **avoir des cheveux raides comme des baguettes de tambour** to have dead straight hair

bah [bɑ] *exclam* bah!

Bahamas [baamas] *nfpl* **les B., l'archipel des B.** the Bahamas

Bahreïn [barajn], **Bahrayn** [barɛ̃] *n* Bahrain

bahut [bay] *nm* (**a**) *(coffre)* chest; *(buffet)* sideboard (**b**) *Fam (collège, lycée)* school (**c**) *Fam (camion)* truck, *Br* lorry

bai, -e [bɛ] *adj (cheval)* bay

baie¹ [bɛ] *nf Géog* bay; **la b. d'Hudson** Hudson Bay

baie² *nf* **b. vitrée** picture window

baie³ *nf (fruit)* berry

baignade [bɛɲad] *nf* (**a**) *(activité)* swimming, *Br* bathing; **b. interdite** *(sur panneau)* no swimming (**b**) *(endroit)* swimming *or Br* bathing place

baigner [beɲe] **1** *vt (pieds, œil, blessure)* to bathe; *(bébé, chien) Br* to bath, *Am* to bathe; *(sujet: mer)* to wash; *(sujet: rivière)* to water; **être baigné de sueur** to be bathed in sweat; **visage baigné de larmes** face streaming with tears; **baigné de lumière** bathed in light
  2 *vi (tremper)* to soak, to steep (**dans** in); **les légumes baignent dans la sauce** the vegetables are swimming in sauce; **il baignait dans son sang** he was lying in a pool of his own blood; *Fam* **ça baigne (dans l'huile)!** everything's hunky dory!
  3 **se baigner** *upr* (**a**) *(se laver)* to have *or* take a bath (**b**) *(nager)* to have a swim

baigneur, -euse [beɲœr, -øz] **1** *nm,f* swimmer, *Br* bather
  2 *nm (poupée)* doll

baignoire [beɲwar] *nf* (**a**) *(dans la salle de bains)* bath (**b**) *Théât* ground-floor box

Baïkal [bajkal] *n voir* **lac**

bail [baj] *(pl* **baux** [bo]*) nm* lease; *Fam* **ça fait un b. que je ne l'ai pas vu** I haven't seen him for ages

bâillement [bajmɑ̃] *nm* yawn

bâiller [baje] *vi* (**a**) *(personne)* to yawn; *Fam* **b. à s'en** *ou* **se décrocher la mâchoire** to yawn one's head off (**b**) *(coutures, col)* to gape; *(porte)* to be ajar

bâillon [bajɔ̃] *nm* gag; **mettre un b. à qn** to gag sb

bâillonner [bajɔne] *vt aussi Fig* to gag

bain [bɛ̃] *nm* (**a**) *(pour se laver)* bath; **prendre un b.** to have *or* take a bath; *Fam Fig* **être/se mettre dans le b.** to be in/get into the swing of things; **b. de bouche** mouthwash; **faire un b. de bouche** to use mouthwash; **b. de boue** mud bath; **prendre un b. de foule** *(personnalité)* to go on a walkabout; **b. moussant** bubble bath; **prendre un b. de pieds** to soak one's feet; **prendre un b. de soleil** to sunbathe; **b. turc** Turkish bath; **b. de vapeur** steam bath
  (**b**) *Can (baignoire)* bathtub, *Br* bath
  (**c**) *(à la piscine)* **petit/grand b.** small/large pool
  (**d**) *(à la mer, en rivière)* swim, *Br* bathe; *Vieilli* **bains de mer** swimming in the sea
  (**e**) *Phot* bath
  (**f**) *Tex* dye

bain-marie *(pl* **bains-marie**) [bɛ̃mari] *nm* bain-marie *(cooking pan set over second pan of boiling water)*; **faire cuire qch au b.** to cook sth in a bain-marie

baïonnette [bajɔnɛt] *nf* bayonet

baisemain [bɛzmɛ̃] *nm* **faire le b. à qn** to kiss sb's hand

baiser¹ [beze] **1** *vt* (**a**) *Litt (embrasser)* to kiss (**b**) *Vulg (coucher avec)* to fuck (**c**) *Vulg (tromper)* to screw; **se faire b.** to get screwed
  2 *vi Vulg* to fuck

baiser² *nm* kiss; **gros baisers** *(dans une lettre)* love and kisses

baisse [bɛs] *nf* fall, drop (**de** in); **être en b.** *(température, actions)* to be falling; *(popularité)* to be on the decline

baisser [bese] **1** *vt* (**a**) *(rideau, store, vitre de voiture)* to lower; **b. la tête** to lower one's head; *(de honte, de découragement)* to hang one's head; **b. les yeux** to look down; *Fig* **b. les bras** to give in (**b**) *(lumière, son, chauffage)* to turn down; *(prix)* to lower; **b. la voix** to lower one's voice; **je vous prie de b. le ton!** please keep your voice down!
  2 *vi* (**a**) *(diminuer) (température, niveau de l'eau, prix)* to fall; *(marée)* to ebb; **elle a baissé dans mon estime** she's gone down in my estimation (**b**) *(s'affaiblir) (malade)* to get weaker; *(enthousiasme)* to fall off; *(feu)* to burn low; *(vue, mémoire)* to fail; **le jour baisse** night is falling
  3 **se baisser** *upr* to bend down; *(pour éviter un coup)* to duck; *Fig* **il n'y a qu'à se b. pour les ramasser** there are loads of them around

baissier [besje] *adj m voir* **marché**

bajoues [baʒu] *nfpl (d'animal)* chops; *Péj (d'une personne)* flabby cheeks

Bakou [baku] *n* Baku

bal *(pl* **bals**) [bal] *nm (populaire)* dance; *(élégant)* ball; **b. costumé** *ou* **masqué** fancy dress ball; **b. musette** = dance to accordion music; **b. populaire** = dance, usually outdoors, open to the public

balade [balad] *nf Fam (à pied)* walk; *(en voiture)* drive; *(à bicyclette, à moto)* ride; **faire une b.** *(à pied)* to go for a walk; *(en voiture)* to go for a drive; *(à bicyclette, à moto)* to go for a ride

balader [balade] *Fam* **1** *vt (personne, chien)* to take for a walk; *(avoir avec soi) (objet)* to drag around
  2 *vi* **envoyer b. qn** to send sb packing
  3 se balader *vpr (à pied)* to go for a walk; *(en voiture)* to go for a drive; *(à bicyclette, à moto)* to go for a ride

baladeur, -euse [baladœr, -øz] **1** *adj Fam* **avoir les mains baladeuses** to have wandering hands
  2 *nm* personal stereo, Walkman®
  3 *nf* **baladeuse** *(lampe)* inspection lamp

baladin [baladɛ̃] *nm* strolling player

balafre [balafr] *nf* **(a)** *(coupure)* gash **(b)** *(cicatrice)* scar

balafré [balafre] *nm* scarface

balafrer [balafre] *vt* to gash; **visage balafré** scarred face

balai [balɛ] *nm* **(a)** *(de ménage)* broom; **passer le b.** to give the floor a sweep; **donner un coup de b.** *(balayer)* to give the floor a sweep; *Fig (dans une entreprise)* to have a shake-out; **du b.!** clear off!; **b. mécanique** carpet sweeper **(b)** *Aut (d'essuie-glace)* blade **(c)** *(percussion)* brush **(d)** *Fam (an)* **avoir quarante/cinquante balais** to be forty/fifty

balai-brosse *(pl* **balais-brosses**) [balɛbrɔs] *nm* long-handled scrubbing brush

balaise [balɛz] = **balèze**

balalaïka [balalaika] *nf* balalaika

balance [balɑ̃s] *nf* **(a)** *(appareil)* (pair of) scales; *(publique)* weighing machine; *Fig* **ce facteur pèse dans la b.** this factor carries some weight; **faire pencher la b.** to tip the scales **(b)** *Astron & Astrol* **la B.** Libra; **être B.** to be a Libran **(c)** *Écon* balance; **b. commerciale** balance of trade; **b. des paiements** balance of payments **(d)** *Fam (mouchard)* squealer

balancé, -e [balɑ̃se] *adj Fam* **être bien b.** *(personne)* to have a good figure

balancelle [balɑ̃sɛl] *nf (de jardin) Br* swing hammock, *Am* glider

balancement [balɑ̃smɑ̃] *nm* swaying

balancer [16] [balɑ̃se] **1** *vt* **(a)** *(bras, jambes, trompe, pendule)* to swing; *(hanches)* to sway **(b)** *Fam (projectile, objet)* to chuck, to throw; **b. des vannes/remarques** to make snide/unpleasant remarks **(c)** *Com (compte)* to balance **(d)** *Fam (se débarrasser de) (objet)* to chuck *or* throw out; **b. qn** to give sb the push; **elle a tout balancé** *(tout abandonné)* she's given it all up **(e)** *Fam (dénoncer)* to squeal on
  2 *vi Litt (hésiter)* to waver
  3 se balancer *vpr* **(a)** *(arbres, blés)* to sway; **se b. sur sa chaise** to rock backwards and forwards on one's chair; **se b. d'un pied sur l'autre** to rock from one foot to the other **(b)** *(sur une balançoire)* to swing **(c)** *très Fam* **je m'en balance!** I don't give a toss! **(d)** *Fam* **il s'est balancé du haut de la tour Eiffel** he chucked himself off the top of the Eiffel Tower

balancier [balɑ̃sje] *nm* **(a)** *(d'un funambule)* balancing pole **(b)** *(d'horloge)* pendulum

balançoire [balɑ̃swar] *nf (suspendue)* swing; *(bascule)* seesaw

balayage [balɛjaʒ] *nm* **(a)** *(pour nettoyer)* sweeping **(b)** *Rad, Élec & TV* scanning

balayer [53] [balɛje] *vt* **(a)** *(nettoyer)* to sweep; *(saletés)* to sweep up; *Fig (objections, obstacles)* to brush aside; **le vent a balayé les nuages** the wind has swept the clouds away; *Fig* **b. devant sa porte** to put

one's own house in order **(b)** *Rad, Élec & TV* to scan; *(sujet: projecteurs)* to sweep

balayette [balɛjɛt] *nf* small brush; *(des WC)* toilet brush

balayeur, -euse [balɛjœr, -øz] **1** *nm,f* road-sweeper
  2 *nf* **balayeuse** *Can (aspirateur)* vacuum cleaner

balbutiement [balbysimɑ̃] *nm* **(a)** *(en parlant)* stammering **(b)** **balbutiements** *(d'une science, d'une discipline)* early stages

balbutier [66] [balbysje] **1** *vi* to stammer
  2 *vt* to stammer (out)

balcon [balkɔ̃] *nm* **(a)** *(d'édifice)* balcony **(b)** *(dans un théâtre)* circle; **premier/deuxième b.** dress/upper circle

baldaquin [baldakɛ̃] *nm* canopy

Bâle [bal] *n* Basel

Baléares [balear] *nfpl* **les (îles) B.** the Balearic Islands

baleine [balɛn] *nf* **(a)** *(animal)* whale; **b. blanche/bleue** white/blue whale **(b)** *(d'un parapluie)* rib; *(d'un corset)* (whale)bone

baleineau, -x [baleno] *nm* whale calf

baleinière [balɛnjer] *nf* whaleboat

balèze [balɛz] *adj Fam (grand et fort)* hefty; *(intelligent)* brainy; **b. en maths** brilliant at maths

balisage [balizaʒ] *nm* **(a)** *(signaux) Naut & Rad* beacons; *Aviat* lights **(b)** *(action) Naut & Rad* beaconing; *Aviat* lighting

balise [baliz] *nf Naut & Rad* beacon; *Aviat* light; *(de piste de ski, d'épave)* marker; *Ordinat* tag; *Naut* **b. flottante** buoy; *Rad* **b. radar** radar beacon

baliser [balize] *vt (chenal)* to beacon; *(aéroport)* to equip with lights; *(route)* to mark out with beacons; *(piste de ski)* to mark out

balistique [balistik] **1** *adj (missile)* ballistic
  2 *nf* ballistics *(singulier)*

balivernes [balivern] *nfpl* twaddle

balkanisation [balkanizasjɔ̃] *nf aussi Fig* Balkanization

Balkans [balkɑ̃] *nmpl* **les B.** the Balkans

ballade [balad] *nf* ballad

ballant, -e [balɑ̃, -ɑ̃t] *adj (bras, jambes)* dangling; **ne reste pas là, les bras ballants** don't just stand there like an idiot

ballast [balast] *nm* **(a)** *Constr (d'une route, d'une voie ferrée)* ballast **(b)** *Naut* ballast tank

balle¹ [bal] *nf* **(a)** *(pour jouer)* ball; **jouer à la b.** to play ball; *Fig* **prendre** *ou* **saisir la b. au bond** to seize the opportunity; *Fig* **se renvoyer la b.** to pass the buck; *Fig* **la b. est dans votre camp** the ball's in your court; **b. de golf/de tennis** golf/tennis ball; **b. de break/de match** break/match point **(b)** *(d'arme)* bullet; **b. à blanc** blank; **b. perdue** stray bullet **(c)** *Fam* **balles** *(francs)* francs

balle² *nf (de coton, de laine)* bale

balle³ *nf (de blé)* husk

ballerine [balrin] *nf* **(a)** *(danseuse)* ballerina **(b)** *(chaussure)* pump

ballet [balɛ] *nm* ballet

ballon [balɔ̃] *nm* **(a)** *(aéronef)* balloon; **b. d'essai** pilot balloon **(b)** *(balle)* ball; **jouer au b.** to play with a ball; **b. de football** football; **le b. ovale** rugby; **le b. rond** football **(c)** *(pour boire)* **(verre) b.** round wine glass **(d)** **b. (de baudruche)** balloon; **souffler dans le b.** *(d'alcootest)* to blow into the bag; **b. d'oxygène** oxygen bottle **(e)** *Suisse (petit pain)* (bread) roll

ballonné, -e [balɔne] *adj (ventre, personne)* bloated

ballon-panier [balɔ̃panje] *nm inv Can Sport* basketball

ballon-sonde *(pl* **ballons-sondes)** [balɔ̃sɔ̃d] *nm Météo* sounding balloon

ballot [balo] *nm* (**a**) *(paquet)* bundle (**b**) *Fam (imbécile)* twit

ballottage [balɔtaʒ] *nm Pol* **il y a b.** there will be a second ballot

ballottement [balɔtmã] *nm (de train)* rocking; *(des passagers)* shaking; *(de navire)* tossing

ballotter [balɔte] **1** *vt (bateau)* to toss about; *(passagers)* to shake about; *Fig* **un enfant ballotté entre son père et sa mère** a child passed backwards and forwards between its father and mother
2 *vi (bagages, bateau)* to be tossed about; *(poitrine)* to bounce up and down

ball-trap [baltrap] *nm (sport)* clay-pigeon shooting

balluchon [balyʃɔ̃] *nm Fam (de vêtements)* bundle; **faire son b.** to pack one's bags

balnéaire [balneɛr] *adj voir* **station**

balourd, -e [balur, -urd] **1** *adj (personne)* oafish
2 *nm,f* clumsy oaf

balsa [balza] *nm* balsawood

balte [balt] **1** *adj* Baltic; **les pays Baltes** the Baltic states
2 *nmf* Balt

Baltique [baltik] *nf* **la (mer) B.** the Baltic (Sea)

baluchon [balyʃɔ̃] = **balluchon**

balustrade [balystrad] *nf* (**a**) *Archit* balustrade (**b**) *(clôture)* railing

bambin [bãbɛ̃] *nm Fam* toddler

bambou [bãbu] *nm (plante)* bamboo; *Fam* **c'est le coup de b.!** it's a rip-off!

bamboula [bãbula] *nf Fam* spree; **faire la b.** to live it up

ban [bã] *nm* (**a**) *(applaudissements)* round of applause (**b**) **bans** *(de mariage)* banns; **publier les bans** to publish the (wedding) banns (**c**) **être au b. de la société** to be an outcast from society; **le b. et l'arrière-b.** *(tout le monde)* the world and his wife (**d**) *Suisse* **mettre qch au b.** to forbid access to sth

banal, -e, -als, -ales [banal] *adj (objet, gens, occupation)* ordinary; *(idée, remarque, style)* trite, banal; *(accident, exemple)* common; **pas b.** unusual

banalisation [banalizasjɔ̃] *nf (généralisation)* spread; *Péj (perte d'originalité)* trivialization; **la b. des transports aériens** the fact that air travel has become commonplace *or* an everyday phenomenon

banaliser [banalize] **1** *vt (rendre commun)* to trivialize; **véhicule banalisé** unmarked police car
2 **se banaliser** *vpr* to become more common

banalité [banalite] *nf* (**a**) *(d'un objet, de gens, d'une occupation)* ordinariness; *(d'une idée, d'une remarque, d'un style)* triteness, banality; *(d'un accident, d'un exemple)* commonness (**b**) **banalités** *(propos banals)* platitudes

banane [banan] *nf* (**a**) *(fruit)* banana; **b. plantain** plantain (**b**) *(coiffure)* quiff (**c**) *(petit sac) Br* bum bag, *Am* fanny pack

bananier, -ère [bananje, -ɛr] **1** *adj (plantation, production)* banana
2 *nm (arbre)* banana tree

banc [bã] *nm* (**a**) *(siège)* bench; **ils se sont connus sur les bancs de l'école** they got to know each other at school; **b. des accusés** dock; **b. d'église** pew; **b. des témoins** *Br* witness box, *Am* witness stand (**b**) *(de roche)* layer; *Can* **b. de neige** snowdrift; *(entassé mécaniquement)* bank of snow; **b. de sable** sandbank (**c**) *(de poissons)* shoal; **b. d'huîtres** oyster bed (**d**) *(établi)* (work)bench (**e**) **b. d'essai** *Ind* test bed; *Ordinat* benchtest; *Fig* testing ground; *Ordinat* **b. de mémoire** memory bank

bancaire [bãkɛr] *adj (opération)* banking; *(chèque, compte)* bank

bancal, -e, -als, -ales [bãkal] *adj (meuble)* wobbly; *Fig (raisonnement, projet)* unsound

bandage [bãdaʒ] *nm (pansement)* bandage; *(action)* bandaging

bandana [bãdana] *nm* bandana

bande¹ [bãd] *nf* (**a**) *(de tissu, de papier, de terre)* strip; *(motif)* stripe; **b. dessinée** comic strip
(**b**) *(pansement)* bandage; **b. Velpeau**® crêpe bandage
(**c**) *(magnétique)* tape; *(pellicule)* film; *Ordinat* **b. en cassettes** cassette tape; *Ordinat* **b. de défilement** scroll bar; *Ordinat* **b. de données** data tape; **b. originale** *(d'un film)* original soundtrack; **b. sonore** soundtrack
(**d**) *Aut* **b. d'arrêt d'urgence** *Br* hard shoulder, *Am* shoulder; **b. médiane** *(sur la route)* central line; **b. de roulement** *(de pneu)* tread
(**e**) *Rad* **b. (de fréquence)** (frequency) band; *Phys & Tél* **b. passante** pass-band
(**f**) *(d'une mitrailleuse)* cartridge belt
(**g**) *Naut* **donner de la b.** to list

bande² *nf (de personnes)* band, group; *(de voleurs)* gang, band; **faire b. à part** *(agir seul)* to do one's own thing; **viens avec nous, ne fais pas b. à part** come with us, don't stay all on your own; **faire qch en b.** to do sth in a group; **une b. d'incapables/d'imbéciles** a bunch of incompetents/idiots

bande-annonce *(pl* **bandes-annonces)** [bãdanɔ̃s] *nf* trailer (**de** for)

bandeau, -x [bãdo] *nm* (**a**) *(pour les cheveux)* headband (**b**) *(sur les yeux)* blindfold; **mettre un b. à qn** to blindfold sb (**c**) *Ordinat (dans un site Web)* banner

bandelette [bãdlɛt] *nf (de tissu)* strip; **bandelettes** *(de momie)* bandages

bander [bãde] **1** *vt* (**a**) *(blessure, main)* to bandage; **b. les yeux à qn** to blindfold sb (**b**) *(ressort)* to tighten; *(arc)* to bend; *(muscles)* to flex
2 *vi Vulg* to have a hard-on

banderille [bãdrij] *nf* banderilla

banderole [bãdrɔl] *nf* banner

bande-son *(pl* **bandes-son)** [bãdsɔ̃] *nf* soundtrack

bandit [bãdi] *nm (escroc)* crook; *Vieilli (brigand)* bandit; **b. de grand chemin** highwayman

banditisme [bãditism] *nm* crime; **le grand b.** organized crime

bandoulière [bãduljɛr] *nf (d'un sac)* shoulder strap; **en b.** over one's shoulder

bang [bãg] *nm inv Aviat* sonic boom; *Astron* **le big b.** the big bang

Bangkok [bãkɔk] *n* Bangkok

Bangladesh [bãgladɛʃ, bɛ̃gladɛʃ] *nm* **le B.** Bangladesh

banjo [bãdʒo] *nm* banjo

banlieue [bãljø] *nf* suburbs; **la b. parisienne/marseillaise** the suburbs of Paris/Marseilles; **la grande/**

proche b. the outer/inner suburbs; **vivre en b.** to live in the suburbs; **de b.** suburban

---

Banlieue

In France the word "banlieue" often refers not to the upmarket areas of a city, as the word "suburbia" suggests in English-speaking countries, but to the impoverished suburban areas on the outskirts of some cities. These neighbourhoods are culturally and ethnically diverse and are frequently associated with social problems such as delinquency, unemployment and unrest.

---

banlieusard, -e [bãljøzar, -ard] *nm,f* suburbanite

bannière [banjɛr] *nf* (**a**) *(drapeau)* banner; **la b. étoi-lée** the Star-spangled Banner (**b**) *Ordinat (dans un site Web)* banner

bannir [banir] *vt (personne, idée)* to banish (**de** from); *(sujet de conversation)* to ban (**de** from); **vous devez b. le sucre de votre alimentation** you must exclude sugar from your diet

bannissement [banismã] *nm* banishment

banque [bãk] *nf* (**a**) *(établissement)* bank; **la b.** *(activité)* banking; **employé/directeur de b.** bank clerk/manager; **b. d'affaires** *Br* merchant bank, *Am* investment bank; **b. centrale** central bank; **B. centrale européenne** European central bank; **B. européenne pour la reconstruction et le développement** European Bank for Reconstruction and Development; **la B. de France** the Bank of France; **B. internationale pour la reconstruction et le développement** International Bank for Reconstruction and Development; **la B. mondiale** the World Bank; **b. à domicile** telebanking, home banking (**b**) *(au jeu)* bank; **faire sauter la b.** to break the bank (**c**) *Ordinat* **b. de données** data bank; *Méd* **b. d'organes/du sperme** organ/sperm bank

banquer [bãke] *vi Fam* to cough up

banqueroute [bãkrut] *nf Jur* bankruptcy; **faire b.** to go bankrupt

banquet [bãkɛ] *nm* banquet

banquette [bãkɛt] *nf* (**a**) *(siège)* seat; **la b. arrière** *(d'une voiture)* the back seat (**b**) *(d'un couloir d'autobus)* = kerb separating a bus lane from the rest of the roadway

banquier, -ère [bãkje, -ɛr] *nm,f* banker

banquise [bãkiz] *nf* ice floe

bantou, -e [bãtu] **1** *adj* Bantu
  2 *nm,f* **B.** Bantu

baobab [baɔbab] *nm* baobab (tree)

baptême [batɛm] *nm* (**a**) *Rel* baptism, christening; **donner le b. à qn** to baptize *or* christen sb (**b**) *(d'un navire)* naming; *(d'une cloche)* blessing (**c**) **b. de l'air** first flight; **b. du feu** baptism of fire (**d**) *Belg* = bizutage

baptiser [batize] *vt* (**a**) *Rel* to baptize, to christen (**b**) *(nommer)* to name; *(surnommer)* to christen (**c**) *(navire)* to name; *(cloche)* to bless

baptismal, -e, -aux, -ales [batismal, -o] *adj* baptismal

baptistère [batistɛr] *nm Rel* baptistry

baquet [bakɛ] *nm (cuve)* tub

bar¹ [bar] *nm (café, comptoir)* bar

bar² *nm (poisson)* bass

bar³ *nm Phys* bar

barachois [baraʃwa] *nm Can (dans une rivière)* sandbar

baragouiner [baragwine] *Fam* **1** *vt (langue étrangère)* to speak badly; **qu'est-ce qu'il baragouine?** what's he jabbering about?
  2 *vi* to jabber

baraque [barak] *nf* (**a**) *(cabane)* hut, shack; *(de forain)* stall, stand (**b**) *Fam (maison)* place

baraqué, -e [barake] *adj Fam* hefty

baraquement [barakmã] *nm* shacks; *Mil* camp

baratin [baratɛ̃] *nm Fam* (**a**) *(d'un vendeur)* sales talk, patter; *(d'un séducteur)* smooth talk (**b**) *(verbiage)* waffle

baratiner [baratine] *Fam* **1** *vt (sujet: vendeur)* to give the sales talk to; *(sujet: séducteur) Br* to chat up, *Am* to hit on
  2 *vi* to waffle

baratineur, -euse [baratinœr, -øz] *nm,f Fam* smooth talker

baratte [barat] *nf* churn

Barbade [barbad] *nf* **la B.** Barbados

barbant, -e [barbã, -ãt] *adj Fam* boring

barbare [barbar] **1** *adj (cruel, sauvage)* barbaric
  2 *nmf* barbarian

barbarie [barbari] *nf* (**a**) *(cruauté)* barbarity (**b**) *(manque de civilisation)* barbarism

barbarisme [barbarism] *nm* barbarism

barbe [barb] *nf* (**a**) *(d'homme)* beard; **b. de trois jours** stubble; *Fig* **à la b. de qn** right under sb's nose; **parler dans sa b.** to mutter, to mumble; **rire dans sa b.** to laugh up one's sleeve; *Fam* **la b.!** what a pain *or* drag!; *Fam* **quelle b.!** what a drag!; **b. à papa** *Br* candy floss, *Am* cotton candy (**b**) *(de chèvre, d'épi)* beard; *(de plume, d'hameçon)* barb (**c**) *Tech (de métal)* burr; *(de papier)* ragged edge

barbecue [barbəkju] *nm* barbecue; **faire un b.** to have a barbecue

barbelé [barbəle] **1** *adj m voir* **fil**
  2 *nmpl* **barbelés** barbed wire

barber [barbe] *Fam* **1** *vt* **b. qn** to bore sb stiff
  2 se barber *vpr* to be bored stiff

barbeux, -euse [barbœ, -øz] *adj Can Fam* **être b.** to be a pain in the neck

barbiche [barbiʃ] *nf* goatee (beard)

barbichette [barbiʃet] *nf Fam* small goatee (beard)

barbier [barbje] *nm* (**a**) *Vieilli* barber (**b**) *Can (coiffeur pour hommes)* (men's) hairdresser

barbiturique [barbityrik] *nm* barbiturate

barboter [barbɔte] **1** *vi* to splash about
  2 *vt Fam (voler)* to pinch

barboteuse [barbɔtøz] *nf* (**a**) *(vêtement)* romper-suit (**b**) *Can (piscine gonflable) Br* paddling pool, *Am* wading pool

barbouiller [barbuje] *vt* (**a**) *(salir)* to smear (**de** with); *(peindre)* to daub (**b**) *Fam* **b. l'estomac** *ou* **le cœur à qn** to make sb feel queasy; **se sentir barbouillé** to feel queasy

barbouze [barbuz] *nf Fam (agent secret)* secret agent

barbu, -e [barby] **1** *adj* bearded
  2 *nm* bearded man

Barcelone [barsəlɔn] *n* Barcelona

barda [barda] *nm Fam* (**a**) *(affaires)* gear; *Mil* kit (**b**) *Can (pagaille)* shambles (**c**) *Can (bruit)* **faire du b.** to make a racket

barde¹ [bard] *nf Culin (sur un rôti)* bard

barde² *nm* bard

barder¹ [barde] *v impersonnel Fam* **ça va b.!** there's going to be trouble!

barder² *vt* (**a**) *Culin* to bard (**b**) **bardé de fer/cuir** steel-/leather-clad; **être bardé de décorations** to be covered with decorations; **être bardé de diplômes** to have a whole string of qualifications

barème [barɛm] *nm* (**a**) *(de notes, de salaires, de prix)* scale (**b**) *(pour calcul rapide)* ready reckoner

barge [barʒ] *nf (péniche)* barge

baril [baril] *nm (de vin, de pétrole)* barrel; *(de poudre)* keg; *(de lessive)* drum

barillet [barijɛ] *nm (de revolver)* cylinder

bariolé, -e [barjɔle] *adj* multicoloured

barjo(t) [barʒo] *adj Fam* nutty

barman [barman] *(pl* **barmans** *ou* **barmen** [barmɛn]*)* *nm Br* barman, *Am* bartender

baromètre [barɔmɛtr] *nm aussi Fig* barometer

baron [barɔ̃] *nm (seigneur)* baron; *Fig* **les barons de la finance/de l'industrie** financial/industrial tycoons

baronne [barɔn] *nf* baroness

baroque [barɔk] **1** *adj (architecture, art, musique)* baroque; *(idées)* bizarre, odd
  2 *nm* **le b.** the Baroque

baroud [barud] *nm* **b. d'honneur** last stand

barouder [barude] *vi Fam (voyager)* to knock about

baroudeur [barudœr] *nm Fam* (**a**) *(combattant)* fighter (**b**) *(voyageur)* keen traveller

barouf(le) [baruf(l)] *nm Fam* din, row

barque [bark] *nf* boat; *Fig* **bien mener** *ou* **bien conduire sa b.** to manage one's affairs well; *Fig* **c'est elle qui mène la b.** she's the boss

barquette [barkɛt] *nf* (**a**) *(pour plat à emporter)* container; *(de fruits)* punnet (**b**) *(gâteau)* pastry boat

barrage [baraʒ] *nm (sur l'eau)* dam; **b. de police** police roadblock; **b. routier** roadblock

barre [bar] *nf* (**a**) *(de métal)* bar, rod; *(de bois)* rod; **b. d'appui** *(d'une fenêtre)* rail; **b. de céréales** cereal *ou* muesli bar; **b. de chocolat** *ou* **chocolatée** bar of chocolate; **b. à mine** = metal bar used for breaking stone surfaces
  (**b**) *(pour la danse)* barre; *Sport* **barres asymétriques** asymmetric bars; **b. fixe** horizontal bar; **barres parallèles** parallel bars; **b. transversale** *(de but)* crossbar; *Fig* **placer la b. trop haut** to set too high a standard
  (**c**) *(trait)* line, stroke; *(d'un t)* cross; **b. oblique** oblique, slash; *Mus* **b. de mesure** bar (line)
  (**d**) *Naut (à l'arrière)* tiller; *(volant)* helm; *aussi Fig* **être à** *ou* **tenir la b.** to be at the helm
  (**e**) *Jur (de tribunal)* bar; **b. des témoins** *Br* witness box, *Am* witness stand; **être appelé à la b.** to be called to the witness box
  (**f**) *(de clavier)* **b. d'espacement** space bar
  (**g**) *Ordinat* **b. d'outils** tool bar; **b. de sélection** menu bar; **b. de titre** title bar
  (**h**) **b. HLM** large block of council flats
  (**i**) *Can* **la b. du jour** dawn, daybreak

barreau, -x [baro] *nm* (**a**) *(d'une fenêtre, d'une cage)* bar; *(d'une échelle, d'une chaise)* rung; *Fig* **b. de chaise** fat cigar; **être derrière les barreaux** to be behind bars
  (**b**) *Jur* **le b.** the bar

barrer [bare] **1** *vt* (**a**) *(route, passage, chemin)* to block off; *(porte, fenêtre)* to bar; *Can (fermer à clef)* to lock; **route barrée** *(sur panneau)* road closed; **b. le passage** *ou* **la route à qn** to bar sb's way (**b**) *(chèque)* to cross (**c**) *(mot, paragraphe)* to cross out (**d**) *Naut*

(bateau) to steer; *(à l'aviron)* to cox (**e**) *Fam* **on est mal barrés** things don't look good
  2 se barrer *vpr Fam* to clear off, to beat it

barrette [barɛt] *nf* (**a**) *(pour les cheveux) Br* (hair) slide, *Am* barrette (**b**) *(broche)* brooch (**c**) *(de haschich)* thin strip (**d**) *Ordinat* **b. de mémoire vive** RAM module

barreur [barœr] *nm Naut* helmsman; *(à l'aviron)* cox

barricade [barikad] *nf* barricade

barricader [barikade] **1** *vt (rue, porte)* to barricade
  2 se barricader *vpr* to barricade oneself in

barrière [barjɛr] *nf (obstacle)* barrier; *(clôture)* fence; *(d'un passage à niveau)* gate; *Aut* **b. de dégel** = ban on the use of a road by heavy traffic during a thaw; *Com* **barrières douanières** trade barriers; *Belg* **b. Nadar** crowd barrier; **la Grande B. de Corail** the Great Barrier Reef

barrique [barik] *nf* barrel; *Fam Fig* **plein** *ou* **rond comme une b.** blind drunk

barrir [barir] *vi (éléphant)* to trumpet

barrissements [barismɑ̃] *nmpl (d'un éléphant)* trumpeting

bar-tabac *(pl* **bars-tabacs***)* [bartaba] *nm* = bar that also sells cigarettes and tobacco

baryton [baritɔ̃] *nm Mus* baritone

baryum [barjɔm] *nm Chim* barium

bas¹ [bɑ], **basse** [bɑs] **1** *adj* (**a**) *(dans l'espace, en quantité, en intensité)* low; *(marée)* out, low; **à b. prix** cheaply; **avoir la vue basse** to be short-sighted
  (**b**) *(dans une hiérarchie)* low; *Péj ou Hum* **le b. peuple** the hoi polloi; **les b. quartiers** the poor districts
  (**c**) *(note)* low; *(instrument de musique)* bass
  (**d**) *(dans le temps)* late; **le b. Moyen Âge** the late Middle Ages
  (**e**) *Péj (acte)* mean, low; *(besognes)* menial
  2 *adv* (**a**) *(dans l'espace)* low (down); **voir plus b.** *(dans un article)* see below; *Fig* **mettre qn plus b. que terre** to treat sb like dirt; **tomber b.** *(température, prix d'une action)* to plummet; *Fam* **b. les mains** *ou* **les pattes!** hands off!, keep your paws off!
  (**b**) *(dans une hiérarchie)* low
  (**c**) *(parler)* quietly; *(chanter) (dans le registre)* low; *(doucement)* softly; **rire tout b.** to chuckle to oneself
  (**d**) **en b.** at the bottom; *(à l'étage inférieur)* downstairs; **les gens d'en b.** the people below *or* downstairs; **la tête en b.** upside down; **en b. de** at the bottom of
  (**e**) **à b. la dictature/la police!** down with dictatorship/the police!
  3 *nm (partie inférieure)* bottom; **l'étagère du b.** the bottom shelf; **le b. du dos** the small of the back; **au b. de** at the bottom of; **de b. en haut** upwards
  4 *nf* **basse** *Mus* (**a**) *(partie)* bass part; *(voix, chanteur)* bass (**b**) *(contrebasse)* (double) bass; *(guitare)* bass (guitar)

bas² *nm (vêtement)* stocking; *Can* sock; **b. de contention** elastic stocking; *Fig* **b. de laine** nest egg; **b. nylon** nylons; **b. résille** fishnet stockings; **b. à varices** support stocking

basalte [bazalt] *nm* basalt

basané, -e [bazane] *adj (bronzé)* tanned; *(tanné)* weatherbeaten; *(naturellement)* swarthy

bas-côté *(pl* **bas-côtés***)* [bakote] *nm* (**a**) *(d'une route)* verge (**b**) *(d'une église)* (side) aisle

basculant, -e [baskylɑ̃, -ɑ̃t] *adj* **benne basculante** *(de camion)* tipping body; **pont b.** drawbridge

bascule [baskyl] *nf* (**a**) *(balançoire)* seesaw (**b**) *(balance)* weighing machine (**c**) *Can* **donner la b. à qn** to give sb the bumps

basculer [baskyle] **1** *vt* (**a**) *(brouette, charrette)* to tip up; *(chargement)* to tip over (**b**) *Ordinat* to toggle
2 *vi* (**a**) *(tomber)* to topple over; **faire b.** *(personne)* to knock over; *(chargement)* to tip over; **le pays a basculé dans l'anarchie** the country tipped over into anarchy (**b**) *Ordinat* to toggle

base [baz] *nf* (**a**) *(partie inférieure)* base; *Fig (d'un syndicat, d'un parti politique)* rank and file; **b. de maquillage** foundation (**b**) *Mil (d'opérations)* base; **b. aérienne/navale** air/naval base; **b. de lancement** launch site (**c**) *(principe)* basis; **jeter** *ou* **poser les bases de qch** to lay the foundations for sth; **de b.** basic; **denrées de b.** staple commodities; **à b. d'amidon/de gin** starch-/gin-based (**d**) *Math & Chim* base (**e**) *Ordinat* **b. de données** database

base-ball [bɛzbol] *nm* baseball

baser [baze] **1** *vt* to base; **être basé sur qch** to be based on sth
2 se baser *vpr* **se b. sur qch** *(sujet: personne)* to base one's argument on sth; **sur quoi te bases-tu pour dire que...?** what basis do you have for saying that...?

bas-fond *(pl* **bas-fonds)** [bufɔ̃] *nm (dans la mer, la rivière)* shallow; **les bas-fonds** *(d'une ville)* the rough areas

basic [bazik] *nm Ordinat* BASIC

basilic [bazilik] *nm (plante)* basil

basilique [bazilik] *nf* basilica

basket [baskɛt] **1** *nm ou nf (chaussure)* **baskets** *Br* trainers, *Am* sneakers; *Fam* **être bien dans ses baskets** to be *Br* sorted *or Am* very together
2 *nm (sport)* basketball

basket-ball [baskɛtbol] *nm* basketball

basketteur, -euse [baskɛtœr, -øz] *nm,f* basketball player

basque¹ [bask] **1** *adj* Basque
2 *nmf* **B.** Basque
3 *nm (langue)* Basque

basque² *nf (d'une veste)* tail; *Fig* **être toujours pendu aux basques de qn** to be always at sb's heels

bas-relief *(pl* **bas-reliefs)** [barəljɛf] *nm* bas-relief

basse [bas] *voir* **bas¹**

basse-cour *(pl* **basses-cours)** [baskur] *nf* (**a**) *(cour)* farmyard (**b**) *(volaille)* poultry

bassement [basmã] *adv* **être b. intéressé** to have one's own interests at heart

bassesse [basɛs] *nf* (**a**) *(d'une action, d'un caractère)* lowness (**b**) *(action)* low act

basset [basɛ] *nm (chien)* basset (hound)

bassin [basɛ̃] *nm* (**a**) *(récipient)* basin, bowl; **b. (hygiénique)** bedpan (**b**) *(dans un jardin)* ornamental lake; *(de fontaine)* basin; *(réservoir)* tank; **petit b.** *(de la piscine)* children's pool; **grand b.** *(de la piscine)* large pool (**c**) *(d'un port)* dock, basin (**d**) *Géol* basin; **b. houiller** coal basin; **b. minier** mining area; **le B. parisien** the Paris Basin (**e**) *(partie du corps)* pelvis

bassine [basin] *nf* (**a**) *(en plastique)* basin, bowl; *(contenu)* basinful, bowlful (**b**) *(en cuivre)* pan; *(contenu)* panful

bassiner [basine] *vt Fam (ennuyer)* to bore stiff

bassiste [basist] *nmf (contrebassiste)* double bass player; *(guitariste)* bass guitarist

basson [basɔ̃] *nm* (**a**) *(instrument)* bassoon (**b**) *(joueur)* bassoonist

basta [basta] *exclam Fam* that'll do!

bastide [bastid] *nf* (**a**) *(maison)* country house; *(ferme)* farm (**b**) *Hist (ville fortifiée)* fortified town

bastille [bastij] *nf* fortress; *Hist* **la B.** the Bastille; **la prise de la B.** the storming of the Bastille

bastingage [bastɛ̃gaʒ] *nm Naut (garde-corps)* rail

bastion [bastjɔ̃] *nm aussi Fig* bastion

baston [bastɔ̃] *nm ou nf Fam* punch-up

bastonner [bastɔne] **se bastonner** *vpr Fam* to fight

bastringue [bastrɛ̃g] *nm Fam* (**a**) *(dancing)* (seedy) dance hall (**b**) *(affaires)* gear, stuff; **et tout le b.** and the whole caboodle

bas-ventre *(pl* **bas-ventres)** [bavɑ̃tr] *nm* lower abdomen

bât [ba] *nm* packsaddle; *Fig* **c'est là que le b. blesse** there's the rub

bataclan [bataklã] *nm Fam (affaires)* stuff, gear; **et tout le b.** and the whole caboodle

bataille [bataj] *nf* (**a**) *(lutte)* battle, fight; *(électorale)* contest; **b. terrestre/aérienne/navale** land/air/naval battle; **cheveux en b.** dishevelled hair (**b**) *(jeu de cartes)* beggar-my-neighbour

batailler [bataje] *vi Fam* **b. pour faire qch** to battle to do sth

batailleur, -euse [batajœr, -øz] *adj* aggressive

bataillon [batajɔ̃] *nm Mil* battalion; *Fam* **un b. de** a troop of

bâtard, -e [batar, -ard] **1** *adj (enfant)* illegitimate; *Péj* bastard; *(style, solution)* hybrid
2 *nm,f (enfant)* illegitimate child; *Péj* bastard
3 *nm (chien)* mongrel; *(pain)* = small French stick

batavia [batavja] *nf* batavia lettuce

bateau, -x [bato] **1** *nm* (**a**) *(embarcation)* boat; **faire du b.** to go boating; **prendre le b.** to go/come by boat; **en** *ou* **par b.** by boat; *Fam Fig* **mener qn en b., monter un b. à qn** to wind sb up; **b. à moteur** motorboat; **b. de pêche** fishing boat; **b. de plaisance** pleasure boat; **b. à vapeur** steamboat, steamer; **b. à voiles** *Br* sailing boat, *Am* sailboat (**b**) *(sur le trottoir)* driveway entrance (**c**) **encolure b.** boat neck
2 *adj inv Fam (banal)* hackneyed

bateau-mouche *(pl* **bateaux-mouches)** [batomuʃ] *nm* river boat *(on the Seine)*

bateleur, -euse [batlœr, -øz] *nm,f Vieilli (jongleur)* juggler; *(acrobate)* acrobat

batelier, -ère [batalje, -ɛr] *nm,f* boatman, *f* boatwoman; *(sur un bac)* ferryman, *f* ferrywoman

bat-flanc [baflã] *nm inv (dans un dortoir, une prison)* wooden partition

bâti, -e [bati] **1** *adj (personne)* **être bien b.** to be well-built; **être mal b.** to have an odd shape
2 *nm* (**a**) *Constr* frame, framework (**b**) *(en couture)* tacking, basting

batifoler [batifole] *vi Fam* to lark about

batik [batik] *nm* batik

bâtiment [batimã] *nm* (**a**) *(immeuble)* building; **b. d'habitation** residential building (**b**) *(secteur)* **le b.** building; **être dans le b.** to be in the building trade; **bâtiments et travaux publics** building and civil engineering (**c**) *Naut* ship; **b. de guerre** warship, battleship

bâtir [batir] **1** *vt* (**a**) *(maison, ville)* to build; *Fig (fortune, hypothèse)* to build (up); **(se) faire b. une maison** to have a house built; **terrain bâti** developed *or*

built-up site (**b**) *(en couture)* to tack, to baste
  2 se bâtir *vpr* **se b. une réputation (de)** to build up a reputation (as)
bâtisse [batis] *nf* ugly building
batiste [batist] *nf* batiste
bâton [batɔ̃] *nm* (**a**) *(en bois, de colle, de craie)* stick; *(d'agent de police)* Br truncheon, Am nightstick; *(de majorette)* baton; **mener une vie de b. de chaise** to lead a wild life; **mettre des bâtons dans les roues à qn** to put a spoke in sb's wheel; **parler à bâtons rompus** to talk about this and that; **conversation à bâtons rompus** rambling conversation; **b. de rouge à lèvres** lipstick; **bâtons de ski** ski sticks *or* poles (**b**) *(trait vertical)* vertical line (**c**) *Can & Suisse* **b. (de hockey)** *Br* ice hockey stick, *Am* hockey stick
bâtonnet [batɔnɛ] *nm* stick
batracien [batrasjɛ̃] *nm Zool* amphibian
battage [bataʒ] *nm* (**a**) *Fam (publicité)* hype; **faire du b. autour de qch** to hype sth up (**b**) *(du blé)* threshing
battant, -e [batɑ̃, -ɑ̃t] **1** *adj (pluie)* lashing; **le cœur b.** with a pounding heart
  2 *nm,f (personne combative)* fighter
  3 *nm* (**a**) *(d'une cloche)* clapper, tongue (**b**) *(d'une porte, d'un volet)* leaf; **porte à double b.** double door
batte [bat] *nf* bat; **b. de base-ball/de cricket** baseball/cricket bat
battement [batmɑ̃] *nm* (**a**) *(de tambour)* beat, beating; *(de mains)* clapping; *(d'ailes, de voiles)* flapping; *(de porte)* banging; **j'entendais les battements de son cœur** I could hear his heart beating (**b**) *(entre deux événements)* gap; **deux heures de b.** a two-hour gap
batterie [batri] *nf* (**a**) *(dans un orchestre)* drums; **être à la b.** to be on drums (**b**) *Mil* battery; *Fig* **dévoiler ses batteries** to show one's hand; **b. antiaérienne/anti-chars** anti-aircraft/antitank battery (**c**) *(ensemble, groupe)* battery; *(de tests, de questions)* series; **élevage en b.** battery farming; **poulet de b.** battery hen; **b. de cuisine** kitchen utensils (**d**) *Élec* battery; **fonctionner sur b.** to be battery-operated *or* battery-powered; **b. de secours** emergency battery
batteur [batœr] *nm* (**a**) *(dans un groupe)* drummer (**b**) *(au cricket)* batsman; *(au base-ball)* batter, striker (**c**) *(de cuisine)* mixer
batteuse [batøz] *nf (machine agricole)* threshing machine, thresher
battoir [batwar] *nm* (**a**) *(pour les tapis)* (carpet) beater; *(pour le linge)* beetle (**b**) *Fam (grande main)* great paw *or* mitt
battre [11] [batr] **1** *vt* (**a**) *(frapper) (personne, chien, tapis)* to beat; *(blé)* to thresh; *(métal)* to hammer; **b. qn à coups de poings** to punch sb; **b. le tambour** to beat the drum; **b. le rappel** *Mil* to call to arms; *Fig* to call everyone together; **b. la campagne** to scour *or* comb the countryside; *(esprit)* to wander; *Prov* **il faut b. le fer quand il** *ou* **pendant qu'il est chaud** strike while the iron is hot
    (**b**) *(cartes)* to shuffle; *(beurre)* to churn; *(œufs, préparation culinaire)* to beat, to whisk; **b. les blancs en neige** to beat the whites stiffly
    (**c**) *(adversaire)* to beat; *(record)* to break; **b. qn à plate(s) couture(s)** to beat sb hollow; *Fig* **b. tous les records** to take some beating
    (**d**) *Mus* **b. la mesure** to beat time
    (**e**) *Naut* **b. pavillon français/britannique** to fly the French/British flag

  2 *vi* (**a**) *(cœur)* to beat; *(porte, volet)* to bang; *(voile)* to flap; **il a le cœur qui bat** *(d'émotion)* his heart is pounding (**b**) **b. en retraite** to beat a retreat
  3 **battre de** *vt ind* **b. des mains** to clap one's hands; **b. des cils** to flutter one's eyelashes
  4 se battre *vpr aussi Fig* to fight (**avec/contre** with/against); **se b. comme des chiffonniers** to fight like cat and dog; **se b. au couteau** to fight with knives; *très Fam* **je m'en bats l'œil** I don't give a toss
battu, -e [baty] *adj (femme, enfant)* battered; **un air** *ou* **regard de chien b.** a hangdog look; **avoir les yeux battus** to have dark circles under one's eyes
battue [baty] *nf (à la chasse)* beat; *(pour retrouver quelqu'un)* search
batture [batyr] *nf Can* sandbank
baud [bo] *nm Tél & Ordinat* baud
baudet [bodɛ] *nm* ass, donkey; **chargé comme un b.** loaded down like a packhorse
baudrier [bodrije] *nm* shoulder strap; *(pour épée)* baldric; *(d'escalade)* harness
baudroie [bodrwa] *nf* monkfish
baudruche [bodryʃ] *nf* **(ballon de) b.** balloon
baume [bom] *nm aussi Fig* balm; **mettre du b. au cœur de qn** *(événement)* to be a consolation for sb
baux [bo] *voir* **bail**
bauxite [boksit] *nf* bauxite
bavard, -e [bavar, -ard] **1** *adj* (**a**) *(qui parle beaucoup)* chatty; *(style, essai)* wordy; **il est b. comme une pie** he'd talk the hind legs off a donkey (**b**) *(indiscret)* indiscreet
  2 *nm,f* (**a**) *(qui parle beaucoup)* chatterbox (**b**) *(indiscret)* gossip
bavardage [bavardaʒ] *nm* (**a**) *(action)* chatting; *(commérage)* gossiping (**b**) *Ordinat (sur Internet)* chat (**c**) **bavardages** *(paroles)* chat; *(commérage)* gossip
bavarder [bavarde] *vi* (**a**) *(parler)* to chat; *(commérer)* to gossip (**b**) *Ordinat (sur Internet)* to chat
bavardoir [bavardwar] *nm Can Ordinat* chat room
bavarois, -e [bavarwa, -az] **1** *adj* Bavarian
  2 *nm,f* **B.** Bavarian
  3 *nm Culin* bavarois, = dessert consisting of set custard and whipped cream mixed with fruit purée
bave [bav] *nf (de personne)* dribble; *(de chien)* slaver; *(de cheval, de chien enragé)* froth, foam; *(d'escargot)* slime; *(de crapaud)* spittle
baver [bave] *vi (personne)* to dribble; *(chien)* to slaver; *(chien enragé)* to foam at the mouth; *(stylo)* to leak, to run; *(encre)* to smudge; *Fam* **en b. (des ronds de chapeaux)** to have a hard time of it; *Fam* **en faire b. (des ronds de chapeaux) à qn** to give sb a hard time
bavette [bavɛt] *nf* (**a**) *(d'un bébé, d'un tablier)* bib (**b**) *Culin* skirt (of beef) (**c**) *Fam* **tailler une b.** to have a chat
baveux, -euse [bavø, -øz] **1** *adj (bouche, enfant)* dribbling; *(omelette)* runny
  2 *nm,f Can (morveux)* pain, pest
Bavière [bavjɛr] *nf* **la B.** Bavaria
bavoir [bavwar] *nm* bib
bavure [bavyr] *nf* (**a**) *(tache)* smudge, smear (**b**) *(erreur)* slip-up; **sans bavure(s)** faultless; **b. policière** case of police misconduct
bayer [53] [baje] *vi* **b. aux corneilles** to stare into space
bazar [bazar] *nm* (**a**) *(marché)* bazaar (**b**) *(magasin)* general store (**c**) *Fam (désordre)* shambles *(singulier)*; *(bruit)* racket; *(affaires)* stuff, gear; **et tout le b.** and

the whole caboodle; **mettre du** *ou* **le b. dans qch** to make a shambles of sth (**d**) *Belg Fam (chose)* thing, thingy

bazarder [bazarde] *vt Fam (se débarrasser de)* to get shot of; *(jeter)* to chuck out; *(vendre)* to flog

bazooka [bazuka] *nm* bazooka

BCBG [besebeʒe] *adj inv (abrév* **bon chic bon genre***) Br* ≃ Sloany, *Am* ≃ preppy

BCE [beseə] *nf (abrév* **Banque centrale européenne***) European central bank

BCG® [beseʒe] *nm Méd* BCG

BD [bede] *nf* (**a**) *(abrév* **bande dessinée***) comic strip, cartoon (**b**) *Ordinat (abrév* **base de données***) dbase

---

BD

This is a common abbreviation for "bande dessinée", or "comic book". Considered a serious and important art form in France, the comic book has become popular among teenagers and intellectuals alike. An annual festival of comic book art is held in Angoulême.

---

bd *abrév* **boulevard**

beach-volley [bitʃvɔlɛ] *nm Sport* beach volleyball

béant, -e [beɑ̃, -ɑ̃t] *adj (bouche, porte)* wide open; *(blessure, gouffre)* gaping

béat, -e [bea, -at] *adj Rel* blessed; *(heureux)* blissful; *Péj (niais)* inane; **être b. d'admiration** to be open-mouthed in admiration; **elle nous observait d'un air b.** she watched us open-mouthed

béatement [beatmɑ̃] *adv (sourire)* inanely

béatifier [66] [beatifje] *vt Rel* to beatify

béatitude [beatityd] *nf* (**a**) *Rel* beatitude (**b**) *(bonheur parfait)* bliss

beau, belle [bo, bɛl]

---

bel is used before masculine singular nouns beginning with a vowel or h mute.

---

1 *adj* (**a**) *(d'apparence) (femme, enfant)* beautiful, good-looking; *(homme)* handsome, good-looking; *(objet, maison)* lovely, beautiful; **b. comme un dieu** like a Greek god; **ce n'est pas b. à voir** it's not a pretty sight; **se faire b.** to smarten oneself up

(**b**) *(de qualité) (œuvre, spectacle, discours)* fine; **avoir une belle situation** to have a good job

(**c**) *(moralement)* fine, noble; **un b. geste** a noble gesture; **ce n'est pas b. de mentir** it isn't nice to tell lies

(**d**) *(bien)* **c'est trop b. pour être vrai** it's too good to be true; **ce serait trop b.!** that would be too much (to hope for)!; **le plus b. jour de ma vie** the best day of my life

(**e**) *Ironique* **une belle grippe** a nasty dose of the flu; **une belle correction** a good thrashing; **te voilà b.!** you're in a fine mess!; **te voilà dans un bel état!** look at the state of you!; **j'ai eu une belle peur** I had an awful fright; **vous avez fait du b. travail!** well done!; *très Fam* **un b. salaud** a real *or* right bastard; **j'en ai entendu de belles sur votre compte!** I've heard some unpleasant things about you!; **il en a fait de belles** he got up to some real tricks

(**f**) *(intensif)* **au b. milieu de la rue** right *or* bang in the middle of the road; **une belle somme** a tidy sum; **un b. poulet** a nice big chicken

(**g**) *(locutions)* **bel et bien** *(complètement)* well and truly; **il est bel et bien venu** he really did come; **il s'est bel et bien trompé** he has indeed made a mis-take; **de plus belle** with a vengeance; **il reprit l'entraî-nement de plus belle** he resumed training with a vengeance *or* more enthusiastically than ever

2 *adv* **il fait b.** it's fine; **il ferait b. voir ça!** that'll be the day!; **j'ai b. le lui expliquer...** no matter how many times I explain it to him...; **j'ai b. pousser, la porte ne bouge pas** no matter how hard I push *or* try as I might, I can't get the door to open

3 *nm* **le b.** *(beauté)* beauty; **mais le plus b., c'est que...** but the best bit *or* part is that ...; *Fam Ironique* **c'est du b.!** that's great!; **le temps est au b. (fixe)** the weather is set fair; *Fig* **avoir le moral au b. fixe** to be permanently in a good mood; **un vieux b.** an old roué; **faire le b.** *(chien)* to sit up and beg; *Can (homme)* to strut about

4 *nf* **belle** (**a**) *(partie)* decider (**b**) *Hum (amie)* lady friend (**c**) *Fam (locutions)* **se faire la b.** to run away, *Br* to do a runner; *(de prison)* to escape; *Belg* **avoir b. à faire qch** to have no trouble doing sth

beaucoup [boku] *adv* (**a**) *(intensément, en grande quantité)* a lot; **ça te plaît? – pas b.** do you like it? – not much *or* not a lot

(**b**) *(une grande quantité, un grand nombre)* **il reste encore b. à faire** there's still a lot to do; **c'est déjà b. qu'il veuille bien vous parler** it's quite something that he condescended to speak to you; **il y est pour b.** he has had a lot *or* a great deal to do with it; **b. pensent que...** a lot of *or* many people think that...; **b. d'entre nous** a lot of *or* many of us; **de b.** *(de loin)* by far; **il s'en faut de b. que je sois riche** I'm far from rich

(**c**) **b. de** *(quantité)* a lot of; *(nombre)* a lot of, many; **b. de vin/chance** a lot of wine/luck; **b. de fautes** a lot of *or* many mistakes; **pas b. de** *(argent, courage)* not much; *(gens, problèmes)* not many; **avec b. de soin** with great care, very carefully; **j'en veux b.!** I want a lot!

(**d**) *(avec des comparatifs)* a lot, much; **b. moins/plus vite** a lot *or* much slower/faster; **il parle b. trop** he talks far too much; **b. moins d'enfants** a lot *or* many fewer children; **b. moins de temps** a lot *or* much less time

beauf [bof] *Fam* **1** *adj Péj* **il est un peu b.** he's a bit of a narrow-minded average Frenchman

2 *nm* (**a**) *(beau-frère)* brother-in-law (**b**) *Péj* = stereotypical narrow-minded, average Frenchman

beau-fils *(pl* **beaux-fils***)* [bofis] *nm* (**a**) *(gendre)* son-in-law (**b**) *(après remariage)* stepson

beau-frère *(pl* **beaux-frères***)* [bofrɛr] *nm* brother-in-law

beaujolais [boʒɔlɛ] *nm* Beaujolais

beau-père *(pl* **beaux-pères***)* [bopɛr] *nm* (**a**) *(père du conjoint)* father-in-law (**b**) *(après remariage)* step-father

beaupré [bopre] *nm Naut* bowsprit

beauté [bote] *nf* beauty; **être en b.** to be looking magnificent; **de toute b.** magnificent; **finir en b.** to end on a high note; **faire qch pour la b. du geste** to do sth for the sake of it; **se refaire une b.** to put one's face on

beaux-arts [bozar] *nmpl* fine art; **école des b., B.** art school

beaux-parents [boparɑ̃] *nmpl* parents-in-law

bébé [bebe] *nm* (**a**) *(nourrisson)* baby; **faire le b.** to be-have like a baby; **être très b.** to be very babyish (**b**) *(animal)* **b. gazelle/lapin** baby gazelle/rabbit

bébé-éprouvette (*pl* bébés-éprouvette) [bebeepruvɛt] *nm* test-tube baby

bébelle [bebɛl] *nf Can (gadget)* gadget; *(bibelot)* ornament; *(jouet)* toy

bébête [bebɛt] *Fam* **1** *adj* silly
  2 *nf* creepy-crawly

bec [bɛk] *nm* (**a**) *(d'oiseau, de tortue, de pieuvre)* beak (**b**) *Fam (bouche)* mouth; **il n'a pas ouvert le b. de la journée** he hasn't opened his mouth all day; **la clope au b.** with a fag in one's mouth; **rester le b. dans l'eau** to be left high and dry; **b. fin** gourmet; *Can* **faire le b. fin** to be picky (**c**) *(de pot)* lip; *(de cafetière)* spout; *(d'instrument à vent)* mouthpiece; **b. Bunsen** Bunsen burner; **b. de gaz** *(réverbère)* gas lamp; **b. verseur** spout (**d**) *Belg, Suisse & Can (baiser)* **donner un b. à qn** to give sb a kiss

bécane [bekan] *nf Fam (vélo)* bike; *(machine, ordinateur)* machine

bécarre [bekar] *adj & nm Mus* natural

bécasse [bekas] *nf* (**a**) *(oiseau)* woodcock (**b**) *Fam (idiote)* silly thing

bec-de-lièvre (*pl* becs-de-lièvre) [bɛkdəljɛvr] *nm* harelip

béchamel [beʃamɛl] *nf* **(sauce) b.** béchamel sauce

bêche [bɛʃ] *nf* spade

bêcher [beʃe] *vt* to dig, to turn over

bêcheur, -euse [beʃœr, -øz] *nm,f Fam (snob)* stuck-up person

bécosses [bekɔs] *nfpl Can Fam* privy, *Am* john

bécoter [bekɔte] *Fam* **1** *vt* to snog
  2 se bécoter *vpr* to snog

becqueter [42] [bɛkte] **1** *vt (sujet: oiseau)* to peck at
  2 *vi très Fam (personne)* to eat

becter [bɛkte] *vi* = becqueter

bedaine [bədɛn] *nf Fam* pot(-belly), paunch; **prendre de la b.** to get a pot(-belly) *or* a paunch

bédé [bede] *nf Fam* comic strip, cartoon

bedeau, -x [bədo] *nm* verger

bedon [bədɔ̃] *nm Fam* pot(-belly), paunch

bedonnant, -e [bədɔnɑ̃, -ɑ̃t] *adj Fam* pot-bellied, paunchy

bédouin, -e [bedwɛ̃, -in] **1** *adj* Bedouin
  2 *nm,f* **B.** Bedouin

bée [be] *adjf* **bouche b.** open-mouthed; **j'en suis restée bouche b.** I was speechless; **regarder qch bouche b.** to gape at sth

beffroi [befrwa] *nm* belfry

bégaiement [begɛmɑ̃] *nm* stuttering, stammering

bégayer [53] [begeje] **1** *vi* to stutter, to stammer
  2 *vt* to stammer (out)

bégonia [begɔnja] *nm* begonia

bègue [bɛg] **1** *adj* **être b.** to stutter, to stammer
  2 *nmf* stutterer, stammerer

bégueule [begœl] *adj* prudish

béguin [begɛ̃] *nm Fam (personne)* crush; **avoir le b. pour qn** to have a crush on sb; **avoir le b. pour qch** to have taken a fancy to sth

BEI [beəi] *nf (abrév* **Banque européenne d'investissement**) EIB

beige [bɛʒ] *adj & nm* beige

beigne¹ [bɛɲ] *nf Fam* clout; **filer une b. à qn** to give sb a clout

beigne² *nm Can* doughnut

beignet [beɲɛ] *nm (salé)* fritter; *(au sucre, à la confiture)* doughnut; **b. de** *ou* **aux pommes** apple fritter

bel [bɛl] *voir* beau

bêlement [bɛlmɑ̃] *nm aussi Fig* bleat; **des bêlements** bleating

bêler [bɛle] *vi aussi Fig* to bleat

bel-étage, bel étage [beletaʒ] (*pl* beaux-étages) [bozetaʒ] *nm Belg* (**a**) *(rez-de-chaussée surélevé)* mezzanine *Br* ground *or Am* first floor (**b**) *(maison)* house with mezzanine *Br* ground *or Am* first floor

belette [bəlɛt] *nf* weasel

Belfast [bɛlfast] *n* Belfast

belge [bɛlʒ] **1** *adj* Belgian
  2 *nmf* **B.** Belgian

belgicisme [bɛlʒisism] *nm (mot)* Belgian-French word; *(tournure)* Belgian-French expression

Belgique [bɛlʒik] *nf* **la B.** Belgium

Belgrade [bɛlgrad] *n* Belgrade

bélier [belje] *nm* (**a**) *(animal)* ram (**b**) *Mil* battering ram (**c**) *Astron & Astrol* **le B.** Aries; **être B.** to be (an) Aries

Belize [beliz] *nm* **le B.** Belize

belladone [beladɔn] *nf* belladonna, deadly nightshade

bellâtre [belɑtr] *nm Péj* smoothie

belle [bɛl] *voir* beau

belle-famille (*pl* belles-familles) [bɛlfamij] *nf* in-laws

belle-fille (*pl* belles-filles) [bɛlfij] *nf* (**a**) *(épouse du fils)* daughter-in-law (**b**) *(après remariage)* stepdaughter

belle-mère (*pl* belles-mères) [bɛlmɛr] *nf* (**a**) *(mère du conjoint)* mother-in-law (**b**) *(après remariage)* stepmother

belle-sœur (*pl* belles-sœurs) [bɛlsœr] *nf* sister-in-law

belligérant, -e [beliʒerɑ̃, -ɑ̃t] **1** *adj* belligerent
  2 *nm* **les belligérants** the warring nations

belliqueux, -euse [belikø, -øz] *adj (pays, peuple)* warlike; *(personne, humeur)* aggressive

belote [bəlɔt] *nf* = card game

bélouga [beluga], **béluga** [belyga] *nm* beluga whale

belvédère [bɛlvedɛr] *nm* (**a**) *(construction)* belvedere, gazebo (**b**) *(sur un site naturel)* viewpoint

bémol [bemɔl] *Mus* **1** *nm* flat; *Fam Fig* **mettre un b.** to tone it down
  2 *adj* flat; **mi b.** E flat

ben [bɛ̃] *adv Fam* **b. oui!** well, yes!; **b. voilà, euh…** yeah, well, er…

bénédictin, -e [benediktɛ̃, -in] *adj, nm,f & nf* Benedictine

bénédiction [benediksjɔ̃] *nf Rel* blessing, benediction; *(d'une église)* consecration; *Fig* blessing

bénéfice [benefis] *nm* (**a**) *(gain)* profit; **b. d'exploitation** operating profit (**b**) *(avantage)* benefit, advantage; **tirer un certain b. de qch** to derive some benefit *or* advantage from sth; **avoir le b. de l'âge** to have the benefit of age; **accorder** *ou* **laisser le b. du doute à qn** to give sb the benefit of the doubt; **au b. de** *(œuvre charitable)* in aid of

bénéficiaire [benefisjɛr] **1** *adj Com (entreprise)* profit-making; *(compte)* in credit
  2 *nmf (d'un chèque)* payee; *Jur* beneficiary

bénéficier [66] [benefisje] **bénéficier de** *vt ind* (**a**) *(profiter de)* to benefit from; **faire b. qn de son expérience** to give sb the benefit of one's experience (**b**) *(avoir)* to have; **cette carte d'abonnement vous fait b. d'une remise** this season ticket entitles you to a 20 per cent reduction

bénéfique [benefik] *adj* beneficial (**à** to)

Benelux [benelyks] *nm* **le B.** Benelux

benêt [bɔnɛ] **1** *adj m* simple
  2 *nm* simpleton

bénévolat [benevɔla] *nm* voluntary work

bénévole [benevɔl] **1** *adj (travail, infirmière)* voluntary
  2 *nmf* volunteer, voluntary worker

Bengale [bɛ̃gal] *nm* **le B.** Bengal

Bénin [benɛ̃] *nm* **le B.** Benin

bénin, -igne [benɛ̃, -iɲ] *adj (accident, opération)* minor; *(tumeur)* benign

béninois, -e [beninwa, -az] **1** *adj* Beninese
  2 *nm,f* **B.** Beninese

bénir [benir] *vt aussi Fig* to bless; *(église)* to consecrate; **(que) Dieu vous bénisse!** (may) God bless you!; **être béni des dieux** to have been touched by God

bénit, -e [beni, -it] *adj voir* **eau, pain**

bénitier [benitje] *nm Rel* holy-water stoup

benjamin, -e [bɛ̃ʒamɛ̃, -in] *nm,f* **(a)** *(le plus jeune)* youngest **(b)** *Sport* junior *(10 to 12 years old)*

benjoin [bɛ̃ʒwɛ̃] *nm* (gum) benzoin, benjamin

benne [bɛn] *nf (de camion)* tipping *or* dump body; *(dans une mine)* tub, truck; *(de téléphérique)* (cable) car; **b. à ordures** bin lorry

benzine [bɛ̃zin] *nf* benzine

BEP [beəpe] *nm Scol (abrév* **brevet d'études professionnelles)** = vocational diploma taken at age eighteen

BEPC [beəpese] *nm Anciennement Scol (abrév* **brevet d'études du premier cycle)** = school-leaving certificate taken at age fifteen

béquille [bekij] *nf* **(a)** *(pour marcher)* crutch; **marcher avec des béquilles** to be on crutches **(b)** *(d'un vélo, d'une moto)* stand

berbère [bɛrbɛr] **1** *adj* Berber
  2 *nmf* **B.** Berber
  3 *nm (langue)* Berber

bercail [bɛrkaj] *nm (de l'Église)* fold; *Hum* **rentrer au b.** to return to the fold

berçante [bɛrsɑ̃t] *adj f & nf Can* **(chaise) b.** rocking chair

berce [bɛrs] *nf Belg & Suisse (berceau)* cradle

berceau, -x [bɛrso] *nm (de bébé)* cradle; *Fig (d'une civilisation, d'un mouvement)* birthplace; **dès le b.** from the cradle, from birth; *Fam* **il les prend au b.** he's a cradle-snatcher

bercer [16] [bɛrse] **1** *vt* **(a)** *(bébé, passager)* to rock; *Fig* **mon enfance a été bercée par la musique de Debussy** I was brought up listening to Debussy **(b)** *Fig* **b. qn de promesses** to delude sb with promises
  2 se bercer *vpr* **se b. d'illusions** to delude oneself

berceuse [bɛrsøz] *nf* **(a)** *(chanson)* lullaby **(b)** *Can (fauteuil à bascule)* rocking-chair

BERD [bɛrd] *nf (abrév* **Banque européenne pour la reconstruction et le développement)** EBRD

béret [berɛ] *nm* beret

bergamote [bɛrgamɔt] *nf* bergamot; **thé à la b.** bergamot-flavoured tea

berge¹ [bɛrʒ] *nf (bord)* bank

berge² *nf Fam (an)* **il a quarante berges** he's forty

berger, -ère [bɛrʒe, -ɛr] **1** *nm,f* shepherd, *f* shepherdess
  2 *nm (chien)* **b. allemand** German shepherd, *Br*

Alsatian; **b. des Pyrénées** Pyrenean mountain dog
  3 *nf* **bergère** *(fauteuil)* wing chair

bergerie [bɛrʒəri] *nf* sheepfold

bergeronnette [bɛrʒərɔnɛt] *nf* wagtail

Béring [beriŋ] *n voir* **détroit**

berk [bɛrk] *exclam* yuk!

Berlin [bɛrlɛ̃] *n* Berlin; *Hist* **B.-Ouest /-Est** West/East Berlin

berline [bɛrlin] *nf Aut Br* (four-door) saloon, *Am* (four-door) sedan

berlingot [bɛrlɛ̃go] *nm* **(a)** *(bonbon) Br* boiled sweet, *Am* hard candy **(b)** *(de lait)* carton; *(de produit d'entretien)* pack

berlinois, -e [bɛrlinwa, -az] **1** *adj* from Berlin
  2 *nm,f* **B.** Berliner

berloque [bɛrlɔk] *nf Belg* **battre la b.** to beat *or* pound wildly

berlue [bɛrly] *nf Fam* **avoir la b.** to be seeing things

berme [bɛrm] *nf Belg & Suisse (terre-plein)* **b. centrale** *Br* central reservation, *Am* median (strip)

bermuda [bɛrmyda] *nm* Bermuda shorts, Bermudas

Bermudes [bɛrmyd] *nfpl* **les (îles) B.** Bermuda

bernard-l'(h)ermite [bɛrnarlɛrmit] *nm inv* hermit crab

Berne [bɛrn] *n* Bern

berne [bɛrn] **en berne** *adj Naut* at *Br* half mast *or Am* half staff; *Mil* furled

berner [bɛrne] *vt* to fool

bernois, -e [bɛrnwa, -az] **1** *adj* Bernese
  2 *nm,f* **B.** Bernese

berzingue [bɛrzɛ̃g] **à tout(e) b.** *adv Fam* at full speed, double quick

besace [bəzas] *nf (de mendiant)* bag; *(de pèlerin)* scrip; **sac b.** = large, soft handbag

bésef [bezɛf] = **bézef**

besogne [bəzɔɲ] *nf* job, task; **aller vite en b.** to get things done quickly; *Fig & Péj* to jump the gun

besoin [bəzwɛ̃] *nm* **(a)** *(nécessité)* need (**de qch** for sth); **avoir b. de qn/qch** to need sb/sth; **avoir b. de faire qch** to need to do sth; **j'ai b. que tu m'aides** I need you to help me; **éprouver le b. de faire qch** to feel the need to do sth; **pour les besoins de la cause** for the sake of the cause; **au b.** if necessary, if need be; **en cas de b.** if need be; **si b. est** if necessary, if need be **(b)** **faire ses besoins** *(personne)* to relieve oneself; *(animal)* to do its business **(c)** *(misère)* **être dans le b.** to be in need

bestial, -e, -aux, -ales [bɛstjal, -o] *adj* bestial

bestiaux [bɛstjo] *nmpl* livestock

bestiole [bɛstjɔl] *nf* small animal; *(insecte)* creepy-crawly

best-seller *(pl* **best-sellers)** [bɛstsɛlœr] *nm* best-seller

bêta, -asse [bɛta, -as] *Fam* **1** *adj* silly
  2 *nm,f* silly-billy

bêtabloquant [betablɔkɑ̃] *nm Méd* beta-blocker

bétail [betaj] *nm* livestock; **gros b.** cattle and horses

bétaillère [betajɛr] *nf* cattle truck

bêta-test *(pl* **bêta-tests)** [betatɛst] *nm Ordinat* beta test

bête [bɛt] **1** *adj* stupid, silly; **c'est b., on a loupé le film!** what a pity *or* a shame, we've missed the film!; **ce n'est pas b.** *(suggestion)* that's not a bad idea; **rester tout b.** *(décontenancé)* to be open-mouthed; *Fam* **être b. comme ses pieds** to be as thick as two short planks; **être b. à pleurer** to be pathetically stupid;

c'est b. comme chou, c'est tout b. it's as easy as pie 2 *nf* (**a**) *(animal)* animal; travailler comme une b. to work flat out; elle m'a regardé comme une b. curieuse she looked at me as if I was from another planet; *Péj* b. à concours *Br* swot, *Am* grind; b. à cornes horned animal; b. fauve big cat; b. féroce wild animal; b. noire *(personne)* bête noire; *(chose)* pet hate; *Can* b. puante skunk; b. de somme beast of burden (**b**) *(insecte)* insect; *Fig* chercher la petite b. to nit-pick; b. à bon Dieu *Br* ladybird, *Am* ladybug

bêtement [bɛtmɑ̃] *adv (rire, regarder)* stupidly; mourir b. to die senselessly; tout b. quite simply, purely and simply

bêtifier [66] [betifje] *vi (avec un enfant)* to use baby-talk

bêtise [betiz] *nf* (**a**) *(manque d'intelligence)* stupidity, silliness (**b**) *(action idiote)* stupid thing (to do); *(parole idiote)* stupid thing to say; dire/faire une b. to say/do something stupid; dire des bêtises to talk nonsense (**c**) *(chose sans importance)* trivial thing; se disputer pour des bêtises to argue over nothing (**d**) *Can* bêtises *(injures)* insults (**e**) bêtises de Cambrai *Br* ≃ mint humbugs, *Am* ≃ hard mint candies

bêtisier [betizje] *nm (écrit)* collection of howlers; *(à la télévision)* collection of humorous out-takes

béton [betɔ̃] *nm* (**a**) *(matériau)* concrete; *Fig* des muscles en b. rock-hard muscles; un alibi en b. a cast-iron alibi; b. armé reinforced concrete (**b**) *Fam* laisse b.! drop it!

bétonner [betɔne] *vt* to concrete

bétonneuse [betɔnøz], **bétonnière** [betɔnjɛr] *nf* cement mixer, concrete mixer

bette [bɛt] *nf* (Swiss) chard

betterave [bɛtrav] *nf* b. (rouge) *Br* beetroot, *Am* beet; b. fourragère mangel-wurzel; b. sucrière sugar beet

beuglement [bøgləmɑ̃] *nm (d'une vache)* moo; *(d'un taureau)* bellow; *(de la radio, de la télé)* blaring; des beuglements mooing/bellowing; pousser des beuglements *(personne)* to bellow

beugler [bøgle] 1 *vi (vache)* to moo; *(taureau, personne)* to bellow; *(radio, télé)* to blare 2 *vt (chanson)* to bawl out, to bellow out

beur [bœr] 1 *nmf* = North African born in France of immigrant parents 2 *adj inv* = of North Africans born in France of immigrant parents

beurre [bœr] *nm* butter; au b. *(pâtisserie)* made with butter; *Fam* ça compte pour du b. that doesn't count; *Fam* faire son b. to make a packet; ça mettra du b. dans les épinards that will make life a bit easier; elle veut le b. et l'argent du b. she wants to have her cake and eat it; b. d'anchois anchovy paste; b. de cacahouètes peanut butter; b. de cacao cocoa butter; b. salé/demi-sel salted/slightly salted butter

beurré, -e [bœre] *adj très Fam (ivre)* plastered, legless

beurrer [bœre] *vt* to butter

beurrier [bœrje] *nm* butter dish

beuverie [bøvri] *nf* binge, drinking session

bévue [bevy] *nf* slip-up

Beyrouth [berut] *n* Beirut

bézef [bezɛf] *adv Fam* il n'y en a pas b. *(pain, confiture)* there's not much or a lot (of it); *(légumes, livres)* there aren't many or a lot (of them)

Bhoutan [butɑ̃] *nm* le B. Bhutan

bi- [bi] *préf* bi-

biais [bjɛ] *nm* (**a**) *(d'un mur)* slant; regarder qn de b. to look sideways at sb; en b. at an angle; tailler un tissu dans le b. to cut material on the bias (**b**) *(moyen)* way; par le b. de through (**c**) *(aspect)* angle; par quel b. envisager la chose? from what angle should we look at the issue?

biaiser [bjeze] *vi (ruser)* to dodge the issue

biathlon [biatlɔ̃] *nm* biathlon

bibelot [biblo] *nm* curio, knick-knack

biberon [bibrɔ̃] *nm* (baby's or feeding) bottle; nourrir ou élever un enfant au b. to bottle-feed a child; c'est l'heure du b. it's the baby's feeding time

bibi¹ [bibi] *nm (chapeau)* (woman's) hat

bibi² *pron Fam (moi)* yours truly; la vaisselle, c'est encore pour b.! yours truly gets stuck with the washing-up again!

bibine [bibin] *nf Fam (boisson)* dishwater

bibite [bibit] *nf Can Fam* bug, insect

bible [bibl] *nf aussi Fig* bible; la B. the Bible

bibliographie [bibliɔgrafi] *nf* bibliography

bibliographique [bibliɔgrafik] *adj* bibliographical

bibliophile [bibliɔfil] *nmf* book-lover

bibliothécaire [bibliɔtekɛr] *nmf* librarian

bibliothèque [bibliɔtɛk] *nf* (**a**) *(bâtiment, salle)* library; b. municipale public library; b. de prêt lending library; b. universitaire university library (**b**) *(meuble)* bookcase

biblique [biblik] *adj* biblical

Bic® [bik] 1 *adj* stylo B., pointe B. ballpoint (pen), *Br* Biro® 2 *nm* ballpoint (pen), *Br* Biro®

bicarbonate [bikarbɔnat] *nm Chim* bicarbonate; b. de soude bicarbonate of soda

bicentenaire [bisɑ̃tnɛr] *nm Br* bicentenary, *Am* bicentennial

biceps [bisɛps] *nm* biceps; *Fam* avoir des b. to have big biceps

biche [biʃ] *nf* (**a**) *(animal)* hind, doe (**b**) *Fam* ma b. darling

bicher [biʃe] *vi Fam Vieilli (se réjouir)* to be tickled pink

bichonner [biʃɔne] 1 *vt* (**a**) *(préparer)* to doll up (**b**) *(soigner)* to pamper 2 se bichonner *vpr* to doll oneself up

bicolore [bikɔlɔr] *adj* two-colour(ed)

bicoque [bikɔk] *nf Fam (maison)* house, place

bicorne [bikɔrn] *nm* cocked hat

bicyclette [bisiklɛt] *nf* bicycle; aller en ville à ou en b. to cycle into town, to go into town by bicycle; faire de la b. to go cycling; il ne sait pas faire de la b. he can't ride a bicycle

bidasse [bidas] *nm très Fam Br* squaddie, *Am* G.I.

bide [bid] *nm Fam* (**a**) *(ventre)* belly; avoir/prendre du b. to have/develop a belly (**b**) *(échec)* flop, washout; faire un b. *Br* to flop, *Am* to bomb

bidet [bidɛ] *nm* (**a**) *(de toilette)* bidet (**b**) *Hum (cheval)* nag

bidimensionnel, -elle [bidimɑ̃sjɔnɛl] *adj* bidimensional

bidoche [bidɔʃ] *nf très Fam* meat

bidon [bidɔ̃] 1 *adj inv Fam (excuse, argument)* phoney, fake; *(élections)* rigged 2 *nm* (**a**) *(d'huile, d'essence)* can; *(de lait)* churn; *(gourde)* water bottle; b. d'essence petrol can, jerry can (**b**) *Fam (ventre)* belly (**c**) *Fam (bluff)* c'est du b.

it's a load of tosh (**d**) *Belg Fam* **bidons** *(vêtements)* gear, togs; *(affaires)* gear

bidonnant, -e [bidɔnã, -ãt] *adj Fam* hilarious

bidonner [bidɔne] **se bidonner** *vpr Fam* to laugh one's head off

bidonville [bidɔ̃vil] *nm* shantytown

bidouiller [biduje] *vt Fam* to patch up; *Ordinat (programme)* to modify

bidule [bidyl] *nm Fam* thingy, whatsit; **B.** *(personne)* what's-his-name, *f* what's-her-name

bielle [bjɛl] *nf Aut* connecting rod, con-rod

biélorusse [bjelorys] **1** *adj* Byelorussian
2 *nmf* **B.** Byelorussian

Biélorussie [bjelorysi] *nf* **la B.** Belarus

bien [bjɛ̃] **1** *adv* (**a**) *(convenablement)* well; **un livre b. écrit** a well-written book; **écoutez-moi b.** listen carefully; *Ironique* **ça commence b.!** that's a good start!
(**b**) *(moralement)* right; **se conduire** *ou* **se tenir b.** to behave (well); **vous avez b. fait** you did the right thing; **tu fais b. de me le dire** it's a good thing you've told me; **tu ferais b. de te méfier** you would be wise to beware
(**c**) *(emphatique)* **regarder qn b. en face** to look sb right in the face; **c'est b. cela** that's right; **c'est b. une erreur** that's definitely a mistake; **est-ce b. le train pour Paris?** is this the right train for Paris?; **j'ai b. dû lire dix de ses livres** I must have read at least ten of his books; **j'irais b. avec vous mais...** I'd love to go with you but...; **j'y suis b. obligé** I just have to; **je sais b.** I'm well aware of it; **je vous l'avais b. dit!** I told you so!; **c'est b. ce que je pensais** that's what I thought; **nous verrons b.!** we'll see!; **qu'est-ce que ça peut b. être/vouloir dire?** what on earth can it be/mean?; **est-ce b. raisonnable?** is that really reasonable?; **B. à vous** *(dans une lettre)* Yours
(**d**) *(très)* very; **vous arrivez b. tard** you're very late; **que ce soit b. clair, je...** let's get this clear, I...
(**e**) *(beaucoup)* (*réfléchir, changer*) a lot, a great deal; **b. plus** much *or* a lot more; **b. moins** much *or* a lot less; **b. des gens** a lot of people; **b. d'autres** many others; **b. des fois** often; **avoir b. de la peine** *ou* **du mal à faire qch** to have a lot of difficulty doing sth; **tu as b. de la chance!** you're really lucky!
(**f**) *(locutions)* **b. que** although, though; **b. que je le sache** although I know it; **b. entendu, b. sûr, b. évidemment** of course; **b. sûr que je viendrai** of course I'll come; **b. sûr que non!** of course not!
2 *exclam* **eh b.!** well!; **b.! je vous appelle demain!** OK, I'll call you tomorrow!
3 *adj inv* (**a**) *(satisfaisant)* good; **c'est b.!** *(bravo)* good!
(**b**) *(à l'aise)* comfortable; **être b. avec qn** *(en bons termes)* to be on good terms with sb; **se mettre b. avec qn** to get into sb's good books; *Fam* **nous voilà b.!** we're in a right mess!
(**c**) *(en forme)* well
(**d**) *(moral)* decent; **ce n'est pas b. de vous moquer de lui** it's not nice *or* kind of you to make fun of him
(**e**) *(beau)* (*personne*) good-looking, attractive; **elle est b. sur cette photo** she looks good in this photo
4 *nm* (**a**) *Phil & Rel* good; **le b. et le mal** good and evil, right and wrong; **faire le b.** to do good; **faire du b. à qn** to do sb good; **grand b. vous fasse!** much good may it do you!; **dire du b. de qn** to speak well of sb; **c'est pour ton b.** it's for your own good; **c'était en tout b. tout honneur** it was quite innocent
(**b**) *(chose matérielle)* possession; *Jur* assets; **biens** possessions, property; **avoir du b.** to have property; *Prov* **b. mal acquis ne profite jamais** ill-gotten gains never prosper; **biens de consommation** consumer goods; **biens immobiliers** *ou* **immeubles** real estate *or* property

bien-aimé, -e (*mpl* **bien-aimés**, *fpl* **bien-aimées**) [bjɛ̃neme] *adj* beloved

bien-être [bjɛ̃nɛtr] *nm* well-being

bienfaisance [bjɛ̃fəzãs] *nf* **œuvre de b.** charity, charitable organization

bienfaisant, -e [bjɛ̃fəzã, -ãt] *adj* (**a**) *(personne)* charitable (**b**) (*remède*) beneficial; *(vent, pluie)* refreshing

bienfait [bjɛ̃fɛ] *nm* (**a**) *(acte)* kindness (**b**) *(avantage)* benefit

bienfaiteur, -trice [bjɛ̃fɛtœr, -tris] *nm,f* benefactor, *f* benefactress

bien-fondé [bjɛ̃fɔ̃de] *nm* validity; *Jur* cogency

bienheureux, -euse [bjɛ̃nørø, -øz] *adj* blissful; *Rel* blessed

biennal, -e, -aux, -ales [bjenal, -o] *adj* biennial

bien-pensant, -e (*mpl* **bien-pensants**, *fpl* **bien-pensantes**) [bjɛ̃pãsã, -ãt] *adj & nm,f* conformist

bienséance [bjɛ̃seãs] *nf* propriety, decorum

bientôt [bjɛ̃to] *adv* soon; **il est b. deux heures** it's nearly two o'clock; **on est b. arrivés?** will we soon be there?; *Fam* **tu n'as pas b. fini?** have you quite finished?; **à b.!** see you soon!

bienveillance [bjɛ̃vejãs] *nf* kindness; **avec b.** kindly

bienveillant, -e [bjɛ̃vejã, -ãt] *adj* kind

bienvenu, -e [bjɛ̃vny] **1** *adj (remarque)* apposite; *(repas, explication)* welcome
2 *nm,f* **soyez le b.!** welcome!; **vous serez toujours la bienvenue** you're always welcome

bienvenue [bjɛ̃vny] **1** *nf* welcome; **souhaiter la b. à qn** to welcome sb
2 *exclam* welcome! (**à** to); *Can (de rien)* you're welcome!

bière¹ [bjɛr] *nf (boisson)* beer; *Fam* **ce n'est pas de la petite b.** it's no small thing; **b. blonde** lager; **b. brune** *Br* brown ale, *Am* dark beer; **b. pression** *Br* draught beer, *Am* draft beer

bière² *nf (cercueil)* coffin; **assister à la mise en b.** to be present when the body is placed in the coffin

biffer [bife] *vt* to cross out; **b. un nom d'une liste** to cross a name off a list

biffure [bifyr] *nf* crossing out

bifidus [bifidys] *nm* live culture

bifocal, -e, -aux, -ales [bifɔkal, -o] *adj (lentille)* bifocal; **lunettes bifocales** bifocals

bifteck [biftɛk] *nm* (beef)steak; **b. haché** *Br* mince, *Am* mincemeat; *Fam* **gagner son b.** to earn one's bread and butter

bifurcation [bifyrkasjɔ̃] *nf* fork

bifurquer [bifyrke] *vi (route, chemin)* to fork; *(automobiliste)* to turn off; **bifurquez à droite** take the right fork

bigame [bigam] *adj* bigamous

bigamie [bigami] *nf* bigamy

bigarré, -e [bigare] *adj (tissu)* multicoloured; **une foule bigarrée** a motley crew

bigarreau, -x [bigaro] *nm* = type of cherry

bigler [bigle] *Fam* **1** *vi* (**a**) *(loucher)* to have a squint
(**b**) **b. sur qch** to have a good look at sth
2 *vt (personne)* to eye up

bigleux, -euse [biglø, -øz] *adj Fam (qui louche)* cross-eyed; *(myope)* short-sighted

bigophone [bigɔfɔn] *nm Fam Br* blower, *Am* horn

bigorneau, -x [bigɔrno] *nm* winkle

bigot, -e [bigo, -ɔt] **1** *nm,f* (religious) bigot
2 *adj* sanctimonious

bigoterie [bigɔtri] *nf* (religious) bigotry

bigoudi [bigudi] *nm* (hair) curler *or* roller; **se mettre des bigoudis** to put one's hair in curlers

bigre [bigr] *exclam Fam Vieilli* gosh!

bigrement [bigrəmã] *adv Fam (très)* awfully; *(beaucoup)* a heck of a lot

bihebdomadaire [biɛbdɔmadɛr] *adj* twice-weekly

bijou, -x [biʒu] *nm* jewel; *Fig* **des bijoux** jewellery, jewels; **b. de famille** family jewel; **un b. fantaisie** a piece of costume jewellery

bijouterie [biʒutri] *nf (boutique)* jeweller's (shop); *(commerce, fabrication)* jeweller's trade

bijoutier, -ère [biʒutje, -ɛr] *nm,f* jeweller

bikini® [bikini] *nm* bikini

bilan [bilã] *nm* (**a**) *Fin* balance sheet; **faire** *ou* **dresser un b.** to draw up a balance sheet; *Com* **déposer son b.** to file one's petition (in bankruptcy); *Com* **un dépôt de b.** a petition in bankruptcy; **b. comptable** balance sheet (**b**) *(appréciation) (d'une situation, de faits)* assessment, evaluation; *(résultats)* results; *(d'une catastrophe)* toll; **faire le b. de la situation** to take stock of the situation; **accident sur l'autoroute, b. quatre morts** *(titre)* motorway accident, four dead; **b. de santé** complete check-up

bilatéral, -e, -aux, -ales [bilateral, -o] *adj* bilateral

bilboquet [bilbɔkɛ] *nm* cup-and-ball

bile [bil] *nf* bile; **décharger sa b. sur qn** to vent one's spleen on sb; *Fam* **se faire de la b. (pour)** to fret (about)

biler [bile] **se biler** *vpr Fam* to fret

biliaire [biljɛr] *adj* biliary

bilingue [bilɛ̃g] *adj* bilingual

billard [bijar] *nm* (**a**) *(jeu)* billiards; **faire un b.** *ou* **une partie de b.** to have a game of billiards; **b. américain** pool; **b. électrique** pinball (**b**) *(table)* billiard table (**c**) *Fam* **passer sur le b.** to go under the knife

bille¹ [bij] *nf* (**a**) *(de verre)* marble; *Fig* **reprendre ses billes** to pull out; *Fam* **toucher sa b. en qch** to know a thing or two about sth (**b**) *(de billard)* (billiard) ball; *Fig* **y aller b. en tête** not to beat about the bush (**c**) *Tech* ball (**d**) *très Fam (visage)* mug; **avoir une bonne b.** to look pleasant enough

bille² *nf (pièce de bois)* billet

billet [bijɛ] *nm* (**a**) *(argent)* **b. (de banque)** *Br* (bank)note, *Am* bill; **un b. de 100 euros** a 100-euro note; **un faux b.** a forged banknote; **le b. vert** the dollar; *Fam* **je te fiche mon b. qu'il ne viendra pas!** I bet my bottom dollar he won't come! (**b**) *(pour voyager, pour le cinéma)* ticket; **b. d'avion/de train** plane/train ticket; **b. de première/de seconde** first-/second-class ticket; **b. simple** *Br* single *or Am* one-way ticket; **b. aller (et) retour** *Br* return *or Am* round-trip ticket (**c**) *Com & Fin (effet)* bill; **b. au porteur** bill payable to bearer (**d**) *Litt (lettre)* note; *Scol* **b. d'absence** absence slip; **b. doux** love letter; *Scol* **b. de retard** = note given to pupil who is late, specifying the time of arrival

billetterie [bijɛtri] *nf* (**a**) *(lieu)* ticket office (**b**) *(de billets de transport)* **b.automatique** ticket machine

billion [biljɔ̃] *nm* trillion

billot [bijo] *nm* block

bimensuel, -elle [bimãsɥɛl] **1** *adj Br* fortnightly, *Am* semimonthly
2 *nm Br* fortnightly *or Am* semimonthly magazine

bimestriel, -elle [bimɛstriɛl] *adj & nm* bimonthly

bimoteur [bimɔtœr] *adj & nm* **(avion) b.** twin-engine aircraft

binaire [binɛr] *adj Math* binary; **langage b.** binary notation

biner [bine] *vt* to hoe

binette¹ [binɛt] *nf (outil)* hoe

binette² *nf très Fam (visage)* mug

binette³ *nf Can Ordinat* smiley, emoticon

biniou [binju] *nm* Breton bagpipes

binoclard, -e [binɔklar, -ard] *nm,f Fam* specs wearer

binocle [binɔkl] *nm* pince-nez *inv*; *Fam* **binocles** *(lunettes)* specs

binôme [binom] *nm* (**a**) *Math* binomial (**b**) *Scol (étudiant)* partner; **travailler en b.** to work in pairs *or* twos

bio [bjo] *adj inv Fam (produit, yaourt)* organic

biocarburant [bjokarbyrã] *nm* biofuel

biochimie [bjoʃimi] *nf* biochemistry

biodégradable [bjodegradabl] *adj* biodegradable

biodiversité [bjodivɛrsite] *nf* biodiversity

biographe [bjograf] *nmf* biographer

biographie [bjografi] *nf* biography

biographique [bjografik] *adj* biographical

bio-industrie *(pl* **bio-industries)** [bjoɛ̃dystri] *nf* biotechnology industry

biologie [bjolɔʒi] *nf* biology

biologique [bjolɔʒik] *adj* biological; *(sans engrais chimiques)* organic

biologiste [bjolɔʒist] *nmf* biologist

biomasse [bjomas] *nf* biomass

biophysique [bjofizik] *nf* biophysics *(singulier)*

biopsie [bjɔpsi] *nf* biopsy

biorythme [bjoritm] *nm* biorhythm

biosphère [bjosfɛr] *nf* biosphere

biotechnique [bjotɛknik], **biotechnologie** [bjotɛknolɔʒi] *nf* biotechnology

bip [bip] **1** *exclam* beep!
2 *nm* (**a**) *(son)* beep; **faire b.** to beep (**b**) *(appareil)* beeper, pager

biparti, -e [biparti], **bipartite** [bipartit] *adj* bipartite

bipède [bipɛd] *adj & nm* biped

biper [bipe] *vt* to page

biplace [biplas] *adj & nm Aut & Aviat* two-seater

biplan [biplã] *nm* biplane

bipolaire [bipɔlɛr] *adj Élec & Phys* bipolar

bique [bik] *nf Fam* (**a**) *(chèvre)* nanny goat (**b**) *Péj (femme)* **vieille b.** old bag

biquet, -ette [bikɛ, -ɛt] *nm,f* (**a**) *(chevreau)* kid (**b**) *Fam* **mon b.** my pet

bircher [birʃɛr] *nm Suisse* muesli

BIRD [bird] *nf (abrév* **banque internationale pour la reconstruction et le développement)** IBRD

biréacteur [bireaktœr] *nm* twin-engine jet

birman, -e [birmã, -an] **1** *adj* Burmese
2 *nm,f* **B.** Burmese
3 *nm (langue)* Burmese

Birmanie [birmani] *nf* **la B.** Burma

bis¹, -e [bi, biz] *adj* greyish-brown

bis² [bis] *adv* (**a**) *Théât* encore; *Mus* repeat (**b**) *(d'une adresse)* **10 b.** ≃ 10A

bisaïeul, -e [bizajœl] *nm,f Litt* great-grandfather, *f* great-grandmother

bisannuel, -elle [bizanɥɛl] *adj* biennial

bisbille [bisbij] *nf Fam* squabble; **être en b. avec qn** to be at odds with sb

bisbrouille [bisbruj] *nf Belg* tiff

biscornu, -e [biskɔrny] *adj* (**a**) *(chapeau)* misshapen; *(bâtiment, objet)* oddly shaped (**b**) *Fam (idées)* cranky; *(raisonnement, esprit)* tortuous

biscoteaux [biskɔto] *nmpl Fam* biceps; **avoir des b.** to have bulging biceps

biscotte [biskɔt] *nf* rusk

biscuit [biskɥi] *nm* (**a**) *(gâteau) Br* biscuit, *Am* cookie; **b. à la cuiller** *Br* sponge finger, *Am* lady finger; **biscuits salés** crackers (**b**) *(porcelaine)* biscuit

bise¹ [biz] *nf (vent)* north wind

bise² *nf Fam (baiser)* kiss; **donner** *ou* **faire une b. à qn** to give sb a kiss; **se faire la b.** to give each other a kiss; **grosses bises** *(sur une lettre)* love and kisses

biseau, -x [bizo] *nm* (**a**) *(bord)* bevel; **taillé en b.** bevel-edged (**b**) *(outil)* bevel

biseauter [bizote] *vt* (**a**) *(tailler)* to bevel (**b**) *(cartes à jouer)* to mark

bisexualité [bisɛksɥalite] *nf* bisexuality

bisexuel, -elle [bisɛksɥɛl] *adj* bisexual

bismuth [bismyt] *nm* bismuth

bison [bizõ] *nm* bison

Bison Futé [bizõfyte] *n* = organization which advises drivers of driving conditions on French motorways

bisou [bizu] *nm Fam* kiss

bisque [bisk] *nf Culin* **b. de homard** lobster bisque

bisquer [biske] *vi Fam* **faire b. qn** to wind sb up

bissectrice [bisɛktris] *nf* bisector

bisser [bise] *vt* (**a**) *(sujet: artiste) (chanson)* to give an encore of (**b**) *(sujet: spectateur) (chanson)* to call for an encore of; **b. un chanteur** to call on a singer to give an encore (**c**) *Belg Scol (redoubler)* to repeat

bissextile [bisɛkstil] *adj* **année b.** leap year

bistouri [bisturi] *nm* lancet

bistro(t) [bistro] *nm Fam* bar

Bistrot

This word can refer either to a small café or to a cosy restaurant, especially one frequented by regulars. These establishments are usually less classy than bistros in English-speaking countries. The "style bistrot" refers to a style of furnishing inspired by the chairs, tables and zinc countertops typical of the traditional "bistrot".

BIT [beite] *nm (abrév* **Bureau international du travail)** ILO

bit [bit] *nm Ordinat* bit; **b. d'arrêt** stop bit; **b. de contrôle** control bit; **b. de départ** start bit

bite [bit] *nf Vulg* cock

bitoniau [bitɔnjo] *nm Fam* thingy

bitte¹ [bit] = **bite**

bitte² *nf Naut* **b. d'amarrage** bollard

biture [bityr] *nf très Fam* **prendre une b.** to get plastered

bitturer [bityre] **se bitturer** *vpr très Fam* to get plastered

bitume [bitym] *nm (revêtement)* asphalt

bitumer [bityme] *vt (route)* to asphalt

bitum(in)eux, -euse [bitym(in)ø, -øz] *adj* bituminous

biture [bityr] = **bitture**

biturer [bityre] = **bitturer**

bivouac [bivwak] *nm* bivouac

bivouaquer [bivwake] *vi* to bivouac

bizarre [bizar] *adj* strange, odd

bizarrement [bizarmã] *adv* strangely, oddly

bizarrerie [bizarri] *nf (d'une situation, d'une idée, d'une attitude)* strangeness, oddness; **bizarreries** oddities; *(d'une personne)* eccentricities

bizarroïde [bizarɔid] *adj Fam* weird

bizut [bizy] *nm Fam Scol & Univ* = first-year student on whom practical jokes are played

bizutage [bizytaʒ] *nm Fam Scol & Univ* = practical jokes played on first-year students, *Br* ≃ ragging, *Am* ≃ hazing

Bizutage

In some French schools and colleges, students in fancy-dress take to the streets and play practical jokes, sometimes of a very cruel nature, on each other and on passers-by at the beginning of the school year. This is part of the traditional initiation ceremony known as "bizutage". As a consequence of the excessive behaviour to which it has often led, a law was passed in 1998 to make it an offence.

bizuter [bizyte] *vt Fam Scol & Univ (étudiant)* to play practical jokes on, *Br* ≃ to rag, *Am* ≃ to haze

bizuth [bizy] = **bizut**

bla-bla [blabla] *nm Fam* claptrap

black [blak] *Fam* **1** *adj* black **2** *nmf* **B.** Black

blackbouler [blakbule] *vt Fam (à un examen)* to fail; **se faire b.** to fail, *Am* to flunk

blafard, -e [blafar, -ard] *adj* pallid

blague [blag] *nf* (**a**) *(plaisanterie)* joke; **faire une b. à qn** to play a joke on sb; **b. à part** joking apart; **sans b.?** no kidding? (**b**) *(mensonge)* **raconter des blagues** to lie

blaguer [blage] *vi Fam* to joke; **aimer b.** to like a joke

blagueur, -euse [blagœr, -øz] *Fam* **1** *adj* **il est très b.** he really likes a joke **2** *nm,f (qui dit des blagues)* joker; *(qui fait des blagues)* practical joker

blair [blɛr] *nm très Fam Br* conk, *Am* schnozzle

blaireau, -x [blɛro] *nm* (**a**) *(animal)* badger (**b**) *(pinceau)* shaving brush (**c**) *Fam Pej (personne)* jerk, *Br* prat

blairer [blere] *vt Fam* **je ne peux pas le b.** I can't stick him

blâme [blɑm] *nm* (**a**) *(reproche)* blame (**b**) *(sanction)* reprimand

blâmer [blɑme] *vt* (**a**) *(désapprouver)* to blame (**b**) *(sanctionner)* to reprimand

blanc, blanche [blɑ̃, blɑ̃ʃ] **1** *adj* (**a**) *(couleur)* white; **b. comme neige** snow-white, as white as snow; *Fig* (as) pure as the driven snow
(**b**) *(peau)* pale; *(pas bronzé)* white; **b. comme un linge** as white as a sheet
(**c**) *(page)* blank
(**d**) *(sourd)* **d'une voix blanche** in a toneless voice
2 *nm* (**a**) *(couleur)* white; **le b. est à la mode** white is in; **b. cassé** off-white

(**b**) *(partie blanche) (d'une cible)* bull's-eye; **le b. des yeux** the whites of the eyes; **regarder qn dans le b. des yeux** to look sb straight in the eye; **b. d'œuf** egg white; **b. de poulet** chicken breast

(**c**) *(espace)* blank

(**d**) *(aux dominos)* blank

(**e**) **chauffé à b.** white-hot; **tirer à b.** to fire a blank/blanks

(**f**) *(linge)* **(articles de) b.** linen; **je lave le b. séparément** I wash my whites separately

(**g**) *(vin)* white wine

3 *nm,f* **B.** White (man), *f* White (woman); **les Blancs** the Whites

4 *nf* **blanche** *Mus Br* minim, *Am* half note

blanc-bec *(pl* **blancs-becs)** [blɑ̃bɛk] *nm* total novice

blanchâtre [blɑ̃ʃɑtr] *adj* whitish

blanche [blɑ̃ʃ] *voir* **blanc**

Blanche-Neige [blɑ̃ʃnɛʒ] *npr* Snow White

blancheur [blɑ̃ʃœr] *nf* whiteness

blanchiment [blɑ̃ʃimɑ̃] *nm (d'argent)* laundering

blanchir [blɑ̃ʃir] **1** *vt* (**a**) *(rendre blanc)* to whiten; *(linge)* to launder; **b. à la chaux** to whitewash (**b**) *(disculper)* to clear (**c**) *(argent)* to launder (**d**) *Culin* to blanch

2 *vi* (**a**) *(devenir blanc)* to turn *or* go white (**b**) *(pâlir)* to blanch

blanchissage [blɑ̃ʃisaʒ] *nm* (**a**) *(du linge)* laundering (**b**) *Can Sport* shutout

blanchissement [blɑ̃ʃismɑ̃] *nm* whitening

blanchisserie [blɑ̃ʃisri] *nf* laundry

blanchisseur, -euse [blɑ̃ʃisœr, -øz] *nm,f* laundryman, *f* laundrywoman

blanchon [blɑ̃ʃɔ̃] *nm Can* whitecoat *(seal pup)*

blanquette¹ [blɑ̃kɛt] *nf Culin* **b. (de veau)** = veal stew in a white sauce

blanquette² *nf* **b. de Limoux** = sparkling white wine from Limoux

blasé, -e [blaze] *adj* blasé

blason [blazɔ̃] *nm* coat of arms

blasphème [blasfɛm] *nm* blasphemy

blasphémer [34] [blasfeme] *vi* to blaspheme

blatte [blat] *nf* cockroach

blazer [blazɛr, blazœr] *nm* blazer

bld *abrév* **boulevard**

blé [ble] *nm* (**a**) *(céréale)* wheat, *Br* corn; **b. dur** durum wheat; **b. en herbe** wheat in the blade; *Fig* **manger son b. en herbe** to eat one's seed corn; *Can* **b. d'Inde** *Br* maize, *Am* (Indian) corn (**b**) *Fam (argent)* bread

bled [blɛd] *nm* (**a**) *(en Afrique du Nord)* **le b.** the interior of the country (**b**) *Fam (lieu isolé)* dump, hole; **dans un b. perdu** in the middle of nowhere

blême [blɛm] *adj (personne, matin)* pale; **b. de colère** livid with anger; **devenir b.** to turn *or* go pale

blêmir [blemir] *vi* to turn *or* go pale; **b. de colère** to turn livid with anger

blennorragie [blɛnoraʒi] *nf* gonorrhoea

blessant, -e [blɛsɑ̃, -ɑ̃t] *adj* hurtful

blessé, -e [blese] **1** *adj (par arme)* wounded; *(dans un accident)* injured; *(moralement)* hurt; **être b. dans son amour-propre** to have had one's pride hurt; **êtes-vous b.?** are you hurt?

2 *nm,f (victime d'un accident)* injured person; *(victime d'une agression)* wounded person; **les blessés** the injured/wounded

blesser [blese] **1** *vt* (**a**) *(par arme)* to wound; *(dans un accident)* to injure, to hurt; *(sujet: chaussures)* to hurt; **il a été blessé au bras** *(par arme)* he was wounded in the arm; *(dans un accident)* his arm was injured (**b**) *(moralement)* to hurt

2 se blesser *vpr (avec une arme)* to wound oneself; *(accidentellement)* to hurt *or* injure oneself (**avec** with); **se b. à la tête** *(avec une arme)* to wound oneself in the head; *(accidentellement)* to hurt one's head

blessure [blesyr] *nf (par arme)* wound; *(dans un accident)* injury; *Fig (morale)* wound, hurt

blette [blɛt] = **bette**

bleu, -e [blø] **1** *adj* blue; *(bifteck)* very rare; **b. de froid** blue with cold

2 *nm* (**a**) *(couleur)* blue; **le b. est à la mode** blue is in; **b. canard** peacock blue; **b. ciel** sky blue; **b. électrique** electric blue; **b. marine** navy (blue); **b. nuit** midnight blue; **b. de Prusse** Prussian blue; **b. roi** royal blue

(**b**) *(ecchymose)* bruise; **se faire un b.** to bruise oneself

(**c**) *Fam (novice)* novice; *Mil* rookie

(**d**) *(fromage)* blue cheese; **b. d'Auvergne/Bresse** = blue cheese from Auvergne/Bresse

(**e**) **b. (de chauffe** *ou* **de travail)** overalls; *(salopette)* dungarees

(**f**) *Suisse Fam (permis de conduire) Br* driving licence, *Am* driver's license

bleuâtre [bløɑtr] *adj* bluish

bleuet [bløɛ] *nm* (**a**) *(plante)* cornflower (**b**) *Can (baie)* blueberry

bleuetière [bløtjɛr] *nf Can* blueberry field

bleuté, -e [bløte] *adj* bluish; *(verres)* blue-tinted

blindage [blɛ̃daʒ] *nm Mil* armour-plating

blinde [blɛ̃d] **à toute blinde** *adv Fam* at full speed, like lightning

blindé, -e [blɛ̃de] **1** *adj* (**a**) *(véhicule militaire)* armoured, armour-plated; *(voiture)* bulletproof; **porte blindée** steel security door (**b**) *Fam* **je suis b.** I'm hardened to it

2 *nm Mil* armoured vehicle

blinder [blɛ̃de] *vt* (**a**) *(véhicule)* to armour-plate; *(porte)* to reinforce with steel (**b**) *Fam (personne)* to harden (**contre** to)

blini [blini] *nm* blini

blizzard [blizar] *nm* blizzard

bloc [blɔk] *nm* (**a**) *(de bois, de pierre)* block

(**b**) *(de maisons)* block

(**c**) *Pol* bloc; **faire b. (avec/contre qn)** to join forces (with/against sb); *Écon* **b. monétaire** monetary bloc

(**d**) *(de papier)* pad; **b. de papier à lettres** writing pad

(**e**) *(ensemble d'éléments)* unit; **b. opératoire** operating theatre

(**f**) *très Fam (prison)* clink; **être au b.** to be in the clink

(**g**) *Ordinat* block; **b. d'alimentation secteur** mains power unit; **b. de données** data block; **b. de touches** keypad

(**h**) *(locutions)* **tout refuser en b.** to reject everything in its entirety; **serrer qch à b.** to screw sth as tightly as possible

blocage [blɔkaʒ] *nm* (**a**) *(d'un mécanisme)* jamming; *(des freins)* locking; *(des prix, des salaires)* freezing; *Psy (mental)* block; *Psy* **faire un b.** to get a (mental) block (**b**) *Ordinat (dans réseau)* lockout; **b. majuscule** caps lock

bloc-appartement (*pl* **blocs-appartements**) [blɔkapartəmã] *nm Can Br* block of flats, *Am* apartment building

blockhaus [blɔkos] *nm* blockhouse

bloc-moteur (*pl* **blocs-moteurs**) [blɔkmɔtœr] *nm* engine block

bloc-notes (*pl* **blocs-notes**) [blɔknɔt] *nm* notepad

blocus [blɔkys] *nm* blockade; **lever/forcer le b.** to raise/run the blockade

blond, -e [blɔ̃, -ɔ̃d] **1** *adj* (*cheveux*) fair, blond; (*personne*) fair-haired, blond; (*sable, blés*) golden; **être b. comme les blés** (*sujet: personne*) to have goldenblond hair
2 *nm,f* (*personne*) **un b.** a fair-haired man; **une blonde** a blonde, a fair-haired woman; **une blonde décolorée** a peroxide blonde
3 *nm* (*couleur*) **b. cendré** ash blond; **b. platine** platinum blond; **b. vénitien** strawberry blond
4 *nf* **blonde** (**a**) (*bière*) lager (**b**) (*cigarette*) Virginia cigarette (**c**) *Can Fam* (*amie*) girlfriend

blondinet, -ette [blɔ̃dinε, -εt] *nm,f* fair-haired child

blondir [blɔ̃dir] **1** *vt* (*cheveux*) to bleach
2 *vi* (*cheveux, personne*) to go *or* turn blond; **faire b. des oignons** to cook onions until they turn pale yellow

bloquer [blɔke] **1** *vt* (**a**) (*mécanisme, porte*) to jam; **il m'a bloqué contre un mur** he jammed me up against a wall; *Fam* **je suis bloqué à l'hôpital** I'm stuck in hospital (**b**) (*réunir*) to group together; (*jours de congé*) to lump together (**c**) (*compte en banque*) to block; (*prix, salaires*) to freeze (**d**) (*route, ballon*) to block; **b. le chemin** *ou* **le passage à qn** to block sb's way (**e**) *Belg Fam* (*sujet*) to bone up on (**f**) *Can Fam* (*examen*) to fail (**g**) *Psy* **ça me bloque de me sentir observé** I get a (mental) block if I feel I'm being watched; **être bloqué** to have a (mental) block
2 se bloquer *vpr* (**a**) (*machine, ascenseur*) to get stuck (**b**) *Psy* to get a (mental) block

blottir [blɔtir] **se blottir** *vpr* to snuggle up; **se b. contre qn/dans les bras de qn** to snuggle up to sb/in sb's arms; **blottis les uns contre les autres** huddled up together

blousant, -e [bluzã, -ãt] *adj* loose-fitting

blouse [bluz] *nf* (**a**) (*tablier*) overall; **b. de laboratoire/blanche** lab/white coat; **les blouses blanches** doctors and nurses (**b**) (*de femme*) blouse

blouser [bluze] **1** *vt Fam* (*personne*) to con
2 *vi* (*corsage*) to be loose-fitting

blouson [bluzɔ̃] *nm* (lumber-)jacket; (*plus léger*) blouson; **b. en** *ou* **de cuir** leather jacket; **b. d'aviateur** bomber jacket; *Fam Vieilli* **b. noir** young hoodlum (*wearing a black leather jacket*)

blue-jean [bludʒin] (*pl* **blue-jeans**) [bludʒins] *nm Vieilli* jeans

blues [bluz] *nm* blues

bluff [blœf] *nm* bluff; **y aller au b.** to try and bluff

bluffer [blœfe] **1** *vt* (*aux cartes*) to bluff; *Fam* (*personne*) to take in
2 *vi* (*aux cartes*) & *Fam* to bluff

blush [blœʃ] *nm* blusher

BN [beεn] *nf* (*abrév* **Bibliothèque nationale**) = the former French national library

BNF [beεnεf] *nf* (*abrév* **bibliothèque nationale de France**) = French national library, comprising the "Bibliothèque de France" and the "Bibliothèque nationale"

BO [beo] **1** *nf* (*abrév* **bande originale**) (original) soundtrack
2 *nm* (*abrév* **bulletin officiel**) = official listing of all new laws and decrees

boa [bɔa] *nm* (**a**) (*serpent*) boa; **b. constricteur** boa constrictor (**b**) (*en plumes*) boa

boat people [botpipœl] *nmpl* boat people

bob [bɔb] *nm Fam* (*chapeau*) sun hat

bobard [bɔbar] *nm Fam* tall story

bobine [bɔbin] *nf* (**a**) (*de ruban, de fil*) reel; (*de machine à coudre*) bobbin; (*de machine à écrire, d'appareil photo*) spool; (*de film, de papier*) roll (**b**) *Élec* coil (**c**) *Fam* (*visage*) mug

bobo [bobo] *nm* (*langage enfantin*) (*coupure*) cut; (*piqûre*) sting; **ça fait b.?** does it hurt?; **se faire b.** to hurt oneself

bobsleigh [bɔbslε(g)] *nm* bobsleigh

bocage [bɔkaʒ] *nm* bocage (*countryside with many hedges, trees and small fields*)

bocal, -aux [bɔkal, -o] *nm* jar; (*aquarium*) (fish)bowl

Boche [bɔʃ] *nmf Fam Péj* Kraut, = offensive term referring to a German

bock [bɔk] *nm* beer glass

body [bɔdi] *nm* (*vêtement*) body

body-building [bɔdibildiŋ] *nm* body building; **faire du b.** to do body building

bœuf [bœf, *pl* bø] **1** *nm* (**a**) (*animal*) bullock; (*de trait*) ox; *Fam* **on n'est pas des bœufs** we're not superhuman (**b**) (*viande*) beef; **b. bourguignon** bœuf bourguignon; **b. mode** stewed beef (**c**) *Fam* (*improvisation*) jam session; **faire un b.** to jam
2 *adj inv Fam* **avoir un succès b.** to be incredibly successful; **faire un effet b.** to make a really big impression

bof [bɔf] *exclam Fam* **ça te plaît? – b., pas tellement** do you like it? – not really, no; **il est chouette, hein, mon nouveau pull? – b.** my new sweater's great, isn't it? – I suppose so

Bogota [bogota] *n* Bogota

bogue [bɔg] *nf* (**a**) (*de châtaigne*) *Br* burr, *Am* shuck (**b**) *Ordinat* bug; **dépourvu/plein de bogues** bug-free/-ridden; **b. de l'an 2000** millennium bug; **b. de logiciel** software bug

bohème [bɔεm] **1** *adj* bohemian
2 *nmf* **mener une vie de b.** to lead a bohemian life

Bohême [bɔεm] *nf* **la B.** Bohemia

bohémien, -enne [bɔεmjε̃, -εn] *nm,f* gypsy

boire¹ [12] [bwar] **1** *vt* (**a**) (*sujet: personne*) to drink; *Fig* **b. les paroles de qn** to drink in sb's every word (**b**) (*sujet: plante, matière poreuse*) to soak up, to absorb
2 *vi* (*personne*) to drink; (*plante*) to soak up *or* absorb water; *Can* (*bébé*) to feed; **b. comme un trou** to drink like a fish; **b. à la bouteille** to drink from the bottle; **b. au succès de qn/qch** to drink to the success of sb/sth; **donner à b. à qn** to give sb a drink; **faire b. qn** to give sb something to drink; **faire b. les chevaux** to water the horses; *Fig* **il y a à b. et à manger là-dedans** it's a bit of a mixed bag; *Prov* **qui a bu boira** old habits die hard
3 se boire *vpr* to be drunk

boire² *nm* **le b. et le manger** food and drink

bois [bwa] *nm* (**a**) (*forêt*) wood (**b**) (*matériau*) wood; **des meubles en b.** wooden furniture; *Fig* **elle n'est pas de b.** she's only human; *Fig* **je vais leur faire voir de quel b. je me chauffe!** I'll show them (what I'm made of)!; **petit b.** kindling; **b. de charpente** *ou* **de construction** *Br* timber, *Am* lumber; **b. de chauffage**

firewood; **b. mort** deadwood; *Can* **b. de poêle** firewood; *Can* **b. rond** log; **b. de rose** rosewood (**c**) *(de chaise, de raquette)* frame; **faire un b.** *(au tennis)* to hit the ball off the frame; **b. de lit** bed frame (**d**) *Mus* **les b.** the woodwind (**e**) **les b.** *(d'un cerf)* the antlers

boisé, -e [bwaze] *adj (région)* wooded

boisement [bwazmɑ̃] *nm* afforestation

boiseries [bwazri] *nfpl* panelling

boisson [bwasɔ̃] *nf* drink; *Can (spiritueux)* hard liquor, spirits; **b. alcoolisée/non alcoolisée** alcoholic/soft drink; **b. chaude** hot drink; **b. gazeuse** fizzy drink

boîte [bwat] *nf* (**a**) *(récipient)* box; **des haricots en b.** canned *or Br* tinned beans; **mettre qch en b.** *(marchandises)* to box sth; *(aliments)* to can sth, *Br* to tin sth; *Fam* **mettre qn en b.** to pull sb's leg; **b. d'allumettes** *(pleine)* box of matches; *(vide)* matchbox; **b. à bijoux** jewel box; **b. de conserve** can, *Br* tin; **b. à couture** *ou* **ouvrage** sewing box; **b. à gants** glove compartment; **b. à** *ou* **aux lettres** *Br* postbox, *Am* mailbox; *(chez soi) Br* letterbox, *Am* mailbox; *Ordinat* **b. à lettres électronique** mailbox; **b. à musique** music box; *Aviat* **b. noire** black box; **b. à outils** toolbox; **b. postale** Post Office Box; *Aut* **b. de vitesses** gearbox; *Ordinat* **b. vocale** voice mail (**b**) *Fam (entreprise)* firm; *(école)* school (**c**) **b. (de nuit)** nightclub; **aller** *ou* **sortir en b.** to go to a nightclub

boiter [bwate] *vi* to limp

boiteux, -euse [bwatø, -øz] *adj (personne, cheval, explication)* lame; *(raisonnement)* shaky; *(phrase)* badly constructed

boîtier [bwatje] *nm* case; *Phot* (camera) body; *Ordinat* **b. de commande** command box; *Ordinat* **b. commutateur** data switch

boitiller [bwatije] *vi* to limp slightly

boive *etc voir* **boire**

bol [bɔl] *nm* (**a**) *(récipient)* bowl (**b**) *(contenu)* bowl(ful); **prendre un b. d'air frais** *ou* **pur** to get a good breath of fresh air (**c**) *Fam (chance)* luck; **avoir du b.** to be lucky; **ne pas avoir de b.** to be unlucky; **manque de b., il avait déjà demandé!** just my luck, he'd already asked! (**d**) **le B. d'or** = 24-hour motorcycle race

bolchevique [bɔlʃəvik, bɔlʃevik] *adj & nmf* Bolshevik

bolduc [bɔldyk] *nm* gift-wrap ribbon

bolée [bɔle] *nf* bowl(ful)

boléro [bɔlero] *nm (vêtement, pièce musicale)* bolero

bolet [bɔlɛ] *nm* boletus

bolide [bɔlid] *nm (voiture)* racing car; **comme un b.** like a rocket

Bolivie [bɔlivi] *nf* **la B.** Bolivia

bolivien, -enne [bɔlivjɛ̃, -ɛn] **1** *adj* Bolivian **2** *nm,f* **B.** Bolivian

bolognais, -e [bɔlɔɲɛ, -ɛz] *adj* Bolognese; *Culin* **spaghetti bolognaise** spaghetti bolognese

Bologne [bɔlɔɲ] *n* Bologna

bombage [bɔ̃baʒ] *nm Fam* (aerosol) graffiti; **faire des bombages sur un mur** to spray-paint a wall with graffiti

bombance [bɔ̃bɑ̃s] *nf Fam* **faire b.** to feast

bombardement [bɔ̃bardəmɑ̃] *nm (avec des obus)* shelling; *(avec des bombes)* bombing; **b. aérien** air raid

bombarder [bɔ̃barde] *vt* (**a**) *(avec des obus)* to shell; *(avec des bombes)* to bomb; **b. qn de questions/de lettres** to bombard sb with questions/letters (**b**) *Fam*

on l'a bombardé ministre he's been pitchforked into the post of minister

bombardier [bɔ̃bardje] *nm (avion)* bomber; *(aviateur)* bombardier

bombe [bɔ̃b] *nf* (**a**) *(explosif)* bomb; *Fig* **faire l'effet d'une b.** to be a bombshell; **b. atomique** atom(ic) bomb; **b. à eau** water bomb; *Culin* **b. glacée** bombe glacée; **b. H** H bomb; **b. à hydrogène** hydrogen bomb; **b. incendiaire** incendiary device, fire bomb; **b. lacrymogène** tear-gas grenade; **b. à retardement** time bomb (**b**) *(atomiseur)* spray, aerosol (**c**) *(chapeau)* riding hat (**d**) *Can (bouilloire)* kettle (**e**) *Fam* **faire la b.** to live it up

bombé, -e [bɔ̃be] *adj* bulging

bomber [bɔ̃be] **1** *vt (gonfler)* **b. qch** to cause sth to bulge; **b. le torse** to throw out one's chest; *Fig* to swagger (around) **2** *vi (mur)* to bulge; *(planche)* to warp

bombonne [bɔ̃bɔn] = **bonbonne**

bôme [bom] *nf Naut* boom

bon¹, bonne [bɔ̃, bɔn] **1** *adj* (**a**) *(agréable)* good; **passer une bonne soirée** to spend a pleasant evening; **l'eau est bonne** *(en se baignant)* the water's great; **de bons petits plats** nice little meals; **souhaiter une** *ou* **la bonne année à qn** to wish sb a happy New Year; **bonnes vacances!** have a good holiday!

(**b**) *(satisfaisant) (travail, qualité)* good; **c'est b.** *(d'accord)* that's fine; **c'est b., j'ai compris** all right *or* OK, I understand

(**c**) *(correct)* right; **c'est la bonne réponse/le b. bus** that's the right answer/bus; **un intellectuel, au b. sens du terme** an intellectual in the true sense of the word

(**d**) *(compétent)* good (**en** at); **un b. médecin/père** a good doctor/father

(**e**) *(profitable) (investissement, conseil, idée)* good; **cet exercice est b. pour le dos** this exercise is good for the back; **c'est b. à savoir** it's worth knowing; **il serait b. que vous lui en parliez** it would be a good idea if you spoke to her about it; **à quoi b.?** what's the point *or* the use?; **à quoi b. se plaindre?** what's the point *or* the use of complaining?; **quand b. vous semble** whenever you like

(**f**) *(apte)* **b. à manger** fit *or* safe to eat; **b. pour le service** *Mil* fit for duty; *Fig* serviceable; **elle n'est bonne à rien** she's useless; **tu es b. pour une contravention** you're in for a fine

(**g**) *(valable) (billet, abonnement)* valid; **la balle est bonne** *(au tennis)* the ball is in *or* good; **les yaourts sont-ils encore bons?** are the yoghurts still all right to eat?

(**h**) *(moralement)* good; *(généreux)* good, kind (**envers** *ou* **avec** to)

(**i**) *(en intensif)* good; **j'ai attendu deux bonnes heures** I waited for a good two hours; **il m'a fallu un b. moment pour comprendre** it took me a while to understand; **un b. rhume** a bad cold

(**j**) *(locutions)* **elle est bien bonne!** that's a good one!; **il en a de bonnes!** he must be joking *or* kidding!; *Fam* **avoir qn à la bonne** to have a soft spot for sb; **pour de b.** *(partir, revenir)* for good

2 *exclam (d'accord)* right!, fine!; **b., on y va?** right, shall we go?; **allons b.!** what!; **ah b., je ne le savais pas** really? I didn't know; **sors d'ici! – b., b., c'est pas la peine de crier!** get out of here! – OK, OK, no need to shout!

3 *adv (sentir)* good, nice; **il fait b.** it's lovely; **un pays**

où il fait b. vivre a country that's good to live in
4 *nm,f* les bons et les méchants *(dans un film)* the goodies and the baddies; un b. à rien a good-for-nothing
5 *nm* cela a du b. it has some good points

bon² *nm* (a) *(papier)* voucher, coupon; b. d'achat gift voucher; b. de commande order form; b. de garantie guarantee; b. de livraison delivery note; b. de réduction money-off coupon (b) *Fin* bond; b. du Trésor treasury bond

bonard, -e [bɔnar, -ard] *adj Fam* c'est b.! that's pretty good!

bonasse [bɔnas] *adj* soft; d'un ton b. meekly

bonbon [bɔ̃bɔ̃] **1** *nm* (a) *(sucrerie)* *Br* sweet, *Am* candy; b. à la menthe mint (b) *Belg Br* biscuit, *Am* cookie
2 *adv Fam* coûter b. to cost an arm and a leg *or* a bundle

bonbonne [bɔ̃bɔn] *nf* demijohn; *(de gaz)* cylinder

bonbonnière [bɔ̃bɔnjɛr] *nf Br* sweet *or Am* candy box

bond [bɔ̃] *nm* (a) *(saut)* leap, jump; faire un b. to leap up; *Fig* to shoot up; faire un b. en avant/en arrière to leap forwards/back; franchir qch d'un b. to clear sth at one leap; se lever d'un b. to jump to one's feet (b) *(d'une balle)* bounce; faire faux b. à qn to leave sb in the lurch

bonde [bɔ̃d] *nf* (a) *(bouchon)* *(d'un évier, d'une baignoire)* plug; *(d'un tonneau)* bung; *(d'un bassin)* sluice gate (b) *(trou)* *(d'un évier, d'une baignoire)* plughole; *(d'un tonneau)* bunghole; *(d'un bassin)* drainage hole

bondé, -e [bɔ̃de] *adj* packed, crammed

bondir [bɔ̃dir] *vi* to leap, to jump; b. sur to pounce on; *Fig* cela me fait b. it makes me hopping mad

bon enfant [bɔ̃nɑ̃fɑ̃] *adj inv* easy-going

bonheur [bɔnœr] *nm* (a) *(bien-être)* happiness; faire le b. de qn to make sb happy (b) *(chance)* good fortune, (good) luck; j'ai le b. de la connaître I have the good fortune to know her; porter b. à qn to bring sb (good) luck; il ne connaît pas son b. he doesn't know how lucky he is; par b. luckily; au petit b. (la chance) at random (c) *Litt (réussite)* avec b. felicitously

bonhomie [bɔnɔmi] *nf* good-naturedness; avec b. good-naturedly

bonhomme [bɔnɔm] *(pl* bonshommes [bɔ̃zɔm]*)* *nm Fam* (a) *(homme)* fellow, guy; c'est un sacré b. he's a hell of a guy; on se retrouvera, mon b.! I'll get even with you, my friend!; aller son petit b. de chemin to be jogging along nicely; b. de neige snowman (b) *(figure)* man; dessiner des bonshommes to draw little men *or* people

boniche [bɔniʃ] *nf Fam* maid, *Br* skivvy

bonification [bɔnifikasjɔ̃] *nf* (a) *(d'une terre, d'un vin)* improvement (b) *Com* bonus (c) *Sport* advantage

bonifier [66] [bɔnifje] **1** *vt (terre, caractère)* to improve
2 se bonifier *vpr* to improve

boniment [bɔnimɑ̃] *nm* (a) *(discours)* sales talk, patter; *Fam* faire du b. à qn *Br* to chat sb up, *Am* to hit on sb (b) *Fam (mensonges)* tall story; tout ça, c'est du b. that's all claptrap

bonite [bɔnit] *nf* bonito

bonjour [bɔ̃ʒur] *nm* hello; *(le matin)* good morning; *(l'après-midi)* good afternoon; dire b. à qn to say hello/good morning/good afternoon to sb; dis b. à ta mère de ma part say hello to your mother for me; facile ou simple comme b. easy as pie; *Fam* b. l'am-

biance! there was one hell of an atmosphere!; *Fam* b. la soirée! what an evening!; *Fam* le périphérique à six heures du soir, b.! the ring road at six o'clock at night, forget it!

bon marché [bɔ̃marʃe] *adj inv* cheap; acheter/vendre qch (à) b. to buy/sell sth cheap(ly)

bonnard, -e [bɔnar, -ard] = bonard, -e

bonne [bɔn] **1** *voir* bon¹
2 *nf (domestique)* maid, *Vieilli* maidservant; *Fam* dis-donc, je ne suis pas ta b.! I'm not your maid, you know!; b. à tout faire maid, *Vieilli* maidservant; b. d'enfants nanny

Bonne-Espérance [bɔnɛsperɑ̃s] *voir* cap

bonne-main *(pl* bonnes-mains*)* [bɔnmɛ̃] *nf Suisse* tip

bonnement [bɔnmɑ̃] *adv* tout b. simply

bonnet [bɔnɛ] *nm* (a) *(coiffure)* hat; c'est b. blanc et blanc b. it's six of one and half a dozen of the other; b. d'âne dunce's cap; b. de bain bathing cap; b. de nuit nightcap; *Fig Péj* wet blanket; b. de ski ski cap (b) *(d'un soutien-gorge)* cup; quelle profondeur de b.? what size cup?

bonneterie [bɔnɛtri] *nf* (a) *(bas)* hosiery (b) *(commerce)* hosiery trade; *(magasin)* hosier's (shop)

bonniche [bɔniʃ] = boniche

bonsaï [bɔnzaj, bɔ̃zaj] *nm* bonsai

bonsoir [bɔ̃swar] *nm* good evening; *(quand on se quitte tard, quand on se couche)* goodnight; dire b. à qn to say good evening/goodnight to sb

bonté [bɔ̃te] *nf* (a) *(gentillesse)* kindness, goodness; une femme d'une grande b. a very kind woman; un sourire plein de b. a kind smile; avoir la b. de faire qch to be so good as to do sth; faire qch par b. d'âme to do sth out of the goodness of one's heart; *Vieilli* b. divine! good heavens! (b) *(acte)* remercier qn pour ses bontés to thank sb for his/her kindness

bonus [bɔnys] *nm (prime de salaire)* bonus; *(d'assurance)* no-claims bonus

bon vivant [bɔ̃vivɑ̃] *adj m* être b. to enjoy life

bonze [bɔ̃z] *nm* Buddhist priest

bookmaker [bukmɛkœr] *nm* bookmaker

booléen, -enne [buleɛ̃, -ɛn] *adj Math & Ordinat* Boolean

boom [bum] *nm* boom

boomerang [bumrɑ̃g] *nm* boomerang

booter [bute] *vi Ordinat* b. (sur le lecteur B) to boot up (off the B drive)

boots [buts] *nmpl* ankle boots

borborygmes [bɔrbɔrigm] *nmpl* rumbling

bord [bɔr] *nm* (a) *(limite)* edge; *(d'un chapeau)* brim; *(d'une tasse, d'un verre)* rim; un chapeau à larges bords a wide-brimmed hat; le b. du trottoir *Br* the kerb, *Am* the curb; sur le ou au b. de *(route)* at the side of; *(lac, rivière)* beside; aller au b. de la mer to go to the seaside; une maison en b. de mer a house beside the sea; *Can* l'autre b. *(outre-Atlantique)* Europe; au b. des larmes/de la catastrophe on the verge of tears/of disaster; *Fam* un peu voleur sur les bords a bit light-fingered; b. à b. edge to edge; *Ordinat* b. de reliure inside margin (b) à b. de *(bateau, avion)* on board; prendre qn à son b. to take sb on board; par-dessus b. overboard; *Fig* être du même b. to be on the same side

bordages [bɔrdaʒ] *nmpl Can (glace)* inshore ice

bordeaux [bɔrdo] **1** *nm* Bordeaux (wine); b. rouge claret
2 *adj inv* maroon

bordée [bɔrde] *nf* (**a**) *Naut (de coups de feu)* broadside; *Fig* **b. de jurons** torrent of swearwords (**b**) *Fam* **être en b.** to be on a binge (**c**) *Can* **b. (de neige)** heavy snowfall

bordel [bɔrdɛl] *nm très Fam (hôtel de passe)* brothel; *(désordre)* mess; *(vacarme)* racket; **mettre** *ou* **foutre le b. dans qch** to make a mess of sth; **mettre** *ou* **foutre le b. en classe** to create mayhem in the classroom; **et tout le b.** and the whole damn lot; *Vulg* **b.!** shit!

bordelais, -e [bɔrdəlɛ, -ɛz] **1** *adj* of Bordeaux **2** *nm,f* **B.** = person from Bordeaux **3** *nm* **le B.** *(région)* the Bordeaux region

bordélique [bɔrdelik] *adj Fam (pièce, organisation)* shambolic; **être b.** *(personne)* to be a slob

border [bɔrde] *vt* (**a**) *(garnir)* **b. qch de** to edge sth with (**b**) *(sujet: arbres) (route)* to line; *(sujet: bateau) (côte)* to skirt (**c**) *(lit, draps)* to tuck in; **b. qn (dans son lit)** to tuck sb in

bordereau, -x [bɔrdəro] *nm (liste)* schedule; **b. de livraison** delivery note

bordure [bɔrdyr] *nf* (**a**) *(bord)* edge; *(d'un vêtement)* border; **en b. de route/de mer** by the roadside/the sea (**b**) *(d'un miroir, d'un tableau)* frame

boréal, -e, -als *ou* **-aux, -ales** [bɔreal, -o] *adj* northern

borgne [bɔrɲ] **1** *adj* (**a**) *(personne)* one-eyed; *(mur)* blind; *(fenêtre)* obstructed (**b**) *(louche)* shady **2** *nmf* one-eyed man, *f* one-eyed woman

borne [bɔrn] *nf* (**a**) *(limite)* boundary marker; *(pierre)* boundary stone; *Fig* **sans bornes** boundless; **b. d'incendie** *Br* (fire) hydrant, *Am* fireplug; **b. kilométrique** kilometre marker, ≃ milestone (**b**) *Fam (kilomètre)* kilometre (**c**) *Élec* terminal (**d**) *Ordinat* **b. (interactive)** terminal

borné, -e [bɔrne] *adj (esprit)* narrow; *(personne)* narrow-minded

borne-fontaine (*pl* **bornes-fontaines**) [bɔrnfɔ̃tɛn] *nf Can (bouche d'incendie) Br* (fire) hydrant, *Am* fireplug

borner [bɔrne] **1** *vt (terrain)* to mark out **2 se borner** *vpr* (**a**) **se b. à qch/à faire qch** *(personne)* to restrict oneself to sth/to doing sth (**b**) **se b. à qch** *(choses)* to be limited to sth

borsalino [bɔrsalino] *nm* fedora

bosniaque [bɔsnjak] **1** *adj* Bosnian **2** *nmf* **B.** Bosnian

Bosnie [bɔsni] *nf* **la B.** Bosnia; **la B.-Herzégovine** Bosnia-Herzegovina

bosquet [bɔskɛ] *nm* copse, grove

bosse [bɔs] *nf* (**a**) *(d'un bossu, d'un chameau)* hump; *Fig* **avoir la b. du commerce/des maths** to have a good head for business/maths; *Fam* **il a roulé sa b.** he's knocked about a bit (**b**) *(sur la tête)* bump, lump; *(sur le sol)* bump; *(sur une piste de ski)* mogul; **se faire une b.** to get a bump

bosselé, -e [bɔsle] *adj (casserole, pare-chocs)* dented

bosser [bɔse] *Fam* **1** *vi* to work **2** *vt Scol* to bone up on, *Br* to swot up

bosseur, -euse [bɔsœr, -øz] *Fam* **1** *adj* hardworking **2** *nm,f* hard worker

bossu, -e [bɔsy] **1** *adj (personne)* hunchbacked; *(animal)* humped **2** *nm,f* hunchback

bot [bo] *adj m voir* **pied**

botanique [bɔtanik] **1** *adj* botanical **2** *nf* botany

botaniste [bɔtanist] *nmf* botanist

Botswana [bɔtswana] *nm* **le B.** Botswana

botte¹ [bɔt] *nf (de fleurs, de carottes, de radis)* bunch; *(de foin, de paille)* bale

botte² *nf (chaussure)* boot; *Fig* **sous la b. de** under the heel of; *Fam* **en avoir plein les bottes (de)** to be fed up to the back teeth (with); **bottes de** *ou* **en caoutchouc** rubber boots, *Br* wellingtons; **bottes de cavalier** *ou* **de cheval** riding boots

botte³ *nf (en escrime)* thrust; **porter une b. à qn** to make a thrust at sb; *Fig* **b. secrète** secret weapon; *Fam* **il lui a proposé la b.** he asked her straight out to sleep with him

botter [bɔte] *vt* (**a**) *(chausser)* **botté de cuir** wearing leather boots (**b**) *Fam* **b. les fesses** *ou* **le derrière à qn** to boot sb up the backside (**c**) *Fam (plaire à)* **ça me botte** I dig it (**d**) *Sport* **b. la balle en touche** to kick the ball into touch; *Fig* to dodge the issue

bottier [bɔtje] *nm* bootmaker

bottillon [bɔtijɔ̃] *nm* ankle boot

Bottin® [bɔtɛ̃] *nm (annuaire téléphonique)* phone book, telephone directory; **B. mondain** ≃ Who's Who

bottine [bɔtin] *nf* ankle boot

botulisme [bɔtylism] *nm Méd* botulism

boubou [bubu] *nm* = long traditional African robe

bouc [buk] *nm (animal)* (billy) goat; *(barbe)* goatee (beard); *Fam* **puer comme un b., puer le b.** to stink to high heaven; **b. émissaire** scapegoat

boucan [bukã] *nm Fam* row, din; **faire du b.** to kick up a row

boucane [bukan] *nf Can* smoke

boucané, -e [bukane] *adj (teint)* weatherbeaten

boucanier [bukanje] *nm* buccaneer

bouche [buʃ] *nf* (**a**) *(de personne, d'animal)* mouth; **avoir/parler la b. pleine** to have/to talk with one's mouth full; **une pipe à la b.** with a pipe in his mouth; *Fig* **faire la fine b.** to be fussy; **c'est une fine b.** he's a gourmet; **elle n'a pas ouvert la b. de la soirée** she didn't say a word all evening; **b. cousue!** mum's the word!; **de b. à oreille** by word of mouth (**b**) *(d'une rivière, d'un cratère, d'un four)* mouth; *(d'un fusil, d'un canon)* muzzle; **b. d'égout** manhole; **b. d'incendie** *Br* (fire) hydrant, *Am* fireplug; **b. de métro** *Br* underground *orAm* subway entrance

bouché, e [buʃe] *adj (conduite, rue)* blocked; *(temps)* cloudy, overcast; **j'ai le nez b.** my nose is stuffed up; **j'ai les oreilles bouchées** my ears are blocked up; *Fam* **être b.** *(personne)* to be dense; *Fam* **être b. à l'émeri** to be a complete moron

bouche-à-bouche [buʃabuʃ] *nm inv* mouth-to-mouth resuscitation, *Br* kiss of life; **faire du b. à qn** to give sb mouth-to-mouth resuscitation

bouchée [buʃe] *nf* (**a**) *(quantité)* mouthful; *Fig* **ne faire qu'une b. de qn/qch** to make short work of sb/sth; **acheter qch pour une b. de pain** to buy sth for a song; **mettre les bouchées doubles** to really get a move on (**b**) *Culin* **b. (au chocolat)** chocolate; **b. à la reine** chicken vol-au-vent

boucher¹ [buʃe] **1** *vt (fente, trou)* to fill in; *(conduite, fenêtre)* to block up; *(vue)* to block; *(bouteille)* to cork; **b. le passage à qn** to block sb's way; *Fam* **elle/ça m'en a bouché un coin** she/that took the wind out of my sails **2 se boucher** *vpr (conduite)* to get blocked up; **se b. le nez** to hold one's nose; **se b. les oreilles** to put one's fingers in one's ears

boucher², -ère¹ [buʃe, -ɛr] *nm,f aussi Fig* butcher
bouchère² [buʃer] *nf Suisse* cold sore
boucherie [buʃri] *nf (boutique)* butcher's (shop); *(activité)* butchery; *Fig (massacre)* slaughter; **b. chevaline** horse butcher's (shop)
bouche-trou (*pl* **bouche-trous**) [buʃtru] *nm Fam* stopgap; **servir de b.** to act as a stopgap
bouchon [buʃɔ̃] *nm* (**a**) *(à vis)* cap, top; *(d'un tonneau)* stopper; **b. (de liège)** cork; **vin qui sent le b.** corked wine; *Aut* **b. de réservoir** *Br* petrol cap, *Am* fuel cap (**b**) *(embouteillage)* hold-up, traffic jam; **3 kilomètres de b.** a 3-kilometre tailback (**c**) *(d'une ligne de pêche)* float (**d**) *(de paille)* wisp (**e**) **tu pousses le b. un peu loin!** you're going a bit too far!
bouchonné, -e [buʃɔne] *adj (vin)* corked
bouchonner [buʃɔne] **1** *vt (cheval)* to rub down
  2 *vi Fam* **ça bouchonne** *(sur la route)* there's congestion
bouchot [buʃo] *nm* mussel bank
boucle [bukl] *nf* (**a**) *(de ceinture, de chaussure, de harnais)* buckle; **b. d'oreille** earring (**b**) *(nœud, méandre, looping)* loop; **faire une b.** *(en marchant, en voiture)* to loop back (**c**) *(de cheveux)* curl (**d**) *Sport* lap (**e**) *Ordinat* loop
bouclé, -e [bukle] *adj (cheveux)* curly; *(personne)* curly-haired; *Ordinat* **système b.** looped system
boucler [bukle] **1** *vt* (**a**) *(ceinture, valise)* to buckle; *Fam (dossier, travail)* to finish off; **b. sa valise** *(se préparer à partir)* to pack one's bags; **avoir du mal à b. ses fins de mois** to find it hard to make ends meet at the end of the month; *Fam* **boucle-la!** belt up! (**b**) *(quartier)* to seal off; *Fam (chambre, maison)* to lock up; *Fam (prisonnier)* to bang up (**c**) **b. la boucle** *Aviat* to loop the loop; *Fig* to come full circle
  2 *vi (cheveux)* to be curly; *(personne)* to have curly hair
bouclette [buklɛt] *nf (de cheveux)* small curl; *(de laine, de moquette)* curl
bouclier [buklije] *nm aussi Fig* shield; **b. atomique** *ou* **nucléaire** nuclear shield; **b. thermique** *(d'engin spatial)* heat shield
Bouddha [buda] *npr* Buddha
bouddhisme [budism] *nm* Buddhism
bouddhiste [budist] *adj & nmf* Buddhist
bouder [bude] **1** *vi* to sulk
  2 *vt* **b. qn/qch** to refuse to have anything to do with sb/sth; **en été, les Parisiens boudent les salles de cinéma** Parisians stay away from the cinema in summer
boudeur, -euse [budœr, -øz] **1** *adj* sulky
  2 *nm,f* sulky person
boudin [budɛ̃] *nm* (**a**) *(charcuterie)* **b. (noir)** *Br* black pudding, *Am* blood sausage; **b. blanc** white pudding (**b**) *(de pâte à modeler, de terre)* roll (**c**) *(traversin)* bolster (**d**) *Fam Péj (femme)* fat lump
boudiné, -e [budine] *adj* (**a**) **je suis b. dans ce pantalon** I'm bursting out of these trousers (**b**) *(doigts)* podgy
boudoir [budwar] *nm* (**a**) *(salon)* boudoir (**b**) *(biscuit)* *Br* sponge finger, *Am* lady finger
boue [bu] *nf* (**a**) *(terre détrempée)* mud; *Fig* **traîner qn dans la b.** to drag sb through the mud (**b**) *(dans une rivière)* silt; *(dans l'océan)* ooze; *Méd* **boues activées** activated sludge
bouée [bwe] *nf Naut* buoy; *(pour nager)* rubber ring; **b. de sauvetage** lifebelt; *Fig* lifeline

boueux, -euse [buø, -øz] **1** *adj* muddy
  2 *nm Fam Br* dustman, *Am* garbage man
bouffant, -e [bufɑ̃, -ɑ̃t] **1** *adj (manche)* puff(ed); *(jupe)* full; *(pantalon)* baggy; **cheveux bouffants** bouffant hair-do
  2 *nm (des cheveux)* body
bouffe [buf] *nf Fam (nourriture)* grub; *(repas)* meal; **on se fait une b. samedi?** do you fancy getting together for a meal on Saturday?
bouffée [bufe] *nf* (**a**) *(de fumée)* puff; *(de parfum)* whiff; *(d'air)* breath; *aussi Fig* **une b. d'air pur** a breath of fresh air; *Méd* **b. de chaleur** *Br* hot flush, *Am* hot flash (**b**) *(d'éloquence, de colère)* outburst; *(d'orgueil)* fit
bouffer [bufe] **1** *vt Fam* (**a**) *(manger)* to eat; *Fig* **je l'aurais bouffé** I could have killed him; **elle se laisse b. par ses enfants/son travail** she has no time for anything but her children/her work; **b. du curé** to rant against the clergy; **elle a bouffé du lion!** she's full of beans! (**b**) *(argent, économies)* to blow; **b. de l'essence** *(voiture)* to be heavy on petrol
  2 *vi* (**a**) *Fam (manger)* to eat (**b**) *(manche, jupe)* to puff out; *(cheveux)* to have body; **faire b. ses cheveux** to give body to one's hair
  3 **se bouffer** *vpr Fam* **se bouffer le nez** *(une fois)* to have a go at one another; *(constamment)* to be at daggers drawn
bouffi, -e [bufi] *adj (yeux, visage)* puffy, swollen; **b. d'orgueil** puffed up with pride
bouffon, -onne [bufɔ̃, -ɔn] **1** *nm* buffoon; *Hist* jester
  2 *adj* farcical
bouge [buʒ] *nm Péj (maison)* hovel; *(bar)* dive
bougeoir [buʒwar] *nm (plat)* candleholder; *(haut)* candlestick
bougeotte [buʒɔt] *nf Fam* **avoir la b.** to be fidgety; *(envie de voyager)* to have itchy feet
bouger [45] [buʒe] **1** *vt* to move, to shift
  2 *vi (remuer, se déplacer)* to move; **rester sans b.** to keep still; **ne bougeons plus!** *(pour une photo)* hold it there!; **je n'ai pas bougé (de chez moi) pendant deux jours** I haven't been out for two days; *Fig* **ce chemisier ne bouge pas au lavage** *(ne déteint pas)* this blouse doesn't run in the wash; *(ne rétrécit pas)* this blouse doesn't shrink in the wash; *Fam* **ça bouge pas mal, dans cette ville** there's a lot going on in this town
  3 **se bouger** *vpr Fam (se déplacer)* to move; *(s'activer)* to get a move on; **bouge-toi de là!** shift yourself!
bougie [buʒi] *nf* (**a**) *(en cire)* candle; **s'éclairer à la b.** to use candles for lighting (**b**) *Aut* **b. (d'allumage)** spark plug
bougnat [buɲa] *nm Fam Vieilli* coal-merchant
bougnoul(e) [buɲul] *nmf Br* wog, = racist term referring to a North African person
bougon, -onne [bugɔ̃, -ɔn] *Fam* **1** *adj* grumpy
  2 *nm,f* grumbler
bougonner [bugɔne] *vi Fam* to grumble
bougre [bugr] *nm Fam* (**a**) *Vieilli (individu)* **le pauvre b.** the poor devil; **ce n'est pas un mauvais b.** he's not a bad sort (**b**) **b. d'imbécile** damn(ed) fool
bougrement [bugrəmɑ̃] *adv* damn(ed)
boui-boui (*pl* **bouis-bouis**) [bwibwi] *nm Fam* dingy café
bouillabaisse [bujabɛs] *nf* bouillabaisse *(Provençal fish soup)*

bouillant, -e [bujɑ̃, -ɑ̃t] *adj* (**a**) *(qui bout)* boiling; *(très chaud, fiévreux)* boiling hot (**b**) *Fig (ardent)* fiery
bouille [buj] *nf Fam (visage)* mug; **il a une bonne b.** he looks a good sort
bouilleur [bujœr] *nm* **b. de cru** home distiller
bouilli, -e [buji] **1** *adj* boiled
2 *nm* boiled meat; *Can* = beans, cabbage, potatoes, salt pork and ham cooked together for several hours; **b. de bœuf** boiled beef
bouillie [buji] *nf (pour bébés)* baby food; *(à base de céréales)* baby cereal; **b. de légumes** mashed vegetables; **réduire qch en b.** *(légumes, fruits)* to mash sth; *(au mixer)* to liquidize sth; *Fam (voiture, visage)* to smash sth up; *Fam* **mettre** *ou* **réduire qn en b.** to beat sb to a pulp
bouilloire [bujwar] *nf* kettle
bouillir [13] [bujir] *vi* to boil; **faire b. qch** to boil sth; **b. de colère** to seethe with anger; **b. d'impatience** to burst with impatience; **cela me fait b.** that makes my blood boil
bouillon [bujɔ̃] *nm* (**a**) *(d'un liquide en ébullition)* bubble; **bouillir à gros bouillons** to boil hard; **le sang sortait à gros bouillons** the blood was gushing out (**b**) *Culin (liquide)* stock; *Fam* **boire un b.** *(en nageant)* to get a mouthful; *(professionnellement)* to come to grief; **b. cube** stock cube; **b. de culture** culture medium; **b. de légumes** vegetable stock
bouillonnant, -e [bujɔnɑ̃, -ɑ̃t] *adj* bubbling; *(torrent)* foaming; *Fig* **b. de colère** seething; *Fig* **b. de vie/d'idées** bubbling over with life/ideas
bouillonner [bujɔne] *vi (eau, soupe, bain)* to bubble; *(torrent)* to foam; **b. de colère** to seethe with anger; **b. d'idées** to bubble over with ideas
bouillotte [bujɔt] *nf* hot-water bottle
boul. *abrév* **boulevard**
boulanger, -ère [bulɑ̃ʒe, -ɛr] *nm,f* baker
boulangerie [bulɑ̃ʒri] *nf (magasin)* baker's (shop); *(industrie)* bakery trade; **b.-pâtisserie** baker's and confectioner's (shop)
boule [bul] *nf* (**a**) *(sphère)* ball; *Fam (tête)* nut; **se rouler** *ou* **se mettre en b.** *(animal)* to roll up into a ball; *Fig* **se mettre en b.** *(en colère)* to fly off the handle; *Fam* **avoir la b. à zéro** to be a skinhead; *Fam* **avoir les boules** *(être énervé)* to be pissed off; *(être déprimé)* to be down in the dumps; *Fam* **foutre les boules à qn** *(faire peur à)* to put the wind up sb; *(énerver)* to upset sb; *Fam* **perdre la b.** to go off one's head; *Suisse* **b. de Berlin** doughnut; **b. de neige** snowball; *Fig* **faire b. de neige** to snowball; **c'est une b. de nerfs** he's/she's a bundle of nerves; **b. puante** stink bomb; **b. Quiès**® earplug (**b**) *(de pétanque, de bowling)* bowl; *(de billard)* ball; **jouer aux boules** to play bowls (**c**) *(de machine à écrire)* golf ball
bouleau, -x [bulo] *nm* (silver) birch; *(bois)* birch(-wood)
bouledogue [buldɔg] *nm* bulldog
bouler [bule] *vi Fam* **envoyer b. qn** to send sb packing
boulet [bulɛ] *nm* (**a**) *(projectile)* **b. (de canon)** cannonball; **passer comme un b. (de canon)** to hurtle past; **tirer à boulets rouges sur qn** to go for sb hammer and tongs (**b**) *(de bagnard)* ball and chain; *Fig* **c'est un b. qu'il traînera toute sa vie** it'll be a millstone round his neck all his life
boulette [bulɛt] *nf* (**a**) *(de papier, de pâte)* small ball (**b**) *Culin* meatball (**c**) *Fam (gaffe) Br* boob, *Am* booboo; **faire une b.** to blunder, to put one's foot in it

boulevard [bulvar] *nm* boulevard; **les Grands Boulevards** *(à Paris)* the main boulevards; **b. périphérique** *Br* ring road, *Am* beltway
bouleversant, -e [bulvɛrsɑ̃, -ɑ̃t] *adj (émouvant)* deeply moving; *(perturbant)* distressing
bouleversement [bulvɛrsəmɑ̃] *nm* (**a**) *(de projets, d'habitudes)* disruption; **bouleversements politiques/économiques** political/economic upheavals (**b**) *(d'une personne)* emotion
bouleverser [bulvɛrse] *vt* (**a**) *(projets, habitudes)* to disrupt; *(vie)* to turn upside down (**b**) *(émouvoir)* to move deeply; *(perturber)* to distress
boulier [bulje] *nm* abacus
boulimie [bulimi] *nf Méd* bulimia
boulimique [bulimik] *adj & nmf Méd* bulimic; **être b.** to be bulimic, to have bulimia
bouliste [bulist] *nmf* bowls player
boulocher [bulɔʃe] *vi (vêtement)* to pill
boulodrome [bulɔdrom] *nm* bowling alley
boulon [bulɔ̃] *nm* bolt
boulonner [bulɔne] **1** *vt* to bolt
2 *vi Fam (travailler)* to slog away
boulot¹, -otte [bulo, -ɔt] *adj Fam* tubby
boulot² [bulo] *Fam* **1** *nm (travail, lieu de travail)* work; *(emploi)* job; **allez, au b.!** come on, get to work!; **refaire les peintures dans une maison, c'est du b.** to repaint a whole house is quite a job; *Fig* **faire le sale b.** to do the dirty work
2 *adj inv* **être b. b.** to be a workaholic
boum [bum] **1** *exclam* bang!
2 *nm Fam* (**a**) *(bruit)* bang (**b**) *(succès)* **le b. du multimédia/de l'informatique** the multimedia/computer boom; **en plein b.** in full swing
3 *nf Fam (fête)* party *(for young people)*
boumer [bume] *vi Fam Vieilli* **ça boume?** how's things?
bouquet¹ [bukɛ] *nm* (**a**) *(fleurs)* bunch of flowers; *(imposant)* bouquet; *(petit)* posy; *(d'arbres)* clump; **un b. de roses** a bunch/bouquet of roses; **le b. de la mariée** the bride's bouquet; *Culin* **b. garni** bouquet garni *(bunch of mixed herbs)* (**b**) *(d'un vin)* bouquet, nose (**c**) *(d'un feu d'artifice)* **b. (final)** grand finale; *Fam Fig* **ça, c'est le b.!** that takes the *Br* biscuit *or Am* cake! (**d**) *TV* (multichannel) package; **b. numérique** digital package
bouquet² *nm (crevette)* prawn
bouquetin [buktɛ̃] *nm* ibex
bouquin [bukɛ̃] *nm Fam* book
bouquiner [bukine] *vi Fam* to read
bouquiniste [bukinist] *nmf* second-hand bookseller
bourbeux, -euse [burbø, -øz] *adj* muddy
bourbier [burbje] *nm aussi Fig* quagmire
bourbon [burbɔ̃] *nm (whisky)* bourbon
bourde [burd] *nf Fam* (**a**) *(balivernes)* fib (**b**) *(gaffe)* blunder; **faire une b.** to put one's foot in it
bourdon [burdɔ̃] *nm* (**a**) *(insecte)* bumblebee; *Fam* **avoir le b.** to be down (in the dumps) (**b**) *(cloche)* great bell (**c**) *Mus (de cornemuse)* drone; *(d'orgue)* bourdon stop
bourdonnement [burdɔnmɑ̃] *nm (d'insectes)* buzz(ing); *(de machine, de moteur)* hum(ming); **avoir des bourdonnements d'oreilles** to have a buzzing in one's ears
bourdonner [burdɔne] *vi (insectes, oreilles)* to buzz; *(machine, moteur)* to hum

bourg [bur] *nm* market town
bourgade [burgad] *nf* village
bourge [burʒ] *Fam* **1** *adj* (**a**) *(de la bourgeoisie)* upper-class (**b**) *Péj* snobby
  2 *nmf* (**a**) *(de la bourgeoisie)* upper-class person (**b**) *Péj* snob
bourgeois, -e [burʒwa, -az] **1** *adj* (**a**) *(personne)* middle-class; **cuisine bourgeoise** home cooking (**b**) *Péj (conventionnel)* middle-class, bourgeois
  2 *nm,f* (**a**) *(de la classe moyenne)* middle-class person; **les grands/petits b.** the upper/lower middle class (**b**) *Hist (roturier)* commoner (**c**) *Suisse (citoyen)* citizen
bourgeoisie [burʒwazi] *nf* middle class, bourgeoisie; **la haute/petite b.** the upper/lower middle class
bourgeon [burʒɔ̃] *nm* bud; **en bourgeons** in bud
bourgeonner [burʒɔne] *vi* (**a**) *(plante, arbre)* to bud (**b**) *Fam (avoir des boutons)* to come out in spots
bourgmestre [burgmɛstr] *nm* burgomaster
Bourgogne [burgɔɲ] **1** *nf* **la B.** Burgundy
  2 *nm* burgundy
bourguignon, -onne [burgiɲɔ̃, -ɔn] **1** *adj* Burgundian
  2 *nm,f* **B.** Burgundian
bourlinguer [burlɛ̃ge] *vi (personne) (naviguer)* to sail the seven seas; *Fam (voyager)* to knock about
bourrade [burad] *nf* push, shove
bourrasque [burask] *nf* squall, gust (of wind); **b. de neige** snow flurry; **souffler en bourrasques** to gust
bourratif, -ive [buratif, -iv] *adj Fam* stodgy
bourre [bur] *nf* (**a**) *(pour rembourrer)* stuffing, padding; *(de coton, de soie)* waste (**b**) *(des bourgeons)* down (**c**) *(d'arme à feu)* wad (**d**) *Fam* **de première b.** first-rate; **à la b.** in a rush
bourré, -e [bure] *adj* (**a**) *(plein)* packed, crammed (**de** with); **b. à craquer** full to bursting; *Fam* **être b. de complexes** to be a mass of complexes; *Fam* **être b. de fric** to have pots of money (**b**) *très Fam (ivre)* plastered
bourreau, -x [buro] *nm* (**a**) *(exécuteur)* executioner; *(qui pend)* hangman; *(tortionnaire)* torturer (**b**) *Fig* tormentor; **b. des cœurs** ladykiller; **b. d'enfants** child-beater; *Hum* child tormentor; **b. de travail** workaholic
bourrée¹ [bure] *nf (danse)* bourrée
bourrée² *nf Suisse* (**a**) *(grande affluence)* crowd (**b**) *(grande quantité)* **une b. de** masses of, loads of
bourrelé, -e [burle] *adj* **b. de remords** stricken with remorse
bourrelet [burlɛ] *nm* (**a**) *Fam* **b. (de graisse)** *(au ventre)* spare tyre (**b**) *(contre les courants d'air)* weather strip, *Br* draught excluder
bourrer [bure] **1** *vt* (**a**) *(chaise, coussin)* to stuff, to pad (**b**) *(placard, sac)* to cram (**de** with); *(pipe)* to fill; **ça bourre** *(aliment)* it's filling; **b. qn de qch** *(gaver)* to fill sb up with sth; **b. qn de coups** to beat sb up; *Fam* **b. le crâne à qn** *(élève)* to stuff sb's head with facts; *(politiquement)* to brainwash sb; *Fam* **b. le mou à qn** to pull the wool over sb's eyes
  2 se bourrer *vpr* (**a**) **se b. de qch** *(se gaver)* to stuff oneself with sth (**b**) *très Fam* **se b. la gueule** to get plastered
bourriche [buriʃ] *nf (d'huîtres)* basket
bourrichon [buriʃɔ̃] *nm Fam* **se monter le b.** to get worked up

bourricot [buriko] *nm* (small) donkey
bourrin [burɛ̃] *nm Fam (cheval)* nag
bourrique [burik] *nf (ânesse)* she-ass; *Fam (personne têtue)* pigheaded individual; **faire tourner qn en b.** to drive sb crazy
bourru, -e [bury] *adj* surly
bourse [burs] *nf* (**a**) *(porte-monnaie)* purse; **la b. ou la vie!** your money or your life!; **sans b. délier** without spending a penny; **faire b. commune** to pool one's money (**b**) *Scol & Univ* **b. (d'études)** grant (**c**) *Fin* **la B. (des valeurs)** the Stock Exchange, the Stock Market; **jouer à la B.** to play the market; **b. de commerce** commodities exchange (**d**) *Anat* **bourses** scrotum
boursicoter [bursikɔte] *vi* to dabble on the Stock Market
boursier, -ère [bursje, -ɛr] **1** *adj* (**a**) *Fin* Stock Exchange, Stock Market (**b**) *Scol & Univ* **étudiant b.** grant holder
  2 *nm,f* (**a**) *Scol & Univ* grant holder (**b**) *Fin* (Stock Exchange) operator (**c**) *Suisse* treasurer
boursouflé, -e [bursufle] *adj (visage, yeux)* swollen, puffy; *(peinture)* blistered; *Fig (style, discours)* turgid
bous *voir* **bouillir**
bousculade [buskylad] *nf (agitation)* pushing and shoving; **être pris dans la b.** to be caught up in the rush
bousculer [buskyle] **1** *vt* (**a**) *(pousser)* to jostle; *Fig (habitudes)* to disrupt; *(préjugés)* to overturn (**b**) *(presser)* to rush
  2 se bousculer *vpr (foule)* to push and shove; **les idées se bousculaient dans sa tête** his head was buzzing with ideas; *Fig* **les candidats ne se bousculent pas au portillon** applicants aren't exactly queuing up for the job
bouse [buz] *nf* **de la b. (de vache)** cow dung; **une b.** a cowpat
bouseux [buzø] *nm Fam Péj* yokel
bousiller [buzije] *Fam* **1** *vt (voiture, appareil photo)* to wreck; *(travail)* to botch (up), to bungle
  2 se bousiller *vpr* **se b. la santé** to ruin one's health
boussole [busɔl] *nf* compass; **s'orienter à la b.** to use a compass to get one's bearings; *Fam Fig* **perdre la b.** to go off one's head
boustifaille [bustifɑj] *nf très Fam* grub
bout¹ [bu] *voir* **bouillir**
bout² *nm* (**a**) *(extrémité)* end; **b. à b.** end to end; **de b. en b., d'un b. à l'autre** *(dans l'espace)* from one end to the other; *(reprendre un travail, lire)* from start to finish; **à l'autre b., au b. du fil** *(au téléphone)* on the other end; *Fig* **je n'en vois pas le b.** I'm nowhere near the end of it; *Fig* **voir le b. du tunnel** to see the light at the end of the tunnel; **au b. de la rue** at the end of the street; **aller au b. du monde** to go to the ends of the earth; *Fig* **ce n'est pas le b. du monde** it's not exactly difficult; **au b. d'une heure/de quelques jours** after an hour/a few days
  (**b**) *(du doigt, du nez)* tip, end; *(d'une pipe)* mouthpiece; *(d'une chaussure)* toe; **b. filtre** *(d'une cigarette)* filter tip; **b. du sein** nipple
  (**c**) *(morceau)* bit; **elle en connaît un b. sur la question** she knows a thing or two about it; **faire un b. de chemin** to go part of the way; **un b. de temps** a little while; **ça fait un bon b. de temps que je ne l'ai pas vu** I haven't seen him for quite a while; *Fig* **b. de chou** little child; *Cin & TV* **b. d'essai** screen test
  (**d**) *(locutions)* **être à b.** *(épuisé)* to be exhausted;

boutade [butad] *nf (trait d'esprit)* quip

boute-en-train [butãtrɛ̃] *nm inv* live wire

bouteille [butɛj] *nf* bottle; *(de gaz, d'oxygène)* cylinder; *(contenu)* bottle(ful); **c'est une bonne b.** it's a good bottle of wine; **mettre du vin en bouteilles** to bottle wine; *Fam* **prendre de la b.** to be getting long in the tooth

boutique [butik] *nf Br* shop, *Am* store; **fermer b.** to shut up shop; **parler b.** to talk shop; **b. hors taxes** duty-free shop; **b. (de mode)** fashion shop, boutique

boutiquier, -ère [butikje, -ɛr] *nm,f Br* shopkeeper, *Am* storekeeper

bouton [butɔ̃] *nm* (**a**) *(de fleur)* bud; **b. de rose** rosebud; **en b.** in bud (**b**) *(sur un vêtement)* button; *(de col)* stud; **boutons de manchette** cufflinks (**c**) *(de porte, de radio)* knob; *(qu'on pousse) & Ordinat* button; *(interrupteur) Ordinat* switch; **b. de réinitialisation** reset button (**d**) *(sur le visage)* spot

bouton-d'or *(pl* **boutons-d'or**) [butɔ̃dɔr] *nm* buttercup

boutonnage [butɔnaʒ] *nm* buttoning (up); **veste à double b.** double-breasted jacket

boutonner [butɔne] **1** *vt (vêtement)* to button (up), to fasten (up)
2 se boutonner *vpr (vêtement)* to button (up)

boutonneux, -euse [butɔnø, -øz] *adj* spotty

boutonnière [butɔnjɛr] *nf (de vêtement)* buttonhole; **porter une fleur à la b.** to wear a *Br* buttonhole *or Am* boutonnière

bouton-pression *(pl* **boutons-pression**) [butɔ̃presjɔ̃] *nm Br* press stud, *Am* snap fastener

bouture [butyr] *nf* cutting; **faire des boutures** to take cuttings

bouturer [butyre] *vt* to propagate by cuttings

bouvier, -ère [buvje, -ɛr] **1** *nm,f* cowherd
2 *nm (chien)* sheepdog

bouvreuil [buvrœj] *nm* bullfinch

bovin, -e [bɔvɛ̃, -in] **1** *adj aussi Fig* bovine
2 *nm Zool* bovine

bowling [bulin] *nm* (**a**) *(jeu)* (tenpin) bowling (**b**) *(lieu)* (tenpin) bowling alley

box *(pl* **boxes**) [bɔks] *nm (dans un dortoir)* cubicle; *(dans une écurie)* stall; *(garage)* lock-up (garage); *Jur* **b. des accusés** dock

boxe [bɔks] *nf* boxing; **faire de la b.** to box; **b. anglaise** boxing; **b. française** kick boxing

boxer¹ [bɔkse] **1** *vi* to box
2 *vt Fam (frapper)* to punch up

boxer² [bɔksɛr] *nm (chien)* boxer

boxeur [bɔksœr] *nm* boxer

box-office *(pl* **box-offices**) [bɔksɔfis] *nm* box office; **être en tête du b.** to be a box-office hit

boyau, -x [bwajo] *nm* (**a**) *(d'animal)* gut; *(corde)* (cat)gut (**b**) *(de vélo)* tubular tyre (**c**) *(allée)* narrow alleyway; *(de mine)* narrow gallery; *Mil* communication trench

boycott(age) [bɔjkɔt(aʒ)] *nm* boycott(ing)

boycotter [bɔjkɔte] *vt* to boycott

boys band [bɔjzbɑ̃d] *nm* boy band

boy-scout *(pl* **boy-scouts**) [bɔjskut] *nm Vieilli* boy scout; *Fig* **mentalité de b.** boy-scout mentality

BP [bepe] *nf (abrév* **boîte postale**) PO Box

bracelet [braslɛ] *nm* (**a**) *(bijou)* bracelet; *(rigide)* bangle; *(de montre)* strap (**b**) *(élastique)* rubber *or* elastic band

bracelet-montre *(pl* **bracelets-montres**) [braslɛmɔ̃tr] *nm* wristwatch

braconnage [brakɔnaʒ] *nm* poaching

braconner [brakɔne] *vi* to poach

braconnier [brakɔnje] *nm* poacher

brader [brade] *vt (solder)* to sell off

braderie [bradri] *nf (liquidation)* clearance sale; *(vente par des particuliers) Br* ≃ car boot sale, *Am* ≃ garage sale; *(magasin)* discount store

braguette [bragɛt] *nf* flies

braille [braj] *nm* Braille; **lire en b.** to read Braille

braillements [brajmɑ̃] *nmpl* yelling; *(d'enfant)* howling

brailler [braje] **1** *vi* to yell; *(enfant)* to howl
2 *vt (chanson)* to bawl out; *(slogan)* to chant

braire [28] [brɛr] *vi (âne)* to bray; *Fam Fig* to yell

braise [brɛz] *nf (charbons)* (glowing) embers; **des yeux de b.** glowing eyes

braiser [brɛze] *vt Culin* to braise

bramer [brame] *vi (cerf)* to bell; *Fig (hurler)* to howl

brancard [brɑ̃kar] *nm* (**a**) *(d'une civière, d'une charrette)* shaft; *Fig* **ruer dans les brancards** to kick over the traces (**b**) *(civière)* stretcher

brancardier, -ère [brɑ̃kardje, -ɛr] *nm,f* stretcher bearer

branchage [brɑ̃ʃaʒ] *nm (des arbres)* branches; **branchages** *(coupés)* cut branches

branche [brɑ̃ʃ] *nf* (**a**) *(d'un arbre)* branch; *(de céleri)* stick; *Fig (de l'industrie, de la science, d'une famille)* branch; *(professionnelle)* line of business; **la b. maternelle** the mother's side; *Fam* **vieille b.** old stick (**b**) *(d'un compas)* leg; *(de lunettes)* side piece; *(d'un chandelier)* branch (**c**) *Suisse Univ (matière)* subject

branché, -e [brɑ̃ʃe] *adj Fam (à la mode)* trendy, hip; **il est b. tennis/techno** he's really into tennis/techno music

branchement [brɑ̃ʃmɑ̃] *nm (sur un réseau)* connecting (up) (**sur** to); *(à une prise)* plugging in; *(assemblage de fils)* connection

brancher [brɑ̃ʃe] **1** *vt* (**a**) *(à un réseau)* to connect (up) (**sur** to); *(à une prise)* to plug in; *Fig* **b. qn sur un sujet** to get sb onto a subject (**b**) *Fam (plaire à)* **l'art moderne, ça ne me branche pas tellement** I'm not really into modern art; **on se fait un resto ce soir, ça te branche?** fancy going to a restaurant tonight?
2 se brancher *vpr* (**a**) *(appareil électrique)* to plug in (**b**) *Can Fam (personne)* to decide, to make up one's mind (**c**) **se b. sur** *(une station de radio)* to tune in to

branchie [brɑ̃ʃi] *nf* gill

brandade [brɑ̃dad] *nf Culin* **b. (de morue)** = salt cod puréed with garlic, oil and cream

brandebourg [brɑ̃dbur] *nm* frog *(on uniform)*

brandir [brɑ̃dir] *vt* to brandish

brandy [brɑ̃di] *nm* brandy

branlant, -e [brɑ̃lɑ̃, -ɑ̃t] *adj (dent)* loose; *(chaise, escalier)* rickety

branle [brɑ̃l] *nm* **mettre qch en b.** *(processus)* to set sth in motion; **se mettre en b.** *(partir)* to get moving; *(entrer en fonctionnement)* to get going

branle-bas [brɑ̃lba] *nm inv* **b. (de combat)** *(agitation)* commotion

branlée [brɑ̃le] *nf Fam* thrashing; **prendre** *ou* **recevoir une b.** to get a thrashing

branler [brɑ̃le] **1** *vt Vulg (masturber)* to jerk off, *Br* to wank off; *Fig* **mais qu'est-ce qu'il branle?** what the hell's he up to?
  2 *vi (dent)* to be loose; *(chaise, escalier)* to be rickety
  3 se branler *vpr Vulg (se masturber)* to jerk off, *Br* to wank; *Fig* **je m'en branle!** I don't give a shit!

branleur, -euse¹ [brɑ̃lœr, -øz] *nm,f Vulg (bon à rien)* nerd, *Br* wanker

branleux, -euse² [brɑ̃lø, øz] *adj Can Fam (qui hésite)* dithering; *(lâche)* cowardly

branque [brɑ̃k] *Fam* **1** *adj* bonkers, nuts
  2 *nmf (imbécile)* dope, jerk; *(fou)* headcase, *Br* nutter

braquage [brakaʒ] *nm* **(a)** *Aut (des roues)* turning; **(angle de) b.** steering lock **(b)** *Fam (vol)* hold-up; **faire un b.** to do a hold-up

braque [brak] *nm (chien)* pointer

braquer [brake] **1** *vt* **(a)** *(diriger)* to point (**sur** at); *(regard)* to fix (**sur** on) **(b)** *(rendre hostile)* **b. qn contre qn/qch** to turn sb against sb/sth **(c)** *Fam (banque)* to hold up
  2 *vi Aut* to turn the (steering) wheel; **b. à fond** to apply full lock; **voiture qui braque mal** car that has a poor lock
  3 se braquer *vpr* to dig one's heels in; **se b. contre qn** to set one's face against sb

braquet [brakɛ] *nm* gear ratio; **changer de b.** to change gear

bras [brɑ] *nm* **(a)** *(membre)* arm; **donner le b. à qn** to give sb one's arm; **un panier au b.** with a basket on one's arm; **les b. croisés** with one's arms folded; *Fig* **rester les b. croisés** *(être passif)* to stand by with one's arms folded; **b. dessus, b. dessous** arm in arm; **être le b. droit de qn** to be sb's right-hand man/ woman; **accueillir qn à b. ouverts** to welcome sb with open arms; *Fam* **tomber sur qn à bras raccourcis** to get stuck into sb; *Fig* **avoir le b. long** to have a lot of influence; *Fig* **avoir qn/qch sur les b.** to have sb/sth on one's hands; **les b. m'en tombent!** I'm flabbergasted!; **en b. de chemise** in (one's) shirtsleeves; **une partie de b. de fer** an arm-wrestling match; *Fig* **un b. de fer entre la direction et les syndicats** a trial of strength between the management and the unions; **faire un b. d'honneur à qn** ≃ to stick two fingers up at sb
  (b) *(d'un fauteuil, d'un levier, d'une ancre)* arm; *(d'une grue)* jib; *(d'une croix)* limb; *Can* **b. d'escalier** banister; **b. de lecture** pickup arm
  (c) *(de fleuve)* arm; **b. de mer** arm of the sea; *Can* **b. de vitesse** *Br* gear lever, *Am* stick shift

brasero [brazero] *nm* brazier

brasier [brazje] *nm (incendie)* blaze, inferno

Brasilia [brazilja] *n* Brasilia

bras-le-corps [brɑlkɔr] **à bras-le-corps** *adv* **saisir qn à b.** to seize sb round the waist; **prendre un problème à b.** to get to grips with a problem

brassage [brasaʒ] *nm* **(a)** *(de la bière)* brewing **(b)** *(mélange)* mixing

brassard [brasar] *nm* armband; **b. de deuil** black armband

brasse [bras] *nf Sport (style)* breaststroke; *(mouvement)* stroke; **nager la b.** to swim breaststroke; **b. coulée** = breaststroke in which face is submerged; **b. papillon** butterfly (stroke)

brassée [brase] *nf* armful

brasser [brase] *vt* **(a)** *(bière)* to brew **(b)** *(mélanger)* to mix; *Fig* **b. de l'argent** to handle large amounts of money; **b. de l'air** *ou* **du vent** to work without getting anything done

brasserie [brasri] *nf* **(a)** *(fabrique)* brewery; *(industrie)* brewing **(b)** *(restaurant)* brasserie

brasseur, -euse [brasœr, -øz] *nm,f* **(a)** *(fabricant de bière)* brewer **(b)** *Fig* **b. d'affaires** big businessman

brassière [brasjɛr] *nf* **(a)** *(de bébé)* *Br* vest, *Am* undershirt **(b)** *Can (soutien-gorge)* bra

Bratislava [bratislava] *n* Bratislava

bravade [bravad] *nf* bravado; **par b.** out of bravado

brave [brav] **1** *adj* **(a)** *(courageux)* brave, courageous **(b)** *(bon)* good; **de braves gens** good people **(c)** *Péj* **il est bien b.** *(pas futé)* he means well
  2 *nm* **(a)** *(héros)* brave man **(b)** *Vieilli* **mon b.** my good man

bravement [bravmɑ̃] *adv* **(a)** *(courageusement)* bravely, courageously **(b)** *(avec résolution)* boldly

braver [brave] *vt (mort, danger)* to brave; *(personne, lois, règlements)* to defy

bravo [bravo] **1** *exclam* bravo!; *(dans un débat)* hear, hear!; *Ironique* well done!
  2 *nm* **un grand b. à toute l'équipe technique** a big hand for all the technical crew; **des bravos** cheers

bravoure [bravur] *nf* bravery, courage

Brazzaville [brazavil] *n* Brazzaville

break¹ [brɛk] *nm (voiture) Br* estate car, *Am* station wagon

break² *nm (pause)* & *Sport* break

brebis [brəbi] *nf* **(a)** *(animal)* ewe; *Fig* **b. galeuse** black sheep **(b)** *Rel* sheep

brèche [brɛʃ] *nf (dans un mur, une haie)* gap; *(dans la coque d'un bateau)* hole; *Mil* breach; *Fig* **être toujours sur la b.** to be always on the go; **battre qch en b.** to demolish sth

bréchet [breʃɛ] *nm* breastbone

bredouille [brəduj] *adj* empty-handed

bredouiller [brəduje] *vt* & *vi* to mumble, to mutter

bref, -ève [brɛf, brɛv] **1** *adj* brief, short; *Ling (voyelle)* short; **soyez b.!** be brief!
  2 *adv* in short; **une cousine ou une tante, enfin b., quelqu'un de sa famille** a cousin or an aunt, well anyway, one of his relatives; **l'actualité en b.** the news in brief
  3 *nf* **brève** *(nouvelle)* short news item

brelan [brəlɑ̃] *nm* three of a kind; **b. d'as** three aces

breloque [brələk] *nf (sur un bracelet)* charm

brème [brɛm] *nf* bream

Brême [brɛm] *n* Bremen

Brésil [brezil] *nm* **le B.** Brazil

brésilien, -enne [breziljɛ̃, -ɛn] **1** *adj* Brazilian
  2 *nm,f* **B.** Brazilian

Bretagne [brətaɲ] *nf* **la B.** Brittany

bretelle [brətɛl] *nf* **(a)** *(de soutien-gorge, de robe)* (shoulder) strap; **(paire de) bretelles** *(pour pantalon)* (pair of) *Br* braces *or* *Am* suspenders **(b)** *(lanière)* strap; *(de fusil)* sling **(c)** *(route)* **b. (d'accès)** access road; **b. (d'autoroute)** *Br* (motorway) slip road, *Am* (highway) access road

breton, -onne [brətɔ̃, -ɔn] **1** *adj* Breton

2 *nm,f* **B.** Breton

3 *nm (langue)* Breton

bretzel [brɛdzɛl] *nm* pretzel

breuvage [brœvaʒ] *nm (potion)* potion; *Hum (boisson)* concoction

brève [brɛv] *voir* **bref**

brevet [brəvɛ] *nm (certificat)* certificate; *(diplôme)* diploma; *Scol* **b. (des collèges)** = general exam taken at fifteen; **b. d'études professionnelles** = vocational diploma; **b. (d'invention)** patent; **b. de pilote** *Aviat* pilot's licence; *Mil* wings; **b. de technicien supérieur** = advanced vocational training certificate

breveter [42] [brəvte] *vt (invention)* to patent; **faire b. qch** to take out a patent on sth

bréviaire [brevjer] *nm Rel* breviary

briard [brijar] *nm (chien)* Briard

bribes [brib] *nfpl* **b. de conversation** snatches of conversation; **des b. de finlandais** a few scraps of Finnish

bric-à-brac [brikabrak] *nm inv (vieux objets)* odds and ends, bric-à-brac; *(mélange)* jumble (**de** of); **(boutique de) b.** second-hand shop

bric et de broc [brikedəbrɔk] **de bric et de broc** *adv* haphazardly

brick [brik] *nm (carton)* carton

bricolage [brikɔlaʒ] *nm* **(a)** *(travail)* do-it-yourself, *Br* DIY; **faire du b.** to do some DIY **(b)** *Péj (réparation)* botch-up

bricole [brikɔl] *nf (objet)* trinket; *(chose sans importance)* trifle; *Fam* **il va lui arriver des bricoles** he's going to get into a pickle

bricoler [brikɔle] **1** *vt (construire)* to put together; *(réparer)* to tinker with

2 *vi* to do do-it-yourself *or Br* DIY; **j'ai passé la matinée à b. dans la maison** I spent the morning doing odd jobs about the house

bricoleur, -euse [brikɔlœr, -øz] **1** *adj* **être b.** to be good with one's hands

2 *nm,f* handyman, *f* handywoman

bride [brid] *nf* **(a)** *(de harnais)* bridle; *Fig* **lâcher la b. à qn** to give sb his/her head; *Fig* **avoir la b. sur le cou** to have a free rein; **aller à b. abattue** to ride full tilt **(b)** *(de boutonnière)* bar

bridé, -e [bride] *adj (yeux)* slanting

brider [bride] *vt (cheval)* to bridle; *(personne, passions, impulsion)* to curb, to restrain

bridge [bridʒ] *nm (jeu, prothèse)* bridge

brie [bri] *nm* Brie

brièvement [brievmɑ̃] *adv* briefly

brièveté [brievte] *nf* brevity, briefness

brigade [brigad] *nf* **(a)** *Mil* brigade; *(de police, de gendarmerie)* squad; **b. antigang** organized crime squad; *Hist* **les Brigades internationales** the International Brigades; **b. des stupéfiants** *ou Fam* **des stups** drug squad **(b)** *(d'ouvriers)* team

brigadier [brigadje] *nm* **(a)** *Mil* corporal; *(d'artillerie)* bombardier **(b)** **b. (de police)** (police) sergeant

brigand [brigɑ̃] *nm (bandit)* brigand; *(personne malhonnête)* crook; **petit b.!** *(enfant)* little rascal! *or* rogue!

briguer [brige] *vt (honneur, poste)* to solicit

brillamment [brijamɑ̃] *adv* brilliantly

brillant, -e [brijɑ̃, -ɑ̃t] **1** *adj* **(a)** *(lumière, couleur)* bright, brilliant; *(pierre précieuse)* sparkling;

(cheveux, chaussures, cuir) shiny; **les yeux brillants de fièvre** eyes bright with fever **(b)** *(carrière, élève, avenir)* brilliant; *(conversation)* sparkling

2 *nm* **(a)** *(d'un métal)* brilliance, brightness; *(d'une pierre précieuse)* sparkle; *(d'un papier, d'un tissu, de cheveux)* shininess **(b)** *(diamant)* brilliant **(c)** **b. à lèvres** lip gloss

brillantine [brijãtin] *nf* brilliantine

briller [brije] *vi* **(a)** *(soleil, étoiles, yeux)* to shine; *(bougie)* to glimmer; *(pierre précieuse)* to sparkle; *(eau, satin)* to shimmer; *(braises)* to glow; **faire b. ses chaussures** to shine or polish one's shoes; **des yeux qui brillent de colère/de joie** eyes shining with anger/happiness; **b. de mille feux** to sparkle brilliantly; *Prov* **tout ce qui brille n'est pas or** all that glitters is not gold **(b)** *(exceller)* to shine; **b. par son absence** to be conspicuous by one's absence; **elle ne brille pas par sa ponctualité** she's not noted for her punctuality

brimade [brimad] *nf* instance of bullying; **faire subir des brimades à qn** to bully sb

brimbaler [brɛ̃bale] = **bringuebaler**

brimer [brime] *vt* to bully; **se sentir brimé** to feel victimized

brin [brɛ̃] **1** *nm* **(a)** *(de persil, de romarin)* sprig; *(de mimosa, de muguet)* spray; *(de paille)* wisp; **un b. d'herbe** a blade of grass **(b)** *Fam (petite quantité)* **un b. de qch** a bit of sth; **un b. d'ironie/de jalousie** a touch of irony/jealousy; **un b. de toilette** to have a quick wash (and brush-up); **un beau b. de fille** a fine-looking girl **(c)** *(de laine, corde, fil)* strand

2 *adv Fam* **un b.** *(un peu)* a bit

brindille [brɛ̃dij] *nf* twig

bringue¹ [brɛ̃g] *nf Fam* **grande b.** *(fille)* beanpole

bringue² *nf Fam (fête)* binge; **faire la b.** to go on a binge

bringue³ *nf Suisse* **(a)** *(querelle)* row **(b)** *(rengaine)* refrain

bringuebaler [brɛ̃gbale], **brinquebaler** [brɛ̃kbale] *vt & vi Fam* to shake about

brio [brijo] *nm* brilliance; **avec b.** brilliantly

brioche [brijɔʃ] *nf* brioche; *Fam Fig* **avoir/prendre de la b.** to have/develop a paunch

brioché, -e [brijɔʃe] *adj* **pain b.** = milk bread

brique [brik] **1** *nf* **(a)** *(de construction)* brick; **mur ou en briques** brick wall **(b)** *très Fam (10 000 francs)* 10,000 francs

2 *adj inv* **(rouge) b.** brick-red

briquer [brike] *vt* **(a)** *(nettoyer)* to scrub down; *(pont de navire)* to holystone **(b)** *Suisse (briser)* to break, to smash

briquet [brikɛ] *nm (cigarette)* lighter

briqueterie [briketri] *nf* brickyard

briquette [brikɛt] *nf* **(a)** *(petite brique)* small brick **(b)** *(de jus de fruit)* small carton **(c)** *(de charbon)* briquette

bris [bri] *nm (de verre, de scellés)* breaking; **b. de glaces** broken windows

brisant [brizɑ̃] *nm (écueil)* reef; **brisants** *(vagues)* breakers

brise [briz] *nf* breeze; *Naut* **forte b.** stiff breeze

brise-glace [brizglas] *nm inv* **(a)** *(navire)* ice breaker **(b)** *(d'une pile de pont)* ice breaker; *(d'un navire)* ice beam

brise-lames [brizlam] *nm inv* breakwater

briser [brize] **1** *vt (casser)* to break; *(opposition, résistance, espérances)* to crush; *(carrière)* to wreck;

(grève) to break; **b. qn** *(sujet: effort, marche)* to shatter sb; **brisé par la douleur** crushed by grief; **la voix brisée par l'émotion** his/her voice choked with emotion; **cela me brise le cœur** it breaks my heart
  2 se briser *vpr (vagues, porcelaine, verre)* to break; *(voix)* to break; *Fig (espoirs)* to be shattered

brise-tout [briztu] *nmf inv* clumsy person *(who is always breaking things)*

briseur, -euse [brizœr, -øz] *nm,f* **b. de grève** strike breaker

brise-vent [brizvã] *nm inv* windbreak

bristol [bristɔl] *nm* Bristol board; *(carte de visite)* visiting card

britannique [britanik] **1** *adj* British; **les îles Britanniques** the British Isles
  2 *nmf* **B.** Briton; **les Britanniques** the British

broc [bro] *nm* pitcher, jug

brocante [brɔkãt] *nf (commerce)* secondhand trade; *(magasin)* secondhand shop; *(marché aux puces)* secondhand market

brocanteur, -euse [brɔkãtœr, -øz] *nm,f* secondhand dealer

brocarder [brɔkarde] *vt Litt* to gibe at

brocart [brɔkar] *nm* brocade

broche [brɔʃ] *nf* (a) *(pour rôtir)* spit; **faire cuire qch à la b.** to spit-roast sth (b) *(bijou)* brooch (c) *Tech, Élec & Méd* pin

brocher [brɔʃe] *vt* (a) *(livre)* to stitch (b) *(tissu)* to brocade

brochet [brɔʃɛ] *nm* pike

brochette [brɔʃɛt] *nf (broche)* skewer; *(plat)* kebab

brochure [brɔʃyr] *nf* brochure, pamphlet

brocoli [brɔkɔli] *nm* broccoli; **des brocolis** broccoli

brodequin [brɔdkɛ̃] *nm* laced boot

broder [brɔde] *vt & vi aussi Fig* to embroider

broderie [brɔdri] *nf* (a) *(ouvrage)* piece of embroidery; **broderies** embroidery; **b. anglaise** broderie anglaise (b) *(activité)* embroidery

broie *voir* **broyer**

bromure [brɔmyr] *nm* bromide

bronche [brɔ̃ʃ] *nf* bronchial tube; **être fragile des bronches** to have a weak chest

broncher [brɔ̃ʃe] *vi* (a) *(réagir)* **sans b.** without batting an eyelid; **il n'a pas bronché** he didn't bat an eyelid (b) *(cheval)* to stumble

bronchite [brɔ̃ʃit] *nf* bronchitis; **avoir une b.** to have bronchitis

broncho-pneumonie *(pl* **broncho-pneumonies**) [brɔ̃kɔpnømɔni] *nf Méd* bronchopneumonia

bronzage [brɔ̃zaʒ] *nm (activité)* tanning; *(hâle)* (sun)tan; **b. intégral** all-over tan

bronze [brɔ̃z] *nm (métal, objet d'art)* bronze

bronzé, -e [brɔ̃ze] *adj (peau)* (sun)tanned; *Euph ou Péj (personne)* coloured

bronzer [brɔ̃ze] *vi (personne)* to go brown, to tan

bronzette [brɔ̃zɛt] *nf Fam* sunbathing; **faire b.** to do a bit of sunbathing

brosse [brɔs] *nf* (a) *(ustensile)* brush; **donner un coup de b. à qch** to give sth a brush; **donner un coup de b. à qn** *(coiffer)* to give sb's hair a brush; **avoir les cheveux en b.** to have a crew cut; *Can Fam* **être en b.** to be smashed *or Br* pissed; *Fig* **manier la b. à reluire** to bow and scrape; **b. à cheveux** hairbrush; **b. à dents** toothbrush; **b. à habits** clothes brush; **b. à ongles** nailbrush (b) *(pinceau large)* (paint)brush

brosser [brɔse] **1** *vt* (a) *(tapis, manteau, cheveux)* to brush; *(sol)* to scrub; *(cheval)* to brush down; *Belg* **b. un cours** to skip a lecture (b) *(décrire)* **b. un tableau optimiste de la situation** to paint an optimistic picture of the situation
  2 se brosser *vpr (se nettoyer)* to brush oneself down; **se b. les dents/les cheveux** to brush one's teeth/one's hair; *Fam* **tu peux toujours te b.!** not a chance!

brou [bru] *nm* (a) *(enveloppe)* husk, *Am* shuck (b) *(teinture)* **b. de noix** walnut stain

broue [bru] *nf Can* froth; *très Fam Fig* **faire** *ou* **péter de la b.** to talk big

brouette [bruɛt] *nf* wheelbarrow

brouhaha [bruaa] *nm* hubbub

brouillard [brujar] *nm* fog; **il y a du b.** it's foggy; *Fig* **être dans le b.** to be in a fog; **b. givrant** freezing fog

brouille [bruj] *nf* quarrel, disagreement

brouillé, -e [bruje] *adj* (a) *(teint)* blotchy (b) **être b. avec qn** to have fallen out with sb; **être b. avec les dates/la grammaire** to be hopeless at dates/grammar

brouiller [bruje] **1** *vt* (a) *(rendre trouble)* *(idées)* to muddle up; *(vue)* to blur; **yeux brouillés de larmes** eyes blurred with tears; *Fig* **b. les cartes** to confuse the issue; *Fig* **b. les pistes** to cover one's tracks (b) *(fâcher)* **b. qn avec qn** to set sb against sb (c) *Rad & Élec (accidentellement)* to cause interference to; *(intentionnellement)* to jam
  2 se brouiller *vpr* (a) *(idées, dates)* to get muddled up (b) *(vue)* to get blurred (c) *(se détériorer)* **le temps se brouille** it's clouding over (d) *(se disputer)* to fall out *(avec qn* with sb)

brouillon, -onne [brujɔ̃, -ɔn] **1** *adj (mal organisé)* disorganized, unmethodical; *(mal présenté)* untidy
  2 *nm (ébauche)* (rough) draft; **(papier) b.** *Br* scrap *or Am* scratch paper; **faire un exercice au b.** to do an exercise in rough; **(cahier de) b.** rough book; *Ordinat* **version b.** draft version

broussaille [brusaj] *nf* **broussailles** scrub; **en b.** *(cheveux)* tousled; *(sourcils)* bushy

broussailleux, -euse [brusajø, -øz] *adj (terrain)* scrubby; *(cheveux)* tousled; *(sourcils)* bushy

brousse [brus] *nf* **la b.** the bush

brouter [brute] **1** *vt (herbe)* to graze
  2 *vi* (a) *(animal)* to graze (b) *(embrayage)* to judder

broutille [brutij] *nf* trifle

broyer [32] [brwaje] *vt (pierre, aliments, couleurs)* to grind; *(membre, main, personne)* to crush; *Fig* **b. du noir** to be down in the dumps

broyeur, -euse [brwajœr, -øz] **1** *adj (appareil)* grinding
  2 *nm (machine)* grinder; **b. à ordures** *Br* waste *orAm* garbage disposal unit

bru [bry] *nf* daughter-in-law

brugnon [bryɲɔ̃] *nm* nectarine

bruine [brɥin] *nf* drizzle

bruiner [brɥine] *v impersonnel* to drizzle

bruire [brɥir] *vi Litt (feuilles, étoffe)* to rustle; *(ruisseau, vent)* to murmur

bruissement [brɥismã] *nm (des feuilles, d'une étoffe)* rustle, rustling; *(d'un ruisseau, du vent)* murmur(ing)

bruit [brɥi] *nm* (a) *(son)* sound, noise; **b. de pas** (sound of) footsteps; **des bruits de voix** the sound of voices; **sans b.** without a sound (b) *(vacarme)* noise; **faire du b.** *(être bruyant)* to make a noise; *Fig (affaire, histoire)* to cause a sensation; **b. de fond**

background noise; **beaucoup de b. pour rien** a lot of fuss over nothing (**c**) *(rumeur)* rumour; **faire courir un b.** to spread a rumour; **le b. court que...** rumour has it that...

bruitage [bʀɥitaʒ] *nm* sound effects

bruiteur, -euse [bʀɥitœʀ, -øz] *nm,f* sound-effects man, *f* woman

brûlant, -e [bʀylɑ̃, -ɑ̃t] *adj (plat, casserole)* red-hot; *(café)* boiling (hot); *(soleil)* scorching; *Fig* **b. de désir** burning with desire; **question brûlante** burning question; **le sujet est d'une actualité brûlante** it's one of the burning issues of the day

brûlé, -e [bʀyle] **1** *nm,f (accidenté)* burns victim; *Méd* **les grands brûlés** people with third-degree burns
2 *nm* **sentir le b.** to smell burnt; **une odeur de b.** a burnt smell; **avoir un goût de b.** to taste burnt

brûle-parfum *(pl* brûle-parfums) [bʀylpaʀfœ̃] *nm* perfume burner

brûle-pourpoint [bʀylpuʀpwɛ̃] **à brûle-pourpoint** *adv* point-blank

brûler [bʀyle] **1** *vt (a) (sujet: flamme, acide)* to burn; *(sujet: eau bouillante)* to scald; *(sujet: fer à repasser)* to scorch; *(café)* to roast; **gazon brûlé par le soleil** lawn scorched by the sun; **être brûlé vif** *(dans un accident)* to be burnt alive; *(être supplicié)* to be burnt at the stake; **l'argent lui brûle les doigts** money burns a hole in his pocket (**b**) *(consommer) (électricité, combustible)* to use; *(calories)* to burn (**c**) **b. un feu rouge** to go through a red light; **b. un stop** to go straight past a stop sign
2 *vi (a) (flamber, être carbonisé)* to burn; *(être très chaud)* to be red-hot; *(liquide)* to be boiling (hot); *(blessure)* to be smart; **attention, ça brûle!** careful, it's hot!; **tu brûles** *(dans un jeu)* you're getting hot (**b**) *Fig* **b. de faire qch** to be burning to do sth; **b. d'impatience** to be bursting with impatience; **b. de désir** to be burning with desire
3 se brûler *vpr (par accident)* to burn oneself (**avec** on); **se b. la langue/la main** to burn one's tongue/hand

brûleur [bʀylœʀ] *nm* burner

brûlot [bʀylo] *nm* (**a**) *(article polémique)* scathing article (**b**) *Can (moustique)* gnat, midge

brûlure [bʀylyʀ] *nf (blessure)* burn; *(sensation)* burning; **b. de cigarette** cigarette burn; **brûlures d'estomac** heartburn

brume [bʀym] *nf* mist, haze; **b. de chaleur** heat haze

brumeux, -euse [bʀymø, -øz] *adj* misty, hazy; *Fig (idées, explication)* hazy

Brumisateur® [bʀymizatœʀ] *nm* atomizer, spray

brun, -e [bʀœ̃, bʀyn] **1** *adj (cheveux)* dark, brown; *(peau, personne) (naturellement)* dark; *(bronzé)* brown; **être b. de peau** to be dark-skinned; *Can* **il fait b.** it's getting dark
2 *nm,f (personne)* dark-haired man, *f* dark-haired woman
3 *nm (couleur)* brown
4 *nf* **brune** (**a**) *(bière)* brown ale (**b**) *(cigarette)* brown tobacco cigarette (**c**) *Litt* **à la b.** at dusk

brunante [bʀynɑ̃t] *nf Can* dusk

brunâtre [bʀynɑtʀ] *adj* brownish

Brunei [bʀynei] *nm* **le B.** Brunei

brunir [bʀyniʀ] *vi (peau, personne)* to tan; *(cheveux)* to darken

brushing® [bʀœʃiŋ] *nm* blow-dry; **se faire faire un b.** to have a blow-dry

brusque [bʀysk] *adj* abrupt

brusquement [bʀyskəmɑ̃] *adv* abruptly

brusquer [bʀyske] *vt* (**a**) **b. qn** *(être impoli envers)* to be abrupt with sb; *(maltraiter)* to treat sb harshly (**b**) *(hâter) (décision)* to rush; **il ne faut rien b.** we mustn't rush things

brusquerie [bʀyskəʀi] *nf* abruptness; **avec b.** abruptly

brut, -e [bʀyt] **1** *adj* (**a**) *(pétrole, minerai)* crude; *(sucre)* unrefined; *(pierre précieuse)* uncut; *(champagne)* extra-dry; *(cidre)* dry; **à l'état b.** in its raw state (**b**) *(bénéfice, poids, salaire)* gross
2 *nm* (**a**) *(pétrole)* crude (oil) (**b**) *(champagne)* extra-dry champagne
3 *adv* gross

brutal, -e, -aux, -ales [bʀytal, -o] *adj* (**a**) *(personne, paroles, manières)* brutal; *(choc)* violent; **être b. avec qn** to be rough with sb (**b**) *(changement)* abrupt

brutalement [bʀytalmɑ̃] *adv (violemment)* brutally; *(avec brusquerie)* roughly; *(soudainement)* abruptly

brutaliser [bʀytalize] *vt* to ill-treat

brutalité [bʀytalite] *nf (violence, brusquerie)* brutality; *(soudaineté)* abruptness; **brutalités** brutality

brute [bʀyt] *nf (personne violente)* brute; *(personne grossière)* boor; **taper sur qch comme une b.** to bang at sth like a madman; **une b. épaisse** a great brute; **grosse b.!** you big brute!

Bruxelles [bʀysɛl, bʀyksɛl] *n* Brussels

bruxellois, -e [bʀysɛlwa, -az, bʀyksɛlwa, -az] **1** *adj* Brussels
2 *nm,f* **B.** = person from Brussels

bruyamment [bʀɥijamɑ̃] *adv (parler, rire)* loudly; *(manger)* noisily

bruyant, -e [bʀɥijɑ̃, -ɑ̃t] *adj (rue, voisin)* noisy; *(rire, applaudissements)* loud

bruyère [bʀyjɛʀ] *nf (plante)* heather; *(terre)* heath; **pipe de b.** briar pipe; **terre de b.** peat

BTP [betepe] *nm (abrév* **bâtiment et travaux publics)** construction industry

BTS [betees] *nm (abrév* **brevet de technicien supérieur)** = advanced vocational training certificate

bu, -e *pp voir* **boire**

buanderette [bɥɑ̃dʀɛt] *nf Can Br* launderette, *Am* Laundromat®

buanderie [bɥɑ̃dʀi] *nf* (**a**) *(pièce)* laundry (room) (**b**) *Can (laverie)* (dry) cleaner's, laundry

Buba [byba] *nf (abrév* **Bundesbank) la Buba** the Bundesbank

bubonique [bybɔnik] *adj voir* **peste**

Bucarest [bykaʀɛst] *n* Bucharest

buccal, -e, -aux, -ales [bykal, -o] *adj* buccal; **par voie buccale** orally

bûche [byʃ] *nf* (**a**) *(morceau de bois)* log; **b. de Noël** Yule log (**b**) *Fam (chute)* fall; **prendre une b.** to come a cropper

bûcher¹ [byʃe] **1** *nm* (**a**) *(pour le bois)* woodshed (**b**) *(de supplice)* stake (**c**) *(funéraire)* (funeral) pyre
2 *vt Can (arbre)* to fell, to cut down

bûcher² *Fam Scol* **1** *vt* to bone up on, *Br* to swot up
2 *vi Br* to swot, *Am* to grind

bûcheron [byʃʀɔ̃] *nm* woodcutter

bûcheur, -euse [byʃœʀ, -øz] *Fam Scol* **1** *adj* hardworking
2 *nm,f Br* swot, *Am* grind

bucolique [bykɔlik] *adj* pastoral

Budapest [bydapɛst] *n* Budapest

budget [bydʒɛ] *nm* budget
budgétaire [bydʒetɛr] *adj (dépenses, contrôle)* budgetary; *(année)* financial; **déficit/excédent b.** budget deficit/surplus
buée [bɥe] *nf (sur les vitres)* condensation; *(sur un miroir)* mist
Buenos Aires [bɥenɔzɛr] *n* Buenos Aires
buffet [byfɛ] *nm* (**a**) *(meuble) (bas)* sideboard; *(haut)* dresser (**b**) *(repas)* buffet; **b. campagnard** = cold buffet made with country produce; **b. froid** cold buffet (**c**) *Fam (ventre)* belly
buffle [byfl] *nm* buffalo
building [bildiŋ] *nm* tower block
buis [bɥi] *nm (arbre)* box (tree); *(bois)* box(wood)
buisson [bɥisɔ̃] *nm* bush
buissonnière [bɥisɔnjɛr] *adj f voir* **école**
bulbe [bylb] *nm* (**a**) *Bot* bulb (**b**) *Anat* **b. pileux** hair bulb; **b. rachidien** medulla oblongata (**c**) *Archit* onion dome
bulgare [bylgar] **1** *adj* Bulgarian
  2 *nmf* **B.** Bulgarian
  3 *nm (langue)* Bulgarian
Bulgarie [bylgari] *nf* **la B.** Bulgaria
bulldozer [byldozœr] *nm* bulldozer
bulle [byl] *nf* (**a**) *(d'air, de savon, stérile)* bubble; *(de bandes dessinées)* balloon; **faire des bulles** to blow bubbles; *Fam* **coincer la b.** to sleep, *Br* to kip; *Ordinat* **b. d'aide** help pop-up (**b**) *(lettre du pape)* papal bull
buller [byle] *vi Fam* to laze around
bulletin [byltɛ̃] *nm (communiqué)* bulletin; *(d'entreprise)* newsletter; *(formulaire)* form; *Scol* **b. (scolaire)** (school) report; **b. blanc** blank ballot paper; **b. d'informations** news bulletin; **b. météorologique** weather report; **b. officiel** official listing of all new laws and decrees; **b. de paie** *ou* **de salaire** pay slip; *Méd* **b. de santé** medical bulletin; **b. trimestriel** end-of-term report; *Suisse* **b. de versement** money order; **b. de vote** ballot paper; **b. (de vote) nul** spoiled ballot paper
bulletin-réponse *(pl* **bulletins-réponse)** [byltɛ̃repɔ̃s] *nm* reply form
bungalow [bœ̃galo] *nm* bungalow
bunker [bunkœr] *nm Mil* bunker; *(en golf) Br* bunker, *Am* sand trap
buraliste [byralist] *nmf* (**a**) *(de bureau de tabac)* tobacconist (**b**) *(dans un bureau)* clerk
bure [byr] *nf (étoffe)* frieze; *(habit religieux)* frock
bureau, -x [byro] *nm* (**a**) *(meuble)* desk
  (**b**) *(lieu)* office; *(à la maison)* study
  (**c**) *(comité)* committee
  (**d**) *(agence)* office; **b. de change** bureau de change; **b. d'études** design office; *(de recherche)* R & D department; **B. international du travail** International Labour Office; **b. de poste** post office; **b. de tabac** tobacconist's (shop)
  (**e**) *(organisme)* **b. d'aide sociale** welfare office
bureaucrate [byrokrat] *nmf* bureaucrat
bureaucratie [byrokrasi] *nf (système)* bureaucracy; *(ensemble des fonctionnaires)* bureaucrats
bureaucratique [byrokratik] *adj* bureaucratic
Bureautique® [byrotik] *nf* office automation
burette [byrɛt] *nf* (**a**) *(pour l'huile)* oilcan; *(de chimiste)* burette (**b**) *très Fam* **burettes** *(testicules)* balls, *Br* bollocks

burin [byrɛ̃] *nm* (**a**) *(de graveur)* burin (**b**) *(pour découper)* (cold) chisel
buriné, -e [byrine] *adj (visage)* deeply lined
Burkina [byrkina] *nm* **le B.** Burkina Faso
burkinabé [byrkinabe] **1** *adj* of Burkina Faso
  2 *nmf* **B.** = person from Burkina Faso
burlesque [byrlɛsk] **1** *adj* (**a**) *(ridicule)* ludicrous, ridiculous (**b**) *(film, genre)* burlesque
  2 *nm (genre)* **le b.** the burlesque
Burundi [burundi] *nm* **le B.** Burundi
bus [bys] *nm (autobus)* & *Ordinat* bus
buse [byz] *nf* (**a**) *(oiseau)* buzzard (**b**) *(conduit)* duct (**c**) *Belg (échec)* failure
busqué, -e [byske] *adj (nez)* hook(ed)
buste [byst] *nm (torse)* chest; *(seins, sculpture)* bust
bustier [bystje] *nm (corsage)* bustier; *(soutien-gorge)* long-line (strapless) bra
but [by, byt] *nm* (**a**) *(objectif)* aim, goal; *(intention)* purpose; *(d'un trajet)* destination, goal; **dans ce b.** with this aim in view; **dans le b. de faire qch** with the aim of doing sth; **c'est le b. de l'opération** that's the point of the operation; **errer sans b.** to wander about aimlessly (**b**) *Sport* goal; **marquer un b.** to score a goal; **gagner/perdre (par) 3 buts à 1** to win/lose by 3 goals to 1; **les buts** *(zone)* the goal (**c**) **demander/dire qch de b. en blanc** to ask/say sth straight out
butane [bytan] *nm* butane
buté, -e [byte] *adj* stubborn, obstinate
butée [byte] *nf* (**a**) *(pièce)* **b. (d'arrêt)** stop (**b**) *Archit* abutment
buter [byte] **1** *vt* (**a**) *(braquer)* **b. qn** to put sb's back up (**b**) *très Fam (tuer)* to bump off
  2 *vi* **b. contre qch** *(cogner)* to bump into sth; *(trébucher)* to stumble over sth; **b. sur un problème/une difficulté** to come up against a problem/a difficulty
  3 se buter *vpr (s'entêter)* to dig one's heels in
buteur [bytœr] *nm (au football)* goalscorer; *(au rugby)* kicker
butin [bytɛ̃] *nm* (**a**) *(d'une armée)* booty; *(de pillards)* spoils; *(de voleur)* loot (**b**) *Can Fam (affaires personnelles)* gear, stuff
butiner [bytine] **1** *vi (abeille)* to gather pollen
  2 *vt (sujet: abeille)* to gather pollen from; *(renseignements)* to gather
butineur [bytinœr] *nm Ordinat* browser
butoir [bytwar] *nm Rail* buffer; *(de porte)* door stop; **date b.** deadline
butte [byt] *nf (colline)* hillock; *Fig* **être en b. à qch** to be exposed to sth
buvable [byvabl] *adj* (**a**) *(potable)* drinkable (**b**) *(médicament)* to be taken orally
buvard [byvar] *nm (feuille)* sheet of blotting paper; *(sous-main)* blotter; **(papier) b.** blotting paper
buvette [byvɛt] *nf (dans une gare, à une fête)* refreshment bar
buveur, -euse [byvœr, -øz] *nm,f* drinker; **un gros b.** a heavy drinker
buviez *etc voir* **boire**
Byzance [bizɑ̃s] *n* Byzantium; *Fam* **c'est B.** it's the last word in luxury; *Fam* **ce n'est pas B.** it's not exactly luxurious

C

C¹, c [se] *nm inv* C, c; **c cédille** c cedilla
C² (*abrév* **Celsius**) C
c' *voir* ce
C4 [sekatr] *nm inv Belg* = official document given to an employee who is being laid off by his or her employer, *Br* = P45
CA [sea] *nm* (**a**) *Élec* (*abrév* **courant alternatif**) AC (**b**) *Com* (*abrév* **chiffre d'affaires**) turnover
ça [sa] *pron démonstratif* (**a**) (*en désignant*) (*cela*) that; (*ceci*) this; **donne-moi ça** give that to me; **c'est bien vrai ça!** that's very true!; **écoute-moi ça!** just listen to this!; **ce n'est pas si facile que ça** it isn't as easy as that; **ça oui!** oh yes!; **à part ça** apart from that; **qui/quand/où ça?** who/when/where?; **c'est ça!** that's right!; *Ironique* if you say so!; **comment ça, elle est partie?** what do you mean she's gone?; **ça alors!, ça par exemple!** my goodness!; **ça y est, j'ai fini** that's it, I'm finished; **et insolent avec ça!** and you're/she's/*etc* rude! (**b**) (*sujet indéterminé*) it; **ça m'ennuie/me choque** it annoys/shocks me; **ça m'amuse** I find it funny; **ça me ferait plaisir** I'd enjoy it (**c**) *Fam* **ça criait dans tous les coins** there was shouting going on everywhere; *Hum* **ça travaille là-dedans!** you're not just a pretty face!
çà [sa] **çà et là** *adv* here and there
cabale [kabal] *nf* (**a**) (*complot, comploteurs*) cabal; **monter une c. contre qn** to plot against sb (**b**) *Rel* cabbala
cabalistique [kabalistik] *adj* cabbalistic
caban [kabã] *nm* reefer
cabane [kaban] *nf* (**a**) (*baraque*) hut; (*en rondins*) cabin; (*à outils*) shed; **c. à lapins** rabbit hutch; *Can* **c. à sucre** sugar shack (**b**) *très Fam* (*prison*) **en c.** in the clink; **faire de la c.** to do time
cabanon [kabanɔ̃] *nm* (**a**) (*petite cabane*) hut, shed (**b**) (*en Provence*) (*maison de campagne*) (country) cottage
cabaret [kabarɛ] *nm* cabaret
cabas [kaba] *nm* shopping bag
cabestan [kabɛstã] *nm* capstan
cabillaud [kabijo] *nm* (fresh) cod
cabine [kabin] *nf* (**a**) (*de bateau, de vaisseau spatial*) cabin; **c. de pilotage** (*de petit avion*) cockpit; (*de gros avion*) flight deck (**b**) **c. de douche** (*pièce*) shower room; (*installation*) shower cubicle; **c. de bain(s)** (*de plage*) beach hut; (*de piscine*) changing cubicle; **c. d'essayage** fitting room; **c. Internet** Internet booth (**c**) (*de grue, de locomotive, de camion*) cab; (*d'ascenseur*) *Br* cage, *Am* car; **c. téléphonique** phone box
cabinet [kabinɛ] *nm* (**a**) (*petite pièce*) small room; *Fam* **les cabinets** *Br* the loo, *Am* the john; **c. noir** cubbyhole;

c. de toilette (small) bathroom; **c. de travail** study (**b**) (*de pub*) agency; (*d'architectes, de notaire*) office; (*de médecin*) *Br* surgery, practice, *Am* office; **c. dentaire** dental surgery *or* practice (**c**) (*entreprise*) **c. conseil** consultancy; **c. juridique** law firm (**d**) *Pol* (*d'un ministre*) departmental staff
câble [kabl] *nm* (**a**) (*fil*) cable; **c. métallique** wire cable (**b**) *TV* **le c.** cable TV; **avoir le c.** to have cable TV (**c**) *Vieilli* (*message*) cable
câblé, -e [kable] *adj* (**a**) *TV* (*ville, région*) with cable television; *Ordinat & Tél* hard-wired; **réseau c.** cable (TV) network; **l'immeuble est c.** the building is wired for cable TV (**b**) (*à fonctionnement fixe*) cabled
câbler [kable] *vt* (**a**) *TV* (*ville, quartier*) to install cable television in (**b**) *Vieilli* (*message*) to cable
câblo-opérateur (*pl* **câblo-opérateurs**) [kablɔɔperatœr] *nm* cable company
cabochard, -e [kabɔʃar, -ard] *Fam* **1** *adj* pigheaded **2** *nm,f* pigheaded person
caboche [kabɔʃ] *nf Fam* (*tête*) nut; **mets-le-toi dans la c.!** get that into your thick skull!
cabosser [kabɔse] *vt* (*métal, voiture*) to bash up; (*chapeau*) to bash in; **un vieux chapeau cabossé** a battered old hat
cabot [kabo] *nm Fam* (**a**) (*chien*) pooch (**b**) (*acteur*) ham (actor)
cabotage [kabɔtaʒ] *nm Naut* coasting
caboteur [kabɔtœr] *nm Naut* coaster
cabotin, -e [kabɔtɛ̃, -in] **1** *adj* (*acteur*) ham **2** *nm,f* (**a**) (*acteur*) ham (actor, *f* actress) (**b**) (*vantard*) show-off
cabrer [kabre] **se cabrer** *vpr* (*cheval*) to rear (up); *Fig* (*personne*) to recoil
cabriole [kabrijɔl] *nf* (*saut, bond*) caper; (*en danse*) cabriole; (*en équitation*) capriole; (*de gymnaste*) somersault; **faire des cabrioles** to caper about
cabriolet [kabrijɔlɛ] *nm* (**a**) (*auto*) convertible (**b**) (*voiture à cheval*) cabriolet
CAC [kak] *n* (*abrév* **Compagnie des agents de change**) **le C.-40** = the Paris Stock Exchange index
caca [kaka] *nm* (*langage enfantin*) (*excrément*) poo; **faire c.** to do a poo; **c. d'oie** yellowish green
cacah(o)uète [kakawɛt] *nf* peanut
cacao [kakao] *nm* (*boisson, poudre*) cocoa; (*fève*) cocoa bean
cacaoui [kakawi] *nm Can* long-tailed duck
cacatoès [kakatɔɛs] *nm* cockatoo
cacatois [kakatwa] *nm Naut* (*voile*) royal sail; (**mât de**) **c.** royal mast
cachalot [kaʃalo] *nm* sperm whale

cache [kaʃ] **1** *nf* hiding place; **c. d'armes** arms cache **2** *nm (sur un texte)* masking card

caché, -e [kaʃe] *adj* hidden; *(sentiment)* secret

cache-cache [kaʃkaʃ] *nm* **jouer à c.** to play hide-and-seek

cache-col [kaʃkɔl] *nm inv Vieilli* scarf

Cachemire [kaʃmir] *nm* **le C.** Kashmir

cachemire [kaʃmir] *nm (laine)* cashmere; **à impression c.** paisley

cache-nez [kaʃne] *nm inv* scarf

cache-pot [kaʃpo] *nm inv* flowerpot holder

cacher [kaʃe] **1** *vt* to hide; **il ne cache pas que…** he makes no secret of the fact that…; **c. qch à qn** *(omettre de lui dire)* to hide sth from sb; **pour ne rien te c.** to be completely open with you; **je ne vous cache pas que j'ai été surpris** I won't pretend (that) I wasn't surprised; **le mur nous cache la vue** the wall hides our view

2 se cacher *vpr (personne, soleil)* to hide; **se c. de qn** to hide from sb; **sa timidité se cache derrière une certaine rudesse** his shyness is hidden behind a bluff exterior; **je ne m'en cache pas** I make no secret of it; **en se cachant** secretly; **sans se c.** openly

cache-sexe [kaʃsɛks] *nm inv* G-string; *(d'indigène)* apron

cachet [kaʃɛ] *nm* (**a**) *(médicament)* tablet, pill (**b**) *(tampon)* stamp; *(sceau)* seal; *(de fabricant)* (trade)-mark; **c. de la poste** postmark (**c**) *(style) (d'un endroit)* character; *(d'un vêtement)* style (**d**) *(salaire)* fee

cacheter [42] *vt* to seal

cachette [kaʃɛt] *nf* (**a**) hiding place; **en c.** secretly; **boire en c.** *(habituellement)* to be a secret drinker; **faire qch en c. de qn** to do sth without sb's knowing (**b**) *Can* **jouer à la c.** to play hide-and-seek

cachot [kaʃo] *nm* (**a**) *(cellule)* dungeon (**b**) *(isolement)* solitary confinement

cachotterie [kaʃɔtri] *nf* **faire des cachotteries** to be secretive

cachottier, -ère [kaʃɔtje, -ɛr] **1** *adj* secretive **2** *nm,f* secretive person; **petit c.!** you secretive little thing!

cachou [kaʃu] *nm (bonbon)* cachou *(liquorice sweet)*

cacophonie [kakɔfɔni] *nf* cacophony

cactus [kaktys] *nm* cactus

c-à-d. *(abrév* **c'est-à-dire)** i.e.

cadastre [kadastr] *nm (registre)* cadastre; *(administration)* cadastral survey office

cadavérique [kadaverik] *adj (teint)* deathly pale; *Méd* cadaveric

cadavre [kadavr] *nm* (**a**) *(de personne)* corpse, (dead) body; *(d'animal)* carcass, body; *Fam* **c'est un c. ambulant** he's a walking skeleton (**b**) *Fam (bouteille)* empty

caddie [kadi] *nm* (**a**) *Sport* caddie (**b**) *(chariot) Br* trolley, *Am* cart

cadeau, -x [kado] *nm* present, gift; *(avec un achat)* free gift; **en c.** as a present; **en c. avec** *(achat)* free with; **faire un c. à qn** to give sb a present; **faire c. de qch à qn** *(donner)* to make sb a present of sth; *Fam Fig* **il ne lui a pas fait de cadeaux** he didn't spare him/her; *Fam* **ton frère, ce n'est pas un c.** your brother's a real pain; **c'est un c. empoisonné** it's more trouble than it's worth

cadenas [kadna] *nm* padlock

cadenasser [kadnase] **1** *vt (porte, pièce)* to padlock **2 se cadenasser** *vpr (personne)* to lock oneself away

cadence [kadɑ̃s] *nf (rythme régulier)* rhythm; *(vitesse)* rate; **en c.** in time; **c. de production** rate of production; **c. de tir** rate of fire

cadencé, -e [kadɑ̃se] *adj* (**a**) *(rythmé)* rhythmic(al); **marcher au pas c.** to walk in time (**b**) *Ordinat* **c. à** running at

cadet, -ette [kadɛ, -ɛt] **1** *adj (de deux)* younger; *(de plus de deux)* youngest **2** *nm,f* (**a**) *(de deux)* younger (one); *(de plus de deux)* youngest (one); **il est mon c. de deux ans** he's two years younger than I am; **c'est le c. de mes soucis** that's the least of my worries (**b**) *Sport* junior *(16 to 18 years old)* (**c**) *Hist & Mil* cadet

cadrage [kadraʒ] *nm Cin & Phot (de l'image)* centring; *(plan)* frame; *Ordinat* positioning

cadran [kadrɑ̃] *nm (d'horloge, de baromètre)* face; *(d'instrument, de téléphone)* dial; *Fig* **faire le tour du c.** *(dormir)* to sleep round the clock; *Aut* **cadrans (de bord)** display panels; **c. solaire** sundial

cadre [kadr] *nm* (**a**) *(de tableau, de porte, de vélo)* frame (**b**) *(domaine)* limits; *(structure)* framework; **dans le c. de** within the framework of (**c**) *(décor)* setting; **c. (de vie)** environment (**d**) *(dans un formulaire)* box; *Ordinat (pour graphique)* box; **c. réservé à l'administration** *(sur formulaire)* for official use only (**e**) *(dans une entreprise)* executive, manager; **les cadres** the management; *Mil* the officers; **c. moyen** middle manager; **c. supérieur** senior executive; **jeune c. dynamique** dynamic young executive (**f**) **être rayé des cadres** to be dismissed (**g**) *Can (tableau)* painting, picture

---

Cadre

In French companies, employees are divided into two categories, "employés" and "cadres". "Cadres", who are better qualified, tend to occupy more senior posts and consequently enjoy higher salaries, more benefits and more prestige. They are also expected to work longer hours.

---

cadre-adresse *(pl* **cadres-adresses)** [kadradrɛs] *nm* address space

cadrer [kadre] **1** *vt (photo)* to centre; *(plan)* to frame; *Ordinat* to position **2** *vi (correspondre)* to tally (**avec** with)

cadreur [kadrœr] *nm TV & Cin* cameraman

caduc, caduque [kadyk] *adj* (**a**) *(feuille)* deciduous (**b**) *Jur (accord)* lapsed; *(loi)* null and void

caducée [kadyse] *nm* caduceus

CAF [seaɛf] *(abrév* **Caisse d'allocations familiales)** = child benefit office

cafard [kafar] *nm* (**a**) *(insecte)* cockroach (**b**) *Fam* **avoir le c.** *ou* **un coup de c.** to feel down *or* low (**c**) *Fam (rapporteur)* sneak

cafarder [kafarde] *vi Fam* (**a**) *(rapporter)* to sneak (**b**) *(avoir le cafard)* to feel down *or* low

cafardeur, -euse [kafardœr, -øz] *nm,f Fam* sneak

cafardeux, -euse [kafardø, -øz] *adj Fam* **se sentir** *ou* **être c.** to feel down *or* low

café [kafe] **1** *nm* (**a**) *(produit, boisson)* coffee; **glace au c.** coffee ice cream; **c. crème** white coffee; **c. décaféiné** decaffeinated coffee; **c. en grains** coffee beans; **c. au lait** white coffee; **c. liégeois** = coffee ice cream topped with whipped cream; **c. moulu** ground coffee; *Suisse* **c. nature** black coffee; **c. noir** black coffee; **c. en poudre** *ou* **instantané** instant coffee (**b**) *(bar)* café *(also serving alcoholic drinks)*; **c. tabac** = café-cum-tobacconist's

2 *adj inv (couleur)* **c. (au lait)** coffee-coloured

Café

In French cafés, a small cup of strong black coffee is called "un (petit) café", "un express" or, colloquially, "un petit noir". This may be served "serré" (extra-strong), "léger" (weak) or "allongé" (diluted with hot water). An "express" with a tiny amount of milk added is called "une noisette". A large cup of black coffee is "un grand café", "un double express" or, colloquially, "un grand noir". Coffee with frothy, steam-heated milk is called "un (grand/petit) crème". The term "café au lait" is almost never used in cafés.

---

caféine [kafein] *nf* caffeine

cafétéria [kafeterja] *nf* cafeteria

café-théâtre *(pl* **cafés-théâtres)** [kafeteatr] *nm Br* ≃ pub theatre

cafetier [kaftje] *nm* café owner

cafetière [kaftjɛr] *nf (récipient)* coffee pot; *(électrique)* coffee machine; **c. à pression** percolator

cafouillage [kafujaʒ] *nm Fam* (**a**) *(confusion)* muddle, shambles (**b**) *(de moteur de voiture)* misfiring

cafouiller [kafuje] *vi Fam* (**a**) *(personne)* to get into a muddle; *(projet)* to fall apart (**b**) *(moteur de voiture)* to misfire; *(poste de télévision)* to be on the blink

cafter [kafte] *vi Fam* to sneak, to tell tales, *Am* to snitch

cage [kaʒ] *nf* (**a**) *(pour oiseaux, dans un zoo)* cage; *(pour poules)* coop; *(pour lapins)* hutch; **mettre un oiseau en c.** to put a bird in a cage; *Fam Fig* **c. à lapins** rabbit hutch (**b**) *(de foot)* goal (**c**) **c. d'ascenseur** lift *or Am* elevator shaft; **c. d'escalier** stairwell (**d**) *Anat* **c. thoracique** rib cage

cageot [kaʒo] *nm* (**a**) *(caisse)* crate (**b**) *Fam Péj (femme)* dog

cagette [kaʒɛt] *nf* crate

cagibi [kaʒibi] *nm Fam* storage room

cagnard [kaɲar] *nm Fam* blazing sunshine

cagneux, -euse [kaɲø, -øz] *adj* **avoir les genoux c.** to have knock-knees

cagnotte [kaɲɔt] *nf (caisse commune)* kitty; *(de jeux)* pool; *(économies)* nest egg

cagoule [kagul] *nf (de moine)* cowl; *(de pénitent, de terroriste)* hood

cahier [kaje] *nm* (**a**) *(livre)* notebook; *(d'écolier)* exercise book; **c. de brouillon** rough book; **c. de textes** homework book (**b**) *Typ* signature (**c**) *(d'un journal)* section (**d**) **Cahiers de...** *(revue)* Journal of... (**e**) *Com* **c. des charges** *(d'un contrat)* terms and conditions; *(de fabrication)* specifications

cahin-caha [kaɛ̃kaa] *adv Fam* **aller c.** *(se déplacer)* to struggle along; **ça va, la santé? – ça va, c.** how are you keeping? – oh, so-so

cahot [kao] *nm (secousse)* jolt

cahoter [kaɔte] **1** *vt* **être cahoté** *(dans un véhicule)* to be jolted about

2 *vi* to jolt along

cahoteux, -euse [kaɔtø, -øz] *adj* bumpy

cahute [kayt] *nf* shack

caïd [kaid] *nm Fam (chef de bande)* gang leader; **un c. de la drogue** a drugs baron; **faire le c., jouer les caïds** to act high and mighty

caillasse [kajas] *nf Fam* loose stones

caille [kaj] *nf* quail; *Fam* **ma petite c.** my little dove

caillé [kaje] *nm* curds

caillebotis [kajbɔti] *nm* (**a**) *Naut* grating (**b**) *(plancher)* duckboard

caillebotte [kajbɔt] *nf* curds

cailler [kaje] **1** *vt (lait)* to curdle; *(sang)* to clot

2 *vi* (**a**) *(lait)* to curdle; *(sang)* to clot; **faire c. du lait** to curdle milk (**b**) *Fam* **ça caille** it's freezing

3 **se cailler** *upr Fam* **on se (les) caille** it's freezing

caillot [kajo] *nm (de sang)* clot

caillou, -x [kaju] *nm* (**a**) *(petite pierre)* stone; *(sur la plage)* (**b**) *Fam (pierre précieuse)* stone (**c**) *Fam (tête)* nut, pebble; **il n'a plus un poil sur le c.** he's as bald as a coot

caillouteux, -euse [kajutø, -øz] *adj (route)* stony; *(plage)* pebbly

caïman [kaimã] *nm* cayman

Caire [kɛr] *voir* **Le Caire**

cairote [kerɔt] **1** *adj* of Cairo

2 *nmf* **C.** person from Cairo, Cairene

caisse [kɛs] *nf* (**a**) *(pour marchandises)* case; *(à outils)* box; *(de champagne, de vin)* case; *(pour plantes)* tub; *(de fruits)* crate

(**b**) *Com & Fin (coffre)* cash box; *(d'une caisse enregistreuse)* till; *(où l'on paie) (dans un magasin)* cash desk; *(dans un supermarché)* checkout; **les caisses de l'État** the coffers of the State; **tenir la c.** *(dans un restaurant, dans un magasin)* to be the cashier; **passer à la c.** *(se faire licencier)* to be paid off; *Fam (payer)* to pay; *Fam (se faire payer)* to be paid; **c. (enregistreuse)** cash register; *Pol* **c. noire** slush fund

(**c**) *(argent)* cash (in hand); **faire la** *ou* **sa c.** to do the till

(**d**) *(organisme)* **c. d'allocations familiales** = child benefit office; **c. d'épargne** savings bank; *Can* **c. populaire** credit union; **c. primaire d'assurance maladie** = French government department dealing with health insurance; **c. de retraite** pension fund

(**e**) *Mus* **c. claire** snare drum; **c. de résonance** sound box

(**f**) *(de piano, d'horloge)* case; *(de véhicule)* body

(**g**) *très Fam (voiture)* car

caissette [kɛsɛt] *nf* small box

caissier, -ère [kɛsje, -ɛr] *nm,f* cashier; *(dans un supermarché)* checkout operator

caisson [kɛsɔ̃] *nm* (**a**) *très Fam* **se faire sauter le c.** to blow one's brains out (**b**) *Archit* **plafond à caissons** coffered ceiling (**c**) *(de plongée)* caisson

cajoler [kaʒɔle] *vt* to cuddle

cajolerie [kaʒɔlri] *nf* cuddle

cajou [kaʒu] *nm voir* **noix**

cake [kɛk] *nm* fruit cake

cal *(pl* **cals)** [kal] *nm (durillon)* callus

calamar [kalamar] = **calmar**

calamine [kalamin] *nf (dépôt)* carbon deposits

calamité [kalamite] *nf (fléau)* calamity; *(malheur)* great misfortune; *Fam* **ce mec, c'est une vraie c.!** this guy is a real disaster!

calamiteux, -euse [kalamitø -øz] *adj* calamitous

calancher [kalɑ̃ʃe] *vi très Fam* to croak, *Br* to snuff it, *Am* to check out

calandre [kalɑ̃dr] *nf* (**a**) *(machine)* calender (**b**) *Aut* radiator grille

calanque [kalɑ̃k] *nf* deep narrow creek *(in the Mediterranean)*

calao [kalao] *nm* hornbill

calcaire [kalkɛr] **1** *adj (sol, terrain)* chalky; *(roche)* calcareous; *(eau)* hard
2 *nm* (**a**) *Géol* limestone (**b**) *(dépôt)* fur

calcification [kalsifikasjɔ̃] *nf Méd* calcification

calciner [kalsine] **1** *vt (brûler)* to char; **calciné** *(trop cuit)* burnt to a cinder
2 se calciner *vpr* to burn

calcium [kalsjɔm] *nm* calcium

calcul¹ [kalkyl] *nm* (**a**) *(compte)* calculation; **faire un c.** to make a calculation (**b**) *Scol* **le c.** arithmetic; **c. mental** mental arithmetic (**c**) *Math* **c. différentiel/intégral** differential/integral calculus (**d**) *(prévision)* calculation; **agir par c.** to act from selfish motives; **faire un mauvais c.** to miscalculate

calcul² *nm Méd* stone, *Spéc* calculus; **c. biliaire/rénal** gall/kidney stone

calculateur, -trice [kalkylatœr, -tris] **1** *adj (personne, politique)* calculating
2 *nm Ordinat* (desktop) calculator; **c. (électronique)** (electronic) computer
3 *nf* **calculatrice (de poche)** (pocket) calculator

calculé, -e [kalkyle] *adj (insulte, risque)* calculated; *(méchanceté)* premeditated; *(insolence)* deliberate

calculer [kalkyle] **1** *vt (compter) (prix, superficie)* to work out, to calculate; *(comportement, propos)* to plan; *(conséquences, chances)* to weigh (up); **tout bien calculé** taking everything into account
2 *vi* to calculate; *Péj (économiser)* to count every penny

calculette [kalkylɛt] *nf* (pocket) calculator

Calcutta [kalkyta] *n* Calcutta

caldoche [kaldɔʃ] **1** *adj* White New Caledonian
2 *nmf* C. New Caledonian

cale¹ [kal] *nf Naut* (**a**) *(de navire)* hold; **à fond de c.** down in the hold (**b**) *(rampe)* **c. sèche** dry dock

cale² *nf (pour meuble, pour porte)* wedge; *(pour bloquer une roue)* chock

calé, -e [kale] *adj Fam* (**a**) *(personne)* **être c. en qch** to be well up in sth (**b**) *(problème, question, devoir)* tough (**c**) *Belg (prêt)* ready

calebasse [kalbas] *nf* calabash

calèche [kalɛʃ] *nf* barouche

calecif [kalsif] *nm Fam Br* pants, *Am* shorts

caleçon [kalsɔ̃] *nm* boxer shorts; *(de femme)* leggings; *Vieilli* **c. de bain** bathing trunks; *Vieilli* **c. long** long johns

calédonien, -enne [kaledɔnjɛ̃, -ɛn] **1** *adj* Caledonian
2 *nm,f* C. Caledonian

calembour [kalɑ̃bur] *nm* pun, play on words; **faire des calembours** to make puns

calendes [kalɑ̃d] *nfpl* **renvoyer qch aux c. grecques** to put sth off indefinitely

calendrier [kalɑ̃drije] *nm* (**a**) *(système, tableau)* calendar (**b**) *(de voyage, de travail)* timetable

cale-pied (*pl* cale-pieds) [kalpje] *nm* toe clip

calepin [kalpɛ̃] *nm* (**a**) *(carnet)* notebook (**b**) *Belg (serviette)* briefcase

caler¹ [kale] **1** *vt* (**a**) *(meuble, porte)* to wedge; *(roue)* to chock; *(chargement)* to secure; **c. un malade avec des coussins** to prop up a patient with cushions (**b**) *Fam (remplir)* **ça cale (l'estomac)** it fills you up; **je suis calé** I'm full up
2 *vi (moteur)* to stall

3 se caler *vpr (dans un fauteuil)* to settle oneself comfortably

caler² *vi* (**a**) *Fam (abandonner)* to give up (**b**) *Can (se dégarnir)* to have a receding hairline

calfater [kalfate] *vt Naut* to caulk

calfeutrer [kalføtre] **1** *vt* (**a**) *(brèches)* to block up (**b**) *(pièce, fenêtre)* to draught-proof
2 se calfeutrer *vpr (pour avoir chaud)* to make oneself snug; *(pour être seul)* to shut oneself away

calibre [kalibr] *nm* (**a**) *(d'arme à feu, de tuyau, de balle)* calibre; *(d'œufs, de fruits)* grade; *Fig* **sa sœur est d'un autre c.** his sister is of quite a different calibre (**b**) *(outil)* gauge (**c**) *très Fam (revolver)* shooter

calibrer [kalibre] *vt (pièce)* to gauge; *(instrument de mesure)* to calibrate; *Com (œufs, fruits)* to grade

calice¹ [kalis] *nm Rel* chalice; *Fig* **boire le c. jusqu'à la lie** to drain the cup to the dregs

calice² *nm Bot* calyx

calife [kalif] *nm* caliph

Californie [kalifɔrni] *nf* **la C.** California

californien, -enne [kalifɔrnjɛ̃, -ɛn] **1** *adj* Californian
2 *nm,f* C. Californian

califourchon [kalifurʃɔ̃] **à califourchon** *adv* astride; **se mettre à c. sur qch** to sit astride sth

câlin, -e [kɑlɛ̃, -in] **1** *adj* affectionate
2 *nm* cuddle; **faire un c. à qn** to give sb a cuddle

câliner [kɑline] *vt* to cuddle

calisson [kalisɔ̃] *nm* = lozenge-shaped sweet made of marzipan

calleux, -euse [kalø, -øz] *adj* callous

call-girl (*pl* call-girls) [kolgœrl] *nf* call girl

calligramme [kaligram] *nm* calligram

calligraphe [kaligraf] *nmf* calligrapher

calligraphie [kaligrafi] *nf* calligraphy

calmant, -e [kalmɑ̃, -ɑ̃t] *Méd* **1** *adj (pour les nerfs)* sedative; *(pour la douleur)* painkilling
2 *nm (pour les nerfs)* sedative; *(pour la douleur)* painkiller; **sous calmants** under sedation

calmar [kalmar] *nm* squid

calme [kalm] **1** *adj* (**a**) *(personne) (qui garde son sang-froid)* calm; *(tranquille)* quiet (**b**) *(mer)* calm; *(ciel)* clear; **les affaires sont calmes en août** business is quiet in August
2 *nm (absence d'agitation)* calm, calmness; *(sang-froid)* composure; *(du paysage)* peace and quiet; **être au c.** to have peace and quiet; **du c.!** *(taisez-vous)* keep quiet!; *(ne vous affolez pas)* keep calm!; **garder/perdre son c.** to keep/lose one's composure; *Naut* **c. plat** dead calm; **c'est le c. plat dans ma vie sentimentale** my love life is in the doldrums

calmement [kalməmɑ̃] *adv* calmly

calmer [kalme] **1** *vt (personne)* to calm (down); *(craintes)* to calm; *(douleur)* to soothe; *(fièvre)* to reduce; *(soif)* to quench; *(faim)* to appease; *(ardeur, passion)* to cool; *Fig* **c. le jeu** to calm things down
2 se calmer *vpr (personne)* to calm down; *(tempête, vent)* to die down; *(mer)* to become calm; *(pluie)* to ease off; *(douleur, fièvre)* to subside

calomnie [kalɔmni] *nf (en paroles)* slander; *(par écrit)* libel

calomnier [66] [kalɔmnje] *vt (en paroles)* to slander; *(par écrit)* to libel

calomnieux, -euse [kalɔmnjø, -øz] *adj (paroles)* slanderous; *(écrits)* libellous

calorie [kalɔri] *nf* calorie; **régime basses calories** low-calorie diet

calorifère [kalɔrifɛr] **1** *adj* heat-conveying
2 *nm Vieilli* (slow-combustion) stove; *Can* radiator

calorifique [kalɔrifik] *adj* calorific

calorifuge [kalɔrifyʒ] **1** *adj* (heat-)insulating
2 *nm* heat insulation; *(pour chaudière, tuyau)* lagging

calorique [kalɔrik] *adj* calorific

calot [kalo] *nm (coiffure militaire) Br* forage cap, *Am* garrison cap

calotte [kalɔt] *nf* (**a**) *(chapeau rond)* skullcap; *Rel* calotte; *(de chapeau)* crown; *très Fam Péj* **la c.** *(le clergé)* the clergy (**b**) *Fam (gifle)* clout (**c**) *Anat* **c. crânienne** skullcap (**d**) *Géol* **c. glaciaire** ice cap

calque [kalk] *nm (copie)* tracing; *Fig (de poème, de portrait)* exact copy; *(traduction)* calque; **prendre un c. de qch** to make a tracing of sth; **(papier) c.** tracing paper

calquer [kalke] *vt (reproduire)* to trace; *Fig* to copy exactly; **expression calquée sur l'anglais** expression copied from the English; **il calque sa conduite sur celle de son frère** he models his behaviour on his brother's

calumet [kalymɛ] *nm* peace pipe; *Fig* **fumer le c. de la paix** to bury the hatchet

calvados [kalvados] *nm* Calvados

calvaire [kalvɛr] *nm* (**a**) *(du Christ)* calvary; *Fig (épreuve pénible)* ordeal (**b**) *(croix)* calvary

calviniste [kalvinist] *adj & nmf* Calvinist

calvitie [kalvisi] *nf* baldness; **avoir un début de c.** to be starting to go bald; **c. précoce** premature baldness

camaïeu, -x [kamajø] *nm (peinture)* monochrome; *(gravure)* tint drawing; **un c. de bleu** *(papiers peints, vêtements)* different shades of blue

camarade [kamarad] *nmf* friend; *Pol (terme d'adresse)* comrade; **c. de classe** classmate; **c. d'école** school friend

camaraderie [kamaradri] *nf* camaraderie

camber [kãbe] *vt Suisse* to stride over

cambiste [kãbist] *nmf Fin* foreign exchange dealer

Cambodge [kãbɔdʒ] *nm* **le C.** Cambodia

cambodgien, -enne [kãbɔdʒjɛ̃, -ɛn] **1** *adj* Cambodian
2 *nm,f* **C.** Cambodian

cambouis [kãbwi] *nm* dirty oil

cambré, -e [kãbre] *adj (pied)* with a high instep; *(personne)* with an arched back

cambrer [kãbre] **1** *vt (dos, pied)* to arch; **c. la taille** *ou* **les reins** to arch one's back
2 **se cambrer** *vpr* to arch one's back

cambrien, -enne [kãbrijɛ̃, -ɛn] *Géol* **1** *adj* Cambrian
2 *nm* **le C.** the Cambrian period

cambriolage [kãbrijɔlaʒ] *nm* burglary, break-in

cambrioler [kãbrijɔle] *vt (maison, personne) Br* to burgle, *Am* to burglarize

cambrioleur, -euse [kãbrijɔlœr, -øz] *nm,f* burglar

cambrousse [kãbrus], **cambrouse** [kãbruz] *nf Fam* country; **en pleine c.** in the middle of nowhere

cambrure [kãbryr] *nf (du pied, du dos)* arch; **c. des reins** small of the back

cambuse [kãbyz] *nf* (**a**) *Naut* storeroom (**b**) *Fam Vieilli (chambre, maison)* dump, *Br* hole

came¹ [kam] *nf Tech* cam

came² *nf très Fam (drogue)* dope

camé, -e [kame] *très Fam* **1** *adj* high
2 *nm,f* junkie

camée [kame] *nm* cameo

caméléon [kameleɔ̃] *nm aussi Fig* chameleon

camélia [kamelja] *nm* camellia

camelote [kamlɔt] *nf Fam* (**a**) *(pacotille)* junk (**b**) *(marchandise)* stuff

camembert [kamãbɛr] *nm* (**a**) *(fromage)* Camembert (**b**) *(diagramme)* pie-chart

camer [kame] **se camer** *vpr très Fam* to do drugs; **se c. à l'héroïne** to do heroin

caméra [kamera] *nf Cin & TV* camera; **c. cachée** *ou* **invisible** *(émission)* candid camera; **c. de télévision** television camera; **c. Internet** webcam; **c. vidéo** video camera

cameraman [kameraman] *(pl* **cameramans** *ou* **cameramen** [kameramɛn]) *nm Cin & TV* cameraman

Cameroun [kamrun] *nm* **le C.** Cameroon

camerounais, -e [kamrunɛ, -ɛz] **1** *adj* Cameroonian
2 *nm,f* **C.** Cameroonian

Caméscope® [kameskɔp] *nm* camcorder

camion [kamjɔ̃] *nm Br* lorry, *Am* truck; **c. à benne** dump truck; **c. de déménagement** removal van; **c. de dépannage** breakdown truck; **c. frigorifique** *ou* **réfrigéré** refrigerated lorry

camion-benne *(pl* **camions-bennes**) [kamjɔ̃bɛn] *nm* dumper truck

camion-citerne *(pl* **camions-citernes**) [kamjɔ̃sitɛrn] *nm* tanker

camionnette [kamjɔnɛt] *nf* van; **c. de livraison** delivery van

camionneur [kamjɔnœr] *nm* (**a**) *(conducteur) Br* lorry driver, *Am* truck driver (**b**) *(transporteur) Br* haulier, *Am* trucker

camisole [kamizɔl] *nf* (**a**) *Can (tricot de corps) Br* vest, *Am* undershirt (**b**) *(chemise de nuit)* nightshirt (**c**) **c. de force** straitjacket

camomille [kamɔmij] *nf* camomile; *(tisane)* camomile tea

camouflage [kamuflaʒ] *nm Mil* camouflage; *(de la vérité, d'intentions)* disguising; *(de bénéfices)* concealment

camoufler [kamufle] **1** *vt Mil* to camouflage; *(vérité, intentions)* to disguise; *(bénéfices)* to conceal; **c. un meurtre en suicide** to make a murder look like suicide
2 **se camoufler** *vpr* to camouflage oneself

camp [kã] *nm* (**a**) *(campement)* camp; **établir un c.** to pitch camp; **lever le c.** to strike camp; *Fam Fig (partir)* to hit the road; **c. (de vacances)** *Br* (children's) holiday camp, *Am* summer camp; **c. de concentration** concentration camp; **c. de loisirs** holiday camp; **c. de prisonniers** prison camp (**b**) *(parti)* camp, side (**c**) *(de jeux)* side; **faire deux camps** to form two teams

campagnard, -e [kãpaɲar, -ard] *adj* country

campagne [kãpaɲ] *nf* (**a**) *(par opposition à la ville)* country; *(paysage)* countryside; **à la c.** in the country; **en pleine c.** deep in the countryside; **en rase c.** in the open country (**b**) *Mil, Pol & Com* campaign; *Pol* **entrer en c.** to go on the campaign trail; **faire c. pour/contre** to campaign for/against; **partir en c. contre le tabac** to launch an anti-smoking campaign; **c. électorale** election campaign; **c. de presse** press campaign; **c. publicitaire** *ou* **de publicité** advertising campaign

campanile [kɑ̃panil] *nm Archit* bell tower
campanule [kɑ̃panyl] *nf* campanula
campement [kɑ̃pmɑ̃] *nm (installation)* camp; *(lieu)* camping place; **établir un c.** to pitch camp
camper [kɑ̃pe] **1** *vi* (**a**) *(faire du camping)* to camp (**b**) *Fig (chez quelqu'un)* to camp out
 2 *vt* (**a**) *Vieilli* **c. son chapeau sur sa tête** to plant one's hat on one's head (**b**) *(décrire)* to put in context; **c. un personnage** *(sujet: acteur)* to play a part effectively
 3 se camper *vpr* **se c. devant qn** to plant oneself in front of sb
campeur, -euse [kɑ̃pœr, -øz] *nm,f* camper
camphre [kɑ̃fr] *nm* camphor
camphré, -e [kɑ̃fre] *adj* camphorated
camping [kɑ̃piŋ] *nm* (**a**) *(activité)* camping; **faire du c.** to go camping; **c. à la ferme** farm camping; **c. sauvage** unauthorized camping (**b**) *(lieu)* camp site; **c. aménagé** camp site with facilities
camping-car *(pl* **camping-cars**) [kɑ̃piŋkar] *nm* camper
camping-caravaning [kɑ̃piŋkaravaniŋ] *nm* camping-caravanning
Camping-Gaz® [kɑ̃piŋgaz] *nm inv* camping stove
campus [kɑ̃pys] *nm* campus; **habiter sur le c.** to live on campus
camus [kamy] *adj m (nez)* flat
Canada [kanada] *nm* **le C.** Canada
Canadair® [kanadɛr] *nm* fire-fighting plane
canadianisme [kanadjanism] *nm Ling* Canadianism
canadien, -enne [kanadjɛ̃, -ɛn] **1** *adj* Canadian
 2 *nm,f* **C.** Canadian
 3 *nf* **canadienne** *(veste)* sheepskin jacket; *(tente)* ridge tent
canaille [kanaj] **1** *adj (chanson, paroles)* vulgar; *(air)* roguish
 2 *nf (crapule)* scoundrel; **petite c.!** *(à un enfant)* you little devil!
canal, -aux [kanal, -o] *nm* (**a**) *(cours d'eau)* canal; **c. d'irrigation** irrigation canal; **le c. de Panama/de Suez** the Panama/Suez Canal (**b**) *(conduite)* conduit (**c**) *Anat & Bot* duct (**d**) *Rad & TV* channel; *TV* **C.+** = French pay television channel (**e**) *Fig (moyen)* channel; **par le c. de la poste** through the post (**f**) *Com* channel; **c. de distribution** distribution channel

> **Canal+**
> Canal+, France's first private television channel, was established in 1982 and started broadcasting in 1984. It broadcasts programmes that have to be unscrambled using a special decoding unit, although for part of the day its programmes can be seen without this device. Canal+ also plays a prominent role in funding international films.

canalisation [kanalizasjɔ̃] *nf* (**a**) *(conduite)* pipe; *(pour pétrole)* pipeline (**b**) *(de rivière)* canalization
canaliser [kanalize] *vt* (**a**) *(région, rivière)* to canalize (**b**) *(énergie)* to channel; *(trafic, foule)* to direct
canapé [kanape] *nm* (**a**) *(meuble)* sofa, couch; **c. convertible** sofa bed; **c. deux places** two-seater sofa (**b**) *(pour l'apéritif)* canapé
canapé-lit *(pl* **canapés-lits**) [kanapeli] *nm* sofa bed
canaque [kanak] **1** *adj* Kanak *(of New Caledonia)*
 2 *nmf* **C.** Kanak *(from New Caledonia)*

canard [kanar] *nm* (**a**) *(oiseau)* duck; *(mâle)* drake; *Fam* **mon petit c.** my pet; **marcher en c.** to walk with one's feet turned out; **c. laqué** Peking duck; **c. à l'orange** duck à l'orange; **c. sauvage** wild duck (**b**) *Fam (journal)* rag (**c**) *(morceau de sucre)* = sugar lump dipped in coffee or alcoholic drink (**d**) *Mus* false note (**e**) *Can (bouilloire)* kettle
canarder [kanarde] *vt Fam* to snipe at
canari [kanari] *nm* canary
Canaries [kanari] *nfpl* **les (îles) C.** the Canary Islands
canasson [kanasɔ̃] *nm Fam (cheval)* nag
cancan [kɑ̃kɑ̃] *nm* (**a**) **cancans** *(ragots)* gossip (**sur** about) (**b**) *(danse)* cancan
cancaner [kɑ̃kane] *vi* (**a**) *(médire)* to gossip (**sur** about) (**b**) *(canard)* to quack
cancanier, -ère [kɑ̃kanje, -ɛr] *Fam* **1** *adj* gossipy
 2 *nm,f* gossip
cancer [kɑ̃sɛr] *nm* (**a**) *Méd & Fig* cancer; **c. du poumon/du sein** lung/breast cancer; **avoir un c.** to have cancer (**b**) *Astron & Astrol* **le C.** Cancer; **être C.** to be (a) Cancer
cancéreux, -euse [kɑ̃serø, -øz] **1** *adj (tumeur)* cancerous
 2 *nm,f* cancer sufferer
cancérigène [kɑ̃seriʒɛn] *adj* carcinogenic; **produit c.** carcinogen
cancérologie [kɑ̃serɔlɔʒi] *nf* cancerology
cancérologue [kɑ̃serɔlɔg] *nmf* cancer specialist
cancre [kɑ̃kr] *nm Fam* dunce
cancrelat [kɑ̃krəla] *nm* cockroach
candélabre [kɑ̃delabr] *nm (chandelier)* candelabra
candeur [kɑ̃dœr] *nf* guilelessness; **un regard plein de c.** a guileless look
candi [kɑ̃di] *adj m voir* **sucre**
candidat, -e [kɑ̃dida, -at] *nm,f (à un poste)* applicant (**à** for); *(à un examen)* candidate (**à** for); **être c. aux élections** to stand *or* run for election
candidature [kɑ̃didatyr] *nf (aux élections)* candidature; *(à un poste)* application (**à** for); **poser sa c. à un poste** to apply for a post; **c. spontanée** unsolicited application
candide [kɑ̃did] *adj* guileless
candidement [kɑ̃didmɑ̃] *adv* guilelessly
candidose [kɑ̃didoz] *nf Méd* candidiasis
cane [kan] *nf* (female) duck
caneton [kantɔ̃] *nm* (male) duckling
canette¹ [kanɛt] *nf (petite cane)* (female) duckling
canette² = **cannette**
canevas [kanva] *nm* (**a**) *(trame)* canvas (**b**) *(de film, de roman)* outline
caniche [kaniʃ] *nm* poodle
canicule [kanikyl] *nf* heatwave
canif [kanif] *nm* penknife
canin, -e [kanɛ̃, -in] **1** *adj* canine; **exposition canine** dog show
 2 *nf* **canine** canine (tooth)
caniveau, -x [kanivo] *nm* gutter
cannabis [kanabis] *nm* cannabis
cannage [kanaʒ] *nm (partie en rotin)* canework
canne [kan] *nf* (**a**) *(tige)* cane; **c. à pêche** fishing rod; **c. à sucre** sugar cane (**b**) *(pour s'appuyer)* (walking) stick; **c. blanche** white stick (**c**) *très Fam (jambe)* leg, pin (**d**) *Suisse (au hockey sur glace) Br* ice hockey stick, *Am* hockey stick
canné, -e [kane] *adj (chaise)* cane

canneberge [kanbɛrʒ] *nf* cranberry

cannelé, -e [kanle] *adj (colonne)* fluted; *(pneu)* grooved

cannelle [kanɛl] *nf* cinnamon; **bâton de c.** cinnamon stick; **à la c.** cinnamon(-flavoured)

cannellonis [kanɛlɔni] *nmpl* cannelloni

cannelure [kanlyr] *nf (rainure)* groove; *(de colonne)* fluting

cannette [kanɛt] *nf* (**a**) *(petite bouteille)* bottle; *(boîte)* can (**b**) *Tex* spool

cannibale [kanibal] **1** *nmf* cannibal
    2 *adj (pratiques)* cannibalistic; **tribu c.** tribe of cannibals

cannibalisme [kanibalism] *nm* cannibalism

canoë [kanɔe] *nm* canoe; **faire du c.** to go canoeing

canoë-kayak [kanɔekajak] *nm* canoeing

canon¹ [kanɔ̃] *nm* (**a**) *(pièce d'artillerie)* gun; *Hist* cannon (**b**) *(de carabine)* barrel (**c**) *Anciennement (mesure)* = wine measure equivalent to 0.058 l; *Fam* **boire un c.** to have a glass of wine

canon² **1** *nm* (**a**) *Rel & Fig (règle)* canon (**b**) *Mus* canon; **c. à deux/trois voix** canon for two/three voices; **chanter qch en c.** to sing sth in canon (**c**) *Fam (personne)* stunner
    2 *adj inv Fam (beau)* stunning

canonique [kanɔnik] *adj* canonical; *Fig* **être d'un âge c.** to be advanced in years

canoniser [kanɔnize] *vt Rel* to canonize

canonnade [kanɔnad] *nf* gunfire; **une c.** a burst of gunfire

canot [kano] *nm Naut* (**a**) *(petit bateau)* boat; **c. pneumatique** rubber dinghy; **c. de sauvetage** lifeboat (**b**) *Can (canoë)* canoe

canotage [kanɔtaʒ] *nm* boating; *Can (en canoë)* canoeing; **faire du c.** to go boating/canoeing

canoter [kanɔte] *vi Naut* to go boating; *Can (en canoë)* to go canoeing

canotier [kanɔtje] *nm* (**a**) *(rameur)* rower (**b**) *(chapeau)* boater

cantal, -als [kɑ̃tal] *nm* Cantal

cantate [kɑ̃tat] *nf* cantata

cantatrice [kɑ̃tatris] *nf (chanteuse d'opéra)* opera singer; *(de concert)* (concert) singer

cantine [kɑ̃tin] *nf* (**a**) *(réfectoire)* canteen; *(à l'école)* dining hall; **déjeuner à la c.** *(de l'école)* to have school meals (**b**) *(malle)* trunk (**c**) *Suisse (boîte)* lunchbox (**d**) *Suisse (tente)* marquee

cantique [kɑ̃tik] *nm Rel* hymn; **le C. des cantiques** the Song of Solomon

canton [kɑ̃tɔ̃] *nm (en France)* canton *(administrative division of a department)*; *(en Suisse)* canton *(semiautonomous administrative region of Switzerland)*; *Can* **les cantons de l'Est** the Eastern Townships

cantonade [kɑ̃tɔnad] *nf* **à la cantonade** *adv* to everybody present; *(au théâtre)* off

cantonais, -e [kɑ̃tɔnɛ, -ɛz] **1** *adj* Cantonese
    2 *nm,f* **C.** Cantonese
    3 *nm (langue)* Cantonese

cantonal, -e, -aux, -ales [kɑ̃tɔnal, -o] *adj* cantonal; **les (élections) cantonales** the cantonal elections

cantonnement [kɑ̃tɔnmɑ̃] *nm Mil (des troupes)* quartering; *(lieu)* quarters

cantonner [kɑ̃tɔne] **1** *vt* (**a**) *Mil (troupes)* to quarter (**b**) **c. qn dans/à** to confine sb to

2 se cantonner *vpr (se limiter)* **se c. dans/à** to confine oneself to

cantonnier [kɑ̃tɔnje] *nm* roadmender; *Rail* lineman

canular [kanylar] *nm Fam* hoax; **monter un c.** to play a hoax

canule [kanyl] *nf Méd* cannula

canyon [kanjɔ̃] *nm* canyon; **le Grand C.** the Grand Canyon

canyoning [kanjɔniŋ] *nm* canyoning

CAO [seao] *nf Ordinat (abrév* **conception assistée par ordinateur***)* CAD

caoutchouc [kautʃu] *nm* (**a**) *(substance)* rubber; **c. Mousse®** foam rubber; **c. synthétique** synthetic rubber (**b**) *(plante)* rubber plant

caoutchouteux, -euse [kautʃutø, -øz] *adj Péj* rubbery

CAP [seape] *nm (abrév* **certificat d'aptitude professionnelle***)* = vocational training certificate

Cap [kap] *voir* **Le Cap**

cap [kap] *nm* (**a**) *Géog* cape, headland; **passer** *ou* **franchir** *ou* **doubler un c.** to round a cape; **quand on a franchi le c. de la quarantaine** when you've turned forty; **notre usine va passer le c. des mille employés** our factory will soon pass the thousand-employee mark; **le c. de Bonne-Espérance** the Cape of Good Hope; **le c. Horn** Cape Horn (**b**) *Naut & Aviat (direction)* course; **mettre le c. sur...** to set course for...

capable [kapabl] *adj* (**a**) *(susceptible)* **être c. de qch** to be capable of sth; **être c. de faire qch** to be capable of doing sth, to be able to do sth; **il est c. de tout** he's capable of anything; **c. du meilleur comme du pire** capable of the best as well as the worst; **elle est bien c. d'oublier les clefs!** she's quite capable of forgetting the keys! (**b**) *(compétent)* capable, able (**c**) *Jur* competent (**de faire** to do)

capacité [kapasite] *nf* (**a**) *(contenance)* capacity; **c. d'accueil** *(d'un hôtel)* accommodation capacity (**b**) *(aptitude)* ability, capability; **de grandes capacités (intellectuelles)** great intellectual abilities; *Ordinat* **c. d'adressage** address capability; **c. de concentration** attention span; *Ordinat* **c. de mémoire** memory capacity (**c**) *Jur* capacity; **avoir c. pour faire qch** to be (legally) entitled to do sth (**d**) *Univ* **c. en droit** = certificate entitling holder to practise in some branches of the legal profession

cape [kap] *nf (vêtement)* cape; *(plus longue)* cloak; **film/roman de c. et d'épée** swashbuckling film/novel; *Fig* **rire sous c.** to laugh up one's sleeve

capeline [kaplin] *nf (chapeau)* floppy hat

CAPES [kapɛs] *nm (abrév* **certificat d'aptitude au professorat de l'enseignement du second degré***)* = postgraduate teaching certificate

---

CAPES

This is a required qualification for state teachers in France. Candidates who pass this competitive exam become "professeurs certifiés" and are entitled to teach in secondary education.

CAPET [kapɛt] *nm (abrév* **certificat d'aptitude au professorat de l'enseignement technique***)* = postgraduate technical teaching certificate

capétien, -enne [kapesjɛ̃, -ɛn] **1** *adj* Capetian
    2 *nmpl* **les Capétiens** the Capetians

capharnaüm [kafarnaɔm] *nm Fam (pièce en désordre)* pigsty; *(désordre)* mess

capillaire [kapilɛr] **1** *adj* capillary

2 *nm* (**a**) *(plante)* maidenhair (fern) (**b**) *Anat* capillary

capillarité [kapilarite] *nf Phys* capillarity

capilotade [kapilɔtad] **en capilotade** *adv* **j'ai le dos en c.** my back's killing me

capitaine [kapitɛn] *nm* (**a**) *Mil & Naut* captain; *Aviat Br* flight lieutenant, *Am* captain; **c. de gendarmerie** police superintendent; **c. des pompiers** fire chief; **c. de port** harbour master (**b**) *Sport* captain

capitainerie [kapitɛnri] *nf* harbour master's office

capital, -e, -aux, -ales [kapital, -o] **1** *adj* (**a**) *(essentiel)* major; **il est c. qu'il soit présent à la réunion** it is essential for him to be at the meeting (**b**) *Typ* **lettre capitale** capital letter

2 *nm Fin* capital; *Fig (culturel, artistique)* wealth; **posséder un c.** to have some capital; **capitaux propres** equity; **c. social** (issued) share capital

3 *nf* **capitale** (**a**) *(ville)* capital (city) (**b**) *Typ* capital; **écrire en capitales d'imprimerie** to write in block letters

capitalisable [kapitalizabl] *adj (intérêts)* capitalizable

capitalisation [kapitalizasjɔ̃] *nf (d'intérêts)* capitalization

capitaliser [kapitalize] **1** *vt (intérêts)* to capitalize

2 *vi* (**a**) *Fin* to save (**b**) **c. sur qch** *(jouer sur)* to capitalize on sth

capitalisme [kapitalism] *nm* capitalism; **c. sauvage** ruthless capitalism

capitaliste [kapitalist] *adj & nmf* capitalist

capite [kapit] *nf Suisse (dans un vignoble, un jardin)* shed

capiteux, -euse [kapitø, -øz] *adj (vin, parfum)* heady; *(charme)* sensuous; *(femme)* alluring

capitonnage [kapitɔnaʒ] *nm (action, matière)* padding, stuffing

capitonné, -e [kapitɔne] *adj (siège, cellule)* padded

capitulation [kapitylasjɔ̃] *nf* surrender; **c. sans conditions** unconditional surrender

capituler [kapityle] *vi* to surrender

caporal, -aux [kapɔral, -o] *nm Mil Br* lance corporal, *Am* private first class

capot¹ [kapo] *nm Aut Br* bonnet, *Am* hood; *Aviat (de moteur d'avion)* cowl; *Naut (bâche)* tarpaulin; *Ordinat* **c. d'imprimante** printer hood

capot² *adj inv* **être c.** *(aux cartes)* to have made no tricks at all

capote [kapɔt] *nf* (**a**) *Aut (de décapotable) Br* hood, *Am* top; **baisser la c.** to put the hood down (**b**) *Mil (manteau)* greatcoat (**c**) *Fam* **c. (anglaise)** rubber

capoté, -e [kapɔte] *adj Can Fam* annoyed

capoter [kapɔte] *vi Naut* to capsize; *Aut & Aviat* to overturn; *Fig (échouer) (projet)* to fall through

cappuccino [kaputʃino] *nm* cappuccino

câpre [kɑpr] *nf* caper

caprice [kapris] *nm* (**a**) *(fantaisie)* whim, caprice; **on lui passe tous ses caprices** they indulge her every whim; **par un c. du destin** by a whim of fate (**b**) *(crise de colère)* tantrum; **faire un c.** to throw a tantrum

capricieux, -euse [kaprisjø, -øz] *adj (personne, courant, vent)* capricious; *(moteur)* temperamental; *(temps)* changeable

capricorne [kaprikɔrn] *nm* (**a**) *(insecte)* capricorn beetle (**b**) *Astron & Astrol* **le C.** Capricorn; **être C.** to be (a) Capricorn

caprin, -e [kaprɛ̃, -in] *adj Zool* goat, *Spéc* caprine

capsule [kapsyl] *nf* (**a**) *Anat, Bot & Méd* capsule (**b**) *(de bouteille)* cap, top (**c**) **c. (spatiale)** (space) capsule

capter [kapte] *vt* (**a**) *(l'attention de quelqu'un)* to gain, to capture (**b**) *(courant électrique)* to pick up; *(eaux)* to harness (**c**) *Rad & Tél (messages, station)* to pick up

capteur [kaptœr] *nm Phys* sensor; *Ordinat* **c. photosensible** photosensitive sensor; **c. solaire** solar panel

captif, -ive [kaptif, -iv] *adj & nm,f* captive

captivant, -e [kaptivɑ̃, -ɑ̃t] *adj* captivating

captiver [kaptive] *vt* to captivate

captivité [kaptivite] *nf* captivity; **en c.** in captivity

capture [kaptyr] *nf* (**a**) *(d'un ennemi, d'un animal)* capture (**b**) *(proie)* catch (**c**) *Ordinat* **c. vidéo** video capture

capturer [kaptyre] *vt* to capture

capuche [kapyʃ] *nf* hood; *(de poche)* rainhood

capuchon [kapyʃɔ̃] *nm* (**a**) *(de manteau)* hood; *(de moine)* cowl (**b**) *(de stylo, de tube de dentifrice)* cap, top; *(de cheminée)* cowl

capucine [kapysin] *nf* nasturtium

capverdien, -enne [kapvɛrdjɛ̃, -ɛn] **1** *adj* of Cape Verde

2 *nm,f* **C.** = person from Cape Verde

Cap-Vert [kapvɛr] *nm* **le C., les îles du C.** Cape Verde

caquelon [kaklɔ̃] *nm* fondue dish

caquet [kakɛ] *nm* (**a**) *(de poules)* cackle (**b**) *Fam (bavardage)* prattle; **quel c. elle a!** she doesn't half prattle on!; **rabattre** *ou* **rabaisser le c. à qn** to shut sb up

caqueter [42] [kakte] *vi* (**a**) *(poule)* to cackle (**b**) *Fam (bavarder)* to prattle

car¹ [kar] *conj* for, because

car² *nm (véhicule)* bus, *Br* coach; **c. de police** police van; **c. de ramassage scolaire** school bus

carabine [karabin] *nf* rifle; **c. à air comprimé** air gun

carabiné, -e [karabine] *adj Fam (vent)* stiff; *(orage, fièvre)* violent; *(rhume)* stinking

carabinier [karabinje] *nm* (**a**) *(en Espagne)* frontier guard (**b**) *(en Italie)* carabiniere (**c**) *Hist* carabineer

Caracas [karakas] *n* Caracas

caraco [karako] *nm* camisole

caracoler [karakɔle] *vi (cheval)* to caracole; *Fam (sautiller)* to prance about; **c. en tête des sondages** to be riding high in the opinion polls

caractère [karaktɛr] *nm* (**a**) *(nature)* character, nature; *(détermination, style)* character; **avoir du c.** to have character; **avoir bon c.** to be good-natured; **avoir mauvais** *ou* **sale c.** to be bad-tempered; *Fam* **avoir un c. de cochon** to have a foul temper; **ce n'est pas dans son c. de...** it's not in his nature to... (**b**) *(attribut)* characteristic, feature; *(aspect)* nature, character; **publication à c. officiel** publication of an official nature; *Biol* **c. héréditaire/acquis** hereditary/acquired characteristic (**c**) *(signe)* character, letter; *Typ* **caractères** *(en métal)* type; **en petits caractères** in small print; **écrivez en caractères d'imprimerie** *(sur formulaire)* write in block letters (**d**) *Ordinat* character; **c. de changement de ligne** line feed character; **c. de changement de page** page break character; **c. de contrôle** control character; **c. d'effacement** delete character; **c. imprimable** printable character; **c. d'interruption** break character; **c. en mode point**

bitmap character; **c. de retour arrière** backspace character; **c. à sept bits** seven-bit character

caractériel, -elle [karakterjɛl] *Psy* **1** *adj (troubles)* emotional; **enfant c.** problem child

 2 *nm,f* emotionally disturbed person; *(enfant)* problem child

caractérisé, -e [karakterize] *adj* **une rougeole caractérisée** a clear case of measles; **c'est de la méchanceté caractérisée** it's sheer spite

caractériser [karakterize] **1** *vt* to characterize; **avec la bonté qui la caractérise, elle...** with characteristic kindness, she...

 2 se caractériser *vpr* **se c. par** to be characterized by

caractéristique [karakteristik] **1** *adj* characteristic (**de** of)

 2 *nf (particularité)* characteristic, feature; **caractéristiques** *(d'une voiture, d'un avion)* specifications

carafe [karaf] *nf* (**a**) *(pour le vin, l'eau)* carafe; *(pour le whisky)* decanter (**b**) *Fam* **rester en c.** to be (left) stranded

carafon [karafɔ̃] *nm (pour le vin)* small carafe; *(pour le whisky)* small decanter

Caraïbes [karaib] *nfpl* **les C.** the Caribbean

carambolage [karɑ̃bɔlaʒ] *nm* (multiple) pile-up

caramboler [karɑ̃bɔle] **se caramboler** *vpr Fam* to collide

caramel [karamɛl] *nm (sucre brûlé)* caramel; **des caramels** *(mous)* fudge; *(durs)* toffees

caraméliser [karamelize] **1** *vt* (**a**) *(sucre)* to caramelize (**b**) *(mets, moule)* to coat with caramel

 2 *vi* to caramelize

 3 se caraméliser *vpr (sucre, oignons)* to caramelize

carapace [karapas] *nf aussi Fig* shell

carapater [karapate] **se carapater** *vpr Fam* to beat it

carat [kara] *nm* carat; **or (à) 18 carats** 18-carat gold; *Fam* **tu as jusqu'à trois heures, dernier c.** you've got until three o'clock at the latest

caravanage [karavanaʒ] = **caravaning**

caravane [karavan] *nf* (**a**) *(de tourisme)* caravan, *Am* trailer (**b**) *(du désert)* caravan

caravaning [karavaniŋ] *nm* caravanning; **faire du c.** to go caravanning

carbonate [karbɔnat] *nm Chim* carbonate; **c. de soude** sodium carbonate; *(dans le commerce)* washing soda

carbone [karbɔn] *nm Chim* carbon; **c. 14** carbon-14; **datation au c. 14** carbon dating; **(papier) c.** carbon (paper)

carbonique [karbɔnik] *adj* carbonic; **gaz c.** carbon dioxide; **neige c.** dry ice

carbonisé, -e [karbɔnize] *adj (nourriture)* burnt to a cinder; *(corps)* charred; **mourir c.** to burn to death

carburant [karbyrɑ̃] *nm* fuel

carburateur [karbyratœr] *nm Aut* carburettor

carbure [karbyr] *nm Chim* carbide; **c. d'hydrogène** hydrogen carbide

carburer [karbyre] *vi* (**a**) *(moteur)* **mal c.** to be badly tuned (**b**) *Fam* **ça carbure ici** everyone here's working like mad; **il carbure au café** coffee keeps him going

carcajou [karkaʒu] *nm* wolverine

carcan [karkɑ̃] *nm Fig* yoke; **le c. des horaires** scheduling constraints; **le c. des conventions** the straitjacket of convention

carcasse [karkas] *nf* (**a**) *(d'animal mort)* carcass; *Fam (de personne)* body (**b**) *(de maison, de bateau)* shell; **à c. radiale** *(pneu)* radial-ply

carcéral, -e, -aux, -ales [karseral, -o] *adj* prison

carcinogène [karsinɔʒɛn] *adj Méd* carcinogenic

cardan [kardɑ̃] *nm* universal joint

carder [karde] *vt* to card

cardiaque [kardjak] **1** *adj (arrêt, massage)* cardiac; **être c.** to have a heart condition

 2 *nmf* person with a heart condition

cardigan [kardigɑ̃] *nm* cardigan

cardinal, -e, -aux, -ales [kardinal, -o] **1** *adj (point, nombre, vertu)* cardinal

 2 *nm (religieux)* cardinal

cardiologie [kardjɔlɔʒi] *nf* cardiology

cardiologue [kardjɔlɔg] *nmf* cardiologist

cardio-training [kardjɔtreniŋ] *nm* cardio-training, CV training

cardio-vasculaire *(pl* **cardio-vasculaires**) [kardjɔvaskylɛr] *adj* cardiovascular

carême [karɛm] *nm* (**a**) *(période)* **le c.** Lent (**b**) *(jeûne)* fast; **faire c.** to fast

carence [karɑ̃s] *nf (manque)* deficiency; **c. en vitamine E** vitamin E deficiency; **c. alimentaire** nutritional deficiency; **c. affective** emotional deprivation

carène [karɛn] *nf* hull

caréner [34] [karene] *vt* (**a**) *Naut* to careen (**b**) *Aviat & Aut* to streamline

caressant, -e [karɛsɑ̃, -ɑ̃t] *adj* affectionate; **d'une voix caressante** affectionately

caresse [karɛs] *nf* caress; **faire des caresses à** *(personne)* to caress; *(animal)* to stroke

caresser [karese] *vt (personne)* to caress; *(animal)* to stroke; *Fig (espoir, rêve)* to cherish

car-ferry *(pl* **car-ferrys**) [karferi] *nm* car ferry

cargaison [kargɛzɔ̃] *nf* cargo; *Fam* **il est arrivé avec une c. de cadeaux** he arrived weighed down with presents

cargo [kargo] *nm Naut* freighter

cariatide [karjatid] *nf* caryatid

caribou [karibu] *nm* caribou

caricatural, -e, -aux, -ales [karikatyral, -o] *adj (récit, description)* caricatured

caricature [karikatyr] *nf* caricature

caricaturer [karikatyre] *vt* to caricature

caricaturiste [karikatyrist] *nmf* caricaturist

caricole [karikɔl] *Belg* periwinkle

carie [kari] *nf* **c. (dentaire)** tooth decay, *Spéc* dental caries; **avoir une c.** to have a cavity

carié, -e [karje] *adj* decayed

carier [66] [karje] **se carier** *vpr* to rot, to decay

carillon [karijɔ̃] *nm* (**a**) *(sonnerie)* chimes; **c. électrique** doorbell (**b**) *(ensemble de cloches)* bells (**c**) *(horloge)* chiming clock

carillonner [karijɔne] **1** *vi (cloches)* to chime; **c. à la porte** to ring the (door)bell loudly

 2 *vt (air)* to chime; *(fête religieuse)* to announce with a peal of bells

carioca [karjɔka] **1** *adj* of Rio de Janeiro

 2 *nmf* **C.** person from Rio de Janeiro

caritatif, -ive [karitatif, -iv] *adj* charitable; **association caritative** charity

carlingue [karlɛ̃g] *nf* (**a**) *Aviat* cabin (**b**) *Naut* keelson

carmélite [karmelit] *nf* Carmelite (nun)

carmin [karmɛ̃] **1** *nm* carmine
  2 *adj inv* **(rouge) c.** carmine, crimson
carnage [karnaʒ] *nm* carnage
carnassier, -ère [karnasje, -ɛr] **1** *adj (animal)* flesh-eating; *Fig (sourire)* cruel
  2 *nm* carnivore
carnaval, -als [karnaval] *nm* carnival; **un masque de c.** a carnival mask
carnet [karnɛ] *nm* **(a)** *(cahier)* notebook; *(de tickets de métro)* = book of ten tickets; *Scol* **c. (de notes)** report card; **c. d'adresses** address book; **c. de chèques** cheque book; *Scol* **c. de correspondance** = book of forms to be completed by parents of schoolchildren in the event of absence; *Journ* **c. mondain** society column; *Journ* **c. rose** births column; **c. de santé** health record; **c. de timbres** book of stamps **(b)** *Fin* **c. de banque** bank book, *Br* savings book; *Belg & Suisse* **c. d'épargne** *(livret d'épargne)* savings account
carnivore [karnivɔr] **1** *adj (animal)* carnivorous
  2 *nm* carnivore
Caroline [karɔlin] *nf* **la C. du Nord/du Sud** North/South Carolina
carolingien, -enne [karɔlɛ̃ʒjɛ̃, -ɛn] **1** *adj* Carolingian
  2 *nmpl* **les Carolingiens** the Carolingians
carotène [karɔtɛn] *nm* carotene
carotide [karɔtid] *nf* carotid
carotte [karɔt] **1** *nf* **(a)** *(légume)* carrot; *Suisse* **c. rouge** beetroot; **la c. et ou ou le bâton** the carrot and the stick; *Fam* **les carottes sont cuites** you've/he's/*etc* had it **(b)** *(enseigne)* tobacconist's sign
  2 *adj inv* **cheveux (roux) c.** carroty hair
carotter [karɔte] *vt Fam (objet, argent)* to pinch, *Br* to nick; **il m'a carotté 50 euros** he cheated me out of 50 euros
caroube [karub] *nf* carob (bean)
Carpates [karpat] *nfpl* **les C.** the Carpathians
carpe¹ [karp] *nm Anat* carpus
carpe² *nf* carp
carpette [karpɛt] *nf* rug; *Fam Péj* **c'est une vraie c.** he's a doormat
carquois [karkwa] *nm* quiver
carre [kar] *nf (de patin, de ski)* edge
carré, -e [kare] **1** *adj* **(a)** *(figure, jardin, visage)* square; *(épaules)* square, broad **(b)** *Math* **10 mètres carrés** 10 square metres **(c)** *(tranché) (personne)* straightforward; **être c. en affaires** to be straightforward in one's business dealings
  2 *nm* **(a)** *(forme)* square; *Can (place)* (public) square; **c. de soie** silk scarf; *Naut* **c. des officiers** wardroom; **c. de valets** *(aux cartes)* four jacks; **avoir une coupe au c. ou un c.** to have one's hair in a bob; *Fam* **faire la tête au c. à qn** to punch sb's face in **(b)** *Math (d'un nombre)* square; **élever au c.** to square; **le c. de six, six au c.** six squared **(c)** *Culin* **c. d'agneau** rack of lamb **(d)** *Rail* **c. Jeunes** = reduced-rate railcard for young people within France
carreau, -x [karo] *nm* **(a)** *(motif)* square; *(sur du tissu)* check; **tissu à carreaux** check(ed) material **(b)** *(de céramique)* tile **(c)** *(vitre)* (window) pane; *Fam* **carreaux** *(lunettes)* specs, glasses **(d)** *(carte)* diamond; *(couleur)* diamonds; *Fam* **se tenir à c.** to keep a low profile **(e)** *(locutions) Fam* **rester sur le c.** *(être tué)* to be killed; *(être blessé)* to be badly injured; *(être éliminé)* to be given the boot
carreauté, -e [karɔte] *adj Can (chemise)* check(ed)

carrefour [karfur] *nm* **(a)** *(croisement)* crossroads *(singulier)*; *Fig* **être à un c.** to be at a crossroads **(b)** *(réunion)* forum
carrelage [karlaʒ] *nm (carreaux)* tiles; *(sol)* (tiled) floor
carreler [42] [karle] *vt* to tile
carrelet [karlɛ] *nm* plaice
carreleur [karlœr] *nm* tiler
carrément [karemɑ̃] *adv Fam* **(a)** *(franchement)* straight out; **vas-y c.** get on with it **(b)** *(très)* really; **c'était c. immangeable** it was absolutely inedible
carrière¹ [karjɛr] *nf (profession)* career; **faire c. (dans)** to make a career (in)
carrière² *nf (lieu)* quarry
carriériste [karjerist] *nmf Péj* careerist
carriole [karjɔl] *nf* **(a)** *(petite charrette)* light cart **(b)** *Can* sleigh, sled
carrossable [karɔsabl] *adj (chemin, route)* suitable for motor vehicles
carrosse [karɔs] *nm* **(a)** *(véhicule)* (horse-drawn) coach **(b)** *Can (voiture d'enfant) Br* pram, *Am* baby carriage
carrosser [karɔse] *vt* to fit the body to; **une voiture bien carrossée** a sturdily built car
carrosserie [karɔsri] *nf (de voiture)* bodywork
carrossier [karɔsje] *nm* coachbuilder
carrousel [karuzɛl] *nm* **(a)** *(d'une aérogare)* carousel **(b)** *Can, Belg & Suisse (manège)* merry-go-round
carrure [karyr] *nf (de personne)* build; *(de vêtement)* width across the shoulders; **un homme à la forte c.** a broad-shouldered man; *Fig* **un homme d'une c. exceptionnelle** a man of exceptional qualities; **elle est d'une autre c. que son prédécesseur** she is of quite a different calibre from her predecessor
cartable [kartabl] *nm* school bag
carte [kart] *nf* **(a)** *(géographique)* map; *Naut* chart; **faire la c. d'une région** to map (out) an area; *Astrol* **c. du ciel** astronomical chart; **c. d'état-major** *Br* ≃ Ordnance Survey map, *Am* ≃ Geological Survey map; **c. routière** road map
  (b) *(carton)* card; **c. (à jouer)** (playing) card; **jouer aux cartes** to play cards; **donner les cartes** to deal (the cards); *Fig* **donner c. blanche à qn** to give sb carte-blanche; *Fig* **jouer cartes sur table** to put one's cards on the table; **c. d'anniversaire** birthday card; **c. maîtresse** trump card; **c. postale** postcard; **c. de visite** *Br* visiting *or Am* calling card; **c. de vœux** greetings card
  (c) *(document officiel)* card; **c. d'abonnement** *(de bibliothèque)* library card; *(de transports, de théâtre)* season ticket; **c. d'adhérent** membership card; **c. d'électeur** voting card; **c. d'embarquement** boarding pass; **c. d'étudiant** student card; **c. de fidélité** loyalty card; *Aut* **c. grise** ≃ (vehicle) registration document; **c. d'identité** identity card; *Rail* **c. Jeunes** = reduced-rate railcard for young people, valid in certain European countries; **C. Orange** *(à Paris)* = combined monthly season ticket for the underground, bus and suburban train; **c. de presse** press card; **c. de Sécurité sociale** ≃ National Insurance Card; **c. de séjour** residence permit; *Rail* **C. Vermeil** = reduced-rate railcard for people over sixty within France; *Aut* **c. verte** green card
  (d) *(document informatisé)* card; **c. bancaire** bank card; **c. Bleue®** debit card, *Br* ≃ Switch® card; **c. de crédit** credit card; **c. de paiement** payment card; **c. à**

puce smart card; **c. de téléphone** phonecard
(**e**) *(de restaurant)* menu; **manger à la c.** to eat à la
carte; **c. des vins** wine list
(**f**) *Ordinat* card; *(de clavier)* map; **c. accélératrice**
accelerator card; **c. à circuit imprimé** *ou* **de circuits
imprimés** printed circuit board, PCB; **c. à circuit(s) in-
tégré(s)** integrated circuit card, IC card; **c. d'extension** expansion card *or* board; **c. mémoire** memory
card; **c. mère** motherboard; **c. modem** modem card;
c. de polices de caractères font card; **c. processeur**
processor card; **c. réseau** network card; **c. SCSI** SCSI
card; **c. son** *ou* **sonore** sound card; **c. unité centrale**
CPU board; **c. vidéo** video card; **c. vocale** voice card
carte-adaptateur *(pl* **cartes-adaptateurs)** [kart-
adaptatœr] *nf Ordinat* **c. réseau** network adaptor card
cartel [kartɛl] *nm Écon* cartel; **c. de l'acier/de la drogue** steel/drug cartel
carte-lettre *(pl* **cartes-lettres)** [kartəlɛtr] *nf* letter-
card
carter [kartɛr] *nm (d'engrenages)* casing; *(de bicyclette)*
chain guard; *Aut (de vilebrequin)* crankcase
carte-réponse *(pl* **cartes-réponses)** [kartrepɔ̃s] *nf*
reply card
carterie [kartəri] *nf* card shop
cartésien, -enne [kartezjɛ̃, -ɛn] *adj* (**a**) *Math* Car-
tesian (**b**) *(logique)* logical
carte-vue *(pl* **cartes-vues)** [kartəvy] *nf Belg* (picture)
postcard
cartilage [kartilaʒ] *nm* cartilage
cartilagineux, -euse [kartilaʒinø, -øz] *adj* cartilagin-
ous; *(viande)* gristly
cartographe [kartɔgraf] *nmf* cartographer
cartographie [kartɔgrafi] *nf* cartography
cartomancien, -enne [kartɔmɑ̃sjɛ̃, -ɛn] *nm,f* fortune-teller *(who uses cards)*
carton [kartɔ̃] *nm* (**a**) *(matière)* cardboard; *(feuille)*
piece of cardboard; **c. d'invitation** invitation (card);
c. jaune/rouge *(au football)* yellow/red card (**b**)
(boîte) (cardboard) box; **faire des cartons** to pack
one's things up in cardboard boxes; **c. à chapeau(x)**
hatbox (**c**) *Art (dessin)* cartoon, sketch; **c. à dessin**
portfolio (**d**) *(locutions)* **faire un c.** *(au tir)* to have a
shot; *Fam (sur quelqu'un)* to shoot somebody; *Fam (à
un examen)* to pass with flying colours; *Fam Scol* **(se)
prendre un c.** *(une mauvaise note)* to get a bad mark
cartonner [kartɔne] **1** *vt (livre)* to case; **livre cartonné**
hardback (book)
2 *vi Fam* (**a**) *(à l'école)* to get excellent marks (**en** in)
(**b**) *(musique)* to be mind-blowing
cartonneux, -euse [kartɔnø, -øz] *adj* like cardboard
carton-pâte [kartɔ̃pɑt] *nm* pasteboard
cartouche [kartuʃ] *nf (de fusil, de stylo, d'imprimante)*
cartridge; *(de cigarettes)* carton; *Ordinat* **c. Zip**® Zip®
disk
cartouchière [kartuʃjɛr] *nf* cartridge belt
caryatide [karjatid] = **cariatide**
cas [kɑ] *nm* (**a**) *(situation)* case, situation; *Jur & Méd*
case; **c. particulier** exception; **envisager tous les c.
possibles** to consider all the possibilities; **examiner
qch au c. par c.** to examine sth on a case by case basis; **c'est le c. de le dire** you can say that again; **en
pareil c.** in a similar situation; **si tel est votre c.** if that
applies to you; **il parle trois langues mais ce n'est pas
mon c.** he speaks three languages but I don't; *Fam*
c'est un c.! he is a case!; **un c. social** a person with
social problems

(**b**) *Gram* case
(**c**) *(locutions)* **en aucun c.** under no circumstances,
on no account; **en tout c., dans tous les c.** in any
case, anyway; **dans ce c.** *(puisqu'il en est ainsi)* in that
case; **dans tous les c. de figure** in all cases; **le c.
échéant** if necessary, if need be; **selon le c.** as the
case may be; **en c. d'urgence** in an emergency; **en c.
de besoin** if need be; **j'ai pris un pull supplémentaire
en c. de besoin** I took an extra sweater just in case; **au
c. où il viendrait** in case he comes; *Fam* **je te le laisse
au c. où** I'll leave it for you just in case; **faire grand c.
de qn/qch** to have a high opinion of sb/sth; **faire peu
de c. de qch** to have a low opinion of sth; **ne faire aucun c. de qch** to take no notice of sth
Casablanca [kazablɑ̃ka] *n* Casablanca
casanier, -ère [kazanje, -ɛr] *adj* home-loving; *Péj*
stay-at-home
casaque [kazak] *nf (de jockey)* blouse; *Fig* **tourner c.**
(partir) to turn tail; *(changer d'opinion)* to change
sides
cascade [kaskad] *nf* (**a**) *(chute d'eau)* waterfall; *Fig* **des
rires en c.** peals of laughter; *Ordinat* **ouvrir des fenêtres en c.** to cascade windows (**b**) *(au cinéma)* stunt
cascadeur, -euse [kaskadœr, -øz] *nm,f* stuntman, *f*
stuntwoman
case [kɑz] *nf* (**a**) *(de tiroir)* compartment; *(de formulaire)* box; *(de mots croisés, de damier)* square; *Fam* **il
lui manque une c., il a une c. de vide** he's got a screw
loose; **c. départ** *(dans les jeux)* start; *Fig* **retour à la c.
départ** back to square one (**b**) *(hutte)* hut (**c**) *Ordinat*
button; *(en forme de boîte)* box (**d**) *Suisse* **c. (postale)**
postbox
casemate [kazmat] *nf* blockhouse
caser [kɑze] **1** *vt* (**a**) *(placer)* to fit in (**b**) *Fam* **c. qn** *(établir)* to fix sb up with a job; *(marier)* to marry sb off
2 se caser *vpr Fam (trouver un emploi)* to get oneself
a job; *(se marier)* to get married and settle down
caserne [kazɛrn] *nf* barracks; **c. de pompiers** fire
station
cash [kaʃ] *adv Fam* **payer c.** to pay cash (down)
cash-flow *(pl* **cash-flows)** [kaʃflo] *nm Com* cash flow
casier [kazje] *nm* (**a**) *(compartiment)* compartment;
(pour le courrier) pigeonhole; *(à vêtements)* locker; **c.
à bouteilles** bottle rack (**b**) *Jur* **c. judiciaire** police *or*
criminal record; **avoir un c. (judiciaire)** to have a record (**c**) *(pour pêcher)* pot; **casiers à homards** lobster
pots
casino [kazino] *nm* casino
Caspienne [kaspjɛn] *adj f voir* **mer**
casque [kask] *nm* (**a**) *(de soldat, de pompier)* helmet;
(de motocycliste) (crash) helmet; **le port du c. est obligatoire** *(sur panneau)* safety helmets must be worn;
c. intégral full-face crash helmet; **les Casques bleus**
the Blue Berets (**b**) *(écouteurs)* headphones, headset
(**c**) *(de salon de coiffure)* hood hairdryer
casqué, -e [kaske] *adj* helmeted
casquer [kaske] *vi Fam (payer)* to fork out
casquette [kaskɛt] *nf* cap
cassable [kasabl] *adj* breakable
cassant, -e [kasɑ̃, -ɑ̃t] *adj* brittle; *Fig (personne, ton)*
brusque
cassation [kasasjɔ̃] *nf Jur* annulment
casse¹ [kas] *nf Typ* case; **bas/haut de c.** lower/upper
case
casse² *nf* (**a**) *(action de casser)* **il va y avoir de la c.**
something will get broken; *Fam (des ennuis)* there'll

be trouble; **aller** *ou* **partir à la c.** *(voiture)* to go for scrap (**b**) *(objets cassés)* breakages

casse³ *nm très Fam (cambriolage)* break-in

cassé, -e [kase] *adj (objet, jambe)* broken; *(voix)* cracked; *très Fam (ivre)* smashed, plastered; *(drogué)* stoned

casse-cou [kasku] **1** *adj inv (personne)* reckless
  2 *nmf inv (personne)* daredevil

casse-croûte [kaskrut] *nm inv* (**a**) *Fam (repas)* snack, bite (**b**) *Can (snack)* snack bar

casse-cul [kasky] *très Fam* **1** *adj inv* damned annoying
  2 *nmf inv* pain in the arse

casse-gueule [kasgœl] *très Fam* **1** *adj inv (endroit)* dangerous; *(entreprise)* risky
  2 *nm inv (endroit)* danger spot; *(entreprise)* risky business

casse-noisettes [kasnwazɛt] *nm inv* nutcrackers

casse-noix [kasnwa] *nm inv* nutcrackers

casse-pieds [kaspje] *Fam* **1** *adj inv* damned annoying; **ce qu'il peut être c.!** he can be a real pain (in the neck)!
  2 *nmf inv* pain (in the neck)

casse-pipe [kaspip] *nm inv Fam* **aller au c.** to go to the front

casser [kase] **1** *vt* (**a**) *(briser)* to break; *(noix)* to crack; *(voix)* to strain; *(chaussures)* to break in; *Fam (personne)* to humiliate; **c. les prix** to slash prices; *aussi Fig* **c. le moral des troupes** to discourage the ranks; *Fig* **c. du sucre sur le dos de qn** to talk about sb behind his/her back; *Fam* **c. la croûte** *ou* **la graine** to have a bite to eat; *Fam* **ça ne casse pas trois pattes à un canard, ça ne casse pas des briques** it's nothing to write home about; *Fam* **c. la baraque** *(pièce, acteur)* to bring the house down; *Fam* **à tout c.** *(au maximum)* at the very most
  (**b**) *Fam (locutions avec parties du corps)* **c. les pieds à qn** *(ennuyer)* to bore the pants off sb; *(agacer)* to get on sb's nerves; **ça fait deux mois qu'elle me casse les pieds pour que j'y aille** she's been bugging me to go for two months now; **c. les oreilles à qn** to deafen sb; **c. la figure** *ou très Fam* **la gueule à qn** to smash sb's face in; *Fam* **c. sa pipe** to kick the bucket; *Vulg* **il nous casse les couilles, il nous les casse** he gets on our tits
  (**c**) *Jur (verdict)* to quash; *(mariage)* to annul; *(fiançailles)* to break off
  2 *vi* (**a**) *(se briser)* to break; **attention, ça casse!** be careful, it's fragile!
  (**b**) *Fam (se séparer)* to split up
  3 se casser *vpr* (**a**) *(se briser)* to break
  (**b**) **se c. une** *ou* **la jambe** to break one's leg; *Fig* **se c. le nez** to fail; *Fig* **se c. la tête** to rack one's brains; *Fam* **se c. la figure** *ou très Fam* **la gueule** *(tomber)* to fall flat on one's face; *(échouer)* to fail
  (**c**) *Fam (se fatiguer)* **il ne s'est pas cassé pour m'aider** he didn't exactly strain himself helping me; *Vulg* **se c. le cul à faire qch** to bust a gut trying to do sth
  (**d**) *Fam (partir)* to split, to clear off; **tu viens? on se casse** we're off, are you coming?; **casse-toi!** get lost!

casserole [kasrɔl] *nf* (**a**) *(de cuisine)* (sauce)pan; *très Fam* **passer à la c.** *(sexuellement)* to be given a good seeing-to; *(être tué)* to get bumped off (**b**) *Fam* **chanter comme une c.** to be a rotten singer

casse-tête [kasɛt] *nm inv* (**a**) *(jeu)* puzzle (**b**) *(problème)* headache

cassette [kasɛt] *nf* (**a**) *(magnétique)* cassette, tape; **enregistrer qch sur c.** to tape sth; **c. vidéo** video

(cassette) (**b**) *Ordinat* **c. à bande magnétique** mag tape cassette

casseur, -euse [kasœr, -øz] *nm,f* (**a**) *(manifestant)* rioter (**b**) *très Fam (cambrioleur)* burglar

cassis [kasis] *nm* (**a**) *(baie)* blackcurrant (**b**) *(arbuste)* blackcurrant bush (**c**) *(liqueur)* blackcurrant liqueur (**d**) *Fam (tête)* nut

cassonade [kasɔnad] *nf* brown sugar

cassoulet [kasulɛ] *nm* cassoulet *(stew of beans, pork, goose etc, a speciality of Languedoc)*

cassure [kasyr] *nf* break; *Géol* fault

castagne [kastaɲ] *nf Fam* fighting; **aimer la c.** *(la bagarre)* to like fighting, *Br* to like a good scrap

castagnettes [kastaɲɛt] *nfpl* castanets; *Fam Fig* **ses dents/genoux jouaient des castagnettes** his teeth were chattering/knees were knocking

caste [kast] *nf* caste

castillan, -e [kastijɑ̃, -an] **1** *adj* Castilian
  2 *nm,f* **C.** Castilian
  3 *nm (langue)* Castilian

Castille [kastij] *nf* **la C.** Castile

casting [kastiŋ] *nm Cin & Théât* casting

castor [kastɔr] *nm* beaver

castrat [kastra] *nm Mus* castrato

castrer [kastre] *vt* to castrate; *(chat, chien)* to neuter

cataclysme [kataklism] *nm* cataclysm

cataclysmique [kataklismik] *adj* cataclysmic

catacombes [katakɔ̃b] *nfpl* catacombs

catadioptre [katadjɔptr] *nm (de véhicule)* reflector; *(sur la route)* cat's-eye®

catafalque [katafalk] *nm* catafalque

catalan, -e [katalɑ̃, -an] **1** *adj* Catalan
  2 *nm,f* **C.** Catalan
  3 *nm (langue)* Catalan

Catalogne [katalɔɲ] *nf* **la C.** Catalonia

catalogue [katalɔg] *nm* catalogue; **faire le c. de** to catalogue; **acheter sur c.** to buy things from a catalogue

cataloguer [katalɔge] *vt* to catalogue; *Fig & Péj* to label

catalyser [katalize] *vt aussi Fig* to catalyse

catalyseur [katalizœr] *nm aussi Fig* catalyst

catalytique [katalitik] *adj Chim* catalytic

catamaran [katamarɑ̃] *nm Naut* catamaran

Cataphote® [katafɔt] = **catadioptre**

cataplasme [kataplasm] *nm* poultice

catapulte [katapylt] *nf* catapult

catapulter [katapylte] *vt* to catapult; *Fig* **c. qn à un poste** to catapult sb into a post

cataracte [katarakt] *nf (maladie, chute d'eau)* cataract

catastrophe [katastrɔf] *nf* disaster, catastrophe; **c. ferroviaire/aérienne** rail/air disaster; **c'est la c.!** it's a disaster!; **c.! il est déjà là!** panic stations! he's here already!; **en c.** *(à toute vitesse)* in a mad rush *or* panic

catastrophé, -e [katastrɔfe] *adj Fam* stunned

catastrophique [katastrɔfik] *adj* disastrous, catastrophic

catch [katʃ] *nm* wrestling; **faire du c.** to wrestle

catcheur, -euse [katʃœr, -øz] *nm,f* wrestler

catéchisme [kateʃism] *nm* catechism

catégorie [kategɔri] *nf* category, type; *(d'hôtel, de personnel)* grade; *(de boxeur)* class; **c. sociale** social class; **c. socioprofessionnelle** socio-professional group

catégorique [kategɔrik] *adj (réponse, refus)* categoric(al); **je suis absolument c., c'est lui** I'm absolutely positive it's him

catégoriquement [kategɔrikmã] *adv* categorically

catégoriser [kategɔrize] *vt* to categorize

Cathares [katar] *nmpl Hist* **les C.** the Cathars

catharsis [katarsis] *nf* catharsis

cathédrale [katedral] *nf* cathedral

cathéter [kateter] *nm Méd* catheter

catho [kato] *adj Fam* Catholic

cathode [katɔd] *nf Élec* cathode

cathodique [katɔdik] *adj Élec* cathodic; **tube c.** cathode ray tube

catholicisme [katɔlisism] *nm* (Roman) Catholicism

catholique [katɔlik] **1** *adj* (Roman) Catholic; *Fam* **ce n'est pas très c.** it's a bit shady
2 *nmf* (Roman) Catholic

catimini [katimini] **en catimini** *adv* on the sly

catin [katɛ̃] *nf* (**a**) *Vieilli (prostituée)* trollop (**b**) *Can (poupée)* doll

catogan [katɔgã] *nm (nœud)* hair ribbon *(for ponytail)*; *(queue de cheval)* ponytail

Caucase [kokaz] *nm* **le C.** the Caucasus

caucasien, -enne [kokazjɛ̃, -ɛn] *adj* Caucasian

cauchemar [kɔʃmar] *nm aussi Fig* nightmare; **une vision de c.** a nightmarish vision; **faire un c.** to have a nightmare

cauchemarder [kɔʃmarde] *vi* to have nightmares

cauchemardesque [kɔʃmardɛsk] *adj* nightmarish

causal, -e, -als *ou* **-aux, -ales** [kozal, -o] *adj* causal

causant, -e [kozã, -ãt] *adj Fam* chatty

cause [koz] *nf* (**a**) *(origine)* cause; **quelle est la c. de son départ?** why is he leaving?; **il s'est mis en colère, et pour c.** he got angry, and with good reason; **fermé pour c. d'inventaire/de décès** *(sur panneau)* closed for stocktaking/due to bereavement; **à c. de** because of
(**b**) *Jur* case; *Fig* **la c. est entendue** there's nothing more to be said; **être en c.** *(sujet à caution)* to be in question; **mettre qch en c.** to doubt sth, to question sth; **mettre qn en c.** *(impliquer)* to implicate sb; **mettre qn hors de c.** to clear sb; **en tout état de c.** in any case
(**c**) *(parti)* cause; **faire c. commune avec qn** to join forces with sb; **c'est pour une bonne c.** it's all in a good cause

causer¹ [koze] *vt (provoquer)* to cause; **c. des ennuis à qn** to cause sb problems

causer² *vi* (**a**) *(parler)* to chat, to talk (**de** about); **c. affaires** to talk business; **c. avec** *ou* **à qn** to chat with sb; *Fam* **je ne lui cause plus!** I'm not talking to him!; *Ironique* **cause toujours(, tu m'intéresses)!** riveting! (**b**) *(cancaner)* to talk, to gossip; **on en cause au village** it's the talk of the village

causerie [kozri] *nf* (**a**) *(discussion)* chat, talk (**b**) *(conférence)* (informal) talk

causette [kozɛt] *nf Fam* little chat; **faire la c.** *ou* **un brin de c. avec qn** to have a little chat with sb

causse [kos] *nm* = limestone plateau in central and southern France

caustique [kostik] *adj aussi Fig* caustic

cautériser [koterize] *vt* to cauterize

caution [kosjõ] *nf* (**a**) *(pour appartement)* deposit; *Jur* bail; *Fig (appui)* support, backing; *Jur* **sous c.** on bail;

sujet à c. *(information)* unconfirmed (**b**) *(personne)* guarantor

cautionner [kosjone] *vt (personne)* to stand surety for; *Jur* to stand bail for; *Fig (approuver)* to support, to back

cavalcade [kavalkad] *nf Fam (bousculade)* stampede

cavale [kaval] *nf Fam (évasion)* escape; **être en c.** to be on the run

cavaler [kavale] *vi Fam (se démener)* to rush around; *(fuir)* to run off; **c. après qn** to chase after sb

cavalerie [kavalri] *nf Mil* cavalry

cavaleur, -euse [kavalœr, -øz] *Fam* **1** *adj (homme)* womanizing; *(femme)* man-chasing
2 *nm,f (homme)* skirt-chaser; *(femme)* man-chaser

cavalier, -ère [kavalje, -ɛr] **1** *adj (manière, personne)* cavalier
2 *nm,f* (**a**) *(à cheval)* rider, horseman, *f* horsewoman (**b**) *(de bal)* partner; *Fig* **faire c. seul** to go it alone
3 *nm* (**a**) *(aux échecs)* knight (**b**) *(accompagnateur)* escort (**c**) *Can (amoureux)* boyfriend (**d**) *Ordinat* jumper

cavalièrement [kavaljɛrmã] *adv* in a cavalier manner

cave¹ [kav] *adj (joues, yeux)* hollow, sunken

cave² *nf* (**a**) *(cellier)* cellar; **c. à charbon/vin** coal/wine cellar; *Fig* **de la c. au grenier** from top to bottom (**b**) *Can (sous-sol)* basement

caveau, -x [kavo] *nm* (**a**) *(petite cave)* small cellar (**b**) *(funéraire)* burial vault

caverne [kavɛrn] *nf* cave, cavern; **homme des cavernes** caveman

caverneux, -euse [kavɛrnø, -øz] *adj (voix)* deep

caviar [kavjar] *nm* caviar

caviarder [kavjarde] *vt* to censor

caviste [kavist] *nm* cellarman

cavité [kavite] *nf* cavity, hollow; **c. buccale** oral cavity

Cayenne [kajɛn]*n* (**a**) *(ville)* Cayenne (**b**) **poivre de C.** cayenne pepper

CB [sibi] *nf (abrév* **citizen band***)* CB

CC [sese] *nm (abrév* **compte courant***)* CA

CCI [sesei] *nf (abrév* **Chambre de commerce et d'industrie***)* Chamber of Commerce and Industry

CCP [sesepe] *nm (abrév* **compte courant postal, compte chèque postal***) Br* ≃ Giro account, *Am* ≃ Post Office checking account

CD [sede] *nm* (**a**) *(abrév* **Compact Disc***)* CD (**b**) *(abrév* **corps diplomatique***)* CD

CDD [sedede] *nm (abrév* **contrat à durée déterminée***)* fixed-term contract

CDI [sedei] *nm inv* (**a**) *(abrév* **centre des impôts***)* tax office (**b**) *(abrév* **contrat à durée indéterminée***)* permanent contract (**c**) *(abrév* **centre de documentation et d'information***)* school library *(with special resources on how to find information)*

CD-I [sedei] *(abrév* **Compact Disc interactif***)* CDI

CD-Rom [sederɔm] *nm inv* CD-Rom; **C. interactif** interactive CD-Rom

CE [seə] **1** *nm* (**a**) *(abrév* **Conseil de l'Europe***)* Council of Europe (**b**) *(abrév* **cours élémentaire***)* **CE1** = second year of primary school; **CE2** = third year of primary school
2 *nf (abrév* **Communauté européenne***)* EC

ce¹ [sə] *pron démonstratif*

ce becomes c' before a vowel.

(**a**) *(pour désigner)* **c'est mon père** that's my father; *(au téléphone)* it's my father; **ce sont** *ou Fam* **c'est mes amis** those are my friends; *(qui arrivent)* there are my friends; **c'était mon idée** it was my idea; **c'est le plus beau jour de ma vie** this is the best day of my life; **c'est moi** it's me; **qui est-ce?**, *Fam* **qui c'est?** who is it?; **c'est lui qui l'a écrit** HE wrote it; **qui a fait ça? – c'est moi!** who did that? – I did!; **c'est un bon traducteur** he's a good translator; **c'est la première voiture que j'aie eue** that was my first car; **c'est ici que je suis né** this is where I was born, I was born here; **c'est jeudi aujourd'hui** today's Thursday, it's Thursday today; **c'était il y a longtemps** it was a long time ago

(**b**) *(pour qualifier ou pour expliquer)* **c'est facile/joli** it's easy/nice; **c'est exact!** that's right!; **c'est que maman est déjà partie** the thing is, Mum's already left; **s'il chante, (alors) c'est qu'il est de bonne humeur** if he's singing, it means he's in a good mood; *Fam* **c'est bizarre qu'il n'ait pas appelé** it's strange that he hasn't called!; *Fam* **ce qu'il est pénible!** he's such a pain!

(**c**) *(avec des pronoms relatifs)* **ce qui..., ce que...** what...; **je sais ce qui s'est passé** I know what happened; **ce que je crois, c'est que...** what I think is...; **voici ce dont il s'agit** this is what it's all about; **voilà ce à quoi j'avais pensé** this is what I thought of; **ce qui compte, c'est que...** what counts is that...; **j'ai appris tout ce qui se trouve dans le chapitre 4** I've learned everything in chapter 4; **j'ai oublié tout ce qu'elle m'a dit** I've forgotten everything she told me; **pour ce qui est de la qualité** with regards to *or* as regards quality

(**d**) *(locutions)* **ce faisant** in so doing, whilst doing so; **il y est allé, et ce malgré mon interdiction** he went despite the fact that I had forbidden him; **sur ce, je m'en vais** on that note, I'm leaving; **... et, sur ce, il sortit son album de photos** ... whereupon he brought out his photo album

ce², **cet**, **cette**, **ces** [sə, sɛt, se] *adj démonstratif*

> **cet** is used before a masculine singular noun or adjective beginning with a vowel or mute h.

(**a**) *(par référence)* **ce garçon** this boy; **cet enfant** this child; **cette fille** this girl; **ces gens/animaux/couleurs** these people/animals/colours (**b**) *(en désignant)* **ce vin-ci** this wine; **ce vin-là** that wine; **ces voitures-ci** these cars; **ces voitures-là** those cars (**c**) *Fam (intensif)* **alors, cette lettre, tu me la montres?** so do I get to see this *or* that letter of yours?; **et ce café, il arrive?** is that coffee on its way or what?; **je lui ai envoyé une de ces lettres!** I wrote him such a letter!; **j'ai une de ces faims!** I'm so hungry!

CEA [seəa] *nm (abrév* **commissariat à l'énergie atomique***)* = French atomic energy commission, *Br* ≃ AEA, *Am* ≃ AEC

ceci [səsi] *pron démonstratif* this; **c. (étant) dit** having said that; **c. n'explique pas cela** that's no explanation

cécité [sesite] *nf* blindness; **être atteint de c.** to be blind

CED [seəde] *nf (abrév* **Communauté européenne de défense***)* EDC

céder [34] [sede] **1** *vt* (**a**) *(donner) (objet, droit)* to give up (**à** to); *(dans un testament)* to leave (**à** to); **c. sa place à qn** to give up one's seat to sb; **c. du terrain** to give ground; **cédez le passage** *(sur panneau) Br* give way, *Am* yield (**b**) *(vendre)* to sell; **à c.** *(sur panneau)* for sale

2 *vi* (**a**) *(plancher, branche)* to give way (**b**) *(se soumettre)* to give in (**devant** to)

3 céder à *vt ind (personne, tentation, revendication)* to give in to

cédérom [sederɔm] *nm Ordinat* CD-Rom

Cedex [sedɛks] *nm (abrév* **Courrier d'entreprise à distribution exceptionnelle***)* = postal code ensuring rapid delivery of business mail

cédille [sedij] *nf* cedilla

cédrat [sedra] *nm (fruit)* citron

cèdre [sɛdr] *nm (arbre, bois)* cedar; **c. du Liban** cedar of Lebanon

CEE [seəə] *nf (abrév* **Communauté économique européenne***)* EEC

CEEA [seəəa] *nf (abrév* **Communauté européenne de l'énergie atomique***)* Euratom

cégep [seʒɛp] *nm Can (abrév* **collège d'enseignement général et professionnel***)* = college of further education

CEI [seəi] *nf (abrév* **Communauté d'États indépendants***)* CIS

ceindre [54] [sɛdr] *vt Litt* (**a**) *(épée)* to strap on (**b**) *(sujet: couronne)* to encircle

ceinture [sɛtyr] *nf* (**a**) *(accessoire)* belt; **être c. noire de judo** to be a black belt in judo; *Fam* **se serrer la c.**, **faire c.** to tighten one's belt; **c. de chasteté** chastity belt; **c. de sécurité** seat belt; **attacher sa c. (de sécurité)** to fasten one's seat belt (**b**) *(taille) (de vêtement)* waistband; *(d'une personne)* waist; **frapper au-dessous de la c.** to hit below the belt (**c**) **la petite C.** = circular bus route around centre of Paris

ceinturer [sɛtyre] *vt* to grab around the waist

ceinturon [sɛtyrɔ̃] *nm* belt

cela [səla, sla] *pron démonstratif* that; **c'est cela!** *(c'est exact)* that's right!; **c'est pour c. que je viens** that's what I've come for *or* why I've come; **il y a deux ans de c.** that was two years ago; **et pourquoi c.?** why is that?; **s'il n'y avait que c.** if that were the only problem; **et avec c.?** *(dans un magasin)* (will there be) anything else?; **c. (étant) dit** having said that

célébration [selebrasjɔ̃] *nf* celebration

célèbre [selɛbr] *adj* famous (**pour** for); **se rendre c. par qch** to become famous for sth; **tristement c.** notorious

célébrer [34] [selebre] *vt* (**a**) *(fêter) (anniversaire, victoire, messe)* to celebrate (**b**) *(vanter)* **c. les mérites/le talent de qn** to extol sb's merits/talent

célébrité [selebrite] *nf (notoriété)* fame; *(personne)* celebrity

céleri [selri] *nm* celery; *Culin* **c. rémoulade** = grated celeriac in mayonnaise

céleri-rave *(pl* **céleris-raves***)* [selrirav] *nm* celeriac

céleste [selɛst] *adj* (**a**) *(du firmament) (phénomènes, corps)* celestial, heavenly (**b**) *Rel* heavenly

célibat [seliba] *nm* single life; *(des prêtres)* celibacy

célibataire [selibatɛr] **1** *adj (non marié)* unmarried, single

2 *nm* bachelor; **un c. endurci** a confirmed bachelor

3 *nf* single woman

celle [sɛl] *voir* **celui**

cellier [selje] *nm* storeroom; *(cave)* cellar

Cellophane® [selɔfan] *nf* cellophane®; **sous C.** cellophane-wrapped

cellulaire [selylɛr] **1** *adj* (**a**) *Biol* cell (**b**) *Jur* **régime c.** solitary confinement (**c**) *Tél* cellular

2 *nm Can Tél* mobile (phone), cellphone

cellule [selyl] *nf* (**a**) *(d'une prison, d'un couvent)* cell; *Hum* **il a passé la nuit en c. de dégrisement** he spent the night in the cells to sober up (**b**) *Biol* cell; **c. nerveuse** nerve cell (**c**) *Fig (élément)* unit; *(de parti politique)* cell (**d**) *Élec* **c. photoélectrique** photoelectric cell

cellulite [selylit] *nf* cellulite

Celluloïd® [selylɔid] *nm* celluloid®

cellulose [selyloz] *nf* cellulose

celte [selt] **1** *adj* Celtic
  2 *nmf* **C.** Celt

celtique [seltik] *adj & nm* Celtic

celui, celle [səlɥi, sɛl] *(mpl* ceux [sø], *fpl* celles*) pron démonstratif* the one; **mon livre et c. de Paul** my book and Paul's; **mes livres et ceux de Paul** my books and Paul's; **c. que je t'ai donné** the one I gave you; **celles dont je t'ai parlé** the ones I talked to you about; **c.-ci** this one; *(ce dernier)* the latter; **c.-là** that one; *(le premier)* the former; **ceux-ci** these ones; *(ces derniers)* the latter; **ceux-là** those ones; *(les premiers)* the former; **ah, c.-là, quel idiot!** he's such an idiot, that one!; **autre exemple, plus technique c.-là** another example, a more technical one this time; **elle est bien bonne, celle-là!** that's a good one!

cendre [sɑ̃dr] *nf* ash(es); **faire cuire des pommes de terre sous la c.** to roast potatoes in the ashes; **réduire qch en cendres** to reduce sth to ashes; **cendres** *(après incinération)* ashes; *Rel* **le mercredi des Cendres** Ash Wednesday

cendré, -e [sɑ̃dre] *adj voir* **blond**

cendrée [sɑ̃dre] *nf Sport (piste)* cinder track; *(mâchefer)* cinders

cendrier [sɑ̃drije] *nm* ashtray

Cendrillon [sɑ̃drijɔ̃] *npr* Cinderella

Cène [sɛn] *nf* **la C.** the Last Supper

censé, -e [sɑ̃se] *adj* **être c. faire qch** to be supposed to do sth

censeur [sɑ̃sœr] *nm* (**a**) *Scol (d'un lycée) Br* deputy head, *Am* assistant principal (**b**) *(dans les médias)* censor (**c**) *Litt (juge)* critic

censure [sɑ̃syr] *nf (activité)* censorship; *(personnes)* (board of) censors

censurer [sɑ̃syre] *vt* (**a**) *(film, livre, scène)* to censor (**b**) *Litt (critiquer)* to censure

cent¹ [sɑ̃] **1** *adj* **a** *or* **one hundred**; **deux cents hommes** two hundred men; **deux c. cinquante** two hundred and fifty; **je te l'ai dit c. fois** I've told you a hundred times; **vous avez c. fois raison** you're absolutely right; *Fam* **je ne vais pas t'attendre (pendant) c. sept ans** I'm not going to wait for you forever; **faire les c. pas** to pace up and down; *Fam* **être aux c. coups** to be frantic; *Fam* **faire les quatre cents coups** to get up to all sorts of tricks
  2 *nm* (**a**) *(nombre)* hundred; a hundred; **pour c.** per cent; **c. pour c.** a hundred per cent; *voir aussi* **trois** (**b**) *(division de l'euro)* cent

cent² [sɛnt] *nm (monnaie)* cent

centaine [sɑ̃tɛn] *nf* **une c. (de)** about a hundred, a hundred or so; **des centaines de livres** hundreds of books; **plusieurs centaines de personnes** several hundred people

centaure [sɑ̃tɔr] *nm* centaur

centenaire [sɑ̃tnɛr] **1** *adj (personne, arbre)* hundred-year-old; **être c.** *(avoir cent ans)* to be a hundred (years old); *(avoir plus de cent ans)* to be over a hundred (years old); **plusieurs fois c.** hundreds of years old

  2 *nmf (vieillard)* centenarian
  3 *nm (anniversaire)* centenary, *Am & Can* centennial

centième [sɑ̃tjɛm] **1** *nmf, nm & adj* hundredth; *voir aussi* **cinquième**
  2 *nf Théât* hundredth performance

centigrade [sɑ̃tigrad] *adj* **degré c.** degree centigrade

centigramme [sɑ̃tigram] *nm* centigram

centilitre [sɑ̃tilitr] *nm* centilitre

centime [sɑ̃tim] *nm* centime; **je ne lui donnerai pas un c.!** I won't give him a penny!

centimètre [sɑ̃timɛtr] *nm* (**a**) *(unité de mesure)* centimetre (**b**) *(ruban)* tape measure

centrafricain, -e [sɑ̃trafrikɛ̃, -ɛn] **1** *adj* of the Central African Republic
  2 *nm,f* **C.** person from the Central African Republic

central, -e, -aux, -ales [sɑ̃tral, -o] **1** *adj* (**a**) *(au centre)* central (**b**) *(principal)* central, main (**c**) **(l'École) Centrale** = "Grande École" specializing in engineering
  2 *nm* **c. téléphonique** telephone exchange
  3 *nf* **centrale** (**a**) *(usine)* **centrale (électrique)** power station; **centrale thermique/nucléaire** thermal/nuclear power station (**b**) *(prison)* county jail (**c**) *(groupement)* **centrale (syndicale)** group of affiliated trade unions; *Com* **centrale d'achat** (central) purchasing group

centralisation [sɑ̃tralizasjɔ̃] *nf* centralization

centraliser [sɑ̃tralize] *vt* to centralize

centralisme [sɑ̃tralism] *nm Pol* centralism

centre [sɑ̃tr] *nm* (**a**) *(milieu)* centre; **il se prend pour le c. du monde** he thinks the world revolves round him; **cette question est au c. du débat** this question is at the heart of the debate; *Phys* **c. de gravité** centre of gravity; **c. d'intérêt** centre of interest
  (**b**) *Pol* centre; **le c. droit/gauche** the centre right/left
  (**c**) *(au football) (passe)* cross; **faire un c.** to make a cross
  (**d**) *(organisme, lieu)* centre; **les grands centres urbains** large conurbations; **c. aéré** outdoor activity centre; **c. d'appels** call centre; **c. commercial** shopping centre; **c. culturel** arts centre; **c. hospitalier** hospital complex; **c. des impôts** tax office; **c. de loisirs** leisure centre; **c. de tri** sorting office

centré, -e [sɑ̃tre] *adj Suisse (magasin, appartement)* central

centrer [sɑ̃tre] *vt (ballon, mécanisme)* to centre; **c. une discussion sur un sujet** to focus a discussion on a subject

centre-ville *(pl* centres-villes*)* [sɑ̃trəvil] *nm* town centre; *(d'une grande ville) Br* city centre, *Am* downtown area; **aller au c.** to go into town; **habiter au c.** to live in the town/city centre, *Am* to live downtown

centrifuge [sɑ̃trifyʒ] *adj* centrifugal

centrifuger [45] [sɑ̃trifyʒe] *vt* to centrifuge

centrifugeur [sɑ̃trifyʒœr] *nm,* **centrifugeuse** [sɑ̃trifyʒøz] *nf (en chimie, en biologie)* centrifuge; *(pour jus de fruits)* juice extractor

centripète [sɑ̃tripɛt] *adj* centripetal

centrisme [sɑ̃trism] *nm Pol* centrism

centriste [sɑ̃trist] *adj & nmf Pol* centrist

centuple [sɑ̃typl] *nm* **le c. de dix** a hundred times ten; **je te le rendrai au c.** I'll repay you a hundred times over

cep [sɛp] *nm* **c. (de vigne)** vine-stock

cépage [sepaʒ] *nm* variety of vine

cèpe [sɛp] *nm* cep

cependant [səpɑ̃dɑ̃] **1** *conj* however, nevertheless; **le directeur, c., n'est pas d'accord** the manager, however, does not agree; **c., vous ne m'avez pas averti** nevertheless, you didn't tell me

     2 *adv Litt* meanwhile; **c. que** while

céphalée [sefale] *nf Méd* headache, *Spéc* cephalalgia

céramique [seramik] *nf (art)* ceramics *(singulier)*; *(matière, objet)* ceramic

cerceau, -x [sɛrso] *nm* hoop

cercle [sɛrkl] *nm* (**a**) *(figure)* circle; **en c.** in a circle; **c. vicieux** vicious circle; **décrire des cercles** *(avion, oiseau)* to circle (**b**) *(groupe de personnes)* circle (**c**) *(association)* club; **c. littéraire** literary society (**d**) *(objet circulaire)* hoop, ring (**e**) *Géog* **c. (polaire) arctique** Arctic Circle

cerclé, -e [sɛrkle] *adj* **lunettes cerclées d'écaille** horn-rimmed spectacles; **un tonneau c. de fer** a barrel with iron hoops

cercueil [sɛrkœj] *nm* coffin

céréale [sereal] *nf* cereal, grain; **céréales** *(au petit déjeuner)* cereal

céréalier, -ère [serealje, -ɛr] *adj (production, culture)* cereal; *(région)* cereal-growing

cérébral, -e, -aux, -ales [serebral, -o] *adj* cerebral; **hémorragie cérébrale** brain haemorrhage

cérémonial, -als [seremɔnjal] *nm* ceremonial

cérémonie [seremɔni] *nf* ceremony; **habit de c.** dress suit; **uniforme de c.** dress uniform; *Fig* **sans cérémonies** *(réception, repas)* informal; *(recevoir quelqu'un)* informally; *(renvoyer quelqu'un)* unceremoniously; **faire des cérémonies** to stand on ceremony; **sans plus de c.** without further ado

cérémonieux, -euse [seremɔnjø, -øz] *adj* ceremonious

cerf [sɛr] *nm* stag

cerfeuil [sɛrfœj] *nm* chervil

cerf-volant (*pl* **cerfs-volants**) [sɛrvɔlɑ̃] *nm* (**a**) *(jeu)* kite (**b**) *(insecte)* stag beetle

cerise [səriz] **1** *nf* cherry

     2 *adj inv* **(rouge) c.** cherry(-red)

cerisier [sərizje] *nm (arbre)* cherry tree; *(bois)* cherry-wood

CERN [sɛrn] *nm (abrév* **Conseil européen pour la recherche nucléaire**) CERN

cerne [sɛrn] *nm* ring

cerné, -e [sɛrne] *adj* **avoir les yeux cernés** to have rings under one's eyes

cerner [sɛrne] *vt* (**a**) *(encercler)* to surround (**b**) *(définir)* *(problème)* to identify; **une personne difficile à c.** a difficult person to figure out

certain, -e [sɛrtɛ̃, -ɛn] **1** *adj (sûr)* certain; **il viendra, c'est c.** he'll definitely come; **être c. de qch** to be certain of sth; **aller à une mort certaine** to be heading for certain death

     2 *adj indéfini (avant le nom)* certain; **il a un c. charme** he has a certain charm; **un c. temps** a while; **jusqu'à un c. point** up to a (certain) point; **d'une certaine façon** in a way; **dans une certaine mesure** to a certain extent; **dans certaines circonstances** in some *or* certain circumstances; **d'un c. âge** elderly; **avoir un c. âge** to be getting on; **cela demande un c. culot/courage** it takes some nerve/courage; **une certaine Martine** someone called Martine

     3 *pron indéfini* **certains pensent que...** some (people)

think (that)...; **certaines d'entre nous/vous** some of us/you

certainement [sɛrtɛnmɑ̃] *adv (probablement)* most probably; **c.!** *(bien sûr)* of course!; **c. pas!** certainly not!

certes [sɛrt] *adv* certainly; **il n'est pas sans défauts, c., mais...** he has his faults, certainly, but...; **c. oui!** yes indeed!; **c. non!** certainly not!

certificat [sɛrtifika] *nm* certificate; **c. d'assurance** insurance certificate; **c. de garantie** certificate of guarantee; **c. médical** medical certificate; **c. de scolarité** school attendance record; **c. de travail** certificate of employment

certifié, -e [sɛrtifje] *adj* **professeur c.** = qualified (graduate) teacher

certifier [66] [sɛrtifje] *vt* (**a**) *(authentifier)* to certify; *(signature)* to witness (**b**) *(assurer)* **c. à qn que...** to assure sb that...

certitude [sɛrtityd] *nf* certainty; **j'en ai la c.** I'm certain of it

cérumen [serymɛn] *nm* earwax, *Spéc* cerumen

cerveau, -x [sɛrvo] *nm Anat & Fig* brain; *(esprit)* mind, brains; *Fam (personne intelligente)* brainy person; *(d'un projet)* mastermind

cervelas [sɛrvəla] *nm* saveloy

cervelet [sɛrvəlɛ] *nm Anat* cerebellum

cervelle [sɛrvɛl] *nf Anat (substance)* brain; **se brûler** *ou* **se faire sauter la c.** to blow one's brains out; **il n'a rien dans la c.** he's got nothing between his ears; **avoir une c. de moineau** to be bird-brained; *Culin* **c. d'agneau** lamb's brains

cervical, -e, -aux, -ales [sɛrvikal, -o] *adj Anat* cervical

CES [seəɛs] *nm* (**a**) *(abrév* **contrat emploi-solidarité**) = short-term contract subsidized by the government (**b**) *(abrév* **collège d'enseignement secondaire**) = former secondary school for pupils aged 12 to 15

ces [se] *voir* **ce²**

César [sezar] **1** *npr* **Jules C.** Julius Caesar

     2 *nm Cin* = French cinema award

césarienne [sezarjɛn] *nf* Caesarean (section)

cessant, -e [sesɑ̃, -ɑ̃t] *adj* **toutes affaires cessantes** forthwith

cessation [sesasjɔ̃] *nf* cessation; **c. des hostilités** cease-fire; **c. de paiements** suspension of payments

cesse [sɛs] *nf* (**a**) **sans c.** constantly, continually (**b**) *Litt* **il n'aura (pas) de c. qu'il ne réussisse** he won't rest until he has succeeded

cesser [sese] **1** *vi* to stop, to cease; *(vent)* to die down; **faire c. qch** to put a stop to sth; **il faudra que ça cesse** this has to stop

     2 *vt (interrompre)* to stop; *Mil* **cessez le feu!** cease fire!; **c. de faire qch** to stop doing sth; **il ne cesse de me contredire** he's forever contradicting me

cessez-le-feu [seselfø] *nm inv* cease-fire

cession [sesjɔ̃] *nf Jur* transfer

c'est-à-dire [sɛtadir] *conj* that is (to say); **vous l'avez prévenu? – eh bien, c. que non** did you let him know? – well, actually, no; **c. que je n'étais pas au courant** the thing is that no one told me; **il faut aller de l'avant! – c.?** we must forge ahead! – what do you mean by that?

césure [sezyr] *nf (en poésie)* caesura; *Ordinat* break, hyphenation

cet [sɛt] *voir* **ce²**

cétacé [setase] *nm* cetacean

cette [sɛt] *voir* **ce²**

ceux [sø] *voir* **celui**

Ceylan [selɑ̃] *n* Ceylon

cf (*abrév* **confer**) cf

CFA [seefa] (*abrév* **Communauté financière africaine**) franc C. CFA franc

CFAO [seefao] *nf* (*abrév* **conception et fabrication assistées par ordinateur**) CADCAM

CFC [seefse] *nm* (*abrév* **chlorofluorocarbone**) CFC

CFDT [seefdete] *nf* (*abrév* **Confédération française démocratique du travail**) = French trade union

CFTC [seeftese] *nf* (*abrév* **Confédération française des travailleurs chrétiens**) = French trade union

CGC [seʒese] *nf* (*abrév* **Confédération générale des cadres**) = French trade union for managerial staff

CGT [seʒete] *nf* (*abrév* **Confédération générale du travail**) = French trade union

chacal, -als [ʃakal] *nm* jackal; *Fig* vulture

chacun, -e [ʃakœ̃, -yn] *pron indéfini* (**a**) (*chaque personne*) each (one), every one; **3 euros c.** 3 euros each; **nous avons pris c. notre chapeau** each of us took our hat (**b**) (*tout le monde*) everyone, everybody; **c. pour soi** every man for himself; **c. ses goûts** everyone to their own taste; **c. son tour** (*dans une file d'attente*) each in turn; **c. son tour!** wait your turn!; **tout un c.** everyone

chagrin, -e [ʃagrɛ̃, -in] **1** *nm* (*peine*) grief, sorrow; **avoir du c.** to be upset; **avoir un gros c.** (*langage enfantin*) to be very unhappy; **faire du c. à qn** to distress sb; **un c. d'amour** an unhappy love affair
2 *adj Litt* woeful; **esprits chagrins** malcontents

chagriner [ʃagrine] **1** *vt* (*peiner*) to grieve; (*contrarier*) to bother
2 se chagriner *vpr Can* **le temps se chagrine** it's getting cloudy

chahut [ʃay] *nm Fam* racket, din; **faire du c.** to make a racket

chahuter [ʃayte] *Fam* **1** *vi* (*faire du tapage*) to make a racket; (*jouer brutalement*) to be rowdy
2 *vt* (*professeur*) to bait; (*orateur*) to heckle; **se faire c.** (*professeur*) to get baited; (*orateur*) to get heckled

chai [ʃɛ] *nm* wine and spirits storehouse

chaîne [ʃɛn] *nf* (**a**) (*pour attacher, pour décorer*) chain; **faire la c.** to form a chain; **chaînes** *Aut* (snow) chains; *Fig* (*contraintes*) chains, shackles
(**b**) (*de transmission*) chain; **c. de vélo** bicycle chain
(**c**) (*série*) (*d'hôtels, de magasins*) chain; **c. alimentaire** food chain; **c. de montagnes** range *or* chain of mountains
(**d**) *TV* channel; **c. de télévision** television channel
(**e**) (*dans l'industrie*) **c. (de montage)** assembly line, production line; **travail à la c.** assembly line work; **travailler à la c.** to work on the assembly line
(**f**) *Tex* warp
(**g**) *Ordinat* string; **c. de caractères** character string; **c. de recherche** search string
(**h**) **c. (haute-fidélité)** hi-fi
(**i**) *Can* **c. du trottoir** *Br* kerb, *Am* curb

chaînette [ʃɛnɛt] *nf* small chain

chaînon [ʃɛnɔ̃] *nm* link; *Fig* **le c. manquant** the missing link

chair [ʃɛr] **1** *nf* (*d'humain, d'animal, de fruit*) flesh; **en c. et en os** in the flesh; **être bien en c.** to be plump; **la c. est faible** the flesh is weak; **c. à canon** cannon fodder; **avoir la c. de poule** to have *Br* goose pimples *or*

Am goose bumps; **donner la c. de poule à qn** to give sb goose pimples; **c. à saucisse** sausagemeat; *Fam Fig* **je vais en faire de la c. à saucisse** I'll make mincemeat of him
2 *adj inv* (**couleur**) **c.** flesh-coloured

chaire [ʃɛr] *nf* (**a**) (*dans une église*) pulpit (**b**) *Univ* (*fonction, tribune*) chair; **être titulaire d'une c.** to hold a chair

chaise [ʃɛz] *nf* chair; *Fig* **être assis** *ou très Fam* **avoir le cul entre deux chaises** to be in an awkward position; *Can* **c. berçante** rocking chair; **chaises musicales** musical chairs; **c. électrique** electric chair; **c. haute** high chair; **c. longue** deckchair; **c. à porteurs** sedan chair; **c. roulante** wheelchair

chaland [ʃalɑ̃] *nm* barge

châle [ʃal] *nm* shawl

chalet [ʃalɛ] *nm* (**a**) (*de montagne*) chalet (**b**) *Can* cottage

chaleur [ʃalœr] *nf* (**a**) (*température*) heat; **les grandes chaleurs** the hot season; **il fait une c. terrible** it's terribly hot; **coup de c.** heatstroke (**b**) (*d'une personne, d'une couleur, d'une voix, d'un accueil*) warmth; **c. humaine** human warmth; **avec c.** warmly (**c**) *Zool* **être en c.** to be *Br* on heat *or Am* in heat

chaleureusement [ʃalørøzmɑ̃] *adv* warmly

chaleureux, -euse [ʃalørø, -øz] *adj* (*accueil, atmosphère*) warm; (*paroles*) glowing

challenge [ʃalɑ̃ʒ] *nm* (**a**) *Sport* tournament (**b**) (*défi*) challenge

challenger [tʃalɑ̃ʒœr] *nm* challenger

chaloupe [ʃalup] *nf* (**a**) *Naut* launch; (*à rames*) *Br* rowing boat, *Am* rowboat; **c. à moteur** motor launch; **c. de sauvetage** lifeboat (**b**) *Can* (*couvre-chaussure*) rubber overshoe

chaloupé, -e [ʃalupe] *adj* swaying

chalumeau, -x [ʃalymo] *nm* (**a**) *Tech Br* blowlamp, *Am* blowtorch (**b**) *Can* spout (*for collecting sap of maple tree*)

chalut [ʃaly] *nm* trawl; **pêcher au c.** to trawl

chalutier [ʃalytje] *nm* trawler

chamade [ʃamad] *nf* **battre la c.** to beat wildly

chamailler [ʃamaje] **se chamailler** *vpr* to squabble

chamailleur, -euse [ʃamajœr, -øz] **1** *adj* quarrelsome
2 *nm,f* squabbler

chamarré, -e [ʃamare] *adj* richly coloured

chambardement [ʃɑ̃bardəmɑ̃] *nm Fam* upheaval

chambarder [ʃɑ̃barde] *vt Fam* (*projets, maison*) to turn upside down

chambouler [ʃɑ̃bule] *vt Fam* (*projets, maison*) to turn upside down

chambranle [ʃɑ̃brɑ̃l] *nm* (*d'une porte, d'une fenêtre*) frame

chambre [ʃɑ̃br] *nf* (**a**) (*pièce*) bedroom; (*d'un hôtel*) room; **c. à un lit/deux lits** single/twin room; **vous auriez une c. (de) libre?** do you have any vacancies?; **faire c. à part** to sleep in separate rooms; **faire sa c.** to tidy (up) one's room; **garder la c.** to keep to one's room; **sportif/politicien en c.** armchair sportsman/politician; **c. d'amis** spare room; **c. de bonne** maid's room; **c. à coucher** (*pièce*) bedroom; (*mobilier*) bedroom furniture; **c. forte** strongroom; **c. frigorifique** *ou* **froide** cold store; **c. à gaz** gas chamber; **c. d'hôte** ≃ guest house; **c. meublée** furnished room, *Br* bedsit(ter)
(**b**) *Jur* (*d'un tribunal*) division; **c. d'accusation** Court

of Criminal Appeal; **C. de commerce** Chamber of Commerce

(**c**) *Pol* **la C.** the House; **siéger à la C.** to sit in the House; **C. des députés** = lower chamber of Parliament

(**d**) *Tech (d'un fusil, d'un appareil photo)* chamber; **c. à air** inner tube

chambrée [ʃãbre] *nf* (**a**) *(occupants d'une chambre)* room(ful) (**b**) *Mil* barrackroom

chambrer [ʃãbre] *vt* (**a**) **c. qch** *(bouteille, vin)* to bring sth to room temperature (**b**) *Fam* **c. qn** to pull sb's leg

chambreur, -euse [ʃãbrœr, -øz] *nm,f Can & Suisse* lodger

chameau, -x [ʃamo] *nm* (**a**) *(animal)* camel (**b**) *Fam (homme)* bastard; *(femme)* cow

chamelier [ʃaməlje] *nm* camel-driver

chamelle [ʃamɛl] *nf* she-camel

chamois [ʃamwa] *nm* (**a**) *(animal)* chamois (**b**) *Sport* **c. d'or/d'argent/de bronze** = gold/silver/bronze skiing proficiency medal

chamoisette [ʃamwazɛt] *nf Belg* duster

champ [ʃã] *nm* (**a**) *(étendue)* field; **c. de blé** field of wheat, wheatfield; **prendre** *ou* **couper à travers champs** to cut across country; **à tout bout de c.** at every possible opportunity; *Fig* **laisser le c. libre à qn** to leave the field free for sb; **c. de bataille** battlefield; **c. de courses** *Br* racecourse, *Am* racetrack; **c. de foire** fairground; **mort** *ou* **tombé au c. d'honneur** killed in action; **c. de mines** minefield; **c. de tir** rifle range; *Mil* practice ground; *(d'un fusil)* field of fire

(**b**) *Fig (portée)* scope; **c. d'action** field of activity; **élargir le c. de ses activités** to extend the scope of one's activities

(**c**) *Phot* shot, picture; *(d'un instrument optique)* field; **être dans le c.** to be in shot; **c. visuel** field of vision (**d**) *Élec & Rad* field; **c. magnétique** magnetic field (**e**) *Ordinat* field; **c. numérique** numeric field; **c. de texte** text field

champagne [ʃãpaɲ] *nm* champagne

champenois, -e [ʃãpənwa, -az] **1** *adj* (**a**) *(de la région)* of Champagne (**b**) **méthode champenoise** champagne method

2 *nm,f* **C.** person from Champagne

champêtre [ʃãpɛtr] *adj* rustic, rural

champignon [ʃãpiɲɔ̃] *nm* (**a**) *(plante)* mushroom; *Fig* **pousser comme un c.** *(enfant)* to shoot up; *(ville)* to mushroom; **c. atomique** mushroom cloud; **c. hallucinogène** magic mushroom; **c. de Paris** button mushroom; **c. vénéneux** poisonous mushroom, toadstool (**b**) *Méd* fungus (**c**) *Fam (accélérateur)* **appuyer sur le c.** *Br* to put one's foot down, *Am* to step on the gas

champion, -onne [ʃãpjɔ̃, -ɔn] **1** *nm,f* (**a**) *(dans une discipline)* champion; **le c. du monde d'escrime** the world fencing champion; *Fam* **c'est un c. du bricolage** he's an ace handyman (**b**) *(d'une cause)* champion

2 *adj* (**a**) *Sport* **l'équipe championne du monde** the world champions (**b**) *Fam* great; **pour les gaffes, il est c.!** he's a great one for putting his foot in it!

championnat [ʃãpjɔna] *nm* championship; **le championnat du monde d'athlétisme** the world athletics championships

champlure [ʃãplyr] *nf Can (robinet) Br* tap, *Am* faucet

chance [ʃãs] *nf* (**a**) *(sort favorable)* (good) luck; **souhaiter bonne c. à qn** to wish sb luck; **bonne c.!** good luck!; **quelle c.!** what a stroke of luck!; **avec un peu**

de c.... with a bit of luck...; **avoir de la c.** to be lucky *or* fortunate; **ne pas avoir de c.** to be unlucky; **porter c. à qn** to bring sb luck; **c'est mon jour de c.** it's my lucky day; **c'est bien ma c.!** just my luck!; **pas de c.!** hard luck!; **par c.** luckily, fortunately (**b**) *(possibilité)* chance; **avoir des chances de faire qch** to stand a (good) chance of doing sth; **avoir peu de chances de faire qch** to have little chance of doing sth; **donner une** *ou* **sa c. à qn** to give sb a chance; **elle a une c. sur deux de gagner** she has a fifty-fifty chance of winning; *Fam* **il y a des chances** probably; **il y a de grandes** *ou* **fortes chances (pour) qu'on le lui propose** there's every chance that she will be offered it

chancelant, -e [ʃãslã, -ãt] *adj (pas)* unsteady; *(mémoire)* shaky; *(santé)* delicate; *(pouvoir, gouvernement)* tottering; *(détermination)* wavering

chanceler [42] [ʃãsle] *vi (personne)* to stagger, to totter; *(objet)* to wobble; *(régime, gouvernement)* to totter; **l'uppercut le fit c.** the uppercut sent him reeling

chancelier [ʃãsəlje] *nm Pol* chancellor; *(d'ambassade)* chief secretary

chancellerie [ʃãsɛlri] *nf* (**a**) *(d'une ambassade)* chancery (**b**) *(ministère de la Justice)* ≃ *Br* Lord Chancellor's Department, ≃ *Am* Department of Justice

chanceux, -euse [ʃãsø, -øz] *adj* lucky

chancre [ʃãkr] *nm Méd & Fig* canker

chandail [ʃãdaj] *nm* sweater, jumper

Chandeleur [ʃãdlœr] *nf* **la C.** Candlemas

chandelier [ʃãdəlje] *nm (à une branche)* candlestick; *(à plusieurs branches)* candelabra

chandelle [ʃãdɛl] *nf* (**a**) *(bougie)* candle; **s'éclairer à la c.** to use candlelight; **un dîner aux chandelles** a candlelit dinner; **faire des économies de bouts de c.** to make cheeseparing economies; **brûler la c. par les deux bouts** to burn the candle at both ends; **le jeu n'en vaut pas la c.** the game is not worth the candle; **tenir la c.** *Br* to play gooseberry, *Am* to feel like a fifth wheel; **voir trente-six chandelles** to see stars; **devoir une fière c. à qn** to owe sb a great debt (**b**) *(en gymnastique)* **faire la c.** to do a shoulder stand (**c**) *Aviat* **(montée en) c.** vertical climb

chanfrein [ʃãfrɛ̃] *nm (de cheval)* nose

change [ʃãʒ] *nm* (**a**) *Fin* exchange; **le c. est avantageux** the exchange rate is good; *Fig* **gagner/ne pas perdre au c.** to gain on/not to lose on the exchange (**b**) *Fig* **donner le c. à qn** to put sb off the scent (**c**) *(couche-culotte)* **c. (complet)** disposable *Br* nappy *or Am* diaper

changeant, -e [ʃãʒã, -ãt] *adj (temps)* unsettled; **d'humeur changeante** moody

changement [ʃãʒmã] *nm* (**a**) *(modification)* change; **ça va te faire un drôle de c.** it'll be quite a change for you; **c. de décor** *Théât* scene change; *Fig* change of scenery; **c. de direction** *(sur un écriteau)* under new management (**b**) *(dans les transports)* change; **il y a un c. à Valence** you have to change at Valence (**c**) **c. de vitesse** *(action)* change of gear; *(levier) Br* gear lever, *Am* gear shift; *Ordinat* **c. de ligne** line feed

changer [45] [ʃãʒe] **1** *vt* (**a**) *(remplacer) (draps, couche de bébé, roue)* to change; **c. qch contre qch** to change *or* exchange sth for sth

(**b**) *(enfant, bébé)* to change

(**c**) *(convertir) (argent)* to change (**en** into)

(**d**) *(transformer)* **c. qn/qch en** to change sb/sth into

(**e**) *(modifier)* to change, to alter; **ça va les c.!** that'll be a change for them!; **ça lui changera les idées** that'll take his mind off things; **ça nous change du café du coin!** that makes a change from the local!; **cela ne change rien à l'affaire** that makes no difference; **sa nouvelle coiffure la change** she looks different with her new hairstyle; **mais cela change tout!** that changes everything!; **c. qch de place** to move sth

2 *vi* (**a**) *(se modifier)* to change; **c. en bien** *ou* **en mieux** to change for the better; **c. en mal** *ou* **en pire** to change for the worse; *Ironique* **pour c.** for a change (**b**) *(dans les transports)* to change

3 changer de *vt ind* to change; **c. de train/de travail** to change trains/jobs; **c. de place avec qn** to change places with sb; **c. de coiffure** to change one's hairstyle; **c. de vêtements** to change (one's clothes), to get changed; **c. de couleur** to change colour; *Aut* **c. de vitesse** to change gear; **je te prie de c. de ton!** don't talk to me in that tone of voice!; *Fam Fig* **change de disque!** put another record on!

4 se changer *vpr* (**a**) *(mettre d'autres vêtements)* to change (**b**) **se c. les idées** to change one's ideas (**c**) *(se transformer)* **se c. en** to change *or* turn into

chanoine [ʃanwan] *nm Rel* canon

chanson [ʃɑ̃sɔ̃] *nf* (**a**) *(air)* song; **la c. française** French song; *Fam* **c'est toujours la même c.!** it's always the same old story!; *Fam* **on connaît la c.!** I've heard that one before!; **c. d'amour** love song; **c. à boire** drinking song (**b**) *(genre littéraire)* song; **c. de geste** chanson de geste

chansonnette [ʃɑ̃sɔnɛt] *nf* ditty

chansonnier [ʃɑ̃sɔnje] *nm* satirical cabaret singer

chant [ʃɑ̃] *nm* (**a**) *(chanson)* song; *(d'un instrument de musique, de la mer, du vent)* sound; *(d'un oiseau)* singing; *(du grillon, de la cigale)* chirping; *(du coq)* crowing; **au c. du coq** at cockcrow; *Fig* **c. du cygne** swan song; **c. funèbre** dirge; **c. de Noël** Christmas carol; **c. sacré** hymn (**b**) *(art)* singing; **leçon/professeur de c.** singing lesson/teacher; **apprendre le c.** to take singing lessons; **c. choral** choral singing; **c. grégorien** Gregorian chant (**c**) *(d'un poème)* canto

chantage [ʃɑ̃taʒ] *nm* blackmail; **faire du c. à qn** to blackmail sb; **il lui fait du c. au suicide** he's blackmailing her with suicide threats

chantant, -e [ʃɑ̃tɑ̃, -ɑ̃t] *adj (musique, air)* tuneful; *(accent, voix)* lilting

chanter [ʃɑ̃te] **1** *vt (chanson)* to sing; *Fam* **qu'est-ce que vous me chantez là?** what are you on about?; *Fam* **elle le chante sur tous les tons** she's always going on about it

2 *vi* (**a**) *(personne, oiseau)* to sing; *(coq)* to crow; *(grillon, cigale)* to chirp; **c. juste/faux** to sing in tune/out of tune (**b**) **faire c. qn** *(exercer un chantage sur)* to blackmail sb (**c**) *(plaire)* **viens, si ça te chante** come along, if you fancy the idea; **il vient quand ça lui chante** he comes when he feels like it

chanterelle¹ [ʃɑ̃trɛl] *nf Mus (corde)* top string

chanterelle² *nf (champignon)* chanterelle

chanteur, -euse [ʃɑ̃tœr, -øz] *nm,f* singer; **c. de charme** crooner; **c. des rues** street singer

chantier [ʃɑ̃tje] *nm* (**a**) *(lieu de construction)* (building) site; *(sur la route)* roadworks; **c. interdit au public** *(sur panneau)* no admittance to the public; **mettre qch en c.** to get sth under way; **c. naval** shipyard (**b**) *Fam (désordre)* **quel c.!** what a shambles!; **ils**

ont tout laissé en c. they left the place in a complete shambles

chantilly [ʃɑ̃tiji] *nf* **(crème) c.** whipped cream

chantonner [ʃɑ̃tɔne] *vt & vi* to sing softly; *(sans paroles)* to hum

chantre [ʃɑ̃tr] *nm (défenseur)* champion

chanvre [ʃɑ̃vr] *nm* hemp; **c. indien** Indian hemp

chaos [kao] *nm* chaos

chaotique [kaɔtik] *adj* chaotic

chaparder [ʃaparde] *vt Fam* to pinch

chapardeur, -euse [ʃapardœr, -øz] *nm,f Fam* thief

chape [ʃap] *nf (de béton)* screed; *(d'un pneu)* tread; **la chaleur pèse sur la ville comme une c. de plomb** the heat lies on the town like a lead weight

chapeau, -x [ʃapo] *nm* (**a**) *(coiffure)* hat; *Fig* **porter le c.** to carry the can; *Fig* **tirer son c. à qn** to take off one's hat to sb; **c.!** well done!; **c. melon** bowler hat; **c. mou** *Br* trilby, *Am* fedora; **c. de paille** straw hat (**b**) *(d'un champignon)* cap (**c**) *(partie supérieure)* *(de vol-au-vent, de bouchée à la reine)* lid; **prendre un virage sur les chapeaux de roues** to take a corner at top speed; **démarrer sur les chapeaux de roues** *(projet, soirée)* to get off to a cracking start (**d**) *Typ & Journ* lead-in

chapeauter [ʃapote] *vt (contrôler)* to head

chapelain [ʃaplɛ̃] *nm Rel* chaplain

chapelet [ʃaplɛ] *nm (de prière)* rosary; *Fig (d'invectives, d'insultes)* stream; *(d'objets)* string; **dire son c.** to say the rosary

chapelier, -ère [ʃapəlje, -ɛr] *nm,f* hatter

chapelle [ʃapɛl] *nf* (**a**) *Rel* chapel; **c. ardente** chapel of rest (**b**) *Belg (café)* café

chapelure [ʃaplyr] *nf* breadcrumbs

chaperon [ʃaprɔ̃] *nm* (**a**) *(personne)* chaperon (**b**) **le Petit C. rouge** Little Red Riding Hood

chaperonner [ʃaprɔne] *vt aussi Fig* to chaperon

chapiteau, -x [ʃapito] *nm* (**a**) *Archit (d'une colonne)* capital (**b**) *(d'un cirque)* big top; **sous c.** in a marquee

chapitre [ʃapitr] *nm* (**a**) *(d'un livre)* chapter; *(d'un budget)* item; **inscrire une somme au c. des recettes/dépenses** to enter a sum under revenue/expenditure; **elle est sévère sur le c. de la discipline** she is strict in the matter of discipline; **en voilà assez sur ce c.** that's enough of that; **et maintenant, au c. des faits divers…** and now for the news in brief… (**b**) *Rel (assemblée)* chapter; *Fig* **avoir voix au c.** to have a say in the matter

chapitrer [ʃapitre] *vt* **c. qn** *(réprimander)* to tell sb off; *(faire la morale à)* to lecture sb

chapon [ʃapɔ̃] *nm (coq)* capon

chaptaliser [ʃaptalize] *vt* to chaptalize

chaque [ʃak] *adj indéfini* each, every; **c. femme doit pouvoir travailler et élever ses enfants** every woman should be able to work as well as bring up her children; **ces livres coûtent 15 euros c.** these books cost 15 euros each; **c. chose à sa place** everything in its place; **c. chose en son temps** all in good time; **c. fois qu'il vient** every time *or* whenever he comes; **j'y pense à c. instant** I think about it all the time

char [ʃar] *nm* (**a**) *Mil* **c. (d'assaut** *ou* **de combat)** tank (**b**) *(romain)* chariot (**c**) **c. de carnaval** float (**d**) *Can Fam (voiture)* car (**e**) *Sport* **c. à voile** sand yacht; **faire du c. à voile** to go sand yachting (**f**) *Fam* **arrête ton c.!** come off it!

charabia [ʃarabja] *nm Fam* gibberish

charade [ʃarad] *nf* (**a**) *(devinette)* riddle (**b**) *(mime)* (game of) charades

charançon [ʃarɑ̃sɔ̃] *nm* weevil

charbon [ʃarbɔ̃] *nm* (**a**) *(combustible)* coal; **c. (de bois)** charcoal; **chauffage au c.** coal-fired heating; *Fig* **être sur des charbons ardents** to be on tenter-hooks (**b**) *Art* charcoal; **dessin au c.** charcoal drawing (**c**) *Méd (médicament)* charcoal

charbonnage [ʃarbɔnaʒ] *nm* (**a**) *(exploitation)* coal mining (**b**) **charbonnages** *(houillères)* collieries

charbonneux, -euse [ʃarbɔnø, -øz] *adj (noir)* coal-black; *(yeux)* heavy with black make-up

charbonnier, -ère [ʃarbɔnje, -ɛr] **1** *adj (industrie)* coal
2 *nm,f* (**a**) *(marchand de charbon)* coal merchant; *Prov* **c. est maître dans sa maison** *ou* **chez soi** a man is master in his own home (**b**) *Naut* coaler
3 *nf* **charbonnière** *(mésange)* great tit

charcuter [ʃarkyte] *Fam* **1** *vt* **c. qn** to hack sb about
2 se charcuter *vpr* to cut oneself to ribbons; **se c. le menton/le doigt** to cut one's chin/finger to ribbons

charcuterie [ʃarkytri] *nf* (**a**) *(magasin)* pork butcher's (shop) (**b**) *(activité)* cooked meats trade (**c**) *(produits)* cooked meats

> ### Charcuterie
> A "charcuterie" sells mainly food prepared with pork: sausages, pâtés, ham etc, collectively also known as "charcuterie". Ready-prepared dishes to take away are usually also sold.

charcutier, -ère [ʃarkytje, -ɛr] *nm,f* (**a**) *(commerçant, fabricant)* pork butcher (**b**) *Fam Péj (chirurgien)* butcher

chardon [ʃardɔ̃] *nm (plante)* thistle

chardonneret [ʃardɔnrɛ] *nm* goldfinch

charentais, -e [ʃarɑ̃tɛ, -ɛz] **1** *adj* of Charente
2 *nm,f* **C.** person from Charente
3 *nf* **charentaise** *(chausson)* slipper

charge [ʃarʒ] *nf* (**a**) *(poids)* load; *(sur bateau)* cargo; *Fig* **être une c. pour qn** to be a burden to sb; **c. utile** *(d'un véhicule)* capacity
(**b**) *(responsabilité)* responsibility; **être en c. de qch** to be in charge of sth; **prendre qn/qch en c.** to take charge of sb/sth; **se prendre en c.** to be responsible for oneself
(**c**) *(fonction)* office; *(d'avoué)* practice
(**d**) *(obligation financière)* **être à la c. de qn** *(personne)* to be dependent on sb; *(appel, transport, réparations)* to be chargeable to sb; **avoir deux enfants à c.** to have two dependent children; **prendre un client en c.** *(taxi)* to pick up a fare; **être pris en c. à cent pour cent par la Sécurité sociale** to have one's medical expenses fully paid for by Social Security; **charges (locatives)** *(d'un appartement)* maintenance charges; **charges d'exploitation** operating costs; **charges sociales** *Br* national insurance contributions, *Am* social security charges *(paid by the employer)*
(**e**) *(d'une arme, d'explosifs)* charge
(**f**) *Constr (pression)* load
(**g**) *Élec (d'une batterie, d'une particule)* charge
(**h**) *Mil* charge; *Fig* **revenir à la c.** to return to the attack
(**i**) *Jur (preuve)* charge

> ### Charges
> Householders and tenants in blocks of flats are required to pay "charges", a monthly contribution to pay for the general upkeep of the building. In estate agencies, rent is expressed either including this sum ("charges comprises" or "cc") or excluding it ("hors charges" or "charges en sus"). Sometimes, the "charges" include heating costs.

chargé, -e [ʃarʒe] **1** *adj* (**a**) *(camion, navire)* loaded, laden (**de** with); *(revolver, appareil photo)* loaded; *Fig (style)* ornate; **la voiture est trop chargée** the car is overloaded; **être c. comme un bourricot** *ou* **un mulet** to be loaded down; **avoir la langue chargée** to have a furred tongue; **un regard c. de reconnaissance** a look full of gratitude
(**b**) *(occupé) (journée, programme)* full
(**c**) *(responsable)* **être c. de qch** *(mission)* to be entrusted with sth; *(tâche)* to be responsible for sth; **être c. de famille** to have family responsibilities; **être c. de faire qch** to be responsible for doing sth
(**d**) *Phys* charged
2 *nm* **c. d'affaires** chargé-d'affaires; **c. de mission** official representative
3 *nm,f Univ* **c. de cours** = part-time lecturer; *Can* lecturer

chargement [ʃarʒəmɑ̃] *nm* (**a**) *(action)* loading; *Élec (d'une batterie)* charging; **machine à laver à c. frontal** front-loading washing machine (**b**) *(marchandises)* load; *(sur bateau)* cargo

charger [45] [ʃarʒe] **1** *vt* (**a**) *(camion, navire, marchandises)* to load
(**b**) *(remplir)* to fill (**de** with)
(**c**) *(fusil, appareil photo)* to load; *Élec (batterie)* to charge; *Ordinat* to load (up)
(**d**) *(donner une responsabilité à)* **c. qn de qch** to entrust sb with sth; **c. qn de faire qch** to give sb the responsibility for doing sth; **il m'a chargé de vous transmettre un message** he asked me to give you a message
(**e**) *(attaquer)* to charge (at)
2 *vi* (**a**) *Ordinat* to load up (**b**) *Mil* to charge
3 se charger *vpr* (**a**) *(s'alourdir)* to weigh oneself down (**b**) **se c. de qn/qch** *(prendre la responsabilité de)* to take care of sb/sth; **se c. de faire qch** to undertake to do sth; **laisse tomber, je m'en charge** don't worry about it, I'll take care of it

chargeur [ʃarʒœr] *nm (d'arme)* magazine; *Phot* cartridge; *Élec (battery)* charger; *Ordinat* loader; **c. automatique** self loader

chariot [ʃarjo] *nm (petite charrette)* wagon; *(de supermarché)* Br trolley, *Am* cart; *(pour diapositives)* cartridge; *(pour la manutention)* truck; *(d'hôpital)* Br trolley, *Am* gurney; *Cin* dolly; *(d'une machine à écrire)* carriage; **c. à bagages** luggage trolley

charismatique [karismatik] *adj* charismatic

charisme [karism] *nm* charisma

charitable [ʃaritabl] *adj* charitable (**envers** towards); *(conseil)* friendly

charité [ʃarite] *nf* (**a**) *(altruisme)* charity; **faites-moi** *ou* **ayez la c. de...** please be kind enough to...; *Prov* **c. bien ordonnée commence par soi-même** charity begins at home (**b**) *(don)* charity; **faire la c. à qn** to give money to sb; **demander la c.** to ask for charity;

la **c.**, **Messieurs Dames** *(dans la rue)* can you spare some change, please?

charlatan [ʃarlatã] *nm Péj (mauvais médecin)* quack; *(escroc)* charlatan

Charles [ʃarl] *npr* **C. Quint** Charles the Fifth

charlot [ʃarlo] *nm Fam (personne peu sérieuse)* clown

charlotte [ʃarlɔt] *nf Culin* charlotte; **c. aux poires/au chocolat** pear/chocolate charlotte

charmant, -e [ʃarmã, -ãt] *adj (personne, chose, soirée)* charming, delightful; *Ironique* **et voilà qu'il pleut, ah, c'est c.!** now it's raining, marvellous!

charme¹ [ʃarm] *nm* (**a**) *(attrait)* charm; **avoir du c.** to have charm; **c'est ce qui en fait le c.** that's what makes it so attractive; **faire du c. à qn** to turn on the charm with sb; **charmes** *(d'une femme)* charms; **vivre de ses charmes** to sell one's charms (**b**) *(magie)* spell; **être/tomber sous le c.** to be/fall under the spell; *Fig* **se porter comme un c.** to be as fit as a fiddle

charme² *nm (arbre)* hornbeam

charmer [ʃarme] *vt* (**a**) *(plaire à)* to charm; **j'ai été charmé de vous rencontrer** it's been a pleasure to meet you (**b**) *(envoûter)* to charm

charmeur, -euse [ʃarmœr, -øz] **1** *nm,f* charmer; **c. de serpents** snake charmer
  2 *adj (regard, sourire)* charming

charnel, -elle [ʃarnɛl] *adj* carnal

charnier [ʃarnje] *nm* mass grave

charnière [ʃarnjɛr] *nf (de porte, de fenêtre)* hinge; *Fig* **à la c. de deux grandes périodes** at the junction of two great eras; **époque/œuvre c.** transitional period/work

charnu, -e [ʃarny] *adj (partie du corps, lèvres)* fleshy; *(fruit)* pulpy; *Hum* **la partie charnue de son anatomie** his posterior

charognard [ʃarɔɲar] *nm* (**a**) *Zool* carrion-eater (**b**) *(exploiteur)* vulture

charogne [ʃarɔɲ] *nf* (**a**) *(d'animal)* carrion (**b**) *Fam (homme)* bastard; *(femme)* bitch

charpente [ʃarpãt] *nf (d'un bâtiment, d'un roman)* framework; *(du corps)* frame; **avoir une solide c.** *(personne)* to be solidly built

charpenterie [ʃarpãtri] *nf (métier)* carpentry

charpentier [ʃarpãtje] *nm* carpenter

charpie [ʃarpi] *nf* **mettre qch en c.** to tear sth to shreds; *Fam* **mettre qn en c.** to make mincemeat out of sb

charretier [ʃartje] *nm* **jurer comme un c.** to swear like a trooper

charrette [ʃarɛt] *nf* (**a**) *(véhicule)* cart (**b**) *(de licenciements)* round of redundancies (**c**) *Suisse Fam* **c. de Paul!** blinking Paul!

charrier [66] [ʃarje] **1** *vt* (**a**) *(transporter)* to cart (**b**) *(entraîner)* to carry along (**c**) *Fam (se moquer de)* **c. qn** *Br* to have sb on, *Am* to put sb on; **se faire c.** to be had on
  2 *vi Fam (exagérer)* to go too far; **faut pas c.!** *(n'exagère pas)* come off it!

charrue [ʃary] *nf* (**a**) *(pour labourer)* plough; *Fig* **mettre la c. avant les bœufs** to put the cart before the horse (**b**) *Can* snowplough

charte [ʃart] *nf* charter

charter [ʃartɛr] *nm* **(avion) c.** charter plane

chartreux, -euse [ʃartrø, -øz] **1** *nm,f Rel* Carthusian
  2 *nf* **chartreuse** (**a**) *(couvent)* Carthusian monastery (**b**) *(alcool)* Chartreuse

chas [ʃa] *nm* eye

chasse [ʃas] *nf* (**a**) *(activité)* hunting; *(au fusil)* shooting; **aller à la c.** to go hunting/shooting; **la c. est ouverte/fermée** the shooting season has begun/ended; *Prov* **qui va à la c. perd sa place** if you leave your place someone will take it; **c. à courre** hunting; **c. au lapin** rabbit shooting
  (**b**) *(événement)* hunt; *(au fusil)* shoot
  (**c**) *(réserve)* **c. gardée** private game preserve; *Fig (domaine)* preserve
  (**d**) *(poursuite)* chase; **donner la c. à qn/qch, prendre qn/qch en c.** to give chase to sb/sth; **c. à l'homme** manhunt; *Pol* **c. aux sorcières** witch hunt; **c. au trésor** treasure hunt
  (**e**) **c. (d'eau)** flush; **tirer la c. (d'eau)** to flush the toilet
  (**f**) **être en c.** *(chienne, chatte)* to be *Br* on heat *or Am* in heat

châsse [ʃas] *nf Rel* shrine

chassé-croisé *(pl* **chassés-croisés)** [ʃasekrwaze] *nm (de personnes)* comings and goings; *(de conversations)* babble

chasse-neige [ʃasnɛʒ] *nm inv* (**a**) *(engin)* snowplough (**b**) *(en ski)* snowplough; **descendre une piste en c.** to snowplough down a ski slope

chasser [ʃase] **1** *vt* (**a**) *(animaux)* to hunt; **c. le renard/la perdrix** to go foxhunting/partridge shooting (**b**) *(expulser)* to drive *or* chase away (**de** from); *(employé)* to dismiss; *(mouches)* to brush away; *(sujet: vent)* *(nuages)* to blow away; *(idées noires)* to forget; **je ne veux pas vous c. mais il est tard** I'm not trying to get rid of you but it's getting late; *Fig* **c. qn/qch de son esprit** to dismiss sb/sth from one's thoughts
  2 *vi* (**a**) *(aller à la chasse)* to hunt, to go hunting; *(au fusil)* to shoot, to go shooting (**b**) *Aut* to skid

chasseur, -euse [ʃasœr, -øz] **1** *nm,f* hunter; **c. de primes** bounty hunter; *aussi Fig* **c. de têtes** headhunter
  2 *nm* (**a**) *(dans un hôtel) Br* pageboy, *Am* bellboy (**b**) *(avion de chasse)* fighter (**c**) *Mil* **les chasseurs alpins** the mountain light infantry

châssis [ʃasi] *nm* (**a**) *(charpente)* frame (**b**) *Art* stretcher (**c**) *(de jardin)* (cold) frame (**d**) *Aut* chassis (**e**) *Can (fenêtre)* window

chaste [ʃast] *adj* chaste

chastement [ʃastəmã] *adv* chastely

chasteté [ʃastəte] *nf* chastity

chasuble [ʃazybl] *nf* (**a**) **(robe) c.** *Br* pinafore dress, *Am* jumper (**b**) *Rel* chasuble

chat, chatte [ʃa, ʃat] **1** *nm,f* cat; **petit c.** kitten; *Fam* **mon petit c., ma petite chatte** my pet; *Fig* **il n'y avait pas un c.** there wasn't a soul there; **appeler un c. un c.** to call a spade a spade; **avoir un c. dans la gorge** to have a frog in one's throat; **jouer au c. et à la souris avec qn** to play cat-and-mouse with sb; *Prov* **c. échaudé craint l'eau froide** once bitten, twice shy; **quand le c. n'est pas là, les souris dansent** when the cat's away the mice will play; **c. de gouttière** alley cat; **c. persan** Persian (cat); **c. sauvage** wildcat; *Can (raton laveur)* raccoon; **c. siamois** Siamese (cat)
  2 *nf* **chatte** *Vulg (sexe féminin)* pussy

châtaigne [ʃatɛɲ] *nf* (**a**) *(fruit)* (sweet) chestnut (**b**) *très Fam (coup de poing)* clout; **flanquer une c. à qn** to clout sb; **se prendre une c.** *(décharge)* to get a shock

châtaignier [ʃatɛɲe] *nm (arbre, bois)* chestnut

châtain [ʃatɛ̃] **1** *adj (cheveux)* (chestnut-)brown; *(personne)* brown-haired
 2 *nm* chestnut brown

château, -x [ʃato] *nm* (**a**) *(forteresse)* castle; *(manoir)* mansion; *(de famille aristocratique)* stately home; *(palais)* palace; **les châteaux de la Loire** the châteaux of the Loire; *Fig* **bâtir des châteaux en Espagne** to build castles in the air; **c. de cartes** house of cards; **c. d'eau** water tower; **c. fort** castle; **c. gonflable** bouncy castle (**b**) *(exploitation vinicole)* château; **mis en bouteille au c.** *(sur bouteille)* = indicates that wine was bottled at source

châtelain [ʃatlɛ̃] *nm (au Moyen Âge)* lord of the manor; *(propriétaire d'un château)* château owner

châtelaine [ʃatlɛn] *nf (au Moyen Âge)* lady of the manor; *(propriétaire d'un château)* (woman) château owner; *(épouse du propriétaire)* wife of a château owner

chat-huant *(pl* **chats-huants)** [ʃayɑ̃] *nm* tawny owl

châtié, -e [ʃatje] *adj (style)* polished; *(langage)* refined

châtier [66] [ʃatje] *vt Litt (personne)* to chastise; *Prov* **qui aime bien châtie bien** spare the rod and spoil the child

chatière [ʃatjɛr] *nf* (**a**) *(pour chat)* cat flap (**b**) *(pour aération)* ventilation hole

châtiment [ʃatimɑ̃] *nm* (**a**) *Litt* chastisement (**b**) **c. corporel** corporal punishment

chaton¹ [ʃatɔ̃] *nm* (**a**) *(petit chat)* kitten (**b**) *Bot* catkin

chaton² *nm* (**a**) *(d'une bague)* bezel (**b**) *(pierre)* stone

chatouille [ʃatuj] *nf* **faire des chatouilles à qn** to tickle sb; **craindre les chatouilles** to be ticklish

chatouiller [ʃatuje] *vt* to tickle; *Fig (curiosité)* to arouse; *(amour-propre)* to flatter; **ah, ça chatouille!** oh, that tickles!

chatouilleux, -euse [ʃatujø, -øz] *adj* ticklish; *Fig* sensitive (**sur** about)

chatoyant, -e [ʃatwajɑ̃, -ɑ̃t] *adj* shimmering; *(pierre, imagination)* sparkling

chatoyer [32] [ʃatwaje] *vi* to shimmer; *(pierre)* to sparkle

châtrer [ʃatre] *vt (homme, taureau)* to castrate; *(étalon)* to geld; *(chat)* to neuter

chatte [ʃat] *nf voir* **chat**

chatterton [ʃatɛrtɔn] *nm Br* insulating tape, *Am* friction tape

chaud, -e [ʃo, ʃod] **1** *adj* (**a**) *(modérément)* warm; *(intensément)* hot; *Fig (voix)* sultry; *(couleur)* warm; **la soupe est toute chaude** the soup is piping hot; **l'été va être c.** it'll be a hot summer; *Fig* there'll be a lot of unrest this summer; **l'alerte fut chaude** it was a close thing; **une nouvelle toute chaude** some hot news (**b**) *(passionné) (discussion)* heated; *(partisan)* keen; **elle n'est pas chaude pour le projet** she's not keen on the plan; **je ne suis pas très c. pour aller au cinéma** I don't really feel like going to the cinema
 2 *adv* **j'aime manger c.** I like my food hot
 3 *nm (modéré)* warmth; *(intense)* heat; **garder** *ou* **tenir qch au c.** to keep sth warm; **chez soi, au c.** at home, in the warmth; **avoir c.** to be *or* feel hot; *Fam (échapper de justesse)* to have a narrow escape; **il fait c.** it's hot; *Fig* **cela ne me fait ni c. ni froid** it's all the same to me; **interroger les spectateurs à c.** to question the audience on the spot; **attraper un c. et froid** to catch a chill

chaudement [ʃodmɑ̃] *adv (s'habiller, féliciter, recommander)* warmly

chaudière [ʃodjɛr] *nf* (**a**) *(de chauffage)* boiler; **c. à mazout/à gaz** oil-fired/gas boiler (**b**) *Can (seau)* bucket

chaudron [ʃodrɔ̃] *nm* cauldron

chaudronnier, -ère [ʃodrɔnje, -ɛr] *nm,f* boiler maker

chauffage [ʃofaʒ] *nm (d'une pièce, d'un bâtiment)* heating; *(appareils)* heating (system); *(dans une voiture)* heater; **c. à l'électricité/au gaz/au mazout** electric/gas/oil-fired heating; **c. central** central heating

chauffagiste [ʃofaʒist] *nm* heating engineer

chauffant, -e [ʃofɑ̃, -ɑ̃t] *adj voir* **couverture, plaque**

chauffard [ʃofar] *nm* reckless driver

chauffe-biberon *(pl* **chauffe-biberons)** [ʃofbibrɔ̃] *nm* bottle-warmer

chauffe-eau [ʃofo] *nm inv* water heater; **c. électrique** immersion heater

chauffe-plat *(pl* **chauffe-plats)** [ʃofpla] *nm* hot plate

chauffer [ʃofe] **1** *vt (pièce, bâtiment)* to heat (up); *(moteur)* to warm up; **c. une maison au gaz** to heat a house with gas; **la chambre n'est pas chauffée** there's no heating in the bedroom; *Fig* **c. la salle** to warm up one's audience
 2 *vi* (**a**) *(devenir chaud)* to heat up; **ce radiateur chauffe bien/mal** this radiator gives out/doesn't give out a lot of heat; **faire c. qch, mettre qch à c.** to heat sth up (**b**) *(s'échauffer) (moteur)* to overheat (**c**) *Fam* **ça va c. s'il est en retard!** there'll be trouble if he's late!; **tu chauffes!** *(dans un jeu)* you're getting warmer!
 3 se chauffer *vpr* to warm oneself; **se c. (les muscles)** to warm up; **se c. au mazout/à l'électricité** to have oil-fired/electric heating

chaufferette [ʃofrɛt] *nf (pour les pieds)* footwarmer

chaufferie [ʃofri] *nf* boiler room

chauffeur [ʃofœr] *nm (de voiture, de bus)* driver; *(employé)* chauffeur; **les chauffeurs du dimanche** Sunday drivers; **c. de camion** *Br* lorry driver, *Am* truck driver; **c. de taxi** taxi driver

chauffeuse [ʃoføz] *nf (fauteuil)* low armless chair

chauler [ʃole] *vt (murs)* to whitewash; *(terres)* to treat with lime

chaume [ʃom] *nm* (**a**) *(pour toits)* thatch (**b**) *(des céréales)* stubble

chaumière [ʃomjɛr] *nf (maison pauvre)* cottage; *(maison à toit de chaume)* thatched cottage

chaussée [ʃose] *nf (route)* roadway

chausse-pied *(pl* **chausse-pieds)** [ʃospje] *nm* shoehorn

chausser [ʃose] *vt* **1** (**a**) *(chaussures, lunettes, skis)* to put on; **chaussé de pantoufles** wearing slippers; **elle chausse du 37** she takes a size 37 (**b**) *(mettre des chaussures à)* to put shoes on (**c**) *(aller à)* to fit; **souliers qui chaussent bien** shoes that fit well
 2 se chausser *vpr (mettre ses chaussures)* to put one's shoes on

chausses [ʃos] *nfpl (vêtement)* breeches

chaussette [ʃosɛt] *nf* sock; **en chaussettes** in one's socks; **laisser tomber qn comme une vieille c.** to cast sb aside like an old rag

chausseur [ʃosœr] *nm (magasin)* shoe shop; *(fabricant)* shoe manufacturer

chausson [ʃosɔ̃] *nm* (**a**) *(pantoufle)* slipper; *(de danse)* ballet shoe; *(de bébé)* bootee (**b**) *Culin* **c. aux pommes** apple turnover

chaussure [ʃosyr] *nf* shoe; **(l'industrie de) la c.** the shoe industry; **chaussures de ville/de sport/habillées** town/sports/dress shoes; **chaussures à lacets** lace-up shoes; **chaussures de marche** *ou* **de montagne** walking boots; **chaussures montantes** ankle boots; **chaussures de ski** ski boots; **chaussures à talons** high-heeled shoes; *Fig* **trouver c. à son pied** to find the right woman/man

chauve [ʃov] **1** *adj* bald
2 *nm* bald(-headed) man

chauve-souris *(pl* **chauves-souris)** [ʃovsuri] *nf* bat

chauvin, -e [ʃovɛ̃, -in] **1** *adj* chauvinistic
2 *nm,f* chauvinist

chauvinisme [ʃovinism] *nm* chauvinism

chaux [ʃo] *nf* lime; **blanchir un mur à la c.** to whitewash a wall; **c. vive** quicklime

chavirer [ʃavire] **1** *vi* **(a)** *(bateau)* to capsize; **faire c. un bateau** to capsize a boat **(b)** *(tourner)* **tout chavire autour de moi** everything's spinning
2 *vt* *(bouleverser)* to overwhelm

check-up [tʃɛkœp] *nm inv Méd* check-up; **se faire faire un c.** to have a check-up

chef [ʃɛf] *nm* **(a)** *(d'un parti politique, d'une bande)* leader; *(d'une tribu)* chief; *Fam (patron)* boss; **ingénieur/rédacteur en c.** chief engineer/editor; **se débrouiller comme un c.** to be getting on very well; **c. d'atelier** (shop) foreman; **c. d'entreprise** company head; **c. d'État** head of state; **c. de famille** head of the family; **c. de file** leader; **c. de gare** station manager; **le c. du gouvernement** the head of government; **c. d'orchestre** conductor; **c. de service** departmental head; *Belg Univ* **c. de travaux** *Br* ≃ (senior) lecturer, *Am* ≃ assistant professor **(b)** *(cuisinier)* chef **(c)** *Jur* **c. d'accusation** charge **(d)** *(tête)* head; **faire qch de son propre c.** to do sth on one's own authority

chefaillon [ʃɛfajɔ̃] *nm Fam Péj* little Hitler

chef-garde *(pl* **chefs-gardes)** [ʃɛfgard] *nm Belg Rail* ticket inspector

chef-d'œuvre *(pl* **chefs-d'œuvre)** [ʃɛdœvr] *nm* masterpiece

chef-lieu *(pl* **chefs-lieux)** [ʃɛfljø] *nm* = administrative centre of a "département"

cheik(h) [ʃɛk] *nm* sheik(h)

chelem [ʃlɛm] *nm Sport* **grand c.** grand slam

chemin [ʃəmɛ̃] *nm* **(a)** *(route étroite)* path, track; **c. de grande randonnée** hiking trail; **c. de ronde** parapet walk; **c. de terre** track; **c. de traverse** path across the fields
(b) *(itinéraire)* way **(de** to); *Fig (de la gloire, du bonheur)* road **(de** to); **sur le c. du retour** on the way back; **en c.** on the way; **se mettre en c.** to set out *or* off; **nous ne pouvons pas nous arrêter en si bon c.** we can't give up now when we're doing so well; **ne pas y aller par quatre chemins** to get straight to the point; **prendre le c. des écoliers** to take the long way round; **suivre le droit c.** to stay on the straight and narrow **(c)** *(distance)* way; *aussi Fig* **avoir beaucoup de c. à faire** to have a long way to go; **nous avons fait la moitié du c. ensemble/à pied** we went half the way together/on foot; *Fig* **faire son c.** *(idée)* to gain ground **(d)** *Ordinat* path; **c. d'accès** path

chemin de fer *(pl* **chemins de fer)** [ʃəmɛ̃dfɛr] *nm Br* railway, *Am* railroad; *Ordinat (affichage)* thumbnail; **les chemins de fer** *(société d'exploitation)* the railway

cheminée [ʃəmine] *nf* **(a)** *(dans une maison)* fireplace; *(dessus)* mantelpiece **(b)** *(conduit) (de maison, d'usine)* chimney; *(de bateau à vapeur)* funnel **(c)** *Géol* chimney

cheminement [ʃəminmɑ̃] *nm (de personnes)* movement; *Fig* **le c. de la pensée** the development of thought

cheminer [ʃəmine] *vi (personne)* to make one's way; *Fig (idée)* to gain ground

cheminot [ʃəmino] *nm Br* railwayman, *Am* railroader

chemise [ʃəmiz] *nf* **(a)** *(vêtement)* shirt; **c. à manches longues/courtes** long-/short-sleeved shirt; *Fig* **changer de qch comme de c.** to change sth at the drop of a hat; **c. de nuit** *(de femme)* nightdress; *(d'homme)* nightshirt **(b)** *(classeur)* folder

chemisette [ʃəmizɛt] *nf (d'homme)* short-sleeved shirt

chemisier [ʃəmizje] *nm* **(a)** *(corsage)* blouse **(b)** *(fabricant)* shirt-maker; *(marchand)* men's outfitter

chenal, -aux [ʃənal, -o] *nm (d'une rivière, d'un port)* channel

chenapan [ʃənapɑ̃] *nm Vieilli* scoundrel

chêne [ʃɛn] *nm* oak; **table en c. massif** solid oak table; **c. vert** holm oak

chêne-liège *(pl* **chênes-lièges)** [ʃɛnljɛʒ] *nm* cork oak

chenet [ʃənɛ] *nm* firedog

chenil [ʃənil] *nm* **(a)** *(abri, élevage)* kennels **(b)** *Suisse (désordre)* shambles

chenille [ʃənij] *nf* **(a)** *(insecte)* caterpillar **(b)** *(de char, d'autoneige)* caterpillar track; **véhicule à chenilles** tracked vehicle **(c)** *(tissu)* chenille

chenu, -e [ʃəny] *adj Litt (personne, tête)* hoary; *(arbre)* leafless

cheptel [ʃɛptɛl] *nm (d'un agriculteur)* livestock

chèque [ʃɛk] *nm* **c. (bancaire)** *Br* cheque, *Am* check; **c. de 60 euros** cheque for 60 euros; **faire un c. à qn** to write sb a cheque; **payer qch par c.** to pay for sth by cheque; **c. barré** crossed cheque; **c. en blanc** blank cheque; *Fam* **c. en bois** rubber cheque; **c. sans provision** bad cheque; **j'ai fait un c. sans provision** my cheque bounced; **c. de voyage** traveller's cheque

chèque-cadeau *(pl* **chèques-cadeaux)** [ʃɛkkado] *nm* gift token

chèque-repas *(pl* **chèques-repas)** [ʃɛkrəpa], **chèque-restaurant** *(pl* **chèques-restaurant)** [ʃɛkrɛstɔrɑ̃] *nm* luncheon voucher

chéquier [ʃekje] *nm Br* cheque book, *Am* check book

cher, -ère [ʃɛr] **1** *adj* **(a)** *(coûteux)* dear, expensive; *Fam* **pas c.** cheap; **la vie est chère en ville** it's expensive to live in town **(b)** *(aimé)* dear; *Litt* **être c. à qn** to be dear to sb; **c'est mon vœu le plus c.** it's my dearest wish; **il a retrouvé sa chère maison/son c. bureau** he's back in his beloved house/office; **C. Monsieur** *(dans une lettre)* Dear Mr X; *(officiel)* Dear Sir
2 *adv* **payer qch c./trop c.** to pay a high price/too much for sth; *Fam* **je l'ai eu pour pas c.** I got it cheap; **coûter c.** to cost a lot; **je donnerais c. pour savoir ce qu'il leur a dit** I'd give anything to know what he said to them
3 *nm,f* **mon c., ma chère** my dear

chercher [ʃɛrʃe] **1** *vt* **(a)** *(objet, personne, emploi, solution)* to look for; *(dans un dictionnaire)* to look up; *(dans ses souvenirs)* to try to think of; **c. qn du regard** *ou* **des yeux** to look around for sb; **c. ses mots** to search for words; **cherche!** *(à un chien)* fetch!; *Fig* **où va-t-il donc c. tout cela?** where on earth does he get that from?; **il l'a bien cherché** he was asking for it; **c. midi à quatorze heures** to look for problems where there are none

(b) *(prendre)* **aller/venir c. qn/qch** to (go/come and) fetch sb/sth

(c) *(essayer)* **c. à faire qch** to try to do sth

(d) *Fam (atteindre)* **cela va c. dans les 10 000 euros** you're talking about something like 10,000 euros

(e) *Fam (provoquer)* to get at; **tu me cherches?** are you looking for a fight?

2 se chercher *vpr (chercher son identité)* to try to find oneself

chercheur, -euse [ʃɛrʃœr, -øz] *nm,f* **(a)** *(scientifique)* researcher **(b) c. d'or** gold digger

chère [ʃɛr] *nf Litt* **aimer la bonne c.** to be a lover of good food

chèrement [ʃɛrmã] *adv* **vendre c. sa peau** to sell one's life dearly

chéri, -e [ʃeri] **1** *adj* dear; **à notre grand-mère chérie** *(sur une couronne mortuaire)* to our beloved grand-mother

2 *nm,f* darling; **mon c., ma chérie** darling

chérir [ʃerir] *vt Litt* to cherish

cherra *etc voir* choir

cherry *(pl* **cherrys** *ou* **cherries**) [ʃeri] *nm* cherry brandy

cherté [ʃɛrte] *nf* high cost; **la c. de la vie** the high cost of living

chérubin [ʃerybɛ̃] *nm aussi Fig* cherub

chétif, -ive [ʃetif, -iv] *adj (personne)* puny, sickly; *(arbuste)* stunted

cheval, -aux [ʃəval, -o] *nm* **(a)** *(animal)* horse; *Péj (femme)* carthorse; **à c.** on horseback; **monter à c.** to ride; *aussi Fig* **être à c. sur qch** to straddle sth; **être à c. sur l'étiquette** to be a stickler for etiquette; *Fam* **ce n'est pas un mauvais c.** he's not such a bad sort; **monter sur ses grands chevaux** to get on one's high horse; **petits chevaux** = type of board game; **c. d'arçons** (vaulting) horse; **c. à bascule** rocking horse; **c'est son c. de bataille** that's her hobby-horse; **chevaux de bois** *Br* roundabout, *Am* carousel; **c. de course** racehorse; **c. de labour** workhorse; **c. de trait** carthorse **(b)** *Aut* horsepower; **une automobile de 20 chevaux** a 20-horsepower car

chevalerie [ʃəvalri] *nf* **(a)** *(dignité)* knighthood **(b)** *(institution)* chivalry

chevalet [ʃəvalɛ] *nm* **(a)** *(de peintre)* easel; *(de menuisier, de charpentier)* trestle **(b)** *Mus (de violon)* bridge

chevalier [ʃəvalje] *nm* **(a)** *(seigneur)* knight; **c. servant** faithful admirer **(b)** *(de la Légion d'honneur)* chevalier

chevalière [ʃəvaljɛr] *nf* signet ring

chevalin, -e [ʃəvalɛ̃, -in] *adj* equine; *Fig (traits)* horsey

cheval-vapeur [ʃəvalvapœr] *(pl* **chevaux-vapeur** [ʃəvovapœr]*) nm* horsepower

chevauchée [ʃəvoʃe] *nf (course)* ride

chevaucher [ʃəvoʃe] **1** *vt (mur, chaise)* to straddle; *Litt (cheval, âne)* to ride

2 *vi Litt* to ride

3 se chevaucher *vpr* to overlap

chevelu, -e [ʃəvly] *adj Péj* long-haired

chevelure [ʃəvlyr] *nf* (head of) hair; **femme à la c. rousse/blonde** red-haired/blonde woman

chevet [ʃəvɛ] *nm* **(a)** *(tête de lit)* bedhead; **rester au c. de qn** to stay at sb's bedside **(b)** *Archit (d'une église)* chevet

cheveu, -x [ʃəvø] *nm* **(a)** *(poil)* hair; **avoir le c. terne** to have dull hair; **un c. blanc** a grey hair; **arriver comme un c. sur la soupe** to come at an awkward moment; **il s'en est fallu d'un c. qu'il n'éclate de rire** he very nearly burst out laughing; **rater qch d'un c.** to miss sth by a whisker; **à un c. près, je ratais mon train** I caught my train by a hair's breadth **(b) cheveux** hair; **avoir les cheveux longs/courts** to have long/short hair; **un vieillard à cheveux blancs** a white-haired old man; **argument tiré par les cheveux** far-fetched argument; **cheveux d'ange** *(pâtes)* angel-hair pasta

cheville [ʃəvij] *nf* **(a)** *(partie du corps)* ankle; *Fig* **il ne vous arrive pas à la c.** he can't hold a candle to you; *Fam Péj* **tu as les chevilles qui enflent** you're getting too big for your *Br* boots *or Am* britches **(b)** *(pour accrocher)* peg; *(pour boucher un trou)* plug; *(de violon, de guitare)* peg; *Fam* **être en c. avec qn** to be in cahoots with sb; *Fig* **c. ouvrière** mainspring

chèvre [ʃɛvr] **1** *nf* goat; *Fam* **devenir c.** to go round the bend; *Fam* **rendre qn c.** to drive sb round the bend

2 *nm* goat's cheese

chevreau, -x [ʃəvro] *nm* kid; **gants en c.** kid gloves

chèvrefeuille [ʃɛvrəfœj] *nm* honeysuckle

chevreuil [ʃəvrœj] *nm* roe deer; *Can* deer; *(gibier)* venison

chevron [ʃəvrɔ̃] *nm* **(a)** *Constr (d'un toit)* rafter **(b)** *Mil* stripe, chevron **(c)** *(motif)* **tissu à chevrons** herringbone-pattern material

chevronné, -e [ʃəvrɔne] *adj (qui a de l'expérience)* experienced

chevrotant, -e [ʃəvrɔtã, -ãt] *adj (voix)* quavering

chevroter [ʃəvrɔte] *vi (voix)* to quaver

chevrotine [ʃəvrɔtin] *nf* buckshot

chewing-gum *(pl* **chewing-gums**) [ʃwiŋɡɔm] *nm* chewing-gum

chez [ʃe] *prép* **(a)** *(dans la maison de)* **il n'est pas c. lui** he's not at home, he's not in; **elle est rentrée c. elle** she's gone home; **faites comme c. vous** make yourself at home; **je vais c. ma sœur** I'm going to my sister's; **venez c. nous** come to our place; **il vit c. nous** he lives with us; **aller c. le dentiste** to go to the dentist; **chez...** *(sur une lettre)* c/o... **(b)** *(en, dans)* **c'est devenu une habitude c. moi** it's become a habit with me; **ce que j'admire c. cet homme, c'est...** what I admire about the man is...; **c. les Espagnols, on dîne tard** the Spaniards have dinner late **(c)** *(au temps de)* **during the time of (d)** *(parmi)* among; **cette expression est courante c. les jeunes** this expression is common among young people

chez-soi [ʃeswa] *nm inv* **son petit c.** one's own little home

chialer [ʃjale] *vi très Fam* to blubber

chiant, -e [ʃjã, -ãt] *adj très Fam* damned annoying

chianti [kjãti] *nm* Chianti

chiasse [ʃjas] *nf Vulg* **avoir la c.** *(la diarrhée)* to have the shits; *(avoir peur)* to be shit-scared

chic [ʃik] **1** *adj inv* **(a)** *(élégant)* stylish, smart; **les gens c.** the smart set **(b)** *Fam Vieilli (aimable)* decent

2 *nm* **(a)** *(savoir-faire)* **avoir le c. pour faire qch** to have the knack of doing sth **(b)** *(élégance)* style; **bon c. bon genre** ≃ *Br* Sloany, *Am* preppy

3 *exclam Fam Vieilli* **c. (alors)!** great!

Chicago [ʃikago] *n* Chicago

chicaner [ʃikane] **1** vt (chercher querelle à) to quibble with (**sur** about)
2 chicaner sur vt ind to quibble over
3 se chicaner vpr to squabble
chicaneur, -euse [ʃikanœr, -øz], **chicanier, -ère** [ʃikanje, -ɛr] nm,f quibbler
chiche [ʃiʃ] adj (repas) scanty; (personne) mean; **être c. de louanges** to be sparing in one's praise; Fam **tu n'es pas c. d'y aller!** I bet you don't go!; Fam **c.!** (pour défier) I dare you!; (pour relever le défi) you're on!
chichement [ʃiʃmɑ̃] adv meanly
chichi [ʃiʃi] nm Fam **faire du c.** ou **des chichis** (se donner des airs) to put on airs; (compliquer les choses) to make a fuss; **repas sans c.** informal meal
chicorée [ʃikɔre] nf (**a**) (plante) **c. (frisée)** endive; **c. sauvage** chicory (**b**) (en poudre) chicory
chicos [ʃikos] adj Fam smart
chicot [ʃiko] nm (dent) stump
chié, -e¹ [ʃje] adj Fam (culotté) **il est c., lui!** he's got a nerve!
chiée² [ʃje] nf très Fam **(toute) une c. de** a hell of a lot of
chien, chienne [ʃjɛ̃, ʃjɛn] **1** nm,f dog, f bitch; **jeune c.** puppy, pup; **(attention) c. méchant** (sur écriteau) beware of the dog; **traiter qn comme un c.** to treat sb like a dog; Fam **quel temps de c.!** what foul weather!; Fam **vie de c.** dog's life; Fam **chienne de vie!** life's a bitch!; **être comme c. et chat** to fight like cat and dog; **entre c. et loup** at dusk; **se regarder en chiens de faïence** to stare at one another; **c. d'arrêt** pointer; **c. d'aveugle** guide dog; **c. de berger** sheepdog; **c. de chasse** retriever; **c. de garde** guard dog; **c. policier** police dog; **c. de race** pedigree dog; **c. savant** (dans un cirque) performing dog; Fig performing monkey; **c. de traîneau** husky
2 nm (**a**) Fam (style) **avoir du c.** to have a certain something (**b**) (d'un fusil) hammer; **dormir en c. de fusil** to sleep curled up
chiendent [ʃjɛ̃dɑ̃] nm couch grass; **brosse en** ou **de c.** scrubbing brush; **pousser comme du c.** to sprout up
chien-loup (pl **chiens-loups**) [ʃjɛ̃lu] nm wolfhound
chienne [ʃjɛn] nf voir **chien**
chier [66] [ʃje] vi Vulg to shit, to crap; **faire c. qn** (énerver) to piss sb off; (ennuyer) to bore sb shitless; **se faire c.** (s'ennuyer) to be bored shitless; **se faire c. (à faire qch)** (avoir du mal) to bust a gut (doing sth); **je me suis fait c. à l'attendre** I did myself in waiting for him
chiffe [ʃif] nf Fam **c'est une c. molle** he's a drip
chiffon [ʃifɔ̃] nm rag; **c. à poussière** duster; **passer un coup de c.** to have a dust; **passer un coup de c. sur qch** to give sth a dust; Fam **parler chiffons** to talk clothes
chiffonner [ʃifɔne] **1** vt (**a**) (robe, morceau de papier) to crumple (**b**) Fam (ennuyer) to bother
2 se chiffonner vpr to crumple
chiffonnier, -ère [ʃifɔnje, -ɛr] **1** nm,f rag picker; **se disputer comme des chiffonniers** to go at it hammer and tongs
2 nm (meuble) chiffonier
chiffrable [ʃifrabl] adj **facilement/difficilement c.** easy/difficult to calculate; **ne pas être c.** to be impossible to calculate
chiffre [ʃifr] nm (**a**) (nombre) figure, number; **chiffres arabes/romains** Arabic/Roman numerals; **nombre à trois chiffres** three-figure number; Ordinat **c. binaire**

binary digit; Ordinat **c. ASCII** ASCII number (**b**) (total) total; **c. d'affaires (annuel)** (annual) turnover; **faire un c. d'affaires de 4 millions d'euros** to have a turnover of 4 million euros
chiffrement [ʃifrəmɑ̃] nm Ordinat **c. de données** data encryption
chiffrer [ʃifre] **1** vt (**a**) (montant, coût) to work out, to calculate; (réparations) to assess (**b**) **message chiffré** coded message
2 se chiffrer vpr **se c. à** to add up to, to amount to
chignole [ʃiɲɔl] nf hand drill; (électrique) electric drill
chignon [ʃiɲɔ̃] nm bun, chignon; **se faire un c.** to put one's hair in a bun
chihuahua [ʃiwawa] nm chihuahua
chiite [ʃiit] adj & nmf Rel Shiite
Chili [ʃili] nm **le C.** Chile
chili (con carne) [ʃili(kɔnkarne)] nm Culin chilli (con carne)
chilien, -enne [ʃiljɛ̃, -ɛn] **1** adj Chilean
2 nm,f **C.** Chilean
chimère [ʃimɛr] nf (monstre) chimera; Fig (rêve) pipe dream
chimie [ʃimi] nf chemistry
chimiothérapie [ʃimjoterapi] nf Méd chemotherapy; **faire une c.** to have chemotherapy
chimique [ʃimik] adj chemical
chimiste [ʃimist] nmf chemist; **ingénieur c.** chemical engineer
chimpanzé [ʃɛ̃pɑ̃ze] nm chimpanzee
chinchilla [ʃɛ̃ʃila] nm (animal, fourrure) chinchilla; **veste en c.** chinchilla jacket
Chine [ʃin] nf **la C.** China
chiné, -e [ʃine] adj (tissu) flecked
chiner [ʃine] **1** vt Fam (personne) to kid
2 vi to hunt for second-hand goods
chinetoque [ʃintɔk] nmf très Fam Chink, = racist term used to refer to a Chinese
chinois, -e [ʃinwa, -az] **1** adj Chinese
2 nm,f **C.** Chinese; **les C.** the Chinese
3 nm (**a**) (langue) Chinese; Fam Fig **c'est du c.** it's all Greek to me (**b**) (ustensile) conical strainer
chinoiserie [ʃinwazri] nf (**a**) (objet) Chinese curio (**b**) Fam **chinoiseries** (complications) pointless complications
chintz [ʃints] nm chintz; **des rideaux en c.** chintz curtains
chiot [ʃjo] nm puppy, pup
chiottes [ʃjɔt] nfpl très Fam Br bog, Am john; Vulg **aux c., l'arbitre!** the referee's a wanker!
chiper [ʃipe] vt Fam to pinch, to swipe
chipie [ʃipi] nf Fam minx
chipolata [ʃipɔlata] nf chipolata (sausage)
chipoter [ʃipɔte] vi (**a**) (picorer) to pick at one's food (**b**) (contester) to quibble (**sur** about)
chips [ʃips] nf Br crisp, Am chip; **des (pommes) c.** crisps, Am chips
chique [ʃik] nf (**a**) (de tabac) quid (**b**) Fam **avoir la c.** (la joue enflée) to have a swollen cheek (due to toothache) (**c**) Belg sweet
chiqué [ʃike] nm Fam **faire du c.** to put on an act; **c'est du c.** it's all put on
chiquenaude [ʃiknod] nf flick; **d'une c., il l'envoya sur le bureau** he flicked it onto the desk
chiquer [ʃike] **1** vt to chew
2 vi to chew tobacco

chiromancien, -enne [kirɔmɑ̃sjɛ̃, -ɛn] *nm,f* palmist

chirurgical, -e, -aux, -ales [ʃiryrʒikal, -o] *adj* surgical

chirurgie [ʃiryrʒi] *nf* surgery; **c. esthétique** plastic surgery

chirurgien [ʃiryrʒjɛ̃] *nm* surgeon

chirurgien-dentiste (*pl* **chirurgiens-dentistes**) [ʃiryrʒjɛ̃dɑ̃tist] *nm* dental surgeon

chiure [ʃjyr] *nf* **c. de mouche** fly-speck

ch-l. (*abrév* **chef-lieu**) = administrative centre of a "département"

chleuh, -e [ʃlø] *adj & nm,f très Fam* Kraut, = offensive term used to refer to a German

chlinguer [ʃlɛ̃ge] *vi très Fam* to stink

chlorate [klɔrat] *nm Chim* chlorate

chlore [klɔr] *nm* chlorine

chlorer [klɔre] *vt* to chlorinate

chlorhydrique [klɔridrik] *adj* (*acide*) hydrochloric

chlorofluorocarbure [klɔrɔflyɔrɔkarbyr] *nm Chim* chlorofluorocarbon

chloroforme [klɔrɔfɔrm] *nm* chloroform

chloroformer [klɔrɔfɔrme] *vt* to chloroform

chlorophylle [klɔrɔfil] *nf* chlorophyll

chlorure [klɔryr] *nm Chim* chloride; **c. de sodium** sodium chloride

chnoque [ʃnɔk] = **schnock**

choc [ʃɔk] *nm* (**a**) (*coup*) impact; *Fig* (*conflit*) clash; (*forte impression*) impact; *Écon* **c. pétrolier** oil crisis (**b**) *Méd* shock; **c. opératoire** post-operative shock (**c**) (*émotion brutale*) shock; **faire un c. à qn** to give sb a shock; **être en état de c.** to be in a state of shock; **être sous le c.** to be in shock (**d**) **équipe de c.** team of troubleshooters; **troupes de c.** shock troops

-choc [ʃɔk] *suff* **image-c.** shocking image; **prix-chocs** (*sur une vitrine*) drastic reductions

chochotte [ʃɔʃɔt] *nf Fam Péj* la-di-da type; (*homme*) namby-pamby; **faire sa c.** to put on airs

chocolat [ʃɔkɔla] **1** *nm* (**a**) (*produit*) chocolate; **gâteau au c.** chocolate cake; **c. blanc** white chocolate; **un c. (chaud)** a hot chocolate; **c. à cuire** cooking chocolate; **c. au lait** milk chocolate; **c. noir** *ou* **à croquer** plain *or* dark chocolate; **c. aux noisettes** hazelnut chocolate; **c. en poudre** drinking chocolate (**b**) (*bonbon*) chocolate
  2 *adj inv* chocolate-coloured; *Fam* **être c.** to have lost out

chocolaté, -e [ʃɔkɔlate] *adj* chocolate

chocolatier, -ère [ʃɔkɔlatje, -ɛr] **1** *nm,f* (*fabricant*) chocolate-maker; (*vendeur*) chocolate-seller
  2 *adj* (*industrie*) chocolate

chocottes [ʃɔkɔt] *nfpl Fam* **avoir les c.** to have the jitters

chœur [kœr] *nm* choir; (*d'opéra*) chorus; **les chœurs** the chorus; **chanter en c.** to sing in chorus; **répétez tous en c.** repeat all together now

choir [14] [ʃwar] *vi* (*aux être*) *Litt* (*tomber*) to fall; **se laisser c.** to sink down; *Fam* **laisser c. qn** to drop sb

choisi, -e [ʃwazi] *adj* (**a**) (*sélectionné*) **morceaux choisis de...** selected extracts from... (**b**) (*langage, termes*) careful

choisir [ʃwazir] *vt* to choose, to pick; **c. de faire qch** to choose to do sth; **il a bien choisi son moment!** he really picked his moment!; **à toi de c., cette fois** it's your turn to choose now

choix [ʃwa] *nm* choice; **un grand c. de cravates** a wide choice *or* selection of ties; **avoir le c.** to have a choice; **faire son c.** to take one's pick; **faire le bon c.** to make the right choice; **mon c. est fait** I've made my choice; **laisser le c. à qn** to let sb choose; **viande ou poisson au c.** (*sur un menu*) choice of meat or fish; **de premier c.** top-grade; **de second c.** second-grade

choléra [kɔlera] *nm* cholera; **avoir le c.** to have cholera

cholestérol [kɔlesterɔl] *nm* cholesterol; **taux de c.** cholesterol level; *Fam* **avoir du c.** to have a high cholesterol level

cholestérolémie [kɔlesterɔlemi] *nf Méd* cholesterol level

chômage [ʃomaʒ] *nm* unemployment; **être au c.** to be unemployed, to be out of work; **toucher le c.** to claim unemployment benefit; **s'inscrire au c.** to sign on; **le c. des jeunes** youth unemployment; **être en c. technique** to have been laid off; **c. de longue durée** long-term unemployment

chômé, -e [ʃome] *adj* **jour c.** public holiday, *Br* bank holiday

chômedu [ʃomdy] *nm Fam* unemployment; **être au c.** to be unemployed

chômer [ʃome] *vi* **vous n'avez pas chômé!** you've not been idle!

chômeur, -euse [ʃomœr, -øz] *nm,f* unemployed person; **les chômeurs** the unemployed; **les chômeurs de longue durée** the long-term unemployed

chope [ʃɔp] *nf* (*récipient*) beer mug, tankard; (*contenu*) ≃ pint

choper [ʃɔpe] *vt Fam* (**a**) (*arrêter, prendre*) to nab; **se faire c.** to get nabbed (**b**) (*maladie*) to catch

chopine [ʃɔpin] *nf Fam* (*bouteille*) half-litre bottle; **tu viens boire une c.?** are you coming for a drink?

choquant, -e [ʃɔkɑ̃, -ɑ̃t] *adj* shocking

choquer [ʃɔke] *vt* (**a**) (*indigner*) to shock (**b**) (*traumatiser*) **c. qn** to shake sb badly

choral, -e, -aux *ou* **-als, -ales** [kɔral] **1** *adj* choral **2** *nf* **chorale** (*club*) choral society; (*chanteurs*) choir

chorégraphe [kɔregraf] *nmf* choreographer

chorégraphie [kɔregrafi] *nf* choreography; **faire la c. d'un spectacle** to choreograph a show

chorégraphier [kɔregrafje] *vt* to choreograph

chorégraphique [kɔregrafik] *adj* choreographic

choriste [kɔrist] *nmf* choir member; (*d'église*) chorister; (*d'opéra*) chorus member; (*d'un chanteur*) backing singer

chorizo [tʃorizo] *nm* chorizo

chorus [kɔrys] *nm* (*de jazz*) chorus

chose [ʃoz] **1** *nf*; (**a**) (*objet, parole, événement*) thing; **il s'est passé une c. incroyable** something unbelievable has happened; **je vais te dire une c.** I'm going to tell you something; **il a très bien pris la c.** he took it very well
  (**b**) (*locutions*) **avant toute c.** first of all; **les choses étant ce qu'elles sont** with things as they are; **aller au fond des choses** to get to the heart of the matter; **bien faire les choses** to do things in style; **il ne fait pas les choses à moitié** he doesn't do things by halves; **parler de choses et d'autres** to talk about this and that; **c'est c. faite** it's done; **de deux choses l'une, soit il parle, soit...** either he talks or...; **c. curieuse, personne n'en savait rien** curiously enough, nobody knew anything about it; **et, c. rare, il a demandé pardon** he apologized for once; **dites bien des choses de ma**

part à… remember me to…

2 *nm Fam (truc)* whatsit, thingummy; **Monsieur/Madame C.** Mr/Mrs thingummy

3 *adj inv Fam* **se sentir tout c.** to feel a bit funny

chou¹, -x [ʃu] *nm* (**a**) *(légume)* cabbage; **faire ses choux gras de qch** to have a field day with sth; **faire c. blanc** to draw a blank; **mon petit c.** darling; **c. de Bruxelles** Brussels sprout; **c. rouge** red cabbage (**b**) *(gâteau)* **c. à la crème** cream puff

chou² *adj inv Fam (mignon)* cute; *(gentil)* nice, kind

chouchou, -oute [ʃuʃu, -ut] **1** *nm,f Fam* **c'est le c. (de la maîtresse)** he's teacher's pet; **c'est le c. de sa maman** he's his mother's little blue-eyed boy

2 *nm (pour les cheveux)* scrunchie

chouchouter [ʃuʃute] *vt Fam* to pamper; **elle aime se faire c.** she enjoys being pampered

choucroute [ʃukrut] *nf (chou)* sauerkraut; **c. (garnie)** = sauerkraut served with different types of sausages and bacon

chouette¹ [ʃwɛt] *nf* owl; **c. hulotte** tawny owl; *Fam Péj* **une vieille c.** an old shrew

chouette² *Fam* **1** *adj* great, terrific; **il a été très c. avec elle** he's been really nice to her

2 *exclam* great!, terrific!

chou-fleur *(pl* **choux-fleurs)** [ʃuflœr] *nm* cauliflower; **oreille en c.** cauliflower ear

chouia [ʃuja] *nm Fam* **un c. (de qch)** a tiny bit (of sth)

chouraver [ʃurave], **chourer** [ʃure] *vt très Fam* to swipe; **se faire c. qch** to have sth swiped

choyer [32] [ʃwaje] *vt* to pamper

CHR [seaʃɛr] *nm (abrév* **centre hospitalier régional)** regional hospital

chrétien, -enne [kretjɛ̃, -ɛn] *adj & nm,f* Christian

chrétienté [kretjɛ̃te] *nf* Christendom

Christ [krist] *nm* (**a**) **le C.** Christ (**b**) *(crucifix)* **c.** crucifix

christianisme [kristjanism] *nm* Christianity

chromatique [krɔmatik] *adj* (**a**) *(des couleurs) & Mus* chromatic (**b**) *Biol* chromosomal

chrome [krom] *nm Chim* chromium; **chromes** *(d'une voiture)* chrome

chromé, -e [krome] *adj* chromium-plated; **acier c.** chrome steel

chromosome [krɔmozom] *nm* chromosome

chromosomique [krɔmozomik] *adj* chromosomal

chronique¹ [krɔnik] *adj* chronic

chronique² *nf* (**a**) *Journ* column; **tenir la c. sportive** to write the sports column (**b**) *(annale)* chronicle

chroniqueur, -euse [krɔnikœr, -øz] *nm,f Journ* columnist; **c. sportif** sports reporter

chrono [krono] *nm Fam* stopwatch; **faire du 220 km/h c.** to be timed at 220 kph

chronologie [krɔnɔlɔʒi] *nf* chronology

chronologique [krɔnɔlɔʒik] *adj* chronological

chronomètre [krɔnɔmɛtr] *nm (montre de précision)* chronometer; *(pour le sport)* stopwatch

chronométrer [34] [krɔnɔmetre] *vt Sport* to time

chrysalide [krizalid] *nf* chrysalis

chrysanthème [krizɑ̃tɛm] *nm* chrysanthemum

Chrysanthèmes

Chrysanthemums are often associated with funerals in France, and so are never offered as gifts. They are traditionally used to decorate graves, especially on All Saints' Day.

---

ch'timi [ʃtimi] **1** *nmf Fam* Northerner *(from Northern France)*

2 *nm (patois)* = dialect spoken in Northern France

CHU [seaʃy] *nm inv (abrév* **centre hospitalo-universitaire)** teaching hospital

chu *voir* **choir**

chuchotement [ʃyʃɔtmɑ̃] *nm* whisper; **des chuchotements** whispering

chuchoter [ʃyʃɔte] *vt & vi* to whisper

chuintement [ʃɥɛ̃tmɑ̃] *nm* hissing

chuinter [ʃɥɛ̃te] *vi (siffler)* to hiss

chut [ʃyt] *exclam* sh!, hush!

chute [ʃyt] *nf* (**a**) *(fait de tomber) & Fig* fall; *(diminution)* drop, fall; **faire une c. (de cheval/moto)** to have a fall (from one's horse/motorbike); **prévenir la c. des cheveux** to prevent hair loss; **il m'a entraîné dans sa c.** he has dragged me down with him; **c. libre** free fall; **descendre en c. libre** to be in free fall; **c. de neige** snowfall (**b**) **c. d'eau** waterfall; **les chutes Victoria** the Victoria Falls (**c**) *(d'histoire drôle)* punchline (**d**) *(de tissu, de métal)* scrap; *(de bois)* off-cut

chuter [ʃyte] *vi (diminuer)* to fall, to drop; *Fam (tomber)* to fall (down)

Chypre [ʃipr] *n* Cyprus

chypriote [ʃiprijɔt] **1** *adj* Cypriot

2 *nmf* **C.** Cypriot

ci¹ [si] *adv* **ce livre-ci** this book; **ces jours-ci** these days; **de-ci de-là** here and there; **par-ci par-là** here and there

ci² *pron démonstratif Fam* **faire ci et ça** to do this and that

CIA [seia] *nf* **la C.** the CIA

ciao [tʃao] *exclam Fam* ciao!

ci-après [siaprɛ] *adv* below; *Jur* hereinafter

cibiste [sibist] *nmf* CB user

cible [sibl] *nf aussi Fig* target

ciblé, -e [sible] *adj* well-targeted

ciboire [sibwar] *nm Rel* ciborium

ciboulette [sibulɛt] *nf* chives

ciboulot [sibulo] *nm très Fam (tête)* nut; **il n'a rien dans le c.** he doesn't have much upstairs; **se creuser le c.** to rack one's brains

cicatrice [sikatris] *nf aussi Fig* scar

cicatrisant, -e [sikatrizɑ̃, -ɑ̃t] *adj* healing

cicatrisation [sikatrizasjɔ̃] *nf* healing

cicatriser [sikatrize] **1** *vt & vi* to heal

2 **se cicatriser** *vpr* to heal

ci-contre [sikɔ̃tr] *adv* opposite

ci-dessous [sidəsu] *adv* below

ci-dessus [sidəsy] *adv* above

ci-devant [sidəvɑ̃] *adv Vieilli* formerly

CIDEX [sideks] *nm (abrév* **courrier individuel à distribution exceptionelle)** = system grouping letter boxes in country areas

CIDJ [seideʒi] *nm (abrév* **centre d'information et de documentation de la jeunesse)** = library offering careers information and literature to young people

cidre [sidr] *nm* cider; **c. bouché** = traditionally-made cider, fermented twice; **c. doux/brut** sweet/dry cider

Cie *(abrév* **compagnie)** Co

ciel [sjɛl] *nm* (**a**) *(air)* sky; **les ciels de Turner** Turner's skies; **à c. ouvert** open-air; **sous d'autres cieux** in other climes; **lever les bras/les yeux au c.** to raise one's arms/one's eyes heavenwards; *Fam* **être au septième c.** to be in seventh heaven; *Fam* **tomber**

du c. (à qn) *(héritage)* to be a godsend (to sb); *(solution)* to come (to sb) out of the blue (**b**) *(pl* **cieux** [sjø]) *(paradis)* heaven; **il est au c.** he's in heaven; **notre Père qui êtes aux cieux** our Father which art in Heaven (**c**) **c. de lit** canopy

cierge [sjɛrʒ] *nm Rel* candle; **brûler un c.** to light a candle

cigale [sigal] *nf* cicada

cigare [sigar] *nm* (**a**) *(à fumer)* cigar (**b**) *très Fam (tête)* **ne rien avoir dans le c.** to be completely brainless

cigarette [sigarɛt] *nf* cigarette; *Culin* **c. russe** = short-cake biscuit shaped like a brandy snap

ci-gît [siʒi] *voir* **gésir**

cigogne [sigɔɲ] *nf* stork

ciguë [sigy] *nf* hemlock

ci-inclus, -e *(mpl* **ci-inclus**, *fpl* **ci-incluses**) [siɛkly, -yz] **1** *adj* **la copie ci-incluse** the enclosed copy
    2 *adv* **(vous trouverez) c. copie de votre lettre** please find enclosed a copy of your letter

ci-joint, -e *(mpl* **ci-joints**, *fpl* **ci-jointes**) [siʒwɛ̃, -ɛ̃t] **1** *adj* **les pièces ci-jointes** the enclosed documents
    2 *adv* **(vous trouverez) c. copie de votre lettre** please find enclosed a copy of your letter

cil [sil] *nm* eyelash; **faux cils** false eyelashes

ciller [sije] *vi* to blink; *Fig* **il n'a pas cillé** he didn't bat an eyelid

cime [sim] *nf (d'une montagne)* summit; *(pic)* peak; *(d'un arbre, d'un mât)* top

ciment [simɑ̃] *nm* cement

cimenter [simɑ̃te] *vt aussi Fig* to cement

cimetière [simtjɛr] *nm* cemetery; *(d'église)* graveyard; **c. de voitures** scrapyard

ciné [sine] *nm Fam Br* pictures, *Am* movies

cinéaste [sineast] *nmf* film maker

ciné-club *(pl* **ciné-clubs**) [sineklœb] *nm* film club

cinéma [sinema] *nm* (**a**) *(art, industrie) Br* cinema, *Am* movies; **faire du c.** to be a film actor, to act in films; *Fam (faire semblant)* to put on an act; *Fam* **c'est du c.** it's all an act; *Fam* **arrête ton c.!** stop making such a fuss!; **c. d'art et d'essai** art films; **c. muet** silent films; **c. parlant** talking films (**b**) *(salle) Br* cinema, *Am* movie theater; **aller au c.** to go to the cinema

CinémaScope® [sinemaskɔp] *nm* CinemaScope®

cinémathèque [sinematɛk] *nf* film library

cinématographie [sinematɔgrafi] *nf* cinematography

cinématographique [sinematɔgrafik] *adj* cinema, film

ciné-parc *(pl* **cinés-parcs**) [sinepark] *nm Can* drive-in movie theater

cinéphile [sinefil] **1** *adj* **être c.** to be a film *or Am* movie buff
    2 *nmf Br* film *or Am* movie enthusiast

cinéraire [sinerɛr] *adj (urne)* cinerary

cinétique [sinetik] *adj (énergie)* kinetic

cinglant, -e [sɛ̃glɑ̃, -ɑ̃t] *adj (pluie)* lashing; *(vent, remarque)* cutting

cinglé, -e [sɛ̃gle] *Fam* **1** *adj* crazy
    2 *nm,f* loony

cingler¹ [sɛ̃gle] *vi Naut* **c. vers** to make for

cingler² *vt (frapper)* to lash; **la grêle lui cinglait le visage** the hail was stinging his face

cinoche [sinɔʃ] *nm Fam Br* cinema, *Am* movie theater

cinq [sɛ̃k] **1** *adj inv* five
    2 *nm inv* five; **recevoir qn c. sur c.** to receive sb loud and clear; *Fam* **c'était moins c.** it was a close shave; *voir aussi* **trois**

cinquantaine [sɛ̃kɑ̃tɛn] *nf* **une c. de personnes** about fifty people, fifty or so people; **avoir la c.** to be about fifty

cinquante [sɛ̃kɑ̃t] *adj & nm inv* fifty; *voir aussi* **trois**

cinquantenaire [sɛ̃kɑ̃tnɛr] **1** *nm (anniversaire)* fiftieth anniversary, golden jubilee
    2 *adj* **être c.** to be fifty years old

cinquantième [sɛ̃kɑ̃tjɛm] *nmf, nm & adj* fiftieth; *voir aussi* **cinquième**

cinquième [sɛ̃kjɛm] **1** *adj* fifth; **le c. jour** the fifth day; **arriver c.** to finish fifth
    2 *nmf* fifth; **le c. en partant de la droite** the fifth from the right; **arriver le c.** to finish fifth
    3 *nm* (**a**) *(fraction)* fifth (**b**) *(étage)* fifth floor; **habiter au c.** to live on the *Br* fifth *or Am* sixth floor (**c**) *(arrondissement)* fifth arrondissement
    4 *nf* (**a**) *(classe) Br* ≃ second year of secondary school, *Am* ≃ sixth grade (**b**) *(vitesse)* fifth (gear); **passer la c.** to go into fifth (gear)

cinquièmement [sɛ̃kjɛmmɑ̃] *adv* fifthly

cintre [sɛ̃tr] *nm* (coat)hanger

cintré, -e [sɛ̃tre] *adj (veste)* fitted; *(taille)* nipped-in

CIO [seio] *nm (abrév* **Comité international olympique**) IOC

cirage [siraʒ] *nm* (shoe) polish; *Fam* **être dans le c.** to be feeling woozy

circoncire [sirkɔ̃sir] *vt* to circumcise

circoncision [sirkɔ̃sizjɔ̃] *nf* circumcision

circonférence [sirkɔ̃ferɑ̃s] *nf* circumference; **avoir 10 centimètres de c.** to have a circumference of 10 centimetres

circonflexe [sirkɔ̃flɛks] *adj voir* **accent**

circonlocution [sirkɔ̃lɔkysjɔ̃] *nf* circumlocution; **parler par circonlocutions** to speak in a roundabout way

circonscription [sirkɔ̃skripsjɔ̃] *nf* division, district; **c. électorale** *(au niveau municipal)* ward; *(au niveau national)* constituency

circonscrire [30] [sirkɔ̃skrir] *vt Math* to circumscribe; *(encercler)* to encircle; *(incendie)* to contain

circonspect, -e [sirkɔ̃spɛ, -ɛkt] *adj* circumspect, cautious

circonstance [sirkɔ̃stɑ̃s] *nf* circumstance; **dans les circonstances actuelles** in the present circumstances; **en pareille c.** under such circumstances; **être à la hauteur des circonstances** to be equal to the occasion; **des paroles de c.** appropriate words; **habillé pour la c.** appropriately dressed; **circonstances aggravantes** aggravating circumstances; *Jur* **circonstances atténuantes** extenuating circumstances

circonstancié, -e [sirkɔ̃stɑ̃sje] *adj* detailed

circonstanciel, -elle [sirkɔ̃stɑ̃sjɛl] *adj voir* **complément**

circonvolution [sirkɔ̃vɔlysjɔ̃] *nf* convolution

circuit [sirkɥi] *nm* (**a**) *(chemin)* way; *(boucle)* tour; *Fig* **ça fait longtemps que je ne suis plus dans le c.** I've been out of circulation for ages; **c. touristique** (organized) tour (**b**) *(de course automobile, de cyclisme)* circuit; **c. automobile** racing circuit (**c**) *Élec* circuit (**d**) *Tech* **c. de refroidissement** cooling system (**e**) *Ordinat* **c. de commande** command circuit; **c. imprimé** printed circuit; **c. intégré** integrated circuit; **c. de liaison** link circuit; **c. logique** logic circuit (**f**) *Écon* **c. de**

distribution distribution network; **circuits de vente** commercial channels

circulaire [sirkylɛr] **1** *nf* circular **2** *adj* circular; **billet c.** round-trip ticket

circulation [sirkylasjɔ̃] *nf* (**a**) *(d'autos, d'avions)* traffic; **c. interdite** *(sur panneau)* no thoroughfare; **c. aérienne** air traffic; **c. routière** road traffic (**b**) *(du sang, de l'information, des marchandises)* circulation; *Méd* **avoir une mauvaise c.** to have bad circulation; **mettre qch en c.** to put sth into circulation; **retirer un produit de la c.** to take a product off the market (**c**) *Fin (des billets, des capitaux)* circulation (**d**) *Pol & Écon* **libre c. des personnes et des biens** free movement of persons and goods

circulatoire [sirkylatwar] *adj* circulatory

circuler [sirkyle] *vi* (**a**) *(sang, air, rumeur)* to circulate; **faire c. un plat** to pass *or* hand a dish round; **faire c. une pétition** to circulate a petition (**b**) *(voyageur)* to travel; *(train, autobus)* to run; **on circule très mal dans Paris** it's very difficult to drive about in Paris; **circulez, il n'y a rien à voir!** move along now, there's nothing to see!

cire [sir] *nf* wax; *(pour le bois)* polish; *(dans l'oreille)* (ear)wax; **c. d'abeille** beeswax; **c. à cacheter** sealing wax; **personnage en c.** waxwork (model)

ciré [sire] *nm* oilskin

cirer [sire] *vt (chaussures, meubles)* to polish; *Fam* **c. les pompes à qn** to lick sb's boots; *très Fam* **il en a rien à c. (de tes histoires)** he doesn't give a damn (about your stories)

cireur, -euse [sirœr, -øz] **1** *nm,f (de chaussures)* shoeblack **2** *nf* **cireuse** *(machine)* (floor) polisher

cireux, -euse [sirø, -øz] *adj* waxy

cirque [sirk] *nm* (**a**) *(spectacle)* circus; *Fam* **quel c. dans ce bureau!** it's like a zoo in this office!; *Fam* **faire tout un c.** to make a scene (**b**) *Géol* corrie

cirrhose [siroz] *nf* **c. (du foie)** cirrhosis (of the liver); **avoir une c.** to have cirrhosis

cisaille [sizaj] *nf* **c., cisailles** *(de jardinier)* shears

cisailler [sizaje] *vt (branches, haie)* to prune

ciseau, -x [sizo] *nm* (**a**) *(de jardin)* shears; **(une paire de) ciseaux** *(pour papier, pour tissu)* (a pair of) scissors; **des ciseaux à ongles** nail scissors (**b**) *Sport* **sauter en ciseaux** to do a scissors jump (**c**) *Tech* chisel

ciseler [39] [sizle] *vt (or, argent)* to chase; *(marbre)* to chisel; *(bijou)* to engrave a design on

Cisjordanie [sisʒɔrdani] *nf* **la C.** the West Bank

cisjordanien, -enne [sisʒɔrdanjɛ̃, -ɛn] **1** *adj* from the West Bank **2** *nm,f* **C.** person from the West Bank

cistercien, -enne [sistɛrsjɛ̃, -ɛn] *adj & nm Rel* Cistercian

citadelle [sitadɛl] *nf* citadel

citadin, -e [sitadɛ̃, -in] **1** *nm,f* city-dweller **2** *adj* city

citation [sitasjɔ̃] *nf* (**a**) *(extrait)* quotation; **fin de c.** unquote (**b**) *Jur* **c. à comparaître** *(d'un accusé)* summons; *(d'un témoin)* subpoena

cité [site] *nf* (**a**) *(ville)* city (**b**) *(groupe d'immeubles)* (housing) *Br* estate *or Am* development; **c. universitaire** *Br* halls of residence, *Am* dormitory complex

cité-dortoir *(pl* **cités-dortoirs)** [sitedɔrtwar] *nf* dormitory town

citer [site] *vt* (**a**) *(rapporter)* to quote; *(auteur)* to quote (from); **c. qn en exemple** to quote sb as an example; **il**

a dit, je cite… he said, and I quote,… (**b**) *(énumérer)* to name (**c**) *Jur (personne en justice)* to summons; *(témoin)* to subpoena (**d**) *Mil* **c. qn (à l'ordre du jour)** to mention sb in dispatches

citerne [sitɛrn] *nf* tank; **c. à mazout** oil tank

cithare [sitar] *nf (instrument moderne)* zither

citizen band [sitizənbãd] *nf* Citizens' Band, CB

citoyen, -enne [sitwajɛ̃, -ɛn] *nm,f* citizen; **c. d'honneur** freeman *(of a city)*

citoyenneté [sitwajente] *nf* citizenship; **la c. française** French citizenship

citrique [sitrik] *adj (acide)* citric

citron [sitrɔ̃] *nm* (**a**) *(fruit)* lemon; **un c. givré** = lemon sorbet served inside the skin of a whole lemon; **un c. pressé** = freshly squeezed lemon juice served with water and sugar; **c. vert** lime (**b**) *Fam (tête)* nut

citronnade [sitrɔnad] *nf Br* lemon squash, *Am* lemonade

citronnelle [sitrɔnɛl] *nf (plante, huile)* citronella

citronnier [sitrɔnje] *nm* lemon tree

citrouille [sitruj] *nf* (**a**) *(plante)* pumpkin (**b**) *Fam (tête)* nut

civelle [sivɛl] *nf* elver

civet [sivɛ] *nm Culin* **c. de lapin** rabbit stew; **c. de lièvre** ≃ jugged hare

civière [sivjɛr] *nf* stretcher

civil, -e [sivil] **1** *adj* (**a**) *(du citoyen, non ecclésiastique)* civil (**b**) *(non militaire)* civilian; **dans la vie civile** in civilian life (**c**) *Litt (courtois)* civil **2** *nm* (**a**) *(personne) (non ecclésiastique)* layman, civilian (**b**) **dans le c.** in civilian life; **en c.** *(policier)* in plain clothes; *(militaire)* in civilian clothes (**c**) *Jur* **poursuivre qn au c.** to bring a civil action against sb

civilement [sivilmã] *adv* (**a**) *Jur* **se marier c.** to have a civil wedding (**b**) *Litt (avec courtoisie)* civilly

civilisation [sivilizasjɔ̃] *nf* civilization

civilisé, -e [sivilize] *adj* civilized

civilité [sivilite] *nf Litt* (**a**) *(courtoisie)* civility (**b**) **civilités** *(politesses)* courtesies

civique [sivik] *adj* civic; **avoir le sens c.** to have a sense of civic responsibility

civisme [sivism] *nm* sense of civic responsibility

cl *(abrév* **centilitre(s))** cl

clac [klak] *exclam (d'un fouet)* crack!; *(d'un objet qui se casse)* snap!; *(d'une porte)* slam!

clafoutis [klafuti] *nm* clafoutis *(fruit, usually cherries, baked in a dish of batter)*

claie [klɛ] *nf* (**a**) *(treillis)* rack (**b**) *(clôture)* fence

clair, -e [klɛr] **1** *adj* (**a**) *(transparent)* (eau, teint, voix) clear; **par temps c.** on a clear day (**b**) *(pièce, couleur)* light (**c**) *(sens, explication)* clear; **il a été très c. là-dessus** he was very clear about it; **il est c. qu'il a tort** he's clearly wrong; **être c. comme de l'eau de roche** to be crystal clear; **avoir les idées claires** to have a clear head; **c'est c. et net** there are no two ways about it; *Fam* **un individu pas très c.** a bit of a shady character (**d**) *(soupe)* thin **2** *adv* clearly; **il fait c.** it's light; *Fig* **je commence à y voir c.** I'm beginning to understand **3** *nm* (**a**) *(lumière)* **c. de lune** moonlight; **au c. de lune** in the moonlight (**b**) **en c.** *(autrement dit)* in plain language; **émission en c.** non-crypted broadcast (**c**) *Fig* **tirer une affaire au c.** to clear a matter up; **passer le plus c. de son temps à faire qch** to spend the better part of one's time doing sth

clairement [klɛrmã] *adv* clearly

claire-voie *(pl* **claires-voies)** [klɛrvwa] *nf* (**a**) *(treillage)* à **c.** open-work (**b**) *Archit* clerestory

clairière [klɛrjɛr] *nf* clearing, glade

clair-obscur *(pl* **clairs-obscurs)** [klɛrɔpskyr] *nm (en peinture)* chiaroscuro

clairon [klɛrɔ̃] *nm* (**a**) *(instrument)* bugle; **sonner le c.** to sound the bugle (**b**) *(joueur)* bugler

claironner [klɛrɔne] *vt (nouvelle)* to trumpet forth

clairsemé, -e [klɛrsəme] *adj (population, cheveux, gazon)* sparse; *(arbres)* scattered

clairvoyant, -e [klɛrvwajã, -ãt] *adj* perceptive

clamer [klame] *vt* to proclaim

clameur [klamœr] *nf* clamour; **une c. de joie** a shout of joy; **les clameurs de la foule** the clamour of the crowd

clamser [klamse] *vi très Fam (mourir)* to kick the bucket

clan [klã] *nm (tribu)* clan; *Péj (groupe)* clique

clandestin, -e [klãdɛstɛ̃, -in] **1** *adj (réunion, atelier)* clandestine; *(travailleur, immigré)* illegal; *(mouvement)* underground
2 *nm,f (voyageur)* stowaway; *(immigré)* illegal immigrant; *(travailleur)* illegal worker

clandestinement [klãdɛstinmã] *adv (secrètement)* clandestinely; *(illégalement)* illegally

clandestinité [klãdɛstinite] *nf* **dans la c.** *(secrètement)* clandestinely; *(illégalement)* illegally; **entrer dans/sortir de la c.** to go into/to come out of hiding

clap [klap] *nm Cin* clapperboard; **c. de fin** end board

clapet [klapɛ] *nm* (**a**) *Tech* valve (**b**) *Fam* **ferme ton c.!** shut your trap!

clapier [klapje] *nm* (rabbit) hutch

clapoter [klapɔte] *vi* to lap

clapotis [klapɔti] *nm* lapping

claquage [klakaʒ] *nm (blessure)* pulled muscle; **se faire un c.** to pull a muscle

claque¹ [klak] *nf* (**a**) *(gifle)* slap; **donner une c. à qn** to give sb a slap; *Fam Fig* **il va se prendre une c.** it'll be a slap in the face for him; **une paire de claques** a slap (**b**) *Fam* **j'en ai ma c.** I've had it up to here (**c**) *Can* **claques** galoshes

claque² *nm très Fam (maison de passe) Br* knocking shop, *Am* cathouse

claqué, -e [klake] *adj Fam (fatigué) Br* shattered, *Am* bushed

claquement [klakmã] *nm (de porte)* slam(ming); *(de dents)* chattering; *(d'un fouet)* crack(ing); *(d'un drapeau)* flap(ping); *(de doigts)* snap(ping); *(de talons, de la langue)* click(ing); *(de sabots)* clatter(ing)

claquer [klake] **1** *vt* (**a**) *(porte)* to slam; **c. la langue** to click one's tongue (**b**) *Fam (dépenser)* to blow; **il claque un fric monstre chez le coiffeur** he spends a fortune at the hairdresser's
2 *vi* (**a**) *(porte)* to slam; *(drapeau)* to flap; *(talons)* to click; *(sabots)* to clatter; **c. des mains** to clap; **c. des doigts** to snap one's fingers; **elle claque des dents** her teeth are chattering; **faire c. sa langue** to click one's tongue (**b**) *(ampoule électrique)* to go; *(élastique)* to snap; *Fam (personne)* to kick the bucket
3 se claquer *vpr* **se c. un muscle** to pull a muscle

claquettes [klakɛt] *nfpl* tap dancing; **faire des c.** to do tap dancing; **danseur de c.** tap dancer

clarification [klarifikasjɔ̃] *nf aussi Fig* clarification

clarifier [66] [klarifje] **1** *vt (liquide, situation)* to clarify
2 se clarifier *vpr (situation)* to become clear

clarinette [klarinɛt] *nf* clarinet

clarinettiste [klarinɛtist] *nmf* clarinettist

clarté [klarte] *nf* (**a**) *(lumière)* light (**b**) *(transparence)* clearness (**c**) *Fig (du style)* clarity; **avec c.** clearly; **manquer de c.** *(personne)* not to make oneself clear; *(texte, argument)* to be unclear

classe [klas] **1** *nf* (**a**) *(catégorie)* class; *(dans une hiérarchie)* grade; **c. affaires/économique** business/economy class; **c. d'âge** age group; **la c. dirigeante** the ruling class; **les classes moyennes** the middle class(es); **la c. ouvrière** the working class(es); **c. sociale** social class
(**b**) *(qualité)* class; **un sportif de c. internationale** a world-class sportsman; **avoir de la c.** *(personne)* to have class; *(objet, vêtement)* to be classy; *Fam* **ce type, c'est la c.!** he's got real class!
(**c**) *(à l'école) (niveau)* year; *(groupe d'élèves)* class; **les grandes classes, les classes supérieures** the senior school; **les petites classes** the junior school; **c. de mer/de neige** school study trip to the seaside/to the mountains; **partir en c. de mer** to go on a school study trip to the seaside; **c. préparatoire (aux grandes écoles)** = preparatory class for the entrance examinations for the Grandes Écoles; **c. unique** = class where pupils belonging to different years are taught together by one teacher; **c. verte** school study trip to the countryside
(**d**) *(leçon)* class; **la c. de français** the French class; **aller en c.** to go to school; **être en c.** *(à l'école)* to be at school; *(en cours)* to be in class; **faire la c.** to teach
(**e**) *(pièce)* **(salle de) c.** classroom
(**f**) *Mil (de conscrits)* levy; **faire ses classes** to undergo basic training
2 *adj inv Fam* classy

Classes préparatoires

This term refers to the two years of intensive preparation required for students who have passed their baccalauréat and wish to enter the "grandes écoles". These two years of study are extremely competitive and highly demanding. Students are completely immersed in their subject, which can be in humanities, economics or the sciences, and do little other than study for the "grandes écoles" exams. For students who are not successful in these exams, two years of "prépas" are considered equivalent to a **DEUG** *(see box at this entry)*, and these students often go on to study at a university.

---

classé, -e [klase] *adj (monument)* listed

classement [klasmã] *nm* (**a**) *(dans une classe ou une course)* position, place; *(liste d'équipes, de concurrents)* classification; *(au foot, au rugby)* table; *(des plantes)* classification; **être troisième au c.** to be in third place; **c. général** overall classification (**b**) *(rangement) (de documents)* filing; *(d'articles)* sorting out; **faire du c.** to do some filing; **c. (par ordre) alphabétique** alphabetical classification

classer [klase] **1** *vt* (**a**) *(classifier)* to classify; *(étudiants)* to grade; **être classés par pays** to be classified according to country (**b**) *(ranger) (documents)* to file; *(articles)* to sort out; **c. une affaire** to consider a matter closed; **c'est une affaire classée** the matter's closed

2 se classer *vpr* **se c. parmi les meilleurs** to rank among the best; *Sport* **se c. troisième** to be placed third

classeur [klasœr] *nm* (**a**) *(dossier)* ring binder (**b**) *(meuble)* filing cabinet (**c**) *Ordinat* filer

classicisme [klasisism] *nm* classicism

classification [klasifikasjɔ̃] *nf* classification; *Chim* **c. périodique des éléments** periodic table

classifier [66] [klasifje] *vt* to classify

classique [klasik] **1** *adj* (**a**) *(période)* classical; *(beauté)* classic (**b**) *(conventionnel) (vêtement, style, exemple, plaisanterie)* classic; *(arme, guerre)* conventional; *Fam* **c'est le coup c.** it's the same old story
2 *nm* (**a**) *(auteur)* classical author; **connaître ses classiques** to be well-read (**b**) *(œuvre, film, chanson)* classic; **c'est un c. du genre** it's a classic of its kind (**c**) *(style musical)* **le c.** classical music

claudication [klodikasjɔ̃] *nf* limp

clause [kloz] *nf Jur* clause; **c. d'exclusivité** exclusivity clause; **c. de la nation la plus favorisée** most-favoured-nation status

claustrophobe [klostrɔfɔb] *adj* claustrophobic

claustrophobie [klostrɔfɔbi] *nf* claustrophobia

clavecin [klavsɛ̃] *nm* harpsichord

claveciniste [klavsinist] *nmf* harpsichordist

clavicule [klavikyl] *nf* collarbone, *Spéc* clavicle

clavier [klavje] *nm* keyboard; *Ordinat* **c. multifonction** multifunctional keyboard; **c. numérique** numerical *or* numeric keypad

claviste [klavist] *nmf Ordinat* keyboarder; *Typ* typesetter

clé [kle] = **clef**

clean [klin] *adj inv Fam* (**a**) *(BCBG)* clean-cut (**b**) *(qui ne se drogue pas)* clean

clébard [klebar], **clebs** [klɛps] *nm Fam* pooch

clef [kle] **1** *nf* (**a**) *(d'une porte, d'un cadenas)* key; **fermer qch à c.** to lock sth; **tenir/mettre qch sous c.** to keep/put sth under lock and key; **usine clefs en main** turnkey factory; **prix clefs en main** *(d'une voiture)* on-the-road price; *(d'une maison)* all-inclusive price; *Fig* **mettre la c. sous la porte** to move away; *(commerçant)* to shut up shop; **prendre la c. des champs** *(prisonnier)* to make a bid for freedom; **c. de contact** ignition key; **c. passe-partout** passkey, master key
(**b**) *(outil)* spanner; **c. anglaise** monkey wrench; **c. à molette** adjustable spanner; **c. plate** open-end *Br* spanner *or Am* wrench
(**c**) *Mus (d'un instrument à cordes)* peg; *(d'un instrument à vent)* key; **c. de sol/de fa** treble/bass clef; **il y a une forte somme d'argent à la c.** there is a large sum of money at the end of it
(**d**) *(moyen d'accès, solution)* key; **la c. du mystère** the key to the mystery
(**e**) **c. de voûte** *(d'une arche)* keystone; *Fig* cornerstone
(**f**) *Ordinat* key; *(du DOS)* switch; **c. de contrôle** control key; **c. gigogne** dongle; **c. à puce** computerized key
2 *adj (vital)* key; **un secteur(-)c. de la recherche** a key area of research

clématite [klematit] *nf* clematis

clémence [klemɑ̃s] *nf* (**a**) *(de la température)* mildness (**b**) *(d'un juge, d'un maître)* clemency (**envers** towards)

clément, -e [klemɑ̃, -ɑ̃t] *adj* (**a**) *(température)* mild (**b**) *(juge, maître)* clement (**envers** towards)

clémentine [klemɑ̃tin] *nf* clementine

Cléopâtre [kleɔpɑtr] *npr* Cleopatra

cleptomane [klɛptɔman] *adj & nmf* kleptomaniac

cleptomanie [klɛptɔmani] *nf* kleptomania

clerc [klɛr] *nm* (**a**) *(dans un bureau)* **c. de notaire** ≃ solicitor's clerk (**b**) *Rel* cleric (**c**) *Litt* **il n'est pas besoin d'être grand c. pour...** you don't have to be a genius in order to...

clergé [klɛrʒe] *nm* clergy

clérical, -e, -aux, -ales [klerikal, -o] *adj* clerical

clic [klik] *nm* (**a**) *(bruit)* click; **faire c.** to click (**b**) *Ordinat* click; **double c.** double click

clic-clac [klikklak] *nm inv* (**a**) *(d'un appareil photo)* click; *(des talons)* click-clack (**b**) *(canapé)* spring-action sofa bed

cliché [kliʃe] *nm* (**a**) *(photo)* photo; *(négatif)* negative (**b**) *(lieu commun)* cliché

client, -e [klijɑ̃, -ɑ̃t] *nm,f (d'un magasin, d'une entreprise)* customer; *(d'un médecin)* patient; *(d'un avocat)* client; *(d'un hôtel)* guest; *(d'un taxi)* fare; **ici, le c. est roi** the customer is always right

clientèle [klijɑ̃tɛl] *nf* (**a**) *(d'un magasin, d'une entreprise)* customers; *(d'un médecin, d'un avocat)* practice; *(d'un hôtel)* clientèle; *(d'un taxi)* fares; **c. de passage** passing trade (**b**) *(fait d'acheter)* custom; **accorder sa c. à** to give one's custom to

cligner [kliɲe] *vi* **c. des yeux** to blink; **c. de l'œil** to wink

clignotant, -e [kliɲɔtɑ̃, -ɑ̃t] **1** *adj (étoile)* twinkling; *(lumière)* flashing
2 *nm (de voiture) Br* indicator, *Am* turn signal; **mettre son c. (à gauche/droite)** to indicate (left/right)

clignoter [kliɲɔte] *vi (étoile)* to twinkle; *(lumière, voyant)* to flash; *Ordinat (marqueur)* to flash, to blink

clignoteur [kliɲɔtœr] *nm Belg Aut Br* indicator, *Am* turn signal

clim [klim] *nf Fam (climatisation)* air-conditioning

climat [klima] *nm aussi Fig* climate; **sous des climats plus ensoleillés** in sunnier climes; **c. de détente** relaxed climate

climatique [klimatik] *adj (conditions)* climatic

climatisation [klimatizasjɔ̃] *nf* air conditioning

climatisé, -e [klimatize] *adj* air-conditioned

climatiser [klimatize] *vt* to air-condition

climatiseur [klimatizœr] *nm* air-conditioner

clin d'œil *(pl* **clins d'œil)** [klɛ̃dœj] *nm* wink; **faire un c. à qn** to wink at sb; **en un c.** in a flash

clinique [klinik] **1** *nf* (**a**) *(hôpital privé)* clinic (**b**) *(médecine)* clinical medicine
2 *adj* clinical

clinquant, -e [klɛ̃kɑ̃, -ɑ̃t] **1** *adj* flashy
2 *nm (éclat trompeur)* flashiness

clip [klip] *nm* (**a**) *(vidéo)* (music) video (**b**) *(bijou)* clip

clique [klik] *nf* (**a**) *Fam (gang)* clique, gang; **et toute la c.** and the rest of the gang (**b**) *(d'une fanfare militaire)* drum-and-bugle band

cliquer [klike] *vi Ordinat* to click (**sur** on); **c. deux fois** to double-click

cliques [klik] *nfpl Fam* **prendre ses c. et ses claques** to pack one's bags and go

cliqueter [42] [klikte] *vi (chaînes)* to rattle; *(épées, aiguilles à tricoter)* to click; *(monnaie, clefs)* to jingle

cliquetis [klikti] *nm (de chaînes)* rattling; *(de pièces de monnaie, de clefs)* jingling; *(d'épées, d'aiguilles à tricoter)* clicking

clitoris [klitɔris] *nm* clitoris

clivage [klivaʒ] *nm (dans la société)* divide; *(dans un parti politique)* split

cloaque [klɔak] *nm aussi Fig* cesspool

clochard, -e [klɔʃar, -ard] *nm,f* tramp, *Am* hobo

clochardiser [klɔʃardize] **1** *vt* to turn into a tramp
  2 se clochardiser *vpr* to turn into a tramp

cloche [klɔʃ] **1** *nf* (**a**) *(d'église, de bétail)* bell; **déménager à la c. de bois** to do a moonlight flit; *Fig* **entendre plusieurs sons de c.** to hear several different versions of events (**b**) *(pour couvrir)* Chim bell jar; *(pour cultures)* cloche; *(pour garder au chaud)* dish cover; **c. à fromage(s)** covered cheese dish; **c. à plongeur** diving bell (**c**) *Fam (imbécile)* twit (**d**) **(chapeau) c.** cloche (hat) (**e**) *Fam* **être de la c.** *(être clochard)* to be a tramp *or Am* hobo (**f**) *Belg Méd* blister
  2 *adj Fam* stupid

cloche-pied [klɔʃpje] **à cloche-pied** *adv* **sauter à c.** to hop

clocher¹ [klɔʃe] *nm (d'une église)* bell tower, steeple

clocher² *vi Fam* **il y a quelque chose qui cloche** there's something wrong somewhere; **il y a quelque chose qui cloche dans son histoire** there's something not quite right about her story

clochette [klɔʃet] *nf* (**a**) *(petite cloche)* small bell (**b**) *(fleur)* bell-flower; *(corolle)* bell shaped flower

clodo [klodo] *nm Fam* tramp, *Am* bum

cloison [klwazɔ̃] *nf* (**a**) *(entre des pièces)* partition (**b**) *Anat* **c. nasale** nasal septum

cloisonner [klwazɔne] *vt (pièce)* to partition (off); *Fig* to compartmentalize

cloître [klwatr] *nm* (**a**) *(partie d'un monastère)* cloister (**b**) *(bâtiment) (pour moines)* monastery; *(pour religieuses)* convent

cloîtrer [klwatre] **1** *vt Rel* to cloister; *Fig* to shut up *or* away; **nonne cloîtrée** nun in an enclosed order
  2 se cloîtrer *vpr (moine)* to enter a monastery; *(religieuse)* to enter a convent; *Fig* to shut oneself away

clonage [klɔnaʒ] *nm Biol* cloning; **c. humain** human cloning

clone [klɔn] *nm Biol* clone

clope [klɔp] *nf Fam Br* fag, *Am* smoke

clopin-clopant [klɔpɛ̃klɔpɑ̃] *adv* **aller c.** to hobble along; *Fig (commerce)* to struggle along

clopiner [klɔpine] *vi* to hobble

clopinettes [klɔpinɛt] *nfpl Fam* **des c.** *Br* sweet FA, *Am* zilch; **travailler pour des c.** to work for peanuts

cloporte [klɔpɔrt] *nm (insecte)* woodlouse

cloque [klɔk] *nf* (**a**) *(sur la peau, sur la peinture)* blister; **faire des cloques** to blister (**b**) *très Fam* **être en c.** *(enceinte) Br* to be up the spout, to be knocked up

clore [15] [klɔr] **1** *vt (réunion, discussion)* to conclude, to end; *(débat, compte)* to close; *Ordinat* **c. une session** to log off, to log out
  2 se clore *vpr (réunion, film, livre)* to end (**sur** with)

clos, -e [klo, kloz] **1** *pp voir* **clore**
  2 *adj* (**a**) *(fermé) (porte, volets)* closed (**b**) *(achevé)* finished, concluded; **l'incident est c.** the matter is closed; **les inscriptions seront closes le 5 mars** the closing date for applications is 5 March (**c**) *(clôturé) (jardin)* enclosed
  3 *nm* enclosure; **c. (de vigne)** vineyard

clôture [klotyr] *nf* (**a**) *(barrière)* fence (**b**) *(d'une réunion, d'une discussion)* conclusion, end; *(d'un débat, d'un compte)* closing; **c. des inscriptions le 3 mars** closing date for applications is 3 March; **c. de la**

chasse close of the hunting season; *Fin* **c. de l'exercice** end of the financial year (**c**) *(à la Bourse)* close; **à la c.** at the close (**d**) *Ordinat* close; **c. de session** logging off

clôturer [klotyre] **1** *vt* (**a**) *(champ, terrain)* to enclose, to fence in (**b**) *(session, débats)* to close (**c**) *Fin (comptes)* to close
  2 *vi (valeur, indice)* **c. à** to close at

clou [klu] *nm* (**a**) *(pointe)* nail; **être maigre comme un c.** to be as thin as a rake; *Fam* **ça ne vaut pas un c.** it's not worth a penny; *Fam* **des clous!** not a sausage!; *Fam* **travailler pour des clous** to work for peanuts (**b**) *Culin* **c. de girofle** clove (**c**) *(d'un spectacle)* main attraction; **ç'a été le c. de la soirée** it was the highlight of the evening (**d**) **les clous** *(passage piéton) Br* the pedestrian crossing, *Am* the crosswalk (**e**) *Fam* **(vieux) c.** *(voiture)* old banger; *(vélo)* old boneshaker (**f**) *Fam* **mettre qn au c.** *(en prison)* to lock sb up; *Vieilli* **mettre qch au c.** *(en gage)* to pawn sth

clouer [klue] *vt* (**a**) *(au mur)* to nail up; *(ensemble)* to nail together; *(caisse)* to nail down; *Fam* **c. le bec à qn** to shut sb up (**b**) *Fig (immobiliser)* **c. qn au sol** to pin sb down; **rester cloué sur place** to be rooted to the spot; **être cloué au lit** to be stuck in bed

clouté, -e [klute] *adj (chaussures)* studded

clown [klun] *nm aussi Fig* clown; **faire le c.** to clown around

club [klœb] *nm* (**a**) *(culturel, sportif, politique)* club; **c. automobile** car club; **c. de foot** football club; **c. d'investissement** investment club; **c. de vacances** *Br* holiday club, *Am* vacation center (**b**) *(canne de golf)* club

CM [seɛm] *nm (abrév* **cours moyen)** **CM1** = fourth year of primary school; **CM2** = fifth year of primary school

cm *(abrév* **centimètre(s)**) cm

CNPF [seɛnpeɛf] *nm (abrév* **Conseil national du patronat français)** = national employers' association

CNRS [seɛnɛres] *nm (abrév* **Centre national de la recherche scientifique)** = national organization for scientific research

coach [kotʃ] *nm (entraîneur)* coach

coagulant, -e [kɔagylɑ̃, -ɑ̃t] **1** *adj* coagulating
  2 *nm* coagulant

coagulation [kɔagylasjɔ̃] *nf* coagulation

coaguler [kɔagyle] **1** *vt & vi (sang)* to clot; *(lait)* to curdle
  2 se coaguler *vpr (sang)* to clot; *(lait)* to curdle

coaliser [kɔalize] **se coaliser** *vpr* to unite; *(partis, pays)* to form a coalition

coalition [kɔalisjɔ̃] *nf* (**a**) *(alliance)* coalition (**b**) *Fig & Péj* conspiracy; **former une c. contre** to join forces against

coaltar [kɔltar] *nm* coaltar; *Fam* **être dans le c.** to be in a daze

coasser [kɔase] *vi (grenouille)* to croak

coassurance [kɔasyrɑ̃s] *nf* mutual assurance

coauteur [kootœr] *nm* (**a**) *(d'un livre)* co-author (**b**) *Jur* accomplice

COB [kɔb] *nf Fin (abrév* **Commission des opérations de Bourse)** = French Stock Exchange watchdog

cobalt [kɔbalt] *nm* cobalt

cobaye [kɔbaj] *nm aussi Fig* guinea pig

cobol [kɔbɔl] *nm Ordinat* COBOL

cobra [kɔbra] *nm* cobra

Coca® [kɔka] *nm inv Fam (boisson)* Coke®

coca [kɔka] **1** *nm (plante)* coca
2 *nf (feuilles)* coca
Coca-Cola® [kɔkakɔla] *nm inv* Coca-Cola®
cocagne [kɔkaɲ] *nf voir* **mât, pays**
cocaïne [kɔkain] *nf* cocaine
cocaïnomane [kɔkainɔman] *nmf* cocaine addict
cocarde [kɔkard] *nf (insigne)* rosette; *Hist (sur un chapeau)* cockade
cocasse [kɔkas] *adj Fam* comical
coccinelle [kɔksinɛl] *nf* (**a**) *(insecte) Br* ladybird, *Am* ladybug (**b**) *(voiture)* beetle
coccyx [kɔksis] *nm* coccyx
coche [kɔʃ] *nm Vieilli* stagecoach; *Fam* **rater** *ou* **louper le c.** to miss the boat
cochenille [kɔʃnij] *nf* cochineal
cocher¹ [kɔʃe] *nm* coachman
cocher² *vt Br* to tick (off), *Am* to check
cochère [kɔʃɛr] *adj f voir* **porte**
cochon, -onne [kɔʃɔ̃, -ɔn] **1** *nm* (**a**) *(animal, personne sale)* pig; *(viande)* pork; **sale comme un c.** filthy; **gros** *ou* **gras comme un c.** as round as a barrel; **manger comme un c.** to eat like a pig; **tu écris comme un c.** your writing's an absolute mess; *Fig* **nous n'avons pas gardé les cochons ensemble!** but we hardly know each other!; *Fam Fig* **eh ben, mon c.!** you old devil!; **c. de lait** suck(l)ing pig (**b**) **c. d'Inde** guinea pig (**c**) *(personne malfaisante)* swine (**d**) *(personne grivoise)* dirty devil; **un vieux c.** a dirty old man (**e**) *Can (tirelire)* piggy bank
2 *adj (histoire, film)* dirty
cochonner [kɔʃɔne] *vt Fam (travail)* to bungle, to botch
cochonnerie [kɔʃɔnri] *nf* (**a**) *(chose sans valeur)* trash, rubbish (**b**) *(nourriture de mauvaise qualité)* muck (**c**) *(saleté)* mess; **faire des cochonneries** to make a mess (**d**) *(obscénité)* smutty remark; **dire des cochonneries** to say smutty things
cochonnet [kɔʃɔnɛ] *nm* (**a**) *(aux boules)* jack (**b**) *(petit cochon)* piglet
cocker [kɔkɛr] *nm* cocker spaniel
cockpit [kɔkpit] *nm Naut & Aviat* cockpit
cocktail [kɔktɛl] *nm (boisson) & Fig* cocktail; *(soirée)* cocktail party; **c. de fruits** fruit cocktail; **c. Molotov** Molotov cocktail
coco¹ [koko] *nm* (**a**) *(plante)* coconut (**b**) *Fam* **mets-toi ça dans le c.!** *(dans la tête)* get that into your thick skull!; *(dans l'estomac)* get that inside you!
coco² *nm* (**a**) *Fam (type)* **un drôle de c.** a strange character; **toi, mon c., je t'ai à l'œil** just watch it, mate (**b**) *(terme d'affection)* **mon petit c.** my pet
coco³ *adj & nmf Fam (communiste)* commie
cocon [kɔkɔ̃] *nm aussi Fig* cocoon; *Fig* **le c. familial** the family nest
cocorico [kɔkɔriko] **1** *exclam* cock-a-doodle-doo!
2 *nm (cri du coq)* cock-a-doodle-doo; *aussi Fig* **faire c.** to crow
cocoter [kɔkɔte] *vi Fam* to stink
cocotier [kɔkɔtje] *nm (arbre)* coconut palm
cocotte [kɔkɔt] *nf* (**a**) *(marmite)* large casserole dish (**b**) *(poule)* hen (**c**) *(pliage)* paper bird (**d**) *(terme d'affection)* **ma c.** darling (**e**) *Fam* **hue, c.!** gee up! (**f**) *Fam Vieilli* tart (**g**) *Can (de pin)* pine cone
Cocotte-Minute® *(pl* **Cocottes-Minute***)* [kɔkɔtminyt] *nf* pressure cooker

cocu, -e [kɔky] **1** *adj* **un mari c.** a cuckold; **je suis c./cocue** my wife's/husband's cheating on me
2 *nm* cuckold; **faire son mari c.** to cheat on one's husband
cocufier [66] [kɔkyfje] *vt* to be unfaithful to
coda [kɔda] *nf Mus* coda
codage [kɔdaʒ] *nm* coding
code [kɔd] *nm* (**a**) *(symboles)* code; **mettre qch en c.** to put sth into code; **c. confidentiel** security code; *(d'une carte bancaire)* PIN; **c. postal** *Br* postcode, *Am* zip code (**b**) *Ordinat* code; **c. abrégé** shortcode; **c. d'accès** access code; **c. d'arrêt** stop code; **c. d'autorisation d'accès** access authorization code; **c. de caractère** character code; **c. de commande** command code; **c. de contrôle** control code; **c. de départ** start code; **c. d'erreur** error code; **c. d'imprimante** printer code; **c. natif** source code; **c. objet** object code; **c. source** source code (**c**) *(ensemble de lois, livre)* code; **passer le c.** *(du permis de conduire)* to sit the written part of one's driving test; **c. civil** civil code, ≃ common law; **c. de la nationalité** = laws governing French nationality; **c. pénal** penal code; **c. de la route** Highway Code; **c. du travail** employment legislation (**d**) *(phare)* **codes** *Br* dipped headlights, *Am* low beams; **se mettre en codes** *Br* to dip one's headlights, *Am* to switch on one's low beams; **rouler en codes** to drive with *Br* dipped headlights *or Am* low beams (**e**) *Biol* **c. génétique** genetic code

---

Code postal

In France, the first two numbers of a given post code correspond to the administrative code number of the relevant "département". Thus all postal codes for Paris begin with 75.

---

code-barres *(pl* **codes-barres***)* [kɔdbar] *nm* bar code
codéine [kɔdein] *nf* codeine
coder [kɔde] *vt* to code
codétenu, -e [kɔdetny] *nm,f* fellow prisoner
CODEVI [kɔdevi] *nm* = type of government savings account
codicille [kɔdisil] *nm Jur* codicil
codification [kɔdifikasjɔ̃] *nf Ordinat* **c. binaire** binary code; **c. décimale** decimal coding
codifier [66] [kɔdifje] *vt* to codify
codirecteur, -trice [kɔdirɛktœr, -tris] *nm,f* joint manager, *f* joint manageress
coédition [kɔedisjɔ̃] *nf* joint publication
coefficient [kɔefisjɑ̃] *nm* coefficient; *Aut* **c. aérodynamique** *ou* **de pénétration dans l'air** drag coefficient
coentreprise [kɔɑ̃trəpriz] *nf* joint venture
coéquipier, -ère [kɔekipje, -ɛr] *nm,f* team-mate
coercitif, -ive [kɔɛrsitif, -iv] *adj* coercive
coercition [kɔɛrsisjɔ̃] *nf* coercion
cœur [kœr] *nm* (**a**) *(organe)* heart; **être malade du c.** to have a weak heart; **être opéré à c. ouvert** to have open-heart surgery; **recevoir une balle en plein c.** to get a bullet right in the heart; **en (forme de) c.** heart-shaped
    (**b**) *(poitrine)* **serrer** *ou* **presser qn contre son c.** to hold sb close
    (**c**) *(estomac)* **avoir mal au c.** to feel sick; **soulever le c. à qn** to turn sb's stomach; *Fig* **avoir le c. solide** *ou* **bien accroché** to have a strong stomach
    (**d**) *(symbole de la bonté)* **avoir bon c.** to be kind-hearted; **ne pas avoir de c.** to be heartless; **avoir un**

c. d'or/de pierre to have a heart of gold/stone; **avoir le c. sur la main** to be very generous; **à votre bon c., M'sieurs Dames** can you spare a few coins?

(**e**) *(siège des sentiments)* **donner son c. à qn** to lose one's heart to sb; **de tout (son) c.** with all one's heart; **aller droit au c. de qn** to go straight to sb's heart; **avoir le c. brisé** to be broken-hearted; *Fig* **ça (me) fait mal au c.** it's sickening; **faire qch le c. léger** to do sth with a light heart; **avoir le c. gros** *ou* **serré** to have a heavy heart; **si tu aimes les pâtes, tu vas t'en donner à c. joie** if you like pasta, you'll be able to eat it to your heart's content; **ne pas porter qn dans son c.** to be not very fond of sb; **du fond du c.** from the bottom of one's heart; **au fond de mon c.** in my heart of hearts; *Prov* **le c. a ses raisons que la raison ne connaît point** the heart has its reasons

(**f**) *(pensées intimes)* **dire ce qu'on a sur le c.** to say what's on one's mind; **en avoir le c. net** to get to the bottom of it; **ouvrir son c. à qn** to open one's heart to sb

(**g**) **par c.** by heart; *Fam* **connaître qn par c.** to know sb inside out

(**h**) *(courage)* courage; **ne pas avoir le c. de faire qch** not to have the heart to do sth; *Fam* **avoir du c. au ventre** to have plenty of guts

(**i**) *(envie, désir)* **ils n'ont pas le c. à l'ouvrage** their hearts aren't in it; **le c. n'y est pas** his/my/*etc* heart isn't in it; **elle n'a plus le c. à rien** she hasn't the heart for anything any more; **avoir le c. à rire** to be in the mood for laughing; **si le c. vous en dit** if you feel like it; **avoir à c. de faire qch** to have one's heart set on doing sth; **ce projet lui tient à c.** this project is close to his heart; **de bon c.** *(volontiers)* willingly; *(rire)* heartily; **y aller de bon c.** to get down to it

(**j**) *(personne)* **c'est un c. d'or** she's got a heart of gold; **merci, mon c.** thank you, darling

(**k**) *(centre)* heart; *(d'un réacteur nucléaire)* core; **fromage fait à c.** ripe cheese; **au c. de l'hiver/l'été** in the depths of winter/height of summer; **au c. de la ville** in the heart of the town; **au c. du débat** at the heart of the debate; **c. d'artichaut** artichoke heart; *Fig* **avoir un c. d'artichaut** to fall in love with every girl/man one meets; **c. de palmier** palm heart

(**l**) *(objet en forme de cœur)* heart; *(carte)* heart; *(couleur)* hearts

coexistence [kɔɛgzistɑ̃s] *nf* coexistence (**avec** with); *Pol* **c. pacifique** peaceful coexistence

coexister [kɔɛgziste] *vi* to coexist (**avec** with)

coffrage [kɔfraʒ] *nm (pour ouvrages en béton)* formwork

coffre [kɔfr] *nm* (**a**) *(meuble)* chest; **c. à jouets** toy box; **c. à linge** linen chest (**b**) *(pour objets de valeur)* safe; *(à la banque)* safe deposit box; **les coffres de l'État** the coffers of the State (**c**) *Fam* **avoir du c.** *(avoir du souffle)* to have a lot of puff; *(avoir de la voix)* to have a powerful voice (**d**) *(d'une voiture)* Br boot, *Am* trunk; **c. à bagages** *(d'un avion)* baggage compartment

coffre-fort *(pl* **coffres-forts***)* [kɔfrəfɔr] *nm* safe

coffrer [kɔfre] *vt Fam (mettre en prison)* to put inside; **se faire c.** to get put inside

coffret [kɔfrɛ] *nm* (**a**) *(petit coffre)* box; **c. à bijoux** jewellery box (**b**) *(de livres, de disques)* box; **c. cadeau** gift box (**c**) *Ordinat* case

cogérant, -e [kɔʒerɑ̃, -ɑ̃t] *nm,f* joint manager, *f* joint manageress

cogestion [kɔʒɛstjɔ̃] *nf* joint management

cogitation [kɔʒitasjɔ̃] *nf Hum* cogitation

cogiter [kɔʒite] *vi Hum* to cogitate

cognac [kɔɲak] *nm* cognac

cognement [kɔɲəmɑ̃] *nm (bruit)* banging; *(d'un moteur)* knocking

cogner [kɔɲe] **1** *vt* (**a**) *(heurter)* to knock (**b**) *Fam (battre)* to knock about

2 *vi* (**a**) *(buter)* to bang (**sur/contre** on); **sa tête a cogné contre le mur** he banged his head on the wall; **c. du poing sur la table** to bang (one's fist) on the table; **c. à une porte** to bang on a door (**b**) *Fam (frapper)* **il cogne dur** he knows how to use his fists; **se faire c. dessus** to get knocked about (**c**) *Fam* **ça cogne** *(il fait chaud)* it's scorching (**d**) *(moteur)* to knock

3 se cogner *vpr* to bang oneself; **se c. à** *ou* **contre qch** to bang into sth; **se c. la tête contre qch** to bang one's head on sth; *Fig* **se c. la tête contre les murs** to bang one's head against a brick wall

cohabitation [koabitasjɔ̃] *nf* living together, cohabitation; *Pol* cohabitation

---

Cohabitation

Originally, this term refers to the period (1986–1988) during which the socialist President (François Mitterrand) had a right-wing Prime Minister (Jacques Chirac), following the victory of the RPR in the legislative elections and Mitterrand's decision not to resign as President. It has since been used to refer to the similar situation which arose following the 1993 elections (with Édouard Balladur as Prime Minister) and more recently the 1997 elections (with the left-wing government of Lionel Jospin co-ruling with the President Jacques Chirac).

---

cohabiter [koabite] *vi* to live together; **c. avec qn** to live with sb

cohérence [kɔerɑ̃s] *nf (d'une argumentation, d'un discours)* coherence; *(d'une attitude)* consistency

cohérent, -e [kɔerɑ̃, -ɑ̃t] *adj (argumentation, discours)* coherent; *(attitude)* consistent

cohéritier, -ère [kɔeritje, -ɛr] *nm,f* joint heir, *f* joint heiress

cohésion [kɔezjɔ̃] *nf* cohesion

cohorte [kɔɔrt] *nf (de gens)* horde

cohue [kɔy] *nf* crowd

coi, coite [kwa, kwat] *adj* **se tenir c.** to keep quiet; **en rester c.** to be speechless

coiffe [kwaf] *nf (coiffure régionale, religieuse)* headdress

coiffé, -e [kwafe] *adj* (**a**) **je ne suis pas encore coiffée** I haven't done my hair yet; **elle est bien coiffée** her hair is lovely; **il est mal c.** his hair's a mess (**b**) **être c. de qch** to be wearing sth *(on one's head)*

coiffer [kwafe] **1** *vt* (**a**) *(peigner)* **c. qn** to do sb's hair; **il coiffe bien** he's a good hairdresser; **se faire c. (chez/par qn)** to have one's hair done (at sb's/by sb) (**b**) *(mettre un chapeau à)* **c. qn de qch** to put sth on sb's head; *Fig* **c. sainte Catherine** to be twenty-five and still unmarried (**c**) *(service)* to head (**d**) *Sport & Fig* **se faire c. (au poteau)** to be pipped at the post

2 se coiffer *vpr* (**a**) *(se peigner)* to do one's hair (**b**) *(mettre)* **se c. de qch** to put sth on

coiffeur, -euse [kwafœr, -øz] **1** *nm,f* hairdresser
2 *nf* **coiffeuse** *(meuble)* dressing-table

coiffure [kwafyr] *nf* (**a**) *(coupe de cheveux)* hairstyle (**b**) *(activité)* hairdressing (**c**) *(chapeau)* headgear; *(de costume régional)* headdress

coin [kwɛ̃] *nm* (**a**) *(angle)* corner; **faire le c.** to be on the corner; **à tous les coins de rue** on every street corner; **aux quatre coins du monde** in all corners of the earth; **mettre un enfant au c.** *(pour le punir)* to make a child stand in the corner; *Fig* **rester dans son c.** to keep to oneself; **les coins et les recoins de qch** the nooks and crannies of sth; **je ne voudrais pas le rencontrer au c. d'un bois** I wouldn't like to meet him on a dark night; *Aviat & Rail* **c. fenêtre/couloir** window/aisle seat; **au c. du feu** by the fire(side); **lancer un regard en c. à qn** to give sb a sidelong glance; **sourire en c.** half smile; **regarder qn du c. de l'œil** to look at sb out of the corner of one's eye (**b**) *(endroit quelconque)* spot, place; **un petit c. tranquille** a quiet little spot; *Euph* **le petit c.** the smallest room (in the house); **dans un c. de ma mémoire** in a corner of my mind; **j'ai dû le mettre dans un c.** I must have put it somewhere; **chercher qch dans tous les coins** to look high and low for sth (**c**) *(voisinage)* **du c.** local; **il habite dans le c.** he lives around here (**d**) *(parcelle)* patch; **c. de ciel bleu** patch of blue sky (**e**) *(cale)* wedge

coincé, -e [kwɛ̃se] *adj* (**a**) *(fermeture, porte, mécanisme)* jammed, stuck (**b**) *Fam (inhibé)* hung up (**c**) *(acculé)* **il faut que je paie, je suis c.** I'll have to pay, I've no choice

coincer [16] [kwɛ̃se] **1** *vt* (**a**) *(accidentellement) (tiroir, clef)* to jam; **j'ai coincé mes cheveux dans ma fermeture Éclair®** I got my hair caught in my zip; **la voiture est coincée entre deux camions** *(en stationnement)* the car is boxed in by two lorries; **être coincé** *(personne) (dans un embouteillage, un endroit)* to be stuck; *(être occupé)* to be tied up (**b**) *(volontairement) (porte)* to wedge; **elle l'a coincé dans le couloir** she cornered him in the corridor; **il m'a coincé** *(je n'ai pas su répondre)* he had me cornered (**c**) *Fam (arrêter)* to nick; **se faire c.** to get nicked

2 *vi (tiroir, mécanisme)* to jam, to stick; *Fam* **ça coince** there's a hitch

3 se coincer *vpr (tiroir, mécanisme)* to jam, to stick; **se c. le doigt dans la porte** to catch one's finger in the door; **je me suis coincé le dos** my back's seized up

coïncidence [kɔɛ̃sidɑ̃s] *nf* coincidence

coïncider [kɔɛ̃side] *vi (événements, versions)* to coincide (**avec** with); **leurs intérêts coïncident** they have similar interests; **tous les témoignages coïncident** the witnesses all bear each other out

coin-coin [kwɛ̃kwɛ̃] **1** *nm inv (des canards)* quacking **2** *exclam* quack! quack!

coin-cuisine (*pl* **coins-cuisines**) [kwɛ̃kɥizin] *nm* kitchen area

coïnculpé, -e [kɔɛ̃kylpe] *nm,f* co-defendant

coing [kwɛ̃] *nm* quince

coin-repas (*pl* **coins-repas**) [kwɛ̃rəpɑ] *nm* dining area

coït [kɔit] *nm* coitus

coite [kwat] *voir* **coi**

coke [kɔk] **1** *nm (combustible)* coke **2** *nf Fam (cocaïne)* coke

col [kɔl] *nm* (**a**) *(d'une robe, d'une chemise)* collar; **c. de fourrure/de dentelle** fur/lace collar; **c. blanc** *(employé de bureau)* white-collar worker; **c. bleu** *(ouvrier)* blue-collar worker; **c. cheminée** *ou* **montant** *Br* turtleneck, *Am* mock turtleneck; **c. rond** round neck; **c.**

roulé *Br* polo neck, *Am* turtleneck; **c. en V** V-neck; **faux c.** false collar (**b**) *(d'une bouteille)* neck (**c**) *Géog* col (**d**) *Anat (d'un os)* neck; **c. de l'utérus** cervix

colchique [kɔlʃik] *nm* autumn crocus

coléoptère [kɔleɔptɛr] *nm* beetle, *Spéc* coleopteran

colère [kɔlɛr] *nf* anger; **être en c. (contre qn)** to be angry (with sb); **mettre qn en c.** to make sb angry; **se mettre en c.** to get angry; **se mettre dans une c. bleue** *ou* **noire** to fly into a towering rage; **piquer une c.** to fly into a rage; **passer sa c. sur qn** to take one's anger out on sb; **avec c.** angrily; *Litt* **la c. de Dieu** the wrath of God; **c. froide** cold fury

coléreux, -euse [kɔlerø, -øz], **colérique** [kɔlerik] *adj (personne)* quick-tempered; *(disposition)* irritable

colibri [kɔlibri] *nm* humming-bird

colifichet [kɔlifiʃɛ] *nm* trinket, knick-knack

colimaçon [kɔlimasɔ̃] *nm voir* **escalier**

colin [kɔlɛ̃] *nm (merlu)* hake; *(lieu noir)* coley

colin-maillard [kɔlɛ̃majar] *nm* blindman's-buff; **jouer à c.** to play blindman's-buff

colique [kɔlik] *nf* (**a**) *(diarrhée)* diarrhoea; **avoir la c.** to have diarrhoea (**b**) *(douleur)* **coliques** stomach pains, colic; **c. néphrétique** renal colic

colis [kɔli] *nm* parcel; **par c. postal** by parcel post

Colisée [kɔlize] *nm* **le C.** the Coliseum

colistier, -ère [kɔlistje, -ɛr] *nm,f Pol* fellow candidate

colite [kɔlit] *nf Méd* colitis

collabo [kɔlabo] *nmf Fam Hist* collaborator

collaborateur, -trice [kɔlabɔratœr, -tris] *nm,f* (**a**) *(aide)* assistant (**b**) *Journ* contributor (**de** to) (**c**) *Hist* collaborator

collaboration [kɔlabɔrasjɔ̃] *nf* (**a**) *(aide)* collaboration (**à** on); **travailler en étroite c. (avec qn)** to work closely (with sb) (**b**) *Journ* contribution (**c**) *Hist* collaboration

collaborer [kɔlabɔre] *vi* (**a**) *(travailler ensemble)* to collaborate (**avec** with); **c. à qch** *(projet)* to take part in sth; *(journal)* to contribute to sth (**b**) *Hist* to collaborate

collage [kɔlaʒ] *nm* (**a**) *(d'affiches)* sticking up; *(de bois)* gluing; *(de papier)* pasting (**b**) *(composition)* collage

collagène [kɔlaʒɛn] *nm* collagen

collant, -e [kɔlɑ̃, -ɑ̃t] **1** *adj* (**a**) *(adhésif)* sticky (**b**) *(poisseux)* sticky (**c**) *(moulant)* skin-tight (**d**) *Fam (personne)* **qu'est-ce qu'il est c.!** you just can't shake him off! **2** *nm* (**a**) *(bas) Br* (pair of) tights, *Am* pantihose; **c. de danse** dance tights (**b**) *Can* **c. à mouches** flypaper

collation [kɔlasjɔ̃] *nf (repas)* light meal

colle [kɔl] *nf* (**a**) *(transparente)* glue; *(blanche)* paste; **c. à bois** woodworking glue; **c. forte** strong glue; **de la c. en pot/stick/tube** a pot/stick/tube of glue (**b**) *Fam (question difficile)* poser; **là, tu me poses une c.** you've got me there (**c**) *Fam (punition)* detention (**d**) *Fam (examen oral)* oral test (**e**) *très Fam* **vivre** *ou* **être à la c.** to be shacked up together

collecte [kɔlɛkt] *nf* collection; **faire une c. (au profit de)** to make a collection (in aid of)

collecter [kɔlɛkte] *vt* to collect

collecteur, -trice [kɔlɛktœr, -tris] **1** *nm,f* collector; **c. d'impôts** tax collector **2** *nm* (**a**) *(d'eaux pluviales)* main sewer (**b**) *Aut* **c. d'échappement** exhaust manifold

collectif, -ive [kɔlɛktif, -iv] **1** *adj (action, travail, responsabilité)* collective; *(billet)* group; *(licenciements)* mass

2 *nm* (**a**) *Fin* **c. budgétaire** bill of supply (**b**) *(association)* collective

collection [kɔlɛksjɔ̃] *nf* (**a**) *(action)* collecting; **faire la c. de qch** to collect sth (**b**) *(série) (de timbres, de papillons, d'œuvres d'art)* collection; *(de périodiques)* series; *(d'échantillons)* line; **j'en ai toute une c.** I've got a whole collection of them (**c**) *(de haute couture, de prêt-à-porter)* collection

collectionner [kɔlɛksjɔne] *vt* to collect

collectionneur, -euse [kɔlɛksjɔnœr, -øz] *nm,f* collector

collectivisme [kɔlɛktivism] *nm Écon* collectivism

collectivité [kɔlɛktivite] *nf* (**a**) *(groupe)* community (**b**) **collectivités locales** local communities

collège [kɔlɛʒ] *nm* (**a**) *(école)* school; **c. d'enseignement secondaire** = former secondary school for pupils aged 12 to 15; **c. d'enseignement technique** technical school; **le C. de France** the Collège de France *(prestigious higher education institution)* (**b**) *Pol* **c. électoral** electoral college

collégial, -e, -aux, -ales [kɔleʒjal, -o] **1** *adj* collegiate
2 *nf* **collégiale** collegiate church

collégien, -enne [kɔleʒjɛ̃, -ɛn] *nm,f* schoolboy, *f* schoolgirl; **je me suis fait avoir comme un c.** I fell for it like a fool

collègue [kɔlɛg] *nmf* **c. (de travail)** colleague; *Fam* **salut, c.!** how's things?

coller [kɔle] **1** *vt* (**a**) *(faire adhérer)* to stick (**à/sur** to/ on); **il avait les cheveux collés par la sueur/la peinture** his hair was matted with sweat/paint; **il est resté collé à la télé toute la soirée** he was glued to the TV all evening
  (**b**) *(appuyer)* **c. qch à** *ou* **contre qch** to press sth against sth
  (**c**) *Fam (mettre)* to stick; **colle ton sac là** stick *or* dump your bag over there; **ils ont collé le bébé à la grand-mère** they've dumped the baby on the grand-mother; **on m'a collé à la comptabilité sans que j'aie dit oui** I got shoved in accounts without any say in the matter; **c. une gifle à qn** to slap sb in the face; **si tu continues, je t'en colle une!** if you don't stop, I'll slap you one!; **c. une contravention à qn** to slap a fine on sb
  (**d**) *Fam (retenir en punition)* to keep in; **se faire c.** to be kept in
  (**e**) *(refuser) (candidat)* to fail; **se faire c.** to fail
  (**f**) *Fam (suivre)* to follow closely; **il me colle!** he sticks to me like glue!
  (**g**) *Ordinat* to paste
2 *vi Fam* (**a**) *(coïncider)* to tally (**avec** with) (**b**) *(aller bien)* **ça colle!** that's OK!; **ça ne va pas c. pour mercredi** it's no go for Wednesday; **ça ne colle pas entre eux** they don't hit it off
3 **coller à** *vt ind aussi Fig* to stick to; *Fam* **c. aux fesses à qn** to stick to sb's tail; **sa réputation lui colle à la peau** he can't shake off his reputation
4 **se coller** *vpr* (**a**) *(adhérer les uns aux autres)* to stick (**b**) *(s'aplatir)* **se c. contre un mur** to flatten oneself against a wall; **se c. contre qn** to cling to sb; *Fam* **se c. devant la télé** to plonk oneself down in front of the TV; *Fam* **c'est encore toi qui t'y colles** you're landed with it again

collerette [kɔlrɛt] *nf* (**a**) *(de vêtement)* collar; *Hist (fraise)* ruff (**b**) *Bot (de champignon)* annulus (**c**) *(de tuyau)* flange

collet [kɔlɛ] *nm* (**a**) *(de vêtement)* collar; **saisir** *ou* **prendre qn au c.** to grab sb by the scruff of the neck; **mettre la main au c. à qn** *(l'arrêter)* to get hold of sb; **être c. monté** to be strait-laced (**b**) *(piège)* snare

colleter [42] [kɔlte] **se colleter** *vpr Fam* to tussle (**avec qn** with sb); **se c. avec qch** to grapple with sth

collier [kɔlje] *nm* (**a**) *(bijou)* necklace; **c. de perles** pearl necklace; **c. de fleurs** garland of flowers (**b**) *(de chien)* collar; *Fig* **donner un coup de c.** to put one's back into it (**c**) *(barbe)* **c. (de barbe)** fringe of beard (**d**) *Culin (de bœuf, de mouton)* neck (**e**) *Tech* collar; **c. de serrage** clamp collar (**f**) *Zool (d'oiseau)* collar

collimateur [kɔlimatœr] *nm Fig* **avoir qn dans le c.** to keep one's eye on sb

colline [kɔlin] *nf* hill

collision [kɔlizjɔ̃] *nf (entre véhicules, entre objets)* collision; **entrer en c. avec qch** to collide with sth; *Aut* **c. frontale/latérale** head-on/side-on collision

colloque [kɔlɔk] *nm (conférence)* seminar

collusion [kɔlyzjɔ̃] *nf* collusion

collutoire [kɔlytwar] *nm* throat spray

collyre [kɔlir] *nm* eyewash

colmater [kɔlmate] *vt* to fill in

colo [kɔlo] *nf Fam Br* (children's) holiday camp, *Am* summer camp

colocataire [kɔlɔkater] *nmf Br* flatmate, *Am* roommate

Colomb [kɔlɔ̃] *npr* **Christophe C.** Christopher Columbus

colombage [kɔlɔ̃baʒ] *nm Constr* half-timbering; **maison à colombages** half-timbered house

colombe [kɔlɔ̃b] *nf* dove

Colombie [kɔlɔ̃bi] *nf* **la C.** Colombia

Colombie-Britannique [kɔlɔ̃bibritanik] *nf* **la C.** British Columbia

colombien, -enne [kɔlɔ̃bjɛ̃, -ɛn] **1** *adj* Colombian
2 *nm,f* **C.** Colombian

colombier [kɔlɔ̃bje] *nm (pigeonnier)* dovecote

colon [kɔlɔ̃] *nm* (**a**) *(pionnier)* settler, colonist (**b**) *(dans une colonie de vacances)* child (at camp)

côlon [kɔlɔ̃] *nm* colon

colonel [kɔlɔnɛl] *nm (dans l'armée de terre)* colonel; *(dans l'armée de l'air) Br* group captain, *Am* colonel

colonial, -e, -aux, -ales [kɔlɔnjal, -o] **1** *adj* colonial
2 *nf Hist* **la coloniale** the Colonial Army

colonialisme [kɔlɔnjalism] *nm* colonialism

colonialiste [kɔlɔnjalist] *adj & nmf* colonialist

colonie [kɔlɔni] *nf* (**a**) *(territoire, immigrés)* colony (**b**) **c. (de vacances)** *Br* (children's) holiday camp, *Am* summer camp; **envoyer ses enfants en c.** to send one's children to camp

---

Colonie de vacances

The "colonie de vacances" or "colo" is an integral part of childhood for many French people. The children's parents do not stay with them at the "colonie", the group being supervised by "moniteurs" or "animateurs" (group leaders), who organize games and activities.

---

colonisation [kɔlɔnizasjɔ̃] *nf* colonization

coloniser [kɔlɔnize] *vt* to colonize

colonnade [kɔlɔnad] *nf* colonnade

colonne [kɔlɔn] *nf* (**a**) *(pilier)* column, pillar; **c. Morris** = pillar used to advertise forthcoming events (**b**) *(file)* column; **en c. par deux/trois** in columns of two/three (**c**) *(d'un dictionnaire, d'un journal)* column (**d**) *(de fumée, de mercure)* column (**e**) *Anat* **c. vertébrale** spine, spinal column (**f**) *Aut* **c. de direction** steering column

coloquinte [kɔlɔkɛ̃t] *nf (plante)* bitter apple

colorant, -e [kɔlɔrɑ̃, -ɑ̃t] **1** *adj* colouring
   2 *nm* (**a**) *(pour teindre)* colorant (**b**) *(alimentaire)* colouring; **sans colorants** *(sur étiquette)* no artificial colouring

coloration [kɔlɔrasjɔ̃] *nf* (**a**) *(fait de colorer)* colouring; **se faire faire une c.** to have one's hair tinted (**b**) *(de la peau)* colouring (**c**) *Fig* **c. politique** political colour

coloré, -e [kɔlɔre] *adj* coloured; *(teint)* ruddy; *Fig (style)* colourful

colorer [kɔlɔre] **1** *vt* to colour; *Fig (récit)* to lend colour to; **c. qch en vert** to colour sth green
   2 se colorer *vpr (visage)* to become flushed

coloriage [kɔlɔrjaʒ] *nm (action)* colouring (in); *(dessin)* drawing; **album** *ou* **livre de c.** colouring (in) book

colorier [66] [kɔlɔrje] *vt* to colour (in)

coloris [kɔlɔri] *nm* shade

coloriser [kɔlɔrize] *vt Cin* to colourize

colossal, -e, -aux, -ales [kɔlɔsal, -o] *adj* colossal, huge

colosse [kɔlɔs] *nm (homme)* giant; *Fig* **un c. aux pieds d'argile** a giant with feet of clay

colostomie [kɔlɔstɔmi] *nf Méd* colostomy

colporter [kɔlpɔrte] *vt (marchandises)* to hawk; *(nouvelle, rumeurs)* to spread

colporteur, -euse [kɔlpɔrtœr, -øz] *nm,f* hawker

colt [kɔlt] *nm* Colt®

coltiner [kɔltine] **se coltiner** *vpr Fam* **se c. qn/qch** to get landed with sb/sth

colvert [kɔlvɛr] *nm* mallard

colza [kɔlza] *nm* rape

coma [kɔma] *nm* coma; **être/tomber dans le c.** to be in/go into a coma

comateux, -euse [kɔmatø, -øz] **1** *adj* comatose
   2 *nm,f* patient in a coma

combat [kɔ̃ba] *nm* (**a**) *Mil (bataille)* fight; *(activité)* combat; **c. aérien** dog fight; *aussi Fig* **c. d'arrière-garde** rearguard action; **c. naval** naval engagement (**b**) *(dispute)* fight; **c. de boxe** boxing match; **c. de coqs** cockfight (**c**) *Fig (lutte)* fight (**contre** against)

combatif, -ive [kɔ̃batif, -iv] *adj* combative

combativité [kɔ̃bativite] *nf* combativeness

combattant, -e [kɔ̃batɑ̃, -ɑ̃t] **1** *nm,f* combatant; **anciens combattants** veterans
   2 *adj (troupes, unité)* fighting

combattre [11] [kɔ̃batr] **1** *vt (ennemi)* to fight (against); *(maladie, inflation, racisme)* to fight
   2 *vi* to fight (**pour/contre** for/against)

combi [kɔ̃bi] *nm Belg* police van

combien [kɔ̃bjɛ̃] **1** *adv* (**a**) *(comme)* how (much); **j'ai pu constater c. tu avais changé** I could see how much you'd changed (**b**) *(en nombre)* how many; **c. sont-ils?** how many (of them) are there?; **c. de** how many; **c. de gens furent tués dans cette guerre!** what a lot of people were killed in that war! (**c**) *(en quantité, en poids)* how much; **ça fait c.?** *(d'argent)* how much is that?; **c. y a-t-il d'ici à Londres?** how far is it to London?; **à c. sommes-nous de Paris?** how far are we from Paris?; **c.

mesure-t-il? how tall is he?; **elle est enceinte – de c.?** she's pregnant – how far gone is she?; **c. de** how much; **c. de temps** how long
   2 *nm inv Fam* **le c. sommes-nous?** what's the date (today)?; **il y a un car tous les c.?** how often do the buses run?; **tu chausses du c.?** what size shoe do you take?

combientième [kɔ̃bjɛ̃tjɛm] *Fam* **1** *nmf* **c'est le c. sur la liste?** where is it on the list?
   2 *adj* **tu as été reçu c. à l'examen?** where did you come in the exam?; **c'est la c. fois que tu viens?** how often have you been now?

combinaison [kɔ̃binɛzɔ̃] *nf* (**a**) *(assemblage)* combination; **la c. gagnante** *(au tiercé)* the winning combination; *Ordinat* **c. de touches** key combination (**b**) *(vêtement) (de travail)* Br boiler suit, Am coveralls; *Aviat* flying suit; *(de femme)* catsuit; *(sous-vêtement)* slip; **c. de plongée** wet suit; **c. de ski** ski suit; **c. spatiale** space suit

combine [kɔ̃bin] *nf Fam* trick; **il a une c. pour entrer sans payer** he knows a way of getting in without paying; **mettre qn dans la c.** to let sb in on it

combiné, -e [kɔ̃bine] **1** *adj (action, efforts)* combined
   2 *nm* (**a**) **c. (téléphonique)** receiver (**b**) *(en ski)* **c. alpin** alpine competition

combiner [kɔ̃bine] **1** *vt* (**a**) *(unir)* to combine (**b**) *Fam (plan)* to concoct; **qu'est-ce que tu combines encore?** what are you cooking up now?
   2 se combiner *vpr* to combine

comble [kɔ̃bl] **1** *adj* (jam-)packed; **faire salle c.** *(au théâtre)* to have a full house
   2 *nm* (**a**) *(maximum)* **le c. de** the height of; *(du désespoir)* the depth of; **ça, c'est le** *ou* **un c.!** that's the last straw!; **être au c. de la joie** to be overjoyed (**b**) *Archit (en bois)* roof timbers; *(en métal)* roof structure; **les combles** *(grenier)* the attic; **loger sous les combles** to live in an attic

combler [kɔ̃ble] *vt* (**a**) *(puits, fossé, trou)* to fill in; *(perte)* to make good; *(découvert)* to pay off; *(lacune)* to fill; **c. son retard** to make up for lost time (**b**) *(satisfaire)* to satisfy; **c. qn de cadeaux** to shower sb with gifts; **un mari comblé** a happily married man

combustible [kɔ̃bystibl] **1** *nm* fuel
   2 *adj* combustible

combustion [kɔ̃bystjɔ̃] *nf* combustion

comédie [kɔmedi] *nf (pièce, film, genre)* comedy; **jouer** *ou* **faire la c.** to act; *Fig* to put on an act; **allons, pas de c.!** *(caprice)* come on, stop your nonsense!; **c'est une vraie c. quand il faut aller à l'école** it's a real fuss when it's time to go to school; **c. de mœurs** comedy of manners; **c. musicale** musical

Comédie-Française [kɔmedifrɑ̃sɛz] *nf* **la C.** = state-run theatre company presenting plays from the established repertoire

---

Comédie–Française

This state-subsidized company dates back to the seventeenth century; the theatre itself, officially called "le Théâtre-Français" or "le Français", is situated in the rue Richelieu in Paris. Its repertoire consists mainly of classical works, although modern plays are sometimes staged. Actors who perform in the Comédie-Française fall into two categories: the "sociétaires" who are fully-fledged members of the company, and the "pensionnaires" who work with the company on a fixed salary but are not shareholders in it.

comédien, -enne [kɔmedjɛ̃, -ɛn] **1** *nm,f (acteur)* actor, *f* actress; *Fig* **c'est une comédienne** she's always putting on an act; **comédiens ambulants** strolling players
2 *adj* **elle est très comédienne** she's always putting on an act

comédon [kɔmedɔ̃] *nm* blackhead

comestible [kɔmɛstibl] *adj* edible; **denrées comestibles** foodstuffs

comète [kɔmɛt] *nf* comet; *Fig* **tirer** *ou* **faire des plans sur la c.** to build castles in the air

comice [kɔmis] *nm* **c. agricole** agricultural association; **comices agricoles** *(foire)* agricultural show

comique [kɔmik] **1** *adj* (**a**) *(acteur, film, rôle)* comedy; **le genre c.** comedy (**b**) *(amusant)* comical, funny
2 *nm* (**a**) *(genre)* comedy (**b**) *(acteur)* comic actor; *Péj (bouffon)* comedian (**c**) **le c. de l'histoire, c'est que...** the funny part is that...

comité [kɔmite] *nm* committee; **faire partie d'un c.** to sit on a committee; *Fig* **nous serons en petit c.** we'll just have a small get-together; **c. d'entreprise** works council; **C. international olympique** International Olympic Committee

> ### Comité d'entreprise
> The "Comité d'entreprise" or "CE" looks after the general welfare of company employees and organizes subsidised leisure activities, outings, holidays etc. It also deals with industrial problems.

commandant [kɔmɑ̃dɑ̃] *nm* (**a**) *(officier) (d'unité)* commander; *(de camp, de base)* commandant; *(de bateau)* captain *(whatever his rank)*; *Aviat* **c. de bord** captain; **c. en chef** commander-in-chief; *Naut* executive officer (**b**) *(rang) (dans l'armée de terre)* major; *(dans l'armée de l'air) Br* squadron leader, *Am* major

commande [kɔmɑ̃d] *nf* (**a**) *Com* order; **faire** *ou* **passer une c.** to put in *or* place an order; **sur c.** *aussi Fig* to order; **on ne peut pas rire sur c.** you can't laugh to order; **ouvrage de c.** commissioned work (**b**) *(action, manette)* control; *(mécanisme)* drive; **c. à distance** remote control; **commandes** *(d'un avion)* controls; **prendre les commandes** *(d'un avion)* to take over the controls; *(d'une société)* to take control (**c**) *Ordinat* command; **c. d'annulation/d'effacement** undo/delete command; **à c. vocale** voice-activated

commandement [kɔmɑ̃dmɑ̃] *nm* (**a**) *(ordre) Mil* command; **à mon c.** when I give the command; *Rel* **les dix commandements** the Ten Commandments (**b**) *(pouvoir)* command; **avoir/prendre le c.** to be in/take command; **c. suprême, haut c.** high command

commander [kɔmɑ̃de] **1** *vt* (**a**) *(diriger, ordonner)* to command; *Fam* **sans vous c., est-ce que vous pourriez fermer la fenêtre?** I wonder if you'd mind closing the window (**b**) *(marchandises, dîner)* to order; *(peinture, ouvrage)* to commission; **c. qch à qn** to order/commission sth from sb (**c**) *(mouvement, valve)* to control; *(machine)* to drive (**d**) *Ordinat* to drive; **commandé par menu** menu-driven
2 *vi* **c. à qn de faire qch** to order sb to do sth; **qui est-ce qui commande ici?** who's in charge here?
3 se commander *vpr* **ces choses-là ne se commandent pas** *(sont incontrôlables)* these things are beyond our control

commanditaire [kɔmɑ̃ditɛr] *adj & nm Com* **(associé) c.** *Br* sleeping *or Am* silent partner; **les commanditaires de l'attentat** the people behind the attack

commandite [kɔmɑ̃dit] *nf Com* **(société en) c.** mixed liability company

commandité [kɔmɑ̃dite] *adj & nm Com* **(associé) c.** active partner

commanditer [kɔmɑ̃dite] *vt Com* to finance; *(meurtre, attentat)* to be behind

commando [kɔmɑ̃do] *nm (groupe)* commando (unit)

comme [kɔm] **1** *adv* (**a**) *(devant un nom, un pronom)* like; **il n'est pas c. les autres** he isn't like the others; **c. ça** like that; *(du coup)* that way; **c'est c. ça, un point c'est tout!** too bad, that's the way it is!; **alors c. ça, vous venez de Paris?** you come from Paris, don't you?; *Fam* **c. ça!** *(formidable)* great!, fab!; **quelque chose c. deux cents personnes** something like two hundred people
(**b**) *(devant une proposition)* as; **il écrit c. il parle** he writes as he speaks; **insolent c. il est...** insolent as he is...; **il leva la main c. pour me frapper** he lifted his hand as if *or* as though to strike me; **c. il faut** *(se conduire)* properly; **des gens très c. il faut** very respectable people; **c. si** as if, as though; **c. si je ne le savais pas!** as if I didn't know!
(**c**) *(dans des images)* as; **doux c. un agneau** (as) gentle as a lamb
(**d**) *(et)* **les femmes c. les hommes** men and women alike; **tout le monde fera la vaisselle, toi c. les autres** everyone's going to do the washing-up, and you're no exception
(**e**) *(tel que)* such as, like; **les bois durs c. le chêne** hard woods like *or* such as oak; **P c. pomme** P as in pomme
(**f**) *(en tant que)* as; **je l'ai eue c. professeur** she was my teacher; **qu'est-ce que vous avez c. desserts?** what have you got in the way of desserts?; **ce n'est pas mal c. film** it's not a bad film
(**g**) *(en quelque sorte)* **elle a eu c. une hésitation** she seemed to hesitate; **j'étais c. hypnotisé** it was as if *or* as though I was hypnotized
(**h**) *(comment)* how; **tu sais bien c. il est** you know what he's like; *Fam* **elle a fait les carreaux, faut voir c.!** you should see the way she's done the windows!
(**i**) *(exclamatif)* how; **c. tu as grandi!** how you've grown!; **c. elle est bête!** she's so stupid!; **c. elle a de beaux cheveux!** what lovely hair she has!
(**j**) *Fam (locutions)* **c'est tout c.** it amounts to the same thing; **c. ci c. ça** so-so; **c. qui dirait** as it were; **c. quoi** *(disant que)* to the effect that; *(ce qui prouve que)* which goes to show that; **drôle c. tout** as funny as anything
2 *conj* (**a**) *(puisque)* as, since; **c. vous êtes mon ami, je vais tout vous dire** as you're my friend I'll tell you everything
(**b**) *(alors que)* **c. il allait frapper, la porte s'ouvrit** he was just about to knock when the door opened

commémoratif, -ive [kɔmemɔratif, -iv] *adj (plaque, cérémonie)* commemorative; *(service)* memorial; **monument c.** memorial

commémoration [kɔmemɔrasjɔ̃] *nf* commemoration; **en c. de** in commemoration of

commémorer [kɔmemɔre] *vt* to commemorate

commencement [kɔmɑ̃smɑ̃] *nm* beginning, start; **au c.** at the beginning *or* start; **il faut un c. à tout** you've got to start somewhere; *Fam* **c'est le c. de la fin** it's the beginning of the end

commencer [16] [kɔmãse] **1** vt (**a**) (entreprendre) to begin, to start; (traitement, régime) to go on, to start; **nous avons mal commencé l'année** we've made a bad start to the year (**b**) (être au début de) to begin, to start

2 vi to begin, to start; **pour c., je dois vous dire...** to begin with, I must tell you...; Ironique **ça commence bien!** that's a good start!; **c. par qch/par faire qch** to begin or start with sth/by doing sth; **par où c.?** where shall I begin?; **à c. par...** beginning with...

3 commencer à vt ind **c. à faire qch** to begin or start to do sth, to begin or start doing sth; Fam **je commence à en avoir assez!** I've had just about enough!; Fam **ça commence à bien faire** it's getting a bit too much

comment [kɔmã] **1** adv how; **c. allez-vous?** how are you?; **c.?** (pour faire répéter) I beg your pardon?; **c. ça, tu ne veux pas?** what do you mean, you don't want to?; **c. faire?** what can I/we/etc do?; **c. est-il, ce garçon?** what's this young man like?; **elle me dira c. faire** she'll tell me how to do it

2 exclam what!; **mais c. donc!** why, of course!; Fam **ça vous a plu? – et c.!** did you like it? – you bet I did!

commentaire [kɔmãtɛr] nm (**a**) (remarque) comment, remark; **faire des commentaires** to make comments; **cela se passe de c.** it speaks for itself; Fam **sans c.!** no comment!; Scol **c. de texte** textual commentary (**b**) (à la radio, à la télévision) commentary; **c. sportif** sports commentary

commentateur, -trice [kɔmãtatœr, -tris] nm,f (à la radio, à la télévision) commentator; **c. sportif** sports commentator

commenter [kɔmãte] vt (expliquer, donner son avis sur) to comment on; (à la radio, à la télévision) (compétition) to commentate on; **c. l'actualité** to comment on current affairs

commérage [kɔmeraʒ] nm (piece of) gossip; **commérages** gossip

commerçant, -e [kɔmɛrsã, -ãt] **1** nm,f trader; (qui tient un magasin) shopkeeper; **petits commerçants** small traders

2 adj **quartier c.** shopping area; **rue très commerçante** busy shopping street; **il n'est pas très c.** he doesn't look after his customers very well

commerce [kɔmɛrs] nm (**a**) **le c.** (activité, secteur) trade; (affaires) business; **ça se trouve dans le c.** you can buy it in the shops; **faire du c. avec** to do business with; **hors c.** not for (general) sale; **c. électronique** e-commerce; **c. en** ou **de gros/de détail** wholesale/retail trade; **c. intérieur/extérieur** home/foreign trade; **c. international** world trade; **c. maritime** seaborne trade; **le petit c.** small traders (**b**) (magasin) business

commercer [16] [kɔmɛrse] vi to trade (**avec** with)

commercial, -e, -aux, -ales [kɔmɛrsjal, -o] **1** adj (rapports, pratiques) business, commercial; (embargo, tribunal) trade; (droit) commercial; Péj (film, chanson) commercial; **suivre une formation commerciale** to do a business studies course

2 nm,f salesman, f saleswoman

3 nf **commerciale** (voiture) Br estate car, Am station wagon

commercialisation [kɔmɛrsjalizasjɔ̃] nf marketing

commercialiser [kɔmɛrsjalize] vt (produit) to market

commère [kɔmɛr] nf gossip

commettre [47] [kɔmɛtr] **1** vt (**a**) (crime, péché, injustice) to commit; (erreur) to make; Hum **il a déjà**

commis deux pièces de théâtre he's already to blame for two plays (**b**) Jur **avocat commis d'office** counsel appointed by the court

2 se commettre vpr Litt **se c. avec qn** to compromise oneself by associating with sb

commis¹, -e voir **commettre**

commis² [kɔmi] nm (**a**) (employé) clerk; (dans un magasin) (shop) assistant (**b**) Vieilli **c. voyageur** commercial traveller

commisération [kɔmizerasjɔ̃] nf commiseration; **témoigner de la c. à qn** to commiserate with sb

commissaire [kɔmisɛr] nm (**a**) **c. (de police)** Br ≃ (police) superintendent, Am ≃ (police) captain (**b**) Fin **c. aux comptes** government auditor (**c**) (membre d'une commission) commissioner (**d**) Sport steward (**e**) (d'une exposition) organizer

commissaire-priseur (pl **commissaires-priseurs**) [kɔmisɛrprizœr] nm auctioneer

commissariat [kɔmisarja] nm (**a**) **c. (de police)** police station (**b**) (fonction) commissionership (**c**) (service) commission; **le C. à l'énergie atomique** the Atomic Energy Commission

commission [kɔmisjɔ̃] nf (**a**) (course) **faire les commissions** to go shopping (**b**) (service) errand; (message) message; **faire une c.** to run an errand; **faire une c. à qn** to give sb a message (**c**) (comité) commission, committee; **c. d'enquête** board of inquiry; **C. européenne** European Commission; **C. des opérations de Bourse** = French Stock Exchange watchdog (**d**) (pourcentage) Com commission; Fin brokerage; **être payé à la c.** to be paid on a commission basis; **c. bancaire** bank commission (**e**) Fam **la petite/grosse c.** number one/two

commissionnaire [kɔmisjɔnɛr] nm (**a**) (messager) messenger; (à l'hôtel, au théâtre) commissionaire (**b**) Com (commission) agent

commissionner [kɔmisjɔne] vt to commission

commissures [kɔmisyr] nfpl **c. des lèvres** ou **de la bouche** corners of the mouth

commode [kɔmɔd] **1** adj (**a**) (heure, lieu) convenient; (outil, système) handy (**b**) **pas c.** (difficile) tricky (**c**) **pas c.** (peu aimable) awkward

2 nf chest of drawers

commodément [kɔmɔdemã] adv (assis, installé) comfortably

commodité [kɔmɔdite] nf (**a**) (facilité) convenience; **pour plus de c.** for greater convenience; **les commodités de la vie moderne** the comforts of modern life (**b**) Vieilli **commodités** (toilettes) Br toilet, Am rest room

commotion [kɔmɔsjɔ̃] nf (**a**) Méd **c. cérébrale** concussion (**b**) (émotion) shock

commotionner [kɔmɔsjɔne] vt (**a**) Méd to concuss (**b**) (choquer) to shake (up)

commuer [kɔmɥe] vt Jur (peine) to commute (**en** to)

commun, -e [kɔmœ̃, -yn] **1** adj (**a**) (non exclusif) common (**à** to); (travail) joint; (ami) mutual; **jardin c. à deux maisons** garden shared by two houses; **en c.** (travailler) together; (vivre) communally; **avoir des choses en c.** (se ressembler) to have things in common; **nous n'avons aucun point c.** we have nothing in common; **se mettre** ou **mettre de l'argent en c. pour acheter un cadeau** to club together to buy a present (**b**) (répandu) common; **il est d'une force peu commune** he's unusually strong (**c**) (vulgaire) common

2 nm (**a**) (majorité) **le c. des mortels** the ordinary man; **hors du c.** out of the ordinary (**b**) **communs** (dépendances) outbuildings

communal, -e, -aux, -ales [kɔmynal, -o] adj (de la commune) (terrain, salle) Br ≃ council, Am ≃ district; **école communale** ≃ local Br primary or Am grade school; Belg **maison communale** town hall

communautaire [kɔmynotɛr] adj (en commun) communal; (de la Communauté européenne) Community

communauté [kɔmynote] nf (**a**) (collectivité) & Rel community; (de hippies) commune; **vivre en c.** to live in a commune; **la C. économique européenne** the European Economic Community; **la C. d'États indépendants** the Commonwealth of Independent States (**b**) (d'intérêts, d'idées) similarity; Jur **être mariés sous le régime de la c.** to be married on the basis of a joint settlement of property

commune [kɔmyn] nf (**a**) (municipalité) commune (smallest territorial division) (**b**) (administration) local authority, Br (town) council (**c**) Hist **la C. (de Paris)** the Commune (in 1789 and 1871)

> **Commune**
> There are over 36,000 "communes" or administrative districts in France, some with less than 25 inhabitants. Each "commune" has an elected mayor and a town council.

communément [kɔmynemã] adv commonly

communiant, -e [kɔmynjã, -ãt] nm,f Rel communicant; **premier c.** person taking his first communion

communicatif, -ive [kɔmynikatif, -iv] adj (**a**) (qui parle) communicative; **peu c.** uncommunicative (**b**) (rire, bonne humeur) infectious

communication [kɔmynikasjõ] nf (**a**) (échange) communication; **entrer** ou **se mettre en c. avec qn** to get in touch or in contact with sb; **toutes les communications sont coupées** all lines of communication are cut; **c. de masse** mass communication (**b**) **c. (téléphonique)** (telephone) call; **je vous passe la c.** I'll put you through; **la c. est mauvaise** the line is bad (**c**) (message) communication, message; **faire une c.** (dans un colloque) to read a paper

communier [66] [kɔmynje] vi Rel to receive Communion

communion [kɔmynjõ] nf (**a**) (communauté) communion; **être en c. avec la nature** to commune with nature (**b**) Rel Communion; **première c.** first Communion; **c. solennelle** solemn Communion; **faire sa c.** to make one's first/solemn Communion

communiqué [kɔmynike] nm communiqué; **c. de presse** press release

communiquer [kɔmynike] **1** vt to communicate (**à** to); (maladie) to pass on (**à** to)
2 vi (**a**) (être en relation) to communicate (**avec** with) (**b**) (pièce) to communicate (**avec** with); **porte qui communique avec le jardin** door that leads into the garden
3 se communiquer vpr (se transmettre) to spread (**à** to)

communisme [kɔmynism] nm communism

communiste [kɔmynist] adj & nmf communist

commutateur [kɔmytatœr] nm Élec (bouton) switch; Ordinat **c. de données** data switch

commutation [kɔmytasjõ] nf (**a**) Jur (de peine) commutation (**b**) (changement) & Gram substitution;

(entre documents) switching (**c**) Ordinat **c. de message/de paquets** message/packet switching

Comores [kɔmɔr] nfpl **les C., l'archipel des C.** the Comoros

comorien, -enne [kɔmɔrjẽ, -ɛn] **1** adj Comoran
2 nm,f **C.** Comoran

compact, -e [kõpakt] **1** adj (**a**) (de petit format) compact (**b**) (masse, terre) compact; (foule) dense
2 nm (CD) compact disc

Compact Disc® (pl **Compact Discs**) [kõpaktdisk] nm compact disc

compacter [kõpakte] vt Ordinat (fichier, données) to compress; (base de données) to pack

compacteur [kõpaktœr] nm Ordinat **c. de données** data compressor; **c. d'exécutables** execute file compressor

compagne [kõpaɲ] nf (**a**) (camarade) companion; **mes compagnes de captivité** my fellow captives (**b**) (concubine) partner

compagnie [kõpaɲi] nf (**a**) (présence) company; **tenir c. à qn** to keep sb company; **en c. de qn** with sb (**b**) (groupe) **et toute la c.** and everybody; Fam **salut, la c.!** hi, guys or everybody! (**c**) Com & Théât company; ComThomas et C. Thomas and Company; **c. aérienne** airline; **c. d'assurances** insurance company; **c. maritime** shipping line; **c. pétrolière** oil company; **c. de transports** carrier (**d**) Mil company (**e**) (de perdrix) covey

compagnon [kõpaɲõ] nm (**a**) (camarade) companion; **c. de voyage** travelling companion (**b**) (ouvrier) journeyman (**c**) (concubin) partner

comparable [kõparabl] adj comparable (**à** ou **avec** to or with); **ce n'est pas c.** there's no comparison

comparaison [kõparɛzõ] nf (**a**) (action de comparer) comparison; **faire la c. entre** to make a comparison between; **c'est sans c. avec...** it can't be compared with...; **il est sans c. le plus grand** he is by far the tallest; **en c. de...** in comparison with...; **par c.** by comparison; **par c. avec** ou **à** compared with or to (**b**) (figure de style) simile

comparaître [50a] [kõparɛtr] vi Jur **c. (en justice)** to appear (in court); **être appelé à c.** to be summoned to appear

comparatif, -ive [kõparatif, -iv] **1** adj comparative
2 nm Gram comparative; **c. de supériorité/d'infériorité** comparative of greater/lesser degree

comparativement [kõparativmã] adv comparatively

comparé, -e [kõpare] adj (anatomie, histoire, littérature) comparative; **c. à** compared with or to

comparer [kõpare] **1** vt to compare (**à** ou **avec** to or with)
2 se comparer vpr (**a**) (soi-même) **se c. à** ou **avec** to compare oneself to or with (**b**) (être comparé) **Händel ne peut pas se c. à Mozart** Handel can't be compared with Mozart

comparse [kõpars] nmf Péj associate

compartiment [kõpartimã] nm (de wagon, de boîte, de tiroir) compartment; **c. fumeurs** smoking compartment, smoker; **c. non-fumeurs** no-smoking compartment, non-smoker; **c. à bagages** (d'autocar) luggage compartment

compartimenter [kõpartimãte] vt (diviser en espaces) to partition; Fig **une société compartimentée** a compartmentalized society

comparution [kõparysjõ] nf Jur appearance

compas [kɔ̃pa] *nm* (**a**) *Math* (pair of) compasses; *Fig* **avoir le c. dans l'œil** to have an accurate eye; **c. à pointes sèches** dividers (**b**) *Naut* compass

compassé, -e [kɔ̃pase] *adj* stiff, starchy

compassion [kɔ̃pasjɔ̃] *nf* compassion; **avec c.** compassionately

compatibilité [kɔ̃patibilite] *nf* compatibility

compatible [kɔ̃patibl] *adj aussi Ordinat* compatible (**avec** with)

compatir [kɔ̃patir] *vi* to sympathize; **c. au chagrin de qn** to sympathize with sb in his/her grief

compatissant, -e [kɔ̃patisã, -ãt] *adj* compassionate, sympathetic

compatriote [kɔ̃patrijɔt] *nmf* compatriot

compensable [kɔ̃pãsabl] *adj (chèque)* clearable

compensation [kɔ̃pãsasjɔ̃] *nf* (**a**) *(d'une perte, d'un inconvénient)* compensation; **en c. de qch** as compensation for sth (**b**) *(de chèque)* clearing

compensé, -e [kɔ̃pãse] *adj* **chaussures à semelles compensées** platform shoes

compenser [kɔ̃pãse] **1** *vt* (**a**) *(perte, défaut)* to compensate for, to make up for (**b**) *(chèque)* to clear
2 se compenser *vpr* to make up for each other

compère [kɔ̃pɛr] *nm Vieilli (camarade)* friend

compétence [kɔ̃petãs] *nf* (**a**) *(capacité)* competence; **compétences** *(connaissances)* ability; **cela n'entre pas dans mes compétences** it's beyond my capabilities (**b**) *Jur (d'un tribunal, d'un maire)* competence; **cela n'est pas de sa c.** that doesn't come within her province

compétent, -e [kɔ̃petã, -ãt] *adj* (**a**) *(capable)* competent; **c. en qch** conversant with sth (**b**) *Jur (tribunal, autorité)* competent; **adressez-vous au service c.** apply to the relevant department

compétitif, -ive [kɔ̃petitif, -iv] *adj* competitive

compétition [kɔ̃petisjɔ̃] *nf* (**a**) *(rivalité)* competition; **être en c. avec qn** to compete with sb (**b**) *Sport (épreuve)* **c. (sportive)** (sporting) event; **faire de la c.** to go in for competitive sport

compétitivité [kɔ̃petitivite] *nf* competitiveness

compilateur [kɔ̃pilatœr] *nm Ordinat* compiler; **c. croisé** cross-compiler

compilation [kɔ̃pilasjɔ̃] *nf* compilation

compiler [kɔ̃pile] *vt aussi Ordinat* to compile

complaire [55a] [kɔ̃plɛr] **se complaire** *vpr* **se c. dans qch/à faire qch** to delight or revel in sth/in doing sth

complaisance [kɔ̃plɛzãs] *nf* (**a**) *(bienveillance)* kindness; **faire qch par c.** to do sth out of kindness (**b**) *Péj (indulgence)* indulgence; **certificat médical de c.** = medical certificate to which one is not entitled (**c**) *(autosatisfaction)* complacency, smugness

complaisant, -e [kɔ̃plɛzã, -ãt] *adj* (**a**) *(bienveillant)* obliging, kind (**envers** towards) (**b**) *Péj (indulgent)* indulgent (**c**) *(satisfait)* complacent, smug

complément [kɔ̃plemã] *nm* (**a**) *(reste)* rest, remainder; **demander un c. d'information** to ask for further information (**b**) *Gram* complement; **c. d'attribution** indirect object; **c. circonstanciel de temps/de manière** adverbial phrase of time/of manner; **c. de nom** possessive phrase; **c. d'objet direct/indirect** direct/indirect object

complémentaire [kɔ̃plemãtɛr] *adj (couleur)* complementary; **pour tout renseignement c., s'adresser à…** for further information, apply to…

complet, -ète [kɔ̃plɛ, -ɛt] **1** *adj* (**a**) *(entier, intégral) (tenue, service)* complete, whole; **deux jours complets** two full or whole days; **formation très complète** thorough training; *Fam* **c'est c.!** that's the last straw! (**b**) *(détaillé)* full (**c**) *(absolu)* complete; **un c. abruti** a complete moron; **ce fut un échec c.** it was a complete failure (**d**) *(bus, salle de théâtre)* full; **c.** *(sur panneau) (parking)* full; *(pension, hôtel)* no vacancies (**e**) *(pain, pâtes)* wholemeal; *(riz)* brown
2 *nm* (**a**) **c.(-veston)** suit (**b**) **est-ce que nous sommes au c.?** are we all here?; **j'ai invité la famille au (grand) c. pour Noël** I've invited the whole family for Christmas

complètement [kɔ̃plɛtmã] *adv* (**a**) *(terminé, guéri)* completely, totally; **je n'ai pas c. fini** I haven't quite finished (**b**) *(vraiment) (perdu, idiot)* completely, totally

compléter [34] [kɔ̃plete] **1** *vt (collection, formation)* to complete; *(somme)* to make up; *(formulaire)* to complete, to fill in
2 se compléter *vpr* to complement one another

complexe [kɔ̃plɛks] **1** *adj (compliqué)* complex
2 *nm* (**a**) *(ensemble de bâtiments, d'industries)* complex; **c. hôtelier** hotel complex; **c. sportif** sports complex (**b**) *(gêne)* hang-up; *Psy* complex; **avoir des complexes (à cause de qch)** to have a hang-up (about sth); **être sans c.** to have no hang-ups; **c. d'infériorité** inferiority complex; **c. d'Œdipe** Oedipus complex

complexé, -e [kɔ̃plɛkse] *adj* hung up (**par** about)

complexer [kɔ̃plɛkse] *vt* **c. qn** to give sb a hang-up

complexité [kɔ̃plɛksite] *nf* complexity

complication [kɔ̃plikasjɔ̃] *nf* (**a**) *(ennui)* complication; **faire des complications** to create complications (**b**) *(complexité)* complexity (**c**) *Méd* **complications** complications

complice [kɔ̃plis] **1** *nmf* accomplice
2 *adj (regard, sourire)* knowing; **être c. de qch** to be party to sth

complicité [kɔ̃plisite] *nf* complicity; **agir en c. avec qn** to act in collusion with sb; **accusé de c. de meurtre** accused of being an accessory to murder

compliment [kɔ̃plimã] *nm* compliment; **faire des compliments à qn (sur qch)** to pay sb compliments (on sth); **(je vous fais) mes compliments!** I congratulate you!; *Ironique* **mes compliments!** congratulations!

complimenter [kɔ̃plimãte] *vt* **c. qn pour** *(courage, présence d'esprit)* to congratulate sb on; **c. qn sur** *(toilette, coiffure)* to compliment sb on

compliqué, -e [kɔ̃plike] *adj* complicated; **ce n'est pourtant pas c.!** it's quite simple!

compliquer [kɔ̃plike] **1** *vt* to complicate; **c. les choses** to complicate matters
2 se compliquer *vpr (situation, problème)* to get complicated; **se c. l'existence** to make life complicated for oneself

complot [kɔ̃plo] *nm* plot, conspiracy

comploter [kɔ̃plɔte] **1** *vt* to plot; **c. de faire qch** to plot to do sth
2 *vi* to plot (**contre** against)

comportement [kɔ̃pɔrtəmã] *nm* behaviour; *Écon* **c. d'achat** buying behaviour

comporter [kɔ̃pɔrte] **1** *vt* (**a**) *(être constitué de)* to consist of, to be made up of (**b**) *(contenir)* to contain (**c**) *(difficultés, inconvénients)* to involve

2 se comporter *vpr* (**a**) *(agir)* to behave (**vis-à-vis de** *ou* **envers** towards) (**b**) *(fonctionner) (voiture)* to handle

composant [kɔ̃pozɑ̃] *nm* component

composante [kɔ̃pozɑ̃t] *nf* component

composé, -e [kɔ̃poze] *adj & nm* compound

composer [kɔ̃poze] **1** *vt* (**a**) *(symphonie, poème)* to compose, to write; *(bouquet)* to make up (**b**) *(faire partie de)* to make up; **être composé de qch** to be made up *or* composed of sth (**c**) *(numéro de téléphone)* to dial (**d**) *Typ* to set (**e**) **c. son visage** to compose one's features

2 *vi* (**a**) *(s'entendre)* to compromise (**avec** with) (**b**) *Scol* to take a test

3 se composer *vpr* (**a**) **se c. de qch** to be made up *or* composed of sth (**b**) **se c. un visage de circonstance** to put on a suitable expression

composite [kɔ̃pozit] *adj* composite

compositeur, -trice [kɔ̃pozitœr, -tris] *nm,f* (**a**) *Mus* composer (**b**) *Typ* typesetter

composition [kɔ̃pozisjɔ̃] *nf* (**a**) *(d'une symphonie, d'un poème)* composition, writing; **un poème de ma c.** a poem I wrote (myself); *Cin & Théât* **rôle de c.** character part (**b**) *(éléments)* composition; *(d'un aliment)* ingredients; **la c. des équipes n'est pas encore connue** the teams haven't been announced yet (**c**) *(œuvre musicale, littéraire)* composition (**d**) *(rédaction)* essay; *(examen)* test (**e**) *(caractère)* **être de bonne c.** to be good-natured (**f**) *Typ* typesetting

compost [kɔ̃pɔst] *nm* compost

composter [kɔ̃pɔste] *vt* (**a**) *(pour dater)* to date-stamp (**b**) *(pour valider)* to punch

> ### Composter
> Rail passengers in France are required to insert their ticket into a special punching machine ("composteur") on the platform before beginning their journey. The words "à composter" printed across the ticket mean that the passenger must do this before getting on the train.

compote [kɔ̃pɔt] *nf* compote, stewed fruit; **c. de pommes** apple compote, stewed apples; *Fam* **j'ai les jambes en c.** my legs feel like jelly

compotier [kɔ̃pɔtje] *nm* fruit dish

compréhensible [kɔ̃preɑ̃sibl] *adj* (**a**) *(clair)* comprehensible (**par** to) (**b**) *(justifié)* understandable

compréhensif, -ive [kɔ̃preɑ̃sif, -iv] *adj* understanding

compréhension [kɔ̃preɑ̃sjɔ̃] *nf* (**a**) *(fait de comprendre)* comprehension, understanding (**b**) *(bienveillance)* understanding

comprendre [58] [kɔ̃prɑ̃dr] **1** *vt* (**a**) *(par l'esprit)* to understand; **dois-je c. que...?** am I to understand that...?; **mal c. qn/qch** to misunderstand sb/sth; **je ne le comprends pas** *(il est étrange, il n'articule pas)* I can't understand him; **il faut la c.** you have to see things from her point of view; **je n'y comprends rien** I can't make head nor tail of it; **c'est à n'y rien c.** it's incomprehensible; **ne cherche pas, il n'y a rien à c.** don't even try to understand; **va y c. quelque chose!** YOU try to make head or tail of it!; **faire c. à qn que...** to give sb to understand that...; *(avec autorité)* to make it clear to sb that...; **se faire c.** to make oneself understood; **me suis-je bien fait c.?** have I made myself clear?; **elle comprend vite** she's quick on the uptake; **ça va, j'ai compris!** OK, I understand!; **tu**

comprends... you see... (**b**) *(être composé de)* to consist of, to be made up of (**c**) *(inclure)* to include

2 se comprendre *vpr* *(l'un l'autre)* to understand each other; **ça se comprend** it's understandable; **je me comprends!** I know what I mean!

comprenure [kɔ̃prənyr] *nf Belg & Can Fam* **être dur de c.** to be slow on the uptake

compresse [kɔ̃prɛs] *nf* compress

compresser [kɔ̃prese] *vt* to compress; *Ordinat* to zip

compresseur [kɔ̃presœr] *nm* (**a**) *Tech (de gaz, de vapeur)* compressor; *(de moteur)* supercharger (**b**) *Ordinat* **c. de données** data compressor

compression [kɔ̃presjɔ̃] *nf* (**a**) *(de gaz, de vapeur)* compression (**b**) *(réduction)* reduction; **c. des dépenses** spending cuts

comprimé, -e [kɔ̃prime] **1** *adj (gaz)* compressed

2 *nm (médicament)* tablet; **un c. d'aspirine** an aspirin

comprimer [kɔ̃prime] *vt* (**a**) *(gaz, artère, fichier informatique)* to compress; **cette jupe me comprime la taille** this skirt is too tight round my waist (**b**) *Fig (dépenses)* to reduce

compris, -e [kɔ̃pri, -iz] **1** *pp voir* **comprendre**

2 *adj* (**a**) *(enregistré)* **bien c.** (fully) understood; **mal c.** misunderstood; **alors, c'est c.?** so, do you understand?; *Fam* **tu fais tes devoirs immédiatement, c.?** you'll do your homework right now, (is that) understood? (**b**) *(inclus)* included; **service non c.** service not included; **tout c.** all in; **y c.** including (**c**) *(situé)* **être c. entre** to be between

compromettant, -e [kɔ̃prɔmɛtɑ̃, -ɑ̃t] *adj* compromising

compromettre [47] [kɔ̃prɔmɛtr] **1** *vt* (**a**) *(personne, réputation)* to compromise; **être compromis dans qch** to be implicated in sth (**b**) *(sécurité, vacances, chances)* to jeopardize

2 se compromettre *vpr* to compromise oneself; **se c. dans qch** to be implicated in sth

compromis [kɔ̃prɔmi] *nm (arrangement)* compromise

compromission [kɔ̃prɔmisjɔ̃] *nf Péj* compromise

comptabiliser [kɔ̃tabilize] *vt (recettes, dépenses)* to enter in the accounts; *(points)* to count

comptabilité [kɔ̃tabilite] *nf* (**a**) *(livres)* accounts; *(technique)* book-keeping, accounting; **tenir la c.** to keep the accounts (**b**) *(service)* accounts department

comptable [kɔ̃tabl] **1** *adj (travail, technique)* book-keeping, accounting

2 *nmf* accountant; **c. agréé** *Br* chartered accountant, *Am* certified public accountant

comptage [kɔ̃taʒ] *nm* counting

comptant [kɔ̃tɑ̃] **1** *adv* **payer c.** to pay (in) cash

2 *nm* cash; **payer/acheter au c.** to pay (in)/buy for cash

compte [kɔ̃t] *nm* (**a**) *(dans une banque, chez un commerçant)* account; **comptes** *(comptabilité)* accounts; **tenir les comptes** to keep the accounts; **faire ses comptes** to do one's accounts; **verser une somme sur son c.** to pay a sum into one's account; **se mettre** *ou* **s'installer à son c.** to start one's own business; **faire qch pour le c. de qn** to do sth on sb's behalf; **c. en banque** *ou* **bancaire** bank account; **c. chèques** *Br* current account, *Am* checking account; **c. chèques postal** ≃ giro account; **c. courant** *Br* current account, *Am* checking account; **c. de dépôt** deposit account; **c. épargne** savings account; **c. épargne logement** savings account *(for purchasing a* *property);* **c. étranger** non-resident *or* foreign account; **c. joint** joint account

(**b**) *(calcul)* calculation; **faire le c. de** *(dépenses)* to add up; *(temps restant)* to calculate; *(objets, personnes)* to count; **le c. y est** *(somme)* it's the right amount; *(objets, personnes)* they're all here; **c. à rebours** countdown

(**c**) *(explication)* **demander des comptes à qn** to ask sb for an explanation; **rendre des comptes** to explain oneself; **je n'ai de comptes à rendre à personne** I'm not answerable to anyone; **rendre c. de qch** to account for sth

(**d**) *(locutions) Fam* **avoir son c.** to have had enough; **être loin du c.** *(se tromper)* to be wide of the mark; *Fam* **régler son c. à qn** to sort sb out; **on réglera nos comptes plus tard** we'll settle scores later; **apprendre qch sur le c. de qn** to learn sth about sb; **j'en ai appris de belles sur son c.!** I heard some fine things about him!; *Fam* **son c. est bon** he's for it; **tenir c. de qch** to take sth into account; **il n'a tenu aucun c. de mes conseils** he took no heed of my advice; **c. tenu de** considering; **s'en tirer à bon c.** to get off lightly; **y trouver son c.** to get something out of it; **à ce c.-là** in that case; **au bout du c., en fin de c.** in the end; **tout c. fait** all things considered; *Prov* **les bons comptes font les bons amis** pay your debts and keep your friends

compte-gouttes [kɔ̃tgut] *nm inv* dropper; *Fig* **au c.** in dribs and drabs

compter [kɔ̃te] **1** *vt* (**a**) *(dénombrer)* to count; **on ne compte plus les mécontents** we've lost count of the malcontents; *Fig* **c. les points** to watch from the sidelines (**b**) *(donner avec parcimonie)* **il compte chaque sou** he begrudges every penny he spends; **ses jours sont comptés** his days are numbered (**c**) *(inclure)* to include; **sans c....** not counting...; **sans c. que...** besides the fact that...; **je le compte parmi mes meilleurs amis** I number him among my best friends (**d**) *(prévoir)* to allow; **j'ai compté 200 grammes par personne** I've allowed 200 grams per person; **c. faire qch** *(espérer)* to expect to do sth; *(avoir l'intention de)* to intend to do sth (**e**) *(facturer)* **c. qch à qn** to charge sb for sth (**f**) *Can (marquer)* to score

2 *vi* (**a**) *(calculer)* to count; **dépenser sans c.** *(dépenser trop)* to spend money like water; **à c. du 1er janvier** (with effect) from 1 January (**b**) *(être parcimonieux)* to count the pennies (**c**) *(être important)* to count, to matter; **il compte beaucoup pour elle** he means a lot to her; **c. double** to count double; **à table, il compte pour deux** he eats enough for two (**d**) *(figurer)* **c. parmi les meilleurs** to rank among the best (**e**) **c. avec qn/qch** to reckon with sb/sth (**f**) **c. sur qn/qch** to count *or* rely on sb/sth; **j'y compte bien!** I should hope so!; *Fam* **compte là-dessus et bois de l'eau!** you'll be lucky!

3 se compter *vpr* **les membres de cette secte se comptent par milliers** this sect has thousands of members

compte rendu (*pl* **comptes rendus**) [kɔ̃trɑ̃dy] *nm* report; *(d'un roman, d'un film)* review; *(d'une réunion)* minutes

compte-tours [kɔ̃ttur] *nm inv* rev counter

compteur [kɔ̃tœr] *nm* meter; **c. d'eau/d'électricité/à gaz** water/electricity/gas meter; **c. (de) Geiger** Geiger counter; *Aut* **c. kilométrique** *Br* mileometer, *Am* odometer; *Can* **c. de stationnement** parking meter; *Aut* **c. de vitesse** speedometer

comptine [kɔ̃tin] *nf* nursery rhyme

comptoir [kɔ̃twar] *nm* (**a**) *(dans un magasin)* counter; *(dans un bar)* bar; **prendre une consommation au c.** to have a drink at the bar; **c. d'enregistrement** check-in desk; **c. d'information** information desk; **c. de réception** reception desk; **c. de vente** sales counter (**b**) *(dans un pays éloigné)* trading post

compulser [kɔ̃pylse] *vt (documents, livres)* to consult

comte [kɔ̃t] *nm* count; *(en Grande-Bretagne)* earl

comté [kɔ̃te] *nm* (**a**) *Hist* earldom (**b**) *(subdivision administrative)* county (**c**) *(fromage)* = type of hard cheese (**d**) *Can Pol* riding

comtesse [kɔ̃tɛs] *nf* countess

con, conne [kɔ̃, kɔn] **1** *adj très Fam* (**a**) *(stupide)* bloody stupid; *Fam* **être c. comme la lune** *ou* **un balai** to be as daft as a brush; **c'est pas c.!** that's pretty smart! (**b**) *(facile)* **c'est tout c.!** it's dead easy!

2 *nm,f très Fam* stupid bastard; **faire le c.** to arse around; **pauvre c.!** stupid bastard!; **à la c.** *(ordinateur, voiture)* bloody useless; *(idée, histoire)* bloody stupid **3** *nm Vulg (sexe)* cunt

conard [kɔnar] *nm très Fam* jerk

conasse [kɔnas] *nf très Fam* silly bitch

concasser [kɔ̃kase] *vt (roche)* to crush; *(poivre)* to grind

concave [kɔ̃kav] *adj* concave

concéder [34] [kɔ̃sede] *vt* (**a**) *(privilège, droit, terrain, concession)* **c. qch à qn** to grant sb sth, to grant sth to sb (**b**) *(reconnaître)* **c. qu'on a tort** to admit that one is wrong; **il fait chaud, je vous le concède** it's warm, I grant you (**c**) *Sport (point, but, victoire)* to concede

concentration [kɔ̃sɑ̃trasjɔ̃] *nf* concentration

concentrationnaire [kɔ̃sɑ̃trasjɔnɛr] *adj* of concentration camps; **la vie c.** life in a concentration camp

concentré, -e [kɔ̃sɑ̃tre] **1** *adj* (**a**) *(solution)* concentrated; *(lait)* condensed (**b**) *(intellectuellement)* **il était très c.** he was concentrating hard

2 *nm Chim & Culin* concentrate; **c. de tomate** tomato purée

concentrer [kɔ̃sɑ̃tre] **1** *vt (troupes, forces, efforts)* to concentrate; *(rayons du soleil)* to focus

2 se concentrer *vpr* (**a**) *(être attentif)* to concentrate (**sur** on) (**b**) *(s'assembler) (foule)* to gather; **la population se concentre dans les grandes villes** the population is concentrated in the big cities

concentrique [kɔ̃sɑ̃trik] *adj* concentric

concept [kɔ̃sɛpt] *nm* concept

conception [kɔ̃sɛpsjɔ̃] *nf* (**a**) *(d'un enfant, d'une idée)* conception (**b**) *(idée)* concept (**c**) *(création)* design; **c. assistée par ordinateur** computer-aided *or* -assisted design

concernant [kɔ̃sɛrnɑ̃] *prép* concerning

concerner [kɔ̃sɛrne] *vt* to concern; **en ce qui me concerne** as far as I am concerned; **cela ne vous concerne pas** *(cela ne vous regarde pas)* it's none of your business; *(vous n'êtes pas visé)* it doesn't concern you

concert [kɔ̃sɛr] *nm* (**a**) *(de musique)* concert (**b**) *(accord)* **agir de c. avec qn** to act jointly with sb

concertation [kɔ̃sɛrtasjɔ̃] *nf* consultation

concerté, -e [kɔ̃sɛrte] *adj (action)* concerted

concerter [kɔ̃sɛrte] **1** *vt (projet)* to devise together **2 se concerter** *vpr* to consult together

concertiste [kɔ̃sɛrtist] *nmf* concert performer

concerto [kɔ̃sɛrto] *nm* concerto; **c. pour violon** violin concerto

concession [kɔ̃sɛsjɔ̃] *nf* (**a**) *(compromis)* concession; **faire des concessions** to make concessions; **sans concessions** uncompromising (**b**) *(attribution)* *(de terrain)* granting (**c**) *(terrain)* concession; *(au cimetière)* plot (**d**) *(droit exclusif de vente)* dealership

concessionnaire [kɔ̃sɛsjɔnɛr] *nmf* dealer

concevable [kɔ̃səvabl] *adj* conceivable

concevoir [60] [kɔ̃səvwar] **1** *vt* (**a**) *(enfant, plan, idée)* to conceive; *(produit)* to design (**b**) *(comprendre)* to understand; **je conçois que tu sois fâché, mais...** I can understand *or* see why you are angry, but...; **c'est ainsi que je conçois l'amour** this is my idea of love (**c**) *(éprouver)* **c. de l'amitié pour qn** to take a liking to sb
2 se concevoir *vpr* **ça se conçoit** that's understandable

concierge [kɔ̃sjɛrʒ] *nmf (d'immeuble, d'appartements) & Scol Br* caretaker, *Am* janitor; *(dans un hôtel)* porter; *Fam* **c'est une vraie c.** she's a terrible gossip

concile [kɔ̃sil] *nm Rel* council

conciliabule [kɔ̃siljabyl] *nm (conversation)* confab

conciliant, -e [kɔ̃siljã, -ãt] *adj* conciliatory

conciliation [kɔ̃siljasjɔ̃] *nf* reconciliation

concilier [66] [kɔ̃silje] **1** *vt (deux choses)* to reconcile; **c. sa vie professionnelle et sa vie de famille** to combine one's professional life with one's family life
2 se concilier *vpr* (**a**) *(être compatible)* **se c. avec** to go with (**b**) **se c. qn** *ou* **la faveur de qn** to win sb's goodwill

concis, -e [kɔ̃si, -iz] *adj* concise

concision [kɔ̃sizjɔ̃] *nf* conciseness; **avec c.** concisely

concitoyen, -enne [kɔ̃sitwajɛ̃, -ɛn] *nm,f* fellow citizen

concluant, -e [kɔ̃klyã, -ãt] *adj* conclusive; **peu c.** inconclusive

conclure [17] [kɔ̃klyr] **1** *vt* (**a**) *(terminer)* to conclude, to end (**par** with) (**b**) *(accord, pacte)* to finalize; *(marché)* to clinch; **marché conclu!, affaire conclue!** it's a deal! (**c**) *(déduire)* to conclude (**de** from); **dois-je en c. que...?** am I to conclude that...?
2 conclure à *vt ind* **ils ont conclu au suicide/meurtre** they concluded it was suicide/murder

conclusion [kɔ̃klyzjɔ̃] *nf* (**a**) *(fin)* (d'un discours, d'une réunion)* conclusion, end (**b**) *(déduction)* conclusion; **tirer une c. de qch** to draw a conclusion from sth; *Fam* **c., l'échafaudage s'est écroulé** the result was that the scaffolding collapsed

concocter [kɔ̃kɔkte] *vt Fam* to concoct

concombre [kɔ̃kɔ̃br] *nm* cucumber

concordance [kɔ̃kɔrdãs] *nf* (**a**) *(de preuves, de témoignages, de dates)* tallying (**b**) *Gram* **c. des temps** sequence of tenses

concorder [kɔ̃kɔrde] *vi (preuves, dates, témoignages)* to tally (**avec** with)

concourir [22] [kɔ̃kurir] *vi* (**a**) *Sport* to compete (**b**) *(lignes)* to converge
2 concourir à *vt ind* **c. à qch/à faire qch** to contribute to sth/to doing sth

concours [kɔ̃kur] *nm* (**a**) *(compétition)* competition, contest; *(examen)* competitive examination; **c. agricole/hippique** agricultural/horse show; **c. de beauté** beauty contest; **c. d'entrée (à)** entrance examination (to) (**b**) *(aide)* aid, assistance; **avec le c. de** with the participation of, in association with (**c**) **c. de circonstances** combination of circumstances; **par un heureux c. de circonstances** by a lucky coincidence

Concours
Unlike an ordinary examination, passing a "concours" does not lead to a degree, but rather to a teaching post in the state education system (for example the **CAPES** and **agrégation**), an appointment or promotion in the civil service, or a place in a **Grande École** ("ENA", "Centrale", "ENS", etc). "Concours" are extremely competitive examinations, and the quota of successful candidates is determined in advance. They are usually held over a period of several days, and comprise a series of written and oral examinations requiring a high level of preparation.

concret, -ète [kɔ̃krɛ, -ɛt] **1** *adj* concrete
2 *nm* **ce que je veux, c'est du c.** what I want is something concrete *or* something I can get my teeth into

concrètement [kɔ̃krɛtmã] *adv* in concrete terms

concrétiser [kɔ̃kretize] **1** *vt (rêve)* to realize; *(projet, promesse)* to carry out
2 se concrétiser *vpr* to materialize

conçu, -e *voir* concevoir

concubin, -e [kɔ̃kybɛ̃, -in] *nm,f Jur* cohabitant

concubinage [kɔ̃kybinaʒ] *nm* cohabitation; **vivre en c.** to cohabit

concupiscent, -e [kɔ̃kypisã, -ãt] *adj* concupiscent

concurrence [kɔ̃kyrãs] *nf* (**a**) *(rivalité, concurrents)* competition; **faire c. à** to compete with; **faire jouer la c.** to shop around (**b**) **jusqu'à c. de...** up to...

concurrencer [16] [kɔ̃kyrãse] *vt* to compete with

concurrent, -e [kɔ̃kyrã, -ãt] **1** *adj (industries, produits)* competing, rival
2 *nm,f* (**a**) *Com* competitor (**b**) *(dans une épreuve, un concours)* competitor

concurrentiel, -elle [kɔ̃kyrãsjɛl] *adj* competitive

condamnation [kɔ̃danasjɔ̃] *nf* (**a**) *Jur (jugement)* conviction (**pour** for); *(peine)* sentence (**à** to); **c. à mort** death sentence (**b**) *(critique)* condemnation

condamné, -e [kɔ̃dane] **1** *adj (malade)* terminally ill
2 *nm,f* convicted person; **un c. à mort** a condemned man

condamner [kɔ̃dane] *vt* (**a**) *Jur* to sentence (**à** to); **c. qn à 1000 euros d'amende** to fine sb 1,000 euros (**b**) *(obliger à)* **c. qn à qch** to force sb into sth; **être condamné à la solitude** to be condemned to loneliness; **je suis condamnée à les attendre** I have to wait for them (**c**) *(blâmer)* to condemn (**d**) *(porte)* to block up; *(pièce)* to seal up (**e**) *(interdire)* to forbid

condensateur [kɔ̃dãsatœr] *nm Élec* condenser

condensation [kɔ̃dãsasjɔ̃] *nf* condensation

condensé, -e [kɔ̃dãse] **1** *adj* condensed
2 *nm* digest

condenser [kɔ̃dãse] **1** *vt (article, récit)* to condense
2 se condenser *vpr* to condense

condescendant, -e [kɔ̃desãdã, -ãt] *adj* condescending

condescendre [kɔ̃desãdr] *vi* **c. à faire qch** to condescend to do sth

condiment [kɔ̃dimã] *nm* condiment

condisciple [kɔ̃disipl] *nmf Univ* fellow student; *Scol* schoolmate

condition [kɔ̃disjɔ̃] *nf* (**a**) *(stipulation)* condition; **sans c.** unconditionally; **à une c....** on one condition...; **à c. que tu viennes avec moi** providing that *or* on condition that you come with me; **tu peux y aller à c. de rentrer pour minuit** you can go providing that *or* on condition that you're home by midnight (**b**) **conditions** *(circonstances)* conditions; *(d'une vente, d'un accord)* terms; **dans ces conditions, je n'y vais pas** if that's the way it is, I'm not going; **conditions atmosphériques** atmospheric conditions; **conditions de paiement** terms of payment; **conditions de vie/travail** living/working conditions (**c**) *(état)* condition; **être en bonne/mauvaise c. physique** to be in good/bad shape (**d**) *(sort)* condition; **la c. humaine** the human condition; **la c. des ouvriers/des paysans** the workers'/farmers' lot (**e**) *(classe sociale)* station, status; **une personne de c. modeste** a person from a humble background

conditionnel, -elle [kɔ̃disjɔnɛl] **1** *adj* conditional
  2 *nm Gram* conditional

conditionnement [kɔ̃disjɔnmɑ̃] *nm* (**a**) *(fait d'emballer, emballage)* packaging (**b**) *Psy* conditioning

conditionner [kɔ̃disjɔne] *vt* (**a**) *(être la condition de)* to govern (**b**) *(emballer)* to package (**c**) *Psy (personne)* to condition

condoléances [kɔ̃dɔleɑ̃s] *nfpl* condolences; **présenter ses c. à qn** to offer one's condolences to sb; **toutes mes c.** (please accept) my condolences

condominium [kɔ̃dɔminjɔm] *nm Pol* condominium

condor [kɔ̃dɔr] *nm* condor

conducteur, -trice [kɔ̃dyktœr, -tris] **1** *nm,f (d'une voiture, d'un train)* driver; *(de machine)* operator; **c. de travaux** clerk of works
  2 *nm Élec & Phys* conductor
  3 *adj Élec & Phys* conductive

conduction [kɔ̃dyksjɔ̃] *nf Élec* conduction

conductivité [kɔ̃dyktivite] *nf Élec* conductivity

conduire [18] [kɔ̃dɥir] **1** *vt* (**a**) *(emmener)* to take; *(en voiture)* to drive, to take (**b**) *(mener) (troupeau, aveugle)* to lead (**c**) *(entraîner)* **c. qn à faire qch** to lead sb to do sth; **c. qn au désespoir/suicide** to drive sb to despair/suicide (**d**) *(voiture, camion)* to drive; *(moto)* to ride; *(bateau)* to steer (**e**) *(acheminer) (eau, gaz)* to carry (**f**) *(diriger) (opérations)* to manage, to run
  2 *vi* (**a**) *(en voiture)* to drive; *(en moto)* to ride; **elle conduit bien** she's a good driver (**b**) *(sujet: porte, couloir, études)* **c. à** to lead to
  3 se conduire *vpr (se comporter)* to behave; **se c. mal** *(d'un enfant)* to misbehave; **se c. bien/mal avec qn** to behave well/badly towards sb

conduit [kɔ̃dɥi] *nm* (**a**) *(tuyau)* conduit, pipe; **c. d'aération** air duct; **c. de ventilation** ventilation shaft (**b**) *Anat* **c. auditif** auditory canal

conduite [kɔ̃dɥit] *nf* (**a**) *(de voiture, de camion)* driving; *(de moto)* riding; **leçons de c.** driving lessons; **c. à gauche/droite** *(position du volant)* left-/right-hand drive; *(sur la route)* driving on the left/right; **c. accompagnée** = learning to drive accompanied by someone holding a full driving licence; **c. intérieure** *Br* saloon (car), *Am* sedan; **c. sur route** driving on the open road (**b**) *(des affaires, des opérations)* management, running; *(d'une armée)* command; *(de travaux)* supervision (**c**) *(comportement)* behaviour, conduct; *Hum* **s'acheter une c.** to turn over a new leaf (**d**) *(tuyau)* pipe; **c. d'eau/de gaz** water/gas main

cône [kon] *nm* cone

confection [kɔ̃fɛksjɔ̃] *nf* (**a**) *(d'un vêtement, d'un repas)* making (**b**) *(industrie)* (ready-made) clothing industry; **vêtements de c.** ready-made clothes

confectionner [kɔ̃fɛksjɔne] *vt* to make

confédération [kɔ̃federasjɔ̃] *nf* confederation; **la C. helvétique** the Swiss Confederation

conférence [kɔ̃ferɑ̃s] *nf* (**a**) *(congrès, colloque)* conference; **c. de presse** press conference; **c. au sommet** summit (conference) (**b**) *(exposé)* lecture; **faire une c. sur...** to give a lecture on...

conférencier, -ère [kɔ̃ferɑ̃sje, -ɛr] *nm,f* lecturer

conférer [34] [kɔ̃fere] **1** *vt (titre)* to confer (**à** on); **l'âge confère certains privilèges** age brings with it certain privileges
  2 *vi* to confer (**avec** with)

confesser [kɔ̃fese] **1** *vt* (**a**) *Rel* to confess (**b**) *(reconnaître)* to confess, to admit
  2 se confesser *vpr* to confess; **(aller) se c.** to go to confession

confession [kɔ̃fesjɔ̃] *nf* (**a**) *Rel & Fig* confession; *Fam* **on lui donnerait le bon Dieu sans c.** he/she looks as though butter wouldn't melt in his/her mouth (**b**) *(croyance)* denomination

confessionnal, -aux [kɔ̃fesjɔnal, -o] *nm* confessional

confetti [kɔ̃feti] *nm* (piece of) confetti; **confettis** confetti

confiance [kɔ̃fjɑ̃s] *nf* (**a**) *(foi)* trust, confidence; **avoir c. en qn/qch, faire c. à qn/qch** to trust sb/sth, to have confidence in sb/sth; **faites-moi c.** trust me; *Fam (croyez-moi)* believe me; **se sentir en c. (avec qn)** to feel safe (with sb); **digne de c.** trustworthy; **de c.** *(mission)* of trust; *(personne)* trustworthy (**b**) *(assurance)* confidence; **c. en soi** self-confidence; **avoir c. en soi** to be self-confident

confiant, -e [kɔ̃fjɑ̃, -ɑ̃t] *adj* (**a**) *(qui fait confiance)* trusting (**b**) *(optimiste)* confident (**dans** in) (**c**) *(qui a confiance en soi)* self-confident

confidence [kɔ̃fidɑ̃s] *nf* confidence; **faire une c./des confidences à qn** to confide in sb; **mettre qn dans la c.** to let sb into the secret

confident, -e [kɔ̃fidɑ̃, -ɑ̃t] *nm,f* confidant, *f* confidante

confidentiel, -elle [kɔ̃fidɑ̃sjɛl] *adj* confidential

confidentiellement [kɔ̃fidɑ̃sjɛlmɑ̃] *adv* confidentially

confier [66] [kɔ̃fje] **1** *vt* (**a**) *(laisser)* **c. qch à qn** to entrust sb with sth; **je leur ai confié les enfants** I left the children with them (**b**) *(dire)* **c. qch à qn** to confide sth to sb; **c. un secret à qn** to share a secret with sb
  2 se confier *vpr* **se c. à qn** to confide in sb

configuration [kɔ̃figyrasjɔ̃] *nf* (**a**) *(disposition)* configuration; *(de bâtiment)* layout; **la c. du terrain** the lie of the land (**b**) *Ordinat* configuration; **c. matérielle** hardware configuration

configurer [kɔ̃figyre] *vt Ordinat* to configure

confiné, -e [kɔ̃fine] *adj* (**a**) *(atmosphère)* enclosed; *(air)* stale (**b**) *(enfermé)* shut up

confiner [kɔ̃fine] **1** *vt (enfermer)* to confine, to shut up
  2 confiner à *vt ind* to border on
  3 se confiner *vpr* **se c. chez soi** to shut oneself up indoors

confins [kɔ̃fɛ̃] *nmpl (de région, d'État)* confines, borders; **aux c. de** on the edge of

confire [19a] [kɔ̃fir] *vt (dans du sucre)* to preserve, to candy; *(dans du vinaigre)* to pickle

confirmation [kɔ̃firmasjɔ̃] *nf* confirmation

confirmer [kɔ̃firme] **1** *vt (nouvelle, jugement)* to confirm; **c. qn dans son opinion** to confirm sb in his/her opinion

2 se confirmer *vpr (nouvelle, bruit)* to be confirmed; *(tendance)* to continue

confiserie [kɔ̃fizri] *nf* (**a**) *(magasin) Br* sweetshop, *Am* candy store (**b**) *(bonbon)* **confiseries** *Br* sweets, *Am* candy (**c**) *(secteur)* confectionery

confiseur, -euse [kɔ̃fizœr, -øz] *nm,f* confectioner

confisquer [kɔ̃fiske] *vt* to confiscate; **c. qch à qn** to confiscate sth from sb

confit, -e [kɔ̃fi, -it] **1** *adj (fruits)* crystallized, candied
2 *nm* **c. d'oie/de canard** potted goose/duck

confiture [kɔ̃fityr] *nf* jam; **c. de fraises** strawberry jam; **c. d'oranges** (orange) marmalade; *Fig* **ce serait donner de la c. aux cochons** that would be throwing pearls before swine

conflictuel, -elle [kɔ̃fliktɥɛl] *adj (témoignages, intérêts)* conflicting; **situation conflictuelle** situation of potential conflict; **ils ont des rapports conflictuels** they have a tempestuous relationship

conflit [kɔ̃fli] *nm* conflict; **c. armé** armed conflict; **conflits sociaux** industrial disputes

confluent [kɔ̃flyɑ̃] *nm* confluence; **au c. du Cher et de la Loire** where the Cher and the Loire meet

confondre [kɔ̃fɔ̃dr] **1** *vt* (**a**) *(personnes, noms, dates)* to confuse, to mix up; **je l'ai confondu avec son frère** I mistook him for his brother; **toutes catégories confondues** all categories taken together (**b**) *(sidérer)* to astound (**c**) *(démasquer)* to confound
2 se confondre *vpr* (**a**) *(couleurs, formes)* to merge, to blend (**en** into) (**b**) *(être similaire) (intérêts)* to merge (**c**) *(se répandre)* **se c. en excuses** to apologize profusely; **se c. en remerciements** to be profuse in one's thanks

conforme [kɔ̃fɔrm] *adj* (**a**) *(identique)* **copie c. à l'original** exact copy; **pour copie c.** *(sur document)* certified true copy; *Fig* **c'est la copie c. de sa mère** she's the image of her mother (**b**) *(qui correspond)* **être c. à** to be in accordance with

conformément [kɔ̃fɔrmemɑ̃] **conformément à** *prép* in accordance with

conformer [kɔ̃fɔrme] **1** *vt* to model (**à** on)
2 se conformer *vpr* **se c. à qch** to conform to sth

conformisme [kɔ̃fɔrmism] *nm* conformism

conformiste [kɔ̃fɔrmist] *adj & nmf* conformist

conformité [kɔ̃fɔrmite] *nf (d'un produit aux normes)* compliance (**à** with); **en c. avec** in accordance with

confort [kɔ̃fɔr] *nm* comfort; **maison/hôtel tout c.** house/hotel with every modern convenience; **améliorer le c. d'écoute** to improve the sound quality; **c. d'emploi** *(d'un ordinateur)* user-friendliness

confortable [kɔ̃fɔrtabl] *adj* comfortable

confortablement [kɔ̃fɔrtabləmɑ̃] *adv* comfortably; **installe-toi c.** make yourself comfortable

conforter [kɔ̃fɔrte] *vt (position, avance)* to consolidate; **c. qn dans son opinion** to confirm sb's opinion

confrère [kɔ̃frɛr] *nm (de profession)* colleague; *(de société)* fellow member

confrérie [kɔ̃freri] *nf Rel* brotherhood

confrontation [kɔ̃frɔ̃tasjɔ̃] *nf* (**a**) *(face-à-face)* confrontation; *Fig (d'opinions, d'idéaux)* clash, conflict (**b**) *(comparaison)* comparison

confronter [kɔ̃frɔ̃te] *vt* (**a**) *(personnes)* to confront; **être confronté à** to be confronted with (**b**) *(comparer)* to compare

confucianisme [kɔ̃fysjanism] *nm* Confucianism

confus, -e [kɔ̃fy, -yz] *adj* (**a**) *(indistinct) (masse, explication, idées)* confused; *(bruit)* indistinct; *(style, texte)* obscure (**b**) *(embarrassé)* embarrassed

confusément [kɔ̃fyzemɑ̃] *adv* vaguely

confusion [kɔ̃fyzjɔ̃] *nf* (**a**) *(désordre)* confusion; **jeter la c. dans les esprits** to confuse people (**b**) *(méprise)* mix-up, confusion (**c**) *(gêne)* embarrassment

congé [kɔ̃ʒe] *nm* (**a**) *(vacances) Br* holiday, *Am* vacation; **en c.** on holiday; **un jour/une semaine de c.** a day/a week off; **congés payés** paid holiday (**b**) *(arrêt de travail)* leave; **c. de maladie** sick leave; **c. de maternité** maternity leave; **c. de paternité** paternity leave; **être en c. de maladie/maternité** to be on sick/maternity leave; **c. sans solde** unpaid leave (**c**) *(avis de renvoi)* notice; **donner son c. à qn** to give sb his notice; **demander son c.** to hand in one's notice (**d**) **prendre c. de qn** to take one's leave of sb

congédier [66] [kɔ̃ʒedje] *vt* to dismiss

congélateur [kɔ̃ʒelatœr] *nm* freezer

congélation [kɔ̃ʒelasjɔ̃] *nf* freezing

congeler [39] [kɔ̃ʒle] **1** *vt (aliments)* to freeze
2 se congeler *vpr* to freeze

congénital, -e, -aux, -ales [kɔ̃ʒenital, -o] *adj* congenital

congère [kɔ̃ʒɛr] *nf* snowdrift

congestion [kɔ̃ʒɛstjɔ̃] *nf* congestion; **c. cérébrale** stroke; **c. pulmonaire** congestion of the lungs

congestionné, -e [kɔ̃ʒɛstjɔne] *adj (visage)* flushed; *(routes)* congested

conglomérat [kɔ̃ɡlɔmera] *nm* conglomerate

Congo [kɔ̃ɡo] *nm* **le C.** the Congo

congolais, -e [kɔ̃ɡɔlɛ, -ɛz] **1** *adj* Congolese
2 *nm,f* **C.** Congolese
3 *nm (pâtisserie)* coconut cake

congratuler [kɔ̃ɡratyle] **1** *vt* to congratulate
2 se congratuler *vpr* to congratulate each other

congre [kɔ̃ɡr] *nm* conger (eel)

congrégation [kɔ̃ɡreɡasjɔ̃] *nf Rel* congregation

congrès [kɔ̃ɡrɛ] *nm* conference; **le C.** *(aux États-Unis)* Congress

congru, -e [kɔ̃ɡry] *adj voir* **portion**

conifère [kɔnifɛr] *nm* conifer

conique [kɔnik] *adj* conical

conjecture [kɔ̃ʒɛktyr] *nf* conjecture

conjecturer [kɔ̃ʒɛktyre] *vi* to conjecture

conjoint, -e [kɔ̃ʒwɛ̃, -ɛ̃t] **1** *adj* joint
2 *nm* spouse; **les conjoints** the husband and wife

conjointement [kɔ̃ʒwɛ̃tmɑ̃] *adv* jointly

conjonctif, -ive [kɔ̃ʒɔ̃ktif, -iv] *adj* (**a**) *Gram* conjunctive (**b**) *Anat* connective

conjonction [kɔ̃ʒɔ̃ksjɔ̃] *nf* (**a**) *(union)* union; **la c. de nos efforts** our combined efforts (**b**) *Gram* conjunction; **c. de coordination/subordination** coordinating/subordinating conjunction

conjonctivite [kɔ̃ʒɔ̃ktivit] *nf* conjunctivitis

conjoncture [kɔ̃ʒɔ̃ktyr] *nf (situation)* circumstances, situation; **dans la c. actuelle** in the present circumstances

conjugaison [kɔ̃ʒyɡɛzɔ̃] *nf* (**a**) *(d'un verbe)* conjugation (**b**) *(union)* combination

conjugal, -e, -aux, -ales [kɔ̃ʒyɡal, -o] *adj (devoir)* conjugal; **bonheur c.** wedded bliss; **le domicile c.** the matrimonial home; **le lit c.** the marital bed; **la vie conjugale** married life

conjuguer [kɔ̃ʒyge] *vt* (**a**) *(verbe)* to conjugate (**b**) *(unir)* to combine

conjurer [kɔ̃ʒyre] **1** *vt* (**a**) *(implorer)* **c. qn de faire qch** to beg *or* implore sb to do sth; **je t'en conjure** I beg you (**b**) *(écarter) (danger, mauvais sort)* to avert, to ward off

  2 se conjurer *vpr* to conspire (together) (**contre** against)

connaissance [kɔnɛsɑ̃s] *nf* (**a**) *(fait de connaître)* knowledge; **avoir c. de qch** to be aware of sth; **prendre c. de qch** to acquaint oneself with sth; **à ma c.** to my knowledge; **en (toute) c. de cause** with full knowledge of the facts (**b**) *(contact)* **faire la c. de qn** to make sb's acquaintance; **faire c. avec qn** to get to know sb; **quelqu'un de ma c.** someone I know, an acquaintance of mine (**c**) *(personne)* acquaintance (**d**) *(savoir)* knowledge; **elle a de bonnes connaissances en astronomie** she has a good knowledge of astronomy (**e**) *(conscience)* consciousness; **sans c.** unconscious

connaisseur, -euse [kɔnɛsœr, -øz] **1** *nm,f* connoisseur, expert

  2 *adj* expert

connaître [20] [kɔnɛtr] **1** *vt* (**a**) *(personne, détails, endroit)* to know; **c. qn de nom/de vue** to know sb by name/by sight; **il n'y connaît rien** he doesn't know anything about it; **c'est ce livre qui l'a fait c.** this is the book that made her name; **tu connais la nouvelle?** have you heard the news?; **c'est mal le c.** you/they/*etc* don't know him; *Fam* **je connais la musique** *ou* **la chanson** I've heard it all before; *Fam* **si tu fais ça, je ne te connais plus** if you do that, I'll have nothing more to do with you (**b**) *(rencontrer)* to meet (**c**) *(éprouver) (famine, guerre civile)* to experience; *(amour, peur, faim)* to know; **c. des moments difficiles** to go through some difficult times; **c. un destin tragique** to have a tragic fate; **c. un succès considérable** to enjoy considerable success (**d**) *(avoir)* **ne pas c. de limites** to know no bounds

  2 se connaître *vpr* (**a**) **se c. (soi-même)** to know oneself (**b**) **s'y c. en qch** to know a lot about sth (**c**) *(mutuellement) (se rencontrer)* to meet

connard [kɔnar] = **conard**

conne [kɔn] *voir* **con**

connecter [kɔnɛkte] *vt Élec* to connect; *Ordinat* **connecté** *(sur Internet)* on line; **connecté en anneau/bus/étoile** in a ring/bus/star configuration

connerie [kɔnri] *nf très Fam* (**a**) *(acte stupide)* **faire une c./des conneries** to do a bloody stupid thing/some bloody stupid things (**b**) *(remarque stupide)* bloody stupid thing; **dire** *ou* **raconter des conneries** to talk bullshit (**c**) *(caractère stupide)* stupidity

connexion [kɔnɛksjɔ̃] *nf* connection

connivence [kɔnivɑ̃s] *nf* connivance; **agir/être de c. avec qn** to act/be in connivance with sb; **des regards de c.** conniving looks

connotation [kɔnɔtasjɔ̃] *nf* connotation

connu, -e [kɔny] **1** *adj (écrivain, chanteur)* well-known; **c'est bien c.!** everyone knows that!

  2 *pp voir* **connaître**

conquérant, -e [kɔ̃kerɑ̃, -ɑ̃t] **1** *adj (air)* triumphant

  2 *nm,f* conqueror

conquérir [7] [kɔ̃kerir] *vt (pays, territoire, sommet)* to conquer; *(marché)* to capture; **ils ont été conquis par son charme** they were won over by his charm

conquête [kɔ̃kɛt] *nf* conquest; **faire la c. de** *(pays)* to conquer; *(personne)* to make a conquest of; **se lancer à la c. de** *(pouvoir)* to make a bid for; *(sommet)* to set out to conquer

conquis, -e *voir* **conquérir**

conquistador [kɔ̃kistadɔr] *nm* conquistador

consacré, -e [kɔ̃sakre] *adj (coutume)* established; **selon l'expression consacrée** as the saying goes; **c. par l'usage** sanctioned by usage

consacrer [kɔ̃sakre] **1** *vt* (**a**) *Rel* to consecrate (**b**) *(temps, énergie)* **c. qch à** to devote sth to; **combien de temps pouvez-vous me c.?** how much time can you spare me? (**c**) *(entériner) (coutume)* to establish; *(usage)* to sanction

  2 se consacrer *vpr* **se c. à son travail/sa famille** to devote oneself to one's work/family

consanguin, -e [kɔ̃sɑ̃gɛ̃, -in] *adj* **frère c.** half-brother *(on the father's side)*; **sœur consanguine** half-sister *(on the father's side)*; **mariage c.** intermarriage

consciemment [kɔ̃sjamɑ̃] *adv* consciously

conscience [kɔ̃sjɑ̃s] *nf* (**a**) *(esprit)* consciousness; **perdre/reprendre c.** to lose/regain consciousness; **avoir/prendre c. de qch** to be/become aware *or* conscious of sth (**b**) *(morale)* conscience; **avoir bonne/mauvaise c.** to have a clear/bad conscience; **se donner bonne c.** to ease one's conscience; **avoir la c. tranquille, avoir sa c. pour soi** to have a clear conscience; **avoir qch sur la c.** to have sth on one's conscience (**c**) **c. professionnelle** professional integrity

consciencieusement [kɔ̃sjɑ̃sjøzmɑ̃] *adv* conscientiously

consciencieux, -euse [kɔ̃sjɑ̃sjø, -øz] *adj* conscientious

conscient, -e [kɔ̃sjɑ̃, -ɑ̃t] *adj* (**a**) *(décision, choix)* conscious; **être c. de qch** to be aware *or* conscious of sth (**b**) *(lucide)* conscious

consécration [kɔ̃sekrasjɔ̃] *nf* (**a**) *(d'une église, d'un évêque)* consecration; *(d'un prêtre)* ordination (**b**) *(aboutissement) (des efforts, d'une œuvre)* recognition; *(d'une carrière)* crowning moment

consécutif, -ive [kɔ̃sekytif, -iv] *adj* consecutive; **c. à** resulting from

consécutivement [kɔ̃sekytivmɑ̃] *adv* consecutively; **c. à** following

conseil [kɔ̃sɛj] *nm* (**a**) *(recommandation)* piece of advice; **des conseils** advice; **donner un c. à qn** to give sb a piece of advice; **être de bon c.** to give good advice (**b**) *(assemblée)* council, committee; *(d'une entreprise)* board; *(réunion)* meeting; **c. d'administration** board of directors; **c. de classe** = staff meeting with participation of class representatives to discuss school matters; **C. constitutionnel** = independent body which pronounces on the constitutionality of government decisions; **c. de discipline** disciplinary committee; **C. d'État** Council of State; **C. de l'Europe** Council of Europe; *Can* **C. Exécutif** ≃ Cabinet; **C. général** regional council; **c. de guerre** *(réunion)* council of war; *(tribunal)* court martial; **le c. des ministres** ≃ the Cabinet; *UE* the (European) Council of Ministers; **c. municipal** local council; *Can* **C. national des autochtones du Canada** Native Council of Canada; **C. de sécurité** *(de l'ONU)* Security Council (**c**) *(personne)* consultant (**en** in)

Conseil de classe

The French school year is divided into three terms. In secondary schools, a "conseil de classe", or staff meeting, is held at the end of each term to discuss the progress made by pupils in a given class. A report containing the marks obtained during the term with teachers' comments is filled in for each pupil. The "conseil de classe" is initially held behind closed doors, attended by the teachers of a given class and the head teacher, and then with two elected class representatives present. During the last "conseil de classe" of the year, decisions are taken such as which pupils repeat a year and which should change courses.

conseiller¹ [kɔ̃seje] vt (**a**) (guider) (personne) to advise; **il m'a bien conseillé** he gave me good or sound advice (**b**) (recommander) **c. qch à qn** to recommend sth to sb; **c. à qn de faire qch** to advise sb to do sth; **il est conseillé de ne pas fumer** it is advisable not to smoke

conseiller², -ère [kɔ̃seje, -ɛr] nm,f (**a**) (spécialiste) adviser, consultant; **c. d'orientation** careers adviser; **c. technique** technical adviser (**b**) Pol (d'un chef d'État) advisor; **c. général** regional councillor; **c. municipal** local councillor

consensuel, -elle [kɔ̃sɑ̃sɥɛl] adj consensual

consensus [kɔ̃sɛ̃sys] nm consensus (of opinion)

consentant, -e [kɔ̃sɑ̃tɑ̃, -ɑ̃t] adj consenting; **être c.** to consent

consentement [kɔ̃sɑ̃təmɑ̃] nm consent; **donner son c. à qch** to give one's consent to sth; **divorce par c. mutuel** divorce by mutual consent

consentir [64a] [kɔ̃sɑ̃tir] **1** vi to consent, to agree (**à qch/à faire qch** to sth/to do sth); **je consens (à ce) qu'il vienne** I consent to his coming
2 vt **c. un prêt à qn** to grant sb a loan; **c. une remise à qn** to allow sb a discount

conséquence [kɔ̃sekɑ̃s] nf consequence; **une erreur sans c.** an inconsequential mistake; **tirer les conséquences de qch** to draw conclusions from sth; **la baisse des taxes a eu pour c. de créer des emplois** the tax reduction resulted in the creation of jobs; **agir en c.** to take appropriate action; **en c. (de quoi)** consequently

conséquent, -e [kɔ̃sekɑ̃, -ɑ̃t] adj (**a**) (cohérent) consistent (**b**) Fam (somme) tidy (**c**) **par c.** consequently

conservateur, -trice [kɔ̃sɛrvatœr, -tris] **1** adj Pol Conservative
2 nm,f (**a**) (de musée) curator; (de bibliothèque) librarian (**b**) Pol Conservative
3 nm (alimentaire) preservative; **sans c.** (sur emballage) free of preservatives

conservation [kɔ̃sɛrvasjɔ̃] nf (de fruits, de viande) preserving; (de bâtiments) preservation; (d'archives) keeping

conservatoire [kɔ̃sɛrvatwar] nm (de musique, d'art dramatique) school, academy; **le C. (de Paris)** the (Paris) Conservatoire; **le C. des arts et métiers** = museum and college of applied sciences

conserve [kɔ̃sɛrv] nf (aliment) canned or Br tinned food; (en bocal) preserve; (boîte) can, Br tin; **en c.** canned, Br tinned; (en bocal) preserved; **mettre qch en c.** to can sth, Br to tin sth; (en bocal) to preserve sth

conserver [kɔ̃sɛrve] **1** vt (**a**) (aliment) to keep; (dans le sel, le vinaigre) to preserve; **c. à l'abri de la lumière** (sur emballage) keep away from direct sunlight; **c. au froid** (sur emballage) keep in a cold place; **être bien conservé** (personne) to be well preserved (**b**) (garder) (objet, emploi, sang-froid) to keep; (droits) to retain; **c. un bon souvenir de qch** to have good memories of sth
2 **se conserver** vpr (aliment) to keep

considérable [kɔ̃siderabl] adj considerable

considérablement [kɔ̃siderabləmɑ̃] adv considerably

considération [kɔ̃siderasjɔ̃] nf (**a**) (examen) **prendre qch en c.** to take sth into consideration; (offre, demande d'emploi) to consider sth (**b**) (estime) regard, esteem; **agir avec/sans c.** to act considerately/inconsiderately; **jouir d'une grande c.** to be highly regarded (**c**) **considérations (sur)** (observations) observations (on); **je ne peux pas entrer dans ces considérations** I can't go into that

considérer [34] [kɔ̃sidere] **1** vt (**a**) (étudier, regarder) to consider; **tout bien considéré** all things considered (**b**) (estimer) **c. que** to consider that; **c. qn/qch comme...** to regard sb/sth as...
2 **se considérer** vpr **se c. désavantagé** to consider oneself disadvantaged; **se c. comme un artiste/un révolutionnaire** to consider oneself an artist/a revolutionary

consigne [kɔ̃siɲ] nf (**a**) (ordres) orders; **avoir pour c. de...** to have orders to...; **passer la c.** to pass on the orders; **consignes en cas d'incendie** fire notice (**b**) (punition) Mil confinement to barracks; Scol detention (**c**) (pour les bagages) **c. (à bagages)** Br left-luggage office, Am checkroom; **c. automatique** lockers (**d**) (de bouteille) deposit

consigner [kɔ̃siɲe] vt (**a**) (bouteille, emballage) to charge a deposit on; **bouteille consignée** returnable bottle (**b**) (noter) to record (**c**) (punir) (soldat) to confine to barracks; (élève) to keep in (**d**) (laisser à la consigne) Br to deposit in the left-luggage office, Am to check

consistance [kɔ̃sistɑ̃s] nf (d'un corps) consistency; **sans c.** (pâte, fromage) too soft; Fig (personne) bland; (personnage de fiction) insubstantial

consistant, -e [kɔ̃sistɑ̃, -ɑ̃t] adj (substance) firm; (sauce, soupe) thick; (repas) substantial; (argument) sound

consister [kɔ̃siste] vi **c. en qch** to consist of sth; **c. à faire qch** to consist in doing sth

consœur [kɔ̃sœr] nf (female) colleague

consolation [kɔ̃sɔlasjɔ̃] nf consolation, comfort

console [kɔ̃sɔl] nf console; **c. de jeux** games console; **c. de visualisation** (visual) display unit

consoler [kɔ̃sɔle] **1** vt to console, to comfort; **si ça peut te c.** if that's any consolation to you
2 **se consoler** vpr to console oneself; (l'un l'autre) to console each other; **se c. d'une perte/d'un échec** to get over a loss/a failure; **elles se sont consolées mutuellement** they consoled each other

consolidation [kɔ̃sɔlidasjɔ̃] nf (**a**) aussi Fig (renforcement) strengthening (**b**) Méd (d'une fracture) knitting

consolider [kɔ̃sɔlide] **1** vt (**a**) aussi Fig (renforcer) to strengthen (**b**) (fracture) to knit (**c**) Fin (dette) to fund; (bilan) to consolidate
2 **se consolider** vpr (**a**) (régime) to strengthen its

position; *(amitié, liens)* to become stronger (**b**) *(fracture)* to knit

consommateur, -trice [kɔsɔmatœr, -tris] *nm,f Écon* consumer; *(dans un restaurant, un café)* customer; **je suis un grand c. de café** I'm a great coffee drinker; *Écon* **c. final** end-user

consommation [kɔsɔmasjɔ̃] *nf* (**a**) *(d'électricité, de pétrole, de nourriture)* consumption; *(d'une voiture)* (fuel) consumption; **faire une grande c. de qch** to consume great quantities of sth (**b**) *(dans un café)* drink (**c**) *(du mariage)* consummation

consommé, -e [kɔsɔme] **1** *nm Culin* consommé
2 *adj (accompli)* consummate

consommer [kɔsɔme] **1** *vt* (**a**) *(électricité, pétrole, nourriture)* to consume; **à c. avant fin novembre** *(sur emballage)* best before end November; **cette voiture consomme trop (d'essence)** this car is heavy on fuel; **c. au bar** to drink at the bar (**b**) *(mariage)* to consummate
2 se consommer *vpr* **ce plat se consomme froid** this dish is eaten cold

consonance [kɔsɔnɑ̃s] *nf Mus & Ling* consonance; **langue à c. germanique** German-sounding language

consonne [kɔsɔn] *nf* consonant

consortium [kɔsɔrsjɔm] *nm Com & Fin* consortium

conspirateur, -trice [kɔspiratœr, -tris] **1** *nm,f* conspirator
2 *adj* conspiratorial

conspiration [kɔspirasjɔ̃] *nf* conspiracy, plot

conspirer [kɔspire] *vi* (**a**) *(comploter)* to conspire, to plot (**contre** against) (**b**) *(contribuer)* to conspire (**à faire qch** to do sth)

constamment [kɔstamɑ̃] *adv* constantly

constance [kɔstɑ̃s] *nf* (**a**) *(dans une tâche)* perseverance; *(en amour)* constancy; **travailler avec c.** to work steadily (**b**) *(de la température, d'un phénomène)* constancy

constant, -e [kɔstɑ̃, -ɑ̃t] **1** *adj* (**a**) *(souci, température, va-et-vient)* constant; *(effort)* persistent; *(amitié, intérêt)* steady (**b**) *(personne)* **être c. dans ses opinions** to stick to one's opinions; **être c. dans ses amitiés** to be faithful to one's friends (**c**) *Écon* **en francs constants** in real terms
2 *nf* **constante** (**a**) *(en sciences)* constant (**b**) *(caractéristique)* stable *or* permanent trait

constat [kɔsta] *nm* (**a**) *Jur* official report; **dresser un c. d'accident** to write out an accident report; **c. amiable** = report of road accident agreed by parties involved (**b**) *(bilan)* assessment; **faire un c. d'échec** to acknowledge failure

constatation [kɔstatasjɔ̃] *nf* (**a**) *(observation)* observation; **c'est une simple c.** it's a simple statement of fact (**b**) **constatations** *(d'une enquête)* findings

constater [kɔstate] *vt* (**a**) *(observer)* to note (**que** that); **vous pouvez c. vous-même qu'elle est partie** you can see for yourself that she's gone (**b**) *Jur (enregistrer)* to record; *(décès)* to certify; *(dégâts)* to assess

constellation [kɔstelasjɔ̃] *nf* constellation

constellé, -e [kɔstele] *adj* **un ciel c. d'étoiles** a star-studded sky; **c. de taches** spattered with stains

consternant, -e [kɔsternɑ̃, -ɑ̃t] *adj (nouvelle)* dismaying; **d'une bêtise consternante** appallingly stupid

consternation [kɔsternasjɔ̃] *nf* dismay, consternation; **jeter la c. dans/parmi** to fill with dismay; **à la c. générale** to everyone's dismay

consterner [kɔsterne] *vt* to dismay

constipation [kɔstipasjɔ̃] *nf* constipation

constipé, -e [kɔstipe] *adj* constipated; *Fam (mal à l'aise)* ill at ease

constituer [kɔstitɥe] **1** *vt* (**a**) *(composer)* to make up; **être constitué de** to be made up of (**b**) *(équivaloir à)* to constitute (**c**) *(comité, gouvernement, équipe)* to form; *(bibliothèque, fortune, stocks)* to build up; **c. une rente/une dot à qn** to settle an annuity/a dowry on sb
2 se constituer *vpr* (**a**) *(devenir)* **se c. prisonnier** to give oneself up; *Jur* **se c. partie civile** to bring a civil suit for damages (**b**) *(se réunir)* **se c. en commission/en association** to form a committee/an association

constitution [kɔstitysjɔ̃] *nf* (**a**) *(physique, d'un pays)* constitution; **avoir une bonne c.** to have a sound constitution (**b**) *(de comité, de société, de gouvernement)* formation; *(de stocks, de bibliothèque)* building up

constitutionnel, -elle [kɔstitysjɔnɛl] *adj* constitutional

constructeur [kɔstryktœr] *nm (bâtisseur)* builder; **c. automobile** car manufacturer; **c. naval** shipbuilder

constructif, -ive [kɔstryktif, -iv] *adj* constructive

construction [kɔstryksjɔ̃] *nf* (**a**) *(d'une maison, d'une route, d'un voilier)* building, construction; *(d'une phrase)* structure; **en c.** under construction; **c. navale** shipbuilding (**b**) *(bâtiment)* building

construire [18] [kɔstrɥir] **1** *vt* to build, to construct; *(roman, phrase, théorie)* to construct
2 se construire *vpr Gram* **"après que" se construit avec l'indicatif** "après que" takes the indicative

consul [kɔsyl] *nm* consul; **le c. de France** the French consul; **c. général** consul general

consulaire [kɔsylɛr] *adj* consular

consulat [kɔsyla] *nm (lieu)* consulate; *(charge)* consulship

consultant, -e [kɔsyltɑ̃, -ɑ̃t] **1** *nm,f* consultant
2 *adj* consulting; **médecin c.** consultant

consultation [kɔsyltasjɔ̃] *nf* (**a**) *(d'un expert, d'un médecin)* consultation; **le médecin est en c.** the doctor is with a patient; **heures de c.** consulting *or Br* surgery hours (**b**) *(de livre)* consultation (**c**) *Pol* **c. populaire** consultation of the people

consulter [kɔsylte] **1** *vt* to consult
2 *vi (docteur)* to see patients, *Br* to take surgery
3 se consulter *vpr* to consult each other

consumer [kɔsyme] **1** *vt (brûler)* to consume; *Fig* **consumé par le remords** consumed with remorse
2 se consumer *vpr (brûler)* to burn; *Fig* **se c. d'inquiétude/de chagrin** to be consumed with worry/with grief

contact [kɔtakt] *nm* (**a**) *(relation, personne)* contact; **garder/perdre le c. avec qn** to keep in touch/lose touch with sb; **prendre c.** *ou* **se mettre en c. avec qn** to get in touch *or* in contact with sb; **être/entrer en c. avec qn** to be in/come into contact with sb; **être d'un c. facile/difficile** to be approachable/unapproachable; **il a changé à mon c.** he's changed since he met me (**b**) *(toucher)* contact; **au c. agréable** pleasant to the touch; **être/entrer en c. avec qch** to be in/come into contact with sth; **au c. de qch** on contact with sth (**c**) *Élec* contact (**d**) *Aut* contact; **mettre/couper le c.** to switch the ignition on/off

contacter [kɔtakte] *vt* to contact

contagieux, -euse [kɔ̃taʒjø, -øz] *adj (maladie, virus, personne)* contagious; *(rire, enthousiasme)* infectious

contagion [kɔ̃taʒjɔ̃] *nf Méd* contagion

container [kɔ̃tɛner] *nm* container

contamination [kɔ̃taminasjɔ̃] *nf (pollution)* contamination; *Méd* infection

contaminer [kɔ̃tamine] *vt (polluer)* to contaminate; *Méd* to infect

conte [kɔ̃t] *nm* story, tale; **c. de fées** fairy tale; *Fig* **elle vit un c. de fées** her life is a fairy tale

contemplatif, -ive [kɔ̃tɑ̃platif, -iv] *adj & nm,f* contemplative

contemplation [kɔ̃tɑ̃plasjɔ̃] *nf* contemplation; **être en c. devant qch** to gaze at sth

contempler [kɔ̃tɑ̃ple] **1** *vt* to contemplate, to gaze at
2 se contempler *vpr (soi-même)* to gaze at oneself

contemporain, -e [kɔ̃tɑ̃pɔrɛ̃, -ɛn] **1** *adj* (**a**) *(moderne)* contemporary (**b**) *(du même âge)* contemporary (**de** with); **être c. de qn** to be a contemporary of sb; **ils sont contemporains** they are contemporaries
2 *nm,f* contemporary

contenance [kɔ̃tnɑ̃s] *nf* (**a**) *(d'un récipient)* capacity (**b**) *(allure)* attitude, bearing; **faire qch pour se donner une c.** to do sth to give an impression of composure; **faire bonne c.** to put on a bold front; **perdre c.** to lose one's composure

contenant [kɔ̃tnɑ̃] *nm* container

conteneur [kɔ̃tnœr] *nm* container

contenir [70] [kɔ̃tnir] **1** *vt* (**a**) *(renfermer)* to contain; **le théâtre contient mille places** the theatre holds *or* seats a thousand (**b**) *(foule, ennemi)* to contain, to keep in check; *(colère)* to curb; *(larmes)* to hold back
2 se contenir *vpr* to contain oneself

content, -e [kɔ̃tɑ̃, -ɑ̃t] **1** *adj (satisfait)* happy, content (**de** with); *(joyeux)* glad (**de faire** to do); **je suis très c. de vous voir** I'm very pleased *or* glad to see you; **être c. de soi** to be pleased with oneself; **tu peux être c. de toi, tu as vu ce que tu as fait!** I hope you're happy, just look what you've done!; **non c. de mentir, il vole!** not content with lying, he steals as well!; **je suis vraiment c. que vous soyez venu** I'm so glad you've come; *Fam* **et si tu n'es pas c., c'est pareil** you can like it or lump it
2 *nm* **manger tout son c.** to eat one's fill; **avoir son c. de qch** to have had one's fill of sth

contentement [kɔ̃tɑ̃tmɑ̃] *nm (état)* satisfaction, contentment; **un sourire de c.** a contented smile

contenter [kɔ̃tɑ̃te] **1** *vt (personne)* to satisfy, to please
2 se contenter *vpr* **se c. de qch/de faire qch** to content oneself with sth/with doing sth; **se c. de peu** to be easily satisfied; **je me contenterai de faire remarquer que...** I will merely point out that...

contentieux [kɔ̃tɑ̃sjø] *nm (querelle)* dispute; *Jur* litigation; *(service)* legal department; **avoir un c. avec qn** to be in dispute with sb

contenu, -e [kɔ̃tny] **1** *nm (d'un paquet, d'une bouteille, d'une boîte)* contents; *(d'une lettre, d'un livre)* content
2 *adj (émotion)* restrained

conter [kɔ̃te] *vt* to tell; **elle ne s'en laisse pas c.** you can't fool her

contestataire [kɔ̃tɛstatɛr] **1** *adj Pol* anti-establishment; *(mécontent)* rebellious
2 *nmf Pol* protester; *(mécontent)* rebel

contestation [kɔ̃tɛstasjɔ̃] *nf* (**a**) *(protestation)* protest; **il y a matière ou sujet à c.** there are grounds for dispute; **sans c. possible** beyond dispute (**b**) *Pol* protest

conteste [kɔ̃tɛst] **sans conteste** *adv* indisputably

contester [kɔ̃tɛste] *vt* to dispute; **je lui conteste le droit de...** I dispute his right to...; **elle est très contestée** she is very controversial; **faire qch sans c.** to do sth without protest

conteur, -euse [kɔ̃tœr, -øz] *nm,f* storyteller

contexte [kɔ̃tɛkst] *nm* context; **dans le c. de** in the context of; **hors c.** out of context

contigu, -ë [kɔ̃tigy] *adj (maisons, pièces)* adjoining; **c. à qch** adjoining sth

continent [kɔ̃tinɑ̃] *nm* (**a**) *(étendue)* continent; **l'Ancien/le Nouveau C.** the Old/the New World (**b**) *(par rapport à une île)* mainland

continental, -e, -aux, -ales [kɔ̃tinɑ̃tal, -o] **1** *adj (climat, plateau)* continental; *(par rapport à une île)* mainland
2 *nm,f* mainlander

contingent [kɔ̃tɛ̃ʒɑ̃] *nm* (**a**) *Mil* contingent; **les soldats du c.** the conscripted soldiers (**b**) *(quota)* quota

continu, -e [kɔ̃tiny] *adj (ligne, effort)* continuous; *(soin, attention)* constant; **en c.** continuously; *Ordinat* **papier en c.** continuous paper

continuation [kɔ̃tinɥasjɔ̃] *nf* continuation; **bonne c.!** all the best!

continuel, -elle [kɔ̃tinɥɛl] *adj (ininterrompu)* continuous; *(qui se répète)* continual

continuellement [kɔ̃tinɥɛlmɑ̃] *adv (de façon ininterrompue)* continuously; *(de façon répétitive)* continually

continuer [kɔ̃tinɥe] **1** *vt (études, efforts, politique)* to continue (with), to carry on with; *(trait, route)* to continue; **c. sa route** *ou* **son chemin** to continue on one's way; **continuez!** carry on!; **si tu continues comme ça,...** if you carry on like that,...
2 *vi* to continue
3 continuer à *ou* **de** *vt ind* **c. à** *ou* **de faire qch** to continue doing sth, to carry on doing sth; **si tu continues à m'embêter, je vais me fâcher** if you carry on *or* keep on annoying me I'm going to get cross; **je continue à** *ou* **de me demander si...** I keep wondering if...
4 se continuer *vpr* to continue

continuité [kɔ̃tinɥite] *nf (d'une action)* continuity; *(d'une tradition, d'une politique)* continuation

contondant, -e [kɔ̃tɔ̃dɑ̃, -ɑ̃t] *adj* blunt

contorsion [kɔ̃tɔrsjɔ̃] *nf* contortion

contorsionner [kɔ̃tɔrsjɔne] **se contorsionner** *vpr* to contort oneself

contorsionniste [kɔ̃tɔrsjɔnist] *nmf* contortionist

contour [kɔ̃tur] *nm* (**a**) *(silhouette)* outline (**b**) *Suisse (virage)* bend

contourner [kɔ̃turne] *vt* to go round; *Fig (loi, difficulté)* to get round

contraceptif, -ive [kɔ̃trasɛptif, -iv] *Méd* **1** *adj* contraceptive
2 *nm* contraceptive; **c. oral** oral contraceptive

contraception [kɔ̃trasɛpsjɔ̃] *nf* contraception

contractant, -e [kɔ̃traktɑ̃, -ɑ̃t] *adj Jur (partie)* contracting

contracté, -e [kɔ̃trakte] *adj* (**a**) *(muscles, visage, personne)* tense (**b**) *Ling* contracted

contracter¹ [kɔ̃trakte] *vt* (**a**) *(alliance, dette)* to contract; *(assurance)* to take out (**b**) *(habitude, goût, manie)* to acquire; *(maladie)* to contract

contracter² 1 *vt (muscles, visage)* to tense; **visage contracté par la douleur** face drawn with pain
   2 **se contracter** *vpr* (**a**) *(cœur, muscle)* to contract; *(personne)* to tense (up) (**b**) *Ling* to contract

contraction [kɔ̃traksjɔ̃] *nf* (**a**) *(d'un muscle, d'un gaz, d'un mot)* contraction; **contractions** *(à l'accouchement)* contractions (**b**) *Scol* **c. de texte** précis; **faire une c. de texte** to summarize a text

contractuel, -elle [kɔ̃traktɥɛl] 1 *adj (obligations)* contractual; **agent c.** = contractor working for the local council
   2 *nm,f (auxiliaire de police) Br* ≃ traffic warden, *Am* ≃ traffic policeman, *f* traffic policewoman

contracture [kɔ̃traktyr] *nf Méd* spasm

contradiction [kɔ̃tradiksjɔ̃] *nf* (**a**) *(opposition)* contradiction; **avoir l'esprit de c.** to be contrary; **il ne supporte pas la c.** he can't stand being contradicted (**b**) *(illogisme)* contradiction; **être en c. avec qch** to contradict sth; **être en c. avec soi-même** to contradict oneself

contradictoire [kɔ̃tradiktwar] *adj* contradictory (**avec** to); **débat c.** debate

contraignant, -e [kɔ̃trɛɲɑ̃, -ɑ̃t] *adj* restricting

contraindre [23] [kɔ̃trɛ̃dr] 1 *vt (obliger)* **c. qn à faire qch** to force *or* compel sb to do sth; **être contraint de faire qch** to be forced *or* compelled to do sth; **contraint et forcé** under duress
   2 **se contraindre** *vpr* **se c. à faire qch** to force oneself to do sth

contrainte [kɔ̃trɛ̃t] *nf* (**a**) *(obligation, limitation, retenue)* constraint; **parler sans c.** to speak freely (**b**) *(force)* force; **obtenir qch par la c.** to get sth by force; **faire qch sous la c.** to do sth under duress (**c**) *Tech* stress

contraire [kɔ̃trɛr] 1 *adj* (**a**) *(opposé) (intérêts, avis)* conflicting; **vent c.** headwind; **c. à** contrary to; **en sens c.** in the opposite direction (**b**) *(défavorable)* **le sort nous/m' est c.** fate is against us/me
   2 *nm* opposite; **le c. de** the opposite of; **sa sœur est tout le c. de lui** his sister is the exact opposite of him; **(bien) au c.** on the contrary

contrairement [kɔ̃trɛrmɑ̃] **contrairement à** *prép* contrary to; **c. à moi,...** unlike me,...

contralto [kɔ̃tralto] *nm Mus* contralto

contrariant, -e [kɔ̃trarjɑ̃, -ɑ̃t] *adj* (**a**) *(personne)* contrary; **elle n'est pas contrariante** she's easy-going; *Péj* she says yes to everything (**b**) *(situation)* annoying, irritating

contrarier [66] [kɔ̃trarje] *vt* (**a**) *(ennuyer)* to annoy, to irritate (**b**) *(contrecarrer) (projets, desseins)* to thwart, to frustrate

contrariété [kɔ̃trarjete] *nf* annoyance; **éprouver une vive c.** to feel extremely annoyed

contraste [kɔ̃trast] *nm* contrast; **faire c. (avec)** to contrast (with); **par c. avec** in contrast to; **effet de c.** contrasting effect

contrasté, -e [kɔ̃traste] *adj* (**a**) *(différencié)* contrasting; **photo bien/mal contrastée** photo with the right amount of/with not enough contrast (**b**) *Ordinat* highlighted

contraster [kɔ̃traste] *vi* to contrast (**avec** with)

contrat [kɔ̃tra] *nm* (**a**) *(accord)* contract, agreement; **passer un c. (avec qn)** to enter into an agreement

(with sb); **c. d'assurance** contract of insurance; **c. collectif** collective agreement; **c. à durée déterminée/indéterminée** fixed-term/permanent contract; **c. emploi-solidarité** = short-term contract subsidized by the government; **c. de mariage** marriage contract; **c. de travail** *Br* contract of employment, *Am* labor contract (**b**) *(au bridge)* contract

contravention [kɔ̃travɑ̃sjɔ̃] *nf (envers un règlement)* contravention; *(amende)* fine; *(pour stationnement non autorisé) (amende)* parking fine; *(avis)* (parking) ticket; **être en c.** to be in breach of the law

contre [kɔ̃tr] 1 *prép* (**a**) *(se battre, jouer)* against; **se fâcher c. qn** to get angry with sb; **la campagne c. l'avortement** the anti-abortion campaign; **je suis c.!** I'm against it!; **je n'ai rien c., je ne suis pas c.** I've got nothing against it; **par c.** on the other hand
   (**b**) *(pour se protéger de)* **sirop c. la toux** cough mixture; **être assuré c. le vol** to be insured against theft
   (**c**) *(en échange de)* (in exchange) for; **échanger une chose c. une autre** to exchange one thing for another
   (**d**) *(en proportion de)* to; **parier à cinq c. un** to bet five to one; **10 voix c. 2** 10 votes to 2
   (**e**) *(en contact avec)* against; **s'appuyer c. qch** to lean against sth; **leur maison est tout c. la mienne** their house is right next to mine; **joue c. joue** cheek to cheek; **le radiateur est allumé, assieds-toi tout c.** the heater is on, sit right next to it
   (**f**) *(en dépit de)* **c. toute logique** against all logic; **c. toute attente** against all expectations
   (**g**) *(en comparaison de)* compared to; **la livre était à 9 francs c. 8 francs le mois précédent** the pound stood at 9 francs compared to 8 francs the previous month
   2 *nm* (**a**) **peser le pour et le c.** to weigh up the pros and cons
   (**b**) *(au volley, au basket)* block

contre-allée *(pl* **contre-allées)** [kɔ̃trale] *nf* side road

contre-attaque *(pl* **contre-attaques)** [kɔ̃tratak] *nf* counter-attack

contre-attaquer [kɔ̃tratake] *vi* to counter-attack

contrebalancer [16] [kɔ̃trəbalɑ̃se] 1 *vt (poids)* to counterbalance; *(inconvénient)* to offset
   2 **se contrebalancer** *vpr Fam* **se c. de qch** not to give a damn about sth

contrebande [kɔ̃trəbɑ̃d] *nf* (**a**) *(activité)* smuggling; **faire de la c.** to smuggle goods; **faire entrer des marchandises en c.** to smuggle in goods; **de c.** smuggled (**b**) *(marchandises)* contraband

contrebandier, -ère [kɔ̃trəbɑ̃dje, -ɛr] *nm,f* smuggler

contrebas [kɔ̃trəba] **en contrebas** *adv* (down) below; **en c. de** below

contrebasse [kɔ̃trəbas] *nf (instrument)* (double) bass; *(musicien)* (double) bass player

contrebassiste [kɔ̃trəbasist] *nmf* (double) bass player

contre-braquer [kɔ̃trəbrake] *vi Aut* to steer into the skid

contrecarrer [kɔ̃trəkare] *vt* to thwart

contrechamp [kɔ̃trəʃɑ̃] *nm Cin* reverse shot

contre-chant *(pl* **contre-chants)** [kɔ̃trəʃɑ̃] *nm Mus* counterpoint

contrecœur [kɔ̃trəkœr] **à contrecœur** *adv* reluctantly, unwillingly

contrecoup [kɔ̃trəku] *nm (conséquence)* repercussions

contre-courant [kɔ̃trəkurɑ̃] **à contre-courant** *adv (nager)* against the current; *(sur la route)* in the wrong direction; *Fig* **aller à c. de qch** to go against the current of sth

contredanse [kɔ̃trədɑ̃s] *nf Fam (amende)* parking fine; *(avis)* (parking) ticket; **flanquer une c. à qn** to give sb a (parking) ticket

contredire [27b] [kɔ̃trədir] **1** *vt* to contradict **2 se contredire** *vpr (soi-même)* to contradict oneself; *(l'un l'autre)* to contradict each other

contrée [kɔ̃tre] *nf Litt (région)* region; *(pays)* land

contre-emploi (*pl* **contre-emplois**) [kɔ̃trɑ̃plwa] *nm Théât & Cin* miscasting; **utiliser qn à c.** to miscast sb

contre-enquête (*pl* **contre-enquêtes**) [kɔ̃trɑ̃kɛt] *nf Jur* counter-inquiry

contre-espionnage [kɔ̃trɛspjɔnaʒ] *nm* counter-espionage

contre-exemple (*pl* **contre-exemples**) [kɔ̃trɛgzɑ̃pl] *nm* counter-example

contre-expertise (*pl* **contre-expertises**) [kɔ̃trɛkspɛrtiz] *nf* second valuation

contrefaçon [kɔ̃trəfasɔ̃] *nf* (**a**) *(pratique)* counterfeiting; *(de signature)* forging (**b**) *(produit)* fake, imitation

contrefaire [36] [kɔ̃trəfɛr] *vt* (**a**) *(voix, écriture)* to disguise (**b**) *(pièce, produit de marque)* to counterfeit; *(signature)* to forge

contrefait, -e [kɔ̃trəfɛ, -ɛt] *adj* (**a**) *(difforme)* deformed, misshapen (**b**) *(falsifié) (signature, argent)* counterfeit, forged

contreficher [kɔ̃trəfiʃe] **se contreficher** *vpr très Fam* **se c. de qch** not to give a damn about sth

contre-filet (*pl* **contre-filets**) [kɔ̃trəfilɛ] *nm Culin* sirloin

contrefort [kɔ̃trəfɔr] *nm* (**a**) *Archit* buttress (**b**) *Géog* **contreforts** foothills (**c**) *(de chaussure)* stiffener

contre-indication (*pl* **contre-indications**) [kɔ̃trɛ̃dikasjɔ̃] *nf* contraindication

contre-interrogatoire (*pl* **contre-interrogatoires**) [kɔ̃trɛ̃terɔgatwar] *nm Jur* cross-examination

contre-jour (*pl* **contre-jours**) [kɔ̃trəʒur] *nm* (**a**) *(éclairage défavorable)* light from behind; **à c.** against the light (**b**) *Art, Cin & Phot* backlighting

contre-la-montre [kɔ̃trəlamɔ̃tr] *nm inv Sport* timetrial

contremaître, -maîtresse [kɔ̃trəmɛtr, -mɛtrɛs] *nm,f* foreman, *f* forewoman

contre-manifestation (*pl* **contre-manifestations**) [kɔ̃trəmanifɛstasjɔ̃] *nf* counter-demonstration

contremarche [kɔ̃trəmarʃ] *nf (d'un escalier)* riser

contremarque [kɔ̃trəmark] *nf (au spectacle)* passout ticket

contre-mesure (*pl* **contre-mesures**) [kɔ̃trəməzyr] *nf* countermeasure

contre-offensive (*pl* **contre-offensives**) [kɔ̃trɔfɑ̃siv] *nf* counter-offensive

contrepartie [kɔ̃trəparti] *nf (compensation)* compensation; **en c. (de)** in return (for)

contre-performance (*pl* **contre-performances**) [kɔ̃trəpɛrfɔrmɑ̃s] *nf* substandard performance

contrepèterie [kɔ̃trəpɛtri] *nf* spoonerism

contre-pied [kɔ̃trəpje] *nm* (**a**) **prendre le c. de qch** *(faire le contraire)* to do the opposite of sth; *(dire le contraire)* to take the opposite view to sth (**b**) *Sport*

prendre son adversaire à c. to wrong-foot one's opponent; **prendre la balle à c.** to take the ball on the wrong foot

contreplaqué [kɔ̃trəplake] *nm* plywood

contre-plongée (*pl* **contre-plongées**) [kɔ̃trəplɔ̃ʒe] *nf Cin & TV* low-angle shot; **filmer qch en c.** to film sth from below

contrepoids [kɔ̃trəpwa] *nm aussi Fig* counterbalance; *Fig* **faire c. à qch** to counterbalance sth

contre-poil [kɔ̃trəpwal] **à contre-poil** *adv* the wrong way; *Fam* **prendre qn à c.** to rub sb up the wrong way

contrepoison [kɔ̃trəpwazɔ̃] *nm* antidote

contre-pouvoir (*pl* **contre-pouvoirs**) [kɔ̃trəpuvwar] *nm* anti-establishment force

contre-proposition (*pl* **contre-propositions**) [kɔ̃trəprɔpozisjɔ̃] *nf* counter-proposal

contrer [kɔ̃tre] *vt* (**a**) *(attaque, argument, personne)* to counter (**b**) *(au volley, au basket)* to block (**c**) *(aux cartes)* to double

contre-révolution (*pl* **contre-révolutions**) [kɔ̃trərevɔlysjɔ̃] *nf* counter-revolution

contre-révolutionnaire (*pl* **contre-révolutionnaires**) [kɔ̃trərevɔlysjɔnɛr] *adj & nmf* counter-revolutionary

contresens [kɔ̃trəsɑ̃s] *nm* (**a**) *(mauvaise compréhension)* misinterpretation; *(mauvaise traduction)* mistranslation; **faire un c.** *(mal comprendre)* to make a mistake in interpretation; *(mal traduire)* to make a mistake in translation (**b**) *Aut* **à c.** the wrong way; **prendre une rue à c.** to go the wrong way down a street

contresigner [kɔ̃trəsiɲe] *vt* to countersign

contretemps [kɔ̃trətɑ̃] *nm* (**a**) *(ennui)* hitch, mishap (**b**) *Mus* offbeat; **à c.** off the beat; *Fig* at the wrong moment

contre-ténor (*pl* **contre-ténors**) [kɔ̃trətenɔr] *nm* counter-tenor

contre-torpilleur (*pl* **contre-torpilleurs**) [kɔ̃trətɔrpijœr] *nm* destroyer

contrevenant, -e [kɔ̃trəvənɑ̃, -ɑ̃t] *nm,f* offender

contrevenir [70] [kɔ̃trəvənir] **contrevenir à** *vt ind* to contravene

contrevent [kɔ̃trəvɑ̃] *nm (volet)* (outside) shutter

contrevérité [kɔ̃trəverite] *nf* untruth, falsehood

contribuable [kɔ̃tribɥabl] *nmf* taxpayer

contribuer [kɔ̃tribɥe] **contribuer à** *vt ind* to contribute to; **c. financièrement à qch** to contribute (money) to sth; **c. à faire qch** to help (to) do sth

contribution [kɔ̃tribysjɔ̃] *nf* (**a**) *(impôt)* tax; **contributions** *(à l'État)* taxes; *(à la collectivité locale)* Br rates, *Am* local taxes; **(bureau des) contributions** tax office, *Br* Inland Revenue, *Am* Internal Revenue; **contributions directes/indirectes** direct/indirect taxation; **c. sociale généralisée** = income-based tax deducted at source (**b**) *(collaboration, aide financière)* contribution (**à** to); **mettre qn à c.** to call on sb's services

contrit, -e [kɔ̃tri, -it] *adj* contrite

contrôle [kɔ̃trol] *nm* (**a**) *(vérification)* checking; *Scol* test; *Scol & Univ* **c. des connaissances** assessment; *Univ* **c. continu** continuous assessment; **c. douanier** customs control; **c. fiscal** tax inspection; **c. d'identité** identity check; **c. de police** police check; **c. radar** *(sur la route)* radar speed check; *Aut* **c. technique** test of roadworthiness, *Br* ≃ MOT (test)

(**b**) *(surveillance) (d'opérations)* monitoring; *Fin* **c. des changes** exchange control; **sous c. judiciaire** on probation; **sous c. médical** under medical supervision;

c. des prix price control (**c**) *(maîtrise)* control; **avoir le c. de qch** to have control of sth, to be in control of sth; **perdre le c. de son véhicule** to lose control of one's vehicle; **prendre le c. d'une entreprise** to take over a company; **c. de soi** self-control; **sous c. serbe** under Serb control; **c. des naissances** birth control (**d**) *Ordinat* **touche c.** control key; **c. d'accès** access control; **faire un c. croisé de** to cross-check

contrôler [kɔ̃trole] **1** *vt* (**a**) *(vérifier)* to check (**b**) *(surveiller) (opérations)* to monitor (**c**) *(maîtriser)* to control (**d**) *Ordinat* **contrôlé par le logiciel** software-controlled; **contrôlé par menu** menu-driven, menu-controlled
2 se contrôler *vpr* to control oneself

contrôleur, -euse [kɔ̃trolœr, -øz] **1** *nm,f (dans les trains, les bus)* ticket inspector; **c. aérien** air-traffic controller; **c. des impôts** tax inspector
2 *nm Ordinat* **c. d'affichage** display *or* screen controller

contrordre [kɔ̃trɔrdr] *nm* countermand; **il y a c.** the orders have been changed; **sauf c.** unless otherwise directed

controverse [kɔ̃trɔvɛrs] *nf* controversy; **prêter à c.** to be controversial

controversé, -e [kɔ̃trɔvɛrse] *adj* controversial

contumace [kɔ̃tymas] **par contumace** *adv Jur* in absentia

contusion [kɔ̃tyzjɔ̃] *nf* bruise, *Spéc* contusion
contusionné, -e [kɔ̃tyzjɔne] *adj* bruised
convaincant, -e [kɔ̃vɛ̃kã, -ãt] *adj* convincing
convaincre [68] [kɔ̃vɛ̃kr] *vt* (**a**) *(persuader)* to convince (**de/que** of/that); **c. qn de faire qch** to persuade sb to do sth; **se laisser c.** to let oneself be persuaded (**b**) *(prouver la culpabilité de)* **être convaincu de meurtre** to be convicted *or* found guilty of murder

convaincu, -e [kɔ̃vɛ̃ky] *adj* convinced; *(pacifiste, partisan)* committed; **être c. de/que** to be convinced of/that; **d'un ton c.** with conviction

convalescence [kɔ̃valesɑ̃s] *nf* convalescence; **être en c.** to be convalescing

convalescent, -e [kɔ̃valesɑ̃, -ãt] *adj & nm,f* convalescent

convecteur [kɔ̃vɛktœr] *nm* convector (heater)

convenable [kɔ̃vnabl] *adj* (**a**) *(décent)* decent, respectable; **il n'est pas c. de faire du bruit en mangeant** it is not polite to make a noise when eating (**b**) *(acceptable) (salaire, délai)* decent (**c**) *(approprié)* appropriate, suitable

convenablement [kɔ̃vnabləmɑ̃] *adv* decently

convenance [kɔ̃vnɑ̃s] *nf* (**a**) *(fait de convenir)* **pour (des raisons de) c. personnelle** for personal reasons; **trouver qch à sa c.** to find sth to one's liking; **il le fera à sa c.** he'll do it at his own convenience (**b**) **les convenances** the proprieties; **contraire aux convenances** improper

convenir [70] [kɔ̃vnir] **1 convenir à** *vt ind (aller à, plaire à)* to suit; **il est difficile de trouver le mot qui convient** it's hard to find the right word
2 convenir de *vt ind* (**a**) *(reconnaître)* to admit; **j'ai eu tort, j'en conviens** I was wrong, I admit it; **il convient qu'il a eu tort** he admits that he was wrong (**b**) *(décider de)* to agree on; **c. de faire qch** to agree to do sth
3 *v impersonnel* (**a**) **il convient de…** *(il est souhaitable de)* it is advisable to…; *(il est de bon ton de)* it is

proper to… (**b**) *(être décidé)* **il fut convenu qu'ils le feraient venir** it was agreed that they would send for him

convention [kɔ̃vɑ̃sjɔ̃] *nf* (**a**) *(accord)* agreement; **c. collective** collective agreement (**b**) *(règle arbitraire)* convention; **les conventions (sociales)** the (social) conventions; *Péj* **amabilité/sourire de c.** superficial courtesy/smile (**c**) *Pol (assemblée)* assembly; *Hist* **la C.** the French National Convention *(1792–95)*

conventionné, -e [kɔ̃vɑ̃sjone] *adj (médecin, clinique)* attached to the health system, *Br* ≃ NHS; **médecin non c.** private doctor

conventionnel, -elle [kɔ̃vɑ̃sjonɛl] *adj* (**a**) *(style, personne, armes)* conventional (**b**) *Jur (clause)* contractual

convenu, -e [kɔ̃vny] *adj* (**a**) *(décidé)* agreed; **comme c.** as agreed (**b**) *Péj (peu original)* conventional

convergence [kɔ̃vɛrʒɑ̃s] *nf* convergence
convergent, -e [kɔ̃vɛrʒɑ̃, -ãt] *adj* convergent
converger [45] [kɔ̃vɛrʒe] *vi (routes, lignes)* to converge (**vers** on); **c. vers** *(efforts)* to be focused on; **leurs opinions convergent** they are of like mind

conversation [kɔ̃vɛrsasjɔ̃] *nf* (**a**) *(discussion)* conversation; **être en grande c. (avec qn)** to be deep in conversation (with sb); **engager la c.** to start a conversation; **faire la c. (à qn)** to make conversation (with sb); **n'avoir aucune c.** to be a poor conversationalist; **c. téléphonique** telephone conversation (**b**) *(pourparlers)* **conversations diplomatiques** diplomatic talks *or* negotiations

conversationnel, -elle [kɔ̃vɛrsasjonɛl] *adj Ordinat* **mode c.** conversational *or* interactive mode

converser [kɔ̃vɛrse] *vi Formel* to converse (**avec** with)

conversion [kɔ̃vɛrsjɔ̃] *nf* (**a**) *(changement)* conversion (**en** into); *Ordinat* **c. de fichier** file conversion (**b**) *(à une doctrine)* conversion (**à** to)

converti, -e [kɔ̃vɛrti] **1** *nm,f Rel* convert; *Fig* **prêcher un c.** to preach to the converted
2 *adj* converted

convertibilité [kɔ̃vɛrtibilite] *nf Fin* convertibility
convertible [kɔ̃vɛrtibl] **1** *adj* convertible (**en** into)
2 *nm (canapé)* sofa bed

convertir [kɔ̃vɛrtir] **1** *vt* (**a**) *(changer)* to convert (**en** into) (**b**) *(à une doctrine)* to convert (**à** to)
2 se convertir *vpr* (**a**) *(à une doctrine)* to be converted (**à** to) (**b**) **se c. en** *(se changer en)* to be converted into

convertisseur [kɔ̃vɛrtisœr] *nm Tech* converter; *Ordinat* **c. analogique numérique** digitizer

convexe [kɔ̃vɛks] *adj* convex

conviction [kɔ̃viksjɔ̃] *nf* (**a**) *(certitude)* conviction; **avoir la c. que…** to be convinced that… (**b**) **convictions** *(opinions)* convictions

convier [66] [kɔ̃vje] *vt Formel (inviter)* to invite (**à** to); **c. qn à faire qch** to invite sb to do sth

convive [kɔ̃viv] *nmf* guest

convivial, -e, -aux, -ales [kɔ̃vivjal, -o] *adj* convivial; *Ordinat* user-friendly

convivialité [kɔ̃vivjalite] *nf* conviviality; *Ordinat* user-friendliness

convocation [kɔ̃vɔkasjɔ̃] *nf* (**a**) *(lettre)* notice to attend; *Jur* summons; **c. à un examen** notification of an examination (**b**) *(d'une assemblée)* convening

convoi [kɔ̃vwa] *nm* (**a**) *(de véhicules, de troupes, de prisonniers)* convoy; **c. exceptionnel** *(sur un camion) (dangereux)* dangerous load; *(large)* wide load (**b**) *(train)* train; **c. de marchandises** goods *or* freight train; **c. postal** mail train (**c**) *(cortège)* **c. funèbre** funeral procession

convoiter [kɔ̃vwate] *vt (poste, richesse)* to covet; *(femme)* to lust after

convoitise [kɔ̃vwatiz] *nf* covetousness; **regarder qch avec c.** to look covetously at sth; **exciter les convoitises** to excite envy

convoler [kɔ̃vɔle] *vi Hum* **c. (en justes noces)** to marry

convoquer [kɔ̃vɔke] *vt* (**a**) *(assemblée)* to convene; **c. les actionnaires** to call the shareholders to a meeting (**b**) *(témoin)* to summon; *(employé)* to call in; **c. qn à un examen** to notify sb of an examination

convoyer [32] [kɔ̃vwaje] *vt (troupes)* to convoy; *(fonds)* to transport under armed guard

convoyeur [kɔ̃vwajœr] *nm* (**a**) *(personne)* **c. de fonds** security guard (**b**) *Ind* conveyer

convulser [kɔ̃vylse] **1** *vt* to convulse
  2 se convulser *vpr* to be convulsed

convulsif, -ive [kɔ̃vylsif, -iv] *adj* convulsive

convulsion [kɔ̃vylsjɔ̃] *nf* convulsion; **être pris de convulsions** to go into convulsions

convulsivement [kɔ̃vylsivmɑ̃] *adv* convulsively

cookie [kuki] *nm* (**a**) *(biscuit)* *Br* biscuit, *Am* cookie (**b**) *Ordinat* cookie

cool [kul] *adj inv Fam* cool

coopérant, -e [kɔɔperɑ̃, -ɑ̃t] **1** *nm,f (à l'étranger)* aid worker
  2 *nm (pendant le service militaire)* = man doing voluntary work overseas instead of military service

coopératif, -ive [kɔɔperatif, -iv] **1** *adj (société, personne)* co-operative
  2 *nf* **coopérative** *(association, magasin)* co-operative, co-op; **coopérative d'achat** wholesale co-operative

coopération [kɔɔperasjɔ̃] *nf* (**a**) *(appui)* co-operation; **en c. avec qn** in co-operation with sb (**b**) *Pol* overseas development; *Anciennement (comme alternative au service militaire)* = voluntary work overseas instead of military service

coopérer [34] [kɔɔpere] *vi* to co-operate (**à** in)

cooptation [kɔɔptasjɔ̃] *nf* co-option; **par c.** by co-option

coordinateur, -trice [kɔɔrdinatœr, -tris] = **coordonnateur**

coordination [kɔɔrdinasjɔ̃] *nf (d'un projet, des mouvements)* co-ordination

coordonnateur, -trice [kɔɔrdɔnatœr, -tris] *nm,f* co-ordinator

coordonné, -e [kɔɔrdɔne] **1** *adj (mouvement, efforts)* co-ordinated; *(draps, vêtements)* matching
  2 *nmpl* **coordonnés** *(vêtements)* co-ordinates
  3 *nfpl* **coordonnées** (**a**) *Math, Géog & Astron* co-ordinates (**b**) *(d'une personne)* address and phone number

coordonner [kɔɔrdɔne] *vt* to co-ordinate (**à** *ou* **avec** with)

copain, copine [kɔpɛ̃, kɔpin] *Fam* **1** *nm,f* (**a**) *(camarade)* pal, mate; **salut les copains!** *(en arrivant)* hi guys!; *(en partant)* see you guys!; **c. de classe** classmate (**b**) *(fiancé)* **(petit) c.** boyfriend; **(petite) copine** girlfriend
  2 *adj* **ils sont très copains** they're great pals; **être copains comme cochons** to be thick as thieves; **ils sont très c.-c.** they're very pally

copeau, -x [kɔpo] *nm (de bois, de chocolat)* shaving; *(de métal)* cutting

Copenhague [kɔpɛnag] *n* Copenhagen

copie [kɔpi] *nf* (**a**) *(double, manuscrit)* copy (**b**) *Scol (d'examen)* paper; **rendre c. blanche** to hand in a blank paper; *Fig* **revoir sa c.** to go back to the drawing board; **c. simple/double** single/double sheet of paper (**c**) *(d'une œuvre d'art)* copy, reproduction; *(d'un roman, d'un style)* imitation (**d**) *TV & Cin* copy (**e**) *Ordinat* **c. sur papier** hard copy, printout; **c. de sauvegarde** *ou* **de secours** backup (copy), security copy

copier [66] [kɔpje] *vt* (**a**) *(texte, musique, document informatique)* to copy; **c. qch au propre** *ou* **au net** to make a fair copy of sth, to copy sth out neatly (**b**) *(œuvre d'art)* to copy, to reproduce; *(personne, style)* to imitate (**c**) *(à un devoir sur table)* to copy (**sur** from)

copier-coller [kɔpjekɔle] *nm inv Ordinat* copy-and-paste

copieur, -euse [kɔpjœr, -øz] **1** *nm,f (élève)* copier
  2 *nm (photocopieuse)* (photo)copier

copieusement [kɔpjøzmɑ̃] *adv (manger, boire)* copiously; **il s'est servi c.** he took a generous helping; **un repas c. arrosé** a meal washed down with a lot of wine; **je me suis fait c. insulter** I got well and truly insulted

copieux, -euse [kɔpjø, -øz] *adj (repas)* copious; *(portion, part, pourboire)* generous

copilote [kɔpilɔt] *nmf (d'avion)* co-pilot; *(de rallye automobile)* navigator

copinage [kɔpinaʒ] *nm Fam* **obtenir un poste par c.** to get a job through one's connections

copiste [kɔpist] *nmf (scribe)* copyist

coprésentateur, -trice [kɔprezɑ̃tatœr, -tris] *nm,f* co-presenter

coprésidence [kɔprezidɑ̃s] *nf* co-chairmanship

coprésident, -e [kɔprezidɑ̃, -ɑ̃t] *nm,f* co-chairman, *f* co-chairwoman

coprocesseur [kɔprɔsesœr] *nm Ordinat* co-processor; **c. arithmétique** maths co-processor

coproduction [kɔprɔdyksjɔ̃] *nf* coproduction

coproduire [18] [kɔprɔdɥir] *vt* to coproduce

copropriétaire [kɔprɔprijetɛr] *nmf* co-owner, joint owner

copropriété [kɔprɔprijete] *nf* co-ownership, joint ownership; **acheter/posséder une maison en c.** to buy/own a house jointly

copte [kɔpt] **1** *adj* Coptic
  2 *nmf* **C.** Copt

copulation [kɔpylasjɔ̃] *nf* copulation

copuler [kɔpyle] *vi* to copulate

copyright [kɔpirajt] *nm* copyright

coq¹ [kɔk] *nm* (**a**) *(oiseau)* cock, *Am* rooster; **jeune c.** cockerel; *Fig* young upstart; **le c. gaulois** the French cockerel; *Fig* **le c. du village** the local Casanova; *Fig* **passer** *ou* **sauter du c. à l'âne** to jump from one subject to another; **être comme un c. en pâte** to be in clover; **c. de bruyère** capercaillie; **c. de combat** fighting cock; *Culin* **c. au vin** coq au vin *(chicken cooked in red wine)* (**b**) *(girouette)* weathercock

coq² *nm Naut* (ship's) cook

coq-à-l'âne [kɔkalan] *nm inv* **faire un c.** to jump from one subject to another

coquard, coquart [kɔkar] *nm Fam* shiner

coque [kɔk] *nf* (**a**) *(d'une noix, d'un fruit)* shell; *Fig* **c. de noix** flimsy craft (**b**) *(d'un navire)* hull; *(d'un avion)* fuselage; *(d'une voiture)* body (**c**) *(mollusque)* cockle

coquelet [kɔklɛ] *nm* cockerel

coquelicot [kɔkliko] *nm* (red) poppy

coqueluche [kɔklyʃ] *nf (maladie)* whooping cough; **avoir la c.** to have whooping cough; **il est devenu la c. de ces dames** he's become a heart-throb

coquet, -ette [kɔkɛ, -ɛt] **1** *adj (ville, intérieur)* charming; **elle est coquette** she's very clothes-conscious; *Fam* **une coquette somme** a tidy sum
2 *nf* **coquette** *Vieilli* coquette

coquetier [kɔktje] *nm* egg-cup; *Fam* **gagner** *ou* **décrocher le c.** to hit the jackpot

coquetterie [kɔketri] *nf* (**a**) *(vestimentaire)* consciousness of one's appearance; *Vieilli (désir de plaire)* coquetry; **avec c.** *(s'habiller)* stylishly (**b**) *Fam* **avoir une c. dans l'œil** to have a cast in one's eye

coquillage [kɔkijaʒ] *nm* (**a**) *(mollusque)* shellfish; **manger des coquillages** to eat shellfish (**b**) *(coque vide)* shell

coquille [kɔkij] *nf* (**a**) *(de mollusque, d'œuf, de noix)* shell; *Fig* **rentrer dans/sortir de sa c.** to withdraw into/to come out of one's shell; *Fig* **c. de noix** flimsy craft; **c. d'œuf** *(couleur)* eggshell; **c. Saint-Jacques** *Culin* scallop; *(coquillage)* scallop shell (**b**) *Typ* misprint

coquillettes [kɔkijɛt] *nfpl* pasta shells

coquin, -e [kɔkɛ̃, -in] **1** *adj (sourire, air)* mischievous; *(sous-vêtement)* naughty; *(histoire)* risqué
2 *nm,f (garnement)* rascal; **petit c.!** little rascal *or* scamp!

cor [kɔr] *nm* (**a**) *(instrument)* horn; **c. de chasse** hunting horn; **sonner du c.** to sound *or* blow the horn; *Fig* **réclamer qch à c. et à cri** to clamour for sth (**b**) *(durillon)* corn

corail, -aux [kɔraj, -o] **1** *nm* coral
2 *adj inv* **(rouge) c.** coral(-red)

Coran [kɔrɑ̃] *nm* **le C.** the Koran

coranique [kɔranik] *adj* Koranic

corbeau, -x [kɔrbo] *nm* (**a**) *(oiseau)* crow (**b**) *(auteur de lettres anonymes)* poison-pen letter writer

corbeille [kɔrbɛj] *nf* (**a**) *(panier)* basket; **c. à linge** laundry basket; **c. de mariage** wedding presents; **c. à ouvrage** workbasket; **c. à pain** breadbasket; **c. à papier** wastepaper basket (**b**) *(à la Bourse de Paris)* trading floor (**c**) *Théât* dress circle (**d**) *Ordinat* wastebasket, *Am* trash

corbillard [kɔrbijar] *nm* hearse

cordage [kɔrdaʒ] *nm (corde)* rope; *(d'une raquette)* stringing; *Naut* **cordages** rigging

corde [kɔrd] *nf* (**a**) *(lien)* rope; **échelle de c.** rope ladder; **c. à linge** clothes *or* washing line; **c. lisse** climbing rope; **c. à nœuds** knotted climbing rope; **c. raide** tightrope; *Fig* **être sur la c. raide** to be walking a tightrope; **c. à sauter** *Br* skipping rope, *Am* jump-rope; **il ne vaut pas la c. pour le pendre** hanging's too good for him
(**b**) *(d'instrument, de raquette)* string; **les cordes** *(d'un orchestre)* the strings; *Fig* **avoir plus d'une c. à son arc** to have more than one string to one's bow; *Fig* **j'ai dû toucher la c. sensible** I must have touched a raw nerve
(**c**) *Sport* **tenir la c.** *(coureur)* to be on the inside; *(cheval)* to hug the rails; **les cordes** *(d'un ring)* the ropes

(**d**) *Anat* **cordes vocales** vocal cords; *Fig* **ce n'est pas dans mes cordes** it's not in my line

cordeau, -x [kɔrdo] *nm (corde)* string; *Fig* **tiré au c.** as straight as a die

cordée [kɔrde] *nf (d'alpinistes)* roped party; **premier de c.** leader

cordelette [kɔrdəlɛt] *nf* cord

cordelière [kɔrdəljɛr] *nf (ceinture)* cord

cordial, -e, -aux, -ales [kɔrdjal, -o] **1** *adj (accueil, personne)* cordial
2 *nm (médicament)* tonic

cordialement [kɔrdjalmɑ̃] *adv* cordially; **détester c. qn** to heartily dislike sb; **bien c.** *(dans une lettre)* best wishes

cordier [kɔrdje] *nm (de violon)* tailpiece

cordillère [kɔrdijɛr] *nf* mountain range; **la c. des Andes** the Andes

cordon [kɔrdɔ̃] *nm* (**a**) *(lien)* cord, string; *Fig* **tenir les cordons de la bourse** to hold the purse-strings; *Anat* **c. ombilical** umbilical cord; *aussi Fig* **couper le c. (ombilical)** to cut the umbilical cord (**b**) *(de policiers, de soldats)* cordon

cordon-bleu *(pl* **cordons-bleus**) [kɔrdɔ̃blø] *nm Fam* cordon bleu (cook)

cordonnerie [kɔrdɔnri] *nf* (**a**) *(métier)* shoe-repairing (**b**) *(boutique)* shoe repairer's (shop)

cordonnier, -ère [kɔrdɔnje, -ɛr] *nm,f* shoe repairer; *Prov* **les cordonniers sont toujours les plus mal chaussés** the shoemaker's wife is always the worst shod

Corée [kɔre] *nf* **la C. du Nord/du Sud** North/South Korea

coréen, -enne [kɔreɛ̃, -ɛn] **1** *adj* Korean
2 *nm,f* **C.** Korean

Corfou [kɔrfu] *n* Corfu

coriace [kɔrjas] *adj* (**a**) *(viande)* tough (**b**) *(personne, adversaire)* tough

coriandre [kɔrjɑ̃dr] *nf* coriander

Corinthe [kɔrɛ̃t] *n voir* **raisin**

cormoran [kɔrmɔrɑ̃] *nm* cormorant

corne [kɔrn] *nf* (**a**) *(d'animal)* horn; **c. d'abondance** horn of plenty, cornucopia; **c. de brume** foghorn; **la C. de l'Afrique** the Horn of Africa; *Fam Fig* **avoir** *ou* **porter des cornes** to be a cuckold; *Fam Fig* **faire porter des cornes à qn** to cuckold sb (**b**) *(matériau)* horn; **peigne de c.** horn comb (**c**) *(d'un croissant)* end; **faire une c. à une page** to turn down the corner of a page (**d**) *(aux pieds, aux mains)* hard skin

corned-beef [kɔrnbif] *nm* corned beef

cornée [kɔrne] *nf* cornea

cornéen, -enne [kɔrneɛ̃, -ɛn] *adj* corneal

corneille [kɔrnɛj] *nf* crow

cornemuse [kɔrnəmyz] *nf* bagpipes

corner¹ [kɔrne] *vt* (**a**) *(page)* to turn down the corner of; *(abîmer)* to make dog-eared (**b**) *Fam* **c. qch aux oreilles de qn** to shout sth into sb's ear

corner² [kɔrnɛr] *nm (au football)* corner; **tirer un c.** to take a corner

cornet [kɔrnɛ] *nm* (**a**) *(de papier)* cone; *(de marrons, de frites)* cornet; **mettre les mains en c.** to cup one's hands together; **c. (à pistons)** cornet; **c. de glace** ice cream cone *or Br* cornet (**b**) *Suisse (sac en papier)* paper bag; *(sac en plastique)* plastic bag

cornette [kɔrnɛt] *nf (coiffe)* cornet

cornettiste [kɔrnetist] *nmf* cornetist

corn flakes [kɔrnflɛks] nmpl cornflakes

corniaud [kɔrnjo] nm (**a**) (chien) mongrel (**b**) Fam (personne) twit

corniche [kɔrniʃ] nf (**a**) (de bâtiment) cornice (**b**) (de rochers) ledge; (de glace, de neige) cornice; (**route de**) **c.** coast road

cornichon [kɔrniʃɔ̃] nm gherkin

Cornouailles [kɔrnwaj] nf **la C.** Cornwall

cornu, -e [kɔrny] adj (animal, diable) horned

corollaire [kɔrɔlɛr] nm (suite) consequence

corolle [kɔrɔl] nf corolla

coron [kɔrɔ̃] nm mining village

coronaire [kɔrɔnɛr] adj coronary

coronarien, -enne [kɔrɔnarjɛ̃, -ɛn] adj coronary

corporation [kɔrpɔrasjɔ̃] nf corporate body

corporatiste [kɔrpɔratist] adj corporatist

corporel, -elle [kɔrpɔrɛl] adj (punition) corporal; (besoins) bodily; (hygiène) personal

corps [kɔr] nm (**a**) (organisme) body; **trembler de tout son c.** to tremble all over; **lutter c. à c.** to fight hand to hand; Fig **faire qch à son c. défendant** to do sth reluctantly; Fig **se jeter à c. perdu dans qch** to throw oneself into sth; Fig **se donner c. et âme à qn/qch** to give oneself body and soul to sb/sth

(**b**) (cadavre) body, corpse

(**c**) Chim & Phys body; Astron **c. céleste** heavenly body; **c. composé** compound; **c. gras** fat; **c. simple** element

(**d**) (consistance) **avoir du c.** (vin) to have body; Fig **prendre c.** (projet, idée) to take shape

(**e**) (partie principale) main part; (d'un texte) body; Naut **perdu c. et biens** lost with all hands; Jur **le c. du délit** the corpus delicti

(**f**) (groupe) **c. d'armée** army corps; **c. de ballet** corps de ballet; **c. diplomatique** diplomatic corps; **c. électoral** electorate; **plaisanterie de c. de garde** barrackroom joke; **le c. médical/enseignant** the medical/teaching profession; **c. de métier** trade; Hist corporation; **les grands c. de l'État** = the highest sections of the French administration (Conseil d'État, Cour des comptes etc)

corpulence [kɔrpylɑ̃s] nf stoutness, corpulence

corpulent, -e [kɔrpylɑ̃, -ɑ̃t] adj stout, corpulent

corpus [kɔrpys] nm Jur & Ling corpus

corpuscule [kɔrpyskyl] nm corpuscle

correct, -e [kɔrɛkt] adj (**a**) (sans fautes) correct (**b**) (courtois) (personne) correct; **cela n'est pas c. de sa part** that's not right of him; **elle a été correcte avec moi** she behaved properly towards me (**c**) Fam (acceptable) (repas, travail, salaire) reasonable

correctement [kɔrɛktəmɑ̃] adv (**a**) (sans faire d'erreur, décemment) correctly (**b**) Fam (de façon acceptable) reasonably; **gagner c. sa vie** to make a reasonable living

correcteur, -trice [kɔrɛktœr, -tris] **1** nm,f (de copies d'examen) examiner; (en typographie) proofreader; (dans la presse) copy reader

2 nm Ordinat checker; **c. liquide** correcting fluid; Ordinat **c. d'orthographe** ou **orthographique** spellchecker

3 adj (verres) correcting

correction [kɔrɛksjɔ̃] nf (**a**) (d'une faute) correction; Scol (d'un exercice) correcting, marking; Typ (d'épreuves) proofreading (**b**) (punition) beating (**c**) (décence, courtoisie) correctness

correctionnel, -elle [kɔrɛksjɔnɛl] Jur **1** adj **peine correctionnelle** = penalty of more than five days' (but less than five years') imprisonment; **tribunal c.** criminal court

2 nf **correctionnelle** criminal court; **passer en correctionnelle** to go before the criminal court

corrélation [kɔrelasjɔ̃] nf correlation; **être en c. étroite** to be closely connected or related

correspondance [kɔrɛspɔ̃dɑ̃s] nf (**a**) (lettres, échange de lettres) correspondence (**b**) (entre trains, avions) connection; **assurer la c. avec...** (train, bateau) to connect with... (**c**) (entre deux choses) correspondence; (d'idées, de principes) conformity

correspondant, -e [kɔrɛspɔ̃dɑ̃, -ɑ̃t] **1** adj corresponding (**à** to)

2 nm,f (**a**) (journaliste) correspondent; **c. de guerre** war correspondent; **c. permanent à Londres** London correspondent (**b**) (au téléphone) caller; (par lettre) penfriend; **le numéro de votre c. a changé** (au téléphone) the number you have dialled has been changed

correspondre [kɔrɛspɔ̃dr] vi (**a**) (être conforme, équivaloir) **c. à qch** to correspond to sth; **les vis et les écrous qui correspondent** the screws and the nuts that go with them (**b**) (par lettres) **c. avec qn** to correspond with sb

corrida [kɔrida] nf bullfight; Fam (problèmes) hassle

corridor [kɔridɔr] nm corridor

corrigé, -e [kɔriʒe] **1** adj corrected; **en données corrigées des variations saisonnières** seasonally adjusted

2 nm Scol (d'un exercice) correct answers (**de** to); (à la fin d'un ouvrage) key (**de** to)

corriger [45] [kɔriʒe] **1** vt (**a**) (erreur, faute d'orthographe, myopie, défauts) to correct; (exercice, examen) to correct, to mark; (épreuves typographiques) to read; (article de journal) to sub-edit; **c. qn de qch** to cure sb of sth (**b**) (pour punir) **c. qn** to give sb a beating

2 se corriger vpr (personne) to mend one's ways; **se c. de qch** to cure oneself of sth

corroborer [kɔrɔbɔre] vt to corroborate

corroder [kɔrɔde] vt to corrode

corrompre [kɔrɔ̃pr] vt (**a**) (personne, goût) to corrupt (**b**) (soudoyer) to bribe

corrompu, -e [kɔrɔ̃py] adj corrupt

corrosif, -ive [kɔrozif, -iv] adj corrosive; Fig (propos, humour) caustic

corrosion [kɔrozjɔ̃] nf (d'un métal) corrosion

corruption [kɔrypsjɔ̃] nf (perversion) corruption; (fait de soudoyer) bribery

corsage [kɔrsaʒ] nm blouse

corsaire [kɔrsɛr] **1** nm (**a**) Hist (navire, homme) corsair (**b**) (pantalon) breeches

2 adj **pantalon c.** breeches

Corse [kɔrs] nf **la C.** Corsica

La Corse

Since the 1970s, the Corsican independence movement has become more radical, with the FLNC (the Corsican Liberation Movement) engaged in a bloody conflict against the French government. In 1982, as part of the law on decentralization, Corsica was attributed a "statut spécial" (special statute) allowing for the election of its own assembly, and became a "collectivité locale" in 1991. In 2001 a devolution bill was passed granting Corsica partial control of its own affairs and making the teaching of the Corsican language mandatory in schools.

corse [kɔrs] **1** *adj* Corsican
  2 *nmf* **C.** Corsican
  3 *nm (langue)* Corsican

corsé, -e [kɔrse] *adj (vin)* full-bodied; *(sauce, plat)* spicy; *(café)* full-flavoured; *Fig (histoire)* spicy

corser [kɔrse] **1** *vt (plat)* to spice up; *Fig (récit)* to liven up
  2 se corser *vpr (intrigue)* to thicken; **ça se corse** things are getting complicated

corset [kɔrsɛ] *nm* corset; **c. orthopédique** surgical corset

cortège [kɔrtɛʒ] *nm* procession; *Fig* **la vie de famille et son c. de problèmes** family life and its attendant problems; **c. funèbre** funeral cortège

cortex [kɔrtɛks] *nm Anat & Bot* cortex

corticoïde [kɔrtikɔid] *nm* corticoid

cortisone [kɔrtizɔn] *nf* cortisone

corvée [kɔrve] *nf (a) (obligation pénible)* chore; **je suis de c. de vaisselle ce soir** I'm on washing-up duty tonight; **quelle c.!** what a drag! **(b)** *Mil* fatigue duty; **être de c.** to be on fatigue duty **(c)** *Hist* corvée

corvette [kɔrvɛt] *nf* corvette

coryza [kɔriza] *nm* head cold, *Spéc* coryza

cosaque [kɔzak] *nm* cossack

cosignataire [kosiɲater] *adj & nmf* cosignatory

cosinus [kɔsinys] *nm* cosine

cosmétique [kɔsmetik] *adj & nm* cosmetic

cosmique [kɔsmik] *adj* cosmic

cosmologie [kɔsmɔlɔʒi] *nf* cosmology

cosmonaute [kɔsmɔnot] *nmf* cosmonaut

cosmopolite [kɔsmɔpɔlit] *adj* cosmopolitan

cosmos [kɔsmos] *nm (univers)* cosmos; *(espace)* outer space

cosse [kɔs] *nf (de petits pois)* pod

cossu, -e [kɔsy] *adj (maison, intérieur)* opulent; *(personne)* well-to-do

costard [kɔstar] *nm Fam* suit; **tailler un c. à qn** *Br* to slag sb off, *Am* to bad-mouth sb

Costa Rica [kɔstarika] *nm* **le C.** Costa Rica

costaud, -e [kɔsto, -od] *Fam* **1** *adj (a) (fort, solide) (personne)* sturdy **(b)** *(problème)* tough **(c)** *(alcool, café)* strong
  2 *nm,f* sturdy man, *f* woman

costume [kɔstym] *nm (habit)* costume; *(complet)* suit

costumé, -e [kɔstyme] *adj voir* **bal**

costumier, -ère [kɔstymje, -ɛr] *nm,f (de théâtre)* wardrobe master, *f* wardrobe mistress; *(de cinéma)* costume supervisor

cotation [kɔtasjɔ̃] *nf* **c. (en Bourse)** quotation (on the Stock Exchange)

cote [kɔt] *nf (a) (d'une action) (valeur)* quotation; *(liste)* share index; *(d'un cheval)* odds; **hors c.** *(actions)* unlisted; *(marché)* *Br* unofficial, *Am* over-the-counter; **c. de popularité** popularity rating; *Fam* **avoir la c. (avec** *ou* **auprès de)** to be popular (with) **(b)** *(servant à classer)* classification mark **(c)** *(altitude)* altitude; **atteindre la c. d'alerte** *(fleuve)* to reach danger level; *Fig* to reach crisis point

coté, -e [kɔte] *adj (a) (estimé)* **bien/très/mal c.** highly/very highly/not highly thought of **(b)** **action cotée en Bourse** share quoted on the Stock Exchange; **être c. à 100 euros** to be trading at 100 euros; **être c. à l'argus** to be listed in the car buyer's guide

côte [kot] *nf (a) (os)* rib; **c. à c.** side by side; *Fam* **on lui voit les côtes** he's nothing but skin and bone; **c.**

d'agneau/de porc lamb/pork chop; **c. de bœuf** rib of beef **(b)** *(de melon, de feuille)* rib; **tissu à côtes** ribbed material **(c)** *(d'une montagne)* slope; **monter/ descendre une c.** to go up/down a hill **(d)** *(rivage)* coast; **la C. (d'Azur)** the (French) Riviera

côté [kote] *nm (a) (du corps humain)* side; **couché sur le c.** lying on one's side; *Fig* **être aux côtés de qn** to be at sb's side
  (b) *(d'une route, d'un triangle, d'une feuille)* side; **de l'autre c. (de qch)** on the other side (of sth); **siège c. couloir/fenêtre** aisle/window seat; *Théât* **c. jardin/ cour** on stage left/right
  (c) *(aspect)* side; **il a de bons côtés** he's got a good side to him; **prendre la vie du bon c.** to look on the bright side of life
  (d) *(endroit)* **de tous côtés** *(cerné)* on all sides; *(affluer)* from all directions; **du c. de** *(près de)* near; **ils s'en allèrent chacun de son c.** they went their separate ways; **de quel c.?** *(direction)* which way?; *(position)* which side?; *Fig* **être du c. de qn** to be on sb's side; **ma tante du c. maternel** my aunt on my mother's side; **d'un c...., d'un autre c....** on the one hand..., on the other hand...
  (e) *(en ce qui concerne)* *Fam* **c. argent, ça va** things are OK moneywise; **de ce c., il n'y a rien à craindre** there's nothing to worry about on that score
  (f) **à c.** *(près)* nearby; **à c. de** *(près de)* next to; *(comparé à)* compared with; **les voisins d'à c.** the next-door neighbours; **à c. l'un de l'autre** side by side; *Fig* **passer à c. de qch** to miss out on sth
  (g) **faire un saut de c.** to leap to one side *or* aside; *Fig* **mettre qch de c.** to put sth aside; *Fig* **laisser qn/ qch de c.** to leave sb/sth out

coteau, -x [kɔto] *nm (versant)* hillside; *(colline)* hill

Côte d'Ivoire [kotdivwar] *nf* **la C.** the Ivory Coast

côtelé, -e [kotle] *adj voir* **velours**

côtelette [kotlɛt, kɔtlɛt] *nf* chop; **c. d'agneau/de porc** lamb/pork chop

coter [kɔte] *vt (a) (prix, actions)* to quote **(b)** *(documents)* to classify

côtier, -ère [kotje, -ɛr] *adj (fleuve, navigation)* coastal; *(pêche)* inshore

cotillon [kɔtijɔ̃] *nm* **accessoires de c., cotillons** party novelties

cotisation [kɔtizasjɔ̃] *nf (a) (à une caisse)* contribution; **cotisations de Sécurité Sociale** ≃ National Insurance contributions **(b)** *(à un club)* subscription

cotiser [kɔtize] **1** *vi (à une caisse de retraite, à une mutuelle)* to contribute (**à** to)
  2 se cotiser *vpr* to club together

coton [kɔtɔ̃] **1** *nm (a) (plante, tissu)* cotton; **chemise 100% c.** 100% cotton shirt; *Fam* **filer un mauvais c.** *(financièrement, physiquement)* to be in a bad way **(b)** **c. (hydrophile)** *Br* cotton wool, *Am* absorbent cotton; **un c.** a piece of *Br* cotton wool *or Am* absorbent cotton; *Fig* **élever un enfant dans du c.** to wrap a child in cotton wool; *Fam* **j'ai les jambes en c.** my legs feel like jelly
  2 *adj Fam* tough, tricky

cotonnade [kɔtɔnad] *nf* cotton fabric

cotonneux, -euse [kɔtɔnø, -øz] *adj (feuille)* downy; *(nuage)* fluffy; *(fruit)* mushy

Coton-Tige® *(pl* **Cotons-Tiges)** [kɔtɔ̃tiʒ] *nm* cotton bud

côtoyer [32] [kotwaje] *vt (a) (personnes)* to mix with **(b)** *(rivière, forêt)* to border on

cotte [kɔt] *nf* **c. de mailles** coat of mail

cou [ku] *nm* neck; **tendre le c.** to crane one's neck; **avoir un c. de taureau** to have a neck like a bull; **se jeter au c. de qn** to throw one's arms round sb's neck; *Fam* **endetté jusqu'au c.** up to one's eyes in debt

couac [kwak] *nm (fausse note)* false note; *Fig* discordant note; **faire un c.** to play a false note; *(chanteur)* to sing a false note

couchage [kuʃaʒ] *nm voir* **sac**

couchant, -e [kuʃɑ̃, -ɑ̃t] **1** *adj* **le soleil c.** the setting sun

2 *nm (ouest)* west; **dans la direction du c.** in a westerly direction

couche [kuʃ] *nf* (**a**) *(de peinture)* coat; *(de beurre, de crème, de poussière)* layer; *(classe sociale)* level; *Géol* layer, stratum; **la c. d'ozone** the ozone layer; *Fam* **il en tient une c.!** he's really stupid! (**b**) *(de bébé)* Br nappy, Am diaper (**c**) *Vieilli* **femme en couches** woman in labour; **mourir en couches** to die in childbirth (**d**) *Litt (lit)* bed

couché, -e [kuʃe] *adj* (**a**) *(allongé)* lying (down); *(au lit)* in bed (**b**) *(écriture)* slanting, sloping

couche-culotte *(pl* **couches-culottes)** [kuʃkylɔt] *nf* disposable Br nappy *or* Am diaper

coucher¹ [kuʃe] *nm* (**a**) *(fait d'aller au lit)* **l'heure du c.** bedtime; **prendre deux comprimés au c.** take two tablets at bedtime (**b**) *(gîte)* accommodation (**c**) *(du soleil)* setting; **un superbe c. de soleil** a magnificent sunset; **au c. du soleil** at sunset

coucher² **1** *vt* (**a**) *(mettre au lit)* **c. qn** to put sb to bed (**b**) *(allonger, poser)* to lay down (**c**) *(écrire)* **c. qn sur son testament** to mention sb in one's will

2 *vi* (**a**) *(passer la nuit)* to sleep; *Fig* **c. sous les ponts** to sleep rough (**b**) *Fam* **c. avec qn** to sleep with sb; **c. ensemble** to sleep together (**c**) *(à un chien)* **couché!** (lie) down!

3 **se coucher** *vpr* (**a**) *(au lit)* to go to bed; **aller se c.** to go to bed; *Fam* **se c. avec les poules** to go to bed early; *Prov* **comme on fait son lit, on se couche** as we make our bed, so we must lie in it (**b**) *(s'allonger)* to lie down; **se c. à plat ventre** to lie flat on one's stomach (**c**) **se c. sur le flanc** *(navire)* to keel over (**d**) *(soleil, lune)* to set, to go down

coucheries [kuʃri] *nf Fam* sleeping around

couchette [kuʃɛt] *nf (de navire)* bunk; *(de train)* couchette

coucheur [kuʃœr] *nm Fam* **c'est un mauvais c.** he's an awkward customer

couci-couça [kusikusa] *adv Fam* so-so

coucou [kuku] **1** *nm* (**a**) *(oiseau)* cuckoo (**b**) *(horloge)* cuckoo clock (**c**) *(plante)* cowslip (**d**) *Fam (avion)* old crate

2 *exclam (langage enfantin)* peekaboo!; *(bonjour)* cooee!

coude [kud] *nm* (**a**) *(articulation)* elbow; **être au c. à c.** to be neck and neck; **jouer des coudes** to push and shove; *Fig* **se manœuvre**; *Fig* **se serrer les coudes** to stick together; *Fig* **garder qch sous le c.** to hold on to sth; *Fam* **lever le c.** to booze (**b**) *(tournant)* sharp bend; *(de barre, de tuyau)* bend; *(d'arbre)* crank

coudé, -e [kude] *adj* bent

coudée [kude] *nf* **avoir les coudées franches** to have plenty of elbow room

cou-de-pied *(pl* **cous-de-pied)** [kudpje] *nm* instep

coudre [21] [kudr] *vt (ourlet)* to sew; *(bouton)* to sew on; *(deux morceaux d'étoffe)* to sew together; *(jupe,*

plaie) to sew up; **c. un bouton à une robe** to sew a button on a dress; **je ne sais pas c.** I can't sew

coudrier [kudrije] *nm* hazel (tree); **b. de coudrier** hazel stick *or* switch

couenne [kwan] *nf* rind

couette¹ [kwɛt] *nf (édredon)* duvet, continental quilt

couette² *nf (coiffure)* bunch; **se faire des couettes** to put one's hair in bunches

couille [kuj] *nf Vulg (testicule)* ball; *(problème)* balls-up

couillon, -onne [kujɔ̃, -ɔn] *très Fam* **1** *adj* damned stupid

2 *nm,f* twat, Br wally

couillonner [kujɔne] *vt très Fam (personne)* to con; **se faire c.** to be conned

couiner [kwine] *vi (animal)* to squeak; *(enfant)* to whine

coulant, -e [kulɑ̃, -ɑ̃t] *adj (fromage)* runny; *Fig (style)* flowing; *Fam (personne)* easy-going

coulée [kule] *nf* **c. de boue** mudslide; **c. de lave** lava flow

coulemelle [kulmɛl] *nf* parasol mushroom

couler [kule] **1** *vt* (**a**) *(liquide, cire, ciment)* to pour; *(métal, statue)* to cast (**b**) *(navire)* to sink; *Fig* **c. qn** to bring sb down (**c**) *(passer)* **c. des jours heureux** to lead a happy life; *Fam* **se la c. douce** to take things easy

2 *vi* (**a**) *(liquide, rivière)* to flow, to run; *(fromage, maquillage)* to run; *(style)* to flow; **la sueur coule sur son front** sweat is trickling down his forehead; **cette affaire a fait c. beaucoup d'encre** a lot has been written about this affair; **faire c. un bain à qn** to run a bath for sb; *Fig* **c. de source** to be obvious (**b**) *(navire)* to sink, to go down; *(entreprise)* to go under (**c**) *(tonneau, stylo)* to leak; *(nez)* to run; **avoir le nez qui coule** to have a runny nose

3 **se couler** *vpr (se glisser)* to slip

couleur [kulœr] **1** *nf* (**a**) *(teinte, orientation politique)* colour; **de quelle c. est...?** what colour is...?; **de c.** coloured; **de c. jaune/verte** yellow-/green-coloured; **télévision/photographie en c.** *ou* **couleurs** colour television/photography; **les couleurs** *(linge)* coloureds; *Fig* **pour faire c. locale** to add a bit of local colour; *Fam* **elle nous en a fait voir de toutes les couleurs** she gave us a hard time; *Fam* **je n'en ai pas encore vu la c.** I've seen no sign of it yet

(**b**) *(teint)* **prendre des couleurs** to get some colour in one's cheeks

(**c**) *Mil* **couleurs** *(drapeau)* colours

(**d**) **couleurs** *(d'un club, d'une écurie)* colours; **défendre les couleurs de** to represent

(**e**) *(peinture)* paint; **une boîte de couleurs** a paintbox

(**f**) *(aux cartes)* suit; **annoncer la c.** to call (trumps); *Fam* to lay one's cards on the table

(**g**) *(en coiffure)* dye; **se faire une c.** to dye one's hair; **se faire faire une c.** to have one's hair dyed

2 *adj inv (télévision, pellicule)* colour; **une chevelure c. de feu** flame-coloured hair

couleuvre [kulœvr] *nf* **c. (à collier)** grass snake; *Fig* **avaler des couleuvres** *(se faire humilier)* to eat humble pie; *(être naïf)* to swallow anything

coulis [kuli] *nm* **c. de tomates/framboises** tomato/raspberry coulis

coulissant, -e [kulisɑ̃, -ɑ̃t] *adj* sliding

coulisse [kulis] *nf* (**a**) *(glissière)* runner; **porte à c.** sliding door (**b**) *Théât* **les coulisses** the wings; **en coulisses, dans les coulisses** in the wings; *Fig* behind the scenes

coulisser [kulise] *vi* to slide

couloir [kulwar] *nm* (**a**) *(de maison)* corridor, passage; *(de train)* corridor; *(en athlétisme, en natation)* lane; *(au tennis) Br* tramlines, *Am* alley; **c. aérien** air corridor; **c. d'autobus** bus lane; **c. à vélos** cycle lane (**b**) *Géog* gully

coulommiers [kulɔmje] *nm* = type of soft cheese

coulon [kulɔ̃] *nm Belg* pigeon

coulpe [kulp] *nf* **battre sa c.** to beat one's breast

coup [ku] *nm* (**a**) *(choc)* blow; **donner un c. à qn** to hit sb; **se donner un c. contre qch** to knock against sth; **j'ai pris un coup sur la tête** I got a knock *or* a bang on the head; **donner un c. de bâton à qn** to hit sb with a stick; **donner un c. de coude à qn** to nudge sb; **donner un c. de couteau à qn** to knife sb; **donner un c. de griffe à qn/qch** to claw at sb/sth; **c. de pied** kick; **donner un c. de pied à qn/qch** to kick sb/sth; **c. de poing** punch; **donner un c. de poing à qn** to punch sb; **c. de poing américain** knuckle-duster; *Fig* **donner un c. de pouce à qn** to push sb; **c. de tête** header; *Fam* **faire qch sur un c. de tête** to do sth on the spur of the moment; **rendre c. pour c.** to give as good as one gets; *Fig* **tous les coups sont permis** there are no holds barred; *Fig* **c'était un c. bas** that was below the belt; *Jur* **coups et blessures** grievous bodily harm

(**b**) *(choc émotionnel)* blow; **ça m'a fait un c.** *(émotion)* it gave me a shock; *(déception)* it was a blow; **accuser le c.** to show that one has been affected; *Fam* **tenir le c.** to hold out; *Fam* **en prendre un c.** to be devastated; **un c. dur** a setback

(**c**) *(action soudaine, événement soudain)* **c. de vent** gust of wind; *Fam* **passer en c. de vent** to pay a flying visit; **donner un c. de frein** to brake; **donner un c. de volant** to turn the wheel sharply; **donner un c. d'arrêt à qch** to call a halt to sth; *Fam* **prendre un c. de vieux** to age; *Fam* **avoir un c. de barre** *ou* **de pompe** to have the munchies; **c. de chance** *ou Fam* **de bol** *ou* **de pot** stroke of luck; *Fam* **avoir un c. de cœur pour qch** to absolutely love sth; **c. d'État** coup (d'État); *Fig* **ç'a été le c. de foudre** it was love at first sight; **avoir le c. de foudre pour qn** to fall head over heels in love with sb; **attraper un c. de froid** to catch a cold; *Fam* **pousser un c. de gueule** to yell; *Fam* **un c. de pub** a publicity stunt; **prendre un c. de soleil** to get sunburned; **c. de théâtre** coup de théâtre; *(dans la vie)* sudden turn of events

(**d**) *(bruit)* **c. de feu** shot; **c. de fusil** shot; **c. de sifflet** whistle; **c. de sonnette** ring; **c. de tonnerre** clap of thunder; **tirer deux coups** to fire twice; **l'horloge sonna trois coups** the clock struck three; *Fig* **sur le c. de midi** on the stroke of twelve; **les trois coups** *(au théâtre)* = the three knocks given just before the curtain rises

(**e**) *(influence)* **sous le c. de la colère** in a fit of anger; **tomber sous le c. de la loi** to be an offence

(**f**) *(essai)* attempt, go; *Fig* **réussir son c.** to be a great success; **d'un seul c.** in one go; **du premier c.** at the first attempt; *Fam* **à tous les coups, le patron va nous repérer** the boss is bound to see us; **il n'en est pas à son c. d'essai** it's not the first time he's done it; **c. de maître** masterstroke

(**g**) *(au golf)* stroke; *(aux échecs)* move; **c. droit** *(au tennis)* forehand; *Fig* **faire c. double** to kill two birds

with one stone; **c. d'envoi** *(au football, au rugby)* kick-off; *Fig* **donner le c. d'envoi de qch** to launch sth; **c. franc** *(au football)* free kick; **c. de pied de réparation** penalty kick

(**h**) *Fam (tour, combine)* **réussir un bon c.** to do well for oneself; **faire un sale c. à qn** to play a dirty trick on sb; **être sur un c.** to be on to a good thing; **être dans le c.** *(impliqué)* to be involved; *(à la mode)* to be trendy; **c. fourré, c. de Jarnac** dirty trick; **c. monté** put-up job

(**i**) *Vulg* **tirer un c.** to have a screw

(**j**) *(locutions)* **tout à c., tout d'un c.** suddenly, all of a sudden; **à c. sûr** for certain, definitely; **au c. par c.** step by step; **c. sur c.** one after the other; **après c.** after the event; *Fam* **du c.** and so; **pleurer un bon c.** to have a good cry; **mourir sur le c.** to die on the spot; **sur le c., je n'ai pas compris** at the time I didn't understand; **faire les quatre cents coups** to sow one's wild oats; **donner le c. de grâce à qn** to finish sb off; **avoir le c. de main (pour faire qch)** to have the knack (of doing sth); **donner un c. de main à qn** to give sb a hand; *Fam* **boire un c.** to have a drink; *Fam* **avoir un c. dans le nez** to be smashed; *Fam* **valoir le c.** to be worth it; *Fam* **il va falloir en mettre un c.** we're going to have to pull out all the stops

coupable [kupabl] **1** *adj (personne)* guilty (**de** of); *(action, négligence)* culpable; *(faiblesse)* reprehensible; **se sentir c. (de faire qch)** to feel guilty (about doing sth)

2 *nmf* culprit

coupant, -e [kupɑ̃, -ɑ̃t] *adj* sharp

coupe¹ [kup] *nf* (**a**) *(récipient)* bowl; **c. à champagne** champagne glass; **la c. est pleine** that's the limit; *Prov* **il y a loin de la c. aux lèvres** there's many a slip 'twixt cup and lip (**b**) *(trophée)* cup; **la C. du monde de football** the Football World Cup; **la c. Davis** the Davis Cup

coupe² *nf* (**a**) *(action) (du blé)* cutting; *(de tissu)* cutting out; *(d'arbres)* cutting down; **c. (de cheveux)** haircut; **acheter du fromage à la c.** to buy cheese from the fresh cheese counter; **c. sombre** *(dans une forêt)* slight thinning; *(du personnel, des dépenses)* drastic cut (**b**) *(d'un vêtement)* cut (**c**) *(plan)* section (**d**) *(aux cartes)* cut; *Fig* **être sous la c. de qn** to be under sb's thumb; **tomber sous la c. de qn** to fall into sb's clutches

coupé, -e [kupe] **1** *adj* (**a**) *(taillé)* cut; **un costume mal c.** a badly cut suit (**b**) *(au tennis)* **une balle coupée** a slice (**c**) *(castré) (chat)* neutered (**d**) *(dilué)* **c. d'eau** watered down, diluted

2 *nm (voiture)* coupé; **c. sport** sports coupé

coupe-coupe [kupkup] *nm inv* machete

coupe-faim [kupfɛ̃] *nm inv* appetite suppressant

coupe-feu [kupfø] *nm inv* firebreak; *Ordinat* **mur c.** firewall; **porte c.** fire-door

coupe-gorge [kupgɔrʒ] *nm inv* dangerous back alley

coupe-légumes [kuplegym] *nm inv* vegetable slicer

coupelle [kupɛl] *nf* (**a**) *(petite coupe)* small dish (**b**) *(de laboratoire)* cupel

coupe-ongles [kupɔ̃gl] *nm inv* nail clippers

coupe-papier [kuppapje] *nm inv* paper knife, letter opener

couper [kupe] **1** *vt* (**a**) *(trancher)* to cut; *(arbre)* to cut down; *(vêtement)* to cut out; **c. qch en morceaux** to cut sth up (into pieces); **c. qch en trois** to cut sth into three; **c. les cheveux à qn** to cut sb's hair; **c. la tête à**

qn to cut off sb's head; **c. les cheveux en quatre** to split hairs; **un brouillard à c. au couteau** fog you could cut with a knife; **j'en donnerais ma main** *ou* **ma tête à c.** I'd stake my life on it

(**b**) *(supprimer, raccourcir)* to cut; **c. dans le vif** to take drastic measures

(**c**) *(traverser)* to cut across; **c. la route à qn** to cut in in front of sb; **c. à travers champs** to cut across country; **c. par le jardin** to cut through the garden

(**d**) *(séparer)* to divide (**en deux** in two); **être coupé du monde** to be cut off from the outside world

(**e**) *(interrompre) (personne)* to cut in on; *(son)* to turn right down; **c. l'eau** *(pour réparation)* to turn off the water; *(pour non-paiement)* to cut off the water; **c. le courant** *ou* **l'électricité** *(pour réparation)* to switch off the current; *(pour non-paiement)* to cut off the power; **c. le téléphone à qn** to cut off sb's telephone; **nous avons été coupés, la communication a été coupée** we were cut off; **c. le contact** *(d'une voiture)* to switch off the ignition; **c. l'appétit à qn** to spoil sb's appetite; **ces bas me coupent la circulation** these stockings are cutting off my circulation; *Fam* **ça te la coupe!** that's taken the wind out of your sails!

(**f**) *(châtrer) (chat)* to neuter

(**g**) **c. du vin** *(en mélangeant)* to blend wine; *(avec de l'eau)* to water down wine

(**h**) *(paquet de cartes)* to cut; *(prendre avec l'atout)* to trump; **à toi de c.** it's your turn to cut; **c. à carreau** to trump with a diamond

(**i**) *(au tennis) (balle)* to slice

2 *vi (être tranchant)* to be sharp; **le couteau coupe bien** the knife cuts well

3 couper à *vt ind* (**a**) *Fam* **c. à qch** *(se dérober)* to get out of sth (**b**) **c. court à qch** to cut sth short

4 se couper *vpr* (**a**) *(se blesser)* to cut oneself; **se c. le** *ou* **au doigt** to cut one's finger; **se c. les veines** to slash one's wrists (**b**) *(tailler)* **se c. les ongles/les cheveux** to cut one's nails/hair (**c**) *(routes)* to intersect, to cross (**d**) **se c. de qn** to cut oneself off from sb

couper-coller [kupekɔle] *nm inv Ordinat* cut and paste

couperet [kuprɛ] *nm* (**a**) *(pour la viande)* cleaver (**b**) *(de la guillotine)* blade

couperose [kuproz] *nf* blotches

couperosé, -e [kuproze] *adj* blotchy

coupe-vent [kupvɑ̃] *nm inv* (**a**) *(dispositif)* windbreak (**b**) *(blouson) Br* windcheater, *Am* Windbreaker®

couple [kupl] *nm (de personnes)* couple; *(d'animaux)* pair; **vivre en c.** to live together; **un c. sans enfants** a childless couple

couplet [kuplɛ] *nm (de chanson)* verse; *Fam* tirade (**sur** about)

coupole [kupɔl] *nf* dome, cupola

coupon [kupɔ̃] *nm* (**a**) *(ticket)* **c. de réduction** money-off coupon (**b**) *(de tissu)* remnant (**c**) *Fin* **c. d'action** coupon

coupon-réponse *(pl* **coupons-réponse**) [kupɔ̃repɔ̃s] *nm* reply coupon

coupure [kupyr] *nf* (**a**) *(blessure)* cut (**b**) *(suppression)* cut (**c**) **c. (de courant)** power cut (**d**) *Fig (séparation)* break (**e**) *(pause)* break (**f**) **c. de journal** *ou* **de presse** newspaper *or* press cutting (**g**) *Fin* denomination; **50 000 euros en petites coupures** 50,000 euros in small notes *or* denominations

cour [kur] *nf* (**a**) *(de maison, de ferme)* yard; *Can* **c. à bois** lumber yard; **c. d'honneur** main courtyard; **c. de récréation** *Br* playground, *Am* schoolyard; *Fig* **jouer dans la c. des grands** to be up there with the leaders (**b**) *(de souverain)* court; **vivre à la c.** to live at court (**c**) *(tribunal)* court; **Messieurs, la C.!** all rise!; **Haute C.** High Court *(for impeachment of president or ministers)*; **c. d'appel** court of appeal; **c. d'assises** court of assises; **c. de cassation** ≃ Supreme Court of Appeal; **la C. des comptes** the Audit Office; **la C. internationale de justice** the International Court of Justice; **c. martiale** court martial; **passer en c. martiale (pour qch)** to be court-martialled (for sth); *Can* **la C. suprême** the Supreme Court (**d**) **faire la c. à qn** to court sb

courage [kuraʒ] *nm* courage, bravery; **avec c.** bravely, courageously; **perdre c.** to lose heart; **prendre son c. à deux mains** to pluck up courage; **avoir/se sentir le c. de ses opinions** to have the courage of one's convictions; **avoir/se sentir le c. de faire qch** to be/to feel up to doing sth; **bon c.!** good luck!

courageusement [kuraʒøzmɑ̃] *adv (bravement)* courageously, bravely; *(résolument)* with a will

courageux, -euse [kuraʒø, -øz] *adj* (**a**) *(brave)* courageous, brave (**b**) *(énergique)* energetic

courailler [kuraje] *vi Can Fam* to chase women

courailleur [kurajœr] *nm Can Fam* womanizer

couramment [kuramɑ̃] *adv* (**a**) *(parler)* fluently (**b**) *(généralement)* commonly; **ce mot s'emploie c.** this word is in common use

courant, -e [kurɑ̃, -ɑ̃t] **1** *adj* (**a**) *(commun)* common; **dans la vie courante** in everyday life (**b**) *(en cours)* current; **le 5 c.** the 5th inst.

2 *nm* (**a**) *(dans une rivière)* current; *Fig (tendance)* trend; **suivre/remonter le c.** to go with/against the current; **c. d'air** draught; **c. de pensée** way of thinking (**b**) *Élec* **c. (électrique)** (electric) current; **c. continu/ alternatif** direct/alternating current; *Fig* **le c. ne passe pas** we're/they're/you're not on the same wavelength (**c**) *(durée)* **dans le c. de** in the course of; **c. janvier** during the month of January (**d**) **être au c. (de qch)** to know (about sth); **mettre qn au c. (de qch)** to tell sb (about sth); **tenir qn au c. (de qch)** to keep sb up-to-date (on sth)

3 *nf* **courante** *Fam* **avoir la courante** to have the runs

courbatu, -e [kurbaty] *adj* aching (all over)

courbature [kurbatyr] *nf* ache; **avoir des courbatures** to be aching (all over)

courbaturé, -e [kurbatyre] *adj* aching (all over)

courbe [kurb] **1** *adj* curved

2 *nf* curve; *(graphe)* graph; **c. de niveau** contour (line); **c. des prix/des salaires** price/salary curve; **c. de température** temperature curve

courber [kurbe] **1** *vt* to bend; **c. la tête** to bow *or* bend one's head; *Fig* **c. l'échine** to submit

2 *vi* to bend

3 se courber *vpr (personne)* to bend down, to stoop; **se c. en deux** to bend double

courbette [kurbɛt] *nf (salut)* bow; *Fig* **faire des courbettes (à qn)** to bow and scrape (to sb)

courbure [kurbyr] *nf (d'une surface, d'une ligne)* curvature; *(d'un morceau de bois, du dos)* curve

coureur, -euse [kurœr, -øz] **1** *nm,f (à pied)* runner; **c. (automobile)** (racing) driver; **c. (cycliste)** (racing) cyclist

2 adj (homme) womanizing; (femme) manhunting
3 nm **c. (de jupons)** womanizer
4 nf **coureuse** (dévergondée) manhunter
courge [kurʒ] nf (**a**) (plante) Br marrow, Am squash (**b**) Fam (imbécile) wally
courgette [kurʒɛt] nf Br courgette, Am zucchini
courir [22] [kurir] **1** vi (**a**) (personne) to run; **monter/descendre la colline en courant** to run up/down the hill; **arriver en courant** to come running (up); **je cours le prévenir** I'll run and warn him; **c. après qn/qch** to run after sb/sth; **c. après la gloire** to chase after glory; **c. à sa perte** to be heading for disaster; **l'assassin court toujours** the murderer is still at large; Fam **tu peux toujours c.!** not a chance!; Fam **laisse c.!** forget it!; Prov **rien ne sert de c., il faut partir à point** slow and steady wins the race
(**b**) (se propager) **le bruit court que...** rumour has it that...; **faire c. un bruit** to spread a rumour
(**c**) (eau, ruisseau) to rush
(**d**) (participer à une course) (à pied) to run; (automobile) to drive; (cycliste) to ride
2 vt (**a**) (tenter) **c. un risque** to run a risk (**b**) Sport **c. le 100 mètres** to run the 100 metres (**c**) (parcourir, fréquenter) **c. le monde** to roam the world; **c. les théâtres** to go to the theatre all the time; **ça ne court pas les rues** (personnes) they're not thick on the ground; (objets) you don't see that every day (**d**) (chasser) **c. les filles** to chase women; Fig **c. deux lièvres à la fois** to have two irons in the fire
3 v impersonnel **il court des bruits sur lui** there are rumours going round about him
courlis [kurli] nm curlew
couronne [kurɔn] nf (**a**) (de fleurs, de lauriers) wreath; **c. funéraire** ou **mortuaire** (funeral) wreath (**b**) (de souverain) crown; (de noble) coronet; **la C. de France** the French Crown (**c**) (monnaie) crown (**d**) (pain) ring-shaped loaf; (de dent) crown; **se faire poser une c.** to have a tooth crowned
couronnement [kurɔnmã] nm (de souverain) coronation; Fig (réussite) crowning achievement
couronner [kurɔne] vt (**a**) (sacrer) to crown; Fig **mes efforts furent couronnés de succès** my efforts were crowned with success; **et pour c. le tout...** and to crown it all... (**b**) (dent) to crown
courra etc voir **courir**
courre [kur] voir **chasse**
courriel [kurjɛl] nm Can Ordinat e-mail
courrier [kurje] nm (**a**) (lettres) mail, Br post; **c. électronique** electronic mail, e-mail; **c. interne** internal mail (**b**) Journ **c. du cœur** problem page; **c. des lecteurs** letters to the Editor (**c**) Vieilli (messager) courier
courroie [kurwa] nf (**a**) (de cuir, de toile) strap (**b**) Méc belt; **c. de transmission** driving belt; **c. de ventilateur** fanbelt
courroucé, -e [kuruse] adj Litt incensed
courroux [kuru] nm Litt ire, wrath
cours¹ [kur] nm (**a**) (leçon) Univ lecture; Scol lesson; (ensemble des leçons) course; **aller en c.** Univ to go to lectures; Scol to go to school; **prendre** ou **suivre un c.** to take or do a course; **donner des c.** Univ to give lectures; Scol to give classes; **c. par correspondance** correspondence course; **c. intensif** crash course; **c. magistral** lecture; **c. particulier** private lesson; **c. du soir** evening class
(**b**) (classe) **c. élémentaire** = second and third years of primary school; **c. moyen** = fourth and fifth years

of primary school; **c. préparatoire** = first year of primary school
(**c**) (de rivière, d'un astre) course; **suivre le c. de ses pensées** to follow one's train of thought; **donner libre c. à qch** to give free rein to sth; **c. d'eau** waterway
(**d**) (évolution) course; **suivre son c.** to run its course; **en c.** (affaires) in hand; (travaux) in progress, (année) current; **en c. de route** on the way; **au c. de qch** in the course of sth
(**e**) (d'une monnaie) currency; **avoir c.** (monnaie) to be legal tender; (pratique) to be current
(**f**) Fin (d'une action) price; (de devises) rate; **c. des changes** exchange rates; **c. pivot** central rate
cours² voir **courir**
course [kurs] nf (**a**) Sport (épreuve) race; (discipline) racing; **faire la c. avec qn** to race with sb; **les courses (de chevaux)** the races; Fam **ça va encore être la c.** it's going to be another mad rush; **la c. aux armements** the arms race; **c. automobile** motor race; (discipline) motor racing; **c. de chevaux** horse race; Sport & Fig **c. contre la montre** race against the clock; **c. cycliste** cycle race; **c. de haies** (en athlétisme) hurdles; (course de chevaux) steeplechase; **c. d'obstacles** steeplechase; **c. d'orientation** orienteering; **c. à pied** race; (discipline) running; **c. de taureaux** (corrida) bullfight
(**b**) (action de courir) running
(**c**) (achat) **faire une c.** to get something from the shops; **courses** shopping; **faire des courses** to go shopping
(**d**) (trajet en taxi) journey; (prix) fare
(**e**) (de planète, de projectile) course
(**f**) Suisse (trajet) trip (by train or boat); (excursion) excursion
courser [kurse] vt Fam to chase after
coursier, -ère [kursje, -ɛr] nm,f messenger; (en moto) motorcycle courier
coursive [kursiv] nf Naut gangway
court¹, -e [kur, kurt] **1** adj short; Fam **15 euros, c'est un peu c.** 15 euros, it's not very much
2 adv short; **pour faire c.** to cut a long story short; **on l'appelle Charles tout c.** people just call him Charles; **prendre qn de c.** (en lui laissant peu de temps) to give sb short notice; (sans le prévenir) to catch sb unawares; **à c. de** short of
court² nm **c. (de tennis)** (tennis) court
court³ voir **courir**
court-bouillon (pl **courts-bouillons**) [kurbujɔ̃] nm court-bouillon
court-circuit (pl **courts-circuits**) [kursirkчi] nm short circuit
court-circuiter [kursirkчite] vt Élec & Fam Fig to short-circuit
courtier, -ère [kurtje, -ɛr] nm,f broker; **c. d'assurances** insurance broker
courtisan [kurtizã] nm (**a**) Hist courtier (**b**) Péj (flatteur) sycophant
courtisane [kurtizan] nf Litt courtesan
courtiser [kurtize] vt (**a**) (femme) to court (**b**) (flatter) to fawn on
courtois, -e [kurtwa, -az] adj (poli) courteous (**envers** ou **avec** towards)
courtoisement [kurtwazmã] adv courteously
courtoisie [kurtwazi] nf courtesy (**envers** towards)

court-vêtu, -e (*mpl* **court-vêtus,** *fpl* **court-vêtues**) [kurvety] *adj* in a short skirt; **être c.** to be wearing a short skirt

couru, -e [kury] *adj* (**a**) (*lieu, spectacle*) popular (**b**) *Fam* **c'est c. (d'avance)** it's a sure thing

cousais *etc voir* **coudre**

couscous [kuskus] *nm* couscous

cousin¹, -e [kuzɛ̃, -in] *nm,f* cousin; **c. germain** first cousin

cousin² *nm* (*insecte*) mosquito

coussin [kusɛ̃] *nm* (**a**) (*de siège*) cushion; *Belg & Suisse* (*oreiller*) pillow (**b**) **c. d'air** air cushion

coussinet [kusinɛ] *nm* (**a**) (*coussin*) small cushion (**b**) (*d'animal*) pad

cousu¹, -e [kuzy] *adj* sewn; **c. (à la) main** hand-sewn; *Fam Fig* **c'est du c. main** it's first-rate; **une histoire cousue de fil blanc** a blatant lie

cousu², -e *voir* **coudre**

coût [ku] *nm aussi Fig* cost; **le c. de la vie** the cost of living

coûtant [kutã] *adj m voir* **prix**

couteau, -x [kuto] *nm* (**a**) (*ustensile*) knife; **être à couteaux tirés (avec qn)** to be at daggers drawn (with sb); *Fig* **avoir le c. sous la gorge** to have a gun at one's head; **c. de cuisine** kitchen knife; **c. à fromage** cheese-knife; **c. à pain** breadknife; **c. suisse** Swiss army knife (**b**) (*mollusque*) razor shell (**c**) *Fig* **deuxième** *ou* **second c.** (*en politique, dans la Mafia*) minion

couteau-scie (*pl* **couteaux-scies**) [kutosi] *nm* serrated knife

coutelas [kutla] *nm* large knife

coûter [kute] *vi* to cost; **combien ça coûte?** how much is it?, how much does it cost?; **ça coûte 100 euros** it costs 100 euros, it's 100 euros; **c. les yeux de la tête** to cost a fortune; **ça ne coûte rien d'essayer** there's no harm in trying; **c. cher** to cost a lot, to be expensive; **cela vous coûtera cher** it'll cost you a lot; *Fig* you'll pay for that; **c. la vie à qn** to cost sb his/her life; **ça m'a beaucoup coûté** it was very painful for me; **coûte que coûte** at all costs

coûteux, -euse [kutø, -øz] *adj* costly, expensive; **peu c.** inexpensive

coutume [kutym] *nf* (**a**) (*habitude*) custom; **avoir c. de faire qch** to be accustomed to doing sth; **plus aimable que de c.** nicer than usual; **comme de c.** as usual; **une fois n'est pas c.** it won't hurt for once (**b**) (*tradition*) custom

coutumier, -ère [kutymje, -ɛr] *adj* (**a**) (*habituel*) customary, usual (**b**) (*personne*) **il est c. du fait** it's not the first time he's done that (**c**) *Jur* **droit c.** common law

couture [kutyr] **1** *nf* (**a**) (*de vêtement*) seam; *Fig* **examiner qn/qch sous toutes les coutures** to examine sb/sth from every angle (**b**) (*activité*) sewing, needlework; **faire de la c.** to sew
2 *adj inv* (*collection*) designer

couturier [kutyrje] *nm* fashion designer, couturier; **grand c.** big fashion designer

couturière [kutyrjɛr] *nf* dressmaker

couvaison [kuvɛzɔ̃] *nf* incubation

couvée [kuve] *nf* (**a**) (*œufs*) clutch (**b**) (*d'oisillons, d'enfants*) brood

couvent [kuvã] *nm* (**a**) (*communauté religieuse*) (*de femmes*) convent; (*d'hommes*) monastery (**b**) (*pensionnat*) convent school

couver [kuve] **1** *vt* (**a**) (*œufs*) to sit on; *Fig* (*personne*) to mollycoddle; **c. qn des yeux** to look fondly at sb (**b**) (*maladie*) to be coming down with
2 *vi* (*poule*) to brood; (*feu, passion*) to smoulder; (*émeute*) to be brewing

couvercle [kuvɛrkl] *nm* lid; (*qui se visse*) cap, top

couvert¹, -e [kuvɛr, -ɛrt] **1** *adj* (**a**) (*allée, marché*) covered; (*piscine*) indoor; (*ciel*) overcast (**b**) (*jonché, plein*) **c. de** covered with *or* in (**c**) (*habillé*) covered up; **chaudement** *ou* **bien c.** warmly dressed (**d**) (*ciel*) overcast
2 *pp voir* **couvrir**

couvert² *nm* (**a**) (*ustensiles*) **un c. en argent** a silver knife, fork and spoon; **couverts** cutlery (**b**) (*pour chaque convive*) place setting; **mettre le c.** to set *or Br* lay the table; **mettre trois couverts** to set *or Br* lay the table for three; **mets deux couverts de plus** set *or Br* lay two extra places (**c**) **sous le c. de** (*sous l'apparence de*) under the cover of

couverture [kuvɛrtyr] *nf* (**a**) (*de lit*) blanket; *Fig* **tirer la c. à soi** to take all the credit; **c. chauffante** electric blanket (**b**) (*d'un livre, d'un magazine, d'un cahier*) cover; **en c.** on the cover (**c**) (*protection*) **c. sociale** social security cover (**d**) (*d'un bâtiment*) roofing (**e**) (*d'un événement médiatique*) coverage

couveuse [kuvøz] *nf* (**a**) (*pour nouveau-nés*) incubator (**b**) (*poule*) brooder

couvre-chef (*pl* **couvre-chefs**) [kuvrəʃɛf] *nm Hum* hat

couvre-feu (*pl* **couvre-feux**) [kuvrəfø] *nm Mil* curfew

couvre-lit (*pl* **couvre-lits**) [kuvrəli] *nm* bedspread

couvre-pied(s) (*pl* **couvre-pieds**) [kuvrəpje] *nm* quilt

couvreur [kuvrœr] *nm* roofer

couvrir [52] [kuvrir] **1** *vt* (**a**) (*casserole, meuble, livre*) to cover (**de** with) (**b**) **c. qn de** (*cadeaux, honneurs, compliments*) to shower sb with (**c**) (*protéger, justifier*) to cover; **être couvert par ses supérieurs** to be acting with the authority of one's superiors (**d**) (*parcourir, englober*) & *Journ* to cover (**e**) (*bruit, voix*) to drown (out) (**f**) (*sujet: assurance*) to cover (**g**) *Zool* (*femelle*) to cover
2 **se couvrir** *vpr* (**a**) (*pour sortir*) to wrap up; (*pour cacher sa nudité*) to cover oneself up; (*mettre son chapeau*) to put on one's hat (**b**) (*ciel*) to cloud over; **le temps** *ou* **ça se couvre** it's clouding over (**c**) **se c. de** (*honte, ridicule*) to cover oneself with; **se c. de feuilles** (*arbre*) to come into leaf; **se c. de boutons** (*visage*) to come out *or* to become covered in spots

covoiturage [kɔvwatyraʒ] *nm* car-pooling (*for commuting to the workplace*)

cow-boy (*pl* **cow-boys**) [kobɔj] *nm* cowboy

coyote [kɔjɔt] *nm* coyote

CP [sepe] *nm* (*abrév* **cours préparatoire**) = first year of primary school

CPAM [sepeaɛm] *nf* (*abrév* **caisse primaire d'assurance maladie**) = French government department dealing with health insurance

cpp *Ordinat* (*abrév* **caractères par pouce**) cpi

cps *Ordinat* (*abrév* **caractères par seconde**) cps

crabe [krab] *nm* crab; **marcher en c.** to walk sideways

crac [krak] **1** *exclam* (*bruit de cassure*) crack!; *Fam* **et c., elle est tombée malade!** and what do you know, she fell ill!
2 *nm* crack

crachat [kraʃa] *nm* gob of spit; **crachats** spit

craché, -e [kraʃe] *adj Fam* **c'est sa mère tout c.**, **c'est le portrait (tout) c. de sa mère** he's the spitting image of his mother; **c'est lui tout c.!** that's just like him!

cracher [kraʃe] **1** *vi* (**a**) *(personne)* to spit; **c. sur qn** to spit at sb; *Fam Fig* **ne pas c. sur qch** not to say no to sth; *Fam Fig* **c. dans la soupe** to bite the hand that feeds (**b**) *(stylo)* to splutter (**c**) *(haut-parleur, téléphone, radio)* to crackle
2 *vt* (**a**) *(chewing-gum, nourriture)* to spit out; **c. du sang** to spit blood (**b**) *(fumée)* to belch out (**c**) *très Fam (somme d'argent)* to cough up

cracheur, -euse [kraʃœr, -øz] *nm,f* **c. de feu** fire-eater

crachin [kraʃɛ̃] *nm* (fine) drizzle

crachoir [kraʃwar] *nm* spittoon; *Fam Fig* **tenir le c.** to monopolize the conversation; *Fam Fig* **tenir le c. à qn** to listen to sb rambling on and on

crachoter [kraʃɔte] *vi (feu)* to splutter; *(radio, téléphone)* to crackle

crack [krak] *nm* (**a**) *Fam (personne)* ace (**en** at) (**b**) *(drogue)* crack

cracker [krakœr] *nm* cracker

Cracovie [krakɔvi] *n* Cracow

cracra [krakra] *adj Inv Fam* filthy

crade [krad], **cradingue** [kradɛ̃g], **crado** [krado] *adj Fam* filthy

craie [krɛ] *nf (matière)* chalk; *(bâtonnet)* stick of chalk

craignais *etc voir* **craindre**

craignos [krɛɲos] *adj Fam (laid)* hideous; *(louche)* dodgy

craindre [23] [krɛ̃dr] **1** *vt* (**a**) *(redouter)* to fear, to be afraid of; **ne craignez rien!** *(n'ayez pas peur)* don't be frightened!; *(ne vous inquiétez pas)* don't worry!; **je crains qu'il (ne) soit parti** I'm afraid he's left; **c. de faire qch** to be afraid of doing sth (**b**) *(ne pas supporter)* **ces plantes craignent le gel** these plants don't like frost; **craint l'humidité/la chaleur** *(sur emballage)* keep dry/cool
2 *vi Fam* **ça craint!** *(c'est ennuyeux)* what a pain!; *(c'est très laid)* it's hideous!; *(c'est louche)* it's dodgy

craint, -e *voir* **craindre**

crainte [krɛ̃t] *nf* fear; **de c. de tomber** for fear of falling; **de c. qu'on ne l'entende** for fear of being overheard; **soyez sans c., n'ayez c.** have no fear

craintif, -ive [krɛ̃tif, -iv] *adj* timid

cramer [krame] *Fam* **1** *vi & vt* to burn
2 **se cramer** *vpr* to burn oneself; **se c. les doigts** to burn one's fingers

cramoisi, -e [kramwazi] *adj* crimson

crampe [krɑ̃p] *nf* cramp; **j'ai une c. au pied** I've got cramp in my foot; **crampes d'estomac** stomach cramps

crampon [krɑ̃pɔ̃] *nm* (**a**) *(de chaussure de sport)* stud; *(pour alpinisme)* crampon; **crampons** *(chaussures)* boots with studs (**b**) *Constr* cramp (iron) (**c**) *Fam (personne)* leech

cramponner [krɑ̃pɔne] **se cramponner** *vpr* to hold on; **se c. à** to hold on to; *Fig (vie, espoir)* to cling to; *(fonction)* to hang on to

cran [krɑ̃] *nm* (**a**) *(entaille)* notch; *(de ceinture)* hole; **serrer sa ceinture d'un c.** to take one's belt in a notch; **c. de sûreté** *ou* **d'arrêt** safety catch; **(couteau à) c. d'arrêt** *Br* flick knife, *Am* switchblade (**b**) *Fig (degré)* **avancer/reculer d'un c.** to go up/come down a notch (**c**) *Fam* **être à c.** to be wound up (**d**) *Fam (courage)*

guts; **avoir du c.** to have guts (**e**) *(dans les cheveux)* crimp

crâne [krɑn] *nm* skull, *Spéc* cranium; *Fam* **avoir mal au c.** to have a headache; *Fam* **mets-toi ça dans le c.!** get that into your head!

crâner [krɑne] *vi Fam* to swagger, to show off

crâneur, -euse [krɑnœr, -øz] *Fam* **1** *adj* swaggering; **être c.** to be a show-off
2 *nm,f* show-off

crânien, -enne [krɑnjɛ̃, -ɛn] *adj Anat* cranial

crapahuter [krapayte] *vi Fam* (**a**) *(marcher)* to traipse about (**b**) *Mil (soldat)* to trudge along

crapaud [krapo] *nm* (**a**) *(animal)* toad (**b**) *(défaut)* flaw

crapule [krapyl] *nf* scoundrel, villain

crapuleux, -euse [krapylø, -øz] *adj voir* **crime**

craquant, -e [krakɑ̃, -ɑ̃t] *adj Fam (personne)* gorgeous

craque [krak] *nf Fam (mensonge)* fib, lie

craqueler [42] [krakle] **1** *vt* to crack
2 **se craqueler** *vpr* to crack

craquement [krakmɑ̃] *nm (de branche)* crack; *(d'escalier, de plancher)* creak; **des craquements** cracking/creaking

craquer [krake] **1** *vi* (**a**) *(branche)* to crack; *(escalier, plancher)* to creak; **faire c. ses doigts** to crack one's fingers (**b**) *(se déchirer)* to rip; *(se casser)* to snap (**c**) *(perdre le contrôle de soi)* to crack up (**d**) *Fam (succomber)* **c. pour qn** to fall for sb; **ce mec me fait c.** I really fancy that guy
2 *vt* (**a**) *(allumette)* to strike (**b**) *(déchirer)* to rip

crasse [kras] **1** *adj (ignorance)* crass
2 *nf* (**a**) *(saleté)* filth (**b**) *Fam (mauvais tour)* dirty trick; **faire une c. à qn** to play a dirty trick on sb

crasseux, -euse [krasø, -øz] *adj* filthy

cratère [krater] *nm* crater

cravache [kravaʃ] *nf* (riding) crop; *Fig* **mener qn à la c.** to rule sb with a rod of iron

cravacher [kravaʃe] **1** *vt (cheval)* to use the crop on
2 *vi Fam (travailler vite)* to work like mad

cravate [kravat] *nf* tie; *Fam* **s'en jeter un derrière la c.** to knock back a drink

crawl [krol] *nm* crawl; **nager le c.** to do the crawl

crayeux, -euse [krɛjø, -øz] *adj (matière, teint)* chalky

crayon [krɛjɔ̃] *nm* (**a**) *(pour écrire)* pencil; **écrire au c.** to write in pencil; **c. de couleur** coloured pencil, crayon; **c. gras** soft lead pencil; *Ordinat* **c. lumineux** *ou* **optique** light pen (**b**) *(bâton)* stick; **c. à lèvres** lip pencil (**c**) *(œuvre)* pencil-drawing

créance [kreɑ̃s] *nf* debt; **c. douteuse** bad debt

créancier, -ère [kreɑ̃sje, -ɛr] *nm,f* creditor

créateur, -trice [kreatœr, -tris] **1** *adj (génie)* creative; **industrie créatrice d'emplois** job-creating industry
2 *nm,f* creator; **c. (de mode)** (fashion) designer; *Rel* **le C.** the Creator

créatif, -ive [kreatif, -iv] *adj* creative

création [kreasjɔ̃] *nf* (**a**) *(fait de créer)* creation; **c. d'emplois** job creation (**b**) *(produit)* new product; *(d'un couturier)* creation (**c**) *(univers)* **la c.** creation (**d**) *(première représentation) (d'une pièce)* first production; *(d'un rôle)* creation; *(d'une œuvre musicale)* first performance

créativité [kreativite] *nf* creativity

créature [kreatyr] *nf* (**a**) *(être vivant)* creature; *Hum* **une c. de rêve** *(femme)* a magnificent woman (**b**) *Péj (protégé)* creature

crécelle [krɛsɛl] *nf* rattle; **une voix de c.** a rasping voice

crèche [krɛʃ] *nf* (**a**) *(garderie)* crèche, day nursery (**b**) *(de Noël)* crib

---

Crèche

State-subsidized care for children under three years of age of working families is well established in France, although this is subject to the availability of places.

---

crécher [34] [kreʃe] *vi Fam (habiter)* to live; *(temporairement)* to crash

crédibilité [kredibilite] *nf* credibility

crédible [kredibl] *adj* credible

crédit [kredi] *nm* (**a**) *(prêt)* credit; **à c.** on credit; **faire c. à qn** to give sb credit; **la maison ne fait pas c.** *(sur panneau)* we do not give credit; **c. à la consommation** consumer credit; **c. gratuit** interest-free credit; **c. immobilier** home loan, mortgage (**b**) *(en comptabilité)* credit side; **porter une somme au c. de qn** to credit sb with a sum (**c**) **crédits** *(somme d'argent)* funds (**d**) *Litt (influence)* credit

crédit-bail *(pl* **crédits-bails***)* [kredibaj] *nm* leasing

créditer [kredite] *vt* (**a**) *Fin (compte)* to credit (**de** with) (**b**) *Fig* **c. qn de qch** to give sb credit for sth

créditeur, -trice [kreditœr, -tris] *adj (solde, compte)* credit; **être c.** to be in credit

crédit-relais *(pl* **crédits-relais***)* [kredirəlɛ] *nm* bridging loan

credo [kredo] *nm inv* credo, creed

crédule [kredyl] *adj* credulous

crédulité [kredylite] *nf* credulity

créer [24] [kree] **1** *vt* (**a**) *(emplois, poste)* to create; *(entreprise)* to set up (**b**) *(œuvre, nouveau produit, vêtement)* to create (**c**) *(difficultés, problème)* to create (**à** for) (**d**) *(interpréter pour la première fois) (rôle)* to create; *(pièce de théâtre)* to produce for the first time; *(œuvre musicale)* to perform for the first time
2 se créer *vpr* (**a**) *(être créé)* to be created (**b**) *(pour soi-même)* **se c. une clientèle** to build up a clientèle; **se c. des problèmes** to create problems for oneself

crémaillère [kremajɛr] *nf (dans la cheminée)* trammel (hook); **pendre la c.** to have a housewarming (party)

crémant [kremã] *nm* slightly sparkling champagne

crémation [kremasjɔ̃] *nf* cremation

crématoire [krematwar] *adj voir* **four**

crématorium [krematɔrjɔm] *nm* crematorium

crème [krɛm] **1** *nf* (**a**) *(du lait, dessert)* cream; *Fig* **c'est la c. des hommes** he's the best of men; **c. anglaise** custard; **c. au beurre** = butter, sugar, eggs and cream, baked together and used as a cake filling; **c. brûlée** crème brûlée; **c. (au) caramel** caramel custard, crème caramel; **c. Chantilly** whipped cream *(with sugar added)*; **c. fouettée** whipped cream; **c. fraîche** crème fraîche; **c. glacée** ice cream; **c. pâtissière** confectioner's custard; **c. renversée** crème caramel *(turned out of its mould)* (**b**) *(produit cosmétique)* cream; **c. antirides** anti-wrinkle cream; **c. hydratante** moisturizing cream; **c. à raser** shaving cream (**c**) *(liqueur)* **c. de menthe** crème de menthe; **c. de cassis** blackcurrant liqueur
2 *nm Fam* **un grand c.** a large white coffee
3 *adj inv* cream(-coloured)

crémerie [krɛmri] *nf (magasin)* dairy; *Fam* **changer de c.** to go somewhere else, to move on

crémeux, -euse [kremø, -øz] *adj* creamy

crémier, -ère [kremje, -ɛr] *nm,f* dairyman, *f* dairywoman

crémone [kremɔn] *nf* espagnolette

créneau, -x [kreno] *nm* (**a**) *(de rempart)* crenel; *Fig* **monter au c.** to step into the breach (**b**) *(manœuvre)* **faire un c.** to reverse into a (parking) space (**c**) *Com* niche (**d**) *(dans un programme, un emploi du temps)* slot; **c. horaire** time slot

crénelé, -e [krɛnle] *adj* crenellated

créole [kreɔl] **1** *adj* Creole
2 *nmf* **C.** Creole
3 *nm (langue)* Creole
4 *nfpl* **créoles** *(boucles d'oreille)* hoop earrings

crêpe [krɛp] **1** *nf* pancake
2 *nm* (**a**) *(tissu)* crêpe (**b**) *(caoutchouc)* crêpe (rubber); **semelles (de) c.** crêpe soles

crêper [krepe] **1** *vt* (**a**) *(cheveux)* to backcomb (**b**) *(tissu)* to crimp
2 se crêper *vpr Fam Fig* **se c. le chignon** to have a dust-up

crêperie [krɛpri] *nf* pancake restaurant

crépi, -e [krepi] *adj & nm Constr* roughcast

crépir [krepir] *vt Constr* to roughcast

crépitement [krepitmã] *nm (du feu)* crackling

crépiter [krepite] *vi (feu)* to crackle

crépon [krepɔ̃] *nm (papier)* crêpe paper

crépu, -e [krepy] *adj* frizzy

crépuscule [krepyskyl] *nm aussi Fig* twilight; **au c.** at twilight

crescendo [kreʃɛndo] **1** *adv* crescendo; **aller c.** to get louder and louder; *Fig (difficultés)* to get worse and worse
2 *nm* crescendo

cresson [kresɔ̃, krəsɔ̃] *nm* watercress

crétacé, -e [kretase] *Géol* **1** *adj* Cretaceous
2 *nm* **le C.** the Cretaceous period

Crète [krɛt] *nf* **la C.** Crete

crête [krɛt] *nf* (**a**) *(d'oiseau)* crest; *(de coq)* comb (**b**) *(de montagne, de vague, de toit)* crest

crétin, -e [kretɛ̃, -in] *nm,f Fam* cretin

crétois, -e [kretwa, -az] **1** *adj* Cretan
2 *nm,f* **C.** Cretan

cretonne [krətɔn] *nf* cretonne

cretons [krətɔ̃] *nmpl Can* potted pork

creuser [krøze] **1** *vt* (**a**) *(trou, tranchée, puits)* to dig; *Fig* **c. l'écart entre** to widen the gap between; *Fig* **c. un abîme entre deux personnes** to create a gulf between two people (**b**) *(évider)* to hollow (out); **c. la terre** to dig (**c**) *(problème, question)* to look into (**d**) *(donner faim à)* **c. qn** to give sb an appetite; **le grand air, ça creuse** the fresh air gives you an appetite (**e**) *(cambrer)* **c. les reins** to arch one's back (**f**) *(amaigrir)* **il avait le visage creusé par la fatigue/la maladie** his face was gaunt with exhaustion/illness
2 *vi* to dig
3 se creuser *vpr* (**a**) *(s'agrandir) (écart)* to widen (**b**) **se c. (la tête** *ou* **la cervelle) (pour faire qch)** to rack one's brains (to do sth) (**c**) *(visage)* to grow hollow

creuset [krøze] *nm* (**a**) *Chim* crucible (**b**) *Fig* melting pot

creux, -euse [krø, krøz] **1** *adj* (**a**) *(vide) (arbre, mur, dent)* hollow; *(chemin)* sunken; *Fig* **avoir le ventre c.** to be hungry (**b**) *(période, heures)* off-peak (**c**) *(joues)* hollow; *(visage)* gaunt (**d**) *Péj (débat, discours,* *personne)* hollow

2 *adv* **sonner c.** to sound hollow; *Fig* to sound empty

3 *nm* (**a**) *(de la main, dans le sol, sur une route)* hollow; **le c. des reins** the small of the back (**b**) *(d'une vague, d'une courbe)* trough; *Fig* **être au c. de la vague** to have hit rock bottom (**c**) *Fam* **avoir un (petit) c.** to be feeling (a bit) peckish

crevaison [krəvɛzɔ̃] *nf (d'un pneu)* puncture, flat

crevant, -e [krəvɑ̃, -ɑ̃t] *adj Fam* (**a**) *(fatigant)* exhausting (**b**) *(drôle)* priceless

crevasse [krəvas] *nf* (**a**) *(sur la peau)* crack; **avoir des crevasses aux mains** to have chapped hands (**b**) *(dans un mur, le sol)* crack; *(dans un glacier)* crevasse

crevé, -e [krəve] *adj* (**a**) *(éclaté)* *(ballon, pneu)* burst (**b**) *Fam (fatigué)* dead beat (**c**) *très Fam (mort)* dead

crève [krɛv] *nf très Fam* **avoir la c.** *(gros rhume)* to have a stinking cold; **attraper la c.** to catch one's death of cold

crève-cœur [krɛvkœr] *nm inv* heartbreak; **c'est un c. de partir** it's heartbreaking to leave

crève-la-faim [krɛvlafɛ̃] *nm inv Fam* down-and-out

crever [46] [krəve] **1** *vt* (**a**) *(ballon, sac, pneu)* to burst; **c. un œil à qn** to put sb's eye out; **ça me crève le cœur** I'm heartbroken about it; *Fig* **ça crève les yeux** it sticks out a mile; *Fig* **c. l'écran** to have great screen presence (**b**) *Fam (épuiser)* to wear out (**c**) *très Fam* **c. la dalle** to be bloody starving

2 *vi* (**a**) *(éclater)* to burst; **mon pneu a** *ou Fam* **j'ai crevé** I've got a puncture; **c. de** *(jalousie, orgueil)* to be bursting with (**b**) *(mourir) (bête, plante)* to die; *très Fam (personne)* to kick the bucket; *Fam* **il fait une chaleur à c.** it's boiling hot; *Fam* **c. d'envie de faire qch** to be dying to do sth; *Fam* **c. de faim** *(mourir)* to starve to death; *(avoir faim)* to be starving; *Fam* **c. de soif** to be parched; *Fam* **c. de froid/de chaud** to be freezing/boiling; *Fam* **c. de rire** to split one's sides laughing; *Fam* **qu'il crève!** he can go to hell!; *Fam* **plutôt c.!** I'd rather die!

3 se crever *vpr Fam* to wear oneself out

crevette [krəvɛt] *nf* **c. (rose)** prawn; **c. grise** shrimp

cri [kri] *nm* (**a**) *(d'une personne)* cry, shout; *(perçant)* scream; **j'ai entendu des cris** I heard shouting; *Fig* **pousser les hauts cris** to kick up a fuss; **c'est le c. du cœur** it's a cry from the heart; *Mil* **c. de guerre** war cry (**b**) *(d'un animal, d'un oiseau)* cry

criailler [kriaje] *vi* (**a**) *(crier sans arrêt)* to bawl (**b**) *(faisan, pintade)* to cry; *(oie)* to honk

criant, -e [krijɑ̃, -ɑ̃t] *adj (erreur)* glaring; *(preuve, contraste)* striking; *(vérité)* obvious; *(abus, injustice)* blatant; **c. de vérité** *(témoignage, reportage)* obviously true

criard, -e [krijar, -ard] *adj* (**a**) *(aigu) (voix)* shrill (**b**) *(couleur)* loud (**c**) *(enfant)* noisy

crible [kribl] *nm* sieve; *Fig* **passer qch au c.** to go through sth with a fine-tooth comb

criblé, -e [krible] *adj* **c. de** *(trous, balles)* riddled with; *Fig* **être c. de dettes** to be up to one's eyes in debt

cric [krik] *nm* jack

cricket [krikɛt] *nm* cricket

criée [krije] *nf (vente)* (sale by) auction; *(salle)* auction room; *(dehors)* auction area; **à la c.** by auction

crier [66] [krije] **1** *vi* (**a**) *(personne)* to shout, to cry (out); *(fort)* to scream; *(parler très fort)* to shout; **c. de douleur** to cry out *or* scream with pain; **c. contre** *ou* **après qn** to shout at sb; **c. au secours** to shout for help; **c. au scandale** to protest, to be up in arms; **c.**

qch sur les toits to shout sth from the rooftops (**b**) *(souris)* to squeak; *(oiseau)* to call

2 *vt (ordre, injures)* to shout (**à** at); **c. à qn de faire qch** to shout to sb to do sth; **c. son innocence** to protest one's innocence

crime [krim] *nm* (**a**) *Jur & Fig* crime; **ce n'est pas un c.!** it's not a crime!; **c. crapuleux** crime committed for financial gain; **c. d'État** treason; **crimes de guerre** war crimes; **c. contre l'humanité** crime against humanity (**b**) *(meurtre)* murder; **c. passionnel** crime of passion

criminalité [kriminalite] *nf* crime

criminel, -elle [kriminɛl] **1** *adj (acte)* criminal; *Fam* **ce serait c. de la jeter** it would be criminal to throw it away

2 *nm,f* (**a**) *(malfaiteur)* criminal; **c. de guerre** war criminal (**b**) *(assassin)* murderer

criminologie [kriminɔlɔʒi] *nf* criminology

crin [krɛ̃] *nm* horsehair; *Fig* **à tout c., à tous crins** out-and-out

crinière [krinjɛr] *nf aussi Fig* mane

crinoline [krinɔlin] *nf* crinoline

crique [krik] *nf* creek

criquet [krikɛ] *nm* locust

crise [kriz] *nf* (**a**) *(marasme, période d'instabilité)* crisis; **c. de l'énergie** energy crisis; **c. du logement** housing crisis *or* shortage (**b**) *(d'une maladie)* attack; **c. cardiaque** heart attack; **c. de foie** bilious attack (**c**) *(accès)* **c. de colère** fit of anger; **c. de conscience** attack of conscience; **c. de larmes** crying fit; **c. de nerfs** attack of nerves, fit of hysterics; *Fam* **la c. (de rire)!** what a hoot! (**d**) *Fam (colère)* fit of rage; **piquer** *ou* **faire une c.** to throw a fit

crispant, -e [krispɑ̃, -ɑ̃t] *adj Fam* irritating, annoying

crispé, -e [krispe] *adj (visage, personne)* tense; *(sourire, rire)* forced

crisper [krispe] **1** *vt* (**a**) *(poings, mains)* to clench; *(corps)* to tense (**b**) *(énerver)* to irritate, to annoy

2 se crisper *vpr (muscle, visage)* to tense; *(sourire)* to become strained; *(personne)* to get tense

crissement [krismɑ̃] *nm (de la craie sur le tableau)* squeak; *(des pneus, des freins)* squeal; *(du gravier, de la neige)* crunch

crisser [krise] *vi (pneus, freins)* to squeal; *(gravier, neige)* to crunch; *(craie)* to squeak

cristal, -aux [kristal, -o] *nm* crystal; **c. de roche** rock crystal; **cristaux** *(verre)* crystal(ware); *(de sel, de glace)* crystals; *Tech* **cristaux liquides** liquid crystal

cristallin, -e [kristalɛ̃, -in] **1** *adj* (**a**) *(roche)* crystalline (**b**) *Fig (eau, voix)* crystal-clear; *(son, note)* ringing

2 *nm (de l'œil)* crystalline lens

cristalliser [kristalize] **1** *vi* to crystallize

2 se cristalliser *vpr* to crystallize

critère [kritɛr] *nm* criterion; *Ordinat* **c. de tri** sort criterion; *UE* **critères de convergence** convergence criteria

critérium [kriterjɔm] *nm Sport* heat

critique¹ [kritik] *adj (décisif, crucial)* critical

critique² [kritik] **1** *adj (esprit, personne, édition)* critical

2 *nmf* critic; **c. d'art/de cinéma** art/film critic; **c. gastronomique** restaurant critic

3 *nf* (**a**) *(condamnation)* criticism; **si je peux me permettre de vous faire une c.,...** if I could just make one criticism,...; **il n'accepte pas la c.** he can't take criticism (**b**) *(article)* critical article; *Théât & Cin* review; **faire la c. de qch** to review sth (**c**) **la c.** *(l'ensemble des critiques)* the critics

critiquer [kritike] *vt (personne, attitude)* to criticize (**pour** for); **ce n'est pas pour te c., mais…** I don't mean to criticize, but…; **c'est facile de c.** it's easy to criticize

croassement [krɔasmɑ̃] *nm* caw; **des croassements** cawing

croasser [krɔase] *vi* to caw

croate [krɔat] **1** *adj* Croatian
2 *nmf* **C.** Croat, Croatian

Croatie [krɔasi] *nf* **la C.** Croatia

croc [kro] *nm* (**a**) *(de loup, de chien)* fang; *Fam* **avoir les crocs** to be famished (**b**) *(crochet)* hook

croc-en-jambe *(pl* **crocs-en-jambe)** [krɔkɑ̃ʒɑ̃b] *nm* trip; **faire un c. à qn** to trip sb up

croche [krɔʃ] *nf Mus Br* quaver, *Am* eighth note

croche-pied *(pl* **croche-pieds)** [krɔʃpje] = **croc-en-jambe**

crochet [krɔʃɛ] *nm* (**a**) *(pour accrocher)* hook; *Fig* **vivre aux crochets de qn** to live off sb (**b**) *(pour tricoter)* crochet hook; *(technique)* crochet; **faire du c.** to (do) crochet (**c**) *(détour)* **faire un c. (par)** *(personne)* to make a detour (through) (**d**) *Typ* square bracket; **entre crochets** in square brackets (**e**) *(coup de poing)* **c. du gauche/du droit** left/right hook (**f**) *(d'un serpent)* fang

crocheter [39] [krɔʃte] *vt (serrure)* to pick; *(porte)* to pick the lock on

crochu, -e [krɔʃy] *adj (nez, bec)* hooked; *(doigts)* claw-like

crocodile [krɔkɔdil] *nm* crocodile; **en c.** *(sac, chaussures)* crocodile(-skin)

crocus [krɔkys] *nm* crocus

croire [25] [krwar] **1** *vt* (**a**) *(accepter, faire confiance à)* to believe; *Fam Ironique* **c'est ça, je te crois!** is that so?; *Fam* **faut pas c.!** don't you believe it!; **croyez-moi, ce n'était pas facile** believe (you) me, it wasn't easy; **à l'en c.,…** to hear him, you'd think…; **si on en croit la rumeur,…** if the rumour is to be believed,…; **je n'en croyais pas mes yeux/mes oreilles** I couldn't believe my eyes/my ears (**b**) *(penser)* to think; **je crois que oui** I think so; **je crois que non** I don't think so; **je ne crois pas** I don't think so; **vous croyez?** do you really think so?; **je vous croyais anglais/riche** I thought you were English/rich; **j'ai cru nécessaire de…** I thought it necessary to…; **j'ai cru bien faire** I thought *or* believed I was doing the right thing; **elle ne croyait pas si bien dire** she didn't know how right she was; **je n'aurais pas cru cela de lui** I would never have thought it of him; **on croirait qu'il dort** you'd think he was asleep
2 *vi (avoir la foi)* to be a believer
3 croire à *vt ind* (**a**) *(envisager)* **le médecin crut à une rougeole** the doctor thought it was measles (**b**) *(accepter)* to believe; **veuillez c.** *ou* **je vous prie de c. à l'expression de mes sentiments distingués** yours sincerely (**c**) *(avoir confiance en, adhérer à)* to believe in
4 croire en *vt ind (personne, talent, Dieu)* to believe in
5 se croire *vpr* **il se croit intelligent** he thinks he's clever; **il se croit tout permis** he thinks he can get away with anything; **on se serait cru en octobre** it felt like October; *Fam* **se c. sorti de la cuisse de Jupiter** to think a lot of oneself; *Fam* **il s'y croit** he thinks a lot of himself

croisade [krwazad] *nf Hist & Fig* crusade; **partir en c.** to go on a crusade

croisé, -e [krwaze] **1** *adj (manteau, veste)* double-breasted
2 *nm Hist* crusader

croisement [krwazmɑ̃] *nm* (**a**) *(carrefour)* crossroads *(singulier),* intersection (**b**) *(d'animaux)* crossing; *(animal)* cross (**entre** between)

croiser [krwaze] **1** *vt* (**a**) *(couper)* *(ligne, route)* to cross; **c. le regard de qn** to meet sb's gaze (**b**) *(passer à côté de)* *(véhicule, personne)* to pass (**c**) *(mettre l'un sur l'autre)* **c. les jambes** to cross one's legs; **c. les bras** to fold one's arms; *Fig* **c. les doigts** to keep one's fingers crossed; **je croise les doigts** fingers crossed (**d**) *(animaux, espèces)* to cross(breed)
2 *vi (navire)* to cruise
3 se croiser *vpr* (**a**) *(lignes, routes)* to cross, to intersect; *(regards)* to meet (**b**) *(personnes)* *(dans la rue)* to walk past each other; *(se voir rapidement)* to meet briefly; *(lettres)* to cross

croiseur [krwazœr] *nm Naut* cruiser

croisière [krwazjɛr] *nf* cruise; **faire une c.** to go on a cruise

croisillon [krwazijɔ̃] *nm* (**a**) *(de croix)* crosspiece (**b**) **croisillons** *(de fenêtre, de barrière)* latticework; *(sur une tarte)* lattice

croissais *etc voir* **croître**

croissance [krwasɑ̃s] *nf (d'un enfant) & Écon* growth; **en pleine c.** growing rapidly; **finir sa c.** *(enfant)* to stop growing

croissant¹, -e [krwasɑ̃, -ɑ̃t] *adj (plante, tendance, angoisse)* growing; *(ordre)* ascending; *(chaleur, température)* increasing

croissant² *nm* (**a**) *(arc de cercle)* crescent; **un c. de lune** a crescent moon; **en c.** crescent-shaped (**b**) *(pâtisserie)* croissant; **c. au beurre/ordinaire** croissant made with/without butter

croissant³ *voir* **croître**

croître [4b] [krwatr] *vi* (**a**) *(enfant, plantes)* to grow (**b**) *(vente, chiffre)* to grow, to increase (**de** by); *(jours)* to get longer; *(lune)* to wax; **aller croissant** *(succès)* to grow and grow; *(suspense)* to get worse and worse

croix [krwa] *nf* cross; **signer d'une c.** to make one's mark; *Fam Fig* **faire une c. sur qch** to say goodbye to sth; **en (forme de) c.** cross-shaped; **les bras en c.** with one's arms stretched out at the sides; **c. de bois c. de fer, si je mens je vais en enfer** cross my heart and hope to die; **c'est la c. et la bannière** it's the devil of a job; **c. gammée** swastika; **la c. de Lorraine** the cross of Lorraine *(symbol of the Gaullist movement);* **la C.-Rouge** the Red Cross

croquant, -e [krɔkɑ̃, -ɑ̃t] *adj* crisp, crunchy

croque-au-sel [krɔkosɛl] **à la croque-au-sel** *adv* = raw and seasoned only with salt

croque-madame [krɔkmadam] *nm inv* = toasted cheese and ham sandwich topped with fried egg

croque-monsieur [krɔkməsjø] *nm inv* = toasted cheese and ham sandwich

croque-mort *(pl* **croque-morts)** [krɔkmɔr] *nm Fam* undertaker

croquer [krɔke] **1** *vt* (**a**) *(pomme, bonbon)* to crunch; *Fig (fortune, héritage)* to squander; **à sucer ou à c.** *(sur boîte de médicaments)* may be sucked or chewed; *Fig* **c. la vie à belles dents** to make the most of life; **il est à c.** *(enfant)* he looks good enough to eat; **joli** *ou*

mignon à c. as pretty as a picture (**b**) *(faire un croquis de)* to sketch

2 *vi* (**a**) *(pomme, salade)* to be crunchy (**b**) *(mordre)* **c. dans** to bite into

croquet [kɔkɛ] *nm (jeu)* croquet

croquette [kɔkɛt] *nf (de pomme de terre, de viande, de poisson)* croquette; **croquettes** *(pour chien, chat)* biscuits

croquis [kɔki] *nm* sketch; **faire un c. de qch** to make a sketch of sth

cross [kɔs] *nm (sport)* cross-country running; *(événement)* cross-country run

crosse [kɔs] *nf* (**a**) *(de fusil)* butt; *(de pistolet)* grip; *(d'évêque)* crook (**b**) *(de hockey)* stick; *Fam Fig* **chercher des crosses à qn** to try to pick a fight with sb (**c**) *Can (jeu)* lacrosse

crotte [kɔt] *nf* (**a**) *(de cheval, de mouton, de lapin)* dung, droppings; **une c. de chien** dog dirt; *Fam* **c.!** blast! (**b**) **une c. de chocolat** a chocolate (**c**) *Vieilli (boue)* mud

crotter [kɔte] 1 *vt (chaussures, manteau)* to cover in mud

2 **se crotter** *vpr* to get covered in mud

crottin [kɔtɛ̃] *nm* (**a**) *(excrément) (de cheval)* dung (**b**) *(fromage)* small goat's-milk cheese

croulant, -e [krulɑ̃, -ɑ̃t] 1 *adj (bâtiment)* crumbling

2 *nm,f très Fam* **(vieux) c.** (old) wrinkly

crouler [krule] *vi (bâtiment)* to crumble; **c. sous le poids de qch** to give way under the weight of sth; **c. sous le travail** to be snowed under with work; **la salle croulait sous les applaudissements** the audience brought the house down

croupe [krup] *nf* rump; **monter en c.** to ride behind

croupi, -e [krupi] *adj (eau)* stagnant

croupier [krupje] *nm* croupier

croupion [krupjɔ̃] *nm (d'oiseau)* rump; *(d'une volaille) Br* parson's *or Am* pope's nose

croupir [krupir] *vi* (**a**) *(eau)* to stagnate (**b**) *(végéter)* **c. en prison** to rot in prison

croupissant, -e [krupisɑ̃, -ɑ̃t] *adj (eau, vie)* stagnant

CROUS [krus] *nm (abrév* **Centre régional des œuvres universitaires et scolaires)** = organization responsible for student accommodation and catering etc

croustillant, -e [krustijɑ̃, -ɑ̃t] *adj* (**a**) *(biscuit, pâte)* crisp; *(pain)* crusty (**b**) *Fig (histoire, détails)* spicy

croustiller [krustije] *vi (biscuit, pâte)* to be crisp; *(pain)* to be crusty

croustilles [krustij] *nfpl Can Br* crisps, *Am* chips

croûte [krut] *nf* (**a**) *(de pain, de tarte)* crust; *(de fromage)* rind; *(d'une plaie)* scab; **la c. terrestre** the earth's crust; *Fam* **gagner sa c.** to earn one's bread and butter (**b**) *Fam (mauvaise peinture)* daub

croûton [krutɔ̃] *nm* (**a**) *(de pain)* end (**b**) *(dans la soupe, les salades)* crouton (**c**) *Fam* **(vieux) c.** old fossil

croyable [krwajabl] *adj* believable, credible; **ce n'est pas c.!** it's unbelievable!, it's incredible!

croyais *etc voir* **croire**

croyance [krwajɑ̃s] *nf* belief (**en** in)

croyant, -e [krwajɑ̃, -ɑ̃t] 1 *adj* **être c.** to be a believer

2 *nm,f* believer

CRS [seɛrɛs] *nm (abrév* **compagnie républicaine de sécurité)** = French riot policeman; **les C.** = French riot police

CRS

The CRS is the Minister of the Interior's police force, whose primary responsibility is to ensure public order at demonstrations and to quell riots. They have been criticized for certain strong-arm tactics.

cru¹, -e [kry] *adj* (**a**) *(viande, poisson, légumes)* raw; *(lait)* unpasteurized (**b**) *(couleur, lumière)* garish (**c**) *(licencieux) (langage)* crude (**d**) *(direct) (réponse, personne)* blunt (**e**) **monter à c.** to ride bareback (**f**) *Belg, Can & Suisse (temps, bâtiment)* damp and cold

cru² *nm (terroir)* vineyard, *(vin)* wine; **un grand c.** a vintage wine; **du c.** local; *Fig* **une histoire de son (propre) c.** a story of his/her own invention

cru³, -e *voir* **croire**

cruauté [kryote] *nf* (**a**) *(dureté)* cruelty (**envers** to) (**b**) *(acte)* (act of) cruelty

cruche [kryʃ] 1 *nf* (**a**) *(récipient, contenu) Br* jug, *Am* pitcher; *Prov* **tant va la c. à l'eau qu'à la fin elle se casse** the pitcher has gone to the well once too often (**b**) *Fam (imbécile)* ass

2 *adj Fam (bête)* dumb, stupid

cruchon [kryʃɔ̃] *nm (récipient, contenu)* small *Br* jug *or Am* pitcher

crucial, -e, -aux, -ales [krysjal, -o] *adj* crucial

crucifier [66] [krysifje] *vt* to crucify

crucifix [krysifi] *nm* crucifix

crucifixion [krysifiksjɔ̃] *nf* crucifixion

cruciforme [krysiform] *adj* cruciform; **vis/tournevis c.** Phillips® screw/screwdriver

cruciverbiste [krysiverbist] *nmf* crossword enthusiast

crudité [krydite] *nf* (**a**) **crudités** *(légumes)* assorted raw vegetables (**b**) *(d'une couleur, d'une lumière)* garishness (**c**) *(d'une expression)* crudeness

crue [kry] *nf (montée)* swelling; *(inondation)* flood; **rivière en c.** river in spate

cruel, -elle [kryɛl] *adj* cruel (**envers** *ou* **avec** to)

cruellement [kryɛlmɑ̃] *adv* cruelly; **être c. éprouvé** to be deeply affected; **faire c. défaut** to be sadly lacking

crûment [krymɑ̃] *adv* (**a**) *(parler) (sans détours)* bluntly; *(grossièrement)* crudely (**b**) **éclairé c.** garishly lit

crustacé [krystase] *nm Zool* crustacean; **crustacés** crustaceans; *Culin* seafood

cruzado [kruzado] *nm* cruzado

cryogénie [krijoʒeni] *nf* cryogenics *(singulier)*

cryogénique [krijoʒenik] *adj* cryogenic

cryothérapie [krijoterapi] *nf* cryotherapy

cryptage [kriptaʒ] *nm* encoding

crypte [kript] *nf* crypt

crypté, -e [kripte] *adj (message)* & *TV* coded

crypter [kripte] *vt* to encode

CSA [seɛsa] *nm (abrév* **Conseil supérieur de l'audiovisuel)** = organization regulating French broadcasting, *Br* ≃ ITC

CSG [seɛsʒe] *nf (abrév* **Contribution sociale généralisée)** = income-based tax deducted at source

Cuba [kyba] *n* Cuba

cubain, -e [kybɛ̃, -ɛn] 1 *adj* Cuban

2 *nm,f* **C.** Cuban

cube [kyb] **1** *nm* cube; *(de jeu)* building block; **élever un nombre au c.** to cube a number

2 *adj (mètre, centimètre)* cubic

cubique [kybik] *adj* cubic

cubisme [kybism] *nm* cubism

cubiste [kybist] *adj & nmf* Cubist

cubitus [kybitys] *nm* ulna

cucul [kyky] *adj inv Fam* **c. (la praline)** *(personne, décoration)* twee; *(film, livre)* corny

cueillette [kœjɛt] *nf (action)* gathering, picking; *(fruits, noisettes, baies)* harvest

cueillir [5] [kœjir] *vt (fleurs, fruits)* to gather, to pick; *Fig* **la mort l'a cueilli en pleine jeunesse** he was cut down in his prime; *Fam* **c. qn** to pick sb up

cui-cui [kɥikɥi] **1** *nm* cheeping

2 *exclam* cheep!

cuiller, cuillère [kɥijɛr] *nf* (**a**) *(couvert)* spoon; *(contenu)* spoon(ful); *Fam Fig* **il n'y va pas avec le dos de la c.** he doesn't go in for half measures; *Fam Fig* **en deux** *ou* **trois coups de c. à pot** in two shakes (of a lamb's tail); *Fam* **être à ramasser à la petite c.** *(épuisé)* to be all in; *(déprimé)* to be down in the dumps; **c. à café, petite c.** teaspoon; **c. à soupe,** *Can* **c. à table** soup spoon; *(pour mesurer)* tablespoon (**b**) *(pour la pêche)* spoon (bait); **pêcher la truite à la c.** to troll for trout

cuillerée [kɥijere] *nf* spoonful; **une c. à café** a teaspoonful; **une c. à soupe** a tablespoonful

cuir [kɥir] *nm* (**a**) *(matière)* leather; *(veste)* leather jacket; **chaussures/pantalon en c.** leather shoes/ trousers (**b**) *(d'un éléphant, d'un rhinocéros)* hide (**c**) **c. chevelu** scalp

cuirasse [kɥiras] *nf* (**a**) *(protection)* breastplate; *Fig* **trouver le défaut dans la c. de qn** to find the chink in sb's armour (**b**) *(d'un navire de guerre, d'un blindé)* armour (plating)

cuirassé [kɥirase] *nm* battleship

cuirassier [kɥirasje] *nm* cuirassier

cuire [18] [kɥir] **1** *vt* (**a**) *(aliment)* to cook; **c. qch à l'eau** to boil sth; **c. qch à la vapeur** to steam sth; **c. qch au four** to bake sth (**b**) *(briques, poterie)* to fire (**c**) *(chauffer) (sujet: soleil)* to bake

2 *vi* (**a**) *(aliments, plat)* to cook; **faire trop c. qch** to overcook sth (**b**) *(brûler)* **les joues me cuisent** my cheeks are burning (**c**) *Fam (avoir très chaud)* to be boiling

3 *v impersonnel* **il vous en cuira** you'll regret it

cuisais *etc voir* **cuire**

cuisant, -e [kɥizã, -ãt] *adj (douleur)* burning; *(froid)* biting; *(déception, échec)* bitter

cuisine [kɥizin] *nf* (**a**) *(pièce)* kitchen; *(sur un navire)* galley (**b**) *(art)* cooking, cookery; **faire la c.** to do the cooking; **bien faire la c.** to be a good cook; **c. au beurre/à l'huile** cooking with butter/oil; **la c. française/chinoise** French/Chinese cooking *or* cuisine (**c**) *(meubles)* kitchen (furniture); **c. intégrée,** *Suisse* **c. agencée** fitted kitchen (**d**) *Fam (magouilles)* scheming

cuisiner [kɥizine] **1** *vi* to cook; **bien c.** to be a good cook

2 *vt* (**a**) *(préparer)* to cook; **plats cuisinés** ready-cooked meals (**b**) *Fam (interroger)* to grill

cuisinette [kɥizinɛt] *nf Offic & Can & Suisse* kitchenette

cuisinier, -ère [kɥizinje, -ɛr] **1** *nm,f* cook

2 *nf* **cuisinière** stove, *Br* cooker; **cuisinière électrique/**

à gaz electric/gas stove *or Br* cooker; **c. mixte** combined gas and electric stove *or Br* cooker

cuissardes [kɥisard] *nfpl (bottes de femme)* thigh boots; *(de pêche)* waders

cuisse [kɥis] *nf* thigh; **cuisses de grenouilles** frogs' legs; **c. de poulet** chicken leg

cuisson [kɥisɔ̃] *nf* (**a**) *(d'aliments)* cooking; *(de pain, de gâteau)* baking; **temps de c.** cooking time; **c. à la vapeur** steaming (**b**) *(des briques, de la porcelaine)* firing

cuissot [kɥiso] *nm (de venaison)* haunch

cuistot [kɥisto] *nm Fam* cook

cuit, -e [kɥi, kɥit] *adj* (**a**) *(aliment)* cooked; **bien c.** well done; **c. à point** done to a turn; **trop c.** overcooked; **pas assez c.** undercooked; **c. au four** baked; **c. à la vapeur** steamed (**b**) *Fam Fig* **être c.** to have had it; **c'est c.!** we've had it!; **c'est du tout c.** it's a cinch

cuite [kɥit] *nf Fam* **avoir/prendre une c.** to be/get plastered

cuivre [kɥivr] *nm* (**a**) *(métal)* **c. (rouge)** copper; **c. jaune** brass; **les cuivres** *(objets)* copper(ware); *(en cuivre jaune)* brasses (**b**) *Mus* **les cuivres** the brass (section)

cuivré, -e [kɥivre] *adj (peau, teint) (naturellement)* copper-coloured; *(par le soleil)* bronzed

cul [ky] **1** *nm* (**a**) *Fam (d'une personne)* backside, *Br* bum; **en rester** *ou* **tomber sur le c.** to be flabbergasted; **c'est à se taper le c. par terre** it's an absolute scream; **de c.** *(magazine, film)* porn; **être comme c. et chemise** to be as thick as thieves; *Vulg* **l'avoir dans le c.** to be screwed up; *Vulg* **en avoir plein le c.** to be pissed off; **avoir qn au c.** to have sb on one's tail (**b**) *Fam (chance)* **avoir du c.** to be jammy (**c**) *(d'un sac, d'un tonneau, d'une bouteille)* bottom; **boire c. sec** to down one's drink in one go; **c. sec!** bottoms up!

2 *adj Fam (personne, décoration)* twee; *(livre)* corny

culasse [kylas] *nf* (**a**) *(de fusil, de pistolet)* breech (**b**) *(de moteur)* cylinder head

culbute [kylbyt] *nf* (**a**) *(cabriole)* somersault; **faire la c.** to do a somersault (**b**) *(chute)* tumble; **faire la c.** to take a tumble

culbuter [kylbyte] **1** *vi (vase, statue)* to topple over; *(personne)* to take a tumble; *(voiture)* to overturn

2 *vt (objet)* to knock over

cul-de-jatte *(pl* **culs-de-jatte)** [kydʒat] *nmf* legless cripple

cul-de-poule [kydpul] *nm* **avoir la bouche en c.** to have pursed lips

cul-de-sac *(pl* **culs-de-sac)** [kydsak] *nm* dead end, cul-de-sac; *Fig* dead end

culinaire [kylinɛr] *adj* culinary

culminant, -e [kylminã, -ãt] *adj* **point c.** *(d'une chaîne de montagnes)* highest point; *(de la gloire, d'une carrière)* height, peak

culminer [kylmine] *vi* (**a**) **le mont Blanc culmine à 4807 mètres** Mont Blanc is 4,807 metres at its highest point (**b**) *(crise, tension)* to peak

culot [kylo] *nm* (**a**) *Fam (audace)* cheek, nerve; **il a un de ces culots!** he's got a nerve!; **y aller au c.** to brazen it out (**b**) *(de douille, de cartouche)* base

culotte [kylɔt] *nf* (**a**) *(sous-vêtement) (de femme)* panties, knickers; *(d'enfant)* pants (**b**) *(pantalon)* **c. courte** short trousers; **c. de cheval** jodhpurs; *Fam Fig* jodhpur thighs; **c. de golf** plus-fours; *Fam Fig* **c'est elle qui porte la c.** she's the one who wears the trousers; *Fam* **faire dans sa c.** to dirty one's pants; *Fig* to wet oneself (**c**) *(de bœuf)* rump

culotté, -e [kylɔte] *adj Fam* cheeky

culpabiliser [kylpabilize] **1** *vt* **c. qn** to make sb feel guilty

2 *vi* to feel guilty

culpabilité [kylpabilite] *nf* guilt

culte [kylt] *nm* (**a**) *(vénération)* worship; *Fig* cult; *Fig* **vouer un c. à qn** to (hero-)worship sb; **c. de la personnalité** personality cult (**b**) *(religion)* religion; **liberté du c.** freedom of worship (**c**) *(service protestant)* (church) service

cul-terreux *(pl* **culs-terreux**) [kytɛrø] *nm Fam Péj* country bumpkin, yokel

cultivable [kyltivabl] *adj* suitable for cultivation

cultivateur, -trice [kyltivatœr, -tris] **1** *nm,f* farmer; **petits cultivateurs** small farmers, *Br* smallholders

2 *nm (machine)* cultivator

cultivé, -e [kyltive] *adj* (**a**) *(terre, champs)* cultivated (**b**) *(personne)* cultured, cultivated

cultiver [kyltive] **1** *vt* (**a**) *(sol, champ)* to cultivate, to farm; *(plantes)* to grow (**b**) *(art, relations, amitié, image)* to cultivate

2 se cultiver *vpr* to improve one's mind

culture [kyltyr] *nf* (**a**) *(du sol)* cultivation; *(de plantes)* growing; **cultures** land under cultivation (**b**) *(espèce cultivée)* crop (**c**) *(connaissances)* culture; **un homme d'une grande c.** a highly cultured man; **c. générale** general knowledge (**d**) *(civilisation)* culture (**e**) *Biol* **c. microbienne/de tissus** bacteria/tissue culture (**f**) **c. physique** physical training

culturel, -elle [kyltyrɛl] *adj* cultural

culturisme [kyltyrism] *nm* body-building

culturiste [kyltyrist] *nmf* body-builder

cumin [kymɛ̃] *nm* cumin

cumul [kymyl] *nm* **c. des fonctions** plurality of offices; **c. des traitements** drawing of more than one salary

cumulable [kymylabl] *adj (fonctions)* which can be held concurrently; *(traitements)* which can be drawn concurrently

cumulatif, -ive [kymylatif, -iv] *adj* cumulative

cumuler [kymyle] *vt* **c. des fonctions** to hold more than one office; **c. plusieurs traitements** to draw several salaries; **c. plusieurs emplois** to have several jobs

cumulo-nimbus [kymylonɛ̃bys] *nm inv* cumulo-nimbus

cumulus [kymylys] *nm inv* cumulus

cupide [kypid] *adj* avaricious

cupidité [kypidite] *nf* cupidity

Cupidon [kypidɔ̃] *npr* Cupid

curable [kyrabl] *adj (maladie)* curable

curaçao [kyraso] *nm* curaçao (liqueur)

curage [kyraʒ] *nm* cleaning out

curare [kyrar] *nm* curare

cure [kyr] *nf* (**a**) *(traitement)* (course of) treatment; **c. d'amaigrissement** (course of) slimming treatment; **faire une c. de désintoxication** *(alcoolique)* to receive treatment for alcohol dependency; *(toxicomane)* to receive treatment for drug dependency; **faire une c. de vitamines** to go/be on a course of vitamins; **faire une c. de fruits** to eat a lot of fruit; **faire une c. de repos/de sommeil** to go/be on a rest cure/sleep cure (**b**) *(dans une ville d'eau)* **c. (thermale)** spa

cure; **faire une c.** to take the waters (**c**) *(fonction de curé)* office of a parish priest

curé [kyre] *nm* parish priest; **aller à l'école chez les curés** to be educated by priests

cure-dents [kyrdɑ̃] *nm inv* toothpick

curée [kyre] *nf (lutte)* scramble; **ce fut la c. entre les héritiers** the heirs started to fight over the spoils

cure-pipe *(pl* **cure-pipes**) [kyrpip] *nm* pipe-cleaner

curer [kyre] **1** *vt* to clean out

2 se curer *vpr* **se c. les ongles/les oreilles** to clean one's nails/one's ears

curetage [kyrtaʒ] *nm (en chirurgie)* D&C

curieusement [kyrjøzmɑ̃] *adv (bizarrement)* curiously (enough)

curieux, -euse [kyrjø, -øz] **1** *adj* (**a**) *(intéressé)* curious; **je serais c. de voir cela** I'd be curious to see that (**b**) *(indiscret)* curious, inquisitive (**c**) *(étrange)* curious, strange; **chose curieuse,...** curiously enough,...

2 *nm,f* inquisitive person; *(badaud)* onlooker

curiosité [kyrjozite] *nf* (**a**) *(intellectuelle)* curiosity; **avec c.** curiously (**b**) *(indiscrétion)* curiosity, inquisitiveness; **par c.** out of curiosity; *Prov* **la c. est un vilain défaut** curiosity killed the cat (**c**) *(objet)* curio; **les curiosités d'une ville** the interesting sights of a town

curiste [kyrist] *nmf* = patient taking a spa cure

curriculum vitae [kyrikylɔmvite] *nm inv Br* curriculum vitae, *Am* résumé

curry [kyri] *nm* curry; **poulet au c., c. de poulet** chicken curry

curseur [kyrsœr] *nm aussi Ordinat* cursor

cursif, -ive [kyrsif, -iv] *adj (écriture)* cursive

cursus [kyrsys] *nm Univ* degree course

cutané, -e [kytane] *adj* skin, *Spéc* cutaneous

cuti [kyti] *nf* skin test; **virer sa c.** to have a positive skin test; *Fam Fig* to change radically

cuti-réaction *(pl* **cuti-réactions**) [kytireaksjɔ̃] *nf* skin test

cutter [kœtœr, kytɛr] *nm* Stanley knife®

cuve [kyv] *nf (réservoir)* (storage) tank; *(de machine à laver)* tub; *(pour la fermentation des alcools, du vin)* vat; *(en photographie)* tank

cuvée [kyve] *nf* (**a**) *(quantité)* vatful (**b**) *(produit)* vintage; *Fig* batch

cuver [kyve] *vt Fam* **c. (son vin)** to sleep it off

cuvette [kyvɛt] *nf* (**a**) *(récipient)* basin, bowl (**b**) *(de W.-C.)* bowl (**c**) *Géog* basin

CV¹ [seve] *Aut (abrév* **cheval-vapeur**) hp

CV² *nm (abrév* **curriculum vitae**) *Br* CV, *Am* résumé

cyanure [sjanyr] *nm* cyanide

cybercafé [sibɛrkafe] *nm* cybercafé

cyberespace [sibɛrɛspas] *nm* cyberspace

cybernétique [sibɛrnetik] **1** *adj* cybernetic

2 *nf* cybernetics *(singulier)*

cybersexe [sibɛrsɛks] *nm* cybersex

cyclable [siklabl] *adj voir* **piste**

cyclamen [siklamɛn] *nm* cyclamen

cycle [sikl] *nm* (**a**) *(suite, mouvement)* cycle; **c. menstruel** menstrual cycle (**b**) *(dans l'éducation)* **premier/second c.** *Scol* lower/upper classes *(in secondary school)*; *Univ* first/last two years *(of degree course)*; *Univ* **troisième c.** postgraduate studies; **c. I/II/III** = subdivisions of primary school (between the ages of 2 and 4, 5 and 7, and 8 and 10 respectively) (**c**) *(bicyclette)* cycle

cyclique [siklik] *adj* cyclical

cyclisme [siklism] *nm* cycling
cycliste [siklist] **1** *nmf* cyclist
  2 *adj voir* **coureur, course**
cyclo-cross [siklokrɔs] *nm inv* cyclo-cross
cyclomoteur [siklomɔtœr] *nm* moped
cyclone [siklon] *nm* cyclone
cyclope [siklɔp] *nm* cyclops
cyclothymique [siklotimik] *adj Psy* manic-depressive
cyclotourisme [sikloturism] *nm* bicycle touring
cygne [siɲ] *nm* swan
cylindre [silɛ̃dr] *nm* (**a**) *aussi Aut* cylinder; **une quatre cylindres** a four-cylinder car (**b**) *(rouleau)* roller
cylindrée [silɛ̃dre] *nf* (cubic) capacity; **petite/grosse c.** *(moto)* motorbike with a small/large engine; *(voiture)* car with a small/large engine

cylindrique [silɛ̃drik] *adj* cylindrical
cymbale [sɛ̃bal] *nf* cymbal
cynique [sinik] **1** *adj* cynical
  2 *nmf* cynic
cyniquement [sinikmɑ̃] *adv* cynically
cynisme [sinism] *nm* cynicism
cyprès [siprɛ] *nm* cypress (tree)
cypriote [siprijɔt] **1** *adj* Cypriot
  2 *nmf* **C.** Cypriot
cyrillique [sirilik] *adj (alphabet, caractères)* Cyrillic
cystite [sistit] *nf* cystitis
cytomégalovirus [sitomegalovirys] *nm Méd* cytomegalovirus, CMV
cytoplasme [sitɔplasm] *nm Biol* cytoplasm

D

D¹, d [de] *nm inv* D, d

D² [de] *nf* (*abrév* **route départementale**) = designation of secondary road

DAB [deabe] *nm* (*abrév* **distributeur automatique de billets**) ATM

dactylo [daktilo] **1** *nmf* (*abrév* **dactylographe**) typist
2 *nf* (*abrév* **dactylographie**) typing

dactylographe [daktilograf] *nmf* typist

dactylographie [daktilografi] *nf* typing

dactylographier [66] [daktilografje] *vt* to type

dada [dada] *nm* (**a**) (*langage enfantin*) (*cheval*) geegee; **à d.** on horseback (**b**) *Fam* (*sujet favori*) hobbyhorse

dadais [dadɛ] *nm Fam* **un grand d.** a great gawk

dague [dag] *nf* (*épée*) dagger

dahlia [dalja] *nm* dahlia

daigner [deɲe] *vt* **d. faire qch** to deign to do sth

daim [dɛ̃] *nm* (**a**) (*animal*) (*fallow*) deer; (*mâle*) buck (**b**) (*peau*) suede; **gants/veste en d.** suede gloves/jacket

dais [dɛ] *nm* canopy

Dakar [dakar] *n* Dakar

dalaï-lama [dalailama] *nm* dalai lama

dallage [dalaʒ] *nm* (*action, revêtement*) paving

dalle [dal] *nf* (**a**) (*de pierre*) paving stone; (*de marbre*) slab; (*de moquette, de lino*) tile (**b**) *Fam* **que d.** (*rien*) damn all; **j'y vois que d.** I can't see a damn thing (**c**) *Fam* **avoir** *ou* **crever la d.** to be starving

daller [dale] *vt* to pave

dalmatien, -enne [dalmasjɛ̃, -ɛn] *nm,f* (*chien*) Dalmatian

daltonien, -enne [daltɔnjɛ̃, -ɛn] **1** *adj* colour-blind
2 *nm,f* colour-blind person

daltonisme [daltɔnism] *nm* colour blindness

dam [dã] *nm* **au grand d. de qn** to the great displeasure of sb

damage [damaʒ] *nm* (*de la terre, de la neige*) packing down

Damas [damas] *n* Damascus; *Fig* **trouver son chemin de D.** to see the light

damas [damas] *nm* damask

damassine [damasin] *nf Suisse* (*fruit*) plum; (*eau de vie*) plum brandy

dame [dam] *nf* (**a**) (*femme*) lady; **d. de compagnie** lady's companion; **d. d'honneur** lady-in-waiting (**b**) (*aux cartes, aux échecs*) queen; (*au jeu de dames*) king (**c**) **dames** (*jeu*) *Br* draughts, *Am* checkers

damer [dame] *vt* (**a**) *Fam Fig* **d. le pion à qn** to put one over on sb (**b**) (*terre, neige*) to pack down

dameuse [damøz] *nf* piste basher

damier [damje] *nm Br* draughtboard, *Am* checkerboard; **tissu à damiers** checked material

damnation [danasjɔ̃] *nf* damnation

damné, -e [dane] **1** *adj* damned
2 *nm,f* damned soul; *Fig* **souffrir comme un d.** to suffer sheer torture

damner [dane] **1** *vt* to damn
2 se damner *vpr* to damn oneself; **il se damnerait pour...** he'd sell his soul to the devil for...

Damoclès [damɔklɛs] *n voir* **épée**

dancing [dãsiŋ] *nm Vieilli* dance hall

dandinement [dãdinmã] *nm* waddle

dandiner [dãdine] **se dandiner** *vpr* to waddle; **se d. d'un pied sur l'autre** to shift from foot to foot

dandy [dãdi] *nm* dandy

Danemark [danmark] *nm* **le D.** Denmark

danger [dãʒe] *nm* danger; **être en d.** to be in danger; **mettre en d. la vie de qn** to endanger sb's life; **d. de mort** (*sur panneau*) danger of death; **hors de d.** out of danger; **d. public** public menace

dangereusement [dãʒrøzmã] *adv* dangerously

dangereux, -euse [dãʒrø, -øz] *adj* dangerous

danois, -e [danwa, -az] **1** *adj* Danish
2 *nm,f* **D.** Dane
3 *nm* (**a**) (*langue*) Danish (**b**) (*chien*) Great Dane

dans [dã] *prép* (**a**) (*à l'intérieur de*) in; **d. une boîte** in(side) a box; **il est d. sa chambre** he's in his room; **lire qch d. un journal** to read sth in a newspaper; **tomber d. l'escalier** to fall down the stairs; **il pleut d. tout le pays** it's raining all over the country; **être d. le commerce/l'informatique** to be in business/computers; **travailler d. le bruit/la saleté** to work in noisy/dirty surroundings
(**b**) (*avec mouvement*) into; **il est entré d. leur chambre** he went into their room
(**c**) (*exprime la temporalité*) in; **d. vingt ans** in twenty years, in twenty years' time; **d. peu de temps** soon, shortly
(**d**) (*indique une provenance*) out of; **boire d. un verre** to drink out of a glass; **découper un article d. le journal** to cut an article out of the paper
(**e**) (*indique une approximation*) **d. les quarante ans/les 3000 euros** about forty (years old)/3,000 euros
(**f**) (*pour indiquer un état*) in; **d. mon excitation/ma hâte** in my excitement/hurry

dansant, -e [dãsã, -ãt] *adj voir* **soirée, thé**

danse [dãs] *nf* (*ensemble de mouvements, musique*) dance; **la d.** (*art*) dancing; **d. classique** ballet; **d. contemporaine** contemporary dance; **d. folklorique** folk dance/dancing; *Méd* **d. de Saint-Guy** St Vitus's dance; **la d. du ventre** belly-dancing

danser [dɑ̃se] **1** *vi* to dance; **le bouchon/le bateau danse sur l'eau** the cork/the boat is bobbing up and down on the water; *Fig* **avec lui je ne sais jamais sur quel pied d.** I never know where I am with him **2** *vt (valse, tango)* to dance

danseur, -euse [dɑ̃sœr, -øz] *nm,f* dancer; **d. (classique** *ou* **de ballet)** ballet-dancer; **d. étoile** lead dancer; **danseuse étoile** prima ballerina; **être en danseuse** *(en cyclisme)* to stand on the pedals

Danube [danyb] *nm* **le D.** the Danube

dard [dar] *nm (d'insecte, de scorpion)* sting

darder [darde] *vt* **il a dardé sur moi un regard furieux** he shot a furious look at me; **le soleil darde ses rayons** the sun is beating down

dare-dare [dardar] *adv Fam* at the double

darne [darn] *nf (de poisson)* steak

dartre [dartr] *nf* dry patch of skin

darwinisme [darwinism] *nm* Darwinism

datation [datasjɔ̃] *nf* dating

date [dat] *nf* date; **prendre d. pour qch** to fix a date for sth; **faire d.** to be a landmark; **amitié de fraîche/longue d.** recent/long-standing friendship; **je la connais de longue d.** I've known her (for) a long time; **d. limite** deadline; **d. limite de consommation/de vente/de fraîcheur** use-by/sell-by/best-before date; **d. de naissance** date of birth

dater [date] **1** *vt (lettre)* to date **2** *vi* **à d. du 15** as from the 15th; **ça date un peu** it's a bit dated; **ça ne date pas d'hier** that's nothing new

dateur [datœr] *adj m* **tampon** *ou* **timbre d.** date stamp

datte [dat] *nf* date

dattier [datje] *nm* date palm

dauphin [dofɛ̃] *nm* **(a)** *(animal)* dolphin **(b)** *Hist* **D.** Dauphin **(c)** *Fig (successeur)* heir apparent

daurade [dɔrad] *nf* sea bream

davantage [davɑ̃taʒ] *adv* more; **elle est jolie, mais tu l'es bien d.** she's pretty but you're even prettier; **nous ne resterons pas d.** we won't stay any longer

DCA [desea] *nf Mil (abrév* **Défense contre avions)** anti-aircraft defence

DD *Ordinat (abrév* **disque dur)** HD

DDASS [das] *nf (abrév* **Direction départementale de l'action sanitaire et sociale)** = local social work department, one of whose tasks is to deal with children who have been abandoned or ill-treated

DDT [dedete] *nm (abrév* **dichloro-diphényl-trichloréthane)** DDT

de [də]

de becomes **d'** before vowel and h mute; **de + le** contracts to form **du**, and **de + les** to form **des**.

1 *prép* **(a)** *(indique l'origine)* from; **venir/être de** to come/be from; **sortir de chez soi** to leave the house; **l'idée est de vous** it's your idea; **de vous à moi...** between ourselves...

(b) *(indique une progression)* **de... à...** from... to...; **du matin au soir** from morning till night; **de vingt à trente personnes** between twenty and thirty people; **de... en...** from... to...; **errer de ville en ville** to go from town to town

(c) *(introduit l'agent, l'auteur)* by; *(introduit l'instrument)* with; **accompagné de ses amis** accompanied by his friends; **la statue est de Rodin** the statue is by Rodin; **un concerto de Beethoven** a Beethoven

concerto; **armé de pierres** armed with stones; **couvert de puces** covered in fleas

(d) *(indique la manière)* **d'un air amusé** with an amused expression; **d'une voix douce** gently, in a gentle voice

(e) *(indique la cause)* **sauter de joie** to jump for joy; **resplendissant de santé** blooming with health

(f) *(introduit une mesure)* **un enfant de dix ans** a child of ten, a ten-year-old child; **il est plus grand que moi de 5 cm** he's 5 cm taller than I am; **une pièce de 20 centimes** a 20-centime coin; **la terrasse fait 20 mètres de long** the terrace is 20 metres long; **20 euros de l'heure** 20 euros an hour

(g) *(indique l'appartenance)* of; **le livre de Pierre** Pierre's book; **le toit de la maison** the roof of the house; **le règlement de l'école** the school rules

(h) *(pour préciser la nature, la matière)* **un problème d'algèbre** an algebra problem; **un hôtel de la rive gauche** a hotel on the left bank; **le journal d'hier** yesterday's paper; **à quatre heures de l'après-midi** at four (o'clock) in the afternoon; **une robe de soie** a silk dress; **un verre de vin** a glass of wine

(i) *(dans, parmi)* of; **l'un d'eux** one of them; **le meilleur élève de la classe** the best pupil in the class; **la moitié de ses économies** half (of) her savings

(j) *(pendant)* **je ne l'ai pas vu de la soirée** I haven't seen him all evening; **de nuit** by night

(k) *(introduit un infinitif)* **il est honteux de mentir** it is shameful to lie; **j'aime mieux attendre que de me faire mouiller** I would rather wait than get wet

(l) *(pour insister)* **c'est d'un ridicule!** it's utterly ridiculous!

(m) *(dans un titre)* **de l'amour** (on) love

2 *art partitif* some; **je bois du café tous les matins** I drink coffee every morning; **donnez-moi du vin** give me some wine; **c'est du Bach** it's Bach; **avez-vous du pain?** have you any bread?

3 *art indéfini* **je n'ai plus d'amis/de problèmes** I haven't got any friends/problems any more

dé¹ [de] *nm (pour joueur)* dice; **joueur aux dés** to play dice; **couper qch en dés** *(légumes)* to dice sth

dé² *nm* **dé (à coudre)** thimble

DEA [deəa] *nm (abrév* **diplôme d'études approfondies)** = postgraduate qualification which is a prerequisite for PhD candidates

dealer [dilœr] *nm Fam (de drogue)* dealer

déambulateur [deɑ̃bylatœr] *nm* Zimmer® (frame)

déambuler [deɑ̃byle] *vi* to stroll (about)

débâcle [debakl] *nf* **(a)** *(d'un cours d'eau gelé)* breaking up **(b)** *Mil* rout; *Fig (d'une affaire, d'une monnaie)* collapse

déballage [debalaʒ] *nm* **(a)** *(action)* unpacking **(b)** *Fam (aveu)* outpouring

déballer [debale] *vt* **(a)** *(affaires, produits, caisses)* to unpack **(b)** *Fam (sa vie privée, ses sentiments)* to pour out

débandade [debɑ̃dad] *nf (d'une armée, d'une équipe)* rout; **c'est la d. dans l'entreprise** the company's in disarray

débaptiser [debatize] *vt (personne, rue)* to rename

débarbouillage [debarbujaʒ] *nm* face wash

débarbouiller [debarbuje] **1** *vt* **d. qn** to wash sb's face **2** **se débarbouiller** *vpr* to wash one's face

débarbouillette [debarbujɛt] *nf Can* (face) flannel, face cloth, *Am* washrag

débarcadère [debarkadɛr] *nm* landing stage; *(pour les marchandises)* wharf

débardeur [debardœr] *nm* (**a**) *(vêtement)* vest (**b**) *(personne)* docker, stevedore

débarquement [debarkəmã] *nm* (**a**) *(de cargaison)* unloading; *(de passagers)* landing (**b**) *(de troupes)* landing; *Hist* **le D.** the Normandy landings

débarquer [debarke] **1** *vt (cargaison)* to unload; *(passagers)* to land
    2 *vi* (**a**) *(d'un bateau, d'un avion)* to disembark (**b**) *Fam Fig (arriver)* to turn up; **il a toujours l'air de d.** he never seems to know what's going on

débarras [debara] *nm* (**a**) *(endroit)* junk room (**b**) *Fam* **bon d.!** good riddance!

débarrasser [debarase] **1** *vt (table, bureau, pièce)* to clear; **d. qn de qch** to relieve sb of sth; **d. qn de qn** to rid sb of sb; *Fam Fig* **d. le plancher** to clear out
    2 se débarrasser *vpr* **se d. de** to get rid of

débat [deba] *nm* debate; *Pol* **débats (parlementaires)** (parliamentary) proceedings

débattre [11] [debatr] **1** *vt (discuter)* to debate, to discuss; **prix à d.** price negotiable
    2 débattre de *vt ind* to discuss
    3 se débattre *vpr* to struggle; **se d. contre les difficultés** to be up against difficulties

débauche [deboʃ] *nf* debauchery; **lieu de d.** den of vice; *Fig* **une d. de couleurs** a riot of colour

débauché, -e [deboʃe] **1** *adj* debauched
    2 *nm,f* debauchee

débaucher [deboʃe] *vt* (**a**) *(inciter à la débauche)* to corrupt (**b**) *(licencier)* to lay off

débecter [debɛkte] *vt très Fam* to sicken

débile [debil] **1** *adj* (**a**) *(qui manque de vigueur) (enfant)* sickly; *(corps)* weak; *(santé)* poor (**b**) *Fam (stupide)* stupid
    2 *nmf* **d. mental** mental defective; *Fam Fig* complete idiot

débilitant, -e [debilitã, -ãt] *adj* debilitating; *Fig* demoralizing

débilité [debilite] *nf* (**a**) *(faiblesse)* debility; **d. mentale** mental deficiency (**b**) *Fam (stupidité)* stupidity

débiliter [debilite] *vt* to debilitate

débiner [debine] *Fam* **1** *vt* to run down
    2 se débiner *vpr* to clear off

débit [debi] *nm* (**a**) *Fin* debit (**b**) *(ventes)* turnover (**c**) *(commerce)* **d. de boissons** bar; **d. de tabac** tobacconist's (shop) (**d**) *(de bois)* cutting up (**e**) *(d'une rivière, de liquide)* flow; *(d'une machine)* output; *Ordinat* **d. de données** data throughput (**f**) *(d'un orateur)* delivery; *Fam* **il a un de ces débits!** he's really got the gift of the gab!

débitant, -e [debitã, -ãt] *nm,f* **d. de boissons** bar owner; **d. de tabac** tobacconist

débiter [debite] *vt* (**a**) *(sujet: usine)* to produce; *(sujet: cours d'eau)* to have a flow rate of (**b**) *Fin (somme, compte)* to debit; **d. une somme d'un compte** to debit an account with an amount, to debit an amount to an account (**c**) *(bois, viande)* to cut up (**d**) *(vendre)* to sell (**e**) *Péj (dire)* to spout

débiteur, -trice [debitœr, -tris] **1** *adj (compte)* debit
    2 *nm,f* debtor

déblaiement [deblɛmã] *nm* clearing

déblatérer [34] [deblatere] *vi Fam* **d. contre** *ou* **sur qn/qch** to rail against sb/sth

déblayage [deblɛjaʒ] *nm* clearing

déblayer [53] [debleje] *vt* (**a**) *(terre, gravats, neige)* to clear (**b**) *(terrain)* to clear; *Fig* **d. le terrain** *(faire des préparatifs)* to prepare the ground

déblocage [deblɔkaʒ] *nm* *(d'une porte, d'un tiroir, d'un mécanisme)* unjamming; *(des prix, des salaires)* unfreezing

débloquer [deblɔke] **1** *vt* (**a**) *(porte, tiroir, mécanisme)* to unjam; *(prix, salaires)* to unfreeze; **d. des fonds** to release funds (**b**) *Psy* **d. qn** *(lui ôter ses complexes)* to rid sb of his/her complexes; *(le rendre moins timide)* to make sb less inhibited
    2 *vi Fam (être fou)* to be off one's rocker; *(raconter n'importe quoi)* to talk drivel; *(être gâteux)* to be gaga

déboguer [debɔge] *vt Ordinat* to debug

débogueur [debɔgœr] *nm Ordinat* debugger

déboires [debwar] *nmpl (déceptions)* disappointments; *(ennuis)* problems; **essuyer des d.** to suffer disappointments *or* setbacks

déboisement [debwazmã] *nm* deforestation

déboiser [debwaze] *vt* to deforest

déboîtement [debwatmã] *nm* (**a**) *(d'un membre, d'une articulation)* dislocation (**b**) *(en voiture)* pulling out

déboîter [debwate] **1** *vt* (**a**) *(objets encastrés)* to disconnect (**b**) *(articulation, membre)* to dislocate
    2 *vi (en voiture)* to pull out
    3 se déboîter *vpr (articulation, membre)* to become dislocated; **se d. l'épaule/le genou** to dislocate one's shoulder/knee

débonnaire [debɔnɛr] *adj (personne)* good-natured, easy-going; **répondre d'un ton d.** to answer good-naturedly

débordant, -e [debɔrdã, -ãt] *adj (activité)* tireless; *(imagination)* boundless; **d. de santé/d'enthousiasme** bursting with health/with enthusiasm

débordé, -e [debɔrde] *adj* **d. (de travail)** snowed under (with work)

débordement [debɔrdəmã] *nm* (**a**) *(d'une rivière)* overflowing; *Fig (d'enthousiasme, de joie)* outburst (**b**) **débordements** *(excès)* excesses (**c**) *Mil (de l'ennemi)* outflanking

déborder [debɔrde] **1** *vi* (**a**) *(liquide, rivière, baignoire)* to overflow; **l'eau déborde du vase** the vase is overflowing; **les papiers débordent de la corbeille** the wastepaper basket is overflowing with paper; **d. sur le temps prévu** to overrun (**b**) *Fig* **d. de vie** to be bursting with vitality; **d. d'imagination** to have boundless imagination
    2 *vt (dépasser) (alignement)* to stick out from; *(limite)* to go beyond; *Mil (l'ennemi)* to outflank; *Sport (coureur)* to overtake; **cela déborde le cadre de...** that is beyond the scope of...

débouchage [debuʃaʒ] *nm* (**a**) *(d'un tuyau, d'un évier)* unblocking (**b**) *(d'une bouteille)* uncorking

débouché [debuʃe] *nm (professionnel)* opening, job opportunity; *Com* outlet

déboucher [debuʃe] **1** *vt* (**a**) *(tuyau, évier)* to unblock (**b**) *(bouteille)* to uncork
    2 *vi* (**a**) *(dans l'espace) (personne, voiture)* to emerge (**de** from), to come out (**de** of); **d. dans/sur** to lead to (**b**) *Fig* **d. sur qch** *(avoir pour résultat)* to lead to sth
    3 se déboucher *vpr (tuyau, évier, oreilles)* to clear; **la bouteille se débouche facilement** the bottle opens easily

débouler [debule] *Fam* **1** *vt* **d. l'escalier** to race down the stairs

2 *vi* (**a**) *(descendre)* to race down (**b**) *(arriver)* to turn up

déboulonner [debulɔne] *vt* (**a**) *Tech* to unbolt; *(statue)* to take down (**b**) *Fam Fig (critiquer)* to debunk; *(de son poste)* to kick out

débourser [deburse] *vt (argent)* to lay out; **sans rien d.** without spending a penny

déboussoler [debusɔle] *vt Fam* to throw

debout [dəbu] *adv* (**a**) *(verticalement) (chose)* upright; *(personne)* standing; **cent ans plus tard, la maison est encore d.** the house is still standing a hundred years later; **elle est d. toute la journée** she's on her feet all day; **mettre qch d.** to stand sth up; **se mettre d.** to stand up; **rester d.** to stand; **tenir d.** *(objet)* to stay upright; *(personne)* to stay on one's feet; **il ne tient plus d.** *(fatigué)* he's dead on his feet; *(ivre)* he's legless; *Fig* **un argument qui ne tient pas d.** an argument that won't stand up; **se tenir d.** to stand; **conte** *ou* **histoire à dormir d.** cock-and-bull story (**b**) *(hors du lit)* **être d.** to be up; **allons, d.!** come on, get up!

débouter [debute] *vt Jur* to nonsuit

déboutonner [debutɔne] **1** *vt* to unbutton
2 se déboutonner *vpr (personne)* to undo one's coat/jacket/*etc*; *(vêtement)* to unbutton; *Fig (se confier)* to open up

débraillé, -e [debraje] *adj* slovenly

débrancher [debrãʃe] *vt (appareil électrique)* to unplug; *(tuyau)* to diconnect

débrayage [debrɛjaʒ] *nm* (**a**) *Aut* declutching (**b**) *(grève)* stoppage

débrayer [53] [debrɛje] *vi* (**a**) *Aut* to release the clutch (**b**) *(se mettre en grève)* to stop work

débridé, -e [debride] *adj (passion)* unbridled; *(imagination)* vivid

débris [debri] **1** *nmpl (d'un avion, d'une voiture)* debris, wreckage; *(de verre, de bois)* fragments; **d. de métal** scrap (metal)
2 *nm Fam* **un vieux d.** an old wreck

débrouillard, -e [debrujar, -ard] *Fam* **1** *adj* resourceful
2 *nm,f* resourceful person

débrouillardise [debrujardiz] *nf* resourcefulness

débrouiller [debruje] **1** *vt (fil, mystère)* to unravel
2 se débrouiller *vpr* to manage, to cope; *(dans une langue, un domaine)* to get by; **débrouillez-vous!** you'll just have to manage!; **elle s'est débrouillée pour rencontrer le directeur** she worked it so that she got to meet the director; **débrouille-toi pour arriver à l'heure** make sure you get there on time

débroussailler [debrusaje] *vt* to clear of undergrowth; *Fig (question)* to clarify

débusquer [debyske] *vt* to flush out

début [deby] *nm* (**a**) *(commencement)* beginning, start; **au d. (de)** at the start *or* beginning (of); **au tout d., tout au d.** at the very start *or* beginning; **dès le d.** from the start; **je le savais depuis le d.** I knew all along; **du d. à la fin** from start to finish; **en d. de** at the start of; *Hum* **il faut** *ou* **il y a un d. à tout** there's a first time for everything (**b**) **débuts** *(d'un acteur, d'un chanteur)* debut, first appearance; **faire ses débuts** to make one's debut; **faire des débuts prometteurs** to get off to a promising start; **en être à ses débuts** *(société, projet)* to be in its early stages (**c**) *Ordinat* home; **aller au d.** *(commande)* go top

débutant, -e [debytã, -ãt] **1** *adj* novice
2 *nm,f (dans une discipline)* beginner; **grand d.** complete beginner

débuter [debyte] **1** *vi* (**a**) *(commencer)* to begin, to start (**par** with) (**b**) *(dans le spectacle)* to make one's debut; *(dans la vie professionnelle)* to start out; **mal/bien d. dans la vie** to get off to a bad/good start in life
2 *vt Fam* to start, to begin (**par** with)

deçà [dəsa] **en deçà de** *prép (dans l'espace)* (on) this side of; **rester (très) en d. de la vérité** to be (very) short of the truth

déca [deka] *nm Fam (café)* decaf

décacheter [42] [dekaʃte] *vt* to unseal, to open

décadenasser [dekadnase] *vt* to take the padlock off

décadence [dekadãs] *nf (état)* decadence; *(processus)* decline; **tomber en d.** to go into decline

décadent, -e [dekadã, -ãt] *adj* decadent

décaféiné [dekafeine] **1** *adj m (café)* decaffeinated
2 *nm* decaffeinated coffee

décagonal, -e, -aux, -ales [dekagɔnal, -o] *adj* decagonal

décagone [dekagon] *nm Math* decagon

décalage [dekalaʒ] *nm* (**a**) *(désaccord)* gap (**b**) *(dans le temps)* time lag; **d. horaire** time difference; **souffrir du d. horaire** to have jet lag

décalaminer [dekalamine] *vt* to decoke

décalcification [dekalsifikasjɔ̃] *nf Méd* decalcification

décalcifier [66] [dekalsifje] *Méd* **1** *vt* to decalcify
2 se décalcifier *vpr* to become decalcified

décalcomanie [dekalkɔmani] *nf (procédé) Br* transfer process, *Am* decal; *(image) Br* transfer, *Am* decal; **faire de la d.** to do *Br* transfers *or Am* decals

décalé, -e [dekale] *adj (humour, style)* offbeat, quirky

décaler [dekale] **1** *vt* (**a**) *(dans l'espace)* to move, to shift (**de** from) (**b**) *(dans le temps) (avancer)* to bring forward (**de** by); *(reculer)* to put back (**de** by)
2 se décaler *vpr* to move, to shift; **vous pourriez vous d. d'un rang/vers la gauche?** could you move up a row/move to the left?

décalitre [dekalitr] *nm* decalitre

décalquer [dekalke] *vt* to trace

décamètre [dekamɛtr] *nm* decametre

décamper [dekãpe] *vi Fam* to clear off

décan [dekã] *nm* = one of three divisions of each sign of the zodiac

décaniller [dekanije] *vi Fam* to clear off

décanter [dekãte] **1** *vt (vin)* to decant
2 se décanter *vpr (vin)* to settle; *Fig (situation)* to become clearer

décapage [dekapaʒ] *nm (avec un produit)* stripping; *(au papier de verre)* sanding (down); *(d'un four)* cleaning

décapant, -e [dekapã, -ãt] **1** *adj* (**a**) **produit d.** *(pour vernis, peinture)* paint stripper; *(pour four)* oven cleaner
(**b**) *Fig (humour)* caustic
2 *nm (pour vernis, peinture)* paint stripper; *(pour four)* oven cleaner

décaper [dekape] *vt* (**a**) *(avec un produit)* to strip; *(au papier de verre)* to sand (down); *(four)* to clean (**b**) *Fam Fig* **ça décape!** *(alcool)* it takes the roof of your mouth off!

décapeuse [dekapøz] *nf* scraper

décapitation [dekapitasjɔ̃] *nf* decapitation

décapiter [dekapite] *vt (personne)* to decapitate; *(arbre)* to pollard

décapotable [dekapɔtabl] **1** *adj* convertible; *(coupé)* drop-head
2 *nf* convertible

décapoter [dekapɔte] *vt* to lower the top of

décapsuler [dekapsyle] *vt* to take the top off

décapsuleur [dekapsylœr] *nm* bottle opener

décarcasser [dekarkase] **se décarcasser** *vpr Fam* to sweat blood (**pour faire** to do)

décasyllabe [dekasilab] **1** *adj* decasyllabic
2 *nm* decasyllable

décathlon [dekatlɔ̃] *nm* decathlon

décati, -e [dekati] *adj (visage)* age-worn; *(personne)* decrepit

décatir [dekatir] **se décatir** *vpr* to become decrepit

décédé, -e [desede] *adj* deceased

décéder [34] [desede] *vi* to die

décelable [deslabl] *adj* detectable

déceler [39] [desle] *vt* (**a**) *(découvrir)* to detect (**b**) *(indiquer)* to indicate

décélération [deselerasjɔ̃] *nf* deceleration

décélérer [34] [deselere] *vi* to decelerate

décembre [desɑ̃br] *nm* December; *voir aussi* **janvier**

décemment [desamɑ̃] *adv* (**a**) *(convenablement) (se comporter)* properly; *(s'habiller)* decently (**b**) *(passablement)* reasonably well (**c**) *(raisonnablement)* reasonably; **je ne pouvais pas d. refuser** I couldn't reasonably refuse

décence [desɑ̃s] *nf* (**a**) *(bienséance) (de comportement)* propriety; *(d'habillement)* decency (**b**) *(tact)* decency; **avoir la d. de faire qch** to have the decency to do sth

décennal, -e, -aux, -ales [desenal, -o] *adj* ten-year

décennie [deseni] *nf* decade

décent, -e [desɑ̃, -ɑ̃t] *adj* (**a**) *(comportement)* proper; *(vêtements)* decent; **peu d.** improper/indecent (**b**) *(passable)* reasonable

décentralisation [desɑ̃tralizasjɔ̃] *nf* decentralization

décentraliser [desɑ̃tralize] *vt* to decentralize

décentré, -e [desɑ̃tre] *adj* (**a**) **être d.** to be off-centre (**b**) *Suisse (quartier, endroit)* outlying

décentrer [desɑ̃tre] **1** *vt* to move off centre
2 se décentrer *vpr* to move off centre

déception [desɛpsjɔ̃] *nf* disappointment; **d. sentimentale** disappointment in love

décerner [deserne] *vt (prix, médaille)* to award (**à** to)

décès [desɛ] *nm* death; **fermé pour cause de d.** *(sur la porte d'un magasin)* closed due to bereavement

décevant, -e [desəvɑ̃, -ɑ̃t] *adj* disappointing

décevoir [60] [desəvwar] *vt* to disappoint; **il/ce voyage m'a beaucoup déçu** I was very disappointed in him/with the trip

déchaîné, -e [deʃene] *adj (passion)* unbridled; *(mer, vent)* raging; *(personne)* wild

déchaînement [deʃenmɑ̃] *nm (des éléments)* fury; *(des passions)* outburst

déchaîner [deʃene] **1** *vt (passions, colère)* to unleash; **d. l'hilarité** to provoke laughter
2 se déchaîner *vpr (tempête, vent)* to rage; *(personne)* to fly into a rage (**contre** with)

déchanter [deʃɑ̃te] *vi Fam* to become disillusioned

décharge [deʃarʒ] *nf* (**a**) *(tirs)* discharge (**b**) **d. (électrique)** (electric) shock; **prendre une d.** to get an electric shock; **d. d'adrénaline** rush of adrenaline

(**c**) *(d'ordures)* **d. (publique)** *Br* rubbish *or Am* garbage dump; **d. interdite** *(sur panneau)* no dumping (**d**) *Jur (d'un accusé)* acquittal; *(d'une obligation)* discharge; *Fig* **dire qch à la d. de qn** to say sth in sb's defence

déchargement [deʃarʒəmɑ̃] *nm* unloading

décharger [45] [deʃarʒe] **1** *vt* (**a**) *(vider) (camion, bateau, cargaison)* to unload; *(sujet: camion) (sable, gravier)* to dump; *(arme à feu)* to fire, to discharge; *Fig* **d. sa conscience** to unburden one's conscience (**de** of) (**b**) *(soulager)* **d. qn de qch** *(tâche, responsabilité)* to relieve sb of sth; *Jur (d'une accusation)* to acquit sb of sth
2 se décharger *vpr* (**a**) *(personne)* **se d. d'une tâche/d'une responsabilité sur qn** to offload a task/a responsibility onto sb (**b**) *(pile, batterie)* to go flat

décharné, -e [deʃarne] *adj (corps, membres, visage)* emaciated; *Fig (arbre)* bare

déchaussé, -e [deʃose] *adj* (**a**) *(sans chaussures)* barefoot (**b**) *(dent)* loose

déchausser [deʃose] **1** *vt (enlever ses chaussures à)* **d. qn** to take off sb's shoes; **d. ses skis** to take off one's skis
2 se déchausser *vpr* (**a**) *(enlever ses chaussures)* to take off one's shoes (**b**) *(dent)* to work loose

dèche [dɛʃ] *nf Fam* **être dans la d.** to be stony broke; **c'est la d.** I'm/we're/*etc* stony broke

déchéance [deʃeɑ̃s] *nf* (**a**) *(physique, morale)* decline (**b**) *Jur (de droits)* forfeiture; **d. de l'autorité parentale** loss of parental rights

déchet [deʃɛ] *nm* (**a**) **déchets** waste; **déchets radioactifs/industriels** radioactive/industrial waste (**b**) *(perte)* **il y a du d.** there's some wastage (**c**) *Péj (personne)* down-and-out; **un d. de la société** a social outcast

déchiffrable [deʃifrabl] *adj* decipherable

déchiffrage [deʃifraʒ] *nm Mus* sight-reading

déchiffrement [deʃifrəmɑ̃] *nm* deciphering; *Ordinat* decryption

déchiffrer [deʃifre] *vt* (**a**) *(inscription, écriture, message)* to decipher; *(signaux)* to interpret; *Fig (pensées, sentiments, mystère)* to fathom (**b**) *(musique)* to sight-read

déchiqueté, -e [deʃikte] *adj* (**a**) *(irrégulier)* jagged (**b**) *(vêtements, papiers)* torn to shreds; *(corps) (dans une explosion)* blown to pieces

déchiqueter [42] [deʃikte] *vt (vêtements, papiers)* to tear to shreds; *(sujet: explosion) (corps)* to blow to pieces

déchirant, -e [deʃirɑ̃, -ɑ̃t] *adj (spectacle, adieux)* heartrending

déchiré, -e [deʃire] *adj aussi Méd & Fig* torn; **être d. entre deux personnes** to be torn between two people

déchirement [deʃirmɑ̃] *nm (peine)* heartbreak

déchirer [deʃire] **1** *vt* (**a**) *(accidentellement)* to tear; *(volontairement)* to tear up; *(enveloppe)* to tear open (**b**) *Fig (famille, pays)* to tear apart; *(silence)* to pierce; **des sons qui déchirent le tympan** ear-splitting sounds
2 se déchirer *vpr* (**a**) *(tissu, papier)* to tear (**b**) *Méd* **se d. un muscle** to tear a muscle (**c**) *Fig (couple)* to tear each other apart

déchirure [deʃiryr] *nf (dans un tissu) & Méd* tear; *Fig (peine)* heartbreak; **se faire une d. musculaire** to tear a muscle

déchoir [14] [deʃwar] *vi* **ce serait d. (que de...)** it would be demeaning (to...); **par ce mariage il déchoit de son rang** he is marrying beneath him

déchu, -e [deʃy] *adj (dépossédé) (roi)* deposed; **être d. de qch** *(droit, nationalité)* to be stripped of sth

décibel [desibɛl] *nm* decibel

décidé, -e [deside] *adj* (**a**) *(fixé)* settled (**b**) *(caractère, personne, manière)* determined; **d'un ton d.** in a decisive tone; **être d. à faire qch** to be determined to do sth

décidément [desidemɑ̃] *adv* really; **d. je n'ai pas de chance!, je n'ai d. pas de chance!** I really don't have any luck!

décider [deside] **1** *vt* (**a**) *(déterminer)* **d. que/quand/si** to decide that/when/if; **il fut décidé qu'on attendrait** it was decided that we/they/*etc* should wait; **c'est moi qui décide ici** I'm the one who makes the decisions here; **je déciderai pour toi** I'll decide for you (**b**) *(convaincre)* **d. qn à faire qch** to persuade sb to do sth
2 décider de *vt ind* **d. de qch** to decide on sth; **un événement qui a décidé de sa carrière** an event that determined his career; **d. de faire qch** to decide to do sth
3 se décider *vpr* (**a**) *(prendre une décision)* to make up one's mind, to come to a decision; **bon, décide-toi!** right, make up your mind!; **se d. à faire qch** to make up one's mind to do sth; **je ne peux pas me d. à le faire** I can't bring myself to do it; *Fig* **il ne se décide pas à faire beau** the weather can't make up its mind whether to be fine or not; **se d. pour qn/qch** to decide on sb/sth (**b**) *(problème, question)* to be settled

décideur, -euse [desidœr, -øz] *nm,f* decision-maker

décigramme [desigram] *nm* decigram

décilitre [desilitr] *nm* decilitre

décimal, -e, -aux, -ales [desimal, -o] **1** *adj* decimal **2** *nf* **décimale** decimal

décimer [desime] *vt* to decimate

décimètre [desimetr] *nm* decimetre; **double d.** *(règle)* ruler *(20 cm long)*

décisif, -ive [desizif, -iv] *adj (bataille, argument)* decisive; *(preuve)* conclusive; *(moment)* critical

décision [desizjɔ̃] *nf* (**a**) *(choix)* decision; *Jur* ruling; **arriver à/prendre une d.** to come to/to make a decision; **prendre la d. de faire qch** to decide to do sth; **la d. ne m'appartient pas** it's not my decision (**b**) *(détermination)* determination; **avec d.** decisively; **esprit de d.** decisiveness

déclamation [deklamasjɔ̃] *nf (éloquence)* declamation

déclamatoire [deklamatwar] *adj Péj (style)* declamatory; *(discours)* bombastic

déclamer [deklame] *vt (discours, vers)* to declaim; *Péj* to spout

déclaration [deklarasjɔ̃] *nf* (**a**) *(annonce orale, écrite)* statement; **d. (d'amour)** declaration of love; **faire une** *ou* **sa d. à qn** to declare one's love to sb; **le chef de l'État a une importante d. à faire** the President has an important announcement to make; **faire une d. à la police** to make a statement to the police; **D. des droits de l'homme** Declaration of Human Rights; **d. de guerre** declaration of war; *Hist* **D. d'indépendance** Declaration of Independence; **d. de principe** statement of principle (**b**) *(acte officiel) (de naissance, de décès)* registration; *(à une compagnie d'assurances)* claim (**de** for); *(à la police)* report; **d. en douane** customs declaration; **d. d'impôts** tax return; **faire sa d. d'impôts** to fill in one's tax return; **d. de revenus** income tax return (**c**) *Ordinat* **d. de champ** field definition

---

Déclaration d'impôts

People in France are required to declare their taxable earnings at the beginning of the year. Thrice-yearly tax payments ("tiers provisionnels") are based on one third of the previous year's total, the final payment being adjusted according to the actual tax owed. It is also possible to pay tax on a monthly basis. This is known as "mensualisation".

---

déclaré, -e [deklare] *adj (ennemi, intention)* declared; *(partisan)* avowed

déclarer [deklare] **1** *vt (annoncer)* to declare; *(revenus, décès, naissance)* to register; *(à une compagnie d'assurances)* to make a claim for; *(à la police)* to report; **d. que** to declare (that); **d. forfait** *(en sport)* to scratch; **d. la guerre à qn** to declare war on sb; **rien à d.** *(en douane)* nothing to declare; **être déclaré coupable** to be found guilty
2 se déclarer *vpr* (**a**) *(feu, maladie, guerre)* to break out (**b**) *(se prononcer)* **se d. pour/contre qch** to declare oneself in favour of/against sth (**c**) *(se dire)* **se d. satisfait/surpris** to declare oneself satisfied/surprised; **se d. coupable** to admit one's guilt (**d**) *(faire une déclaration d'amour)* to declare one's love (**à** to)

déclasser [deklase] *vt* (**a**) *(faire changer de classe)* *Sport* to relegate; *(hôtel)* to downgrade; *(passagers)* to transfer from one class to another (**b**) *(déranger)* to get out of order

déclenchement [deklɑ̃ʃmɑ̃] *nm (d'un appareil)* starting; *(d'un mécanisme)* activation; *(d'une sonnerie)* setting off; *(d'un événement)* triggering

déclencher [deklɑ̃ʃe] **1** *vt (appareil)* to start; *(mécanisme)* to activate; *(sonnerie)* to set off; *(événement, critiques, questions)* to trigger; *Mil (attaque)* to launch
2 se déclencher *vpr* (**a**) *(sonnerie, sirène, bombe)* to go off (**b**) *(commencer) (douleur, incendie)* to start

déclencheur [deklɑ̃ʃœr] *nm Phot* shutter release

déclic [deklik] *nm (bruit)* click; **la vue de cette photo a été pour elle un véritable d.** when she looked at the photo things fell into place

déclin [deklɛ̃] *nm (du talent, de la santé, d'une civilisation)* decline; *(de la beauté)* fading; *(du jour)* close; **être en d.** to be in decline; **le soleil est à son d.** the sun is setting; **au d. de sa vie** in her declining years

déclinaison [deklinɛzɔ̃] *nf Gram* declension

déclinant, -e [deklinɑ̃, -ɑ̃t] *adj (beauté, lumière)* fading; *(pouvoirs)* declining

décliner [dekline] **1** *vi (jour)* to draw to a close; *(talent, santé)* to decline; *(beauté)* to fade
2 *vt* (**a**) *Formel (refuser) (offre, invitation)* to decline; **d. toute responsabilité** to accept no liability (**b**) *Gram* to decline (**c**) *(réciter) (identité)* to state
3 se décliner *vpr Gram* to be declined

déclivité [deklivite] *nf* slope, incline

décloisonnement [deklwazɔnmɑ̃] *nm* decompartmentalization

décloisonner [deklwazɔne] *vt* to decompartmentalize

déco [deko] *nf Fam (d'une pièce)* décor; *(métier)* (interior) decorating; **j'aime beaucoup faire de la d.** I love decorating

décocher [dekɔʃe] *vt* (**a**) *(flèche)* to shoot; **d. un coup/ une ruade à qn** to hit out at/to kick sb (**b**) *Fig (remarque)* to fire off (**à** at); *(sourire, œillade)* to flash (**à** at)

décoction [dekɔksjɔ̃] *nf* decoction

décodage [dekɔdaʒ] *nm* decoding

décoder [dekɔde] *vt* to decode

décodeur [dekɔdœr] *nm TV* decoder; **d. numérique** set-top box

décoiffer [dekwafe] **1** *vt (ébouriffer)* **d. qn** to mess up sb's hair; **tu es tout décoiffé** your hair's in a mess; *Fam Fig* **un film qui décoiffe** a mind-blowing film
　2 se décoiffer *vpr* (**a**) *(se dépeigner)* to mess up one's hair (**b**) *(ôter son chapeau)* to remove one's hat

décoincer [16] [dekwɛ̃se] **1** *vt (tiroir, mécanisme)* to loosen; *Fam Fig (personne)* to loosen up
　2 se décoincer *vpr (tiroir, mécanisme)* to loosen; *Fam Fig (personne)* to loosen up

déçois *etc voir* **décevoir**

décolérer [34] [dekɔlere] *vi* to calm down; **il ne décolérait pas** he was still angry; **il n'a pas décoléré depuis huit jours** he's been angry for a week

décollage [dekɔlaʒ] *nm* (**a**) *aussi Fig (démarrage)* takeoff (**b**) *(d'un timbre, de papier peint, d'une affiche)* peeling off

décollement [dekɔlmɑ̃] *nm* (**a**) *Méd* **d. de la rétine** detachment of the retina (**b**) *(d'un timbre, de papier peint, d'une affiche)* peeling off

décoller [dekɔle] **1** *vt (timbre, papier peint, affiche)* to peel off; **d. une enveloppe à la vapeur** to steam open an envelope; *Fam Fig* **d. qn de la télé/du bar** to tear sb away from theTV/the bar
　2 *vi* (**a**) *(avion, fusée, économie)* to take off (**b**) *Fam (partir)* to leave; **bon, on décolle?** shall we get moving?; **je ne décollerai pas d'ici tant que...** I'm not budging until...; *Sport* **d. du peloton** to pull away from the pack
　3 se décoller *vpr (se détacher)* to peel off; *Méd (rétine)* to become detached

décolleté, -e [dekɔlte] **1** *adj (vêtement)* low-cut; **une femme très décolletée** a woman in a very low-cut dress; **robe décolletée dans le dos** dress cut low at the back
　2 *nm (de vêtement)* low neckline; *(haut des seins)* cleavage

décolonisation [dekɔlɔnizasjɔ̃] *nf* decolonization

décoloniser [dekɔlɔnize] *vt* to decolonize

décolorant, -e [dekɔlɔrɑ̃, -ɑ̃t] **1** *adj* bleaching
　2 *nm* bleaching agent

décoloration [dekɔlɔrasjɔ̃] *nf (d'un tissu)* fading; *(des cheveux)* bleaching; **se faire faire une d.** to have one's hair bleached

décolorer [dekɔlɔre] **1** *vt (tissu)* to fade; *(cheveux)* to bleach
　2 se décolorer *vpr (tissu)* to fade; **se d. les cheveux** to bleach one's hair

décombres [dekɔ̃br] *nmpl* ruins, debris

décommander [dekɔmɑ̃de] **1** *vt (réunion, dîner)* to cancel, to call off; *(invité)* to put off
　2 se décommander *vpr* to cancel

décomplexer [dekɔ̃plɛkse] *vt Fam* **d. qn** to cure sb of his/her hang-ups

décomposer [dekɔ̃poze] **1** *vt* (**a**) *(élément chimique)* to decompose; *(problème, phrase, mouvement)* to break down (**en** into) (**b**) *(matière organique)* to decompose (**c**) *(traits, visage)* to distort; **il est arrivé complètement décomposé** *(par l'émotion)* he arrived quite distraught

　2 se décomposer *vpr* (**a**) *(corps, viande, feuilles)* to decompose; *Fig (tomber en décadence)* to decay (**b**) *(visage, traits)* to become distorted

décomposition [dekɔ̃pozisjɔ̃] *nf* (**a**) *(d'un élément chimique)* decomposition; *(d'un problème, d'une phrase, d'un mouvement)* breaking down (**en** into) (**b**) *(de viande, de feuilles, de corps)* decomposition; *Fig (décadence)* decay; **en d.** *(cadavre)* decomposing; *Fig (société)* decaying

décompresser [dekɔ̃prese] **1** *vt Tech* to decompress; *Ordinat* to decompress, to unzip
　2 *vi Fam* to unwind

décompression [dekɔ̃prɛsjɔ̃] *nf* decompression; *Ordinat* decompression, unbundling; **avoir un accident de d.** *(plongeur)* to get the bends

décompte [dekɔ̃t] *nm (sur une somme à payer)* deduction; *(calcul)* calculation; **faire le d. des voix** to count the votes; **faire le d. des points** to add *or* to reckon up the score

décompter [dekɔ̃te] *vt* to deduct (**de** from)

déconcentrer [dekɔ̃sɑ̃tre] **1** *vt* (**a**) *(pouvoirs, administration)* to devolve, to decentralize (**b**) *(distraire)* to distract
　2 se déconcentrer *vpr* to lose concentration

déconcertant, -e [dekɔ̃sɛrtɑ̃, -ɑ̃t] *adj* disconcerting

déconcerté, -e [dekɔ̃sɛrte] *adj* disconcerted

déconcerter [dekɔ̃sɛrte] *vt* to disconcert

déconfit, -e [dekɔ̃fi, -it] *adj (personne, mine)* crestfallen

déconfiture [dekɔ̃fityr] *nf (échec)* defeat

décongeler [39] [dekɔ̃ʒle] *vt* to defrost, to thaw

décongestionner [dekɔ̃ʒɛstjɔne] *vt aussi Fig* to relieve congestion in

déconnecter [dekɔnɛkte] *vt (fil)* to disconnect; *Fig* **déconnecté de la réalité** out of touch with the real world

déconner [dekɔne] *vi très Fam* (**a**) *(dire des bêtises)* to talk garbage; *(faire des bêtises)* to piss around; **faire qch pour d.** *(pour rire)* to do sth for a laugh; **sans d., c'était super** no kidding, it was great; **sans d.!** *(en réponse)* no kidding! (**b**) *(mal fonctionner)* to play up

déconneur, -euse [dekɔnœr, -øz] *nm,f très Fam* clown

déconseiller [dekɔ̃seje] *vt* **d. qch à qn** to advise sb against sth; **d. à qn de faire qch** to advise sb against doing sth; **un livre à d. aux jeunes** an unsuitable book for young people; **il est déconseillé de faire qch** it is inadvisable to do sth

déconsidérer [34] [dekɔ̃sidere] **1** *vt* to discredit
　2 se déconsidérer *vpr* to bring discredit on oneself

décontamination [dekɔ̃taminasjɔ̃] *nf* decontamination

décontaminer [dekɔ̃tamine] *vt* to decontaminate

décontenancer [16] [dekɔ̃tnɑ̃se] **1** *vt* to disconcert
　2 se décontenancer *vpr* to become disconcerted

décontracté, -e [dekɔ̃trakte] *adj (ambiance, attitude, personne)* relaxed; *(vêtement)* casual; *Péj (désinvolte)* casual

décontracter [dekɔ̃trakte] **1** *vt (muscle)* to relax; *(personne)* to put at ease
　2 se décontracter *vpr* to relax

décontraction [dekɔ̃traksjɔ̃] *nf* relaxation; **faire qch avec d.** to do sth casually

déconvenue [dekɔ̃vny] *nf Formel* disappointment; **quelle ne fut pas ma d. quand...** I was so disappointed when...

décor [dekɔr] *nm* (**a**) *(d'une maison, d'un restaurant)* décor (**b**) *Théât, Cin & TV* **décors** set, scenery; **en d. naturel** on location; *Fam* **aller/envoyer qn dans le d.** *(en voiture)* to go/knock sb off the road (**c**) *(environnement)* surroundings; *Fig* **il aurait besoin d'un changement** *ou* **de changer de d.** he needs a change of scene

décorateur, -trice [dekɔratœr, -tris] *nm,f* (**a**) *(d'intérieur)* (interior) decorator (**b**) *Théât* set designer

décoratif, -ive [dekɔratif, -iv] *adj* decorative; *(arbre)* ornamental; *Péj* **n'avoir qu'un rôle d.** to have a purely decorative role

décoration [dekɔrasjɔ̃] *nf* (**a**) *(d'une maison, d'un restaurant)* decoration; **faire de la d.** to decorate; **d. d'intérieur** interior decorating; **décorations de Noël** Christmas decorations (**b**) *(médaille)* decoration

décorer [dekɔre] *vt* (**a**) *(pièce, maison)* to decorate (**de** with) (**b**) *(médailler)* to decorate (**de** with)

décorticage [dekɔrtikaʒ] *nm* *(de crevettes, de noisettes)* shelling; *(de riz, d'orge)* hulling; *Fig (d'un texte, d'un auteur)* detailed analysis

décortiquer [dekɔrtike] *vt* *(crevettes, noisettes)* to shell; *(riz, orge)* to hull; *Fig (texte)* to analyse in detail

décorum [dekɔrɔm] *nm* decorum

découcher [dekuʃe] *vi* to stay out all night

découdre [21] [dekudr] **1** *vt* *(vêtement, poche, ourlet)* to unpick, to unstitch; *(bouton)* to take off
2 *vi* **en d.** to fight
3 se découdre *vpr (vêtement, poche, ourlet)* to come unstitched; *(bouton)* to come off

découler [dekule] *vi* to follow (**de** from); **il en découle que…** it follows that…

découpage [dekupaʒ] *nm* (**a**) *(de gâteau)* cutting up; *(de viande)* carving; *(de métaux, du cuir)* punching; *Ordinat (de fichier, d'image)* splitting; *Pol* **d. électoral** division into constituencies (**b**) *(image découpée)* cutout; **faire du d.** *ou* **des découpages** to do some cutting out (**c**) *Fig (d'un texte)* division (**en** into); *Cin (scénario)* shooting script

découpé, -e [dekupe] *adj (irrégulier)* jagged

découper [dekupe] **1** *vt* (**a**) *(gâteau, papier)* to cut up; *(viande)* to carve; *(métaux, cuir)* to punch; *Ordinat (fichier, image)* to split; *(disque dur)* to partition; **d. un article dans un journal** to cut an article out of a newspaper (**b**) *Fig (texte)* to divide (**en** into)
2 se découper *vpr* **se d. sur** to stand out against

décourageant, -e [dekuraʒɑ̃, -ɑ̃t] *adj (nouvelle, situation, travail)* disheartening; *(personne)* hopeless

découragement [dekuraʒmɑ̃] *nm* discouragement

décourager [45] [dekuraʒe] **1** *vt* (**a**) *(démoraliser)* to discourage, to dishearten; **se laisser d.** to be discouraged *or* disheartened (**b**) *(dissuader)* to discourage; **d. qn de faire qch** to discourage sb from doing sth
2 se décourager *vpr* to get discouraged *or* disheartened

décousu, -e [dekuzy] *adj (ourlet, poche, vêtement)* unstitched; *Fig (phrases, idées)* disjointed; *(conversation)* rambling; *(travail)* unmethodical

découvert, -e [dekuver, -ɛrt] **1** *adj (épaules)* bare; *(terrain)* open; **dormir d.** to sleep without any covers; **la tête découverte** bareheaded
2 *nm* **Fin d. (bancaire)** overdraft; **être à d. (de 200 euros)** *(personne, compte)* to be overdrawn (by 200 euros) (**b**) **agir à d.** to act openly; **s'avancer à d.** to move forward without cover

découverte [dekuvert] *nf* discovery; **aller** *ou* **partir à la d. de qch** to go off to explore sth; **faire une d.** to make a discovery; *Hum* **ce n'est pas une d.!** that's nothing new!

découvrir [52] [dekuvrir] **1** *vt* (**a**) *(trouver)* to discover (**b**) *(mettre à jour) (secret, complot)* to uncover; **d. qch à qn** *(projets, secrets)* to disclose *or* reveal sth to sb (**c**) *(apprendre à connaître) (domaine, art, sentiment)* to discover; *(personne)* to get to know (**d**) *(casserole, statue)* to uncover; *(dents, bras)* to bare; **une robe avec un décolleté qui découvre les épaules** an off-the-shoulder dress; *aussi Fig* **d. son jeu** to show one's hand (**e**) *(apercevoir)* to have a view of
2 se découvrir *vpr* (**a**) *(enlever son chapeau)* to take off one's hat (**b**) *(en dormant)* **le malade s'est découvert** the patient threw off his bedclothes (**c**) *(ciel)* to clear (**d**) *(se trouver)* to discover; **se d. des parents éloignés** to discover some distant relatives; **il s'est découvert une passion pour le jardinage** he discovered he had a passion for gardening

décrasser [dekrase] **1** *vt* to clean; *Fam Fig* **d. qn** to knock the rough edges off sb
2 se décrasser *vpr* to clean oneself up; *Fig (en faisant de l'exercice)* to clean out one's system

décrêper [dekrepe] *vt (cheveux)* to straighten; **se faire d. les cheveux** to have one's hair straightened

décrépit, -ite [dekrepi, -it] *adj (maison, mur, personne)* decrepit

décrépitude [dekrepityd] *nf* decrepitude; *(décadence)* decay; **tomber en d.** *(civilisation)* to decay; *(institution)* to become obsolete

décret [dekrɛ] *nm* decree

décréter [34] [dekrete] *vt* (**a**) *Jur (état d'urgence, nomination)* to decree (**b**) *(décider)* **d. que** to vow (that)

décrié, -e [dekrije] *adj* disparaged

décrire [30] [dekrir] *vt* (**a**) *(représenter)* to describe (**b**) **d. un cercle** to circle; **d. une courbe** to curve

décrispation [dekrispasjɔ̃] *nf Pol* détente

décrisper [dekrispe] **1** *vt (personne)* to relax; *(atmosphère)* to lighten
2 se décrisper *vpr* to relax

décrocher [dekrɔʃe] **1** *vt* (**a**) *(détacher) (vêtement d'une patère, rideaux, tableau)* to take down (**de** from); *(wagons)* to uncouple; *(combiné)* to pick up; **d. (le téléphone)** *(pour répondre)* to pick up the phone; *(pour ne pas être dérangé)* to take the phone off the hook; **décrochez** *(dans cabine téléphonique)* lift the receiver (**b**) *(recevoir) (poste, prix, contrat)* to land; *Fam* **d. la timbale** to hit the jackpot
2 *vi Fam* (**a**) *(ne plus se concentrer)* to switch off; *(être à la traîne)* to fail to keep up (**b**) *(arrêter de se droguer)* to kick the habit
3 se décrocher *vpr (rideau, tableau)* to come unhooked (**de** from); *(vêtement)* to fall down (**de** from); *(collier)* to come undone; *(wagon)* to come uncoupled (**de** from); **se d. la mâchoire** to dislocate one's jaw

décrocheur, -euse [dekrɔʃœr, -øz] *nm,f Can* dropout

décroiser [dekrwaze] *vt (jambes, bras)* to uncross

décroissant, -e [dekrwasɑ̃, -ɑ̃t] *adj* decreasing; **par ordre d.** in descending order

décroître [4a] [dekrwatr] *vi (forces, population, nombre, intensité)* to decrease; *(journées)* to draw in, to get shorter; *(lune)* to wane; *(eaux)* to subside; **aller (en) décroissant** to be decreasing

décrotter [dekʀɔte] *vt (chaussures, semelles)* to clean the mud off; *Fam Fig (personne)* to knock the rough edges off

décrue [dekʀy] *nf (de rivière)* drop in level

décrypter [dekʀipte] *vt* to decipher

déçu, -e [desy] **1** *pp voir* **décevoir**
2 *adj* disappointed; *Fig & Ironique* **elle ne va pas être déçue (du voyage)** she's in for a disappointment

déculottée [dekylɔte] *nf Fam* hammering

déculotter [dekylɔte] **1** *vt* **d. qn** *(enlever son slip)* to take sb's underpants off; *(enlever son pantalon)* to take sb's trousers off
2 **se déculotter** *vpr (enlever son slip)* to take one's underpants off; *(enlever son pantalon)* to take off one's trousers; *Fig (s'abaisser)* to grovel (**devant** to)

déculpabiliser [dekylpabilize] **1** *vt* **d. qn** to stop sb feeling guilty
2 **se déculpabiliser** *vpr* to stop feeling guilty

décuple [dekypl] *nm* **le d. de qch** ten times sth

décupler [dekyple] **1** *vt* to increase tenfold; *Fig* **la terreur décupla ses forces** terror gave her the strength of ten people
2 *vi* to increase tenfold

dédaigner [dedeɲe] *vt (offre)* to scorn; *(injure, conseil, gloire)* to disregard; *(personne)* to despise; **il ne dédaigne pas un cigare de temps en temps** he is not averse to the occasional cigar

dédaigneusement [dedeɲøzmɑ̃] *adv* scornfully, disdainfully

dédaigneux, -euse [dedeɲø, -øz] *adj* scornful, disdainful (**de** of)

dédain [dedɛ̃] *nm* scorn, disdain (**pour qn/de qch** for sb/sth); **avec d.** scornfully, with disdain

dédale [dedal] *nm aussi Fig* maze

dedans [dədɑ̃] **1** *adv* inside; **la lettre est d.** the letter is inside; **c'est un bon film mais il y a trop de violence d.** it's a good film but there's too much violence in it; **de d.** *(depuis l'intérieur)* from inside; **en d.** *(d'un objet)* (on the) inside; *(en son for intérieur)* inwardly; **marcher les pieds en d.** to be pigeon-toed; **en d. de** inside
2 *nm (d'une maison, d'une boîte)* inside; **du d.** *(depuis l'intérieur)* from inside

dédicace [dedikas] *nf (a) (de livre, de photo)* dedication; *(b) (à la radio)* dedication

dédicacer [16] [dedikase] *vt (a) (signer)* to sign (**à** for); *(écrire dans) (livre)* to write a dedication in (**à** to); *(photo)* to write a dedication on (**à** to) *(b) (chanson)* to dedicate (**à** to)

dédier [66] [dedje] *vt* to dedicate (**à** to)

dédire [27a] [dedir] **se dédire** *vpr* **se d. d'une déclaration** to retract *or* to withdraw a statement; **se d. d'une promesse** to go back on one's word

dédommagement [dedɔmaʒmɑ̃] *nm* compensation; **500 000 euros de d.** 500,000 euros (in) compensation; **en d. de qch** in compensation for sth

dédommager [45] [dedɔmaʒe] *vt (financièrement)* to compensate (**de** for); **pour me d., il m'a invité au restaurant** he took me out for a meal to make up for it

dédouanement [dedwanmɑ̃] *nm* clearance through customs

dédouaner [dedwane] **1** *vt (marchandise)* to clear (through customs); *Fig (personne)* to clear
2 **se dédouaner** *vpr* to clear one's name

dédoublement [dedublomɑ̃] *nm* **d. de la personnalité** split personality

dédoubler [deduble] **1** *vt (partager)* to divide *or* split into two
2 **se dédoubler** *vpr Psy* to have a split personality; *Hum* **je ne peux pas me d.** I can't be in two places at once

dédramatiser [dedramatize] *vt* **d. qch** to make sth less dramatic

déductible [dedyktibl] *adj* deductible; **d. des impôts** tax-deductible

déduction [dedyksjɔ̃] *nf (a) (soustraction, abattement)* deduction; **d. faite des frais d'essence** after deduction of petrol costs *(b) (conclusion)* deduction

déduire [18] [deɥir] *vt (a) (enlever)* to deduct (**de** from) *(b) (conclure)* to deduce, to infer (**de** from)

déesse [deɛs] *nf* goddess

défaillance [defajɑ̃s] *nf (a) (insuffisance) (morale)* failing; *(physique)* deficiency; *(d'une machine)* failure; **avoir des défaillances en** *(intellectuelles)* to have problems with; **courage sans d.** unfailing courage; **d. cardiaque** heart failure *(b) (évanouissement)* fainting fit; *(faiblesse)* feeling of weakness; **avoir une d.** *(s'évanouir)* to faint; *(se sentir faible)* to feel weak

défaillant, -e [defajɑ̃, -ɑ̃t] *adj (a) (forces, mémoire, santé)* failing; *(cœur)* weak; *(voix)* faltering *(b) (qui s'évanouit)* faint

défaillir [35] [defajir] *vi (a) (faiblir) (mémoire, forces)* to fail; **à cette nouvelle, son cœur défaillit** her heart sank at the news *(b) (s'évanouir)* to faint; **d. de faim/de bonheur** to feel faint with hunger/happiness

défaire [36] [defɛr] **1** *vt (a) (ouvrir, détacher)* to undo; *(valise)* to unpack; **d. le lit** *(enlever les draps)* to strip the bed; *(le mettre en désordre)* to rumple the bedclothes; **d. ses cheveux** to let one's hair down *(b) (désassembler) (puzzle)* to take apart; *(ourlet)* to undo
2 **se défaire** *vpr (a) (se dénouer) (vêtement, nœud)* to come undone; *(cheveux)* to come down *(b) (se désagréger) (puzzle)* to come apart; *(ourlet)* to come undone; *Fig (alliance, mariage)* to break up *(c)* **se d. de qn/qch** to get rid of sb/sth; **je ne veux pas m'en d.** I don't want to part with it *(d) (s'altérer) (visage)* to drop

défait, -e [defɛ, -ɛt] *adj (traits, visage)* haggard; **il est arrivé à l'hôpital, complètement d.** he arrived at the hospital in total distress

défaite [defɛt] *nf* defeat

défaitisme [defetism] *nm* defeatism

défaitiste [defetist] *adj & nmf* defeatist

défalquer [defalke] *vt* to deduct (**de** from)

défausser [defose] **se défausser** *vpr (aux cartes)* to discard; **se d. à cœur** to discard a heart/some hearts; **se d. d'un dix** to discard a ten

défaut [defo] *nm (a) (imperfection) (d'une personne)* fault, shortcoming; *(d'une pierre précieuse, d'un verre, d'un tissu)* flaw; *(d'une machine)* defect; *(d'un raisonnement)* flaw; *(inconvénient)* drawback; **c'est là son moindre d.** that's the least of his faults; **sans d.** faultless, flawless; **prendre qn en d.** to catch sb napping; **d. de fabrication** manufacturing fault; **d. de prononciation** *ou* **d'élocution** speech impediment *(b) (manque)* lack; **le courage lui a fait d.** his courage failed him; **l'argent lui fait cruellement d.** she is very short of money; **le bon sens lui fait cruellement d.** he is sadly lacking in common sense; **ou à d.,…** or, failing that,…; **à d. de qch** for lack of sth; **à d. d'un salaire conséquent, elle a au moins un travail intéressant** she might not have a very good salary, but at least her work is interesting *(c) Jur* default; **faire d.** to default; **d. de paiement** default on payment (**d**) *Math* **total approché par d.** total rounded down; *Ordinat* **lecteur/clavier par d.** default drive/keyboard

défaveur [defavœr] *nf* **être en d. (auprès de qn)** to be in disfavour (with sb); **s'attirer la d. de qn** to incur sb's disfavour

défavorable [defavɔrabl] *adj* unfavourable (**à** to)

défavorisé, -e [defavɔrize] *adj (milieu, pays)* under-privileged

défavoriser [defavɔrize] *vt* to put at a disadvantage (**par rapport à** compared to)

défectif, -ive [defɛktif, -iv] *adj* defective

défection [defɛksjɔ̃] *nf* (**a**) *(d'un espion, d'un soldat)* defection (**b**) *(annulation)* cancellation

défectueux, -euse [defɛktɥø, -øz] *adj* defective, faulty

défendable [defɑ̃dabl] *adj* defensible

défendre [defɑ̃dr] **1** *vt* (**a**) *(soutenir)* to defend (**contre** against) (**b**) *(protéger) (personne, pays, propriété)* to defend (**contre** against *ou* from); *(intérêts)* to protect; **d. qn contre le froid** *ou* **du froid** to protect sb from the cold; *Fig* **d. son bifteck** to look after number one; *Sport* **Durant défendra les buts de l'équipe d'Aix** Durant will be in goal for Aix (**c**) *(interdire)* to forbid, to prohibit; **ce médicament est défendu aux enfants** this medicine must not be given to children; **d. à qn de faire qch** to forbid sb to do sth; **il m'est défendu de fumer** I'm not allowed to smoke; **il est défendu de fumer** smoking is prohibited
2 se défendre *vpr* (**a**) *(se protéger)* to defend oneself (**de** *ou* **contre** against); **se d. comme un beau diable** to fight like a mad thing (**b**) *Fam (se débrouiller)* **je me défends (en anglais/en tennis)** I can get by (in English/at tennis) (**c**) *(se justifier)* **ça se défend** there's something to be said for it (**d**) *(s'empêcher)* **se d. de faire qch** to refrain from doing sth; **on ne peut se d. de les aimer** you can't help liking them

défenestrer [defənɛstre] **1** *vt* **d. qn** to throw sb out of a window
2 se défenestrer *vpr* to jump out of the window

défense¹ [defɑ̃s] *nf* (**a**) *(soutien) (d'une théorie, d'une politique, d'un accusé)* defence; **prendre la d. de qn** to come to sb's defence; **sans d.** defenceless; *Jur* **assurer la d. de qn** to defend sb; **qu'avez-vous à dire pour votre d.?** what do you have to say in your defence?; **d. des consommateurs** consumer protection (**b**) *(protection) (d'une personne, d'un pays, en sport)* defence; **d. aérienne/nationale/passive** air/national/civil defence; *Méd* **défenses immunitaires** immune defences (**c**) *(interdiction)* **d. d'entrer/de fumer** *(sur panneau)* no entry/smoking; **et d. d'en parler à ton père!** don't go telling your father about it!

défense² *nf (d'éléphant, de sanglier)* tusk

défenseur [defɑ̃sœr] *nm* (**a**) *(d'une personne, d'une ville, d'une cause, en sport)* defender; **jouer les défenseurs de la veuve et de l'orphelin** to protect the weak and oppressed (**b**) *Jur* counsel for the defence

défensif, -ive [defɑ̃sif, -iv] **1** *adj* defensive
2 *nf* **être** *ou* **se tenir sur la défensive** to be on the defensive

déféquer [34] [defeke] *vi* to defecate

déférence [deferɑ̃s] *nf* deference (**pour** for)

déférer [34] [defere] *vtJur* **d. une affaire à un tribunal** to refer a case to a court; **d. qn à la justice** to hand sb over to the police

déferlante [defɛrlɑ̃t] *adj f & nf* **(vague) d.** breaker; *Fig* tidal wave

déferlement [defɛrləmɑ̃] *nm (des vagues)* breaking; *Fig (de personnes)* invasion; *(d'enthousiasme, de violence, de racisme)* wave

déferler [defɛrle] *vi (vagues)* to break; **la foule déferle dans les rues** the crowd is surging along the streets; **les vacanciers déferlent sur les routes** holiday-makers are taking to the roads in droves

défi [defi] *nm* (**a**) *(acte de provocation)* challenge (**à** to); **lancer** *ou* **jeter un d. à qn** to throw out a challenge to sb; **mettre qn au d. de faire qch** to defy sb to do sth; **relever un d.** to take up a challenge (**b**) *(bravade)* defiance

défiance [defjɑ̃s] *nf* mistrust

déficience [defisjɑ̃s] *nf* deficiency; **d. immunologique** immune deficiency

déficient, -e [defisjɑ̃, -ɑ̃t] **1** *adj* deficient; *(raisonnement, théorie)* weak
2 *nm,f* **d. moteur** person with motor deficiency; **d. mental** mentally deficient person

déficit [defisit] *nm* (**a**) *Fin* deficit; **être en d.** to be in deficit; **d. budgétaire/commercial** budget/trade deficit (**b**) *Méd (mental)* deficiency; **d. immunitaire** immunodeficiency

déficitaire [defisitɛr] *adj (entreprise)* loss-making; *(compte)* in debit; *(budget)* in deficit

défier [66] [defje] **1** *vt* (**a**) *(provoquer)* to challenge; **d. qn aux échecs** to challenge sb to a game of chess (**b**) *(inciter)* **d. qn de faire qch** to defy sb to do sth (**c**) *(braver) (personne, danger, mort)* to defy (**d**) *(résister à)* **d. l'imagination** to defy the imagination; **des prix qui défient toute concurrence** unbeatable prices
2 se défier *vpr Litt* **se d. de** to mistrust

défigurer [defigyre] *vt (personne, paysage)* to disfigure; *Fig (vérité, sens)* to distort; *(pensée, intentions)* to misrepresent

défilé [defile] *nm* (**a**) *Géog* (mountain) pass (**b**) *(de manifestants)* march; *(de chars de carnaval)* procession; *Mil* parade; **un d. ininterrompu de touristes/ voitures** an endless stream of tourists/cars; **d. aérien** flypast; **d. de mode** fashion show

défilement [defiləmɑ̃] *nm Ordinat* scrolling

défiler¹ [defile] **se défiler** *vpr Fam (se dérober)* to slope off

défiler² *vi* (**a**) *(manifestants)* to march; *(chars de carnaval)* to drive in procession; *(touristes, voitures)* to stream; *Mil* to parade (**b**) *(avancer) (bande)* to wind on; *Ordinat* **faire d. un document** to scroll through a document; *Ordinat* **d. vers le bas/le haut** to scroll down/up (**c**) *(se succéder) (images, souvenirs)* to pass; **le paysage défile à toute vitesse** the countryside is speeding past

défini, -e [defini] *adj* (**a**) *(précis)* definite; **bien d.** clearly defined; *Ordinat* **d. par l'utilisateur** user-defined
(**b**) *Gram* definite

définir [definir] **1** *vt* to define
2 se définir *vpr* (**a**) *(concept)* **se d. comme** to be defined as (**b**) *(soi-même)* to describe oneself (**comme** as)

définissable [definisabl] *adj* definable

définitif, -ive [definitif, -iv] *adj* (**a**) *(irrévocable) (jugement, décision, version)* final (**b**) *(pour toujours) (séparation, fermeture)* permanent (**c**) *(qui fait autorité)* definitive (**d**) **en définitive** *(à la fin)* in the end

définition [definisjɔ̃] *nf* (**a**) *(d'un mot, de conditions)* definition; *(de mots croisés)* clue; **par d.** by definition (**b**) *(d'une image sur écran)* definition

définitivement [definitivmɑ̃] *adv* *(décider)* definitely; *(partir, s'installer)* for good; *(nommé)* permanently

défiscaliser [defiskalize] *vt* to exempt from tax

déflagration [deflagrasjɔ̃] *nf* *(explosion)* explosion

déflation [deflasjɔ̃] *nf Écon* deflation

déflecteur [deflektœr] *nm (d'une voiture) Br* quarterlight, *Am* vent

déflocage [deflɔkaʒ] *nm* removal of asbestos

déflorer [deflɔre] *vt* (**a**) *(vierge)* to deflower (**b**) *Fig (sujet)* to spoil

défoliant [defɔljɑ̃] *nm* defoliant

défonce [defɔ̃s] *nf Fam* **la d.** getting high

défoncé, -e [defɔ̃se] *adj* (**a**) *(chemin)* bumpy (**b**) *Fam (drogué)* high (**à** on)

défoncer [16] [defɔ̃se] **1** *vt (boîte, porte)* to smash in; *(matelas)* to ruin; *(mur)* to knock down; *(tonneau, bateau)* to stave in; *(chaussée)* to break up
   2 se défoncer *vpr Fam* (**a**) *(se droguer)* to get high (**à** on) (**b**) *(faire un grand effort)* to sweat blood (**pour faire qch** to do sth)

déforestation [defɔrestasjɔ̃] *nf* deforestation

déformant, -e [defɔrmɑ̃, -ɑ̃t] *adj (glace)* distorting

déformation [defɔrmasjɔ̃] *nf (d'un membre)* deformation; *(d'un vêtement, de chaussures)* putting out of shape; *(de métal)* buckling; *(de bois)* warping; *(des traits, d'une image, des faits)* distortion; *(de propos)* twisting; **d. professionnelle** = habits acquired through the type of work one does; *Hum* **ne fais pas attention, c'est la d. professionnelle!** don't worry, it's just my job!

déformer [defɔrme] **1** *vt (membre)* to deform; *(vêtement, chaussures)* to put out of shape; *(métal)* to buckle; *(bois)* to warp; *(traits, image, faits)* to distort; *(propos)* to twist; *(pensée)* to misrepresent
   2 se déformer *vpr (corps, vêtement, chaussures)* to get out of shape; *(bois)* to warp; *(métal)* to buckle

défoulement [defulmɑ̃] *nm Fam* letting off steam; **avoir besoin de d.** to need to let off steam

défouler [defule] *Fam* **1** *vt (agressivité)* to vent (**sur** on); **d. qn** to help sb let off steam; **ça défoule** it helps you let off steam
   2 se défouler *vpr* to let off steam; **se d. sur qn** to take it out on sb

défraîchi, -e [defreʃi] *adj (fleur, beauté)* faded; *(vêtement)* shabby

défrayer [53] [defreje] *vt* (**a**) *(rembourser)* **d. qn** to pay sb's expenses (**b**) **d. la chronique** to be widely talked about

défrichage [defriʃaʒ], **défrichement** [defriʃmɑ̃] *nm (de terrain)* clearing

défricher [defriʃe] *vt* to clear; *Fig (domaine)* to open up; *Fig* **d. le terrain** to prepare the ground

défriser [defrize] *vt (cheveux)* to straighten; *Fam Fig (agacer)* to bug

défroisser [defrwase] *vt* to smooth out

défroqué, -e [defrɔke] *adj* defrocked

défunt, -e [defɛ̃, -ɑ̃t] **1** *adj* **mon d. mari** my late husband; *Litt* **des amours défuntes** lost loves
   2 *nm,f* deceased; **prier pour les défunts** to pray for the dead

dégagé, -e [degaʒe] *adj (ton, air)* casual; *(ciel, route)* clear; *(vue)* open; **une coupe avec la nuque très dégagée** a haircut that is very short at the back

dégagement [degaʒmɑ̃] *nm* (**a**) *(d'une route, des poumons)* clearing (**b**) *(au football)* clearance (**c**) *(de vapeur, de gaz, de chaleur)* emission

dégager [45] [degaʒe] **1** *vt* (**a**) *(libérer)* to free (**de** from); *(d'une voiture accidentée, de décombres)* to pull clear (**de** of); **une robe qui dégage les épaules** an off-the-shoulder dress (**b**) *(désencombrer) (route, passage)* to clear; *Fam* **dégage!** clear off! (**c**) *Fam (enlever)* to clear away; **tu vas me d. toutes ces bricoles de tes étagères** I want you to clear all these odds and ends off your shelves (**d**) *(laisser échapper) (vapeur, odeur, chaleur)* to emit; *Fig (impression)* to give off (**e**) *(au football)* **d. (le ballon) en touche** to kick the ball into touch (**f**) *Fin (crédits)* to release; *(profit)* to show
   2 se dégager *vpr* (**a**) *(se libérer)* to free oneself (**de** from); *(d'une situation difficile)* to extricate oneself (**de** from) (**b**) *(se débloquer) (ciel, nez)* to clear (**c**) *(gaz, odeur, chaleur)* to be given off (**de** by); *Fig* **le magnétisme qui se dégage d'elle** the magnetism she radiates

dégaine [degen] *nf Fam (démarche)* awkward way of walking; *(apparence)* strange appearance

dégainer [degene] *vt (arme)* to draw

dégarni, -e [degarni] *adj (personne)* balding; **avoir le front d.** to have a receding hairline

dégarnir [degarnir] **1** *vt (frigidaire, rayons)* to empty
   2 se dégarnir *vpr (personne)* to go bald; *(arbre)* to lose its leaves; *(salle)* to empty; *(rayons)* to be emptied

dégât [dega] *nm* damage; **faire du d.** *ou* **des dégâts** to cause damage; *Fig* **limiter les dégâts** to limit the damage; **dégâts des eaux** water damage; **dégâts matériels** material damage

dégel [deʒel] *nm Météo & Pol* thaw; *Écon (des prix, des salaires, des crédits)* unfreezing

dégeler [39] [deʒle] **1** *vt* (**a**) *(réchauffer)* to thaw; *(surgelé)* to defrost; *Fig (public)* to warm up; **d. l'atmosphère** to make the atmosphere less chilly (**b**) *Écon (prix, salaires, crédits)* to unfreeze
   2 *vi (étang, surgelé)* to thaw; **faire d. qch** *(surgelé)* to defrost sth
   3 *v impersonnel* to thaw
   4 se dégeler *vpr* (**a**) *(étang)* to thaw (**b**) *Fig (atmosphère)* to become less chilly; *(personne)* to thaw out, to relax

dégénératif, -ive [deʒeneratif, -iv] *adj* degenerative

dégénéré, -e [deʒenere] **1** *adj* (**a**) *(arriéré)* mentally defective (**b**) *(dépravé)* degenerate
   2 *nm,f* (**a**) *(arriéré)* mental defective (**b**) *(dépravé)* degenerate

dégénérer [34] [deʒenere] *vi (mal tourner) (situation, conversation)* to degenerate (**en** into); **son rhume a dégénéré en bronchite** his cold developed into bronchitis

dégénérescence [deʒeneresɑ̃s] *nf Méd & Fig* degeneration

dégingandé, -e [deʒɛ̃gɑ̃de] *adj* gangling, lanky

dégivrage [deʒivraʒ] *nm* (**a**) *(action) (d'un pare-brise)* de-icing; *(d'un réfrigérateur)* defrosting (**b**) *(dispositif) (d'un pare-brise)* de-icer; *(d'un réfrigérateur)* defroster

dégivrer [deʒivre] *vt (pare-brise)* to de-ice; *(réfrigérateur)* to defrost

déglacer [deglase] *vt Culin (poêle à frire)* to deglaze

déglinguer [deglɛ̃ge] *Fam* **1** *vt (appareil)* to bust; **ma moto est toute déglinguée** my motorbike is falling to pieces

2 se déglinguer *vpr (appareil)* to go wrong; *(véhicule)* to fall to pieces

déglutir [deglytir] *vi* to swallow

déglutition [deglytisjɔ̃] *nf* swallowing

dégobiller [degɔbije] *très Fam* **1** *vi* to puke

2 *vt* to puke up

dégonflé, -e [degɔ̃fle] **1** *adj* **(a)** *(pneu, ballon)* flat **(b)** *Fam (lâche)* chicken

2 *nm,f Fam* chicken

dégonfler [degɔ̃fle] **1** *vt (pneu, ballon)* to let the air out of, to deflate

2 *vi (partie du corps)* to go down

3 se dégonfler *vpr* **(a)** *(pneu, ballon)* to go flat **(b)** *Fam (personne)* to chicken out

dégorger [45] [degɔrʒe] **1** *vt* **(a)** *(évacuer)* to discharge; **la rue a dégorgé un flot de gens** a crowd of people surged from the street **(b)** *(passage, tuyau, évier)* to unblock

2 *vi* **faire d. des concombres** = to remove water from cucumbers by sprinkling them with salt

dégot(t)er [degɔte] *vt Fam* to dig up

dégouliner [deguline] *vi (liquide)* to trickle; **je dégouline** I'm dripping wet

dégoupiller [degupije] *vt* to pull the pin out of

dégourdi, -e [degurdi] **1** *adj* smart, bright

2 *nm,f* **c'est un d.** he's a smart one

dégourdir [degurdir] **1** *vt (membres)* to remove the stiffness from; *Fig* **d. qn** to teach sb a thing or two

2 se dégourdir *vpr* **(a)** *(membres)* **se d. les jambes** to stretch one's legs **(b)** *Fig* to learn a thing or two

dégoût [degu] *nm* **(a)** *(aversion)* disgust, distaste; **éprouver du d. pour qch** to be disgusted by sth; **prendre qch en d.** to take a strong dislike to sth **(b)** *(lassitude)* weariness; **le d. de la vie** world-weariness

dégoûtant, -e [degutɑ̃, -ɑ̃t] **1** *adj* disgusting

2 *nm,f* disgusting person; **un vieux d.** a dirty old man

dégoûté, -e [degute] **1** *adj* **(a)** *(écœuré) (air)* disgusted; *Ironique* **vous n'êtes pas d.!** you're not fussy! **(b)** *(choqué)* disgusted **(c)** *(las)* weary; **être d. de qch** to be weary *or* sick of sth

2 *nm,f* **faire le d.** to turn up one's nose

dégoûter [degute] *vt* **d. qn** *(physiquement)* to turn sb's stomach; *(moralement)* to disgust sb, to make sb sick; **d. qn de qch** to put sb off sth; **c'est à vous d. de l'Espagne/des hommes!** it's enough to put you off Spain/men for life!

dégoutter [degute] **dégoutter de** *vt ind (laisser couler)* to drip with

dégradant, -e [degradɑ̃] *adj* degrading

dégradation [degradasjɔ̃] *nf (d'un monument)* defacement; *(de matériel scolaire, de l'environnement)* damage (**de** to); *Fig (de la santé, de relations, d'une situation)* deterioration

dégradé [degrade] *nm (de couleurs)* gradation; **un d. de bleus** blues shading off into each other; **se faire faire un d.** *(chez le coiffeur)* to have one's hair layered; *Ordinat* **d. de couleur** colour scale

dégrader [degrade] **1** *vt* **(a)** *(abîmer) (monument)* to deface; *(matériel, maison)* to damage; *Ordinat (données)* to corrupt **(b)** *Fig (humilier)* to degrade **(c)** *Mil* to demote

2 se dégrader *vpr* **(a)** *(se détériorer) (santé, relations, situation)* to deteriorate; *(bâtiment)* to fall into disrepair **(b)** *(s'abaisser)* to degrade oneself

dégrafer [degrafe] **1** *vt (vêtement, bracelet)* to undo

2 se dégrafer *vpr* **(a)** *(vêtement, bracelet)* to come undone **(b)** *(femme)* to undo one's dress

dégraissage [degrɛsaʒ] *nm (d'une entreprise)* downsizing

dégraisser [degrese] **1** *vt (bouillon)* to skim the fat off; *Fig (entreprise)* to downsize; **d. les effectifs** to cut back on staff

2 *vi (entreprise)* to downsize

degré [dəgre] *nm* **(a)** *(d'un angle, de chaleur)* degree; *(de boisson alcoolisée)* proof; **combien de degrés fait ce whisky?** what proof is this whisky?; **d. Celsius** degree Celsius; **d. Fahrenheit** degree Fahrenheit **(b)** *(stade, niveau)* stage; **d. de parenté** family relationship; **cousins au second d.** second cousins; **brûlure au deuxième/troisième d.** second/third degree burn; **au plus haut d.** *(extrêmement)* in the extreme; **jusqu'à un certain d.** up to a point; **par degrés** by degrees; **prendre une plaisanterie au premier d.** to take a joke seriously **(c)** *(d'escalier)* step; *(d'échelle)* rung

dégressif, -ive [degresif, -iv] *adj* **tarif d.** tapering rate; **impôt d.** degressive taxation

dégrèvement [degrɛvmɑ̃] *nm* **d. (fiscal)** tax relief

dégriffé, -e [degrife] **1** *adj* = with its designer label removed and reduced in price

2 *nm* = reduced-price designer item with its label removed

dégringolade [degrɛ̃gɔlad] *nf Fam (chute)* tumble; *Fig (d'une entreprise)* collapse; *(des prix, des cours)* slump (**de** in)

dégringoler [degrɛ̃gɔle] *Fam* **1** *vt* to rush down

2 *vi (personne)* to tumble; *Fig (entreprise)* to collapse; *(prix, cours)* to slump

dégripper [degripe] *vt (mécanisme)* to unjam

dégriser [degrize] **1** *vt* to sober up; *Fig* to bring down to earth

2 se dégriser *vpr* to sober up

dégrossir [degrosir] *vt (bois)* to trim; *(pierre)* to rough-hew; *Fig (travail)* to rough out; **d. qn** to knock the rough edges off sb; **être mal dégrossi** to be uncouth

dégrouper [degrupe] *vt* to divide into groups

déguenillé, -e [degənije] *adj* ragged

déguerpir [degɛrpir] *vi* to clear off; **faire d. qn** to chase sb away

dégueulasse [degœlas] *très Fam* **1** *adj (sale)* filthy; *(mauvais, désagréable)* disgusting; **c'est pas d.** *(bon)* it's not bad at all; **être d. avec qn** to be mean to sb; **se balader en d.** to go around in sloppy old clothes

2 *nmf* **un gros d.** *(sale)* a filthy pig; *(débauché)* a filthy swine

dégueulasser [degœlase] *vt très Fam* to mess up

dégueuler [degœle] *vi très Fam* to puke

dégueulis [degœli] *nm très Fam* puke

déguisé, -e [degize] *adj (pour tromper)* disguised; *(pour s'amuser)* dressed up; **avec une joie non déguisée** with unconcealed delight

déguisement [degizmɑ̃] *nm (pour tromper)* disguise; *(pour s'amuser)* fancy dress

déguiser [degize] **1** *vt* **(a)** *(costumer)* to dress up; **d. qn en clown** to dress sb up as a clown **(b)** *(voix, écriture, vérité, pensée)* to disguise

2 se déguiser *vpr (pour tromper)* to disguise oneself;

(pour s'amuser) to dress up; **se d. en pompier** to dress up as a fireman

dégurgiter [degyrʒite] *vt aussi Fig* to regurgitate

dégustation [degystasjɔ̃] *nf* tasting; **d. de vin** wine tasting; **d. d'huîtres** *(panneau devant un restaurant)* oysters served here

déguster [degyste] *vt* (**a**) *(tester) (vin, alcool)* to taste (**b**) *(savourer) (aliment, livre)* to savour (**c**) *très Fam* **toute sa vie, elle a dégusté** *(souffert)* she's had a rough time of it all her life; **tu vas d.!** you're in for it!

déhanché, -e [deɑ̃ʃe] *adj* lopsided

déhanchement [deɑ̃ʃmɑ̃] *nm (en marchant)* swaying of the hips; *(à l'arrêt)* standing with one's weight on one foot

déhancher [deɑ̃ʃe] **se déhancher** *vpr (en marchant)* to sway one's hips; *(à l'arrêt)* to stand with one's weight on one foot

dehors [dəɔr] **1** *adv (à l'extérieur)* outside; *(en plein air)* out of doors; *(pas chez soi)* out; *Fam* **ficher** *ou* **foutre qn d.** to kick sb out; **ne pas mettre le nez** *ou* **les pieds d.** not to set foot outside; **en d.** *(s'ouvrir, tourner)* outwards; **marcher les pieds en d.** to walk with one's feet turned out; **en d. de** *(à l'extérieur de)* outside; *(à part)* apart from; **rester en d. d'une dispute** to keep out of an argument; **en d. du sujet** *(remarque)* irrelevant

2 *nm* (**a**) *(extérieur)* outside; **au d.** on the outside; *(se pencher, se répandre)* out (**b**) *(apparence)* **une maison aux d. imposants** a house with an imposing exterior; **sous des d. aimables** under a pleasant exterior

déhoussable [deusabl] *adj (canapé, siège)* with loose covers

déjà [deʒa] *adv* (**a**) *(dès maintenant)* already; *(si tôt)* yet; **il est d. trois heures** it's already three o'clock; **faut-il que vous partiez d.?** do you have to go so soon?

(**b**) *(auparavant)* before; **j'avais d. lu ce livre** I'd read that book before; **d. en 1900** as early as 1900

(**c**) *(intensif)* **j'aurais dû le faire il y a d. trois jours** I should have done it three days ago as it is; **c'est d. ça!**, **c'est d. pas mal!** that's not bad at all!; **vous avez d. trop de travail** you have too much work as it is; **d. que je n'en ai pas beaucoup, si tu m'en prends la moitié…** I haven't got much as it is, so if you take half…

(**d**) *(interrogatif)* **qu'est-ce que vous faites, d.?** what did you say your job was?; **c'est quoi, d., ton nom?** what was your name again?

déjanté, -e [deʒɑ̃te] *adj très Fam* **être (complètement) d.** to be off one's rocker *or Br* trolley

déjanter [deʒɑ̃te] **1** *vi très Fam (être fou)* to be off one's rocker; *(devenir fou)* to flip one's lid

2 se déjanter *vpr (pneu)* to come off the rim

déjà-vu [deʒavy] *nm inv* **une impression de d.** a feeling of déjà vu; **c'est du d.** *(ce n'est pas original)* it's the same old thing

déjeuner [deʒœne] **1** *nm* (**a**) *(repas de midi)* lunch; **prendre son d.** to have lunch; **d. d'affaires/de travail** business/working lunch (**b**) *(repas du matin)* **(petit) d.** breakfast (**c**) *(tasse et soucoupe)* breakfast cup and saucer

2 *vi* (**a**) *(le matin)* to have breakfast (**b**) *(à midi)* to have lunch; **nous avons les Dupont à d. dimanche** the Duponts are coming for lunch on Sunday; **d. d'un sandwich** to have a sandwich for lunch

déjouer [deʒwe] *vt (complot, plans)* to foil

délabré, -e [delabre] *adj (bâtiment, meuble)* dilapidated; *(santé)* ruined

délabrement [delabrəmɑ̃] *nm (d'un bâtiment, d'un meuble)* dilapidated state; *(d'une entreprise)* ruin; **dans un état de grand d.** *(bâtiment)* in a state of total disrepair

délabrer [delabre] **se délabrer** *vpr (bâtiment)* to fall into disrepair; *(meuble)* to fall to pieces; *(entreprise)* to go to rack and ruin; *(santé)* to deteriorate

délacer [16] [delase] **1** *vt (chaussures)* to untie; *(corset)* to unlace

2 se délacer *vpr (chaussures)* to come untied; *(corset)* to come unlaced; *(femme)* to unlace one's corset

délai [delɛ] *nm* (**a**) *(laps de temps)* time allowed; **dans un d. de dix jours** within ten days; **il faut compter un d. de dix jours** you should allow ten days; **respecter** *ou* **tenir les délais** to meet the deadline; **dans les délais** on time; **dans les plus brefs délais** as soon as possible; **lundi dernier d.** by Monday at the very latest; **d. de livraison: un mois** allow one month for delivery; **d. de paiement** *(fixé par contrat)* term of payment (**b**) *(prolongation)* extension; **laisser à qn un d. de réflexion** to give sb time to think; **sans d.** without delay, immediately

délaisser [delese] *vt (abandonner)* to desert, to abandon; *(négliger)* to neglect

délassant, -e [delɑsɑ̃, -ɑ̃t] *adj (bain, massage)* relaxing; *(lecture)* entertaining

délassement [delɑsmɑ̃] *nm* relaxation

délasser [delɑse] **1** *vt* to relax

2 se délasser *vpr* to relax

délateur, -trice [delatœr, -tris] *nm,f* informer

délation [delɑsjɔ̃] *nf* denouncement

délavé, -e [delave] *adj (tissu, jean)* faded; *(couleur)* watery

délayage [delɛjaʒ] *nm Péj* padding

délayer [53] [deleje] *vt* (**a**) *(poudre)* to add water to; *(peinture)* to thin; *(liquide)* to water down; **d. de la farine dans du lait** to mix flour with milk (**b**) *Fig (discours, texte)* to pad out

Delco® [delko] *nm Aut* distributor

délectable [delɛktabl] *adj* delectable

délecter [delɛkte] **se délecter** *vpr* **se d. de qch/à faire qch** to take delight in sth/in doing sth

délégation [delegasjɔ̃] *nf* (**a**) *(action de déléguer) (de représentants)* delegation; **agir par d.** to act on the authority invested in one; **d. de pouvoir** delegation of authority (**b**) *(groupe)* delegation

délégué, -e [delege] *nm,f* delegate; *Scol* **d. (de classe)** class representative *(at class meetings)*; **d. du personnel** staff representative; **d. syndical** union representative; *(d'usine)* shop steward

déléguer [34] [delege] *vt* (**a**) *(personne)* to delegate (**b**) *(transmettre) (pouvoirs)* to delegate (**à** to); **c'est un patron qui sait d.** he's a boss who knows how to delegate

délestage [delɛstaʒ] *nm (d'un navire, d'un ballon)* unballasting; **pour assurer le d. des grandes artères** to relieve congestion on the main roads; **itinéraire de d.** relief route

délester [delɛste] *vt (navire, ballon)* to unballast; *(voie de communication)* to relieve congestion on; *aussi Hum* **d. qn de qch** to relieve sb of sth

délibération [deliberasjɔ̃] *nf* (**a**) *(débat)* deliberation; **être en d.** to be under discussion (**b**) *(réflexion)* deliberation; **après mûre d.** after careful consideration

délibéré, -e [delibere] **1** *adj (intentionnel)* deliberate **2** *nmJur (de juges)* consultation
délibérément [deliberemã] *adv* deliberately
délibérer [34] [delibere] *vi* (**a**) *(discuter)* to deliberate (**de** *ou* **sur** on); *Jur (jury)* to consider its verdict (**b**) *(réfléchir)* to deliberate
délicat, -e [delika, -at] *adj* (**a**) *(fragile, fin, difficile)* delicate; *(peau)* sensitive; *(travail)* fine (**b**) *(raffiné)* *(goûts)* refined; *(gestes)* graceful; *(plat)* sophisticated; **avoir le palais d.** to have a discerning palate (**c**) *(plein de tact)* tactful; **quelle attention délicate!** how thoughtful!; **peu d.** *(peu scrupuleux)* unscrupulous (**d**) *(exigeant)* fussy; **faire le d.** turn up one's nose
délicatement [delikatmã] *adv (légèrement)* gently; *(finement)* finely
délicatesse [delikatɛs] *nf* (**a**) *(d'un objet)* fragility; *(d'une fleur, d'un tissu, d'un coloris)* delicacy; *(de la peau)* sensitivity; *(de la santé)* frailty (**b**) *(des goûts)* refinement; *(des gestes)* gracefulness; *(d'un plat)* sophistication; **avec d.** *(légèrement)* gently; *(finement)* finely (**c**) *(difficulté)* delicacy (**d**) *(tact)* tact; **avec d.** tactfully
délice [delis] *nm (plaisir)* delight; **cette tarte est un vrai d.** this tart is absolutely delicious
délices [delis] *nfpl Litt ou Hum* delights; **faire ses d. de qch** to delight in sth
délicieusement [delisjøzmã] *adv (agréablement)* delightfully; **d. bon** *(plat)* absolutely delicious
délicieux, -euse [delisjø, -øz] *adj (nourriture, sensation, chaleur)* delicious; *(personne, robe)* delightful
délictueux, -euse [deliktɥø, -øz] *adj Jur* **acte d.** offence
délié, -e [delje] **1** *adj (taille)* slim; *(doigts)* nimble **2** *nm (de l'écriture)* thin stroke
délier [66] [delje] **1** *vt* to untie; **d. qn d'une promesse** to release sb from a promise; *Fig* **le vin lui a délié la langue** the wine loosened his tongue **2 se délier** *vpr (se défaire)* to come untied; *Fig* **sa langue s'est déliée** she found her tongue
délimiter [delimite] *vt (territoire)* to demarcate; *(responsabilité, sujet)* to define
délinquance [delɛ̃kãs] *nf* delinquency; **d. juvénile** juvenile delinquency; **la petite d. des banlieues** petty crime in the suburbs
délinquant, -e [delɛ̃kã, -ãt] **1** *adj* delinquent **2** *nm,f* offender; **d. juvénile** juvenile delinquent; **d. sexuel** sex offender
déliquescence [delikɛsãs] *nf Péj (d'une civilisation, des mœurs)* decay; **tomber en d.** to fall into decay
déliquescent, -e [delikɛsã, -ãt] *adj Péj (civilisation, mœurs)* decadent
délirant, -e [delirã, -ãt] *adj Méd* delirious; *Fig (joie, imagination)* frenzied; **c'est d. de leur demander de tout payer!** it's crazy asking them to pay for everything!
délire [delir] *nm* (**a**) *Méd* delirium; **avoir le d.** to be delirious; *Fig* **c'est du d.!** it's crazy!; **d. de grandeur** delusions of grandeur; **d. de persécution** persecution complex (**b**) *(frénésie)* frenzy; **foule en d.** frenzied crowd; *Fam* **cette soirée, c'est le d.!** it's a wild party!
délirer [delire] *vi (être malade)* to be delirious; *(dire n'importe quoi)* to rave
delirium tremens [delirjɔmtremɛ̃s] *nm* delirium tremens; **avoir le d.** to have delirium tremens
délit [deli] *nm* offence; **d. de fuite** failure to report an accident; **d. d'initié** insider dealing *or* trading

délivrance [delivrãs] *nf* (**a**) *(soulagement)* relief; **leur départ fut une vraie d.** it was a real relief when they left (**b**) *(accouchement)* delivery (**c**) *(d'un certificat, d'un passeport, d'un permis)* issue
délivrer [delivre] **1** *vt* (**a**) *(libérer) (captif, otage)* to rescue; *(ville)* to liberate; *(peuple)* to set free; **d. qn de ses liens** to free sb from his bonds (**b**) *(soulager)* **d. qn d'un secret trop lourd** to share the burden of a secret with sb; **d. qn d'un grand poids** to take a weight off sb's shoulders (**c**) *(remettre) (marchandises)* to deliver; *(certificat, passeport, permis)* to issue **2 se délivrer** *vpr* to free oneself (**de** from)
délocalisation [delɔkalizasjɔ̃] *nf* relocation
délocaliser [delɔkalize] *vt* to relocate
déloger [45] [delɔʒe] *vt (envahisseur)* to drive out (**de** from); *(locataire)* to evict; *(objet coincé)* to dislodge (**de** from)
déloyal, -e, -aux, -ales [delwajal, -o] *adj (ami)* disloyal, unfaithful; *(adversaire, pratique, concurrence)* unfair; *(coup)* illegal
delta [dɛlta] *nm* (**a**) *(d'un fleuve)* delta (**b**) *Aviat* **(aile) d.** delta wing
deltaplane [dɛltaplan] *nm* hang-glider; **faire du d.** to go hang-gliding
déluge [delyʒ] *nm (de pluie)* downpour; *(d'injures)* torrent; *(de larmes)* flood; *Rel* **le D.** the Flood; **noyer qn sous un d. de compliments** to shower sb with compliments; **après moi le d.!** when I'm gone I don't care what happens!
déluré, -e [delyre] *adj (vif)* sharp, smart; *Péj (provocant)* forward
démagogie [demagɔʒi] *nf* demagogy
démagogique [demagɔʒik] *adj* demagogic
démagogue [demagɔg] *nmf* demagogue
demain [dəmɛ̃] **1** *adv* tomorrow; **d. soir** tomorrow evening; **d. en huit** a week tomorrow, tomorrow week; **à d.!** see you tomorrow!; **le journal de d.** tomorrow's paper; *Fam* **ce n'est pas pour d., ce n'est pas d. la veille** that won't happen for a long time yet; *Fig* **d. il fera jour** tomorrow is another day; *Fig* **de d.** *(de l'avenir)* of tomorrow **2** *nm* tomorrow; **tu as tout d. pour y réfléchir** you've got all tomorrow to think about it
demande [dəmãd] *nf* (**a**) *(requête)* request (**de** for); *(formulaire)* application form; **faire une d. de qch** *(de permis, de prêt)* to apply for sth; **faire qch à** *ou* **sur la d. de qn** to do sth at sb's request; **à la d. générale** by popular demand; **sur d.** on request; **demandes d'emploi** *(titre de rubrique)* situations wanted; **d. (en mariage)** proposal (of marriage); **faire sa d. (en mariage)** to propose; **d. de rançon** ransom demand (**b**) *Écon* demand; **d. des consommateurs** consumer demand (**c**) *Jur* **d. en divorce** divorce petition; **d. de dommages-intérêts** claim for damages (**d**) *(besoin) (de soins, d'affection)* need
demander [dəmãde] **1** *vt* (**a**) *(réclamer) (augmentation, addition, preuves)* to ask for; *(dommages et intérêts)* to claim; **d. qch à qn** to ask sb for sth; *(service)* to ask sb sth; **d. à qn de faire qch** to ask sb to do sth; **d. à manger/boire** to ask for something to eat/drink; **d. son avis à qn** to ask sb's opinion; **d. le divorce** to file for divorce; **d. la main de qn** to ask for sb's hand (in marriage); **d. qn en mariage** to propose to sb; **d. la parole** to ask to speak; **d. la permission de faire qch** to ask (for) permission to do sth; **combien demandez-vous de l'heure?** how much do you charge an hour?;

combien en demande-t-elle? how much is she asking for it?; **je ne demande pas mieux que de vous aider** I'll be only too pleased to help you; **il ne demande que ça** he'd be only too pleased; *Hum* **que demande le peuple?** what more could I/he/*etc* ask?; **je ne demande qu'une seule chose: qu'on me laisse tranquille** all I ask is to be left alone; **on demande un maçon** *(dans une petite annonce)* builder wanted; **être très demandé** to be in great demand; **il n'y a qu'à** *ou* **il suffit de d.** you/he/*etc* only have/has to ask (**b**) *(nécessiter) (tact, réflexion, attention)* to require; **ça demande de gros sacrifices** great sacrifices are called for

(**c**) *(exiger)* to demand; **en d. trop à qn** to ask too much of sb; **d. l'impossible** to ask the impossible

(**d**) *(s'enquérir de) (prix, cause, raison)* to ask; **d. qch à qn** to ask sb sth; **il m'a demandé de tes nouvelles** he asked after you; *Fam* **je ne t'ai rien demandé!** I didn't ask for your advice!; **je vous (le) demande, je vous demande un peu!** I ask you!

(**e**) *(appeler) (médecin, prêtre)* to ask for; **on vous demande** you're wanted; **on vous demande au téléphone** there's a call for you

2 demander à *vt ind* **d. à faire qch** to ask to do sth; **les suspects ne demandaient qu'à parler** the suspects were only too willing to speak; **demande à ce qu'on vienne te chercher** ask someone to come and collect you

3 se demander *vpr* to wonder, to ask oneself; **je me demande pourquoi elle a dit ça** I wonder why she said that; **c'est à se d. si...** it makes you wonder whether...; **des choses comme ça, ça ne se demande pas!** you don't ask that sort of question!

demandeur, -euse [dəmãdœr, -øz] *nm,f* **d. d'asile** asylum seeker; **d. d'emploi** job seeker

démangeaison [demãʒɛzɔ̃] *nf* itch; **avoir une d.** to have an itch, to be itching; **j'ai des démangeaisons dans les jambes** my legs are itchy

démanger [45] [demãʒe] *vi* to itch; **l'épaule me démange** my shoulder's itching; *Fig* **méfie-toi, la main me démange!** *(à un enfant)* watch out or you'll feel the back of my hand!; **ça me démange de lui dire ce que je pense** I'm itching to tell him/her what I think

démantèlement [demãtɛlmã] *nm* breaking up

démanteler [39] [demãtle] *vt* to break up

démantibuler [demãtibyle] *Fam* **1** *vt* to break up
2 se démantibuler *vpr* to come to pieces

démaquillage [demakijaʒ] *nm* removal of make-up

démaquillant, -e [demakijã, -ãt] **1** *adj* cleansing
2 *nm* cleanser; **d. pour les yeux** eye make-up remover

démaquiller [demakije] **1** *vt* **d. qn** to remove sb's make-up
2 se démaquiller *vpr* to remove one's make-up; **se d. les yeux** to remove one's eye make-up

démarcation [demarkasjɔ̃] *nf* demarcation

démarchage [demarʃaʒ] *nm (porte-à-porte)* door-to-door selling; **d. électoral** canvassing; **d. par téléphone** telesales

démarche [demarʃ] *nf* (**a**) *(allure)* gait, walk (**b**) *(requête)* step; **faire une d. auprès de qn** to approach sb; **faire les démarches nécessaires pour faire qch** to take the necessary steps to do sth (**c**) *Fig (cheminement)* process; **d. intellectuelle** thought process

démarcher [demarʃe] *vt* to canvass for

démarcheur, -euse [demarʃœr, -øz] *nm,f* door-to-door salesman, *f* saleswoman

démarque [demark] *nf Com* markdown; **la d. inconnue** shrinkage

démarquer [demarke] **1** *vt (marchandises)* to mark down
2 se démarquer *vpr Sport* to lose one's marker; *Fig* **se d. de qn** *(se distinguer)* to distinguish oneself from sb

démarrage [demaraʒ] *nm (d'un moteur)* starting; *(d'une entreprise)* start-up; *(d'un projet, d'une campagne publicitaire)* start; **faire un d.** *(coureur)* to put on a spurt; *Ordinat* **d. à chaud/froid** warm/cold start; **d. en côte** hill start

démarrer [demare] **1** *vi* (**a**) *(véhicule)* to move off; *(moteur)* to start; *(conducteur)* to drive off (**b**) *(commencer)* to start; **bien/mal d.** to get off to a good/bad start (**c**) *(commencer à réussir)* to take off
2 *vt* to start; *Ordinat* to boot (up), to start up

démarreur [demarœr] *nm Aut* starter (motor)

démasquer [demaske] *vt aussi Fig* to unmask

démâter [demɑte] **1** *vt* to dismast
2 *vi* to lose its mast

démêlant [demelã] *adj m & nm* **(produit) d.** conditioner

démêlé [demele] *nm* disagreement (**avec** with); **avoir des démêlés avec la justice** to be in trouble with the law

démêler [demele] **1** *vt (fil, laine, cheveux)* to untangle; *(mystère)* to unravel; **d. le vrai du faux** to disentangle the truth from the lies
2 se démêler *vpr* **se d. de** to extricate oneself from

démembrement [demãbrəmã] *nm (d'un empire)* breaking up; *(d'une propriété agricole)* division

démembrer [demãbre] *vt (empire)* to break up; *(propriété agricole)* to divide (up)

déménagement [demenaʒmã] *nm* move; **c'est pour quand le d.?** when are you/we/*etc* moving?

déménager [45] [demenaʒe] **1** *vi* (**a**) *(personne, entreprise)* to move; **où déménage-t-il?** where's he moving to?; **d. à la cloche de bois** to do a moonlight flit; *Fam* **allez, déménagez!** beat it! (**b**) *Fam Fig (musique)* to be mind-blowing; *(cocktail)* to pack a punch
2 *vt (meubles)* to move

déménageur [demenaʒœr] *nm Br* removal man, *Am* furniture mover; **avoir des épaules de d.** to have strong broad shoulders

démence [demãs] *nf* insanity; *Méd* dementia; *Fam* **c'est de la d.!** it's madness!

démener [46] [demne] **se démener** *vpr* (**a**) *(s'agiter)* to thrash about; **se d. comme un beau diable** *(pour se libérer)* to struggle like a madman (**b**) *(se dépenser)* to exert oneself (**c**) *(faire des efforts)* **se d. pour faire qch** to go to great lengths to do sth

dément, -e [demã, -ãt] **1** *adj (fou)* insane; *Fam (formidable)* terrific; *Fam* **c'est d.!** it's unreal!
2 *nm,f* lunatic; *Méd* demented person

démenti [demãti] *nm* denial; *Journ* disclaimer; **opposer un d. formel à qch** to issue a firm denial of sth

démentiel, -elle [demãsjɛl] *adj (idée, projet)* insane; *Fam (incroyable)* crazy

démentir [64a] [demãtir] **1** *vt* to deny; *(être en contradiction avec)* to belie
2 se démentir *vpr (cesser)* **leur honnêteté ne s'est jamais démentie** they've always been unfailing in their honesty

démerder [demɛrde] **se démerder** *vpr très Fam* to get by, to manage; **démerde-toi tout seul!** sort it out yourself!; **elle est assez grande pour se d. seule** she's old enough to take care of herself; **elle se démerde pas mal en cuisine/tennis** she's not a bad cook/tennis player; **se d. pour faire qch** to manage to do sth

démériter [demerite] *vi* to be at fault; **je ne vois pas en quoi il a démérité** I don't see how he is at fault

démesure [deməzyr] *nf* excess

démesuré, -e [deməzyre] *adj (en taille)* enormous; *(orgueil, ambition)* excessive

démesurément [deməzyremã] *adv* enormously

démettre¹ [47] [demɛtr] **1** *vt* **il m'a démis l'épaule** he dislocated my shoulder

2 se démettre *vpr* **se d. l'épaule/le genou** to dislocate one's shoulder/knee

démettre² **1** *vt* **d. qn de ses fonctions** to remove sb from his/her post

2 se démettre *vpr* **se d. de ses fonctions** to resign from one's post

demeurant [dəmœrã] **au demeurant** *adv (malgré tout)* for all that; *(d'ailleurs)* after all

demeure [dəmœr] *nf* **(a)** *(château)* mansion; *Litt (résidence)* (place of) residence; *Euph* **dernière d.** last resting place **(b)** **mettre qn en d. de faire qch** to instruct sb to do sth; *Jur* to give sb notice to do sth **(c)** **à d.** permanently

demeuré, -e [dəmœre] **1** *adj Vieilli* mentally retarded; *Fam Péj* halfwitted

2 *nm,f Vieilli* mentally retarded person; *Fam Péj* half-wit

demeurer [dəmœre] *vi* **(a)** *(aux* **être)** *(rester)* to remain; **d. convaincu que...** to remain convinced that...; **d. fidèle à qn** to remain faithful to sb; **demeurons-en là** let's leave it at that; **il n'en demeure pas moins que...** the fact remains that... **(b)** *Formel (aux* **avoir)** *(habiter)* to reside

demi, -e [dəmi] **1** *adj* **(a)** *(après un nom)* **deux heures et demie** *(durée)* two and a half hours; *(moment)* half past two; **un litre/kilo et d.** a litre/kilo and a half; **il gagne trois fois et demie ce que je gagne** he earns three and a half times as much as I do **(b)** *(avant un nom ou un adjectif)* half; **une d.-cuillère de sucre** half a teaspoon of sugar

2 *nm* **(a)** *(moitié)* half **(b)** *(bière)* **un d.** a beer, ≃ a half **(c)** *Sport (au football)* midfielder; **d. de mêlée** *(au rugby)* scrum half; **d. d'ouverture** *(au rugby)* fly half

3 *nf* **demie** *(heure)* **il est la demie** it's half past; **à la demie** at half past

4 *adv* half; **d. plein** half full; **à d.** half; **à d. mort** half dead; **faire les choses à d.** to do things by halves; **croire qn à d.** to half believe sb; **ouvrir qch à d.** to half open sth

demiard [dəmjar] *nm Can* half pint

demi-cercle (*pl* **demi-cercles**) [dəmisɛrkl] *nm* semicircle, half circle; **en d.** in a semicircle

demi-dieu (*pl* **demi-dieux**) [dəmidjø] *nm* demigod

demi-douzaine (*pl* **demi-douzaines**) [dəmiduzɛn] *nf* half-dozen; **une d. d'œufs/de stylos** half a dozen eggs/pens

demi-droite (*pl* **demi-droites**) [dəmidrwat] *nf Math* half-line

demi-écrémé, -e (*mpl* **demi-écrémés**, *fpl* **demi-écrémées**) [dəmiekreme] *adj* semi-skimmed

demi-finale (*pl* **demi-finales**) [dəmifinal] *nf* semi-final

demi-fond [dəmifɔ̃] *nm inv Sport* **(course de) d.** middle-distance race

demi-frère (*pl* **demi-frères**) [dəmifrɛr] *nm* half-brother

demi-gros [dəmigro] *nm inv* **(commerce de) d.** cash and carry

demi-heure (*pl* **demi-heures**) [dəmijœr] *nf* **une d.** half an hour; **toutes les demi-heures** every half-hour

demi-jour (*pl* **demi-jours**) [dəmiʒur] *nm* half-light

demi-journée (*pl* **demi-journées**) [dəmiʒurne] *nf* half-day

démilitariser [demilitarize] *vt* to demilitarize

demi-litre (*pl* **demi-litres**) [dəmilitr] *nm* half-litre; **un d. de vin** half a litre of wine

demi-lune (*pl* **demi-lunes**) [dəmilyn] *nf* half-moon

demi-mesure (*pl* **demi-mesures**) [dəmiməzyr] *nf* *(compromis)* half-measure

demi-mort, -e (*mpl* **demi-morts**, *fpl* **demi-mortes**) [dəmimɔr, -mɔrt] *adj* half-dead

demi-mot [dəmimo] **à demi-mot** *adv* **comprendre à d.** to take the hint; **nous nous comprenons à d.** we don't have to spell everything out to each other

déminage [deminaʒ] *nm* mine clearance; *(en mer)* minesweeping

déminer [demine] *vt* to clear of mines

démineur [deminœr] *nm (personne)* bomb disposal expert; *(navire)* minesweeper

demi-pause (*pl* **demi-pauses**) [dəmipoz] *nf Mus Br* minim rest, *Am* half-note rest

demi-pension [dəmipɑ̃sjɔ̃] *nf (à l'hôtel) Br* half-board, *Am* breakfast and one meal; **sept jours en d.** seven days *Br* half-board *or Am* breakfast and one meal; *Scol* **être en d.** to be a *Br* day boarder *or Am* day student

demi-pensionnaire (*pl* **demi-pensionnaires**) [dəmipɑ̃sjɔnɛr] *nmf (écolier) Br* day boarder, *Am* day student

demi-portion (*pl* **demi-portions**) [dəmipɔrsjɔ̃] *nf Fam Péj* weed

demi-queue (*pl* **demi-queues**) [dəmikø] *adj & nm* **(piano) d.** baby grand (piano)

démis, -e [demi, -iz] *adj (membre)* dislocated

demi-saison (*pl* **demi-saisons**) [dəmisɛzɔ̃] *nf* spring or autumn; **vêtements de d.** spring or autumn clothes

demi-sel (*pl* **demi-sels**) [dəmisɛl] *adj inv (beurre)* slightly salted; **fromage d.** slightly salted cream cheese

demi-sœur (*pl* **demi-sœurs**) [dəmisœr] *nf* half-sister

demi-sommeil (*pl* **demi-sommeils**) [dəmisɔmɛj] *nm* half-sleep; **être dans un d.** to be half-asleep

demi-soupir (*pl* **demi-soupirs**) [dəmisupir] *nm Mus Br* quaver rest, *Am* eighth-note rest

démission [demisjɔ̃] *nf* resignation; *Fig* renunciation; **donner sa d.** to hand in one's resignation

démissionnaire [demisjɔnɛr] *adj* resigning

démissionner [demisjɔne] *vi* to resign (**de** from); *Fig* to give up

demi-tarif [dəmitarif] **1** *nm (pl* **demi-tarifs**) half-price

2 *adj inv* **billet d.** *(de transports)* half-fare (ticket); *(de spectacle)* half-price ticket

demi-teinte (*pl* **demi-teintes**) [dəmitɛ̃t] *nf* halftone; *Fig* **être tout en demi-teintes** to be subtle in character

demi-ton (*pl* **demi-tons**) [dəmitɔ̃] *nm Mus Br* semitone, *Am* half step

demi-tour (*pl* **demi-tours**) [dəmitur] *nm* half-turn; (*en voiture*) U-turn; *Mil* about-turn; **faire d.** to turn back; **faire un d.** (*en voiture*) to do a U-turn; *Mil* **d. droite!** right about-turn!

démiurge [demjyrʒ] *nm* demiurge

demi-volée (*pl* **demi-volées**) [dəmivɔle] *nf* (*au tennis, au football*) half-volley

démobilisation [demɔbilizasjɔ̃] *nf* (**a**) (*de troupes*) demobilization (**b**) *Fig* (*désintérêt*) apathy

démobiliser [demɔbilize] *vt* (**a**) (*troupes*) to demobilize (**b**) *Fig* (*désintéresser*) to demotivate

démocrate [demɔkrat] **1** *adj* democratic
   2 *nmf* democrat

démocrate-chrétien, -enne (*mpl* **démocrates-chrétiens**, *fpl* **démocrates-chrétiennes**) [demɔkratkretjɛ̃, -ɛn] *adj & nm,f Pol* Christian Democrat

démocratie [demɔkrasi] *nf* democracy

démocratique [demɔkratik] *adj* democratic

démocratiquement [demɔkratikmɑ̃] *adv* democratically

démocratisation [demɔkratizasjɔ̃] *nf* democratization

démocratiser [demɔkratize] **1** *vt* to democratize
   2 se démocratiser *vpr* to become (more) democratic

démodé, -e [demɔde] *adj* old-fashioned

démoder [demɔde] **se démoder** *vpr* to go out of fashion

démographie [demɔgrafi] *nf* demography

démographique [demɔgrafik] *adj* demographic

demoiselle [dəmwazɛl] *nf* (**a**) (*jeune fille*) young lady; **d. de compagnie** lady's companion; **d. d'honneur** (*d'une souveraine*) lady-in-waiting; (*d'une mariée*) bridesmaid (**b**) *Vieilli* (*célibataire*) maiden lady; **c'est une vieille d.** she's never married (**c**) (*insecte*) dragonfly

démolir [demɔlir] *vt* (**a**) (*abattre*) to demolish, to pull down; (*mettre en pièces*) to demolish, to wreck; **d. une porte à coups de hache** to smash in a door with an axe; **l'alcool lui a démoli le foie** alcohol has ruined his liver (**b**) *Fig* (*théorie, adversaire*) to demolish; (*autorité*) to undermine; (*auteur, cinéaste, roman, film*) to slate (**c**) *Fam* (*battre*) to beat up; **d. le portrait à qn** to smash sb's face in; **se faire d. (le portrait)** to get beaten up

démolition [demɔlisjɔ̃] *nf* demolition; **chantier de d.** demolition site; **entreprise de d.** demolition contractors; **en d.** being demolished

démon [demɔ̃] *nm aussi Fig* demon, devil; **le d.** the Devil; **le d. de midi** the mid-life crisis; *Can* **être en d.** to be furious *or* mad

démoniaque [demɔnjak] *adj* demonic; *Fig* (*pervers*) fiendish

démonstratif, -ive [demɔ̃stratif, -iv] **1** *adj* (*affectueux*) *& Gram* demonstrative
   2 *nm Gram* demonstrative

démonstration [demɔ̃strasjɔ̃] *nf* (**a**) *Math* demonstration; **d. par l'absurde** reductio ad absurdum; **faire la d. de qch** to demonstrate sth (**b**) (*d'appareil*) demonstration; **être en d.** to be a display model (**c**) (*manifestation*) show; **d. de force** show of force; **faire de grandes démonstrations d'amitié** to make a great show of friendship

démontable [demɔ̃tabl] *adj* that can be dismantled

démontage [demɔ̃taʒ] *nm* dismantling

démonté, -e [demɔ̃te] *adj* (*mer*) raging

démonter [demɔ̃te] **1** *vt* (**a**) (*machine, meuble, tente*) to dismantle; (*pneu*) to remove (**b**) *Fam* (*déconcerter*) to throw; **se laisser d.** to get thrown (**c**) *Can* (*décourager*) to discourage
   2 se démonter *vpr* (**a**) (*machine, meuble*) to come apart (**b**) *Fam* **elle ne s'est pas démontée pour si peu** she wasn't so easily thrown

démontrable [demɔ̃trabl] *adj* demonstrable

démontrer [demɔ̃tre] *vt* to demonstrate; *Fam* **d. qch par A plus B** to prove sth conclusively

démoralisant, -e [demɔralizɑ̃, -ɑ̃t] *adj* demoralizing

démoralisation [demɔralizasjɔ̃] *nf* demoralization

démoraliser [demɔralize] **1** *vt* to demoralize
   2 se démoraliser *vpr* to become demoralized

démordre [demɔrdr] **démordre de** *vt ind* **ne pas d. de qch** to stick to sth; **elle n'en démord pas** she's sticking to her guns

démotiver [demɔtive] *vt* to demotivate; **se laisser d. par qch** to be put off by sth

démoulage [demulaʒ] *nm* (*d'un moulage*) removal from the mould; (*d'un gâteau*) turning out

démouler [demule] *vt* (*moulage*) to remove from the mould; (*gâteau*) to turn out

démuni, -e [demyni] *adj* (*pauvre*) destitute, penniless

démunir [demynir] **1** *vt* **d. qn de qch** to deprive sb of sth
   2 se démunir *vpr* **se d. de qch** to part with sth

démystification [demistifikasjɔ̃] *nf* demystification

démystifier [66] [demistifje] *vt* to demystify

dénatalité [denatalite] *nf* fall in the birth rate

dénationaliser [denasjɔnalize] *vt* to denationalize

dénaturé, -e [denatyre] *adj* (**a**) (*parents, goût, mœurs*) unnatural (**b**) *Chim* denatured

dénaturer [denatyre] *vt* (*faits, propos*) to distort; *Chim* to denature

dénégation [denegasjɔ̃] *nf* denial

déneiger [45] [deneʒe] *vt* to clear the snow from

déneigeuse [deneʒøz] *nf Can* snowblower

déni [deni] *nm Jur* **d. de justice** denial of justice

déniaiser [denjeze] *vt Fam* **d. qn** (*dépuceler*) to initiate sb sexually; (*dégourdir*) to teach sb a thing or two

dénicher [deniʃe] *vt Fam* (*objet*) to unearth; (*personne*) to track down

denier [dənje] *nm* (**a**) (*monnaie française*) denier; *Fig* **deniers** funds; **le d. du culte** contribution to parish costs (**b**) (*de bas*) **bas de 30 deniers** 30-denier stockings

dénier [66] [denje] *vt* (**a**) (*nier*) (*faute, responsabilité*) to deny (**b**) (*refuser*) **d. à qn le droit de faire qch** to deny sb the right to do sth

dénigrement [denigrəmɑ̃] *nm* denigration; **une campagne de d.** a smear campaign

dénigrer [denigre] *vt* to denigrate

dénivelé [denivle] *nm* difference in level

dénivellation [denivelasjɔ̃] *nf* difference in level

dénombrable [denɔ̃brabl] *adj* countable

dénombrer [denɔ̃bre] *vt* to count

dénominateur [denɔminatœr] *nm Math* denominator; **le plus petit d. commun** the lowest common denominator

dénomination [denɔminasjɔ̃] *nf* designation

dénommé, -e [denɔme] *adj* **un d. Charles** someone by the name of Charles

dénoncer [16] [denɔ̃se] **1** *vt* (**a**) *(trahir) (malfaiteur)* to denounce (**à** to); *(élève)* to tell on (**à** to) (**b**) *(protester contre) (abus)* to denounce (**c**) *(annuler) (traité, contrat)* to terminate
  2 se dénoncer *vpr (malfaiteur)* to give oneself up (**à** to); *(élève)* to own up (**à** to)

dénonciation [denɔ̃sjasjɔ̃] *nf* denunciation

dénoter [denɔte] *vt* to denote, to indicate

dénouement [denumã] *nm (d'un livre)* ending; *(d'une pièce)* dénouement; *(d'une affaire)* outcome

dénouer [denwe] **1** *vt (nœud)* to untie, to undo; *(cheveux)* to undo, to let down; *Fig (intrigue)* to unravel
  2 se dénouer *vpr (nœud)* to come undone; *(cheveux)* to come down

dénoyauter [denwajote] *vt Br* to stone, *Am* to pit

denrée [dɑ̃re] *nf* foodstuff; **denrées alimentaires** foodstuffs; **denrées de consommation courante** staple foods; **denrées périssables** perishable goods

dense [dɑ̃s] *adj* dense

densité [dɑ̃site] *nf* (**a**) *(de population) & Phys* density (**b**) *Ordinat* **à double d.** double-density

dent [dɑ̃] *nf* (**a**) *(d'homme, d'animal)* tooth; **faire ses dents** *(enfant)* to be teething; **se faire les dents sur qch** *(chat, enfant)* to cut one's teeth on sth; **manger du bout des dents** to pick at one's food; **mordre à belles dents dans qch** to take a good bite out of sth; **parler entre ses dents** to mumble, to mutter; *Fig* **se casser les dents sur qch** to come a cropper over sth; *aussi Fig* **serrer les dents** to grit one's teeth; *Fig* **avoir les dents longues** to have great ambitions; *Fig* **avoir la d. dure** to have a sharp tongue; *Fig* **il n'a pas desserré les dents de la soirée** he hasn't opened his mouth all evening; *Fam* **être sur les dents** *(sur le qui-vive)* to be on the alert; *(surmené)* to be overworked; *Fam* **avoir une d. contre qn** to have a grudge against sb; *Fam* **avoir la d.** to be starving; **d. de lait/de sagesse** milk/wisdom tooth
  (**b**) *(de peigne, de scie)* tooth; *(de roue)* cog; *(de fourchette)* prong; *(de timbre)* perforation; **en dents de scie** serrated; *Fig (évolution, progrès)* uneven

dentaire [dɑ̃tɛr] *adj* dental

denté, -e [dɑ̃te] *adj Tech* toothed; *(feuille)* jagged

dentelé, -e [dɑ̃tle] *adj (rivage, feuille)* jagged

dentelle [dɑ̃tɛl] *nf* lace; **robe de** *ou* **en d.** lace dress; **des crêpes d.** very thin pancakes; *Fam* **ne pas faire dans la d.** *(en paroles)* not to beat about the bush; *(en actions)* not to mess about

dentellière [dɑ̃təljɛr] *nf (personne)* lacemaker

dentelure [dɑ̃tlyr] *nf (d'un rivage, d'une feuille)* jagged outline; **dentelures** *(d'un timbre)* perforations

dentier [dɑ̃tje] *nm* (set of) false teeth, dentures

dentifrice [dɑ̃tifris] **1** *nm* toothpaste
  2 *adj* **pâte d.** toothpaste

dentiste [dɑ̃tist] *nmf* dentist

dentition [dɑ̃tisjɔ̃] *nf* (**a**) *(croissance)* dentition (**b**) *(denture)* set of teeth

denture [dɑ̃tyr] *nf* set of teeth

dénudé, -e [denyde] *adj (campagne, arbre, fil)* bare

dénuder [denyde] **1** *vt (colline, arbre, fil)* to strip; **cette robe laisse le dos** this dress leaves the back bare
  2 se dénuder *vpr* (**a**) *(colline)* to grow bare; *(arbre)* to lose its leaves (**b**) *(se déshabiller)* to strip (naked)

dénué, -e [denɥe] *adj* **d. de** *(intelligence, intérêt)* devoid of; **d. de tout fondement** totally without foundation

dénuement [denymã] *nm* destitution; **être dans le d.** to be destitute

déodorant [deɔdɔrɑ̃] *nm* deodorant

déodoriser [deɔdɔrize] *vt* to deodorize

déontologie [deɔ̃tɔlɔʒi] *nf* professional ethics

dépannage [depanaʒ] *nm (d'une machine)* (emergency) repairs; *(remorquage)* recovery; *Ordinat* trouble-shooting; **service de d.** breakdown service

dépanner [depane] *vt (machine)* to repair; *Fam (personne)* to help out (**de** with)

dépanneur [depanœr] *nm* (**a**) *(de voitures)* breakdown mechanic; *(de téléviseurs)* (television) repairman (**b**) *Can (magasin) Br* corner shop, *Am* convenience store

dépanneuse [depanøz] *nf (véhicule) Br* breakdown lorry, *Am* wrecker

dépareillé, -e [depareje] *adj (gant)* odd; *(service de table)* incomplete

déparer [depare] *vt* to spoil, to mar; **ce tableau ne dépare pas dans le salon** this painting looks pretty good in the living room

départ [depar] *nm* (**a**) *(d'une personne, d'un véhicule, d'un bateau)* departure; **les grands départs** the great holiday exodus; **être sur le d.** to be on the point of leaving; **excursions au d. de Nice** trips departing from Nice; **je regrette votre d.** I'm sorry you're leaving; **d. volontaire** *(d'employé)* voluntary redundancy (**b**) *(d'une course)* start; **ligne de d.** starting line; **faux d.** false start; **donner le d. (d'une course)** to give the starting signal (for a race); *aussi Fig* **prendre un bon/mauvais d.** to get off to a good/bad start (**c**) *(début)* start, beginning; **salaire de d.** starting salary; **au d.** at first, to start with

départager [45] [departaʒe] *vt* to decide between

département [departəmã] *nm* (**a**) *(de la France)* department *(division of local government)* (**b**) *(dans un ministère)* department; **le d. d'anglais** *(d'une faculté)* the English department

---

Départment

A "département" is the chief administrative division of France. There are 95 "départements" in metropolitan France and 4 overseas and each is administered by a "conseil général" and a "préfet". The number of the "département" corresponds to the first two figures in a postcode and the last two figures on a car registration number.

---

départemental, -e, -aux, -ales [departəmãtal, -o] **1** *adj* departmental
  2 *nf* **départementale** secondary road, *Br* B road

départir [64a] [departir] **se départir** *vpr Litt* **il ne s'est jamais départi de son calme/sa bonne humeur** his calm/his good humour never deserted him

dépassé, -e [depase] *adj* (**a**) *(démodé) (vêtement, technique)* old-fashioned (**b**) *(perdu)* overwhelmed; **être d. par les événements** to be overtaken by events

dépassement [depasmã] *nm* (**a**) *(en voiture) Br* overtaking, *Am* passing (**b**) *Fin* **il y a un d. de crédit de plusieurs millions** the budget has been exceeded by several million

dépasser [depase] **1** *vt* (**a**) *(aller plus loin que)* to go past (**b**) *(doubler)* *Br* to overtake, *Am* to pass (**c**) *(excéder)* *(limite de vitesse, temps imparti, poids)* to exceed; **d. la date limite de vente** *(produit)* to be past its sell-by date; **d. dix minutes** to last longer than ten minutes; **ne pas d. la dose prescrite** *(sur notice)* do not exceed the stated dose; **cela dépasse l'entendement** it's beyond belief (**d**) *(surpasser)* to outstrip; **d. qn d'une tête** to stand a head taller than sb; **d. qn en beauté** to be more beautiful than sb; **d. les espérances de qn** to exceed sb's expectations (**e**) *(exagérer)* **d. les bornes** to overstep the mark; **cela me dépasse** it's beyond me

2 *vi* (**a**) *(en voiture)* *Br* to overtake, *Am* to pass (**b**) *(se voir)* to stick out (**de** of); *(jupon)* to show

3 se dépasser *vpr* to surpass oneself

dépassionner [depasjɔne] *vt (débat)* to take the heat out of

dépatouiller [depatuje] **se dépatouiller** *vpr Fam* to cope, to manage; **se d. d'une situation** to get out of *or* to wriggle one's way out of a situation

dépaysé, -e [depeize] *adj* out of one's element

dépaysement [depeizmã] *nm (positif)* change of scene; *(négatif)* disorientation

dépayser [depɛize] *vt (positivement)* to be a change of scene for; *(négativement)* to disorientate

dépecer [16/34] [depɔse] *vt (sujet: boucher)* to cut up; *(sujet: animal)* to tear up

dépêche [depɛʃ] *nf* dispatch; **d. d'agence** agency news item

dépêcher [depeʃe] **1** *vt (messager)* to dispatch

2 se dépêcher *vpr* to hurry; **dépêchez-vous!** hurry up!; **se d. de faire qch** to hurry to do sth; **dépêche-toi de finir ton travail** hurry up and finish your work

dépeindre [54] [depɛ̃dr] *vt* to depict

dépenaillé, -e [depɔnaje] *adj* ragged

dépénalisation [depenalizasjɔ̃] *nf* decriminalization

dépénaliser [depenalize] *vt* to decriminalize

dépendance [depãdãs] *nf* (**a**) *(asservissement)* dependence (**à** on); **être sous la d. de qn** to be under sb's domination (**b**) *(bâtiment)* outbuilding

dépendant, -e [depãdã, -ãt] *adj* dependent (**de** on)

dépendre [depãdr] *vi* to depend (**de** on); **cela ne dépend pas de nous** it's not up to us; *Fam* **ça dépend (des fois)** it depends

dépens [depã] *nmpl* (**a**) **aux d. de** at the expense of; **apprendre qch à ses d.** to learn sth to one's cost (**b**) *Jur* **être condamné aux d.** to be ordered to pay costs

dépense [depãs] *nf* (**a**) *(frais)* expenditure, expense; **dépenses** spending; **les dépenses du ménage** household expenses; **faire des dépenses** to spend money; **pousser (les gens) à la d.** to encourage people to spend; **il ne regarde pas à la d.** he spares no expense (**b**) **d. physique** physical exertion

dépenser [depãse] **1** *vt (de l'argent)* to spend; *Fig* **d. toute son énergie (à faire qch)** to use up all one's energy (in doing sth)

2 *vi* to spend (money); **d. sans compter** to spend lavishly

3 se dépenser *vpr* to burn up energy

dépensier, -ère [depãsje, -er] *adj* extravagant

déperdition [deperdisjɔ̃] *nf (de chaleur, d'énergie)* loss

dépérir [deperir] *vi (personne)* to waste away; *(plante)* to wither; *(arbre)* to decay

dépêtrer [depetre] *Fam* **1** *vt* **d. qn de qch** to free sb from sth

2 se dépêtrer *vpr (se dégager)* to free oneself (**de** from); *Fig* **se d. de qch** to get oneself out of sth; *Fig* **se d. de qn** to get rid of sb

dépeuplement [depœplɔmã] *nm (d'un pays)* depopulation

dépeupler [depœple] **1** *vt (pays)* to depopulate

2 se dépeupler *vpr (pays)* to become depopulated

déphasé, -e [defaze] *adj* (**a**) *Élec* out of phase (**b**) *Fam (désorienté)* disorientated

dépiauter [depjote] *vt Fam (animal)* to skin; *Fig* **d. un texte** to pull a text to pieces

dépilatoire [depilatwar] *adj* **crème d.** hair-removing cream

dépistage [depistaʒ] *nm (d'une maladie)* screening; **d. du sida** AIDS screening

dépister [depiste] *vt (gibier, criminel)* to track down; *(maladie)* to detect

dépit [depi] *nm* (**a**) *(ressentiment)* spite; **par d.** out of spite (**b**) **en d. de** in spite of, despite; **en d. du bon sens** contrary to common sense

dépité, -e [depite] *adj* annoyed

déplacé, -e [deplase] *adj* (**a**) *(dérangé)* out of place; **avoir une vertèbre déplacée** to have a slipped disc (**b**) *(inconvenant)* *(observation)* uncalled-for

déplacement [deplasmã] *nm* (**a**) *(réarrangement)* moving; *(mutation)* transfer; **d. de vertèbre** slipped disc; *Ordinat* **d. du curseur** cursor movement; *Ordinat* **d. entre fichiers** movement between files (**b**) *(voyage)* trip; **déplacements** travel; **être en d.** to be on a (business) trip; *Fig* **valoir le d.** to be worth the trip

déplacer [16] [deplase] **1** *vt (objet)* to move; *(fonctionnaire, service)* to transfer; *Fig* **d. le problème** *(volontairement)* to avoid the issue; *(involontairement)* to miss the point

2 se déplacer *vpr* (**a**) *(changer de place)* to move around (**b**) *(voyager)* to travel (**c**) **se d. une vertèbre** to slip a disc

déplafonner [deplafɔne] *vt (prix, crédit)* to remove the ceiling on

déplaire [55a] [deplɛr] **1** *vi* **d. à qn** *(irriter)* to displease sb; **cet homme/cette maison me déplaît** I don't like that man/that house; **cela ne me déplairait pas** I wouldn't mind it; *Ironique* **ne vous/leur en déplaise** whether you/they like it or not

2 se déplaire *vpr* **il se déplaît à Paris** he doesn't like it in Paris; **elle ne se déplaît pas à Paris** she quite likes it in Paris

déplaisant, -e [deplɛzã, -ãt] *adj* unpleasant

déplaisir [deplezir] *nm* displeasure, annoyance; **à son grand d.** to his great annoyance

dépliant [deplijã] *nm* leaflet; *(d'un livre)* fold-out page

déplier [66] [deplije] **1** *vt (journal, lettre, mouchoir)* to unfold; *(canapé)* to open out; **d. les jambes** to stretch one's legs

2 se déplier *vpr* to unfold, to open out

déplisser [deplise] **1** *vt* to take the creases out of

2 se déplisser *vpr* to lose its creases

déploiement [deplwamã] *nm (d'ailes)* spreading; *(de troupes)* deployment; *Fig (de force)* display

déplorable [deplɔrabl] *adj* deplorable

déplorer [deplɔre] *vt* to deplore; **nous devrons travailler plus, (et) je le déplore, mais...** we'll have to do more work, I'm sorry to say, but...; **d. la mort de qn** to mourn sb's death; **d. la perte de qch** to lament the loss of sth

déployer [32] [deplwaje] **1** *vt (journal, carte)* to unfold, to open out; *(voiles, ailes)* to spread; *(troupes, police)* to deploy; *Fig (étaler)* to display
2 se déployer *vpr (voile)* to unfurl; *(troupes, police)* to deploy

déplumé, -e [deplyme] *adj* featherless; *Fam (chauve)* bald

déplumer [deplyme] **se déplumer** *vpr (oiseau)* to moult; *Fam (personne)* to go bald

dépoitraillé, -e [depwatraje] *adj Fam* with one's shirt open

dépoli, -e [depɔli] *adj (verre)* frosted

dépolitiser [depɔlitize] *vt* to depoliticize

dépolluer [depɔlɥe] *vt* to clean up

déportation [depɔrtasjɔ̃] *nf (en camp de concentration)* internment

déporté, -e [depɔrte] *nm,f (de camp de concentration)* internee

déporter [depɔrte] **1** *vt* **d. qn** *(en camp de concentration)* to send sb to a concentration camp
2 se déporter *vpr* **se d. vers la droite/gauche** to veer off to the right/left

déposer [depoze] **1** *vt* **(a)** *(mettre à terre)* to put down; *aussi Fig* **d. les armes** to lay down one's arms **(b)** *(laisser) (personne)* to drop (off); **d. qch chez qn** to drop sth off at sb's house; **d. une gerbe sur une tombe** to lay a wreath on a grave; **d. un baiser sur le front de qn** to plant a kiss on sb's forehead; **d. la clé à la réception** to leave the key at reception; **d. une caution** to leave a deposit; **d. de l'argent (à la banque)** to deposit money (at the bank); *Jur* **d. une plainte (contre qn)** to lodge a complaint (against sb); *Pol* **d. un projet de loi** to introduce a bill **(c)** *(marque, brevet)* to register; **marque déposée** registered trademark **(d)** *(monarque)* to depose
2 *vi Jur* **d. (en justice)** to give evidence **(contre** against)
3 se déposer *vpr (substance)* to settle

dépositaire [depozitɛr] *nmf* **(a)** *(de papiers)* depositary; *Fig (d'un secret)* guardian **(b)** *Com (de produits)* agent

déposition [depozisjɔ̃] *nf* **(a)** *Jur* statement *(made by witness)*; **faire/recueillir une d.** to make/take a statement **(b)** *(d'un monarque)* deposing

déposséder [34] [depɔsede] *vt* to dispossess, to deprive **(de** of)

dépôt [depo] *nm* **(a)** *(action)* depositing; *(somme)* deposit; **faire un d.** *(à la banque)* to make a deposit; **mettre qch en d.** to put sth into storage; *Fin* **d. d'espèces** cash deposit; *Jur* **d. légal** registration of copyright; *Fin* **d. à vue** cash deposit **(b)** *(entrepôt)* depot; *(de trains)* engine shed; **d. de munitions** munitions depot; **d. d'ordures** *Br* rubbish dump, *Am* garbage dump **(c)** *(prison)* prison **(d)** *(substance)* deposit; *(limon)* silt; *(de bouilloire)* fur

dépoter [depɔte] *vt (plantes)* to repot

dépotoir [depɔtwar] *nm (dépôt d'ordures)* dump; *Fam (chambre)* dump; *(classe)* dumping ground

dépôt-vente (*pl* **dépôts-ventes**) [depovɑ̃t] *nm* second-hand shop *(where items are sold on commission)*

dépouille [depuj] *nf* **(a)** *(d'animal)* skin, hide; **d. (mortelle)** (mortal) remains **(b)** **dépouilles** *(trésor de guerre)* spoils, booty

dépouillé, -e [depuje] *adj (style)* bald; *(arbre)* bare

dépouillement [depujmɑ̃] *nm* **(a)** *(examen)* **d. du scrutin** counting of the votes; **d. du courrier** sorting through the mail **(b)** *(pauvreté)* poverty; *(sobriété)* austerity

dépouiller [depuje] **1** *vt* **(a)** *(priver)* to deprive **(de** of); **d. qn de ses vêtements** to strip sb; **se faire d.** *(dans une affaire)* to lose all one's money **(b)** *(examiner) (courrier)* to sort through; **d. le scrutin** to count the votes **(c)** *(animal)* to skin
2 se dépouiller *vpr* **se d. de qch** to rid oneself of sth; **les arbres se dépouillent de leurs feuilles** the trees are shedding their leaves

dépourvu, -e [depurvy] *adj* **(a)** **d. de qch** devoid of sth **(b)** **être pris au d.** to be caught off (one's) guard

dépoussiérer [34] [depusjere] *vt* to dust; *Fig (institution)* to dust down

dépravation [depravasjɔ̃] *nf* depravity

dépravé, -e [deprave] **1** *adj* depraved
2 *nm,f* degenerate

dépraver [deprave] *vt* to deprave

dépréciation [depresjasjɔ̃] *nf* depreciation

déprécier [66] [depresje] **1** *vt* to undervalue
2 se déprécier *vpr (valeurs, marchandises)* to depreciate

déprédation [depredasjɔ̃] *nf* depredation

dépressif, -ive [deprɛsif, -iv] *adj* depressive

dépression [depresjɔ̃] *nf* **(a)** *(creux)* depression; **d. (atmosphérique)** low, trough **(b)** *Psy* depression; **faire de la d.** to be suffering from depression; **faire une d.** to be depressed; **d. nerveuse** nervous breakdown

dépressurisation [depresyrizasjɔ̃] *nf* depressurization

dépressuriser [depresyrize] *vt (avion)* to depressurize

déprimant, -e [deprimɑ̃, -ɑ̃t] *adj* depressing

déprime [deprim] *nf Fam* depression; **avoir un (petit) coup de d.** to be feeling (a bit) low

déprimé, -e [deprime] *adj Psy* depressed

déprimer [deprime] **1** *vt (démoraliser)* to depress
2 *vi Fam* to be feeling low

déprogrammer [deprɔgrame] *vt (émission)* to cancel; *Ordinat* to remove from a program

dépuceler [42] [depysle] *vt Fam* to deflower

depuis [dəpɥi] **1** *prép* **(a)** *(indiquant le point de départ)* **d. hier/ce matin/1995** since yesterday/this morning/1995; **d. l'âge de cinq ans** from the age of five; **d. leur rencontre** since they met; **d. ce temps-là** since then; **d. quand êtes-vous ici?** how long have you been here? **(b)** *(durée)* for; **je suis ici d. trois jours** I've been here for three days; **d. combien de temps êtes-vous mariés?** how long have you been married (for)?; **il l'aime d. toujours** he has always loved her; **d. longtemps** for a long time; **d. la nuit des temps** since the dawn of time **(c)** *(lieu)* from; **il ne m'a pas parlé d. Rouen** he hasn't spoken to me since (we left) Rouen
2 *adv* since (then)
3 *conj* **d. que** since; **d. que le monde est monde** since the world began

député, -e [depyte] *nm,f Pol* deputy, *Br* ≃ MP, *Am* ≃ representative **(de** for); **d. (du Parlement) européen** Member of the European Parliament, MEP

déraciné, -e [derasine] **1** *adj* uprooted
2 *nm,f* person who has been uprooted

déraciner [derasine] *vt (arbre, personne)* to uproot

déraillement [derɑjmɑ̃] *nm* derailment

dérailler [derɑje] *vi* (**a**) *(train, tram)* to leave the rails; **faire d. un train** to derail a train (**b**) *Fam (personne)* to talk drivel

dérailleur [derɑjœr] *nm (de bicyclette)* derailleur (gears)

déraison [derɛzɔ̃] *nf Litt* folly

déraisonnable [derɛzɔnabl] *adj* foolish

déraisonner [derɛzɔne] *vi Litt* to talk nonsense

dérangé, -e [derɑ̃ʒe] *adj (fou)* deranged

dérangeant, -e [derɑ̃ʒɑ̃, -ɑ̃t] *adj (film, personnage)* disturbing

dérangement [derɑ̃ʒmɑ̃] *nm* (**a**) *(gêne)* trouble; **je ne veux pas vous causer de d.** I don't want to put you to any trouble; **excusez-moi pour le d.** I'm sorry to trouble you (**b**) *(panne)* **la ligne est en d.** the line is out of order

déranger [45] [derɑ̃ʒe] **1** *vt* (**a**) *(papiers, livres)* to disturb; *(pièce)* to mess up (**b**) *(gêner) (personne)* to disturb; **ne pas d.** *(sur panneau)* do not disturb; **cela vous dérange si j'ouvre la fenêtre?** would you mind if I opened the window?; *Ironique* **je ne te dérange pas trop?** am I in your way?; *Fam* **et alors, ça te dérange?** what's it to you? (**c**) *(perturber)* to upset; **avoir le cerveau dérangé** to be deranged
2 *vi (choquer)* to be disturbing
3 se déranger *vpr* **merci de vous être dérangé** thank you for your trouble; **ne vous dérangez pas pour moi** please don't go to any trouble on my account

dérapage [derapaʒ] *nm (en voiture)* skid; *(à skis)* sideslip; *Fig* mistake; *Fig* **le d. des prix** spiralling prices; **le d. de l'économie** the downward spiral of the economy

déraper [derape] *vi (voiture)* to skid; *(à skis)* to sideslip; *Fig (prix)* to be rising uncontrollably; *(situation)* to go wrong

dératé, -e [derate] *nm,f Fam* **courir comme un d.** to run flat out

dératiser [deratize] *vt* **d. qch** to clear sth of rats

derechef [dərəʃɛf] *adv Litt* once more

déréglé, -e [deregle] *adj* (**a**) *(mécanisme)* not working properly (**b**) *(estomac)* upset

dérèglement [dereglǝmɑ̃] *nm (d'un mécanisme)* malfunctioning; **d. hormonal** hormone disorder

dérégler [34] [deregle] **1** *vt (mécanisme)* to cause to malfunction
2 se dérégler *vpr (mécanisme)* to go wrong; **elle s'est déréglé le système digestif** she's ruined her digestive system

dérider [deride] **1** *vt* to cheer up
2 se dérider *vpr* to cheer up

dérision [derizjɔ̃] *nf* derision; **tourner qch en d.** to deride sth

dérisoire [derizwar] *adj (salaire, somme)* derisory; *(prix)* rock-bottom

dérivatif [derivatif] *nm* distraction (**à** from)

dérivation [derivasjɔ̃] *nf* (**a**) *(route, cours d'eau)* diversion; *Élec* **monté en d.** shunt connected (**b**) *Math* derivation

dérive [deriv] *nf Naut & Aviat* drift; **à la d., en d.** adrift; **aller à la d.** to drift, to go adrift; *Fig* to go downhill; **la d. des continents** continental drift

dérivé, -e [derive] **1** *adj* (**a**) *(sens, fonction)* derived; **produit d.** *Chim* by-product; *Fin* derivative (**b**) *Élec* **courant d.** shunt current
2 *nm* (**a**) *Chim* derivative (**b**) *(produit)* by-product
3 *nf Math* **dérivée** derivative

dériver¹ [derive] **1** *vt* (**a**) *(cours d'eau)* to divert; *Élec (courant)* to shunt (**b**) *Math (fonction)* to derive
2 dériver de *vt ind (mot)* to be derived from

dériver² *vi Naut & Aviat* to drift

dériveur [derivœr] *nm Naut* sailing dinghy *(with centreboard)*

dermatite [dɛrmatit] *nf Méd* dermatitis

dermato [dɛrmato] *nmf Fam* dermatologist

dermatologie [dɛrmatɔlɔʒi] *nf* dermatology

dermatologique [dɛrmatɔlɔʒik] *adj* dermatological

dermatologiste [dɛrmatɔlɔʒist], **dermatologue** [dɛrmatɔlɔg] *nmf* dermatologist

derme [dɛrm] *nm* dermis

dernier, -ère [dɛrnje, -ɛr] **1** *adj* (**a**) *(ultime)* last; *(marquant la fin)* final; **au d. moment** at the last moment (**b**) *(passé)* last; *(le plus récent) (livre, nouvelles, mode)* latest; **au cours des dernières années** over the past *or* last few years (**c**) *(dans l'espace)* last; **le d. rang** the back *or* last row; **la dernière marche de l'escalier** *(en haut)* the top step; *(en bas)* the bottom step; **au d. étage** on the top floor (**d**) *Litt (extrême)* utmost; **de la dernière importance** of the utmost importance; **c'est du d. chic** it's the height of elegance (**e**) *(le pire)* worst; **de d. ordre** very inferior; **être reçu d. au concours** to come last in the competition; **c'était la dernière chose à faire** that's the last thing you/he/*etc* should have done
2 *nm,f* (**a**) *(dans un classement)* last; **les six derniers** the last six; **arriver dans les derniers** to be one of the last to finish; **il est arrivé le d.** *ou* **bon d.** he came in last; **c'est le d. de sa classe** he's bottom of his class; *Fam* **c'est le d. de mes soucis** that's the least of my worries (**b**) *(dans une chronologie) (l'ultime)* last; *(le plus récent)* latest; **le d. en date** the most recent; **ce d. répondit...** the latter answered...; **c'est toujours le d. à sortir** he's always last out; **comment va la petite dernière?** how's the little one? (**c**) *Péj* **on la traite comme la dernière des dernières** they treat her like the lowest of the low; **c'est vraiment le d. des menteurs** he's the world's biggest liar
3 *nf* **dernière** (**a**) *(spectacle)* last night (**b**) *(nouveauté)* **tu as entendu la dernière de ton frère?** have you heard your brother's latest?
4 *adv* **en d.** last (of all); **il sort toujours en d.** he's always last out

dernièrement [dɛrnjɛrmɑ̃] *adv* lately, recently

dernier-né, dernière-née *(mpl* **derniers-nés,** *fpl* **dernières-nées)** [dɛrnjene, dɛrnjɛrne] *nm,f* youngest (child)

dérobade [derɔbad] *nf* (**a**) *(esquive)* evasion (**b**) *(d'un cheval)* swerve

dérobé, -e [derɔbe] *adj* (**a**) *(escalier, porte)* hidden, secret (**b**) *(volé)* stolen

dérobée [derɔbe] **à la dérobée** *adv* secretly, on the sly; **regarder qn à la d.** to steal a glance at sb

dérober [derɔbe] **1** *vt* (**a**) *(voler)* to steal (**à** from) (**b**) *(cacher)* to hide (**à** from)
2 se dérober *vpr* (**a**) *(s'échapper)* to slip away (**à**

from); **se d. à la curiosité de qn** to avoid sb's prying eyes (**b**) *(éviter de répondre)* to be evasive (**c**) *(manquer) (sol, jambes)* to give way (**sous** beneath) (**d**) *(cheval)* to swerve

dérogation [derɔgasjɔ̃] *nf* exemption (**à** from); *Jur* waiver; *(à une loi)* derogation (**à** of)

déroger [45] [derɔʒe] *vi* **d. à l'usage/à la loi** to depart from custom/the law

dérouillée [deruje] *nf très Fam* thrashing, hammering; **prendre une d.** to get thrashed *or* hammered

dérouiller [deruje] **1** *vi très Fam* (**a**) *(être battu)* to get a belting (**b**) *(souffrir)* to have a hard time of it
3 se dérouiller *vpr Fam* **se d. les jambes** to stretch one's legs

déroulement [derulmã] *nm (d'événement)* unfolding; **pendant tout le d. de la cérémonie** throughout the ceremony

dérouler [derule] **1** *vt (rouleau)* to unroll; *(store)* to let down; *(câble)* to unwind; *Ordinat* **d. un menu** to pull down a menu
2 se dérouler *vpr* (**a**) *(rouleau)* to unroll; *(store)* to come down; *(câble)* to unwind (**b**) *Fig (événement)* to unfold; **la manifestation s'est déroulée dans le calme** the demonstration passed off peacefully

déroutant, -e [derutã, -ãt] *adj* disconcerting

déroute [derut] *nf aussi Fig* rout; **l'ennemi fut mis en d.** the enemy was routed

dérouter [derute] *vt* (**a**) *(navire, avion)* to divert, to reroute (**b**) *(égarer) (poursuivants)* to throw off the scent (**c**) *Fig (étonner)* to throw

derrière [derjer] **1** *prép* behind; **les uns d. les autres** one behind the other; **sortir de d. un buisson** to come out from behind a bush; *aussi Fig* **les autres sont loin d. elle** the others are way behind her; *Fig* **il faut toujours être d. elle** you always have to be at her back; *Fig* **c'est lui qui est d. tout ça** he's the one behind it all
2 *adv* behind; **aller** *ou* **monter d.** *(en voiture)* to sit in the back
3 *nm* (**a**) *(de bâtiment)* back, rear; **le mur de d.** the back wall (**b**) *(de personne)* behind, backside; *(d'animal)* hindquarters; **recevoir des coups de pied dans le** *ou* **au d.** to get kicked in the behind

des [de] *voir* **de, un**

dès [de] *prép (à partir de)* from; **d. 1840** as far back as 1840; **d. le matin** first thing in the morning; **d. leur arrivée** as soon as they arrive/arrived; **d. maintenant, d. à présent** from now on; **d. que tu seras là** as soon as you're here; **d. lors** *(dans le temps)* from then on; *(par conséquent)* consequently; **d. lors que...** since...

désabusé, -e [dezabyze] *adj* disillusioned

désaccord [dezakɔr] *nm* disagreement; **être en d. avec qn (sur qch)** to disagree with sb (about sth)

désaccordé, -e [dezakɔrde] *adj* out of tune

désaccoutumer [dezakutyme] **se désaccoutumer** *vpr* to get out of the habit (**de** of)

désaffecté, -e [dezafɛkte] *adj* disused

désaffection [dezafɛksjɔ̃] *nf* disaffection (**à l'égard de** with)

désagréable [dezagreabl] *adj* unpleasant

désagrégation [dezagregasjɔ̃] *nf (désintégration)* disintegration

désagréger [59] [dezagreʒe] **1** *vt (désintégrer)* to cause to disintegrate
2 se désagréger *vpr* to disintegrate

désagrément [dezagremã] *nm* (**a**) *(gêne)* trouble; **causer du d. à qn** to inconvenience sb (**b**) *(souci, aspect négatif)* problem

désaltérant, -e [dezalterã, -ãt] *adj* thirst-quenching

désaltérer [34] [dezaltere] **1** *vt* **d. qn** to quench sb's thirst; **c'est une boisson qui désaltère** it's a thirst-quenching drink
2 se désaltérer *vpr* to quench one's thirst

désambiguïser [dezãbiguize] *vt (situation)* to clarify; *(mot)* to disambiguate

désamorçage [dezamɔrsaʒ] *nm* (**a**) *(d'une bombe, d'un conflit)* defusing (**b**) *(d'une pompe)* draining

désamorcer [16] [dezamɔrse] *vt* (**a**) *(bombe, conflit, querelle)* to defuse (**b**) *(pompe)* to drain

désappointer [dezapwɛte] *vt Litt* to disappoint

désapprobateur, -trice [dezaprɔbatœr, -tris] *adj* disapproving

désapprobation [dezaprɔbasjɔ̃] *nf* disapproval

désapprouver [dezapruve] *vt* to disapprove of

désarçonner [dezarsɔne] *vt* (**a**) *(jeter bas)* to unseat, to throw (**b**) *Fig (déconcerter)* to throw

désargenté, -e [dezarʒãte] *adj Fam (personne)* broke

désarmant, -e [dezarmã, -ãt] *adj* disarming

désarmé, -e [dezarme] *adj (touché)* disarmed; *(sans défense)* defenceless, helpless

désarmement [dezarməmã] *nm* (**a**) *(d'un pays, d'une région)* disarmament; **d. multilatéral** multilateral disarmament (**b**) *(de soldats)* disarming

désarmer [dezarme] **1** *vt* (**a**) *(malfaiteur)* to disarm (**b**) *Fig (toucher)* to disarm (**c**) *(navire)* to lay up
2 *vi* (**a**) *(pays, région)* to disarm (**b**) *(cesser)* **sa colère ne désarme pas** he is still angry

désarroi [dezarwa] *nm* confusion; **jeter qn dans le d.** to throw sb into confusion; **il est en plein d.** *ou* **dans un grand d.** he's in a state of utter confusion

désarticuler [dezartikyle] **1** *vt* to dislocate
2 se désarticuler *vpr* to contort oneself; **se d. l'épaule** to dislocate one's shoulder

désastre [dezastr] *nm* disaster

désastreux, -euse [dezastrø, -øz] *adj* disastrous

désavantage [dezavãtaʒ] *nm* disadvantage; **avoir un d. par rapport à qn** to be at a disadvantage compared with sb; **voir qn à son d.** to see sb in an unfavourable light

désavantager [45] [dezavãtaʒe] *vt* to put at a disadvantage, to disadvantage; **être désavantagé par rapport à qn** to be at a disadvantage compared with sb

désavantageux, -euse [dezavãtaʒø, -øz] *adj* disadvantageous

désaveu [dezavø] *nm* (**a**) *(reniement)* disowning (**b**) *(condamnation)* disapproval

désavouer [dezavwe] *vt* (**a**) *(renier)* to disown (**b**) *(condamner)* to disapprove of (**c**) *Jur (enfant)* to disown

désaxé, -e [dezakse] **1** *adj (psychiquement)* unbalanced, unhinged
2 *nm,f* lunatic

desceller [desele] *vt* (**a**) *(pierre)* to loosen (**b**) *(acte, document)* to unseal

descendance [desãdãs] *nf* (**a**) *(filiation)* descent (**b**) *(postérité)* descendants

descendant, -e [desãdã, -ãt] **1** *adj (mouvement)* downward
2 *nm,f* descendant

descendre [desɑ̃dr] **1** *vi* (*aux* **être**) (**a**) (*en s'approchant*) to come down; (*en s'éloignant*) to go down; **d. de qch** to come down from sth; **faire d. qn de qch** to get sb down from sth; **aider qn à d.** to help sb down; **d. à 150 m de profondeur** to go down to a depth of 150 m; **d. en dessous des dix secondes** to get below ten seconds; **d. à Marseille/dans le Midi** to go down to Marseilles/to the South; *Fig* **d. dans la rue** to take to the streets
  (**b**) (*d'un escalier*) (*en s'approchant*) to come downstairs; (*en s'éloignant*) to go downstairs; **d. à la cave** to go down to the cellar
  (**c**) (*d'un véhicule*) **d. d'un train/d'une voiture** to get off a train/out of a car; **d. de cheval/de vélo/de moto** to dismount; **tout le monde descend!** (*au terminus*) all change!
  (**d**) (*baisser*) (*marée*) to go out; **faire d. la fièvre** to reduce fever
  (**e**) (*tomber*) (*brouillard*) to come down
  (**f**) (*s'étendre*) to go down; (*route, rue*) to go downhill; **d. jusqu'à la taille/jusqu'aux chevilles** to come down to the waist/to the ankles; **ce chemin descend au village** this path goes down to the village
  (**g**) (*loger*) **d. chez qn** to stay with sb; **d. à l'hôtel** to put up *or* stay at a hotel
  (**h**) (*être issu*) **d. de** to be descended from
  2 *vt* (*aux* **avoir**) (**a**) (*dévaler*) **d. un escalier/la rue/la rivière** (*en s'éloignant*) to go down a staircase/the street/the river; (*en s'approchant*) to come down a staircase/the street/the river
  (**b**) (*porter vers le bas*) (*en s'éloignant*) to take down; (*en s'approchant*) to bring down; **d. la poubelle** to take the rubbish down; **peux-tu me d. mon pull?** can you bring me down my sweater?
  (**c**) (*abaisser*) (*store, étagère*) to lower
  (**d**) *Fam* (*abattre*) (*avion, personne*) to shoot down
  (**e**) *Fam* (*consommer*) (*repas, boisson*) to put away; **qu'est-ce qu'il descend!** he's really putting it away!

descente [desɑ̃t] *nf* (**a**) (*action de descendre*) descent; **d. en rappel** abseiling
  (**b**) (*sortie*) **accueillir qn à sa d. du train** to meet sb off the train
  (**c**) (*incursion*) raid; **d. de police** police raid
  (**d**) (*route en pente*) slope; **ralentir dans la d.** to slow down when going downhill
  (**e**) (*en ski*) (*course*) downhill (race); **faire de la d.** to do downhill (skiing)
  (**f**) **d. de lit** bedside rug
  (**g**) (*tuyau*) downpipe
  (**h**) *Fam* **il a une bonne d.** he can really put it away

descriptible [dɛskriptibl] *adj* describable
descriptif, -ive [dɛskriptif, -iv] **1** *adj* descriptive
  2 *nm* description
description [dɛskripsjɔ̃] *nf* description; **faire la d. de** to give a description of; **d. de poste** job description
désembourber [dezɑ̃burbe] *vt* to pull out of the mud
désembuage [dezɑ̃bɥaʒ] *nm* demisting
désemparé, -e [dezɑ̃pare] *adj* (*personne*) at a loss
désemparer [dezɑ̃pare] *vi* **sans d.** without stopping
désemplir [dezɑ̃plir] *vi* **ne pas d.** to be always full
désenchanté, -e [dezɑ̃ʃɑ̃te] *adj* (*personne*) disillusioned; (*sourire*) wistful
désenchantement [dezɑ̃ʃɑ̃tmɑ̃] *nm* disillusion
désenchanter [dezɑ̃ʃɑ̃te] *vt* to disillusion
désenclaver [dezɑ̃klave] *vt* (*région*) to open up

désencombrer [dezɑ̃kɔ̃bre] *vt* (*passage*) to clear (**de** of)
désendettement [dezɑ̃dɛtmɑ̃] *nm* debt clearing
désenfler [dezɑ̃fle] *vi* to go down, to become less swollen
désengagement [dezɑ̃gaʒmɑ̃] *nm* disengagement
désengager [45] [dezɑ̃gaʒe] **1** *vt* (*d'une obligation*) to free (**de** from); *Mil* (*d'un conflit*) to withdraw
  2 se désengager *vpr* (*d'une obligation*) to free oneself (**de** from); *Mil* (*d'un conflit*) to withdraw
désensabler [dezɑ̃sable] *vt* (**a**) (*chenal, port*) to clear of sand (**b**) (*bateau*) to get off the sand; (*voiture*) to dig out of the sand
désensibiliser [dezɑ̃sibilize] *vt aussi Fig* to desensitize
désépaissir [dezepesir] *vt* (**a**) (*sauce*) to thin down (**b**) (*cheveux*) to thin out
déséquilibre [dezekilibr] *nm* imbalance; **être en d.** to be unsteady
déséquilibré, -e [dezekilibre] **1** *adj* unbalanced
  2 *nm,f* unbalanced person
déséquilibrer [dezekilibre] *vt* (**a**) (*objet, personne*) to throw off balance (**b**) *Psy* to unbalance
désert, -e [dezɛr, -ɛrt] **1** *adj* (*lieu*) deserted; (*pays, région*) uninhabited
  2 *nm* desert; **d. culturel** cultural desert *or* wasteland; **le d. de Gobi** the Gobi Desert; **d. de sable** sandy desert
déserter [dezɛrte] **1** *vt* (**a**) (*lieu, fonction*) to desert; *Mil* **d. son poste** to desert one's post (**b**) *Fig* (*cause*) to desert, to abandon
  2 *vi* (*soldat*) to desert
déserteur [dezɛrtœr] *nm* deserter
désertification [dezɛrtifikasjɔ̃] *nf* (**a**) (*transformation en désert*) desertification (**b**) (*dépeuplement*) depopulation
désertion [dezɛrsjɔ̃] *nf* desertion
désertique [dezɛrtik] *adj* desert
désespérant, -e [dezɛsperɑ̃, -ɑ̃t] *adj* (*situation, personne*) hopeless; **être d'une lenteur/bêtise désespérante** to be incredibly slow/stupid
désespéré, -e [dezɛspere] **1** *adj* (**a**) (*qui ne laisse aucun espoir*) desperate; (*inconsolable*) in despair (**b**) (*exprimant le désespoir*) desperate (**c**) (*extrême*) (*mesure, solution*) desperate
  2 *nm,f* desperate person
désespérément [dezɛsperemɑ̃] *adv* desperately
désespérer [34] [dezɛspere] **1** *vt* (*personne*) to drive to despair
  2 *vi* to despair
  3 désespérer de *vt ind* to despair of; **d. de faire qch** to despair of doing sth; **il ne désespère pas d'y arriver** he hasn't given up hope of getting there
  4 se désespérer *vpr* to despair
désespoir [dezɛspwar] *nm* despair; **être au d.** to be in despair; **être au d. de faire qch** to be extremely sorry to do sth; **faire** *ou* **être le d. de qn** (*personne*) to be the despair of sb; **réduire qn au d.** to drive sb to despair
déshabillé [dezabije] *nm* negligee
déshabiller [dezabije] **1** *vt* (*personne*) to undress; **d. qn du regard** to undress sb with one's eyes
  2 se déshabiller *vpr* (**a**) (*pour être nu*) to undress, to take off one's clothes (**b**) (*ôter son manteau*) to take off one's coat
déshabituer [dezabitɥe] **1** *vt* **d. qn de qch/de faire qch** to get sb out of the habit of sth/of doing sth

2 **se déshabituer** *vpr* **se d. de qch/de faire qch** to get out of the habit of sth/of doing sth

désherbage [dezεrbaʒ] *nm* weeding

désherbant [dezεrbã] *nm* weedkiller

désherber [dezεrbe] *vt* to weed

déshérité, -e [dezerite] **1** *adj (démuni)* deprived
2 *nm,f* **les déshérités** the underprivileged

déshériter [dezerite] *vt* to disinherit

déshonneur [dezɔnœr] *nm* dishonour

déshonorant, -e [dezɔnɔrã, -ãt] *adj* dishonourable

déshonorer [dezɔnɔre] **1** *vt* to disgrace; **se croire/ sentir déshonoré de faire qch** to think/feel it beneath oneself to do sth
2 **se déshonorer** *vpr* to disgrace oneself

déshumaniser [dezymanize] *vt* to dehumanize

déshydratation [dezidratasjɔ̃] *nf* dehydration

déshydraté, -e [dezidrate] *adj* dehydrated

déshydrater [dezidrate] **1** *vt* to dehydrate
2 **se déshydrater** *vpr* to become dehydrated

desiderata [deziderata] *nmpl* desiderata

design [dizajn] **1** *nm* design; **d. industriel** industrial design
2 *adj inv* designer; **un intérieur d.** a designer interior

désignation [deziɲasjɔ̃] *nf* (**a**) *(appellation)* designation (**b**) *(choix)* appointment

désigner [deziɲe] *vt* (**a**) *(montrer)* to point out; **d. qn/ qch du doigt** to point to sb/sth (**b**) *(dénommer)* to refer to (**c**) *(choisir)* to designate, to appoint (**d**) **il est tout désigné pour le faire** he's just the man for the job

désillusion [dezilyzjɔ̃] *nf* disillusion

désillusionner [dezilyzjɔne] *vt* to disillusion

désincrustant, -e [dezɛ̃krystã, -ãt] **1** *adj* (**a**) *Tech (substance)* scaling (**b**) *(masque, savon)* cleansing
2 *nm* (**a**) *Tech* scale preventive (**b**) *(savon)* cleanser

désindustrialisation [dezɛ̃dystrijalizasjɔ̃] *nf* de-industrialization

désinence [dezinãs] *nf Gram* ending

désinfectant, -e [dezɛ̃fɛktã, -ãt] *adj & nm* disinfectant

désinfecter [dezɛ̃fɛkte] *vt* to disinfect

désinfection [dezɛ̃fɛksjɔ̃] *nf* disinfection

désinflation [dezɛ̃flasjɔ̃] *nf Écon* disinflation

désinformation [dezɛ̃fɔrmasjɔ̃] *nf* disinformation

désinformer [dezɛ̃fɔrme] *vt* to disinform

désintégration [dezɛ̃tegrasjɔ̃] *nf* (**a**) *(des roches)* weathering (**b**) *(d'un groupe, de la famille)* break-up (**c**) *Phys (de matière)* disintegration

désintégrer [34] [dezɛ̃tegre] **1** *vt* (**a**) *(roches)* to weather (**b**) *(groupe, famille)* to break up (**c**) *Phys (matière)* to disintegrate; *(atome)* to split
2 **se désintégrer** *vpr* (**a**) *(roches)* to weather (**b**) *(groupe, famille)* to break up (**c**) *Phys (matière)* to disintegrate

désintéressé, -e [dezɛ̃terese] *adj* disinterested

désintéresser [dezɛ̃terese] **se désintéresser** *vpr* **se d. de qn/qch** *(ne pas s'y intéresser)* to have no interest in sb/sth; *(s'en détacher)* to lose interest in sb/sth

désintérêt [dezɛ̃tere] *nm* disinterest

désintoxication [dezɛ̃tɔksikasjɔ̃] *nf Méd* detoxification

désintoxiquer [dezɛ̃tɔksike] **1** *vt (alcoolique)* to treat for alcoholism; *(drogué)* to treat for drug addiction
2 **se désintoxiquer** *vpr* (**a**) *(alcoolique)* to come off

alcohol; *(drogué)* to come off drugs (**b**) *Fig (se remettre en forme)* to clean out one's system; *(perdre une habitude)* to get out of the habit

désinvolte [dezɛ̃vɔlt] *adj* (**a**) *(négligeant)* casual, off-hand (**b**) *(à l'aise) (manière)* unselfconscious; *(mouvements)* easy

désinvolture [dezɛ̃vɔltyr] *nf* (**a**) *(excès de liberté)* casualness; **avec d.** casually (**b**) *(naturel) (de manières)* unselfconsciousness; *(de mouvement)* ease

désir [dezir] *nm* (**a**) *(souhait)* desire; **selon le d. de qn** in accordance with sb's wishes; **prendre ses désirs pour des réalités** to indulge in wishful thinking; **tes désirs sont des ordres** your wish is my command (**b**) **d. (sexuel)** (sexual) desire

désirable [dezirabl] *adj* desirable

désirer [dezire] *vt* (**a**) *(souhaiter)* to wish; **d. faire qch** to wish to do sth; **je désire qu'il vienne** I want him to come; **cela laisse à d.** it leaves a lot to be desired; **elle se fait d.** *(elle n'arrive pas)* she's keeping us waiting; **que désirez-vous?**, *Fam* **vous désirez?** *(dans un magasin)* can I help you?; *(qu'est-ce que je vous sers?)* what would you like? (**b**) *(sexuellement)* to desire

désireux, -euse [dezirø, -øz] *adj* **être d. de faire qch** to be anxious to do sth

désistement [dezistəmã] *nm* withdrawal

désister [deziste] **se désister** *vpr* to withdraw

désobéir [dezɔbeir] *vi* to disobey; **d. à qn/qch** to disobey sb/sth

désobéissance [dezɔbeisãs] *nf* disobedience (**à** to); **d. civile** civil disobedience

désobéissant, -e [dezɔbeisã, -ãt] *adj* disobedient (**à** to)

désobligeant, -e [dezɔbliʒã, -ãt] *adj* disagreeable

désodorisant, -e [dezɔdɔrizã, -ãt] *adj & nm* deodorant

désodoriser [dezɔdɔrize] *vt* to deodorize

désœuvré, -e [dezœvre] *adj* idle

désœuvrement [dezœvrəmã] *nm* idleness; **par d.** for something to do

désolant, -e [dezɔlã, -ãt] *adj* (**a**) *(affligeant)* distressing (**b**) *(contrariant)* annoying

désolé, -e [dezɔle] *adj* (**a**) *(navré)* sorry; **je suis d. de vous déranger** I'm sorry to disturb you; **d., je n'ai pas le temps** sorry, I haven't got the time (**b**) *(affligé)* upset (**c**) *(région)* desolate

désoler [dezɔle] **1** *vt* (**a**) *(navrer)* to upset (**b**) *(affliger)* to distress
2 **se désoler** *vpr* to be upset

désolidariser [desɔlidarize] **se désolidariser** *vpr* **se d. de** to dissociate oneself from

désopilant, -e [dezɔpilã, -ãt] *adj* hilarious

désordonné, -e [dezɔrdɔne] *adj* (**a**) *(chambre, bureau, personne)* untidy (**b**) *(désorganisé) (personne, article, pensées)* disorganized; *(mouvements)* uncoordinated (**c**) *(vie)* disorderly

désordre [dezɔrdr] *nm* (**a**) *(manque d'ordre)* untidiness, mess; **en d.** untidy; **mettre qch en d.** to make a mess of sth (**b**) *(manque d'organisation)* disorder (**c**) *(trouble)* commotion; **mettre le d. dans une réunion** to disrupt a meeting (**d**) *(agitation)* **désordres** disturbances (**e**) *Méd* disorder

désorganisation [dezɔrganizasjɔ̃] *nf* disorganization

désorganisé, -e [dezɔrganize] *adj (personne)* disorganized

désorganiser [dezɔrganize] *vt* to disrupt

désorienté, -e [dezɔrjɑ̃te] *adj* (**a**) *(égaré)* disorientated (**b**) *(déconcerté)* bewildered

désorienter [dezɔrjɑ̃te] *vt (déconcerter)* to bewilder

désormais [dezɔrmɛ] *adv* from now on, in future

désosser [dezɔse] **1** *vt (viande, poisson)* to bone
2 se désosser *vpr* to contort oneself

despote [dɛspɔt] *nm aussi Fig* despot

despotique [dɛspɔtik] *adj* despotic

desquamation [dɛskwamasjɔ̃] *nf* peeling, *Spéc* desquamation

desquels, desquelles [dekɛl] *voir* **lequel**

DESS [deɛsɛs] *nm (abrév* **diplôme d'études supérieures spécialisées**) = postgraduate diploma

dessaisir [desezir] **1** *vt* (**a**) *(déposséder)* **d. qn de qch** to confiscate sth from sb (**b**) **d. un juge d'une affaire** to withdraw a judge from a case
2 se dessaisir *vpr* **se d. de qch** to relinquish sth, to part with sth

dessaler [desale] **1** *vt* (**a**) *(viande, poisson)* to remove the salt from *(by soaking)*; *(eau de mer)* to desalinate (**b**) *Fam* **d. qn** to teach sb a thing or two
2 *vi* (**a**) *(voilier)* to capsize (**b**) **mettre qch à d.** *(viande, poisson)* to soak sth to remove the salt
3 se dessaler *vpr Fam* to learn a thing or two

dessaouler [desule] *Fam* = **dessoûler**

dessèchement [desɛʃmɑ̃] *nm (de la peau)* drying up; *(de la végétation)* withering

dessécher [34] [deseʃe] **1** *vt (déshydrater) (peau)* to dry up; *(végétation)* to wither
2 se dessécher *vpr (peau)* to dry up; *(végétation)* to wither

dessein [desɛ̃] *nm* intention, purpose; **à d.** intentionally; **dans ce d.** with this intention; **dans le d. de faire qch** with the intention of doing sth

desseller [desele] *vt (cheval)* to unsaddle

desserrer [desere] **1** *vt* (**a**) *(relâcher) (vis, ceinture, nœud)* to loosen; *(frein à main)* to release (**b**) *(décrisper) (poing)* to unclench; *(étreinte)* to relax; *Fig* **il n'a pas desserré les dents** he didn't open his mouth
2 se desserrer *vpr* (**a**) *(vis, ceinture, nœud)* to come loose (**b**) *(étreinte)* to relax

dessert [desɛr] *nm* dessert; **qu'est-ce qu'il y a comme ou au d.?** what's for dessert?

desserte [desɛrt] *nf (meuble)* sideboard

desservir¹ [63] [desɛrvir] *vt* (**a**) *(passer par) (ville, localité)* to serve; **ce train dessert les gares de...** *(annonce)* this train stops at...; **ville bien desservie** town with efficient public transport (**b**) *(conduire à) (pièce)* to lead to

desservir² *vt* (**a**) *(débarrasser) (table)* to clear; **vous pouvez d.** you may clear the table (**b**) *(nuire à)* **d. qn** to do sb a disservice

dessiller [desije] *vt Fig & Litt* **d. les yeux de qn** to open sb's eyes

dessin [desɛ̃] *nm* (**a**) *(technique, art)* drawing; **faire du d.** to draw; **d. industriel** industrial drawing (**b**) *(représentation)* drawing; **faire un d.** to do a drawing; *Fam Fig* **tu veux que je te fasse un d.?** do you want me to spell it out for you?; *Cin* **d. animé** cartoon; **d. humoristique** cartoon (**c**) *(motif) (sur tissu)* design, pattern; **un tissu à dessins géométriques** a fabric with geometric patterns *or* a geometric design (**d**) *(contour) (de la bouche, du visage)* outline

dessinateur, -trice [desinatœr, -tris] *nm,f* (**a**) *(artiste)* drawer; **d. de bandes dessinées** cartoonist; **d.**

humoristique cartoonist (**b**) *(concepteur)* designer (**c**) *Tech* **d. industriel** draughtsman

dessiner [desine] **1** *vt* (**a**) *(faire un dessin de)* to draw; **d. à l'encre/à la craie** to draw in ink/chalk (**b**) *(concevoir)* to design (**c**) *Fig (tracer) (lignes)* to outline; **vêtement qui dessine la taille** garment that shows off the waist; **visage bien dessiné** finely chiselled face
2 se dessiner *vpr* (**a**) *(apparaître)* to stand out; **se d. à l'horizon** to stand out on the horizon; **un sourire se dessine sur ses lèvres** a smile flickers over her lips (**b**) *Fig (prendre forme) (changement, résultat)* to become apparent; *(projet)* to take shape

dessoûler [desule] *vt & vi Fam* to sober up

dessous [dəsu] **1** *adv* (**a**) *(sous)* underneath (**b**) **en d.** underneath; **l'appartement d'en d.** the downstairs flat, the flat downstairs; **en d. de** below; **tu es très en d. de la vérité** you're not even close; *Fam* **être en d. de tout** to be worse than useless (**c**) **prendre/porter qch par (en) d.** to take hold of/carry sth from underneath; *Fig* **regarder qn par en d.** to look at sb furtively
2 *nm (partie inférieure) (d'une assiette, d'une table)* underside; *(du pied)* bottom; **les gens du d.** the people below; **avoir le d.** to get the worst of it
3 *nmpl* (**a**) *(partie cachée) (d'une affaire)* hidden side (**b**) *(sous-vêtements)* underwear

dessous-de-plat [dəsudpla] *nm inv* table mat

dessous-de-table [dəsudtabl] *nm inv* backhander; **verser un d. à qn** to give sb a backhander

dessous-de-verre [dəsudvɛr] *nm inv* coaster; *(en carton)* beer mat

dessus [dəsy] **1** *adv* on (it/them); **il a marché d.** he trod on it; **mais il n'y a pas l'adresse d.** but the address isn't on it
2 *nm* (**a**) *(d'une table, du pied)* top; *(d'une assiette)* upper side; **l'étage du d.** the top floor (**b**) *Fig* **avoir le d.** to have the upper hand; **reprendre le d.** *(se remettre)* to get over it

dessus-de-lit [dəsydli] *nm inv* bedspread

déstabiliser [destabilize] *vt* to destabilize

destin [dɛstɛ̃] *nm* fate, destiny

destinataire [dɛstinatɛr] *nmf (d'une lettre)* addressee; *(de marchandises)* consignee; *(d'un mandat postal)* payee

destination [dɛstinasjɔ̃] *nf* destination; **trains/vols à d. de Paris** trains/flights to Paris; **arriver à d.** to reach one's destination

destinée [dɛstine] *nf* (**a**) *(vie)* destiny (**b**) *Litt* **être promis à de grandes ou hautes destinées** to be destined for great things (**c**) *(fatalité)* fate, destiny

destiner [dɛstine] **1** *vt* (**a**) *(réserver)* **d. qch à qn** *(bien, somme d'argent, emploi)* to intend sth for sb (**b**) *(adresser)* **être destiné à qn** *(remarque, paquet)* to be meant for sb (**c**) *(assigner)* **d. une somme d'argent à qch** to allot *or* assign a sum of money to sth; **cet argent est destiné à la recherche contre le sida** this money is going towards AIDS research (**d**) *(concevoir pour)* **destiné à qch** (intended) for sth; **cette salle est destinée aux répétitions** this room is for rehearsing in (**e**) *(vouer)* **d. qn à qch** to destine sb for sth; *Litt* **le sort les destinait à se rencontrer** they were destined to meet
2 se destiner *vpr* **se d. à qch** to intend to take up sth

destituer [dɛstitɥe] *vt (renvoyer) (officier)* to discharge; *(fonctionnaire)* to remove from office; *(souverain)* to depose

destitution [dɛstitysjɔ̃] *nf (d'un officier)* discharge; *(d'un fonctionnaire)* removal from office; *(d'un souverain)* deposition

destructeur, -trice [dɛstryktœr, -tris] *adj* destructive

destruction [dɛstryksjɔ̃] *nf* destruction

désuet, -ète [dezɥɛ, -ɛt, desɥɛ, -ɛt] *adj* **(a)** *(dépassé)* obsolete **(b)** *(démodé)* old-fashioned

désuétude [dezɥetyd, desɥetyd] *nf* disuse; **tomber en d.** *(mot, expression, pratique)* to become obsolete

désuni, -e [dezyni] *adj (famille, amis, amants)* divided

désunir [dezynir] *vt (personnes, famille)* to divide

désynchronisé, -e [desɛ̃krɔnize] *adj* out of synch

détachable [detaʃabl] *adj* detachable

détachant, -e [detaʃɑ̃, -ɑ̃t] **1** *adj* stain-removing **2** *nm* stain remover

détaché, -e [detaʃe] *adj* **(a)** *(ton, air, manière)* detached **(b)** *(fonctionnaire)* seconded

détachement [detaʃmɑ̃] *nm* **(a)** *(indifférence)* detachment (**de** from) **(b)** *(d'un fonctionnaire)* secondment; **être en d.** to be on secondment **(c)** *(troupes)* detachment

détacher¹ [detaʃe] **1** *vt* **(a)** *(défaire) (étiquette, page perforée)* to detach; *(ceinture, liens)* to undo; *(rideau)* to take down; *(wagon)* to uncouple; **d. ses yeux de qch** to take one's eyes off sth **(b)** *(libérer) (prisonnier, animal)* to untie **(c)** *(déléguer) (fonctionnaire)* to second; *(militaire)* to detach **(d)** *Fig* **d. qn de qch** to turn sb away from sth **(e)** *(faire sonner)* **d. les syllabes d'un mot** to pronounce each syllable of a word separately; *Mus* **d. les notes** to detach the notes

2 se détacher *vpr* **(a)** *(étiquette, bouton, page)* to come off; *(ceinture)* to come undone; *(écorce)* to peel off **(b)** *(se libérer) (animal)* to get loose **(c)** *Fig* **se d. de qn** *(en devenant adulte)* to break away from sb; *(par manque d'intérêt)* to grow apart from sb; **se d. de qch** to turn one's back on sth **(d)** *(se séparer) (groupe de coureurs)* to break away (**de** from) **(e)** *(ressortir)* to stand out (**sur** against)

détacher² *vt (nettoyer)* to remove the stains from

détail [detaj] *nm* **(a)** *(élément)* detail **(b)** *(énumération) (d'un compte, d'un inventaire)* items; *(d'une facture)* breakdown; **elle m'a fait le d. de sa soirée** she gave me a detailed account of her party; *Fam Fig* **il n'a pas fait de d.!** he didn't make any exceptions!; *Fam Fig* **il n'a pas fait dans le d.** he didn't go into detail; **en d.** in detail; **se perdre dans les détails** to get bogged down in detail **(c)** *Com* retail; **vendre/acheter au d.** to sell/buy retail

détaillant, -e [detajɑ̃, -ɑ̃t] *nm,f Com* retailer

détaillé, -e [detaje] *adj (récit, description)* detailed; *(facture)* itemized

détaler [detale] *vi Fam (personne)* to take off; **faire d. qn** to send sb packing

détartrage [detartraʒ] *nm* **(a)** *(de dents)* scaling; **se faire faire un d.** to have one's teeth scaled **(b)** *(de bouilloire, de cafetière, de chaudière)* descaling

détartrer [detartre] *vt* **(a)** *(dents)* to scale **(b)** *(bouilloire, cafetière, chaudière)* to descale

détaxe [detaks] *nf* tax refund

détaxer [detakse] *vt* to exempt from tax; **marchandises détaxées** duty-free goods

détectable [detɛktabl] *adj* detectable

détecter [detɛkte] *vt* to detect

détecteur, -trice [detɛktœr, -tris] **1** *adj* detecting **2** *nm* detector; **d. de faux billets** forged banknote detector; **d. de fumée** smoke detector; **d. de mensonges**

lie detector; **d. de mines** mine detector; *Ordinat* **d. de virus** virus detector

détection [detɛksjɔ̃] *nf* detection; *Ordinat* **d. d'erreurs** error detection; *Ordinat* **d. virale** virus detection

détective [detɛktiv] *nm* detective; **d. privé** private detective

déteindre [54] [detɛ̃dr] *vi (tissu)* to run (**sur** over); **d. au lavage** to run in the wash; *Fig* **cela a déteint sur eux** it's rubbed off on them

dételer [42] [detle] **1** *vt (chevaux)* to unharness; *(bœufs)* to unyoke **2** *vi Fam* to stop working; **sans d.** non-stop

détendre [detɑ̃dr] **1** *vt* **(a)** *(relâcher) (corde)* to slacken; *(arc)* to unbend; *(ressort)* to release **(b)** *(décontracter) (personne)* to relax; **le sport, ça détend** sport is relaxing **(c)** **d. l'atmosphère** to make the atmosphere less tense

2 se détendre *vpr* **(a)** *(corde)* to slacken; *(arc)* to unbend; *(ressort)* to lose its tension **(b)** *(se relaxer) (personne, visage)* to relax **(c)** *(atmosphère, situation)* to become less tense

détendu, -e [detɑ̃dy] *adj (personne, conversation)* relaxed

détenir [70] [detnir] *vt* **(a)** *(avoir en sa possession) (passeport, titres, pouvoir, record du monde)* to hold; *(secret, preuve)* to have **(b)** *(garder prisonnier)* to hold

détente [detɑ̃t] *nf* **(a)** *(relaxation)* relaxation **(b)** *Pol* détente **(c)** *(d'une arme)* trigger **(d)** *(d'un athlète)* spring; **avoir de la d.** to jump well **(e)** *(d'un gaz)* expansion **(f)** **être dur** *ou* **long à la d.** to be slow on the uptake

détenteur, -trice [detɑ̃tœr, -tris] *nm,f (d'argent, de titres, de record)* holder; *(d'arme)* possessor

détention [detɑ̃sjɔ̃] *nf* **(a)** *(de titres)* holding; *(d'armes)* possession **(b)** *(incarcération)* detention; **d. provisoire** detention pending trial

détenu, -e [detny] *nm,f* prisoner

détergent, -e [detɛrʒɑ̃, -ɑ̃t] *adj & nm* detergent

détérioration [deterjɔrasjɔ̃] *nf* deterioration

détériorer [deterjɔre] **1** *vt* to damage **2 se détériorer** *vpr* to deteriorate

déterminant, -e [detɛrminɑ̃, -ɑ̃t] **1** *adj* decisive **2** *nm* **(a)** *Ling* determiner **(b)** *Math* determinant

détermination [detɛrminasjɔ̃] *nf* **(a)** *(fermeté)* determination **(b)** *(d'une date, d'un lieu, d'un prix)* determination, fixing; *(du sang, d'une bactérie)* typing

déterminé, -e [detɛrmine] *adj* **(a)** *(résolu)* determined; **être d. à faire qch** to be determined to do sth **(b)** *(défini)* specific

déterminer [detɛrmine] **1** *vt* **(a)** *(définir)* to determine, to fix; *(sang, bactérie)* to type **(b)** *(décider)* **d. qn à faire qch** to induce sb to do sth **(c)** *(causer) (changement)* to cause; *(action, décision)* to determine **(d)** *Gram* to determine

2 se déterminer *vpr* **se d. à faire qch** to make up one's mind to do sth

déterré, -e [detere] *nm,f Fam* **avoir une mine de d.** to look like death warmed up

déterrer [detere] *vt aussi Fig* to dig up

détestable [detɛstabl] *adj* foul

détester [detɛste] **1** *vt* to detest, to hate; **je déteste être dérangé** I hate being disturbed; **ne pas d. faire qch** to quite like doing sth

2 se détester *vpr (soi-même)* to hate oneself; *(l'un l'autre)* to hate each other

détonant, -e [detɔnɑ̃, -ɑ̃t] **1** *adj aussi Fig* explosive **2** *nm* explosive

détonateur [detɔnatœr] *nm* detonator; *Fig* **servir de d. à qch** to spark sth off

détonation [detɔnasjɔ̃] *nf (bruit)* explosion; *(bruit d'arme à feu)* bang

détoner [detɔne] *vi (explosif)* to detonate; **faire d. qch** to detonate sth

détonner [detɔne] *vi* (**a**) *(chanteur)* to sing out of tune; *(instrumentiste)* to play out of tune (**b**) *(trancher) (couleurs)* to clash; **il détonne dans ce milieu** he's out of place in that environment

détordre [detɔrdr] *vt (fil)* to untwist

détour [detur] *nm* (**a**) *(parcours)* detour; **faire un d. (par)** to make a detour (via); **valoir le d.** *(site)* to be worth the trip (**b**) *Fig (biais)* roundabout means; **user de détours pour faire qch** to do sth in a roundabout way; **sans d.** without beating about the bush (**c**) *(tracé) (d'une route, d'une rivière)* bend; **faire un d.** to bend; *Fig* **au d. de la conversation** in the course of the conversation

détourné, -e [deturne] *adj aussi Fig (indirect)* roundabout, indirect

détournement [deturnəmɑ̃] *nm* (**a**) **d. d'avion** hijacking (**b**) *(d'un cours d'eau)* diversion (**c**) **d. de fonds** embezzlement

détourner [deturne] **1** *vt* (**a**) *(circulation, rivière)* to divert; *(avion)* to hijack (**b**) *(éloigner)* **d. qn de** *(ami, famille)* to take sb away from; *(préoccupation, engagement)* to divert sb from; **d. qn du droit chemin** to lead sb astray; **d. l'attention de qn** to divert *or* distract sb's attention; **d. la conversation** to change the subject; **d. les soupçons** to avert suspicion (**c**) *(voler) (fonds)* to embezzle (**à** from) (**d**) *(tourner)* **d. la tête** to turn one's head away; **d. les yeux** *ou* **le regard** to look away **2** **se détourner** *vpr aussi Fig* to turn away (**de** from)

détracteur, -trice [detraktœr, -tris] *nm,f* detractor

détraqué, -e [detrake] **1** *adj (appareil)* out of order; *(estomac)* upset; *(temps)* unsettled; *Fam (personne) (psychologiquement)* unhinged **2** *nm,f Fam* maniac

détraquer [detrake] **1** *vt (appareil)* to put out of order; *(santé)* to ruin; *(estomac)* to upset **2** **se détraquer** *vpr (appareil, santé)* to break down; *(temps)* to become unsettled; **se d. l'estomac** to upset one's stomach

détrempé, -e [detrɑ̃pe] *adj (terre, sol)* sodden, waterlogged

détresse [detrɛs] *nf* (**a**) *(angoisse)* distress (**b**) *(dénuement)* financial difficulties; **les familles dans la d.** families in dire need *or* straits (**c**) *(perdition)* **en d.** *(navire)* in distress; *(voiture, avion)* in difficulties (**d**) *Méd* **d. respiratoire** respiratory distress

détriment [detrimɑ̃] *nm* **au d. de** to the detriment of; **je l'ai appris à mon d.** I found it out to my cost

détritus [detritys] *nm Br* rubbish, *Am* garbage

détroit [detrwa] *nm* strait; **le d. de Béring** the Bering Strait; **le d. de Gibraltar** the Strait of Gibraltar

détromper [detrɔ̃pe] **1** *vt* **d. qn** to put sb right (**sur** about) **2** **se détromper** *vpr* to realize that one was wrong; **détrompez-vous!** think again!

détrôner [detrone] *vt* (**a**) *(monarque)* to dethrone (**b**) *(théorie, méthode, produit)* to supersede

détrousser [detruse] *vt Hum* **d. qn** to relieve sb of his valuables

détruire [18] [detrɥir] **1** *vt* (**a**) *(démolir) (édifice, empire, avion)* to destroy (**b**) *(anéantir) (espoir, mariage, santé)* to ruin, to wreck (**c**) *(tuer)* to kill **2** **se détruire** *vpr (se faire du mal)* to ruin one's health

dette [dɛt] *nf aussi Fig* debt; **avoir des dettes** to be in debt; **être couvert** *ou* **criblé de dettes** to be crippled with debt; **d. extérieure** foreign debt; **la d. publique** *ou* **de l'État** the National Debt; **payer sa d. à la société** to pay one's debt to society

DEUG [dœg] *nm (abrév* **diplôme d'études universitaires générales)** = degree gained after a two-year course

> **DEUG**
> In French universities, students take the "DEUG" or the "DEUST" ("diplôme d'études universitaires scientifiques et techniques") after two years of courses. They may then take further courses leading to the "licence" (the equivalent of a bachelor's degree). Most students who obtain the "DEUG" choose to do this, while the majority of students who obtain the "DEUST" leave university and go straight into employment.

deuil [dœj] *nm* (**a**) *(décès)* bereavement; **il y a eu un d. dans leur famille** there has been a death in their family (**b**) *(tristesse)* mourning; **être en d.** to be in mourning; **journée de d. national** day of national mourning (**c**) *(tenue)* **porter le d. (de qn)** to be in mourning (for sb); **prendre/quitter le d.** to go into/come out of mourning; *Fam Fig* **avoir les ongles en d.** to have dirty fingernails (**d**) **faire son d. de qch** to give sth up as lost

Deutsche Mark [dɔjtʃmark, dœtʃmark] *nm* Deutschmark

deux [dø] **1** *adj inv* (**a**) *(chiffre)* two; **d. fois** twice; **des d. côtés du fleuve** on either side *or* on both sides of the river; **tous (les) d.** both; **tous les d. jours** every other day, every two days; **nous/vous/eux d.** the two of us/you/them; **vivre à d.** to live together; **les ordinateurs et moi, ça fait d.** I know absolutely nothing about computers (**b**) *(peu de)* **c'est à d. pas d'ici** it's only a short distance away, it's two minutes away; **je reviens dans d. minutes** I'll be back in a minute; **tu peux venir? – d. secondes!** can you come here? – just a minute! **2** *nm inv* two; **casser qch en d.** to break sth in two; **marcher par d.** to walk in pairs *or* twos; *(dans une procession)* to march two abreast; *Fam* **en moins de d.** in next to no time; *voir aussi* **trois**

deuxième [døzjɛm] *adj & nmf* second; *voir aussi* **cinquième**

deuxièmement [døzjɛmmɑ̃] *adv* secondly

deux-mâts [døma] *nm* two-master

deux-pièces [døpjɛs] *nm* (**a**) *(maillot de bain)* two-piece (swimsuit) (**b**) *(tailleur)* two-piece (**c**) *(appartement)* two-room *Br* flat *or Am* apartment

deux-points [døpwɛ̃] *nm* colon

deux-roues [døru] *nm* two-wheeled vehicle

deux-temps [døtɑ̃] *nm (moteur)* two-stroke (engine)

deuzio [døzjo] *adv Fam* second

dévaler [devale] **1** *vt (escalier, pente)* to hurtle down **2** *vi (personne, pierres)* to hurtle down; *(eau, lave, boue)* to rush down

dévaliser [devalize] *vt* (**a**) *(cambrioler) (banque)* to rob; *(maison)* to burgle; *Fig (commerçant)* to clean out (**b**) *(vider) (réfrigérateur, placard)* to raid

dévalorisation [devalɔrizasjɔ̃] *nf* (**a**) *(action) (de la monnaie)* devaluation; *(de marchandises)* marking down; *(résultat) (de la monnaie)* depreciation; *(de marchandises)* mark-down (**b**) *Fig (d'une personne, d'une politique)* discrediting; *(d'un diplôme, d'une profession)* devaluation

dévaloriser [devalɔrize] **1** *vt* (**a**) *(monnaie)* to devalue (**b**) *(personne, politique)* to discredit; *(qualification, diplôme)* to devalue
2 se dévaloriser *vpr* (**a**) *(monnaie)* to depreciate (**b**) *(personne)* to put oneself down

dévaluation [devalɥasjɔ̃] *nf Fin* devaluation

dévaluer [devalɥe] **1** *vt (monnaie)* to devalue
2 se dévaluer *vpr* to fall in value

devancer [16] [dəvɑ̃se] *vt* (**a**) *(être devant) (concurrent)* to be/get ahead of; **d. son époque** to be ahead of one's time (**b**) *(arriver avant)* to arrive before (**c**) *(prévoir) (personne, critiques)* to forestall; *(demande)* to anticipate (**d**) *(faire avant) Mil* **d. l'appel** to enlist before call-up; *Fin* **d. une échéance** to settle an account early

devant [dəvɑ̃] **1** *prép* (**a**) *(en face de, en avant de)* in front of; **assis d. moi** sitting in front of me; **marcher droit d. soi** to walk straight on; **regardez d. vous!** look where you're going!; **passer d. qn/qch** *(dans la rue)* to go past sb/sth; **passer d. qn** *(dans une file d'attente)* to go in front of sb; **avoir du temps/de l'argent d. soi** to have time/money to spare; **tu as la vie d. toi** you've got your whole life ahead of you; **d. derrière** back to front
(**b**) *(face à)* **d. le danger** in the face of danger; **égaux d. la loi** equal in the eyes of the law; **que faire d. tant d'injustice?** what can one do faced with so much injustice?
2 *adv* (**a**) *(en face)* in front; **je cherchais la gare et j'étais juste d.** I was looking for the station when I was standing right in front of it; **où est Martin? – je crois qu'il est d.** where's Martin? – he's up ahead, I think
(**b**) *(en avant) (dans les premiers rangs)* at the front; *(en voiture)* in the front; **aller d.** to go in front; **marcher/courir d.** to walk on/run on ahead; **passez d.!** you go ahead of me!
3 *nm* front; *Fig* **prendre les devants** to make the first move

devanture [dəvɑ̃tyr] *nf (vitrine)* window; *(façade)* front

dévastateur, -trice [devastatœr, -tris] *adj* devastating

dévastation [devastasjɔ̃] *nf* devastation

dévaster [devaste] *vt* to devastate

déveine [devɛn] *nf Fam* bad luck; **être dans la d.** to be down on one's luck

développement [devlɔpmɑ̃] *nm* development; *(de pellicule)* developing; *(en cyclisme)* gear ratio; **en plein d.** *(entreprise, pays)* growing fast; **développements** *(d'une affaire)* developments; *Fig* **se lancer dans de grands développements** to go into detailed explanation

développer [devlɔpe] **1** *vt* to develop
2 se développer *vpr* to develop; *(s'étendre)* to spread

devenir¹ [dəvnir] *nm Litt* (**a**) *(évolution)* evolution; **être en perpétuel d.** to be constantly evolving (**b**) *(futur)* future

devenir² [70] *(aux être) vi* to become; **il devint général** he became a general; **il était devenu (un) homme** he had grown into a man; **ça devient difficile** it's getting difficult; **d. vieux** to get or grow old; **d. fou** to go mad; **c'est à d. fou!** it's enough to drive you mad!; **d. tout rouge** to go all red; **que devient-il?** how is he getting on?; **qu'est-il devenu?** what's become of him?

dévergondé, -e [devɛrgɔ̃de] **1** *adj* shameless
2 *nm,f* shameless person

dévergonder [devɛrgɔ̃de] **se dévergonder** *vpr* to get into bad ways

déversement [devɛrsəmɑ̃] *nm (écoulement)* discharge; *(action)* pouring

déverser¹ [devɛrse] **1** *vt* (**a**) *(eau)* to pour; *(sable, gravier, déchets)* to dump; *Fig (touristes, voyageurs)* to disgorge (**b**) **d. sa colère sur qn** to vent one's anger on sb; **d. des insultes sur qn** to shower sb with abuse
2 se déverser *vpr (rivière)* to empty (**dans** into)

dévestiture [devɛstityr] *nf Suisse* access; **(chemin de) d.** access road

dévêtir [71] [devetir] **1** *vt* to undress
2 se dévêtir *vpr* to undress

devez *voir* devoir

déviation [devjasjɔ̃] *nf* (**a**) *(itinéraire modifié) Br* diversion, *Am* detour (**b**) *(modification)* deviation (**par rapport à** from)

dévier [66] [devje] **1** *vt* (**a**) *(circulation)* to divert (**b**) *(balle, coup)* to deflect
2 *vi (véhicule, missile)* to veer (**vers** towards); *(balle)* to deflect (**vers** towards); **d. de sa route** *(véhicule, missile)* to veer off course; *Fig* **d. de son sujet** to digress

devin [dəvɛ̃] *nm* soothsayer; *Fam* **je ne suis pas d.!** I'm not a mind-reader!

deviner [dəvine] *vt (énigme, secret)* to guess; *(futur)* to predict; *(pensée)* to read; **devine qui j'ai vu** guess who I saw; **je ne pouvais pas d.!** how was I supposed to know?

devinette [dəvinɛt] *nf* riddle; **jouer aux devinettes** to play at riddles; *Fig* to speak in riddles; **poser une d. à qn** to ask sb a riddle

devis [dəvi] *nm* estimate, quote; **faire faire un d. pour qch** to get an estimate *or* a quote for sth

dévisager [45] [devizaʒe] *vt* to stare at

devise [dəviz] *nf* (**a**) *(d'une personne)* motto (**b**) *(monnaie)* currency; **devises étrangères** foreign currency; **d. forte** hard currency (**c**) *(en héraldique)* device

deviser [dəvize] *vi Litt* to converse

dévisser [devise] **1** *vt* to unscrew
2 *vi (alpiniste)* to fall
3 se dévisser *vpr* to unscrew; *(par accident)* to come unscrewed; *Fig* **se d. la tête** *ou* **le cou** to screw one's head round

de visu [devizy] *adv* with one's own eyes

dévitaliser [devitalize] *vt (dent)* to remove the nerve from

dévoiler [devwale] **1** *vt (visage, statue, plaque)* to unveil; *Fig (nom, secret, complot)* to disclose
2 se dévoiler *vpr (secret, complot)* to come to light

devoir¹ [dəvwar] *nm* (**a**) *(obligation)* duty; **faire qch par d.** to do sth out of a sense of duty; **un homme/ une femme de d.** a man/a woman with a sense of duty; **faire** ou **remplir son d. (envers)** to do one's duty (by); **il est de mon d. de vous le dire** it is my duty to tell you

(**b**) *(exercices) (en classe)* test; **devoirs** *(à la maison)* homework; **faire ses devoirs** to do one's homework; **devoirs de vacances** holiday homework

(**c**) *Formel* **rendre les derniers devoirs à qn** to pay one's last respects to sb

devoir² [26] **1** *vt (être redevable de)* **d. qch à qn** to owe sb sth, to owe sth to sb; **il me doit mille euros** he owes me a thousand euros; **je lui dois bien cela** it's the least I can do for him, I owe him that at least

2 *v aux* (**a**) *(indique l'obligation)* **d. faire qch** to have to do sth; **vous devez être là à trois heures** you must or you have to be there by three o'clock; **elle a cru d. refuser** she thought it advisable to refuse; **les commandes doivent être adressées à...** orders should be sent to...; **vous devriez rester** you should stay, you ought to stay; **il aurait dû m'avertir** he should have warned me, he ought to have warned me

(**b**) *(indique la nécessité)* **tu dois absolument lui en parler** you really must talk to him about it; **finalement, j'ai dû céder** I had to give way in the end; **il ne devait plus les revoir** *(il ne les reverrait plus)* he was (destined) never to see them again; **cela devait arriver!** it was bound to or it had to happen!

(**c**) *(indique l'intention)* **je devais partir lundi, mais...** I was meant to leave on Monday, but...; **le train doit arriver à midi** the train is due (to arrive) at twelve o'clock

(**d**) *(indique la supposition)* **vous devez avoir faim** you must be hungry; **il ne doit pas avoir plus de 40 ans** he can't be more than 40; **il a dû me prendre pour un autre** he must have mistaken me for someone else; **la pollution devrait s'accroître d'ici la fin du siècle** pollution is expected to increase by the end of the century

3 se devoir *vpr* **je me dois à ma famille/mon travail** I must devote myself to my family/my work; **je me dois de le faire** it's my duty to do it; **comme il se doit** as is (only) right and proper

dévolu, -e [devɔly] **1** *adj (somme, responsabilités)* assigned (**à** to)

2 *nm* **jeter son d. sur** to set one's heart on

devons voir **devoir**

dévorant, -e [devɔrɑ̃, -ɑ̃t] *adj (jalousie, passion)* consuming; *(envie)* overwhelming; *(curiosité)* burning; **avoir une faim dévorante** to be ravenous

dévorer [devɔre] *vt* (**a**) *(proie, nourriture, livre)* to devour; **être dévoré par les moustiques** to be eaten alive by mosquitoes; **d. qn des yeux** ou **du regard** to devour sb with one's eyes (**b**) *Fig (détruire)* **l'ambition/la jalousie la dévore** she is consumed by ambition/jealousy; **dévoré de remords** consumed with remorse (**c**) *Fig (fortune, kilomètres)* to eat up

dévot, -e [devo, -ɔt] **1** *adj* devout

2 *nm,f* devout person

dévotion [devosjɔ̃] *nf* (**a**) *(ferveur)* devoutness (**b**) *(adoration)* devotion; **avoir une d. pour** to be devoted to (**c**) **dévotions** *(prières)* devotions

dévoué, -e [devwe] *adj* devoted (**à** to)

dévouement [devumɑ̃] *nm* (**a**) *(abnégation)* devotion to duty (**b**) *(amour)* devotion (**à** to); **avec d.** devotedly

dévouer [devwe] **se dévouer** *vpr (se sacrifier)* to volunteer (**pour faire qch** to do sth); *(se consacrer)* to devote oneself (**à** to); **il faut que quelqu'un se dévoue** somebody has to do it; *Hum* **vous voulez que je finisse la tarte? bon, je me dévoue!** you want me to finish the tart? oh well, if I must!

dévoyé, -e [devwaje] *adj & nm,f* delinquent

dévoyer [32] [devwaje] **se dévoyer** *vpr Litt* to go astray

devra etc voir **devoir**

dextérité [dɛksterite] *nf* dexterity, skill; **avec d.** skilfully

dézipper [dezipe] *vt Ordinat* to unzip

DGSE [deʒeɛsə] *nf (abrév* **direction générale de la sécurité extérieure)** = French military intelligence service, *Br* ≃ MI6

diabète [djabɛt] *nm* diabetes; **avoir du d.** to have diabetes

diabétique [djabetik] *adj & nmf* diabetic

diable [djabl] *nm* (**a**) *(démon)* devil; **le d.** the Devil; **un petit d.** *(enfant)* a little devil; **avoir une faim de tous les diables** to be absolutely ravenous; **un bruit de tous les diables** a hell of a din; *Fig* **avoir le d. au corps** to be possessed; *Can Fam* **être au d.** to be fed up; *Fig* **tirer le d. par la queue** to live from hand to mouth; **au d. l'avarice!** to hell with the expense!; **allez au d.!** go to hell!, **au d. (vauvert)** miles away; **que le d. l'emporte!** he can go to hell!; **ce serait bien le d. si...** it would be surprising if... (**b**) *(marque la surprise, l'agacement)* **d.!** goodness me!; **où d. est-elle allée?** where the devil has she gone?; **que d.!** for goodness sake! (**c**) *(chariot)* (two-wheeled) trolley (**d**) *(jouet)* jack-in-the-box

diablement [djabləmɑ̃] *adv Fam* damned

diablesse [djablɛs] *nf (démon, méchante femme)* she-devil; *Vieilli (jeune fille)* devil

diablotin [djablɔtɛ̃] *nm* imp

diabolique [djabɔlik] *adj* diabolical

diaboliser [djabɔlize] *vt* to demonize

diabolo [djabɔlo] *nm (boisson)* **d. menthe/fraise** mint/strawberry syrup and lemonade

diadème [djadɛm] *nm* tiara

diagnostic [djagnɔstik] *nm* diagnosis; **faire un d.** to make a diagnosis; **ce médecin a un d. très sûr** this doctor makes very reliable diagnoses; *Ordinat* **d. d'autotest** self-test diagnosis

diagnostiquer [djagnɔstike] *vt* to diagnose

diagonal, -e, -aux, -ales [djagɔnal, -o] **1** *adj* diagonal

2 *nf* **diagonale** diagonal; **en diagonale** diagonally; *Fig* **lire qch en diagonale** to skim through sth

diagonalement [djagɔnalmɑ̃] *adv* diagonally

diagramme [djagram] *nm* diagram

dialecte [djalɛkt] *nm* (**a**) *(variante régionale)* dialect (**b**) *Suisse* Swiss German

dialectique [djalɛktik] **1** *adj* dialectical

2 *nf* dialectics *(singulier)*

dialogue [djalɔg] *nm* dialogue; *(conversation)* conversation; **c'est un d. de sourds** it's a dialogue of the deaf; *Ordinat* **mode de d.** interactive mode

dialoguer [djalɔge] *vi* to communicate; *(avec un ordinateur)* to interact

dialyse [djaliz] *nf Méd* dialysis

diamant [djamɑ̃] *nm* diamond

diamantaire [djamɑ̃tɛr] *nm (tailleur)* diamond cutter; *(vendeur)* diamond merchant

diamétralement [djametralmã] *adv* **d. opposés** diametrically opposed

diamètre [djamɛtr] *nm* diameter

diapason [djapazɔ̃] *nm Mus* (**a**) *(note)* pitch; *Fig* **se mettre au d.** to fall in with the others (**b**) *(appareil)* tuning fork

diaphane [djafan] *adj* diaphanous

diaphragme [djafragm] *nm* diaphragm

diapo [djapo] *nf Fam* slide

diaporama [djaporama] *nm* slide show

diapositive [djapozitiv] *nf* slide

diarrhée [djare] *nf* diarrhoea; **avoir la d.** to have diarrhoea

diaspora [djaspɔra] *nf* diaspora

diatonique [djatɔnik] *adj* diatonic

diatribe [djatrib] *nf* diatribe (**contre** against)

dichotomie [dikɔtɔmi] *nf* dichotomy

dico [diko] *nm Fam* dictionary

Dictaphone® [diktafɔn] *nm* Dictaphone®

dictateur [diktatœr] *nm* dictator

dictatorial, -e, -aux, -ales [diktatɔrjal, -o] *adj* dictatorial

dictature [diktatyr] *nf* dictatorship

dictée [dikte] *nf* dictation; **écrire qch sous la d. de qn** to write sth at sb's dictation; **d. musicale** musical dictation

dicter [dikte] *vt* to dictate

diction [diksjɔ̃] *nf* diction

dictionnaire [diksjɔnɛr] *nm* dictionary; **d. électronique** electronic dictionary; **d. de langue** language dictionary

dicton [diktɔ̃] *nm* saying

didactique [didaktik] **1** *adj* (**a**) *(ouvrage, voyage)* educational (**b**) *(terme, langage)* technical
2 *nf* didactics *(singulier)*

dièse [djɛz] *Mus* **1** *nm* sharp
2 *adj* sharp; **fa d.** F sharp

diesel [djezɛl] **1** *adj* **moteur d.** diesel engine
2 *nm (carburant)* diesel
3 *nf (voiture)* diesel

diète [djɛt] *nf* (**a**) *(régime) (partiel)* diet; *(total)* fast; **être à la d.** *(partielle)* to be on a diet; *(totale)* to be fasting (**b**) *Hist* diet

diététicien, -enne [djetetisjɛ̃, -ɛn] *nm,f* dietitian

diététique [djetetik] **1** *adj (menu, repas)* diet; *(magasin, restaurant)* health food
2 *nf* dietetics *(singulier)*

dieu, -x [djø] **1** *nm* (**a**) *(divinité)* god; *Fam* **comme un d.** *(chanter, jouer)* like a god (**b**) *(dans la religion chrétienne)* **D.** God; **le bon D.** God; **D. merci!, D. soit loué!** thank God!; **D. sait si j'ai travaillé** God knows I've worked hard enough; **D. seul le sait** God only knows
2 *exclam* **mon D.!** (good) God!; **D. qu'elle est petite!** God, she's small!; *Fam* **c'est pas D. possible!** it's just not possible!; *Fam* **bon D.!** for God's sake!; *très Fam* **nom de D.!** Christ almighty!

diffamation [difamasjɔ̃] *nf (paroles)* slander; *(écrits)* libel; **procès en d.** slander/libel trial

diffamatoire [difamatwar] *adj (paroles)* slanderous; *(écrits)* libellous

différé, -e [difere] **1** *adj Ordinat* **traitement d.** off-line processing
2 *nm* **en d.** *(émission)* pre-recorded

différemment [diferamɑ̃] *adv* differently

différence [diferɑ̃s] *nf* difference (**entre** between); **d. d'âge/de prix** age/price difference; **faire la d. (entre)** to make a distinction (between); **cela ne fait aucune** *ou* **pas de d.** it makes no difference; **à la d. de** unlike

différenciation [diferɑ̃sjasjɔ̃] *nf* differentiation

différencier [66] [diferɑ̃sje] **1** *vt* to differentiate (**de** *ou* **d'avec** from)
2 se différencier *vpr* (**a**) *(être différent)* to differ (**de/par** from/in) (**b**) *(chercher à être différent)* to differentiate oneself (**de** from)

différend [diferɑ̃] *nm* difference of opinion, disagreement (**entre** between); *Jur* dispute; **avoir un d. avec qn** to have a disagreement with sb

différent, -e [diferɑ̃, -ɑ̃t] *adj* different (**de** from); **différents cas** *(plusieurs)* various cases

différentiel, -elle [diferɑ̃sjɛl] **1** *adj & nm* differential
2 *nf* **différentielle** *Math* differential

différer [34] [difere] **1** *vt (jugement, paiement)* to defer; *(décision, départ)* to postpone
2 *vi (être différent)* to differ (**par** in)

difficile [difisil] **1** *adj* difficult; *(exigeant)* fussy; **le plus d. est fait** the most difficult part is over; **il est d. de le joindre** it's difficult to contact him; **il m'est d. d'accepter** it's difficult for me to accept; **être d. à vivre** to be difficult to get on with; **être d. sur qch** to be particular about sth
2 *nmf* **faire le d.** to be fussy

difficilement [difisilmɑ̃] *adv* with difficulty, not easily; **on peut d. le lui dire** you can hardly tell him that

difficulté [difikylte] *nf* difficulty; **être en d.** to be in difficulty *or* trouble; **faire des difficultés** to create difficulties; **avoir de la d. à faire qch** to have difficulty (in) doing sth; **avoir des difficultés en anglais** to have difficulties with English

difforme [difɔrm] *adj* deformed, misshapen

difformité [difɔrmite] *nf* deformity

diffus, -e [dify, -yz] *adj (lumière)* diffuse; *(impression, souvenir)* vague; *(douleur)* dull

diffuser [difyze] *vt* (**a**) *(lumière, chaleur)* to diffuse; *(livres)* to distribute; *(idée, nouvelle)* to spread (**b**) *(émission)* to broadcast

diffuseur [difyzœr] *nm (de lumière, de chaleur)* diffuser; **d. de parfum** room freshener

diffusion [difyzjɔ̃] *nf* (**a**) *(de lumière, de chaleur)* diffusion; *(de livres)* distribution; *(d'une idée, d'une nouvelle)* spreading (**b**) *(d'une émission)* broadcasting

digérer [34] [diʒere] *vt* (**a**) *(aliment)* to digest; **je ne digère pas le lait** I can't digest milk (**b**) *(assimiler intellectuellement)* to digest; *Fam (accepter)* to stomach, to take; **des vérités dures à d.** unpalatable truths

digeste [diʒest] *adj aussi Fig* easily digestible

digestif, -ive [diʒestif, -iv] **1** *adj* digestive
2 *nm* liqueur

digestion [diʒestjɔ̃] *nf* digestion; **avoir une d. difficile** to have problems with one's digestion

Digicode® [diʒikɔd] *nm* door code *(for entry to a building)*

digital¹, -e, -aux, -ales [diʒital, -o] *adj (numérique)* digital

digital², -e, -aux, -ales 1 *adj voir* **empreinte**
2 *nf* **digitale** *Bot* digitalis

digne [diɲ] *adj* (**a**) *(méritant)* **d. de** worthy of; **d. d'éloges** praiseworthy; **d. de foi** reliable; **être d. de faire qch** to be fit to do sth (**b**) *(approprié)* **d. de** worthy of; **peu d. de qn** unworthy of sb; **d. de ce**

nom worthy of the name; *Hum* **tu es bien le d. fils de ton père** you're your father's son all right (**c**) *(grave)* dignified

dignement [diɲəmɑ̃] *adv* (**a**) *(avec dignité)* with dignity (**b**) *(de façon appropriée)* fittingly; **être d. récompensé** to be justly rewarded

dignitaire [diɲiter] *nm* dignitary

dignité [diɲite] *nf* dignity

digression [digresjɔ̃] *nf* digression; **faire une d.** to digress

digue [dig] *nf* (**a**) *(dans un port)* dike; *(contre l'érosion)* sea wall (**b**) *Can (de billes de bois)* logjam

dilapider [dilapide] *vt (fortune)* to squander; *(fonds publics)* to embezzle

dilatation [dilatasjɔ̃] *nf* (**a**) *(des pupilles)* dilation; *(de l'estomac)* distension (**b**) *(d'un gaz)* expansion

dilater [dilate] **1** *vt* (**a**) *(pupilles)* to dilate; *(estomac)* to distend (**b**) *(gaz)* to expand
  2 se dilater *vpr* (**a**) *(pupilles)* to dilate; *(estomac)* to distend (**b**) *(gaz)* to expand

dilemme [dilem] *nm* dilemma

dilettante [diletɑ̃t] *nmf* dilettante; **faire qch en d.** to dabble in sth

diligence [diliʒɑ̃s] *nf* (**a**) *(véhicule)* (stage)coach (**b**) *Litt (soin)* diligence

diligent, -e [diliʒɑ̃, -ɑ̃t] *adj Litt (zélé)* diligent

diluant [dilɥɑ̃] *nm* thinner

diluer [dilɥe] *vt (boisson)* to dilute; *(peinture)* to thin down; *Fig (discours, dissertation)* to pad out

dilution [dilysjɔ̃] *nf (de peinture)* thinning down; *(d'une boisson)* dilution

diluvien, -enne [dilyvjɛ̃, -ɛn] *adj (pluies)* torrential

dimanche [dimɑ̃ʃ] *nm* Sunday; **le d. des Rameaux/ de Pâques** Palm/Easter Sunday; *Fig* **conducteur du d.** Sunday driver; *voir aussi* **samedi**

dîme [dim] *nf Hist* tithe

dimension [dimɑ̃sjɔ̃] *nf* (**a**) *(grandeur)* dimension, size; **à deux/trois dimensions** two-/three-dimensional; **prendre les dimensions de qch** *(objet)* to take the measurements of sth (**b**) *(importance)* magnitude (**c**) *(aspect)* dimension

diminué, -e [diminɥe] *adj* **être d.** to have gone downhill

diminuer [diminɥe] **1** *vt* (**a**) *(réduire)* to reduce, to decrease (**b**) *(affaiblir)* to weaken (**c**) *(dénigrer) (personne)* to belittle; *(action)* to undermine
  2 *vi* to decrease; *(fièvre)* to drop
  3 se diminuer *vpr* to belittle oneself

diminutif, -ive [diminytif, -iv] *adj & nm* diminutive

diminution [diminysjɔ̃] *nf* reduction, decrease; **être en d.** *(effectifs)* to be dwindling; *(naissances, ventes)* to be falling

dinar [dinar] *nm* dinar

dinde [dɛ̃d] *nf* (**a**) *(volaille, viande)* turkey (**b**) *Fam (femme sotte)* silly goose

dindon [dɛ̃dɔ̃] *nm* turkey (cock); *Fig* **être le d. de la farce** to be made a fool of

dindonneau, -x [dɛ̃dɔno] *nm* turkey poult

dîner¹ [dine] *nm* (**a**) *(repas du soir)* dinner; *(soirée)* dinner party; **il y a des pâtes pour le** *ou* **au** *ou* **à d.** it's pasta for dinner (**b**) *(repas de midi)* lunch

dîner² *vi* (**a**) *(le soir)* to have dinner, to dine; **il dîna d'une tranche de jambon** he had a slice of ham for dinner (**b**) *(à midi)* to have lunch

dînette [dinɛt] *nf (service)* doll's teaset; **jouer à la d.** to have a dolls' tea party

dingo [dɛ̃go] **1** *Fam adj* crazy
  2 *nm (chien sauvage d'Australie)* dingo
  3 *nmf Fam* nutcase

dingue [dɛ̃g] *Fam* **1** *adj* (**a**) *(fou)* crazy; **être d. de qn/ qch** to be crazy about sb/sth (**b**) *(incroyable)* incredible
  2 *nmf (fou)* nutcase; **être un(e) d. de moto/cinéma** to be a motorbike/film nut

dinguer [dɛ̃ge] *vi Fam* **aller d. contre qch** to go crashing into sth; **envoyer d. qn** *(éconduire)* to send sb packing, **envoyer d. qch** to send sth flying

dinosaure [dinozɔr] *nm aussi Fig* dinosaur

diocèse [djɔsɛz] *nm Rel* diocese

diode [djɔd] *nf Élec* diode; **d. électroluminescente** light-emitting diode

dioxyde [djɔksid] *nm Chim* dioxide; **d. de carbone** carbon dioxide

diphtérie [difteri] *nf Méd* diphtheria; **avoir la d.** to have diphtheria

diphtongue [diftɔ̃g] *nf Ling* diphthong

diplomate [diplɔmat] **1** *adj* diplomatic
  2 *nm Culin* ≃ trifle
  3 *nmf* diplomat

diplomatie [diplɔmasi] *nf* (**a**) *(habileté)* diplomacy; **user de d.** to be diplomatic (**b**) *(service)* diplomatic service

diplomatique [diplɔmatik] *adj* diplomatic

diplomatiquement [diplɔmatikmɑ̃] *adv* diplomatically

diplôme [diplom] *nm* diploma; *Univ* degree; **avoir des diplômes** to have qualifications

diplômé, -e [diplome] **1** *adj* qualified; *Univ* graduate; **un ingénieur d. de l'École polytechnique** an engineering graduate of the École Polytechnique
  2 *nm,f* holder of a diploma; *Univ* graduate

dire¹ [dir] *nm* **au d. de qn** according to sb; **selon ses dires** according to him

dire² [27a] **1** *vt* (**a**) *(exprimer)* to say; **comment dit-on "soleil" en anglais?** how do you say "soleil" in English?; **il ne savait plus quoi d.** he didn't know what to say; **je sais ce que je dis!** I know what I'm talking about!; **laisse-les d., ils sont stupides!** let them talk, they're stupid!; **elle a dit qu'elle arriverait en retard** she said she would be late; **comment dirais-je?** how shall I put it?; **comme on dit** as the saying goes; **cela dit...** having said that...; **il est un peu lent, pour ne pas d. complètement idiot** he's a bit slow, or to put it bluntly he's a complete idiot; **qui dit mieux?** *(à une vente aux enchères)* any advance?; **c'est vite dit** it's easier said than done
  (**b**) *(communiquer)* **d. qch à qn** to tell sb sth; **d. à qn que...** to tell sb (that)...; **je t'ai déjà dit que oui!** I've already said yes!; **je vous l'avais bien dit!** I told you so!; *Fam* **c'est elle, je te dis** it's her, I tell you; **je lui ai fait d. de venir** I sent for him; **elle ne se le fit pas d. deux fois** she didn't wait to be told twice
  (**c**) *(ordonner)* **d. à qn de faire qch** to tell sb to do sth; **faites ce qu'on vous dit** do as you're told; **taisez-vous, j'ai dit!** be quiet, I said!
  (**d**) *(prétendre)* to say; **à ce qu'elle dit** according to her; **on le dit mort** he is said to have died
  (**e**) *(langage enfantin) (rapporter)* to tell; **je vais le d. à ma mère** I'm going to tell my mum on you
  (**f**) *(décider)* **disons à quatre heures** let's say four

o'clock; **il est dit que je resterai célibataire** I'm destined to stay single

(**g**) *(penser)* **alors, qu'est-ce que tu en dis?** well, what do you think?; **qu'est-ce que tu dirais d'aller au cinéma?** how about going to the cinema?; **on dirait qu'il pleut** it looks as if it's raining; **on dirait du Mozart** it sounds like Mozart; **on dirait du gin** *(au goût)* it tastes like gin; **on aurait dit qu'elle était hypnotisée** it looked as if she was hypnotized; **et d. que...!** and to think (that)...!

(**h**) *(objecter)* to say; **j'ai eu une augmentation conséquente, je n'ai rien à d.** I got a decent rise, I can't complain; **vous avez beau d.,...** you can say what you like, but...; **ce n'est pas pour d., mais...** I don't want to be rude, but...

(**i**) *(indiquer) (sujet: statistiques)* to show; **que dit le baromètre?** what does the barometer say?; **qu'est-ce qui vous dit qu'il viendra?** what makes you think he'll come?; **ce nom ne me dit rien** the name doesn't ring a bell; **quelque chose me dit que...** something tells me (that)...

(**j**) *(plaire)* **ça te dit de partir en vacances avec nous?** do you fancy coming on holiday with us?; **ça ne me dit trop rien de manger chinois** I don't really fancy Chinese food; **ça ne me dit rien qui vaille** I don't like the look of it

(**k**) *(prière, messe)* to say; *(poésie)* to recite

(**l**) *(signifier)* **qui dit bordeaux dit bon vin** Bordeaux is synonymous with good wine

(**m**) *(locutions)* **c'est (tout) d.** need I say more?; **c'est d. s'il t'aime** that shows how much he loves you; **c'est beaucoup d.** that's saying (quite) a lot; **c'est peu d.** that's putting it mildly; **il n'y a pas à d.,...** there are no two ways about it,...; **pour ainsi d.** so to speak, as it were; **pour tout (vous) d.,...** to be honest (with you),...; **quelques jours, je ne dis pas, mais un mois!** a few days, that's fair enough, but a whole month!; *Fam* **je te dis pas la tête qu'il a faite!** you should have seen his face!; *Fam* **je ne te dis que ça** say no more, enough said; **c'est moi qui vous le dis** let me tell you, believe me; *Fam* **à qui le dites-vous!** you're telling ME!; **vous m'en direz tant!** you don't say!; *Fam* **je ne te le fais pas d.!** tell me something I don't know!; *Fam* **tu l'as dit (, bouffi)!** you can say that again!; **cela va sans d.** that goes without saying; **dis donc!** *(au fait)* hey!; *(marque la surprise)* gosh!; *(marque l'indignation)* do you mind!; **tu me le donnes, dis?** give it to me, yeah?

2 se dire *vpr* (**a**) *(l'un à l'autre)* **on se dit bonjour** we say hello

(**b**) *(penser)* **se d. que...** to think that...; **dis-toi bien que ça aurait pu être plus grave** it could have been worse, you know; **je me disais bien que je l'avais déjà vu quelque part** I knew I'd seen him somewhere before

(**c**) *(être exprimé)* **comment ça se dit en anglais?** how do you say that in English?; **ça se dit en français?** can you say that in French?

(**d**) *(se prétendre)* **elle se dit écossaise** she says she's Scottish

direct, -e [dirɛkt] **1** *adj* direct

2 *nm* (**a**) *(à la radio, à la télévision)* live broadcasting; **en d. de l'Opéra de Paris** live from the Paris Opera House (**b**) *(en boxe)* jab; **d. du droit/du gauche** straight right/left (**c**) *(train)* direct train (**pour** to) **3** *adv Fam* straight

directement [dirɛktəmā] *adv* (**a**) *(sans détour)* straight (**b**) *(sans intermédiaire)* directly

directeur, -trice [dirɛktœr, -tris] **1** *nm,f* (**a**) *(d'un magasin, d'un service)* manager; **d. artistique** *(d'un film)* artistic director, *(à la télévision)* production designer; *(d'un journal)* art editor; **d. commercial** sales director; **d. général** *(d'une entreprise)* managing director; **d. de la rédaction** editorial director; **d. des ressources humaines** *ou* **du personnel** personnel manager (**b**) *(d'une école) Br* headmaster, *f* headmistress, *Am* principal (**c**) *(d'une prison) Br* governor, *Am* warden (**d**) *Univ* **d. de thèse** thesis supervisor

2 *adj (équipe, instances)* management; *(idée)* main; *(principe, force)* guiding

direction [dirɛksjɔ̃] *nf* (**a**) *(d'une entreprise, d'un théâtre)* management; *(d'une école)* running; *(d'un parti, d'un pays)* leadership; **sous la d. de qn** under the supervision of sb; *(orchestre)* conducted by sb (**b**) *(ensemble des cadres)* management; **d. commerciale** sales management; **d. générale** general management; **d. des ressources humaines** *ou* **du personnel** *(service)* personnel department (**c**) *(orientation)* direction; **toutes/autres directions** *(sur panneau)* all/other directions; **quelle d. ont-ils prise?** which way did they go?; **le train en d. de Strasbourg** the train to Strasbourg, the Strasbourg train (**d**) *(d'un véhicule)* steering; **d. assistée** power steering

directive [dirɛktiv] *nf* directive

directoire [dirɛktwar] *nm* (**a**) *Com (d'une société anonyme)* board of directors (**b**) *Hist* **le D.** the (French) Directory

dirham [diram] *nm* dirham

dirigeable [diriʒabl] *adj & nm* **(ballon) d.** dirigible, airship

dirigeant, -e [diriʒā, āt] **1** *adj voir* **classe**
2 *nm,f (d'un parti, d'un pays)* leader; *(d'une entreprise)* manager; **d. syndical** union leader

diriger [45] [diriʒe] **1** *vt* (**a**) *(entreprise, équipe, projet)* to manage, to run; *(pays, parti)* to lead; *(séance)* to conduct; *(travaux)* to supervise; *(acteurs)* to direct; *(orchestre)* to conduct (**b**) *(arme, télescope, lumière)* to point (**sur** at) (**c**) *(pas)* to direct (**vers** towards); *(regard)* to turn (**vers** to); *(attention)* to turn (**sur** to); *(conversation)* to steer (**sur** onto) (**d**) *(orienter professionnellement)* to steer (**sur** *ou* **vers** towards)

2 se diriger *vpr* (**a**) *(aller)* **se d. vers** *(endroit)* to head for; *(personne)* to go up to; *(carrière, secteur)* to go into (**b**) *(s'orienter)* to find one's way around

dirigisme [diriʒism] *nm* state control

dirlo [dirlo] *nm Fam Br* head, *Am* principal

disais *etc voir* **dire**

discernement [disɛrnəmā] *nm (jugement)* discernment; **sans d.** rashly

discerner [disɛrne] *vt* (**a**) *(percevoir)* to make out (**b**) *(différencier)* **d. qch de** to distinguish sth from (**c**) *(deviner)* to discern

disciple [disipl] *nmf* disciple

disciplinaire [disipliner] *adj* disciplinary

discipline [disiplin] *nf (ordre, matière)* discipline

discipliné, -e [disipline] *adj* disciplined

discipliner [disipline] **1** *vt (enfant)* to control
2 se discipliner *vpr* to discipline oneself

disc-jockey *(pl* disc-jockeys) [diskʒɔkɛ] *nm* disc jockey

discographie [diskɔgrafi] *nf* discography

discontinu, -e [diskɔ̃tiny] *adj* intermittent; *(ligne)* broken

discontinuer [diskɔ̃tinɥe] **sans discontinuer** *adv* without stopping

disconvenir [70] [diskɔ̃vnir] *vi Litt* **ne pas d. de qch** not to deny sth

discordant, -e [diskɔrdɑ̃, -ɑ̃t] *adj* (**a**) *(son, bruit)* discordant (**b**) *(couleurs)* clashing; *(opinions)* conflicting

discorde [diskɔrd] *nf* discord; **semer la d.** to make trouble

discothèque [diskɔtɛk] *nf* (**a**) *(boîte de nuit)* disco (**b**) *(organisme)* record library; *(collection)* record collection

discount [diskunt] *nm (rabais)* discount

discourir [22] [diskurir] *vi* **d. sur qch** to discourse on sth; *Péj* to air one's opinions on sth

discours [diskur] *nm* (**a**) *(allocution)* speech; **prononcer** *ou* **faire un d.** to make a speech; **d. de clôture/d'ouverture** closing/opening speech (**b**) *Gram* speech; **d. indirect/direct** reported *or* indirect/direct speech (**c**) *(paroles)* talk; **il m'a tenu un grand d. sur la tolérance** he gave me a great long speech about tolerance; **tous ces beaux d. ne nous avancent à rien** all this talking isn't getting us anywhere

discrédit [diskredi] *nm* discredit; **jeter le d. sur qn** to bring discredit on sb

discréditer [diskredite] **1** *vt* to discredit
2 se discréditer *vpr (personne)* to discredit oneself; **se d. auprès de** *ou* **aux yeux de qn** to discredit oneself with sb

discret, -ète [diskrɛ, -ɛt] *adj* (**a**) *(plein de retenue)* discreet; **tu sauras rester d.?** you'll keep it to yourself, won't you? (**b**) *(sobre) (personne)* unassuming; *(vêtements)* simple; *(maquillage)* natural (**c**) *(endroit)* quiet

discrètement [diskrɛtmɑ̃] *adv* (**a**) *(avec retenue)* discreetly; **il lui a parlé d.** he had a quiet word with her (**b**) *(sobrement) (habillé)* simply; **être d. maquillée** to be wearing natural make-up

discrétion [diskresjɔ̃] *nf* (**a**) *(retenue)* discretion; **manquer de d.** to be tactless (**b**) *(sobriété)* simplicity; **avec d.** *(s'habiller)* simply; *(se maquiller)* discreetly (**c**) **champagne à d.** unlimited champagne

discrimination [diskriminasjɔ̃] *nf* discrimination; **d. raciale/sexuelle** racial/sexual discrimination; **sans d. d'âge ni de sexe** regardless of age or sex

discriminatoire [diskriminatwar] *adj* discriminatory

disculper [diskylpe] **1** *vt* to exonerate (**de** from)
2 se disculper *vpr* to exonerate oneself (**de** from)

discussion [diskysjɔ̃] *nf* discussion; **avoir une d.** (**sur** *ou* **à propos de**) to have a discussion (about); **pas de d., au travail!** don't argue, get to work!

discutable [diskytabl] *adj* questionable

discutailler [diskytaje] *vi Fam Péj* to quibble

discuté, -e [diskyte] *adj (question)* disputed; *(livre, sujet)* much discussed

discuter [diskyte] **1** *vt (examiner)* to discuss; *(contester)* to question; *Fam* **d. le coup, d. le bout de gras** to have a chat
2 *vi* (**a**) *(parler)* to discuss; **d. avec qn sur** *ou* **de qch** to discuss sth with sb (**b**) *(protester)* to argue; **suismoi sans d.** follow me and don't argue
3 se discuter *vpr* **ça se discute** that's debatable

dise *etc voir* **dire**

disette [dizɛt] *nf* food shortage

diseuse [dizøz] *nf* **d. de bonne aventure** fortune teller

disgrâce [disgrɑs] *nf* **tomber en d.** to fall into disfavour

disgracieux, -euse [disgrasjø, -øz] *adj (personne)* ungainly; *(visage, moue)* ugly

disjoindre [43] [disʒwɛ̃dr] **1** *vt* to separate
2 se disjoindre *vpr* to come apart

disjoint, -e [disʒwɛ̃, -ɛt] *adj (pièces)* separated

disjoncter [disʒɔ̃kte] **1** *vt (circuit électrique)* to break
2 *vi (circuit électrique)* to fuse; *Fam Fig* to crack up

disjoncteur [disʒɔ̃ktœr] *nm* circuit breaker

dislocation [dislɔkasjɔ̃] *nf (d'une articulation)* dislocation

disloquer [dislɔke] **1** *vt* (**a**) *(épaule, genou)* to dislocate (**b**) *(empire, État)* to break up
2 se disloquer *vpr (empire, État)* to break up; **se d. l'épaule** to dislocate one's shoulder

disparaître [20] [disparɛtr] *vi* (**a**) *(devenir invisible)* to disappear, to vanish; **d. dans la foule** to disappear into the crowd; *Fam* **d. de la circulation** to drop out of circulation; *Fam* **disparais!** clear off! (**b**) *(mourir)* to die
(**c**) *(douleur, sentiment)* to disappear; *(maladie, tradition)* to die out; **faire d. qch** to get rid of sth

disparate [disparat] *adj (éléments)* disparate; *(couleurs, objets, mobilier)* ill-matched

disparité [disparite] *nf (d'éléments)* disparity; *(de couleurs, d'objets, de mobilier)* mismatch; *(des salaires, des revenus)* inequality

disparition [disparisjɔ̃] *nf* (**a**) *(absence)* disappearance (**b**) *(décès)* death

disparu, -e [dispary] **1** *adj (personne)* missing; **être porté d.** to be reported missing
2 *nm,f (mort)* dead person; *(absent)* missing person

dispensaire [dispɑ̃sɛr] *nm* community health centre

dispense [dispɑ̃s] *nf* (**a**) *(d'une obligation)* exemption (**b**) *(certificat)* certificate of exemption

dispenser [dispɑ̃se] **1** *vt* (**a**) **d. qn de qch/de faire qch** to exempt sb from sth/from doing sth; **se faire d. de qch** to be excused *or* let off sth; *Euph* **je vous dispense de vos commentaires** you can keep your remarks to yourself (**b**) *(soins, charité, faveurs)* to dispense
2 se dispenser *vpr* **se d. de qch/de faire qch** to get out of sth/of doing sth; **tu pourrais te d. de ce genre de commentaire!** you can keep that sort of remark to yourself!

dispersé, -e [dispɛrse] *adj (épars)* scattered

disperser [dispɛrse] **1** *vt (foule, famille, feuilles)* to scatter
2 se disperser *vpr (nuages, foule, famille)* to scatter, to disperse; *Fig (intellectuellement)* to spread oneself too thinly

dispersion [dispɛrsjɔ̃] *nf* (**a**) *(de manifestants, de nuages, d'une armée)* scattering, dispersal; *Fig (inattention)* lack of focus (**b**) *Suisse (peinture)* emulsion (paint)

disponibilité [dispɔnibilite] *nf* (**a**) *(d'une personne, de places, d'un capital)* availability; **d. d'esprit** receptiveness (**b**) *(d'un fonctionnaire)* leave of absence; **être en d.** to be on leave of absence (**c**) *Fin* **disponibilités** available funds

disponible [dispɔnibl] *adj* (**a**) *(personne, place, capital)* available; **êtes-vous d. ce soir?** are you free tonight?
(**b**) *(fonctionnaire)* on leave of absence

dispos, -e [dispo, -oz] *adj (personne)* fit and well

disposé, -e [dispoze] *adj (personne)* être bien/mal d. to be in a good/bad mood; être bien d. envers qn to be well disposed towards sb; être d. à faire qch to feel disposed *or* willing to do sth

disposer [dispoze] 1 *vt* (a) *(objets, fleurs)* to arrange; *(table)* to lay, to set (b) d. qn à (faire) qch to dispose *or* incline sb to (do) sth
2 *vi* (a) *Formel* vous pouvez d. you may go (b) *(décider) Prov* l'homme propose, Dieu dispose man proposes, God disposes
3 disposer de *vt ind* to have at one's disposal; les renseignements dont je dispose the information at my disposal; le droit des peuples à d. d'eux-mêmes the right of people to self-determination
4 se disposer *vpr* se d. à faire qch to get ready to do sth

dispositif [dispozitif] *nm* (a) *(appareil)* device (b) *(ensemble de moyens)* system; d. policier police presence (c) *Ordinat* d. d'alimentation power unit; *(pour papier)* sheet feed; d. d'alimentation papier *(d'une imprimante)* sheet feed, paper feed

disposition [dispozisjɔ̃] *nf* (a) *(arrangement)* arrangement (b) *(disponibilité)* à la d. de qn at sb's disposal; mettre qch à la d. de qn to put sth at sb's disposal; je suis *ou* je me tiens à votre d. I am at your service (c) *(tendance)* tendency (à to) (d) *(intentions)* être dans de bonnes/mauvaises dispositions to be in a good/bad mood; être dans de bonnes dispositions à l'égard de qn to be favourably disposed towards sb (e) *(dons)* avoir des dispositions pour qch to have an aptitude for sth (f) dispositions *(préparatifs)* arrangements; prendre des dispositions pour faire qch to make arrangements to do sth; prendre ses dispositions to make arrangements (g) *Jur* dispositions *(d'une loi)* clauses

disproportion [disprɔpɔrsjɔ̃] *nf* disproportion (entre between)

disproportionné, -e [disprɔpɔrsjɔne] *adj* disproportionate (par rapport à to)

dispute [dispyt] *nf* quarrel, argument

disputé, -e [dispyte] *adj (question)* controversial; *(match)* hard-fought; ce poste sera très d. there will be a lot of competition for this post

disputer [dispyte] 1 *vt* (a) *(match)* to play; *(combat)* to fight (b) *(se battre pour)* d. qch à qn to fight with sb over sth (c) *Fam (réprimander)* to tell off; se faire d. to get told off
2 se disputer *vpr* (a) *(se quereller)* to quarrel, to argue (pour/avec over/with) (b) *(avoir lieu)* le match se disputera à Wimbledon the match will be played at Wɪmbledon (c) *(se battre pour)* se d. qch to fight over sth

disquaire [diskɛr] *nmf* record dealer

disqualification [diskalifikasjɔ̃] *nf* disqualification

disqualifier [66] [diskalifje] *vt (sportif)* to disqualify

disque [disk] *nm* (a) *(enregistrement)* record; mettre un d. to play a record; d. audionumérique compact disc; d. compact compact disc, CD; d. compact vidéo video compact disc; d. laser laser disc; d. vidéo numérique digital video disc (b) *Ordinat* disk; d. amovible removable disk; d. dur hard disk; d. fixe fixed disk (c) *(cartilage)* disc (d) *(objet rond)* disc; d. de stationnement parking disc (e) *(en sport)* discus (f) *Tech* disc; d. d'embrayage clutch plate

disquette [diskɛt] *nf Ordinat* diskette, floppy (disk); sur d. on diskette, on floppy; d. de démonstration,

Fam d. démo demo disk; d. haute densité high-density disk; d. optique optical disk, floptical disk

dissection [disɛksjɔ̃] *nf aussi Fig* dissection

dissemblable [disãblabl] *adj* dissimilar

dissémination [diseminasjɔ̃] *nf* (a) *(de graines, de peuple)* scattering; *(de germes)* spreading

disséminer [disemine] 1 *vt (graines, peuple)* to scatter; *(germes)* to spread; les écoles sont très disséminées the schools are very thin on the ground
2 se disséminer *vpr* to be scattered

dissension [disãsjɔ̃] *nf* dissension

disséquer [34] [diseke] *vt aussi Fig* to dissect

dissertation [disɛrtasjɔ̃] *nf* essay; faire une d. to write an essay

disserter [disɛrte] *vi (parler)* d. sur qch to discourse on sth, *Péj* to hold forth on sth; *(écrire)* to write about sth

dissidence [disidãs] *nf* dissidence; la d. *(les opposants)* the dissidents

dissident, -e [disidã, -ãt] 1 *adj (en politique)* dissident; *(en religion)* dissenting
2 *nm,f (en politique)* dissident; *(en religion)* dissenter

dissimulateur, -trice [disimylatœr, -tris] 1 *adj* dissembling
2 *nm,f* dissembler

dissimulation [disimylasjɔ̃] *nf* (a) *(hypocrisie)* dissembling, deceit; agir avec d. to act in an underhand way (b) *(des sentiments, de la vérité)* concealment

dissimuler [disimyle] 1 *vt* to cover up, to conceal; *(sujet: rideau)* to screen off; d. qch à qn to conceal sth from sb; avec un plaisir non dissimulé with unconcealed delight
2 se dissimuler *vpr* to be hidden

dissipation [disipasjɔ̃] *nf* (a) *(de craintes, de soupçons)* dispelling; *(d'un malentendu)* clearing up; après d. des brouillards matinaux after the early fog has cleared (b) *(à l'école)* unruly behaviour (c) *Litt (débauche)* dissipation

dissipé, -e [disipe] *adj* (a) *(élève)* unruly (b) *Litt (débauché)* dissipated

dissiper [disipe] 1 *vt* (a) *(nuages)* to disperse; *(brouillard)* to clear; *(malentendu)* to clear up; *(craintes, soupçons)* to dispel (b) *(distraire)* to lead astray
2 se dissiper *vpr* (a) *(nuages)* to disperse; *(brouillard)* to clear; *(craintes, soupçons)* to vanish (b) *(se laisser distraire)* to be unruly

dissociable [disɔsjabl] *adj* separable

dissocier [66] [disɔsje] 1 *vt* to separate
2 se dissocier *vpr* se d. de qch to dissociate oneself from sth

dissolu, -e [disɔly] *adj Litt* dissolute

dissolution [disɔlysjɔ̃] *nf* (a) *(d'un parlement, d'un mariage)* dissolution; *(d'une association)* breaking up (b) *(dans un liquide)* dissolving

dissolvais *etc voir* **dissoudre**

dissolvant, -e [disɔlvã, -ãt] *adj & nm* (produit) d. solvent; *(pour ongles)* nail polish remover

dissonant, -e [disɔnã, -ãt] *adj (sons)* dissonant; *Fig* clashing

dissoudre [3a] [disudr] 1 *vt* (a) *(substance)* to dissolve (b) *(parlement, mariage)* to dissolve; *(association)* to break up
2 se dissoudre *vpr (substance)* to dissolve; *(association)* to break up

dissuader [disyade] *vt* d. qn de faire qch to dissuade sb from doing sth

dissuasif, -ive [disɥazif, -iv] *adj* deterrent; *(prix)* prohibitive; **avoir un effet d.** to be a deterrent

dissuasion [disɥazjɔ̃] *nf* dissuasion; *Mil* **force de d.** deterrent

dissymétrie [disimetri] *nf* asymmetry

distance [distɑ̃s] *nf* distance; **suivre qn à d.** to follow sb at a distance; **à quelle d. sommes-nous de la ville?** how far are we from the town?; **à une courte d. (de)** a short distance away (from); **à d.** *(déclencher)* by remote control; *(rester, observer)* at a distance; *aussi Fig* **tenir qn à d.** to keep sb at a distance; **conserver** *ou* **garder ses distances, se tenir à d.** to hold oneself aloof; **prendre ses distances, prendre de la d.** to stand back; *Sport & Fig* **tenir la d.** to go the distance

distancer [16] [distɑ̃se] *vt aussi Fig* to outstrip, to outdistance; **se laisser d.** to fall *or* lag behind; **d. qn de deux points/de 10 mètres** to go two points/10 metres ahead of sb

distant, -e [distɑ̃, -ɑ̃t] *adj* (a) *(éloigné)* distant; **nos deux maisons sont distantes d'un kilomètre** our two houses are a kilometre apart (b) *Fig (froid)* distant, standoffish (**avec** with)

distendre [distɑ̃dr] **1** *vt (corde, élastique, vêtement)* to stretch; *(muscle)* to strain

2 se distendre *vpr (corde, élastique, vetement)* to stretch; *(muscle)* to slacken

distillation [distilasjɔ̃] *nf* distillation

distiller [distile] *vt* (a) *(alcool, pétrole)* to distil; **eau distillée** distilled water (b) *(poison)* to distil; *Fig (colère, ennui)* to exude

distillerie [distilri] *nf (lieu)* distillery; *(procédé)* distilling

distinct, -e [distɛ̃, -ɛ̃kt] *adj* (a) *(séparé)* distinct, separate (**de** from) (b) *(clair) (silhouette, voix)* distinct, clear

distinctement [distɛ̃ktəmɑ̃] *adv* distinctly, clearly

distinctif, -ive [distɛ̃ktif, -iv] *adj* distinctive

distinction [distɛ̃ksjɔ̃] *nf* (a) *(différence)* distinction; **faire une d. entre deux choses** to make a distinction between two things; **sans d.** without distinction, indiscriminately; **sans d. de race ou de couleur** regardless of race or colour (b) *(élégance)* distinction; **avoir de la d.** to be distinguished

distingué, -e [distɛ̃ge] *adj* distinguished

distinguer [distɛ̃ge] **1** *vt* (a) *(différencier)* to distinguish (**de** from); **il a appris à d. les champignons** he has learnt how to tell the various kinds of mushroom apart; **on peut à peine les d. l'un de l'autre** you can hardly tell them apart (b) *(discerner) (objet, silhouette)* to make out; *(personne)* to pick out; **d. une nuance d'amertume dans la voix de qn** to detect a trace of bitterness in sb's voice

2 se distinguer *vpr* (a) *(s'illustrer)* to distinguish oneself (**par** by); **on ne peut vraiment pas dire qu'il se distingue par son intelligence** he hardly stands out as being very intelligent (b) *(se différencier)* **se d. de qn/qch (par)** to be distinguishable from sb/sth (by) (c) *(être perçu)* **au loin se distinguait la côte** the coastline could be made out in the distance

distinguo [distɛ̃go] *nm* distinction; **faire un d. entre** to make a distinction between

distordre [distɔrdr] *vt* to distort

distorsion [distɔrsjɔ̃] *nf* distortion; *(entre deux facteurs, deux salaires)* imbalance

distraction [distraksjɔ̃] *nf* (a) *(inattention)* absent-mindedness; **par d.** inadvertently, absent-mindedly (b) *(loisir)* activity; **ça manque de distractions, ici** there's nothing to do here

distraire [28] [distrɛr] **1** *vt* (a) *(détourner)* to distract (**de** from) (b) *(divertir)* to entertain, to amuse

2 se distraire *vpr (s'occuper)* to amuse oneself; *(se détendre)* to enjoy oneself

distrait, -e [distrɛ, -ɛt] *adj* (a) *(étourdi)* absent-minded; **d'un air d.** absent-mindedly (b) *(inattentif)* inattentive; **d'une oreille distraite** with only half an ear

distraitement [distrɛtmɑ̃] *adv* absent-mindedly

distrayais *etc voir* **distraire**

distrayant, -e [distrɛjɑ̃, -ɑ̃t] *adj* entertaining

distribuer [distribɥe] *vt* (a) *(donner) (prix, bonbons, provisions, vivres)* to distribute (**à** to); *(dividendes)* to pay (**à** to); *(cartes)* to deal (**à** to); *(courrier)* to deliver (**à** to); *(eau, gaz, électricité)* to supply (**à** to); *(sourires, compliments)* to bestow (**à** on); **d. des coups** to lash out with one's fists (b) *(répartir) (tâches)* to allocate; **d. les rôles** to cast a play (c) *(commercialiser)* to distribute

distributeur, -trice [distribytœr, -tris] **1** *nm,f Com* distributor; **d. agréé** authorized distributor

2 *nm (appareil)* (vending) machine; **d. (automatique) de billets** cash dispenser *or* machine; **d. (automatique) de boissons/de cigarettes** drinks/cigarette machine

distribution [distribysjɔ̃] *nf* (a) *(remise)* distribution; *(de lettres, de marchandises)* delivery; **la d. des prix** *(à l'école)* prizegiving (b) *(répartition) (de tâches)* allocation; *(d'une maison, d'un appartement)* layout; *(d'un film, d'une pièce) (action)* casting; *(acteurs)* cast (c) *Com* distribution; **grande d.** large-scale distribution (d) *(approvisionnement)* supply; **d. des eaux** water supply

district [distrikt] *nm* district

dit, -e [di, dit] **1** *pp voir* **dire**

2 *adj* (a) *(décidé)* **à l'heure dite** at the agreed time (b) *(appelé)* known as

dithyrambique [ditirɑ̃bik] *adj* eulogistic

diurétique [djyretik] *adj & nm* diuretic

diurne [djyrn] *adj* diurnal

diva [diva] *nf* diva

divagations [divagasjɔ̃] *nfpl* raving

divaguer [divage] *vi* to rave

divan [divɑ̃] *nm* divan, couch

divergence [divɛrʒɑ̃s] *nf (de lignes, de rayons)* divergence; *(d'opinions)* difference

divergent, -e [divɛrʒɑ̃, -ɑ̃t] *adj (lignes)* divergent; *(opinions)* differing

diverger [45] [divɛrʒe] *vi (opinions, lignes, rayons)* to diverge (**de** from)

divers, -e [divɛr, -ɛrs] *adj* (a) *(différents)* varied; **d. (rubrique)** miscellaneous (b) *(plusieurs)* various; **diverses solutions sont possibles** there are various possible solutions

diversement [divɛrsəmɑ̃] *adv* in various ways

diversification [divɛrsifikasjɔ̃] *nf* diversification

diversifier [66] [divɛrsifje] **1** *vt (économie, cultures, activités)* to diversify; *(intérêts, couleurs)* to vary

2 se diversifier *vpr (entreprise, activités)* to diversify

diversion [divɛrsjɔ̃] *nf* diversion; **faire d.** to create a diversion

diversité [divɛrsite] *nf (variété)* variety, diversity

divertir [divɛrtir] **1** *vt (amuser)* to entertain, to amuse **2 se divertir** *vpr* to enjoy oneself; **se d. de qch** to laugh at sth

divertissant, -e [divɛrtisã, -ãt] *adj* amusing, entertaining

divertissement [divɛrtismã] *nm* (**a**) *(amusement)* entertainment, amusement (**b**) *Mus* divertimento

dividende [dividãd] *nm Math & Fin* dividend

divin, -e [divɛ̃, -in] *adj aussi Fig* divine; **le d. Enfant** the Holy Child

divinement [divinmã] *adv* divinely

divinité [divinite] *nf* (**a**) *(nature de Dieu)* divinity (**b**) *(dieu)* deity

diviser [divize] **1** *vt* (**a**) *(partager)* to divide (**en/entre** into/among); **d. 15 par 3** to divide 15 by 3 (**b**) *(opposer)* to divide; **l'opinion est divisée au sujet de cette affaire** opinion on the matter is divided; **d. pour mieux régner** divide and rule **2 se diviser** *vpr* to divide (**en** into); **l'examen se divise en trois parties** the examination is divided into three parts; **le chemin se divise en deux** the road divides *or* forks

diviseur [divizœr] *nm Math* divisor; **plus grand commun d.** highest common factor

divisible [divizibl] *adj* divisible

division [divizjɔ̃] *nf* (**a**) *(séparation) & Math* division (**en** into); **faire une d.** to do a division; *Biol* **d. cellulaire** cell division; **d. du travail** division of labour (**b**) *(partie)* part, section; *Mil* division; **d. blindée** armoured division (**c**) *(désaccord)* division

divisionnaire [divizjɔnɛr] **1** *adj* divisional **2** *nm* (**a**) *(commissaire) Br* ≃ chief superintendent, *Am* ≃ police chief (**b**) *Mil* major general

divorce [divɔrs] *nm* divorce; *Fig (désaccord)* gulf; **demander le d.** to ask for a divorce; **obtenir le d.** to get a divorce

divorcé, -e [divɔrse] **1** *adj* divorced **2** *nm,f* divorcee

divorcer [16] [divɔrse] *vi* to get divorced, to get a divorce; **d. d'avec** *ou* **de qn** to divorce sb

divulgation [divylgasjɔ̃] *nf* disclosure (**de** of)

divulguer [divylge] *vt* to divulge, to disclose

dix [dis] *adj & nm inv* ten; *voir aussi* **trois**

dix-huit [dizɥit] *adj & nm inv* eighteen; *voir aussi* **trois**

dix-huitième [dizɥitjɛm] *nmf, nm & adj* eighteenth; *voir aussi* **cinquième**

dixième [dizjɛm] *nmf, nm & adj* tenth; *voir aussi* **cinquième**

dixit [diksit] **d. Paul** so Paul says

dix-neuf [diznœf] *adj & nm inv* nineteen; *voir aussi* **trois**

dix-neuvième [diznœvjɛm] *nmf, nm & adj* nineteenth; *voir aussi* **cinquième**

dix-sept [dis(s)ɛt] *adj & nm inv* seventeen; *voir aussi* **trois**

dix-septième [dis(s)ɛtjɛm] *nmf, nm & adj* seventeenth; *voir aussi* **cinquième**

dizaine [dizɛn] *nf* **une d. (de)** about ten, ten or so; *Math* **la colonne des dizaines** the tens column

Djibouti [dʒibuti] *n* Djibouti

do [do] *nm inv (note)* C; *(chantée)* doh

doberman [dɔbɛrman] *nm* doberman

docile [dɔsil] *adj (enfant, animal)* docile

docilement [dɔsilmã] *adv* docilely

docilité [dɔsilite] *nf* docility

dock [dɔk] *nm* (**a**) *(bassin)* dock (**b**) *(entrepôt)* warehouse

docker [dɔkɛr] *nm* docker

docte [dɔkt] *adj Litt* learned

docteur [dɔktœr] *nm* (**a**) *(médecin)* doctor (**b**) *Univ* **être d. ès lettres/ès sciences** ≃ to have a PhD in arts/science; **être d. en droit** ≃ to have an LLD

doctoral, -e, -aux, -ales [dɔktɔral, -o] *adj Péj (air, ton)* pompous

doctorat [dɔktɔra] *nm Univ* doctorate; **d. d'État** = highest postgraduate research degree; **d. de 3e cycle** ≃ PhD

doctoresse [dɔktɔrɛs] *nf Vieilli* lady doctor

doctrine [dɔktrin] *nf* doctrine

document [dɔkymã] *nm* document

documentaire [dɔkymãtɛr] *adj & nm* documentary

documentaliste [dɔkymãtalist] *nmf (d'archives)* archivist; *(dans les écoles)* librarian

documentation [dɔkymãtasjɔ̃] *nf (action)* research; *(documents)* documentation (**sur** on)

documenté, -e [dɔkymãte] *adj (personne)* well-informed; *(étude, thèse)* documented

documenter [dɔkymãte] **se documenter** *vpr* to gather information *or* material (**sur** on)

dodeliner [dɔdəline] *vi* **il dodelinait de la tête** his head kept nodding

dodo [dodo] *nm (langage enfantin)* **faire d.** to sleep; **aller au d.** to go to bye-byes

dodu, -e [dɔdy] *adj* plump, chubby

doge [dɔʒ] *nm Hist* doge

dogmatique [dɔgmatik] *adj* dogmatic

dogmatisme [dɔgmatism] *nm* dogmatism

dogme [dɔgm] *nm* dogma

dogue [dɔg] *nm* mastiff

doigt [dwa] *nm* (**a**) *(de la main)* finger; **d. de pied** toe; **le petit d.** the little finger; **lever le d.** *(en classe)* to put one's hand up; **porter une bague au d.** to wear a ring on one's finger; **faire signe à qn du d.** to beckon to sb; **être comme les (deux) doigts de la main** to be very close; **on peut les compter sur les doigts de la main** you can count them on the fingers of one hand; *Fig* **se faire taper sur les doigts** to get a rap over the knuckles; **filer** *ou* **glisser entre les doigts de qn** to slip through sb's fingers; **vous avez mis le d. dessus** you've put your finger on it; **obéir à qn au d. et à l'œil** to obey sb blindly; **savoir qch sur le bout des doigts** to have sth at one's fingertips; **mon petit d. me l'a dit** a little bird told me; **avoir des doigts de fée** to have nimble fingers; *Fig* **ne pas lever** *ou* **bouger le petit d.** not to lift a finger; *Fam* **tu te mets le d. dans l'œil (jusqu'au coude)** you couldn't be more wrong (if you tried); *Fam* **faire qch les doigts dans le nez** to do sth standing on one's head; *Fam* **gagner les doigts dans le nez** to win hands down (**b**) *(petite quantité) (d'alcool)* drop; **être à deux doigts de qch/de faire qch** to be within a hair's breadth of sth/of doing sth

doigté [dwate] *nm* (**a**) *Mus (d'un morceau de musique)* fingering (**b**) *Fig (adresse)* dexterity; *(tact)* tact

dois, doive *etc voir* **devoir**

doléances [dɔleãs] *nfpl* complaints; **présenter ses doléances** to air one's grievances

dollar [dɔlar] *nm* dollar

dolmen [dɔlmɛn] *nm* dolmen

domaine [dɔmɛn] *nm* (**a**) *(propriété)* estate, property; **être du d. public** to be in the public domain; **d. skiable** skiing area (**b**) *(matière)* field, domain; **c'est du d. du possible** it's within the realms of possibility

domanial, -e, -aux, -ales [dɔmanjal, -o] *adj* state-owned

dôme [dom] *nm Archit & Géog* dome

domestication [dɔmɛstikasjɔ̃] *nf* domestication

domestique [dɔmɛstik] **1** *adj (vie, soucis, querelle)* domestic; *(tâches, déchets)* household; **accidents domestiques** accidents in the home
2 *nmf* servant

domestiquer [dɔmɛstike] *vt (animal)* to domesticate; *(éléments)* to harness

domicile [dɔmisil] *nm* (place of) residence, home; **sans d. fixe** of no fixed abode; **travailler à d.** to work from home; **livrer à d.** to do home deliveries; *Jur* **d. conjugal** marital home

domicilié, -e [dɔmisilje] *adj* **d. à** resident at

dominant, -e [dɔminɑ̃, -ɑ̃t] **1** *adj (opinion)* prevailing; *(couleur, trait, idée)* dominant; *Biol* **caractère d.** dominant characteristic
2 *nf* **dominante** *(ce qui domine)* chief characteristic; **une tenue pâle, avec une dominante de rose** a pale, mainly pink outfit

dominateur, -trice [dɔminatœr, -tris] *adj (personne, ton, attitude)* domineering

domination [dɔminasjɔ̃] *nf* domination (**sur** over); **être sous la d. de qn** to be dominated by sb

dominer [dɔmine] **1** *vt* (**a**) *(assujettir) (personne)* to dominate; *(empire)* to rule over (**b**) *(surpasser) (adversaire, concurrent)* to surpass (**c**) *(prédominer dans)* to be the dominant feature of (**d**) *(maîtriser) (timidité, passions, larmes, sujet)* to master; *(paresse, envie)* to overcome; *(match)* to dominate; **d. la situation** to keep the situation under control (**e**) *(surplomber)* to dominate; **de leur terrasse, on domine la mer** their balcony overlooks the sea
2 *vi* (**a**) *(l'emporter)* to be dominant (**b**) *(prédominer)* to predominate
3 se dominer *vpr* to control oneself

dominicain, -e [dɔminikɛ̃, -ɛn] **1** *adj* Dominican
2 *nm,f* (**a**) *Rel* Dominican (**b**) *(de la République Dominicaine)* **D.** Dominican

dominical, -e, -aux, -ales [dɔminikal, -o] *adj* Sunday; **repos d.** day of rest; **ouverture dominicale des magasins** Sunday opening

Dominique [dɔminik] *nf* **la D.** Dominica

domino [dɔmino] *nm (plaquette)* domino; **jouer aux dominos** to play dominoes

dommage [dɔmaʒ] *nm* (**a**) *(préjudice)* harm; **causer un d. à qn** to do sb harm; **d. corporel** physical injury; **dommages et intérêts, dommages-intérêts** damages; **d. matériel** material damage (**b**) **dommages** *(dégâts matériels)* damage (**c**) **(quel) d.!** what a pity!, what a shame!; **c'est (bien) d. qu'elle ne soit pas venue** it's a (great) pity that she didn't come (**d**) *Can* **beau d!** of course!, you bet!

dommageable [dɔmaʒabl] *adj* detrimental (**à** to)

dompter [dɔ̃(p)te] *vt (fauve, fleuve, nature)* to tame; *(sentiments, passions, personne)* to subdue

dompteur, -euse [dɔ̃(p)tœr, -øz] *nm,f* tamer

DOM-TOM [dɔmtɔm] *nmpl (abrév* **départements et territoires d'outre-mer)** = French overseas departments and territories

DON [deoɛn] *nm Ordinat (abrév* **disque optique numérique)** CD

don [dɔ̃] *nm* (**a**) *(cadeau)* gift; *(à un musée, une œuvre)* donation; **faire d. à qn de qch** to make a gift of sth to sb; **d. du sang/de sperme** blood/sperm donation; *Fig* **d. du ciel** godsend; **le d. de soi** self-sacrifice (**b**) *(aptitude)* gift, talent; *aussi Ironique* **avoir le d. de faire qch** to have a knack for doing sth

donateur, -trice [dɔnatœr, -tris] *nm,f* donor

donation [dɔnasjɔ̃] *nf* donation; *Jur* **d. entre vifs** donation inter vivos

donc [dɔ̃k] *conj* (**a**) *(marque la conséquence)* so (**b**) *(emphatique)* **tu le savais d. depuis le début?** so you knew from the start?; **que voulez-vous d.?** whatever do you want?; **mais taisez-vous d.!** do be quiet!; **allons d.!** come on! (**c**) *(après interruption ou digression)* **je disais d. que...** I was saying, then, that...

dondon [dɔ̃dɔ̃] *nf Fam Péj* **grosse d.** great lump of a woman/girl

donjon [dɔ̃ʒɔ̃] *nm* keep

don Juan *(pl* **dons Juans)** [dɔ̃ʒɥɑ̃] *nm* Don Juan

donne [dɔn] *nf (aux cartes)* deal

donné, -e [dɔne] *adj* (**a**) *(offert)* given; *Fam* **c'est d.** it's dirt cheap; *Fam* **ce n'est pas d.** it doesn't come cheap (**b**) *(défini)* given; **à un moment d.** *(dans le passé)* at one point; *(dans le futur)* at some point; **étant d. la situation** given the situation; **étant d. que...** seeing that...

donnée [dɔne] *nf* (**a**) *(élément)* piece of information; **avoir toutes les données du problème** to have all the data *or* information on the problem (**b**) *Ordinat* **données** data; **données numériques** digital data

donner [dɔne] **1** *vt* (**a**) *(offrir, distribuer)* to give; **d. qch à qn** to give sth to sb, to give sb sth; **d. à boire à qn** to give sb something to drink; **d. à manger à** *(animal)* to feed; **c'est à qui de d.?** *(aux cartes)* whose deal is it?
(**b**) *(faire don de) (temps, vie)* to give; *(corps, organe)* to donate; **d. son sang** to give blood
(**c**) *(céder)* to give; *Fam (dénoncer)* to grass on (**à** to); **en d. à qn pour son argent** to give sb their money's worth
(**d**) *(payer)* **je lui donne 15 euros de l'heure** I pay him 15 euros an hour; **je vous en donne 10 euros** I'll give you 10 euros for it
(**e**) *(confier)* **d. qch à garder à qn** to give sb sth to look after; **d. un vêtement à nettoyer** to hand in a garment to be dry-cleaned
(**f**) *(avis, ordre, conseil)* to give; **d. l'heure à qn** to tell sb the time; **tu lui donneras le bonjour de ma part** say hello to her for me; **d. des** *ou* **de ses nouvelles à qn** to keep in touch with sb
(**g**) *(chance, délai, occasion)* to give; **je vous donne une semaine, pas plus** I'll give you a week and no more
(**h**) *(causer)* **d. de l'appétit à qn** to give sb an appetite; **d. des boutons à qn** to bring sb out in a rash; **d. mal à la tête à qn** to give sb a headache; **d. faim/sommeil/chaud à qn** to make sb hungry/sleepy/hot; **d. du souci à qn** to cause sb worry; **toute cette histoire m'a donné à réfléchir** the whole business made me think again
(**i**) *(produire) (récoltes)* to yield; *(fruits)* to bear; **les blés vont d. cette année** there will be a good crop of wheat this year; **ça n'a rien donné** nothing came of it; **qu'est-ce que ça donne?** *(comment ça se présente?)* how does it look?

(**j**) *(administrer)* to give; **d. un baiser/une gifle à qn** to give sb a kiss/a slap in the face; **tu peux d. un coup de balai dans la cuisine?** can you give the kitchen a sweep?

(**k**) *(bal, dîner, conférence)* to give; *(pièce de théâtre)* to put on, to perform; **qu'est-ce qu'on donne au cinéma?** what's on at the cinema?

(**l**) *(attribuer)* **je lui donne vingt ans** I'd say she's twenty; **les médecins lui donnent deux jours (à vivre)** the doctors give him two days (to live)

(**m**) *(maladie)* to give

2 *vi (cogner)* **d. de la tête contre qch** to hit one's head against sth; *Fig* **je ne savais pas où d. de la tête** I didn't know where to start

3 *v impersonnel* **le spectacle le plus épouvantable qu'il m'ait été donné de voir** the most horrifying sight I've ever been unfortunate enough to witness; **il n'est pas donné à tout le monde d'être écrivain** not everyone can be a writer

4 donner dans *vt ind* (**a**) *(tomber)* **d. dans le piège** *ou* **le panneau** to fall into the trap

(**b**) *(avoir un penchant pour)* to have a tendency for

5 donner sur *vt ind (sujet: fenêtre)* to look onto; *(sujet: porte)* to lead into

6 se donner *vpr* (**a**) *(faire don de soi)* to give of oneself; **se d. à qch** to devote oneself to sth; **se d. en spectacle** to make an exhibition of oneself

(**b**) *(à soi-même)* **se d. un coup de peigne/brosse** to give one's hair a quick comb/brush; **se d. un coup de marteau sur le pouce** to hit one's thumb with a hammer; **se d. le temps de réfléchir** to give oneself time to think; **se d. pour tâche de faire qch** to set oneself the task of doing sth

(**c**) *Litt (sexuellement)* to give oneself (**à** to)

(**d**) *(l'un l'autre)* **se d. des coups** to exchange blows; **se d. des baisers** to kiss (each other)

donneur, -euse [dɔnœr, -øz] *nm,f* (**a**) *(d'organe)* donor; **d. de sang** blood donor (**b**) *(aux cartes)* dealer

dont [dɔ̃] *pron relatif* (**a**) *(introduit le complément du verbe)* **la famille d. je descends** the family I'm descended from; **la façon d. il me regardait** the way (in which) he looked at me; **le livre d. j'ai besoin** the book (that) I need; **un film d. on parle beaucoup** a film that is being talked about a lot; **l'homme d. elle se moque** the man she's making fun of

(**b**) *(introduit le complément du nom)* **la dame d. je connais le fils** the woman whose son I know; **la maison d. on voit le toit** the house whose roof can be seen; **un film d. voici le résumé** a film of which this is a summary; **quelques-uns étaient là, d. votre frère** there were a few people there, including your brother

(**c**) *(introduit le complément de l'adjectif)* **la femme d. il est amoureux** the woman he is in love with; **le groupe d'enfants d. vous êtes responsable** the group of children you are responsible for; **le souvenir d. elle est si honteuse** the memory she is so ashamed of

dopage [dɔpaʒ] *nm doping; (de sportif)* drug-taking

doper [dɔpe] **1** *vt (droguer)* to dope

2 se doper *vpr* to take drugs

dorade [dɔrad] *nf* sea bream

doré, -e [dɔre] **1** *adj* (**a**) *(recouvert d'or)* gilded, gilt; **d. sur tranche** gilt-edged (**b**) *(couleur d'or)* (blé, lumière, peau, cheveux) golden; *(gâteau passé au jaune d'œuf)* glazed; *(viande, pommes de terre, gâteau cuit)* browned

2 *nm Can (poisson)* wall-eyed pike, yellow pike

dorénavant [dɔrenavɑ̃] *adv* from now on

dorer [dɔre] **1** *vt* (**a**) *(recouvrir d'or)* to gild; *Fig* **d. la pilule à qn** to sweeten the pill for sb (**b**) *(donner une couleur dorée à) (peau)* to turn golden; *(gâteau)* to glaze; *(viande, pommes de terre)* to brown

2 *vi (plat, gâteau)* to brown

3 se dorer *vpr* **se d. au soleil** to sunbathe; *Fig* **se d. la pilule** to catch some rays

dorloter [dɔrlɔte] *vt* to pamper, to coddle

dormant, -e [dɔrmɑ̃, -ɑ̃t] **1** *adj* **eaux dormantes** stagnant water

2 *nm Can Rail Br* sleeper, *Am* tie

dormeur, -euse [dɔrmœr, -øz] *nm,f (personne endormie)* sleeper; **être un gros d.** to need a lot of sleep

dormir [29] [dɔrmir] *vi* (**a**) *(sommeiller)* to sleep; **elle dort** she's sleeping, she's asleep; **d. profondément** to be fast asleep; **je n'ai pas dormi de la nuit** I didn't sleep a wink (all night); **le café m'empêche de d.** coffee keeps me awake; *Fam* **ce n'est pas ça qui va m'empêcher de d.** I won't lose any sleep over it; **d. à poings fermés, d. comme un loir** to sleep like a log; **ne d. que d'un œil** to sleep with one eye open; **vous pouvez d. tranquille** *ou* **sur vos deux oreilles** you can rest easy; **avoir envie de d.** to be *or* feel sleepy; **d. debout** to be asleep on one's feet; *Prov* **qui dort, dîne** he who sleeps forgets his hunger (**b**) *Fig (ville, forêt)* to be sleeping; *(capitaux)* to lie idle

dorsal, -e, -aux, -ales [dɔrsal, -o] *adj* dorsal

dortoir [dɔrtwar] *nm* dormitory

dorure [dɔryr] *nf* (**a**) *(couche d'or)* gilding (**b**) *(ornement)* gilt

doryphore [dɔrifɔr] *nm* Colorado beetle

DOS [dɔs] *nm Ordinat* DOS

dos [do] *nm* (**a**) *(d'une personne, d'un animal)* back; **sur le d.** on one's back; **je n'ai rien à me mettre sur le d.** I haven't a thing to wear; **à d. d'âne** on a donkey; **je ne l'ai vu que de d.** I only saw him from the back; **d. à d.** back to back; **faire le gros d.** *(chat)* to arch its back; **faire qch derrière** *ou* **dans le d. de qn** to do sth behind sb's back; *Fam* **je l'ai tout le temps sur le d.** she's always on my back; **s'enrichir sur le d. de qn** to get rich off sb; **avoir bon d.** *(personne)* to have a broad back; **elle a bon d., la grève des postes, dis plutôt que tu n'as pas écrit** why don't you admit you haven't written instead of blaming it on the postal strike?; *Fam* **en avoir plein le d.** to be sick of it, to be fed up with it; **se mettre qn à d.** to get sb's back up; **tourner le d. à qn** *(debout)* to stand with one's back to sb; *(assis)* to sit with one's back to sb; *(volontairement)* to turn one's back on sb; **dès qu'il a le d. tourné** as soon as his back is turned

(**b**) *(d'une chaise, d'une page, d'un chèque, de la main)* back; *(d'un livre)* spine; **voir au d.** (please) turn over, PTO

(**c**) **d. (crawlé)** backstroke

dosage [dozaʒ] *nm (d'ingrédients)* proportioning; *(de médicaments)* dosage

dos-d'âne [dodan] *nm inv* bump; **pont en d.** humpbacked bridge

dose [doz] *nf (d'un élément dans un mélange)* proportion; *(de médicament)* dose; *Fig* **à petites doses** in small doses; *Fam* **il faut une sacrée d. de culot pour faire cela** it takes a hell of a nerve to do that; **forcer la d.** to overdo it; *Fam* **avoir sa d. (de qch)** to have had more than enough (of sth)

doser [doze] *vt (médicament, ingrédient)* to measure out

doseur [dozœr] *nm* measure

dossard [dosar] *nm* number *(worn by competitor)*

dossier [dosje] *nm* (**a**) *(d'un siège)* back (**b**) *(documents)* file, dossier; *(d'un prisonnier, d'un malade, d'un élève)* record; *(chemise)* folder, file; *Ordinat (répertoire)* folder; *(fichier)* file; **constituer un d. sur qn/qch** to build up a file on sb/sth; *Ordinat* **d. système** system folder (**c**) *Fig (sujet)* question

dot [dɔt] *nf* dowry

dotation [dɔtasjɔ̃] *nf (fonds)* (d'hôpital, de collège) endowment; *(versés à un chef d'État)* allowance

doter [dɔte] *vt (équiper)* to equip (**de** with); **elle est dotée d'une intelligence remarquable** she is endowed with great intelligence

douairière [dwɛrjɛr] *adj & nf* dowager

douane [dwan] *nf* customs; **passer à la d.** to go through customs; **droits de d.** customs duty

douanier, -ère [dwanje, -ɛr] **1** *adj* customs; **union douanière** customs union; **barrières douanières** tariff barriers
2 *nm* customs officer

doublage [dublaʒ] *nm* (**a**) *(d'un vêtement)* lining (**b**) *(d'un film, d'une voix)* dubbing; *(par une doublure)* doubling

double [dubl] **1** *adj* (**a**) *(quantité, lit, chambre)* double; **en d. exemplaire** in duplicate; **fermer une porte à d. tour** to double-lock a door; **avoir la d. nationalité** to have dual nationality; *Mus* **d. croche** *Br* semi-quaver, *Am* sixteenth note; *Ordinat* **d. densité** double density; **d. mètre** 2-metre rule; **d. vitrage** double glazing (**b**) *(ambigu)* **mener une d. vie** to lead a double life; **mot à d. sens** ambiguous word
2 *adv* double
3 *nm* (**a**) **le d. (de)** *(quantité, prix)* twice as much (as); *(nombre)* twice as many (as); **dix est le d. de cinq** ten is two times five; **mettre qch en d.** to fold sth in two *or* half (**b**) *(exemplaire)* duplicate, copy; *(d'une clef)* duplicate; *Ordinat* backup; **avoir qch en d.** to have two of sth; **faire qch en d.** *(lettre, devoir)* to make two copies of sth (**c**) *(personne)* double (**d**) *(au tennis)* **d. messieurs/dames/mixte** men's/ladies'/ mixed doubles

doublé, -e [duble] **1** *adj* (**a**) *(veste, gants)* lined (**de** with) (**b**) *(film)* dubbed
2 *nm (victoires)* double

doublement¹ [dubləmɑ̃] *adv* doubly

doublement² *nm (d'un nombre, d'une somme, d'une lettre)* doubling

doubler [duble] **1** *vt* (**a**) *(multiplier par deux)* to double (**b**) *(plier)* to fold in two *or* in half (**c**) *(vêtement)* to line (**d**) *(film, voix)* to dub; *(sujet: acteur)* to dub the voice of; *(sujet: cascadeur)* to stand in for (**e**) *(passer) (véhicule)* *Br* to overtake, *Am* to pass (**f**) *Fam (trahir)* to double-cross
2 *vi* (**a**) *(population, salaire)* to double; **d. de valeur** to double in value (**b**) *(véhicule)* *Br* to overtake, *Am* to pass
3 se doubler *upr* **se doubler de** to be coupled with

doublure [dublyr] *nf* (**a**) *(d'un vêtement, d'un sac)* lining (**b**) *(au théâtre)* understudy; *(au cinéma)* stand-in

douce [dus] *voir* **doux**

douceâtre [dusɑtr] *adj (saveur)* sickly sweet; *(ton)* smarmy

doucement [dusmɑ̃] *adv (délicatement)* gently; *(bas)* softly; **allez-y d.!** gently does it!; *Fam* **(allez-y) d. avec le vin!** go easy on the wine!

doucereux, -euse [dusrø, -øz] *adj (personne, voix, ton)* smarmy

douceur [dusœr] *nf* (**a**) *(d'un son, d'une matière)* softness; *(d'un climat)* mildness; *(du miel, d'un parfum)* sweetness (**b**) *(de caractère)* gentleness; *(d'un sourire)* sweetness; **traiter qn avec d.** to treat sb gently; **en d.** gently; **la voiture a démarré en d.** the car started smoothly (**c**) **douceurs** *(sucreries)* *Br* sweets, *Am* candy

douche [duʃ] *nf* shower; **prendre une d.** to have *or* take a shower; *Fig* **avec lui, c'est la d. écossaise** you never know where you are with him; *Fig* **d. froide** terrible disappointment

doucher [duʃe] **1** *vt (pour laver)* **d. qn** to give sb a shower
2 se doucher *upr* to have *or* take a shower

doudoune [dudun] *nf (anorak)* padded jacket

doué, -e [dwe] *adj* gifted, talented; **être d. pour** to have a gift for

douille [duj] *nf (d'une ampoule)* lamp socket; *(d'une cartouche)* case

douillet, -ette [dujɛ, -ɛt] *adj* (**a**) *(lit)* cosy (**b**) *(délicat)* **ne sois pas si d.!** don't be such a baby!

douillettement [dujɛtmɑ̃] *adv (confortablement)* cosily

douleur [dulœr] *nf (physique)* pain; *(diffuse)* ache; *(morale)* sorrow, grief; **nous avons la d. de vous faire part de...** we regret to inform you of...; *Fam* **j'ai compris ma d.** my worst fears came true

douloureux, -euse [dulurø, -øz] *adj* (**a**) *(coup, maladie, opération)* painful; *(au contact)* sore, tender; **mon dos est d.** my back is sore *or* aching (**b**) *(perte, événement)* sad; *(séparation, circonstances)* painful

doute [dut] *nm* (**a**) *(incertitude)* doubt; **être dans le d. (au sujet de qch)** to be doubtful (about sth); **mettre qch en d.** to question sth, to cast doubt on sth; **mettre en d. la parole de qn** to doubt sb's word; **il n'y a pas de** *ou* **aucun d.** there's no doubt about it; **sans d.** no doubt, probably; **sans aucun d.** without (any) doubt (**b**) *(soupçon)* doubt; **avoir des doutes sur** *ou* **au sujet de qn/qch** to have doubts about sb/sth

douter [dute] **1** *vi* to doubt; **d. de qn/qch** to doubt sb/ sth; **elle ne doute de rien** she isn't backward in coming forward; **j'en doute** I doubt it
2 *vt* **je doute qu'il soit assez fort** I doubt whether he's strong enough; **je n'ai jamais douté que tu viendrais** I never doubted that you'd come
3 se douter *upr* **se d. de qch** to suspect sth; **je m'en doutais (bien)** I thought as much; *Fam* **on s'en serait douté!** I might have known!

douteux, -euse [dutø, -øz] *adj* (**a**) *(incertain)* doubtful (**b**) *(suspect)* dubious; **vêtements d.** *ou* **d'une propreté douteuse** dubious clothes; **d'un goût d.** *(plaisanteries, vêtements)* in dubious taste

douve [duv] *nf (d'un château)* moat

Douvres [duvr] *n* Dover

doux, douce [du, dus] **1** *adj* (**a**) *(au toucher)* soft; *(au goût)* mild (**b**) *(couleur, son, lumière)* soft; *(climat, hiver, tabac)* mild; *(vin, cidre)* sweet; *(pente)* gentle; **les médecines douces** alternative forms of medicine (**c**) *(nature, regard, voix)* gentle; **faire les yeux d. à qn** to make sheep's eyes at sb; **d. comme un agneau** as gentle as a lamb
2 *adv* *Fam* **filer d.** to toe the line
3 *nf* **douce** *Fam* **en d.** on the quiet

douzaine [duzɛn] *nf* une d. (de) *(environ)* around a dozen, a dozen or so; **trois douzaines d'œufs** three dozen eggs

douze [duz] *adj & nm inv* twelve; *voir aussi* **trois**

douzième [duzjɛm] *nmf, nm & adj* twelfth; *voir aussi* **cinquième**

doyen, -enne [dwajɛ̃, -ɛn] *nm,f* (**a**) *(personne la plus âgée)* most senior member (**b**) *(d'une faculté)* dean

drachme [drakm] *nf* drachma

draconien, -enne [drakɔnjɛ̃, -ɛn] *adj* *(règlement)* draconian; *(régime)* very strict

dragage [dragaʒ] *nm* *(nettoyage)* dredging

dragée [draʒe] *nf* *(confiserie)* sugared almond; *(médicament)* sugar-coated pill

dragon [dragɔ̃] *nm* (**a**) *(animal mythologique, femme acariâtre)* dragon (**b**) *(soldat)* dragoon

draguer [drage] **1** *vt* (**a**) *(nettoyer)* to dredge (**b**) *Fam (hommes, femmes)* to chat up, *Am* to hit on
  2 *vi Fam* to go on the pull

dragueur, -euse [dragœr, -øz] **1** *nm* *(bateau)* dredger; **d. de mines** minesweeper
  2 *nm,f Fam* chat-up merchant

drain [drɛ̃] *nm* (**a**) *(conduit)* drain (**b**) *Méd* drainage tube

drainage [drɛnaʒ] *nm* *(d'un champ, d'une plaie)* draining

drainer [drɛne] *vt* *(sol, abcès)* to drain

dramatique [dramatik] **1** *adj* (**a**) *(de théâtre)* dramatic; **auteur d.** playwright (**b**) *(grave)* tragic
  2 *nf* TV drama

dramatiser [dramatize] *vt* to dramatize

dramaturge [dramatyrʒ] *nm* dramatist, playwright

drame [dram] *nm* (**a**) *(genre littéraire, pièce)* drama (**b**) *Fig* tragedy; **faire un d. de qch** to make a drama out of sth

drap [dra] *nm* (**a**) *(linge)* **d. (de lit)** sheet; **d. de dessous/dessus** bottom/top sheet; *Fig* **être dans de beaux draps** to be in a real mess; **d. de bain** bath sheet (**b**) *(tissu)* cloth (**c**) *Belg (serviette)* towel

drapeau, -x [drapo] *nm* flag; *Fig* **être sous les drapeaux** to be in the armed forces; **d. blanc** white flag; **d. tricolore** tricolour

draper [drape] **1** *vt* *(étoffe)* to drape
  2 *se draper vpr* **se d. dans** to drape oneself in; *Fig* **se d. dans sa dignité** to stand on one's dignity

draperie [drapri] *nf* *(tenture)* drapery

drap-housse *(pl* **draps-housses***)* [draus] *nm* fitted sheet

drapier, -ère [drapje, -ɛr] **1** *nm,f (marchand)* draper; *(fabricant)* cloth manufacturer
  2 *adj* cloth

drastique [drastik] *adj* drastic

drave [drav] *nf Can (de rondins)* drive

draver [drave] *vt Can (rondins)* to float, to drive

draveur [dravœr] *nm Can* driver, raftsman

Dresde [drɛzd] *n* Dresden

dressage [drɛsaʒ] *nm* *(d'un animal)* training; *(d'un cheval)* breaking in

dresser [drese] **1** *vt* (**a**) *(élever)* to put up, to erect; **d. la tête** to raise *or* lift one's head; *(pour regarder)* to look up; **d. les oreilles** to prick up *or* cock its ears; *Fig* **d. l'oreille** to prick up one's ears (**b**) *(plan, rapport, liste)* to prepare, to draw up (**c**) *(animal)* to train (**à faire qch** to do sth); *(cheval)* to break in; *Fam* **ça va le d.!** that'll put him in his place! (**d**) *(exciter)* **d. qn contre qn** to set sb against sb

2 se dresser *vpr* (**a**) *(se lever)* to stand up, to rise (**b**) *(monument)* to stand; *(montagne)* to rise up; *Fig* **les obstacles qui se dressent sur notre chemin** the obstacles that stand in our way

dresseur, -euse [drɛsœr, -øz] *nm,f (d'animaux)* trainer

DRH [deɛraʃ] *nf (abrév* **direction des ressources humaines)** human resources department

dribble [dribl] *nm* dribble

dribbler [drible] **1** *vi* to dribble
  2 *vt (joueur)* to dribble round

drille [drij] *nm Fam* **c'est un joyeux d.** he's always good for a laugh

drogue [drɔg] *nf* (**a**) *(stupéfiant)* drug; **d. dure/douce** hard/soft drug (**b**) *Vieilli (médicament)* medicine

drogué, -e [drɔge] *nm,f* drug addict

droguer [drɔge] **1** *vt* (**a**) *(victime)* to drug; *(cheval)* to dope (**b**) *(malade)* to dose with drugs
  2 se droguer *vpr* to take drugs; **se d. à qch** to be on sth

droguerie [drɔgri] *nf* hardware *Br* shop *or Am* store

droguiste [drɔgist] *nmf* hardware dealer

droit¹, -e [drwa, drwat] **1** *adj* (**a**) *(rectiligne, vertical)* straight; **se tenir d.** *(debout)* to stand (up) straight; *(assis)* to sit (up) straight; **d. comme un i** *ou* **un piquet** as straight as a poker (**b**) *(honnête)* upright
  2 *nf* **droite** straight line
  3 *adv* **écrire/marcher d.** to write/walk straight; **aller d. devant soi** to go straight ahead; **aller d. au but** to get to the point; **aller d. à la catastrophe** to be heading straight for disaster; **c'est tout d.** it's straight ahead

droit², -e *adj (main, jambe, gant)* right; **du côté d.** on the right-hand side
  2 *nf* **droite** (**a**) *(côté)* right; **tourner à droite** to turn (to the) right; **rouler à droite** to drive on the right; **le placard de droite** the right-hand cupboard, the cupboard on the right; **à ma droite, le château** to *or* on my right is the castle; *Fig* **courir à droite et à gauche** to run about all over the place (**b**) *Pol* **la droite** the right (wing); **de droite** *(candidat, journal)* right-wing; **voter à droite** to vote for the right

droit³ *nm* (**a**) *(prérogative)* right; **avoir d. à qch** to have a right to sth; **avoir le d. de faire qch** to have the right to do sth; **donner d. à qch à qn** *(carte, abonnement)* to entitle sb to sth; **être dans son (bon) d.** to be within one's rights; **avoir des droits sur qn/qch** to have rights over sb/sth; **tous droits (de reproduction) réservés** *(sur livre)* all rights reserved; **de quel d. me critiques-tu?** what gives you the right to criticize me?; **d. d'aînesse** birthright; **d. d'asile** right of asylum; **avoir un d. de regard sur qch** to have the right to know about sth; **d. de réponse** right of reply; **d. de visite** *(d'un parent)* visiting rights; **d. de vote** right to vote; **les droits de l'homme** human rights
  (**b**) *(en argent)* fee; *(imposition)* duty; *(taxe)* tax; **droits d'auteur** royalties; **droits de douane** (customs) duty; **d. d'entrée** admission fee; **droits d'inscription** registration fee; **droits de succession** death duties; **d. de timbre** stamp duty
  (**c**) *Jur* law; **faire son d.** to study *or* read law; **d. administratif** administrative law; **d. des affaires** business law; **d. canon** canon law; **d. civil** civil law; **d. commercial** commercial law; **d. commun** common law; **d. communautaire** Community law; **d. constitutionnel** constitutional law; **d. international** international law; **d. pénal**

criminal law; **d. privé** private law; **d. public** public law; **d. du travail** labour laws

droitier, -ère [drwatje, -ɛr] **1** *adj* right-handed **2** *nm,f* right-handed person

droiture [drwatyr] *nf* rectitude

drôle [drol] *adj* (**a**) *(amusant)* funny (**b**) *(étrange)* funny; **un d. de type** a funny sort; **faire une d. de tête** to pull a face; *Fam* **ça me fait tout d. de te voir ici** it feels really funny seeing you here (**c**) *Fam (en intensif)* **il faut un d. de courage pour faire ça** you need a hell of a lot of courage to do that; **j'ai eu une d. de grippe!** I had a bad case of flu

drôlement [drolmã] *adv* funnily; *Fam (très)* awfully; *Fam* **les prix ont d. augmenté** prices have gone up an awful lot; *Fam* **elle est d. bien** *(remarquable)* she's a terrific person; *(belle)* she's great-looking

drôlerie [drolri] *nf* funniness

dromadaire [drɔmadɛr] *nm* dromedary

dru, -e [dry] **1** *adj (herbe, blé, cheveux, barbe)* thick; *(pluie)* heavy **2** *adv* **pousser d.** to grow thickly; **tomber d.** *(pluie)* to fall heavily

druide [drɥid] *nm* druid

DST [dɛɛste] *nf (abrév* **Direction de la surveillance du territoire)** = French Secret Service

DTP [detepe] *nm (abrév* **diphtérie, tétanos, polio)** diphtheria, tetanus and polio vaccination

du [dy] *voir* **de**

dû, due *(mpl* **dus,** *fpl* **dues)** [dy] **1** *pp voir* **devoir 2** *adj* (**a**) *(que l'on doit)* due, owed; **en port dû** carriage forward (**b**) *(causé)* **être dû à qch** to be due to sth (**c**) **en bonne et due forme** in due form **3** *nm* due

dualisme [dɥalism] *nm* dualism

dualité [dɥalite] *nf* duality

dubitatif, -ive [dybitatif, -iv] *adj* doubtful

Dublin [dyblɛ̃] *n* Dublin

dublinois, -e [dyblinwa, -az] **1** *adj* of Dublin **2** *nm,f* **D.** Dubliner

duc [dyk] *nm* duke

ducal, -e, -aux, -ales [dykal, -o] *adj* ducal

duché [dyʃe] *nm* duchy

duchesse [dyʃɛs] *nf (femme)* duchess

due *voir* **dû**

duel [dɥɛl] *nm* duel; **se battre en d.** to fight a duel

dulcinée [dylsine] *nf Litt ou Hum* ladylove

dûment [dymã] *adv* duly

dumping [dœmpiŋ] *nm* dumping; **faire du d.** to dump

dune [dyn] *nf* dune

Dunkerque [dœ̃kɛrk] *n* Dunkirk

duo [dɥo] *nm (chanson)* duet; *(de comiques, de musiciens)* duo

duodénum [dɥɔdenɔm] *nm* duodenum

dupe [dyp] **1** *nf* dupe **2** *adj* **être d. (de)** to be taken in (by)

duper [dype] *vt* to dupe, to fool

duperie [dypri] *nf* deception

duplex [dyplɛks] *nm* (**a**) **(émission en) d.** link-up (**b**) *(appartement) Br* maisonette, *Am* duplex

duplicata [dyplikata] *nm* duplicate

duplication [dyplikasjɔ̃] *nf* (**a**) *Biol* doubling (**b**) *Ordinat* **d. de logiciel** software copying

duplicité [dyplisite] *nf* duplicity

duquel [dykɛl] *voir* **lequel**

dur, -e [dyr] **1** *adj* (**a**) *(rigide)* hard; *(viande)* tough; *(pain)* stale (**b**) *(difficile, pénible) (travail, hiver)* hard; *(scène, film)* distressing (**c**) *(sévère, cruel)* harsh (**avec** with) (**d**) *Fam* **être d. de la feuille** to be hard of hearing **2** *nm,f Fam (personne)* tough type; *Pol* hard liner; **un d. à cuire** a hard-boiled type; **jouer les durs** to act tough **3** *nm* **bâtiment en d.** permanent building **4** *nf Fam* **élever qn à la dure** to bring sb up the hard way **5** *adv (travailler)* hard

durable [dyrabl] *adj* lasting

durablement [dyrabləmã] *adv* for a long time

duraille [dyraj] *adj Fam* hard

durant [dyrã] *prép* **d. le mois de mai** during May; **d. plusieurs années** for several years; **d. toute sa vie, sa vie d.** throughout his life; **parler des heures d.** to talk for hours on end

durcir [dyrsir] **1** *vt aussi Fig* to harden **2** *vi* to harden **3 se durcir** *vpr aussi Fig* to harden

durcissement [dyrsismã] *nm aussi Fig* hardening

durée [dyre] *nf (d'un règne, d'une guerre, d'un séjour)* duration, length; *(d'une note)* length, value; **de courte d.** *(bonheur, soulagement)* short-lived; **d. de connexion** *(sur Internet)* on-line time; **d. de projection** *(d'un film)* running time; **d. de validité** *(d'un billet)* period of validity; **d. de vie** *(de personne)* lifespan; *(d'une pile)* life; *(d'une machine)* useful life; **d. de vol** flight time

durement [dyrmã] *adv (répondre, parler)* harshly; **d. éprouvé** sorely tried

durer [dyre] *vi* to last; **voilà trois ans que cela dure** it's been going on for three years; **ça ne peut pas d.** this can't go on; *Hum* **faire d. le plaisir** to prolong the agony

dureté [dyrte] *nf* (**a**) *(rigidité)* hardness; *(d'une viande)* toughness (**b**) *(d'un hiver)* severity (**c**) *(cruauté) (d'une personne)* harshness; **parler avec d.** to speak harshly

durillon [dyrijɔ̃] *nm (de la main)* callus; *(du pied)* corn

Durit® [dyrit] *nf* hose (connection)

DUT [deyte] *nm (abrév* **diplôme universitaire de technologie)** = post-baccalauréat technical qualification awarded after two years

duvet [dyvɛ] *nm* (**a**) *(poil)* down (**b**) *(sac de couchage)* sleeping bag (**c**) *Belg & Suisse* duvet, continental quilt

duveteux, -euse [dyvtø, -øz] *adj* downy

DVD [devede] *nm (abrév* **digital versatile disc)** DVD

dynamique [dinamik] **1** *adj* dynamic **2** *nf* (**a**) *(science)* dynamics *(singulier)* (**b**) *(progrès)* dynamic

dynamiser [dinamize] *vt* to energize

dynamisme [dinamism] *nm* dynamism

dynamite [dinamit] *nf aussi Fig* dynamite

dynamiter [dinamite] *vt* to dynamite

dynamo [dinamo] *nf* dynamo

dynastie [dinasti] *nf* dynasty

dysenterie [disãtri] *nf* dysentery

dysfonctionnement [disfɔ̃ksjɔnmã] *nm* dysfunction

dyslexie [dislɛksi] *nf* dyslexia

dyslexique [dislɛksik] *adj* dyslexic

E

E¹, e [ə] *nm inv* E, e

E² (*abrév* **Est**) E

EAO [əao] *nm inv* (*abrév* **enseignement assisté par ordinateur**) CAL

eau, -x [o] *nf* (**a**) (*liquide*) water; **laver qch à grande e.** to wash sth down; **prendre l'e.** to let in water; **avoir l'e. courante** to have running water; *Fig* **mettre de l'e. dans son vin** to tone it down a bit; *Fig* **apporter de l'e. au moulin de qn** to strengthen sb's case; *Fig* **dans ces eaux-là** or thereabouts; *Can* **s'en aller à l'e.** to be going bankrupt; *Fam* **s'en aller en e. de boudin** to go down the tubes; *Fam* **il y a de l'e. dans le gaz** there's trouble brewing; **e. bénite** holy water; **e. de Cologne** eau de Cologne; **e. douce** fresh water; **e. de Javel** bleach; **e. lourde** heavy water; **e. de mer** *ou* **salée** salt water; **e. minérale** mineral water; **e. oxygénée** hydrogen peroxide; **e. de pluie** rainwater; **e. du robinet** tap water; *Fig* **roman/film à l'e. de rose** sentimental novel/film; **e. de source** spring water; **eaux thermales** hot springs; *Vieilli* **prendre les eaux** to take the waters; **e. de toilette** toilet water; *aussi Fig* **e. de vaisselle** dishwater

(**b**) (*étendue*) water; **au bord de l'e.** by the water's edge; **tomber à l'e.** to fall into the water; *Fig* to fall through; *Fig* **se jeter à l'e.** to take the plunge; **les eaux territoriales françaises** French waters

(**c**) (*sécrétion*) **être tout en e.** to be dripping with perspiration; **j'en ai l'e. à la bouche!** my mouth's watering!; **elle a perdu les eaux** her waters have broken

(**d**) (*d'une pierre précieuse*) **un diamant de la plus belle e.** a diamond of the first water

eau-de-vie (*pl* **eaux-de-vie**) [odvi] *nf* brandy

eau-forte (*pl* **eaux-fortes**) [ofɔrt] *nf* (*estampe*) etching

ébahi, -e [ebai] *adj* astounded

ébats [eba] *nmpl* frolicking; **é. amoureux** lovemaking

ébattre [11] [ebatr] **s'ébattre** *upr* to frolic

ébauche [eboʃ] *nf* (*dessin*) rough sketch; (*d'un roman*) outline; (*d'une lettre*) draft; *Fig* **l'é. d'un sourire** the ghost of a smile

ébaucher [eboʃe] *vt* (*tableau, roman*) to rough out; (*lettre*) to draft; *Fig* **é. un sourire** to give a faint smile; *Fig* **é. un geste** to make a movement

ébène [ebɛn] *nf* ebony; (**d'un noir) d'é., (noir) é.** jet black

ébéniste [ebenist] *nmf* cabinet maker

éberlué, -e [ebɛrlɥe] *adj* flabbergasted

éblouir [ebluir] *vt aussi Fig* to dazzle

éblouissant, -e [ebluisã, -ãt] *adj aussi Fig* dazzling; **d'une beauté éblouissante** dazzlingly beautiful

éblouissement [ebluismã] *nm* dazzle, glare; (*malaise*) fit of dizziness; *Fig* **ce fut un é.** it was dazzling

éborgner [ebɔrɲe] **1** *vt* **é. qn** to put sb's eye out

  2 s'éborgner *upr* to put one's eye out

éboueur [ebwœr] *nm Br* dustman, *Am* garbage man

ébouillanter [ebujãte] **1** *vt* to scald

  2 s'ébouillanter *upr* to scald oneself

éboulement [ebulmã] *nm* (**a**) (*écroulement*) collapse; (*de mine*) cave-in; **deux personnes sont mortes dans l'é. de la falaise** two people were killed when the cliff collapsed (**b**) (*gravats*) mass of fallen rocks

ébouler [ebule] **s'ébouler** *upr* (*falaise, remblai*) to collapse; (*tunnel*) to cave in

éboulis [ebuli] *nm* mass of fallen rocks

ébouriffé, -e [eburife] *adj* (*cheveux, personne*) dishevelled

ébouriffer [eburife] *vt* (*cheveux*) to ruffle; **é. qn** to ruffle sb's hair

ébranler [ebrãle] **1** *vt aussi Fig* to shake

  2 s'ébranler *upr* to move off

Èbre [ɛbr] *nm* **l'È.** the Ebro

ébrécher [34] [ebreʃe] *vt* (*verre, porcelaine*) to chip; (*lame*) to nick

ébriété [ebriete] *nf* **en état d'é.** in a state of inebriation

ébrouer [ebrue] **s'ébrouer** *upr* (**a**) (*cheval*) to snort (**b**) (*chien*) to shake itself

ébruiter [ebrɥite] **1** *vt* (*secret*) to give away; (*nouvelle*) to spread

  2 s'ébruiter *upr* (*nouvelle*) to spread

EBS [əbeɛs] *nf* (*abrév* **encéphalite bovine spongiforme**) BSE

ébullition [ebylisjɔ̃] *nf* boiling; **arriver à é.** to come to the boil; **amener qch à é.** to bring sth to the boil; *Fig* **en é.** in turmoil

écaille [ekaj] *nf* (*de poisson*) scale; (*de tortue, d'huître*) shell; (*de peinture*) flake; **peigne en é.** tortoiseshell comb; **des lunettes d'é.** *ou* **en é.** tortoiseshell-rimmed glasses

écailler [ekaje] **1** *vt* (**a**) (*poisson*) to scale (**b**) (*huître*) to open

  2 s'écailler *upr* (*émail, vernis à ongles*) to chip (off); (*peinture*) to peel (off)

écarlate [ekarlat] *adj* scarlet; *Fig* **devenir é.** to go bright red

écarquiller [ekarkije] *vt* **é. les yeux** to open one's eyes wide

écart [ekar] *nm* (**a**) (*entre deux chiffres*) difference (**entre** between); (*en distance, en temps, dans un classement*) gap (**entre** between); **ils ont trois ans d'é.** there's a three-year gap between them; **é. de niveau**

(dans une classe) difference in ability; **é. de salaires** wage differential (**b**) **faire le grand é.** to do the splits (**c**) *(déviation)* **faire un é.** *(personne)* to jump aside; *(cheval)* to shy; *(voiture)* to swerve; *Fig* **écarts de conduite** misbehaviour; *Fig* **écarts de langage** bad language (**d**) **mettre qn à l'é.** to keep sb out of things; **tenir qn à l'é. de qch** to keep sb out of sth; **se tenir à l'é.** to keep out of things; **un terrain à l'é. de la ville** a piece of land away from the town

écarté, -e [ekarte] *adj* (**a**) *(loin l'un de l'autre) (bras, pieds)* apart; *(yeux)* widely spaced; **avoir les dents écartées** to be gap-toothed (**b**) *Can (personne)* lost

écarteler [39] [ekartəle] *vt* to quarter; *Fig* **être écartelé (entre)** to be torn (between)

écartement [ekartəmã] *nm (distance)* space, gap

écarter [ekarte] **1** *vt* (**a**) *(séparer) (doigts, bras, jambes)* to spread; *(rideaux)* to draw (back); *(personnes, objets)* to move apart (**b**) *(repousser) (objet, branches)* to move aside; *(danger, soupçons)* to avert; **é. qn/qch de** to move sb/sth away from; **é. qn de son chemin** to push sb out of one's way (**c**) *(exclure) (candidat, proposition)* to turn down

2 s'écarter *vpr* (**a**) *(se séparer) (personnes)* to move apart; *(foule)* to part; *(routes)* to diverge (**b**) *(s'éloigner) (piéton)* to move away (**de** from); *(voiture)* to swerve (**de** from); *Fig* **s'é. du sujet** to wander from the subject (**c**) *Can (s'égarer)* to get lost

ecchymose [ekimoz] *nf* bruise

ecclésiastique [eklezjastik] **1** *adj* ecclesiastical **2** *nm* clergyman

écervelé, -e [eservəle] **1** *adj* scatterbrained **2** *nm,f* scatterbrain

ECG [əseʒe] *nm Méd (abrév* **électrocardiogramme**) ECG

échafaud [eʃafo] *nm* scaffold; *Fig* **monter à l'é.** to go to the scaffold

échafaudage [eʃafodaʒ] *nm* scaffolding; **des échafaudages** scaffolding

échafauder [eʃafode] *vt (empiler)* to pile up; *Fig (système, argumentation)* to put together, to construct

échalas [eʃala] *nm Fam* **grand é.** beanpole

échalote [eʃalɔt] *nf* shallot

échancré, -e [eʃãkre] *adj* (**a**) *(vêtement)* low-cut (**b**) *(littoral)* jagged, indented

échancrer [eʃãkre] *vt* to cut out the neckline of

échancrure [eʃãkryr] *nf (décolleté)* low neckline

échange [eʃãʒ] *nm* (**a**) *(d'objets, de prisonniers, d'idées)* exchange; **voulez-vous (me) faire l'é.?** could you exchange it/them (for me)?; **recevoir/donner qch en é. (de qch)** to receive/give sth in exchange (for sth); **de violents échanges** *(physiques)* violent clashes; *(verbaux)* violent exchanges; **échanges culturels** cultural exchanges (**b**) **échanges commerciaux** trade; **échanges internationaux** international trade (**c**) *(au tennis)* rally; **faire des échanges** to knock up (**d**) *Ordinat* **é. de données** data exchange; **é. de données informatisé** electronic data interchange

échanger [45] [eʃãʒe] *vt (objets, articles)* to exchange, to swap (**contre** for); *Fig (coups, idées)* to exchange; *(injures)* to trade

échangeur [eʃãʒœr] *nm* interchange

échantillon [eʃãtijɔ̃] *nm* sample; **prélever un é. de qch** to take a sample of sth; **é. gratuit** free sample

échantillonnage [eʃãtijɔnaʒ] *nm* (**a**) *(action)* sampling (**b**) *(échantillons)* selection of samples

échantillonner [eʃãtijɔne] *vt (pour sondage)* to sample

échappatoire [eʃapatwar] *nf* way out

échappée [eʃape] *nf* (**a**) *(de coureurs)* breakaway; **être dans l'é.** to be part of the breakaway group (**b**) *(espace libre)* **une é. sur la mer** a sea view

échappement [eʃapmã] *nm* (**a**) *(de voiture)* exhaust; **des gaz d'é.** exhaust fumes (**b**) *Ordinat* escape

échapper [eʃape] **1 échapper à** *vt ind* **é. à qn** *(sujet: personne)* to get away from sb; **é. à qch** *(punition, mort)* to escape sth; *(corvée)* to get out of sth; **son nom m'échappe** her name escapes me; **je n'aurais pas dû le dire mais ça m'a échappé** I shouldn't have said it but it just slipped out; **rien ne lui échappe** he doesn't miss a thing; **la victoire nous a échappé** victory eluded us; **le vase m'a échappé des mains** the vase slipped out of my hands

2 *vi* **laisser é.** *(personne, animal)* to let escape; *(objet)* to drop; *(de l'air)* to let out; *(de la vapeur)* to let off; *(larme)* to let fall; *(secret, soupir, cri)* to let out; *(détail)* to overlook

3 *vt* **il l'a échappé belle** he had a narrow escape

4 s'échapper *vpr* (**a**) *(s'évader)* to escape (**de** from) (**b**) *(sortir) (eau, gaz)* to escape (**de** from); **un cri s'échappa de ses lèvres** she let out a cry

écharde [eʃard] *nf* splinter

écharpe [eʃarp] *nf* scarf; **l'é. tricolore** the tricolour sash; **avoir le bras en é.** to have one's arm in a sling

écharper [eʃarpe] *vt Fam* **se faire é.** to get torn to pieces

échasse [eʃas] *nf* (**a**) *(bâton)* stilt; **être monté sur des échasses** to be on stilts (**b**) *(oiseau)* stilt

échassier [eʃasje] *nm* wader

échaudé, -e [eʃode] *adj Fig* **être é.** to get one's fingers burnt

échauffement [eʃofmã] *nm* (**a**) *(d'un moteur)* overheating (**b**) *(excitation)* overexcitement (**c**) *(d'athlète)* warm-up

échauffer [eʃofe] **1** *vt* (**a**) *(moteur)* to overheat (**b**) *(exciter)* **é. les esprits** to get people worked up; **les esprits sont échauffés** feelings are running high; *Fam* **é. les oreilles à qn** to get up sb's nose (**c**) *(athlète)* to warm up

2 s'échauffer *vpr* (**a**) *(moteur)* to get overheated (**b**) *(athlète)* to warm up (**c**) *(s'énerver) (personne)* to get worked up

échauffourée [eʃofure] *nf* brawl; *Mil* skirmish

échéance [eʃeãs] *nf (de dette, de facture)* date of payment; **à courte/longue é.** *(prêt)* short-/long-term; **venir à é.** to fall due; **faire face à ses échéances** to meet one's financial obligations; *Fig* **une é. électorale** an election

échéancier [eʃeãsje] *nm* (**a**) *(livre)* billbook (**b**) *(calendrier)* timetable

échéant [eʃeã] *adj m voir* **cas**

échec [eʃɛk] *nm* (**a**) *(défaite)* failure; *(revers)* setback; **subir un é.** *(défaite)* to fail; *(revers)* to suffer a setback; *Can* **mettre en é.** *(au hockey)* to check; **faire é. à qch** to foil sth; **faire é. à qn** to frustrate sb; **l'é. scolaire** doing badly at school (**b**) *(jeu)* **échecs** chess; **é.!** check!; **é. et mat!** checkmate!

échelle [eʃɛl] *nf* (**a**) *(pour grimper)* ladder; **l'é. des pompiers** the fireman's ladder; *Fig* **l'é. sociale** the social ladder; *Fig* **é. des salaires** salary scale; **é. des valeurs** scale of values; **faire la courte é. à qn** to give sb *Br* a leg up *or Am* a boost; **5 sur l'é. de Richter** 5 on the Richter scale (**b**) *(d'une carte)* scale; **l'é. est de 1/10 000**

the scale is 1:10,000; *Fig* **sur une grande é.** on a large scale; **à l'é. nationale** on a national scale; *Ordinat* **intégration à grande/petite é.** large-/small-scale integration (**c**) *(dans un collant) Br* ladder, *Am* run; **faire une é. à son collant** *Br* to ladder one's tights, *Am* to get a run in one's pantyhose

échelon [eʃlɔ̃] *nm* (**a**) *(d'une échelle)* rung (**b**) *(d'une hiérarchie)* grade; **gravir tous les échelons** to climb to the top of the ladder (**c**) *(niveau)* level; **à l'é. national** on a national level; **à tous les échelons** at every level

échelonnement [eʃlɔnmɑ̃] *nm* (**a**) *(de paiements)* spreading; *(de vacances)* staggering (**b**) *(d'objets)* spacing

échelonner [eʃlɔne] **1** *vt* (**a**) *(paiements)* to spread; *(vacances)* to stagger (**b**) *(objets)* to space out
2 s'échelonner *vpr* (**a**) **les paiements s'échelonnent sur deux ans** the payments are spread over two years (**b**) *(objets)* to be spaced out

écheveau, -x [eʃvo] *nm (de fil)* skein; *Fig* **démêler l'é. d'une affaire compliquée** to untangle a complicated business

échevelé, -e [eʃəvle] *adj (personne)* dishevelled; *Fig (course)* mad

échevin [eʃəvɛ̃] *nm Belg* deputy mayor

échine [eʃin] *nf* (**a**) *(colonne vertébrale)* spine, backbone (**b**) *(de porc)* loin

échiné, -e [eʃine] *adj Can* exhausted

échiner [eʃine] **s'échiner** *vpr* **s'é. à faire qch** to wear oneself out doing sth

échiquier [eʃikje] *nm (d'échecs)* chessboard; *Fig* **l'é. politique** the political scene

écho [eko] *nm* (**a**) *(bruit)* echo; **il y a de l'é.** there's an echo; *Fig* **trouver un é.** to get a response; *Fig* **se faire l'é. de qch** to echo sth; *Fig* **j'en ai eu de très bons échos** I've had some very good feedback (**b**) **les échos** *(de journal)* gossip column

échographie [ekografi] *nf* (ultrasound) scan; **passer une é.** to have a scan

échoir [14] [eʃwar] **1** *vi (dette)* to fall due; *(investissement)* to mature
2 échoir à *vt ind* to fall to

échoppe [eʃɔp] *nf* shop

échotier, -ère [ekɔtje, -ɛr] *nm,f* gossip columnist

échouer [eʃwe] **1** *vi* (**a**) *(navire)* to run aground; *(baleine)* to get stranded; **navire échoué** stranded ship; *Fam* **é. dans un bar** to land up in a bar (**b**) *(rater) (projet, personne)* to fail; **é. à un examen** to fail an exam; **faire é.** *(projet)* to wreck; *(complot)* to foil
2 *vt (navire)* to beach
3 s'échouer *vpr (navire)* to run aground; *(baleine)* to get stranded

éclabousser [eklabuse] **1** *vt* to splash, to spatter (**avec** with); *Fig* **le scandale a éclaboussé certains de ses collègues** the scandal tarnished the reputation of some of his colleagues
2 s'éclabousser *vpr* to splash oneself

éclaboussure [eklabusyr] *nf* splash

éclair [ekler] **1** *nm* (**a**) *(lumière)* flash; *(pendant un orage)* flash of lightning; **éclairs** lightning; **être rapide comme l'é.** to be as quick as a flash; *Fig* **en un é.** in a flash (**b**) *Fig (de lucidité, de génie)* flash; **lancer des éclairs** *(yeux)* to flash (**c**) *(gâteau)* éclair
2 *adj inv (visite, attaque)* lightning

éclairage [ekleraʒ] *nm* lighting; *(par projecteurs)* floodlighting

éclairagiste [ekleraʒist] *nmf (de cinéma, de théâtre)* lighting technician

éclaircie [eklersi] *nf* sunny spell

éclaircir [eklersir] **1** *vt* (**a**) *(rendre plus clair) (couleur, cheveux)* to lighten; *(teint)* to clear (**b**) *(rendre moins épais) (sauce)* to thin (**c**) *Fig (élucider) (mystère)* to clear up
2 s'éclaircir *vpr* (**a**) *(temps, ciel)* to clear; *(visage)* to brighten up (**b**) *(se dissiper) (brouillard)* to clear; *Fig (mystère)* to be cleared up (**c**) *(cheveux)* to thin (**d**) **s'é. la voix** to clear one's throat

éclaircissement [eklersismɑ̃] *nm* (**a**) *(explication)* explanation; **demander des éclaircissements (à qn) sur qch** to ask (sb) for an explanation of sth (**b**) *(de cheveux)* lightening

éclairé, -e [eklere] *adj* lit; *Fig* enlightened

éclairer [eklere] **1** *vt* (**a**) *(pièce, vitrine)* to light; **e. qn** to give sb some light; **éclairé au néon** neon-lit; *Fig* **é. qch d'un jour nouveau** to shed *or* throw new light on sth; *Fig* **un sourire éclairait son visage** a smile lit up her face (**b**) *Fig (informer)* to enlighten; *Fam* **é. la lanterne de qn (sur qch)** to put sb in the picture (about sth)
2 *vi* **cette lampe éclaire mal** this lamp doesn't give much light
3 s'éclairer *vpr* (**a**) *(personne)* **s'é. au pétrole/gaz** to use oil lamps/gaslight; **s'é. à la bougie** to use candles for lighting (**b**) *(devenir lumineux) (bâtiment, visage)* to light up (**c**) *Fig* **tout s'éclaire!** everything's becoming clear!

éclaireur, -euse [eklerœr, -øz] **1** *nm Mil* scout; *Mil & Fig* **partir en é.** to go off for a scout around
2 *nm,f* (boy) scout, *f* (girl) guide

éclat [ekla] *nm* (**a**) *(fragment) (de bois, de verre)* splinter; *(de pierre)* chip; **é. d'obus** piece of shrapnel; **des éclats d'obus** shrapnel; **des éclats de verre** *(bris)* broken glass; *(projeté)* flying glass; **voler en éclats** to shatter (**b**) *(son)* **é. de rire** burst of laughter; **partir d'un grand é. de rire** to burst out laughing; **rire aux éclats** to roar with laughter; **des éclats de voix** loud voices (**c**) *Fig (scandale)* scandal; **faire un é.** to create a scandal (**d**) *(du soleil)* glare; *(d'un diamant)* flash; *(de couleurs)* brilliance; **l'é. de ses yeux** the sparkle in her eyes; *Fig* **l'é. de la jeunesse** the bloom of youth (**e**) *(d'une cérémonie, d'une époque)* splendour; **action *ou* coup d'é.** brilliant feat

éclatant, -e [eklatɑ̃, -ɑ̃t] *adj* (**a**) *(lumière, couleur, succès)* brilliant; *(teint)* glowing; *(preuve)* striking; **être é. de santé** to be glowing with health; **être dans une forme éclatante** to be on brilliant form (**b**) *(son, rire)* loud

éclate [eklat] *nf Fam* **c'est l'é.** it's a laugh *or* hoot

éclaté, -e [eklate] *adj (vision)* fragmented

éclatement [eklatmɑ̃] *nm (d'un obus, d'un pneu)* bursting; *(d'un verre)* shattering; *Fig (d'un groupe)* break-up

éclater [eklate] **1** *vi* (**a**) *(exploser) (obus, pneu, ballon)* to burst; *(verre)* to shatter; *Fig (groupe)* to break up; **faire é. qch** to burst/shatter sth; **faire é. un pétard** to let off a firework (**b**) *Fig* **é. de rire** to burst out laughing; **é. en sanglots** to burst into tears; **é. en applaudissements** to burst into applause (**c**) *(se déclencher) (guerre, incendie)* to break out; *(orage, scandale)* to break
2 *vt Fam* **é. la tête à qn** to smash sb's head in
3 s'éclater *vpr Fam* to have a really good time

éclectique [eklɛktik] *adj* eclectic

éclipse [eklips] *nf (de soleil, de lune)* eclipse

éclipser [eklipse] **1** *vt aussi Fig* to eclipse
  2 s'éclipser *vpr Fam (s'esquiver)* to slip away

éclopé, -e [eklɔpe] **1** *adj* lame
  2 *nm,f* lame person

éclore [15] [eklɔr] *vi* (**a**) *(œuf, poussin)* to hatch (**b**) *(fleur)* to open (**c**) *Fig (talent)* to be born, to appear

éclosion [eklozjɔ̃] *nf* (**a**) *(d'œuf, de poussin)* hatching (**b**) *(de fleurs)* opening (**c**) *Fig (d'un talent)* birth

écluse [eklyz] *nf* lock; **(porte d')é.** lock gate

éclusier, -ère [eklyzje, -ɛr] *nm,f* lock keeper

écœurant, -e [ekœrã, -ãt] *adj* (**a**) *(nourriture)* nauseating; *Fig (révoltant)* disgusting (**b**) *Fam (décourageant)* sickening

écœurement [ekœrmã] *nm* (**a**) *(nausée)* nausea; *Fig (indignation)* disgust; **manger qch jusqu'à l'é.** to eat sth until one feels sick (**b**) *Fam (découragement)* discouragement

écœurer [ekœre] *vt* (**a**) **é. qn** *(donner la nausée à)* to make sb feel sick; *Fig (indigner)* to disgust sb (**b**) *Fam (décourager)* to sicken

écolabel [ekolabɛl] *nm* ecolabel

école [ekɔl] *nf* (**a**) *(établissement, enseignement)* school; **être à l'é.** to be at school; **aller à l'é.** to go to school; **reprendre l'é.** to go back to school; **faire l'é. buissonnière** to play *Br* truant *or Am* hookey; *Fig* **être à bonne é.** to be in good hands; *Fam* **je n'ai pas é. aujourd'hui** I don't have any classes today; **les grandes écoles** = university-level colleges specializing in professional training; **É. des beaux-arts** = art school in Paris; **é. de commerce** business school; **é. de conduite** driving school; **é. de danse** dancing school; **é. de dessin** art school; **é. hôtelière** hotel school; **é. libre** independent *or* private school; **é. maternelle**, *Suisse* **é. enfantine** nursery school; **é. militaire** military academy; **é. de musique** music school; **É. nationale d'administration** = university-level college preparing students for senior posts in law and economics; *Anciennement* **é. normale** teacher training college; **É. normale supérieure** = university-level college preparing students for senior posts in teaching; **é. primaire** *(bâtiment)* primary school; *(enseignement)* primary education; **é. privée** private school; **é. publique** *Br* state *or Am* public school; *Can & Suisse* **é. secondaire** *Br* secondary school, *Am* high school (**b**) *(de pensée, d'art)* school; **faire é.** to win a following

---

Grandes écoles

These are highly selective establishments which exist in parallel to the universities. Admission is usually only possible after two years of intensive preparatory studies ("écoles préparatoires") and a competitive examination ("**concours**"). Graduates from these institutions typically go on to work in senior and executive posts in the civil service or the private sector. The "grandes écoles" include HEC (management), Polytechnique, Centrale, the École des Mines and the École des Ponts et Chaussées (engineering), the ENA (senior civil service) and the École normale supérieure (humanities or science). Having been to a "grande école" is comparable in prestige to having an Oxbridge degree in Britain or a degree from Harvard or Yale in the US.

écolier, -ère [ekɔlje, -ɛr] *nm,f* schoolchild, schoolboy, *f* schoolgirl *(at primary school)*

écolo [ekɔlo] *adj & nmf Fam* green

écologie [ekɔlɔʒi] *nf* ecology

écologique [ekɔlɔʒik] *adj* ecological; *(produit)* eco-friendly, environmentally-friendly; *(politique, parti)* green

écologiste [ekɔlɔʒist] *adj & nmf* environmentalist

écomusée [ekomyze] *nm* living museum *(showing man in his natural and social environment)*

éconduire [18] [ekɔ̃dɥir] *vt Litt* (**a**) *(congédier)* to dismiss (**b**) *(refuser) (prétendant)* to reject

économat [ekɔnɔma] *nm* (**a**) *(fonction)* bursarship (**b**) *(bureau)* bursar's office

économe [ekɔnɔm] **1** *adj* economical, thrifty
  2 *nmf (de collège)* bursar
  3 *nm* **(couteau)** é. potato peeler

économie [ekɔnɔmi] *nf* (**a**) *(système)* economy; **é. dirigée** planned economy; **é. libérale** open market economy; **é. de marché** market economy (**b**) *(gain)* saving; *(vertu)* economy, thrift; **avoir le sens de l'é.** to be thrifty; **faire une é. de temps/de 20%** to save time/20%; **faire l'é. d'un coup de fil** to save oneself a phone call (**c**) *(discipline)* economics *(singulier)*; **il enseigne l'é.** he teaches economics; **économies** savings; **faire des économies** to save money; **faire des économies de chauffage** to save money on heating; **faire des économies d'énergie** to save energy; **prendre sur ses économies** to dip into one's savings; **il n'y a pas de petites économies** every little helps

économique [ekɔnɔmik] *adj* (**a**) *(relatif à l'économie)* economic (**b**) *(avantageux)* economical

économiser [ekɔnɔmize] *vt (argent, temps, énergie)* to save; *(électricité, nourriture)* to economize on, to save on; **é. ses forces** to conserve one's strength; **é. sa salive** to save one's breath; **é. pour ses vacances** to save up for one's holidays

économiseur [ekɔnɔmizœr] *nm Ordinat* **é. d'écran** screen saver

économiste [ekɔnɔmist] *nmf* economist

écoper [ekɔpe] **1** *vt (barque)* to bale (out); **nous avons dû é.** we had to bale out
  2 écoper de *vt ind Fam (être puni)* **é. d'une amende/ de cinq ans de prison** to get a fine/five years in prison; **c'est encore moi qui vais é.** I'm going to get the blame again

écoproduit [ekoprɔdɥi] *nm* eco-friendly *or* environmentally-friendly product

écorce [ekɔrs] *nf* (**a**) *(d'arbre)* bark; *(d'orange)* peel (**b**) **l'é. terrestre** the earth's crust

écorché, -e [ekɔrʃe] **1** *nm* anatomical model
  2 *nm,f Fig* **é. (vif)** tortured soul

écorcher [ekɔrʃe] **1** *vt* (**a**) *(animal)* to skin; *(criminel)* to flay (**b**) *(érafler)* to graze; *Fig (nom)* to mispronounce; *Fig* **é. les oreilles à qn** to grate on sb's ears
  2 s'écorcher *vpr* to graze oneself; **s'é. le genou** to graze one's knee

écorchure [ekɔrʃyr] *nf* graze

écorecharge *(pl* **écorecharges)** [ekɔrəʃarʒ] *nf* eco-refill

écorner [ekɔrne] *vt (meuble)* to damage the corner(s) of; *(livre)* to dog-ear

écossais, -e [ekɔsɛ, -ɛz] **1** *adj (coutume, lande, personne)* Scottish; *(whisky)* Scotch; **une jupe écossaise** a tartan skirt

2 *nm,f* **É.** Scot
3 *nm (tissu)* tartan
Écosse [ekɔs] *nf* **l'É.** Scotland
écosser [ekɔse] *vt* to shell
écosystème [ekosistɛm] *nm* ecosystem
écot [eko] *nm* **payer son é.** to pay one's share
écoulement [ekulmã] *nm* (**a**) *(de liquide)* flow (**b**) *(de blessure)* discharge (**c**) *(de marchandises)* sale; *(de faux billets)* circulation (**d**) *(du temps)* passage
écouler [ekule] **1** *vt (marchandises)* to dispose of; *(faux billets)* to circulate
2 s'écouler *vpr* (**a**) *(liquide)* to flow out, to run out (**de** of) (**b**) *(marchandises)* to sell (**c**) *(temps)* to pass
écourter [ekurte] *vt (robe, texte)* to shorten; *(visite, discours)* to cut short
écoute [ekut] *nf* (**a**) *(d'une radio)* **être à l'é. (de)** to be listening in (to); **rester à l'é.** to stay tuned; **heure de grande é.** *Rad* peak listening time; *TV* peak viewing time; **indice d'é.** ratings; **écoutes téléphoniques** telephone tapping; **elle est sur é.** her phone's been tapped (**b**) **être à l'é. des autres** to be willing to lend a sympathetic ear
écouter [ekute] **1** *vt* (**a**) *(entendre)* to listen to; **é. qn jusqu'au bout** to hear sb out; **savoir é.** to be a good listener; **é. aux portes** to listen at doors; **faire é. qch à qn** to play sb sth; **écoute, ça suffit maintenant!** listen or look here, that's quite enough now! (**b**) *(suivre) (personne)* to listen to; **é. sa conscience** to listen to one's conscience
2 s'écouter *vpr* **il s'écoute trop** he coddles himself; **si je m'écoutais** if I did what I wanted; **s'é. parler** to like the sound of one's own voice
écouteur [ekutœr] *nm (du téléphone)* earpiece; **écouteurs** *(casque)* headphones
écoutille [ekutij] *nf Naut* hatchway
écouvillon [ekuvijɔ̃] *nm (pour bouteille, biberon)* bottle brush
écrabouiller [ekrabuje] *vt Fam* to squash, to crush; **se faire é. par une voiture** to get flattened by a car
écran [ekrã] *nm* (**a**) *(de télévision, de cinéma)* screen; **porter une pièce à l'é.** to adapt a play for the screen; **prochainement sur vos écrans** coming soon to a cinema near you; **le grand/petit é.** the big/small screen; **é. panoramique** wide screen; **é. plat** flat screen (**b**) *Ordinat* screen, display; **à l'é.** on screen; **é. d'accueil** logo screen; **é. d'aide** help screen; **é. couleur** colour screen *or* display; **é. à cristaux liquides** liquid crystal screen; **é. à fenêtres** split screen; **é. monochrome** monochrome screen; **é. rétro-éclairé** back-lit screen; **é. tactile** touch-sensitive screen; **é. de visualisation** VDU (**c**) *(pour protéger)* screen; **on ne peut pas voir le lac car les arbres font é.** you can't see the lake because it's screened by the trees; **é. de fumée** smoke screen; **é. total** sun block
écrasant, -e [ekrazã, -ãt] *adj (poids, défaite, responsabilité)* crushing; *(majorité, victoire)* overwhelming
écrasé, -e [ekraze] *adj (nez)* flat; *Fig* **é. de travail** snowed under with work
écraser [ekraze] **1** *vt* (**a**) *(fruit, ail, membre)* to crush; *(insecte)* to squash; *(cigarette)* to stub out; *(piéton, chien)* to run over; **se faire é.** *(par une voiture)* to get run over; *Fam* **é. l'accélérateur** *ou* **le champignon** to put one's foot down (**b**) *(vaincre) (adversaire, troupes)* to crush; **se faire é.** to be crushed (**c**) *Fam* **en é.** to sleep like a log (**d**) *très Fam* **écrase!** shut it!

2 s'écraser *vpr* (**a**) *(avion)* to crash (**b**) *Fam (ne rien dire)* to keep quiet
écrémage [ekremaʒ] *nm (sélection)* creaming off
écrémer [34] [ekreme] *vt (lait)* to skim; *Fig (sélectionner)* to cream off the best of
écrevisse [ekrəvis] *nf* crayfish
écrier [66] [ekrije] **s'écrier** *vpr* to cry out, to exclaim
écrin [ekrɛ̃] *nm (jewel)* case
écrire [30] [ekrir] **1** *vt (lettre, livre, chanson)* to write; *(noter)* to write down; **é. à qn** to write to sb; **é. un mot à qn** to drop sb a line; **je leur ai écrit de venir** I've written asking them to come; **il écrit bien** his handwriting is good; *(écrivain)* he writes well; **ce stylo écrit très bien** this pen writes very well
2 s'écrire *vpr* (**a**) *(s'orthographier)* to be spelt; **comment ça s'écrit?** how do you spell it? (**b**) *(correspondre)* to write to each other
écrit [ekri] *nm* (**a**) **mettre qch par é.** to put sth down in writing (**b**) *(texte)* (written) document; **écrits** *(œuvre)* writings (**c**) *(examen)* written examination
écriteau, -x [ekrito] *nm* notice
écritoire [ekritwar] *nf* writing case
écriture [ekrityr] *nf* (**a**) *(système, caractères)* writing; *Ordinat* write (**b**) *(façon d'écrire)* (hand)writing; **elle a une belle é.** she has good handwriting (**c**) *(littérature)* writing; *TV & Cin* **é. de scénarios** scriptwriting (**d**) **écritures** *(comptabilité)* accounts; **tenir les écritures** to keep the accounts (**e**) *Rel* **l'É. sainte, les saintes Écritures** the Scriptures
écrivain [ekrivɛ̃] *nm* writer; **é. public** (public) letter writer
écrivais *etc voir* **écrire**
écrou [ekru] *nm (de boulon)* nut
écrouer [ekrue] *vt Jur* to imprison
écroulé, -e [ekrule] *adj Fam* **é. (de rire)** doubled up with laughter
écroulement [ekrulmã] *nm* collapse
écrouler [ekrule] **s'écrouler** *vpr (bâtiment, prix, empire)* to collapse; *(espoirs)* to crumble away; **s'é. sur une chaise** to flop onto a chair; **s'é. de fatigue** to collapse with exhaustion
écru, -e [ekry] *adj (beige)* ecru; *(naturel)* unbleached
ecsta [ɛksta] *nf Fam* E
ecstasy [ɛkstazi] *nf* ecstasy
ECU, ÉCU [eky] *nm (abrév* **European Currency Unit)** ECU
écu [eky] *nm* (**a**) *Hist* crown (**b**) *(bouclier)* shield
écueil [ekœj] *nm (rocher)* reef; *Fig (danger)* pitfall
écuelle [ekɥɛl] *nf* bowl
éculé, -e [ekyle] *adj (chaussure)* down-at-heel; *Fig (plaisanterie, argument)* hackneyed
écume [ekym] *nf (bave, sur la mer)* foam; *(sur la soupe, la confiture)* scum; **avoir l'é. à la bouche** to be foaming at the mouth; **é. (de mer)** *(magnésite)* meerschaum
écumer [ekyme] **1** *vt* (**a**) *(soupe, confiture)* to skim (**b**) *(piller)* to plunder; *Fig (parcourir)* to scour; **é. les mers** *(pirates)* to scour the seas
2 *vi* **é. (de rage)** to foam (with rage)
écumoire [ekymwar] *nf* skimmer; *Fig* **troué comme une é.** riddled with holes
écureuil [ekyrœj] *nm* squirrel; **é. roux/gris** red/grey squirrel
écurie [ekyri] *nf* stable; **é. (de courses)** *(de chevaux, de voitures)* (racing) stable

écusson [ekysɔ̃] *nm* (**a**) *(armoiries)* escutcheon (**b**) *(de tissu)* badge

écuyer, -ère [ekɥije, -ɛr] **1** *nm Hist (gentilhomme)* squire
  2 *nm,f* rider; **é. de cirque** circus rider

eczéma [egzema] *nm* eczema; **avoir** *ou* **faire de l'é.** to have eczema

édam [edam] *nm* Edam

edelweiss [edɛlvɛs] *nm* edelweiss

Éden [edɛn] *nm* **l'É.** Eden; *Fig* **un é.** a paradise

édenté, -e [edɑ̃te] *adj* toothless

EDF [ədɛf] *nf (abrév* **Électricité de France)** French electricity company

EDI [ədei] *nm Ordinat (abrév* **échange de données informatisé)** EDI

édifiant, -e [edifjɑ̃, -ɑ̃t] *adj* edifying

édification [edifikasjɔ̃] *nf* (**a**) *(d'un monument)* erection; *Fig (d'un empire, d'une fortune)* building up (**b**) *(instruction morale)* edification

édifice [edifis] *nm* building; *Fig* **apporter sa pierre à l'é.** to make a contribution; *Fig* **l'é. social** the social fabric

édifier [66] [edifje] *vt* (**a**) *(monument)* to erect; *Fig (empire, fortune)* to build up (**b**) *(instruire)* to edify

Édimbourg [edɛ̃bur] *n* Edinburgh

édimbourgeois, -e [edɛ̃burʒwa, -az] **1** *adj* of Edinburgh
  2 *nm,f* **É.** person from Edinburgh

édit [edi] *nm Hist* edict

éditer [edite] *vt* (**a**) *(publier)* to publish (**b**) *(commenter) (texte)* to edit (**c**) *Ordinat* to edit; **pouvant être édité** editable

éditeur, -trice [editœr, -tris] **1** *nm,f* (**a**) *(d'une maison d'édition)* publisher (**b**) *(commentateur)* editor
  2 *nm Ordinat (de programme)* editor; **é. d'icônes** icon editor; **é. de logiciel** software company; **é. de texte** text editor

édition [edisjɔ̃] *nf* (**a**) *(activité)* publishing (**b**) *(texte, exemplaire)* edition; *Hum* **où est le sucre? – dans le placard, troisième é.!** where's the sugar? – for the third time, it's in the cupboard!; **é. originale** first edition (**c**) *(d'un journal)* edition; **dernière é.** final edition; **é. spéciale** special edition (**d**) *Ordinat* editing; **é. de liens** linking; **é. pleine page** full page editing; **é. électronique** electronic publishing

édito [edito] *nm Fam* editorial, *Br* leader

éditorial, -e, -aux, -ales [editɔrjal, -o] **1** *adj* editorial
  2 *nm* editorial, *Br* leader

éditorialiste [editɔrjalist] *nmf* editorial writer, *Br* leader writer

édredon [edrədɔ̃] *nm* eiderdown

éducateur, -trice [edykatœr, -tris] *nm,f* teacher; **é. spécialisé** special needs teacher

éducatif, -ive [edykatif, -iv] *adj* educational

éducation [edykasjɔ̃] *nf* (**a**) *(enseignement)* education; *(par les parents)* upbringing; **faire l'é. de qn** to educate sb; **é. manuelle et technique** handicraft classes; **l'É. nationale** the Department of Education; **é. physique** physical training *or* education; **é. religieuse** religious instruction; **é. sexuelle** sex education (**b**) *(savoir-vivre)* good manners; **avoir de l'é.** to have good manners; **manquer d'é.** to have no manners (**c**) *Fig (des réflexes, du goût)* training

édulcorant, -e [edylkɔrɑ̃, -ɑ̃t] **1** *adj* sweetening
  2 *nm* sweetener; **é. de synthèse** artificial sweetener

édulcorer [edylkɔre] *vt (discours, compte rendu)* to water down; *(roman pornographique)* to tone down

éduquer [edyke] *vt* (**a**) *(donner un enseignement à) (enfant, peuple)* to educate; *(élever)* to bring up; **mal éduqué** ill-mannered (**b**) *Fig (réflexes, goût)* to train

EEE [əəə] *nm Pol (abrév* **Espace économique européen)** EEA

EEG *nm (abrév* **électroencéphalogramme)** EEG

effaçable [efasabl] *adj* erasable

effacé, -e [efase] *adj* (**a**) *(personne, manières)* self-effacing (**b**) *(menton)* receding

effacement [efasmɑ̃] *nm* (**a**) *(d'un mot, d'un message, d'une bande)* erasing; *Ordinat* deletion; *(d'une tache)* removal; *(par le temps) (d'une inscription)* wearing away; *(des souvenirs)* fading (**b**) *(d'une personne)* self-effacement

effacer [16] [efase] **1** *vt* (**a**) *(mot, enregistrement, bande)* to erase; *(tableau)* to clean; *Ordinat (données)* to erase, to delete; *(écran)* to clear; *(tache, traces)* to remove; *(sujet: temps) (inscription)* to wear away (**b**) *Fig* **e. qch de sa mémoire** to erase sth from one's memory; **on efface tout et on recommence** we'll wipe the slate clean and make a fresh start
  2 s'effacer *vpr* (**a**) *(disparaître) (inscription)* to wear away; *Fig (sentiment, souvenir)* to fade (away) (**b**) *(s'écarter)* to move aside; *Fig (se faire discret)* to keep in the background

effaceur [efasœr] *nm* **e. (d'encre)** ink eraser

effarant, -e [efarɑ̃, -ɑ̃t] *adj* astounding

effaré, -e [efare] *adj* astounded

effarement [efarmɑ̃] *nm* astonishment

effarer [efare] *vt* to astound

effaroucher [efaruʃe] **1** *vt* (**a**) *(effrayer)* to scare; *(faire reculer)* to scare away (**b**) *(choquer)* to shock
  2 s'effaroucher *vpr* (**a**) *(s'effrayer)* to take fright (**de** at) (**b**) *(s'offusquer)* to be shocked (**de** by)

effectif, -ive [efɛktif, -iv] **1** *adj (réel)* effective
  2 *nm (employés)* staff; *(d'un club, d'un bataillon)* strength; *(d'une classe)* size

effectivement [efɛktivmɑ̃] *adv* (**a**) *(en effet)* actually; **c'est pratique, hein? – e.!** it's practical, isn't it? – yes it is! (**b**) *(réellement, de manière effective)* actually

effectuer [efɛktɥe] **1** *vt (mouvement, opération)* to perform; *(paiement, parcours, calcul, réservation)* to make; *(démarches)* to take; *(commande)* to place
  2 s'effectuer *vpr (mouvement, opération)* to be performed; *(paiement, parcours)* to be made

efféminé, -e [efemine] *adj* effeminate

effervescence [efɛrvɛsɑ̃s] *nf* excitement; **être en e.** *(ville, bureau)* to be buzzing with excitement

effervescent, -e [efɛrvɛsɑ̃, -ɑ̃t] *adj (médicament)* effervescent

effet [efɛ] *nm* (**a**) *(résultat, conséquence)* effect (**sur** on); **avoir pour e. de faire qch** to have the effect of doing sth; **faire e.** to take effect; **à cet e.** with that in mind; **rester** *ou* **demeurer sans e.** to have no effect; **sous l'e. de l'alcool/la drogue** under the influence of alcohol/drugs; **les feuilles sont tombées sous l'e. de la chaleur** the heat caused the leaves to drop off; **e. pervers** undesired effect; *Méd* side effect; **e. de serre** greenhouse effect; **e. secondaire** side effect; *Ordinat* **e. de transition** melt
  (**b**) *(impression)* impression; **quel e. ça te fait qu'elle revienne?** how do you feel about her coming

back?; **ne faire aucun e. à qn** to make no impression on sb; **elle me fait l'e. d'une fille plutôt équilibrée** she strikes me as being a fairly well-balanced girl; **il me fait de l'e.** he does something for me; **faire un drôle d'e. à qn** to give sb a funny feeling; **faire bon/mauvais e. (à qn)** to make a good/bad impression (on sb)

(**c**) *(but recherché)* **manquer son e.** *(plaisanterie)* to fall flat; **faire des effets de voix** to make striking use of one's voice; *Cin* **effets spéciaux** special effects; **e. de style** stylistic effect

(**d**) *(application)* **prendre e.** to take effect

(**e**) *(au tennis)* spin; **donner de l'e. à une balle** to put spin on a ball

(**f**) *Fin* bill; **e. de commerce** bill of exchange

(**g**) **effets (personnels)** *(affaires)* belongings

(**h**) **en e., je m'en souviens** yes, I do remember; **en e., c'est ce que je me suis dit** that's just what I thought; **mais c'est monstrueux! – en e.!** it's abominable! – isn't it just!; **j'ai dû partir, en e. j'étais pressé** I had to leave because I was in a hurry

effeuiller [efœje] *vt (fleur)* to pull the petals off; *(sujet: vent) (arbre)* to blow the leaves off; *Fig* **e. la marguerite** to play "he/she loves me, he/she loves me not"

efficace [efikas] *adj (méthode, remède)* effective; *(personne)* efficient

efficacement [efikasmã] *adv (avec succès)* effectively; *(de façon productive)* efficiently

efficacité [efikasite] *nf (d'une méthode, d'un remède)* effectiveness; *(d'une personne)* efficiency

effigie [efiʒi] *nf* effigy; **à l'e. de qn** bearing the image of sb

effilé, -e [efile] *adj (frange)* ragged; *(doigts)* tapering; *(outil, lame)* tapered; *(amandes)* slivered

effilocher [efilɔʃe] **s'effilocher** *vpr* to fray

efflanqué, -e [eflãke] *adj* skinny

effleurement [eflœrmã] *nm* light touch

effleurer [eflœre] *vt (frôler)* to touch lightly; *(accidentellement)* to brush (against); *(surface de l'eau)* to skim; *Fig (sujet)* to touch on; **cette idée ne m'a jamais effleuré** the idea never crossed my mind

effluent [eflyã] *nm* **e. urbain** (sewage) effluent; **effluents radioactifs** radioactive waste

effluve [eflyv] *nm* emanation

effondré, -e [efɔ̃dre] *adj (peiné)* grief-stricken; *(déçu)* shattered

effondrement [efɔ̃drəmã] *nm (d'un bâtiment, d'un mur, d'un toit)* collapse; *Fig (d'un plan)* falling through; *(d'un empire, des prix)* collapse; *(d'une personne)* dejection

effondrer [efɔ̃dre] **s'effondrer** *vpr (bâtiment, mur, toit)* to collapse; *Fig (plan)* to fall through; *(empire, prix)* to collapse; *(personne)* to go to pieces; **s'e. dans un fauteuil** to sink *or* slump into an armchair

efforcer [16] [efɔrse] **s'efforcer** *vpr* **s'e. de faire qch** to do one's best to do sth

effort [efɔr] *nm* (**a**) *(physique, intellectuel)* effort; **allons, encore un (petit) e.** come on, try again; **son médecin lui a interdit tout e.** her doctor has forbidden any exertion; **sans e.** effortlessly; **faire un e. (pour faire qch)** to make an effort (to do sth); **faire des efforts** to make an effort; **faire l'e. de faire qch** to make the effort to do sth; **après l'e., le réconfort** I/you/*etc* deserve this; **il est partisan du moindre e.** he doesn't believe in exerting himself (**b**) *Tech* strain, stress

effraction [efraksjɔ̃] *nfJur* breaking and entering; **entrer par e.** to break in

effraie [efrɛ] *nf (oiseau)* barn owl

effranger [45] [efrãʒe] **1** *vt* to fray

  2 s'effranger *vpr* to fray

effrayant, -e [efrɛjã, -ãt] *adj* frightening; *(chaleur, appétit)* tremendous

effrayer [53] [efrɛje] **1** *vt (faire peur à)* to frighten, to scare; *(inquiéter)* to alarm

  2 s'effrayer *vpr* to be frightened (**de** at); **elle s'effraie pour un rien** the least little thing frightens her

effréné, -e [efrene] *adj (passion, luxe)* unbridled; *(galop, course)* frantic

effritement [efritmã] *nm (d'un mur, d'un revêtement)* crumbling; *(de la roche)* weathering; *Fig (de l'autorité, d'une majorité, de fonds)* erosion

effriter [efrite] **1** *vt (pain, fromage)* to crumble; *(roche)* to weather

  2 s'effriter *vpr (mur, revêtement)* to crumble; *(roche)* to weather; *Fig (autorité, majorité, fonds)* to be eroded

effroi [efrwa] *nm Litt* terror, dread

effronté, -e [efrɔ̃te] *adj (personne, manières)* impudent; *(mensonge, menteur)* brazen

effrontément [efrɔ̃temã] *adv* impudently; *(mentir)* brazenly

effronterie [efrɔ̃tri] *nf (d'une personne, de manières)* impudence; *(d'un mensonge)* brazenness

effroyable [efrwajabl] *adj* dreadful

effroyablement [efrwajabləmã] *adv* dreadfully

effusion [efyzjɔ̃] *nf* (**a**) **e. de sang** bloodshed (**b**) *(exubérance)* effusiveness; **avec e.** effusively

égailler [egaje] **s'égailler** *vpr* to disperse

égal, -e, -aux, -ales [egal, -o] **1** *adj* (**a**) *(équivalent)* equal (**à** to); **la partie n'est pas égale** they/we/you are not evenly matched; **ils sont de force/d'intelligence égale** they are equally strong/intelligent; **à prix é., tu peux trouver mieux** for the same price, you can find something better (**b**) *(constant) (respiration, son)* even; *(allure, pouls)* steady; *(sol)* level; *(climat)* equable; **être d'humeur égale** to be even-tempered; **rester é. à soi-même** to be still one's old self (**c**) **cela m'est é.** it's all the same to me; *(cela ne m'intéresse pas)* I don't care

  2 *nm,f* equal; **être l'é. de qn** to be sb's equal; **traiter qn d'é. à é.** to treat sb as an equal; **sans é.** unequalled

également [egalmã] *adv (aussi)* as well, too

égaler [egale] *vt (personne, score, record)* to equal; **deux et deux égalent quatre** two and two equal four

égalisation [egalizasjɔ̃] *nf* (**a**) *(équilibrage)* equalization; *Sport (but/point d')é.* equalizer (**b**) *(d'une surface)* levelling

égaliser [egalize] **1** *vt* (**a**) *(salaires, pression)* to equalize; *(cheveux)* to trim (**b**) *(sol)* to level

  2 *vi Sport* to equalize

égalitaire [egaliter] *adj* egalitarian

égalité [egalite] *nf* (**a**) *(entre des quantités, des personnes)* equality; *(au tennis)* deuce; **être à é.** *(équipes)* to be level; **é. des chances** equal opportunities; **é. des salaires** equal pay (**b**) *(constance) (de la respiration, d'un son)* evenness; *(de l'allure, du pouls)* steadiness; *(du sol)* levelness; *(du climat)* equability; **é. d'humeur** even-temperedness

égard [egar] *nm* (**a**) *(respect)* consideration; **par é. pour qn** out of consideration for sb; **égards** *(attentions)* consideration (**b**) *(aspect)* **à cet é.,...** in this respect,...; **je n'ai pas d'opinion à cet é.** I've no opinion on that score; **à certains/tous les égards** in some/all respects (**c**) *(locutions)* **à l'é. de qn** towards sb; **eu é. à** considering

égaré, -e [egare] *adj* (**a**) *(personne, animal)* lost (**b**) *(hagard) (air, regard)* distraught

égarement [egarmã] *nm* (**a**) *(folie)* distraction (**b**) **égarements** *(dérèglements de conduite)* wild behaviour

égarer [egare] **1** *vt (objet)* to mislay; *(personne) (volontairement)* to mislead; *(soupçons)* to avert
2 s'égarer *vpr* (**a**) *(se perdre) (personne, lettre)* to get lost (**b**) *(sortir du sujet)* to wander from the point

égayer [53] [egeje] **1** *vt (personne)* to cheer up; *(conversation)* to liven up; *(pièce, vêtement)* to brighten up
2 s'égayer *vpr (s'animer)* to cheer up

Égée [eʒe] *n voir* **mer**

égérie [eʒeri] *nf* muse

égide [eʒid] *nf* **sous l'é. de** under the aegis of

églantier [eglãtje] *nm* wild rose (bush)

églantine [eglãtin] *nf* wild rose

églefin [egləfɛ̃] *nm* haddock

église [egliz] *nf* (**a**) *(bâtiment)* church; **aller à l'é.** *(à la messe)* to go to church; **se marier à l'é.** to get married in church, to have a church wedding (**b**) **l'É.** the Church; **l'É. catholique** the Catholic Church; **l'É. anglicane** the Church of England, the Anglican Church

ego [ego] *nm inv* ego

égocentrique [egosɑ̃trik] **1** *adj* self-centred, egocentric
2 *nmf* self-centred person

égoïsme [egɔism] *nm* selfishness, egoism

égoïste [egɔist] **1** *adj* selfish, egoistic
2 *nmf* selfish person, egoist

égorger [45] [egɔrʒe] *vt* to cut the throat of

égosiller [egozije] **s'égosiller** *vpr (en parlant)* to shout oneself hoarse; *(en chantant)* to sing at the top of one's voice

égout [egu] *nm* sewer

égoutier [egutje] *nm* sewerman

égoutter [egute] **1** *vt* to drain
2 *vi* **laisser é. qch** to leave sth to drain
3 s'égoutter *vpr* to drain

égouttoir [egutwar] *nm* (**a**) *(dans l'évier)* draining board; *(mobile)* drainer (**b**) *(passoire)* colander

égratigner [egratiɲe] **1** *vt* to scratch; *Fig* to have a dig at
2 s'égratigner *vpr* to scratch oneself; **s'é. la joue** to scratch one's cheek

égratignure [egratiɲyr] *nf* scratch; *Fig* dig

égrener [46] [egrəne] *vt* (**a**) *(maïs, pois)* to shell; *(grappe)* to pick the grapes off (**b**) *Fig* **é. son chapelet** to tell one's beads

égrillard, -e [egrijar, -ard] *adj* bawdy

Égypte [eʒipt] *nf* **l'É.** Egypt

égyptien, -enne [eʒipsjɛ̃, -ɛn] **1** *adj* Egyptian
2 *nm,f* **É.** Egyptian

eh [e] *exclam* hey!; **eh bien** well; **eh oui!** that's right!

éhonté, -e [eɔ̃te] *adj* shameless

éjaculation [eʒakylasjɔ̃] *nf* ejaculation; **é. précoce** premature ejaculation

éjaculer [eʒakyle] *vi* to ejaculate

éjectable [eʒɛktabl] *adj* **siège é.** ejector seat

éjecter [eʒɛkte] *vt (cartouche, pilote)* to eject; *Fam (expulser)* to throw out (**de** of)

éjection [eʒɛksjɔ̃] *nf (d'une cartouche, du pilote)* ejection; *Fam (expulsion)* throwing out

élaboration [elabɔrasjɔ̃] *nf (d'un plan, d'une idée)* development; *(d'une constitution, d'une loi)* drawing up

élaboré, -e [elabɔre] *adj (technique, machine)* sophisticated; *(plan)* elaborate

élaborer [elabɔre] *vt (plan, idée)* to develop; *(constitution, loi)* to draw up

élagage [elagaʒ] *nm aussi Fig* pruning

élaguer [elage] *vt aussi Fig* to prune

élan¹ [elɑ̃] *nm* (**a**) *(course)* run-up; *(vitesse)* momentum; *Fig (impulsion)* boost; **prendre de l'é.** *ou* **son é.** to take a run-up; **saut sans/avec é.** standing/running jump; *Fig* **d'un seul é.** all in one go; *Fig* **emporté par son é.** carried away (**b**) *(transport) (d'enthousiasme)* burst; *(de tendresse, de passion)* surge (**c**) *(ferveur)* fervour

élan² *nm (cerf)* elk

élancé, -e [elɑ̃se] *adj* slim, slender

élancement [elɑ̃smɑ̃] *nm (douleur)* shooting pain

élancer [16] [elɑ̃se] **1** *vi* **la jambe m'élance** I've got shooting pains in my leg
2 s'élancer *vpr (se précipiter)* to rush forward; *Sport* to take a run-up

élargir [elarʒir] **1** *vt* (**a**) *(route, rue)* to widen; *(vêtement)* to let out; *(trou)* to enlarge (**b**) *Fig (groupe, gamme de produits)* to expand; *(connaissances, débat)* to broaden (**c**) *Jur (prisonnier)* to release
2 *vi Fam (personne)* to get bigger
3 s'élargir *vpr* (**a**) *(route, rue)* to widen; *(chaussures, vêtement)* to stretch; *(trou)* to enlarge (**b**) *Fig (groupe, gamme de produits)* to expand; *(connaissances, débat)* to broaden

élargissement [elarʒismɑ̃] *nm* (**a**) *(d'une route, d'une rue)* widening; *(d'un trou)* enlargement (**b**) *Fig (d'un groupe, d'une gamme de produits)* expansion; *(des connaissances, d'un débat)* broadening (**c**) *Jur (d'un prisonnier)* release

élastique [elastik] **1** *adj (corps, matière)* elastic; *Fig (démarche)* springy; *(règlement, principes)* flexible; *(conscience)* accommodating
2 *nm* (**a**) *(pour la couture)* elastic (**b**) *(de bureau)* elastic *or* rubber band (**c**) *(jeu)* **jouer à l'é.** to play elastics

électeur, -trice [elɛktœr, -tris] *nm,f* voter, elector; **mes électeurs** the people who voted for me

élection [elɛksjɔ̃] *nf* (**a**) *(d'un candidat)* election; **élections législatives** general election; **élections municipales** local elections; **é. présidentielle, élections présidentielles** presidential election (**b**) *(choix)* **mon pays d'é.** my adopted country

---

Élections

All French citizens of eighteen or over are entitled to vote in elections, which take place on a Sunday. Polling stations are often set up in local schools. Voters collect leaflets (each corresponding to the different political parties or candidates), go to a booth and put their chosen leaflet into the envelope provided, which is then placed in the ballot box ("l'urne") supervised by an "assesseur", who then utters the words "a voté!". Unlike Britain with its first-past-the-post system, the French electoral system is based on a type of proportional representation. As from 2002 presidential elections take place every five years. General elections are also held every five years.

électoral, -e, -aux, -ales [elɛktɔral, -o] *adj (campagne, comité, promesses)* election

électorat [elɛktɔra] *nm* voters, electorate; **l'é. communiste/féminin** communist/female voters

électricien, -enne [elɛktrisjɛ̃, -ɛn] *nm,f* electrician

électricité [elɛktrisite] *nf* electricity; *(installation)* wiring; *Fig* **il y a de l'é. dans l'air** the atmosphere is electric; **é. statique** static (electricity)

électrifier [66] [elɛktrifje] *vt (chemin de fer)* to electrify; *(village)* to bring electricity to

électrique [elɛktrik] *adj aussi Fig* electric

électrisant, -e [elɛktrizɑ̃, -ɑ̃t] *adj (exaltant)* electrifying

électriser [elɛktrize] *vt aussi Fig* to electrify

électroaimant [elɛktrɔɛmɑ̃] *nm* electromagnet

électrocardiogramme [elɛktrokardjɔgram] *nm* electrocardiogram

électrochoc [elɛktrɔʃɔk] *nm* electric shock; **traitement par électrochocs** electric shock treatment; **faire des électrochocs à qn** to give sb electric shock treatment

électrocuter [elɛktrɔkyte] **1** *vt* to electrocute; **se faire é.** to be electrocuted
2 s'électrocuter *vpr* to electrocute oneself

électrocution [elɛktrokysjɔ̃] *nf* electrocution

électrode [elɛktrɔd] *nf* electrode

électroencéphalogramme [elɛktrɔɑ̃sefalɔgram] *nm* electroencephalogram

électrogène [elɛktrɔʒɛn] *adj* **groupe é.** generating unit

électrolyse [elɛktrɔliz] *nf* electrolysis

électroménager [elɛktromenaʒe] **1** *adj m* **appareils électroménagers** household appliances
2 *nm* household appliances

électron [elɛktrɔ̃] *nm* electron; **é. libre** free electron; *Fig* maverick

électronicien, -enne [elɛktrɔnisjɛ̃, -ɛn] *nm,f* electronics engineer

électronique [elɛktrɔnik] **1** *adj (composant, jeu)* electronic; *(microscope, télescope)* electron; *(industrie)* electronics
2 *nf* electronics *(singulier)*

électrophone [elɛktrɔfɔn] *nm* record player

élégamment [elegamɑ̃] *adv (vêtu, maquillée)* elegantly, smartly

élégance [elegɑ̃s] *nf (d'une personne, d'un restaurant, d'un style)* elegance, smartness; *(d'un geste, d'un comportement)* courtesy; *(d'une méthode, d'une solution)* neatness; **habillé avec é.** elegantly *or* smartly dressed; **savoir perdre avec é.** to be a good loser

élégant, -e [elegɑ̃, -ɑ̃t] *adj (vêtements, restaurant, style)* elegant, smart; *(geste, comportement)* courteous; *(méthode, solution)* neat; **un procédé peu é.** callous behaviour

élégie [eleʒi] *nf* elegy

élément [elemɑ̃] *nm* (**a**) *(partie) (d'une structure, d'un problème)* element; *(meuble)* unit; *Ordinat* **é. de menu** menu item (**b**) *(personne)* element; **j'ai de bons éléments dans ma classe** I've got some good pupils in my class (**c**) *(naturel)* element; **les quatre éléments** the four elements; *Fig* **être dans son é.** to be in one's element (**d**) *Chim* element (**e**) *(d'une batterie, d'un accumulateur)* cell

élémentaire [elemɑ̃tɛr] *adj* (**a**) *(de base) (connaissance, cours, problème)* elementary; *(minimal) (habitation)* basic; **c'est é.!** *(évident)* it's elementary! (**b**) *Chim & Phys* elementary

éléphant [elefɑ̃] *nm* elephant; **é. mâle/femelle** bull/cow elephant; **é. de mer** sea elephant; **é. d'Afrique/d'Asie** African/Indian elephant

éléphanteau, -x [elefɑ̃to] *nm* baby elephant

élevage [elvaʒ] *nm* (**a**) *(production)* breeding; *(d'abeilles, de volaille)* keeping; **faire de l'é.** *(de bétail)* to breed cattle; **é. intensif/en batterie** intensive/battery farming (**b**) *(ferme)* farm; **é. de poulets/de visons** poultry/mink farm

élévateur, -trice [elevatœr, -tris] **1** *adj* **chariot é.** forklift truck
2 *nm (appareil)* elevator

élévation [elevasjɔ̃] *nf* (**a**) *(action d'élever) (du niveau d'eau, de la voix, des prix, de la température)* raising; *(d'une statue)* erection; *Rel (de l'hostie)* elevation (**b**) *(dans l'air)* rising (up) (**c**) *(augmentation)* rise (**de** in) (**d**) *Litt (des sentiments)* nobility (**e**) *Archit (projection)* elevation (**f**) *(relief)* rise

élevé, -e [elve] *adj* (**a**) *(haut, important)* high; *(rythme, pouls)* rapid; *Fig (style, esprit)* elevated (**b**) *(éduqué)* **bien/mal é.** well-/ill-mannered; **c'est très mal é. de parler la bouche pleine** it's very bad manners to speak with your mouth full

élève [elɛv] *nmf* student, pupil; **é. infirmière** student nurse; *Mil* **é. officier** cadet

élever¹ [46] [elve] *vt* (**a**) *(éduquer)* to bring up, to raise; **bébé élevé au sein/au biberon** breast-/bottle-fed baby (**b**) *(faire l'élevage de)* to breed; *(abeilles, volaille)* to keep

élever² **1** *vt* (**a**) *(faire monter) (niveau d'eau, voix, prix, température)* to raise; **é. un nombre au carré/au cube** to square/cube a number; **é. un nombre à la puissance 4** to raise a number to the power of 4 (**b**) *(dresser) (monument, statue)* to erect; *(bras, poing, yeux)* to raise; *Fig (objection)* to raise (**c**) *(rehausser) (plafond, plancher)* to raise; **é. qch de 20 cm** to raise sth by 20 cm (**d**) *(promouvoir)* to promote (**au rang de** to) (**e**) *(édifier) (esprit)* to improve; **é. le débat** to raise the tone of the debate
2 s'élever *vpr* (**a**) *(avec mouvement)* to rise (up); *(cri)* to go up (**b**) *(se dresser) (bâtiment, montagnes)* to stand (**c**) *(monter) (température, prix)* to rise (**d**) *(protester)* **s'é. contre** to rise up against (**e**) **s'é. à** *(atteindre)* to amount to

éleveur, -euse [elvœr, -øz] *nm,f (de bovins)* cattle farmer; **é. de chevaux/chiens** horse/dog breeder; **é. de moutons/poulets** sheep/poultry farmer

elfe [ɛlf] *nm* elf

éligibilité [eliʒibilite] *nf* eligibility

éligible [eliʒibl] *adj* eligible

élimé, -e [elime] *adj* worn, threadbare

élimination [eliminasjɔ̃] *nf* elimination; **procéder par é.** to use a process of elimination

éliminatoire [eliminatwar] *adj* **5 est une note é.** 5 counts as a fail; **il a eu une note é.** he didn't get a pass mark; **(épreuve) é.** qualifying heat

éliminer [elimine] *vt (candidat, suspect, toxines)* to eliminate (**de** from); *Sport (pour faute, dopage)* to disqualify; *(possibilité, théorie)* to rule out; **faites de l'exercice pour é.** do some exercise to clear your system

élire [44] [elir] *vt* (**a**) *(candidat, représentant)* to elect (**b**) **é. domicile** to take up residence

élision [elizjɔ̃] *nf Ling* elision

élite [elit] *nf* elite; **d'é.** *(personnel)* top; *(régiment)* crack

élitisme [elitism] *nm* elitism

élitiste [elitist] *adj & nmf* elitist

élixir [eliksir] *nm* elixir; **é. d'amour** elixir of love

elle [εl] *pron personnel* (**a**) *(sujet) (personne)* she; *(chose, animal)* it; **ton amie viendra-t-e.?** is your friend coming?; **e., e. n'aurait pas levé le petit doigt** SHE wouldn't have raised a finger; **la France, e., a exprimé clairement sa position** France, for its part, has clearly expressed its position; **si j'étais e., je me méfierais** if I were her, I'd be careful

(**b**) *(objet direct) (personne)* her; *(chose)* it; **et e., tu l'oublies?** and what about her, have you forgotten her?

(**c**) *(avec préposition) (personne)* her; *(réfléchi)* herself; *(chose, animal)* it; **dis-le-lui, à e.** tell HER; **ce n'est pas à moi, c'est à e.** it's not mine, it's hers; **elle possède une entreprise à e.** she has her own company; *Fam* **une relation à e.** a relation of her; **e. ne pense qu'à e.** she only thinks about herself

(**d**) *(dans les comparaisons)* her; **il boit plus qu'e.** he drinks more than she does *or* than her

elle-même [εlmεm] *pron personnel (personne)* herself; *(chose, animal)* itself

elles [εl] *pron personnel* (**a**) *(sujet)* they; **nos chambres sont-e. prêtes?** are our rooms ready?; **e., e. seraient déjà parties** THEY would have left by now; **mes filles, e., ont fait des études** my daughters, for their part, have been to university; **si j'étais e., je me méfierais** if I were them, I'd be careful

(**b**) *(objet direct)* them; **et e., tu les oublies?** and what about them, have you forgotten them?

(**c**) *(avec préposition)* them; *(réfléchi)* themselves; **dis-le-leur, à e.** tell THEM; **cette voiture est à e.** this car is theirs; **e. ont un appartement à e.** they have their own flat; *Fam* **un parent à e.** a relative of theirs; **e. ne pensent qu'à e.** they only think about themselves

(**d**) *(dans les comparaisons)* them; **je mange plus qu'e.** I eat more than they do *or* than them

elles-mêmes [εlmεm] *pron personnel* themselves

ellipse [elips] *nf* (**a**) *Gram* ellipsis (**b**) *(courbe)* ellipse

elliptique [eliptik] *adj* elliptical

élocution [elɔkysjɔ̃] *nf* (**a**) *(diction)* diction (**b**) *Belg Scol (exposé)* talk, presentation

éloge [elɔʒ] *nm* (**a**) *(louange)* praise; **faire l'é. de qn/qch** to praise sb/sth; **digne d'éloges** praiseworthy (**b**) *(discours)* eulogy; **é. funèbre** funeral oration

élogieux, -euse [elɔʒjø, -øz] *adj (discours, article)* complimentary; **parler de qn/qch en termes é.** to speak very highly of sb/sth

éloigné, -e [elwaɲe] *adj (dans l'espace, dans le temps)* distant, remote; *(parent)* distant; **ils sont éloignés d'un kilomètre** they're one kilometre apart; **être é. de qch** to be a long way (away) from sth; **se tenir é. de** to keep away from

éloignement [elwaɲəmɑ̃] *nm* (**a**) *(séparation)* separation; **l'é. est difficile à vivre** being apart is difficult (**b**) *(distance) (dans l'espace, dans le temps)* distance, remoteness

éloigner [elwaɲe] **1** *vt* (**a**) *(dans l'espace) (personne, objet)* to move away (**de** from); *(moustiques)* to keep away; **ce trajet nous éloigne du centre-ville** this route takes us away from the centre of town (**b**) *(distraire, détourner) (crainte, pensée)* to dismiss;

(soupçons) to avert; *(personne) (de son travail, d'une autre personne)* to keep away (**de** from)

2 s'éloigner *vpr* (**a**) *(s'écarter)* to move away (**de** from); *(partir)* to go away (**de** from); *(orage)* to pass (**b**) *(se distraire, se détourner)* **s'é. de** *(vérité, sujet)* to wander from; *(famille, amis)* to distance oneself from; *(dans un couple)* to grow away from

élongation [elɔ̃gasjɔ̃] *nf* pulled muscle; **se faire une é.** to pull a muscle

éloquence [elɔkɑ̃s] *nf (expressivité)* eloquence

éloquent, -e [elɔkɑ̃, -ɑ̃t] *adj aussi Fig* eloquent; **ces chiffres sont éloquents** these figures speak for themselves

élu, -e [ely] **1** *adj (à un poste)* elected; *Rel* chosen

2 *nm,f* (**a**) *Rel* **les élus** the chosen ones (**b**) *(responsable)* elected representative (**c**) *Hum* **qui est l'heureuse élue?** who's the lucky lady?; **l'é. de son cœur** her beloved

élucider [elyside] *vt* to elucidate

élucubrations [elykybrasjɔ̃] *nfpl Péj* flights of fancy

éluder [elyde] *vt* to evade

Élysée [elize] *nm* (**le palais de**) **l'É.** the Élysée Palace *(residence of the President of the French Republic)*

> ### Élysée
> This eighteenth-century palace near the Champs-Élysées in Paris is the official residence of the French President. The name is often used to refer to the presidency itself.

émacié, -e [emasje] *adj* emaciated

émail, -aux [emaj, -o] *nm* enamel; *(sur porcelaine)* glaze; **en é.** *(ustensile de cuisine)* enamel

e-mail [imεl] *(pl* **e-mails***) nm Ordinat* e-mail; **envoyer un e. à qn** to e-mail sb

émaillé, -e [emaje] *adj* (**a**) *(métal, ustensile de cuisine)* enamelled (**b**) *(porcelaine)* glazed (**c**) *Fig* **é. de** *(plein de)* studded with

émanation [emanasjɔ̃] *nf* **émanations** emanations; **émanations toxiques** toxic fumes; *Fig* **être l'é. de qch** to emanate from sth

émancipation [emɑ̃sipasjɔ̃] *nf* emancipation; *Fig (de l'esprit, de la pensée)* liberation

émancipé, -e [emɑ̃sipe] *adj* emancipated

émanciper [emɑ̃sipe] **1** *vt* to emancipate

2 s'émanciper *vpr* to become emancipated

émaner [emane] **émaner de** *vt ind aussi Fig* to emanate from

émarger [45] [emarʒe] **1** *vi* to draw one's salary

2 *vt (apposer ses initiales sur)* to initial; *(signer)* to sign

émasculation [emaskylasjɔ̃] *nf* emasculation

émasculer [emaskyle] *vt* to emasculate

emballage [ɑ̃balaʒ] *nm* (**a**) *(action)* packing; *(dans du papier)* wrapping; **e. sous vide** vacuum-packing (**b**) *(contenant)* packaging; *(papier)* wrapping

emballé, -e [ɑ̃bale] *adj Fam (enthousiaste)* mad keen (**par** on)

emballer [ɑ̃bale] **1** *vt* (**a**) *(empaqueter)* to pack; *(dans du papier)* to wrap; *(pour la vente)* to package (**b**) *(moteur)* to race (**c**) *Fam (enthousiasmer)* to grab (**d**) *Fam (séduire)* to pick up

2 s'emballer *vpr* (**a**) *(moteur)* to race; *(cheval)* to bolt (**b**) *Fam (s'enthousiasmer)* to get carried away (**c**) *(cours, monnaie)* to spiral out of control

embarcadère [ɑ̃barkadεr] *nm* landing stage

embarcation [ãbarkasjɔ̃] *nf* (small) boat

embardée [ãbarde] *nf (d'une voiture)* swerve; *(d'un bateau)* yaw; **faire une e.** *(voiture)* to swerve; *(bateau)* to yaw

embargo [ãbargo] *nm* embargo; **mettre l'e. sur** to put an embargo on; **lever l'e. sur** to lift the embargo on

embarquement [ãbarkəmã] *nm (de passagers)* boarding; *(de marchandises)* loading; **e. immédiat porte 5** *(annonce)* now boarding at gate 5

embarquer [ãbarke] **1** *vt* (**a**) *(passagers)* to take on board; *(marchandises)* to load (**b**) *Fam (emporter)* to take (with one) (**c**) *Fam (entraîner)* (*en week-end, au cinéma)* to take off; *(arrêter)* to nick; **se laisser e. dans** *(affaire, discussion)* to get caught up in
   2 *vi (sur un bateau) (monter)* to go on board, to board; *(pour une destination)* to embark
   3 s'embarquer *vpr* (**a**) *(sur un bateau) (monter)* to go on board, to board; *(pour une destination)* to embark (**b**) *Fam Fig* **s'e. dans** *(entreprise, discussion)* to embark on

embarras [ãbara] *nm* (**a**) *(situation difficile)* **mettre qn dans l'e.** to put sb in an awkward situation; **tirer qn d'e.** to get sb out of an awkward situation; **n'avoir que l'e. du choix** to be spoilt for choice (**b**) *(difficulté financière)* **être dans l'e.** to be in financial difficulties (**c**) *(gêne)* embarrassment (**d**) *(obstacle)* **être un e. pour qn** to be a bother to sb (**e**) *Méd* **e. gastrique** upset stomach

embarrassant, -e [ãbarasã, -ãt] *adj* (**a**) *(qui gêne) (question, situation)* embarrassing (**b**) *(qui encombre)* cumbersome

embarrassé, -e [ãbarase] *adj* (**a**) *(gêné)* embarrassed; **je suis très e. de devoir le leur dire** I'm very embarrassed about having to tell them (**b**) *(encombré) (table, pièce)* cluttered (**de** with); **avoir les mains embarrassées** to have one's hands full

embarrasser [ãbarase] **1** *vt* (**a**) *(gêner)* to embarrass (**b**) *(encombrer) (table, pièce)* to clutter up (**de** with); **e. qn** *(vêtement, achats)* to hamper sb; *(empêcher le passage de)* to be in sb's way
   2 s'embarrasser *vpr (s'encombrer)* **s'e. de** to burden oneself with; *Fig* **elle ne s'embarrasse pas de douceur** she doesn't worry about being gentle

embauche [ãboʃ] *nf* (**a**) *(action)* taking on, hiring (**b**) *(emploi)* employment

embaucher [ãboʃe] *vt* (**a**) *(engager)* to take on, to hire; **l'entreprise embauche en ce moment** the company is currently recruiting people (**b**) *Fam (pour corvée)* to recruit (**pour faire** to do)

embaumer [ãbome] *vt* (**a**) *(corps)* to embalm (**b**) *(répandre une odeur de)* to be fragrant with; **son parfum embaumait la pièce** the scent of her perfume filled the room; **le chèvrefeuille embaumait** there was a fragrant smell of honeysuckle

embaumeur [ãbomœr] *nm (de corps)* embalmer

embellie [ãbɛli] *nf (éclaircie)* bright spell; *Naut* calm spell, lull; *Fig (de l'économie, d'une situation etc)* improvement; **courte e.** bright interval

embellir [ãbɛlir] **1** *vt (pièce, parc, personne)* to make more attractive; *Fig (histoire, vérité)* to embellish
   2 *vi* to grow more attractive

embellissement [ãbɛlismã] *nm (d'un lieu)* improvement; *(d'un récit)* embellishment

emberlificoter [ãbɛrlifikɔte] *Fam* **1** *vt* (**a**) *(fil)* to tangle up (**b**) *(duper)* to take in
   2 s'emberlificoter *vpr* **s'e. dans** *(vêtements, mensonges)* to get tangled up in

embêtant, -e [ãbɛtã, -ãt] *adj Fam* annoying

embêtement [ãbɛtmã] *nm Fam* problem; **faire des embêtements à qn** to make trouble for sb

embêter [ãbɛte] *Fam* **1** *vt (contrarier, agacer)* to annoy; *(ennuyer)* to bore
   2 s'embêter *vpr (s'ennuyer)* to be bored; *Ironique* **tu ne t'embêtes pas!** you don't do badly for yourself!; **s'e. à faire qch** *(prendre la peine de le faire)* to bother doing sth

emblée [ãble] **d'emblée** *adv* right away, straight away

emblématique [ãblematik] *adj* emblematic; *Fig* symbolic

emblème [ãblɛm] *nm aussi Fig* emblem

embobiner [ãbɔbine] *vt Fam (duper)* to take in

emboîter [ãbwate] **1** *vt (assembler)* to fit together; **e. qch dans qch** to fit sth into sth; **e. le pas à qn** to follow close on sb's heels; *Fig* to follow sb's lead
   2 s'emboîter *vpr* to fit together

embolie [ãbɔli] *nf* embolism; **e. gazeuse/pulmonaire** air/pulmonary embolism; **e. cérébrale** clot on the brain, *Spéc* cerebral embolism

embonpoint [ãbɔ̃pwɛ̃] *nm* stoutness; **avoir/prendre de l'e.** to be/get stout

embouché, -e [ãbuʃe] *adj Fam* **mal e.** foul-tempered

embouchure [ãbuʃyr] *nf* (**a**) *(d'un instrument à vent)* mouthpiece (**b**) *(d'un cours d'eau)* mouth

embourber [ãburbe] **s'embourber** *vpr* (**a**) *(véhicule)* to get stuck in the mud (**b**) *Fig & Péj* to get bogged down

embourgeoisement [ãburʒwazmã] *nm (d'une personne)* attainment of middle-class respectability; *(d'un quartier)* gentrification

embourgeoiser [ãburʒwaze] **s'embourgeoiser** *vpr (personne)* to become middle-class; *(quartier)* to become gentrified

embout [ãbu] *nm (d'un parapluie, d'une canne)* tip; *(d'un tuyau)* nozzle

embouteillage [ãbuteja3] *nm* traffic jam, hold-up

embouteiller [ãbuteje] *vt (route)* to clog up

emboutir [ãbutir] *vt* (**a**) *(véhicule)* to crash into (**b**) *(métal)* to stamp

embranchement [ãbrãʃmã] *nm* (**a**) *(croisement)* junction; *(bifurcation) (d'une route)* fork (**b**) *(voie secondaire) (de route)* side road; *(de chemin de fer)* branch line (**c**) *Bot & Zool* subkingdom

embraser [ãbraze] *Litt* **1** *vt* (**a**) *(incendier)* to set ablaze (**b**) *(éclairer)* to set aglow (**c**) *Fig (exalter) (foule)* to set alight
   2 s'embraser *vpr* (**a**) *(prendre feu)* to blaze up (**b**) *(rougeoyer)* to glow

embrassade [ãbrasad] *nf* embrace, hug

embrasser [ãbrase] **1** *vt* (**a**) *(donner un baiser à)* to kiss (**b**) *(étreindre)* to embrace, to hug; **qui trop embrasse mal étreint** one shouldn't spread oneself too thinly (**c**) *(adopter) (religion, doctrine, cause)* to embrace; *(carrière)* to take up (**d**) *(englober) (sujets, questions)* to embrace, to take in; **e. qch du regard** to take sth in at a glance
   2 s'embrasser *vpr* to kiss (each other)

embrasure [ãbrazyr] *nf Constr* aperture; **se tenir dans l'e. de la porte** to stand in the doorway

embrayage [ãbrɛja3] *nm* (**a**) *(mécanisme)* clutch (**b**) *(action)* engaging the clutch

embrayer [53] [ɑ̃breje] *vi* (**a**) *Aut* to engage the clutch (**b**) *Fam (commencer)* to get going (**sur** on)
embrigadement [ɑ̃brigadmɑ̃] *nm* dragooning (**dans** into)
embrigader [ɑ̃brigade] *vt* to dragoon (**dans** into)
embringuer [ɑ̃brɛ̃ge] *Fam* **1** *vt* **e. qn dans qch** to get sb mixed up in sth
2 s'embringuer *vpr* **s'e. dans qch** to get mixed up in sth
embrocher [ɑ̃brɔʃe] *vt* (**a**) *Culin (viande)* to put on a spit (**b**) *Fam (transpercer)* **e. qn** to skewer sb
embrouillamini [ɑ̃brujamini] *nm Fam* muddle
embrouillé, -e [ɑ̃bruje] *adj* (**a**) *(fils)* tangled (**b**) *Fig (idées, raisonnement, esprit)* muddled; *(affaire)* complicated
embrouiller [ɑ̃bruje] **1** *vt* (**a**) *(fils)* to tangle (up) (**b**) *Fig (personne, situation, idées)* to muddle (up)
2 s'embrouiller *vpr (personne, idées)* to get muddled (up)
embroussaillé, -e [ɑ̃brusaje] *adj (allée, jardin)* overgrown; *(cheveux)* messed up
embrumé, -e [ɑ̃bryme] *adj (horizon)* hazy; *(esprit)* fuddled
embruns [ɑ̃brɛ̃] *nmpl* spray
embryologie [ɑ̃brijɔlɔʒi] *nf* embryology
embryon [ɑ̃brijɔ̃] *nm* embryo
embryonnaire [ɑ̃brijɔnɛr] *adj* embryonic
embûches [ɑ̃byʃ] *nfpl* traps; **semé d'e.** full of pitfalls
embuer [ɑ̃bɥe] *vt (miroir, vitre)* to mist up; **yeux embués de larmes** eyes misted over with tears
embuscade [ɑ̃byskad] *nf* ambush; **tendre une e. à qn** to set an ambush for sb; **tomber dans une e.** to be ambushed
embusquer [ɑ̃byske] **s'embusquer** *vpr* (**a**) *(se mettre en embuscade)* to lie in ambush (**b**) *(se faire affecter loin du front)* to get a cushy posting
éméché, -e [emeʃe] *adj Fam* tipsy
émeraude [emrod] **1** *nf (pierre)* emerald
2 *nm & adj inv* emerald green
émergence [emɛrʒɑ̃s] *nf (apparition)* emergence
émerger [45] [emɛrʒe] *vi* (**a**) *(apparaître)* to emerge (**de** from) (**b**) *Fam (se lever)* to surface
émeri [emri] *nm* emery; **papier** *ou* **toile é.** emery paper
émérite [emerit] *adj* (**a**) *(expert)* highly skilled (**b**) *(professeur)* emeritus
émerveillement [emɛrvɛjmɑ̃] *nm* wonder
émerveiller [emɛrveje] **1** *vt (enchanter)* to fill with wonder; **être émerveillé par** to marvel at
2 s'émerveiller *vpr* **s'é. de** *ou* **devant** *(s'enchanter de)* to marvel at
émetteur, -trice [emetœr, -tris] **1** *adj* (**a**) *Fin (banque, organisme)* issuing (**b**) *Rad* **poste é.** transmitter; **station émettrice** transmitting station
2 *nm* transmitter
émettre [47] [emɛtr] **1** *vt* (**a**) *(cri, rot, soupir)* to give; *(son, lumière)* to give out, to emit; *(fumée, chaleur)* to give off, to emit (**b**) *Fig (opinion, objection, idée)* to voice (**c**) *Rad & TV* to transmit, to broadcast (**d**) *(billets de banque, actions, timbres-poste)* to issue
2 *vi Rad & TV* to transmit, to broadcast
émeu [emø] *nm* emu
émeus, émeut *voir* **émouvoir**
émeute [emøt] *nf* riot
émeutier, -ère [emøtje, -ɛr] *nm,f* rioter

émeuve *etc voir* **émouvoir**
émietter [emjete] **1** *vt* (**a**) *(pain)* to crumble (**b**) *Fig (domaine, empire)* to break up
2 s'émietter *vpr (pain, roche)* to crumble
émigrant, -e [emigrɑ̃, -ɑ̃t] *nm,f* emigrant
émigration [emigrasjɔ̃] *nf* emigration
émigré, -e [emigre] **1** *nm,f* emigrant; *Hist* émigré
2 *adj (travailleur, population)* migrant
émigrer [emigre] *vi* to emigrate
émincer [16] [emɛ̃se] *vt (viande, légumes)* to slice thinly
éminemment [eminamɑ̃] *adv* eminently
éminence [eminɑ̃s] *nf* (**a**) *(de relief)* hill (**b**) *Rel* **É.** Eminence; *Fig* **l'é. grise** the éminence grise
éminent, -e [eminɑ̃, -ɑ̃t] *adj (personne)* eminent; **il nous a rendu d'éminents services** he rendered us outstanding service
émir [emir] *nm* emir
émirat [emira] *nm* emirate; **les Émirats arabes unis** the United Arab Emirates
émissaire [emisɛr] *nm (envoyé)* emissary
émission [emisjɔ̃] *nf* (**a**) *(de son, de substance)* emission (**b**) *Rad & TV (action)* transmission, broadcasting; *(ce qui est diffusé)* programme (**c**) *(de billets de banque, d'actions, de timbres-poste)* issue
emmagasiner [ɑ̃magazine] *vt (marchandises)* to store; *(électricité, chaleur, connaissances)* to store up
emmailloter [ɑ̃majɔte] *vt (nourrisson)* to swaddle
emmancher [ɑ̃mɑ̃ʃe] **1** *vt* (**a**) *(outil)* to fit a handle on (**b**) *(tuyaux)* to fit together; *(pièce)* to fit (**dans** into)
2 s'emmancher *vpr (pièces)* to fit together; *Fam Fig* **bien/mal s'e.** to get off to a good/bad start
emmanchure [ɑ̃mɑ̃ʃyr] *nf* armhole
emmêler [ɑ̃mele] **1** *vt (fils, cheveux)* to tangle
2 s'emmêler *vpr (fils, cheveux)* to get tangled; *Fam* **s'e. les pédales** *ou* **les pinceaux** to get all muddled up
emménager [45] [ɑ̃menaʒe] *vi* to move in
emmener [46] [ɑ̃mne] *vt* (**a**) *(prendre avec soi) (personne)* to take; *(prisonnier)* to take away; *Fam (objet)* to take; **e. qn en voiture** to give sb a *Br* lift *or Am* ride (**b**) *(entraîner) (équipier, peloton, sprint)* to lead
emmenthal [emɛ̃tal] *nm* Emmenthal
emmerdant, -e [ɑ̃mɛrdɑ̃, -ɑ̃t] *adj très Fam* (**a**) *(contrariant, agaçant)* damn *or Br* bloody annoying (**b**) *(ennuyeux) Br* bloody *or Am* godawful boring
emmerdement [ɑ̃mɛrdəmɑ̃] *nm très Fam* bloody nuisance; **avoir des emmerdements** to have a hell of a lot of trouble
emmerder [ɑ̃mɛrde] **1** *vt très Fam* **e. qn** *(contrarier, agacer)* to get on sb's nerves; *(ennuyer)* to bore sb stiff; **je l'emmerde!** sod him!
2 s'emmerder *vpr très Fam (s'ennuyer)* to be bored stiff; **s'e. à faire qch** *(prendre la peine de le faire)* to bother doing sth; *Ironique* **tu ne t'emmerdes pas!** you're not doing badly for yourself!; *(tu as du culot)* you've got a bloody nerve!
emmerdeur, -euse [ɑ̃mɛrdœr, -øz] *nm,f très Fam* pain in the arse
emmitoufler [ɑ̃mitufle] **1** *vt* to wrap up (**dans** in)
2 s'emmitoufler *vpr* to wrap oneself up (**dans** in)
emmurer [ɑ̃myre] *vt* to wall up
émoi [emwa] *nm (trouble)* emotion; *(plaisir)* excitement; **être (tout) en é.** *(troublé)* to be in a flutter
émollient, -e [emɔljɑ̃, -ɑ̃t] *adj & nm* emollient
émoluments [emɔlymɑ̃] *nmpl* remuneration

émonder [emɔ̃de] vt (arbre, texte) to prune
émoticon [emɔtikɔ̃] nm Ordinat smiley, emoticon
émotif, -ive [emɔtif, -iv] **1** adj emotional
  2 nm,f emotional person
émotion [emɔsjɔ̃] nf emotion; (frayeur) fright; **donner des émotions à qn** to give sb a real fright
émotivité [emotivite] nf **être d'une grande é.** to be highly emotional
émoulu, -e [emuly] adj **frais é. de l'université** fresh from university
émoussé, -e [emuse] adj (pointe, lame) blunt; Fig (sentiment, intérêt) blunted
émoustiller [emustije] vt to arouse
émouvant, -e [emuvɑ̃, -ɑ̃t] adj moving
émouvoir [31a] [emuvwar] **1** vt (toucher) to move, to touch; (troubler) to upset
  2 s'émouvoir vpr (être touché) to be moved or touched; **s'é. de qch** (s'en inquiéter) to be concerned about sth
empailler [ɑ̃paje] vt (a) (animal) to stuff (b) **e. une chaise** to bottom a chair with straw
empaler [ɑ̃pale] **1** vt to impale
  2 s'empaler vpr to impale oneself
empaqueter [42] [ɑ̃pakte] vt to pack
emparer [ɑ̃pare] s'emparer vpr **s'e. de** (lieu, personne, objet) to seize; (sujet: sentiment, doute) to take hold of
empâter [ɑ̃pate] **1** vt to bloat
  2 s'empâter vpr to become bloated
empattement [ɑ̃patmɑ̃] nm (a) (d'une voiture) wheelbase (b) Typ serif
empêché, -e [ɑ̃peʃe] adj (retenu) held up, detained
empêchement [ɑ̃peʃmɑ̃] nm hitch; **il a eu un e.** something came up
empêcher [ɑ̃peʃe] **1** vt (action, événement) to prevent, to stop; (mouvement, passage) to obstruct; **e. qn de faire qch** to prevent or stop sb (from) doing sth; Fam **ça ne m'empêchera pas de dormir** I won't lose any sleep over it; **il n'y a rien qui t'en empêche** there's nothing stopping you; **cela n'empêche que...**, **il n'empêche que...**, all the same,...; Fam **(il) n'empêche** all the same
  2 s'empêcher vpr **je ne peux pas m'en e.** I can't help it; **je ne pouvais pas m'e. de rire** I couldn't help laughing
empêcheur, -euse [ɑ̃peʃœr, -øz] nm,f Fam **e. de tourner en rond** spoilsport
empennage [ɑ̃penaʒ] nm (de flèche) feathering, feathers; (d'avion) tail section
empereur [ɑ̃prœr] nm emperor
empesé, -e [ɑ̃pəze] adj (a) (col, chemise) starched (b) Fig (personne, air, style) stiff
empester [ɑ̃peste] **1** vt (frigo, pièce) to stink out; **e. l'alcool/le parfum/le fromage** to stink of alcohol/perfume/cheese
  2 vi to stink
empêtrer [ɑ̃petre] s'empêtrer vpr to get entangled; **s'e. les pieds dans qch** to get one's feet caught in sth; Fig **s'e. dans** (explications, mensonges) to get tangled up in; Fig **s'e. dans une affaire** to get mixed up in a business; **s'e. de qn** to land oneself with sb
emphase [ɑ̃faz] nf pomposity; **avec e.** pompously
emphatique [ɑ̃fatik] adj pompous
emphysème [ɑ̃fizɛm] nm emphysema
empiècement [ɑ̃pjɛsmɑ̃] nm (d'un vêtement) yoke
empiétement [ɑ̃pjetmɑ̃] nm encroachment (**sur** on)

empiéter [34] [ɑ̃pjete] vi **e. sur** (terrain, horaire, vie privée) to encroach on
empiffrer [ɑ̃pifre] s'empiffrer vpr Fam to stuff oneself (**de** with)
empiler [ɑ̃pile] **1** vt (livres, bois, boîtes) to stack, to pile (up)
  2 s'empiler vpr (a) (livres, dossiers) to pile up (b) (passagers) **s'e. dans** to cram into
empire [ɑ̃pir] nm (a) Hist & Fig empire; **un e. commercial** a business empire; **pas pour un e.!** not for all the tea in China!; **le premier E.**, **l'E.** the First Empire; **le second E.** the Second Empire; **style/meubles E.** Empire style/furniture; **L'E. du milieu** the Middle Kingdom, the Celestial Empire (b) Litt (influence) influence; **avoir de l'e. sur qn** to have influence over sb; **faire qch sous l'e. de la boisson/de la colère** to do sth under the influence of drink/in a fit of anger
empirer [ɑ̃pire] vi to worsen, to get worse
empirique [ɑ̃pirik] adj empirical
emplacement [ɑ̃plasmɑ̃] nm (a) (endroit) site, location; (sur un marché, dans un parking) space (b) Ordinat slot; **e. pour carte d'extension** expansion slot; **e. (pour) périphériques** extension slot
emplafonner [ɑ̃plafone] vt Fam to crash into
emplâtre [ɑ̃plɑtr] nm (a) (pansement) plaster (b) Fam (personne) drip
emplette [ɑ̃plɛt] nf purchase; **faire ses emplettes** to go shopping; **faire l'e. de qch** to purchase sth
emplir [ɑ̃plir] **1** vt to fill (**de** with)
  2 s'emplir vpr to fill (up) (**de** with)
emploi [ɑ̃plwa] nm (a) (utilisation) use; **prêt à l'e.** ready to use; **e. du temps** timetable, schedule; **faire double e.** to be redundant (b) (situation) job; (embauche) employment; **être sans e.** to be out of work, to be unemployed; **la crise/situation de l'e.** the employment crisis/situation; Fig **la physique** ou **la tête** ou Fam **la gueule de l'e.** he looks the part
emploi-jeunes [ɑ̃plwaʒœn] nm inv = job, usually in the public sector or in education, created for a young person as part of a programme to combat unemployment
employé, -e [ɑ̃plwaje] nm,f employee; **e. de banque** bank clerk; **e. de bureau** office worker; **e. de maison** domestic employee
employer [32] [ɑ̃plwaje] **1** vt (a) (utiliser) (outil, mot, technique, force) to use; **e. les grands moyens** to take drastic measures; **e. son temps à faire qch** to spend one's time doing sth (b) (faire travailler) (personne) to employ; **elle l'emploie comme secrétaire** she employs her as a secretary
  2 s'employer vpr (a) (personne) **s'e. à faire qch** to work on doing sth; **je m'y emploie** I'm working on it (b) (être utilisé) to be used
employeur, -euse [ɑ̃plwajœr, -øz] nm,f employer
empocher [ɑ̃pɔʃe] vt to pocket
empoignade [ɑ̃pwaɲad] nf Fam dust-up
empoigne [ɑ̃pwaɲ] nf voir **foire**
empoigner [ɑ̃pwaɲe] **1** vt to grab (hold of)
  2 s'empoigner vpr to have a dust-up
empoisonnant, -e [ɑ̃pwazɔnɑ̃, -ɑ̃t] adj Fam irritating
empoisonnement [ɑ̃pwazɔnmɑ̃] nm (a) (par une substance nocive) poisoning (b) Fam (ennui) problem
empoisonner [ɑ̃pwazɔne] **1** vt (a) (avec une substance nocive) (personne, nourriture, lieu) to poison; Fig **empoisonné** (paroles) poisonous (b) (empester) (lieu) to stink out (c) Fam (irriter) **e. qn** to get on sb's

nerves (**d**) *(altérer) (existence, relations)* to poison; **e. la vie de qn** to make sb's life a misery

2 s'empoisonner *vpr* to poison oneself; **s'e. l'existence** to make one's life a misery

emporté, -e [ɑ̃pɔrte] *adj* quick-tempered

emportement [ɑ̃pɔrtəmɑ̃] *nm* anger

emporte-pièce [ɑ̃pɔrtəpjɛs] **1** *nm inv Tech* punch; *Culin* pastry cutter

2 à l'emporte-pièce *adj (jugement, style)* incisive

emporter [ɑ̃pɔrte] **1** *vt* (**a**) *(prendre avec soi)* to take; **plats à e.** *ou Suisse* **à l'e.** take-away meals

(**b**) *(transporter)* to take away

(**c**) *(entraîner) (sujet: courant)* to sweep away; *(sujet: vent)* to blow off; **il a eu une jambe emportée par un obus** a shell took one of his legs off; **e. qn** *(maladie)* to carry sb off; **e. la bouche** *ou Fam* **la gueule** *(moutarde, plat épicé)* to take the roof of your mouth off; *Fig* **se laisser e. par la colère/son imagination** to let one's anger/one's imagination get the better of one

(**d**) *(conquérir) (position)* to take

(**e**) **l'e.** *(gagner)* to win; *(prédominer)* to prevail; **l'e. sur qn** to beat sb; **l'e. sur qch** to prevail over sth

2 s'emporter *vpr* to lose one's temper (**contre qn** with sb)

empoté, -e [ɑ̃pɔte] *Fam* **1** *adj* cack-handed

2 *nm,f* cack-handed idiot

empourprer [ɑ̃purpre] **1** *vt* to tinge with crimson

2 s'empourprer *vpr* to turn crimson

empoussiéré, -e [ɑ̃pusjere] *adj* dusty

empreinte [ɑ̃prɛ̃t] *nf* (**a**) *(trace) (de pas)* footprint; *(d'animal)* track; **e. digitale** fingerprint; **e. génétique** genetic fingerprint (**b**) *Fig (de l'éducation, du milieu)* stamp, mark

empressé, -e [ɑ̃prese] **1** *adj (prévenant)* attentive

2 *nm,f Péj* **faire l'e. auprès de qn** to dance attendance on sb

empressement [ɑ̃prɛsmɑ̃] *nm* (**a**) *(prévenance)* attentiveness (**b**) *(hâte)* eagerness (**à faire qch** to do sth); **il montre peu d'e. à faire les travaux** he doesn't seem very eager to do the work; **avec e.** eagerly; **mettre beaucoup d'e. à faire qch** to hasten to do sth

empresser [ɑ̃prese] **s'empresser** *vpr* (**a**) *(se dépêcher)* **s'e. de faire qch** to hasten to do sth (**b**) *(être prévenant)* **s'e. auprès de qn** to be attentive to sb

emprise [ɑ̃priz] *nf* hold (**sur** over); **avoir de l'e. sur qn** to have a hold over sb; **sous l'e. de la colère** in a fit of anger

emprisonnement [ɑ̃prizɔnmɑ̃] *nm* imprisonment; **peine d'e.** prison sentence

emprisonner [ɑ̃prizɔne] *vt* to imprison

emprunt [ɑ̃prœ̃] *nm* (**a**) *(action)* borrowing (**b**) *(somme)* loan; **faire un e.** *(auprès d'une banque)* to take out a loan; **e. d'État** government loan; **lancer un e.** to issue a bond (**c**) *Ling* borrowing

emprunté, -e [ɑ̃prœ̃te] *adj* self-conscious, awkward

emprunter [ɑ̃prœ̃te] *vt* (**a**) *(objet, argent)* to borrow (**à** from) (**b**) *(route, chemin)* to take

emprunteur, -euse [ɑ̃prœ̃tœr, -øz] *nm,f* borrower

empuantir [ɑ̃pɥɑ̃tir] *vt (lieu)* to stink out

ému, -e [emy] **1** *pp voir* **émouvoir**

2 *adj (touché)* moved, touched; *(intimidé)* nervous; **voix émue** voice filled with emotion; **garder un souvenir é. de qch** to have fond memories of sth

émulation [emylasjɔ̃] *nf aussi Ordinat* emulation

émule [emyl] *nmf* emulator; **j'ai fait des émules** people followed my example

émuler [emyle] *vt Ordinat* to emulate

émulsifiant [emylsifjɑ̃] *nm* emulsifier

émulsion [emylsjɔ̃] *nf* emulsion

en¹ [ɑ̃] *prép* (**a**) *(indique la date ou la durée)* in; **en 1800** in 1800; **en hiver/été** in winter/summer; **en une minute/trois jours** in a minute/three days

(**b**) *(indique la destination)* to; **aller en Allemagne** to go to Germany; **partir en vacances** to go on *Br* holiday *or Am* vacation

(**c**) *(indique le lieu)* in; **vivre en France** to live in France; **en altitude** at altitude; **se promener en forêt** to walk in the forest; **en pleine mer** out at sea; **il y a quelque chose en lui qui me déplaît** there's something about him I don't like

(**d**) *(indique le moyen)* by; **en voiture/avion/train** by car/plane/train

(**e**) *(décrit un état)* in; **écrit en français** written in French; **en ruines** ruined; **être en colère/en larmes** to be angry/crying; **être en transe/en danger** to be in a trance/in danger; **être en arrêt maladie** to be on sick leave; **en trois parties** in three parts; **montre en or/en argent** gold/silver watch; **disponible en rouge/38** available in red/in size 38; **être bon en physique** to be good at physics; **payer en euros** to pay in euros; **la même chose en mieux/en moins bien** the same thing but better/but not as good

(**f**) *(indique une transformation, une progression)* into; **traduire qch en français** to translate sth into French; **transformer une chambre en bureau** to convert a bedroom into an office; **casser qch en deux** to break sth in two *or* in half; **peindre qch en rouge** to paint sth red; **réduire qch en poudre** to reduce sth to a powder; **se mettre en colère** to get angry; **aller de ville en ville** to go from town to town; **de jour en jour** by the day; **changer en bien/mal** to change for the better/for the worse

(**g**) *(en tant que)* as; **parler à qn en ami** to speak to sb as a friend; **parler en connaisseur** to speak as an expert; **agir en traître** to be disloyal

(**h**) *(avec un participe présent)* **entrer en criant** to come in shouting; **il s'est coupé en se rasant** he cut himself shaving; **c'est impoli de lire en mangeant** it's rude to read while you're eating; **traverser en courant** to run across; **répondre en maugréant** to grumble in reply; **dire qch en plaisantant** to say sth as a joke; **elle s'est cassé la jambe en tombant** she fell and broke her leg; **c'est en s'entraînant qu'il s'améliorera** he'll only get better if he practices

en² *pron* (**a**) *(avec les adjectifs construits avec de)* **il en est bien capable** he's quite capable of it; **et ta voiture? – j'en suis très content** how's your car? – I'm very pleased with it

(**b**) *(avec les verbes construits avec de)* **qu'en penses-tu?** what do you think of it?; **je ne m'en souviens plus** I can't remember; **on en reparlera** we'll talk about it later; **j'espère en tirer 200 euros** I hope to get 200 euros for it

(**c**) *(remplace le complément du nom)* **nous en avons la possibilité** we can do it; **elle en a mangé un morceau** she ate a piece of it; **j'en ai acheté 3 kilos** I bought 3 kilos

(**d**) *(remplace le nom)* **il y en a plusieurs** there are several of them; **elle en a cassé deux** she broke two of them; **est-ce que tu en veux?** do you want some?; **je n'en ai jamais vu** I've never seen one/any; **est-ce de l'or? – non, ce n'en est pas** is it gold? – no, it's not

(**e**) *(indique la cause)* **il en a perdu la raison** it made him lose his mind; **j'en suis tout retourné** I'm really upset about it

(**f**) *Fam (pour insister)* **il en a fait une histoire!** he made a real song and dance about it; **des balayeurs, il en faut** someone has to sweep the streets

(**g**) *(indique la provenance)* from there; **justement, j'en viens** I've just come from there

ENA [ena] *nf (abrév* **École nationale d'administration)** = university-level college preparing students for senior posts in law and economics

enamouré, -e [ãnamure], **énamouré, -e** [enamure] *adj Vieilli ou Hum* amorous

enamourer [ãnamure], **énamourer** [enamure] **s'enamourer** *vpr* **s'e. de** to become enamoured of

énarque [enark] *nmf* = graduate of the ENA

encabaner [ãkabane] **s'encabaner** *vpr Can* to shut oneself away

encadré [ãkadre] *nm (dans un texte)* box; *Ordinat* **e. graphique** graphics box; *Ordinat* **e. texte** text box

encadrement [ãkadrəmã] *nm* (**a**) *(cadre)* frame; **dans l'e. de la porte** in the doorway (**b**) *(fonction) (de personnel)* management; *(d'élèves, d'enfants)* supervision; *(personnes qui encadrent) (du personnel)* management; *Mil* officers (**c**) *Écon* **e. du crédit** credit squeeze

encadrer [ãkadre] *vt* (**a**) *(tableau, photo)* to frame (**b**) *(entourer) (mots, paragraphe)* to circle; **encadré par deux gendarmes** flanked by two policemen (**c**) *(guider) (personnel, équipe)* to manage; *(enfants, handicapés)* to supervise; *Mil (soldats)* to officer (**d**) *Fam (supporter)* **je ne peux pas l'e.** I can't stand him

encadreur, -euse [ãkadrœr, -øz] *nm,f* picture framer

encaissé, -e [ãkese] *adj (vallée)* deep; *(rivière)* with steep sides; *(route)* cut into the hillside

encaissement [ãkesmã] *nm* (**a**) *(d'un chèque)* cashing; *(d'argent)* collection (**b**) *(d'une vallée)* depth

encaisser [ãkese] *vt* (**a**) *(chèque)* to cash; *(argent)* to collect (**b**) *Fam (supporter) (coups, critiques)* to take; **je ne peux pas l'e.** I can't stand her; **il sait e.** he can take it; **qu'est-ce qu'il a encaissé!** he took a lot of punishment!

encanailler [ãkanaje] **s'encanailler** *vpr* to slum it

encart [ãkar] *nm (feuille)* insert; **e. publicitaire** advertising insert

en-cas [ãka] *nm inv* snack

encastrable [ãkastrabl] *adj (machine à laver, cuisinière)* that can be built in

encastré, -e [ãkastre] *adj* built-in

encastrer [ãkastre] **1** *vt* to build in

2 s'encastrer *vpr (éléments)* to fit together; *(machine à laver, cuisinière)* to fit (**dans** into); **la voiture s'est encastrée sous un camion** the car embedded itself under a lorry

encaustique [ãkɔstik] *nf* wax, polish

enceinte¹ [ãsɛ̃t] *nf* (**a**) *(mur)* (surrounding) wall; *(palissade)* fence (**b**) *(espace)* enclosure; *(d'église, de couvent)* precinct(s); **dans l'e. du parc** within the park (**c**) *(baffle)* **e. (acoustique)** speaker

enceinte² *adj f* pregnant; **e. de cinq mois** five months pregnant; **être e. de jumeaux** to be expecting twins; **elle est e. de Marc** she's pregnant by Marc

encens [ãsã] *nm* incense

encenser [ãsãse] *vt* **e. qn** to praise sb to the skies

encensoir [ãsãswar] *nm* censer

encéphalite [ãsefalit] *nf* encephalitis; **e. bovine spongiforme** bovine spongiform encephalopathy

encéphalogramme [ãsefalɔgram] *nm* encephalogram

encercler [ãserkle] *vt* (**a**) *(ennemi, lieu)* to encircle, to surround (**b**) *(mot)* to circle, to ring

enchaînement [ãʃenmã] *nm* (**a**) *(série) (d'événements, de circonstances)* series, chain (**b**) *(liaison) (d'idées, de séquences)* linking (**c**) *(en danse)* sequence (of steps); *(en ballet)* enchaînement (**d**) *Ordinat* concatenation

enchaîner [ãʃene] **1** *vt* (**a**) *(animal, prisonnier)* to chain up; *Fig (peuple)* to enslave; *(presse)* to curb; **e. qn à** to chain sb (up) to (**b**) *(lier) (épisodes, séquences)* to link (up)

2 *vi* to move on; **e. sur un sujet** to move on to a subject

3 s'enchaîner *vpr* (**a**) *(personne)* **s'e. à** to chain oneself (up) to (**b**) *(séquences, épisodes)* to be linked together; **les événements se sont enchaînés rapidement** events happened very quickly

enchanté, -e [ãʃãte] *adj* (**a**) *(ravi)* delighted (**de** with); **e. (de faire votre connaissance)!** pleased to meet you! (**b**) *(magique)* enchanted

enchantement [ãʃãtmã] *nm* (**a**) *(sortilège)* (magic) spell; **comme par e.** as if by magic (**b**) *(ravissement, merveille)* delight

enchanter [ãʃãte] *vt* (**a**) *(ravir)* to delight; **cette idée ne l'enchante pas** she's not keen on the idea (**b**) *(ensorceler)* to bewitch

enchanteur, -eresse [ãʃãtœr, -trɛs] **1** *adj (sourire)* bewitching; *(spectacle, endroit)* enchanting, delightful

2 *nm* (**a**) *(sorcier)* sorcerer (**b**) *Fig (charmeur)* charmer

3 *nf* **enchanteresse** sorceress

enchâsser [ãʃase] *vt* (**a**) *(bijou)* to set (**b**) *(relique)* to enshrine

enchère [ãʃɛr] *nf* bid; **les enchères** the bidding; **vente aux enchères** auction; **faire monter les enchères** to up the bidding; *Fig* to raise the stakes; **vendre qch aux enchères** to sell sth at auction

enchérir [ãʃerir] *vi* to make a higher bid; **e. sur qn** to outbid sb; *Fig* to go one better than sb

enchevêtré, -e [ãʃəvetre] *adj (branchages, fils, explications)* tangled

enchevêtrement [ãʃəvetrəmã] *nm (de fils, branchages)* tangle

enchevêtrer [ãʃəvetre] **1** *vt (fils, branchages)* to tangle (up)

2 s'enchevêtrer *vpr (fils)* to get tangled (up)

enclave [ãklav] *nf* enclave

enclenchement [ãklãʃmã] *nm (d'une vitesse, d'un mécanisme)* engaging

enclencher [ãklãʃe] **1** *vt (vitesse, mécanisme)* to engage; *Fig (processus)* to get under way

2 s'enclencher *vpr (vitesse, mécanisme)* to engage; *Fig (processus)* to get under way

enclin, -e [ãklɛ̃, -in] *adj* **être e. à faire qch** to be inclined to do sth; **être e. à la paresse/la méfiance** to be inclined to be lazy/distrustful; **il est peu e. à partager ses secrets** he is reluctant to share his secrets; **peu e. au bavardage** not very talkative

enclos [ãklo] *nm (espace)* enclosure; *(pour chevaux)* paddock

enclume [ãklym] *nf* anvil; *Fig* **être entre le l'e. et marteau** to be between the devil and the deep blue sea

encoche [ãkɔʃ] *nf* notch; *Ordinat* **e. de protection contre l'écriture** write-protect notch

encodage [ãkɔdaʒ] *nm Ling & Ordinat* encoding

encoder [ãkɔde] *vt Ling & Ordinat* to encode

encoignure [ãkwaɲyr] *nf* (**a**) *(d'une pièce)* corner (**b**) *(meuble)* corner cupboard

encoller [ãkɔle] *vt (papier peint)* to paste

encolure [ãkɔlyr] *nf* (**a**) *(d'animal)* neck; **gagner d'une e.** to win by a neck (**b**) *(tour de cou)* collar size (**c**) *(d'un vêtement)* neck

encombrant, -e [ãkɔ̃brã, -ãt] *adj (meuble, valise, paquet)* cumbersome, bulky; *Fig (personne, témoin)* undesirable

encombre [ãkɔ̃br] *nm* **sans e.** without mishap

encombrement [ãkɔ̃brəmã] *nm* (**a**) *(état) (d'une pièce)* clutter; *(de lignes téléphoniques)* jamming; *(embouteillage)* traffic jam (**b**) *(volume) (d'un objet)* (overall) dimensions (**c**) *Ordinat* **faible e. sur le disque dur** low use of hard disk space

encombrer [ãkɔ̃bre] **1** *vt (pièce)* to clutter (up); *(passage, route)* to block; *(lignes téléphoniques)* to jam; **tu m'encombres, sors d'ici!** you're getting under my feet, get out!
2 s'encombrer *vpr* **s'e. de** *(colis, équipement)* to load oneself down with; *Fig (obligations, personne)* to saddle oneself with; **elle ne s'encombre pas de scrupules** she is quite unscrupulous

encontre [ãkɔ̃tr] **à l'encontre de** *prép* **aller à l'e. de** to go against

encorbellement [ãkɔrbɛlmã] *nm* corbelled structure

encorder [ãkɔrde] **s'encorder** *vpr* to rope up

encore [ãkɔr] *adv* (**a**) *(toujours)* still; **pas e.** not yet; **elle n'est pas e. arrivée** she hasn't arrived yet; **je n'avais e. jamais vu ça** I'd never seen that before; **qu'il m'appelle par mon prénom, passe e., mais...** his calling me by my Christian name is one thing, but...; **e. heureux que les enfants n'aient pas été là!** it's just as well the children weren't there!
(**b**) *(davantage)* more; **en voulez-vous e.?** would you like some more?; **e. une tasse de café** another cup of coffee; **e. trois mois** three more months, another three months; **e. plus/moins** even more/less; **e. plus froid** even colder; **c'est e. pire/mieux** it's even worse/better; **mais e.?** and apart from that?
(**c**) *(de nouveau)* again; **il a e. cassé un verre** he's broken another glass; **qu'est-ce qu'il a e. fait?** what's he done this time?; **quoi e.?** now what?; **et puis quoi e.?** is that all?; **e. une fois** once more, once again; **e. vous!** you again!
(**d**) *(restrictif)* **si e....** if only...; **il vous en donnera 10 euros, et e.!** he'll give you 10 euros for it, if that!; **et e., ce n'est même pas sûr** even then, it's not certain; **e. faudrait-il qu'elle accepte/qu'il le sache!** she has to agree/he has to know about it first!
(**e**) *(seulement)* only; **hier e. elle me disait que...** only yesterday she was telling me that...
(**f**) **e. que** although, even though

encorner [ãkɔrne] *vt* to gore

encoubler [ãkuble] **s'encoubler** *vpr Suisse* to trip over

encourageant, -e [ãkuraʒã, -ãt] *adj* encouraging

encouragement [ãkuraʒmã] *nm* encouragement; **des encouragements** encouragement

encourager [45] [ãkuraʒe] *vt* (**a**) *(personne)* to encourage; *(athlète, équipe)* to cheer on; **e. qn à faire qch** to encourage sb to do sth (**b**) *(promouvoir) (arts)* to encourage

encourir [22] [ãkurir] *vt* to incur

encrasser [ãkrase] **1** *vt (vêtements, mains)* to dirty; *Aut (bougie)* to soot up; *(moteur)* to clog
2 s'encrasser *vpr* to get dirty; *Aut (bougie)* to soot up; *(moteur)* to get clogged

encre [ãkr] *nf* ink; *Fig* **nuit d'e.** inky black night; **e. de Chine** Indian ink; **e. sympathique** invisible ink

encrier [ãkrije] *nm* inkpot; *(de pupitre)* inkwell

encroûter [ãkrute] **s'encroûter** *vpr Fam (personne)* to get into a rut

enculé, -e [ãkyle] *nm,f Vulg Br* arsehole, *Am* asshole

enculer [ãkyle] *vt Vulg* to bugger; **va te faire e.!** fuck off!; *Fig* **e. les mouches** to nit-pick

encyclique [ãsiklik] *nf Rel* encyclical

encyclopédie [ãsiklɔpedi] *nf* encyclopedia

encyclopédique [ãsiklɔpedik] *adj* encyclopedic

endémie [ãdemi] *nf* endemic disease

endémique [ãdemik] *adj* endemic

endetté, -e [ãdɛte] *adj* in debt; **très e.** heavily in debt

endettement [ãdɛtmã] *nm* debt

endetter [ãdɛte] **1** *vt* **e. qn** to get sb into debt
2 s'endetter *vpr* to get into debt

endeuiller [ãdœje] *vt (famille, nation)* to plunge into mourning; *(événement)* to cast a gloom over

endiablé, -e [ãdjable] *adj (personne, musique, rythme)* wild

endiguer [ãdige] *vt* (**a**) *(cours d'eau)* to dyke (up) (**b**) *Fig (révolte, inflation, chômage)* to contain

endimanché, -e [ãdimãʃe] *adj* in one's Sunday best

endive [ãdiv] *nf* chicory

endocrine [ãdɔkrin] *adj (glande)* endocrine

endoctrinement [ãdɔktrinmã] *nm* indoctrination

endoctriner [ãdɔktrine] *vt* to indoctrinate

endogène [ãdɔʒɛn] *adj Biol & Géol* endogenous

endolori, -e [ãdɔlɔri] *adj* painful

endommager [45] [ãdɔmaʒe] *vt* (**a**) *(abîmer)* to damage (**b**) *Ordinat* to corrupt

endormi, -e [ãdɔrmi] **1** *adj* (**a**) *(qui dort) (personne)* sleeping; *(voix, village)* sleepy; **être e.** *(personne)* to be asleep *or* sleeping; **avoir l'air e.** to look sleepy (**b**) *(inerte, lent) (personne)* sluggish (**c**) *Fig (passion, intérêt)* dormant
2 *nm,f (personne inerte, lente)* slowcoach

endormir [29] [ãdɔrmir] **1** *vt* (**a**) **e. qn** *(bébé)* to send sb to sleep; *(anesthésier)* to put sb to sleep; *(ennuyer)* to send sb to sleep (**b**) *(apaiser) (douleur)* to deaden; **e. les soupçons** to allay suspicion (**c**) *(mettre en confiance) (électeurs, public)* to lull into a false sense of security
2 s'endormir *vpr* to fall asleep, to go to sleep

endossable [ãdosabl] *adj (chèque)* endorsable

endossement [ãdosmã] *nm (d'un chèque)* endorsement

endosser [ãdose] *vt* (**a**) *(vêtement)* to put on (**b**) *(responsabilité)* to assume (**c**) *(chèque)* to endorse

endroit [ãdrwa] *nm* (**a**) *(lieu)* place, spot; **à quel e.?** where?; **c'est à cet e. que...** this is where...; **par endroits** here and there, in places (**b**) *(d'un vêtement)* right side; **à l'e.** the right way round (**c**) *Litt* **à l'e. de** *(personne)* towards; *(événement, objet)* with regard to

enduire [18] [ãdɥir] **1** *vt* to coat, to cover (**de** with)
2 s'enduire *vpr* **s'e. de** to cover oneself with

enduit [ãdɥi] *nm* coating; *(pour boucher)* filler

endurance [ãdyrãs] *nf* (**a**) *(physique)* stamina (**b**) *Sport* **épreuve/course d'e.** endurance race

endurant, -e [ãdyrã, -ãt] *adj* tough

endurci, -e [ãdyrsi] *adj* (**a**) *(dur) (personne)* hard (**b**) *(invétéré) (criminel)* hardened; *(célibataire)* confirmed

endurcir [ãdyrsir] **1** *vt* (**a**) *(moralement)* to harden (**b**) *(physiquement)* to toughen (up)
2 s'endurcir *vpr* (**a**) *(moralement)* to become hard (**b**) *(physiquement)* to toughen up

endurer [ãdyre] *vt* to endure, to bear

enduro [ãdyro] *nm Sport* enduro

énergétique [enɛrʒetik] *adj* (**a**) *(nourriture)* energy-giving (**b**) *(ressources, besoins)* energy

énergie [enɛrʒi] *nf* (**a**) *(dynamisme)* energy; **mettre toute son é. à qch/à faire qch** to devote all one's energy to sth/to doing sth; **avec é.** *(nier)* strongly; *(refuser, répondre)* forcefully; **sans é.** *(enfant)* listless; *(jouer)* listlessly (**b**) *(force)* energy, power; **é. hydro-électrique** hydroelectric power; **é. nucléaire** *ou* **atomique** nuclear power; **é. solaire** solar power *or* energy

énergique [enɛrʒik] *adj* (**a**) *(personne)* energetic, dynamic; *(geste)* brisk; *(visage)* strong (**b**) *(mesures)* strong; *(remède)* powerful

énergiquement [enɛrʒikmã] *adv* *(nier)* strongly; *(refuser)* forcefully; **serrer é. la main à qn** to shake sb's hand warmly

énergumène [enɛrɡymɛn] *nmf* eccentric

énervant, -e [enɛrvã, -ãt] *adj* irritating

énervé, -e [enɛrve] *adj* *(agacé)* irritated; *(excité)* edgy, agitated

énervement [enɛrvəmã] *nm* *(agacement)* irritation; *(excitation)* agitation

énerver [enɛrve] **1** *vt* **é. qn** *(agacer)* to get on sb's nerves, to irritate sb; *(exciter)* to make sb nervous
2 s'énerver *vpr* to get worked up

enfance [ãfãs] *nf* *(jeunesse)* childhood; *(de garçon)* boyhood; *(de fille)* girlhood; **la petite e.** early childhood; *Fam* **c'est l'e. de l'art** it's child's play

enfant [ãfã] *nmf* child; **faire l'e.** to act like a child; **je l'ai connu e.** I knew him when he was a child; **il lui a fait un e.** she had a child by him; **viens ici, mon e.** come here, my child; *Fam* **salut, les enfants!** hi guys!; *Fam* **il n'y a plus d'enfants!** honestly, kids nowadays!; **e. en bas âge** infant; **e. bleu** blue baby; *Rel* **e. de chœur** altar boy; *Fig* **ce n'est pas un e. de chœur** he's no angel; **e. terrible** enfant terrible; **e. trouvé** foundling; **e.unique** only child

enfantement [ãfãtmã] *nm Litt* childbirth

enfanter [ãfãte] *vt Litt* to give birth to

enfantillages [ãfãtijaʒ] *nmpl* childish behaviour; **faire des e.** to be childish

enfantin, -e [ãfãtɛ̃, -in] *adj* *(voix)* child's; *(littérature)* children's; *(très facile)* childishly simple; *Péj (remarque, conduite)* childish

enfarger [ãfarʒe] *vi Can* to trip

enfariné, -e [ãfarine] *adj* *(visage, cheveux)* covered with flour; *Fam* **arriver la gueule enfarinée** to arrive blithely ignorant of the facts

enfer [ãfer] *nm aussi Fig* **l'e.** hell; **aller à un train d'e.** to go like a bat out of hell; *Fig* **elle a vécu un véritable e.** she's been through sheer hell; *Fam* **c'est l'e. pour se garer ici** it's hell trying to park here; *Fam* **une soirée d'e.** one hell of a party; **l'e. est pavé de bonnes intentions** the road to hell is paved with good intentions

enfermement [ãfɛrməmã] *nm* imprisonment

enfermer [ãfɛrme] **1** *vt (personne, chose)* to shut up; **e. qn/qch à clef** to lock sb/sth up; **je suis enfermé toute la journée** I'm cooped up all day; *Fam* **elle est bonne à e.** she should be locked up
2 s'enfermer *vpr* to shut oneself up; **s'e. à clef** to lock oneself in; *Fig* **s'e. dans le silence** to retreat into silence

enferrer [ãfere] **s'enferrer** *vpr Fig* to get tangled up (**dans** in)

enfiévré, -e [ãfjevre] *adj (front, imagination)* fevered

enfiévrer [34] [ãfjevre] **1** *vt (personne, imagination)* to excite
2 s'enfiévrer *vpr* to get excited

enfilade [ãfilad] *nf (de portes, de pièces)* series; **être en e.** to be adjoining

enfiler [ãfile] **1** *vt* (**a**) *(aiguille, perles)* to thread (**b**) *(vêtements)* to slip on
2 s'enfiler *vpr* (**a**) *(gants, bottes)* to go on (**b**) *Fam (boisson, nourriture)* to put away

enfin [ãfɛ̃] *adv* (**a**) *(en dernier lieu)* finally, lastly
(**b**) *(à la fin)* at last, finally
(**c**) *(de résignation)* **e., n'en parlons plus!** look, let's forget about it!; **e., ce qui est fait est fait!** what's done is done!
(**d**) *(d'exaspération)* **e. quoi, tu n'as plus dix ans!** for God's sake, you're not ten any more!; **mais e., je te l'avais dit!** but I told you, for God's sake!
(**e**) *(d'hésitation, pour résumer)* well; **e., je ne dis pas non, mais…** well, I'm not saying no, but…; **elle n'est pas mal, e. pour son âge** she's not bad, for her age that is; **e. (bref), c'était la panique!** in short, it was panic!

enflammé, -e [ãflame] *adj* (**a**) *(brindille, torche, allumette)* burning (**b**) *(joues) (de froid)* glowing; *(de fièvre, de gêne)* burning (**c**) *Fig (discours)* fiery, passionate

enflammer [ãflame] **1** *vt* (**a**) *(mettre le feu à)* to set light to; *(allumette)* to strike (**b**) *Fig (imagination)* to stir; **la colère enflammait son regard** her eyes were blazing with anger
2 s'enflammer *vpr* (**a**) *(prendre feu)* to catch fire (**b**) *Fig (imagination)* to be stirred

enflé, -e [ãfle] *adj (rivière, membre)* swollen

enfler [ãfle] **1** *vt* (**a**) *(rivière, membre)* to swell; **e. les joues** to puff out one's cheeks (**b**) *Fig (exagérer) (histoire, succès)* to exaggerate
2 *vi (membre)* to swell (up)

enflure [ãflyr] *nf* (**a**) *(d'un membre)* swelling (**b**) *très Fam (imbécile)* jerk, *Br* git

enfoiré, -e [ãfware] *nm,f Vulg* bugger, bastard

enfoncé, -e [ãfɔ̃se] *adj (yeux)* deep-set

enfoncement [ãfɔ̃smã] *nm (dans le sol)* dip; *(dans un mur)* recess

enfoncer [16] [ãfɔ̃se] **1** *vt* (**a**) *(clou)* to bang in; *(pieu)* to drive in; *(aiguille)* to stick in, to push in; **e. un couteau dans qch** to stick a knife into sth; **e. la main dans sa poche** to thrust one's hand into one's pocket; **e. son chapeau sur sa tête** to jam one's hat on one's head (**b**) *(porte)* to break down (**c**) *Fam (personne)* to humiliate
2 s'enfoncer *vpr (clou, couteau)* to go in; *(bateau)* to sink; **s'e. dans son fauteuil** to sink into one's armchair; **s'e. dans un bois** to go into the depths of a wood; *Fam* **enfonce-toi ça dans le crâne!** can't you get it into your thick head?

enfouir [ãfwir] **1** vt to bury (**dans/sous** in/under)
  2 s'**enfouir** vpr to bury oneself
enfourcher [ãfurʃe] vt (cheval, vélo) to get on, to mount
enfourner [ãfurne] vt (pain) to put in the oven; (poteries, briques) to put in the kiln; Fam (manger) to stuff down
enfreindre [54] [ãfrɛ̃dr] vt to infringe, to break
enfuir [38] [ãfɥir] s'**enfuir** vpr to run away (**de** from); (d'une prison) to escape (**de** from)
enfumé, -e [ãfyme] adj (pièce, atmosphère) smoky
enfumer [ãfyme] vt (**a**) (pièce) to fill with smoke (**b**) (personne, abeilles) to smoke out
enfuyais etc voir **enfuir**
engagé, -e [ãɡaʒe] **1** adj (littérature, écrivain) committed
  2 nm (soldat) **e. (volontaire)** enlisted man
engageant, -e [ãɡaʒã, -ãt] adj (manière, sourire) engaging
engagement [ãɡaʒmã] nm (**a**) (promesse) undertaking, commitment; **prendre un e.** to enter into an undertaking; **prendre l'e. de faire qch** to undertake to do sth; **tenir ses engagements** to honour one's commitments; **sans e. (de votre part)** without obligation (on your part) (**b**) (à une cause) commitment (**c**) (coup d'envoi) (au football, au rugby) kick-off; (au hockey) bully-off; (au basket) tip-off (**d**) (commencement) start; (de poursuites) institution (**e**) (d'un employé) appointment; (d'un soldat) enlistment
engager [45] [ãɡaʒe] **1** vt (**a**) (lier) to commit; **e. sa parole** to give one's word; **cela ne vous engage à rien** it doesn't commit you to anything; **cela n'engage que moi** that's just my opinion (**b**) (mettre en gage) to pawn (**c**) (embaucher) (employé) to appoint; (soldat) to enlist (**d**) (commencer) (conversation, négociations) to begin, to start; (poursuites) to institute; **e. la partie** to start the match; **la partie est maintenant bien engagée** the match is now well under way (**e**) (introduire) (clef) to insert (**dans** in) (**f**) (inciter) **e. qn à faire qch** to urge sb to do sth
  2 s'**engager** vpr (**a**) (promettre) s'**e. à faire qch** to promise to do sth, to undertake to do sth (**b**) (prendre position) to commit oneself (**c**) (se lancer) s'**e. dans une aventure** to get involved in an adventure (**d**) (soldat) to enlist, to join up (**e**) (pénétrer) s'**e. dans une rue** to turn into a street; s'**e. dans une forêt** to enter a forest (**f**) (commencer) (négociations, conversation) to begin
engeance [ãʒãs] nf Fam crew, bunch
engelure [ãʒlyr] nf chilblain
engendrer [ãʒãdre] vt to father; Fig (maladie, pauvreté) to cause
engin [ãʒɛ̃] nm (machine) machine; (outil) device; Fam (objet) thing; **e. blindé** armoured vehicle; **e. de mort** deadly weapon; **e. spatial** spacecraft
englober [ãɡlɔbe] vt to include (**dans** in)
engloutir [ãɡlutir] vt (**a**) (avaler) (boisson) to gulp down; (nourriture) to wolf down (**b**) (submerger) (bateau, village) to submerge; Fig (fortune) to swallow up
engoncé, -e [ãɡɔ̃se] adj **il avait l'air e. dans son manteau** his coat looked too tight for him
engorgement [ãɡɔrʒəmã] nm (blocage) blocking; (d'un marché) glutting; Méd (d'un organe) congestion
engorger [45] [ãɡɔrʒe] **1** vt (bloquer) to block, to clog; (marché) to glut

2 s'**engorger** vpr (tuyau) to be blocked or clogged; Méd (organe) to become engorged or congested
engouement [ãɡumã] nm craze (**pour** for)
engouffrer [ãɡufre] **1** vt Fam (nourriture) to devour
  2 s'**engouffrer** vpr s'**e. dans** to rush in to; **le vent s'engouffra par la porte** the wind rushed in through the door
engourdi, -e [ãɡurdi] adj numb (**par** with)
engourdir [ãɡurdir] **1** vt (**a**) (membre) to numb (**b**) (douleur) to dull
  2 s'**engourdir** vpr to go numb, to go to sleep
engourdissement [ãɡurdismã] nm numbness
engrais [ãɡrɛ] nm fertilizer
engraisser [ãɡrese] **1** vt (animaux, personne) to fatten up
  2 vi Fam to get fatter
engranger [45] [ãɡrãʒe] vt (céréales) to bring in; Fig to build up
engrenage [ãɡrənaʒ] nm (**a**) (roues dentées) gears (**b**) Fig (d'événements) chain; **l'e. de la violence** the cycle of violence; **être pris dans un e.** to get caught up in a system; **mettre le doigt dans l'e.** to get caught up in it
engrosser [ãɡrose] vt très Fam (femme) to knock up; **se faire e. (par)** to get knocked up (by)
engueulade [ãɡœlad] nf Fam (réprimande) earbashing; (querelle) row, Br slanging match
engueuler [ãɡœle] Fam **1** vt **e. qn** to give sb an earbashing; **se faire e.** to get an earbashing; **e. qn comme du poisson pourri** to call sb every name under the sun
  2 s'**engueuler** vpr to have a row or Br slanging match
enguirlander [ãɡirlãde] vt (**a**) Fam **e. qn** to give sb an earbashing; **se faire e.** to get an earbashing (**b**) (décorer) to garland (**de** with)
enhardir [ãardir] **1** vt to embolden
  2 s'**enhardir** vpr to become bolder; s'**e. à faire qch** to pluck up the courage to do sth
énième [enjɛm] adj **après une é. tentative** after countless attempts; **pour la é. fois** for the umpteenth time
énigmatique [eniɡmatik] adj enigmatic
énigme [eniɡm] nf (mystère) enigma, mystery; (devinette) riddle
enivrant, -e [ãnivrã, -ãt] adj (parfum) heady; (vitesse) exhilarating
enivrement [ãnivrəmã] nm (**a**) (par l'alcool) intoxication (**b**) Fig exhilaration
enivrer [ãnivre] **1** vt (**a**) (soûler) to intoxicate, to make drunk (**b**) Fig (exalter) to exhilarate; **enivré par le succès** intoxicated with success
  2 s'**enivrer** vpr (se soûler) to become intoxicated (**de** with), to get drunk (**de** on)
enjambée [ãʒãbe] nf stride; **marcher à grandes enjambées** to stride along
enjambement [ãʒãbmã] nm enjambment
enjamber [ãʒãbe] vt (obstacle) to step over; (sujet: pont) (rivière) to span
enjeu, -x [ãʒø] nm (au jeu) stake; Fig (d'une guerre) stakes; **quel est l'e. de cette élection?** what's at stake in this election?
enjoignais etc voir **enjoindre**
enjoindre [43] [ãʒwɛ̃dr] vt Litt **e. à qn de faire qch** to enjoin sb to do sth
enjôler [ãʒole] vt to cajole

enjôleur, -euse [ãʒolœr, -øz] **1** *adj* cajoling **2** *nm,f* charmer

enjoliver [ãʒɔlive] *vt* to embellish

enjoliveur [ãʒɔlivœr] *nm* hubcap

enjoué, -e [ãʒwe] *adj* playful

enjouement [ãʒumã] *nm* playfulness

enlacement [ãlasmã] *nm* (**a**) *(de rubans, de branches)* intertwining (**b**) *(étreinte)* embrace

enlacer [16] [ãlase] **1** *vt* (**a**) *(rubans, branches)* to intertwine (**b**) *(étreindre)* to embrace **2** *s'enlacer vpr (s'étreindre)* to embrace

enlaidir [ãledir] **1** *vt (personne)* to make ugly, to disfigure; *(paysage, ville)* to disfigure **2** *s'enlaidir vpr* to make oneself look ugly

enlevé, -e [ãlve] *adj (style, rythme)* lively

enlèvement [ãlɛvmã] *nm* (**a**) *(de meubles, d'une tache)* removal, removing; *(de bagages)* collection; **e. des ordures** *Br* rubbish *or Am* garbage collection (**b**) *(kidnapping)* kidnapping, abduction

enlever [46] [ãlve] **1** *vt* (**a**) *(vêtements, couvercle)* to remove, to take off; *(meubles)* to remove, to take away; *(tapis)* to take up; *(rideaux)* to take down; *(papier peint, étiquette, tache)* to remove; **e. qch à qn** to take sth away from sb; **elle me l'a enlevé des mains** she took it from me; **e. à qn la garde d'un enfant** to remove a child from sb's care; **e. à qn le goût de qch** to take away sb's taste for sth (**b**) *(kidnapper)* to kidnap, to abduct (**c**) *(remporter) (prix)* to carry off; *(victoire, contrat)* to win **2** *s'enlever vpr (couvercle, peinture)* to come off; *(tache)* to come out

enlisement [ãlizmã] *nm* sinking

enliser [ãlize] **1** *vt* **e. une voiture** to get a car stuck **2** *s'enliser vpr (personne, voiture)* to get stuck; *Fig* **s'e. dans ses explications** to get bogged down in explanations

enluminure [ãlyminyr] *nf* illumination

enneigé, -e [ãneʒe] *adj (montagne, champ, route)* snow-covered; *(village)* snowbound

enneigement [ãnɛʒmã] *nm* snow cover

ennemi, -e [ɛnmi] **1** *nm,f* enemy; **se faire un e. de qn** to make an enemy of sb; **passer à l'e.** to defect; *Prov* **le mieux est l'e. du bien** it's better to leave well alone; **e. public numéro un** public enemy number one **2** *adj* **en pays e.** in enemy country

ennui [ãɥi] *nm* (**a**) *(souci)* worry; *(problème)* problem; **avoir des ennuis** *(soucis)* to be worried; *(problèmes)* to have problems; **avoir des ennuis de santé** to have health problems; **avoir des ennuis avec la police** to be in trouble with the police; **attirer des ennuis à qn** to get sb into trouble; **faire des ennuis à qn** to bother sb (**b**) *(lassitude)* boredom; **il est d'un e.!** his conversation is so boring!

ennuyé, -e [ãɥije] *adj* (**a**) *(contrarié)* annoyed (**de** about) (**b**) *(las)* bored

ennuyer [32] [ãɥije] **1** *vt* (**a**) *(contrarier)* to bother; **cela vous ennuierait-il d'attendre?** would you mind waiting? (**b**) *(agacer)* to annoy, to irritate (**c**) *(lasser)* to bore (**avec** with) **2** *s'ennuyer vpr* to be bored; **qu'est-ce qu'on s'ennuie ici!** it's so boring here!; **s'e. à cent sous de l'heure** to be bored to death

ennuyeux, -euse [ãɥijø, -øz] *adj* (**a**) *(contrariant)* annoying, irritating; **comme c'est e.!** it's so annoying! (**b**) *(lassant)* boring

énoncé [enɔ̃se] *nm* (**a**) *(des faits)* statement; *(d'une sentence)* pronouncement (**b**) *(d'une question)* wording

énoncer [16] [enɔ̃se] *vt (opinion, conditions)* to state

énonciation [enɔ̃sjasjɔ̃] *nf (de faits)* statement

enorgueillir [ãnɔrgœjir] **1** *vt* to make proud **2** *s'enorgueillir vpr* **s'e. de qch/de faire qch** to pride oneself on sth/on doing sth

énorme [enɔrm] *adj* enormous, huge

énormément [enɔrmemã] *adv (lire, travailler, pleurer)* an awful lot; **je le regrette é.** I'm extremely sorry; **s'amuser é.** to have a great time; **il n'a pas é. d'argent** he hasn't got a huge amount of money

énormité [enɔrmite] *nf* (**a**) *(d'une demande, d'un crime)* enormity, outrageousness (**b**) *(d'une personne, d'une somme)* huge size (**c**) *(erreur)* glaring mistake; *(propos choquants)* outrageous statement

enquérir [7] [ãkerir] *s'enquérir vpr* to inquire (**de** about)

enquête [ãkɛt] *nf* (**a**) *(recherches)* inquiry; *(de journalistes, de policiers)* investigation (**sur** into); *Fam* **faire sa petite e.** to do a bit of investigating (**b**) *(sondage)* survey

enquêter [ãkete] *vi* (**a**) *(faire des recherches)* to hold an inquiry; *(police, journaliste)* to investigate; **e. sur qch** to investigate sth (**b**) *(faire un sondage)* to conduct a survey *(sur/auprès de* into/among)

enquêteur, -trice [ãkɛtœr, -tris] *nm,f* (**a**) *(policier)* investigator (**b**) *(sondeur)* researcher

enquiers, enquiert *voir* **enquérir**

enquiquinant, -e [ãkikinã, -ãt] *adj Fam (agaçant)* irritating, annoying

enquiquiner [ãkikine] *vt Fam (agacer)* to irritate, to annoy

enquiquineur, -euse [ãkikinœr, -øz] *nm,f Fam* nuisance, pain

enquis, -e *voir* **enquérir**

enraciné, -e [ãrasine] *adj (habitude, haine)* deep-rooted, deep-seated

enraciner [ãrasine] *s'enraciner vpr aussi Fig* to take root

enragé, -e [ãraʒe] **1** *adj (animal)* rabid **2** *nm,f Fam* fanatic

enrager [45] [ãraʒe] *vi* to be furious; **e. de devoir faire qch** to be really angry at having to do sth; **faire e. qn** *(taquiner)* to tease sb

enrayer [ãreje] [53] **1** *vt (machine)* to jam; *Fig (épidémie)* to check; *(inflation)* to curb **2** *s'enrayer vpr (machine)* to jam

enrégimenter [ãreʒimãte] *vt Péj (dans une organisation)* to enrol

enregistrement [ãrəʒistrəmã] *nm* (**a**) *(d'une naissance, d'un acte)* registration; *(de bagages)* check-in (**b**) *(disque)* recording; **e. vidéo** video recording; **e. sur bande/cassette** tape/cassette recording (**c**) *Ordinat (de données)* logging, recording; **e. de transactions** transaction logging

enregistrer [ãrəʒistre] **1** *vt* (**a**) *(naissance, acte)* to register; *(bagages)* to check in; **les meilleures ventes jamais enregistrées** the best sales ever recorded (**b**) *(disque, émission)* to record, to tape; *(données)* to store; *Ordinat* **programme enregistré** stored programme (**c**) *Fam (mémoriser)* to note, to register **2** *s'enregistrer vpr (personne)* to record oneself

enregistreur, -euse [ãrəʒistrœr, -øz] **1** *adj (appareil)* recording
2 *nm* recorder, recording device; *Belg* tape recorder
enrhumé, -e [ãryme] *adj* **être e.** to have a cold
enrhumer [ãryme] **s'enrhumer** *vpr* to catch a cold
enrichi, -e [ãriʃi] *adj* (**a**) *(personne)* wealthy (**b**) *(céréales)* enriched (**en** with)
enrichir [ãriʃir] **1** *vt (personne, pays)* to make richer; *Fig (collection)* to enhance (**de** with); *(esprit)* to enrich, to improve
2 s'enrichir *vpr* (**a**) *(personne, pays)* to get richer; *Fig (collection)* to be enhanced (**de** by) (**b**) **s'e. l'esprit** to improve one's mind
enrichissant, -e [ãriʃisã, -ãt] *adj (expérience)* rewarding
enrichissement [ãriʃismã] *nm* (**a**) *(en argent)* acquiring of wealth (**b**) *(de l'esprit, d'une collection)* enrichment
enrober [ãrɔbe] *vt* (**a**) *(bonbon)* to coat (**de** with) (**b**) *Hum* **il est un peu enrobé** he's a bit chubby
enrôlement [ãrolmã] *nm* enrolment; *(d'un soldat)* enlistment
enrôler [ãrole] **1** *vt* to enrol, to recruit; *(soldat)* to enlist
2 s'enrôler *vpr* to enrol; *(soldat)* to enlist
enroué, -e [ãrwe] *adj* hoarse, husky; **avoir la voix enrouée** to have a husky voice
enrouer [ãrwe] **1** *vt (voix, personne)* to make hoarse
2 s'enrouer *vpr* to get hoarse
enrouler [ãrule] **1** *vt* (**a**) *(rouler) (carte, tapis)* to roll up; *(câble, ruban)* to wind (**b**) *(envelopper)* to wrap up (**dans** in)
2 s'enrouler *vpr* (**a**) *(serpent)* to coil up; *(fil)* to wind (**b**) **s'e. dans une couverture** to wrap oneself up in a blanket
ENS [əɛnɛs] *nf (abrév* **École normale supérieure)** = university-level college preparing students for senior posts in teaching
ENSA [ɛnsa] *nf (abrév* **École nationale supérieure d'agronomie)** = one of five competitive-entry agricultural engineering schools
ensablement [ãsabləmã] *nm* (**a**) *(d'un port)* silting up (**b**) *(dépôt) (dû à l'eau)* sandbank; *(dû au vent)* sand dune
ensabler [ãsable] **1** *vt (port)* to silt up
2 s'ensabler *vpr* (**a**) *(véhicule)* to get stuck in the sand (**b**) *(port)* to silt up
ensanglanter [ãsãglãte] *vt* to cover with blood; **des mains ensanglantées** bloodstained *or* bloody hands; **un festival ensanglanté par un attentat** a festival marred by an attempted murder
enseignant, -e [ãsɛɲã, -ãt] **1** *nm,f* teacher
2 *adj* **le corps e.** the teaching profession
enseigne [ãsɛɲ] **1** *nf* (**a**) *(panonceau)* sign; **e. lumineuse** illuminated sign; *Fig* **nous sommes tous logés à la même e.** we're all in the same boat (**b**) *Littà* à **telle e. que…** so much so that…
2 *nm* **e. (de vaisseau)** *Br* sub-lieutenant, *Am* ensign
enseignement [ãsɛɲmã] *nm* (**a**) *(profession)* teaching; **être dans l'e.** to be a teacher (**b**) *(formation)* education; *Fig* **tirer un e. de qch** to learn a lesson from sth; **e. assisté par ordinateur** computer-aided learning; **e. par correspondance** distance learning; **e. primaire/secondaire** primary/secondary education; **e. professionnel/technique** vocational/technical education; **e. supérieur** higher education

enseigner [ãsɛɲe] **1** *vt* to teach; **e. qch à qn** to teach sb sth
2 *vi* to be a teacher, to teach
ensemble [ãsãbl] **1** *adv* together; **aller bien e.** *(personnes)* to be well matched; *(couleurs)* to go together; **ils sont partis tous e.** they left en masse; *Hum* **ne répondez pas tous e.** don't all answer at once
2 *nm* (**a**) *(totalité)* **l'e. des personnes présentes** all the people present; **l'e. de sa fortune** his whole fortune; **dans l'e.** on the whole (**b**) *(unité)* unity; **avec un parfait e.** *(répondre)* as one; *(danser)* in unison (**c**) *(groupe) (de gens)* group; *(d'objets, de faits)* set; *(de services)* package (**d**) *(tenue)* outfit; **e. pantalon** *Br* trouser suit, *Am* pant suit (**e**) *(immeubles)* block; **grand e.** residential estate (**f**) *Math* set
ensemblier [ãsãblije] *nm* interior designer; *(pour la télévision)* set designer
ensemencer [16] [ãsəmãse] *vt* (**a**) *(champ)* to sow (**b**) *Biol* to culture
ensevelir [ãsəvlir] *vt Litt* to bury
ensoleillé, -e [ãsɔleje] *adj* sunny
ensoleillement [ãsɔlejmã] *nm* **en raison de l'e. d'une pièce** because the room gets a lot of sun; **cinq heures d'e. par jour** five hours of sunshine a day; **jouir d'un e. exceptionnel** to get a lot of sun
ensommeillé, -e [ãsɔmeje] *adj* sleepy
ensorceler [42] [ãsɔrsəle] *vt* to cast *or* put a spell on; *Fig* to bewitch, to captivate
ensorcellement [ãsɔrsɛlmã] *nm (action)* bewitching; *(état)* bewitchment; *Fig (charme)* charm
ensuite [ãsɥit] *adv (plus tard)* later; *(puis)* then, next; **et e., qu'est-ce qu'on fait?** what do you do next?; *Fam* **d'abord, c'est très cher, et e. ça ne te va pas du tout** for one thing it's very expensive, and for another it doesn't suit you at all
ensuivre [65] [ãsɥivr] **s'ensuivre** *vpr* **jusqu'à ce que mort s'ensuive** until dead; **il s'ensuit que…** it follows that…; **et tout ce qui s'ensuit** and all that goes with it
entacher [ãtaʃe] *vt (réputation)* to sully
entaille [ãtaj] *nf* (**a**) *(dans du bois)* notch; *(longue)* groove (**b**) *(blessure)* gash; **se faire une e. au doigt** to cut one's finger open
entailler [ãtaje] *vt (blesser)* to gash
entame [ãtam] *nf* (**a**) *(de pain, de jambon)* first slice (**b**) *(aux cartes)* lead
entamer [ãtame] *vt* (**a**) *(blesser)* to cut into; *Fig (conviction, détermination)* to undermine (**b**) *(commencer) (pain, jambon)* to start on; *(bouteille, pot de confiture)* to open; *(travail, recherches, conversation, négociations)* to start; *(démarches)* to initiate; *(poursuites)* to institute (**c**) *(aux cartes)* **e. à trèfle** to open clubs
entartrer [ãtartre] **1** *vt (chaudière)* to fur (up)
2 s'entartrer *vpr (chaudière)* to fur (up); *(dents)* to scale up
entassement [ãtasmã] *nm* (**a**) *(de pierres) (action)* piling up; *(tas)* pile (**b**) *(de passagers, du bétail)* crowding together
entasser [ãtase] **1** *vt* (**a**) *(pierres, livres, vêtements)* to pile up (**b**) *(passagers, bétail)* to crowd together
2 s'entasser *vpr* (**a**) *(objets)* to pile up (**b**) *(personnes)* to crowd together
entendement [ãtãdmã] *nm* **dépasser l'e.** to be beyond comprehension
entendeur [ãtãdœr] *nm* **à bon e., salut!** mark my words!

entendre [ãtãdr] **1** *vt* (**a**) *(ouïr)* to hear; **je n'entends rien (de ce que tu dis)** I can't hear a thing (you're saying); **je l'entends rire** I can hear him laughing; **e. dire que...** to hear that...; **e. qn dire qch** to hear sb say sth; **e. parler de** *(connaître l'existence de)* to hear of; *(être au courant de)* to hear about; **elle ne veut pas en e. parler!** she doesn't want to hear another word about it!; **il va m'e.!** I'll give him a talking-to!; **elle répétait à qui voulait l'e. que...** she'd tell anyone who'd listen that...; *Fam* **ce qu'il ne faut pas e.!** I've heard it all now!
(**b**) *(écouter) (témoin, suppliant)* to hear; **e. qn en confession** to hear sb's confession; **à vous e., il a eu tort** from what you say, he was in the wrong; **il n'a rien voulu e.** he wouldn't listen; **que Dieu vous entende** may God answer your prayers
(**c**) *(comprendre)* to understand; **laisser e. qch** to imply sth; **elle m'a laissé e. que...** she gave me to understand that...; **ce n'est pas ainsi qu'il l'entend** he doesn't see it like that
(**d**) *(vouloir dire)* to mean; **qu'entendez-vous par là?** what do you mean by that?
(**e**) *(vouloir)* **e. faire qch** to intend *or* mean to do sth; **faites comme vous l'entendez** do as you think best; **il ne l'entendait pas ainsi** he wouldn't hear of it
2 *vi* to hear; **e. mal** to be hard of hearing; **j'ai mal entendu!** *(je n'ai pas entendu)* I didn't hear you properly!; *(je suis choqué)* I don't think I heard you right!; **tu entends?** *(menace)* got it?
3 **s'entendre** *vpr* (**a**) *(sympathiser)* to get on (**avec** with)
(**b**) *(se mettre d'accord)* to agree; **entendons-nous bien!** let's be clear about this!
(**c**) *(être entendu)* to be heard; **on ne s'entend plus ici** you can't hear yourself think in here
(**d**) *(être compris)* to be understood
(**e**) **s'e. aux affaires** to have a good head for business; **il s'y entend** he knows what he's talking about
entendu, -e [ãtãdy] *adj* (**a**) *(complice) (sourire)* knowing; **d'un air e.** knowingly (**b**) *(décidé)* (**c'est**) **e.!** fine!, all right! (**c**) **bien e.** of course
entente [ãtãt] *nf* (**a**) *(accord)* agreement, understanding (**entre** between) (**b**) *(harmonie)* **bonne e.** harmony
entériner [ãterine] *vt* to ratify
entérite [ãterit] *nf Méd* enteritis
enterrement [ãtɛrmã] *nm* (**a**) *(mise en terre)* burial (**b**) *(cérémonie)* funeral; *Fam* **faire une tête d'e.** to look miserable (**c**) *(cortège)* funeral procession
enterrer [ãtere] **1** *vt* (**a**) *(trésor, corps)* to bury; *Hum* **il nous enterrera tous** he'll outlive us all (**b**) *Fig (projet)* to scrap; *(affaire)* to bury; **e. sa vie de garçon** to have a stag party
2 **s'enterrer** *vpr Fig* to hide oneself away
entêtant, -e [ãtɛtã, -ãt] *adj (parfum, musique)* heady
en-tête (*pl* **en-têtes**) [ãtɛt] *nm* heading; *Ordinat* header
entêté, -e [ãtete] **1** *adj* obstinate, stubborn
2 *nm,f* obstinate *or* stubborn person
entêtement [ãtɛtmã] *nm* obstinacy, stubbornness; **e. à faire qch** persistence in doing sth
entêter [ãtete] **s'entêter** *vpr* to persist; **s'e. à faire qch** to persist in doing sth
enthousiasmant, -e [ãtuzjasmã, -ãt] *adj* exciting
enthousiasme [ãtuzjasm] *nm* enthusiasm (**pour** for); **avec e.** enthusiastically; **sans e.** unenthusiastically

enthousiasmer [ãtuzjasme] **1** *vt (personne)* to fill with enthusiasm
2 **s'enthousiasmer** *vpr* to get enthusiastic (**pour** about)
enthousiaste [ãtuzjast] **1** *adj* enthusiastic
2 *nmf* enthusiast
enticher [ãtiʃe] **s'enticher** *vpr* **s'e. de qn/qch** to become infatuated with sb/sth
entier, -ère [ãtje, -ɛr] **1** *adj* (**a**) *(complet)* whole, entire; **la France entière** the whole of France; **il a mangé le gâteau tout e.** he ate the whole cake; **des heures entières** for hours on end; **le mystère reste e.** the mystery remains unsolved (**b**) *(responsabilité)* full; *(confiance)* complete; **jouir d'une entière liberté** to have absolute freedom; **donner entière satisfaction à qn** *(produit)* to give sb complete satisfaction (**c**) *(sans compromis) (personne)* uncompromising (**d**) *Math (nombre)* whole
2 *nm* (**a**) **j'ai écouté le disque en e.** I listened to the whole record; **elle a lu le livre en e.** she read the whole book; **le pays dans son e.** the whole country (**b**) *Math (nombre)* integer, whole number
entièrement [ãtjɛrmã] *adv* entirely; **je ne l'ai pas lu e.** I didn't read all of it
entité [ãtite] *nf* entity
entonner [ãtɔne] *vt* to start singing
entonnoir [ãtɔnwar] *nm* funnel
entorse [ãtɔrs] *nf* sprain, wrench; **se faire une e. au poignet** to sprain one's wrist; *Fig* **faire une e. au règlement** to stretch the rules; **faire une e. a son régime** to break one's diet
entortiller [ãtɔrtije] **1** *vt (envelopper)* to wrap (**dans** in); *(enrouler)* to wind (**autour de** round)
2 **s'entortiller** *vpr* (**a**) *(serpent, lierre)* to coil (**autour de** round) (**b**) *(s'empêtrer)* to get tangled up (**dans** in) (**c**) *(s'enrouler)* to wrap oneself up (**dans** in)
entour [ãtur] *nm* **à l'e. de** round
entourage [ãturaʒ] *nm (amis)* circle (of friends); *(de ministre, de souverain)* entourage; **dans son e. proche** amongst those close to him
entourer [ãture] **1** *vt* (**a**) *(border, enceindre)* to surround (**de** with) (**b**) *(être autour de)* to surround; **les gens qui vous entourent** the people around *or* about you; **le monde qui nous entoure** the world about us; **entouré de mystère** shrouded in mystery; **un rang de perles entourait son cou** she had a string of pearls round her neck (**c**) *(soutenir) (personne)* to rally round; **elle est très entourée** she has a lot of people she can turn to for support
2 **s'entourer** *vpr* **s'e. d'amis/de belles choses** to surround oneself with friends/with beautiful things
entouloupe [ãturlup], **entourloupette** [ãturlupɛt] *nf Fam* dirty trick; **faire une e. à qn** to play a dirty trick on sb
entournure [ãturnyr] *nf Fam* **être gêné aux entournures** *(mal à l'aise)* to feel awkward; *(financièrement)* to feel the pinch
entracte [ãtrakt] *nm* intermission, *Br* interval
entraide [ãtrɛd] *nf* mutual aid
entraider [ãtrede] **s'entraider** *vpr* to help one another
entrailles [ãtraj] *nfpl* entrails
entrain [ãtrɛ̃] *nm* get-up-and-go; **être plein d'e.** to be full of life; **travailler avec e.** to beaver away; **faire qch sans e.** to do sth half-heartedly
entraînant, -e [ãtrɛnã, -ãt] *adj (air, rythme)* lively

entraînement [ɑ̃trɛnmɑ̃] *nm* (**a**) *(en sport)* training; **un e.** a training session; **à l'e.** in training; **avoir de l'e.** to be well trained; **manquer d'e.** to be out of practice (**b**) *Tech* drive

entraîner [ɑ̃trene] **1** *vt* (**a**) *(sujet: rivière)* to carry away; *(sujet: locomotive)* to pull; **e. qn quelque part** to take sb off somewhere; **il l'a entraîné dans sa chute** he dragged him down with him (**b**) *(exercer une influence sur)* to influence; **e. qn à faire qch** to lead sb to do sth; **e. qn dans un piège** to lure sb into a trap; **se laisser e.** to allow oneself to be led astray (**c**) *(causer) (dépense, modification)* to entail, to lead to; **e. un retard** to result in a delay (**d**) *(athlète, équipe)* to coach, to train; *(cheval)* to train; **e. qn à faire qch** to train sb to do sth (**e**) *Tech* to drive
2 s'entraîner *vpr (athlète)* to train; **s'e. à faire qch** to practise doing sth

entraîneur [ɑ̃trɛnœr] *nm (d'un athlète, d'une équipe)* coach; *(d'un cheval)* trainer

entraîneuse [ɑ̃trɛnøz] *nf* (**a**) *(de boîte de nuit)* hostess (**b**) *(d'un athlète, d'une équipe)* coach; *(d'un cheval)* trainer

entrapercevoir [60] [ɑ̃trapɛrsəvwar] *vt* to catch a fleeting glimpse of

entrave [ɑ̃trav] *nf (obstacle)* hindrance, impediment (**à** to)

entraver [ɑ̃trave] *vt* (**a**) *(mouvement, processus)* to hinder, to impede (**b**) *Fam* **j'y entrave que dalle** it beats me

entre [ɑ̃tr] *prép* (**a**) *(au milieu de)* between; *Fig* **e. les deux** *(ni l'un ni l'autre)* in between; **être e. la vie et la mort** to hover between life and death; **être e. deux âges** to be middle-aged; *Fig* **faire qch e. deux portes** to do sth in passing
(**b**) *(parmi)* among(st); **hésiter e. plusieurs solutions** to hesitate between several solutions; **plusieurs d'e. nous** several of us; **être dangereux e. tous** to be extremely dangerous; **e. autres** among others
(**c**) *(rapport réciproque) (deux personnes)* between; *(plus de deux personnes)* among(st); **se marier e. cousins** to intermarry with cousins; **ils se battent e. eux** they fight with each other; **qu'y a-t-il e. eux exactement?** what exactly is going on between them?; **soit dit e. nous** between you and me; *Fam* **il faut que je te parle e. quat'z'yeux** I've got to talk to you in private
(**d**) *(dans)* **tenir qch e. ses mains** to hold sth in one's hands; **e. ces murs** within these walls
(**e**) *(à travers)* through; **se faufiler e. les arbres** to thread one's way through the trees

entrebâillement [ɑ̃trəbajmɑ̃] *nm* **par l'e. de la porte** through the half-open door

entrebâiller [ɑ̃trəbaje] *vt (porte, fenêtre)* to half-open; **la porte était entrebâillée** the door was ajar

entrechat [ɑ̃trəʃa] *nm (pas de danse)* entrechat

entrechoquer [ɑ̃trəʃɔke] **1** *vt* to knock together; **e. des verres** to chink glasses
2 s'entrechoquer *vpr* to knock against one another; *(verres)* to chink

entrecôte [ɑ̃trəkot] *nf* rib steak; **e. à la bordelaise** rib steak in a shallots and red wine sauce

entrecoupé, -e [ɑ̃trəkupe] *adj (voix)* broken

entrecouper [ɑ̃trəkupe] *vt* to interrupt (**de** with)

entrecroiser [ɑ̃trəkrwaze] **1** *vt (ligne)* to intersect; *(fils)* to interlace

2 s'entrecroiser *vpr (lignes, routes)* to intersect; *(fils)* to interlace

entre-déchirer [ɑ̃trədeʃire] **s'entre-déchirer** *vpr* to tear each other to pieces

entre-deux [ɑ̃trədø] *nm inv* (**a**) *(intervalle)* intervening period (**b**) *Sport* jump ball

entre-deux-guerres [ɑ̃trədøgɛr] *nm inv* **l'e.** the inter-war period

entre-dévorer [ɑ̃trədevɔre] **s'entre-dévorer** *vpr* to devour one another *or* each other

entrée [ɑ̃tre] *nf* (**a**) *(action)* entry, entrance; *(de marchandises)* import; **faire son e.** to make one's entrance; **l'e. de la Norvège dans la CE** Norway's entry into the EC; **avant mon e. à l'université** before I went to university; **e. en scène** entrance (on to the stage); **e. en fonction** assumption of one's duties; **e. en matière** introduction; **e. en vigueur** coming into force; *Fig* **à l'e. de l'hiver** at the beginning of winter; *Fig* **d'e. (de jeu)** from the outset
(**b**) *(accès)* admission, admittance (**dans** *ou* **de** to); **avoir ses entrées dans un lieu** to have contacts in a place; **e. à l'hôpital** admission into hospital; **e. interdite** *(sur panneau)* no admittance, no entry; **e. libre** *(dans un musée)* admission free; *(dans une boutique)* browsers welcome
(**c**) *(voie d'accès)* way in, entrance (**de** to); *(vestibule)* entrance hall; **e. des artistes** stage door; **e. principale** main entrance; **e. de service** service entrance
(**d**) *(hors-d'œuvre)* starter
(**e**) **faire 1000 entrées** *(film)* to sell 1,000 tickets
(**f**) *Ordinat (processus)* input, entry; *(information)* entry; *(touche)* enter (key); **données d'e.** input (data); **e. (par le) clavier** keyboard input; **e. de gamme** entry level; **e. de papier** paper input; **e./sortie** input/output; **e./sortie parallèles** parallel input/output

entrefaites [ɑ̃trəfɛt] *nfpl* **sur ces e.** at that moment

entrefilet [ɑ̃trəfilɛ] *nm* short (news) item

entrejambe [ɑ̃trəʒɑ̃b] *nm* crotch

entrelacer [16] [ɑ̃trəlase] **1** *vt (rubans, branches)* to intertwine; *Ordinat* **écran entrelacé** interlaced screen
2 s'entrelacer *vpr* to intertwine

entrelacs [ɑ̃trəla] *nm* interlaced design, tracery

entrelarder [ɑ̃trəlarde] *vt Culin (viande)* to lard; *Fig* **e. un discours de citations** to lace a speech with quotations

entremêler [ɑ̃trəmele] **1** *vt* to interweave (**de** with)
2 s'entremêler *vpr* to be interwoven

entremets [ɑ̃trəmɛ] *nm* dessert, *Br* sweet

entremetteur, -euse [ɑ̃trəmɛtœr, -øz] *nm,f* go-between

entremise [ɑ̃trəmiz] *nf* intervention; **par l'e. de qn** through sb

entrepont [ɑ̃trəpɔ̃] *nm* 'tweendecks; *(pour voyageurs)* steerage

entreposer [ɑ̃trəpoze] *vt* to store; *(marchandises)* to warehouse

entrepôt [ɑ̃trəpo] *nm* warehouse

entreprenant, -e [ɑ̃trəprənɑ̃, -ɑ̃t] *adj* enterprising; *(auprès des femmes)* forward

entreprendre [58] [ɑ̃trəprɑ̃dr] *vt* (**a**) *(commencer)* to undertake; **e. des démarches** to take steps; **e. de faire qch** to undertake to do sth (**b**) *(entretenir)* **e. qn sur qch** to engage sb in conversation about sth

entrepreneur, -euse [ɑ̃trəprənœr, -øz] *nm,f* (**a**) *(dans le bâtiment)* contractor (**b**) *(patron)* entrepreneur (**c**) **e. de pompes funèbres** *Br* undertaker, *Am* mortician

entrepris, -e *voir* entreprendre

entreprise [ãtrəpriz] *nf* (**a**) *(action, initiative)* enterprise, undertaking; **la libre e.** free enterprise (**b**) *(firme)* company, firm; **e. privée** private company; **e. publique** public corporation

entrer [ãtre] **1** *vi* (*aux* être) (**a**) *(aller)* to go in, to enter; *(venir)* to come in, to enter; **e. dans qch** to go/come into sth, to enter sth; **e. dans une voiture/un ascenseur** to get into a car/lift; **e. par la fenêtre** to get in *or* enter through the window; **e. en courant** to run in; **e. sans payer** to get in without paying; **e. en gare** to come into the station; **e. au port** to come into harbour; **laisser e. qn/qch** to let sb/sth in; **empêcher qn d'e.** to keep sb out; **faire e. qn** to let sb in; *(sujet: secrétaire, majordome)* to show sb in; **faire e. qch dans une pièce** to get sth into a room; *Théât* **Hamlet entre en scène** enter Hamlet; **entrez!** come/go in!

(**b**) *(pénétrer) (eau, air)* to go/come in; **le clou entra dans le mur** the nail went into the wall; **la clef n'entre pas dans la serrure** the key won't go in the lock

(**c**) *(heurter)* **e. dans qch** to go into sth, to run into sth; *Fam* **e. dans le décor** to go off the road

(**d**) *(faire tenir)* **faire e. qch dans qch** to insert sth in sth; **on n'y entrera jamais à vingt** we'll never get twenty people in; **il n'entre pas dans le carton** it won't go in the box

(**e**) *(devenir membre)* **e. dans l'armée** to join the army; **e. en religion** to take (holy) orders; **e. aux PTT/chez Renault** to start working for the Post Office/for Renault; **e. au service de qn** to enter sb's service; **e. dans la Communauté européenne** to join the European Community

(**f**) *(être admis)* **e. à l'université** to go to university; **e. à l'hôpital** to go into hospital; **e. en maternelle** to start nursery school

(**g**) *(faire partie de)* **e. dans une catégorie** to fall into a category; **e. dans la légende** to become a legend; **e. dans l'histoire** to go down in history; **e. en ligne de compte** to be taken into account; **e. dans les projets de qn** to be part of sb's plans; **e. dans la vie de qn** to come into sb's life; **e. dans la composition de qch** to go into the making of sth; **cela n'entre pas dans mes idées** I don't go along with that

(**h**) *(commencer)* **e. dans une colère terrible** to get extremely angry; **e. en campagne** *Mil* to take the field; *Pol* to go on the campaign trail; **e. en guerre** to enter the war; **e. en fonction** to take up one's duties; **e. en vigueur** to come into force *or* effect; **e. dans la vie active** to start one's working life; **e. dans une ère nouvelle** to enter a new era; **e. dans les détails** to go into detail; **on entre dans l'hiver** winter is just beginning

(**i**) *Ordinat* to log in *or* on

2 *vt* (*aux* avoir) (**a**) *(introduire)* **e. des marchandises en fraude** to smuggle in goods

(**b**) *(enfoncer)* **e. ses ongles dans le cou de qn** to sink one's nails into sb's neck

(**c**) *Ordinat (données)* to enter, to input; *(au clavier)* to key in

3 *v impersonnel* **il n'entre pas dans mes projets de le faire** it's not part of my plans to do it

entresol [ãtrəsɔl] *nm* mezzanine (floor)

entre-temps [ãtrətã] *adv* meanwhile, in the meantime

entretenir [70] [ãtrətənir] **1** *vt* (**a**) *(soigner) (maison, jardin, routes, machine)* to maintain; **une moquette facile à e.** a carpet which is easy to look after; **e. sa**

---

forme to keep fit (**b**) *(payer pour) (famille, maîtresse)* to maintain, to support (**c**) *(maintenir)* **e. une correspondance avec qn** to keep up a correspondence with sb; **e. de bonnes relations avec qn** to remain on good terms with sb; **cela entretient leur amitié** that keeps their friendship going *or* alive (**d**) *(parler à)* **e. qn de qch** to converse with sb about sth

2 s'entretenir *vpr* **s'e. avec qn (de qch)** to converse with sb (about sth)

entretenu, -e [ãtrətəny] *adj* (**a**) **bien/mal e.** *(maison, jardin)* well-kept/badly kept (**b**) **une femme entretenue** a kept woman

entretien [ãtrətjɛ̃] *nm* (**a**) *(soins) (d'une maison, d'un jardin, des routes, d'une machine)* maintenance; **facile/difficile d'e., d'e. facile/difficile** easy/difficult to maintain; **produits d'e.** (household) cleaning materials (**b**) *(subsistance) (d'une famille, d'une armée)* support, maintenance (**c**) *(conversation)* conversation; *(audience)* interview; **entretiens** *(négociations)* discussions, talks

entre-tuer [ãtrətɥe] **s'entre-tuer** *vpr* to kill each other

entreverrai *etc voir* entrevoir

entrevoir [73a] [ãtrəvwar] *vt (rapidement)* to catch sight of, to catch a glimpse of; *(indistinctement)* to make out; **e. des difficultés** to foresee difficulties

entrevoyons *etc voir* entrevoir

entrevu, -e *voir* entrevoir

entrevue [ãtrəvy] *nf (rendez-vous)* interview; *(réunion)* meeting

entrouvert, -e [ãtruvɛr, -ɛrt] *adj* half-open

entrouvrir [52] [ãtruvrir] **1** *vt* to half-open

2 s'entrouvrir *vpr* to half-open

entuber [ãtybe] *vt Fam (duper)* to con; **se faire e.** to be conned

énumération [enymerasjɔ̃] *nf* listing

énumérer [34] [enymere] *vt* to list

envahir [ãvair] *vt (pays)* to invade; *(marché)* to flood; **un jardin envahi par les mauvaises herbes** a garden overgrown with weeds; *Fig* **un doute m'a envahi** I was overcome with doubt; *Fam* **e. qn** *(sujet: personne)* to intrude on sb

envahissant, -e [ãvaisã, -ãt] *adj (plantes)* invasive; *(odeur)* overwhelming; *Fam (personne)* intrusive

envahisseur [ãvaisœr] *nm* invader

enveloppant, -e [ãvlɔpã, -ãt] *adj* (**a**) *(couvrant)* **regard e.** look that takes/took everything in (**b**) *Fig (séduisant) (manières)* captivating

enveloppe [ãvlɔp] *nf* (**a**) *(de lettre)* envelope; **e. à fenêtre** window envelope; **envoyer qch sous e.** to send sth under cover; *Fig* **e. budgétaire** budget; *Fig* **l'e. de la recherche** the research budget (**b**) *(de paquet)* wrapping (**c**) *(de graines)* husk (**d**) *Fig (apparence)* **sous une e. de rudesse** beneath a rough exterior

enveloppé, -e [ãvlɔpe] *adj Fam* **(bien) e.** *(personne)* well-padded

envelopper [ãvlɔpe] **1** *vt* (**a**) *(marchandises, bébé)* to wrap (up); **enveloppé dans des bandages** swathed in bandages (**b**) *(entourer)* **e. qch du regard** to take sth in with one's gaze; **la nuit nous enveloppa** darkness closed in on us; **enveloppé de mystère/brume** shrouded in mystery/mist

2 s'envelopper *vpr* **s'e. dans une couverture** to wrap oneself up in a blanket

envenimer [ãvənime] **1** *vt (plaie)* to make septic; *Fig (querelle, discussion)* to embitter

2 s'envenimer *vpr (plaie)* to turn septic; *Fig (querelle, discussion)* to get acrimonious

envergure [ãvergyr] *nf* (**a**) *(d'un oiseau, d'un avion)* wingspan (**b**) *Fig (ampleur)* scope; **de grande e., d'e.** *(réforme)* far-reaching; *(opération)* large-scale (**c**) *(de personne)* calibre; **manquer d'e.** to be of a low calibre

enverrai *etc voir* **envoyer**

envers¹ [ãver] *nm (d'un document, d'une assiette)* back; *(d'une médaille, d'une pièce)* reverse; **à l'e.** *(l'extérieur à l'intérieur)* inside out; *(de haut en bas)* the wrong way up, upside down; *(devant derrière)* the wrong way round, back to front; *Fig* **l'e. du décor** the other side of the picture; *Fam* **c'est le monde à l'e.!** what's the world coming to!

envers² *prép* towards; **e. et contre tous** in the face of all opposition

envi [ãvi] **à l'envi** *adv* **faire qch à l'e.** to vie with one another in doing sth

enviable [ãvjabl] *adj* enviable

envie [ãvi] *nf* (**a**) *(désir)* desire; *(caprice)* craving (**de** for); **avoir (très) e. de qch/de faire qch** to (really) want sth/to do sth; **avoir e. de dormir** to feel sleepy; **avoir envie de rire/pleurer** to feel like laughing/crying; **être pris d'une terrible e. de rire** to have a terrible urge to laugh; **donner à qn l'e. de faire qch** to make sb want to do sth; **il a e. que je le fasse** he wants me to do it; **je vais lui ôter l'e. de s'amuser** I'll stop her messing around; **ce gâteau me fait e.** that cake is tempting; **avoir e. de qn** *(sexuellement)* to want or desire sb; **faire e. à qn** *(sujet: personne)* to tempt sb; *Fam* **ça lui a pris comme une e. de pisser** he just got a sudden urge (**b**) *(jalousie)* envy; **regarder qch avec e.** to look enviously at sth (**c**) *(au doigt)* hangnail; *(sur la peau)* birthmark

envier [66] [ãvje] *vt* to envy; **e. qch à qn** to envy sb sth; **n'avoir rien à e. à personne** to have no cause to be envious of anyone

envieux, -euse [ãvjø, -øz] **1** *adj* envious (**de** of)
  2 *nm,f* envious person; **faire des e.** to make people envious

environ [ãvirõ] **1** *adv (à peu près)* about, around
  2 environs *nmpl (alentours)* surrounding area; **aux** *ou* **dans les environs de Paris** in the vicinity of Paris; **aux environs de cinq heures** round about five o'clock

environnant, -e [ãvironã, -ãt] *adj* surrounding

environnement [ãvironmã] *nm* (**a**) *(milieu)* environment (**b**) *Ordinat* environment; **e. partagé** shared environment

environner [ãvirone] **1** *vt* to surround; **environné de qch** surrounded by sth
  2 s'environner *vpr* **s'e. de** to surround oneself with

envisageable [ãvizaʒabl] *adj* conceivable

envisager [45] [ãvizaʒe] *vt (considérer) (question, situation, solution)* to consider; *(projeter) (conséquence, événement)* to envisage; **e. l'avenir** to foresee the future; **e. de faire qch** to consider doing sth

envoi [ãvwa] *nm* (**a**) *(action)* sending; **e. recommandé** recorded delivery (**b**) *(colis)* parcel; *(lettre)* letter; *(marchandises)* consignment (**de** of)

envol [ãvɔl] *nm (d'avion)* take-off; *(d'oiseau)* taking off

envolée [ãvɔle] *nf* flight; *Fig* **e. lyrique** flight of fancy; *Fig* **l'e. du dollar** the soaring price of the dollar

envoler [ãvɔle] **s'envoler** *vpr* (**a**) *(oiseau)* to fly away; *(avion)* to take off; **je m'envole dans une heure** my plane leaves in an hour; *Fig* **s'e. dans les sondages** to shoot up the opinion polls (**b**) *(emporté par le vent)*

(chapeau) to blow off; *(papiers)* to blow away (**c**) *Fam (disparaître) (personne, sac)* to vanish

envoûtant, -e [ãvutã, -ãt] *adj (fascinant)* bewitching

envoûtement [ãvutmã] *nm aussi Fig* bewitchment

envoûter [ãvute] *vt aussi Fig* to bewitch

envoyé, -e [ãvwaje] *nm,f (messager)* messenger; *(d'un gouvernement)* envoy; **e. spécial** *(journaliste)* special correspondent

envoyer [33] [ãvwaje] **1** *vt* to send; *(lancer)* to throw; **e. qch par courrier** to mail sth, *Br* to post sth; **e. qch à qn** to send sb sth; *(lancer)* to throw sth to sb; **e. un baiser à qn** to blow sb a kiss; **e. chercher qn** to send for sb; **e. qn faire qch** to send sb to do sth; *Fam* **e. promener** *ou* **balader** *ou* **paître qn, e. qn sur les roses** to send sb packing; *Fam* **je vais tout e. promener** I'm going to chuck it all in; *Fig* **e. des fleurs à qn** to pat sb on the back
  2 s'envoyer *vpr* (**a**) *(l'un l'autre)* **ils s'envoient des cartes postales** they send postcards to each other; *Fig* **s'e. des fleurs** *(mutuellement)* to sing one another's praises, to pat one another on the back; *(à soi-même)* to pat oneself on the back (**b**) *Fam* **s'e. un verre de vin** to knock back a glass of wine; *très Fam* **s'e. qn** *Br* to have it off with sb, *Am* to make it with sb; *très Fam* **s'e. en l'air** *Br* to have it off, *Am* to make it

envoyeur, -euse [ãvwajœr, -øz] *nm,f* sender; **retour à l'e.** return to sender

enzyme [ãzim] *nf* enzyme; **lessive aux enzymes** biological washing powder

éolien, -enne [eɔljẽ, -ɛn] **1** *adj* **énergie éolienne** wind energy; **moteur é.** wind-powered engine
  2 *nf* **éolienne** wind turbine

épagneul, -e [epaɲœl] *nm,f* spaniel; **é. breton** Brittany spaniel

épais, -aisse [epɛ, -ɛs] **1** *adj* thick; **é. de 2 mètres** 2 metres thick; *Fam* **elle n'est pas bien épaisse** she hasn't got much on her
  2 *adv* (**a**) *(pousser)* thick(ly) (**b**) *Fam (beaucoup)* **il n'y en a pas é.** there's not much of it
  3 *nm* **au plus é. de la forêt** in the depths of the forest

épaisseur [epɛsœr] *nf* thickness; *Fig (d'une personne)* depth; **avoir 2 mètres d'é.** to be 2 metres thick

épaissir [epesir] **1** *vt (sauce, peinture)* to thicken; *(ombre, mystère)* to deepen
  2 *vi (sauce)* to thicken; *(personne)* to fill out
  3 s'épaissir *vpr (cheveux, brouillard, sauce)* to thicken; *(personne)* to fill out; *(ombre, mystère)* to deepen

épaississant [epesisã] *nm (substance)* thickener

épaississement [epesismã] *nm (du brouillard, d'une sauce)* thickening

épanchement [epãʃmã] *nm* (**a**) **é. de synovie** water on the knee (**b**) *Fig (de sentiments)* outpouring

épancher [epãʃe] **1** *vt* **é. sa bile** to vent one's spleen; **é. son cœur** to pour out one's heart
  2 s'épancher *vpr (personne)* to pour out one's heart

épandage [epãdaʒ] *nm Agr* manure spreading, manuring

épandre [epãdr] **1** *vt Agr* to spread
  2 s'épandre *vpr Litt* to spread (**sur** over)

épanoui, -e [epanwi] *adj (fleur)* in full bloom; *(visage, sourire)* beaming; *(personne)* well-adjusted

épanouir [epanwir] **1** *vt (fleur, pétales)* to open out
  2 s'épanouir *vpr* (**a**) *(fleur)* to bloom (**b**) *(visage)* to light up (**c**) *(personne)* to blossom

épanouissant, -e [epanwisã, -ãt] *adj (travail, vie)* fulfilling

épanouissement [epanwismã] *nm* (**a**) *(action) (d'une fleur)* blooming; *(d'un visage)* lighting up; *(d'une personne)* blossoming (**b**) *(plénitude)* full bloom

épargnant, -e [eparɲã, -ãt] *nm,f* saver; **les petits épargnants** small investors

épargne [eparɲ] *nf* (**a**) *(action, vertu)* saving (**b**) *(sommes)* savings (**c**) *(épargnants)* **l'é. privée** private investors

épargner [eparɲe] **1** *vt* (**a**) *(argent, provisions)* to save (**b**) *(énergie, temps)* to save; **é. à qn la peine de faire qch** to save sb the trouble of doing sth; **épargne-moi les détails!** spare me the details! (**c**) *(prisonnier)* to spare
2 *vi* to save (**sur** on)
3 s'épargner *vpr* **s'é. la peine de faire qch** to save oneself the trouble of doing sth

éparpiller [eparpije] **1** *vt (objets, foule)* to scatter
2 s'éparpiller *vpr (objets, foule)* to scatter; *Fig (personne)* to take on too much

épars, -e [epar, -ars] *adj (maisons)* scattered; *(végétation, population, informations)* sparse; *(cheveux)* thin

épatant, -e [epatã, -ãt] *adj Fam* splendid

épaté, -e [epate] *adj Fam* dumbfounded

épater [epate] *vt Fam* to astound

épaule [epol] *nf* shoulder; **être large d'épaules** to be broad-shouldered; *Culin* **é. d'agneau** shoulder of lamb

épauler [epole] **1** *vt* (**a**) *(fusil)* to raise to one's shoulder (**b**) *(aider)* **é. qn** to back sb up
2 *vi* to take aim

épaulette [epolɛt] *nf* (**a**) *(rembourrage)* shoulder pad (**b**) *(bretelle)* shoulder strap

épave [epav] *nf aussi Fig* wreck

épée [epe] *nf* sword; *Sport* épée; **coup d'é.** swordthrust; *Fig* **un coup d'é. dans l'eau** a wasted effort; *Fig* **une é. de Damoclès** a Sword of Damocles

épeler [42] [eple] *vt & vi* to spell

éperdu, -e [epɛrdy] *adj (regard)* distraught; *(amour)* passionate

éperdument [epɛrdymã] *adv (aimer)* madly; **é. amoureux** head over heels in love, madly in love; *Fam* **je m'en fiche é.** I couldn't care less

éperlan [epɛrlã] *nm* smelt

éperon [eprɔ̃] *nm* spur

éperonner [eprɔne] *vt* to spur on

épervier [epɛrvje] *nm* sparrowhawk

épeurant, -e [epœrã, -ãt] *adj Can* scary, frightening

éphèbe [efɛb] *nm* Adonis

éphémère [efemɛr] **1** *adj* short-lived, ephemeral
2 *nm* mayfly

épi [epi] *nm* (**a**) *(de grain)* ear; *(de fleur)* spike; **é. de maïs** corncob (**b**) *(de cheveux)* tuft of hair

épice [epis] *nf* spice; **quatre épices** allspice

épicé, -e [epise] *adj* spicy

épicéa [episea] *nm* spruce

épicentre [episãtr] *nm* epicentre

épicer [epise] *vt* to spice

épicerie [episri] *nf* (**a**) *(magasin)* grocer's (shop); **é. fine** delicatessen (**b**) *(produits)* groceries (**c**) *Can Fig* **liste d'é.** *(de griefs)* shopping list

épicier, -ère [episje, -ɛr] *nm,f* grocer; *Péj* **d'é.** *(mentalité)* small-town, parochial

épicurien, -enne [epikyrjɛ̃, -ɛn] **1** *adj* epicurean; *Phil* Epicurean
2 *nm,f* epicure; *Phil* Epicurean

épidémie [epidemi] *nf* epidemic

épidémique [epidemik] *adj* epidemic

épiderme [epidɛrm] *nm* skin, *Spéc* epidermis

épidermique [epidɛrmik] *adj* epidermal; *Fig* **une réaction é.** a kneejerk reaction

épier [66] [epje] *vt (espionner) (personne, activités)* to spy on; *(observer) (signe, occasion)* to watch out for

épilation [epilasjɔ̃] *nf (des jambes)* removal of unwanted hair; *(des sourcils)* plucking

épilatoire [epilatwar] *adj (crème)* hair-removing

épilepsie [epilɛpsi] *nf* epilepsy; **crise d'é.** epileptic fit

épileptique [epilɛptik] *adj & nmf* epileptic

épiler [epile] **1** *vt (jambes)* to remove the unwanted hair from; *(sourcils)* to pluck
2 s'épiler *vpr* **s'é. les jambes** to remove the unwanted hair from one's legs; **s'é. les sourcils** to pluck one's eyebrows; **s'é. les jambes à la cire** to wax one's legs

épilogue [epilɔg] *nm* epilogue

épiloguer [epilɔge] *vi* to hold forth (**sur** about)

épinard [epinar] *nm (plante)* spinach; **épinards** spinach; **épinards en branches** leaf spinach

épine [epin] *nf (piquant)* thorn; *(d'un animal)* spine, prickle; *Fig* **tirer une é. du pied à qn** *(tirer d'embarras)* to get sb out of a mess; *(soulager)* to relieve sb's mind; **é. dorsale** backbone

épinette [epinɛt] *nf* (**a**) *Can Bot* spruce (**b**) *(instrument)* spinet

épineux, -euse [epinø, -øz] *adj (arbuste, problème)* thorny; *(poisson)* spiny

épingle [epɛ̃gl] *nf* pin; **attacher qch avec des épingles** *(cheveux)* to pin sth up; *(tissu, feuilles)* to pin sth together; *Fig* **tirer son é. du jeu** to extricate oneself; *Fig* **être tiré à quatre épingles** to be dressed up to the nines; *Fig* **chercher une é. dans une botte de foin** to look for a needle in a haystack; *Fig* **monter qch en é.** to make too much of sth; **é. à chapeau** hatpin; **é. à cheveux** hairpin; **virage en é. à cheveux** hairpin *Br* bend *or Am* turn; **é. à linge** clothes *Br* peg *or Am* pin; **é. de** *ou* **à nourrice, é. de sûreté** safety pin

épingler [epɛ̃gle] *vt* (**a**) *(attacher)* to pin (**à/sur** to/on) (**b**) *Fam (arrêter)* to nab; **se faire é.** to get nabbed

épinoche [epinɔʃ] *nf* stickleback

Épiphanie [epifani] *nf Rel* **l'É.** Epiphany

épique [epik] *adj* epic

épiscopal, -e, -aux, -ales [episkɔpal, -o] *adj* episcopal

épiscopat [episkɔpa] *nm (fonction, évêques)* episcopate

épisode [epizɔd] *nm aussi Fig* episode

épisodique [epizɔdik] *adj (intermittent)* occasional; *(accessoire)* minor

épisodiquement [epizɔdikmã] *adv* occasionally

épistémologie [epistemɔlɔʒi] *nf* epistemology

épistolaire [epistɔlɛr] *adj* epistolary; **être en relation é. avec qn** to correspond with sb

épitaphe [epitaf] *nf* epitaph

épithélium [epiteljɔm] *nm* epithelium

épithète [epitɛt] *nf* epithet; *Gram* attribute

épître [epitr] *nf* epistle

éploré, -e [eplɔre] *adj* tearful

épluchage [eplyʃaʒ] *nm* peeling; *Fig* detailed examination

épluche-légumes [eplyʃlegym] *nm inv* potato peeler

éplucher [eplyʃe] *vt (peler)* to peel; *Fig (texte, journal)* to go through in detail

épluchette [eplyʃɛt] *nf Can* **é. de blé d'Inde** corn-husking party

épluchure [eplyʃyr] *nf (pelure)* peeling

éponge [epɔ̃ʒ] **1** *nf* sponge; **donner un coup d'é. à qch** to wipe sth with a sponge; **d'un coup d'é.** with a sponge; **jeter l'é.** *(à la boxe) & Fig* to throw in the towel; *Fig* **passer l'é.** to forget all about it
2 *adj inv* **tissu é.** (terry) towelling; **serviette é.** terry towel

éponger [45] [epɔ̃ʒe] **1** *vt* (**a**) *(liquide)* to mop up (**b**) *(surface)* to sponge (down); *(le front de quelqu'un)* to mop (**c**) *Fig (déficit)* to mop up
2 s'éponger *vpr* **s'é. le front** to mop one's brow

épopée [epɔpe] *nf aussi Fig* epic

époque [epɔk] *nf* (**a**) *(historique)* era, age; *Géol* period; **la Belle É.** ≃ the Edwardian era; **quelle é. (nous vivons)!** what times we live in!; **être de son é.** to be in tune with the times; **meubles d'é.** period furniture (**b**) *(moment précis)* time; **à l'é.** at the time

---

La Belle Époque

This refers to the period of apparent stability and prosperity from the closing years of the 19th century to the beginning of the First World War, which found its expression in café and theatre society, fashion, art and architecture. Its chief surviving monument is the area on the south side of the Champs-Élysées containing the "Petit Palais" and the "Grand Palais", erected at the time of the Universal Exhibition of 1900.

épouiller [epuje] *vt* to delouse

époumoner [epumɔne] **s'époumoner** *vpr (en criant)* to shout oneself hoarse; *(en chantant)* to sing oneself hoarse

épouse [epuz] *nf* wife

épouser [epuze] *vt* to marry; *Fig (cause)* to espouse; *Fig* **é. la forme de qch** to take on the exact shape of sth

épousseter [42] [epuste] *vt* to dust

époustouflant, -e [epustuflɑ̃, -ɑ̃t] *adj Fam* astounding

époustoufler [epustufle] *vt Fam* to astound

épouvantable [epuvɑ̃tabl] *adj* dreadful, appalling

épouvantail [epuvɑ̃taj] *nm (de jardin)* scarecrow; *Péj (personne laide)* fright; *(personne terrifiante)* bogy

épouvante [epuvɑ̃t] *nf* terror

épouvanté, -e [epuvɑ̃te] *adj* terror-stricken

épouvanter [epuvɑ̃te] *vt* to terrify

époux [epu] *nm* husband; **les é.** the married couple; **les é. Thomas** Mr and Mrs Thomas

éprendre [58] [eprɑ̃dr] **s'éprendre** *vpr* **s'é. de qn** to fall in love with sb

épreuve [eprœv] *nf* (**a**) *(essai)* test; **mettre qn/qch à l'é.** to put sb/sth to the test; **à l'é. du feu** fireproof; **à l'é. des balles** bulletproof; **un courage à toute é.** unfailing courage; **être mis à rude é.** *(personne, patience)* to be severely tested; **les bateaux furent mis à rude é. par la tempête** the boats took a battering from the storm; *Fig* **é. de force** trial of strength (**b**)

(examen) (écrit) (examination) paper; *(oral)* test (**c**) *(d'athlétisme)* event; **é. contre la montre** time trial; **é. éliminatoire** heat (**d**) *(adversité)* trial, ordeal; **dans l'é.** in adversity (**e**) *Typ* proof (**f**) *Phot* print

épris, -e [epri, -iz] *adj* **é. de qn** in love with sb; **é. de qch** passionate about sth

éprouvant, -e [epruvɑ̃, -ɑ̃t] *adj* trying

éprouvé, -e [epruve] *adj* (**a**) *(testé) (remède)* proven, well-tried; *(matériaux)* tested (**b**) *(famille)* sorely tried; *(région)* hard-hit

éprouver [epruve] *vt* (**a**) *(essayer) (méthode, personne, courage)* to test (**b**) *(ressentir) (sensation, sentiment, douleur)* to feel (**c**) *(subir) (perte)* to suffer; *(difficultés)* to meet with

éprouvette [epruvɛt] **1** *nf* test tube
2 *adj* **bébé é.** test-tube baby

EPS [əpees] *nf (abrév* **éducation physique et sportive**) PE

épuisant, -e [epɥizɑ̃, -ɑ̃t] *adj* exhausting

épuisé, -e [epɥize] *adj* (**a**) *(très fatigué)* exhausted (**b**) *(sol)* exhausted (**c**) *(livre, édition)* out of print; *(marchandises)* sold out

épuisement [epɥizmɑ̃] *nm* (**a**) *(fatigue)* exhaustion; **danser jusqu'à l'é.** to dance till one drops (**b**) *(d'un sol, d'un stock, de ressources)* exhaustion; **jusqu'à. é. des stocks** while stocks last

épuiser [epɥize] **1** *vt* (**a**) *(fatiguer)* to exhaust (**b**) *(sol, stock, ressources, sujet)* to exhaust
2 s'épuiser *vpr* (**a**) *(se fatiguer)* to exhaust oneself, to wear oneself out; **s'é. à faire qch** to wear oneself out doing sth (**b**) *(source)* to dry up; *(stock, ressources)* to run out

épuisette [epɥizɛt] *nf* landing net

épuration [epyrasjɔ̃] *nf (de l'eau, du gaz)* purification; *(du pétrole, d'un minerai)* refining; *Fig (d'une langue)* refining; *Pol* purge

épurer [epyre] *vt (eau, gaz)* to purify; *(pétrole, minerai)* to refine; *Fig (langue)* to refine; *Pol (parti)* to purge

équarrir [ekarir] *vt* (**a**) *(bois, pierre)* to square (**b**) *(animal)* to quarter

équarrissage [ekarisaʒ] *nm* (**a**) *(du bois, de la pierre)* squaring (**b**) *(d'animaux)* quartering

Équateur [ekwatœr] *nm* **l'É.** Ecuador

équateur [ekwatœr] *nm* equator; **sous l'é.** at the equator

équation [ekwasjɔ̃] *nf* equation; **é. du premier/deuxième degré** simple/quadratic equation

équatorial, -e, -aux, -ales [ekwatɔrjal, -o] *adj* equatorial

équatorien, -enne [ekwatɔrjɛ̃, -ɛn] **1** *adj* Ecuadorian **2** *nm,f* **É.** Ecuadorian

équerre [ekɛr] *nf* **é. (à dessin)** set square; **en é., à l'é.** at right angles; **d'é.** square, straight

équestre [ekɛstr] *adj (statue, sports)* equestrian; *(exercices)* horseriding

équidés [ekɥide, ekide] *nmpl* horse family, *Spéc* Equidae

équidistant, -e [ekɥidistɑ̃, -ɑ̃t] *adj* equidistant (**de** from)

équilatéral, -e, -aux, -ales [ekɥilateral, -o] *adj* equilateral

équilibrage [ekilibraʒ] *nm* balancing

équilibre [ekilibr] *nm* (**a**) *(d'un corps, d'un objet)* balance; **mettre qch en é.** to balance sth; **perdre l'é.** to lose one's balance; **faire perdre l'é. à qn** to throw sb off balance; **faire de l'é. sur qch** to balance on sth; **être en é. instable** to be precariously balanced (**b**) *(mental)* (mental) balance, equilibrium (**c**) **budget en é.** balanced budget; **é. budgétaire** balanced budget (**d**) *(d'un ensemble)* balance

équilibré, -e [ekilibre] *adj (chargement, alimentation)* balanced; *(personne)* well-balanced; *(vie)* stable

équilibrer [ekilibre] **1** *vt (charge, composition)* to balance; *(bateau, avion)* to trim; **é. un budget** to balance a budget
2 s'équilibrer *vpr (l'un l'autre)* to balance each other out

équilibriste [ekilibrist] *nmf (funambule)* tightrope walker

équinoxe [ekinɔks] *nm* equinox

équipage [ekipaʒ] *nm* (**a**) *(d'un navire, d'un avion)* crew; **les hommes d'é.** the crew; **les membres de l'é.** the crew (**b**) *(voiture et chevaux)* equipage

équipe [ekip] *nf* (**a**) *Sport* team; **une é. de football** a football team (**b**) *(de chercheurs, de médecins)* team; *(d'ouvriers)* gang; *(à l'usine)* shift; *Mil* working party; **travailler en é.** to work as a team; **faire é. avec qn** to team up with sb; **é. dirigeante** management team; **é. de jour/nuit** day/night shift; **é. de secours** rescue team

équipée [ekipe] *nf (frasque)* escapade; *(promenade, voyage)* jaunt

équipement [ekipmã] *nm* (**a**) *(action) (d'un atelier, d'une cuisine)* equipping, fitting out (**de** with) (**b**) *(matériel)* equipment; *(de soldat)* kit (**c**) *(installations)* facilities; **équipements collectifs** public facilities; *Ordinat* **é. informatique** computer equipment

équiper [ekipe] **1** *vt (atelier, cuisine)* to equip, to fit out (**de** with); *(sportif, armée)* to equip, *Br* to kit out (**de** with); **appartement avec cuisine équipée** flat with cooking facilities
2 s'équiper *vpr* to equip oneself (**de** with)

équipier, -ère [ekipje, -ɛr] *nm,f* team member

équitable [ekitabl] *adj* fair

équitablement [ekitabləmã] *adv* fairly

équitation [ekitasjɔ̃] *nf* (horse)riding; **faire de l'é.** to go (horse)riding

équivalence [ekivalãs] *nf* equivalence; *Univ* **avoir/obtenir une é.** to have/get an equivalent diploma

équivalent, -e [ekivalã, -ãt] **1** *adj* equivalent (**à** to)
2 *nm* equivalent; **sans é.** without equal

équivaloir [69] [ekivalwar] *vi* **é. à qch** *(valoir)* to be equivalent to sth; *(revenir à)* to amount to sth

équivaut *voir* **équivaloir**

équivoque [ekivɔk] **1** *adj* (**a**) *(ambigu) (terme, attitude)* equivocal, ambiguous (**b**) *(douteux) (conduite, passé)* dubious
2 *nf* ambiguity; **sans é.** *(réponse, situation)* unequivocal; *(répondre)* unequivocally

érable [erabl] *nm (arbre, bois)* maple; **sirop d'é.** maple syrup

érablière [erablijɛr] *nf Can* maple grove

éradication [eradikasjɔ̃] *nf* eradication

éradiquer [eradike] *vt* to eradicate

érafler [erafle] **1** *vt (genou)* to graze; *(cuir)* to scuff; *(bois, meuble)* to scratch
2 s'érafler *vpr* **s'é. le coude** to graze one's elbow

éraflure [eraflyr] *nf (au genou)* graze; *(sur cuir)* scuff mark; *(sur bois, sur meuble)* scratch

éraillé, -e [eraje] *adj* (**a**) *(voix)* hoarse (**b**) *(surface)* scratched

ère [ɛr] *nf* era; **en l'an 1150 de notre è.** in the year 1150 AD; **avant notre è.** BC

érection [erɛksjɔ̃] *nf* (**a**) *(construction)* erection (**b**) *(gonflement)* erection; **être en é.** *(personne)* to have an erection; *(verge)* to be erect

éreintant, -e [erɛ̃tã, -ãt] *adj Fam* exhausting

éreinté, -e [erɛ̃te] *adj Fam* exhausted

éreinter [erɛ̃te] **1** *vt* (**a**) *(fatiguer) (personne, animal)* to exhaust, to wear out (**b**) *(critiquer) (livre, auteur)* to pull to pieces
2 s'éreinter *vpr* **s'é. à faire qch** to wear oneself out doing sth

érémiste [eremist] = **RMiste**

Erevan [erevan] *n* Yerevan

ergot [ɛrgo] *nm* (**a**) *(d'un coq)* spur (**b**) *(d'un chien)* dewclaw (**c**) *Tech* pin

ergoter [ɛrgɔte] *vi* to quibble (**sur** about)

Érié [erje] *n voir* **lac**

ériger [45] [eriʒe] **1** *vt* (**a**) *(dresser) (statue, temple, mât)* to erect (**b**) *(créer) (tribunal)* to establish, to set up (**c**) *Fig* **é. qn en qch** to set sb up as sth; **é. qch en qch** to elevate sth to the status of sth
2 s'ériger *vpr* **s'é. en qch** to set oneself up as sth

ermitage [ɛrmitaʒ] *nm* hermitage

ermite [ɛrmit] *nm* hermit; **vivre en e.** to live the life of a recluse

érogène [erɔʒɛn] *adj* erogenous

érosion [erozjɔ̃] *nf* erosion

érotique [erɔtik] *adj* erotic

érotisme [erɔtism] *nm* eroticism

errance [erãs] *nf Litt* roving, wandering

errant, -e [erã, -ãt] *adj (vie)* roving, wandering; **chevalier e.** knight-errant; **chien e.** stray dog

errata [erata] *nmpl voir* **erratum**

erratique [eratik] *adj* erratic

erratum [eratɔm] *(pl* **errata** [erata]) *nm* erratum

errements [ermã] *nmpl* bad ways; **retomber dans ses e. passés** to fall back into one's bad old ways

errer [ere] *vi (marcher)* to wander; **e. par les rues** to roam the streets; **e. comme une âme en peine** to wander about like a lost soul

erreur [erœr] *nf* (**a**) *(faute)* mistake, error; **faire** *ou* **commettre une e.** to make a mistake; **faire e.** to be mistaken; **être dans l'e.** to be mistaken; **induire qn en e.** to mislead sb; **par e.** by mistake; **sauf e. de ma part** if I'm not mistaken; **il y a e. sur la personne** you've/they've/etc got the wrong person; **il n'y a pas d'e. (possible)** there's no doubt about it; **l'e. est humaine** to err is human; **e. de calcul** miscalculation; **e. de jeunesse** youthful indiscretion; **e. judiciaire** miscarriage of justice; **e. de jugement** error of judgement (**b**) *Ordinat* error; **message d'e.** error message; **correction des erreurs** error correction; **e. d'analyse (syntaxique)** parse error; **e. de disque** disk error; **e. d'échantillonnage** sampling error; **e. d'écriture** write error; **e. de lecture** read error; **e. de logiciel** software *or* system error; **e. de programmation** programming error; **e. de saisie** keying error

erroné, -e [erɔne] *adj* erroneous

ersatz [ɛrzats] *nm inv* ersatz, substitute

éructer [erykte] **1** *vi* to belch
2 *vt Fig* **é. des injures** to hurl abuse

érudit, -e [erydi, -it] **1** *adj* erudite, scholarly **2** *nm,f* scholar

érudition [erydisjɔ̃] *nf* erudition, scholarship

éruption [erypsjɔ̃] *nf* (**a**) *(d'un volcan)* eruption; **entrer en é.** to erupt (**b**) *(de boutons)* rash

érythème [eritɛm] *nm Méd* rash; **é. fessier** *Br* nappy *or Am* diaper rash; **é. solaire** sunburn

Érythrée [eritre] *nf* l'**É.** Eritrea

érythréen, -enne [eritreɛ̃, -ɛn] **1** *adj* Eritrean **2** *nm,f* É. Eritrean

E/S *Ordinat (abrév* **entrée/sortie)** I/O

es *voir* **être²**

ès [es] *prép* **docteur ès lettres/sciences** ≃ PhD; **licencié ès lettres** ≃ BA; **licencié ès sciences** ≃ BSc

ESB [əɛsbe] *nf (abrév* **encéphalite spongiforme bovine)** BSE

esbroufe [ɛzbruf] *nf Fam* bluffing; **faire de l'e.** to bluff

escabeau, -x [ɛskabo] *nm* (**a**) *(tabouret)* stool (**b**) *(marchepied)* stepladder

escadre [ɛskadr] *nf Naut* squadron; *Aviat* **e. aérienne** wing; **chef d'e.** *Naut* squadron commander; *Aviat* wing commander

escadrille [ɛskadrij] *nf* (**a**) *Naut* flotilla (**b**) *Aviat (unité)* flight

escadron [ɛskadrɔ̃] *nm* (**a**) *Mil* squadron; **chef d'e. major** (**b**) *Aviat* squadron (**c**) *Fig (groupe) (de personnes)* troop, band

escalade [ɛskalad] *nf* (**a**) *(d'un mur, d'une falaise)* climbing, scaling; *Sport* climbing; **faire de l'e.** to go climbing (**b**) *Fig (d'une guerre, des prix, de la violence)* escalation

escalader [ɛskalade] *vt* to climb, to scale

escalator® [ɛskalatɔr] *nm* escalator

escale [ɛskal] *nf* (**a**) *(arrêt)* stopover; **faire e.** *(en bateau)* to put into port; *(en avion)* to touch down; **faire e. à Athènes** *(en bateau)* to put in at Athens; *(en avion)* to stop over at Athens; **vol sans e.** nonstop flight; **e. technique** refuelling stop (**b**) *(lieu) (pour bateau)* port of call; *(pour avion)* stopover

escalier [ɛskalje] *nm (marches)* stairs; *(cage)* staircase; **dans l'e., dans les escaliers** on the stairs; **monter en e.** *(en ski)* to sidestep; **e. en colimaçon** spiral staircase; **e. mécanique, e. roulant,** *Can* **e. mobile** escalator; **e. de secours** fire escape; **e. de service** backstairs

escalope [ɛskalɔp] *nf* escalope

escamotable [ɛskamɔtabl] *adj (antenne, train d'atterrissage, phares)* retractable; *(meuble)* foldaway

escamotage [ɛskamɔtaʒ] *nm* (**a**) *(par un illusionniste)* vanishing (**b**) *(d'un train d'atterrissage)* retraction (**c**) *Fig (d'un problème)* dodging

escamoter [ɛskamɔte] *vt* (**a**) **e. qch** *(sujet: illusionniste)* to make sth vanish (**b**) *(voler)* to sneak off with (**c**) *(train d'atterrissage)* to retract (**d**) *Fig (problème)* to dodge

escampette [ɛskãpɛt] *nf Fam* **prendre la poudre d'e.** to make off

escapade [ɛskapad] *nf* jaunt; **faire une e.** to go on a jaunt

escarbille [ɛskarbij] *nf* cinder

escargot [ɛskargo] *nm* snail; **aller à une allure d'e.** *ou* **à la vitesse d'un e.** to go at a snail's pace; **marcher comme un e.** to walk at a snail's pace; *Fig* **opération e.** = slowing down of traffic by protesting truck drivers

escarmouche [ɛskarmuʃ] *nf* skirmish

escarpé, -e [ɛskarpe] *adj (route, montagne)* steep

escarpement [ɛskarpəmã] *nm (versant)* steep slope; *Géog* escarpment

escarpin [ɛskarpɛ̃] *nm* pump, *Br* court shoe

escarpolette [ɛskarpɔlɛt] *nf Vieilli (balançoire)* swing

escarre [ɛskar] *nf Méd* scab; *(due aux draps)* bedsore

escient [ɛsjã] *nm* **à bon e.** wisely; **à mauvais e.** unwisely

esclaffer [ɛsklafe] **s'esclaffer** *vpr* to burst out laughing, to roar with laughter

esclandre [ɛsklãdr] *nm (scandale, tapage)* scene; **faire** *ou* **causer un e.** to make a scene

esclavage [ɛsklavaʒ] *nm* slavery; **réduire qn en e.** to enslave sb

esclavagisme [ɛsklavaʒism] *nm* slavery; *(doctrine)* pro-slavery

esclave [ɛsklav] **1** *nmf* slave; **être vendu comme e.** to be sold into slavery; *Fig* **être l'e. de qn/qch** to be a slave to sb/sth **2** *adj Fig* **être e. de ses habitudes** to be a slave to one's habits

escogriffe [ɛskɔgrif] *nm* **(grand) e.** beanpole

escompte [ɛskɔ̃t] *nm* discount; *Fin* **taux d'e.** (bank) discount rate

escompter [ɛskɔ̃te] *vt (espérer)* to expect, to anticipate (**que** that); **e. faire qch** to expect to do sth

escorte [ɛskɔrt] *nf* escort; **sous (bonne) e.** under escort

escorter [ɛskɔrte] *vt* to escort

escouade [ɛskwad] *nf Mil* squad

escrime [ɛskrim] *nf Sport* fencing; **faire de l'e.** to fence

escrimer [ɛskrime] **s'escrimer** *vpr* to fight; **s'e. à faire qch** to struggle to do sth

escrimeur, -euse [ɛskrimœr, -øz] *nm,f* fencer

escroc [ɛskro] *nm* crook, swindler

escroquer [ɛskrɔke] *vt (personne)* to swindle, to cheat; **e. qch à qn, e. qn de qch** to swindle *or* to cheat sb out of sth

escroquerie [ɛskrɔkri] *nf (action)* swindling; *(résultat)* swindle; *(délit)* fraud; *Fam* **mais c'est de l'e.!** it's a rip-off!

escudo [ɛskydo] *nm* escudo

eskimo [ɛskimo] = **esquimau**

ésotérique [ezɔterik] *adj* esoteric

espace [ɛspas] *nm* (**a**) *(étendue, distance)* space; **laisser de l'e.** to leave space; **e. blanc** space; **E. économique européen** European economic area; **e. publicitaire** advertising space; **e. de rangement** storage space; **e. vital** living space; **espaces verts** parks, green spaces (**b**) *(durée)* **en l'e. d'une semaine** within a week (**c**) *(atmosphère)* space; **e. aérien** airspace (**d**) *Math* space; **e. à trois/quatre dimensions** three-/four-dimensional space (**e**) *Ordinat* **e. disque** disk space; **e. mémoire** memory space; **e. de stockage** storage space

espacement [ɛspasmã] *nm (action)* spacing out; *(résultat)* spacing; *(distance)* space; *Ordinat* **e. arrière** backspace

espacer [16] [ɛspase] **1** *vt (objets, paiements, visites)* to space out **2** **s'espacer** *vpr* (**a**) *(visites, lettres)* to become less frequent (**b**) *(personnes)* **espacez-vous** space yourselves out

espace-temps (*pl* espaces-temps) [ɛspastã] *nm Math & Phys* space-time (continuum)

espadon [ɛspadɔ̃] *nm* swordfish

espadrille [ɛspadrij] *nf* espadrille

Espagne [ɛspaɲ] *nf* l'E. Spain

espagnol, -e [ɛspaɲɔl] **1** *adj* Spanish
2 *nm,f* E. Spaniard; **les Espagnols** the Spanish
3 *nm* (*langue*) Spanish

espagnolette [ɛspaɲɔlɛt] *nf* window fastener (*long vertical bar with pivoting central catch*)

espalier [ɛspalje] *nm* (**a**) (*mur*) espalier wall (**b**) (*de gymnase*) wall bars

espèce [ɛspɛs] *nf* (**a**) (*sorte*) kind, sort; **les gens de son e.** people like her, people of her kind; **de la pire e.** of the worst sort; **cela n'a aucune e. d'importance** that's of no importance whatsoever; *Fam* **cette e. d'idiot** that stupid idiot; *Fam* **e. d'idiot!** you idiot! (**b**) *Jur* **cas d'e.** specific case; **la loi applicable en l'e.** the law applicable to the case in point (**c**) **espèces** (*argent*) cash; **payer en espèces** to pay in cash; **espèces sonnantes et trébuchantes** hard cash (**d**) *Bot & Zool* species; **l'e. humaine** the human race, mankind

espérance [ɛsperãs] *nf* hope; **dans l'e. de faire qch** in the hope of doing sth; **dans l'e. que...** in the hope that...; **au-delà de nos espérances** beyond our expectations; **répondre aux espérances de qn** to live up to sb's expectations; **e. de vie** life expectancy

espérer [34] [ɛspere] **1** *vt* to hope for; **e. faire qch** to hope to do sth; **e. que** to hope that; **je ne vous espérais plus** I'd given you up
2 *vi* **j'espère bien** I hope so; **espérons!** let's hope so!

espiègle [ɛspjɛgl] *adj* mischievous

espion, -onne [ɛspjɔ̃, -ɔn] *nm,f* spy

espionnage [ɛspjɔnaʒ] *nm* espionage, spying; **faire de l'e.** to spy; **l'e. industriel** industrial espionage

espionner [ɛspjɔne] **1** *vt* to spy on
2 *vi* to spy

esplanade [ɛsplanad] *nf* esplanade

espoir [ɛspwar] *nm* (**a**) (*espérance*) hope; **avoir l'e. de faire qch** to have hopes of doing sth; **avoir bon e.** to be full of hope; **reprendre e.** to become hopeful again; **nourrir l'e. de faire qch** to live in hope of doing sth; **dans l'e. de faire qch** in the hope of doing sth; **dans l'e. de vous voir bientôt** hoping to see you soon; **tous les espoirs sont permis** things look hopeful; **c'est sans e.** it's hopeless; *Ironique* **l'e. fait vivre** hope springs eternal (**b**) (*personne*) hope; **un e. du tennis français** one of the most promising French tennis players

esprit [ɛspri] *nm* (**a**) (*intellectuel*) mind; **avoir l'e. large/étroit** to be broad-/narrow-minded; **avoir l'e. tranquille** to be easy in one's mind; **avoir l'e. mal tourné** to have a dirty mind; **avoir l'e. d'analyse/scientifique** to have an analytical/a scientific (turn of) mind; **perdre l'e.** to go out of one's mind; **reprendre ses esprits** to regain consciousness; **elle avait l'e. ailleurs** her thoughts were elsewhere; **elle n'a pas l'e. à ce qu'elle fait** her mind isn't on what she's doing; **je n'ai pas l'e. à plaisanter** I'm not in the mood for joking; **une pareille idée ne me serait jamais venue à l'e.** such an idea would never have crossed my mind; **qu'avez-vous à l'e.?** what are you thinking about?

(**b**) (*attitude mentale*) spirit; **avoir mauvais e.** to be a malicious sort; **faire du mauvais e.** to be malicious; **e. de caste** class-consciousness; **e. de clocher** parochialism; **e. de compétition** competitive spirit; **e. de corps** esprit de corps; **e. d'entreprise** enterprise spirit; **e. d'équipe** team spirit; **e. de famille** family feeling

(**c**) (*humour*) wit; **avoir de l'e.** to be witty; **mots** *ou* **traits d'e.** witticisms; **faire de l'e.** to display one's wit

(**d**) (*personne*) **un e. fort** a freethinker; *Prov* **les grands esprits se rencontrent** great minds think alike

(**e**) (*sens*) spirit; **l'e. de la loi** the spirit of the law

(**f**) (*fantôme*) spirit; **e., es-tu là?** (*dans une séance de spiritisme*) is there anybody there?; **e. frappeur** poltergeist

(**g**) *Chim* (volatile) spirit

esquif [ɛskif] *nm* skiff; **un frêle e.** a frail barque

esquimau, -aude, -x, -audes [ɛskimo, -od] **1** *adj* Eskimo, *Am* Inuit
2 *nm,f* E. Eskimo, *Am* Inuit
3 *nm* (*glace*) E.® *Br* ≃ choc-ice (*on a stick*), *Am* ≃ ice-cream bar

esquinté, -e [ɛskɛ̃te] *adj Fam* (*abîmé*) wrecked, knackered

esquinter [ɛskɛ̃te] *Fam* **1** *vt* (*abîmer*) to wreck; (*blesser*) to hurt
2 **s'esquinter** *upr* (*s'abîmer*) **s'e. la jambe** to hurt one's leg; **s'e. la santé/les yeux (à faire qch)** to ruin one's health/eyes (doing sth)

esquisse [ɛskis] *nf* (*dessin*) sketch; *Fig* (*d'un projet, d'un roman*) outline; (*d'un sourire*) suggestion

esquisser [ɛskise] **1** *vt* (*dessiner*) to sketch; *Fig* (*plan, roman*) to outline; *Fig* **e. un sourire** to give a slight smile
2 **s'esquisser** *upr* (*idée, projet*) to take shape

esquiver [ɛskive] **1** *vt aussi Fig* to dodge, to evade
2 **s'esquiver** *upr* to slip away

essai [ɛsɛ] *nm* (**a**) (*tentative*) try; **faire un e.** to have a try (**b**) (*test*) (*d'un produit, d'une voiture*) test, trial; **à l'e.** on a trial basis; *Ordinat* **e. approfondi** beta test; **e. nucléaire** nuclear test; *Ordinat* **e. de performance** benchmark (**c**) (*ouvrage*) essay (**d**) (*au rugby*) try

essaim [ɛsɛ̃] *nm aussi Fig* swarm

essaimer [ɛseme] *vi* (*abeilles*) to swarm; *Fig* (*population, famille*) to spread; (*entreprise*) to expand

essayage [ɛsejaʒ] *nm* fitting

essayer [53] [ɛseje] **1** *vt* (**a**) (*pour la première fois*) (*gadget, restaurant*) to try (out); (*voiture*) to test-drive; (*vin, plat*) to try, to taste; (*vêtement, chaussures*) to try on (**b**) (*tester*) (*machine, produit*) to test (**c**) (*tenter*) **e. de faire qch** to try to do sth
2 **s'essayer** *upr* **s'e. à qch/à faire qch** to try one's hand at sth/at doing sth

ESSEC [ɛsɛk] *nf* (*abrév* École supérieure des sciences économiques et commerciales) = university-level business school

essence [esãs] *nf* (**a**) (*combustible*) *Br* petrol, *Am* gas(oline); **e. ordinaire** *Br* two-star petrol, *Am* regular gas; **e. sans plomb** unleaded (*Br* petrol *or Am* gas) (**b**) (*extrait*) (*de plantes, de café*) essence; **e. de térébenthine** spirits of turpentine (**c**) (*caractère fondamental*) essence; **par e.** essentially (**d**) (*espèce*) species

essentiel, -elle [esãsjɛl] **1** *adj* (**a**) (*nécessaire*) essential, necessary (**à/pour** for) (**b**) (*principal*) (*condition, caractère*) essential; (*raison*) basic, main
2 *nm* **l'e.** (*le plus important*) the main thing; (*le*

minimum) the essentials; **l'e. de** *(la majeure partie de)* the majority of

essentiellement [esãsjɛlmã] *adv* (**a**) *(principalement)* essentially, mainly (**b**) *(par nature)* essentially

esseulé, -e [esœle] *adj* isolated

essieu, -x [esjø] *nm* axle

essor [esɔr] *nm* (**a**) *(d'un oiseau)* flight; **prendre son e.** to fly off (**b**) *Fig (d'une industrie, d'une économie)* (rapid) growth; **en plein e.** booming; **prendre son e.** to take off

essorage [esɔraʒ] *nm (à la machine)* spin-drying; *(à la main)* wringing

essorer [esɔre] *vt (vêtements) (à la machine)* to spin (-dry); *(à la main)* to wring out; *(salade)* to spin

essoreuse [esɔrøz] *nf (à tambour)* spin-drier

essoufflé, -e [esufle] *adj* out of breath

essoufflement [esufləmã] *nm* breathlessness; *Fig (de l'économie, d'une activité)* running down

essouffler [esufle] **1** *vt* to make out of breath
   2 s'essouffler *vpr* to get out of breath; *Fig (économie, activité)* to run down

essuie [esɥi] *nm Belg (essuie-mains)* hand towel; *(torchon)* cloth, tea towel; *(serviette de bain)* bath towel

essuie-glace *(pl* **essuie-glaces)** [esɥiglas] *nm Br* windscreen *or Am* windshield wiper

essuie-mains [esɥimɛ̃] *nm inv* hand towel

essuie-tout [esɥitu] *nm inv* kitchen paper

essuyer [32] [esɥije] **1** *vt* (**a**) *(surface)* to wipe; *(liquide)* to wipe up; *(larmes)* to wipe away; **e. la vaisselle** to dry the dishes, to dry up (**b**) *(subir) (défaite, perte, insultes)* to suffer; *(refus)* to meet with; *(tempête)* to run into
   2 s'essuyer *vpr* to wipe oneself; *(après un bain)* to dry oneself; **s'e. la bouche/les yeux** to wipe one's mouth/eyes

est¹ [ɛ] *voir* **être²**

est² [ɛst] **1** *nm* east; **un vent d'e.** an easterly wind; **le vent d'e.** the east wind; **à l'e.** in the east; **à l'e. de** (to the) east of; *Géog & Pol* **l'E.** the East
   2 *adj inv (côte, face, régions)* eastern

estafilade [ɛstafilad] *nf* gash

estaminet [ɛstaminɛ] *nm Belg* (small) café

estampe [ɛstãp] *nf* print

estampille [ɛstãpij] *nf (sur un document)* stamp; *(sur un produit)* mark

est-ce que [ɛskə] *adv interrogatif* **e. je peux entrer?** can I come in?; **est-ce qu'il est là?** is he here?; **e. tu la connais?** do you know her?; **est-ce qu'il connaissait la réponse?** did he know the answer?

esthète [ɛstɛt] *nmf* aesthete

esthéticien, -enne [ɛstetisjɛ̃, -ɛn] *nm,f* beautician

esthétique [ɛstetik] **1** *adj* aesthetic; *(beau)* aesthetically pleasing
   2 *nf (beauté)* aesthetic quality

estimable [ɛstimabl] *adj* (**a**) *(digne de respect)* estimable (**b**) *(assez bon)* fairly good

estimation [ɛstimasjɔ̃] *nf* (**a**) *(détermination) (d'un prix, d'une distance, d'un poids)* estimation; *(de marchandises, d'une œuvre d'art)* valuation; *(de dommages, de besoins)* assessment (**b**) *(valeur, quantité estimée)* estimate

estime [ɛstim] *nf* (**a**) *(respect)* esteem, regard; **avoir de l'e. pour qn/qch** to esteem sb/sth; **baisser/remonter dans l'e. de qn** to go down/up in sb's estimation;

avoir un succès d'e. to be a critical (though not a popular) success (**b**) *Naut* **à l'e.** by dead reckoning

estimer [ɛstime] **1** *vt* (**a**) *(déterminer) (prix, distance, poids)* to estimate; *(marchandises, œuvre d'art)* to value; *(dommages, besoins)* to assess (**b**) *(considérer)* to consider, to think *(que* that); **il n'a pas estimé nécessaire de me prévenir** he didn't consider it necessary to warn me (**c**) *(respecter) (personne)* to have a high opinion of; **e. qn à sa juste valeur** to value sb
   2 s'estimer *vpr* **s'e. satisfait/heureux** to consider oneself satisfied/lucky

estival, -e, -aux, -ales [ɛstival, -o] *adj* summer

estivant, -e [ɛstivã, -ãt] *nm,f Br* holidaymaker, *Am* vacationer

estocade [ɛstɔkad] *nf aussi Fig* death-blow; **donner l'e. à** to deal the death-blow to

estomac [ɛstɔma] *nm* (**a**) *(ventre)* stomach; **avoir l'e. vide** to have an empty stomach; **avoir l'e. dans les talons** to be starving (**b**) *Fam Fig (courage)* guts

estomaquer [ɛstɔmake] *vt Fam* to flabbergast

estomper [ɛstɔ̃pe] **1** *vt Art (dessin)* to shade off; *Fig (paysage, contour, souvenir)* to blur
   2 s'estomper *vpr (paysage, contour, souvenir)* to become blurred; *(peine)* to ease; *(rides)* to be smoothed out

Estonie [ɛstɔni] *nf* **l'E.** Estonia

estonien, -enne [ɛstɔnjɛ̃, -ɛn] **1** *adj* Estonian
   2 *nm,f* **E.** Estonian
   3 *nm (langue)* Estonian

estourbir [ɛsturbir] *vt Fam* (**a**) *(tuer)* to bump off (**b**) *(étonner)* to astound

estrade [ɛstrad] *nf* platform

estragon [ɛstragɔ̃] *nm* tarragon

estropié, -e [ɛstrɔpje] **1** *adj* crippled
   2 *nm,f* cripple

estropier [66] [ɛstrɔpje] *vt* (**a**) *(personne)* to cripple, to maim (**b**) *Fig (morceau de musique, langue étrangère)* to murder; *(mot, nom)* to mispronounce; *(texte)* to mutilate

estuaire [ɛstɥɛr] *nm* estuary

estudiantin, -e [ɛstydjãtɛ̃, -in] *adj* student

esturgeon [ɛstyrʒɔ̃] *nm* sturgeon

et [e] **1** *conj* (**a**) *(exprime l'addition, la simultanéité)* and; **et son frère et sa sœur** both his brother and his sister; **et d'un, il pleut, et de deux, je n'ai pas envie d'y aller** in the first place it's raining, and in the second place I don't want to go; **j'aime le café, et vous?** I like coffee, do you?; **et moi, alors?** what about me? (**b**) *(dans les nombres, les heures)* **vingt/trente et un** twenty-/thirty-one; **une livre et demie** a pound and a half; **il est quatre heures et demie/et quart** it's half/a quarter past four
   2 *nm (symbole)* **et commercial** ampersand

ETA [ətea] *nf (abrév* **Euskadi ta Askatasuna**) ETA

étable [etabl] *nf* cowshed

établi¹ [etabli] *nm* workbench

établi², -e *adj* established; **considérer qch comme une chose établie** to take sth for granted

établir [etablir] **1** *vt* (**a**) *(paix, relations, principe)* to establish; *(agence)* to set up; *(camp)* to pitch; *(prix)* to fix; *(devis, liste)* to draw up; *(record)* to set (**b**) *(démontrer)* to establish, to prove (**c**) *(autorité, réputation)* to establish (**sur** on)
   2 s'établir *vpr* (**a**) *(dans une ville, un pays)* to settle (**b**) *(pour exercer un métier)* to set up in business (**c**) *(s'instaurer)* to become established

établissement [etablismã] *nm* (**a**) *(de la paix, de relations, d'un principe)* establishment; *(d'une agence)* setting up; *(d'un camp)* pitching; *(d'un prix)* fixing; *(d'un devis, d'une liste)* drawing up (**b**) *(démonstration)* establishment (**c**) *(installation) (d'une personne)* settlement (**d**) *(institution)* establishment, institution; *(école)* school; **é. bancaire** bank; **é. de crédit** credit institution; **é. financier** financial institution; **é. hospitalier** hospital; **é. scolaire** school (**e**) *(entreprise)* business, firm; **les établissements Martin** Martin & Co

étage [etaʒ] *nm* (**a**) *(d'un bâtiment)* floor, storey; **à deux étages** two-storeyed; **au troisième é.** on the *Br* third *or Am* fourth floor; **à l'é.** upstairs (**b**) *(d'un terrain)* level; *(d'un gâteau)* tier (**c**) *(d'une fusée)* stage

étager [45] [etaʒe] **s'étager** *vpr* to rise in tiers

étagère [etaʒɛr] *nf (meuble)* (set of) shelves; *(planche)* shelf

étai [etɛ] *nm Constr* prop

étain [etɛ̃] *nm* (**a**) *(métal)* tin (**b**) *(matériau pour vaisselle)* pewter; **un é.** a piece of pewter

étais, était *voir* **être²**

étal (*pl* **étals**) [etal] *nm* (**a**) *(au marché)* stall (**b**) *(de boucher)* butcher's block

étalage [etalaʒ] *nm* (**a**) *(vitrine)* window display (**b**) *Fig (ostentation)* display; **faire é. de son savoir/sa richesse** to show off one's knowledge/wealth

étalagiste [etalaʒist] *nmf* window dresser

étalement [etalmã] *nm (dans le temps)* staggering (**sur** over)

étaler [etale] **1** *vt* (**a**) *(étendre) (journal, papiers)* to spread out; *(nappe, beurre)* to spread; *(peinture, pommade)* to apply (**sur** to); *(cartes)* to lay down (**b**) *Fig (montrer) (richesse, connaissances)* to show off; *(vie privée)* to make a display of; **é. une affaire au grand jour** to make a matter public (**c**) *(dans le temps)* to stagger (**sur** over)

 2 s'étaler *vpr* (**a**) *(village, parc)* to spread out (**b**) *(dans le temps)* to be spread (**sur** over) (**c**) *(se vautrer)* to sprawl (**d**) *Fam (tomber)* to fall flat on the ground; **s'é. de tout son long** to fall flat on one's face

étalon¹ [etalɔ̃] *nm (cheval)* stallion

étalon² *nm (de mesure, monétaire)* standard; *Fig (modèle)* yardstick; *Écon* **l'é.-or** the gold standard

étamine [etamin] *nf Bot* stamen

étanche [etɑ̃ʃ] *adj (bateau, récipient)* watertight; *(montre, bottes)* waterproof

étanchéité [etɑ̃ʃeite] *nf (d'un bateau, d'un récipient)* watertightness; *(d'une montre, de bottes)* waterproofness

étancher [etɑ̃ʃe] *vt* (**a**) *(liquide)* to stop the flow of; *(sang)* to staunch; *(larmes)* to dry (**b**) *(soif)* to quench

étang [etɑ̃] *nm* pond, pool

étant *voir* **être²**

étape [etap] *nf* (**a**) *(lieu)* stopover; **faire é.** to stop; *Fig* **brûler les étapes** *(dans la hiérarchie)* to shoot to the top; *(dans une tâche)* to cut corners (**b**) *(distance)* stage (**c**) *Fig (phase)* stage, step; **par étapes** in stages

état [eta] *nm* (**a**) *(façon d'être)* state, condition; *Phys* state; **l'é. des routes** road conditions; **à l'é. solide/naturel** in its solid/natural state; **à l'é. neuf** as good as new; **à l'é. pur** *(substance)* unalloyed; *Fig (bêtise, incompétence)* sheer, downright; **dans l'é. actuel des choses** as things stand; **être dans un triste é.** to be in a sorry state; **être dans tous ses états** to be in a state; **en bon/mauvais é.** in good/bad condition; **remettre**

qch en é. to repair sth; *(moteur)* to overhaul sth; **laisser les choses en l'é.** to leave things as they are; **être en é. de marche** to be in working order; *(voiture)* to be roadworthy; **être/se sentir en é. de faire qch** to be/feel up to doing sth; **é. d'alerte** state of alert; **faire qch sans états d'âme** *(sans scrupules)* to have no qualms about doing sth; **é. de choses** state of affairs; **é. d'esprit** state of mind; **c'est un é. de fait** it's an undeniable fact; **l'é. de guerre a été déclaré** a state of war has been declared; **é. de santé** state of health; **être dans un é. second** to be spaced out; **é. de siège** martial law; **é. d'urgence** state of emergency

 (**b**) *Vieilli ou Hum (profession)* **épicier de son é.** grocer by trade

 (**c**) *(autorité centrale)* **l'É.** the State; **É. membre** member state

 (**d**) *(inventaire) (des dépenses, des ventes)* statement; **faire é. de qch** to mention sth; **é. civil** *(à la mairie)* register office; **é. des lieux** inventory of fixtures *(in rented premises)*; **dresser** *ou* **faire un é. des lieux** to draw up an inventory of fixtures; *Fig* to take stock of the situation; **états de service** service record

 (**e**) *Hist* **les États généraux** the States General

 (**f**) *Ordinat* **é. d'attente** wait state; **en é. de veille** in standby mode

étatique [etatik] *adj* state

étatiser [etatize] *vt* to bring under state control

état-major (*pl* **états-majors**) [etamaʒɔr] *nm* (**a**) *Mil (officiers)* (general) staff; *(lieu)* headquarters (**b**) *(d'une firme)* management; *(d'un parti politique)* leadership

États-Unis [etazyni] *nmpl* **les É. (d'Amérique)** the United States (of America)

étau, -x [eto] *nm* (**a**) *Tech* vice (**b**) *Fig (restrictions)* stranglehold; **l'é. se resserre** the net is closing in

étayer [53] [eteje] *vt* (**a**) *(mur, plafond)* to shore up (**b**) *Fig (argumentation, théorie)* to support

etc [ɛtsetera] *adv* etc

et cætera, et cetera [ɛtsetera] *adv* et cetera

été¹ [ete] *nm* summer; **en é.** in (the) summer; **un jour d'é.** a summer's day; **é. indien** *ou Can* **des Indiens** Indian summer

été² *voir* **être²**

éteindre [54] [etɛ̃dr] **1** *vt (incendie, bougie, cigarette)* to put out, to extinguish; *(gaz)* to turn off; *(lumière, radio, radiateur)* to switch off, to turn off; **éteins dans le salon, s'il te plaît** can you switch the light off in the lounge, please?

 2 s'éteindre *vpr* (**a**) *(incendie, cigarette, lampe)* to go out (**b**) *(passion)* to fade; *(son, rires, voix)* to die away (**c**) *(disparaître) (personne)* to pass away; *(race)* to die out

éteint, -e [etɛ̃, -ɛ̃t] *adj* (**a**) **être é.** *(incendie, cigarette)* to be out; *(lampe, électricité, radio)* to be off (**b**) *(race, famille, volcan)* extinct (**c**) *(terne) (couleur)* dull; *(regard)* blank; *(voix)* faint; *(personne)* subdued

étendard [etɑ̃dar] *nm* (**a**) *(drapeau)* standard (**b**) *Fig (symbole)* **lever l'é. de la révolte** to raise the standard of revolt; **se ranger sous l'é. de qn** to join sb's camp

étendoir [etɑ̃dwar] *nm (à linge)* clothes-line

étendre [etɑ̃dr] **1** *vt* (**a**) *(déployer) (carte, nappe)* to spread out; *(linge)* to hang up; *(beurre, pommade, ailes)* to spread; *(pâte)* to roll out; **é. les bras** to open one's arms wide; *Fam* **se faire é.** *(être assommé)* to be knocked out; *(à un examen)* to fail (**b**) *(coucher)* to lay down (**c**) *(influence, pouvoir, connaissances)* to extend (**à** to) (**d**) *(diluer)* to dilute (**e**) *Ordinat (mémoire)* to upgrade

2 s'étendre *vpr* (**a**) *(s'allonger)* to lie down (**b**) *(aller)* to stretch (**c**) *(incendie, épidémie, grève)* to spread; *(pouvoir, influence, connaissances)* to grow (**d**) *(s'attarder)* **s'é. sur un sujet** to dwell on a subject

étendu, -e [etɑ̃dy] **1** *adj* (**a**) *(large, important) (plaine, connaissances)* extensive; *(pouvoirs)* far-reaching (**b**) *(bras, jambes)* outstretched (**c**) *(personne)* lying (**d**) *(dilué)* diluted (**de** with)

2 *nf* **étendue** *(d'un champ, d'une région)* area; *(d'une grève, d'une épidémie, d'un problème)* scale, extent; *(d'eau, de sable, de terre)* expanse; *(des connaissances, du vocabulaire, des pouvoirs)* range

éternel, -elle [etɛrnɛl] **1** *adj* eternal; *(discussion, bavardages)* never-ending; **tu es un é. mécontent** you're never satisfied

2 *nm* (**a**) **l'É.** *(Dieu)* the Lord; *Hum* **c'est un grand fumeur/paresseux devant l'É.** he's an incurable smoker/incurably lazy (**b**) **l'é. féminin** the archetypal female

éternellement [etɛrnɛlmɑ̃] *adv* for ever; *(reconnaissant)* eternally; **elle est é. mécontente** she's never satisfied

éterniser [etɛrnize] **s'éterniser** *vpr (durer)* to drag on (for ever); *(chez quelqu'un)* to outstay one's welcome

éternité [etɛrnite] *nf* eternity; **il y a une é.** *ou* **des éternités que je ne vous ai vu** I haven't seen you for ages

éternuement [etɛrnymɑ̃] *nm* sneeze

éternuer [etɛrnɥe] *vi* to sneeze

êtes *voir* **être²**

éther [etɛr] *nm* ether

éthéré, -e [etere] *adj* ethereal

Éthiopie [etjɔpi] *nf* **l'É.** Ethiopia

éthiopien, -enne [etjɔpjɛ̃, -ɛn] **1** *adj* Ethiopian
2 *nm,f* **É.** Ethiopian

éthique [etik] **1** *adj* ethical
2 *nf* ethics *(singulier)*

ethnie [ɛtni] *nf* ethnic group

ethnique [ɛtnik] *adj* ethnic

ethnologie [ɛtnɔlɔʒi] *nf* ethnology

ethnologique [ɛtnɔlɔʒik] *adj* ethnological

ethnologue [ɛtnɔlɔg] *nmf* ethnologist

éthylique [etilik] *adj* **alcool é.** ethyl alcohol; **coma é.** alcohol-induced coma

éthylisme [etilism] *nm Méd* alcoholism

étiez *voir* **être²**

étincelant, -e [etɛ̃slɑ̃, -ɑ̃t] *adj* sparkling; *(étoile)* twinkling

étinceler [42] [etɛ̃sle] *vi (diamant, métal, lac)* to sparkle; *(étoile)* to twinkle; *(yeux) (de joie)* to sparkle (**de** with); *(de colère)* to glint (**de** with)

étincelle [etɛ̃sɛl] *nf aussi Fig* spark; **lancer des étincelles** to throw out sparks; *(diamant, yeux)* to sparkle; *Fig* **ça va faire des étincelles** sparks will fly; **avoir une é. de génie** to have a stroke of genius

étioler [etjɔle] **s'étioler** *vpr (plante)* to wilt; *(personne)* to grow sickly; *(esprit, mémoire)* to deteriorate

étions *voir* **être²**

étiqueter [42] [etikte] *vt aussi Fig* to label (**comme** as)

étiquette [etiket] *nf* (**a**) *(sur une valise, un produit)* label (**b**) *Fig (d'une personne)* label; **coller une é. à qn** to label sb; **é. politique** political affiliation (**c**) *(protocole)* **l'é.** etiquette

étirement [etirmɑ̃] *nm (des membres, du corps)* stretching; **faire des étirements** to do stretching exercises

étirer [etire] **1** *vt* to stretch
2 s'étirer *vpr (personne, tissu, vêtement)* to stretch; *(journée, réunion)* to drag on (for ever)

étoffe [etɔf] *nf* material, fabric; *Fig* **avoir l'é. d'un chef d'État** to have the makings of a statesman; **avoir l'é. d'un héros** to be the stuff heroes are made of

étoffer [etɔfe] **1** *vt (discours, livre, personnage)* to flesh out
2 s'étoffer *vpr (personne)* to fill out

étoile [etwal] *nf* (**a**) *(astre)* star; **un ciel sans étoiles** a starless sky; **coucher** *ou* **dormir à la belle é.** to sleep out (in the open); **né sous une bonne/mauvaise é.** born under a lucky/an unlucky star; **l'é. du berger** *(vue le matin)* the morning star; *(vue le soir)* the evening star; **é. filante** shooting star; **l'é. Polaire** the Pole star (**b**) *(ornement, objet)* star; *(astérisque)* asterisk; **hôtel trois étoiles** three-star hotel; **é. de David** Star of David (**c**) *(vedette)* star (**d**) **é. de mer** starfish (**e**) *Ordinat* **connecté en é.** in a star configuration

étoilé, -e [etwale] *adj* (**a**) *(ciel, nuit)* starry (**b**) *(pare-brise)* starred

étonnamment [etɔnamɑ̃] *adv* surprisingly

étonnant, -e [etɔnɑ̃, -ɑ̃t] *adj* surprising; **ce n'est pas é. qu'il soit malade** it's not surprising that he's ill; **chose étonnante, elle est arrivée à l'heure** amazingly enough, she arrived on time

étonné, -e [etɔne] *adj* surprised (**de** at)

étonnement [etɔnmɑ̃] *nm* surprise; **à mon grand é.** to my amazement

étonner [etɔne] **1** *vt* to surprise; **elle n'est pas venue? ça m'étonne** she didn't come? I'm surprised; *Fam* **alors ça, ça m'étonnerait!** that'll be the day!; **ça m'étonne de toi** I'm surprised at you; *Fam* **tu m'étonnes!** you don't say!; **tu m'étonneras toujours!** you never cease to amaze me!
2 s'étonner *vpr* to be surprised (**de** at); **je ne m'étonne plus de rien** nothing surprises me any more

étouffant, -e [etufɑ̃, -ɑ̃t] *adj (air, chaleur, atmosphère)* stifling; *(temps)* oppressive

étouffe-chrétien [etufkretjɛ̃] *Fam* **1** *adj inv* stodgy
2 *nm inv* **c'est de l'é., cette tarte** this tart is pure stodge

étouffée [etufe] **à l'étouffée 1** *adj* braised
2 *adv* **cuire qch à l'é.** to braise sth

étouffement [etufmɑ̃] *nm (asphyxie)* suffocation

étouffer [etufe] **1** *vt* (**a**) *(personne)* to suffocate; *Euph* **ce ne sont pas les scrupules qui l'étouffent** she's not exactly overscrupulous (**b**) *Fig (cri, bâillement, rire)* to stifle; *(son)* to muffle; *(feu)* to smother; *(révolte)* to suppress; *(scandale, affaire)* to hush up
2 *vi* to suffocate; **é. de rire/colère** to choke with laughter/anger; **on étouffe ici** it's stuffy in here
3 s'étouffer *vpr* to suffocate; *(en mangeant)* to choke (**avec** on)

étourderie [eturdəri] *nf* (**a**) *(caractère)* absent-mindedness (**b**) *(faute)* careless mistake

étourdi, -e [eturdi] **1** *adj (distrait)* scatterbrained
2 *nm,f* scatterbrain

étourdir [eturdir] *vt (assommer)* to stun, to daze; *Fig (sujet: vin, éloges)* to make dizzy

étourdissant, -e [eturdisɑ̃, -ɑ̃t] *adj (bruit)* deafening; *(nouvelles, succès)* staggering; *(beauté)* stunning

étourdissement [eturdismã] *nm* **avoir un é.** to feel dizzy

étourneau, -x [eturno] *nm* starling

étrange [etrãʒ] *adj* strange, odd; **chose é., il est revenu** strangely enough, he came back

étrangement [etrãʒmã] *adv* strangely, oddly; **ressembler é. à qch** to look suspiciously like sth

étranger, -ère [etrãʒe, -ɛr] **1** *adj* (**a**) *(d'un autre pays)* foreign (**b**) *(inconnu)* strange, unfamiliar (**à** to) (**c**) *(extérieur)* **des éléments étrangers** outsiders; **elle est étrangère à cette société/au projet** she isn't involved with this company/the plan

2 *nm,f* (**a**) *(d'un autre pays)* foreigner (**b**) *(d'un autre groupe)* stranger, outsider

3 *nm* **l'é.** *(pays étrangers)* foreign countries; **aller/vivre à l'é.** to go/live abroad

étrangeté [etrãʒte] *nf* strangeness, oddness

étranglé, -e [etrãgle] *adj (passage, vallée)* narrow; *(voix)* choked; *Méd (hernie)* strangulated

étranglement [etrãgləmã] *nm* (**a**) *(d'une personne)* strangling, strangulation; **mourir par é.** to be strangled (**b**) *(partie resserrée) (d'une rivière)* narrow part; *(d'une route)* bottleneck

étrangler [etrãgle] **1** *vt* (**a**) *(personne)* to strangle; *Fig (ruiner)* to cripple (**b**) *(resserrer) (taille, tube)* to constrict

2 s'étrangler *vpr* (**a**) *(en mangeant)* to choke (**avec** on); **s'é. de colère/rire** to choke with anger/laughter (**b**) *(voix)* to choke; **les mots s'étranglèrent dans sa gorge** the words stuck in her throat

étrave [etrav] *nf Naut* stem

être¹ [ɛtr] *nm (personne, âme)* being; **un ê. cher** a loved one; **c'est un ê. méprisable** he's a despicable creature; **ê. humain** human being; **ê. vivant** living creature

être² [2] **1** *vi* (**a**) *(indique la nature)* to be; **ê. professeur/informaticien** to be a teacher/computer expert; **ceci est un reptile** this is a reptile

(**b**) *(indique l'état)* to be; **ê. bien/mal** *(en bonne/mauvaise santé)* to be well/ill; **le temps est à l'orage** there's a storm brewing; **il serait mieux avec les cheveux courts** he would look better with short hair

(**c**) *(indique le lieu)* to be; **elle est chez elle** she's at home; **Rabat est au Maroc** Rabat is in Morocco; **j'en suis au chapitre IV** I'm on chapter IV; **où en es-tu dans ton travail?** how far have you got with your work?; **je ne sais plus où j'en suis** I don't know what I'm doing any more; **j'en suis à me demander si...** I'm beginning to wonder whether...

(**d**) *(indique le moment)* **nous sommes mercredi/le 16** it's Wednesday/the 16th today

(**e**) *(indique l'appartenance)* **ê. à qn** to belong to sb; *Fig* **je suis à vous** I'm all yours; **elle est de la famille** she's one of the family

(**f**) *(indique la provenance)* to be; **je suis de Lyon/du sud** I'm from Lyons/from the South; **l'enfant n'est pas de lui** it's not his child; **ce tableau est de Cézanne** this picture is by Cézanne

(**g**) *(indique l'obligation)* **ceci est à lire pour demain** this has to be read for tomorrow; **ce film est à voir absolument** this film is unmissable

(**h**) *(aller)* to go; **as-tu déjà été à Brighton?** have you ever been to Brighton?; *Fam* **ç'a été** it went OK

(**i**) *(exister)* to be; **la plus belle voiture qui soit** the most beautiful car in the world; *Litt* **elle n'est plus** she is no longer with us

(**j**) *(locutions)* **ê. tout le temps à se plaindre/à médire** to be always complaining/criticizing; **ne serait-ce que** if only

2 *v aux* (**a**) *(avec des verbes à l'actif)* to have/to be; **je suis sorti hier soir** I went out last night; **es-tu déjà allé en Chine?** have you ever been to China?; **elle est née en 1967** she was born in 1967; **j'étais parti très tôt** I had left very early; **il serait parti plus tôt s'il avait pu** he would have left earlier if he could; **ils se sont aimés** they loved each other; **nous nous étions trompés** we had made a mistake

(**b**) *(avec des verbes au passif)* to be; **nous y sommes/étions toujours bien reçus** we are/were always warmly welcomed

3 *v impersonnel* to be; **il est cinq heures** it's five (o'clock); **il est difficile de juger** it's hard to tell; **il m'est impossible de vous répondre** it's impossible for me to give you an answer

étreindre [54] [etrɛdr] *vt* to embrace; *(sujet: peur, douleur)* to grip

étreinte [etrɛt] *nf (embrassade)* embrace; *(sexuelle)* coupling

étrenner [etrene] *vt (objet)* to use for the first time, to christen; *(vêtement)* to wear for the first time

étrennes [etren] *nfpl* New Year's gift; *(pour facteur, éboueur) Br* ≃ Christmas box, *Am* ≃ Christmas bonus

étrier [etrije] *nm* (**a**) *(en équitation)* stirrup; **vider les étriers** to be thrown; *Fig* **mettre le pied à l'é. à qn** to give sb a helping hand (**b**) *(sur table d'examen)* stirrup

étriller [etrije] *vt* (**a**) *(cheval)* to curry (**b**) *Fig (critiquer)* to pan

étriper [etripe] **1** *vt (poisson, volaille)* to gut; *Fam Fig* **je vais l'é.!** I'll murder him!

2 s'étriper *vpr Fam (se battre)* to tear each other apart

étriqué, -e [etrike] *adj* (**a**) *(vêtement)* tight (**b**) *Fig (esprit, vie)* narrow

étroit, -e [etrwa, -at] *adj* (**a**) *(peu large)* narrow; *Fig* **avoir l'esprit é.** to be narrow-minded (**b**) *(serré)* tight; *Fig (liens, collaboration, surveillance)* close (**c**) *(logement, pièce)* poky; **être à l'é.** to be cramped for room

étroitement [etrwatmã] *adv (nouer, tenir)* tightly; *Fig (unir, collaborer, surveiller)* closely

étroitesse [etrwatɛs] *nf* narrowness; *(d'un logement, d'une pièce)* pokiness; *Fig* **é. d'esprit** narrow-mindedness

étron [etrõ] *nm* piece of excrement

étrusque [etrysk] **1** *adj* Etruscan

2 *nmf* É. Etruscan

étude [etyd] *nf* (**a**) *(examen)* study, survey; **mettre qch à l'é.** to study *or* investigate sth; **é. de cas** case study; **é. de faisabilité** feasibility study; **faire une é. de marché** to do market research (**b**) **études** *(éducation)* studies; **j'ai arrêté mes études à seize ans** I left school when I was sixteen; **faire des études (de français/de droit)** to study French/law; **elle a fait ses études à Oxford** she studied at Oxford (**c**) *Scol (heure)* study period; *(salle)* study room (**d**) *(morceau de musique, peinture)* study (**e**) *(bureau)* office

étudiant, -e [etydjã, -ãt] **1** *nm,f* student; **é. en médecine/en droit** medical/law student; **é. de première/seconde année** first-/second-year student, *Am* freshman/sophomore

2 *adj (vie, mouvement)* student

étudié, -e [etydje] *adj* (**a**) *(recherché) (tenue, style)* carefully chosen (**b**) *Péj (affecté)* studied (**c**) *Com* **prix très étudiés** very reasonable prices

étudier [66] [etydje] **1** *vt* to study; *(leçon)* to prepare **2** *vi* to study **3** **s'étudier** *vpr (l'un l'autre)* to study each other

étui [etɥi] *nm* case; *(de revolver)* holster; **é. à lunettes** glasses case

étuve [etyv] *nf* (**a**) *(aux thermes)* steam room; *Fig* oven (**b**) *(pour sécher)* drying oven; *(pour stériliser)* sterilizer

étuvée [etyve] **à l'étuvée 1** *adj* braised **2** *adv* **cuire qch à l'é.** to braise sth

étymologie [etimɔlɔʒi] *nf* etymology

EU [øy] *nmpl (abrév* **États-Unis**) USA

eu, -e *pp voir* **avoir¹**

eucalyptus [økaliptys] *nm* eucalyptus

eucharistie [økaristi] *nf Rel* **l'e.** the Eucharist

euh [ø] *exclam* er!

eunuque [ønyk] *nm* eunuch

euphémisme [øfemism] *nm* euphemism

euphorie [øfɔri] *nf* euphoria

euphorique [øfɔrik] *adj* euphoric

euphorisant, -e [øfɔrizã, -ãt] **1** *adj (effet, atmosphère)* exhilarating; *(médicament)* antidepressant; *(drogue)* that produces a feeling of euphoria **2** *nm* antidepressant; *(drogue)* drug that produces a feeling of euphoria

Euphrate [øfrat] *nm* **l'E.** the Euphrates

eurasien, -enne [ørazjɛ̃, -ɛn] **1** *adj* Eurasian **2** *nm,f* **E.** Eurasian

eurêka [øreka] *exclam* eureka!

euro [øro] *nm (monnaie)* Euro

euro- [øro] *préf* Euro-

Eurocorps [ørokɔr] *nm Mil* Eurocorps

eurocrate [ørokrat] *nmf* Eurocrat

eurodéputé, -e [ørodepyte] *nm,f* Euro MP

eurodevise [ørodəviz] *nf* Eurocurrency

eurodollar [ørodɔlar] *nm* Eurodollar

Europe [ørɔp] *nf* **l'E.** Europe; **l'E. centrale** central Europe; **l'E. de l'Est/de l'Ouest** Eastern/Western Europe; **l'E. du Nord** Northern Europe; **l'E. occidentale** Western Europe; **l'E. sociale** social Europe *(a united Europe committed to a progressive social and welfare policy)*; **l'E. verte** European agriculture

européen, -enne [ørope̯ɛ̃, -ɛn] **1** *adj* European **2** *nm,f* **E.** European

eurosceptique [ørosɛptik] *nmf Pol* Eurosceptic

Eurovision [ørovizjɔ̃] *nf* Eurovision

eut *voir* **avoir¹**

euthanasie [øtanazi] *nf* euthanasia

eux [ø] *pron personnel* (**a**) *(sujet)* they; **ils apprécient mon travail, e.!** THEY like my work!; **les enfants, e., se sont amusés** the children, for their part, enjoyed themselves; **si j'étais e., je me méfierais** if I were them, I'd be careful (**b**) *(objet direct)* them; **et e., tu les oublies?** and what about them, have you forgotten them? (**c**) *(avec préposition)* them; *(réfléchi)* themselves; **dis-le-leur, à e.** tell THEM; **ils ne pensent qu'à e.** they only think of themselves; **les deux maisons sont à e.** both houses are theirs; **ils ont leurs méthodes à e.** they have their own methods; *Fam* **un copain à e.** a friend of theirs

(**d**) *(dans les comparaisons)* them; **je dépense plus qu'e.** I spend more than they do *or* than them

eux-mêmes [ømɛm] *pron personnel* themselves

évacuation [evakɥasjɔ̃] *nf* (**a**) *(de matières du corps)* discharge; *(des eaux de pluie, des eaux usées)* drainage (**b**) *(de personnes, d'un lieu)* evacuation

évacuer [evakɥe] *vt* (**a**) *(matières du corps)* to discharge; *(eaux de pluie, eaux usées)* to drain off (**b**) *(personnes, lieu)* to evacuate; **faire é. une salle** to evacuate a hall (**c**) *Fig (problème)* to solve

évadé, -e [evade] *nm,f* escaped prisoner

évader [evade] **s'évader** *vpr aussi Fig* to escape (**de** from)

évaluation [evalɥasjɔ̃] *nf (d'une propriété, d'un bien)* valuation; *(de dommages)* assessment; *(d'un poids, d'un nombre, des risques)* estimation

évaluer [evalɥe] *vt (propriété, bien)* to value; *(dommages)* to assess; *(poids, nombre, risques)* to estimate

évangéliser [evãʒelize] *vt* to evangelize

évangéliste [evãʒelist] *nm (prédicateur)* evangelist; *(de la Bible)* Evangelist

évangile [evãʒil] *nm Rel* **l'É.** the Gospel; **l'É. selon saint Marc** the Gospel according to St Mark; *Fig* **prendre qch pour parole d'é.** to take sth as gospel (truth)

évanoui, -e [evanwi] *adj* unconscious; **tomber é.** to fall down in a faint

évanouir [evanwir] **s'évanouir** *vpr* (**a**) *(perdre conscience)* to faint (**b**) *(disparaître)* to fade (away)

évanouissement [evanwismã] *nm (syncope)* fainting fit

évaporation [evapɔrasjɔ̃] *nf* evaporation

évaporé, -e [evapɔre] *Péj* **1** *adj* scatterbrained **2** *nm,f* airhead

évaporer [evapɔre] **s'évaporer** *vpr* (**a**) *(liquide)* to evaporate (**b**) *Fig (disparaître)* to vanish (into thin air)

évasé, -e [evaze] *adj (récipient)* wide-mouthed; *(jupe)* flared

évaser [evaze] **s'évaser** *vpr* to widen; *(jupe)* to be flared

évasif, -ive [evazif, -iv] *adj* evasive

évasion [evazjɔ̃] *nf* (**a**) *(fuite)* escape (**de** from); **é. de capitaux** flight of capital; **é. fiscale** tax evasion (**b**) *Fig (distraction)* escapism; **avoir besoin d'é.** to need to escape

Ève [ɛv] *npr* Eve; *Fam* **je ne le connais ni d'È. ni d'Adam** I don't know him from Adam

évêché [eveʃe] *nm (diocèse)* bishopric; *(palais)* bishop's palace

éveil [evɛj] *nm* awakening; **être en é.** to be alert

éveillé, -e [eveje] *adj* (**a**) *(non endormi)* awake (**b**) *(vif)* alert

éveiller [eveje] **1** *vt* (**a**) *(curiosité, soupçons, jalousie)* to arouse; *(intelligence, imagination)* to stimulate (**b**) *Litt (personne)* to wake **2** **s'éveiller** *vpr* (**a**) *Litt (personne)* to awake (**b**) *Fig (curiosité, soupçons, jalousie)* to be aroused; *(intelligence, imagination)* to develop

événement [evɛnmã] *nm* event; **attendre la suite des événements** to wait and see what happens; **créer l'é.** to make big news; *Hum* **quand il fait la vaisselle, c'est (tout) un é.** it's a major event when he does the washing-up

éventail [evãtaj] *nm* (**a**) *(pour se rafraîchir)* fan; **en é.** fan-shaped (**b**) *(choix)* range

éventaire [evãtɛr] *nm* (**a**) *(étal)* stall (**b**) *(d'un marchand ambulant)* tray

éventé, -e [evãte] *adj (vin, parfum)* stale; *(bière)* flat

éventer [evãte] **1** *vt* (**a**) *(avec un éventail)* to fan (**b**) *(secret, complot)* to discover
   2 s'éventer *vpr* (**a**) *(avec un éventail)* to fan oneself (**b**) *(vin, parfum)* to go stale; *(bière)* to go flat

éventrer [evãtre] *vt (personne, animal)* to disembowel; *(colis, matelas)* to rip open; *(fût, boîte)* to break open

éventualité [evãtɥalite] *nf* (**a**) *(circonstance)* eventuality; **parer à toute é.** to be prepared for all eventualities; **dans l'é. de** in the event of (**b**) *(possibilité)* possibility

éventuel, -elle [evãtɥɛl] *adj* possible

éventuellement [evãtɥɛlmã] *adv* possibly; **j'aurais é. besoin de votre concours** I may need your help

évêque [evɛk] *nm* bishop

Everest [evərɛst] *nm* **l'E., le mont E.** (Mount) Everest

évertuer [evɛrtɥe] **s'évertuer** *vpr* **s'é. à faire qch** to endeavour to do sth

éviction [eviksjɔ̃] *nf (d'un rival, d'une tête de parti)* ousting; *(d'un locataire)* eviction

évidemment [evidamã] *adv* of course, obviously

évidence [evidãs] *nf* (**a**) *(d'un fait, de la vérité)* obviousness; **c'est une é.!** obviously!; **nier l'é.** to deny the obvious; **se rendre à l'é.** to face facts; **de toute é., à l'é.** obviously (**b**) **en é.** *(visible)* in a prominent position; **mettre qch en é.** to highlight sth; **se mettre en é.** to try to get oneself noticed

évident, -e [evidã, -ãt] *adj* obvious; **tu crois qu'on va réussir? – c'est é.!** do you think we'll succeed? – of course (we will)!; **elle va se rendre compte, c'est é.** she's bound to notice; *Fam* **c'est pas é.** *(pas facile)* it's not so easy!

évider [evide] *vt* to hollow out

évier [evje] *nm* sink

évincer [16] [evɛ̃se] *vt (rival)* to oust (**de** from)

éviter [evite] **1** *vt* (**a**) *(s'écarter de)* to avoid; **é. de faire qch** to avoid doing sth; **il faut é. qu'il le voie** he mustn't be allowed to see it; **évite que ça se sache** don't let it get out (**b**) *(épargner)* **é. qch à qn** to save *or* spare sb sth; **ça m'évitera d'avoir à le faire** it will save me having to do it
   2 s'éviter *vpr* (**a**) **s'é. qch** to avoid sth (**b**) *(se fuir mutuellement)* to avoid each other

évocateur, -trice [evɔkatœr, -tris] *adj* evocative (**de** of)

évocation [evɔkasjɔ̃] *nf* evocation; **le pouvoir d'é. d'un lieu/mot** the evocative power of a place/word

évolué, -e [evɔlɥe] *adj (société)* advanced; *(personne)* broadminded; *Ordinat (langage)* high-level

évoluer [evɔlɥe] *vi* (**a**) *(se déplacer)* to move around; *Fig* **é. dans le milieu des artistes** to move in artistic circles (**b**) *(se développer)* to develop (**c**) *Ordinat* **faire é.** to upgrade

évolutif, -ive [evɔlytif, -iv] *adj* progressive; *Ordinat* upgradeable

évolution [evɔlysjɔ̃] *nf* (**a**) *(développement)* development (**b**) *Biol* evolution (**c**) **évolutions** *(déplacements)* movements

évoquer [evɔke] *vt* (**a**) *(se remémorer) (passé)* to recall, to evoke (**b**) *(faire penser à)* to be reminiscent of; **son nom ne m'évoque rien** her name means nothing to me (**c**) *(aborder)* to touch on, to mention (**d**) *(par la magie)* to call up, to invoke

ex [ɛks] *nmf Fam* ex

ex- [ɛks] *préf* ex-; **ex-femme/-ministre** ex-wife/minister

exacerbation [ɛgzasɛrbasjɔ̃] *nf* exacerbation

exacerber [ɛgzasɛrbe] **1** *vt* to exacerbate
   2 s'exacerber *vpr* to become acute

exact, -e [ɛgzakt] *adj* (**a**) *(quantité, poids, nombre)* exact, precise; *(rapport, description)* exact, accurate; *(mot, réponse, heure, date)* right, correct; **c'est e.** *(vrai)* it's quite true; **il s'appelle bien Martin? – e.!** his name's Martin? – that's right! (**b**) *(ponctuel)* punctual, on time

exactement [ɛgzaktəmã] *adv* exactly

exactions [ɛgzaksjɔ̃] *nfpl* atrocities

exactitude [ɛgzaktityd] *nf* (**a**) *(précision, fidélité)* exactness; *(justesse)* correctness; **avec. e.** accurately (**b**) *(ponctualité)* punctuality; *Prov* **l'e. est la politesse des rois** punctuality is the politeness of kings

ex æquo [ɛgzeko] **1** *adj inv* **être e.** to tie, to be equally placed (**avec** with)
   2 *nmf inv* **il y a deux e.** there's a two-way tie; **départager les e.** to break the tie
   3 *adv* **être troisième e.** to tie for third place

exagération [ɛgzaʒerasjɔ̃] *nf* exaggeration

exagéré, -e [ɛgzaʒere] *adj (récit, geste)* exaggerated; *(prix, salaire, pessimisme)* excessive; **il n'est pas e. de dire que…** it's no exaggeration to say that…

exagérément [ɛgzaʒeremã] *adv* excessively

exagérer [34] [ɛgzaʒere] **1** *vt* to exaggerate; **il ne faut rien e., n'exagérons rien** let's not exaggerate
   2 *vi (amplifier)* to exaggerate; *(abuser)* to go too far

exaltant, -e [ɛgzaltã, -ãt] *adj* stirring

exaltation [ɛgzaltasjɔ̃] *nf (excitation)* intense excitement

exalté, -e [ɛgzalte] **1** *adj (discours, sentiment)* impassioned; *(personne)* fanatical
   2 *nm,f* fanatic

exalter [ɛgzalte] *vt* (**a**) *(exciter) (imagination)* to stir; *(ressentiment, orgueil)* to intensify (**b**) *(louer) (personne)* to exalt

exam [ɛgzam] *nm Fam* exam

examen [ɛgzamɛ̃] *nm* (**a**) *(d'un document, de faits)* examination; *(d'une machine)* checking; *(d'un local)* inspection; *(d'une demande)* consideration; **e. de conscience** soul-searching (**b**) **e. (médical)** (medical) examination; **e. de la vue** sight *or* eye test (**c**) *Scol & Univ* exam, examination; **e. blanc** mock exam; **e. d'entrée** entrance exam; **e. de passage** *Br* end-of-year exam, *Am* final exam

examinateur, -trice [ɛgzaminatœr, -tris] *nm,f* examiner

examiner [ɛgzamine] **1** *vt* (**a**) *(étudier) (document, faits)* to examine; *(machine)* to check; *(local)* to inspect; *(demande)* to consider (**b**) *(observer)* to examine; *(horizon)* to scan; **e. qn de la tête aux pieds** to eye sb up and down (**c**) *(patient)* to examine; **se faire e. par un médecin** to be examined by a doctor
   2 s'examiner *vpr* (**a**) *(dans une glace)* to examine oneself (**b**) *(l'un l'autre)* to examine each other

exaspérant, -e [ɛgzasperã, -ãt] *adj* exasperating

exaspération [ɛgzasperasjɔ̃] *nf* exasperation

exaspérer [34] [ɛgzaspere] *vt* (**a**) *(personne)* to exasperate (**b**) *Litt (douleur, sentiment)* to aggravate

exaucement [ɛgzosmã] *nm* granting

exaucer [16] [ɛgzose] *vt* (**a**) *(souhait)* to grant (**b**) **e. qn** to grant sb's wish

excavateur [ɛkskavatœr] *nm* excavator, (mechanical) digger

excavation [ɛkskavasjɔ̃] *nf* (**a**) *(trou)* excavation; *(creusée par une bombe)* crater (**b**) *(action)* excavation

excavatrice [ɛkskavatris] *nf* = **excavateur**

excédant, -e [ɛksedɑ̃, -ɑ̃t] *adj* exasperating

excédent [ɛksedɑ̃] *nm* surplus; **budget en e.** surplus budget; **e. de poids** excess weight; **e. de bagages** excess baggage; **être en e.** to show a surplus

excédentaire [ɛksedɑ̃tɛr] *adj (production, poids)* excess; *(budget)* surplus; **balance commerciale e.** trade surplus

excéder [34] [ɛksede] *vt* (**a**) *(quantité, somme, limite)* to exceed; *(forces, compétences)* to be beyond; **e. ses pouvoirs** to exceed one's powers (**b**) *(irriter)* to exasperate

excellence [ɛksɛlɑ̃s] *nf* excellence; *Scol* **prix d'e.** class prize *(for all-round standard)*; **par e.** par excellence; **Son/Votre E.** *(titre)* His/Her/Your Excellency

excellent, -e [ɛksɛlɑ̃, -ɑ̃t] *adj* excellent (**en** at)

exceller [ɛksele] *vi* to excel (**en** at)

excentré, -e [ɛksɑ̃tre] *adj* (**a**) *(quartier)* outlying (**b**) *Tech* off centre

excentricité [ɛksɑ̃trisite] *nf (de caractère, acte bizarre)* eccentricity

excentrique [ɛksɑ̃trik] **1** *adj (bizarre)* eccentric
2 *nmf (personne)* eccentric

excepté, -e [ɛksɛpte] **1** *prép* except, apart from
2 *adj* **les femmes exceptées** except for *or* apart from the women

excepter [ɛksɛpte] *vt* to except (**de** from); **sans e. les enfants** not forgetting the children

exception [ɛksɛpsjɔ̃] *nf* exception (**à** to); **c'est l'e. qui confirme la règle** it's the exception that proves the rule; **à quelques exceptions près** with a few exceptions; **un être d'e.** an exceptional person

exceptionnel, -elle [ɛksɛpsjɔnɛl] *adj* exceptional; **ne rien avoir d'e.** to be nothing special

exceptionnellement [ɛksɛpsjɔnɛlmɑ̃] *adv* exceptionally

excès [ɛksɛ] *nm* (**a**) *(excédent)* excess; **pécher par e. de zèle** to be overzealous; **avec e.** excessively, to excess; **sans e.** in moderation; **(jusqu')à l'e.** to excess, excessively; **tomber dans l'e. inverse** to go to the other extreme; **e. de vitesse** speeding; **faire un e. de vitesse** to speed (**b**) *(abus)* excess; **faire des e.** to overindulge

excessif, -ive [ɛksɛsif, -iv] *adj* excessive; **il est e.** he does things to excess

excessivement [ɛksɛsivmɑ̃] *adv (extrêmement)* extremely; *(avec excès)* excessively

excision [ɛksizjɔ̃] *nf* excision

excitant, -e [ɛksitɑ̃, -ɑ̃t] **1** *adj (fascinant, provocant)* exciting; *(tonique)* stimulating
2 *nm* stimulant

excitation [ɛksitasjɔ̃] *nf* (**a**) *(incitation)* incitement (**à** to) (**b**) *(état)* excitement (**c**) *Méd* excitation

excité, -e [ɛksite] **1** *adj* excited
2 *nm,f (personne)* hothead

exciter [ɛksite] **1** *vt* (**a**) *(attiser) (curiosité, jalousie, pitié)* to arouse (**b**) *(encourager)* to urge on; **e. qn à la révolte** to incite sb to revolt (**c**) *(énerver)* to excite (**d**) *(nerf, muscle)* to excite
2 **s'exciter** *vpr* to get excited

exclamation [ɛksklamasjɔ̃] *nf* exclamation

exclamer [ɛksklame] **s'exclamer** *vpr* **s'e. de joie/douleur** to cry out with joy/pain; **"jamais!" s'exclama-t-il** "never!" he exclaimed

exclu, -e [ɛkskly] **1** *adj* (**a**) *(non compris)* **TVA exclue** excluding VAT (**b**) *(impensable)* out of the question; **il est e. qu'elle vienne avec nous** there's no question of her coming with us
2 *nm,f* outcast

exclure [17] [ɛksklyr] *vt* (**a**) *(expulser)* **e. qn de qch** *(parti, école)* to expel sb from sth; *(fonction publique)* to remove sb from sth; *(salle, réunion)* to eject sb from sth (**b**) *(mettre à l'écart)* **e. qn de qch** to exclude sb from sth (**c**) *(ne pas considérer) (hypothèse, solution)* to rule out; **cela n'exclut pas que vous puissiez enseigner** that doesn't rule out the possibility of your teaching

exclusif, -ive [ɛksklyzif, -iv] *adj* exclusive; *(but, mission)* sole; **être e. dans ses amitiés** to be selective in one's choice of friends

exclusion [ɛksklyzjɔ̃] *nf* (**a**) *(d'un parti, d'une école)* expulsion; *(d'une fonction publique)* removal; *(d'une salle, d'une réunion)* ejection (**de** from) (**b**) **à l'e.** with the exception of

exclusivement [ɛksklyzivmɑ̃] *adv* exclusively

exclusivité [ɛksklyzivite] *nf* (**a**) *(droit)* exclusive rights (**de** to); **en e.** exclusively; **film en première e.** recent release; *Fig* **ne pas avoir l'e. de l'intelligence** not to have a monopoly on intelligence (**b**) *(information)* exclusive, scoop

excommunier [66] [ɛkskɔmynje] *vt* to excommunicate

excréments [ɛkskremɑ̃] *nmpl* excrement

excrétion [ɛkskresjɔ̃] *nf* (**a**) *(action)* excretion (**b**) **excrétions** *(déchets)* excreta

excroissance [ɛkskrwasɑ̃s] *nf* excrescence

excursion [ɛkskyrsjɔ̃] *nf (en car, en voiture)* excursion, trip; *(d'une journée)* day trip; *(de plusieurs jours)* tour; **faire une e., partir en e.** to go on a trip/a tour

excursionniste [ɛkskyrsjɔnist] *nmf* *Br* day-tripper, *Am* excursionist

excusable [ɛkskyzabl] *adj* excusable, forgivable

excuse [ɛkskyz] *nf* (**a**) *(raison)* excuse; **trouver des excuses à qn** to find excuses for sb; **ce n'est pas une e.!** that's no excuse! (**b**) **excuses** *(regrets)* apology; **faire** *ou* **présenter ses excuses à qn** to make one's apologies to sb

excuser [ɛkskyze] **1** *vt* (**a**) *(justifier) (personne, action)* to excuse; **e. qn auprès de qn** to apologize for sb to sb (**b**) *(pardonner) (personne, erreur, colère)* to excuse; **excusez-moi** *(j'ai fait une faute)* I'm sorry; *(pour attirer l'attention)* excuse me; **excuse-moi de te déranger** I'm sorry to disturb you; **excuse-moi de ne pas t'avoir téléphoné** I'm sorry I didn't phone you; *Formel* **je vous prie de m'e.** I do beg your pardon; *Hum* **excusez du peu!** you please! (**c**) *(dispenser)* to excuse; **se faire e.** to ask to be excused
2 **s'excuser** *vpr* to apologize; **s'e. auprès de qn** to apologize to sb; **s'e. de qch/de faire qch** to apologize for sth/for doing sth; **je m'excuse!** I'm sorry!

exécrable [ɛgzekrabl] *adj* atrocious

exécrer [34] [ɛgzekre] *vt* *Litt* to loathe

exécutable [ɛgzekytabl] *adj* (**a**) *(réalisable)* possible, feasible (**b**) *Ordinat* executable

exécutant, -e [εgzekytã, -ãt] *nm,f* (**a**) *(employé)* subordinate; **ce n'est qu'un simple e.** he just carries out orders (**b**) *(musicien)* performer

exécuter [εgzekyte] **1** *vt* (**a**) *(effectuer) (travail, ordres)* to carry out; *(danse, morceau de musique)* to perform; *(peinture)* to execute (**b**) *Ordinat (programme)* to run; *(commande)* to execute (**c**) *(mettre à mort)* to execute; *Fam (battre)* to slaughter; *Fam (critiquer)* to savage
2 s'exécuter *vpr* to comply

exécuteur, -trice [εgzekytœr, -tris] *nm,f Jur* **e. testamentaire** executor; **exécutrice testamentaire** executrix

exécutif, -ive [εgzekytif, -iv] **1** *adj (pouvoir)* executive
2 *nm* **l'e.** the executive

exécution [εgzekysjɔ̃] *nf* (**a**) *(d'un travail, d'ordres)* carrying out; *(d'une danse, d'un morceau de musique)* performance; *(d'une peinture)* execution; **mettre qch à e.** to carry sth out (**b**) *Ordinat* execution (**c**) *(mise à mort)* execution

exécutoire [εgzekytwar] *adj* (**a**) **jugement e.** enforceable decision (**b**) **formule e.** executory formula

exégèse [εgzeʒεz] *nf* exegesis; **faire l'e. de** to write a critical interpretation of

exemplaire¹ [εgzãplεr] *adj* (**a**) *(comportement, courage)* exemplary (**b**) *(punition)* exemplary

exemplaire² *nm (livre, gravure)* copy; **en deux/trois exemplaires** in duplicate/triplicate; **photocopier qch en vingt exemplaires** to make twenty photocopies of sth; **le livre a été tiré à dix mille exemplaires** ten thousand copies of the book were printed

exemple [εgzãpl] *nm* (**a**) *(modèle)* example (**pour** for); **donner l'e. (à qn)** to set (sb) an example; **suivre l'e. de qn** to follow sb's example; **prendre qn en e.** to model oneself on sb; **citer qn/qch en e.** to quote sb/sth as an example; **faire un e.** *(en punissant)* to set an example (**b**) *(cas, mot, phrase)* example; **être l'e. même de la bêtise** to be stupidity itself (**c**) **par e.** for example, for instance; *Fam* **ah ça par e.!** *(stupeur)* oh no!

exempt, -e [εgzã, -ãt] *adj* **e. de** *(service militaire)* exempt from; *(danger, problème)* free from; **e. de droits de douane** duty-free; **sa remarque n'était pas exempte d'une certaine amertume** her remark wasn't without a trace of bitterness

exempter [εgzãte] *vt (dispenser)* to exempt (**de** from)

exemption [εgzãpsjɔ̃] *nf* exemption (**de** from)

exercé, -e [εgzεrse] *adj (œil, oreille)* trained; *(main)* practised

exercer [16] [εgzεrse] **1** *vt* (**a**) *(entraîner) (corps, esprit, mémoire)* to train; **e. qn à qch/à faire qch** to train sb in sth/to do sth (**b**) *(user de) (autorité, talent, droit)* to exercise; **e. une influence sur qn** to exert an influence on sb; **e. une pression sur qn/qch** to exert pressure on sb/sth; **e. un contrôle sur qch** to exercise control over sth (**c**) *(profession)* to practise; **e. ses fonctions** to carry out one's duties; **e. le métier de journaliste** to work as a journalist
2 *vi (médecin, juriste)* to practise
3 s'exercer *vpr* (**a**) *(s'entraîner)* to practise; **s'e. à qch/à faire qch** to practise sth/doing sth (**b**) *(se manifester) (autorité, pouvoir)* to make itself felt

exercice [εgzεrsis] *nm* (**a**) *(entraînement sportif ou scolaire)* exercise; **faire des exercices** to do (some) exercises; **prendre de l'e.** to (take) exercise (**b**) *Mil* drill;

être à l'e. to be on parade (**c**) *(du pouvoir, d'un droit)* exercise (**d**) *(d'une profession)* practice; **dans l'e. de ses fonctions** in the exercise of one's duties; **être en e.** *(avocat, médecin)* to be in practice; *(président)* to be in office; **le président en e.** the incumbent president (**e**) **l'e. du culte** public worship (**f**) *(en comptabilité) Br* financial year, *Am* fiscal year

exergue [εgzεrg] *nm (de médaille)* inscription; *(d'un texte)* epigraph; **en e.** *(citation)* as an epigraph

exfoliant, -e [εksfɔljã, -ãt] **1** *adj* exfoliating
2 *nm* exfoliant

exhaler [εgzale] **1** *vt (odeur)* to give off; *Fig (joie, colère)* to give vent to; *Fig* **cette maison exhale la tristesse** sadness pervades this house
2 s'exhaler *vpr (odeur)* to be given off

exhausser [εgzose] *vt (mur, édifice)* to heighten; **e. une maison d'un étage** to add a storey to a house

exhaustif, -ive [εgzostif, -iv] *adj* exhaustive

exhiber [εgzibe] **1** *vt* (**a**) *(documents, passeport)* to produce (**b**) *Péj (savoir, richesses)* to show off, to flaunt
2 s'exhiber *vpr* to flaunt oneself

exhibition [εgzibisjɔ̃] *nf Péj (de savoir, de richesses)* flaunting

exhibitionniste [εgzibisjɔnist] *nmf* exhibitionist

exhortation [εgzɔrtasjɔ̃] *nf* exhortation (**à** to)

exhorter [εgzɔrte] *vt* **e. qn à qch/à faire qch** to exhort sb to sth/to do sth

exhumation [εgzymasjɔ̃] *nf (d'un corps)* exhumation; *(d'un trésor, de vestiges)* excavation

exhumer [εgzyme] *vt (corps)* to exhume; *(trésor, vestiges)* to excavate

exigeant, -e [εgziʒã, -ãt] *adj (personne, travail)* exacting

exigence [εgziʒãs] *nf* (**a**) *(caractère)* exacting nature (**b**) *(condition)* requirement, demand; **satisfaire aux exigences de qch** to meet the requirements of sth (**c**) **exigences** *(salaire)* expected salary; **quelles sont vos exigences?** what salary do you expect?

exiger [45] [εgziʒe] *vt* (**a**) *(demander en insistant)* to demand (**de** from); **e. que qch soit fait** to demand that sth be done (**b**) *(nécessiter) (soin, action)* to require

exigible [εgziʒibl] *adj (dette, impôt)* payable

exigu, -uë [εgzigy] *adj (cramped, tiny*

exiguïté [εgziɡyite] *nf* crampedness

exil [εgzil] *nm* exile; **envoyer qn en e.** to send sb into exile; **être en e.** to be in exile

exilé, -e [εgzile] *nm,f* exile

exiler [εgzile] **1** *vt* to exile (**de** from)
2 s'exiler *vpr* to go into exile; *Fig* **s'e. de la ville** to cut oneself off from the town

existant, -e [εgzistã, -ãt] *adj* existing

existence [εgzistãs] *nf* (**a**) *Phil (être)* existence (**b**) *(vie)* life; **mener une e. tranquille** to lead a quiet life; **dans l'e.** in life (**c**) *(présence)* existence (**de** of) (**d**) *(durée) (d'une institution)* life

existentialisme [εgzistãsjalism] *nm Phil* existentialism

existentiel, -elle [εgzistãsjεl] *adj* existential

exister [εgziste] **1** *vi* to exist; **rien n'existe pour lui que l'art** art is all that matters to him; **et l'amitié, cela existe, non?** there's such a thing as friendship, isn't there?
2 *v impersonnel* **il existe** there is/are

exode [εgzɔd] *nm* exodus; **e. rural** rural depopulation

exogène [εgzɔʒεn] *adj Biol & Géol* exogenous

exonération [εgzɔnerasjɔ̃] *nf* exemption; **e. fiscale** tax exemption

exonérer [34] [εgzɔnere] *vt (personne)* to exempt; *(marchandises)* to exempt from tax; **être exonéré d'impôts** to be exempt from tax

exorbitant, -e [εgzɔrbitɑ̃, -ɑ̃t] *adj (prix, demande)* exorbitant

exorbité, -e [εgzɔrbite] *adj (yeux)* protruding; *Fig* **ils regardaient, les yeux exorbités** they watched with bulging eyes

exorciser [εgzɔrsize] *vt aussi Fig* to exorcize

exorcisme [εgzɔrsism] *nm* exorcism

exorciste [εgzɔrsist] *nmf* exorcist

exotique [εgzɔtik] *adj* exotic; **poisson e.** tropical fish

expansé, -e [εkspɑ̃se] *adj (polystyrène)* expanded

expansif, -ive [εkspɑ̃sif, -iv] *adj (exubérant)* expansive

expansion [εkspɑ̃sjɔ̃] *nf* **(a)** *(de gaz, de l'univers)* expansion; **l'univers en e.** the expanding universe **(b)** *(développement)* *(d'une ville, d'une industrie)* expansion; **taux d'e.** growth rate; **être en pleine e.** *(économie, entreprise)* to be booming

expansionnisme [εkspɑ̃sjɔnism] *nm* expansionism

expatriation [εkspatrijasjɔ̃] *nf* expatriation

expatrié, -e [εkspatrije] *adj & nm,f* expatriate

expatrier [66] [εkspatrije] **1** *vt (personne)* to expatriate
2 s'expatrier *vpr* to leave one's country

expectative [εkspεktativ] *nf* **être dans l'e.** to be waiting to see what happens

expectorant, -e [εkspεktɔrɑ̃, -ɑ̃t] *adj & nm* expectorant

expectorer [εkspεktɔre] *vt* to expectorate

expédient [εkspedjɑ̃] *nm* expedient; **vivre d'expédients** to live by one's wits

expédier [66] [εkspedje] *vt* **(a)** *(envoyer)* to send, to dispatch; **e. qch par bateau/par avion/par le train** to send sth by sea/air/rail **(b)** *(se débarrasser de)* to dispose of; **elle les a expédiés en colonie de vacances** she packed them off to camp **(c)** *(faire rapidement)* *(tâche)* to deal promptly with; *(devoirs, dissertation)* to dash off; **e. les affaires courantes** to deal with the day-to-day matters

expéditeur, -trice [εkspeditœr, -tris] **1** *nm,f* sender
2 *adj (bureau, gare)* dispatching

expéditif, -ive [εkspeditif, -iv] *adj* hasty

expédition [εkspedisjɔ̃] *nf* **(a)** *(envoi)* dispatch, sending **(b)** *(marchandises)* consignment **(c)** *(voyage, opération militaire)* *& Fig* expedition; **partir en e.** to go on an expedition

expéditionnaire [εkspedisjɔnεr] *adj Mil* expeditionary

expérience [εksperjɑ̃s] *nf* **(a)** *(pratique)* experience; **avoir de l'e.** to have experience; **avoir l'e. de qch** to have experience of sth; **savoir qch par e.** to know sth from experience; **faire l'e. de qch** to experience sth; **tenter l'e.** to give it a try **(b)** *(test scientifique)* experiment; **e. en laboratoire** laboratory experiment; **faire une e. (sur)** to carry out an experiment (on)

expérimental, -e, -aux, -ales [εksperimɑ̃tal, -o] *adj* experimental

expérimentalement [εksperimɑ̃talmɑ̃] *adv* experimentally

expérimentation [εksperimɑ̃tasjɔ̃] *nf* experimentation; **e. sur l'homme** human experiments

expérimenté, -e [εksperimɑ̃te] *adj* experienced

expérimenter [εksperimɑ̃te] *vt (remède, vaccin)* to test, to try out (**sur** on)

expert, -e [εkspεr, -εrt] **1** *adj* expert, skilled (**en/dans** in); **être e. en la matière** to be an expert on the subject
2 *nm* expert; *(d'assurance)* valuer

expert-comptable (*pl* **experts-comptables**) [εkspεrkɔ̃tabl] *nm Br* ≃ chartered accountant, *Am* ≃ certified public accountant, CPA

expertise [εkspεrtiz] *nf* **(a)** *(évaluation)* *(d'une œuvre d'art)* valuation; *(de dommages)* assessment **(b)** *(rapport)* expert's report (**de** on) **(c)** *(compétence)* expertise

expertiser [εkspεrtize] *vt (œuvre d'art)* to value; *(dommages)* to assess

expiation [εkspjasjɔ̃] *nf* expiation (**de** of)

expiatoire [εkspjatwar] *adj* expiatory

expier [66] [εkspje] *vt* to atone for, to expiate

expiration [εkspirasjɔ̃] *nf* **(a)** *(respiration)* breathing out **(b)** *(d'un contrat, d'un bail)* *Br* expiry, *Am* expiration; **venir** *ou* **arriver à e.** to expire

expirer [εkspire] **1** *vi* **(a)** *Litt (mourir)* to expire **(b)** *(contrat, bail)* to expire **(c)** *(respirer)* to breathe out
2 *vt* to breathe out

explicatif, -ive [εksplikatif, -iv] *adj* explanatory; **notice explicative** directions for use

explication [εksplikasjɔ̃] *nf* explanation; **donner une e. à qch** to give an explanation for sth; **exiger des explications** to demand an explanation; **avoir une e. avec qn** *(discuter)* to talk things over with sb; *(se disputer)* to have it out with sb; **e. de textes** critical *or* textual analysis

explicite [εksplisit] *adj* explicit

explicitement [εksplisitmɑ̃] *adv* explicitly

expliquer [εksplike] **1** *vt* to explain; *(texte)* to analyse
2 s'expliquer *vpr* **(a)** *(communiquer ses idées, se justifier)* to explain oneself; **je m'explique** let me explain **(b)** *(comprendre)* **je ne m'explique pas pourquoi il...** I can't understand why he... **(c)** *(être explicable)* **cela s'explique facilement** that's easily explained; **tout s'explique!** there's a reason for everything! **(d)** *(se parler)* to talk things over; **s'e. avec qn** *(discuter)* to talk things over with sb; *(se disputer)* to have it out with sb

exploit [εksplwa] *nm* feat

exploitant, -e [εksplwatɑ̃, -ɑ̃t] *nm,f* **(a)** **e. (agricole)** farmer; **petits exploitants** small farmers **(b)** *Cin* exhibitor

exploitation [εksplwatasjɔ̃] *nf* **(a)** *(d'une mine, d'une forêt)* working; *(d'une ligne de chemin de fer, d'une ferme)* running; *(d'une terre)* farming; *(des ressources naturelles, d'un brevet)* *& Fig Péj* exploitation; *Ordinat* **système d'e.** operating system; *Fig* **c'est de l'e.!** it's exploitation!; **l'e. de l'homme par l'homme** man's exploitation of man **(b)** *(entreprise)* concern; **e. agricole** farm; **e. minière** mine

exploiter [εksplwate] *vt* **(a)** *(mine, forêt)* to work; *(ressources naturelles, brevet)* to exploit; *(ligne de chemin de fer, ferme)* to run; *(terre)* to farm; *Fig (situation, talent, idée)* to exploit **(b)** *Péj (abuser de)* *(personne)* to exploit

exploiteur, -euse [εksplwatœr, -øz] *nm,f Péj* exploiter

explorateur, -trice [ɛksplɔratœr, -tris] *nm,f (personne)* explorer

exploration [ɛksplɔrasjɔ̃] *nf* exploration; **partir en e.** to go off exploring

exploratoire [ɛksplɔratwar] *adj* exploratory

explorer [ɛksplɔre] *vt* to explore

exploser [ɛksploze] *vi* (**a**) *(bombe, avion, chaudière)* to explode; **faire e. une bombe** to explode a bomb (**b**) *Fig (se mettre en colère)* to explode

explosif, -ive [ɛksplozif, -iv] **1** *adj aussi Fig* explosive **2** *nm* explosive

explosion [ɛksplozjɔ̃] *nf aussi Fig* explosion; **une e. de joie** an outburst of joy; **e. démographique** population explosion

exponentiel, -elle [ɛkspɔnɑ̃sjɛl] **1** *adj* exponential **2** *nf* **exponentielle** exponential

export [ɛkspɔr] *nm* export; *Ordinat* **e. de données** data export

exportateur, -trice [ɛkspɔrtatœr, -tris] **1** *adj* exporting; **pays e. de vin** wine-exporting country **2** *nm,f* exporter

exportation [ɛkspɔrtasjɔ̃] *nf (action)* export(ation); *(produit)* export; *Ordinat (d'un fichier)* exporting; *Ordinat (données exportées)* exported data

exporter [ɛkspɔrte] *vt aussi Ordinat* to export (**vers** to)

exposant, -e [ɛkspozɑ̃, -ɑ̃t] **1** *nm,f (artiste, firme)* exhibitor **2** *nm* (**a**) *Math* exponent (**b**) *Typ (chiffre, lettre)* superscript; **3 en e.** superscript 3

exposé [ɛkspoze] *nm (de faits, d'une situation)* account; *Scol & Univ* talk; **après un bref e. de la situation** after outlining the situation; **faire un e.** to give a talk

exposer [ɛkspoze] **1** *vt* (**a**) *(montrer) (marchandises)* to display; *(œuvres d'art)* to exhibit (**b**) *(expliquer) (raisons, projet)* to set out; *(griefs, point de vue)* to air; **je leur ai exposé ma situation** I explained my situation to them (**c**) *(présenter)* **e. qch à la lumière/au soleil** to expose sth to the light/to the sun; **e. un film** to expose a film; **e. qn à la critique/au danger** to expose sb to criticism/to danger; **exposé au nord** facing north **2** *s'exposer vpr* **s'e. au danger** to put oneself in danger; **s'e. à la critique/à des poursuites** to lay oneself open to criticism/to prosecution; **ne t'expose pas trop longtemps** don't stay in the sun too long

exposition [ɛkspozisjɔ̃] *nf* (**a**) *(action) (de marchandises, de fleurs)* display; *(d'œuvres d'art)* exhibition (**b**) *(de musée)* exhibition (**c**) *(salon, foire)* exhibition, show; **l'E. universelle** the World Fair (**d**) *(de faits, de raisons)* exposition (**e**) *(au froid, au danger, au soleil)* exposure (**à** to); *(d'une maison)* aspect; *Phot* exposure; **durée d'e.** exposure time

exprès¹, -esse [ɛksprɛs] *adj (explicite)* express

exprès² *adj inv* **lettre/paquet e.** special delivery letter/parcel; **en e.** by special delivery

exprès³ [ɛksprɛ] *adv (à dessein)* on purpose, deliberately; *(spécialement)* specially; **je l'ai allumé sans le faire e.** I switched it on without meaning to; **c'est fait e.** it's deliberate; **on dirait un fait e.** you'd think it was done on purpose; **comme (par) un fait e., il pleuvait** and wouldn't you know it, it was raining

express [ɛksprɛs] **1** *adj (train)* express **2** *nm* (**a**) *(train)* express (**b**) *(café)* espresso

expressément [ɛksprɛsemɑ̃] *adv* (**a**) *(catégoriquement)* expressly (**b**) *(spécialement)* specially

expressif, -ive [ɛksprɛsif, -iv] *adj* expressive

expression [ɛksprɛsjɔ̃] *nf* (**a**) *(d'un sentiment, d'une opinion)* expression; *(du visage)* expression, look; **l'e. de son visage** the expression or look on her face; **sans e.** expressionless; **e. corporelle** self-expression through movement (**b**) *(locution)* expression (**c**) *Math* expression; *Fig* **réduit à sa plus simple e.** reduced to its simplest form; *Ordinat* **e. logique** logical expression

expressionnisme [ɛksprɛsjɔnism] *nm* expressionism

expressionniste [ɛksprɛsjɔnist] *adj & nmf* expressionist

exprimable [ɛksprimabl] *adj* expressible

exprimer [ɛksprime] **1** *vt* (**a**) *(sentiment, opinion)* & *Math* to express (**b**) *(jus)* to squeeze (**de** from) **2** *s'exprimer vpr (en parlant, en agissant)* to express oneself; **s'e. par gestes** to use sign language; **si je peux m'e. ainsi** if I can put it like that; **le président ne s'est pas encore exprimé sur ce sujet** the president has yet to voice an opinion on the matter

expropriation [ɛksprɔprijasjɔ̃] *nf* expropriation

exproprier [66] [ɛksprɔprije] *vt* to expropriate

expulser [ɛkspylse] *vt (étranger)* to deport, to expel (**de** from); *(locataire)* to evict (**de** from); *(élève, membre de parti)* to expel (**de** from); *(joueur)* to send off

expulsion [ɛkspylsjɔ̃] *nf (d'un étranger)* deportation (**de** from); *(d'un locataire)* eviction (**de** from); *(d'un élève, d'un membre de parti)* expulsion (**de** from); *(d'un joueur)* sending off

expurger [45] [ɛkspyrʒe] *vt* to expurgate

exquis, -e [ɛkski, -iz] *adj* exquisite; *(personne, sourire, temps)* delightful

exsangue [ɛksɑ̃g, ɛgzɑ̃g] *adj (patient, visage)* anaemic; *Fig (pays, région)* bled white

extase [ɛkstaz] *nf* (**a**) *Rel & Psy* ecstasy (**b**) *(admiration)* rapture, ecstasy; **être en e. devant qn/qch** to be in raptures over sb/sth

extasier [66] [ɛkstazje] **s'extasier** *vpr (s'exclamer)* to go into raptures (**sur/devant** about/over); *(être en extase)* to be in raptures (**sur/devant** about/over)

extatique [ɛkstatik] *adj* ecstatic

extenseur [ɛkstɑ̃sœr] **1** *adj m (muscle)* extensor **2** *nm (appareil)* chest expander

extensible [ɛkstɑ̃sibl] *adj* (**a**) *(métal)* tensile; *(vêtement, tissu)* stretch (**b**) *Ordinat* upgradeable

extensif, -ive [ɛkstɑ̃sif, -iv] *adj* **culture extensive** extensive farming

extension [ɛkstɑ̃sjɔ̃] *nf* (**a**) *(d'un muscle, d'un ressort)* stretching; **être en e.** *(ressort)* to be released; *(gymnaste)* to be fully stretched (**b**) *Fig (d'un territoire, d'une firme)* expansion; *(d'un contrat)* extension; *(d'une maladie, d'une langue)* spread; **prendre de l'e.** *(entreprise)* to expand; *(maladie, incendie)* to spread (**c**) **par e.** by extension (**d**) *Ordinat* expansion; **e. mémoire** memory upgrade

exténuer [ɛkstenɥe] **1** *vt* to exhaust **2** *s'exténuer vpr* **s'e. à faire qch** to exhaust oneself doing sth

extérieur, -e [ɛksterjœr] **1** *adj* (**a**) *(surface, partie)* outer, external; *(escalier, éclairage, intérêts)* outside; *(signe, fragilité)* outward; *(facteur, cause)* external; **le monde e.** the outside world; **sans aide extérieure** without outside help (**b**) *(étranger) (commerce, politique)* foreign, external **2** *nm* (**a**) *(d'un bâtiment, d'une boîte)* outside, exterior;

vu de l'e. seen from the outside; **à l'e.** *(d'un bâtiment)* outside; *(d'une boîte)* on the outside; **à l'e. de la gare/ville** outside the station/town; *Fig* **juger de l'e.** to judge by appearances; **match à l'e.** away match; **jouer à l'e.** to play away (**b**) **l'e.** *(pays étrangers)* foreign countries; **à l'e.** abroad; **de l'e.** from abroad (**c**) *Cin* location shot; **tourner en e.** to film on location (**d**) *Belg Sport (joueur)* winger

extérieurement [ɛkstɛrjœrmã] *adv* (**a**) *(dehors)* on the outside, externally (**b**) *(en apparence)* outwardly

extérioriser [ɛkstɛrjɔrize] **1** *vt (sentiment)* to express; *Psy* to externalize
　2 s'extérioriser *vpr (sentiment)* to express itself; *(personne)* to express oneself

exterminateur, -trice [ɛkstɛrminatœr, -tris] **1** *adj (rage)* destructive
　2 *nm,f* exterminator

extermination [ɛkstɛrminasjɔ̃] *nf* extermination

exterminer [ɛkstɛrmine] *vt* to exterminate

externaliser [ɛkstɛrnalize] *vt Écon* to outsource

externat [ɛkstɛrna] *nm* (**a**) *(école)* day school (**b**) *(élèves)* day pupils (**c**) *(à l'hôpital)* non-resident (medical) studentship

externe [ɛkstɛrn] **1** *adj* (**a**) *(surface, partie)* external, outer; *(cause)* external; *Ordinat* **dispositif e.** external device; **à usage e.** *(médicament)* for external use only (**b**) **élève e.** day pupil
　2 *nmf* (**a**) *(élève)* day pupil (**b**) *(étudiant en médecine)* **e. (des hôpitaux)** non-resident medical student, *Am* extern

extincteur [ɛkstɛ̃ktœr] *nm* fire extinguisher

extinction [ɛkstɛ̃ksjɔ̃] *nf* (**a**) **e. des feux** lights out (**b**) *(d'une espèce)* extinction; **espèce en voie d'e.** endangered species (**c**) **e. de voix** loss of voice; **avoir une e. de voix** to have lost one's voice

extirper [ɛkstirpe] **1** *vt (plante)* to root up; *Fig (vices)* to eradicate, to root out; **e. qn de son lit** to drag sb out of bed; **je n'ai pas pu lui e. le moindre renseignement** I couldn't get a single piece of information out of him
　2 s'extirper *vpr* **s'e. de qch** to extricate oneself from sth; **s'e. de son lit** to drag oneself out of bed

extorquer [ɛkstɔrke] *vt (argent, promesse)* to extort (**à** from)

extorsion [ɛkstɔrsjɔ̃] *nf* extortion; **e. de fonds** extortion of funds

extra [ɛkstra] **1** *adj inv* (**a**) *(de qualité supérieure)* top-quality (**b**) *Fam (remarquable)* great, neat
　2 *nm inv* (**a**) *(gâterie)* (special) treat; **s'offrir un e.** to treat oneself (**b**) *(serviteur)* extra hand; **faire des e. chez qn** to do occasional work for sb

extra- [ɛkstra] *préf* extra-

extraconjugal, -e, -aux, -ales [ɛkstrakɔ̃ʒygal, -o] *adj* extramarital

extracteur [ɛkstraktœr] *nm* extractor

extraction [ɛkstraksjɔ̃] *nf aussi Math* extraction; *(d'une balle)* removal; *Fig* **de haute/basse e.** of noble/humble extraction

extrader [ɛkstrade] *vt* to extradite

extradition [ɛkstradisjɔ̃] *nf* extradition

extrafin, -e [ɛkstrafɛ̃, -in] *adj* (**a**) *(petit pois)* extra-fine (**b**) *(de qualité supérieure)* top-quality

extrafort, -e [ɛkstrafɔr, -ɔrt] **1** *adj* extra-strong
　2 *nm* bias binding

extraire [28] [ɛkstrɛr] **1** *vt aussi Math* to extract (**de** from); *(balle)* to remove (**de** from); *(épingle, clou)* to

pull out (**de** of); *(personne)* to free (**de** from); **cette citation est extraite de...** this quotation is taken from...
　2 s'extraire *vpr* **s'e. de qch** to extricate oneself from sth

extrait [ɛkstrɛ] *nm* (**a**) *(essence)* extract (**b**) *(de texte, de film)* extract; *(d'un acte)* abstract; **e. de casier judiciaire** = documentary evidence showing whether one has a criminal record; **e. de naissance** birth certificate

extralucide [ɛkstralysid] *adj & nmf* **(voyante) e.** clairvoyant

extraordinaire [ɛkstraɔrdinɛr] *adj* (**a**) *(spécial) (mesures, messager, mission)* special (**b**) *(étonnant, remarquable)* extraordinary; *Fam (excellent)* fantastic; **cela n'a rien d'e.** that's nothing out of the ordinary; **si par e.** if by some remote chance

extraordinairement [ɛkstraɔrdinɛrmã] *adv* extraordinarily

extraplat, -e [ɛkstrapla, -at] *adj (montre, calculette)* slimline

extrapoler [ɛkstrapɔle] *vi* to extrapolate

extrascolaire [ɛkstraskɔlɛr] *adj (activités)* extra-curricular

extraterrestre [ɛkstratɛrɛstr] *adj & nmf* extraterrestrial

extra-utérin, -e [ɛkstrayterɛ̃, -in] *adj voir* **grossesse**

extravagance [ɛkstravagãs] *nf* (**a**) *(d'un comportement, de vêtements)* extravagance; *(d'une personne)* eccentricity; **des idées d'une telle e.** such extravagant ideas (**b**) *(action, remarque)* piece of nonsense

extravagant, -e [ɛkstravagã, -ãt] *adj (idée, comportement, vêtements)* extravagant; *(personne)* eccentric

extraverti, -e [ɛkstravɛrti] *adj & nm,f* extrovert

extrême [ɛkstrɛm] **1** *adj* (**a**) *(point, limite)* furthest; *(jeunesse, vieillesse, froid, plaisir)* extreme; **en cas d'e. urgence** if it's extremely urgent; **d'une maigreur e.** extremely thin; *Pol* **e. droite/gauche** far *or* extreme right/left (**b**) *(excessif)* extreme
　2 *nm* extreme; **passer d'un e. à l'autre** to go from one extreme to the other; **prudent à l'e.** cautious in the extreme

extrêmement [ɛkstrɛmmã] *adv* extremely

extrême-onction (*pl* **extrêmes-onctions**) [ɛkstrɛmɔ̃ksjɔ̃] *nf Rel* extreme unction

Extrême-Orient [ɛkstrɛmɔrjã] *nm* **l'E.** the Far East

extrémisme [ɛkstremism] *nm* extremism

extrémité [ɛkstremite] *nf* (**a**) *(bout) (d'une jambe, d'une corde)* end; *(d'un doigt)* tip; *(d'une aiguille, d'une épée)* point; **les extrémités** *(pieds et mains)* the extremities (**b**) *(acte désespéré)* **se livrer à une e.** to do something desperate (**c**) *(situation désespérée)* extremity; **être à la dernière e.** to be on the point of death

exubérance [ɛgzyberãs] *nf (d'une personne)* exuberance; *(d'une végétation)* lushness; **avec e.** exuberantly

exubérant, -e [ɛgzyberã, -ãt] *adj (personne, joie)* exuberant; *(végétation)* lush

exultation [ɛgzyltasjɔ̃] *nf* exultation

exulter [ɛgzylte] *vi* to exult, to rejoice

exutoire [ɛgzytwar] *nm* outlet (**à** for)

ex-voto [ɛksvɔto] *nm inv Rel* votive offering

F

F¹, f [ɛf] *nm inv* F, f; **un F2/F3** *(appartement)* a two-/three-roomed *Br* flat *or Am* apartment

F² (**a**) *(abrév* **franc(s)**) F, fr (**b**) *(abrév* **Fahrenheit**) F

fa [fa] *nm inv (note de musique)* F; *(chantée)* fa

fable [fabl] *nf* (**a**) *(récit)* fable (**b**) *(invention)* story

fabricant, -e [fabrikã, -ãt] *nm,f* manufacturer

fabrication [fabrikasjɔ̃] *nf (industrielle)* manufacture; *(manuelle)* making; **f. artisanale** production by craftsmen; **bombe de f. artisanale** home-made bomb; **f. assistée par ordinateur** computer-aided manufacture; **de f. française** French-made

fabrique [fabrik] *nf* factory

fabriquer [fabrike] *vt* (**a**) *(industriellement)* to manufacture; *(manuellement)* to make; *Fam* **qu'est-ce qu'elle fabrique?** what's she up to? (**b**) *(inventer)* to make up, to fabricate

fabulation [fabylasjɔ̃] *nf* fantasizing

fabuleusement [fabyløzmã] *adv* fabulously

fabuleux, -euse [fabylø, -øz] *adj* fabulous

fac [fak] *nf Fam* uni; **à la f.** at uni; **être en f. d'allemand** to be studying German at uni

façade [fasad] *nf aussi Fig* façade

face [fas] *nf* (**a**) *(visage)* face; *Fig* **perdre/sauver la f.** to lose/save face

   (**b**) *(côté) (d'un disque)* side; *(d'une pièce de monnaie)* head (side); **changer un disque de f.** to turn a record over

   (**c**) *Fig (aspect)* side; **changer la f. des choses** to change the face of things

   (**d**) *(locutions)* **f. à** *(dans l'espace)* facing; *(difficultés, situation)* faced with; *(adversaire)* confronted with; **f. à f. (avec)** face to face (with); **faire f. à** *(lieu, personne)* to face, to be opposite; *(responsabilités, dépenses)* to meet; *(situation, difficultés)* to face up to; **de f.** face on; *(attaquer)* from the front; **en f.** opposite; *(de l'autre côté de la rue)* across the road; **regarder qn en f.** to look sb in the face; **dire qch en f. à qn** to tell sb sth to his face; **la maison (d')en f.** the house across the road; **en f. de** opposite, facing; **l'un en f. de l'autre** opposite *or* facing each other

face-à-face [fasafas] *nm inv (public)* face-to-face debate; *(privé)* one-to-one meeting

facétie [fasesi] *nf Litt* joke

facétieux, -euse [fasesjø, -øz] *adj Litt (personne)* mischievous

facette [fasɛt] *nf aussi Fig* facet; **à facettes** facetted; *(personnalité)* multi-faceted

fâché, -e [faʃe] *adj* (**a**) *(en colère)* angry (**contre** with) (**b**) *(brouillé)* on bad terms (**avec** with); *Fam* **elle est fâchée avec les maths** she's hopeless at maths (**c**)

(contrarié) sorry; **je ne suis pas f. que ça soit terminé** I'm not sorry that it's finished

fâcher [faʃe] **1** *vt (mettre en colère)* to make angry, to anger

   2 se fâcher *vpr* (**a**) *(se mettre en colère)* to get angry (**contre** with) (**b**) *(se brouiller)* to fall out (**avec** with)

fâcheux, -euse [faʃø, -øz] *adj* unfortunate

facho [faʃo] *adj & nmf Fam* fascist

faciès [fasjɛs] *nm* features

facile [fasil] **1** *adj* (**a**) *(simple)* easy; **être f. à faire** to be easy to do; **c'est f. à dire** that's easily said; **f. d'emploi** easy to use (**b**) *(agréable)* easy-going; **être f. à vivre** to be easy to get on with (**c**) *Péj (superficiel)* facile (**d**) *Péj (femme, fille)* easy

   2 *adv Fam (au moins)* easily

facilement [fasilmã] *adv* easily

facilité [fasilite] *nf* (**a**) *(simplicité)* easiness; **choisir la f.** to take the easy way out (**b**) *(aisance)* ease; **avoir des facilités pour qch** to have a talent for sth (**c**) **facilités de paiement** payment facilities

faciliter [fasilite] *vt* to make easier; **f. qch à qn** to make sth easier for sb; **tu ne me facilites pas la tâche!** you're not making things easy for me!

façon [fasɔ̃] *nf* (**a**) *(manière)* way, manner; **faire qch à sa f.** to do sth (in) one's own way; **de cette f.** (in) this way; **de f. à faire qch** so as to do sth; **de f. à ce qu'il t'entende** so that he hears you; **de telle f. que** in such a way that; **d'une** *ou* **de f. générale** generally speaking; **d'une f. ou d'une autre** one way or another; **de toute f.** anyway, in any case; *Formel* **vous ne me dérangez en aucune f.** you're not disturbing me in the least; **c'est une f. de parler** in a manner of speaking; **je ne tolère pas ces façons de parler!** I won't tolerate that sort of language!; *Can* **avoir de la f.** *(avoir des manières agréables)* to have pleasant manners; *(être beau parleur)* to speak well

   (**b**) *(imitation)* **f. cuir** imitation leather

   (**c**) *(fabrication)* making; *(facture)* craftsmanship, workmanship; *(main-d'œuvre)* labour

   (**d**) **façons** *(comportement)* manners, behaviour; **en voilà des façons!** what a way to behave!; **faire des façons** *(minauder)* to put on airs; **faire des façons pour accepter qch** to make a fuss about accepting sth; **sans façons** *(personne, repas)* unpretentious; **non merci, sans façons!** no thanks, really!

façonner [fasɔne] *vt* (**a**) *(travailler)* to shape (**b**) *(fabriquer)* to make (**c**) *Fig (personne, caractère)* to mould

fac-similé (*pl* **fac-similés**) [faksimile] *nm* facsimile

facteur¹, -trice [faktœr, -tris] **1** *nm,f (employé des Postes) Br* postman, *Am* mailman

2 *nm (de pianos, de clavecins)* maker; *(d'orgues)* builder

facteur² *nm* (**a**) *(élément)* factor; **le f. temps** the time factor (**b**) *Math* factor

factice [faktis] *adj* (**a**) *(faux)* imitation (**b**) *Fig (sourire)* forced; *(gaieté)* false

faction [faksjɔ̃] *nf* (**a**) *(groupe)* faction (**b**) *Mil* guard duty; **être de** *ou* **en f.** to be on guard duty

factotum [faktɔtɔm] *nm* factotum

factuel, -elle [faktɥɛl] *adj* factual

facturation [faktyrasjɔ̃] *nf* invoicing, billing

facture¹ [faktyr] *nf* (**a**) *(style) (d'une œuvre)* construction; *(d'un artiste)* style (**b**) *(de pianos, de clavecins)* making; *(d'orgues)* building

facture² *nf (document)* invoice, bill; **faire** *ou* **dresser une f.** to make out an invoice; **f. d'électricité/de gaz** electricity/gas bill; **f. détaillée** itemized invoice

facturer [faktyre] *vt* to invoice

facturette [faktyrɛt] *nf* credit card sales slip

facultatif, -ive [fakyltatif, -iv] *adj* optional

faculté [fakylte] *nf* (**a**) *(de médecine, de droit)* faculty (**b**) *(pouvoir)* capacity (**de** for) (**c**) **facultés mentales** faculties; **ne plus avoir toutes ses facultés** to no longer have all one's faculties

fada [fada] *Fam* **1** *adj* crazy
   2 *nmf* nutcase

fadaise [fadɛz] *nf* silly remark; **dire des fadaises** to talk nonsense

fadasse [fadas] *adj Fam* insipid

fade [fad] *adj* insipid

fadeur [fadœr] *nf* insipidness

fagot [fago] *nm* bundle of firewood; *Fig* **de derrière les fagots** *(bouteille de vin)* for special occasions; *(compliment, idée)* remarkable

fagoté, -e [fagɔte] *adj Péj* **mal/bizarrement f.** badly/oddly dressed

faiblard, -e [fɛblar, -ard] *adj Fam* a bit weak

faible [fɛbl] **1** *adj* (**a**) *(physiquement, moralement)* weak; (**b**) *(raisonnement, plaisanterie)* weak; **être f. en qch** *(élève)* to be weak at sth (**c**) *(voix, odeur, lumière)* faint; *(vent)* light; **et le terme est f.!** and that's putting it mildly! (**d**) *(quantité)* small; *(prix, revenu)* low; *(avantage, chance, espoir)* slight; *(vitesse)* low; **à une f. hauteur/profondeur** not very high up/deep down
   2 *nmf* weakling; **les faibles d'esprit** the feeble-minded
   3 *nm* **avoir un f. pour qn/qch** to have a soft spot for sb/a weakness for sth

faiblement [fɛbləmã] *adv (résister, protester)* weakly, feebly; *(éclairer)* faintly

faiblesse [fɛblɛs] *nf* (**a**) *(physique, morale)* weakness; **avoir la f. de faire qch** to be weak enough to do sth; **donner des signes de f.** *(appareil)* to be showing signs of wear and tear; *(personne)* to be looking weak (**b**) *(médiocrité)* weakness (**en** at) (**c**) *(malaise)* **avoir une f.** to feel faint

faiblir [fɛblir] *vi* (**a**) *(devenir faible) (personne, monnaie)* to weaken; *(lumière)* to grow weaker; *(vent)* to drop (**b**) *(niveau scolaire)* to decrease; *(élève)* to get weaker

faïence [fajãs] *nf* (**a**) *(matière)* earthenware (**b**) *(objet)* piece of earthenware; **faïences** earthenware

faïencerie [fajãsri] *nf* (**a**) *(articles)* earthenware (**b**) *(fabrique)* pottery (works) (**c**) *(commerce)* pottery (trade)

faille [faj] *nf* (**a**) *(dans un raisonnement)* flaw; *(dans une amitié)* rift; **sans f.** *(raisonnement)* flawless; *(fidélité)* unwavering (**b**) *Géol* fault

faillir [35] [fajir] **1** *vi* **j'ai failli tomber** I nearly *or* almost fell; **j'ai bien failli me noyer** I very nearly drowned
   2 faillir à *vt ind Litt (réputation)* not to live up to; *(devoir)* to fail in

faillite [fajit] *nf* (**a**) *(d'entreprise)* bankruptcy; **être en f.** to be bankrupt; **faire f.** to go bankrupt (**b**) *(échec)* failure

faim [fɛ̃] *nf* hunger; **avoir f.** to be hungry; *Fig* **avoir f. de qch** to hunger for sth; *Fam* **avoir une grosse/petite f.** to be very hungry/a bit hungry; **avoir une f. de loup** to be ravenous; **rester sur sa f.** to remain hungry; *Fig* to be left unsatisfied

fainéant, -e [fɛneã, -ãt] **1** *adj* lazy, idle
   2 *nm,f* idler

fainéanter [fɛneãte] *vi* to idle about

fainéantise [fɛneãtiz] *nf* laziness, idleness

faire [36] [fɛr] **1** *vt* (**a**) *(fabriquer, produire)* to make; *(tache, trace)* to leave; **f. du bruit** to make some noise; **f. de la fumée** to give off smoke; **f. une erreur** to make a mistake; **f. de la betterave/du colza** to grow beetroot/rape; *Fam* **f. des femmes comme ça, on n'en fait plus** they don't make women like that any more; **f. un enfant à qn** to make sb pregnant; **f. des compliments à qn** to compliment sb; **je ferai de lui un homme/un avocat** I'll make a man/a lawyer of him; **qu'est-ce que je vais f. de lui?** what am I going to do with him?; **qu'est-ce que tu vas f. de ce vieux bidon?** what are you going to do with that old can?; **qu'est-ce que j'ai fait de mes lunettes?** what have I done with my glasses?
   (**b**) *(effectuer) (changements, effort, grimace, mouvement)* to make; **f. le ménage/la vaisselle** to do the housework/the washing-up; **f. un pas en avant** to step forward; **faire demi-tour** to turn round; **f. une école de commerce** to study at a business school; **f. une licence** to study for a degree; **c'est moi qui fais tout ici** I have to do everything round here; **voilà une bonne chose de faite** that's one thing out of the way; **ce qui est fait est fait** what's done is done; **c'est bien fait pour elle** it serves her right
   (**c**) *(occasionner)* **f. de la peine à qn** to hurt sb; **qu'est-ce que tu lui as fait?** what have you done to her? *Fam* **f. des ennuis à qn** to make trouble for sb; **ça m'a fait quelque chose/un choc** it upset/shocked me; **ça a fait du scandale** it caused a scandal; **ça fait rien** it doesn't matter; **qu'est-ce que ça peut faire?** what difference does it make?; **ça fait mauvais effet** it gives a bad impression; **le médicament n'a pas fait effet** the medicine didn't take effect
   (**d**) *(changer)* **on ne peut rien y f.** nothing can be done about it; *Fam* **rien à f.!** nothing doing!
   (**e**) *(subir)* to have; **f. une dépression** to have depression; *Fam* **f. une pneumonie/une grippe** to have pneumonia/flu; *Fam* **il m'a encore fait une grippe!** he's gone and got the flu again!
   (**f**) *(pratiquer)* **f. du tennis/football** to play tennis/football; **f. de la voile** to sail; **f. du violon/piano** to play the violin/the piano; **f. du russe/de l'espagnol** to do Russian/Spanish
   (**g**) *(constituer)* to make; **il ferait un excellent mari/pompier** he would make an excellent husband/

fireman; **f. l'affaire** to do the trick; **c'est cela qui fait ton charme** that's what gives you your charm; **cette chambre fait aussi bureau** this bedroom also serves as an office

(**h**) *(s'occuper à)* to do; **qu'est-ce qu'il fait dans la vie?** what does he do for a job?; **qu'est-ce que tu fais demain?** what are you doing tomorrow?; **f. des études** to study; **qu'est-ce que tu fais ici?** what are you doing here?

(**i**) *(parcourir)* to do; **f. 100 kilomètres par jour** to do 100 kilometres a day; **il a fait toute la ville pour la retrouver** he searched the whole town for her; **f. du cent à l'heure** to do 100 km/h

(**j**) *(indique une mesure, une quantité)* to be; **la table fait 1 mètre de long** the table is 1 metre long; **deux et deux font quatre** two and two are *or* make four; **combien ça fait en dollars?** how much is that in dollars?; **le bébé fait 5 kilos** the baby weighs 5 kilos

(**k**) *(agir comme)* **f. l'imbécile** to play the fool; **f. l'innocent** to play the innocent; **f. l'important** to act important; **il fait celui qui n'a pas entendu** he pretends he hasn't heard

(**l**) *(sembler)* to look; **il fait jeune/anglais** he looks young/English

(**m**) *(dire)* to say; **"à bientôt!", fit-elle** "see you soon!", she said; **ça a fait plouf** it went splash

(**n**) *(suivi d'un infinitif)* **f. voir qch à qn** to show sb sth; **f. traverser qn** to help sb across; **f. faire qch à qn** to make sb do sth; **elle m'a fait ranger ma chambre** she made me tidy up my bedroom; **f. réparer qch** to get *or* have sth repaired; **f. construire une maison** to have a house built; **elle ne fait que se plaindre** she's always complaining; **je ne fais que répéter ses paroles** I'm just repeating what she said

(**o**) *(pour remplacer un verbe)* **il devait arroser les plantes mais il ne l'a pas fait** he was meant to water the plants but he didn't; **mais faites donc!** please do!

2 *vi* (**a**) *(agir)* to do; **f. vite** to be quick; **fais comme tu voudras** do as you like; **f. pour le mieux** to do one's best; **f. comme chez soi** to make oneself at home; **comment f.?** how can I/we do it?; *Fam* **il faut f. avec** it'll have to do

(**b**) *Fam (faire ses besoins)* to go to the toilet

3 *v impersonnel* (**a**) *(indique un état)* to be; **il fait froid/chaud** it's cold/hot; **il fait beau** it's fine; **il fait 20 degrés** it's 20 degrees; **il fait jour/nuit** it's light/night

(**b**) *(indique la distance, la durée)* **ça fait un mois qu'il est parti** he's been gone for a month; **ça fait une heure que je t'attends** I've been waiting for you for an hour; **ça fait 200 kilomètres que nous roulons** we've been driving for 200 kilometres

4 se faire *vpr* (**a**) *(avoir lieu)* **finalement ça ne s'est jamais fait** nothing happened in the end; **comment se fait-il que...?** how is it that...?

(**b**) *(être pratiqué)* to be done; **ça se fait beaucoup cette année** it's the in thing this year

(**c**) *(être acceptable)* **ça se fait** it's the done thing; **ça ne se fait pas** it's not the done thing

(**d**) *(être fabriqué)* to be made

(**e**) *(se confectionner)* **se f. un lit** to make a bed for oneself; **se f. une bibliothèque** to build up a library; **se f. un œuf sur le plat** to make oneself a fried egg; **se f. les ongles** to do one's nails

(**f**) *(fromage, vin)* to mature; *(chaussures)* to wear in

(**g**) *(provoquer)* **se f. mal** to hurt oneself; **se f. une entorse au poignet** to sprain one's wrist; **se f. du**

souci to worry; **se f. une opinion** to form an opinion; **se f. des amis/des ennemis** to make friends/enemies; *Fam* **s'en f.** to worry; **elle ne s'en fait pas celle-là!** *(elle a du culot)* she's got a nerve!; *(elle a beaucoup d'argent)* she hasn't got a care in the world!

(**h**) *(s'ériger en)* **se f. le défenseur des opprimés** to become established as a defender of the oppressed

(**i**) *(devenir)* **se f. vieux** to get old; **se f. beau** to do oneself up; **se f. moine** to become a monk; **il se fait tard** it's getting late

(**j**) *(avec un infinitif)* **se f. insulter** to get abused; **se f. couper les cheveux** to have one's hair cut; **se f. prêter qch** to borrow sth; **se f. refaire le nez** to have a nose job

(**k**) *(s'habituer)* **se f. à qch** to get used to sth

(**l**) *(l'un l'autre)* **se f. des cadeaux** to give each other presents; **se f. des reproches** to blame each other

(**m**) *Fam* **il faut se le f. celui-là!** what a pain in the neck!

faire-part [fɛrpar] *nm inv* announcement

faire-valoir [fɛrvalwar] *nm inv (personne)* foil

fair-play [fɛrplɛ] **1** *adj inv* **être f.** to play fair
  2 *nm* fair play

fais *voir* **faire**

faisabilité [fəzabilite] *nf* feasibility

faisable [fəzabl] *adj* feasible

faisan [fəzã] *nm* pheasant

faisandé, -e [fəzãde] *adj (gibier)* high

faisane [fəzan] *adj f & nf* **(poule) f.** hen pheasant

faisceau, -x [fɛso] *nm* (**a**) *(rayons)* beam; **f. hertzien** electromagnetic wave; **f. lumineux** beam of light (**b**) *Fig (de preuves)* body

faiseur, -euse [fəzœr, -øz] **1** *nm,f* maker; **f. d'embarras** fusspot; **f. de miracles** miracle worker
  2 *nf* **faiseuse d'anges** backstreet abortionist

faisons *voir* **faire**

faisselle [fɛsɛl] *nf (fromage)* = type of soft white cheese; *(récipient)* cheese drainer

fait¹, -e *pp voir* **faire**

fait², -e [fɛ, fɛt] *adj* (**a**) *(fabriqué)* **tout f.** *(idée, expression)* fixed

(**b**) *(adapté)* **être f. pour qn/qch** to be made for sb/sth; **ils sont faits l'un pour l'autre** they're made for each other; **être f. pour faire qch** *(personne)* to be cut out to do sth

(**c**) *(bâti)* *Litt ou Hum* **être bien f. de sa personne** to be good-looking

(**d**) *(maquillé)* **avoir les ongles/les yeux faits** to be wearing nail polish/eye make-up

(**e**) *(fromage)* ripe

fait³ *nm* (**a**) *(acte)* act; **les faits et gestes de qn** sb's every move; **prendre qn sur le f.** to catch sb in the act *or* red-handed; **prendre f. et cause pour qn** to stand up for sb

(**b**) *(réalité)* fact; **le f. d'habiter en ville** living in town; **mettre qn devant le f. accompli** to present sb with a fait accompli; **c'est un f. acquis** it's an established fact

(**c**) *(point précis)* **aller droit au f.** to get straight to the point; **en venir au f.** to come to the point

(**d**) *(événement)* event; **un f. nouveau s'est produit** there was a new development; **un f. divers** a news item; **faits divers** *(rubrique)* ≃ news in brief

(**e**) *(locutions)* **au f.** *(à propos)* by the way; **être au f. de qch** to know *or* be informed about sth; **en f., de f.** in fact, as a matter of fact; **de ce f.** for that reason;

expert en f. de vins expert as regards wine *or* when it comes to wine

faîte [fɛt] *nm* (**a**) *(d'un toit)* ridge; *(d'un arbre, d'une maison)* top; *(d'une montagne)* summit (**b**) *Fig* **le f. de la gloire** the height of glory

faites *voir* **faire**

faîtier, -ère [fɛtje, -ɛr] *adj Suisse (organisation, association)* umbrella

faitout *nm*, **fait-tout** *nm inv* [fɛtu] stewpot

fakir [fakir] *nm* fakir

falaise [falɛz] *nf* cliff

fallacieux, -euse [falasjø, -øz] *adj (prétexte)* false; *(argument, raisonnement)* specious; *(apparence)* misleading

falloir [37] [falwar] **1** *v impersonnel* (**a**) *(être nécessaire)* **faut-il tout cela?** is all that necessary?; **je l'ai fait parce qu'il le fallait** I did it because I had to; **il lui faut un nouveau pardessus** he needs a new coat; **il me faudrait un kilo de pommes** I need a kilo of apples; **je lui ai tout donné, qu'est-ce qu'il lui faut de plus!** I've given him everything, what more does he want!; **il m'a fallu trois jours pour le faire** it took me three days to do it; **il faut partir** I/we/you/*etc* must go *or* have to go; **il lui faut se dépêcher** she has to hurry; **il fallait le dire!** why didn't you say so?; **je vous en prie, il ne fallait pas!** you shouldn't have!; **il faudrait qu'elle reste** she ought to stay; **il ne faudrait pas que je vous mette en retard** I'd better not make you late; **il faut toujours que tu fasses des histoires!** why do you always have to cause such a fuss!; **il a fallu qu'elle le raconte à tout le quartier!** she had to go and tell the whole neighbourhood!

(**b**) *(locutions) Fam* **il faut ce qu'il faut!** you might as well do things in style!; **il faut voir** *(il faut attendre)* we'll have to wait and see; *(il faut réfléchir)* I/we will have to think about it; *Fam* **elle lui a répondu, faut voir comment!** you wouldn't believe the way she answered him!

2 s'en falloir *vpr* **il s'en est fallu de peu** *ou* **peu s'en est fallu qu'elle ne meure** she very nearly died; **5 livres ou peu s'en faut** the best part of £5; **loin** *ou* **tant s'en faut** far from it

fallu *voir* **falloir**

falot¹ [falo] *nm (lanterne)* lantern

falot², **-e** [falo, -ɔt] *adj* dreary, drab

falsification [falsifikasjɔ̃] *nf (de documents, de comptes)* falsification; *(d'une signature)* forging

falsifier [66] [falsifje] *vt (document, comptes)* to falsify; *(signature)* to forge

falzar [falzar] *nm Fam Br* trousers, *Am* pants

famé, -e [fame] *adj* **mal f.** disreputable

famélique [famelik] *adj* half-starved

fameusement [famøzmã] *adv Fam (très)* incredibly

fameux, -euse [famø, -øz] *adj* (**a**) *(célèbre)* famous (**pour** for); **c'est donc ça, ton f. régime!** so this is your famous diet! (**b**) *Fam (excellent)* brilliant; **pas f.** not much good

familial, -e, -aux, -ales [familjal, -o] **1** *adj (vie, atmosphère)* family; *(entreprise, hôtel)* family-run; *(paquet, format)* family-size

2 *nf* **familiale** *(auto) Br* estate car, *Am* station wagon

familiariser [familjarize] **1** *vt* **f. qn avec qch** to familiarize sb with sth, to get sb used to sth

2 se familiariser *vpr* **se f. avec qch** *(en le pratiquant)* to familiarize oneself with sth; *(en s'y habituant)* to get used to sth; *(lieu)* to get to know sth

familiarité [familjarite] *nf* (**a**) *(désinvolture)* informality (**b**) **familiarités** *(libertés)* familiarities

familier, -ère [familje, -ɛr] **1** *adj* (**a**) *(désinvolte)* informal (**avec** with) (**b**) *(langage, expression)* colloquial (**c**) *(connu)* familiar (**à** to)

2 *nm,f (client)* regular visitor (**de** to)

familièrement [familjɛrmã] *adv* familiarly; **parler f. à qn** to be familiar with sb

famille [famij] *nf* (**a**) *(proches)* family; **de bonne f.** from a good family; **en f.** with one's family; **c'est de f.** it runs in the family; *Fam* **un repas des familles** a cosy little meal; **f. monoparentale** one-parent family; **f. nombreuse,** *Suisse* **grande f.** large family (**b**) *(d'animaux, de langues, de plantes)* family; **f. littéraire/politique** literary/political circle

famine [famin] *nf* famine; **crier f.** to be starving

fan [fan], **fana** [fana] *nmf Fam* fan

fanal, -aux [fanal, -o] *nm (lanterne)* lantern

fanatique [fanatik] **1** *adj* fanatical (**de** about)

2 *nmf* fanatic; **f. de football** football fanatic

fanatiser [fanatize] *vt* to make fanatical

fanatisme [fanatism] *nm* fanaticism

faner [fane] **1** *vi (fleur)* to wither; *Fig (beauté, teint)* to fade

2 se faner *vpr (fleur)* to wither; *Fig (beauté, teint)* to fade

fanes [fan] *nfpl (de carottes, de radis)* tops

fanfare [fɑ̃far] *nf (orchestre)* brass band; **réveil en f.** brutal awakening

fanfaron, -onne [fɑ̃farɔ̃, -ɔn] **1** *adj* boastful

2 *nm,f* braggart; **faire le f.** to brag, to boast

fanfaronnades [fɑ̃farɔnad] *nfpl* bragging, boasting

fanfaronner [fɑ̃farɔne] *vi* to brag, to boast

fanfreluches [fɑ̃frəlyʃ] *nfpl Péj* frills

fange [fɑ̃ʒ] *nf Litt* mire; **élevé dans la f.** brought up in the gutter

fanion [fanjɔ̃] *nm (d'un club)* pennant; *(balise)* flag; **fanions** *(guirlandes)* bunting

fanon [fanɔ̃] *nm (de baleine)* whalebone

fantaisie [fɑ̃tezi] **1** *adj inv* **collants f.** patterned tights; **kirsch f.** kirsch-flavoured liqueur

2 *nf* (**a**) *(envie)* whim; **faire qch à sa f.** to do sth as the fancy takes one (**b**) *(créativité)* imagination (**c**) *(œuvre musicale)* fantasia

fantaisiste [fɑ̃tezist] **1** *adj (personne)* eccentric; *(interprétation)* fanciful; *(horaires, mode de vie)* unorthodox

2 *nmf (comédien)* variety artist

fantasmagorique [fɑ̃tasmagɔrik] *adj* phantasmagorical

fantasme [fɑ̃tasm] *nm* fantasy

fantasmer [fɑ̃tasme] *vi* to fantasize (**sur** about)

fantasque [fɑ̃task] *adj* whimsical

fantassin [fɑ̃tasɛ̃] *nm* foot soldier, infantryman

fantastique [fɑ̃tastik] **1** *adj* (**a**) *(littérature, conte, film)* fantasy (**b**) *Fam (excellent)* fantastic (**c**) *(créature)* fantastic

2 *nm* **le f.** the fantastic; *(littérature)* fantasy literature

fantoche [fɑ̃tɔʃ] **1** *nm* puppet

2 *adj* **gouvernement f.** puppet government

fantomatique [fɑ̃tɔmatik] *adj* ghostly

fantôme [fɑ̃tom] **1** *nm* ghost, phantom

2 *adj (ville, train)* ghost

fanzine [fɑ̃zin] *nm* fanzine

FAO [εfao] *nf* (**a**) (*abrév* **fabrication assistée par ordinateur**) CAM (**b**) (*abrév* **Food and Agricultural Organization**) FAO

faon [fã] *nm* fawn

far [far] *nm* **f. breton** custard flan with prunes

faramineux, -euse [faraminø, -øz] *adj Fam* phenomenal

farandole [farãdɔl] *nf* farandole

farce [fars] *nf* (**a**) (*tour*) (practical) joke, prank; **faire une f. à qn** to play a (practical) joke on sb; **magasin de farces et attrapes** joke shop; *Can Fam* **c'est pas des farces!** it's true!, I'm not joking! (**b**) (*préparation culinaire*) stuffing (**c**) (*pièce de théâtre*) farce

farceur, -euse [farsœr, -øz] *1 adj* mischievous
2 nm,f (practical) joker, prankster

farcir [farsir] *1 vt* (**a**) (*volaille, légume*) to stuff (**b**) *Fam* (*remplir*) to cram (**de** with)
2 se farcir vpr Fam **se f. qch** (*corvée*) to get landed with sth; **se f. qn/qch** (*supporter*) to put up with sb/sth

fard [far] *nm* make-up; *Fam* **piquer un f.** to go red; **f. à joues** blusher; **f. à paupières** eye shadow

fardeau, -x [fardo] *nm* load; *Fig* burden

farder [farde] *1 vt* (*maquiller*) to make up
2 se farder vpr to put on one's make-up; **se f. les yeux** to put eye shadow on

farfadet [farfadε] *nm* goblin

farfelu, -e [farfəly] *Fam 1 adj* (*personne, idée*) weird
2 nm,f weirdo

farfouiller [farfuje] *vi Fam* to rummage (**dans** through)

farine [farin] *nf* flour; **f. de blé** wheat flour; **f. de maïs** *Br* cornflour, *Am* cornstarch

farineux, -euse [farinø, -øz] *1 adj* (**a**) *Péj* (*pommes de terre, banane*) floury (**b**) (*contenant de la fécule*) starchy
2 nmpl starchy food

farniente [farnjente] *nm* idleness

farouche [faruʃ] *adj* (**a**) (*animal*) timid; (*personne*) shy (**b**) (*haine, air, regard*) fierce

farouchement [faruʃmã] *adv* fiercely

fart [fart] *nm* (ski) wax

fascicule [fasikyl] *nm* (*d'une publication*) instalment; (*brochure*) brochure

fascinant, -e [fasinã, -ãt] *adj* fascinating

fascination [fasinasjɔ̃] *nf* fascination; **exercer une f. sur qn** to fascinate sb

fasciner [fasine] *vt* (**a**) (*impressionner*) to fascinate (**b**) (*charmer*) to captivate

fascisme [faʃism] *nm* fascism

fasciste [faʃist] *adj & nmf* fascist

fasse *etc voir* **faire**

faste¹ [fast] *nm* splendour

faste² *adj* (*jour*) lucky; (*période*) good

fast-food (*pl* **fast-foods**) [fastfud] *nm* fast-food restaurant

fastidieux, -euse [fastidjø, -øz] *adj* tedious

fastoche [fastɔʃ] *adj Fam* dead easy

fastueux, -euse [fastɥø, -øz] *adj* sumptuous

fat [fa(t)] *nm* conceited person

fatal, -e, -als, -ales [fatal] *adj* (**a**) (*mortel*) fatal; *Fig* fatal (**à** for); **le choc lui a été f.** the shock killed him; *Ordinat* **erreur fatale** fatal error (**b**) (*inévitable*) inevitable

fatalement [fatalmã] *adv* inevitably

fatalisme [fatalism] *nm* fatalism

fataliste [fatalist] *1 adj* fatalistic
2 nmf fatalist

fatalité [fatalite] *nf* (**a**) (*malédiction*) bad luck (**b**) (*inévitabilité*) inevitability

fatidique [fatidik] *adj* fateful

fatigant, -e [fatigã, -ãt] *adj* (**a**) (*épuisant*) tiring; **c'est f. pour le cœur/les yeux** it's a strain on the heart/the eyes (**b**) (*ennuyeux*) tiresome

fatigue [fatig] *nf* tiredness; **tomber** *ou* **être mort de f.** to be dead tired; **f. nerveuse** nervous exhaustion; **f. oculaire** eyestrain

fatigué, -e [fatige] *adj* (**a**) (*las*) tired; **f. par sa promenade** tired from one's walk; **f. par le voyage** travelworn; **f. de qn/qch** tired of sb/sth; **f. de faire qch** tired *or* weary of doing sth (**b**) (*estomac, foie*) upset; (*cœur*) strained

fatiguer [fatige] *1 vt* (**a**) (*personne*) to tire (out); (*yeux, cœur*) to strain; (*estomac, foie*) to upset; *Ironique* **si ça ne te fatigue pas trop** if it's not too much of an effort (**b**) (*ennuyer*) to wear out (**c**) *Fam* **f. la salade** to toss the salad
2 vi (*personne*) to get tired; (*moteur, voiture*) to labour
3 se fatiguer vpr (**a**) (*s'épuiser*) to get tired; **se f. à faire qch** to tire oneself out doing sth; **se f. les yeux/ le cœur** to strain one's eyes/heart; *Ironique* **tu ne t'es pas fatigué** you didn't exactly strain yourself; **ne te fatigue pas, je m'en charge** don't bother, I'll see to it (**b**) (*se lasser*) **se f. de qn/qch** to get tired of sb/sth

fatras [fatra] *nm* jumble, muddle

fatwa [fatwa] *nf Rel* fatwa; **prononcer une f. contre qn** to declare *or* issue a fatwa against sb

faubourg [fobur] *nm* suburb

fauche [foʃ] *nf Fam* thieving; **il y a de la f.** there are thieves about

fauché, -e [foʃe] *adj Fam* **f. (comme les blés)** (flat) broke

faucher [foʃe] *vt* (**a**) (*herbe, champ*) to mow; (*blé*) to reap (**b**) (*piéton*) to mow down; **se faire f. par une voiture** to be mown down by a car (**c**) *Fam* (*voler*) to pinch; **se faire f. qch** to get sth pinched

faucheur, -euse [foʃœr, -øz] *1 nm,f* (*de blé*) reaper; (*d'herbe*) mower
2 nm (*insecte*) *Br* harvestman, *Am* daddy-long-legs
3 nf **faucheuse** (*machine*) (*pour le blé*) reaper; (*pour l'herbe*) mower; **la Faucheuse** (*la Mort*) the Grim Reaper

faucheux [foʃø] *nm Br* harvestman, *Am* daddy-long-legs

faucille [fosij] *nf* sickle; **la f. et le marteau** the hammer and sickle

faucon [fokɔ̃] *nm* falcon, hawk; **f. pèlerin** peregrine falcon

faudra *etc voir* **falloir**

faufiler [fofile] *1 vt* to tack, to baste
2 se faufiler vpr (*à travers la foule*) to work one's way (**à travers** through); **il s'était faufilé parmi les invités** he had slipped in with the guests

faune [fon] *nf* (*animaux*) fauna, animal life; *Fig & Péj* **la f. des boîtes de nuit** the nightclub set; **elle fréquente une f. bizarre** she mixes with a funny crowd

faussaire [fosεr] *nmf* forger

fausse [fos] *adj voir* **faux¹**

faussement [fosmã] *adv* (**a**) (*injustement*) wrongly, falsely (**b**) (*de façon hypocrite*) deceptively

fausser [fose] **1** *vt* (**a**) *(clef, axe)* to buckle, to bend (**b**) *(réalité, résultat)* to distort (**c**) **f. compagnie à qn** to give sb the slip
2 se fausser *vpr* (**a**) *(voix)* to become strained (**b**) *(clef, axe)* to buckle, to bend
fausset [fosɛ] *nm Mus* falsetto; **voix de f.** falsetto voice
fausseté [foste] *nf* (**a**) *(d'une information, d'un raisonnement)* falseness (**b**) *(hypocrisie)* duplicity
faut *voir* **falloir**
faute [fot] *nf* (**a**) *(erreur)* mistake, error; *(au football)* foul; *(au tennis)* fault; **faire une f.** to make a mistake *or* an error; **être en f.** to be at fault; **prendre qn en f.** to catch sb out; **c'est de ma f.!** it's my fault!; **f. d'étourderie** *ou* **d'inattention** careless mistake; **f. de français** grammatical mistake; **f. de frappe** typing mistake; **f. d'orthographe** spelling mistake; **f. professionnelle** professional misconduct (**b**) *(manque)* **sans f.** without fail; **f. de temps** for lack of time; **f. de mieux** for lack *or* want of anything better; **f. de quoi** failing which, otherwise; **ce n'est pas f. d'avoir essayé** it's not for want of trying
fauteuil [fotœj] *nm* (**a**) *(siège)* armchair, easy chair; **f. à bascule** rocking chair; **f. d'orchestre** seat in the *Br* stalls *or Am* orchestra; **f. pivotant** swivel chair; **f. roulant** wheelchair (**b**) *Fig (à l'Académie française)* seat
fauteur [fotœr] *nm* **f. de troubles** troublemaker
fautif, -ive [fotif, -iv] **1** *adj* (**a**) *(coupable)* at fault, in the wrong (**b**) *(incorrect)* faulty
2 *nm,f (coupable)* person at fault *or* in the wrong
fauve [fov] **1** *adj* (**a**) *(roux)* fawn (**b**) *(odeur)* musky (**c**) *(en peinture)* Fauvist
2 *nm* (**a**) *(grand félin)* big cat; **sentir le f.** to smell of sweat (**b**) *(couleur)* fawn (**c**) *(en peinture)* Fauvist
fauvette [fovɛt] *nf* warbler
fauvisme [fovism] *nm* Fauvism
faux¹, fausse [fo, fos] **1** *adj* (**a**) *(incorrect)* wrong; **c'est un f. problème** that's not the real problem; *Fam* **t'as tout f.** you're completely wrong; **f. ami** false friend; **faire une fausse couche** to have a miscarriage; **faire une fausse note** to hit a wrong note; **faire fausse route** to take the wrong road; *Fig* to be on the wrong track; **faire un f. sens** *(en traduisant)* to give an inaccurate translation; *(en français)* to give an inaccurate definition (**b**) *(mensonger)* false, untrue; *Fam* **c'est un f. jeton** *ou* **cul** he's two-faced; **f. témoignage** perjury (**c**) *(injustifié) (alerte, espoirs)* false (**d**) *(postiche)* false (**e**) *(billet, pièce, document)* forged; *(tableau, bijoux)* fake; *(plafond)* false (**f**) *Péj (hypocrite)* false
2 *adv (chanter, sonner)* out of tune, off key; *Fig* **sonner f.** not to ring true
3 *nm* (**a**) *(tableau, sculpture)* fake (**b**) *(document)* forgery; **f. en écriture** forgery
faux² *nf* scythe
faux-cul [foky] *très Fam* **1** *adj* **il est f.** he's a two-faced bastard
2 *nmf* two-faced bastard, *f* two-faced bitch
faux-filet *(pl* **faux-filets)** [fofilɛ] *nm* sirloin
faux-fuyant *(pl* **faux-fuyants)** [fofɥijɑ̃] *nm (prétexte)* subterfuge
faux-monnayeur *(pl* **faux-monnayeurs)** [fomɔnɛjœr] *nm* forger, counterfeiter
faux-semblant *(pl* **faux-semblants)** [fosɑ̃blɑ̃] *nm* pretence, sham

faveur [favœr] *nf* (**a**) *(considération)* favour; **avoir la f. de qn** to be in favour with sb; **de f.** *(marques)* of favour; *(régime, traitement)* special (**b**) *(privilège)* favour; **faire une f. à qn** to do sb a favour (**c**) **être en f. de qch** *(être favorable à)* to be in favour of sth; **en ma/sa f.** *(à mon/son avantage)* in my/her favour, to my/her advantage (**d**) *(ruban)* favour
favorable [favɔrabl] *adj* favourable (**à** to)
favorablement [favɔrabləmɑ̃] *adv* favourably
favori, -ite [favɔri, -it] *adj & nm,f* favourite
favoris [favɔri] *nmpl* sideburns
favorisé, -e [favɔrize] *adj (milieu, famille)* fortunate
favoriser [favɔrize] *vt* (**a**) *(avantager) (personne)* to favour (**b**) *(encourager) (croissance, emploi)* to encourage, to promote
favoritisme [favɔritism] *nm* favouritism
fax [faks] *nm (appareil)* fax (machine); *(message)* fax; **envoyer qch par f.** to send sth by fax; **f. modem** fax modem
faxer [fakse] *vt* to fax
fayot [fajo] *nm Fam* (**a**) *(haricot sec)* bean (**b**) *(élève)* crawler
fayotage [fajotaʒ] *nm Fam* crawling
fayoter [fajote] *vi Fam* to crawl
fébrile [febril] *adj aussi Fig* feverish
fébrilement [febrilmɑ̃] *adv* feverishly
fébrilité [febrilite] *nf* feverishness
fécond, -e [fekɔ̃, -ɔ̃d] *adj (femme, femelle, terre, imagination)* fertile; *(écrivain)* prolific; *Fig* **f. en qch** *(période, moment)* full of sth
fécondation [fekɔ̃dasjɔ̃] *nf (d'une femme, d'une femelle)* impregnation; *(d'un œuf, d'un ovule)* fertilization; **f. artificielle** artificial insemination; **f. in vitro** in vitro fertilization
féconder [fekɔ̃de] *vt (femme, femelle)* to impregnate; *(œuf, ovule)* to fertilize
fécondité [fekɔ̃dite] *nf* (**a**) *(d'une femme, d'une femelle)* fertility (**b**) *(d'un écrivain)* productiveness
fécule [fekyl] *nf* starch
féculent, -e [fekylɑ̃, -ɑ̃t] **1** *adj* starchy
2 *nm* starchy food
FED [ɛføde] *nm (abrév Fonds européen de développement)* EDF
FEDER [fedɛr] *nm (abrév Fonds européen de développement régional)* ERDF
fédéral, -e, -aux, -ales [federal, -o] *adj* federal
fédéralisme [federalism] *nm* federalism
fédéraliste [federalist] *adj & nmf* federalist
fédérateur, -trice [federatœr, -tris] *adj* federal
fédération [federasjɔ̃] *nf* federation
fédéré, -e [federe] *adj* federate
fée [fe] *nf* fairy; *Hum* **f. du logis** wonderful housewife; *Suisse* **f. verte** absinthe
feed-back [fidbak] *nm* feedback
féerie [feri, feeri] *nf (spectacle magnifique)* enchanting display
féerique [ferik, feerik] *adj (personnage, monde)* fairy; *(vision)* enchanting
feignais *etc voir* **feindre**
feignant, -e [feɲɑ̃, -ɑ̃t] *Fam* **1** *adj* bone idle
2 *nm,f* idler
feindre [54] [fɛ̃dr] *vt (maladie, sentiment)* to feign; **inutile de f.** it's no use pretending; **f. de faire qch** to pretend to do sth
feint, -e [fɛ̃, fɛ̃t] *adj (maladie, joie)* feigned

feinte [fɛ̃t] nf (**a**) (ruse) ruse (**b**) (au football, au rugby) dummy

feinter [fɛ̃te] **1** vt Fam (duper) to take in **2** vi (au football, au rugby) to dummy

fêlé, -e [fele] adj (**a**) (verre, voix) cracked (**b**) Fam (fou) cracked, bonkers

fêler [fele] vt to crack

félicitations [felisitasjɔ̃] nfpl congratulations (**pour** on)

féliciter [felisite] **1** vt to congratulate (**de/pour** on); **f. qn d'avoir fait qch** to congratulate sb on having done sth
2 se féliciter vpr se **f. de qch/d'avoir fait qch** to congratulate oneself on sth/on having done sth

félin, -e [felɛ̃, -in] adj & nm feline

fêlure [felyr] nf aussi Fig crack

femelle [fəmɛl] adj & nf female

féminin, -e [feminɛ̃, -in] **1** adj (personne, charme, visage) feminine; (hormone, population, sexe) female; (équipe, magazine, mode) women's
2 nm feminine; **au f.** in the feminine

féminiser [feminize] **1** vt (**a**) (ouvrir aux femmes) to increase the number of women in (**b**) (rendre efféminé) to make effeminate
2 se féminiser vpr (**a**) (profession, institution, carrière) to attract more women (**b**) (homme) to become effeminate

féminisme [feminism] nm feminism

féministe [feminist] adj & nmf feminist

féminité [feminite] nf femininity

femme [fam] nf (**a**) (adulte de sexe féminin) woman; **des femmes, de la f.** (libération, émancipation, droits) women's; **la f. de ma vie** the love of my life; **elle est très f.** she's very feminine; Fam **une bonne f.** a woman; **f. d'affaires** businesswoman; **f. de chambre** (dans un hôtel) (chamber)maid; **f. fatale** femme fatale; **f. au foyer** housewife; **f. de ménage,** Belg **f. d'ouvrage** cleaning lady; **f. du monde** society woman; **f. de tête** forceful woman (**b**) (épouse) wife

femmelette [famlɛt] nf Péj (homme) weakling

fémur [femyr] nm thighbone, Spéc femur

FEN [fɛn] nf (abrév **Fédération de l'Éducation Nationale**) = largest French teachers' union

fenaison [fənɛzɔ̃] nf haymaking

fendant, -e [fɑ̃dɑ̃, -ɑ̃t] adj Fam hilarious

fendiller [fɑ̃dije] **1** vt (bois, vernis) to crack; (peau, lèvres) to chap
2 se fendiller vpr (bois, vernis) to crack; (peau, lèvres) to chap

fendre [fɑ̃dr] **1** vt (**a**) (bois) to split; (pierre, sol) to crack; **f. le cœur à qn** to break sb's heart (**b**) (traverser) (flots, mer) to plough through; (air) to cut through
2 se fendre vpr (**a**) (bois) to split; (pierre, sol) to crack (**b**) Fam se **f. de qch** (d'une somme) to fork out sth; (d'un cadeau) to fork out on sth; **tu ne t'es pas fendu** (ce n'était pas cher) it didn't break the bank; (tu ne t'es pas fatigué) you didn't strain yourself (**c**) Fam se **f. la pipe** ou **la pêche** ou **la poire** to split one's sides (laughing)

fendu, -e [fɑ̃dy] adj (jupe) slit

fenêtre [fənɛtr] nf (**a**) (ouverture) window; **f. à guillotine** sash window (**b**) Ordinat window; **f. d'aide** help window; **f. déroulante** pull-down window

fennec [fenɛk] nm fennec

fenouil [fənuj] nm fennel

fente [fɑ̃t] nf (**a**) (dans le bois) split; (dans le sol, dans un mur) crack (**b**) (d'une tirelire, d'une boîte aux lettres) slot

féodal, -e, -aux, -ales [feɔdal, -o] adj feudal

féodalité [feɔdalite] nf feudalism

fer [fɛr] nm (**a**) (métal) iron; Fig de **f.** (discipline, volonté) iron; (santé) cast-iron; **croire qch dur comme f.** to believe very firmly in sth; **f. forgé** wrought iron (**b**) (objet en fer) **f.** à cheval horseshoe; Fam **les quatre fers en l'air** flat on one's back; Fig **f. de lance** spearhead (**c**) (outil) **f.** à repasser iron; **donner un coup de f.** à **qch** to iron sth; **marquer qch au f. rouge** to brand sth; **f.** à **souder** soldering iron (**d**) **fers** (chaînes) irons

ferai etc voir **faire**

fer-blanc (pl **fers-blancs**) [fɛrblɑ̃] nm tin(plate); **en f.** tin

ferblanterie [fɛrblɑ̃tri] nf (**a**) (commerce) tinplate trade (**b**) (articles) tinware

férié, -e [ferje] adj **lundi prochain est f.** next Monday is a (public) holiday

férir [ferir] vt **sans coup f.** without any difficulty

ferme¹ [fɛrm] **1** adj (**a**) (dur) firm (**b**) Jur **trois ans de prison f., trois ans fermes** three years' imprisonment
2 adv (travailler) hard; (discuter) keenly; **s'ennuyer f.** to be bored stiff

ferme² nf farm; **produits de la f.** farm produce

fermé, -e [fɛrme] adj (**a**) (porte, récipient, boutique) closed, shut; (route) closed (**b**) (expression, visage) impassive; **être f.** à **qch** (ne pas être sensible à) to have no appreciation of sth (**c**) (société, club, milieu) exclusive, select

fermement [fɛrməmɑ̃] adv firmly

ferment [fɛrmɑ̃] nm aussi Fig ferment

fermentation [fɛrmɑ̃tasjɔ̃] nf fermentation

fermenter [fɛrmɑ̃te] vi to ferment

fermer [fɛrme] **1** vt (**a**) (porte, boîte, livre) to close, to shut; (maison) to shut up; (rideaux) to close, to draw; (vêtement) to fasten, to do up; (parenthèse) to close; (enveloppe) to seal; **f. sa porte** à **qn** to close one's door to sb; **f. les yeux/la bouche** to close one's eyes/one's mouth; Fig **f. les yeux sur qch** to turn a blind eye to sth; Fam **je n'ai pas fermé l'œil** I didn't sleep a wink; Fam **f. sa gueule, la f.** to shut up, to shut one's mouth (**b**) (frontière, pays) to close off (**c**) (robinet, eau, électricité) to turn off (**d**) (compte bancaire) to close (**e**) (entreprise) (temporairement) to close, to shut; (définitivement) to close down; **f. boutique** to shut up shop (**f**) Ordinat (fichier, fenêtre) to close; (commande) to end
2 vi (**a**) (porte, boîte) to close, to shut; **f. bien/mal** to close/not to close properly (**b**) (entreprise, magasin) (temporairement) to close, to shut; (définitivement) to close down
3 se fermer vpr (**a**) (porte, boîte, yeux) to close, to shut; (vêtement) to fasten, to do up (**b**) (visage) to freeze; (personne) to clam up

fermeté [fɛrməte] nf firmness; **avec f.** firmly

fermeture [fɛrmətyr] nf (**a**) (d'une porte) closing, shutting; (d'une route, d'une frontière, d'un débat) closing (**b**) (cessation d'activité) closing; **heure de f.** closing time (**c**) (d'un compte bancaire) closing (**d**) **f. Éclair®** ou **à glissière** Br zip, Am zipper (**e**) Ordinat (d'un fichier, d'une fenêtre) closing; (d'une commande) ending

fermier, -ère [fɛrmje, -ɛr] **1** *adj (poulet)* free-range; *(beurre)* dairy
2 *nm,f* farmer

fermoir [fɛrmwar] *nm (de collier, de sac)* clasp; *Can (fermeture à glissière) Br* zip, *Am* zipper

féroce [fɛrɔs] *adj (animal, personne, critique)* ferocious; *(joie, moquerie)* savage; *(appétit)* ravenous

férocement [fɛrɔsmã] *adv* ferociously

férocité [fɛrɔsite] *nf* ferocity

Féroé [fɛrɔe] *nfpl* **les (îles) F.** the Faroe Islands, the Faroes

ferraille [fɛrɑj] *nf* **(a)** *(débris de fer)* scrap (iron); **mettre qch à la f.** to put sth on the scrap heap **(b)** *Fam (petite monnaie)* small change

ferré, -e [fɛre] *adj* **(a)** *(chaussure)* hobnailed; *(canne)* metal-tipped **(b)** *(calé)* **être f. en qch** to be well up in sth

ferrer [fɛre] *vt* **(a)** *(cheval)* to shoe **(b)** *(poisson)* to strike

ferreux, -euse [fɛrø, -øz] *adj* ferrous

ferronnerie [fɛrɔnri] *nf* **(a)** *(objets)* **f. (d'art)** (decorative) ironwork **(b)** *(travail)* ironwork **(c)** *(atelier)* ironworks *(singulier)*

ferronnier, -ère [fɛrɔnje, -ɛr] *nm,f* **f. (d'art)** worker in wrought iron

ferroviaire [fɛrɔvjɛr] *adj (réseau, trafic, ligne) Br* railway, *Am* railroad; *(transports)* rail

ferrugineux, -euse [fɛryʒinø, -øz] *adj* ferruginous

ferrure [fɛryr] *nf* **(a)** *(garniture)* fitting **(b)** *(d'un cheval)* shoeing

ferry [fɛri] *nm* ferry

ferry-boat *(pl* ferry-boats) [fɛribot] *nm* ferry

fertile [fɛrtil] *adj aussi Fig* fertile; *Fig* **f. en qch** *(période)* full of sth

fertilisation [fɛrtilizasjɔ̃] *nf* fertilization

fertiliser [fɛrtilize] *vt* to fertilize

fertilité [fɛrtilite] *nf* fertility

féru, -e [fery] *adj* **f. de qch** passionately interested in sth

férule [fɛryl] *nf Litt* **être sous la f. de qn** to be under sb's sway

fervent, -e [fɛrvã, -ãt] **1** *adj* fervent; *(catholique)* devout
2 *nm,f* devotee (**de** of)

ferveur [fɛrvœr] *nf* fervour; **avec f.** fervently

fesse [fɛs] *nf* buttock; **fesses** *Br* bottom, *Am* butt

fessée [fese] *nf* spanking; **donner une f. à qn** to give sb a spanking

fessier, -ère [fesje, -ɛr] **1** *adj (muscle)* buttock, *Spéc* gluteal
2 *nm (muscle)* gluteal muscle

festif, -ive [fɛstif, -iv] *adj* festive

festin [fɛstɛ̃] *nm* feast, banquet

festival, -als [fɛstival] *nm* festival; **le f. d'Avignon** = theatre festival held in Avignon; **le f. de Cannes** the Cannes film festival

festivités [fɛstivite] *nfpl* festivities

feston [fɛstɔ̃] *nm* **(a)** *(en broderie)* scallop; **à festons** scalloped **(b)** *(guirlande) & Archit* festoon

festoyer [32] [fɛstwaje] *vi* to feast

feta [feta] *nf* feta cheese

fêtard, -e [fɛtar, -ard] *nm,f Fam* party animal

fête [fɛt] *nf* **(a)** *(célébration publique)* fête, fair; *(événement culturel)* festival; **f. foraine** funfair; **la f. des Mères/Pères** Mother's/Father's Day; **la f. de la Musique** = annual music festival held on 21 June; **la f. des Rois** Twelfth Night
(b) *(soirée)* party; **organiser** *ou* **faire une f.** to have a party
(c) *(manifestation de joie)* **en f.** in a festive mood; **avoir le cœur en f.** to be over the moon; *Fam* **faire la f.** to party; **être de la f.** to be one of the party; **faire f. à qn** to make a fuss of sb
(d) *(du saint dont on porte le nom)* saint's day; *Ironique* **ça va être ta f.!** you're in for it!; *Fam* **faire sa f. à qn** to give sb a good hiding
(e) *(jour chômé)* holiday; **les fêtes (de fin d'année)** the Christmas and New Year holidays; **f. légale** *Br* bank holiday, *Am* legal holiday; **f. nationale** national holiday; **la f. du Travail** Labour Day

---

Fête de la musique

This annual event takes place throughout France on 21 June, the summer solstice. Both amateur and professional musicians take to the streets and there are many impromptu live performances, with bars and restaurants as well as museums and hospitals serving as free venues for jazz, classical, rock and many other styles of music. The festival was originally launched in 1982 by the minister of culture, Jack Lang, following the election of François Mitterand's socialist government. Such has been its success and popularity in France that the event has now spread to many other European countries.

Fête-Dieu *(pl* Fêtes-Dieu) [fɛtdjø] *nf* **la F.** Corpus Christi

fêter [fete] **1** *vt* **(a)** *(anniversaire, événement)* to celebrate **(b)** *(personne)* to fête
2 se fêter *vpr* **ça se fête!** this calls for a celebration!

fétiche [fetiʃ] **1** *adj* lucky
2 *nm (objet de culte)* fetish; *(mascotte)* mascot

fétichisme [fetiʃism] *nm* fetishism

fétichiste [fetiʃist] **1** *adj* fetishistic
2 *nmf* fetishist

fétide [fetid] *adj* fetid

fétu [fety] *nm* **f. (de paille)** wisp of straw

feu¹, -x [fø] **1** *nm* **(a)** *(élément, flammes, incendie)* fire; **mettre (le) f. à qch** to set fire to sth; **prendre f.** to catch fire; **allumer** *ou* **faire un f.** to make a fire; **au f.!** fire!; **en f.** *(lieu)* on fire; *Fig (joues, visage)* burning; **mettre une ville à f. et à sang** to ransack a town; **être tout f. tout flamme** to be burning with enthusiasm; **faire f. de tout bois** to use every available means; **ne pas faire long f.** not to last long; **dans le f. de l'action** in the heat of the action; *Fig* **sous le f. des projecteurs** in the limelight; *Vulg* **avoir le f. au cul** *(être pressé)* to be in a mad rush; *(sexuellement)* to be always gagging for it; **f. d'artifice** *(spectacle)* fireworks display; **f. de Bengale** Bengal light; **f. de camp** campfire; **f. de cheminée** fire in the hearth; **f. follet** will-o'-the-wisp; **f. de forêt** forest fire; **f. de joie** bonfire; *Fig* **f. de paille** flash in the pan; *Can* **f. sauvage** cold sore
(b) *(pour allumer une cigarette)* **avez-vous du f.?** have you got a light?
(c) *(brûleur)* burner; **à f. doux** *ou* **à petit f.** over a low heat; **à f. vif** over a high heat
(d) *(sur la chaussée)* **f. rouge/vert** red/green light; **feux de signalisation** *ou* **tricolores** traffic lights; *Fig* **donner le f. vert à qn** to give sb the green light

(**e**) *(phare)* **feux de brouillard** *ou* **antibrouillard** fog lamps; **feux de croisement** dipped headlights, *Am* low beams; **feux de détresse** hazard (warning) lights; **feux de position** sidelights; **feux de stationnement** parking lights

(**f**) *(tirs)* **faire f.** to fire, to shoot; **ouvrir le f.** to open fire; *Fig* **être pris entre deux feux** to be caught in the crossfire

2 *adj inv* **noir et f.** black-and-tan

feu², **-e** *adj* **f. M. Perrin** the late Mr Perrin; **f. mon mari** my late husband

feuillage [fœjaʒ] *nm* leaves, foliage

feuille [fœj] *nf* (**a**) *(de plante, d'arbre)* leaf; **f. morte** dead leaf; **f. de vigne** fig leaf (**b**) *(de papier)* sheet; **f. volante** loose sheet (**c**) *(journal)* paper; *Péj* **f. de chou** rag (**d**) *(document)* **f. d'impôt** tax return; **f. de maladie** = form given by doctor to patient for claiming reimbursement from Social Security; **f. de paie** *ou* **paye** payslip; **f. de soins** medical expenses claim form (**e**) *Ordinat* **f. de calcul** spreadsheet

feuillet [fœjɛ] *nm* leaf

feuilleté, **-e** [fœjte] **1** *adj* (**a**) *(pâte)* flaky (**b**) *(verre)* laminated

2 *nm* **f. au jambon/au fromage** ham/cheese pasty

feuilleter [42] [fœjte] *vt* (**a**) *(livre)* to leaf through (**b**) *Ordinat* **f. en arrière** to page up; **f. en avant** to page down

feuilleton [fœjtɔ̃] *nm* serial; **f. télévisé** television serial

feuillu, **-e** [fœjy] **1** *adj* (**a**) *(ayant beaucoup de feuilles)* leafy (**b**) *Bot* broad-leaved

2 *nm* *Bot* broad-leaved tree

feutre [føtr] *nm* (**a**) *(matière)* felt (**b**) *(chapeau)* felt hat (**c**) *(stylo)* felt-tip (pen)

feutré, **-e** [føtre] *adj* (**a**) *(garni de feutre)* felt(-covered) (**b**) *(assourdi)* muffled; **à pas feutrés** stealthily (**c**) *(vêtement)* matted

feutrer [føtre] **1** *vt* (**a**) *(garnir de feutre)* to cover with felt (**b**) *(assourdir)* to muffle (**c**) *(vêtement)* to mat

2 *vi* *(vêtement)* to felt

3 **se feutrer** *vpr* *(vêtement)* to felt

feutrine [føtrin] *nf* felt

fève [fɛv] *nf* (**a**) *(plante, graine)* broad bean (**b**) *(dans la galette des Rois)* charm (**c**) *Can (haricot)* bean

février [fevrije] *nm* February; *voir aussi* **janvier**

FF *nm (abrév* **franc(s) français**) FF

FFI [ɛfɛfi] *nfpl Hist (abrév* **Forces françaises de l'intérieur**) = French Resistance forces in France during World War Two

FFL [ɛfɛfɛl] *nfpl Hist (abrév* **Forces françaises libres**) Free French Army

fiabilité [fjabilite] *nf* reliability

fiable [fjabl] *adj* reliable

fiacre [fjakr] *nm* hackney carriage

fiançailles [fjɑ̃saj] *nfpl* engagement

fiancé, **-e** [fjɑ̃se] *nm,f* fiancé, *f* fiancée

fiancer [16] [fjɑ̃se] **se fiancer** *vpr* to get engaged (**avec** to); **être fiancés** to be engaged

fiasco [fjasko] *nm* fiasco

fibre [fibr] *nf* fibre; *Fig* **avoir la f. maternelle** to be the maternal sort; **f. optique** fibre optics *(singulier)*; **f. de verre** fibreglass

fibreux, **-euse** [fibrø, -øz] *adj (tissu)* fibrous; *(viande)* stringy

fibrome [fibrom] *nm* fibroma

fibroscopie [fibrɔskɔpi] *nf Méd* fibre-optic endoscopy

ficelé, **-e** [fisəle] *adj Fam* (**a**) *(construit)* **bien/mal f.** *(scénario)* well/poorly put together (**b**) *(habillé)* got up

ficeler [42] [fisəle] *vt* (**a**) *(attacher)* to tie up; **ficelé comme un saucisson** trussed up like a chicken (**b**) *Fam (construire)* to put together

ficelle [fisɛl] *nf* (**a**) *(cordelette)* string; *Fig* **les ficelles du métier** the tricks of the trade (**b**) *(pain)* small French stick

fiche¹ [fiʃ] *nf* (**a**) *(formulaire)* form; **f. d'état civil** = administrative record of birth details and marital status; **f. de paie** payslip; **f. signalétique** personal details card (**b**) *(carte)* (index) card; **mettre qch sur fiches** to card-index sth; **f. cartonnée** index card; **f. cuisine** *(dans un magazine)* recipe card (**c**) *(prise)* plug; *(broche)* pin (**d**) *Ordinat* **f. d'état** report form

fiche² = **ficher³**

ficher¹ [fiʃe] *vt (mettre sur fiches) (informations)* to file; *(personne)* to put on file

ficher² **1** *vt (enfoncer)* **f. qch dans qch** to stick sth into sth

2 **se ficher** *vpr (balle, clou)* **se f. dans qch** to go into sth

ficher³ *Fam* **1** *vt* (**a**) *(mettre)* to stick; **f. qn par terre** to send sb sprawling; **f. qch par terre** *(exprès)* to chuck sth on the floor; *(accidentellement)* to knock sth over; *Fig* to mess sth up; **f. qn à la porte** to kick sb out; **f. une gifle à qn** to give sb a slap in the face (**b**) *Fam (faire)* to do; **qu'est-ce que tu fiches?** what are you up to? (**c**) *Fam* **f. le camp** to clear off

2 **se ficher** *vpr* (**a**) *(se mettre)* **se f. un coup** to wallop oneself; **se f. par terre** to go sprawling; **se f. dedans** to screw up (**b**) *(se moquer)* **se f. de qn** to poke fun at sb; **se f. du monde** to take the piss; **se f. de qch** not to give a damn about sth; **je m'en fiche** I don't give a damn

fichier [fiʃje] *nm* (**a**) *(ensemble de fiches)* (card-index) file (**b**) *(boîte)* card-index box; *(meuble)* card-index cabinet (**c**) *Ordinat* file; **f. joint** *(de courrier électronique)* attachment

fichu¹, **-e** [fiʃy] *adj Fam* (**a**) *(insupportable)* damn; *(caractère)* rotten (**b**) *(abîmé)* **être f.** to have had it; **c'est f. maintenant!** *(c'est raté)* we can forget it!; **c'est f. pour dimanche** we can forget Sunday (**c**) **être bien/mal f.** *(bien/mal bâti)* to have/not to have a nice body; *(bien/mal conçu)* to be well/badly designed; **être mal f.** *(malade)* to be under the weather (**d**) *(capable)* **être f. de faire qch** to be capable of doing sth

fichu² *nm* headscarf

fictif, **-ive** [fiktif, -iv] *adj* fictitious

fiction [fiksjɔ̃] *nf* fiction; **œuvre de f.** work of fiction; **la réalité dépasse la f.** truth is stranger than fiction

ficus [fikys] *nm* ficus

fidèle [fidɛl] **1** *adj* (**a**) *(ami, époux)* faithful; *(lecteur, auditeur, client)* regular; **être f. à qn** to be faithful to sb; **être f. à qch** to be loyal *or* true to sth; *Fig* **être f. au poste** to be always there (**b**) *(copie, traduction, récit)* faithful (**à** to); *(mémoire, souvenir)* reliable

2 *nmf* (**a**) *(croyant)* believer; **les fidèles** the faithful; *(à l'église)* the congregation (**b**) *(partisan)* loyal supporter (**de** of) (**c**) *(d'un programme télévisé)* regular viewer (**de** of); *(d'un programme radio)* regular listener (**de** to)

fidèlement [fidɛlmɑ̃] *adv* faithfully

fidélisation [fidelizasjɔ̃] *nf* f. de la clientèle building of customer loyalty

fidéliser [fidelize] *vt* to win the loyalty of; **f. la clientèle** to create customer loyalty

fidélité [fidelite] *nf* (**a**) *(d'un époux, d'un ami)* faithfulness (**à** to); *(d'un client, à un principe)* loyalty (**à** to) (**b**) *(d'une traduction, d'une reproduction)* faithfulness

Fidji [fidʒi] *nfpl* **les îles F.** Fiji

fiduciaire [fidysjɛr] *adj Fin* **monnaie f.** paper money

fief [fjɛf] *nm* fief; *Fig* **un f. du parti socialiste** a safe Socialist seat

fieffé, -e [fjefe] *adj* inveterate

fiel [fjɛl] *nm aussi Fig* gall

fier¹, fière [fjɛr] **1** *adj* (**a**) *(satisfait)* proud (**de** of); **être f. de faire qch** to be proud to do sth; **f. comme un paon** proud as a peacock (**b**) *(hautain, noble)* proud
2 *nm,f Péj* **faire le f.** to put on airs

fier² [66] [fje] **se fier** *vpr* **se f. à qn/qch** *(avoir confiance en)* to trust sb/sth; *(compter sur)* to rely on sb/sth

fièrement [fjɛrmɑ̃] *adv* proudly

fierté [fjɛrte] *nf* (**a**) *(satisfaction)* pride; **avec f.** proudly; **tirer f. de qch** to take pride in sth (**b**) *(amour-propre)* pride

fiesta [fjɛsta] *nf Fam* wild party

fièvre [fjɛvr] *nf* (**a**) *(élévation de la température)* fever; **avoir de la f.** to have a fever *or* a temperature; **elle a 40 de f.** she's got a temperature of 40 degrees; **avoir une f. de cheval** to have a raging fever (**b**) *(excitation)* frenzy; **dans la f. de la campagne électorale** in the heat *or* excitement of the election campaign

fiévreusement [fjevrøzmɑ̃] *adv* feverishly

fiévreux, -euse [fjevrø, -øz] *adj aussi Fig* feverish

fifre [fifr] *nm (instrument)* fife; *(joueur)* fife player

figé, -e [fiʒe] *adj* (**a**) *(locution)* set (**b**) *(sourire)* fixed (**c**) *(sauce)* congealed

figer [45] [fiʒe] **1** *vt* (**a**) *(immobiliser)* to paralyse; **figé sur place** rooted to the spot (**b**) *(solidifier)* to congeal
2 se figer *vpr (huile, sauce)* to congeal; *(regard, traits, sourire)* to freeze

fignoler [fiɲɔle] *vt Fam* to put the finishing touches to; **il ne reste plus qu'à f.** it's just a matter now of adding the finishing touches

figue [fig] *nf* fig; **f. de Barbarie** prickly pear

figuier [figje] *nm* fig tree; **f. de Barbarie** prickly pear

figurant, -e [figyrɑ̃, -ɑ̃t] *nm,f (dans une pièce de théâtre)* walk-on; *(dans un film)* extra

figuratif, -ive [figyratif, -iv] *adj* figurative

figuration [figyrasjɔ̃] *nf* **faire de la f.** to play bit parts

figure [figyr] *nf* (**a**) *(visage)* face; **faire bonne f.** to make a good impression; **faire f. d'intellectuel/de patriarche** to be seen as an intellectual/a patriarch (**b**) *(représentation)* figure; *aussi Fig* **f. de proue** figurehead (**c**) *(personnage)* figure (**d**) *(en danse, en patinage artistique)* figure; **figures imposées** compulsory figures; **figures libres** freestyle (**e**) *Ling* **f. de rhétorique** figure of speech; **f. de style** stylistic device

figuré, -e [figyre] **1** *adj (sens)* figurative
2 *nm* **au f.** in the figurative sense

figurer [figyre] **1** *vt* to represent
2 *vi* (**a**) *(apparaître)* to appear (**sur/dans** on/in) (**b**) *(faire partie)* to figure (**parmi** among)
3 se figurer *vpr* **se f. que** to imagine that; **il se figure qu'il va gagner de l'argent** he thinks *or* believes that

he's going to make money; **je suis à sec, figure-toi** believe it or not, I'm broke

figurine [figyrin] *nf* figurine

fil [fil] *nm* (**a**) *(brin, de toile d'araignée)* thread; **de f. en aiguille** little by little, bit by bit; *Fig* **ne tenir qu'à un f.** to hang by a thread; **f. conducteur** unifying thread; **f. à coudre** (sewing) thread; **f. dentaire** dental floss; **f. d'Écosse** lisle thread; **f. à plomb** plumb line; *Fig* **f. rouge** recurring theme
(**b**) *(métallique, électrique)* wire; *Fig* **donner du f. à retordre à qn** to give sb trouble; **f. de fer** wire; **f. de fer barbelé** barbed wire
(**c**) *Fam (téléphone)* **au bout du f.** on the line; **coup de f.** call; **donner** *ou* **passer un coup de f. à qn** to give sb a call, to call sb (up)
(**d**) *(cours)* **au f. de l'eau** with the current; **au f. des jours/semaines** with the passing days/weeks; **perdre/reprendre le f. de qch** to lose/pick up the thread of sth
(**e**) *(tissu)* linen
(**f**) *(tranchant)* edge

filaire [filɛr] *adj Tél (téléphone)* corded, plug-in

filament [filamɑ̃] *nm* (**a**) *(d'une ampoule électrique)* filament (**b**) *(de viande)* fibre (**c**) *Biol* filament

filandreux, -euse [filɑ̃drø, -øz] *adj (viande, légumes)* stringy

filant, -e [filɑ̃, -ɑ̃t] *adj voir* **étoile**

filasse [filas] **1** *nf* tow
2 *adj inv* tow-coloured

filature [filatyr] *nf* (**a**) *(fabrique)* (spinning) mill (**b**) *(surveillance)* shadowing; **prendre qn en f.** to shadow sb

file [fil] *nf* (**a**) *(queue) Br* queue, *Am* line; **en f. indienne** in single file; **trois jours à la f.** three days in a row; **f. (d'attente)** *Br* queue, *Am* line (**b**) *(sur la route)* lane; **se garer en double f.** to double-park (**c**) *Ordinat* **f. d'attente** print queue

filé, -e [file] *adj* (**a**) *(bas, collant)* with a run, *Br* laddered (**b**) *(verre)* spun (**c**) *(métaphore)* extended

filer [file] **1** *vt* (**a**) *(coton, verre)* to spin (**b**) *(développer)* *(image, métaphore)* to draw *or* to spin out (**c**) *Fam (donner)* **f. qch à qn** to give sb sth (**d**) *(surveiller) (suspect)* to shadow, to tail (**e**) *(bas, collant)* to put a run in, *Br* to ladder (**f**) **f. le parfait amour** to live love's dream
2 *vi* (**a**) *(passer vite) (temps)* to fly; *(véhicule)* to speed along; **f. entre les mains** *ou* **les doigts à qn** *(argent)* to run through sb's fingers like water; *(personne)* to slip through sb's fingers (**b**) *Fam (partir)* **il faut que je file** I must dash; **allez, file!** off you go! (**c**) *(bas, collant)* to run, *Br* to ladder

filet¹ [filɛ] *nm* (**a**) *(de lumière)* thin streak; *(d'air)* thin stream; *(d'eau)* trickle (**b**) *(petite quantité)* dash (**c**) *(d'une vis)* thread (**d**) *(de viande, de poisson)* fillet; **f. mignon** filet mignon *(small fillet steak)*

filet² *nm* (**a**) *(en mailles)* net; **f. à bagages** luggage rack; **f. à papillons** butterfly net; **f. de pêche** fishing net; **f. à provisions** string bag (**b**) *(au cirque)* (safety) net; **travailler sans f.** *(trapéziste)* to work without a net; *Fig* to take risks (**c**) *(au tennis)* net

filial, -e, -aux, -ales [filjal, -o] **1** *adj* filial
2 *nf* **filiale** subsidiary (company)

filiation [filjasjɔ̃] *nf* (**a**) *(lien de parenté)* filiation (**b**) *Fig (relation)* relationship (**avec** to)

filière [filjɛr] *nf* (**a**) *(voie obligée)* channels (**b**) *(domaine d'études)* field of study; **suivre une f. scientifique/**

commerciale to study scientific/business subjects (**c**) *(organisation clandestine)* network

filiforme [filifɔrm] *adj* spindly

filigrane [filigran] *nm (dessin)* watermark; *Fig* **en f.** implicit

filin [filɛ̃] *nm* rope

fille [fij] *nf* (**a**) *(descendante)* daughter (**b**) *(enfant)* girl; **petite f.** little girl (**c**) *(femme)* **salut les filles!** hi, girls!; **f. de joie** prostitute; **jeune f.** girl; **vieille f.** old maid

fillette [fijɛt] *nf* little girl

filleul, -e [fijœl] *nm,f* godson, *f* goddaughter

film [film] *nm* (**a**) *(œuvre)* film, movie; **f. d'action** action film; **f. d'animation** animated film; **f. d'aventures** adventure film; **f. d'épouvante** *ou* **d'horreur** horror film; **f. policier** detective film (**b**) *(déroulement)* **revoir le f. de sa vie** to see one's life flashing before one's eyes (**c**) *(emballage)* film; **f. alimentaire** clingfilm (**d**) *(fine pellicule)* film

filmer [filme] *vt* to film

filmographie [filmɔgrafi] *nf* filmography

filon [filɔ̃] *nm* (**a**) *(de minéraux)* vein, seam (**b**) *Fam* **trouver le f.** to strike it rich

filou [filu] *nm (escroc)* rogue; *(enfant)* rascal

fils [fis] *nm* son; **f. de famille** young man of good social standing; *Péj* **f. à papa** daddy's boy

filtrage [filtraʒ] *nm* (**a**) *(contrôle)* screening (**b**) *(d'un liquide)* filtering

filtrant, -e [filtrɑ̃, -ɑ̃t] *adj (pouvoir)* filtering; *(verres, papier)* filter

filtre [filtr] **1** *adj (cigarette, café, papier)* filter
2 *nm* filter; **f. à air** air filter; **f. à café** coffee filter; *Phot* **f. coloré** colour filter; *Ordinat* **f. écran** screen filter

filtrer [filtre] **1** *vt* (**a**) *(liquide, son, lumière)* to filter (**b**) *(informations, visiteurs)* to screen
2 *vi (liquide)* to filter (**à travers** through); *(nouvelle)* to leak out; **laisser f. qch** to let sth filter through; *Fig* to leak sth

fin¹ [fɛ̃] *nf* (**a**) *(conclusion)* end; **"f."** *(au cinéma)* "the end"; **f. juillet** at the end of July; **à la f.** in the end; *Fam* **tu m'ennuies à la f.!** you're really annoying me!; **en f. de qch, à la f. de qch** at the end of sth; **chômeur en f. de droits** = unemployed person about to lose their entitlement to benefit; **mettre f. à qch** to put an end to sth; **prendre f.** to come to an end; **toucher** *ou* **tirer à sa f.** to draw to a close; **avoir des fins de mois difficiles** to be always short of money at the end of the month; **f. de série** discontinued line; **f. de semaine** end of the week, *Can* weekend (**b**) *(mort)* end, death (**c**) *(but)* end, aim; **arriver** *ou* **parvenir à ses fins** to achieve one's ends; **à cette f.** to this end; **à toutes fins utiles** just in case (**d**) *Ordinat* **f. de ligne** line end; **f. de page** pagebreak; **f. de session** logoff

fin², fine [fɛ̃, fin] **1** *adj* (**a**) *(papier, tranche, taille)* thin; *(cheveux, sable, pointe)* fine; **une petite pluie fine** drizzle (**b**) *(traits)* fine (**c**) *(de première qualité)* fine (**d**) **fines herbes** mixed herbs (**e**) **un f. connaisseur** a connoisseur (**f**) *(vue, odorat)* keen; **avoir l'ouïe fine** to have keen hearing (**g**) *(subtil)* subtle (**h**) *Can (gentil)* kind, sweet(-natured) (**i**) **le f. mot de l'histoire** the truth of the matter
2 *nm* **le f. du f.** the ultimate
3 *adv* (**a**) **f. prêt** all ready (**b**) *(finement)* finely

final, -e, -als *ou* **-aux, -ales** [final, -o] *adj* final

finale [final] **1** *nf* (**a**) *(compétition sportive)* final; **aller/ être en f.** to go through to/to be in the finals (**b**) *(de mot)* final syllable
2 *nm (d'un morceau de musique)* finale

finalement [finalmɑ̃] *adv* in the end, finally

finaliser [finalize] *vt* to finalize

finaliste [finalist] *adj & nmf* finalist

finalité [finalite] *nf* (**a**) *(objectif)* aim (**b**) *(en biologie)* finality

finance [finɑ̃s] *nf* (**a**) *(profession)* finance; **la haute f.** high finance (**b**) *(argent)* **moyennant f.** for a fee; **finances** finances

financement [finɑ̃smɑ̃] *nm* financing

financer [16] [finɑ̃se] *vt* to finance

financier, -ère [finɑ̃sje, -ɛr] **1** *adj* financial
2 *nm* (**a**) *Fin* financier (**b**) *(gâteau)* = rectangular sponge finger made with almonds

financièrement [finɑ̃sjɛrmɑ̃] *adv* financially

finasser [finase] *vi Fam* to resort to trickery

finaud, -e [fino, -od] **1** *adj* crafty
2 *nm,f* crafty devil

fine [fin] *nf* liqueur brandy

finement [finmɑ̃] *adv* (**a**) *(adroitement)* cleverly (**b**) *(délicatement)* finely

finesse [fines] *nf* (**a**) *(minceur)* fineness; *(de la taille)* slenderness, slimness (**b**) *(d'un visage)* fineness; *(d'un travail fait à la main)* delicacy (**c**) *(subtilité)* subtlety

fini, -e [fini] **1** *adj* (**a**) *(usé, à bout)* finished (**b**) *Péj (imbécile, escroc)* absolute (**c**) *(espace, temps, nombre)* finite
2 *nm (d'un objet manufacturé)* finish

finir [finir] **1** *vt* to finish; *(vie)* to end; **f. son assiette** to finish what's on one's plate
2 *vi* to end, to finish; **f. bien/mal** to end well/badly; *(film, roman)* to have a happy/sad ending; **mal f.** *(personne)* to come to a bad end; **f. de faire qch** to finish doing sth; **f. par faire qch** to end up doing sth; **en f. avec qn/qch** to have done with sb/sth; **à n'en plus f.** endless; **pour f.** *(en résumé)* to cut a long story short; *(finalement)* in the end

finish [finiʃ] *nm inv* finish

finition [finisjɔ̃] *nf* finishing touch; **travail de f.** finishing touches; **les finitions de cette robe sont mal faites** this dress is badly finished

finlandais, -e [fɛ̃lɑ̃dɛ, -ɛz] **1** *adj* Finnish
2 *nm,f* **F.** Finn

Finlande [fɛ̃lɑ̃d] *nf* **la F.** Finland

finnois, -e [finwa, -az] **1** *adj* Finnish
2 *nm (langue)* Finnish

fiole [fjɔl] *nf (flacon)* phial

fioriture [fjɔrityr] *nf (dessin)* flourish

fioul [fjul] *nm* fuel oil

firmament [firmamɑ̃] *nm Litt* firmament

firme [firm] *nf* firm

FIS [fis] *nm (abrév* **Front islamique du salut**) **le F.** the Islamic Salvation Front

fisc [fisk] *nm Br* ≃ Inland Revenue, *Am* ≃ Internal Revenue

fiscal, -e, -aux, -ales [fiskal, -o] *adj* tax

fiscaliser [fiskalize] *vt* to tax

fiscalité [fiskalite] *nf* tax system

fissure [fisyr] *nf aussi Fig* crack

fissurer [fisyre] **1** *vt* to crack; *Fig* to split
2 se fissurer *vpr* to crack; *Fig* to split

fiston [fistɔ̃] *nm Fam* son, lad
FIV [ɛfive] *nf* (*abrév* **fécondation in vitro**) IVF
fivete [fivɛt] *nf* (*abrév* **fécondation in vitro et transfert embryonnaire**) GIFT
fixateur, -trice [fiksatœr, -tris] *Phot* **1** *adj* fixing
    2 *nm* fixer
fixatif [fiksatif] *nm* fixative
fixation [fiksasjɔ̃] *nf* (**a**) (*action*) fixing (**b**) (*de skis*) (ski) binding (**c**) (*obsession*) fixation; **faire une f. sur qn/qch** to become fixated on sb/sth
fixe [fiks] **1** *adj* (**a**) (*immobile*) (*étagère, planche, regard*) fixed (**b**) (*arrêté*) (*prix, frais*) fixed
    2 *nm* fixed salary
fixement [fiksəmã] *adv* fixedly; **regarder f. qn/qch** to stare at sb/sth
fixer [fikse] **1** *vt* (**a**) (*immobiliser*) to fix; **f. son attention/son regard sur qch** to focus one's attention/one's gaze on sth; **f. qn (du regard)** to stare at sb (**b**) (*déterminer*) (*date, heure, rendez-vous*) to fix; (*prix, salaire*) to fix, to set (**à** at); **f. son choix sur qch** to decide on sth (**c**) (*informer*) **maintenant, tu es fixé** now you know
    2 se fixer *vpr* (**a**) (*s'installer*) to settle down (**b**) **son choix s'est fixé sur celui-ci** she decided on this one (**c**) **se f. un objectif** to set oneself a target
fixité [fiksite] *nf* (*du regard*) fixedness
fjord [fjɔrd] *nm* fjord
flacon [flakɔ̃] *nm* (small) bottle
flagada [flagada] *adj inv Fam* washed-out
flageller [flaʒele] *vt* to flog, to whip
flageoler [flaʒɔle] *vi* (*jambes*) to shake, to tremble
flageolet [flaʒɔlɛ] *nm* (*haricot*) flageolet (bean)
flagornerie [flagɔrnəri] *nf Péj* fawning, toadying
flagrant, -e [flagrã, -ãt] *adj* flagrant, blatant; **en f. délit** red-handed; **être pris en f. délit d'adultère** to be caught in flagrante
flair [flɛr] *nm* sense of smell; **avoir du f.** to have a good sense of smell; *Fig* to have good intuition
flairer [flere] *vt aussi Fig* to smell
flamand, -e [flamã, -ãd] **1** *adj* Flemish
    2 *nm,f* **F.** Fleming
    3 *nm* (*langue*) Flemish
flamant [flamã] *nm* **f. rose** flamingo
flambant [flãbã] *adv* (**a**) (*locution*) **f. neuf** brand new (**b**) *Can Fam* (*complètement*) totally; **f. nu** stark naked, *Br* starkers
flambeau, -x [flãbo] *nm* (*torche*) torch; *Fig* **passer le f. à qn** to pass the torch on to sb
flambée [flãbe] *nf* (**a**) (*feu*) blaze (**b**) (*de violence*) flare-up; (*des prix*) upsurge
flamber [flãbe] **1** *vi* (**a**) (*brûler*) to blaze (**b**) *Fam* (*parier*) to gamble for big money
    2 *vt* (**a**) (*volaille*) to singe (**b**) (*crêpes*) to flambé
flambeur, -euse [flãbœr, -øz] *nm,f Fam* big-time gambler
flamboyant, -e [flãbwajã, -ãt] *adj* (**a**) (*regard*) blazing; **d'un rouge f.** flaming red (**b**) *Archit* flamboyant
flamboyer [32] [flãbwaje] *vi* to blaze
flamme [flam] *nf* (**a**) (*feu*) flame; **en flammes** on fire, ablaze; *Fig* **descendre qn/qch en flammes** to shoot sb/sth down in flames (**b**) *Fig* (*enthousiasme*) fire (**c**) *Litt* (*amour*) passion
flammèche [flamɛʃ] *nf* spark
flan [flã] *nm* (*dessert*) baked custard

flanc [flã] *nm* side; (*d'une armée*) flank; **être sur le f.** (*malade*) to be laid up; (*épuisé*) to be worn out; *Fam* **tirer au f.** to shirk, *Br* to skive
flancher [flãʃe] *vi Fam* to give in
Flandre [flãdr] *nf* **la F., les Flandres** Flanders
flanelle [flanɛl] *nf* flannel
flâner [flane, flane] *vi* (**a**) (*se promener*) to stroll, to saunter (**b**) (*perdre son temps*) to hang about
flânerie [flɑ̃ri, flɑnri] *nf* (*promenade*) stroll
flâneur, -euse [flɑ̃nœr, flɑnœr, -øz] *nm,f* (*promeneur*) stroller
flanquer¹ [flãke] *vt* (**a**) (*être à coté de*) to flank (**b**) (*accompagner*) **flanqué de** flanked by
flanquer² *Fam* **1** *vt* (**a**) (*jeter*) to chuck; **f. qn à la porte ou dehors** to kick sb out; (*licencier*) to fire sb, *Br* to sack sb; **f. qch par terre** to fling sth on the ground; *Fig* to mess sth up (**b**) **f. qch à qn** (*coup de pied, gifle*) to give sb sth; **f. la trouille** *ou* **les jetons à qn** to put the wind up sb
    2 se flanquer *vpr* **se f. par terre** to go sprawling
flapi, -e [flapi] *adj Fam* dead beat
flaque [flak] *nf* (*d'huile, de sang*) pool; **f. (d'eau)** puddle
flash [flaʃ] *nm* (**a**) (*sur un appareil photo*) flash (**b**) (*à la radio, à la télévision*) flash; **f. d'information** newsflash; **f. publicitaire** commercial
flash-back [flaʃbak] *nm inv* flashback
flasher [flaʃe] *vi Fam* **f. sur qn/qch** to fall for sb/sth in a big way
flasque¹ [flask] *adj* (*chair*) flabby
flasque² *nf* flask
flatter [flate] **1** *vt* (**a**) (*complimenter*) to flatter (**b**) (*avantager*) to flatter (**c**) (*caresser*) (*animal*) to stroke
    2 se flatter *vpr* to flatter oneself; **se f. de faire qch** to pride oneself on doing sth; **je ne m'en flatterais pas** it's not something I'd be proud of
flatterie [flatri] *nf* flattery
flatteur, -euse [flatœr, -øz] **1** *adj* (*remarque, portrait, couleur*) flattering; (*personne*) full of flattery
    2 *nm,f* flatterer
flatulence [flatylãs] *nf* flatulence
FLE [flə] *nm* (*abrév* **français langue étrangère**) French as a foreign language
fléau, -x [fleo] *nm* (**a**) (*calamité*) scourge; *Fig* (*chose pénible*) pain (**b**) (*à céréales*) flail (**c**) (*d'une balance à plateaux*) beam
fléchage [fleʃaʒ] *nm* signposting
flèche [flɛʃ] *nf* (**a**) (*projectile, signe*) arrow; **partir comme une f.** to shoot off; **monter en f.** (*avion, prix*) to shoot up (**b**) (*attaque verbale*) jibe (**c**) (*d'une église*) spire (**d**) *Ordinat* **f. de défilement** scroll arrow; **flèches verticales** up and down arrow keys
flécher [34] [fleʃe] *vt* (*route, direction*) to arrow; **itinéraire fléché** signposted route
fléchette [fleʃɛt] *nf* dart; **jouer aux fléchettes** to play darts
fléchir [fleʃir] **1** *vt* (**a**) (*bras, jambe, genou*) to bend (**b**) (*faire céder*) to sway
    2 *vi* (**a**) (*ployer*) (*branche*) to bend; (*jambes*) to give way; (*poutre*) to sag (**b**) (*faiblir*) to weaken (**c**) (*baisser*) (*prix, devises*) to fall
fléchissement [fleʃismã] *nm* (**a**) (*du genou*) bending; (*d'une poutre*) sagging (**b**) (*de prix, de devises, de résultats*) drop (**de** in)
flegmatique [flɛgmatik] *adj* phlegmatic

flegme [flɛgm] *nm* phlegm

flemmard, -e [flɛmar, -ard] *Fam* **1** *adj* lazy
2 *nm,f* lazybones

flemmarder [flemarde] *vi Fam* to laze about

flemmardise [flemardiz] *nf Fam* laziness

flemme [flɛm] *nf Fam* laziness; **j'ai la f. (de le faire)** I can't be bothered (to do it)

flétan [fletã] *nm* halibut

flétri, -e [fletri] *adj* withered

flétrir [fletrir] **1** *vt (peau, plantes)* to wither
2 se flétrir *upr (visage, plantes)* to wither

fleur [flœr] *nf* **(a)** *(plante)* flower; **à fleurs** *(tissu)* floral; **en fleurs** *(arbre)* in flower; **être f. bleue** to be a romantic; *Fam* **faire une f. à qn** to do sb a favour; **fleurs des champs** wild flowers **(b)** *Can (farine)* flour **(c)** *(locutions)* **dans la f. de l'âge** in the prime of life; **la fine f. de qch** the cream of sth; **à f. d'eau** just above the surface of the water; **avoir les nerfs à f. de peau** to be all on edge

fleurdelisé [flœrdəlize] *nm Can (drapeau du Québec)* flag of Quebec

fleurer [flœre] **1** *vt Litt* to smell of
2 *vi* **f. bon** to smell nice

fleuret [flœrɛ] *nm (épée)* foil

fleurette [flœrɛt] *nf Vieilli* **conter f. à qn** to whisper sweet nothings to sb

fleuri, -e [flœri] *adj* **(a)** *(couvert de fleurs) (arbre)* in flower **(b)** *(orné de fleurs) (tissu, robe)* floral; *(vaisselle)* flower-patterned **(c)** *(style)* flowery **(d)** *(teint)* florid

fleurir [flœrir] **1** *vi* **(a)** *(plantes)* to flower **(b)** *(art, commerce)* to flourish
2 *vt (table)* to decorate with flowers; *(tombe)* to lay flowers on

fleuriste [flœrist] *nmf (commerçant)* florist

fleuron [flœrɔ̃] *nm (d'une collection)* jewel

fleuve [flœv] *nm* river; **le f. Jaune** the Yellow River

flexibilité [flɛksibilite] *nf aussi Fig* flexibility

flexible [flɛksibl] **1** *adj aussi Fig* flexible
2 *nm (tuyau)* hose(pipe)

flexion [flɛksjɔ̃] *nf (fléchissement)* bending; **être en f.** *(muscle, membre)* to be flexed

flibustier [flibystje] *nm* buccaneer

flic [flik] *nm Fam* cop

flingue [flɛ̃g] *nm Fam* shooter

flinguer [flɛ̃ge] *Fam* **1** *vt* to gun down
2 se flinguer *upr* to blow one's brains out

flippant, -e [flipã, -ãt] *adj Fam (déprimant)* grim; *(effrayant)* creepy

flipper¹ [flipœr] *nm (appareil)* pinball machine; *(jeu)* pinball; **jouer au f.** to play pinball

flipper² [flipe] *vi Fam (déprimer)* to feel down

flirt [flœrt] *nm* **(a)** *(amourette)* flirtation **(b)** *(personne)* boyfriend, *f* girlfriend

flirter [flœrte] *vi aussi Fig* to flirt (**avec** with)

FLN [ɛfɛlɛn] *nm (abrév* **Front de libération nationale)** National Liberation Front *(in Algeria)*

FLNC [ɛfɛlɛnse] *nm (abrév* **Front de libération nationale de la Corse)** Corsican liberation front

FLNKS [ɛfɛlɛnkaɛs] *nm (abrév* **Front de libération nationale kanak et socialiste)** Kanak national liberation front *(in New Caledonia)*

flocon [flɔkɔ̃] *nm* flake; **flocons d'avoine** oat flakes; **f. de neige** snowflake

floconneux, -euse [flɔkɔnø, -øz] *adj* fluffy

flonflons [flɔ̃flɔ̃] *nmpl* tiddly-om-pom-pom

flop [flɔp] *nm Fam* flop; **faire un f.** to flop

flopée [flɔpe] *nf Fam* **une f. ou des flopées de qch** loads of sth, masses of sth

floraison [flɔrɛzɔ̃] *nf* flowering

floral, -e, -aux, -ales [flɔral, -o] *adj* floral

floralies [flɔrali] *nfpl* flower show

flore [flɔr] *nf* flora; **f. intestinale** intestinal flora

Floride [flɔrid] *nf* **la F.** Florida

florilège [flɔrilɛʒ] *nm* anthology

florin [flɔrɛ̃] *nm* florin

florissant, -e [flɔrisã, -ãt] *adj (affaire)* flourishing; *(santé)* blooming

flot [flo] *nm* **(a)** *(marée)* flood (tide) **(b)** *(quantité importante)* stream (**de** of) **(c)** *Litt* **les flots** *(la mer)* the waves **(d)** *(locutions)* **couler à flots** to flow freely; **être à f.** *(bateau)* to be afloat; *Fig (personne)* to have one's head above water; **remettre à f.** *(personne, entreprise)* to get back on an even keel

flottaison [flɔtɛzɔ̃] *nf* floating

flotte [flɔt] *nf* **(a)** *(bateaux)* fleet **(b)** *Fam (pluie)* rain **(c)** *Fam (eau)* water

flottement [flɔtmã] *nm* **(a)** *(d'un drapeau)* fluttering **(b)** *(d'une monnaie)* fluctuation **(c)** *(hésitation)* wavering

flotter [flɔte] **1** *vi* **(a)** *(embarcation)* to float; *Fig* **il flotte dans sa veste** his jacket is far too baggy for him **(b)** *(drapeau)* to flutter; **f. au** *ou* **dans le vent** *(cheveux)* to stream in the wind
2 *v impersonnel Fam* **il flotte** it's raining

flotteur [flɔtœr] *nm* float

flottille [flɔtij] *nf (de bateaux)* flotilla

flou, -e [flu] **1** *adj* **(a)** *(contour, photographie)* blurred, fuzzy **(b)** *(idée, réponse)* vague
2 *nm (d'un contour, d'une photographie)* fuzziness; *(d'une idée, d'une réponse)* vagueness; **f. artistique** *(en photographie)* soft-focus effect; *Fig* deliberate vagueness

flouer [flue] *vt Fam* to swindle

flouse, flouze [fluz] *nm Fam (argent)* bread

fluctuant, -e [flyktµã, -ãt] *adj* fluctuating

fluctuation [flyktµasjɔ̃] *nf* fluctuation

fluctuer [flyktµe] *vi* to fluctuate

fluet, -ette [flyɛ, -ɛt] *adj* thin

fluide [flµid] **1** *adj (liquide)* fluid; *(circulation)* flowing freely; *(style, pensée)* flowing
2 *nm* **(a)** *(substance)* fluid **(b)** *(pouvoir surnaturel)* occult power

fluidifier [66] [flµidifje] *vt (sang)* to thin

fluidité [flµidite] *nf (d'un corps)* fluidity; *(de la circulation)* free flow

fluo [flyo] *adj inv Fam* fluorescent

fluor [flyɔr] *nm* fluorine; **dentifrice au f.** fluoride toothpaste

fluorescent, -e [flyɔresã, -ãt] *adj* fluorescent

flûte [flyt] **1** *nf* **(a)** *(instrument)* flute; **f. à bec** recorder; **f. de Pan** panpipes; **f. traversière** concert flute **(b)** *(pain)* small French stick **(c)** *(verre)* **f. à champagne** champagne flute
2 *exclam Fam* damn!

flûtiste [flytist] *nmf Br* flautist, *Am* flutist

fluvial, -e, -aux, -ales [flyvjal, -o] *adj* river; *(alluvions)* fluvial

flux [fly] *nm* (**a**) *(de paroles)* flow (**b**) *(marée montante)* flow; **le f. et le reflux** the ebb and flow; **f. migratoire** flow of migrants (**c**) *(électrique, magnétique)* flux

fluxion [flyksjɔ̃] *nf* inflammation; **f. de poitrine** pneumonia

FM [ɛfɛm] *nf (abrév* **frequency modulation***)* FM

FME [ɛfɛmə] *nm (abrév* **fonds monétaire européen***)* EMF

FMI [ɛfɛmi] *nm (abrév* **Fonds monétaire international***)* IMF

FN [ɛfɛn] *nm (abrév* **Front national***)* = French political party of the extreme right

FNSEA [ɛfɛnɛsəa] *nf (abrév* **Fédération nationale des syndicats d'exploitants agricoles***)* = French farmers' union

FO [ɛfo] *nf (abrév* **Force ouvrière***)* = French trade union

foc [fɔk] *nm* jib

focal, -e, -aux, -ales [fɔkal, -o] *adj* focal

focaliser [fɔkalize] **1** *vt* to focus (**sur** on)
  2 se focaliser *vpr* to focus (**sur** on)

fœtal, -e, -aux, -ales [fetal, -o] *adj* foetal

fœtus [fetys] *nm* foetus

fofolle [fɔfɔl] *adj voir* **foufou**

foi [fwa] *nf* (**a**) *(confiance)* faith, trust; **avoir f. en qn/qch** to have faith in sb/sth; **les candidatures devront nous parvenir le 1ᵉʳ mars dernier délai, le cachet de la poste faisant f.** ≃ applications should be postmarked no later than 1 March (**b**) *(croyance religieuse)* faith; **avoir/perdre la f.** to have/lose faith (**c**) *(locutions)* **bonne f.** sincerity; **mauvaise f.** insincerity; **être de bonne/mauvaise f.** to be sincere/insincere; **ma f., oui!** yes indeed!

foie [fwa] *nm* liver; *très Fam* **avoir les foies** to be scared shitless; **f. gras** foie gras; **f. de veau/volaille** calf's/chicken liver

foin [fwɛ̃] *nm (fourrage)* hay; **faire les foins** to make hay; *Fam* **faire du f.** *(causer un scandale)* to kick up a fuss; *(faire du bruit)* to make a din; *Can Fam* **avoir du f.** to be loaded

foire [fwar] *nf* (**a**) *(fête foraine)* funfair; *Fam* **faire la f.** to muck about; *Fam* **c'est la f., ici** it's bedlam in here; **f. d'empoigne** free-for-all (**b**) *(salon international, professionnel)* (trade) fair

foirer [fware] *vi très Fam* to be a cock-up; **il a tout fait f.** he *Br* ballsed *or Am* balled *or Br* cocked everything up

foireux, -euse [fwarø, -øz] *adj très Fam (projet, affaire)* hopeless

fois [fwa] *nf* time; **une f.** once; **il était une f. un roi** once upon a time there was a king; **deux f.** twice; **deux f. par jour/mois** twice a day/month; **ça coûte trois f. rien** it costs next to nothing; **trois f. quatre douze** three times four is twelve; **trois f. plus grand** three times as big; **neuf f. sur dix** nine times out of ten; **combien de f.?** how many times?, how often?; **toutes les f.** *ou* **chaque f. que** every time (that), whenever; **encore une f.** once more, once again; **une (bonne) f. pour toutes** once and for all; **une f. que** once, as soon as; **pour cette f.** this once; **pour une f.** for once; **pour une f. que j'étais à l'heure, personne n'était là** the one time I was on time and no one was there; **à la f. utile et pas cher** both useful and inexpensive; **une chose à la f.** one thing at a time; **l'autre f.** *(il y a peu)* the other day; *Fam* **des f.**

(parfois) sometimes; *Fam* **des f. qu'il viendrait** in case he comes; *Fam* **non, mais des f.!** really now!

foison [fwazɔ̃] *nf* **à f.** in abundance

foisonnement [fwazɔnmɑ̃] *nm (abondance)* abundance

foisonner [fwazɔne] *vi* to abound (**de** *ou* **en** in); **f. d'idées** *(personne)* to have plenty of ideas

fol [fɔl] *voir* **fou**

folâtre [fɔlatr] *adj (personne)* playful

folâtrer [fɔlatre] *vi (personne)* to romp, to frolic

foldingue [fɔldɛ̃g] *adj Fam* nutty

folichon, -onne [fɔliʃɔ̃, -ɔn] *adj Fam* **ce n'est pas f.** it's not much fun

folie [fɔli] *nf* madness; **aimer qn à la f.** to be madly in love with sb; **aimer qch à la f.** to adore sth; **faire des folies** *(faire des achats extravagants)* to go mad; **c'est de la f.!** it's madness!; **c'est de la f. douce** it's sheer madness; **la f. des grandeurs** delusions of grandeur

folio [fɔljo] *nm* folio

folk [fɔlk] *adj & nm* folk

folklo [fɔlklo] *adj inv Fam (personne)* eccentric; *(endroit, soirée)* bizarre

folklore [fɔlklɔr] *nm* folklore

folklorique [fɔlklɔrik] *adj* (**a**) *(costume)* traditional; *(danse)* folk (**b**) *Fam (personne)* eccentric; *(endroit, soirée)* bizarre

folle [fɔl] *adj voir* **fou**

follement [fɔlmɑ̃] *adv* madly

follet [fɔlɛ] *adj m voir* **feu**

fomenter [fɔmɑ̃te] *vt* to foment

foncé, -e [fɔ̃se] *adj* dark

foncer [16] [fɔ̃se] **1** *vt* to darken
  2 *vi* (**a**) *(s'assombrir)* to darken (**b**) *(se hâter)* to get a move on; **f. sur qn/qch** *(se précipiter sur)* to swoop on sb/sth (**c**) *Fam (s'y mettre)* to get one's head down

fonceur, -euse [fɔ̃sœr, -øz] *Fam* **1** *adj* go-getting
  2 *nm,f* go-getter

foncier, -ère [fɔ̃sje, -ɛr] *adj* (**a**) *(impôt, crédit)* land (**b**) *(fondamental)* fundamental, basic

foncièrement [fɔ̃sjɛrmɑ̃] *adv* fundamentally, basically

fonction [fɔ̃ksjɔ̃] *nf* (**a**) *(poste)* office; **entrer en fonctions, prendre ses fonctions** to take up one's duties; **être en f.** to be in office; **de f.** *(voiture, appartement)* company; **la f. publique** the civil service (**b**) *(rôle)* function; **faire f. de qch** to act as sth (**c**) *Ordinat* **f. de comptage de mots** word count facility; **f. d'éditeur de texte** text editing feature; **f. multimédia** multimedia facility; **f. recherche et remplacement** search and replace function; **f. de sauvegarde** save function (**d**) **en f. de** according to

fonctionnaire [fɔ̃ksjɔnɛr] *nmf* ≃ civil servant; **haut f.** ≃ senior civil servant

---

Fonctionnaire

This term covers a broader range of public service employees than the term "civil servant", from high-ranking members of the state administration to public-sector teachers and post office workers. "Fonctionnaires", of whom there are more than four and a half million in France, are normally recruited through competitive state examination and enjoy greater job security and other privileges to which private sector employees are not automatically entitled.

fonctionnariat [fɔ̃ksjɔnarja] *nm* employment by the state

fonctionnel, -elle [fɔ̃ksjɔnɛl] *adj* functional

fonctionnement [fɔ̃ksjɔnmɑ̃] *nm (d'une machine)* working, functioning; **en état de f.** in (good) working order; *Ordinat* **f. en réseau** networking

fonctionner [fɔ̃ksjɔne] *vi (machine, mécanisme)* to work, to function; *Ordinat* to run; **faire f. qch** to operate sth

fond [fɔ̃] *nm* (**a**) *(d'un récipient, de la mer, de l'océan)* bottom; *(d'un espace clos, de la gorge)* back; **être assis au f. de la classe** to be sitting at the back of the class; **c'est au f. du couloir/de la salle** it's at the (far) end of the corridor/hall; **la pièce du f.** the room at the end, the far room; **au fin f. de qch** in the depths of sth; **il n'en reste qu'un f.** there's only a drop left; **du f. du cœur** from the bottom of one's heart; **tu connais le f. de ma pensée** you know what my feelings really are; **à f.** *(à bloc)* all the way; *(complètement)* thoroughly; *(totalement)* totally; **à f. de train** at full tilt; *Fam* **à f. la caisse** *(très vite)* hell for leather; **au f., dans le f.** when it comes down to it; **de f. en comble** from top to bottom; **f. d'artichaut** artichoke heart; **f. de bouteille** *(contenu)* dregs; **f. de teint** foundation (cream)

(**b**) *(substance essentielle)* **le f. du problème** the heart of the problem; **avoir un bon/mauvais f.** to be basically a good/bad person; **le f. et la forme** form and content

(**c**) *(arrière-plan)* background; **f. sonore** background music; **il y avait du jazz en f. sonore** there was jazz playing in the background

fondamental, -e, -aux, -ales [fɔ̃damɑ̃tal, -o] *adj* basic, fundamental

fondamentalement [fɔ̃damɑ̃talmɑ̃] *adv* fundamentally, basically

fondamentalisme [fɔ̃damɑ̃talism] *nm* fundamentalism

fondamentaliste [fɔ̃damɑ̃talist] *nmf* fundamentalist

fondant, -e [fɔ̃dɑ̃, -ɑ̃t] **1** *adj* (**a**) *(neige)* melting (**b**) *(poire)* that melts in the mouth; *(viande)* very tender
2 *nm (bonbon)* fondant

fondateur, -trice [fɔ̃datœr, -tris] **1** *adj (mythe)* underlying; **membre f.** founder member
2 *nm,f* founder

fondation [fɔ̃dasjɔ̃] *nf* (**a**) *(d'une ville, d'un hôpital)* founding (**b**) *(établissement)* foundation (**c**) **fondations** *(d'une construction)* foundations

fondé, -e [fɔ̃de] **1** *adj (reproches, doutes)* well-founded, justified; **être f. à faire qch** to have good reason to do sth
2 *nm,f* **f. de pouvoir** agent *(holding power of attorney)*; *(mandant)* proxy

fondement [fɔ̃dmɑ̃] *nm* foundation

fonder [fɔ̃de] **1** *vt* (**a**) *(créer) (ville, hôpital)* to found; *(société, journal)* to start, to set up; **f. un foyer** to start a family (**b**) *(baser)* **f. qch sur qch** to base sth on sth; **f. de grands espoirs sur qn** to pin one's hopes on sb
2 se fonder *vpr* **se f. sur qch** *(sujet: remarque, théorie)* to be based on sth; **sur quoi se fonde-t-il pour le nier?** what are his grounds for denying it?; **pour son livre, elle s'est fondée sur plusieurs articles** she based her book on several articles

fonderie [fɔ̃dri] *nf (usine)* foundry

fondre [fɔ̃dr] **1** *vt* (**a**) *(rendre liquide) (métal)* to melt down; *(sucre, sel)* to dissolve; *(neige, cire)* to melt (**b**) *(fabriquer) (cloche, arme)* to cast (**c**) *(combiner)*

(couleurs) to blend; *(sociétés)* to merge
2 *vi* (**a**) *(se liquéfier)* to melt; *(sucre)* to dissolve; **faire f. qch** to melt sth; *(sucre)* to dissolve sth; **f. dans la bouche** to melt in the mouth; **f. en larmes** to dissolve into tears; *Fig* **je fonds** my heart melts (**b**) *Fig (diminuer)* to melt away (**c**) *Fam (maigrir)* to lose weight
3 fondre sur *vt ind* to swoop on
4 se fondre *vpr* **se f. dans** to merge into

fonds [fɔ̃] **1** *nm* (**a**) *(capital)* funds; *(organisme)* fund; **prêter son argent à f. perdu** to lend one's money without security; **f. commun de placement** mutual fund; **F. européen de développement** European Development Fund; **F. européen de développement régional** European Regional Development Fund; **F. monétaire européen** European Monetary Fund; **F. monétaire international** International Monetary Fund; **f. de roulement** working capital (**b**) *(d'un musée, d'une bibliothèque)* collection; *(ressources)* resource (**c**) **f. de commerce** business
2 *nmpl (ressources financières)* funds; **être en f.** to be in funds; **f. publics** government funds; *(valeurs)* government stocks

fondu, -e [fɔ̃dy] **1** *adj Fam (fou)* round the bend, out to lunch
2 *nm,f Fam* **un f. d'informatique/de skateboard** a computer/skateboard freak
3 *nm* (**a**) *(de couleurs)* blending (**b**) *Cin* fade-out; **f. enchaîné** dissolve

fondue [fɔ̃dy] *nf* **f. (savoyarde)** (cheese) fondue; **f. bourguignonne** fondue bourguignonne, = fondue consisting of cubes of raw beef cooked in hot oil

fongicide [fɔ̃ʒisid] **1** *adj* fungicidal
2 *nm* fungicide

font *voir* **faire**

fontaine [fɔ̃tɛn] *nf (source naturelle)* spring; *(construction publique)* fountain

fonte [fɔ̃t] *nf* (**a**) *(de métaux)* melting down; **la f. des neiges** the thaw (**b**) *(alliage)* cast iron; **poêle en f.** cast-iron stove (**c**) *Typ* font

fonts [fɔ̃] *nmpl* **f. baptismaux** font

foot [fut] *nm Fam Br* football, *Am* soccer

football [futbol] *nm Br* football, *Am* soccer

footballeur, -euse [futbolœr, -øz] *nm,f Br* footballer, *Am* soccer player

footing [futiŋ] *nm* jogging; **faire du f.** to go jogging

for [fɔr] *nm* **dans** *ou* **en son f. intérieur** in one's heart of hearts, deep (down) inside

forage [fɔraʒ] *nm* drilling, boring

forain, -e [fɔrɛ̃, -ɛn] **1** *adj voir* **fête, marchand**
2 *nm* fairground stallholder

forçat [fɔrsa] *nm (prisonnier)* convict; **travailler comme un f.** to work like a slave

force [fɔrs] *nf* (**a**) *(vigueur)* strength; **ne pas se sentir/ne pas être de f. à faire qch** not to feel/not to be up to doing sth; **de f. égale, de même f.** equally matched; **dans la f. de l'âge** in the prime of life; **être à bout de forces** to have no strength left; **c'est au-dessus de ses forces** it's too much for him; **de toutes ses forces** *(pousser, frapper)* with all one's strength; *(vouloir)* with all one's heart; **f. de caractère** strength of character; **c'est une f. de la nature** *(personne)* she's a force to be reckoned with; **les forces vives du pays** the country's resources

(**b**) *(violence)* force; **faire qch de** *ou* **par la f.** to do sth by force; **par la f. des choses** through force of circumstance

(c) *(puissance)* **f. centrifuge/centripète** centrifugal/centripetal force; *aussi Fig* **f. d'inertie** inertia; **f. motrice** motive power; *Fig* driving force

(d) *(organisation)* **les forces armées** the armed forces; **les forces aériennes** the airforce; **f. de dissuasion** deterrent; **f. de frappe** strike force; **les forces de police** *ou* **de l'ordre** the police (force)

(e) *(locutions)* **à f.** in the end; **à f. de volonté** through sheer willpower; **à f. d'insister, tu vas finir par m'agacer** if you keep going on about it, I'm going to get annoyed; **en f.** in force

forcé, -e [fɔrse] *adj* forced; *Fam* **c'est f.!** it's inevitable!

forcément [fɔrsemũ] *adv* inevitably; **elle sera f. déçue** she's bound to be disappointed; **pas f.** not necessarily

forcené, -e [fɔrsəne] **1** *adj (partisan, individualisme)* fanatical; *(haine, lutte)* frenzied
2 *nm,f* maniac

forceps [fɔrsɛps] *nm* forceps

forcer [16] [fɔrse] **1** *vt* (a) *(obliger)* to force; **f. qn à faire qch** to force sb to do sth; **f. la main à qn** to force sb's hand; **f. le respect/l'admiration** to command respect/admiration (b) *(faire céder) (porte)* to force (open) (c) *(voix)* to strain; *Fig* **f. la dose** to overdo it
2 *vi (appuyer, tirer)* to force it; *(se surmener)* to overdo it; *Fam* **f. sur qch** to overdo sth
3 se forcer *vpr (s'obliger)* to force oneself (**à faire qch** to do sth)

forcing [fɔrsiŋ] *nm Sport* sustained pressure; **faire le f.** to put the pressure on; *Fam Fig* **faire du f.** to put on a lot of pressure

forcir [fɔrsir] *vi* (a) *(vent, tempête)* to get stronger (b) *(personne)* to get bigger

forer [fɔre] *vt* to drill, to bore

forestier, -ère [fɔrɛstje, -ɛr] **1** *adj (zone, chemin)* forest; **exploitation forestière** *(activité)* forestry
2 *nm* forester

forêt [fɔrɛ] *nf* forest; **F.-noire** *(gâteau)* Black Forest gateau; **f. vierge** virgin forest

foreuse [fɔrøz] *nf* drill

forfait¹ [fɔrfɛ] *nm (crime)* heinous crime

forfait² *nm* (a) *(contrat)* fixed-price contract; **travailler au f.** to work for a flat fee (b) **être au f.** *(fiscalement)* to pay an estimated amount of tax (c) *(prix global)* all-in price; **f. week-end** weekend package (d) *(de ski)* pass

forfait³ *nm voir* **déclarer**

forfaitaire [fɔrfɛtɛr] *adj (indemnités)* basic; *(prix)* all-in

forfanterie [fɔrfɑ̃tri] *nf* bragging

forge [fɔrʒ] *nf* forge

forger [45] [fɔrʒe] **1** *vt* (a) *(métal)* to forge; *Fig (caractère)* to form; *Prov* **c'est en forgeant qu'on devient forgeron** practice makes perfect (b) *(inventer) (histoire, excuse)* to make up
2 se forger *vpr* **se f. une réputation** to carve out a reputation for oneself

forgeron [fɔrʒərɔ̃] *nm* (black)smith

formaliser [fɔrmalize] **1** *vt* to formalize
2 se formaliser *vpr* to take offence (**de** at)

formalisme [fɔrmalism] *nm* formalism

formalité [fɔrmalite] *nf* formality; **les formalités d'usage** the usual formalities

format [fɔrma] *nm* format; *Ordinat* **f. d'écran** screen format; *Ordinat* **f. de fichier** file format; *Ordinat* **f.**

d'impression print format; **f. de papier** paper format; **f. de poche** pocket format

formatage [fɔrmataʒ] *nm Ordinat* formatting

formater [fɔrmate] *vt Ordinat* to format

formateur, -trice [fɔrmatœr, -tris] **1** *adj* formative
2 *nm,f* trainer

formation [fɔrmasjɔ̃] *nf* (a) *(de roches, d'un mot)* formation; *(du caractère)* forming (b) *(éducation)* training; **f. continue** *ou* **permanente** continuing education; **f. professionnelle** vocational training; **être en f.** to be undergoing training (c) *(groupe)* group

forme [fɔrm] *nf* (a) *(configuration)* shape, form; **formes** *(d'une femme)* curves; **en f. de qch** in the shape of sth; **en f. de L** L-shaped; **sous f. de qch** in the form of sth; **sous toutes ses formes** in all its forms; **sans f.** shapeless; **prendre f.** to take shape (b) *(manière)* form; **en bonne et due f.** in due form; **sans autre f. de procès** without further ado (c) *(convention)* **de pure f.** purely formal; **pour la f.** as a matter of form; **dans les formes** in the accepted way; **respecter les formes** to observe the proprieties (d) *(bonne santé physique)* form; **être en (pleine) f.** to be on (top) form

formel, -elle [fɔrmɛl] *adj* (a) *(personne)* positive; *(ordre)* express; *(démenti, refus)* flat; *(interdiction)* strict (b) *(apparent)* formal (c) *(soutenu)* formal

formellement [fɔrmɛlmɑ̃] *adv* (a) *(interdire)* strictly; *(affirmer)* categorically; *(identifier)* positively (b) *(du point de vue de la forme)* formally

former [fɔrme] **1** *vt* (a) *(créer) (gouvernement, projet)* to form (b) *(constituer)* to form; **ils forment une bonne équipe/un beau couple** they make a good team/a lovely couple (c) *(tracer) (lettre)* to form (d) *(entraîner)* to train (e) *(développer) (caractère)* to form; *(esprit, goût, jugement)* to develop
2 se former *vpr* (a) *(apparaître)* to form; *(association, liens)* to be formed (b) *(mûrir) (goût)* to develop (c) *(apprendre son métier)* to train oneself

Formica® [fɔrmika] *nm* Formica®; **en F.** Formica®

formidable [fɔrmidabl] *adj* (a) *(fantastique)* great, fantastic (b) *(gigantesque)* tremendous

formol [fɔrmɔl] *nm* formalin

formulaire [fɔrmylɛr] *nm* form; **remplir un f.** to fill in *or* out a form; *Ordinat* **f. de saisie** input form

formulation [fɔrmylasjɔ̃] *nf* formulation, wording

formule [fɔrmyl] *nf* (a) *(expression)* expression, phrase; **selon la f. consacrée** as the expression goes; **f. magique** magic formula; **f. de politesse** polite phrase; *(au début d'une lettre)* standard opening; *(à la fin d'une lettre)* standard ending (b) *(solution)* method; **nouvelle f.** *(menu, abonnement)* new-style (c) *(en mathématique, en chimie)* formula (d) *(automobile)* **f. 1/2** Formula 1/2

formuler [fɔrmyle] *vt* to formulate

forniquer [fɔrnike] *vi* to fornicate

FORPRONU [fɔrprɔny] *nf (abrév* **Force de protection des Nations unies)** **la F.** UNPROFOR

forsythia [fɔrsisja] *nm* forsythia

fort, -e [fɔr, fɔrt] **1** *adj* (a) *(vigoureux)* strong; **f. comme un Turc** *ou* **un bœuf** as strong as an ox; **c'est une forte tête** she's very strong-minded; **c'est plus f. que moi!** I can't help it!; *Fam* **c'est un peu f.!** that's a bit much!; **le plus f., c'est que...** the best of it is,... (b) *(doué)* **être f. en qch** to be good at sth (c) *(boisson, odeur, voix, lumière, accent)* strong; *(mer)* heavy; *(voix)* loud (d) *(robuste) (personne)* large (e) *(considérable) (somme d'argent)* large; *(pente)* steep; **il y a**

de fortes chances (pour) que ça réussisse there's a good chance it will work
2 *adv* (**a**) *(parler, crier, chanter)* loud, loudly; *(frapper, tirer)* hard; *(sentir)* strong; *Fam* **y aller f.** to overdo it; *Fam* **faire (très) f.** to do (really) brilliantly (**b**) *(très)* very (**c**) *(beaucoup)* very much; **avoir f. à faire (avec qn/qch)** to have one's work cut out (with sb/sth)
3 *nm* (**a**) *(spécialité)* strong point (**b**) *(citadelle)* fort (**c**) **au plus f. de qch** *(hiver)* in the depths of sth; *(été, épidémie, tempête)* at the height of sth
fortement [fɔrtəmɑ̃] *adv* (**a**) *(avec force)* *(tirer, pousser)* hard (**b**) *(intensément)* *(désirer, souhaiter, influencer)* strongly; *(impressionner, irriter)* greatly; *(insister)* firmly (**c**) *(très)* *(épicé)* highly; *(conseillé)* strongly
forteresse [fɔrtəres] *nf* fortress
fortifiant, -e [fɔrtifjɑ̃, -ɑ̃t] **1** *adj (nourriture, boisson)* fortifying
2 *nm* tonic
fortification [fɔrtifikasjɔ̃] *nf* fortification
fortifier [66] [fɔrtifje] *vt (ville, mur)* to fortify; *(muscles, corps, sentiment)* to strengthen
fortuit, -e [fɔrtɥi, -it] *adj* chance, fortuitous
fortune [fɔrtyn] *nf* (**a**) *(richesse)* fortune; **faire f.** to make one's fortune (**b**) *(hasard)* fortune, chance; **de f.** *(moyens, installation)* makeshift; **faire contre mauvaise f. bon cœur** to make the best of it
fortuné, -e [fɔrtyne] *adj (riche)* wealthy
forum [fɔrɔm] *nm* forum; *Ordinat* **f. de discussion** newsgroup
fosse [fos] *nf* (**a**) *(creux)* pit; **f. d'aisances** cesspool; **f. aux lions** lions' den; **f. d'orchestre** orchestra pit; **f. septique** septic tank (**b**) *(tombe)* grave; **f. commune** mass grave
fossé [fose] *nm (le long de la route)* ditch; *(autour d'un château)* moat; *Fig (entre personnes)* gulf
fossette [fosɛt] *nf* dimple
fossile [fosil] **1** *adj* fossil
2 *nm Fam aussi Fig* fossil
fossoyeur [foswajœr] *nm* gravedigger; *Fig* destroyer
fou, folle [fu, fɔl]

> **fol** is used before masculine singular nouns beginning with a vowel or h mute.

1 *adj* (**a**) *(dément)* mad, insane; **f. de joie** beside oneself with joy; **f. à lier** raving mad; **être f. (amoureux) de qn/qch** to be mad about sb/sth (**b**) *(énorme)* tremendous; *(prix)* exorbitant (**c**) *(incroyable)* incredible (**d**) *(train)* runaway; *(boussole, aiguille)* crazy; **f. rire** uncontrollable giggling; **avoir un** *ou* **le f. rire** to have the giggles
2 *nm,f* madman, *f* madwoman; *Fam* **comme un f.** like mad; **entrer/sortir comme un f.** to storm in/out; **faire le f.** to play *or* act the fool; **un f. furieux** a maniac; **un f. du volant** a reckless driver; *Prov* **plus on est de fous, plus on rit** the more the merrier
3 *nm* (**a**) *(aux échecs)* bishop (**b**) *(bouffon)* jester (**c**) **f. de Bassan** gannet
foudre [fudr] **1** *nf* lightning; *Litt* **s'attirer les foudres de qn** to bring down sb's wrath on one
2 *nm* (**a**) *(tonneau)* tun (**b**) **un f. de guerre** a great warrior; *Fig* **ce n'est pas un f. de guerre** he's no bright spark
foudroyant, -e [fudrwajɑ̃, -ɑ̃t] *adj (maladie)* violent; *(crise cardiaque)* massive; *(révélation, nouvelle)* devastating; *(succès)* stunning; *(vitesse, progrès)* lightning; *(regard)* withering

foudroyer [32] [fudrwaje] *vt* to strike; **être foudroyé** to be struck by lightning; **f. qn du regard** to give sb a withering look
fouet [fwɛ] *nm (pour punir)* whip; *(de cuisine)* whisk; **de plein f.** head-on
fouetter [fwete] **1** *vt* (**a**) *(punir)* to whip; *Fam* **il n'y a pas de quoi f. un chat** it's nothing to make a fuss about; *Fam* **avoir d'autres chats à f.** to have other fish to fry
(**b**) *(cingler)* to lash (against) (**c**) *(battre)* *(œufs)* to beat, to whisk; *(crème)* to whip
2 *vi Fam (puer)* to stink
foufou, fofolle [fufu, fɔfɔl] *adj Fam* daft
fougasse [fugas] *nf* = type of flat bread often made with olives, herbs, bacon etc
fougère [fuʒɛr] *nf* fern
fougue [fug] *nf* fire, spirit
fougueusement [fugøzmɑ̃] *adv (s'élancer)* impetuously; *(s'embrasser)* passionately
fougueux, -euse [fugø, -øz] *adj (personne, tempérament)* fiery, ardent; *(cheval)* spirited
fouille [fuj] *nf* (**a**) *(d'une maison, d'une personne)* search; **faire une f.** to make a search; **f. corporelle** *(rapide)* frisking; *(approfondie)* body search (**b**) **fouilles** *(archéologiques)* excavations, dig (**c**) *Fam (poche)* pocket
fouillé, -e [fuje] *adj (approfondi)* detailed
fouiller [fuje] **1** *vt* (**a**) *(maison, personne)* to search (**b**) *(problème)* to go thoroughly into
2 *vi* to search (**dans** in)
fouillis [fuji] *nm* jumble, muddle
fouine [fwin] *nf* stone marten
fouiner [fwine] *vi* to nose about (**dans** in)
foulard [fular] *nm* scarf
foule [ful] *nf (de gens)* crowd; **il ne supporte pas la f.** he can't stand crowds; *Fig* **une f. de qch** lots of sth
foulée [fule] *nf (d'un coureur)* stride; *Fig* **dans la f., j'ai vérifié les comptes** while I was at it, I checked the accounts
fouler [fule] **1** *vt (sol)* to tread; *(raisins)* to press; *Fig* **f. qch aux pieds** to trample sth underfoot
2 **se fouler** *vpr* (**a**) **se f. la cheville** to sprain one's ankle (**b**) *Fam (se fatiguer)* to strain oneself
foulure [fulyr] *nf* sprain; **se faire une f. à la cheville** to sprain one's ankle
four [fur] *nm* (**a**) *(de cuisine)* oven; **f. à gaz/électrique/à micro-ondes** gas/electric/microwave oven; **cuit au f.** *(pain)* baked; *(viande)* roasted; **il fait noir comme dans un f.** it's pitch black; **on ne peut être à la fois au f. et au moulin** you can't be in two places at once (**b**) **petits fours** *(gâteaux)* petits fours (**c**) *(industriel)* kiln; *Hist* **les fours crématoires** the gas ovens (**d**) *Fam (fiasco)* flop; **faire un f.** to flop
fourbe [furb] **1** *adj* deceitful
2 *nmf* cheat
fourbi [furbi] *nm Fam* (**a**) *(désordre)* mess (**b**) *(truc)* thingy
fourbu, -e [furby] *adj* exhausted
fourche [furʃ] *nf* (**a**) *(outil)* fork (**b**) *(de bicyclette, sur une route)* fork; *(des cheveux)* split end; **faire une f.** to fork (**c**) *Belg Scol* break, gap *(in one's timetable)*
fourcher [furʃe] *vi* **sa langue a fourché** she made a slip of the tongue

fourchette [furʃɛt] *nf* (**a**) *(ustensile)* fork; *Fam* **avoir un joli** *ou* **bon coup de f.** to have a hearty appetite (**b**) *(écart)* bracket; **f. de prix** price bracket

fourchu, -e [furʃy] *adj (tronc, route)* forked; **aux pieds fourchus** cloven-hoofed; **avoir les cheveux fourchus** to have split ends

fourgon [furgɔ̃] *nm* (**a**) *(véhicule)* van; **f. cellulaire** *Br* police van, *Am* patrol wagon; **f. funèbre** *ou* **funéraire** hearse (**b**) *(d'un train)* **f. à bétail** cattle truck

fourgonnette [furgɔnɛt] *nf* small van

fourguer [furge] *vt Fam* **f. qch à qn** to unload sth onto sb

fourmi [furmi] *nf* ant; *Fig (personne travailleuse)* busy bee; **avoir des fourmis (dans les jambes)** to have pins and needles (in one's legs); **travail de f.** painstaking work

fourmilière [furmiljɛr] *nf* anthill; *Fig* hive of activity

fourmillement [furmijmã] *nm* (**a**) *(sensation)* pins and needles (**b**) *(agitation)* swarming

fourmiller [furmije] **1** *vi* to swarm, to teem
2 fourmiller de *vt ind* to swarm with, to teem with

fournaise [furnɛz] *nf* (**a**) *(endroit surchauffé)* **c'est une vraie f. ici!** this place is like a furnace! (**b**) *Litt (feu)* blaze (**c**) *Can (poêle à bois)* (wood-burning) stove; *(poêle au charbon)* (coal-burning) stove; *(chaudière de chauffage central) Br* boiler, *Am* (central heating) furnace

fourneau, -x [furno] *nm* (**a**) *(de cuisine)* stove; **être aux fourneaux** to be cooking (**b**) *(de verrier, de fondeur)* furnace (**c**) *(d'une pipe)* bowl

fournée [furne] *nf aussi Fig* batch

fourni, -e [furni] *adj* (**a**) *(magasin)* **bien/mal f.** well/poorly stocked (**b**) *(barbe, sourcils)* bushy; **peu f.** sparse

fournil [furni] *nm* bakehouse

fournir [furnir] **1** *vt* (**a**) *(approvisionner)* to supply (**en** with) (**b**) *(procurer)* **f. qch à qn** to provide sb with sth (**c**) *(présenter) (preuve, alibi)* to provide; *(documents)* to provide; **pièces à f.** required documents (**d**) *(effort)* to make
2 se fournir *vpr* **se f. en qch** to get in supplies of sth; **se f. chez qn** to get one's supplies from sb

fournisseur, -euse [furnisœr, -øz] *nm,f* supplier; *Ordinat* **f. d'accès** access provider

fournitures [furnityr] *nfpl* **f. de bureau** office supplies; **f. scolaires** educational stationery

fourrage [furaʒ] *nm* fodder

fourrager¹ [45] [furaʒe] *vi Fam (fouiller)* to rummage (**dans** in)

fourrager², -ère [furaʒe, -ɛr] *adj (plante)* fodder

fourre [fur] *nf Suisse (d'un oreiller)* pillowcase; *(pour un édredon)* quilt cover; *(d'un disque)* sleeve; *(d'un livre)* jacket

fourreau, -x [furo] *nm* (**a**) *(d'épée)* sheath, scabbard; *(de parapluie)* cover (**b**) **(robe) f.** sheath dress; **jupe f.** pencil skirt

fourrer [fure] **1** *vt* (**a**) *(gâteau, bonbon)* to fill (**à** with); **bonbon fourré** *Br* soft-centred sweet, *Am* soft-centered candy (**b**) *Fam (mettre)* to stick
2 se fourrer *vpr Fam* **où est-il allé se f.?** where's he got to?; **ne pas savoir où se f.** not to know where to put oneself; **se f. dans une sale affaire** to get involved in a nasty business

fourre-tout [furtu] **1** *adj inv (placard)* junk; **un texte/une loi f.** a ragbag of a text/a law
2 *nm inv* (**a**) *(pièce)* junk room; *(placard)* junk cupboard
(**b**) *(sac) Br* holdall, *Am* carryall

fourreur [furœr] *nm* furrier

fourrière [furjɛr] *nf* pound; **mettre en f.** *ou* **à la f.** *(voiture)* to impound; *(chien)* to put in the pound

fourrure [furyr] *nf* fur; **de** *ou* **en f.** fur

fourvoyer [32] [furvwaje] *Litt* **se fourvoyer** *vpr* to lose one's way; *Fig* to go astray

foutaise [futez] *nf Fam* bullshit

foutoir [futwar] *nm Fam* dump

foutre [futr] *très Fam* **1** *vt* (**a**) *(mettre)* to stick; **f. qch par terre** to chuck sth on the ground; **f. qn à la porte** to kick sb out; **f. qch en l'air** *(le faire échouer)* to screw sth up (**b**) *(faire)* to do; **ne rien f.** to do damn all; **je n'en ai rien à f.!** I couldn't give a damn!; **qu'est-ce que ça peut f.?** what the hell does it matter? (**c**) *(donner) (correction, gifle)* to give; **f. la trouille à qn** to put the wind up sb (**d**) *(locutions)* **f. le camp** to piss off; **fous(-moi) le camp!** piss off!; **je t'en foutrais, du champagne!** champagne, you'll be bloody lucky!; *Vulg* **va te faire f.!** fuck off!
2 se foutre *vpr* (**a**) *(se mettre)* **se f. un coup** to bang oneself; **se f. par terre** to go sprawling; **se f. dedans** to screw up (**b**) **se f. de (la gueule de) qn** *(se moquer de)* to take the piss out of sb; **se f. du monde** to take the piss (**c**) **se f. de qn/qch** *(être indifférent à)* not to give a damn about sb/sth; **je m'en fous** I don't give a damn

foutu, -e [futy] *adj Fam* (**a**) *(maudit)* damn (**b**) *(en mauvais état, perdu)* **être f.** to have had it; **c'est f.!** forget it! (**c**) **être bien/mal f.** *(bien/mal bâti)* to have/not to have a nice body; *(bien/mal conçu)* to be well/badly designed; **être mal f.** *(malade)* to be under the weather (**d**) *(capable)* **être f. de faire qch** to be quite likely to do sth; **elle n'est même pas foutue d'être à l'heure** she can't even be bothered to turn up on time

fox [fɔks], **fox-terrier** (*pl* **fox-terriers**) [fɔkstɛrje] *nm* fox terrier

foyer [fwaje] *nm* (**a**) *(domicile)* home; **le f. conjugal** the marital home (**b**) *(famille)* family (**c**) *(résidence) (d'étudiants)* residence; *(de travailleurs, de délinquants)* hostel (**d**) *(de chaleur, d'infection)* source; *(d'incendie, de conflits)* seat (**e**) *(âtre)* hearth (**f**) *(de lunettes)* focus

fracas [fraka] *nm* crash

fracassant, -e [frakasã, -ãt] *adj (bruit)* deafening; *(nouvelle, révélation)* shattering; *(succès)* resounding

fracasser [frakase] **1** *vt* to smash
2 se fracasser *vpr* to smash

fraction [fraksjɔ̃] *nf* (**a**) *(partie)* part, fraction; **pendant une f. de seconde** for a fraction of a second (**b**) *Math* fraction

fractionnement [fraksjɔnmã] *nm* splitting up

fractionner [fraksjɔne] **1** *vt* to split up (**en** into)
2 se fractionner *vpr* to split up (**en** into)

fracture [fraktyr] *nf* fracture; **f. du crâne** fractured skull; *Fig* **la f. sociale** the gap between the haves and the have-nots in society

fracturer [fraktyre] **1** *vt* (**a**) *(serrure, porte)* to break open (**b**) *(os)* to fracture
2 se fracturer *vpr* **se f. le tibia** to fracture one's tibia

fragile [fraʒil] *adj (matériau, objet)* fragile; *(santé, estomac, équilibre)* delicate; *(personne) (physiquement)* frail; *(mentalement)* sensitive; *(bonheur)* precarious; *(hypothèse)* shaky

fragiliser [fraʒilize] *vt* to weaken

fragilité [fraʒilite] *nf (d'un matériau, d'un objet)* fragility; *(d'une personne) (physique)* frailty; *(mentale)* sensitivity; *(du bonheur)* precariousness; *(d'une hypothèse)* shakiness; *(de la santé, de l'estomac, d'un équilibre)* delicacy

fragment [fragmɑ̃] *nm (d'un objet, de conversation)* fragment; *(d'un livre)* extract; *(de vérité)* shred

fragmentaire [fragmɑ̃tɛr] *adj* fragmentary

fragmenter [fragmɑ̃te] *vt* to fragment

fraîche [frɛʃ] *adj voir* **frais¹**

fraîchement [frɛʃmɑ̃] *adv* (a) *(recevoir, accueillir)* coolly (b) *(récemment)* newly

fraîcheur [frɛʃœr] *nf (de la température, d'un accueil)* coolness; *(d'aliments, du teint)* freshness

fraîchir [frɛʃir] *vi (temps)* to freshen

frais¹, fraîche [frɛ, frɛʃ] 1 *adj* (a) *(vent, air, accueil)* cool (b) *(aliments, fleurs, teint)* fresh; **f. et dispos** hale and hearty (c) *(souvenir, nouvelles)* recent; *(encre, peinture)* wet
2 *adv* **servir/boire f.** *(sur étiquette)* serve/drink chilled; **f. émoulu de** fresh out of
3 *nm* **prendre le f.** to get a breath of fresh air; **mettre/conserver qch au f.** to put/keep sth in a cool place; **il fait f.** it's cool; *Can Fam Péj* **faire le f.** to show off
4 *nf* **à la fraîche** in the cool part of the day; *Can* **prendre la f.** *(sortir prendre l'air)* to go for a stroll; *(prendre froid)* to catch a chill

frais² *nmpl* expenses, costs; **faire de gros f.** to go to great expense; **tous f. payés** all expenses paid; **rentrer dans ses f.** to cover one's expenses; *Fig* **faire les f. de qch** *(être victime de)* to pay the price for sth; **faire les f. de la conversation** to keep the conversation going; **faire qch à ses f.** to do sth at one's own expense; **aux f. de la société** at the company's expense; **aux f. de la princesse** at the firm's/government's/*etc* expense; **à grands/peu de f.** at great/little cost; **se mettre en f.** to go to great expense; **en être pour ses f.** to have been wasting one's time; **f. de déplacement** travelling expenses; **f. généraux** overheads; **f. d'inscription** membership fee; **f. de port** postage and packing; **f. de scolarité** school fees; *Can Tél* **appeler qn a f. virés** *Br* to make a reverse-charge call to sb, *Am* to call sb collect; **faux f.** incidental expenses

fraise¹ [frɛz] *nf (fruit)* strawberry; **glace à la f.** strawberry(-flavoured) ice-cream; **f. des bois** wild strawberry

fraise² *nf (de dentiste)* drill

fraise³ *nf (collerette)* ruff

fraisier [frɛzje] *nm* (a) *(plante)* strawberry plant (b) *(gâteau)* strawberry cream cake

framboise [frɑ̃bwaz] *nf* raspberry

framboisier [frɑ̃bwazje] *nm* raspberry bush

franc¹ [frɑ̃] *nm* franc; **f. français/suisse/belge** French/Swiss/Belgian franc; **f. CFA** CFA franc; **ancien/nouveau f.** old/new franc; **f. symbolique** nominal sum

franc², franche [frɑ̃, frɑ̃ʃ] 1 *adj* (a) *(sincère)* frank (b) *(zone, ville, port)* free (c) *(net) (couleur)* pure; *(rupture)* clean
2 *adv (parler)* frankly

français, -e [frɑ̃sɛ, -ɛz] 1 *adj* French
2 *nm,f* **F.** Frenchman, *f* Frenchwoman; **les F.** the French
3 *nm (langue)* French; **parler f.** to speak French; *(correctement)* to speak properly; *Fam* **tu ne comprends pas le f.?** don't you understand plain English?

France [frɑ̃s] *nf* la **F.** France; *TV* **F. 2/3** = second/third French state-owned TV channel; **F. Télécom** = state-owned telecommunications company

Francfort [frɑ̃kfɔr] *n* Frankfurt

franche [frɑ̃ʃ] *adj voir* **franc**

franchement [frɑ̃ʃmɑ̃] *adv* (a) *(sincèrement)* frankly (b) *(tout à fait, vraiment)* really (c) *(carrément)* **y aller f.** to get on with it

franchir [frɑ̃ʃir] *vt (obstacle, difficulté)* to get over; *(porte)* to go through; *(fossé)* to jump (over); *(ligne d'arrivée, rivière, frontière)* to cross; *Fig (cap, seuil, niveau)* to pass

franchise [frɑ̃ʃiz] *nf* (a) *(sincérité)* frankness; **en toute f.** quite frankly (b) *(exonération)* exemption; **f. postale** ≃ postage paid (c) *(d'assurance) Br* excess, *Am* deductible (d) *Com* franchise

franchouillard, -e [frɑ̃ʃujar, -ard] *adj Fam* typically French

francilien, -enne [frɑ̃siljɛ̃, -ɛn] 1 *adj* of the Île-de-France
2 *nm,f* **F.** person from the Île-de-France

franciscain, -e [frɑ̃siskɛ̃, -ɛn] *adj & nm,f* Franciscan

franciser [frɑ̃size] *vt* to gallicize

franc-maçon, -onne *(pl* **francs-maçons, francmaçonnes)** [frɑ̃masɔ̃, -ɔn] *nm,f* freemason

franc-maçonnerie [frɑ̃masɔnri] *nf* freemasonry

franco [frɑ̃ko] *adv* (a) *Fam (franchement)* **y aller f.** to get on with it (b) *Com* **f. (de port)** postage paid; **f. à bord** free on board

francophile [frɑ̃kɔfil] *adj & nmf* Francophile

francophobe [frɑ̃kɔfɔb] *adj & nmf* Francophobe

francophone [frɑ̃kɔfɔn] 1 *adj* French-speaking
2 *nmf* French speaker

francophonie [frɑ̃kɔfɔni] *nf* French-speaking world

franc-parler [frɑ̃parle] *nm* outspokenness; **avoir son f.** to speak one's mind

franc-tireur *(pl* **francs-tireurs)** [frɑ̃tirœr] *nm (combattant)* irregular (soldier); *Fig* maverick

frange [frɑ̃ʒ] *nf* fringe

frangin, -e [frɑ̃ʒɛ̃, -in] *nm,f Fam* brother, *f* sister

frangipane [frɑ̃ʒipan] *nf* = almond-flavoured confectioner's custard

franglais [frɑ̃glɛ] *nm* Franglais

franquette [frɑ̃kɛt] *nf* **à la bonne f.** without ceremony

frappant, -e [frapɑ̃, -ɑ̃t] *adj* striking

frappe [frap] *nf* (a) *(sur un clavier d'ordinateur)* keying; *(sur une machine à écrire)* typing; *Ordinat* **f. en continu** type-ahead; *Ordinat* **f. au kilomètre** continuous input (b) *(de monnaie)* minting (c) *(au base-ball)* hit; *(au football)* kick; *(en boxe)* punch (d) *Fam (voyou)* hoodlum (e) *Mil* strike; **frappe aérienne** air-strike

frappé, -e [frape] *adj* (a) *(champagne)* chilled; *(café)* iced (b) *Fam (fou)* crazy

frapper [frape] 1 *vt* (a) *(donner un ou des coups à)* to hit, to strike; *Fig (faire une forte impression sur)* to strike (b) *(monnaie)* to mint (c) *(champagne)* to put on ice (d) *Can (entrer en collision avec)* to hit
2 *vi* (a) *(donner un coup)* to strike, to hit; **f. du poing sur la table** to bang (on) the table; **f. des mains** *ou* **dans ses mains** to clap (one's hands); **f. à la porte** to knock on *or* at the door; *Fig* **tu frappes à la bonne/mauvaise porte** you've come to the right/wrong place; **entrez sans f.** *(sur écriteau)* go straight in (b)

Fam (agir) to strike
3 se frapper *vpr* (**a**) *Fam (se faire du souci)* to get oneself worked up (**b**) *Can (entrer en collision)* to collide

frasques [frask] *nfpl* carryings-on

fraternel, -elle [fratɛrnɛl] *adj* fraternal, brotherly

fraterniser [fratɛrnize] *vi* to fraternize

fraternité [fratɛrnite] *nf* fraternity, brotherhood

fratricide [fratrisid] **1** *adj* fratricidal
2 *nmf (personne)* fratricide
3 *nm (crime)* fratricide

fraude [frod] *nf* fraud; **passer qch en f.** to smuggle sth in; **f. électorale** electoral fraud; **f. fiscale** tax evasion

frauder [frode] **1** *vt (douane)* to defraud; **f. le fisc** to evade tax
2 *vi* to cheat (**sur** on)

fraudeur, -euse [frodœr, -øz] *nm,f* defrauder

frauduleux, -euse [frodylø, -øz] *adj* fraudulent

frayer [53] [freje] **1** *vi (poisson)* to spawn; *Fig* **f. avec qn** to mix with sb
2 se frayer *vpr* **se f. un chemin** to clear a way (for oneself)

frayeur [frejœr] *nf* fright; **faire une f. à qn** to give sb a fright

fredaines [frədɛn] *nfpl* pranks, escapades

fredonner [frədɔne] *vt & vi* to hum

free-lance [frilɑ̃s] **1** *adj inv* freelance
2 *nm (travail)* freelance work; **travailler en f.** to work freelance
3 *nmf (pl* **free-lances***)* freelance, freelancer

freezer [frizœr] *nm* freezer compartment

frégate [fregat] *nf* (**a**) *(oiseau)* frigate bird (**b**) *(navire)* frigate

frein [frɛ̃] *nm* (**a**) *(de voiture)* brake; **donner un coup de f.** to put on the brakes; *Fig* **mettre un f. à qch** to curb sth; **freins à disque** disc brakes; **f. à main** *Br* handbrake, *Am* parking brake; **f. moteur** engine brake (**b**) *(mors)* bit

freinage [frɛnaʒ] *nm* braking

freiner [frene] **1** *vt* (**a**) *(véhicule, processus)* to slow down; *(chute)* to break; *(inflation, production)* to curb (**b**) *(personne)* to restrain
2 *vi* to brake
3 se freiner *vpr* to restrain oneself

frelaté, -e [frəlate] *adj (vin)* adulterated

frelater [frəlate] *vt* to adulterate

frêle [frɛl] *adj* frail

frelon [frəlɔ̃] *nm* hornet

freluquet [frəlykɛ] *nm Fam* whippersnapper

frémir [fremir] *vi* (**a**) *(personne)* to tremble (**de** with) (**b**) *(eau chaude)* to simmer; *(feuillage)* to rustle

frémissant, -e [fremisɑ̃, -ɑ̃t] *adj (eau)* simmering; *(voix)* trembling; *(feuillage)* rustling

frémissement [fremismɑ̃] *nm* (**a**) *(de peur)* shudder; *(de plaisir, de joie)* thrill; *(de colère, d'impatience)* quiver (**b**) *(de l'eau)* simmering; *(des feuilles)* rustle

french cancan (*pl* **french cancans**) [frɛ̃ʃkɑ̃kɑ̃] *nm* cancan

frêne [frɛn] *nm* ash

frénésie [frenezi] *nf* frenzy

frénétique [frenetik] *adj* frenzied

frénétiquement [frenetikmɑ̃] *adv* frenziedly

fréquemment [frekamɑ̃] *adv* frequently

fréquence [frekɑ̃s] *nf* frequency; **basse/haute f.** low/high frequency

fréquent, -e [frekɑ̃, -ɑ̃t] *adj* frequent

fréquentable [frekɑ̃tabl] *adj* **des gens peu fréquentables** people you wouldn't want to associate with

fréquentation [frekɑ̃tasjɔ̃] *nf* (**a**) *(d'un lieu)* frequenting; **la f. de qn** seeing sb regularly (**b**) **fréquentations** *(relations)* company; **avoir de mauvaises fréquentations** to keep bad company

fréquenté, -e [frekɑ̃te] *adj* **très f.** very busy; **bien/mal f.** of good/ill repute

fréquenter [frekɑ̃te] **1** *vt* (**a**) *(lieu)* to frequent (**b**) *(personne) (voir régulièrement)* to see regularly; *(sortir avec)* to go out with
2 se fréquenter *vpr (se voir régulièrement)* to see each other regularly; *(sortir ensemble)* to go out with each other

frère [frɛr] **1** *adj (pays, peuple)* fellow
2 *nm* brother; **faux f.** false friend; **frères d'armes** brothers-in-arms

frérot [frero] *nm Fam* kid brother

fresque [frɛsk] *nf* fresco

fret [frɛ, frɛt] *nm* freight

frétillant, -e [fretijɑ̃, -ɑ̃t] *adj (poisson)* wriggling; *(personne) (de joie)* quivering (**de** with)

frétiller [fretije] *vi (poisson, personne)* to wriggle; **f. de joie** to quiver with joy

fretin [frətɛ̃] *nm aussi Fig* **menu f.** small fry

freudien, -enne [frødjɛ̃, -ɛn] *adj* Freudian

freux [frø] *nm* rook

FRF *(abrév* **franc(s) français***)* FF

friable [frijabl] *adj* crumbly

friand, -e [frijɑ̃, -ɑ̃d] **1** *adj* **être f. de qch** to be fond of sth
2 *nm (salé)* = small savoury pastry; *(sucré)* = small almond cake

friandise [frijɑ̃diz] *nf* titbit, delicacy

fric [frik] *nm Fam* dough

fricassée [frikase] *nf (ragoût)* fricassee; *Belg* fried egg and bacon

friche [friʃ] *nf* fallow land; **en f.** fallow; **f. industrielle** industrial wasteland

frichti [friʃti] *nm Fam* grub

fricot [friko] *nm Fam* grub; **faire le f.** to do the cooking

fricoter [frikɔte] *Fam* **1** *vt* (**a**) *(manigancer)* to cook up (**b**) *(plat)* to cook
2 *vi (avoir des activités suspectes)* to be on the fiddle

friction [friksjɔ̃] *nf* (**a**) *(massage)* rubdown; *(du cuir chevelu)* scalp massage (**b**) *(heurt)* friction

frictionner [friksjɔne] **1** *vt (partie du corps)* to rub; *(personne)* to rub down
2 se frictionner *vpr* to rub oneself

Frigidaire® [friʒidɛr] *nm* fridge

frigide [friʒid] *adj* frigid

frigidité [friʒidite] *nf* frigidity

frigo [frigo] *nm Fam* fridge

frigorifié, -e [frigɔrifje] *adj Fam (personne)* frozen stiff

frigorifier [66] [frigɔrifje] *vt (aliment)* to refrigerate

frigorifique [frigɔrifik] *adj voir* **camion**

frileux, -euse [frilø, -øz] *adj (personne)* sensitive to the cold; *(attitude, réponse)* timid

frime [frim] *nf Fam* show

frimer [frime] *vi Fam* to show off

frimeur, -euse [frimœr, -øz] *nm,f Fam* show-off

frimousse [frimus] *nf Fam* sweet little face

fringale [frɛ̃gal] *nf Fam (faim)* hunger; *Fig (envie)* craving (**de** for); **avoir la f.** to be starving

fringant, -e [frɛ̃gɑ̃, -ɑ̃t] *adj (personne)* dashing

fringuer [frɛ̃ge] *Fam* **1** *vt* to dress
2 se fringuer *vpr (se vêtir)* to get dressed; *(choisir ses vêtements)* to dress; **il se fringue super bien** he dresses really well, he's a really natty dresser

fringues [frɛ̃g] *nfpl Fam* gear

fripé, -e [fripe] *adj* crumpled

friper [fripe] **1** *vt* to crumple
2 se friper *vpr* to get crumpled

friperie [fripri] *nf* second-hand clothes shop

fripes [frip] *nfpl* second-hand clothes

fripier, -ère [fripje, -ɛr] *nm,f* second-hand clothes dealer

fripon, -onne [fripɔ̃, -ɔn] *Fam* **1** *adj* mischievous
2 *nm,f* rascal

fripouille [fripuj] *nf Fam* rogue

friqué, -e [frike] *adj Fam* loaded

frire [19a] [frir] **1** *vt* to fry
2 *vi* to fry; **faire f. qch** to fry sth

Frisbee® [frizbi] *nm* Frisbee®

frise [friz] *nf* frieze

frisé, -e [frize] **1** *adj (cheveux)* curly; *(personne)* curly-haired
2 *nf* **frisée** *(salade)* curly endive

friser [frize] **1** *vt* (**a**) *(cheveux)* to curl (**b**) *(approcher)* **f. la catastrophe** to come within an inch of disaster; **elle doit f. la quarantaine** she must be getting on for forty; **cela frise le ridicule** it's verging on the ridiculous
2 *vi (cheveux)* to curl; *(personne)* to have curly hair

frisette [frizɛt] *nf (de cheveux)* small curl

frisotter [frizɔte] **1** *vt (cheveux)* to frizz
2 *vi* to be frizzy

frisquet, -ette [friskɛ, -ɛt] *adj Fam* chilly; **il fait f.** it's chilly

frisson [frisɔ̃] *nm (de froid, de peur)* shiver; *(de plaisir)* thrill; **avoir des frissons** to shiver; **donner des frissons** *ou* **le f. à qn** *(de peur)* to give sb the shivers

frissonner [frisɔne] *vi* (**a**) *(personne) (de froid, de peur)* to shiver (**b**) *Litt (feuillage)* to quiver; *(eau)* to ripple

frit, -e [fri, frit] **1** *adj* fried
2 *nf* **frite** (**a**) *(de pomme de terre) Br* chip, *Am* (French) fry (**b**) *Fam* **avoir la frite** to be on form

friteuse [fritøz] *nf* deep frier, *Br* chip pan; **f. électrique** electric frier

friture [frityr] *nf* (**a**) *(mode de cuisson)* frying (**b**) *(corps gras)* frying fat (**c**) *(aliments)* fried food; **f. (de poissons)** fried fish (**d**) *Rad & Tél* crackling (**e**) *Belg (friterie) Br* chip stall, *Am* French fry vendor

frivole [frivɔl] *adj* frivolous

frivolité [frivɔlite] *nf* frivolity

froc [frɔk] *nm* (**a**) *Fam (pantalon) Br* trousers, *Am* pants (**b**) *(habit religieux)* habit

froid, -e [frwa, frwad] **1** *adj aussi Fig* cold
2 *adv* **boire/manger qch f.** to drink/eat sth cold
3 *nm* cold; **les grands froids** the coldest part of the winter; **il fait f.** it's cold; *Fam* **il fait un f. de canard** it's freezing (cold); *Fig* **ça fait f. dans le dos** it sends a shiver down your spine; **avoir f.** to be cold; **j'ai f. aux mains** my hands are cold, I've got cold hands; **ne pas avoir f. aux yeux** to have plenty of nerve; **à f.** *(répondre)* off the top of one's head; *(humour)* deadpan;

être en f. (avec qn) to be on bad terms (with sb); **prendre f.** to catch cold

froidement [frwadmɑ̃] *adv (accueillir, recevoir)* coldly; *(abattre)* cold-bloodedly; *(répondre)* coolly

froideur [frwadœr] *nf* coldness; **avec f.** coldly

froissement [frwasmɑ̃] *nm* (**a**) *(bruit)* rustle (**b**) *(de muscle)* straining

froisser [frwase] **1** *vt* (**a**) *(tissu, papier)* to crumple, to crease (**b**) *Fig (sentiment, personne)* to offend
2 se froisser *vpr* (**a**) *(tissu)* to crease, to crumple (**b**) **se f. un muscle** to strain a muscle (**c**) *Fig (personne)* to take offence (**de** at)

frôlement [frolmɑ̃] *nm (contact)* brushing (**contre** against); *(son)* rustle

frôler [frole] **1** *vt* (**a**) *(effleurer)* to brush (against), to touch lightly (**b**) *Fig (la mort, la catastrophe)* to come close to; *(le ridicule)* to border on
2 se frôler *vpr* to brush (against) each other

fromage [frɔmaʒ] *nm* (**a**) *(produit laitier)* cheese; *Fam Fig* **faire tout un f. de qch** to make a great fuss about sth; **f. blanc** fromage frais; **f. de brebis** sheep's *ou* ewe's milk cheese; **f. de chèvre** goat's cheese; **f. frais** soft cheese; **f. à pâte molle/dure** soft/hard cheese; **f. à tartiner** cheese spread (**b**) **f. de tête** *Br* brawn, *Am* headcheese

fromager, -ère [frɔmaʒe, -ɛr] **1** *adj* cheese
2 *nm,f (commerçant)* cheese seller; *(fabricant)* cheesemaker

fromagerie [frɔmaʒri] *nf (lieu de fabrication)* cheese dairy; *(magasin)* cheese shop

froment [frɔmɑ̃] *nm* wheat

fronce [frɔ̃s] *nf* gather

froncement [frɔ̃smɑ̃] *nm* **f. de(s) sourcils** frown

froncer [16] [frɔ̃se] *vt* (**a**) *(nez, front)* to wrinkle; **f. les sourcils** to frown (**b**) *(tissu)* to gather

fronde [frɔ̃d] *nf* (**a**) *(arme)* sling; *(jouet) Br* catapult, *Am* slingshot (**b**) *(révolte)* rebellion

frondeur, -euse [frɔ̃dœr, -øz] **1** *adj* rebellious
2 *nm,f* rebel

front [frɔ̃] *nm* (**a**) *(partie du visage)* forehead (**b**) *(avant)* front; **faire f.** to face up to things; **faire f. à qn/qch** to face up to sb/sth; **de f.** *(marcher, avancer)* side by side; *(heurter, aborder un problème)* head-on; **mener plusieurs choses de f.** to have several things on the go at once; **f. de mer** seafront (**c**) *(audace)* **avoir le f. de faire qch** to have the nerve to do sth (**d**) *Mil & Météo* front

frontal, -e, -aux, -ales [frɔ̃tal, -o] *adj* (**a**) *(attaque, choc)* head-on; **machine à laver à chargement f.** front-loading washing machine (**b**) *Ordinat* front-end; **ordinateur f.** front end (**c**) *(os)* frontal

frontalier, -ère [frɔ̃talje, -ɛr] **1** *adj (région)* border, frontier
2 *nm,f (habitant)* person living near the border; *(travailleur)* cross-border commuter

frontière [frɔ̃tjɛr] **1** *adj (ville, poste)* border, frontier
2 *nf (entre pays)* border, frontier; *Fig (des langues)* boundary; *(de la connaissance)* frontier

frontispice [frɔ̃tispis] *nm* frontispiece

fronton [frɔ̃tɔ̃] *nm* (**a**) *(sur monument)* pediment (**b**) *(de pelote basque)* fronton

frottement [frɔtmɑ̃] *nm* (**a**) *(d'une chose contre une autre)* rubbing; *Tech* friction (**b**) *(heurt)* friction

frotter [frɔte] **1** *vt* to rub; *(allumette)* to strike; *(parquet)* to scrub; *Belg Fam* **f. la manche à qn** to soft-soap sb

2 *vi* to rub (**contre** against)
3 **se frotter** *vpr* to rub oneself; *aussi Fig* **se f. les mains** to rub one's hands; *Fig* **se f. à qn/qch** to be in contact with sb/sth; *Fig* **se f. à qn** (*l'attaquer*) to meddle with sb

frottis [frɔti] *nm Méd* smear; **f. vaginal** cervical smear

froufrou [frufru] *nm* (**a**) (*bruit*) rustling (**b**) **froufrous** (*vêtements*) frills; **robe à froufrous** frilly dress

froufrouter [frufrute] *vi* to rustle

froussard, -e [frusar, -ard] *adj & nm,f Fam* chicken

frousse [frus] *nf Fam* fear; **avoir la f.** to be scared; **flanquer la f. à qn** to put the wind up sb

fructifier [66] [fryktifje] *vi* (*arbres, idée*) to bear fruit; (*terre*) to be productive; (*placements, capital*) to yield a profit; **faire f. qch** (*idée, projet*) to bring sth to fruition

fructose [fryktoz] *nm* fructose

fructueux, -euse [fryktɥø, -øz] *adj* fruitful, profitable

frugal, -e, -aux, -ales [frygal, -o] *adj* frugal

frugalité [frygalite] *nf* frugality

fruit [frɥi] *nm aussi Fig* fruit; **des fruits** (some) fruit; **un f.** some fruit, a piece of fruit; **fruits confits** crystalized fruit; *Fig* **le f. défendu** the forbidden fruit; **fruits de mer** seafood; **f. de la passion** passion fruit; **fruits rouges** red berries and currants; **fruits secs** dried fruit; *Suisse* **petits fruits** fruits of the forest; *Fig* **porter ses fruits** (*d'une action, d'un investissement*) to bear fruit

fruité, -e [frɥite] *adj* fruity

fruitier, -ère [frɥitje, -ɛr] **1** *adj voir* **arbre**
   2 *nm,f* fruit seller, *Br* fruiterer

frusques [frysk] *nfpl Fam* gear

fruste [fryst] *adj* (*style, personne*) rough

frustrant, -e [frystrɑ̃, -ɑ̃t] *adj* frustrating

frustration [frystrasjɔ̃] *nf* frustration

frustré, -e [frystre] **1** *adj* frustrated
   2 *nm,f* frustrated person

frustrer [frystre] *vt* (**a**) (*décevoir*) to frustrate (**b**) (*priver*) **f. qn de qch** to deprive sb of sth

FTP [ɛftepe] *nmpl* (*abrév* **Francs-tireurs et partisans**) = French Communist resistance group in the Second World War

fuchsia [fyʃja] **1** *adj inv* (**rose**) **f.** fuchsia
   2 *nm* (*fleur, couleur*) fuchsia

fuel [fjul] *nm* fuel oil

fugace [fygas] *adj* fleeting

fugitif, -ive [fyʒitif, -iv] **1** *adj* (*fugace*) fleeting
   2 *nm,f* fugitive, runaway

fugue [fyg] *nf* (**a**) (*composition musicale*) fugue (**b**) (*d'un enfant*) **faire une f.** to run away

fuguer [fyge] *vi* to run away

fugueur, -euse [fygœr, -øz] **1** *adj* who runs away a lot
   2 *nm,f* runaway

fui *voir* **fuir**

fuir [38] [fɥir] **1** *vt* (*pays*) to flee; (*personne*) to run away from; (*guerre*) to escape; (*responsabilités*) to shirk
   2 *vi* (**a**) (*s'échapper*) to run away, to flee (**devant** from); **f. de son pays** to flee one's country (**b**) (*robinet, gaz, eau*) to leak (**c**) (*s'écouler rapidement*) to fly by

fuis, fuit *voir* **fuir**

fuite [fɥit] *nf* (**a**) (*escapade*) flight (**devant** from); *Fig* (*devant des difficultés, des problèmes*) avoidance (**devant** of); **prendre la f.** to take flight; **être en f.** to be on the run; **mettre qn en f.** to put sb to flight; **la f. des capitaux** the flight of capital; **la f. des cerveaux** the brain drain (**b**) (*de liquide, de gaz, d'informations*) leak

fulgurant, -e [fylgyrɑ̃, -ɑ̃t] *adj* (**a**) (*attaque, changement, rapidité*) lightning; (*succès*) spectacular (**b**) (*douleur*) searing

fulminer [fylmine] *vi* to fulminate (**contre** against)

fumant, -e [fymɑ̃, -ɑ̃t] *adj* (**a**) (*âtre, cendres*) smoking; (*potage*) steaming (**b**) *Fam* (*remarquable*) **faire un coup f.** to pull off a masterstroke

fumé, -e [fyme] *adj* (**a**) (*poisson, viande*) smoked (**b**) (*verres*) tinted

fume-cigare [fymsigar] *nm inv* cigar holder

fumée [fyme] *nf* (*de feu, de cigarette*) smoke; (*d'un liquide chaud*) steam; *Prov* **il n'y a pas de f. sans feu** there's no smoke without fire

fumer [fyme] **1** *vt* (**a**) (*poisson, viande*) to smoke (**b**) (*tabac, cigarette*) to smoke; **f. la pipe** to smoke a pipe
   2 *vi* (**a**) (*feu, moteur*) to smoke; (*liquide, plat*) to steam (**b**) (*fumeur*) to smoke; **f. comme un pompier** *ou* **un sapeur** to smoke like a chimney

fumet [fyme] *nm* (*d'un mets*) aroma

fumeur, -euse [fymœr, -øz] *nm,f* smoker; **fumeurs** (*sur panneau*) smoking

fumeux, -euse [fymø, -øz] *adj* (*idées, explications, projets*) hazy

fumier [fymje] *nm* (**a**) (*engrais*) manure, dung (**b**) *très Fam* (*injure*) bastard

fumigation [fymigasjɔ̃] *nf* fumigation; *Méd* inhalation; **faire des fumigations de désinfectant** to fumigate with disinfectant

fumiste [fymist] **1** *nmf Fam* (*sur qui on ne peut compter*) clown
   2 *nm* (*technicien*) heating engineer
   3 *adj Fam* unreliable

fumisterie [fymistəri] *nf* (**a**) (*métier*) heating engineering (**b**) *Fam* (*farce*) con

fumoir [fymwar] *nm* smoking room

funambule [fynɑ̃byl] *nmf* tightrope walker

funboard [fœnbɔrd] *nm* funboard

funèbre [fynɛbr] *adj* (**a**) (*cérémonie, marche*) funeral; **hymne** *ou* **chant f.** dirge (**b**) (*lugubre*) funereal

funérailles [fyneraj] *nfpl* funeral; **f. nationales** state funeral

funéraire [fynerɛr] *adj* (*dépenses, urne*) funeral; **pierre f.** tombstone, gravestone

funeste [fynɛst] *adj* (**a**) (*erreur, conséquences, influence*) disastrous (**b**) *Litt* (*accident*) fatal

funiculaire [fynikylɛr] *nm* funicular (railway)

fur [fyr] *nm* **au f. et à mesure** as one goes along, bit by bit; **au f. et à mesure de leurs recherches** as they progressed with their research

furax [fyraks] *adj inv Fam* livid

furet [fyrɛ] *nm* ferret

fureter [39] [fyrte] *vi* (*chercher*) to ferret about

fureur [fyrœr] *nf* (**a**) (*colère*) fury, rage (**b**) (*passion*) passion; **faire f.** to be all the rage

furibard, -e [fyribar, -ard] *adj Fam* livid

furibond, -e [fyribɔ̃, -ɔ̃d] *adj* furious

furie [fyri] *nf* (**a**) (*rage*) fury; **en f.** infuriated; **la f. du jeu** a passion for gambling (**b**) *Fig* (*femme*) shrew; **comme une f.** like a wild thing

furieux, -euse [fyrjø, -øz] **1** adj (**a**) (en colère) furious (**contre** with); Fig (tempête) raging; (combat) violent (**b**) Fam (intense) (envie) overwhelming, tremendous

furoncle [fyrɔ̃kl] nm boil

furtif, -ive [fyrtif, -iv] adj furtive, stealthy

furtivement [fyrtivmɑ̃] adv furtively, stealthily; **entrer f.** to sneak in

fusain [fyzɛ̃] nm (crayon, dessin) charcoal

fuseau, -x [fyzo] nm (**a**) (pantalon) ski pants (**b**) (pour filer la laine) spindle; (pour faire de la dentelle) bobbin (**c**) **f. horaire** time zone

fusée [fyze] nf (**a**) (projectile) rocket; **il est parti comme une f.** he shot off like a rocket; **f. éclairante** flare (**b**) (d'axe) spindle; Aut stub axle

fuselage [fyzlaʒ] nm (d'un avion) fuselage

fuselé, -e [fyzle] adj (colonne, doigts) tapering; (voiture) streamlined

fuser [fyze] vi **des rires/cris fusèrent de toutes parts** laughter was/cries were suddenly heard from all sides

fusible [fyzibl] nm fuse

fusil [fyzi] nm (**a**) (arme) gun, rifle; **f. à air comprimé** air gun; **f. de chasse** shotgun; **f. à lunette** rifle with telescopic sight; Fig **changer son f. d'épaule** to change tack; **coup de f.** gunshot; Fam **c'est le coup de f. dans ce restaurant** the prices in this restaurant are extortionate; Can **partir/entrer en coup de f.** to storm in/out (**b**) (personne) shot (**c**) (pour aiguiser) steel

fusilier [fyzilje] nm fusilier; **f. marin** marine

fusillade [fyzijad] nf (tir) gunfire

fusiller [fyzije] vt (**a**) (par un peloton d'exécution) to shoot; Fig **f. qn du regard** to look daggers at sb (**b**) Fam (abîmer) to wreck

fusil-mitrailleur (pl **fusils-mitrailleurs**) [fyzimitrajœr] nm light machine-gun

fusion [fyzjɔ̃] nf (**a**) (par la chaleur) melting, Spéc fusion; (en métallurgie) smelting; **point de f.** melting point; **métal/roche en f.** molten metal/rock (**b**) (de sociétés) merger; Ordinat **f. de fichiers** file merge

fusionner [fyzjɔne] vi & vt aussi Ordinat to merge

fustiger [45] [fystiʒe] vt (critiquer) to castigate

fût [fy] nm (**a**) (tonneau) cask, barrel (**b**) (d'arbre) bole (**c**) (de colonne) shaft (**d**) (de fusil) stock

futaie [fytɛ] nf forest (producing timber from full-grown trees)

futal, -als [fytal] nm, **fute** [fyt] nm Fam Br trousers, Am pants

futé, -e [fyte] **1** adj crafty; **il n'est pas très f.** he's not very bright; aussi Ironique **ça, c'est f.!** that was clever! **2** nm,f crafty devil

futile [fytil] adj (argument, occupation, prétexte) trivial, trifling; (personne) frivolous

futilement [fytilmɑ̃] adv frivolously

futilité [fytilite] nf triviality

futon [fytɔ̃] nm futon

futur, -e [fytyr] **1** adj future; **un f. artiste** a budding artist; **mon f. emploi/appartement** my next job/flat; **mon f. mari** my husband-to-be **2** nm,f Hum **mon f./ma future** my intended **3** nm (**a**) (avenir) future (**b**) Gram future (tense); **au f.** in the future (tense); **f. antérieur** future perfect

futurisme [fytyrism] nm futurism

futuriste [fytyrist] **1** adj futuristic **2** nmf futurist

fuyant, -e [fɥijɑ̃, -ɑ̃t] adj (**a**) (ligne, menton) receding; **lignes fuyantes** perspective lines (**b**) (personne, attitude) evasive; (yeux) shifty

fuyard, -e [fɥijar, -ard] nm,f fugitive, runaway

fuyez etc voir **fuir**

G

G¹, g [ʒe] *nm inv* G, g; **le G8** the G8

G² [ʒe] *nm Belg Fam (abrév* **GSM**) mobile (phone)

g. (**a**) *(abrév* **gauche**) L (**b**) *(abrév* **gramme(s)**) g

gabardine [gabardin] *nf* gabardine

gabarit [gabari] *nm* (**a**) *(dimension)* size (**b**) *Fam (corpulence)* **un grand/petit g.** a huge/tiny man, *f* woman (**c**) *(valeur)* calibre (**d**) *(instrument)* gauge (**e**) *Ordinat* template

Gabon [gabɔ̃] *nm* **le G.** Gabon

gabonais, -e [gabɔnɛ, -ɛz] **1** *adj* Gabonese
  2 *nm,f* **G.** Gabonese

gâcher [gɑʃe] *vt* (**a**) *(gaspiller)* to waste (**b**) *(gâter) (plaisir, soirée)* to spoil (**c**) *(mélanger) (mortier, plâtre)* to mix

gâchette [gɑʃɛt, gaʃɛt] *nf* trigger; *Fam* **avoir la g. facile** to be trigger-happy; **appuyer sur la g.** to pull the trigger

gâchis [gɑʃi] *nm* waste

gadelle [gadɛl] *nf Can Bot* currant; **g. rouge** redcurrant

gadget [gadʒɛt] *nm* gadget

gadoue [gadu] *nf* mud

gaélique [gaelik] *adj & nm* Gaelic

gaffe [gaf] *nf* (**a**) *Fam (maladresse)* blunder; **faire une g.** to put one's foot in it (**b**) *(perche)* boathook (**c**) *Fam* **faire g.** to be careful

gaffer [gafe] **1** *vt (objet flottant)* to hook; *(poisson)* to gaff
  2 *vi Fam* to put one's foot in it

gaffeur, -euse [gafœr, -øz] *nm,f Fam* blunderer

gag [gag] *nm* gag

gaga [gaga] *adj Fam* gaga

gage [gaʒ] *nm* (**a**) *(chez le prêteur sur gages)* pledge; *Fig (garantie)* guarantee; **laisser qch en g.** to leave sth as security; **mettre qch en g.** to pawn sth (**b**) *(preuve)* token; **en g. de notre amitié** as a token of our friendship (**c**) *(dans un jeu)* forfeit (**d**) *Vieilli (salaire)* **gages** wages

gager [45] [gaʒe] *vt Litt* **g. que...** to wager that...

gageure [gaʒyr] *nf* (**a**) *(action difficile)* challenge (**b**) *Litt (pari)* wager

gagnant, -e [gaɲɑ̃, -ɑ̃t] **1** *adj* winning
  2 *nm,f* winner; **partir g.** to have a strong probability of winning

gagne-pain [gaɲpɛ̃] *nm inv* livelihood

gagne-petit [gaɲpəti] *nmf inv* low wage earner

gagner [gaɲe] **1** *vt* (**a**) *(remporter) (course, prix, guerre)* to win; **rien n'est encore gagné!** it's not in the bag yet! (**b**) *(comme rémunération)* to earn; **g. sa vie** to earn one's living (**c**) *(obtenir)* to gain; **g. du**

temps *(aller plus vite)* to save time; *(temporiser)* to gain time; **g. de l'espace** to save space; **chercher à g. du temps** to play for time; **c'est toujours ça de gagné** that's something, anyway; **tu as tout à g.** you've got everything to gain; **et moi, qu'est-ce que j'y gagne?** and what do I get out of it? (**d**) *(se concilier)* **g. qn à une cause** to win sb over to a cause; **g. la confiance/l'estime de qn** to win *or* gain sb's confidence/respect (**e**) *(atteindre) (ville, sortie, porte)* to reach, to get to; *(sujet: maladie, infection)* to spread to; *(sujet: sentiment, sommeil)* to overcome; **le rire gagna l'assemblée tout entière** laughter spread through the whole audience (**f**) *(s'étendre à) (sujet: feu, épidémie)* to spread to; **g. du terrain** to gain ground (**g**) *(battre)* **g. qn de vitesse** to outstrip sb
  2 *vi* (**a**) *(être vainqueur)* to win; **g. haut la main** to win hands down (**b**) *(profiter)* **g. à qch/à faire qch** to benefit from sth/from doing sth; **j'ai gagné au change** I got the best of the deal (**c**) *(croître)* to increase; **g. en intensité/en vigueur** to increase in intensity/in strength

gagneur, -euse [gaɲœr, -øz] *nm,f* winner

gai, -e [gɛ] *adj* (**a**) *(personne, voix, décor, musique)* cheerful; **g. comme un pinson** happy as a lark; *Fam* **être un peu g.** *(ivre)* to be tipsy; *Ironique* **ça va être g.!** that'll be fun! (**b**) *Belg (agréable)* nice, pleasant (**c**) *(homosexuel)* = **gay**

gaiement [gemɑ̃] *adv* cheerfully; *Ironique* **allons-y g.!** let's get on with it!

gaieté [gete] *nf* cheerfulness, gaiety; **je ne le fais pas de g. de cœur** I don't enjoy doing it

gaillard, -e [gajar, -ard] **1** *adj* (**a**) *(vigoureux) (personne)* strong; *(vieillard)* sprightly (**b**) *(jovial) (humeur)* merry; *(grivois) (histoire, commentaire)* bawdy
  2 *nm* (**a**) *(homme)* hearty type; **un grand et solide g.** a great strapping man; **toi mon g., tu ne perds rien pour attendre!** just you wait, chum! (**b**) *Naut* **g. d'avant** forecastle; **g. d'arrière** poop

gaîment [gemɑ̃] = **gaiement**

gain [gɛ̃] *nm* (**a**) *(succès)* winning; **avoir** *ou* **obtenir g. de cause** to win one's case; **donner g. de cause à qn** to decide in favour of sb (**b**) *(profit)* gain, profit; **l'appât du g.** the lure of money (**c**) *(économie)* **ça fait un sacré g. de temps/de place** that saves an awful lot of time/space (**d**) **gains** *(au jeu)* winnings; *(à la Bourse)* profit (**e**) *Suisse* **par g. de paix** as a conciliatory gesture

gaine [gɛn] *nf* (**a**) *(étui)* sheath (**b**) *Anat & Bot* sheath (**c**) *(sous-vêtement)* girdle

gainer [gene] *vt* to sheathe (**de** in)

Gal *Mil (abrév* **Général**) Gen

gala [gala] *nm* gala; **en habit** *ou* **tenue de g.** in gala dress; *Fig* in one's best clothes

galamment [galamã] *adv* gallantly

galant, -e [galã, -ãt] **1** *adj (homme)* gallant; **rendez-vous g.** romantic rendezvous
2 *nm Vieilli & Litt* gallant

galanterie [galãtri] *nf* gallantry; **dire des galanteries à qn** to pay sb compliments

Galapagos [galapagos] *nfpl* **les (îles) G.** the Galapagos (Islands)

galaxie [galaksi] *nf* galaxy

galbe [galb] *nm* curve

galbé, -e [galbe] *adj* shapely

gale [gal] *nf* (**a**) *Méd* scabies; *Fig* **je n'ai pas la g.!** I haven't got the plague! (**b**) *(de chien, de chat)* mange (**c**) *Bot* scab

galère [galɛr] *nf* (**a**) *(navire)* galley (**b**) *Fam (situation pénible)* hassle; **je me suis mis dans une g. pas possible** I got myself into a terrible mess; **être dans la même g.** to be in the same boat

galérer [34] [galere] *vi Fam* to have a hard time

galerie [galri] *nf* (**a**) *(passage, salle)* gallery; *Can (véranda)* porch; **g. d'art/de portraits** art/portrait gallery; **g. marchande** shopping arcade, *Am* mall (**b**) *(dans une mine)* gallery; *(de taupe)* tunnel (**c**) *(de voiture)* roof rack (**d**) *(de théâtre)* balcony; *Fig* **c'est pour (épater) la g.** it's just showing off

galérien [galerjɛ̃] *nm* galley slave

galet [galɛ] *nm* (**a**) *(caillou)* pebble; **plage de galets** shingle beach (**b**) *Tech* roller

galette [galɛt] *nf* (**a**) *(crêpe de blé noir)* buckwheat pancake; **g. des Rois** Twelfth Night cake (**b**) *(biscuit rond sablé)* butter biscuit (**c**) *Belg (gaufrette)* wafer (**d**) *Fam (argent)* dough

galeux, -euse [galø, -øz] *adj (chien)* mangy; *(mur)* peeling

Galice [galis] *nf* **la G.** Galicia

galicien, -enne [galisjɛ̃, -ɛn] **1** *adj* Galician
2 *nm,f* **G.** Galician

Galilée¹ [galile] *nf (région)* **la G.** Galilee

Galilée² *npr* Galileo

galimatias [galimatja] *nm* gibberish

galion [galjɔ̃] *nm* galleon

galipette [galipɛt] *nf Fam* somersault; **faire des galipettes** to do somersaults; *(ébats amoureux)* to have a romp *or Br* a bit of slap and tickle

galipote [galipɔt] *nf Can* **courir la g.** to chase women

Galles [gal] *voir* **pays**

gallicisme [galisism] *nm* Gallicism

gallois, -e [galwa, -az] **1** *adj* Welsh
2 *nm,f* **G.** Welshman; *f* Welshwoman; **les G.** the Welsh
3 *nm (langue)* Welsh

gallon [galɔ̃] *nm* gallon

gallo-romain, -e *(mpl* **gallo-romains,** *fpl* **gallo-romaines)* [galorɔmɛ̃, -ɛn] *adj* Gallo-Roman

galoche [galɔʃ] *nf* clog *(with leather upper)*

galon [galɔ̃] *nm* (**a**) *(en couture)* braid (**b**) *(de militaire)* stripe; *Fam* **prendre du g.** to get promoted (**c**) *Can* **g. (à mesurer)** measuring tape

galop [galo] *nm* gallop; **au g.** at a gallop; *Fig* **allez, au travail et au g.!** come on, to work, and be quick about it!; **g. d'essai** trial run

galopade [galɔpad] *nf* (**a**) *(de cheval)* gallop (**b**) *(de personnes)* stampede

galopant, -e [galɔpã, -ãt] *adj (inflation)* galloping; **phtisie galopante** galloping consumption

galoper [galɔpe] *vi (cheval)* to gallop; *(enfant)* to charge

galopin [galɔpɛ̃] *nm Fam* urchin; **espèce de petit g.!** you little rascal!

galure [galyr] *nm,* **galurin** [galyrɛ̃] *nm Fam* hat

galvaniser [galvanize] *vt* to galvanize

galvauder [galvode] **1** *vt (nom, réputation)* to bring into disrepute; *(talents, dons)* to prostitute; *(mot)* to overuse
2 se galvauder *vpr* to damage one's reputation

gambade [gãbad] *nf* leap

gambader [gãbade] *vi* to leap *or* frisk about

gambas [gãbas] *nfpl* large prawns

gamberger [45] [gãbɛrʒe] *vi Fam* to think hard

gambette [gãbɛt] *nf Fam (jambe)* pin

Gambie [gãbi] *nf* **la G.** the Gambia

gamelle [gamɛl] *nf (de soldat)* mess tin; *(d'ouvrier)* billy(can); *(d'animal)* bowl; *Hum (assiette)* plate; *Fam aussi Fig* **(se) ramasser** *ou* **(se) prendre une g.** to come a cropper

gamète [gamɛt] *nm* gamete

gamin, -e [gamɛ̃, -in] **1** *nm,f (enfant)* kid; **une gamine de dix ans** a girl of ten
2 *adj* (**a**) *(jeune)* **elle était encore toute gamine** she was still just a child (**b**) *(puéril)* childish

gaminerie [gaminri] *nf (acte)* childish prank; *(comportement)* childishness

gamme [gam] *nf* (**a**) *(de couleurs, de prix, d'articles)* range; **produit bas/haut de g.** bottom-of-the-range/top-of-the-range product (**b**) *Mus* scale

gammée [game] *adj f voir* **croix**

ganache [ganaʃ] *nf* (**a**) *Fam (imbécile)* **vieille g.** old fool (**b**) *(d'un cheval)* lower jaw

Gand [gã] *n* Ghent

gang [gãg] *nm* gang

Gange [gãʒ] *nm* **le G.** the Ganges

ganglion [gãglijɔ̃] *nm* ganglion; **j'ai des ganglions** I've got swollen glands

gangrène [gãgrɛn] *nf* (**a**) *Méd* gangrene (**b**) *Fig* canker

gangrener [46] [gãgrəne] **1** *vt* (**a**) *Méd* to turn gangrenous (**b**) *Fig* to corrupt
2 se gangrener *vpr* (**a**) *Méd* to go gangrenous (**b**) *Fig* to become corrupt

gangster [gãgstɛr] *nm* gangster

gangstérisme [gãgsterism] *nm* gangsterism

gangue [gãg] *nf (de minerai)* gangue; *(couche) (de boue, de glace)* layer; *Fig (carcan)* straitjacket

gant [gã] *nm* glove; **g. de boxe** boxing glove; **gants de caoutchouc** rubber gloves; **g. de toilette** ≃ facecloth; *Fig* **cela vous va comme un g.** it fits you like a glove; **prendre** *ou* **mettre des gants avec qn** to handle sb with kid gloves; **jeter le g. à qn** to throw down the gauntlet to sb; **relever le g.** to take up the gauntlet

ganté, -e [gãte] *adj (personne)* wearing gloves; *(main)* gloved

gantelet [gãtlɛ] *nm* gauntlet

garage [garaʒ] *nm (pour se garer, pour les réparations)* garage; **g. de** *ou* **à bicyclettes** bicycle shed; **g. d'autobus** bus depot; *Can* **vente de g.** garage sale

garagiste [garaʒist] *nmf (propriétaire)* garage owner; *(mécanicien)* garage mechanic

garant, -e [garã, -ãt] *nm,f* guarantor; **se porter g. de qn** *(à la banque)* to stand guarantor for sb; **se porter g. de qch** to vouch for sth

garantie [garãti] *nf* (**a**) *(précaution)* guarantee, safeguard (**contre** against) (**b**) *(de produit)* guarantee; **être sous g.** to be under guarantee (**c**) *(certitude)* guarantee

garantir [garãtir] *vt* (**a**) *(promettre)* to guarantee; **g. à qn que** to give sb a guarantee that; **je te le garantis** I can vouch for it (**b**) *Fin (émission d'actions)* to underwrite; *(emprunt)* to secure (**c**) *(protéger)* to protect (**de** from)

garce [gars] *nf Fam* bitch

garçon [garsɔ̃] *nm* (**a**) *(enfant mâle, fils)* boy; *(jeune homme)* young man; **un mauvais g.** a bad sort; **vieux g.** confirmed bachelor; **g. manqué** tomboy (**b**) *(serveur)* waiter; **g. d'ascenseur** *Br* lift attendant, *Am* elevator operator; **g. de café** waiter; **g. d'honneur** best man

garçonne [garsɔn] *nf* **être coiffée à la g.** to have an urchin cut

garçonnet [garsɔnɛ] *nm* little boy

garçonnière [garsɔnjɛr] *nf* bachelor *Br* flat *or Am* apartment

garde¹ [gard] *nf* (**a**) *(protection)* care; *Jur* **g. des enfants** *(après un divorce)* custody of the children (**b**) *(surveillance)* guarding; **être de g.** to be on duty; **monter la g.** to mount guard; **médecin de g.** duty doctor; **pharmacie de g.** emergency chemist (**c**) *(méfiance)* **mettre qn en g. contre qn/qch** to warn sb against sb/sth; **être** *ou* **se tenir sur ses gardes** to be on one's guard; **prendre g. à qn/qch** to watch out for sb/sth; **prendre g. que… (ne)** + *subjunctive* to be careful that…; **prendre g. de ne pas faire qch** to be careful not to do sth (**d**) *(groupe de soldats)* **la g.** the guard; **g. d'honneur** guard of honour; **la G. républicaine** the Republican Guard *(of Paris)* (**e**) *Jur* **g. à vue** police custody; **il a été mis/est resté en g. à vue** he was put/was held in police custody (**f**) *(en boxe, en escrime)* guard; **se mettre en g.** to take one's guard; **en g.!** on guard! (**g**) *Aut* **g. au sol** ground clearance (**h**) *(d'une épée)* hilt

garde² 1 *nm* (**a**) *(soldat) (sentinelle)* guard; *(dans une garde)* guardsman; **g. mobile** = member of the security police (**b**) *(dans un domaine particulier)* **g. champêtre** rural policeman; **g. du corps** bodyguard; **g. forestier** *Br* forest warden, *Am* ranger (**c**) **le g. des Sceaux** the (French) Minister of Justice

2 *nmf* **g. de nuit** *(pour un malade)* night nurse *(privately employed)*; **g. d'enfants** childminder

garde-à-vous [gardavu] *nm inv Mil* (position of) attention; **se mettre/être au g.** to stand to attention; **g.!** attention!

garde-barrière *(pl* **gardes-barrière(s)**) [gardəbarjɛr] *nmf Br* level-crossing *or Am* grade-crossing keeper

garde-boue [gardəbu] *nm inv* mudguard

garde-chasse *(pl* **gardes-chasse(s)**) [gardəʃas] *nm* gamekeeper

garde-chiourme *(pl* **gardes-chiourme(s)**) [gardəʃjurm] *nm (personne autoritaire et brutale)* martinet

garde-côte *(pl* **garde-côtes**) [gardəkot] *nm (bateau)* coastguard vessel

garde-feu [gardəfø] *nm inv* (**a**) *(grille)* fireguard (**b**) *Can (personne)* forest warden

garde-fou *(pl* **garde-fous**) [gardəfu] *nm (mur)* parapet; *(rambarde)* railing; *Fig* safeguard

garde-malade *(pl* **gardes-malade(s)**) [gardəmalad] *nmf* nurse

garde-manger [gardəmãʒe] *nm inv* larder

garde-meuble *(pl* **garde-meubles**) [gardəmœbl] *nm* furniture repository; **mettre une table au g.** to put a table into storage

gardénia [gardenja] *nm* gardenia

garder [garde] 1 *vt* (**a**) *(conserver)* to keep; **g. qn à dîner** to get sb to stay for dinner; **g. la chambre** to keep to *or* stay in one's room; **devoir g. le lit** to be confined to bed; **g. la tête froide** to keep a cool head (**b**) *(surveiller) (maison, sac, enfants)* to look after, to mind; *Jur* **g. qn à vue** to hold sb in custody (**c**) *(protéger)* to protect (**de** from); **que Dieu nous garde!** God protect us!

2 **se garder** *upr* (**a**) *(se méfier)* **se g. de qn/qch** to beware of sb/sth (**b**) *(s'abstenir)* **se g. de faire qch** to be careful not to do sth (**c**) *Fam (conserver)* **tes réflexions, tu peux te les g.!** you can keep your thoughts to yourself! (**d**) *(se conserver) (denrées)* to keep

garderie [gardəri] *nf Br* day nursery, *Am* daycare center; *(dans un magasin, une université)* *Br* crèche, *Am* baby-sitting service; *(le soir, après l'école)* childminding service

garde-robe *(pl* **garde-robes**) [gardərɔb] *nf (armoire, vêtements)* wardrobe

gardien, -enne [gardjɛ̃, -ɛn] 1 *nm,f (concierge)* caretaker, *Am* janitor; *(de musée, de parking)* attendant; *Fig (de libertés, traditions)* guardian; **g. de but** goalkeeper; **g. de nuit** night watchman; **g. de la paix** policeman; **g. de prison** prison *Br* warder *or Am* guard

2 **gardienne** *nf* (**a**) *(personne)* **gardienne d'enfants** childminder (**b**) *Belg (école)* nursery school, kindergarten

gardiennage [gardjɛnaʒ] *nm (d'un bâtiment)* caretaking; *(de locaux)* guarding; **société de g.** security firm

gardon [gardɔ̃] *nm* roach; *Fig* **frais comme un g.** fresh as a daisy

gare¹ [gar] *nf* station; **g. maritime** harbour station; **g. de marchandises** goods station; **g. routière** bus station; **g. de triage** marshalling yard

gare² *exclam* (**a**) *(menace)* **g. à toi si on l'apprend** woe betide you if anyone finds out; *Fam* **si je te reprends à voler du gâteau, g. à tes fesses!** if I catch you stealing cake again, you've had it! (**b**) *(attention)* **g. aux orties!** mind the nettles!; **sans crier g.** without warning

garer [gare] 1 *vt (voiture)* to park

2 **se garer** *upr* (**a**) *(automobiliste)* to park (**b**) **se g. de qn/qch** to steer clear of sb/sth; *Fam* **garez-vous!** get out of the way!

gargariser [gargarize] **se gargariser** *upr* to gargle; *Fam Péj* **se g. de qch** to revel in sth

gargarisme [gargarism] *nm (produit)* mouthwash; *(action)* gargling; **faire des gargarismes** to gargle

gargote [gargɔt] *nf Péj* cheap restaurant

gargouillement [gargujmã] *nm* gurgling; *(d'estomac)* rumbling

gargouiller [garguje] *vi* (**a**) *(eau)* to gurgle (**b**) *(estomac)* to rumble

gargouillis [garguji] = **gargouillement**

garnement [garnəmã] *nm* scamp, rascal

garni, -e [garni] *adj* (**a**) **bien g.** *(bourse)* well-lined (**b**) *(plat, viande)* with vegetables

garnir [garnir] *vt* (**a**) *(munir)* to fit out (**de** with); *(commode, tiroir)* to line; *(siège) (rembourrer)* to stuff; *(couvrir)* to cover (**b**) *(embellir) (robe, chapeau)* to trim (**de** with); (**c**) *Culin (plat)* to garnish (**d**) *(remplir)* to fill (**de** with); *(cave)* to stock (**de** with)

garnison [garnizɔ̃] *nf* garrison; **ville de g.** garrison town; **être en g. à** to be garrisoned at

garniture [garnityr] *nf* (**a**) *(ornement) (d'un chapeau, d'une robe)* trimming; **g. de lit** bedding; **g. de cheminée** mantelpiece ornaments (**b**) *(d'un plat)* garnish; *(légumes)* vegetables; *(d'un vol-au-vent)* filling (**c**) *Aut* **g. d'embrayage** clutch lining; **g. de frein** brake lining; *(de disque de frein)* brake pad

Garonne [garɔn] *nf* **la G.** the Garonne

garrigue [garig] *nf* scrubland *(typical of southern France)*

garrocher [garɔʃe] *vt Can Fam* to throw

garrot[1] [garo] *nm* (**a**) *Méd* tourniquet (**b**) *(supplice)* garrotte

garrot[2] *nm (de quadrupède)* withers; **mesurer 1,20 m au g.** to be 12 hands high

garrotter [garɔte] *vt (prisonnier)* to tie up; *Fig (opposants)* to muzzle

gars [gɑ] *nm Fam (jeune homme)* lad, *(homme)* guy

Gascogne [gaskɔɲ] *nf* **la G.** Gascony

gas-oil, gasoil [gazɔjl, gazwal] *nm* diesel oil

gaspillage [gaspijaʒ] *nm (d'argent, de nourriture, de temps)* wasting; **c'est du g.** it's a waste; **quel g.!** what a waste!

gaspiller [gaspije] *vt* to waste

gastéropode [gasterɔpɔd] *nm Zool* gastropod

gastrique [gastrik] *adj* gastric; **embarras g.** upset stomach

gastrite [gastrit] *nf Méd* gastritis

gastro-entérite (*pl* **gastro-entérites**) [gastrɔɑ̃terit] *nf Méd* gastroenteritis

gastro-entérologue (*pl* **gastro-entérologues**) [gastrɔɑ̃terɔlɔg] *nmf Méd* gastroenterologist

gastro-intestinal, -e, -aux, -ales [gastrɔɛ̃testinal, -o] *adj Méd* gastrointestinal

gastronome [gastrɔnɔm] *nmf* gastronome, gourmet

gastronomie [gastrɔnɔmi] *nf* gastronomy

gastronomique [gastrɔnɔmik] *adj* gastronomic

gastropode [gastrɔpɔd] *nm Zool* gastropod

gâté, -e [gɑte] *adj* (**a**) *(pourri) (fruit, dents)* bad (**b**) *Fig (enfant)* spoilt

gâteau, -x [gɑto] *nm* cake; *Suisse (tarte)* tart; **faire un g.** to make *or* bake a cake; *Fam* **c'est du g.** it's a piece of cake; *Fam* **ce n'est pas du g.** it's no easy thing; *Fam* **se partager le g.** to share out the cake; **g. d'anniversaire** birthday cake; **g. de riz** rice pudding; **g. sec** *Br* biscuit, *Am* cookie

gâter [gɑte] **1** *vt* (**a**) *(gâcher)* to spoil (**b**) *(choyer) (personne)* to spoil; **on n'est pas gâtés!** just our luck!
2 se gâter *vpr (affaires, temps)* to take a turn for the worse; *(aliment)* to go bad

gâterie [gɑtri] *nf (petit cadeau, friandise)* treat

gâteux, -euse [gɑtø, -øz] *Fam* **1** *nm,f* old dodderer
2 *adj (sénile)* senile; **avec leurs petits-enfants, ils sont complètement g.** they're totally besotted with their grandchildren

gâtisme [gɑtism] *nm* senility

GATT [gat] *nm Écon (abrév* **General Agreement on Tariffs and Trade**) **le G.** GATT

gauche [goʃ] **1** *adj* (**a**) *(par opposition à droit)* left (**b**) *(maladroit) (personne, attitude, démarche, style)* awkward, clumsy (**c**) *Tech (déformé)* warped
2 *nf* (**a**) *(côté)* left; **à ma g.** on my left; **le tiroir de g.** the left-hand drawer; **à g. (de)** on the left (of); **tournez à g.** turn left; **conduire à g.** to drive on the left; *Fam* **mettre de l'argent à g.** to put some money away (**b**) *Pol* **la g.** the left; **politique/gouvernement de g.** left-wing politics/government; **voter à g.** to vote for the left; *Fam* **la g. caviar** champagne socialism; **la g. plurielle** = the rainbow coalition of socialists, communists and environmentalists in the government of Lionel Jospin *(elected in 1997)*
3 *nm (en boxe)* left; **un crochet du g.** a left hook; **un direct du g.** a straight left

gaucher, -ère [goʃe, -ɛr] **1** *adj* left-handed
2 *nm,f* left-hander

gauchisant, -e [goʃizɑ̃, -ɑ̃t] *adj* leftish

gauchisme [goʃism] *nm* leftism

gauchiste [goʃist] *adj & nmf* leftist

gaufre [gofr] *nf* waffle

gaufrette [gofrɛt] *nf* wafer (biscuit)

Gaule [gol] *nf* **la G.** Gaul

gaule [gol] *nf* pole; *(pour pêcher)* fishing rod

gauler [gole] *vt* (**a**) *(arbre fruitier, noyer)* to beat; *(fruits, noix)* to bring down *(using a pole)* (**b**) *Fam (attraper)* to nab; **se faire g.** to get nabbed

gaullisme [golism] *nm* Gaullism

Gaullisme

The political ideology inspired by the ideas of General de Gaulle includes nationalism, independence from foreign powers, and a strong executive. Gaullists are strongly committed to the defence of France's prestige on the international scene.

---

gaulliste [golist] *adj & nmf* Gaullist

gaulois, -e [golwa, -az] **1** *adj* Gallic; **esprit g.** bawdy humour
3 *nm,f* **les G.** the Gauls
4 *nf* **Gauloise**® Gauloise *(popular brand of cigarette)*

gauloiserie [golwazri] *nf (plaisanterie)* bawdy joke; *(caractère)* bawdiness

gausser [gose] **se gausser** *vpr Litt* **se g. de qn** to mock sb; **vous vous gaussez!** you jest!

gaver [gave] **1** *vt (engraisser) (volaille)* to force-feed; *(personne) (de nourriture)* to stuff (**de** with); *Fig* **g. qn de qch** to force-feed sb sth
2 se gaver *vpr Fam* to stuff oneself (**de** with); *Fig* **se g. de romans policiers/jeux vidéo** to read detective novels/play video games till they're coming out of one's ears

gay [gɛ] *adj & nmf* gay *(homosexual)*; **il/elle est g.** he's/she's gay

gaz [gaz] *nm* gas; *Fam* **il y a de l'eau dans le g.** things aren't going too well; *Fam* **mettre les g.** *Br* to put one's foot down, *Am* to step on the gas; *Aviat* to open up the throttle; **avoir des g.** to have wind; **g. carbonique** carbon dioxide; **g. de combat** poison gas; **g. d'échappement** exhaust fumes; **g. à effet de serre** greenhouse gas; **g. hilarant** laughing gas; **g. lacrymogène** tear gas; **g. naturel** natural gas; **g. de ville** town gas; **avoir le g. de ville** to be connected to the gas supply

Gaza [gaza] *n* **la bande de G.** the Gaza Strip
gaze [gaz] *nf* gauze
gazé, -e [gaze] **1** *adj* gassed
   2 *nm,f* (*poison*) gas victim
gazéifier [66] [gazeifje] *vt* to gasify; (*boissons*) to carbonate
gazelle [gazɛl] *nf* gazelle; **avoir des yeux de g.** to be
   doe-eyed
gazer [gaze] **1** *vt* (*asphyxier*) to gas
   2 *vi Fam* **ça gaze!** everything's OK!; **ça gaze?** how's
   things?
gazette [gazɛt] *nf* (*journal*) newspaper
gazeux, -euse [gazø, -øz] *adj* (**a**) (*eau, boisson*) fizzy
   (**b**) *Chim* gaseous
gazinière [gazinjer] *nf* gas cooker
gazoduc [gazɔdyk] *nm* gas pipeline
gazole [gazɔl] *nm* diesel oil
gazomètre [gazɔmetr] *nm* gasometer
gazon [gazɔ̃] *nm* (**a**) (*herbe*) grass, turf (**b**) (*surface*)
   lawn
gazonner [gazɔne] *vt* to turf
gazouillement [gazujmã] *nm* (*des oiseaux*) twittering, chirping; (*d'un bébé*) gurgling; (*d'un ruisseau*)
   babbling
gazouiller [gazuje] *vi* (*oiseau*) to twitter, to chirp;
   (*bébé*) to gurgle; (*eau*) to babble
gazouillis [gazuji] = **gazouillement**
GDF [ʒedeef] *nm* (*abrév* **Gaz de France**) = French gas
   company
geai [ʒɛ] *nm* jay
géant, -e [ʒeã, -ãt] **1** *adj* (**a**) (*arbre, écran*) giant, gigantic; (*paquet*) giant(-size) (**b**) *Fam* (*formidable*) **c'est g.!**
   it's fantastic!
   2 *nm,f* giant; *Fig* **les géants de la littérature classique** the giants *or* great names of classical literature;
   Fig **avancer** *ou* **aller à pas de g.** to make great strides
geignard, -e [ʒɛɲar, -ard] *Fam* **1** *adj* whining
   2 *nm,f* whiner
geindre [54] [ʒɛ̃dr] *vi* (**a**) (*gémir*) to moan, to groan
   (**de** with) (**b**) *Fam* (*se plaindre constamment*) to whine
gel [ʒɛl] *nm* (**a**) (*verglas*) frost; *Fig* **g. des négociations**
   suspension of negotiations; **g. des prix/salaires**
   price/wage freeze (**b**) (*produit cosmétique*) gel; **g.
   coiffant** hair gel; **g. douche** shower gel
gélatine [ʒelatin] *nf* gelatine
gélatineux, -euse [ʒelatinø, -øz] *adj* gelatinous
gelé, -e [ʒəle] *adj* (**a**) (*lac, rivière*) frozen; (*plante*)
   frost-nipped (**b**) *Méd* (*orteil, doigt*) frostbitten (**c**) (*très
   froid*) frozen; **j'ai les pieds gelés/les mains gelées** my
   feet/hands are frozen (**d**) (*bloqué*) (*fonds*) frozen;
   (*négociations*) suspended
gelée [ʒəle] *nf* (**a**) (*gel*) frost; **g. blanche** hoarfrost (**b**)
   Culin jelly; **g. royale** royal jelly
geler [39] [ʒəle] **1** *vt* (**a**) (*lac, rivière, liquide*) to freeze;
   fleurs/salades gelées par le froid flowers/lettuces
   nipped by the frost (**b**) *Fin* (*bloquer*) (*crédits, capital*)
   to freeze
   2 *vi* (*lac, rivière*) to freeze (over); **on gèle dans cette
   salle** it's freezing in this room
   3 *v impersonnel* **il gèle** it's freezing; **il gèle à pierre
   fendre** it's freezing hard; **il a gelé blanc cette nuit**
   there was a frost last night
   4 **se geler** *vpr Fam* to freeze
gélifiant [ʒelifjã] *nm* gelling agent
gélule [ʒelyl] *nf* capsule

gelure [ʒəlyr] *nf* frostbite
Gémeaux [ʒemo] *nmpl Astron & Astrol* Gemini; **être
   G.** to be (a) Gemini
gémir [ʒemir] *vi* (*personne*) to groan, to moan (**de**
   with); (*vent*) to moan
gémissant, -e [ʒemisã, -ãt] *adj* (*personne*) groaning;
   (*voix*) wailing
gémissement [ʒemismã] *nm* (*d'une personne*) groan,
   moan; (*de vent*) moaning
gemme [ʒem] *nf* (**a**) (*pierre*) gem(stone) (**b**) (*résine*)
   pine resin
gênant, -e [ʒenã, -ãt] *adj* (**a**) (*témoin, situation, silence*) awkward; (*bruit, lumière*) irritating (**b**) (*encombrant*) (*objet*) cumbersome
gencive [ʒãsiv] *nf* gum
gendarme [ʒãdarm] *nm* gendarme, policeman;
   jouer aux gendarmes et aux voleurs to play cops
   and robbers; *Fam* **faire le g.** to lay down the law; **g.
   couché** sleeping policeman; **g. mobile** = member of
   the flying squad
gendarmerie [ʒãdarməri] *nf* (**a**) (*corps*) (*en France*)
   gendarmerie, police force; **g. mobile** = flying squad;
   g. nationale national police force; **la G. royale du Canada** the Royal Canadian Mounted Police (**b**) (*lieu*)
   gendarmes' headquarters
gendre [ʒãdr] *nm* son-in-law
gène [ʒɛn] *nm* gene
gêne [ʒɛn] *nf* (**a**) (*confusion*) embarrassment; **ressentir de la g.** to feel embarrassed; **où (il) y a de la g., (il
   n')y a pas de plaisir** we don't need to stand on ceremony (**b**) (*dérangement*) inconvenience (**c**) (*difficulté
   physique*) discomfort; **g. respiratoire** difficulty in
   breathing (**d**) (*manque d'argent*) **être dans la g.** to be
   in financial difficulties
gêné, -e [ʒene] *adj* (**a**) (*embarrassé*) embarrassed;
   Fam **il n'est pas g., lui!** he's got a nerve! (**b**) (*serré*) **être
   g. dans un vêtement** to be uncomfortable in a gar-
   ment (**c**) (*qui manque d'argent*) in financial difficulties
généalogie [ʒenealɔʒi] *nf* genealogy
généalogique [ʒenealɔʒik] *adj* genealogical; **arbre
   g.** family tree
gêner [ʒene] **1** *vt* (**a**) (*perturber*) (*sujet: bruit, fumée,
   chaleur*) to bother; (*opérations, déroulement*) to hamper; **g. la circulation** to hold up the traffic; **g. le passage** to be in the way; **pousse-toi, tu me gênes!**
   move over, you're in my way!; **ça te gêne si je fume?**
   do you mind if I smoke?; **cela ne te gênerait pas de
   me prêter ta voiture?** would you mind lending me
   your car?; **ce qui me gêne, c'est que...** what bothers
   me is that...; **sa présence me gêne** I feel awkward in
   her presence (**b**) (*être source d'inconfort*) **cette cein-
   ture/ce col me gêne** this belt/this collar is uncomfortable (**c**) (*embarrasser*) to embarrass; **ça me gênerait
   de le rencontrer** I'd feel uncomfortable meeting him;
   Fam **et alors, ça te gêne?** what's it to you?
   2 **se gêner** *vpr* (**a**) **je ne me suis pas gêné pour le lui
   dire** I didn't hesitate to tell him so; **elle aurait tort de
   se g.** she shouldn't feel bad about it; *aussi Ironique* **ne
   vous gênez pas pour moi!** don't mind me! (**b**) (*dans
   un lieu*) to be in each other's way (**c**) *Suisse* (*être intimidé*) to be shy
général, -e, -aux, -ales [ʒeneral, -o] **1** *adj* general;
   assemblée/amnistie générale general assembly/
   amnesty; **l'intérêt g.** the general interest; **à la surprise générale** to everyone's surprise; **à la demande**

générale by popular request; **d'une façon générale** generally speaking; **en g.** *(globalement)* in general; *(habituellement)* as a rule, generally
  2 *nm* (**a**) *Mil* general (**b**) *(ce qui est universel)* **passer du g. au particulier** to go from the general to the particular
  3 *nf* **générale** (**a**) *Théât* dress rehearsal (**b**) *(femme de général)* general's wife

généralement [ʒeneralmã] *adv* generally

généralisation [ʒeneralizasjɔ̃] *nf* generalization

généraliser [ʒeneralize] **1** *vt* to generalize; *Méd* **un cancer généralisé** a generalized cancer
  2 *vi* to generalize
  3 se généraliser *vpr (utilisation, usage, phénomène)* to become widespread; *(conflit, grève)* to spread

généraliste [ʒeneralist] *adj & nmf* (**médecin**) **g.** general practitioner, GP

généralité [ʒeneralite] *nf* (**a**) *(notion générale)* generality; **s'en tenir à des généralités** to confine oneself to generalities (**b**) *(majorité)* **la g. de** the majority of

générateur, -trice [ʒeneratœr, -tris] **1** *adj (machine)* generating; *(organe)* generative; **être g. de** to generate
  2 *nm* generator; *Ordinat* **g. de caractères** character generator; **g. d'effets numériques** digital effects generator; **g. d'effets spéciaux** (special) effects generator; **g. graphique** graphics generator
  3 *nf* **génératrice** generator

génération [ʒenerasjɔ̃] *nf* (**a**) *(classe d'âge, degrés de filiation)* generation (**b**) *(action de produire)* generation; *Biol* **g. spontanée** spontaneous generation

générer [34] [ʒenere] *vt* to generate

généreusement [ʒenerøzmã] *adv* generously

généreux, -euse [ʒenerø, -øz] *adj* generous; **une terre généreuse** a fertile soil; **elle a des formes généreuses** she has generous curves

générique [ʒenerik] **1** *adj* generic
  2 *nm* *Cin & TV* credits; **g. de fin** closing credits

générosité [ʒenerozite] *nf* generosity; **avec g.** generously

Gênes [ʒɛn] *n* Genoa

genèse [ʒənɛz] *nf* genesis; **la G.** Genesis

genêt [ʒɔnɛ] *nm* broom

généticien, -enne [ʒenetisjɛ̃, -ɛn] *nm,f* geneticist

génétique [ʒenetik] **1** *adj* genetic
  2 *nf* genetics *(singulier)*

génétiquement [ʒenetikmã] *adv* genetically; **g. modifié** genetically modified

gêneur, -euse [ʒɛnœr, -øz] *nm,f* nuisance

Genève [ʒənɛv] *n* Geneva

genevois, -e [ʒənvwa, -az] **1** *adj* Genevan
  2 *nm,f* **G.** Genevan

genévrier [ʒənevrije] *nm* juniper

génial, -e, -aux, -ales [ʒenjal, -o] *adj* (**a**) *(invention, œuvre, artiste)* brilliant (**b**) *Fam (extraordinaire)* fantastic, great

génialement [ʒenjalmã] *adv* brilliantly

génie¹ [ʒeni] *nm* (**a**) *(qualité, personne)* genius; **avoir du g.** to be a genius; **une idée/invention de g.** a brilliant idea/invention; **un trait de g.** a stroke of genius; **avoir le g. de qch/pour faire qch** to have a genius for sth/for doing sth (**b**) *(être mythique)* genie; **son bon/mauvais g.** his good/evil genius

génie² *nm Mil* **le (corps du) g.** ≃ the Engineers; **g. civil** civil engineering; *(corps)* civil engineers; **g. génétique** genetic engineering

genièvre [ʒənjɛvr] *nm (fruit)* juniper berry; *(arbre)* juniper (tree)

génique [ʒenik] *adj Méd* **thérapie g.** gene therapy

génisse [ʒenis] *nf* heifer

génital, -e, -aux, -ales [ʒenital, -o] *adj (glandes, hormones)* genital

géniteur, -trice [ʒenitœr, -tris] *nm,f Hum* parent

génocide [ʒenɔsid] *nm* genocide

génoise [ʒenwaz] *nf (gâteau)* sponge cake

génome [ʒenom] *nm Biol* genome

génotype [ʒenɔtip] *nm Biol* genotype

genou, -x [ʒənu] *nm* knee; **enfoncé jusqu'aux genoux dans la boue** knee-deep in mud; **avoir les genoux en dedans** to be knock-kneed; **être à genoux** to be kneeling (down), to be on one's knees; **se mettre à genoux** to kneel (down); *Fig* **être à genoux devant qn** to worship sb; *Fig* **demander qch à genoux** to ask for sth on bended knee; *Fig* **être sur les genoux** to be on one's last legs; **tenir un enfant sur ses genoux** to hold a child on one's knee *or* one's lap

genouillère [ʒənujɛr] *nf (protection du genou)* knee-pad; *Méd* knee bandage

genre [ʒãr] *nm* (**a**) *(sorte)* kind, sort; **en tout g., en tous genres** of all kinds; **très bon dans son g.** very good in its own way; **c'est ce qu'on fait de mieux dans le g.** it's the best of its kind; **c'est tout à fait son g. d'arriver en retard** it's just like him to be late; **ce n'est pas le g. (de femme) à se plaindre** she's not the sort (of woman) to complain; **tu vois le g.** you know the sort; **un vin blanc g. sauternes** a white wine similar to Sauternes (**b**) *(artistique, littéraire)* genre; **le g. comique** comedy (**c**) *(race)* **le g. humain** the human race (**d**) *(goût)* **ça fait bon/mauvais g.** it's in good/bad taste (**e**) *Gram* gender

gens [ʒã] *nmpl (individus)* people; **les g. du pays** *ou* **du coin** the local people; **jeunes g.** *(garçons et filles)* young people; *(jeunes hommes)* young men; **g. de lettres** men and women of letters; **g. du voyage** travelling people

gent [ʒã] *nf Vieilli ou Hum* **la g. féminine/masculine** the fair/male sex

gentiane [ʒãsjan] *nf (plante)* gentian

gentil, -ille [ʒãti, -ij] *adj* (**a**) *(aimable)* kind, nice (**avec** to); *(sage)* good; **sois g., ferme la fenêtre** do me a favour and close the window (**b**) *(considérable)* **une gentille somme** a nice little sum

gentilhomme [ʒãtijɔm] *(pl* **gentilshommes** [ʒãtizɔm]*) nm* gentleman

gentillesse [ʒãtijɛs] *nf (bonté)* kindness; **auriez-vous la g. de…?** would you be so kind as to…?; **elle a eu la g. de venir elle-même** she was kind enough to come herself; **dire des gentillesses à qn** to say kind things to sb

gentillet, -ette [ʒãtijɛ, -ɛt] *adj Péj (roman, film)* pleasant enough

gentiment [ʒãtimã] *adv (aimablement)* kindly; *(sagement)* nicely

génuflexion [ʒenyflɛksjɔ̃] *nf* genuflexion; **faire une g.** to genuflect

géo [ʒeo] *nf Fam Scol* geog

géographe [ʒeɔgraf] *nmf* geographer

géographie [ʒeɔgrafi] *nf* geography; **g. humaine/physique** human/physical geography

géographique [ʒeɔgrafik] *adj* geographic(al)
geôle [ʒol] *nf Litt* jail, *Br* gaol
geôlier, -ère [ʒolje, -ɛr] *nm,f Litt* jailer, *Br* gaoler
géologie [ʒeɔlɔʒi] *nf* geology
géologique [ʒeɔlɔʒik] *adj* geological
géologue [ʒeɔlɔg] *nmf* geologist
géomètre [ʒeɔmɛtr] *nm* (**arpenteur**) g. (land) surveyor
géométrie [ʒeɔmetri] *nf* geometry; **g. dans l'espace** solid geometry; **à g. variable** *(avion)* swing-wing; *Fig* that varies according to circumstances
géométrique [ʒeɔmetrik] *adj* geometric(al)
géophysicien, -enne [ʒeofizisjɛ̃, -ɛn] *nm,f* geophysicist
géophysique [ʒeofizik] **1** *adj* geophysical
  2 *nf* geophysics *(singulier)*
géopolitique [ʒeopɔlitik] **1** *adj* geopolitical
  2 *nf* geopolitics *(singulier)*
Géorgie [ʒeɔrʒi] *nf* **la G.** *(aux États-Unis, dans le Caucase)* Georgia
géorgien, -enne [ʒeɔrʒjɛ̃, -ɛn] **1** *adj* Georgian
  2 *nm,f* **G.** Georgian
géostationnaire [ʒeostasjɔnɛr] *adj voir* **satellite**
géothermie [ʒeotɛrmi] *nf* geothermics *(singulier)*
géothermique [ʒeotɛrmik] *adj* geothermal
gérance [ʒerɑ̃s] *nf* management; **prendre un commerce en g.** to take over the management of a business
géranium [ʒeranjɔm] *nm* geranium
gérant, -e [ʒerɑ̃, -ɑ̃t] *nm,f* manager
gerbe [ʒɛrb] *nf (de blé)* sheaf; *(d'étincelles)* shower; *(d'eau)* spray; **g. (de fleurs)** spray of flowers
gerber [ʒɛrbe] *vi Vulg (vomir)* to puke, to barf; *Fig* **ça me fait g.** it makes me want to throw up *or* puke
gercé, -e [ʒɛrse] *adj* chapped
gercer [16] [ʒɛrse] **1** *vt & vi* to chap
  2 se gercer *vpr* to chap
gerçure [ʒɛrsyr] *nf* **avoir des gerçures (aux mains/lèvres)** to have chapped hands/lips
gérer [34] [ʒere] *vt* to manage
gériatrie [ʒerjatri] *nf Méd* geriatrics *(singulier)*
gériatrique [ʒerjatrik] *adj Méd* geriatric
germain, -e [ʒermɛ̃, -ɛn] *adj voir* **cousin**
germanique [ʒermanik] *adj* (**a**) *Hist (relatif aux Germains)* Germanic (**b**) *(allemand)* German (**c**) *(langue)* Germanic
germanophone [ʒermanɔfɔn] **1** *adj* German-speaking
  2 *nmf* German speaker
germe [ʒɛrm] *nm (embryon, virus)* germ; *(de pomme de terre)* eye; *Fig* **les germes de** *(origine)* the seeds of; **germes de soja** bean sprouts
germer [ʒɛrme] *vi (plante, idée)* to germinate; *(pommes de terre)* to sprout
germination [ʒerminasjɔ̃] *nf Biol* germination
gérondif [ʒerɔ̃dif] *nm Gram* gerund; *(cas latin)* gerundive
gérontologie [ʒerɔ̃tɔlɔʒi] *nf Méd* gerontology
gérontologue [ʒerɔ̃tɔlɔg] *nmf Méd* gerontologist
gésier [ʒezje] *nm* gizzard
gésir [40] [ʒezir] *vi Litt* to lie; **ci-gît…** *(sur une tombe)* here lies…
gestation [ʒɛstasjɔ̃] *nf Biol* gestation; *Fig* **en g.** in preparation

geste [ʒɛst] *nm* (**a**) *(mouvement)* gesture; **faire un g.** to make a gesture; **pas un g. ou je tire!** one move and I'll shoot!; **il lui montra la porte d'un g.** he motioned her towards the door; **d'un g. de la main** with a wave of the hand; **écarter qn d'un g.** to wave sb aside; **joindre le g. à la parole** to suit the action to the word (**b**) *(action)* gesture; **un beau g.** a fine gesture; **faire un g.** to make a gesture
gesticuler [ʒɛstikyle] *vi* to gesticulate
gestion [ʒɛstjɔ̃] *nf* management; **g. de bases de données** database management; *Ordinat* **g. des couleurs** colour management; **g. d'entreprise** business management; *Ordinat* **g. de fichiers** file management; *Ordinat* **g. de mémoire** memory management; *Ordinat* **g. sonore** sound handling, sound management; **g. des stocks** stock control
gestionnaire [ʒɛstjɔnɛr] **1** *nmf (dirigeant)* administrator
  2 *nm Ordinat* manager, driver; **g. de fichiers** file manager; **g. de périphérique** device driver; **g. de projets** project management package; **g. de réseau** network manager
gestuel, -elle [ʒɛstɥɛl] **1** *adj* gestural
  2 *nf* **gestuelle** body language
geyser [ʒezɛr] *nm* geyser
Ghana [gana] *nm* **le G.** Ghana
ghanéen, -enne [ganeɛ̃, -ɛn] **1** *adj* Ghanaian
  2 *nm,f* **G.** Ghanaian
ghetto [gɛto] *nm* ghetto
GIA [ʒeia] *nm (abrév* **Groupes islamiques armés***)* GIA
gibecière [ʒibsjɛr] *nf (de chasseur)* game bag
gibelotte [ʒiblɔt] *nf Culin* **g. (de lapin)** fricassee of rabbit cooked in white wine
gibet [ʒibɛ] *nm* gibbet, gallows *(singulier)*
gibier [ʒibje] *nm* game; *aussi Fig* **gros g.** big game; **g. à plumes** game birds; **g. à poil** game animals; *Fig* **g. de potence** gallows bird
giboulée [ʒibule] *nf* sudden shower; **giboulées de mars** ≃ April showers
Gibraltar [ʒibraltar] *n* Gibraltar
giclée [ʒikle] *nf* (**a**) *(d'eau, de sang)* spurt (**b**) *Suisse (petite quantité)* spot, smidgen (**c**) *Suisse (averse)* (rain) shower
gicler [ʒikle] *vi* (**a**) *(eau, sang)* to spurt out; *(boue)* to splash up (**b**) *Suisse (pleuvoir)* to rain
gicleur [ʒiklœr] *nm Aut* jet
GIE [ʒeiə] *nm (abrév* **groupement d'intérêt économique***)* economic interest group
gifle [ʒifl] *nf aussi Fig* slap in the face; **donner une g. à qn** to give sb a slap in the face
gifler [ʒifle] *vt (sujet: personne)* to slap in the face; *(sujet: vent)* to lash
gigahertz [ʒigaɛrts] *nm Phys* gigahertz
gigantesque [ʒigɑ̃tɛsk] *adj* gigantic
gigaoctet [ʒigaɔktɛ] *nm Ordinat* gigabyte
GIGN [ʒeiʒeɛn] *nm (abrév* **Groupe d'intervention de la gendarmerie nationale***)* = special task force of the gendarmerie
gigogne [ʒigɔɲ] *adj* **tables gigognes** nest of tables; **lits gigognes** beds that fit one underneath the other; **poupées gigognes** nest of (Russian) dolls
gigolo [ʒigɔlo] *nm Fam* gigolo
gigot [ʒigo] *nm (d'agneau, de mouton)* leg
gigoter [ʒigɔte] *vi* to wriggle, to fidget
gigue¹ [ʒig] *nf (danse)* jig

gigue² *nf Fam* **une grande g.** *(fille)* a beanpole (of a girl)

gilet [ʒilɛ] *nm (sans manches) Br* waistcoat, *Am* vest; *(veste en laine)* cardigan; **g. pare-balles** bulletproof jacket; **g. de sauvetage** life jacket

gin [dʒin] *nm* gin; **g. tonic** gin and tonic

gingembre [ʒɛ̃ʒɑ̃br] *nm* ginger

gingivite [ʒɛ̃ʒivit] *nf Méd* gingivitis

ginseng [ʒɛsɑ̃, ʒinsɑ̃g] *nm* ginseng

girafe [ʒiraf] *nf* giraffe; *Fig (personne)* beanpole

giratoire [ʒiratwar] **1** *adj (mouvement)* gyratory
   2 *nm Suisse (rond-point) Br* roundabout, *Am* traffic circle

girofle [ʒirɔfl] *nm voir* **clou**

giroflée [ʒirɔfle] *nf* stock

girolle [ʒirɔl] *nf* chanterelle (mushroom)

giron [ʒirɔ̃] *nm (partie du corps)* lap; *Fig* bosom

gironde [ʒirɔ̃d] *adj f Fam* curvy; *Péj* on the plump side

girondin, -e [ʒirɔ̃dɛ̃, -in] **1** *adj* of the Gironde
   2 *nm,f* **G.** person from the Gironde

girouette [ʒirwɛt] *nf aussi Fig* weathercock

gisais *etc voir* **gésir**

gisement [ʒizmɑ̃] *nm (de minerai)* deposit; **g. de pétrole** oilfield

gît *voir* **gésir**

gitan, -e [ʒitɑ̃, -an] **1** *adj* gypsy
   2 *nm,f* gypsy
   3 *nf* **Gitane**® Gitane® *(popular brand of cigarette)*

gîte¹ [ʒit] *nm* (**a**) *(logement)* lodging; **offrir le g. et le couvert à qn** to offer sb board and lodging (**b**) *(en montagne, à la campagne)* **g. d'étape** = transit accommodation for hikers, cyclists etc; **g. rural** gîte, = self-catering holiday cottage or apartment (**c**) *(du lièvre)* form (**d**) *Culin* shank

gîte² *nf Naut* list; **donner de la g.** to list

gîter [ʒite] *vi Naut* to list

givre [ʒivr] *nm* frost

givré, -e [ʒivre] *adj* (**a**) *(couvert de givre)* covered with frost (**b**) *Fam (fou)* crazy

glabre [glabr] *adj (rasé)* clean-shaven; *(imberbe) (personne)* smooth-chinned; *(visage)* hairless

glaçage [glasaʒ] *nm (d'un gâteau)* icing

glaçant, -e [glasɑ̃, -ɑ̃t] *adj (manières, accueil)* frosty

glace [glas] *nf* (**a**) *(eau à l'état solide)* ice; **glaces** *(du pôle)* ice fields; *(en mer)* ice floes; **le navire est pris dans les glaces** the ship is icebound; *Fig* **rester de g.** to remain impassive; *Fig* **rompre la g.** to break the ice; **g. pilée** crushed ice (**b**) *(de voiture)* window (**c**) *(miroir)* mirror; **g. sans tain** two-way mirror (**d**) *(crème congelée)* ice cream; **g. à la vanille/à la fraise** vanilla/strawberry ice cream; **g. à l'italienne** soft ice cream

glacé, -e [glase] *adj* (**a**) *(rivière, lac)* frozen (**b**) *(très froid) (pièce, eau, personne)* freezing (cold); *(avec des glaçons) (café)* iced; **j'ai les pieds glacés** my feet are freezing (**c**) *Fig (accueil, politesse, regard)* frosty (**d**) *(brillant) (papier, épreuve)* glossy (**e**) *Culin (fruits)* glacé

glacer [16] [glase] **1** *vt* (**a**) *(refroidir, intimider)* to chill; *Fig* **à vous g. le sang** spine-chilling (**b**) *(gâteau)* to ice
   2 se glacer *vpr (sang)* to run cold

glaciaire [glasjɛr] *adj Géol (vallée)* glacial; **période g.** Ice Age

glacial, -e, -als *ou* **-aux, -ales** [glasjal, -o] *adj (température, froid, air, vent)* freezing, icy; *Fig (ton, accueil, sourire)* frosty; *(personne)* cold

glacier¹ [glasje] *nm (étendue de glace)* glacier

glacier² *nm (vendeur)* ice-cream seller; *(fabricant)* ice-cream maker

glacière [glasjɛr] *nf (de pique-nique)* cool box; **cette chambre est une vraie g.!** this room's like an icebox!

glaçon [glasɔ̃] *nm (pour rafraîchir une boisson)* ice cube; *(pendant)* icicle; *Fig (personne)* cold fish; **glaçons** *(sur une rivière)* drift ice; **avec ou sans glaçons?** with or without ice?; **un whisky avec des glaçons** a whisky on the rocks; **j'ai les pieds comme des glaçons** my feet are like blocks of ice

gladiateur [gladjatœr] *nm* gladiator

glaïeul [glajœl] *nm* gladiolus; **des glaïeuls** gladioli

glaire [glɛr] *nf (crachat)* phlegm; **g. cervicale** cervical mucus

glaise [glɛz] *nf* **(terre) g.** clay

glaive [glɛv] *nm (épée)* broadsword; *Fig (symbole)* sword

gland [glɑ̃] *nm* (**a**) *(de chêne)* acorn (**b**) *(de passementerie)* tassel (**c**) *Anat* glans (**d**) *très Fam (personne) Br* prat, *Am* jerk

glande [glɑ̃d] *nf (organe)* gland; *très Fam* **foutre les glandes à qn** *(énerver)* to piss sb off; *(mettre mal à l'aise)* to put the wind up sb; **glandes lacrymales** tear glands; **glandes sudoripares** sweat glands

glander [glɑ̃de] *vi très Fam (ne rien faire)* to loaf around; *(attendre)* to hang around; **mais qu'est-ce qu'il glande?** *(que fait-il?)* what the hell's he up to?; **j'en ai rien à g.** I don't give a shit

glandeur, -euse [glɑ̃dœr, -øz] *nm,f très Fam* layabout

glandouiller [glɑ̃duje] *vi très Fam (ne rien faire)* to loaf around; *(attendre)* to hang around

glandulaire [glɑ̃dylɛr], **glanduleux, -euse** [glɑ̃dylø, -øz] *adj* glandular

glaner [glane] *vt aussi Fig* to glean

glapir [glapir] *vi (chien)* to yap; *(renard)* to bark; *(personne, radio)* to shriek

glapissements [glapismɑ̃] *nmpl (d'un chien)* yapping; *(d'un renard)* barking; *(d'une personne, de la radio)* shrieking

glas [glɑ] *nm* knell; **sonner le g.** to toll the knell; *Fig* **sonner le g. de qch** to sound the death knell for sth

glaucome [glokom] *nm Méd* glaucoma

glauque [glok] *adj (eau)* murky; *(ambiance, personne)* creepy

glissade [glisad] *nf* sliding; *(de patineur)* gliding; *(pas de danse)* glissade; **faire une g./des glissades** to slide

glissant, -e [glisɑ̃, -ɑ̃t] *adj* slippery; *Fig* **être sur un terrain g.** to be on dangerous ground

glisse [glis] *nf* **sports de g.** = sports involving sliding motion, eg skiing, surfing, windsurfing

glissement [glismɑ̃] *nm (action)* sliding; *(variation électorale)* swing (**à** to); **g. de sens** shift in meaning; **g. de terrain** landslide; *(moins important)* landslip

glisser¹ [glise] **1** *vi* (**a**) *(par accident)* to slip; *(roue)* to skid; **le couteau lui a glissé des mains** the knife slipped out of her hands; *Aviat* **g. sur l'aile** to sideslip (**b**) *(volontairement)* to slide; **se laisser g. le long d'une corde** to slide down a rope; *Ordinat* **faire g. sur** *(pointeur)* to drag (**c**) *(avancer régulièrement)* to glide; *Fig (dans le sommeil, vers le désespoir)* to slip (**d**) **g. sur** *(sujet)* to skip over (**e**) *(avoir une surface glissante)* to be slippery

2 *vt (introduire)* to slip; **g. un mot à l'oreille de qn** to drop a word in sb's ear
3 se glisser *vpr* to slip (**dans** into)
glisser² *nm Ordinat* **g. d'icônes** icon drag
glissière [glisjɛr] *nf* (**a**) *Tech* runner, slide; **à g.** sliding (**b**) **g. de sécurité** crash barrier (**c**) *Ind (pour le charbon)* chute
global, -e, -aux, -ales [glɔbal, -o] *adj (somme)* total; *(paiement)* lump; *(vision)* overall; *Scol* **méthode globale** word recognition method
globalement [glɔbalmã] *adv* overall
globalité [glɔbalite] *nf* **prendre un problème dans sa g.** to tackle a problem as a whole
globe [glɔb] *nm* (**a**) *(sphère)* globe; **g. oculaire** eyeball (**b**) *(terre)* globe; **faire le tour du g.** to go round the world; **g. terrestre** *(terre)* earth; *(mappemonde)* globe (**c**) *(en verre) (d'une pendule)* glass dome
globe-trotter *(pl* **globe-trotters**) [glɔbtrɔtœr] *nmf* globetrotter
globulaire [glɔbylɛr] *adj Méd* **numération g.** blood count
globule [glɔbyl] *nm (du sang)* corpuscle; **globules blancs/rouges** white/red corpuscles
globuleux, -euse [glɔbylø, -øz] *adj (yeux)* protruding
gloire [glwar] *nf* (**a**) *(renom)* glory; **tirer g. de qch** to glory in sth (**b**) *(personne célèbre)* celebrity; **il est la g. de notre école** he is the pride of our school (**c**) *(manifestation de respect)* **rendre g. à** to glorify; **g. à...!** glory to...!; **à la g. de qn** in praise of sb
glorieux, -euse [glɔrjø, -øz] *adj* glorious; **être promis à un avenir g.** to have a glorious future ahead of one; *Fam* **ce n'est pas très g.** *(pas très bon)* it's not exactly brilliant
glorifier [66] [glɔrifje] **1** *vt* to glorify
2 se glorifier *vpr* **se g. de (faire) qch** to glory in (doing) sth
gloriole [glɔrjɔl] *nf Fam* **faire qch par g.** to do sth in order to show off
glose [gloz] *nf (explication)* gloss
gloser [gloze] **gloser sur** *vt ind (discourir sur)* to ramble on about
glossaire [glɔsɛr] *nm (ouvrage)* glossary
glotte [glɔt] *nf Anat* glottis
glouglou [gluglu] *nm* (**a**) *(bruit d'un liquide)* gurgle; **faire g.** to gurgle (**b**) *(cri de la dinde)* gobble
gloussements [glusmã] *nmpl (d'une poule)* clucking; *(d'une dinde)* gobbling; *(d'une personne)* chuckling
glousser [gluse] *vi (poule)* to cluck; *(dinde)* to gobble; *(personne)* to chuckle
glouton, -onne [glutõ, -ɔn] **1** *adj* greedy, gluttonous
2 *nm,f* glutton
3 *nm (animal)* wolverine
gloutonnement [glutɔnmã] *adv* greedily
gloutonnerie [glutɔnri] *nf* gluttony, greed
glu [gly] *nf (colle)* glue
gluant, -e [glyã, -ãt] *adj* slimy
glucide [glysid] *nm* carbohydrate
glucose [glykoz] *nm* glucose
gluten [glytɛn] *nm* gluten
glycémie [glisemi] *nf Méd* glycaemia
glycérine [gliserin] *nf* glycerine
glycine [glisin] *nf (plante)* wisteria
gnangnan [ɲãɲã] *adj inv Fam Péj (personne)* drippy; *(livre, film)* soppy

gnognot(t)e [ɲɔɲɔt] *nf Fam (mauvaise qualité)* **c'est de la g.** it's a load of rubbish; **c'est pas de la g., cette voiture** that car's quite something
gnole, gnôle [ɲol] *nf Fam* hooch
gnome [gnom] *nm* gnome; *Fig & Péj (homme)* midget
gnon [ɲɔ̃] *nm Fam (coup de poing)* thump; **se prendre un g.** to get thumped
GO 1 *Rad (abrév* **grandes ondes**) LW
2 [ʒeo] *nm (abrév* **gentil organisateur**) activity organizer *(at Club Méditerranée holiday villages)*
Go *nm Ordinat (abrév* **gigaoctet(s)**) GB
go [go] **tout de go** *adv* straight away
goal [gol] *nm* goalkeeper
gobelet [gɔblɛ] *nm (en argent, en étain)* tumbler; **g. en plastique/carton** plastic/paper cup
gober [gɔbe] *vt (nourriture)* to gulp down; *Fig (croire)* to swallow
goberger [gɔbɛrʒe] **se goberger** *vpr Fam* to have a good time
Gobi [gɔbi] *n voir* **désert**
godasse [gɔdas] *nf Fam* shoe
godelureau, -x [gɔdlyro] *nm Péj & Vieilli* popinjay
godet [gɔdɛ] *nm* (**a**) *(récipient)* pot; *Fam* **boire un g.** to have a jar (**b**) *(d'une noria)* scoop; *(d'un excavateur, d'une roue à eau)* bucket (**c**) *(d'une jupe)* **à godets** flared
godiche [gɔdiʃ] *Fam* **1** *adj* clumsy
2 *nf* clumsy oaf
godille [gɔdij] *nf* (**a**) *Naut* scull; **avancer à la g.** to scull (**b**) *(en ski)* wedeln; **faire de la g.** to wedeln
godiller [gɔdije] *vi* (**a**) *Naut* to scull (**b**) *(en ski)* to wedeln
godillot [gɔdijo] *nm Mil* boot; *Fam (gros soulier)* clodhopper
goéland [gɔelã] *nm* gull
goélette [gɔelɛt] *nf (navire)* schooner
goémon [gɔemɔ̃] *nm* wrack
gogo¹ [gogo] **à gogo** *adv Fam* galore
gogo² *nm Fam* sucker, mug
goguenard, -e [gɔgnar, -ard] *adj* mocking
goguette [gɔgɛt] *nf Fam* **être en g.** *(faire la noce)* to be out for a good time
goinfre [gwɛ̃fr] *Fam* **1** *nmf* pig
2 *adj* piggish
goinfrer [gwɛ̃fre] **se goinfrer** *vpr Fam* to pig oneself (**de** on)
goinfrerie [gwɛ̃frəri] *nf* piggishness
goitre [gwatr] *nm Méd* goitre
golden [gɔldɛn] *nf* Golden Delicious (apple)
golf [gɔlf] *nm* golf; **(terrain de) g.** golf course; **g. miniature** miniature golf
golfe [gɔlf] *nm* gulf, bay; **le G.** the Gulf; **le g. Persique** the Persian Gulf; **les États** *ou* **les pays du G.** the Gulf States; **le g. du Bengale** the Bay of Bengal; **le g. de Gascogne** the Bay of Biscay; **le g. du Mexique** the Gulf of Mexico
golfeur, -euse [gɔlfœr, -øz] *nm,f* golfer
Gomina® [gɔmina] *nf* hair cream
gominé, -e [gɔmine] *adj (cheveux)* plastered-down
gommage [gɔmaʒ] *nm* (**a**) *(pour effacer)* rubbing out, erasing (**b**) *(nettoyage de la peau)* face scrub; **se faire un g.** to give oneself a face scrub
gomme [gɔm] *nf* (**a**) *(pour effacer)* eraser, *Br* rubber (**b**) *(substance)* gum; **g. à mâcher** chewing gum (**c**)

Fam (locutions) **mettre (toute) la g.** to get a move on; *(en voiture)* to step on it; **à la g.** useless

gommé, -e [gɔme] *adj (papier, enveloppe)* gummed

gommer [gɔme] *vt (effacer)* to rub out, to erase; *Fig (souvenir)* to erase

gond [gɔ̃] *nm (de porte)* hinge; **sortir de ses gonds** *(porte)* to come off its hinges; *Fig* to fly off the handle

gondole [gɔ̃dɔl] *nf (barque, présentoir)* gondola

gondoler [gɔ̃dɔle] **1** *vi (bois, disque)* to warp; *(papier)* to crinkle

2 se gondoler *vpr* (a) *(bois, disque)* to warp; *(papier)* to crinkle (b) *Fam (rire)* to fall about laughing

gondolier [gɔ̃dɔlje] *nm* gondolier

gonflable [gɔ̃flabl] *adj* inflatable

gonflage [gɔ̃flaʒ] *nm* **g. (des pneus)** tyre pressure

gonflant, -e [gɔ̃flɑ̃, -ɑ̃t] *adj* (a) *(coiffure)* bouffant (b) *très Fam (énervant)* maddening

gonflé, -e [gɔ̃fle] *adj* (a) *(boursouflé)* swollen (b) *Fam* **être g.** *(personne)* to have a lot of nerve; **c'est g., ce qu'il a fait là** what he did took some nerve; **g. à bloc** *(sûr de soi)* raring to go

gonflement [gɔ̃fləmɑ̃] *nm (d'une partie du corps)* swelling

gonfler [gɔ̃fle] **1** *vt* (a) *(pneu, ballon, matelas pneumatique)* to blow up, to inflate; *(ses joues)* to puff out; *(sujet: vent) (voiles)* to fill (b) *(faire augmenter de volume)* to swell (c) *Fig (grossir) (résultats, conséquences)* to exaggerate; *Fam (moteur)* to soup up (d) *très Fam (énerver)* **g. qn** to get up sb's nose *or Br* on sb's tits

2 *vi* to swell; *(gâteau, pâte)* to rise

3 se gonfler *vpr (voiles, poumons)* to fill; *Fig* **se g. de joie** *(cœur)* to fill with joy

gonflette [gɔ̃flɛt] *nf Fam Péj* pumping iron; **faire de la g.** to pump iron

gong [gɔ̃g] *nm* (a) *(percussion)* gong (b) *(en boxe)* bell; *Fig* **sauvé par le g.** saved by the bell

gonzesse [gɔ̃zɛs] *nf très Fam* chick, *Br* bird

goret [gɔrɛ] *nm* piglet; *Fam (enfant malpropre)* little pig

gorge [gɔrʒ] *nf* (a) *(gosier, cou)* throat; **avoir mal à la g.** to have a sore throat; **avoir la g. serrée** to have a lump in one's throat; *Fig* **cela m'est resté en travers de la g.** it stuck in my throat; **trancher la g. à qn** to cut sb's throat; *Fig* **être pris à la g.** to be in a stranglehold; **faire des gorges chaudes de qch** to laugh sth to scorn; **rire à g. déployée** to roar with laughter (b) *Litt (poitrine)* bosom (c) *(vallée)* gorge (d) *(d'une poulie)* groove

gorgé, -e [gɔrʒe] *adj* **une éponge gorgée d'eau** a sponge full of water; **sol g. d'eau** waterlogged earth

gorgée [gɔrʒe] *nf* mouthful; **boire qch à petites gorgées** to sip sth; **avaler qch d'une g.** to swallow sth in one gulp

gorger [45] [gɔrʒe] **se gorger** *vpr* to gorge oneself (**de** on *or* with); **se g. d'eau** *(sol)* to get waterlogged

gorgonzola [gɔrgɔ̃zɔla] *nm* Gorgonzola

gorille [gɔrij] *nm (animal)* gorilla; *Fam (garde du corps)* gorilla

gosier [gozje] *nm* throat; *Fam* **avoir le g. sec** to be parched

gosse [gɔs] *nmf* (a) *Fam (enfant)* kid; **g. de riches** rich kid (b) *Fam* **être beau g.** to be good-looking (c) *Can Fam* **gosses** balls

gosser [gɔse] *vt Can Fam* to whittle

gotha [gɔta] *nm* **le g. du show-business/de la finance** the show-business/financial elite

gothique [gɔtik] **1** *adj* Gothic; **écriture g.** Gothic script

2 *nm (style)* Gothic

gouache [gwaʃ] *nf* gouache

gouailleur, -euse [gwajœr, -øz] *adj (ton)* bantering

gouda [guda] *nm* Gouda

goudron [gudrɔ̃] *nm* tar; **goudrons** *(dans les cigarettes)* tar

goudronner [gudrɔne] *vt* to tar

gouffre [gufr] *nm* abyss; *Géol* sinkhole, *Br* swallow hole; *Fig* **être au bord du g.** to be on the edge of the abyss; *Fig* **un g. les sépare** there is a gulf between them; *Fig* **cette voiture est un g.** this car just swallows up money

gougère [guʒɛr] *nf Culin* gougère *(choux pastry with cheese)*

gouine [gwin] *nf très Fam* dyke, = offensive term used to refer to a lesbian

goujat [guʒa] *nm* boor

goujon [guʒɔ̃] *nm (poisson)* gudgeon

goulache, goulasch [gulaʃ] *nm* goulash

goulafre [gulafr] *adj Belg* greedy

goulée [gule] *nf (de liquide)* gulp; *(d'air)* lungful

goulet [gulɛ] *nm (défilé)* gully; **g. d'étranglement** bottleneck

gouleyant, -e [gulɛjɑ̃, -ɑ̃t] *adj (vin)* easy-drinking

goulot [gulo] *nm (d'une bouteille)* neck; **boire au g.** to drink straight from the bottle

goulu, -e [guly] **1** *adj* greedy, gluttonous

2 *nm,f* glutton

goulûment [gulymɑ̃] *adv* greedily

goupille [gupij] *nf (d'une grenade)* pin

goupiller [gupije] *Fam* **1** *vt (arranger)* to fix (up)

2 se goupiller *vpr* **bien se g.** to work out well; **ça s'est mal goupillé** it didn't work out

goupillon [gupijɔ̃] *nm* (a) *(pour eau bénite)* sprinkler (b) *(pour biberons, bouteilles)* bottle brush

gourd, -e [gur, gurd] *adj* numb (with cold)

gourde [gurd] **1** *nf* (a) *(récipient)* flask (b) *Fam (femme niaise)* dope

2 *adj Fam* dopey

gourdin [gurdɛ̃] *nm* club, cudgel

gourer [gure] **se gourer** *vpr Fam Br* to boob, *Am* to goof; **se g. d'adresse/de jour** to get the wrong address/day

gourgane [gurgan] *nf Can* broad bean

gourmand, -e [gurmɑ̃, -ɑ̃d] **1** *adj (personne)* who likes his/her food; *(à l'excès)* greedy; *Fig (intéressé) (regard)* greedy; **cet enfant est très g.** *(de sucreries)* that child has a sweet tooth

2 *nm,f* person who likes his/her food; **quel g.!** he certainly likes his food!

gourmandise [gurmɑ̃diz] *nf* (a) *(d'une personne)* love of food; *Fig* **avec g.** greedily (b) **gourmandises** *(sucreries)* delicacies

gourmet [gurmɛ] *nm* gourmet; **un fin g.** a great gourmet

gourmette [gurmɛt] *nf (bracelet)* chain (bracelet)

gourou [guru] *nm aussi Fig* guru

gousse [gus] *nf (de haricot, de petit pois)* pod; **g. d'ail** clove of garlic; **g. de vanille** vanilla pod

gousset [gusɛ] *nm (poche)* fob (pocket)

goût [gu] *nm* (**a**) *(saveur)* taste; **avoir un g. de banane/d'alcool** to taste of banana/alcohol; **manquer de g., ne pas avoir de g.** to be tasteless (**b**) *(sens)* taste (**c**) *(préférence, convenance)* taste; **avoir des goûts de luxe** to have expensive tastes; **trouver qn/qch à son g.** to find sb/sth to one's taste; **avoir du g. pour** *ou* **le g. de qch** to have a taste for sth; **elle n'a plus (de) g. à rien** she doesn't want to do anything any more; **faire qch par g.** to do sth because one likes to; **prendre g. à qch** to acquire a taste for sth; **chacun ses goûts** each to his own; **des goûts et des couleurs on ne discute pas, tous les goûts sont dans la nature** there's no accounting for taste (**d**) *(discernement, jugement)* taste; **s'habiller avec g.** to have good dress sense; **de bon g.** tasteful; **d'un g. douteux** in doubtful taste; **de mauvais g.** in bad taste (**e**) *(style)* **quelque chose dans ce g.-là** something of that sort

goûter¹ [gute] *nm* (afternoon) tea; **l'heure du g.** tea-time

goûter² **1** *vt* (**a**) *(essayer)* *(nourriture, boisson)* to taste, to try (**b**) *(apprécier)* to enjoy, to appreciate (**c**) *Belg & Can (avoir un goût de)* to taste of; **ce fruit goûte le pourri** this fruit tastes rotten
2 *vi (à quatre heures)* to have tea
3 goûter à *vt ind (aliment)* to taste, to try; *Fig* to have a taste of

goûteur, -euse [gutœr, -øz] *nm,f* taster

goutte [gut] **1** *nf* (**a**) *(de liquide)* drop; **couler g. à g.** to drip; **il suait à grosses gouttes** the sweat was pouring off him; **gouttes** *(pour les yeux, les oreilles)* drops; *Fig* **c'est la g. d'eau qui fait déborder le vase** it's the straw that breaks/broke the camel's back; *Fam* **avoir la g. au nez** to have a runny nose; **se ressembler comme deux gouttes d'eau** to be as like as two peas in a pod (**b**) *(petite quantité)* drop; **encore une g. de café?** a drop more coffee?; *Fam* **boire la g.** to have a nip (**c**) *Méd (maladie)* gout; **avoir la g.** to have gout
2 *adv Vieilli* **je n'y vois/entends g.** I can't see/understand anything

goutte-à-goutte [gutagut] *nm inv Méd* drip; **on lui a mis un g.** she was put on a drip

gouttelette [gutlɛt] *nf* droplet

goutter [gute] *vi* to drip

gouttière [gutjɛr] *nf* (**a**) *(le long du toit)* gutter (**b**) *(le long du mur)* drainpipe

gouvernail [guvɛrnaj] *nm Naut* rudder; **tenir le g.** to be at the helm

gouvernant, -e [guvɛrnɑ̃, -ɑ̃t] **1** *adj (classe, parti)* governing, ruling
2 *nm* **les gouvernants** those in power

gouvernante [guvɛrnɑ̃t] *nf (d'enfants)* governess; *(d'une personne, d'un hôtel)* housekeeper

gouverne [guvɛrn] *nf* (**a**) *Aviat* **gouvernes** control surfaces (**b**) **pour votre g.** for your guidance

gouvernement [guvɛrnəmɑ̃] *nm* government; **sous le g. Giscard** during Giscard's term of office

gouvernemental, -e, -aux, -ales [guvɛrnəmɑ̃tal, -o] *adj* government; *(parti)* governing

gouverner [guvɛrne] **1** *vt* (**a**) *(diriger) (pays)* to govern, to rule; **un parti qui gouverne depuis des années** a party which has been in power for years (**b**) *(bateau)* to steer
2 se gouverner *vpr* **le droit des peuples à se g. eux-mêmes** the right of peoples to self-government

gouverneur [guvɛrnœr] *nm* governor; *Can* **G. Général** governor-general; *Can* **Lieutenant-G.** lieutenant-governor

goyave [gɔjav] *nf* guava

GR [ʒeɛr] *nm (abrév* **(sentier de) grande randonnée**) = long-distance hiking path

grabat [graba] *nm* pallet

grabataire [grabatɛr] **1** *adj* bedridden
2 *nmf* bedridden invalid

grabuge [grabyʒ] *nm Fam* rumpus; **il va y avoir du g.** there'll be a rumpus

grâce [grɑs] *nf* (**a**) *(charme)* grace; **avec g.** gracefully (**b**) **g. à qn/qch** *(avec l'aide de)* thanks to sb/sth (**c**) *Litt (bienveillance, faveur)* favour; **faites-moi la g. d'oublier cette histoire** do me the favour of forgetting this matter; **trouver g. aux yeux de qn** to find favour in sb's eyes; **de g.!** for pity's sake! (**d**) *(volonté)* **de bonne g.** willingly, readily; **de mauvaise g.** unwillingly, grudgingly (**e**) *(acquittement)* pardon; **demander** *ou* **crier g.** to beg for mercy; **faire g. à qn de qch** *(dette, tâche)* to let sb off sth; **je vous fais g. des détails** I'll spare you the details; **g. présidentielle** presidential pardon (**f**) *(remerciements)* **rendre g. à** to give thanks to (**g**) *Rel* grace

gracier [66] [grasje] *vt* to pardon

gracieusement [grasjøzmɑ̃] *adv* (**a**) *(avec grâce)* gracefully (**b**) *(aimablement)* graciously (**c**) *(gratuitement)* free of charge

gracieux, -euse [grasjø, -øz] *adj* (**a**) *(qui a du charme)* graceful (**b**) *(aimable)* gracious (**c**) *(gratuit)* **à titre g.** free of charge

gracile [grasil] *adj* slender

gradation [gradasjɔ̃] *nf* gradation

grade [grad] *nm* (**a**) *(dans l'armée, dans l'administration)* rank; **monter en g.** to be promoted; *Fam* **en prendre pour son g.** to be hauled over the coals (**b**) *Belg Scol & Univ (mention)* distinction

gradé, -e [grade] *nm,f Mil* non-commissioned officer, NCO

gradin [gradɛ̃] *nm (d'amphithéâtre, de stade)* row of seats; **les gradins** *(d'un stade) Br* the terraces, *Am* the bleachers

graduation [graduasjɔ̃] *nf* graduation

gradué, -e [gradye] *adj* (**a**) *(qui porte une graduation)* graduated (**b**) *(progressif) (exercices, problèmes)* graded

graduel, -elle [graduɛl] *adj* gradual

graduellement [graduɛlmɑ̃] *adv* gradually

graduer [gradye] *vt* (**a**) *(diviser en degrés)* to graduate (**b**) *(augmenter)* to increase gradually

graffiti [grafiti] *nm* piece of graffiti; **des graffitis** graffiti

graillé, -e [graje] *adj Can (pour faire quelque chose)* well-equipped; *Fam (bien monté)* well-hung

grailler [graje] *vi très Fam (manger)* to eat

graillon [grajɔ̃] *nm* **sentir le g.** to smell of burnt fat

grain¹ [grɛ̃] *nm* (**a**) *(graine, fruit, céréales)* grain; **g. de café** coffee bean; **g. de poivre** peppercorn; **g. de raisin** grape (**b**) *(de sable, de poudre)* grain; *(de poussière)* speck; *(de chapelet)* bead; *Fig* **un g. de qch** *(un peu de)* a hint of sth; **pas un g. de bon sens/de vérité** not a grain of common sense/of truth; *Fam* **il a un g.** he's not quite right in the head; **mettre son g. de sel** to stick one's oar in; **g. de beauté** mole (**c**) *(d'un tissu, d'une photographie)* grain; *(de la peau)* rough side

grain² *nm Naut* squall; *Fig* **veiller au g.** to keep a weather eye open

graine [grɛn] *nf* seed; **monter en g.** to run to seed; *Fig (personne)* to shoot up; **regarde un peu ce qu'a fait ton cousin et prends-en de la g.!** just look at what your cousin's done and take a leaf out of his book!; **c'est de la mauvaise g.** he's a bad lot; **g. de voyou/voleur** little lout/thief

graissage [gresaʒ] *nm (d'une machine, d'un engrenage)* greasing

graisse [grɛs] *nf (d'animal, de personne)* fat; *(lubrifiant)* grease; **graisses animales/végétales** animal/vegetable fat

graisser [grese] *vt (machine, engrenage)* to grease; *(bottes)* to oil, *Br* to dubbin; **g. la patte à qn** to grease sb's palm

graisseux, -euse [gresø, -øz] *adj* **(a)** *(taché de graisse)* greasy **(b)** *(tumeur, tissu)* fatty

grammaire [gramɛr] *nf* **(a)** *(science, règles)* grammar; **faute/règle de g.** grammatical error/rule **(b)** *(livre)* grammar (book)

grammairien, -enne [gramɛrjɛ̃, -ɛn] *nm,f* grammarian

grammatical, -e, -aux, -ales [gramatikal, -o] *adj* grammatical

gramme [gram] *nm* gram; *aussi Fig* **pas un g. de** not an ounce of

grand, -e [grɑ̃, grɑ̃d] **1** *adj* **(a)** *(en taille)* big, large; *(en hauteur)* tall; *(en longueur)* long; *Phot* **g. angle** wide-angle lens
  (b) *(principal)* chief, main; **grandes lignes** *(de train)* main lines
  (c) *(adulte, plus âgé)* big; **tu es g. maintenant** you're a big boy now
  (d) *(en quantité, en intensité)* *(bruit)* loud; *(coup)* heavy; *(froid)* severe; *(différence, catastrophe)* big; **le g. amour** true love; **un acteur sans g. talent** a rather untalented actor; **il fait g. jour** it's broad daylight; **c'est un g. buveur** he's a big drinker; **les grands blessés** the seriously wounded
  (e) *(puissant, prestigieux)* great; **une grande dame de la littérature** a great literary lady
  (f) *(dans un titre, un grade)* grand; **g. prêtre** high priest; **g. reporter** chief reporter
  2 *adv* **ouvrir g. la bouche/la fenêtre** to open one's mouth/the window wide; **g. ouvert** wide open
  3 *nm,f* **les grands** *(enfants)* the older ones; **grands et petits** old and young, grown-ups and children; **les grands de ce monde** those in high places; **les grands du pétrole** the oil giants; **mon g.** mate, pal; **ma grande** dear

grand-chose [grɑ̃ʃoz] **1** *pron indéfini* **pas g.** not much; **ce ne sont que quelques fleurs, ce n'est pas g.** it's just a few flowers, nothing much
  2 *nmf inv Fam (personne)* **un pas g.** a dead loss

grand-duc *(pl* **grands-ducs)** [grɑ̃dyk] *nm (noble)* grand duke; *Fam* **faire la tournée des grands-ducs** to go out on the town

grand-duché *(pl* **grands-duchés)** [grɑ̃dyʃe] *nm* grand duchy

Grande-Bretagne [grɑ̃dbrətaɲ] *nf* **la G.** Great Britain

grande-duchesse *(pl* **grandes-duchesses)** [grɑ̃ddyʃɛs] *nf* grand duchess

grandement [grɑ̃dmɑ̃] *adv (beaucoup)* greatly; **se tromper g.** to be greatly mistaken; **avoir g. le temps**

to have ample time; **avoir g. de quoi vivre** to have plenty to live on

grandeur [grɑ̃dœr] *nf* **(a)** *(taille)* size; *(d'un arbre)* height, size; **g. nature** life-size **(b)** *(importance)* importance **(c)** *Math* magnitude **(d)** *(gloire)* greatness, grandeur; **g. et décadence d'un empire** rise and fall of an empire **(e)** *(des sentiments)* nobility; **g. d'âme** magnanimity **(f)** *Can* **à la g. de** throughout

grand-guignol [grɑ̃giɲɔl] *nm Péj* **c'est du g.** it's all blood and gore

grandiloquence [grɑ̃dilɔkɑ̃s] *nf* grandiloquence

grandiloquent, -e [grɑ̃dilɔkɑ̃, -ɑ̃t] *adj* grandiloquent

grandiose [grɑ̃djoz] *adj* imposing

grandir [grɑ̃dir] **1** *vi (en taille)* to grow; *(en âge)* to grow up; *(en importance)* to increase, to grow
  2 *vt* **g. qn** *(sujet: talons)* to make sb look taller; *Fig (sujet: expérience, épreuve)* to improve sb's standing
  3 **se grandir** *vpr (en taille)* to make oneself taller

grandissant, -e [grɑ̃disɑ̃, -ɑ̃t] *adj* growing

grand-maman *(pl* **grand-mamans** *ou* **grands-mamans)** [grɑ̃mamɑ̃] *Suisse & Can (en langage enfantin)* granny, grandma

grand-mère *(pl* **grand-mères** *ou* **grands-mères)** [grɑ̃mɛr] *nf* grandmother; *Fam (vieille femme)* old granny

grand-oncle [grɑ̃tɔ̃kl] *(pl* **grands-oncles** [grɑ̃zɔ̃kl]*) nm* great-uncle

grand-papa *(pl* **grands-papas)** [grɑ̃papa] *Suisse & Can (en langage enfantin)* grandpa, grandad

grand-peine [grɑ̃pɛn] **à grand-peine** *adv* with great difficulty

grand-père *(pl* **grands-pères)** [grɑ̃pɛr] *nm* grandfather; *Fam (vieil homme)* granddad

grand-route *(pl* **grand-routes)** [grɑ̃rut] *nf* main road

grand-rue *(pl* **grand-rues)** [grɑ̃ry] *nf* high street, main street

grands-parents [grɑ̃parɑ̃] *nmpl* grandparents

grand-tante *(pl* **grand-tantes** *ou* **grands-tantes)** [grɑ̃tɑ̃t] *nf* great-aunt

grand-voile *(pl* **grand-voiles** *ou* **grands-voiles)** [grɑ̃vwal] *nf* mainsail

grange [grɑ̃ʒ] *nf* barn

granit(e) [granit] *nm* granite

granule [granyl] *nm* granule

granulé [granyle] *nm* granule

granuleux, -euse [granylø, -øz] *adj* granular

graphe [graf] *nm* graph

graphie [grafi] *nf Ling* written form

graphique [grafik] **1** *adj* graphic
  2 *nm* diagram; *(sur un axe)* graph; *Ordinat* graphic; *Ordinat* **g. de gestion** management chart; **g. à** *ou* **en barres** bar chart

graphisme [grafism] *nm* **(a)** *(écriture)* handwriting **(b)** *Art (style)* style of drawing

graphiste [grafist] *nmf* graphic designer

graphite [grafit] *nm* graphite

graphologie [grafɔlɔʒi] *nf* graphology

graphologue [grafɔlɔg] *nmf* graphologist

grappe [grap] *nf (de raisin)* bunch; *(de fleurs, de gens)* cluster; *Vulg* **lâche-moi la g.!** piss off!

grappiller [grapije] *vt (renseignements)* to glean; *(argent)* to make on the side

grappin [grapɛ̃] *nm Naut* grappling hook *or* iron; *Fam Fig* **mettre le g. sur qn/qch** to get one's hands on sb/sth

gras, grasse [grɑ, grɑs] **1** *adj* (**a**) *(nourriture, tissu)* fatty (**b**) *(gros) (personne, animal)* fat; *(poulet)* plump (**c**) *(graisseux) (chiffon, cheveux, peau)* greasy (**d**) *(épais) (terre)* heavy, clayey; *(crayon)* soft lead; *(toux)* loose; *(rire)* throaty (**e**) *Typ* bold; **caractères g.** bold type (**f**) *Fig (bénéfices, récompense)* handsome; **faire la grasse matinée** to have a lie-in (**g**) *(graveleux) (histoire)* dirty, smutty
2 *adv* **manger g.** to eat fatty food
3 *nm* (**a**) *(de la jambe, du bras)* fleshy part (**b**) *(du jambon, de la viande)* fat (**c**) *Typ* bold; **en g.** in bold

gras-double (*pl* **gras-doubles**) [grɑdubl] *nm* tripe

grassement [grɑsmɑ̃] *adv (récompenser, payer)* handsomely

grasseyer [grɑseje] *vi* to pronounce one's r's at the back of the throat

grassouillet, -ette [grɑsujɛ, -ɛt] *adj* plump, chubby

gratifiant, -e [gratifjɑ̃, -ɑ̃t] *adj* rewarding, gratifying

gratification [gratifikasjɔ̃] *nf* (**a**) *(prime)* bonus (**b**) *(satisfaction)* gratification

gratifier [66] [gratifje] *vt* (**a**) **g. qn de qch** *(récompense)* to present sb with sth; *Ironique (sourire)* to bestow sth on sb (**b**) *(valoriser)* to gratify

gratin [gratɛ̃] *nm* (**a**) *(plat)* gratin *(baked dish with a topping of grated cheese and sometimes breadcrumbs)*; **au g.** au gratin; **chou-fleur au g.** cauliflower cheese; **g. dauphinois** = sliced potatoes baked with cream and browned on top (**b**) *Fam Fig* **le g.** *(le beau monde)* the upper crust

gratiné, -e [gratine] **1** *adj* (**a**) *(au gratin)* au gratin *(topped with grated cheese and sometimes breadcrumbs)* (**b**) *Fam Fig (addition)* huge; *(examen, problème)* tough
2 *nf* **gratinée** *Culin* onion soup au gratin

gratiner [gratine] **1** *vt* to brown
2 *vi* **faire g. qch** to brown sth

gratis [gratis] **1** *adv* free (of charge)
2 *adj* free

gratitude [gratityd] *nf* gratitude

gratos [gratos] *adj Fam* free (of charge)

gratouiller [gratuje] *vt Fam (démanger)* **ça (me) gratouille** it makes me itch

gratte [grat] *nf Can* snowplough

gratte-ciel [gratsjɛl] *nm inv* skyscraper

gratte-papier [gratpapje] *nm inv Péj* pen-pusher

gratter [grate] **1** *vt (avec les ongles)* to scratch; *(avec un objet)* to scrape; *(effacer) (mot, inscription)* to scratch out; *(tache)* to scrape off; *Fam* **ça me gratte** it makes me itch; **pull qui gratte** scratchy jumper; *Fig* **g. les fonds de tiroir** to scrape around for money
2 *vi* **g. à la porte** to tap lightly at the door
3 **se gratter** *vpr* to scratch oneself; **se g. jusqu'au sang** to scratch oneself raw; **se g. la tête/l'oreille** to scratch one's head/ear; *très Fam* **tu peux toujours te g.!** you can take a running jump!

gratteux, -euse [gratø, -øz] *Can* **1** *adj* stingy, mean
2 *nm,f* miser

grattoir [gratwar] *nm* scraper; *(de boîte d'allumettes)* striking surface

grattouiller [gratuje] = **gratouiller**

gratuit, -e [gratɥi, -it] *adj* (**a**) *(billet, entrée, échantillon)* free; **à titre g.** free of charge (**b**) *(acte, violence)* gratuitous

gratuité [gratɥite] *nf* (**a**) *(fait de ne pas payer)* **la g. de l'enseignement/des soins hospitaliers** free education/hospital care (**b**) *(d'un acte, de la violence)* gratuitousness

gratuitement [gratɥitmɑ̃] *adv* (**a**) *(sans payer)* free (of charge) (**b**) *(sans motif)* gratuitously

gravats [grava] *nmpl* rubble

grave [grav] **1** *adj* (**a**) *(sérieux, dramatique)* serious; **ce n'est pas g.** *(ça n'a pas d'importance)* it doesn't matter; **un accident qui a fait deux blessés graves** an accident in which two people were seriously injured (**b**) *(solennel) (visage, ton, expression)* grave, solemn (**c**) *(note, voix)* low, deep (**d**) *Fam (dérangé)* off one's rocker
2 *nm* **le g., les graves** *(notes)* the low notes; **les graves** *(sur une chaîne stéréo)* the bass
3 *adv Fam* in a bad way; **il me prend la tête g.** he really bugs me

graveleux, -euse [gravlø, -øz] *adj* (**a**) *(histoire, chanson)* smutty, dirty (**b**) *(terre)* gravelly

gravement [gravmɑ̃] *adv* (**a**) *(malade, blessé)* seriously (**b**) *(avec dignité)* gravely, solemnly

graver [grave] *vt (matériau, motif)* to engrave; *(sur bois)* to carve; *(disque)* to make; *Fig* **rester gravé dans la mémoire de qn** to be engraved on sb's memory

graveur, -euse [gravœr, -øz] **1** *nm,f* engraver; **g. sur bois** woodcarver
2 *nm Ordinat (de CD-ROM)* writer, burner

gravier [gravje] *nm* gravel

gravillon [gravijɔ̃] *nm (caillou)* piece of gravel; **du g., des gravillons** gravel; **gravillons** *(sur panneau)* loose chippings

gravir [gravir] *vt* to climb; *Fig* **g. les échelons** to climb the ladder

gravissime [gravisim] *adj* extremely serious

gravitation [gravitasjɔ̃] *nf* gravitation

gravité [gravite] *nf* (**a**) *Phys* gravity (**b**) *(solennité)* gravity (**c**) *(importance)* seriousness; **sans g.** *(blessure, problème)* minor

graviter [gravite] *vi* **g. autour de qch** to orbit sth; *Fig* **g. autour de qn** to hover around sb

gravure [gravyr] *nf* (**a**) *(action)* engraving; **g. sur bois** woodcarving (**b**) *(ouvrage)* engraving; **g. sur bois** woodcut; *Fig* **c'est une vraie g. de mode** she dresses like a fashion model

gré [gre] *nm* (**a**) *(goût)* **à mon/son g.** for my/his/her liking (**b**) *(volonté)* **contre son g.** against one's will; **de son propre g., de son plein g.** of one's own free will; **de bon g.** willingly, gladly; **bon g. mal g.** whether we/you/*etc* like it or not; **faites-le venir de g. ou de force** make him come whether he wants to or not; **au g. des flots** at the mercy of the waves; **au g. des événements/des circonstances** *(agir, changer d'avis)* according to how events turn out/to the circumstances (**c**) *Formel (gratitude)* **nous vous saurions g. de bien vouloir…** we would be grateful if you would kindly…

grec, grecque [grɛk] **1** *adj* Greek
2 *nm,f* **G.** Greek
3 *nm (langue)* Greek; **g. ancien/moderne** ancient/modern Greek
4 *nf* **grecque** (**a**) *Culin* **à la grecque** *(légumes)* = marinated in olive oil, lemon juice and herbs and served cold (**b**) *(motif)* Greek key pattern

Grèce [grɛs] *nf* **la G.** Greece

gredin, -e [grədɛ̃, -in] *nm,f Fam Vieilli* rascal

gréement [gremã] *nm* (**a**) Naut rigging (**b**) Can *(ustensiles)* gear, equipment

greffe¹ [grɛf] *nf* (**a**) *(de peau, de tissu)* graft; *(d'organe)* transplant; **g. du cœur/du rein** heart/kidney transplant (**b**) Bot *(action)* grafting; *(bouture)* graft

greffe² *nmJur* clerk of the court's office

greffé, -e [grɛfe] *nm,f Méd* **g. cardiaque** *ou* **du cœur** heart transplant patient

greffer [grefe] *vt (peau, tissu, bouture)* to graft; *(organe)* to transplant

greffier, -ère [grefje, -ɛr] *nm Jur* clerk (of the court)

greffon [grɛfɔ̃] *nm (de tissu, de peau)* graft; *(d'organe)* transplant; *(bouture)* graft

grégaire [gregɛr] *adj* gregarious; **l'instinct g.** the herd instinct

grège [grɛʒ] *adj (beige)* whitish-beige

grégorien, -enne [gregɔrjɛ̃, -ɛn] *adj* Gregorian

grêle¹ [grɛl] *adj (jambes, mains)* skinny; *(tige, silhouette)* slender; *(voix, son)* shrill

grêle² *nf aussi Fig* hail

grêlé, -e [grele] *adj (peau)* pockmarked

grêler [grele] *v impersonnel* to hail

grêlon [grɛlɔ̃] *nm* hailstone

grelot [grəlo] *nm* (small) bell

grelotter [grəlɔte] *vi* to shiver (**de** with)

Grenade [grənad] *nf (aux Antilles)* **la G.** Grenada

grenade [grənad] *nf* (**a**) *(projectile)* grenade; **g. lacrymogène** tear-gas grenade (**b**) *(fruit)* pomegranate

grenadine [grənadin] *nf* grenadine

grenaille [grənaj] *nf* (**a**) *(plombs)* shot (**b**) Belg *(revêtement)* grit, fine gravel; **grenailles errantes** *(sur panneau)* loose chippings

grenat [grəna] **1** *nm* garnet
2 *adj inv* dark red

grenier [grənje] *nm* (**a**) *(sous les combles)* attic (**b**) *(pour grain, fourrage)* granary; **g. à blé** wheat loft; **g. à foin** hayloft

grenouille [grənuj] *nf (animal)* frog; *Fig & Péj* **g. de bénitier** Bible basher

grenouillère [grənujɛr] *nf (pour bébé)* Babygro®

grès [grɛ] *nm* (**a**) *(pierre)* sandstone (**b**) *(céramique)* stoneware; **cruche en g.** stoneware jug

grésil [grezil, grezi] *nm* fine hail

grésillement [grezijmã] *nm (du feu, d'une radio)* crackling; *(de l'huile)* sizzling

grésiller [grezije] *vi (feu, radio)* to crackle; *(huile)* to sizzle

gressin [gresɛ̃] *nm* bread stick

grève¹ [grɛv] *nf (arrêt du travail)* strike; **se mettre en g.** to go out on strike, to strike; **être en g., faire g.** to be on strike; **g. des Postes** postal strike; **g. de la faim** hunger strike; **g. générale** general strike; **g. sauvage** wildcat strike; **g. sur le tas** sit-down strike; **g. tournante** staggered strike; **g. du zèle** work-to-rule, go-slow

grève² *nf (le long de la mer)* shore; *(d'un fleuve)* bank

grever [46] [grəve] *vt (pouvoir d'achat)* to restrict; *(budget)* to put a strain on

gréviste [grevist] *nmf* striker; **g. de la faim** hunger striker

gribouillage [gribujaʒ] *nm (écriture)* scribble, scrawl; *(dessin)* doodle

gribouille [gribuj] *nm Can (dispute)* quarrel, fight

gribouiller [gribuje] *vt & vi (écrire)* to scrawl, to scribble; *(dessiner)* to doodle

gribouillis [gribuji] = **gribouillage**

grief [grijɛf] *nm* grievance, ground for complaint; **faire** *ou* **tenir g. à qn de qch** to hold sth against sb

grièvement [grijɛvmã] *adv* seriously, badly

griffe [grif] *nf* (**a**) *(d'animal)* claw; **faire ses griffes** *(chat)* to sharpen its claws; *Fig* **montrer les griffes** to show one's claws; **arracher qn des griffes de qn** to snatch sb out of sb's clutches (**b**) *(sur un bijou)* claw (**c**) *(sur vêtements)* label; *Fig (style)* stamp (**d**) *Belg (rayure)* scratch

griffé, -e [grife] *adj (vêtement)* designer

griffer [grife] *vt* to scratch

griffon [grifɔ̃] *nm* (**a**) *(chien)* griffon (**b**) *(créature mythique)* griffin

griffonner [grifɔne] *vt & vi (écrire)* to scrawl, to scribble; *(dessiner)* to sketch quickly

griffure [grifyr] *nf* scratch

grignoter [griɲɔte] **1** *vt* to nibble; *Fig (libertés)* to erode; *(capital, économies)* to eat into
2 *vi* to nibble

gril [gril] *nm (de cuisine) Br* grill, *Am* broiler; **faire cuire qch sur le g.** to grill sth; *Fig* **être sur le g.** to be on tenterhooks

grillade [grijad] *nf (viande)* piece of grilled meat; *(poisson)* piece of grilled fish; **faire des grillades** to have a barbecue

grillage [grijaʒ] *nm (de fenêtre, de porte)* wire mesh; *(clôture)* wire netting

grillagé, -e [grijaʒe] *adj (fenêtre)* covered with wire mesh; *(jardin)* surrounded with wire netting

grille [grij] *nf* (**a**) *(à l'entrée d'un parc, d'un jardin)* gate; *(clôture basse)* railings (**b**) *(d'une cage, d'une fenêtre)* screen, netting; *Aut* **g. de radiateur** radiator grille (**c**) *(d'un évier, d'un égout)* grating, grate (**d**) *(tableau)* *(de mots croisés)* grid; **une g. de Loto** a Loto card, ≃ *Br* a National Lottery playslip; *Rad & TV* **g. des programmes** programme schedule; **g. des salaires** salary scale

grille-pain [grijpɛ̃] *nm inv* toaster

griller [grije] **1** *vt* (**a**) *(rôtir) (viande)* to grill; *(pain)* to toast; *(café, marrons)* to roast (**b**) *(brûler)* to scorch, to burn; *(ampoule, fusible)* to blow; *Fam (cigarette)* to smoke (**c**) *Fam (dépasser)* **g. un concurrent** to leave a competitor standing; **g. un feu rouge** to jump the lights (**d**) *Fam (discréditer)* **il est grillé** his game's up
2 *vi* (**a**) *(viande)* to grill; *(pain)* to toast; *(marrons)* to roast; *Fig* **g. d'impatience** to be burning with impatience (**b**) *(ampoule, fusible)* to blow
3 se griller *vpr* **se g. au soleil** to roast in the sun; *Fam* **se g. auprès de qn** to blot one's copybook with sb

grillon [grijɔ̃] *nm* cricket

grimaçant, -e [grimasã, -ãt] *adj* grimacing

grimace [grimas] *nf* grimace; **faire une g. (à qn)** to make *or* pull a face (at sb); **faire la g.** to make *or* pull a face; **faire une g. de douleur** to wince with pain

grimacer [16] [grimase] *vi* to make *or* pull a face; **g. de douleur** to wince with pain

grimer [grime] **1** *vt* to make up
2 se grimer *vpr* to put one's make-up on

grimpant, -e [grɛ̃pã, -ãt] *adj (plante)* climbing

grimpe [grɛ̃p] *nf Fam* rock-climbing; **faire de la g.** to go rock-climbing

grimpée [grɛ̃pe] *nf* (stiff) climb

grimper [grɛ̃pe] **1** *vi aussi Fig* to climb; **g. aux arbres** to climb trees; **ça grimpe** it's steep

2 *vt (montagne, escalier)* to climb; *Fig* **g. les échelons** to climb the ladder

grimpeur, -euse [grɛ̃pœr, -øz] *nm,f* climber

grinçant, -e [grɛ̃sɑ̃, -ɑ̃t] *adj (qui grince)* creaking; *Fig (caustique)* caustic

grincement [grɛ̃smɑ̃] *nm (d'une porte, de roues)* creaking; **grincements de dents** grinding of teeth; *Fig* gnashing of teeth

grincer [16] [grɛ̃se] *vi (porte, roues)* to creak; **g. des dents** to grind one's teeth

grincheux, -euse [grɛ̃ʃø, -øz] **1** *adj* grumpy
2 *nm,f* grumpy person

gringalet [grɛ̃galɛ] **1** *nm* weakling
2 *adj m* puny

griotte [grijɔt] *nf* morello (cherry)

grippal, -e, -aux, -ales [gripal, -o] *adj* **soulage les états grippaux** *(sur médicament)* relieves flu symptoms

grippe [grip] *nf* **(a)** *(maladie)* flu; **avoir la g.** to have (the) flu; **g. intestinale** gastric flu **(b)** **prendre qn/ qch en g.** to take a dislike to sb/sth

grippé, -e [gripe] *adj* **(a)** *(malade)* **être g.** to have (the) flu **(b)** *(moteur, mécanisme)* seized-up

grippe-sou (*pl* **grippe-sous** *ou* **grippe-sou**) [gripsu] *nm* skinflint, miser

gris, -e [gri, griz] **1** *adj* **(a)** *(couleur, temps)* grey; **il fait g. ce matin** it's a grey *or* dull morning; **g. ardoise** slate grey; **g. perle** pearl grey **(b)** *(ivre)* tipsy
2 *nm* **(a)** *(couleur)* grey; *Ordinat* **tons de g.** shades of grey; **s'habiller en g.** to wear grey **(b)** *(tabac)* shag

grisaille [grizaj] *nf (caractère morne)* dreariness

grisant, -e [grizɑ̃, -ɑ̃t] *adj (succès, atmosphère)* intoxicating; *(aventure, soirée)* exhilarating

grisâtre [grizɑtr] *adj* greyish

grisé [grize] *nm Ordinat* grey tone

griser [grize] **1** *vt* **(a)** *(enivrer)* to make tipsy; *Fig* to intoxicate **(b)** *Ordinat* to shade
2 se griser *vpr* **se g. de qch** *(air pur)* to get drunk on sth; *(paroles)* to get carried away by sth

grisonnant, -e [grizɔnɑ̃, -ɑ̃t] *adj (cheveux, personne)* greying; **avoir les tempes grisonnantes** to be greying at the temples

grisonner [grizɔne] *vi (cheveux, personne)* to go grey

grisou [grizu] *nm* firedamp; **coup de g.** firedamp explosion

grive [griv] *nf* thrush

grivois, -e [grivwa, -az] *adj* bawdy

grivoiserie [grivwazri] *nf (plaisanterie)* bawdy joke; *(histoire)* bawdy story; *(acte)* rude gesture

grizzli, grizzly [grizli] *nm* grizzly (bear)

Groenland [grɔɛnlɑ̃d] *nm* **le G.** Greenland

grog [grɔg] *nm* hot toddy

groggy [grɔgi] *adj inv Fam* groggy

grogne [grɔɲ] *nf Fam* discontent

grognement [grɔɲmɑ̃] *nm (d'un cochon)* grunt; *(d'un chien, d'un ours, d'une personne)* growl; **pousser des grognements** to grunt/to growl

grogner [grɔɲe] *vi* **(a)** *(gronder)* *(cochon)* to grunt; *(chien, personne)* to growl **(b)** *(protester)* to grumble

grognon [grɔɲɔ̃] *adj* grumpy

groin [grwɛ̃] *nm* snout

grol(l)e [grɔl] *nf très Fam* shoe

grommeler [42] [grɔmle] *vt & vi* to mutter

grommellements [grɔmɛlmɑ̃] *nmpl* muttering

grondement [grɔ̃dmɑ̃] *nm* **(a)** *(d'un chien)* growl **(b)** *(du tonnerre)* rumble; *(d'un torrent, des vagues, d'un moteur)* roar; *(des canons)* booming

gronder [grɔ̃de] **1** *vi* **(a)** *(chien)* to growl **(b)** *(tonnerre)* to rumble; *(torrent, vagues, moteur)* to roar; *(canons)* to boom; **la révolte/le mécontentement gronde** there are rumblings of rebellion/discontent
2 *vt (réprimander)* to scold, to tell off; **se faire g.** to get told off

groom [grum] *nm Br* page, *Am* bellhop

gros, grosse [gro, gros] **1** *adj* **(a)** *(corpulent)* big, fat **(b)** *(important, abondant)* big; *(rhume)* bad; *(dépenses, averse, mer)* heavy; *(somme)* large; *(faute)* serious; **g. buveur/mangeur** big drinker/eater; **avoir un g. chagrin** to be very upset; **la plus grosse partie de qch** the majority of sth; **un mensonge g. comme une maison** a whopper of a lie; *très Fam* **g. lard** big fat slob; *Fam* **g. nigaud** *ou* **bêta!** you great twit!; *Fam* **g. bonnet, grosse légume** big shot, bigwig **(c)** *(épais)* *(morceau, caractères)* big, large; *(toile)* coarse; *(pull, chaussettes, corde)* thick; *(chaussures)* strong, stout **(d)** *(peu subtil)* *(voix)* gruff; *(rire)* coarse; **c'est un peu g.!** that's a bit much!; **g. mot** swearword **(e)** *Mus* **grosse caisse** bass drum
2 *adv (beaucoup)* *(gagner, rapporter, risquer)* a lot; **je donnerais g. pour savoir qui a fait ça** I'd give a lot to know who did that
3 *nm,f* fat man, *f* fat woman
4 *nm* **(a)** *(partie la plus importante)* bulk; **le g. de** the majority of; **le plus g. est fait** the bulk of the work has been done **(b)** *Com* wholesale (trade); **faire du g.** to sell wholesale; **de g.** *(commerce, boucher)* wholesale **(c)** **en g.** *(en grosses lettres)* in big *or* large letters; *(approximativement)* roughly; *Com* wholesale

groseille [grozɛj] *nf* **g. (rouge)** redcurrant; **g. à maquereau** gooseberry

groseillier [grozeje] *nm* redcurrant bush; **g. à maquereau** gooseberry bush

grosse [gros] *voir* **gros**

grossesse [grosɛs] *nf* pregnancy; **g. extra-utérine** ectopic pregnancy; **g. nerveuse** phantom pregnancy; **g. à risque** high-risk pregnancy

grosseur [grosœr] *nf* **(a)** *(taille, volume)* size; **de la g. d'un œuf** the size of an egg **(b)** *Méd* lump

grossier, -ère [grosje, -ɛr] *adj* **(a)** *(impoli)* *(personne)* rude (**envers** to); *(langage, plaisanterie)* crude; **un g. personnage** an uncouth individual **(b)** *(peu raffiné)* *(nourriture, tissu)* coarse, rough; *(dessin)* crude, rough; *(goûts, traits du visage)* coarse; *(ruse)* crude **(c)** *(important)* *(erreur)* gross

grossièrement [grosjɛrmɑ̃] *adv* **(a)** *(de façon impolie)* rudely **(b)** *(sans raffinement)* crudely **(c)** *(approximativement)* roughly

grossièreté [grosjɛrte] *nf* **(a)** *(incorrection)* coarseness **(b)** *(parole grossière)* coarse remark; *(obscénité)* rude joke; **dire des grossièretés** to swear; **il aime raconter des grossièretés** he likes telling rude jokes **(c)** *(caractère rudimentaire)* *(d'un dessin)* crudeness; *(d'un tissu, des goûts)* coarseness

grossir [grosir] **1** *vi (personne, animal)* to put on weight, to get fatter; *(mer)* to get rough; *(rivière)* to swell; **g. de 2 kilos** *(personne)* to put on 2 kilos
2 *vt (sujet: loupe, microscope)* to magnify; *Fig (exagérer)* to exaggerate; **g. qn** *(sujet: vêtement)* to make

sb look fat; **g. les rangs de qch** to swell the ranks of sth

grossissant, -e [grosisã, -ãt] *adj* **miroir g.** distorting mirror

grossissement [grosismã] *nm* (**a**) *(augmentation de taille)* increase in size (**b**) *(pouvoir grossissant)* magnification

grossiste [grosist] *nmf* wholesaler

grosso modo [grosomɔdo] *adv* roughly; **g. c'est une comédie** broadly speaking it's a comedy

grotesque [grɔtɛsk] *adj* ludicrous, ridiculous

grotte [grɔt] *nf* cave; **g. artificielle** grotto

grouillant, -e [grujã, -ãt] *adj* swarming (**de** with)

grouiller [gruje] **1** *vi (se presser)* to swarm around; **g. de** to swarm with
2 **se grouiller** *vpr Fam* to get a move on

groupe [grup] *nm* (**a**) *(de gens, de choses)* group; *(de musiciens)* group, band; **en g.** in a group; **se mettre par groupes de trois** to get into *or* form groups of three; *Pol* **le G. des 8** the Group of Eight; **g. d'âge** age group; *Ordinat* **g. de discussion** discussion group; *Scol* **g. de niveau** stream; *Pol* **g. de pression** pressure group (**b**) *(industriel, de presse)* group; *(hospitalier, scolaire)* complex (**c**) *Gram* **g. verbal/nominal** verbal/nominal group (**d**) *Mil* **g. de combat** unit (**e**) *Méd* **g. sanguin** blood group (**f**) *Élec* **g. électrogène** generator

groupement [grupmã] *nm (association)* group; **g. d'achat** purchasing co-operative; **g. de consommateurs** consumer group

grouper [grupe] **1** *vt* to group (together); *(moyens, ressources)* to pool
2 **se grouper** *vpr (dans une association)* to form a group; *(dans un lieu)* to gather; **rester groupés** to keep together

groupie [grupi] *nf Fam* groupie

groupuscule [grupyskyl] *nm* small group

gruau [gryo] *nm* (**a**) **g. (d'avoine)** groats; **(farine de) g.** (fine) wheat flour (**b**) *Can Culin* porridge

grue [gry] *nf* (**a**) *(oiseau)* crane; **faire le pied de g.** to hang about (**b**) *(machine)* crane; *TV & Cin* cherry picker (**c**) *très Fam Vieilli (prostituée)* tart

gruger [45] [gryʒe] *vt (rouler)* to swindle

grumeau, -x [grymo] *nm (dans une sauce, une pâte)* lump

grumeleux, -euse [grymlø, -øz] *adj (sauce, pâte)* lumpy

gruyère [gryjɛr] *nm* Gruyère (cheese)

GSM [ʒeɛsɛm] *nm Tél (abrév* **global system for mobile communications**) (**a**) *(système)* GSM; **réseau G.** GSM network (**b**) *Belg (téléphone portable)* mobile phone

Guadeloupe [gwadlup] *nf* **la G.** Guadeloupe

guadeloupéen, -enne [gwadlupeɛ̃, -ɛn] **1** *adj* of Guadeloupe
2 *nm,f* **G.** person from Guadeloupe

Guatemala [gwatemala] *nm* **le G.** Guatemala

guatémaltèque [gwatemaltɛk] **1** *adj* Guatemalan
2 *nmf* **G.** Guatemalan

gué [ge] *nm* ford; **passer une rivière à g.** to ford a river

guéguerre [gegɛr] *nf Fam* squabble

guenilles [gɡnij] *nfpl* (old) rags; **en g.** in rags

guenon [gɡnɔ̃] *nf* female monkey

guépard [gepar] *nm* cheetah

guêpe [gɛp] *nf* wasp; *Fam* **pas folle, la g.!** she's nobody's fool!

guêpier [gepje] *nm* wasps' nest; *Fig (situation)* sticky situation; **se fourrer dans un g.** to get oneself into a sticky situation

guêpière [gepjɛr] *nf* basque

guère [gɛr] *adv* **ne... g.** *(pas beaucoup)* not much; *(pas longtemps)* hardly, scarcely; **il n'a g. d'argent/d'amis** he hasn't got much money/many friends; **il n'y a g. qu'elle qui soit au courant** she's about the only one who knows what's going on; **il ne mange g. que du pain** he eats hardly anything but bread; **il n'y a g. plus de six ans** just over six years ago; **et celui-là, comment le trouvez-vous? – g. mieux!** and what do you think of that one? – not much better!

guéri, -e [geri] *adj aussi Fig* cured (**de** of)

guéridon [geridɔ̃] *nm* pedestal table

guérilla [gerija] *nf* guerrilla warfare

guérillero [gerijero] *nm* guerrilla

guérir [gerir] **1** *vt (personne, maladie)* to cure; *Fig* **g. qn de qch** *(timidité, habitude)* to cure sb of sth
2 *vi (personne)* to get better, to recover; *(blessure)* to heal
3 **se guérir** *vpr (soi-même)* to cure oneself; *Fig* **se g. de qch** *(timidité, habitude)* to cure oneself of sth

guérison [gerizɔ̃] *nf (rétablissement)* recovery

guérissable [gerisabl] *adj* curable

guérisseur, -euse [gerisœr, -øz] **1** *nm,f* healer
2 *nm (d'une tribu)* medicine man

guérite [gerit] *nf Mil* sentry box

guerre [gɛr] *nf* (**a**) *(conflit)* war; *(technique)* warfare; **en temps de g.** in wartime; **être en g. (contre)** to be at war (with); **faire la g.** *(soldat)* to fight; **la drôle de g.** the phoney war; **la Grande G.** the Great War; **la Première/la Seconde G. mondiale** the First/Second World War, World War One/Two; **la g. de 14** the 1914–18 War; **la g. de 70** the Franco-Prussian War; **la g. d'Algérie** the Algerian War of Independence; **la g. de Cent Ans** the Hundred Years' War; **g. civile** civil war; **la g. de Corée** the Korean War; **g. éclair** blitzkrieg; **la g. d'Espagne** the Spanish Civil War; **la g. froide** the cold war; **la g. du Golfe** the Gulf War; **la g. d'Indochine** the first Indo-Chinese War *(1946–1954)*; **g. sainte** holy war; **la g. de Sécession** the American Civil War; **la g. du Việt Nam** the Vietnam War (**b**) *(locutions)* **elle fait la g. à son fils pour qu'il ne fume pas** she's fighting a running battle with her son about smoking; **faire la g. à qch** to wage war on sth; **partir en g. contre** to declare war on sth; **il est en g. ouverte contre sa hiérarchie** there's open war between him and his superiors; **à la g. comme à la g.** we'll/you'll/*etc* have to do the best we/you/*etc* can; **c'est de bonne g.** that's fair enough; **de g. lasse** for the sake of peace and quiet

guerrier, -ère [gɛrje, -ɛr] **1** *adj* warlike; *(chant)* war
2 *nm,f* warrior

guerroyer [32] [gɛrwaje] *vi Litt* to wage war (**contre** on)

guet [gɛ] *nm* **poste de g.** lookout post; **faire le g.** to be on the lookout

guet-apens *(pl* **guets-apens)** [gɛtapã] *nm (piège)* ambush; *Fig* trap; **tomber dans un g.** to be ambushed; *Fig* to fall into a trap

guêtre [gɛtr] *nf* gaiter; *Belg Fig* **il a la police à ses guêtres** the police are on his tail *or* hot on his heels

guetter [gete] *vt (occasion)* to watch out for; *(proie)* to lie in wait for; **il guette le facteur** he's on the lookout for the postman; **la dépression le guette** he's on the verge of a nervous breakdown

gueulante [gœlɑ̃t] *nf très Fam* **pousser une g.** to kick up a stink

gueulard, -e [gœlar, -ard] *très Fam* **1** *adj (personne)* loudmouthed, *Br* gobby; *(bébé)* screaming; *(couleur)* garish

2 *nm,f (personne)* loudmouth; *(bébé)* screaming kid

gueule [gœl] *nf* (**a**) *(d'un animal)* mouth; *Fig* **se jeter dans la g. du loup** to put one's head in the lion's mouth (**b**) *très Fam (bouche)* mouth; **ça emporte** *ou* **arrache la g.** it takes the roof of your mouth off; **une grande g.** *(personne)* a loudmouth; **(ferme) ta g.!** shut your mouth *or* face!, shut it!; **avoir la g. de bois** to have a hangover (**c**) *très Fam (visage)* mug, face; **avoir une sale g.** *(mine patibulaire)* to look shady; *(mauvaise mine)* to look rotten; **faire la g.** to sulk; **faire la g. à qn** to be in a huff with sb; **faire une g. d'enterrement** to look really pissed off; **se foutre de** *ou* **se payer la g. de qn** to take the piss out of sb; **(s')en prendre plein la g.** to get a right mouthful (of abuse) (**d**) *Fam (allure)* **avoir une drôle de g.** to look odd; **ce tableau a de la g.** that's some picture

gueuler [gœle] *très Fam* **1** *vi* to yell, to bawl; *(radio, télévision)* to blare; *(protester)* to kick up a fuss; **si je suis en retard, ça va g. à la maison** if I'm late, I'll get an earbashing when I get home

2 *vt* to bawl out, to yell out

gueuleton [gœltɔ̃] *nm Fam* blowout; **faire un g.** to have a blowout

gueux, gueuse [gø, gøz] *nm,f Vieilli (mendiant)* beggar

gueuze, gueuse [gøz] *nf* = type of strong double-fermented Belgian beer

gugusse [gygys] *nm Fam* twit; **faire le g.** to act the fool

gui [gi] *nm* mistletoe

guibol(l)e [gibɔl] *nf Fam (jambe)* pin, leg

guichet [giʃɛ] *nm* (**a**) *(de gare, de poste, de banque)* window; *(de théâtre)* box office; **on joue à guichets fermés** the performance is sold out; **g. automatique** *(de banque)* cash dispenser (**b**) *(de porte de prison)* hatch; *(de confessionnal)* grille (**c**) *(au cricket)* wicket

guichetier, -ère [giʃtje, -ɛr] *nm,f (de gare)* ticket clerk; *(de poste, de banque)* counter clerk

guide [gid] **1** *nm* (**a**) *(personne)* guide; **g. de haute montagne** mountain guide; **g.-interprète** bilingual tour guide (**b**) *(manuel)* guide (book); **g. de conversation** phrase book; **g. gastronomique** restaurant guide; **g. touristique** tourist guide (**c**) *Belg (indicateur de chemin de fer)* railway timetable; *(annuaire)* telephone directory

2 *nf (scout) Br* (Girl) Guide, *Am* Girl Scout

guider [gide] *vt* to guide; **se laisser g. par son intuition** to be guided by one's intuition

guidon [gidɔ̃] *nm* handlebars

guigne¹ [giɲ] *nf (cerise)* sweet cherry; *Fam* **se soucier de qn/qch comme d'une g.** not to give a fig about sb/sth

guigne² *nf Fam (malchance)* bad luck; **avoir la g.** to be out of luck

guigner [giɲe] *vt Fam (avoir des vues sur)* to have one's eye on

guignol [giɲɔl] *nm* (**a**) **G.** *(personnage)* ≃ Punch (**b**) *Péj (personne)* clown, joker; **faire le g.** to clown around (**c**) *(spectacle)* ≃ Punch and Judy show

Guillaume [gijom] *npr* **G. le Conquérant** William the Conqueror

guillemets [gijmɛ] *nmpl* inverted commas, quotation marks; **entre g.** in inverted commas, in quotation marks

guilleret, -ette [gijrɛ, -ɛt] *adj* jaunty, lively

guillotine [gijɔtin] *nf* guillotine

guillotiner [gijɔtine] *vt* to guillotine

guimauve [gimov] *nf (confiserie)* marshmallow; *Fig & Péj* **c'est de la g.** it's pure schmaltz

guimbarde [gɛ̃bard] *nf* (**a**) *Fam (vieille voiture)* jalopy (**b**) *(instrument de musique)* Jew's harp

guindé, -e [gɛ̃de] *adj (personne, air)* stiff; *(atmosphère)* strained; *(style)* stilted; *(réception)* posh

Guinée [gine] *nf* **la G.** Guinea; **la G. équatoriale** Equatorial Guinea

Guinée-Bissau [ginebiso] *nf* **la G.** Guinea-Bissau

guinéen, -enne [gineɛ̃, -ɛn] **1** *adj* Guinean

2 *nm,f* **G.** Guinean

guingois [gɛ̃gwa] **de guingois** *adv* askew, lopsided

guinguette [gɛ̃gɛt] *nf* riverside café

guirlande [girlɑ̃d] *nf (de fleurs)* garland; **g. lumineuse** string of lights; **g. de Noël** piece of tinsel; **g. de papier** paper chain

guise [giz] *nf* **faire qch à sa g.** to do sth as one likes; **n'en faire qu'à sa g.** to do just as one likes; **en g. de** by way of

guitare [gitar] *nf* guitar; **g. basse** bass guitar; **g. électrique** electric guitar; **g. sèche** acoustic guitar

guitariste [gitarist] *nmf* guitarist

gus [gys] *nm Fam* guy

gustatif, -ive [gystatif, -iv] *adj* **papilles gustatives** taste buds

guttural, -e, -aux, -ales [gytyral, -o] *adj* guttural

Guyana [gɥijana] *nm* **le G.** Guyana

guyanais, -e [gɥijanɛ, -ɛz] **1** *adj* Guianese

2 *nm,f* **G.** Guianese

Guyane [gɥijan] *nf* **la G.** Guiana; **la G. française** French Guiana

gym [ʒim] *nf Fam* gym

gymkhana [ʒimkana] *nm* rally

gymnase [ʒimnaz] *nm* (**a**) *(salle)* gymnasium (**b**) *Suisse (lycée) Br* ≃ secondary school, *Am* ≃ high school

gymnaste [ʒimnast] *nmf* gymnast

gymnastique [ʒimnastik] *nf* gymnastics; *Fig* **il faut faire toute une g. pour sortir de cette auto** you have to be a contortionist to get out of this car; **g. respiratoire** breathing exercises; **g. rythmique** eurhythmics *(singulier)*

gynécologie [ʒinekɔlɔʒi] *nf* gynaecology

gynécologique [ʒinekɔlɔʒik] *adj* gynaecological

gynécologue [ʒinekɔlɔg] *nmf* gynaecologist

gypse [ʒips] *nm* gypsum

gyrophare [ʒirofar] *nm* flashing light

H

H, h [aʃ] *nm inv* H, h; **h. aspiré** aspirate h; **h muet** mute h

*ha [ɑ] *exclam* ah!; **ha, ha!** *(rire)* ha-ha!

habile [abil] *adj* (**a**) *(personne)* skilful; *(manœuvre, film, roman)* clever; **être h. de ses mains** to be good with one's hands; **être h. en affaires** to be a good businessman/businesswoman (**b**) *Jur* **h. à faire qch** able to do sth

habilement [abilmɑ̃] *adv* skilfully

habileté [abilte] *nf* skill

habiliter [abilite] *vtJur* **h. qn à faire qch** to enable sb to do sth; **être habilité à faire qch** to be authorized to do sth

habillage [abijaʒ] *nm* (**a**) *(d'une personne)* dressing (**b**) **h. intérieur** *(d'une voiture)* trim (**c**) *TV & Rad* station identification

habillé, -e [abije] *adj* (**a**) *(vêtu)* dressed; **h. en femme/cosmonaute** dressed (up) as a woman/spaceman; **s'endormir tout h.** to go to sleep with one's clothes on (**b**) *(élégant) (personne, tenue)* smart; **soirée habillée** formal occasion

habillement [abijmɑ̃] *nm* (**a**) *(vêtements)* clothes (**b**) *(industrie)* clothing industry

habiller [abije] **1** *vt* (**a**) *(vêtir)* to dress; **h. qn en soldat/cow-boy** to dress sb up as a soldier/cowboy (**b**) *(fournir en vêtements)* to clothe (**c**) *(garnir)* to cover (**d**) *(aller à)* **un rien t'habille** you look good in anything

2 s'habiller *vpr* (**a**) *(se vêtir)* to get dressed, to dress; **elle s'habille n'importe comment** she wears any old thing; **comment vous habillez-vous pour la soirée?** what are you wearing to the party?; **s'h. en femme/cosmonaute** to dress up as a woman/spaceman (**b**) *(se fournir)* **elle s'habille chez Dior** she buys her clothes from Dior (**c**) *(élégamment)* to dress up

habilleur, -euse [abijœr, -øz] *nm,f* dresser

habit [abi] **1** *nm* (**a**) *(vêtement)* **habits** clothes; **habits du dimanche** Sunday best (**b**) *(tenue)* **h. (de soirée)** evening dress, tails; **l'h. vert** = the green coat worn by a member of the Académie française (**c**) *(religieux)* habit; *Prov* **l'h. ne fait pas le moine** appearances can be deceptive

2 *nm ou nf Can* suit; **h. de neige** snowsuit

habitable [abitabl] *adj* (in)habitable

habitacle [abitakl] *nm (d'un avion)* cockpit; *(d'une voiture)* passenger compartment

habitant, -e [abitɑ̃, -ɑ̃t] **1** *nm,f* (**a**) *(d'une ville)* inhabitant, resident; *(d'une maison)* occupant; **loger chez l'h.** *(en voyage)* to stay with local people (**b**) *Can (fermier)* small-scale farmer

2 *adj Can (nourriture, objets)* rustic; *Péj* **il est un peu h.** he's a bit of a country bumpkin

habitat [abita] *nm (d'un animal, d'une plante)* habitat; *(de personnes) (mode de peuplement)* settlement; *(conditions de logement)* housing conditions

habitation [abitasjɔ̃] *nf* (**a**) *(fait de résider)* living; **locaux à usage d'h.** premises for residential use (**b**) *(lieu)* dwelling; **h. à loyer modéré** *Br* ≃ council flat/house, *Am* ≃ public housing unit

habiter [abite] **1** *vt (maison, lieu)* to live in; *Fig (âme, personne)* to possess; **la région n'est pas habitée** the area is uninhabited

2 *vi* to live (**à/en** in)

habitude [abityd] *nf* (**a**) *(comportement répété)* habit; **avoir l'h.** *ou* **avoir pour h. de faire qch** to be in the habit of doing sth; **ça ne la gênera pas, elle a l'h.** that won't bother her, she's used to it; **avoir l'h. de qch** to be used to sth; **prendre l'h. de faire qch** to get into the habit of doing sth; **faire qch par h.** to do sth out of habit; **ce n'est pas dans mes habitudes** I don't make a habit of it; **d'h.** usually; **meilleur/plus tôt que d'h.** better/earlier than usual; **comme d'h.** as usual (**b**) **habitudes** *(coutumes)* customs

habitué, -e [abitɥe] *nm,f (d'une maison)* regular visitor; *(d'un restaurant, d'un magasin)* regular (customer)

habituel, -elle [abitɥɛl] *adj* usual, customary

habituellement [abitɥɛlmɑ̃] *adv* usually

habituer [abitɥe] **1** *vt* **h. qn à qch/à faire qch** to get sb used to sth/to doing sth; **être habitué à qn/à qch/à faire qch** to be used *or* accustomed to sb/to sth/to doing sth

2 s'habituer *vpr* **s'h. à qn/à qch/à faire qch** to get used *or* accustomed to sb/to sth/to doing sth; **tu finiras par t'h.** you'll get used to it in the end

*hâbleur, -euse [ɑblœr, -øz] *adj* boastful

*hache [aʃ] *nf* axe; *Fig* **enterrer la h. de guerre** to bury the hatchet

*haché, -e [aʃe] **1** *adj* (**a**) *(viande) Br* minced, *Am* ground; *(légumes, herbes)* chopped (**b**) *(style, phrases)* jerky

2 *nm Br* mince, *Am* ground meat

*hacher [aʃe] *vt* to chop (up); *(viande) (dans un hachoir) Br* to mince, *Am* to grind; **h. menu qch** to chop sth (up) finely; *Fig* **h. qn menu (comme chair à pâté)** to make mincemeat of sb; *Fig* **se faire h.** *(se faire battre)* to be massacred

*hachette [aʃɛt] *nf* hatchet

*hachis [aʃi] *nm* **h. d'herbes** chopped herbs; **h. Parmentier** ≃ cottage pie; **h. de viande** *Br* mince, *Am* ground meat

*hachisch [aʃiʃ] *nm* hashish

---

*hachoir [aʃwar] *nm* (**a**) *(couteau)* chopper (**b**) *(machine) Br* mincer, *Am* grinder

*hachurer [aʃyre] *vt* to hatch

*hachures [aʃyr] *nfpl* hatching

*hagard, -e [agar, -ard] *adj (visage)* haggard; *(expression, regard, yeux)* wild

*haie [ɛ] *nf* (**a**) *(clôture)* hedge; **h. vive** quickset hedge (**b**) *(en athlétisme)* hurdle; *(en équitation)* fence; **400 mètres haies** 400 metre hurdles (**c**) *(d'arbres, de pieux, de curieux)* line, row; **h. d'honneur** guard of honour; **faire une h. d'honneur** to form a guard of honour

*haillons [ajɔ̃] *nmpl (vêtements)* rags; **en h.** in rags (and tatters)

*haine [ɛn] *nf* hate, hatred; **sa h. de/pour** his hatred of/for; **être avoir la h.** *(être révolté)* to be full of rage; *(être furieux)* to be bloody furious

*haineux, -euse [ɛnø, -øz] *adj* full of hatred

*haïr [41] [air] **1** *vt* to hate
  2 se haïr *vpr (soi-même)* to hate oneself; *(l'un l'autre)* to hate each other

*hais *voir* **haïr**

*haïssable [aisabl] *adj* hateful

*hait *voir* **haïr**

Haïti [aiti] *n* Haiti

haïtien, -enne [aisjɛ̃, -ɛn] **1** *adj* Haitian
  2 *nm,f* **H.** Haitian

*halage [alaʒ] *nm* towing; **chemin de h.** towpath

*hâle [ɑl] *nm* (sun)tan

*hâlé, -e [ɑle] *adj* (sun)tanned

haleine [alɛn] *nf* breath; **avoir mauvaise h.** to have bad breath; **courir à perdre h.** to run until one is out of breath; **reprendre h.** to get one's breath (back); **tenir qn en h.** to keep sb in suspense; **hors d'h.** out of breath, breathless; **travail de longue h.** long job

*haler [ale] *vt* to tow

*haletant, -e [alətɑ̃, -ɑ̃t] *adj (coureur, malade, voix)* panting, gasping; *Fig (suspense)* unbearable; **respiration haletante** panting, gasping

*halètement [alɛtmɑ̃] *nm (d'un coureur, d'un malade)* panting, gasping

*haleter [39] [aləte] *vi (coureur, malade)* to pant, to gasp

*hall [ol] *nm (d'une maison)* entrance hall; *(d'un hôtel)* foyer, lobby; *(d'un aéroport)* lounge; **h. d'accueil** reception hall; **h. d'entrée** entrance hall; **h. de gare** station concourse; *Péj* **littérature/roman de h. de gare** trashy literature/novel

*halle [al] *nf* (**a**) *(marché)* (covered) market; **h. au poisson** fish market (**b**) *Suisse (bâtiment)* hall; **h. de fête** community centre

---

Les Halles

"Les Halles" refers to the central Paris wholesale food markets, dating from the Second Empire, and historically comparable to the markets at Covent Garden in London. Once a tourist attraction and also a source of traffic congestion, they were moved to the outskirts, mainly to Rungis, near Orly, in the 1960s. After much delay and controversy, the site (infamously known as the "trou des Halles") was redeveloped in the late 1970s with a Metro station and a modern shopping centre, the "Forum des Halles".

---

*hallebarde [albard] *nf* halberd; *Fam* **il pleut** *ou* **tombe des hallebardes** it's raining cats and dogs

hallucinant, -e [alysinɑ̃, -ɑ̃t] *adj (extraordinaire)* striking; *(incroyable)* incredible

hallucination [alysinasjɔ̃] *nf* hallucination; **avoir des hallucinations** *(malade, ivrogne)* to have hallucinations; *Fig (se tromper)* to see things

halluciner [alysine] *vi (avoir des hallucinations)* to hallucinate; *Fam Fig* **j'hallucine!** I don't believe it!

hallucinogène [alysinɔʒɛn] **1** *adj* hallucinogenic
  2 *nm* hallucinogen

*halo [alo] *nm aussi Fig* halo

halogène [alɔʒɛn] *nm Chim* halogen; **(lampe à) h.** halogen lamp

*halte [alt] *nf* (**a**) *(arrêt)* stop; **faire h.** to stop; **h.(-là)!** stop!; *Fig* **h.-là, je ne suis pas d'accord!** hold on, I don't agree!; **h. à l'armement!** stop the arms build-up! (**b**) *(lieu)* stopping place; *Rail* halt; *Can (point de vue)* viewing point, *Am* scenic overlook; *(aire de repos routière) Br* service area, *Am* rest area

*halte-garderie *(pl* **haltes-garderies)** [altəgardəri] *nf* crèche

haltère [altɛr] *nm* dumbbell; **faire des haltères** to do weightlifting

haltérophile [alterɔfil] *nmf* weightlifter

haltérophilie [alterɔfili] *nf* weightlifting

*hamac [amak] *nm* hammock

*Hambourg [ɑ̃bur] *n* Hamburg

*hamburger [ɑ̃burgœr] *nm* burger

*hameau, -x [amo] *nm* hamlet

hameçon [amsɔ̃] *nm* (fish-)hook; *Fig* **mordre à l'h.** to swallow the bait

*hammam [amam] *nm* Turkish baths

*hampe [ɑ̃p] *nf (d'un drapeau)* pole

*hamster [amstɛr] *nm* hamster

*hanche [ɑ̃ʃ] *nf* hip

*hand [ɑ̃d] *nm Fam* handball

*handball [ɑ̃dbal] *nm* handball

*handballeur, -euse [ɑ̃dbalœr, -øz] *nm,f* handball player

*handicap [ɑ̃dikap] *nm (physique, mental)* disability; *Sport & Fig* handicap; *Fig* **partir avec un h.** to start at a disadvantage

*handicapé, -e [ɑ̃dikape] **1** *adj* disabled
  2 *nm,f* disabled person; **les handicapés** the disabled; **h. mental** mentally handicapped person; **h. moteur** person with motor impairment

*handicaper [ɑ̃dikape] *vt (physiquement, mentalement)* to disable; *Fig* to handicap

*hangar [ɑ̃gar] *nm* shed; *(pour les trains, les bus)* depot; *(pour les avions)* hangar; **h. à bateaux** boathouse

*hanneton [antɔ̃] *nm* cockchafer; *Fam* **pas piqué des hannetons** *(difficile)* tough; *(bon, beau)* incredible

Hanoi [anɔj] *n* Hanoi

*Hanovre [anɔvr] *n* Hanover

*hanté, -e [ɑ̃te] *adj* haunted

*hanter [ɑ̃te] *vt (sujet: fantôme, pensée)* to haunt; *Fig (bars, musées)* to hang round

*hantise [ɑ̃tiz] *nf* obsession; **avoir la h. de qch** to really dread sth

*happer [ape] *vt (dans sa gueule, son bec)* to snap up; *(sujet: véhicule)* to hit

---

*hara-kiri [arakiri] *nm* hara-kiri; **(se) faire h.** to commit hara-kiri

*harangue [arɑ̃g] *nf* harangue

*haranguer [arɑ̃ge] *vt* to harangue

*haras [ara] *nm* stud farm

*harassant, -e [arasɑ̃, -ɑ̃t] *adj* exhausting

*harassé, -e [arase] *adj* exhausted

*harasser [arase] *vt* to exhaust

*harcèlement [arsɛlmɑ̃] *nm* harassment; **h. sexuel** sexual harassment

*harceler [39/42] [arsəle] *vt (importuner)* to harass; *(insister auprès de)* to pester; **h. qn de questions** to pester sb with questions; **être harcelé de remords/regrets** to be plagued by remorse/regrets

*harde [ard] *nf (de cerfs)* herd

*hardes [ard] *nfpl (haillons)* rags

*hardi, -e [ardi] *adj (audacieux, original)* bold; *(osé)* brazen

*hardiesse [ardjɛs] *nf (audace, originalité)* boldness; *(caractère osé)* brazenness

*hardiment [ardimɑ̃] *adv (avec audace)* boldly

*hard-rock [ardrɔk] *nm* hard rock

*harem [arɛm] *nm* harem

*hareng [arɑ̃] *nm* herring; **h. saur** smoked herring

*harfang [arfɑ̃] *nm Can* snowy owl

*hargne [arɲ] *nf* bad temper; **avec h.** bad-temperedly

*hargneux, -euse [arɲø, -øz] *adj (personne)* bad-tempered; **d'un ton h.** bad-temperedly

*haricot [ariko] *nm* (a) *(légume)* bean; **haricots en grains** dried beans; *Fam* **c'est la fin des haricots** we've/they've/*etc* had it now; *Fam* **courir sur le h. à qn** *Br* to get up sb's nose, *Am* to tee sb off; **h. beurre** butter bean; **h. blanc** haricot bean; **h. rouge** red kidney bean; **h. vert** green bean (b) *Culin* **h. de mouton** mutton stew

*harissa [arisa] *nf Culin* harissa *(hot pepper purée)*

*harki [arki] *nm* harki *(Algerian soldier who fought on the French side during the Franco-Algerian War)*

harmonica [armɔnika] *nm* harmonica, mouth organ

harmonie [armɔni] *nf* (a) *(accord) & Mus* harmony; **être en h. avec qch** to be in harmony with sth; **vivre en h.** to live in harmony (b) *(fanfare)* brass band

harmonieux, -euse [armɔnjø, -øz] *adj* harmonious

harmonique [armɔnik] *adj Mus* harmonic

harmonisation [armɔnizasjɔ̃] *nf* harmonization

harmoniser [armɔnize] **1** *vt* to harmonize (**avec** with) **2 s'harmoniser** *vpr* to go well together

harmonium [armɔnjɔm] *nm* harmonium

*harnachement [arnaʃmɑ̃] *nm* (a) *(action)* harnessing (b) *(harnais)* harness; *Fig (vêtements)* get-up

*harnacher [arnaʃe] *vt (cheval)* to harness; *Fig* **il fallait voir comment elle était harnachée** you should have seen the get-up she was wearing

*harnais [arnɛ] *nm* (a) *(de cheval)* harness (b) **h. de sécurité** *(d'alpiniste, d'élagueur)* safety harness

*haro [aro] *nm* **crier h. sur** to rail against; **crier h. sur le baudet** to scream for blood

*harpe [arp] *nf* harp

*harpie [arpi] *nf aussi Fig* harpy

*harpiste [arpist] *nmf* harpist

*harpon [arpɔ̃] *nm* harpoon; **pêche au h.** harpoon fishing

*harponner [arpɔne] *vt* (a) *(poisson)* to harpoon (b) *Fam (sujet: police)* to nab; *(sujet: importun)* to corner

*hasard [azar] *nm* (a) *(sort)* chance, luck; **le h. a voulu que je sois à l'étranger** as it happened I was abroad; **coup de h.** stroke of luck; **par un heureux h.** by a happy coincidence; **ne rien laisser au h.** to leave nothing to chance; **le h. fait bien les choses!** what a stroke of luck!; **au h.** *(choisir, répondre)* at random; *(marcher)* aimlessly; **au h. de ses voyages/lectures** in the course of her travels/reading; **à tout h.** *(par précaution)* just in case; *(pour voir)* on the off chance; **par h.** by accident, by chance; **si par h. vous le voyez** if you (should) happen to see him; **comme par h.** as if by chance (b) **hasards** *(dangers)* hazards

*hasarder [azarde] **1** *vt (opinion, remarque)* to venture **2 se hasarder** *vpr (dans l'obscurité, dans la jungle)* to venture; **se h. à faire qch** to risk doing sth

*hasardeux, -euse [azardø, -øz] *adj* risky, hazardous

*hasch [aʃ] *nm Fam* hash, pot

*haschisch [aʃiʃ] *nm* hashish

*hâte [ɑt] *nf* haste; **avoir h. de faire qch** *(avoir envie)* to be eager to do sth; **à la h.** hastily; **en h.** in a hurry, hurriedly

*hâter [ɑte] **1** *vt (accélérer)* to hasten; *(avancer)* to bring forward **2 se hâter** *vpr* to hurry; **se h. de faire qch** to hurry to do sth

*hâtif, -ive [ɑtif, -iv] *adj (trop rapide)* hasty

*hâtivement [ɑtivmɑ̃] *adv* hastily

*hauban [obɑ̃] *nm* (a) *Naut* shroud (b) *(d'un pont)* stay

*hausse [os] *nf* rise, increase (**de** in); **être en h.** to be rising; **être à la h.** *(marché)* to be rising; **jouer à la h.** *(en Bourse)* to speculate on a rising market

*haussement [osmɑ̃] *nm* **h. d'épaules** shrug; **avec un h. de sourcils** with raised eyebrows

*hausser [ose] **1** *vt* to raise; **h. la voix/les sourcils** to raise one's voice/eyebrows; **h. les épaules** to shrug (one's shoulders) **2 se hausser** *vpr* to raise oneself (up); **se h. sur la pointe des pieds** to stand on tiptoe

*haussier [osje] *adj m voir* **marché**

*haut, -e [o, ot] **1** *adj* (a) *(dans l'espace, en quantité, en intensité)* high; **une femme de haute taille** a tall woman; **un mur h. de 3 mètres** a 3-metre high wall (b) *(dans une hiérarchie)* high; **la haute couture** high fashion; **les hauts salaires** the highly paid; **un athlète de h. niveau** a top-ranking athlete; **une montre de haute précision** a high-precision timepiece; **de hauts faits** daring deeds (c) *(note)* high (d) *(dans le temps)* early; **le h. Moyen Âge** the early Middle Ages (e) **h. en couleur** *(récit, personnage)* colourful **2** *adv* (a) *(dans l'espace)* high; **comme il est dit plus h.** as mentioned above; **h. les mains!** hands up!; **gagner h. la main** to win hands down; **h. les cœurs!** cheer up! (b) *(dans une hiérarchie)* highly (c) *(dans la gamme)* high (d) *(fort)* **dire qch tout h.** to say sth out loud; **dire tout h. ce que tout le monde pense tout bas** to say what everyone is thinking (but is too afraid to say) (e) **en h.** at the top; *(à l'étage supérieur)* upstairs; **les gens d'en h.** the people above *or* upstairs; **en h. de** at the top of

---

The symbol * indicates that the initial **h** is aspirate and that hence there is no liaison, eg **les haricots** [leariko] and not [lezariko], or contraction in spelling, eg **la haine** and not **l'haine**.

3 nm (**a**) (hauteur) le mur fait 3 mètres de h. the wall is 3 metres high (**b**) (partie supérieure) top; Can (d'un immeuble) top floor; l'étagère du h. the top shelf; regarder qn de h. en bas to look sb up and down; connaître des hauts et des bas to have one's ups and downs (**c**) (corsage) top **4** nf Fam haute upper crust

*__hautain, -e__ [otɛ̃, -ɛn] adj haughty

*__hautbois__ [obwa] nm oboe

*__haut-commissaire__ (pl hauts-commissaires) [okɔmisɛr] nm high commissioner

*__haut-commissariat__ (pl hauts-commissariats) [okɔmisarja] nm high commission

*__haut-de-chausses__ (pl hauts-de-chausses) [odəʃos] nm breeches

*__haut-de-forme__ (pl hauts-de-forme) [odəfɔrm] nm top hat

*__haute-contre__ (pl hautes-contre) [otkɔ̃tr] nm counter tenor

*__haute-fidélité__ [otfidelite] nf hi-fi; chaîne h. hi-fi (system)

*__hautement__ [otmɑ̃] adv (très) highly

*__hauteur__ [otœr] nf (**a**) (dimension) height (**b**) (altitude) altitude; prendre de la h. to climb, to gain height; à la h. de qch (dans l'espace) level with sth; à la h. du Mans near Le Mans; Fig être ou se montrer à la h. de qch to be equal to or up to sth; être à la h. to be up to it; à h. des yeux at eye level; l'eau nous arrivait à h. des épaules the water came up to our shoulders; contribuer à h. de deux millions to contribute two million (**c**) (colline) hill; hauteurs heights; il y a de la neige sur les hauteurs there's snow on the higher slopes (**d**) (d'une note de musique) pitch

*__haut-fond__ (pl hauts-fonds) [ofɔ̃] nm shallow

*__haut-fourneau__ (pl hauts-fourneaux) [ofurno] nm blast furnace

*__haut-le-cœur__ [oləkœr] nm inv avoir un h. to retch; cette vision me donna un h. the sight of it made me feel sick

*__haut-parleur__ (pl haut-parleurs) [oparlœr] nm (loud)speaker

*__Havane__ [avan] **1** voir La Havane **2** nm h. Havana (cigar)

*__hâve__ [ɑv] adj (visage) gaunt; (joues) sunken

*__havre__ [ɑvr] nm Litt haven

Hawaii [awai] n Hawaii

hawaiien, -enne [awajɛ̃, -ɛn] **1** adj Hawaiian **2** nm,f H. Hawaiian

*__Haye__ [ɛ] voir La Haye

*__hayon__ [ajɔ̃] nm (d'une voiture) hatchback

HCR [aʃseer] nm (abrév Haut-Commissariat des Nations unies pour les réfugiés) UNHCR

*__hé__ [e] exclam (pour interpeller) hey!

hebdo [ɛbdo] nm Fam weekly; h. télé TV magazine programme

hebdomadaire [ɛbdɔmadɛr] adj & nm weekly

hébergement [ebɛrʒəmɑ̃] nm (d'un ami) putting up; (d'un sans-abri, d'un réfugié) taking in; (d'un fugitif) harbouring

héberger [45] [ebɛrʒe] vt (**a**) (ami) to put up; (sans-abri, réfugié) to take in; (fugitif) to harbour (**b**) (site Web) to host

hébété, -e [ebete] adj dazed

hébreu, -x [ebrø] **1** adj m Hebrew **2** nm (langue) Hebrew; Fam c'est de l'h. pour moi it's all Greek to me **3** nmpl les Hébreux the Hebrews

Hébrides [ebrid] nfpl les H. the Hebrides

HEC [aʃəse] nf (abrév Hautes études commerciales) = prestigious business school in Paris

hécatombe [ekatɔ̃b] nf (tuerie) slaughter, massacre; Fig ç'a été une h. cette année à l'examen! the exam results were disastrous this year!

hectare [ɛktar] nm hectare

hectogramme [ɛktɔgram] nm hectogram

hectolitre [ɛktɔlitr] nm hectolitre

hectomètre [ɛktɔmɛtr] nm hectometre

hédonisme [edɔnism] nm hedonism

hédoniste [edɔnist] **1** adj hedonistic **2** nmf hedonist

hégémonie [eʒemɔni] nf hegemony

*__hein__ [ɛ̃] exclam Fam (**a**) (pour faire répéter) eh?, what? (**b**) (pour insister) il fait beau aujourd'hui, h.? it's a nice day, isn't it?; ce n'est pas très bon, h.? it's not very good, is it?; ne refais jamais ça, h.! don't ever do that again, OK?; h. qu'il fait bien la cuisine! he does cook well, doesn't he?

*__hélas__ [elɑs] exclam unfortunately

*__héler__ [34] [ele] vt to hail

hélice [elis] nf (**a**) (d'un hélicoptère, d'un bateau) propeller (**b**) Math & Biol helix

hélico [eliko] nm Fam chopper

hélicoïdal, -e, -aux, -ales [elikɔidal, -o] adj helical

hélicoptère [elikɔptɛr] nm helicopter

héliomarin, -e [eljɔmarɛ̃, -in] adj Méd cure héliomarine = course of treatment based on sun and sea air; centre h. = seaside convalescent home where heliotherapy is used

héliothérapie [eljɔterapi] nf Méd heliotherapy

héliport [elipɔr] nm heliport

héliporté, -e [elipɔrte] adj (matériel) transported by helicopter; (troupes) airborne

hélium [eljɔm] nm helium

*__Helsinki__ [ɛlsinki] n Helsinki

helvétique [ɛlvetik] adj Swiss

hématie [emasi] nf Biol red blood corpuscle

hématologie [ematɔlɔʒi] nf Méd haematology

hématome [ematom] nm bruise, Spéc haematoma; se faire un h. to bruise oneself

hémicycle [emisikl] nm l'h. (de l'Assemblée nationale) the chamber

hémiplégie [emipleʒi] nf Méd hemiplegia

hémiplégique [emipleʒik] adj & nmf Méd hemiplegic

hémisphère [emisfɛr] nm hemisphere; l'h. Nord/Sud the Northern/Southern hemisphere

hémisphérique [emisferik] adj hemispheric(al)

hémistiche [emistiʃ] nm hemistich

hémoglobine [emɔglɔbin] nf haemoglobin; Fig (dans un film) blood and gore

hémophile [emɔfil] Méd **1** adj haemophilic **2** nm haemophiliac

hémophilie [emɔfili] nf Méd haemophilia

hémorragie [emɔraʒi] nf haemorrhage, bleeding; Fig (des capitaux) drain; h. interne internal bleeding

hémorroïdes [emɔrɔid] nfpl haemorrhoids, piles

The symbol * indicates that the initial **h** is aspirate and that hence there is no liaison, eg **les haricots** [leariko] and not [lezariko], or contraction in spelling, eg **la haine** and not **l'haine**.

*henné [ene] *nm* henna; **se faire un h.** to henna one's hair

*hennir [enir] *vi* to neigh, to whinny; *Fig (personne)* to bray

*hennissement [enismã] *nm* neigh, whinny; *Fig (d'une personne)* braying; **hennissements** neighing, whinnying; *Fig* braying

*hep [ɛp] *exclam* hey!

hépatique [epatik] *adj Méd* hepatic

hépatite [epatit] *nf* hepatitis; **h. A/B/C** hepatitis A/B/C

heptathlon [ɛptatlɔ̃] *nm* heptathlon

héraldique [eraldik] **1** *adj* heraldic
    2 *nf* heraldry

herbage [ɛrbaʒ] *nm* pasture

herbe [ɛrb] *nf* (**a**) *(de gazon)* grass; *Fig* **couper l'h. sous le pied à qn** to cut the ground from under sb's feet; **en h.** *(céréale)* green; *Fig (débutant)* budding (**b**) *(plante)* herb; **fines herbes** mixed herbs; **omelette/fromage aux fines herbes** omelette/cheese with herbs; **mauvaise h.** weed; **herbes folles** wild grass; *Can* **h. à la puce** poison ivy (**c**) *Fam (drogue)* grass

herbeux, -euse [ɛrbø, -øz] *adj* grassy

herbicide [ɛrbisid] *adj & nm* **(produit) h.** weedkiller

herbier [ɛrbje] *nm (collection)* herbarium

herbivore [ɛrbivɔr] *Zool* **1** *adj* herbivorous
    2 *nm* herbivore

herboriser [ɛrbɔrize] *vi* to collect plants

herboriste [ɛrbɔrist] *nmf* herbalist

herboristerie [ɛrbɔristəri] *nf (boutique)* herbalist's (shop); *(commerce)* herb trade

herbu, -e [ɛrby] *adj* grassy

herculéen, -enne [ɛrkyleɛ̃, -ɛn] *adj* Herculean

*hère [ɛr] *nm* **pauvre h.** poor creature

héréditaire [ereditɛr] *adj (maladie, titre)* hereditary; **c'est h.!** it runs in the family!

hérédité [eredite] *nf Biol* heredity; **avoir une lourde h.** to come from a family with a history of mental/physical illness

hérésie [erezi] *nf* heresy; *Fig* **c'est une h.** *ou* **de l'h.!** that's sacrilege!

hérétique [eretik] **1** *adj* heretical
    2 *nmf* heretic

*hérissé, -e [erise] *adj* (**a**) *(cheveux)* spiky; *(moustache)* bristly (**b**) *(garni)* **h. de** bristling with

*hérisser [erise] **1** *vt* (**a**) *(ses plumes)* to ruffle up; **h. ses poils** to bristle (**b**) *Fig (mettre en colère)* **h. qn** to get sb's back up
    2 se hérisser *vpr (animal)* to bristle; *(poils, cheveux)* to stand on end; *Fig (personne)* to bristle

*hérisson [erisɔ̃] *nm* hedgehog

héritage [eritaʒ] *nm* inheritance; *Fig (spirituel, intellectuel)* heritage; **faire un h.** to come into an inheritance

hériter [erite] **1** *vt* to inherit (**de** from)
    2 hériter de *vt ind (fortune, objet, qualité)* to inherit; **h. de qn** to receive an inheritance from sb; *Fig* **h. de qn/qch** *(se retrouver avec)* to be landed with sb/sth

héritier, -ère [eritje, -ɛr] *nm,f* heir, *f* heiress (**de** to)

hermaphrodite [ɛrmafrɔdit] *nm & adj* hermaphrodite

hermétique [ɛrmetik] *adj* (**a**) *(récipient)* hermetically sealed; *(joint) (à l'air)* airtight; *(à l'eau)* watertight (**b**)

Fig (abscons) abstruse; *(visage)* impenetrable; **être h. à qch** to be impervious to sth

hermétiquement [ɛrmetikmã] *adv* hermetically

hermine [ɛrmin] *nf (animal)* stoat; *(fourrure)* ermine

*hernie [ɛrni] *nf* hernia; **h. discale** slipped disc

héroïne¹ [erɔin] *nf (personnage)* heroine

héroïne² *nf (drogue)* heroin

héroïnomane [erɔinɔman] *nmf* heroin addict

héroïque [erɔik] *adj* heroic

héroïquement [erɔikmã] *adv* heroically

héroïsme [erɔism] *nm* heroism

*héron [erɔ̃] *nm* heron; **h. cendré** grey heron

*héros [ero] *nm* hero; **mourir en h.** to die a hero's death

herpès [ɛrpɛs] *nm Méd* herpes; *(buccal)* cold sore

*herse [ɛrs] *nf* (**a**) *(pour labourer)* harrow (**b**) *(de forteresse)* portcullis

hertz [ɛrts] *nm* hertz

hertzien, -enne [ɛrtsjɛ̃, -ɛn] *adj* Hertzian; *Rad* **réseau h.** radio relay system; *TV* **diffusion hertzienne** terrestrial broadcasting

hésitant, -e [ezitã, -ãt] *adj* hesitant

hésitation [ezitasjɔ̃] *nf* hesitation; **avoir une h.** to hesitate; **avec h.** hesitatingly; **sans h.** without hesitation

hésiter [ezite] *vi* to hesitate (**sur/entre** over/between); **je ne sais pas, j'hésite** I don't know, I can't make up my mind; **h. à faire qch** to hesitate to do sth

hétéro [etero] *adj & nmf Fam* straight, hetero

hétéroclite [eterɔklit] *adj* motley

hétérogène [eterɔʒɛn] *adj* mixed

hétérogénéité [eterɔʒeneite] *nf* heterogeneity

hétérosexualité [eterɔseksɥalite] *nf* heterosexuality

hétérosexuel, -elle [eterɔseksɥɛl] *adj & nm,f* heterosexual

*hêtre [ɛtr] *nm* beech

*heu [ø] *exclam* er

heure [œr] *nf* (**a**) *(soixante minutes)* hour; **5 euros l'h. ou de l'h.** 5 euros an hour; *Scol* **h. de cours** period; **heures supplémentaires** overtime; **faire des heures supplémentaires** to do overtime
    (**b**) *(de la journée)* time; **à h. fixe** at regular intervals; **à toute h.** at any time; **à toute h. du jour ou de la nuit** at any hour of the day or night; **quelle h. est-il?** what time is it?, what's the time?; **quelle h. avez-vous?** what time do you make it?; **il est deux heures** it's two o'clock; **cinq heures moins dix** ten to five; **trois heures vingt** twenty past three; **vingt heures quarante** eight forty pm; **à quelle h....?** what time...?; **ils devraient être arrivés à l'h. qu'il est** they ought to have arrived by now; **être à l'h.** *(personne)* to be on time; *(montre)* to be right; **mettre sa montre à l'h.** to set one's watch; **à la bonne h.!** marvellous!; **de bonne h.** early; **heures d'affluence** peak hours; **heures de bureau** office hours; **h. d'été** *Br* summer time, *Am* daylight-saving time; **heures d'ouverture** opening hours; **heures de pointe** rush hour
    (**c**) *(moment précis)* time; **l'h. du dîner/déjeuner** dinner/lunch time; **il est** *ou* **c'est l'h. (de faire qch)** it's time (to do sth); **son h. est venue** his time has come; **avoir son h. de gloire** to have one's moment of glory; **l'h. H** zero hour
    (**d**) *(moment présent)* **l'h. est grave** these are difficult times; **à l'h. actuelle** currently; **pour l'h.** for the present, for the time being; *Litt* **sur l'h.** at once

---

The symbol * indicates that the initial **h** is aspirate and that hence there is no liaison, eg **les haricots** [leariko] and not [lezariko], or contraction in spelling, eg **la haine** and not **l'haine**.

heureusement [œrøzmɑ̃] *adv* (**a**) *(par bonheur)* fortunately, luckily; **h. que j'étais là** it's a good thing I was there (**b**) *(avec succès)* successfully

heureux, -euse [œrø, -øz] **1** *adj* (**a**) *(satisfait)* happy (**de qch** with sth); **être h. en ménage** to be happily married; **vivre h.** to live happily; **être h. de faire qch** to be happy to do sth; **h. anniversaire!** happy birthday! (**b**) *(favorable) (dénouement)* successful; *(juste) (formule, style)* apt; *(choix)* happy (**c**) *(favorisé)* lucky; **par un h. concours de circonstances** by a lucky *or* fortunate coincidence; **h. au jeu/en amour** lucky at cards/in love; **s'estimer h. (de faire qch)** to consider oneself lucky (to do sth) (**d**) *(situation)* **c'est h. que vous soyez libre** it's a good thing you're free; *Fam* **encore h. (qu'il ait gardé le ticket de caisse)!** it's just as well (he held on to the receipt)!
    2 *nm,f* **si tu le lui donnes, tu vas faire un h.** if you give it to him, you'll make him a happy man; **faire des h.** to make some people happy

*heurt [œr] *nm (choc)* collision; *Fig (conflit)* clash; **sans heurts** smoothly, without a hitch

*heurter [œrte] **1** *vt* (**a**) *(cogner)* to hit; *(entrer en collision avec)* to collide with (**b**) *(choquer)* to offend
    2 *vi* (**a**) **h. contre qch** to hit sth (**b**) *Suisse* to knock; **h. à la porte** to knock at the door
    3 se heurter *vpr* (**a**) *(se cogner)* to collide (**à** *ou* **contre** with); *Fig* **se h. à qch** to meet with sth (**b**) *(couleurs, intérêts, personnes)* to clash

*heurtoir [œrtwar] *nm* (door) knocker

hévéa [evea] *nm* rubber tree

hexagonal, -e, -aux, -ales [ɛgzagɔnal, -o] *adj* hexagonal; *Fig* French

hexagone [ɛgzagɔn] *nm* hexagon; *Fig* **l'H.** France

hiatus [jatys] *nm* (**a**) *Ling & Anat* hiatus (**b**) *(décalage)* gap

hibernation [ibɛrnasjɔ̃] *nf* hibernation; *Méd* **h. artificielle** induced hypothermia

hiberner [ibɛrne] *vi* to hibernate

*hibou, -x [ibu] *nm* owl

*hic [ik] *nm inv Fam* **voilà le h.!** that's the snag!; **le h., c'est que...** the snag is...

*hideusement [idøzmɑ̃] *adv* hideously

*hideux, -euse [idø, -øz] *adj* hideous

hier [jɛr] *adv* yesterday; **h. matin/soir** yesterday morning/evening; **je m'en souviens comme si c'était h.** I remember it as if it were yesterday; **le journal d'h.** yesterday's paper; **cela ne date pas d'h.** that's nothing new; **je ne suis pas né d'h.** I wasn't born yesterday

*hiérarchie [jerarʃi] *nf* hierarchy

*hiérarchique [jerarʃik] *adj* hierarchical; **c'est mon supérieur h.** he's immediately above me in rank; **par la voie h.** through the official channels

*hiérarchisé, -e [jerarʃize] *adj* hierarchical

*hiéroglyphe [jerɔglif] *nm* hieroglyph

*hi-fi [ifi] *adj inv & nf inv* hi-fi

*hi-han [ĩɑ̃] *exclam* hee-haw!

hilarant, -e [ilarɑ̃, -ɑ̃t] *adj* hilarious

hilare [ilar] *adj* grinning

hilarité [ilarite] *nf* hilarity, mirth; **provoquer l'h. générale** to be the source of much hilarity

Himalaya [imalaja] *nm* **l'H.** the Himalayas

*hindi [indi] *nm* Hindi

hindou, -e [ɛ̃du] **1** *adj* Hindu
    2 *nm,f* **H.** Hindu

hindouisme [ɛ̃duism] *nm* Hinduism

*hippie [ipi] *adj & nmf* hippy

hippique [ipik] *adj* **concours h.** horse show; **sport h.** equestrianism

hippisme [ipism] *nm* horse riding; *(courses)* horse racing

hippocampe [ipɔkɑ̃p] *nm* sea horse

hippodrome [ipɔdrom] *nm Br* racecourse, *Am* racetrack

hippopotame [ipɔpɔtam] *nm* hippopotamus

*hippy [ipi] = **hippie**

hirondelle [irɔ̃dɛl] *nf* swallow; *Prov* **une h. ne fait pas le printemps** one swallow doesn't make a summer; **h. de mer** tern

hirsute [irsyt] *adj (personne)* hairy; *(barbe)* shaggy; *(cheveux)* unkempt

hispanique [ispanik] *adj* Hispanic

hispano-américain, -e (*mpl* **hispano-américains**, *fpl* **hispano-américaines**) [ispanɔamerikɛ̃, -ɛn] **1** *adj* Spanish-American
    2 *nm,f* **H.** Spanish-American, Hispanic

hispanophone [ispanɔfɔn] **1** *adj* Spanish-speaking
    2 *nmf* Spanish speaker

*hisser [ise] **1** *vt* to hoist (up); **ho! hisse!** heave-ho!
    2 se hisser *vpr* to heave oneself up; **se h. sur la pointe des pieds** to stand on tiptoe; *Fig* **se h. jusqu'au pouvoir** to rise to power

histogramme [istɔgram] *nm* bar chart, histogram

histoire [istwar] *nf* (**a**) *(discipline)* history; **l'h. de France** French history; **h. de l'art** history of art; **sachez, pour la petite h., que...** let me tell you in passing that...; *Fig* **c'est de l'h. ancienne** that's all ancient history
    (**b**) *(récit)* story; *Fam (mensonge)* fib, story; **raconter des histoires** *(mentir)* to tell fibs; **c'est toujours la même h.** it's always the same old story; **c'est une autre h.** it's quite a different matter; **une h. drôle** a joke, a funny story; **il m'est arrivé une drôle d'h.** a funny thing happened to me; **elle l'a dit, h. de dire quelque chose** she said it just for the sake of saying something; **c'est toute une h.** *(à raconter)* it's a long story; **c'est une h. de fous!** it's crazy!
    (**c**) *(problème)* fuss; **c'est toute une h. pour lui faire prendre son bain** it's quite a business getting her to have a bath; *Fam* **en voilà une h.!** what a fuss!, what a song and dance!; **faire des histoires** to make a fuss; **s'attirer des histoires** to get oneself into trouble; **faire des histoires à qn** to make trouble for sb; **au lit, et pas d'histoires!** off to bed now, and no fuss!

histologie [istɔlɔʒi] *nf* histology

historien, -enne [istɔrjɛ̃, -ɛn] *nm,f* historian

historique [istɔrik] **1** *adj (qui concerne l'histoire)* historical; *(important)* historic
    2 *nm* historical account; *Ordinat (de document)* log; **faire l'h. des événements** to give a chronological account of events

historiquement [istɔrikmɑ̃] *adv* historically

*hit-parade (*pl* **hit-parades**) [itparad] *nm* charts

HIV [aʃive] *nm* HIV

hiver [ivɛr] *nm* winter; **en h.** in winter; **une soirée d'h.** a winter's night; **h. nucléaire** nuclear winter

hivernal, -e, -aux, -ales [ivɛrnal, -o] *adj* winter; *(temps)* wintry

hiverner [ivɛrne] *vi* to overwinter

---

*__HLM__ [aʃɛlɛm] *nm ou nf* (*abrév* **habitation à loyer modéré**) *Br* ≃ block of council flats, *Am* ≃ low-rent apartment building

*__hochement__ [ɔʃmã] *nm* **h. de tête** (*négatif*) shake of the head; (*affirmatif*) nod

*__hocher__ [ɔʃe] *vt* **h. la tête** (*pour dire non*) to shake one's head; (*pour dire oui*) to nod

*__hochet__ [ɔʃɛ] *nm* (child's) rattle

*__hockey__ [ɔkɛ] *nm* (**a**) (*sport*) hockey; **h. sur gazon** *Br* hockey, *Am* field hockey; **h. sur glace** ice hockey, *Am* hockey (**b**) *Can* (*crosse*) ice hockey stick

*__holà__ [ɔla] **1** *exclam* (*pour appeler*) stop!, hold on!; **h., on se calme, hein!** hey, cool it, OK?
2 *nm* **mettre le h. à qch** to put a stop to sth

*__holding__ [ɔldiŋ] *nm* holding company

*__hold-up__ [ɔldœp] *nm inv Fam* hold-up

*__hollandais, -e__ [ɔlãdɛ, -ɛz] **1** *adj* Dutch
2 *nm,f* **H.** Dutchman, *f* Dutchwoman; **les H.** the Dutch
3 *nm* (*langue*) Dutch

*__Hollande__ [ɔlãd] *nf* **la H.** Holland

holocauste [ɔlokost] *nm* holocaust

hologramme [ɔlɔgram] *nm* hologram

holographie [ɔlɔgrafi] *nf* holography

*__homard__ [ɔmar] *nm* lobster

homélie [ɔmeli] *nf* homily

homéopathe [ɔmeɔpat] *nmf* homoeopath

homéopathie [ɔmeɔpati] *nf* homoeopathy

homéopathique [ɔmeɔpatik] *adj* homoeopathic; *Fig* **à dose h.** in small doses

Homère [ɔmɛr] *npr* Homer

homicide [ɔmisid] **1** *adj* homicidal
2 *nm* homicide; **h. involontaire** *ou* **par imprudence** manslaughter (*through negligence*)

hommage [ɔmaʒ] *nm* homage; **rendre h. à qn** to pay homage to sb; **hommages** respects; **mes hommages!** how do you do!

hommasse [ɔmas] *adj Péj* mannish

homme [ɔm] *nm* (**a**) (*adulte*) man; **rayon hommes** men's department; **parler à qn d'h. à h.** to have a man-to-man talk with sb; **il n'est pas h. à laisser passer cela** he's not the sort of man to let something like that happen; **comme un seul h.** in unison; *Fam* **mon h.** my man; **jeune h.** young man; **h. d'affaires** businessman; **h. de barre** helmsman; **h. de confiance** right-hand man; **h. d'église** man of the church; **h. d'équipage** crewman; **h. d'État** statesman; **h. à femmes** ladies' man; *Suisse* **h. du feu** *Br* fireman, *Am* fire fighter; **c'est l'h. fort du parti** he's the kingpin of the party; **h. de loi** lawyer; **h. de main** henchman; **h. du monde** gentleman; **h. de paille** figurehead; **h. de peine** labourer; **h. politique** politician; **h. à tout faire** handyman; **h. de troupe** private (**b**) (*genre humain*) **l'h.** man, mankind; **de mémoire d'h.** within living memory; **les premiers hommes** early man

homme-grenouille (*pl* **hommes-grenouilles**) [ɔmgrənuj] *nm* frogman

homme-orchestre (*pl* **hommes-orchestres**) [ɔmɔrkɛstr] *nm* one-man band

homme-sandwich (*pl* **hommes-sandwichs**) [ɔmsãdwitʃ] *nm* sandwich man

homo [ɔmo] *adj & nmf* gay

homogène [ɔmɔʒɛn] *adj* homogeneous

homogénéisation [ɔmɔʒeneizasjõ] *nf* homogenization

homogénéiser [ɔmɔʒeneize] *vt* to homogenize

homogénéité [ɔmɔʒeneite] *nf* homogeneity

homologue [ɔmɔlɔg] *nmf* counterpart, opposite number

homologuer [ɔmɔlɔge] *vt* (*accord, décision, record*) to ratify; (*testament*) to prove

homonyme [ɔmɔnim] **1** *nm* (*mot*) homonym
2 *nmf* (*personne*) namesake

homophobe [ɔmɔfɔb] **1** *adj* homophobic
2 *nmf* homophobe

homophobie [ɔmɔfɔbi] *nf* homophobia

homosexualité [ɔmɔsɛksɥalite] *nf* homosexuality

homosexuel, -elle [ɔmɔsɛksɥel] *adj & nm,f* homosexual

*__Honduras__ [õdyras] *nm* **le H.** Honduras

*__hondurien, -enne__ [õdyrjɛ̃, -ɛn] **1** *adj* Honduran
2 *nm,f* **H.** Honduran

*__Hongrie__ [õgri] *nf* **la H.** Hungary

*__hongrois, -e__ [õgrwa, -az] **1** *adj* Hungarian
2 *nm,f* **H.** Hungarian
3 *nm* (*langue*) Hungarian

honnête [ɔnɛt] *adj* (**a**) (*intègre*) (*personne, conduite*) honest; **peu h.** dishonest; **être h. avec soi-même** to be honest with oneself (**b**) (*décent*) (*vie, gens*) decent; (*intentions*) honourable (**c**) (*acceptable*) (*prix, note, résultat*) fair; **un repas/film h. sans plus** an OK meal/film, but nothing to write home about

honnêtement [ɔnɛtmã] *adv* (**a**) (*avec intégrité*) (*agir, se comporter*) honestly (**b**) (*franchement*) to be honest; **h., qu'est-ce que tu en penses?** be honest, what do you think? (**c**) (*raisonnablement*) decently

honnêteté [ɔnɛtte] *nf* (**a**) (*intégrité*) honesty (**b**) (*décence*) decency

honneur [ɔnœr] *nm* honour; **mettre un point d'h. à faire qch** to make it a point of honour to do sth; **déclarer/jurer sur l'h. que…** to state/swear on one's honour that…; **sauver l'h.** to save one's honour; **en tout bien tout h.** with no ulterior motive; **en l'h. de qn** in sb's honour; **à qui ai-je l'h.?** to whom have I the honour (of speaking)?; *Fam* **en quel h. devrais-je t'aider?** give me one good reason why I should help you!; **à vous l'h.** after you; **être à l'h.** to have pride of place; **c'est tout à ton h.** it's to your credit; **faire h. à qn/qch** to be a credit to sb/sth; **faire h. à un repas** to do justice to a meal; **rechercher les honneurs** to court fame

*__honnir__ [ɔnir] *vt* to disgrace

honorable [ɔnɔrabl] *adj* (**a**) (*profession, personne, intentions*) honourable (**b**) (*performance, résultat*) creditable, respectable

honorablement [ɔnɔrabləmã] *adv* (**a**) (*de façon respectable*) honourably (**b**) (*correctement*) **il s'en est h. tiré** he did quite creditably; **gagner h. sa vie** to earn a good living

honoraire [ɔnɔrɛr] **1** *adj* (*fonction, membre*) honorary
2 *nmpl* **honoraires** fee, fees

honorer [ɔnɔre] **1** *vt* (**a**) (*rendre hommage à*) to honour; **h. qn de sa confiance** to put one's trust in sb (**b**) (*acquitter*) (*facture, dette, engagements*) to honour (**c**) (*valoir de l'estime à*) (*personne, chose*) to be a credit to (**d**) *Hum* (*sexuellement*) to honour
2 **s'honorer** *vpr* **s'h. de qch/d'avoir fait qch** to pride oneself on sth/on having done sth

honorifique [ɔnɔrifik] *adj* honorary

*__honoris causa__ [ɔnɔriskoza] *adj* honoris causa; **docteur h.** doctor honoris causa, honorary doctor

---

The symbol * indicates that the initial **h** is aspirate and that hence there is no liaison, eg **les haricots** [leariko] and not [lezariko], or contraction in spelling, eg **la haine** and not **l'haine**.

*honte [ɔ̃t] *nf* (**a**) *(sentiment)* shame; **à ma grande h.** to my shame; **sans h.** shamelessly; **avoir h. (de)** to be ashamed (of); **avoir h. pour qn** to feel embarrassed for sb; **faire h. à qn** to make sb ashamed (**b**) *(chose scandaleuse)* disgrace; **c'est une h.!** it's a disgrace!

*honteux, -euse [ɔ̃tø, øz] *adj* (**a**) *(personne, air)* ashamed (**b**) *(conduite, acte)* shameful, disgraceful; **c'est h.!** it's a disgrace!

*hop [ɔp] *exclam* **allez h., saute!** go on, jump!; **allez h., tout le monde dehors!** come on, everybody out!; **h.-là!** oops(-a-daisy)!

hôpital, -aux [ɔpital, -o] *nm* hospital; *Prov* **c'est l'h. qui se moque de la charité** it's the pot calling the kettle black; **h. de campagne** field hospital; **h. de jour** day hospital; **h. militaire** military hospital; **h. psychiatrique** psychiatric hospital

*hoquet [ɔkɛ] *nm* hiccup; **avoir le h.** to have the hiccups

*hoqueter [42] [ɔkəte] *vi* to hiccup

horaire [ɔrɛr] **1** *adj* hourly
2 *nm* (**a**) *(des services de transport)* timetable, schedule; **être en retard sur l'h.** to be running late (**b**) *(emploi du temps)* timetable, schedule; **h. variable** *ou* **flexible** flexible hours, flexitime; **horaires de travail** working hours

*horde [ɔrd] *nf* horde

horizon [ɔrizɔ̃] *nm aussi Fig* horizon; **ouvrir de nouveaux horizons à qn** to open up new horizons *or* prospects to sb; **à l'h.** on the horizon; **à l'h. 2020** in the year 2020; **h. intellectuel** intellectual horizons

horizontal, -e, -aux, -ales [ɔrizɔ̃tal, -o] **1** *adj* horizontal
2 *nf* **horizontale** horizontal line; **à l'horizontale** horizontal

horizontalement [ɔrizɔ̃talmɑ̃] *adv* horizontally; *(dans les mots croisés)* across

horloge [ɔrlɔʒ] *nf* clock; **réglé comme une h.** as regular as clockwork; **h. biologique** biological clock; **l'h. parlante** the speaking clock; *Ordinat* **h. du système** system clock; *Ordinat* **h. en temps réel** real-time clock

horloger, -ère [ɔrlɔʒe, -ɛr] **1** *adj* **l'industrie horlogère** the watchmaking industry
2 *nm,f* watchmaker

horloger-bijoutier (*pl* **horlogers-bijoutiers**) [ɔrlɔʒebiʒutje] *nm* jeweller and watchmaker

horlogerie [ɔrlɔʒri] *nf (industrie)* watchmaking; *(magasin)* watchmaker's (shop); **l'h.** *(ouvrages)* clocks and watches

*hormis [ɔrmi] *prép Litt* except, save

hormonal, -e, -aux, -ales [ɔrmɔnal, -o] *adj* hormonal

hormone [ɔrmɔn] *nf* hormone

hormonothérapie [ɔrmɔnoterapi] *nf* hormone therapy

horodateur [ɔrɔdatœr] *nm* time and date stamping machine; *(de stationnement)* pay and display machine

horoscope [ɔrɔskɔp] *nm* horoscope

horreur [ɔrœr] *nf* (**a**) *(effroi)* horror (**b**) *(répugnance)* disgust; **avoir h. de qn/qch** to hate sb/sth; **avoir h. de faire qch** to hate doing sth; **avoir qn/qch en h.** to loathe sb/sth; **faire h. à qn** to disgust sb; *Fam* **c'est l'h.** it's the pits, it sucks (**c**) *(caractère horrible)* horror; **quelle h.!** how horrible!, how awful! (**d**) *(chose ou personne exécrable)* **être une h.** to be a nightmare (**e**)

horreurs *(atrocités)* horrors; *(calomnies)* horrible things

horrible [ɔribl] *adj* (**a**) *(effrayant)* horrible (**b**) *(très laid)* hideous

horriblement [ɔribləmɑ̃] *adv (brûlé, défiguré)* horribly; *(cher, froid)* terribly

horrifiant, -e [ɔrifjɑ̃, -ɑ̃t] *adj* horrifying

horrifier [66] [ɔrifje] *vt* to horrify

horripilant, -e [ɔripilɑ̃, -ɑ̃t] *adj* exasperating

horripiler [ɔripile] *vt* to exasperate

*hors [ɔr] *prép* (**a**) *(dehors)* **h. de** outside; **h. d'ici!** get out (of here)!; **ça l'a mise h. d'elle** that infuriated her; **être h. de soi** to be beside oneself (**b**) *Litt (sauf)* except, save (**c**) *(en conjonction avec un nom)* **h. antenne** off-air; **h. d'atteinte** out of reach; **h. de combat** out of action; **h. jeu** offside; **mettre qn/qch h. la loi** to outlaw sb/sth; **h. pair** unrivalled; **h. piste** off piste; **h. de prix** extortionate; **h. de question** out of the question; **h. saison** off-season; **numéro h. série** special issue; **h. service** out of order; **h. sujet** not relevant; **h. taxe** net of tax; *(exempt de taxe)* tax-free; **boutique h. taxe** duty-free shop; **h. d'usage** *(vêtement)* worn out; *(machine)* beyond repair

*hors-bord [ɔrbɔr] *nm inv* speedboat; **moteur h.** outboard motor

*hors-d'œuvre [ɔrdœvr] *nm inv* (**a**) *(plat)* hors d'œuvre, starter (**b**) *Fig* starter, taster

*hors-jeu [ɔrʒø] *nm inv* offside

*hors-la-loi [ɔrlalwa] *nm inv* outlaw

*hors-piste [ɔrpist] *nm inv (en ski)* off-piste skiing; **faire du h.** to ski off piste

hortensia [ɔrtɑ̃sja] *nm* hydrangea

horticole [ɔrtikɔl] *adj* horticultural; **exposition h.** flower show

horticulteur [ɔrtikyltœr] *nm* nurseryman

horticulture [ɔrtikyltyr] *nf* horticulture

hospice [ɔspis] *nm* (**a**) *(asile)* home (**b**) *(monastère)* hospice

hospitalier¹, -ère [ɔspitalje, -ɛr] *adj (accueillant)* hospitable

hospitalier², -ère *adj (relatif aux hôpitaux)* hospital; **en milieu h.** in a hospital environment; **personnel h.** hospital staff

hospitalisation [ɔspitalizasjɔ̃] *nf* hospitalization; **h. à domicile** home care

hospitaliser [ɔspitalize] *vt* to hospitalize; **faire h. qn** to have sb hospitalized

hospitalité [ɔspitalite] *nf* hospitality

hospitalo-universitaire [ɔspitaloyniversiter] *adj* **centre h.** teaching hospital

hostie [ɔsti] *nf Rel* host

hostile [ɔstil] *adj* hostile (**à** towards)

hostilité [ɔstilite] *nf* hostility (**contre** *ou* **envers** towards); **hostilités** hostilities; **reprendre les hostilités** to reopen *or* to resume hostilities

hosto [ɔsto] *nm Fam* hospital

hôte [ot] *nm* (**a**) *(personne qui invite)* host (**b**) *(invité)* guest, visitor; **h. payant** paying guest (**c**) *Biol* host

hôtel [otɛl] *nm* (**a**) *(pour l'hébergement)* hotel; **h. de passe** = hotel used as a brothel (**b**) *(bâtiment)* **h. des impôts** tax office; **l'h. de la Monnaie** ≃ the Royal Mint; **h. (particulier)** mansion, town house; **h. des ventes** saleroom; **h. de ville** town hall

---

hôtelier, -ère [otəlje, -ɛr] **1** *adj* l'industrie hôtelière the hotel industry **2** *nm,f* hotel keeper, hotelier

hôtellerie [otɛlri] *nf* (a) *(hôtel)* inn (b) *(secteur)* l'h. the hotel industry

hôtel-restaurant *(pl* hôtels-restaurants) [otɛlrɛstɔrã] *nm* hotel and restaurant

hôtesse [otɛs] *nf* (a) *(personne qui reçoit)* hostess (b) *(dans un avion)* hostess, stewardess; **h. d'accueil** receptionist; **h. de l'air** air hostess

*****hotte** [ɔt] *nf* (a) *(panier)* basket; **la h. du Père Noël** Santa Claus's sack (b) *(pour la ventilation)* hood; **h. aspirante** extractor hood

*****hou** [u] *exclam* boo!; **h.! la vilaine!** tut-tut, you naughty girl!

*****houblon** [ublɔ̃] *nm* hops

*****houe** [u] *nf* hoe

*****houille** [uj] *nf* coal; **h. blanche** hydroelectric power

*****houiller, -ère** [uje, -ɛr] **1** *adj (terrain)* rich in coal; **bassin h.** coalfield; **production houillère** coal output **2** *nf* **houillère** coalmine, colliery

*****houle** [ul] *nf* swell

*****houlette** [ulɛt] *nf* (a) *(de berger)* crook; *Fig* **sous la h. de** under the leadership of (b) *(petite bêche)* trowel

*****houleux, -euse** [ulø, -øz] *adj (mer)* choppy; *Fig (réunion)* stormy

houmous [umus] *nm Culin* houmous, hummus

*****houppette** [upɛt] *nf (de plumes)* small tuft; *(de cheveux)* quiff; *(à poudre)* powder puff

*****hourra** [ura] **1** *exclam* hurrah!; **hip, hip, hip, h.!** hip, hip, hooray! **2** *nm* hurrah; **pousser des hourras** to cheer

*****houspiller** [uspije] *vt* to tell off

*****housse** [us] *nf* cover; *(contre la poussière)* dust sheet; *(dans une voiture)* seat cover

*****houx** [u] *nm* holly

hovercraft [ɔvɛrkraft] *nm* hovercraft

*****HS** [aʃɛs] *adj Fam (abrév* **hors service***) (personne)* bushed, *Br* knackered, *Am* beat

HT (a) *(abrév* **haute tension***)* HT (b) *(abrév* **hors taxe***)* exclusive of tax

*****HTML** [aʃteemɛl] *nm Ordinat (abrév* **HyperText Markup Language***)* HTML

*****hublot** [yblo] *nm (de bateau)* porthole; *(dans un avion, une machine à laver)* window

*****huche** [yʃ] *nf* chest; **h. à pain** bread bin

*****hue** [y, hy] *exclam (à un cheval)* gee up!; **tirer à h. et à dia** to pull in opposite directions

*****huées** [ɥe] *nfpl* booing; **quitter la scène sous les h.** to be booed off the stage

*****huer** [ɥe] **1** *vt* to boo **2** *vi (hibou, chouette)* to hoot

huile [ɥil] *nf* (a) *(liquide)* oil; *Fig* **jeter de l'h. sur le feu** to add fuel to the fire; **une mer d'h.** a glassy sea; **h. d'amandes douces** almond oil; **h. d'arachide** groundnut oil; *Can* **h. de chauffage** heating oil; *Fig* **h. de coude** elbow grease; **h. essentielle** essential oil; **h. de foie de morue** cod liver oil; **h. de moteur** engine oil; **h. d'olive** olive oil; **h. de ricin** castor oil; **h. solaire** suntan oil; **h. de tournesol** sunflower oil; **h. végétale** vegetable oil; **h. de vidange** sump oil (b) *(peinture)* oil painting (c) *Fam (personne importante)* big shot

huiler [ɥile] *vt* to oil; *Fig* **une mécanique bien huilée** a well-oiled machine

huileux, -euse [ɥilø, -øz] *adj* oily

huis [ɥi] *nm* **à h. clos** behind closed doors; *Jur* in camera

huissier [ɥisje] *nm* (a) *Jur* bailiff (b) *(portier)* usher

*****huit** [ɥit] *adj & nm inv* eight; **h. jours** a week; **aujourd'hui/demain en h.** a week today/tomorrow; **donner ses h. jours à qn** to give sb a week's notice; *voir aussi* **trois**

*****huitaine** [ɥitɛn] *nf* (a) *(environ huit)* (about) eight (b) *(semaine)* week; **sous h.** within a week; **dans une h. de jours** in a week or so

*****huitante** [ɥitãt] *adj inv Suisse* eighty

*****huitième** [ɥitjɛm] *adj, nm & nmf* eighth; *voir aussi* **cinquième**

huître [ɥitr] *nf* oyster; **h. perlière** pearl oyster

*****hulotte** [ylɔt] *nf* tawny owl

*****hululement** [ylylmã] *nm* hoot; **des hululements** hooting

*****hululer** [ylyle] *vi* to hoot

*****hum** [œm] *exclam* hm!

humain, -e [ymɛ̃, -ɛn] **1** *adj* (a) *(relatif à l'homme)* human; **c'est h.** it's only human; **des pertes humaines énormes** a huge loss of life (b) *(compatissant)* humane **2** *nm* human (being)

humainement [ymɛnmã] *adv* (a) *(relatif à l'homme)* in human terms; **h. possible** humanly possible (b) *(avec bonté)* humanely

humaniser [ymanize] *vt* to make more human

humanisme [ymanism] *nm* humanism

humaniste [ymanist] *adj & nmf* humanist

humanitaire [ymanitɛr] *adj* humanitarian; **organisation h.** relief *or* aid organization

humanité [ymanite] *nf* (a) *(genre humain)* humanity, mankind (b) *(bonté)* humanity; **avec h.** humanely

humanoïde [ymanɔid] *nm* humanoid

humble [œ̃bl] *adj* humble; **à mon h. avis** in my humble opinion

humblement [œ̃bləmã] *adv* humbly

humecter [ymɛkte] *vt* to moisten

*****humer** [yme] *vt (air)* to breathe in; *(parfum)* to smell

humérus [ymerys] *nm* humerus

humeur [ymœr] *nf* (a) *(disposition)* mood; **être de bonne/mauvaise h.** to be in a good/bad mood; **mettre qn de bonne/mauvaise h.** to put sb in a good/bad mood; **être d'une h. massacrante** to be in a foul mood; **plein de bonne h.** good-humoured; **être/ne pas être d'h. à faire qch** to be/not be in the mood to do sth (b) *(caractère)* temper, temperament; **d'h. égale** even-tempered; **d'humeur inégale** *ou* **changeante** temperamental (c) *Litt (mauvaise humeur)* bad mood; **geste d'h.** ill-tempered gesture; **avec h.** irritably (d) *Anat* **h. aqueuse** aqueous humour; **h. vitrée** vitreous humour

humide [ymid] *adj (maison, linge)* damp, wet; *(climat)* humid; **les yeux humides (de larmes)** eyes moist with tears

humidificateur [ymidifikatœr] *nm* humidifier

humidifier [66] [ymidifje] *vt* to dampen; *(air)* to humidify

humidité [ymidite] *nf (d'une maison)* dampness; *(du climat, d'une région)* humidity; **il faut beaucoup d'h. à cette plante** this plant needs a lot of moisture; **craint l'h.** *(sur un paquet)* store in a dry place

humiliant, -e [ymiljã, -ãt] *adj* humiliating

humiliation [ymiljasjɔ̃] *nf* humiliation

The symbol * indicates that the initial **h** is aspirate and that hence there is no liaison, eg **les haricots** [leariko] and not [lezariko], or contraction in spelling, eg **la haine** and not **l'haine**.

humilier [66] [ymilje] **1** *vt* to humiliate
 2 s'humilier *vpr* to humiliate oneself
humilité [ymilite] *nf* humility
humoriste [ymɔrist] *nmf* humorist
humoristique [ymɔristik] *adj* humorous; **dessin h.** cartoon
humour [ymur] *nm* humour; **avoir (le sens) de l'h.** to have a (good) sense of humour; **h. noir** black humour
***huppe¹** [yp] *nf (oiseau)* hoopoe
***huppe²** *nf (d'un oiseau)* crest
***huppé, -e** [ype] *adj* (**a**) *Fam (gens, endroit, quartier)* smart (**b**) *(oiseau)* crested
***hurlement** [yrləmã] *nm (d'un loup, d'un chien)* howl; *(d'une personne)* scream; *(du vent)* roaring; *(d'une sirène)* wail
***hurler** [yrle] **1** *vi (loup, chien)* to howl; *(personne)* to howl, to scream; *(vent, tempête)* to roar; *(sirène)* to wail; *(radio)* to blare; **j'ai dû h. pour qu'il m'entende** I had to shout for him to hear me; **h. de douleur/rage** to howl with pain/rage; **c'est à h. de rire** it's screamingly funny; **h. à la lune** to bay at the moon; **il faut h. avec les loups** if you can't beat them join them
 2 *vt (insultes, instructions)* to yell
hurluberlu [yrlybɛrly] *nm* oddball
***Huron** [yrɔ̃] *n voir* **lac**
***husky** *(pl* **huskies)** [œski] *nm* husky
***hussard** [ysar] *nm* hussar
***hussarde** [ysard] *nf* **à la h.** roughly
***hutte** [yt] *nf* hut
hybride [ibrid] *adj & nm* hybrid
hydratant, -e [idratã, -ãt] *adj* moisturizing
hydratation [idratasjɔ̃] *nf (de la peau)* moisturizing
hydrate [idrat] *nm* hydrate; **h. de carbone** carbohydrate
hydrater [idrate] **1** *vt (peau)* to moisturize; *(organisme)* to hydrate
 2 s'hydrater *vpr* to take in water
hydraulique [idrolik] **1** *adj* hydraulic
 2 *nf (science)* hydraulics *(singulier)*
hydravion [idravjɔ̃] *nm* seaplane
hydre [idr] *nf* hydra
hydrocarbure [idrɔkarbyr] *nm* hydrocarbon
hydrocution [idrɔkysjɔ̃] *nf* = loss of consciousness caused by immersion in cold water
hydroélectricité [idrɔelɛktrisite] *nf* hydroelectricity
hydroélectrique [idrɔelɛktrik] *adj* hydroelectric
hydrogène [idrɔʒɛn] *nm* hydrogen
hydroglisseur [idrɔglisœr] *nm* jetfoil
hydrographie [idrɔgrafi] *nf* hydrography
hydrolyse [idrɔliz] *nf* hydrolysis
hydromel [idrɔmɛl] *nm* mead
hydrophile [idrɔfil] *adj (coton)* absorbent
hydrothérapie [idrɔterapi] *nf* hydrotherapy
hydroxyde [idrɔksid] *nm* hydroxide
hyène [jɛn] *nf* hyena
Hygiaphone® [iʒjafɔn] *nm (au guichet)* grille; **parlez dans l'H.** speak into the grille
hygiène [iʒjɛn] *nf* hygiene; **par mesure d'h.** for hygiene reasons; **h. alimentaire** diet; **h. corporelle** personal hygiene; **h. mentale** mental health; **avoir une bonne h. de vie** to live healthily

hygiénique [iʒjenik] *adj* (**a**) *(propre)* hygienic; **peu h.** unhygienic (**b**) *(bon pour la santé)* healthy; **une promenade h.** a bracing walk
hymne [imn] *nm* hymn; **h. national** national anthem
hyper [ipɛr] *nm Fam (abrév* **hypermarché**) hypermarket, superstore
hyper- [ipɛr] *préf Fam* very, *Br* dead, *Am* real
hyperactif, -ive [ipɛraktif, -iv] *adj* hyperactive
hyperbole [ipɛrbɔl] *nf* (**a**) *(figure de style)* hyperbole (**b**) *Math* hyperbola
hyperbolique [ipɛrbɔlik] *adj* hyperbolic
hyperglycémie [ipɛrglisemi] *nf* hyperglycemia
hyperlien [ipɛrljɛ̃] *nm Ordinat* hyperlink
hypermarché [ipɛrmarʃe] *nm* hypermarket, superstore
hypermétrope [ipɛrmetrɔp] *adj* longsighted
hypernerveux, -euse [ipɛrnɛrvø, -øz] **1** *adj* highly-strung
 2 *nm,f* highly-strung person
hyperréaliste [ipɛrealist] *adj* hyperrealistic
hypersensibilité [ipɛrsãsibilite] *nf* hypersensitivity
hypersensible [ipɛrsãsibl] *adj* hypersensitive
hypertendu, -e [ipɛrtãdy] *adj* **être h.** to have high blood pressure
hypertension [ipɛrtãsjɔ̃] *nf* high blood pressure, *Spéc* hypertension
hypertexte [ipɛrtɛkst] *nm Ordinat* hypertext
hypertrophie [ipɛrtrɔfi] *nf* enlargement, *Spéc* hypertrophy
hypertrophié, -e [ipɛrtrɔfje] *adj* enlarged, *Spéc* hypertrophied
hypnose [ipnoz] *nf* hypnosis; **sous h.** under hypnosis; **être en état d'h.** to be under hypnosis
hypnotique [ipnɔtik] *adj* hypnotic
hypnotiser [ipnɔtize] *vt* to hypnotize
hypnotisme [ipnɔtism] *nm* hypnotism
hypoallergénique [ipɔalɛrʒenik] *adj* hypoallergenic
hypocalorique [ipɔkalɔrik] *adj (régime, aliment)* low-calorie
hypocondriaque [ipɔkɔ̃drijak] *adj & nmf* hypochondriac
hypocrisie [ipɔkrizi] *nf* hypocrisy
hypocrite [ipɔkrit] **1** *adj* hypocritical
 2 *nmf* hypocrite
hypocritement [ipɔkritmã] *adv* hypocritically
hypodermique [ipɔdermik] *adj* hypodermic
hypoglycémie [ipɔglisemi] *nf* hypoglycemia
hypokhâgne [ipɔkɑɲ] *nf* = first-year arts class preparing students for the entrance examination for the "École normale supérieure"
hypophyse [ipɔfiz] *nf* pituitary gland
hypotendu, -e [ipɔtãdy] *adj* **être h.** to have low blood pressure
hypotension [ipɔtãsjɔ̃] *nf* low blood pressure, *Spéc* hypotension
hypoténuse [ipɔtenyz] *nf* hypotenuse
hypothalamus [ipɔtalamys] *nm* hypothalamus
hypothécaire [ipɔtekɛr] *adj* **contrat h.** mortgage deed; **prêt h.** mortgage (loan)
hypothèque [ipɔtɛk] *nf* mortgage
hypothéquer [34] [ipɔteke] *vt (propriété)* to mortgage; *Fig* **h. son avenir** to sign away one's future

hypothermie [ipɔtɛrmi] *nf* hypothermia
hypothèse [ipɔtɛz] *nf* hypothesis; **dans l'h. où nous échouerions** should we fail; **ils ont écarté l'h. du suicide** they have ruled out the possibility of suicide
hypothétique [ipɔtetik] *adj* hypothetical

hystérectomie [isterɛktɔmi] *nf* hysterectomy
hystérie [isteri] *nf* hysteria; **h. collective** mass hysteria
hystérique [isterik] **1** *adj* hysterical
   2 *nmf* hysterical person

I

I, i [i] *nm inv* I, i
ibère [ibɛr] **1** *adj* Iberian
  2 *nmf* **I.** Iberian
ibérique [iberik] *adj* Iberian
ibis [ibis] *nm* ibis
iceberg [ajsbɛrg, isbɛrg] *nm* iceberg; *Fig* **la partie ca-chée de l'i.** the hidden aspects of the problem; *Fig* **la partie visible de l'i.** the tip of the iceberg
ichtyologie [iktjɔlɔʒi] *nf* ichthyology
ici [isi] *adv* (**a**) *(dans l'espace)* here; **i. et là** here and there; **i. même** on this very spot; **les gens d'i.** the people from round here, the locals; **c'est i.** this is the place; **c'est i. que ça s'est passé** this is where it happened; *Fig* **je reprends i. ses propres paroles** and here I'm using her own words; **i. Thomas** *(au téléphone)* this isThomas
  (**b**) *(dans le temps)* **jusqu'i.** until now, up to now; **d'i. lundi/demain** by Monday/tomorrow; **d'i. là** by that time, by then; **d'i. peu** before long; **d'i. à ce que vous ayez fini, je serai parti** by the time you've finished, I'll have gone; **d'i. à ce qu'il la quitte, il n'y a pas loin** he will have left her before long
icône [ikon] *nf Rel & Ordinat* icon; *Ordinat* **i. de la corbeille** wastebasket icon, *Am* trash icon
iconoclaste [ikɔnɔklast] **1** *adj* iconoclastic
  2 *nmf* iconoclast
iconographie [ikɔnɔgrafi] *nf* (**a**) *(dans un domaine particulier)* iconography (**b**) *(dans l'édition)* illustrations, art work
iconographique [ikɔnɔgrafik] *adj* iconographic
idéal, -e, -als *ou* **-aux, -ales** [ideal, -o] **1** *adj* ideal
  2 *nm* ideal; **l'i.** the ideal thing; **dans l'i.** ideally; **l'i. serait que tu y ailles tout seul** it would be best if you went alone
idéalement [idealmɑ̃] *adv* ideally
idéalisation [idealizasjɔ̃] *nf* idealization
idéaliser [idealize] *vt* to idealize
idéalisme [idealism] *nm* idealism
idéaliste [idealist] **1** *adj* idealistic
  2 *nmf* idealist
idée [ide] *nf* (**a**) *(inspiration)* idea; **i. de génie, i. lumineuse** brilliant idea; **avoir la bonne i. de faire qch** to have the bright idea of doing sth; **avoir une i. derrière la tête** to be up to something; **donner des idées à qn** to put ideas into sb's head; **quelle drôle d'i.!, en voilà une i.!** the very idea!; **se faire des idées** to imagine things; **i. fixe** obsession; **idées noires** black thoughts; **i. reçue** generally accepted idea (**b**) *(notion)* idea; **pour vous donner une i.** to give you an idea; **as-tu une i. du prix que ça coûte?** have you any idea how much it costs?; **je n'en ai pas la moindre i.** I haven't

got the faintest idea; *Fam* **on n'a pas i. de faire des choses pareilles!** whoever heard of such a thing! (**c**) *(opinion)* view, opinion; **avoir une haute i. de qn/qch** to have a high opinion of sb/sth; **se faire une i. de qn/qch** to get an idea of sb/sth; **avoir sa petite i. sur qch** to have one's pet theory about sth; **avoir les idées larges** to be broad-minded; **fais à ton i.** do as you like; **changer d'i.** to change one's mind (**d**) *(esprit)* **ça ne m'est jamais venu à l'i.** it's never occurred to me; **je ne peux pas lui ôter cela de l'i.** I can't get her to change her mind about it; **se mettre dans l'i. que/de faire qch** to get it into one's head that/to do sth; **cela m'était sorti de l'i.** it had slipped my mind
idem [idɛm] *adv* ditto
identification [idɑ̃tifikasjɔ̃] *nf* identification (**avec** *ou* **à** with); *Ordinat* **i. de l'utilisateur** user identification
identifier [66] [idɑ̃tifje] **1** *vt* to identify
  2 s'identifier *vpr* **s'i. à** *ou* **avec** to identify with
identique [idɑ̃tik] *adj* identical (**à** to)
identitaire [idɑ̃titɛr] *adj* **les revendications identitaires des minorités ethniques** ethnic minorities' demands for recognition; **obsession i.** obsession with issues of identity
identité [idɑ̃tite] *nf* identity; **papiers** *ou* **pièces d'i.** identity papers
idéogramme [ideɔgram] *nm* ideogram
idéologie [ideɔlɔʒi] *nf* ideology
idéologique [ideɔlɔʒik] *adj* ideological
idiomatique [idjɔmatik] *adj* idiomatic; **expression i.** idiom
idiome [idjom] *nm* idiom
idiot, -e [idjo, -ɔt] **1** *adj (stupide)* idiotic, stupid; *(regrettable)* stupid, silly; **ce système n'est pas i.** this system is pretty smart
  2 *nm,f* idiot; *Fam* **l'i. du village** the village idiot; **faire l'i.** *(faire des bêtises)* to act the fool; *(feindre de ne pas comprendre)* to act dumb
idiotie [idjɔsi] *nf (chose, parole idiote)* stupid thing; *(caractère stupide)* stupidity; **ne dites pas d'idioties!** don't talk rubbish!
idolâtrer [idɔlatre] *vt* to idolize
idolâtrie [idɔlatri] *nf* idolatry
idole [idɔl] *nf* idol; **i. des jeunes** teenage idol
idylle [idil] *nf* (**a**) *(aventure)* romance (**b**) *(poème)* idyll
idyllique [idilik] *adj* idyllic
IEP [iəpe] *nm (abrév* **Institut d'études politiques)** = higher education establishment for political science students

if [if] *nm* yew

IFOP [ifɔp] *nm* (*abrév* **Institut français d'opinion publique**) = French market research institute

IGF [iʒɛɛf] *nm inv* (*abrév* **impôt sur les grandes fortunes**) wealth tax

igloo, iglou [iglu] *nm* igloo

IGN [iʒɛɛn] *nm* (*abrév* **Institut géographique national**) *Br* ≃ Ordnance Survey, *Am* ≃ United States Geological Survey

> **IGN**
> Created in 1940, this state agency is responsible for the official map of France and for keeping a geographical database. It is organized into regional offices and sponsors a school which trains 200 students a year.

ignare [iɲar] **1** *adj* ignorant
2 *nmf* ignoramus

ignifuge [iɲnifyʒ] **1** *adj* fireproof
2 *nm* fireproofing material

ignifugé, -e [iɲnifyʒe] *adj* fireproofed

ignoble [iɲnɔbl] *adj* (**a**) (*personne, conduite*) vile (**b**) (*habitation, quartier*) filthy; (*nourriture*) disgusting

ignominie [iɲnɔmini] *nf* (**a**) (*caractère*) ignominy; **se couvrir d'i.** to bring shame upon oneself (**b**) (*action*) shameful thing; **c'est une i.!** it's a disgrace!

ignorance [iɲnɔrɑ̃s] *nf* ignorance; **être/tenir qn dans l'i.** to be/keep sb in the dark

ignorant, -e [iɲnɔrɑ̃, -ɑ̃t] **1** *adj* ignorant (**de** of)
2 *nm,f* ignoramus; **faire l'i.** to pretend one doesn't know

ignoré, -e [iɲnɔre] *adj* unknown; (*négligé*) ignored; **vivre i.** to live in obscurity

ignorer [iɲnɔre] **1** *vt* (**a**) (*ne pas savoir*) not to know (about); **j'ignorais qu'il était malade** I was unaware that he was ill; **il ignore tout de cela** he knows nothing about it; **ne rien i. de qch** to know all about sth; **personne n'ignore que…** everybody knows that…; **i. la peur/la jalousie** to feel no fear/jealousy (**b**) (*mépriser*) (*personne, conseil, interdiction*) to ignore
2 **s'ignorer** *vpr* (**a**) (*se mépriser l'un l'autre*) to ignore each other (**b**) (*se méconnaître*) **c'est un artiste qui s'ignore** he's an artist but he doesn't know it

iguane [igwan] *nm* iguana

il [il] *pron personnel* (**a**) (*personne*) he; (*chose, animal*) it; **ton père est-il toujours à l'hôpital?** is your father still in hospital?
(**b**) (*impersonnel*) it; **il est six heures** it's six o'clock; **il pleut** it's raining; **il existe de nombreuses possibilités** there are many possibilities

île [il] *nf* island; **dans une î.** on an island; **î. déserte** desert island; **les îles Anglo-Normandes** the Channel Islands; *Culin* **î. flottante** floating island (*beaten egg whites served on custard*); **les îles Salomon** the Solomon Islands; **les îles de la Société** the Society Islands; **les îles Sous-le-Vent** the Leeward Islands

Île-de-France [ildəfrɑ̃s] *nf* **l'Î.** = administrative region including Paris

iliaque [iljak] *adj Anat* iliac; **os i.** ilium

illégal, -e, -aux, -ales [ilegal, -o] *adj* illegal

illégalement [ilegalmɑ̃] *adv* illegally

illégalité [ilegalite] *nf* illegality; **vivre dans l'i.** to live outside the law; **être dans l'i.** to break the law

illégitime [ileʒitim] *adj* (*enfant*) illegitimate; (*union*) unlawful; (*demande*) unwarranted

illettré, -e [iletre] *adj & nm,f* illiterate

illettrisme [iletrism] *nm* illiteracy

illicite [ilisit] *adj* illicit, unlawful

illico [iliko] *adv Fam* **i. (presto)** pronto

illimité, -e [ilimite] *adj* (*pouvoirs, moyens, crédit*) unlimited; (*confiance*) boundless

illisible [ilizibl] *adj* (**a**) (*indéchiffrable*) illegible; *Ordinat* (*fichier, disquette*) unreadable (**b**) (*incompréhensible*) unreadable

illogique [ilɔʒik] *adj* illogical

illumination [ilyminasjɔ̃] *nf* (**a**) (*action d'illuminer*) illumination; (*par projecteurs*) floodlighting (**b**) (*lumière*) **illuminations** illuminations (**c**) (*inspiration*) flash of inspiration

illuminé, -e [ilymine] **1** *adj* (*éclairé*) lit up, illuminated; (*par projecteurs*) floodlit
2 *nm,f Péj* fanatic

illuminer [ilymine] **1** *vt* (*éclairer*) to light up, to illuminate; (*par projecteurs*) to floodlight; *Fig* (*visage, yeux*) to light up
2 **s'illuminer** *vpr aussi Fig* to light up (**de** with)

illusion [ilyzjɔ̃] *nf* illusion; **se faire des illusions** to delude oneself; **je ne me fais aucune i. sur ses intentions** I have no illusions about her intentions; **perdre ses illusions** to become disillusioned; **enlever** *ou* **faire perdre ses illusions à qn** to disillusion sb; **faire i.** to take people in; **i. d'optique** optical illusion

illusionner [ilyzjɔne] **s'illusionner** *vpr* to delude oneself (**sur** about)

illusionniste [ilyzjɔnist] *nmf* conjurer

illusoire [ilyzwar] *adj* illusory

illustrateur, -trice [ilystratœr, -tris] *nm,f* illustrator

illustration [ilystrasjɔ̃] *nf* illustration

illustre [ilystr] *adj* illustrious; *Hum* **un i. inconnu** a famous person no one has ever heard of

illustré, -e [ilystre] **1** *adj* illustrated
2 *nm Vieilli* (*pour enfants*) comic

illustrer [ilystre] **1** *vt* (*livre, récit*) to illustrate (**de** with)
2 **s'illustrer** *vpr* to distinguish oneself (**par** by)

îlot [ilo] *nm* (*île*) small island; (*groupe d'immeubles*) block; *Fig* **î. de verdure** island of greenery

îlotage [ilotaʒ] *nm* community policing

ils [il] *pron personnel* they; **les magasins sont-i. ouverts le dimanche?** are the shops open on Sunday?

image [imaʒ] *nf* (**a**) (*dans un miroir*) reflection, image; (*à la télévision*) picture; **vingt-quatre images par seconde** twenty-four frames a second; **être à l'i.** to be on camera; **nous n'avons plus d'i.** the picture's gone; **i. d'archives** library picture; *Cin & TV* stock shot; *Ordinat* **i. bitmap** bitmap image; **images de synthèse** computer-generated images; *Ordinat* **i. vectorielle** outline image (**b**) *Fig* image; **soigner son i.** to cultivate one's image; **donner une bonne/mauvaise i. de** to present a good/bad image of; **i. de marque** (*d'un produit*) brand image; (*d'un homme politique, d'une entreprise*) public image (**c**) (*dessin*) picture; (*récompense scolaire*) ≃ gold star

imagé, -e [imaʒe] *adj* vivid

imagerie [imaʒri] *nf* imagery; *Méd* **i. médicale** medical imaging; *Méd* **i. par résonance magnétique** magnetic resonance imaging

imaginable [imaʒinabl] *adj* imaginable

imaginaire [imaʒinɛr] **1** *adj (personnage, pays, animal)* imaginary
  2 *nm* **l'i.** the imagination
imaginatif, -ive [imaʒinatif, -iv] *adj* imaginative
imagination [imaʒinasjɔ̃] *nf* imagination; **avoir de l'i.** to be imaginative
imaginer [imaʒine] **1** *vt* **(a)** *(inventer)* to devise **(b)** *(se figurer)* to imagine; **tu l'imagines avec des enfants!** just imagine him with children!; **j'imagine qu'elle viendra vers neuf heures** she'll come about nine o'clock, I should imagine
  2 s'imaginer *vpr* **(a)** *(croire)* **s'i. que** to think that; **il s'imagine tout savoir** he thinks he knows it all **(b)** *(se figurer)* to imagine; *(soi-même)* to picture oneself; **tu t'imagines la tête qu'elle va faire** you can imagine how she'll take it; **je me l'imaginais bien plus grand** I imagined him much taller
imam [imam] *nm* imam
imbattable [ɛ̃batabl] *adj* unbeatable
imbécile [ɛ̃besil] **1** *adj* idiotic, stupid
  2 *nmf* idiot, fool; **c'est un i. heureux** he's living in blissful ignorance; **faire l'i.** *(faire des bêtises)* to play *or* act the fool; *(feindre de ne pas comprendre)* to act stupid
imbécillité [ɛ̃besilite] *nf* **(a)** *(caractère stupide)* idiocy, stupidity **(b)** *(parole, chose stupide)* idiotic thing; **dire des imbécillités** to talk nonsense
imberbe [ɛ̃bɛrb] *adj* beardless
imbiber [ɛ̃bibe] **1** *vt* **i. qch de qch** to soak sth in sth; **imbibé d'eau** *(coton, éponge)* saturated (with water); *(terrain)* waterlogged
  2 s'imbiber *vpr* **s'i. de qch** to become soaked with sth
imbrication [ɛ̃brikasjɔ̃] *nf* overlapping; *Fig (ensemble complexe)* web; *Ordinat* embedding; *(de commandes)* nesting
imbriquer [ɛ̃brike] **1** *vt* to overlap; *Ordinat* to embed; *(commandes)* to nest
  2 s'imbriquer *vpr (s'emboîter)* to overlap; *Fig (problèmes, situations)* to be interwoven
imbroglio [ɛ̃brɔljo] *nm* imbroglio
imbu, -e [ɛ̃by] *adj* **i. de sa personne** *ou* **de soi-même** full of oneself
imbuvable [ɛ̃byvabl] *adj* undrinkable; *Fig (personne)* insufferable
imitateur, -trice [imitatœr, -tris] *nm,f (amateur)* mimic; *(professionnel)* impersonator, impressionist
imitation [imitasjɔ̃] *nf* **(a)** *(d'une personne)* impersonation, impression; *(d'un produit, d'un style)* imitation; *(d'une signature, d'un billet)* forgery **(b)** *(copie)* imitation; **bijoux en i. argent** imitation silver jewellery
imiter [imite] *vt (personne) (singer)* to imitate; *(faire une imitation de)* to impersonate; *(produit, style)* to imitate; *(signature)* to forge; *(billet, pièce de monnaie)* to counterfeit; **il leva son verre et tout le monde l'imita** he raised his glass and everyone did the same
immaculé, -e [imakyle] *adj (draps, linge, réputation)* spotless; **d'un blanc i.** spotlessly white; *Rel* **l'Immaculée Conception** the Immaculate Conception
immangeable [ɛ̃mɑ̃ʒabl] *adj* inedible
immanquablement [ɛ̃mɑ̃kabləmɑ̃] *adv* inevitably
immatériel, -elle [imaterjɛl] *adj Phil* immaterial; *Fin (actif)* intangible; *Litt (pâleur, minceur)* ethereal
immatriculation [imatrikylasjɔ̃] *nf* registration (**à** with); **(numéro d')i.** *Br* registration number, *Am* license number

---

Immatriculation
The last two numbers on French number plates refer to the "département" where the vehicle was registered. Vehicles from the Val-de-Marne, for example, bear the number 94.

---

immatriculer [imatrikyle] *vt* to register (**à** with); **la voiture est immatriculée en Dordogne** the car has a Dordogne *Br* number plate *or Am* license plate
immature [imatyr] *adj* immature
immaturité [imatyrite] *nf* immaturity
immédiat, -e [imedja, -at] **1** *adj* immediate; *(contact)* direct; *(mort)* instantaneous
  2 *nm* **dans l'i.** for the time being
immédiatement [imedjatmɑ̃] *adv* immediately
immémorial, -e, -aux, -ales [imemɔrjal, -o] *adj Litt* age-old; **en des temps immémoriaux** in ancient times
immense [imɑ̃s] *adj* immense
immensément [imɑ̃semɑ̃] *adv* immensely
immensité [imɑ̃site] *nf* immensity
immerger [45] [imerʒe] *vt* to immerse (**dans** in)
immérité, -e [imerite] *adj* unmerited, undeserved
immersion [imersjɔ̃] *nf* immersion (**dans** in)
immettable [ɛ̃mɛtabl] *adj* unwearable
immeuble [imœbl] **1** *nm (bâtiment)* building; *(d'appartements) Br* block of flats, *Am* apartment block
  2 *adj voir* **bien**
immigrant, -e [imigrɑ̃, -ɑ̃t] *adj & nm,f* immigrant
immigration [imigrasjɔ̃] *nf* immigration
immigré, -e [imigre] *adj & nm,f* immigrant
immigrer [imigre] *vi* to immigrate
imminence [iminɑ̃s] *nf* imminence
imminent, -e [iminɑ̃, -ɑ̃t] *adj* imminent
immiscer [16] [imise] **s'immiscer** *vpr* to interfere (**dans** in)
immobile [imɔbil] *adj* motionless, still; *Fig (figé)* unchanging
immobilier, -ère [imɔbilje, -ɛr] **1** *adj Br* property, *Am* real-estate
  2 *nm* **l'i.** *Br* property, *Am* real estate
immobilisation [imɔbilizasjɔ̃] *nf* **(a)** *(fait de ne plus bouger)* immobilization **(b)** *Fin* **immobilisations** fixed assets
immobiliser [imɔbilize] **1** *vt* **(a)** *(blessé)* to immobilize; *(train)* to bring to a standstill; *(véhicule) (avec un sabot)* to clamp **(b)** *(capital)* to tie up
  2 s'immobiliser *vpr* to come to a stop
immobilisme [imɔbilism] *nm* opposition to change
immobilité [imɔbilite] *nf* stillness; *(d'un visage)* immobility
immodéré, -e [imɔdere] *adj* immoderate
immodérément [imɔderemɑ̃] *adv* immoderately
immoler [imɔle] *Litt* **1** *vt aussi Fig* to sacrifice (**à** to)
  2 s'immoler *vpr* to sacrifice oneself; **s'i. par le feu** to die by setting fire to oneself
immonde [imɔ̃d] *adj (sale)* foul; *(ignoble, laid)* vile
immondices [imɔ̃dis] *nfpl* refuse
immoral, -e, -aux, -ales [imɔral, -o] *adj* immoral
immoralité [imɔralite] *nf* immorality
immortaliser [imɔrtalize] *vt* to immortalize
immortalité [imɔrtalite] *nf* immortality
immortel, -elle [imɔrtɛl] **1** *adj (dieu, être)* immortal; *(amour)* everlasting

2 *nm,f (membre de l'Académie française)* member of the Académie Française

3 *nf* **immortelle** *(plante)* everlasting flower

immuable [imɥabl] *adj (vérité)* unchanging, immutable; *(opinion, sourire)* fixed

immunisation [imynizasjɔ̃] *nf* immunization (**contre** against)

immuniser [imynize] *vt* to immunize (**contre** against)

immunitaire [imynitɛr] *adj (système, réactions, défenses)* immune

immunité [imynite] *nf* immunity; **i. parlementaire/ diplomatique** parliamentary/diplomatic immunity

immunodéficitaire [imynɔdefisitɛr] *adj Méd* immunodeficient

immunodépresseur [imynɔdeprɛsœr] *adj m & nm Méd* immunosuppressive

immunologie [imynɔlɔʒi] *nf* immunology

immunologique [imynɔlɔʒik] *adj* immunological

immunosuppresseur [imynɔsyprɛsœr] *adj m & nm Méd* immunosuppressive

impact [ɛ̃pakt] *nm* impact; **avoir un i. sur qch** to have an impact on sth

impair, -e [ɛ̃pɛr] **1** *adj (nombre, jours)* odd; *(côté d'une rue)* odd-numbered

2 *nm* (**a**) *(à la roulette)* odd numbers (**b**) *(maladresse)* blunder; **faire** *ou* **commettre un i.** to make a blunder

impalpable [ɛ̃palpabl] *adj* impalpable

imparable [ɛ̃parabl] *adj (coup)* unstoppable; *Fig (argument, logique)* irrefutable

impardonnable [ɛ̃pardɔnabl] *adj* unforgivable; **j'ai encore pris votre parapluie, je suis i.** I've taken your umbrella again, how unforgivable of me!

imparfait, -e [ɛ̃parfɛ, -ɛt] **1** *adj* (**a**) *(qui a des défauts)* imperfect (**b**) *(inachevé)* unfinished

2 *nm Gram* imperfect (tense); **à l'i.** in the imperfect (tense)

impartial, -e, -aux, -ales [ɛ̃parsjal, -o] *adj* impartial, unbiased

impartialité [ɛ̃parsjalite] *nf* impartiality

impartir [ɛ̃partir] *vt Litt* **i. qch à qn** *(droit)* to grant sth to sb; *(tâche)* to assign sth to sb; **dans le délai imparti** within the time allowed; **le temps qui vous est imparti** the time allotted to you

impasse [ɛ̃pas] *nf* (**a**) *(cul-de-sac)* dead end, cul-de-sac; *Fig* impasse, deadlock; *Fig* **être dans une i.** to be deadlocked; *Fig* **sortir de l'i.** to break the deadlock (**b**) **faire une i.** *(en révisant)* = to miss out part of a subject when revising

impassibilité [ɛ̃pasibilite] *nf* impassiveness

impassible [ɛ̃pasibl] *adj* impassive

impatiemment [ɛ̃pasjamɑ̃] *adv* impatiently

impatience [ɛ̃pasjɑ̃s] *nf* impatience; **avec i.** impatiently

impatient, -e [ɛ̃pasjɑ̃, -ɑ̃t] **1** *adj* impatient; **d'un air i.** impatiently; **être i. de faire qch** to be impatient to do sth

2 *nf* **impatiente** *(plante)* Busy Lizzie

impatienter [ɛ̃pasjɑ̃te] **1** *vt* to annoy, to irritate

2 s'impatienter *vpr* to get impatient (**de/contre** at/with)

impavide [ɛ̃pavid] *adj Litt* impassive

impayable [ɛ̃pɛjabl] *adj Fam (histoire, personne)* priceless

impayé, -e [ɛ̃peje] **1** *adj* unpaid

2 *nm* outstanding payment

impec [ɛ̃pɛk] *adj Fam* spotless; **i.!** *(parfait)* great!

impeccable [ɛ̃pekabl] *adj* impeccable; **d'une propreté i.** impeccably clean; *Fam* **i.!** *(parfait)* great!

impeccablement [ɛ̃pekabləmɑ̃] *adv* impeccably

impénétrable [ɛ̃penetrabl] *adj* (**a**) *(forêt, citadelle)* impenetrable (**b**) *(visage, caractère, air)* inscrutable; *(mystère, texte)* impenetrable; **les voies du Seigneur sont impénétrables** God works in mysterious ways

impénitent, -e [ɛ̃penitɑ̃, -ɑ̃t] *adj* unrepentant

impensable [ɛ̃pɑ̃sabl] *adj* unthinkable; **il est i. que vous ne soyez pas remplacé** it's unthinkable that they're not going to replace you

imper [ɛ̃pɛr] *nm Fam* raincoat, *Br* mac

impératif, -ive [ɛ̃peratif, -iv] **1** *adj* (**a**) *(ton, geste)* imperious (**b**) *(nécessité, besoin)* imperative; **il est i. de connaître l'anglais** it is imperative to know English

2 *nm* (**a**) *(exigence)* requirement; **savoir nager est un i.** it is essential to be able to swim; **les impératifs de la mode** the dictates of fashion (**b**) *Gram* imperative (mood); **à l'i.** in the imperative (mood)

impérativement [ɛ̃perativmɑ̃] *adv* **il faut i. que je la voie** it is imperative that I see her

impératrice [ɛ̃peratris] *nf* empress

imperceptible [ɛ̃pɛrsɛptibl] *adj* imperceptible (**à** to)

imperceptiblement [ɛ̃pɛrsɛptibləmɑ̃] *adv* imperceptibly

imperdable [ɛ̃pɛrdabl] *adj* **le match/le procès est i.** the match/the case can't be lost

imperfectible [ɛ̃pɛrfɛktibl] *adj* imperfectible

imperfection [ɛ̃pɛrfɛksjɔ̃] *nf* imperfection

impérial, -e, -aux, -ales [ɛ̃perjal, -o] **1** *adj aussi Fig* imperial

2 *nf* **impériale** *(d'un bus)* top deck

impérialisme [ɛ̃perjalism] *nm* imperialism

impérialiste [ɛ̃perjalist] *adj & nmf* imperialist

impérieux, -euse [ɛ̃perjø, -øz] *adj* (**a**) *(autoritaire)* imperious (**b**) *(nécessité, désir, besoin)* urgent, pressing

impérissable [ɛ̃perisabl] *adj (œuvre, souvenir)* enduring; **ça ne m'a pas laissé un souvenir i.** it didn't make a lasting impression on me

imperméabilisant, -e [ɛ̃pɛrmeabilizɑ̃, -ɑ̃t] **1** *adj* waterproofing

2 *nm* waterproofing agent

imperméabiliser [ɛ̃pɛrmeabilize] *vt* to waterproof

imperméable [ɛ̃pɛrmeabl] **1** *adj* impermeable; *(à l'eau)* waterproof; *Fig* **être i. à qch** to be impervious to sth

2 *nm* raincoat, *Br* mackintosh

impersonnel, -elle [ɛ̃pɛrsɔnɛl] *adj* impersonal

impertinemment [ɛ̃pɛrtinamɑ̃] *adv* impertinently

impertinence [ɛ̃pɛrtinɑ̃s] *nf* impertinence; **avec i.** impertinently

impertinent, -e [ɛ̃pɛrtinɑ̃, -ɑ̃t] **1** *adj* impertinent

2 *nm,f* impertinent person; **un petit i.** an impertinent little boy

imperturbable [ɛ̃pɛrtyrbabl] *adj (personne)* imperturbable; *(optimisme)* unshakeable

imperturbablement [ɛ̃pɛrtyrbabləmɑ̃] *adv* imperturbably

impétigo [ɛ̃petigo] *nm* impetigo

impétueusement [ɛ̃petɥøzmɑ̃] *adv* impetuously

impétueux, -euse [ε̃petɥø, -øz] *adj* (**a**) *(personne)* impetuous; *(tempérament)* fiery (**b**) *Litt (torrent)* raging

impétuosité [ε̃petɥozite] *nf (fougue)* impetuosity

impie [ε̃pi] *Litt* **1** *adj* impious
2 *nmf* impious person

impitoyable [ε̃pitwajabl] *adj* merciless

impitoyablement [ε̃pitwajabləmã] *adv* mercilessly

implacable [ε̃plakabl] *adj (personne, vengeance, logique)* implacable; *(avancée)* relentless

implant [ε̃plã] *nm* implant; **i. mammaire** breast implant; **implants (capillaires)** hair graft

implantation [ε̃plãtasjɔ̃] *nf* (**a**) *(installation)* establishment (**b**) *(des cheveux)* line; *(des dents)* arch

implanter [ε̃plãte] **1** *vt* (**a**) *(installer)* to establish (**b**) *(chirurgicalement)* to implant
2 s'implanter *vpr* to become established

implication [ε̃plikasjɔ̃] *nf* (**a**) *(engagement)* involvement (**b**) **implications** *(conséquences)* implications

implicite [ε̃plisit] *adj* implicit

implicitement [ε̃plisitmã] *adv* implicitly

impliquer [ε̃plike] **1** *vt* (**a**) *(compromettre)* to implicate (**dans** in) (**b**) *(supposer)* to imply; **i. que** to imply that
2 s'impliquer *vpr* to get involved (**dans** in)

implorer [ε̃plɔre] *vt* to implore, to beseech; **i. le pardon de qn** to beg sb's forgiveness; **i. qn de faire qch** to implore *or* beseech sb to do sth

imploser [ε̃ploze] *vi* to implode

implosion [ε̃plozjɔ̃] *nf* implosion

impoli, -e [ε̃pɔli] *adj* impolite, rude

impoliment [ε̃pɔlimã] *adv* impolitely, rudely

impolitesse [ε̃pɔlitεs] *nf* (**a**) *(d'une personne, d'une remarque)* impoliteness, rudeness (**b**) *(acte)* impolite act; *(remarque)* rude remark

impondérable [ε̃pɔ̃derabl] *adj & nm* imponderable

impopulaire [ε̃pɔpylεr] *adj* unpopular

import [ε̃pɔr] *nm* (**a**) *Com* import; *Ordinat* **i. de données** data import (**b**) *Belg (montant)* amount; **une facture d'un i. de 2000 euros** a bill for 2000 euros

importable [ε̃pɔrtabl] *adj (vêtement)* unwearable

importance [ε̃pɔrtãs] *nf* (**a**) *(d'un événement, d'un acte, d'une personne)* importance; **avoir de l'i. (pour)** to be important (to); **sans i.** unimportant; **cela n'a aucune i.** it's of no importance; **c'est d'une i. capitale** it's extremely important; **de la première** *ou* **de la plus haute i.** extremely important; **attacher** *ou* **donner de l'i. à qch** to attach importance to sth; **et alors, quelle i.?** well, so what? (**b**) *(d'une ville, d'une somme, d'un projet)* size; *(de dégâts, d'une catastrophe)* extent; **prendre de l'i.** *(société)* to expand; *(mouvement, parti)* to gain ground

important, -e [ε̃pɔrtã, -ãt] **1** *adj* (**a**) *(événement, acte, personne)* important (**pour** to); **il est i. que vous le sachiez** it's important for you to know; **peu i.** unimportant; **se donner des airs importants** to give oneself airs (**b**) *(ville, projet)* large; *(somme d'argent, dégâts, retard)* considerable; *(chiffre)* high
2 *nm,f Péj* **faire l'i.** to act important
3 *nm* **l'i., c'est que tu sois satisfait** the important thing is that you're satisfied

importateur, -trice [ε̃pɔrtatœr, -tris] **1** *nm,f* importer
2 *adj* importing; **les pays importateurs de pétrole** oil-importing countries

importation [ε̃pɔrtasjɔ̃] *nf* (**a**) *(de marchandises)* importing; **articles** *ou* **produits d'i.** imports; **licence d'i.** import licence (**b**) *(produit)* import

importer¹ [ε̃pɔrte] *vt* (**a**) *(marchandises)* to import (**b**) *Ordinat* to download

importer² **1** *vi* *(compter)* to matter (**à** to); **ce qui importe, c'est que tu viennes** the important thing is that you come
2 *v impersonnel* (**a**) *(être important)* **il importe que vous y soyez** it's important that you're there; **peu importe** it doesn't matter; **peu m'importe** I don't mind; **qu'importe?** what does it matter? (**b**) **faire qch n'importe où/quand/comment** to do sth anywhere/any time/anyhow; *Fam* **n'importe comment, c'est trop tard** anyway, it's too late; **n'importe** never mind; **n'importe quel gamin** any child; **n'importe qui** anyone, anybody; **n'importe qui d'autre** anyone else; **n'importe quoi** anything; *Péj* **dire/écrire n'importe quoi** to talk/write nonsense; *Fam* **n'importe quoi!** rubbish!

import-export [ε̃pɔrεkspɔr] *nm* import-export business

importun, -e [ε̃pɔrtœ̃, -yn] **1** *adj (personne, visiteur, question)* importunate; *(arrivée, remarque)* ill-timed
2 *nm,f (personne)* nuisance

importuner [ε̃pɔrtyne] *vt Formel* to bother

imposable [ε̃pozabl] *adj* taxable

imposant, -e [ε̃pozã, -ãt] *adj* imposing

imposé, -e [ε̃poze] *adj (taxé)* taxed; **être i. à la source** to be taxed at source

imposer [ε̃poze] **1** *vt* (**a**) *(une condition)* to impose (**à** on); **i. une tâche à qn** to set sb a task; **i. le respect** to command respect; **i. sa loi** to lay down the law; **i. le silence à qn** to make sb be quiet; **i. sa présence à qn** to impose on sb (**b**) *(soumettre à l'impôt)* to tax
2 *vi* **en i.** to be impressive; **en i. à qn** to impress sb
3 s'imposer *vpr* (**a**) *(faire reconnaître sa valeur)* to assert oneself; *(gagner)* to win (**b**) *(déranger)* **je ne voulais pas m'i.** I didn't want to impose (**c**) *(être nécessaire)* to be essential; **prendre les mesures qui s'imposent** to take the necessary steps (**d**) *(se contraindre)* **s'i. un sacrifice** to force oneself to make a sacrifice; **s'i. de faire qch** to make it a rule to do sth

imposition [ε̃pozisjɔ̃] *nf (taxation)* taxation

impossibilité [ε̃pɔsibilite] *nf* impossibility; **être** *ou* **se trouver dans l'i. de faire qch** to find it impossible to do sth

impossible [ε̃pɔsibl] **1** *adj* impossible; **i. à lire** impossible to read; **il est i. qu'il revienne avant lundi** he can't possibly be back before Monday; **il m'est i. de le faire** it's impossible for me to do it; **i. n'est pas français** there's no such word as can't; **rendre la vie i. à qn** to make life impossible for sb; **tu es i.!** you're impossible!
2 *nm* **tenter/demander l'i.** to attempt/to ask the impossible; **faire l'i. pour faire qch** to do everything possible to do sth

imposteur [ε̃pɔstœr] *nm* impostor

imposture [ε̃pɔstyr] *nf* deception

impôt [ε̃po] *nm* tax; **payer 1000 euros d'impôts** to pay 1,000 euros in tax; *Fam* **les impôts m'ont envoyé une lettre** the tax man has sent me a letter; **i. direct/indirect** direct/indirect tax; **i. foncier** land tax; **i. sur les grandes fortunes** wealth tax; **impôts locaux** local taxes; **i. sur le revenu** income tax; **i. sur les sociétés** corporation tax

Impôts locaux
These are taxes levied to finance local, departmental or regional government. The best-known are the "taxe d'habitation" (paid by rent-paying tenants), the "taxe foncière" (paid by homeowners) and the "taxe professionnelle" (paid by the self-employed). The rate of each tax is decided at local level.

impotence [ɛpɔtɑ̃s] *nf (infirmité)* disability; *(due à la vieillesse)* infirmity

impotent, -e [ɛpɔtɑ̃, -ɑ̃t] **1** *adj (infirme)* disabled; *(à cause de la vieillesse)* infirm
  2 *nm,f (infirme)* disabled person; *(vieillard)* infirm person

impraticable [ɛpratikabl] *adj* **(a)** *(où l'on ne peut pas passer)* impassable **(b)** *(terrain de sport)* unfit for play **(c)** *(irréalisable)* impracticable

imprécation [ɛprekasjɔ̃] *nf Litt* imprecation

imprécis, -e [ɛpresi, -iz] *adj* imprecise

imprécision [ɛpresizjɔ̃] *nf* imprecision

imprégner [34] [ɛpreɲe] **1** *vt* **(a)** *(sujet: eau, odeur)* to impregnate **(b)** *Fig (influencer)* **être imprégné de qch** to be full of sth
  2 s'imprégner *vpr* **(a)** *(s'imbiber)* to become impregnated (**de** with); **s'i. d'eau** to become soaked with water **(b)** *Fig* **s'i. d'un auteur** to immerse oneself in an author

imprenable [ɛprənabl] *adj* **(a)** *(forteresse, ville)* impregnable **(b)** *(vue)* unobstructed

imprésario [ɛpresarjo] *nm* manager

imprescriptible [ɛpreskriptibl] *adj Jur* imprescriptible

impression [ɛpresjɔ̃] *nf* **(a)** *(sensation)* impression; **donner à qn l'i. que** to give sb the impression that; **faire bonne/mauvaise/forte i. (à qn)** to make a good/bad/strong impression (on sb); **ça m'a fait une drôle d'i.** it gave me a funny feeling; **j'ai l'i. de l'avoir déjà vue** I've a feeling that I've seen her before; **j'ai l'i. qu'elle est timide** I have the impression that she's shy **(b)** *(action d'imprimer)* printing; *(copie)* printout; *Ordinat* **i. écran** screen dump; **i. laser** laser printing; *(copie)* laser printout **(c)** *(motif)* **tissu à impressions florales** material with a floral pattern

impressionnable [ɛpresjɔnabl] *adj (personne)* impressionable

impressionnant, -e [ɛpresjɔnɑ̃, -ɑ̃t] *adj (imposant)* impressive; *(bouleversant)* upsetting

impressionner [ɛpresjɔne] *vt* **(a)** *(frapper)* to impress; *(bouleverser)* to upset; **se laisser i.** to let oneself be overawed **(b)** *Phot (pellicule)* to expose

impressionnisme [ɛpresjɔnism] *nm* impressionism

impressionniste [ɛpresjɔnist] *adj & nmf* impressionist

imprévisible [ɛprevizibl] *adj (temps, réaction, personne)* unpredictable; *(événement)* unforeseeable

imprévoyance [ɛprevwajɑ̃s] *nf* lack of foresight

imprévoyant, -e [ɛprevwajɑ̃, -ɑ̃t] *adj* lacking in foresight

imprévu, -e [ɛprevy] **1** *adj* unexpected, unforeseen
  2 *nm* **(a)** *(surprise)* **aimer l'i.** to like the unexpected; **un voyage plein d'i.** a journey full of surprises **(b)** *(incident)* unexpected *or* unforeseen event; **sauf i., à moins d'un i.** unless something unexpected happens

imprimable [ɛprimabl] *adj* printable

imprimante [ɛprimɑ̃t] *nf* printer; **i. à aiguilles** 24 pin printer; **i. feuille à feuille** sheet-fed printer; **i. graphique** graphics printer; **i. à jet d'encre** ink-jet printer; **i. (à) laser** laser printer

imprimé, -e [ɛprime] **1** *adj* printed
  2 *nm* **(a)** *(formulaire)* form; **imprimés** *(journaux, prospectus)* printed matter **(b)** *(sur un tissu)* print; **un i. à fleurs/à motifs géométriques** a floral/geometric print

imprimer [ɛprime] *vt* **(a)** *(livre)* to print; *Ordinat* to print (out); *Ordinat* **i. un écran** to do a print screen **(b)** *(motif, empreinte, tissu)* to print **(c)** *(mouvement)* to impart (**à** to)

imprimerie [ɛprimri] *nf* **(a)** *(technique)* printing **(b)** *(atelier, usine)* printing works; **l'I. nationale** = French government printing office, *Br* ≃ Her Majesty's Stationery Office

imprimeur [ɛprimœr] *nm* printer

improbable [ɛprɔbabl] *adj* improbable, unlikely

improductif, -ive [ɛprɔdyktif, -iv] *adj* unproductive

impromptu, -e [ɛprɔ̃pty] *adj & nm* impromptu

imprononçable [ɛprɔnɔ̃sabl] *adj* unpronounceable

impropre [ɛprɔpr] *adj* **(a)** *(incorrect)* incorrect **(b)** *(inadapté)* **i. à qch** unfit for sth; **i. à la consommation** unfit for human consumption

improprement [ɛprɔprəmɑ̃] *adv* incorrectly

improvisation [ɛprɔvizasjɔ̃] *nf* improvisation; **faire une i.** to improvise

improvisé, -e [ɛprɔvize] *adj* improvised

improviser [ɛprɔvize] **1** *vt & vi* to improvise
  2 s'improviser *vpr* **un départ en vacances, ça ne s'improvise pas** going on holiday isn't something you can do just like that

improviste [ɛprɔvist] **à l'improviste** *adv* unexpectedly

imprudemment [ɛprydamɑ̃] *adv (parler, agir)* rashly; *(conduire)* recklessly

imprudence [ɛprydɑ̃s] *nf* **(a)** *(d'un acte, d'une personne)* rashness **(b)** *(acte)* **commettre une i.** to act rashly

imprudent, -e [ɛprydɑ̃, -ɑ̃t] **1** *adj* rash; *(conducteur)* reckless
  2 *nm,f* rash person

impubliable [ɛpyblijabl] *adj* unpublishable

impudence [ɛpydɑ̃s] *nf* impudence

impudent, -e [ɛpydɑ̃, -ɑ̃t] *adj* impudent

impudeur [ɛpydœr] *nf* shamelessness

impudique [ɛpydik] *adj* shameless

impuissance [ɛpɥisɑ̃s] *nf* **(a)** *(incapacité)* powerlessness (**à faire qch** to do sth) **(b)** *(sexuelle)* impotence

impuissant, -e [ɛpɥisɑ̃, -ɑ̃t] **1** *adj* **(a)** *(désarmé)* powerless **(b)** *(sexuellement)* impotent
  2 *nm* impotent man

impulsif, -ive [ɛpylsif, -iv] **1** *adj* impulsive
  2 *nm,f* impulsive person

impulsion [ɛpylsjɔ̃] *nf* **(a)** *Tech* impulse **(b)** *Fig (élan)* impulse; **faire qch sous l'i. de la colère** to do sth in a fit of anger **(c)** *(essor)* impetus

impulsivité [ɛpylsivite] *nf* impulsiveness

impunément [ɛpynemɑ̃] *adv* with impunity

impuni, -e [ɛpyni] *adj* unpunished

impunité [ɛpynite] *nf* impunity; **agir en toute i.** to act with impunity

impur, -e [ɛpyr] *adj* impure

imputable [ɛ̃pytabl] *adj* (**a**) *(erreur)* attributable (**à** to) (**b**) *Fin* chargeable (**sur** to)

imputer [ɛ̃pyte] *vt* (**a**) *(crime, erreur)* **i. qch à qn** to attribute sth to sb (**b**) *Fin* **i. des frais sur un compte** to charge expenses to an account

inabordable [inabɔrdabl] *adj (endroit)* inaccessible; *(prix, marchandises)* unaffordable; *(personne)* unapproachable

inacceptable [inaksɛptabl] *adj* unacceptable

inaccessible [inaksesibl] *adj* (**a**) *(lieu)* inaccessible; *(objectif)* unattainable (**b**) *(personne)* unapproachable (**c**) *(insensible)* **i. à la pitié** incapable of pity; **i. à la flatterie** impervious to flattery

inachevé, -e [inaʃəve] *adj* unfinished

inactif, -ive [inaktif, -iv] **1** *adj* (**a**) *(personne)* inactive; *Écon* **la population inactive** the non-working population (**b**) *(remède)* ineffective
2 *nm,f* **un i.** a person without paid employment; **les inactifs** the non-working population

inaction [inaksjɔ̃] *nf* inaction

inactivité [inaktivite] *nf* inactivity

inadapté, -e [inadapte] **1** *adj (personne) (socialement)* maladjusted; *(physiquement, mentalement)* handicapped; *(matériel)* unsuitable (**à** for)
2 *nm,f (socialement)* maladjusted person; *(physiquement, mentalement)* handicapped person; **les inadaptés** the maladjusted/handicapped

inadéquation [inadekwasjɔ̃] *nf* inadequacy

inadmissible [inadmisibl] *adj* inadmissible

inadvertance [inadvɛrtɑ̃s] **par inadvertance** *adv* inadvertently

inaliénable [inaljenabl] *adj Jur (droit)* inalienable

inaltérable [inalterabl] *adj* (**a**) *(métal, revêtement)* stable (**b**) *Fig (constant)* unwavering

inamical, -e, -aux, -ales [inamikal, -o] *adj* unfriendly

inamovible [inamɔvibl] *adj* (**a**) *(four, autoradio)* built-in (**b**) *(juge, magistrat)* permanent

inanimé, -e [inanime] *adj* (**a**) *(mort)* lifeless; *(inconscient)* unconscious; **tomber i.** to fall down in a faint (**b**) *(objet)* inanimate

inanité [inanite] *nf (d'un effort)* futility; *(d'une conversation)* inanity

inanition [inanisjɔ̃] *nf* starvation; **mourir d'i.** to die of starvation

inaperçu, -e [inapɛrsy] *adj* **passer i.** to go unnoticed

inapplicable [inaplikabl] *adj (réforme, loi)* unenforceable; *(théorie)* inapplicable

inappréciable [inapresjabl] *adj (précieux)* invaluable

inapte [inapt] *adj (pour raisons médicales)* unfit; *(intellectuellement)* unsuited; **être i. à qch/à faire qch** *(pour raisons médicales)* to be unfit for sth/to do sth; *(intellectuellement)* to be unsuited for sth/to do sth; **être i. (au service)** *(appelé)* to be unfit (for service)

inaptitude [inaptityd] *nf (intellectuelle)* inaptitude; *(médicale, militaire)* unfitness (**à** for)

inarticulé, -e [inartikyle] *adj (son, cris)* inarticulate

inassouvi, -e [inasuvi] *adj (faim, désir, vengeance)* unsatisfied; *(soif)* unquenched

inattaquable [inatakabl] *adj* unassailable

inattendu, -e [inatɑ̃dy] *adj* unexpected

inattentif, -ive [inatɑ̃tif, -iv] *adj (distrait)* inattentive; **i. à qch** *(indifférent)* heedless of sth

inattention [inatɑ̃sjɔ̃] *nf* lack of attention; **un moment d'i.** a lapse of concentration

inaudible [inodibl] *adj* inaudible

inaugural, -e, -aux, -ales [inogyral, -o] *adj (discours, séance)* inaugural

inauguration [inogyrasjɔ̃] *nf (d'un bâtiment, d'une route)* (official) opening, inauguration; *(d'une statue, d'un monument)* unveiling

inaugurer [inogyre] *vt (bâtiment, route)* to officially open, to inaugurate; *(statue, monument)* to unveil; *Fig (politique, méthode)* to implement; *(époque)* to usher in

inavouable [inavwabl] *adj* shameful

inavoué, -e [inavwe] *adj* unconfessed

INC [iɛnse] *nm (abrév* **Institut national de la consommation**) = national institute for consumer advice, *Br* ≃ National Consumer Council

inca [ɛ̃ka] **1** *adj* Inca
2 *nmf* **I.** Inca

incalculable [ɛ̃kalkylabl] *adj* incalculable; **un nombre i. de fois** countless times

incandescence [ɛ̃kɑ̃desɑ̃s] *nf* incandescence

incandescent, -e [ɛ̃kɑ̃desɑ̃, -ɑ̃t] *adj* incandescent

incantation [ɛ̃kɑ̃tasjɔ̃] *nf* incantation

incantatoire [ɛ̃kɑ̃tatwar] *adj* incantatory

incapable [ɛ̃kapabl] **1** *adj* (**a**) *(incompétent)* incapable, incompetent; *Jur* incompetent (**b**) **être i. de faire qch** to be incapable of doing sth; **i. de lâcheté** incapable of cowardice
2 *nmf* (**a**) *(incompétent)* incompetent; **espèce d'i.!** you useless idiot! (**b**) *Jur* incompetent person

incapacité [ɛ̃kapasite] *nf* (**a**) *(impossibilité)* **i. à faire qch** inability to do sth; **être dans l'i. de faire qch** to be unable to do sth (**b**) *(incompétence)* incompetence (**c**) *(invalidité)* disability; **i. de travail** unfitness for work (**d**) *Jur* incompetence

incarcération [ɛ̃karserasjɔ̃] *nf* incarceration

incarcérer [34] [ɛ̃karsere] *vt* to incarcerate

incarnation [ɛ̃karnasjɔ̃] *nf aussi Fig* incarnation

incarné, -e [ɛ̃karne] *adj* (**a**) *Rel & Fig* incarnate (**b**) *(ongle)* ingrowing

incarner [ɛ̃karne] **1** *vt* (**a**) *(représenter)* to embody (**b**) *Théât & Cin* **i. (le rôle de) qn** to play (the part of) sb
2 **s'incarner** *vpr* (**a**) *Rel* to become incarnate (**b**) *(ongle)* to become ingrown

incartade [ɛ̃kartad] *nf* indiscretion

incassable [ɛ̃kasabl] *adj* unbreakable

incendiaire [ɛ̃sɑ̃djɛr] **1** *adj (bombe)* incendiary; *Fig (discours)* inflammatory
2 *nmf (personne)* arsonist, fire-raiser

incendie [ɛ̃sɑ̃di] *nm* fire; **i. de forêt** forest fire; **un i. criminel** arson

incendier [66] [ɛ̃sɑ̃dje] *vt* (**a**) *(mettre le feu à)* to set on fire (**b**) *Fam (accabler de reproches)* **i. qn** to haul sb over the coals; **se faire i.** to get hauled over the coals

incertain, -e [ɛ̃sɛrtɛ̃, -ɛn] *adj (fait, donnée, résultat)* uncertain; *(temps)* unsettled; *(mémoire)* unreliable; *(personne)* indecisive; *(démarche, pas)* unsteady; *(couleur)* vague

incertitude [ɛ̃sɛrtityd] *nf* uncertainty; **être dans l'i. (quant à)** to be uncertain (about)

incessamment [ɛ̃sesamɑ̃] *adv* very soon; **il doit arriver i.** he'll be here any minute now; *Hum* **i. sous peu** very soon

incessant, -e [ɛ̃sesɑ̃, -ɑ̃t] *adj* incessant, constant

incessible [ɛ̃sesibl] *adj (pension, titre de propriété)* non-transferable; *(droit)* inalienable

inceste [ɛ̃sɛst] *nm* incest
incestueux, -euse [ɛ̃sɛstɥø, -øz] *adj* incestuous; **enfant i.** child of an incestuous relationship
inchangé, -e [ɛ̃ʃɑ̃ʒe] *adj* unchanged
incidemment [ɛ̃sidamɑ̃] *adv* in passing
incidence [ɛ̃sidɑ̃s] *nf* (**a**) *(répercussion)* impact (**sur** on) (**b**) *Méd & Phys* incidence
incident, -e [ɛ̃sidɑ̃, -ɑ̃t] **1** *nm* (**a**) *(événement sans conséquence)* hitch; **se dérouler sans i.** to go off without incident; **i. de parcours** minor setback; **i. technique** technical hitch (**b**) *(événement plus grave)* incident; **i. diplomatique** diplomatic incident
  2 *adj (question, remarque)* incidental
incinérateur [ɛ̃sineratœr] *nm* incinerator
incinération [ɛ̃sinerasjɔ̃] *nf (de déchets)* incineration; *(d'une personne)* cremation
incinérer [34] [ɛ̃sinere] *vt (déchets)* to incinerate; *(personne)* to cremate
inciser [ɛ̃size] *vt (peau)* to make an incision in; *(abcès)* to lance
incisif, -ive [ɛ̃sizif, -iv] **1** *adj (remarque, personne, style)* incisive
  2 *nf* **incisive** incisor
incision [ɛ̃sizjɔ̃] *nf* incision; **pratiquer une i. dans** to make an incision in
incitation [ɛ̃sitasjɔ̃] *nf (à la violence, l'émeute)* incitement; *(encouragement)* incentive; **i. fiscale** tax incentive; **i. à l'achat** incentive to buy; **i. de mineurs à la débauche** corruption of minors
inciter [ɛ̃site] *vt* **i. qn à faire qch** to encourage sb to do sth; **i. qn à la prudence/la clémence** *(sujet: événement)* to incline sb to be cautious/merciful
inclassable [ɛ̃klasabl] *adj* unclassifiable; **un film/ peintre i.** a film/painter that cannot be pigeonholed
inclinable [ɛ̃klinabl] *adj (siège, dossier)* reclining
inclinaison [ɛ̃klinɛzɔ̃] *nf (d'un toit)* slope; *(d'une pente)* incline; *(de la tête, d'un chapeau)* tilt
inclination [ɛ̃klinasjɔ̃] *nf* (**a**) **i. de la tête** *(pour saluer)* nod (**b**) *(tendance)* inclination (**pour** for)
incliné, -e [ɛ̃kline] *adj (mât, toit)* sloping; *(table à dessin, dossier)* tilted
incliner [ɛ̃kline] **1** *vt* (**a**) *(pencher)* to tilt; **i. la tête** *(en avant)* to bow one's head; *(en signe de salut)* to nod; *(sur le côté)* to tilt one's head to one side (**b**) *(pousser)* **i. qn à faire qch** to incline sb to do sth; **i. qn à la prudence/la clémence** to incline sb to be cautious/merciful
  2 *vi* **j'incline à penser qu'elle a tort** I'm inclined to think she's wrong
  3 **s'incliner** *vpr* (**a**) *(terrain)* to slant, to slope; *(bateau)* to heel *or* keel over; *(avion)* to bank (**b**) *(se pencher) (en avant)* to lean forward; *(sur le côté)* to lean to one side; *(pour saluer)* to bow; *Fig* **s'i. devant qch** to bow to sth (**c**) *(se soumettre)* to give in (**devant** to) (**d**) *(être battu)* to lose (**devant** to)
inclure [17] [ɛ̃klyr] *vt* (**a**) *(dans un courrier)* to enclose (**dans** with) (**b**) *(englober, insérer)* & *Math* to include
inclus, -e [ɛ̃kly, -yz] *adj* (**a**) *(compris)* **jusqu'à la page 5 incluse** up to and including page 5; **jusqu'au mardi i.** *Br* up to and including Tuesday, *Am* through Tuesday; **du 7 au 18 i.** from the 7th to the 18th inclusive; **ils seront trente-cinq, professeurs i.** there will be thirty-five of them, including the teachers (**b**) *(dent)* impacted
inclusion [ɛ̃klyzjɔ̃] *nf* (**a**) *(dans un courrier)* enclosure (**dans** with) (**b**) *(insertion)* insertion (**c**) *(objet décoratif)*

= flower, shell etc set into plastic and used as a paperweight, an ornament, jewellery etc (**d**) *(d'une dent)* impacting (**e**) *Ordinat (de fichier)* insertion
incognito [ɛ̃kɔnito] **1** *adv* incognito
  2 *nm* **garder l'i.** to remain incognito
incohérence [ɛ̃kɔerɑ̃s] *nf (d'une personne, dans un film, une histoire)* inconsistency; *(d'un discours, d'idées)* incoherence
incohérent, -e [ɛ̃kɔerɑ̃, -ɑ̃t] *adj (personne, histoire, attitude)* inconsistent; *(idées, argumentation, discours)* incoherent; **tenir des propos incohérents** to talk incoherently
incollable [ɛ̃kɔlabl] *adj* (**a**) *(riz)* non-stick (**b**) *Fam (personne)* **elle est i. sur la question/en histoire** you can't catch her out on the subject/on history
incolore [ɛ̃kɔlɔr] *adj* colourless
incomber [ɛ̃kɔ̃be] **incomber à** *vt ind (responsabilité)* to lie with; *(devoirs)* to fall to; **il m'incombe/il lui incombe de...** it falls to me/to him to...
incombustible [ɛ̃kɔ̃bystibl] *adj* incombustible
incommensurable [ɛ̃kɔmɑ̃syrabl] *adj (richesse)* immeasurable; *(espace)* boundless; *Hum* **être d'une bêtise i.** to be incredibly stupid
incommodant, -e [ɛ̃kɔmɔdɑ̃, -ɑ̃t] *adj* discomforting
incommode [ɛ̃kɔmɔd] *adj (horaire, arrangement)* inconvenient; *(situation)* awkward
incommoder [ɛ̃kɔmɔde] *vt* to bother
incomparable [ɛ̃kɔ̃parabl] *adj (sans pareil)* beyond compare, matchless
incomparablement [ɛ̃kɔ̃parabləmɑ̃] *adv* incomparably
incompatibilité [ɛ̃kɔ̃patibilite] *nf* incompatibility; **i. d'humeur** *ou* **de caractère** mutual incompatibility
incompatible [ɛ̃kɔ̃patibl] *adj* incompatible (**avec** with)
incompétence [ɛ̃kɔ̃petɑ̃s] *nf* incompetence
incompétent, -e [ɛ̃kɔ̃petɑ̃, -ɑ̃t] *adj* incompetent
incomplet, -ète [ɛ̃kɔ̃plɛ, -ɛt] *adj* incomplete
incompréhensible [ɛ̃kɔ̃prẽsibl] *adj* incomprehensible
incompréhension [ɛ̃kɔ̃prẽsjɔ̃] *nf* incomprehension
incompressible [ɛ̃kɔ̃prɛsibl] *adj* (**a**) *(matériau)* incompressible (**b**) *Jur (peine)* to be served in full (**c**) *(dépenses)* which cannot be reduced
incompris, -e [ɛ̃kɔ̃pri, -iz] **1** *adj* misunderstood
  2 *nm,f* **être un i.** to be misunderstood
inconcevable [ɛ̃kɔ̃səvabl] *adj* inconceivable
inconciliable [ɛ̃kɔ̃siljabl] *adj (théorie)* irreconcilable (**avec** with); *(mode de vie, activité)* incompatible (**avec** with)
inconditionnel, -elle [ɛ̃kɔ̃disjɔnɛl] **1** *adj (soutien, retrait)* unconditional; *(obéissance)* unquestioning, unconditional; *(supporter)* staunch
  2 *nm,f* fan; **c'est un i. de la pêche/du hard rock** he's absolutely mad about fishing/hard rock
inconfort [ɛ̃kɔ̃fɔr] *nm (matériel)* discomfort; *(moral)* awkwardness
inconfortable [ɛ̃kɔ̃fɔrtabl] *adj aussi Fig* uncomfortable
incongru, -e [ɛ̃kɔ̃gry] *adj* inappropriate; *(bruit)* rude
incongruité [ɛ̃kɔ̃gryite] *nf* (**a**) *(manque d'à-propos)* inappropriateness (**b**) *(remarque déplacée)* inappropriate remark
inconnu, -e [ɛ̃kɔny] **1** *adj (auteur, civilisation, destination)* unknown (**de** to); *(lieu, visage)* strange; **il**

m'est i. I've never heard of him/it; **né de père i.** *(sur document administratif)* father unknown; **i. à cette adresse** not known at this address; *Fam* **Durand? i. au bataillon!** Durand? never heard of him!
 2 *nm,f (étranger)* stranger; *(personne non célèbre)* unknown
 3 *nm* **la peur de l'i.** the fear of the unknown
 4 *nf* **inconnue** *Math & Fig* unknown (quantity)
inconsciemment [ɛ̃kɔ̃sjamɑ̃] *adv* (**a**) *(sans réfléchir)* without thinking (**b**) *(dans l'inconscient)* subconsciously
inconscience [ɛ̃kɔ̃sjɑ̃s] *nf* (**a**) *(perte de connaissance)* unconsciousness; **sombrer** *ou* **tomber dans l'i.** to lose consciousness (**b**) *(manque de jugement)* recklessness; **c'est de l'i.!** it's sheer madness!
inconscient, -e [ɛ̃kɔ̃sjɑ̃, -ɑ̃t] **1** *adj* (**a**) *(évanoui)* unconscious (**b**) *(acte)* unconscious; **i. du danger** oblivious to the danger (**c**) *(irréfléchi) (personne)* reckless
 2 *nm* **l'i.** the unconscious, the subconscious; **l'i. collectif** the collective unconscious
inconséquence [ɛ̃kɔ̃sekɑ̃s] *nf (caractère)* recklessness; *(acte)* reckless act
inconséquent, -e [ɛ̃kɔ̃sekɑ̃, -ɑ̃t] *adj* (**a**) *(irréfléchi)* reckless (**b**) *(illogique)* inconsistent
inconsidéré, -e [ɛ̃kɔ̃sidere] *adj (acte, remarque)* ill-considered; *(dépenses)* reckless
inconsistance [ɛ̃kɔ̃sistɑ̃s] *nf* (**a**) *(d'une pâte, d'une soupe)* thinness (**b**) *(d'une personne, d'une conduite)* inconsistency (**c**) *(d'une intrigue, d'un film, d'un roman)* thinness
inconsistant, -e [ɛ̃kɔ̃sistɑ̃, -ɑ̃t] *adj* (**a**) *(pâte, crème, soupe)* thin (**b**) *(conduite, personne)* inconsistent (**c**) *(intrigue, film, roman)* thin
inconsolable [ɛ̃kɔ̃sɔlabl] *adj* inconsolable
inconstance [ɛ̃kɔ̃stɑ̃s] *nf (instabilité)* changeableness; *(infidélité)* fickleness
inconstant, -e [ɛ̃kɔ̃stɑ̃, -ɑ̃t] *adj (instable)* changeable; *(infidèle)* fickle
inconstitutionnel, -elle [ɛ̃kɔ̃stitysjɔnɛl] *adj* unconstitutional
incontestable [ɛ̃kɔ̃tɛstabl] *adj* indisputable
incontestablement [ɛ̃kɔ̃tɛstabləmɑ̃] *adv* indisputably
incontesté, -e [ɛ̃kɔ̃tɛste] *adj* undisputed
incontinence [ɛ̃kɔ̃tinɑ̃s] *nf* *Méd* incontinence; **i. verbale** verbal diarrhoea
incontinent, -e [ɛ̃kɔ̃tinɑ̃, -ɑ̃t] *adj Méd* incontinent
incontournable [ɛ̃kɔ̃turnabl] *adj (film, artiste)* that cannot be ignored; **son argument était i.** there was no getting away from her argument
incontrôlable [ɛ̃kɔ̃trolabl] *adj* (**a**) *(incendie, bâillements)* uncontrollable; **des éléments incontrôlables** rowdy elements (**b**) *(affirmation)* unverifiable
incontrôlé, -e [ɛ̃kɔ̃trole] *adj (éléments, bande)* uncontrolled
inconvenance [ɛ̃kɔ̃vənɑ̃s] *nf (indécence)* impropriety; **dire/commettre une i.** to say/to do something improper
inconvenant, -e [ɛ̃kɔ̃vənɑ̃, -ɑ̃t] *adj (propos, remarque, acte)* improper
inconvénient [ɛ̃kɔ̃venjɑ̃] *nm* drawback, disadvantage; **je n'y vois pas d'i.** I have no objection
inconvertible [ɛ̃kɔ̃vɛrtibl] *adj (monnaie)* non-convertible

incorporation [ɛ̃kɔrpɔrasjɔ̃] *nf* (**a**) *(mélange)* blending, mixing (**de qch dans qch** of sth into sth) (**b**) *Mil* conscription
incorporé, -e [ɛ̃kɔrpɔre] *adj (flash, micro)* built-in
incorporer [ɛ̃kɔrpɔre] **1** *vt* (**a**) *(mélanger)* **i. qch à qch** to blend *or* mix sth into sth (**b**) *(insérer)* to insert (**à** in) (**c**) *(troupes)* to draft
 2 s'incorporer *vpr* **s'i. dans un groupe** to join a group
incorrect, -e [ɛ̃kɔrɛkt] *adj* (**a**) *(erroné)* incorrect, wrong (**b**) *(personne)* impolite; *(attitude)* improper (**c**) *(tenue) (déplacée)* unsuitable; *(indécente)* improper
incorrectement [ɛ̃kɔrɛktəmɑ̃] *adv* (**a**) *(en faisant des erreurs)* incorrectly, wrongly (**b**) *(impoliment)* impolitely (**c**) *(habillé) (de façon déplacée)* unsuitably; *(de façon indécente)* improperly
incorrection [ɛ̃kɔrɛksjɔ̃] *nf* (**a**) *(impolitesse)* impoliteness (**b**) *(action)* impolite action; *(propos)* impolite remark (**c**) *(grammaticale)* mistake
incorrigible [ɛ̃kɔriʒibl] *adj* incorrigible
incorruptible [ɛ̃kɔryptibl] **1** *adj* incorruptible
 2 *nmf* incorruptible person
incrédule [ɛ̃kredyl] *adj (sceptique)* incredulous; **d'un air i.** with a look of disbelief
incrédulité [ɛ̃kredylite] *nf* incredulity
increvable [ɛ̃krəvabl] *adj* (**a**) *(pneu)* puncture-proof (**b**) *Fam (personne)* tireless; *(voiture, moteur)* indestructible
incriminer [ɛ̃krimine] *vt (personne)* to accuse; *(sujet: événement)* to condemn; *(comportement, décision)* to condemn
incrochetable [ɛ̃krɔʃtabl] *adj* unpickable
incroyable [ɛ̃krwajabl] *adj* incredible; **c'est i., ça!** I don't believe it!; **d'une bêtise i.** incredibly stupid
incroyablement [ɛ̃krwajabləmɑ̃] *adv* incredibly
incroyance [ɛ̃krwajɑ̃s] *nf* unbelief
incroyant, -e [ɛ̃krwajɑ̃, -ɑ̃t] **1** *adj* unbelieving
 2 *nm,f* unbeliever
incrustation [ɛ̃krystasjɔ̃] *nf* (**a**) *(ornement)* inlay (**b**) *(dépôt calcaire)* fur, scale (**c**) *TV (image)* inset
incruste [ɛ̃kryst] *nf Fam* **si on l'invite, il va encore taper l'i.** if we invite him, we'll never get rid of him; **elle a tapé l'i. à ma soirée** she gatecrashed my party
incruster [ɛ̃kryste] **1** *vt* (**a**) *(bois, métal)* to inlay (**de** with) (**b**) *(entartrer)* to scale, to fur up
 2 s'incruster *vpr* (**a**) *(adhérer)* to become encrusted (**b**) *(chaudière, bouilloire)* to fur up (**c**) *Fam (s'imposer)* **quand on l'invite, il s'incruste** once you invite him you can't get rid of him
incubateur [ɛ̃kybatœr] *nm* incubator
incubation [ɛ̃kybasjɔ̃] *nf* incubation; **période d'i.** incubation period
incuber [ɛ̃kybe] *vt* to incubate, to hatch
inculpation [ɛ̃kylpasjɔ̃] *nf* indictment; **sous l'i. d'assassinat** charged with murder
inculpé, -e [ɛ̃kylpe] *nm,f* **l'i.** the accused
inculper [ɛ̃kylpe] *vt* to indict, to charge (**de** with)
inculquer [ɛ̃kylke] *vt* to instil (**à qn** in sb)
inculte [ɛ̃kylt] *adj (terre, personne)* uncultivated
incultivable [ɛ̃kyltivabl] *adj* untillable
inculture [ɛ̃kyltyr] *nf* lack of culture
incurable [ɛ̃kyrabl] **1** *adj* incurable; **d'une paresse i.** incurably lazy
 2 *nmf* person with an incurable disease

incurie [ɛ̃kyri] *nf Formel* negligence
incursion [ɛ̃kyrsjɔ̃] *nf* (**a**) *(invasion)* raid, incursion (**b**) *Fig (entrée soudaine)* intrusion; **faire une i. dans une pièce/une réunion** to burst into a room/a meeting
incurvé, -e [ɛ̃kyrve] *adj* bent, curved
indatable [ɛ̃databl] *adj* that cannot be dated
Inde [ɛ̃d] *nf* **l'I.** India
indéboulonnable [ɛ̃debulɔnabl] *adj* **il est i.!** they'll never be able to sack him!
indécence [ɛ̃desɑ̃s] *nf* indecency
indécent, -e [ɛ̃desɑ̃, -ɑ̃t] *adj* indecent
indéchiffrable [ɛ̃deʃifrabl] *adj* (**a**) *(illisible)* indecipherable (**b**) *(incompréhensible)* impenetrable
indéchirable [ɛ̃deʃirabl] *adj* tearproof
indécis, -e [ɛ̃desi, -iz] **1** *adj* (**a**) *(personne) (de caractère)* indecisive; *(ponctuellement)* undecided; **je suis encore indécise** I haven't made my mind up yet (**b**) *(peu net) (victoire, bataille)* inconclusive; *(contour)* vague
2 *nm,f* indecisive person; *Pol* **les i.** the floating voters
indécision [ɛ̃desizjɔ̃] *nf (de caractère)* indecisiveness; *(ponctuelle)* indecision
indécrottable [ɛ̃dekrɔtabl] *adj Fam (incorrigible)* hopeless; **être d'une bêtise i.** to be hopelessly stupid
indéfendable [ɛ̃defɑ̃dabl] *adj* indefensible
indéfini, -e [ɛ̃defini] *adj* (**a**) *(illimité)* indefinite (**b**) *(imprécis) (tristesse, malaise)* vague, undefined (**c**) *Gram (pronom, article)* indefinite
indéfiniment [ɛ̃definimɑ̃] *adv* indefinitely
indéfinissable [ɛ̃definisabl] *adj* indefinable
indéformable [ɛ̃defɔrmabl] *adj* that keeps its shape
indélébile [ɛ̃delebil] *adj* indelible
indélicat, -e [ɛ̃delika, -at] *adj* (**a**) *(sans tact)* tactless, insensitive (**b**) *(malhonnête)* dishonest
indélicatesse [ɛ̃delikates] *nf* (**a**) *(manque de tact)* tactlessness (**b**) *(malhonnêteté)* dishonesty; *(acte malhonnête)* dishonest act; **commettre une i.** to behave dishonestly
indemne [ɛ̃demn] *adj* (**a**) *(physiquement)* unhurt, unharmed; **elle est sortie i. de la collision** she was unhurt in the collision (**b**) *(moralement)* unscathed; **il est sorti i. du scandale** he emerged unscathed from the scandal
indemnisation [ɛ̃demnizasjɔ̃] *nf* compensation
indemniser [ɛ̃demnize] *vt* to compensate (**de** for)
indemnité [ɛ̃demnite] *nf* (**a**) *(pour perte encourue)* compensation; *(pour délai, non-livraison)* penalty (**b**) *(allocation)* allowance; **i. journalière** daily allowance; **i. de licenciement** severance pay, redundancy payment; **i. parlementaire** = salary paid to member of French parliament; **i. de transport** travel allowance
indémodable [ɛ̃demɔdabl] *adj* perennially fashionable
indémontrable [ɛ̃demɔ̃trabl] *adj* unprovable
indéniable [ɛ̃denjabl] *adj* undeniable
indéniablement [ɛ̃denjabləmɑ̃] *adv* undeniably
indépendamment [ɛ̃depɑ̃damɑ̃] *adv* independently; **i. de** apart from
indépendance [ɛ̃depɑ̃dɑ̃s] *nf* independence; **accéder à l'i.** to gain independence
indépendant, -e [ɛ̃depɑ̃dɑ̃, -ɑ̃t] **1** *adj* (**a**) *(personne, pays, vie)* independent (**de** of); *(travailleur)*

self-employed, freelance; *(appartement)* self-contained; **i. de ma volonté** beyond my control (**b**) *Gram* **proposition indépendante** main clause
2 *nm,f (travailleur)* self-employed person, freelancer; **travailler en i.** to work on a freelance basis
indépendantisme [ɛ̃depɑ̃dɑ̃tism] *nm* independence movement
indépendantiste [ɛ̃depɑ̃dɑ̃tist] *nmf Pol (partisan de l'indépendance)* supporter of independence; *(activiste)* freedom fighter
indéracinable [ɛ̃derasinabl] *adj (préjugés)* deep-rooted
indescriptible [ɛ̃dɛskriptibl] *adj* indescribable
indésirable [ɛ̃dezirabl] *adj & nmf* undesirable
indestructible [ɛ̃dɛstryktibl] *adj* indestructible
indétectable [ɛ̃detɛktabl] *adj* undetectable
indéterminé, -e [ɛ̃detɛrmine] *adj* (**a**) *(date, heure)* unspecified; *(raison)* unknown (**b**) *(personne)* undecided
index [ɛ̃dɛks] *nm* (**a**) *(doigt)* forefinger, index finger (**b**) *(de livre)* index; *Fig* **mettre qn/qch à l'i.** to blacklist sb/sth (**c**) *Ordinat* index
indexation [ɛ̃dɛksasjɔ̃] *nf Écon* index-linking (**sur** to); *Ordinat* indexing
indexer [ɛ̃dɛkse] *vt* (**a**) *Écon* to index-link (**sur** to) (**b**) *aussi Ordinat (ajouter un index à)* to index
indic [ɛ̃dik] *nm Fam* grass, informer
indicateur, -trice [ɛ̃dikatœr, -tris] **1** *adj voir* **panneau, poteau**
2 *nm* (**a**) *(livre)* **i. des rues de Paris** Paris street finder; **i. des chemins de fer** railway timetable (**b**) *(instrument)* indicator, gauge; *Aviat* **i. d'altitude** altimeter; **i. de niveau de carburant** fuel gauge (**c**) *(informateur)* informer (**d**) *Écon* indicator
indicatif, -ive [ɛ̃dikatif, -iv] **1** *adj* indicative (**de** of); **à titre i.** as a guide
2 *nm* (**a**) *Gram* indicative (mood); **à l'i.** in the indicative (**b**) *Tél* dialling code; *TV & Rad* theme tune
indication [ɛ̃dikasjɔ̃] *nf* (**a**) *(action)* indication (**b**) *(renseignement)* (piece of) information (**c**) *(directive)* instruction, direction; **sauf i. contraire** unless otherwise specified; *Théât* **indications scéniques** stage directions (**d**) *(sur notice pharmaceutique)* **indications:...** suitable for...
indice [ɛ̃dis] *nm* (**a**) *(signe)* sign, indication (**de** of); *(dans une enquête)* clue (**de** to) (**b**) *(chiffre indicateur)* & *Math* index; *Typ* subscript; *Aut* **i. d'octane** octane rating; **i. des prix** price index; **i. de protection** *(d'une crème solaire)* protection factor
indicible [ɛ̃disibl] *adj Litt* indescribable
indien, -enne [ɛ̃djɛ̃, -ɛn] **1** *adj* Indian
2 *nm,f* **I.** *(d'Inde, d'Amérique)* Indian
indifféremment [ɛ̃diferamɑ̃] *adv (sans distinction)* equally
indifférence [ɛ̃diferɑ̃s] *nf* indifference
indifférencié, -e [ɛ̃diferɑ̃sje] *adj* undifferentiated
indifférent, -e [ɛ̃diferɑ̃, -ɑ̃t] *adj* (**a**) *(peu ou pas intéressé)* indifferent (**à** to); **laisser qn i.** to leave sb cold; **il m'est i.** I'm indifferent to him (**b**) *(sans importance)* irrelevant; **cela m'est i.** it makes no difference to me; **parler de choses indifférentes** to chat about nothing in particular
indifférer [34] [ɛ̃difere] *vt* **cela m'indiffère** it's a matter of complete indifference to me
indigence [ɛ̃diʒɑ̃s] *nf* destitution

indigène [ɛ̃diʒɛn] **1** *adj* native; *Bot & Zool* native, indigenous (**de** to)
2 *nmf* (**a**) *(autochtone) & Bot & Zool* native (**b**) *Suisse (citoyen)* citizen

indigent, -e [ɛ̃diʒɑ̃, -ɑ̃t] **1** *adj* destitute
2 *nm,f* pauper; **les indigents** the poor

indigeste [ɛ̃diʒɛst] *adj aussi Fig* indigestible

indigestion [ɛ̃diʒɛstjɔ̃] *nf* **avoir une i.** to have a stomach upset; **faire une i. de chocolat** to make oneself sick from eating chocolate; *Fig* **j'en ai une i.** I'm fed up with it

indignation [ɛ̃diɲasjɔ̃] *nf* indignation

indigne [ɛ̃diɲ] *adj (personne)* unworthy (**de** of); *(action, conduite)* shameful

indigner [ɛ̃diɲe] **1** *vt* to outrage
2 **s'indigner** *vpr* to be indignant (**de** at)

indignité [ɛ̃diɲite] *nf* (**a**) *(d'une personne)* unworthiness; *(d'une action)* shamefulness (**b**) *(action)* shameful act

indigo [ɛ̃digo] *nm & adj inv* indigo

indiqué, -e [ɛ̃dike] *adj (recommandé)* advisable; **il est tout à fait i. pour ce poste** he's the right person for the job

indiquer [ɛ̃dike] *vt* (**a**) *(montrer) (sujet: personne)* to point out; **i. qch du doigt** to point to *or* at sth; **i. le chemin à qn** to tell sb the way, to direct sb (**b**) *(marquer) (sujet: panneau, étiquette, carte)* to show, to indicate; *(sujet: compteur)* to show, to read (**c**) *(donner) (date, adresse)* to give; **à l'heure indiquée** at the agreed time; **pourriez-vous m'i. le prix de ce vase?** could you tell me how much this vase costs? (**d**) *(recommander)* to recommend; **elle m'a indiqué un excellent dentiste/hôtel** she recommended an excellent dentist/hotel to me (**e**) *(dénoter)* to point to, to indicate

indirect, -e [ɛ̃dirɛkt] *adj aussi Gram* indirect

indirectement [ɛ̃dirɛktəmɑ̃] *adv* indirectly

indiscipline [ɛ̃disiplin] *nf* indiscipline

indiscipliné, -e [ɛ̃disipline] *adj* undisciplined; *(cheveux)* unmanageable

indiscret, -ète [ɛ̃diskrɛ, -ɛt] **1** *adj* (**a**) *(qui parle trop)* indiscreet (**b**) *(curieux)* inquisitive; **à l'abri des regards indiscrets** safe from prying eyes
2 *nm,f* (**a**) *(qui parle trop)* indiscreet person (**b**) *(curieux)* inquisitive person

indiscrétion [ɛ̃diskresjɔ̃] *nf* (**a**) *(manque de discrétion)* indiscretion (**b**) *(curiosité)* inquisitiveness; **sans i., combien l'avez-vous payé?** if you don't mind me asking, how much did you pay for it? (**c**) *(remarque)* indiscreet remark; **commettre une i.** to say something one shouldn't

indiscutable [ɛ̃diskytabl] *adj* indisputable

indiscutablement [ɛ̃diskytabləmɑ̃] *adv* indisputably

indispensable [ɛ̃dispɑ̃sabl] **1** *adj* indispensable, essential (**à qch** for sth); **i. à qn** indispensable to sb; **il est i. que tu y ailles** it is essential that you go
2 *nm* **l'i.** the essentials

indisponibilité [ɛ̃disponibilite] *nf* unavailability

indisponible [ɛ̃disponibl] *adj* unavailable

indisposé, -e [ɛ̃dispoze] *adj* indisposed, unwell; *Euph* **elle est indisposée** it's her time of the month

indisposer [ɛ̃dispoze] *vt* (**a**) *(rendre malade)* **i. qn** *(odeur, climat)* to make sb feel ill; *(nourriture)* to disagree with sb (**b**) *(contrarier)* to annoy

indisposition [ɛ̃dispozisjɔ̃] *nf* indisposition, slight illness

indissociable [ɛ̃disɔsjabl] *adj* indissociable (**de** from)

indissoluble [ɛ̃disɔlybl] *adj* indissoluble

indistinct, -e [ɛ̃distɛ̃, -ɛkt] *adj* indistinct

indistinctement [ɛ̃distɛ̃ktəmɑ̃] *adv* (**a**) *(voir, parler)* indistinctly (**b**) *(indifféremment)* equally

individu [ɛ̃dividy] *nm* (**a**) *(être humain)* individual (**b**) *Péj (homme)* individual, character; **un drôle d'i.** a strange individual *or* character

individualiser [ɛ̃dividɥalize] *vt* (**a**) *(différencier)* to make individual (**b**) *(adapter)* to adapt to individual circumstances

individualisme [ɛ̃dividɥalism] *nm* individualism

individualiste [ɛ̃dividɥalist] **1** *adj* individualistic
2 *nmf* individualist

individualité [ɛ̃dividɥalite] *nf* individuality

individuel, -elle [ɛ̃dividɥɛl] *adj* individual; *(liberté, responsabilité)* personal; *(maison)* detached; *(chambre)* single

individuellement [ɛ̃dividɥɛlmɑ̃] *adv* individually

indivisible [ɛ̃divizibl] *adj* indivisible

Indochine [ɛ̃dɔʃin] *nf* **l'I.** Indochina

indocile [ɛ̃dɔsil] *adj* disobedient

indo-européen, -enne *(mpl* **indo-européens**, *fpl* **indo-européennes**) [ɛ̃doørɔpeɛ̃, -ɛn] **1** *adj* Indo-European
2 *nm,f* **I.** Indo-European
3 *nm (langue)* Indo-European

indolence [ɛ̃dɔlɑ̃s] *nf* laziness

indolent, -e [ɛ̃dɔlɑ̃, -ɑ̃t] *adj* lazy

indolore [ɛ̃dɔlɔr] *adj* painless

indomptable [ɛ̃dɔ̃tabl] *adj* (**a**) *(animal)* untamable (**b**) *Fig (orgueil, caractère)* indomitable; *(passion)* uncontrollable

indompté, -e [ɛ̃dɔ̃te] *adj* (**a**) *(animal)* untamed (**b**) *Fig (passion, orgueil)* uncontrolled

Indonésie [ɛ̃dɔnezi] *nf* **l'I.** Indonesia

indonésien, -enne [ɛ̃dɔnezjɛ̃, -ɛn] **1** *adj* Indonesian
2 *nm,f* **I.** Indonesian

indu, -e [ɛ̃dy] *adj* **à une heure indue** at an ungodly hour; **il rentre à des heures indues** he comes home at all hours of the night

indubitable [ɛ̃dybitabl] *adj* indisputable, indubitable; **c'est i.** there's no doubt about it

indubitablement [ɛ̃dybitabləmɑ̃] *adv* undoubtedly

induire [18] [ɛ̃dɥir] *vt* (**a**) *(entraîner)* **i. qn à faire qch** to induce sb to do sth; **i. qn en erreur** to mislead sb (**b**) *(conclure)* to infer (**de** from)

indulgence [ɛ̃dylʒɑ̃s] *nf* (**a**) *(bienveillance)* indulgence, leniency; **faire preuve d'i. envers qn** to be indulgent towards sb; **rires sans i.** merciless laughter; **faire de qn un portrait sans i.** to describe sb warts and all (**b**) *Rel* indulgence

indulgent, -e [ɛ̃dylʒɑ̃, -ɑ̃t] *adj* indulgent

indûment [ɛ̃dymɑ̃] *adv* unduly

industrialisation [ɛ̃dystrijalizasjɔ̃] *nf* industrialization

industrialiser [ɛ̃dystrijalize] **1** *vt* to industrialize
2 **s'industrialiser** *vpr* to become industrialized

industrie [ɛ̃dystri] *nf* industry; **travailler dans l'i.** to work in industry; **l'i. alimentaire** the food industry; **l'i. automobile** the car industry; **l'i. lourde** heavy industry; **l'i. pharmaceutique** the pharmaceutical industry

industriel, -elle [ɛ̃dystrijɛl] **1** *adj* industrial; *Fam* **des magazines en quantité industrielle** vast quantities of magazines
2 *nm* manufacturer, industrialist

industriellement [ɛ̃dystrijɛlmɑ̃] *adv* industrially

industrieux, -euse [ɛ̃dystrijø, -øz] *adj Litt (habile)* skilful, ingenious; *(travailleur)* industrious

inébranlable [inebrɑ̃labl] *adj (mur, rocher)* immovable; *Fig* unshakeable

inédit, -e [inedi, -it] **1** *adj* (**a**) *(livre)* previously unpublished; *(disque)* previously unreleased (**b**) *(spectacle, projet, idée)* new, original
2 *nm (texte)* previously unpublished work; *(disque)* previously unreleased record

ineffable [inefabl] *adj* ineffable, unutterable

ineffaçable [inefasabl] *adj aussi Fig* indelible

inefficace [inefikas] *adj (personne)* inefficient; *(remède, méthode, loi)* ineffective

inefficacité [inefikasite] *nf (de personne)* inefficiency; *(d'un remède, d'une méthode, d'une loi)* ineffectiveness

inégal, -e, -aux, -ales [inegal, -o] *adj* (**a**) *(non égal) (parts, partage, force, lutte)* unequal (**b**) *(irrégulier) (sol)* uneven; *(pouls)* irregular, *Fig (travail, écrivain, style, qualité)* inconsistent; *(humeur)* changeable

inégalable [inegalabl] *adj* incomparable, matchless

inégalé, -e [inegale] *adj (qualité, personne)* unequalled; *(record)* unbeaten

inégalement [inegalmɑ̃] *adv* (**a**) *(injustement)* unequally (**b**) *(irrégulièrement)* unevenly

inégalitaire [inegaliter] *adj* unequal

inégalité [inegalite] *nf* (**a**) *(injustice)* inequality (**entre** between) (**b**) *(différence)* disparity (**de** in) (**c**) *(du sol)* unevenness; *Fig* **i. d'humeur** moodiness

inélégant, -e [inelegɑ̃, -ɑ̃t] *adj Litt (mal habillé)* inelegant; *(discourtois)* discourteous

inéligible [ineliʒibl] *adj* ineligible

inéluctable [inelyktabl] *adj* inescapable

inemployable [inɑ̃plwajabl] *adj* unusable

inemployé, -e [inɑ̃plwaje] *adj (objet, machine, talent)* unused; *(ressources)* untapped; *(forces)* unchannelled

inénarrable [inenarabl] *adj* comical

inepte [inɛpt] *adj (remarque, réponse, histoire)* inane; *(personne)* inept

ineptie [inɛpsi] *nf* (**a**) *(d'un comportement, d'un film)* inanity (**b**) *(action)* stupid thing; *(remarque)* stupid comment; **dire des inepties** to talk nonsense

inépuisable [inepɥizabl] *adj (réserves, sujet, curiosité)* inexhaustible; *(imagination)* limitless; **sur ce sujet-là, elle est i.** you can never get her off the subject

inerte [inɛrt] *adj* (**a**) *(masse, corps, matière)* inert (**b**) *(personne) (inanimé)* lifeless; *(passif)* apathetic

inertie [inɛrsi] *nf* (**a**) *Phys* inertia (**b**) *(manque de réaction)* apathy

inespéré, -e [inɛspere] *adj* unexpected, unhoped-for

inesthétique [inɛstetik] *adj* unaesthetic

inestimable [inɛstimabl] *adj (dégâts, coût, richesse)* incalculable; *(aide, chance)* invaluable; *(œuvre d'art)* priceless; **d'une valeur i.** priceless

inévitable [inevitabl] *adj* inevitable, unavoidable

inévitablement [inevitabləmɑ̃] *adv* inevitably, unavoidably

inexact, -e [inɛgzakt] *adj* (**a**) *(incorrect) (réponse, description, détail)* inaccurate; *(somme, calcul)* wrong, incorrect (**b**) *(manquant de ponctualité)* unpunctual

inexactitude [inɛgzaktityd] *nf* (**a**) *(caractère erroné, erreur)* inaccuracy (**b**) *(manque de ponctualité)* unpunctuality

inexcusable [inɛkskyzabl] *adj* inexcusable, unforgivable

inexhaustible [inɛgzostibl] *adj Litt* inexhaustible

inexistant, -e [inɛgzistɑ̃, -ɑ̃t] *adj* non-existent; *Hum* **il est totalement i.** he's a complete nonentity

inexistence [inɛgzistɑ̃s] *nf* non-existence

inexorable [inɛgzɔrabl] *adj (destin)* inexorable; *(juge)* pitiless; *(volonté)* inflexible

inexorablement [inɛgzɔrabləmɑ̃] *adv* inexorably

inexpérience [inɛksperjɑ̃s] *nf* inexperience

inexpérimenté, -e [inɛksperimɑ̃te] *adj* inexperienced

inexplicable [inɛksplikabl] *adj* inexplicable

inexpliqué, -e [inɛksplike] *adj* unexplained

inexploité, -e [inɛksplwate] *adj (mine)* unworked; *(terre)* undeveloped; *(ressources)* untapped

inexploré, -e [inɛksplɔre] *adj* unexplored

inexpressif, -ive [inɛkspresif, -iv] *adj* inexpressive, expressionless

inexprimable [inɛksprimabl] *adj* inexpressible

inexprimé, -e [inɛksprime] *adj* unexpressed

in extenso [inɛkstɛ̃so] *adv* in full

in extremis [inɛkstremis] *adv* at the last minute

inextricable [inɛkstrikabl] *adj* inextricable

inextricablement [inɛkstrikabləmɑ̃] *adv* inextricably

infaillibilité [ɛ̃fajibilite] *nf* infallibility

infaillible [ɛ̃fajibl] *adj* infallible

infailliblement [ɛ̃fajibləmɑ̃] *adv* infallibly

infaisable [ɛ̃fəzabl] *adj* not feasible, impossible

infamant, -e [ɛ̃famɑ̃, -ɑ̃t] *adj* (**a**) *(déclaration, accusation)* defamatory, slanderous (**b**) *Jur (peine)* involving loss of civil rights

infâme [ɛ̃fɑm] *adj (mensonge, personne)* despicable; *(acte, crime)* unspeakable; *(taudis)* squalid; *(odeur, nourriture)* revolting

infamie [ɛ̃fami] *nf* (**a**) *(caractère infâme)* infamy (**b**) *(action)* unspeakable act; *(remarque)* slanderous remark

infant, -e [ɛ̃fɑ̃, -ɑ̃t] *nm,f* infante, *f* infanta

infanterie [ɛ̃fɑ̃tri] *nf* infantry; **i. de marine** marine corps, marines

infanticide [ɛ̃fɑ̃tisid] **1** *adj* infanticidal
2 *nmf (personne)* child-killer, infanticide
3 *nm (crime)* infanticide

infantile [ɛ̃fɑ̃til] *adj* (**a**) *(maladie)* childhood (**b**) *Péj (comportement, personne)* childish, infantile

infantiliser [ɛ̃fɑ̃tilize] *vt Péj* **la télévision infantilise les gens** television makes people behave like children

infarctus [ɛ̃farktys] *nm* heart attack; **i. du myocarde** myocardial infarction, coronary thrombosis

infatigable [ɛ̃fatigabl] *adj* tireless

infatué, -e [ɛ̃fatɥe] *adj Litt* conceited; **i. de soi-même** full of oneself

infécond, -e [ɛ̃fekɔ̃, -ɔ̃d] *adj* infertile

infect, -e [ɛ̃fɛkt] *adj* foul

infecter [ɛ̃fɛkte] **1** vt (**a**) (plaie, blessure) to infect (**b**) (atmosphère, eau, sol) to contaminate
2 s'infecter vpr to become infected, to go septic
infectieux, -euse [ɛ̃fɛksjø, -øz] adj infectious
infection [ɛ̃fɛksjɔ̃] nf (**a**) Méd & Ordinat infection (**b**) (puanteur) stench, stink; **quelle i. dans cette pièce!** this room stinks!
inférieur, -e [ɛ̃ferjœr] **1** adj (**a**) (qui est en bas) (étagère, niveau) bottom; (étages, lèvre, paupière, membres, mâchoire) lower; **partie inférieure** bottom (part); **allez voir à l'étage i.** go and look on the floor below (**b**) (dans une hiérarchie) (qualité, marchandises, intelligence) inferior; **d'un rang i.** of a lower rank; **être rétrogradé à l'échelon i.** to be demoted to the grade below (**c**) (dans une comparaison) **i. à** (qualité) inferior to; (quantité) less than; **i. ou égal à** less than or equal to; **note inférieure à douze** mark below twelve; **i. en nombre** fewer in number; **i. à la moyenne** below average
2 nm,f inferior
infériorité [ɛ̃ferjɔrite] nf inferiority
infernal, -e, -aux, -ales [ɛ̃fɛrnal, -o] adj (**a**) (de l'enfer) infernal; Fig (cruauté, méchanceté) diabolical (**b**) Fam (insupportable) (chaleur, bruit) infernal; **à une vitesse infernale** at breakneck speed; **des cadences infernales** an impossible rate of work; **cet enfant est i.** this child's a little devil
infertile [ɛ̃fɛrtil] adj infertile
infertilité [ɛ̃fɛrtilite] nf infertility
infester [ɛ̃fɛste] vt (sujet: vermine) to infest; Fig (sujet: personnes) to overrun; **infesté de** infested/overrun with
infidèle [ɛ̃fidɛl] **1** adj (**a**) (déloyal) unfaithful (à to) (**b**) (inexact) (traduction, rapport) inaccurate (**c**) Rel infidel
2 nmf Rel infidel
infidélité [ɛ̃fidelite] nf (**a**) (déloyauté) unfaithfulness (à to); **faire des infidélités à** to be unfaithful to (**b**) (manque d'exactitude) (dans une traduction, un compte rendu) inaccuracy
infiltration [ɛ̃filtrasjɔ̃] nf (**a**) (d'un liquide) infiltration; **il y a des infiltrations dans le plafond** there are some leaks in the ceiling (**b**) (d'espions) infiltration (**c**) (piqûre) **faire des infiltrations à qn** to give sb injections
infiltrer [ɛ̃filtre] **1** vt (noyauter) (parti, pays) to infiltrate
2 s'infiltrer vpr (**a**) (fluide) to infiltrate; **s'i. dans** to seep into (**b**) (espion) **s'i. dans** to infiltrate
infime [ɛ̃fim] adj tiny
infini, -e [ɛ̃fini] **1** adj infinite; **ça prend un temps i.** it takes an eternity
2 nm **l'i.** infinity; **à l'i.** (s'étendre, se refléter) to infinity; (discutailler) ad infinitum
infiniment [ɛ̃finimɑ̃] adv (énormément) infinitely; **i. petit** infinitesimal; **i. reconnaissant** extremely grateful; **je regrette i.** I'm extremely sorry
infinité [ɛ̃finite] nf infinity; **une i. de** an infinite number of
infinitésimal, -e, -aux, -ales [ɛ̃finitezimal, -o] adj infinitesimal
infinitif, -ive [ɛ̃finitif, -iv] **1** adj infinitive
2 nm infinitive; **à l'i.** in the infinitive
infirmation [ɛ̃firmasjɔ̃] nf Jur invalidation
infirme [ɛ̃firm] **1** adj disabled
2 nmf disabled person; **les infirmes** the disabled
infirmer [ɛ̃firme] vt to invalidate

infirmerie [ɛ̃firmɔri] nf (d'une prison, d'une caserne) infirmary; (à l'école, dans un bateau) sick bay
infirmier [ɛ̃firmje] nm (male) nurse
infirmière [ɛ̃firmjɛr] nf nurse; **i. de jour/nuit** day/night nurse
infirmité [ɛ̃firmite] nf disability
inflammable [ɛ̃flamabl] adj inflammable, flammable
inflammation [ɛ̃flamasjɔ̃] nf Méd inflammation; **j'ai une i. au genou** my knee is inflamed
inflation [ɛ̃flasjɔ̃] nf inflation
inflationniste [ɛ̃flasjɔnist] adj inflationary
infléchir [ɛ̃fleʃir] **1** vt (**a**) (rayon) to bend (**b**) (politique) to change the direction of; **i. le cours des événements** to change the course of events
2 s'infléchir vpr (**a**) (dévier) (route, ligne) to bend (**b**) (changer) (politique) to change direction
inflexibilité [ɛ̃flɛksibilite] nf inflexibility
inflexible [ɛ̃flɛksibl] adj inflexible
inflexion [ɛ̃flɛksjɔ̃] nf (**a**) (mouvement) **i. du corps** bend of the body; (pour saluer) bow; **i. de (la) tête** tilt of the head; (pour saluer, acquiescer) nod (**b**) (de la voix) inflection (**c**) (de courbe, rayon) inflection
infliger [45] [ɛ̃fliʒe] vt **i. qch à qn** (correction, punition) to inflict sth on sb; (peine, amende) to impose sth on sb
influençable [ɛ̃flyɑ̃sabl] adj easily influenced
influence [ɛ̃flyɑ̃s] nf influence (sur on); **trafic d'i.** corruption (involving a public official)
influencer [16] [ɛ̃flyɑ̃se] vt to influence; **il ne faut pas te laisser i.** you mustn't let yourself be influenced; **il se laisse facilement i.** he's easily influenced
influent, -e [ɛ̃flyɑ̃, -ɑ̃t] adj influential
influer [ɛ̃flye] vi **i. sur** to influence
influx [ɛ̃fly] nm **i. nerveux** nerve impulse
info [ɛ̃fo] nf Fam (nouvelle) news item; **les infos** the news (singulier)
Infographie® [ɛ̃fɔɡrafi] nf computer graphics
informateur, -trice [ɛ̃fɔrmatœr, -tris] nm,f informant; (de police) informer
informaticien, -enne [ɛ̃fɔrmatisjɛ̃, -ɛn] **1** nm,f computer scientist
2 adj **ingénieur i.** computer engineer
information [ɛ̃fɔrmasjɔ̃] nf (**a**) (renseignement) (piece of) information; **informations** information; **pour votre i.** for your information; **à titre d'i.** for information; **assurer l'i. du public en matière de santé** to ensure that the public is kept informed about health matters; **le droit à l'i.** freedom of information (**b**) (nouvelle) news item; **une i. de dernière minute** some late news; **les informations** the news (singulier) (**c**) (médias) **l'i.** the media (**d**) Ordinat data, information; **traitement de l'i.** data processing; **théorie de l'i.** information theory (**e**) Jur (enquête) inquiry; (instruction préparatoire) preliminary investigation; **ouvrir une i.** to begin legal proceedings
informatique [ɛ̃fɔrmatik] nf (traitement de l'information) data processing; (science) computer science, computing; **travailler dans l'i.** to work in computers; **société/magazine/cours d'i.** computer company/magazine/course
informatisation [ɛ̃fɔrmatizasjɔ̃] nf computerization
informatiser [ɛ̃fɔrmatize] **1** vt to computerize
2 s'informatiser vpr to become computerized;

depuis que je me suis informatisé since I got a computer

informe [ɛ̃fɔrm] *adj (masse, objet, vêtement)* shapeless; *(monstre, être)* misshapen

informé, -e [ɛ̃fɔrme] **1** *adj* informed; **bien i.** well-informed; **mal i.** ill-informed; **dans les milieux informés** in informed circles
    2 *nmJur* inquiry; **jusqu'à plus ample i.** until we have further information

informel, -elle [ɛ̃fɔrmɛl] *adj* informal

informer [ɛ̃fɔrme] **1** *vt* to inform (**de** of); **i. qn que…** to inform sb that…; **nous informons les voyageurs que…** we would like to inform passengers that…
    2 **s'informer** *vpr (se renseigner)* to inquire, to ask (**de/au sujet de** about); *(se tenir au courant)* to keep oneself informed

inforoute [ɛ̃fɔrut] *nf Can Ordinat* information superhighway, infohighway

infortune [ɛ̃fɔrtyn] *nf* misfortune; **compagnons d'i.** companions in adversity

infortuné, -e [ɛ̃fɔrtyne] **1** *adj* unfortunate
    2 *nm,f* unfortunate wretch

infoutu, -e [ɛ̃futy] *adj Fam* **être i. de faire qch** to be downright incapable of doing sth

infraction [ɛ̃fraksjɔ̃] *nf (à un règlement, à la loi)* infringement (**à** of); *(délit)* offence; **être en i.** to be committing an offence

infranchissable [ɛ̃frɑ̃ʃisabl] *adj (rivière, col, gouffre)* impassable; *(obstacle, difficulté)* insurmountable

infrarouge [ɛ̃fraruʒ] *adj & nm* infrared

infrastructure [ɛ̃frastryktyr] *nf* **(a)** *Constr* substructure **(b)** *(d'équipements)* infrastructure; **i. routière/touristique** road/tourist infrastructure

infructueux, -euse [ɛ̃fryktɥø, -øz] *adj* fruitless

infumable [ɛ̃fymabl] *adj* unsmokable

infuse [ɛ̃fyz] *adj f voir* **science**

infuser [ɛ̃fyze] **1** *vi (thé)* to brew; *(tisane)* to infuse; **faire i. qch** to brew sth
    2 *vt* **(a)** *(faire pénétrer)* to instil (**dans** into) **(b)** *(herbes)* to infuse; *(thé)* to brew

infusion [ɛ̃fyzjɔ̃] *nf* **(a)** *(boisson)* herb tea; **une i. de camomille** some camomile tea **(b)** *(processus)* infusion; *(de thé)* brewing

ingénier [66] [ɛ̃ʒenje] **s'ingénier** *vpr* **s'i. à faire qch** to strive to do sth; **il s'ingénie à me contredire** he goes out of his way to contradict me

ingénierie [ɛ̃ʒeniri] *nf* engineering

ingénieur [ɛ̃ʒenjœr] *nm* engineer; **i. agronome** agricultural engineer; **i. électronicien** electronics engineer; **i. des mines** mining engineer; **i. du son** sound engineer; **i. des travaux publics** civil engineer

ingénieur-conseil *(pl* **ingénieurs-conseils***)* [ɛ̃ʒenjœrkɔ̃sɛj] *nm* consultant engineer

ingénieusement [ɛ̃ʒenjøzmɑ̃] *adv* ingeniously

ingénieux, -euse [ɛ̃ʒenjø, -øz] *adj* ingenious

ingéniosité [ɛ̃ʒenjozite] *nf* ingenuity

ingénu, -e [ɛ̃ʒeny] **1** *adj* ingenuous
    2 *nm,f* ingenuous person

ingénuité [ɛ̃ʒenɥite] *nf* ingenuousness

ingérence [ɛ̃ʒerɑ̃s] *nf* interference (**dans** in)

ingérer [34] [ɛ̃ʒere] *vt* to ingest

ingestion [ɛ̃ʒestjɔ̃] *nf* ingestion

ingrat, -e [ɛ̃gra, -at] **1** *adj (personne)* ungrateful (**envers** to); *(sol, terre)* barren; *(tâche)* thankless; *(travail,*

sujet) unrewarding; *(physique, visage)* unattractive
    2 *nm,f* ungrateful person

ingratitude [ɛ̃gratityd] *nf* ingratitude

ingrédient [ɛ̃gredjɑ̃] *nm* ingredient

inguérissable [ɛ̃gerisabl] *adj* incurable

ingurgiter [ɛ̃gyrʒite] *vt (aliment, boisson)* to gulp down; *Fam Fig (connaissances)* to cram into one's head

inhabitable [inabitabl] *adj* uninhabitable

inhabité, -e [inabite] *adj* uninhabited

inhabituel, -elle [inabitɥɛl] *adj* unusual

inhalation [inalasjɔ̃] *nf* **(a)** *(respiration)* breathing in, inhalation **(b)** *Méd* (steam) inhalation; **le mieux pour les rhumes, c'est de faire des inhalations** inhaling steam is the best thing for a cold

inhaler [inale] *vt* to inhale

inhérent, -e [inerɑ̃, -ɑ̃t] *adj* inherent (**à** in)

inhiber [inibe] *vt* to inhibit

inhibition [inibisjɔ̃] *nf* inhibition

inhospitalier, -ère [inɔspitalje, -ɛr] *adj* inhospitable

inhumain, -e [inymɛ̃, -ɛn] *adj* inhuman

inhumanité [inymanite] *nf* inhumanity

inhumation [inymasjɔ̃] *nf* burial

inhumer [inyme] *vt* to bury

inimaginable [inimaʒinabl] *adj* unimaginable

inimitable [inimitabl] *adj* inimitable

inimitié [inimitje] *nf* enmity

ininflammable [inɛ̃flamabl] *adj* non-flammable

inintelligent, -e [inɛ̃teliʒɑ̃, -ɑ̃t] *adj* unintelligent

inintelligible [inɛ̃teliʒibl] *adj* unintelligible

inintéressant, -e [inɛ̃teresɑ̃, -ɑ̃t] *adj* uninteresting

ininterrompu, -e [inɛ̃terɔ̃py] *adj* continuous

inique [inik] *adj* iniquitous

iniquité [inikite] *nf* iniquity

initial, -e, -aux, -ales [inisjal, -o] **1** *adj* initial
    2 *nf* **initiale** initial

initialement [inisjalmɑ̃] *adv* initially

initialisation [inisjalizasjɔ̃] *nf Ordinat* initialization

initialiser [inisjalize] *vt Ordinat (disque)* to initialize; *(ordinateur)* to boot (up)

initiateur, -trice [inisjatœr, -tris] **1** *nm,f (d'un projet, d'une réforme)* initiator
    2 *adj* initiatory

initiation [inisjasjɔ̃] *nf* **(a)** *(formation)* introduction (**à** to) **(b)** *(rituels)* initiation (**à** into)

initiatique [inisjatik] *adj* initiatory

initiative [inisjativ] *nf* initiative; **à l'i. de qn** on sb's initiative; **prendre l'i. de faire qch** to take the initiative in doing sth; **faire qch de sa propre i.** to do sth on one's own initiative; **il n'a aucune i.** he's got no initiative

initié, -e [inisje] *nm,f* initiate

initier [66] [inisje] **1** *vt* **(a)** *(former)* to introduce (**à** to) **(b)** *(rituellement)* to initiate (**à** into)
    2 **s'initier** *vpr* **s'i. à qch** to start learning sth

injectable [ɛ̃ʒɛktabl] *adj* injectable

injecté, -e [ɛ̃ʒɛkte] *adj* **yeux injectés de sang** bloodshot eyes

injecter [ɛ̃ʒɛkte] *vt (substance, capitaux)* to inject (**dans** into)

injection [ɛ̃ʒɛksjɔ̃] *nf (de substance, de capital)* injection; **moteur à i.** fuel-injection engine

injonction [ɛ̃ʒɔ̃ksjɔ̃] *nf* injunction; **i. de payer** order to pay; **recevoir l'i. de faire qch** to get the order to do sth

injure [ɛ̃ʒyr] *nf* insult; **injures** abuse, insults; **faire i. à qn** to insult sb

injurier [66] [ɛ̃ʒyrje] *vt* to insult, to abuse

injurieux, -euse [ɛ̃ʒyrjø, -øz] *adj* insulting, abusive

injuste [ɛ̃ʒyst] *adj* unfair (**envers** *ou* **avec** to *or* towards)

injustement [ɛ̃ʒystəmɑ̃] *adv* unjustly, unfairly

injustice [ɛ̃ʒystis] *nf* (**a**) *(iniquité)* injustice, unfairness (**envers** towards); **i. sociale** social injustice (**b**) *(acte, parole)* injustice

injustifiable [ɛ̃ʒystifjabl] *adj* unjustifiable

injustifié, -e [ɛ̃ʒystifje] *adj* unjustified

inlassable [ɛ̃lɑsabl] *adj* untiring

inlassablement [ɛ̃lɑsabləmɑ̃] *adv* untiringly; *(répéter)* ceaselessly

inné, -e [ine] *adj* innate, inborn

innocemment [inɔsamɑ̃] *adv* innocently

innocence [inɔsɑ̃s] *nf* innocence; **en toute i.** in all innocence

innocent, -e [inɔsɑ̃, -ɑ̃t] **1** *adj* innocent (**de** of) **2** *nm,f (non coupable)* innocent person; *(idiot)* simpleton; **ne fais pas l'i.!** don't act the innocent!; *Prov* **aux innocents les mains pleines** fortune favours fools

innocenter [inɔsɑ̃te] *vt* to clear (**de** of)

innocuité [inɔkɥite] *nf* harmlessness

innombrable [inɔ̃brabl] *adj* innumerable, countless; *(foule)* huge

innommable [inɔmabl] *adj Péj (conduite, actes)* unspeakable; *(nourriture, odeur)* vile

innovateur, -trice [inɔvatœr, -tris] **1** *adj* innovative **2** *nm,f* innovator

innovation [inɔvasjɔ̃] *nf* innovation

innover [inɔve] *vi* to innovate

inoccupé, -e [inɔkype] *adj* unoccupied

inoculation [inɔkylasjɔ̃] *nf Méd* inoculation

inoculer [inɔkyle] *vt* (**a**) **i. un virus/un vaccin à qn** to inoculate sb with a virus/a vaccine; **i. une maladie à qn** to infect sb with a disease; *Fig* **elle nous a inoculé sa gaieté** she infected us with her cheerfulness (**b**) **i. qn (contre une maladie)** to inoculate sb (against a disease)

inodore [inɔdɔr] *adj* odourless

inoffensif, -ive [inɔfɑ̃sif, -iv] *adj* harmless

inondation [inɔ̃dasjɔ̃] *nf* flood; *(action)* flooding

inondé, -e [inɔ̃de] *adj (lieu)* flooded; **populations inondées** flood victims; **visage i. de larmes** face streaming with tears; **i. de lumière** flooded with light

inonder [inɔ̃de] *vt (lieu)* to flood; *Fig (marché)* to flood, to inundate (**de** with); **être inondé de réclamations** to be inundated with complaints

inopérable [inɔperabl] *adj* inoperable

inopérant, -e [inɔperɑ̃, -ɑ̃t] *adj* ineffective

inopiné, -e [inɔpine] *adj* unexpected

inopportun, -e [inɔpɔrtœ̃, -yn] *adj* inopportune

inoubliable [inublijabl] *adj* unforgettable

inouï, -e [inwi] *adj* (**a**) *(ahurissant)* incredible; **il leur est arrivé une histoire inouïe** something incredible happened to them; **c'est/vous êtes i.!** it's/you're incredible! (**b**) *(nouveau)* unheard-of

Inox® [inɔks] *nm* stainless steel

inoxydable [inɔksidabl] *adj (métal)* rustproof; **acier i.** stainless steel

inqualifiable [ɛ̃kalifjabl] *adj* unspeakable

inquiet, -ète [ɛ̃kjɛ, -ɛt] **1** *adj (anxieux) (personne, air, voix)* worried, anxious (**au sujet de** about); *(attente)* anxious **2** *nm,f* worrier

inquiétant, -e [ɛ̃kjetɑ̃, -ɑ̃t] *adj* (**a**) *(alarmant)* worrying (**b**) *(qui effraie) (air, sourire)* frightening

inquiéter [34] [ɛ̃kjete] **1** *vt* to worry; **être inquiété par la police** to be bothered by the police **2 s'inquiéter** *vpr* (**a**) *(se faire du souci)* to worry; **il n'y a pas de quoi s'i.** there's nothing to worry about; **s'i. pour qn** to be worried about sb; **ne t'inquiète pas pour elle!** don't (you) worry about her! (**b**) **s'i. de** *(se faire du souci pour)* to bother about; *(s'informer de)* to inquire about; **sans s'i. de rien** without a care in the world

inquiétude [ɛ̃kjetyd] *nf* anxiety, worry; **sujet d'i.** cause for anxiety; **éprouver quelques inquiétudes** to feel a bit worried; **soyez sans i.** rest easy

inquisiteur, -trice [ɛ̃kizitœr, -tris] **1** *adj (regard)* inquisitive **2** *nm* inquisitor; **le Grand I.** the Inquisitor General

inquisition [ɛ̃kizisjɔ̃] *nf* inquisition; **l'I.** the Inquisition

insaisissable [ɛ̃sezisabl] *adj* (**a**) *(personne)* elusive (**b**) *(son, différence, nuance)* imperceptible

insalubre [ɛ̃salybr] *adj (climat, habitation, pays)* insalubrious; *(occupation)* unhealthy

insanité [ɛ̃sanite] *nf (de raisonnement, de propos)* insanity; **des insanités** complete nonsense

insatiable [ɛ̃sasjabl] *adj* insatiable

insatisfait, -e [ɛ̃satisfɛ, -ɛt] **1** *adj (personne)* dissatisfied; *(désir)* unsatisfied **2** *nm,f* **c'est un éternel i.** he's never satisfied

inscription [ɛ̃skripsjɔ̃] *nf* (**a**) *(action) (dans un journal, un registre)* entering; *(immatriculation)* registration (**b**) *(sur une tombe, un mur)* inscription; *(dans un livre de comptes)* entry

inscrire [30] [ɛ̃skrir] **1** *vt* (**a**) *(renseignements, date)* to write down; *(dans un journal, dans un registre)* to enter (**b**) *(pour participer)* **i. qn à un club/à une activité** to enrol sb in a club/for an activity; **i. un enfant dans une école** to enrol a child at a school (**c**) *(dans la pierre)* to inscribe **2 s'inscrire** *vpr (à l'université) Br* to matriculate, *Am* to register (**à** at); *(à un tournoi, à un concours)* to enter (**à** for); *(à une activité)* to enrol (**à** for); *(dans une école)* to enrol (**dans** at); **s'i. dans un club/à un parti** to join a club/party; **s'i. sur les listes électorales** to register to vote; **s'i. en faux contre qch** to deny sth; **s'i. dans le cadre de** to come within the framework of

inscrit, -e [ɛ̃skri, -it] **1** *adj (électeur, candidat)* registered **2** *nm,f (à l'université)* registered student; *(à un concours)* registered entrant; *(électeur)* registered voter

insécable [ɛ̃sekabl] *adj* indivisible

insecte [ɛ̃sɛkt] *nm* insect

insecticide [ɛ̃sɛktisid] **1** *adj* insecticidal **2** *nm* insecticide

insectivore [ɛ̃sɛktivɔr] **1** *adj* insectivorous **2** *nm* insectivore

insécurité [ɛ̃sekyrite] *nf* insecurity

INSEE [inse] *nm (abrév* **Institut national de la statistique et des études économiques**) = French national institute of statistics and information about the economy

insémination [ɛ̃seminasjɔ̃] *nf* insemination; **i. artificielle** artificial insemination

inséminer [ɛ̃semine] *vt* to inseminate

insensé, -e [ɛ̃sɑ̃se] **1** *adj (projet, idée)* crazy; *(action, espoir, dépenses)* wild; **c'est i.!** it's crazy!
   2 *nm,f* madman, *f* madwoman

insensibilité [ɛ̃sɑ̃sibilite] *nf* insensitivity (**à** to)

insensible [ɛ̃sɑ̃sibl] *adj (à la douleur, au froid)* insensitive (**à** to); **i. à la critique** impervious to criticism; **elle demeura i. à leurs larmes** she remained unmoved by their tears

insensiblement [ɛ̃sɑ̃sibləmɑ̃] *adv* imperceptibly

inséparable [ɛ̃separabl] *adj* inseparable

insérer [34] [ɛ̃sere] **1** *vt* to insert (**dans** in); **i. une annonce dans un journal** to put an advertisement in a paper
   2 s'insérer *vpr* (**a**) *(s'attacher)* to be attached (**sur** to) (**b**) *(s'intégrer)* **s'i. dans** *(réformes, politique)* to fit into

insertion [ɛ̃sɛrsjɔ̃] *nf* insertion; **i. sociale** (social) integration; **i. professionnelle** integration into the job market; *Ordinat* **mode d'i.** insert mode; *Ordinat* **i. de ligne** line insert; **i. publicitaire** advertisement

insidieusement [ɛ̃sidjøzmɑ̃] *adv* insidiously

insidieux, -euse [ɛ̃sidjø, -øz] *adj* insidious

insigne¹ [ɛ̃siɲ] *nm* badge; **insignes de la royauté** insignia of royalty

insigne² *adj* (**a**) *Formal (remarquable)* signal (**b**) *Hum (indiscrétion, maladresse)* remarkable

insignifiant, -e [ɛ̃siɲifjɑ̃, -ɑ̃t] *adj* insignificant

insinuation [ɛ̃sinɥasjɔ̃] *nf* insinuation

insinuer [ɛ̃sinɥe] **1** *vt* to insinuate; **que voulez-vous i.?** what are you insinuating?
   2 s'insinuer *vpr* **s'i. dans** *(froid, odeur)* to creep into; *(personne)* to worm one's way into; **le doute/l'idée qui s'insinue dans mon esprit** the doubt/the idea that is creeping into my mind; **s'i. dans les bonnes grâces de qn** to insinuate oneself into sb's favour

insipide [ɛ̃sipid] *adj* insipid

insistance [ɛ̃sistɑ̃s] *nf* insistence; **avec i.** insistently

insistant, -e [ɛ̃sistɑ̃, -ɑ̃t] *adj* insistent

insister [ɛ̃siste] *vi* (**a**) *(persévérer)* to insist; **elle a beaucoup insisté** she was very insistent; **i. pour faire qch** to insist on doing sth; **elle a essayé la planche à voile mais elle n'a pas insisté** she tried windsurfing but soon gave it up; **j'ai dit non, n'insistez pas!** *ou* **inutile d'i.!** I said no, don't go on about it!; **ça ne répond pas – insiste encore un peu** there's no answer – hang on a bit (**b**) *(mettre l'accent sur)* **i. sur qch** to stress sth; **nous insistons particulièrement sur la ponctualité** we lay particular stress on punctuality

insolation [ɛ̃sɔlasjɔ̃] *nf* (**a**) *Méd* sunstroke; **attraper une i.** to get sunstroke (**b**) *(ensoleillement)* sunshine

insolence [ɛ̃sɔlɑ̃s] *nf* (**a**) *(impertinence)* insolence (**b**) *(remarque, action)* impertinence

insolent, -e [ɛ̃sɔlɑ̃, -ɑ̃t] **1** *adj* (**a**) *(impertinent)* insolent (**envers** *ou* **avec** to) (**b**) *(dans la victoire)* haughty (**c**) *(succès)* outrageous; *(luxe)* unashamed
   2 *nm,f* insolent person

insolite [ɛ̃sɔlit] **1** *adj* unusual, strange
   2 *nm* **l'i.** the unusual

insoluble [ɛ̃sɔlybl] *adj* insoluble

insolvable [ɛ̃sɔlvabl] *adj* insolvent

insomniaque [ɛ̃sɔmnjak] *adj & nmf* insomniac

insomnie [ɛ̃sɔmni] *nf* insomnia; **avoir des insomnies** to have insomnia; **j'ai eu une i. la nuit dernière** I couldn't sleep last night

insondable [ɛ̃sɔ̃dabl] *adj (océan, gouffre, mystère)* unfathomable; *(bêtise)* immense

insonorisation [ɛ̃sɔnɔrizasjɔ̃] *nf* soundproofing

insonoriser [ɛ̃sɔnɔrize] *vt* to soundproof

insouciance [ɛ̃susjɑ̃s] *nf* carefree attitude; **vivre dans l'i.** to live a carefree life

insouciant, -e [ɛ̃susjɑ̃, -ɑ̃t] *adj* carefree; **i. de son avenir** unconcerned about his future

insoumis, -e [ɛ̃sumi, -iz] **1** *adj* (**a**) *(peuple, tribus)* unsubdued (**b**) *(personne)* rebellious (**c**) *Mil (soldat)* absentee
   2 *nm Mil* absentee

insoupçonnable [ɛ̃supsɔnabl] *adj (personne)* beyond suspicion

insoupçonné, -e [ɛ̃supsɔne] *adj* unsuspected (**de** by)

insoutenable [ɛ̃sutnabl] *adj* (**a**) *(spectacle, odeur)* unbearable (**b**) *(opinion, position)* untenable

inspecter [ɛ̃spɛkte] *vt* to inspect

inspecteur, -trice [ɛ̃spɛktœr, -tris] *nm,f* inspector; **i. d'Académie** school inspector; **i. de police** police inspector; **i. du travail** factory inspector; *Hum* **i. des travaux finis** idler, *Br* skiver *(who arrives after the work has been done)*

inspection [ɛ̃spɛksjɔ̃] *nf* (**a**) *(examen)* inspection; **faire l'i. de** to inspect (**b**) *(service)* inspectorate; **i. académique** school inspectorate; **i. du travail** factory inspectorate

inspiration [ɛ̃spirasjɔ̃] *nf* (**a**) *(créatrice)* inspiration; **avoir de l'i.** to be inspired; **un poème d'i. romantique** a poem in the romantic style (**b**) *(idée)* inspiration (**c**) *(d'air)* breathing in

inspiré, -e [ɛ̃spire] *adj (style, poète, artiste, air)* inspired (**de** by); **être bien/mal i. de faire qch** to do the right/wrong thing in doing sth

inspirer [ɛ̃spire] **1** *vt* (**a**) *(donner de l'inspiration à)* to inspire; **ça m'a inspiré une chanson** it inspired me to write a song; *Hum* **ça ne m'inspire pas** it doesn't exactly inspire me (**b**) *(susciter)* **à qn** to inspire confidence in sb; **ça m'inspire la plus grande inquiétude** it gives me great cause for concern (**c**) *(air)* to breathe in
   2 *vi* to breathe in
   3 s'inspirer *vpr* **s'i. de** to be inspired by; **une toile inspirée de Renoir** a painting inspired by Renoir

instabilité [ɛ̃stabilite] *nf* instability; *(du temps)* changeability

instable [ɛ̃stabl] *adj* unstable; *(temps)* changeable

installateur, -trice [ɛ̃stalatœr, -tris] *nm,f* fitter

installation [ɛ̃stalasjɔ̃] *nf* (**a**) *(fait d'installer) (d'une machine, du chauffage, d'un ascenseur)* installation; *(d'une cuisine)* fitting out; *(de rideaux)* putting up (**b**) *(emménagement)* move; **prévoir son i. dans une région** to plan to settle in an area (**c**) *(d'un ecclésiastique, d'un magistrat)* installation (**d**) *Ordinat* **programme d'i.** installation program; **i. en réseau** network installation (**e**) *(équipements)* **installations** *(d'une maison, d'un atelier)* fittings; **l'i. électrique** the wiring; **installations sanitaires** sanitary fittings; **installations touristiques** tourist facilities

installer [ɛ̃stale] **1** *vt* (**a**) *(mettre en place) (machine, chauffage, ascenseur)* to install, to put in; *(cuisine)* to fit out; *(rideaux)* to put up (**b**) *(placer)* **i. qn dans un**

fauteuil/devant la télévision to settle sb down in an armchair/in front of the television; **je les ai installés dans la chambre bleue** I've put them in the blue room (**c**) *(aménager)* **les nouveaux bureaux sont très bien installés** the new offices are very well fitted out; **il a installé son bureau au grenier** he set up his office in the attic (**d**) *(dans une fonction)* *(ecclésiastique, magistrat)* to install
2 s'installer *vpr (supermarché, cirque)* to be set up; *(personne)* *(dans un fauteuil)* to settle down; *(dans un bureau)* to install oneself; **confortablement installé dans un fauteuil** comfortably installed in an armchair; **s'i. à la campagne** to settle in the country; **des bourgeois bien installés** comfortably off middle-class people; **s'i. comme médecin** to set up as a doctor; **un climat d'insécurité s'est installé dans le pays** a climate of insecurity has taken hold of the country
instamment [ɛ̃stamɑ̃] *adv* earnestly
instance [ɛ̃stɑ̃s] *nf* (**a**) *Litt (insistance)* plea, entreaty; **demander à qn de faire qch avec i.** to plead with sb to do sth (**b**) *Jur* proceedings; **en seconde i.** on appeal (**c**) *(autorité)* authority; **les instances internationales** the international authorities; **l'i. compétente** the relevant authority (**d**) *(cours)* **être en i. de divorce** to be waiting for a divorce; **courrier en i.** mail waiting to go out; **être en i.** *(affaire)* to be pending
instant [ɛ̃stɑ̃] *nm* moment, instant; **à chaque** *ou* **tout i.** all the time; **pendant un i.** for a moment; **un i.!** one moment!; **sans perdre un i.** without wasting a second; **d'un i. à l'autre** at any moment; **à l'i.** (just) a moment ago; **à l'i. même où** at the very moment that; **j'en reviens à l'i.** I've just come back from there; **pour l'i.** for the moment; **dans un i.** in a moment; **en un i.** in no time at all
instantané, -e [ɛ̃stɑ̃tane] **1** *adj (mort, riposte)* instantaneous; *(café, soupe)* instant
2 *nm (photo)* snap
instantanément [ɛ̃stɑ̃tanemɑ̃] *adv* instantaneously
instar [ɛ̃star] **à l'instar de** *prép* following the example of; **à l'i. de ses parents, il sera enseignant** like his parents, he's going to be a teacher
instauration [ɛ̃stɔrasjɔ̃] *nf* establishment
instaurer [ɛ̃stɔre] **1** *vt* to establish
2 s'instaurer *vpr* to be established
instigateur, -trice [ɛ̃stigatœr, -tris] *nm,f* instigator
instigation [ɛ̃stigasjɔ̃] *nf* instigation; **à l'i. de qn** at sb's instigation
instinct [ɛ̃stɛ̃] *nm* instinct; **faire qch d'i.** to do sth by instinct
instinctif, -ive [ɛ̃stɛ̃ktif, -iv] *adj* instinctive
instinctivement [ɛ̃stɛ̃ktivmɑ̃] *adv* instinctively
instit [ɛ̃stit] *nmf Fam* (primary school) teacher
instituer [ɛ̃stitɥe] *vt* to establish
institut [ɛ̃stity] *nm* institute; **i. de beauté** beauty salon; **i. médico-légal** institute of forensic medicine
instituteur, -trice [ɛ̃stitytœr, -tris] *nm,f* (primary school) teacher
institution [ɛ̃stitysjɔ̃] *nf* (**a**) *(création)* establishment (**b**) *(école)* private school (**c**) *(coutume)* institution (**d**) *Pol* **institutions** institutions
institutionnaliser [ɛ̃stitysjɔnalize] *vt* to institutionalize
institutionnel, -elle [ɛ̃stitysjɔnɛl] *adj* institutional
instructeur [ɛ̃stryktœr] **1** *nm* instructor
2 *adj m Jur* **juge i.** examining magistrate
instructif, -ive [ɛ̃stryktif, -iv] *adj* instructive

instruction [ɛ̃stryksjɔ̃] *nf* (**a**) *(éducation)* education; *Mil* training; **avoir de l'i.** to be well educated; **sans i.** uneducated; **i. civique** civics *(singulier)*; **i. musicale** musical training; **i. religieuse** religious instruction (**b**) *Ordinat* instruction (**c**) *(circulaire)* memo (**d**) *Jur (d'une affaire)* preliminary investigation (**e**) **instructions** *(directives)* instructions
instruire [18] [ɛ̃strɥir] **1** *vt* (**a**) *(enseigner à)* to teach, to educate; **i. par le jeu** to teach through play (**b**) *(soldats)* to train (**c**) *(informer)* **i. qn de qch** to inform sb of sth (**d**) *Jur (affaire)* to investigate
2 s'instruire *vpr* to educate oneself; **s'i. de** to find out about
instruit, -e [ɛ̃strɥi, -it] *adj* educated
instrument [ɛ̃strymɑ̃] *nm* (**a**) *(outil)* instrument; **i. de mesure/de précision** measuring/precision instrument; *Fig* **il n'a été qu'un i.** he was merely a tool (**b**) **i. (de musique)** (musical) instrument; **i. à vent/cordes** wind/string instrument
instrumental, -e, -aux, -ales [ɛ̃strymɑ̃tal, -o] *adj* instrumental
instrumentiste [ɛ̃strymɑ̃tist] *nmf* instrumentalist
insu [ɛ̃sy] **à l'insu de** *prép* without the knowledge of; **à leur i.** without their knowing; **je l'ai fait à mon i.** I did it without realizing
insubmersible [ɛ̃sybmɛrsibl] *adj* unsinkable
insubordination [ɛ̃sybɔrdinasjɔ̃] *nf* insubordination
insuccès [ɛ̃syksɛ] *nm* failure
insuffisamment [ɛ̃syfizamɑ̃] *adv* insufficiently, inadequately
insuffisance [ɛ̃syfizɑ̃s] *nf* (**a**) *(manque)* insufficiency; *(de personnel, de réserves)* shortage; *(de moyens)* inadequacy (**b**) *Méd (d'un organe)* insufficiency; **i. cardiaque** cardiac insufficiency; **i. respiratoire** respiratory failure *or* insufficiency (**c**) **insuffisances** *(faiblesses)* shortcomings
insuffisant, -e [ɛ̃syfizɑ̃, -ɑ̃t] *adj (quantité)* insufficient; *(moyens, mesures)* inadequate; **tes résultats sont insuffisants** your results are not good enough
insuffler [ɛ̃syfle] *vt Méd* to insufflate (**dans** into); **ce succès a insufflé un nouvel élan à l'entreprise** this success breathed new life into the company
insulaire [ɛ̃sylɛr] **1** *adj* island; *Péj (mentalité)* insular
2 *nmf* islander
insuline [ɛ̃sylin] *nf* insulin
insulte [ɛ̃sylt] *nf* insult; **il nous a fait l'i. de refuser** he insulted us by refusing
insulter [ɛ̃sylte] *vt* to insult
insupportable [ɛ̃sypɔrtabl] *adj* unbearable
insurgé, -e [ɛ̃syrʒe] *adj & nm,f* insurgent
insurger [45] [ɛ̃syrʒe] **s'insurger** *vpr* to rise up (**contre** against)
insurmontable [ɛ̃syrmɔ̃tabl] *adj (difficulté, obstacle)* insurmountable; *(aversion, dégoût)* unconquerable
insurrection [ɛ̃syrɛksjɔ̃] *nf* uprising, rebellion; **en état d'i.** in a state of rebellion
insurrectionnel, -elle [ɛ̃syrɛksjɔnɛl] *adj* insurrectionary
intact, -e [ɛ̃takt] *adj* intact
intangible [ɛ̃tɑ̃ʒibl] *adj (loi, institution)* sacred
intarissable [ɛ̃tarisabl] *adj* inexhaustible
intégral, -e, -aux, -ales [ɛ̃tegral, -o] **1** *adj* (**a**) *(paiement, remboursement)* full; *(texte)* unabridged; *Fam* **un fumiste/crétin/menteur i.** a complete clown/idiot/liar (**b**) *Math* **calcul i.** integral calculus

2 *nf* **intégrale** (**a**) *Math* integral (**b**) *(totalité)* **l'intégrale des symphonies de Beethoven/des œuvres de Shakespeare** the complete Beethoven symphonies/works of Shakespeare

intégralement [ɛ̃tegralmɑ̃] *adv (citer, rembourser)* fully, in full

intégralité [ɛ̃tegralite] *nf* **l'i.** the whole (**de** of); **dans son i.** in its entirety

intégrante [ɛ̃tegrɑ̃t] *adj f* **une partie i. de** an integral part of; **faire partie i. de** to be an integral part of

intégration [ɛ̃tegrasjɔ̃] *nf (au sein d'un groupe)* & *Math* integration; *(dans une grande école)* admission; *Écon* **i. horizontale/verticale** horizontal/vertical integration

intègre [ɛ̃tegr] *adj* upright, honest

intégrer [34] [ɛ̃tegre] **1** *vt (incorporer)* to integrate (**à/dans** into)
  2 s'intégrer *vpr* to become integrated (**à/dans** into); **cette sculpture s'intègre bien au paysage** this sculpture blends in well with the countryside

intégrisme [ɛ̃tegrism] *nm* fundamentalism

intégriste [ɛ̃tegrist] *adj* & *nmf* fundamentalist

intégrité [ɛ̃tegrite] *nf* integrity; *Ordinat* **i. des données** data integrity

intellect [ɛ̃telɛkt] *nm* intellect

intellectuel, -elle [ɛ̃telɛktɥel] **1** *adj* intellectual; *(fatigue)* mental; *(travail)* non-manual
  2 *nm,f* intellectual

intelligemment [ɛ̃teliʒamɑ̃] *adv* intelligently

intelligence [ɛ̃teliʒɑ̃s] *nf* (**a**) *(intellect)* intelligence; **avoir l'i. de faire qch** to have the intelligence to do sth; **i. artificielle** artificial intelligence (**b**) *(compréhension)* understanding (**c**) *(entente)* **vivre en bonne/mauvaise i. avec qn** to be on good/bad terms with sb (**d**) *(connivence)* **un regard/sourire d'i.** a knowing look/smile; **faire des signes d'i. à qn** to signal to sb

intelligent, -e [ɛ̃teliʒɑ̃, -ɑ̃t] *adj* intelligent, clever; *Ordinat* smart, intelligent

intelligentsia [inteligdʒɛnsja] *nf* **l'i.** the intelligentsia

intelligible [ɛ̃teliʒibl] *adj (compréhensible)* intelligible; *(clair)* clear; **à haute et i. voix** in a loud, clear voice

intello [ɛ̃telo] *nmf Fam souvent Péj* intellectual, highbrow

intempéries [ɛ̃tɑ̃peri] *nfpl* bad weather; **exposé aux i.** exposed to the elements

intempestif, -ive [ɛ̃tɑ̃pɛstif, -iv] *adj* untimely, ill-timed

intemporel, -elle [ɛ̃tɑ̃pɔrɛl] *adj (hors du temps)* timeless

intenable [ɛ̃tənabl] *adj (chaleur, situation)* intolerable, unbearable; *(position)* untenable; *Fam (enfant)* uncontrollable

intendance [ɛ̃tɑ̃dɑ̃s] *nf* (**a**) *Scol* bursary; *(bureau)* bursar's office (**b**) *Mil* commissariat (**c**) *(d'un domaine)* stewardship (**d**) *Fig (questions matérielles)* practical matters

intendant [ɛ̃tɑ̃dɑ̃] *nm* (**a**) *Scol* bursar (**b**) *Mil* quartermaster (**c**) *(d'un domaine)* steward

intendante [ɛ̃tɑ̃dɑ̃t] *nf* (**a**) *Scol* (woman) bursar (**b**) *(d'une maison)* housekeeper

intense [ɛ̃tɑ̃s] *adj* intense

intensément [ɛ̃tɑ̃semɑ̃] *adv* intensely

intensif, -ive [ɛ̃tɑ̃sif, -iv] *adj* intensive

intensification [ɛ̃tɑ̃sifikasjɔ̃] *nf* intensification

intensifier [66] [ɛ̃tɑ̃sifje] **1** *vt* to intensify
  2 s'intensifier *vpr* to intensify

intensité [ɛ̃tɑ̃site] *nf* intensity

intenter [ɛ̃tɑ̃te] *vt Jur* **i. une action contre qn** to bring an action against sb; **i. un procès à** *ou* **contre qn** to institute proceedings against sb

intention [ɛ̃tɑ̃sjɔ̃] *nf (projet)* intention; *Jur* intent; **avoir l'i. de faire qch** to intend to do sth; **dans l'i. de faire qch** with a view to *or* with the intention of doing sth; **elle a de bonnes intentions** she means well; **c'est l'i. qui compte** it's the thought that counts; **à l'i. de...** *(pour)* for...; *(en l'honneur de)* in honour of...; *(sur une lettre)* for the attention of...

intentionné, -e [ɛ̃tɑ̃sjɔne] *adj* **bien/mal i.** well-/ill-intentioned; **bien/mal i. envers qn** well-/ill-disposed towards sb

intentionnel, -elle [ɛ̃tɑ̃sjɔnɛl] *adj* intentional, deliberate

intentionnellement [ɛ̃tɑ̃sjɔnɛlmɑ̃] *adv* intentionally, deliberately

interactif, -ive [ɛ̃tɛraktif, -iv] *adj Ordinat* interactive

interaction [ɛ̃tɛraksjɔ̃] *nf* interaction

interallié, -e [ɛ̃tɛralje] *adj* allied

interbancaire [ɛ̃tɛrbɑ̃kɛr] *adj* interbank

intercalaire [ɛ̃tɛrkalɛr] **1** *adj (jour)* intercalary; **feuillet i.** insert
  2 *nm (feuillet)* insert; *(dans un classeur)* divider

intercaler [ɛ̃tɛrkale] **1** *vt (dans un texte, un film)* to insert, to include; *(dans un programme, entre deux événements)* to slot in
  2 s'intercaler *vpr* to come in between

intercéder [34] [ɛ̃tɛrsede] *vi* to intercede (**en faveur de/auprès de** on behalf of/with)

intercepter [ɛ̃tɛrsɛpte] *vt (lettre, avion, ballon, personne)* to intercept; *(bruit, lumière)* to shut out

interchangeable [ɛ̃tɛrʃɑ̃ʒabl] *adj* interchangeable

interclasse [ɛ̃tɛrklas] *nm* = short break between classes

intercontinental, -e, -aux, -ales [ɛ̃tɛrkɔ̃tinɑ̃tal, -o] *adj* intercontinental

intercours [ɛ̃tɛrkur] *nm Belg Scol* = short break between classes

interdépartemental, -e, -aux, -ales [ɛ̃tɛrdepartəmɑ̃tal, -o] *adj* = shared by several French départements

interdépendant, -e [ɛ̃tɛrdepɑ̃dɑ̃, -ɑ̃t] *adj* interdependent

interdiction [ɛ̃tɛrdiksjɔ̃] *nf* (**a**) *(défense)* ban, banning; **i. de fumer/stationner** *(sur panneau)* no smoking/parking (**b**) *(suspension)* banning; **i. de séjour** = order banning former prisoner from certain areas

interdire [27b] [ɛ̃tɛrdir] **1** *vt* (**a**) *(défendre) (stationnement, port d'armes)* to ban; **i. qch à qn** to forbid sb sth; **le centre-ville est interdit aux camions** lorries are not allowed in the town centre; **i. à qn de faire qch** *(personne)* to forbid sb to do sth; *(règlement)* to prohibit sb from doing sth; **il nous est interdit de révéler...** we are not allowed to reveal... (**b**) *(empêcher)* to prevent, to stop (**de faire qch** from doing sth)
  2 s'interdire *vpr* **s'i. l'alcool** to abstain from drinking; **il s'interdit d'y penser** he doesn't let himself think about it

interdit, -e [ɛ̃tɛrdi, -it] **1** *adj* (**a**) *(défendu)* forbidden; **il est i. de fumer** smoking is not allowed; **i. au public** *(sur un écriteau)* no unauthorized entry; **un film i.**

aux moins de 18 ans an 18 film; **i. de séjour** = banned from living in certain areas; **être i. de chéquier** to have (had) one's chequebook facilities withdrawn; *Ordinat* **i. d'écriture** *(disquette)* write-protected (**b**) *(déconcerté)* disconcerted, taken aback
2 *nm,f Jur* **i. de séjour** = former prisoner banned from certain areas
3 *nm (social)* taboo; *(religieux)* interdict; **frapper qn/qch d'i.** to impose a ban on sb/sth

intéressant, -e [ēterɛsã, -ãt] **1** *adj* (**a**) *(attirant)* interesting (**b**) *(avantageux)* worthwhile; *(prix)* attractive; *(lucratif)* profitable
2 *nm,f Fam* **faire l'i.** to show off

intéressé, -e [ēterese] **1** *adj* (**a**) *(concerné)* **les parties intéressées** the interested parties, the persons concerned (**b**) *(égoïste) (personne)* self-seeking; *(sentiment)* self-interested; *(conseil)* biased; **agir dans un but i.** to have an axe to grind
2 *nm,f* **l'i.** the person concerned

intéresser [ēterese] **1** *vt* (**a**) *(captiver)* to interest; **l'art m'intéresse beaucoup** I'm very interested in art; **est-ce que ça t'intéresse d'aller au cinéma?** would you like to go to the cinema? (**b**) *Ind & Com* **i. les employés (aux bénéfices)** to operate a profit-sharing scheme; **être intéressé dans une affaire** to have a financial interest in a business (**c**) *(concerner)* to concern, to affect
2 s'intéresser *vpr* **s'i. à qn/qch** to take an interest in sb/sth, to be interested in sb/sth

intérêt [ēterɛ] *nm* (**a**) *(avantage)* interest; **c'est dans mon i. de le faire** it's in my interest to do it; **elle a tout i. à se taire** she'd be well-advised to remain silent; **on a i. à réserver si on veut avoir des places** we'd better book if we want seats; *Fam* **tu n'as pas i. à recommencer!** you'd better not do it again!; **agir dans/contre l'i. de qn** to act in/against sb's interest(s); **agir par i. personnel** to act out of self-interest; **faire un mariage d'i.** to marry for money; **l'i. des vacances en groupe, c'est de faire des rencontres** the advantage of group holidays is that you meet people; *Fam* **tu viens à la réunion du syndicat? – y a i.!** are you coming to the union meeting? – you bet (I am)! (**b**) *(attrait)* interest; **sans i.** uninteresting (**c**) *(curiosité)* interest (**pour** in); **éprouver de l'i. pour qch** to be interested or to take an interest in sth (**d**) *Fin* interest; **i. fixe** fixed interest; **i. variable** variable-rate interest

interface [ēterfas] *nf Ordinat* interface; **i. graphique** graphic interface; **i. d'imprimante** printer interface; **i. numérique** digital interface; **i. parallèle** parallel interface; **i. utilisateur** user interface; **i. vidéo numérique** digital video interface

interférence [ēterferãs] *nf (d'ondes)* interference; *Fig (d'événements)* combination

interférer [34] [ēterfere] *vi aussi Fig* to interfere

intergouvernemental, -e, -aux, -ales [ēterguvɛrnəmãtal, -o] *adj* intergovernmental

intérieur, -e [ēterjœr] **1** *adj* (**a**) *(dans l'espace) (escalier)* interior, inside; *(cour)* inner; *(poche)* inside; *(partie)* inside, internal; *(mer)* inland (**b**) *(national)* domestic (**c**) *(vie, sentiments, force)* inner
2 *nm* (**a**) *(dedans)* inside, interior; **à l'i.** inside; **à l'i. de la gare** inside the station; **fermé de l'i.** locked from the inside; **tourné en i.** *(film)* shot indoors (**b**) *(d'un pays)* interior; **dans l'i. du pays** inland (**c**) *(maison)* home; **femme d'i.** houseproud housewife

intérieurement [ēterjœrmã] *adv* inwardly

intérim [ēterim] *nm (travail intérimaire)* temporary work, temping; **faire de l'i.** to temp; **par i.,** *Belg* **ad i.** acting; **assurer l'i. (de qn)** to stand in (for sb)

intérimaire [ēterimɛr] **1** *adj (fonction, employé)* temporary; *(directeur, ministre)* acting; *(cabinet, gouvernement)* caretaker
2 *nmf (travailleur)* temporary worker; *(secrétaire)* temp

intérioriser [ēterjorize] *vt* to internalize

interjection [ēterʒɛksjõ] *nf* interjection

interligne [ēterliɲ] *nm* line spacing; **dans l'i.** in the space between the lines; **simple/double i.** single/double spacing

interlocuteur, -trice [ēterlɔkytœr, -tris] *nm,f* (**a**) *(dans une conversation)* speaker; **mon i.** the person I was/am speaking to (**b**) *(dans une négociation)* discussion partner

interloqué, -e [ēterlɔke] *adj* taken aback

interlude [ēterlyd] *nm* interlude

intermède [ētermɛd] *nm aussi Fig* interlude

intermédiaire [ētermedjɛr] **1** *adj* intermediate; **i. entre** halfway between; **trouver une solution i.** to find a compromise solution; **pointure i.** size in-between
2 *nmf (personne)* intermediary, go-between; *Com* middleman; **sans i.** directly
3 *nm* **par l'i. de** through; **sans l'i. de** without

interminable [ēterminabl] *adj* interminable

interministériel, -elle [ēterministerjɛl] *adj* interministerial

intermittence [ētermitãs] *nf* **par i.** intermittently, on and off

intermittent, -e [ētermitã, -ãt] **1** *adj (lumière, bruit, tir)* intermittent, sporadic; *(travail)* casual
2 *nm,f* casual worker

internat [ēterna] *nm* (**a**) *Scol (système)* boarding; *(pensionnat)* boarding school (**b**) *Méd (concours)* entrance examination for *Br* a housemanship or *Am* an internship; *(formation) Br* clinicals, *Am* internship

international, -e, -aux, -ales [ēternasjɔnal, -o] **1** *adj & nm,f* international
2 *nf* **l'Internationale** *(groupement)* the International; *(chant)* the Internationale

internationalisation [ēternasjɔnalizasjõ] *nf* internationalization

internationaliser [ēternasjɔnalize] **1** *vt* to internationalize
2 s'internationaliser *vpr* to become international

internaute [ēternot] *nmf* Internet surfer

interne [ētɛrn] **1** *adj (structure, paroi, hémorragie)* internal; *(côté)* inner; *(de l'entreprise)* in-house
2 *nmf (élève)* boarder; **i. (des hôpitaux)** *Br* house doctor, *Am* intern

internement [ētɛrnəmã] *nm (emprisonnement)* internment; *(hospitalisation)* confinement

interner [ētɛrne] *vt (emprisonner)* to intern; *(hospitaliser)* to commit

Internet [ētɛrnɛt] *nm* **l'I.** the Internet; **sur I.** on the Internet

interparlementaire [ētɛrparləmãtɛr] *adj (réunion)* interparliamentary; *(commission)* joint

interpellation [ēterpelasjõ] *nf (appel)* calling out; *(au Parlement)* question; **la police a procédé à plusieurs interpellations** the police took several people in for questioning

interpeller [ēterpəle] **1** *vt* (**a**) *(appeler)* to call (out) to; *(sujet: police)* to take in for questioning; *(ministre)* to

question; *(à une réunion, un spectacle)* to heckle; *(sujet: sentinelle)* to challenge (**b**) *(toucher)* **ce roman m'a interpellé** I can really relate to this novel
  2 s'interpeller *vpr (s'appeler)* to call (out) to each other; *(s'insulter)* to shout insults at each other

Interphone® [ɛ̃tɛrfɔn] *nm (de bureau)* intercom; *(d'immeuble)* Entryphone®; **à l'I.** on the intercom/ Entryphone®

interplanétaire [ɛ̃tɛrplanetɛr] *adj* interplanetary

interpolation [ɛ̃tɛrpɔlasjɔ̃] *nf* interpolation

interpoler [ɛ̃tɛrpɔle] *vt* to interpolate

interposé, -e [ɛ̃tɛrpoze] *adj* **par personne interposée** through an intermediary

interposer [ɛ̃tɛrpoze] **1** *vt* to interpose (**entre** between)
  2 s'interposer *vpr (intervenir)* to intervene

interprétariat [ɛ̃tɛrpretarja] *nm* interpreting

interprétation [ɛ̃tɛrpretasjɔ̃] *nf* (**a**) *(d'un texte, d'un rêve, d'un rôle)* interpretation (**b**) *(traduction)* interpreting

interprète [ɛ̃tɛrprɛt] *nmf (dans une autre langue)* interpreter; *(d'un rôle, d'une œuvre musicale)* performer; *(porte-parole)* spokesman, *f* spokeswoman; **i. de conférence** conference interpreter

interpréter [34] [ɛ̃tɛrprete] *vt* (**a**) *(rôle, œuvre musicale)* to perform, to interpret (**b**) *(texte, paroles, geste, rêve)* to interpret; **mal i. les paroles de qn** to misinterpret sb's words

interro [ɛ̃tero] *nf Fam Scol (abrév* **interrogation**) test

interrogateur, -trice [ɛ̃tɛrɔgatœr, -tris] **1** *adj* questioning
  2 *nm,f (examinateur)* (oral) examiner

interrogatif, -ive [ɛ̃tɛrɔgatif, -iv] **1** *adj* (**a**) *(air, ton)* inquiring, questioning (**b**) *(pronom, phrase)* interrogative
  2 *nm* interrogative
  3 *nf* **interrogative** interrogative (clause)

interrogation [ɛ̃tɛrɔgasjɔ̃] *nf* (**a**) *(question)* question; **i. directe/indirecte** direct/indirect question (**b**) *Scol* test; **i. écrite/orale** written/oral test (**c**) *(d'un prisonnier, d'un suspect)* questioning, interrogation (**d**) *Ordinat (d'une base de données) (question)* inquiry, query; *(activité)* interrogation; **i. à distance** remote interrogation

interrogatoire [ɛ̃tɛrɔgatwar] *nm* questioning

interroger [45] [ɛ̃tɛrɔʒe] **1** *vt* (**a**) *(personne)* to question; *(candidat, élève)* to test; **i. qn du regard** to look at sb questioningly (**b**) *Ordinat (base de données)* to query, to interrogate
  2 s'interroger *vpr* to ask oneself, to wonder (**sur** about)

interrompre [ɛ̃tɛrɔ̃pr] **1** *vt* to interrupt; *(trafic)* to hold up; *(grossesse)* to terminate
  2 s'interrompre *vpr* to break off

interrupteur [ɛ̃teryptœr] *nm* switch; **i. à bascule** toggle switch; *Ordinat* **i. DIP** *ou* **à plusieurs positions** DIP switch

interruption [ɛ̃terypsjɔ̃] *nf (arrêt)* interruption; *(de négociations)* breaking off; **sans i.** non-stop, continuously; *Ordinat* **fonction d'i.** interrupt function; **i. volontaire de grossesse** termination (of pregnancy)

intersection [ɛ̃tɛrsɛksjɔ̃] *nf* intersection, junction; **à l'i. des deux routes** where the two roads intersect *or* meet

intersidéral, -e, -aux, -ales [ɛ̃tɛrsideral, -o] *adj* interstellar

interstice [ɛ̃tɛrstis] *nm* chink, crack

intersyndical, -e, -aux, -ales [ɛ̃tɛrsɛ̃dikal, -o] **1** *adj* interunion
  2 *nf* **intersyndicale** *(association)* interunion group

intertitre [ɛ̃tɛrtitr] *nm Journ* subheading; *Cin* subtitle

interurbain, -e [ɛ̃tɛryrbɛ̃, -ɛn] **1** *adj* interurban; *Vieilli Tél* **appel i.** trunk call
  2 *nm Vieilli Tél* long-distance service

intervalle [ɛ̃tɛrval] *nm* (**a**) *(dans le temps, en musique)* interval; **un i. d'une heure** a one-hour interval; **à deux mois d'i.** two months apart; **par intervalles** at intervals, now and then; **dans l'i.** in the meantime, meanwhile (**b**) *(dans l'espace)* gap, space; **à 2 mètres d'i.** 2 metres apart (**c**) *Math* interval

intervenant, -e [ɛ̃tɛrvənã, -ãt] *nm,f (dans une conférence, un débat)* speaker, contributor

intervenir [70] [ɛ̃tɛrvənir] *vi* (**a**) *(agir, prendre la parole)* to intervene (**dans** in); **i. pour faire qch** to intervene *or* step in to do sth; **i. en faveur de qn** to intervene on sb's behalf; **i. auprès de qn** to intercede with sb; **faire i. qn** to bring sb in (**b**) *(arriver) (événement, changement)* to occur; *(accord)* to be reached (**c**) *(jouer un rôle)* to play a part (**dans** in)

intervention [ɛ̃tɛrvãsjɔ̃] *nf* (**a**) *(intercession, ingérence)* intervention (**en faveur de/auprès de** on behalf of/with) (**b**) *(prise de parole)* intervention; *(discours)* speech (**c**) *(opération)* **i. (chirurgicale)** operation

interventionniste [ɛ̃tɛrvãsjɔnist] *adj & nmf* interventionist

interversion [ɛ̃tɛrvɛrsjɔ̃] *nf* inversion, reversal

intervertir [ɛ̃tɛrvɛrtir] *vt (l'ordre de qch)* to invert, to reverse; *(objets, éléments)* to switch (round); *(rôles)* to reverse

intervienne *voir* **intervenir**

interview [ɛ̃tɛrvju] *nm ou nf* interview

interviewer [ɛ̃tɛrvjuve] *vt* to interview

intestin¹, -e [ɛ̃tɛstɛ̃, -in] *adj Litt* internal

intestin² *nm* intestine; **intestins** intestines, bowels; **gros i.** large intestine; **i. grêle** small intestine

intestinal, -e, -aux, -ales [ɛ̃tɛstinal, -o] *adj* intestinal

intime [ɛ̃tim] **1** *adj* intimate; *(hygiène, toilette)* personal; **être i. avec qn** to be close to sb; **avoir l'i. conviction que...** to be thoroughly convinced that...
  2 *nmf* close friend; **pour les intimes** to my/her/*etc* friends

intimement [ɛ̃timmã] *adv* intimately; **i. liés** *(amis)* very close; *(phénomènes)* closely linked; **être i. persuadé que...** to be thoroughly convinced that...

intimer [ɛ̃time] *vt* (**a**) *(ordonner)* **i. à qn l'ordre de faire qch** to order sb to do sth (**b**) *Jur* to summon before the Court of Appeal

intimidant, -e [ɛ̃timidã, -ãt] *adj* intimidating

intimidation [ɛ̃timidasjɔ̃] *nf* intimidation

intimider [ɛ̃timide] *vt* to intimidate; **ne te laisse pas i. par eux!** don't let them intimidate you!

intimité [ɛ̃timite] *nf (vie privée)* privacy; *(familiarité)* intimacy, closeness; **dans l'i.** in private; **le mariage a eu lieu dans la plus stricte i.** only close family and friends attended the wedding

intitulé [ɛ̃tityle] *nm (de livre)* title; *(de chapitre)* heading, title

intituler [ɛ̃tityle] **1** *vt (livre, chanson)* to give a title to; **un livre intitulé...** a book entitled *or* called...

2 s'intituler *vpr (livre, chanson)* to be entitled, to be called; *(personne)* to call oneself

intolérable [ɛ̃tɔlerabl] *adj* intolerable

intolérance [ɛ̃tɔlerɑ̃s] *nf* intolerance; *Méd* **i. à qch** intolerance to sth

intolérant, -e [ɛ̃tɔlerɑ̃, -ɑ̃t] *adj* intolerant

intonation [ɛ̃tɔnasjɔ̃] *nf* intonation

intouchable [ɛ̃tuʃabl] *adj & nmf* untouchable

intox [ɛ̃tɔks] *nf Fam* brainwashing

intoxication [ɛ̃tɔksikasjɔ̃] *nf (empoisonnement)* poisoning; *Fig* brainwashing; **i. alimentaire** food poisoning

intoxiquer [ɛ̃tɔksike] **1** *vt (empoisonner)* to poison; *Fig* to brainwash

2 s'intoxiquer *vpr* to poison oneself

intradermique [ɛ̃tradɛrmik] *Méd* **1** *adj* intradermal

2 *nf* intradermal injection

intraduisible [ɛ̃tradɥizibl] *adj* untranslatable

intraitable [ɛ̃tretabl] *adj* uncompromising, inflexible (**sur** about)

intra-muros [ɛ̃tramyros] **1** *adj inv* **Londres/Paris i.** inner London/Paris

2 *adv* within the city

intramusculaire [ɛ̃tramyskylɛr] **1** *adj* intramuscular

2 *nf* intramuscular injection

Intranet [ɛ̃tranet] *nm Ordinat* Intranet

intransigeance [ɛ̃trɑ̃ziʒɑ̃s] *nf* intransigence

intransigeant, -e [ɛ̃trɑ̃ziʒɑ̃, -ɑ̃t] *adj (personne)* intransigent, uncompromising (**envers/sur** with/about); *(morale)* uncompromising

intransitif, -ive [ɛ̃trɑ̃zitif, -iv] *adj & nm Gram* intransitive

intransmissible [ɛ̃trɑ̃smisibl] *adj* (**a**) *Biol* intransmissible (**b**) *Jur* untransferable

intransportable [ɛ̃trɑ̃spɔrtabl] *adj (objet)* untransportable; *(blessé)* unfit to travel

intraveineux, -euse [ɛ̃travɛnø, -øz] **1** *adj* intravenous

2 *nf* **intraveineuse** intravenous injection

intrépide [ɛ̃trepid] *adj* intrepid, fearless

intrépidité [ɛ̃trepidite] *nf* fearlessness

intrigant, -e [ɛ̃trigɑ̃, -ɑ̃t] **1** *adj* scheming, plotting

2 *nm,f* schemer

intrigue [ɛ̃trig] *nf (machination)* intrigue; *(liaison amoureuse)* (love) affair; *(d'un roman, d'un film)* plot

intriguer [ɛ̃trige] **1** *vt* to intrigue

2 *vi* to scheme, to intrigue

intrinsèque [ɛ̃trɛ̃sɛk] *adj* intrinsic

intrinsèquement [ɛ̃trɛ̃sɛkmɑ̃] *adv* intrinsically

intro [ɛ̃tro] *nf Fam* intro; *(musicale)* theme tune

introductif, -ive [ɛ̃trɔdyktif, -iv] *adj* (**a**) *(discours, exposé)* introductory, opening (**b**) *Jur* introductory

introduction [ɛ̃trɔdyksjɔ̃] *nf* introduction; *(insertion)* insertion, introduction (**dans** into); *(au rugby)* put-in; **i. en Bourse** listing on the stock market

introduire [18] [ɛ̃trɔdɥir] **1** *vt (dans une serrure, dans un trou)* to insert (**dans** into); *(marchandises)* to bring in; *(coutume, réforme, mesures, mode)* to introduce; *(étranger, visiteur)* to show in; **i. qn auprès de qn** *(faire entrer)* to show sb in to see sb; *(présenter)* to introduce sb to sb; **i. en Bourse** to list on the stock market; **i. sur le marché** to launch onto the market

2 s'introduire *vpr* **s'i. dans une maison** to get into a house; **l'eau s'introduit partout** there's water coming in everywhere

intronisation [ɛ̃trɔnizasjɔ̃] *nf* enthronement; *Fig* establishment

introniser [ɛ̃trɔnize] *vt* to enthrone; *Fig* to establish

introspection [ɛ̃trɔspɛksjɔ̃] *nf* introspection

introuvable [ɛ̃truvabl] *adj (produit, denrées)* unobtainable; *(personne)* nowhere to be found

introversion [ɛ̃trɔvɛrsjɔ̃] *nf* introversion

introverti, -e [ɛ̃trɔvɛrti] **1** *adj* introverted

2 *nm,f* introvert

intrus, -e [ɛ̃try, -yz] *nm,f aussi Ordinat* intruder

intrusion [ɛ̃tryzjɔ̃] *nf* intrusion (**dans** into)

intuitif, -ive [ɛ̃tɥitif, -iv] **1** *adj* intuitive

2 *nm,f* **c'est un i.** he's an intuitive sort

intuition [ɛ̃tɥisjɔ̃] *nf* intuition; **avoir l'i. de qch/que** to sense sth/that

intuitivement [ɛ̃tɥitivmɑ̃] *adv* intuitively

inuit [inɥit] **1** *adj inv* Inuit

2 *nmf inv* **les I.** the Inuit *or* Inuits

inusable [inyzabl] *adj aussi Fig* hard-wearing

inusité, -e [inyzite] *adj (mot)* uncommon

inutile [inytil] *adj (qui ne sert à rien)* useless; *(effort)* vain, pointless; *(précautions, démarche, bagages)* unnecessary; **c'est i.!** *(ça ne sert à rien)* it's pointless!; *(ce n'est pas nécessaire)* you/he/etc needn't bother!; **i. de dire que...** needless to say,...; **c'est i. d'attendre** there's no point in waiting; **i. d'insister, je ne viens pas** don't go on about it, I'm not coming

inutilement [inytilmɑ̃] *adv* needlessly, unnecessarily

inutilisable [inytilizabl] *adj* unusable

inutilisé, -e [inytilize] *adj* unused

inutilité [inytilite] *nf (d'un objet)* uselessness; *(d'un effort, d'un argument)* pointlessness

invaincu, -e [ɛ̃vɛ̃ky] *adj* undefeated

invalidant, -e [ɛ̃validɑ̃, -ɑ̃t] *adj* disabling

invalidation [ɛ̃validasjɔ̃] *nf Jur* invalidation

invalide [ɛ̃valid] **1** *adj* disabled

2 *nmf* disabled person, invalid; **i. de guerre** disabled ex-serviceman/ex-servicewoman

invalider [ɛ̃valide] *vt Jur* to invalidate

invalidité [ɛ̃validite] *nf* disability

invariable [ɛ̃varjabl] *adj* invariable

invariablement [ɛ̃varjabləmɑ̃] *adv* invariably

invasion [ɛ̃vazjɔ̃] *nf aussi Fig* invasion

invective [ɛ̃vɛktiv] *nf* invective; **invectives** abuse

invectiver [ɛ̃vɛktive] **1** *vt* to hurl abuse at

2 s'invectiver *vpr* to hurl abuse at each other

invendable [ɛ̃vɑ̃dabl] *adj* unsellable

invendu, -e [ɛ̃vɑ̃dy] **1** *adj* unsold

2 *nm* **invendus** unsold goods; *(journaux, livres)* unsold copies; *(revendus moins cher)* remainders

inventaire [ɛ̃vɑ̃tɛr] *nm* (**a**) *(liste)* inventory (**b**) *(de marchandises)* stocklist; **faire** *ou* **dresser l'i. (des stocks)** to stocktake; **fermé pour cause d'i.** *(sur un écriteau)* closed for stocktaking (**c**) *Fig (de peintures, de richesses artistiques)* survey

inventer [ɛ̃vɑ̃te] **1** *vt (machine)* to invent; *(concept, moyen)* to think up; *(histoire, excuse)* to make up; *(expression)* to coin; **qu'est-ce qu'il va encore i.?** what's he going to come out with next?; *Fam* **il n'a pas inventé la poudre** *ou* **le fil à couper le beurre** he'll never set the Thames on fire

2 s'inventer *vpr* **ça ne s'invente pas** you can't make something like that up; **s'i. un passé** to invent a past for oneself

inventeur, -trice [ɛ̃vɑ̃tœr, -tris] *nm,f* (**a**) *(d'une machine, d'un procédé)* inventor (**b**) *Jur (d'un trésor)* finder

inventif, -ive [ɛ̃vɑ̃tif, -iv] *adj* inventive

invention [ɛ̃vɑ̃sjɔ̃] *nf* (**a**) *(action)* invention; *(faculté)* inventiveness (**b**) *(chose découverte, mensonge)* invention (**c**) *Jur (d'un trésor)* finding

inventorier [66] [ɛ̃vɑ̃tɔrje] *vt* to make an inventory of; *(marchandises)* to make a stocklist of

invérifiable [ɛ̃verifjabl] *adj* unverifiable

inverse [ɛ̃vɛrs] **1** *adj aussi Math* inverse; **en sens i. (de)** in the opposite direction (to); **dans l'ordre i.** in reverse order; **dans le sens i. des aiguilles d'une montre** *Br* anticlockwise, *Am* counterclockwise
2 *nm* **l'i.** the opposite, the reverse; **faire l'i. (de)** to do the opposite (of); **à l'i. de** contrary to

inversement [ɛ̃vɛrsəmɑ̃] *adv* **et i.** and vice versa; **i., on peut dire que...** conversely, one can say that...; **i. proportionnel (à)** inversely proportional (to)

inverser [ɛ̃vɛrse] *vt (ordre, tendance)* to reverse; *(deux mots)* to invert

inversion [ɛ̃vɛrsjɔ̃] *nf (d'ordre, de mots)* inversion; *Ordinat* **i. vidéo** reverse video

invertébré, -e [ɛ̃vɛrtebre] *adj & nm* invertebrate

inverti, -e [ɛ̃vɛrti] **1** *adj (sucre)* invert
2 *nm,f Vieilli (homosexuel)* homosexual, invert

investigateur, -trice [ɛ̃vɛstigatœr, -tris] **1** *adj (regard)* searching
2 *nm,f* investigator

investigation [ɛ̃vɛstigasjɔ̃] *nf* investigation

investir [ɛ̃vɛstir] **1** *vt* (**a**) *(argent, temps, énergie)* to invest (**dans** in) (**b**) *(ville, édifice)* to besiege (**c**) *(charger)* **i. qn d'une mission** to entrust sb with a mission
2 *vi* to invest (**dans** in)
3 **s'investir** *vpr* **s'i. dans qch** to put a lot into sth

investissement [ɛ̃vɛstismɑ̃] *nm* investment; **i. à court/long terme** short-/long-term investment

investisseur [ɛ̃vɛstisœr] *nm* investor; **les investisseurs institutionnels** institutional investors

investiture [ɛ̃vɛstityr] *nf (d'un candidat)* nomination; *(d'un gouvernement)* voting in; *(d'un évêque)* investiture

invétéré, -e [ɛ̃vetere] *adj* inveterate

invincible [ɛ̃vɛ̃sibl] *adj (armée, adversaire)* invincible; *(peur)* unconquerable

inviolabilité [ɛ̃vjɔlabilite] *nf Jur* inviolability; *(d'un parlementaire)* immunity; **i. diplomatique** diplomatic immunity

inviolable [ɛ̃vjɔlabl] *adj (coffre)* burglarproof; *(droit, asile)* inviolable; *(parlementaire)* immune

invisibilité [ɛ̃vizibilite] *nf* invisibility

invisible [ɛ̃vizibl] *adj* invisible

invitation [ɛ̃vitasjɔ̃] *nf* invitation; **venir à** *ou* **sur l'i. de qn** to come at sb's invitation; **sur i.** by invitation

invite [ɛ̃vit] *nf* (**a**) *(invitation)* invitation (**b**) *Ordinat* prompt; **i. du DOS** DOS prompt; **i. du système** system prompt

invité, -e [ɛ̃vite] *nm,f* guest

inviter [ɛ̃vite] **1** *vt* (**a**) *(convier)* to invite; **i. qn à dîner** to invite *or* ask sb to dinner (**b**) **i. qn à faire qch** *(inciter)* to urge sb to do sth; *(prier)* to request sb to do sth; **je vous invite à me suivre** would you be so kind as to follow me
2 *vi (payer)* **ce soir, c'est moi qui invite!** it's my treat tonight!
3 **s'inviter** *vpr* to invite oneself

in vitro [invitro] *adj inv & adv* in vitro

invivable [ɛ̃vivabl] *adj* unbearable

in vivo [invivo] *adj inv & adv* in vivo

invocation [ɛ̃vɔkasjɔ̃] *nf* invocation

involontaire [ɛ̃vɔlɔ̃tɛr] *adj (mouvement, geste)* involuntary; *(erreur, réaction)* unintentional; *(témoin)* unwilling

involontairement [ɛ̃vɔlɔ̃tɛrmɑ̃] *adv* involuntarily, unintentionally

invoquer [ɛ̃vɔke] *vt* (**a**) *(raison, argument)* to put forward; *(prétexte, excuse)* to plead; *(loi, texte)* to refer to (**b**) *(Dieu, divinité, esprit)* to invoke; **i. l'aide de qn** to call upon sb's help

invraisemblable [ɛ̃vrɛsɑ̃blabl] *adj* (**a**) *(hypothèse)* unlikely (**b**) *(excuses, alibi)* implausible (**c**) *(extraordinaire)* incredible

invraisemblance [ɛ̃vrɛsɑ̃blɑ̃s] *nf (improbabilité)* unlikelihood; *(d'un récit, d'une excuse)* implausibility; **des invraisemblances** implausibilities

invulnérabilité [ɛ̃vylnerabilite] *nf* invulnerability

invulnérable [ɛ̃vylnerabl] *adj* invulnerable

iode [jɔd] *nm* iodine

iodé, -e [jɔde] *adj (eau, air)* iodized

ion [jɔ̃] *nm* ion

iota [jɔta] *nm inv* iota; **ça n'a pas changé d'un i.** it hasn't changed one iota; **ne pas bouger d'un i.** not to budge an inch

ipso facto [ipsofakto] *adv* ipso facto

Ipsos [ipsos] *nm* = French market research institute

ira, irai *etc voir* **aller**

Irak [irak] *nm* **l'I.** Iraq

irakien, -enne [irakjɛ̃, -ɛn] **1** *adj* Iraqi
2 *nm,f* **I.** Iraqi

Iran [irɑ̃] *nm* **l'I.** Iran

iranien, -enne [iranjɛ̃, -ɛn] **1** *adj* Iranian
2 *nm,f* **I.** Iranian
3 *nm (langue)* Iranian

Iraq [irak] = **Irak**

iraquien, -enne [irakjɛ̃, -ɛn] = **irakien**

irascible [irasibl] *adj Litt* irascible

iriez *etc voir* **aller**

iris [iris] *nm* (**a**) *(de l'œil)* iris (**b**) *(fleur)* iris

irisé, -e [irize] *adj* iridescent

irlandais, -e [irlɑ̃dɛ, -ɛz] **1** *adj* Irish
2 *nm,f* **I.** Irishman, *f* Irishwoman; **I. du Nord** person from Northern Ireland; **les I.** the Irish
3 *nm (langue)* Irish

Irlande [irlɑ̃d] *nf* **l'I.** Ireland, Eire; **l'I. du Nord** Northern Ireland, Ulster

IRM [iɛrɛm] *nf Méd (abrév* **imagerie par résonance magnétique)** MRI

ironie [irɔni] *nf* irony; **l'i. du sort a voulu que...** as fate would have it,...

ironique [irɔnik] *adj* ironic(al)

ironiquement [irɔnikmɑ̃] *adv* ironically

ironiser [irɔnize] *vi* to be ironical (**sur** about)

irradiation [iradjasjɔ̃] *nf Phys & Méd* irradiation

irradier [66] [iradje] **1** *vi (rayons)* to radiate; *(douleur)* to spread
2 *vt* to irradiate

irraisonné, -e [irɛzɔne] *adj* irrational

irrationnel, -elle [irasjɔnɛl] *adj* irrational

irrattrapable [iratrapabl] *adj (retard)* that cannot be made up; *(erreur)* irredeemable

irréalisable [irealizabl] *adj (rêve)* unrealizable; *(projet)* impracticable

irréaliste [irealist] *adj* unrealistic

irréalité [irealite] *nf* unreality

irrecevable [irəsəvabl] *adj (inacceptable)* unacceptable; *Jur (preuve, demande)* inadmissible

irrécupérable [irekyperabl] *adj (argent)* irrecoverable; *(personne)* irredeemable; *(appareil, voiture)* beyond repair

irrécusable [irekyzabl] *adj* (**a**) *(indéniable) (preuve, signe)* indisputable (**b**) *Jur (témoignage, juge)* unimpeachable

irréductible [iredyktibl] **1** *adj* (**a**) *(volonté, optimisme)* indomitable, invincible; *(attachement, fidélité)* unshakeable; *(opposition, ennemi)* implacable (**b**) *(fracture, fraction)* irreducible
2 *nmf* die-hard

irréel, -elle [ireɛl] **1** *adj* unreal
2 *nm* **l'i.** the unreal; *Gram* **l'i. du présent/passé** the hypothetical present/past

irréfléchi, -e [irefleʃi] *adj* rash

irréfutable [irefytabl] *adj* irrefutable

irrégularité [iregylarite] *nf* (**a**) *(du sol, d'un terrain)* unevenness; *(du pouls, de traits, d'horaires)* irregularity (**b**) *(acte)* irregularity

irrégulier, -ère [iregylje, -ɛr] *adj* (**a**) *(sol, terrain)* uneven; *(rythme, respiration, traits, verbe)* irregular; *(résultats, athlète)* inconsistent (**b**) *(malhonnête) (procédure, situation)* irregular; **être en situation irrégulière** *(étranger)* not to have one's residence papers in order; *(voyageur)* not to hold a valid ticket

irrégulièrement [iregyljɛrmɑ̃] *adv* irregularly

irréligieux, -euse [ireliʒjø, -øz] *adj* irreligious

irrémédiable [iremedjabl] *adj (préjudice, perte, problème)* irreparable; *(désastre)* irreversible

irrémissible [iremisibl] *adj Litt* (**a**) *(impardonnable)* unpardonable (**b**) *(irrémédiable)* irreversible

irremplaçable [irɑ̃plasabl] *adj* irreplaceable

irréparable [ireparabl] **1** *adj (tort, perte, erreur)* irreparable; *(affront)* unpardonable; *(vêtement, voiture, télévision)* beyond repair
2 *nm* **commettre l'i.** to go beyond the point of no return

irrépressible [irepresibl] *adj* irrepressible

irréprochable [ireproʃabl] *adj (personne, conduite)* irreproachable; *(tenue, travail)* impeccable; **d'une propreté i.** impeccably clean

irrésistible [irezistibl] *adj (personne, charme)* irresistible; *(envie, besoin)* compelling

irrésolu, -e [irezɔly] *adj* (**a**) *(personne)* indecisive; *(pas)* uncertain (**b**) *(problème)* unresolved

irrespect [irɛspɛ] *nm* disrespect (**envers** towards)

irrespectueux, -euse [irɛspɛktɥø, -øz] *adj* disrespectful (**envers** towards)

irrespirable [irɛspirabl] *adj (air)* unbreathable; *Fig (atmosphère)* unbearable

irresponsable [irɛspɔ̃sabl] **1** *adj* irresponsible
2 *nmf* irresponsible person

irrévérence [ireverɑ̃s] *nf* irreverence

irrévérencieux, -euse [ireverɑ̃sjø, -øz] *adj* irreverent

irréversible [irevɛrsibl] *adj* irreversible

irrévocabilité [irevɔkabilite] *nf* irrevocability

irrévocable [irevɔkabl] *adj* irrevocable

irrévocablement [irevɔkabləmɑ̃] *adv* irrevocably

irrigation [irigasjɔ̃] *nf* irrigation; **l'i. du cerveau** the blood supply to the brain

irriguer [irige] *vt* to irrigate; **le cerveau n'est plus irrigué** the brain is no longer being supplied with blood

irritable [iritabl] *adj* irritable

irritant, -e [iritɑ̃, -ɑ̃t] *adj* (**a**) *(personne, comportement)* irritating (**b**) *(substance)* irritant (**pour** to)

irritation [iritasjɔ̃] *nf aussi Méd* irritation

irrité, -e [irite] *adj* (**a**) *(énervé)* irritated (**contre** with) (**b**) *(enflammé)* irritated, inflamed

irriter [irite] **1** *vt (énerver, enflammer)* to irritate
2 s'irriter *vpr* (**a**) *(s'énerver)* **s'i. contre qn/de qch** to get irritated with sb/at sth (**b**) *(s'enflammer)* to become irritated *or* inflamed

irruption [irypsjɔ̃] *nf* (**a**) *(entrée)* irruption; **faire i. dans** to burst into (**b**) *(invasion)* invasion (**c**) *(émergence)* upsurge

islam [islam] *nm* **l'i.** Islam

islamique [islamik] *adj* Islamic

islamiste [islamist] *nmf* Islamic fundamentalist

islandais, -e [islɑ̃dɛ, -ɛz] **1** *adj* Icelandic
2 *nm,f* **I.** Icelander
3 *nm (langue)* Icelandic

Islande [islɑ̃d] *nf* **l'I.** Iceland

isobare [izɔbar] **1** *adj* isobaric
2 *nf* isobar

isocèle [izɔsɛl] *adj* isosceles

isolant, -e [izɔlɑ̃, -ɑ̃t] **1** *adj (contre le froid, en électricité)* insulating; *(contre le bruit)* soundproofing
2 *nm (contre le froid, en électricité)* insulating material; *(contre le bruit)* soundproofing (material)

isolation [izɔlasjɔ̃] *nf (électrique)* insulation; **i. acoustique** *ou* **phonique** soundproofing; **i. thermique** (thermal) insulation

isolationniste [izɔlasjɔnist] *adj & nmf* isolationist

isolé, -e [izɔle] *adj* (**a**) *(personne, cas, endroit, maison)* isolated (**b**) *(protégé) (en électricité, du froid)* insulated; *(du bruit)* soundproofed

isolement [izɔlmɑ̃] *nm* (**a**) *(d'une personne, d'une maison)* isolation (**b**) *(isolation)* insulation

isolément [izɔlemɑ̃] *adv (agir)* in isolation; *(interroger des gens)* individually

isoler [izɔle] **1** *vt* (**a**) *(séparer)* to isolate (**de** from) (**b**) *(protéger) (du froid, d'un courant électrique)* to insulate; *(du bruit)* to soundproof
2 s'isoler *vpr* to isolate oneself

isoloir [izɔlwar] *nm* polling booth

isotherme [izɔtɛrm] **1** *adj* maintained at a constant temperature; **boîte/sac i.** cool box/bag; **bouteille i.** vacuum flask
2 *nf* isotherm

Israël [israɛl] *n* Israel

israélien, -enne [israeljɛ̃, -ɛn] **1** *adj* Israeli
2 *nm,f* **I.** Israeli

israélite [israelit] **1** *adj* Jewish
2 *nmf* Jew

issu, -e [isy] *adj* **être i. de** *(être originaire de)* to come from; *(résulter de)* to stem from

issue [isy] *nf* (**a**) *(sortie)* exit; *Fig (solution)* way out; **i. de secours** emergency exit (**b**) *(fin)* outcome; **à l'i. de** at the end of

Istanbul [istɑ̃bul] *n* Istanbul

isthme [ism] *nm* isthmus

Italie [itali] *nf* **l'I.** Italy

italien, -enne [italjɛ̃, -ɛn] **1** *adj* Italian **2** *nm,f* **I.** Italian **3** *nm (langue)* Italian **4** *nf* **italienne** *Ordinat* **imprimer à l'italienne** to print landscape

italique [italik] **1** *adj* italic **2** *nm* **en italique(s)** in italics

Ithaque [itak] *nf* Ithaca

itinéraire [itinerɛr] *nm* route, itinerary; **i. bis** = alternative route recommended when roads are highly congested, especially at peak holiday times; **i. touristique** tourist route

itinérant, -e [itinerɑ̃, -ɑ̃t] *adj (comédiens, exposition)* travelling; *(ambassadeur)* roving

itou [itu] *adv Fam Vieilli* likewise, too; **et moi i.!** me too!

IUFM [iyɛfɛm] *nm (abrév* **Institut universitaire de formation des maîtres)** ≃ teacher training college

IUT [iyte] *nm (abrév* **Institut universitaire de technologie)** = vocational higher education college

IVG [iveʒe] *nf (abrév* **interruption volontaire de grossesse)** termination (of pregnancy)

ivoire [ivwar] *nm* ivory

ivoirien, -enne [ivwarjɛ̃, -ɛn] **1** *adj* of the Ivory Coast **2** *nm, f* **I.** person from the Ivory Coast

ivre [ivr] *adj* drunk; **i. mort** blind drunk; **i. de joie** beside oneself with joy

ivresse [ivrɛs] *nf (ébriété)* drunkenness; *(extase)* exhilaration; **conduite en état d'i.** drink-driving

ivrogne [ivrɔɲ] *nmf* drunkard

ivrognerie [ivrɔɲri] *nf* drunkenness

J

J, j [ʒi] *nm inv* J, j

j' [ʒ] *voir* **je**

jabot [ʒabo] *nm* (**a**) *(d'oiseau)* crop (**b**) *(de chemise)* frill, ruffle

jacassements [ʒakasmɑ̃] *nmpl (d'une pie, d'une personne)* chattering

jacasser [ʒakase] *vi (pie, personne)* to chatter

jachère [ʒaʃɛr] *nf* leaving land fallow; **laisser en j.** *(champ)* to leave fallow; *Fig (talent)* to leave undeveloped

jacinthe [ʒasɛ̃t] *nf* hyacinth

jacquard [ʒakar] *adj (pull)* argyle

jacquet [ʒakɛ] *nm* backgammon

jacter [ʒakte] *vi Fam* to gab

Jacuzzi® [ʒakuzi] *nm* Jacuzzi®

jade [ʒad] *nm* (**a**) *(pierre)* jade; **un collier en j.** a jade necklace (**b**) *(objet)* jade object

jadis [ʒadis] *Litt* **1** *adv* in times past, formerly; **les chevaliers de j.** the knights of old
  2 *adj* **au temps j.** in the olden days

jaguar [ʒagwar] *nm* jaguar

jaillir [ʒajir] *vi* (**a**) *(source, liquide)* to gush out; *(étincelles, flammes, foule)* to shoot out; *(lumière)* to flash (**b**) *(rires, cris)* to burst out

jais [ʒɛ] *nm* jet; **(d'un noir) de j.** jet-black

Jakarta [dʒakarta] *n* Jakarta

jalon [ʒalɔ̃] *nm* ranging pole; *Fig (référence)* milestone, landmark; *Fig* **poser des jalons** to pave the way, to prepare the ground

jalonner [ʒalɔne] *vt (marquer) (parcelle, piste d'atterrissage)* to mark out; *(ponctuer) (route, côte)* to line (**de** with); *Fig* to punctuate

jalousement [ʒaluzmɑ̃] *adv* jealously

jalouser [ʒaluze] *vt* to be jealous of

jalousie [ʒaluzi] *nf* (**a**) *(sentiment)* jealousy; **éprouver de la j. envers qn** to feel jealous of sb; **être malade de j.** to be green with envy (**b**) *(store)* Venetian blind

jaloux, -ouse [ʒalu, -uz] **1** *adj* jealous (**de** of); **j. comme un tigre** wildly jealous
  2 *nm,f* **c'est un j.** he's a jealous man; **faire des j.** to make people jealous

jamaïcain, -e, jamaïquain, -e [ʒamaikɛ̃, -ɛn] **1** *adj* Jamaican
  2 *nm,f* **J.** Jamaican

Jamaïque [ʒamaik] *nf* **la J.** Jamaica

jamais [ʒamɛ] *adv* (**a**) *(positif)* ever; **plus que j.** more than ever; **à (tout) j.** for good, for ever; **si j. elle revenait** if she ever came back; **le film le plus drôle que j'aie j. vu** the funniest film I've ever seen (**b**) *(négatif)* never; **je ne l'ai j. vu** I've never seen him; **il a passé**

toute sa vie sans j. boire un verre d'alcool he's spent all his life without ever touching a drop of alcohol; **j. plus** never again; **j., au grand j., je ne le dirai** I shall never ever tell; **elle n'a j. que dix minutes de retard** she's only ten minutes late; *Fam* **j. de la vie!** not on your life!; *Prov* **j. deux sans trois** things come in threes

jambe [ʒɑ̃b] *nf* leg; **jambes nues** bare-legged; **traîner la j.** *(de fatigue)* to drag one's feet; *(en boitant)* to drag one foot behind one; **à toutes jambes** as fast as one can; **prendre ses jambes à son cou** to take to one's heels; **être dans les jambes de qn** to be under sb's feet; **traiter qn par-dessous** *ou* **par-dessus la j.** to treat sb in an offhand manner; *Fam* **ça me fait une belle j.!** a fat lot of good that does me!; *Fam* **tenir la j. à qn** to bend sb's ear; **j. de bois** wooden leg

jambière [ʒɑ̃bjɛr] *nf* (**a**) *(de sport)* (shin) pad (**b**) *(pour tenir chaud)* legwarmer

jambon [ʒɑ̃bɔ̃] *nm* ham; **j. blanc** boiled ham; **j. cru** raw ham; **j. fumé** smoked ham; **j. de Parme** Parma ham; **j. d'York** boiled ham on the bone

jambonneau, -x [ʒɑ̃bɔno] *nm* knuckle of ham

jante [ʒɑ̃t] *nf* rim

janvier [ʒɑ̃vje] *nm* January; **en j., au mois de j.** in January; **nous sommes le 7 j.** it's the 7th of January, it's January the 7th; **j'y vais le 7 j.** I'm going on the 7th of January *or* January the 7th

Japon [ʒapɔ̃] *nm* **le J.** Japan

japonais, -e [ʒapɔnɛ, -ɛz] **1** *adj* Japanese
  2 *nm,f* **J.** Japanese; **les J.** the Japanese
  3 *nm (langue)* Japanese

jappement [ʒapmɑ̃] *nm* yap, yelp; **jappements** yapping, yelping

japper [ʒape] *vi* to yap, to yelp

jaquette [ʒakɛt] *nf* (**a**) *(d'homme)* morning coat; *(de femme)* jacket; *Can (chemise de nuit)* nightdress (**b**) *(de livre)* (dust) jacket, (dust) cover

jardin [ʒardɛ̃] *nm* garden; *Fig* **c'est mon j. secret** I keep it very much to myself; **j. botanique** botanical garden(s); **j. d'enfants** kindergarten; **j. potager** vegetable garden; **j. public** gardens; **j. zoologique** zoological gardens

jardinage [ʒardinaʒ] *nm* gardening

jardiner [ʒardine] *vi* to do some gardening

jardinet [ʒardinɛ] *nm* small garden

jardinier, -ère [ʒardinje, -ɛr] **1** *nm,f* gardener
  2 *nf* **jardinière** (**a**) *(pour balcon)* window box; *(intérieure)* jardinière (**b**) *Culin* **jardinière (de légumes)** mixed vegetables

jargon [ʒargɔ̃] *nm* (**a**) *(argot, de métier)* jargon (**b**) *(langage incompréhensible)* gibberish

jarre [ʒar] *nf* (**a**) *(vase)* (earthenware) jar (**b**) *Can (bocal)* preserving jar

jarret [ʒarɛ] *nm* (**a**) *(de personne)* back of the knee; *(de cheval)* hock (**b**) *(pièce de viande) (de veau)* knuckle; *(de bœuf)* shin

jarretelle [ʒartɛl] *nf Br* suspender, *Am* garter

jarretière [ʒartjɛr] *nf* garter

jars [ʒar] *nm* (**a**) *Zool* gander (**b**) *Can* **faire le j.** to show off

jaser [ʒaze] *vi* (**a**) *(médire)* to gossip; **cela va faire j.** that'll set tongues wagging (**b**) *Can (bavarder)* to chatter (**de** about)

jasmin [ʒasmɛ̃] *nm* jasmine

jatte [ʒat] *nf* (**a**) *(petite)* bowl; *(grande)* basin (**b**) *Belg (récipient)* coffee cup; *(contenu)* cup of coffee

jauge [ʒoʒ] *nf* (**a**) *(instrument de mesure)* gauge; **j. d'essence** *Br* petrol *or Am* gas gauge; **j. de niveau d'huile** oil-level indicator; *(manuelle)* dipstick (**b**) *(de navire)* tonnage

jauger [45] [ʒoʒe] **1** *vt* (**a**) *(mesurer) (tonneau, réservoir)* to measure the capacity of; *(navire)* to measure the tonnage of (**b**) *Fig (personne, situation)* to size up
2 *vi* **j. 300 tonneaux** to have a tonnage of 300 tons

jaunâtre [ʒonɑtr] *adj* yellowish

jaune [ʒon] **1** *adj (couleur, objet)* yellow; *(teint)* sallow; **j. canari** canary yellow; **j. citron** lemon yellow; **j. moutarde** mustard yellow; **j. d'or** golden yellow; **j. paille** straw-coloured
2 *nm* (**a**) *(couleur)* yellow (**b**) **j. d'œuf** (egg) yolk
3 *nmf Péj* (**a**) *(non gréviste)* strikebreaker (**b**) *Can (lâche)* yellowbelly
4 *adv* **rire j.** to give a forced laugh

jauni, -e [ʒoni] *adj* yellowed

jaunir [ʒonir] *vt & vi* to turn yellow

jaunisse [ʒonis] *nf* jaundice; *Fam Fig* **en faire une j.** to get into a state about it

Java® [ʒava] *nm Ordinat* Java®

java [ʒava] *nf* (**a**) *(danse)* = type of popular waltz (**b**) *Fam (fête)* **faire la j.** to live it up

Javel [ʒavɛl] *n voir* **eau**

javelot [ʒavlo] *nm* javelin

jazz [dʒaz] *nm* jazz

J.-C. *(abrév* **Jésus-Christ)** JC; **av. J.-C.** BC; **ap. J.-C.** AD

je [ʒə]

> **j'** is used before a word beginning with a vowel or h mute.

pron personnel I

jean [dʒin] *nm (pantalon)* jeans; *(tissu)* denim; **un j.** (a pair of) jeans; **veste en j.** denim jacket

Jeanne [ʒan] *npr* **J. d'Arc** Joan of Arc

Jeep® [dʒip] *nf* Jeep®

Jéhovah [ʒeova] *npr* Jehovah

je-m'en-foutisme [ʒmɑ̃futism] *nm très Fam* couldn't-care-less attitude

je-m'en-foutiste *(pl* **je-m'en-foutistes)** [ʒmɑ̃futist] *nmf très Fam* couldn't-care-less type

je-ne-sais-quoi [ʒənsɛkwa] *nm inv* **un j.** a certain something

jérémiades [ʒeremjad] *nfpl* whining

jerrican(e), jerrycan [dʒerikan, ʒerikan] *nm* jerry can

Jérusalem [ʒeryzalɛm] *n* Jerusalem

jésuite [ʒezɥit] **1** *adj* Jesuit; *Fig & Péj* jesuitical
2 *nm* Jesuit

Jésus(-Christ) [ʒezy(kri)] *npr* Jesus (Christ)

jet¹ [ʒɛ] *nm* (**a**) *(lancer) (de pierre)* throwing; *Fig* **faire qch d'un seul j.** to do sth in one go (**b**) *(de liquide, de vapeur)* jet; **premier j.** *(d'un roman)* first draft; **j. d'eau** *(fontaine)* fountain

jet² [dʒɛt] *nm (avion)* jet

jetable [ʒətablə] *adj* disposable

jeté, -e [ʒəte] **1** *nm* (**a**) *(en danse)* jeté (**b**) **j. de lit** bedspread
2 *adj très Fam* crazy

jetée [ʒəte] *nf* jetty, pier

jeter [42] [ʒəte] **1** *vt* (**a**) *(lancer)* to throw; *(plus fort)* to fling, to hurl; *(filets)* to cast; **j. qch à qn** to throw sb sth, to throw sth to sb; **j. qn à terre** to throw sb to the ground; **j. qch à terre** *ou* **par terre** to throw sth on the ground; **j. qn en prison** to throw sb in prison; **j. les bras autour de qn** to throw one's arms around sb; **j. quelques idées sur le papier** to jot down a few ideas; **j. le trouble dans l'esprit de qn** to trouble sb; **ça a jeté un froid** it cast a chill
(**b**) *(se défaire de)* to throw away *or* out; **j. son argent par les fenêtres** to throw one's money down the drain; *Fam* **se faire j. (de)** to get chucked out (of)
(**c**) *(émettre) (cri)* to utter; **j. un regard à qn** to glance at sb; **j. un coup d'œil (sur qch)** to have a quick glance (at sth)
(**d**) *(établir)* **j. les fondements de qch** to lay the foundations for sth
(**e**) *Fam* **ça (en) jette!** it's really something!
3 se jeter *vpr* (**a**) *(fleuve, rivière)* **se j. dans** to flow into
(**b**) *(personne)* to throw oneself; **se j. dans le vide** *(suicidaire)* to jump; **se j. sur qn** to throw oneself at sb; *Fig* to pounce on sb; **se j. sur** *(nourriture)* to pounce on; *(occasion)* to jump at; **se j. à l'eau** to plunge into the water; *Fig* to take the plunge; **se j. par la fenêtre** to throw oneself out of the window; **se j. aux pieds de qn** to throw oneself at sb's feet; *Fig* **se j. à la tête de qn** *(le draguer)* to throw oneself at sb

jeton [ʒətɔ̃] *nm* (**a**) *(au jeu)* chip; *(pour téléphone, machine)* token; **j. de présence** *(objet)* token *(issued as voucher for attendance at meeting)*; *(honoraires)* director's fees (**b**) *Fam* **avoir les jetons** to have the jitters

jeu, -x [ʒø] *nm* (**a**) *(amusement)* play; **faire qch par j.** to do sth for fun; *Fig* **entrer en j.** to come into play; *Fig* **c'est un j. d'enfant** it's child's play; *Prov* **jeux de mains, jeux de vilains** all this fooling around is going to end in tears; **j. de mots** play on words, pun; **j. de rôles** role-playing
(**b**) *(activité)* game; **mettre la balle en j.** to bring the ball into play; *Fig* **jouer le j.** to play the game; *Fig* **jouer franc j. (avec qn)** to play fair (with sb); *Fig* **se prendre au j.** to get caught up in it; *Fig* **faire le j. de qn** to play into sb's hands; **on aurait beau j. de répondre** it would be quite easy to answer; **j. d'adresse** game of skill; **j. de cartes** card game; **j. électronique** computer game; **le j. de l'oie** = board game similar to snakes and ladders; **les jeux Olympiques** the Olympic Games, the Olympics; **jeux de société** *(charades, devinettes)* parlour games; *(petits chevaux, jeu de l'oie)* board games; **j. télévisé** (television) game show; *(avec questions)* (television) quiz show; **j. vidéo** video game
(**c**) *(au casino)* **le j.** gambling; **se ruiner au j.** to

bankrupt oneself gambling; **mettre qch en j.** *(argent, voiture, carrière)* to stake sth; *Fig* **être en j.** to be at stake; **les jeux sont faits** *(à la roulette)* les jeux sont faits; **faites vos jeux!** place your bets!; **jeux de hasard** games of chance

(**d**) *(cartes en main)* hand; **avoir du j.** to have a good hand; **cacher son j.** to hide one's hand; *Fig* to keep one's cards close to one's chest; *Fig* **sortir le grand j.** to pull out all the stops

(**e**) *(au tennis)* game; **j., set et match** game, set and match; **j. Noah** game (to) Noah; **j. blanc** love game

(**f**) *(d'un acteur)* acting; *(d'un musicien)* playing; **j. de jambes** *(d'un boxeur, d'un tennisman)* footwork

(**g**) *(d'outils, de clefs)* set; **j. de boules/quilles** set of bowls/skittles; **j. de cartes** *Br* pack *or Am* deck of cards; **j. d'échecs** chess set

(**h**) **il y a du j.** *(ça bouge)* there's a bit of play; **le vis a** *ou* **prend du j.** the screw is loose

(**i**) *(mécanisme)* **le j. de l'offre et de la demande** the system of supply and demand

jeu-concours *(pl* **jeux-concours**) [ʒøkɔ̃kur] *nm* competition

jeudi [ʒødi] *nm* Thursday; **le j. saint** Maundy Thursday; *Fam* **la semaine des quatre jeudis**, *Can* **dans la semaine des trois jeudis** when pigs fly; *voir aussi* **samedi**

jeun [ʒœ̃] **à jeun 1** *adj* **être à j.** *(sans avoir mangé ni bu)* not to have eaten or drunk anything; *(pas ivre)* to be sober

2 *adv* **prendre qch à j.** to take sth on an empty stomach

jeune [ʒœn] **1** *adj (personne, vin, pays)* young; *(apparence, allure)* youthful; *(coiffure, vêtement)* that makes one look young; **être j. d'esprit** to have a youthful outlook; **faire plus j. que son âge** to look younger than one's age; **elle n'est plus toute j.** she's not as young as she was

2 *nmf* **un j.** a youngster; **une j.** a girl; *Fam* **un petit j.** a young guy; **les jeunes** young people

3 *adv* **s'habiller j.** to dress in a youthful style; **ça fait j.** it makes you/her/*etc* look young

jeûne [ʒøn] *nm* (**a**) *(période)* fast; **rompre le j.** to break one's fast (**b**) *(pratique)* fasting

jeûner [ʒøne] *vi* to fast

jeunesse [ʒœnɛs] *nf* (**a**) *(période)* youth (**b**) *(d'apparence, d'esprit)* youthfulness (**c**) *(jeunes gens)* young people

jeunot, -otte [ʒœno, -ɔt] *Fam* **1** *adj* youngish

2 *nm,f Péj* youngster; **un petit j.** a young little fellow

JF (**a**) *(abrév* **jeune fille**) girl (**b**) *(abrév* **jeune femme**) young woman

JH *(abrév* **jeune homme**) young man

jingle [dʒingəl] *nm* jingle

JO [ʒio] **1** *nm (abrév* **Journal officiel**) = French government publication, *Br* ≃ Hansard, *Am* ≃ Federal Register

2 *nmpl (abrév* **jeux Olympiques**) Olympic Games

joaillerie [ʒɔajri] *nf* (**a**) *(magasin)* jeweller's shop (**b**) *(bijoux)* jewellery

joaillier, -ère [ʒɔaje, -ɛr] *nm,f* jeweller

job [dʒɔb] *nm Fam* job

jockey [ʒɔkɛ] *nm* jockey

Joconde [ʒɔkɔ̃d] *nf* **la J.** the Mona Lisa

joggeur, -euse [dʒɔgœr, -øz] *nm,f* jogger

jogging [dʒɔgiŋ] *nm* (**a**) *(vêtement)* track suit (**b**) *(activité)* jogging; *(course)* run; **faire du j.** to go jogging, to jog

Johannesburg [ʒɔanɛsbur] *n* Johannesburg

joie [ʒwa] *nf* joy, delight; **avec j.** *(volontiers)* with pleasure, gladly; *Fam* **c'est pas la j.!** it's no fun!; **faire la j. de qn** to make sb happy; **se faire une j. de faire qch** *(envisager)* to look forward to doing sth; *(faire avec plaisir)* to be delighted to do sth; **faire une fausse j. à qn** to falsely raise sb's hopes; **j. de vivre** joie de vivre

joignable [ʒwaɲabl] *adj* contactable

joignais *etc voir* **joindre**

joindre [43] [ʒwɛ̃dr] **1** *vt* (**a**) *(réunir)* to join; **j. les mains** to put one's hands together; *Fam Fig* **j. les deux bouts** to make ends meet (**b**) *(ajouter)* to add (**à** to); *(dans une lettre, un colis)* to enclose (**à** with); **j. le geste à la parole** to suit the action to the word; **j. l'utile à l'agréable** to combine business with pleasure (**c**) *(contacter)* to contact

2 se joindre *vpr* **se j. à qn** to join sb; **se j. à qch** to join in sth

joint, -e [ʒwɛ̃, -ɛ̃t] **1** *pp de* **joindre**

2 *adj* **sauter à pieds joints** to jump from a standing position; **les mains jointes** with hands together; **pièces jointes** *(dans une lettre)* enclosures

3 *nm* (**a**) *(d'étanchéité)* seal; *(articulation)* joint; **j. de culasse** cylinder head gasket; **j. de dilatation** expansion joint (**b**) *Fam (à fumer)* joint

jointure [ʒwɛ̃tyr] *nf (articulation)* joint

jojo [ʒɔʒo] *Fam* **1** *nm voir* **affreux**

2 *adj inv* **ne pas être j.** *(physiquement)* not to look very nice; *(moralement)* not to be very nice

jojoba [ʒɔʒoba] *nm* jojoba

joker [ʒɔkɛr] *nm (aux cartes)* joker; *Ordinat* wild-card

joli, -e [ʒɔli] **1** *adj* (**a**) *(personne, ville, voix)* pretty, attractive; **il est j. garçon** he's good-looking; **j. comme un cœur** pretty as a picture; **faire le j. cœur** to flirt (**b**) *(situation, somme)* nice; **c'est bien j. tout ça mais...** that's all well and good but...; *Fam* **c'est pas j. j.** *(blâmable)* that's not very nice; *(laid)* it's not a pretty sight

2 *nm Ironique* **c'est du j.!** marvellous!

joliment [ʒɔlimɑ̃] *adv* (**a**) *(bien)* nicely; **c'est j. dit** that's nicely put; *Ironique* **te voilà j. arrangé!** you're in a right mess! (**b**) *Fam (extrêmement)* really; **elle s'est j. fait engueuler** she got a good telling-off

jonc [ʒɔ̃] *nm (plante)* rush

joncher [ʒɔ̃ʃe] *vt* to strew (**de** with)

jonction [ʒɔ̃ksjɔ̃] *nf* junction

jongler [ʒɔ̃gle] *vi* (**a**) *(avec des balles)* & *Fig* to juggle (**avec** with) (**b**) *Can (rêvasser)* to daydream

jongleur, -euse [ʒɔ̃glœr, -øz] *nm,f* juggler

jonquille [ʒɔ̃kij] *nf* daffodil

Jordanie [ʒɔrdani] *nf* **la J.** Jordan

jordanien, -enne [ʒɔrdanjɛ̃, -ɛn] **1** *adj* Jordanian

2 *nm,f* **J.** Jordanian

jos-connaissant [djokɔnɛsɑ̃] *nm Can Fam Péj* know-all

jouable [ʒwabl] *adj* playable

joual, -e [ʒwal] *Can* **1** *nm* joual *(French-Canadian dialect)*

2 *adj* **langue jouale** joual

joue [ʒu] *nf (de personne, d'animal)* cheek; **j. contre j.** cheek to cheek; **mettre qn en j.** to take aim at sb; **tenir qn en j.** to keep sb in one's sights; **en j.!** take aim!

jouer [ʒwe] **1** vt (**a**) (parier) to stake (**sur** on); (cheval) to back, to bet on
(**b**) (participer à) **j. la finale** to play in the final
(**c**) (carte) to play; (pion, pièce) to move
(**d**) (rôle) to act, to play; **j. la surprise** to pretend to be surprised; **j. les héros** to play the hero; Hum **j. la fille de l'air** to vanish into thin air
(**e**) (air) to play; **j. du Bach** to play (some) Bach
2 vi (**a**) (s'amuser) to play; Fig **j. sur les mots** to play with words; Fig **j. avec les sentiments de qn** to play with sb's feelings; Fig **j. avec son avenir** to risk one's future; Fig **j. avec le feu** to play with fire; **c'est à qui de j.?** whose turn is it?; (aux échecs, aux dames) whose move is it?; Fig **maintenant à vous de j.** now it's your turn
(**b**) (acteur) to act; (troupe) to perform; **il joue très mal** he's a very bad actor
(**c**) (parier) to gamble; **j. en Bourse** to speculate on the stock market
(**d**) (fonctionner) **j. en faveur/défaveur de qn** to work in sb's favour/against sb; **faire j. un ressort** to release a spring; Fig **faire j. ses relations pour obtenir qch** to pull a few strings to get sth
(**e**) (bois) to warp; (pièce) to work loose
(**f**) Suisse (convenir) to be alright; **avec un peu de chance ça pouvait j.** with a bit of luck it could work out
3 jouer à vt ind (**a**) (pratiquer) to play; **j. au tennis/aux cartes** to play tennis/cards; **j. aux gendarmes et aux voleurs** to play cops and robbers; **j. à la marchande** to play at shops; Fig **j. au plus fin** to try to outwit each other
(**b**) (parier sur) **j. aux courses** to bet on or back horses
4 jouer de vt ind **j. du piano/de la harpe** to play the piano/the harp; Fig **j. des coudes** to elbow one's way through
5 se jouer vpr (**a**) (match) to be played
(**b**) (se décider) **son sort est en train de se j.** his fate is hanging in the balance
(**c**) **se j. de qn** to trifle with sb; **se j. des lois** to make a mockery of the law; **se j. des difficultés** to make light of difficulties
(**d**) (pièce de théâtre, film) to be on

jouet [ʒwɛ] nm toy; Fig **être le j. des dieux** to be the plaything of the gods

joueur, -euse [ʒwœr, -øz] **1** nm,f (**a**) (d'un jeu, d'un sport, d'un instrument de musique) player; **j. de tennis/cartes** tennis/card player; **être beau/mauvais j.** to be a good/bad loser (**b**) (au casino) gambler
2 adj (enfant, chien) playful

joufflu, -e [ʒufly] adj (bébé, angelot) chubby-cheeked; (visage) chubby

joug [ʒu] nm aussi Fig yoke

jouir [ʒwir] vi (**a**) (profiter) **j. de qch** to enjoy sth (**b**) (sexuellement) to come (**c**) (être en possession) **j. d'une bonne réputation** to have a good reputation; **j. d'une bonne santé** to enjoy good health

jouissance [ʒwisɑ̃s] nf (**a**) (plaisir) enjoyment; (sexuel) orgasm (**b**) Jur (usage) use

jouisseur, -euse [ʒwisœr, -øz] nm,f sensualist

jouissif, -ive [ʒwisif, -iv] adj très Fam orgasmic

joujou, -x [ʒuʒu] nm (langage enfantin) toy; **faire j.** to play

joule [ʒul] nm joule

jour [ʒur] nm (**a**) (clarté) daylight; **au petit j.** at daybreak; **en plein j.** in broad daylight; Fig **au grand j.** publicly; **travailler le** ou **de j.** to work days; **j. et nuit** day and night; Fig **elle et son mari, c'est le j. et la nuit** she and her husband are like chalk and cheese; **elle est belle comme le j.** she's a real beauty; **il fait j.** it's light
(**b**) (journée) day; **huit jours** a week; **quinze jours** two weeks, Br a fortnight; **un j. ou l'autre** one day; **de j. en j.** day by day; **du j. au lendemain** overnight; **nous l'attendons d'un j. à l'autre** we're expecting him any day (now); **un de ces jours** one of these days; **un beau j., elle décida de…** one day, she decided to…; **vivre au j. le j.** (sans faire de projets) to live from day to day; (financièrement) to live from hand to mouth; **mettre qch à j.** to update sth, to bring sth up to date; **tenir qch à j.** to keep sth up to date; **décidément, ce n'est pas mon j.!** it just isn't my day today!; **il y a les jours avec et les jours sans** there are good days and bad days; **le j. de l'an** New Year's Day; **j. de congé** day off; **j. férié** public holiday, Br bank holiday; **le jour J** D-day; **le j. de Noël** Christmas Day; **j. ouvrable** working day; **j. de repos** day off
(**c**) (date) day; **quel j. sommes-nous?** what's the date (today)?; **le j. de mes vingt ans** my twentieth birthday; **il y a six ans j. pour j.** six years ago to the day; **à ce j., nous n'avons toujours pas reçu votre lettre** to date we still have not received your letter
(**d**) (époque) **passer des jours heureux** to have a good time; **de nos jours** these days, nowadays; **les beaux jours** the fine days of summer; **pour mes vieux jours** for my old age
(**e**) (vie) **donner le j. à un enfant** to give birth to a child; **mettre fin à ses jours** to put an end to one's life; **ses jours ne sont plus en danger** we no longer fear for her life; **il vit le j. à Paris** he was born in Paris; **jusqu'à mon dernier j.** to my dying day
(**f**) (éclairage) light; Fig **voir qch sous un j. nouveau/sous son vrai j.** to see sth in a new light/in its true light; Fig **présenter qch sous un j. favorable** to present sth in a favourable light
(**g**) (ouverture) gap

Jourdain [ʒurdɛ̃] nm **le J.** the River Jordan

journal, -aux [ʒurnal, -o] nm (**a**) (publication) paper, newspaper; **j. (télévisé)** (television) news (**b**) (récit d'événements, d'expériences) journal; Ordinat log; **tenir un j.** to keep a journal; **j. de bord** log (book); **j. intime** diary; **J. officiel** = French government publication, Br ≃ Hansard, Am ≃ Federal Register

---

Journal officiel

This bulletin prints information about new laws and summaries of parliamentary debates, and informs the public of any important government business. When new companies are established, they are obliged by law to publish an announcement in the "Journal officiel".

---

journalier, -ère [ʒurnalje, -ɛr] **1** adj daily
2 nm,f (ouvrier agricole) day labourer

journalisme [ʒurnalism] nm journalism; **j. d'investigation** investigative journalism

journaliste [ʒurnalist] nmf journalist; **elle est j. au Monde** she's a journalist with Le Monde; **j. sportif** sports journalist

journalistique [ʒurnalistik] adj journalistic

journée [ʒurne] *nf* (**a**) *(par opposition à nuit)* day(-time); **pendant la j.** in the daytime, during the day; **dans la j.** in the course of the day; **toute la j.** all day (**b**) *(unité de temps)* day; **j. de travail** *(jour non chômé)* working day; *(quantité de travail)* day's work; **faire la j. continue** *(personne)* to work through lunch; **j. portes ouvertes** *Br* open day, *Am* open house

journellement [ʒurnɛlmã] *adv* daily

joute [ʒut] *nf (combat médiéval)* joust; *Fig* **joutes oratoires** verbal jousting

jouvence [ʒuvãs] *nf Litt* **cela a été un bain** *ou* **une cure de j.** it has rejuvenated me

jouvenceau, -x [ʒuvãso] *nm Hum* stripling

jouvencelle [ʒuvãsɛl] *nf Hum* maiden

jouxter [ʒukste] *vt* to adjoin

jovial, -e, -als *ou* **-aux, -ales** [ʒɔvjal, -o] *adj* jovial, jolly

jovialité [ʒɔvjalite] *nf* joviality, jolliness

joyau, -x [ʒwajo] *nm aussi Fig* jewel

joyeusement [ʒwajøzmã] *adv* joyfully

joyeux, -euse [ʒwajø, -øz] *adj* joyful; **j. anniversaire!** happy birthday!; **j. Noël!** Happy *or* Merry Christmas!

JT [ʒite] *nm (abrév* **journal télévisé)** TV news

jubilation [ʒybilasjɔ̃] *nf* jubilation

jubilé [ʒybile] *nm* jubilee

jubiler [ʒybile] *vi* to be jubilant; *(méchamment)* to gloat

jucher [ʒyʃe] **1** *vt* to perch (**sur** on)
2 se jucher *vpr* to perch (**sur** on)

judaïque [ʒydaik] *adj* Jewish; *(loi)* Judaic

judaïsme [ʒydaism] *nm* Judaism

judas [ʒyda] *nm (ouverture)* peephole

judéo-chrétien, -enne *(mpl* **judéo-chrétiens**, *fpl* **judéo-chrétiennes)** [ʒydeɔkretjɛ̃, -ɛn] *adj* Judaeo-Christian

judiciaire [ʒydisjɛr] *adj (pouvoir, enquête, acte)* judicial; *(aide, autorité)* legal

judicieusement [ʒydisjøzmã] *adv* judiciously

judicieux, -euse [ʒydisjø, -øz] *adj* judicious; **peu j.** injudicious

judo [ʒydo] *nm* judo

judoka [ʒydɔka] *nmf Sport* judoka

juge [ʒyʒ] *nm* judge; **Monsieur le J.** Your Honour; **les juges** the bench; **je vous laisse j.** I'll let you be the judge; *Fig* **être à la fois j. et partie** to sit in judgement on oneself; **j. d'instruction** examining magistrate; **j. de ligne** line judge; **j. de touche** *(au football)* linesman; *(au rugby)* touch judge

jugé [ʒyʒe] **au jugé** *adv (tirer)* blind; *(calculer)* roughly

jugement [ʒyʒmã] *nm* (**a**) *Jur (d'une affaire)* trial; **passer en j.** to stand trial (**b**) *Jur (décision)* decision; *(dans des affaires criminelles)* sentence (**c**) *(opinion)* judgement; **porter un j. sur qch** to pass judgement on sth; **j. de valeur** value judgement (**d**) *(discernement)* judgement

jugeote [ʒyʒɔt] *nf Fam* common sense

juger¹ [45] [ʒyʒe] **1** *vt* (**a**) *(affaire, prévenu)* to try; *(demande, litige)* to adjudicate (**b**) *(évaluer, condamner)* to judge (**sur** by); **à toi de j.** it's for you to judge (**c**) *(croire)* **j. que** to consider that; **on le jugeait fou** people considered him mad; **j. superflu de faire qch** to consider it superfluous to do sth
2 juger de *vi ind* to judge; **jugez de ma surprise!** imagine my surprise!; **à en j. par...** judging by...

juger² = **jugé**

jugulaire [ʒygylɛr] *nf* (**a**) *(veine)* jugular (vein) (**b**) *(de casque)* chin strap

juguler [ʒygyle] *vt (rébellion)* to quell; *(inflation, épidémie)* to check

juif, -ive [ʒɥif, -iv] **1** *adj* Jewish
2 *nm,f* **J.** Jew

juillet [ʒɥijɛ] *nm* July; **le 14-J.** Bastille Day *(day of national celebration in France)*; *voir aussi* **janvier**

La fête du 14 juillet

The celebrations to mark the anniversary of the storming of the Bastille begin on 13 July with outdoor public dances ("les bals du 14 Juillet") and firework displays, and continue on the 14th with a military parade in the morning. Firework displays are also held in the evening of "Bastille Day".

---

juin [ʒɥɛ̃] *nm* June; *voir aussi* **janvier**

juke-box [dʒykbɔks, ʒykbɔks] *nm inv* jukebox

Jules [ʒyl] *npr* **J. César** Julius Caesar

jules [ʒyl] *nm Fam (mari, petit ami)* guy

julienne [ʒyljɛn] *nf* **j. de légumes** julienne of vegetables *(cut into thin strips)*

jumbo [dʒœmbo], **jumbo-jet** *(pl* **jumbo-jets)** [dʒœmbodʒɛt] *nm* jumbo (jet)

jumeau, -elle, -x, -elles [ʒymo, -ɛl] **1** *adj (frère, sœur)* twin
2 *nm,f* twin; *(sosie)* double; **vrais/faux jumeaux** identical/fraternal twins

jumelage [ʒymlaʒ] *nm (de villes)* twinning

jumelé, -e [ʒymle] *adj (villes)* twinned; *(maisons)* semi-detached

jumelles [ʒymɛl] *nfpl* **(paire de) j.** (pair of) binoculars; **j. de théâtre** opera glasses

jument [ʒymã] *nf* mare

jungle [ʒɔ̃gl, ʒœ̃gl] *nf aussi Fig* jungle

junior [ʒynjɔr] **1** *adj (mode, taille)* junior
2 *nmf Sport* junior *(19 to 20 years old)*

junte [ʒœ̃t] *nf* junta

jupe [ʒyp] *nf* skirt; *Fam* **être dans les** *ou* **pendu aux jupes de sa mère** to be clinging to one's mother's skirts; **j. droite** straight skirt; **j. plissée** pleated skirt

jupe-culotte *(pl* **jupes-culottes)** [ʒypkylɔt] *nf* culottes

jupette [ʒypɛt] *nf* skirt

Jupiter [ʒypitɛr] *npr (dieu, planète)* Jupiter

jupon [ʒypɔ̃] *nm* underskirt, petticoat

Jura [ʒyra] *nm* **le J.** the Jura (Mountains)

jurassique [ʒyrasik] *Géol* **1** *adj* Jurassic
2 *nm* **le J.** the Jurassic period

juré, -e [ʒyre] **1** *adj* **ennemi j.** sworn enemy
2 *nm,f* juror; **les jurés** the jury

jurer [ʒyre] **1** *vt* to swear; **je le jure** I swear; **je te jure que c'est vrai!** I swear it's true!; **j. qch sur la tête de qn** to swear sth on sb's grave; **j'aurais juré qu'il était là** I could have sworn that it was there; **j. de faire qch** to swear to do sth; **ne j. que par** to swear by; *Prov* **il ne faut j. de rien** you never can tell
2 *vi* (**a**) *(dire des gros mots)* to swear (**b**) *(couleurs, vêtements)* to clash (**avec** with)
3 se jurer *vpr* (**a**) *(l'un à l'autre)* **se j. fidélité** to swear to be faithful to each other (**b**) *(à soi-même)* **se j. que** to swear (to oneself) that; **se j. de faire qch** to swear to do sth

juridiction [ʒyridiksjɔ̃] *nf (compétence)* jurisdiction; *(tribunaux)* courts

juridique [ʒyridik] *adj* legal

jurisprudence [ʒyrisprydɑ̃s] *nf* case law; **faire j.** to set a (legal) precedent

juriste [ʒyrist] *nmf* legal expert; **j. d'entreprise** company lawyer

juron [ʒyrɔ̃] *nm* swearword

jury [ʒyri] *nm* (**a**) *(d'un tribunal)* jury (**b**) *(pour l'attribution d'un prix)* (panel of) judges; *(d'examen)* board of examiners

jus [ʒy] *nm* (**a**) *(de fruits, de légumes)* juice; *(de viande)* juices; **j. d'orange/de fruit** orange/fruit juice; *Can Fam* **j. de bras** elbow grease; *Fam Hum* **j. de chaussettes** *(café)* dishwater (**b**) *Fam (courant électrique)* juice; **prendre le j.** to get an electric shock

jusant [ʒyzɑ̃] *nm* ebb tide

jusque [ʒysk, ʒyskə] *prép* (**a**) **jusqu'à** *(délimite un espace)* as far as; *(délimite une mesure)* up to; **jusqu'ici** as far as here; **j.-là** as far as there; *Fam* **s'en mettre j.-là** to stuff oneself; **jusqu'où?** how far?; **avoir de l'eau jusqu'à la taille** to have water right up to one's waist; **compter jusqu'à dix** to count (up) to ten; **jusqu'au bout (de la rue)** to the end (of the street); **j. dans les campagnes** right into the countryside; *Fig* **aller jusqu'au bout d'un raisonnement** to follow an argument through; **aller jusqu'à faire qch** to go so far as to do sth

(**b**) *(indique le temps)* until, till; **jusqu'ici, jusqu'à maintenant, jusqu'à présent** until now, up to now; **j.-là, jusqu'alors** until then, up to then; **jusqu'à ce que** + *subjunctive* until, till; **jusqu'à (l'âge de) quinze ans** up to the age of fifteen; **jusqu'à nouvel ordre** until further notice; **jusqu'au jour** *ou* **moment où...** until the time when...; **si nous remontons jusqu'en** *ou* **jusqu'à 1800** if we go right back to 1800

(**c**) *(également)* **jusqu'à** even

justaucorps [ʒystokɔr] *nm (de sport)* leotard

juste [ʒyst] **1** *adj* (**a**) *(équitable)* fair (**avec** *ou* **envers** to); **à j. titre** rightly

(**b**) *(exact) (calcul, réponse)* right, correct; *(raisonnement)* sound; *(note)* right; **arriver à l'heure j.** to arrive right on time; **avez-vous l'heure j.?** do you have the right time?

(**c**) *(trop petit) (chaussures, vêtement)* tight; **une bouteille pour six, c'est un peu j.** one bottle isn't quite enough for six people

(**d**) *Fam (financièrement)* **être (un peu) j.** to be (a bit) strapped for cash

2 *adv* (**a**) *(avec exactitude) (viser, parler)* accurately; *(chanter)* in tune; *Fam* **tomber j.** to guess right; **tout j.!** that's right!

(**b**) *(précisément)* just; **à dix heures j.** on the stroke of ten; **j. au coin/en face/à côté** just *or* right on the corner/opposite/next door; **arriver j. à temps** to arrive just in time; **ça fait 10 francs tout j.** that's 10 francs exactly

(**c**) *(à peine)* just; **c'est tout j. s'il sait lire** he can barely read; **avoir j. le temps (de faire qch)** to have just enough time (to do sth); **ils ont tout j. fini de manger** they've only just finished eating

(**d**) *(trop peu)* **calculer trop j. (pour)** not to allow enough (for)

(**e**) **au j.** *(exactement)* exactly

justement [ʒystəmɑ̃] *adv* (**a**) *(précisément)* exactly; **j'allais j. t'appeler** I was just going to ring you (**b**) *(avec justesse)* rightly (**c**) *(avec justice)* justly

justesse [ʒystɛs] *nf* (**a**) *(précision) (d'une expression, d'une remarque)* aptness (**b**) **de j.** (only) just; **j'ai eu mon train de j.** I (only) just caught my train

justice [ʒystis] *nf* (**a**) *(équité)* justice; **faire** *ou* **rendre j. à qn** to do justice to sb; **se faire j.** *(se venger)* to take the law into one's own hands; *(se tuer)* to take one's own life (**b**) *Jur* **la j.** the law; **aller en j.** to go to court; **passer en j.** to stand trial, to appear in court

justicier, -ère [ʒystisje, -ɛr] *nm,f* righter of wrongs

justifiable [ʒystifjabl] *adj* justifiable

justificatif, -ive [ʒystifikatif, -iv] **1** *adj* justificatory; **pièces justificatives** *(d'un dossier)* supporting documents

2 *nm* written proof

justification [ʒystifikasjɔ̃] *nf* (**a**) *(explication)* justification (**de** for *ou* of) (**b**) *(preuve)* proof (**c**) *Typ & Ordinat* justification

justifié, -e [ʒystifje] *adj* (**a**) *(légitime)* justified; **peu j.** unjustified (**b**) *Typ & Ordinat* justified; **j. à droite/à gauche** right-/left-justified

justifier [66] [ʒystifje] **1** *vt* (**a**) *(légitimer, démontrer)* to justify (**b**) *Typ & Ordinat* to justify; **j. à droite/gauche** to right-/left-justify

2 **se justifier** *vpr* to justify oneself

jute [ʒyt] *nm* jute; **(toile de) j.** hessian

juter [ʒyte] *vi* to be juicy

juteux, -euse [ʒytø, -øz] *adj aussi Fam Fig* juicy

juvénile [ʒyvenil] *adj* youthful

juxtaposer [ʒykstapoze] *vt* to juxtapose

juxtaposition [ʒykstapozisjɔ̃] *nf* juxtaposition

K

K, k¹ [kɑ] *nm inv* K, k
k² (*abrév* **kilo(s)**) k
K7 [kaset] *nf* (*abrév* **cassette**) tape
Kaboul [kabul] *n* Kabul
kaki¹ [kaki] *adj inv & nm inv* (*couleur*) khaki
kaki² *nm* (*arbre, fruit*) persimmon
kaléidoscope [kaleidɔskɔp] *nm aussi Fig* kaleido-scope
kamikaze [kamikaz] *nm* kamikaze; *Fig* **être k.** to have a death wish
kanak, -e [kanak] = **canaque**
kangourou [kɑ̃guru] *nm* kangaroo
kapok [kapɔk] *nm* kapok
karaoké [karaɔke] *nm* karaoke
karaté [karate] *nm* karate
karatéka [karateka] *nmf* karate expert
karma [karma] *nm* karma
kart [kart] *nm* (go-)kart
karting [kartiŋ] *nm* karting, go-kart racing; **faire du k.** to go karting
kasher [kaʃer] *adj inv Rel* kosher
Katmandou [katmɑ̃du] *n* Katmandu
kayak [kajak] *nm* (**a**) (*embarcation de sport*) canoe, kayak; **faire du k.** to go canoeing (**b**) (*esquimau*) kayak
kayakiste [kajakist] *nmf* canoeist
kazakh, -e [kazak] **1** *adj* Kazakh
  2 *nm,f* **K.** Kazakh
Kazakhstan [kazakstɑ̃] *nm* **le K.** Kazakhstan
keffieh [kefje] *nm* kaffiyeh
kendo [kendo] *nm* kendo
Kenya [kenja] *nm* **le K.** Kenya
kenyan, -e [kenjɑ̃, -an] **1** *adj* Kenyan
  2 *nm,f* **K.** Kenyan
képi [kepi] *nm* kepi
kératine [keratin] *nf* keratin
kermesse [kermes] *nf* (**a**) (*dans les Flandres*) village fair (**b**) (*fête de bienfaisance*) (charity) fête
kern [kern] *nm Belg Pol* inner cabinet
kérosène [kerozen] *nm* kerosene
ketchup [ketʃœp] *nm* (tomato) ketchup
keuf [kœf] *nm très Fam* cop
kF [kɑɛf] *nm* (*abrév* **kilofranc(s)**) thousand francs
kg (*abrév* **kilogramme(s)**) kg
KGB [kɑgebe] *nm* **le K.** the KGB
khâgne [kɑɲ] *nf* = second-year arts class preparing students for the entrance examination for the "École normale supérieure"

khâgneux, -euse [kɑɲø, -øz] *nm,f* = student in the "khâgne"
Khartoum [kartum] *n* Khartoum
khmer, -ère [kmɛr] **1** *adj* Khmer
  2 *nm,f* **K.** Khmer; **les Khmers rouges** the Khmer Rouge
khôl [kol] *nm* kohl
kibboutz [kibuts] *nm inv* kibbutz
kidnapper [kidnape] *vt* to kidnap
kidnappeur, -euse [kidnapœr, -øz] *nm,f* kidnapper
kidnapping [kidnapiŋ] *nm* kidnapping
kif-kif [kifkif] *adj inv Fam* **c'est k. (bourricot)** it's six and half a dozen
kiki [kiki] *nm Fam* (**a**) (*cou*) **serrer le k. à qn** to wring sb's neck (**b**) (*langage enfantin*) (*pénis*) willy (**c**) **c'est parti mon k.!** here we go!
kilo [kilo] *nm* kilo
kilobaud [kilɔbo] *nm Ordinat* kilobaud
kilocalorie [kilɔkalɔri] *nf* kilocalorie
kilofranc [kilɔfrɑ̃] *nm* thousand francs
kilogramme [kilɔgram] *nm* kilogram(me)
kilohertz [kilɔɛrts] *nm* kilohertz
kilojoule [kilɔʒul] *nm* kilojoule
kilométrage [kilɔmetraʒ] *nm* (*distance*) ≃ mileage; **k. illimité** (*de voiture de location*) unlimited mileage
kilomètre [kilɔmetr] *nm* kilometre; **100 kilomètres à l'heure, 100 kilomètres-heure** 100 kilometres per *or* an hour; **taper du texte au k.** to type text straight in (*and leave the formatting etc until later*); **k. zéro** = point near Notre-Dame from which distances from Paris are measured
kilométrique [kilɔmetrik] *adj voir* **borne**
kilo-octet (*pl* **kilo-octets**) [kilɔɔktɛ] *nm Ordinat* kilo-byte
kilovolt [kilɔvɔlt] *nm* kilovolt
kilowatt [kilɔwat] *nm* kilowatt
kilowattheure [kilɔwatœr] *nm Phys* kilowatt-hour
kilt [kilt] *nm* kilt
kimono [kimono] *nm* kimono
kiné [kine] *Fam* **1** *nmf* (*médecin*) physio
  2 *nf* (*discipline*) physio
kinésiste [kinezist] *nmf Belg Br* physiotherapist, *Am* physical therapist
kinésithérapeute [kineziterapøt] *nmf Br* physio-therapist, *Am* physical therapist
kinésithérapie [kineziterapi] *nf Br* physiotherapy, *Am* physical therapy
Kinshasa [kinʃasa] *n* Kinshasa
kiosque [kjɔsk] *nm* (**a**) (*pavillon*) pavilion; (*point de vente*) kiosk; **k. à journaux** newspaper kiosk,

newsstand; **k. à musique** bandstand (**b**) *(sur Minitel ®)* **K.**® = service accessible on the Minitel® information network

kippa [kipa] *nf* kippa

kir [kir] *nm* kir *(white wine with blackcurrant liqueur)*; **k. royal** kir royal *(champagne with blackcurrant liqueur)*

kirghiz, -e [kirgiz] **1** *adj* Kirg(h)iz
   2 *nm,f* **K.** Kirg(h)iz
   3 *nm (langue)* Kirg(h)iz

Kirghizistan [kirgizistã] *nm* **le K.** Kirg(h)izia, Kirg(h)izstan

kirsch [kirʃ] *nm* kirsch

kit [kit] *nm* (self-assembly) kit; **en k.** in kit form; *Ordinat* **k. d'extension** *ou* **d'évolution** upgrade kit

kitch [kitʃ] = **kitsch**

kitchenette [kitʃənɛt] *nf* kitchenette

kitsch [kitʃ] *adj inv & nm inv* kitsch

kiwi [kiwi] *nm* (**a**) *(fruit)* kiwi fruit (**b**) *(oiseau)* kiwi

Klaxon® [klaksɔn] *nm* horn; **donner un coup de K.** to sound one's horn

klaxonner [klaksɔne] **1** *vi* to sound one's horn
   2 *vt* to sound one's horn at

klebs [klɛps] = **clebs**

Kleenex® [klinɛks] *nm inv* tissue, Kleenex®

kleptomane [klɛptɔman] *adj & nmf* kleptomaniac

kleptomanie [klɛptɔmani] *nf* kleptomania

klondike [klɔndajk] *nm Can Fam* plum job, high-paying job

km *(abrév **kilomètre(s)**)* km

km/h *(abrév **kilomètres à l'heure, kilomètres-heure**)* kph

Ko *nm (abrév **kilo-octet(s)**)* K, KB

K-O [kao] **1** *nm inv* knockout
   2 *adj inv* (**a**) *(assommé)* knocked out; **mettre qn K.** to knock sb out (**b**) *Fam (fatigué)* shattered

koala [kɔala] *nm* koala (bear)

kop [kɔp] *nm Belg Sport (club de supporters)* fan club; *(groupement de supporters)* fans

kopeck [kɔpɛk] *nm* kopeck; *Fam* **ça ne vaut pas un k.** it's not worth a bean

koter [kɔte] *vi Belg Fam* to rent a room

kouglof [kuglɔf] *nm* kugelhopf

Koweït [kɔwɛjt, kɔwɛt] *nm* **le K.** Kuwait

koweïtien, -enne [kɔwɛjtjɛ̃, kɔwɛtjɛ̃, -ɛn] **1** *adj* Kuwaiti
   2 *nm,f* **K.** Kuwaiti

krach [krak] *nm* **k. (boursier)** (stock market) crash

kraft [kraft] *nm voir* **papier**

Kremlin [krɛmlɛ̃] *nm* **le K.** the Kremlin

kumquat [kɔmkwat, kumkwat] *nm (fruit)* kumquat

kung-fu [kuŋfu] *nm inv* kung fu

kurde [kyrd] **1** *adj* Kurdish
   2 *nmf* **K.** Kurd
   3 *nm (langue)* Kurdish

Kurdistan [kyrdistã] *nm* **le K.** Kurdistan

kW *(abrév **kilowatt(s)**)* kW

K-way® [kawɛ] *nm inv* cagoule

kWh *(abrév **kilowattheure(s)**)* kWh

kyrielle [kirjɛl] *nf (de mots, de fautes)* string; *(d'insultes)* stream; *(d'enfants)* crowd; **elle a toute une k. d'amis** she has masses of friends

kyste [kist] *nm* cyst

L

L, l¹ [ɛl] *nm inv* L, l

l² (*abrév* **litre(s)**) l

l' [l] **1** *art défini voir* **le¹**
  2 *pron personnel voir* **la², le²**

la¹ [la] *art défini voir* **le¹**

la² [la]

> **l'** is used before a word beginning with a vowel or h mute.

pron personnel (femme, fille) her; *(chose, idée)* it; *(animal)* it, her; **je la connais bien** I know her well; **il te la rendra demain** he'll give it back to you tomorrow; **et ta cousine, tu l'as vue?** have you seen your cousin?; **la voilà** here she/it is

la³ *nm inv (note)* A; *(chantée)* la

là [la] **1** *adv* **(a)** *(là-bas)* there; *(ici)* here; **il est là** *(présent)* he's in; *(près d'ici)* he's here; *(là-bas)* he's there; **est-ce que Paul est là?** *(au téléphone)* is Paul there?; **je suis là pour ça** that's what I'm here for; **à quelques mètres de là** a few metres away; **de là à Paris, il n'y a que quelques kilomètres** it's only a few kilometres (away) from Paris; **là en bas/haut** down/up there; **qui va là?** who goes there?
  (b) *(à ce point)* **restons-en là** let's leave it at that; **la question n'est pas là** that's not the point; **c'est bien là le problème** that's the problem; **je sais bien qu'il est bizarre mais de là à dire qu'il est fou...** I know he's strange, but to say he's mad...; **je ne vois là aucune raison de s'inquiéter** I can't see any cause for concern; **de là sa réaction** hence his/her reaction
  (c) *(avec un relatif)* **c'est là que j'habite** that's where I live; **c'est là que j'ai compris** that's when I understood
  (d) **ce vin-là** that wine; **ces vins-là** those wines
  2 *exclam* **oh là là!** my goodness!; **alors là, je n'aurais jamais cru!** I'd never have expected that!

là-bas [laba] *adv* over there; *(dans cette région, dans ce pays)* there

label [labɛl] *nm* **(a)** *Com* quality label **(b)** *Ordinat* **l. de volume** volume label

labeur [labœr] *nm Litt* labour

labo [labo] *nm Fam* lab; **l. photo** darkroom

laborantin, -e [labɔrɑ̃tɛ̃, -in] *nm,f* laboratory assistant

laboratoire [labɔratwar] *nm* laboratory; **l. d'analyses (médicales)** pathology laboratory

laborieusement [labɔrjøzmɑ̃] *adv* laboriously

laborieux, -euse [labɔrjø, -øz] *adj* **(a)** *(difficile)* laborious; *Péj (style)* laboured; *Fam* **il n'a pas encore fini? c'est l.!** hasn't he finished yet? he's making heavy weather of it! **(b)** *Litt* **les masses laborieuses** the toiling masses

labour [labur] *nm* **(a)** *(labourage)* ploughing **(b)** **labours** *(champs)* ploughed land

labourage [laburaʒ] *nm* ploughing

labourer [labure] *vt* **(a)** *(terre)* to plough **(b)** *Fig (griffer)* to claw; **visage labouré de rides** face furrowed with wrinkles

laboureur [laburœr] *nm* ploughman

labrador [labradɔr] *nm* labrador

labyrinthe [labirɛ̃t] *nm* maze, labyrinth

lac [lak] *nm* lake; **les Grands Lacs** the Great Lakes; **le l. Baïkal** Lake Baikal; **le l. Érié** Lake Erie; **le l. Huron** Lake Huron; **le l. Léman** *ou* **de Genève** Lake Geneva; **le l. Michigan** Lake Michigan; **le l. Ontario** Lake Ontario; **le l. Supérieur** Lake Superior

lacer [16] [lase] **1** *vt (chaussures)* to tie (up); *(corset)* to lace up
  2 se lacer *vpr (chaussures)* to tie (up); *(corset)* to lace up

lacérer [34] [lasere] *vt (déchirer)* to tear to shreds; *(blesser)* to lacerate

lacet [lasɛ] *nm* **(a)** *(de chaussure, de corset)* lace; **faire ses lacets** to tie one's laces **(b)** *(tournant)* sharp bend; **faire des lacets** to twist and turn **(c)** *(collet)* snare

lâche [laʃ] **1** *adj* **(a)** *(ressort, nœud)* loose; *(vêtement)* loose-fitting; *(discipline)* lax **(b)** *Péj (personne, acte, attitude)* cowardly
  2 *nmf* coward

lâchement [laʃmɑ̃] *adv (sans courage)* in a cowardly way

lâcher [laʃe] **1** *vt* **(a)** *(desserrer)* *(corde, ceinture)* to loosen
  (b) *(ne plus tenir)* to let go of; *(laisser tomber)* to drop; *Fam Fig (cesser d'importuner)* to leave alone; **l. prise** to let go; *Fam* **il ne m'a pas lâché d'une semelle** he stuck to me like a leech; *Fam* **lâche-moi les baskets** *ou* **la grappe!** get off my back!; *Can Fam* **l. son fou** to let one's hair down
  (c) *Fam (abandonner)* *(associé)* to walk out on; *(ami)* to let down; *(amant)* to chuck, to dump; *(emploi)* to chuck in; **la voiture nous a lâchés** the car died on us
  (d) *(distancer)* *(poursuivant)* to shake off; *(dans une course)* to leave behind
  (e) *(libérer)* to release; **l. un chien sur qn** to set a dog on sb
  (f) *(laisser échapper)* *(juron, cri, pet)* to let out; *(sottise, plaisanterie)* to come out with; *Fam* **l. le morceau** to spill the beans
  2 *vi (corde, câble)* to break; *(mécanisme, pièce)* to go; *(moteur)* to die; *(freins)* to fail; *Fig* **ses nerfs ont lâché** he/she broke down
  3 *nm (de colombes, de ballons)* release

lâcheté [lɑʃte] *nf* cowardice

lâcheur, -euse [lɑʃœr, -øz] *nm,f Fam* unreliable person

lacis [lasi] *nm (de nerfs, de fils)* network; *(de ruelles)* maze

laconique [lakɔnik] *adj* laconic

laconiquement [lakɔnikmɑ̃] *adv* laconically

lacrymal, -e, -aux, -ales [lakrimal, -o] *adj* tear, *Spéc* lachrymal

lacrymogène [lakrimɔʒɛn] *adj voir* gaz, grenade

lacté, -e [lakte] *adj (produit)* which contains milk; *(régime)* milk

lactique [laktik] *adj Chim* lactic

lactose [laktoz] *nm Chim* lactose

lacune [lakyn] *nf (dans une liste, ses connaissances, ses souvenirs)* gap; **avoir des lacunes en qch** to have a patchy knowledge of sth

lacustre [lakystr] *adj* lakeside

lad [lad] *nm* stable lad

là-dedans [ladədɑ̃] *adv* inside, in there; **il y a l. quelque chose que je ne comprends pas** there's something here I don't understand; **elle n'a rien à voir l.!** she's got nothing to do with it!; *Fam* **il y en a l.!** he's/she's got a lot up top!

là-dessous [latsu] *adv* underneath, under there; *Fig* **il y a quelque chose l.** there's something behind it

là-dessus [latsy] *adv* on there; *(sur ces mots)* with that; **tout le monde est d'accord l.** everybody agrees about it; **c'est l. que tu dois te concentrer** that's what you have to concentrate on

lagon [lagɔ̃] *nm* lagoon

lagopède [lagɔpɛd] *nm* **l. d'Écosse** grouse

lagune [lagyn] *nf* lagoon

là-haut [lao] *adv* up there; *(à un étage supérieur)* upstairs

La Havane [laavan] *n* Havana

La Haye [laɛ] *n* The Hague

laïc [laik] = **laïque**

laïciser [laisize] *vt* to secularize

laïcité [laisite] *nf (des écoles)* secularity; *Pol* secularism

laid, -e [lɛ, lɛd] **(a)** *adj (personne, visage, bâtiment)* ugly; **l. comme un pou** *ou* **à faire peur** as ugly as sin **(b)** *(langage enfantin) (méprisable)* not nice

laideron [lɛdrɔ̃] *nm Péj (fille)* ugly girl; *(femme)* ugly woman

laideur [lɛdœr] *nf* **(a)** *(d'une personne, d'un visage, d'un bâtiment)* ugliness **(b)** *(bassesse)* meanness

laie [lɛ] *nf (animal)* wild sow

lainage [lɛnaʒ] *nm* **(a)** *(étoffe)* woollen fabric **(b)** *(vêtement en laine)* jumper; **lainages** woollens

laine [lɛn] *nf* **(a)** *(tissu)* wool; **en l.** woollen; **l. d'agneau** lambswool; **l. vierge** new wool; **(en) pure l.** pure wool **(b)** *(vêtement)* **(petite) l.** sweater, *Br* woolly **(c)** **l. de verre** glass wool

laineux, -euse [lɛnø, -øz] *adj (tissu)* fleecy; *(mouton, cheveux)* woolly

lainier, -ère [lɛnje, -ɛr] *adj* wool

laïque [laik] **1** *adj (État)* secular; *(école, enseignement)* non-religious
   2 *nmf* layman, *f* laywoman

laisse [lɛs] *nf (pour chien)* lead, leash; **tenir un chien en l.** to keep a dog on a lead

laissé-pour-compte, laissée-pour-compte *(mpl* **laissés-pour-compte**, *fpl* **laissées-pour-compte**) [lesepurkɔ̃t] *nm,f* reject

laisser [lese] **1** *vt* **(a)** *(permettre à)* **l. qn faire qch** to let sb do sth; **laissez-le faire!** leave him alone!; **le toit laissait passer la pluie** the roof let the rain in; **l. sécher la peinture** to let the paint dry; *Fig* **laissez-moi rire!** don't make me laugh!; *aussi Fig* **l. tomber qn/qch** to drop sb/sth; *Fam* **l. courir** to leave things alone; **l. dire** to let people talk; **laisse faire!** never mind!
   (b) *(quitter) (mari, femme)* to leave; **l. qn tout seul** to leave sb all on their own; **bon, je vous laisse!** well, I'll be off!; **il a laissé une veuve et trois enfants** he left a widow and three children
   (c) *(ne pas prendre)* to leave; **l. qch à qn** *(le lui réserver)* to leave sth for sb
   (d) *(maintenir)* **l. qch ouvert/fermé** to leave sth open/closed
   (e) *(oublier)* to leave
   (f) *(traces, impression, souvenir)* to leave
   (g) *(ne pas s'occuper de) (personne)* to leave; **laisse, je m'en occupe** don't bother about that, I'll see to it
   (h) *(donner)* **l. qch à qn** *(en héritage)* to leave sb sth; *(pour qu'il s'en occupe)* to leave sth to sb; **l. le choix à qn** to give sb a choice; **cela nous laisse le temps de...** that leaves us time to...; **ils ont laissé les enfants à la grand-mère** they left the children with their grandmother; **je vous le laisse pour 100 francs** I'll let you have it for 100 francs
   (i) *(perdre) (fortune, vie, membre)* to lose
   (j) *Formel* **cela n'a pas laissé de le surprendre** it could not fail to surprise him
   2 **se laisser** *vpr* **se l. décourager/embrasser** to let oneself be discouraged/kissed; **ne te laisse pas faire!** don't let her walk all over you!; **se l. aller** to let oneself go; **se l. aller au découragement** to let oneself get discouraged; **ce vin se laisse boire** this wine is very drinkable; **je me suis laissé dire que...** I hear that...; **se l. vivre** to take life as it comes

laisser-aller [leseale] *nm inv (relâchement)* carelessness; **il y a du l. dans cette maison!** things are a bit too easy-going *or* slack in this house!

laissez-passer [lesepase] *nm inv* pass

lait [lɛ] *nm* **(a)** *(aliment)* milk; **petit l.** whey; *Fig* **boire du petit l.** to lap it up; **l. de brebis/de chèvre/de vache** sheep's/goat's/cow's milk; *Belg* **l. battu** buttermilk; **l. caillé** curd; **l. condensé** condensed milk; **l. cru** unpasteurized milk; **l. demi-écrémé** semi-skimmed milk; **l. écrémé** skimmed milk; **l. entier** whole milk; **l. longue conservation** long-life milk; **l. maternel** mother's milk; **l. maternisé** baby formula milk; **l. en poudre** powdered milk; **l. de soja** soya milk **(b)** *(cosmétique)* **l. après-soleil** after-sun (lotion); **l. bronzant** suntan lotion; **l. démaquillant** *ou* **de toilette** cleansing lotion

laitage [lɛtaʒ] *nm* dairy product

laitance [lɛtɑ̃s] *nf (de poisson)* milt; *Culin* soft roe

laiterie [lɛtri] *nf* dairy

laiteux, -euse [lɛtø, -øz] *adj (teint)* creamy; *(couleur, lumière)* milky

laitier¹, -ère [lɛtje, -ɛr] **1** *adj* dairy
   2 *nm,f (livreur)* milkman, *f* milkwoman
   3 *nf* **laitière** *(vache)* dairy cow

laitier² *nm Ind* slag

laiton [lɛtɔ̃] *nm* brass

laitue [lɛty] *nf* lettuce

laïus [lajys] *nm (discours)* speech

lama¹ [lama] *nm Rel* lama; **le Grand l.** the Dalai Lama

lama² *nm (animal)* llama

lambda [lɑ̃bda] *adj inv (moyen)* average

lambeau, -x [lɑ̃bo] *nm (de tissu, de papier, de viande)* scrap; **vêtements en lambeaux** clothes in tatters; **tomber en lambeaux** to fall to pieces

lambin, -e [lɑ̃bɛ̃, -in] *Fam* **1** *adj* slow **2** *nm,f Br* slowcoach, *Am* slowpoke

lambiner [lɑ̃bine] *vi Fam* to dawdle

lambris [lɑ̃bri] *nm (en bois)* panelling; *(en marbre, en stuc)* lining

lambrissé, -e [lɑ̃brise] *adj (de bois)* panelled; *(de marbre, de stuc)* lined

lambswool [lɑ̃bswul] *nm* lambswool; **en l.** lambswool

lame [lam] *nf* (a) *(d'épée, de couteau)* blade; *(épée)* sword; *Fig* **une fine l.** a fine swordsman; **visage en l. de couteau** hatchet face; **l. de rasoir** razor blade (b) *(bande) (de métal, de verre, de parquet)* strip; *(de store)* slat (c) *(vague)* wave; **l. de fond** groundswell

lamé, -e [lame] **1** *adj* lamé; **l. or** gold lamé **2** *nm* lamé; **en l.** lamé

La Mecque [lamɛk] *n* Mecca

lamelle [lamɛl] *nf* (a) *(de métal, de verre)* thin strip; *Bot (de champignon)* gill; *Culin* **couper en (fines) lamelles** to cut into (wafer-)thin slices (b) *(de microscope)* cover glass

lamentable [lamɑ̃tabl] *adj* appalling, awful; *(personne)* hopeless, pathetic

lamentablement [lamɑ̃tabləmɑ̃] *adv (échouer)* miserably

lamentations [lamɑ̃tasjɔ̃] *nfpl* (a) *(cris, pleurs)* wailing (b) *Péj (plaintes)* moaning, complaining

lamenter [lamɑ̃te] **se lamenter** *vpr* to moan; **se l. sur qch** to bemoan sth

laminage [laminaʒ] *nm (du métal)* rolling; **l. à chaud/ à froid** hot-/cold-rolling

laminer [lamine] *vt* (a) *(métal)* to roll (b) *Fig (revenus)* to erode; *(parti politique)* to annihilate

laminoir [laminwar] *nm Ind* rolling mill

lampadaire [lɑ̃padɛr] *nm* (a) *(d'intérieur) Br* standard lamp, *Am* floor lamp (b) *(réverbère)* lamppost

lampe [lɑ̃p] *nf* (a) *(appareil d'éclairage)* lamp; **l. à alcool** spirit lamp; **l. de bureau** desk lamp; **l. de chevet** bedside lamp; **l. à pétrole** oil lamp; **l. de poche** *Br* torch, *Am* flashlight (b) *Fam* **s'en mettre plein la l.** to have a good blowout

lampée [lɑ̃pe] *nf Fam* gulp

lampe-tempête *(pl* **lampes-tempête)** [lɑ̃ptɑ̃pɛt] *nf* hurricane lamp

lampion [lɑ̃pjɔ̃] *nm* paper lantern

lampiste [lɑ̃pist] *nm (subalterne)* underling

lamproie [lɑ̃prwa] *nf* lamprey

lance [lɑ̃s] *nf* (a) *(pique)* spear (b) *(tuyau)* **l. d'incendie** fire hose

lancée [lɑ̃se] *nf* **continuer sur sa l.** to keep going; **j'ai fait les exercices 5 et 6, et sur ma l. j'ai aussi fait le 7** I did exercises 5 and 6, and while I was at it I did 7 as well

lance-flammes [lɑ̃sflam] *nm inv* flamethrower

lancement [lɑ̃smɑ̃] *nm* (a) *(d'une fusée, d'un projet, d'un produit)* launch(ing) (b) *Ordinat (d'impression)* start; *(de programme)* running

lance-missiles [lɑ̃smisil] *nm inv* missile launcher

lance-pierre *(pl* **lance-pierres)** [lɑ̃spjɛr] *nm Br* catapult, *Am* slingshot; *Fam Fig* **manger avec un l.** to wolf one's food down; *Fam Fig* **être payé avec un l.** to be paid peanuts

lancer [16] [lɑ̃se] **1** *vt* (a) *(projeter)* to throw (**à** to); *(flèche)* to shoot; *(fusée)* to launch; *(bombe)* to drop; *(étincelles)* to shoot out; *Fig (idée, proposition)* to throw out; *(remarque)* to come out with; *(plaisanterie)* to crack; *(juron)* to let out; **l. un coup d'œil à qn** to dart *or* shoot a glance at sb; **l. le poids** to put the shot (b) *(envoyer) (signaux de détresse, SOS)* to send out (c) *(projet, produit, artiste)* to launch; *(mode)* to start; *Fin* **l. un emprunt** to issue a bond (d) *(faire démarrer) (moteur)* to start (up); **être lancé** *(dans une course, dans un travail)* to have got going; **l. qn sur un sujet** to start sb (off) on a subject (e) *Ordinat (impression)* to start; *(programme)* to run, to start (up)
2 *nm* (a) **(pêche au) l.** rod-and-reel fishing (b) *Sport* **l. du javelot/du disque/du marteau** throwing the javelin/the discus/the hammer; **l. du poids** putting the shot; **l. franc** *(au basket)* free throw
3 **se lancer** *vpr* (a) *(se jeter)* **se l. dans le vide** to throw oneself off; **se l. en avant** to rush forward; **se l. à la poursuite de qn** to rush off in pursuit of sb (b) *(s'engager)* **se l. dans** *(affaire, discussion, aventure)* to embark on; *(dépenses)* to get involved in; *(domaine)* to launch out into (c) *(se faire connaître)* to make a name for oneself

lance-roquettes [lɑ̃srɔket] *nm inv* rocket launcher

lance-torpilles [lɑ̃stɔrpij] *nm inv* torpedo tube

lanceur, -euse [lɑ̃sœr, -øz] *nm,f (au cricket)* bowler; *(au base-ball)* pitcher; **l. de javelot/disque/marteau** javelin/discus/hammer thrower; **l. de poids** shot putter

lancinant, -e [lɑ̃sinɑ̃, -ɑ̃t] *adj (douleur)* shooting; *(souvenir, air, musique)* haunting; *(regret)* nagging

landau [lɑ̃do] *nm (voiture d'enfant) Br* pram, *Am* baby carriage

lande [lɑ̃d] *nf* moor, heath

langage [lɑ̃gaʒ] *nm* (a) *(langue, vocabulaire)* language; *Fig* **changer de l.** to change one's tune; **l. chiffré** cipher, code (b) *Ordinat* language; **l. de description de page** page description language; **l. d'imprimante par pages** page printer language; **l. d'interrogation** query language; **l. machine** machine language; **l. naturel** natural language; **l. à objets** object-oriented language; **l. de programmation** programming language; **l. utilisateur** user language

lange [lɑ̃ʒ] *nm (couche) Br* nappy, *Am* diaper; *Vieilli* **langes** swaddling clothes

langer [45] [lɑ̃ʒe] *vt (mettre une couche à)* to put a *Br* nappy *or Am* diaper on; *Vieilli* to wrap in swaddling clothes

langoureusement [lɑ̃gurøzmɑ̃] *adv* languorously

langoureux, -euse [lɑ̃gurø, -øz] *adj* languorous

langouste [lɑ̃gust] *nf* crayfish

langoustine [lɑ̃gustin] *nf* Dublin Bay prawn

langue [lɑ̃g] *nf* (a) *(organe)* tongue; **tirer la l. à qn** to stick one's tongue out at sb; *Fig* **j'ai tiré la l.** *(peiné)* it was hard going; **avoir la l. bien pendue** to have the gift of the gab; **ne pas avoir la l. dans sa poche** never to be at a loss for words; **donner sa l. au chat** to give up; **tu as avalé *or* perdu ta l.?** has the cat got your tongue?; *Culin* **l. de bœuf** ox tongue (b) *(langage, style, jargon)* language; **peuples/pays**

de l. **anglaise** English-speaking people/countries; **parler la l. de bois** to come out with clichés; **l. étrangère** foreign language; **l. maternelle** native language, mother tongue; **l. morte** dead language; **l. d'oc** = medieval French dialect spoken in Southern France; **l. d'oïl** = medieval French dialect spoken in Northern France; **langues vivantes** *(matière)* modern languages

(**c**) *(personne)* **une mauvaise l.** a backbiter; **une l. de vipère** a spiteful gossip

(**d**) *(bande)* **l. de terre** strip of land

langue-de-chat *(pl* **langues-de-chat**) [lɑ̃gdəʃa] *nf* finger biscuit

languedocien, -enne [lɑ̃gdɔsjɛ̃, -ɛn] **1** *adj* of the Languedoc

2 *nm,f* **L.** person from the Languedoc

languette [lɑ̃gɛt] *nf (de bois, de métal, de chaussure)* tongue

langueur [lɑ̃gœr] *nf* (**a**) *(apathie)* listlessness (**b**) *(mélancolie, rêverie)* languor

languir [lɑ̃gir] *vi* (**a**) *Litt ou Hum (dépérir)* to languish (**b**) *(attendre avec impatience)* **ne nous faites pas l.** don't keep us in suspense; *Litt* **l. de faire qch** to long to do sth (**c**) *(conversation)* to be flagging

lanière [lanjɛr] *nf (de sac, de sandale)* strap; *(de fouet)* lash; **découper qch en lanières** to cut sth into strips

lanoline [lanɔlin] *nf* lanolin

La Nouvelle-Orléans [lanuvɛlɔrleɑ̃] *n* New Orleans

lanterne [lɑ̃tɛrn] *nf* (**a**) *(lampe)* lantern; *Fig* **éclairer la l. de qn** to enlighten sb; **l. chinoise** Chinese lantern (**b**) *(de véhicule) Br* sidelight, *Am* parking light

lanterner [lɑ̃tɛrne] *vi Fam* to dawdle; **faire l. qn** to keep sb hanging about

Laos [laɔs] *nm* **le L.** Laos

laotien, -enne [laɔsjɛ̃, -ɛn] **1** *adj* Laotian

2 *nm,f* **L.** Laotian

lapalissade [lapalisad] *nf* statement of the obvious

laper [lape] *vt* to lap up

lapidaire [lapidɛr] *adj (style, formule)* concise, succinct

lapidation [lapidasjɔ̃] *nf* stoning

lapider [lapide] *vt (mettre à mort)* to stone (to death); *Fig (critiquer)* to lambast

lapin [lapɛ̃] *nm* rabbit; **manteau en (peau de) l.** rabbitskin coat; **poser un l. à qn** to stand sb up; **mon petit l.** sweetheart; **l. de garenne** wild rabbit; *Fam* **un chaud l.** a randy devil; *Can Fam* **en criant l.** in a flash

lapine [lapin] *nf* doe (rabbit)

lapis [lapis], **lapis-lazuli** [lapislazyli] *nm inv* lapis lazuli

lapon, -one *ou* **-onne** [lapɔ̃, -ɔn] **1** *adj* Lapp

2 *nm,f* **L.** Lapp, Laplander

Laponie [lapɔni] *nf* **la L.** Lapland

laps [laps] *nm* **un l. de temps** a period of time; **un l. de temps de trois heures** a period of three hours

lapsus [lapsys] *nm (oral)* slip of the tongue; *(écrit)* slip of the pen; **faire un l.** to make a slip (of the tongue/pen); **un l. révélateur** a Freudian slip

laquais [lakɛ] *nm* footman; *Fig & Péj* lackey

laque [lak] **1** *nf* (**a**) *(vernis)* lacquer (**b**) *(pour les cheveux)* hair spray, lacquer (**c**) *(peinture)* gloss (paint)

2 *nm (objet)* piece of lacquerwork; **des laques** lacquerware, lacquerwork

laquelle [lakɛl] *voir* **lequel**

laquer [lake] *vt* (**a**) *(vernir)* to lacquer (**b**) *(cheveux)* to lacquer (**c**) *(peindre)* to paint with gloss

larbin [larbɛ̃] *nm Fam* flunkey

larcin [larsɛ̃] *nm (vol)* petty theft

lard [lar] *nm* (**a**) *(du porc) (viande)* bacon; *(gras)* fat; *Fig* **se demander si c'est du l. ou du cochon** to wonder what to make of it; **l. fumé** smoked bacon; **l. maigre** streaky bacon (**b**) *Fam (graisse)* **faire du l.** to sit around and get fat; **rentrer dans le l. à qn** to lay into sb

larder [larde] *vt Culin* to lard; *Fig* **l. qn de coups de couteau** to hack at sb with a knife; **l. un texte de citations** to pepper a text with quotations

lardon [lardɔ̃] *nm* (**a**) *Culin* piece of chopped bacon (**b**) *très Fam (enfant)* kid

large [larʒ] **1** *adj* (**a**) *(route, porte, chaussures)* wide; *(vêtement)* loose-fitting; *(visage, nez, geste)* broad; **l. d'épaules** broad-shouldered; **l. de 10 mètres** 10 metres wide; **terme employé dans son sens l.** term used in its broad sense; **avoir l'esprit l.**, **être l. d'esprit** to be broad-minded (**b**) *(considérable)* large; *(ressources)* ample; **dans une l. mesure** to a large extent (**c**) *(généreux)* generous

2 *nm* (**a**) *(espace)* **être au l.** to have plenty of room (**b**) *(haute mer)* open sea; **au l. de** off; **prendre le l.** to take to the open sea; *Fig (s'enfuir)* to beat it (**c**) *(largeur)* **faire 10 mètres de l.** to be 10 metres wide

3 *adv* **compter l.** to allow for more

largement [larʒəmɑ̃] *adv* (**a**) *(répandu, critiqué)* widely (**b**) *(abondamment) (récompenser, payer, servir)* generously; *(dépasser)* by a long way; **avoir l. de quoi vivre** to have easily enough to live on; **avoir l. le temps** to have plenty of time; **c'est l. suffisant, ça suffit l.** it's more than enough

largesse [larʒɛs] *nf* (**a**) *(générosité)* generosity (**envers** towards) (**b**) **largesses** *(dons)* generous gifts

largeur [larʒœr] *nf* (**a**) *(dimension)* width, breadth; *(de voie ferrée)* gauge; **en l., dans la l.** widthwise; **les policiers barraient la rue sur toute sa l.** the policemen blocked off the whole width of the street; *Rad* **l. de bande** bandwidth; *Ordinat* **l. de papier** paper width (**b**) *Fig* **l. d'esprit** *ou* **de vues** broadmindedness

largué, -e [large] *adj Fam (qui ne comprend plus)* lost

larguer [large] *vt* (**a**) *(amarres)* to cast off; *(cordage)* to loose; *(voile)* to unfurl (**b**) *(par avion) (parachutiste, vivres, bombe)* to drop (**c**) *Fam (abandonner) (personne)* to chuck; **il a tout largué pour partir vivre aux Caraïbes** he chucked everything in and went to live in the Caribbean

larme [larm] *nf* (**a**) *(pleur)* tear; **larmes de joie** tears of joy; **avoir facilement la l. à l'œil** to be easily moved to tears; **avoir les larmes aux yeux** to have tears in one's eyes; **en larmes** in tears; **larmes de crocodile** crocodile tears (**b**) *(petite quantité)* drop

larmoyant, -e [larmwajɑ̃, -ɑ̃t] *adj* (**a**) *(pleurnicheur) (voix, ton)* tearful (**b**) *Péj (histoire, film, sentimentalité)* mawkish

larmoyer [32] [larmwaje] *vi* (**a**) *(yeux)* to water (**b**) *Péj (personne)* to snivel

larron [larɔ̃] *nm* **s'entendre comme larrons en foire** to be as thick as thieves

larve [larv] *nf* (**a**) *(de batracien, de poisson)* larva; *(d'insecte)* grub (**b**) *Fam (personne apathique)* wimp

larvé, -e [larve] *adj (guerre, conflit)* latent

laryngite [larɛ̃ʒit] *nf Méd* laryngitis

laryngologie [larɛ̃gɔlɔʒi] *nf Méd* laryngology

laryngologiste [larɛ̃gɔlɔʒist], **laryngologue** [larɛ̃-gɔlɔg] *nmf Méd* throat specialist, *Spéc* laryngologist

larynx [larɛ̃ks] *nm Anat* larynx

las, lasse [lɑ, lɑs] *adj Litt* weary; **être l. de qch/de faire qch** to be weary of sth/of doing sth

lasagnes [lazaɲ] *nfpl* lasagne

lascar [laskar] *nm Fam* rascal

lascif, -ive [lasif, -iv] *adj* lascivious

lascivement [lasivmɑ̃] *adv* lasciviously

laser [lazɛr] *nm* laser

lassant, -e [lɑsɑ̃, -ɑ̃t] *adj* tiresome

lasser [lɑse] **1** *vt* to tire
  2 se lasser *upr* **se l. (de qch/de faire qch)** to get tired (of sth/of doing sth)

lassitude [lɑsityd] *nf* weariness

lasso [laso] *nm* lasso; **prendre un animal au l.** to lasso an animal

latent, -e [latɑ̃, -ɑ̃t] *adj* latent; **à l'état l.** latent

latéral, -e, -aux, -ales [lateral, -o] *adj (entrée, rue, vent, choc)* side

latéralement [lateralmɑ̃] *adv (se déplacer)* sideways; *(être situé)* at the side

latex [latɛks] *nm* latex

latin, -e [latɛ̃, -in] **1** *adj* Latin; *(langue)* Romance
  2 *nm* Latin; **l. de cuisine** dog Latin; *Fig* **j'y perds mon l.** I can't make head or tail of it

latiniste [latinist] *nmf (spécialiste)* Latinist; *(étudiant)* Latin student

latino [latino] *nmf Fam* Latino

latino-américain, -e *(mpl* **latino-américains,** *fpl* **latino-américaines)** [latinoamerikɛ̃, -ɛn] **1** *adj* Latin-American
  2 *nm,f* **L.-A.** Latin-American

latitude [latityd] *nf (a) Géog* latitude; **à 30° de l. nord** at latitude 30° north; **sous ces latitudes** in these latitudes *(b) (liberté)* latitude, scope; **avoir/donner à qn toute l. pour agir** to have/to give sb total freedom of action

latrines [latrin] *nfpl* latrines

latte [lat] *nf* lath; *Fam* **donner un coup de l. à qn** to give sb a kick

lattis [lati] *nm* lathing

laudanum [lodanɔm] *nm* laudanum

lauréat, -e [lɔrea, -at] **1** *adj* (prize)winning
  2 *nm,f* (prize)winner

laurier [lɔrje] *nm (a) (plante)* laurel; *Culin* bay leaves *(b) Fig (gloire)* **lauriers** laurels; **se reposer** *ou* **s'endormir sur ses lauriers** to rest on one's laurels; **être couvert de lauriers** to be covered with glory

laurier-rose *(pl* **lauriers-roses)** [lɔrjeroz] *nm* oleander

lavable [lavabl] *adj* washable; **l. en machine/à la main** machine-/hand-washable

lavabo [lavabo] *nm (a) (cuvette)* washbasin *(b)* **lavabos** *(toilettes)* toilets

lavage [lavaʒ] *nm* washing; **l. de cerveau** brainwashing; **faire subir un l. de cerveau à qn** to brainwash sb; **faire un l. d'estomac à qn** to pump sb's stomach (out)

lavande [lavɑ̃d] **1** *nf (fleur)* lavender; **(eau de) l.** lavender water
  2 *adj inv* **(bleu) l.** lavender blue

lavandière [lavɑ̃djɛr] *nf (a) (blanchisseuse)* washerwoman *(b) (oiseau)* wagtail

lave [lav] *nf* lava

lave-autos [lavoto] *nm inv Can* carwash

lave-glace *(pl* **lave-glaces)** [lavglas] *nm Br* windscreen *or Am* windshield washer

lave-linge [lavlɛ̃ʒ] *nm inv* washing machine

lave-mains [lavmɛ̃] *nm inv* handbasin

lavement [lavmɑ̃] *nm* enema

laver [lave] **1** *vt (a) (nettoyer)* to wash; *(plaie)* to bathe; **l. qch à l'eau froide** to wash sth in cold water; **il faut l. son linge sale en famille** one shouldn't wash one's dirty linen in public *(b) (disculper)* **l. qn d'une accusation/de tout soupçon** to clear sb of an accusation/of all suspicion *(c) (venger)* **l'affront a été lavé dans le sang** the insult was paid for in blood
  2 se laver *upr (a) (se nettoyer)* to wash (oneself), to have a wash; **se l. les dents** to clean *or* brush one's teeth; **se l. les cheveux/les mains** to wash one's hair/one's hands; *Fig* **je m'en lave les mains** I wash my hands of it *(b) (pouvoir être lavé)* **se l. à la main/à la machine** to be hand-/machine-washable

laverie [lavri] *nf* **l. automatique** *Br* launderette, *Am* Laundromat®

lavette [lavɛt] *nf (a) (de vaisselle)* dishcloth *(b) Belg & Suisse (gant de toilette) Br* face cloth, *Am* washcloth *(c) Fam Fig (homme)* drip

laveur, -euse [lavœr, -øz] *nm,f* washer; **l. de vitres** window cleaner

lave-vaisselle [lavvesɛl] *nm inv* dishwasher

lave-vitre *(pl* **lave-vitres)** [lavvitr] *nm Br* windscreen *or Am* windshield washer

lavis [lavi] *nm (a) (procédé)* washing *(b) (dessin)* wash drawing

lavoir [lavwar] *nm (a) (établissement)* **l. (public)** (public) washhouse *(b) (bassin)* washtub *(c) Belg (blanchisserie)* **l. (automatique)** self-service laundry

lavomatic [lavomatik] *nm Br* launderette, *Am* Laundromat®

laxatif, -ive [laksatif, -iv] *adj & nm* laxative

laxisme [laksism] *nm* laxness

laxiste [laksist] **1** *adj* lax
  2 *nmf* lax person

layette [lɛjɛt] *nf* baby clothes

le¹, la, les [lə, la, le]

---

l' is used instead of **le** or **la** before a word beginning with a vowel or h mute.

---

article défini (a) (pour définir les noms) the; **le soleil** the sun; **la lune** the moon; **l'étoile** the star; **les planètes** the planets; **le pull que je me suis acheté** the jumper I bought myself; **le Paris de 1900** Paris in 1900, the Paris of 1900; **oh, la jolie robe!** what a lovely dress!; **debout, les enfants!** get up, children!

  (b) *(avec des notions ou des généralités)* **le français** French; **la biologie** biology; **l'amour** love; **l'homme et la femme** man and woman; **the chien est l'ami de l'homme** a dog is a man's best friend; **aider les pauvres** to help the poor; **fumer la pipe** to smoke a pipe

  (c) *(avec les noms de lieux)* **la France** France; **les États-Unis** the United States; **le mont Blanc** Mont Blanc; **les Alpes** the Alps; **la Seine** the Seine

  (d) *(avec les noms de personnes)* **la reine d'Angleterre** the Queen of England; **le roi Henri IV** King Henry IV; **le Docteur Goron** Doctor Goron

  (e) *(avec les parties du corps)* **avoir les yeux verts** to have green eyes; **avoir mal à la gorge** to have a sore throat; **hausser les épaules** to shrug one's shoulders; **se laver les pieds** to wash one's feet

(**f**) *(avec un adjectif)* **je préfère le rouge** I prefer the red one

(**g**) *(distributif)* **50 francs le mètre** 50 francs a metre; **35 francs de l'heure** 35 francs an hour

(**h**) *(dans un complément de temps)* **le dimanche, il ne travaille pas** he doesn't work on Sundays; **il va à l'école le matin** he goes to school in the mornings; **il y fait vraiment froid l'hiver** it's really cold there in the winter; **je n'ai rien mangé de la journée** I haven't eaten all day; **Londres, le 9 novembre 1997** *(dans une lettre)* 9 November 1997; **je suis arrivé le 10** I arrived on the 10th

le²

> **l'** is used before a word beginning with a vowel or h mute.

pron personnel (**a**) *(homme, garçon)* him; *(chose, idée)* it; *(animal)* it, him; **elle l'admire** she admires him; **je te le rendrai demain** I'll give it back to you tomorrow; **et lui, tu le connais?** do you know him?; **le voici** here it/he is

(**b**) *(remplace une proposition)* **elle me l'a dit** she told me; **il me l'a confirmé** he confirmed it

(**c**) *(remplace un adjectif, un nom)* **est-ce qu'elle est disponible? – oui, je crois qu'elle l'est** is she available? – yes, I think she is; **jaloux, il l'est sans aucun doute** he's undoubtedly jealous; **son frère est médecin, il voudrait l'être aussi** his brother is a doctor and he'd like to be one too

leader [lidœr] *nm* leader

leasing [liziŋ] *nm* leasing; **acheter une auto en l.** to buy a car on a leasing basis

Le Caire [ləkɛr] *n* Cairo

Le Cap [ləkap] *n* CapeTown

lèche [lɛʃ] *nf très Fam* bootlicking; **faire de la l.** to be a bootlicker

lèche-bottes [lɛʃbɔt] *Fam* **1** *adj inv* **elle est l.** she's a bootlicker

2 *nmf inv* bootlicker

lèche-cul [lɛʃky] *nm inv Vulg Br* arse-licker, *Am* brown-nose

lécher [34] [leʃe] **1** *vt* (**a**) *(avec la langue)* to lick; *Fam* **l. les bottes à qn** to lick sb's boots (**b**) *(fignoler)* *(travail, style)* to polish (**c**) *(effleurer)* *(sujet: vagues)* to lap against; *(sujet: flammes)* to lick

2 se lécher *vpr* **se l. les doigts** to lick one's fingers

lèche-vitrines [lɛʃvitrin] *nm Fam* window-shopping; **faire du l.** to go window-shopping

leçon [ləsɔ̃] *nf* (**a**) *(cours, contenu)* lesson; **leçons de chant** singing lessons; **l. de choses** general science *(in primary school)*; **l. particulière** private lesson; **le bricolage en dix leçons** DIY in ten easy lessons (**b**) *(conseil)* **faire la l. à qn** to give sb a lecture; **donner une l. à qn** to teach sb a lesson; **je n'ai pas de l. à recevoir de toi** I don't need your advice; **que cela te serve de l.!** let that be a lesson to you!

lecteur, -trice [lɛktœr, -tris] **1** *nm,f* (**a**) *(personne qui lit)* reader (**b**) *(dans l'édition)* (publisher's) reader (**c**) *Univ* foreign language assistant

2 *nm* (**a**) *(dispositif)* **l. de cassettes** cassette player; **l. de disques compacts** compact disc player, CD player; **l. optique** optical reader (**b**) *Ordinat* **l. (de disquettes)** (disk) drive, floppy (disk) drive; **l. de bandes** tape drive *or* reader; **l. de CD-ROM** *ou* **de disque**

optique CD-ROM drive; **l. de disque dur** hard disk drive; **l. Zip®** Zip® drive

lecteur-encodeur *(pl* **lecteurs-encodeurs)** [lɛktœrãkɔdœr] *nm Ordinat* reader-encoder

lectorat [lɛktɔra] *nm* (**a**) *Univ* assistantship (**b**) *(lecteurs)* readership

lecture [lɛktyr] *nf* (**a**) *(action de lire)* reading; **faire la l. à qn** to read aloud to sb; *Pol* **en deuxième l.** at the second reading (**b**) *(ce qu'on lit)* reading; **elle m'a apporté de la l.** she brought me something to read; **avoir de mauvaises lectures** to read the wrong things; **livre de l.** reading book (**c**) *(interprétation)* reading (**d**) *Ordinat* read(ing); **l. optique** optical reading; **l. au scanneur** scan; **en l. seule** in read-only mode; **l. sur disque** reading to disk

ledit, ladite [lədi, ladit] *(mpl* **lesdits** [ledi], *fpl* **lesdites** [ledit]) *adj* the aforementioned

légal, -e, -aux, -ales [legal, -o] *adj* legal

légalement [legalmã] *adv* legally

légalisation [legalizasjɔ̃] *nf* legalization; *(de signature)* authentication

légaliser [legalize] *vt* *(rendre légal)* to legalize; *(authentifier)* to authenticate

légalité [legalite] *nf* (**a**) *(de mesure, décision)* legality (**b**) *(situation légale)* **la l.** the law; **agir en toute l.** to act within the law

légataire [legater] *nmf* legatee; **l. universel** sole legatee

légendaire [leʒãder] *adj* legendary

légende [leʒãd] *nf* (**a**) *(histoire, fable)* legend; *Fig (mensonge)* fairy tale; **entrer dans la l.** to become a legend; **de l.** *(personnage, pays)* fairy-tale (**b**) *(d'un dessin, d'une photo)* caption; *(d'une carte)* key

léger, -ère [leʒe, -ɛr] **1** *adj* (**a**) *(de peu de poids)* light; **l. comme une plume** as light as a feather; **avoir le cœur l.** to be light-hearted (**b**) *(blessure, amélioration, nuance)* slight; *(brise, vin, parfum)* light; *(tabac)* mild; *(thé, café)* weak; **il y a eu quelques blessés légers** some people were slightly injured (**c**) *(insuffisant)* *(preuves, arguments)* lightweight; *Fam* **ses résultats sont un peu légers** his marks are a bit on the low side (**d**) *(désinvolte)* *(personne)* thoughtless; *(en amour)* fickle; **femme légère** *ou* **de mœurs légères** loose woman

2 *nf* **à la légère** *(agir, parler)* thoughtlessly; **prendre qch à la légère** to make light of sth

3 *adv* **je vais manger l.** I'll have a light meal; **s'habiller l.** to wear light clothes

légèrement [leʒɛrmã] *adv* (**a**) *(habillé)* lightly (**b**) *(un peu)* slightly; **ça sent l. le moisi** there's a slight smell of mildew; **pourrais-tu l. baisser le volume?** could you turn the volume down a bit *or* slightly? (**c**) *(avec désinvolture)* *(agir)* thoughtlessly

légèreté [leʒɛrte] *nf* (**a**) *(d'un objet, d'un danseur, d'une démarche)* lightness (**b**) *(faiblesse)* *(d'une blessure, d'une nuance)* slightness; *(d'un vin)* lightness (**c**) *(désinvolture)* thoughtlessness; **avec l.** *(agir, parler)* thoughtlessly (**d**) *(en amour)* fickleness; *(des mœurs)* looseness

légiférer [34] [leʒifere] *vi* to legislate (**sur** on)

légion [leʒjɔ̃] *nf* legion; *Fig (multitude)* huge number; **ils sont l.** they are legion; **la L. (étrangère)** the Foreign Legion; **la L. d'honneur** the Legion of Honour

Légion d'honneur

Intended to reward not only acts of military bravery but also outstanding civilian achievements, the Legion of Honour is the highest distinction that can be conferred by the French state. It can be awarded regardless of the nationality of its recipients.

It is divided into five ranks ("chevalier","officier", "commandeur", "grand officier" and "grand-croix"). The order of the Legion of Honour is currently made up of one-third civilians and two-thirds soldiers. Among the most recent recipients of this award are the twenty-two players of the victorious French football team in the 1998 World Cup.

légionnaire [leʒjɔnɛr] nm (**a**) Hist legionary (**b**) (à la Légion étrangère) legionnaire

législateur, -trice [leʒislatœr, -tris] Jur**1** nm,f legislator

  2 nm (corps législatif) legislature

  3 adj legislative

législatif, -ive [leʒislatif, -iv] **1** adj legislative; **le pouvoir l.** the legislature

  2 nm **le l.** legislative power

  3 nfpl **les législatives** the parliamentary elections

législation [leʒislasjɔ̃] nf legislation

législature [leʒislatyr] nf (**a**) (durée) term of office (**b**) (corps) legislature

légiste [leʒist] nm jurist

légitime [leʒitim] adj (**a**) (légal) (pouvoir, enfant) legitimate; (action) lawful; (propriétaire) legal; (héritier) rightful (**b**) (juste) (récompense, motif, désir) legitimate (**c**) (justifié) (colère, action) justified; **l. défense** self-defence; **elle était en état de l. défense** she was acting in self-defence

légitimement [leʒitimmɑ̃] adv legitimately; Jur lawfully

légitimer [leʒitime] vt (**a**) (enfant, union) to legitimize (**b**) (action, demande) to justify (**c**) (titre, pouvoir) to recognize

légitimité [leʒitimite] nf legitimacy

legs [lɛ, lɛg] nm (**a**) Jur legacy, bequest; **faire un l. à qn** to leave sb a legacy (**b**) Fig (héritage) legacy

léguer [34] [lege] vt (**a**) Jur to bequeath (**à** to) (**b**) (tradition, qualité) to pass on (**à** to)

légume [legym] **1** nm (**a**) (aliment) vegetable; **légumes verts** green vegetables, greens; **légumes secs** pulses (**b**) Fam Fig (personne végétative) vegetable

  2 nf Fam **grosse l.** bigwig

leitmotiv [lajtmɔtif, lɛtmɔtif] nm leitmotiv

Léman [lemɑ̃] nm **le lac L.** Lake Geneva

lendemain [lɑ̃dmɛ̃] nm (**a**) (jour suivant) **le l.** the next day; **le l. matin/soir** the next morning/evening; **le l. de la bataille** the day after the battle (**b**) (avenir) **penser au l.** to think of the future; **des lendemains prometteurs** a promising future; **sans l.** (succès, aventures) short-lived (**c**) (période qui suit) **au l. de la guerre/de ce scandale** soon after the war/this scandal

lent, -e [lɑ̃, lɑ̃t] adj slow; **être l. à comprendre** to be slow to understand; **avoir l'esprit l.** to be slow-witted

lente [lɑ̃t] nf nit

lentement [lɑ̃tmɑ̃] adv slowly; **l. mais sûrement** slowly but surely

lenteur [lɑ̃tœr] nf slowness; **avec l.** slowly; **les lenteurs de la justice** the slowness of the law

lentille [lɑ̃tij] nf (**a**) (plante) lentil; **l. d'eau** duckweed (**b**) (en optique) lens; **lentilles de contact** contact lenses

léopard [leɔpar] nm (animal) leopard; (fourrure) leopard skin

LEP [ɛləpe, lɛp] nm Anciennement (abrév **lycée d'enseignement professionnel**) ≃ technical college

lèpre [lɛpr] nf leprosy

lépreux, -euse [leprø, -øz] **1** adj leprous

  2 nm,f leper

lequel, laquelle [ləkɛl, lakɛl] (mpl **lesquels** [lekɛl], fpl **lesquelles** [lekɛl])

> **lequel** and **lesquel(le)s** contract with **à** to form **auquel** and **auxquel(le)s**, and with **de** to form **duquel** and **desquel(le)s**.

1 pron relatif (personne) who; (après une préposition) whom; (chose) which; **il était avec sa sœur, laquelle m'a reconnu** he was with his sister, who recognized me; **l'actrice à laquelle je pense** the actress (that) I'm thinking of or of whom I'm thinking; **le stylo avec l. j'écris** the pen I'm writing with or with which I'm writing

  2 adj relatif **j'ai vu son adversaire, l. adversaire est impressionnant** I've seen his opponent, he's impressive; **auquel cas** in which case

  3 pron interrogatif which (one)

les [le] **1** art défini voir **le¹**

  2 pron personnel them; **l. voilà** here they are

lesbienne [lɛsbjɛn] nf lesbian

lèse-majesté [lɛzmaʒɛste] nf inv **crime de l.** high treason, crime of lese-majesty

léser [34] [leze] vt (**a**) (désavantager) (personne) to wrong; (intérêts) to harm; **la partie lésée** the injured party (**b**) Méd to injure

lésiner [lezine] vi to skimp (**sur** on); **ne pas l. sur les moyens** not to spare any expense

lésion [lezjɔ̃] nf lesion

lesquels, lesquelles [lekɛl] voir **lequel**

lessivable [lesivabl] adj washable

lessivage [lesivaʒ] nm washing

lessive [lesiv] nf (**a**) (produit) (en poudre) washing powder; (liquide) liquid detergent (**b**) (action de laver) wash(ing); **faire la l.** to do the washing; **j'ai fait trois lessives ce matin** I've done three washes this morning (**c**) (linge propre) washing

lessivé, -e [lesive] adj Fam washed out

lessiver [lesive] vt (**a**) (nettoyer) to wash (**b**) Fam (fatiguer) to wear out

lessiveuse [lesivøz] nf (**a**) Anciennement boiler (for clothes) (**b**) Belg (machine à laver) washing machine

lest [lɛst] nm (de bateau, ballon) ballast; **lâcher du l.** to discharge ballast; Fig (faire des concessions) to make concessions

leste [lɛst] adj (**a**) (agile) nimble (**b**) (grivois) risqué

lestement [lɛstəmɑ̃] adv (avec agilité) nimbly

lester [lɛste] vt (**a**) (bateau, ballon) to ballast (**b**) Fam (poche, portefeuille) to stuff

letchi [lɛtʃi] nm lychee

léthargie [letarʒi] nf lethargy

léthargique [letarʒik] adj lethargic

letton, -onne ou **-one** [lɛtɔ̃, -ɔn] **1** adj Latvian

  2 nm,f **L.** Latvian

  3 nm (langue) Latvian

Lettonie [lɛtɔni] *nf* la L. Latvia
lettre [lɛtr] *nf* (**a**) *(de l'alphabet)* letter; **l. majuscule/minuscule** capital/small letter; **écrire qch en toutes lettres** to write sth out in full; **au pied de la l.** literally; **à la l.** *(suivre, exécuter)* to the letter; **il fut surréaliste avant la l.** he was a surrealist before the word had been invented; **rester l. morte** to remain a dead letter; **gagner ses lettres de noblesse** to prove one's/its worth
(**b**) *(missive)* letter; **l. de change** bill of exchange; **l. ouverte (à)** open letter (to); **l. recommandée** registered letter; *Fam* **c'est passé comme une l. à la poste** it went off without a hitch; *Fam* **la nouvelle est passée comme une l. à la poste** the news was received without any fuss
(**c**) **lettres** *(littérature)* literature; *(à l'université)* arts subjects; **homme/femme de lettres** man/woman of letters; **avoir des lettres** to be well-read; **faculté de lettres** faculty of arts; **lettres classiques** classics; **lettres modernes** *(à l'université)* French
lettré, -e [letre] **1** *adj* (**a**) *(cultivé)* well-read (**b**) *Belg (sachant lire et écrire)* **il est l.** he can read and write
2 *nm,f* (**a**) *(personne cultivée)* well-read person (**b**) *Belg (personne sachant lire et écrire)* = person who can read and write
leu [lø] *nm* **à la queue l. l.** in single file
leucémie [løsemi] *nf* leukaemia; **avoir une l.** to have leukaemia
leucocyte [løkɔsit] *nm* leucocyte
leur¹, leurs [lœr] **1** *adj possessif* their; **l. chien** *(il y a un chien)* their dog; *(chacun a son chien)* their dogs; **leurs enfants** their children; **l. père et l. mère** their mother and father; **un de leurs amis** one of their friends, a friend of theirs; *Fam* **ils ont eu l. vendredi** they got Friday off
2 *pron possessif* **le l., la l., les leurs** theirs; *(en insistant)* their own; **ils te prêtent le l.** you can borrow theirs; **ils n'en ont pas besoin, ils ont le l.** they don't need it, they've got their own
3 *nm* **il faut qu'ils y mettent du l.** they have to do their share
4 *nmpl* **les leurs** *(leur famille)* their family; **nous serons des leurs ce soir** we'll be joining them tonight
leur² *pron personnel* to them; **donne-l. ta carte de visite** give them your business card; **je le l. ai montré** I showed it to them
leurre [lœr] *nm* (**a**) *(à la chasse)* decoy (**b**) *(illusion)* illusion
leurrer [lœre] **1** *vt (tromper)* to delude
2 se leurrer *vpr* to delude oneself (**sur** about)
levage [ləvaʒ] *nm* lifting; **appareil de l.** lifting apparatus
levain [ləvɛ̃] *nm* leaven; **pain au/sans l.** leavened/unleavened bread
levant [ləvɑ̃] **1** *adj m* **soleil l.** rising sun; **au soleil l.** at sunrise
2 *nm* (**a**) *Litt* **le l.** the east (**b**) **le L.** the Levant (**c**) *Belg Fam* **bien/mal l.** in a good/bad mood
levé, -e [ləve] **1** *adj* (**a**) *(en l'air)* (main, poing) raised (**b**) *(personne, soleil)* up
2 *nm (de terrain)* survey
levée [ləve] *nf* (**a**) *(d'une interdiction, de sanctions)* lifting; *(d'une séance)* close; *(d'un siège)* raising; *(de scellés)* breaking (**b**) *(de troupes)* levying (**c**) *(de lettres)* collection (**d**) *(aux cartes)* trick; **faire une l.** to take a trick (**e**) *(remblai)* levee (**f**) **l. de boucliers**

general outcry; **l. du corps** = removal of the coffin; **l. d'écrou** release from prison
lever¹ [46] [ləve] **1** *vt* (**a**) *(objet)* to lift, to raise, **l. son verre (à qn/qch)** to raise one's glass (to sb/sth)
(**b**) *(bras, main, jambe)* to raise, to lift; **l. la tête** to look up; **l. les yeux au ciel** to raise one's eyes to heaven; **l. les bras au ciel** to throw up one's hands; **l. la main sur qn** to raise one's hand to sb; **l. le doigt** to put one's hand up; **il n'a pas levé le petit doigt** he didn't lift a finger; *Fam* **l. le pied** *(ralentir)* to slow down
(**c**) *(faire cesser)* (embargo, peine, interdiction) to lift; *(difficulté, doute, ambiguïté)* to remove; *(siège)* to raise; *(séance)* to close
(**d**) *(débusquer)* (perdrix) to flush; *très Fam (femme)* to pull; **l. un lièvre** to start a hare; *Fig* to open a can of worms
(**e**) *(faire sortir du lit)* (enfant, malade) to get up
(**f**) *(collecter)* (courrier, impôts) to collect
(**g**) *(enrôler)* (troupes, armée) to raise, to levy
(**h**) *(plan)* to draw
2 *vi* (**a**) *(blé, grain)* to shoot
(**b**) *(pâte)* to rise
3 se lever *vpr* (**a**) *(se mettre debout)* to stand up, to get up; **se l. de sa chaise** to get up from one's chair; **se l. de table** to leave the table
(**b**) *(quitter le lit)* to get up; *Fam* **se l. du pied gauche** to get out of bed on the wrong side
(**c**) *(apparaître)* (soleil, lune) to rise; *(vent)* to get up; *(jour)* to break
(**d**) *(s'éclaircir)* (brouillard, brume) to lift, to clear
(**e**) *(monter)* (rideau de théâtre) to go up, to rise
lever² *nm* (**a**) *(du lit)* getting up; **demain, l. six heures trente** tomorrow, get up six thirty; **au l., buvez un jus d'orange** first thing in the morning, have a drink of orange juice (**b**) *(apparition)* **le l. du jour** daybreak; **le l. du soleil** sunrise (**c**) **l. de rideau** *(début du spectacle)* curtain up; *(première partie)* curtain raiser (**d**) *(de terrain)* survey
lève-tard [lɛvtar] *nmf inv Fam* late riser
lève-tôt [lɛvto] *nmf inv Fam* early riser
lève-vitre *(pl* **lève-vitres**) [lɛvvitr] *nm* window winder
levier [ləvje] *nm aussi Fig* lever; **faire l.** to act as a lever; **l. de commande** control lever; *Fig* **être aux leviers de commande** to be in control; **l. (de changement) de vitesse** *Br* gear lever, *Am* gearshift
lévitation [levitasjɔ̃] *nf* levitation; **être en l.** to be levitating
lèvre [lɛvr] *nf* (**a**) *(de la bouche)* lip; **un cigare aux lèvres** with a cigar in his mouth; **le sourire aux lèvres** with a smile on her lips; **manger du bout des lèvres** to pick at one's food; **rire du bout des lèvres** to force a laugh; **accepter du bout des lèvres** to accept grudgingly; *Fig* **nous étions tous suspendus à ses lèvres** we were all hanging on her every word (**b**) *(de la vulve)* **lèvres** labia; **les grandes/petites lèvres** the labia majora/minora (**c**) *(bord)* (de plaie) lip; *(de cratère)* rim
levrette [ləvrɛt] *nf* greyhound bitch
lévrier [levrije] *nm* greyhound; **l. afghan** Afghan hound
levure [ləvyr] *nf* yeast; **l. de boulanger** fresh *or* baker's yeast; **l. chimique** baking powder
lexical, -e, -aux, -ales [lɛksikal, -o] *adj* lexical
lexicographe [lɛksikɔgraf] *nmf* lexicographer
lexicographie [lɛksikɔgrafi] *nf* lexicography

lexique [lɛksik] *nm* (**a**) *(dictionnaire)* lexicon; *(glossaire)* glossary (**b**) *(mots d'un auteur)* vocabulary
lézard [lezar] *nm (animal)* lizard; *(cuir)* lizard skin
lézarde [lezard] *nf* crack
lézarder [lezarde] **1** *vt* to crack
2 *vi Fam* to lounge in the sun
3 se lézarder *vpr* to crack
liaison [ljɛzɔ̃] *nf* (**a**) *(dans les transports)* **l. aérienne/maritime/ferroviaire/routière** air/sea/rail/road link; **toutes les liaisons Paris-Téhéran sont suspendues** all services between Paris and Teheran have been suspended (**b**) *Tél* link; **l. radio/téléphonique** radio/telephone link; **l. par satellite** satellite link; **établir une l. radio** to establish radio contact; *Ordinat* **l. par modem** modem link; *Ordinat* **l. spécialisée** dedicated line (**c**) *(entre des personnes)* contact; **assurer la l. entre deux personnes/services** to liaise between two people/departments; **être en l. avec qn** to be in contact with sb; **travailler en l. (étroite) avec qn** to work (closely) with sb (**d**) *(relation amoureuse)* (love) affair (**e**) *(enchaînement logique)* connection (**f**) *Ling* liaison *(sounding of final consonant before initial vowel sound)*; **faire la l.** to make the liaison
liane [ljan] *nf* creeper
liant, -e [ljã, -ãt] **1** *adj* sociable
2 *nm Tech* binder
liasse [ljas] *nf (de lettres, de papiers)* bundle; *(de billets)* wad
Liban [libã] *nm* **le L.** (the) Lebanon
libanais, -e [libanɛ, -ɛz] **1** *adj* Lebanese
2 *nm,f* **L.** Lebanese; **les L.** the Lebanese
libations [libasjɔ̃] *nfpl* libations; **faire des l.** *(boire)* to drink copious amounts (of alcohol)
libellé [libele] *nm* wording
libeller [libele] *vt (document, acte, contrat)* to word; **l. un chèque à l'ordre de** to make out a cheque to
libellule [libelyl] *nf* dragonfly
libéral, -e, -aux, -ales [liberal, -o] **1** *adj* (**a**) *Pol & (aux idées larges)* liberal (**b**) *Écon* free-market
2 *nm,f Pol* Liberal
libéralisation [liberalizasjɔ̃] *nf* (**a**) *(d'un régime, des mœurs)* liberalization (**b**) *Écon* deregulation
libéraliser [liberalize] **1** *vt* (**a**) *(régime, mœurs)* to liberalize (**b**) *Écon* to deregulate
2 se libéraliser *vpr (régime)* to become more liberal; *(mœurs)* to become freer
libéralisme [liberalism] *nm* (**a**) *Pol* liberalism (**b**) *Écon* free-market economics
libéralité [liberalite] *nf* (**a**) *(générosité)* generosity (**b**) *(cadeau)* generous gift; **vivre des libéralités de ses amis** to live off the generosity of one's friends
libérateur, -trice [liberatœr, -tris] **1** *adj* liberating
2 *nm,f* liberator
libération [liberasjɔ̃] *nf* (**a**) *(mise en liberté) (d'un prisonnier)* release; *(d'un soldat)* discharge; **l. conditionnelle** (release on) parole (**b**) *(affranchissement)* liberation (**c**) *(fin de l'Occupation)* **la L.** the Liberation *(from the Germans in 1944–45)* (**d**) *(d'énergie, d'une substance)* release
libéré, -e [libere] **1** *adj* liberated; **jeune homme l. des obligations militaires** young man who has carried out his national service duties
2 *nm,f* released prisoner
libérer [34] [libere] **1** *vt* (**a**) *(rendre sa liberté à) (otage, prisonnier)* to free, to release; *(pays, peuple)* to liberate

(**b**) *(laisser partir) (élèves, étudiants)* to let go; *(soldat)* to discharge
(**c**) *(soulager)* **l. qn d'un souci** *ou* **d'un poids** to take a weight off sb's mind
(**d**) *(rendre disponible) (appartement, chambre d'hôtel)* to vacate
(**e**) *(débloquer) (prix)* to free; *(cran de sûreté)* to release; *(instincts, passions)* to unleash; **l. le passage** to clear the way
(**f**) *(décharger)* **l. qn de qch** *(dette)* to free sb from sth; *(engagement)* to release sb from sth
(**g**) *(émettre) (substance, énergie)* to release
2 se libérer *vpr* (**a**) *(s'affranchir)* to free oneself (**de** from) (**b**) *(se rendre disponible)* **je tâcherai de me l. ce jour-là** I'll try and be free that day; **je n'ai pas pu me l. plus tôt** I couldn't get away any earlier; **il y a un poste qui vient de se l.** a job vacancy has just come up
Liberia [liberja] *nm* **le L.** Liberia
libérien, -enne [liberjɛ̃, -ɛn] **1** *adj* Liberian
2 *nm,f* **L.** Liberian
libertaire [libɛrtɛr] *adj & nmf* libertarian
liberté [libɛrte] *nf* (**a**) *(condition)* freedom, liberty; **en l.** *(fugitif)* at large; *(animal)* in the wild; **rendre sa l. à qn/un animal** to let sb/an animal go; **reprendre sa l.** to regain one's freedom; **mettre qn en l.** to set sb free; **(mise en) l. provisoire** *ou* **sous caution** (release on) bail; **l. conditionnelle** parole; **l. surveillée** probation; **mettre qn en l. provisoire/conditionnelle/surveillée** to release sb on bail/parole/probation
(**b**) *(droit de l'individu)* freedom, liberty; **l., égalité, fraternité** liberty, equality, fraternity; **l. d'expression** freedom of expression *or* speech; **l. d'opinion** freedom of opinion; **l. de la presse** freedom of the press
(**c**) *(absence de contrainte)* freedom; **l. d'entreprise** free enterprise; **avoir toute l. d'action** to have complete freedom of action; **avoir toute l. pour faire qch** to have complete freedom to do sth; **en toute l.** *(s'exprimer, agir)* freely; **prendre la l. de faire qch** to take the liberty of doing sth
(**d**) *(familiarités)* **prendre** *ou* **se permettre des libertés avec** to take liberties with
libertin, -e [libɛrtɛ̃, -in] **1** *adj (personne)* dissolute; *(livre, propos)* licentious
2 *nm,f* libertine
libertinage [libɛrtinaʒ] *nm* licentiousness
libidineux, -euse [libidinø, -øz] *adj* lustful
libido [libido] *nf* libido
libraire [librɛr] *nmf* bookseller
librairie [libreri] *nf (magasin)* bookshop; *(activité)* bookselling
librairie-papeterie *(pl* **librairies-papeteries)** [libreripapɛtri] *nf* bookshop and stationer's
libre [libr] *adj* (**a**) *(non soumis) (personne, pays)* free; **être l. de faire qch** to be free to do sth; **l. à vous de le faire** you're quite at liberty to do it; **donner l. cours à son enthousiasme/son imagination** to give one's enthusiasm/imagination free rein; **l. de** *(souci, contrainte, préjugé)* free from; **l. arbitre** free will; **l. pensée** free thinking; **l. penseur** free thinker
(**b**) *(disponible) (personne, siège)* free; *(appartement, chambre)* available; *(toilettes)* vacant; **je n'ai pas eu une minute de l. aujourd'hui** I haven't had a spare minute today; **être l. comme l'air** to be as free as a bird; **avoir les mains libres** to have one's hands free; *Fig* to have a free hand; **l. de suite** *(dans une annonce)*

available immediately; **la ligne n'est pas l.** the line's *Br* engaged *or Am* busy

(**c**) *(non bloqué) (route)* clear; *Fig* **la voie est l.** the coast is clear

(**d**) *(privé)* **enseignement/école l.** independent Catholic education/school; **radio l.** independent radio

(**e**) *(non réglementé) (prix)* free; *(honoraires)* unrestricted; **la l. entreprise** free enterprise; **il pratique les honoraires libres** there are no restrictions on his fees

libre-échange [librɛʃɑ̃ʒ] *nm* free trade

librement [librəmɑ̃] *adv* freely

libre-service *(pl* **libres-services**) [librəsɛrvis] *nm* (**a**) *(principe)* self-service; **station-service en l.** self-service *Br* petrol *or Am* gas station (**b**) *(magasin)* self-service shop; *(restaurant)* self-service restaurant

Libreville [librəvil] *n* Libreville

Libye [libi] *nf* **la L.** Libya

libyen, -enne [libjɛ̃, -ɛn] **1** *adj* Libyan
2 *nm,f* **L.** Libyan

lice [lis] *nf* **entrer en l.** to enter the fray

licence [lisɑ̃s] *nf* (**a**) *Univ* (bachelor's) degree; **l. ès** *ou* **de lettres/ès** *ou* **de sciences/en droit** arts/science/law degree; **faire une l.** to do a degree (**b**) *(dans le commerce)* licence (**c**) *Sport* permit *(giving right of entry into competition)* (**d**) *(liberté)* licence; **l. poétique** poetic licence (**e**) *(dérèglement)* licentiousness

licencié, -e [lisɑ̃sje] *nm,f* (**a**) *Univ* **l. ès lettres/ès** *ou* **en sciences/en droit** arts/science/law graduate (**b**) *Sport* permit holder

licenciement [lisɑ̃simɑ̃] *nm (pour raisons économiques)* redundancy; *(pour faute professionnelle)* dismissal; **l. collectif** mass redundancies; **l. économique** redundancy

licencier [66] [lisɑ̃sje] *vt (pour raisons économiques)* to make redundant; *(pour faute professionnelle)* to dismiss; **se faire l.** to be made redundant

lichen [likɛn] *nm* lichen

lichette [liʃɛt] *nf Fam (de pain, fromage)* tiny bit

licol [likɔl] *nm* halter

licorne [likɔrn] *nf* unicorn

licou [liku] *nm* halter

LICRA [likra] *nf (abrév* **Ligue internationale contre le racisme et l'antisémitisme)** = anti-racist movement

lie [li] *nf* dregs; *Litt* **boire la coupe** *ou* **le calice jusqu'à la l.** to drink one's cup of sorrow to the dregs; *Fig* **la l. de la société** the dregs of society

lié, -e [lje] *adj* (**a**) *(attaché)* bound; **avoir les mains liées** to have one's hands tied; *Fig* **j'ai les mains liées** my hands are tied; *Fig* **être pieds et poings liés** to be bound hand and foot (**b**) *(en relation étroite)* **être (très) l. avec qn** to be (great) friends with sb

liège [ljɛʒ] *nm* cork; **bouchon de l.** cork

liégeois, -e [ljeʒwa, -az] **1** *adj* (**a**) *(de Liège)* of Liège (**b**) *Culin* **café/chocolat l.** coffee/chocolate ice cream topped with crème Chantilly
2 *nm,f* **L.** person from Liège

lien [ljɛ̃] *nm* (**a**) *(attache)* bond; *aussi Fig* **se libérer de ses liens** to free oneself from one's bonds (**b**) *(relation)* link, connection; **l. de parenté** *ou* **de famille** family relationship; **il y a un l. de parenté entre ces deux familles** the two families are related; **les liens du mariage** the bonds of marriage; **l. d'amitié** bond of friendship; **l. social** social *or* civic bond; **la crise**

du l. social the breakdown of a sense of community in society (**c**) *Ordinat* **l. hypertexte** hypertext link

lier [66] [lje] **1** *vt* (**a**) *(attacher)* to tie up; *(sujet: contrat, serment)* to be binding on (**b**) *(unir) (personnes)* to bind together (**c**) *(établir un rapport entre) (événements, paragraphes)* to connect, to link; **tout est lié** everything's connected (**d**) *Culin (sauce)* to thicken (**e**) **l. amitié/conversation avec qn** to strike up a friendship/conversation with sb
2 se lier *upr* **se l. (d'amitié) avec qn** to strike up a friendship with sb

lierre [ljɛr] *nm* ivy

liesse [ljɛs] *nf* jubilation; **en l.** jubilant

lieu¹, -x [ljø] *nm* (**a**) *(endroit)* place; **en l. sûr** in a safe place; **un l. de passage** a busy place; **les lieux** *(local)* the premises; *(d'un accident, d'un crime)* the scene; **quitter les lieux** to vacate the premises; **un haut l. de** a mecca for; **en haut l.** in high places; **l. de naissance** place of birth; **l. de perdition** den of vice; **l. public** public place; **l. de rendez-vous** meeting place; **l. saint** holy place (**b**) *(pour indiquer un ordre)* **en premier l.** in the first place; **en dernier l.** last(ly) (**c**) **l. commun** commonplace (**d**) *(locutions)* **avoir l.** to take place; **il y a l. de supposer que...** there is reason to suppose that...; **il n'y a pas l. de s'inquiéter** there's no need to worry; **s'il y a l.** if necessary; **donner l. à qch** to give rise to sth; **tenir l. de qch** to take the place of sth; **au l. de** instead of; **au l. de te plaindre** instead of complaining; **au l. de cela** instead

lieu² *(pl* **lieus)** *nm (poisson)* **l. jaune** pollack; **l. noir** coalfish

lieu-dit *(pl* **lieux-dits)** [ljødi] *nm* locality

lieue [ljø] *nf* league; *Naut* **l. marine** league; **j'étais à cent** *ou* **mille lieues de penser que...** I never dreamt for a single moment that...

lieutenant [ljøtnɑ̃] *nm (dans l'armée de terre)* lieutenant; *(dans l'armée de l'air) Br* flying officer, *Am* first lieutenant; *(dans la marine marchande)* mate

lieutenant-colonel *(pl* **lieutenants-colonels)** [ljøtnɑ̃kɔlɔnɛl] *nm (dans l'armée de terre)* lieutenant-colonel; *(dans l'armée de l'air) Br* wing commander, *Am* lieutenant-colonel

lièvre [ljɛvr] *nm* hare; **courir deux lièvres à la fois** to try to do two things at once

lifter [lifte] *vt (balle)* to put topspin on

liftier, -ère [liftje, -ɛr] *nm,f Br* lift attendant, *Am* elevator operator

lifting [liftiŋ] *nm* face lift; **se faire faire un l.** to have a face lift

ligament [ligamɑ̃] *nm* ligament

ligature [ligatyr] *nf Méd* ligature; **l. des trompes** tying of tubes

ligaturer [ligatyre] *vt Méd* to ligature

ligne [liɲ] *nf* (**a**) *(trait)* line; **l. droite** straight line; **avancer en l. droite** to advance in a straight line; **lire les lignes de la main à qn** to read sb's palm; **l. d'arrivée** finishing line; **l. blanche** *(sur la route) Br* white line, *Am* yellow line; **l. continue** *(sur la route)* continuous line; **l. de démarcation** demarcation line; **l. de départ** starting line; **l. discontinue** *(sur la route)* broken line; **l. de flottaison** waterline; **l. d'horizon** horizon; **l. jaune** *(sur la route) Br* white line, *Am* yellow line; **l. de mire** line of sight; *Fig* **avoir qn dans sa l. de mire** to have sb in one's sights; **l. de touche** touchline

(**b**) *(d'écriture)* line; **lire entre les lignes** to read between the lines; **aller à la l.** to begin a new paragraph; **à la l.** *(en dictant)* new paragraph; *Fig* **entrer en l. de compte** to be taken into consideration

(**c**) *(contour, silhouette, d'objet)* line; *(de personne)* figure; **avoir la l.** to have a good figure

(**d**) *(rangée)* line; **se mettre en l.** to line up; *Mil & Fig* **en première l.** in the front line; *Mil* **les lignes ennemies** the enemy lines; *Fig* **sur toute la l.** completely

(**e**) *(orientation)* line; **l. d'action/de conduite** line of action/conduct; **la l. du parti** the party line; **l. directrice** guideline

(**f**) *(dans les transports)* **l. de chemin de fer** *Br* railway *or Am* railroad line; **grandes lignes** main lines; **l. maritime/aérienne** shipping/air route; **l. d'autobus** bus service; *(parcours)* bus route; **lignes de banlieue** suburban lines; **l. de métro** *Br* underground *or Am* subway line

(**g**) *Élec* **l. électrique** power line; **l. à haute tension** high tension line

(**h**) *Tél* **l. (téléphonique)** (telephone) line; **rappelez plus tard, elle est en l.** call back later, her line's *Br* engaged *or Am* busy; **vous êtes en l.** you're through; **l. extérieure** outside line

(**i**) *(fil)* line; *(de pêche)* (fishing) line

(**j**) *(de produits)* line, range

(**k**) *(filiation)* **descendre en l. directe** *ou* **en droite l. de...** to be directly descended from...

(**l**) *Ordinat* line; **en l.** on line; **hors l.** off line; **changer de l.** to do a line feed; **l. d'état** status line

(**m**) *Belg* *(raie des cheveux)* *Br* parting, *Am* part

lignée [liɲe] *nf* descendants; *Fig* **dans la l. de** in the tradition of

lignite [liɲit] *nm* lignite

ligoter [ligɔte] *vt* to tie up (**à** to)

ligue [lig] *nf* league

liguer [lige] **1** *vt* **être ligués contre** to be lined up against

2 se liguer *vpr (États)* to form a league (**avec/contre** with/against); *(personnes)* to gang up (**avec/contre** with/against)

lilas [lila] *nm & adj inv* lilac

lilliputien, -enne [lilipysjɛ̃, -ɛn] *adj (minuscule)* Lilliputian

Lima [lima] *n* Lima

limace [limas] *nf* slug; *Fam (personne lente)* *Br* slowcoach, *Am* slowpoke

limaille [limaj] *nf* filings

limande [limɑ̃d] *nf* dab; **l.-sole** lemon sole

lime [lim] *nf (outil)* file; **l. à ongles** nail file

limer [lime] **1** *vt* to file; *(barreaux de cellule)* to file through

2 se limer *vpr* **se l. les ongles** to file one's nails

limier [limje] *nm (chien)* bloodhound; *Fig* sleuth; **un fin l.** a supersleuth

limitatif, -ive [limitatif, -iv] *adj* restrictive

limitation [limitasjɔ̃] *nf* limitation; **l. des naissances** birth control; **l. de vitesse** speed limit

limite [limit] **1** *nf* (**a**) *(frontière)* boundary (**b**) *(maximum)* limit; **ma patience a des limites!** there are limits to my patience!; **mettre une l./des limites à qch** to set a limit/limits to sth; **c'est à la l. de la vulgarité/du supportable** it's bordering on vulgarity/the unacceptable; **dans la l. des stocks disponibles** while stocks last; **à la l., on pourrait changer d'hôtel** if it came to it, we could change hotels; **sans limites** unbounded, limitless

2 *adj* **cas l.** borderline case; **vitesse l.** maximum speed; *Fam* **je ne lui ai pas mis une claque, mais c'était l.** I didn't slap him, but it was touch and go; *Fam* **je suis un peu l. financièrement** I'm a bit short of cash

limité, -e [limite] *adj (réduit)* limited; *Fam Péj (obtus)* thick

limiter [limite] **1** *vt* (**a**) *(délimiter) (pays, territoire)* to bound (**b**) *(restreindre)* to limit, to restrict (**à** to); *Fam* **l. les dégâts** to limit the damage

2 se limiter *vpr (personne)* to limit oneself; **se l. à qch/à faire qch** *(personne)* to limit *or* restrict oneself to sth/to doing sth; **son œuvre se limite à quelques essais** his works amount to no more than a few essays

limitrophe [limitrɔf] *adj* neighbouring; **être l. de** *(pays)* to border on; *(région)* to adjoin

limogeage [limɔʒaʒ] *nm* dismissal

limoger [45] [limɔʒe] *vt* to dismiss; **se faire l.** to be dismissed

limon [limɔ̃] *nm (alluvions)* silt

limonade [limɔnad] *nf (boisson gazeuse)* lemonade

limousine [limuzin] *nf* limousine

limpide [lɛ̃pid] *adj (eau, diamant, regard)* limpid; *(explication)* lucid

limpidité [lɛ̃pidite] *nf (de l'eau, d'un diamant, d'un regard)* limpidity; *(d'une explication)* lucidity

lin [lɛ̃] *nm* (**a**) *(tissu)* linen (**b**) *(plante)* flax

linceul [lɛ̃sœl] *nm* shroud

linéaire [lineɛr] **1** *adj* (**a**) *(récit)* & *Math* linear (**b**) *(dessin)* line

2 *nm (dans un magasin)* shelf space

linge [lɛ̃ʒ] *nm* (**a**) *(draps, serviettes, nappes)* linen; **l. de maison** household linen; **l. de table** table linen (**b**) *(lessive)* washing (**c**) *(dessous)* **l. (de corps)** underwear; *Fam Fig* **du beau l.** top-drawer people (**d**) *(morceau de tissu)* cloth (**e**) *Suisse (serviette)* towel

lingerie [lɛ̃ʒri] *nf* (**a**) *(dessous)* underwear, lingerie (**b**) *(pièce)* linen room

lingot [lɛ̃go] *nm (de métal)* ingot; **l. (d'or)** gold bar *or* ingot

linguiste [lɛ̃gɥist] *nmf* linguist

linguistique [lɛ̃gɥistik] **1** *adj* linguistic

2 *nf* linguistics *(singulier)*

lino [lino] *nm Fam* lino

linoléum [linɔleɔm] *nm* linoleum

linotte [linɔt] *nf voir* **tête**

linteau, -x [lɛ̃to] *nm Constr* lintel

lion [ljɔ̃] *nm* (**a**) *(animal)* lion; **tourner comme un l. en cage** to prowl around (**b**) *Astron & Astrol* **le L.** Leo; **être L.** to be (a) Leo

lionceau, -x [ljɔ̃so] *nm* lion cub

lionne [ljɔn] *nf* lioness

lipide [lipid] *nm* lipid

liposome [lipozom] *nm Chim* liposome

liposuccion [liposysjɔ̃] *nf* liposuction

liquéfaction [likefaksjɔ̃] *nf* liquefaction

liquéfier [66] [likefje] **1** *vt* to liquefy

2 se liquéfier *vpr* to liquefy

liquette [likɛt] *nf* grandad shirt

liqueur [likœr] *nf* (**a**) *(spiritueux)* liqueur (**b**) *Can* **l. (douce)** soft drink

liquidation [likidasjɔ̃] *nf* (**a**) *Jur* liquidation; **être en l.** to have gone into liquidation; **l. judiciaire** official receivership (**b**) *(d'une dette, en Bourse)* settlement (**c**)

Com (de stocks) selling off; **l. totale** *(sur une vitrine)* stock clearance (**d**) *Fam (meurtre)* liquidation

liquide [likid] **1** *adj (non solide)* liquid; *(trop fluide)* thin

2 *nm* (**a**) *(substance)* liquid, fluid; **l. correcteur** correction fluid; **l. de frein** brake fluid; **l. vaisselle** washing-up liquid (**b**) *(espèces)* cash; **payer en l.** to pay cash

liquider [likide] *vt* (**a**) *Jur (affaire)* to liquidate (**b**) *Fin (dette)* to settle (**c**) *Fam (tuer)* to liquidate (**d**) *Fam (travail, restes, bouteille)* to polish off (**e**) *(stocks)* to sell off; **on liquide** *(sur une vitrine)* stock clearance

liquidités [likidite] *nfpl Fin* liquid assets

liquoreux, -euse [likɔrø, -øz] *adj (vin)* syrupy

lire¹ [44] [lir] **1** *vt* (**a**) *(déchiffrer, interpréter)* to read; **l. qch à qn** to read sth to sb; **lu et approuvé** read and approved; **l. dans les pensées de qn** to read sb's thoughts (**b**) *Fig (deviner) (sur un visage, dans un regard)* to read

2 se lire *vpr (se deviner)* to show

lire² *nf (monnaie)* lira

lis [lis] *nm* lily; **l. blanc** white lily

lisais *etc voir* **lire**

Lisbonne [lizbɔn] *n* Lisbon

lise *etc voir* **lire**

liseré [lizre], **liséré** [lizere] *nm* border, edging

liseron [lizrɔ̃] *nm* bindweed, convolvulus

lisibilité [lizibilite] *nf (d'une écriture)* legibility; *(d'un roman, d'un fichier informatique)* readability

lisible [lizibl] *adj (écriture)* legible; *(roman, fichier informatique)* readable

lisiblement [lizibləmɑ̃] *adv* legibly

lisière [lizjɛr] *nf (d'un champ, d'une forêt)* edge

lisiez *etc voir* **lire**

lissage [lisaʒ] *nm Ordinat* **l. de courbes/des caractères** curve/character smoothing

lisse [lis] *adj (surface, peau, eau)* smooth; *(pneu)* bald; *(cheveux)* sleek

lisser [lise] *vt (cheveux)* to smooth down; *(vêtement)* to smooth out; *(sujet: oiseau) (plumes)* to preen

liste [list] *nf (a)* list; **l. d'attente** waiting list; *Ordinat* **l. de diffusion** distribution *or* discussion *or* mailing list; **l. électorale** electoral roll; *Ordinat* **l. de fichiers à imprimer** print list, print queue; **l. de mariage** wedding list; **l. noire** blacklist; **être sur (la) l. rouge** *(du téléphone)* *Br* to be ex-directory, *Am* to be unlisted

listing [listiŋ] *nm Ordinat* listing, printout

lit [li] *nm* (**a**) *(meuble)* bed; **être au l.** to be in bed; **aller au l.** to go to bed; **mettre qn au lit** to put sb to bed; **au l., les enfants!** bedtime, children!; **faire son l.** to make one's bed; **faire l. à part** to sleep in separate beds; **enfant d'un premier l.** child from a first marriage; **l. à baldaquin** four-poster (bed); **l. de camp** *Br* camp bed, *Am* cot; **l. conjugal** marital bed; **grand l.** double bed; **l. d'enfant** *Br* cot, *Am* crib; **lits jumeaux** twin beds; **être sur son l. de mort** to be on one's death bed; **l. une place/deux places** single/double bed; **lits superposés** bunk beds (**b**) *(couche) (d'argile, de pierres)* bed, layer; *Culin* bed (**c**) *(de rivière)* bed; **sortir de son l.** to burst its banks

litanie [litani] *nf aussi Fig* litany

litchi [litʃi] *nm* lychee

literie [litri] *nf* bedding

lithium [litjɔm] *nm Chim* lithium; **piles au l.** lithium batteries

lithographie [litografi] *nf* (**a**) *(technique)* lithography (**b**) *(œuvre)* lithograph

litière [litjɛr] *nf* (**a**) *(pour cheval, pour chat)* litter (**b**) *(palanquin)* litter

litige [litiʒ] *nm (conflit)* dispute; *(procès)* lawsuit

litigieux, -euse [litiʒjø, -øz] *adj (question, cas)* contentious

litote [litɔt] *nf* understatement, *Spéc* litotes

litre [litr] *nm* litre

litron [litrɔ̃] *nm Fam* bottle of wine

littéraire [literɛr] **1** *adj* literary

2 *nmf* (**a**) *(doué pour la littérature)* literary person (**b**) *(étudiant)* student of literature

littéral, -e, -aux, -ales [literal, -o] *adj (traduction, sens)* literal

littéralement [literalmɑ̃] *adv* literally

littérature [literatyr] *nf (œuvres, documentation)* literature; *(métier)* writing

littoral, -e, -aux, -ales [litɔral, -o] **1** *adj* coastal

2 *nm* coast(line)

Lituanie [lituani] *nf* **la L.** Lithuania

lituanien, -enne [lituanjɛ̃, -ɛn] **1** *adj* Lithuanian

2 *nm,f* **L.** Lithuanian

3 *nm (langue)* Lithuanian

liturgie [lityrʒi] *nf* liturgy

liturgique [lityrʒik] *adj* liturgical

livide [livid] *adj (pâle)* pallid

living [liviŋ], **living-room** (*pl* living-rooms) [liviŋrum] *nm Vieilli* living room

livraison [livrezɔ̃] *nf* (**a**) *(de marchandises)* delivery; **payable à la l.** payable on delivery; **faire la l. de pain/journaux** to deliver the bread/the newspapers; **prendre l. de qch** to take delivery of sth; **l. à domicile** home delivery (**b**) *(d'ouvrage publié en fascicules)* part

livre¹ [livr] *nm* (**a**) *(ouvrage, partie d'un ouvrage)* book; **l. d'histoire/d'anglais** history/English book; **l. de chevet** bedside book; **l. de classe** *ou* **scolaire** schoolbook; **l. de cuisine** *ou* **de recettes** cookery book, cookbook; **l. pour enfants** children's book; **l. d'images** picture book; **l. de poche** paperback; **l. de prières** prayer book (**b**) *(édition)* **l'industrie du l., le l.** the book trade (**c**) *(registre)* **l. de bord** *Naut* log(-book); *Scol* (teacher's) record book; **l. de comptes** account book; **l. d'or** visitors' book; **grand l.** ledger

livre² *nf* (**a**) *(unité de poids)* half kilo; ≃ pound; *Can* pound (**b**) *(monnaie)* **l. (sterling)** pound (sterling); **l. irlandaise** Irish pound, punt

livre-cassette (*pl* livres-cassettes) [livrəkasɛt] *nm* audio book

livrée [livre] *nf (de domestique)* livery

livrer [livre] **1** *vt* (**a**) *(marchandises)* to deliver; **nous livrons à domicile** we deliver; **vous serez livré dès demain** you'll receive delivery tomorrow (**b**) *(abandonner)* **l. un village au pillage/un pays à l'anarchie** to abandon a village to pillage/a country to anarchy; **livré à soi-même** left to oneself (**c**) *(remettre)* **l. qn à qn** *(coupable, complice)* to hand sb over to sb; **l. un secret à qn** to reveal a secret to sb (**d**) *(locutions)* **l. bataille** to join battle; **l. passage à qn** to let sb pass

2 se livrer *vpr* (**a**) *(se rendre)* to give oneself up (**à** to) (**b**) *(se confier)* to open up; **se l. à qn** to confide in sb (**c**) *(s'abandonner)* **se l. à qch** *(vice, spéculations)* to indulge in sth; *(désespoir)* to give way to sth (**d**) *(s'occuper)* **se l. à qch** *(occupations, recherches)* to be engaged in sth; *(étude, lecture)* to devote oneself to sth

livret [livrɛ] *nm* (**a**) *(petit livre)* booklet; **l. (de caisse) d'épargne** bankbook, passbook; **l. de famille** family record book *(for registration of births and deaths)*; **l. militaire** service record; **l. scolaire** (school) report book (**b**) *Mus (d'opéra)* libretto (**c**) *Suisse* multiplication table

livreur, -euse [livrœr, -øz] *nm,f* delivery man, *f* delivery woman

lob [lɔb] *nm* lob; **faire un l.** to hit a lob

lobe [lɔb] *nm* (**a**) *Anat & Bot* lobe (**b**) *Archit* foil

lober [lɔbe] *vt & vi* to lob

lobotomie [lɔbɔtɔmi] *nf Méd* lobotomy

local, -e, -aux, -ales [lɔkal, -o] **1** *adj aussi Méd* local; *(averses)* scattered

2 *nm* (**a**) *(lieu) (de société, d'organisation)* premises; *(sans usage précis)* place; **locaux commerciaux** business premises (**b**) *Can Tél* extension

localement [lɔkalmã] *adv* locally

localisation [lɔkalizasjõ] *nf* (**a**) *(repérage)* location; *(d'un appel téléphonique)* tracing (**b**) *Ordinat* **l. de logiciel** software localization

localisé, -e [lɔkalize] *adj (circonscrit)* localized

localiser [lɔkalize] *vt (repérer) (bruit, gène, personne)* to locate; *(appel téléphonique)* to trace

localité [lɔkalite] *nf (ville)* town; *(village)* village

locataire [lɔkatɛr] *nmf* tenant; *(chez le propriétaire)* lodger

locatif, -ive [lɔkatif, -iv] *adj voir* **charge**

location [lɔkasjõ] *nf* (**a**) *(de voiture, d'équipement, de costume) (par le locataire)* renting, *Br* hiring; *(par le propriétaire)* renting out, *Br* hiring out; **prendre qch en l.** to rent sth, *Br* to hire sth; **donner qch en l.** to rent sth out, *Br* to hire sth out; **l. de voitures** car rental, *Br* car hire (**b**) *(de logement) (par le locataire)* renting; *(par le propriétaire)* renting out, *Br* letting (out) (**c**) *(appartement, maison)* rented accommodation (**d**) *(de places de spectacle)* booking

location-vente *(pl* **locations-ventes**) [lɔkasjõvãt] *nf Br* hire purchase, *Am* installment plan; **acheter qch en l.** to buy sth on *Br* hire purchase *or Am* on the installment plan

loche [lɔʃ] *nf (poisson)* loach

locomoteur, -trice [lɔkɔmɔtœr, -tris] *adj* locomotor

locomotion [lɔkɔmɔsjõ] *nf* locomotion; **moyen de l.** means of transport

locomotive [lɔkɔmɔtiv] *nf* (**a**) *(de train)* locomotive, engine; **l. à vapeur** steam engine (**b**) *Fig (leader)* pacemaker; *(entreprise, secteur)* powerhouse

locuteur, -trice [lɔkytœr, -tris] *nm,f Ling* speaker

locution [lɔkysjõ] *nf* expression, phrase

loft [lɔft] *nm* converted loft

logarithme [lɔgaritm] *nm* logarithm

loge [lɔʒ] *nf* (**a**) *(d'artiste)* dressing room (**b**) *(sièges)* box; *Fig* **être aux premières loges** to have a ringside seat (**c**) *(maçonnique, de concierge)* lodge (**d**) *Belg* **l. foraine** stall

logement [lɔʒmã] *nm* (**a**) *(habitation)* accommodation; *(maison)* house; *(appartement) Br* flat, *Am* apartment; **l. de fonction** accommodation that goes with the job; **logements sociaux** *Br* ≃ council flats, *Am* ≃ low-rent housing (**b**) *(action)* housing; **la crise du l.** the housing shortage

loger [45] [lɔʒe] **1** *vi (en permanence)* to live; *(temporairement)* to stay; **l. chez l'habitant** *(en vacances)* to stay in a private house

2 *vt* (**a**) *(héberger)* to put up; **être logé et nourri** to have board and lodging (**b**) *(contenir) (sujet: hôtel, maison)* to accommodate (**c**) *(placer)* to put

3 se loger *vpr* (**a**) **(trouver à) se l.** *(en permanence)* to find somewhere to live; *(temporairement)* to find accommodation (**b**) *(se placer)* to lodge itself

logeur, -euse [lɔʒœr, -øz] *nm,f* landlord, *f* landlady *(of furnished apartments)*

loggia [lɔdʒja] *nf Archit* loggia

logiciel [lɔʒisjel] *nm Ordinat* software; **un l.** a (software) package; **l. d'application** application software; **l. bureautique** business software (package); **l. de communication** communications package, comms package, communications software; **l. de compression de données** data compression software; **l. de comptabilité** accounts package, accounts software; **l. de décompression** decompression software, decompressor; **l. de dessin** art package, drawing program; **l. d'exploitation** operating system software; **l. grapheur** graphics package, graphics software; **l. de jeu** games software; **l. de mise en page** desktop publishing package; **l. de navigation** browser; **l. public** freeware; **l. de reconnaissance de caractères** OCR software, character recognition software; **l. de reconnaissance vocale** voice recognition software; **l. de réseau** network software; **l. de SGBD** DBMS software; **l. de télémaintenance** remote access software; **logiciels de traitement de texte** word-processing software, word-processing software packages

logique [lɔʒik] **1** *adj* logical

2 *nf* logic; **en toute l.,...** logically,...; *Ordinat* **l. câblée** wired logic; **l. floue** fuzzy logic

logiquement [lɔʒikmã] *adv* (**a**) *(avec cohérence)* logically (**b**) *(normalement)* **l., il devrait bientôt être là** if all goes well, he should soon be here

logis [lɔʒi] *nm Litt (maison)* dwelling, abode

logistique [lɔʒistik] **1** *adj* logistic

2 *nf* logistics *(singulier)*

logo [logo] *nm* logo

logopède [logopɛd] *nmf Belg & Suisse* speech therapist

loi [lwa] *nf* law; **nul n'est censé igorer la l.** ignorance of the law is no excuse; **faire la** *ou* **sa l.** to lay down the law; *Pol* **l. de finances** Finance Act; **la l. de la jungle** the law of the jungle; **l. martiale** martial law; **la l. de l'offre et de la demande** the law of supply and demand; **la l. du plus fort** the law of the strongest; **la l. du talion** an eye for an eye

loi-cadre *(pl* **lois-cadres**) [lwakadr] *nf* outline law

loin [lwɛ̃] **1** *adv* (**a**) *(dans l'espace)* far (**de** from); **la poste est l.** the post office is a long way away; **c'est encore l., le théâtre/Annecy?** is it far to the theatre/Annecy?; **il y a l. d'ici à Paris** it's a long way to Paris; **plus l.** further (on); **voir plus l.** *(dans un texte)* see below; **de l.** *(reconnaître, admirer)* from a distance; *Prov* **l. des yeux, l. du cœur** out of sight, out of mind (**b**) *(dans le temps)* far away (**de** from); **comme c'est l., tout ça!** that all happened such a long time ago!; **ce jour est encore l.** that day is still a long way off; **d'aussi l.** *ou* **du plus l. qu'elle se souvienne** for as long as she can remember

(**c**) *Fig* **de là à l'accuser de mensonge il n'y a pas l.** it's practically calling him a liar; **aller l.** *(réussir)* to go far; **aller trop l.** *(exagérer)* to go too far; **nous étions l. de penser que...** we never thought for a moment that...; **elle est l. d'être bête** she's far from stupid; **je**

ne suis pas fâché, **l. de là!** I'm not angry, far from it!; **l. de moi l'idée d'insinuer que…** far be it from me to insinuate that…; **l. de moi cette idée!** I wouldn't dream of it!, perish the thought!; **pas l. de** *(presque)* not far off; **de l.** *(de beaucoup)* by far; **de l. en l.** *(de temps en temps)* every now and then
  (d) *Suisse (absent)* **il est l.** he's not here
  2 *nm* **au l.** in the distance
lointain, -e [lwɛ̃tɛ̃, -ɛn] **1** *adj (dans l'espace, dans le temps)* distant; *(ressemblance)* vague; *(air, regard)* faraway; **dans un avenir l.** in the distant future
  2 *nm* **dans le l., au l.** in the distance
loir [lwar] *nm* dormouse
Loire [lwar] *nf* **la L.** the Loire
loisir [lwazir] *nm* **(a)** *(temps libre)* leisure; **activités de l.** leisure *or* spare-time activities; **loisirs** spare time; **avoir des loisirs** to have some spare time **(b)** *(activité)* pastime; **les loisirs** leisure *or* spare-time activities **(c)** *Formel (possibilité, temps nécessaire)* **avoir le l. de faire qch** to have time to do sth; **donner** *ou* **laisser à qn le l. de faire qch** to give sb the opportunity to do sth; *Litt* **à l.** at one's leisure
lolo [lolo] *nm Fam* **(a)** *(langage enfantin) (lait)* milk **(b)** *(sein)* boob
lombaire [lɔ̃bɛr] *Anat* **1** *adj* lumbar
  2 *nf* lumbar vertebra
lombalgie [lɔ̃balʒi] *nf Méd* lumbago
lombric [lɔ̃brik] *nm* earthworm
Lomé [lɔme] *n* Lomé
londonien, -enne [lɔ̃dɔnjɛ̃, -ɛn] **1** *adj* London
  2 *nm,f* **L.** Londoner
Londres [lɔ̃dr] *n* London
long, longue [lɔ̃, lɔ̃g] **1** *adj* **(a)** *(dans l'espace)* long; *(personne)* tall; **l. de 5 mètres** 5 metres long **(b)** *(dans le temps)* long; **dix jours, c'est l.** ten days is a long time; **ce ne sera pas l.** it won't take long; **pendant de longues années** for many years; **longue durée** *(pile)* long-life; *(cassette)* extended play; **de longue durée** *(chômage, chômeur)* long-term **(c)** *(lent)* slow; **être l. à faire qch** to be slow to do sth
  2 *nm* **(a)** *(dans l'espace)* **faire 2 mètres de l.** to be 2 metres long; **(tout) le l. de** (all) along; **de tout son l.** *(être étendu)* at full length; *(tomber)* flat on one's face; **de l. en large** up and down, to and fro; **en l.** *(couper, fendre)* lengthwise; *Fam* **expliquer qch en l. et en large** *ou* **en l., en large et en travers** to explain sth in great detail **(b)** *(dans le temps)* **tout au l. de** throughout
  3 *adv* **(a)** *(beaucoup)* **en dire l.** *(être révélateur)* to speak volumes; **en savoir l. (sur)** to know a lot (about) **(b)** **s'habiller l.** to wear long clothes
long-courrier *(pl* **long-courriers)** [lɔ̃kurje] **1** *adj (navire)* ocean-going; *(avion)* long-haul
  2 *nm (navire)* ocean-going ship; *(avion)* long-haul aircraft
longe¹ [lɔ̃ʒ] *nf (pour guider)* leading rein; *(pour attacher)* tether
longe² *nf Culin (de veau, de porc)* loin
longer [45] [lɔ̃ʒe] *vt* **(a)** *(sujet: personne, voiture) (route, rivière)* to go along; *(mur, côte)* to hug **(b)** *(sujet: sentier, canal, voie ferrée)* to run alongside
longévité [lɔ̃ʒevite] *nf (longue vie)* longevity; *(espérance de vie)* life expectancy
longiligne [lɔ̃ʒiliɲ] *adj* willowy
longitude [lɔ̃ʒityd] *nf Géog* longitude; **à 10° de l. ouest** at longitude 10° west

longitudinal, -e, -aux, -ales [lɔ̃ʒitydinal, -o] *adj* longitudinal, lengthwise
longtemps [lɔ̃tɑ̃] *adv* **(a)** *(attendre, rester)* (for) a long time; **ça ne durera pas l.** it won't last (for) long; *Fig* **tu peux attendre l.** you'll have a long wait **(b)** *(avec une préposition, avec "il y a")* **avant l.** before long; **pas avant l.** not for a long time; **cela existe depuis l.** it has existed for a long time; **pendant l.** for a long time; **je n'en ai pas pour l.** I won't be long; **il n'en a plus pour l.** *(il va bientôt mourir)* he doesn't have much longer to live; **il y a l.** a long time ago; **il y a l. qu'il est mort** he's been dead for a long time; **il y a l. que je ne l'ai pas vue** it's a long time since I saw her; **l. avant/après** long before/after
longue [lɔ̃g] **1** *adj voir* **long**
  2 *nf* **à la l.** in the end
longuement [lɔ̃gmɑ̃] *adv (attendre, réfléchir, s'attarder)* for a long time; *(parler, expliquer)* at length; **il a l. insisté pour que je vienne** he kept on insisting I should come
longuet, -ette [lɔ̃gɛ, -ɛt] *adj Fam* longish
longueur [lɔ̃gœr] *nf* **(a)** *(dimension, durée)* & *Sport* length; **jardin de 100 mètres de l.** *ou* **d'une l. de 100 mètres** garden 100 metres long; **en l., dans le sens de la l.** *(couper, fendre)* lengthwise; **avoir une l. d'avance sur** *Sport* to be one length ahead of; *Fig* to have a clear lead over; **à l. de journée/de semaine/d'année** all day/week/year long **(b)** *Péj (développement trop long)* **longueurs** drawn-out passages; **il y a des longueurs dans le film** the film is a little tedious in parts **(c)** *Rad* **l. d'ondes** wavelength; *Fig* **être sur la même l. d'ondes** to be on the same wavelength
longue-vue *(pl* **longues-vues)** [lɔ̃gvy] *nf* telescope
look [luk] *nm Fam* look; **avoir un l. d'enfer** to look out of this world
looping [lupiŋ] *nm Aviat* loop; **faire un l./des loopings** to loop the loop
lopin [lɔpɛ̃] *nm* **l. de terre** patch *or* plot of land
loquace [lɔkas] *adj* talkative
loque [lɔk] *nf* **(a)** *(vêtement)* rag; **être en loques** to be in rags; **tomber en loques** to fall to pieces **(b)** *Belg (serpillière)* mop **(c)** *Fig (personne)* wreck
loquet [lɔkɛ] *nm* latch
lordose [lɔrdoz] *nf Méd* hollow-back, *Spéc* lordosis
lorgner [lɔrɲe] *vt* **(a)** *(regarder indiscrètement)* to eye; *(avec concupiscence)* to eye up **(b)** *(convoiter)* to have one's eye on
lorgnette [lɔrɲɛt] *nf* opera glasses; *Fig* **regarder** *ou* **voir les choses par le petit bout de la l.** to take a narrow-minded view of things
lorgnon [lɔrɲɔ̃] *nm (avec tige)* lorgnette; *(avec ressort)* pince-nez
lorrain, -e [lɔrɛ̃, -ɛn] **1** *adj* of Lorraine
  2 *nm,f* **L.** person from Lorraine
lors [lɔr] *adv* **l. de** *(pendant)* during; *(au moment de)* at the time of; *Litt* **depuis l.** from that time
lorsque [lɔrsk] *conj* when
losange [lɔzɑ̃ʒ] *nm (forme)* diamond; *(en géométrie)* rhombus
Los Angeles [lɔsɑ̃dʒələs] *n* Los Angeles
lot [lo] *nm* **(a)** *(dans une loterie)* prize; **gros l.** jackpot; *Fam Fig* **tirer le gros l.** to hit the jackpot; **l. de consolation** consolation prize **(b)** *Com (de marchandises)* batch; *(de serviettes, de casseroles)* set; *(de chaussettes, de savonnettes)* pack; *Fig* **dans le l., il y en aura bien un de bon** *(choses, personnes)* at least one out of

this lot should be some good; **se détacher** *ou* **être au-dessus du l.** to stand out from the crowd (**c**) *(de terrain)* plot (**d**) *Litt (sort)* lot (**e**) *Ordinat* **traitement par lots** batch processing

loterie [lɔtri] *nf* lottery; **gagner à la l.** to win on the lottery; **l. nationale** national lottery

loti, -e [lɔti] *adj* **être bien/mal l.** to be well/badly off

lotion [losjɔ̃] *nf* lotion; **l. après-rasage** aftershave (lotion); **l. capillaire** hair lotion; **l. tonique** toner

lotissement [lɔtismã] *nm (ensemble résidentiel)* housing estate

loto [lɔto] *nm* (**a**) *(jeu de hasard)* lotto (**b**) *(jeu national)* national lottery; **jouer au l.** to do the lottery

> **Loto**
> "Loto" is a popular game of chance with large cash prizes. Printed grids ("bulletins") are available at tobacconists or special kiosks. Players mark six numbers on the grid and pay a fee. The twice-weekly prize draw is broadcast on television. "Loto Sportif" is a version of "Loto" in which players bet on the football results.

lotte [lɔt] *nf (de rivière)* burbot; *(de mer)* monkfish

lotus [lɔtys] *nm* lotus; **fleur de l.** lotus; **position du l.** lotus position

louable [lwabl] *adj (admirable)* praiseworthy, laudable

louage [lwaʒ] *nm* **contrat de l.** rental agreement; **voiture de l.** hired carriage

louange [lwãʒ] *nf* praise; **digne de louange(s)** praiseworthy; **chanter les louanges de qn** to sing sb's praises

loubard [lubar] *nm Fam* hooligan

louche¹ [luʃ] *adj* dodgy

louche² *nf* ladle

loucher [luʃe] *vi (volontairement)* to squint; *(être atteint de strabisme)* to have a squint; **l. de l'œil gauche** to have a squint in one's left eye; *Fig* **l. sur qch** *(regarder)* to eye sth; *(convoiter)* to have one's eye on sth

louer¹ [lwe] *vt* (**a**) *(donner en location) (logement)* to rent out, *Br* to let (out) (**à** to); *(équipement, véhicule, costume)* to rent out, *Br* to hire out (**à** to); **maison à l.** house *Br* to let *or Am* for rent (**b**) *(prendre en location) (logement)* to rent (**à** from); *(équipement, véhicule, costume)* to rent, *Br* to hire (**à** from); *(place de spectacle)* to book

louer² **1** *vt (exalter)* to praise; **l. qn de** *ou* **pour qch** to praise sb for sth; **louons le Seigneur!** praise the Lord! **2 se louer** *vpr* **se l. de qch** to be very satisfied with sth; **je n'ai qu'à me l. de lui/de ses services** I have nothing but praise for him/for his work; **se l. d'avoir fait qch** to congratulate oneself on having done sth

loufdingue [lufdɛ̃g], **loufoque** [lufɔk] *adj Fam* crazy

louis [lwi] *nm* **l. (d'or)** louis(-d'or)

Louisiane [lwizjan] *nf* **la L.** Louisiana

loukoum [lukum] *nm* piece of Turkish delight; **des loukoums** Turkish delight

loup [lu] *nm* (**a**) *(mammifère)* wolf; *Fig* **il est connu comme le l. blanc** everybody knows him; **quand on parle du l. on en voit la queue** talk of the devil; *Fig* **jeune l.** young go-getter; *(en politique)* Young Turk; *Fam* **mon petit l., mon gros l.** darling, pet (**b**) *(poisson)* bass (**c**) *(demi-masque)* eye mask (**d**) **(vieux) l. de mer** *(marin)* old salt, sea dog

loupe [lup] *nf* (**a**) *(instrument d'optique)* magnifying glass; **regarder qch à la l.** to look at sth through a magnifying glass; *Fig* to put sth under the microscope (**b**) *Bot* knur; **l. d'érable/de noyer** *(en ébénisterie)* burr maple/walnut

louper [lupe] *Fam* **1** *vt* (**a**) *(ne pas réussir) (travail, plat)* to botch, to bungle; *(examen)* to flunk; **l. son entrée** *(au théâtre)* to fluff one's entrance; **loupé!** missed!; **la soirée est loupée** the party's a flop (**b**) *(ne pas prendre) (son tour, occasion, train)* to miss; **il n'en loupe pas une!** *(en actions)* it's one stupid thing after another!; *(en paroles)* he's always opening his big mouth!; **je ne vais pas le l.!** I won't let him get away with it!

2 *vi* **je lui ai dit qu'il attraperait froid et ça n'a pas loupé** I told him he'd catch cold and sure enough he did

3 se louper *vpr* (**a**) *(ne pas se rencontrer)* to miss each other (**b**) *(manquer son suicide)* to bungle it; *Ironique* **il ne s'est pas loupé!** he made a proper job of it!

loup-garou *(pl* **loups-garous)** [lugaru] *nm* werewolf; *(pour faire peur aux enfants)* bogeyman

loupiote [lupjɔt] *nf Fam (lampe)* small light

loup-marin [lumarɛ̃] *nm Can* seal

lourd, -e [lur, lurd] **1** *adj* (**a**) *(pesant)* heavy; **j'ai la tête lourde** I've got a thick head; **avoir l'estomac l.** to feel bloated; **yeux lourds de fatigue** eyes heavy with tiredness (**b**) *(à l'aspect pesant) (personne)* heavily built; *(tentures)* heavy (**c**) *(peu subtil) (personne, plaisanterie)* unsubtle; *(mouvement, style)* heavy (**d**) *(perte, dépenses, responsabilité)* heavy (**e**) *(temps)* close; *(parfum)* heavy (**f**) *(plein)* **l. de conséquences** fraught with consequences; **l. de menaces** ominous **2** *adv* **peser l.** to weigh a lot, to be heavy; *Fam* **pas l.** not much

lourdaud, -e [lurdo, -od] **1** *adj* oafish **2** *nm,f* oaf

lourdement [lurdəmã] *adv* heavily; **se tromper l.** to be greatly mistaken; **insister l.** to keep on insisting

lourder [lurde] *vt Fam* **l. qn** to give sb the boot; **se faire l. (par qn)** to get the boot (from sb)

lourdeur [lurdœr] *nf (poids, manque de subtilité)* heaviness; *(de la bureaucratie)* unwieldiness; *(d'une responsabilité, d'une tâche)* weight; *(du temps)* closeness; **l. d'esprit** slow-wittedness; **j'ai des lourdeurs d'estomac** I feel bloated

lourdingue [lurdɛ̃g] *adj Fam (style)* heavy; *(personne, plaisanterie)* unsubtle

loustic [lustik] *nm Fam* **un drôle de l.** *(louche)* a dodgy character

loutre [lutr] *nf* otter; *(fourrure)* otter skin

louve [luv] *nf* she-wolf

louveteau, -x [luvto] *nm* (**a**) *(animal)* wolf cub (**b**) *(jeune scout)* Cub (Scout)

louvoyer [32] [luvwaje] *vi Naut* to tack; *Fig* to hedge

Louvre [luvr] *nm* **le (palais du) L.** the Louvre

> **Louvre**
> This former royal palace became a museum in 1791–1793. It houses one of the richest art collections in the world. The museum was extended in 1989, with the construction of the glass "pyramide du Louvre" in the main courtyard, and again in 1993 when the Richelieu wing, formerly occupied by the ministry of finance, was inaugurated.

lover [lɔve] **se lover** *vpr (serpent)* to coil up; *(personne)* to curl up

loyal, -e, -aux, -ales [lwajal, -o] **1** *adj* (**a**) *(honnête)* fair (**b**) *(fidèle) (serviteur, ami)* loyal; **après vingt-cinq ans de bons et loyaux services** after twenty-five years of good and faithful service
  2 *nf* **loyale** *Fam* **se battre à la loyale** to fight cleanly

loyalement [lwajalmɑ̃] *adv* (**a**) *(honnêtement)* fairly (**b**) *(fidèlement)* loyally

loyaliste [lwajalist] *adj & nmf Pol* loyalist

loyauté [lwajote] *nf* (**a**) *(honnêteté)* fairness (**b**) *(fidélité)* loyalty (**envers** to)

loyer [lwaje] *nm* rent; **j'ai trois loyers de retard** I'm three months behind with the rent; *Can* **être a l.** to be in rented accommodation

LP [ɛlpe] *nm (abrév* **lycée professionnel**) vocational secondary school

LSD [ɛlɛsde] *nm* LSD

lu, -e *voir* **lire**

lubie [lybi] *nf* whim, fad

lubrifiant, -e [lybrifjɑ̃, -ɑ̃t] **1** *adj* lubricating
  2 *nm* lubricant

lubrifier [66] [lybrifje] *vt* to lubricate

lubrique [lybrik] *adj* lustful, lecherous

lucarne [lykarn] *nf* (**a**) *(dans un toit)* skylight; *(en saillie)* dormer (window) (**b**) *(au football)* top corner

lucide [lysid] *adj* lucid

lucidement [lysidmɑ̃] *adv* lucidly

lucidité [lysidite] *nf* lucidity

Lucifer [lysifɛr] *npr* Lucifer

luciole [lysjɔl] *nf* firefly

lucratif, -ive [lykratif, -iv] *adj* lucrative; **à but l.** profit-making; **sans but l.** *Br* non-profit-making, *Am* not-for-profit

lucre [lykr] *nm Litt* lucre

ludique [lydik] *adj* play(ful), *Spéc* ludic

ludothèque [lydɔtɛk] *nf* toy and game library

luette [lɥɛt] *nf* (**a**) *Anat* uvula (**b**) *Can Fam (locution)* **se mouiller** *ou* **se rincer la l.** *(prendre un verre)* to wet one's whistle; *(se soûler)* to get sloshed *or* drunk

lueur [lɥœr] *nf* (**a**) *(lumière faible)* glow; **à la l. d'une bougie/des étoiles** by candlelight/starlight; **à la l. des derniers événements** in the light of recent events (**b**) *Fig (de lucidité, de colère)* flash; *(d'intelligence, d'espoir)* glimmer

luge [lyʒ] *nf* toboggan, *Br* sledge, *Am* sled; **faire de la l.** to go tobogganing *or Br* sledging *or Am* sledding

luger [lyʒe] *vi* (**a**) *(descendre en luge)* to toboggan, *Br* to sledge, *Am* to sled (**b**) *Suisse (déraper)* to skid

lugubre [lygybr] *adj* gloomy; *(son, cri)* mournful

lui [lɥi] *pron personnel* (**a**) *(sujet) (personne)* he; *(chose, animal)* it; **l., il aurait fait un effort** HE would have made an effort; **mon frère, l., n'est pas venu** as for my brother, he didn't come; **si j'étais l., je me méfierais** if I were him I'd be careful
  (**b**) *(objet direct) (personne)* him; *(chose, animal)* it; **et l., tu le connais?** and what about him, do you know him?
  (**c**) *(objet indirect) (homme)* to him; *(femme)* to her; *(chose, animal)* to it; **donnez-le-l.** give it to him/her/it, give him/her/it it; **je l. ai serré la main** I shook his/her hand; **il l. jeta une pierre** he threw a stone at him/her/it
  (**d**) *(avec préposition) (personne)* him; *(chose, animal)* it; **elle pense encore à l.** she still thinks about

him; **dis-le-lui, à l.** tell HIM; **ce livre est à l.** this book is his
  (**e**) *(réfléchi) (personne)* himself; *(chose, animal)* itself; **il ne pense qu'à l.** he thinks only of himself; **il a un appartement à l.** he's got his own flat; **un ami à l.** a friend of his
  (**f**) *(dans les comparaisons)* him; **elle gagne plus que l.** she earns more than him *or* than he does

lui-même [lɥimɛm] *pron personnel (personne)* himself; *(chose, animal)* itself

luire [18] [lɥir] *vi (métal, astre, yeux)* to shine; *(surface de l'eau, trottoir mouillé)* to glisten; *(flamme, braises)* to glow

luisais *etc voir* **luire**

luisant, -e [lɥizɑ̃, -ɑ̃t] **1** *adj (étoile, métal, yeux)* shining; *(surface, pelage, peau)* shiny; *(braise)* glowing; **front l. de sueur** forehead glistening with sweat
  2 *nm* sheen

lumbago [lɔ̃bago] *nm* lumbago

lumière [lymjɛr] *nf* (**a**) *(clarté)* light; **à la l. de la lune** by moonlight; **il y a de la l. chez lui** there's a light on/there are lights on at his place; *Fig* **j'ai besoin de tes lumières** I need the benefit of your knowledge; **l. d'ambiance** subdued lighting (**b**) *(locutions)* **à la l. de son exposé,...** in the light of his account,...; **faire (toute) la l. sur qch** to get (right) to the bottom of sth; **mettre qch en l.** to bring sth out; *Fam* **ce n'est pas une l.** she's not very bright

lumignon [lymiɲɔ̃] *nm* small light

luminaire [lyminɛr] *nm* **magasin de luminaires** lighting shop

luminescent, -e [lyminɛsɑ̃, -ɑ̃t] *adj* luminescent

lumineux, -euse [lyminø, -øz] *adj* (**a**) *(corps, cadran)* luminous; *(pièce, ciel)* bright (**b**) *(radieux) (regard)* radiant; *(teint)* glowing (**c**) *(explication, propos)* lucid; *(idée)* brilliant

luminosité [lyminozite] *nf* (**a**) *(du ciel)* brightness; *(d'un regard, du teint)* radiance; *Phot* **la l.** the amount of light available (**b**) *(d'un écran)* brightness

lump [lœ̃p] *nm* **œufs de l.** lumpfish roe

lunaire [lynɛr] *adj* lunar; *Fig* **un visage l.** a moon face

lunatique [lynatik] *adj* quirky

lunch *(pl* **lunchs** *ou* **lunches**) [lœ̃tʃ] *nm* buffet lunch

lundi [lœ̃di] *nm* Monday; **le l. de Pâques/de la Pentecôte** Easter/Whit Monday; *voir aussi* **samedi**

lune [lyn] *nf* (**a**) *(astre)* moon; *Fig* **je ne te demande pas la l.** I'm not asking for the moon; **être dans la l.** to be miles away; **la nouvelle/pleine l.** the new/full moon; **l. de miel** honeymoon (**b**) *Fam (derrière)* bottom

luné, -e [lyne] *adj Fam* **être bien/mal l.** to be in a good/bad mood

lunette [lynɛt] *nf* (**a**) *(pour la vue)* **lunettes** glasses, spectacles; **lunettes noires** dark glasses; **lunettes de soleil**, *Belg* **lunettes solaires** sunglasses; **lunettes de vue** corrective glasses (**b**) *(instrument d'optique)* telescope (**c**) *(siège des W.-C.)* seat (**d**) *(de voiture)* **l. arrière** rear window

lupin [lypɛ̃] *nm* lupin

lurette [lyrɛt] *nf* **il y a belle l.** ages ago; **il y a belle l. que je ne l'ai pas vu** I haven't seen him for ages

luron [lyrɔ̃] *nm* **c'est un gai** *ou* **joyeux l.** he's a bit of a lad

lusophone [lyzɔfɔn] **1** *adj* Portuguese-speaking
  2 *nmf* Portuguese speaker

lustre¹ [lystr] *nm* (**a**) *(lampe)* chandelier (**b**) *(brillant)* lustre (**c**) *(prestige)* lustre

lustre² *nm* **ça dure depuis des lustres** it's been going on for ages

lustrer [lystre] *vt (glace, meuble, voiture)* to polish; **lustré par l'usure** shiny with wear

lustrine [lystrin] *nf* cotton lustre

luth [lyt] *nm* lute

luthier [lytje] *nm* stringed-instrument maker

lutin [lytɛ̃] *nm* imp, elf

lutrin [lytrɛ̃] *nm* (**a**) *(à la messe)* lectern; *(pour soutenir un livre, des feuilles)* reading stand (**b**) *Belg, Can & Suisse (pupitre à musique)* music stand

lutte [lyt] *nf* (**a**) *(combat)* fight, struggle; *(antagonisme)* conflict; *(contre une maladie, contre la pollution)* fight; **entrer/être en l. contre qn** to enter into/to be in conflict with sb; **gagner de haute l.** to win after a hard struggle; **l. armée** armed struggle; **la l. des classes** the class struggle (**b**) *Sport* wrestling; **faire de la l.** to wrestle

lutter [lyte] *vi* (**a**) *(se battre)* to struggle, to fight; **l. contre** *(adversaire, oppresseur)* to fight against; *(maladie, incendie, tentation)* to fight; *(sommeil)* to fight off (**b**) *(rivaliser)* **l. de vitesse avec qn** to race sb (**c**) *Sport* to wrestle (**avec** *ou* **contre** with)

lutteur, -euse [lytœr, -øz] *nm,f Sport* wrestler

luxation [lyksasjɔ̃] *nf Méd* dislocation

luxe [lyks] *nm* (**a**) *(abondance, richesse)* luxury; *(d'une maison, de l'ameublement)* luxuriousness (**b**) *(qualité)* **de l.** *(produits)* luxury; *(voiture, édition)* de luxe; **boutique de l.** luxury goods shop (**c**) *(bien superflu)* luxury; *Fig* **s'offrir** *ou* **se payer le l. de faire qch** to give oneself the luxury of doing sth; **je vais faire nettoyer ce vieil imperméable, ce ne sera pas du l.** I'm going to have this old raincoat cleaned, and not before time (**d**) *(profusion)* **un l. de précautions/de détails** a wealth of precautions/details

Luxembourg [lyksãbur] **1** *n (ville)* Luxembourg **2** *nm* **le L.** Luxembourg

luxembourgeois, -e [lyksãburʒwa, -az] **1** *adj* of Luxembourg **2** *nm,f* **L.** Luxembourger

luxer [lykse] **se luxer** *vpr* **se l. l'épaule/le poignet** to dislocate one's shoulder/one's wrist

luxueux, -euse [lyksɥø, -øz] *adj* luxurious

luxure [lyksyr] *nf Litt* lust

luxuriant, -e [lyksyrjã, -ãt] *adj (végétation, forêt, chevelure)* luxuriant; *(imagination)* fertile

luzerne [lyzɛrn] *nf Br* lucerne, *Am* alfalfa

lycée [lise] *nm Br* ≃ secondary school, *Am* ≃ high school *(for pupils aged fifteen to eighteen)*; **l. professionnel** vocational secondary school; **l. technique** technical school

lycéen, -enne [liseɛ̃, -ɛn] *nm,f Br* ≃ secondary school pupil, *Am* ≃ high school pupil

Lycra® [likra] *nm* Lycra®

lymphatique [lɛ̃fatik] *adj* (**a**) *Biol* lymphatic (**b**) *(personne)* lethargic

lymphe [lɛ̃f] *nf* lymph

lymphocyte [lɛ̃fɔsit] *nm Biol* lymphocyte

lyncher [lɛ̃ʃe] *vt* to lynch

lynx [lɛ̃ks] *nm* lynx; *Fig* **avoir des yeux de l.** to have eyes like a hawk

Lyon [ljɔ̃] *n* Lyons

lyonnais, -e [ljɔnɛ, -ɛz] **1** *adj* of Lyons **2** *nm,f* **L.** person from Lyons

lyophilisé, -e [ljɔfilize] *adj* freeze-dried

lyre [lir] *nf* lyre

lyrique [lirik] *adj* (**a**) *(poème, poète)* lyric (**b**) *(passionné)* lyrical

lyrisme [lirism] *nm* lyricism; **parler de qch avec l.** to wax lyrical about sth

lys [lis] = **lis**

M

M, m¹ [ɛm] *nm inv* M, m
m² (**a**) **M.** *(abrév* **Monsieur**) Mr (**b**) *(abrév* **mètre(s)**) m;
1 m 50 1.5 m (**c**) *Gram (abrév* **masculin**) m
m' [m] *voir* **me**
ma [ma] *voir* **mon**
MA [ɛma] *nm (abrév* **maître auxiliaire**) *Br* supply *or Am*
substitute teacher
maboule, -e [mabul] *Fam* **1** *adj (fou)* crazy, *Br* bonkers
  2 *nm,f* nutcase
mac [mak] *nm très Fam (maquereau)* pimp
macabre [makabr] *adj (découverte, histoire)* macabre,
gruesome; *(humour)* macabre
macadam [makadam] *nm* (**a**) *(revêtement)* macadam;
m. goudronné tarmac(adam) (**b**) *(route)* road
macaque [makak] *nm* (**a**) *(singe)* macaque; **m. rhésus**
rhesus monkey (**b**) *Fam (personne laide)* pig
macareux [makarø] *nm* puffin
macaron [makarɔ̃] *nm* (**a**) *Culin* macaroon (**b**) **macarons** *(coiffure)* coils *(over the ears)* (**c**) *(badge)* badge;
(décoration) rosette; *(autocollant)* sticker; *Journ* **m.
de presse** press badge
macaroni [makarɔni] *nm* (**a**) *(pâte)* piece of macaroni;
des macaronis macaroni (**b**) *(Italien)* Eyetie, = racist
term used to refer to an Italian
Macédoine [masedwan] *nf* **la M.** Macedonia
macédoine [masedwan] *nf* **m. de fruits** fruit salad; **m.
de légumes** mixed vegetables
macédonien, -enne [masedɔnjɛ̃, -ɛn] **1** *adj* Macedonian
  2 *nm,f* **M.** Macedonian
macération [maserasjɔ̃] *nf* steeping
macérer [34] [masere] **1** *vt* to steep
  2 *vi* to steep; **faire m. qch** to steep sth; *Fig* **laisser m.
qn** to leave sb to stew
mâche [maʃ] *nf* lamb's lettuce
mâcher [maʃe] *vt (nourriture)* to chew; **ne pas m. ses
mots** not to mince one's words
machette [maʃɛt] *nf* machete
machiavélique [makjavelik] *adj* Machiavellian
machin [maʃɛ̃] *nm Fam* (**a**) *(objet)* thingy, thingummy
(**b**) *(personne)* what's-his-name, *f* what's-her-name;
monsieur M. Mr What's-his-name; **madame M.** Mrs
What's-her-name
machinal, -e, -aux, -ales [maʃinal, -o] *adj (action,
geste, travail)* mechanical; *(réaction)* automatic
machinalement [maʃinalmɑ̃] *adv (agir)* mechanically; *(réagir, répondre)* automatically
machination [maʃinasjɔ̃] *nf* conspiracy

machine [maʃin] *nf* (**a**) *(appareil)* machine; **m. à café**
coffee machine; **m. à calculer** calculator; *(plus
grande)* calculating machine; **m. à coudre** sewing
machine; **m. à écrire** typewriter; **écrire qch à la m.**
to type sth; **m. à laver,** *Belg* **m. à lessiver** washing machine; **m. à sous** slot machine, *Br* fruit machine; **m. à
tricoter** knitting machine (**b**) *(dans un bateau)* **stopper les machines** to stop engines; **faire m. arrière** to
reverse engines; *Fig* to backtrack (**c**) *(locomotive)* engine; *Fam (moto)* machine (**d**) *(organisation)* machinery
machine-outil *(pl* **machines-outils**) [maʃinuti] *nf*
machine tool
machiner [maʃine] *vt* to plot
machinisme [maʃinism] *nm* mechanization
machiniste [maʃinist] *nmf* (**a**) *(dans un théâtre)* scene-
shifter, stagehand; *(au cinéma, à la télévision)* grip (**b**)
(conducteur d'autobus) driver
machisme [matʃism, maʃism] *nm* machismo
macho [matʃo] *adj & nm Fam* macho
mâchoire [maʃwar] *nf* (**a**) *(d'une personne, d'un animal)* jaw (**b**) *(d'une poulie)* flange (**c**) **mâchoires** *(d'un
étau, d'une tenaille)* jaws; *(de frein)* shoes
mâchonner [maʃɔne] *vt* (**a**) *(mâcher)* to chew (**b**)
(marmonner) to mutter
mâchouiller [maʃuje] *vt Fam* to chew away at
maçon [masɔ̃] *nm* (**a**) *(d'ouvrage en briques)* bricklayer; *(d'ouvrage en pierre)* (stone)mason (**b**) *(franc-
maçon)* mason
maçonnerie [masɔnri] *nf* (**a**) *(de briques)* brickwork;
(de pierres) masonry, stonework (**b**) *(franc-maçonnerie)* masonry
maçonnique [masɔnik] *adj* masonic
macramé [makrame] *nm* macramé
macrobiotique [makrobjɔtik] **1** *adj* macrobiotic
  2 *nf* macrobiotics *(singulier)*
macro-commande *(pl* **macro-commandes**) [ma-
krokɔmɑ̃d] *nf Ordinat* macro(-command)
macroéconomie [makroekɔnɔmi] *nf* macro-eco-
nomics *(singulier)*
macrolangage [makrolɑ̃gaʒ] *nm Ordinat* macro-lan-
guage
maculer [makyle] *vt* to stain (**de** with)
Madagascar [madagaskar] *n* Madagascar
madame [madam] *(pl* **mesdames** [medam]) *nf* (**a**) *(titre)* Mrs; **M. Martin** Mrs Martin; **M. le Ministre** the
Minister (**b**) *(en apostrophe)* madam; *(à l'école)* Miss;
M. le Ministre Madam Minister; **au revoir, m.** goodbye; **M.,** *(dans une lettre)* Dear Madam,; *Fam* **et en
plus, M. exige des excuses!** and so Her Ladyship

wants an apology as well, does she?; **par ici, mesdames** this way, ladies; **mesdames, messieurs** ladies and gentlemen

madeleine [madlɛn] *nf (gâteau)* madeleine

mademoiselle [madmwazɛl] *(pl* **mesdemoiselles** [medmwazɛl]) *nf* (**a**) *(suivi d'un nom)* Miss; **M. Martin** Miss Martin; **Mesdemoiselles Martin et Durand** the Misses Martin and Durand (**b**) *(en apostrophe) (à l'école)* Miss; **merci m.** thank you; *Fam* **et en plus, M. se plaint!** so, Her Ladyship is complaining as well, is she?; **mesdemoiselles, un peu de silence je vous prie!** *(dans une classe)* let's have some quiet, girls, please! (**c**) *(dans une lettre)* **M.** Dear Madam (**d**) *(utilisé seul)* **M. se plaint que...** *(dans un magasin)* this young lady is complaining that...

Madère [madɛr] *n* Madeira

madère [madɛr] *nm* Madeira (wine)

madone [madɔn] *nf* Madonna

madras [madrɑs] *nm (tissu)* madras (cotton)

Madrid [madrid] *n* Madrid

madrier [madrije] *nm* beam

madrilène [madrilɛn] **1** *adj* of Madrid
  2 *nmf* **M.** person from Madrid

maestria [maɛstrija] *nf* mastery

maf(f)ia [mafja] *nf* Mafia; **la M.** the Mafia

maf(f)ieux, -euse [mafjø, -øz] **1** *adj* Mafia
  2 *nm,f* Mafioso

maf(f)ioso [mafjozo] *(pl* **maf(f)iosi** [mafjozi]) *nm* Mafioso

maganer [magane] *vt Can (chose)* to spoil, to waste; *(personne)* to manhandle

magasin [magazɛ̃] *nm* (**a**) *(boutique) Br* shop, *Am* store; **avoir qch en m.** to have sth in stock; **courir** *ou* **faire les magasins** to go shopping; **grand m.** department store; *Can* **m. général** general store (**b**) *(entrepôt)* warehouse (**c**) *(d'un appareil photo, d'une arme)* magazine

magasinage [magazinaʒ] *nm* (**a**) *(mise en dépôt)* warehousing (**b**) *(droits)* warehouse charges (**c**) *Can* **faire du m.** to go shopping

magasiner [magazine] *vi Can* to go shopping

magasinier [magazinje] *nm* warehouseman

magazine [magazin] *nm* (**a**) *(journal)* magazine (**b**) *(émission à la radio ou à la télévision)* magazine programme

mage [maʒ] *nm* magus

Maghreb [magrɛb] *nm* **le M.** the Maghreb

maghrébin, -e [magrebɛ̃, -in] **1** *adj* of the Maghreb
  2 *nm,f* **M.** person from the Maghreb

Maghrébin

This term usually refers to people from Algeria, Morocco and Tunisia, although it can also refer to Libyans and Mauritanians. It has a particular resonance in contemporary France, where immigrants from these countries constitute the largest ethnic minority.

---

magicien, -enne [maʒisjɛ̃, -ɛn] *nm,f* magician

magie [maʒi] *nf* magic; **m. blanche/noire** white/black magic

magique [maʒik] *adj* (**a**) *(surnaturel)* magic (**b**) *(extraordinaire)* magical

magiquement [maʒikmɑ̃] *adv* magically

magistère [maʒistɛr] *nm* (**a**) *(diplôme)* = post-graduate vocational qualification (**b**) *(autorité)* authority

magistral, -e, -aux, -ales [maʒistral, -o] *adj* (**a**) *(admirable) (interprétation, démonstration)* masterly; *(réussite)* brilliant (**b**) *(énorme) (correction, dispute)* proper; *(erreur)* colossal (**c**) *(docte) (ton)* magisterial

magistralement [maʒistralmɑ̃] *adv* authoritatively

magistrat [maʒistra] *nm (qui rend la justice)* judge; *(qui applique la loi) Br* public prosecutor, *Am* prosecuting attorney

magistrature [maʒistratyr] *nf* **la m.** the judicial authorities; **la m. assise** the Bench *or* judges; **la m. debout** the (body of) *Br* public prosecutors *or Am* prosecuting attorneys

magma [magma] *nm* (**a**) *Géol* magma (**b**) *(ensemble confus)* jumble

magnanime [maɲanim] *adj* magnanimous

magnanimité [maɲanimite] *nf* magnanimity

magnat [magna] *nm* magnate, tycoon; **m. de la presse** press baron

magner [maɲe] **se magner** *vpr Fam* to get a move on

magnésium [maɲezjɔm] *nm* magnesium

magnétique [maɲetik] *adj* magnetic

magnétiser [maɲetize] *vt* (**a**) *(matériau, corps)* to magnetize (**b**) *(personne, foule)* to hypnotize

magnétisme [maɲetism] *nm (d'un matériau, de la terre, d'une personne)* magnetism

magnéto [maɲeto] *nm Fam* tape recorder

magnétophone [maɲetɔfɔn] *nm* tape recorder

magnétoscope [maɲetɔskɔp] *nm* video(recorder)

magnificence [maɲifisɑ̃s] *nf* magnificence

magnifier [66] [maɲifje] *vt* to magnify, to glorify

magnifique [maɲifik] *adj* magnificent

magnifiquement [maɲifikmɑ̃] *adv* magnificently

magnitude [maɲityd] *nf* magnitude

magnolia [maɲɔlja] *nm* magnolia (tree)

magnum [magnɔm] *nm* magnum

magot [mago] *nm Fam* hoard

magouille [maguj] *nf Fam* scheming; **faire des magouilles** to scheme

magouiller [maguje] *vt & vi Fam* to scheme

magouilleur, -euse [magujœr, -øz] *nm,f Fam* schemer

magret [magrɛ] *nm (de canard)* fillet

Mahomet [maɔmɛ] *npr* Mohammed

mai [mɛ] *nm* May; **le premier m.** *(fête)* May Day; **le huit m.** *(fête)* VE day; *voir aussi* **janvier**

Mai 68

The events of May 1968 came about when student protests, coupled with widespread industrial unrest, culminated in a general strike and rioting. De Gaulle's government survived the crisis, but the issues raised made the events a turning point in French social history.

---

maigre [mɛgr] **1** *adj* (**a**) *(très mince) (personne, partie du corps)* thin (**b**) *(sans gras) (viande)* lean; *(fromage, yaourt)* low-fat (**c**) *(peu abondant) (filet d'eau)* thin; *(repas, salaire)* meagre; *(végétation, barbe)* sparse (**d**) *(peu conséquent) (conclusions, explication)* thin; *(succès)* very limited
  2 *nm (de viande)* lean part
  3 *nmf* thin person
  4 *adv* **faire m.** not to eat meat

maigrelet, -ette [mɛgrəlɛ, -ɛt] *adj* skinny

maigreur [mɛgrœr] *nf (d'une personne)* thinness

maigrichon, -onne [mɛgriʃɔ̃, -ɔn] *adj* skinny

maigrir [mɛgrir] *vi* to get thinner

mailing [mɛliŋ] *nm* mailshot

maillage [majaʒ] *nm* networking

maille [maj] *nf* (a) *(de tricot)* stitch; **m. à l'endroit/à l'envers** plain/purl stitch (b) *(de filet)* mesh; *Fig* **passer entre les mailles du filet** to slip through the net (c) *(tissu)* knitted fabric (d) *(de chaîne)* link (e) **avoir m. à partir avec qn** to have a set-to with sb

maillet [majɛ] *nm* mallet

maillon [majɔ̃] *nm* link

maillot [majo] *nm (de footballeur, de coureur cycliste)* shirt, jersey; **m. de bain** *(pour femmes)* swimsuit; *(pour hommes)* (swimming) trunks; **m. de corps** *Br* vest, *Am* undershirt; **m. jaune** yellow jersey *(in the Tour de France)*

main [mɛ̃] **1** *nf* hand; **avoir qch en m.** *(situation)* to have sth in hand; *(voiture)* to have the feel of sth; **avoir la m. heureuse** to be lucky; **avoir la m. leste** to be quick to raise one's hand; **avoir la m. lourde** *(être brutal)* to be heavy-handed; **il a eu la m. lourde avec le sel** he was a bit heavy-handed with the salt; **donner la m. à qn** to hold sb's hand; **faire m. basse sur qch** to get one's hands on sth; **mettre la m. sur qch** *(trouver ce que l'on cherchait)* to lay one's hands on sth; **mettre la m. à la pâte** *ou* **à l'ouvrage** to lend a hand; **mettre la dernière m. à qch** to put the finishing touches to sth; **en mettre sa m. au feu** *ou* **à couper** to stake one's life on it; **ne pas y aller de m. morte** *(en frappant, en insultant)* not to pull one's punches; *(forcer une description, une action)* to overdo it; **prendre qn par la m.** to take sb's hand; *Fig* **se prendre par la m.** to take oneself in hand; **prendre qn/qch en m.** to take sb/sth in hand; **prendre qn la m. dans le sac** to catch sb red-handed; **à la m.** *(faire, fabriquer)* by hand; *(tenir, avoir)* in one's hand; **écrit à la m.** handwritten; **fait à la m.** *(pull, poterie)* handmade; **à deux mains** in both hands; **à quatre mains** *(morceau)* for four hands; *(jouer)* four-handed; **à m. armée** *(vol, attaque)* armed; **à main(s) nue(s)** with bare hands; **à pleines mains** by the handful; **de m. en m.** from hand to hand; **de la m. à la m.** cash in hand; **de m. de maître** with a master's hand; **de première m.** firsthand; **de seconde m.** secondhand; **en mains propres** in person; **haut les mains!, les mains en l'air!** hands up!; **les mains vides** empty-handed; *Fig* **les mains dans les poches** unprepared; **sous la m.** handy; **m. courante** handrail

2 *adv* **tricoté/fait/cousu m.** hand-knitted/-made/-sewn

main-d'œuvre [mɛ̃dœvr] *nf* labour

main-forte [mɛ̃fɔrt] *voir* **prêter**

mainmise [mɛ̃miz] *nf* seizure (**sur** of)

maint, -e [mɛ̃, mɛ̃t] *adj indéfini Litt* many a; **maintes et maintes fois, en maintes et maintes occasions** time and (time) again

maintenance [mɛ̃tnɑ̃s] *nf* maintenance

maintenant [mɛ̃tnɑ̃] *adv* now

maintenir [70] [mɛ̃tnir] **1** *vt* (a) *(soutenir)* to hold in position (b) *(empêcher d'avancer)* *(foule)* to hold back; **m. qn à distance** to keep sb at a distance (c) *(conserver)* *(tradition, paix)* to maintain, to keep; *(décision)* to abide by; **m. qn en vie** to keep sb alive (d) *(affirmer)* to maintain (**que** that)

2 se maintenir *vpr* to hold up

maintien [mɛ̃tjɛ̃] *nm* (a) *(conservation)* maintenance; *(de la loi)* upholding; **m. de l'ordre** maintenance of law and order (b) *(allure, posture)* bearing

maintiendrai *etc voir* **maintenir**

maire [mɛr] *nm* mayor

Maire

In France, the mayor has obligations not only to the community but also to national government. He or she is responsible for promulgating national law as well as supervising the local police and officiating at civic occasions. Mayors are elected by the "conseil municipal" (and thus indirectly by the town's residents).

---

mairie [mɛri] *nf (lieu) Br* town hall, *Am* city hall; *(administration) Br* town council, *Am* city hall

---

Mairie

Also called the "hôtel de ville", this is the centre of municipal government. The "mairie" serves as a vital information source for town residents. People go there to ask about taxes, to get married in a civil ceremony, to enrol in certain community-sponsored classes, etc.

---

mais [mɛ] **1** *conj* (a) *(marque l'opposition ou la transition)* but; **non seulement..., m. aussi** *ou* **encore...** not only... but also...; **m. qu'est-ce qui t'arrive?** whatever's the matter with you?; **m. j'y pense, je ne l'ai pas encore appelée!** I've just thought, I haven't rung her yet! (b) *(emphatique)* **m. oui!** of course!; **m. non!** of course not!; **m. enfin** well really; **elle ne fait rien, m. vraiment rien** she does nothing all day, and I mean nothing; **j'ai faim, m. faim!** I'm so hungry!

2 *nm* **il y a un m.** there's a but

maïs [mais] *nm Br* maize, *Am* corn

maison [mezɔ̃] **1** *nf* (a) *(habitation)* house; **m. de campagne** *(résidence secondaire)* house in the country; **m. individuelle** detached house; **m. de poupée** doll's house (b) *(foyer)* home; **à la m.** at home; **toute la m. dort** the whole house is asleep (c) *(entreprise)* company; **m. de couture** fashion house; **m. d'édition** publishing house; **m. mère** parent company (d) *(lignée)* house (e) *(institution)* **m. d'arrêt** remand centre; **m. close** *ou* **de passe** brothel; **m. de correction** *ou* **de redressement** detention centre; **m. de la culture** arts centre; **m. des jeunes et de la culture** = youth club and arts centre; **m. de repos** rest *or* convalescent home; **m. de retraite** old people's home

2 *adj inv* (a) *(artisanal)* home-made (b) *(au sein de l'entreprise)* in-house (c) *Fam (en intensif)* almighty

Maison-Blanche [mezɔ̃blɑ̃ʃ] *nf* **la M.** the White House

maisonnée [mezɔne] *nf* household

maisonnette [mezɔnɛt] *nf* small house

maître [mɛtr] **1** *nm* (a) *(de situation, de chien)* master; **m. de maison** host; **en m.** authoritatively; **être m. de son destin** to be master of one's own destiny; **être m. de soi** to have self-control; **il n'était plus m. de ses actes** he didn't know what he was doing

(b) *(dans des fonctions)* **m. (d'école)** *(Br* primary school *orAm* elementary school) teacher; **m. assistant** = assistant lecturer; **m. de conférence** *Br* (senior) lecturer, *Am* assistant professor; **m. d'hôtel** *(dans une maison)* butler; *(dans un restaurant)* head waiter; **m.**

nageur swimming instructor; **m. d'œuvre** project manager (**c**) *(titre octroyé à un peintre, à un musicien)* maestro; **les grands maîtres** the great masters; **être passé m. dans l'art de qch/de faire qch** to be a past master at sth/at doing sth (**d**) *(titre donné à un avocat)* = form of address for lawyer (**e**) **m. chanteur** blackmailer **2** *adj* **m. mot** key word

maîtresse [metres] **1** *nf* mistress; **être m. de son destin** to be mistress of one's own destiny; **être m. de soi** to have self-control; **m.** (**d'école**) *(Br* primary school *or Am* elementary school) teacher; **m. de maison** hostess **2** *adj* main, principal; **m. femme** capable woman

maîtrise [metriz] *nf* (**a**) *(diplôme universitaire)* ≃ master's degree (**de** in) (**b**) *(contrôle) (de ses passions)* mastery; **m. de soi** self-control (**c**) *(connaissance)* mastery (**d**) *(école de chant)* choir school

maîtriser [metrize] **1** *vt* (**a**) *(soumettre) (agresseur)* to overpower; *(élèves, animal)* to control; *(flammes, opposition)* to subdue; *(incendie, épidémie)* to control (**b**) *(contrôler) (passion)* to control; *(peur)* to overcome (**c**) *(connaître parfaitement) (sujet, langue)* to master; **il ne maîtrise pas la langue** he hasn't mastered the language (**d**) *(rester maître de) (véhicule)* to have under control **2 se maîtriser** *vpr* to control oneself

Maïzena® [maizena] *nf Br* cornflour, *Am* cornstarch

majesté [maʒeste] *nf* (**a**) *(noblesse)* majesty (**b**) **Sa M. (le Roi)** His Majesty (the King); **Sa M. (la Reine)** Her Majesty (the Queen) (**c**) *Art* **Christ en m.** Christ in majesty

majestueux, -euse [maʒɛstɥø, -øz] *adj* majestic

majeur, -e [maʒœr] **1** *adj* (**a**) *(principal)* major (**b**) *(personne)* of age (**c**) *Mus (mode, intervalle)* major **2** *nm (doigt)* middle finger

major [maʒɔr] *nm* (**a**) *(d'une promotion)* top student (**b**) *Mil (officier)* regimental adjutant *(with administrative duties)*; *Belg, Can & Suisse* ≃ major

majoration [maʒɔrasjɔ̃] *nf (d'une facture)* surcharge (**de** on); *(d'un prix)* increase (**de** in)

majordome [maʒɔrdɔm] *nm* butler

majorer [maʒɔre] *vt (facture)* to put a surcharge on; *(prix)* to increase

majorette [maʒɔrɛt] *nf* (drum) majorette

majoritaire [maʒɔritɛr] *adj* majority; **être m.** to be in the majority

majorité [maʒɔrite] *nf* (**a**) *(supériorité en nombre)* majority; **en m.** for the most part; **avoir la m.** to be in the majority (**b**) *(dans des élections)* majority; **m. relative/absolue** relative/absolute majority (**c**) *(parti politique)* majority party (**d**) **m. civile** majority, coming of age

Majorque [maʒɔrk] *n* Majorca

majorquin, -e [maʒɔrkɛ̃, -in] **1** *adj* Majorcan **2** *nm,f* **M.** Majorcan

majuscule [maʒyskyl] **1** *adj (lettre)* capital **2** *nf* capital letter

mal¹, maux [mal, mo] *nm* (**a**) *(douleur)* pain, ache; **avoir m. à l'estomac/à la tête/au dos** to have stomach ache/a headache/backache; **avoir m. à la gorge** to have a sore throat; **j'ai m. au bras** my arm hurts, I have a sore arm; **avoir m. aux dents** to have toothache; **avoir des maux d'estomac/de tête** to get

stomach ache/headaches; **où avez-vous m.?** where does it hurt?; **faire m. à qn** to hurt sb; **mon genou/ œil me fait m.** my knee/eye hurts; **se faire m.** to hurt oneself; *Fam* **attraper du m.** to catch cold; **ça fait m. au cœur de voir ça!** it's sickening to see things like that!; *Fam* **ça me ferait m.!** I'm not having it!; **être en m. de qch** to crave sth; **être en m. d'enfants** to be broody; **m. de cœur** sickness; **m. de dents** toothache; **m. de gorge** sore throat; **m. de mer** seasickness; **avoir le m. de mer** to be seasick; **m. du pays** homesickness; **avoir le m. du pays** to be homesick; *Litt* **m. du siècle** world-weariness; **m. de tête** headache; **m. des transports** travel-sickness; *Prov* **aux grands maux les grands remèdes** desperate situations call for desperate remedies

(**b**) *(préjudice)* harm; **faire du m. à qn** to harm sb; **ça n'a jamais fait de m. à personne!** it never did anyone any harm!; **vouloir du m. à qn** to mean to harm sb; **cela fera plus de m. que de bien** it will do more harm than good; **le m. est fait** the damage has been done; **un m. nécessaire** a necessary evil; **il n'y a pas de m. à cela** there's no harm in that; *Fam* **il n'y a pas de m.** there's no harm done; **dire du m. de qn** to speak ill of sb; **ne pas penser à m.** to mean well

(**c**) *(contraire du bien)* wrong; **le bien et le m.** right and wrong, good and evil; **voir le m. partout** to always see the bad side

(**d**) *(difficulté)* **avoir du m. à faire qch** to have difficulty *or* trouble doing sth; *Fam* **avoir un m. de chien à faire qch** to have a hell of a job doing sth; **non sans m.** not without difficulty; **se donner du m. pour faire qch** to take pains to do sth; **donner du m. à qn** to give sb trouble

mal² **1** *adv* (**a**) *(médiocrement)* badly; *(incorrectement)* wrongly; **elle chante m.** she's a bad singer; **la porte est m. fermée** the door isn't closed properly; **il travaille m. à l'école** he's a poor student; **cette lampe éclaire m.** this lamp doesn't give much light; **m. comprendre** to misunderstand; **m. interpréter** to misinterpret; **m. choisir** to make the wrong choice; **ça va m. finir** it'll end in tears; **on y mange m.** the food's not very good there; **on dort m. dans ce canapé-lit** this sofa bed isn't very comfortable; **je ne pensais pas m. faire** I didn't think I was doing anything wrong; **aller de m. en pis** to go from bad to worse; **on voit m. d'ici** you can't see very well from here; *Fam* **se mettre m. avec qn** to fall out with sb; *Fam* **être m. avec qn** to be on bad terms with sb; **vous ne feriez pas m. de...** you would be wise to...

(**b**) *(en mauvaise santé)* **se sentir m.** to feel ill; **se trouver m.** to faint; **aller m.** to be ill; **être au plus m.** to be at death's door; **être m. en point** to be in a bad way

(**c**) *(une certaine quantité)* **pas m. de** quite a lot of; **il y en a pas m.** there is/are quite a lot; **cela m'a pris pas m. de temps** it took me quite a while

2 *adj inv (contraire à la morale)* bad; **c'est très m. de faire ça** it's very naughty to do that; **c'est pas m.** it's not bad, it's quite good; **elle n'est pas m.** she's not bad; **on n'est pas m. ici** we've found a nice place here

malabar [malabar] *nm Fam* hulk

malade [malad] **1** *adj* (**a**) *(souffrant)* ill, sick; *(nauséeux)* sick; **tomber m.** to fall *or* be taken ill; **je suis m. en bateau/voiture/avion** I suffer from seasickness/ carsickness/airsickness; **être m. du cœur/du foie** to have heart/liver trouble; **être m. d'inquiétude/de jalousie** to be sick with worry/jealousy (**b**) *(qui*

fonctionne mal) (organe, dent) bad; *Fig (industrie)* ailing (**c**) *(dérangé intellectuellement)* mad
　2 *nmf* sick person; *(dans un hôpital)* patient; **un m. mental** a mentally ill person; *(dans un hôpital)* a mental patient; **un m. imaginaire** a hypochondriac
maladie [maladi] *nf* illness, disease; *Fig* **en faire une m.** to make a song and dance about it; **la m. d'Alzheimer** Alzheimer's disease; **m. bleue** cyanosis; **la m. de Parkinson** Parkinson's disease; **m. sexuellement transmissible** sexually transmitted disease; **m. de la vache folle** mad cow disease
maladif, -ive [maladif, -iv] *adj* (**a**) *(personne, teint)* sickly (**b**) *(curiosité, pensées)* morbid (**c**) *(susceptibilité, jalousie)* pathological
maladresse [maladrɛs] *nf* (**a**) *(manque d'habileté physique)* clumsiness, awkwardness (**b**) *(manque de tact)* tactlessness; *(bévue)* blunder
maladroit, -e [maladrwa, -at] **1** *adj* (**a**) *(inhabile)* clumsy, awkward (**b**) *(manquant de tact)* tactless
　2 *nm,f* (**a**) *(personne inhabile)* clumsy or awkward person (**b**) *(personne sans tact)* tactless person
maladroitement [maladrwatmã] *adv* (**a**) *(de façon gauche)* clumsily (**b**) *(sans tact)* tactlessly
malais, -e [malɛ, -ɛz] **1** *adj* Malaysian
　2 *nm,f* **M.** Malaysian
　3 *nm (langue)* Malay
malaise [malɛz] *nm* (**a**) *(trouble physique)* feeling of sickness; *(étourdissement)* dizzy spell; **avoir un m.** to feel faint (**b**) *(inconfort moral)* uneasiness (**c**) *(état de crise)* unrest
malaisé, -e [malɛze] *adj* difficult
Malaisie [malɛzi] *nf* **la M.** Malaysia
malaria [malarja] *nf* malaria; **avoir la m.** to have malaria
malavisé, -e [malavize] *adj Litt* unwise (**de faire qch** to do sth)
Malawi [malawi] *nm* **le M.** Malawi
malaxer [malakse] *vt* to knead
malchance [malʃãs] *nf* bad luck; **par m.** as bad luck would have it
malchanceux, -euse [malʃãsø, -øz] **1** *adj* unlucky
　2 *nm,f* unlucky person
malcommode [malkɔmɔd] *adj* (**a**) *(appareil)* impractical; *(vêtement)* unsuitable (**b**) *Can (personne) (indiscipliné)* unruly; *(hargneux)* cantankerous
Maldives [maldiv] *nfpl* **les (îles) M.** the Maldives
maldonne [maldɔn] *nf* misdeal; *Fig* **il y a m.** something's gone wrong somewhere
mâle [mal] **1** *adj* (**a**) *(du sexe masculin)* male (**b**) *(viril) (courage, assurance)* manly; *(style)* virile (**c**) **prise m.** plug
　2 *nm* male
malédiction [malediksjɔ̃] *nf* curse
maléfice [malefis] *nm* evil spell
maléfique [malefik] *adj* evil
malencontreusement [malãkɔ̃trøzmã] *adv* unfortunately
malencontreux, -euse [malãkɔ̃trø, -øz] *adj* unfortunate
malentendant, -e [malãtãdã, -ãt] **1** *adj* hard of hearing
　2 *nm,f* person who is hard of hearing
malentendu [malãtãdy] *nm* misunderstanding
mal-en-train [malãtrɛ̃] *adj Can* unwell, *Br* poorly; **avoir l'air m.** to look peaky or out-of-sorts

malfaçon [malfasɔ̃] *nf* defect
malfaisant, -e [malfəzã, -ãt] *adj* harmful
malfaiteur [malfɛtœr] *nm* criminal
malfamé, -e [malfame] *adj* disreputable
malformation [malfɔrmasjɔ̃] *nf* malformation
malfrat [malfra] *nm Fam* crook
malgache [malgaʃ] **1** *adj* Madagascan
　2 *nmf* **M.** Madagascan
　3 *nm (langue)* Malagasy
malgré [malgre] *prép (en dépit de)* in spite of, despite; **m. tout** *(en dépit de tout)* in spite of or despite everything; *(pourtant)* all the same
malhabile [malabil] *adj* clumsy, awkward
malheur [malœr] **1** *nm* (**a**) *(drame, catastrophe)* misfortune; **le m., c'est que...** the unfortunate thing is that...; **faire un m.** to be a big hit; **un m. n'arrive jamais seul** it never rains but it pours (**b**) *(chagrin, infortune)* misfortune; **faire le m. de qn** to cause sb a lot of unhappiness (**c**) *(malchance)* bad luck; **par m.** unfortunately; **porter m. à qn** to bring sb bad luck; **avoir le m. de faire qch** to make the big mistake of doing sth
　2 *exclam* hell!
malheureusement [malørøzmã] *adv* unfortunately; **m. pour toi, il ne reste plus de petites tailles** you're out of luck, there are no small sizes left
malheureux, -euse [malørø, -øz] **1** *adj* (**a**) *(triste)* unhappy, miserable (**b**) *(malchanceux) (personne)* unlucky; *(candidat, tentative)* unsuccessful; *(amour)* unrequited; **m. au jeu/en amour** unlucky at gambling/in love (**c**) *(regrettable)* unfortunate (**d**) *(négligeable)* miserable, wretched
　2 *nm,f* (**a**) *(personne infortunée)* poor wretch (**b**) *(indigent)* poor or needy person; **les m.** the poor, the needy
malhonnête [malɔnɛt] *adj* (**a**) *(personne, pratique)* dishonest (**b**) *(indécent) (proposition)* indecent
malhonnêteté [malɔnɛtte] *nf* dishonesty
Mali [mali] *nm* **le M.** Mali
malice [malis] *nf* (**a**) *(espièglerie)* mischief (**b**) *(méchanceté)* malice; **sans m.** without malice
malicieusement [malisjøzmã] *adv* mischievously
malicieux, -euse [malisjø, -øz] *adj (espiègle)* mischievous
malien, -enne [maljɛ̃, -ɛn] **1** *adj* Malian
　2 *nm,f* **M.** Malian
malignité [maliɲite] *nf* (**a**) *(méchanceté)* malice (**b**) *(d'une tumeur)* malignancy
malin, -igne [malɛ̃, -iɲ] **1** *adj* (**a**) *(rusé) (personne)* crafty; *(regard)* knowing; *Ironique* **c'est m.!** that's clever! (**b**) *(méchant) (plaisir)* perverse, malicious; **prendre un m. plaisir à faire qch** to take a perverse or malicious pleasure in doing sth (**c**) *(tumeur)* malignant
　2 *nm,f* crafty person; **faire le m.** to show off
malingre [malɛ̃gr] *adj* puny
malintentionné, -e [malɛ̃tãsjɔne] *adj* ill-intentioned
malle [mal] *nf* (**a**) *(valise)* trunk; *Fam* **se faire la m.** to clear off (**b**) *(de voiture) Br* boot, *Am* trunk (**c**) *Can* **mettre une lettre à la m.** to mail *or Br* post a letter
malléable [maleabl] *adj* malleable
mallette [malɛt] *nf (porte-documents)* briefcase
malmener [46] [malməne] *vt* (**a**) *(brutaliser) (personne)* to manhandle, to treat roughly; *(verbalement)*

to attack; *(matériel, véhicule)* to mistreat **(b)** *(dominer)* **m. qn** to give sb a hard time

malnutrition [malnytrisjɔ̃] *nf* malnutrition

malodorant, -e [malɔdɔrã, -ãt] *adj* smelly

malotru, -e [malɔtry] *nm,f* lout

Malouines [malwin] *nfpl* **les (îles) M.** the Falkland Islands, the Falklands

malpoli, -e [malpɔli] *Fam* **1** *adj* rude
2 *nm,f* rude person

malpropre [malprɔpr] *adj* **(a)** *(sale) (mains)* dirty; *(apparence, travail)* slovenly **(b)** *(inconvenant)* smutty **(c)** *(malhonnête)* despicable

malsain, -e [malsɛ̃, -ɛn] *adj* **(a)** *(dangereux pour la santé)* unhealthy **(b)** *(pernicieux)* unhealthy; *(personne)* unwholesome

malséant, -e [malseã, -ãt] *adj* Litt unseemly

malt [malt] *nm* malt

maltais, -e [maltɛ, -ɛz] **1** *adj* Maltese
2 *nm,f* **M.** Maltese; **les M.** the Maltese
3 *nm (langue)* Maltese

Malte [malt] *n* Malta

maltraitance [maltrɛtãs] *nf* ill-treatment

maltraiter [maltrɛte] *vt* **(a)** *(brutaliser)* to ill-treat **(b)** *(verbalement)* to attack

malus [malys] *nm* partial loss of no-claims bonus *(due to insurance claim)*

malveillance [malvɛjãs] *nf* spite

malveillant, -e [malvɛjã, -ãt] *adj* spiteful

malvenu, -e [malvəny] *adj* out of place, inappropriate

malversation [malvɛrsasjɔ̃] *nf* embezzlement

maman [mamã] *nf Br* mum, *Am* mom; *(langage enfantin) Br* mummy, *Am* mommy

mamelle [mamɛl] *nf (de vache)* udder; *(de chienne, de truie)* teat

mamelon [mamlɔ̃] *nm* **(a)** *(du sein)* nipple **(b)** *(colline)* hillock

mamie [mami] *nf* grandma, gran(ny)

mammaire [mamɛr] *adj* mammary

mammifère [mamifɛr] **1** *adj* mammalian
2 *nm* mammal

mammographie [mamɔgrafi] *nf* mammography

mammouth [mamut] *nm* mammoth

mamours [mamur] *nmpl Fam* kissing and cuddling; **faire des m. à qn** to kiss and cuddle sb

manager¹ [manadʒɛr] *nm* manager

manager² [45] [manadʒe] *vt* to manage

manant [manã] *nm* **(a)** *Hist (villageois)* villager; *(paysan)* peasant **(b)** *Litt (mufle)* churl, boor

Manche [mãʃ] *nf* **la M.** the (English) Channel

manche¹ [mãʃ] *nf* **(a)** *(de vêtement)* sleeve; **en manches de chemise** in one's shirtsleeves; **manches longues/courtes** long/short sleeves; **manches ballon/kimono/raglan** puff/kimono/raglan sleeves **(b)** *(de jeu, de compétition)* round; *(au tennis)* set **(c)** *Fam* **faire la m.** to beg

manche² *nm* **(a)** *(d'outil)* handle; **m. à balai** broomstick; *(d'avion)* joystick **(b)** *(de guitare)* neck **(c)** *Fam* **s'y prendre comme un m.** to make a right mess of things

manchette [mãʃɛt] *nf* **(a)** *(extrémité de la manche)* cuff **(b)** *(de journal)* headline **(c)** *(au catch)* forearm smash; *(au volley-ball)* dig

manchon [mãʃɔ̃] *nm* **(a)** *(vêtement)* muff **(b)** *Tech* sleeve

manchot¹, -e [mãʃo, -ɔt] **1** *adj (privé d'un bras)* one-armed; *Fam* **il n'est pas m.** *(adroit)* he's clever with his hands; *(il peut le faire lui-même)* he's got hands, hasn't he?
2 *nm,f* one-armed person

manchot² *nm (oiseau)* penguin

mandale [mãdal] *nf très Fam* clout, slap

mandarin [mãdarɛ̃] *nm* **(a)** *(de Chine)* mandarin **(b)** *Fig & Péj (personnage influent)* mandarin **(c)** *(langue)* Mandarin (Chinese)

mandarine [mãdarin] *nf (fruit)* mandarin (orange)

mandat [mãda] *nm* **(a)** *(mission) (de député)* mandate; *(de président)* term of office **(b)** *(ordre)* warrant; **m. d'amener** = summons; **m. d'arrêt** arrest warrant; **m. de dépôt** committal order; **m. de perquisition** search warrant **(c)** *(mode de paiement)* order; **m. postal** *Br* postal order, *Am* money order **(d)** *(autorité)* mandate **(e)** *(procuration)* power of attorney

mandataire [mãdatɛr] *nmf (d'électeurs)* representative; *(dans une réunion)* proxy

mandat-carte *(pl* **mandats-cartes***)* [mãdakart] *nm Br* postal order, *Am* money order *(in postcard form)*

mandater [mãdate] *vt* **(a)** *(représentant)* to commission; *(membre parlementaire)* to give a mandate to **(b)** *(frais)* to pay by order

mandat-lettre *(pl* **mandats-lettres***)* [mãdalɛtr] *nm Br* postal order, *Am* money order *(in letter-card form)*

mandibule [mãdibyl] *nf* mandible

mandoline [mãdɔlin] *nf* mandolin

mandrin [mãdrɛ̃] *nm (pour percer)* punch; *(pour élargir un trou)* drift

manège [manɛʒ] *nm* **(a)** *(attraction foraine) Br* roundabout, merry-go-round, *Am* carousel **(b)** *(en équitation)* riding school **(c)** *(manigances)* game

manette [manɛt] *nf* lever; **m. de jeux** joystick; *Fam* **à fond les manettes** at full speed

manga [mãga] *nm* manga

manganèse [mãganɛz] *nm* manganese

mangeable [mãʒabl] *adj* **(a)** *(comestible)* edible **(b)** *(médiocre)* eatable

mangeoire [mãʒwar] *nf* manger

manger [45] [mãʒe] **1** *vt* **(a)** *(aliments)* to eat; **m. qn/qch des yeux** to look at sb/sth longingly; **m. ses mots** to mumble; **ça ne mange pas de pain** it doesn't cost anything; **je ne mange pas de ce pain-là** I don't go in for that sort of thing **(b)** *(attaquer)* to eat away **(c)** *(consommer)* to get through **(d)** *(dépenser)* to get through
2 *vi* to eat; **donner à m. à qn** to give sb something to eat; **m. comme quatre** *ou* **comme un ogre** to eat like a horse; **m. comme un oiseau** to eat like a sparrow; **m. à sa faim** to eat one's fill
3 **se manger** *vpr* to be eaten

mange-tout [mãʒtu] *nm inv (pois) Br* mangetout, *Am* snow pea; *(haricot) Br* runner bean, *Am* string bean

mangeur, -euse [mãʒœr, -øz] *nm,f* **gros m.** big eater; **tigre/requin m. d'hommes** man-eating tiger/shark; *Can Fam Péj* **m. de balustrades** sanctimonious man, *f* woman

mangue [mãg] *nf* mango

maniable [manjabl] *adj (outil)* handy; *(véhicule)* easy to handle

maniaque [manjak] **1** *adj* **(a)** *(pointilleux)* fussy **(b)** *(fou)* manic
2 *nmf* **(a)** *(pointilleux) Br* fusspot, *Am* fussbudget;

être un m. de qch to be fanatical about *or* obsessed with sth (**b**) *(fou)* maniac

manichéen, -enne [manikeɛ̃, -ɛn] *adj* Manichean

manichéisme [manikeism] *nm* Manicheism

manie [mani] *nf* (**a**) *(habitude)* odd habit (**b**) *(idée fixe)* mania, obsession (**c**) *Méd* mania

maniement [manimɑ̃] *nm* handling

manier [66] [manje] *vt* (**a**) *(manipuler) (objet)* to handle (**b**) *(utiliser) (véhicule)* to handle; *(outil, ironie)* to use

manière [manjɛr] *nf* (**a**) *(façon)* way, manner; **faire qch à sa m.** to do sth one's (own) way; **de m. à faire qch** so as to do sth; **de m. que** + *subjunctive* so that, in such a way that; **d'une** *ou* **de m. générale** generally speaking; **en aucune m.** under no circumstances; **de toute m.** in any case; **d'une certaine m.** in a manner of speaking, in a sense; **c'est sa m. d'être** that's the way he is; **la m. forte** strong-arm tactics (**b**) *(conduite)* **manières** manners; **faire des manières** *(agir de façon pompeuse)* to put on airs and graces; *(se faire prier)* to make a fuss (**c**) *(d'une œuvre)* **à la m. de** in the style of

maniéré, -e [manjere] *adj* affected

maniérisme [manjerism] *nm* mannerism

manif [manif] *nf Fam* demo

manifestant, -e [manifestɑ̃, -ɑ̃t] *nm,f* demonstrator

manifestation [manifɛstasjɔ̃] *nf* (**a**) *(de sentiments)* display (**b**) *(rassemblement politique)* demonstration (**c**) *(événement organisé)* event

manifeste¹ [manifɛst] *adj* obvious, manifest

manifeste² *nm* manifesto

manifestement [manifɛstəmɑ̃] *adv* obviously, manifestly

manifester [manifɛste] **1** *vt (exprimer)* to show
2 *vi* to demonstrate
3 se manifester *vpr* (**a**) *(personne)* to make oneself known (**b**) *(maladie)* to show *or* manifest itself (**par in**)

manigancer [16] [manigɑ̃se] *vt* to scheme

manigances [manigɑ̃s] *nfpl* scheming

Manille [manij] *n* Manila

manioc [manjɔk] *nm* manioc, cassava

manipulateur, -trice [manipylatœr, -tris] **1** *nm,f* (**a**) *(de machines)* operator; **m. de laboratoire** laboratory technician; **m. radio(graphe)** X-ray technician (**b**) *Péj (de personnes)* manipulator
2 *nm (appareil de transmission)* (sending) key

manipulation [manipylasjɔ̃] *nf* (**a**) *(d'appareils, de produits)* handling; **m. génétique** genetic engineering (**b**) **manipulations** *(en science)* experiments, practical work (**c**) *Péj (de personnes)* manipulation (**d**) *Ordinat* **m. de colonnes** column handling

manipuler [manipyle] *vt* (**a**) *(appareils, produits)* to handle (**b**) *Péj (personnes)* to manipulate (**c**) *(statistiques)* to massage

manivelle [manivɛl] *nf* crank

manne [man] *nf (dans la Bible)* manna; *Fig (don inespéré)* godsend

mannequin [manikɛ̃] *nm* (**a**) *(personne)* model (**b**) *(de magasin, de couturier)* dummy

manœuvre¹ [manœvr] *nf* (**a**) *(conduite, direction) (de machines)* operation; *(de véhicules)* manoeuvring; **faire une m.** to (do a) manoeuvre; **faire une fausse m.** *(en voiture)* to manoeuvre badly; *Fig* to get it wrong (**b**) *(intrigue)* manoeuvre; **manœuvres** manoeuvring

(**c**) *Mil (dans une bataille)* manoeuvre; **être en manœuvres** to be on manoeuvres (**d**) *(d'un bateau)* manoeuvre

manœuvre² *nm (ouvrier)* unskilled worker

manœuvrer [manœvre] **1** *vt* (**a**) *(faire fonctionner) (machine)* to operate; *(véhicule)* to manoeuvre (**b**) *(influencer)* to influence
2 *vi aussi Fig* to manoeuvre

manoir [manwar] *nm* manor house

manomètre [manɔmɛtr] *nm* pressure gauge, manometer

manquant, -e [mɑ̃kɑ̃, -ɑ̃t] *adj* missing

manque [mɑ̃k] **1** *nm* (**a**) *(insuffisance)* lack; **par m. de** through lack of; **m. de chance!** bad luck!; **m. à gagner** loss of earnings (**b**) *(lacune)* gap (**c**) *(d'un drogué)* withdrawal symptoms; **être en (état de) m.** to have withdrawal symptoms
2 *nf Fam* **à la m.** useless, pathetic

manqué, -e [mɑ̃ke] **1** *adj* (**a**) *(occasion, rendez-vous)* missed (**b**) *(tentative, expérience)* unsuccessful (**c**) *(personne)* **c'est un poète/un médecin m.** he should have been a poet/doctor
2 *nm (gâteau)* = sponge cake with almond-flavoured or fruit-flavoured icing

manquement [mɑ̃kmɑ̃] *nm* breach (**à** of)

manquer [mɑ̃ke] **1** *vt* (**a**) *(cible, train, occasion)* to miss (**b**) *(échouer à)* to fail
2 *vi* (**a**) *(faire défaut)* to be lacking; **le temps/la place me manque** I don't have enough time/room; **elle me manque** I miss her (**b**) *(échouer)* to fail; **ça n'a pas manqué, il est arrivé en retard** sure enough, he was late (**c**) *(être absent)* to be missing (**à** from)
3 *v impersonnel* **il ne manque personne** there's no one missing; **il manque quelques pages** there are a few pages missing; **il manque un bouton à ta veste** there's a button missing from your jacket; **il me manque 10 euros** I'm 10 euros short; **il ne manquait plus que cela!** that's all I/he/*etc* needed!
4 manquer à *vt ind (devoir, honneur)* to fail in; *(parole, promesses)* to break
5 manquer de *vt ind* (**a**) *(argent, main-d'œuvre)* to be short of, to lack; *(temps)* to be short of; *(courage, bon sens, charme)* to lack; **ne m. de rien** to have all that one needs; **m. de respect à qn** to show a lack of respect towards sb; **on manque d'air ici** there isn't enough air in here (**b**) *(faillir)* **m. (de) faire qch** to almost do sth (**c**) *(à la forme négative)* **ne pas m. de faire qch** to be sure to do sth; **je n'y manquerai pas** I certainly will
6 se manquer *vpr* to miss each other *(by not being in the same place at the same time)*

mansarde [mɑ̃sard] *nf* attic

mansardé, -e [mɑ̃sarde] *adj (chambre)* attic

mante [mɑ̃t] *nf* mantis; **m. religieuse** praying mantis

manteau, -x [mɑ̃to] *nm* coat; **m. de fourrure** fur coat; *Fig* **sous le m.** secretly

mantille [mɑ̃tij] *nf* mantilla

manucure [manykyr] **1** *nmf (personne)* manicurist
2 *nf (soin)* manicure; **se faire faire une m.** to have a manicure

manuel¹, -elle [manɥɛl] **1** *adj (travail, activité)* manual; **être m.** *(personne)* to be good with one's hands
2 *nm,f* (**a**) *(travailleur)* manual worker (**b**) *(personne adroite de ses mains)* **c'est un m.** he's good with his hands

manuel² nm (d'utilisation, d'entretien) manual, handbook; (scolaire) textbook

manuellement [manɥɛlmɑ̃] adv manually

manufacture [manyfaktyr] nf (usine) factory

manufacturer [manyfaktyre] vt to manufacture

manu militari [manymilitari] adv by force

manuscrit, -e [manyskri, -it] **1** adj handwritten
2 nm manuscript

manutention [manytɑ̃sjɔ̃] nf handling

manutentionnaire [manytɑ̃sjɔnɛr] nmf warehouseman, f warehousewoman

maous, -ousse [maus] adj Fam enormous

mappemonde [mapmɔ̃d] nf (a) (carte) map of the world (in two hemispheres) (b) (globe) globe

maquereau¹, -x [makro] nm (poisson) mackerel

maquereau², -x nm très Fam (souteneur) pimp

maquerelle [makrɛl] nf très Fam madam

maquette [makɛt] nf (a) (de livre) dummy (b) (d'une construction architecturale) (scale) model; (de mise en page) paste-up (c) (jouet) model; **m. d'avion/de bateau** model plane/boat

maquettiste [makɛtist] nmf (a) (dans une entreprise) model maker (b) (graphiste) graphic designer

maquignon [makiɲɔ̃] nm (a) (marchand de chevaux) horse dealer (b) Fig (entremetteur malhonnête) crooked dealer

maquillage [makijaʒ] nm (a) (de visage) (action) making up; (produits) make-up (b) (de documents) forging; (de photos) faking; (de comptes) falsification

maquiller [makije] **1** vt (a) (personne, visage) to make up (b) (documents) to forge; (photos) to fake; (comptes) to falsify; **m. un meurtre en suicide** to make a murder look like a suicide
2 se maquiller vpr to put one's make-up on

maquilleur, -euse [makijœr, -øz] nm,f make-up artist

maquis [maki] nm (a) (végétation) maquis (b) Fig (d'une procédure, de l'administration) jungle (c) Hist maquis (Resistance movement in World War II); **prendre le m.** to take to the hills

maquisard [makizar] nm Hist member of the maquis, Resistance fighter (in World War II)

marabout [marabu] nm (a) (sorcier) witchdoctor (b) (oiseau) marabou (c) Can (personne acariâtre) bad-tempered person

maracas [marakas] nfpl maracas

maraîcher, -ère [mareʃe, -ɛr] **1** adj **culture maraîchère** Br market gardening, Am truck farming; **produits maraîchers** Br market garden produce, Am truck
2 nm,f Br market gardener, Am truck farmer

marais [marɛ] nm marsh; **m. salant** saltern

marasme [marasm] nm (a) (ralentissement) stagnation (b) (découragement) depression

marathon [maratɔ̃] nm marathon

marathonien, -enne [maratɔnjɛ̃, -ɛn] nm,f marathon runner

marâtre [marɑtr] nf (a) (belle-mère) stepmother (b) (mère cruelle) cruel mother

maraude [marod] nf (a) (vol) pilfering (b) **un taxi en m.** a cruising taxi

marauder [marode] vi (a) (voler) to pilfer (b) (taxi) to cruise for fares (c) (rôdeur) to prowl around

maraudeur, -euse [marodœr, -øz] nm,f pilferer

marbre [marbr] nm (a) (roche) marble; **en** ou **de m.** marble; Fig **rester de m.** to remain impassive (b) (statue) marble (statue) (c) (table de traçage) faceplate (d) (de presse) bed

marbré, -e [marbre] adj (a) (surface, couverture de livre) marbled; (pierre) veined (b) (peau) blotchy (c) **gâteau m.** marble cake

marbrier [marbrije] nm monumental mason

marbrière [marbrijer] nf marble quarry

marbrure [marbryr] nf (a) (sur un livre) marbling (b) (sur la peau) mottling

marc [mar] nm (a) (de raisins, d'olives) marc (b) (eau-de-vie) marc (brandy) (c) (de café) grounds

marcassin [markasɛ̃] nm young wild boar

marchand, -e [marʃɑ̃, -ɑ̃d] **1** adj (prix) trade
2 nm,f (dans un magasin) Br shopkeeper, Am storekeeper; (de vin) merchant; (de meubles, de chevaux) dealer; **m. ambulant** street vendor; **m. forain** travelling stallholder; **m. de glaces** ice cream seller; **m. de journaux** Br newsagent, Am newsdealer; **m. de légumes** greengrocer; **m. de tableaux** art dealer; **m. de tapis** carpet dealer

marchandage [marʃɑ̃daʒ] nm haggling

marchander [marʃɑ̃de] **1** vt to haggle over
2 vi to haggle

marchandisage [marʃɑ̃dizaʒ] nm merchandizing

marchandise [marʃɑ̃diz] nf commodity; **marchandises** goods, merchandise

marche [marʃ] nf (a) (d'escalier) step, stair
(b) (action de marcher) walking; (promenade) walk; (allure) pace; **faire de la m.** to go walking; **faire une m.** to go for a walk; **à deux heures de m.** two hours' walk away; **m. à pied** walking
(c) (défilé, manifestation) march; **ouvrir la m.** to lead the way; **fermer la m.** to bring up the rear
(d) (morceau de musique) march; **m. funèbre** funeral march
(e) (déplacement) **être en m.** (véhicule) to be moving; (mouvement, progrès) to be on the march; **se mettre en m.** (véhicule) to move off; (personne) to set off or out; **dans le sens de la m.** (en voyage) facing forward; **dans le sens contraire de la m.** facing backwards; **m. avant/arrière** (vitesse) forward/reverse gear; **faire m. arrière** (véhicule) to reverse; Fig to backtrack
(f) (fonctionnement) running, working; **mettre qch en m.** to start sth; **se mettre en m.** to start
(g) (des événements, de l'histoire) course; (du temps) march; **m. à suivre** procedure

marché [marʃe] nm (a) (accord) deal, bargain; (plus officiel) contract; **m. conclu!** it's a deal!; **par-dessus le m.** into the bargain; **bon m.** cheap (b) (lieu public de vente) market; **faire son m.** to go shopping; **M. commun** Common Market; **m. noir** black market; **m. aux puces** flea market; **M. unique (européen)** Single (European) Market (c) (débouché économique) market (d) Fin market; **m. des changes** foreign exchange market; **m. haussier/baissier** bull/bear market; **m. à terme** futures market

marchepied [marʃəpje] nm (a) (de train) step (b) (escabeau) steps (c) Fig stepping-stone

marcher [marʃe] vi (a) (se déplacer à pied) to walk; (mettre le pied) to step (**dans/sur** in/on); aussi Fig **m. sur les pieds de qn** to tread on sb's toes; Fig **m. droit** to keep on the straight and narrow (b) (fonctionner) (machine) to work, to run; (plans) to work; **faire m.**

qch to work or operate sth; **comment ça marche?** how does it work?; Fig **les affaires marchent (bien)** business is doing well; **ça marche!** (d'accord) sure! (**c**) (avancer) to march (**vers/sur** towards/on) (**d**) Fam (croire sans réserve) to fall for it; **faire m. qn** to pull sb's leg (**e**) Fam (accepter) to go along with it

marchette [marʃɛt] nf Can (chariot d'enfant) baby-walker; (support de marche) walking frame

marcheur, -euse [marʃœr, -øz] nm,f walker

mardi [mardi] nm Tuesday; **M. gras** Shrove Tuesday; voir aussi **samedi**

Mardi gras

This is a very popular festival, falling on the eve of Ash Wednesday, at the end of the carnival. On this day, "crêpes" are prepared and eaten, and children dress up at school.

---

mare [mar] nf (**a**) (étendue d'eau) pond (**b**) (grande quantité) pool

marécage [mareka3] nm marsh, bog

marécageux, -euse [mareka3ø, -øz] adj (**a**) (terrain) marshy, boggy (**b**) (plante) marsh

maréchal, -aux [mareʃal, -o] nm **m. (de France)** (officier général) field marshal; (d'un roi) marshal; **m. des logis** sergeant

maréchal-ferrant [mareʃalferã] (pl **maréchaux-ferrants** [mareʃoferã]) nm blacksmith

marée [mare] nf (**a**) (de la mer) tide; **à m. haute/basse** at high/low tide; **à la m. montante/descendante** when the tide comes in/goes out; **m. noire** oil slick (**b**) Fig (de personnes) surging mass (**c**) (fruits de la pêche) fresh seafood

marelle [marɛl] nf hopscotch

marémoteur, -trice [maremɔtœr, -tris] adj (énergie) tidal; **usine marémotrice** tidal power station

mareyeur, -euse [marɛjœr, -øz] nm,f fish wholesaler

margarine [margarin] nf margarine

marge [mar3] nf (**a**) (de page) margin; **en m. de** on the fringes of; **vivre en m. (de la société)** to live on the fringes of society (**b**) (liberté d'action) leeway; **avoir de la m.** to have some leeway; (temps) to have time to spare; **m. d'erreur** margin of error; **m. de négociation/manœuvre** room for negotiation/manoeuvre; **m. de sécurité** safety margin (**c**) (commerciale) **m. (bénéficiaire)** profit margin

margelle [mar3ɛl] nf (de puits) coping, curb

marger [45] [mar3e] vt (page) to feed in; Ordinat to set the margins for

marginal, -e, -aux, -ales [mar3inal, -o] **1** adj (**a**) (personne, mode de vie) on the fringes of society (**b**) (secondaire) (occupations, importance) marginal
2 nm,f dropout

marginalisation [mar3inalizasjõ] nf marginalization

marginaliser [mar3inalize] **1** vt to marginalize
2 se marginaliser vpr to become marginalized

marguerite [margərit] nf (**a**) (fleur) daisy (**b**) (de machine à écrire) daisy wheel

mari [mari] nm husband

mariage [marja3] nm (**a**) (cérémonie) wedding; (union) marriage; **m. d'amour** love match; **m. blanc** marriage in name only (primarily in order to acquire nationality); **m. civil** ≃ registry office wedding; Can **m. obligé** shotgun wedding; **m. de raison** marriage of convenience (**b**) (de choses) combination, marriage; (de couleurs) blend(ing)

Mariage

In France, a civil ceremony (which takes place at the "mairie") is required of all couples wishing to marry, though some choose to have a church wedding as well. The traditional wedding involves a long and sumptuous meal at which the wedding cake, a "pièce montée" is served.

Marianne [marjan] nf = young woman symbolizing the French Republic

marié, -e [marje] **1** adj married; **non m.** unmarried, single
2 nm,f groom; f bride; **les mariés** the bride and groom; **les jeunes mariés** the newly-weds

marie-jeanne [mari3an] nf inv Fam (cannabis) Mary-Jane, pot

marier [66] [marje] **1** vt (**a**) (sujet: prêtre) to marry; (sujet: père) to marry off (**b**) (qualités) to combine; (sociétés) to merge; (couleurs) to blend; (styles) to harmonize
2 se marier vpr (**a**) (personnes) to get married, to marry; **se m. avec qn** to marry sb (**b**) (couleurs) to blend (**avec** with); (styles) to go together (**avec** with)

marieur, -euse [marjœr, -øz] nm,f Fam matchmaker

marihuana [marirwana], **marijuana** [mari3ɥana] nf marijuana

marin, -e [marɛ̃, -in] **1** adj (**a**) (air, brise) sea; (plante, animal) marine (**b**) (carte) sea; (mille) nautical
2 nm seaman, sailor; **m. pêcheur** (deep-sea) fisherman; **m. d'eau douce** landlubber

marina [marina] nf marina

marinade [marinad] nf (mélange aromatique) marinade; **m. de poissons/de gibier** marinated fish/game

marine [marin] **1** nf (**a**) (flotte) navy; **la m. de guerre** the navy; **la m. marchande** the merchant navy; **la M. nationale** the French navy (**b**) (navigation) seamanship (**c**) (tableau) seascape
2 adj inv navy (blue)
3 nm (fusilier) Br (Royal) Marine, Am marine

mariner [marine] **1** vt to marinate
2 vi (**a**) (aliment) to marinate; **faire m. qch** to marinate sth; **harengs marinés** pickled herrings (**b**) Fam Fig (personne) to hang around; **faire ou laisser m. qn** (dans un lieu) to keep sb hanging around; (dans une situation) to leave sb to stew

maringouin [marɛ̃gwɛ̃] nm Can mosquito

marinier [marinje] nm Br bargee, Am bargeman

marinière [marinjɛr] nf blouse

mariole [marjɔl] nm Fam sly devil; **faire le m.** to try to be clever

marionnette [marjɔnɛt] nf puppet

marionnettiste [marjɔnetist] nmf puppeteer

marital, -e, -aux, -ales [marital, -o] adj marital

maritalement [maritalmã] adv **vivre m.** to cohabit

maritime [maritim] adj (**a**) (navigation, plante, trafic) maritime; (ville) seaside (**b**) Can **les Maritimes** the Maritimes

marivaudage [marivoda3] nm Litt light-hearted banter

marjolaine [mar3ɔlɛn] nf marjoram

mark [mark] nm (German) mark

marketing [marketiŋ] nm marketing

marmaille [marmɑj] nf Fam brood, kids

marmelade [marməlad] *nf* compote; **m. (d'oranges)** (orange) marmalade; *Fig* **en m.** reduced to a pulp

marmite [marmit] *nf* (cooking) pot; *Fig* **faire bouillir la m.** to bring home the bacon

marmonner [marmɔne] *vt & vi* to mumble, to mutter

marmot [marmo] *nm Fam* kid

marmotte [marmɔt] *nf* marmot

marmotter [marmɔte] *vt* to mumble, to mutter

marner [marne] *vi Fam* to slog

Maroc [marɔk] *nm* **le M.** Morocco

marocain, -e [marɔkɛ̃, -ɛn] **1** *adj* Moroccan
2 *nm,f* **M.** Moroccan

maronite [marɔnit] *adj & nmf* Maronite

maroquin [marɔkɛ̃] *nm* morocco (leather)

maroquinerie [marɔkinri] *nf* (**a**) *(fabrication)* leather tanning (**b**) *(magasin)* leather goods shop (**c**) *(articles)* leather goods

maroquinier [marɔkinje] *nm* (**a**) *(fabricant)* leather worker (**b**) *(commerçant)* dealer in leather goods

marotte [marɔt] *nf (idée fixe)* craze

marquant, -e [markɑ̃, -ɑ̃t] *adj (incident, personne, journée)* remarkable; *(épisode)* significant

marque [mark] *nf* (**a**) *(signe, trace)* mark (**b**) *(de produits, d'appareils)* brand; *(de voiture)* make; **de m.** *(produits)* branded; *(vêtements)* designer; **m. déposée** registered trademark (**c**) *(preuve) (d'amitié)* token; *(de confiance)* sign (**d**) *(cachet)* stamp; **porter la m. du génie** to bear the stamp of genius (**e**) *Ordinat* marker; **m. d'insertion** insertion marker (**f**) **de m.** *(important)* distinguished, prominent (**g**) **marques** *(repères)* marks; **à vos marques! prêts? partez!** on your marks! get set! go!

marqué, -e [marke] *adj* (**a**) *(visage)* lined; **il est très m.** his face is very lined (**b**) *(différence, penchant)* marked

marque-page *(pl* **marque-pages**) [markpaʒ] *nm* bookmark

marquer [marke] **1** *vt* (**a**) *(faire un signe sur)* to mark (**b**) *(écrire)* to write (**c**) *(délimiter)* to mark (**d**) *Sport (adversaire)* to mark; *(but, essai)* to score (**e**) *(indiquer)* to show (**f**) *(accentuer)* to mark; **m. le pas** to mark time; *Fig* **m. le coup** to mark the occasion (**g**) *(impressionner)* to make an impression on (**h**) *Ordinat* to mark
2 *vi (laisser une trace)* to leave a mark

marqueterie [markətri] *nf* marquetry

marqueur [markœr] *nm* (**a**) *(stylo)* (felt-tip) marker (**b**) *(biologique, génétique)* marker

marquis [marki] *nm* marquis

marquise [markiz] *nf* (**a**) *(auvent)* canopy (**b**) *(canapé)* (two-seater) sofa (**c**) *(personne)* marchioness

Marquises [markiz] *nfpl* **les (îles) M.** the Marquesas Islands

marraine [marɛn] *nf* (**a**) *(d'un enfant)* godmother (**b**) *(d'un bateau)* = woman who launches a new boat

Marrakech [marakɛʃ] *n* Marrakesh

marrant, -e [marɑ̃, -ɑ̃t] *adj Fam* funny

marre [mar] *adv Fam* **en avoir m. (de qn/qch)** to be fed up (with sb/sth); **en avoir m. de faire qch** to be fed up with doing sth

marrer [mare] **se marrer** *vpr Fam* to have a good laugh

marron¹ [marɔ̃] **1** *adj inv (couleur)* brown
2 *nm* (**a**) *(fruit)* chestnut; **marrons chauds** roast chestnuts; **marrons glacés** marrons glacés; **m. d'Inde**

horse chestnut (**b**) *(couleur)* brown (**c**) *Fam (coup de poing)* thump; **flanquer un m. à qn** to wallop sb

marron², -onne [marɔ̃, -ɔn] *adj (médecin, homme de loi)* quack

marronnier [marɔnje] *nm* horse chestnut (tree); **m. d'Inde** horse chestnut (tree)

Mars [mars] *npr (dieu, planète)* Mars

mars [mars] *nm* March; *voir aussi* **janvier**

marseillais, -e [marsɛjɛ, -ɛz] **1** *adj* of Marseilles
2 *nm,f* **M.** person from Marseilles
3 *nf* **la Marseillaise** the Marseillaise

Marseille [marsɛj] *n* Marseilles

marsouin [marswɛ̃] *nm* (**a**) *Zool* porpoise (**b**) *Can Fam (malin)* rascal

marsupial, -e, -aux, -ales [marsypjal, -o] *adj & nm* marsupial

marteau, -x [marto] **1** *adj Fam* crazy
2 *nm* (**a**) *(outil)* hammer; **m. piqueur** pneumatic drill; *Fig* **être entre le m. et l'enclume** to be between the devil and the deep blue sea (**b**) *(de porte)* (door) knocker (**c**) *(de piano)* hammer

martel [martɛl] *nm* **se mettre m. en tête** to worry oneself sick

martèlement [martɛlmɑ̃] *nm* hammering

marteler [39] [martəle] *vt* (**a**) *(métal, pieu)* to hammer; **m. la table à coups de poing** to hammer on the table (**b**) *(mot, phrase)* to hammer out

martial, -e, -aux, -ales [marsjal, -o] *adj* martial

martien, -enne [marsjɛ̃, -ɛn] *adj & nm,f* Martian

martinet¹ [martinɛ] *nm (fouet)* strap

martinet² *nm (oiseau)* swift

martingale [martɛ̃gal] *nf (sur un vêtement)* half belt

martiniquais, -e [martinikɛ, ɛz] **1** *adj* Martinican
2 *nm,f* **M.** Martinican

Martinique [martinik] *nf* **la M.** Martinique

martin-pêcheur *(pl* **martins-pêcheurs**) [martɛ̃-pɛʃœr] *nm* kingfisher

martyr, -e [martir] **1** *adj (enfant)* battered; *(peuple)* martyred
2 *nm,f* martyr

martyre [martir] *nm* martyrdom

martyriser [martirize] *vt (maltraiter)* to batter; *(harceler)* to bully

marxisme [marksism] *nm* Marxism

marxisme-léninisme [marksismleninism] *nm* Marxism-Leninism

marxiste [marksist] *adj & nmf* Marxist

marxiste-léniniste [marksistleninist] *(pl* **marxistes-léninistes**) *adj & nmf* Marxist-Leninist

mas [mɑ, mɑs] *nm (en Provence) (ferme)* farm; *(maison)* farmhouse

mascara [maskara] *nm* mascara

mascarade [maskarad] *nf* masquerade; *Fig* sham

mascotte [maskɔt] *nf* mascot

masculin, -e [maskylɛ̃, -in] **1** *adj* (**a**) *(sexe, mode, métier)* male; *(trait de caractère, femme)* masculine (**b**) *(nom, genre)* masculine (**c**) *(rime)* masculine
2 *nm* masculine; **au m.** in the masculine

masculinité [maskylinite] *nf* masculinity

maskinongé [maskinɔ̃ʒe] *nm Can* muskellunge

maso [mazo] *Fam* **1** *adj* masochistic
2 *nmf* masochist

masochisme [mazɔʃism] *nm* masochism

masochiste [mazɔʃist] **1** *adj* masochistic
2 *nmf* masochist

masquage [maskaʒ] *nm Ordinat* masking

masque [mask] *nm* (**a**) *(déguisement)* mask; **m. à gaz/oxygène** gas/oxygen mask; **m. de plongée** diving mask (**b**) *(apparence)* façade; **lever le m.** to remove one's mask (**c**) *(soin cosmétique)* **m. (de beauté)** face pack (**d**) *Ordinat* mask; **m. d'entrée, m. de saisie** input mask

masqué, -e [maske] *adj (personne)* masked

masquer [maske] *vt* to mask

massacrante [masakrãt] *adj f voir* **humeur**

massacre [masakr] *nm* (**a**) *(tuerie)* massacre (**b**) *Fig (travail mal fait)* mess; **faire un m.** *(travailler mal)* to make a complete mess; *(remporter un grand succès)* to be a runaway success

massacrer [masakre] *vt* (**a**) *(tuer, exterminer)* to massacre (**b**) *Fam (abîmer) (travail)* to make a mess of; *(mal interpréter) (morceau de musique, texte)* to murder

massage [masaʒ] *nm* massage; **faire un m. à qn** to give sb a massage

masse¹ [mas] *nf* (**a**) *(volume)* mass; **m. d'air** air mass; **taillé/sculpté dans la m.** carved/sculpted from the block; **tomber comme une m.** to fall in a heap (**b**) *(grande quantité)* mass; **de m.** *(culture, communication)* mass; **en m.** en masse; **une m. de** masses of; *Fam* **pas des masses** not much; *(nombre)* not many; **m. monétaire** money supply; **m. salariale** wage bill (**c**) **les masses** *(le peuple)* the masses; **masses laborieuses** working masses (**d**) *Phys* mass (**e**) *Élec Br* earth, *Am* ground; **mettre qch à la m.** *Br* to earth sth, *Am* to ground sth; *Fam Fig* **être à la m.** to be off one's head

masse² *nf (marteau)* sledgehammer

massepain [maspẽ] *nm* marzipan

masser¹ [mase] **1** *vt (rassembler)* to assemble; *(troupes)* to mass
2 se masser *vpr* to assemble

masser² 1 *vt (faire un massage à)* to massage; **se faire m.** to have a massage
2 se masser *vpr* to massage oneself; **se m. le pied** to massage one's foot

masseur, -euse [masœr, -øz] *nm,f* masseur, *f* masseuse

massicot [masiko] *nm* guillotine

massif, -ive [masif, -iv] **1** *adj* (**a**) *(formes, meuble, porte)* massive; *(personne)* heavily built (**b**) *(argent, or, bois)* solid (**c**) *(dose)* massive
2 *nm* (**a**) *(de plantes, d'arbres)* clump; **m. de fleurs** flower bed (**b**) *(ensemble de montagnes)* massif; **le M. central** the Massif Central *(mountains in central France)*

massivement [masivmã] *adv (répondre, voter)* en masse

mass media, mass-média(s) [masmedja] *nmpl* mass media

massue [masy] **1** *adj inv (argument)* sledgehammer
2 *nf* club

mastectomie [mastɛktɔmi] *nf* mastectomy

mastic [mastik] *nm (pour fenêtres)* putty; *(pour bois)* mastic

mastication [mastikasjɔ̃] *nf* chewing

mastiquer¹ [mastike] *vt (mâcher)* to chew

mastiquer² *vt (fissures)* to fill (in); *(vitre)* to put putty round

mastoc [mastɔk] *adj inv Fam (personne)* hulking; *(construction)* clumsy

mastodonte [mastɔdɔ̃t] *nm* (**a**) *Fam (personne)* colossus; *(objet)* hulking great thing (**b**) *(animal)* mastodon

masturbation [mastyrbasjɔ̃] *nf* masturbation

masturber [mastyrbe] **1** *vt* to masturbate
2 se masturber *vpr* to masturbate

m'as-tu-vu [matyvy] *nmf inv Fam* show-off

masure [mazyr] *nf* hovel

mat¹, -e [mat] *adj (métal, couleur)* matt; *(teint)* darkish; *(son)* dull

mat² 1 *adj inv (aux échecs)* checkmated
2 *nm* checkmate

mat' [mat] *nm Fam* **deux/trois heures du m.** two/three a.m. or in the morning

mât [mɑ] *nm* (**a**) *(d'un voilier)* mast (**b**) *(poteau)* pole; **m. de cocagne** greasy pole

matador [matadɔr] *nm* matador

match *(pl* **matchs** *ou* **matches)** [matʃ] *nm Br* match, *Am* game; **m. aller/retour** first/return leg; **un m. amical** a friendly; **m. nul** draw; **faire m. nul** to draw

matelas [matlɑ] *nm* mattress; **m. pneumatique** air bed

matelassé, -e [matlase] *adj (tissu, blouson)* quilted; *(enveloppe)* padded

matelot [matlo] *nm* sailor

mater¹ [mate] *vt (se rendre maître de) (personne)* to bring to heel; *(rébellion)* to put down

mater² *vt Fam (regarder)* to ogle

matérialisation [materjalizasjɔ̃] *nf* materialization

matérialiser [materjalize] **se matérialiser** *vpr* to materialize

matérialisme [materjalism] *nm* materialism

matérialiste [materjalist] **1** *adj* materialistic
2 *nmf* materialist

matériau, -x [materjo] *nm* (**a**) *(substance)* material (**b**) **matériaux** *(de construction)* material(s); *(documents)* material

matériel¹, -elle [materjɛl] *adj (confort, besoins, dégâts)* material; *(organisation, problème)* practical

matériel² *nm* (**a**) *(pour une activité, un sport)* equipment; **m. de bureau** office equipment; **m. pédagogique** teaching material; **m. agricole** farm equipment (**b**) *(d'une entreprise)* plant; **m. d'exploitation** working plant (**c**) *Ordinat* **m. (informatique)** (computer) hardware

matériellement [materjɛlmã] *adv* (**a**) *(sur le plan matériel)* materially (**b**) **c'est m. impossible** it's physically impossible

maternel, -elle [matɛrnɛl] *adj* (**a**) *(personne, attitude, gestes)* maternal (**b**) *(langue)* native

maternelle [matɛrnɛl] *nf* nursery (school)

Maternelle

Nursery education for children from two to six years old is provided by the state and is available to all families in France. Although it is not compulsory, a vast majority of children attend nursery schools and are thus well-prepared for entry into primary school.

---

materner [matɛrne] *vt* to mother

maternisé, -e [matɛrnize] *adj* **lait m.** milk suitable for infants

maternité [matɛrnite] *nf* (**a**) *(fait d'être mère)* motherhood (**b**) *(hôpital)* maternity hospital (**c**) *(tableau)* Madonna and Child

mathématicien, -enne [matematisjɛ̃, -ɛn] *nm,f* mathematician

mathématique [matematik] **1** *adj* (**a**) *(science)* mathematical (**b**) *(esprit)* logical; *(rigueur)* mathematical (**c**) *Fig (inévitable)* inevitable
  2 *nfpl* **les mathématiques** mathematics *(singulier)*

mathématiquement [matematikmɑ̃] *adv* mathematically

matheux, -euse [matø, -øz] *nm,f Fam* mathematician

maths [mat] *nfpl Fam Br* maths, *Am* math; **M. Sup/Spé** = first/second year of classes preparing students for entrance to science-oriented "grandes écoles"

matière [matjɛr] *nf* (**a**) *(substance)* material; **matières grasses** fat; **m. grise** grey matter; *Fam* **faire fonctionner sa m. grise** to exercise one's grey matter; **m. plastique** plastic; **matières premières** raw materials (**b**) *(sujet) (scolaire)* subject; *(pour en faire un film, un livre, une étude)* material; **il n'y a pas m. à rire** it's no laughing matter; **donner m. à qch** to give cause for sth; **en m. de** as regards (**c**) *(d'un corps physique)* matter

Matignon [matiɲɔ̃] *n* (**l'hôtel**) **M.** = French Prime Minister's offices

> **Matignon**
> The name of the Prime Minister's offices is often used to refer to the Prime Minister and his or her administrative staff, for example "L'Élysée et Matignon ont fini par se mettre d'accord".

matin [matɛ̃] *nm* morning; **ce m.**, *Can* **à m.** this morning; **quatre heures du m.** four o'clock in the morning, 4 am; **le jeudi 2 au m.** on the morning of Thursday the 2nd; **faire qch le m.** to do sth in the morning; **être du m.** to be a morning person; **tous les lundis m.** every Monday morning; **de grand** *ou* **bon m.** early in the morning, in the early morning; **au petit m.** in the small *or* early hours; **du m. au soir** from morning till night

matinal, -e, -aux, -ales [matinal, -o] *adj* (**a**) *(heure)* early; *(excursion, activité)* morning (**b**) *(personne)* **être m.** to be an early riser

mâtiné, -e [matine] *adj* crossbred; **m. de** crossed with; *Fig* mixed with

matinée [matine] *nf* (**a**) *(matin)* morning; **dans la m.** in (the course of) the morning; **en fin de m.** towards the end of the morning (**b**) *(au théâtre, cinéma)* matinée

maton, -onne [matɔ̃, -ɔn] *nm,f Fam* screw *(prison warder)*

matos [matos] *nm Fam* gear

matou [matu] *nm* tom (cat)

matraquage [matrakaʒ] *nm* (**a**) *(avec une matraque)* bludgeoning (**b**) *(insistance)* **m. publicitaire** hype

matraque [matrak] *nf* bludgeon; *(d'agent de police) Br* truncheon, *Am* nightstick

matraquer [matrake] *vt* (**a**) *(frapper)* to club (**b**) *Fig (harceler)* to bombard (**c**) *Fam (faire payer très cher)* to rip off, to fleece

matriarcal, -e, -aux, -ales [matrijarkal, -o] *adj* matriarchal

matrice [matris] *nf* (**a**) *(moule)* matrix, die; *(de disque)* matrix (**b**) *Math* matrix (**c**) *Ordinat* array; **m. d'aiguilles** dot matrix

matricide [matrisid] *nm* matricide

matriciel, -elle [matrisjɛl] *Ordinat* **1** *adj* **imprimante matricielle** dot matrix printer
  2 *nf* **matricelle** dot matrix

matricule [matrikyl] **1** *nm (numéro)* number
  2 *nf (registre)* register

matrimonial, -e, -aux, -ales [matrimɔnjal, -o] *adj* matrimonial

matrone [matrɔn] *nf* (**a**) *Péj (femme corpulente)* stout woman (**b**) *Can (gardienne de prison)* prison wardress

mature [matyr] *adj* mature

mâture [mɑtyr] *nf* masts

maturité [matyrite] *nf* (**a**) *(de personne)* maturity; *(de fruit)* ripeness; **manquer de m.** to be immature; **arriver** *ou* **venir à m.** *(fromage, vin)* to mature; *(fruit)* to ripen (**b**) *Suisse (baccalauréat)* school-leaving diploma *(from a 'gymnase', granting admission to university)*

maudire [modir] *vt* to curse

maudit, -e [modi, -it] *adj* (**a**) *(damné)* cursed (**b**) *(avant le nom) (insupportable)* damn(ed)

maugréer [24] [mogree] *vi* to grumble (**contre** about *or* at)

maure [mɔr] **1** *adj* Moorish
  2 *nm* **M.** Moor

mauresque [mɔrɛsk] **1** *adj* Moorish
  2 *nf* **M.** Moorish woman

Maurice [mɔris] *n* **l'île M.** Mauritius

mauricien, -enne [mɔrisjɛ̃, -ɛn] **1** *adj* Mauritian
  2 *nm,f* **M.** Mauritian

Mauritanie [mɔritani] *nf* **la M.** Mauritania

mauritanien, -enne [mɔritanjɛ̃, -ɛn] **1** *adj* Mauritanian
  2 *nm,f* **M.** Mauritanian

mausolée [mozɔle] *nm* mausoleum

maussade [mosad] *adj* (**a**) *(de mauvaise humeur)* sullen (**b**) *(temps, paysage)* gloomy

mauvais, -e [mɔvɛ, -ɛz] **1** *adj* (**a**) *(défectueux) (santé, vue, excuse)* poor (**b**) *(incompétent) (élève, professeur, mère)* bad (**en** at) (**c**) *(nuisible)* bad (**pour** for) (**d**) *(inapproprié) (clef, numéro, moment)* wrong (**e**) *(méchant) (personne)* bad, nasty; *(chien)* vicious (**f**) *(mer)* rough (**g**) *Fam* **la trouver** *ou* **l'avoir mauvaise** to be hacked off *or* bummed
  2 *adv* (**a**) **sentir m.** to smell (bad) (**b**) **il fait m.** the weather's bad

mauve [mov] **1** *adj* mauve
  2 *nm (couleur)* mauve

mauviette [movjɛt] *nf Fam* wimp

max [maks] *nm Fam* **un m. de gens** *(le plus possible)* as many people as possible; *(énormément)* loads of people

max. *(abrév* **maximum***)* max

maxi [maksi] *adv Fam* max, tops; **on sera vingt m.** there'll be twenty of us max *or* tops

maxillaire [maksilɛr] *nm* jawbone, *Spéc* maxilla

maxima [maksima] *voir* **maximum**

maximal, -e, -aux, -ales [maksimal, -o] *adj* maximum

maxime [maksim] *nf* maxim

maximiser [maksimize] *vt* to maximize

maximum [maksimɔm] *(pl* **maximums** *ou* **maxima** [maksima]*)* **1** *adj* maximum
  2 *nm* maximum; **faire le m. (pour faire qch)** to do one's very best (to do sth); **au m.** at the most; *Fam* **un m.** *(beaucoup)* loads; *Fam* **un m. de gens** *(le plus*

possible) as many people as possible; (énormément) loads of people

maya [maja] **1** adj Maya, Mayan

2 nmf **M.** Maya, Mayan

3 nm (langue) Mayan

mayonnaise [majɔnɛz] nf mayonnaise

mazout [mazut] nm (fuel) oil

mazouté, -e [mazute] adj (plage) oil-polluted; (oiseau) covered in oil

Mbps Ordinat (abrév **mégabits par seconde**) mbps

me [mə]

---
m' is used before a word beginning with a vowel or h mute.
---

pron personnel (**a**) (objet direct) me; **il est venu me chercher** he came to fetch me; **me voici** here I am (**b**) (objet indirect) to me; **il m'a écrit** he wrote to me; **elle m'a serré la main** she shook my hand; **ils m'ont lancé des cailloux** they threw stones at me (**c**) (dans les réfléchis) myself; **je vais me doucher** I'm going to have a shower (**d**) (dans les pronominaux) **je me suis trompé** I made a mistake

mea culpa [meakylpa] nm inv **faire son m.** to own up

méandre [meɑ̃dr] nm (de rivière) meander; (de route) bend; Fig **méandres** (d'un raisonnement) intricacies

mec [mɛk] nm Fam (homme quelconque) guy, Br bloke; (amoureux) man

mécanicien, -enne [mekanisjɛ̃, -ɛn] nm,f (**a**) (garage or motor) mechanic (**b**) (conducteur de train) Br train driver, Am engineer

mécanique [mekanik] **1** adj mechanical

2 nf (**a**) (science du mouvement) mechanics (singulier) (**b**) (des moteurs, des machines) mechanical engineering (**c**) (mécanisme) mechanism

mécaniquement [mekanikmɑ̃] adv mechanically

mécanisation [mekanizasjɔ̃] nf mechanization

mécanisme [mekanism] nm (**a**) (d'une machine, d'une montre, d'un moteur) mechanism (**b**) (de la pensée, de la parole) mechanics

mécénat [mesena] nm sponsorship; **m. d'entreprise** corporate sponsorship

mécène [mesɛn] nm sponsor

méchamment [meʃamɑ̃] adv (**a**) (avec méchanceté) nastily (**b**) Fam (en intensif) **être m. déçu/embêté** to be terribly disappointed/annoyed

méchanceté [meʃɑ̃ste] nf (**a**) (d'une personne, d'une remarque) nastiness; (d'un enfant) naughtiness (**b**) (action) nasty action; (parole) nasty remark

méchant, -e [meʃɑ̃, -ɑ̃t] **1** adj (**a**) (personne, remarque) nasty; (enfant) naughty; (animal) vicious; **attention chien m.** (sur panneau) beware of the dog (**b**) (désagréable) (affaire) unpleasant; (blessure, grippe) nasty; (humeur) foul

2 nm,f Fam baddie, baddy

mèche¹ [meʃ] nf (**a**) (de bougie, de lampe) wick; (de charge explosive) fuse (**b**) (de perceuse) bit (**c**) (de cheveux) strand; (boucle) lock; **se faire des mèches** to get highlights (in one's hair)

mèche² nf **être de m. avec qn** to be in cahoots with sb

méchoui [meʃwi] nm spit-roasted lamb

méconduite [mekɔ̃dɥit] nf Belg misbehaviour

méconnaissable [mekɔnɛsabl] adj unrecognizable

méconnaître [20] [mekɔnɛtr] vt (**a**) (faits) to fail to take account of (**b**) (talent, artiste) to fail to recognize

méconnu, -e [mekɔny] adj (talent, artiste) unrecognized

mécontent, -e [mekɔ̃tɑ̃, -ɑ̃t] **1** adj (insatisfait) displeased (**de** with); (contrarié) annoyed

2 nm,f grumbler; (électeur) malcontent

mécontentement [mekɔ̃tɑ̃tmɑ̃] nm (insatisfaction) displeasure; (contrariété) annoyance

mécontenter [mekɔ̃tɑ̃te] vt (ne pas satisfaire) to displease; (contrarier) to annoy

Mecque [mɛk] n voir **La Mecque**

médaille [medaj] nf (**a**) (prix, décoration) medal; **la m. d'or/d'argent/de bronze** the gold/silver/bronze medal (**b**) (bijou) (avec le nom) pendant (with name engraved on it); (à l'effigie d'un saint) medal (**c**) (de chat, de chien) identity disc

médaillé, -e [medaje] **1** adj (sportif) holding a medal; (soldat) decorated

2 nm,f (sportif) medallist; (soldat) medal-holder

médaillon [medajɔ̃] nm (**a**) (bijou) locket (**b**) (de poisson, de viande) medallion

médecin [medsɛ̃] nm doctor; **m. généraliste** general practitioner, GP; **m. légiste** Br forensic scientist, Am medical examiner; **m. traitant** consulting physician; **m. du travail** = doctor who carries out the annual medical examination, required by law, of a company's employees

médecine [medsin] nf medicine; **exercer la m.** to practise medicine; **m. douce** ou **parallèle** alternative medicine; **m. générale** general medicine; **m. du travail** industrial medicine

média [medja] nm medium; **les médias** the media

médian, -e [medjɑ̃, -an] **1** adj median

2 nf **médiane** median

médiateur, -trice [medjatœr, -tris] **1** adj mediating

2 nm,f mediator

3 nm **le M. (de la République)** ≃ Ombudsman, Parliamentary Commissioner for Administration

médiathèque [medjatɛk] nf media library

médiation [medjasjɔ̃] nf mediation

médiatique [medjatik] adj (événement, campagne) media; **il est très m.** (il passe bien à la télé) he comes over well on television

médiatisation [medjatizasjɔ̃] nf media coverage

médiatiser [medjatize] vt to give media coverage to

médiator [medjatɔr] nm Mus plectrum

médiatrice [medjatris] nf median

médical, -e, -aux, -ales [medikal, -o] adj medical

médicalisé, -e [medikalize] adj **logement m.** nursing home

médicaliser [medikalize] vt (**a**) (région, pays, population) to make medical care available to (**b**) (grossesse) to treat as a medical matter

médicament [medikamɑ̃] nm medicine; **m. de confort** = medication prescribed to relieve pain and symptoms rather than as a cure for the illness

médicinal, -e, -aux, -ales [medisinal, -o] adj medicinal

médico-légal, -e (mpl **médico-légaux**, fpl **médico-légales**) [medikolegal, -o] adj forensic

médico-social, -e (mpl **médico-sociaux**, fpl **médico-sociales**) [medikosɔsjal, -o] adj **centre m.** health centre

médiéval, -e, -aux, -ales [medjeval, -o] adj medieval

médiocre [medjɔkr] adj mediocre

médiocrement [medjɔkrəmɑ̃] adv indifferently

médiocrité [medjɔkrite] nf mediocrity

médire [27b] [medir] **médire de** *vt ind* to speak ill of

médisance [medizɑ̃s] *nf* (**a**) *(action)* scandalmongering, gossiping (**b**) *(propos)* piece of scandal *or* gossip; **médisances** scandal, gossip

médisant, -e [medizɑ̃, -ɑ̃t] *adj (paroles)* slanderous; *(personne)* scandalmongering

méditation [meditasjɔ̃] *nf* meditation

méditer [medite] **1** *vt* (**a**) *(considérer par une profonde réflexion)* to contemplate (**b**) *(préparer)* to mull over
2 *vi* to meditate
3 méditer sur *vt ind* to meditate on

Méditerranée [mediterane] *nf* **la (mer) M.** the Mediterranean (Sea)

méditerranéen, -enne [mediteraneɛ̃, -ɛn] **1** *adj* Mediterranean
2 *nm,f* **M.** person from a Mediterranean country

médium [medjɔm] *nmf (voyant)* medium

médius [medjys] *nm* middle finger

méduse [medyz] *nf* jellyfish

méduser [medyze] *vt* to dumbfound

meeting [mitiŋ] *nm* meeting; **m. aérien** air show

méfait [mefɛ] *nm* misdemeanour; **les méfaits du tabac** the damage caused by smoking

méfiance [mefjɑ̃s] *nf (manque de confiance)* distrust; *(suspicion)* mistrust, suspicion; **m.!** be careful!

méfiant, -e [mefjɑ̃, -ɑ̃t] *adj (n'ayant pas confiance)* distrustful; *(suspicieux)* suspicious (**à l'égard de** *ou* **avec** of)

méfier [66] [mefje] **se méfier** *vpr* to be careful; **se m. de qn** not to trust sb; **se m. de qch** *(faire attention à)* to watch out for sth; *(douter de)* to be wary of sth

méga¹ [mega] *nm Ordinat* megabyte, meg

méga² *adj inv Fam* mega

mégabit [megabit] *nm Ordinat* megabit

mégalo [megalo] *adj & nmf Fam* megalomaniac

mégalomane [megaloman] *adj & nmf* megalomaniac

mégalomanie [megalomani] *nf* megalomania

mégalopole [megalopol] *nf* megalopolis

mégaoctet *(pl* **mégaoctets**) [megaɔktɛ] *nm Ordinat* megabyte

mégaphone [megafɔn] *nm Br* megaphone, *Am* bullhorn

mégarde [megard] **par mégarde** *adv* inadvertently, accidentally

mégère [meʒɛr] *nf (femme)* shrew

mégot [mego] *nm* fag butt or end

mégoter [megote] *vi Fam* to skimp (**sur** on)

meilleur, -e [mejœr] **1** *adj* (**a**) *(comparatif de bon)* better (**que** than) (**b**) *(superlatif de bon)* **le m. élève** *(de la classe)* the best pupil; *(parmi deux élèves)* the better pupil
2 *nm,f (personne)* **le m.** *(de tous)* the best; *(des deux)* the better; *Fam* **alors ça, c'est la meilleure!** that's just great!
3 *nm (ce qu'il y a de mieux)* **le m.** the best; **pour le m. et pour le pire** for better and for worse
4 *adv* **il fait m.** it's warmer

méjuger [45] [meʒyʒe] **1** *vt Litt (mal juger)* to misjudge; *(sous-estimer)* to underestimate
2 méjuger de *vt ind (mal juger)* to misjudge; *(sous-estimer)* to underestimate

mél [mel] *nm (courrier électronique)* e-mail; *(adresse électronique)* e-mail address

mélancolie [melɑ̃kɔli] *nf* melancholy

mélancolique [melɑ̃kɔlik] *adj* melancholy

Mélanésie [melanezi] *nf* **la M.** Melanesia

mélanésien, -enne [melanezjɛ̃, -ɛn] **1** *adj* Melanesian
2 *nm,f* **M.** Melanesian
3 *nm (langue)* Melanesian

mélange [melɑ̃ʒ] *nm* (**a**) *(action)* mixing (**b**) *(résultat)* mixture; **je ne fais jamais de mélanges** I never mix my drinks

mélanger [45] [melɑ̃ʒe] **1** *vt* (**a**) *(mettre ensemble)* to mix (**b**) *(confondre, déranger)* to mix up; **je mélange tout en français** I get everything in French mixed up (**c**) *(cartes)* to shuffle
2 se mélanger *vpr* (**a**) *(s'incorporer)* to mix (**b**) *(se confondre)* to get mixed up (**c**) *Fam* **se m. les pédales** *ou* **les pinceaux** to get into a muddle

mélangeur [melɑ̃ʒœr] *nm* **(robinet) m.** *Br* mixer tap, *Am* mixing faucet

mélanome [melanom] *nm Méd* melanoma

mêlant [mɛlɑ̃] *adj m Can* **c'est pas m.** there's no doubt about it

mélasse [melas] *nf Br* (black) treacle, *Am* molasses *(singulier)*; *Fam* **être dans la m.** to be in a mess

Melba [mɛlba] *adj inv* **pêche M.** peach Melba

mêlé, -e [mele] *adj* (**a**) *(mélangé)* mixed (**de** with) (**b**) *Can (embrouillé)* mixed-up; *(désorienté)* disoriented; **être m. dans ses papiers** to be confused

mêlée [mele] *nf* (**a**) *(conflit)* fray, mêlée (**b**) *(au rugby)* scrum, scrummage

mêler [mele] **1** *vt* (**a**) *(mettre ensemble)* to mix (**à** *ou* **avec** with) (**b**) *(impliquer)* **m. qn à qch** *(affaire, conversation)* to involve sb in sth
2 se mêler *vpr* (**a**) *(substances)* to combine (**b**) *(se joindre)* **se m. à qch** *(foule)* to mingle with sth; *(cortège)* to join sth; *(conversation)* to join in sth (**c**) *(s'occuper)* **se m. de qch** to get involved in sth; **mêle-toi de tes affaires!** mind your own business!

mélèze [melɛz] *nm* larch (tree)

méli-mélo *(pl* **mélis-mélos**) [melimelo] *nm Fam* jumble

mélo [melo] *Fam* **1** *adj (qui tient du mélodrame)* melodramatic; *(qui donne dans la sensiblerie)* sentimental
2 *nm* melodrama

mélodie [melɔdi] *nf* (**a**) *(composition musicale)* melody, tune (**b**) *(de vers, d'une langue)* melodiousness, tunefulness

mélodieusement [melɔdjøzmɑ̃] *adv* melodiously, tunefully

mélodieux, -euse [melɔdjø, -øz] *adj* melodious, tuneful

mélodique [melɔdik] *adj* melodic

mélodiste [melɔdist] *nmf* melody writer

mélodramatique [melɔdramatik] *adj* melodramatic

mélodrame [melɔdram] *nm* melodrama

mélomane [melɔman] **1** *adj* music-loving
2 *nmf* music lover

melon [məlɔ̃] *nm* (**a**) *(fruit)* melon (**b**) *(chapeau) Br* bowler (hat), *Am* derby

membrane [mɑ̃bran] *nf* membrane

membre [mɑ̃br] **1** *adj (État, pays)* member
2 *nm* (**a**) *(partie du corps)* limb; **m. supérieur/inférieur** upper/lower limb; **m. viril** male member (**b**) *(d'une association, d'un groupe)* member

mémé [meme] *nf (grand-mère)* gran(ny), grandma; *Fam (vieille femme)* old dear

même [mɛm] **1** *adj indéfini* (**a**) *(avant le nom) (identique)* same; **j'ai la m. voiture que toi** I have the same car as you (do)

(**b**) *(après le nom, pour insister)* **je l'ai fait le jour m.** I did it that (very) same day; **c'est cela m.** that's it exactly; **c'est la gentillesse m.** she's kindness itself *or* personified

2 *pron indéfini* **le/la m.** the same (one); **j'ai les mêmes que lui** I have the same (ones) as him; **cela revient au m.** it comes *or* amounts to the same thing

3 *adv* (**a**) *(pour insister)* even; **il n'est m. pas beau** he's not even good-looking; **m. moi, je le sais!** even I know that!; **m. si je l'avais, je ne te le donnerais pas** even if I had it, I wouldn't give it to you; **elle habite ici m.** she lives in this very place; **aujourd'hui m.** this very day; **je pense m. qu'il sera d'accord** I think he'll actually agree

(**b**) **être à m. de faire qch** to be able *or* in a position to do sth; **dormir à m. le sol** to sleep on the bare ground; **porter un pull-over à m. la peau** to wear a jumper next to one's bare skin; **de m.** likewise; **Joyeux Noël – vous de m.** Merry Christmas – same to you; **il en est de m. des autres** the same goes for the others; **faire de m.** to follow suit; **de m. que qn** just like sb; **de m. que qch** just like sth; *(aussi bien que qch)* as well as sth; **tout de m.**, *Fam* **quand m.** all the same; *Fam* **enfin, quand m.!** honestly!; *Fam* **m. que je te l'avais déjà dit!** but I already TOLD you!

mémento [memɛ̃to] *nm* (**a**) *(pour réviser)* revision notes; **m. de chimie** chemistry revision notes (**b**) *(carnet)* diary

mémère [memɛr] *nf Fam Péj* old biddy, *Br* old dear; **une grosse m.** a fat old bag

mémo [memo] *nm* memo

mémoire¹ [memwar] *nf* (**a**) *(faculté)* memory; **avoir de la m.** to have a good memory; **avoir la m. des noms/dates** to have a good memory for names/dates; **avoir la m. courte** to have a short memory; **se rafraîchir la m.** to refresh one's memory; **à la m. de qn** *(monument)* in memory of sb; **de m.** *(citer)* from memory; **de m. d'homme** within living memory; **pour m.** for the record; **si j'ai bonne m.** if I remember correctly; **avoir une m. d'éléphant** to have a memory like an elephant; **la m. collective** collective memory

(**b**) *Ordinat* memory; **mettre un dossier en m.** to write a file to memory; **carte d'extension de m.** memory expansion card; **m. cache** cache memory; **m. centrale** main memory; **m. à disque** disk memory, RAM disc; **m. étendue** extended memory; **m. expansée** expanded memory; **m. haute** high memory; **m. de masse** mass storage; **m. morte** read-only memory; **m. non effaçable** non-erasable memory; **m. paginée** expanded memory; **m. permanente** permanent memory; **m. tampon** buffer (store *or* memory); **m. vidéo** video memory; **m. vive** random access memory, RAM; **m. vive dynamique** DRAM, dynamic random access memory; **m. vive statique** static RAM, static random access memory

mémoire² *nm* (**a**) *(thèse)* thesis, dissertation (**b**) *(rapport)* report (**c**) **Mémoires** *(chronique)* memoirs

mémorable [memɔrabl] *adj* memorable

mémorandum [memɔrɑ̃dɔm] *nm* (**a**) *(note)* memorandum (**b**) *(carnet)* notebook

mémorial, -aux [memɔrjal, -o] *nm (monument)* memorial

mémoriser [memɔrize] *vt* to memorize

menaçant, -e [mənasɑ̃, -ɑ̃t] *adj* threatening, menacing

menace [mənas] *nf* threat (**de** of); **menaces de mort** death threats

menacer [16] [mənase] **1** *vt* to threaten (**de** with); **m. qn du poing** to shake one's fist at sb; **m. de faire qch** to threaten to do sth

2 *vi (tempête, orage, révolution)* to be brewing; **la pluie menace** it's threatening to rain

ménage [menaʒ] *nm* (**a**) *(nettoyage)* **faire le m.** *(à la maison)* to do the housework; *Fig* to have a shake-up; **faire des ménages** to go out cleaning (**b**) *(couple)* **se mettre en m.** to move in together; **se mettre en m. avec qn** to move in with sb; **faire bon/mauvais m. (avec qn)** to get on well/badly (with sb); **m. à trois** ménage à trois (**c**) *Écon* household

ménagement [menaʒmɑ̃] *nm* care, caution; *(tact)* consideration; **sans m.** *(annoncer)* bluntly

ménager¹, -ère [menaʒe, -ɛr] **1** *adj* (**a**) *(de la maison) (équipement, appareils)* household (**b**) *Can (économe)* thrifty, careful (with money)

2 *nf* **ménagère** *(femme)* housewife

ménager² [45] **1** *vt* (**a**) *(utiliser avec parcimonie) (argent)* to use sparingly; *(forces)* to conserve, to save; *(santé)* to take care of; **ne pas m. sa peine** to put in a lot of effort (**b**) *(traiter avec soin)* to treat carefully; *Fig* **m. la chèvre et le chou** to keep everyone happy (**c**) *(arranger) (entrevue, réunion)* to arrange, to organize; *(sortie)* to provide; *(réconciliation)* to bring about

2 **se ménager** *vpr* (**a**) *(prendre soin de soi)* to take care of oneself, to look after oneself (**b**) *(se réserver)* to set aside

ménagerie [menaʒri] *nf* menagerie

mendiant, -e [mɑ̃djɑ̃, -ɑ̃t] **1** *adj (moine, ordre)* mendicant

2 *nm,f* beggar

mendicité [mɑ̃disite] *nf* begging

mendier [66] [mɑ̃dje] **1** *vt* to beg for
2 *vi* to beg

mener [46] [məne] **1** *vt* (**a**) *(accompagner)* to take (**à** to) (**b**) *(cortège, course)* to lead; **m. qch à bien** to bring sth to a successful conclusion; *Fig* **m. la danse** to call the tune (**c**) *(vie)* to lead; **m. la vie dure à qn** to give sb a hard time (**d**) *(débat, enquête)* to lead (**e**) *(contrôler) (personne)* **m. qn à la baguette** to have sb under one's thumb; **m. qn par le bout du nez** to lead sb by the nose

2 *vi* (**a**) *(dans un match, une compétition)* to lead; **m. par 2 buts à 1** to lead by 2 goals to 1 (**b**) **m. à un lieu** to lead to a place; *Fig* **cela ne mène à rien** this is getting us nowhere (**c**) *Fam* **elle n'en menait pas large** her heart was in her mouth

meneur, -euse [mənœr, -øz] **1** *nm,f (de parti politique)* leader; *(agitateur)* ringleader; **m. d'hommes** born leader; **m. de jeu** question master, quiz master; *Sport* play maker

2 *nf* **meneuse de revue** principal chorus girl; *Can* **m. de claques** cheerleader

menhir [menir] *nm* menhir

méninges [menɛ̃ʒ] *nfpl Fam* brains

méningite [menɛ̃ʒit] *nf* meningitis; **avoir une m.** to have meningitis

ménisque [menisk] *nm* meniscus

ménopause [menɔpoz] *nf* menopause

menotte [mənɔt] *nf* (**a**) *Fam (petite main)* little hand (**b**) **menottes** *(bracelets métalliques)* handcuffs; **mettre** *ou*

passer les menottes à qn to handcuff sb, to put handcuffs on sb

mensonge [mɑ̃sɔ̃ʒ] *nm* (**a**) *(propos)* lie; **petit m., pieux m.** white lie (**b**) *(acte)* lying

mensonger, -ère [mɑ̃sɔ̃ʒe, -ɛr] *adj (propos)* untrue; *(publicité)* misleading

menstruation [mɑ̃stryasjɔ̃] *nf* menstruation

menstruel, -elle [mɑ̃stryɛl] *adj* menstrual

mensualiser [mɑ̃sɥalize] *vt* to pay monthly; **être mensualisé** *(pour les impôts)* = to pay one's income tax in advance monthly instalments, the amount paid being an estimation based on previous years

mensualité [mɑ̃sɥalite] *nf* monthly payment

mensuel, -elle [mɑ̃sɥɛl] **1** *adj* monthly
   2 *nm (publication)* monthly (magazine)

mensuellement [mɑ̃sɥɛlmɑ̃] *adv* monthly, every month

mensuration [mɑ̃syrasjɔ̃] *nf* (**a**) *(action)* measurement, measuring (**b**) **mensurations** *(dimensions)* measurements

mental, -e, -aux, -ales [mɑ̃tal, -o] **1** *adj* mental
   2 *nm* mental attitude

mentalement [mɑ̃talmɑ̃] *adv* mentally

mentalité [mɑ̃talite] *nf* mentality; **les mentalités ont changé** (people's) attitudes have changed; *Ironique* **jolie m.!** that's a nice way of thinking!

menteur, -euse [mɑ̃tœr, -øz] **1** *adj (personne)* untruthful, lying
   2 *nm,f* liar

menthe [mɑ̃t] *nf (plante)* mint; **dentifrice a la m.** mint *or* mint-flavoured toothpaste; **m. à l'eau** peppermint cordial

menthol [mɑ̃tɔl] *nm* menthol

mentholé, -e [mɑ̃tɔle] *adj* menthol, mentholated

mention [mɑ̃sjɔ̃] *nf* (**a**) *(fait de citer)* mention; **faire m. de qn/qch** to mention sb/sth (**b**) **rayer la m. inutile** *(sur formulaire)* delete where applicable (**c**) *(à un examen)* **m. passable** ≃ C; **m. assez bien** ≃ B; **m. bien/très bien** ≃ A

mentionner [mɑ̃sjɔne] *vt* to mention

mentir [64b] [mɑ̃tir] *vi* to lie (**à** to); **sans m.** honestly

menton [mɑ̃tɔ̃] *nm* chin; **m. en galoche** protruding chin; **m. fuyant** receding chin; **double m.** double chin

mentor [mɑ̃tɔr] *nm* mentor

menu¹, -e [məny] **1** *adj* (**a**) *(détail, monnaie)* small (**b**) *(taille)* slim; *(personne)* petite
   2 *adv* small, fine

menu² *nm* (**a**) *(au restaurant)* set menu, fixed-price menu (**b**) *Ordinat* menu; **contrôlé par m.** menu-driven; **m. d'aide** help menu; **m. déroulant** pull-down menu; **m. fichier** file menu; **m. primaire/secondaire/principal** primary/secondary/main menu

menuet [mənɥɛ] *nm* minuet

menuiserie [mənɥizri] *nf* (**a**) *(atelier)* (joiner's) workshop (**b**) *(travail du bois, résultat)* joinery, woodwork

menuisier [mənɥizje] *nm* joiner, carpenter

méprendre [58] [meprɑ̃dr] **se méprendre** *vpr* to be mistaken (**sur** about); **elle te ressemble à s'y m.** she looks exactly like you

mépris¹, -e *voir* **méprendre**

mépris² [mepri] *nm* contempt, scorn; **avec m.** scornfully, contemptuously; **avoir du m. pour qn** to despise sb; **au m. de qch** regardless of sth

méprisable [meprizabl] *adj* contemptible, despicable

méprisant, -e [meprizɑ̃, -ɑ̃t] *adj* scornful, contemptuous

méprise [mepriz] *nf* mistake

mépriser [meprize] *vt* (**a**) *(dédaigner) (personne, argent)* to despise (**b**) *(ignorer) (conseil, offre, danger)* to disregard

mer [mɛr] *nf* (**a**) *(étendue d'eau)* sea; **en haute** *ou* **pleine m.** (out) at sea; **au bord de la m.** at the seaside; **aller à la m.** to go to the seaside; **prendre la m.** to set sail, to put (out) to sea; *Fam* **ce n'est pas la m. à boire** it's no big deal; **une m. d'huile** a sea as calm as a millpond; **la m. Adriatique** the Adriatic Sea; **la m. d'Aral** the Aral Sea; **la m. Caspienne** the Caspian Sea; **la m. de Chine** the China Sea; **la m. de Corail** the Coral Sea; **la m. Égée** the Aegean Sea; **la m. d'Irlande** the Irish Sea; **la m. Morte** the Dead Sea; **la m. Noire** the Black Sea; **la m. du Nord** the North Sea; **la m. Rouge** the Red Sea; **la m. des Sargasses** the Sargasso Sea (**b**) *(marée)* tide

mercantile [mɛrkɑ̃til] *adj* mercenary

mercatique [mɛrkatik] *nf* marketing

mercenaire [mɛrsənɛr] *adj & nm* mercenary

mercerie [mɛrsəri] *nf* (**a**) *(magasin)* *Br* haberdasher's (shop), *Am* notions store (**b**) *(articles)* *Br* haberdashery, *Am* notions

merchandising [mɛrʃɑ̃dajziŋ] *nm* merchandising

merci [mɛrsi] **1** *exclam* thank you, thanks (**de** *ou* **pour** for); **(non) m.** no thank you, no thanks; **dire m. (à qn)** to say thank you *or* thanks (to sb); **m. bien, m. beaucoup** thank you *or* thanks very much
   2 *nm* thank you
   3 *nf* **être à la m. de qn/qch** to be at the mercy of sb/sth; **sans m.** merciless

mercier, -ère [mɛrsje, -ɛr] *nm,f Br* haberdasher, *Am* notions dealer

mercredi [mɛrkrədi] *nm* Wednesday; **le m. des Cendres** Ash Wednesday; *voir aussi* **samedi**

Mercure [mɛrkyr] *npr (dieu, planète)* Mercury

mercure [mɛrkyr] *nm* mercury

Mercurochrome® [mɛrkyrɔkrom] *nm* Mercurochrome®

merde [mɛrd] *Vulg* **1** *nf* shit; *Fig* **être dans la m.** to be in the shit; **ne pas se prendre pour de la m.** to think the sun shines out of one's arse; **c'est de la m.** *(c'est de la mauvaise qualité)* it's shit; **de m.** *(voiture, idée)* shitty
   2 *exclam* shit!; *Fig* **dire m. à qn** *(l'envoyer au diable)* to tell sb to bugger off; **je te dis m.!** *(bonne chance)* break a leg!; **m. alors!** oh shit!

merder [mɛrde] *vi très Fam (ne pas fonctionner) (projet)* to go down the pan; **ça merde entre eux** things between them are really screwed up; **j'ai merdé à l'examen** I really screwed up in the exam

merdeux, -euse [mɛrdø, -øz] *très Fam* **1** *adj* **se sentir m.** to feel shitty
   2 *nm,f (enfant)* **un petit m.** a little shit

merdier [mɛrdje] *nm Vulg* **être dans le m.** to be in the shit

merdique [mɛrdik] *adj très Fam* shitty

mère [mɛr] **1** *adj voir* **maison**
   2 *nf* (**a**) *(parent)* mother; **elle est m. de trois enfants** she is the mother of three children; **m. célibataire** single mother; **être m. de famille** to be a wife and mother; **m. nourricière** foster mother; **m. patrie**

mother country, motherland; **m. porteuse** surrogate mother; **m. poule** mother hen (**b**) *Fam (femme)* **la m. Martin** old Mrs Martin

merguez [mɛrgɛz] *nf* merguez *(spicy North African sausage)*

méridien, -enne [meridjɛ̃, -ɛn] **1** *adj (ligne)* meridian, meridional
  2 *nm Géog* meridian
  3 *nf* **méridienne** *(canapé)* day bed

méridional, -e, -aux, -ales [meridjɔnal, -o] **1** *adj (du Sud)* southern; *(du sud de la France)* from the South of France
  2 *nm,f (du Sud)* southerner; *(du sud de la France)* person from the South of France

meringue [mərɛ̃g] *nf* meringue

mérinos [merinos] *nm* (**a**) *Zool* merino (**b**) *Tex* **(laine** *f*) **m.** merino wool

merisier [mərizje] *nm (arbre)* wild cherry (tree); *(bois)* cherry(wood)

méritant, -e [meritɑ̃, -ɑ̃t] *adj* deserving

mérite [merit] *nm* merit; *(honneur)* credit; **avoir du m. (à faire qch)** to deserve credit (for doing sth); **au moins, son livre a le m. de la clarté** at least her book has the merit of being clearly written; **tout le m. lui revient** he deserves all the credit

mériter [merite] *vt* (**a**) *(après une action)* to deserve; **m. d'être puni/récompensé** to deserve to be punished/rewarded; **elle mérite qu'on le lui dise** she deserves to be told (**b**) *(demander)* to be worth; **m. réflexion** to be worth thinking about; **ce livre mérite d'être lu** this book is worth reading

méritoire [meritwar] *adj* commendable, praiseworthy

merlan [mɛrlɑ̃] *nm* (**a**) *(poisson)* whiting (**b**) *très Fam (coiffeur)* hairdresser

merle [mɛrl] *nm* blackbird

merlu [mɛrly] *nm* hake

mérou [meru] *nm* grouper

mérovingien, -enne [merɔvɛ̃ʒjɛ̃, -ɛn] **1** *adj* Merovingian
  2 *nmpl* **les Mérovingiens** the Merovingians

merveille [mɛrvɛj] *nf* (**a**) *(chose remarquable)* marvel, wonder; **à m.** wonderfully (well); **se porter à m.** to be in the best of health; *Fig* **faire des merveilles** to work wonders; **les Sept Merveilles du monde** the Seven Wonders of the World (**b**) *(gâteau)* = sweet fritter

merveilleusement [mɛrvɛjøzmɑ̃] *adv* marvellously, wonderfully

merveilleux, -euse [mɛrvɛjø, -øz] **1** *adj* marvellous, wonderful
  2 *nm* **le m.** the supernatural

mes [me] *voir* **mon**

mésalliance [mezaljɑ̃s] *nf* unsuitable marriage; **faire une m.** to marry beneath oneself

mésallier [66] [mezalje] **se mésallier** *vpr* to marry beneath oneself

mésange [mezɑ̃ʒ] *nf* tit; **m. bleue** blue tit; **m. charbonnière** coal tit

mésaventure [mezavɑ̃tyr] *nf* misadventure

mesdames [medam] *nfpl voir* **madame**

mésentente [mezɑ̃tɑ̃t] *nf* disagreement

mésestimer [mezɛstime] *vt* to underestimate

mésothérapie [mezoterapi] *nf* = treatment consisting of injecting minute quantities of medication into the affected area

mesquin, -e [mɛskɛ̃, -in] *adj* mean, petty

mesquinement [mɛskinmɑ̃] *adv* meanly

mesquinerie [mɛskinri] *nf* (**a**) *(d'un caractère, d'un procédé)* meanness, pettiness (**b**) *(action)* mean *or* petty thing (to do)

mess [mɛs] *nm* mess

message [mesaʒ] *nm* message; *Ordinat* **m. d'accueil** welcome message; *Ordinat* **m. d'alerte** warning message, alert box; *Ordinat* **m. électronique** e-mail; **envoyer un m. électronique à qn** to e-mail sb; *Ordinat* **m. d'erreur** error message; *Ordinat* **m. d'invite** *(du système)* prompt; **m. publicitaire** advertisement; **m. texte** text message

messager, -ère [mesaʒe, -ɛr] *nm,f* messenger

messagerie [mesaʒri] *nf* (**a**) *(service de transports)* courier company; **messageries aériennes** air freight company (**b**) *(service télématique)* **m. électronique** electronic mail service, e-mail; **m. vocale** voice mail (**c**) *(entreprise de routage)* **m. de presse** newspaper distributing service

messe [mɛs] *nf (office religieux, composition musicale)* mass; **aller à la m.** to go to mass; *Fig* **faire des messes basses** to whisper; **m. de minuit** midnight mass

messeigneurs [mesɛɲœr] *nmpl voir* **monseigneur**

Messie [mesi] *nm* **le M.** the Messiah

messieurs [mesjø] *nmpl voir* **monsieur**

mesurable [məzyrabl] *adj* measurable

mesure [məzyr] *nf* (**a**) *(dimension)* measurement; *(action)* measurement, measuring; **prendre les mesures de qn/qch** to measure sb/sth; *Fig* **prendre la m. de qn/qch** to size sb/sth up; **sur m.** *(costume)* made to measure; *(rôle, emploi)* ideal; **donner toute sa m.** to show what one is capable of; **être à la m. de qn/qch** to measure up to sb/sth; **être sans commune m. avec qch** to be out of proportion to sth; **elle a trouvé quelqu'un/un homme à sa m.** she met her match
  (**b**) *(moyen)* measure; **prendre des mesures** to take measures; **m. de sécurité** safety measure *or* precaution; **par m. d'économie** as a way to save money
  (**c**) *(quantité, unité)* measure; **sans commune m.** unrivalled
  (**d**) *(modération)* moderation; **sans m.** *(ambition, jalousie)* limitless
  (**e**) *Mus (temps)* time; *(division)* bar; **m. à quatre temps** four-four time, common time; **battre la m.** to beat time; **en m.** in time
  (**f**) *(locutions)* **à m. que** as; **(au fur et) à m.** as one goes along; **dans une certaine m.** to some *or* a certain extent; **dans une large m.** to a large extent; **dans la m. où** in so far as; **dans la m. du possible** as far as is possible; **être en m. de faire qch** to be in a position to do sth

mesuré, -e [məzyre] *adj (pas)* measured; *(langage, personne)* restrained

mesurer [məzyre] **1** *vt* (**a**) *(dimensions, taille)* to measure; *(tissu)* to measure off (**b**) *(déterminer)* to assess (**c**) *(limiter)* to limit; **m. l'argent à qn** to ration out money to sb (**d**) **m. ses paroles** to moderate one's language
  2 *vi* to measure; **m. 2 mètres** *(personne)* to be 2 metres tall; *(tour, colonne)* to be 2 metres high
  3 se mesurer *vpr* **se m. avec** *ou* **à qn** to pit oneself against sb

met *voir* **mettre**

métabolique [metabɔlik] *adj* metabolic

métabolisme [metabɔlism] *nm* metabolism

métairie [meteri] *nf* small farm *(worked by share-cropper)*

métal, -aux [metal, -o] *nm* metal

métallique [metalik] *adj* metallic

métallisé, -e [metalize] *adj (peinture, couleur)* metallic

métallo [metalo] *nm Fam* metalworker

métallurgie [metalyrʒi] *nf* (**a**) *(industrie)* metallurgical industry (**b**) *(procédé)* metallurgy

métallurgique [metalyrʒik] *adj* metallurgical

métallurgiste [metalyrʒist] *nm* (**a**) *(ouvrier)* metalworker (**b**) *(chef d'entreprise)* metallurgist

métamorphose [metamɔrfoz] *nf aussi Fig* metamorphosis

métamorphoser [metamɔrfoze] **1** *vt* to transform (**en** into)
  2 se métamorphoser *vpr Biol* to metamorphose; *Fig* to be transformed (**en** into)

métaphore [metafɔr] *nf* metaphor

métaphorique [metafɔrik] *adj* metaphorical

métaphoriquement [metafɔrikmɑ̃] *adv* metaphorically

métaphysique [metafizik] **1** *adj* metaphysical
  2 *nf* metaphysics *(singulier)*

métastase [metastɑz] *nf* metastasis

métayer, -ère [meteje, -ɛr] *nm,f* sharecropper

météo [meteo] *Fam* **1** *adj* weather
  2 *nf (bulletin)* weather forecast; *(organisme) Br* weather centre, *Am* weather bureau

météore [meteɔr] *nm* meteor

météorite [meteɔrit] *nf* meteorite

météorologie [meteɔrɔlɔʒi] *nf* meteorology

météorologique [meteɔrɔlɔʒik] *adj (bulletin, prévisions)* weather

météorologiste [meteɔrɔlɔʒist], **météorologue** [meteɔrɔlɔg] *nmf* meteorologist

métèque [metɛk] *nm* = racist term used to refer to any dark-skinned foreigner living in France, especially one from the Mediterranean

méthadone [metadɔn] *nf* methadone

méthane [metan] *nm* methane

méthanol [metanɔl] *nm* methanol

méthode [metɔd] *nf* (**a**) *(démarche)* method; **m. pour faire qch** method of doing sth (**b**) *(ordre)* method; **avec m.** methodically (**c**) *(livre)* book; **m. d'anglais** English course book; **m. de piano** piano tutor

méthodique [metɔdik] *adj* methodical

méthodiquement [metɔdikmɑ̃] *adv* methodically

méthodiste [metɔdist] *adj & nmf* Methodist

méthodologie [metɔdɔlɔʒi] *nf* methodology

méthodologique [metɔdɔlɔʒik] *adj* methodological

méthylène [metilɛn] *nm* methylene

méticuleusement [metikyløzmɑ̃] *adv* meticulously

méticuleux, -euse [metikylø, -øz] *adj* meticulous

méticulosité [metikylozite] *nf* meticulousness

métier [metje] *nm* (**a**) *(manuel, commercial)* trade; *(intellectuel)* profession; **exercer un m.** to have a job; **j'exerce le m. de journaliste** I'm a journalist by profession; **quel m. veux-tu faire plus tard?** what do you want to be when you grow up?; **il n'est pas** *ou* **il n'y a pas de sot m.** a job's a job; **être du m.** to be in the business; **connaître son m.** to know what one is doing (**b**) *(savoir-faire, expérience)* experience; **avoir du m.** to have experience; **elle a plusieurs années de**

m. she has several years' experience (**c**) *(machine)* **m. à tisser** loom

métis, -isse [metis] **1** *adj (personne)* half-caste
  2 *nm,f (personne)* half-caste
  3 *nm (tissu)* linen and cotton mixture

métissage [metisaʒ] *nm* crossbreeding

métisser [metise] *vt* to cross(breed); **une population très métissée** a highly intermixed population; **musique métissée** crossover *or* fusion music

métrage [metraʒ] *nm* (**a**) *(action)* measuring (**b**) *(coupon de tissu)* length (**c**) *(longueur d'un film)* footage, length; **long/moyen/court m.** feature/medium-length/short film

mètre¹ [mɛtr] *nm* (**a**) *(unité de longueur)* metre; **m. carré/cube** square/cubic metre (**b**) *(pour mesurer)* tape measure; *(en bois, en métal)* rule; **m. à ruban** tape measure

mètre² *nm (en poésie)* metre

métreur [metrœr] *nm* quantity surveyor

métrique¹ [metrik] *adj (système)* metric

métrique² **1** *adj (en poésie)* metrical
  2 *nf* metrics *(singulier)*

métro [metro] *nm Br* underground, *Am* subway; **le premier/dernier m.** the first/last train; **m. aerien** elevated *or* overhead railway

métronome [metrɔnɔm] *nm* metronome

métropole [metrɔpɔl] *nf* (**a**) *(grande ville)* metropolis (**b**) *(pays)* mother country

métropolitain, -e [metrɔpɔlitɛ̃, -ɛn] **1** *adj (non insulaire)* metropolitan
  2 *nm Vieilli (métro) Br* underground, *Am* subway

mets¹ [mɛ] *voir* **mettre**

mets² *nm* dish

mettable [metabl] *adj* wearable

mette *etc voir* **mettre**

metteur [metœr] *nm* **m. en scène** director

mettre [47] [mɛtr] **1** *vt* (**a**) *(placer)* to put; **m. qch sur/dans qch** to put sth on/in sth; **m. qn à mal** *(verbalement)* to berate sb; *(physiquement)* to beat sb up
  (**b**) *(vêtement, chaussures, lunettes, pansement)* to put on
  (**c**) *(moquette)* to lay; *(papier peint, étagères)* to put up
  (**d**) *(allumer)* to put on, to switch on; **m. qch en marche** to turn sth on; **m. qch plus fort** to turn sth up; **m. de la musique** to put some music on; **m. le réveil (à cinq heures)** to set the alarm (for five o'clock); **faire m. le téléphone** to get the phone put in
  (**e**) **elle y a mis beaucoup d'argent** she's spent a lot of money on it
  (**f**) **elle a mis du temps/deux ans à le faire** it took her a while/two years to do it; **combien de temps met-on pour y aller?** how long does it take to get there?
  (**g**) **ça va prendre, mettons, trois mois** it will take, (let's) say, three months; **mettons que je n'ai rien dit** pretend I didn't say anything
  (**h**) *(écrire)* to put
  (**i**) *Fam* **qu'est-ce qu'on leur a mis!** we really thrashed them!; **m. les bouts** *ou* **les voiles** to make a move; *Vulg* **va te faire m.!** go fuck yourself!
  2 *vi* **m. bas** to give birth
  3 se mettre *vpr* (**a**) *(se placer)* **mets-toi là!** *(va là-bas)* stand there!; *(assieds-toi là-bas)* sit there!; **se m. au soleil** *(s'asseoir)* to sit in the sun; *(s'allonger)* to lie in the sun; **se m. au lit** to get into bed; **se m. sur le dos/**

ventre to lie on one's back/stomach; *(en se tournant)* to turn (over) onto one's back/stomach; *Belg* **mettez-vous!** take a seat!, sit down!; *Fig* **se m. en avant** to push oneself forward; *Fig* **je ne savais plus où me m.** I didn't know where to put myself
(**b**) *(maquillage, vêtement)* to put on; **je n'ai plus rien à me m.** I haven't a thing to wear
(**c**) *(commencer)* **se m. à qch** *(activité)* to take sth up; **se m. au travail** to get (down) to work; **se m. à faire qch** to begin *or* to start doing sth; **le temps s'est mis à la pluie** it turned to rain; *Fam* **si tu t'y mets aussi!** don't YOU start!
(**d**) **il a fallu se m. à trois pour la déplacer** it took three of us to move it
(**e**) *Fam* **qu'est-ce qu'ils se sont mis!** they really laid into each other!

meuble [mœbl] **1** *adj* (**a**) *(sol, terre, roche)* soft (**b**) *(biens)* movable
2 *nm* piece of furniture; **meubles** furniture; **être dans ses meubles** to have a place of one's own; *Fam* **faire partie des meubles** to be part of the furniture

meublé, -e [mœble] **1** *adj* furnished; **non m.** unfurnished
2 *nm* *(chambre)* furnished room; *(appartement)* furnished *Br* flat *or Am* apartment

meubler [mœble] **1** *vt* (**a**) *(pièce, maison)* to furnish (**de** with) (**b**) *(remplir)* to fill (**de** with); **m. la conversation** to make conversation
2 se meubler *vpr* to furnish one's home

meuf [mœf] *nf très Fam Br* bird, *Am* chick

meuglement [møgləmã] *nm* moo; **des meuglements** mooing

meugler [møgle] *vi* to moo

meule [møl] *nf* (**a**) *(d'herbe, de céréales)* stack; **m. de foin** haystack (**b**) *(de moulin)* millstone (**c**) *(de fromage)* round

meunier, -ère [mønje, -ɛr] **1** *adj* (**a**) *(industrie)* flour-milling (**b**) **(à la) meunière** *(poisson)* = coated with flour and fried in butter
2 *nm,f* miller, *f* miller's wife

meurs, meurt *voir* **mourir**

meurtre [mœrtr] *nm* murder

meurtri, -e [mœrtri] *adj* bruised

meurtrier, -ère [mœrtrije, -ɛr] **1** *adj (guerre, attentat, colère)* murderous; *(arme, épidémie)* deadly
2 *nm,f* murderer
3 *nf* **meurtrière** *Archit* loophole

meurtrir [mœrtrir] *vt* to bruise

meurtrissure [mœrtrisyr] *nf* bruise

meute [møt] *nf aussi Fig* pack

MEV [mɛv] *nf Ordinat (abrév* **mémoire vive)** RAM

mexicain, -e [mɛksikɛ̃, -ɛn] **1** *adj* Mexican
2 *nm,f* **M.** Mexican

Mexico [mɛksiko] *n* Mexico City

Mexique [mɛksik] *nm* **le M.** Mexico

mézigue [mezig] *pron personnel Fam* yours truly

mezzanine [mɛdzanin] *nf* (**a**) *(entre deux étages)* mezzanine (floor) (**b**) *(au théâtre) Br* dress circle, *Am* mezzanine

mezzo-soprano *(pl* **mezzo-sopranos)** [mɛdzo-soprano] **1** *nm (voix)* mezzo-soprano
2 *nf (cantatrice)* mezzo-soprano

MF [ɛmɛf] *nf Rad (abrév* **modulation de fréquence)** FM

mg *(abrév* **milligramme(s)**) mg

Mgr *Rel (abrév* **Monseigneur)** Mgr

mi [mi] *nm inv (note)* E; *(chantée)* mi

mi- [mi] *adv* **la mi-avril** mid-April; **à mi-hauteur** *(en montant)* halfway up; *(en descendant)* halfway down; **elle avait de l'eau jusqu'à mi-jambe** the water was halfway up her legs; **mi-amusé, mi-intrigué** half-amused, half-puzzled; **mi-figue, mi-raisin** *(sourire)* half-hearted; *(plaisanterie)* half-serious

miam-miam [mjammjam] *exclam* yum yum!

miaou [mjau] *exclam* miaow!

miasme [mjasm] *nm* miasma

miaulement [mjolmã] *nm* miaowing

miauler [mjole] *vi* to miaow

mi-bas [miba] *nm inv (en laine)* knee sock; *(en voile)* popsock

mica [mika] *nm* mica

mi-carême *(pl* **mi-carêmes)** [mikarɛm] *nf* = third Thursday in Lent

miche [miʃ] *nf* (**a**) *(pain)* round loaf (**b**) *Fam* **miches** *(fesses) Br* bum, *Am* butt

Michel-Ange [mikɛlãʒ] *npr* Michelangelo

micheline [miʃlin] *nf* railcar

mi-chemin [miʃmɛ̃] **à mi-chemin** *adv* halfway

Michigan [miʃigã] *n voir* **lac**

mi-clos, -e *(mpl* **mi-clos,** *fpl* **mi-closes)** [miklo, mikloz] *adj* half-closed

micmac [mikmak] *nm Fam* (**a**) *(complications)* muddle (**b**) *Can (désordre)* mess

mi-côte [mikot] **à mi-côte** *adv* halfway up the hill

mi-course [mikurs] **à mi-course** *adv* at the halfway mark

micro [mikro] **1** *nm* (**a**) *(microphone)* mike (**b**) *Ordinat* micro(computer)
2 *nf Ordinat* microcomputing

microbe [mikrɔb] *nm* (**a**) *(germe)* microbe, germ (**b**) *Fam (personne chétive)* little squirt

microbien, -enne [mikrɔbjɛ̃, -ɛn] *adj* microbial

microbiologie [mikrɔbjɔlɔʒi] *nf* microbiology

microchirurgie [mikroʃiryrʒi] *nf* microsurgery

microcircuit [mikrosirkɥi] *nm Ordinat* microcircuit; **microcircuits** microcircuitry

microclimat [mikroklima] *nm* microclimate

microcosme [mikrɔkɔsm] *nm* microcosm

microéconomie [mikroekɔnɔmi] *nf* microeconomics *(singulier)*

microéconomique [mikroekɔnɔmik] *adj* microeconomic

microédition [mikroedisjɔ̃] *nf Ordinat* desktop publishing, DTP

microfiche [mikrofiʃ] *nf* microfiche

microfilm [mikrofilm] *nm* microfilm

micro-informatique [mikroɛ̃fɔrmatik] *nf Ordinat* microcomputing

micron [mikrɔ̃] *nm* micron

Micronésie [mikronezi] *nf* **la M.** Micronesia

micro-ondes [mikroɔ̃d] *nm inv* microwave

micro-ordinateur *(pl* **micro-ordinateurs)** [mikro-ɔrdinatœr] *nm Ordinat* microcomputer

micro-organisme *(pl* **micro-organismes)** [mikro-ɔrganism] *nm* micro-organism

microphone [mikrɔfɔn] *nm* microphone

micropilule [mikropilyl] *nf* mini pill

microprocesseur [mikroprɔsɛsœr] *nm Ordinat* microprocessor

microscope [mikrɔskɔp] *nm* microscope; **au m.** under a microscope; **m. électronique** electron microscope

microscopique [mikrɔskɔpik] *adj* microscopic

microsillon [mikrɔsijɔ̃] *nm (de disque)* groove

micro-trottoir [mikrotrɔtwar] *(pl* micros-trottoirs) *nm* street interview, *Br* vox pop

midi [midi] *nm* (**a**) *(heure)* twelve o'clock, midday; **m. et demie** half past twelve; **entre m. et deux** at lunchtime (**b**) *(moment du déjeuner)* lunchtime (**c**) *(partie sud)* south; **le M. (de la France)** the South of France

midinette [midinɛt] *nf* silly young girl

mi-distance [midistãs] **à mi-distance** *adv* halfway (**de** in)

mie [mi] *nf (de pain)* soft part

miel [mjɛl] *nm* honey

mielleusement [mjɛløzmã] *adv (parler)* in honeyed tones

mielleux, -euse [mjɛlø, -øz] *adj (discours, sourire)* sugary; *(personne)* smooth

mien, mienne [mjɛ̃, mjɛn] **1** *pron possessif* **le m., la mienne, les miens, les miennes** mine; *(en insistant)* my own; **je te prête le m.** you can borrow mine; **je n'en ai pas besoin, j'ai le m.** I don't need it, I've got my own
2 *nm* **j'y ai mis du m.** I did my share
3 *nmpl* **les miens** *(ma famille)* my family

miette [mjɛt] *nf (de pain, de gâteau)* crumb; *Fig* **en miettes** in pieces; **mettre qch en miettes** *(briser)* to smash sth to pieces; **ne pas perdre une m. de qch** *(conversation)* not to miss a word of sth; **après le partage, ma cousine n'a eu que des miettes** my cousin had to make do with what little was left over after the inheritance was shared out

mieux [mjø] **1** *adv* (**a**) *(comparatif)* better; **m. que** better than; **il vaut m. les surveiller** it's best to watch them; **vous feriez m. de m'écouter** you'd do better to listen to me; **elle va m.** she's (feeling) better; **c'est on ne peut m.** it couldn't be better; **j'espérais m. de votre part** I expected better of you; **plus on se voit et m. on s'apprécie** the more we see each other, the more we like each other; **de m. en m.** better and better; **faire qch à qui m. m.** to try to outdo each other in doing sth (**b**) *(superlatif)* **c'est elle qui s'exprime le m.** she expresses herself (the) best; **le plus tôt sera le m.** the sooner the better; **le m. serait de…** the best thing would be to…; **ils s'entendent le m. du monde** they get on extremely well; **être au m. avec qn** to be on the best of terms with sb; **un service des m. organisés** an extremely well-organized department
2 *adj* better; *(plus beau)* better-looking; **si tu n'as rien de m. à faire** if you've nothing better to do; **c'est le m. (de tous)** *(le plus beau)* he's the best-looking (of all)
3 *nm* **espérer m.** to hope for better things; **il y a un m. ou du m.** there's been a change for the better; **faire ou agir pour le m.** to act for the best; **faire de son m.** to do one's best; **fais du m. que tu peux** do the best you can

mièvre [mjɛvr] *adj* insipid

mièvrerie [mjɛvrəri] *nf* insipidness

mignon, -onne [miɲɔ̃, -ɔn] **1** *adj* (**a**) *(joli, charmant)* cute (**b**) *(gentil)* nice
2 *nm (favori)* minion
3 *nm,f* **mon m.** darling

migraine [migrɛn] *nf (douleur violente)* migraine; *(mal de tête)* headache; **avoir des migraines** to get migraines/headaches

migraineux, -euse [migrɛnø, -øz] *nm,f* migraine sufferer

migrant, -e [migrã, -ãt] *adj & nm,f* migrant

migrateur, -trice [migratœr, -tris] *adj (animaux)* migratory

migration [migrasjɔ̃] *nf* migration

migratoire [migratwar] *adj* migratory

migrer [migre] *vi aussi Ordinat* to migrate (**vers** to)

mijaurée [miʒɔre] *nf (jeune fille)* affected girl; **faire la ou sa m.** to give oneself airs

mijoter [miʒɔte] **1** *vt* (**a**) *(faire cuire)* to simmer; *(préparer avec soin)* to cook up (**b**) *(tramer)* to cook up
2 *vi* to simmer; **faire m.** to simmer

mikado [mikado] *nm (jeu)* jack-straws, spillikins

mil¹ [mil] *adj inv* **l'an m.** the year one thousand

mil² [mij, mil] *nm (céréale)* millet

Milan [milã] *n* Milan

mildiou [mildju] *nm (des céréales)* mildew; *(de la vigne)* brown rot

mile [majl] *nm* mile

milice [milis] *nf* militia

milicien, -enne [milisjɛ̃, -ɛn] *nm,f* militiaman, *f* militiawoman

milieu, -x [miljø] *nm* (**a**) *(centre)* middle; **au m. de** in the middle of; **en plein ou au beau m. de qch** right in the middle of sth; **la table du m.** the middle table (**b**) *(environnement)* environment; *(social)* background; *Phys* medium; **le m. familial** the home environment; **dans les milieux autorisés** in official circles (**c**) *(position intermédiaire)* middle course; **le juste m.** the happy medium (**d**) *(pègre)* **le m.** the underworld

militaire [militɛr] **1** *adj* military; *(port)* naval
2 *nm* serviceman; **m. de carrière** professional soldier

militant, -e [militã, -ãt] *adj & nm,f* militant

militantisme [militãtism] *nm* militancy

militarisation [militarizasjɔ̃] *nf* militarization

militariser [militarize] *vt* to militarize

militariste [militarist] **1** *adj* militaristic
2 *nmf* militarist

militer [milite] *vi* to campaign (**pour** ou **en faveur de/contre** for/against)

milk-shake *(pl* milk-shakes) [milkʃɛk] *nm* milk shake

mille¹ [mil] **1** *adj inv* (**a**) *(cardinal)* a *ou* one thousand; **deux m.** two thousand; **l'an m.** the year one thousand (**b**) *Fig (nombreux) (exemples, occasions)* countless; **je vous l'ai dit m. fois** I've told you a thousand times; **vous avez m. fois raison** you're absolutely right; **c'est m. fois trop grand** it's far too big
2 *nm inv* (**a**) *(nombre)* a *ou* one thousand; **plusieurs centaines de m.** several hundred thousand; **cinq pour m.** five per thousand (**b**) *(locutions)* **mettre (en plein) dans le m.** to hit the bull's-eye; **gagner des m. et des cents** to make a mint; *voir aussi* **trois**

mille² *nm* **m. (marin** ou **nautique)** nautical mile

mille-feuille *(pl* mille-feuilles) [milfœj] *nm Br* ≃ vanilla slice, millefeuille, *Am* ≃ napoleon

millénaire [milenɛr] **1** *adj* thousand-year-old
2 *nm* millennium

mille-pattes [milpat] *nm inv* centipede, millipede

millepertuis [milpɛrtɥi] *nm* St John's wort

millésime [milezim] *nm (de vin, de voiture)* year; *(sur pièce de monnaie)* date

millésimé, -e [milezime] *adj (vin)* vintage; *(pièce de monnaie)* dated

millet [mijɛ] *nm* millet

milliard [miljar] *nm* billion

milliardaire [miljardɛr] **1** *adj* billionaire; **être m.** to be a billionaire; **être plusieurs fois m.** to be worth billions
   2 *nmf* billionaire

millibar [milibar] *nm* millibar

millième [miljɛm] *nmf, nm & adj* thousandth; *voir aussi* **cinquième**

millier [milje] *nm* thousand; **un m. de personnes** a thousand people; **des milliers de personnes** thousands of people; **par milliers** in thousands

milligramme [miligram] *nm* milligram(me)

millilitre [mililitr] *nm* millilitre

millimètre [milimɛtr] *nm* millimetre

millimétré, -e [milimetre], **millimétrique** [milimetrik] *adj voir* **papier**

million [miljɔ̃] *nm* million; **un m. de francs** a million francs; **quatre millions d'hommes** four million men; **par millions** in millions

millionnaire [miljɔnɛr] **1** *adj* millionaire; **être m.** to be a millionaire
   2 *nmf* millionaire

millivolt [milivɔlt] *nm* millivolt

mime [mim] **1** *nm (art)* mime
   2 *nmf (artiste)* mime (artist)

mimer [mime] *vt* (**a**) *(exprimer)* to mime (**b**) *(imiter)* to mimic

mimétisme [mimetism] *nm* mimicry

mimi [mimi] **1** *nm (langage enfantin)* kiss; **faire un m. à qn** to give sb a kiss
   2 *adj inv Fam (mignon)* sweet

mimique [mimik] *nf* expression

mimolette [mimɔlɛt] *nf* = type of Dutch hard cheese

mimosa [mimoza] *nm* mimosa

min *(abrév* **minute(s))** min

min. *(abrév* **minimum)** min

minable [minabl] **1** *adj* (**a**) *(mesquin, pauvre)* shabby (**b**) *(incompétent, insuffisant)* pathetic
   2 *nmf* failure, loser

minaret [minarɛ] *nm* minaret

minauder [minode] *vi* to simper

minauderie [minodri] *nf* simpering; **faire des minauderies** to simper

mince [mɛ̃s] **1** *adj* (**a**) *(fin) (tranche, mur)* thin; *(taille, personne)* slim (**b**) *(insuffisant)* slight; **c'est un peu m., comme excuse!** it's a bit of a poor excuse!
   2 *exclam Fam* **m. (alors)!** *(surprise)* well, blow me!; *(déception)* blast!

minceur [mɛ̃sœr] *nf* (**a**) *(d'une tranche, d'un tissu)* thinness; *(de la taille, d'une personne)* slimness (**b**) *(insuffisance)* slightness

mincir [mɛ̃sir] *vi* to get slimmer

mine¹ [min] *nf* (**a**) *(gisement)* mine; *Fig* **une m. de renseignements** a mine of information; **m. de charbon** coalmine; *aussi Fig* **m. d'or** goldmine (**b**) *(de crayon)* lead (**c**) *(explosif)* mine (**d**) **les Mines** = government department responsible for supervising all construction projects involving tunnelling; **École des Mines**, *Fam* **les Mines** = university-level institute for geological engineers

mine² *nf* (**a**) *(expression)* look; **avoir bonne/mauvaise m.** to look well/ill; **avoir une m. de papier mâché** *ou* **de déterré** to look like death warmed up; **faire** *ou* **avoir triste m.** to look down in the dumps; **faire grise m.** not to look pleased; **faire m. de faire qch** to make as if to do sth (**b**) *(allure)* appearance; **juger les gens sur la m.** to judge people by appearances; *Fam* **ne pas payer de m.** not to be much to look at; *Fam* **m. de rien, il n'est pas bête** you wouldn't think it to look at him, but he's not stupid (**c**) *Péj* **mines** *(simagrées)* faces; **faire des mines** to make faces

miner¹ [mine] *vt* (**a**) *(creuser)* to eat away (**b**) *(ruiner moralement)* to wear down

miner² *vt (poser des explosifs dans)* to mine

minerai [minrɛ] *nm* ore; **m. de fer** iron ore

minéral, -e, -aux, -ales [mineral, -o] *adj & nm* mineral

minéralogique [mineralɔʒik] *adj* (**a**) **plaque m.** *Br* number or *Am* license plate (**b**) *Géol* mineralogical

minerve [minɛrv] *nf* (surgical) collar

minestrone [minɛstron] *nm* minestrone

minet, -ette [minɛ, -ɛt] *nm,f Fam* (**a**) *(chat)* pussy cat (**b**) *(personne coquette)* trendy

mineur¹ [minœr] *nm (ouvrier)* miner; **m. de fond** underground worker

mineur², -e 1 *adj* (**a**) *(secondaire)* minor (**b**) *(qui n'a pas la majorité légale)* underage (**c**) *Mus* minor
   2 *nm,f* minor

mini [mini] *Fam* **1** *adj inv (jupe, robe)* mini
   2 *nm* (**a**) *(mode)* **le m.** miniskirts (**b**) *(mini-ordinateur)* mini

miniature [minjatyr] **1** *nf* miniature; **en m.** in miniature
   2 *adj* miniature

miniaturiser [minjatyrize] *vt* to miniaturize

minibus [minibys] *nm* minibus

minichaîne [miniʃɛn] *nf* mini-hifi

MiniDisc® [minidisk] *nm* MiniDisc®

minier, -ère [minje, -ɛr] *adj* mining

minigolf [minigɔlf] *nm* crazy golf

minijupe [miniʒyp] *nf* miniskirt

minima [minima] *voir* **minimum**

minimal, -e, -aux, -ales [minimal, -o] *adj* minimum; *(art)* minimal

minimaliste [minimalist] *adj & nmf* minimalist

minime [minim] **1** *adj* minimal
   2 *nmf Sport* junior *(13 to 15 years old)*

mini-message [minimesaʒ] *nm* text message

minimex [minimɛks] *nm Belg (abrév* **minimum de moyens d'existence)** *Br* ≃ income support, *Am* ≃ welfare

minimiser [minimize] *vt* to minimize

minimum [minimɔm] *(pl* **minimums** *ou* **minima** [minima]) **1** *adj* minimum
   2 *nm* minimum; **avec un m. d'efforts** with a minimum of effort; **en un m. de temps** in as short a time as possible; **réduire qch au m.** to minimize sth; **faire le m. (pour faire qch)** to do the bare minimum (to do sth); **c'est vraiment le m. que tu puisses faire pour elle** it's the very least you can do for her; **au m.** at the very least; **le m. vital** a minimum to live on; **le strict m.** the absolute minimum; **m. vieillesse** basic state pension

mini-ordinateur *(pl* **mini-ordinateurs)** [miniɔrdinatœr] *nm* minicomputer

minipilule [minipilyl] *nf* mini pill

mini-slip [minislip] (*pl* **mini-slips**) *nm* tanga

ministère [ministεr] *nm* (**a**) (*département*) government department, *Br* ministry; **m. des Affaires étrangères** *Br* ≃ Foreign Office, *Am* ≃ State Department; **m. de la Défense (nationale)** *Br* ≃ Ministry of Defence, *Am* ≃ Department of Defense; **m. de l'Éducation nationale** Department of Education (**b**) (*gouvernement*) government (**c**) *Jur* **le m. public** ≃ the Crown Prosecution Service (**d**) *Rel* ministry

ministériel, -elle [ministerjεl] *adj* (*arrêté, décret, entourage*) ministerial; (*crise, remaniement*) cabinet

ministre [ministr] *nm* (**a**) (*homme d'État*) secretary, *Br* minister; **m. des Affaires étrangères** *Br* ≃ Foreign Secretary, *Am* ≃ Secretary of State; **m. de la Défense (nationale)** ≃ Secretary of State for Defence; **m. de l'Éducation nationale** ≃ Secretary of State for Education; **m. d'État** ≃ secretary of state, *Br* ≃ cabinet minister; **Premier m.** Prime Minister; *Can* (*d'une province*) Premier (**b**) (*pasteur*) minister; **m. du culte** minister

Minitel® [minitεl] *nm* = consumer information network accessible via home computer terminal; **le M. rose** = dating and erotic entertainment service available on Minitel®

Minitel®

The domestic viewdata service run by France Télécom has become a familiar part of French life. The basic monitor and keyboard are given free of charge, and the subscriber is charged for the services used on his or her ordinary telephone bill. The subscriber dials a four-figure number (typically 3615); a code word then gives access to the particular service required. Some Minitel® services are purely informative (the weather, road conditions, news etc); others are interactive (enabling users to carry out bank transactions, book tickets for travel, register for and obtain the results of nationwide examinations, for example).
The Minitel® also serves as an electronic telephone directory. Nowadays the services offered by Minitel® are increasingly available on the Internet.

---

minitéliste [minitelist] *nmf* Minitel® user

minois [minwa] *nm* pretty face

minorer [minɔre] *vt* (**a**) (*minimiser*) to downplay (**b**) (*faire baisser*) to reduce

minoritaire [minɔritεr] *adj* minority; **être m.** to be in the minority

minorité [minɔrite] *nf* (**a**) (*de choses, de personnes*) minority; **être en m.** to be in the minority; **m. ethnique** ethnic minority (**b**) (*avant la majorité légale*) minority

Minorque [minɔrk] *n* Minorca

minorquin, -e [minɔrkε̃, -in] **1** *adj* Minorcan **2** *nm,f* **M.** Minorcan

minoterie [minɔtri] *nf* (*moulin*) flour mill; (*activité*) flour-milling

minou [minu] *nm* (**a**) *Fam* (*chat*) pussy cat (**b**) *Can* (*boule de poussière*) piece of fluff, *Am* dust ball *or* kitten

Minsk [minsk] *n* Minsk

minuit [minɥi] *nm* midnight, twelve o'clock

minuscule [minyskyl] **1** *adj* (**a**) (*très petit*) tiny, minute (**b**) (*lettre*) small **2** *nf* small letter

minute [minyt] **1** *nf* (**a**) (*unité de temps*) minute; **une m. de silence** a minute's silence; **de dernière m.** last-minute; **faire qch à la m.** to do sth this very minute; **d'une m. à l'autre** any minute (**b**) (*court moment*) minute, moment; **la m. de vérité** the moment of truth; **m.!** hold on a minute! (**c**) (*de contrat*) minute; (*d'acte notarié, de jugement*) record
2 *adj* (*sur panneau*) **nettoyage m.** dry-cleaning while you wait; **talons m.** heel bar

minuter [minyte] *vt* to time

minuterie [minytri] *nf* (*pour l'éclairage*) time switch; (*d'un four*) timer

minuteur [minytœr] *nm* timer

minutie [minysi] *nf* meticulousness; **avec m.** meticulously

minutieusement [minysjøzmɑ̃] *adv* meticulously

minutieux, -euse [minysjø, -øz] *adj* meticulous

mioche [mjɔʃ] *nmf Fam* kid

MIPS [mips] *nm Ordinat* (*abrév* **million d'instructions par seconde**) MIPS

mirabelle [mirabεl] *nf* mirabelle plum

miracle [mirakl] **1** *nm* miracle; **faire un m.** to perform a miracle; *Fig* **faire des miracles** to work miracles; **par m.** by a miracle, miraculously
2 *adj inv* miracle

miraculé, -e [mirakyle] **1** *adj* (*malade*) miraculously cured; (*rescapé*) miraculously saved
2 *nm,f* (*malade*) miraculously cured person; (*rescapé*) miraculous survivor

miraculeusement [mirakyløzmɑ̃] *adv* miraculously

miraculeux, -euse [mirakylø, -øz] *adj* miraculous

mirador [miradɔr] *nm* watchtower

mirage [miraʒ] *nm* mirage

mire [mir] *nf* test card

mirer [mire] **se mirer** *vpr Litt* (**a**) (*se regarder*) to gaze at oneself (**b**) (*se refléter*) to be reflected

mirettes [mirεt] *nfpl Fam* eyes

mirifique [mirifik] *adj* wonderful

miro [miro] *adj Fam* short-sighted

mirobolant, -e [mirɔbɔlɑ̃, -ɑ̃t] *adj* fabulous

miroir [mirwar] *nm* mirror; *Fig* **m. aux alouettes** lure; **m. de courtoisie** vanity mirror; **m. grossissant** magnifying mirror; **m. de poche** pocket mirror

miroiter [mirwate] *vi* to shimmer; *Fig* **faire m. qch à qn** to lure sb with the prospect of sth

miroton [mirɔtɔ̃] *nm* = beef boiled in sauce with onions

mis, -e *pp voir* **mettre**

misanthrope [mizɑ̃trɔp] **1** *adj* misanthropic **2** *nmf* misanthropist, misanthrope

mise [miz] *nf* (**a**) (*placement*) putting; **m. en accusation** committal (for trial); **m. en application** implementation; **m. en demeure** formal demand; **m. en disponibilité** leave of absence; *Can* layoff; **m. en examen** indictment; **m. à feu** (*d'une fusée*) launch; **m. de fonds** investment; **m. en garde** warning; **m. à jour** updating; **m. en liberté provisoire** release on bail; **m. à mort** killing; **m. en page(s)** page make-up; **m. à pied** suspension; *Can* layoff; **m. en place** putting into place; **m. en plis** set (*hairstyle*); **m. au point** (*d'un objectif*) focusing; (*d'une technique*) perfecting; (*d'un moteur*) tuning; (*d'un document, d'un rapport*) finalization; *Fig* **faire une m. au point** to make things clear; **m. en route** start-up; **m. en scène** *(d'une pièce de théâtre)* production; *(d'un film)* direction; **m. en service** *(d'une machine)* commissioning; **m. en vigueur** implementation

(**b**) *(habillement)* attire

(**c**) *(au jeu)* stake; *(à une vente aux enchères)* bid; *Fig* **sauver la m. à qn** to get sb out of a tight spot

(**d**) **être de m.** to be appropriate

(**e**) *Ordinat* **m. en attente des fichiers à imprimer** printer spooling; **m. en forme** formatting; **m. en mémoire** saving; **m. à niveau** upgrade; **m. en relation** *(avec un service)* log-on; **m. en réseau** networking; **m. sous tension** power-up

(**f**) *Suisse (vente)* auction (sale)

miser [mize] *vt* to stake (**sur** on); **m. sur qn/qch** *(parier)* to bet on sb/sth; *(compter sur)* to count on sb/sth; **m. sur tous les tableaux** to hedge one's bets

misérabilisme [mizerabilism] *nm* sordid realism

misérabiliste [mizerabilist] *adj* sordidly realistic

misérable [mizerabl] **1** *adj* (**a**) *(indigent) (personne)* poor; *(condition, existence)* wretched (**b**) *(pitoyable, insignifiant)* miserable

2 *nmf* (**a**) *(personne indigente)* poor wretch (**b**) *(coquin, fripouille)* scoundrel

misérablement [mizerabləmã] *adv* (**a**) *(pauvrement)* wretchedly (**b**) *(pitoyablement)* miserably

misère [mizɛr] *nf* (**a**) *(indigence)* extreme poverty; **être dans la m.** to be poverty-stricken; **être dans une m. noire** to be destitute; **salaire de m.** starvation wage (**b**) *(ennui)* trouble; **faire des misères à qn** to give sb trouble (**c**) *(vétille)* **payer qch une m.** to pay next to nothing for sth

miséreux, -euse [mizerø, -øz] *adj* poverty-stricken

miséricorde [mizerikɔrd] **1** *nf* mercy

2 *exclam Vieilli* mercy!

miséricordieux, -euse [mizerikɔrdjø, -øz] *adj* merciful (**envers** to)

misogyne [mizɔʒin] **1** *adj* misogynous

2 *nmf* misogynist

misogynie [mizɔʒini] *nf* misogyny

miss *(pl* **miss** *ou* **misses**) [mis] *nf (reine de beauté)* beauty queen; **M. Monde/France** Miss World/France

missel [misɛl] *nm* missal

missile [misil] *nm* missile

mission [misjɔ̃] *nf* (**a**) *(tâche)* mission; *(d'un employé)* task; **partir en m.** *(cadre)* to go away on business; *(diplomate)* to go off on a mission (**b**) *(groupe)* delegation; **m. scientifique** scientific expedition (**c**) *Rel (vocation, organisation)* mission; *(bâtiment)* mission (station)

missionnaire [misjɔnɛr] *adj & nmf* missionary

Mississippi [misisipi] *nm (fleuve)* **le M.** the Mississippi

missive [misiv] *nf Litt* missive

mistral [mistral] *nm* mistral

mitaine [mitɛn] *nf* fingerless glove; *Can & Suisse (moufle)* mitten

mite [mit] *nf* moth; **rongé aux mites** moth-eaten

mité, -e [mite] *adj* moth-eaten

mi-temps [mitã] **1** *nf inv (moitié)* half; *(pause)* half-time

2 *nm inv* part-time job; **travailler** *ou* **être à m.** to work part-time

miteux, -euse [mitø, -øz] *adj* shabby

mitigé, -e [mitiʒe] *adj (enthousiasme, accueil)* luke-warm; *(sentiments, impressions)* mixed

mitigeur [mitiʒœr] *nm* mixer *Br* tap *orAm* faucet

mitonner [mitɔne] **1** *vt* (**a**) *(cuire à feu doux)* to simmer (**b**) *Fig (projet)* to concoct

2 *vi* to simmer

mitoyen, -enne [mitwajɛ̃, -ɛn] *adj (mur)* party; **maisons mitoyennes** *(deux)* semi-detached houses; *(rangée)* terraced houses

mitrailler [mitraje] *vt* to machine-gun; *Fig* **m. qn de questions** to bombard sb with questions

mitraillette [mitrajɛt] *nf* submachine gun

mitrailleuse [mitrajøz] *nf* machine gun

mitre [mitr] *nf* (**a**) *(d'évêque)* mitre (**b**) *(de cheminée)* cowl

mi-voix [mivwa] **à mi-voix** *adv* in a low voice

mixage [miksaʒ] *nm* mixing

mixer¹ [mikse] *vt* (**a**) *(film)* to mix (**b**) *(ingrédients) (mélanger)* to mix; *(réduire à l'état liquide)* to blend

mixer², **mixeur** [miksœr] *nm (pour mélanger)* mixer; *(pour réduire à l'état liquide)* blender

mixité [miksite] *nf* coeducation

mixte [mikst] *adj* (**a**) *(des deux sexes)* mixed; **double m.** *(au tennis)* mixed doubles (**b**) *(combiné) (commission)* joint; *(mariage)* mixed; *(cuisinière)* gas-and-electric

mixture [mikstyr] *nf* (**a**) *(pharmaceutique)* mixture (**b**) *Fig* concoction

MJC [ɛmʒise] *nf (abrév* **maison des jeunes et de la culture**) community centre

ml *(abrév* **millilitre(s)**) ml

MLF [ɛmɛlɛf] *nm (abrév* **Mouvement de libération des femmes**) ≃ Women's Liberation Movement

Mlle *(abrév* **Mademoiselle**) Miss

Mlles *(abrév* **Mesdemoiselles**) **M. Armand et Duchêne** Miss Armand and Miss Duchêne

MM *(abrév* **Messieurs**) Messrs

mm *(abrév* **millimètre(s)**) mm

Mme *(abrév* **Madame**) Mrs

Mmes *(abrév* **Mesdames**) **M. Binoche et Huppert** Mrs Binoche and Mrs Huppert

Mo *nm Ordinat (abrév* **méga-octet(s)**) Mb

mobile [mɔbil] **1** *adj* (**a**) *(cloison)* movable; *(feuillets)* loose; *(cible)* moving (**b**) *(expression, regard)* shifting; *(visage)* lively (**c**) *(personne âgée, main d'œuvre, population)* mobile

2 *nm* (**a**) *(motif)* motive (**de** for) (**b**) *(objet décoratif)* mobile (**c**) *(objet en mouvement)* moving body (**d**) *(téléphone)* mobile (phone)

mobilier, -ère [mɔbilje, -ɛr] **1** *adj Jur* movable

2 *nm* furniture

mobilisation [mɔbilizasjɔ̃] *nf* mobilization; **m. générale** general mobilization

mobiliser [mɔbilize] **1** *vt* to mobilize; *Fig (énergie, courage)* to summon up

2 se mobiliser *vpr* to mobilize (**contre/en faveur de** against/in support of)

mobilité [mɔbilite] *nf* mobility

Mobylette® [mɔbilɛt] *nf* moped

mocassin [mɔkasɛ̃] *nm* moccasin

moche [mɔʃ] *adj Fam* (**a**) *(laid)* ugly (**b**) *(moralement)* rotten

modal, -e, -aux, -ales [mɔdal, -o] *adj* modal

modalité [mɔdalite] *nf* (**a**) *(manière)* mode; **modalités de paiement** conditions of payment (**b**) *(d'un acte juridique)* clause

mode¹ [mɔd] **1** *adj inv* **c'est très m.** it's very fashionable

2 *nf* (**a**) *(vestimentaire, de consommation)* fashion; **à la m.** fashionable; **revenir à la m.** to come back into fashion (**b**) *(manière)* **à la m. de Lyon/Provence** Lyons/Provence style

mode² *nm* (**a**) *(manière)* **m. de** means of; **m. de cuisson** cooking instructions; **m. d'emploi** instructions; **m. de paiement** means of payment; **m. de transport** mode of transport; **m. de vie** way of life (**b**) *Gram* mood (**c**) *Mus* mode (**d**) *Ordinat* mode; **m. paysage/portrait** landscape/portrait mode

modèle [mɔdɛl] **1** *adj (parfait)* model; *(appartement, maison)* show

2 *nm* (**a**) *(exemple)* model; **prendre qn pour m.** to take sb as one's model; **m. de lettre** standard letter (**b**) *(personne)* **m. de générosité/fidélité** model of generosity/fidelity; **m. de vertu** paragon of virtue (**c**) *(exemplaire) (de voiture, d'appareil)* model; *(de robe)* style; *(de tricot)* pattern; **vous n'auriez pas un plus grand m.?** do you have it in a larger size?; **m. déposé** registered design (**d**) *(d'un peintre, d'un sculpteur)* model (**e**) *(maquette)* **m. réduit** small-scale model

modeler [39] [mɔdle] **1** *vt (argile, pot)* to model; *Fig (relief, caractère, destinée)* to shape; **m. sa personnalité sur celle de qn** to model oneself on sb

2 se modeler *vpr* **se m. sur qn** to model oneself on sb

modélisme [mɔdelism] *nm* model-making

modem [mɔdɛm] *nm Ordinat* modem; **carte m.** modem card; **m. fax** fax modem

modérateur, -trice [mɔderatœr, -tris] **1** *adj* moderating

2 *nm* (**a**) *(personne)* moderator (**b**) *(de moteur)* regulator

modération [mɔderasjɔ̃] *nf* (**a**) *(retenue)* moderation; **avec m.** in moderation; **à consommer avec m.** *(dans les publicités)* drink in moderation *(health warning on all products advertising alcoholic drinks)* (**b**) *(réduction)* reduction

modéré, -e [mɔdere] *adj & nm,f* moderate

modérément [mɔderemɑ̃] *adv* moderately; *Euph* **j'ai m. apprécié sa remarque** I didn't much appreciate her remark

modérer [34] [mɔdere] **1** *vt* (**a**) *(passions, désirs, envies)* to moderate, to restrain; *Hum* **modère tes ardeurs!** control yourself!; **je te prie de m. ton langage!** please mind your language! (**b**) *(prix, vitesse)* to reduce

2 se modérer *vpr (personne)* to calm down

moderne [mɔdɛrn] **1** *adj* modern

2 *nm* **le m.** the modern style

modernisation [mɔdɛrnizasjɔ̃] *nf* modernization

moderniser [mɔdɛrnize] **1** *vt* to modernize

2 se moderniser *vpr* to modernize

modernisme [mɔdɛrnism] *nm* modernism

moderniste [mɔdɛrnist] *adj & nmf* modernist

modernité [mɔdɛrnite] *nf* modernity

modeste [mɔdɛst] **1** *adj* modest

2 *nmf* **faire le m.** to be modest

modestement [mɔdɛstəmɑ̃] *adv* modestly; **être m. logé** to live in modest surroundings

modestie [mɔdɛsti] *nf* modesty; **fausse m.** false modesty

modicité [mɔdisite] *nf* lowness

modifiable [mɔdifjabl] *adj* modifiable

modification [mɔdifikasjɔ̃] *nf* alteration, modification; **apporter** *ou* **faire une m. à qch** to make an alteration to sth

modifier [66] [mɔdifje] **1** *vt* to alter, to modify; *Gram* to modify

2 se modifier *vpr* to alter

modique [mɔdik] *adj* modest

modiste [mɔdist] *nmf* milliner

modulable [mɔdylabl] *adj (horaires)* flexible; *(éclairage, chauffage)* adjustable

modulaire [mɔdylɛr] *adj* modular

modulation [mɔdylasjɔ̃] *nf* (**a**) *(des sons, de la voix)* modulation (**b**) *(adaptation)* adjustment (**en fonction de** in relation to) (**c**) *Rad* modulation; **m. de fréquence** frequency modulation

module [mɔdyl] *nm* (**a**) *(élément d'un tout)* unit; **m. (d'enseignement)** module (**b**) *(d'un vaisseau spatial)* module; **m. lunaire/de commande** lunar/command module (**c**) *Ordinat* **m. d'extension** plug-in

moduler [mɔdyle] **1** *vt* (**a**) *(sons, amplitude, voix)* to modulate (**b**) *(adapter)* to adjust (**en fonction de** in relation to)

2 *vi* to modulate

modus vivendi [mɔdysvivɛ̃di] *nm inv* modus vivendi

moelle [mwal] *nf* marrow; *Fig* **jusqu'à la m.** to the core; **m. épinière** spinal cord; **m. osseuse** bone marrow

moelleusement [mwaløzmɑ̃] *adv* snugly

moelleux, -euse [mwalø, -øz] *adj* (**a**) *(au toucher)* soft (**b**) *(fromage, vin)* smooth; *(gâteau)* spongy

moellon [mwalɔ̃] *nm* quarry stone

mœurs [mœr, mœrs] *nfpl* (**a**) *(coutumes)* customs; **entrer** *ou* **passer dans les m.** to become part of everyday life (**b**) *(d'animaux)* habits (**c**) *(sens moral)* morals; **bonnes m.** morality; **contraire aux bonnes m.** contrary to accepted standards of behaviour; **femme de m. légères** *ou* **faciles** woman of easy virtue

mohair [mɔɛr] *nm* mohair; **un pull en m.** a mohair sweater

moi [mwa] **1** *pron personnel* (**a**) *(sujet)* I; **qui vient avec nous? – m.** who's coming with us? – I am *or* me; **m., quand je serai grand...** when I grow up,...; **m., je n'aurais pas fait comme ça** I wouldn't have done it like that

(**b**) *(objet direct)* me; **et m., tu m'oublies?** and what about me, have you forgotten me?

(**c**) *(avec préposition)* me; **fais-m. voir, à m.** show ME; **ce livre est à m.** this book is mine; **j'ai mes petits secrets à m.** I've got my own little secrets; *Fam* **un ami à m.** a friend of mine; **à m.!** help!; **je ne le fais pas que pour m.** I'm not doing it just for myself

(**d**) *(dans les comparaisons)* me; **elle boit plus que m.** she drinks more than me *or* than I do

2 *nm* ego, self

moignon [mwaɲɔ̃] *nm* stump

moi-même [mwamɛm] *pron personnel* myself

moindre [mwɛ̃dr] *adj* (**a**) *(comparatif)* lesser; *(prix)* lower; *(quantité)* smaller; *(vitesse)* slower; **c'est un m. mal** it's not as bad as it might have been (**b**) *(superlatif)* **le/la m.** the least; **pas la m. chance/idée** not the slightest chance/idea; **au m. reproche** at the slightest reproach; **dans les moindres détails** in the smallest detail; **c'est la m. des choses** it's the least I/he/*etc* can do; **on a fait venir un expert, et non des moindres** we called in an expert, and not just any old one

moine [mwan] *nm* monk

moineau, -x [mwano] *nm* sparrow

moins [mwɛ̃] **1** *adv* (**a**) *(comparatif)* less; **je gagne m. que vous** I earn less than you (do); **elle est m. intelligente que sa sœur** she's not as intelligent as her sister; **il n'est pas m. nerveux que toi** he's no less nervous than you (are); **m. de** *(argent, patience)* less; *(hommes, occasions)* fewer; *(avec un nombre)* less than; **elle a m. de vingt ans** she's under twenty; **m. tu feras d'exercice, plus tu grossiras** the less exercise you do, the fatter you'll get; **de m. en m.** less and less; **celui-ci coûte 10 francs de m. que l'autre** this one costs 10 francs less than the other one; **il y a eu 20% de visiteurs de m.** *ou* **en m.** there have been 20% fewer visitors; **il n'en est pas m. vrai que…** the fact remains that…

(**b**) *(superlatif)* **le m.** the least; **c'est celui qui me plaît le m.** that's the one I like (the) least; **les élèves les m. appliqués** the least industrious pupils; **pas le m. du monde** not in the least *or* slightest

(**c**) *(locutions)* **à m. d'un imprévu/d'un miracle** barring unforeseen circumstances/a miracle; **à m. de partir tout de suite** unless I/you/*etc* leave at once; **à m. que…** + *subjunctive* unless…; **au m.** at least; *Fam* **tu as fait ton travail, au m.?** you've done your work, I hope?; **du m.** at least; **c'est pour le m. surprenant** it's surprising, to say the least; *Fam* **un m. que rien** a nobody

2 *prép (dans les calculs, les températures)* minus; **une heure m. cinq** five (minutes) to one; **il est m. vingt** it's twenty to; *Fam* **il était m. une** it was a close shave *or* a near thing

3 *nm (signe)* minus (sign)

moins-value *(pl* **moins-values**) [mwɛ̃valy] *nf Fin* depreciation; *(après une vente)* capital loss

moire [mwar] *nf* moire

moiré, -e [mware] *adj* (**a**) *(tissu)* watered, moiré (**b**) *(aux reflets changeants)* shimmering

mois [mwa] *nm* (**a**) *(période)* month; **au m. d'août** in August; **un m. de vacances/salaire** a month's holiday/wages (**b**) *(paie mensuelle)* monthly salary; **treizième m.** extra month's salary *(paid as an annual bonus)*

Moïse [mɔiz] *npr* Moses

moisi, -e [mwazi] **1** *adj (aliment)* mouldy; *(mur, livre)* mildewed **2** *nm (sur un aliment)* mould; *(sur un mur, un tissu)* mildew

moisir [mwazir] *vi* (**a**) *(aliment)* to go mouldy; *(mur, livre)* to go mildewed (**b**) *(personne) (stagner)* to moulder away; *(attendre longtemps)* to hang about; **m. en prison** to rot in prison

moisissure [mwazisyr] *nf* mould

moisson [mwasɔ̃] *nf* (**a**) *(récolte, époque)* harvest; **faire la m.** *ou* **les moissons** to harvest (**b**) *Fig (de documents, d'idées)* wealth

moissonner [mwasɔne] *vt* (**a**) *(céréales)* to harvest; *(champ)* to reap (**b**) *Fig (informations, idées)* to collect, to gather

moissonneur, -euse [mwasɔnœr, -øz] **1** *nm,f* harvester **2** *nf* **moissonneuse** *(machine)* harvester

moissonneuse-batteuse *(pl* **moissonneuses-batteuses**) [mwasɔ̃ɔzbatøz] *nf* combine harvester

moite [mwat] *adj (mains, front, chaleur)* sticky; *(atmosphère, air)* muggy

moiteur [mwatœr] *nf (des mains, du front)* stickiness; *(d'atmosphère, d'air)* mugginess

moitié [mwatje] *nf* (**a**) *(d'un tout)* half; **la m. des livres/de la journée** half (of) the books/the day; **m. anglais, m. écossais** half English, half Scottish; **c'est m. moins cher** it's half the price; *Fam* **m.-m.** fifty-fifty; **faire m.-m.** to go halves; **à m. plein/vide** half-full/-empty; **à m. mort** half-dead; **vendre qch à m. prix** to sell sth (at) half-price; **ne pas faire les choses à m.** not to do things by halves (**b**) *Fam (époux, épouse)* **ma m.** my better half

moka [mɔka] *nm* (**a**) *(café)* mocha (**b**) *(gâteau)* coffee cake

molaire [mɔlɛr] *nf* molar

moldave [mɔldav] **1** *adj* Moldavian **2** *nmf* **M.** Moldavian

Moldavie [mɔldavi] *nf* **la M.** Moldavia

mole [mɔl] *nf Phys* mole

moléculaire [mɔlekylɛr] *adj* molecular

molécule [mɔlekyl] *nf* molecule

moleskine [mɔlɛskin] *nf* imitation leather

molester [mɔlɛste] *vt* to manhandle

molette [mɔlɛt] *nf* (**a**) *(de briquet, de clé)* wheel; *(de jumelles)* focus wheel (**b**) *(pour couper le verre)* cutting wheel

Molières [mɔljɛr] *nmpl* **les M.** *(cérémonie)* = French theatre awards ceremony

mollard [mɔlar] *nm très Fam* gob of spit

mollasson, -onne [mɔlasɔ̃, -ɔn] *Fam* **1** *adj (personne)* lethargic **2** *nm,f* lazy lump

molle [mɔl] *voir* **mou¹**

mollement [mɔlmɑ̃] *adv* (**a**) *(avec abandon)* languidly; *(avec lenteur)* gently (**b**) *(sans énergie)* feebly

mollesse [mɔlɛs] *nf* (**a**) *(d'un coussin, d'un matelas)* softness; *(de tissus, de muscles)* flabbiness (**b**) *(d'une personne)* lethargy; *(d'un gouvernement)* laxness; *(du style)* limpness

mollet¹ [mɔlɛ] *adj m (œuf)* soft-boiled

mollet² *nm* calf; **avoir des mollets de coq** to have spindly legs

molleton [mɔltɔ̃] *nm* (**a**) *(tissu) (en coton)* flannelette; *(en laine)* flannel (**b**) *(sous-nappe)* table felt

molletonné, -e [mɔltɔne] *adj* fleece-lined

mollir [mɔlir] *vi* (**a**) *(faiblir) (vent)* to die down; *(courage, enthousiasme)* to flag; **sentir ses jambes m.** to feel one's legs give way (**b**) *(devenir moins ferme) (matière)* to soften; *(sol)* to give way (**sous** beneath)

mollo [mɔlo] *adv Fam* **y aller m.** to take it easy

mollusque [mɔlysk] *nm* (**a**) *(animal)* mollusc (**b**) *Fam (personne)* lazy lump

molosse [mɔlɔs] *nm* big dog

môme [mom] *nmf Fam (enfant)* kid

moment [mɔmɑ̃] *nm* (**a**) *(point précis dans le temps)* moment; **arriver au bon m.** to arrive at just the right time; **le m. venu** *(dans le passé)* when the time came; *(dans l'avenir)* when the time comes; **c'est le m. ou jamais** it's now or never; **c'est le m. ou jamais de le faire** now's the time to do it; **au m. de qch** at the time of sth; **au m. où j'allais me coucher, le téléphone a sonné** just as I was going to bed, the phone rang; **à quel m.**

de sa vie? at what point in his life?; **à un m. donné** at one point; **dans ces moments-là** at times like that; **d'un m. à l'autre** (at) any moment; **en ce m.** at the moment, just now; **jusqu'au m. où…** until…; **par moments** at times, now and again; **pour le m.** for the moment, for the time being; **sur le m.** at the time; **à tout m., à tous moments** *(sans cesse)* constantly; *(n'importe quand)* (at) any moment; **à ce m.-là** then; *(dans ces conditions)* in that case

  (**b**) *(durée)* moment; **un m.!** just a moment!; **je suis à vous dans un m.** I'll be with you in a moment; **passer un bon m.** to have a good time; **ce n'est qu'un mauvais m. à passer** it'll soon be over with; **j'en ai pour un m.** I'll be a while; **ne pas avoir un m. à soi** not to have a moment to oneself; **dans un m. de bonté** in a moment of kindness

  (**c**) *(temps présent)* **du m.** *(disque, star)* of the moment

  (**d**) *(locutions)* **du m. que…** seeing that…

momentané, -e [mɔmɑ̃tane] *adj (bref)* brief; *(temporaire)* temporary

momentanément [mɔmɑ̃tanemɑ̃] *adv (brièvement)* briefly; *(temporairement)* temporarily

momie [mɔmi] *nf* mummy

momifier [66] [mɔmifje] **1** *vt* to mummify

  2 se momifier *vpr* to become fossilized

mon, ma, mes [mɔ̃, ma, me]

ma becomes **mon** before a word beginning with a vowel or mute h.

adj possessif (**a**) *(marquant la possession)* my; **m. chien** my dog; **ma voiture** my car; **m. ami/amie** my friend; **mes enfants** my children; **mon père et ma mère** my mother and father; **un de mes amis** one of my friends, a friend of mine; *Fam* **j'ai eu m. vendredi** I got Friday off (**b**) *(en s'adressant à quelqu'un)* **non, m. général** no, General

monacal, -e, -aux, -ales [mɔnakal, -o] *adj* monastic

Monaco [mɔnako] *n* Monaco

monarchie [mɔnarʃi] *nf* monarchy

monarchique [mɔnarʃik] *adj* monarchical

monarchiste [mɔnarʃist] *adj & nmf* monarchist

monarque [mɔnark] *nm* monarch

monastère [mɔnastɛr] *nm (d'hommes)* monastery; *(de femmes)* convent

monastique [mɔnastik] *adj* monastic

monceau, -x [mɔ̃so] *nm* heap, pile

mondain, -e [mɔ̃dɛ̃, -ɛn] **1** *adj* (**a**) *(soirée, journaliste)* society (**b**) *Péj (personne)* **être très m.** to be a great socialite

  2 *nm,f* socialite

  3 *nf Fam Vieilli* **la mondaine** the drugs squad

mondanités [mɔ̃danite] *nfpl* (**a**) *(événements)* society life (**b**) *(politesses)* social niceties; *(conversations superficielles)* social chitchat

monde [mɔ̃d] *nm* (**a**) *(univers, humanité)* world; **l'autre m.** the next world; **dans le m. entier** *(connu, en vente)* worldwide, all over the world; **personne au m.** no one in the world; **pour rien au m.** not for anything in the world; **mettre un enfant au m.** to bring a child into the world; **venir au m.** to come into the world; *Litt* **il n'est plus de ce m.** he is no longer of this world; **les meilleurs amis du m.** the best friends in the world; **en ce bas m.** here on earth; *Fam* **c'est (quand même) un m.!** that's a bit much!; *Fam* **se faire un m. de qch** to get worked up about sth; **comme le m. est**

petit! it's a small world!; **c'est le m. à l'envers** the world's gone mad

  (**b**) *(milieu)* world; **être du même m.** to belong to the same crowd; **le (beau) m.** (fashionable) society

  (**c**) *(gens)* people; **tout le m.** everyone, everybody; **il y a du m.** *(beaucoup de gens)* there are a lot of people; **peu de m., pas grand m.** not many people; **avoir du m. à dîner** to have people to dinner; **comment va tout votre petit m.?** how are all the family?; *Can* **le grand m.** the grown-ups, the adults

  (**d**) *(vie séculière)* world

mondial, -e, -aux, -ales [mɔ̃djal, -o] *adj* world, global; **guerre mondiale** world war

mondialement [mɔ̃djalmɑ̃] *adv* throughout the world

mondialisation [mɔ̃djalizasjɔ̃] *nf* globalization

mondialiser [mɔ̃djalize] **1** *vt* to globalize

  2 se mondialiser *vpr* to become globalized

monégasque [mɔnegask] **1** *adj* Monegasque

  2 *nmf* **M.** Monegasque

monétaire [mɔnetɛr] *adj (unité, système, questions)* monetary; *(marché)* money

monétarisme [mɔnetarism] *nm* monetarism

monétariste [mɔnetarist] *adj & nmf* monetarist

Monétique® [mɔnetik] *nf* electronic banking, e-banking

mongol, -e [mɔ̃gɔl] **1** *adj* Mongolian

  2 *nm,f* **M.** Mongolian

  3 *nm (langue)* Mongolian

Mongolie [mɔ̃gɔli] *nf* **la M.** Mongolia

mongolien, -enne [mɔ̃gɔljɛ̃, -ɛn] **1** *adj* **être m.** to have Down's syndrome

  2 *nm,f (bébé)* Down's syndrome baby; *(personne)* person with Down's syndrome

mongolisme [mɔ̃gɔlism] *nm* Down's syndrome

moniteur, -trice [mɔnitœr, -tris] **1** *nm,f* (**a**) *(d'activités sportives, d'auto-école)* instructor (**b**) *(dans une colonie de vacances) Br* assistant, *Am* (camp) counselor

  2 *nm aussi Ordinat* monitor; **m. cardiaque** heart monitor

monitoring [mɔnitɔriŋ] *nm* monitoring

monnaie [mɔnɛ] *nf* (**a**) *(argent)* money; *(d'un pays)* currency; **m. électronique** plastic money; *UE* **m. unique** single currency; **fausse m.** counterfeit money; **c'est m. courante dans ce milieu** it's common in these circles; *Fam* **payer qn en m. de singe** to fob sb off (**b**) *(pièces)* change; **avoir la m. de 100 francs** to have change for 100 francs; **faire (de) la m.** to get some change; **faire la m. de 100 francs** to get change for 100 francs; **petite** *ou* **menue m.** small change

monnayable [mɔnɛjabl] *adj* convertible into cash; *Fig* **être m.** *(expérience, information)* to be worth money

monnayer [53] [mɔneje] **1** *vt* (**a**) *(terrains, biens)* to convert into cash (**b**) *(expérience, information)* to cash in on

  2 se monnayer *vpr* **ici tout se monnaye** money can buy you anything here

monnayeur [mɔnɛjœr] *nm (appareil)* change machine

monochrome [mɔnokrom] *adj* monochrome

monocle [mɔnɔkl] *nm* monocle

monocoque [mɔnokɔk] *nm* monohull

monocorde [mɔnokɔrd] *adj* monotonous

monoculture [mɔnokyltyr] *nf* monoculture

monogame [mɔnɔgam] *adj* monogamous

monogamie [mɔnɔgami] *nf* monogamy

monogramme [mɔnɔgram] *nm* monogram

monoï [mɔnɔj] *nm inv* scented coconut oil

monokini [mɔnɔkini] *nm* monokini; **faire du m.** to go topless

monolingue [mɔnɔlɛ̃g] *adj* monolingual

monolithe [mɔnɔlit] *nm* monolith

monolithique [mɔnɔlitik] *adj aussi Fig* monolithic

monologue [mɔnɔlɔg] *nm* monologue; **m. intérieur** interior monologue

monologuer [mɔnɔlɔge] *vi* (**a**) *(monopoliser la parole)* to carry on a monologue (**b**) *(au théâtre)* to soliloquize

monôme [mɔnom] *nm Math* monomial

mononucléose [mɔnɔnykleoz] *nf* **m. (infectieuse)** glandular fever

monoparental, -e, -aux, -ales [mɔnɔparɑ̃tal, -o] *adj (famille)* single-parent, one-parent

monoplace [mɔnɔplas] *adj & nm* single-seater

monopole [mɔnɔpɔl] *nm* monopoly; **avoir le m. de qch** to have a monopoly on sth; **m. d'État** state monopoly

monopoliser [mɔnɔpɔlize] *vt* to monopolize

monoposte [mɔnɔpɔst] *nm Ordinat* stand-alone

monoski [mɔnɔski] *nm* monoski; **faire du m.** to monoski

monospace [mɔnɔspas] *nm* people carrier, people mover

monosyllabe [mɔnɔsilab] **1** *adj* monosyllabic **2** *nm* monosyllable

monosyllabique [mɔnɔsilabik] *adj* monosyllabic

mono-tâche [mɔnɔtaʃ] *adj inv Ordinat* single-tasking

monothéisme [mɔnɔteism] *nm* monotheism

monotone [mɔnɔtɔn] *adj* monotonous

monotonie [mɔnɔtɔni] *nf* monotony

monoxyde [mɔnɔksid] *nm* **m. de carbone** carbon monoxide

monseigneur [mɔ̃sɛɲœr] *(pl* **messeigneurs** [mesɛɲœr]*) nm* (**a**) *(titre) (d'un prince)* His Royal Highness; *(d'un cardinal)* His Eminence; *(d'un évêque)* His Lordship (**b**) *(en s'adressant au prince)* Your Royal Highness; *(au cardinal)* Your Eminence; *(à l'évêque)* Your Lordship

monsieur [məsjø] *(pl* **messieurs** [mesjø]*) nm* (**a**) *(titre)* **M. Robert Marceau** Mr Robert Marceau; **M. le Ministre** the Minister; *Fam* **m. je-sais-tout** Mr Know-it-all; **m. météo** the weatherman; **m. tout-le-monde** the man in the street (**b**) *(en apostrophe)* sir; **M. le Ministre** Minister; **au revoir, m.** goodbye; **M.,...***(dans une lettre)* Dear Sir,...; *Fam* **et en plus, M. exige des excuses!** His Lordship wants an apology as well, does he?; **que prendront ces messieurs?** what will you have, gentlemen?; **bonsoir, messieurs-dames!** good evening everybody! (**c**) *(homme quelconque)* gentleman

monstre [mɔ̃str] **1** *adj Fam* huge; **j'ai un boulot m.** I've got loads *or* tons *or* piles of work to do **2** *nm* monster; **m. d'ingratitude/d'égoïsme** ungrateful/selfish monster; **petit m.!** you little monster!; **m. sacré** giant

monstrueusement [mɔ̃stryøzmɑ̃] *adv* monstrously

monstrueux, -euse [mɔ̃stryø, -øz] *adj* (**a**) *(malformé)* monstrous (**b**) *(énorme)* huge; **être d'un égoïsme m.** to be extremely selfish (**c**) *(scandaleux)* monstrous

monstruosité [mɔ̃stryozite] *nf* monstrosity

mont [mɔ̃] *nm* mountain; *Fig* **être toujours par monts et par vaux** to be always on the move; **le m. Blanc** Mont Blanc

montage [mɔ̃taʒ] *nm* (**a**) *(pose) (de bijou)* mounting; *(d'appareils)* assembling (**b**) *(d'un film)* editing; *(image truquée)* montage; **m. vidéo** video(tape) editing (**c**) *Écon* **m. financier** financial arrangement (**d**) *(d'installation électrique)* wiring (up)

montagnard, -e [mɔ̃taɲar, -ard] **1** *adj* mountain **2** *nm,f* mountain dweller

montagne [mɔ̃taɲ] *nf* (**a**) *(élévation)* mountain; *(région)* mountains; **à la m.** in the mountains; *Fig* **se faire une m. de qch** to make a great song and dance about sth; **en haute m.** high in the mountains (**b**) **faire de la m.** *(alpinisme)* to go mountain climbing; *(randonnée)* to go hill walking (**c**) *Fig (grande quantité)* **une m. de** a mountain of (**d**) **montagnes russes** *(attraction foraine)* big dipper, rollercoaster

montagneux, -euse [mɔ̃taɲø, -øz] *adj* mountainous

montant [mɔ̃tɑ̃] *nm* (**a**) *(somme)* amount; **versement d'un m. de 500 francs** payment of 500 francs; **montants compensatoires** subsidies (**b**) *(d'échelle)* upright; *(de lit)* post; *(de fenêtre)* jamb

mont-de-piété *(pl* **monts-de-piété)** [mɔ̃dpjete] *nm* pawnshop

monté, -e [mɔ̃te] *adj (équipé)* **être bien m. (en qch)** to be well stocked (with sth); *Fam Fig* **être bien m.** to be well-hung

monte-charge *(pl* **monte-charges)** [mɔ̃tʃarʒ] *nm* goods *Br* lift *or Am* elevator

montée [mɔ̃te] *nf* (**a**) *(côte)* slope, hill (**b**) *(d'une côte)* climb; *(d'un avion)* ascent; **la m. des eaux** the rise in the water level (**c**) *(des prix)* rise (**de** in) (**d**) *(apparition) (du nationalisme, du fascisme)* rise, growth

monte-plats [mɔ̃tpla] *nm inv* dumb waiter

monter [mɔ̃te] **1** *vt (aux* avoir*)* (**a**) *(colline, escalier) (en s'éloignant)* to go up, to climb (up); *(en s'approchant)* to come up, to climb (up); **m. la rue en courant** to run up the street
  (**b**) *(porter en haut) (en s'éloignant)* to take up; *(en s'approchant)* to bring up
  (**c**) *(son, chauffage)* to turn up
  (**d**) *(assembler) (meuble)* to assemble; *(tente)* to put up; *(bijou, photo)* to mount
  (**e**) *(pièce de théâtre)* to put on, to stage
  (**f**) *(film)* to edit
  (**g**) *(créer) (entreprise, magasin)* to set up; *(complot)* to hatch; **m. un coup** to plan a job
  (**h**) *(trousseau)* to put together
  (**i**) *(en tricot)* **m. les mailles** to cast on
  (**j**) *(cheval)* to ride
  (**k**) *(locutions)* **m. la garde** to mount guard; **m. (la tête à) qn contre qn** to set sb against sb
  2 *vi (aux* être*)* (**a**) *(aller vers le haut)* to go up; *(venir vers le haut)* to come up; *(oiseau)* to fly up; *(avion)* to climb; **m. se coucher** to go (up) to bed; **faire m. qn** to show sb up; **m. sur qch** to climb onto sth; **m. à qch** to climb (up) sth; **m. à Paris** *(y déménager)* to move up to Paris; *(en visite)* to go up to Paris; **m. à la tête à qn** *(sang)* to rush to sb's head; *Fig* to go to sb's head; **les larmes lui sont montées aux yeux** his eyes filled with tears

(**b**) *(prendre place)* **m. dans qch** *(voiture, barque)* to get in sth; *(train, autobus, avion)* to get on sth; **m. sur qch** to get on sth; **m. à bord** to go on board; **m. à bicyclette** to ride a bicycle; **m. à cheval** to ride, to go riding; **m. en voiture** to get into a car

(**c**) *(route)* to climb

(**d**) *(prix, baromètre, marée)* to rise; **m. en flèche** *(prix)* to soar; **faire m. les prix** to put up prices; **m. à** *(s'élever à)* to amount to, to come to

3 se monter *vpr* (**a**) *(s'élever)* **se m. à** to come to, to amount to

(**b**) *(s'équiper)* **se m. en qch** to provide oneself with sth

(**c**) *Fam* **se m. la tête** *(s'exalter)* to get carried away with oneself

monteur, -euse [mɔ̃tœr, -øz] *nm,f Cin* editor

Montevideo [mɔ̃tevideo] *n* Montevideo

montgolfière [mɔ̃gɔlfjɛr] *nf* hot-air balloon

monticule [mɔ̃tikyl] *nm* hillock, mound

montre [mɔ̃tr] *nf* (**a**) *(instrument)* watch; **à ma m. il est midi** by my watch it's twelve o'clock; **m. en main** exactly; **m. de plongée** diver's watch; **m. à quartz** quartz watch (**b**) *(preuve)* **faire m. de qch** to show sth

Montréal [mɔ̃real] *n* Montreal

montréalais, -e [mɔ̃realɛ, -ɛz] **1** *adj* of Montreal **2** *nm,f* **M.** Montrealer

montre-bracelet *(pl* **montres-bracelets)** [mɔ̃trəbraslɛ] *nf* wristwatch

montrer [mɔ̃tre] **1** *vt* (**a**) *(révéler)* to show (**à** to); **tu devrais m. ça au médecin** you should let the doctor take a look at it; **m. le chemin à qn** to show sb the way; **m. les dents** to show *or* bare one's teeth (**b**) *(désigner)* to point out; **m. qn/qch du doigt** to point at sb/sth; *Fig* to point the finger at sb/sth (**c**) *(faire preuve de)* to show

2 se montrer *vpr* (**a**) *(se présenter) (personne)* to show oneself (**b**) *(s'avérer)* **se m. gentil/courageux** to be kind/courageous

montreur, -euse [mɔ̃trœr, -øz] *nm,f* **m. d'ours** bear leader

monture [mɔ̃tyr] *nf* (**a**) *(de lunettes)* frame; *(de bijou)* setting (**b**) *(cheval)* mount

monument [mɔnymã] *nm* (**a**) *(statue)* monument; **m. funéraire** monument *(over a tomb)*; **m. aux morts** war memorial (**b**) *(édifice public)* monument; **m. classé** listed building; **être classé m. historique** to be a listed building (**c**) *Fig (livre, film)* masterpiece

monumental, -e, -aux, -ales [mɔnymãtal, -o] *adj* monumental

moquer [mɔke] **se moquer** *vpr* (**a**) *(rire)* **se m. de qn/ qch** to make fun of sb/sth; *Fig* **il se moque du monde** who does he think he is? (**b**) *(ignorer)* **se m. de qch** not to care about sth; *Fam* **se m. de qch comme de l'an quarante** *ou* **comme de sa première chemise** not to give two hoots about sth

moquerie [mɔkri] *nf* mockery

moquette [mɔkɛt] *nf* (fitted) carpet; **poser de la m.** to fit a carpet

moqueur, -euse [mɔkœr, -øz] **1** *adj (remarque, rires)* mocking; *(personne)* given to mockery **2** *nm* **les moqueurs** mocking people

moraine [mɔrɛn] *nf* moraine

moral, -e, -aux, -ales [mɔral, -o] **1** *adj* moral **2** *nm* morale; **avoir le m.** to be in good spirits; **avoir le m. au beau fixe** to be in fine spirits; **avoir un m.**

d'acier to be very resilient; *Fam* **avoir le m. à zéro** to feel really down; **remonter le m. à qn** to cheer sb up

morale [mɔral] *nf* (**a**) *(bien)* morals; **contraire à la m.** immoral (**b**) *(règles)* morality; **faire une leçon de m. à qn, faire la m. à qn** to lecture sb (**c**) *(d'une histoire)* moral

moralement [mɔralmã] *adv* morally

moralisateur, -trice [mɔralizatœr, -tris] **1** *adj (discours, personne)* moralizing **2** *nm,f* moralizer

moraliste [mɔralist] **1** *adj* moralistic **2** *nmf* moralist

moralité [mɔralite] *nf* (**a**) *(conduite, attitude)* morality; **être d'une m. irréprochable** to have impeccable moral standards (**b**) *(d'une histoire)* moral; **m.: quand on veut, on peut** the moral of the story is, you can do anything if you put your mind to it

moratoire [mɔratwar] *nm Jur* moratorium

morbide [mɔrbid] *adj* morbid

morbidité [mɔrbidite] *nf* morbidness

morceau, -x [mɔrso] *nm* (**a**) *(de nourriture)* piece, bit; *Fam* **le gros m.** *(le plus difficile)* the big one; *Fam* **manger un m.** to have a bite to eat; *Fam Fig* **lâcher** *ou* **cracher le m.** to spill the beans; **m. de choix** choice morsel; **bas morceaux** *(de viande)* cheap cuts

(**b**) *(de savon, de tissu, de papier)* piece, bit; *(de sucre)* lump; *(de terre)* piece; **en morceaux** in pieces; **mettre qch en morceaux** to tear sth to pieces; **tomber en morceaux** to fall to pieces

(**c**) *(de musique)* piece

(**d**) *(extrait)* **m. d'anthologie** anthology piece; **m. de bravoure** purple passage; **morceaux choisis** selected passages *or* extracts

morceler [42] [mɔrsəle] *vt* to divide up

morcellement [mɔrsɛlmã] *nm* dividing up

mordant, -e [mɔrdã, -ãt] **1** *adj* (**a**) *(esprit, remarque, ton)* biting, caustic (**b**) *(froid)* biting **2** *nm (causticité)* bite

mordicus [mɔrdikys] *adv Fam* stubbornly

mordiller [mɔrdije] *vt* to nibble

mordoré, -e [mɔrdɔre] *adj (couleur)* bronze

mordre [mɔrdr] **1** *vt* (**a**) *(sujet: personne, animal)* to bite; **m. qn au bras** to bite sb's arm, to bite sb on the arm; **se faire m. par un chien** to be bitten by a dog (**b**) *(entamer) (sujet: lime)* to bite into; *(sujet: acide)* to eat into

2 *vi (personne, chien)* to bite; **m. dans une pomme** to bite into an apple; **ça mord?** *(poissons)* are the fish biting?

3 mordre à *vt ind* (**a**) *(poisson) & Fig* **m. à l'appât** *ou* **à l'hameçon** to rise to the bait (**b**) *Fam (prendre goût à)* to take to

4 mordre sur *vt ind (déborder)* **m. sur qch** to encroach (up)on sth; **m. sur la ligne** *(sportif)* to have one's foot over the line

5 se mordre *vpr* **se m. la langue** to bite one's tongue; *Fig* **se m. les doigts d'avoir fait qch** to kick oneself for doing sth; **vous vous en mordrez les doigts** you'll be sorry

mordu, -e [mɔrdy] *Fam* **1** *adj* (**a**) *(amoureux)* madly in love (**b**) *(passionné)* **être m. de qch** to be mad on sth **2** *nm,f* fanatic; **un m. de bridge/cinéma** a bridge/ film fanatic

morfal, -e, -als, -ales [mɔrfal] *nm,f Fam* greedy-guts

morfler [mɔrfle] *vi Fam* (**a**) *(être abîmé)* to get smashed up; *(être blessé)* to get injured (**b**) *(être puni, pâtir)* to catch it

morfondre [mɔrfɔ̃dr] **se morfondre** *vpr* (**a**) *(languir)* to mope (**b**) *Can (s'épuiser)* to wear oneself out

morgue¹ [mɔrg] *nf (arrogance)* haughtiness; **plein de m.** haughty

morgue² *nf (dans un hôpital)* mortuary; *(pour les corps non identifiés)* morgue

moribond, -e [mɔribɔ̃, -ɔ̃d] **1** *adj* dying
2 *nm,f* dying man, *f* dying woman

morille [mɔrij] *nf* morel

mormon, -e [mɔrmɔ̃, -ɔn] *adj & nm,f* Mormon

morne [mɔrn] *adj (personne, regard)* glum; *(silence)* gloomy; *(temps)* dismal, dreary

morose [mɔroz] *adj (personne, humeur)* morose; *(temps)* miserable

morosité [mɔrozite] *nf (d'une personne, de l'humeur)* moroseness; *(du temps)* miserable nature

morphine [mɔrfin] *nf* morphine

morphologie [mɔrfɔlɔʒi] *nf* morphology

morphologique [mɔrfɔlɔʒik] *adj* morphological

morpion [mɔrpjɔ̃] *nm* (**a**) *très Fam (pou)* crab (**b**) *Fam (enfant)* kid (**c**) *(jeu) Br* noughts and crosses, *Am* tick-tack-toe

mors [mɔr] *nm* bit; *Fig* **prendre le m. aux dents** to take the bit between one's teeth

morse¹ [mɔrs] *nm (animal)* walrus

morse² *nm (code)* Morse (code)

morsure [mɔrsyr] *nf* bite

mort¹, -e [mɔr, mɔrt] **1** *pp voir* **mourir**
2 *adj* (**a**) *(personne, feuille, langue)* dead; **plus m. que vif** more dead than alive; **m. de peur/d'inquiétude/de froid** frightened/worried/frozen to death; *Fam* **être m. de rire** to fall about laughing; *Fam* **être m. (de fatigue)** to be dead tired (**b**) *(hors d'usage) (pile)* dead; *Fam* **être m.** *(voiture, chaussures)* to have had it
3 *nm,f* dead man, *f* dead woman; **les morts** the dead; *Rel* **le jour** *ou* **la fête des morts** All Souls' Day; **faire le m.** to pretend to be dead; *Fig* to lie low; **l'accident a fait trois morts** three people were killed in the accident
4 *nm (aux cartes)* dummy

mort² *nf* death; **trouver la m. dans un accident** to die in an accident; **se donner la m.** to take one's own life; **mettre qn à m.** to put sb to death; **en vouloir à qn à m.** to have a huge grudge against sb; **la m. dans l'âme** with a heavy heart; *Fam* **c'est pas la m.!** it won't kill you/him/*etc*!

mortadelle [mɔrtadɛl] *nf* mortadella

mortaise [mɔrtɛz] *nf* mortise

mortalité [mɔrtalite] *nf* mortality, death rate; **m. infantile** infant mortality

mort-aux-rats [mɔrora] *nf inv* rat poison

mortel, -elle [mɔrtɛl] **1** *adj* (**a**) *(éphémère)* mortal (**b**) *(fatal) (maladie, accident)* fatal; *(dose)* lethal; *(champignon, poison)* deadly (**c**) *(péché, ennemi)* deadly; *(silence)* deathly; **d'une pâleur mortelle** deathly pale (**d**) *Fam (ennuyeux)* deadly boring
2 *nm,f* mortal

mortellement [mɔrtɛlmɑ̃] *adv (blessé)* fatally; *(ennuyeux)* deadly

morte-saison *(pl* **mortes-saisons)** [mɔrtsɛzɔ̃] *nf* off-season; **à la m.** in the off-season

mortier [mɔrtje] *nm* mortar; **tirs de m.** mortar fire

mortifiant, -e [mɔrtifjɑ̃, -ɑ̃t] *adj* mortifying

mortification [mɔrtifikasjɔ̃] *nf* mortification

mortifié, -e [mɔrtifje] *adj* mortified

mortifier [66] [mɔrtifje] **1** *vt* to mortify
2 **se mortifier** *vpr* to mortify oneself

mort-né, -e *(mpl* **mort-nés,** *fpl* **mort-nées)** [mɔrne] **1** *adj aussi Fig* stillborn
2 *nm,f* stillborn child

mortuaire [mɔrtɥɛr] *adj* death

morue [mɔry] *nf* (**a**) *(poisson)* cod (**b**) *très Fam (prostituée)* tart

morve [mɔrv] *nf* snot

morveux, -euse [mɔrvø, -øz] **1** *adj (enfant)* runny-nosed; *(nez)* runny
2 *nm,f Fam Péj (gamin)* brat; *(jeune prétentieux)* upstart

mosaïque [mɔzaik] *nf* (**a**) *(en décoration)* mosaic (**b**) *Fig (de couleurs)* kaleidoscope; *(de populations)* medley

Moscou [mɔsku] *n* Moscow

moscovite [mɔskɔvit] **1** *adj* Muscovite
2 *nmf* **M.** Muscovite

mosquée [mɔske] *nf* mosque

mot [mo] *nm* (**a**) *(parole)* word; **avoir son m. à dire** to have one's say; **avoir toujours le m. pour rire** to be always ready with a joke; **avoir des mots avec qn** to have words with sb; **avoir le dernier m.** to have the last word; **je n'ai pas dit mon dernier m.** I'm not finished yet; **dire un m.** *ou* **deux mots à qn** to have a word with sb; **se donner le m.** to pass the word around; **prendre qn au m.** to take sb at his/her word; **traduire m. à m., faire du m. à m.** to translate word for word; **répéter qch m. pour m.** to repeat sth word for word; **sans m. dire** without (saying) a word; **sur ces mots** and with these words; **en un m.** in a word; **au bas m.** at least; **à mots couverts** in veiled terms; **mots doux, mots d'amour** sweet nothings; **mots croisés** crossword; **faire des mots croisés** to do crosswords; **m. d'ordre** watchword, slogan; **m. de passe** password; **bon m.** witty remark; **gros m.** swear word; **dire des gros mots** to swear
(**b**) *(message écrit)* note; **envoyer un m. à qn** to drop sb a line; **m. d'excuse** note *(explaining absence)*
(**c**) *Ordinat* **m. de 6 bits** 6-bit byte; **m. binaire** binary word

motard, -e [mɔtar, -ard] **1** *nm,f Fam (conducteur de moto)* biker
2 *nm (policier)* motorcycle policeman

mot-clef *(pl* **mots-clefs)** [mokle] *nm* keyword

motel [mɔtɛl] *nm* motel

moteur, -trice [mɔtœr, -tris] **1** *adj* (**a**) *(force, roue)* driving; **à deux/quatre roues motrices** two-/four-wheel drive (**b**) *(nerf, trouble)* motor
2 *nm* engine; *(électrique)* motor; *Fig* driving force; *Cin* **m.!** camera!; **à m.** motor(-driven); **m. à deux/quatre temps** two-/four-stroke engine; **m. à explosion** internal combustion engine; **m. à injection** fuel-injected engine; **m. à réaction** jet engine; *Ordinat* **m. de recherche** search engine
3 *nf Rail* **motrice** engine

motif [mɔtif] *nm* (**a**) *(raison)* reason (**de** for); **elle n'a aucun m. de mécontentement** she has no reason to be unhappy (**b**) *(dessin)* pattern, motif (**c**) *(dans un morceau de musique)* motif

motion [mosjɔ̃] *nf* motion; **m. de censure** motion of censure

motivant, -e [mɔtivɑ̃, -ɑ̃t] *adj (travail)* motivating; *(salaire, rémunération)* attractive

motivation [mɔtivasjɔ̃] *nf* motivation

motivé, -e [mɔtive] *adj* (**a**) *(personne)* motivated (**b**) *(action)* justified

motiver [mɔtive] *vt* (**a**) *(provoquer, stimuler)* to motivate (**b**) *(justifier)* to justify

moto [moto] *nf* motorbike; **faire de la m.** to ride a motorbike; **m. tout terrain** trial bike

motocross [motokrɔs] *nm* motocross

motoculteur [motokyltœr] *nm* motor cultivator

motocyclette [motosiklɛt] *nf* motorcycle

motocycliste [motosiklist] *nm* motorcyclist; *Mil* dispatch rider

motomarine [motomarin] *nf Can* jet ski

motoneige [motonɛʒ] *nf Can* snowmobile

motorisé, -e [mɔtɔrize] *adj* motorized; **être m.** *(personne)* to have transport

motrice [mɔtris] *voir* **moteur**

motricité [mɔtrisite] *nf* motor function

motte [mɔt] *nf* (**a**) *(de terre)* clod, clump (**b**) *(de beurre)* block

motus [mɔtys] *exclam* **m. (et bouche cousue)!** mum's the word!

mou¹, molle [mu, mɔl] **1** *adj* (**a**) *(matelas, substance)* soft; *(chair, ventre)* flabby; **j'ai les jambes molles** my legs are like jelly (**b**) *(personne, gouvernement)* spineless; *(protestation)* feeble; *(poignée de main)* limp
  2 *nm,f Fam* wimp
  3 *nm (d'un cordage, d'un câble)* slack

mou² *nm (abats)* lights, lungs

mouchard, -e [muʃar, -ard] *Fam* **1** *nm,f (informateur) Br* grass, *Am* fink; *(à l'école)* sneak
  2 *nm (de camion)* tachograph

moucharder [muʃarde] *Fam* **1** *vt (personne)* to squeal *or Br* grass on; *(élève)* to sneak on
  2 *vi (élève)* to sneak on people

mouche [muʃ] *nf* (**a**) *(insecte)* fly; **prendre** *ou Suisse* **piquer la m.** to fly off the handle; **elle ne ferait pas de mal à une m.** she wouldn't hurt a fly; **quelle m. te pique?** what's got into you?; **m. tsé-tsé** tsetse fly; **fine m.** sharp customer (**b**) *(de cible)* bull's-eye; **faire m.** to hit the bull's-eye; *Fig* to hit home (**c**) *(accessoire cosmétique)* beauty spot

moucher [muʃe] **1** *vt* (**a**) *(nez)* to blow; **m. un enfant** to blow a child's nose (**b**) *Fig* **m. qn** to put sb in his/her place (**c**) *(chandelle)* to snuff out
  2 se moucher *vpr* to blow one's nose; *Fam* **ne pas se m. du coude** *ou* **du pied** to think one is the bee's knees

moucheron [muʃrɔ̃] *nm* midge

moucheté, -e [muʃte] *adj (cheval)* dappled; *(tissu)* speckled

mouchoir [muʃwar] *nm* handkerchief; **arriver dans un m.** to come in neck and neck; **grand comme un m. de poche** no bigger than a pocket handkerchief; **m. en papier** tissue; **m. en tissu** handkerchief

moudre [48] [mudr] *vt* to grind

moue [mu] *nf* pout; **faire la m.** to pout

mouette [mwɛt] *nf* (sea)gull

moufle [mufl] *nf* mitten, mitt

mouflet, -ette [muflɛ, -ɛt] *nm,f Fam* kid

mouflon [muflɔ̃] *nm* moufflon

mouillage [mujaʒ] *nm* (**a**) *(de bateau) (manœuvre)* anchoring; *(emplacement)* anchorage; **être au m.** to be riding at anchor (**b**) *(du vin)* watering down

mouillé, -e [muje] *adj* (**a**) *(vêtement, personne, pieds)* wet; **tout m.** soaking wet (**b**) *(consonne)* palatalized

mouiller [muje] **1** *vt* (**a**) *(rendre humide)* to wet; **se faire m.** to get wet; *Fig* **m. sa chemise** to work up a sweat (**b**) *(vin, lait)* to water down (**c**) *(ancre)* to drop (**d**) *Fam (compromettre)* to involve (**e**) *Can Fam (fêter)* **il va falloir m. ça!** this calls for a celebration!
  2 *vi (bateau)* to anchor
  3 se mouiller *vpr* (**a**) *(personne)* to get wet; **se m. les pieds** to get one's feet wet (**b**) *Fam (prendre position)* to stick one's neck out

mouillette [mujɛt] *nf* finger *(of bread)*

mouise [mwiz] *nf très Fam* **être dans la m.** to be hard up

moulage [mulaʒ] *nm* (**a**) *(action)* casting (**b**) *(objet)* plaster cast

moule¹ [mul] *nm aussi Fig* mould; *Fig* **être coulé dans le même m.** to be cast in the same mould; **m. à gâteaux** *Br* cake tin, *Am* cake pan; **m. à gaufres** waffle iron; **m. à tarte** flan dish

moule² *nf* mussel; **moules frites** mussels and *Br* chips *or Am* French fries *(speciality of Belgium and the North of France)*; **moules marinières** moules marinières, = mussels in white wine; *Belg* **moules parquées** = mussels served raw

mouler [mule] *vt* (**a**) *(statue)* to mould (**b**) *(sujet: vêtement)* to fit closely

moulin [mulɛ̃] *nm* (**a**) *(bâtiment)* mill; **on y entre comme dans un m.** anyone can just walk in; **m. à eau** watermill; *Can* **m. à scie** sawmill; **m. à vent** windmill (**b**) *(appareil)* **m. à café** coffee grinder; **m. à légumes** vegetable mill *or* grinder; *Fig* **m. à paroles** chatterbox; **m. à poivre** pepper mill

mouliner [muline] *vt (aliment)* to pass through a food mill

moulinet [mulinɛ] *nm* (**a**) *(de canne à pêche)* reel (**b**) *(rotation)* **faire des moulinets (avec les bras)** to circle one's arms

Moulinette® [mulinɛt] *nf* food mill

moult [mult] *adv Hum ou Vieilli* many

moulu, -e [muly] **1** *pp voir* **moudre**
  2 *adj* (**a**) *(café, poivre)* ground (**b**) *Fig* **être m. (de fatigue)** to be shattered

moulure [mulyr] *nf* (ornamental) moulding

moumoute [mumut] *nf Fam* (**a**) *(perruque)* rug, wig (**b**) *(veste)* sheepskin jacket

mourant, -e [murɑ̃, -ɑ̃t] **1** *adj* dying
  2 *nm,f* dying man, *f* dying woman

mourir [49] [murir] *(aux être)* **1** *vi* (**a**) *(personne, animal, plante)* to die; **m. de sa belle mort** *ou* **de mort naturelle** to die a natural death; **m. de vieillesse** to die of old age; **m. assassiné** to be murdered; **m. d'inquiétude/de peur** to be worried/frightened to death; **m. de faim** to starve to death; *Fam (avoir très faim)* to be starving; **m. de soif/d'ennui** to die of thirst/boredom; **s'ennuyer à m.** to be bored to death; **aimer qn à en m.** to be desperately in love with sb; **à m. d'ennui** deadly boring; **à m. de rire** hilarious, hysterical; **m. d'envie de faire qch** to be dying to do sth; *Fig* **tu ne vas pas en m.!** it won't kill you! (**b**) *(coutume, industrie, civilisation)* to die out; *(feu, région)* to die
  2 *v impersonnel* **il meurt des milliers d'enfants**

chaque jour thousands of children die every day **3 se mourir** *vpr Litt (personne)* to be dying
mouroir [murwar] *nm Fam Péj* old people's home
mouron [murɔ̃] *nm Fam* **se faire du m.** to worry
mousquetaire [muskətɛr] *nm* musketeer
mousqueton [muskətɔ̃] *nm* (a) *(anneau)* snap clasp; *(d'alpiniste)* karabiner (b) *(arme)* carbine
moussaka [musaka] *nf* moussaka
moussant, -e [musã, ãt] *adj* **être peu m.** not to produce a lot of lather; **bain m.** bubble bath
mousse¹ [mus] *nf* (a) *(végétation)* moss (b) *(écume)* foam; *(sur un verre de bière)* head; *(de savon)* lather; *Fam* **une m.** *(bière)* a beer; **m. à raser** shaving foam (c) *(plat, dessert)* mousse; **m. au chocolat/de saumon** chocolate/salmon mousse (d) *(matériau synthétique)* foam rubber
mousse² *nm* ship's boy
mousseline [muslin] *nf (tissu)* muslin; **m. de soie** chiffon
mousser [muse] *vi (bière)* to froth; *(savon, lessive)* to lather; *(vin, eau gazeuse)* to fizz; *Fam Fig* **se faire m.** to show off
mousseux, -euse [musø, -øz] **1** *adj* (a) *(vin, cidre)* sparkling (b) *(lait, bière)* frothy
  2 *nm* sparkling wine
mousson [musɔ̃] *nf* monsoon
moussu, -e [musy] *adj* mossy
moustache [mustaʃ] *nf* (a) *(d'un homme)* moustache; **porter la m.** to have a moustache (b) *(de chat, de rongeur)* whiskers
moustachu, -e [mustaʃy] **1** *adj* with a moustache; **être m.** to have a moustache
  2 *nm* man with a moustache
moustiquaire [mustikɛr] *nf* mosquito net
moustique [mustik] *nm* (a) *(insecte)* mosquito (b) *Fam (gamin)* kid, mite
moût [mu] *nm (de raisins)* must; *(de bière)* wort
moutard [mutar] *nm Fam* kid
moutarde [mutard] **1** *adj inv* **(jaune) m.** mustard (yellow)
  2 *nf* mustard; *Fig* **la m. me monte au nez** I'm beginning to lose my temper; **m. forte/de Dijon** strong/Dijon mustard
moutardier [mutardje] *nm (pot)* mustard pot
mouton [mutɔ̃] *nm* (a) *(animal)* sheep; **(peau de) m.** sheepskin; **être frisé comme un m.** to have curly hair; *Fig* **revenons à nos moutons** let's get back to the subject; **compter les moutons** *(pour s'endormir)* to count sheep; *Fig* **m. à cinq pattes** rare bird (b) *(viande)* mutton (c) **moutons** *(écume)* white horses; *(poussière)* fluff (d) *Can* **m. noir** *(nuage)* rain cloud
moutonner [mutɔne] *vi (mer)* to be flecked with foam
moutonneux, -euse [mutɔnø, -øz] *adj* (a) *(mer)* foam-flecked (b) *(ciel)* dotted with fleecy clouds
mouture [mutyr] *nf* (a) *(action de moudre)* grinding (b) *(d'un ouvrage, d'un livre)* version
mouvance [muvãs] *nf* **il faisait partie de la m. surréaliste** he moved in surrealist circles
mouvant, -e [muvã, ãt] *adj (terrain)* unstable; *(cible)* moving; *Fig (situation)* uncertain
mouvement [muvmã] *nm* (a) *(déplacement)* movement, motion; *(des marchandises, des capitaux)* movement; *(geste)* gesture; **faire un m.** to make a movement; **faire un faux m.** *(se faire mal)* to move the wrong way; **en m.** in motion; **ralentir le m.** to slow

down; **suivre le m.** to go with the flow; **il y eut un m. de foule** a ripple ran through the crowd; **m. de tête** *(pour acquiescer)* nod; *(pour nier)* shake of the head (b) *(de gymnastique)* exercise (c) *(élan)* impulse; **m. d'humeur** outburst (of temper); **m. de colère** fit of anger (d) *(politique, artistique)* movement; **m. de grève** strike action; **mouvements sociaux** industrial action (e) *(d'un concerto, d'une symphonie)* movement
mouvementé, -e [muvmãte] *adj (discussion, débat)* animated, lively; *(journée, voyage, vie)* eventful
mouvoir [31b] *(muvwar)* **1** *vt Litt* (a) *(machine)* to drive; *(bateau)* to propel; **mû par la vapeur** steam-driven (b) *(pousser)* **mû par l'intérêt** prompted by self-interest
  2 se mouvoir *vpr* to move
moyen¹, -enne [mwajɛ̃, -ɛn] *adj* (a) *(du milieu)* middle; **trouver un m. terme** to find a happy medium (b) *(coût, taille, vitesse)* average; **de taille moyenne** medium-sized; *(personne)* of average height (c) *(quelconque, médiocre)* average; **le Français m.** the average Frenchman
moyen² *nm* (a) *(façon, possibilité)* means, way; *aussi Hum* **trouver le m. de faire qch** to manage to do sth; **se donner les moyens de faire qch** to provide oneself with the means to do sth; **faire qch par ses propres moyens** to do sth on one's own; **employer les grands moyens** to take extreme measures; **au m. de qch** by means of sth; **par tous les moyens** any way I/you/etc can; **il n'y a pas m. de le lui faire comprendre** it's impossible to make him understand; **faire avec les moyens du bord** to make do with what one has; **moyens de communication/production/transport** means of communication/production/transport (b) **avoir des moyens** *(capacité mentale)* to be bright; **perdre tous ses moyens** to go to pieces (c) **moyens** *(financiers)* means; **j'en ai/je n'en ai pas les moyens** I can/can't afford it
Moyen Âge [mwajɛnaʒ] *nm* **le M.** the Middle Ages
moyenâgeux, -euse [mwajɛnaʒø, -øz] *adj* medieval
moyen-courrier *(pl* **moyen-courriers)** [mwajɛ̃kurje] *nm* **(avion) m.** medium-haul aircraft
moyennant [mwajɛnã] *prép* (in return) for; **faire qch m. finance** to do sth in return for payment; **m. quoi** in return for which
moyenne [mwajɛn] **1** *adj voir* **moyen¹**
  2 *nf* (a) *(niveau le plus courant)* average; **en m.** on average (b) *(à un examen)* pass mark; *(sur une période)* average (mark); **avoir 10 sur 20 de m.** to average 10 out of 20
moyennement [mwajɛnmã] *adv* moderately, fairly
Moyen-Orient [mwajɛnɔrjã] *nm* **le M.** the Middle East
moyeu [mwajø] *nm* hub
mozambicain, -e [mɔzãbikɛ̃, -ɛn] **1** *adj* Mozambican
  2 *nm,f* **M.** Mozambican
Mozambique [mɔzãbik] *nm* **le M.** Mozambique
mozzarella [mɔdzarɛla], **mozzarelle** [mɔdzarɛl] *nf* mozzarella
MRAP [mrap] *nm (abrév* **Mouvement contre le racisme, l'antisémitisme et pour la paix)** = French anti-racist pacifist movement
MRG [ɛmɛrʒe] *nm (abrév* **Mouvement des radicaux de gauche)** = French left-wing political party
MST¹ [ɛmɛste] *nf (abrév* **maladie sexuellement transmissible)** STD

MST² *nf (abrév* **maîtrise de sciences et techniques)** = master's degree in science and technology

mû [my] *voir* **mouvoir**

mucoviscidose [mykovisidoz] *nf* cystic fibrosis

mucus [mykys] *nm* mucus

mue [my] **1** *pp voir* **mouvoir**
  2 *nf* (**a**) *(d'oiseaux, de mammifères)* moulting; *(de reptiles)* sloughing (**b**) *(à la puberté)* breaking of the voice

muer [mɥe] **1** *vi* (**a**) *(mammifère)* to moult; *(serpent)* to slough (**b**) *(voix)* to break; **il commence à m.** his voice is breaking
  2 se muer *vpr* **se m. en** to change into

muesli [mysli] *nm* muesli

muet, -ette [mɥɛ, -ɛt] **1** *adj* (**a**) *(personne)* dumb; *Fig (silencieux)* silent; **m. d'étonnement/de colère** speechless with astonishment/anger; **m. comme la tombe** as quiet as the grave; **il est resté m. comme une carpe** he didn't open his mouth (**b**) *(film, réprobation)* silent; *(rôle)* non-speaking (**c**) *Ling* silent
  2 *nm,f* mute
  3 *nm Cin* **le m.** silent films

muezzin [mɥedzin] *nm* muezzin

mufle [myfl] *nm* (**a**) *Fam (homme)* lout (**b**) *(du bœuf, du bison)* muffle; *(du lion, du taureau)* muzzle

muge [myʒ] *nm* mullet

mugir [myʒir] *vi* (**a**) *(vache)* to moo; *(taureau)* to bellow (**b**) *(vent)* to howl

mugissement [myʒismɑ̃] *nm* (**a**) *(de vache)* moo; *(de taureau)* bellow; **des mugissements** *(de vache)* mooing; *(de taureau)* bellowing (**b**) *(du vent)* howling

muguet [mygɛ] *nm (plante)* lily of the valley

> **Muguet**
> On May Day in France, bunches of lily of the valley are sold in the streets and given as presents. The flowers are supposed to bring good luck.

mulâtre [mylɑtr] *adj & nm* mulatto

mulâtresse [mylɑtrɛs] *nf* mulatto

mule¹ [myl] *nf (animal)* mule; *Fam (personne entêtée)* mule

mule² *nf (chaussure)* mule

mulet¹ [mylɛ] *nm (équidé)* mule

mulet² *nm (poisson)* grey mullet

muletier, -ère [myltje, -ɛr] **1** *adj* **chemin** *ou* **sentier m.** mule track
  2 *nm,f* mule driver

mulot [mylo] *nm* field mouse

multicarte [myltikart] *adj (représentant)* for several companies

multicolore [myltikɔlɔr] *adj* multicoloured

multicoque [myltikɔk] *nm* multihull

multicritère [myltikritɛr] *nm Ordinat* multicriterion

multiculturel, -elle [myltikyltyrɛl] *adj* multicultural

multidisciplinaire [myltidisiplinɛr] *adj* multi-disciplinary

multi-écran *(pl* **multi-écrans)** [myltiekrɑ̃] *nm* split screen

multifonctions [myltifɔ̃ksjɔ̃] *adj* multi-functional

multiforme [myltifɔrm] *adj* multifaceted

multilatéral, -e, -aux, -ales [myltilateral, -o] *adj* multilateral

multimédia [myltimedja] *adj & nm* multimedia

multimilliardaire [myltimiljardɛr] *adj & nmf* multi-millionaire

multimillionnaire [myltimiljɔnɛr] *adj & nmf* multi-millionaire

multinational, -e, -aux, -ales [myltinasjɔnal, -o] **1** *adj* multinational
  2 *nf* **multinationale** multinational (company)

multiple [myltipl] **1** *adj* (**a**) *(nombreux)* many, numerous; **à usages multiples** multipurpose; **à de multiples reprises** repeatedly; *Ordinat* **à accès m.** multi-access (**b**) *(divers)* many, multiple
  2 *nm Math* multiple; **le plus petit commun m.** the lowest common multiple

multiplex [myltiplɛks] *adj inv & nm inv* multiplex

multiplexe [myltiplɛks] *nm* multiplex (cinema)

multiplicateur, -trice [myltiplikatœr, -tris] **1** *adj* multiplying
  2 *nm* multiplier

multiplication [myltiplikasjɔ̃] *nf* (**a**) *(calcul)* multiplication (**b**) *(augmentation)* increase (**de** in)

multiplicité [myltiplisite] *nf* multiplicity

multiplier [66] [myltiplije] **1** *vt* (**a**) *(somme, chiffre)* to multiply (**par** by) (**b**) *(répéter)* **m. les mises en garde** to issue repeated warnings; **m. les erreurs** to make mistake after mistake
  2 se multiplier *vpr* (**a**) *(augmenter)* to increase (**b**) *(se reproduire)* to multiply

multiposte [myltipɔst] *adj Ordinat* multi-station

multiprocesseur [myltiprɔsesœr] *nm Ordinat* multi-processor

multiprogrammation [myltiprɔgramasjɔ̃] *nf Ordinat* multiprogramming

multipropriété [myltiprɔprijete] *nf* time-share; **acheter un appartement en m.** to buy a time-share *Br* flat *orAm* apartment

multiracial, -e, -aux, -ales [myltirasjal, -o] *adj* multiracial

multirisque [myltirisk] *adj* comprehensive

multisalles [myltisal] *adj* **complexe m.** multiplex (cinema)

multitâche [myltitaʃ] *adj Ordinat* multitasking

multithérapie [myltiterapi] *nf Méd* combination therapy

multitraitement [myltitrɛtmɑ̃] *nm Ordinat* multi-processing

multitude [myltityd] *nf* multitude (**de** of)

multi-utilisateurs [myltiytilizatœr] *adj inv Ordinat* multiuser

municipal, -e, -aux, -ales [mynisipal, -o] **1** *adj* municipal
  2 *nfpl* **les municipales** municipal *or* local (government) elections

> **Municipales**
> These are the elections where residents choose the town councils. Electors vote for a list of council members whose leader or "tête de liste" will become the mayor, a ceremonial and political post.

municipalité [mynisipalite] *nf* (**a**) *(commune)* municipality (**b**) *(maire et conseillers)* (local) council

munir [mynir] **1** *vt (personne)* to supply, to provide (**de** with); *(voiture, chambre)* to fit, to equip (**de** with)
  2 se munir *vpr* **se m. de qch** to take sth

munitions [mynisjɔ̃] *nfpl* ammunition, munitions

munster [mœ̃stɛr] *nm* Munster (cheese)
muqueuse [mykøz] *nf* mucous membrane
mur [myr] *nm* (**a**) *(construction)* wall; **l'ennemi est dans nos murs** the enemy is within the gates; **le m. de Berlin** the Berlin Wall; **le M. des lamentations** the Wailing Wall; **m. porteur** load-bearing wall; **m. du son** sound barrier; **franchir le m. du son** to break the sound barrier; **m. de soutènement** retaining wall (**b**) *Fig (résistance)* brick wall
mûr, -e [myr] *adj* (**a**) *(fruit)* ripe; *Fig* **être m. pour qch** to be ripe for sth (**b**) *(personne, esprit)* mature (**c**) *(intense)* **après mûre réflexion** after careful consideration
muraille [myraj] *nf* wall; **la Grande M. de Chine** the Great Wall of China
mural, -e, -aux, -ales [myral, -o] *adj* wall
mûre [myr] *nf* mulberry; *(fruit de la ronce)* blackberry
mûrement [myrmã] *adv* **après avoir m. réfléchi** after careful consideration; **un projet m. réfléchi** a carefully thought-out plan
murène [myrɛn] *nf* moray (eel)
murer [myre] **1** *vt* (**a**) *(ville, jardin)* to wall in (**b**) *(porte, fenêtre, personne)* to wall up
2 se murer *vpr* to shut oneself away; **se m. dans le silence/la solitude** to retreat into silence/solitude
muret [myrɛ] *nm (mur bas)* low wall; *(de pierres sèches)* dry-stone wall
murette [myrɛt] *nf* = **muret**
mûrier [myrje] *nm* (**a**) *(arbre)* mulberry tree (**b**) *(roncier)* blackberry bush
mûrir [myrir] *vi* (**a**) *(fruit)* to ripen (**b**) *(projet, sentiment)* to evolve, to develop (**c**) *(personne)* to mature
murmure [myrmyr] *nm* murmur
murmurer [myrmyre] *vt & vi* to murmur
musaraigne [myzarɛɲ] *nf* shrew
musarder [myzarde] *vi (flâner)* to wander around; *(fainéanter)* to lounge around
musc [mysk] *nm* musk
muscade [myskad] *nf* **m., noix (de) m.** nutmeg
muscat [myska] *nm* (**a**) *(raisin)* muscat grape (**b**) *(vin)* muscatel (wine)
muscle [myskl] *nm* muscle; **être tout en m.** to be all muscle
musclé, -e [myskle] *adj* (**a**) *(personne, bras, jambes)* muscular (**b**) *Fig (campagne électorale, discours)* punchy; *(intervention)* forceful; *(politique, mesure)* tough
muscler [myskle] **1** *vt* to develop the muscles of
2 se muscler *vpr* to develop one's muscles
muscu [mysky] *Fam* = **musculation**
musculaire [myskylɛr] *adj (système, tissu, force)* muscular; *(fibre)* muscle
musculation [myskylasjɔ̃] *nf* body-building; **faire de la m.** to do body-building
musculature [myskylatyr] *nf* musculature
muse [myz] *nf* muse
museau, -x [myzo] *nm* (**a**) *(d'animal)* muzzle, snout (**b**) *Fam (visage)* face
musée [myze] *nm* museum; **m. (de peinture)** art gallery; **m. des horreurs** chamber of horrors
museler [42] [myzle] *vt aussi Fig* to muzzle
muselière [myzəljɛr] *nf* muzzle
musette [myzɛt] **1** *nf* (**a**) *(instrument de musique)* musette (**b**) *(sac)* bag; *(de soldat)* haversack; *(d'écolier)* satchel
2 *nm Fam* **le m.** accordion music

muséum [myzeɔm] *nm* natural history museum
musical, -e, -aux, -ales [myzikal, -o] *adj* musical
musicalement [myzikalmã] *adv* musically
music-hall *(pl* **music-halls**) [myzikol] *nm (genre, salle)* music hall
musicien, -enne [myzisjɛ̃, -ɛn] **1** *adj* musical
2 *nm,f* musician
musicologie [myzikɔlɔʒi] *nf* musicology
musicologue [myzikɔlɔg] *nmf* musicologist
musique [myzik] *nf* (**a**) *(art, notation ou science)* music; **mettre qch en m.** to set sth to music; **faire de la m.** to make music; *Fig* **connaître la m.** to have heard it all before; *Can* **faire face à la m.** to face the music; **m. d'ambiance** *ou* **de fond** background music; **m. de chambre** chamber music; **m. classique** classical music; **m. folklorique** folk music; **m. religieuse** religious music; **m. sacrée** sacred music (**b**) *Belg, Suisse & Can* **m. à bouche** harmonica, mouth organ
musqué, -e [myske] *adj (odeur)* musky
must [mœst] *nm Fam* must
mustang [mystãg] *nm* mustang
musulman, -e [myzylmã, -an] *adj & nm,f* Moslem, Muslim
mutant, -e [mytã, ãt] *adj & nm,f* mutant
mutation [mytasjɔ̃] *nf* (**a**) *(de personnel)* transfer (**b**) *(changement)* change, alteration
muter [myte] *vt* to transfer
mutilation [mytilasjɔ̃] *nf* mutilation
mutilé, -e [mytile] *nm,f* **mutilés de guerre** disabled ex-servicemen
mutiler [mytile] **1** *vt (personne)* to mutilate, to maim; *(partie du corps)* to badly injure; *(paysage)* to disfigure
2 se mutiler *vpr* to mutilate oneself
mutin¹ [mytɛ̃] *nm* mutineer
mutin², -e [mytɛ̃, -in] *adj (espiègle)* mischievous
mutiner [mytine] **se mutiner** *vpr* to mutiny (**contre** against)
mutinerie [mytinri] *nf* mutiny
mutisme [mytism] *nm* silence; **observer un m. absolu** to maintain total silence
mutualité [mytɥalite] *nf* mutual insurance
mutuel, -elle [mytɥɛl] **1** *adj* mutual
2 *nf* **mutuelle** mutual insurance company

> **Mutuelle**
> A "mutuelle" is a non-profit-making health insurance company which provides insurance complementary to that of the **"Sécurité sociale"**. Often these companies are set up for a particular profession: there is a "mutuelle" for students, one for teachers etc.

mutuellement [mytɥɛlmã] *adv* each other, one another
Myanmar [mjanmar] *nm* **le M.** Myanmar
mycose [mikoz] *nf* fungal infection, *Spéc* mycosis
mygale [migal] *nf* trapdoor spider
myocarde [mjɔkard] *nm* myocardium
myopathe [mjɔpat] *nmf* person with muscular dystrophy
myopathie [mjɔpati] *nf* muscular dystrophy
myope [mjɔp] **1** *adj* shortsighted, *Spéc* myopic; *Fig* **m. comme une taupe** as blind as a bat
2 *nmf* shortsighted person
myopie [mjɔpi] *nf* shortsightedness, *Spéc* myopia

myosotis [mjɔzɔtis] *nm* forget-me-not

myriade [mirjad] *nf* myriad (**de** of)

myrrhe [mir] *nf* myrrh

myrtille [mirtij] *nf Br* bilberry, *Am* blueberry

mystère [mistɛr] *nm* (**a**) *(énigme)* mystery; **faire des mystères** to be mysterious; **faire m. de qch** to make a secret of sth; **il n'y a pas de m.** it's quite simple; *Fam* **m. et boule de gomme!** search me! (**b**) *(pièce de théâtre)* mystery (play) (**c**) **Mystère**® *(dessert glacé)* = vanilla ice cream filled with meringue and coated with chopped nuts

mystérieusement [misterjøzmã] *adv* mysteriously

mystérieux, -euse [misterjø, -øz] *adj* mysterious; *(secret)* secret

mysticisme [mistisism] *nm* mysticism

mystification [mistifikasjɔ̃] *nf* hoax

mystifier [66] [mistifje] *vt* to take in

mystique [mistik] **1** *adj* mystical
2 *nmf* mystic

mythe [mit] *nm* myth; **elle fait un m. vivant** she was a legend in her own lifetime

mythique [mitik] *adj* mythical

mythologie [mitɔlɔʒi] *nf* mythology

mythologique [mitɔlɔʒik] *adj* mythological

mythomane [mitɔman] **1** *adj* **être m.** to be a pathological liar
2 *nmf* pathological liar, *Spéc* mythomaniac

mythomanie [mitɔmani] *nf* mythomania

myxomatose [miksɔmatoz] *nf* myxomatosis

N

N¹, n [ɛn] *nm inv* N, n

N² [ɛn] **1** (*abrév* **Nord**) N

2 *nf* (*abrév* **route nationale**) = designation of major road

nabot, -e [nabo, -ɔt] *nm,f Péj* midget

nacelle [nasɛl] *nf* (**a**) (*de montgolfière*) basket; (*de dirigeable*) gondola (**b**) (*de landau*) (*détachable*) carrycot; (*fixe*) carriage

nacre [nakr] *nf* mother-of-pearl; **un collier de** *ou* **en n.** a mother-of-pearl necklace

nacré, -e [nakre] *adj* pearly

nage [naʒ] *nf* (**a**) (*activité*) swimming; (*manière*) stroke; **traverser une rivière à la n.** to swim across a river; **le 100 mètres quatre nages** the 4 x 100 metres relay; **n. indienne** sidestroke; **n. libre** freestyle (**b**) **être en n.** to be bathed in perspiration

nageoire [naʒwar] *nf* (*de poisson*) fin; (*de dauphin, de cétacé*) flipper

nager [45] [naʒe] **1** *vi* to swim; **aller n.** to go for a swim; **n. vers la côte** to swim for the shore, *Fig* **n. entre deux eaux** to sit on the fence; *Fig* **n. dans son sang** to be bathed in blood; *Fig* **n. dans le bonheur** to be on cloud nine; *Fam* **il nage dans ses vêtements** his clothes are far too baggy on him; *Fam* **je nage complètement!** I'm totally at sea!

2 *vt* (**a**) (*la brasse, le crawl*) to do, to swim (**b**) (*disputer*) **n. le 100 mètres** to swim (in) the 100 metres

nageur, -euse [naʒœr, -øz] *nm,f* swimmer

naguère [nagɛr] *adv Litt* not long ago; (*autrefois*) formerly

naïf, -ïve [naif, -iv] **1** *adj* naive

2 *nm,f* (**a**) (*personne*) fool (**b**) (*peintre*) naive painter

nain, -e [nɛ̃, nɛn] **1** *adj* (*personne*) dwarf

2 *nm,f* dwarf

Nairobi [nerobi] *n* Nairobi

naissance [nɛsɑ̃s] *nf* (**a**) *aussi Fig* birth; **sourd/aveugle de n.** deaf/blind from birth, born deaf/blind; **français de n.** French by birth; **donner n. à un enfant** to give birth to a child; **donner n. à une rumeur** to give rise to a rumour; **il était blond à la n.** his hair was blond when he was born (**b**) (*d'ongle*) root; (*du cou*) base; **prendre n.** to originate; (*rivière*) to rise

naissant, -e [nɛsɑ̃, -ɑ̃t] *adj* (*jour*) dawning; (*beauté*) nascent; **une barbe naissante** stubble

naître [50a] [nɛtr] *vi* (*aux* **être**) (**a**) (*personne, animal*) to be born; **enfant à n.** unborn child; **il naît plus de filles que de garçons** more girls are born than boys; **elle est née en 1880** she was born in 1880; *Fam* **je ne suis pas né d'hier** I wasn't born yesterday (**b**) (*espoir*) to arise; (*projet, idée*) to originate (**de** in); **faire n.** (*espoir, doute, soupçons*) to give rise to; (*sourire*) to raise

naïvement [naivmɑ̃] *adv* naively

naïveté [naivte] *nf* naivety; **avoir la n. de croire qch** to be naive enough to believe sth

Namibie [namibi] *nf* **la N.** Namibia

namibien, -enne [namibjɛ̃, -ɛn] **1** *adj* Namibian

2 *nm,f* **N.** Namibian

nana [nana] *nf Fam* girl

nanisme [nanism] *nm* dwarfism

nano- [nano] *préf* nano-

nanti, -e [nɑ̃ti] **1** *adj* well-to-do

2 *nm,f* well-to-do person; **les nantis** the well-to-do

nantir [nɑ̃tir] *vt* **n. qn de qch** to provide sb with sth

napalm [napalm] *nm* napalm

naphtaline [naftalin] *nf* naphthalene; **boules de n.** mothballs; *Can Fig* **sortir qch de la n.** to take sth out of mothballs

Napoléon [napoleɔ̃] **1** *npr* Napoleon

2 *nm* **n.** (*pièce*) 20-franc piece (*bearing the likeness of Napoleon*)

nappage [napaʒ] *nm* coating

nappe [nap] *nf* (**a**) (*de table*) tablecloth; **mettre la n.** to put the tablecloth on; **ôter la n.** to take the tablecloth off (**b**) *Fig* **n. de brouillard** fog patch; **n. d'eau** expanse of water; **n. de pétrole** (*souterraine*) layer of oil; (*de marée noire*) oil slick; **n. phréatique** water table

napper [nape] *vt* to coat (**de** with)

napperon [naprɔ̃] *nm* mat

narcisse [narsis] *nm* (**a**) (*fleur*) narcissus (**b**) (*personne*) narcissist

narcissique [narsisik] *adj* narcissistic

narcissisme [narsisism] *nm* narcissism

narcodollars [narkodɔlar] *nmpl* drug money

narcotique [narkɔtik] *adj & nm* narcotic

narcotrafic [narkɔtrafik] *nm* drug trafficking

narcotrafiquant, -e [narkɔtrafikɑ̃, -ɑ̃t] *nm,f* drug trafficker

narguer [narge] *vt* to taunt

narine [narin] *nf* nostril

narquois, -e [narkwa, -az] *adj* taunting

narquoisement [narkwazmɑ̃] *adv* tauntingly

narrateur, -trice [naratœr, -tris] *nm,f* narrator

narratif, -ive [naratif, -iv] *adj* narrative

narration [narasjɔ̃] *nf* (**a**) (*genre*) narration (**b**) (*récit*) narrative

narrer [nare] *vt Litt* to narrate

narval, -als [narval] *nm* narwhal

nasal, -e, -aux, -ales [nazal, -o] *adj* nasal

nase [naz] *adj Fam* (*personne*) shattered; (*machine, voiture*) kaput

naseau, -x [nazo] *nm* nostril

nasillard, -e [nazijar, -ard] *adj* nasal; (*vieux disque*) tinny

nasse [nas] *nf* pot

natal, -e, -als, -ales [natal] *adj* native; **sa maison natale** the house where she was born

nataliste [natalist] *adj* **politique n.** pro-birth policy

natalité [natalite] *nf* **(taux de) n.** birth rate

natation [natasjɔ̃] *nf* swimming; **faire de la n.** to swim; **n. synchronisée** synchronized swimming

natif, -ive [natif, -iv] **1** *adj* native; **être n. de** to be a native of
  2 *nm,f* native

nation [nasjɔ̃] *nf* nation; **les Nations unies** the United Nations

national, -e, -aux, -ales [nasjɔnal, -o] **1** *adj* national
  2 *nmpl* **nationaux** nationals
  3 *nf* **nationale** *(route) Br* ≃ A road, *Am* ≃ highway

nationalisation [nasjɔnalizasjɔ̃] *nf* nationalization

nationaliser [nasjɔnalize] *vt* to nationalize

nationalisme [nasjɔnalism] *nm* nationalism

nationaliste [nasjɔnalist] *adj & nmf* nationalist

nationalité [nasjɔnalite] *nf* nationality; **être de n. française** to be a French national

national-socialisme [nasjɔnalsɔsjalism] *nm Hist* National Socialism

nativité [nativite] *nf (Noël, peinture)* Nativity

natte [nat] *nf* **(a)** *(de cheveux) Br* plait, *Am* braid **(b)** *(de paille)* mat

natter [nate] *vt (cheveux, paille) Br* to plait, *Am* to braid

naturalisation [natyralizasjɔ̃] *nf* naturalization

naturaliser [natyralize] *vt* to naturalize; **se faire n.** to become naturalized; **il s'est fait n. français** he was granted French citizenship

naturalisme [natyralism] *nm* naturalism

nature [natyr] **1** *nf* **(a)** *(univers)* nature; **contre n.** unnatural; **plus grand que n.** larger than life; **laisser faire la n.** to let nature take its course; *Fam* **elle n'est pas gâtée par la n.** nature hasn't been kind to her **(b)** *(campagne)* country; **en pleine n.** in the middle of the country; *Fig* **disparaître dans la n.** to vanish into thin air **(c)** *(caractère)* nature; **être timide de** *ou* **par n.** to be shy by nature; **être de n. à faire qch** to be likely to do sth; **chez elle, c'est une seconde n.** it's second nature to her; *Fam* **c'est une petite n.** he's a bit fragile **(d)** **payer en n.** to pay in kind **(e)** **n. morte** still life
  2 *adj inv* **(a)** *(omelette)* plain; *(yaourt)* natural; **thé n.** tea without milk **(b)** *Fam (personne)* natural

naturel, -elle [natyrɛl] **1** *adj* natural; *(besoin)* bodily; **mort naturelle** death from natural causes; **mais c'est tout n.** don't mention it
  2 *nm* **(a)** *(caractère)* nature; **être d'un n. peureux** to be timid by nature; *Prov* **chassez le n., il revient au galop** what's bred in the bone will come out in the flesh **(b)** *(simplicité)* naturalness; **avec (beaucoup de) n.** (very) naturally **(c)** **thon au n.** tuna in brine

naturellement [natyrɛlmɑ̃] *adv* naturally

naturisme [natyrism] *nm* naturism

naturiste [natyrist] *adj & nmf* naturist

naufrage [nofraʒ] *nm* (ship)wreck; *Fig (d'entreprise)* failure; **faire n.** *(bateau)* to be wrecked; *(marin)* to be shipwrecked; *Fig (entreprise)* to founder

naufragé, -e [nofraʒe] **1** *adj (bateau)* wrecked; *(marin)* shipwrecked
  2 *nm,f* shipwrecked person

nauséabond, -e [nozeabɔ̃, -ɔ̃d] *adj (odeur)* nauseating; *(personne, pièce)* foul-smelling; *Fig (thèses)* sickening

nausée [noze] *nf* **(a)** *(envie de vomir)* nausea, sickness; **avoir la n., avoir des nausées** to feel sick **(b)** *Fig* disgust; **ça me donne la n.** it makes me sick

nauséeux, -euse [nozeø, -øz] *adj* **se sentir n.** to feel sick *or* nauseous

nautique [notik] *adj* nautical

nautisme [notism] *nm* water sports

naval, -e, -als, -ales [naval] *adj* naval

navet [navɛ] *nm* turnip; *Fam* **c'est un n.** *(film, pièce)* it's a load of rubbish

navette [navɛt] *nf* **(a)** *(véhicule)* shuttle; **faire la n. entre deux endroits/services** to shuttle back and forth between two places/departments; **n. gratuite** courtesy bus **(b)** *(fusée)* **n. (spatiale)** (space) shuttle

navetteur, -euse [navɛtœr, -øz] *nm,f Belg* commuter

navigable [navigabl] *adj* navigable

navigant, -e [naviɡɑ̃, -ɑ̃t] *adj voir* **personnel**

navigateur, -trice [navigatœr, -tris] **1** *nm,f (marin)* navigator; **n. solitaire** lone yachtsman
  2 *nm Ordinat* browser

navigation [navigasjɔ̃] *nf* navigation; **après un mois de n.** after a month at sea; *Ordinat* **n. sur l'Internet** browsing the Internet, Internet surfing

naviguer [navige] *vi* to sail (**vers** to); **n. sur l'Internet** to surf the Net, to browse the Web

navire [navir] *nm* ship; **n.-école** training ship; **n. de guerre** warship

navrant, -e [navrɑ̃, -ɑ̃t] *adj* appalling; **un film n. de bêtise** an appallingly stupid film

navré, -e [navre] *adj (personne, expression, ton)* distressed; **être n. (de qch)** to be terribly sorry (about sth)

navrer [navre] *vt* to appal

naze [naz] = **nase**

nazi, -e [nazi] *adj & nm,f Hist* Nazi

nazisme [nazism] *nm Hist* Nazism

NB *(abrév* **nota bene**) NB

NDLR *(abrév* **note de la rédaction**) Ed

NdT *(abrév* **note du traducteur**) translator's note

ne [nə] *adv* **(a)** *voir* **aucun, guère, jamais, pas, personne, plus, que, rien** **(b)** *(utilisé seul)* **je n'ai que faire de vos conseils** I have no need of your advice; **elle est plus vigoureuse qu'elle n'y paraît** she's stronger than she looks; **qui ne connaît cette œuvre?** who doesn't know this work?

né, -e [ne] **1** *pp voir* **naître**
  2 *adj* born; **Mme Martin, née Dupond** Mrs Martin, née Dupond; **né de parents anglais/inconnus** of English/unknown parentage; **être bien né** to be of noble birth; *Fig* **être né coiffé** to be born with a silver spoon in one's mouth; **c'est un conteur né** he's a born storyteller

néanmoins [neɑ̃mwɛ̃] *adv* nevertheless

néant [neɑ̃] *nm* **(a)** *(ce qui n'existe pas)* nothingness; **réduire qch à n.** to reduce sth to nothing **(b)** *(sur formulaire)* none

nébuleux, -euse [nebylø, -øz] **1** *adj aussi Fig* hazy
  2 *nf* **nébuleuse** *Astron* nebula

nécessaire [nesesɛr] **1** *adj* necessary (**à** for); **n. pour faire qch** necessary to do sth; **il est n. que vous y alliez** you must go; **elles n'ont pas jugé n. de me le dire** they didn't think it necessary to tell me
  2 *nm* **le n.** the necessities; **n'emportez que le strict n.** just take the basic essentials; **faire le n.** to do what's necessary; **n. à chaussures** shoe-cleaning

kit; **n. de couture** sewing kit; **n. de toilette** toilet bag; **n. de voyage** overnight bag

nécessairement [nesesεrmã] *adv* necessarily

nécessité [nesesite] *nf* necessity; **être dans la n. de faire qch** to have no choice but to do sth; **quelle n. y avait-il de le faire?** what need was there to do it?; **faire de n. vertu** to make a virtue out of necessity; **produits de première n.** basic essentials; *Prov* **n. fait loi** needs must

nécessiter [nesesite] *vt* to require, to necessitate

nécessiteux, -euse [nesesitø, -øz] **1** *adj* needy
2 *nm,f* person in need; **les n.** the needy

nec plus ultra [nεkplyzyltra] *nm inv* **le n.** the best there is

nécrologie [nekrɔlɔʒi] *nf* (*notice*) obituary; (*liste*) obituary column

nécrologique [nekrɔlɔʒik] *adj voir* **rubrique**

nécropole [nekrɔpɔl] *nf* necropolis

nécrose [nekroz] *nf* necrosis

nécroser [nekroze] **1** *vt* to necrose
2 se nécroser *vpr* to necrose

nectar [nεktar] *nm* nectar

nectarine [nεktarin] *nf* nectarine

néerlandais, -e [neεrlãdε, -εz] **1** *adj* Dutch
2 *nm,f* **N.** Dutchman; *f* Dutchwoman; **les N.** the Dutch
3 *nm* (*langue*) Dutch

nef [nεf] *nf* (*d'église*) **n. (centrale)** nave; **n. latérale** aisle

néfaste [nefast] *adj* harmful

nèfle [nεfl] *nf* medlar; *Fam* **des nèfles!** no way!

négatif, -ive [negatif, -iv] **1** *adj* negative
2 *nm Phot* negative
3 négative *nf* **dans la n.** if not; **répondre par la n.** to give a negative answer, to answer in the negative

négation [negasjɔ̃] *nf* (**a**) (*fait de nier*) negation (**b**) *Gram* negative

négationnisme [negasjɔnism] *nm* revisionism

négationniste [negasjɔnist] *adj & nmf* revisionist

négativement [negativmã] *adv* (*réagir*) negatively; (*répondre*) in the negative

négligé, -e [negliʒe] **1** *adj* (**a**) (*peu soigné*) slovenly (**b**) (*délaissé*) neglected
2 *nm* (*vêtement*) négligée

négligeable [negliʒabl] *adj* negligible; **un avantage non n.** a not inconsiderable advantage; **une quantité non n. de** a significant quantity of

négligemment [negliʒamã] *adv* (**a**) (*habillé*) carelessly (**b**) (*répondre, lire*) casually

négligence [negliʒãs] *nf* (**a**) (*manque de soin*) carelessness, negligence; (*abandon*) neglect; **avec n.** carelessly (**b**) (*acte négligent*) act of carelessness; (*oubli*) oversight; **par n.** through carelessness

négligent, -e [negliʒã, -ãt] *adj* careless, negligent

négliger [45] [negliʒe] **1** *vt* (**a**) (*délaisser*) to neglect (**b**) (*omettre*) to disregard; **n. de faire qch** to neglect to do sth
2 se négliger *vpr* to neglect oneself

négoce [negɔs] *nm* trade

négociable [negɔsjabl] *adj* negotiable

négociant, -e [negɔsjã, -ãt] *nm,f* merchant, dealer

négociation [negɔsjasjɔ̃] *nf* negotiation; **entamer des négociations sur qch** to enter into negotiations on sth; **être en n. avec qn** to be in negotiation with sb

négocier [66] [negɔsje] **1** *vt* (**a**) (*prêt, salaire, paix*) to negotiate; **prix à n.** price negotiable (**b**) (*virage*) to negotiate
2 *vi* (*discuter*) to negotiate (**avec** with)

nègre [nεgr] **1** *nm* (**a**) *Injurieux* Negro (**b**) *Fig* (*écrivain*) ghost writer; **être le n. de qn** to ghost for sb
2 *adj* (**a**) **l'art n.** Negro art (**b**) *Injurieux* (*personne*) Negro

négresse [negrεs] *nf Injurieux* Negress

neige [nεʒ] *nf* (**a**) (*flocons*) snow; *Can* **banc de n.** snow bank; **être bloqué par la n.** to be snowbound; **aller à la n.** to go on a skiing holiday; **fondre comme n. au soleil** to melt away; **être blanc comme n.** to be as white as snow; *Fig* to be as pure as the driven snow; **n. artificielle** *ou Can* **fabriquée** artificial snow; **n. carbonique** dry ice; **neiges éternelles** perpetual snow; **n. fondue** (*qui tombe*) sleet; (*par terre*) slush (**b**) *très Fam* (*cocaïne*) snow

neiger [45] [neʒe] *v impersonnel* to snow

neigeux, -euse [neʒø, -øz] *adj* (*temps, blanc*) snowy; (*pic, pente*) snow-covered

nem [nεm] *nm* spring roll

néné [nene] *nm Fam* tit, boob

nénette [nenεt] *nf Fam* (**a**) (*jeune fille*) chick (**b**) (*petite amie*) girl (**c**) (*tête*) **se casser la n.** to rack one's brains

nénuphar [nenyfar] *nm* water lily

néo- [neo] *préf* neo-

néo-calédonien, -enne (*mpl* **néo-calédoniens**, *fpl* **néo-calédoniennes**) [neokaledɔnjε̃, -εn] **1** *adj* New Caledonian
2 *nm,f* **N.-C.** New Caledonian

néoclassique [neoklasik] *adj* neoclassical

néocolonialisme [neokɔlɔnjalism] *nm* neocolonialism

néolithique [neolitik] *Géol* **1** *adj* Neolithic
2 *nm* **le N.** the Neolithic period

néologisme [neolɔʒism] *nm* neologism

néon [neɔ̃] *nm* (*gaz*) neon; (*tube*) neon tube; (*enseigne*) neon sign

néonazi, -e [neonazi] *adj & nm,f* neo-Nazi

néonazisme [neonazism] *nm* neo-Nazism

néophyte [neofit] *nmf* (*nouvel adepte*) novice

néo-zélandais, -e (*mpl* **néo-zélandais**, *fpl* **néo-zélandaises**) [neozelãdε, -εz] **1** *adj* New Zealand
2 *nm,f* **N.-Z.** New Zealander

Népal [nepal] *nm* **le N.** Nepal

népalais, -e [nepalε, -εz] **1** *adj* Nepalese
2 *nm,f* **N.** Nepalese; **les N.** the Nepalese
3 *nm* (*langue*) Nepali

néphrétique [nefretik] *adj voir* **colique**

népotisme [nepɔtism] *nm* nepotism

Neptune [nεptyn] *npr* (*dieu, planète*) Neptune

nerf [nεr] *nm* (**a**) (*optique, spinal*) nerve; **viande pleine de nerfs** meat full of gristle; **avoir les nerfs solides** to have strong nerves; **être malade des nerfs** to suffer from nerves; **être sur les nerfs** to live on one's nerves; **être à bout de nerfs** to be at the end of one's tether; **passer ses nerfs sur qn/qch** to take it out on sb/sth; *Fam* **avoir les nerfs en pelote** *ou* **en boule** to be all on edge; *Fam* **porter** *ou* **taper** *ou Can* **tomber sur les nerfs à qn** to get on sb's nerves; *Fam* **c'est un paquet** *ou* **une boule de nerfs** he's a bag of nerves (**b**) (*force*) **un peu de n.!**, **du n.!** get stuck in!; **l'argent est le n. de la guerre** money is the sinews of war

nerveusement [nεrvøzmã] *adv* nervously

nerveux, -euse [nɛrvø, -øz] **1** adj (**a**) (système, maladie) nervous (**b**) (émotif) (personne, rire, toux) nervous (**c**) (dynamique) (personne, style) dynamic; **une conduite nerveuse** a jerky way of driving (**d**) (corps, main) sinewy; (viande) stringy
2 nm,f nervous person
nervosité [nɛrvozite] nf (excitation) nervousness; (irritabilité) irritability
nervure [nɛrvyr] nf (**a**) (de feuille, d'aile d'insecte) vein (**b**) (de voûte) rib
n'est-ce pas [nɛspɑ] adv **tu viendras, n.?** you'll come, won't you?; **tu l'as, n.?** you've got it, haven't you?; **n. qu'elle est mignonne?** she's cute, isn't she?; **le problème, n., c'est qu'il est déjà tard** the problem is that it's already late, don't you think?
Net [nɛt] nm Ordinat **le N.** the Net
net, nette [nɛt] **1** adj (**a**) (propre) clean; Fig (conscience) clear; **faire place nette** to clear everything out (**b**) (précis) (contour) sharp; (différence, souvenir) clear; (écriture) neat; (cassure) clean; **il fait plus froid, c'est très n.** it's noticeably colder (**c**) (prix, salaire, profit) net; **n. d'impôt** net of tax (**d**) Fam **il n'est pas n.** (fou) he's not all there; (louche) he's a bit dodgy
2 adv (**a**) (brutalement) **refuser (tout) n.** to refuse point-blank; **s'arrêter n.** to stop dead; **se casser n.** to break clean through; **tué n.** killed outright (**b**) Com **100 francs n.** 100 francs net; **n. à payer** net payable
netiquette [nɛtikɛt] nf Ordinat netiquette
nettement [nɛtmɑ̃] adv (**a**) (avec précision) clearly (**b**) (incontestablement) distinctly (**c**) (beaucoup) much; **il va n. mieux** he's much better; **il est n. moins bon qu'elle** he's not nearly as good as her
netteté [nɛtte] nf (**a**) (propreté) cleanness (**b**) (précision) (de cassure) cleanness (**c**) (clarté) (de vision, d'objet) distinctness; (d'image) sharpness; (de refus) flatness
nettoiement [nɛtwamɑ̃] nm cleaning; **service du n.** refuse collection service
nettoyage [nɛtwajaʒ] nm cleaning; **faire du n.** to do the cleaning; **faire n. par le vide** to throw everything out; **grand n. de printemps** spring cleaning; **n. à sec** dry-cleaning
nettoyant, -e [nɛtwajɑ̃, -ɑ̃t] **1** adj cleaning
2 nm cleaning product
nettoyer [32] [nɛtwaje] **1** vt (**a**) (rendre propre) to clean; **n. à sec** to dry-clean (**b**) Fam (sujet: cambrioleur) (maison) to clean out; **se faire n. au jeu** to be cleaned out gambling
2 se nettoyer vpr (**a**) **se n. les oreilles/les mains** to clean one's ears/hands (**b**) **le four se nettoie automatiquement** the oven is self-cleaning
neuf¹ [nœf] adj & nm inv nine; voir aussi **trois**
neuf², neuve [nœf, nœv] **1** adj new; **tout n.** brand new; **comme n.** as good as new; **quoi de n.?** what's new?
2 nm **habillé de n.** wearing new clothes; **acheter du n.** (dans l'immobilier) to buy new; **remettre qch à n.** to make sth as good as new; (machine) to recondition sth
neurasthénie [nørasteni] nf depression
neurasthénique [nørastenik] adj & nmf depressive
neurochirurgie [nøroʃiryrʒi] nf neurosurgery
neurochirurgien, -enne [nøroʃiryrʒjɛ̃, -ɛn] nm,f neurosurgeon
neuroleptique [nørolɛptik] adj & nm neuroleptic
neurologie [nørolɔʒi] nf neurology

neurologue [nørolɔg] nmf neurologist
neurone [nøron, nøron] nm neuron
neutraliser [nøtralize] **1** vt to neutralize
2 se neutraliser vpr to neutralize each other
neutralité [nøtralite] nf neutrality; **sortir de sa n.** to abandon one's neutral position
neutre [nøtr] **1** adj (**a**) (ni masculin ni féminin) neuter (**b**) (impartial) neutral (**c**) (ton de voix, couleur) neutral (**d**) Chim & Él neutral
2 nm (**a**) Gram neuter (**b**) Can Aut neutral; **se mettre sur le n.** to go into neutral
neutron [nøtrɔ̃] nm neutron
neuvième [nœvjɛm] nmf, nm & adj ninth; voir aussi **cinquième**
névé [neve] nm névé, firn
neveu, -x [nəvø] nm nephew; Fam **un peu, mon n.!** you bet!, sure thing!
névralgie [nevralʒi] nf neuralgia; **avoir des névralgies** to suffer from neuralgia
névralgique [nevralʒik] adj neuralgic
névrose [nevroz] nf neurosis; **n. post-traumatique** post-traumatic stress disorder
névrosé, -e [nevroze] adj & nm,f neurotic
New York [nujɔrk] n New York
new-yorkais, -e [njujɔrkɛ, -ɛz] (mpl **new-yorkais**, fpl **new-yorkaises**) [njujɔrkɛ, -ɛz] **1** adj of New York
2 nm,f **N.-Y.** New Yorker
nez [ne] nm (**a**) (organe) nose; **n. en trompette** turned-up nose; **parler du n.** to speak through one's nose; **sentir qch à plein n.** to smell strongly of sth; **rire au n. de qn** to laugh in sb's face; **faire qch au n. et à la barbe de qn** to do sth right under sb's nose; **fermer ou claquer la porte au n. de qn** to shut the door in sb's face; **se trouver n. à n. avec qn** to find oneself face to face with sb; **avoir le n. dans son journal** to have one's nose in one's newspaper; **avoir le n. en l'air** to be looking up in the air; Fig (rêvasser) to have one's head in the clouds; Fig **mener qn par le bout du n.** to lead sb by the nose; Fam **fourrer ou mettre son n. dans les affaires de qn** to poke one's nose into sb's affairs; Fam **avoir un verre ou un coup dans le n.** to have had one too many; **je n'ai pas mis le n. dehors de toute la journée** I didn't set foot outside all day; **tu ne vois pas plus loin que le bout de ton n.** you can't see further than the end of your nose; Fam **elle nous a dans le n.** she can't stand us; **ça lui pend au n.** she's got it coming to her; **ça se voit comme le n. au milieu de la figure** it's as plain as the nose on your face; **où est-il? – il est sous ton n. ou tu as le n. dessus** where is it? – it's under your nose (**b**) (odorat) sense of smell; **avoir le n. fin** to have a good nose; Fig **avoir du n.** to be shrewd (**c**) (de bateau, d'avion) nose (**d**) (parfumeur) nose
ni [ni] conj **ni... ni...** neither... nor...; **ni Pierre ni Paul ne sont venus** neither Pierre nor Paul came; **sans argent ni bagages** without money or luggage; **il est parti sans manger ni boire** he left without eating or drinking; **ni l'un ni l'autre** neither (of them); **ni plus ni moins** neither more nor less
niais, -e [njɛ, njɛz] **1** adj silly
2 nm,f fool
niaisage [njɛzaʒ] nm Can idleness
niaisement [njɛzmɑ̃] adv foolishly
niaiser [njɛze] Can **1** vt **n. qn** (faire tourner en bourrique) to drive sb crazy; (se moquer de) to laugh at sb;

(raconter des histoires à) to pull sb's leg

  2 *vi (ne rien faire)* to hang around doing nothing

niaiserie [njɛzri] *nf* (**a**) *(caractère stupide)* silliness (**b**) *(acte, remarque)* silly thing

niaiseux, -euse [njɛzø, -øz] *Can Fam* **1** *adj* silly

  2 *nm,f* fool

Nicaragua [nikaragwa] *nm* **le N.** Nicaragua

nicaraguayen, -enne [nikaragwajɛ̃, -ɛn] **1** *adj* Nicaraguan

  2 *nm,f* **N.** Nicaraguan

niche [niʃ] *nf* (**a**) *(renfoncement)* niche, recess (**b**) *(de chien)* kennel

nichée [niʃe] *nf (d'oisillons)* brood; *(de souris, de chiots)* litter

nicher [niʃe] **1** *vi (oiseau)* to nest (**dans** in)

  2 *vt* **n. sa tête au creux de l'épaule de qn** to nestle one's head against sb's shoulder

  3 se nicher *vpr* (**a**) *(oiseau)* to nest (**b**) *Fam (se cacher)* **où est-elle allée se n.?** where's she hiding (herself)?

nichon [niʃɔ̃] *nm Fam* boob, tit

nickel [nikɛl] **1** *nm* nickel

  2 *adj inv Fam (propre)* spotlessly clean

nicotine [nikɔtin] *nf* nicotine

nid [ni] *nm aussi Fig* nest; *Fig* **n. à poussière** dust trap; *Prov* **petit à petit, l'oiseau fait son n.** slow and steady wins the race

nid-de-poule *(pl* **nids-de-poule**) [nidpul] *nm* pothole

nièce [njɛs] *nf* niece

nier [66] [nje] **1** *vt* to deny; **je nie l'avoir vue** I deny having seen her; **on ne peut pas n. que...** there's no denying that...; **n. l'évidence** to deny the obvious

  2 *vi (accusé)* to deny the charge

niet [njɛt] *exclam Fam* no way!, not a chance!

nigaud, -e [nigo, -od] *nm,f* ninny; **gros n.!** you big ninny!

Niger [niʒɛr] *nm* **le N.** *(pays)* Niger; *(fleuve)* the Niger

Nigeria [niʒɛrja] *nm* **le N.** Nigeria

nigérian, -e [niʒɛrjɑ̃, -an] **1** *adj* Nigerian

  2 *nm,f* **N.** Nigerian

nigérien, -enne [niʒɛrjɛ̃, -ɛn] **1** *adj* Nigerien

  2 *nm,f* **N.** Nigerien

nihilisme [niilism] *nm* nihilism

nihiliste [niilist] **1** *adj* nihilistic

  2 *nmf* nihilist

Nil [nil] *nm* **le N.** the Nile

n'importe [nɛ̃pɔrt] *voir* **importer**

NIP [nip] *nm Can Fin (abrév* **numéro d'identification personnelle)** ≃ PIN (number)

nipper [nipe] *Fam* **1** *vt* to dress; **bien nippé** dolled up

  2 se nipper *vpr* to dress

nippes [nip] *nfpl Fam (vêtements)* gear, togs

nippon, -onne *ou* **-one** [nipɔ̃, -ɔn] **1** *adj* Japanese

  2 *nm,f* **N.** Japanese; **les Nippons** the Japanese

nique [nik] *nf Fam* **faire la n. à qn** to cock a snook at sb

niquer [nike] *vt* (**a**) *très Fam (abîmer)* to knacker (**b**) *Vulg (sexuellement)* to shag, to screw (**c**) *très Fam (escroquer)* **se faire n.** to get shafted

nitrate [nitrat] *nm* nitrate

nitreux, -euse [nitrø, -øz] *adj* nitrous

nitrique [nitrik] *adj* nitric

nitroglycérine [nitrogliserin] *nf* nitroglycerine

niveau, -x [nivo] *nm* (**a**) *(hauteur, étage)* level; **n. de l'eau/de la mer** water/sea level; **au n. de la mer** at sea level; **au n. du carrefour, vous tournez à droite** when you come to the crossroads, turn right; **au n. régional/local** at regional/local level; *Fam* **au n. sentimental** as far as one's love life is concerned; *aussi Fig* **se mettre au n. de qn** to put oneself on sb's level; **l'eau nous arrivait au n. de la taille** the water came up to our waists (**b**) *(degré)* level; *Scol* standard; **avoir le n. (requis), être au n.** to be up to standard; **ne pas avoir le n. pour passer un concours** not to be of a high enough standard to take an examination; **elle a un très bon n. en physique** her physics is of a very high standard; **ils sont d'un n. social différent** they are from different social backgrounds; *Ordinat* **n. d'accès** *(dans un réseau)* access level; *Ordinat* **n. de gris** grey scale; **n. de langue** register; **n. de vie** standard of living

niveler [42] [nivle] *vt* (**a**) *(sol)* to level (**b**) *(fortunes)* to even out

nivellement [nivɛlmɑ̃] *nm (de terrain, des classes sociales)* levelling; **n. par le bas** levelling down

nobiliaire [nɔbiljɛr] *adj* **titre n.** title; **particule n.** nobiliary particle

noble [nɔbl] **1** *adj* noble; **le n. art** *(boxe)* the noble art

  2 *nmf* nobleman, *f* noblewoman; **les nobles** the nobility

noblement [nɔbləmɑ̃] *adv* nobly

noblesse [nɔblɛs] *nf* nobility; **la haute et la petite n.** the nobility and the gentry; **n. oblige** noblesse oblige

noce [nɔs] *nf* (**a**) *(cérémonie du mariage)* wedding; *(ensemble des invités)* wedding party; **noces d'argent/ d'or/de diamant** silver/golden/diamond wedding; **il l'a épousée en secondes noces** she's his second wife (**b**) *Fam* **faire la n.** to live it up (**c**) *Fam* **je n'étais pas à la n.** it was no picnic

noceur, -euse [nɔsœr, -øz] *nm,f Fam* party animal, raver

nocif, -ive [nɔsif, -iv] *adj* harmful

nocivité [nɔsivite] *nf* harmfulness

noctambule [nɔktɑ̃byl] *nmf* night owl

nocturne [nɔktyrn] **1** *adj (animal)* nocturnal; *(attaque, visite)* night; **évasion n.** escape by night

  2 *nm (musique)* nocturne

  3 *nf* (**a**) *(de magasin)* late-night opening (**b**) **match (disputé) en n.** evening game

nodal, -e, -aux, -ales [nɔdal, -o] *adj* nodal

nodule [nɔdyl] *nm Géol & Méd* nodule

Noé [nɔe] *n* Noah

Noël [nɔɛl] *nm* (**a**) *(fête)* Christmas; **à N.** at Christmas (time); **le jour de N.** Christmas Day; **arbre** *ou* **sapin de N.** Christmas tree; **joyeux N.!** Happy *or* Merry Christmas! (**b**) *(chanson)* **n.** (Christmas) carol (**c**) *(cadeau)* **(petit) n.** Christmas present

nœud [nø] *nm* (**a**) *(entrecroisement)* knot; **faire un n. (à qch)** to make *or* tie a knot (in sth); **n. coulant** *(pour serrer)* slipknot; *(pour étrangler)* noose; **n. de vipères** nest of vipers (**b**) *(ornement)* bow; **n. de cravate** tie knot; **faire un n. de cravate** to knot a tie; *Fam* **n. pap** bow tie; **n. papillon** bow tie (**c**) *(de courbe) & Ordinat* node (**d**) *(sur bois)* knot (**e**) *Naut (vitesse)* knot; **filer** *ou* **faire 20 nœuds** to do *or* make 20 knots (**f**) *Vulg (pénis)* cock

noie *etc voir* **noyer**

noir, -e [nwar] **1** *adj* (**a**) *(couleur)* black; **la place était noire de monde** the square was swarming with people

(**b**) *(très sombre)* dark; **il fait tout n.** it's pitch-black
(**c**) *(sale)* black
(**d**) *Fig (pensées, dessein, regard)* black; **être d'une humeur noire** to be in a black mood
2 *nm,f* **N.** Black (man), *f* Black (woman)
3 *nm* (**a**) *(couleur)* black; **en n. et blanc** *(film, photo)* black and white; **être en n.** to be dressed in black; **c'était écrit n. sur blanc** it was there in black and white
(**b**) *(obscurité)* dark; **avoir peur du n.** to be afraid of the dark
(**c**) *(salissure)* **avoir du n. sur le visage** to have a black mark on one's face
(**d**) *(d'une cible)* bull's-eye
(**e**) *(café)* **un (petit) n.** a (small) black coffee
(**f**) *Fig* **voir tout en n.** to look on the black side of everything
(**g**) *Fam* **le travail au n.** moonlighting; **travailler au n.** to moonlight
4 *nf* **noire** *(note de musique) Br* crotchet, *Am* quarter note

noirâtre [nwaratr] *adj* blackish

noirceur [nwarsœr] *nf* (**a**) *(couleur)* blackness; *Litt (d'un crime)* heinousness (**b**) *Can (obscurité)* dark, darkness; **dans la n.** in the dark *or* darkness; **avoir peur dans la n.** to be afraid of the dark

noircir [nwarsir] **1** *vt* to blacken; *Fig* **n. du papier** to write pages and pages; *Fig* **n. (la réputation de) qn** to blacken sb's reputation; *Fig* **n. le tableau** *ou* **la situation** to paint things blacker than they are
2 *vi* to turn *or* go black
3 se noircir *vpr* (**a**) *(ciel)* to darken (**b**) **se n. le visage** to black one's face; *Théât* to black up

noise [nwaz] *nf* **chercher n.** *ou* **des noises à qn** to try to pick a quarrel with sb

noisetier [nwaztje] *nm (arbre)* hazel tree; *(bois)* hazel (wood)

noisette [nwazɛt] **1** *nf* (**a**) *(fruit)* hazelnut (**b**) *(petite quantité) (de beurre)* small knob; *(de gel)* small amount
2 *adj inv* **yeux n.** hazel eyes

noix [nwa] *nf* (**a**) *(fruit)* walnut; **n. de cajou** cashew nut; **n. de coco** coconut; **n. de pécan** pecan (**b**) *(petite quantité) (de beurre)* knob (**c**) **n. de veau** cushion of veal (**d**) *Fam* **à la n.** lousy

nom [nɔ̃] *nm* (**a**) *(de personne, de chose)* name; **un homme du n. de Pierre** a man by the name of Pierre; **n.... prénom...** *(sur formulaire)* surname... first name...; **vos n., prénoms et adresse** your full name and address; **porter le n. de sa mère** to be named after one's mother; **sous le n. de Leduc** under the name of Leduc; **se faire un n.** to make a name for oneself; **appeler les choses par leur n.** to call a spade a spade; **traiter qn de tous les noms** to call sb everything under the sun; **quelqu'un dont je tairai le n.** someone who shall remain nameless; **une impolitesse sans n.** unspeakable rudeness; **un grand n. de la musique** one of the great names in music; **faire une proposition au n. de qn** to make a proposal for sb *or* on behalf of sb; **au n. de la loi/de l'amitié** in the name of the law/of friendship; *Fam* **avoir un n. à coucher dehors** to have a totally unpronounceable name; **n. de baptême** Christian name; *Ordinat* **n. de champ** field name; *Ordinat* **n. de domaine** domain name; **n. d'emprunt** assumed name; **n. de famille** surname; *Ordinat* **n. de fichier** file name; **n. de jeune fille** maiden name; **n. à particule** aristocratic name *(with a nobiliary particle)*; **n. de plume** nom de plume,

pen name; *Fam* **n. à rallonges** *ou* **à tiroirs** long aristocratic name; **n. de scène** *ou* **de théâtre** stage name (**b**) *Gram* noun; **n. commun** common noun; **n. composé** compound (noun); **n. propre** proper noun (**c**) *Fam* **n. d'une pipe!**, **n. d'un chien!** hell!

nomade [nɔmad] **1** *adj* nomadic
2 *nmf* nomad

nomadisme [nɔmadism] *nm* nomadism

nombre [nɔ̃br] *nm aussi Gram* number; **un grand/petit n. d'entre nous** many/a few of us; **le plus grand n.** the majority; **(bon) n. de** a good many; **supérieur en n.** superior in number(s); **nous sommes en n. suffisant** there are enough of us; **venir en n.** to come in large numbers; **ils sont au n. de huit** there are eight of them; **être au n.** *ou* **du n. de** to be among; **faire n.** to make up the numbers; *Phys* **n. atomique** atomic number; *Math* **n. décimal** decimal (number); *Math* **n. entier** whole number, integer; *Math* **n. premier** prime number

nombreux, -euse [nɔ̃brø, -øz] *adj (membres, objets)* numerous, many; *(famille, armée, groupe)* large; **nous sommes peu n.** there aren't many of us; **venir (très) n.** to come in (very) large numbers

nombril [nɔ̃bri, nɔ̃bril] *nm* navel; **une chemise ouverte jusqu'au n.** a shirt open to the waist; **il se prend pour le n. du monde** he thinks the whole world revolves around him; *Fig* **se regarder le n.** to contemplate one's navel; *Can* **ne pas avoir le n. sec** to be (still) wet behind the ears

nombrilisme [nɔ̃brilism] *nm* navel-gazing

nombriliste [nɔ̃brilist] *adj* self-absorbed

nomenclature [nɔmãklatyr] *nf (de termes techniques)* nomenclature; *(d'un dictionnaire)* word list

nominal, -e, -aux, -ales [nɔminal, -o] *adj* (**a**) *(prix, autorité)* & *Fin* nominal (**b**) *(par noms de famille)* **appel n.** roll call; **liste nominale** list of names (**c**) *Gram* noun

nominalement [nɔminalmã] *adv* (**a**) *(de nom seulement)* in name only (**b**) *Gram (employé)* as a noun

nominatif, -ive [nɔminatif, -iv] *adj (carte d'adhérent, billet)* nontransferable; *Fin (titre)* registered

nomination [nɔminasjɔ̃] *nf* (**a**) *(à un poste)* appointment (**à** to) (**b**) *(pour une remise de récompense)* nomination (**à** for)

nominativement [nɔminativmã] *adv* by name

nominé, -e [nɔmine] *adj* nominated (**à** for)

nommé, -e [nɔme] **1** *adj (personne, objet)* named
2 *nm,f* **un n. Bertrand a appelé** someone called Bertrand rang

nommément [nɔmemã] *adv* (**a**) *(par son nom)* by name (**b**) *(spécialement)* especially, in particular

nommer [nɔme] **1** *vt* (**a**) *(donner un prénom à)* to name, to call (**b**) *(donner un nom à)* **on nomme aumôniers les prêtres attachés à un régiment** priests attached to a regiment are called chaplains (**c**) *(désigner)* to name; *Hum* **M. Boivin, pour ne pas le n.** without mentioning any names, Mr Boivin (**d**) *(à un poste)* to appoint (**à** to); **être nommé à Lille** to be posted to Lille
2 se nommer *vpr* (**a**) *(avoir pour nom)* to be called (**b**) *(s'identifier)* to give one's name

non [nɔ̃] **1** *adv* (**a**) *(en réponse, exprime la surprise, l'indignation)* no; **je pense que n.** I don't think so; **faire signe que n.** *(de la tête)* to shake one's head; **n. mais!** honestly! (**b**) *(n'est-ce pas?)* **c'est dégoûtant, n.?** it's disgusting, isn't it?; **il est pas mal, n.?** he's not

bad-looking, is he? **(c)** *(pas)* not; **n. loin** not far; **qu'elle vienne ou n.** whether she comes or not; **elle veut déménager, lui n.** she wants to move house but he doesn't; *Litt* **n. (pas) que je le craigne** not that I fear him
  2 *nm inv* no
nonagénaire [nɔnaʒenɛr] *adj & nmf* nonagenarian
non-agression [nɔnagresjɔ̃] *nf voir* **pacte**
non-alcoolisé, -e [nɔnalkɔlize] *adj* non-alcoholic
non-aligné, -e [nɔnaliɲe] *adj Pol* non-aligned
nonante [nɔnɑ̃t] *adj & nm inv Belg & Suisse* ninety; *voir aussi* **trois**
non-assistance [nɔnasistɑ̃s] *nf Jur* **n. à personne en danger** = failure to assist a person in danger, for example at the scene of an accident
non-autorisé, -e [nɔnɔtɔrize] *adj Ordinat (nom de fichier)* illegal
non-belligérant, -e [nɔbeliʒerɑ̃, -ɑ̃t] *adj* non-belligerent
nonchalamment [nɔ̃ʃalamɑ̃] *adv* nonchalantly
nonchalance [nɔ̃ʃalɑ̃s] *nf* nonchalance; **avec n.** nonchalantly
nonchalant, -e [nɔ̃ʃalɑ̃, -ɑ̃t] *adj* nonchalant
non-conformisme [nɔ̃kɔ̃fɔrmism] *nm* non-conformism
non-conformiste [nɔ̃kɔ̃fɔrmist] *adj & nmf* non-conformist
non-conformité [nɔ̃kɔ̃fɔrmite] *nf* nonconformity
non-connecté, -e [nɔ̃kɔnɛkte] *adj Ordinat* off-line
non-dit [nɔ̃di] *nm* **le n.** what is unspoken; **un film riche en non-dits** a film full of meaningful silences
non-formaté, -e [nɔ̃fɔrmate] *adj Ordinat* unformatted
non-fumeur, -euse [nɔ̃fymœr, -øz] **1** *adj* non-smoking
  2 *nm,f* non-smoker
non-ingérence [nɔnɛ̃ʒerɑ̃s] *nf* noninterference
non-initialisé, -e [nɔninisjalize] *adj Ordinat* uninitialized
non-initié, -e [nɔninisje] *nm,f* uninitiated person; **les non-initiés** the uninitiated
non-inscrit, -e [nɔnɛ̃skri, -it] *nm,f Pol* independent
non-intervention [nɔnɛ̃tɛrvɑ̃sjɔ̃] *nf* non-intervention
non-interventionniste [nɔnɛ̃tɛrvɑ̃sjɔnist] *adj* non-interventionist
non-lieu, -x [nɔ̃ljø] *nm Jur* **bénéficier d'un n.** to be discharged through lack of evidence
nonne [nɔn] *nf* nun
nono, -ote [nɔno, -ɔt] *nm,f Can Fam* idiot
non-paiement [nɔ̃pɛmɑ̃] *nm* non-payment
non-polluant, -e [nɔ̃pɔlɥɑ̃, -ɑ̃t] *adj* environmentally friendly
non-prolifération [nɔ̃prɔliferajɔ̃] *nf* nonproliferation
non-remboursable [nɔ̃rɑ̃bursabl] *adj* non-refundable
non-respect [nɔ̃rɛspɛ] *nm (d'une loi)* non-observance
non-retour [nɔ̃rətur] *nm* **point de n.** point of no return
non-salarié, -e [nɔ̃salarje] *nm,f* self-employed person
non-sens [nɔ̃sɑ̃s] *nm inv* **(a)** *(dans une traduction)* meaningless phrase **(b)** *(absurdité)* **un n.** a nonsense

non-stop [nɔnstɔp] *adj inv & adv Fam* non-stop
non-syndiqué, -e [nɔ̃sɛ̃dike] **1** *adj* non-union
  2 *nm,f* non-union worker
non-violence [nɔ̃vjɔlɑ̃s] *nf* non-violence
non-violent, -e [nɔ̃vjɔlɑ̃, -ɑ̃t] *adj* non-violent
non-voyant, -e *(mpl* **non-voyants,** *fpl* **non-voyantes)** [nɔ̃vwajɑ̃, -ɑ̃t] *nm,f* unsighted person; **les non-voyants** the unsighted
nord [nɔr] **1** *nm* north; **un vent du n.** a northerly *or* north wind; **le vent du n.** the north wind; **au n.** in the north; **au n. de** (to the) north of; *Fig* **il ne perd pas le n.** he's keeping a cool head; **le grand N.** the Frozen North
  2 *adj inv (côte, face)* north; *(régions)* northern
nord-africain, -e *(mpl* **nord-africains,** *fpl* **nord-africaines)** [nɔrafrikɛ̃, -ɛn] **1** *adj* North African
  2 *nm,f* **N.-A.** North African
nord-américain, -e *(mpl* **nord-américains,** *fpl* **nord-américaines)** [nɔramerikɛ̃, -ɛn] **1** *adj* North American
  2 *nm,f* **N.-A.** North American
nord-coréen, -enne *(mpl* **nord-coréens,** *fpl* **nord-coréennes)** [nɔrkɔreɛ̃, -ɛn] **1** *adj* North Korean
  2 *nm,f* **N.-C.** North Korean
nord-est [nɔrɛst] *nm & adj inv* northeast
nordique [nɔrdik] **1** *adj* Nordic, Scandinavian
  2 *nmf* **N.** Scandinavian
nordiste [nɔrdist] *adj & nmf* Unionist
nord-nord-est [nɔrnɔrɛst] *nm & adj inv* north-north-east
nord-nord-ouest [nɔrnɔrwɛst] *nm & adj inv* north-northwest
nord-ouest [nɔrwɛst] *nm & adj inv* northwest
nord-vietnamien, -enne *(mpl* **nord-vietnamiens,** *fpl* **nord-vietnamiennes)** [nɔrvjɛtnamjɛ̃, -ɛn] **1** *adj* North Vietnamese
  2 *nm,f* **N.-V.** North Vietnamese
noria [nɔrja] *nf* noria
normal, -e, -aux, -ales [nɔrmal, -o] **1** *adj* **(a)** *(dans la norme, naturel)* normal; **c'est tout à fait n. que la jeunesse se rebelle** it's only normal for young people to rebel; **ce n'est pas n.** *(que + subjunctive)* it's not right (that); **en temps n.** in normal circumstances **(b)** *(moyen) (poids, taille)* standard
  2 *nf* **normale (a) la normale** normal, the norm; **au-dessus/au-dessous de la normale** above/below average; **température au-dessous des normales saisonnières** temperature below the seasonal average **(b)** *Fam Univ* **Normale Sup'** = university-level college preparing students for senior posts in teaching
normalement [nɔrmalmɑ̃] *adv* normally
normalien, -enne [nɔrmaljɛ̃, -ɛn] *nm,f Univ* = student or former student of the "École normale supérieure"
normalisation [nɔrmalizasjɔ̃] *nf* **(a)** *(des relations diplomatiques)* normalization **(b)** *Ind* standardization
normaliser [nɔrmalize] *vt* **(a)** *(relations diplomatiques)* to normalize **(b)** *Ind* to standardize
normalité [nɔrmalite] *nf* normality
normand, -e [nɔrmɑ̃, -ɑ̃d] *aussi Hist* **1** *adj* Norman
  2 *nm,f* **N.** Norman
Normandie [nɔrmɑ̃di] *nf* **la N.** Normandy
norme [nɔrm] *nf* **(a)** *(règle)* norm; **dans la n.** within the norm **(b)** *Ind & Com* standard
noroît [nɔrwa] *nm* north-wester

Norvège [nɔrvɛʒ] *nf* la N. Norway
norvégien, -enne [nɔrveʒjɛ̃, -ɛn] **1** *adj* Norwegian
2 *nm,f* N. Norwegian
3 *nm (langue)* Norwegian
nos [no] *voir* **notre**
nostalgie [nɔstalʒi] *nf* nostalgia; *(mal du pays)* homesickness; **avoir la n. de qch** to feel nostalgic for sth; **avoir la n. du pays** to be homesick
nostalgique [nɔstalʒik] *adj* nostalgic
nota bene [nɔtabene] *nm inv* nota bene
notable [nɔtabl] *adj & nm* notable
notablement [nɔtabləmɑ̃] *adv* notably
notaire [nɔtɛr] *nm* notary (public)
notamment [nɔtamɑ̃] *adv* notably
notarié, -e [nɔtarje] *adj Jur* **acte n.** notarized deed
notation [nɔtasjɔ̃] *nf* (**a**) *(d'un travail scolaire)* marking (**b**) *(par des symboles)* notation; *Ordinat* **n. hexadécimale** hex *or* hexadecimal code
note [nɔt] *nf* (**a**) *(annotation, communication écrite)* note; **prendre des notes** to take (down) notes; **prendre bonne n. de qch** to take due note of sth; *Typ & Ordinat* **n. de ou en bas de page** footnote; **n. de service** memo (**b**) *(appréciation) Br* mark, *Am* grade (**c**) *Mus* note (**d**) *(facture)* bill; *(dans un hôtel) Br* bill, *Am* check; **n. de frais** expenses; **n. de téléphone** phone bill (**e**) *(nuance)* touch, note
notebook [nɔtbuk] *nm Ordinat* notebook
noter [nɔte] *vt* (**a**) *(mettre par écrit)* to note down, to make a note of (**b**) *(remarquer)* to note; **note bien que…** mind you,…; *Fig* **c'est noté, je note** got it (**c**) *(travail scolaire, élève) Br* to mark, *Am* to grade
notice [nɔtis] *nf (mode d'emploi)* instructions; *(d'un médicament)* directions
notification [nɔtifikasjɔ̃] *nf Jur* notification
notifier [66] [nɔtifje] *vt* **n. qch à qn** to notify sb of sth
notion [nosjɔ̃] *nf* (**a**) *(concept)* notion, concept; **perdre la n. du temps/de la réalité** to lose track of time/all sense of reality (**b**) **notions** *(connaissances sommaires)* basics; **avoir des notions de qch** to know the basics of sth
notoire [nɔtwar] *adj (fait)* well-known; *(criminel, mesquinerie)* notorious
notoriété [nɔtɔrjete] *nf (d'une personne)* fame; **il est de n. publique que…** it's common knowledge that…
notre, nos [nɔtr, no] *adj possessif* our; **n. chien** *(il y a un chien)* our dog; *(chacun a son chien)* our dogs; **nos enfants** our children; **n. père et n. mère** our mother and father; **un de nos amis** one of our friends, a friend of ours; *Fam* **nous avons n. vendredi** we've got Friday off
nôtre [notr] **1** *pron possessif* **le n., la n., les nôtres** ours; *(en insistant)* our own; **nous te prêtons le n.** you can borrow ours; **nous n'en avons pas besoin, nous avons le n.** we don't need it, we've got our own; *Fam* **à la n.!** here's to us!
2 *nm* **il faut y mettre du n.** we have to do our share
3 *nmpl* **les nôtres** *(notre famille)* our family; **serez-vous des nôtres ce soir?** will you be joining us this evening?
nouba [nuba] *nf Fam* party; **faire la n.** to party
noué, -e [nwe] *adj* **avoir l'estomac n.** to have a knot in one's stomach; **avoir la gorge nouée** to have a lump in one's throat
nouer [nwe] **1** *vt* (**a**) *(ficelle, ruban, lacets)* to tie; *(cheveux)* to tie up; *(cravate)* to knot (**b**) *(relations)* to establish (**avec** with)

2 se nouer *vpr* (**a**) *(amitié)* to be formed (**b**) *(intrigue)* to take shape
noueux, -euse [nwø, -øz] *adj (bois)* knotty; *(tronc d'arbre, mains, doigts)* gnarled
nougat [nuga] *nm* nougat
nougatine [nugatin] *nf* nougatine
nouille [nuj] **1** *nf* (**a**) *Culin* **nouilles** noodles; *(pâtes en général)* pasta (**b**) *Fam (personne) (molle)* drip; *(niaise)* dimwit
2 *adj Fam (niais)* dumb, dopey
nounou [nunu] *nf (langage enfantin)* nanny
nounours [nunurs] *nm (langage enfantin)* teddy (bear)
nourri, -e [nuri] *adj (applaudissements)* prolonged; *(feu)* heavy
nourrice [nuris] *nf* (**a**) *(assistante maternelle)* child minder; **n. agréée** registered child minder (**b**) *Vieilli (qui allaite)* wet nurse
nourricier, -ère [nurisje, -ɛr] *adj Litt (terre)* nourishing
nourrir [nurir] **1** *vt* (**a**) *(personnes, animaux)* to feed (**de** with); **le lait nourrit** milk is nourishing (**b**) *(peau, visage, cuir)* to nourish; *(feu)* to feed (**c**) *Litt (entretenir) (idées de vengeance, illusion)* to harbour; *(espoir)* to cherish; *(projet)* to nurse
2 se nourrir *vpr (manger)* to eat; **se n. de qch** to live on sth; *Fig & Litt* to feed on sth
nourrissant, -e [nurisɑ̃, -ɑ̃t] *adj* nourishing
nourrisson [nurisɔ̃] *nm* infant
nourriture [nurityr] *nf* food
nous [nu] **1** *pron personnel* (**a**) *(sujet)* we; **n. deux/tous** both/all of us; **n. autres Français** we French; **n., n. n'aurions pas fait comme ça** WE wouldn't have done it like that
(**b**) *(objet direct)* us; **et n., tu n. oublies?** and what about us, have you forgotten us?
(**c**) *(objet indirect)* to us; **lisez-le-n.** read it to us; **il n. a serré la main** he shook our hands; **les enfants n. ont jeté des pierres** the children threw stones at us
(**d**) *(avec préposition)* us; **n. ne pensons pas qu'à n.** we're not just thinking of ourselves; **tu n. le montres, à n.?** can you show US?; **ce livre est à n.** this book is ours; **n. avons nos règles à n.** we have our own rules; *Fam* **un ami à n.** a friend of ours; **à n. deux** *(sur un ton menaçant)* I want a word with you; *Hum* I'm all yours
(**e**) *(dans les réfléchis)* ourselves; **n. n. sommes habillés** we got dressed
(**f**) *(dans les pronominaux)* **n. n. déciderons demain** we'll decide tomorrow
(**g**) *(réciproque)* each other
(**h**) *(dans les comparaisons)* us; **vous buvez plus que n.** you drink more than us *or* than we do
2 *nm* **le n. de majesté** the royal we
nous-mêmes [numɛm] *pron personnel* ourselves
nouveau, -elle, -x, -elles [nuvo, -ɛl] **1** *adj*

| **nouvel** is used before masculine singular nouns beginning with a vowel or h mute. |

(**a**) *(récent, moderne, autre)* new; *(mode)* latest; **les nouveaux pères** modern fathers; *Fam* **tout n. tout beau** it's all new and exciting; **le nouvel an** the New Year; **nouvelle cuisine** nouvelle cuisine; *Péj* **n. riche** nouveau riche (**b**) *(avec une fonction adverbiale)* **les nouveaux arrivants** the newcomers; **les nouveaux élus** those newly elected; **n. pays industrialisé** newly industrialized country (**c**) **à n., de n.** again

2 *nm* **il y a du n.** there's been a new development; **rien de n. depuis la dernière fois** nothing new since last time

3 *nm,f (personne)* new person; *(à l'école)* new pupil

Nouveau-Brunswick [nuvobrɛ̃zvik] *nm* **le N.** New Brunswick

Nouveau-Mexique [nuvomɛksik] *nm* **le N.** New Mexico

nouveau-né, -e *(mpl* **nouveau-nés,** *fpl* **nouveau-nées)** [nuvone] **1** *adj* newborn
2 *nm,f* newborn baby

nouveauté [nuvote] *nf* **(a)** *(caractère nouveau)* novelty **(b)** *(produit récent) (livre)* new publication; *(disque)* new release; *Fam* **ce n'est pas une n.!** that's nothing new!

nouvel [nuvɛl] *voir* **nouveau**

nouvelle [nuvɛl] *nf* **(a)** *(annonce d'un événement)* **une n.** a piece of news; **je viens d'apprendre la n.** I've just heard the news; *Fam* **première n.!** that's news to me! **(b)** *(information)* **avoir des nouvelles de qn** *(directement)* to have heard from sb; *(indirectement)* to have had news about sb; *Fig* **vous aurez de mes nouvelles!** you'll be hearing from me!; **demander** *ou* **prendre des nouvelles de qn** to inquire *or* ask about sb; **être sans nouvelles de qn** to have no news from sb; **aux dernières nouvelles,...** the last I/we/*etc* heard,...; **les nouvelles vont vite!** (good) news travels fast!; **goûtez cela, vous m'en direz des nouvelles** taste this, you'll love it; **pas de nouvelles, bonnes nouvelles** no news is good news **(c)** *Journ* news item; **les nouvelles** the news **(d)** *(roman court)* short story

Nouvelle-Angleterre [nuvɛlɑ̃glətɛr] *nf* **la N.** New England

Nouvelle-Calédonie [nuvɛlkaledɔni] *nf* **la N.** New Caledonia

Nouvelle-Écosse [nuvɛlekɔs] *nf* **la N.** Nova Scotia

nouvellement [nuvɛlmɑ̃] *adv* newly, recently

Nouvelle-Orléans [nuvɛlɔrleɑ̃] *voir* **La Nouvelle-Orléans**

Nouvelles-Hébrides [nuvɛlzebrid] *nfpl* **les N.** the New Hebrides

Nouvelle-Zélande [nuvɛlzelɑ̃d] *nf* **la N.** New Zealand

novateur, -trice [nɔvatœr, -tris] **1** *adj* innovative
2 *nm,f* innovator

novembre [nɔvɑ̃br] *nm* November; **le onze n.** *(fête) Br* Armistice Day, *Am* Veterans Day; *voir aussi* **janvier**

novice [nɔvis] *nmf aussi Rel* novice

noyade [nwajad] *nf* drowning

noyau, -x [nwajo] *nm* **(a)** *(de fruit)* stone, *Am* pit **(b)** *(centre) (d'atome, de cellule)* nucleus; *(de la terre)* core **(c)** *(petit groupe)* small group; **le n. dur** the hard core **(d)** *Ordinat* node

noyauter [nwajote] *vt* to infiltrate

noyé, -e [nwaje] **1** *adj* **(a)** *(dans l'eau)* **mourir n.** to die by drowning; *Fig* **être n.** *(perdu)* to be out of one's depth **(b)** *(plein)* **yeux noyés de larmes** eyes brimming with tears **(c)** *(perdu)* **le village était n. dans la brume** the village was shrouded in mist; **les points essentiels sont noyés dans le détail** the essential points are buried in too many details
2 *nm,f* drowned person

noyer¹ [nwaje] *nm (arbre)* walnut (tree); *(bois)* walnut

noyer² [32] **1** *vt* **(a)** *(personne, animal)* to drown; *(terres, champs)* to swamp; *Fig* **n. une rébellion dans le sang** to bloodily quash a rebellion; **n. son chagrin**

(dans l'alcool) to drown one's sorrows (in drink); **n. le poisson** to confuse the issue deliberately **(b)** *(moteur)* to flood **(c)** *(diluer) (vin)* to drown
2 se noyer *vpr (accidentellement)* to drown; *(volontairement)* to drown oneself; *Fig* **se n. dans les détails** to get bogged down in details; **se n. dans un verre d'eau** to make a mountain out of a molehill

NPI [ɛnpei] *nm (abrév* **nouveau pays industrialisé)** NIC

nu, -e [ny] **1** *adj* **(a)** *(dévêtu) (personne)* naked; *(partie du corps)* bare; *Art* nude; **être tout nu** to be naked *or* in the nude; **se baigner tout nu** to go swimming in the nude; **nu comme un ver** stark naked; **aller pieds nus** to go barefoot; **se battre à mains nues** to fight with bare fists **(b)** *Fig (paysage, arbre, pièce)* bare; *(style)* plain
2 *nm Art* nude; **mettre qch à nu** *(surface)* to expose sth; *(fil électrique)* to strip sth

nuage [nɥaʒ] *nm* **(a)** *(dans le ciel)* cloud; **sans nuages** *(ciel)* cloudless; *Fig (vie, avenir)* unclouded; *(bonheur)* perfect; *Fig* **être dans les nuages** to have one's head in the clouds; **n. radioactif** cloud of radioactive dust **(b)** *(de lait)* drop **(c)** *Can (foulard)* scarf

nuageux, -euse [nɥaʒø, -øz] *adj* cloudy

nuance [nɥɑ̃s] *nf* **(a)** *(de couleur)* shade **(b)** *(légère trace)* touch, hint **(c)** *(subtilité)* nuance; *(légère différence)* slight difference; **tout en nuances** full of nuances; **j'ai dit peut-être, pas oui, n.!** I said perhaps, not yes, there's a slight difference!; **être sans nuances** *(personne)* to see everything in black and white

nuancé, -e [nɥɑ̃se] *adj* full of nuances

nuancer [16] [nɥɑ̃se] *vt* to qualify

nucléaire [nykleɛr] **1** *adj* nuclear
2 *nm* **le n.** nuclear power

nucléon [nykleɔ̃] *nm Phys* nucleon

nudisme [nydism] *nm* nudism

nudiste [nydist] *nmf* nudist

nudité [nydite] *nf (d'une personne)* nudity, nakedness; *(d'un mur, d'un paysage)* bareness; *(d'un style)* plainness

nue [ny] *nf* **porter qn/qch aux nues** to praise sb/sth to the skies; **tomber des nues** to be taken aback

nuée [nɥe] *nf* **(a)** *(d'insectes, de criquets)* cloud, swarm; *(de personnes)* horde **(b)** *Litt (dans le ciel)* cloud

nui *voir* **nuire**

nuire [18] [nɥir] **1 nuire à** *vt ind* to harm; **nuit gravement à la santé** *(sur paquet de cigarettes)* tobacco seriously damages health; **mettre qn hors d'état de n.** *(en lieu sûr)* to put sb out of harm's way
2 se nuire *vpr* **se n. (à soi-même)** to do oneself harm

nuisais *etc voir* **nuire**

nuisance [nɥizɑ̃s] *nf* nuisance; **nuisances acoustiques** noise pollution

nuise *voir* **nuire**

nuisette [nɥizɛt] *nf* baby doll nightie

nuisible [nɥizibl] *adj* harmful **(à** to); **animaux nuisibles** vermin, pests

nuit [nɥi] *nf* night; **cette n.** *(ce soir)* tonight; *(passée)* last night; **bonne n.!** good night!; **le train/bateau de n.** the night train/boat; **voyager de n.** to travel by *or* at night; **il commence à faire n.** it's getting dark; **il fait n.** it's dark; **il fait n. noire** it's pitch-black; **à la n. tombante** at nightfall; *Fig* **perdu dans la n. des temps** lost in the mists of time; *Prov* **la n. porte conseil** it would be best to sleep on it; *Prov* **la n., tous les chats sont gris** all cats are grey in the dark; **passer une n.**

blanche *(avoir une insomnie)* to have a sleepless night; *(volontairement)* to stay up all night; **n. de noces** wedding night

nuitée [nɥite] *nf* overnight stay

nul, nulle [nyl] **1** *adj* (**a**) *(inexistant) (différence, risques, écart)* nil (**b**) *(non valable) (bulletin de vote)* spoilt; *Jur* **n. et non avenu** null and void (**c**) *Fam (qui ne vaut rien) (réponse, personne)* useless; *(film, livre, chanson, blague)* rubbish; **être n. en qch** to be useless at sth; *Vulg* **c'est n. à chier!** it's a load of crap!
  2 *nm,f Fam* useless idiot
  3 *adj indéfini Litt* no
  4 *pron indéfini Litt* no one, nobody

nullard, -e [nylar, -ard] *nm,f très Fam* useless idiot

nullement [nylmã] *adv* not at all

nulle part [nylpar] *adv* nowhere; **je ne les vois n.** I can't see them anywhere; **n. ailleurs** nowhere else

nullité [nylite] *nf (d'un contrat, d'un mariage)* nullity, invalidity

numéraire [nymerɛr] *nm* cash

numéral, -e, -aux, -ales [nymeral, -o] *adj & nm* numeral

numérateur [nymeratœr] *nm Math* numerator

numération [nymerasjɔ̃] *nf Math* numeration; *Méd* **n. globulaire** blood count

numérique [nymerik] *adj* (**a**) *(valeur, supériorité)* numerical (**b**) *Ordinat (ordinateur, donnée)* digital; **balance à affichage n.** digital scales

numérisation [nymerizasjɔ̃] *nf Ordinat* digitization

numériser [nymerize] *vt Ordinat* to digitize

numériseur [nymerizœr] *nm Ordinat* digitizer; **n. d'image** image digitizer

numéro [nymero] *nm* (**a**) *(chiffre)* number; *Fig* **tirer le bon n.** to strike (it) lucky; **n. azur** = special telephone number for which users are charged at local rate irrespective of distance; **n. de compte** account number; **n. de fax** fax number; **n. d'immatriculation** *(de véhicule) Br* registration number, *Am* license number; *Belg Vieilli & Suisse* **n. postal** *Br* postcode, *Am* zip code; **n. de téléphone** telephone number; **n. vert** *Br* Freefone® number, *Am* toll-free number; **n. de vol** flight number (**b**) *(de périodique)* issue, number; **la suite au prochain n.** (to be) continued in the next issue; *Fig* watch this space; **n. spécial** special issue (**c**) *(spectacle)* act, number; *Fam Fig* **faire son petit n.** to do one's little act (**d**) *Fam (personne)* character

numérotation [nymerɔtasjɔ̃] *nf* numbering

numéroter [nymerɔte] *vt* to number

numismate [nymismat] *nmf* numismatist

numismatique [nymismatik] **1** *adj* numismatic
  2 *nf* numismatics *(singulier)*

nunuche [nynyʃ] *adj Fam* twee

nu-pieds [nypje] **1** *nm inv* sandal
  2 *adv* barefoot

nuptial, -e, -aux, -ales [nypsjal, -o] *adj (anneau, marche)* wedding; *(chambre, cortège)* bridal

nuque [nyk] *nf* nape, back of the neck

nurse [nœrs] *nf Vieilli* nanny

nu-tête [nytɛt] *adv* bareheaded

nutritif, -ive [nytritif, -iv] *adj* nutritious

nutrition [nytrisjɔ̃] *nf* nutrition

nutritionniste [nytrisjɔnist] *nmf* nutritionist

Nylon® [nilɔ̃] *nm* nylon

nymphe [nɛ̃f] *nf (déesse)* nymph

nymphette [nɛ̃fɛt] *nf* nymphet

nymphomane [nɛ̃fɔman] *adj & nf* nymphomaniac

nymphomanie [nɛ̃fɔmani] *nf* nymphomania

O

O¹, o [o] *nm inv* O, o

O² *(abrév* **ouest)** W

ô [o] *exclam Litt* O!

OAS [oaɛs] *nf (abrév* **Organisation de l'armée secrète)** OAS *(terrorist group opposed to Algerian independence)*

oasis [ɔazis] *nf* oasis; *Fig* haven

obédience [ɔbedjɑ̃s] *nf* **d'o. communiste/musulmane** of the Communist/Muslim persuasion

obéir [ɔbeir] *vi* (**a**) *(personne)* to obey; **o. à qn/qch** to obey sb/sth; **o. à une impulsion** to act on an impulse; **o. à qn au doigt et à l'œil** to be at sb's beck and call; **se faire o.** to command obedience (**b**) *(freins, mécanisme)* to respond (**à** to)

obéissance [ɔbeisɑ̃s] *nf* obedience (**à** to); **jurer o. à qn** to swear allegiance to sb

obéissant, -e [ɔbeisɑ̃, -ɑ̃t] *adj* obedient

obélisque [ɔbelisk] *nm* obelisk

obèse [ɔbɛz] **1** *adj* obese
2 *nmf* obese person

obésité [ɔbezite] *nf* obesity

objecter [ɔbʒɛkte] *vt* (**a**) *(rétorquer)* **n'avoir rien à o. à qch** to have no objection to sth; **o. que...** to object that... (**b**) *(invoquer)* **on lui objecta sa jeunesse** his youth was held against him

objecteur [ɔbʒɛktœr] *nm* **o. de conscience** conscientious objector

objectif, -ive [ɔbʒɛktif, -iv] **1** *adj* objective
2 *nm* (**a**) *(but, cible)* objective (**b**) *(d'un appareil photo)* lens; *(d'un microscope)* objective; *Fig* **devant l'o.** in front of the camera

objection [ɔbʒɛksjɔ̃] *nf aussi Jur* objection; **je ne vois pas d'o. à continuer le débat/à ce que vous partiez** I have no objection to our continuing the debate/to your leaving

objectivement [ɔbʒɛktivmɑ̃] *adv* objectively

objectivité [ɔbʒɛktivite] *nf* objectivity; **en toute o.** quite objectively

objet [ɔbʒɛ] *nm* (**a**) *(chose)* object; **(bureau des) objets trouvés** *Br* lost-property office, *Am* lost and found; **femme-o.** sex object; **o. d'art** objet d'art; **objets de valeur** valuables; **o. volant non identifié** unidentified flying object
(**b**) *Gram* object; **o. direct/indirect** direct/indirect object
(**c**) *(sujet)* *(d'une dispute, d'une conversation)* subject; **être** *ou* **faire l'o. de qch** to be the object of sth; *Hum* **l'o. de ses désirs** the object of her desires
(**d**) *(but)* object, aim; **ma visite a pour o. de...** the object of my visit is to...; **sans o.** *(remarque, réclamation)* unjustified
(**e**) *Ordinat* object

---

obligataire [ɔbligatɛr] *Fin* **1** *nmf* bondholder, debenture holder
2 *adj (emprunt, marché)* debenture

obligation [ɔbligasjɔ̃] *nf* (**a**) *(contrainte)* obligation; **tu viens si tu veux, mais ce n'est pas une o.** you can come if you want, but you're not obliged to; **avoir l'o. de faire qch** to be under an obligation to do sth; **être** *ou* **se voir dans l'o. de faire qch** to be obliged to do sth; **sans o. d'achat** no purchase necessary; **être dégagé des obligations militaires** to have done one's military service (**b**) *Fin* bond, debenture; **o. au porteur** bearer bond

obligatoire [ɔbligatwar] *adj* obligatory, compulsory; *Fam (inévitable)* inevitable

obligatoirement [ɔbligatwarmɑ̃] *adv* **vous devez o. montrer votre passeport** you are required to show your passport; **pas o.** not necessarily

obligé, -e [ɔbliʒe] *adj* (**a**) *Fam (inévitable)* inevitable (**b**) *Formel (reconnaissant)* **être o. à qn de qch** to be obliged to sb for sth

obligeance [ɔbliʒɑ̃s] *nf Formel* **avoir l'o. de faire qch** to be so kind as to do sth

obligeant, -e [ɔbliʒɑ̃, -ɑ̃t] *adj* obliging, kind

obliger [45] [ɔbliʒe] **1** *vt* (**a**) *(contraindre)* **o. qn à faire qch** to force sb to do sth; **son état de santé l'oblige au repos** the state of his health means he has to rest; **être obligé de faire qch** to be obliged to do sth; **ne te crois pas obligé de tout manger** don't feel you have to eat everything; **tu y es allé? – bien obligé!** did you go? – I had to! (**b**) *Formel (rendre service à)* **vous m'obligeriez en fermant la porte** I'd be obliged if you would close the door
2 s'obliger *upr* **s'o. à faire qch** to force oneself to do sth

oblique [ɔblik] **1** *adj (ligne)* oblique; *(regard)* sidelong
2 *nf* oblique (line)

obliquement [ɔblikmɑ̃] *adv* obliquely

obliquer [ɔblike] *vi* **o. à gauche/à droite** to bear left/right

oblitérer [34] [ɔblitere] *vt* (**a**) *(timbre)* to cancel (**b**) *Litt (souvenirs, passé)* to obliterate

oblong, -ongue [ɔblɔ̃, -ɔ̃g] *adj* oblong

obnubiler [ɔbnybile] *vt* to obsess

obole [ɔbɔl] *nf* small contribution; **apporter** *ou* **verser son o. à qch** to make a small contribution to sth

obscène [ɔpsɛn] *adj* obscene

obscénité [ɔpsenite] *nf* obscenity; **dire des obscénités** to utter obscenities

obscur, -e [ɔpskyr] *adj* (**a**) *(sombre)* dark (**b**) *(difficile à comprendre)* obscure (**c**) *(pressentiment, impression)* vague (**d**) *(écrivain, peintre)* obscure

obscurantisme [ɔpskyrɑ̃tism] *nm* obscurantism

obscurcir [ɔpskyrsir] **1** *vt* (**a**) *(assombrir)* to darken (**b**) *(rendre confus)* *(faits, sens)* to obscure; *(jugement)* to cloud

2 s'obscurcir *vpr (pièce, ciel)* to darken, to grow dark; *(esprit, vue)* to grow dim

obscurément [ɔpskyremɑ̃] *adv* vaguely

obscurité [ɔpskyrite] *nf* (**a**) *(noirceur)* darkness; **dans l'o.** in the dark (**b**) *(anonymat)* obscurity

obsédant, -e [ɔpsedɑ̃, -ɑ̃t] *adj (souvenir, musique)* haunting; *(pensée)* obsessive

obsédé, -e [ɔpsede] *nm,f* fanatic; **o. (sexuel)** sex maniac; **un o. du cinéma/du rangement** a film/tidiness fanatic

obséder [34] [ɔpsede] *vt* to obsess; **être obsédé par qch** to be obsessed by *or* with sth

obsèques [ɔpsɛk] *nfpl* funeral; **o. nationales** state funeral

obséquieux, -euse [ɔpsekjø, -øz] *adj* obsequious

observateur, -trice [ɔpsɛrvatœr, -tris] **1** *adj* observant

2 *nm,f* observer

observation [ɔpsɛrvasjɔ̃] *nf* (**a**) *(étude, surveillance)* observation; **être en o.** *(à l'hôpital)* to be under observation; **avoir l'esprit d'o.** to be very observant (**b**) *(remarque)* observation; *(critique)* remark (**c**) *(respect)* observance

observatoire [ɔpsɛrvatwar] *nm (astronomique, météorologique)* observatory; *Mil* observation post

observer [ɔpsɛrve] **1** *vt* (**a**) *(regarder)* to watch, to observe; **se sentir observé** to feel one is being watched (**b**) *(remarquer)* to notice; **faire o. qch à qn** to point sth out to sb; **faire o. à qn que...** to point out to sb that... (**c**) *(étudier)* to observe (**d**) *(respecter)* to observe; **o. une minute de silence** to observe a minute's silence

2 s'observer *vpr* (**a**) *(l'un l'autre)* to watch *or* observe each other (**b**) *(phénomène, attitude)* to be seen

obsession [ɔpsɛsjɔ̃] *nf* obsession; **mais c'est une o. ou de l'o.!** you're/he's/*etc* obsessed!

obsessionnel, -elle [ɔpsɛsjɔnɛl] *adj Psy* obsessional

obsidienne [ɔpsidjɛn] *nf* obsidian

obsolète [ɔpsɔlɛt] *adj* obsolete

obstacle [ɔpstakl] *nm aussi Fig* obstacle; *(aux courses)* fence, jump; **faire o. à qch** to stand in the way of sth

obstétricien, -enne [ɔpstetrisjɛ̃, -ɛn] *nm,f* obstetrician

obstétrique [ɔpstetrik] *nf* obstetrics *(singulier)*

obstination [ɔpstinasjɔ̃] *nf* obstinacy, stubbornness

obstiné, -e [ɔpstine] *adj (personne, caractère)* obstinate, stubborn; *(résistance, efforts)* dogged; *(refus)* stubborn

obstinément [ɔpstinemɑ̃] *adv (travailler, avancer)* doggedly; *(refuser)* stubbornly

obstiner [ɔpstine] **s'obstiner** *vpr* to persist; **s'o. à faire qch** *(continuer)* to persist in doing sth; *(vouloir)* to be set on doing sth; **s'o. dans ses convictions** to cling stubbornly to one's convictions

obstruction [ɔpstryksjɔ̃] *nf* obstruction; **faire de l'o.** *Pol* to be obstructive; *Sport* to obstruct

obstructionnisme [ɔpstryksjɔnism] *nm Pol* obstructionism

obstruer [ɔpstrye] *vt* to obstruct

obtempérer [34] [ɔptɑ̃pere] **obtempérer à** *vt ind* to comply with; *Jur* **refus d'o.** obstruction

obtenir [70] [ɔptənir] *vt* to get, to obtain; **o. qch de qn** to get sth from sb; **faire o. qch à qn** to get sth for sb; **o. de faire qch** to get permission to do sth; **j'ai obtenu qu'elle revienne** I got her to come back

obtention [ɔptɑ̃sjɔ̃] *nf* obtaining; **depuis l'o. de son diplôme** since obtaining her diploma

obtenu, -e *voir* obtenir

obtiendrai *etc voir* obtenir

obtienne *voir* obtenir

obturateur [ɔptyratœr] *nm Phot* shutter

obtus, -e [ɔpty, -yz] *adj (angle, personne)* obtuse

obus [ɔby] *nm* shell

OC *nfpl (abrév* **ondes courtes)** SW

oc [ɔk] *voir* langue

ocarina [ɔkarina] *nm* ocarina

occase [ɔkaz] *nf Fam* (**a**) *(affaire)* bargain (**b**) *(article de seconde main)* second-hand item; **d'o.** second-hand

occasion [ɔkazjɔ̃] *nf* (**a**) *(circonstance favorable)* opportunity, chance; **avoir l'o. de faire qch** to have the opportunity *or* chance to do sth; *Hum* **tu as encore perdu l'o. de te taire** why can't you keep your big mouth shut?; **c'est l'o. ou jamais** it's now or never; **c'est l'o. ou jamais d'essayer** now's the time to try; **venez boire un coup à l'o.** come for a drink when you get the chance; **à la première o.** at the first opportunity; *Prov* **l'o. fait le larron** opportunity makes the thief (**b**) *(moment)* occasion; **à plusieurs occasions** on several occasions; **à l'o. de** *(pour fêter)* on the occasion of; **à l'o. d'une visite de routine** during a routine visit; **dans/pour les grandes occasions** on/for special occasions; **être l'o. de qch** to be the occasion of sth (**c**) *(affaire)* bargain (**d**) *(article de seconde main)* second-hand item; **le marché de l'o.** the second-hand market; **d'o.** second-hand

occasionnel, -elle [ɔkazjɔnɛl] *adj* occasional; *(rencontre)* chance; *(aide)* casual

occasionnellement [ɔkazjɔnɛlmɑ̃] *adv* occasionally

occasionner [ɔkazjɔne] *vt* to cause

occident [ɔksidɑ̃] *nm* west; *Pol* **l'O.** the West

occidental, -e, -aux, -ales [ɔksidɑ̃tal, -o] **1** *adj* western; **l'Europe occidentale** Western Europe

2 *nm,f* **O.** Westerner

occidentaliser [ɔksidɑ̃talize] **1** *vt* to westernize

2 s'occidentaliser *vpr* to become westernized

occiput [ɔksipyt] *nm* back of the head

occire [ɔksir] *vt* to slay

occitan, -e [ɔksitɑ̃, -an] **1** *adj* of the langue d'oc

2 *nm (langue)* = language spoken in some parts of southern France

occlusion [ɔklyzjɔ̃] *nf* occlusion; **o. intestinale** intestinal obstruction

occulte [ɔkylt] *adj (surnaturel)* occult; *(secret)* secret; *(cause)* hidden; *(rôle)* clandestine

occulter [ɔkylte] *vt Astron* to occult; *(signal lumineux)* to block out; *Fig (informations, intentions)* to conceal

occupant, -e [ɔkypɑ̃, -ɑ̃t] **1** *adj (armée)* occupying

2 *nm,f (d'une maison)* occupier, occupant; *Mil* **l'o.** the occupying forces

occupation [ɔkypasjɔ̃] *nf* (**a**) *(d'un lieu)* & *Mil* occupation; *Hist* **l'O.** the Occupation; **grève avec o. des locaux** sit-down strike (**b**) *(activité)* occupation; **vaquer à ses occupations** to go about one's business

occupé, -e [ɔkype] *adj (personne)* busy; *(place)* taken; *(ligne téléphonique) Br* engaged, *Am* busy; *(toilettes)* engaged; **en territoire o.** in occupied territory

occuper [ɔkype] **1** *vt* (**a**) *(maison, lieu)* to occupy; *(place)* to take up, to occupy; **le magasin occupe le rez-de-chaussée** the shop takes up *or* occupies the ground floor (**b**) *(par la force)* to occupy (**c**) *(temps)* to fill, to occupy (**d**) *(poste, fonction)* to have, to hold (**e**) **o. qn** *(employer)* to employ sb; *(donner une activité à)* to keep sb busy, to occupy sb
  2 s'occuper *vpr* (**a**) *(avoir une activité)* to keep oneself busy *or* occupied, to occupy oneself; **s'o. en lisant** to spend one's time reading; **on a toujours de quoi s'o.** there's always something to keep you busy (**b**) **s'o. de** *(s'intéresser à)* to be interested in; *(se charger de)* to take care of; **s'o. de faire qch** to see about doing sth; **je m'en occuperai** I'll see to it; *Fam* **occupe-toi de ce qui te regarde** *ou* **de tes affaires** *ou* **de tes oignons!** mind your own business!; *Fam* **t'occupe (pas)!** keep your nose out!; *Ironique* **je vais m'o. de lui** I'll take care of him; **est-ce qu'on s'occupe de vous?** *(dans un magasin)* are you being attended to?

occurrence [ɔkyrãs] *nf* (**a**) *(circonstance)* **en l'o.** in this case (**b**) *Ling* occurrence

OCDE [osedeə] *nf (abrév* **Organisation de coopération et de développement économiques)** OECD

océan [ɔseã] *nm* ocean; **l'O.** *(l'Atlantique)* the Atlantic; **l'o. Atlantique/Pacifique/Indien** the Atlantic/Pacific/Indian Ocean; **l'o. (Glacial) Arctique** the Arctic Ocean; *Fig* **un o. de fleurs/couleurs** a sea of flowers/colour

Océanie [ɔseani] *nf* **l'O.** Oceania

océanique [ɔseanik] *adj* oceanic

océanographie [ɔseanɔgrafi] *nf* oceanography

ocelot [ɔslo] *nm* ocelot

ocre [ɔkr] *nm & adj inv* ochre

octane [ɔktan] *nm* octane

octante [ɔktãt] *adj & nm inv Belg & Suisse* eighty; *voir aussi* **trois**

octave [ɔktav] *nf* octave

octet [ɔktɛ] *nm Ordinat* byte; **milliard d'octets** gigabyte

octobre [ɔktɔbr] *nm* October; *voir aussi* **janvier**

octogénaire [ɔktɔʒenɛr] *adj & nmf* octogenarian

octogonal, -e, -aux, -ales [ɔktɔgɔnal, -o] *adj* octagonal

octogone [ɔktɔgɔn] *nm* octagon

octroyer [32] [ɔktrwaje] **1** *vt* **o. qch à qn** to grant sb sth
  2 s'octroyer *vpr* **s'o. qch** to grant oneself sth

oculaire [ɔkylɛr] **1** *adj* **hygiène o.** eye care; **témoin o.** eyewitness
  2 *nm* eyepiece

oculiste [ɔkylist] *nmf* eye specialist

ode [ɔd] *nf* ode

odeur [ɔdœr] *nf* smell; **une o. de brûlé** a smell of burning; **sans o.** odourless; **bonne/mauvaise o.** pleasant/unpleasant smell; *Fig* **ne pas être en o. de sainteté auprès de qn** to be in sb's bad books; *Prov* **l'argent n'a pas d'o.** money has no smell

odieux, -euse [ɔdjø, -øz] *adj (comportement)* odious; *(crime)* heinous; **être o. avec qn** to be horrible to sb

odorant, -e [ɔdɔrã, -ãt] *adj (agréable)* sweet-smelling, fragrant; *(désagréable)* strong-smelling

odorat [ɔdɔra] *nm* (sense of) smell

odyssée [ɔdise] *nf* odyssey; **l'O.** the Odyssey

œcuménique [ekymenik, økymenik] *adj* ecumenical

œdème [edɛm, ødɛm] *nm* oedema; **avoir un o. aux poumons** to have pulmonary oedema

œil [œj] *(pl* **yeux** [jø]*) nm* (**a**) *(organe)* eye; **avoir les yeux bleus** to have blue eyes; **o. de verre** glass eye; **un o. au beurre noir, un o. poché** a black eye; **j'ai le soleil dans les yeux** *ou* **dans l'o.** the sun's in my eyes; **visible à l'o. nu** visible to the naked eye; **voir qch de ses (propres) yeux** to see sth with one's own eyes; **je n'ai pas fermé l'o. de la nuit** I didn't sleep a wink all night; **faire qch les yeux fermés** to do sth with one's eyes closed; **ouvrir de grands yeux** to look surprised; **faire les gros yeux (à qn)** to glare (at sb); *Fam* **avoir de petits yeux** to look tired; **ouvrir des yeux ronds** to gape in amazement; *Fam* **entre quat'z'yeux** in private; **les yeux dans les yeux** gazing into each other's eyes; **o. pour o., dent pour dent** an eye for an eye, a tooth for a tooth; **je ne le fais pas pour ses beaux yeux** I'm not doing it just to please him; **tu as les yeux plus gros** *ou* **grands que le ventre** your eyes are bigger than your belly; **n'avoir plus que les** *ou* **ses yeux pour pleurer** to have nothing left but the clothes on one's back; *Fam* **mon o.!** my foot!; *Fam* **à l'o.** free; **faire les yeux doux à qn** to make eyes at sb; *Fam* **faire de l'o. à qn** to give sb the eye; **le mauvais o.** the evil eye; **sous mes/leurs yeux** right before my/their eyes; **avoir qch sous les yeux** to have sth right in front of one; *Can Fam* **tomber dans l'o. à qn** to catch sb's eye
  (**b**) *(vue)* **yeux** (eye)sight, eyes; **avoir de bons/mauvais yeux** to have good/bad (eye)sight; **avoir des yeux de lynx** to be eagle-eyed
  (**c**) *(attention)* **avoir l'o. sur qch** to keep an eye on sth; **avoir qn à l'o.** to keep an eye on sb; **avoir l'o. à tout** to keep an eye on everything; *Fam* **ouvrir l'o. (et le bon)** to keep one's eyes open *or* peeled; **ne pas avoir les yeux en face des trous** to be half-asleep; *Fam* **ne pas avoir les yeux dans sa poche** to have sharp eyes; **fermer les yeux sur qch** to turn a blind eye to sth; **coup d'o.** glance; **au** *ou* **du premier coup d'o.** at a glance; **jeter un coup d'o. sur qch** to have a glance at sth; **avoir le coup d'o., avoir l'o.** to have a good eye; **ça vaut** *ou* **ça mérite le coup d'o.** it's worth a look
  (**d**) *(point de vue)* **voir qch d'un autre o.** to look at sth differently; **voir qch d'un bon/mauvais o.** to look favourably/unfavourably on sth; **aux yeux de la loi** in the eyes of the law; **à mes yeux** in my eyes
  (**e**) *(dans la soupe)* speck of fat
  (**f**) *(d'un cyclone)* eye

œil-de-bœuf *(pl* **œils-de-bœuf)** [œjdəbœf] *nm* bull's-eye (window)

œillade [œjad] *nf* wink; **lancer une o. à qn** to wink at sb

œillère [œjɛr] *nf Br* blinker, *Am* blinder; *Fig* **avoir des œillères** to wear *Br* blinkers *or Am* blinders

œillet [œjɛ] *nm* (**a**) *(fleur)* carnation (**b**) *(trou) (de vêtement, de chaussure)* eyelet (**c**) *(en papeterie)* reinforcement ring

œnologie [enɔlɔʒi, ønɔlɔʒi] *nf* oenology

œnologue [enɔlɔg, ønɔlɔg] *nmf* oenologist

œsophage [ezɔfaʒ, øzɔfaʒ] *nm* oesophagus

œstrogène [ɛstrɔʒɛn, østrɔʒɛn] *adj & nm* oestrogen

œuf [œf, *pl* ø] *nm* egg; **œufs** *(de poisson)* spawn, hard roe; *Fig* **mettre tous ses œufs dans le même panier** to put all one's eggs in one basket; *Fam Fig* **marcher**

sur des œufs *(avancer)* to walk carefully; *(être prudent)* to be walking on eggs; *Fam* **va te faire cuire un o.!** take a running jump!; **étouffer** *ou* **tuer qch dans l'o.** to nip sth in the bud; **œufs brouillés** scrambled eggs; **o. en chocolat** chocolate egg; **o. à la coque** boiled egg; **o. dur** hard-boiled egg; **o. mollet** soft-boiled egg; **œufs à la neige** floating islands *(beaten egg whites served on custard)*; **œufs en neige** beaten egg whites; **o. de Pâques** Easter egg; **o. au plat** *ou* **sur le plat** fried egg; **o. poché** poached egg; **o. à repriser** darning egg

œuvre [œvr] **1** *nf* (**a**) *(travail)* work; **être à l'o.** to be at work; **se mettre à l'o.** to get down to work; **mettre qch en o.** *(traité, loi, système)* to implement sth; **mettre tout en o.** to do everything possible; **les bonnes œuvres** charitable work (**b**) *(création)* work; *(ensemble de créations)* works; **o. d'art** work of art; **œuvres complètes/choisies** complete/selected works
  2 *nm Constr* **gros o.** fabric; **à pied d'o.** on site; *Fig* ready to start work

œuvrer [œvre] *vi* to work (**pour** for)
offensant, -e [ɔfɑ̃sɑ̃, -ɑ̃t] *adj* offensive
offense [ɔfɑ̃s] *nf* (**a**) *(affront)* insult (**b**) *Rel* transgression
offenser [ɔfɑ̃se] **1** *vt* (**a**) *(insulter)* to offend; **sans vouloir vous o....** with all due respect... (**b**) *Litt (bon goût, délicatesse)* to offend against
  2 s'offenser *vpr* to take offence (**de** at)
offensif, -ive [ɔfɑ̃sif, -iv] *adj* offensive
offensive [ɔfɑ̃siv] *nf* offensive; **passer à l'o.** to go on the offensive; **o. de charme** charm offensive
offert, -e *voir* offrir
office [ɔfis] *nm* (**a**) *(charge)* office; **faire o. de secrétaire/témoin** to act as secretary/witness; **d'o.** without having any say in the matter; **être commis d'o.** to be appointed by the court (**b**) *(assistance)* **recourir aux bons offices de qn** to turn to sb for assistance (**c**) *Rel* service (**d**) *(pièce)* pantry (**e**) *(agence)* **o. du tourisme** tourist information centre; *Suisse* **o. de poste** post office
officialiser [ɔfisjalize] *vt* to make official
officiel, -elle [ɔfisjɛl] *adj & nm* official
officiellement [ɔfisjɛlmɑ̃] *adv* officially
officier¹ [ɔfisje] *nm* officer; **o. de réserve** reserve officer
officier² [66] *vi* to officiate
officieusement [ɔfisjøzmɑ̃] *adv* unofficially; *(en confidence)* off-the-record
officieux, -euse [ɔfisjø, -øz] *adj* unofficial; *(confidentiel)* off-the-record
off-line [ɔflajn] *adj Ordinat* off-line
offrande [ɔfrɑ̃d] *nf* offering; **en o.** as an offering
offrant [ɔfrɑ̃] *nm* **vendre au plus o.** to sell to the highest bidder
offre [ɔfr] *nf* offer; *(dans un appel d'offres)* tender; *(dans une vente aux enchères)* bid; **o. d'emploi** job offer; **o. spéciale** special offer; **o. publique d'achat** takeover bid; **faire** *ou* **lancer une o. publique d'achat (sur)** to make a takeover bid (for); **l'o. et la demande** supply and demand
offrir [52] [ɔfrir] **1** *vt* (**a**) *(cadeau)* to give (**à** to); **c'est pour o.** it's a gift; **je t'offre un verre** I'll buy you a drink; **o. la main de sa fille à qn** to offer one's daughter's hand in marriage to sb (**b**) *(proposer)* to offer; **o. de faire qch** to offer to do sth; **combien t'en a-t-elle offert?** how much did she offer you for it? (**c**)

(présenter) (avantage, garantie) to offer; **o. une résistance acharnée** to put up stiff resistance
  2 s'offrir *vpr* (**a**) *(se proposer) (sexuellement)* to offer oneself; **s'o. pour faire qch** to offer to do sth; **s'o. aux regards** *(spectacle, vue)* to meet our/your/*etc* eyes (**b**) *(se présenter) (occasion, possibilité)* to present itself (**c**) *(s'acheter)* **s'o. un bon cigare/une semaine de vacances** to treat oneself to a good cigar/a week's holiday; **je ne peux pas m'o. de vacances** I can't afford a holiday
offset [ɔfsɛt] *nm inv* offset
offusquer [ɔfyske] **1** *vt* to offend
  2 s'offusquer *vpr* to take offence (**de** at)
ogive [ɔʒiv] *nf* (**a**) *Archit* (diagonal) rib (**b**) *Mil (d'un obus)* head; *(d'une roquette)* nose cone; **o. nucléaire** nuclear warhead
OGM [ɔʒeɛm] *nm (abrév* **organisme génétiquement modifié**) genetically modified organism, GMO
ogre [ɔgr] *nm* ogre
ogresse [ɔgrɛs] *nf* ogress
oh [o] *exclam* oh!; *(pour interpeller)* hey!; **oh! hisse!** heave-ho!
ohé [ɔe] *exclam* hey!
ohm [om] *nm* ohm
oie [wa] *nf* goose; **o. sauvage** wild goose; *Fig* **une o. blanche** an innocent young thing
oignon [ɔɲɔ̃] *nm* (**a**) *(légume)* onion; **oignons blancs** *(pour les salades)* spring onions; **petits oignons** *(au vinaigre)* pickling onions; *Fam Fig* **aux petits oignons** first-rate; *Fam* **mêle-toi de tes oignons** mind your own business; *Fam* **ce ne sont pas tes oignons** it's none of your business (**b**) *Bot* bulb (**c**) *Méd* bunion
oindre [43] [wɛ̃dr] *vt* (**a**) *(enduire)* to oil (**b**) *Rel* to anoint
oiseau, -x [wazo] *nm* bird; *Fam Fig* **c'est un drôle d'o.** he's an odd character; **o. de malheur, o. de mauvais augure** bird of ill omen; **o. marin** sea bird; **o. nocturne** nocturnal bird; *Fig* **o. de nuit** night owl; **o. de proie** bird of prey; **l'o. rare** the ideal person
oiseau-lyre *(pl* **oiseaux-lyres**) [wazolir] *nm* lyrebird
oiseau-mouche *(pl* **oiseaux-mouches**) [wazomuʃ] *nm* hummingbird
oiseleur [wazlœr] *nm* bird catcher
oiseux, -euse [wazø, -øz] *adj (conversation)* idle; *(débat)* pointless; *(explication)* unsatisfactory
oisif, -ive [wazif, -iv] **1** *adj* idle
  2 *nm,f* person of leisure
oisillon [wazijɔ̃] *nm* fledgling
oisiveté [wazivte] *nf* idleness; *Prov* **l'o. est (la) mère de tous les vices** the Devil finds work for idle hands to do
OIT [oite] *nf (abrév* **Organisation internationale du travail**) ILO
okapi [ɔkapi] *nm* okapi
oléagineux, -euse [ɔleaʒinø, -øz] **1** *adj* oil-yielding
  2 *nmpl* oil-yielding plants
oléoduc [ɔleɔdyk] *nm* pipeline
olé olé [ɔleɔle] *adj inv Fam (propos, spectacle)* risqué; *(gens)* wild
olfactif, -ive [ɔlfaktif, -iv] *adj* olfactory
olibrius [ɔlibrijys] *nm Fam* oddball
oligarchie [ɔligarʃi] *nf* oligarchy
oligarchique [ɔligarʃik] *adj* oligarchic
oligoélément [ɔligoelemɑ̃] *nm* trace element
olivâtre [ɔlivɑtr] *adj* olive-greenish; *(teint)* sallow

olive [ɔliv] **1** *nf* olive
  2 *adj inv* olive (green)
oliveraie [ɔlivrɛ] *nf* olive grove
olivier [ɔlivje] *nm (arbre)* olive tree; *(bois)* olive (wood)
OLP [ɔɛlpe] *nf (abrév* **Organisation de libération de la Palestine)** PLO
olympiade [ɔlɛ̃pjad] *nf* Olympiad
olympique [ɔlɛ̃pik] *adj* Olympic
ombilical, -e, -aux, -ales [ɔ̃bilikal, -o] *adj* umbilical
omble [ɔ̃bl] *nm* **o.(-chevalier)** char
ombrage [ɔ̃braʒ] *nm* shade; **prendre o. de qch** to take umbrage at sth; **porter o. à qn** to give offence to sb
ombragé, -e [ɔ̃braʒe] *adj* shady
ombrageux, -euse [ɔ̃braʒø, -øz] *adj (personne)* touchy
ombre¹ [ɔ̃br] *nf* **(a)** *(forme)* shadow; **ombres chinoises** shadow play; *Fig* **jeter une o. sur qch** to cast a shadow over sth
  (b) *(zone sombre)* shade; **40 degrés à l'o.** 40 degrees in the shade; **faire de l'o. à qn** to be in sb's light; *Fig* to put sb in the shade; *Fig* **il y a une o. au tableau** there's a fly in the ointment
  (c) *(obscurité)* darkness; *Fig (anonymat)* obscurity; *Fig* **rester dans/sortir de l'o.** to remain in/emerge from obscurity; *Fig* **laisser qch dans l'o.** to keep sth dark; *Fig* **travailler dans l'o.** to work behind the scenes; *Fam* **mettre qn à l'o.** to put sb inside
  (d) *Litt (fantôme)* shade; *Fig* **n'être plus que l'o. de soi-même** to be a mere shadow of one's former self
  (e) *(trace)* hint; **vous n'avez pas l'o. d'une chance** you haven't the ghost of a chance; **il n'y a pas l'o. d'un doute** there isn't the shadow of a doubt; **pas l'o. d'un** not a single one
  (f) **o. à paupières** eye shadow
ombre² *nm (poisson)* char; **o. de rivière** grayling
ombré [ɔ̃bre] *nm Ordinat* shading
ombrelle [ɔ̃brɛl] *nf* sunshade, parasol
OMC [ɔɛmse] *nf (abrév* **Organisation mondiale du commerce)** WTO
omelette [ɔmlɛt] *nf* omelette; *Fig* **on ne fait pas d'o. sans casser des œufs** you can't make an omelette without breaking eggs; **o. norvégienne** baked Alaska
omettre [47] [ɔmɛtr] *vt* to omit; **o. de faire qch** to omit to do sth
omis, -e *voir* **omettre**
omission [ɔmisjɔ̃] *nf (d'un mot, d'un détail)* omission; *(oubli)* oversight
omnibus [ɔmnibys] *nm* slow train
omnipotence [ɔmnipɔtɑ̃s] *nf* omnipotence
omnipotent, -e [ɔmnipɔtɑ̃, -ɑ̃t] *adj* omnipotent
omniprésence [ɔmniprezɑ̃s] *nf* omnipresence
omniprésent, -e [ɔmniprezɑ̃, -ɑ̃t] *adj* omnipresent
omniscience [ɔmnisjɑ̃s] *nf* omniscience
omniscient, -e [ɔmnisjɑ̃, -ɑ̃t] *adj* omniscient
omnisports [ɔmnispɔr] *adj inv* **stade/centre o.** sports stadium/centre
omnivore [ɔmnivɔr] **1** *adj* omnivorous
  2 *nm* omnivore
omoplate [ɔmɔplat] *nf* shoulder blade, *Spéc* scapula
OMS [ɔɛmɛs] *nf (abrév* **Organisation mondiale de la santé)** WHO
on [ɔ̃] *pron indéfini* **(a)** *(indéterminé)* you, people; *(quelqu'un)* somebody, someone; **on ne sait jamais** you never know; **on nous prend parfois pour deux**

sœurs people sometimes take us for sisters; **on dit qu'il est malade, on le dit malade** they say he's ill; **on sonne** there's somebody at the door; **dans tous les pays où l'on parle français** in every country where French is spoken; **on m'a volé mon sac** my bag's been stolen, someone's stolen my bag **(b)** *Fam (nous)* we; **on ne s'est plus jamais quittés** we've been together ever since
onanisme [ɔnanism] *nm* onanism
once [ɔ̃s] *nf aussi Fig* ounce
oncle [ɔ̃kl] *nm* uncle; **o. d'Amérique** rich uncle
onctueux, -euse [ɔ̃ktɥø, -øz] *adj aussi Fig & Péj* smooth
onctuosité [ɔ̃ktɥozite] *nf* smoothness
onde [ɔ̃d] *nf* **(a)** *Phys* wave; *Rad* **grandes ondes** long wave; *Rad* **ondes courtes/moyennes** short/medium wave; **o. de choc** shock wave; **sur les ondes** on the radio; **passer sur les ondes** to be on the radio; **o. sonore** sound wave **(b)** *Litt (eau)* waters; **l'o. limpide du ruisseau** the clear waters of the stream
ondée [ɔ̃de] *nf* sudden downpour
on-dit [ɔ̃di] *nm inv* rumour, hearsay; **ce ne sont que des o.** it's only hearsay
ondoyant, -e [ɔ̃dwajɑ̃, -ɑ̃t] *adj Litt* undulating
ondoyer [32] [ɔ̃dwaje] *vi (blés)* to sway; *(drapeau)* to wave; *(surface de l'eau)* to ripple; *(flamme)* to flicker
ondulant, -e [ɔ̃dylɑ̃, -ɑ̃t] *adj (plaine)* rolling, undulating; *(vagues)* rippling; *(chevelure)* wavy; *(démarche)* swaying
ondulation [ɔ̃dylasjɔ̃] *nf (des vagues)* ripple; **les ondulations de la plaine** the rolling or undulating plain; **les ondulations de sa chevelure** her wavy hair
ondulé, -e [ɔ̃dyle] *adj (sol)* undulating; *(cheveux)* wavy; *(tôle, carton)* corrugated
onduler [ɔ̃dyle] *vi* to undulate; *(cheveux)* to be wavy; **o. des hanches** to sway one's hips
onduleur [ɔ̃dylœr] *nm Ordinat* uninterruptible power supply, UPS
onéreux, -euse [ɔnerø, -øz] *adj* costly
ONF [ɔɛnɛf] *nm (abrév* **Office national des forêts)** *Br* ≃ Forestry Commission, *Am* ≃ National Forestry Service
ONG [ɔɛnʒe] *nf (abrév* **organisation non gouvernementale)** NGO
ongle [ɔ̃gl] *nm (finger)*nail; *(des orteils)* (toe)nail; *(d'un animal)* claw; *(d'un oiseau de proie)* talon; **se faire les ongles** to do one's nails; **o. incarné** ingrowing nail; *Fig* **jusqu'au bout des ongles** to one's fingertips
onglée [ɔ̃gle] *nf* **j'ai l'o.** my fingers are numb with cold
onglet [ɔ̃glɛ] *nm* **(a)** *(d'un répertoire)* tab; *(d'un canif)* thumbnail groove; **dictionnaire à onglets** thumb-indexed dictionary **(b)** *Culin* flank of beef
onguent [ɔ̃gɑ̃] *nm Litt* ointment
onirique [ɔnirik] *adj* dreamlike
onomatopée [ɔnɔmatɔpe] *nf* onomatopoeia
ont *voir* **avoir**
Ontario [ɔ̃tarjo] *n voir* **lac**
ONU [ɔny, ɔɛny] *nf (abrév* **Organisation des Nations unies)** UN
onyx [ɔniks] *nm* onyx
onze [ɔ̃z] *adj & nm inv* eleven; *voir aussi* **trois**
onzième [ɔ̃zjɛm] *nmf, nm & adj* eleventh; *voir aussi* **cinquième**
OPA [ɔpea] *nf (abrév* **offre publique d'achat)** takeover bid; **lancer une O. (sur)** to make a takeover bid (for)

opacité [ɔpasite] *nf* opacity

opale [ɔpal] *nf* opal

opaque [ɔpak] *adj aussi Fig* opaque

OPEP [ɔpɛp] *nf (abrév* **Organisation des pays exportateurs de pétrole)** OPEC

opéra [ɔpera] *nm* (**a**) *(genre, œuvre)* opera (**b**) *(lieu)* opera house; **aller à l'o.** to go to the opera; **l'O. (de Paris)** the Paris Opera House; **o. bouffe** comic opera

opérable [ɔperabl] *adj* operable

opérateur, -trice [ɔperatœr, -tris] **1** *nm,f (personne)* operator; *Cin* cameraman; **o. de saisie** keyboarder
2 *nm* (**a**) *Math* operator (**b**) *Ordinat* **o. logique** logical operator

opération [ɔperasjɔ̃] *nf* (**a**) **o. (chirurgicale)** operation; **o. à cœur ouvert** open-heart surgery (**b**) *Math* operation; **faire des opérations** to do some calculations (**c**) *(transaction)* deal, transaction; **o. financière** financial transaction (**d**) *(action)* operation; **o. de police** police operation

opérationnel, -elle [ɔperasjɔnɛl] *adj* operational

opératoire [ɔperatwar] *adj (procédure)* operating

opérer [34] [ɔpere] **1** *vt* (**a**) *(réforme, restructuration)* to carry out; *(changement, distinction)* to make (**b**) *(patient)* to operate on; **se faire o.** to have an operation; **se faire o. des amygdales** to have one's tonsils (taken) out; **se faire o. du cœur/de la hanche** to have a heart/hip operation; **se faire o. d'une tumeur** to have an operation to remove a tumour
2 *vi* (**a**) *(être efficace)* to work (**b**) *(procéder)* to operate
3 s'opérer *vpr (changement, transformation)* to take place

opérette [ɔperɛt] *nf* operetta

ophtalmo [ɔftalmo] *nmf Fam* ophthalmologist

ophtalmologie [ɔftalmɔlɔʒi] *nf Méd* ophthalmology

ophtalmologiste [ɔftalmɔlɔʒist], **ophtalmologue** [ɔftalmɔlɔg] *nmf Méd* ophthalmologist

opiner [ɔpine] *vi* **o. du chef** *ou* **du bonnet** to nod one's assent

opiniâtre [ɔpinjɑtr] *adj* stubborn

opinion [ɔpinjɔ̃] *nf* opinion (**de/sur** of/about); **se faire une o. sur qch** to make up one's mind about sth, to form an opinion about sth; **changer d'o.** to change one's mind; **sans o.** *(dans un sondage)* don't know; **avoir une bonne/mauvaise o. de qn/qch** to have a good/bad opinion of sb/sth; **o. publique** public opinion

opiomane [ɔpjɔman] *nmf* opium addict

opium [ɔpjɔm] *nm* opium

opossum [ɔpɔsɔm] *nm* opossum

opportun, -e [ɔpɔrtœ̃, -yn] *adj (arrivée)* timely, opportune; *(moment, jour)* right

opportunément [ɔpɔrtynemɑ̃] *adv* opportunely

opportunisme [ɔpɔrtynism] *nm* opportunism

opportuniste [ɔpɔrtynist] *adj & nmf* opportunist

opportunité [ɔpɔrtynite] *nf (d'une arrivée)* timeliness; *(d'un projet, d'une décision)* advisability

opposant, -e [ɔpozɑ̃, -ɑ̃t] **1** *adj* opposing
2 *nm,f* opponent (**à** of)

opposé, -e [ɔpoze] **1** *adj* (**a**) *(en contradiction) (armées, caractères, équipe)* opposing; *(intérêts)* conflicting (**b**) *(dans l'espace) (côtés, rivage, direction)* opposite (**c**) *(contre)* **être o. à qch** to be opposed to sth
2 *nm (contraire)* **l'o.** the opposite; **à l'o.** *(côté)* on the opposite side; *(direction)* in the opposite direction; *Fig*

on the other hand; **à l'o. de** *(côté)* on the opposite side to; *(contrairement à)* unlike; **à l'o. de sa mère, elle n'aimait pas la peinture** unlike her mother, she didn't like painting; **son deuxième film est à l'o. du premier** this second film is the complete opposite of the first

opposer [ɔpoze] **1** *vt* (**a**) *(mettre en conflit) (armées, pays)* to bring into conflict (with each other); *(équipes)* to pit against each other; **o. à** *(armée, pays)* to bring into conflict with; *(équipe)* to pit against (**b**) *(objecter) (argument)* to put forward (**à** against); **o. une résistance vigoureuse** to put up stiff resistance (**c**) *(mettre en contraste) (théories, styles, conceptions)* to contrast
2 s'opposer *vpr* (**a**) *(théories, styles, conceptions)* to contrast; *(équipes, adversaires)* to confront each other (**b**) **s'o. à qch** to be opposed to sth; **je m'oppose à ce qu'elle revienne** I'm against *or* opposed to her coming back

opposition [ɔpozisjɔ̃] *nf* (**a**) *(résistance)* opposition; *Pol* **l'o.** the Opposition; **faire o. à un chèque** to stop a cheque (**b**) *(contraste)* contrast; **tout cela est en o. totale avec ce que je pense** all that is the complete opposite of what I think; **par o. à qch** as opposed to sth

oppressant, -e [ɔprɛsɑ̃, -ɑ̃t] *adj* oppressive

oppresser [ɔprese] *vt* (**a**) *(sujet: situation, atmosphère)* to oppress (**b**) *Litt (peuple, nation)* to oppress

oppresseur [ɔprɛsœr] **1** *nm* oppressor
2 *adj* oppressive

oppression [ɔprɛsjɔ̃] *nf* (**a**) *(asservissement)* oppression (**b**) *Méd* tightness of the chest

opprimé, -e [ɔprime] **1** *adj* oppressed
2 *nm,f* **les opprimés** the oppressed

opprimer [ɔprime] *vt (peuple, nation)* to oppress

opprobre [ɔprɔbr] *nm Litt* opprobrium; **jeter l'o. sur qn** to cast opprobrium on sb

opter [ɔpte] *vi* **o. pour qch** to opt for sth; **o. entre deux choses** to choose between two things

opticien, -enne [ɔptisjɛ̃, -ɛn] *nm,f* optician

optimal, -e, -aux, -ales [ɔptimal, -o] *adj* optimum, optimal

optimiser [ɔptimize] *vt* to optimize

optimisme [ɔptimism] *nm* optimism; **avec o.** optimistically

optimiste [ɔptimist] **1** *adj* optimistic
2 *nmf* optimist

option [ɔpsjɔ̃] *nf* (**a**) *(choix)* option (**b**) *(chose facultative)* optional extra; *Scol (matière)* option; **le flash est en o.** the flash is an optional extra; *Scol* **matières à o.** optional subjects (**c**) *(d'achat)* **prendre une o. sur qch** to take (out) an option on sth (**d**) *Ordinat* **o. d'impression** print option; **o. de menu** menu option

optionnel, -elle [ɔpsjɔnɛl] *adj* optional

optique [ɔptik] **1** *adj (nerf)* optic; *(verre)* optical
2 *nf* (**a**) *(science)* optics *(singulier)*; **instruments d'o.** optical instruments (**b**) *(perspective)* perspective; **dans cette o.** from this perspective (**c**) *(d'un projecteur)* optical system

opulence [ɔpylɑ̃s] *nf* (**a**) *(richesse)* opulence (**b**) *(des formes)* fullness

opulent, -e [ɔpylɑ̃, -ɑ̃t] *adj (pays, personne)* opulent; *(pâturage)* abundant; *(poitrine)* full

opuscule [ɔpyskyl] *nm* opuscule

or¹ [ɔr] *nm* (**a**) *(métal)* gold; **montre/dent en or** gold watch/tooth; *Fam* **j'ai une femme en or** my wife is worth her weight in gold; **pour tout l'or du monde**

for all the money in the world; *Fig* **c'est de l'or en barre** it's a safe investment; **le silence est d'or** silence is golden; **or fin** fine gold; **or massif** solid gold; **or noir** black gold; **or pur** pure gold; **l'or vert** agricultural earnings (**b**) *(couleur)* gold; **cheveux d'or** golden hair

or² *conj (pour introduire une précision)* now; *(pour introduire une opposition)* well

oracle [ɔrakl] *nm* oracle

orage [ɔraʒ] *nm* (thunder)storm; *aussi Fig* **il y a de l'o. dans l'air** there's a storm brewing

orageux, -euse [ɔraʒø, -øz] *adj aussi Fig* stormy

oraison [ɔrɛzɔ̃] *nf* prayer; **o. funèbre** funeral oration

oral, -e, -aux, -ales [ɔral, -o] **1** *adj* oral; **par voie orale** orally

2 *nm (examen)* oral; **il n'est pas très bon à l'o.** his oral work isn't very good

oralement [ɔralmã] *adv* orally

orange [ɔrãʒ] **1** *nf* orange; **o. givrée** = orange sorbet served inside the skin of a whole orange; **o. pressée** = freshly-squeezed orange juice served with water and sugar; **o. sanguine** blood orange

2 *nm (couleur)* orange; **passer à l'o.** *(automobiliste)* to go through (the lights) on amber

3 *adj inv* orange

orangé, -e [ɔrãʒe] *adj* orange-coloured

orangeade [ɔrãʒad] *nf Br* orange squash, *Am* orangeade

oranger [ɔrãʒe] *nm* orange tree

orangeraie [ɔrãʒrɛ] *nf* orange grove

orangerie [ɔrãʒri] *nf* orangery

orang-outan *(pl* **orangs-outans**), **orang-outang** *(pl* **orangs-outangs**) [ɔrãutã] *nm* orang-outang, orang-utan

orateur, -trice [ɔratœr, -tris] *nm,f (personne éloquente)* orator; *(personne qui prend la parole)* speaker

oratoire¹ [ɔratwar] *adj* oratorical

oratoire² *nm (chapelle)* oratory

oratorio [ɔratɔrjo] *nm* oratorio

orbite [ɔrbit] *nf* (**a**) *Astron & Fig* orbit; **être en** *ou* **sur o.** to be in orbit; **mettre** *ou* **placer un satellite en** *ou* **sur o.** to put a satellite into orbit (**b**) *(de l'œil)* socket

Orcades [ɔrkad] *nfpl* **les (îles) O.** the Orkneys, the Orkney Islands

orchestral, -e, -aux, -ales [ɔrkɛstral, -o] *adj* orchestral

orchestration [ɔrkɛstrasjɔ̃] *nf aussi Fig* orchestration

orchestre [ɔrkɛstr] *nm* (**a**) *(de musiciens)* orchestra; **o. de chambre** chamber orchestra; **o. de jazz** jazz band (**b**) *(partie de la salle) Br* stalls, *Am* orchestra

orchestrer [ɔrkɛstre] *vt aussi Fig* to orchestrate

orchidée [ɔrkide] *nf* orchid

ordinaire [ɔrdinɛr] **1** *adj* (**a**) *(habituel)* ordinary, usual; **peu** *ou* **pas o.** unusual (**b**) *(commun)* ordinary

2 *nm* (**a**) *(habitude)* **d'o.** usually; **comme à l'o.** as usual; **moins/plus que d'o.** less/more than usual (**b**) *(moyenne)* **ça sort de l'o.** it's out of the ordinary (**c**) *(régime habituel)* standard fare; *Mil* (company) mess (**d**) *(essence) Br* two-star, *Am* regular

ordinal, -e, -aux, -ales [ɔrdinal, -o] *adj* ordinal

ordinariat [ɔrdinarja] *nm Belg Univ* tenured *Br* lectureship *or Am* professorship

ordinateur [ɔrdinatœr] *nm* computer; **o. autonome** stand-alone (computer); **o. bloc-notes** notebook (computer); **o. central** mainframe (computer); **o.**

domestique home computer; **o. individuel** personal computer; **o. de poche** palmtop (computer); **o. portable** laptop (computer)

ordination [ɔrdinasjɔ̃] *nf* ordination

ordonnance [ɔrdɔnãs] *nf* (**a**) *(document)* prescription; **délivré seulement sur o.** available only on prescription (**b**) *(disposition)* arrangement (**c**) *Jur* order, ruling (**d**) *Mil* orderly

ordonné, -e [ɔrdɔne] **1** *adj* (**a**) *(vie)* orderly (**b**) *(personne, armoire, bureau)* tidy

2 *nf* **ordonnée** *Math* ordinate; **axe des ordonnées** Y-axis

ordonner [ɔrdɔne] *vt* (**a**) *(mettre de l'ordre dans)* to organize (**b**) *(commander)* to order; **o. à qn de faire qch** to order sb to do sth (**c**) *Rel* to ordain

ordre [ɔrdr] *nm* (**a**) *(organisation)* order; **par o. alphabétique/chronologique** in alphabetical/chronological order; **procéder par o.** to do things in order; **par o. d'apparition à l'écran** in order of appearance; *Fig* **c'est dans l'o. des choses** it's in the nature of things (**b**) *(de pièce, de personne)* tidiness; **en o.** *(bureau, maison)* tidy; *(comptes)* in order; **mettre de l'o.** to tidy up (**c**) *(discipline)* order; **maintenir/rétablir l'o.** to maintain/restore order; **tout est rentré dans l'o.** everything has returned to normal; **l'o. établi** the established order; **l'o. public** law and order; **troubler l'o. public** to cause a breach of the peace (**d**) *(catégorie)* order; **de premier/second/troisième o.** first-/second-/third-rate; **renseignements/idées d'o. général** general information/ideas; **d'o. privé/pratique** of a private/practical nature; **du même o.** of the same order; **de l'o. de** in the order of (**e**) *(communauté)* order; **o. religieux** religious order; **entrer dans les ordres** to take holy orders; **l'o. des médecins** *Br* ≃ the British Medical Association, *Am* ≃ the American Medical Association (**f**) *(commandement)* order; **donner l'o. à qn de faire qch** to give sb the order to do sth; **je ne suis pas à tes ordres!** I don't take orders from you!; **à vos ordres, mon général!** yes sir!; **sur l'o. de qn** on the order of sb; **jusqu'à nouvel o.** until further notice (**g**) *Fin* order; **à l'o. de…** payable to (the order of)… (**h**) **o. du jour** *(d'un comité)* agenda; *Mil* order of the day

ordure [ɔrdyr] *nf* (**a**) *(saleté)* dirt, filth (**b**) **ordures** *(déchets) Br* rubbish, *Am* garbage; **ordures ménagères** household *Br* rubbish *or Am* garbage; **jeter** *ou* **mettre qch aux ordures** to throw sth in the *Br* dustbin *or Am* garbage can (**c**) *Fam (personne méprisable)* bastard

ordurier, -ère [ɔrdyrje, -ɛr] *adj* filthy

orée [ɔre] *nf* **à l'o. de la forêt/du bois** on the edge of the forest/wood

oreille [ɔrɛj] *nf* (**a**) *(d'une personne, d'un animal)* ear; **o. externe/interne** outer/inner ear; *Fam* **avoir les oreilles en feuilles de chou** to have big sticky-out ears; **il partit l'o. basse** he went off with his tail between his legs; **tirer les oreilles à qn** to pull sb's ears; *Fig* to give sb a telling off; **n'écouter que d'une o., écouter d'une o. distraite** to listen with half an ear; **dire qch à l'o. de qn** to whisper sth in sb's ear; **dresser** *ou* **tendre l'o.** to prick up one's ears; **je n'en crois pas mes oreilles** I can't believe my ears; **les oreilles ont dû lui siffler** his ears must have been burning; **faire la sourde o.** to turn a deaf ear; **ce n'est pas tombé dans l'o. d'un sourd** it didn't fall on deaf ears; *Fig* **elle ne l'entend pas de cette o.** she won't hear of it; **être dur d'o.** to be hard of hearing; **avoir de l'o.** to have a good ear (**b**) *(d'un fauteuil)* wing; *(d'un plat, d'un vase)* handle; *(d'une casquette)* ear flap; **écrou à oreilles** wing nut

oreiller [ɔrɛje] *nm* pillow; **sur l'o.** in bed; **confidences sur l'o.** pillow talk

oreillette [ɔrɛjɛt] *nf* (**a**) *(du cœur)* auricle (**b**) *(d'une casquette)* ear flap

oreillons [ɔrɛjɔ̃] *nmpl* mumps; **avoir les o.** to have mumps

Orénoque [ɔrenɔk] *nm* **l'O.** the Orinoco

ores [ɔr] **d'ores et déjà** *adv* already

orfèvre [ɔrfɛvr] *nm (d'or)* goldsmith; *(d'argent)* silversmith; *Fig* **être o. en la matière** to be an expert in the matter

orfèvrerie [ɔrfɛvrəri] *nf (travail de l'or)* goldsmith's trade; *(travail de l'argent)* silversmith's trade; *(objets)* plate

organe [ɔrgan] *nm* (**a**) *Anat* organ; **organes génitaux** genitals (**b**) *(d'une machine)* part; **organes de transmission** transmission system (**c**) *Fig (instrument)* organ; **o. de publicité** advertising agency; **l'o. officiel du parti** the official organ of the party (**d**) *Hum (voix)* voice

organigramme [ɔrganigram] *nm* organization chart; *Ordinat* (data) flow chart

organique [ɔrganik] *adj* organic

organisateur, -trice [ɔrganizatœr, -tris] **1** *adj* organizing
2 *nm,f* organizer; **o. de conférences/de congrès** conference organizer; **o. de voyages** tour operator

organisation [ɔrganizasjɔ̃] *nf* (**a**) *(action, résultat)* organization (**b**) *(groupement)* organization; **o. à but non lucratif** *Br* non-profit-making *or Am* not-for-profit organization; **o. politique/syndicale** political/trade-union organization; **O. mondiale de la santé** World Health Organization; **O. des Nations unies** United Nations Organization; **O. du Traité de l'Atlantique Nord** North Atlantic Treaty Organization

organisé, -e [ɔrganize] *adj* organized

organiser [ɔrganize] **1** *vt* to organize
2 **s'organiser** *vpr* to get organized

organisme [ɔrganism] *nm* (**a**) *Biol & Zool* organism; *Anat* system (**b**) *(organisation)* organization, body; **o. de crédit** credit institution; **o. international** international organization

organiste [ɔrganist] *nmf* organist

orgasme [ɔrgasm] *nm* orgasm

orge [ɔrʒ] *nf* barley

orgeat [ɔrʒa] *nm* **sirop d'o.** barley water

orgelet [ɔrʒəlɛ] *nm* sty

orgie [ɔrʒi] *nf* orgy

orgue [ɔrg] **1** *nm* organ; **o. de Barbarie** barrel organ
2 *nfpl* (**a**) *Mus* **orgues** organ; **les grandes orgues de la cathédrale** the great organ of the cathedral (**b**) *Géol* **orgues de basalte** basalt columns

orgueil [ɔrgœj] *nm* pride

orgueilleux, -euse [ɔrgœjø, -øz] *Péj* **1** *adj* proud
2 *nm,f* proud person

orient [ɔrjɑ̃] *nm* east; **l'O.** the East, the Orient; **en O.** in the East

orientable [ɔrjɑ̃tabl] *adj (grue)* swivelling; *(lampe, antenne)* adjustable

oriental, -e, -aux, -ales [ɔrjɑ̃tal, -o] **1** *adj (région, côte)* eastern; *(langue)* oriental
2 *nm,f* **O.** Oriental

orientateur, -trice [ɔrjɑ̃tatœr, -tris] = **orienteur**

orientation [ɔrjɑ̃tasjɔ̃] *nf* (**a**) *(détermination de position)* orientation; **avoir le sens de l'o.** to have a good sense of direction (**b**) *Scol* careers guidance; **choisir une o.** to choose a course of study (**c**) *(d'une grue, d'une antenne)* positioning (**d**) *(d'une maison)* aspect (**e**) *(d'une politique, de recherches)* direction

orienté, -e [ɔrjɑ̃te] *adj* (**a**) *(disposé)* **maison/pièce orientée au sud** house/room facing south (**b**) *(peu objectif)* biased (**c**) *Ordinat* **o. ligne** line-orientated; **o. objet** object-orientated

orienter [ɔrjɑ̃te] **1** *vt* (**a**) *(bâtiment)* to orientate; *(canon, fusil, télescope)* to point (**vers** *ou* **sur** at) (**b**) *(voyageur)* to direct, to guide; *Scol* **on l'a bien/mal orientée** she was given good/bad careers advice; **o. la conversation** to steer the conversation to; **o. ses recherches vers** to direct one's research towards
2 **s'orienter** *vpr* (**a**) *(trouver sa route)* to get one's bearings (**b**) *Fig* **s'o. vers** *(sujet: étudiant)* to specialize in; *(sujet: recherches)* to be directed towards

orienteur, -euse [ɔrjɑ̃tœr, -øz] *nm,f Scol* careers adviser

orifice [ɔrifis] *nm* opening; *(du corps)* orifice; *Tech* port

oriflamme [ɔriflam] *nf* (**a**) *Hist* oriflamme (**b**) *(bannière)* banner

origan [ɔrigɑ̃] *nm* oregano

originaire [ɔriʒinɛr] *adj* **être o. de** *(sujet: personne)* to be a native of; *(sujet: coutume, plat)* to originate from

original, -e, -aux, -ales [ɔriʒinal, -o] **1** *adj* (**a**) *(premier, nouveau)* original (**b**) *(excentrique)* eccentric
2 *nm,f (excentrique)* eccentric
3 *nm (œuvre, document)* original; *(d'un fichier, d'une disquette)* master copy

originalité [ɔriʒinalite] *nf* (**a**) *(nouveauté)* originality (**b**) *(excentricité)* eccentricity (**c**) *(trait original)* original feature

origine [ɔriʒin] *nf* origin; **des origines à nos jours** from the earliest times to the present day; **à l'o.** originally; **être à l'o. de qch** to be at the origin of sth; **être d'o. modeste** to be of humble origin; **être d'o. anglaise, être anglais d'o.** to be of English origin

originel, -elle [ɔriʒinɛl] *adj* original

orignal, -aux [ɔriɲal, -o] *nm* moose

oripeaux [ɔripo] *nmpl* rags, tatters

ORL [ɔɛrɛl] *nmf Méd (abrév* **oto-rhino-laryngologiste)** ENT specialist

orme [ɔrm] *nm* elm

ormeau, -x [ɔrmo] *nm* (**a**) *(arbre)* young elm (**b**) *(mollusque)* abalone

ornement [ɔrnəmɑ̃] *nm aussi Mus* ornament

ornemental, -e, -aux, -ales [ɔrnəmɑ̃tal, -o] *adj* ornamental

orner [ɔrne] *vt* to decorate (**de** with); *(vêtement)* to trim (**de** with)

ornière [ɔrnjɛr] *nf* rut; *Fig* **sortir de l'o.** to get out of trouble

ornithologie [ɔrnitɔlɔʒi] *nf* ornithology

ornithologiste [ɔrnitɔlɔʒist], **ornithologue** [ɔrnitɔlɔg] *nmf* ornithologist

oronge [ɔrɔ̃ʒ] *nf* agaric

orphelin, -e [ɔrfəlɛ̃, -in] **1** *adj* orphan(ed); **o. de père** fatherless; **o. de mère** motherless
2 *nm,f* orphan

orphelinat [ɔrfəlina] *nm* orphanage

orque [ɔrk] *nf* killer whale

Orsay [ɔrsɛ] *n voir* **quai**

ORSEC [ɔrsɛk] *(abrév* **organisation des secours)** le plan O. = disaster contingency plan

> **Le plan ORSEC**
>
> This scheme is set in motion whenever there is a major disaster in France, such as flooding or forest fires. Under the provisions of the scheme, the "préfet", or chief of police, is empowered to mobilize both public and private resources to deal with a civil emergency.

orteil [ɔrtɛj] *nm* toe; **gros/petit o.** big/little toe

orthodontiste [ɔrtodɔ̃tist] *nmf* orthodontist

orthodoxe [ɔrtɔdɔks] **1** *adj aussi Rel* orthodox; **peu o.** unorthodox
  2 *nmf Rel (de stricte obédience)* person of orthodox beliefs; *(de l'Église orthodoxe)* member of the Orthodox Church

orthodoxie [ɔrtɔdɔksi] *nf* orthodoxy

orthogonal, -e, -aux, -ales [ɔrtɔgɔnal, -o] *adj* orthogonal

orthographe [ɔrtɔgraf] *nf* spelling; **avoir une bonne o.** to be good at spelling

orthographier [66] [ɔrtɔgrafje] *vt* to spell; **mal o. un mot** to misspell a word

orthographique [ɔrtɔgrafik] *adj* orthographic

orthopédie [ɔrtɔpedi] *nf* orthopaedics *(singulier)*

orthopédique [ɔrtɔpedik] *adj* orthopaedic

orthopédiste [ɔrtɔpedist] *nmf* **(a)** *(médecin)* orthopaedist **(b)** *(fabricant)* maker of orthopaedic apparatus

orthophonie [ɔrtɔfɔni] *nf* speech therapy

orthophoniste [ɔrtɔfɔnist] *nmf* speech therapist

ortie [ɔrti] *nf* nettle

ortolan [ɔrtɔlɑ̃] *nm* ortolan (bunting)

OS [oɛs] *nm (abrév* **ouvrier spécialisé)** semi-skilled worker

os [ɔs, *pl* o] *nm* bone; *Fam Fig (obstacle)* snag; **mouillé** *ou* **trempé jusqu'aux os** soaked to the skin; **il ne fera pas de vieux os** he won't make old bones; *Fam* **tomber sur un os** to hit a snag; *très Fam* **je l'ai dans l'os** I've had it; **os à moelle,** *Belg* **os à la moelle** marrowbone

oscar [ɔskar] *nm (récompense)* Oscar

oscillateur [ɔsilatœr] *nm Phys* oscillator

oscillation [ɔsilasjɔ̃] *nf* **(a)** *(d'un pendule)* swing; *(d'une aiguille)* flickering; *(d'un bateau)* rocking; *Phys* oscillation **(b)** *Fig (du marché, de l'opinion)* fluctuation

osciller [ɔsile] *vi* **(a)** *(pendule)* to swing; *(aiguille)* to flicker; *(bateau)* to rock; *Phys* to oscillate **(b)** *(hésiter)* **o. entre** to waver between

osé, -e [oze] *adj* daring

oseille [ozɛj] *nf* **(a)** *(plante)* sorrel **(b)** *Fam (argent)* dosh

oser [oze] *vt* **o. faire qch** to dare (to) do sth; **j'ose croire que...** I dare say that...; **si j'ose dire** if I may say so; **comment osez-vous!** how dare you!

osier [ozje] *nm* **(a)** *(arbre)* osier **(b)** *(en vannerie)* wicker

Oslo [ɔslo] *n* Oslo

osmose [ɔsmoz] *nf aussi Fig* osmosis

ossature [ɔsatyr] *nf* **(a)** *(d'un homme, d'un animal)* frame **(b)** *Fig (d'un bâtiment, d'un texte)* framework

osselets [ɔslɛ] *nmpl* **jouer aux o.** to play at knucklebones

ossements [ɔsmɑ̃] *nmpl* bones

osseux, -euse [ɔsø, -øz] *adj (visage, main)* bony; *(tissu, greffe)* bone

ossuaire [ɔsɥɛr] *nm* ossuary

ostensible [ɔstɑ̃sibl] *adj* open

ostensiblement [ɔstɑ̃sibləmɑ̃] *adv* openly

ostensoir [ɔstɑ̃swar] *nm Rel* monstrance

ostentation [ɔstɑ̃tasjɔ̃] *nf* ostentation; **sans o.** unostentatiously

ostéopathe [ɔsteɔpat] *nmf* osteopath

ostéoporose [ɔsteɔpɔroz] *nf Méd* osteoporosis

ostracisme [ɔstrasism] *nm* ostracism

ostréiculteur, -trice [ɔstreikyltœr, -tris] *nm,f* oyster farmer

ostréiculture [ɔstreikyltyr] *nf* oyster farming

otage [ɔtaʒ] *nm* hostage; **prendre qn en o.** to take sb hostage

otalgie [ɔtalʒi] *nf Méd* earache, *Spéc* otalgia

OTAN [ɔtɑ̃] *nf (abrév* **Organisation du traité de l'Atlantique Nord)** **l'O.** NATO

otarie [ɔtari] *nf* sea lion

OTASE [ɔtaz] *nf (abrév* **Organisation du traité de l'Asie du Sud-Est)** **l'O.** SEATO

ôter [ote] **1** *vt* **(a)** *(enlever)* to take away, to remove; *(vêtement)* to take off; *(tache)* to remove; *(assiettes)* to clear away; **ô. qch à qn** to take sth away from sb; *(illusions)* to rid sb of sth; **cela lui a ôté l'appétit** it's made him lose his appetite; **je vais t'ô. l'envie de recommencer!** I'll teach you not to start that again!; **tu ne m'ôteras pas de l'idée que...** I'm quite convinced that... **(b)** *Math* **10 ôté de 30 égale 20** 10 from 30 leaves 20
  2 **s'ôter** *vpr* **ôtez-vous de là!** move yourself!; **s'ô. une idée de la tête** to get an idea out of one's head

otite [ɔtit] *nf Méd* ear infection, *Spéc* otitis

oto-rhino *(pl* oto-rhinos*)* [ɔtɔrino] *nmf Fam* ENT specialist

oto-rhino-laryngologiste *(pl* oto-rhino-laryngologistes*)* [ɔtɔrinɔlarɛ̃gɔlɔʒist] *nmf* ear, nose and throat specialist

Ottawa [ɔtawa] *n* Ottawa

ou [u] *conj* or; **ou... ou (bien)...** either... or (else)...

où [u] **1** *adv* **(a)** *(interrogatif, relatif)* where; **d'où vient ce mot?** where does this word come from?; **par où est-il passé?** which way did he go?; **je ne sais pas où aller** I don't know where to go **(b)** *(indéfini)* **où que vous soyez** wherever you may be **(c)** *(exprime la conséquence)* **d'où sa tristesse** hence his sadness
  2 *pron relatif* **(a)** *(dans l'espace)* where; **là où** where; **partout où** wherever **(b)** *(dans le temps)* when **(c)** *(dans lequel, auquel)* **dans l'état où elle est** in the state she's in; **au prix où est le champagne** with champagne the price it is

OUA [oya] *nf (abrév* **Organisation de l'unité africaine)** **l'O.** the OAU

ouache [waʃ] *nf Can* bear's den

ouah [wa] *exclam* **(a)** *(aboiement)* woof! **(b)** *exprime l'admiration)* wow!

ouailles [wɑj] *nfpl Litt ou Hum* flock

ouais [wɛ] *exclam Fam* yeah!

ouananiche [wananiʃ] *nf Can* freshwater salmon

ouaouaron [wawarɔ̃] *nm Can* bullfrog

ouate [wat] *nf* (**a**) *(pour soins) Br* cotton wool, *Am* absorbent cotton (**b**) *(pour rembourrage)* padding

ouatine [watin] *nf* quilting (material)

ouatiné, -e [watine] *adj* quilted

oubli [ubli] *nm* (**a**) *(trou de mémoire)* oversight; *(lacune)* omission (**b**) *(général)* oblivion; **tomber dans l'o.** to sink into oblivion (**c**) *(acte d'oublier)* forgetting

oublier [66] [ublije] **1** *vt* to forget; *(omettre)* to leave out; **o. de faire qch** to forget to do sth; *Hum* **il a oublié d'être bête** he's not lacking in brains

  2 s'oublier *vpr* (**a**) *(se relâcher)* to forget oneself; *Euph (chien)* to make a mess (**b**) *(sortir de la mémoire)* to be forgotten; **c'est comme le vélo, ça ne s'oublie pas** it's like riding a bike, once you learn you never forget

oubliettes [ublijɛt] *nfpl* dungeon; *Fig* **mettre qch aux o.** to shelve sth

ouest [wɛst] **1** *nm* west; **un vent d'o.** a westerly wind; **le vent d'o.** the west wind; **à l'o.** in the west; **à l'o. de** (to the) west of; *Géog & Pol* **l'O.** the West

  2 *adj inv (côte, face)* west; *(régions)* western

ouf [uf] *exclam* phew!; *Fam* **elle n'a pas eu le temps de dire o.** she didn't even have time to catch her breath

Ouganda [ugɑ̃da] *nm* **l'O.** Uganda

ougandais, -e [ugɑ̃dɛ, -ɛz] **1** *adj* Ugandan

  2 *nm,f* **O.** Ugandan

oui [wi] **1** *adv* yes; **répondre par o. ou par non** to answer yes or no; **je crois que o.** I think so; **faire signe que o.** to nod (one's head); **ah, o.?** really?; *Fam* **tu viens, o.?** are you coming?; *Fam* **tu viens, o. ou non?** are you coming or aren't you?

  2 *nm inv Pol* aye; *Fam* **se quereller/pleurer pour un o., pour un non** to quarrel/cry over the slightest thing

ouï-dire [widir] *nm* hearsay; **par o.** by hearsay

ouïe [wi] *nf* (**a**) *(sens)* hearing; **avoir l'o. fine** to have sharp ears; *Hum* **être tout o.** to be all ears (**b**) *(de poisson)* **ouïes** gills (**c**) *Mus* **ouïes** sound holes

ouille [uj] *exclam* ouch!, ow!

ouistiti [wistiti] *nm* marmoset; *Fam Fig* **un drôle de o.** an odd character

ouragan [uragɑ̃] *nm* hurricane; *Fig (de protestations)* storm; **entrer comme un o. dans une pièce** to burst into a room

Oural [ural] *nm* **l'O.** *(montagnes)* the Urals

ourler [urle] *vt* (**a**) *(faire un ourlet à)* to hem (**b**) *(border)* to edge (**de** with)

ourlet [urlɛ] *nm* (**a**) *(d'un vêtement)* hem; **faire un o. à** to put a hem on (**b**) *(de l'oreille)* rim

ours [urs] *nm aussi Fig* bear; *Prov* **il ne faut pas vendre la peau de l'o. avant de l'avoir tué** don't count your chickens before they're hatched; **o. blanc** polar bear; **o. brun** brown bear; *Fig* **o. mal léché** boor; **o. en peluche** teddy bear; **o. polaire** polar bear

ourse [urs] *nf* she-bear; *Astron* **la Grande O.** the Great Bear; **la Petite O.** the Little Bear

oursin [ursɛ̃] *nm* sea urchin

ourson [ursɔ̃] *nm* bear cub

oust(e) [ust] *exclam (pour presser)* get a move on!; *(pour chasser)* scram!

outarde [utard] *nf Can* Canada goose

outil [uti] *nm aussi Fig* tool; **outils pédagogiques** teaching aids; **o. de production** production tool; **o. de travail** tool

outillage [utijaʒ] *nm* (**a**) *(ensemble d'outils)* (set of) tools (**b**) *(industriel, agricole)* equipment

outiller [utije] **1** *vt* to equip

  2 s'outiller *vpr (bricoleur)* to equip oneself; *(usine)* to equip itself

outrage [utraʒ] *nm (au bon goût, au bon sens)* insult (**à** to); *Euph & Litt* **faire subir les derniers outrages à une femme** to violate a woman; *Jur* **o. aux bonnes mœurs** affront to public decency; **o. à magistrat** contempt of court; **o. à la pudeur** public indecency

outrageant, -e [utraʒɑ̃, -ɑ̃t] *adj (proposition, refus)* insulting; *(plaisanterie, propos)* offensive; *(accusation)* outrageous

outrageusement [utraʒøzmɑ̃] *adv (excessivement)* outrageously

outrance [utrɑ̃s] *nf (d'une tenue, d'une attitude, de propos)* extravagance; **à o.** excessively

outre¹ [utr] *nf* wine skin

outre² **1** *prép* (**a**) *(en plus de)* besides (**b**) **o. mesure** unduly

  2 *adv* **en o.** besides; **passer o.** *(malgré une interdiction)* to carry on regardless; **passer o. à qch** to disregard sth

  3 *conj* **o. (le fait) que...** apart from the fact that...

outré, -e [utre] *adj* (**a**) *(indigné)* outraged (**de** *ou* **par** by) (**b**) *(excessif)* overdone

outre-Atlantique [utratlɑ̃tik] *adv* across the Atlantic

outrecuidance [utrəkɥidɑ̃s] *nf Litt* (**a**) *(insolence)* impertinence; **avoir l'o. de faire qch** to have the impertinence to do sth (**b**) *(orgueil)* presumptuousness

outrecuidant, -e [utrəkɥidɑ̃, -ɑ̃t] *adj* (**a**) *(insolent)* impertinent (**b**) *(orgueilleux)* presumptuous

outre-Manche [utrəmɑ̃ʃ] *adv* across the Channel

outre-mer [utrəmɛr] *adv* overseas; **la France d'o.** France's overseas territories and departments

outrepasser [utrəpase] *vt* to exceed, to go beyond

outre-Rhin [utrərɛ̃] *adv* across the Rhine

outre-tombe [utrətɔ̃b] **d'outre-tombe** *adj (voix)* sepulchral

ouvert, -e [uvɛr, -ɛrt] **1** *pp voir* **ouvrir**

  2 *adj* (**a**) *(porte, yeux, plaie, vêtement, magasin)* open; **grand o.** wide open; **être o. à qn** *(lieu, concours)* to be open to sb (**b**) *(gaz, robinet)* on (**c**) *Fig (franc, sans préjugés)* open; **avoir l'esprit o.** to be open-minded; **être o. à toute proposition** to be open to suggestions

ouvertement [uvɛrtəmɑ̃] *adv* openly

ouverture [uvɛrtyr] *nf* (**a**) *(d'une porte, d'une séance, d'un compte)* opening; *(des hostilités)* outbreak; **l'o. de la chasse/de la pêche** the start of the hunting season/fishing season; **à l'o.** *(de la Bourse)* at the start of trading; *Fig* **o. d'esprit** open-mindedness; *Ordinat* **o. de session** log-on (**b**) *(orifice)* opening (**c**) **ouvertures** *(avances)* overtures; **faire des ouvertures à qn** to make overtures to sb (**d**) *Mus* overture (**e**) *Phot* aperture (**f**) *Pol* **politique d'o.** policy of conciliation (**g**) *(aux échecs, aux cartes)* opening

ouvrable [uvrabl] *adj voir* **jour**

ouvrage [uvraʒ] **1** *nm* (**a**) *(travail)* work; **se mettre à l'o.** to get down to work (**b**) *Constr* work; **ouvrages d'art** civil engineering works (**c**) *(livre)* work; **o. de référence** reference work (**d**) *(résultat d'un travail)* piece of work; *(tricot, broderie)* work

  2 *nf Fam* **c'est de la belle o.** that's a nice piece of work

ouvragé, -e [uvraʒe] *adj* elaborate

ouvrant, -e [uvrã, -ãt] *adj voir* **toit**

ouvre-boîtes [uvrəbwat] *nm inv* can opener

ouvre-bouteilles [uvrəbutɛj] *nm inv* bottle opener

ouvreur, -euse [uvrœr, -øz] *nm,f* usher, *f* usherette

ouvrier, -ère [uvrije, -ɛr] **1** *adj (quartier, tradition)* working-class; *(agitation)* industrial
    2 *nm,f* worker; **une famille d'ouvriers** a working-class family; **o. agricole** farm worker; **o. qualifié** skilled worker; **o. spécialisé** semi-skilled worker
    3 *nm (dans les travaux publics, le bâtiment)* workman
    4 *nf* **ouvrière** *(abeille, fourmi)* worker

ouvrir [52] [uvrir] **1** *vt* (**a**) *(porte, boîte, bouteille, rideaux)* to open; *(verrou)* to draw; *(avec une clef)* to unlock; *(robinet, gaz)* to turn on; *(électricité)* to switch on; **o. à qn** to let sb in; **ouvre, c'est moi** open the door, it's me (**b**) *Méd (abcès)* to lance; *(pour opérer)* to open up (**c**) *(lancer) (boutique, compte, débat)* to open; **o. la marche** to lead the way; *Ordinat* **o. une session** to log in, to log on (**d**) *Fig* **cela ouvre l'appétit** it whets the appetite; **o. son cœur à qn** to open one's heart to sb; **o. l'esprit à qn** to broaden sb's mind; **o. qch à qn** *(domaine, profession, perspectives)* to open up sth to sb
    2 *vi (magasin, porte)* to open
    3 s'ouvrir *vpr* (**a**) *(porte, yeux, séance, fleur)* to open; *Fig* **s'o. à qn** *(perspectives, domaine)* to open up for sb (**b**) *(se couper)* **s'o. la main/le menton** to cut open one's hand/chin; **s'o. les veines** to slash one's wrists (**c**) *(s'épancher)* to open up; **s'o. à qn de qch** to open one's heart to sb about sth, to confide in sb about sth

ouzbek [uzbɛk] **1** *adj* Uzbek
    2 *nmf* **O.** Uzbek

Ouzbékistan [uzbekistã] *nm* **l'O.** Uzbekistan

ovaire [ɔvɛr] *nm* ovary

ovale [ɔval] *adj & nm* oval

ovariectomie [ɔvarjɛktɔmi] *nf Méd* ovariectomy

ovarien, -enne [ɔvarjɛ̃, -ɛn] *adj* ovarian

ovation [ɔvasjɔ̃] *nf* ovation; **faire une o. à qn** to give sb an ovation

ovationner [ɔvasjɔne] *vt* **o. qn** to give sb an ovation

overdose [ɔvœrdoz] *nf aussi Fig* overdose; **faire une o. (de qch)** *(drogue)* to take an overdose (of sth); *Fig* to overdose (on sth)

ovin, -e [ɔvɛ̃, -in] *Zool* **1** *adj* ovine
    2 *nm* sheep

ovni [ɔvni] *nm (abrév* **objet volant non identifié)** UFO

ovulation [ɔvylasjɔ̃] *nf* ovulation

ovule [ɔvyl] *nm* ovum

ovuler [ɔvyle] *vi* to ovulate

oxhydrique [ɔksidrik] *adj* oxyhydrogen

oxydant, -e [ɔksidã, -ãt] **1** *adj* oxidizing
    2 *nm* oxidizer

oxydation [ɔksidasjɔ̃] *nf* oxidization

oxyde [ɔksid] *nm Chim* oxide; **o. de carbone** carbon monoxide

oxyder [ɔkside] **1** *vt* to oxidize
    2 s'oxyder *vpr* to oxidize

oxygéné, -e [ɔksiʒene] *adj Chim* oxygenated; *(cheveux)* peroxide blonde, bleached

oxygène [ɔksiʒɛn] *nm* oxygen; *Fig* **j'ai besoin d'o.** I need some fresh air

oxygéner [34] [ɔksiʒene] **1** *vt* (**a**) *Chim (liquide, tissu vivant)* to oxygenate; *(élément, produit chimique)* to oxidize (**b**) *(cheveux)* to bleach, to peroxide
    2 s'oxygéner *vpr (respirer)* to get some fresh air

oyat [ɔja] *nm* marram grass

ozone [ozon] *nm* ozone

P

P, p [pe] *nm inv* P, p
PAC [pak] *nf (abrév* **politique agricole commune**) CAP
PACA [paka] *nf (abrév* **Provence-Alpes-Côte d'Azur**) = region of south-eastern France
pacage [pakaʒ] *nm (champ)* pasture
pacemaker [pɛsmɛkœr] *nm* pacemaker
pacha [paʃa] *nm* pasha; *Fig* **mener une vie de p.** to live like a lord
pachyderme [paʃidɛrm] *nm* pachyderm; *Fig (personne)* lumbering oaf
pacification [pasifikasjɔ̃] *nf* pacification
pacifier [66] [pasifje] *vt* to pacify
pacifique [pasifik] **1** *adj (sans violence, calme)* peaceful; *(qui aime la paix)* peace-loving
    2 *nm* **le P.** *(océan)* the Pacific; **le P. sud** the South Pacific
pacifisme [pasifism] *nm* pacifism
pacifiste [pasifist] *adj & nmf* pacifist
pack [pak] *nm (lot) & Sport* pack; **vendu en p.** sold in packs
pacotille [pakɔtij] *nf* junk; **de p.** *(marchandise)* shoddy; *(bijoux)* paste; *Fig* third-rate
PACS [paks] *nm inv (abrév* **Pacte civil de solidarité**) = bill introduced in the French parliament in 1998 allowing unmarried couples to legally formalize their relationship

PACS
The "Pacte civil de solidarité", more commonly known by its acronym "PACS", is a contract which offers legal recognition to adult cohabiting couples, including homosexuals. The law allows same-sex or heterosexual couples to register their union formally in a magistrates' court. Controversial when first proposed, the "PACS" became law in 1999, after more than 120 hours of parliamentary debate.

pacson [paksɔ̃] *nm Fam (argent)* packet
pacte [pakt] *nm* pact; **p. de non-agression** non-aggression pact; **le p. de Varsovie** the Warsaw Pact
pactiser [paktize] *vi* **p. avec l'ennemi** to make a pact with the enemy
pactole [paktɔl] *nm Fam (au loto)* jackpot; **un joli p.** a nice little sum
paddock [padɔk] *nm* paddock; *Fam (lit)* bed
paella [paɛla] *nf* paella
PAF [paf] *nm (abrév* **paysage audiovisuel français**) = French broadcasting
paf [paf] **1** *exclam (chute)* bang!; *(claque)* slap!; *(coup de poing)* wham!

    2 *adj inv Fam* (**a**) *(saoul)* plastered (**b**) *Belg* **être/rester p.** to be flabbergasted
pagaie [pagɛ] *nf* paddle
pagaïe, pagaille [pagaj] *nf Fam* (**a**) *(désordre)* mess; **en p.** in a mess; **arrête de mettre la p. dans mes affaires** stop messing up my things (**b**) *(confusion)* chaos; **semer la p.** to cause chaos (**c**) **des cadeaux/des jouets en p.** loads of presents/toys
pagayer [53] [pageje] *vi* to paddle
page¹ [paʒ] *nf* (**a**) *(d'un livre, d'un cahier, sur l'Internet)* page; *Fig (extrait)* passage; *(de l'histoire, d'une vie)* chapter; **en première p. (des journaux)** on the front page (of the newspapers); *Typ* **mettre qch en page(s)** to make sth up; **perdre la p.** to lose one's place; *Fig* **tourner la p.** to make a fresh start; *Ordinat* **p. d'accueil** home page; **p. centrale** *(d'un magazine)* centre pages; **p. de garde** flyleaf; **les pages jaunes** *(de l'annuaire)* the Yellow Pages®; *Ordinat* **p. précédente** page up; *Rad & TV* **p. de publicité** commercial break; *Ordinat* **p. suivante** page down (**b**) **être à la p.** *(à la mode)* to be up to date
page² *nm* page(boy)
pager, pageur [paʒœr] *nm Ordinat* pager
pagination [paʒinasjɔ̃] *nf* pagination
paginer [paʒine] *vt* to paginate
pagne [paɲ] *nm* loincloth; *(en paille)* grass skirt
pagode [pagɔd] *nf* pagoda
paie [pɛ] **1** *voir* **payer**
    2 *nf* (**a**) *(salaire)* pay, wages (**b**) *Fam* **ça fait une p.** it's ages ago; **ça fait une p. que je ne l'ai pas vue** I haven't seen her for ages
paiement [pɛmã] *nm* payment; *aussi Fig* **en p. de qch** as payment for sth; **p. à la commande** cash with order; **p. à la livraison** cash on delivery; *Ordinat* **p. sécurisé** secure (electronic) transaction
païen, -enne [pajɛ̃, -ɛn] *adj & nm,f* pagan, heathen
paiera *etc voir* **payer**
paillard, -e [pajar, -ard] *adj* bawdy
paillasse [pajas] *nf* (**a**) *(matelas)* straw mattress (**b**) *(de l'évier)* draining board; *(de laboratoire)* bench
paillasson [pajasɔ̃] *nm aussi Fig* doormat
paille [paj] **1** *nf* (**a**) *(de céréales)* straw; *Fig* **être sur la p.** to be down and out; **tirer à la courte p.** to draw lots; **p. de fer** steel wool (**b**) *(pour boire)* straw; **boire avec une p.** to drink through a straw
    2 *adj inv (jaune)* straw-coloured
paillé, -e [paje] *adj (chaise)* straw-bottomed
pailleté, -e [pajte] *adj* sequined

paillette [pajɛt] *nf* (**a**) *(sur vêtement)* sequin; **paillettes** *(pour se maquiller)* glitter; **à paillettes** sequined (**b**) *(d'or)* speck; *(de savon)* flake

paillote [pajɔt] *nf* straw hut

pain [pɛ̃] *nm* (**a**) *(aliment)* bread; *(miche)* loaf; *Fig* **avoir du p. sur la planche** to have a lot on one's plate; **gagner son p.** to earn one's living; **je ne mange pas de ce p.-là** I'm having nothing to do with that; **ça ne mange pas de p.** it won't cost you/him/*etc* anything; **ôter le p. de la bouche à qn** to take the bread out of sb's mouth; **petit p.** (bread) roll; *Fig* **partir** *ou* **se vendre comme des petits pains** to sell like hot cakes; **p. azyme** unleavened bread; **p. bénit** consecrated bread; **p. bis** brown bread; **p. de campagne** farmhouse bread; **p. au chocolat** chocolate-filled pastry; **p. complet** wholemeal bread; **p. d'épices** ≃ gingerbread; **p. grillé** toast; *Can* **p. d'habitant** *ou* **de famille** *ou* **du pays** homemade bread; **p. au lait** sweet roll; **p. de mie** sliced white bread; **p. perdu** French toast; **p. aux raisins** currant bun; **p. de seigle** rye bread; **p. au** *ou* **de son** bran bread; **p. de sucre** sugarloaf (**b**) *(de savon)* bar (**c**) *Fam (coup de poing)* punch

pair, -e [pɛr] **1** *adj (nombre, jours)* even
 2 *nm* (**a**) *(égal)* **être jugé par ses pairs** to be judged by one's peers; **aller de p. avec qch** to go hand in hand with sth (**b**) *(noble)* peer (**c**) **jeune fille au p.** au pair; **être** *ou* **travailler au p.** to work as an au pair (**d**) *(au jeu)* even numbers

paire [pɛr] *nf* pair; *(de gibier à plumes, de pistolets)* brace; **il a reçu une p. de claques** he got his face slapped; *Fam Fig* **ça, c'est une autre p. de manches** that's a different kettle of fish

paisible [pɛzibl] *adj* peaceful; *(personne)* quiet

paisiblement [pɛzibləmɑ̃] *adv* peacefully

paître [50b] [pɛtr] **1** *vt (herbe)* to crop; *(feuilles)* to feed on
 2 *vi* to feed; *(manger de l'herbe)* to graze; *(manger des feuilles)* to browse; *Fam Fig* **envoyer p. qn** to send sb packing

paix [pɛ] *nf* (**a**) *(entre États)* peace; **faire la p. (avec qn)** to make peace (with sb); *Fig* to make it up (with sb); **vivre en p. avec sa conscience** to have a clear conscience (**b**) *Rel* **à son âme** may his soul rest in peace; **allez en p.** go in peace (**c**) *(tranquillité)* peace; **avoir la p.** to have some peace (and quiet); **faire qch en p.** to do sth in peace (and quiet); **laisser qn en p.** to leave sb in peace; *Fam* **fiche-moi** *ou* **fous-moi la p.!** get off my back!; *Fam* **la p.!** quiet!

Pakistan [pakistɑ̃] *nm* **le P.** Pakistan

pakistanais, -e [pakistanɛ, -ɛz] **1** *adj* Pakistani
 2 *nm,f* **P.** Pakistani

Pal [pal] *adj inv TV (abrév* **phase alternation line)** PAL

palabres [palabr] *nfpl* endless discussion

palace [palas] *nm* luxury hotel

palais¹ [palɛ] *nm* (**a**) *(d'un roi, d'un noble)* palace; **le p. Bourbon** = home of the French parliament; **p. des congrès** conference centre; **le p. de l'Élysée** the Élysée (Palace) *(official residence of the French President)*; **le p. Garnier** = the Paris Opera House; **le p. du Luxembourg** = home of the French Senate; **p. des sports** sports centre (**b**) *(tribunal)* **le P. (de justice)** the law courts

palais² *nm (partie de la bouche, goût)* palate; **avoir le p. fin** to have a refined palate

palan [palɑ̃] *nm* hoist

pale [pal] *nf* blade

pâle [pal] *adj* (**a**) pale; **p. comme un linge** as white as a sheet; **p. comme la mort** deathly pale; *Fam Mil* **se faire porter p.** to report sick (**b**) *Fig (sourire)* faint; *(style)* colourless; **une p. imitation de qch** a pale imitation of sth

palefrenier [palfrənje] *nm* groom

paléolithique [paleɔlitik] *Géol* **1** *adj* Palaeolithic
 2 *nm* **le P.** the Palaeolithic period

paléontologie [paleɔ̃tɔlɔʒi] *nf* palaeontology

paléontologiste [paleɔ̃tɔlɔʒist], **paléontologue** [paleɔ̃tɔlɔg] *nmf* palaeontologist

Palerme [palɛrm] *n* Palermo

Palestine [palɛstin] *nf* **la P.** Palestine

palestinien, -enne [palɛstinjɛ̃, -ɛn] **1** *adj* Palestinian
 2 *nm,f* **P.** Palestinian

palet [palɛ] *nm* (**a**) *(pour hockey)* puck (**b**) *(gâteau sec)* = round butter biscuit

paletot [palto] *nm* (short) overcoat; *Fam Fig* **tomber sur le p. à qn** *(l'attaquer)* to jump on sb; *(pour lui parler)* to buttonhole sb; *Belg Fig* **vieux paletots** old guard

palette [palɛt] *nf* (**a**) *(de peintre)* palette; *Fig (éventail)* range; *Ordinat* **p. graphique** graphics palette; *Ordinat* **p. d'outils** tool palette (**b**) *(pour la manutention)* pallet (**c**) *Culin (de mouton, de porc)* shoulder

palétuvier [paletyvje] *nm* mangrove

pâleur [palœr] *nf (d'une personne)* pallor; *(d'une couleur, de la lumière)* paleness; *(du style)* colourlessness; **d'une p. mortelle** deathly pale

pâlichon, -onne [paliʃɔ̃, -ɔn] *adj Fam* a bit pale

palier [palje] *nm* (**a**) *(d'escalier)* landing (**b**) *(dans une évolution)* plateau; **par paliers** in stages

palindrome [palɛ̃drom] *nm Ling* palindrome

pâlir [palir] *vi (personne)* to turn *ou* go pale; *(lumière, couleur, souvenir)* to fade; **p. de rage** to turn white with anger; *Fig* **faire p. qn de jalousie** to make sb green with envy

palissade [palisad] *nf* fence

palliatif, -ive [paljatif, -iv] **1** *adj* palliative
 2 *nm Méd* palliative; *Fig* stopgap measure

pallier [66] [palje] **1** *vt (manque)* to compensate for; *(erreur, problème)* to lessen the impact of
 2 **pallier à** *vt ind (manque)* to compensate for; *(erreur, problème)* to lessen the impact of

palmarès [palmarɛs] *nm (à un concours)* list of prizewinners; *(d'une compétition sportive)* list of winners; **le p. (de la chanson)** the charts; **être** *ou* **figurer au p.** *(d'un concours, d'une compétition)* to be among the (prize-)winners; *(de la chanson)* to be in the charts; **avoir** *ou* **compter cinquante victoires à son p.** to have fifty wins to one's credit

palme [palm] *nf* (**a**) *(de palmier)* palm (branch) (**b**) *(récompense)* **les palmes académiques** = decoration awarded to teachers; **la P. d'or** *(du festival de Cannes)* the Palme d'or (**c**) *(pour nager)* flipper

palmé, -e [palme] *adj* (**a**) *(feuille)* palmate (**b**) *(pattes)* webbed

palmeraie [palmərɛ] *nf* palm grove

palmier [palmje] *nm* (**a**) *(arbre)* palm (tree); **p. dattier** date palm (**b**) *(gâteau sec)* = sweet heart-shaped pastry

palmipède [palmipɛd] *nm Zool* web-footed bird, *Spéc* palmiped

palombe [palɔ̃b] *nf* wood pigeon

pâlot, -otte [palo, -ɔt] *adj Fam* a bit pale

palourde [palurd] *nf* clam

palpable [palpabl] *adj* palpable

palpation [palpasjɔ̃] *nf Méd* palpation

palper [palpe] *vt* (**a**) *(objet)* to feel (with one's hands); *Méd* to palpate (**b**) *Fam (somme)* to be paid, to get

palpitant, -e [palpitɑ̃, -ɑ̃t] **1** *adj* (**a**) *(cœur, pouls)* fluttering; *(plus fort)* throbbing; *(personne) (d'émotion)* quivering (**b**) *(passionnant)* thrilling
 2 *nm Fam (cœur)* ticker

palpitations [palpitasjɔ̃] *nfpl* palpitations

palpiter [palpite] *vi (cœur, pouls)* to flutter; *(plus fort)* to throb

paludisme [palydism] *nm* malaria

pâmer [pɑme] **se pâmer** *vpr Vieilli* to swoon; *Fig & Hum* **se p. d'aise** to be blissfully happy; *Fig & Hum* **se p. (devant)** to swoon (over)

pamphlet [pɑ̃flɛ] *nm* satirical tract

pamplemousse [pɑ̃pləmus] *nm* grapefruit

pan¹ [pɑ̃] *nm* (**a**) *(de chemise, de manteau)* tail; *(de jupe)* panel (**b**) *(morceau)* section, piece; *Fig (d'une époque)* part; **p. de mur** section of wall

pan² *exclam (coup de feu)* bang!; *(gifle)* whack!; **et p., la voilà qui entre!** and lo and behold, in she walks!

panacée [panase] *nf* panacea

panachage [panaʃaʒ] *nm* mixing; *(de liste électorale)* = voting for candidates from more than one list

panache [panaʃ] *nm* (**a**) *(plume)* plume (**b**) *(brio, éclat)* panache

panaché, -e [panaʃe] **1** *adj* multicoloured; **p. de blanc** streaked with white, with white streaks; **un demi p.** a shandy
 2 *nm (boisson)* shandy

panacher [panaʃe] *vt* to mix

panade [panad] *nf Fam* **être dans la p.** *(avoir des ennuis)* to be in a bit of a mess; *(manquer d'argent)* to be strapped for cash

panafricain, -e [panafrikɛ̃, -ɛn] *adj* Pan-African

panais [panɛ] *nm* parsnip

Panama [panama] *nm* **le P.** Panama

panama [panama] *nm (chapeau)* panama hat

Paname [panam] *n Fam* Paris

panaméen, -enne [panameɛ̃, -ɛn] **1** *adj* Panamanian
 2 *nm,f* **P.** Panamanian

panaméricain, -e [panamerikɛ̃, -ɛn] *adj* Pan-American

panard [panar] *nm Fam* (**a**) *(pied)* foot (**b**) *(plaisir intense)* **quel p.!** great!, terrific!; **ce n'est pas le p.** it's not exactly a load of laughs *or* a barrel of fun

panaris [panari] *nm* whitlow

pan-bagnat *(pl* **pans-bagnats)** [pɑ̃baɲa] *nm* = large bread roll filled with salade niçoise

pancarte [pɑ̃kart] *nf (affiche)* sign, notice; *(pour manifestation)* placard

pancréas [pɑ̃kreas] *nm* pancreas

panda [pɑ̃da] *nm* panda

pané, -e [pane] *adj* coated with breadcrumbs, breaded

panégyrique [paneʒirik] *nm* eulogy; **faire le p. de qn** to eulogize sb

panel [panɛl] *nm (groupe)* panel; *(échantillon)* sample (group)

paneuropéen, -enne [panørɔpeɛ̃, -ɛn] *adj* Pan-European

panier [panje] *nm* (**a**) *(corbeille)* basket; **mettre** *ou* **jeter qch au p.** to throw sth in the wastepaper basket; *Fig* **le dessus du p.** the pick of the bunch; *Fig* **c'est un p. de crabes** they're always at each other's throats; *Fam* **mettre la main au p. à qn** to goose sb; **p. à linge** linen basket; *Fam* **p. percé** *(personne dépensière)* spendthrift; *Can (personne indiscrète)* blabbermouth; **p. à provisions** shopping basket; **p. à salade** salad shaker; *Fam (convoi cellulaire) Br* black Maria, *Am* paddy wagon (**b**) *(au basket-ball)* basket (**c**) *(pour diapositives)* slide magazine (**d**) *(de robe)* hoop

panier-repas *(pl* **paniers-repas)** [panjerəpa] *nm* packed lunch

panique [panik] **1** *nf* panic; **être pris de p.** to panic; **ne pas céder à la p.** not to panic; **il y a eu un début de p.** people started to panic; **il y a eu un mouvement de p.** people panicked
 2 *adj* **peur p.** panic

paniqué, -e [panike] *adj Fam* in a panic

paniquer [panike] *vt & vi Fam* to panic

panislamisme [panislamism] *nm* Pan-Islamism

panne [pan] *nf* breakdown; *Ordinat* failure, crash; **être en p.** *(machine)* to be out of order; *(automobiliste)* to have broken down; **tomber en p.** to break down; **tomber en p. d'essence, tomber en p. sèche** to run out of *Br* petrol *or Am* gas; *Fam* **il m'a fait le coup de la p.** he tried to pull the old "the car won't start" trick on me; **p. (de courant** *ou* **d'électricité)** power failure *or* cut; **p. de moteur** engine failure; **p. de secteur** power failure

panneau, -x [pano] *nm* (**a**) *(pour afficher)* board; **p. d'affichage** *Br* notice board, *Am* bulletin board; **p. publicitaire** *Br* hoarding, *Am* billboard (**b**) *(sur la route)* **p. (de signalisation routière), p. indicateur** road sign (**c**) *(élément plan)* panel (**d**) *Fig* **tomber** *ou* **donner dans le p.** to fall into the trap

panonceau, -x [panɔ̃so] *nm* (**a**) *(de notaire)* plaque (**b**) *(pancarte)* sign

panoplie [panɔpli] *nf* (**a**) *(habit)* outfit; **une p. de Zorro/d'infirmière** a Zorro/nurse's outfit (**b**) *(assortiment)* set

panorama [panɔrama] *nm* panorama; *Fig* overview

panoramique [panɔramik] *adj (vue)* panoramic; *(restaurant)* with panoramic views; *(écran)* wide

panse [pɑ̃s] *nf* (**a**) *(de ruminant)* rumen (**b**) *Fam (ventre)* belly; **s'en mettre plein la p.** to stuff oneself

pansement [pɑ̃smɑ̃] *nm* dressing; **p. (adhésif)** *Br* (sticking) plaster, *Am* Band-aid®; **faire un p. (à qn)** to put a dressing on (sb); **refaire un p. à qn** to change sb's dressing

panser [pɑ̃se] *vt* (**a**) *(blessure)* to dress; *(membre)* to bandage; **p. qn** to dress sb's wounds; *Fig* **p. ses blessures** to lick one's wounds (**b**) *(cheval)* to groom

pantagruélique [pɑ̃tagryelik] *adj* gigantic

pantalon [pɑ̃talɔ̃] *nm Br* trousers, *Am* pants; **un p.** a pair of *Br* trousers *or Am* pants; **p. de golf** plus-fours; **p. à pattes d'éléphant** flares; **p. à pinces** pleated *Br* trousers *or Am* pants; **p. de pyjama** pyjama *Br* trousers *or Am* pants

pantalonnade [pɑ̃talɔnad] *nf (spectacle)* burlesque farce

pantelant, -e [pɑ̃tlɑ̃, -ɑ̃t] *adj Litt (à bout de souffle)* panting

panthère [pɑ̃tɛr] *nf* leopard; **p. noire** panther

pantin [pɑ̃tɛ̃] *nm (jouet)* jumping-jack; *Péj (fantoche)* puppet

pantois, -e [pɑ̃twa, -az] *adj* speechless; **en rester p.** to be speechless

pantomime [pɑ̃tɔmim] *nf (art)* mime; *(spectacle)* mime show

pantouflard, -e [pɑ̃tuflar, -ard] *adj & nm,f Fam* stay-at-home

pantoufle [pɑ̃tufl] *nf* slipper

pantoufler [pɑ̃tufle] *vi Fam* to join the private sector

PAO [peao] *nf Ordinat (abrév* **publication assistée par ordinateur***)* DTP

paon [pɑ̃] *nm* peacock

papa [papa] *nm* dad; *(langage enfantin)* daddy; **p. gâteau** indulgent father; **p. poule** doting father; *Fam Péj* **de p.** old-fashioned; **jouer au p. et à la maman** to play mummies and daddies

papal, -e, -aux, -ales [papal, -o] *adj* papal

paparazzi [paparadzi] *nmpl* paparazzi

papauté [papote] *nf* papacy

papaye [papaj] *nf* papaya

pape [pap] *nm* pope; *Fam* **sérieux comme un p.** deadly serious

papelard [paplar] *nm Fam* piece of paper

paperasse [papras] *nf Péj* papers, *Br* bumf

paperasserie [paprasri] *nf Péj* **(a)** *(documents)* papers, *Br* bumf; **faire de la p.** to do paperwork **(b)** *(d'un système bureaucratique)* red tape

papeterie [papetri] *nf (usine)* paper mill; *(magasin)* stationer's; *(articles)* stationery

papetier, -ère [papətje, -ɛr] *nm,f* **(a)** *(industriel)* paper manufacturer **(b)** *(commerçant)* stationer

papi [papi] *nm* grandpa, granddad

papier [papje] *nm* **(a)** *(pour écrire)* paper; **un p.** a piece of paper; *Fam* **être dans les petits papiers de qn** to be in sb's good books; *Fam* **p. alu** tinfoil; **p. avion** airmail paper; *Ordinat* **p. à bandes perforées** perforated paper; **p. de bonbon** sweet wrapper; **p. cadeau** gift wrap, wrapping paper; *Ordinat* **p. continu** continuous paper *or* stationery; *Ordinat* **p. continu plié en accordéon** fanfold paper; **p. crépon** crêpe paper; *très Fam* **p. cul** bog roll; **p. à dessin** drawing paper; **p. d'emballage** brown paper; **p. à en-tête** headed notepaper; **p. glacé** glazed paper; **papiers gras** litter; **p. hygiénique** toilet paper; **p. journal** newspaper; **p. kraft** brown paper; **p. à lettres** writing paper; *Ordinat* **p. listing** listing paper; **p. mâché** papier-mâché; **p. machine** typing paper; **p. millimétré** *ou* **millimétrique** graph paper; **p. à musique** manuscript paper; *Fig* **être réglé comme du p. à musique** *(événement)* to be as regular as clockwork; **elle est réglée comme du p. à musique** you can set your watch by her; **p. peint** wallpaper; **p. de soie** tissue paper; **p. toilette** toilet paper; **p. de verre** sandpaper; **passer qch au p. de verre** to sandpaper sth **(b)** **papiers** *(documents officiels)* papers; **papiers (d'identité)** (identity) papers; *(d'un automobiliste) Br* driving licence, *Am* driver's license **(c)** *Fam (article de journal)* article

papilles [papij] *nfpl* **p. gustatives** taste buds

papillon [papijɔ̃] *nm* **(a)** *(insecte)* butterfly; **p. de nuit** moth; *Fam* **minute p.!** hold on a minute! **(b)** *(écrou)* wing nut **(c)** *(sur document)* flag **(d)** *Fam (contravention)* (parking) ticket **(e)** *(nage)* butterfly

papillonner [papijɔne] *vi* **(a)** *(paupières)* to flutter **(b)** *(d'une personne à une autre)* to flit about

papillote [papijɔt] *nf* **(a)** *(en papier alu)* **cailles en papillotes** quails en papillotes *(cooked in tinfoil)* **(b)** *(de gigot)* frill **(c)** *(bigoudi)* curlpaper; *Fam* **tu peux en faire des papillotes** you can chuck it away

papilloter [papijɔte] *vi (yeux)* to blink; *(lumière)* to flicker

papoter [papɔte] *vi Fam* to chat

papou, -e [papu] **1** *adj* Papuan
2 *nm,f* **P.** Papuan

Papouasie-Nouvelle-Guinée [papwazinuvɛlgine] *nf* **la P.** Papua New Guinea

papouille [papuj] *nf Fam* **faire des papouilles à qn** to tickle sb

paprika [paprika] *nm* paprika

papyrus [papirys] *nm* papyrus

paqson [paksɔ̃] = **pacson**

Pâque [pɑk] *nf* **P., la P. juive** Passover

paquebot [pakbo] *nm* liner

pâquerette [pɑkrɛt] *nf* daisy

pâques [pɑk] **1** *nfpl* **joyeuses p.!** Happy Easter!
2 *nm* **P.** Easter; *Fam* **à P. ou à la Trinité!** never in a month of Sundays!

> ### Pâques
> In France, Easter is traditionally symbolized not only by eggs but also by bells; according to legend, church bells fly to Rome at Easter. At this time of the year, people offer each other chocolate eggs, bells, fish or hens.

paquet [pakɛ] *nm* **(a)** *(sac)* packet; *(de sucre)* bag; *(de cigarettes)* packet, *Am* pack; *(postal)* parcel, package **(b)** *Fam (grande quantité)* **un p. de** a pile or stack of; **toucher un joli p.** to make a packet; **mettre le p.** to pull out all the stops; *Fam* **c'est un p. de nerfs** she's a bundle *or* a bag of nerves; **p.-cadeau** gift-wrapped parcel; **je vous fais un p.-cadeau?** would you like it gift-wrapped? **(c)** **p. de mer** big wave **(d)** *Ordinat* packet

paquetage [paktaʒ] *nm* (soldier's) pack; **faire son p.** to get one's kit ready

par [par] *prép* **(a)** *(à travers)* through; **p. la porte/le trou de la serrure** through the door/the keyhole; **regarder p. la fenêtre** *(de l'intérieur)* to look out (of) the window; *(de l'extérieur)* to look through the window; **passer p. Calais** to go via Calais; **p. ici/là** this/that way; **p. où est-il passé?** which way did he go?
   (b) *(position)* **p. ici** round about here; **p. là** over there; **p. 200 mètres de fond** at a depth of 200 metres; **p. endroits** in places
   (c) *(pendant)* **p. une belle journée d'automne** on a beautiful autumn day; **p. cette chaleur** in this heat; **p. le passé** in the past; *Litt* **p. deux fois** twice
   (d) *(introduit le complément d'agent)* by; **c'est p. eux que je l'ai appris** I found out from them; **faire faire qch p. qn** to have sth done by sb
   (e) *(indique la cause)* out of; **faire qch p. amitié/pitié** to do sth out of friendship/pity; **p. hasard/erreur** by chance/mistake; **p. malheur** unfortunately, as bad luck would have it; **p. pitié!** for pity's sake!
   (f) *(au moyen de)* with, by; **retenu p. une corde** held by a rope; **fermé p. un cadenas** padlocked; **p. train/avion/voiture/bateau** by train/plane/car/boat; **conduire/prendre qn p. la main** to lead/take sb by the hand; **tenir qn p. la taille** to hold sb round the waist; **pendu p. les pieds** hanging by the feet; **envoyer qch p. la poste** to send sth by post; **répondre p. oui ou p. non** to answer yes or no; **se terminer p. un divorce/une dispute** to end in divorce/an argument; **p. tous les moyens** by every possible means; **il est monté p. l'escalier** he took the stairs up; **obtenir qch**

p. la force to obtain sth by force; **appeler qn p. son nom** to call sb by his/her name

(**g**) *(selon)* according to; **p. ordre de grandeur** according to size

(**h**) *(distributif)* per, a; **deux p. deux** two by two; **p. groupes de six** in groups of six; **deux jours p. semaine** two days a week; **10 000 francs p. an** 10,000 francs a year; **un siège p. personne** one seat per person

(**i**) **de p.** *(à cause de)* due to; **de p. le monde** the world over

para [para] *nm Fam* para

parabole [parabɔl] *nf* (**a**) *(allégorie)* parable (**b**) *(courbe)* parabola (**c**) *(antenne)* (satellite) *or* (parabolic) dish

parabolique [parabɔlik] *adj* parabolic

paracétamol [parasetamɔl] *nm* paracetamol

parachever [46] [paraʃəve] *vt* to complete, to finish off

parachutage [paraʃytaʒ] *nm* parachuting

parachute [paraʃyt] *nm* parachute; **faire du p.** to go parachuting; **p. ascensionnel** parascending

parachuter [paraʃyte] *vt (vivres, soldats)* to parachute in; *Fam (nommer)* to draft in

parachutisme [paraʃytism] *nm* parachuting; **faire du p.** to go parachuting

parachutiste [paraʃytist] *nmf* (**a**) *(sportif)* parachutist (**b**) *(soldat)* paratrooper

parade¹ [parad] *nf* (**a**) *(exhibition)* show, ostentation; **faire p. de qch** to show sth off (**b**) *(défilé)* parade

parade² *nf* (**a**) *(en escrime, boxe)* parry (**b**) *(réplique)* riposte; **Fam je n'ai pas encore trouvé la p.** I haven't come up with a way of handling him/it/*etc* yet

parader [parade] *vi* to show off

paradis [paradi] *nm* heaven; *Fig* paradise; **le p. terrestre** the Garden of Eden; *Fig* heaven on earth; **aller au p.** to go to heaven; **un p. fiscal** a tax haven; *Fam* **le p.** *(d'un théâtre)* the gods; *Fam* **il ne l'emportera pas au p.** he won't get away with it, he'll be sorry

paradisiaque [paradizjak] *adj* heavenly

paradoxal, -e, -aux, -ales [paradɔksal, -o] *adj* paradoxical

paradoxalement [paradɔksalmã] *adv* paradoxically

paradoxe [paradɔks] *nm* paradox

parafe [paraf] = **paraphe**

parafer [parafe] = **parapher**

paraffine [parafin] *nf* paraffin

parafiscalité [parafiskalite] *nf* = taxes paid to the state and used for administration purposes

parages [paraʒ] *nmpl* (**a**) *Naut* waters (**b**) *(alentours)* **dans les p. de...** in the vicinity of...; *Fam* **est-ce qu'elle est dans les p.?** is she around?

paragraphe [paragraf] *nm* (**a**) paragraph (**b**) *Typ* paragraph (sign)

Paraguay [paragwɛ] *nm* **le P.** Paraguay

paraguayen, -enne [paragwɛjɛ̃, -ɛn] **1** *adj* Paraguayan

2 *nm,f* **P.** Paraguayan

paraître [20] [parɛtr] **1** *vi* (**a**) *(apparaître)* to appear; *(étoile, lune)* to appear, to come out; **laisser p. sa déception** to let one's disappointment show; **un faible sourire parut sur ses lèvres** he smiled weakly; **elle ne pense qu'à p.** all she thinks about is showing off

(**b**) *(livre)* to come out, to be published

(**c**) *(sembler)* to seem, to appear; **cette décision me**

paraît bizarre it seems a strange decision to me; **elle paraissait furieuse** *(à la voir)* she looked furious; *(à l'entendre)* she sounded furious

2 *v impersonnel* (**a**) *(sembler)* **il me paraît utile de...** I think it would be useful to...; **demain, il n'y paraîtra plus** there'll be no trace of it tomorrow; **sans qu'il y paraisse** without it being apparent

(**b**) **il paraît que...** *(on dit)* it seems *or* appears that...; **il paraît qu'elle s'en va, elle s'en va, paraît-il** it seems *or* appears that she's leaving, apparently she's leaving; **il paraît que ça fait maigrir** apparently it helps you lose weight; **il paraît que oui** so it would appear, apparently (so); **il paraît que non** it would appear not, apparently not; **à ce qu'il paraît** apparently

3 *nm* **le p.** appearance

parallèle [paralɛl] **1** *adj* parallel (**à** to *or* with); *(police, marché)* unofficial; **mener une vie p.** to lead a secret life; *Ordinat* **imprimante/interface p.** parallel printer/interface

2 *nf* parallel (line)

3 *nm* parallel; **mettre qch en p. avec qch, établir un p. entre qch et qch** to draw a parallel between sth and sth

parallèlement [paralɛlmã] *adv* parallel (**à** to *or* with); *(simultanément)* at the same time (**à** as)

parallélépipède [paralelepipɛd] *nm* parallelepiped

parallélisme [paralelism] *nm* parallelism; **p. (des roues)** (wheel) alignment

parallélogramme [paralelɔgram] *nm* parallelogram

paralysant, -e [paralizã, -ãt] *adj* paralysing

paralysé, -e [paralize] *adj aussi Fig* paralysed

paralyser [paralize] *vt aussi Fig* to paralyse; **le froid lui paralyse les mains** his hands are numb with the cold

paralysie [paralizi] *nf aussi Fig* paralysis; **p. générale** creeping paralysis

paralytique [paralitik] *adj & nmf* paralytic

paramédical, -e, -aux, -ales [paramedikal, -o] **1** *adj* paramedical

2 *nm* **les emplois du p.** paramedical jobs

paramétrable [parametrabl] *adj Ordinat* configurable; **p. par l'utilisateur** user-definable

paramètre [parametr] *nm Math & Fig* parameter; *Ordinat* parameter, setting; *(du DOS)* switch

paramétrer [34] [parametre] *vt Ordinat* to configure

paramilitaire [paramilitɛr] *adj* paramilitary

parano [parano] *Fam* **1** *adj* paranoid

2 *nf* **faire de la p.** to be paranoid

paranoïa [paranɔja] *nf* paranoia

paranoïaque [paranɔjak] *adj & nmf* paranoiac

paranormal, -e, -aux, -ales [paranɔrmal, -o] *adj* paranormal

parapente [parapãt] *nm (activité)* paragliding; *(parachute)* paraglider; **faire du p.** to go paragliding

parapet [parapɛ] *nm* parapet

paraphe [paraf] *nm* initials

parapher [parafe] *vt* to initial

paraphrase [parafraz] *nf* paraphrase

paraphraser [parafraze] *vt* to paraphrase

paraplégie [parapleʒi] *nf* paraplegia

paraplégique [parapleʒik] *adj & nmf* paraplegic

parapluie [paraplɥi] *nm* umbrella

parapsychologie [parapsikɔlɔʒi] *nf* parapsychology

parascolaire [paraskɔlɛr] *adj* extra-curricular

parasite [parazit] **1** *nm aussi Fig* parasite; **parasites** *(à la radio)* interference
2 *adj (insecte, plante)* parasitic
parasol [parasɔl] *nm* parasol, sunshade; *(de plage)* beach umbrella
parastatal, -e, -aux, -ales [parastatal, -o] *adj Belg* semi-public
paratonnerre [paratɔnɛr] *nm* lightning conductor
paravent [paravɑ̃] *nm aussi Fig* screen; *Fig* **servir de p. à qch** to be a screen for sth
parbleu [parblø] *exclam Vieilli* good Lord!; *(évidemment)* good Lord, yes!
parc [park] *nm* (**a**) *(jardin)* park; *(d'un château)* grounds; **p. aquatique** water park; **p. naturel** nature reserve; **p. zoologique** zoo (**b**) *(enclos) (pour enfant)* playpen; **p. d'attractions** theme park; **p. des expositions** exhibition centre; **p. à huîtres** oyster bed; **p. de stationnement** *Br* car park, *Am* parking lot; **p. à thème** theme park (**c**) *(ensemble)* **le p. automobile français** the number of cars in France
parcelle [parsɛl] *nf* small piece; **p. de terrain** plot; *Fig* **pas la moindre p. d'intelligence** not an ounce of intelligence
parce que [parskə] *conj* because; **ce n'est pas parce qu'il fait froid qu'on doit rester à la maison** just because it's cold doesn't mean we have to stay in; **pourquoi ne viens-tu pas? – p.** why aren't you coming? – (just) because
parchemin [parʃəmɛ̃] *nm* parchment
parcimonie [parsimɔni] *nf* thrift; **avec p.** sparingly
parcimonieux, -euse [parsimɔnjø, -øz] *adj* thrifty
parcmètre [parkmɛtr] *nm* (parking) meter
parcourir [22] [parkurir] *vt* (**a**) *(lieu)* to walk round; *(pays)* to walk through; *(rues)* to walk through; *(mer)* to sail; **p. un lieu à la recherche de qn** to scour a place for sb; **p. la terre entière pour retrouver qn** to travel the world to find sb; **p. une distance de plusieurs kilomètres** to cover a distance of several kilometres; **il reste 2 kilomètres à p.** there are 2 kilometres to go; *Fig* **un frisson me parcourut l'échine** *ou* **le dos** a shiver ran down my spine; *Fig* **un murmure a parcouru la foule** a murmur ran through the crowd (**b**) *(regarder) (texte, journal)* to skim through; *Ordinat* to scroll through; **p. qch des yeux** *ou* **du regard** to glance at sth
parcours [parkur] *nm (de défilé, de bus)* route; *(circuit automobile)* circuit; *(d'équitation, de golf, d'un fleuve)* course; *(évolution personnelle)* career, path; **p. du combattant** *Mil* assault course; *Fig* obstacle course; **faire un p. sans faute** *(cheval)* to have a clear round; *Fig (dans une carrière)* to have a copybook career; **refaire le p. pour retrouver qch** to retrace one's steps to find sth; **elle fait plusieurs fois le p. dans la journée** she does the journey several times a day
par-delà [pardəla] *prép & adv* beyond
par-derrière [pardɛrjɛr] **1** *prép* behind
2 *adv (attaquer)* from behind; *(se boutonner)* at the back; **passer p.** to go in the back door; *Fig* **dire des choses de qn p.** to talk about sb behind his/her back
par-dessous [pardəsu] **1** *prép* under, underneath
2 *adv* underneath
pardessus [pardəsy] *nm* overcoat
par-dessus [pardəsy] **1** *prép* over; **p. tout** above all
2 *adv* over; **j'ai mis un T-shirt avec une chemise p.** I wore a T-shirt with a shirt on top *or* over it

par-devant [pardəvɑ̃] **1** *prép Jur* **acte signé p. notaire** deed signed in the presence of a lawyer
2 *adv (attaquer)* from the front; *(se boutonner)* at the front
pardi [pardi] *exclam Fam* of course!
pardon [pardɔ̃] *nm* (**a**) *(grâce)* forgiveness; **accorder son p. à qn** to forgive sb; **demander p. à qn** to apologize to sb; **(je vous demande) p.!** *(pour passer)* excuse me!; *(pour s'excuser)* (I'm) sorry!; **(je vous demande) p.?** *(je n'ai pas entendu)* pardon?; *(je suis indigné)* I beg your pardon!; *Fam* **elle est intelligente, mais sa fille, p.!** she's pretty clever but you should see her daughter! (**b**) *Rel* **le Grand P.** the Day of Atonement, Yom Kippur
pardonnable [pardɔnabl] *adj* forgivable, excusable
pardonner [pardɔne] **1** *vt* to forgive; **p. qch à qn** to forgive sb sth; **elle m'a pardonné d'avoir oublié** she forgave me for forgetting; **pour me/te/etc faire p.** to make it up; **tu es tout pardonné** I'll let you off
2 *vi* (**a**) *(oublier une faute)* to forgive (**b**) **ça ne pardonne pas** it's fatal
3 se pardonner *vpr* **je ne me le pardonnerai jamais** I'll never forgive myself
paré, -e [pare] *adj* (**a**) *(prêt)* prepared (**contre** for) (**b**) *(revêtu)* adorned (**de** with)
pare-avalanches [paravalɑ̃ʃ] *nm inv* avalanche barrier
pare-balles [parbal] *adj inv* bullet-proof
pare-boue [parbu] *nm inv* mudflap
pare-brise [parbriz] *nm inv Br* windscreen, *Am* windshield
pare-chocs [parʃɔk] *nm inv* bumper
pare-feu [parfø] *nm inv* (**a**) *(dans la forêt)* fire-break (**b**) *(de cheminée)* fireguard
pareil, -eille [parɛj] **1** *adj* (**a**) *(identique)* the same; **elles sont presque pareilles** they're almost the same; **ce n'est pas p.** it's not the same (thing); *Litt* **à nul autre p.** unparalleled; **p. que** *ou* **à** the same as, just like; *Fam* **si ça ne te plaît pas, c'est p.** if you don't like it, too bad (**b**) *(tel)* such; **en p. cas** in such cases; **dans des moments pareils** at times like these; **mais je n'ai jamais dit une chose pareille!** but I never said any such thing!
2 *nm,f* **elle n'a pas sa pareille** she's second to none; **sans p.** unparalleled; **mes pareils** my equals
3 *nf* **rendre la pareille à qn** *(se venger de quelqu'un)* to get one's own back on sb, to pay sb back; *(rendre un service à quelqu'un)* to repay sb
4 *nm Fam* **c'est du p. au même** it's six of one and half a dozen of the other
5 *adv Fam* the same; **faire p.** to do the same (thing)
pareillement [parɛjmɑ̃] *adv* (**a**) *(de la même manière)* in a similar manner, in the same way (**b**) *(aussi)* likewise
parement [parmɑ̃] *nm (de manche, de col)* facing
parent, -e [parɑ̃, -ɑ̃t] **1** *adj* related
2 *nm,f (tante, oncle, cousin)* relative, relation
3 *nmpl* **parents** *(père et mère)* parents; **parents adoptifs** adoptive parents; **parents biologiques** biological parents
parental, -e, -aux, -ales [parɑ̃tal, -o] *adj* parental
parenté [parɑ̃te] *nf* relationship; **avoir un lien de p. avec qn** to be related to sb
parenthèse [parɑ̃tɛz] *nf* bracket, parenthesis; *Fig (dans un discours)* digression; **entre parenthèses** in brackets; *Fig (à propos)* incidentally, by the way

parer¹ [pare] **1** *vt* (**a**) *aussi Fig (éviter)* to parry (**b**) *(protéger)* to protect (**contre** against)
2 parer à *vt ind (accident)* to prevent; *(problème)* to avoid; **p. au plus pressé** to attend to the most urgent things first
parer² *Litt* **1** *vt (vêtir)* to adorn (**de** with); *Fig* **p. qn de toutes les vertus** to endow sb with every virtue
2 se parer *vpr* (**a**) *(s'habiller avec élégance)* to get dressed up (**de** in) (**b**) *Can (se préparer)* to get ready
pare-soleil [parsɔlɛj] *nm inv (de voiture)* sun visor
paresse [parɛs] *nf* (**a**) *(indolence)* laziness; **d'une p. incroyable** incredibly lazy (**b**) *(lenteur)* **p. intellectuelle** laziness of mind; **p. intestinale** sluggishness of the bowels
paresser [parɛse] *vi* to laze about *or* around
paresseux, -euse [parɛsø, -øz] **1** *adj* (**a**) *(nonchalant)* lazy (**b**) *(intestin)* sluggish
2 *nm,f* lazy person
3 *nm (animal)* sloth
parfaire [36] [parfɛr] *vt (travail)* to finish off, to complete; *(technique)* to perfect
parfait, -e [parfɛ, -ɛt] **1** *adj* (**a**) *(sans fautes)* perfect (**b**) *(complet) (bonheur)* perfect, complete; *(ressemblance)* exact; *Fam* **un p. imbécile** an utter fool
2 *nm* parfait; **p. au café** coffee parfait
parfaitement [parfɛtmɑ̃] *adv* (**a**) *(sans fautes)* perfectly; **parler p. l'anglais** to speak perfect English (**b**) *(complètement)* completely, thoroughly; *(compréhensible, clair, heureux)* perfectly; **ça m'est p. égal** it makes absolutely no difference to me; **j'ai p. conscience de…** I'm perfectly aware of… (**c**) *(tout à fait)* **vous affirmez que vous l'avez vu? – p.!** you say you saw it? – I certainly did!
parfois [parfwa] *adv* sometimes
parfum [parfœ̃] *nm* (**a**) *(essences)* perfume (**b**) *(senteur) (d'une fleur)* fragrance, scent; *(d'un vin)* bouquet; *Fig* **un p. de scandale** a whiff of scandal (**c**) *(de glace, de yaourt)* flavour (**d**) *Fam* **être au p.** to be in the know; **mettre qn au p.** to fill sb in
parfumer [parfyme] **1** *vt* (**a**) *(embaumer)* to scent (**b**) *(gâteau, glace)* to flavour (**à** with) (**c**) *(mouchoir)* to scent; **je vous parfume?** *(à une cliente)* would you like to try some perfume?
2 se parfumer *vpr* to put perfume on
parfumerie [parfymri] *nf (magasin)* perfumery; *(rayon)* perfume counter; *(produits)* perfumes; *(industrie)* perfume industry
parfumeur, -euse [parfymœr, -øz] *nm,f* perfumer
pari [pari] *nm* bet; **faire un p. avec qn** to make a bet with sb; **p. mutuel** *Br* ≃ tote, *Am* ≃ pari-mutuel
paria [parja] *nm Fig* pariah, (social) outcast
parier [66] [parje] **1** *vt* to bet; **il y a fort** *ou* **gros à p. que…** the odds are that…; **je te parie qu'elle viendra** I bet you she'll come; **je l'aurais parié** I thought as much
2 *vi* to bet; **p. avec qn/sur qch** to bet with sb/on sth; **je te dis qu'elle viendra – on parie?** she'll come, I tell you – (do you) want a bet?
parieur, -euse [parjœr, -øz] *nm,f* better
parigot, -e [parigo, -ɔt] *Fam* **1** *adj* Parisian
2 *nm,f* **P.** Parisian
Paris [pari] *n* Paris
parisien, -enne [parizjɛ̃, -ɛn] **1** *adj* Parisian
2 *nm,f* **P.** Parisian
parité [parite] *nf aussi Ordinat* parity; **nous devons arriver à une p. hommes-femmes au parlement** we

must ensure that there are an equal number of men and women in parliament
parjure [parʒyr] **1** *nm (action)* perjury
2 *nmf (personne)* perjurer
3 *adj* treacherous
parjurer [parʒyre] **se parjurer** *vpr* to perjure oneself
parka [parka] *nm ou nf* parka
parking [parkiŋ] *nm Br* car park, *Am* parking lot; **p. couvert** underground car park; **p. payant** *Br* ≃ pay-and-display car park
parlant, -e [parlɑ̃, -ɑ̃t] *adj (geste)* eloquent, meaningful; *(description)* vivid
parlé, -e [parle] *adj* **le français p.** spoken French; **journal p.** news (programme)
parlement [parləmɑ̃] *nm* **le P.** Parliament; **le P. européen** the European Parliament
parlementaire [parləmɑ̃tɛr] **1** *adj* parliamentary
2 *nmf* member of parliament, *Am* Congressman, *f* Congresswoman
parlementarisme [parləmɑ̃tarism] *nm* parliamentary government
parlementer [parləmɑ̃te] *vi* to negotiate (**avec** with)
parler¹ [parle] **1** *vi* (**a**) *(s'exprimer)* to speak, to talk; *(avouer)* to talk; **elle parle bien** *(oratrice)* she's a good speaker; **p. par signes** to use sign language; **parlez-vous sérieusement?** are you serious?; **les résultats/faits parlent d'eux-mêmes** the results/facts speak for themselves; **p. pour ne rien dire** to talk for the sake of talking; **c'est comme si je parlais à un mur** it's like talking to a brick wall; **p. de qn/qch (à qn)** to talk (to sb) about sb/sth; **p. de** *(sujet: livre, film)* to be about; **on m'a beaucoup parlé de vous** I've heard a lot about you; **n'en parlons plus** let's drop the subject; **faire p. de soi** to be talked about; **p. de faire qch** to talk about doing sth
(**b**) *(locutions)* **je sais de quoi je parle** I know what I'm talking about; *Fam* **tu peux p.!** YOU can talk!; *Fam* **parle pour toi!** speak for yourself!; *Fam* **tu parles!** you bet!; *Fam* **tu parles d'une occasion/d'un idiot!** talk about an opportunity/an idiot!; *Fam* **sa timidité? parlons-en!** his shyness? that's a good one! *or* you've got to be joking!; *Fam* **ne m'en parlez pas!** you're telling me!; **sans p. de…** not to mention…; **trouver à qui p.** to get more than one bargains for
2 *vt (langue)* to speak; **p. (le) français** to speak French; **ici on parle anglais** *(dans un magasin)* English spoken; **p. chiffons/cuisine** to talk about clothes/cooking; **p. affaires/politique** to talk business/politics
3 se parler *vpr* (**a**) *(langue)* to be spoken (**b**) *(l'un à l'autre)* to talk to each other
parler² *nm* speech; *(régional)* dialect; **il a un p. très rude** he has a very abrupt way of speaking
parleur, -euse [parlœr, -øz] *nm,f Péj* **beau p.** smooth talker
parloir [parlwar] *nm* (**a**) *(d'une prison)* visiting room (**b**) *Belg (salon)* parlour
parlot(t)e [parlɔt] *nf Fam* chat; **faire la p. (avec qn)** to chat (with sb), to have a chat (with sb)
Parme [parm] *n* Parma
parmesan [parməzɑ̃] *nm* Parmesan (cheese)
parmi [parmi] *prép* among; **choisir p. plusieurs possibilités** to choose from several possibilities; **nous espérons vous revoir p. nous** we hope to see you back with us
parodie [parɔdi] *nf* parody

parodier [66] [parɔdje] *vt* to parody

parodique [parɔdik] *adj* parodic

paroi [parwa] *nf* (**a**) *(d'une falaise, d'une montagne)* face (**b**) *(d'une pièce, d'une caverne)* wall; *(d'un tunnel, de l'estomac)* lining

paroisse [parwas] *nf* parish

paroissial, -e, -aux, -ales [parwasjal, -o] *adj* parish

paroissien, -enne [parwasjɛ̃, -ɛn] *nm,f* parishioner

parole [parɔl] *nf* (**a**) *(mot)* word; **paroles** *(de chanson)* lyrics, words; **histoire sans paroles** short silent film; **une p. blessante** a hurtful remark; *Ironique* **de belles paroles** fine words; **ce ne sont que des paroles en l'air** they're just empty threats (**b**) *Fig (engagement)* promise, word; **tenir p.** to keep one's promise *or* word; **manquer à sa p.** to break one's promise *or* word; **il n'a qu'une p.** he's a man of his word; **donner sa p. (d'honneur) à qn que...** to give sb one's word that...; **(ma) p. d'honneur!** I give you my word!; **je te crois sur p.** I'll take your word for it (**c**) **la p.** *(faculté de parler)* speech; *(diction)* delivery; **adresser la p. à qn** to speak to sb; **couper la p. à qn** to interrupt sb; **prendre la p.** to speak; **laisser la p. à qn** to let sb speak; **la p. est à M. Renant, M. Renant a la p.** Mr Renant has the floor; **la p. est d'argent mais le silence est d'or** speech is silver, silence is golden (**d**) *(aux cartes)* **p.!** pass!; *(au bridge)* no bid!

parolier, -ère [parɔlje, -ɛr] *nm,f* lyricist

paroxysme [parɔksism] *nm* **atteindre son p.** to reach its peak *or* climax; **être au p. de la joie** to be ecstatically happy

parpaing [parpɛ̃] *nm* breeze block

parquer [parke] *vt (bétail)* to pen in; *(prisonniers)* to confine

parquet [parke] *nm* (**a**) *(sol)* wooden floor; *(avec des motifs)* parquet floor (**b**) *Jur* public prosecutor's office

parrain [parɛ̃] *nm (pour un baptême, d'une organisation criminelle)* godfather; *(d'un sportif, d'un membre d'un club)* sponsor

parrainer [parene] *vt (sportif, nouveau membre)* to sponsor

parricide [parisid] **1** *adj* parricidal
2 *nmf & nm* parricide

pars *voir* **partir**

parsemer [46] [parsəme] *vt* to scatter (**de** with)

part¹ [par] *voir* **partir**

part² *nf* (**a**) *(partie d'un tout)* part; *(d'un marché, d'un héritage, de travail)* share; *(d'un gâteau, d'une pizza)* slice; **diviser qch en parts égales** to divide sth into equal parts; **ils viennent pour une bonne p. des environs de Lille** a good many of them come from the Lille area; **à p. entière** fully-fledged; **pour ma p.** personally, as for me; **faire la p. du feu** to cut one's losses; **la p. du lion** the lion's share
(**b**) *(participation)* share, part; **prendre p. à qch** to take part in sth; *(joie, douleur)* to share sth; **faire p. de qch à qn** to inform sb of sth, to tell sb about sth; **faire la p. des choses** to get things in perspective
(**c**) *(côté)* **de p. et d'autre** on both sides; **de p. en p.** right through; **d'une p...., d'autre p....** on the one hand..., on the other hand...; **de toutes parts** on all sides
(**d**) **de la p. de qn** *(en provenance de)* from sb; *(à la place de)* on sb's behalf; **c'est de la p. de qui?** *(au téléphone)* who's calling?; **ce serait bien aimable de votre p.** that would be very kind of you; **cela m'étonne de sa p.** that surprises me, coming from him
(**e**) *(locutions)* **prendre qn à p.** to take sb aside; **à p. lui/quelques erreurs** apart from him/a few mistakes; **c'est un cas à p.** he's a special case; *Fam* **à p. que...** apart from the fact that...

partage [partaʒ] *nm* (**a**) *(action)* *(d'une fortune, d'un domaine)* dividing up; *(de tâches, de responsabilités)* sharing out; **faire le p. de qch** to divide sth up; **sans p.** *(amour)* total; *Ordinat* **p. d'imprimantes** printer sharing (**b**) *(lot)* **recevoir qch en p.** to be left sth *(in a will)*

partagé, -e [partaʒe] *adj* (**a**) *(entre plusieurs personnes)* shared; *(amour)* mutual; *Ordinat* **travail en temps p.** timesharing (**b**) *(indécis)* **être p.** to be torn; **les avis sont partagés** opinions are divided

partager [45] [partaʒe] **1** *vt* (**a**) *(répartir)* to divide (up); **p. son temps entre** to divide one's time between; **p. qch en deux** to divide sth in two (**b**) *(avoir en commun)* to share (**avec** with); **p. l'avis de qn** to share sb's opinion; **p. la joie de qn** to share (in) sb's joy
2 *vi* to share
3 se partager *vpr* (**a**) *(se répartir)* **ils se le sont partagé** they shared it between them (**b**) *(partager son temps)* to divide one's time (**entre** between)

partageur, -euse [partaʒœr, -øz] *adj* willing to share

partance [partɑ̃s] *nf* **en p.** about to depart; **en p. pour Bordeaux** for Bordeaux

partant¹ [partɑ̃] *conj Litt* consequently, therefore

partant², -e [partɑ̃, -ɑ̃t] **1** *adj Fam* **je suis p.!** count me in!
2 *nm,f (coureur, cheval)* starter

partenaire [partənɛr] *nmf* partner; **les partenaires sociaux** workers and management

partenariat [partənarja] *nm* partnership

parterre [partɛr] *nm* (**a**) *(de fleurs)* flower bed; *(plate-bande)* border (**b**) *(au théâtre) Br* stalls, *Am* orchestra (**c**) *Fam (sol)* floor

parti¹ [parti] *nm* (**a**) *(camp)* side; **prendre le p. de qn** to take sb's side; **prendre p. pour qn** to side with sb; **prendre p. contre qn** to take sides against sb (**b**) **p. (politique)** *(political)* party; **le P. (communiste)** the Communist Party (**c**) *(personne)* **un beau p.** a good match (**d**) *(choix)* **prendre le p. de faire qch** to make up one's mind to do sth; **en prendre son p.** to resign oneself to the fact (**e**) *(profit)* **tirer p. de qch** to make good use of sth (**f**) **p. pris** bias; **avoir un p. pris contre** to be biased against; **être de p. pris** to be biased; **être sans p. pris** to be unbiased

parti², -e *adj Fam (ivre)* tight; *(drogué)* high

partial, -e, -aux, -ales [parsjal, -o] *adj* biased

partialement [parsjalmɑ̃] *adv* in a biased way

partialité [parsjalite] *nf* bias (**envers/contre** in favour of/against)

participant, -e [partisipɑ̃, -ɑ̃t] **1** *adj* participating
2 *nm,f (personne présente)* participant (**à** in); *(sportif)* competitor

participation [partisipasjɔ̃] *nf* (**a**) *(collaboration, en classe)* participation (**à** in); *(argent)* contribution (**à** towards); *(nombre de votants)* turnout (**à** at); **avec la p. de Jean Martin (dans le rôle de...)** with Jean Martin (as...); **p. aux frais** contribution towards costs; **p. aux bénéfices** profit-sharing (**b**) *Fin* interest (**à** in)

participe [partisip] *nm Gram* participle; **p. présent/passé** present/past participle

participer [partisipe] **participer à** *vt ind* (**a**) *(assister à)* to take part in, to participate in; *(spectacle)* to appear in; **p. activement à qch** to take an active part in sth (**b**) *(financièrement)* to contribute to (**c**) **p. aux bénéfices** to share in the profits

particulariser [partikylarize] *vt* to particularize

particularisme [partikylarism] *nm* particularism

particularité [partikylarite] *nf* distinctive feature

particule [partikyl] *nf* particle; **p. élémentaire** elementary *or* fundamental particle

particulier, -ère [partikylje, -ɛr] **1** *adj* (**a**) *(propre)* characteristic (**à** of) (**b**) *(remarquable)* unusual, exceptional; *(soin, intérêt)* particular (**c**) *Péj (bizarre)* peculiar (**d**) *(privé) (maison, voiture)* private; *(salle de bain)* en suite (**e**) **en p.** *(spécialement)* in particular; *(en privé)* in private

2 *nm (individu)* private individual; **un simple p.** an ordinary person; **vente de p. à p.** private sale

particulièrement [partikyljermã] *adv* particularly; **j'attire tout p. votre attention sur...** I would particularly like to draw your attention to...

partie [parti] *nf* (**a**) *(morceau)* part; **la plus grande p. de qch** the greatest part of sth; **en p.** partly, in part; **en grande** *ou* **majeure p.** for the most part; **être en p. remboursé** to be partially refunded; **faire p. de qch** to be part of sth; *Fam* **faire p. des meubles** to be part of the furniture; **les parties communes** the communal areas; *Fam* **les parties** the private parts; **les parties génitales** the genitals

(**b**) *(domaine)* field, subject; **je ne suis pas de la p.** that's not my field

(**c**) *(d'un chanteur, d'un instrument)* part

(**d**) *(fête)* party; **ce n'est pas une p. de plaisir!** it's not my idea of fun!; **p. de campagne** day in the country; **p. de chasse** shooting party; *Fam* **p. de jambes en l'air** roll in the hay; *Can* **p. de sucre** sugaring-off party

(**e**) *(jeu)* game; **faire une p. de cartes** to have a game of cards; *Fig* **ce n'est que p. remise** we'll do it another time

(**f**) *Jur* party; **la p. adverse** the other side; **être p. prenante** to be an interested party; **p. civile** plaintiff; **se constituer** *ou* **se porter p. civile** to institute proceedings *(in a civil case)*

(**g**) *(locutions)* **avoir affaire à forte p.** to have a tough opponent on one's hands; **prendre qn à p.** to take sb to task; **avoir p. liée avec qn** to be hand in glove with sb

partiel, -elle [parsjɛl] **1** *adj* partial; **élection partielle** by-election; **travailler à temps p.** to work part-time

2 *nm Univ* end-of-term exam

3 *nf* **partielle** by-election

partiellement [parsjɛlmã] *adv* partially

partir [64a] [partir] *vi (aux* **être**) (**a**) *(s'en aller)* to go, to leave; *(commencer un voyage)* to set off; *(sans destination particulière)* to go off; *(bateau, avion)* to leave; *(moteur)* to start; *(fusil, pétard)* to go off; *Euph (mourir)* to pass away; **p. en vacances** to go (away) on holiday; **p. en promenade** to go for a stroll; **p. faire ses courses** to go out shopping; **p. en courant** to run off; **p. de rien** to start from nothing; **p. d'un éclat de rire** to burst out laughing; **être bien/mal parti** to have got off to a good/bad start; **faire p.** *(fusil)* to fire; *(feux d'artifice)* to let off; *(moteur)* to start; *Fam* **c'est parti, mon kiki!** here we go!

(**b**) *(disparaître) (douleur, bleu)* to go, to disappear; *(tache)* to come out; *(peinture, vernis)* to come off; **faire p. une tache** to get a stain out

(**c**) *(sortir)* **p. de** *(sujet: route, chemin)* to start from;

en partant du principe que... assuming that...; **ça partait d'un bon sentiment** the thought was there; **et, partant de là,...** on that assumption,...

(**d**) **à p. du village** from the village; **à p. d'aujourd'hui** from today (onwards); **à p. de maintenant** from now on; **à p. de 200 francs** from 200 francs (upwards)

partisan, -e [partizã, -an] **1** *nm* (**a**) *(fidèle)* supporter (**b**) *(combattant)* partisan

2 *adj (esprit)* partisan; **querelles partisanes** sectarian quarrels; **être p. de qch/de faire qch** to be in favour of sth/of doing sth

partitif, -ive [partitif, -iv] *adj & nm Gram* partitive

partition [partisjɔ̃] *nf (musique)* score

partout [partu] *adv* (**a**) *(en tous lieux)* everywhere; **p. où je vais** everywhere I go; **un peu p.** all over the place; **j'ai mal p.** I'm aching all over (**b**) **3 buts p.** *(au football)* 3 all; **15/30 p.** *(au tennis)* 15/30 all; **40 p.** *(au tennis)* deuce

partouze [partuz] *nf Fam* orgy

paru, -e *voir* **paraître**

parure [paryr] *nf (ensemble)* set; **p. de lit** set of bed linen

parution [parysjɔ̃] *nf* appearance, publication

parvenir [70] [parvənir] **parvenir à** *vt ind (aux* **être**) (**a**) *(atteindre) (endroit, personne)* to reach; **p. à ses fins** to achieve one's ends; **faire p. qch à qn** to send sth to sb (**b**) *(réussir)* **p. à faire qch** to manage to do sth

parvenu, -e [parvəny] *nm,f Péj* upstart

parvis [parvi] *nm* square *(in front of a church or a public building)*

pas¹ [pɑ] *nm* (**a**) *(enjambée, de danse)* step; *(allure)* pace; **p. à p.** step by step; **à p. de loup** stealthily; **marcher à grands p.** to stride along; **marcher à petits p.** to toddle along; **marcher d'un p. hésitant** to walk hesitantly; **faire un faux p.** to trip; *Fig* to make a faux pas; **faire un p. (vers)** to take a step (towards); **faire un p. en avant/en arrière** to (take a) step forward/back; **faire les cent p.** to pace up and down; *Fig* **faire le premier p.** to take the first step; **marcher au p.** *(soldat)* to march in step; **rouler au p.** *(en voiture)* to crawl along; **ils habitent à deux p. d'ici** they live a few yards away; **j'y vais de ce p.** I'll do it right away; **p. de deux** pas de deux; **p. de course** *ou* **gymnastique** jog trot

(**b**) *(trace)* footprint; **revenir** *ou* **retourner sur ses p.** to retrace one's steps

(**c**) *(seuil)* **p. de la porte** doorstep

(**d**) *(passage)* **le p. de Calais** the Straits of Dover

(**e**) *(de vis, d'hélice)* pitch

(**f**) *(locutions)* **prendre le p. sur qch** to take precedence over sth; **tirer qn d'un mauvais p.** to get sb out of a tight corner

pas² *adv* not; **je ne sais p.** I don't know; **je ne l'ai p. vue** I haven't seen her; **il est difficile de ne p. le lui dire** it's difficult not to tell him; **qu'elle vienne ou p.** whether she comes or not; **viendra viendra p.?** will she come or won't she?; **p. mal** not bad; **une explication p. claire** an unclear explanation; **p. un n'a réagi** not one of them reacted; **p. de sucre/lecteurs** no sugar/readers; **p. du tout** not at all

pascal¹, -e, -als *ou* **-aux, -ales** [paskal, -o] *adj* Easter; *(agneau)* paschal

pascal², -als *nm* (**a**) *Phys* pascal (**b**) *Fam (billet)* 500-franc note

passable [pasabl] *adj* passable, fair

passablement [pasabləmɑ̃] *adv* fairly

passade [pasad] *nf* passing fancy

passage [pasaʒ] *nm* (**a**) *(d'une route, d'une rivière)* crossing; *(d'un lieu)* passing; **on sourit sur son p.** people smile as he goes by; **les soldats ont tout détruit sur leur p.** the soldiers destroyed everything in their path; **être de p. dans une ville** to be passing through a town; *Fig* **et au p., je te ferai remarquer que…** and incidentally, let me draw your attention to the fact that…; *Fam* **p. à tabac** beating up; *Ordinat* **p. automatique à la ligne suivante** wordwrap (**b**) *(chemin)* passage; *(ruelle)* alley(way); *(galerie commerciale)* (shopping) arcade; **p. clouté** *Br* pedestrian crossing, *Am* crosswalk; **p. à niveau** *Br* level crossing, *Am* grade crossing; **p. pour piétons** *Br* pedestrian crossing, *Am* crosswalk; *(souterrain)* pedestrian subway; **p. souterrain** underpass (**c**) *(extrait)* passage (**d**) *(changement)* change, transition; **le p. de l'autocratie à la démocratie** the changeover *or* transition from autocracy to democracy (**e**) *(moment)* **p. nuageux/pluvieux** cloudy/rainy spell; *Fam* **avoir un p. à vide** to go through a bad patch (**f**) *Psy* **p. à l'acte** acting out

passager, -ère [pasaʒe, -ɛr] **1** *adj* momentary; **des pluies passagères** occasional showers; **ils ont eu une petite brouille passagère** they fell out for a while **2** *nm,f* passenger; **p. clandestin** stowaway

passant¹ [pasɑ̃] *nm (de ceinture)* loop

passant², -e [pasɑ̃, -ɑ̃t] **1** *adj (rue)* busy **2** *nm,f* passer-by

passation [pasasjɔ̃] *nf (d'un accord)* signing; **p. de pouvoirs** transfer of power

passe¹ [pas] *nf* (**a**) *(au football)* pass; **p. en avant/en retrait** forward/back pass (**b**) *(d'une prostituée)* trick; **hôtel de p.** = hotel used by prostitutes and their clients; **maison de p.** brothel (**c**) *(à la roulette)* passe *(any number above 18)* (**d**) *Fig* **être en p. de faire qch** to be on the way to doing sth; **être dans une mauvaise p.** to be going through a bad patch

passe² *nm Fam (clef)* master key

passé, -e [pase] **1** *adj* (**a**) *(écoulé) (temps)* past; **la semaine passée** last week; **il est quatre heures passées** it's gone *or* after four; **elle a quarante ans passés** she's over forty (**b**) *(terminé)* over; **penser à son enfance passée** to think about one's childhood (**c**) *(décoloré)* faded (**d**) **p. de mode** out of fashion **2** *nm* (**a**) *(période)* **le p.** the past; **par le p.** in the past; **tout ça, c'est du p.** that's all in the past (**b**) *Gram* past (tense); **p. antérieur** past anterior; **p. composé** perfect (tense); **p. simple** preterite, past historic; **au p.** in the past (tense) **3** *prép* after

passe-droit *(pl* **passe-droits)** [pasdrwa] *nm* privilege

passéiste [paseist] *Péj* **1** *adj* living in the past **2** *nmf* person who lives in the past

passe-montagne *(pl* **passe-montagnes)** [pasmɔ̃taɲ] *nm* balaclava (helmet)

passe-partout [paspartu] **1** *nm inv* master key **2** *adj inv* all-purpose

passe-plat *(pl* **passe-plats)** [paspla] *nm* serving hatch

passeport [paspɔr] *nm aussi Fig* passport

passer [pase] **1** *vi (aux* **être)** (**a**) *(se déplacer)* to go past; **p. devant qn/qch** to go past sb/sth; **laisser p. qn** to let sb past; *(dans une queue)* to let sb in; **je ne**

peux pas **p.** I can't get by *or* past; **p. sur les détails** to skip the details; **elle nous a fait p. dans son bureau** she showed us into her office; **mais où est-il passé?** where's he got to?; **dire qch en passant** to mention sth in passing; **soit dit en passant** incidentally (**b**) *(évoluer)* **p. de qch à qch** to go from sth to sth; **p. dans la classe supérieure** to move up a class; **p. en première/seconde** *(en voiture)* to change into first/second; **p. capitaine** to be promoted to captain (**c**) *(traverser)* **p. par le village/Paris** to go through the village/Paris; **par où est -il passé?** which way did he go?; **laisser p. qch** *(lumière, air)* to let sth in (**d**) *(apparaître)* **p. à la radio/télévision** to be on the radio/television; **p. au cinéma** to be on at the cinema (**e**) *(aller)* **je suis passé chez elle/à la boucherie** I went round to her house/to the butcher's; **le facteur est déjà passé** the postman's already been; **je ne fais que p.** I'm not staying (**f**) *(disparaître)* to go; **laisser p. qch** *(occasion)* to pass up sth; *(erreur)* to miss sth; **le plus dur est passé** the worst is over; **j'avais mal à la tête mais ça m'a passé** I had a headache but it's gone away; **il était amoureux d'elle mais ça lui a passé** he was in love with her but he's got over it (**g**) *(année, temps)* to pass, to go by (**h**) *(être considéré)* **p. pour un génie** to be considered a genius; **faire p. qn pour** to pass sb off as (**i**) *(être adopté) (loi, proposition)* to be passed, to go through (**j**) **passe!** *(aux cartes)* pass! (**k**) *Fam* **il a bien failli y p.** *(mourir)* he nearly didn't make it; **toute sa fortune y est passée** she spent her entire fortune on it

2 *vt (aux* **avoir)** (**a**) *(pont, rivière, frontière)* to go over; *(porte, douane)* to go through; **il a passé la soixantaine** he's in his sixties (**b**) *(donner) (ballon, témoin)* to pass; **p. qch à qn** to pass *or* give sth to sb; *Fam* **p. son rhume à qn** to give sb one's cold; **p. la parole à qn** to hand over to sb; **pourriez-vous me la p.?** *(au téléphone)* could you put me through to her? (**c**) *(mettre) (vêtement)* to slip on; **p. un coup d'éponge sur qch** to give sth a sponge; **p. la tête par la fenêtre** to lean one's head out of the window; **p. le doigt sur qch** to run one's finger over sth; **p. la seconde/troisième** *(en voiture)* to change into second/third; *Fam* **qu'est-ce qu'il va nous p.!** he's going to make us wish we'd never been born! (**d**) *(film)* to show; *(disque)* to play; *(vidéo)* to put on (**e**) *(temps, vacances)* to spend; **p. son temps à faire qch** to spend one's time doing sth; **pour p. le temps** to pass the time (**f**) *(pardonner)* **elle lui passe tout** she lets him get away with everything (**g**) *(omettre)* to leave out; **p. son tour** to miss a turn; **j'en passe et des meilleures** and that's not the half of it (**h**) *(examen)* to take *or* sit; *(visite médicale)* to have; **faire p. un examen à qn** to take sb for an exam (**i**) *(accord, contrat)* to enter into, to sign; *(commande)* to place (**à** with) (**j**) *(liquide)* to strain; *(café)* to filter

3 se passer *vpr* (**a**) *(se produire)* to happen; **que se passe-t-il?, qu'est-ce qui se passe?** what's happening?; **ça s'est bien passé** it went well; **l'histoire se passe en 1900/en Normandie** the story takes place in 1900/in Normandy; *Fam* **ça ne se passera pas comme ça!** I'm not having it!

(**b**) *(mettre)* **se p. la main dans les cheveux** to run one's fingers through one's hair; **se p. de l'eau sur la figure** to splash one's face with water; **se p. de la crème sur les mains** to put some cream on one's hands

4 se passer de *vt ind (se priver de)* to do without; **il ne peut pas se p. de télévision** he can't live without TV

passereau, -x [pasʁo] *nm* passerine

passerelle [pasʁɛl] *nf* (**a**) *(au-dessus d'une rue, d'un ruisseau)* footbridge (**b**) *(de navire)* bridge; **p. de débarquement** *ou* **d'embarquement** *(de navire)* gangway; *(d'avion) (amovible)* steps (**c**) *Fig (intermédiaire)* link (**d**) *Ordinat* **p. (de connexion) (avec)** gateway (to)

passe-temps [pastɑ̃] *nm inv* pastime

passe-thé [paste] *nm inv* tea-strainer

passeur, -euse [pasœʁ, -øz] *nm,f* (**a**) *(de bac)* ferryman, *f* ferrywoman (**b**) *(d'immigrants clandestins)* smuggler; **il trouva un p. qui l'aida à gagner les États-Unis** he found someone to get him over the border into the United States

passible [pasibl] *adj* liable (**de** to)

passif, -ive [pasif, -iv] **1** *adj* passive

2 *nm* (**a**) *Gram* passive; **au p.** in the passive (**b**) *Fin* liabilities

passion [pasjɔ̃] *nf* (**a**) *(sentiment dévorant)* passion; **avoir une p. pour qn/qch** to have a passion for sb/sth; **avoir la p. de qch** to have a passion for sth; **vivre une p.** to have a passionate love affair; **avec p.** passionately (**b**) *Rel* **la P. selon saint Jean** the St John Passion

passionnant, -e [pasjɔnɑ̃, -ɑ̃t] *adj* fascinating

passionné, -e [pasjɔne] **1** *adj* passionate; **p. de qch** extremely keen on sth

2 *nm,f* enthusiast; **un p. de football** a football enthusiast

passionnel, -elle [pasjɔnɛl] *adj (relation)* passionate

passionnément [pasjɔnemɑ̃] *adv* passionately

passionner [pasjɔne] **1** *vt (sujet: livre, film)* to fascinate; **son métier la passionne** she finds her job fascinating

2 se passionner *vpr* **se p. pour qch** to have a passion for sth

passivement [pasivmɑ̃] *adv* passively

passivité [pasivite] *nf* passivity, passiveness

passoire [paswaʁ] *nf (avec un grillage)* sieve; *(avec de petits trous)* colander; *Fam* **ce gardien de but est une vraie p.!** this goalkeeper is really useless *or* lets everything in!

pastel [pastɛl] *nm & adj inv* pastel

pastèque [pastɛk] *nf* watermelon; *Fam* **j'ai la tête comme une p.** my head's throbbing

pasteur [pastœʁ] *nm* (**a**) *Litt (berger)* shepherd (**b**) *(religieux)* pastor, minister

pasteurisation [pastœʁizasjɔ̃] *nf* pasteurization

pasteuriser [pastœʁize] *vt* to pasteurize

pastiche [pastiʃ] *nm* pastiche

pastille [pastij] *nf (bonbon mou)* pastille; *(médicament)* lozenge; **p. contre la toux** cough sweet *or* lozenge; **p. de menthe** mint; **p. verte** = green label on a low-emission vehicle indicating that it may be driven on days when restrictions are placed on traffic due to high levels of atmospheric pollution

pastis [pastis] *nm* (**a**) *(boisson)* pastis (**b**) *Fam* **être dans le p.** to be in a fix

pastoral, -e, -aux, -ales [pastɔʁal, -o] **1** *adj* pastoral

2 *nf* **pastorale** *(musique)* pastorale

patachon [pataʃɔ̃] *nm Fam* **mener une vie de p.** to lead a wild life

Patagonie [patagɔni] *nf* **la P.** Patagonia

patapouf [patapuf] **1** *exclam* flop!

2 *nm (langage enfantin)* **gros p.** fatty

pataquès [patakɛs] *nm (faute de langage)* malapropism

patate [patat] *nf Fam (pomme de terre)* spud; *Fig (imbécile)* clot; *Can* **patates frites** French fries, *Br* chips; *Fig* **en avoir gros sur la p.** to be down in the mouth

patati [patati] *exclam Fam* **et p. et patata** and so on and so forth

patatras [patatʁa] *exclam Fam* crash!

pataud, -e [pato, -od] *adj Fam* clumsy

Pataugas® [patogas] *nm* canvas walking boot

pataugeoire [patoʒwaʁ] *nf* paddling pool

patauger [45] [patoʒe] *vi (s'embourber)* to squelch (**dans** in); *(barboter)* to splash about (**dans** in); *Fam (s'embrouiller)* to flounder (**dans** in)

pâte [pɑt] **1** *nf* (**a**) *(pour une tarte)* pastry; *(pour le pain)* dough; *(pour un gâteau)* mixture; **p. brisée** shortcrust pastry; **p. à choux** choux pastry; **p. à crêpes** pancake batter; **p. feuilletée** puff *or* flaky pastry; **p. à frire** batter; **p. à pain** bread dough; **p. sablée** rich shortcrust pastry; **p. à tarte** pastry; **p. à tartiner** chocolate spread (**b**) *(mixture)* **p. d'amandes** marzipan; **p. de fruits** fruit jelly; **p. à modeler** modelling clay; **p. à papier** pulp

2 *nfpl* **pâtes (alimentaires)** pasta; **pâtes fraîches** fresh pasta

pâté [pate] *nm* (**a**) *(terrine)* pâté; **p. de campagne** pâté de campagne *(coarse pâté made with pork)*; *Can* **p. chinois** shepherd's pie; **p. en croûte** ≃ pork pie; **p. de foie** liver pâté (**b**) *Belg (gâteau)* cake (**c**) **p. (de sable)** sandpie (**d**) **p. de maisons** block of houses (**e**) *(tache d'encre)* blot; **faire un p. sur qch** to get a blot on sth

pâtée [pate] *nf* (**a**) *(de chat)* cat food; *(de chien)* dog food (**b**) *Fam (défaite)* **prendre la p.** to get thrashed; **mettre la p. à qn** to thrash sb

patelin¹ [patlɛ̃] *nm Fam* village

patelin², -e [patlɛ̃, -in] *adj Litt & Péj* unctuous

patent, -e [patɑ̃, -ɑ̃t] *adj* (**a**) *(évident)* patent (**b**) **lettres patentes** letters patent

patente [patɑ̃t] *nf (impôt)* tax *(paid by self-employed people)*

patenté, -e [patɑ̃te] *adj* licensed

patère [patɛʁ] *nf* (coat) peg

paternaliste [patɛʁnalist] *adj* paternalistic

paternel, -elle [patɛʁnɛl] **1** *adj* paternal; *(ton)* fatherly; **du côté p.** on the father's side; **ma grandmère paternelle** my grandmother on my father's side

2 *nm Fam* **le p.** the old man

paternité [patɛʁnite] *nf* paternity, fatherhood; **recherche de p.** establishment of paternity

pâteux, -euse [patø, -øz] *adj* (**a**) *(nourriture)* doughy; **avoir la langue pâteuse** to have a furry tongue (**b**) *(sauce)* thick

pathétique [patetik] *adj* pathetic, moving

pathogène [patɔʒɛn] *adj* pathogenic

pathologique [patɔlɔʒik] *adj aussi Fam Fig* pathological

patibulaire [patibylɛr] *adj* **avoir une mine p.** to have a sinister look

patiemment [pasjamɑ̃] *adv* patiently

patience [pasjɑ̃s] *nf* (**a**) *(qualité)* patience; **avoir de la p. (avec qn)** to be patient (with sb); **avoir une p. d'ange** to have the patience of a saint; **prendre son mal en p.** to suffer in silence; **perdre p.** to lose patience; **p., j'ai presque fini!** hold on *or* just a minute, I've almost finished!; *Prov* **p. et longueur de temps font plus que force ni que rage** all things take their time (**b**) *(jeu de cartes) Br* patience, *Am* solitaire

patient, -e [pasjɑ̃, -ɑ̃t] **1** *adj* patient
2 *nm,f (malade)* patient

patienter [pasjɑ̃te] *vi* to wait; **faire p. qn** to ask sb to wait

patin [patɛ̃] *nm* (**a**) *(de patineur)* skate; **patins à glace/à roulettes** ice/roller skates; **faire du p. à glace/à roulettes** to go ice-/roller-skating; *Can Fam Fig* **être vite sur ses patins** to be quick off the mark (**b**) *(pour parquet)* cloth pad (**c**) *Tech* shoe; **p. de frein** brake shoe

patinage [patinaʒ] *nm (sport)* skating; **p. artistique** figure skating; **p. de vitesse** speed skating

patine [patin] *nf* patina

patiner¹ [patine] *vi* (**a**) *(faire du patinage)* to skate (**b**) *(glisser) (voiture)* to skid; *(embrayage)* to slip; **ça patine!** it's like a skating rink!

patiner² *vt* to give a patina to

patinette [patinɛt] *nf* scooter

patineur, -euse [patinœr, -øz] *nm,f* skater

patinoire [patinwar] *nf* skating *or* ice rink; **ce trottoir est une vraie p.** this pavement is like an ice rink

pâtir [pɑtir] *vi* to suffer *(de* because of)

pâtisserie [pɑtisri] *nf* (**a**) *(magasin)* cake shop; **p.-confiserie** confectioner's (**b**) *(gâteau)* pastry, cake (**c**) *(confection)* pastry-making; **faire de la p.** to make cakes

pâtissier, -ère [pɑtisje, -ɛr] **1** *nm,f (artisan)* pastry cook; *(commerçant)* confectioner
2 *adj voir* **crème**

patois [patwa] *nm* patois

patraque [patrak] *adj Fam* out of sorts

patriarcal, -e, -aux, -ales [patriarkal, -o] *adj* patriarchal

patriarche [patrijarʃ] *nm* patriarch

patrie [patri] *nf* homeland; **ma seconde p.** my second home; *Fig* **la p. des arts** the cradle of the arts

patrimoine [patrimwan] *nm* heritage; *(biens)* property; **p. culturel** cultural heritage; *Biol* **p. génétique** genotype

patriote [patrijɔt] **1** *adj* patriotic
2 *nmf* patriot

patriotique [patrijɔtik] *adj* patriotic

patriotisme [patrijɔtism] *nm* patriotism

patron, -onne [patrɔ̃, -ɔn] **1** *nm,f* (**a**) *(dirigeant)* boss; *(propriétaire)* owner (**b**) *Rel* patron saint (**de** of)
2 *nm* (**a**) *(médecin)* senior consultant (**b**) *(pour la couture)* pattern

patronage [patrɔnaʒ] *nm* (**a**) *(parrainage)* patronage; **placé sous le p. de...** sponsored by... (**b**) *(organisation)* youth club

patronal, -e, -aux, -ales [patrɔnal, -o] *adj* employers'

patronat [patrɔna] *nm* employers

patronnesse [patrɔnɛs] *adj f* **dame p.** lady bountiful

patronyme [patrɔnim] *nm* patronymic

patrouille [patruj] *nf* patrol

patrouiller [patruje] *vi* to patrol

patte [pat] *nf* (**a**) *(jambe)* leg; *(pied) (de chien, de chat)* paw; *(d'oiseau)* foot; **pattes de devant** forelegs; *(pied)* front paws; **pattes de derrière** hind legs; *(pied)* back paws; **court/haut sur pattes** short-/long-legged; **marcher/se mettre à quatre pattes** to walk/get down on all fours; *Fig* **tirer dans les pattes à qn** to give sb a hard time; *Fig* **retomber sur ses pattes** to land on one's feet; *Fig* **montrer p. blanche** to show one's credentials; *Fam* **bas les pattes!** hands off!; *Fam* **pattes de mouche(s)** cramped handwriting (**b**) *(de cartable, de sac)* tab (**c**) *(de poche)* flap; *(d'épaule)* epaulette (**d**) *Suisse (torchon)* cloth (**e**) **pattes** *(favoris)* sideburns

patte-d'oie (*pl* **pattes-d'oie**) [patdwa] *nf* (**a**) *(carrefour)* crossroads *(singulier)* (**b**) *(ride)* crow's foot

pattemouille [patmuj] *nf* damp cloth *(for ironing clothes)*

pâturage [pɑtyraʒ] *nm (endroit)* pasture; **pâturages** pasture land

paume [pom] *nf* palm

paumé, -e [pome] *Fam* **1** *adj* lost
2 *nm,f* loser

paumer [pome] *Fam* **1** *vt* to lose
2 **se paumer** *vpr* to get lost

paupérisation [poperizasjɔ̃] *nf* impoverishment

paupière [popjɛr] *nf* eyelid

paupiette [popjɛt] *nf* (meat) olive; **paupiettes de veau** veal olives

pause [poz] *nf* (**a**) *(dans une activité)* break; *(en parlant)* pause; **faire une p.** to have a break; *(en parlant)* to pause; **p. de midi** lunch break; **p.-café** coffee break (**b**) *Mus Br* semibreve rest, *Am* whole rest

pauvre [povr] **1** *adj* (**a**) *(personne, sol)* poor; **p. en vitamine C** with a low vitamin C content; **p. de moi!** poor old me! (**b**) *(misérable) (robe, meubles)* shabby; *(sourire)* weak; *(excuse)* poor (**c**) *Péj* sad, pathetic; *Fam* **p. mec!** you sad individual!
2 *nmf* poor man, *f* poor woman; **les pauvres** the poor; *Fig* **p. d'esprit** half-wit

pauvrement [povrəmɑ̃] *adv* poorly

pauvresse [povrɛs] *nf (fille)* poor girl; *(femme)* poor woman

pauvreté [povrəte] *nf aussi Fig* poverty

pavane [pavan] *nf Mus* pavane

pavaner [pavane] **se pavaner** *vpr* to strut about

pavé [pave] *nm* (**a**) *(morceau de grès)* paving stone; *Fam Péj (livre)* massive tome; *Fig* **un p. dans la mare** a bombshell (**b**) *(revêtement)* paving; *Fig* **tenir le haut du p.** to be at the top; *Fig* **battre le p.** to hang about the streets; *Fig* **être sur le p.** to be on the street (**c**) *Ordinat* keypad; **p. numérique** numeric keypad

paver [pave] *vt* to pave *(with small stones)*; *Fig* **l'enfer est pavé de bonnes intentions** the road to hell is paved with good intentions

pavillon [pavijɔ̃] *nm* (**a**) *(petite maison)* detached house; **p. de chasse** hunting lodge (**b**) *(d'hôpital)* wing (**c**) *(partie évasée) (d'un Klaxon®, d'un haut-parleur)* horn; *(d'une trompette)* bell; *(d'un entonnoir)* mouth; **p. de l'oreille** external ear (**d**) *(drapeau)* flag; **p. de complaisance** flag of convenience

pavillonnaire [pavijɔnɛr] *adj* **banlieue p.** suburb *(consisting of houses as opposed to high-rise apartment buildings)*

pavoiser [pavwaze] *vi Fam* to gloat

pavot [pavo] *nm* poppy

payable [pɛjabl] *adj* payable; **p. comptant** payable in cash; **p. à la livraison** payable on delivery; **p. à vue** payable at sight

payant, -e [pɛjã, -ãt] *adj (qui paie) (hôte, élève)* paying; *(où il faut payer)* with a charge for admission; **l'entrée est payante** there is a charge for admission; *Fig* **ça s'est avéré p.** it turned out to be worth it

paye [pɛj] = **paie**

payement [pɛjmã] = **paiement**

payer [53] [peje] **1** *vt* (a) *(somme, dette, loyer, personne)* to pay; *(objet, service)* to pay for; **faire p. qch** *(service)* to charge for sth; *(somme)* to charge sth; **se faire p.** to get *or* be paid; **je le lui ai payé 100 francs** I paid her 100 francs for it; *Fam* **p. qch à qn** *(le lui offrir)* to buy sth for sb; *Fig* **p. les pots cassés** to carry the can (b) *Fig (expier)* to pay for; **il l'a payé de sa vie** he paid for it with his life; **tu me le paieras!** you'll pay for it!; *Fam* **je suis payé pour le savoir** I've learnt it the hard way

2 *vi* (a) *(verser de l'argent)* to pay; **p. en liquide/par carte (de crédit)/par chèque** to pay (in) cash/by credit card/by cheque; **p. de sa poche** to pay out of one's own pocket (b) *Fig* **p. de sa personne** to put oneself out; **il ne paie pas de mine, mais il est doué** he doesn't look it, but he's very clever (c) *(rapporter)* to pay

3 se payer *vpr Fam* **se p. qch** *(s'offrir)* to treat oneself to sth; *(être chargé de)* to be landed or saddled with sth; **se p. du bon temps** to have a fantastic time; **se p. un arbre** to crash into a tree; **je me suis payé un 2 à l'oral** I got a 2 in the oral; **se p. la tête de qn** to take the mickey out of sb; **se p. le culot de faire qch** to have the nerve to do sth

payeur, -euse [pɛjœr, -øz] *nm,f* payer; **mauvais p.** bad debtor, defaulter

pays [pei] *nm* (a) *(nation)* country; **p. de cocagne** land of plenty; **p. en voie de développement** developing country; **les p. de l'Est** Eastern European countries (b) *(région)* region; **voir du p.** to travel around; **revenir au p.** to go back home; **p. de chasse/pêche** hunting/fishing country (c) **le P. basque** the Basque country; **le p. de Galles** Wales

paysage [peizaʒ] *nm* (a) *(site)* landscape; *(vue)* scenery; *Fig (ensemble)* scene; **le p. audiovisuel français** French broadcasting (b) *(peinture)* landscape (painting) (c) *Ordinat* **mode p.** landscape mode

paysager, -ère [peizaʒe, -ɛr] *adj (jardin)* landscaped; *(bureau)* open-plan

paysagiste [peizaʒist] *nmf* (a) *(peintre)* landscape painter (b) **(jardinier) p.** landscape gardener

paysan, -anne [peizã, -an] **1** *adj* country; *Péj* peasant; **syndicat p.** farmers' union

2 *nm,f* farmer; *Péj* peasant

paysannerie [peizanri] *nf* **la p.** the peasantry

Pays-Bas [peibɑ] *nmpl* **les P.** the Netherlands

PC [pese] *nm* (a) *(abrév* **parti communiste)** CP (b) *(abrév* **personal computer)** PC

PCF [peseɛf] *nm (abrév* **parti communiste français)** French Communist Party

PCV [peseve] *nm* **(appel en) P.** *Br* reverse-charge call, *Am* collect call; **appeler en P.** *Br* to reverse the charges, *Am* to call collect

P-DG [pedeʒe] *nm inv (abrév* **président-directeur général)** *Br* chairman and managing director, *Am* chief executive officer

péage [peaʒ] *nm* (a) *(droit)* toll; **pont à p.** toll bridge (b) *(installation)* tollbooth (c) **chaîne (de télévision) à p.** pay channel

peau, -x [po] *nf* (a) *(derme)* skin; **avoir la p. grasse** to have greasy skin; **avoir la p. blanche/noire** to be white/black; **avoir une p. de pêche** to have velvety skin; *Fig* **faire p. neuve** *(personne)* to turn over a new leaf; *(entreprise, parti)* to get a new image; **entrer dans la p. d'un personnage** to get right inside a character; **n'avoir que la p. et les os** to be nothing but skin and bone; **diminuer comme une p. de chagrin** to dwindle away; *Fam* **être bien/mal dans sa p.** to feel/not to feel good about oneself; *Fam* **avoir qch dans la p.** to have sth in one's blood; *Fam* **avoir qn dans la p.** to be crazy about sb; *Fam* **tenir à sa p.** to value one's life; *Fam* **risquer sa p.** to risk one's neck; *Fam* **sauver sa p.** to save one's skin; *Fam* **avoir la p. de qn** to have sb's hide; *Fam* **prendre douze balles dans la p.** to be shot by a firing squad; *Fam* **p. de vache** *(homme)* bastard; *(femme)* cow

(b) *(dépouille) (d'un animal)* skin; *(d'un animal à fourrure)* pelt

(c) *(cuir)* hide, leather; *(d'un tambour)* skin; **p. de chamois** chamois (leather); **p. de mouton** sheepskin; **p. de serpent** snakeskin

(d) *(de fruit, de légume)* skin; *(d'agrume, de pomme)* peel; **p. de banane** banana skin; **p. d'orange** orange peel; *Fig* orange-peel skin

(e) *(du lait)* skin

(f) *(des ongles)* hangnail

peaufiner [pofine] *vt* to polish *(with a chamois leather)*; *Fam Fig (fignoler)* to add the final touches to

Peau-Rouge *(pl* **Peaux-Rouges)** [poruʒ] *nmf* Red Indian

peausserie [posri] *nf* (a) *(commerce)* skin trade (b) *(marchandise)* leatherwear

pécari [pekari] *nm* peccary

peccadille [pekadij] *nf* peccadillo

péché [peʃe] *nm* sin; **les sept péchés capitaux** the seven deadly sins; **p. de jeunesse** youthful indiscretion; **p. mignon** weakness; **le p. originel** original sin

pêche¹ [pɛʃ] **1** *nf* (a) *(fruit)* peach; **p. blanche** white peach; **p. jaune** yellow peach (b) *Fam (coup)* clout (c) *Fam (forme)* **avoir la p.** to be on form

2 *adj inv* peach(-coloured)

pêche² *nf* (a) *(activité)* fishing; **aller à la p.** to go fishing; **p. à la ligne** angling; **p. à la mouche** fly fishing; *Can* **p. sous la glace** ice fishing (b) *(produits pêchés)* catch; **faire une bonne p.** to get a good catch

pécher [34] [peʃe] *vi* to sin; **il pèche par excès de timidité** he's painfully shy; **cette enquête pèche sur un point** the inquiry falls down on one point; **p. par omission** to sin by omission

pêcher¹ [peʃe] *nm* peach tree

pêcher² **1** *vt* (a) *(chercher à prendre)* to fish for; *(prendre)* to catch; **p. la baleine** to go whaling (b) *Fam (trouver)* **où avez-vous pêché cela?** where did you pick that up?

2 *vi* to fish; **p. à la ligne** to go angling; *Fig* **p. en eau trouble** to fish in troubled waters

pécheresse [peʃrɛs] *voir* **pécheur**

pêcherie [peʃri] *nf* fishery, fishing ground

pêcheur, -eresse [peʃœr, peʃrɛs] *nm,f* sinner

pêcheur, -euse [peʃœr, -øz] *nm,f* fisherman, *f* fisherwoman; **p. à la ligne** angler; **p. de baleines** whaler; **p. de corail** coral fisher

pécore [pekɔr] *nmf Fam Péj* country bumpkin, yokel

pectoral, -e, -aux, -ales [pɛktɔral, -o] 1 *adj* pectoral
2 *nm* pectoral muscle

pécule [pekyl] *nm* savings, nest egg

pécuniaire [pekynjɛr] *adj* financial

pédagogie [pedagɔʒi] *nf* (**a**) *(discipline)* pedagogy (**b**) *(qualité du pédagogue)* teaching skills

pédagogique [pedagɔʒik] *adj (voyage, sortie)* educational; *(méthode)* teaching

pédagogue [pedagɔg] 1 *adj* **elle est très p.** she's a very good teacher
2 *nmf* (**a**) *(spécialiste)* educationalist (**b**) *(personne qui sait enseigner)* teacher

pédale [pedal] *nf* (**a**) *(de vélo, de voiture, de piano)* pedal; **p. d'accélérateur** accelerator pedal; **p. d'embrayage** clutch pedal; **p. de frein** brake pedal; *Fam Fig* **mettre la p. douce** to go easy; *Fam Fig* **perdre les pédales** *(s'affoler)* to lose one's head (**b**) *Fam Péj (homosexuel)* queer, = offensive term used to refer to a male homosexual

pédaler [pedale] *vi* to pedal; *Fam* **p. dans la choucroute** *ou* **la semoule** to be all at sea

pédalier [pedalje] *nm* (**a**) *(de vélo)* crank gear (**b**) *(clavier d'orgue)* pedal board

Pédalo® [pedalo] *nm* pedal boat, pedalo; **faire du P.** to go out on a Pedalo

pédant, -e [pedã, -ãt] 1 *adj* pedantic
2 *nm,f* pedant

pédé [pede] *nm très Fam* queer, = offensive term used to refer to a male homosexual

pédéraste [pederast] *nm* (**a**) *(homosexuel)* homosexual (**b**) *(pédophile)* pederast

pédestre [pedɛstr] *adj (voyage)* on foot; **chemin p.** footpath; **randonnée p.** hike

pédiatre [pedjatr] *nmf* paediatrician

pédiatrie [pedjatri] *nf* paediatrics *(singulier)*

pédicure [pedikyr] *nmf* chiropodist

pedigree [pedigre] *nm* pedigree

pédoncule [pedɔ̃kyl] *nm* peduncle

pédophile [pedɔfil] *nmf* paedophile

pègre [pɛgr] *nf* underworld

peignais, peigne *etc voir* **peindre**

peigne [pɛɲ] *nm* (**a**) *(pour les cheveux)* comb; **se donner un coup de p.** to give one's hair a comb; **p. fin** fine-tooth comb; *Fig* **passer qch au p. fin** to go through sth with a fine-tooth comb (**b**) *(pour la laine)* card

peigne-cul *(pl* **peigne-culs)** [pɛɲky] *nm très Fam Péj* creep

peignée [peɲe] *nf Fam* thrashing; **flanquer une p. à qn** to give sb a thrashing

peigner [peɲe] 1 *vt* (**a**) *(cheveux)* to comb; **p. un enfant** to comb a child's hair; *Fam* **p. la girafe** to waste one's time (**b**) *(laine)* to card
2 **se peigner** *vpr* to comb one's hair

peignoir [pɛɲwar] *nm* (**a**) *(vêtement d'intérieur)* housecoat; *(robe de chambre)* dressing gown; **p. (de bain)** bathrobe (**b**) *(chez le coiffeur)* cape

peinard, -e [penar, -ard] *adj Fam (poste)* cushy; *(personne)* nice and comfortable

peindre [54] [pɛ̃dr] 1 *vt* (**a**) *(avec de la peinture)* to paint; **p. qch en vert** to paint sth green (**b**) *(décrire)* to depict
2 *vi* to paint
3 **se peindre** *vpr* **l'émotion/la consternation se peignit sur son visage** emotion/dismay was written on his face

peine [pɛn] *nf* (**a**) *(sanction)* punishment; **p. capitale** capital punishment; **p. de mort** death penalty; **p. de prison** prison sentence; **défense d'entrer sous p. d'amende** *(sur panneau)* trespassers will be prosecuted; **pour la** *ou* **ta p., tu vas descendre la poubelle** just for that, you can take the bin down
(**b**) *(chagrin)* sorrow, sadness; **avoir de la p.** to be upset; **faire de la p. à qn** to upset sb; **elle fait p. à voir** she's a pitiful sight; **p. de cœur** heartache
(**c**) *(effort)* trouble; **se donner de la p. pour faire qch** to go to a lot of trouble to do sth; **donnez-vous** *ou* **prenez la p. d'entrer** please come in; **c'est p. perdue** it's a waste of time; **elle n'est pas au bout de ses peines** her troubles aren't over yet; **en être pour sa p.** to have nothing to show for one's trouble; **ça vaut la p. d'essayer** it's worth a try; **ça ne vaut pas la p.** it's not worth it; **ce n'est pas la p. de débarrasser la table** there's no point (in) clearing the table; **est-ce que ça vaut la p. que tu viennes?** do I need to come?; *Ironique* **c'était bien la p. de se donner tout ce mal!** it was really worth going to all that trouble!
(**d**) *(difficulté)* difficulty; **avoir de la p. à faire qch** to have difficulty doing sth; **j'ai (de la) p. à croire que...** I find it hard to believe that...; **elle serait bien en p. de t'expliquer comment ça marche** she'd be hard put to explain to you how it works; **cela n'a pas été sans p.** it was no easy matter
(**e**) **à p.** hardly, scarcely; **c'est à p. si je le connais** I hardly know him; **il est à p. trois heures** it's only just three o'clock; **à p. étions-nous sortis que...** we'd only just gone out when...; **j'arrive à p.** I've only just arrived; **à p. arrivée, elle alluma une cigarette** no sooner had she arrived than she lit a cigarette

peiner [pene] 1 *vt* to upset, to sadden; **d'un ton peiné** in a sad voice
2 *vi* to labour

peint, -e *voir* **peindre**

peintre [pɛ̃tr] *nm* (**a**) *(artisan, artiste)* painter; **p. en bâtiment** painter and decorator (**b**) *Fig* portrayer

peinture [pɛ̃tyr] *nf* (**a**) *(art, action)* painting; **faire de la p.** to paint; **p. à l'eau** watercolour (painting); **p. à l'huile** oil painting; **p. sur soie** silk painting (**b**) *(tableau)* painting, picture; *Fig (description)* depiction; *Fig* **je ne peux pas le voir en p.** I can't stand the sight of him; **p. murale** mural (**c**) *(matière)* paint; **p. fraîche** *(sur écriteau)* wet paint (**d**) *(surface peinte)* paintwork; **il faudra refaire les peintures** the paintwork will have to be done

peinturer [pɛ̃tyre] *vt Can* to paint

peinturlurer [pɛ̃tyrlyre] *vt Fam* to daub with paint; **se p. le visage** to plaster make-up on one's face

péjoratif, -ive [peʒɔratif, -iv] *adj* pejorative

Pékin [pekɛ̃] *n* Peking, Beijing

pékinois, -e [pekinwa, -az] 1 *adj* of Peking, of Beijing
2 *nm,f* person from Peking or Beijing
3 *nm* (**a**) *(chien)* pekin(g)ese (**b**) *(langue)* Pekingese

PEL [peœl] *nm Fin (abrév* **plan d'épargne-logement**) = savings plan entitling savers to low mortgages, *Br* ≃ building society account, *Am* ≃ savings and loan association account

pelade [pəlad] *nf* alopecia

pelage [pəlaʒ] *nm* coat, fur

pelé, -e [pəle] **1** *adj (personne, fourrure)* bald; *Fig (paysage)* bare; *(tissu)* threadbare
2 *nm Fam* **il y avait trois pelés et un tondu** there was hardly a soul there

pêle-mêle [pɛlmɛl] **1** *adv* higgledy-piggledy
2 *nm inv (cadre)* multiple (photo) frame

peler [39] [pəle] **1** *vt* to peel
2 *vi (peau)* to peel; **j'ai le nez qui pèle** my nose is peeling; *Fam Fig* **je pèle (de froid)** I'm freezing (cold)
3 se peler *vpr Fam* **on se pèle (de froid)** it's freezing (cold)

pèlerin [pɛlrɛ̃] *nm* pilgrim

pèlerinage [pɛlrinaʒ] *nm* pilgrimage; **faire un p., aller en p.** to go on a pilgrimage

pèlerine [pɛlrin] *nf* cape

pélican [pelikɑ̃] *nm* pelican

pelisse [pəlis] *nf* pelisse

pelle [pɛl] *nf* shovel; *(d'enfant)* spade; *Fig* **à la p.** by the bucketful; *Fam* **ramasser** *ou* **se prendre une p.** to fall flat on one's face; **p. mécanique** mechanical shovel; **p. à ordures** dustpan; **p. à tarte** cake slice

pelletée [pɛlte] *nf* shovelful

pelleteuse [pɛltøz] *nf* mechanical shovel

pellicule [pelikyl] *nf* (**a**) *(de glace, de peinture)* thin layer; *(sur un liquide)* film (**b**) *Cin & Phot* film (**c**) *(dans les cheveux)* **pellicules** dandruff; **avoir des pellicules** to have dandruff

pelote [pəlɔt] *nf* (**a**) *(de laine, de ficelle)* ball; *Can* **p. de neige** snowball; *Fig* **avoir les nerfs en p.** to be on edge (**b**) *(sport)* **p. (basque)** pelota (**c**) **p. (à épingles)** pincushion

peloter [pəlɔte] *vt Fam* to pet

peloton [pəlɔtɔ̃] *nm* (**a**) *(en cyclisme)* pack; *aussi Fig* **le p. de tête** the leaders (**b**) *Mil* platoon; **p. d'exécution** firing squad (**c**) *(petite pelote)* small ball

pelotonner [pəlɔtɔne] **se pelotonner** *vpr* to curl up; *(pour avoir chaud)* to snuggle up

pelouse [pəluz] *nf* lawn; **p. interdite** *(sur panneau)* keep off the grass

peluche [pəlyʃ] *nf* (**a**) *(tissu)* plush; **jouet en p.** soft *or* cuddly toy (**b**) *(jouet)* soft *or* cuddly toy (**c**) *(bout d'étoffe)* piece of fluff

pelucheux, -euse [pəlyʃø, -øz] *adj* fluffy

pelure [pəlyr] *nf* (**a**) *(peau) (de fruit)* peel; *(de légumes)* peelings; **p. d'oignon** onion skin (**b**) *Fam (vêtement)* coat

pelvis [pɛlvis] *nm* pelvis

pénal, -e, -aux, -ales [penal, -o] *adj* penal

pénaliser [penalize] *vt* to penalize

pénalité [penalite] *nf* penalty

penalty [penalti] *nm* penalty

pénates [penat] *nmpl Fam* **regagner ses p.** to return home

penaud, -e [pəno, -od] *adj* sheepish; **d'un air p.** sheepishly

penchant [pɑ̃ʃɑ̃] *nm (tendance)* propensity (**pour** for); *(préférence)* penchant (**pour** for)

penché, -e [pɑ̃ʃe] *adj* leaning; *(écriture)* sloping

pencher [pɑ̃ʃe] **1** *vt (récipient, meuble)* to tilt; **p. la tête en avant/en arrière** to lean forward/backwards; **p. la tête à droite** to lean one's head to the right
2 *vi (s'écarter de la position verticale)* to lean over; *(bateau)* to list; **p. vers la droite** to lean to the right; *Fig* **p. pour qch** to incline towards sth
3 se pencher *vpr* to lean over; **se p. en avant/en arrière/sur le côté** to lean forward/backwards/to the side; **se p. par la fenêtre** to lean out of the window; *Fig* **se p. sur un problème** to look into a problem

pendaison [pɑ̃dɛzɔ̃] *nf* hanging; **p. de crémaillère** housewarming (party)

pendant¹, -e [pɑ̃dɑ̃, -ɑ̃t] **1** *adj* (**a**) *(qui pend)* hanging; *(jambes)* dangling; **le chien avait la langue pendante** the dog's tongue was hanging out (**b**) *(en attente)* pending
2 *nm* (**a**) **p. (d'oreille)** drop earring (**b**) *(d'un tableau, d'un bibelot)* matching piece (**de** to); **se faire p.** to go together

pendant² **1** *prép* (**a**) *(au cours de)* during; **p. mon séjour** during my stay (**b**) *(pour une durée de)* **p. dix minutes/deux mois** for ten minutes/two months; **p. tout le trajet** throughout the journey, for the whole journey; **p. ce temps(-là)** in the meantime
2 *conj* **p. que** while; **p. que vous y êtes** while you're at it

pendentif [pɑ̃dɑ̃tif] *nm (bijou)* pendant

penderie [pɑ̃dri] *nf Br* wardrobe, *Am* closet

pendouiller [pɑ̃duje] *vi Fam* to dangle

pendre [pɑ̃dr] **1** *vt* (**a**) *(accrocher)* to hang (up) (**b**) *(mettre à mort)* to hang; **p. qn haut et court** to string sb up; *Fam Fig* **qu'il aille se faire p. ailleurs** let him go hang; *Fig* **je veux bien être pendu si…** I'll be hanged if…
2 *vi* to hang; *(cheveux)* to hang down; *(langue d'un animal)* to hang out; *(bras, jambes)* to dangle; **ton pan de chemise pend** your shirt's hanging out; *Fam* **ça lui pend au nez** she's got it coming to her
3 se pendre *vpr* (**a**) *(se suicider)* to hang oneself (**b**) *(s'accrocher)* **se p. à qch** to hang from sth; **se p. au cou de qn** to throw one's arms round sb's neck

pendu, -e [pɑ̃dy] **1** *adj* (**a**) *(mort)* hanged (**b**) *(accroché)* hanging up; **p. à** hanging from; **p. aux jupes de sa mère** clinging to one's mother's skirts; *Fig* **avoir la langue bien pendue** to be a great talker; **elle est toujours pendue au téléphone** she's never off the phone
2 *nm,f* hanged man, *f* hanged woman; **le p.** *(jeu)* hangman

pendule [pɑ̃dyl] **1** *nf* clock; *Fig* **remettre les pendules à l'heure** to get things straight
2 *nm* pendulum

pendulette [pɑ̃dylɛt] *nf* small clock

pêne [pɛn] *nm* bolt

pénétrant, -e [penetrɑ̃, -ɑ̃t] *adj (vent, froid)* piercing; *(pluie)* soaking; *(odeur, regard, esprit)* penetrating

pénétration [penetrasjɔ̃] *nf* penetration

pénétré, -e [penetre] *adj (air, ton)* earnest; **p. d'un sentiment/d'une idée** imbued with a feeling/an idea; **il est p. de son importance** he's full of his own importance

pénétrer [34] [penetre] **1** *vi* to penetrate; **p. dans une maison** to get into a house
2 *vt* (**a**) *(sujet: balle)* to penetrate; *(sujet: liquide)* to soak into; *Fig (pensée, intentions)* to fathom; *(marché)* to penetrate (**b**) *(sexuellement)* to penetrate

3 se pénétrer *vpr* **se p. d'une idée** to become convinced of an idea

pénible [penibl] *adj* (**a**) *(tâche, voyage, vie)* hard; *(hiver, froid)* severe (**b**) *(spectacle, nouvelles)* painful (**c**) *Fam (personne)* **ce qu'il est p.!** he's such a pain!

péniblement [peniblømã] *adv* with difficulty; **avancer** *ou* **marcher p.** to struggle along

péniche [peniʃ] *nf* barge

pénicilline [penisilin] *nf* penicillin

péninsule [penẽsyl] *nf* peninsula; **la p. Ibérique** the Iberian Peninsula

pénis [penis] *nm* penis

pénitence [penitãs] *nf* (**a**) *Rel (repentir)* penitence; *(peine)* penance; **faire p.** to repent (**b**) *(punition)* punishment; **mettre un enfant en p.** to punish a child

pénitencier [penitãsje] *nm* prison, *Am* penitentiary

pénitent, -e [penitã, -ãt] *adj & nm,f* penitent

pénitentiaire [penitãsjer] *adj* prison

Pennsylvanie [pensilvani] *nf* **la P.** Pennsylvania

pénombre [penɔbr] *nf* half-light

pensable [pãsabl] *adj* **ce n'est pas p.** it's unthinkable

pensant, -e [pãsã, -ãt] *adj* thinking; **mal p.** unorthodox

pense-bête *(pl* **pense-bêtes)** [pãsbɛt] *nm* reminder

pensée¹ [pãse] *nf (fleur)* pansy

pensée² *nf (idée)* thought; *(activité)* thinking; **perdu dans ses pensées** lost in thought; **deviner les pensées de qn** to guess what sb is thinking; **dire le fond de sa p.** to say what one really thinks; **à la p. des vacances,...** at the thought of the holidays,...; **la seule p. de ce repas me met l'eau à la bouche** just thinking about this meal makes my mouth water; **la p. marxiste/bouddhiste** Marxist/Buddhist thought *or* thinking; **je suis avec vous en p.** *ou* **par la p.** you're in my thoughts; **avoir une p. pour qn** to think of sb

penser [pãse] **1** *vi* (**a**) *(songer, réfléchir)* to think; **p. à qn/qch** to think of *or* about sb/sth; **pensez-vous!** what an idea!; **vous n'y pensez pas!** you're not serious!; **n'y pensons plus** let's forget (about) it; **ce n'est même pas la peine d'y p.** it's not even worth thinking about; **ah, j'y pense!** by the way!; **rien que d'y p., ça me donne des frissons** just thinking about it gives me the shivers; **elle l'a fait sans p. à mal** she didn't mean any harm by it

(**b**) *(se souvenir)* **p. à faire qch** to remember to do sth; **fais-moi p. à vérifier que...** remind me to check that...; **elle me fait p. à ma sœur** she reminds me of my sister

2 *vt* (**a**) *(estimer)* to think; **c'est bien ce que je pensais** I thought as much; **je pense que oui/non** I think/don't think so; *Fam* **pensez si j'étais furieux** you can imagine how angry I was; **p. du bien/du mal de qn** to think a lot/not to think much of sb

(**b**) **p. faire qch** *(espérer)* to hope to do sth; *(avoir l'intention)* to be thinking of doing sth

(**c**) *(croire à)* to mean; **elle ne pense pas ce qu'elle dit** she doesn't mean what she says

(**d**) *(concevoir)* **c'est bien/mal pensé** it's well/badly thought out

penseur, -euse [pãsœr, -øz] *nm,f* thinker

pensif, -ive [pãsif, -iv] *adj* pensive, thoughtful; **d'un air p.** thoughtfully

pension [pãsjɔ̃] *nf* (**a**) *(allocation)* pension; **p. alimentaire** maintenance, alimony; **p. de retraite** *(retirement or old age)* pension (**b**) *(pensionnat)* boarding school; **mettre un enfant en p.** to send a child to boarding school (**c**) *(hôtel)* **p. (de famille)** boarding house; **être en p. chez qn** to board with sb; **prendre qn en p.** to take sb in as a lodger; **p. complète** *Br* full board, *Am* American plan (**d**) *Belg (cessation d'activité)* retirement; **l'âge de la p.** retirement age

pensionnaire [pãsjɔner] *nmf (dans une pension de famille, à l'école)* boarder; *(dans une maison privée)* lodger; *Fam (d'une prison)* inmate

pensionnat [pãsjɔna] *nm* boarding school

pensionné, -e [pãsjɔne] *nm,f* pensioner

pensionner [pãsjɔne] **1** *vt* to pension
2 *vi Can (être en pension)* to be a boarder

pensivement [pãsivmã] *adv* thoughtfully, pensively

pensum [pɛ̃sɔm] *nm* (**a**) *(travail ennuyeux)* chore (**b**) *Vieilli Scol* imposition

pentagone [pɛ̃tagɔn] *nm* (**a**) *(figure)* pentagon (**b**) **le P.** *(aux États-Unis)* the Pentagon

pente [pãt] *nf* slope; **en p.** sloping; *Fig* **être sur une mauvaise p.** to be going downhill; *Fig* **remonter la p.** to get back on one's feet

Pentecôte [pãtkot] *nf Rel* Pentecost; *(jours fériés)* Whit(sun)

pentu, -e [pãty] *adj* sloping

pénultième [penyltjɛm] *adj & nf* penultimate

pénurie [penyri] *nf* shortage, scarcity

PEP [pɛp] *nm Fin (abrév* **plan d'épargne populaire)** = personal pension plan

pépé [pepe] *nm (grand-père)* grandpa, grandad; *Fam (vieux monsieur)* grandad

pépée [pepe] *nf Fam* chick

pépère [pepɛr] *Fam* **1** *nm* (**a**) **c'est un gros p.** *(enfant)* he's a chubby little fellow (**b**) *(grand-père)* grandad
2 *adj (endroit)* quiet; *(travail)* cushy; **un petit coin p.** a nice quiet little spot; **être p.** *(dans une situation confortable)* to have it easy

pépie [pepi] *nf Fam* **avoir la p.** to be parched

pépiement [pepimã] *nm* cheeping, chirping

pépier [66] [pepje] *vi* to cheep, to chirp

pépin [pepɛ̃] *nm* (**a**) *(de fruit)* seed, *Br* pip; **sans pépins** seedless (**b**) *Fam (ennui)* hitch; **avoir un p.** to have a problem (**c**) *Fam (parapluie)* umbrella, *Br* brolly

pépinière [pepinjer] *nf* (**a**) *(d'arbustes)* nursery (**b**) *Fig* training ground (**de** for)

pépite [pepit] *nf (d'or)* nugget; **pépites de chocolat** chocolate chips

péquenaud, -e [pekno, -od] *nm,f Fam* peasant, yokel

péquiste [pekist] **1** *adj* of the Parti Québécois
2 *nmf (membre)* member of the Parti Québécois; *(partisan)* supporter of the Parti Québécois

percale [pɛrkal] *nf* percale

perçant, -e [pɛrsã, -ãt] *adj (regard, cri)* piercing; *(voix)* penetrating; *(vue)* sharp

percée [pɛrse] *nf* (**a**) *(ouverture)* opening (**b**) *Mil, Sport & Fig* breakthrough

percement [pɛrsəmã] *nm (d'un trou, d'un passage, d'un tunnel)* boring; *(d'une avenue)* opening; *(d'un canal)* cutting

perce-neige [pɛrsəneʒ] *nm ou nf inv* snowdrop

perce-oreille *(pl* **perce-oreilles)** [pɛrsɔrɛj] *nm* earwig

percepteur [pɛrsɛptœr] *nm* (**a**) *(receveur des impôts)* tax collector (**b**) *Belg (receveur des postes)* postmaster, *f* postmistress

perceptible [pɛrsɛptibl] *adj* (**a**) *(que l'on peut percevoir)* perceptible (**b**) *(impôt)* collectable

perception [pɛrsɛpsjɔ̃] nf (**a**) (par les sens) perception (**b**) (d'impôts, de droits, de loyer) collection (**c**) (bureau) tax office

percer [16] [pɛrse] **1** vt (**a**) (transpercer) (corps, surface, armure) to pierce; (abcès) to lance; **le soleil perce les nuages** the sun's breaking through the clouds (**b**) (découvrir) (complot, secret) to uncover; (mystère, énigme) to solve; **p. qch à jour** to see through sth (**c**) (trouer) to make a hole in; (trou) to make; (avec une perceuse) to drill, to bore; (tunnel) to bore; (avenue) to open; (canal, fenêtre) to cut; (tonneau) to broach; (coffre-fort) to crack; **se faire p. les oreilles** to have one's ears pierced

2 vi (**a**) (apparaître) (soleil) to break through; (dents) to come through (**b**) (être révélé) to get out; **rien n'a percé de leur entretien** nothing's got out about their meeting (**c**) (devenir célèbre) to make a name for oneself

perceuse [pɛrsøz] nf drill

percevable [pɛrsəvabl] adj (impôt) collectable

percevoir [60] [pɛrsəvwar] vt (**a**) (par les sens, l'intellect) to perceive; (bruit) to hear; **être bien/mal perçu** to be well/badly received (**b**) (impôts, loyers) to collect; (intérêts, allocation, commission) to receive

perchaude [pɛrʃod] nf Can yellow perch

perche¹ [pɛrʃ] nf (tige) pole; (pour micro) boom; Fam Fig **une grande p.** (personne) a beanpole; Fig **tendre la p. à qn** to throw sb a line

perche² nf (poisson) perch

percher [pɛrʃe] **1** vi (**a**) (oiseaux) to perch; (poules) to roost (**b**) Fam (personne) to live

2 vt Fam (mettre) to perch

3 se percher vpr to perch

percheron [pɛrʃərɔ̃] nm percheron

perchiste [pɛrʃist] nmf Sport pole vaulter; Cin & TV boom operator

perchman [pɛrʃman] nm ski-lift attendant; Cin & TV boom operator

perchoir [pɛrʃwar] nm aussi Fig perch; (pour les volailles) roost

perclus, -e [pɛrkly, -yz] adj **p. de rhumatismes** crippled with rheumatism

percolateur [pɛrkɔlatœr] nm percolator

perçu, -e voir **percevoir**

percussion [pɛrkysjɔ̃] nf percussion

percussionniste [pɛrkysjɔnist] nmf percussionist

percutant, -e [pɛrkytɑ̃, -ɑ̃t] adj forceful

percuter [pɛrkyte] **1** vt to crash into

2 vi (**a**) **p. contre qch** to crash into sth (**b**) Fam (comprendre) to catch on

3 se percuter vpr to crash into each other

percuteur [pɛrkytœr] nm firing pin

perdant, -e [pɛrdɑ̃, -ɑ̃t] **1** adj losing; **partir p.** to start out with low hopes

2 nm,f loser; **être bon/mauvais p.** to be a good/bad loser

perdition [pɛrdisjɔ̃] nf (**a**) Rel perdition; **lieu de p.** den of iniquity (**b**) Naut **navire en p.** ship in distress; Fig **entreprise en p.** company in difficulties

perdre [pɛrdr] **1** vt (**a**) (égarer) to lose; (habitude) to get out of; (occasion) to miss; aussi Fig **p. qn/qch de vue** to lose sight of sb/sth; **p. de son assurance/sa souplesse** to lose some of one's confidence/suppleness; **il perd son pantalon** his trousers keep slipping down; **tu ne perds rien pour attendre!** just you wait!; **p. son temps** to waste one's time; **il n'y a pas de**

temps à **p.** there's no time to lose; **tu n'as rien perdu en ne venant pas** you didn't miss anything by not coming; **y p.** (dans un échange) to lose out; (dans une vente) to make a loss; **p. au change** to lose out on the deal (**b**) (ruiner) **ta générosité/ton ambition te perdra** your generosity/ambition will be the ruin of you

2 se perdre vpr (**a**) (s'égarer) to get lost; Fig **se p. de vue** to lose touch with each other; **se p. en conjectures/dans les détails** to get lost in conjecture/details; Fam **je m'y perds** I'm lost (**b**) (être gâché) (nourriture, récolte) to go to waste; **il y a des claques qui se perdent** you/they/etc need a good slap (**c**) (disparaître) (usage, tradition) to die out

perdreau, -x [pɛrdro] nm young partridge

perdrix [pɛrdri] nf partridge; **p. des neiges** ptarmigan

perdu, -e [pɛrdy] adj (égaré) lost; (vêtement, récolte) ruined; (endroit) out-of-the-way; (emballage) non-returnable; **p. dans ses pensées** lost in thought; **il est p.** (d'un malade) there's no hope for him; **à mes moments perdus, à mes heures perdues** in my spare time; **un de p., dix de retrouvés** there are plenty more fish in the sea

perdurer [pɛrdyre] vi Litt to continue

père [pɛr] nm (**a**) (géniteur) father; **p. de famille** father; **de p. en fils** from father to son; Prov **tel p., tel fils** like father, like son; **nos pères** our forefathers, our ancestors; Fig **le p. du cubisme** the father of cubism; Fam **(mon) petit p.** Br old chap, Am old buddy; **le p. Paul** old Paul; **le p. Noël** Father Christmas, Santa Claus; aussi Fam Fig **croire au p. Noël** to believe in Father Christmas (**b**) Rel father; **le (révérend) p. Martin** Father Martin; **mon p.** father

pérégrinations [peregrinasjɔ̃] nfpl peregrinations

péremption [perɑ̃psjɔ̃] nf **date de p.** use-by date

péremptoire [perɑ̃ptwar] adj peremptory

pérennité [perenite] nf permanence

péréquation [perekwasjɔ̃] nf equalization

perestroïka [perɛstrɔika] nf perestroika

perfectif, -ive [pɛrfɛktif, -iv] adj & nm perfective

perfection [pɛrfɛksjɔ̃] nf perfection; **à la p.** to perfection

perfectionné, -e [pɛrfɛksjɔne] adj sophisticated

perfectionnement [pɛrfɛksjɔnmɑ̃] nm (**a**) (action) perfecting, improving; (formation) further training; **cours de p.** proficiency course (**b**) (résultat) improvement; **apporter des perfectionnements à qch** to improve sth

perfectionner [pɛrfɛksjɔne] **1** vt to perfect, to improve

2 se perfectionner vpr to improve; **se p. en allemand** to improve one's German

perfectionnisme [pɛrfɛksjɔnism] nm perfectionism

perfectionniste [pɛrfɛksjɔnist] **1** adj **être p.** to be a perfectionist

2 nmf perfectionist

perfide [pɛrfid] adj perfidious; **la p. Albion** perfidious Albion

perfidie [pɛrfidi] nf Litt (**a**) (déloyauté) perfidiousness (**b**) (action) perfidy

perforation [pɛrfɔrasjɔ̃] nf (**a**) (action) perforation; Ordinat punching (**b**) (trou) & Méd perforation; Ordinat punch (hole)

perforatrice [pɛrfɔratris] nf (pour papier) (hole) punch

perforer [pɛrfɔre] vt (**a**) (papier, organe) to perforate; (cuir) to punch; (sujet: missile) to pierce (**b**) Ordinat *(carte, bande)* to punch; **bande perforée** punched tape; **carte perforée** punch card

perforeuse [pɛrfɔrøz] *nf* hole punch

performance [pɛrfɔrmãs] *nf (en sport)* performance; *Fig (exploit)* feat, achievement; **performances** *(d'une voiture, d'un ordinateur)* performance

performant, -e [pɛrfɔrmã, -ãt] *adj (machine)* high-performance; *(personne)* highly efficient

perfusion [pɛrfyzjɔ̃] *nf* drip; **être sous p.** to be on a drip

péricliter [periklite] *vi* to collapse

péridurale [peridyral] *nf* epidural; **accoucher sous p.** to give birth under an epidural

Périgord [perigɔr] *nm* **le P.** Périgord

périgourdin, -e [perigurdɛ̃, -in] **1** *adj* of Périgord **2** *nm,f* **P.** person from Périgord

péril [peril] *nm* peril, danger; **au p. de sa vie** at the risk of one's life; **en p.** in peril; **mettre qch en p.** to imperil *or* endanger sth; **à ses risques et périls** at one's own risk; **il n'y a pas p. en la demeure** it's not a matter of urgency

périlleux, -euse [perijø, -øz] *adj* perilous, dangerous

périmé, -e [perime] *adj (billet, passeport, coupon)* out of date; *(nourriture, article)* past its sell-by date; *(idée, conception)* outdated

périmètre [perimɛtr] *nm* perimeter; **dans un p. de 50 km** within a 50-km radius

périnée [perine] *nm* perineum

période [perjɔd] *nf* period; **p. bleue/blanche/rouge** *(de trains)* = off-peak/peak/high-peak periods of rail schedules during which ticket prices vary accordingly; **p. d'essai** trial period

périodique [perjɔdik] **1** *adj* (a) *(cyclique)* periodic (b) *(hygiénique)* **serviette p.** sanitary *Br* towel *or Am* napkin **2** *nm* periodical

périodiquement [perjɔdikmã] *adv* periodically

péripétie [peripesi] *nf Litt* event

périph [perif] *nm Fam Br* ring road, *Am* beltway

périphérie [periferi] *nf* periphery; *(banlieue)* outskirts; **à la p. des grandes villes** on the outskirts of cities

périphérique [periferik] **1** *adj aussi Ordinat* peripheral; **boulevard p.** *Br* ring road, *Am* beltway; **radio** *ou* **station p.** = private radio station broadcasting from outside national territory **2** *nm* (a) *(route) Br* ring road, *Am* beltway (b) *Ordinat* peripheral; **p. d'impression** printer peripheral; **p. de sortie** output device

périphrase [perifraz] *nf* circumlocution, *Spéc* periphrasis

périple [peripl] *nm (voyage)* tour, journey; *(par mer)* voyage

périr [perir] *vi* to perish

périscolaire [periskɔlɛr] *adj* extracurricular

périscope [periskɔp] *nm* periscope

périssable [perisabl] *adj (denrées, produit)* perishable; *Fig (sentiment)* transient

péristyle [peristil] *nm* peristyle

péritonite [peritɔnit] *nf* peritonitis

perle [pɛrl] *nf* (a) *(naturelle)* pearl; *(de verre, de métal)* & *Fig (de sueur)* bead; **p. fine/de culture** real/cultured pearl; *Fig* **jeter des perles aux pourceaux** to cast pearls before swine; *Fam Fig* **enfiler des perles** to waste one's time on trivia (b) *(personne)* gem,

treasure; **c'est la p. des sœurs** she's the best sister in the world; **ma bonne est une p. rare** my maid is a real gem (c) *Hum (erreur)* howler (d) *Can (prunelle)* pupil *(of the eye)*

perlé, -e [pɛrle] *adj (orné de perles)* set with pearls; *(de perles de verre)* beaded; **grève perlée** *Br* go-slow, *Am* slowdown

perler [pɛrle] *vi (larmes, sueur)* to form in beads

perlimpinpin [pɛrlɛ̃pɛ̃pɛ̃] *nm* **poudre de p.** magic powder

perm [pɛrm] *nf Fam* (a) *Mil* leave; **en p.** on leave (b) *Scol* study room; **avoir deux heures de p.** to have two hours' private study

permanence [pɛrmanãs] *nf* (a) *(continuité)* permanence; **en p.** permanently (b) *(lieu)* duty office; **la p. est assurée le dimanche** there's someone on duty on Sundays; **être de p.** to be on duty (c) *Scol* study room; **avoir deux heures de p.** to have two hours' private study

permanent, -e [pɛrmanã, -ãt] **1** *adj (commission)* standing; *(spectacle)* continuous; *(tribunal)* permanent; **cinéma p.** cinema with continuous showings **2** *nm,f Pol* official **3** *nf* **permanente** perm; **se faire faire une p.** to have a perm, to have one's hair permed

perméable [pɛrmeabl] *adj* permeable (**à** to); *Fig* susceptible (**à** to)

permettre [47] [pɛrmɛtr] **1** *vt* (a) *(autoriser)* to allow, to permit; **p. à qn de faire qch** to allow *or* permit sb to do sth; **p. qch à qn** to allow sb sth; **permettez-moi de...** allow me to...; **permettez!** excuse me!; **vous permettez?** may I?; **il se croit tout permis** he thinks he can do whatever he likes; *Fam* **il est égoïste comme ce n'est pas permis!** he's incredibly selfish! (b) *(rendre possible)* to allow; **p. à qn de faire qch** to allow sb to do sth; **mes moyens ne me le permettent pas** I can't afford it; **si le temps le permet** weather permitting; **si mon emploi du temps le permet** if my schedule allows it **2 se permettre** *vpr* **se p. qch** to allow oneself sth; **se p. de faire qch** to take the liberty of doing sth; **je me permets d'attirer votre attention sur...** may I draw your attention to...

permis, -e [pɛrmi, -iz] **1** *adj* allowed, permitted **2** *nm* permit, licence; **p. de chasse** hunting permit; **p. de conduire** *Br* driving licence, *Am* driver's license; *(examen)* driving test; **p. de construire** planning permission; **p. de séjour** residence permit; **p. de travail** work permit

permissif, -ive [pɛrmisif, -iv] *adj* permissive

permission [pɛrmisjɔ̃] *nf* (a) *(autorisation)* permission; **demander/donner la p. à qn de faire qch** to ask/give sb permission to do sth (b) *Mil (congé)* leave; *(certificat)* pass; **en p.** on leave

permissionnaire [pɛrmisjɔnɛr] *nmf* person on leave

permutation [pɛrmytasjɔ̃] *nf* (a) *(échange)* exchange of posts; *Mil* transfer (b) *(de lettres, de chiffres)* transposition; *Math* permutation

permuter [pɛrmyte] **1** *vt (lettres, chiffres)* to transpose; *Math* to permute **2** *vi* to exchange posts

pernicieux, -euse [pɛrnisjø, -øz] *adj* pernicious

péroné [perɔne] *nm* fibula

péroraison [perɔrɛzɔ̃] *nf* peroration

pérorer [perɔre] *vi Péj* to hold forth

Pérou [peru] *nm* **le P.** Peru; *Fig* **ce n'est pas le P.** *(pas extraordinaire)* it's no great shakes; *(peu d'argent)* it's not a fortune

peroxyde [pɛrɔksid] *nm* peroxide

perpendiculaire [pɛrpɑ̃dikylɛr] *adj & nf* perpendicular **(à** to)

perpète [pɛrpɛt] *nf Fam* **(a)** *(perpétuité)* **condamné à p.** sentenced to life; **prendre p.** to get life; **jusqu'à p.** for ever **(b)** *(distance)* **à p.** miles away

perpétrer [34] [pɛrpetre] *vt* to perpetrate

perpette [pɛrpɛt] = **perpète**

perpétuel, -elle [pɛrpetɥɛl] *adj* perpetual; *(secrétaire, membre)* permanent

perpétuellement [pɛrpetɥɛlmɑ̃] *adv* perpetually

perpétuer [pɛrpetɥe] **1** *vt* to perpetuate
  2 se perpétuer *vpr* to be perpetuated

perpétuité [pɛrpetɥite] *nf* perpetuity; **à p.** *(concession)* in perpetuity; *(emprisonnement)* for life; **être condamné (à la réclusion) à p.** to be sentenced to life (imprisonment)

perplexe [pɛrplɛks] *adj* perplexed, puzzled; **laisser qn p.** to perplex *or* puzzle sb

perplexité [pɛrplɛksite] *nf* perplexity

perquisition [pɛrkizisjɔ̃] *nf* search; **faire une p.** to make a search

perquisitionner [pɛrkizisjɔne] **1** *vi* to make a search
  2 *vt* to search

perron [pɛrɔ̃] *nm* steps *(leading to a building)*

perroquet [pɛrɔkɛ] *nm* **(a)** *(oiseau)* parrot; **p. de mer** puffin **(b)** *(voile)* topgallant

perruche [peryʃ] *nf* budgerigar

perruque [peryk] *nf* wig

perruquier, -ère [perykje, -ɛr] *nm,f* wig maker

pers [pɛr] *adj m Litt* blue-green

persan, -e [pɛrsɑ̃, -an] **1** *adj* Persian
  2 *nm,f* **P.** Persian
  3 *nm (langue)* Persian

perse [pɛrs] **1** *adj* Persian
  2 *nmf* **P.** Persian
  3 *nm (langue)* Persian
  4 *nf* **la P.** Persia

persécuter [pɛrsekyte] *vt* to persecute

persécution [pɛrsekysjɔ̃] *nf* persecution; **manie** *ou* **délire de p.** persecution mania

persévérance [pɛrseverɑ̃s] *nf* perseverance

persévérant, -e [pɛrseverɑ̃, -ɑ̃t] *adj* persevering

persévérer [34] [pɛrsevere] *vi* to persevere (**dans** in)

persienne [pɛrsjɛn] *nf* shutter

persiflage [pɛrsiflaʒ] *nm (propos)* taunts, scoffs

persifler [pɛrsifle] *vt* to mock, to ridicule

persil [pɛrsi] *nm* parsley

persillé, -e [pɛrsije] *adj (viande)* marbled; *(assaisonné de persil)* sprinkled with chopped parsley; *(fromage)* veined

Persique [pɛrsik] *adj voir* **golfe**

persistance [pɛrsistɑ̃s] *nf* persistence (**à faire qch** in doing sth); **avec p.** persistently; **p. dans le mensonge** persistent lying

persistant, -e [pɛrsistɑ̃, -ɑ̃t] *adj* persistent; **à feuillage p.** evergreen

persister [pɛrsiste] *vi* **(a)** *(persévérer)* to persist (**dans** in); **p. à faire qch** to persist in doing sth **(b)** *(continuer)* to persist; **il persiste un doute** there remains a doubt

perso [pɛrso] *adj Fam (abrév* **personnel)** personal, private

personnage [pɛrsɔnaʒ] *nm* **(a)** *(de fiction)* character; *aussi Fig* **jouer un p.** to play a part *or* a role **(b)** *(individu)* character **(c)** *(image publique)* image, persona **(d)** *(personnalité)* important person; **p. célèbre** celebrity; **p. officiel** VIP; **un grand p. de l'État** a state dignitary

personnalisation [pɛrsɔnalizasjɔ̃] *nf* personalization

personnalisé, -e [pɛrsɔnalize] *adj* personalized; *(voiture, crédit)* customized

personnaliser [pɛrsɔnalize] *vt* to personalize; *(voiture)* to customize

personnalité [pɛrsɔnalite] *nf* **(a)** *(caractère)* personality; **avoir de la p.** to have lots of personality; **manquer de p.** to have no personality **(b)** *(personnage important)* personality **(c)** *Jur* **p. juridique** legal personality

personne [pɛrsɔn] **1** *nf* **(a)** *(individu)* person; **deux personnes** two people; **les personnes intéressées** those interested; **les personnes âgées** the elderly, elderly people; **une grande p.** a grown-up; **une jeune p.** a young lady **(b)** *(soi-même)* **en p.** in person, personally; **être bien de sa p.** to be good-looking; **être satisfait de sa petite p.** to be pleased with oneself **(c)** *Jur* **p. morale** legal entity; **p. physique** natural person **(d)** *Gram* person
  2 *pron indéfini* **(a)** *(quiconque)* anyone, anybody; **elle le sait mieux que p.** she knows better than anyone **(b)** *(aucune personne)* no one, nobody; **p. n'est venu** no one has come; **il n'y a p. de blessé** no one has been injured; **p. d'autre** no one else, nobody else; **je n'y suis pour p.** I'm not at home to anyone; **ne connaissez-vous p. qui puisse nous aider?** don't you know anyone who could help us?; *Fam* **dès qu'il s'agit de travailler, il n'y a plus p.** as soon as there's work to be done, you can't see anyone for dust

personnel, -elle [pɛrsɔnɛl] **1** *adj* **(a)** *(à soi)* personal **(b)** *(égoïste)* selfish; *(intérêt)* vested
  2 *nm (d'une firme, d'une école)* staff; *(d'une usine)* workforce; *(dans l'armée)* personnel; **faire partie du p. de...** to be on the staff of...; **manquer de p.** to be understaffed; **un membre du p.** a member of staff; **p. de bureau** office *or* clerical staff; **p. navigant** flight personnel; **p. au sol** ground personnel

personnellement [pɛrsɔnɛlmɑ̃] *adv* personally

personnifier [66] [pɛrsɔnifje] *vt* to personify; **il est la bêtise personnifiée** he's stupidity personified

perspective [pɛrspɛktiv] *nf* **(a)** *(de dessin)* perspective **(b)** *(idée)* prospect; **à la p. de faire qch** at the prospect of doing sth; **en p.** in prospect; **des perspectives de reprise** outlook for recovery; **des perspectives d'avenir** future prospects **(c)** *(point de vue)* viewpoint, point of view

perspicace [pɛrspikas] *adj* shrewd

perspicacité [pɛrspikasite] *nf* shrewdness

persuader [pɛrsɥade] **1** *vt* **p. qn (de qch)** to persuade *or* convince sb (of sth); **p. qn de faire qch** to persuade sb to do sth; **être persuadé de qch/que...** to be convinced of sth/that...
  2 se persuader *vpr* **se p. de qch/que...** to convince oneself of sth/that...

persuasif, -ive [pɛrsɥazif, -iv] *adj* persuasive

persuasion [pɛrsɥazjɔ̃] *nf* persuasion

perte [pɛrt] *nf* **(a)** *(d'un objet, d'une personne, d'un procès)* loss; **de lourdes pertes en hommes et en**

matériel heavy losses of men and equipment; **à p. de vue** as far as the eye can see; **vendre qch à p.** to sell sth at a loss; *aussi Fig* **passer qch par pertes et profits** to write sth off; **p. sèche** dead loss; **ce n'est pas une grosse p.** it's no great loss (**b**) *(gaspillage)* **une p. de temps** a waste of time; **en pure p.** to no purpose (**c**) *(déperdition)* loss; **être en p. de vitesse** to be losing speed; *Fig* to be running out of steam; **pertes blanches** vaginal discharge; **p. de chaleur** heat loss; **p. de connaissance** loss of consciousness; *Ordinat* **p. de données irréparable** irretrievable data loss (**d**) *(destruction)* ruin; **jurer la p. de qn** to swear to ruin sb; **courir à sa p.** to be heading for disaster

pertinemment [pɛrtinamɑ̃] *adv* **savoir qch p.** to know sth for a fact

pertinence [pɛrtinɑ̃s] *nf* pertinence, relevance

pertinent, -e [pɛrtinɑ̃, -ɑ̃t] *adj* pertinent, relevant

perturbant, -e [pɛrtyrbɑ̃, -ɑ̃t] *adj* disturbing, upsetting

perturbateur, -trice [pɛrtyrbatœr, -tris] **1** *adj* disruptive
   2 *nm,f* troublemaker

perturbation [pɛrtyrbasjɔ̃] *nf* disruption; **p. (atmosphérique)** (atmospheric) disturbance

perturber [pɛrtyrbe] *vt (services publics, circulation)* to disrupt; *(personne)* to perturb, to upset

péruvien, -enne [peryvjɛ̃, -ɛn] **1** *adj* Peruvian
   2 *nm,f* **P.** Peruvian

pervenche [pɛrvɑ̃ʃ] *nf* (**a**) *(plante)* periwinkle; **(bleu) p.** periwinkle blue (**b**) *Fam (contractuelle)* Br (female) traffic warden, *Am* meter maid

pervers, -e [pɛrvɛr, -ɛrs] **1** *adj* perverse
   2 *nm,f* pervert

perversion [pɛrvɛrsjɔ̃] *nf* perversion

perversité [pɛrvɛrsite] *nf* perversity

pervertir [pɛrvɛrtir] **1** *vt* to pervert
   2 se pervertir *upr* to become perverted

pesamment [pəzamɑ̃] *adv* heavily

pesant, -e [pəzɑ̃, -ɑ̃t] **1** *adj* heavy; *(sommeil)* deep; *(ambiance)* oppressive; **marcher à pas pesants** to walk heavily
   2 *nm* **valoir son p. d'or** to be worth one's/its weight in gold

pesanteur [pəzɑ̃tœr] *nf* (**a**) *(attraction terrestre)* gravity (**b**) *(lourdeur)* heaviness

pesée [pəze] *nf* (**a**) *(pour connaître le poids)* weighing; *(de boxeur, de chevaux)* weigh-in (**b**) *(pression)* force

pèse-lettre *(pl* **pèse-lettres)** [pɛzlɛtr] *nm* letter scales

pèse-personne *(pl* **pèse-personnes)** [pɛzpɛrsɔn] *nm* scales

peser [46] [pəze] **1** *vt* to weigh; *Fig* **p. le pour et le contre** to weigh up the pros and cons; *Fig* **p. ses mots** to weigh one's words; *Fig* **tout bien pesé** all things considered
   2 *vi (être lourd)* to be heavy; **p. 2 kilos** to weigh 2 kilos; **p. sur qch** to press on sth; *Fig* **p. sur la conscience** to lie heavy on one's conscience; *Fig* **p. sur l'estomac** to lie heavy on the stomach; *Fig* **p. sur** *ou* **dans une décision** to carry weight in a decision; **la solitude me pèse** the solitude is getting me down
   3 se peser *upr* to weigh oneself

peseta [pezeta] *nf* peseta

peso [pezo] *nm* peso

pessimisme [pesimism] *nm* pessimism

pessimiste [pesimist] **1** *adj* pessimistic
   2 *nmf* pessimist

peste [pɛst] *nf* (**a**) *(maladie)* plague; *Fig* **je me méfie de lui comme de la p.** I don't trust him as far as I could throw him; **la p. bubonique** the bubonic plague; *Hist* **la p. noire** the Black Death (**b**) *Fig & Péj (personne)* pest

pester [pɛste] *vi* **p. contre qn/qch** to curse sb/sth

pesticide [pɛstisid] **1** *adj* pesticidal
   2 *nm* pesticide

pestiféré, -e [pɛstifere] **1** *adj* plague-stricken
   2 *nm,f* plague victim; **traiter qn comme un p.** to treat sb like a pariah *or* a leper

pestilentiel, -elle [pɛstilɑ̃sjɛl] *adj* stinking

pet [pɛ] *nm Fam (gaz)* fart; **lâcher un p.** to fart; **ça ne vaut pas un p. (de lapin)** it isn't worth a monkey's fart; **il a toujours un p. de travers** there's always something up with him

pétale [petal] *nm* petal

pétanque [petɑ̃k] *nf* ≃ bowls *(played in the South of France)*

> ### Pétanque
> Originally invented in the South of France, where it has become a local institution, this bowling game is equally popular with tourists. The game, which requires two teams and is played up to a score of thirteen points, is played outdoors on a flat sandy or earth surface. Each team consists of two to three players, each of whom has three steel "boules". Each player tosses or rolls their "boule" so that it ends up as near as possible to the "cochonnet" (a small wooden ball thrown from a distance of 6 to 10 metres), at the same time trying to hit the other team's "boules" so as to scatter them. Players take turns, and whoever ends up closest to the "cochonnet" when all balls are played, wins.

pétant, -e [petɑ̃, -ɑ̃t] *adj Fam* **à une heure pétante** at one o'clock on the dot

Pétaouchnock [petauʃnɔk] *n Fam* **ils l'ont envoyé à P.** they sent him to some place in the back of beyond *or* to Timbuktu

pétarade [petarad] *nf* (**a**) *(de feux d'artifice, d'armes à feu)* crackling (**b**) *(de véhicule)* backfiring

pétarader [petarade] *vi* (**a**) *(feux d'artifice, armes à feu)* to crackle (**b**) *(véhicule)* to backfire

pétard [petar] *nm* (**a**) *(feu d'artifice)* (fire)cracker, *Br* banger (**b**) *Fam (pistolet)* shooter (**c**) *Fam (joint)* joint (**d**) *Fam (postérieur)* butt, *Br* bum, *Am* fanny (**e**) *Fam* **être en p. (contre)** to be raging (at)

pétasse [petas] *nf Vulg* slag

pétaudière [petodjɛr] *nf Fam* bedlam

pété, -e [pete] *adj Fam (ivre)* smashed

péter [34] [pete] *Fam* **1** *vi* (**a**) *(bois qui brûle)* to crackle; *(bouchon)* to pop; *(personne)* to fart; *Vulg* **il pète plus haut que son cul** he thinks he's God's gift to humanity (**b**) *(exploser)* to blow up; *Fig* **je veux que ça pète!** get your finger out! (**c**) *(casser)* to bust
   2 *vt* (**a**) **p. le feu** *ou* **la forme** to be full of beans; **p. les plombs** to blow one's top (**b**) *(casser)* to bust
   3 se péter *upr (se casser)* to bust; **se p. la gueule** to get wasted; *Can* **se p. les bretelles** to be full of oneself

pète-sec [pɛtsɛk] *adj inv Fam* curt

péteux, -euse [petø, -øz] *Fam Péj* **1** *adj (honteux)* sheepish

2 *nm,f* (**a**) *(lâche)* yellowbelly (**b**) *(prétentieux)* up-start

pétillant, -e [petijã, -ãt] *adj (vin, yeux)* sparkling; *(eau)* fizzy

pétillement [petijmã] *nm (du vin, des yeux)* sparkling

pétiller [petije] *vi (vin, yeux)* to sparkle; **p. d'intelligence** *(yeux)* to sparkle with intelligence

petit, -e [pəti, -it] **1** *adj* (**a**) *(de taille réduite)* small, little; *(distance, séjour)* short; *(somme)* small; **tout p.** tiny; **un p. moment** a little while; *Fam* **une petite demi-heure** barely half an hour; *Fig* **se faire tout p.** to make oneself as inconspicuous as possible; **petites et moyennes entreprises** small and medium-sized businesses; *Can* **p. suisse** chipmunk
(**b**) *(peu grave) (problème, erreur)* small; *(accident)* minor; *(rhume)* slight
(**c**) *(jeune)* little, young; **mon p. frère** my little brother; **p. cousin** first cousin once removed; **un p. Anglais** an English boy
(**d**) *(faible) (voix)* small; *(bruit)* little; **avoir une petite santé** to be delicate
(**e**) *(de niveau inférieur) Scol* **les petites classes** the lower classes; **petite route** minor road; **p. commerçant/artisan** small trader/craftsman
(**f**) *(pour insister)* little; **p. crétin/con!** little idiot/bastard!; **mon p. ange** my little angel; **je fumerais bien une petite cigarette** I'd love a cigarette; *Fam* **p. nom** first name
(**g**) *(mesquin)* petty
2 *nm,f* (**a**) *(enfant)* (little) boy, *f* (little) girl; **les petits** the little ones; *Fam* **mon p.** my dear; **pauvre p.!** poor little thing!
(**b**) *(en taille)* **les petits devant, les grands derrière** small people in front and the tall ones behind
3 *nm (d'un chien)* puppy; *(d'un chat)* kitten; **faire** *ou* **avoir des petits** to have puppies/kittens/*etc*; *Fam* **faire des petits** *(argent)* to multiply
4 *adv (écrire)* small; **p. à p.** little by little

petit-beurre *(pl* **petits-beurre)** [pətibœr] *nm* butter *Br* biscuit *or Am* cookie

petit-bourgeois, petite-bourgeoise *(mpl* **petits-bourgeois,** *fpl* **petites-bourgeoises)** [pəti-burʒwa, pətitburʒwaz] *aussi Péj* **1** *adj* lower middle class
2 *nm,f* member of the lower middle class

petite-fille *(pl* **petites-filles)** [pətitj] *nf* grand-daughter

petitesse [pətites] *nf (d'un objet)* smallness; *Péj (mesquinerie)* pettiness

petit-fils *(pl* **petits-fils)** [pətifis] *nm* grandson

pétition [petisjɔ̃] *nf* petition

petit-lait *(pl* **petits-laits)** [pətilɛ] *nm* whey; *Fam* **se boire comme du p.** to go down a treat; *Fig* **boire du p.** to lap it up

petit-nègre [pətinɛgr] *nm Fam (mauvais français)* pidgin French; **c'est du p.** *(mal écrit)* it's gibberish

petits-enfants [pətizãfã] *nmpl* grandchildren

petit-suisse *(pl* **petits-suisses)** [pətisɥis] *nm* = small dessert of thick fromage frais

pétoche [petɔʃ] *nf Fam* jitters; **avoir la p.** to have the jitters; **flanquer la p. à qn** to give sb the jitters

pétoire [petwar] *nf Fam (fusil)* popgun

pétri, -e [petri] *adj* **p. de qch** *(orgueil)* puffed up with sth; *(contradictions)* riddled with sth

pétrifier [66] [petrifje] *vt aussi Fig* to petrify

pétrin [petrɛ̃] *nm* kneading trough; *Fam* **être dans le p.** to be in a mess

pétrir [petrir] *vt (pâte à pain, argile)* to knead

pétrochimique [petroʃimik] *adj* petrochemical

pétrodollar [petrodɔlar] *nm Fin* petrodollar

pétrole [petrɔl] *nm* oil, petroleum

pétrolette [petrɔlɛt] *nf Fam* moped

pétrolier, -ère [petrɔlje, -ɛr] **1** *adj* **l'industrie pétrolière** the oil industry
2 *nm* (oil) tanker

pétrolifère [petrɔlifɛr] *adj* oil-bearing; **gisement p.** oilfield

pétulant, -e [petylã, -ãt] *adj* exuberant

pétunia [petynja] *nm* petunia

peu [pø] **1** *adv* (**a**) *(avec un verbe)* not much; **elle mange/parle p.** she doesn't eat/talk much
(**b**) *(avec un adjectif ou un adverbe)* not very; **il a agi p. honorablement** he didn't behave very honourably; **très/trop p.** very/too little
(**c**) *(avec un nom)* **p. de** *(temps, courage, vin)* little, not much; *(amis, lettres, illusions)* few, not many; **ne te fâche pas pour si p.** don't get angry over such a small thing; **c'est p. de chose** it's nothing; *Fam* **très p. pour moi!** not for me!
(**d**) *(un petit nombre)* few; **p. ont compris** few (people) understood
(**e**) *(indique la durée)* **sous p., avant p., d'ici p.** soon, shortly; **p. après** shortly afterwards; **depuis p.** lately, recently; **c'est ouvert depuis p.** it hasn't been open long; **j'ai manqué le train de p.** I (only) just missed the train; **il y a p.** not very long ago, recently; **p. à p.** little by little, gradually
(**f**) **pour p. que** + *subjunctive* if by chance; **pour p. qu'il ait oublié la clé,...** if by chance he's forgotten the key,...
2 *nm* (**a**) *(petite quantité)* **le p. que je sais d'elle** the little I know about her; **le p. d'argent qu'il me reste** what little money I have left; **son p. d'instruction** what little education he has had
(**b**) **un p.** a little *or* a bit; **un peu grand/ennuyeux** a little *or* a bit big/boring; **un p. de temps/sucre** a bit of *or* a little time/sugar; **je le connais un p.** I know him slightly *or* a little; **un p. plus/moins** a little *or* a bit more/less; **un tout petit p.** a tiny bit; **il est un p. artiste** he's a bit of an artist; **un p. plus et elle tombait** she very nearly fell; **pour un p. je l'aurais jeté dehors** I all but *or* I very nearly threw him out; **écoutez un p.** just listen; **viens un p. ici** come here a minute; *Fam* **tu ferais ça? – un p.!** you'd do that? – you bet!
(**c**) *(de temps)* **un p.** a bit, a little while; **restez encore un p.** stay a bit longer, stay a little (while) longer

peuchère [pøʃɛr] *exclam* heavens!

peuh [pø] *exclam* bah!

peuplade [pœplad] *nf* tribe

peuple [pœpl] *nm* (**a**) *(nation)* people; **le p. français** the French people (**b**) *(citoyens)* people; **les gens du p.** ordinary people (**c**) *Fam (foule)* crowd

peuplé, -e [pœple] *adj* inhabited (**de** by); **très/peu p.** densely/sparsely populated

peuplement [pœpləmã] *nm (d'une région)* populating

peupler [pœple] **1** *vt* (**a**) *(installer une population dans)* to populate (**b**) *(habiter)* to inhabit; *Fig* **peuplé de qch** full of sth
2 **se peupler** *vpr* to become populated

peuplier [pøplije] *nm* poplar

peur [pœr] *nf* fear; *(subite)* fright; **avoir p. (de)** to be afraid *or* frightened (of); *Fam* **avoir une p. bleue de**

qn/qch to be frightened *or* scared to death of sb/sth; **faire p. à** qn to frighten *or* scare sb; **par p. de qch** through fear of sth; **de p. de faire qch** for fear of doing sth; **de p. qu'il ne le fasse** for fear that he would do it; **j'ai bien p. qu'il (ne) soit en retard** I'm very much afraid he's going to be late

peureux, -euse [pœrø, -øz] **1** *adj* fearful
    2 *nm,f* fearful person

peut *voir* **pouvoir**

peut-être [pøtɛtr] *adv* perhaps, maybe; **p. que oui, p. que non** perhaps, perhaps not; **p. (bien) qu'elle viendra, p. viendra-t-elle** perhaps she'll come; **je ne suis p. pas riche, mais...** I may not be rich, but...; *Ironique* **tu le sais mieux que moi, p.?** you think you know better, do you?

peux *voir* **pouvoir**

pèze [pɛz] *nm très Fam (argent)* dosh

pH [peaʃ] *nm Chim* pH

phacochère [fakɔʃɛr] *nm* warthog

phagocyter [fagɔsite] *vt Biol* to phagocytose; *Fig* to swallow up

phalange [falɑ̃ʒ] *nf (du doigt)* phalanx

phallique [falik] *adj* phallic

phallocrate [falɔkrat] *nm Péj* male chauvinist

phalloïde [falɔid] *adj voir* **amanite**

phallus [falys] *nm* phallus

phantasme [fɑ̃tasm] = **fantasme**

pharamineux, -euse [faraminø, -øz] = **faramineux**

pharaon [faraɔ̃] *nm* Pharaoh

phare [far] **1** *nm* **(a)** *(pour navires)* lighthouse; *(pour avions)* beacon **(b)** *(de voiture)* headlight; **faire un appel de phares** to flash one's headlights; **se mettre en phares** *Br* to dip *or Am* to dim one's headlights; **p. antibrouillard** foglight
    2 *adj* **film-p.** seminal film; **épreuve-p.** star event

pharmaceutique [farmasøtik] *adj* pharmaceutical

pharmacie [farmasi] *nf* **(a)** *(science)* pharmacy **(b)** *(magasin) Br* chemist's, *Am* drugstore **(c)** *(médicaments)* pharmaceuticals; **(armoire à) p.** medicine cabinet

pharmacien, -enne [farmasjɛ̃, -ɛn] *nm,f (vendeur) Br* chemist, *Am* druggist; *(chercheur)* pharmacist, *Br* chemist

pharmacologie [farmakɔlɔʒi] *nf* pharmacology

pharyngite [farɛ̃ʒit] *nf Méd* pharyngitis

pharynx [farɛ̃ks] *nm Anat* pharynx

phase [fɑz] *nf* phase; **cancer en p. terminale** terminal cancer; *Phys* **être en p.** to be in phase; *Fam* **être en p. (avec** qn**)** to be on the same wavelength (as sb)

phénicien, -enne [fenisjɛ̃, -ɛn] *Hist* **1** *adj* Phoenician
    2 *nm,f* **P.** Phoenician

phénix [feniks] *nm (animal mythologique)* phoenix; *Fig & Litt* paragon

phénoménal, -e, -aux, -ales [fenɔmenal, -o] *adj Fam* phenomenal

phénomène [fenɔmɛn] *nm* phenomenon; *Fam (personne)* character; **un p. de foire** a freak

Philadelphie [ladɛlfi] *n* Philadelphia

philanthrope [filɑ̃trɔp] *nmf* philanthropist

philanthropique [filɑ̃trɔpik] *adj* philanthropic

philatélie [filateli] *nf* philately, stamp collecting

philatéliste [filatelist] *nmf* philatelist, stamp collector

philharmonique [filarmɔnik] *adj* philharmonic

philippin, -e [filipɛ̃, -in] **1** *adj* Filipino
    2 *nm,f* **P.** Filipino

Philippines [filipin] *nfpl* **les P.** the Philippines

philosophale [filɔzɔfal] *adj f voir* **pierre**

philosophe [filɔzɔf] **1** *nmf* philosopher
    2 *adj* philosophical

philosopher [filɔzɔfe] *vi* to philosophize

philosophie [lɔzɔfi] *nf* philosophy; *Fig* **avec p.** philosophically

philosophique [lɔzɔfik] *adj* philosophical

philtre [filtr] *nm* philtre; **p. d'amour** love potion

phlébite [flebit] *nf Méd* phlebitis

phlébologue [flebɔlɔg] *nmf Méd* vein specialist, *Spéc* phlebologist

Phnom Penh [pnɔmpɛn] *n* Phnom Penh

phobie [fɔbi] *nf* phobia; **avoir la p. de qch** to have a phobia about sth

phonème [fɔnɛm] *nm* phoneme

phonétique [fɔnetik] **1** *adj* phonetic
    2 *nf* phonetics *(singulier)*

phonographe [fɔnɔgraf] *nm Vieilli Br* gramophone, *Am* phonograph

phoque [fɔk] *nm* **(a)** *(animal)* seal; *très Fam* **il est pédé comme un p.** he's a screaming queen **(b)** *(fourrure)* sealskin

phosphate [fɔsfat] *nm* phosphate; **sans phosphates** phosphate-free

phosphore [fɔsfɔr] *nm* phosphorus

phosphorescent, -e [fɔsfɔresɑ̃, -ɑ̃t] *adj* phosphorescent

photo [foto] **1** *nf* **(a)** *(cliché)* photo; **prendre** qn/qch **en p.** to take a photo of sb/sth; *Fam* **tu veux ma p.?** who do you think you're staring at?; **p. d'identité** passport-sized photograph; **p. de mode** fashion photo; **p. souvenir** souvenir photo **(b)** *(activité)* **faire de la p.** *(en amateur)* to take photographs; *(en professionnel)* to be a photographer
    2 *adj inv voir* **appareil**

photocomposition [fotokɔ̃pozisjɔ̃] *nf* photosetting

photocopie [fotokɔpi] *nf* photocopy

photocopier [66] [fotokɔpje] *vt* to photocopy

photocopleur [fotokɔpjœr] *nm, nf* photocopier

photocopieuse [fotokɔpjøz] *nf* photocopier

photoélectrique [fotoelɛktrik] *adj* photoelectric

photo-finish *(pl* **photos-finish)** [fotoniʃ] *nf* photo finish; *(appareil)* photo-finish camera

photogénique [fotoʒenik] *adj* photogenic

photographe [fotograf] *nmf* **(a)** *(professionnel)* photographer; **p. de mode** fashion photographer; **p. de presse** press photographer **(b)** *(commerçant)* **chez le p.** at the photo shop

photographie [fotografi] *nf* **(a)** *(technique)* photography; **faire de la p.** to take photographs **(b)** *(cliché)* photograph; **prendre une p. de** to take a photograph of; **p. aérienne** aerial photograph

photographier [66] [fotografje] *vt* to photograph; **se faire p.** to have one's photograph taken

photographique [fotografik] *adj* photographic

photogravure [fotogravyr] *nf* photogravure

Photomaton® [fotomatɔ̃] *nm* photo booth

photomontage [fotomɔ̃taʒ] *nm* photomontage

photon [fotɔ̃] *nm Phys* photon

photoreportage [fotorəpɔrtaʒ] *nm* photo report

photosensible [fotosɑ̃sibl] *adj* photosensitive

photostyle [fotostil] *nm Ordinat* light pen

photosynthèse [fotosɛ̃tɛz] *nf Biol* photosynthesis

phrase [frɑz] *nf* sentence; *(musicale)* phrase; *Fig* **faire de grandes phrases** to use flowery language

phrasé [frɑze] *nm Mus* phrasing

phraséologie [frazeɔlɔʒi] *nf* phraseology; *Péj* flowery language

phréatique [freatik] *adj voir* **nappe**

phrygien, -enne [friʒjɛ̃, -ɛn] *adj Hist* **bonnet p.** Phrygian cap *(in French Revolution)*

phtisie [ftizi] *nf Vieilli* consumption

phylloxéra, phylloxera [filɔksera] *nm* phylloxera

physicien, -enne [fizisjɛ̃, -ɛn] *nm,f* physicist

physiologie [fizjɔlɔʒi] *nf* physiology

physiologique [fizjɔlɔʒik] *adj* physiological

physionomie [fizjɔnɔmi] *nf* (a) *(traits du visage)* features; **juger les gens à leur p.** to judge people by appearances (b) *(aspect)* face

physionomiste [fizjɔnɔmist] *adj* **être p.** to have a good memory for faces

physiothérapie [fizjɔterapi] *nf* natural medicine

physique [fizik] **1** *adj* physical; *Fam* **je ne le supporte pas, c'est p.** he absolutely repulses me
2 *nf (science)* physics *(singulier)*; **p. nucléaire** nuclear physics
3 *nm (d'une personne)* physique; **avoir un p. avantageux** to have a good physique; **avoir le p. de l'emploi** to look the part

physiquement [fizikmɑ̃] *adv* physically

phytoplancton [fitoplɑ̃ktɔ̃] *nm* phytoplankton

phytothérapie [fitoterapi] *nf* herbal medicine

piaf [pjaf] *nm Fam* sparrow

piaffer [pjafe] *vi (cheval)* to paw the ground; *Fig* **p. d'impatience** to fidget impatiently

piaillement [pjajmɑ̃] *nm (d'un oiseau)* cheeping; *Fam (d'un enfant)* squealing

piailler [pjaje] *vi (oiseau)* to cheep; *Fam (enfant)* to squeal

pianiste [pjanist] *nmf* pianist

piano¹ [pjano] *nm* piano; **jouer** *ou* **faire du p.** to play the piano; **p. demi-queue** baby grand; **p. droit** upright piano; **p. à queue** grand piano

piano² *adv Mus* piano; *Fig* gently

pianoter [pjanɔte] *vi Fam* (a) *(mal jouer)* to tinkle away (b) *(tapoter)* **p. sur qch** *(table)* to drum one's fingers on sth; *Fam (clavier)* to tap away at sth

piastre [pjastr] *nf* piastre; *Can Fam (dollar)* buck

piaule [pjol] *nf Fam* pad

piauler [pjole] *vi (poussins)* to cheep

PIB [peibe] *nm Écon (abrév* **produit intérieur brut)** GDP

pic [pik] *nm* (a) *(pioche)* pick(axe); **p. à glace** ice pick (b) *(sommet)* peak; **couler à p.** to sink like a stone; **tomber à p.** *(falaise)* to go straight down; *Fam* to come at just the right moment

picard, -e [pikar, -ard] **1** *adj* of Picardy
2 *nm,f* **P.** person from Picardy

Picardie [pikardi] *nf* **la P.** Picardy

picaresque [pikarɛsk] *adj* picaresque

pichenette [piʃnɛt] *nf* flick

pichet [piʃɛ] *nm Br* jug, *Am* pitcher

pickpocket [pikpɔkɛt] *nm* pickpocket

pick-up [pikœp] *nm inv* (a) *Vieilli (électrophone)* record player (b) *(véhicule)* pick-up (truck)

picoler [pikɔle] *vi Fam* to booze

picorer [pikɔre] **1** *vt (sujet: oiseau)* to peck (at); *(sujet: personne)* to nibble
2 *vi (oiseau)* to pick about; *(personne)* to pick at one's food

picotement [pikɔtmɑ̃] *nm (dans la gorge, dans le nez)* tickling; *(dans les yeux)* stinging; *(sur la peau)* prickling

picoter [pikɔte] *vt* **j'ai la gorge qui (me) picote** I've got a tickle in my throat; **la fumée me picotait les yeux** the smoke made my eyes sting; **j'ai la peau qui (me) picote** my skin's prickling

Pictes [pikt] *nmpl* **les P.** the Picts

pictogramme [piktɔgram] *nm* pictogram

pictural, -e, -aux, -ales [piktyral, -o] *adj* pictorial

pic-vert (*pl* **pics-verts**) [pivɛr] = **pivert**

pie [pi] **1** *nf* magpie; *Fam (personne)* chatterbox; *Fam* **être bavard comme une p.** to be a real chatterbox
2 *adj inv (cheval)* piebald; *(vache)* black-and-white

pièce [pjɛs] *nf* (a) *(salle)* room
(b) *(élément)* piece; *(d'un mécanisme)* part; **un service complet de trente-six pièces** a complete thirty-six piece service; **coûter 10 francs p.** to cost 10 francs each; **travailler à la p.** to do piecework; *Fig* **être tout d'une p.** to be straightforward; *Fig* **une histoire fabriquée de toutes pièces** a completely made-up story; **mettre qch en pièces** to tear sth to pieces; **p. de bœuf** cut *or* piece of beef; **p. de collection** collector's item; **p. d'eau** ornamental lake; *(plus petite)* ornamental pond; **p. montée** = large tiered cake served at weddings, baptisms etc; **p. de musée** museum piece; **pièces de rechange, pièces détachées** spare parts, spares; **p. de résistance** main dish; *Fig* pièce de résistance
(c) *(argent)* **p. (de monnaie)** coin; **p. de 10 francs** 10-franc piece
(d) **p. (de théâtre)** play
(e) *(raccord)* patch; **mettre une p. à qch** to put a patch on sth
(f) *(document)* document; **juger sur pièces** to judge on the evidence; **p. à conviction** exhibit *(in criminal case)*; **p. d'identité** proof of identity; **p. jointe** *(à une lettre)* enclosure
(g) *(aux échecs)* piece; *(aux dames)* *Br* draught, *Am* checker

---

Pièce

Flats in France are referred to in terms of the total number of rooms they have (excluding the kitchen and bathroom). "Un deux-pièces" is a flat with a living room and one bedroom; "un cinq-pièces" is a flat with five rooms.

---

piécette [pjesɛt] *nf* small coin

pied [pje] *nm* (a) *(d'une personne)* foot; **avoir les pieds plats** to have flat feet; **avoir un p. bot** to have a club foot; **se prendre les pieds dans qch** to get one's feet caught in sth; **avoir p.** to be within one's depth; **perdre p.** to get out of one's depth; **mettre p. à terre** *(de cheval, de vélo)* to dismount; **de p. en cap** from head to toe
(b) *(de cheval)* hoof; *Culin* **p. de porc** pig's trotter
(c) *(de vigne)* stock; *(de céleri, de salade)* head
(d) *(de chaise, de table)* leg; *(de verre)* stem; *(d'appareil photo, de lampadaire)* stand
(e) *(base)* foot
(f) **à p.** on foot; **j'y suis allé à p.** I walked there, I went there on foot; **faire 2 kilomètres à p.** to walk 2

kilometres; **tu en as pour dix minutes à p.** it'll take you ten minutes to walk (there)

(**g**) *(mesure)* foot; *Fig* **six pieds sous terre** six foot under

(**h**) *(locutions)* **mettre qch sur p.** to set sth up; **être sur p.** *(personne)* to be up and about; **être à p. d'œuvre** to be ready to get on with the job; **être sur un p. d'égalité avec qn** to be on an equal footing with sb; *Fig* **être sur le p. de guerre** to be ready for action; **avoir bon p. bon œil** to be hale and hearty; **avoir un p. dans la tombe** to have one foot in the grave; **avoir le p. marin** to be a good sailor; **mettre qn au p. du mur** to get sb with his/her back to the wall; **attendre qn de p. ferme** to be ready and waiting for sb; **se lever du p. gauche** to get out of bed on the wrong side; **faire qch au p. levé** to do sth at a moment's notice; **faire un p. de nez à qn** to cock a snook at sb; *Fam* **il chante/conduit comme un p.** he can't sing/drive to save his life; *Fam* **s'y prendre comme un p.** to make a real mess of it; *Fam* **mettre les pieds dans le plat** to put one's foot in it; *Fam* **je ne remettrai jamais les pieds chez lui** I'll never set foot in his house again; *Fam* **faire des pieds et des mains pour obtenir qch** to move heaven and earth to get sth; *Fam* **faire du p. à qn** to play footsie with sb; *Fam* **ça lui fera les pieds!** that'll teach him a lesson!; *Fam* **prendre son p.** to get one's kicks; *Fam* **c'est le p.!** it's fantastic!

pied-à-terre [pjetatɛr] *nm inv* pied-à-terre

pied-bot *(pl* **pieds-bots)** [pjebo] *nm* club-footed person

pied-de-biche *(pl* **pieds-de-biche)** [pjedbiʃ] *nm (outil)* nail claw

pied-de-poule *(pl* **pieds-de-poule)** [pjedpul] *adj inv & nm* hound's-tooth

piédestal, -aux [pjedɛstal, -o] *nm* pedestal; *Fig* **mettre** *ou* **placer qn sur un p.** to put *or* to set sb on a pedestal

pied-noir *(pl* **pieds-noirs)** [pjenwar] *nmf Fam* = French settler in North Africa

---

Pied noir

This is the name given to the French settlers who settled in North Africa (most notably in Algeria) during the period of French colonial expansion. Most of them resettled in France (mainly on the south coast) after the colonies regained their independence. The largest wave of these settlers to arrive in France was in 1962, following the Algerian war.

---

piège [pjɛʒ] *nm aussi Fig* trap; **tendre un p. (à)** to set a trap (for); **prendre un animal au p.** to catch an animal in a trap; **tomber dans un p.** to fall into a trap; *très Fam* **p. à cons** con

piéger [59] [pjeʒe] *vt* (**a**) *aussi Fig (attraper)* to trap; **se faire p.** to be trapped; **se laisser p.** to fall into a trap (**b**) *(placer une bombe dans)* to booby-trap; **colis piégé** parcel bomb; **lettre piégée** letter bomb; **voiture piégée** car bomb

Piémont [pjemɔ̃] *nm* **le P.** Piedmont

piémontais, -e [pjemɔ̃tɛ, -ɛz] **1** *adj* Piedmontese
2 *nm,f* **P.** Piedmontese
3 *nm (langue)* Piedmontese

piercing [pirsiŋ] *nm* body piercing

pierraille [pjɛraj] *nf* loose stones

pierre [pjɛr] *nf* (**a**) *(matière, caillou)* stone; *(rocher)* rock; **mur de p.** stone wall; **maison en p.** stone(-built)

house; **investir dans la p.** to invest in bricks and mortar; **poser la première p. de qch** to lay the foundation stone for sth; *Fig* **jeter la p. à qn** to reproach sb; *Fig* **faire d'une p. deux coups** to kill two birds with one stone; *Fig* **être malheureux comme les pierres** to be extremely unhappy; *Prov* **p. qui roule n'amasse pas mousse** a rolling stone gathers no moss; **p. d'achoppement** stumbling block; *aussi Fig* **p. angulaire** cornerstone; **p. à briquet** flint *(for lighter)*; **p. philosophale** philosopher's stone; **p. ponce** pumice stone; **p. de taille** dressed stone; **p. tombale** tombstone; *aussi Fig* **p. de touche** touchstone (**b**) *(en bijouterie)* stone; **p. précieuse** precious stone, gem; **p. fine** *ou* **semi-précieuse** semi-precious stone

pierreries [pjɛrri] *nfpl* precious stones, gems

pierreux, -euse [pjɛrø, -øz] *adj (sol, route)* stony; *(lit de rivière)* gravelly

piétaille [pjetaj] *nf Péj* rank and file

piété [pjete] *nf* (**a**) *(ferveur religieuse)* piety (**b**) *(affection)* **p. filiale** filial devotion

piétinement [pjetinmɑ̃] *nm (bruit)* stamping; *(marche sur place)* standing around; *Fig (stagnation)* lack of progress

piétiner [pjetine] **1** *vt* **p. qch** *(en trépignant)* to stamp on sth; *(en marchant)* to trample on sth; *(écraser)* to trample sth underfoot; **ils sont morts piétinés par la foule** they were trampled to death by the crowd
2 *vi* (**a**) **p. d'impatience** to stamp (one's feet) impatiently (**b**) *(faire du surplace)* to stand around; *Fig* to make no progress

piéton, -onne [pjetɔ̃, -ɔn] **1** *nm,f* pedestrian
2 *adj* **rue piétonne** pedestrianized street; **zone piétonne** pedestrian precinct

piétonnier, -ère [pjetɔnje, -ɛr] *adj* pedestrian; **rue piétonnière** pedestrianized street; **zone piétonnière** pedestrian precinct

piètre [pjɛtr] *adj Litt (compagnon)* wretched; *(excuse)* paltry; *(consolation)* small

pieu¹, -x [pjø] *nm (piquet)* stake

pieu², -x *nm Fam (lit)* bed; **se mettre au p., aller au p.** to hit the sack

pieuter [pjøte] **se pieuter** *vpr Fam* to hit the sack

pieuvre [pjœvr] *nf* octopus

pieux, -euse [pjø, -øz] *adj* pious, devout

pif [pif] *nm Fam (nez)* conk, *Br* hooter; *Fig* **faire qch au p.** to do sth by guesswork; **répondre au p.** to hazard a guess; **au p., je dirais...** at a rough guess, I'd say...

pif(f)er [pife] *vt Fam* **je ne peux pas le p.** I can't stomach him

pifomètre [pifɔmɛtr] *nm Fam* **faire qch au p.** to do sth by guesswork; **répondre au p.** to hazard a guess; **au p., je dirais...** at a rough guess, I'd say...

pige [piʒ] *nf* (**a**) *(article)* freelance contribution; **faire des piges** to do freelance work (**b**) *Fam (année)* **elle a quarante-cinq piges** she's forty-five; **à soixante piges** at sixty

pigeon [piʒɔ̃] *nm* (**a**) *(oiseau)* pigeon; **p. d'argile** clay pigeon; **p. ramier** wood pigeon; **p. vole** = children's game with forfeits; ≃ Simon says; **p. voyageur** carrier pigeon, homing pigeon (**b**) *Fam Péj (personne)* sucker

pigeonnant, -e [piʒɔnɑ̃, -ɑ̃t] *adj Fam* **poitrine pigeonnante** high bust; **soutien-gorge p.** uplift bra

pigeonnier [piʒɔnje] *nm* dovecot

piger [45] [piʒe] *Fam* **1** *vt* to get; **ne rien p. à qch** *(maths, anglais)* not to have a clue about sth; **je n'ai**

rien pigé à ce qu'il a dit I didn't get any of what he said
2 *vi* to get it

pigiste [piʒist] *nmf* freelance journalist

pigment [pigmɑ̃] *nm* pigment

pigmentation [pigmɑ̃tasjɔ̃] *nf* pigmentation

pignon¹ [piɲɔ̃] *nm (de mur)* gable; **avoir p. sur rue** to be of some standing

pignon² *nm (petite roue)* pinion

pignon³ *nm (graine)* pine nut

pilage [pilaʒ] *nm* crushing

pile¹ [pil] *nf* (**a**) *(tas)* pile; **en p.** in a pile (**b**) **p. (électrique)** battery; **marcher avec des piles** to work off batteries; **p. atomique** atomic pile

pile² **1** *nf (d'une pièce)* reverse; **p. ou face?** heads or tails?; **tirer à p. ou face** to toss for it
2 *adv Fam* **s'arrêter p.** to stop dead; **tomber p.** to come at just the right time; **à six heures p.** at six on the dot; **nous étions p. dix à table** there were exactly ten of us at the table; **elle est arrivée p. le même jour que moi** she arrived on exactly the same day as I did

piler [pile] **1** *vt* (**a**) *(broyer)* to crush; *(amandes)* to grind (**b**) *Fam (battre)* to thrash
2 *vi Fam* to slam on the brakes

pileux, -euse [pilø, -øz] *adj* hair; **système p.** body hair

pilier [pilje] *nm* (**a**) *(colonne)* pillar (**b**) *(au rugby)* prop (forward) (**c**) *Fig (défenseur)* pillar; *Fam Péj* **c'est un p. de bar** he's always propping up the bar

pillage [pijaʒ] *nm* pillaging, looting; *(lors d'une émeute)* looting

pillard, -e [pijar, -ard] **1** *adj* pillaging, looting; *(lors d'une émeute)* looting
2 *nm,f* pillager; *(lors d'une émeute)* looter

piller [pije] *vt* to pillage, to loot; *(lors d'une émeute)* to loot

pilleur, -euse [pijœr, -øz] *nm,f* pillager; *(lors d'une émeute)* looter; **p. d'épaves** looter of wrecks

pilon [pilɔ̃] *nm* (**a**) *(de pharmacien)* pestle; *Fig* **mettre un livre au p.** to pulp a book (**b**) *(de poulet)* drumstick (**c**) *(jambe de bois)* wooden leg

pilonnage [pilɔnaʒ] *nm (bombardement)* bombardment

pilonner [pilɔne] *vt (bombarder)* to bombard

pilori [pilɔri] *nm* pillory; *aussi Fig* **mettre qn au p.** to pillory sb

pilosité [pilozite] *nf* hairiness

pilotage [pilɔtaʒ] *nm* (**a**) *(d'un navire, d'un avion)* piloting; **p. automatique** automatic piloting (**b**) *Ordinat* control

pilote [pilɔt] **1** *nm* (**a**) *(de navire, d'avion)* pilot; *(de voiture de course)* driver; *(de moto de course)* rider; *Fig* **servir de p. à qn** to show sb round; **p. automatique** automatic pilot, autopilot; **p. de chasse** fighter pilot; **p. d'essai** test pilot; **p. de ligne** airline pilot (**b**) *Ordinat* driver; **p. d'affichage** display driver; **p. d'imprimante** printer driver
2 *adj* **installation(-)p.** pilot plant; **université(-)p.** experimental university

piloter [pilɔte] *vt* (**a**) *(navire)* to pilot; *(avion)* to pilot, to fly; *(voiture)* to drive; *(moto)* to ride; *Fig (projet)* to be in charge of; *(touriste)* to show round (**b**) *Ordinat* to drive; **piloté par menu** menu-driven

pilotis [pilɔti] *nmpl* stilts

pilule [pilyl] *nf* pill, tablet; **la p.** *(contraceptif)* the pill; **prendre la p.** to be on the pill; **p. abortive** abortion pill; **p. du lendemain** morning-after pill

pimbêche [pɛ̃bɛʃ] **1** *nf (fille)* stuck-up girl; *(femme)* stuck-up woman
2 *adj* stuck-up

piment [pimɑ̃] *nm* (**a**) *(piquant)* chilli; **p. doux** (sweet) pepper (**b**) *Fig* spice

pimenter [pimɑ̃te] *vt aussi Fig* to spice up

pimpant, -e [pɛ̃pɑ̃, ɑ̃t] *adj* smart

pin [pɛ̃] *nm* pine; **p. maritime** maritime pine; **p. parasol** umbrella pine; **p. sylvestre** Scots pine

pinacle [pinakl] *nm* **être au p.** to be at the top; **porter qn au p.** to praise sb to the skies

pinailler [pinaje] *vi Fam* to nitpick *(sur* over)

pinailleur, -euse [pinajœr, -øz] *Fam* **1** *adj* nitpicking
2 *nm,f* nitpicker

pinard [pinar] *nm Fam* wine, *Br* plonk

pince [pɛ̃s] *nf* (**a**) *(outil)* pliers; *(de forgeron)* tongs; **p. à cheveux** hair clip; **p. crocodile** crocodile clip; **p. à épiler** tweezers; **p. à linge** clothes peg; **p. à sucre** sugar tongs; **p. à vélo** bicycle clip (**b**) *(des crustacés)* pincer, claw (**c**) *(sur un vêtement)* dart (**d**) *Fam* **serrer la p. à qn** to shake hands with sb (**e**) *Fam* **à pinces** on foot

pincé, -e [pɛ̃se] *adj (air)* stiff, starchy; *(sourire)* tight-lipped; *(lèvres)* pursed

pinceau, -x [pɛ̃so] *nm (brosse)* brush, paintbrush; **avoir un bon coup de p.** to be a good painter

pincée [pɛ̃se] *nf* pinch

pincement [pɛ̃smɑ̃] *nm* (**a**) **avoir un p. au cœur** *(être ému)* to feel a pang of sadness (**b**) *(fait de pincer)* pinching; *(des cordes d'un instrument)* plucking

pince-monseigneur *(pl* **pinces-monseigneur)** [pɛ̃smɔ̃seɲœr] *nf* jemmy

pince-nez [pɛ̃sne] *nm inv* pince-nez

pincer [16] [pɛ̃se] **1** *vt* (**a**) *(serrer)* to pinch, to nip; *(lèvres)* to purse; *(cordes d'un instrument)* to pluck (**b**) *Fam (attraper)* to catch; **se faire p.** to get caught (**c**) *Fam* **en p. pour qn** to be crazy about sb (**d**) *Fam* **ça pince** it's freezing
2 **se pincer** *vpr* **se p. le doigt** to catch one's finger; **se p. le nez** to hold one's nose

pince-sans-rire [pɛ̃sɑ̃rir] **1** *nmf inv* person with a dry sense of humour
2 *adj inv* dry, deadpan

pincette [pɛ̃sɛt] *nf* (**a**) *(petite pince)* tweezers; **pincettes** *(à feu)* (fire) tongs; *Fig* **il n'est pas à prendre avec des pincettes** he's like a bear with a sore head (**b**) *Suisse (pince à linge)* clothes peg

pinçon [pɛ̃sɔ̃] *nm* pinch mark

pinède [pinɛd] *nf* pine wood

pingouin [pɛ̃gwɛ̃] *nm* auk; *(manchot)* penguin

ping-pong [piŋpɔ̃g] *nm* table tennis, Ping-Pong®

pingre [pɛ̃gr] *adj* stingy

pingrerie [pɛ̃grəri] *nf* stinginess

pin's [pinz] *nm inv* badge

pinson [pɛ̃sɔ̃] *nm* chaffinch

pintade [pɛ̃tad] *nf* guinea fowl

pinte [pɛ̃t] *nf (ancienne mesure)* pint *(0.93 litres)*; *(au Royaume-Uni, aux États-Unis)* pint; *Can* quart

pinter [pɛ̃te] *Fam* **1** *vi* to booze
2 **se pinter** *vpr* to get sozzled

pinteur, -euse [pɛ̃tœr, -øz] *nm,f Belg & Suisse Fam* boozer, alkie

pin-up [pinœp] *nf inv* pin-up

pioche [pjɔʃ] *nf* (**a**) *(outil)* pick, pickaxe (**b**) *(aux cartes, aux dominos)* stock, pile

piocher [pjɔʃe] **1** *vt (creuser)* to dig *(with a pick)*
  2 *vi (aux cartes, aux dominos)* to pick up; *Fig* **p. dans qch** *(tas)* to plunge one's hand into sth; *(économies, réserves)* to dip into sth

piolet [pjɔlɛ] *nm* ice axe

pion¹ [pjɔ̃] *nm (de jeu de société)* piece; *(aux échecs)* pawn; *(aux dames) Br* draught, *Am* checker; *Fig* **n'être qu'un p. (sur l'échiquier)** to be only a pawn in the game

pion², pionne [pjɔ̃, pjɔn] *nm,f Fam (surveillant)* supervisor *(paid to supervise pupils outside class hours)*

Pion

In French lycées, the "pions" (officially called "surveillants") are responsible for supervising pupils outside class hours; they are often university students who do the job to make a little extra money.

---

pioncer [16] [pjɔ̃se] *vi Fam* to sleep

pionnier, -ère [pjɔnje, -ɛr] *nm,f aussi Fig* pioneer

pipe [pip] *nf* (**a**) *(de fumeur)* pipe; *Fam Fig* **casser sa p.** to kick the bucket (**b**) *Vulg* **faire** *ou* **tailler une p. à qn** to give sb a blowjob

pipeau, -x [pipo] *nm Mus* (reed) pipe; *Fam* **c'est du p.** it's all claptrap

pipelette [piplɛt] *nf Fam* gossip

pipeline, pipe-line (*pl* **pipe-lines**) [piplin, pajplajn] *nm* pipeline

piper [pipe] *vt* (**a**) *(dés)* to load; *(cartes)* to mark; *Fig* **les dés sont pipés** the dice are loaded (**b**) **ne pas p. (mot)** to keep mum

pipette [pipɛt] *nf* pipette; *Suisse* **ça ne vaut pas p.** it's not worth a bean *or* a red cent

pipi [pipi] *nm Fam* pee; **faire p.** to pee; **faire p. au lit** to wet the bed; *Fam Péj* **c'est du p. de chat** *(boisson)* it's dishwater

piquant, -e [pikɑ̃, ɑ̃t] **1** *adj* (**a**) *(au goût)* spicy, hot; *(moutarde)* hot (**b**) *(plante)* prickly, thorny; *(barbe)* prickly; *(vent)* biting (**c**) *Fig (détail, style, situation)* piquant; *(histoire)* spicy; **une petite brune piquante** a striking little brunette
  2 *nm* (**a**) *(d'une plante)* thorn; *(d'un porc-épic, d'un hérisson)* spine; *(de barbelé)* spike, barb (**b**) *(d'un style, d'une situation)* piquancy; *(d'une histoire)* spice; **avoir du p.** *(femme)* to be striking

pique¹ [pik] **1** *nf (arme)* pike; *(d'un picador)* lance
  2 *nm (carte)* spade; *(couleur)* spades

pique² *nf (méchanceté)* spiteful remark; **envoyer** *ou* **lancer des piques à qn** to have a go at sb

piqué, -e [pike] **1** *adj* (**a**) *(bois)* wormeaten; *(livre)* foxed; *(miroir)* tarnished; *(métal)* pitted; *Fam* **une histoire/angine pas piquée des hannetons** *ou* **des vers** one heck of a story/sore throat (**b**) *(vin)* sour (**c**) *Fam (fou)* bonkers (**d**) *Mus (note)* staccato
  2 *nm* (**a**) *Aviat* **descente en p.** nose dive (**b**) *(tissu)* piqué

pique-assiette (*pl* **pique-assiettes**) [pikasjɛt] *nmf Fam* scrounger, sponger

pique-feu [pikfø] *nm inv* poker

pique-nique (*pl* **pique-niques**) [piknik] *nm* picnic; **faire un p.** to have a picnic

pique-niquer [piknike] *vi* to have a picnic, to picnic

piquer [pike] **1** *vt* (**a**) *(avec une pointe)* to prick; *(sujet: guêpe)* to sting; *(sujet: puce, moustique)* to bite; *(cheval)* to spur on; *(bœuf)* to goad; **la fumée me pique les yeux** the smoke is making my eyes sting; **ça me pique la gorge/le nez** it tickles my throat/nose (**b**) *Fam (faire une piqûre à)* **p. qn** to give sb an injection; **p. un chien** to put a dog down, to put a dog to sleep (**c**) *Fam (voler)* to pinch, *Br* to nick (**à** from); **je me suis fait p. mon stylo** my pen got pinched *or Br* nicked (**d**) *(coudre)* to stitch (**e**) *(enfoncer)* to stick (**dans** into) (**f**) *Fam* **p. un cent mètres** to sprint off; **p. une crise** to throw a fit; **p. une tête** to dive (**g**) *(vexer)* **p. qn au vif** to cut sb to the quick (**h**) *(exciter)* **p. la curiosité de qn** to arouse *or* excite sb's curiosity (**i**) *(sujet: acide, vers)* to eat into; *(sujet: humidité)* to spot, to mark (**j**) *Culin* **p. qch d'ail** to stick garlic into sth
  2 *vi* (**a**) *Aviat* **p. (du nez)** to nosedive; *Fig* **p. du nez** *(s'assoupir)* to nod off; *(baisser les yeux)* to look down (**b**) *(plat)* to be spicy *or* hot; *(vin)* to be sour (**c**) *(guêpe)* to sting; *(puce, moustique)* to bite; *(plante)* to be prickly; **tu piques!** *(à un homme mal rasé)* you're all bristly!
  3 se piquer *vpr* (**a**) *(se blesser)* to prick oneself; **se p. le doigt** to prick one's finger (**b**) *(se faire une piqûre)* to give oneself an injection; *Fam (se droguer)* to shoot up; **se p. à l'héroïne** to shoot heroin (**c**) *(se vexer)* to take offence (**d**) *(vin)* to (turn) sour (**e**) *(locutions)* **se p. au jeu** to get into it; *Litt* **se p. de faire qch** to pride oneself on doing sth

piquet [pikɛ] *nm* (**a**) *(pieu)* stake, post; *(de tente)* peg (**b**) *Vieilli Scol* **mettre** *ou* **envoyer qn au p.** to send sb to stand in the corner (**c**) **p. de grève** picket

piquette [pikɛt] *nf* (**a**) *Péj (vin)* cheap wine, *Br* plonk (**b**) *Fam (défaite)* **prendre une** *ou* **la p.** to get a hammering

piqûre [pikyr] *nf* (**a**) *(de guêpe)* sting; *(de puce, de moustique)* bite; **p. d'épingle** pinprick (**b**) *Méd* injection, shot; **faire une p. à qn** to give sb an injection (**c**) **piqûres** *(d'un tissu, du cuir)* stitching (**d**) *(de rouille, de moisi)* spot, speck

piranha [pirana] *nm* piranha

piratage [pirataʒ] *nm* pirating; **p. informatique** hacking

pirate [pirat] **1** *nm* (**a**) *(des mers)* pirate; **p. de l'air** hijacker, skyjacker; **p. informatique** hacker (**b**) *(escroc)* crook
  2 *adj (radio, enregistrement)* pirate

pirater [pirate] *vt (enregistrement, cassette)* to pirate; *Ordinat* to hack

piraterie [piratri] *nf* (**a**) *(sur les mers)* piracy (**b**) *Fig (escroquerie)* swindling

pire [pir] **1** *adj* (**a**) *(comparatif)* worse; **c'est de p. en p.** it's getting worse and worse; *Can Fam* **p. que p.** dire, as bad as it can get (**b**) *(superlatif)* worst
  2 *nm* **le p., c'est que…** the worst thing about it is…; **craindre le/s'attendre au p.** to fear/to expect the worst; **au p....** if the worst comes to the worst…

pirogue [pirɔg] *nf* dugout (canoe)

pirouette [pirwɛt] *nf* (**a**) *(tour sur soi-même)* pirouette; *(saut périlleux)* somersault; **faire un p.** to pirouette (**b**) *Fig (dérobade)* flippant answer; **s'en tirer par une p.** to answer flippantly

pis¹ [pi] *nm (mamelle)* udder

pis² **1** *adv* **aller de mal en p.** to go from bad to worse
  2 *adj Litt* worse
  3 *nm* (**a**) *Litt (comparatif)* worse; **il y a p.** there is/are

worse (**b**) *Litt (superlatif)* worst; **au p.** if the worst comes to the worst; **au p. aller** at the very worst (**c**) **dire p. que pendre de qn** to call sb every name under the sun

pis-aller [pizale] *nm inv* stopgap (solution)

pisciculture [pisikyltyr] *nf* fish farming

piscine [pisin] *nf* (swimming) pool; **p. couverte/en plein air** indoor/outdoor pool

Pise [piz] *n* Pisa

pisse [pis] *nf très Fam* piss, pee

pisse-froid [pisfrwa] **1** *adj inv* **il est très p.** he's a bit of a cold fish

2 *nm inv Fam* cold fish

pissenlit [pisāli] *nm* dandelion; *Fam* **manger les pissenlits par la racine** to be pushing up the daisies

pisser [pise] **1** *vi* (**a**) *très Fam (uriner)* to piss; **c'est comme si je pissais dans un violon** it's like pissing in the wind; **laisse p.!** forget it!; **c'était à p. de rire** we were wetting ourselves (**b**) *Fam (fuir)* to leak

2 *vt* (**a**) *très Fam* **p. du sang** to piss blood (**b**) *Fam* **son bras pissait le sang** blood was pouring from his arm

pisseux, -euse [pisø, -øz] *adj Fam (couleur)* washed out

pissotière [pisɔtjɛr] *nf Fam* (public) urinal

pistache [pistaʃ] **1** *nf (graine)* pistachio (nut); **glace à la p.** pistachio ice cream

2 *adj inv (couleur)* pistachio (green)

piste [pist] *nf* (**a**) *(trace)* track, trail; *(indices)* lead; **être sur la p. de qn** to be on sb's track; **suivre une fausse p.** to be on the wrong track (**b**) *Sport* track; *(de courses de chevaux)* Br racecourse, Am racetrack; *(de course automobile)* racetrack; *(de ski)* run, piste; *(de cirque)* ring; **p. artificielle** *(de ski)* artificial *or* dry ski slope; **p. de danse** dance floor (**c**) *Aviat* runway; **p. d'atterrissage** landing strip; *(dans la brousse, dans la forêt)* airstrip (**d**) *(chemin)* track, trail; **p. cyclable** cycle path (**e**) *(de magnétophone, de disque)* track; *Ordinat* **p. d'amorçage** boot track; *Ordinat* **p. magnétique** magnetic stripe

pister [piste] *vt (animal)* to track; *(personne)* to tail

pistil [pistil] *nm Bot* pistil

pistolet [pistɔlɛ] *nm* (**a**) *(arme à feu)* pistol, gun; **p. à air comprimé** air pistol; **p. à eau** water pistol (**b**) *(à peinture)* paint gun

pistolet-mitrailleur *(pl* **pistolets-mitrailleurs)** [pistɔlɛmitrajœr] *nm* submachine-gun

piston [pistɔ̃] *nm* (**a**) *Tech* piston (**b**) *Fam Fig (recommandation)* string-pulling; **il a eu la place par p.** someone pulled some strings to get him the job (**c**) *(d'instrument à vent)* valve

pistonner [pistɔne] *vt Fam* to pull strings for; **elle s'est fait p.** she got someone to pull strings for her

pistou [pistu] *nm (sauce)* pesto; *(soupe)* vegetable soup with pesto

pita [pita] *nf* pitta bread

pitance [pitãs] *nf Vieilli (nourriture)* sustenance

pit-bull *(pl* **pit-bulls)** [pitbul] *nm* pit bull (terrier)

piteux, -euse [pitø, -øz] *adj* (**a**) *(mauvais) (résultat)* poor, pitiful; **en p. état** in a sorry state (**b**) *(honteux)* shamefaced

pithiviers [pitivje] *nm Culin* = cake made of puff pastry containing rum and almond-flavoured cream

pitié [pitje] *nf* (**a**) *(compassion)* pity; **avoir p. de qn** to pity sb; **il me faisait p.** I felt sorry for him; **faire p. (à voir)** to be a pitiful sight; **être sans p.** to be ruthless; **(par) p.!** *(pour demander grâce)* (have) mercy!;

(exprime l'agacement) for pity's sake! (**b**) *(tristesse)* **quelle p.!** what a terrible shame!

piton [pitɔ̃] *nm* (**a**) *Tech* eye bolt; *(d'alpiniste)* piton (**b**) *(sommet)* **p. (rocheux)** (rocky) peak

pitoyable [pitwajabl] *adj* (**a**) *(digne de pitié)* pitiful (**b**) *Péj (excuse, plaisanterie)* pathetic

pitre [pitr] *nm* clown; **faire le p.** to clown around

pitrerie [pitrəri] *nf* piece of clowning; **pitreries** clowning

pittoresque [pitɔrɛsk] *adj (lieu)* picturesque; *(description, style)* vivid

pivert [pivɛr] *nm* green woodpecker

pivoine [pivwan] *nf* peony

pivot [pivo] *nm* (**a**) *(axe)* pivot; *(de levier)* fulcrum; *(de compas, de boussole)* centre pin; *(en dentisterie)* post (**b**) *Fig (d'un drame, d'une argumentation)* pivot (**c**) *(au basket)* pivot, post

pivotant, -e [pivɔtã, ãt] *adj (grue, lampe)* swivelling; *(présentoir)* revolving

pivoter [pivɔte] *vi* to pivot, to swivel (**sur** on); **faire p. qch** to swivel sth round

pixel [piksɛl] *nm Ordinat* pixel

pixélisé, -e [pikselize] *adj Ordinat* bit-mapped

pizza [pidza] *nf* pizza

pizzeria [pidzerja] *nf* pizzeria

PJ [peʒi] *nf Fam (abrév* **police judiciaire)** *Br* ≃ CID, *Am* ≃ FBI

placage [plakaʒ] *nm* (**a**) *(bois)* veneer; *(métal)* plating (**b**) *(au rugby)* tackle

placard [plakar] *nm* (**a**) *(armoire)* cupboard; *Fam Fig* **mettre qn au p.** to sideline sb; *Fam Fig* **mettre qch au p.** to put sth on ice, to shelve sth (**b**) *(affiche)* poster (**c**) *Fam (prison)* slammer, clink

placarder [plakarde] *vt (affiche)* to stick up, to put up; **p. un mur d'affiches** to cover a wall with posters

place [plas] *nf* (**a**) *(endroit, rôle)* place; **changer qch de p.** to move sth; *Fig* **se mettre à la p. de qn** to put oneself in sb's position; **mettre qch en p.** to put sth in place; **être en p.** *(objet)* to be in place; *(au pouvoir)* to be in office; **les gens en p.** people in high places; *Fig* **remettre qn à sa p.** to put sb in his/her place; **il ne tient pas en p.** he can't keep still; **à la p. de qn** *(au lieu de)* instead of sb; **à votre p....** if I were you...; **sur p.** on the spot; **faire p. nette** to have a clearout; **p. de parking** parking place *or* space (**b**) *(espace)* room, space; **prendre beaucoup de p.** to take up a lot of room *or* space; **faire de la p. à qn** to make room for sb; *Fig* **faire p. à qn/qch** to make way for sb/sth (**c**) *(siège)* seat; **(voiture à) deux/quatre places** two-/four-seater (car); **prendre p.** to take a seat; **p. assise** seat; **p. debout** *(billet)* standing ticket; **la p. du mort** the passenger seat (**d**) *(poste)* job, post; *Suisse* **p. de travail** job (**e**) *(lieu public)* square; **p. du marché** market place (**f**) *(rang)* place (**g**) *Mil* **p. forte** fortified town (**h**) *Com & Fin* market; **sur la p. de Paris** on the Paris market; **p. financière** financial market (**i**) *Belg (pièce d'habitation)* room

placé, -e [plase] *adj* **être bien/mal p. pour faire qch** to be well/badly placed to do sth

placebo [plasebo] *nm* placebo

placement [plasmã] *nm* (**a**) *(d'argent)* investment; **faire des placements** to invest (money) (**b**) *(à un emploi)* placement, placing

placenta [plasɛ̃ta] *nm* placenta

placer [16] [plase] **1** *vt* (**a**) *(mettre à sa place)* to place, to put; *(faire asseoir)* to seat (**b**) *(procurer un emploi à* to find a job for, to place; **p. qn comme apprenti chez qn** to apprentice sb to sb (**c**) *(vendre)* to sell (**d**) *(dans la conversation)* to get in; *Fam* **avec elle, on ne peut pas en p. une!** you can't get a word in edgeways with her! (**e**) *(argent)* to invest

2 se placer *vpr* (**a**) *(debout)* to stand; *(assis)* to sit (**b**) **se p. sous la protection de qn** to place oneself under sb's protection; **il faut se p. dans son optique** you have to look at things from her point of view (**c**) *(trouver un emploi)* to find a job

placide [plasid] *adj* placid, calm

placoter [plakɔte] *vi Can Fam* to chat

plafond [plafɔ̃] *nm aussi Fig* ceiling; **être haut/bas de p.** to have a high/low ceiling; **prix/vitesse p.** maximum price/speed

plafonner [plafɔne] *vi (quantité, salaire)* to have reached a ceiling (**à** of)

plafonnier [plafɔnje] *nm* ceiling light

plage [plaʒ] *nf* (**a**) *(grève)* beach; **aller en vacances à la p.** to go on holiday to the seaside; **p. de sable/de galets** sandy/pebble beach (**b**) *(surface)* area (**c**) *(dans un emploi du temps, à la télé, à la radio)* slot; **p. horaire** time slot (**d**) *(d'un disque)* track (**e**) **p. arrière** *(d'une voiture)* back shelf

plagiaire [plaʒjɛr] *nmf* plagiarist

plagiat [plaʒja] *nm* plagiarism

plagier [66] [plaʒje] *vt* to plagiarize

plaid [plɛd] *nm* travelling rug

plaider [plede] **1** *vt* to plead; **p. coupable/non coupable** to plead guilty/not guilty; **p. la cause de qn** *Jur* to plead sb's case; *Fig* to plead sb's cause

2 *vi (avocat)* to plead; **p. pour/contre qn** to defend/prosecute sb; *Fig* **p. en faveur de qn/qch** to speak for sb/sth, to defend sb/sth

plaidoirie [pledwari] *nf Jur* speech for the defence

plaidoyer [pledwaje] *nm Jur* speech for the defence; *Fig* plea

plaie [plɛ] *nf* (**a**) *aussi Fig* wound (**b**) *(fléau)* affliction, scourge; *(personne, chose)* pest, nuisance

plaignant, -e [plɛɲɑ̃, -ɑ̃t] *nm,f Jur* plaintiff

plaindre [23] [plɛ̃dr] **1** *vt* to pity, to feel sorry for; **je vous plains de voyager dans ces conditions** I feel sorry for you having to travel in these conditions; **elle n'est pas à p.** she's got nothing to worry about

2 se plaindre *vpr* (**a**) *(protester)* to complain; **se p. de** to complain about; *(douleur)* to complain of (**b**) *(gémir)* to moan

plaine [plɛn] *nf* plain

plain-pied [plɛ̃pje] **de plain-pied** *adv (pièce)* on the same level (**avec** as); *(maison)* single-storey

plainte [plɛ̃t] *nf* (**a**) *(protestation)* complaint (**b**) *(gémissement)* moan (**c**) *Jur* complaint; **porter p. contre qn (auprès de)** to lodge a complaint against sb (with); **p. contre X** complaint against person or persons unknown

plaintif, -ive [plɛ̃tif, -iv] *adj* plaintive

plaire [55a] [plɛr] **1** *vi* (**a**) *(être apprécié)* **cet homme me plaît** I like this man; **ce livre/film m'a plu** I liked *or* enjoyed the book/film; **cette offre devrait lui p.** the offer should appeal to him; **ça plaît beaucoup** it's very popular; **je fais ce qui me plaît** I do whatever I want; **que cela te plaise ou non** whether you like it or not (**b**) *(se rendre agréable)* to please; **rien à faire, elle ne plaît pas** *(physiquement)* no matter what she does, no one finds her attractive

2 *v impersonnel* **s'il te/vous plaît** please; **s'il vous plaît!** *(dit par un client)* excuse me!; *Belg (dit par un serveur)* here you are!; **et pas n'importe qui, s'il vous plaît** and not just anybody, if you please; **comme il vous plaira** just as you like

3 se plaire *vpr* (**a**) *(soi-même)* **elle se plaît dans cette robe** she likes herself in that dress (**b**) *(l'un l'autre)* to like each other (**c**) *(se trouver bien)* **je me plais beaucoup à Paris** I'm very happy in Paris; **se p. à faire qch** to enjoy *or* like doing sth

plaisance [plɛzɑ̃s] *nf* **la (navigation de) p.** boating

plaisancier, -ère [plɛzɑ̃sje, -ɛr] *nm,f* (amateur) yachtsman, *f* yachtswoman

plaisant, -e [plɛzɑ̃, -ɑ̃t] **1** *adj* (**a**) *(agréable)* pleasant, agreeable (**b**) *(drôle)* funny, amusing

2 *nm* **mauvais p.** malicious joker

plaisanter [plɛzɑ̃te] **1** *vi* to joke; **dire qch en plaisantant** to say sth as a joke; **vous plaisantez!** you're joking!; **on ne plaisante pas avec la santé** you shouldn't take any chances with your health

2 *vt* to tease, to poke fun at (**sur** about)

plaisanterie [plɛzɑ̃tri] *nf (acte, propos)* joke; **elle ne comprend pas la p.** she can't take a joke; **par p.** for a joke; **tourner qch en p.** to make a joke out of sth; **les plaisanteries les plus courtes sont les meilleures** brevity is the soul of wit

plaisantin [plɛzɑ̃tɛ̃] *nm* joker

plaise *etc voir* **plaire**

plaisir [plezir] *nm* (**a**) *(sensation agréable)* pleasure; **j'ai le p. de vous apprendre que…** I'm pleased to be able to tell you that…; **faire qch pour le p.** to do sth for fun; *Ironique* **je vous souhaite bien du p.!** the best of luck!; **ça m'a fait p. de te revoir** I was pleased to see you again; **ça me ferait p. que tu viennes** I'd be pleased if you came; **fais-moi p., viens danser** do me a favour, come and dance; **si cela peut te faire p.** if it makes you happy; **il va se faire un p. de te téléphoner demain** he'll be only too pleased to phone you tomorrow; **cela fait p. à voir** it's good to see; **prendre p. à qch/à faire qch** to enjoy sth/doing sth; **les plaisirs de la table** fine food and wine (**b**) *(distraction)* pleasure; **c'est son plus grand p.** it's his greatest pleasure

plan¹, -e [plɑ̃, plan] **1** *adj (terrain, surface)* flat; *Math* plane

2 *nm* (**a**) *Math* plane (**b**) *(surface)* **p. de cuisson** hob; **p. d'eau** lake; **p. incliné** inclined plane; **p. de travail** *(d'une cuisine)* worktop (**c**) *Cin, Phot & Fig* **au premier p.** in the foreground; **au second p.** in the background; **un artiste de premier p.** a leading artist; **sur le même p. (que)** on the same level (as); **sur le p. politique/économique** from a political/an economic point of view; **gros p.** close-up; **en gros p.** in close-up

plan² *nm* (**a**) *(relevé)* plan; *(carte) (de ville)* map; **p. d'occupation des sols** land-use map (**b**) *(projet)* plan; *Fam* **j'ai un bon p. pour les vacances** I've got a great idea for the holidays; **p. de carrière** career strategy; **p. social** = corporate restructuring plan, usually involving job losses (**c**) *(d'un roman, d'un devoir)* plan, framework (**d**) *Fin* **p. d'épargne** savings plan; **p. d'épargne en actions** personal equity plan, PEP; **p. d'épargne-logement** = savings plan entitling savers to low mortgages, *Br* ≃ building society account, *Am* ≃ savings and loan association account; **p. d'épargne-retraite** personal pension plan

plan³ *nm Fam* **laisser qn en p.** to leave sb in the lurch; **tout laisser en p.** to drop everything

planant, -e [planɑ̃, ɑ̃t] *adj Fam* mind-blowing

planche [plɑ̃ʃ] *nf* (**a**) *(pièce de bois)* plank; *(plus large)* board; **faire la p.** *(flotter)* to float on one's back; *Fam* **c'est une vraie p. à pain** she's as flat as a pancake; **p. à découper** chopping board; **p. à dessin** drawing board; **p. à repasser** ironing board; **p. de salut** last hope (**b**) *Théât* **monter sur les planches** to go on the stage, to tread the boards (**c**) *(d'imprimerie, de gravure)* plate, block (**d**) *Sport* **p. (de surf)** surfboard; **p. (à voile)** windsurfer; *Can* **p. à neige** snowboard; **p. à roulettes** skateboard; **faire de la p. à roulettes** to skateboard; **faire de la p. à voile** to go windsurfing

plancher[1] [plɑ̃ʃe] *nm* (**a**) *(sol)* floor; *Fam* **le p. des vaches** dry land, terra firma; *Fig* **mettre le pied au p.** to put one's foot down (**b**) *Fig (minimum)* minimum; **prix p.** bottom price

plancher[2] **1** *vi Fam Scol* to have an exam
2 plancher sur *vt ind* **p. sur un problème** to work on a problem

plancton [plɑ̃ktɔ̃] *nm* plankton

plané [plane] *adj m voir* **vol**

planer [plane] *vi* (**a**) *(oiseau, planeur)* to glide; *(brume, fumée)* to hang; *Fig* **p. sur qn/qch** *(danger)* to hang over sb/sth (**b**) *Fam (se sentir bien)* to be floating on air, to be on a high; *(après s'être drogué)* to be high; *(rêver)* to dream

planétaire [planetɛr] *adj* (**a**) *Astron* planetary (**b**) *(expansion, action)* worldwide

planétarium [planetarjɔm] *nm* planetarium

planète [planɛt] *nf* planet

planeur [planœr] *nm (avion)* glider

planification [planifikasjɔ̃] *nf Écon* planning

planifier [66] [planifje] *vt* to plan

planisphère [planisfɛr] *nm* planisphere

planning [planiŋ] *nm* schedule; **p. familial** family planning; *(lieu)* family planning clinic

planque [plɑ̃k] *nf Fam* (**a**) *(d'un gangster)* hideout; *(pour un butin)* hiding place (**b**) *(travail facile)* cushy job

planqué, -e [plɑ̃ke] *nm,f Fam* person with a cushy job; *Mil* draft dodger

planquer [plɑ̃ke] *Fam* **1** *vt* to hide
2 se planquer *vpr* to hide

plant [plɑ̃] *nm (d'arbre)* sapling; *(de plante)* seedling

plantaire [plɑ̃tɛr] *adj Anat* plantar

plantation [plɑ̃tasjɔ̃] *nf (exploitation agricole)* plantation

plante[1] [plɑ̃t] *nf* **p. du pied** sole (of the foot)

plante[2] *nf (végétal)* plant; *Fam Fig* **une belle p.** *(femme)* a voluptuous woman; **p. d'appartement** house plant; **p. grasse** succulent (plant); **p. potagère** plant grown for food; **p. verte** house plant

planté, -e [plɑ̃te] *adj* (**a**) *(debout)* standing; *Fam* **rester p. (comme un piquet)** *(immobile)* to stand there doing nothing, *Br* to stand there like a lemon (**b**) **bien p.** *(robuste)* sturdy

planter [plɑ̃te] **1** *vt* (**a**) *(graines, fleurs, arbre)* to plant; **une colline plantée d'arbres** a hill planted with trees (**b**) *(clou)* to hammer in; *(tente)* to put up, to pitch; **p. un clou dans qch** to hammer a nail into sth; *Fig* **p. un baiser sur la joue à qn** to plant a kiss on sb's cheek (**c**) *Fam* **p. là qn** to dump sb; **il veut tout p. là** he wants to pack it all in (**d**) *Fam (tuer)* to knife to death
2 *vi Fam Ordinat* to go down, to crash
3 se planter *vpr* (**a**) *(se tenir immobile)* to stand (**b**)

Fam (se tromper) to get it wrong (**c**) *Fam (tomber)* to come a cropper (**d**) *Fam (en voiture)* to crash

planteur [plɑ̃tœr] *nm* (**a**) *(exploitant)* planter (**b**) *(cocktail)* planter's punch

plantigrade [plɑ̃tigrad] *nm Zool* plantigrade

planton [plɑ̃tɔ̃] *nm Mil* orderly

plantureux, -euse [plɑ̃tyrø, -øz] *adj (femme)* buxom; *(poitrine)* ample

plaquage [plakaʒ] = **placage** (**b**)

plaque [plak] *nf* (**a**) *(de métal)* plate, sheet; *(de marbre)* slab; *(de chocolat)* bar; *(de beurre)* pack; *(de verglas)* sheet; **p. chauffante** hotplate; **p. d'égout** manhole cover; *Fig* **p. tournante** hub, centre (**b**) *(sur une porte)* nameplate; *(commémorative)* plaque; **p. d'immatriculation** *ou* **minéralogique** *Br* number plate, *Am* license plate; **p. de rue** street sign (**c**) *(sur la peau)* patch; **p. (dentaire)** (dental) plaque (**d**) *Fam* **être à côté de la p.** to be wide of the mark

plaqué, -e [plake] **1** *adj* **p. or/argent** gold-/silver-plated
2 *nm* (**a**) **p. or/argent** gold/silver plate; **montre en p. or** gold-plated watch (**b**) *(bois)* veneered wood

plaquer [plake] **1** *vt* (**a**) *(cheveux)* to plaster down; **p. qn contre un mur** to pin sb against a wall (**b**) *Fam (petit ami)* to ditch, to chuck; **tout p.** to chuck it all in (**c**) *(au rugby)* to tackle (**d**) *Mus (accord)* to play (**e**) *(bois)* to veneer; *(métal)* to plate
2 se plaquer *vpr* **se p. au sol** to lie flat on the ground; **se p. contre un mur** to flatten oneself against a wall

plaquette [plakɛt] *nf* (**a**) *(de métal)* (small) plate; *(portant une inscription)* (small) plaque; *Ordinat* circuit board; *Aut* **p. de frein** brake pad (**b**) *(de chocolat)* bar; *(de beurre)* pack (**c**) *(petit livre)* booklet (**d**) *Méd* **plaquettes** (blood) platelets

plasma [plasma] *nm Biol & Phys* plasma

plastic [plastik] *nm* plastic explosive

plasticage [plastikaʒ] *nm* bombing (**de** of)

plastifier [66] [plastifje] *vt* to laminate

plastiquage [plastikaʒ] = **plasticage**

plastique [plastik] **1** *adj & nm* plastic
2 *nf* (**a**) *(art)* art of modelling (**b**) *(du corps)* figure

plastiquer [plastike] *vt* to bomb

plastron [plastrɔ̃] *nm* (**a**) *(de chemise)* shirt front (**b**) *(d'escrimeur)* plastron

plat, -e [pla, plat] **1** *adj* (**a**) *(sans relief)* flat, level; *(chaussure)* flat; *(mer)* smooth; *(eau)* still; *Fam* **plate comme une limande** *(femme)* as flat as a pancake (**b**) *Fig (ennuyeux)* flat, dull (**c**) **à p.** *(pneu, batterie)* flat; *Fam* **être à p.** *(épuisé)* to be run down; **mettre qch à p.** to lay sth (down) flat; *Fig* **tomber à p.** *(proposition, plaisanterie)* to fall flat; **se mettre à p. ventre** to lie face down; *Fig* **se mettre à p. ventre devant qn** to grovel to sb
2 *nm* (**a**) *(assiette)* dish; *Fig* **mettre les petits plats dans les grands** to put on a marvellous spread (**b**) *(mets)* dish; *(partie du menu)* course; *Fam* **en faire tout un p.** to make a song and dance about it; **p. cuisiné** ready meal; **p. du jour** today's special, dish of the day; *Fam Fig* **p. de nouilles** *Br* berk, *Am* meathead; **p. principal** *ou* **de résistance** main course (**c**) *(de la main, d'une épée)* flat (**d**) *(en cyclisme, en hippisme)* **sur le p.** on the flat (**e**) **faire un p.** *(en plongeant)* to do a bellyflop (**f**) *Fam* **faire du p. à qn** *Br* to chat sb up, *Am* to hit on sb

platane [platan] *nm* plane tree

plateau, -x [plato] *nm* (**a**) *(plat)* tray; **p. à fromages** cheeseboard; **p. de fruits de mer** seafood platter (**b**) *(d'une balance)* pan; *(d'une platine, d'un four micro-ondes)* turntable (**c**) *Géog* plateau; **haut p.** high plateau (**d**) *TV & Cin* set (**e**) *(de vélo)* chain wheel

plateau-repas *(pl* **plateaux-repas)** [platorəpa] *nm* meal on a tray

plate-bande *(pl* **plates-bandes)** [platbãd] *nf* flower bed; *Fam* **marcher sur les plates-bandes de qn** to tread on sb's toes

plate-forme *(pl* **plates-formes)** [platfɔrm] *nf* (**a**) *(surface plane)* platform; **p. pétrolière** *ou* **de forage** oil rig (**b**) *Géog* **p. continentale** continental shelf (**c**) *Ordinat* platform

platement [platmã] *adv* (**a**) *(s'exprimer, écrire)* dully (**b**) *(s'excuser)* humbly

platine¹ [platin] *nf* *(tourne-disque)* turntable; **p. cassettes** cassette *or* tape deck; **p. laser** CD player

platine² **1** *nm* platinum
2 *adj inv* **cheveux (blonds) p.** platinum blond hair

platiné, -e [platine] *adj* (**a**) *(recouvert de platine)* platinum-plated (**b**) *(cheveux)* platinum blond; **une blonde platinée** a platinum blonde

platitude [platityd] *nf* (**a**) *(manque d'intérêt)* dullness (**b**) *(propos)* platitude; **débiter des platitudes** to talk in platitudes

Platon [platɔ̃] *npr* Plato

platonique [platɔnik] *adj (amour)* platonic

plâtras [platra] *nmpl* (plaster) rubble

plâtre [platr] *nm* plaster; *(sculpture)* plaster cast; *(pour jambe cassée)* plaster (cast); **avoir la jambe dans le p.** to have one's leg in plaster; *Fig* **essuyer les plâtres** to have to put up with the teething problems

plâtrer [platre] *vt* (**a**) *(mur, plafond)* to plaster; *(trou, fissure)* to plaster over (**b**) *(jambe, bras)* to put in plaster

plâtreux, -euse [platrø, -øz] *adj (fromage)* chalky

plâtrier [platrije] *nm* plasterer

plausible [plozibl] *adj* plausible

play-back [plɛbak] *nm inv* miming; **chanter en p.** to mime

play-boy *(pl* **play-boys)** [plɛbɔj] *nm* playboy

plèbe [plɛb] *nf* **la p.** the plebs

plébéien, -enne [plebejɛ̃, -ɛn] *adj & nm,f* plebeian

plébiscite [plebisit] *nm* plebiscite

plébisciter [plebisite] *vt* (**a**) *(élire)* **p. qn/qch** to vote for sb/sth by plebiscite (**b**) *Fig* to endorse

pléiade [plejad] *nf* **une p. de** a host of

plein, -e [plɛ̃, plɛn] **1** *adj* (**a**) *(rempli)* full (**de** of); **il a les doigts pleins d'encre** his fingers are covered with ink; **p. à craquer** full to bursting; **p. comme un œuf** chock-full
(**b**) *(complet) (accord, pouvoirs)* full; **pleine lune** full moon; **pleine mer** high tide; **p. tarif** full price; *(de transports)* full fare; **travailler à p. temps** to work full-time
(**c**) *(solide)* solid
(**d**) *(en intensif)* **une pleine bouteille** a whole bottle; **p. sud** due south; **en p. (milieu du) désert/village** right in the middle of the desert/village; **en p. dans/ devant/sur** right in/in front of/on; **en pleine figure/ poitrine** right in the face/chest; **être en p. travail** to be hard at work; **en p. hiver** in the depths of winter; **en p. soleil** in the full heat of the sun
(**e**) *(animal)* pregnant
(**f**) *Fam (soûl)* plastered

2 *adv* **il avait des larmes p. les yeux** his eyes were full of tears; **elle avait de la colle p. les mains** her hands were covered with glue; **à p.** *(fonctionner)* at full capacity; *Fam* **gentil tout p.** really kind; *Fam* **p. de** *(beaucoup de)* lots *or* loads of
3 *nm* (**a**) *(d'essence)* **faire le p. (d'essence)** to fill up (with *Br* petrol *or Am* gas); **le p., s'il vous plaît** fill her up, please; *Fig* **faire le p. d'air pur/de soleil** to get a good dose of fresh air/of sunshine
(**b**) *(trait)* downstroke
(**c**) **battre son p.** to be in full swing

pleinement [plɛnmã] *adv* fully; **profiter p. de qch** to take full advantage of sth

plein-emploi [plɛ̃ãplwa] *nm* full employment

plénier, -ère [plenje, -ɛr] *adj* plenary

plénipotentiaire [plenipɔtãsjɛr] *adj & nm* plenipotentiary

plénitude [plenityd] *nf* fullness

pléonasme [pleɔnasm] *nm* pleonasm

pléthore [pletɔr] *nf* plethora (**de** of)

pleurer [plœre] **1** *vi* (**a**) *(verser des larmes)* to cry, to weep (**sur/pour** over/for); **p. sur son sort** to bewail one's fate; **p. de joie** to weep for joy; **p. de rage** to cry with rage; **p. à chaudes larmes**, *Fam* **p. comme une madeleine** *ou* **comme un veau** to cry one's eyes out; **bête/triste à p.** terribly stupid/sad; **j'ai les yeux qui pleurent** my eyes are watering (**b**) *Fig & Péj (réclamer plaintivement)* to beg; **aller p. auprès de qn** to go begging to sb
2 *vt* (**a**) *(regretter) (personne disparue)* to mourn (for) (**b**) **p. toutes les larmes de son corps** to cry one's eyes out

pleurésie [plœrezi] *nf* pleurisy

pleureur [plœrœr] *adj m voir* **saule**

pleureuse [plœrøz] *nf* (hired) mourner

pleurnichard, -e [plœrniʃar, -ard] = **pleurnicheur**

pleurnicher [plœrniʃe] *vi Fam* to whine

pleurnicheur, -euse [plœrniʃœr, -øz] *Fam* **1** *nm,f* whine
2 *adj* whining

pleurote [plœrɔt] *nm* oyster mushroom

pleurs [plœr] *nmpl* tears; **en p.** in tears

pleut *voir* **pleuvoir**

pleutre [pløtr] *adj & nm Litt* craven

pleuvoir [56] [pløvwar] **1** *v impersonnel* to rain; **il pleut** it's raining; **il pleut à verse** it's pouring (down); *Fam* **il pleut des cordes** it's coming down in buckets; *Fam* **il pleut comme vache qui pisse** it's chucking it down; **des cadeaux comme s'il en pleuvait** presents galore
2 *vi (obus, coups, insultes)* to rain down (**sur** on)

plèvre [plɛvr] *nf* pleura

Plexiglas® [plɛksiglas] *nm Br* Perspex®, *Am* Plexiglass®

plexus [plɛksys] *nm* plexus; **p. solaire** solar plexus

pli [pli] *nm* (**a**) *(de rideaux, de tissu, de papier)* fold; *(en couture)* pleat; **(faux) p.** crease; *Fig* **ça ne fait pas un p.** there's no doubt about it; *Fig* **prendre le p. (de faire qch)** to get into the habit (of doing sth); *Fig* **prendre un mauvais p.** to get into a bad habit (**b**) *(de la peau) (du ventre, du cou, du menton)* fold; *(de la bouche, des yeux)* wrinkle; *(du front)* line (**c**) *(enveloppe)* envelope; *(lettre)* letter; **sous p. séparé** under separate cover; **p. cacheté** sealed envelope; **envoyer qch sous p. cacheté** to send sth in a sealed envelope (**d**) *(aux cartes)* trick; **faire un p.** to take a trick (**e**) *Géol* fold

pliage [plijaʒ] *nm* folding

pliant, -e [plijɑ̃, -ɑ̃t] **1** *adj (chaise, table)* folding
  2 *nm* folding stool

plie [pli] *nf* plaice

plier [66] [plije] **1** *vt* (**a**) *(draps, vêtements)* to fold; *(page)* to turn down; *(voile)* to furl; *(parapluie, pliant)* to fold up; *Fig* **p. bagage** to pack one's bags (**b**) *(courber) (branche, genou)* to bend; *Fam Fig* **être plié de rire/de douleur** to be doubled up with laughter/with pain; **être plié en deux** *ou* **en quatre** *(de rire)* to be doubled up *or* bent double; **être plié en deux** *(de douleur)* to be doubled up *or* bent double; **p. qn à la discipline/une règle** to impose discipline/a rule on sb
  2 *vi* (**a**) *(se courber)* to bend (over); **p. sous le poids de qch** *(poutre, branches)* to bend under the weight of sth (**b**) *(se soumettre)* to submit, to yield; *(armée, troupes)* to give way
  3 se plier *vpr* (**a**) *(pouvoir être plié) (parapluie, chaise)* to fold up (**b**) *(se soumettre)* **se p. à la discipline** to submit to discipline; **se p. aux lois** to obey the law; **se p. aux caprices/volontés de qn** to give in to sb's whims/wishes

plinthe [plɛ̃t] *nf* (**a**) *(de mur) Br* skirting (board), *Am* baseboard (**b**) *(de colonne)* plinth

plissé, -e [plise] **1** *adj* (**a**) *(visage, front)* wrinkled (**b**) **jupe plissée** pleated skirt
  2 *nm* pleats

plissement [plismɑ̃] *nm* (**a**) *(des yeux)* screwing up (**b**) *Géol* fold

plisser [plise] **1** *vt* (**a**) *(front)* to wrinkle; *(lèvres)* to pucker; *(yeux)* to screw up (**b**) *(tissu, jupe)* to pleat
  2 *vi (vêtement)* to crease
  3 se plisser *vpr (étoffe)* to crease; *(bouche)* to pucker; *(yeux)* to wrinkle up; **son front se plissa** she frowned

pliure [plijyr] *nf (d'un tissu)* fold; *(de papier)* folding; *(du genou)* bend

plomb [plɔ̃] *nm* (**a**) *(métal)* lead; **ciel de p.** leaden sky; **soleil de p.** blazing sun; *Fig* **n'avoir pas de p. dans la tête** to be scatterbrained; **cela lui mettra un peu de p. dans la tête** *ou* **dans la cervelle** that'll knock some sense into him (**b**) *(de chasse)* shot; *Fam Fig* **avoir du p. dans l'aile** to be in a bad way (**c**) *Élec (fusible)* fuse; **faire sauter les plombs** to blow the fuses; *très Fam* **j'ai pété les plombs** I blew my top (**d**) *(pour la pêche)* sinker (**e**) *(sceau)* lead seal

plombage [plɔ̃baʒ] *nm* (**a**) *(fait de mettre des plombs)* weighting with lead (**b**) *(d'une dent)* filling

plombe [plɔ̃b] *nf Fam* hour

plombé, -e [plɔ̃be] *adj (toit)* lead(-covered); *Fig (teint)* livid; *(ciel)* leaden

plomber [plɔ̃be] **1** *vt* (**a**) *(couvrir de plomb)* to cover with lead (**b**) *(mettre des plombs à)* to weight with lead (**c**) *(dent)* to fill
  2 se plomber *vpr (ciel)* to become leaden

plomberie [plɔ̃bri] *nf (installations, métier)* plumbing

plombier [plɔ̃bje] *nm* plumber

plonge [plɔ̃ʒ] *nf Fam* dishwashing, *Br* washing up; **faire la p.** to wash dishes

plongeant, -e [plɔ̃ʒɑ̃, -ɑ̃t] *adj (tir, décolleté)* plunging; **vue plongeante (sur)** bird's-eye view (of)

plongée [plɔ̃ʒe] *nf* (**a**) *(discipline)* diving; **faire de la p.** to dive; **p. sous-marine** skin *or* scuba diving (**b**) *(de sous-marin)* dive (**c**) *Cin & TV* elevated shot; *(verticale)* bird's-eye view

plongeoir [plɔ̃ʒwar] *nm* diving board

plongeon [plɔ̃ʒɔ̃] *nm* (**a**) *(fait de plonger)* dive; **faire un p.** *(nageur, gardien de but)* to dive; *Fam Fig* **faire le p.** to hit the rocks (**b**) *(oiseau) Br* diver, *Am* loon

plonger [45] [plɔ̃ʒe] **1** *vi* (**a**) *(nageur, sous-marin)* to dive (**dans** into) (**b**) *(avion, oiseau)* to dive (**sur** onto)
  2 *vt aussi Fig* to plunge (**dans** into); **plongé dans ses pensées** lost *or* deep in thought; **la pièce fut plongée dans l'obscurité** the room was plunged into darkness
  3 se plonger *vpr* **se p. dans l'étude** to immerse oneself in one's studies

plongeur, -euse [plɔ̃ʒœr, -øz] **1** *nm,f* (**a**) *(dans l'eau)* diver; **p. sous-marin** skin *or* scuba diver (**b**) *Fam (dans un restaurant)* dishwasher, *Br* washer-up
  2 *nm (oiseau)* diver

plot [plo] *nm* (**a**) *Élec* contact (**b**) **p. de départ** starting block

plouc [pluk] *Péj* **1** *nm* yokel, peasant
  2 *adj Fam* naff; **ça fait p.!** that's really naff!

plouf [pluf] *exclam* plop!; *(objet plus lourd)* splash!

ploutocratie [plutɔkrasi] *nf* plutocracy

ployer [32] [plwaje] **1** *vi (courber)* to bend; *(plancher, poutre)* to sag; *(sous un joug, un fardeau)* to bend
  2 *vt* to bend

plu *voir* **plaire, pleuvoir**

pluie [plɥi] *nf* (**a**) *(précipitations)* rain; **pluies acides** acid rain; **p. battante** driving rain; **p. fine** drizzle; **temps de p.** rainy *or* wet weather; **sous la p.** in the rain; **parler de la p. et du beau temps** to talk of this and that; **il n'est pas tombé** *ou* **né de la dernière p.** he wasn't born yesterday; *Fam* **faire la p. et le beau temps** to rule the roost; *Prov* **après la p., le beau temps** it's a long road that has no turning (**b**) *Fig (de coups, de projectiles)* hail, shower; *(d'injures, de compliments)* stream

plumage [plymaʒ] *nm* plumage

plumard [plymar] *nm Fam* bed

plume [plym] *nf* (**a**) *(d'oiseau)* feather; *Fam Fig* **il y a laissé des plumes** he didn't come out of it unscathed; *Fam Fig* **on lui a volé dans les plumes** they laid into him; **léger comme une p.** as light as a feather; *Hum* **perdre ses plumes** to go thin on top (**b**) *(de stylo)* nib; **p. (d'oie)** quill (pen); **écrire au fil de la p.** to write just what comes into one's head; **dessin à la p.** pen (and ink) drawing; **prendre la p.** to put pen to paper; **vivre de sa p.** to live by one's pen; **avoir la p. facile** to have a gift for writing

plumeau, -x [plymo] *nm* feather duster

plumer [plyme] *vt (volaille)* to pluck; *Fam (personne)* to fleece

plumier [plymje] *nm* pencil box

plupart [plypar] *nf* **la p.** most; **la p. des gens/des cas** most people/cases; **la p. d'entre eux** most of them; **la p. du temps** most of the time; *(en général)* in most cases; **pour la p.** for the most part, mostly

pluralisme [plyralism] *nm* pluralism

pluridisciplinaire [plyridisiplinɛr] *adj* multi-disciplinary

pluriel, -elle [plyrjɛl] **1** *adj* plural
  2 *nm* plural; **au p.** in the plural

plus 1 *adv* [ply] (**a**) *(comparatif)* more; **je gagne p. que vous** I earn more than you (do); **il est p. grand que moi** he's taller than I am *or* than me; **elle est p. jolie que belle** she is pretty rather than beautiful; **p. de** *(temps, hommes)* more; *(avec un nombre)* more than; **il a p. de vingt ans** he's over twenty; **p.... p....** the more... the more...; **p.... moins...** the more... the less...; **p. on va vers le sud, p. les jours allongent** the further south you go, the longer the days get; **de p. en p.** more and more; **de p. en p. froid** colder and colder; **celui-ci coûte 10 francs de p. que l'autre** this one costs 10 francs more than the other one; **cette année, il y a trois élèves de** *ou* **en p.** this year there are three more *or* extra pupils; **le vin est en p.** the wine is extra; **de p.** *(aussi)* furthermore; **en p.** *(aussi)* what's more; **en p. de** besides; **sans p. attendre** without further ado

(**b**) *(superlatif)* **le p.** the most; **la p. longue rue** *ou* **la rue la p. longue de la ville** the longest street in the town; **c'est tout ce qu'il y a de p. simple** nothing could be simpler; **une soirée des p. réussies** a most successful evening; **qui peut le p. peut le moins** you've/he's/*etc* done more difficult things than that before

(**c**) *(indique la négation)* **ne... p.** no more, no longer; **je ne les vois p.** I don't see them any more, I no longer see them; **je ne le ferai p.** I won't do it again; **il n'y a p. rien** there's nothing left; **p. que dix minutes!** only ten minutes left!; **non p.** neither; **je ne suis jamais allé en Afrique – moi non p.** I've never been to Africa – neither *or* nor have I

(**d**) *(locutions)* **p. ou moins** more or less; **ni p. ni moins** no more no less; **sans p.** but no more than that

2 *conj* [plys] *(dans les calculs, dans les températures)* plus

3 *nm* [plys] (**a**) *(signe)* plus (sign)
(**b**) *Fig (atout)* plus

plusieurs [plyzjœr] *adj indéfini & pron indéfini* several

plus-que-parfait (*pl* **plus-que-parfaits**) [plyskəparfɛ] *nm* pluperfect, past perfect

plus-value (*pl* **plus-values**) [plyvaly] *nf (bénéfice)* profit; *(augmentation de la valeur)* appreciation; *(excédent) (d'impôts)* surplus; **impôt sur les plus-values** capital gains tax

Pluton [plytɔ̃] *npr (dieu, planète)* Pluto

plutonium [plytɔnjɔm] *nm* plutonium

plutôt [plyto] *adv* rather; *(à la place)* instead; **p. mourir!** I'd rather die!; **n'y va pas en voiture, prends p. le train** don't go by car, take the train instead; **p. que de faire qch** rather than doing sth

pluvial, -e, -aux, -ales [plyvjal, -o] *adj* pluvial; **eau pluviale** rainwater

pluvieux, -euse [plyvjø, -øz] *adj* rainy, wet

PME [peɛmə] *nf (abrév* **petite et moyenne entreprise***)* small business

PMI [peɛmi] *nf (abrév* **petite et moyenne industrie***)* small industrial firm

PMU [peɛmy] *nm (abrév* **Pari mutuel urbain***)* = state-run betting system

PNB [peɛnbe] *nm (abrév* **produit national brut***)* GNP

pneu [pnø] *nm* (**a**) *(de véhicule)* tyre; **avoir un p. à plat/crevé** to have a flat/a puncture; **p. à clous, p. clouté** studded tyre; *Can* **p. d'hiver** winter tyre; **p. neige** snow tyre; **p. pluie** wet-weather tyre; *Can* **p. quatre-saisons** all-season tyre (**b**) *(lettre)* express letter *(sent through a pneumatic dispatch system)*

pneumatique [pnømatik] **1** *adj (qui fonctionne à l'air)* pneumatic; *(gonflable)* inflatable
2 *nm =* **pneu**

pneumonie [pnømɔni] *nf* pneumonia

pneumothorax [pnømotɔraks] *nm* pneumothorax

poche [pɔʃ] *nf* (**a**) *(de vêtement)* pocket; **p. revolver** hip pocket; *Fam* **faire les poches à qn** to go through

sb's pockets; **de p.** pocket; **en être de sa p.** to be out of pocket; **payer de sa p.** to pay out of one's own pocket; *Fig* **connaître un endroit comme sa p.** to know a place like the back of one's hand; *Fam Fig* **se remplir les poches, s'en mettre plein les poches** to make a packet; **sans un sou en p.** without a penny in one's pocket; *Fam* **c'est dans la p.** it's in the bag
(**b**) *(sac)* bag; **p. de glace** ice pack
(**c**) *(amas de substance)* pocket; **p. de pétrole/gaz** pocket of oil/gas
(**d**) *(déformation)* **poches sous les yeux** bags under the eyes; **son pantalon fait des poches aux genoux** his trousers are baggy at the knees
(**e**) *(de kangourou)* pouch
(**f**) *(zone)* **p. de résistance/pauvreté** pocket of resistance/deprivation

pocher [pɔʃe] *vt* (**a**) *(œuf, poisson)* to poach (**b**) *Fam* **p. l'œil à qn** to give sb a black eye

pochette [pɔʃɛt] *nf* (**a**) *(petit sac)* (small) bag; *(d'un disque)* sleeve; *(de photos)* wallet; **p. d'allumettes** book of matches (**b**) *(mouchoir)* pocket handkerchief

pochette-surprise (*pl* **pochettes-surprises**) [pɔʃɛtsyrpriz] *nf* lucky bag; *Fam* **il a eu son permis dans une p.** it's a wonder he passed his driving test

pochoir [pɔʃwar] *nm* stencil

podiatre [pɔdiatr] *nmf Can Br* chiropodist, *Am* podiatrist

podium [pɔdjɔm] *nm* podium; **monter sur le p.** to mount the podium

poêle¹ [pwal] *nf* frying pan; **passer qch à la p.** to fry sth

poêle² [pwal] *nm (appareil de chauffage)* stove; **p. à mazout** oil stove

poêlon [pwalɔ̃] *nm* casserole (dish)

poème [pɔɛm] *nm* poem; *Fam* **ta fille, c'est (tout) un p.!** your daughter's really something else!

poésie [pɔezi] *nf* (**a**) *(art)* poetry (**b**) *(poème)* poem

poète [pɔɛt] *nm aussi Fig* poet

poétesse [pɔetɛs] *nf* poetess

poétique [pɔetik] *adj* poetic

poétiquement [pɔetikmɑ̃] *adv* poetically

pogne [pɔɲ] *nf Fam* paw

pognon [pɔɲɔ̃] *nm Fam* dough

pogrom(e) [pɔgrɔm] *nm* pogrom

poids [pwa] *nm* (**a**) *(masse)* weight; **de tout son p.** with all one's weight; **perdre/prendre du p.** to lose/gain weight; **vendre au p.** to sell by weight; *Fam* **il ne fait pas le p.** he's not up to scratch; **p. net/brut** net/gross weight; **p. léger** *(en boxe)* lightweight; **p. lourd** *(camion) Br* lorry, *Am* truck; *(en boxe)* heavyweight; **p. mouche** flyweight; **p. plume** *(en boxe)* featherweight; *Fig* lightweight (**b**) *Fig (charge pénible)* burden; *Litt* **le p. des ans** the weight of the years; **le p. des impôts** the burden of taxation (**c**) *Fig (importance)* weight; **donner du p. à qch** to give weight to sth; **avoir du p.** to carry weight; **faire deux poids deux mesures** to apply double standards (**d**) *(sport)* shot; **lancer le p.** to put the shot

poignant, -e [pwaɲɑ̃, -ɑ̃t] *adj* poignant

poignard [pwaɲar] *nm* dagger

poignarder [pwaɲarde] *vt* to stab; **se faire p.** to be stabbed

poigne [pwaɲ] *nf* grip; **avoir de la p.** to have a strong grip; *Fig* to be firm

poignée [pwaɲe] *nf* (**a**) *(quantité, petit nombre)* handful (**b**) *(de porte, de sac)* handle; *(d'épée)* hilt (**c**) **p. de main** handshake

poignet [pwaɲɛ] *nm* (**a**) *(du bras)* wrist; *Fig* **faire qch à la force du p.** to do sth by sheer hard work (**b**) *(de chemise)* cuff

poil [pwal] *nm* (**a**) *(d'un animal, d'une personne, d'une plante)* hair; *(pelage)* coat; *(d'une brosse, d'un pinceau)* bristle; **à p. long/ras** long-/short-haired; *Fam* **caresser qn dans le sens du p.** to rub sb up the right way; *Fam* **tomber sur le p. à qn** to lay into sb; *Fam* **à p.** stark naked; *Fam* **se mettre à p.** to strip off; *Fam* **avoir un p. dans la main** to be bone idle; *Fam* **reprendre du p. de la bête** to pick up again; *Fam Fig* **de tous poils** of all sorts; *Fam* **être de bon/mauvais p.** to be in a good/bad mood; *Fam* **au quart de p.** perfectly; *Fam* **à un p. près** very nearly; *Fam* **un p. plus haut/moins vite** a touch higher/slower; *Fam* **au p.** great; *Fam* **tomber au p.** to arrive at just the right moment (**b**) **p. à gratter** itching powder

poiler [pwale] **se poiler** *vpr Fam* to kill oneself laughing

poilu, -e [pwaly] **1** *adj* hairy
2 *nm Fam* poilu *(French soldier in the 1914–1918 war)*

poinçon [pwɛ̃sɔ̃] *nm (de graveur)* style; *(de cordonnier)* awl; *(marque)* hallmark

poinçonner [pwɛ̃sɔne] *vt (perforer)* to punch; *(or, argent)* to hallmark

poinçonneur, -euse [pwɛ̃sɔnœr, -øz] **1** *nm,f (personne)* ticket puncher
2 *nf* **poinçonneuse** punching machine

poindre [43] [pwɛ̃dr] *vi (jour)* to dawn, to break; *(plantes, étoiles)* to appear

poing [pwɛ̃] *nm* fist; **sabre/revolver au p.** sword/revolver in hand; **les poings sur les hanches** hands on hips, arms akimbo; **dormir à poings fermés** to sleep like a log

point¹ [pwɛ̃] *nm* (**a**) *(endroit)* point, spot; *(en géométrie)* point; **les quatre points cardinaux** the (four) points of the compass; *Ordinat* **p. de césure** breakpoint, hyphenation point; **p. chaud** *(zone de conflits)* hot spot, trouble spot; **p. de côté** *(douleur)* stitch; *aussi Fig* **p. de départ** starting point; **p. d'eau** *(dans le désert)* waterhole; **p. de mire** target; *Fig* focus; *Aut* **p. mort** neutral; *Fig* **être au p. mort** to be at a standstill; **p. noir** *(comédon)* blackhead; *(embouteillage)* blackspot; **p. de rencontre** meeting point; **p. de vente** *(magasin)* point of sale, sales outlet; **p. de vue** *(panorama)* viewpoint; *(opinion)* point of view; **du p. de vue international/économique** from an international/economic point of view

(**b**) *(marque)* dot; *(en fin de ligne)* Br full stop, Am period; *Fig* **mettre les points sur les i (à qn)** to make oneself perfectly clear (to sb); *Typ & Ordinat* **points par pouce** dots per inch; **deux points** colon; **p. d'exclamation** exclamation Br mark or Am point; **p. final** Br full stop, Am period; *Fam* **un p., c'est tout!, p. final!** and that's that!; *aussi Fig* **p. d'interrogation** question mark; **points de suspension** suspension points; *Ordinat* **p. de tabulation** tab marker

(**c**) *(aspect, question)* point; **en tous points** in every way, in all respects; **p. faible/fort** weak/strong point

(**d**) *(de couture, de tricot)* stitch; **p. de croix** cross-stitch; **p. mousse** garter stitch

(**e**) *(phase, degré)* point, stage; **traiter un problème en trois points** to deal with a problem in three stages;

(cuit) **à p.** done to a turn; *(steak)* medium-rare; **jusqu'à un certain p.** to a certain extent, up to a (certain) point; **au p. où j'en suis...** at the stage I've reached...; **à tel p. que..., au p. que...** to such an extent that..., so much so that...; **vous n'êtes pas malade à ce p.-là** you're not as ill as all that; **au plus haut p.** extremely

(**f**) *(dans le temps)* point; **être sur le p. de faire qch** to be about to do sth, to be on the point of doing sth; **arriver à p. nommé** to arrive just at the right moment

(**g**) *(dans un score, dans un pourcentage)* point; *(dans une notation)* mark; **bon p.** *Scol* ≃ gold star; *Fig* brownie point

(**h**) **mettre au p.** *(objectif)* to focus; *(moteur)* to tune; *(technique)* to perfect; *(stratégie)* to finalize; **être au p.** to be up to scratch

(**i**) *Naut & Av* **faire le p.** to take one's bearings; *Fig* take stock; *Fig* **faire le p. sur qch** to take stock of sth

point² *adv Vieilli* = **pas²**

pointage [pwɛ̃taʒ] *nm* (**a**) *(contrôle)* *(de noms sur une liste)* ticking off; *(de votes)* counting; *(au travail)* *(à l'arrivée)* clocking in; *(au départ)* clocking out (**b**) *(d'un télescope)* pointing; *(de fusil)* aiming

pointe [pwɛ̃t] *nf* (**a**) *(extrémité)* *(d'aiguille, de couteau)* point; *(de flèche)* tip; *(de balle)* nose; *(de chaussure)* toe; *(de sein)* nipple; **p. d'asperge** asparagus tip; **en p.** pointed; **sur la p. des pieds** on tiptoe; **entrer sur la p. des pieds** to tiptoe in; **faire des pointes** *(en danse)* to go up on points (**b**) *(maximum)* peak; **p. de vitesse** burst of speed; **faire une p. de vitesse** to put on a burst of speed; **vitesse de p.** top speed (**c**) *(summum)* **être à la p. de la technique/de la recherche** to be in the forefront of technology/of research; **de p.** *(secteur, industrie, technique)* state-of-the-art (**d**) *(petite quantité)* *(d'accent, d'ironie)* hint; *(d'ail, de vanille)* dash (**e**) *(raillerie)* dig; **lancer des pointes à qn** to make digs at sb (**f**) *(clou)* nail; *(pour tapis)* tack; *(sur une chaussure de sport)* spike; **chaussures à pointes** spiked shoes

pointer¹ [pwɛ̃te] **1** *vt* (**a**) *(vérifier)* *(noms sur une liste)* to tick off; *(votes)* to count (**b**) *(dresser)* **p. les oreilles** to prick up its ears (**c**) *(diriger)* *(télescope)* to point (**sur** at); *(fusil)* to aim (**sur** at); *Ordinat (curseur)* to position (**sur** on); **j'ai pointé le doigt vers lui** I pointed (my finger) at him
2 *vi* (**a**) *(au travail)* *(à l'arrivée)* to clock in; *(à la sortie)* to clock out; **p. à l'ANPE** *ou* **au chômage** to register unemployed, to sign on (**b**) *(apparaître)* *(plante)* to come up; *(jour)* to dawn (**c**) *(se dresser)* *(clocher, tour, arbre)* to rise (**d**) *(au jeu de boules)* to get one's ball nearest to the jack
3 se pointer *vpr Fam* to show up

pointer² [pwɛ̃ter] *nm (chien)* pointer

pointeur, -euse [pwɛ̃tœr, -øz] **1** *nm,f (contrôleur)* timekeeper; *(en sport)* scorer
2 *nm Ordinat* pointer
3 *nf* **pointeuse** *(machine)* timeclock

pointillé [pwɛ̃tije] *nm* (**a**) *(trait)* dotted line; *(sur une feuille détachable)* perforations; **découper suivant les pointillés** cut along the dotted line; **les frontières sont en p. sur la carte** the frontiers are drawn as dotted lines on the map (**b**) *(technique de dessin)* stippling

pointilleux, -euse [pwɛ̃tijø, -øz] *adj* particular, fussy (**sur** about)

pointu, -e [pwɛ̃ty] **1** *adj* (**a**) *(en forme de pointe)* pointed; *(voix)* shrill (**b**) *Fig (susceptible)* *(ton de la* *voix, humeur)* touchy (**c**) *(accent)* Parisian (**d**) *Fig (spécialisé)* specialized

2 *adv* **parler p.** to speak with a Parisian accent

pointure [pwɛ̃tyr] *nf* size; *Fam Fig* **une (grosse) p. du cinéma français** a big name in French cinema

point-virgule *(pl* **points-virgules**) [pwɛ̃virgyl] *nm* semicolon

poire [pwar] *nf* (**a**) *(fruit)* pear; *Fig* **couper la p. en deux** to meet each other halfway; *(faire la moyenne entre deux quantités)* to split the difference (**b**) *(objet en forme de poire) (d'un appareil photo)* bulb; *(interrupteur)* switch (**c**) *Fam (tête)* mug; **en pleine p.** right in the face (**d**) *Fam (idiot)* sucker, mug; **et moi, bonne p., j'ai accepté** and like the sucker *or* mug I am, I accepted

poireau, -x [pwaro] *nm* leek; *Fam* **faire le p.** to hang around

poireauter [pwarote] *vi Fam* to hang around

poirier [pwarje] *nm* (**a**) *(arbre)* pear tree; **faire le p.** to do a headstand, to stand on one's head (**b**) *(bois)* pear-tree wood

pois [pwa] *nm* (**a**) *(plante)* pea; **petit p.** (garden) pea; **p. cassés** split peas; **p. chiche** chickpea; **p. de senteur** sweet pea (**b**) *(rond)* (polka) dot; **à p.** polka-dot

poison [pwazɔ̃] **1** *nm* poison

2 *nmf Fam (personne)* pest

poisse [pwas] *nf Fam* bad luck

poisseux, -euse [pwasø, -øz] *adj* sticky

poisson [pwasɔ̃] *nm* (**a**) *(animal)* fish; **p. d'eau douce/ de mer** freshwater/saltwater fish; *Prov* **petit p. deviendra grand** great oaks from little acorns grow; **p. d'argent** silverfish; **p. d'avril** April fool; **p. rouge** goldfish; **p. volant** flying fish (**b**) *Astron & Astrol* **les Poissons** Pisces; **être Poissons** to be (a) Pisces

> ### Poisson d'avril
> In France and in French-speaking countries, on the first of April, children cut fish shapes out of paper and stick them on their unsuspecting classmates' backs, and people play practical jokes on one another before crying out "Poisson d'avril!" ("April fool!"). This custom is referred to in Quebec as "courir le poisson d'avril".

poisson-chat *(pl* **poissons-chats**) [pwasɔ̃ʃa] *nm* catfish

poissonnerie [pwasɔnri] *nf* fish shop, *Br* fishmonger's

poissonneux, -euse [pwasɔnø, -øz] *adj* full of fish

poissonnier, -ère [pwasɔnje, -ɛr] *nm,f Br* fishmonger, *Am* fish merchant

poitevin, -e [pwatvɛ̃, -in] *adj (de Poitiers)* of Poitiers; *(du Poitou)* of Poitou

poitrail [pwatraj] *nm (d'animal)* breast; *Fam (poitrine)* chest

poitrinaire [pwatrinɛr] *adj & nmf Vieilli* consumptive

poitrine [pwatrin] *nf* (**a**) *(thorax)* chest; *(seins)* bust; **serrer qn contre sa p.** to hold sb to one's breast; **ne pas avoir beaucoup de p.** to have a small bust (**b**) *Culin (de veau)* breast; *(de bœuf)* brisket; *(de porc)* belly

poivre [pwavr] *nm* pepper; **p. en grains** peppercorns; **p. et sel** *(cheveux, barbe)* pepper-and-salt

poivré, -e [pwavre] *adj* (**a**) *(nourriture, odeur)* peppery (**b**) *Fig (histoire)* spicy

poivrer [pwavre] **1** *vt* to put pepper on/in

2 **se poivrer** *vpr Fam* to get plastered

poivrier [pwavrije] *nm* (**a**) *(plante)* pepper plant (**b**) *(petit pot)* pepper pot; *(moulin)* pepper mill

poivron [pwavrɔ̃] *nm* pepper

poivrot, -e [pwavro, -ɔt] *nm,f Fam* drunk

poix [pwa] *nf* pitch

poker [pɔkɛr] *nm* poker

polaire [pɔlɛr] *adj (faune, expédition)* polar; *(froid)* Arctic

polar [pɔlar] *nm Fam* whodunnit

polarisation [pɔlarizasjɔ̃] *nf* (**a**) *Phys* polarization (**b**) *Fig (focalisation)* focusing

polariser [pɔlarize] **1** *vt Phys* to polarize; *Fig (attention)* to focus

2 **se polariser** *vpr* **se p. sur** to focus on

Polaroid® [pɔlarɔid] *nm* Polaroid® (camera)

pôle [pol] *nm* (**a**) *Géog* pole; **p. Nord/Sud** North/ South Pole (**b**) *Fig* **p. d'intérêt** focus of interest; **p. d'attraction** centre of attention

polémique [pɔlemik] **1** *adj* polemical

2 *nf* controversy; **une vive p. s'ensuivit** a heated debate ensued

polémiquer [pɔlemike] *vi* to debate

poli¹, -e [pɔli] *adj (lisse)* polished

poli², -e *adj (courtois)* polite (**avec** to)

police¹ [pɔlis] *nf* (**a**) *(maintien de l'ordre)* policing; **faire la p.** to keep order (**b**) *(institution)* **la p.** the police; **la p. est prévenue** the police have been called; **appeler p. secours** to call the police *(in an emergency)*; **être de** *ou* **dans la p.** to be in the police; **p. de l'air et des frontières** airport and border police; **p. judiciaire** police investigation department; **p. mondaine** *ou* **des mœurs** vice squad; **p. montée** mounted police; **p. municipale** local police; **la p. nationale** the national police force; **p. secrète** secret police

> ### Police nationale
> The "Police nationale" operates under the authority of the Ministry of the Interior, unlike the "Gendarmerie", which is an army corps.

police² *nf* (**a**) *(d'assurance)* policy; **p. d'assurance** insurance policy (**b**) *Ordinat* **p. (de caractères)** font; **p. bitmap** *ou* **pixélisée** bitmap font; **p. de taille variable** scalable font; **p. vectorielle** outline font

polichinelle [pɔliʃinɛl] *nm* (**a**) *(marionnette)* Punch (**b**) *Fig & Péj* buffoon

policier, -ère [pɔlisje, -ɛr] **1** *adj (enquête, État, régime)* police; *(roman, film)* detective

2 *nm* (**a**) *(personne)* policeman, police officer; **femme p.** policewoman, woman police officer (**b**) *(roman)* detective novel; *(film)* detective film

policlinique [pɔliklinik] *nf* outpatients' clinic

poliment [pɔlimɑ̃] *adv* politely

polio [pɔljo] **1** *nf* polio; **avoir la p.** to have polio

2 *nmf* polio victim

poliomyélite [pɔljɔmjelit] *nf* poliomyelitis

polir [pɔlir] *vt* to polish

polisson, -onne [pɔlisɔ̃, -ɔn] **1** *nm,f (enfant espiègle)* rascal

2 *adj* (**a**) *(espiègle)* naughty (**b**) *(grivois)* saucy

politesse [pɔlitɛs] *nf* politeness; **par p.** out of politeness; **ce serait la moindre des politesses de le**

prévenir it's only polite to warn him; **rendre la p. à qn** to return sb's favour
politicien, -enne [pɔlitisjɛ̃, -ɛn] **1** nm,f politician **2** adj Péj **politique politicienne** politicking
politique [pɔlitik] **1** adj political **2** nf (**a**) (de gouvernement, d'entreprise) policy; **p. intérieure/extérieure** domestic/foreign policy; **la p. du pire** = the policy of presenting one's situation in the worst possible light in order to achieve one's objectives; **la p. agricole commune** the Common Agricultural Policy (**b**) (affaires publiques) politics; **faire de la p.** (en tant que politicien) to be in politics; (en tant que militant) to be involved in politics **3** nm (personne) politician
politiquement [pɔlitikmɑ̃] adv politically
politisation [pɔlitizasjɔ̃] nf politicization
politiser [pɔlitize] vt to politicize
politologue [pɔlitɔlɔg] nmf political scientist
polka [pɔlka] nf polka
pollen [pɔlɛn] nm pollen
polluant, -e [pɔlɥɑ̃, -ɑ̃t] **1** adj polluting; **produit p.** pollutant **2** nm pollutant
pollué, -e [pɔlɥe] adj polluted
polluer [pɔlɥe] vt to pollute
pollueur, -euse [pɔlɥœr, -øz] **1** nm,f polluter **2** adj polluting
pollution [pɔlysjɔ̃] nf pollution
polo [pɔlo] nm (**a**) (sport) polo (**b**) (chemise) polo shirt
polochon [pɔlɔʃɔ̃] nm Fam bolster; **bataille de polochons** pillow fight
Pologne [pɔlɔɲ] nf **la P.** Poland
polonais, -e [pɔlɔnɛ, -ɛz] **1** adj Polish **2** nm,f **P.** Pole **3** nm (langue) Polish **4** nf **polonaise** (danse) polonaise
poltron, -onne [pɔltrɔ̃, -ɔn] **1** adj cowardly **2** nm,f coward
polyamide [pɔliamid] nm polyamide
polychrome [pɔlikrom] adj polychrome
polyclinique [pɔliklinik] nf polyclinic
polycopie [pɔlikɔpi] nf (procédé) duplication; (document) duplicate
polycopié, -e [pɔlikɔpje] **1** adj duplicated **2** nm duplicate; Scol & Univ duplicated course material
polycopier [66] [pɔlikɔpje] vt to duplicate
polyculture [pɔlikyltyr] nf mixed farming
polyester [pɔliɛstɛr] nm polyester
polygame [pɔligam] **1** adj polygamous **2** nm polygamist
polygamie [pɔligami] nf polygamy
polyglotte [pɔliglɔt] adj & nmf polyglot
polygone [pɔligon, pɔligɔn] nm (**a**) (figure) polygon (**b**) Mil **p. de tir** shooting range
polymère [pɔlimɛr] **1** adj polymeric **2** nm polymer
Polynésie [pɔlinezi] nf **la P.** Polynesia; **la P. française** French Polynesia
polynésien, -enne [pɔlinezjɛ̃, -ɛn] **1** adj Polynesian **2** nm,f **P.** Polynesian
polype [pɔlip] nm polyp
polyphonie [pɔlifɔni] nf polyphony
polysémique [pɔlisemik] adj polysemous
polystyrène [pɔlistirɛn] nm polystyrene

polytechnicien, -enne [pɔlitɛknisjɛ̃, -ɛn] nm,f graduate of the "École polytechnique"
Polytechnique [pɔlitɛknik] nf (**l'École**) p., P. = "grande école" specializing in technology

> ### École polytechnique
> Founded in 1794, this prestigious engineering college has close connections with the Ministry of Defence. Formerly situated in the heart of the 5th arrondissement, the college moved to Palaiseau, near Paris, in the 1970s. It is popularly known as "l'X". Students are effectively enlisted in the army and must repay their education through government service.

polythéisme [pɔliteism] nm polytheism
polyvalence [pɔlivalɑ̃s] nf (en chimie) polyvalency; Fig (d'une personne) versatility
polyvalent, -e [pɔlivalɑ̃, -ɑ̃t] **1** adj (**a**) (en chimie) polyvalent (**b**) (salle) multi-purpose; (outil, personne) versatile **2** nm tax inspector
pomélo [pɔmelo] nm pomelo
pommade [pɔmad] nf ointment; Fam **passer de la p. à qn** to butter sb up
pomme [pɔm] nf (**a**) (fruit) apple; Fam **haut comme trois pommes** knee-high to a grasshopper; Fam **tomber dans les pommes** to pass out; Fam **être dans les pommes** to be out for the count; **p. d'Adam** Adam's apple; **p. de discorde** bone of contention; **p. de pin** pine cone; (de sapin) fir cone
(**b**) (partie arrondie) (de bois de lit, de canne) knob; (d'arrosoir) rose; **p. de douche** shower head
(**c**) (pomme de terre) **pommes allumettes** matchstick Br chips or Am potatoes; **pommes chips** (potato) Br crisps or Am chips; **pommes dauphine** dauphine potatoes; **p. de terre** potato; **pommes (de terre) à l'eau** boiled potatoes; **pommes (de terre) frites** Br chips, Am (French) fries; **pommes (de terre) sautées** sauté potatoes; **pommes vapeur** steamed potatoes
(**d**) Fam (personne) **ma p.** yours truly; **ta p.** you; **sa p.** him/her
(**e**) Fam (idiot) mug; **être bonne p.** to be a mug
pommeau, -x [pɔmo] nm (d'un sabre, d'une selle) pommel; (d'une canne, d'un levier de vitesse) knob
pommelé, -e [pɔmle] adj dappled; **gris p.** (cheval) dapple-grey; **ciel p.** mackerel sky
pommer [pɔme] vi (chou, salade) to form a heart
pommeraie [pɔmrɛ] nf apple orchard
pommette [pɔmɛt] nf cheekbone
pommier [pɔmje] nm apple tree; **p. sauvage** crab-apple tree
pompage [pɔ̃paʒ] nm pumping
pompe¹ [pɔ̃p] nf (cérémonie) pomp, ceremony; **en grande p.** with great (pomp and) ceremony
pompe² nf (**a**) (machine) pump; **p. à essence** (distributeur) Br petrol or Am gas pump; (station-service) Br petrol or Am gas station; **p. à incendie** water pump (on a fire engine); **p. à vélo** bicycle pump; Fam **à toute p.** like lightning; Fam **faire des pompes** to do Br press-ups or Am push-ups (**b**) Fam **pompes** (chaussures) shoes; Fig **il est à côté de ses pompes** he's not with it (**c**) **pompes funèbres** undertaker's
pomper [pɔ̃pe] **1** vt (**a**) (puiser) (eau, air) to pump; (faire monter) to pump up; (évacuer) to pump out; Fam Fig **p. qn** (épuiser) to do sb in; Fam **être pompé**

to be done in; *Fam* **tu me pompes l'air** you're getting on my nerves (**b**) *Fam (boisson)* to knock back (**c**) *Fam Scol* to crib (**sur** from)
   2 *vi* (**a**) *(faire marcher une pompe)* to pump (**b**) *Fam Scol* to crib (**sur** from)

pompette [pɔ̃pɛt] *adj Fam* tipsy

pompeux, -euse [pɔ̃pø, -øz] *adj Péj* pompous

pompier¹ [pɔ̃pje] *nm* fireman; **appeler les pompiers** to call the fire *Br* brigade *or Am* department

pompier², -ère [pɔ̃pje, -ɛr] *adj Art* pompier; *Péj (style)* pompous

pompiste [pɔ̃pist] *nmf* pump attendant

pompon [pɔ̃pɔ̃] *nm* pompom, bobble; **bonnet à p.** bobble hat; *Fam* **c'est le p.!** that's the limit!

pomponner [pɔ̃pɔne] **se pomponner** *vpr Fam* to doll oneself up

ponce [pɔ̃s] *adj voir* **pierre**

poncer [16] [pɔ̃se] *vt* (**a**) *(au papier de verre, avec une ponceuse)* to sand (down) (**b**) *(passer à la pierre ponce)* to pumice

ponceuse [pɔ̃søz] *nf* sander

poncho [pɔ̃tʃo] *nm* poncho

poncif [pɔ̃sif] *nm* cliché, commonplace

ponction [pɔ̃ksjɔ̃] *nf Méd* puncture; *(de poumon)* tapping; **p. lombaire** lumbar puncture; *Fig* **faire des ponctions dans ses économies** to draw on one's savings; **p. fiscale** taxation

ponctualité [pɔ̃ktɥalite] *nf* punctuality

ponctuation [pɔ̃ktɥasjɔ̃] *nf* punctuation

ponctuel, -elle [pɔ̃ktɥɛl] *adj* (**a**) *(à l'heure)* punctual (**b**) *(unique) Br* one-off, *Am* one-of-a-kind; *(isolé)* selective

ponctuellement [pɔ̃ktɥɛlmɑ̃] *adv (de façon limitée)* on a *Br* one-off *or Am* one-of-a-kind basis

ponctuer [pɔ̃ktɥe] *vt aussi Fig* to punctuate (**de** with)

pondaison [pɔ̃dɛzɔ̃] *nf* egg-laying time

pondérale [pɔ̃deral] *adj f voir* **surcharge**

pondération [pɔ̃derasjɔ̃] *nf* (**a**) *(modération)* level-headedness (**b**) *Écon* weighting

pondéré, -e [pɔ̃dere] *adj* (**a**) *(personne)* level-headed (**b**) *Écon* weighted

pondeuse [pɔ̃døz] *adj f & nf* **(poule) p.** layer

pondre [pɔ̃dr] *vt* (**a**) *(œuf)* to lay (**b**) *Fam (produire)* to turn out

poney [pɔnɛ] *nm* pony

pont [pɔ̃] *nm* (**a**) *(sur un cours d'eau)* bridge; **les Ponts et Chaussées** the Highways Department; *Fig* **faire un p. d'or à qn** to give sb a golden hello; **p. suspendu** suspension bridge (**b**) *Fig (congés)* long weekend; **le p. du premier mai** the May Day long weekend; **faire le p.** to make a long weekend of it (**c**) *(d'un navire)* deck; **sur le p.** on deck (**d**) *(lien)* **couper les ponts (avec qn)** to break off all relations (with sb); **p. aérien** airlift; *Ordinat* **p. routeur** routing node (**e**) *Ind* **p. roulant** travelling crane

pontage [pɔ̃taʒ] *nm Méd* bypass (operation)

ponte¹ [pɔ̃t] *nf (action)* (egg) laying; *(œufs)* eggs (laid)

ponte² *nm Fam* **(grand) p.** *(personnage important)* big shot

pontife [pɔ̃tif] *nm Rel* pontiff; **le souverain p.** the Supreme Pontiff

pontifiant, -e [pɔ̃tifjɑ̃, -ɑ̃t] *adj Péj* pontificating

pontifical, -e, -aux, -ales [pɔ̃tifikal, -o] *adj* papal

pontifier [66] [pɔ̃tifje] *vi* to pontificate

pont-l'évêque [pɔ̃levɛk] *nm inv* Pont-l'Évêque (cheese)

pont-levis (*pl* **ponts-levis**) [pɔ̃ləvi] *nm* drawbridge

ponton [pɔ̃tɔ̃] *nm* pontoon

pop [pɔp] *adj inv & nf* pop

pop-corn [pɔpkɔrn] *nm inv* popcorn

pope [pɔp] *nm Rel* (Orthodox) priest

popeline [pɔplin] *nf* poplin

popote [pɔpɔt] **1** *nf* (**a**) *Fam (cuisine)* cooking; **faire la p.** to do the cooking (**b**) *Mil* officers' mess
   2 *adj inv Fam* stay-at-home

popotin [pɔpɔtɛ̃] *nm Fam Br* bum, *Am* butt

populace [pɔpylas] *nf* rabble, mob

populaire [pɔpylɛr] *adj* (**a**) *(du peuple, qui plaît)* popular (**b**) *(langue, expression)* vernacular (**c**) *(ouvrier)* working-class; **les classes populaires** the working classes

populariser [pɔpylarize] *vt* to popularize

popularité [pɔpylarite] *nf* popularity

population [pɔpylasjɔ̃] *nf* population; **p. active** working population

populeux, -euse [pɔpylø, -øz] *adj* crowded

populisme [pɔpylism] *nm* populism

populo [pɔpylo] *nm Fam (foule)* crowd (of people)

porc [pɔr] *nm* (**a**) *(animal)* pig, *Am* hog; *Fig (homme grossier ou sale)* pig (**b**) *(viande)* pork (**c**) *(cuir)* pigskin

porcelaine [pɔrsəlɛn] *nf (matière)* porcelain, china; *(objet)* piece of porcelain; **une tasse de** *ou* **en p.** a porcelain *or* china cup

porcelet [pɔrsəlɛ] *nm* piglet

porc-épic (*pl* **porcs-épics**) [pɔrkepik] *nm* porcupine

porche [pɔrʃ] *nm* porch

porcherie [pɔrʃəri] *nf aussi Fig Br* pigsty, *Am* pigpen

porcin, -e [pɔrsɛ̃, -in] **1** *adj* pig; *Péj (visage, yeux)* piggy
   2 *nmpl* **porcins** pigs, *Am* hogs

pore [pɔr] *nm* pore; **elle sue la suffisance par tous les pores** she exudes *or* oozes self-importance

poreux, -euse [pɔrø, -øz] *adj* porous

porno [pɔrno] *adj & nm Fam* porn

pornographie [pɔrnɔgrafi] *nf* pornography

pornographique [pɔrnɔgrafik] *adj* pornographic

port¹ [pɔr] *nm* (**a**) *(pour bateaux)* harbour; *(plus important)* port; *Fig* **arriver à bon p.** to arrive safe and sound; **p. d'attache** home port; *Fig* home base; **p. de commerce** commercial port; **p. de pêche** fishing port; **p. de plaisance** marina (**b**) *Ordinat* port; **p. de communication** comms port, communications port; **p. d'entrée/sortie** input/output port; **p. d'E/S** I/O port; **p. d'extension** expansion port; **p. modem** modem port; **p. parallèle** parallel port; **p. série** serial port; **p. souris** mouse port

port² *nm* (**a**) *(fait de transporter)* carrying; **p. d'armes** carrying of firearms (**b**) *(fait de revêtir)* wearing; **le p. du casque est obligatoire** *(sur panneau)* safety helmets must be worn (**c**) *(de marchandises)* carriage; *(de paquets, de lettres, de télégrammes)* delivery; **p. et emballage** postage and packing; **p. franc** *(de marchandises)* carriage paid; **p. payé** *(de magazine)* postage paid (**d**) *(allure)* bearing; **un gracieux p. de tête** a graceful manner of holding one's head

portabilité [pɔrtabilite] *nf Ordinat* portability

portable [pɔrtabl] **1** *adj* (**a**) *(ordinateur, machine à écrire)* portable; *(téléphone)* mobile (**b**) *(vêtement)* wearable

2 *nm* *(ordinateur)* laptop, portable; *(téléphone)* mobile (phone)

portage [pɔrtaʒ] *nm Can* portage

portager [45] [pɔrtaʒe] *vi Can* to portage

portail [pɔrtaj] *nm aussi Ordinat* portal

portant, -e [pɔrtã, -ãt] *adj* **être bien/mal p.** to be in good/poor health

portatif, -ive [pɔrtatif, -iv] *adj* portable

Port-au-Prince [pɔrɔprɛ̃s] *n* Port-au-Prince

porte [pɔrt] *nf* (**a**) *(de maison, de placard, de véhicule)* door; **à ma p.** on my doorstep; **de p. à p.** door to door; *Fig* **entre deux portes** briefly; **mettre qn à la p.** to throw sb out; *(d'un emploi)* to fire sb; **trouver p. close** to find nobody in; *Fam* **ce n'est pas la p. à côté** it's hardly just around the corner; **c'est la p. ouverte à...** it's leaving the door wide open to...; **(voiture) deux/quatre/cinq portes** two-/four-/five-door car; **p. cochère** carriage entrance; **p. de derrière** back door; **p. d'entrée,** *Belg* **p. de rue** front door; **p. tournante, p. à tambour** revolving door; **p. vitrée** glass door (**b**) *(d'une ville)* gate; **aux portes du désert** at the gateway to the desert; **p. (d'embarquement)** *(dans un aéroport)* (boarding) gate (**c**) *(en ski)* gate

porté, -e [pɔrte] *adj (enclin)* **être p. à faire qch** to be inclined to do sth; *Fam* **être p. sur la bouteille** to be fond of the bottle; *Fam* **être p. sur la chose** to have a one-track mind

porte-à-faux [pɔrtafo] **en porte-à-faux** *adv* overhanging; *Fig* **être en p.** to be awkwardly placed

porte-à-porte [pɔrtapɔrt] *nm* door-to-door selling; **faire du p.** *(pour vendre)* to sell from door to door; *(faire des enquêtes)* to go from door to door

porte-avions [pɔrtavjɔ̃] *nm inv* aircraft carrier

porte-bagages [pɔrtbagaʒ] *nm inv (de bicyclette)* carrier; *(de train)* luggage rack

porte-bébé *(pl* **porte-bébés)** [pɔrtbebe] *nm* baby carrier

porte-bonheur [pɔrtbɔnœr] *nm inv* (lucky) charm

porte-bouteilles [pɔrtbutɛj] *nm inv (pour stocker)* wine rack; *(pour porter)* bottle-carrier

porte-cartes [pɔrtəkart] *nm inv (portefeuille)* cardholder

porte-cigarettes [pɔrtsigarɛt] *nm inv* cigarette case

porte-clefs, porte-clés [pɔrtəkle] *nm inv* key ring

porte-documents [pɔrtdɔkymã] *nm inv* briefcase

porte-drapeau *(pl* **porte-drapeaux** *ou* **porte-drapeau)** [pɔrtdrapo] *nm aussi Fig* standard bearer

portée [pɔrte] *nf* (**a**) *(petits)* litter; *(d'une truie)* farrow (**b**) *(amplitude)* *(d'un fusil, d'un émetteur, de la voix)* range; *Fig (d'un traité)* scope; **à p. de (la) main** within reach, to hand; **à p. de (la) voix** within earshot; **à la p. de toutes les bourses** within everyone's means; **c'est à ma p.** *(objet)* it's within my reach; *Fig (livre)* I can understand it; **hors de ma p.** *(objet)* beyond my reach; *Fig (livre)* beyond me; **hors de p.** out of reach (**c**) *Fig (impact) (de paroles, d'une décision)* significance (**d**) *Mus* stave

portefaix [pɔrtəfɛ] *nm* porter

porte-fenêtre *(pl* **portes-fenêtres)** [pɔrtfənɛtr] *nf* French window

portefeuille [pɔrtəfœj] *nm* (**a**) *(pour l'argent)* wallet, *Am* billfold; **faire un lit en p.** to make an apple-pie bed; **jupe p.** wrapover skirt (**b**) *Fin & Pol* portfolio; **p. d'actions/de titres** share/securities portfolio

porte-jarretelles [pɔrtʒartɛl] *nm inv Br* suspender *or Am* garter belt

porte-malheur [pɔrtmalœr] *nm inv* jinx

portemanteau, -x [pɔrtmãto] *nm (au mur)* coat rack; *(sur pied)* coat stand

portemine [pɔrtəmin] *nm* propelling pencil

porte-monnaie [pɔrtmɔnɛ] *nm inv* purse; **p. électronique** electronic purse

porte-parapluies [pɔrtparaplɥi] *nm inv* umbrella stand

porte-parole [pɔrtparɔl] *nm inv* spokesperson, spokesman, *f* spokeswoman

porte-plume [pɔrtəplym] *nm inv* penholder

porter [pɔrte] **1** *vt* (**a**) *(soutenir)* to carry; **mes jambes ne me portent plus** my legs won't carry me any further; **je ne le porte pas dans mon cœur** he's not exactly my favourite person

(**b**) *(emporter)* to take; *(amener)* to bring

(**c**) *(vêtement, chapeau, lunettes)* to wear; *(signature, date)* to bear; *(prénom, nom)* to have; **p. une moustache/la barbe** to have a moustache/a beard; **p. les cheveux courts/longs** to wear one's hair short/long, to have short/long hair; **p. le nom de qn** to be named after sb; **p. le titre de...** *(livre, film)* to be entitled...

(**d**) *(produire) (fruits)* to bear

(**e**) *(diriger)* **p. un coup à qn** to strike sb; **p. la main à son front** to hold one's hand to one's forehead; **p. son attention sur qch** to turn one's attention to sth, to give sth one's attention; **p. une affaire devant les tribunaux** to bring a matter to court; **p. qch à la connaissance de qn** to bring sth to sb's attention

(**f**) *(inscrire)* to enter; **se faire p. malade** to report sick

(**g**) *(inciter)* **tout (me) porte à croire que...** everything leads me to believe that...

(**h**) *(à un niveau plus élevé)* **p. la température à 100°** to raise the temperature to 100°; **portez le liquide à ébullition** bring the liquid to the boil; **cela portera à 100 francs le prix du billet** that will bring the price of the ticket up to 100 francs

2 *vi* (**a**) *(cogner)* **p. sur/contre qch** to hit sth

(**b**) *(atteindre son objectif) (coup)* to strike home, to hit its target; *(voix)* to carry

3 porter sur *vt ind* (**a**) *(avoir pour sujet)* to be about (**b**) *Fam* **p. sur les nerfs à qn** to get on sb's nerves

4 se porter *vpr* (**a**) *(physiquement)* **se p. bien** to be well; **je ne m'en porte pas plus mal** I'm none the worse for it; *Hum* **moins je le vois, mieux je me porte** the less I see him, the better I feel

(**b**) *(devoir être porté)* to be worn; *(être à la mode)* to be fashionable

(**c**) *(se présenter comme)* **se p. acquéreur de qch** to offer to buy sth; **se p. candidat** to *Br* stand *or Am* run as a candidate; **se p. caution** to stand surety

(**d**) *(aller)* **se p. au secours de qn** to go to sb's assistance

(**e**) **se p. sur** *(sujet: regard, choix)* to fall on

porte-savon *(pl* **porte-savons** *ou* **porte-savon)** [pɔrtsavɔ̃] *nm* soapdish

porte-serviettes [pɔrtsɛrvjɛt] *nm inv* towel rail

porteur, -euse [pɔrtœr, -øz] **1** *nm,f* (**a**) *(d'un message, de nouvelles)* bearer; **par p.** by messenger (**b**) *(de gare, d'aéroport)* porter; **p. d'eau** water carrier (**c**) *Méd* carrier; **p. sain** = carrier who doesn't have the symptoms of the disease (**d**) *(détenteur)* holder; *(d'un chèque)* bearer; **payable au p.** payable to bearer

2 *adj* (**a**) *Élec* **fréquence/onde porteuse** carrier frequency/wave (**b**) *(marché, créneau)* growth

porte-voix [pɔrtəvwa] *nm inv* megaphone; *(électrique) Br* loudhailer, *Am* bullhorn; **mettre ses mains en p.** to cup one's hands round one's mouth

portier [pɔrtje] *nm* porter, doorkeeper; *(dans un hôtel)* commissionaire; **p. de nuit** night porter

portière [pɔrtjɛr] *nf (d'une voiture, d'un train)* door

portillon [pɔrtijɔ̃] *nm* gate; *(d'un passage à niveau)* side gate; **p. (automatique)** *(de gare, de métro)* ticket barrier

portion [pɔrsjɔ̃] *nf* portion; **être réduit à la p. congrue** to get the smallest share

portique [pɔrtik] *nm* (a) *(colonnes)* portico (b) *(pour agrès)* (cross)beam

Porto [pɔrto] *n* Oporto

porto [pɔrto] *nm* port

portoricain, -e [pɔrtɔrikɛ̃, -ɛn] 1 *adj* Puerto Rican
2 *nm,f* **P.** Puerto Rican

Porto Rico [pɔrtoriko] *n* Puerto Rico

portrait [pɔrtrɛ] *nm* (a) *(peinture, dessin, photo)* portrait; **le p.** *(genre)* portrait painting, portraiture; **faire le p. de qn** to do a portrait of sb; *Fig* **c'est le p. vivant de son père, c'est tout le p. de son père** he's the spitting image of his father; *Fam* **il s'est fait abîmer** *ou* **arranger le p.** he got his face rearranged; *Fam* **se faire tirer le p.** to have one's photo taken (b) *(description)* description; **faire le p. de qn/qch** to paint a picture of sb/sth (c) *Ordinat* **mode p.** portrait mode

portraitiste [pɔrtretist] *nmf* portrait painter, portraitist

portrait-robot *(pl* **portraits-robots)** [pɔrtrɛrɔbo] *nm* Photofit® (picture), Identikit picture; *Fig* profile

portuaire [pɔrtɥɛr] *adj* port, harbour

portugais, -e [pɔrtɥgɛ, -ɛz] 1 *adj* Portuguese
2 *nm,f* **P.** Portuguese
3 *nm (langue)* Portuguese
4 *nf* **portugaise** (a) *(huître)* Portuguese oyster (b) *Fam (oreille)* ear; **avoir les portugaises ensablées** to be as deaf as a post

Portugal [pɔrtygal] *nm* **le P.** Portugal

pose [poz] *nf* (a) *(de rideaux, de papier peint)* putting up, hanging; *(d'une vitre)* putting in; *(de moquette, de câbles)* laying; *(d'appareils)* installation; *(d'une bombe)* planting; *Méd (d'un stérilet)* putting in; *(de ventouses)* application (b) *(pour photo, portrait)* pose; **prendre la p.** to pose; **garder la p.** to hold the pose; *Péj* **prendre des poses** to pose (c) *Phot* exposure; **pellicule de 24 poses** 24-exposure film

posé, -e [poze] *adj (réfléchi)* composed, calm

posément [pozemɑ̃] *adv* calmly

poser [poze] 1 *vt* (a) *(mettre)* to put down; **p. qch sur/sous qch** to put sth on/under sth; *Fig* **p. son regard sur qn/qch** to look at sb/sth
(b) *(formuler) (question)* to ask; *(hypothèse)* to put forward; *(principe)* to lay down; **p. une question à qn** to ask sb a question; **p. un problème à qn** to pose a problem for sb; **p. sa candidature** *(aux élections)* to put oneself forward (as a candidate), *Br* to stand (as a candidate); *(à un poste)* to apply
(c) *(rideaux, papier peint)* to put up, to hang; *(vitre)* to put in; *(moquette, câble)* to lay; *(appareil)* to install; *(bombe)* to plant; *Méd* **p. qch à qn** *(stérilet)* to put sth in sb; *(ventouses)* to apply sth to sb
(d) *Math (opération, équation)* to set out; **je pose deux et je retiens un** put down two and carry one
(e) *Can (photographier)* to photograph, to take a photograph of

2 *vi (pour une photo, pour un tableau)* to pose; *Péj* **p. pour la galerie** to play to the gallery
3 **se poser** *vpr* (a) *(oiseau, avion)* to land; *Fig* **se p. sur** *(sujet: regard)* to rest on
(b) *(question, problème)* to arise, to come up
(c) *(à soi-même)* **se p. des questions** to ask oneself questions; *(avoir des doutes)* to have one's doubts
(d) *Fam* **comme bricoleur/cuisinier, il se pose un peu là!** some handyman/cook, I don't think!; **comme enquiquineur, il se pose là!** he's a real pain in the neck!
(e) *(se prétendre)* **se p. en réformateur/redresseur de torts** to set oneself up as a reformer/a righter of wrongs

poseur, -euse [pozœr, -øz] *nm,f* (a) *(de câbles, de carrelage)* layer; **p. d'affiches** billsticker, billposter; **la police recherche les poseurs de bombes** the police are hunting the people who planted the bombs (b) *Péj (pédant)* show-off, poseur

positif, -ive [pozitif, -iv] *adj* positive; **il est p.** *(à l'Alcotest, au contrôle antidopage)* his test result is positive

position [pozisjɔ̃] *nf* (a) *(emplacement)* position; **être en première/deuxième p.** *(dans une course)* to be in first/second place; *(sur une liste)* to be first/second; **arriver en première/deuxième p.** to come first/second (b) *(attitude, en danse)* position; **être/se mettre en p.** to be in/get into position; **en p. debout/assise** in a standing/sitting position (c) *(opinion)* position (**sur** on); **prendre p.** to take a stand; **rester sur ses positions** to stand one's ground (d) *(situation)* position; **être en p. de faire qch** to be in a position to do sth; **p. sociale** social position

positionner [pozisjone] 1 *vt* to position
2 **se positionner** *vpr* to position oneself

positivement [pozitivmɑ̃] *adv* positively

positologie [pozolɔʒi] *nf Méd* dosage

possédé, -e [posede] 1 *adj (du démon)* possessed
2 *nm,f* person possessed; **hurler comme un p.** to scream like one possessed

posséder [34] [posede] *vt* (a) *(biens matériels)* to possess, to own; *(talent, qualité)* to possess, to have (b) *(sujet)* to have a thorough knowledge of; *(langue, technique)* to have mastered (c) *(sujet: démon, passion)* to possess (d) *Fam (tromper)* to take in; **se faire p.** to be taken in (e) *Litt (femme)* to possess

possesseur [posesœr] *nm* owner; *(d'un titre)* holder

possessif, -ive [posesif, -iv] *adj & nm* possessive

possession [posesjɔ̃] *nf* (a) *(fait d'avoir)* ownership, possession; *(d'un titre)* holding; **avoir qch en sa p.** to have sth in one's possession; **être en p. de qch** to be in possession of sth; **prendre p. de qch** to take possession of sth (b) *(bien, territoire)* possession (c) *(par le démon)* possession (d) *(maîtrise)* **être en p. de toutes ses facultés** to be in full possession of one's faculties; **être en pleine p. de ses moyens** to be at the peak of one's powers

possibilité [posibilite] *nf* (a) *(éventualité)* possibility (b) *(moyen, occasion)* opportunity, chance; **avoir la p. de faire qch** to have the opportunity *or* the chance of doing sth (c) **possibilités** *(intellectuelles)* potential; *(financières)* means (d) *Ordinat* **possibilités d'extension** upgradeability

possible [posibl] 1 *adj* (a) *(faisable, vraisemblable)* possible; **il leur est p. de vous héberger** it's possible for them to put you up; **il est p. qu'il soit mort** it's possible that he's dead, he might be dead; **aussitôt que p., dès que p.** as soon as possible; *Fam* **pas p.! I** don't believe it!; **si p.** if possible (**b**) *(comme superlatif)* **elle nous en parle le moins/plus p.** she talks to us about it as little/much as possible; **le moins/plus souvent p.** as infrequently/frequently as possible; **le moins/plus de détails p.** as few/many details as possible; **la boîte la plus grande p.** the largest box possible; **tous les détails possibles (et imaginables)** every possible detail (**c**) *Fam (supportable)* **pas p.** *(personne, situation)* impossible; **ça n'est plus p.!** I've had enough!

2 *nm* **faire tout son p. (pour faire qch)** to do everything one possibly can (to do sth)

postal, -e, -aux, -ales [pɔstal, -o] *adj (tarif, services)* postal; *(train, wagon)* mail

postdater [pɔstdate] *vt* to postdate

poste¹ [pɔst] *nf* (**a**) *(service)* mail, *Br* post; **la P.** the postal service; **mettre qch à la p.** to mail *or Br* post sth; **par la p.** by mail, *Br* by post; **p. aérienne** airmail (**b**) *(lieu)* **(bureau de) p.** post office; **p. restante** *Br* poste restante, *Am* general delivery

poste² *nm* (**a**) *(fonction)* position, post; **p. à pourvoir** vacancy (**b**) *(appareil)* **p. (de radio/télévision)** radio/ television (set); *Rad* **p. émetteur** *(équipement)* transmitter (**c**) *(local)* **p. (de police)** (police) station; **p. d'aiguillage** signal box; **p. d'essence** *Br* petrol *or Am* gas station; *Ordinat* **p. de travail** workstation (**d**) *(d'un soldat)* post; **être à son p.** to be at one's post; **p. de pilotage** cockpit (**e**) *(d'un standard)* extension (**f**) *(comptable)* entry, item

poster¹ [pɔste] **1** *vt (sentinelle, hommes, troupes)* to post, to station

2 se poster *vpr* to take up a position, to station oneself

poster² *vt (courrier)* to mail, *Br* to post

poster³ [pɔstɛr] *nm* poster

postérieur, -e [pɔsterjœr] **1** *adj* (**a**) *(dans le temps)* later, subsequent; **p. à** after (**b**) *(de derrière) (pattes)* back, hind; *Anat* posterior

2 *nm Hum (derrière)* posterior

postérieurement [pɔsterjœrmɑ̃] *adv* later, subsequently; **p. à** after

postérité [pɔsterite] *nf* posterity; **passer à la p.** *(personne)* to go down in history; *(œuvre, mot)* to be handed down to posterity

postface [pɔstfas] *nf* postscript

posthume [pɔstym] *adj* posthumous

postiche [pɔstiʃ] **1** *adj* false

2 *nm* hairpiece

postier, -ère [pɔstje, -ɛr] *nm,f* postal worker

postillon [pɔstijɔ̃] *nm* (**a**) *Hist (cocher)* postilion (**b**) **postillons** *(salive)* shower of spit; **envoyer des postillons** to splutter

postillonner [pɔstijɔne] *vi* to splutter

postindustriel, -elle [pɔstɛ̃dystrijɛl] *adj* post-industrial

postmoderne [pɔstmɔdɛrn] *adj* post-modernist

postopératoire [pɔstɔperatwar] *adj Méd* post-operative

post-scriptum [pɔstskriptɔm] *nm inv* postscript

postsynchroniser [pɔstsɛ̃krɔnize] *vt Cin* to dub

postulant, -e [pɔstylɑ̃, -ɑ̃t] *nm,f (à un emploi)* applicant, candidate (**à** for)

postulat [pɔstyla] *nm* postulate

postuler [pɔstyle] *vi* **p. à** *ou* **pour un emploi** to apply for a job

posture [pɔstyr] *nf* (**a**) *(attitude)* posture (**b**) *(situation)* **être en fâcheuse p.** to be in an awkward situation

pot [po] *nm* (**a**) *(récipient, contenu)* pot; *(en verre)* jar; **p. à eau/à lait** water/milk jug; *Fam* **le p.** *(pour enfant)* the potty; **mettre en p.** *(plante)* to pot; *Fam* **quel p. de colle!** he sticks to you like glue!; **découvrir le p. aux roses** to find out what's been going on; **petit p.** *(pour bébé)* jar of baby food; **p. de chambre** chamber pot; **p. de fleurs** *(récipient)* flowerpot; *(plante)* pot of flowers; *Fam* **c'est un vrai p. de peinture!** *(femme)* she wears make-up an inch thick! (**b**) *Fam (chance)* **avoir du p.** to be lucky; **manque de p.,...** unfortunately,... (**c**) *(tuyau)* **p. (d'échappement)** *Br* exhaust (pipe), *Am* tail pipe; **p. catalytique** catalytic converter (**d**) *Fam (boisson)* drink; **viens, je t'offre un p.** come on, I'll buy you a drink; **ils font un p. pour son départ à la retraite** they're having a little get-together for her retirement (**e**) *Fam* **plein p.** *(à toute vitesse) Br* like the clappers, *Am* like sixty

potable [pɔtabl] *adj* (**a**) *(que l'on peut boire)* drinkable; **eau p./non p.** drinking/non-drinking water (**b**) *Fam (correct)* passable

potache [pɔtaʃ] *nm Fam* schoolboy

potage [pɔtaʒ] *nm* soup; **p. aux légumes** vegetable soup

potager, -ère [pɔtaʒe, -ɛr] **1** *adj voir* **jardin, plante**

2 *nm* vegetable *or* kitchen garden

potasser [pɔtase] *vt Fam (matière)* to bone up on, *Br* to swot up; *(examen)* to bone up for, *Br* to swot up for

potassium [pɔtasjɔm] *nm Chim* potassium

pot-au-feu [pɔtofø] *nm inv* = boiled beef with vegetables

pot-de-vin *(pl* **pots-de-vin)** [pɔdvɛ̃] *nm* bribe

pote [pɔt] *nm Fam* pal

poteau, -x [pɔto] *nm* (**a**) *(piquet)* post; *(de but)* (goal)-post; *Fam* **poteaux** *(jambes)* legs like tree-trunks; **p. (d'exécution)** execution stake; *Belg* **p. d'éclairage** street lamp; **p. électrique** electricity pylon; **p. indicateur** signpost; **p. télégraphique** telegraph pole (**b**) *Fam (ami)* pal

potée [pɔte] *nf* = boiled beef or pork with vegetables

potelé, -e [pɔtle] *adj* chubby, plump

potence [pɔtɑ̃s] *nf* (**a**) *(gibet)* gallows *(singulier)* (**b**) *(pièce de charpente)* bracket

potentiel, -elle [pɔtɑ̃sjɛl] *adj & nm* potential

potentiellement [pɔtɑ̃sjɛlmɑ̃] *adv* potentially

poterie [pɔtri] *nf* (**a**) *(art)* pottery; **faire de la p.** to make pottery (**b**) *(objet)* piece of pottery; *(objets)* pottery

potiche [pɔtiʃ] *nf* (**a**) *(vase)* oriental vase (**b**) *Fig* figurehead

potier, -ère [pɔtje, -ɛr] *nm,f* potter

potin [pɔtɛ̃] *nm Fam* (**a**) **potins** *(ragots)* gossip (**b**) *(bruit)* row; **faire du p.** to kick up a row

potion [posjɔ̃] *nf* potion

potiron [pɔtirɔ̃] *nm* pumpkin

pot-pourri *(pl* **pots-pourris)** [popuri] *nm (chanson)* medley; *(fleurs séchées)* potpourri

pou, -x [pu] *nm* louse; *Fam* **chercher des poux dans la tête à qn** to try and pick a quarrel with sb

poubelle [pubɛl] *nf* (**a**) *(récipient) Br* (dust)bin, *Am* garbage can; **jeter** *ou* **mettre qch à la p.** to throw sth out; **faire les poubelles** to scrounge in *Br* dustbins or *Am* garbage cans (**b**) *Ordinat* wastebasket, *Am* trash (**c**) *Fam (voiture)* heap, banger

pouce [pus] *nm* (**a**) *(doigt)* thumb; *(gros orteil)* big toe; *Fam* **se tourner les pouces** to twiddle one's thumbs; *Suisse* **tenir les pouces à qn** to keep one's fingers crossed for sb; **p.!** *(dans un jeu)* truce!; *Fig* **manger sur le p.** to grab something to eat (**b**) *(mesure)* inch; **ne pas bouger d'un p.** not to move an inch (**c**) *Can* **faire du p.** *(faire du stop)* to hitch(hike)

Poucet [pusɛ] *npr* **le Petit P.** Tom Thumb

poudre [pudr] *nf* (**a**) *(poussière)* powder; **réduire qch en p.** to reduce sth to powder; *Fig* **jeter de la p. aux yeux à qn** to try and dazzle sb; **p. compacte/libre** *(maquillage)* pressed/loose powder; **p. à éternuer** sneezing powder; **p. à laver,** *Belg* **p. à lessiver** washing powder; **p. à récurer** scouring powder; *Vieilli* **p. de riz** face powder (**b**) *(explosif)* (gun)powder (**c**) *Fam (héroïne)* smack, skag; *(cocaine)* cake, charlie

poudrer [pudre] **1** *vt* to powder; **une femme poudrée** a woman with a powdered face
2 se poudrer *vpr* to powder one's face

poudrerie [pudrǝri] *nf* (**a**) *(fabrique de poudre)* (gun)-powder factory (**b**) *Can (neige)* drifting snow

poudreux, -euse [pudrø, -øz] **1** *adj* powdery; **neige poudreuse** powder snow
2 *nf* **poudreuse** powder snow

poudrier [pudrije] *nm* (powder) compact

poudrière [pudrijɛr] *nf (entrepôt)* powder magazine; *Fig* powder keg

pouf [puf] **1** *exclam (chute)* thud!
2 *nm* (**a**) *(meuble)* pouf (**b**) *Belg* **à p.** *(à crédit)* on tick; **taper à p.** *(deviner)* to make a wild guess

pouffer [pufe] *vi* **p. (de rire)** to burst out laughing

pouffiasse [pufjas] *nf Vulg* bitch, *Br* cow

pouilleux, -euse [pujø, -øz] **1** *adj (personne)* filthy; *(quartier, maison)* squalid
2 *nm,f* down-and-out

poulailler [pulaje] *nm* (**a**) *(basse-cour)* hen house (**b**) *(au théâtre)* **le p.** the gods

poulain [pulɛ̃] *nm* foal; *Fig* protégé

poulamon [pulamɔ̃] *nm Can* tomcod

poularde [pulard] *nf* fattened pullet

poulbot [pulbo] *nm Vieilli* = street urchin of Montmartre

poule¹ [pul] *nf* (**a**) *(animal)* hen; *Culin* (boiling) fowl; *Fig* **la p. aux œufs d'or** the goose that lays the golden eggs; **quand les poules auront des dents** when pigs fly; **p. d'eau** moorhen; **p. faisane** hen pheasant; *Péj* **p. mouillée** wimp; **p. au pot** boiled chicken (**b**) *(terme d'affection)* **ma (petite) p.** darling (**c**) *Fam Péj (femme légère)* floozie; *(maîtresse)* mistress

poule² *nf (compétition)* tournament; *(groupe)* group

poulet [pulɛ] *nm* (**a**) *(animal)* chicken; **p. d'élevage** battery-reared chicken; **p. fermier** free-range chicken; **p. de grain** corn-fed chicken; **p. rôti** roast chicken (**b**) *(terme d'affection)* **mon (petit) p.** darling (**c**) *Fam (policier)* cop

poulette [pulɛt] *nf* (**a**) *(jeune poule)* pullet (**b**) *(terme d'affection)* **ma p.** darling

pouliche [puliʃ] *nf* filly

poulie [puli] *nf* pulley

poulpe [pulp] *nm* octopus

pouls [pu] *nm* pulse; **tâter le p. à qn** to feel sb's pulse; **prendre le p. à qn** to take sb's pulse

poumon [pumɔ̃] *nm* lung; **p. d'acier** iron lung; **respirer à pleins poumons** to breathe deeply

poupe [pup] *nf Naut* stern, poop

poupée [pupe] *nf* (**a**) *(jouet)* doll; **jouer à la p.** to play with dolls; **p. mannequin** Barbie doll®; **poupées russes** Russian dolls (**b**) *Fam (jolie fille)* doll (**c**) *(pansement)* finger bandage

poupin, -e [pupɛ̃, -in] *adj (personne)* chubby-cheeked; **visage p.** baby face

poupon [pupɔ̃] *nm* (**a**) *(bébé)* tiny baby (**b**) *(jouet)* baby doll

pouponner [pupɔne] *vi* to play the doting mother/father

pour [pur] **1** *prép* (**a**) *(indique le but, la destination)* for; **tiens, c'est p. toi** look, it's for you; **livres p. enfants** children's books; **p. faire qch** *(in order)* to do sth; **p. ne pas être en retard** so as not to be late; **p. bien faire** to do things properly; **p. que** + *subjunctive* so that, in order that; **j'épargne p. quand je serai vieux** I'm saving for when I'm old; **p. affaires** on business; **je viens p. la machine à laver** I've come about the washing machine; **c'est p. cela qu'il est venu** that's why he came, that's the reason he came; **p. quoi faire?** what for?; **tout ça p. rien!** all that for nothing!; *Fam* **c'est fait p.** that's what it's there for

(**b**) *(indique la direction)* for; **partir p. l'Espagne** to leave for Spain; **le train p. Paris** the Paris train, the train to *or* for Paris

(**c**) *(dans le temps)* for; **j'en ai p. une heure** it'll take me an hour, I'll be an hour; **il sera ici p. midi** he'll be here by midday

(**d**) *(contre)* for; **il me l'a vendu p. trois fois rien** he sold it to me for next to nothing; **donnez-moi p. 100 francs d'essence** give me 100 francs' worth of petrol

(**e**) *(en faveur de)* for, in favour of; **je suis p.** I'm (all) for it, I'm in favour of it

(**f**) *(à la place de)* for

(**g**) *(comme)* for; **j'avais p. ambition de...** my ambition was to...; **laisser qn p. mort** to leave sb for dead

(**h**) *(quant à, par rapport à)* for; **il est grand p. son âge** he's tall for his age; **p. ce qui est de...** as regards..., with regard to...; **p. moi, c'est absurde** in my opinion it's ridiculous, I think it's ridiculous

(**i**) *(indique le résultat)* **être trop faible p. marcher** to be too weak to walk; **cette situation n'était pas p. lui déplaire** the situation was rather to his liking

(**j**) *(à cause de)* for; **on l'apprécie p. sa gentillesse** people like her because she's so kind; **p. avoir désobéi** for having disobeyed, for disobeying

(**k**) *Litt (indique la concession)* **p. être célèbre, il n'en est pas moins modeste** although famous, he's nonetheless modest

(**l**) *(locutions)* **être p. beaucoup dans qch** to have a lot to do with sth; **je n'y suis p. rien!** it's got nothing to do with me!; *Fam* **être p. faire qch** *(être sur le point de)* to be about to do sth; *Fam* **p. une surprise, c'est une surprise!** that's a surprise and a half!; **perdre p. perdre, autant que tu...** if you're going to lose anyway, you might as well...

2 *nm inv* **le p. et le contre** the pros and cons

pourboire [purbwar] *nm* tip; **5 francs/10% de p.** a 5-franc/10% tip; **être payé au p.** to be paid in tips

pourceau, -x [purso] *nm Litt* swine

pourcentage [pursɑ̃taʒ] *nm* percentage; **être payé au p.** to be paid on a commission basis

pourchasser [purʃase] *vt* to pursue

pourfendre [purfɑ̃dr] *vt Hum (injustices, hypocrisie)* to combat

pourlécher [34] [purleʃe] **se pourlécher** *vpr* **se p. (les babines)** to lick one's lips

pourparlers [purparle] *nmpl* talks, negotiations; **entrer/être en p. (avec)** to enter into/be having talks (with); **p. de paix** peace talks *or* negotiations

pourpre [purpr] **1** *adj & nm* crimson
     2 *nf (teinte naturelle)* purple (dye)

pourquoi [purkwa] **1** *adv & conj* why; **c'est p....** that's why…; **p. pas?** why not?
     2 *nm inv (raison)* **le p. de** the reason for; **le p. et le comment** the whys and wherefores

pourrais *etc voir* pouvoir

pourri, -e [puri] **1** *adj* (a) *(bois, dent)* rotten; *(chair)* putrid; *(fruit, œufs)* bad (b) *Fam (corrompu)* corrupt (c) *Fam (déplaisant)* rotten (d) *Fam* **être p. de fric** to be stinking rich
     2 *nm* (a) *(d'un fruit)* bad part; **sentir le p.** to smell rotten (b) *très Fam (personne)* bastard

pourrir [purir] **1** *vi (bois, dent)* to rot; *(corps)* to putrefy; *(aliments)* to go bad; *Fig* **p. en prison** to rot in prison
     2 *vt* (a) *(gâter)* to rot (b) *Fam (enfant)* to spoil

pourriture [purityr] *nf* (a) *(décomposition)* rot (b) *Fam (corruption)* corruption (c) *très Fam (personne)* bastard

poursuite [pursɥit] *nf* (a) *(chasse)* pursuit; **se lancer à la p. de qn** to set off in pursuit of sb; **être à la p. de qch** *(bonheur, paix)* to be in pursuit of sth (b) *(continuation)* continuation (c) *Jur* **poursuites (judiciaires)** (legal) proceedings; *(en droit pénal)* prosecution; **engager des poursuites contre qn** to start proceedings against sb; *(en droit pénal)* to prosecute sb (d) *(course cycliste)* pursuit

poursuivant, -e [pursɥivɑ̃, -ɑ̃t] *nm,f* pursuer

poursuivre [65] [pursɥivr] **1** *vt* (a) *(pourchasser)* to pursue; *(sujet: idée, crainte)* to haunt; *(sujet: malchance)* to dog (b) *(idéal, rêve, but)* to pursue (c) *(harceler)* to pester (**de** with); *(sujet: créancier)* to hound; **p. qn de ses assiduités** to force one's attentions on sb (d) *Jur* **p. qn (en justice)** to bring proceedings against sb; *(en droit pénal)* to prosecute sb (e) *(continuer)* to continue, to go on with; **poursuivez** *(à quelqu'un qui parle)* go on
     2 se poursuivre *vpr (continuer)* to continue, to go on

pourtant [purtɑ̃] *adv* yet; **tout avait p. bien commencé** yet it all started so well; **je ne peux p. pas l'empêcher de venir** still, I can't stop him from coming; **ça n'est p. pas compliqué!** it's hardly complicated!

pourtour [purtur] *nm* circumference, perimeter

pourvoi [purvwa] *nm Jur* appeal; **p. en cassation** appeal to a higher court

pourvoir [73b] [purvwar] **1** *vt* **p. qn de qch** to provide sb with sth; **p. qch de qch** to equip *or* fit sth with sth
     2 pourvoir à *vt ind (besoins)* to provide *or* cater for
     3 se pourvoir *vpr* (a) *(se munir)* **se p. de qch** to provide oneself with sth (b) *Jur* **se p. en cassation** to take one's case to the Court of Appeal

pourvoyeur, -euse [purvwajœr, -øz] *nm,f* supplier

pourvu¹ [purvy] **pourvu que** *conj* (a) *(condition)* **p. que tu y sois** provided (that) *or* so long as you're there (b) *(souhait)* **p. qu'il le fasse!** let's just hope he does it!

pourvu², -e *voir* pourvoir

pousse [pus] *nf* (a) *(des feuilles, des cheveux)* growth (b) *(bourgeon)* shoot; **p. de bambou** bamboo shoot; *Fig* **jeune p.** *(société)* start-up

poussé, -e [puse] *adj (en profondeur)* thorough

pousse-café [puskafe] *nm inv* (glass of) liqueur *(after coffee)*

poussée [puse] *nf* (a) *(pression)* pressure; *(d'un liquide)* upthrust; **la p. de la foule** the pushing and shoving of the crowd (b) *(croissance)* growth; *(de boutons, d'herpès)* eruption; **p. de fièvre** sudden rise in temperature; **p. démographique** sudden population increase; **faire une p. de croissance** to shoot up (c) *Fig (des prix)* upsurge (**de** in)

pousse-pousse [puspus] *nm inv* rickshaw

pousser [puse] **1** *vt* (a) *(soumettre à une force)* to push; *(sujet: vent)* *(embarcation)* to drive; **p. qn du coude** to nudge sb with one's elbow; *Fam* **à la va comme je te pousse** slipshod; *Fam* **faut pas p. Mémé** *ou* **Mémère dans les orties!** don't push your luck!
     (b) *(inciter)* **p. qn à faire qch** *(sujet: faim, jalousie)* to drive sb to do sth; *(sujet: personne)* to urge sb to do sth; **p. qn à qch** to drive sb to sth; **poussé par la curiosité** prompted by curiosity
     (c) *(continuer)* **p. trop loin une plaisanterie** to take a joke too far; **il a poussé la générosité jusqu'à l'héberger** he was so generous that he even put him up
     (d) *(émettre)* **p. un cri** to shout, to give a shout; **p. des cris** to shout; **p. un soupir** to sigh, to heave a sigh; **p. un gémissement** to groan; *Fam* **p. la chansonnette** to sing a song
     2 *vi* (a) *(exercer une pression)* to push; *(aux toilettes)* to strain; *(en accouchant)* to push; *Fam* **faut pas p.!** don't push your luck!
     (b) *(continuer)* **p. jusqu'au bois** to push on as far as the wood
     (c) *(plante, cheveux, ongles)* to grow; *(bourgeon)* to sprout; *(dents)* to come through; *Fam (enfant)* to shoot up; **se laisser p. la barbe** to grow a beard
     3 se pousser *vpr (pour faire de la place)* to move over *or* up

poussette [puset] *nf (pour enfants) Br* pushchair, *Am* stroller

poussière [pusjɛr] *nf* dust; **une p.** a speck of dust; *Fam* **faire la p.** *ou* **les poussières** to do the dusting, to dust; *Fig* **tomber en p.** to crumble to dust; *Fig* **mordre la p.** to bite the dust; *Fam* **10 francs et des poussières** 10 and a bit francs

poussiéreux, -euse [pusjerø, -øz] *adj* dusty; *Fig* stuffy

poussif, -ive [pusif, -iv] *adj (moteur, personne)* wheezy

poussin, -e [pusɛ̃, -in] **1** *nm* chick; *Fam* **mon p.** pet
     2 *nm,f Sport* junior *(9 years old)*

poutre [putr] *nf (en bois)* beam; *(en métal)* girder; **p. apparente** exposed beam; **p. maîtresse** main beam/girder

poutrelle [putrɛl] *nf* girder

pouvoir¹ [puvwar] *nm* (a) *(puissance)* power; **avoir du p. sur qn** to have power *or* influence over sb; **prendre le p.** to assume power; **être au p.** to be in power; **p. absolu** absolute power; **p. exécutif** executive power; **p. judiciaire** judicial power; **p. législatif** legislative power; **les pouvoirs publics** the authorities (b) *(attributions)* power; **il n'est pas en mon p. de…** it is not within my power to… (c) **p. d'achat** purchasing power

pouvoir² [57] **1** *vt* (**a**) *(être capable de)* can, to be able; **p. faire qch** can *or* to be able to do sth; **si je peux** if I can, if I'm able to; **je ne peux pas** I can't, I'm unable to; **comment a-t-il pu dire cela?** how could he say that?; **on n'y peut rien** it can't be helped, there's nothing that can be done about it; **on ne peut plus/moins aimable** extremely friendly/unfriendly; **il n'en peut plus** *(de fatigue)* he's exhausted; *(d'exaspération, d'impatience)* he can't take any more; **dès que je pourrai** as soon as I can; **où peut-il bien être?** where can he be?; **nous ne pouvons rien pour vous** we can't do anything for you

(**b**) *(avoir le droit, la permission de)* can, to be allowed; **vous pouvez partir** you can go; **puis-je entrer?** can I come in?; **si je puis m'exprimer ainsi** if I may use the phrase

(**c**) *(être possible)* **la porte a pu se fermer toute seule** the door might have *or* could have closed on its own; **tout le monde peut se tromper** anyone can make a mistake; **elle peut bien s'excuser, je ne lui pardonnerai pas** she can apologize all she likes, but I won't forgive her; *Fam* **qu'est-ce que ça peut te faire?** what's that got to do with you?

2 *v impersonnel* **cela se peut/se pourrait (bien)** it's quite possible; **il se peut qu'il vienne** he may *or* might come

PPCM [pepeseɛm] *nm Math (abrév* **plus petit commun multiple)** LCM

PQ [peky] *nm* (**a**) *Can Pol (abrév* **Parti Québécois)** PQ (**b**) *Fam (papier hygiénique)* toilet paper, *Br* loo paper

pragmatique [pragmatik] *adj* pragmatic

pragois, -e [pragwa, -az] **1** *adj* of Prague
2 *nm,f* **P.** person from Prague

Prague [prag] *n* Prague

praire [prɛr] *nf* clam

prairie [preri] *nf* meadow; *Géog* **la P.** the Prairies

praline [pralin] *nf* praline

praliné, -e [praline] *adj (chocolat)* praline-filled; *(glace)* praline-flavoured

praticable [pratikabl] *adj* (**a**) *(route)* passable, negotiable; *(terrain)* playable (**b**) *(réalisable)* practicable

praticien, -enne [pratisjɛ̃, -ɛn] *nm,f (médecin)* (medical) practitioner

pratiquant, -e [pratikã, -ãt] **1** *adj* practising; **je ne suis pas p.** I'm not religious
2 *nm,f* practising Christian/Jew/Muslim/*etc*

pratique [pratik] **1** *adj (méthode, personne)* practical; *(outil)* handy; *(date, heure, jour)* convenient; **avoir l'esprit p.** to have a practical turn of mind
2 *nf* (**a**) *(application)* practice; **mettre qch en p.** to put sth into practice; **dans la p.** in practice (**b**) *(expérience)* (practical) experience; **avoir une longue p. de qch** to have had a lot of (practical) experience of sth (**c**) *(d'un sport)* playing; **la p. du yoga** doing yoga (**d**) *(procédé, coutume)* practice

pratiquement [pratikmã] *adv* (**a**) *(concrètement)* in practice (**b**) *(presque)* practically

pratiquer [pratike] **1** *vt* (**a**) *(religion)* to practise; *(activité)* to take part in; *(langue)* to use; *(sport)* to play; **p. la natation** to swim; **les prix pratiqués ici** the prices being asked here (**b**) *(faire) (ouverture)* to make; *(opération chirurgicale)* to carry out
2 *vi* (**a**) *(médecin, avocat)* to practise (**b**) *(être religieux)* to practise one's religion; **il est catholique mais il ne pratique pas** he's a Catholic but he doesn't go to church

3 se pratiquer *vpr (sport)* to be played; *(coutume)* to be practised

pré [pre] *nm* meadow

préadolescent, -e [preadɔlɛsã, -ãt] *nm,f* pre-adolescent

préalable [prealabl] **1** *adj* previous, prior (**à** to); *(accord)* prior; *(formalités)* preliminary
2 *nm (condition)* prerequisite, precondition; **au p.** first, beforehand

préalablement [prealabləmã] *adv* first, beforehand; **p. à...** prior to...

préambule [preãbyl] *nm* preamble (**de** to); **sans p., elle annonça...** without any warning, she announced...

PréAO [preao] *nf Ordinat (abrév* **présentation assistée par ordinateur)** computer-assisted presentation

préau, -x [preo] *nm (de cour d'école)* covered area; *(salle)* hall

préavis [preavi] *nm* (advance) notice; **un p. de trois mois** three months' notice; **p. de grève** strike notice; **déposer un p. de grève** to give notice of strike action; **p. de licenciement** notice (of dismissal)

précaire [prekɛr] *adj (position)* precarious; *(santé)* delicate; **être en équilibre p.** to be precariously balanced; **il a un emploi p.** he's got no job security

précambrien, -enne [prekãbrijɛ̃, -ɛn] *Géol* **1** *adj* Precambrian
2 *nm* **le P.** the Precambrian period

précarité [prekarite] *nf* precariousness; **la p. de l'emploi** the lack of job security

précaution [prekosjɔ̃] *nf* (**a**) *(mesure)* precaution; **par (mesure de) p.** as a precaution; **prendre des** *ou* **ses précautions** to take precautions; *Prov* **deux précautions valent mieux qu'une** better safe than sorry (**b**) *(prudence)* caution, care; **pour plus de p.** to be on the safe side

précautionneux, -euse [prekosjɔnø, -øz] *adj* careful

précédemment [presedamã] *adv* previously, before

précédent, -e [presedã, -ãt] **1** *adj* previous
2 *nm* precedent; **sans p.** unprecedented, without precedent

précéder [34] [presede] **1** *vt* to precede; **je l'ai précédé de dix minutes** I got there ten minutes before he did
2 *vi* **la page qui précède** the preceding *or* previous page; **dans les jours qui précèdent** in the preceding days; **ce qui précède** the foregoing

précepte [presɛpt] *nm* precept

précepteur, -trice [preseptœr, -tris] *nm,f* (private) tutor

préchauffage [preʃofaʒ] *nm* preheating

préchauffer [preʃofe] *vt* to preheat

prêcher [preʃe] **1** *vt* (**a**) *(enseigner)* to preach (**à** to) (**b**) *(prôner)* to advocate; *Hum* **p. la bonne parole** to spread the good word
2 *vi (prononcer un sermon)* to preach; *Fig* **p. dans le désert** to be a voice crying in the wilderness; *Fig* **p. pour sa paroisse** to look after one's own interests

prêchi-prêcha [preʃipreʃa] *nm inv Fam Péj* preachifying

précieusement [presjøzmã] *adv* **garder** *ou* **conserver qch p.** to keep sth safe

précieux, -euse [presjø, -øz] *adj* (**a**) *(coûteux)* precious (**b**) *(conseil, temps)* valuable (**à** to) (**c**) *(style, personne)* precious, affected

préciosité [presjozite] *nf Litt* affectation, preciosity

précipice [presipis] *nm* chasm, abyss; *(d'une falaise, d'un ravin)* precipice; *Fig* abyss; *Fig* **être au bord du p.** to be on the edge of an abyss

précipitamment [presipitamɑ̃] *adv* hurriedly, hastily; **entrer/sortir p.** to rush *or* dash in/out

précipitation [presipitasjɔ̃] *nf* (a) *(hâte)* haste; **dans ma p., j'ai oublié les clés** I was in such a hurry, I forgot the keys (b) *Chim* precipitation (c) **précipitations** *(pluies)* precipitation

précipité, -e [presipite] **1** *adj* hasty, hurried
2 *nm Chim* precipitate

précipiter [presipite] **1** *vt* (a) *(entraîner)* to throw down, to hurl down; *Fig* to plunge; **p. qn dans le vide** to hurl sb over the edge (b) *(hâter)* to speed up; *(événements)* to precipitate; *(la mort de quelqu'un)* to hasten; **il ne faut rien p.** we mustn't rush things (c) *Chim* to precipitate
2 *vi Chim* to precipitate
3 se précipiter *vpr* (a) *(se hâter)* to rush, to hurry (b) *(s'accélérer)* **les événements se sont précipités** things started happening quickly (c) *(se jeter)* to rush (**sur/ vers** at/towards)

précis, -e [presi, -iz] **1** *adj* precise, exact; **à deux heures précises** at two o'clock precisely *or* exactly; **penser à quelque chose de p.** to have something specific in mind
2 *nm* précis, summary; *(livre)* handbook; **p. d'histoire de France** short history of France

précisément [presizemɑ̃] *adv* precisely, exactly

préciser [presize] **1** *vt* (a) *(déterminer) (date)* to specify (b) *(clarifier) (pensée)* to clarify; **je tiens à p. que...** I wish to make it clear that...; **pourriez-vous p.?** could you be more specific?
2 se préciser *vpr* to become clear(er); *(idée)* to take shape

précision [presizjɔ̃] *nf* (a) *(d'une information, d'une description)* accuracy; *(de mouvements)* preciseness, precision; **avec p.** precisely (b) *(détail)* **une p.** a precise detail; **donner** *ou* **apporter des précisions sur qch** to give precise details about sth; **demander des précisions sur qch** to ask for further information about sth

précoce [prekɔs] *adj (enfant)* precocious; *(fruit, été)* early; *(sénilité, calvitie)* premature

précocité [prekɔsite] *nf* precociousness; *(d'un fruit, d'une saison)* earliness

précolombien, -enne [prekɔlɔ̃bjɛ̃, -ɛn] *adj* pre-Columbian

préconçu, -e [prekɔ̃sy] *adj* preconceived

préconiser [prekɔnize] *vt* to advocate; *(remède)* to recommend

précuit, -e [prekɥi, -it] *adj* precooked

précurseur [prekyrsœr] **1** *nm* precursor, forerunner
2 *adj m* **signe p.** forewarning

prédateur [predatœr] *nm* predator

prédécesseur [predesesœr] *nm* predecessor

prédécoupé, -e [predekupe] *adj* precut

prédestination [predɛstinasjɔ̃] *nf* predestination

prédestiné, -e [predɛstine] *adj* predestined (**à qch/à faire qch** for sth/to do sth)

prédestiner [predɛstine] *vt* to predestine (**à qch/à faire qch** for sth/to do sth)

prédicat [predika] *nm Gram* predicate

prédicateur, -trice [predikatœr, -tris] *nm,f* preacher

prédiction [prediksjɔ̃] *nf* prediction

prédilection [predilɛksjɔ̃] *nf* predilection, partiality; **de p.** favourite; **avoir une p. pour qch** to be partial to sth, *Formal* to have a predilection for sth

prédire [27b] [predir] *vt* to predict; **p. qch à qn** to predict sth for sb; **elle m'a prédit que je voyagerais** she predicted that I would travel

prédisposer [predispoze] *vt* to predispose (**à** to)

prédisposition [predispozisjɔ̃] *nf* predisposition (**à** to)

prédominant, -e [predɔminɑ̃, -ɑ̃t] *adj* predominant

prédominer [predɔmine] *vi* to predominate

préélectoral, -e, -aux, -ales [preelɛktɔral, -o] *adj* pre-electoral, pre-election

préemballé, -e [preɑ̃bale] *adj* prepacked

prééminence [preeminɑ̃s] *nf* pre-eminence

prééminent, -e [preeminɑ̃, -ɑ̃t] *adj* pre-eminent

préempter [preɑ̃pte] *vt Jur* to pre-empt

préemption [preɑ̃psjɔ̃] *nf Jur* pre-emption

préenregistré, -e [preɑ̃rəʒistre] *adj* prerecorded

préétablir [preetablir] *vt* to pre-establish

préexistant, -e [preɛgzistɑ̃, -ɑ̃t] *adj* pre-existing

préexister [preɛgziste] *vi* to pre-exist; **p. à qch** to pre-exist sth

préfabrication [prefabrikasjɔ̃] *nf* prefabrication

préfabriqué, -e [prefabrike] **1** *adj* prefabricated
2 *nm* prefabricated material; **c'est du p.** it's prefabricated

préface [prefas] *nf* preface, foreword (**à** *ou* **de** to)

préfacer [16] [prefase] *vt* to preface

préfectoral, -e, -aux, -ales [prefɛktɔral, -o] *adj* = relating to a "préfecture" or "préfet"

préfecture [prefɛktyr] *nf* prefecture; *(ville)* = administrative centre of a "département"; **la P. de police** police headquarters

---

Préfecture

This refers to the main administrative office of each "département". The word has also come to refer to the town where the office is located. One goes to the "préfecture" to obtain a driving licence or a "carte de séjour", for example.

---

préférable [preferabl] *adj* preferable (**à** to); **il serait p. de le revoir** *ou* **que nous le revoyions** it would be preferable to see him again

préféré, -e [prefere] *adj & nm,f* favourite

préférence [preferɑ̃s] *nf* preference; **de p.** preferably; **de p. à** in preference to

préférentiel, -elle [preferɑ̃sjɛl] *adj* preferential

préférer [34] [prefere] *vt* to prefer (**à** to); **je préférerais du thé** I'd prefer tea, I'd rather have tea; **je préférerais que vous veniez** I'd prefer it if you came, I'd rather you came; **p. faire qch** to prefer to do sth

préfet [prefɛ] *nm* (a) *(fonctionnaire)* prefect *(administrative head of a "département")*; **p. de police** = chief commissioner of police (b) *Belg Scol Br* head teacher, *Am & Ir* principal

préfigurer [prefigyre] *vt* to prefigure, to foreshadow

préfixe [prefiks] *nm* prefix

pré-formaté, -e *(mpl* pre-formatés, *fpl* pré-formatées) [preformate] *adj Ordinat* pre-formatted

préhension [preɑ̃sjɔ̃] *nf* gripping

préhistoire [preistwar] *nf* prehistory

préhistorique [preistɔrik] *adj* prehistoric

pré-impression [preɛ̃presjɔ̃] *nf Typ* pre-press

préindustriel, -elle [preɛ̃dystrijɛl] *adj* pre-industrial

préinscription [preɛ̃skripsjɔ̃] *nf* pre-check-in

préjudice [preʒydis] *nm (à une cause)* prejudice, detriment; *(à une personne)* harm, wrong; *Jur* tort; **subir un p. matériel** to sustain damage; **subir un p. moral** to suffer mental distress; **porter p. à qn** to do sb harm; **au p. de qch** to the detriment of sth

préjugé [preʒyʒe] *nm* prejudice, bias (**contre** against); **avoir un p. contre qn/qch** to be prejudiced *or* biased against sb/sth; **n'avoir aucun p.** to be totally unprejudiced *or* unbiased

prélasser [prelase] **se prélasser** *vpr* to lounge

prélat [prela] *nm* prelate

prélavage [prelavaʒ] *nm* pre-wash

prélèvement [prelɛvmɑ̃] *nm* (**a**) *(en argent)* deduction (**sur** from); **faire un p. sur un compte** to debit an account; **p. automatique** direct debit; **prélèvements obligatoires** = tax and social security contributions (**b**) *(extraction) (d'un organe)* removal; *(de sécrétions)* taking a sample; *(d'un échantillon)* taking; **faire un p. de sang** *ou* **sanguin à qn** to take a blood sample from sb (**c**) *(partie prélevée) (de sécrétions)* swab; *(de sang)* sample

prélever [46] [prelve] *vt* (**a**) *(argent)* to deduct (**sur** from); *(impôt)* to levy (**b**) *(organe)* to remove; *(sécrétions, échantillon)* to take; **p. du sang à qn** to take a blood sample from sb

préliminaire [preliminɛr] **1** *adj* preliminary
2 *nmpl* **préliminaires** preliminaries

prélude [prelyd] *nm Mus & Fig* prelude (**de** *ou* **à** to)

prématuré, -e [prematyre] **1** *adj* premature; **être p. de six semaines** to be six weeks premature
2 *nm,f* premature baby

prématurément [prematyremɑ̃] *adv* prematurely

préméditation [premeditasjɔ̃] *nf* premeditation; **meurtre avec p.** premeditated murder

préméditer [premedite] *vt* to premeditate

prémenstruel, -elle [premɑ̃stryɛl] *adj* premenstrual

premier, -ère [prəmje, -ɛr] **1** *adj* (**a**) *(initial, dominant)* first; **les trois premières années** the first three years; **la première marche** the bottom stair; **le p. rang** the front row; **prendre la première place** *(dans une course)* to take the lead; **le p. venu** the first person who comes along; **les premiers arrivés** the first to arrive; **je suis le p. concerné** I'm the one most affected; **en p.** in the first place, firstly; **le p. de l'an** New Year's Day
(**b**) *(original)* primary, original
2 *nm,f* (**a**) *(dans un classement)* first; **arriver le p.** *ou* **en p.** to arrive first; **être le p. de sa classe** to be top of one's class; **être le p. à faire qch** to be (the) first to do sth; *voir aussi* **cinquième**
(**b**) *(acteur)* **jeune p.** (young) romantic lead; *Fig* **avoir des airs de jeune p.** to look like a film star
3 *nm (date)* **le p. janvier** the first of January, January the first; **le p. de l'an** New Year's Day
4 *nf* **première** (**a**) *(d'une pièce)* first *or* opening night; *(d'un film)* première
(**b**) *(classe) Br* ≃ lower sixth, *Am* ≃ eleventh grade
(**c**) *(de train, d'avion)* first class; **voyager en première** to travel first-class
(**d**) *(vitesse)* first (gear)
(**e**) *(de chaussure)* insole
(**f**) *Fam* **de première** *(de très bonne qualité)* first-rate, first-class

premièrement [prəmjɛrmɑ̃] *adv* first, in the first place

prémisse [premis] *nf* premise

prémolaire [premɔlɛr] *nf* premolar

prémonition [premɔnisjɔ̃] *nf* premonition

prémonitoire [premɔnitwar] *adj* premonitory

prémunir [premynir] **se prémunir** *vpr* **se p. contre qch** to be on one's guard against sth

prenant, -e [prənɑ̃, -ɑ̃t] *adj (livre, spectacle)* fascinating; *(travail)* time-consuming

prénatal, -e, -als, -ales [prenatal] *adj* antenatal, prenatal

prendre [58] [prɑ̃dr] **1** *vt* (**a**) *(saisir)* to take; **p. qch dans un tiroir** to take sth out of a drawer; **prends-le par la poignée** take hold of it by the handle; **c'est à p. ou à laisser** take it or leave it; *Fam* **il faut savoir le p.** you have to know how to handle him; *Fam* **c'est toujours ça de pris** that's something at least; *Fam* **qu'est-ce qu'on va p.!** we're in for it!
(**b**) *(enlever)* to take (away); **p. qch à qn** to take sth (away) from sb; **cela m'a pris du temps/deux heures** it took me a while/two hours; **p. 100 francs de l'heure** to take 100 francs an hour
(**c**) *(s'emparer de) (personne, gibier)* to catch; *(ville, région)* to take, to capture; **se laisser p.** to let oneself be *or* get caught; *Fig* to let oneself be taken in; *Prov* **tel est pris qui croyait p.** it's a case of the biter bit
(**d**) *(aller chercher)* to collect, to pick up; **attends, je vais p. mon parapluie** wait till I get my umbrella
(**e**) *(acheter)* to get; *(chambre, studio)* to take; **cette robe me plaît, je la prends** I like this dress, I'll take it
(**f**) *(bonne, assistant)* to take on; *(pensionnaire)* to take in; *(travail)* to take; **être pris** *(élève, candidat)* to be accepted; *(acteur)* to get the part
(**g**) *(repas, boisson, bain)* to have; *(médicament)* to take
(**h**) *(moyen de transport)* to take
(**i**) *(apparence)* to take on, to assume; *(attitude)* to take; *(accent)* to pick up
(**j**) **p. l'eau** *(bateau)* to be leaking, to be letting in water
(**k**) *(personne)* **p. qn comme exemple** to take sb as an example; **p. qn/qch pour** to take sb/sth for
(**l**) *Fam (arriver)* **qu'est-ce qui lui prend?** what's come over him?; **ça te prend souvent?** do you get like that often?
2 *vi* (**a**) *(ciment, flan)* to set
(**b**) *(plante)* to take (root)
(**c**) *(feu)* to catch
(**d**) *(réussir) (vaccin)* to take effect; *(mode)* to catch on; *Fam* **avec moi, ça ne prend pas!** you can't fool me!
(**e**) *(tourner)* **p. à gauche/droite** to go left/right
(**f**) **p. sur soi** to restrain *or* contain oneself
3 **se prendre** *vpr* (**a**) *(s'accrocher)* **se p. dans une porte/à un clou** to get caught in the door/on a nail
(**b**) *(se considérer)* **se p. pour un héros** to consider oneself a hero; **pour qui vous prenez-vous?** who do you think you are?
(**c**) *(locutions)* **s'en p. à qn/qch** to take it out on sb/sth; **ne t'en prends qu'à toi-même** you've only got yourself to blame; **s'y p. bien avec qn** to know how to handle sb; **s'y p. mal avec qn** not to handle sb the right way; **vous vous y prenez mal** you're going about it the wrong way; **s'y p. à deux fois pour faire qch** to take two attempts to do sth

preneur, -euse [prənœr, -øz] *nm,f* (**a**) *(acheteur)* buyer, purchaser; **trouver p.** to find a buyer; **je suis p.!** I'm interested! (**b**) **p. d'otages** hostage taker; **p. de son** sound engineer

prenne *etc voir* **prendre**

prénom [prenɔ̃] *nm Br* first *or Am* given name; *(de chrétiens)* Christian name

prénommé, -e [prenɔme] *adj* **le p. Victor** the man/boy called Victor

prénommer [prenɔme] **1** *vt* to call, to name

2 se prénommer *vpr* **il se prénomme Adam** his *Br* first *or Am* given name is Adam

prénuptial, -e, -aux, -ales [prenypsjal, -o] *adj* premarital; **examen p.** premarital medical check-up

préoccupant, -e [preɔkypɑ̃, -ɑ̃t] *adj* worrying

préoccupation [preɔkypasjɔ̃] *nf* concern, preoccupation; **j'ai d'autres préoccupations** I have other things to worry about

préoccupé, -e [preɔkype] *adj* worried

préoccuper [preɔkype] **1** *vt* to worry; **être préoccupé par qch** to be worried about sth; **sa santé me préoccupe** I'm worried about his health

2 se préoccuper *vpr* **se p. de qn/qch** to concern oneself with sb/sth

prépa [prepa] *nf Fam Scol* preparatory class *(for the entrance exam to the "grandes écoles")*; **faire une p., être en p.** to be studying for the entrance exam to the "grandes écoles"

préparateur, -trice [preparatœr, -tris] *nm,f* laboratory assistant; **p. en pharmacie** pharmacist's *or Br* chemist's assistant

préparatifs [preparatif] *nmpl* preparations (**de** for)

préparation [preparasjɔ̃] *nf* preparation (**à** for); **faire une p. militaire** = to do an officer training course in preparation for military service; **faire une p. aux grandes écoles** to prepare for the entrance exam to the "grandes écoles"

préparatoire [preparatwar] *adj* preparatory

préparer [prepare] **1** *vt* (**a**) *(discours, repas, plat)* to prepare; *(réunion, soirée, vacances)* to make preparations for, to arrange; *(ordonnance)* to make up; **plats tout préparés** ready-cooked meals; *Fig* **je suis sûr qu'il nous prépare quelque chose** I'm sure he's up to something (**b**) *(personne)* **p. qn à qch** to prepare sb for sth; *(entraîner)* to train sb for sth (**c**) *(examen)* to prepare for, to study for

2 se préparer *vpr* (**a**) *(être imminent)* to be in the offing (**b**) *(s'apprêter)* to get ready; **se p. à qch/à faire qch** to prepare *or* get ready for sth/to do sth (**c**) *(se faire)* **se p. qch** *(boisson, plat)* to make oneself sth; **tu te prépares bien des désillusions** you're in for a big disappointment

prépayé, -e [prepeje] *adj* prepaid

prépondérant, -e [prepɔ̃derɑ̃, -ɑ̃t] *adj* predominant

préposé, -e [prepoze] *nm,f* *(employé)* employee; *(dans un vestiaire)* attendant; **p. (des postes)** *Br* postman, *f* postwoman, *Am* mailman, *f* mailwoman

préposer [prepoze] *vt* **p. qn à qch** to appoint sb to sth

préposition [prepozisjɔ̃] *nf Gram* preposition

prépuce [prepys] *nm Anat* foreskin, *Spéc* prepuce

préraphaélite [prerafaelit] *adj & nm* Pre-Raphaelite

préretraite [prerɔtret] *nf* early retirement; *(pension)* early retirement pension; **partir en p.** to take early retirement

prérogative [prerɔgativ] *nf* prerogative

près [prɛ] *adv* (**a**) *(dans l'espace)* near, close; *(dans le temps)* close; **de p.** closely; **voir qch de p.** to see sth close up; **à quelques détails p.** except for a few details; **la longueur, à 5 centimètres p.** the length, to

within 5 centimetres; **à deux minutes p., je ratais le train** two minutes later and I would have missed the train; **je n'en suis pas à 10 francs p.** 10 francs more or less doesn't matter; **à peu de chose(s) p.** more or less (**b**) **p. de** *(dans l'espace)* near (to), close to; *(dans le temps)* close to; *(environ)* nearly, almost; **p. de là** nearby, close by; **p. de chez eux** near (to) *or* close to where they live; *Fam* **être p. de ses sous** to be tightfisted; *Hum* **nous ne sommes pas p. de le revoir** we won't see him again in a hurry

(**c**) **à peu p.** *(pas tout à fait)* nearly, almost; *(approximativement)* about, approximately; **il est à peu p. certain que...** it is fairly certain that...

présage [prezaʒ] *nm* omen, sign; **mauvais p.** bad omen

présager [45] [prezaʒe] *vt* (**a**) *(annoncer)* to presage; **cela ne présage rien de bon** it doesn't bode well (**b**) *(prévoir)* to predict; **ces gros nuages noirs laissent p. un orage** those big black clouds are a sure sign of a storm

pré-salé *(pl* **prés-salés)** [presale] *nm* *(mouton)* salt-meadow sheep; *(viande)* salt-meadow lamb

presbyte [presbit] *adj* long-sighted

presbytère [presbiter] *nm* presbytery

presbytérien, -enne [presbiterjɛ̃, -ɛn] *adj & nm,f* Presbyterian

presbytie [presbisi] *nf* long-sightedness

préscolaire [preskɔler] *adj* preschool

prescription [preskripsjɔ̃] *nf* (**a**) *Jur* **après cinquante ans, il y a p.** the statute of limitations runs out after fifty years (**b**) *(ordonnance)* prescription (**c**) *(instruction)* rule, regulation

prescrire [30] [preskrir] *vt* *(médicament)* to prescribe; **à la date prescrite** on the date specified

préséance [preseɑ̃s] *nf* precedence, priority (**sur** over)

présélection [preseleksjɔ̃] *nf* preselection; *(de candidats)* short-listing

présélectionner [preseleksjɔne] *vt* to preselect; *(candidats)* to short-list

présence [prezɑ̃s] *nf* (**a**) *(dans un lieu)* presence; *(à l'école)* attendance; **il ignore votre p.** he doesn't know you're here; **avoir de la p.** *(acteur)* to have great presence; **les parties en p.** the parties present; **en p. de toute la famille** in front of the whole family; **en p. du virus** when the virus is present (**b**) **avoir la p. d'esprit de faire qch** to have the presence of mind to do sth

présent¹, -e [prezɑ̃, -ɑ̃t] **1** *adj* (**a**) *(physiquement)* present; **les personnes présentes** those present; **Jacques Martelin, ici p., vous le dira** Jacques Martelin, who is here with us, will tell you; **Tardieu? – p.!** Tardieu? – here! *or* present! (**b**) *(situation, moment)* present; **vivre dans l'instant p.** to live in the present

2 *nm* (**a**) *Gram* present (tense); **le p. du subjonctif/de l'indicatif** the present subjunctive/indicative; **au p.** in the present (**b**) *(moment présent)* present; **vivre dans le p.** to live in the present (**c**) **à p.** at present, (just) now; **jusqu'à p.** up to now, until now; **jusqu'à p., je n'ai pas reçu de nouvelles** I've not received any news as yet; **dès à p.** from now on; **à p. que...** now that...

3 *nf* **par la présente** *(par cette lettre)* hereby

présent² *nm Litt (cadeau)* present, gift; **faire p. de qch à qn** to present sth to sb

présentable [prezɑ̃tabl] *adj* presentable

présentateur, -trice [prezɑ̃tatœr, -tris] *nm,f* presenter; *(d'un spectacle télévisé)* compère; **p. de journal télévisé** newscaster, newsreader

présentation [prezɑ̃tasjɔ̃] nf (**a**) (de faits, d'un billet) presentation; **10% de réduction sur p. de la carte** 10% discount on presentation of this card (**b**) (apparence) (d'une personne) appearance; (d'un document) presentation, layout; **recherche hôtesses, excellente p.** (petite annonce) hostesses required, must have smart appearance; Ordinat **p. assistée par ordinateur** computer-aided presentation (**c**) (dans un groupe) introduction (**à** to); **faire les présentations** to make the introductions (**d**) (d'un film) showing, presentation; **p. de mode** fashion show

présenter [prezɑ̃te] **1** vt (**a**) (montrer) to show, to present; (symptôme) to present; (facture) to submit (**b**) (par écrit) to present (**c**) (oralement) (arguments) to present, to set out; (spectacle) to present, to host; **p. ses condoléances à qn** to offer sb one's condolences (**d**) (projet de loi) to bring in, to introduce; **p. sa candidature à un poste** to apply for a job (**e**) (personne) **p. qn à qn** to introduce sb to sb; **je vous présente Marie** this is Marie
2 vi Fam **bien/mal p.** to look/not to look good
3 se présenter vpr (**a**) (occasion, cas) to arise, to present itself; **ça se présente bien** things are looking promising (**b**) (à un poste) to apply (**à** for); **se p. à un examen** to take or Br sit an examination; **se p. aux élections** to be a candidate at or Br stand at the elections (**c**) (arriver) to turn up; **présentez-vous au commissariat à huit heures** be at the police station at eight o'clock; **se p. chez qn** to call on sb (**d**) (dire son nom) to introduce oneself (**à** to) (**e**) **le bébé se présente par la tête/le siège** the baby is presenting normally/in a breech position

présentoir [prezɑ̃twar] nm display unit

préservatif [prezɛrvatif] nm condom; **p. féminin** female condom

préservation [prezɛrvasjɔ̃] nf preservation, protection

préserver [prezɛrve] **1** vt to preserve, to protect (**de** from); **le ciel m'en préserve!** heaven forbid!
2 se préserver vpr to protect oneself (**de** from)

présidence [prezidɑ̃s] nf (**a**) (d'un état) presidency (**b**) (d'un club) chairmanship

président, -e [prezidɑ̃, -ɑ̃t] nm,f (**a**) (d'un état) president; **le p. de la République** the President of the Republic (**b**) (d'une assemblée, d'un club) chairman, f chairwoman; **P. du conseil d'administration** Chairman of the Board; **p.-directeur général** Br chairman and managing director, Am chief executive officer (**c**) (magistrat) presiding judge; **p. du jury** foreman of the jury

présidentiel, -elle [prezidɑ̃sjɛl] **1** adj presidential
2 nfpl **présidentielles** presidential elections

Présidentielles
In France, since 1873, the president has been traditionally elected for a renewable seven-year term ("le septennat"). However, as a result of a referendum held in September 2000 the French parliament ruled that the seven-year term of office was to be replaced in 2002 by a five-year term ("le quinquennat"). Candidates are usually nominated by the main political parties, but anyone who collects the requisite number of sponsors can run. If no candidate wins an outright majority in the first round of voting, a runoff between the two frontrunners is held two weeks later.

présider [prezide] **1** vt (**a**) (conseil) to preside over; (réunion) to chair (**b**) (banquet) to be the guest of honour at
2 présider à vt ind Litt **p. aux destinées de...** to preside over the destinies of...

présomption [prezɔ̃psjɔ̃] nf presumption; **p. d'innocence** presumption of innocence

présomptueux, -euse [prezɔ̃ptɥø, -øz] adj presumptuous

presque [prɛsk] adv (**a**) (à peu près) almost, nearly; **p. jamais/rien** scarcely or hardly ever/anything; **je ne dors p. pas** I hardly or scarcely get any sleep; **rien ou p.** scarcely anything (**b**) (devant un nom) **la p. totalité de son œuvre** nearly or almost all of his work

presqu'île [prɛskil] nf peninsula

pressant, -e [prɛsɑ̃, -ɑ̃t] adj (besoin) pressing, urgent; (demande, vendeur) insistent; Fam Euph **avoir un besoin p.** to need to go (to the toilet)

presse [prɛs] nf (**a**) (ensemble des journaux) press; **travailler dans la p.** to work in journalism; **je l'ai lu dans la p.** I read it in the papers; Fig **avoir bonne/mauvaise p. (auprès de)** to be well/badly thought of (by); **la p. écrite** the print media, the press; **la p. à scandale, la p. à sensation** the popular press, Br the tabloids (**b**) Tech press (**c**) (pour imprimer) (printing) press; **mettre qch sous p.** to send sth to press

pressé, -e [prese] adj (**a**) (personne) in a hurry or rush; **p. de faire qch** in a hurry to do sth; **être p. par le temps** to be pushed for time; **d'un pas p.** hurriedly; **on n'est pas p.** there's no rush (**b**) (urgent) urgent; **aller ou parer au plus p.** to deal with the most urgent thing(s) first

presse-agrumes [prɛsagrym] nm inv juice extractor, juicer

presse-ail [prɛsaj] nm inv garlic press

presse-citron [prɛssitrɔ̃] nm inv lemon squeezer

pressentiment [prɛsɑ̃timɑ̃] nm presentiment; (d'un malheur) foreboding; **j'ai le p. que...** I've a (funny) feeling that...

pressentir [64a] [prɛsɑ̃tir] vt (**a**) (deviner) to have a premonition of, to sense; (malheur) to have a foreboding of (**b**) **p. qn (pour qch)** to sound sb out (about sth)

presse-papiers [prɛspapje] nm inv paperweight; Ordinat clipboard

presse-purée [prɛspyre] nm inv potato masher

presser [prɛse] **1** vt (**a**) (agrume, éponge) to squeeze; (raisin, pommes) to press; **p. qn contre son cœur** to clasp sb in one's arms, to hug sb (**b**) (sonnette, bouton) to press, to push (**c**) (harceler) **p. qn de questions** to ply or bombard sb with questions; **p. qn de faire qch** to urge sb to do sth (**d**) (faire se hâter) (personne) to hurry (up); (travail, mouvement) to speed up; **le pas ou l'allure** to speed up, to quicken one's pace
2 vi **le temps presse** there isn't much time (left); **rien ne presse** there's no hurry or rush; **allons, pressons!** come on, let's get a move on!
3 se presser vpr (**a**) (se dépêcher) to hurry (up); **se p. de faire qch** to hurry to do sth; **faire qch sans se p.** to take one's time doing sth (**b**) (se serrer) **se p. contre** to press (oneself) against; **se p. autour de** to crowd or cluster around

pressing [presiŋ] nm dry cleaner's

pression [presjɔ̃] nf (**a**) Tech pressure; **mettre qch sous p.** to pressurize sth; **sous p.** (récipient) pressurized; Fig **être sous p.** to be under pressure; Méd **p.**

artérielle blood pressure; *Météo* **p. atmosphérique** atmospheric pressure; **zone de hautes/basses pressions** area of high/low pressure (**b**) *(action de presser)* pressure; **d'une simple p. du doigt** at the touch of a button (**c**) *Fig (influence)* pressure; **faire p. sur qn** to put pressure on sb, to pressurize sb; **subir des pressions** to be under pressure; *Fam* **mettre la p. à qn** to pressurize sb, to put pressure on sb (**d**) *(bouton) Br* press stud, *Am* snap fastener (**e**) **bière (à la) p.** draught beer; **une p., s'il vous plaît** *Br* ≃ a half pint of lager, please, *Am* ≃ a beer, please

pressoir [prɛswar] *nm* (**a**) *(instrument)* press (**b**) *(lieu)* press house, press room

pressurer [prɛsyre] *vt (exploiter)* to squeeze

pressurisation [prɛsyrizasjɔ̃] *nf* pressurization

prestance [prɛstɑ̃s] *nf* presence; **avoir de la p.** to have (great) presence

prestataire [prɛstatɛr] **1** *nmf* (**a**) *(bénéficiaire)* person receiving benefits (**b**) *(fournisseur)* **p. de service** service provider
  2 *nm Ordinat* **p. d'accès** access provider

prestation [prɛstasjɔ̃] *nf* (**a**) *(allocation)* benefit; **prestations familiales** family benefits; **prestations sociales** social security benefits (**b**) **prestations** *(services fournis)* services (**c**) *(fait de fournir)* provision; **p. de service** provision of a service (**d**) *(d'un comédien)* performance (**e**) **p. de serment** taking the oath

preste [prɛst] *adj* nimble

prestement [prɛstəmɑ̃] *adv* promptly

prestidigitateur, -trice [prɛstidiʒitatœr, -tris] *nm,f* conjurer, magician

prestidigitation [prɛstidiʒitasjɔ̃] *nf* conjuring, magic

prestige [prɛstiʒ] *nm* prestige; **de p.** *(voiture, hôtel)* luxury; *(réalisation)* prestige; **le p. de l'uniforme** the glamour of a uniform

prestigieux, -euse [prɛstiʒjø, -øz] *adj* prestigious

présumer [prezyme] **1** *vt (supposer)* to presume, to assume; **p. qn innocent** to presume sb (to be) innocent
  2 **présumer de** *vt ind* **trop p. de soi** to be overconfident; **p. de ses forces** to overestimate one's strength

présupposer [presypoze] *vt* to presuppose

présure [prezyr] *nf* rennet

prêt¹, -e [prɛ, prɛt] *adj* ready; **être p. à tout** to be prepared to do anything; **être p. à faire qch** to be ready to do sth

prêt² *nm (action)* lending; *(somme)* loan; **p. bancaire** bank loan; **p. immobilier** home loan, ≃ mortgage

prêt-à-porter [prɛtaportе] *nm* (**a**) *(vêtements)* ready-to-wear clothes (**b**) *(secteur)* ready-to-wear (clothing business)

prétendant, -e [pretɑ̃dɑ̃, -ɑ̃t] **1** *nm,f (à un poste)* applicant, candidate (**à** for); *(à un bien, à un titre)* claimant (**à** to); *(au trône)* pretender (**à** to)
  2 *nm (d'une femme)* suitor

prétendre [pretɑ̃dr] **1** *vt (déclarer)* to maintain, to claim; **on prétend que…** people say that…, it is said that…; **à ce qu'il prétend** according to him; **il ne prétend pas être artiste** he doesn't claim or pretend to be an artist; **on le prétend fou** they say he's mad
  2 **prétendre à** *vt ind* to lay claim to; **p. à la victoire** to aim to win
  3 **se prétendre** *vpr* to claim to be

prétendu, -e [pretɑ̃dy] *adj (coupable, voleur)* alleged; *(progrès, égalité, héros)* so-called

prétendument [pretɑ̃dymɑ̃] *adv* supposedly

prête-nom (*pl* **prête-noms**) [prɛtnɔ̃] *nm Fig* figurehead

prétentieux, -euse [pretɑ̃sjø, -øz] **1** *adj* pretentious
  2 *nm,f* pretentious person

prétention [pretɑ̃sjɔ̃] *nf* (**a**) *(vanité)* pretentiousness, pretension; **sans p.** *(repas, maison, personne)* unpretentious (**b**) *(revendication, ambition)* pretension, claim (**à** to); **avoir la p. de faire qch** to claim or pretend to be able to do sth; **quelles sont vos prétentions?** *(salaire demandé)* what sort of salary are you looking for?

prêter [prɛte] **1** *vt* (**a**) *(temporairement)* to lend, *Am* to loan; **p. qch à qn** to lend sth to sb, to lend sb sth; **p. sur gages** to lend against security; *Prov* **on ne prête qu'aux riches** people don't lend money to those who really need it; *Fig* people are judged according to their reputation (**b**) *(donner)* **p. son appui** *ou* **son concours à qn** to give sb one's support; **p. assistance** *ou* **secours à qn** to lend or give assistance to sb; **p. main-forte à qn** to lend or give sb a hand; **p. l'oreille (à)** to listen or lend an ear (to); **p. attention à qch** to pay attention to sth; **p. serment** to take an oath; **p. le flanc à la critique** to lay oneself open to criticism (**c**) *(attribuer)* **p. qch à qn** *(propos, intentions)* to attribute or ascribe sth to sb
  2 prêter à *vt ind* **p. à confusion** to give rise to confusion; **cela prête à rire** that's laughable
  3 se prêter *vpr* (**a**) *(consentir)* **se p. à** to lend oneself to (**b**) *(convenir)* **se p. à** to lend itself to; **la situation ne s'y prête pas** the situation isn't ideal

prétérit [preterit] *nm* preterite (tense); **au p.** in the preterite

prêteur, -euse [prɛtœr, -øz] **1** *nm,f* lender; **p. sur gages** pawnbroker
  2 *adj* ready or willing to lend things; **je ne suis pas p.** I don't like lending things

prétexte [pretɛkst] *nm* pretext, excuse; **pour toi, tout est p. à rire** you find cause for laughter in everything; **sous p. de faire qch** on the pretext of doing sth; **sous p. que…** on the pretext that…; **sous aucun p.** on no account, under no circumstances

prétexter [pretɛkste] *vt* to give as a pretext or an excuse; **il a prétexté qu'il était malade** he gave the excuse that he was ill; **p. la fatigue** to plead tiredness

Pretoria [pretɔrja] *n* Pretoria

prêtre [prɛtr] *nm* priest

prêtresse [prɛtrɛs] *nf* priestess

prêtrise [pretriz] *nf* priesthood

preuve [prœv] *nf* (**a**) *(pour démontrer)* piece of evidence; **il nous faut des preuves** we need proof or evidence; **faire la p. de qch** to prove sth; **avoir la p. que/de…** to have proof that/of…; **faire p. d'intelligence/de courage** to show intelligence/courage; **faire ses preuves** *(personne)* to prove oneself, to show one's ability; *(technique)* to be tried and tested; **jusqu'à p. du contraire** until there's proof to the contrary; *Fam* **elle ne m'aime pas: la p., elle ne m'écrit jamais** I know she doesn't like me because she never writes to me; **j'en veux pour p.…** the proof of it is…; **p. d'achat** proof of purchase (**b**) *Jur* evidence (**c**) *(témoignage)* **une p. d'amour/d'amitié** a token of love/friendship (**d**) *Math* **faire la p. d'une opération** to prove or test the validity of a mathematical operation; **faire la p. par neuf** to cast out nines

prévaloir [69] [prevalwar] **1** *vi* to prevail (**sur** over); **faire p. son opinion** to win acceptance for one's opinion

2 se prévaloir *vpr* **se p. de qch** *(profiter de)* to take advantage of sth; *(s'enorgueillir)* to pride oneself on sth

prévenant, -e [prevnã, -ãt] *adj (personne)* kind (**envers** *ou* **avec** to), considerate (**envers** *ou* **avec** towards); *(geste)* thoughtful (**envers** *ou* **avec** towards)

prévenir [70] [prevnir] *vt* (**a**) *(informer)* to inform, to let know (**de** about *or* of); *(mettre en garde)* to warn; **tu es prévenu!** you've been warned!; **partir sans p.** to leave without telling anyone *or* without warning (**b**) *(empêcher) (maladie)* to prevent, to guard against; *(danger, accident)* to avert; *Prov* **mieux vaut p. que guérir** prevention is better than cure (**c**) *(devancer) (désir)* to anticipate; *(objection)* to forestall

préventif, -ive [prevãtif, -iv] *adj* preventive; *Jur* **détention préventive** custody; **être en détention préventive** to be remanded in custody

prévention [prevãsjõ] *nf* (**a**) *(pour empêcher)* prevention; **p. routière** road safety (**b**) *Jur* custody; **mettre qn en p.** to remand sb in custody

prévenu, -e [prevny] *nm,f Jur* defendant, accused

prévisible [previzibl] *adj* foreseeable

prévision [previzjõ] *nf* forecast; *(activité)* forecasting; **en p. de qch** in expectation *or* anticipation of sth; **prévisions budgétaires** budget projections *or* forecasts; **prévisions météorologiques** weather forecast

prévisionnel, -elle [previzjɔnɛl] *adj (coûts)* estimated; *(budget)* projected; *(analyse)* preliminary

prévoir [73c] [prevwar] *vt* (**a**) *(météo)* to forecast; *(réaction, difficultés, retards)* to expect, to anticipate; **on ne peut pas tout p.** you can't think of everything (**b**) *(programmer) (sortie, vacances)* to plan; **la réunion est prévue pour demain** the meeting is scheduled for tomorrow; **il faudra p. des vêtements de pluie** we'll have to take waterproof clothes; **qu'est-ce que tu as prévu pour le dessert?** what are you planning to have for dessert?; **comme prévu** as planned; **cela s'est passé comme prévu** it went according to plan; **plus tôt/tard que prévu** sooner/later than expected; **cela n'était pas prévu au programme** that wasn't on the agenda

prévoyance [prevwajãs] *nf* foresight, forethought

prévoyant, -e [prevwajã, -ãt] *adj* far-sighted

prie-Dieu [pridjø] *nm inv* prie-dieu, prayer stool

prier [66] [prije] **1** *vi* to pray (**pour** for)

2 *vt* (**a**) *(dieu)* to pray to (**b**) *(supplier)* to beg; **il ne s'est pas fait p. pour venir** he didn't need much persuading to come; **allez, viens, arrête de te faire p.!** come on, stop being so difficult!; **sans se faire p.** without hesitation (**c**) *(demander à)* **p. qn de faire qch** to ask sb to do sth; **je te prie de te dépêcher!** please hurry up!; **taisez-vous, je vous prie!** please be quiet!; **je te prie de croire qu'elle a été surprise!** she was surprised, believe you me!; **je vous en prie!** *(faites-le)* please do!, of course!; *(taisez-vous)* stop it!; *(il n'y a pas de quoi)* you're welcome!

prière [prijɛr] *nf* (**a**) *Rel* prayer; **faire** *ou* **dire sa p.** to say one's prayers (**b**) *(demande)* request; **p. de ne pas fumer** *(sur écriteau)* no smoking; **p. de fermer la porte** *(sur écriteau)* please close the door

prieuré [prijœre] *nm* priory

primaire [primɛr] **1** *adj* (**a**) *(école, couleur, secteur, ère)* primary (**b**) *Péj (personne)* simple-minded; *(réaction, racisme)* narrow-minded

2 *nm* (**a**) *Scol* primary education; **être en p.** to be at primary school (**b**) *Géol* Primary era (**c**) *Écon* primary sector

primate [primat] *nm Zool* primate

primauté [primote] *nf* primacy

prime¹ [prim] *adj* (**a**) **de p. abord** at first sight; *Litt* **dès sa p. jeunesse** since her early youth (**b**) *Math* **B p.** B prime

prime² *nf (d'assurance)* premium; *(allocation)* grant; *(sur salaire)* bonus; **et vous aurez droit à un stylo en p.** and you will receive a free pen; *Fig* **en p.** into the bargain; **p. d'ancienneté** long-service award; **p. d'assurance** insurance premium; **p. de départ** severance pay, golden handshake; **p. de licenciement** severance allowance; **p. de transport** transport allowance

primer¹ [prime] **1** *vt (avoir la priorité sur)* to take precedence over

2 *vi* to come first; **p. sur** to take precedence over

primer² *vt (attribuer un prix à)* to award a prize to; **primé** *(taureau)* prize(winning); *(roman, film)* prize-winning, award-winning

primeur [primœr] *nf* (**a**) **primeurs** *(fruits et légumes)* (early) fruit and vegetables; **marchand de primeurs** greengrocer *(selling early produce)* (**b**) *(exclusivité)* **avoir la p. d'une nouvelle** to be the first to hear a piece of news

primevère [primvɛr] *nf* primrose

primitif, -ive [primitif, -iv] **1** *adj* primitive; *(originel)* original

2 *nm (artiste)* primitive

primo [primo] *adv* first(ly), in the first place

primordial, -e, -aux, -ales [primɔrdjal, -o] *adj* essential, primordial

prince [prɛ̃s] *nm* prince; **comme un p.** *(traité, élevé, habillé)* like a prince; **être** *ou* **se montrer bon p.** to be very decent; **le p. charmant** Prince Charming

prince-de-galles [prɛ̃sdəgal] *adj inv* Prince of Wales check

princesse [prɛ̃sɛs] *nf* princess

princier, -ère [prɛ̃sje, -ɛr] *adj* princely

principal, -e, -aux, -ales [prɛ̃sipal, -o] **1** *adj aussi Gram* main; *(question, raison, but)* main, principal; *(rôle, acteur)* leading

2 *nm* (**a**) *(ce qui compte le plus)* **le p.** the main thing, the most important thing (**b**) *(d'une école) Br* headmaster, *f* headmistress, *Am* principal

principalement [prɛ̃sipalmã] *adv* mainly, principally

principauté [prɛ̃sipote] *nf* principality

principe [prɛ̃sip] *nm* principle; **un accord de p.** an agreement in principle; **partir du p. que...** to assume that...; **c'est une question de p.** it's a matter of principle; **avoir pour p. de...** to make it a matter of principle to...; **avoir des principes** to have (high) principles; **en p.** in principle, theoretically; **par p.** on principle

printanier, -ère [prɛ̃tanje, -ɛr] *adj* spring

printemps [prɛ̃tã] *nm* spring; **au p.** in (the) spring(time); **une journée de p.** a spring day; *Fig* **ses vingt-six p.** her twenty-six summers

prion [prijõ] *nm Biol* prion

prioritaire [prijɔritɛr] *adj* (that has) priority; **être p.** to have priority; *(en voiture)* to have the right of way

priorité [prijɔrite] *nf* (**a**) *(précédence)* priority; **donner la p. à qn/qch** to give sb/sth priority; **leur dossier sera traité en p.** their file will get priority treatment;

avoir la p. sur to have priority over (**b**) *Aut* right of way, priority; **avoir la p.** to have the right of way; **accorder** *ou* **laisser la p. à une voiture** *Br* to give way *or Am* to yield to a car; **refuser la p.** to refuse to give way; **p. à droite** *(sur panneau)* = give way to vehicles coming from the right

pris, -e [pri, priz] **1** *pp voir* **prendre**
2 *adj* (**a**) *(siège)* occupied, taken; **avoir les mains prises** to have one's hands full (**b**) *(personne)* busy; **je suis déjà p. ce jour-là** I've already got something on that day (**c**) *(saisi)* **p. de peur** seized with fear; **p. de panique** panic-stricken; **p. de remords** racked with guilt (**d**) *(gelé)* frozen (over) (**e**) *(encombré)* **avoir le nez p.** to have a blocked nose; **avoir la gorge prise** to have a sore throat (**f**) **avoir la taille bien prise** to have a trim waist

prise [priz] *nf* (**a**) *(d'une ville, de prisonniers)* taking, capture; *(à la pêche)* catch; *(de drogue)* seize
(**b**) *(de médicaments)* taking
(**c**) *Élec* **p. (de courant** *ou* **électrique)** *(femelle) Br* socket, *Am* outlet; *(mâle)* plug; **p. multiple** adaptor; *Ordinat* **p. péritel** scart connector; **p. de terre** *Br* earth *or Am* ground (connection)
(**d**) *Cin, Phot & TV* **p. de son** sound recording; **p. de vue** *(cliché)* shot; *(de tournage)* take; *(action)* shooting
(**e**) *Tech* **en p.** in gear, engaged; *Fig* **en p. (directe) sur** *ou* **avec qch** in touch with sth
(**f**) *(de judo, de lutte)* hold; *(pour se retenir)* hold; *(plus ferme)* grasp, grip; *(pour le pied)* foothold; *Fig* **avoir p. sur qn** to have a hold on *or* over sb; **lâcher p.** to lose one's grip; *Fig* to give up; **donner p. aux reproches/critiques** to lay oneself open to reproach/criticism; **être aux prises avec des difficultés** to be grappling with difficulties; **être aux prises avec qn** to be at odds with sb
(**g**) *(locutions) Fam* **p. de bec** row, squabble; **p. en charge** *(par un taxi) (d'un passager)* picking up; *(somme)* minimum charge; *(par la Sécurité sociale)* (guaranteed) reimbursement; **p. de conscience** awareness, realization; **p. de contact** initial contact *or* meeting; **p. de notes** note-taking; **p. d'otages** hostage-taking; **p. de position** stance; **p. de pouvoir** (political) takeover; **faire une p. de sang à qn** to take a blood sample from sb

priser¹ [prize] **1** *vt* **p. du tabac** to take snuff
2 *vi* to take snuff

priser² *vt Litt (estimer)* to prize, to value

prisme [prism] *nm* prism

prison [prizɔ̃] *nf* (**a**) *(lieu de détention)* prison, jail; **mettre qn en prison** to put sb in prison; **faire de la p.** to serve a prison sentence (**b**) *(peine)* imprisonment; **cinq ans de p.** five years' imprisonment

prisonnier, -ère [prizɔnje, -ɛr] **1** *nm,f* prisoner; **faire qn p.** to take sb prisoner; **p. de droit commun** common criminal; **p. de guerre** prisoner of war, POW; **p. politique** political prisoner
2 *adj* imprisoned, in prison; **ils sont encore prisonniers sous les décombres** they are still trapped in the rubble; **être p. de** to be a prisoner of; *Fig* to be a slave to

privation [privasjɔ̃] *nf* (**a**) *(action de priver)* deprivation (**b**) **privations** *(manque)* hardship, privation; **s'imposer des privations** to deprive oneself, to go without

privatisation [privatizasjɔ̃] *nf* privatization

privatiser [privatize] *vt* to privatize

privautés [privote] *nfpl* (undue) familiarity; **prendre** *ou* **se permettre des p. avec qn** to be over-familiar with sb

privé, -e [prive] **1** *adj* private; **à titre p.** in a private capacity
2 *nm* (**a**) *(secteur)* **le p.** the private sector; *Scol* the private education system; **mes enfants sont dans le p.** my children go to a private school (**b**) *(intimité)* **dans le p.** privately; **connaître qn dans le p.** to know sb personally; **en p.** in private (**c**) *Fam (détective)* private eye

priver [prive] **1** *vt* **p. qn de qch** to deprive sb of sth; **p. qn de sorties** not to allow sb to go out; **être privé de dessert** to go without pudding; **privé d'eau/d'air/de sommeil** deprived of water/air/sleep; **ça ne le prive pas du tout de ne plus fumer** he doesn't find it a hardship not to smoke any more
2 se priver *vpr* to do *or* go without; **se p. de** to do *or* go without; *(plaisir)* to deprive oneself of, to deny oneself; **ne pas se p. de faire qch** not to hesitate to do sth

privilège [privilɛʒ] *nm* privilege

privilégié, -e [privileʒje] **1** *adj (personne, site)* privileged; *(conditions)* privileged, favourable; *(relations)* special
2 *nm,f* privileged person; **les privilégiés** the privileged

privilégier [66] [privileʒje] *vt (personne, groupe)* to privilege; *(facteur, aspect)* to prioritize

prix [pri] *nm* (**a**) *(coût)* price; **à tout p.** at all costs, at any price; **à aucun p.** not at any price, on no account; **se vendre à p. d'or** to fetch huge prices; **acheter qch à p. d'or** to pay a (small) fortune for sth; **payer qch au p. fort** to pay a high price for sth; **faire un p. à qn** to give sb a good deal; **je vous fais un p. d'ami** I'll let you have it cheap; **y mettre le p.** to pay a high price; **la santé/le bonheur, ça n'a pas de p.** you can't put a price on health/happiness; **mettre à p. la tête de qn** to put a price on sb's head; **c'est mon dernier p.** that's my final offer; **votre p. sera le mien** name your price; **au p. coûtant** at cost price; **p. de revient** cost price; **p. de vente** selling price
(**b**) *(importance)* **attacher beaucoup de p.** *ou* **un grand p. à qch** to set great store by sth
(**c**) *(récompense)* prize; **p. de consolation** consolation prize; **le p. Goncourt** = prestigious French literary prize; **p. Nobel** *(récompense)* Nobel Prize; *(personne)* Nobel *Br* prizewinner *or Am* laureate; **le p. Nobel de la Paix** *(récompense)* the Nobel Peace Prize

pro [pro] *nmf Fam* pro

probabilité [prɔbabilite] *nf* probability, likelihood; **selon toute p.** in all probability *or* likelihood; *Math* **calcul des probabilités** theory of probability

probable [prɔbabl] *adj* probable, likely; **il est p. qu'elle viendra** she'll probably come; **peu p.** improbable, unlikely; **il est peu p. qu'elle vienne** she's not likely *or* she's unlikely to come

probablement [prɔbabləmɑ̃] *adv* probably

probant, -e [prɔbɑ̃, -ɑ̃t] *adj* convincing, conclusive

probité [prɔbite] *nf* probity, integrity

problématique [prɔblematik] **1** *adj* problematic(al)
2 *nf* set of problems

problème [prɔblɛm] *nm* problem; **c'est tout un p.!** it's such a problem!; **peau/cheveux à problèmes**

problem skin/hair; **avoir des problèmes familiaux/ d'argent** to have family/money problems

procédé [prɔsede] *nm* (**a**) *(façon de faire)* method; **échange de bons procédés** exchange of friendly services (**b**) *(technique)* process; **p. de fabrication** manufacturing process; *Péj* **ça sent le p.** it seems rather artificial

procéder [34] [prɔsede] **1** *vi* (**a**) *(agir)* to proceed, to act; **p. par ordre** to do things in order; **p. avec méthode** to proceed methodically; **p. par élimination** to follow a process of elimination (**b**) *Formel* **p. de** *(venir de)* to arise out of, to originate in
2 procéder à *vt ind (recherches, arrestation, vérification)* to carry out; *(élections)* to hold

procédure [prɔsedyr] *nf* (**a**) *(méthode)* procedure (**b**) *Jur* proceedings; **engager une p.** to take proceedings (**c**) *Ordinat* procedure; **p. de chargement** loading procedure

procédurier, -ère [prɔsedyrje, -ɛr] *adj* quibbling

procès [prɔse] *nm Jur (legal)* proceedings; *(civil)* lawsuit; *(criminel)* (criminal) trial; **engager un p.** to take legal action; **faire** *ou* **intenter un p. à qn** to take proceedings against sb; **être en p. avec qn** to be involved in legal proceedings with sb; **gagner/perdre son p.** to win/lose one's case; **faire un p. d'intention à qn** to accuse sb on the basis of assumptions not facts; **faire le p. de qn/qch** *(critiquer)* to attack sb/sth; *Fig* **sans autre forme de p.** without (any) further ceremony, without further ado

processeur [prɔsesœr] *nm Ordinat* processor; **p. central** central processing unit, CPU; **p. de données** data processor

procession [prɔsesjɔ̃] *nf* procession

processus [prɔsesys] *nm* process

procès-verbal [prɔseverbal] *(pl* **procès-verbaux** [prɔseverbo]*) nm* (**a**) *Jur* policeman's report *(about an offence)*; *(amende)* fine (**b**) *(rapport)* (official) report; *(d'une réunion)* minutes; *(d'un témoignage)* record

prochain, -e [prɔʃɛ̃, -ɛn] **1** *adj* (**a**) *(qui suit)* next; **ce sera pour une prochaine fois** *Br* another time, perhaps, *Am* let's take a rain check; **à la prochaine (fois)!** see you (soon)!; *Fam* **je descends à la prochaine** I'm getting off at the next stop (**b**) *(imminent)* imminent; **dans un avenir p.** in the near *or* not too distant future; **un jour p.** one day soon
2 *nm (semblable)* **aimer son p.** to love one's neighbour

prochainement [prɔʃɛnmɑ̃] *adv* shortly, soon; **p. sur vos écrans** coming soon to a cinema near you

proche [prɔʃ] **1** *adj* (**a**) *(dans l'espace)* near, close; **p. de qch** close to *or* near sth (**b**) *(dans l'avenir)* near, imminent; **dans un avenir p.** in the near *or* not too distant future; **la fin est p.** the end is nigh (**c**) *(récent)* recent (**d**) *(semblable, intime)* close (**de** to); **ils sont proches parents** they are closely related (**e**) **de p. en p.** gradually, step by step
2 *nm* close relative *or* relation

Proche-Orient [prɔʃɔrjɑ̃] *nm* **le P.** the Middle East

proclamation [prɔklamasjɔ̃] *nf* proclamation

proclamer [prɔklame] *vt* to proclaim; *(résultats de scrutin)* to declare

procréation [prɔkreasjɔ̃] *nf* procreation

procréer [24] [prɔkree] *vi* to procreate

procuration [prɔkyrasjɔ̃] *nf* proxy, power of attorney; **par p.** by proxy, *Spéc* per pro(curationem); *Fig* **vivre par p.** to live vicariously *or* by proxy

procurer [prɔkyre] **1** *vt* **p. qch à qn** *(sujet: personne)* to get sth for sb; *(sujet: chose)* to bring sb sth
2 se procurer *vpr* to get (hold of), to obtain

procureur [prɔkyrœr] *nm Jur* procurator, proxy; **p. général/de la République** *(système anglais)* ≃ public prosecutor; *(système écossais)* ≃ procurator fiscal; *(système américain)* ≃ district attorney

prodigalité [prɔdigalite] *nf* extravagance, prodigality

prodige [prɔdiʒ] **1** *nm* wonder, marvel; *(personne)* prodigy; **faire des prodiges** to work wonders; **tenir du p.** to be extraordinary, to be something of a miracle
2 *adj* **enfant p.** child prodigy

prodigieusement [prɔdiʒjøzmɑ̃] *adv* prodigiously

prodigieux, -euse [prɔdiʒjø, -øz] *adj* prodigious, extraordinary

prodigue [prɔdig] *adj (dépensier)* wasteful, spendthrift; *(généreux)* lavish, unsparing (**de** in *or* with)

prodiguer [prɔdige] *vt* **p. qch à qn** to lavish sth on sb; **p. des conseils à qn** to pour out advice to sb

producteur, -trice [prɔdyktœr, -tris] **1** *adj* **pays p. de blé/pétrole** wheat-growing/oil-producing country
2 *nm,f* producer

productif, -ive [prɔdyktif, -iv] *adj* productive

production [prɔdyksjɔ̃] *nf* (**a**) *Ind & Cin* production; *(d'électricité)* production, generation (**b**) *(produit)* product; *Cin* production; *(d'une usine)* output; **p. littéraire** literary output

productivité [prɔdyktivite] *nf* productivity

produire [18] [prɔdɥir] **1** *vt* (**a**) *(marchandise, émission, gaz)* to produce; *(chaleur, électricité, odeur)* to generate, to produce (**b**) *(résultat, effet)* to produce, to bring about; *(irritation, sensation)* to cause
2 se produire *vpr* (**a**) *(événement)* to happen (**b**) *(acteur)* to appear

produit [prɔdɥi] *nm* (**a**) *(marchandise)* product; **produits agricoles** agricultural *or* farm produce; **p. de beauté** beauty product; **p. chimique** chemical; **p. de consommation** consumer product; **p. d'entretien** (household) cleaning product; **p. fini** finished product; **p. intérieur brut** gross domestic product; **p. de luxe** luxury product; **p. manufacturé** manufactured product; **produits ménagers** (household) cleaning products; **p. national brut** gross national product (**b**) *(profit)* yield; **p. d'une vente** proceeds of a sale; **le p. de dix années de travail** the result of ten years' work; **vivre du p. de la terre** to live off the land (**c**) *Math (d'une multiplication)* product (**d**) *(création)* **c'est le p. de son imagination** it's the product of his imagination

proéminent, -e [prɔeminɑ̃, -ɑ̃t] *adj* prominent

prof [prɔf] *nmf Fam* teacher

profanateur, -trice [prɔfanatœr, -tris] *nm,f (de tombes)* desecrator

profanation [prɔfanasjɔ̃] *nf* desecration, violation

profane [prɔfan] **1** *adj* non-religious, secular; *Fig* **être p. en la matière** to know nothing about the subject
2 *nmf (non-initié)* layman, *f* laywoman

profaner [prɔfane] *vt (église)* to desecrate; *(tombe)* to desecrate, to violate; *(souvenir, mémoire)* to defile

proférer [34] [prɔfere] *vt* to utter

professer [prɔfese] *vt* to profess

professeur [prɔfesœr] *nm* teacher; *(à l'université)* professor; **p. des écoles** primary school teacher; **p. principal** *Br* class *or* form teacher, *Am* homeroom teacher

profession [prɔfesjɔ̃] *nf* (**a**) *(métier)* profession, occupation; *(d'artisans)* trade; **de p.** *(musicien)* professional;

(menuisier) by trade; **p. libérale** profession; **sans p.** *(dans un questionnaire)* not working; **je suis sans p.** I don't work (**b**) *(déclaration)* **faire p. de qch** to profess sth; **p. de foi** profession of faith

professionnalisation [prɔfɛsjɔnalizasjɔ̃] *nf* professionalization

professionnalisme [prɔfɛsjɔnalism] *nm* professionalism

professionnel, -elle [prɔfɛsjɔnɛl] **1** *adj (attitude, sportif)* professional; *(enseignement)* vocational; *(maladie)* occupational
 2 *nm,f* professional

professionnellement [prɔfɛsjɔnɛlmɑ̃] *adv* professionally

professoral, -e, -aux, -ales [prɔfɛsɔral, -o] *adj* (**a**) *(de professeur)* professorial (**b**) *(pédant)* patronizing, lecturing

professorat [prɔfɛsɔra] *nm* teaching profession *(especially in higher education)*

profil [prɔfil] *nm aussi Fig* profile; **dessiner qn de p.** to draw sb in profile; **se mettre de p.** to turn one's face *(so it is in profile)*; *Fig* **adopter un p. bas** to adopt a low profile; **p. de poste** job description; **avoir le p. de l'emploi** to fit the job description

profilé, -e [prɔfile] **1** *adj (carrosserie)* streamlined
 2 *nm* section

profiler [prɔfile] **se profiler** *vpr* to stand out (in profile), to be outlined (**sur** *ou* **contre** against); *(problèmes)* to emerge, to loom; *(solution)* to emerge; *(événement)* to be in the offing

profit [prɔfi] *nm* (**a**) *(avantage)* profit, benefit; **mettre qch à p.** to put sth to good use; **tirer p. de qch** to take advantage of sth; **ce manteau m'a fait du p.** this coat has served me well; **au p. des pauvres** in aid of the poor; **concert donné au p. des orphelins** benefit concert for orphans; **perdre des voix au p. de qn** to lose votes to sb (**b**) *(gain)* profit; **il n'y a pas de petits profits** every little helps

profitable [prɔfitabl] *adj* profitable

profiter [prɔfite] **1 profiter de** *vt ind* to take advantage of; **je profite d'un moment de calme pour vous dire que...** I'm using these few moments of peace and quiet to tell you that...; **p. de la vie/de sa jeunesse** to make the most of life/one's youth
 2 profiter à *vt ind* to be of benefit to, to benefit; **ses vacances lui ont bien profité** his holiday has done him a lot of good
 3 *vi Fam (enfant, plante)* to thrive

profiteur, -euse [prɔfitœr, -øz] *nm,f Péj* profiteer

profond, -e [prɔfɔ̃, -ɔ̃d] **1** *adj* (**a**) *(trou, lac, voix)* deep; *(décolleté)* plunging; *(forêt)* dense, thick; *(sommeil)* deep, sound (**b**) *(cause)* underlying (**c**) *(paroles)* profound; *(haine, silence, dégoût)* profound, deep; *(soupir)* heavy
 2 *adv* deep
 3 *nm* **au plus p. de mon cœur** in my heart of hearts, deep down; **au plus p. de la nuit** at dead of night

profondément [prɔfɔ̃demɑ̃] *adv (choqué, déçu, ému)* deeply, profoundly; *(aimer, mépriser)* deeply; *(dormir)* soundly; *(creuser)* deep; **p. endormi** sound *or* fast asleep; **j'en suis p. convaincu** I'm quite convinced of it

profondeur [prɔfɔ̃dœr] *nf* (**a**) *(de l'eau, d'un trou)* depth; **faire 10 mètres de p.** to be 10 metres deep; **en p.** *(étude, analyse)* in-depth; *Phot* **p. de champ** depth of field (**b**) *(d'un sentiment)* depth; *(d'un texte)* profoundness, profundity

profusion [prɔfyzjɔ̃] *nf* profusion, abundance; **à p.** in profusion

progéniture [prɔʒenityr] *nf* progeny, offspring

progiciel [prɔʒisjɛl] *nm Ordinat* software package; **p. de communication** comms package

prognathe [prɔgnat] *adj (visage)* undershot, underhung, *Spéc* prognathous

programmable [prɔgramabl] *adj* programmable

programmateur, -trice [prɔgramatœr, -tris] **1** *nm,f Rad & TV* programme planner
 2 *nm Tech* automatic control (device); *Ordinat* programmer

programmation [prɔgramasjɔ̃] *nf* (**a**) *TV & Rad* programme planning (**b**) *Ordinat* programming

programme [prɔgram] *nm* (**a**) *(émissions, œuvres)* programme; *(brochure) (de télévision)* TV guide; *(de cinéma)* cinema guide; *(au concert, au théâtre)* programme (**b**) *(d'activités)* programme (**c**) *Scol* curriculum; *(d'un cours)* syllabus; **les auteurs au** *ou* **du p.** the set books (**d**) *(d'un parti politique)* manifesto; **p. électoral** (election) platform; *Fig* **c'est tout un p.!** that'll be interesting! (**e**) *Ordinat* program; **p. d'amorçage** boot program; **p. d'arrière-plan** background program; **p. d'auto-test** self-test program; **p. de configuration** configuration program; **p. de conversion** conversion program; **p. détecteur de virus** virus detection program; **p. éditeur de liens** link program, linker; **p. d'évaluation de performance** benchmark program; **p. de formatage** formatter

programmer [prɔgrame] *vt* (**a**) *Ordinat* to program (**b**) *TV & Rad* to schedule (**c**) *(vacances, changements)* to plan

programmeur, -euse [prɔgramœr, -øz] *nm,f Ordinat* programmer

progrès [prɔgrɛ] *nm* progress; **faire des p.** to make progress; **être en p.** to be making progress; *Fam* **il y a du** *ou* **un p.** there's been an improvement

progresser [prɔgrese] *vi* (**a**) *(avancer) (armée)* to advance, to progress; *(marcheur)* to make progress (**b**) *(épidémie, incendie)* to spread; *(chômage, délinquance)* to rise, to increase (**c**) *(faire des progrès)* to make progress

progressif, -ive [prɔgresif, -iv] *adj* progressive; *(changement)* gradual

progression [prɔgresjɔ̃] *nf* (**a**) *(avance) (d'une armée)* advance, progress; *(de marcheurs)* progress (**b**) *(d'un incendie, d'une épidémie)* spread; *(de la délinquance, du chômage)* rise, increase; **être en p.** *(secteur économique)* to be growing *or* expanding; *(maladie)* to be spreading; *(chômage, criminalité)* to be rising, to be on the increase

progressiste [prɔgresist] *adj & nmf* progressive

progressivement [prɔgresivmɑ̃] *adv* progressively

prohiber [prɔibe] *vt* to prohibit, to forbid

prohibitif, -ive [prɔibitif, -iv] *adj* prohibitive

prohibition [prɔibisjɔ̃] *nf* prohibition; *Hist* **la P.** Prohibition

proie [prwa] *nf* prey; **être la p. de qn** to fall prey *or* victim to sb; **être en p. à** *(remords, doute)* to be racked *or* tormented by; *(hallucinations)* to suffer from; **lâcher la p. pour l'ombre** to go chasing after rainbows

projecteur [prɔʒɛktœr] *nm* (**a**) *Cin & Phot* projector (**b**) *(dans un stade, sur un monument)* floodlight; *Théât* spotlight; *Fig* **sous les projecteurs de l'actualité** in the limelight

projectile [pɾɔʒɛktil] *nm* missile

projection [pɾɔʒɛksjɔ̃] *nf* (**a**) *(lancer)* projection; *(d'un liquide, de boue)* splashing; *(de graisse)* spattering; *(de cendres, de roches)* spewing out; **des projections de boue** splashes of mud (**b**) *Cin* projection; *(séance)* screening, showing; **p. de diapositives** slide show; **p. privée** private screening (**c**) *Math, Géom* & *(prévision)* projection

projectionniste [pɾɔʒɛksjɔnist] *nmf* projectionist

projet [pɾɔʒɛ] *nm* *(intention)* plan; *(étude)* project; **faire des projets** to make plans; **p. de loi** bill; **en p.** at the planning stage; **c'est resté à l'état de p.** it never got off the ground

projeter [42] [pɾɔʒte] **1** *vt* (**a**) *(lancer)* to project; *(graisse)* to spatter; *(liquide, boue)* to splash; *(cendres, roches)* to spew out; **être projeté au sol** to be hurled to the ground (**b**) *(prévoir)* to plan; **p. de faire qch** to plan to do sth (**c**) *(film)* to show, to screen (**d**) *(faire apparaître) (ombre)* to cast, to throw; *(image)* to project (**e**) *Psy* to project (**sur** onto)
2 se projeter *vpr (ombre)* to be cast

prolétaire [pɾɔletɛɾ] *adj* & *nmf* proletarian

prolétariat [pɾɔletaɾja] *nm* proletariat

prolétarien, -enne [pɾɔletaɾjɛ̃, -ɛn] *adj* proletarian

prolifération [pɾɔlifeɾasjɔ̃] *nf* proliferation

proliférer [34] [pɾɔlifeɾe] *vi* to proliferate

prolifique [pɾɔlifik] *adj* prolific

prolixe [pɾɔliks] *adj* wordy, verbose

prolo [pɾɔlo] *Fam* **1** *adj* plebby
2 *nmf* pleb, prole

prologue [pɾɔlɔg] *nm* prologue (**de** to)

prolongation [pɾɔlɔ̃gasjɔ̃] *nf* *(de discussions)* prolongation; *(d'un congé, d'un séjour)* extension; **jouer les prolongations** *(au football)* to play extra time *or Am* overtime

prolongé, -e [pɾɔlɔ̃ʒe] *adj* *(absence, séjour)* prolonged, lengthy; *(effort)* prolonged, sustained; *(week-end)* long; **pas d'utilisation prolongée sans avis médical** *(sur un médicament)* ≃ if symptoms persist, consult your doctor

prolongement [pɾɔlɔ̃ʒmɑ̃] *nm* (**a**) *(d'une rue)* continuation; *(d'un mur, d'une voie de chemin de fer)* extension; **être dans le p. de qch** *(meuble)* to be flush with sth; *(rue)* to be a continuation of sth (**b**) **prolongements** *(d'une action)* repercussions

prolonger [45] [pɾɔlɔ̃ʒe] **1** *vt (vie, débat, repas)* to prolong; *(séjour, absence)* to prolong, to extend; *(mur, route, voie ferrée)* to extend
2 se prolonger *vpr (séjour, absence)* to be prolonged *or* extended; *(réunion)* to go on; *(rue)* to continue, to extend

promenade [pɾɔmnad] *nf* (**a**) *(marche)* walk; *(courte)* stroll; **faire une p.** to go for a walk/stroll; **faire une p. en voiture** to go for a drive; **faire une p. à bicyclette** to go for a bike ride; **faire une p. à cheval** to go (horse)riding; **l'heure de la p.** *(d'un détenu)* exercise time (**b**) *(avenue)* promenade

promener [46] [pɾɔmne] **1** *vt* (**a**) *(personne, chien)* to take for a walk; *Fig* **p. qn de musée en musée** to take sb from museum to museum; *Fam* **cela te promènera un peu** it'll get you out a bit (**b**) *(passer)* **p. sa main/son regard sur qch** to run one's hand/one's eyes over sth
2 se promener *vpr* (**a**) *(à pied)* to go for a walk; **aller se p.** to go for a walk; *Ordinat* **se p. dans** *(texte)* to

scroll through (**b**) *(mains, regard)* **se p. sur** to wander over

promeneur, -euse [pɾɔmnœɾ, -øz] *nm,f* walker

promesse [pɾɔmɛs] *nf* promise; **faire une p. à qn** to make sb a promise; **tenir sa p.** to keep one's promise; **p. de Gascon** empty promise; **p. d'achat/de vente** undertaking to buy/to sell

prometteur, -euse [pɾɔmɛtœɾ, -øz] *adj* promising

promettre [47] [pɾɔmɛtɾ] **1** *vt* (**a**) *(s'engager à)* to promise; **p. qch à qn** to promise sb sth; **je ne peux rien te p.** I can't promise (you) anything; **tu me le promets?** (do you) promise?; **je te promets de le faire** I promise you I'll do it; **je le ferai, c'est promis** I'll do it, I promise; **p. monts et merveilles à qn** to promise sb the earth *or* the moon (**b**) *(être prometteur)* **la soirée promet d'être amusante** it promises to be an amusing evening; *Fam* **ça ne promet rien de bon** it doesn't look good
2 *vi (projet, enfant)* to be promising; *Fam Ironique* **ça promet!** that's promising!
3 se promettre *vpr* **se p. qch** *(à soi-même)* to promise oneself sth; *(l'un l'autre)* to promise each other sth; **se p. de faire qch** *(à soi-même)* to resolve to do sth; **ils se sont promis de ne jamais se quitter** they promised each other they'd never part

promis, -e [pɾɔmi, -iz] **1** *adj* promised
2 *nm,f Vieilli* betrothed

promiscuité [pɾɔmiskɥite] *nf* overcrowding; **vivre dans la p.** to live in crowded accommodation

promo [pɾɔmo] *nf Fam* promo; **en p.** on special offer

promontoire [pɾɔmɔ̃twaɾ] *nm* promontory, headland

promoteur, -trice [pɾɔmɔtœɾ, -tɾis] *nm,f* (**a**) **p. (immobilier)** property developer (**b**) *(créateur)* originator (**de** of)

promotion [pɾɔmɔsjɔ̃] *nf* (**a**) *(avancement)* promotion; **p. à l'ancienneté** promotion by seniority; **p. interne** internal promotion; **p. sociale** upward social mobility (**b**) *(d'une école)* *Br* year, *Am* class; **premier de sa p.** first in one's *Br* year *or Am* class (**c**) *(dans le commerce)* promotion; **faire la p. de qch** to promote sth; **la p. de la semaine** this week's special offer; **en p.** on special offer

promotionnel, -elle [pɾɔmɔsjɔnɛl] *adj* *(article)* promotional; *(tarif)* special; **vente promotionnelle** special offer

promouvoir [31a] [pɾɔmuvwaɾ] *vt aussi Fig* to promote; **être promu chef du personnel** to be promoted to personnel manager

prompt, -e [pɾɔ̃, pɾɔ̃t] *adj (réaction)* prompt; **p. à faire qch** quick to do sth; **p. à la riposte** quick with a riposte

promptement [pɾɔ̃tmɑ̃, pɾɔ̃ptəmɑ̃] *adv Litt* promptly

promptitude [pɾɔ̃tityd] *nf Litt (d'une réaction)* promptness

promu, -e *voir* **promouvoir**

promulgation [pɾɔmylgasjɔ̃] *nf* promulgation

promulguer [pɾɔmylge] *vt* to promulgate

prôner [pɾone] *vt* to advocate

pronom [pɾɔnɔ̃] *nm Gram* pronoun; **p. personnel/indéfini/interrogatif** personal/indefinite/interrogative pronoun

pronominal, -e, -aux, -ales [pɾɔnɔminal, -o] *adj Gram* pronominal

prononcé, -e [pɾɔnɔ̃se] **1** *adj* pronounced, strong
2 *nm Jur* **le p. du jugement** the verdict

prononcer [16] [prɔnɔ̃se] **1** *vt* (**a**) *(articuler)* to pronounce; **mal p. un mot** to mispronounce a word (**b**) *(dire) (mot)* to utter; *(discours)* to deliver; *(sentence, divorce)* to pronounce

2 se prononcer *vpr* (**a**) *(être articulé)* to be pronounced; **ça s'écrit comme ça se prononce** it's written as it's pronounced (**b**) *(s'exprimer)* to give one's opinion; *(juge)* to give a verdict; **se p. pour** *ou* **en faveur de qn/qch** to express one's support for sb/sth; **se p. contre qn/qch** to express one's opposition to sb/sth; **50 pour cent ne se prononcent pas** *(dans un sondage)* 50 per cent are undecided

prononciation [prɔnɔ̃sjasjɔ̃] *nf* pronunciation; **elle a une bonne/mauvaise p.** her pronunciation is good/bad

pronostic [prɔnɔstik] *nm* forecast; *(d'un médecin)* prognosis

propagande [prɔpagɑ̃d] *nf* propaganda; **faire de la p. pour qn/qch** to put out propaganda for sb/sth; *(pour une élection)* to campaign for sb/sth

propagation [prɔpagasjɔ̃] *nf* spreading

propager [45] [prɔpaʒe] **1** *vt* to spread

2 se propager *vpr* (**a**) *(épidémie, nouvelle, idée)* to spread (**b**) *(lumière, son)* to be propagated

propane [prɔpan] *nm Chim* propane

propension [prɔpɑ̃sjɔ̃] *nf* propensity (**à** for); **p. à faire qch** propensity to do sth

prophète [prɔfɛt] *nm* prophet; **p. de malheur** prophet of doom; *Prov* **nul n'est p. en son pays** no man is a prophet in his own country

prophétie [prɔfesi] *nf* prophecy

prophétique [prɔfetik] *adj* prophetic

prophylactique [prɔfilaktik] *adj* prophylactic

propice [prɔpis] *adj* **le moment p.** the right moment; **p. à qch** good for sth; **un endroit p. au repos** a restful spot; **un endroit p. aux rencontres** a good place to meet people

proportion [prɔpɔrsjɔ̃] *nf* proportion; **respecter les proportions** to get the proportions right; **en p. de qch** in proportion to sth; **hors de (toute) p. avec** out of (all) proportion to; **toutes proportions gardées** relatively speaking

proportionné, -e [prɔpɔrsjɔne] *adj* (**a**) *(bâti)* **bien/mal p.** well-/badly-proportioned (**b**) *(lié)* **être p. à** to be proportionate to

proportionnel, -elle [prɔpɔrsjɔnɛl] **1** *adj* proportional (**à** to); **inversement p. à qch** inversely proportional to sth

2 *nf* **proportionnelle** *Pol* proportional representation; **être élu à la proportionelle** to be elected by proportional representation

proportionnellement [prɔpɔrsjɔnɛlmɑ̃] *adv* proportionally (**à** to)

propos [prɔpo] *nm* (**a**) *(sujet)* **à p. de qn/qch** about sb/sth; **à ce p.,...** talking of which...; **à tout p.** constantly; **à p., avez-vous lu ce livre?** by the way, have you read this book?; **c'est à quel p.?** what's it about?; **arriver fort à p.** to arrive at just the right moment; **juger à p. de faire qch** to think it right to do sth; **hors de p.** *(remarque)* inappropriate (**b**) *(intention)* purpose, intention; **de p. délibéré** deliberately, on purpose (**c**) *(parole)* **des p.** talk, words; **tenir des p. étonnants** to say some surprising things

proposer [prɔpoze] **1** *vt* (*suggérer*) to suggest, to propose; *(offrir)* to offer; *(amendement, loi)* to table; **p. qch à qn** to suggest *or* propose sth to sb; *(argent, travail)* to offer sb sth; **je vous en propose 6000 francs/un bon prix** I'll give you 6,000 francs/a good price for it; **voilà ce que je vous propose** this is what I suggest; **le cinéma Le César vous propose cette semaine...** Le César will be showing the following films this week...; **je leur ai proposé de venir avec moi** I suggested (to them) that they should come with me; **elle m'a proposé de m'aider** she offered to help me; **je propose qu'on y aille demain** I suggest going tomorrow

2 se proposer *vpr* (**a**) *(être volontaire)* to offer one's services; **se p. pour faire qch** to offer to do sth (**b**) **se p. de faire qch** *(en avoir l'intention)* to propose to do sth

proposition [prɔpozisjɔ̃] *nf* (**a**) *(suggestion)* suggestion, proposal; *(offre)* offer; **faire une p. (à qn)** to make a suggestion *or* proposal (to sb); **faire des propositions à une femme** to proposition a woman; **sur la p. de qn** at sb's suggestion; **p. de loi** bill (**b**) *Phil & Math* proposition (**c**) *Gram* clause; **p. principale** main clause

propre [prɔpr] **1** *adj* (**a**) *(impeccable) (personne, linge, maison)* clean; *(bébé)* potty-trained; *(copie d'élève)* neat; **n'utilise pas la serviette des autres, ce n'est pas p.!** don't use other people's towels, it's not hygienic!; **p. comme un sou neuf** spick and span; *Fam* **nous voilà propres!** now we're in a mess!

(**b**) *(à soi)* own; **voir qch de ses propres yeux** to see sth with one's own eyes; **ce sont là ses propres paroles** those are his very words

(**c**) *(particulier)* **être p. à qn/qch** to be characteristic of *or* peculiar to sb/sth

(**d**) *(adapté)* **être p. à qch** to be suitable for sth

(**e**) *(littéral)* **au sens p.** in the literal sense, literally

2 *nm* (**a**) *(caractéristique)* characteristic feature

(**b**) **appartenir en p. à qn** to be sb's sole property

(**c**) *(sens propre)* **au p.** literally

(**d**) **recopier qch au p.** to make a clean copy of sth

(**e**) *(propreté)* **sentir le p.** to smell clean; *Belg* **faire du p.** to spring-clean

(**f**) *Fam* **c'est du p.!** that's a fine way to carry on!

propre-à-rien *(pl* **propres-à-rien)** [prɔprarjɛ̃] *nmf* good-for-nothing

proprement [prɔprəmɑ̃] *adv* (**a**) *(avec propreté)* cleanly; *(vêtu)* tidily; **manger p.** to eat without making a mess (**b**) *(strictement)* strictly; **c'est un problème p. urbain** it's strictly an inner-city problem; **à p. parler** strictly speaking; **voilà la bibliothèque p. dite** there's the actual library (**c**) *Fam (vraiment)* **c'est p. scandaleux!** it's an absolute disgrace!

propreté [prɔprəte] *nf (hygiène)* cleanliness; *(des vêtements, de la vaisselle, d'une maison)* cleanness; *(d'un travail)* neatness

propriétaire [prɔprijetɛr] *nmf* (**a**) *(d'une voiture, d'une propriété, d'un hôtel)* owner; **devenir** *ou* **se rendre p. de qch** to become the owner of sth; **être p.** to be a landowner; *(de maison)* to be a home owner; **p. foncier** landowner (**b**) *(d'une location)* landlord, *f* landlady

propriété [prɔprijete] *nf* (**a**) *(fait de posséder)* ownership; **p. littéraire** copyright; **p. foncière** property ownership; *Jur* **p. intellectuelle** intellectual property (**b**) *(chose ou terre possédée)* property; **p. privée** private property (**c**) *(caractéristique)* property

proprio [prɔprijo] *nmf Fam* landlord, *f* landlady

propulser [prɔpylse] 1 *vt* to propel
  2 **se propulser** *vpr Fam* **se p. en tête du peloton** to shoot to the front of the pack
propulsion [prɔpylsjɔ̃] *nf* propulsion; **sous-marin à p. nucléaire** nuclear-powered submarine
prorata [prɔrata] *nm inv* proportion; **au p. de qch** in proportion to sth
prorogation [prɔrɔgasjɔ̃] *nf (de contrat, de bail)* extension
proroger [45] [prɔrɔʒe] *vt (contrat, bail)* to extend; *(échéance)* to defer
prosaïque [prɔzaik] *adj* prosaic
proscrire [30] [prɔskrir] *vt* to ban, to proscribe
proscrit, -e [prɔskri, -it] 1 *adj* banned, proscribed
  2 *nm,f Litt (banni)* exile
prose [proz] *nf* prose; **en p.** *(écrire)* in prose; *(texte, poème)* prose
prosélytisme [prɔzelitism] *nm* proselytism; **faire du p.** to proselytize
prosodie [prɔzɔdi] *nf* prosody
prospecter [prɔspɛkte] *vt* **(a)** *(terrain)* to prospect **(b)** *(client)* to canvass; *(marché)* to explore
prospecteur, -trice [prɔspɛktœr, -tris] *nm,f* **(a)** *(de terrain)* prospector **(b)** *(de clients)* canvasser
prospection [prɔspɛksjɔ̃] *nf* **(a)** *(de terrain)* prospecting; **faire de la p.** to prospect; **p. minière/pétrolière** mining/oil exploration **(b)** *(de clients)* canvassing; **faire de la p.** to explore the market; **p. téléphonique** telephone canvassing
prospectus [prɔspɛktys] *nm* **(a)** *(brochure)* leaflet **(b)** *Fin* prospectus
prospère [prɔspɛr] *adj* prosperous; *(santé)* glowing
prospérer [34] [prɔspere] *vi* to prosper
prospérité [prɔsperite] *nf* prosperity; **en période de p.** in times of prosperity
prostate [prɔstat] *nf Anat* prostate (gland)
prosterner [prɔsterne] **se prosterner** *vpr (saluer)* to prostrate oneself (**devant** before); *Fig (s'abaisser)* to grovel, to kowtow (**devant** to)
prostitué, -e [prɔstitɥe] *nm,f (homme)* male prostitute; *(femme)* prostitute
prostituer [prɔstitɥe] 1 *vt* to prostitute
  2 **se prostituer** *vpr* to prostitute oneself
prostitution [prɔstitysjɔ̃] *nf* prostitution
prostré, -e [prɔstre] *adj* prostrate
protagoniste [prɔtagɔnist] *nmf* protagonist
protecteur, -trice [prɔtɛktœr, -tris] 1 *adj (qui protège)* protective (**avec** towards); *Péj (ton)* patronizing
  2 *nm,f* **(a)** *(d'une personne)* protector; *(d'une prostituée)* pimp **(b)** *(des arts)* patron
protection [prɔtɛksjɔ̃] *nf* **(a)** *(défense)* protection (**contre** from *or* against); **de p.** *(écran, visière, vernis)* protective; **sous la p. de la police** under police protection; **p. de l'environnement** protection of the environment; **p. sociale** social welfare system; *Ordinat* **p. d'accès logique** logical access protection; **p. contre l'écriture** write-protection; **p. contre la copie** copy protection; **p. de fichiers** file protection; **p. par mot de passe** password protection **(b)** *(serviette hygiénique)* **p. (féminine)** sanitary *Br* towel *or Am* napkin
protectionnisme [prɔtɛksjɔnism] *nm Écon* protectionism
protectionniste [prɔtɛksjɔnist] *adj & nmf* protectionist

protectorat [prɔtɛktɔra] *nm* protectorate
protégé, -e [prɔteʒe] 1 *adj* protected; *Ordinat* **p. contre la copie** copy-protected
  2 *nm,f* protégé, *f* protégée
protège-cahier *(pl* **protège-cahiers)** [prɔteʒkaje] *nm* exercise book cover
protège-dents [prɔteʒdã] *nm inv* gum shield
protéger [59] [prɔteʒe] 1 *vt* to protect (**contre/de** against/from); **ça protège bien** it gives good protection; **que Dieu vous protège!** God keep you!; *Ordinat* **p. contre l'écriture** *ou* **en écriture** to write-protect
  2 **se protéger** *vpr* to protect oneself (**contre/de** against/from)
protège-slip *(pl* **protège-slips)** [prɔteʒslip] *nm* panty-liner
protéine [prɔtein] *nf* protein
protestant, -e [prɔtɛstã, -ãt] *adj & nm,f* Protestant
protestantisme [prɔtɛstãtism] *nm* Protestantism
protestataire [prɔtɛstater] *nmf* protester
protestation [prɔtɛstasjɔ̃] *nf* **(a)** *(plainte)* protest; **émettre des protestations** to voice one's protest; **en signe de p.** as a protest **(b)** **des protestations d'amitié** protestations of friendship
protester [prɔtɛste] 1 *vi* to protest (**contre** against); **p. auprès de qn** to protest to sb
  2 **protester de** *vt ind (innocence, bonne foi)* to protest
prothèse [prɔtɛz] *nf* prosthesis; **p. auditive** hearing aid; **p. dentaire** *(complète)* false teeth, dentures; *(partielle)* bridge
protocole [prɔtɔkɔl] *nm* **(a)** *(usages)* protocol **(b)** **p. d'accord** protocol of agreement **(c)** *Ordinat* protocol; **p. de téléchargement** download protocol; **p. de transmission** transmission protocol
proton [prɔtɔ̃] *nm* proton
prototype [prɔtɔtip] *nm* prototype
protozoaire [prɔtɔzɔɛr] *nm* protozoan; **les protozoaires** the Protozoa
protubérance [prɔtyberãs] *nf* protuberance
protubérant, -e [prɔtyberã, -ãt] *adj* protuberant
proue [pru] *nf* bows, prow
prouesse [prɥɛs] *nf* feat; **faire des prouesses pour obtenir qch** to work wonders to get sth
prouver [pruve] 1 *vt* **(a)** *(établir comme vrai)* to prove; **p. qch à qn** to prove sth to sb; **p. qch par A plus B** to prove sth in a logical fashion; **cela reste à p.** it still has to be proved **(b)** *(être la preuve de)* to prove, to show (**que** that)
  2 **se prouver** *vpr* **se p. qch** *(à soi-même)* to prove sth to oneself
provenance [prɔvnãs] *nf* origin; **marchandises de p. italienne** goods of Italian origin; **en p. de Bordeaux** from Bordeaux
provençal, -e, -aux, -ales [prɔvãsal, -o] 1 *adj* Provençal
  2 *nm,f* **P.** person from Provence
  3 *nm (langue)* Provençal
Provence [prɔvãs] *nf* **la P.** Provence
provenir [70] [prɔvnir] *vi* **p. de** to come from; *(difficultés)* to arise from
proverbe [prɔvɛrb] *nm* proverb; **comme dit le p.** as the proverb goes
proverbial, -e, -aux, -ales [prɔvɛrbjal, -o] *adj* proverbial

providence [prɔvidɑ̃s] *nf* (**a**) *(sort)* providence; **cette auberge est la p. des marcheurs** this inn is a haven for walkers (**b**) **la P.** Providence

providentiel, -elle [prɔvidɑ̃sjɛl] *adj* providential

province [prɔvɛ̃s] **1** *nf* (**a**) *(région)* province; *Can* **les Provinces Maritimes** the Maritime Provinces (**b**) **la p.** the provinces; **de p.** provincial; **en p.** in the provinces; **arriver de sa p.** to be new in town
2 *adj inv Fam Péj* provincial

provincial, -e, -aux, -ales [prɔvɛ̃sjal, -o] *adj & nm,f* provincial

proviseur [prɔvizœr] *nm* (**a**) *(directeur) Br* headmaster, *f* headmistress, *Am* principal (**b**) *Belg (adjoint)* deputy head

provision [prɔvizjɔ̃] *nf* (**a**) *(réserve)* stock, supply; **provisions** *(nourriture)* shopping; **faire des provisions** *ou* **faire p. de qch** to stock up on sth (**b**) *(de compte bancaire)* credit; *(acompte)* deposit

provisionnel, -elle [prɔvizjɔnɛl] *adj voir* **tiers**

provisoire [prɔvizwar] *adj* temporary; **à titre p.** temporarily

provisoirement [prɔvizwarmɑ̃] *adv* temporarily, provisionally

provocant, -e [prɔvɔkɑ̃, -ɑ̃t] *adj* provocative

provocateur, -trice [prɔvɔkatœr, -tris] **1** *adj* provocative; **agent p.** agent provocateur
2 *nm,f* troublemaker

provocation [prɔvɔkasjɔ̃] *nf* provocation; **il l'a dit par p.** he said it to be provocative

provoquer [prɔvɔke] *vt* (**a**) *(personne)* to provoke (**b**) *(réaction)* to provoke; *(incendie, mort, malaise)* to cause; *(jalousie, colère)* to arouse; **p. l'accouchement** to induce labour

proxénète [prɔksenɛt] *nmf* pimp

proxénétisme [prɔksenetism] *nm* pimping

proximité [prɔksimite] *nf* closeness, proximity; **à p.** close by; **à p. de qch** close to sth; **commerces de p.** local shops; **emplois de p.** = employment in the community *(as a way of reducing unemployment)*

prude [pryd] *Péj* **1** *adj* prudish
2 *nf* prude

prudemment [prydamɑ̃] *adv* carefully, cautiously

prudence [prydɑ̃s] *nf* care, caution; **par (mesure de) p.** as a precaution; *Prov* **p. est mère de sûreté** discretion is the better part of valour

prudent, -e [prydɑ̃, -ɑ̃t] *adj (personne)* careful, cautious; *(décision)* wise, sensible

prud'homme [prydɔm] *nm Jur* member of an industrial tribunal; **conseil des prud'hommes** industrial tribunal

prune [pryn] **1** *nf (fruit)* plum; *(liqueur)* plum brandy; *Fam* **pour des prunes** for nothing
2 *adj inv* plum-coloured

pruneau, -x [pryno] *nm* (**a**) *(fruit)* prune (**b**) *Fam (balle)* slug

prunelle [prynɛl] *nf (pupille)* pupil; *Fig* **j'y tiens comme à la p. de mes yeux** it's the apple of my eye

prunier [prynje] *nm* plum tree; *Fam* **secouer qn comme un p.** to shake sb like a rag doll

prurit [pryrit] *nm Méd* pruritus

Prusse [prys] *nf voir* **bleu**

PS [peɛs] *nm* (**a**) *(abrév* **Parti socialiste**) Socialist Party (**b**) *(abrév* **post-scriptum**) PS

psalmodier [66] [psalmɔdje] **1** *vt* to chant; *Fig* to drone out
2 *vi* to chant; *Fig* to drone on

psaume [psom] *nm* psalm

pseudo- [psødo] *préf* pseudo-; **un p.-intellectuel** a pseudo-intellectual

pseudonyme [psødɔnim] *nm (pour un écrivain)* pen name, pseudonym; *(pour la scène)* stage name

psy [psi] *nmf Fam (médecin)* shrink

psychanalyse [psikanaliz] *nf* psychoanalysis; **faire une p.** to be in psychoanalysis

psychanalyser [psikanalize] *vt* to psychoanalyse; **se faire p.** to be psychoanalysed

psychanalyste [psikanalist] *nmf* psychoanalyst

psyché [psiʃe] *nf (miroir)* cheval glass

psychédélique [psikedelik] *adj* psychedelic

psychiatre [psikjatr] *nmf* psychiatrist

psychiatrie [psikjatri] *nf* psychiatry

psychiatrique [psikjatrik] *adj* psychiatric

psychique [psiʃik] *adj* psychic

psychisme [psiʃism] *nm* psyche

psychodrame [psikodram] *nm* role-playing, *Spéc* psychodrama

psychologie [psikolɔʒi] *nf* (**a**) *(étude, mentalité)* psychology; **comprendre la p. de qn** to understand the way sb's mind works (**b**) *(intuition)* perception; **faire preuve de p.** to be very perceptive; **tu manques de p.** you're not very perceptive

psychologique [psikolɔʒik] *adj* psychological

psychologiquement [psikolɔʒikmɑ̃] *adv* psychologically

psychologue [psikolɔg] **1** *nmf* psychologist; *Fig* **être fin p.** to be a good psychologist
2 *adj* **être p.** to be a good psychologist

psychopathe [psikopat] *nmf* psychopath

psychose [psikoz] *nf* psychosis; **p. maniaco-dépressive** manic depression; *Fig* **la p. de la maladie** an obsessive fear of illness

psychosomatique [psikosɔmatik] *adj* psychosomatic

psychothérapeute [psikoterapøt] *nmf* psychotherapist

psychothérapie [psikoterapi] *nf* psychotherapy; **p. de groupe** group therapy

psychotique [psikɔtik] *adj & nmf* psychotic

PTT [petete] *nfpl (abrév* **Postes, Télécommunications et Télédiffusion)** *Anciennement* ≃ Post Office and Telecommunications Service

pu *voir* **pouvoir**

puant, -e [pɥɑ̃, -ɑ̃t] *adj* stinking; *Fig* cocky

puanteur [pɥɑ̃tœr] *nf* stink, stench

pub [pyb] *nf Fam* (**a**) *(secteur)* advertising (**b**) *(message)* ad

pubère [pybɛr] *adj* pubescent

puberté [pybɛrte] *nf* puberty

pubis [pybis] *nm Anat* pubis; *(os)* pubic bone

public, -ique [pyblik] **1** *adj* public
2 *nm (d'un spectacle)* audience; **en p.** in public; *(émission)* before a live audience; **le grand p.** the general public

publication [pyblikasjɔ̃] *nf* (**a**) *(d'un ouvrage, d'une nouvelle)* publication; **p. assistée par ordinateur** desktop publishing (**b**) *(ouvrage)* publication

publiciel [pyblisjɛl] *nm Can Ordinat* public domain software

publiciste [pyblisist] *nmf Fam* advertising executive

publicitaire [pyblisitɛr] **1** *adj* advertising **2** *nmf* advertising executive

publicité [pyblisite] *nf* (**a**) *(secteur)* advertising; **être dans la p.** to be in advertising; **faire de la p. pour qch** to advertise sth; *Fig* **faire de la p. à qn** to be publicity for sb; **p. comparative** comparative advertising; **p. mensongère** misleading advertising (**b**) *(message)* advertisement, advert; **une pleine page de p.** a full page advertisement

publier [66] [pyblije] *vt* to publish; *(communiqué)* to issue

Publiphone® [pyblifɔn] *nm* card phone

publiquement [pyblikmɑ̃] *adv* publicly

puce [pys] *nf* (**a**) *(insecte)* flea; **le marché aux puces, les puces** the flea market; *Fig* **mettre la p. à l'oreille à qn** to make sb suspicious; *Fam* **secouer les puces à qn** to give sb a good telling off; *Fam* **être excité comme une p.** to be jumping up and down with excitement (**b**) *Ordinat* (micro)chip; **p. mémoire** memory chip; **p. de reconnaissance vocale** voice recognition chip (**c**) *(terme affectueux)* **ma p.** sweetie

puceau, -x [pyso] *nm & adj m Fam* virgin

pucelle [pysɛl] *nf & adj f* virgin; **la P. d'Orléans, Jeanne la P.** The Maid of Orléans, Joan of Arc

puceron [pysrɔ̃] *nm* greenfly

pudeur [pydœr] *nf* modesty; **avec p.** modestly; **sans p.** boldly; **par p.** out of a sense of decency; **avoir la p. de faire qch** to have the decency to do sth

pudibond, -e [pydibɔ̃, -ɔ̃d] *adj* prudish

pudique [pydik] *adj* modest

puer [pɥe] **1** *vi* to stink; **il pue des pieds** his feet stink **2** *vt* to stink of; *Fig* **p. la méchanceté/l'hypocrisie** to be oozing spitefulness/hypocrisy

puéricultrice [pɥerikyltris] *nf* nursery nurse

puériculture [pɥerikyltyr] *nf* child care

puéril, -e [pɥeril] *adj* childish, puerile

pugilat [pyʒila] *nm* brawl

pugnace [pygnas] *adj Litt* pugnacious

puis¹ [pɥi] *adv* then; **et p.** *(ensuite)* and then; *(d'ailleurs)* and besides; **et p. c'est tout!** and that's all there is to it!; **et p. après?** *(et ensuite?)* then what?; *Fam (et alors?)* so what?

puis² *voir* **pouvoir**

puisatier [pɥizatje] *nm* well digger

puiser [pɥize] *vt (eau, carte)* to draw (**à** from); *Fig (inspiration, idées)* to draw (**dans/chez** from); **p. dans ses réserves** to draw on one's reserves; **p. dans la caisse** to have one's hand in the till

puisque [pɥiskə] *conj* since, as; **p. c'est comme ça** if that's the way it is; **p. je te dis que je l'ai vu!** I'm telling you I saw him!; **tu en es bien sûr? – mais p. je te le dis!** are you really sure? – I've said I am, haven't I?

puissamment [pɥisamɑ̃] *adv* powerfully

puissance [pɥisɑ̃s] *nf* power; **p. de feu** fire power; **les grandes puissances** the great powers; *Math* **élever un nombre à la p. trois/quatre** to raise a number to the third/fourth power; **dix (à la) p. quatre** ten to the power of four; **en p.** *(meurtrier)* potential

puissant, -e [pɥisɑ̃, -ɑ̃t] *adj* powerful

puisse *etc voir* **pouvoir**

puits [pɥi] *nm* (**a**) *(pour l'eau)* well; **p. de pétrole** oil well; *Fig* **c'est un p. de science** she's a fount of knowledge (**b**) *(de mine)* shaft, pit

pull [pyl] *nm Fam* sweater, *Br* jumper

pull-over *(pl* **pull-overs)** [pylɔvœr] *nm* sweater, *Br* jumper

pulluler [pylyle] *vi* (**a**) *(se reproduire)* to proliferate (**b**) *(exister en profusion)* to abound

pulmonaire [pylmɔnɛr] *adj* pulmonary

pulpe [pylp] *nf* (**a**) *(de fruit)* pulp; **yaourt à la p. de fruits** yoghurt with real fruit (**b**) *(des doigts, des orteils)* pad; *(des dents)* pulp

pulpeux, -euse [pylpø, -øz] *adj* fleshy; *(femme)* curvaceous

pulsar [pylsar] *nm Astron* pulsar

pulsation [pylsasjɔ̃] *nf (de cœur)* & *Mus* beat; **pulsations cardiaques** heartbeats

pulsion [pylsjɔ̃] *nf* impulse; **pulsions sexuelles** sexual urges; **p. de mort** death wish

pulvérisateur [pylverizatœr] *nm* spray

pulvérisation [pylverizasjɔ̃] *nf (de liquides)* spraying

pulvériser [pylverize] *vt* (**a**) *(réduire en poudre)* to pulverize; *Fam (voiture)* to smash up (**b**) *(vaporiser)* to spray (**c**) *Fam (record)* to smash

puma [pyma] *nm* puma

punaise [pynɛz] *nf* (**a**) *(insecte)* bug; *Fam* **oh p.!** good grief! (**b**) *(pour accrocher) Br* drawing pin, *Am* thumbtack

punaiser [pynɛze] *vt Fam* to pin up; **p. qch à qch** to pin sth to sth

punch¹ [pɔ̃ʃ] *nm (boisson)* punch

punch² [pœnʃ] *nm* punch; *Fig (de personne)* drive

punching-ball *(pl* **punching-balls)** [pœnʃiŋbol] *nm* punchball

punir [pynir] *vt (personne, crime)* to punish; **p. qn de mort** to punish sb with death; **p. qn d'un crime** to punish sb for a crime; **me voilà puni de ma gourmandise!** it serves me right for being greedy!

punitif, -ive [pynitif, -iv] *adj* punitive

punition [pynisjɔ̃] *nf* punishment; **p. corporelle** corporal punishment

punk [pœnk] *adj inv & nmf* punk

pupille¹ [pypij] *nmf (orphelin)* ward; **pupilles de la Nation** war orphans

pupille² *nf (de l'œil)* pupil

pupitre [pypitr] *nm* (**a**) *(d'écolier)* desk; *(d'orateur)* lectern; *(de musicien)* music stand (**b**) *Ordinat* **p. (de commande)** console (desk); **p. de visualisation** visual display unit

pupitreur, -euse [pypitrœr, -øz] *nm,f Ordinat* console operator

pur, -e [pyr] *adj* (**a**) *(or, air)* pure; *(ciel)* clear; *(whisky, gin)* straight, neat; **pure laine** pure wool; **biscuits p. beurre** all butter biscuits (**b**) *(recherche, mathématiques, théorie)* pure; **un communiste p. et dur** a hard-line Communist; **la vérité pure et simple** the plain and simple truth; **du vol p. et simple** sheer robbery; **c'est de la folie pure** it's sheer madness (**c**) *(lignes)* clean; *(visage)* clean-cut

purée [pyre] *nf* **1** *nf* purée; **réduire qch en p.** to purée sth; *Fig* to smash sth to a pulp; **p. (de pommes de terre)** mashed potatoes; *Fam Fig* **p. de pois** pea-souper **2** *exclam Fam (colère)* hell!; *(surprise)* wow!

purement [pyrmɑ̃] *adv* purely; **p. et simplement** purely and simply

pureté [pyrte] *nf* purity; *(du ciel)* clearness; *(de lignes)* cleanness

purgatoire [pyrgatwar] *nm* purgatory

purge [pyrʒ] *nf* (**a**) *(pour raisons médicales)* purge (**b**) *(à des fins politiques)* purge (**c**) *(de freins, de radiateur)* bleeding
purger [45] [pyrʒe] *vt* (**a**) *(patient)* to purge (**b**) *(freins, radiateur)* to bleed (**c**) *(peine)* to serve
purifiant, -e [pyrifjɑ̃, -ɑ̃t] *adj* purifying
purificateur, -trice [pyrifikatœr, -tris] *adj* purifying
purification [pyrifikasjɔ̃] *nf* purification; **p. ethnique** ethnic cleansing
purifier [66] [pyrifje] **1** *vt aussi Fig* to purify; *(sang, teint)* to cleanse
  2 se purifier *upr* to be purified
purin [pyrɛ̃] *nm* liquid manure
puriste [pyrist] *nmf* purist
puritain, -e [pyritɛ̃, -ɛn] **1** *nm,f* puritan; *Hist* Puritan
  2 *adj* puritanical; *Hist* Puritan
puritanisme [pyritanism] *nm* puritanism; *Hist* Puritanism
pur-sang [pyrsɑ̃] *nm inv* thoroughbred
purulent, -e [pyrylɑ̃, -ɑ̃t] *adj* suppurating
pus [py] *nm* pus
pusillanime [pyzilanim] *adj Litt* pusillanimous
pustule [pystyl] *nf* pustule
putain [pytɛ̃] *Vulg* **1** *nf* (**a**) *(prostituée)* whore (**b**) **une p. de machine/cravate** a fucking machine/tie
  2 *exclam* fuck!
pute [pyt] *nf Vulg* whore; **fils de p.** son of a bitch
putois [pytwa] *nm* polecat; *Fam* **crier comme un p.** to scream blue murder
putréfaction [pytrefaksjɔ̃] *nf* putrefaction; **matière en p.** putrefying matter
putréfier [66] [pytrefje] **1** *vt* to putrefy
  2 se putréfier *upr* to putrefy
putrescent, -e [pytresɑ̃, -ɑ̃t] *adj* putrescent

putride [pytrid] *adj* putrid
putsch [putʃ] *nm* putsch
putschiste [putʃist] **1** *adj* putsch
  2 *nmf* putschist
puzzle [pœzl] *nm* jigsaw (puzzle); *Fig* puzzle
P.-V. [peve] *nm Fam* (*abrév* **procès-verbal**) (parking) ticket
PVC [pevese] *nm* (*abrév* **polychlorure de vinyle**) PVC; **siège en P.** PVC seat
PVD [pevede] *nm* (*abrév* **pays en voie de développement**) developing country
pygmée [pigme] *nmf* pygmy
pyjama [piʒama] *nm* pyjamas; **un p.** a pair of pyjamas
pylône [pilon] *nm* pylon; *(pour fils télégraphiques)* mast
pyramidal, -e, -aux, -ales [piramidal, -o] *adj* pyramid-shaped
pyramide [piramid] *nf* pyramid; **p. des âges** population pyramid; **structure en p.** pyramid-like structure
pyrénéen, -enne [pireneɛ̃, -ɛn] **1** *adj* Pyrenean
  2 *nm,f* **P.** Pyrenean
  3 *nm (chien)* Pyrenean mountain dog
Pyrénées [pirene] *nfpl* **les P.** the Pyrenees
Pyrex® [pirɛks] *nm* Pyrex®; **plat en P.** Pyrex® dish
pyrogravure [pirogravyr] *nf* poker work, pyrography; *(gravure)* pyrograph
pyrolyse [piroliz] *nf* pyrolysis; **four à p.** self-cleaning oven
pyromane [piroman] *nmf* arsonist; *Psy* pyromaniac
pyromanie [piromani] *nf* pyromania
pyrotechnique [piroteknik] *adj* pyrotechnic
python [pitɔ̃] *nm* python

Q

Q, q [ky] *nm inv* Q, q
Qatar [katar] *nm* **le Q.** Qatar
QCM [kyseɛm] *nm inv* (*abrév* **questionnaire à choix multiple**) multiple-choice questionnaire
QG [kyʒe] *nm inv* (*abrév* **quartier général**) HQ
QI [kyi] *nm inv* (*abrév* **quotient intellectuel**) IQ
quadra [kwadra] *nmf Fam* fortysomething
quadragénaire [kwadraʒenɛr] **1** *adj* **être q.** to be in one's forties
2 *nmf* person in his/her forties
quadrangulaire [kwadrãgylɛr] *adj* quadrangular
quadrature [kwadratyr] *nf* quadrature; **c'est la q. du cercle** it's like trying to square the circle
quadriceps [kwadrisɛps] *nm* quadriceps
quadrilatère [kwadrilatɛr, kadrilatɛr] *nm* quadrilateral
quadrillage [kadrijaʒ] *nm* (**a**) (*par la police*) tight surveillance (**b**) (*d'un tissu*) check pattern; (*sur une carte*) grid
quadrille [kadrij] *nm* quadrille
quadrillé, -e [kadrije] *adj* (*papier*) squared
quadriller [kadrije] *vt* (**a**) (*quartier, ville, région*) to put under tight surveillance (**b**) (*papier*) to mark into squares
quadrimoteur [kwadrimɔtœr, kadrimɔtœr] **1** *adj* four-engined
2 *nm* four-engined plane
quadriparti, -e [kwadriparti], **quadripartite** [kwadripartit] *adj* (*traité*) quadripartite; (*conférence, commission*) (*entre partis*) four-party; (*entre pays*) four-power
quadriphonie [kwadrifoni] *nf* quadraphony
quadrupède [kwadrypɛd, kadrypɛd] *adj & nm* quadruped
quadruple [kwadrypl, kadrypl] **1** *adj* quadruple, fourfold; *Mus* **q. croche** *Br* hemidemisemiquaver, *Am* sixty-fourth note
2 *nm* **le q. (de)** (*quantité, prix*) four times as much (as); (*nombre*) four times as many (as); **douze est le q. de trois** twelve is four times three
quadrupler [kwadryple, kadryple] *vt & vi* to quadruple, to increase fourfold
quadruplés, -ées [kwadryple, kadryple] *nm,f pl* quadruplets
quai [kɛ] *nm* (**a**) (*de gare, de métro*) platform (**b**) (*d'un port*) quay; **se mettre à q.** to berth (**c**) (*d'une rivière, d'un fleuve*) embankment; **le Q. des Orfèvres** Police Headquarters (*in Paris*); **le Q. d'Orsay** the French Foreign Office

qualificatif, -ive [kalifikatif, -iv] *Gram* **1** *adj* (*adjectif*) qualifying
2 *nm* term
qualification [kalifikasjɔ̃] *nf* (**a**) (*formation*) qualification (**b**) (*d'une équipe, d'un sportif*) qualification (**c**) (*désignation*) description
qualifié, -e [kalifje] *adj* (**a**) (*compétent*) qualified (**pour faire qch** to do sth) (**b**) (*délit, vol*) aggravated
qualifier [66] [kalifje] **1** *vt* (**a**) (*appeler*) to describe (**de** as) (**b**) (*autoriser*) **q. qn pour qch/pour faire qch** to qualify sb for sth/to do sth
2 se qualifier *vpr* (*sportif, équipe*) to qualify (**pour** for)
qualitatif, -ive [kalitatif, -iv] *adj* qualitative
qualité [kalite] *nf* (**a**) (*d'un produit*) quality; **de q.** quality; **de bonne/mauvaise q.** of good/poor quality; *Ordinat* **q. brouillon, q. liste rapide, q. listing** draft quality; *Ordinat* **q. courrier** (near) letter quality; **la q. de la vie** the quality of life (**b**) (*d'une personne*) quality; **elle n'a pas que des qualités** she isn't all good (**c**) (*occupation*) occupation; (*fonction*) capacity; **en q. de** in my/her/*etc* capacity as
quand [kɑ̃] **1** *conj* (**a**) (*lorsque*) when; **je lui en parlerai q. je le verrai** I'll mention it to him when I see him; *Fam* **q. je pense que le voyage devait être annulé!** when I think that they were going to cancel the trip!; **q. bien même** even if (**b**) (*alors que*) when
2 *adv* when; **q. viendra-t-il?** when will he come?; **demande-lui q. il va partir** ask him when he's going to leave; **à q. le mariage?** when's the wedding?; **de q. est ce journal?** what's the date of this paper?; **pour q. est la réunion?** when is the meeting?
quant [kɑ̃] **quant à** *prép* as for
quant-à-soi [kɑ̃taswa] *nm inv* **rester sur** *ou* **se tenir sur son q.** to keep oneself to oneself
quantième [kɑ̃tjɛm] *nm* day of the month
quantifiable [kɑ̃tifjabl] *adj* quantifiable
quantifier [66] [kɑ̃tifje] *vt* to quantify
quantitatif, -ive [kɑ̃titatif, -iv] *adj* quantitative
quantitativement [kɑ̃titativmɑ̃] *adv* quantitatively
quantité [kɑ̃tite] *nf* quantity; **en grande/petite q.** in large/small quantities; **en q.** in abundance; **q. de gens/réponses** a great many people/replies
quarantaine [karɑ̃tɛn] *nf* (**a**) (*environ quarante*) **une q. (de)** about forty, forty or so (**b**) (*âge*) **avoir la q.** to be about forty; **approcher de la q.** to be getting on for forty (**c**) (*isolement*) quarantine; **mettre qn en q.** to put sb in quarantine; *Fig* to send sb to Coventry
quarante [karɑ̃t] *adj & nm inv* forty; *Fam* **se ficher de qch comme de l'an q.** not to give two hoots about sth;

Can **vieux comme l'an q.** ancient, as old as the hills; *voir aussi* **trois**

quarante-cinq tours [karɑ̃tsɛtur] *nm inv* single, 45

quarantième [karɑ̃tjɛm] *nmf, nm & adj* fortieth; *voir aussi* **cinquième**

quart¹ [kar] *adj* **le q. monde** *(dans les pays riches)* the underclass

quart² *nm* (**a**) *(fraction)* quarter; **un q. de siècle/de beurre** a quarter (of a) century/kilo of butter; **un q. d'heure** a quarter of an hour; *Fam* **passer un mauvais q. d'heure** to have a bad time of it; **deux heures et q.** (a) quarter past *orAm* after two; **deux heures moins le q.** (a) quarter to *orAm* of two; **il est moins le q.** it's (a) quarter to; **démarrer** *ou* **partir au q. de tour** *(voiture)* to start first time; *(personne)* to fly off the handle; **q. de cercle** quadrant; **q. de finale** quarter final; *Mus* **q. de soupir** *Br* semiquaver *orAm* sixteenth rest (**b**) *(bouteille, pichet)* quarter litre (**c**) *(veille sur un bateau)* watch; **être de q.** to be on watch

quart-arrière [kararjɛr] *nm Can* quarterback

quarte [kart] *nf Mus* fourth

quarté [karte] *nm* = system of betting on four horses in the same race

quartette [kwartɛt] *nm* jazz quartet

quartier [kartje] *nm* (**a**) *(d'une ville)* district, area; **les beaux quartiers** the fashionable districts; **les quartiers nord de la ville** the north side of the town; **de q., du q.** local (**b**) *(morceau) (d'une orange)* segment; *(d'une pomme)* piece (**c**) *(de la lune)* quarter (**d**) *(de viande)* quarter (**e**) *(en héraldique)* quarter; **avoir quatre quartiers de noblesse** to belong to the established nobility (**f**) *(locutions)* **avoir q. libre** to be off duty; **ne pas faire de q.** to give no quarter

quartz [kwarts] *nm* quartz; **horloge/montre à q.** quartz clock/watch

quasi [kazi] *adv* almost, nearly

quasi- [kazi] *préf* **la q.-totalité des membres** almost all the members

quasiment [kazimɑ̃] *adv* almost, nearly; **je n'ai q. rien senti** I hardly felt a thing

quaternaire [kwatɛrnɛr] *Géol* **1** *adj* Quaternary **2** *nm* Quaternary era

quatorze [katɔrz] *adj & nm inv* fourteen; *voir aussi* **trois**

quatorzième [katɔrzjɛm] *nmf, nm & adj* fourteenth; *voir aussi* **cinquième**

quatrain [katrɛ̃] *nm* quatrain

quatre [katr] *adj & nm inv* four; **aux q. coins du monde** throughout the world; **monter l'escalier q. à q.** to rush up the stairs; *Fig* **se mettre en q. pour qn/pour faire qch** to bend over backwards for sb/to do sth; *voir aussi* **trois**

quatre-quarts [katkar, katrəkar] *nm inv* ≃ pound cake

quatre-quatre [katkatr] *nm inv ou nf inv* four-wheel drive

quatre-saisons [katsɛzɔ̃, katrəsɛzɔ̃] *nfpl* **marchand des q.** fruit-and-vegetable merchant *(with outdoor stall)*

quatre-vingt [katrəvɛ̃] *voir* **quatre-vingts**

quatre-vingt-dix [katrəvɛ̃dis] *adj & nm inv* ninety; *voir aussi* **trois**

quatre-vingt-dixième [katrəvɛ̃dizjɛm] *adj, nmf & nm* ninetieth; *voir aussi* **cinquième**

quatre-vingtième [katrəvɛ̃tjɛm] *adj, nmf & nm* eightieth; *voir aussi* **cinquième**

quatre-vingts [katrəvɛ̃] *adj & nm inv* eighty; **quatre-vingt-deux** eighty-two; **page quatre-vingt** page eighty; *voir aussi* **trois**

quatrième [katrijɛm] **1** *adj* fourth; **le q. âge** extreme old age; *Fam* **en q. vitesse** in a hurry, at breakneck speed **2** *nmf* fourth **3** *nf* (**a**) *(classe) Br* ≃ third form, *Am* ≃ ninth grade (**b**) *(vitesse)* fourth (gear); *voir aussi* **cinquième**

quatrièmement [katrijemmɑ̃] *adv* fourthly

quatuor [kwatɥɔr] *nm* quartet; **q. à cordes** string quartet

que¹ [k(ə)]

> En anglais, le pronom relatif objet (voir (**a**)) peut être omis.

pron relatif (**a**) *(objet) (personne)* that, whom; *(chose)* that, which; **l'homme q. vous voyez** the man (that) you see; **la tarte q. j'ai fait cuire** the tart (that) I baked; **c'est le meilleur q. nous ayons** it is the best (that) we have (**b**) *(attribut)* **il mourut en brave soldat qu'il était** he died like the brave soldier he was (**c**) *(dans le temps)* **il y a trois mois q. j'habite Paris** I've been living in Paris for three months; **un jour q. j'étais de service** one day when I was on duty

que² *pron interrogatif* what; **q. voulez-vous?** what do you want?; **il ne savait q. penser** he didn't know what to think

que³ *adv exclamatif* **qu'elle est intelligente!** she's so intelligent!; **q. de monde!** what a lot of people!

que⁴

> La conjonction "that" peut être omise après les verbes d'opinion, ainsi que "say", "know", etc : **je sais que c'est possible** I know (that) it's possible.

conj (**a**) *(complétif)* that; **je pense qu'il a raison** I think (that) he's right; **je veux qu'il vienne** I want him to come; **c'est q. je ne le savais pas** I just didn't know (**b**) *(exprime le souhait)* **qu'elle entre!** let her come in! (**c**) *(exprime l'hypothèse)* **q. la machine chauffe, et il y aura un accident** let the machine get hot and there will be an accident; **qu'il essaie encore une fois!** just let him try again! (**d**) *(dans une alternative)* **q. tu le veuilles ou non** whether you like it or not (**e**) *(relie deux conditionnels)* **il me le dirait lui-même q. je ne le croirais pas** he could tell me himself and I still wouldn't believe it (**f**) *(afin que, pour que)* **approchez qu'on vous entende** come closer so (that) we can hear you (**g**) *(pour ne pas répéter une autre conjonction)* **quand tu iras mieux et q. tu voudras sortir** when you're better and you want to go out; **si ça te plaît et que tu veux l'acheter...** if you like it and you want to buy it... (**h**) *(dans les comparaisons)* **plus/moins grand q. moi** bigger/smaller than me; **aussi grand q. moi** as big as me (**i**) **ne... q.** only; **il n'a qu'une jambe** he's only got one leg; **il ne me reste plus q. 20 francs** I've only got 20 francs left (**j**) *Fam* **ah! q. non!** surely not!; **il va au cercle – qu'il dit!** he goes to the club – so he says!

Québec [kebɛk] **1** *nm (province)* **le Q.** Quebec **2** *n (ville)* Quebec

québécisme [kebesism] *nm* = word or expression peculiar to Quebec French

québécois, -e [kebekwa, -az] **1** *adj* of Quebec
2 *nm,f* **Q.** Quebecker
3 *nm (langue)* Quebec French

quel, quelle [kɛl] **1** *adj interrogatif (personne)* which; *(chose)* which, what; **q. homme?** which man?; **quelle heure est-il?** what time is it?, what's the time?; **q. genre d'homme est-ce?** what sort of a man is he?; **si tu savais à q. point il y tient** if you knew how fond he is of it; **à q. film faites-vous référence?** which *or* what film are you referring to?; **quelles sont ses raisons?** what are his reasons?; *Litt* **q. est cet homme?** who is this man?
2 *adj exclamatif* **q. homme!** what a man!; **quelle surprise!** what a surprise!; **quelle bêtise de sa part!** how stupid of him!
3 *adj relatif* **q. que soit le coupable** whoever the culprit may be; **q. que soit le résultat** whatever the result may be; **q. que soit l'endroit où...** no matter where...
4 *pron interrogatif* which (one)

quelconque [kɛlkɔ̃k] **1** *adj indéfini* **donne-moi un livre q.** give me any book; **sous un prétexte q.** on some pretext or other
2 *adj (insignifiant)* ordinary

quelle [kɛl] *voir* **quel**

quelque [kɛlk] **1** *adj indéfini* some; **quelques** some, a few; **il y a quelques jours** a few days ago; **et quelque(s)** or so; **cent et quelques mètres** a hundred metres plus; **q.... que** + *subjunctive* whatever; **sous q. prétexte que ce soit** on whatever pretext; **de q. côté que vous regardiez** whichever way you look
2 *adv* some, about; **q. dix ans** some *or* about ten years; **les q. 1000 francs qu'il m'a prêtés** the 1,000 francs or so that he lent me

quelque chose [kɛlkəʃoz] *pron indéfini* something; **avez-vous q. à dire?** do you have anything *or* something to say?; **est-ce que je peux te dire q.?** can I tell you something?; **q. d'autre/de neuf** something else/new; **cela m'a fait q.** it touched me; **ça te ferait vraiment q. si je m'en allais?** would it really matter to you if I went away?; *Fam* **ah, mais c'est q., ça!** that's a bit much!; *Fam* **un petit q.** *(cadeau)* a little something

quelquefois [kɛlkəfwa] *adv* sometimes

quelque part [kɛlkəpar] *adv* somewhere; *(dans les questions, les hypothèses)* anywhere; **q. où tu n'es jamais allé** somewhere you've never been before; *Fam* **je lui ai donné un coup de pied q.** I kicked him where it hurts

quelques-uns, quelques-unes [kɛlkəzœ̃, -yn] *pron indéfini* some, a few (**de** of)

quelqu'un [kɛlkœ̃] *pron indéfini* (**a**) *(une personne)* someone, somebody; *(dans les questions, les hypothèses)* anyone, anybody; **q. de trop** one too many; **q. d'important** someone important; **c'est q. de bien** he's a decent person (**b**) *(personne importante)* somebody

quémander [kemɑ̃de] *vt* to beg for (**à** from)

qu'en-dira-t-on [kɑ̃diratɔ̃] *nm* **le q.** gossip

quenelle [kənɛl] *nf Culin* quenelle

quenotte [kənɔt] *nf Fam* tooth

quenouille [kənuj] *nf (pour filer)* distaff; *Fig* **tomber en q.** to go to rack and ruin

quéquette [kekɛt] *nf Fam Br* willy, *Am* peter

querelle [kərɛl] *nf* quarrel; **chercher q. à qn** to try to pick a quarrel with sb; **q. de clocher** petty dispute

quereller [kərɛle] **se quereller** *vpr* to quarrel (**avec** with)

querelleur, -euse [kərɛlœr, -øz] *adj* quarrelsome

quérir [kerir] *vt Litt* **aller q. qn/qch** to go and fetch sb/sth

qu'est-ce que [kɛskə] **1** *pron interrogatif* what; **q. vous voulez?** what do you want?; **q. c'est que ça?** what's that?; *Fam* **q. tu avais besoin d'aller lui dire ça?** what did you have to go and tell him that for?
2 *pron exclamatif* **qu'est-ce qu'il fait beau!** what lovely weather!; **qu'est-ce qu'il fait chaud!** it's so hot!; **qu'est-ce qu'on a rigolé!** we had such a good laugh!; **q. tu as changé!** how you've changed!; **q. j'ai mangé!** I've eaten so much!

qu'est-ce qui [kɛski] *pron interrogatif* what

question [kɛstjɔ̃] *nf* (**a**) *(interrogation)* question (**sur** about); **q. de confiance** vote of confidence; **q. piège** trick question; **q. subsidiaire** tie-break (**b**) *(affaire)* question, matter; **le dossier en q.** the file in question; **remettre qch en q.** to call sth into question; **une q. d'argent/de temps/d'habitude** a question *or* matter of money/of time/of habit; **c'est une q. de vie ou de mort** it's a matter of life or death; **il est q. qu'ils déménagent** there's some talk of them moving; **il n'en est pas q.** it's out of the question; **là n'est pas la q.** that's not the point; *Fam* **pas q.!** no way!, no chance!; *Fam* **q. argent, ça va** moneywise *or* as far as money goes, things are OK

questionnaire [kɛstjɔnɛr] *nm* questionnaire; **q. à choix multiple** multiple-choice questionnaire

questionner [kɛstjɔne] *vt* to question (**sur** about)

quête [kɛt] *nf* (**a**) *(recherche)* quest, search (**de** for); **se mettre en q. de qn/qch** to go in search of sb/sth (**b**) *(collecte)* collection; **faire la q.** *(à l'église)* to take the collection

quêter [kete] **1** *vt* to seek
2 *vi* to collect money (**pour** for)

quêteux, -euse [kɛtø, -øz] *nm,f Can* beggar

quetsche [kwɛtʃ] *nf* (**a**) *(prune)* dark-red plum (**b**) *(eau-de-vie)* plum brandy

queue [kø] *nf* (**a**) *(d'animal)* tail; **n'avoir ni q. ni tête** to have neither rhyme nor reason; **une histoire sans q. ni tête** a shaggy-dog story; **faire une q. de poisson à qn** to cut (in) in front of sb; **finir en q. de poisson** *(pièce de théâtre, projet)* to end up in the air (**b**) *(d'une casserole)* handle; *(d'une comète, d'un cerf-volant)* tail; *(d'un fruit, d'une fleur)* stalk; *(d'une note de musique)* stem (**c**) *(d'une procession)* rear; **de q.** *(voiture, wagon)* rear; **être en q. de peloton** to be at the back of the bunch; **être en q. de classement** to be bottom of the table (**d**) *(file) Br* queue, *Am* line; **à la q. leu leu** in single file; **faire la q.** *Br* to queue (up), *Am* to stand in line (**e**) *(pour le billard)* cue (**f**) *Vulg (pénis)* cock

queue-de-cheval *(pl* **queues-de-cheval)** [kødʃəval] *nf* ponytail

queue-de-pie *(pl* **queues-de-pie)** [kødpi] *nf Fam* tails

qui¹ [ki]

En anglais, le pronom relatif objet peut être omis lorsque la préposition qui l'introduit est rejetée en fin de phrase: **l'amie avec qui j'ai passé mes vacances** the friend (who) I spent my holidays with.

pron relatif (**a**) *(personne)* who, that; *(animal, chose)* which, that; **vous q. êtes du pays, pourriez-vous me dire si...** you being from the country, could you tell me if...; **je le vois q. vient** I can see him coming (**b**) *(ce qui)* **q. plus est** what's more; **voilà q. me plaît** that's what I like (**c**) *(après une préposition)* who, whom; **voilà l'homme à q. je pensais** there's the man (who) I was thinking about; **il cherche quelqu'un avec q. jouer** he's looking for someone to play with; **c'est à q. finira le premier** everyone's trying to be the first to finish (**d**) *(n'importe qui)* whoever; **emmenez q. vous voulez** take whoever you like with you; **q. que vous soyez** whoever you are; **je défie q. que ce soit de le prouver** I challenge anyone to prove it

qui² *pron interrogatif* who; *(complément d'objet ou après une préposition)* who, whom; **q. a dit cela?** who said that?; **savez-vous q. a dit cela?** do you know who said that?; **à q. est-ce?** whose is it?; **de q. parlez-vous?** who are you talking about?; **de q. êtes-vous le fils?** whose son are you?; **q. d'autre?** who else?; *Fam* **q. ça?** who's that?; *Fam* **il est là – q. donc?** he's here – who?

quiche [kiʃ] *nf* quiche; **q. lorraine** quiche lorraine

quiconque [kikɔ̃k] *pron indéfini (sujet)* whoever, anyone who; *(complément)* anyone, anybody; **q. désobéira sera puni** anyone who disobeys will be punished; **sans l'aide de q.** without anyone's help

quidam [kidam] *nm* fellow

quiétude [kjetyd] *nf Litt* peace; **en toute q.** *(sans être dérangé)* without being disturbed; *(sans souci)* with an easy mind

quignon [kiɲɔ̃] *nm* hunk

quille¹ [kij] *nf* (**a**) **quilles** *(jeu)* skittles (**b**) *Fam* **la q.** *(fin du service militaire)* discharge, *Br* demob (**c**) *Fam* **quilles** *(jambes)* pins

quille² *nf (d'un bateau)* keel

quilleur, -euse [kijœr, -øz] *nm,f Can* skittle player

quincaillerie [kɛ̃kajri] *nf* (**a**) *(magasin)* hardware shop, *Br* ironmonger's (**b**) *(ustensiles)* hardware (**c**) *Fam (bijoux voyants)* cheap jewellery

quincaillier, -ère [kɛ̃kaje, -ɛr] *nm,f* hardware dealer, *Br* ironmonger

quinconce [kɛ̃kɔ̃s] **en quinconce** *adv* in staggered rows

quinine [kinin] *nf* quinine

quinquagénaire [kɛ̃kaʒenɛr] **1** *adj* **être q.** to be in one's fifties
2 *nmf* person in his/her fifties

quinquennal, -e, -aux, -ales [kɛ̃kenal, -o] *adj (plan)* five-year; *(exposition, élection)* five-yearly

quinquennat [kɛ̃kena] *nm* five-year term

quintal, -aux [kɛ̃tal, -o] *nm* quintal *(= 100 kg)*

quinte [kɛ̃t] *nf* (**a**) *(accès)* **q. de toux** coughing fit (**b**) *Mus* fifth

quinté [kɛ̃te] *nm* = bet in which the punter predicts the first five horses to finish a race

quintessence [kɛ̃tesɑ̃s] *nf* quintessence

quintet [kɛ̃tɛt] *nm* (jazz) quintet

quintette [kɛ̃tɛt, kɥɛ̃tɛt] *nm* quintet; **q. à cordes** string quintet

quintuple [kɛ̃typl] **1** *adj* quintuple, fivefold
2 *nm* **le q. (de)** *(quantité, prix)* five times as much (as); *(nombre)* five times as many (as); **quinze est le q. de trois** fifteen is five times three

quintupler [kɛ̃typle] *vt & vi* to quintuple, to increase fivefold

quintuplés, -ées [kɛ̃typle] *nm,f pl* quintuplets

quinzaine [kɛ̃zɛn] *nf* (**a**) *(environ quinze)* **une q. (de)** about fifteen, fifteen or so (**b**) *(deux semaines)* two weeks, *Br* fortnight; *Com* = sale lasting two weeks

quinze [kɛ̃z] **1** *adj inv* fifteen; **q. jours** two weeks, *Br* a fortnight
2 *nm inv* fifteen; **demain en q.** two weeks *or Br* a fortnight tomorrow; **les Quinze** *(de l'Europe)* the member countries of the EU; *voir aussi* **trois**

quinzième [kɛ̃zjɛm] *nmf, nm & adj* fifteenth; *voir aussi* **cinquième**

quiproquo [kiprɔko] *nm* mix-up

quittance [kitɑ̃s] *nf* receipt; **q. de loyer** rent receipt

quitte [kit] *adj* (**a**) *(libéré)* **nous sommes quittes** we're quits (**b**) *(locutions)* **en être q. pour qch** to get off with sth; *Belg* **être q. de qch** to be deprived of sth; **q. ou double** double or quits; **q. à faire qch** even if it means doing sth

quitter [kite] **1** *vt* (**a**) *(personne, lieu)* to leave; *(chambre d'hôtel)* to vacate; **q. la route** *(par accident)* to go off the road; *(délibérément)* to turn off the road; **un ami très cher vient de nous q.** we have just lost a very dear friend; *Ordinat* **q. le système** to quit (the system) (**b**) *(fonctions, poste)* to leave (**c**) *(vêtement)* to take off (**d**) *(au téléphone)* **ne quittez pas** hold the line (**e**) **ne pas q. qn/qch des yeux** to keep one's eye on sb/sth
2 **se quitter** *upr* to part; **ils ne se quittent plus** they are inseparable

qui-vive [kiviv] *nm* **être ou se tenir sur le q.** to be on the alert

quoi¹ [kwa] *pron relatif* (**a**) what; **ce à q. je m'oppose** what I object to; **après q.** after which; **sur q.** whereupon; **avoir de q. vivre** to have enough to live on; **avez-vous de q. écrire?** do you have something to write with?; **il n'y a pas de q. être fier** that's nothing to be proud of; **il y a de q. se mettre en colère!** it's enough to make you really angry!; **je suis en colère – il y a de q.** I'm angry – you've every right to be; **il n'y a pas de q.** *(après des remerciements)* don't mention it, not at all (**b**) **q. que tu dises** whatever you say; **q. qu'il advienne** whatever happens; **q. qu'il en soit** be that as it may

quoi² *pron interrogatif* what; **q. d'autre?** what else?; **q. de neuf?** what's new?; **q. de plus simple?** what could be simpler?; **je ne sais q. penser** I don't know what to think; **à q. pensez-vous?** what are you thinking about?; **de q. parlez-vous?** what are you talking about?; **à q. bon?** what's the use?; *Fam* **tu es sourd ou q.?** are you deaf or what?; *Fam* **q.?** *(pardon?)* what?

quoi³ *exclam* what!; **et q. encore!** whatever next!; *Fam* **enfin, c'était nul, q.!** it was crap, basically!; **décide-toi, q.!** well make up your mind!

quoique [kwak] *conj* (al)though; **q. je le sache déjà** (al)though I already know

quolibet [kɔlibɛ] *nm* gibe, jeer

quorum [kwɔrɔm] *nm* quorum; **atteindre le q.** to have a quorum

quota [kɔta] *nm* quota; *Can Fig* **avoir son q.** to be fed-up

quote-part *(pl quotes-parts)* [kɔtpar] *nf* share

quotidien, -enne [kɔtidjɛ̃, -ɛn] **1** *adj (de chaque jour)* *(promenade, repas, entraînement)* daily; *(préoccupations)* everyday; **leurs disputes étaient devenues presque quotidiennes** they'd got to the stage where they were arguing almost every day
  2 *nm* **(a)** *(journal)* daily (paper); **grand q.** national daily (paper) **(b)** *(routine)* daily life; **au q.** on a day-to-day basis

quotidiennement [kɔtidjɛnmã] *adv* daily

quotient [kɔsjã] *nm* quotient; **q. intellectuel** intelligence quotient

R

R, r [ɛr] *nm inv* R, r

rab [rab] *nm Fam (nourriture)* extra; **faire du r.** *(au travail)* to put in a bit of overtime; **en r.** left over

rabâchage [rabɑʃaʒ] *nm* tedious repetition

rabâcher [rabɑʃe] **1** *vi* to say the same thing over and over again
   2 *vt (conseils, recommandations)* to keep on repeating; *(leçon)* to repeat parrot-fashion

rabais [rabɛ] *nm* discount, reduction; **faire un r. à qn (sur qch)** to give sb a discount (on sth); *Fig* **au r.** *(travail)* badly paid

rabaisser [rabese] **1** *vt* **(a)** *(prétentions)* to moderate **(b)** *(personne, valeur, talents)* to belittle
   2 se rabaisser *vpr* to belittle oneself

Rabat [raba] *n* Rabat

rabat [raba] *nm* **(a)** *(de sac à main, d'enveloppe)* flap **(b)** *(de costume officiel)* bands

rabat-joie [rabaʒwa] **1** *adj inv* **être r.** to be a killjoy
   2 *nm inv* killjoy

rabattable [rabatabl] *adj (siège, dossier)* fold-down

rabatteur, -euse [rabatœr, -øz] *nm,f* **(a)** *(à la chasse)* beater **(b)** *Fig* tout

rabattre [11] [rabatr] **1** *vt* **(a)** *(col)* to turn down **(b)** *(couvercle)* to close; *(strapontin) (en se levant)* to fold up; *(pour s'asseoir)* to fold down **(c)** *(gibier, foule)* to drive **(vers** towards) **(d)** *(somme)* to deduct **(de** from) **(e)** *(prétentions)* to moderate
   2 se rabattre *vpr* **(a)** *(strapontin)* to fold down **(b)** *(véhicule)* to pull back in **(c)** *(foule)* **se r. vers qch** to veer off towards sth **(d)** *(avoir recours)* **se r. sur qn/ qch** to fall back on sb/sth

rabbin [rabɛ̃] *nm* rabbi; **grand r.** chief rabbi

rabibocher [rabibɔʃe] *Fam* **1** *vt* to patch things up between
   2 se rabibocher *vpr* to patch things up (**avec** with)

rabiot [rabjo] = **rab**

râble [rɑbl] *nm (de lièvre, lapin)* back; **r. de lièvre** *(plat)* saddle of hare

râblé, -e [rable] *adj* stocky

rabot [rabo] *nm* plane

raboter [rabɔte] *vt* to plane

raboteuse [rabɔtøz] *nf* planing machine

raboteux, -euse [rabɔtø, -øz] *adj* uneven

rabougri, -e [rabugri] *adj (plante, personne)* stunted

rabougrir [rabugrir] **se rabougrir** *vpr* to shrivel up

rabrouer [rabrue] *vt* to snub

racaille [rakaj] *nf (voyous)* scum; *Vieilli (populace)* rabble

raccommodage [rakɔmɔdaʒ] *nm (de vêtements)* mending; *(de bas, de chaussettes)* darning; **faire du r.** to do some mending/darning

raccommoder [rakɔmɔde] **1** *vt* **(a)** *(vêtement)* to mend; *(bas, chaussette)* to darn **(b)** *Fam (personnes)* to patch things up between
   2 se raccommoder *vpr Fam* to patch things up (**avec** with)

raccompagner [rakɔ̃paɲe] *vt* to take back

raccord [rakɔr] *nm* **(a)** *(de papier peint)* join; *(de peinture)* touch-up **(b)** *(pièce d'assemblage)* connection **(c)** *Cin* continuity; *(plan)* link

raccordement [rakɔrdəmã] *nm* **(a)** *(lien)* link, connection **(b)** *Ordinat* link

raccorder [rakɔrde] **1** *vt* **(a)** *(relier) (canalisations, bâtiments, routes)* to link up, to connect (**à** to); *Ordinat* to connect **(b)** *(bande magnétique)* to splice
   2 se raccorder *vpr* to link up; *Ordinat* **se r. à** to link up to

raccourci [rakursi] *nm* short cut; **en r.** *(en bref)* in brief; *(en miniature)* in miniature; *Ordinat* **r. clavier** keyboard shortcut

raccourcir [rakursir] **1** *vt* to shorten (**de** by)
   2 *vi* to get shorter

raccrocher [rakrɔʃe] **1** *vt* to hang up again; **r. l'appareil** *ou* **le téléphone** to hang up
   2 *vi* **(a)** *(au téléphone)* to hang up, to put the phone down; **r. au nez de qn** to hang up on sb, to put the phone down on sb **(b)** *Fam (sportif)* to retire
   3 se raccrocher *vpr* **se r. à qch** to catch hold of sth; *Fig (espérance)* to cling to sth

race [ras] *nf* **(a)** *(ethnie)* race; **la r. blanche/noire** the white/black race; **la r. humaine** the human race **(b)** *(animale)* breed; **de r.** *(chien)* pedigree; *(cheval)* thoroughbred

racé, -e [rase] *adj (animal)* pure-bred; *(cheval, voiture)* thoroughbred; *(personne)* noble-looking

rachat [raʃa] *nm* **(a)** *(d'une voiture, d'un appartement)* repurchase, buying back **(b)** *(d'une société)* buy-out **(c)** *(d'un péché)* atonement

racheter [39] [raʃte] **1** *vt* **(a)** *(acheter davantage de)* to buy some more **(b)** *(remplacer)* to buy another (**à** for) **(c)** *(compagnie)* to buy out **(d)** *(après une vente)* to buy back (**à** from) **(e)** *(otage, prisonnier)* to pay a ransom for **(f)** *(faute, faiblesse)* to make up for; *(péché)* to atone for; *(honneur, réputation)* to retrieve
   2 se racheter *vpr* to make amends, to redeem oneself

rachitique [raʃitik] *adj (malade)* suffering from rickets; *(très maigre)* scrawny

rachitisme [raʃitism] *nm* rickets *(singulier)*

racial, -e, -aux, -ales [rasjal, -o] *adj* racial

racine [rasin] *nf* root; **prendre r.** *(plante, personne)* to take root; **r. carrée/cubique** square/cube root

racisme [rasism] *nm* racism

raciste [rasist] *adj & nmf* racist

racket [rakɛt] *nm Fam* racket

racketter [rakete] *vt Fam (personne)* to extort money from; **se faire r.** to pay protection money

raclage [raklaʒ] *nm* scraping

raclée [rakle] *nf Fam* thrashing; **mettre une r. à qn** *(battre)* to give sb a good thrashing; *(vaincre)* to thrash sb; **prendre une r.** to get a thrashing

raclement [rakləmɑ̃] *nm* scraping (noise)

racler [rakle] **1** *vt* to scrape; *(peinture, boue)* to scrape off; *Fig* **r. les fonds de tiroirs** to scrape some money together; *Fam* **r. la gorge** *ou* **le gosier** *(vin)* to be rough on the throat
  2 se racler *vpr* **se r. la gorge** to clear one's throat

raclette [raklɛt] *nf* (a) *(plat)* raclette *(Swiss dish consisting of potatoes covered in melted cheese)* (b) *(outil)* scraper

racloir [raklwar] *nm* scraper

racolage [rakɔlaʒ] *nm (d'une prostituée)* soliciting; *(d'un publicitaire)* touting for business; **faire du r.** *(prostituée)* to solicit; *(publicitaire)* to tout for business

racoler [rakɔle] **1** *vt (sujet: prostituée)* to solicit; *(sujet: commerçant)* to tout for
  2 *vi (prostituée)* to solicit; *(commerçant)* to tout for business

racoleur, -euse [rakɔlœr, -øz] **1** *adj (publicité, affiche)* eye-catching
  2 *nm,f (politicien)* = canvasser who attempts to recruit party members using unscrupulous means; *(commerçant)* tout
  3 *nf* **racoleuse** streetwalker

racontable [rakɔ̃tabl] *adj* relatable; **ce n'est pas r. devant les enfants** it's not something to be spoken about in front of the children

racontar [rakɔ̃tar] *nm* piece of gossip; **racontars** gossip

raconter [rakɔ̃te] **1** *vt* (a) *(histoire, mensonge)* to tell; *(événement)* to tell about; **r. qch à qn** *(histoire)* to tell sb sth; *(événement)* to tell sb about sth (b) *(dire)* to say; **qu'est-ce qu'il raconte?** what's he talking about?; **alors, qu'est-ce que tu racontes (de beau ou de neuf)?** so what's new?
  2 se raconter *vpr* (a) *(parler de soi)* to talk about oneself (b) *(être raconté)* to be talked about

racornir [rakɔrnir] **1** *vt* (a) *(durcir)* to harden (b) *(ratatiner)* to shrivel
  2 se racornir *vpr* (a) *(durcir)* to harden (b) *(se ratatiner)* to shrivel

radar [radar] *nm* radar; *Fam* **être** *ou* **avancer au r.** to be on automatic pilot

rade [rad] *nf* harbour; **en r. de Toulon** off Toulon; *Fam* **laisser en r.** *(personne)* to leave in the lurch; *(projet)* to jettison; *Fam* **être en r.** *(personne)* to be stranded

radeau, -x [rado] *nm* raft; **r. pneumatique** inflatable raft; **r. de sauvetage** life raft

radial, -e, -aux, -ales [radjal, -o] *adj voir* **carcasse**

radiateur [radjatœr] *nm* radiator; **r. électrique** electric heater

radiation¹ [radjasjɔ̃] *nf (sur une liste)* striking off

radiation² *nf (d'une onde)* radiation

radical, -e, -aux, -ales [radikal, -o] **1** *adj* radical; **c'est r. (contre)** *(médicament, méthode)* it works like magic (on)
  2 *nm (d'un mot)* stem

radicalement [radikalmɑ̃] *adv* radically

radicaliser [radikalize] **1** *vt* to radicalize
  2 se radicaliser *vpr* to become more radical

radier [66] [radje] *vt* to strike off (**de** from)

radiesthésiste [radjestezist] *nmf* diviner

radieux, -euse [radjø, -øz] *adj (soleil, personne)* radiant; *(temps)* glorious

radin, -e [radɛ̃, -in] *Fam* **1** *adj* stingy
  2 *nm,f* skinflint

radiner [radine] **se radiner** *vpr Fam* to roll up; **tu te radines?** are you coming or not?

radio [radjo] **1** *nf* (a) *(poste)* radio; *(station)* radio station; **à la r.** on the radio; **faire de la r.** to be *or* work as a radio presenter; **r. libre** independent radio station; **r. locale** local radio station (b) *(radiotéléphonie)* radio (c) *Méd* X-ray; **passer une r.** to have an X-ray
  2 *nm (opérateur)* radio operator
  3 *adj inv* radio

radioactif, -ive [radjoaktif, -iv] *adj* radioactive

radioactivité [radjoaktivite] *nf* radioactivity

radioamateur [radjoamatœr] *nm* radio ham

radiocassette [radjokasɛt] *nf* radio cassette player

radiodiffuser [radjodifyze] *vt* to broadcast

radiodiffusion [radjodifyzjɔ̃] *nf* broadcasting

radiographie [radjɔgrafi] *nf* (a) *(technique)* radiography (b) *(cliché)* X-ray

radiographier [66] [radjɔgrafje] *vt* to X-ray

radioguidé, -e [radjogide] *adj* radio-controlled; *(missile)* guided

radiologie [radjɔlɔʒi] *nf* radiology

radiologique [radjɔlɔʒik] *adj* radiological

radiologue [radjɔlɔg], **radiologiste** [radjɔlɔʒist] *nmf (médecin)* radiologist; *(technicien)* radiographer

radiophonique [radjofɔnik] *adj (de radio)* radio; *(bon pour la radio)* good for radio

radioreportage [radjorəpɔrtaʒ] *nm (activité)* radio reporting; *(émission)* radio report

radioreporter [radjorəpɔrter] *nmf* radio reporter

radio-réveil *(pl* **radios-réveils)** [radjorevɛj] *nm* radio-alarm (clock)

radioscopie [radjoskɔpi] *nf* radioscopy

radioscopique [radjoskɔpik] *adj (examen)* X-ray

radio-taxi *(pl* **radio-taxis)** [radjotaksi] *nm* radio taxi

radiotélescope [radjotelɛskɔp] *nm* radio telescope

radiotélévisé, -e [radjotelevize] *adj* broadcast on both radio and television

radiothérapie [radjoterapi] *nf* radiotherapy

radis [radi] *nm* radish; *Fam* **ne plus avoir un r.** not to have a bean; **r. noir** black radish

radium [radjɔm] *nm* radium

radius [radjys] *nm* radius

radon [radɔ̃] *nm Chim* radon

radotage [radɔtaʒ] *nm (rabâchage)* going on and on; *(divagations)* rambling

radoter [radɔte] **1** *vi (rabâcher)* to go on and on; *(divaguer)* to ramble on
  2 *vt Fam* **qu'est-ce que tu radotes?** what are you drivelling on about?

radoteur, -euse [radɔtœr, -øz] *nm,f* rambling old fool

radoub [radu] *nm* **bassin de r.** dry dock

radoucir [radusir] **1** *vt* (**a**) *(temps)* to make milder (**b**) *(personne)* to calm down; *(caractère)* to soften
  2 se radoucir *vpr* (**a**) *(temps)* to become milder (**b**) *(personne)* to calm down

radoucissement [radusismɑ̃] *nm* (**a**) *(de la température)* milder spell (**b**) *(d'une personne)* calming down

rafale [rafal] *nf* (**a**) *(de vent, de pluie)* gust; **par** *ou* **en rafales** in gusts (**b**) *(de coups de feu)* burst

raffermir [rafɛrmir] **1** *vt* (**a**) *(peau, muscles)* to firm up (**b**) *(autorité, courage)* to strengthen
  2 se raffermir *vpr* (**a**) *(muscles, peau)* to firm up (**b**) *(gouvernement)* (*devenir plus intransigeant)* to take a stronger line; *(devenir plus fort)* to become stronger; *(autorité)* to strengthen

raffermissement [rafɛrmismɑ̃] *nm* (**a**) *(des muscles, de la peau)* firming up (**b**) *(de l'autorité, du pouvoir)* strengthening

raffinage [rafinaʒ] *nm* refining

raffiné, -e [rafine] *adj* refined

raffinement [rafinmɑ̃] *nm* refinement

raffiner [rafine] **1** *vt* to refine
  2 raffiner sur *vt ind* to be overparticular about

raffinerie [rafinri] *nf* refinery; **r. de pétrole/sucre** oil/sugar refinery

raffoler [rafɔle] **raffoler de** *vt ind Fam* **r. de qch** to be mad about sth

raffut [rafy] *nm Fam (bruit)* din, racket; **faire du r.** *(bruit)* to make a din; *(scandale)* to set tongues wagging; *(pour protester)* to kick up a fuss

rafiot [rafjo] *nm Péj* old tub

rafistolage [rafistɔlaʒ] *nm Fam* patching up

rafistoler [rafistɔle] *vt Fam* to patch up

rafle [rafl] *nf* raid; **la police a fait une r. dans le club** the police raided the club

rafler [rafle] *vt Fam* to swipe

rafraîchir [rafrɛʃir] **1** *vt* (**a**) *(rendre frais)* *(aliment, boisson)* to chill; *(pièce)* to air; *(atmosphère)* to cool (**b**) *(raviver)* *(couleur, maquillage, peintures)* to freshen up; *(appartement)* to brighten up; *Fam* **r. la mémoire à qn** to refresh sb's memory
  2 *vi* to cool down
  3 se rafraîchir *vpr* (**a**) *(temps)* to turn cooler (**b**) *(se mouiller le visage)* to freshen up (**c**) *Fam (boire)* to have a cold drink

rafraîchissant, -e [rafrɛʃisɑ̃, -ɑ̃t] *adj* refreshing

rafraîchissement [rafrɛʃismɑ̃] *nm* (**a**) *(de la température, d'une boisson)* cooling (**b**) *(boisson)* cold drink; **rafraîchissements** refreshments (**c**) *Ordinat* refresh

rafting [raftiŋ] *nm* rafting

ragaillardir [ragajardir] *Fam* **1** *vt* to buck up
  2 se ragaillardir *vpr* to buck up

rage [raʒ] *nf* (**a**) *(maladie)* rabies (**b**) *(colère)* rage; **faire r.** *(tempête)* to rage; **avoir la r. au cœur** to be seething with rage; **ivre** *ou* **fou de r.** furious; **mettre qn en r.** to enrage sb; **r. de dents** raging toothache (**c**) *(passion)* passion (**de qch** for sth); **avoir la r. du jeu** to have a passion for gambling

rageant, -e [raʒɑ̃, -ɑ̃t] *adj Fam* infuriating

rager [45] [raʒe] *vi Fam* to fume; **faire r. qn** to make sb mad

rageur, -euse [raʒœr, -øz] *adj (ton, voix)* furious

rageusement [raʒøzmɑ̃] *adv* furiously

raglan [raglɑ̃] *nm* raglan coat

ragot [rago] *nm Fam* piece of gossip; **ragots** gossip

ragoût [ragu] *nm* stew; **en r.** stewed

ragoûtant, -e [ragutɑ̃, -ɑ̃t] *adj* **peu** *ou* **pas r.** *(plat)* unappetizing; *(personne)* unsavoury

rai [rɛ] *nm (de lumière)* ray

raï [raj] *nm inv* raï,= North African popular music influenced by rock music

raid [rɛd] *nm* raid; **r. aérien** air raid

raide [rɛd] **1** *adj* (**a**) *(membre, articulation)* stiff; *(cheveux)* straight; *(câble)* taut (**b**) *(escalier, pente)* steep (**c**) *(personne, démarche)* stiff; **r. comme un piquet** as stiff as a ramrod (**d**) *(caractère)* inflexible; *(manières)* stiff (**e**) *Fam (difficile à croire)* far-fetched (**f**) *Fam (osé)* risqué (**g**) *Fam (fort)* *(alcool)* rough
  2 *adv* (**a**) *(de façon abrupte)* steeply (**b**) *(brutalement)* **tomber r.** to fall to the ground; **tomber r. mort** to drop dead

raideur [rɛdœr] *nf* (**a**) *(d'un membre, d'une articulation, d'un mouvement)* stiffness; **avoir une r. dans le cou/à l'épaule** to have a stiff neck/shoulder (**b**) *(d'une personne)* stiffness (**c**) *(de caractère)* inflexibility (**d**) *(d'une pente)* steepness

raidillon [rɛdijɔ̃] *nm (chemin)* steep path; *(partie de route)* steep rise

raidir [rɛdir] **1** *vt (bras, jambes)* to brace; *(corde, câble)* to tauten; *(tissu)* to stiffen
  2 se raidir *vpr* (**a**) *(membres, articulations)* to stiffen; *(câble)* to tauten (**b**) *(personne)* to tense up

raidissement [rɛdismɑ̃] *nm* (**a**) *(d'une matière, des muscles)* stiffening; *(d'une corde)* tautening (**b**) *(montée de la tension)* **r. des rapports internationaux** increase of tension in international relations; **le r. des ouvriers face à la direction** the tougher line taken by the workers with the management

raie¹ [rɛ] *nf* (**a**) *(motif)* stripe (**b**) *(dans les cheveux) Br* parting, *Am* part (**c**) *(des fesses)* cleft

raie² *nf (poisson)* skate

raifort [rɛfɔr] *nm* horseradish

rail [raj] *nm* (**a**) *(sur une voie de chemin de fer)* rail; *Fig* **remettre qn sur les rails** to get sb back on the rails (**b**) **le r.** *(les chemins de fer)* rail (**c**) **r. de sécurité** crash barrier (**d**) *(couloir)* *(aérien, maritime)* lane

railler [raje] *vt* to mock

raillerie [rajri] *nf* gibe

railleur, -euse [rajœr, -øz] **1** *adj* mocking
  2 *nm,f* scoffer

rainette [rɛnɛt] *nf* (**a**) *(grenouille)* tree frog (**b**) *(pomme)* pippin

rainure [rɛnyr] *nf* groove

raisin [rɛzɛ̃] *nm* grapes; **raisins de Corinthe** currants; **raisins secs** raisins; **raisins de Smyrne** sultanas

raisinet [rezine] *nm Suisse* redcurrant

raison [rɛzɔ̃] *nf* (**a**) *(motif)* reason (**de** for); **en r. de qch** because of sth; **être absent pour r. de santé** to be absent for health reasons; **à plus forte r.** all the more so; **r. de plus (pour faire qch)** all the more reason (to do sth); **la r. pour laquelle il est venu** the reason (why) he came; **la r. d'État** reasons of State; **r. d'être** raison d'être; **r. de vivre** reason for living (**b**) *(entendement)* reason; **recouvrer la r.** to come to one's senses; **perdre la r.** to take leave of one's senses; **entendre r.** to listen to reason; **de r.** *(âge)* of reason; *(mariage)* of convenience (**c**) *(satisfaction)* satisfaction; **avoir r. de qn/qch** to get the better of sb/sth (**d**) *(proportion)* **à r. de** at the rate of (**e**) *(désignation)* **r. sociale** company name (**f**) *(locutions)* **avoir r. (de faire qch)** to be right (to do sth); **donner r. à qn** *(personne)* to admit that sb is right; *(événement)* to prove sb right; **se faire une r.** to accept the inevitable, to resign oneself; **comme de r.** as one might expect; **plus que de r.** more than is reasonable

raisonnable [rɛzɔnabl] *adj* reasonable

raisonnablement [rɛzɔnabləmã] *adv* (**a**) *(avec bon sens)* reasonably (**b**) *(modérément)* in moderation

raisonné, -e [rɛzɔne] *adj (argumentation, choix)* reasoned

raisonnement [rɛzɔnmã] *nm (argumentation)* argument; *(faculté)* reasoning; **tenir un r.** to use an argument; **r. par l'absurde** reductio ad absurdum

raisonner [rɛzɔne] **1** *vt (personne)* to reason with
2 *vi* (**a**) *(penser)* to reason (**sur** about); *Fam* **r. comme une pantoufle** to talk through one's hat (**b**) *(discuter)* to argue (**avec** with)
3 se raisonner *vpr (personne)* to see reason

raisonneur, -euse [rɛzɔnœr, -øz] **1** *adj* reasoning; *Péj* argumentative
2 *nm,f Péj* arguer

rajeunir [raʒœnir] **1** *vt* (**a**) **r. qn** *(faire paraître plus jeune)* to make sb look younger; *(faire se sentir plus jeune)* to make sb feel younger (**b**) *(donner un âge moins élevé à)* **r. qn** to underestimate how old sb is; **r. qn de trois ans** to take three years off sb's age (**c**) *(robe, veste)* to update (**d**) *(organisation, bureau)* to modernize; *(équipe)* to bring new blood into
2 *vi (physiquement)* to look younger; *(moralement)* to seem younger; **il a rajeuni de dix ans** he looks ten years younger; **ça ne nous rajeunit pas!** we're showing our age!
3 se rajeunir *vpr (se prétendre plus jeune)* to make oneself out to be younger than one is

rajeunissant, -e [raʒœnisã, -ãt] *adj* rejuvenating

rajeunissement [raʒœnismã] *nm* (**a**) *(après un traitement)* rejuvenation (**b**) *(de la population, d'un secteur professionnel)* decrease in age

rajout [raʒu] *nm* addition

rajouter [raʒute] *vt* to add; *Fam* **en r.** to exaggerate

rajuster [raʒyste] **1** *vt (vêtement)* to adjust, to straighten
2 se rajuster *vpr* to tidy oneself up

râle [rɑl] *nm (bruit aux poumons)* rale; *(d'un agonisant)* death rattle

ralenti, -e [ralãti] **1** *adj* slow
2 *nm* (**a**) *(régime du moteur)* idling speed; **au r.** *(vivre, fonctionner)* at a slower pace; **tourner au r.** *(moteur, usine) Br* to tick over, *Am* to turn over (**b**) *Cin* slow motion; **au r.** in slow motion

ralentir [ralãtir] *vt & vi* to slow down

ralentissement [ralãtismã] *nm* slowing down; *(embouteillage)* hold-up

ralentisseur [ralãtisœr] *nm (dos d'âne)* speed bump

râler [rɑle] *vi* (**a**) *Fam (protester)* to moan (**b**) *(mourant)* to give a death rattle

râleur, -euse [rɑlœr, -øz] *Fam* **1** *adj* bad-tempered, grumpy
2 *nm,f* moaner

ralliement [ralimã] *nm* rallying; **cri de r.** rallying cry

rallier [66] [ralje] **1** *vt* (**a**) *(regagner) (lieu)* to return to (**b**) *(gagner à sa cause)* to win over (**à** to) (**c**) *(réunir) (adhérents)* to rally; **r. tous les suffrages** to win general approval (**d**) *(regrouper) (troupes)* to rally
2 se rallier *vpr* **se r. à** *(avis)* to come round to; *(parti)* to join; *(cause)* to rally to

rallonge [ralɔ̃ʒ] *nf* (**a**) *(de table)* extension (**b**) *(électrique)* extension (lead) (**c**) *Fam (d'argent)* extra money; *(de temps)* extra time

rallonger [45] [ralɔ̃ʒe] **1** *vt (vêtement)* to lengthen; *(période, route)* to extend (**de** by)
2 *vi* to get longer

rallumer [ralyme] **1** *vt* (**a**) *(appareil électrique, lumière)* to switch on again (**b**) *(feu, cigarette)* to light again; *(querelle, colère, espoir)* to rekindle
2 se rallumer *vpr* (**a**) *(lumière, appareil électrique)* to come back on (**b**) *(feu, guerre, dispute)* to flare up again; *(espoir)* to rekindle

rallye [rali] *nm* (**a**) *(épreuve sportive)* (car) rally (**b**) *(soirée)* = dance attended by young people from rich families looking for a marriage partner

RAM [ram] *nf Ordinat* RAM

ramadan [ramadã] *nm* Ramadan; **faire le r.** to observe Ramadan

ramage [ramaʒ] *nm* (**a**) *(chant des oiseaux)* song (**b**) **ramages** *(motif)* leafy design

ramassage [ramasaʒ] *nm* (**a**) *(de fruits, de noix)* gathering (**b**) *(d'ordures, de vêtements, de vieux journaux)* collection; **car de r. scolaire** school bus

ramassé, -e [ramase] *adj* (**a**) *(trapu) (personne)* stocky (**b**) *(style)* compact

ramasse-miettes [ramasmjɛt] *nm inv* table tidy *(small brush and pan for clearing crumbs off the table)*

ramasser [ramase] **1** *vt* (**a**) *(prendre par terre) (objet, personne)* to pick up; *(fruits, noix, coquillages)* to gather; *(champignons)* to pick; *(pommes de terre)* to dig up; *Fam* **se faire r. par la police** to get picked up by the police (**b**) *(copies, affaires, informations)* to collect; *(cartes)* to pick up; **r. ses forces** to gather one's strength (**c**) *(enfants, ouvriers, courrier)* to pick up, to collect (**d**) *Fam (gifle)* to get; *(procès-verbal)* to pick up; *(maladie)* to catch
2 se ramasser *vpr* (**a**) *(après une chute)* to pick oneself up (**b**) *(se pelotonner)* to curl up (**c**) *Fam (tomber)* to fall flat on one's face; *(échouer)* to come a cropper (**d**) *(gifle)* to get; *(P-V)* to pick up

ramassette [ramasɛt] *nf Belg* dustpan

ramasseur, -euse [ramasœr, -øz] *nm,f* (**a**) *(de champignons)* picker; *(de fruits)* gatherer (**b**) *(au tennis)* **r. de balles** ball boy, *f* ball girl

ramassis [ramasi] *nm Péj (de choses)* jumble; *(de gens)* bunch; *(d'idées)* hotchpotch; **un r. de mensonges** a tissue of lies

rambarde [rãbard] *nf* (guard)rail

ramdam [ramdam] *nm Fam* racket; **faire du r.** to make a heck of a racket

rame¹ [ram] *nf (pour plantes grimpantes)* stick

rame² *nf (aviron)* oar

rame³ *nf* (**a**) *(de papier)* ream (**b**) *(de wagons)* train; **r. (de métro)** (*Br* underground *or Am* subway) train

rameau, -x [ramo] *nm* (**a**) *(d'arbre)* branch (**b**) **les Rameaux** Palm Sunday

ramener [46] [ramne] **1** *vt* (**a**) *(amener)* to bring back; *(raccompagner)* to take back; **r. qn en voiture** to give sb a lift back; **r. qn à la vie** to bring sb back to life; **r. qn à la raison** to bring sb back to his/her senses (**b**) *Fam (rapporter, revenir avec)* to bring back; **r. tout à soi** to bring everything back to oneself (**c**) *(remettre) (couverture, châle)* to pull up (**sur** over) (**d**) *(rétablir) (ordre, paix)* to restore (**e**) *(réduire)* **r. qch à qch** to reduce sth to sth (**f**) *Fam* **r. sa fraise, la r.** to show off

2 se ramener *vpr* (**a**) *(se réduire)* **se r. à** to boil down to (**b**) *Fam (arriver)* to roll up

ramequin [ramkɛ̃] *nm* ramekin

ramer [rame] *vi* (**a**) *(pagayer)* to row (**b**) *Fam (peiner)* to sweat blood

rameur, -euse [ramœr, -øz] *nm,f* rower

ramier [ramje] *adj m voir* **pigeon**

ramification [ramifikasjɔ̃] *nf (d'une plante)* ramification; *(d'une famille, d'une science)* branch; **ramifications** *(d'une société, d'une affaire)* ramifications

ramifier [66] [ramifje] **se ramifier** *vpr* to branch out (**en** into)

ramolli, -e [ramɔli] *adj Fam (mentalement)* soft-headed

ramollir [ramɔlir] **1** *vt (substance)* to soften; *Fam* **r. qn** *(intellectuellement)* to make sb soft in the head
2 se ramollir *vpr (substance)* to soften; *Fam Fig (personne)* to become unfit

ramollissement [ramɔlismã] *nm* softening; **r. cérébral** softening of the brain

ramon [ramɔ̃] *nm Belg* broom

ramonage [ramɔnaʒ] *nm* chimney sweeping

ramoner [ramɔne] *vt (cheminée)* to sweep

ramoneur [ramɔnœr] *nm* (chimney) sweep

rampant, -e [rɑ̃pɑ̃, -ɑ̃t] *adj* (**a**) *(plante)* creeping; *(animal)* crawling; *Péj (personne, caractère)* grovelling (**b**) **personnel r.** *(de l'aviation)* ground crew (**c**) *(inflation)* rampant

rampe [rɑ̃p] *nf* (**a**) *(d'escalier)* banister, handrail (**b**) *(plan incliné)* slope, incline; **r. d'accès** *(d'un pont)* access ramp; *(d'une autoroute) Br* slip road, *Am* ramp; **r. de lancement** launching ramp (**c**) *(rebord d'une scène de théâtre)* footlights

ramper [rɑ̃pe] *vi (animal, enfant, soldat)* to crawl; *Péj* **r. devant qn** to grovel to sb

ramure [ramyr] *nf* (**a**) *(d'un arbre)* branches (**b**) *(d'un cerf)* antlers

rancard [rɑ̃kar] *nm Fam (rendez-vous)* meeting; *(amoureux)* date

rancarder [rɑ̃karde] *très Fam* **1** *vt* **r. qn sur qch** to tip sb off about sth
2 se rancarder *vpr* to find out (**sur** about)

rancart [rɑ̃kar] *nm Fam* **mettre qch au r.** to chuck sth out; **mettre qn au r.** to put sb on the rubbish heap

rance [rɑ̃s] **1** *adj* rancid
2 *nm* **goût de r.** rancid taste

ranch [rɑ̃tʃ] *nm* ranch

rancir [rɑ̃sir] *vi* to go rancid

rancœur [rɑ̃kœr] *nf* resentment, rancour; **avoir de la r. pour** *ou* **contre qn** to feel resentment towards sb

rançon [rɑ̃sɔ̃] *nf* ransom; *Fig* **la r. de la gloire** the price of fame

rançonner [rɑ̃sɔne] *vt* **r. qn** to hold sb to ransom

rancune [rɑ̃kyn] *nf* spite; **garder r. à qn, avoir de la r. contre qn** to have a grudge against sb, to bear sb a grudge; **sans r.!** no hard feelings!

rancunier, -ère [rɑ̃kynje, -ɛr] **1** *adj* spiteful
2 *nm,f* spiteful person

randonnée [rɑ̃dɔne] *nf* (**a**) *(marche à pied)* **r. (pédestre)** hike; *(activité)* hiking, rambling; *(en montagne)* hill-walking; **faire une r.** to go for a hike; **faire de la r.** to go hiking *or* rambling; *(en montagne)* to go hill-walking (**b**) *(en voiture)* drive; *(à vélo)* ride (**c**) *(excursion à ski)* ski-mountaineering

randonneur, -euse [rɑ̃dɔnœr, -øz] *nm,f (à pied)* hiker, rambler

rang [rɑ̃] *nm* (**a**) *(d'arbres, de sièges)* row; **se mettre en r. (par deux/trois)** to line up (in twos/threes); *Hum* **en r. d'oignons** in a neat row; **en rangs serrés** in serried ranks; *Fig* **se mettre sur les rangs** to put oneself in the running (**b**) *(position sociale)* station; *(de militaire)* rank; **de haut r.** high-ranking (**c**) *(classement)* rank; **par r. de taille** in order of size (**d**) *Can (chemin)* concession road

rangé, -e [rɑ̃ʒe] *adj* (**a**) *(maison, chambre)* tidy (**b**) *(personne)* steady; *(vie)* settled

rangée [rɑ̃ʒe] *nf* row

rangement [rɑ̃ʒmã] *nm* (**a**) *(action)* tidying up; **faire du r.** to do some tidying up; **faire du r. dans ses affaires** to tidy up one's things (**b**) *(placard)* rangements storage space (**c**) *Ordinat* storage

ranger [45] [rɑ̃ʒe] **1** *vt* (**a**) *(pièce, maison)* to tidy (up) (**b**) *(affaires, vêtements)* to put away (**c**) *(mettre)* to put (**d**) *(classer)* to rank (**parmi** among); **r. par** *(ordre alphabétique, taille)* to arrange by (**e**) *(véhicule, vélo)* to park (**f**) *(soldats, élèves)* to line up (**g**) *Ordinat* **r. en mémoire** to store
2 se ranger *vpr* (**a**) *(se disposer)* to line up (**b**) *(s'écarter)* *(piéton)* to stand aside; *(véhicule)* to pull over (**c**) *(prendre position pour)* **se r. du côté de qn** to side with sb, to take sb's side; **se r. à l'opinion de qn** to come round to sb's opinion (**d**) *(se mettre)* to go (**e**) *Fam (s'assagir)* to settle down; **se r. des voitures** to settle down

ranimer [ranime] **1** *vt* (**a**) *(personne)* *(après un évanouissement)* to bring round; *(après un arrêt cardiaque)* to resuscitate (**b**) *(feu)* to rekindle (**c**) *(sentiment, souvenir, espoir)* to reawaken; *(débat)* to revive
2 se ranimer *vpr* (**a**) *(personne)* to come round (**b**) *(feu)* to flicker into life

rap [rap] *nm* **le r.** rap

rapace [rapas] **1** *nm* bird of prey
2 *adj* (**a**) *(oiseau)* predatory (**b**) *(personne)* grasping

rapacité [rapasite] *nf* rapaciousness

rapatrié, -e [rapatrije] **1** *adj* repatriated
2 *nm,f* repatriate

rapatriement [rapatrimã] *nm* repatriation

rapatrier [66] [rapatrije] *vt* to repatriate

râpe [rɑp] *nf* (**a**) *(de cuisine)* grater; **r. à fromage** cheese grater (**b**) *(lime)* rasp (**c**) *Suisse Fam Péj (avare)* miser

râpé, -e [rɑpe] **1** *adj* (**a**) *(fromage, carotte)* grated (**b**) *(vêtement)* threadbare (**c**) *Fam (raté)* **c'est r.!** we've had it!
2 *nm (fromage)* grated cheese

râper [rɑpe] *vt* (**a**) *(carotte, fromage)* to grate (**b**) *(racler)* **ce vin râpe la gorge** this wine's rough on the throat (**c**) *(limer)* to rasp

rapetasser [raptase] *vt Fam (vêtement)* to patch up

rapetisser [raptise] **1** *vt* (**a**) *(rendre plus petit)* to make smaller (**b**) *(dévaluer)* to belittle (**c**) *(faire paraître plus petit)* to make look smaller
2 *vi (vêtement, personne)* to shrink

râpeux, -euse [rɑpø, -øz] *adj (langue)* rough; *(vin)* harsh

raphia [rafja] *nm* raffia

rapiat, -e [rapja, -at] *Fam* **1** *adj (avare)* stingy
2 *nm,f* skinflint

rapide [rapid] **1** *adj* (**a**) *(coureur, voiture, itinéraire)* fast; *(pouls, progrès)* rapid; **r. comme l'éclair** as quick as lightning; **r. comme une flèche** as swift as an arrow (**b**) *(courant)* swift-flowing (**c**) *(prompt)* *(personne, esprit, intelligence)* quick (**d**) *(fait en peu de temps) (lecture, décision)* quick (**e**) *(pente)* steep
  2 *nm* (**a**) *(train)* express (train) (**b**) *(dans un fleuve)* rapid

rapidement [rapidmɑ̃] *adv* quickly, rapidly

rapidité [rapidite] *nf* (**a**) *(d'actions, d'une décision, d'une réponse)* speed; **r. d'esprit** quickness of mind (**b**) *Ordinat* **r. d'impression** print speed; **r. de traitement** processing speed

rapiécer [16/34] [rapjese] *vt* to patch

rapine [rapin] *nf Litt* pillage

raplapla [raplapla] *adj inv Fam* (**a**) *(pneu, coussin)* flat as a pancake (**b**) *(personne)* washed out

rappel [rapεl] *nm* (**a**) *(d'un événement, d'une promesse)* reminder; **r. de couleurs** repeat of colours; **r. à l'ordre** *(à un membre d'une assemblée)* call to order; *(d'un employé)* warning; **le r. des titres (de l'actualité)** the headlines; **dernier r.** *(de facture)* final demand (**b**) *(d'un ambassadeur, de réservistes)* recall (**c**) *(d'un salaire)* back pay (**d**) *(de vaccin)* booster; **faire un r.** to have a booster (**e**) *(au théâtre)* curtain call; *(à un concert)* encore (**f**) *(en alpinisme)* abseiling; **faire une descente** *ou* **descendre en r., faire du r.** to abseil down (**g**) *Ordinat (de texte)* restore

rappeler [42] [rapəle, raple] **1** *vt* (**a**) *(appeler) (personne)* to call back; *(chien)* to call off (**b**) *(au téléphone) (sujet: personne appelée)* to call back; *(sujet: personne qui appelle)* to call again; **r. dix fois** to call ten times (**c**) *(faire revenir) (personne)* to call back; *(ambassadeur)* to recall; **r. qn à l'ordre** *(membre d'une association)* to call sb to order; *(employé)* to warn sb (**d**) *(acteur, chanteur)* to call back (**e**) *(faire penser à)* **r. qn/qch à qn** to remind sb of sb/sth; **cela ne me rappelle rien** it doesn't ring a bell (**f**) *(remettre en mémoire)* **r. qch à qn** to remind sb of sth; **rappelez-moi votre nom** what was your name again?; **r. qn au bon souvenir de qn** to remember sb to sb
  2 se rappeler *vpr* (**a**) **se r. qn/qch** *(se souvenir de)* to remember sb/sth; **rappelle-toi que...** don't forget that... (**b**) *Fam (au téléphone)* **on se rappelle la semaine prochaine** we'll talk again next week

rappeur, -euse [rapœr, -øz] *nm,f* rapper

rappliquer [raplike] *vi Fam* to roll up

rapport [rapɔr] *nm* (**a**) *(relation)* **rapports** relations, relationship; **avoir de bons/mauvais rapports avec qn** to be on good/bad terms with sb; **entretenir des rapports amicaux avec qn** to stay on friendly terms with sb; **mettre qn en r. avec qn** to put sb in touch with sb; **être en r. avec qn** to be in touch with sb; **r. de forces** battle of wills (**b**) *(lien)* connection, link (**avec** with); **avoir un r. avec qch** to have something to do with sth; **n'avoir aucun r. avec qch** to have nothing to do with sth; **faire le r.** to make the connection; **être sans r. avec qch** to be unconnected with sth; **en r. avec** *(lié à)* in keeping with; **par r. à qch** *(en comparaison)* compared with sth (**c**) *(aspect)* **sous ce r.** in this respect; **bien sous tous rapports** nice in every respect (**d**) *(proportion)* ratio, proportion; **en r. avec** in pro-

portion to; **d'un bon r. qualité-prix** good value for money (**e**) *(compte rendu)* report; **faire** *ou* **rédiger un r. sur qch** to draw up a report on sth; **r. annuel** annual report; **r. commercial** market report (**f**) *(profit)* return, yield; **d'un bon r.** profitable; **d'un mauvais r.** unprofitable (**g**) **rapports** *(relations sexuelles)* (sexual) intercourse; **avoir des rapports avec qn** to have sex with sb

rapporter [rapɔrte] **1** *vt* (**a**) *(apporter avec soi)* to bring back; **r. qch à qn** to bring sb sth back (**b**) *(rendre)* to bring back (**à** to); *(remporter)* to take back (**à** to) (**c**) *(ajouter) (poche, pièce)* to sew on (**d**) *(raconter)* to report; **on rapporte que...** it is reported that... (**e**) *(produire) (bénéfice, intérêt)* to yield; **r. (de l'argent)** to be profitable; **r. qch à qn** *(financièrement)* to bring sb in sth; *Fig (moralement)* to bring sb sth (**f**) *Péj (répéter)* to report (**à** to) (**g**) *(sujet: chien)* to retrieve; **rapporte!** fetch!
  2 se rapporter *vpr* (**a**) **se r. à qch** *(concerner)* to relate to sth (**b**) *(se remettre)* **s'en r. à qn/qch** to rely on sb/sth

rapporteur, -euse [rapɔrtœr, -øz] **1** *adj Péj* sneaky
  2 *nm,f Péj* telltale, sneak
  3 *nm* (**a**) *(d'une commission)* reporter (**b**) *(instrument)* protractor

rapproché, -e [raprɔʃe] *adj (dans l'espace, dans le temps)* close; *(yeux)* close-set; **des maisons très rapprochées** houses very close together; **des rendez-vous très rapprochés (dans le temps)** appointments very close to each other

rapprochement [raprɔʃmɑ̃] *nm* (**a**) *(rapport) (de faits, d'idées)* connection; **faire le r. (entre deux choses)** to make a connection (between two things) (**b**) *(de deux objets)* bringing together (**c**) *(réconciliation) (entre personnes)* reconciliation; *(entre pays)* rapprochement

rapprocher [raprɔʃe] **1** *vt* (**a**) *(mettre plus près) (deux ou plusieurs objets)* to move closer together; *(objet)* to move closer (**de** to); **ça te rapprochera (de chez toi)** that'll get you a bit closer (to home) (**b**) *(réunir)* to join (**c**) *(séances)* to group closer together (**d**) *(unir) (personnes)* to bring together (**e**) *(lier) (idées, textes)* to compare (**de** with)
  2 se rapprocher *vpr* (**a**) *(aller plus près)* to get closer (**de** to); **se r. de la vérité** to get close to the truth (**b**) *(devenir proche)* to get closer (**de** to); *(après une brouille)* to become reconciled (**de** with) (**c**) **se r. de qn/qch** *(ressembler à)* to be similar to sb/sth

rapsodie [rapsɔdi] *nf* rhapsody

rapt [rapt] *nm* abduction

raquer [rake] *très Fam* **1** *vt* to fork out
  2 *vi* to pay up, to cough up

raquette [rakεt] *nf* (**a**) *(de tennis, de badminton, de squash)* racket (**b**) *(de ping-pong)* bat (**c**) *(pour marcher dans la neige)* snowshoe

rare [rar] *adj* (**a**) *(peu commun, peu fréquent)* rare; **c'est r. qu'il pleuve ici** it rarely rains here; **cela n'a rien de r.** it's quite common (**b**) *(peu nombreux, peu abondant)* **être r.** to be scarce; **c'est une des rares personnes que je connaisse à s'y opposer** he's one of the few people I know who's against it (**c**) *(exceptionnel)* rare (**d**) *(clairsemé) (végétation)* sparse; **avoir le cheveu r.** to have thinning hair (**e**) **tu te fais r.** we've hardly seen you lately

raréfaction [rarefaksjɔ̃] *nf* (**a**) *(d'une denrée, de l'argent)* growing scarcity (**b**) *(de l'air)* rarefaction

raréfier [66] [rarefje] **se raréfier** *vpr* (**a**) *(denrée, argent)* to become scarce (**b**) *(air)* to become rarefied

rarement [rarmã] *adv* rarely, seldom

rareté [rarte] *nf* (**a**) *(de denrées, de main-d'œuvre)* scarcity; *(de visites)* infrequency; *(d'un phénomène, d'un mot, d'une maladie)* rareness (**b**) *(objet rare)* rarity

RAS [ɛraɛs] *Fam (abrév* **rien à signaler)** everything OK

ras, -e [rɑ, rɑz] **1** *adj* (**a**) *(cheveux)* close-cropped; *(barbe)* short; *(tapis)* short-pile (**b**) *(entier) (mesure)* full; **deux cuillerées rases** two level spoonfuls (**c**) *(locutions)* **à r. bord** to the brim; **en rase campagne** in the open country

2 *nm* (**a**) *(bord)* **à** *ou* **au r. de** level with; **voler au r. du sol/de l'eau** to fly close to the ground/water; *Fam Fig* **au r. des pâquerettes** lowbrow (**b**) **r. du cou** *(pullover)* crew-neck sweater

3 *adv* short; *Fam* **en avoir r. le bol (de qch)** to have had it up to here *or* be fed up to the back teeth (with sth)

rasade [razad] *nf* glassful

rasage [razaʒ] *nm* shaving

rasant, -e [razã, -ãt] *adj* (**a**) *Fam (personne, discours, film)* boring (**b**) *(lumière)* low-angled; *(tir)* grazing

rascasse [raskas] *nf* scorpion fish

rasé, -e [raze] *adj* shaven; **r. de près** close-shaven

rase-mottes [razmɔt] *nm inv Fam* **faire du** *ou* **voler en r.** to hedgehop

raser [raze] **1** *vt* (**a**) *(visage, personne)* to shave; *(moustache, barbe, cheveux)* to shave off (**b**) *(passer très près de) (sol, eau)* to skim; *(filet, trottoir)* to graze; **r. les murs** to hug the walls (**c**) *(détruire) (bâtiment, ville)* to raze to the ground (**d**) *Fam (ennuyer)* to bore

2 se raser *vpr* (**a**) *(se couper la barbe)* to shave, to have a shave; **se r. les jambes** to shave one's legs (**b**) *Fam (s'ennuyer)* to be bored

raseur, -euse [razœr, -øz] *nm,f Fam* bore

rasibus [razibys] *adv Fam* **la balle est passée r.** the bullet whizzed past really close

ras-le-bol [ralbɔl] *Fam* **1** *nm inv* discontent

2 *exclam* enough's enough!

rasoir [razwar] **1** *nm* razor; **r. électrique** electric razor *or* shaver

2 *adj inv Fam* boring

rassasier [66] [rasazje] **1** *vt (faim, curiosité)* to satisfy; **r. qn** to satisfy sb's hunger

2 se rassasier *vpr* **se r. de qch** to get one's fill of sth

rassemblement [rasãbləmã] *nm* (**a**) *(attroupement)* gathering (**b**) *(de documents, d'objets)* collecting, gathering (**c**) *(union politique)* union (**d**) *Mil* fall in, parade; **sonner le r.** to sound the assembly

rassembler [rasãble] **1** *vt* (**a**) *(personnes, choses, documents)* to gather (together) (**b**) *(courage, forces)* to muster, to summon up; **r. ses idées** to collect one's thoughts; **r. ses esprits** to collect oneself

2 se rassembler *vpr (manifestants)* to gather, to assemble; *(famille)* to get together

rasseoir [10a] [raswar] **se rasseoir** *vpr* to sit down again

rasséréner [34] [raserene] **1** *vt* **r. qn** to put sb's mind at rest

2 se rasséréner *vpr* to calm down

rassir [rasir] *vi* to go stale

rassis, -e [rasi, -iz] *adj* (**a**) *(pain)* stale (**b**) *Litt (personne, esprit)* calm

rassurant, -e [rasyrã, -ãt] *adj* reassuring

rassuré, -e [rasyre] *adj* at ease; **me voilà r.!** that's a relief!

rassurer [rasyre] **1** *vt* to reassure; **ah, tu me rassures!** well, that's a relief!

2 se rassurer *vpr* to reassure oneself; **rassurez-vous** rest assured

rasta [rasta] *adj inv & nmf* Rasta

rat [ra] **1** *nm* (**a**) *(animal)* rat; **r. d'égout** sewer rat; *Fam* **être fait comme un r.** to be caught like a rat in a trap; **petit r. (de l'Opéra)** ballet pupil; **mon petit r.** darling; *Fam* **r. de bibliothèque** bookworm; **r. d'hôtel** hotel thief (**b**) *Can (sournois)* tricky customer

2 *adj Fam* (**a**) *(avare)* stingy (**b**) *Can (sournois)* wily, sly

ratage [rataʒ] *nm Fam* botch-up

ratatiné, -e [ratatine] *adj* (**a**) *(fruit)* shrivelled (**b**) *Fam (vieillard)* wizened (**c**) *Fam (véhicule)* smashed-up

ratatiner [ratatine] **1** *vt Fam* (**a**) *(voiture)* to smash up (**b**) *(équipe)* to thrash

2 se ratatiner *vpr* (**a**) *(fruit)* to shrivel up (**b**) *(vieillard)* to become wizened

ratatouille [ratatuj] *nf* ratatouille

rate¹ [rat] *nf (organe)* spleen

rate² *nf (animal)* female rat

raté, -e [rate] **1** *nm,f Fam* loser

2 *nm* misfiring; *Fig* hitch; **avoir des ratés** to misfire

râteau, -x [rɑto] *nm* (**a**) *(de jardin)* rake (**b**) *Suisse Fam Péj (avare)* miser, skinflint

râtelier [rɑtəlje] *nm* (**a**) *(pour le fourrage)* rack; *Fig* **manger à tous les râteliers** to have a finger in every pie (**b**) *(à outils, à armes)* rack (**c**) *Fam (dentier)* (set of) false teeth

rater [rate] **1** *vt* (**a**) *(examen)* to fail; *(vie, plat)* to make a mess of; **c'est raté** it hasn't worked; *Fig* **r. son coup** to make a mess of things (**b**) *(train, avion, personne, occasion)* to miss; **tu n'as pas raté grand-chose** you didn't miss much (**c**) *Fam (locutions)* **ne pas r. qn** to let sb have it; **elle n'en rate pas une** she's always putting her foot in it

2 *vi* to fail; **faire r. qch** to ruin sth; **j'étais sûr qu'elle allait oublier, et ça n'a pas raté** I was sure she was going to forget, and right enough she did

3 se rater *vpr Fam* (**a**) *(ne pas se rencontrer)* to miss each other (**b**) *(personne suicidaire)* to bungle one's suicide attempt

ratiboiser [ratibwaze] *vt Fam* (**a**) *(ruiner)* to clean out; **se faire r.** to be cleaned out (**b**) *(cheveux)* **se faire r.** to get scalped

ratier [ratje] *nm (chien)* ratter

ratière [ratjɛr] *nf* rat trap

ratification [ratifikasjɔ̃] *nf* ratification

ratifier [66] [ratifje] *vt (traité, acte)* to ratify; *(décision)* to confirm

ratio [rasjo] *nm* ratio

ration [rasjɔ̃] *nf (de pain, de nourriture)* ration; *Fig (de critiques, de difficultés)* share; **r. alimentaire** food ration

rationaliser [rasjɔnalize] *vt* to rationalize

rationnel, -elle [rasjɔnɛl] *adj* rational

rationnellement [rasjɔnɛlmã] *adv* rationally

rationnement [rasjɔnmã] *nm* rationing

rationner [rasjɔne] **1** vt to ration
2 se rationner vpr to ration oneself

ratissage [ratisaʒ] nm (**a**) (allée, sol) raking (**b**) Fam (par la police) combing

ratisser [ratise] **1** vt (**a**) (allée, sol) to rake; (feuilles) to rake up (**b**) Fam (quartier) to comb (**c**) Fam (personne) to clean out; **se faire r.** (au jeu) to be cleaned out
2 vi **r. large** to cast one's net wide

raton [ratɔ̃] nm (**a**) (animal) young rat; **r. laveur** raccoon (**b**) Fam (Maghrébin) = racist term used to refer to a North African Arab

ratonnade [ratɔnad] nf = racist attack on North African Arabs

ratoureux, -euse [raturø, -øz] Can **1** adj wily, devious
2 nm,f shady customer

RATP [ɛratepe] nf (abrév Régie autonome des transports parisiens) = Parisian transport authority

rattachement [rataʃmɑ̃] nm (d'une région) uniting (**à** with)

rattacher [rataʃe] **1** vt (**a**) (attacher de nouveau) (lacets, chien, objet) to tie up again (**à** to); (cheveux) to put up again; **r. qch sur qch** to tie sth onto sth again (**b**) (région) to unite (**à** with) (**c**) **être rattaché à** (faire partie de) to be attached to (**d**) (lier) **c'était la seule chose qui nous rattachait l'un à l'autre** it was the only thing that bound us together; **c'est tout ce qui le rattache à la vie** it's the only thing keeping him alive
2 se rattacher vpr **se r. à qch** to be linked to sth

rattrapage [ratrapaʒ] nm **être admis au r., être admis à passer les épreuves de r.** = to be allowed to sit further oral examinations to gain a pass mark in the baccalauréat; **cours de r.** remedial class

rattraper [ratrape] **1** vt (**a**) (prisonnier, chien) to recapture; **se faire r. par la police** to get caught by the police (**b**) (objet ou personne qui tombe) to catch (**c**) (rejoindre) (personne, voiture) to catch up with (**d**) (regagner) **r. le temps perdu** to make up for lost time; **r. son retard** to catch up; **avoir du sommeil à r.** to have to catch up on some sleep (**e**) (rétablir) (erreur) to correct; (situation) to salvage
2 se rattraper vpr (**a**) (se retenir) to catch oneself in time; **se r. à qch** to catch hold of sth (**b**) (se reprendre) to stop oneself (**c**) (se faire pardonner) to make up for it (**d**) (compenser son retard) to catch up

rature [ratyr] nf crossing-out, deletion; **faire une r.** to make a deletion

raturer [ratyre] vt (mot) to cross out, to delete; **les devoirs raturés ne seront pas corrigés** homework with too many crossings-out will not be marked

rauque [rok] adj (cri) raucous; (voix) (enrouée) hoarse; (voilée) husky

ravagé, -e [ravaʒe] adj (**a**) (visage) ravaged, haggard (**b**) Fam (fou) nuts

ravager [45] [ravaʒe] vt to ravage, to devastate

ravages [ravaʒ] nmpl (du feu, de la tempête) devastation; (d'une guerre, d'une maladie) ravages; **faire des r.** to wreak havoc; Fig (mode) to be all the rage; (jeune femme) to break hearts

ravageur, -euse [ravaʒœr, -øz] adj devastating

ravalement [ravalmɑ̃] nm cleaning

ravaler [ravale] **1** vt (**a**) (façade) to clean; **se faire r. la façade** to have a facelift (**b**) (avaler de nouveau) (salive) to swallow; Fig **faire r. ses paroles à qn** to make sb eat his/her words (**c**) (cacher) (sanglot, larmes) to choke back; (colère, indignation, reproches) to stifle

(**d**) (abaisser) **r. qn à** to lower sb to
2 se ravaler vpr to lower oneself; Fam **se r. la façade** to put on the warpaint

ravaudage [ravodaʒ] nm Vieilli (de vêtements) mending, repairing

ravauder [ravode] vt (**a**) Vieilli (vêtements) to mend, to repair (**b**) Can (errer) to wander about; (faire l'idiot) to fool around (**c**) Can (faire du bruit) to make a racket

rave¹ [rav] nf (radis) radish; (navet) turnip

rave² [rɛv] nf (soirée) rave

ravi, -e [ravi] adj delighted (**de** with); **je suis r. de vous voir** I'm delighted to see you; **je suis r. que ça te plaise** I'm delighted you like it; **r. de vous connaître** pleased to meet you

ravier [ravje] nm hors d'oeuvres dish

ravigotant, -e [ravigɔtɑ̃, -ɑ̃t] adj Fam invigorating

ravigote [ravigɔt] nf = highly seasoned oil-and-vinegar dressing with herbs and capers

ravigoter [ravigɔte] vt Fam **r. qn** to put new life into sb

ravin [ravɛ̃] nm ravine

ravine [ravin] nf gully

raviné, -e [ravine] adj (visage) deeply lined

ravinement [ravinmɑ̃] nm gullying

raviner [ravine] vt to gully

ravioli [ravjɔli] nm piece of ravioli; **des raviolis** ravioli

ravir [ravir] vt (**a**) (plaire) to delight; **à r.** (jouer, chanter) delightfully; **belle à r.** ravishingly beautiful; **aller à r. à qn** to suit sb beautifully (**b**) Litt **r. qch à qn** to rob sb of sth

raviser [ravize] **se raviser** vpr to change one's mind

ravissant, -e [ravisɑ̃, -ɑ̃t] adj delightful

ravissement [ravismɑ̃] nm (**a**) (enchantement) rapture, ecstasy; **avec r.** (écouter, contempler) with great delight (**b**) Litt (d'une femme) ravishing

ravisseur, -euse [ravisœr, -øz] nm,f abductor

ravitaillement [ravitajmɑ̃] nm (action) supplying (**en** with); (marchandises) supplies; **r. (en carburant)** refuelling

ravitailler [ravitaje] **1** vt (personne, groupe) to supply; (véhicule) to refuel
2 se ravitailler vpr to get in supplies; **se r. (en carburant)** to refuel

raviver [ravive] vt (**a**) (feu) to rekindle (**b**) (couleur) to brighten up (**c**) (colère, souvenir, querelle) to rekindle; (douleur) to revive

ravoir [ravwar] **1** vt (**a**) (avoir de nouveau) to have back (**b**) Fam (nettoyer) to get clean
2 se ravoir vpr Belg (reprendre haleine) to get one's breath back; (retrouver ses esprits) to come to one's senses

rayé, -e [rɛje] adj (**a**) (tissu) striped (**b**) (disque, parquet, carrosserie de voiture) scratched (**c**) (canon de fusil) rifled

rayer [53] [rɛje] vt (**a**) (verre, carrosserie de voiture, disque) to scratch (**b**) (mention, mot) to cross out; **r. qn du barreau** to strike sb off; **r. qn/le nom de qn d'une liste** to cross sb/sb's name off a list

rayon¹ [rɛjɔ̃] nm (**a**) (faisceau) (de lumière) ray, beam; **r. laser** laser beam; **r. de soleil** sunbeam; Fig **être le r. de soleil de qn** to be sb's ray of sunshine; **rayons X** X-rays (**b**) (d'un cercle) radius; **dans un r. de 2 kilomètres (autour de)** within a radius of 2 kilometres (of); **r. d'action** range (**c**) (de roue) spoke

rayon² nm (**a**) (dans un magasin) department; Fig **c'est mon r.** that's my department (**b**) (d'une étagère) shelf; *Fam Fig* **en connaître un r. (sur qch)** to be well clued up (about sth) (**c**) **r. de miel** honeycomb

rayonnage [rɛjɔnaʒ] *nm* shelving, shelves

rayonnant, -e [rɛjɔnɑ̃, -ɑ̃t] *adj (chaleur, lumière)* radiant; *Fig (visage)* beaming; **r. de bonheur** radiant with happiness; **r. de santé** glowing with health

rayonne [rɛjɔn] *nf* rayon

rayonnement [rɛjɔnmɑ̃] *nm* (**a**) *(du soleil)* radiance (**b**) *(influence)* influence

rayonner [rɛjɔne] *vi* (**a**) *(soleil, visage)* to beam; **r. de joie** to beam with joy (**b**) *(voyager)* to travel around *(from a central base)* (**c**) *(se propager)* to spread its influence (**d**) *(avenues, douleur)* to radiate

rayure [rɛjyr] *nf* (**a**) *(motif)* stripe; **tissu à rayures** striped material (**b**) *(sur miroir, sur carrosserie)* scratch (**c**) *(d'un canon de fusil)* groove

raz de marée [radmare] *nm inv* tidal wave; *Fig* **r. électoral** landslide

razzia [razja] *nf* raid; *Fam* **faire une r. sur qch** to raid sth

RD [ɛrde] *nf (abrév* **route départementale**) secondary road

RDA [ɛrdeɑ] *nf Anciennement (abrév* **République démocratique allemande**) GDR

rdc *(abrév* **rez-de-chaussée**) *Br* ground *or Am* first floor

RDS [ɛrdeɛs] *nm (abrév* **Remboursement de la Dette Sociale**) = contribution paid by every taxpayer in France towards the social security deficit

ré [re] *nm inv (note)* D; *(chantée)* re

réabonnement [reabɔnmɑ̃] *nm* subscription renewal

réabonner [reabɔne] **1** *vt* **r. qn** to renew sb's subscription (**à** to)
2 se réabonner *vpr* to renew one's subscription (**à** to)

réac [reak] *adj & nmf Fam Péj* reactionary

réaccoutumer [reakutyme] **1** *vt* to reaccustom (**à** to)
2 se réaccoutumer *vpr* **se r. à qch** to become reaccustomed to sth

réacteur [reaktœr] *nm* (**a**) *(moteur)* jet engine (**b**) **r. nucléaire** nuclear reactor

réaction [reaksjɔ̃] *nf* (**a**) *(attitude)* reaction; **n'avoir aucune r.** not to react; **il eut une r. de peur/de colère** his reaction was one of fear/anger; **faire qch par r.** to do sth as a reaction; **en r. à qch** in reaction to sth; **rester sans r.** not to react; **r. en chaîne** chain reaction (**b**) *(d'un organe, du corps)* reaction; **r. cutanée** skin reaction

réactionnaire [reaksjɔnɛr] *adj & nmf Péj* reactionary

réactiver [reaktive] *vt (feu, négociations, sentiments)* to revive

réactualisation [reaktɥalizasjɔ̃] *nf* updating

réactualiser [reaktɥalize] *vt* to update

réadaptation [readaptasjɔ̃] *nf* rehabilitation

réadapter [readapte] **1** *vt* to rehabilitate
2 se réadapter *vpr* to readjust

réaffirmer [reafirme] *vt* to reaffirm

réagir [reaʒir] *vi* to react (**à/contre** to/against); **r. sur qch** to affect sth

réajuster [reaʒyste] = **rajuster**

réalisable [realizabl] *adj* (**a**) *(projet, proposition)* feasible; *(rêve)* attainable (**b**) *(avoirs)* realizable

réalisateur, -trice [realizatœr, -tris] *nm,f (d'un film, d'un feuilleton)* director; *(d'une émission de radio ou de télévision)* producer

réalisation [realizasjɔ̃] *nf* (**a**) *(d'un projet)* realization; *(d'un rêve)* fulfilment (**b**) *(d'un film, d'un feuilleton)* direction; *(d'une émission de radio ou de télévision)* production (**c**) *(d'une œuvre d'art)* creation

réaliser [realize] **1** *vt* (**a**) *(comprendre)* to realize (**que** that) (**b**) *(ambition, projet)* to realize; *(rêve)* to fulfil (**c**) *(œuvre d'art)* to create (**d**) *(film, feuilleton)* to direct; *(émission de radio ou de télévision)* to produce (**e**) *(bénéfices)* to make; **r. un chiffre d'affaires de 10 millions de francs** to have a turnover of 10 million francs
2 se réaliser *vpr* *(prédiction, rêve)* to come true (**b**) *(personne)* to fulfil oneself

réalisme [realism] *nm* realism; **faire preuve de r.** to be realistic; **avec r.** realistically

réaliste [realist] **1** *adj (personne, description, portrait)* realistic; *(écrivain, peintre)* realist
2 *nmf* realist

réalité [realite] *nf* reality; **c'est une r.** it's a reality; **en r.** in reality; *Ordinat* **r. virtuelle** virtual reality

réamorcer [16] [reamɔrse] *Ordinat* **1** *vt* to reboot
2 se réamorcer *vpr* to reboot

réanimation [reanimasjɔ̃] *nf* resuscitation; **service de r.** intensive care unit; **en r.** in intensive care

réanimer [reanime] *vt* to resuscitate

réapparaître [20] [reaparɛtr] *vi* to reappear; *(douleur)* to come back, to recur

réapparition [reaparisjɔ̃] *nf* reappearance; *(d'une douleur)* recurrence

réapprovisionner [reaprɔvizjɔne] **1** *vt (magasin)* to restock (**en** with); *(personne)* to resupply (**en** with)
2 se réapprovisionner *vpr* to stock up again (**en** with)

réargenter [rearʒɑ̃te] *vt* to resilver

réarmement [rearmɔmɑ̃] *nm* rearmament

réarmer [rearme] **1** *vt* (**a**) *(région, pays)* to rearm (**b**) *(arme à feu)* to recock; *(appareil photo)* to reset
2 *vi (pays, région)* to rearm

réassortir [reasɔrtir] **1** *vt (magasin)* to restock
2 se réassortir *vpr* to restock

rebaptiser [rəbatize] *vt (rue)* to rename

rébarbatif, -ive [rebarbatif, -iv] *adj* (**a**) *(sujet, tâche)* daunting; *(style)* off-putting (**b**) *(visage, mine)* forbidding

rebâtir [rəbɑtir] *vt* to rebuild

rebattre [11] [rəbatr] *vt* **r. les oreilles à qn de qch** to go on to sb about sth

rebattu, -e [rəbaty] *adj (histoire, sujet)* hackneyed

rebelle [rəbɛl] **1** *adj* (**a**) *(personne, esprit)* rebellious; *(camp, armée, troupes)* rebel; **r. à toute discipline** unamenable to discipline (**b**) *(mèches, boucle)* unruly (**c**) *(fièvre)* stubborn; **r. aux antibiotiques** resistant to antibiotics
2 *nmf* rebel

rebeller [rəbɛle] **se rebeller** *vpr* to rebel (**contre** against)

rébellion [rebɛljɔ̃] *nf* rebellion

rebelote [rəbəlɔt] *exclam Fam* not again!

rebiffer [rəbife] **se rebiffer** *vpr Fam* to hit back (**contre** at)

rebiquer [rəbike] *vi Fam (mèche)* to stick up

reblochon [rəblɔʃɔ̃] *nm* Reblochon *(type of cheese from Savoie)*

reboisement [rəbwazmɑ̃] *nm* reafforestation

reboiser [rəbwaze] *vt* to reafforest

rebond [rəbɔ̃] *nm (d'un ballon)* bounce

rebondi, -e [rəbɔ̃di] *adj (joues, personne)* chubby

rebondir [rəbɔ̃dir] *vi* (**a**) *(ballon)* to bounce; **r. contre** *ou* **sur qch** to bounce off sth (**b**) *Fig (affaire, crise)* to be revived; **faire r. la discussion** to get the discussion going again (**c**) *Can (chèque)* to bounce

rebondissement [rəbɔ̃dismɑ̃] *nm* (**a**) *(d'un ballon)* bounce (**b**) *Fig (d'une affaire)* revival

rebord [rəbɔr] *nm (d'une table, d'un puits)* edge; *(de fenêtre)* sill

reboucher [rəbuʃe] *vt* (**a**) *(bouteille)* to recork; *(tube)* to put the top back on (**b**) *(trou)* to fill in again

rebours [rəbur] **à rebours** *adv* the wrong way; *Fig* the wrong way round

rebouteux, -euse [rəbutø, -øz] *nm,f Fam* bonesetter

reboutonner [rəbutɔne] **1** *vt* to button up again
  2 se reboutonner *vpr* to do oneself up again

rebrousse-poil [rəbruspwal] **à rebrousse-poil** *adv* the wrong way; **prendre qn à r.** to rub sb up the wrong way

rebrousser [rəbruse] *vt* **r. chemin** to turn back

rebuffade [rəbyfad] *nf* rebuff; **essuyer une r.** to meet with a rebuff

rébus [rebys] *nm* rebus

rebut [rəby] *nm* (**article de) r.** reject; **mettre qch au r.** to throw sth out

rebutant, -e [rəbytɑ̃, -ɑ̃t] *adj (tâche, manières, personne) (décourageant)* off-putting; *(repoussant)* repulsive

rebuter [rəbyte] *vt* (**a**) *(décourager)* to put off (**b**) *(déplaire)* to disgust

récalcitrant, -e [rekalsitrɑ̃, -ɑ̃t] *adj & nm,f* recalcitrant

recaler [rəkale] *vt Fam* to fail; **être recalé, se faire r.** to fail

récapitulatif, -ive [rekapitylatif, -iv] **1** *adj* recapitulatory
  2 *nm* recapitulation

récapitulation [rekapitylasjɔ̃] *nf* recapitulation; **faire la r. de qch** to recapitulate sth

récapituler [rekapityle] *vt & vi* to recapitulate

recaser [rəkɑze] *Fam* **1** *vt* (**a**) *(retrouver un emploi à)* to find a new job for (**b**) *(retrouver un logement à)* to rehouse
  2 se recaser *vpr* (**a**) *(retrouver un emploi)* to find a new job (**b**) *(se remarier)* to get hitched again

recel [rəsɛl] *nm* receiving stolen goods; **r. de malfaiteur** harbouring a (known) criminal

receler [39] [rəsəle] *vt* (**a**) *(biens volés)* to receive; *(criminel)* to harbour (**b**) *Litt (renfermer) (secret, trésor)* to conceal

receleur, -euse [rəsəlœr, -øz] *nm,f* receiver

récemment [resamɑ̃] *adv* recently

recensement [rəsɑ̃smɑ̃] *nm (d'objets)* inventory; *(de la population)* census

recenser [rəsɑ̃se] *vt (objets)* to make an inventory of; *(habitants)* to take a census of

récent, -e [resɑ̃, -ɑ̃t] *adj* recent

recentrer [rəsɑ̃tre] *vt* (**a**) *(parti politique)* to reorientate (**b**) *(balle)* to centre again

récépissé [resepise] *nm* receipt

réceptacle [reseptakl] *nm* (**a**) *(d'objets)* receptacle; *(de personnes)* gathering place (**b**) *Ordinat* **r. pour extension** extension slot

récepteur, -trice [reseptœr, -tris] **1** *adj* receiving
  2 *nm* (**a**) *(de téléphone)* receiver (**b**) *Rad & TV* set, receiver (**c**) *Ordinat* **r. de données** data receiver

réceptif, -ive [reseptif, -iv] *adj* receptive (**à** to)

réception [resepsjɔ̃] *nf* (**a**) *(accueil)* reception; **faire une bonne/mauvaise r. à qn** to give sb a good/poor reception (**b**) *(d'une lettre, d'une commande, de biens)* receipt; **à payer à la r.** cash on delivery; **r. des travaux** acceptance of work (**c**) *(soirée)* reception (**d**) *(dans un hôtel)* reception (desk) (**e**) *(d'une radio)* reception (**f**) *(d'un gymnaste)* landing; *(d'un joueur de football)* control

réceptionner [resepsjɔne] **1** *vt* (**a**) *(marchandises livrées)* to take delivery of (**b**) *(ballon)* to take
  2 se réceptionner *vpr* to land

réceptionniste [resepsjɔnist] *nmf* receptionist

récessif, -ive [resesif, -iv] *adj* recessive

récession [resesjɔ̃] *nf* recession

recette [rəsɛt] *nf* (**a**) *(pour plat) & Fig* recipe (**de** for) (**b**) *(bureau)* tax office (**c**) *(gain)* **recettes** takings; **recettes fiscales** tax revenue; **faire r.** to be a success

recevable [rəsəvabl] *adj (excuse, témoignage)* admissible

recevant, -e [rəsəvɑ̃, -ɑ̃t] *adj Can (personne)* hospitable, who likes entertaining

receveur, -euse [rəsəvœr, -øz] *nm,f* (**a**) *(fonctionnaire)* **r. des contributions** tax collector; **r. des Postes** postmaster, *f* postmistress (**b**) *(de bus)* (bus) conductor, *f* (bus) conductress

recevoir [60] [rəsəvwar] **1** *vt* (**a**) *(lettre, coup de téléphone, fleurs)* to receive, to get (**de** from); **r. la visite de qn** to have a visit from sb; **r. des nouvelles de qn** to hear from sb; **je n'ai de conseils à r. de personne!** I don't need advice from anybody!; **nous avons bien reçu votre lettre** we are in receipt of your letter
  (**b**) *(blâme, gifle, coup, balle)* to get; *Fam* **qu'est-ce que j'ai reçu!** I really got it!
  (**c**) *(amis, invités)* to receive, to welcome; **être mal/bien reçu** to get a poor/good reception; **r. qn à dîner** to have sb (round) to dinner; **aimer r.** to enjoy entertaining; **savoir r.** to be a good host/hostess; **ils reçoivent très peu** they don't do much entertaining
  (**d**) *(clients)* to see; **le docteur ne reçoit que sur rendez-vous** the doctor will see patients by appointment only
  (**e**) *(proposition, projet)* to receive
  (**f**) *(élève, candidat)* to admit; **être reçu à l'Académie française** to be admitted to the Académie française; **être reçu à un examen** to pass an exam
  (**g**) *(pluie, soleil, lumière)* to get; **r. des radiations** to be exposed to radiation, to receive a dose of radiation
  (**h**) *(chaîne)* to get; *(station de radio)* to pick up, to receive
  (**i**) *(communion, absolution)* to receive
  2 se recevoir *vpr (gymnaste)* to land

rechange [rəʃɑ̃ʒ] **de rechange** *adj* spare; *Fig* alternative

rechaper [rəʃape] *vt (pneu)* to retread; **pneu rechapé** retread

réchapper [reʃape] *vi* **r. de qch** to survive sth

recharge [rəʃarʒ] *nf* (**a**) *(de stylo, de briquet)* refill; **r. d'encre** ink refill (**b**) *(action) (d'une batterie)* recharging

rechargeable [rəʃarʒabl] *adj (briquet, vaporisateur)* refillable; *(pile)* rechargeable

recharger [45] [rəʃarʒe] **1** vt (**a**) (batterie, pile) to recharge; Fam **r. ses batteries** ou **ses accus** to recharge one's batteries (**b**) (camion, arme, appareil photo) to reload (**c**) (stylo, briquet, vaporisateur) to refill
2 se recharger vpr Ordinat to reload

réchaud [reʃo] nm (portable) stove; **r. à gaz** gas ring

réchauffé, -e [reʃofe] **1** adj (**a**) (plat) reheated, warmed-up (**b**) (plaisanterie) stale
2 nm **c'est du r.** (plaisanterie) that's a stale joke; (nouvelles, politique) that's old hat

réchauffement [reʃofmã] nm warming up; **le r. de la planète** ou **de l'atmosphère** global warming

réchauffer [reʃofe] **1** vt (**a**) (plat) to reheat, to warm up (**b**) (personne) to warm up (**c**) Fig to rekindle; (cœur) to warm
2 se réchauffer vpr (**a**) (temps) to get warmer (**b**) (personne) to get warm; **se r. les pieds/les mains** to warm one's feet/one's hands

rechausser [rəʃose] **se rechausser** vpr to put one's shoes on again

rêche [rɛʃ] adj rough

recherche [rəʃɛrʃ] nf (**a**) (prospection, quête) search (**de** for); (de la célébrité, du pouvoir) quest (**de** for), pursuit (**de** of); **être à la r. de** to be in search of (**b**) **recherches** (par la police) (pour retrouver une personne disparue) search, hunt; **faire des recherches** to make inquiries (**c**) (scientifique) research (**sur** into); **faire de la r.** to do research; **faire des recherches sur qch** to do research into sth (**d**) (raffinement) elegance; **avec r.** elegantly; **sans r.** (style) straightforward (**e**) Ordinat find, search; **r. et remplacement** search and replace; **r. et remplacement global** global search and replace

recherché, -e [rəʃɛrʃe] adj (**a**) (demandé) (objet) sought-after (**b**) (apprécié) (personne) in demand (**c**) (raffiné) elegant; (plat) exquisite (**d**) (criminel) wanted

rechercher [rəʃɛrʃe] vt (**a**) (chercher) (personne, objet, solution) to look for, to search for; (emploi) to look for; (sens, mot) to look up; (faveurs, honneurs) to seek (**b**) Ordinat **r. qch** to search or do a search for sth; **r. et remplacer** to search and replace; **r. vers le bas/haut** to search forwards/backwards

rechigner [rəʃiɲe] vi **r. à qch** to balk at sth; **r. à faire qch** to be reluctant to do sth; **faire qch en rechignant** to do sth with bad grace; **faire qch sans r.** to do sth without (making) a fuss

rechute [rəʃyt] nf relapse; **faire une r.** to have a relapse

rechuter [rəʃyte] vi to have a relapse

récidive [residiv] nf (**a**) (d'un délinquant) repeat offence (**b**) (d'une maladie) recurrence

récidiver [residive] vi (**a**) (délinquant) to reoffend; Fig to do it again (**b**) (maladie) to recur

récidiviste [residivist] nmf repeat offender

récif [resif] nm reef; **r. de corail** ou **corallien** coral reef

récipient [resipjã] nm container

réciproque [resiprɔk] **1** adj (sentiments) mutual; (bénéfices, accord, concessions) reciprocal; **elle ne veut plus me voir, et c'est r.** she doesn't want to see me again, and the feeling's mutual
2 nf **la r.** the reverse

réciproquement [resiprɔkmã] adv mutually; **et r.** and vice versa

récit [resi] nm story; **faire le r. de qch** to give an account of sth

récital, -als [resital] nm recital

récitant, -e [resitã, -ãt] nm,f narrator

récitation [resitasjɔ̃] nf recitation

réciter [resite] vt to recite

réclamation [reklamasjɔ̃] nf complaint; **faire une r.** to make a complaint; **le service des réclamations, les réclamations** the complaints department

réclame [reklam] nf (**a**) (publicité) advertising; **faire de la r. pour qch** to advertise sth (**b**) (annonce) advertisement (**c**) (promotion) **en r.** on special offer

réclamer [reklame] **1** vt (**a**) (demander) to ask for; (droit, allocation) to claim; **la fillette réclame ses parents** the little girl is calling for her parents (**b**) (exiger) to demand; **r. des dommages et intérêts** to claim damages (**c**) (nécessiter) to require
2 se réclamer vpr **se r. de qn** (se recommander) to mention sb's name; **se r. de qch** (d'un parti, d'une idéologie) to identify with sth

reclasser [rəklase] vt (**a**) (fichiers) to reclassify (**b**) (chômeur) to find a new job for (**c**) (personnel, salaires) to regrade

reclus, -e [rəkly, -yz] **1** adj cloistered
2 nm,f recluse

réclusion [reklyzjɔ̃] nf (peine) imprisonment; **r. à perpétuité** life imprisonment

recoiffer [rəkwafe] **se recoiffer** vpr (**a**) (arranger ses cheveux) to redo one's hair (**b**) (remettre son chapeau) to put one's hat back on

recoin [rəkwɛ̃] nm (d'un lieu) nook; (de la mémoire) recess

reçois, reçoit, reçoive etc voir **recevoir**

recoller [rəkɔle] vt (objet cassé) to stick back together; (timbre) to stick back on; (enveloppe) to stick back down; Fam **r. les morceaux** to patch things up

récoltant, -e [rekɔltã, -ãt] **1** adj **apiculteur r.** honey producer; **viticulteur r.** = winegrower who harvests his own grapes
2 nm,f **mis en bouteille chez le r.** estate-bottled

récolte [rekɔlt] nf (**a**) (action) harvesting; **faire la r.** to harvest the crops (**b**) (résultat) harvest (**c**) (d'informations) crop

récolter [rekɔlte] vt (cultures) to harvest; Fig (renseignements, documents) to collect; Fam (ennuis, maladie) to get

recommandable [rəkɔmãdabl] adj (personne, lieu) reputable; **peu r.** (personne, lieu) disreputable

recommandation [rəkɔmãdasjɔ̃] nf (appui, conseil) recommendation

recommandé, -e [rəkɔmãde] **1** adj (**a**) (lettre) registered (**b**) (conseillé) recommended; **ce n'est pas très r.** it's not very advisable
2 nm **en r.** registered

recommander [rəkɔmãde] **1** vt (**a**) (lieu, produit, personne) to recommend (**à** to) (**b**) (conseiller) to advise; **r. à qn de faire qch** to advise sb to do sth; **r. la prudence à qn** to advise sb to be cautious (**c**) (lettre, paquet) to register
2 se recommander vpr (**a**) (demander de l'aide) **se r. à qn** to commend oneself to sb (**b**) **se r. de qn** (pour un emploi) to give sb's name as a reference (**c**) Suisse (insister) **se r. auprès de qn que...** to point out to sb that...

recommencement [rəkɔmãsmã] nm renewal; **la vie est un éternel** ou **perpétuel r.** life is a constant succession of new beginnings

recommencer [16] [rəkɔmɑ̃se] **1** *vt* to start *or* begin again
2 *vi* to start *or* begin again; **ne recommencez pas!** don't do it again!
3 recommencer à *vt ind* **r. à faire qch** to start *or* begin to do sth again

récompense [rekɔ̃pɑ̃s] *nf* reward; *(prix)* award; **1000 francs de r.** 1,000 francs reward; **en r. (de)** as a reward (for)

récompenser [rekɔ̃pɑ̃se] *vt* to reward (**de** for); **ce film a été récompensé à Cannes** this film won an award at Cannes

recomposer [rəkɔ̃poze] *vt (numéro de téléphone)* to redial

recompter [rəkɔ̃te] *vt* to count again

réconciliation [rekɔ̃siljasjɔ̃] *nf* reconciliation

réconcilier [66] [rekɔ̃silje] **1** *vt* to reconcile (**avec** with); **r. qn avec la vie** to renew sb's appetite for life
2 se réconcilier *vpr* to make it up (**avec** with)

reconductible [rəkɔ̃dyktibl] *adj (contrat, bail)* renewable

reconduction [rəkɔ̃dyksjɔ̃] *nf* **(a)** *(d'un bail, d'un contrat)* renewal; **r. tacite** *(d'un accord)* tacit renewal **(b)** *(d'un budget, d'une politique, d'une grève)* continuation

reconduire [18] [rəkɔ̃dɥir] *vt* **(a)** *(personne)* to take sb back; **r. qn (à la porte)** to show sb out; **r. qn à la frontière** to escort sb back to the border **(b)** *(bail, contrat)* to renew **(c)** *(budget, politique, grève)* to continue

réconfort [rekɔ̃fɔr] *nm* comfort

réconfortant, -e [rekɔ̃fɔrtɑ̃, -ɑ̃t] *adj* comforting

réconforter [rekɔ̃fɔrte] *vt* to comfort; **cela me réconforte de le savoir** I'm glad to know it

reconnaissable [rəkɔnɛsabl] *adj* recognizable (**à** by *or* from); **r. entre tous** unmistakable

reconnaissance [rəkɔnɛsɑ̃s] *nf* **(a)** *(action de reconnaître)* recognition; **en r. de qch** in recognition of sth **(b)** *(d'un droit, d'un gouvernement)* recognition; **r. de dette** IOU **(c)** *(gratitude)* gratitude (**pour** for); **avec r.** gratefully **(d)** *Mil* reconnaissance; **partir en r.** to go off on reconnaissance; *Fam Fig* to go and reconnoitre **(e)** *Ordinat* **r. de l'écriture manuscrite** handwriting recognition; **r. optique des caractères** optical character recognition, OCR; **r. de la parole, r. vocale** speech recognition

reconnaissant, -e [rəkɔnɛsɑ̃, -ɑ̃t] *adj* grateful; **être r. à qn de qch** to be grateful to sb for sth; **je vous serais r. de ne plus en parler** I'd be grateful if you didn't mention it again

reconnaître [20] [rəkɔnɛtr] **1** *vt* **(a)** *(identifier)* to recognize (**à** by *or* from); **je te reconnais bien là!** that's just like you! **(b)** *(admettre) (vérité, droit, gouvernement)* to recognize; *(enfant)* to acknowledge; **r. qn pour chef** to recognize sb as leader **(c)** *(avouer) (erreur, faute)* to acknowledge; **je reconnais que j'ai en tort** I admit I was wrong **(d)** *(accorder)* **je lui reconnais des qualités** I recognize her qualities **(e)** *(position, terrain)* to reconnoitre
2 se reconnaître *vpr* **(a)** *(soi-même)* to recognize oneself **(b)** *(l'un l'autre)* to recognize each other **(c)** *(s'avouer)* **se r. vaincu/coupable** to acknowledge defeat/one's guilt **(d)** *(se retrouver)* to find one's way around; **je ne me reconnais plus** I can't find my way around any more **(e)** *(être identifiable)* **le mâle se reconnaît à...** the male can be recognized by...

reconnu, -e [rəkɔny] *adj* recognized

reconquérir [7] [rəkɔ̃kerir] *vt (estime, amitié)* to win back; *(territoire)* to reconquer

reconquête [rəkɔ̃kɛt] *nf* reconquest

reconsidérer [34] [rəkɔ̃sidere] *vt* to reconsider

reconstituant, -e [rəkɔ̃stitɥɑ̃, -ɑ̃t] *adj & nm* tonic

reconstituer [rəkɔ̃stitɥe] *vt* **(a)** *(reformer) (armée, gouvernement)* to reconstitute; *(société, parti)* to revive; *(fortune, forces)* to build up again **(b)** *(rétablir) (objet archéologique, faits)* to piece together; *(bâtiment, quartier)* to restore **(c)** *(avec simulation) (crime)* to reconstruct

reconstitution [rəkɔ̃stitysjɔ̃] *nf (d'un crime, d'une bataille)* reconstruction; **r. historique** historical reconstruction

reconstruction [rəkɔ̃stryksjɔ̃] *nf* reconstruction, rebuilding

reconstruire [rəkɔ̃strɥir] *vt* to reconstruct, to rebuild

reconversion [rəkɔ̃vɛrsjɔ̃] *nf* **(a)** *(d'une usine)* conversion; **r. économique** economic restructuring **(b)** *(d'une personne)* retraining

reconvertir [rəkɔ̃vɛrtir] **1** *vt* **(a)** *(entreprise)* to convert **(b)** *(personne)* to retrain
2 se reconvertir *vpr (entreprise)* to convert (**dans** to); *(personne)* to retrain; **se r. dans qch** to retrain for a new career in sth

recopier [66] [rəkɔpje] *vt* **(a)** *(faire un double de)* to recopy **(b)** *(mettre au propre)* to copy out

record [rəkɔr] **1** *adj inv (chiffre, vitesse)* record
2 *nm* record; **détenir le r. (de qch)** to hold the record (for sth); **battre le r. (de qch)** to break the record (for sth)

recordman [rəkɔrdman] *(pl* **recordmen** [rəkɔrdmɛn]) *nm* (men's) record holder

recordwoman [rəkɔrdwuman] *(pl* **recordwomen** [rəkɔrdwumɛn]) *nf* (women's) record holder

recoucher [rəkuʃe] **1** *vt (personne)* to put to bed again
2 se recoucher *vpr* to go back to bed

recoudre [21] [rəkudr] *vt (bouton)* to sew back on; *(déchirure, plaie)* to sew *or* stitch up; *Fam (personne)* to stitch up

recoupement [rəkupmɑ̃] *nm* crosscheck; **faire le r.** to crosscheck; **par r.** by crosschecking

recouper [rəkupe] **1** *vt* **(a)** *(couper à nouveau) (vêtement)* to recut; **r. du pain** to cut some more bread; **r. une tranche de gâteau** to cut another slice of cake **(b)** *(faire coïncider)* to confirm; **r. des témoignages** to crosscheck testimony
2 se recouper *vpr (témoignages)* to tally

recourbé, -e [rəkurbe] *adj (bec)* curved; *(nez)* hooked

recourber [rəkurbe] **1** *vt* to bend
2 se recourber *vpr* to bend

recourir [22] [rəkurir] **1** *vt (épreuve sportive)* to run again
2 *vi (courir de nouveau)* to run again
3 recourir à *vt ind* **(a)** *(personne)* to turn to **(b)** *(moyen, violence)* to resort to

recours [rəkur] *nm* **(a)** *(personne, chose)* recourse; **en dernier r.** as a last resort; **avoir r. à qn** to turn to sb; **avoir r. à qch** to resort to sth **(b)** *Jur* **r. en cassation** appeal; *Can* **r. collectif** class action; **r. en grâce** petition for reprieve

recouvrement [rəkuvrəmɑ̃] *nm (de dettes, d'une facture)* recovery; *(de l'impôt)* collection

recouvrer [rəkuvre] *vt* **(a)** *(biens, argent, santé)* to recover; *(forces, liberté, vue)* to regain; *(courage, en-*

thousiasme) to get back (**b**) *(percevoir) (dettes)* to recover; *(impôts)* to collect

recouvrir [52] [rəkuvrir] *vt* (**a**) *(couvrir de nouveau) (cahier, toit)* to re-cover; *(enfant)* to cover up again (**b**) *(couvrir complètement)* to cover (**de** with) (**c**) *(tapisser)* to cover (**de** with) (**d**) *(inclure)* to cover

recracher [rəkraʃe] *vt* to spit out

récré [rekre] *nf Fam Br* break, *Am* recess; *(pour les plus jeunes)* playtime

récréatif, -ive [rekreatif, -iv] *adj (activité)* entertaining; *(lecture)* light

récréation [rekreasjɔ̃] *nf* (**a**) *(à l'école) Br* break, *Am* recess; *(pour les plus jeunes)* playtime (**b**) *(détente)* recreation

recréer [24] [rəkree] *vt* to re-create

récrier [66] [rekrije] **se récrier** *vpr (mécontents)* to protest (**contre** about)

récrimination [rekriminasjɔ̃] *nf* recrimination

récriminer [rekrimine] *vi* to make recriminations (**contre** against)

récrire [30] [rekrir] = **réécrire**

récriture [rekrityr] = **réécriture**

recroquevillé, -e [rəkrɔkvije] *adj* huddled up

recroqueviller [rəkrɔkvije] **se recroqueviller** *vpr (personne)* to huddle up; *(papier, feuille morte)* to shrivel up

recru, -e [rəkry] *adj Litt* **r. (de fatigue)** exhausted

recrudescence [rəkrydesɑ̃s] *nf* renewed outbreak

recrue [rəkry] *nf* recruit; **faire une nouvelle r.** to gain a new recruit

recrutement [rəkrytmɑ̃] *nm* recruitment

recruter [rəkryte] **1** *vt* to recruit; **r. par concours** to recruit by competition

2 se recruter *vpr* to be recruited (**parmi** from)

rectal, -e, -aux, -ales [rɛktal, -o] *adj* rectal

rectangle [rɛktɑ̃gl] *nm* rectangle

rectangulaire [rɛktɑ̃gylɛr] *adj* rectangular

recteur [rɛktœr] *nm (d'une académie) Br* director *or Am* commissioner of education

rectificatif, -ive [rɛktifikatif, -iv] **1** *adj (lettre)* of amendment; *(texte, facture)* amended

2 *nm* correction

rectification [rɛktifikasjɔ̃] *nf (d'un texte, d'un calcul, d'une erreur)* correction; *(d'un compte, d'une courbe)* adjustment; *(d'un alignement)* straightening; **faire** *ou* **apporter une r.** to make a correction

rectifier [66] [rɛktifje] *vt* (**a**) *(texte, calcul, erreur)* to correct; *(prix, compte, courbe)* to adjust; *(alignement)* to straighten; **r. le tir** to adjust the range; *Fig* to take a slightly different tack (**b**) *Fam (tuer)* to bump off

rectiligne [rɛktiliɲ] *adj (mouvement, figure)* rectilinear; *(avenue)* straight

rectitude [rɛktityd] *nf (d'un jugement, d'un raisonnement)* soundness

recto [rɛkto] *nm* front, *Spéc* recto; **r. verso** on both sides

rectorat [rɛktɔra] *nm* ≃ *Br* local education authority, *Am* board of education

rectum [rɛktɔm] *nm* rectum

reçu¹, -e *voir* **recevoir**

reçu², -e [rəsy] **1** *nm* receipt

2 *nm,f (à un examen)* successful candidate

recueil [rəkœj] *nm (de poèmes, de chansons, de recettes)* collection; *(de lois)* body; **r. de morceaux choisis** anthology

recueillement [rəkœjmɑ̃] *nm* meditation; **avec r.** meditatively

recueilli, -e [rəkœji] *adj* meditative

recueillir [5] [rəkœjir] **1** *vt* (**a**) *(argent, renseignements)* to collect (**b**) *(votes)* to win; *Fig* **r. le fruit de qch** to reap the fruit of sth (**c**) *(personne, animal)* to take in (**d**) *(miel)* to gather (**e**) *Jur* **r. un héritage** to inherit

2 se recueillir *vpr* to meditate; **se r. pour prier** to gather one's thoughts before praying

recuire [18] [rəkɥir] *vt (plat)* to cook longer

recul [rəkyl] *nm* (**a**) *(mouvement) (d'un glacier, d'une armée)* retreat; *(d'un canon)* recoil; **avoir un mouvement de r.** to recoil (**b**) *(déclin)* decline (**c**) *(baisse)* decline (**de** in) (**d**) *(espace nécessaire)* room to move back (**e**) *Fig (distance)* **considérer qch avec du r.** to consider sth with detachment; **manquer de r.** to be too closely involved; **prendre du r.** to stand back from things

reculade [rəkylad] *nf (d'une armée)* retreat; *Fig & Péj* climbdown

reculé, -e [rəkyle] *adj (endroit, époque)* remote

reculer [rəkyle] **1** *vi* (**a**) *(aller en arrière) (personne)* to move back; *(automobiliste, voiture)* to reverse; *(troupes)* to retreat; *(glacier, eaux)* to recede; **faire r. la foule** to move the crowd back (**b**) *(régresser) (épidémie)* to lose ground; *(chômage)* to decline; *Fig* **faire r. la maladie** to bring the disease under control (**c**) *(renoncer)* to retreat (**devant** in the face of); **il ne recule devant rien** nothing daunts him; **faire r. qn** to put sb off; **il est trop tard pour r.** it's too late to pull out; **c'est r. pour mieux sauter** it's just putting off the evil day

2 *vt* (**a**) *(meuble)* to move back; *(voiture)* to reverse (**b**) *(paiement, décision)* to postpone

reculons [rəkylɔ̃] **à reculons** *adv* backwards; *Fig (avec réticence)* unwillingly, under protest

récupérable [rekyperabl] *adj (déchets)* salvageable; **les heures supplémentaires sont récupérables** additional time off may be taken in lieu

récupération [rekyperasjɔ̃] *nf* (**a**) *(d'une somme d'argent, d'un objet)* recovery; **la r. des heures supplémentaires** time off in lieu; **temps de r.** *(d'un sportif)* recovery time (**b**) *(de déchets)* salvage (**c**) *(d'un parti, d'une pensée)* exploitation

récupérer [34] [rekypere] *vt* (**a**) *(objet prêté ou perdu)* to get back, to recover; *Ordinat (fichier, données)* to retrieve (**b**) *(passer prendre) (personne, affaires, objet)* to collect; *(bagages)* to retrieve, to reclaim (**c**) *(retrouver) (forces)* to recover (**d**) *(recycler)* to salvage (**e**) *(détourner à son profit) (mouvement, idée)* to exploit (**f**) **r. des heures supplémentaires** to take time off in lieu

récurer [rekyre] *vt* to scour; **poudre/tampon à r.** scouring powder/pad

récurrent, -e [rekyrɑ̃, -ɑ̃t] *adj* recurring; *Ordinat* **processus r.** recursive process

récusable [rekyzabl] *adj (témoignage)* impugnable

récuser [rekyze] **1** *vt* to challenge

2 se récuser *vpr* to decline to give an opinion

recyclable [rəsiklabl] *adj* recyclable

recyclage [rəsiklaʒ] *nm* (**a**) *(de matériaux)* recycling (**b**) *(d'une personne)* retraining

recycler [rəsikle] **1** *vt* (**a**) *(matériaux)* to recycle (**b**) *(personne)* to retrain

2 se recycler *vpr (personne)* to retrain

rédacteur, -trice [redaktœr, -tris] *nm,f (d'un journal, d'un dictionnaire)* editor; **r. en chef** editor in chief

rédaction [redaksjɔ̃] *nf* (**a**) *(d'un texte)* writing (**b**) *(poste)* editorship; *(personnel)* editorial staff; *(département)* editorial department; **(salle de) r.** editorial office (**c**) *Scol* essay, composition

rédactionnel, -elle [redaksjɔnɛl] *adj* editorial

reddition [rɛdisjɔ̃] *nf* surrender

redécouvrir [52] [rədekuvrir] *vt (auteur, œuvre)* to rediscover

redéfinir [rədefinir] *vt Ordinat (touche)* to redefine

redemander [rədəmɑ̃de] *vt* (**a**) *(en reposant une question)* to ask again; **r. de l'aide à qn** to ask sb again for help (**b**) *(pour en avoir plus)* **r. du pain/des timbres** to ask for more bread/stamps; **r. un litre/un kilo de qch** to ask for another litre/kilo of sth; **des gens comme ça, on en redemande** there aren't enough people like that in the world; *Ironique* **il en redemande** he's still asking for it (**c**) *(pour récupérer)* **r. qch** to ask for sth back

redémarrer [rədemare] *vi (voiture)* to start again; *(économie, ventes)* to take off again; *Ordinat* to reboot; **faire r. une voiture** to start a car again

rédemption [redɑ̃psjɔ̃] *nf* redemption

redéploiement [rədeplwamɑ̃] *nm* redeployment

redescendre [rədesɑ̃dr, rədesɑ̃dr] **1** *vi (en s'approchant)* to come back down; *(en s'éloignant)* to go back down; **r. de voiture** to get back out of the car
2 *vt* (**a**) *(apporter)* to bring back down; *(emporter)* to take back down (**b**) *(escalier, rivière)* to go/come back down

redevable [rədəvabl] *adj* **être r. de qch à qn** to be indebted to sb for sth; **je vous suis r. de 100 francs** I owe you 100 francs

redevance [rədəvɑ̃s] *nf (pour la télévision)* licence fee

redevenir [70] [rədəvənir] *vi* to become again; **r. silencieux** to fall silent again; **r. normal** to get back to normal

rédhibitoire [redibitwar] *adj (prix)* prohibitive; *(conditions, salaire)* unacceptable

rediffuser [rədifyze] *vt (émission)* to repeat, to rebroadcast; *(film)* to show again

rediffusion [rədifyzjɔ̃] *nf (d'une émission)* repeat, rebroadcasting; *(d'un film)* rerun

rédiger [45] [rediʒe] *vt (contrat)* to draw up; *(article, lettre)* to write; *(ordonnance)* to write out; **savoir r.** to write well; **être bien/mal rédigé** to be well/badly written

redingote [rədɛ̃gɔt] *nf* (**a**) *(manteau cintré)* fitted coat (**b**) *(manteau à basques)* frock coat

redire [27a] [rədir] **1** *vt* (**a**) *(répéter)* to say again, to repeat; **pourrais-tu lui r. que...?** could you tell him again that...?; **on ne le redira jamais assez** it can never be said often enough (**b**) *(révéler)* to repeat (**à to**)
2 redire à *vt ind* **avoir** *ou* **trouver à r. à qch** to find fault with sth; **il n'y a rien à r. à cela** there's nothing wrong with that

redite [rədit] *nf* (useless) repetition

redondance [rədɔ̃dɑ̃s] *nf aussi Ordinat* redundancy; **redondances** redundancy

redondant, -e [rədɔ̃dɑ̃, -ɑ̃t] *adj* redundant

redonner [rədɔne] *vt* (**a**) *(donner davantage de)* **redonne-lui de la soupe** give him some more soup (**b**) *(rendre)* to give back; **r. de l'appétit/du courage à qn** to restore sb's appetite/courage; **r. envie à qn de**

faire qch to make sb want to do sth again; **r. des forces à qn** to give sb back his/her strength (**c**) *(donner de nouveau)* to give again

redorer [rədɔre] *vt* to regild; *Fig* **r. son blason** to restore one's reputation

redoublant, -e [rədublɑ̃, -ɑ̃t] *nm,f (élève)* pupil repeating a year

redoublé, -e [rəduble] *adj* **frapper à coups redoublés** to knock harder

redoublement [rədubləmɑ̃] *nm* (**a**) *(de douleur, de joie, de prudence)* increase (**b**) *(d'une syllabe)* reduplication (**c**) *Scol* = repeating of a year; **le professeur principal décidera des redoublements** the head teacher will decide who will have to repeat the year

redoubler [rəduble] **1** *vt* (**a**) *(douleur, joie, prudence)* to increase; *(efforts)* to redouble (**b**) *Scol* **r. une classe** to repeat a year
2 *vi* (**a**) *Scol* to repeat a year (**b**) *(sentiment)* to intensify (**c**) *(orage)* to intensify, to become more severe; *(vent)* to grow stronger
3 redoubler de *vt ind* **r. de violence** *(orage, vent)* to become more and more severe; **r. d'efforts** to redouble one's efforts; **r. de prudence/d'attention/de douceur** to be twice as cautious/attentive/gentle

redoutable [rədutabl] *adj (adversaire, arme)* formidable; *(maladie)* dreadful

redouter [rədute] *vt* to dread; **r. de faire qch** to dread doing sth; **je redoute qu'il ne soit déjà trop tard** I'm afraid it's already too late

redoux [rədu] *nm* milder weather

redressement [rədrɛsmɑ̃] *nm* (**a**) *(économique, financier)* recovery (**b**) *(correction)* **r. fiscal** tax adjustment (**c**) *Jur* **r. judiciaire** receivership; **être mis en r. judiciaire** to go into receivership

redresser [rədrɛse] **1** *vt* (**a**) *(objet penché)* to put up straight; **r. la tête** to hold up one's head; *(la lever)* to raise one's head (**b**) *(rectifier) (erreur, situation)* to rectify; *(économie, entreprise)* to put back on its feet (**c**) *(bois courbé, tôle cabossée)* to straighten (out)
2 *vi (automobiliste)* to straighten up
3 se redresser *vpr* (**a**) *(personne)* to straighten up (**b**) *(économie, pays, ventes)* to recover

redresseur [rədrɛsœr] *nm* **r. de torts** righter of wrongs

réducteur, -trice [redyktœr, -tris] *adj (simpliste)* simplistic

réduction [redyksjɔ̃] *nf* (**a**) *(des prix, des dépenses, de la production)* reduction (**de in**) (**b**) *(rabais)* reduction; **faire une r. de 600 francs (à qn)** to give (sb) a reduction of 600 francs (**c**) *(reproduction)* small reproduction (**d**) *(d'une fracture)* setting

réduire [18] [redɥir] **1** *vt* (**a**) *(diminuer)* to reduce (**de by**); *(texte)* to shorten, to cut; **réduit de moitié** half size (**b**) *(transformer)* **r. qch en qch** to reduce sth to sth (**c**) *(contraindre)* **r. qn à qch** *(misère, désespoir)* to reduce sb to sth; **en être réduit à faire qch** to be reduced to doing sth (**d**) *(fracture)* to set (**e**) *(photographie, dessin)* to reduce
2 *vi (sauce)* to reduce; **faire r. qch** to reduce sth
3 se réduire *vpr* (**a**) **se r. à** *(se ramener à)* to come down to (**b**) **se r. en** *(se transformer en)* to be reduced to

réduit [redɥi] *nm (pièce)* small room

rééchelonnement [reeʃɔlɔnmɑ̃] *nm* rescheduling

rééchelonner [reeʃɔlɔne] *vt* to reschedule

réécrire [30] [reekrir] *vt* to rewrite

réécriture [reekrityr] *nf* rewriting
rééditer [reedite] *vt* (**a**) *(ouvrage)* to reissue (**b**) *(fait)* to repeat
réédition [reedisjɔ̃] *nf* (**a**) *(d'un ouvrage)* reissue (**b**) *(d'un fait)* repeat
rééducation [reedykasjɔ̃] *nf* (**a**) *(d'une partie du corps)* re-education; *(d'un handicapé, d'un accidenté)* rehabilitation; **faire de la r.** *(chez un kinésithérapeute)* to have physiotherapy (**b**) *(de délinquants)* rehabilitation
rééduquer [reedyke] *vt* *(handicapé, accidenté, délinquant)* to rehabilitate; *(partie du corps)* to re-educate
réel, -elle [reɛl] **1** *adj* real
   2 *nm* (**a**) *(nombre)* real number (**b**) **le r.** *(la réalité)* reality
réélection [reelɛksjɔ̃] *nf* re-election
réélire [44] [reelir] *vt* to re-elect
réellement [reɛlmɑ̃] *adv* really
réembaucher [rɛ̃boʃe] *vt* to take on again
rééquilibrage [reekilibraʒ] *nm* *(de pneus)* balancing; *Fig* **le r. du budget** balancing the budget again
rééquilibrer [reekilibre] *vt* *(pneus)* to balance; *Fig (budget)* to balance again
réessayer [53] [reeseje] **1** *vt* to try again; *(vêtement)* to try on again
   2 *vi* to try again
réévaluer [reevalɥe] *vt* *(monnaie)* to revalue; *(prix)* to reassess
réexamen [reɛgzamɛ̃] *nm* re-examination; *(d'une décision)* reconsideration
réexaminer [reɛgzamine] *vt* to re-examine; *(décision)* to reconsider
réexpédier [66] [reɛkspedje] *vt* (**a**) *(à une autre adresse)* to send on, to forward (**b**) *(à l'expéditeur)* to send back, to return
réexpédition [reɛkspedisjɔ̃] *nf* (**a**) *(à une autre adresse)* forwarding (**b**) *(à l'expéditeur)* return
refaire [36] [rəfɛr] **1** *vt* (**a**) *(faire à nouveau) (travail)* to do again, to redo; *(voyage)* to make again; **r. du riz** to make some more rice; **r. ses lacets** to tie one's laces again; *Hum* **ton éducation est à r.** where were you brought up?; **et si c'était à r.?** and if you had to do it again?; **r. le monde** to put the world to rights; **r. sa vie** to make a new life for oneself (**b**) *(remettre en état) (pièce, appartement)* to do up; **r. la peinture de qch** to repaint sth; **r. la moquette de qch** to recarpet sth; **r. qch à neuf** *(moteur)* to recondition sth; *(appartement)* to renovate sth completely (**c**) *Fam (duper)* to take in; **je me suis fait r. de 100 francs** I was done out of 100 francs
   2 se refaire *vpr* (**a**) *(se changer)* to change the way one is; **on ne se refait pas** you can't change the way you are (**b**) *(se rétablir)* **se r. une santé** to recover (**c**) *Fam (financièrement)* to recoup one's losses (**d**) *(s'habituer)* **se r. à qch** to get used to sth again
réfection [refɛksjɔ̃] *nf* repair
réfectoire [refɛktwar] *nm* refectory, dining hall
référence [referɑ̃s] *nf* (**a**) *(renvoi)* reference (**à** to); **faire r. à qch** to refer to sth; **en r. à** with reference to (**b**) *(sur une lettre, sur un document)* reference; **r. à rappeler** please quote reference (**c**) *(d'employeur)* **références** references
référencer [16] [referɑ̃se] *vt Ordinat* to reference
référendum [referɛ̃dɔm] *nm* referendum; **faire un r.** to hold a referendum

référer [34] [refere] **1 référer à** *vt ind* **en r. à qn** to refer the matter to sb
   2 se référer *vpr* **se r. à qch** to refer to sth; **se r. à un auteur** to refer to an author
refermer [rəfɛrme] **1** *vt* to shut or close again
   2 se refermer *vpr (porte)* to close or shut again; *(fleur, blessure)* to close up
refiler [rəfile] *vt Fam* **r. qch à qn** *(pour s'en débarrasser)* to palm sth off on sb; *(maladie)* to give sb sth
réfléchi, -e [refleʃi] *adj* (**a**) *(personne)* thoughtful (**b**) *(action, opinion)* considered; **c'est tout r.** I've made up my mind; **tout bien r.** all things considered (**c**) *(verbe, pronom)* reflexive
réfléchir [refleʃir] **1** *vt* (**a**) *(image, lumière, son)* to reflect (**b**) **r. que** to realize that
   2 *vi* to think (**à** *ou* **sur** about); **je réfléchis** I'm thinking; *(avant de décider)* I'm thinking about it; **sans r.** without thinking
   3 se réfléchir *vpr* to be reflected
réfléchissant, -e [refleʃisɑ̃, -ɑ̃t] *adj* reflective
réflecteur, -trice [reflɛktœr, -tris] *adj* reflecting
reflet [rəflɛ] *nm* (**a**) *(dans un miroir, dans l'eau)* reflection; *(d'un tissu)* sheen; *(de la lune)* glint; **reflets** *(de cheveux)* highlights (**b**) *Fig (image)* reflection; **être le r. de qn** to be exactly like sb; **être le r. d'une époque** to symbolize an era
refléter [34] [rəflete] **1** *vt aussi Fig* to reflect
   2 se refléter *vpr aussi Fig* to be reflected
refleurir [rəflœrir] **1** *vi* to flower again; *Fig* to flourish again
   2 *vt (tombe)* to put fresh flowers on
réflexe [reflɛks] **1** *adj* reflex
   2 *nm* reflex; **avoir de bons réflexes** to have good reflexes; **devenir un r.** to become automatic; **avoir le r. de faire qch** to do sth instinctively; **r. conditionné** conditioned reflex
réflexion [reflɛksjɔ̃] *nf* (**a**) *(d'une image, de la lumière, du son)* reflection (**b**) *(pensée)* reflection, thought; **r. faite, à la r.** on reflection, on second thoughts (**c**) *(remarque)* remark; **faire une r. à qn** to make a remark to sb
refluer [rəflye] *vi (liquide)* to flow back; *(marée)* to ebb; *(foule)* to surge back
reflux [rəfly] *nm (de la marée)* ebb; *(d'une foule)* backward surge
refondre [rəfɔ̃dr] *vt (ouvrage)* to revise
refonte [rəfɔ̃t] *nf (d'un ouvrage)* revision
reformater [rəfɔrmate] *vt Ordinat (page, disque)* to reformat
réformateur, -trice [refɔrmatœr, -tris] **1** *adj* reforming
   2 *nm,f* reformer
réforme [refɔrm] *nf* reform; *Hist* **la R.** the Reformation
réformé, -e [refɔrme] **1** *adj (protestant)* Protestant
   2 *nm,f (recrue)* recruit rejected as unfit; *(soldat)* soldier discharged as unfit
reformer [rəfɔrme] **1** *vt* to re-form; **r. les rangs** to fall into line again
   2 se reformer *vpr* to re-form
réformer [refɔrme] *vt* (**a**) *(abus, loi)* to reform (**b**) *(recrue)* to reject as unfit; *(soldat)* to discharge as unfit
réformisme [refɔrmism] *nm* reformism
réformiste [refɔrmist] *adj & nmf* reformist
reformuler [rəfɔrmyle] *vt* to reformulate
refoulé, -e [rəfule] *adj* repressed

refouler [Rəfule] **1** vt (**a**) (faire reculer) (foule) to drive or force back; (étranger) to turn away (**b**) (sentiments, colère, souvenir) to repress; (larmes) to hold back **2** vi **l'évier refoule** the water's coming up through the plughole in the sink

réfractaire [Refrakter] adj (**a**) (rebelle) insubordinate; **r. à** (loi, conseils, proposition) unwilling to accept (**b**) (brique, argile) fireproof (**c**) (prêtre) non-juring

réfraction [Refraksjɔ̃] nf refraction

refrain [Rəfrɛ̃] nm (d'une chanson) chorus, refrain; Fam **c'est toujours le même r.** it's always the same old story

refréner [Rəfrene], **réfréner** [Refrene] [34] vt to curb

réfrigérant, -e [RefriʒeRɑ̃, -ɑ̃t] adj (**a**) (appareil, produit) refrigerating (**b**) Fam (accueil, personne) frosty

réfrigérateur [RefriʒeRatœR] nm refrigerator

réfrigération [RefriʒeRasjɔ̃] nf refrigeration

réfrigéré, -e [Refriʒere] adj (**a**) (wagon) refrigerated (**b**) Fam (personne) frozen

réfrigérer [34] [Refriʒere] vt (aliment, boisson) to refrigerate

refroidir [RəfRwadiR] **1** vt (**a**) (eau) to cool (down) (**b**) Fig (amitié) to cool; (enthousiasme) to dampen; Fam **sa réaction m'a refroidi** her reaction dampened my enthusiasm (**c**) très Fam (tuer) to bump off **2** vi (**a**) (devenir froid) to get cold; (devenir moins chaud) to cool down; **laisser r. qch** (volontairement) to let sth cool down; (par négligence) to let sth get cold (**b**) (temps) to get colder **3** se refroidir vpr (**a**) (temps) to get colder (**b**) Fig (amitié, relations) to cool (**c**) (prendre froid) to catch a chill

refroidissement [RəfRwadismɑ̃] nm (**a**) (de la température) drop in temperature; (de l'eau) cooling (**b**) (indisposition) chill (**c**) Fig (dans une amitié, dans des relations) cooling off

refuge [Rəfyʒ] **1** nm (**a**) (lieu) & Fig refuge; **trouver/ chercher r. (auprès de qn)** to find/seek refuge (with sb) (**b**) (en montagne) (mountain) hut (**c**) (sur la route) traffic island **2** adj **valeur r.** safe investment

réfugié, -e [Refyʒje] nm,f refugee

réfugier [66] [Refyʒje] se réfugier vpr to take refuge (**dans** in)

refus [Rəfy] nm (d'une invitation, d'une offre) refusal; (d'une proposition, d'un candidat, d'un manuscrit) rejection; **essuyer un r.** to meet with a refusal; **opposer un r. à qn/qch** to turn sb/sth down; Fam **ce n'est pas de r.** I won't say no; **r. de priorité** (infraction) failure Br to give way or Am to yield

refuser [Rəfyze] **1** vt (**a**) (offre, invitation, demande) to refuse, to turn down; (proposition, marchandises, manuscrit) to reject; **r. qch à qn** to refuse sb sth (**b**) (clients, spectateurs) to turn away (**c**) (candidat) **être refusé** to fail **2** vi to refuse; **r. de faire qch** to refuse to do sth **3** se refuser vpr (**a**) (être rejeté) **une offre pareille, ça ne se refuse pas** you can't refuse an offer like that (**b**) **se r. qch** (se priver de) to deny oneself sth; **ne rien se r.** not to stint oneself (**c**) (résister) **se r. à l'évidence** to shut one's eyes to the facts; **se r. à tout commentaire** to refuse to comment; **se r. à faire qch** to refuse to do sth

réfuter [Refyte] vt to refute

regagner [Rəgaɲe] vt (**a**) (confiance, affection, estime) to regain, to get back (**b**) (argent perdu) to win back; **r.**
le temps perdu to make up for lost time (**c**) **r. du terrain** (reprendre l'avantage) to make up lost ground (**d**) (endroit) to get back to; **r. son foyer** to get back home

regain [Rəgɛ̃] nm (d'intérêt, d'activité) renewal; **un r. d'espoir** renewed hope

régal, -als [Regal] nm treat

régalade [Regalad] nf **boire à la r.** to drink without letting the bottle touch one's lips

régaler [Regale] **1** vt **r. qn** to give sb a delicious meal **2** vi Fam **c'est moi qui régale** (it's) my treat **3** se régaler vpr **je me régale** (en mangeant) I'm really enjoying it; (je m'amuse) I'm having a great time

regard [RəgaR] nm (**a**) (coup d'œil) look; **porter son r. sur qn/qch** to look at sb/sth; **jeter ou lancer un r. à qn** to glance at sb; **jeter un r. à ou sur qch** to glance at sth; **lancer un r. furieux à qn** to glare at sb; **chercher qn/qch du r.** to look round for sb/sth; **interroger qn du r.** to give sb a questioning look; **soustraire qn/qch aux regards (de qn)** to keep sb/sth hidden (from sb); **attirer le r.** to attract attention; **sous les regards de la foule** while the crowd looked on; Fig **porter un nouveau r./un r. critique sur qch** to take a fresh look/a critical look at sth (**b**) (expression) look (**c**) (ouverture) (d'une porte) peephole; (d'un égout) manhole (**d**) (locutions) **au r. de la loi** in the eyes of the law; **en r.** (en face) opposite

regardant, -e [RəgaRdɑ̃, -ɑ̃t] adj (**a**) Fam (avare) careful with money (**b**) (exigeant) particular (**sur** about)

regarder [RəgaRde] **1** vt (**a**) (personne, objet) to look at; (émission, film) to watch; **r. qn droit dans les yeux** to look sb in the eye; **r. qn fixement** to stare at sb; **r. qn faire qch** to watch sb do sth; **regarde où tu marches!** watch where you're going!; Fam **non, mais tu ne m'as pas regardé!** what do you take me for? (**b**) (considérer) to regard, to consider (**comme** as); **r. qch en face** to face up to sth; **r. les choses telles qu'elles sont** to see things as they are (**c**) (concerner) to concern; **cela ne regarde que moi** that's nobody's business but mine; **cela ne vous regarde pas** that's none of your business **2** vi (**a**) (observer) to look; **r. autour de soi/en bas/ en arrière** to look round/down/back; **r. par ou à la fenêtre** (du dedans) to look out of the window; (du dehors) to look in through the window (**b**) (être orienté) **r. sur ou vers** (jardin, rue) to look onto **3** regarder à vt ind (**a**) (apparence, détail) to pay attention to; **r. à la dépense** to be careful with one's money; **y r. à deux fois avant de faire qch** to think twice before doing sth; **y r. de près** to look at it closely (**b**) Belg (veiller sur) to look after **4** se regarder vpr (**a**) (soi-même) to look at oneself; Fam **elle ne s'est pas regardée!** she can talk! (**b**) (l'un l'autre) to look at each other; **se r. dans les yeux** to look into each other's eyes (**c**) (se faire face) to face each other

regarnir [RəgaRniR] vt (garde-manger, étagères) to restock

régate [Regat] nf regatta

régence [Reʒɑ̃s] **1** adj inv **style R.** Regency style **2** nf regency; Hist **la R.** the Regency

régénération [ReʒeneRasjɔ̃] nf (**a**) (d'une cellule, de la peau) regeneration (**b**) Ordinat **r. de l'écran** screen refresh

régénérer [34] [ReʒeneRe] **1** vt to regenerate **2** se régénérer vpr to regenerate

régent, -e [reʒɑ̃, -ɑ̃t] *nm,f* (**a**) *(chef du gouvernement)* regent (**b**) *Belg Scol* (secondary) schoolteacher

régenter [reʒɑ̃te] *vt* **vouloir tout r.** to want to run the whole show

reggae [rege] **1** *adj inv* reggae
2 *nm* **le r.** reggae

régie [reʒi] *nf* (**a**) *(entreprise publique)* state-controlled company (**b**) *Cin & TV (organisation)* production management (**c**) *TV (lieu)* control room

regimber [rəʒɛ̃be] *vi (personne)* to balk (**contre** at); **il est inutile de r.** it's no use protesting

régime [reʒim] *nm* (**a**) **r. (alimentaire)** diet; **être au r.** to be on a diet; **faire** *ou* **suivre un r.** to diet; **se mettre au r.** to go on a diet; **r. amincissant** slimming diet; *Fam* **être au r. sec** to be on an alcohol-free diet; *Hum* to be on the wagon (**b**) *(forme de gouvernement)* government, regime (**c**) *(pénitentiaire, hospitalier)* system; *(de retraite)* scheme; **r. matrimonial** marriage settlement; **r. de Sécurité sociale** = division of social security system applying to some professional groups (**d**) *(d'un moteur)* speed; **r. de croisière** cruising speed; *Fig* **à ce r.** at this rate (**e**) *(d'une rivière, d'un fleuve)* rate of flow (**f**) *(de bananes, de dattes)* bunch

régiment [reʒimɑ̃] *nm (unité militaire)* regiment; *Fig (d'admirateurs, de créanciers)* host; *Fam* **il y en a pour un r.** there's enough for a whole army

région [reʒjɔ̃] *nf* area, region; **la r. parisienne** the Paris area *or* region; **la R.** = administrative area comprising several "départements"; **en r.** *(en province)* in the provinces

régional, -e, -aux, -ales [reʒjɔnal, -o] *adj* regional

régionalisme [reʒjɔnalism] *nm* regionalism

régionaliste [reʒjɔnalist] **1** *adj* regionalist
2 *nmf* regionalist; *(écrivain)* regional writer

régir [reʒir] *vt* (**a**) *(déterminer)* to govern (**b**) *(domaine)* to manage

régisseur [reʒisœr] *nm* (**a**) *(d'un domaine)* manager (**b**) *Cin & TV* assistant production manager; *Théât* stage manager

registre [rəʒistr] *nm* (**a**) *(livre)* register; *(de comptabilité)* account book; **r. du commerce** trade register; **r. de l'état civil** register of births, marriages and deaths (**b**) *(d'une voix, d'un instrument)* register (**c**) *Ordinat* register; **r. d'accès mémoire** memory access register (**d**) *(d'une œuvre)* style

réglable [reglabl] *adj* adjustable

réglage [reglaʒ] *nm* (**a**) *(d'un siège, d'un appareil)* adjustment; **r. automatique** automatic control (**b**) *(d'une radio, d'une télévision)* tuning; **r. du contraste** contrast control

règle [regl] *nf* (**a**) *(de conduite, de grammaire)* rule; *Fig* **la r. du jeu** the rules of the game; **en r.** *(passeport, papiers)* in order; **en r. générale** as a general rule; **dans** *ou* **selon les règles de l'art** according to the book; **r. d'or** golden rule; *Math* **r. de trois** rule of three (**b**) *(pour tracer des lignes)* ruler (**c**) *Ordinat (sur écran)* ruler line (**d**) **règles** *(menstruation)* period; **avoir ses règles** to have one's period

réglé, -e [regle] *adj* (**a**) *(papier)* ruled (**b**) *(organisé)* well-ordered (**c**) *(résolu)* **c'est r.** it's settled (**d**) *(jeune fille)* who has started having periods

règlement [regləmɑ̃] *nm* (**a**) *(résolution)* settlement; **en cours de r.** being settled; **r. à l'amiable** amicable settlement; **r. de comptes** settling of scores (**b**) *(paiement)* payment; **pour r. de tout compte** in full settlement (**c**) *(règle)* regulations; **r. intérieur** *(d'une école)*

school rules; *(d'un bureau)* company rules; **c'est le r.** that's the rule

réglementaire [regləmɑ̃tɛr] *adj (tenue)* regulation; **faire qch dans le temps r.** to do sth in the time allowed

réglementation [regləmɑ̃tasjɔ̃] *nf* (**a**) *(action)* regulation (**b**) *(ensemble de lois)* regulations; **la r. du travail** labour legislation

réglementer [regləmɑ̃te] *vt* to regulate

régler [34] [regle] **1** *vt* (**a**) *(mécanisme, appareil, image)* to adjust; *(radio, moteur)* to tune (**b**) *(journée, emploi du temps)* to plan (**c**) **r. qch sur qch** *(conduite)* to model sth on sth; *(pas)* to adjust sth to sth (**d**) *(résoudre)* *(question, dispute)* to settle; **r. ses affaires** to put one's affairs in order; **r. qch à l'amiable** to settle sth out of court (**e**) *(payer)* *(facture)* to settle, to pay; *(employé, commerçant, loyer)* to pay; *(achats)* to pay for
2 *vi* to pay
3 se régler *vpr* (**a**) **se r. sur qn** to model oneself on sb (**b**) *(se conclure)* to be settled

réglette [reglɛt] *nf* small ruler; *Ordinat* **r. de clavier** key strip

réglisse [reglis] *nf* liquorice

réglo [reglo] *adj inv Fam* on the level

régnant, -e [reɲɑ̃, -ɑ̃t] *adj (prince, famille)* reigning; *(idéologie, opinion)* prevailing

règne [reɲ] *nm* (**a**) *(d'un souverain)* reign; *Fig (de l'argent, de la technologie)* rule (**b**) *(végétal, animal)* kingdom

régner [34] [reɲe] *vi* (**a**) *(souverain)* to reign, to rule (**sur** over); **r. en maître sur qch** to reign supreme over sth (**b**) *(exister)* *(idée)* to prevail; *(silence, atmosphère)* to reign; **faire r. la paix/l'ordre** to keep the peace/law and order; *Ironique* **la confiance règne!** there's confidence for you!

regonfler [rəgɔ̃fle] *vt (ballon, pneu)* to blow up again, to reinflate

regorger [45] [rəgɔrʒe] *vi* **r. de qch** to be overflowing with sth; **r. de monde** to be packed with people

régresser [regrese] *vi* (**a**) *(criminalité, idéologie, production)* to decline (**b**) *(personne)* to regress

régression [regresjɔ̃] *nf* (**a**) *(de la criminalité, d'une idéologie, de la production)* decline; **être en r.** to be on the decline (**b**) *(d'une personne)* regression; **être en r.** to be regressing

regret [rəgrɛ] *nm* regret (**de** for); **avoir des regrets** to have regrets; **à r.** with regret; **j'ai le r.** *ou* **je suis au r. de vous annoncer que...** I regret to tell you that...; **à mon (grand) r.** (much) to my regret

regrettable [rəgrɛtabl] *adj* regrettable

regretter [rəgrɛte] *vt* (**a**) *(avoir des remords sur)* to regret; **je ne regrette rien** I have no regrets; **il me ferait presque r. ma gentillesse** I'm almost sorry I was so kind to him; **r. de faire qch** to regret to do sth; **r. d'avoir fait qch** to regret having done sth; **r. que** + *subjunctive* to be sorry that; **il est à r. que...** it is to be regretted that...; **je regrette!** I'm sorry! (**b**) *(personne, endroit)* to miss; **r. sa jeunesse/son enfance** to wish one was young/a child again

regroupement [rəgrupmɑ̃] *nm* (**a**) *(action)* grouping; *(d'animaux, d'enfants)* round-up; *(de sociétés)* amalgamation; *Mil* regrouping; **le r. familial** = policy of authorizing the families of immigrant workers in possession of long-term work permits to join their relatives in France (**b**) *(groupe)* grouping

regrouper [rəgrupe] **1** *vt* (**a**) *(personnes, objets)* to gather together; *(animaux, enfants)* to round up (**b**) *(sociétés)* to amalgamate
  2 se regrouper *vpr* (**a**) *(personnes)* to gather together (**b**) *(sociétés)* to amalgamate

régularisation [regylarizasjɔ̃] *nf* (**a**) *(d'une situation)* regularization; *(d'un compte)* adjustment (**b**) *(d'un fleuve, d'un fonctionnement, de la circulation)* regulation

régulariser [regylarize] *vt* (**a**) *(situation)* to regularize; *(compte)* to adjust; **ils ont régularisé la situation** *(ils se sont mariés)* they made it official (**b**) *(fleuve, fonctionnement, circulation)* to regulate

régularité [regylarite] *nf* (**a**) *(exactitude)* regularity (**b**) *(constance)* steadiness (**c**) *(d'une décision, d'une situation)* legality

régulateur, -trice [regylatœr, -tris] **1** *adj* regulating
  2 *nm* regulator

régulation [regylasjɔ̃] *nf* control; **r. des naissances** birth control

régulier, -ère [regylje, -ɛr] **1** *adj* (**a**) *(à intervalles fixes)* regular (**b**) *(constant)* steady; *(travail, résultats)* consistent (**c**) *(écriture, ligne, couche)* even; *(traits du visage)* regular (**d**) *(légal)* *(situation)* legitimate; **être en situation régulière** to have one's papers in order (**e**) *Gram* regular (**f**) *Fam (honnête)* on the level (**g**) *(clergé)* regular
  2 *nf* **régulière** *Fam Hum (femme)* steady

régulièrement [regyljɛrmɑ̃] *adv* (**a**) *(à intervalles fixes)* regularly (**b**) *(avec constance)* steadily (**c**) *(réparti, étalé)* evenly (**d**) *(selon la loi)* legitimately

régurgiter [regyrʒite] *vt (nourriture)* to regurgitate

réhabilitation [reabilitasjɔ̃] *nf* (**a**) *(de délinquant)* rehabilitation (**b**) *(de bâtiment, de quartier)* renovation

réhabiliter [reabilite] **1** *vt* (**a**) *(délinquant)* to rehabilitate (**b**) *(personne accusée)* to clear (**c**) *(bâtiment, quartier)* to renovate
  2 se réhabiliter *vpr* to rehabilitate oneself

réhabituer [reabitɥe] **1** *vt* **r. qn à qch/à faire qch** to get sb used to sth/to doing sth again
  2 se réhabituer *vpr* **se r. à qch/à faire qch** to get used to sth/to doing sth again

rehausser [rəose] *vt* (**a**) *(mur, bâtiment)* to make higher (**b**) *(couleur, teint)* to set off; *(détail)* to accentuate

réimplanter [reɛ̃plɑ̃te] **1** *vt* to relocate
  2 se réimplanter *vpr* to relocate

réimpression [reɛ̃presjɔ̃] *nf* reprinting; **en cours de r.** *(ouvrage)* being reprinted

réimprimer [reɛ̃prime] *vt* to reprint

rein [rɛ̃] *nm* (**a**) *(organe)* kidney; **r. artificiel** kidney *or* dialysis machine (**b**) **reins** *(bas du dos)* lower back; **la chute** *ou* **le creux des reins** the small of the back; **avoir mal aux reins** to have a pain in the small of one's back; *Fig* **avoir les reins solides** to be tough; *(financièrement)* to have money behind one

réincarnation [reɛ̃karnasjɔ̃] *nf* reincarnation

réincarner [reɛ̃karne] **se réincarner** *vpr* to be reincarnated (**en** as)

reine [rɛn] *nf* (**a**) *(souveraine, épouse d'un roi)* queen; **un port** *ou* **un maintien de r.** a queenly bearing; **la r. Anne** Queen Anne; **la r. mère** the Queen Mother (**b**) *(femme)* **r. de beauté** beauty queen; **la r. du bal** the belle of the ball (**c**) *(abeille)* queen (bee) (**d**) **la petite r.** *(cyclisme)* cycling

reine-claude (*pl* **reines-claudes**) [rɛnklod] *nf* greengage

reinette [rɛnɛt] *nf* pippin; **r. grise** russet

réinitialiser [reinisjalize] *vt* *Ordinat* to reset; *(mémoire)* to reinitialize

réinscription [reɛ̃skripsjɔ̃] *nf* reregistration

réinscrire [30] [reɛ̃skrir] **1** *vt* to reregister (**à** for)
  2 se réinscrire *vpr* to reregister (**à** for)

réinsérer [34] [reɛ̃sere] **1** *vt* (**a**) *(personne)* to reintegrate (**dans** into) (**b**) *Ordinat (bloc)* to reinsert
  2 se réinsérer *vpr* to reintegrate (**dans** into)

réinsertion [reɛ̃sɛrsjɔ̃] *nf* reintegration; **r. sociale** rehabilitation

réintégrer [34] [reɛ̃tegre] *vt* (**a**) *(fonctionnaire)* **r. qn (dans ses fonctions)** to reinstate sb (**b**) *(lieu)* **r. son domicile** to return to one's home

réintroduire [18] [reɛ̃trɔdɥir] *vt* to reintroduce

réitérer [34] [reitere] *vt (demande, promesse, question)* to repeat, to reiterate; *(démarche)* to repeat

rejaillir [rəʒajir] *vi* to spurt out; *Fig* **r. sur qn** *(scandale)* to reflect on sb

rejet [rəʒɛ] *nm* (**a**) *(de produits chimiques)* discharge (**b**) *(d'une proposition, d'une personne, d'une greffe)* rejection (**c**) *(en poésie)* enjambment

rejeter [42] [rəʒte] *vt* (**a**) *(relancer)* to throw back (**b**) *(candidature, offre, greffe)* to reject; *(témoignage)* to disallow; *(réclamation, accusation)* to dismiss; *(projet de loi)* to throw out (**c**) *(personne)* to reject (**d**) *(repousser)* **r. ses cheveux en arrière** to toss one's hair back; **r. la tête en arrière** to throw one's head back; **r. un mot en fin de phrase** to put a word at the end of a sentence (**e**) *(déchets, gaz toxiques)* to discharge; *(nourriture)* to regurgitate; *(épaves)* to cast up (**f**) *(blâme, responsabilité)* to shift (**sur** on)

rejeton [rəʒtɔ̃] *nm Fam Hum (enfant)* kid

rejoindre [43] [rəʒwɛ̃dr] **1** *vt* (**a**) *(personne) (pour un rendez-vous)* to meet; *(rattraper)* to catch up (with) (**b**) *(aboutir sur) (rue, rivière)* to join (up with) (**c**) *(atteindre) (lieu)* to reach; *(régiment, poste)* to return to (**d**) *(concorder avec)* to coincide with
  2 se rejoindre *vpr* (**a**) *(amis)* to meet up (**b**) *(rivières, routes, lignes)* to join up (**c**) *(propos, idées)* to coincide

rejouer [rəʒwe] *vt (match, point)* to replay; *(morceau de musique)* to play again; *(pièce de théâtre)* to do again

réjoui, -e [reʒwi] *adj* joyful

réjouir [reʒwir] **1** *vt (personne)* to delight
  2 se réjouir *vpr* to be delighted (**de** at); **se r. que** + *subjunctive* to be delighted that; **se r. de faire qch** to be delighted to be doing sth; *Suisse* **se r. de qch/de faire qch** to look forward to sth/to doing sth

réjouissance [reʒwisɑ̃s] *nf* rejoicing; **en signe de r.** to mark the occasion; **réjouissances** festivities

réjouissant, -e [reʒwisɑ̃, -ɑ̃t] *adj* delightful

relâche [rəlɑʃ] *nf* (**a**) *(arrêt)* **sans r.** without a break (**b**) *(au théâtre)* **il y a r. ce soir** there is no performance this evening; **faire r.** to be closed; **r.** *(sur panneau)* closed

relâché, -e [rəlɑʃe] *adj (mœurs, conduite)* lax

relâchement [rəlɑʃmɑ̃] *nm* (**a**) *(des muscles)* relaxing; *(d'une corde)* slackening (**b**) *(de la discipline)* relaxation; *(des mœurs)* laxness; *(des efforts)* let-up; *(de l'attention)* wavering; **il y a du r. dans votre travail** you're letting your work slide

relâcher [rəlɑʃe] **1** *vt* (**a**) *(muscles)* to relax; *(corde, étreinte)* to loosen (**b**) *(discipline)* to relax; *(efforts)* to let up; **r. son attention** to let one's attention waver (**c**) *(prisonnier)* to release, to let go

2 se relâcher *vpr* (**a**) *(muscles)* to relax; *(corde)* to slacken; *(étreinte)* to loosen (**b**) *(discipline, mœurs)* to become lax; *(élève, employé)* to slack off; *(attention)* to waver

relais [rəlɛ] *nm* (**a**) *(épreuve sportive)* (**course de**) r. relay *(race)*; **r. 4 x 100 mètres** 4 x 100-metre relay (**b**) *(relève)* **passer le r. à qn** to hand over to sb; **prendre le r. (de)** to take over (from) (**c**) *(intermédiaire)* intermediary (**d**) *(auberge)* coaching inn; **r. gastronomique** gourmet restaurant (**e**) *(dispositif émetteur)* relay

relance [rəlɑ̃s] *nf* (**a**) *(de l'économie, de la production)* revival (**b**) *(au jeu)* raise

relancer [16] [rəlɑ̃se] *vt* (**a**) *(lancer de nouveau)* to throw again; *(rendre)* to throw back (**b**) *(économie, ventes, production)* to boost (**c**) *(moteur)* to restart; *Ordinat (programme)* to rerun; *(logiciel)* to restart (**d**) *(client)* to follow up

relater [rəlate] *vt Litt (raconter)* to relate

relatif, -ive [rəlatif, -iv] **1** *adj* relative; **r. à** relating to; **tout est r.** it's all relative
2 *nm (pronom)* relative pronoun
3 *nf* **relative** *(proposition)* relative clause

relation [rəlasjɔ̃] *nf* (**a**) *(rapports entre personnes)* relationship; **être en r. avec qn** to be in touch with sb; **mettre qn en r. (avec qn)** to put sb in touch (with sb); **avoir de bonnes/mauvaises relations avec qn** to be on good/bad terms with sb; **r. (amoureuse)** (love) affair; **relations extérieures** foreign affairs; **relations publiques** public relations; **relations sexuelles** (sexual) intercourse (**b**) *(lien)* (entre des phénomènes, des faits) relationship, connection; **être sans r. avec qch** to bear no relation to sth; **en r. avec...** in relation to...; **r. de cause à effet** cause-and-effect relationship (**c**) *(connaissance)* acquaintance; **avoir des relations** to have contacts; **une r. de travail** a colleague (**d**) *(récit)* account

relationnel, -elle [rəlasjɔnɛl] *adj* relational; *Ordinat* **base de données relationnelles** relational database

relativement [rəlativmɑ̃] *adv* (**a**) *(assez)* relatively (**b**) **r. à** *(par rapport à)* compared to

relativiser [rəlativize] *vt* to put into perspective; **il faut r.** you have to put things into perspective

relativisme [rəlativism] *nm* relativism

relativité [rəlativite] *nf* relativity

relax [rəlaks] *adj Fam* laid-back

relaxant, -e [rəlaksɑ̃, -ɑ̃t] *adj* relaxing

relaxation [rəlaksasjɔ̃] *nf* relaxation; **faire de la r.** to do relaxation exercises

relaxer [rəlakse] **1** *vt* (**a**) *(détendre)* to relax (**b**) *(prisonnier)* to release
2 se relaxer *vpr* to relax

relayer [53] [rəleje] **1** *vt (personne)* to take over from
2 se relayer *vpr* (**a**) *(se remplacer)* to take turns; **se r. pour faire qch** to take turns doing sth; **on se relaie toutes les trois heures** we change over every three hours (**b**) *(coureurs)* to take over from each other

relecture [rəlɛktyr] *nf* (**a**) *(d'épreuves)* proofreading (**b**) *(d'un livre, d'un texte)* rereading

reléguer [34] [rəlege] *vt* to relegate (**à/en** to); *Fig* **r. qch au second plan** to push sth into the background

relent [rəlɑ̃] *nm* (**a**) *(odeur)* stench (**b**) *(de scandale)* whiff

relevable [rəlvabl] *adj (dossier, appuie-tête)* adjustable; *(accoudoir)* folding

relevé, -e [rəlve] **1** *adj* (**a**) *(style)* lofty (**b**) *(sauce, plat)* spicy, highly seasoned

2 *nm (d'un compteur)* reading; **r. de compte** bank statement; **r. d'identité bancaire** = document giving details of one's bank account

> ### Relevé d'identité bancaire
> An "RIB" is a small slip of paper with all of a person's bank details. Employers, utility companies and other financial institutions may ask for one to effect standing orders.

relève [rəlɛv] *nf* relief; **assurer** *ou* **prendre la r. (de qn)** to take over (from sb)

relèvement [rəlɛvmɑ̃] *nm* (**a**) *(d'une économie, d'un pays)* recovery (**b**) *(des salaires, des tarifs, d'un impôt)* raising

relever [46] [rəlve] **1** *vt* (**a**) *(objet renversé)* to pick up; *(personne)* to help back up; **r. la tête** to look up; *Fig* to stand up for oneself (**b**) *(économie, pays)* to revive (**c**) *(col)* to turn up; *(manches, bas de pantalon)* to roll up, to turn up; *(voilette, jupe)* to lift (up); *(cheveux)* to put up (**d**) *(augmenter)* to raise (**e**) *(contradiction, erreur)* to pick out; *(traces, empreinte)* to find (**f**) *(prêter attention à)* **r. l'allusion** to pick up on the hint; **je n'ai pas relevé** I let it go (**g**) *(adresse, coordonnées)* to take down; *(compteur)* to read; *(copies)* to collect; **r. le gaz** to read the gas meter (**h**) *(défi)* to accept (**i**) *(sauce, plat)* to spice up (**j**) *(remplacer)* (troupes, sentinelle) to relieve (**k**) *(libérer)* **r. qn de ses fonctions** to relieve sb of his/her duties
2 relever de *vt ind* (**a**) *(dépendre de)* (personne, autorité) to be answerable to; **r. de l'article 7** to come under article 7; **cette affaire relève de la justice** this is a matter for the courts; **son cas relève de la folie** he's well and truly insane (**b**) *(se remettre de)* to be recovering from
3 se relever *vpr* (**a**) *(après une chute)* to get up (**b**) *(accoudoir, siège)* to lift up (**c**) *(se remettre)* **se r. de qch** to get over sth, to recover from sth

relief [rəljɛf] *nm* (**a**) *(d'un paysage, d'une médaille)* relief; **en r.** in relief; *Fig* **mettre qch en r.** *(idées, qualité)* to bring sth out; *(beauté)* to set sth off; *(avantage)* to highlight sth; **sans r.** *(paysage, style)* flat (**b**) *Litt* **reliefs** *(d'un repas)* remains; *Fig (de la gloire)* shreds (**c**) *Ordinat* highlight; **mettre qch en r.** to highlight sth

relier [66] [rəlje] **1** *vt* (**a**) *(mettre en contact)* to connect, to link (**à** to) (**b**) *(idées, faits)* to link together (**c**) *(livre)* to bind
2 se relier *vpr Ordinat* to link up

relieur, -euse [rəljœr, -øz] *nm,f* (book)binder

religieusement [rəliʒjøzmɑ̃] *adv* (**a**) *(selon la religion)* religiously; **se marier r.** to get married in church (**b**) *(avec révérence)* reverently (**c**) *(scrupuleusement)* religiously

religieux, -euse [rəliʒjø, -øz] **1** *adj* religious; *(mariage)* church; *Fig (silence)* respectful
2 *nm (moine)* monk
3 *nf* **religieuse** (**a**) *(sœur)* nun (**b**) *(gâteau)* cream puff

religion [rəliʒjɔ̃] *nf* religion; **entrer en r.** to join a religious order

reliquaire [rəlikɛr] *nm* reliquary

reliquat [rəlika] *nm (d'argent)* remainder; **r. de caisse** cash balance; **r. de compte** account balance

relique [rəlik] *nf* relic

relire [44] [rəlir] **1** *vt* (**a**) *(livre, auteur, notes)* to reread (**b**) *(épreuves)* to proofread
2 se relire *vpr* to read (over) what one has written

reliure [rəljyr] *nf* (**a**) *(activité, art)* bookbinding (**b**) *(couverture)* binding

reloger [45] [rəlɔʒe] *vt* to rehouse

relooker [rəluke] *vt Fam* to revamp

reluire [18] [rəlɥir] *vi (parquet, meuble, métal)* to shine, to gleam; **faire r. qch** to polish sth (up)

reluisant, -e [rəlɥizɑ̃, -ɑ̃t] *adj* (**a**) *(parquet, meuble, métal)* shining, gleaming (**b**) *Fig* **ce qu'il a fait n'est pas très r.** what he did doesn't reflect very well on him

reluquer [rəlyke] *vt Fam* to eye up

remâcher [rəmɑʃe] *vt (colère, échec)* to brood over

remake [rimɛk] *nm* remake

remaniement [rəmanimɑ̃] *nm* (**a**) *(d'un texte)* revision (**b**) **r. ministériel** cabinet reshuffle

remanier [66] [rəmanje] *vt* (**a**) *(texte)* to revise (**b**) *(ministère)* to reshuffle

remariage [rəmarjaʒ] *nm* remarriage

remarier [66] [rəmarje] **se remarier** *vpr* to remarry; **se r. avec qn** to remarry sb

remarquable [rəmarkabl] *adj* remarkable (**par** for)

remarquablement [rəmarkabləmɑ̃] *adv* remarkably

remarque [rəmark] *nf* (**a**) *(orale)* remark; **faire une r.** to make a remark; **faire une r. à qn sur qch** to pass a remark to sb about sth (**b**) *(écrite)* comment

remarqué, -e [rəmarke] *adj (entrée, absence)* conspicuous; *(intervention)* that attracted attention

remarquer [rəmarke] **1** *vt* (**a**) *(observer)* to notice; **faire r. qch à qn** to point sth out to sb; **je vous ferai r. que...** I'd like to point out that...; **se faire r.** to attract attention; *Fam* **remarque, il n'est pas le seul** he's not the only one, mind you (**b**) *(dire)* to remark, to observe
2 se remarquer *vpr (tache, cicatrice)* to show

remballer [rɑ̃bale] *vt (marchandises)* to repack; *Fig (compliment)* to keep to oneself

rembarrer [rɑ̃bare] *vt Fam* to snub; **se faire r.** to be snubbed *or* rebuffed

remblai [rɑ̃blɛ] *nm* embankment

remblayer [53] [rɑ̃bleje] *vt (route, voie ferrée)* to bank (up)

rembobiner [rɑ̃bɔbine] **1** *vt* to rewind
2 se rembobiner *vpr* to rewind

rembourrage [rɑ̃buraʒ] *nm (action, matériau)* stuffing

rembourrer [rɑ̃bure] *vt* to stuff

remboursable [rɑ̃bursabl] *adj (emprunt)* repayable; *(frais)* refundable

remboursement [rɑ̃bursəmɑ̃] *nm (d'un emprunt)* repayment; *(de frais)* refund

rembourser [rɑ̃burse] *vt* (**a**) *(frais, achat)* to refund; *(emprunt, dettes)* to pay back; **ce médicament est remboursé à 70%** 70% of the cost of this medicine will be refunded (**b**) *(personne)* to pay back; **r. qn de qch** to reimburse sb for sth; **se faire r.** to get a refund; *Fam* **remboursez!** *(au théâtre)* give us our money back!

rembrunir [rɑ̃brynir] **se rembrunir** *vpr (visage, personne)* to become sullen

remède [rəmɛd] *nm* remedy, cure (**contre** for); **r. de bonne femme** old wives' remedy; **r. de cheval** kill-or-cure remedy

remédier [66] [rəmedje] **remédier à** *vt ind (erreur, situation)* to remedy; *(inconvénient)* to make up for

remembrement [rəmɑ̃brəmɑ̃] *nm (de terres)* grouping of land

remémorer [rəmemɔre] **se remémorer** *vpr* to remember

remerciement [rəmɛrsimɑ̃] *nm* **lettre de r.** thank-you letter; **remerciements** thanks; *(dans un livre)* acknowledgements

remercier [66] [rəmɛrsje] *vt* (**a**) *(dire merci à)* to thank (**de** *ou* **pour** for); **r. qn d'avoir fait qch** to thank sb for doing sth; **(non,) je vous remercie** no, thank you (**b**) *Euph (congédier)* to ask to leave

remettre [47] [rəmɛtr] **1** *vt* (**a**) **r. qch à qn** *(lettre, télégramme, colis)* to deliver sth to sb; *(rapport)* to submit sth to sb; *(démission)* to hand sth in to sb; *(rançon)* to hand sth over to sb; **r. qn à la justice** to turn sb over to the police; **r. son sort entre les mains de qn** to put one's fate in sb's hands
(**b**) *(retarder)* to postpone (**à** to *or* till); **r. qch à plus tard** to put sth off till later
(**c**) *(replacer)* to put back; **r. qch à sa place** *ou* **en place** to put sth back in its place; **r. qch en cause** *ou* **en question** to call sth into question; **r. qn en liberté** to set sb free
(**d**) *(reconnaître)* **je ne vous remets pas** I can't place you
(**e**) *(dans un état antérieur)* **r. une montre à l'heure** to set a watch to the right time; **r. qch à zéro** to reset sth to zero; **r. qch en marche** *(moteur, machine)* to restart sth; **r. qch en ordre** *(dossiers, maison)* to tidy sth (up)
(**f**) *(rétablir la santé de)* to make better
(**g**) *(manteau, chapeau)* to put back on
(**h**) *(chauffage, télévision)* to turn on again; *(disque, chanson)* to put on again
(**i**) *(ajouter)* *(sel, eau)* to add (**dans** to)
(**j**) *Fam (recommencer)* **on remet ça?** how about another (one)?; **tu ne vas pas r. ça!** you're not going to start that again, are you?; *Belg* **r. le couvert** to start again
(**k**) *Belg & Suisse (céder)* to sell
2 se remettre *vpr* (**a**) *(dans un endroit, dans un état)* **se r. debout** to get up again; **se r. au lit** to go back to bed; **se r. en cause** *ou* **en question** to question oneself; **le temps s'est remis au beau** the weather has brightened up again
(**b**) *(recommencer)* **se r. à qch/à faire qch** to start sth/doing sth again; **se r. au français/au tennis** to take up French/tennis again
(**c**) *(après une maladie, un choc)* to recover (**de** from); *Fig* **voyons, remettez-vous!** come on, pull yourself together!
(**d**) *(faire confiance)* **je m'en remets à vous** I'll leave it to you, it's up to you
(**e**) *(se placer)* **se r. entre les mains de qn** to place oneself in sb's hands
(**f**) *Fam (renouer)* **se r. ensemble** to get back together again

réminiscence [reminisɑ̃s] *nf (souvenir imprécis)* vague recollection

remise [rəmiz] *nf* (**a**) *(dans son lieu ou son état d'origine)* **r. en état** *(d'une maison)* restoration; **r. à neuf** *(d'une machine)* reconditioning; **r. en question** *ou* **cause** questioning (**b**) *(d'une lettre)* delivery (**à** to); *(d'une rançon)* handing over (**à** to); **r. des prix** prize-giving (**c**) *(réduction)* **r. de peine** reduction of sentence (**d**) *(rabais)* discount; **faire une r. à qn** to give sb a discount (**e**) *(appentis)* shed (**f**) *Ordinat* **r. à blanc** *(d'une disquette)* reformatting; **r. en forme** *(de texte)* reformatting

remiser [rəmize] *vt* to put away

rémission [remisjɔ̃] *nf* (**a**) *(d'un péché)* remission; *Fig* **sans r.** *(travailler)* unremittingly; *(punir)* mercilessly (**b**) *(d'une maladie)* remission; **être en r.** to be in remission

remmener [46] [rɑ̃mne] *vt* to take back; **r. qn en voiture** to drive sb back

remodeler [39] [rəmɔdle] *vt* (**a**) *(refaçonner)* to remodel (**b**) *(réorganiser)* to restructure

remontant [rəmɔ̃tɑ̃] *nm* tonic

remontée [rəmɔ̃te] *nf* (**a**) *(d'une pente)* ascent (**b**) *(dans un classement sportif)* recovery (**c**) *(des eaux)* rising (**d**) *(pour skieurs)* **r. mécanique** ski lift

remonte-pente *(pl* **remonte-pentes***)* [rəmɔ̃tpɑ̃t] *nm* ski-tow

remonter [rəmɔ̃te] **1** *vt* (**a**) *(pente, escalier)* *(en s'éloignant)* to go up again, to climb back up; *(en s'approchant)* to come up again, to climb back up; **r. la rue** to go/come up the street; **r. la rivière** to go upstream (**b**) *(hausser)* *(étagère, poster)* to move up; *(pantalon, jupe)* to hitch up; *(manche, chaussettes)* to pull up; *(fermeture éclair)* to do up; *(vitre de voiture)* to wind up (**c**) *(porter en haut)* to take/bring up (**d**) *(horloge, montre)* to wind (up) (**e**) *(revigorer)* *(personne)* to cheer up (**f**) *(pièces d'une machine)* to reassemble

2 *vi* (**a**) *(dans l'espace)* *(personne)* to go/come back up; *(marée)* to flow; *(baromètre)* to rise again; *(route, ruelle)* to climb again; *(jupe)* to ride up; **r. en voiture** to get back in one's car; *Fig* **r. dans les sondages** to improve one's position in the polls (**b**) *(dans le temps)* to go back (**à** to); **ça remonte à loin** *(tradition)* it goes back a long way; *(épisode)* it was a long time ago (**c**) *(actions, monnaie, température)* to go up again, to rise again

3 se remonter *vpr (moralement)* to cheer up; *(physiquement)* to recover one's strength

remontoir [rəmɔ̃twar] *nm* winder

remontrance [rəmɔ̃trɑ̃s] *nf* remonstrance; **faire des remontrances à qn** to remonstrate with sb

remontrer [rəmɔ̃tre] **1** *vt* **en r. à qn** to show one knows better than sb

2 se remontrer *vpr* to show oneself again

remords [rəmɔr] *nm* remorse; **avoir du** *ou* **des r.** to feel remorse; **je n'ai aucun r.!** I'm not the slightest bit sorry!

remorque [rəmɔrk] *nf* (**a**) *(véhicule)* trailer (**b**) **prendre qch en r.** to take sth in tow; *Fig* **être à la r.** to lag behind

remorquer [rəmɔrke] *vt (voiture, bateau)* to tow; *(train)* to pull

remorqueur [rəmɔrkœr] *nm* tug(boat)

rémoulade [remulad] *nf Culin* **(sauce) r.** remoulade (sauce) *(mayonnaise sauce with mustard and herbs)*

rémouleur [remulœr] *nm* knife grinder

remous [rəmu] *nm (d'une rivière)* eddy; *(d'un bateau)* wash; *Fig (de la foule)* ripple; *Fig* **provoquer** *ou* **faire des r.** to cause a stir

rempailler [rɑ̃paje] *vt* to reseat

rempart [rɑ̃par] *nm* rampart; **remparts** walls; **faire un r. de son corps à qn** to shield sb with one's body

rempiler [rɑ̃pile] *vi Fam Hum* to sign up again

remplaçable [rɑ̃plasabl] *adj* replaceable

remplaçant, -e [rɑ̃plasɑ̃, -ɑ̃t] *nm,f (personne)* replacement; *(d'un médecin)* locum (tenens); *(d'un enseignant)* *Br* supply teacher, *Am & Ir* substitute teacher

remplacement [rɑ̃plasmɑ̃] *nm* replacement; **en r. de qn/qch** in place of sb/sth; **faire des remplacements** *(professeur)* to work as *Br* a supply teacher *or Am & Ir* a substitute teacher

remplacer [16] [rɑ̃plase] *vt* (**a**) *(être à la place de)* to take the place of, to replace; *(professionnellement)* to stand in for; **se faire r.** to get somebody to stand in *or* cover for one (**b**) *(substituer)* to replace (**par** with)

remplir [rɑ̃plir] **1** *vt* (**a**) *(récipient)* to fill (**de** with); *(espace, trou)* to fill (in); *Fig (journée, vie)* to take up; **r. qn de joie/colère** to fill sb with joy/anger (**b**) *(formulaire)* to fill in *or* out; *(chèque)* to write, to make out; *(page)* to fill (**c**) *(promesse, rôle, contrat)* to fulfil; *(devoirs, tâche)* to carry out

2 se remplir *vpr* to fill up (**de** with); *Fig* **se r. les poches** to line one's pockets

remplissage [rɑ̃plisaʒ] *nm* (**a**) *(d'un tonneau, d'un réservoir)* filling (up); *(d'un trou, d'un espace)* filling (in) (**b**) *Péj* **faire du r.** *(dans un texte)* to pad

remplumer [rɑ̃plyme] **se remplumer** *vpr Fam* (**a**) *(financièrement)* to be in funds again (**b**) *(grossir)* to put some weight back on

rempocher [rɑ̃pɔʃe] *vt* to put back in one's pocket

remporter [rɑ̃pɔrte] *vt* (**a**) *(reprendre)* to take back *or* away (**b**) *(gagner)* *(prix, victoire)* to win; *(succès)* to achieve; *Fig* **r. tous les suffrages** to meet with universal approval

rempoter [rɑ̃pɔte] *vt* to repot

remuant, -e [rəmɥɑ̃, -ɑ̃t] *adj* hyperactive

remue-ménage [rəmymenaʒ] *nm inv* commotion; **faire du r.** to cause a commotion *or* stir

remuer [rəmɥe] **1** *vt* (**a**) *(partie du corps)* to move around; *(lèvres)* to move; **r. la queue** *(chien)* to wag its tail; **r. les oreilles** *(chien)* to waggle its ears (**b**) *(mobilier, objets)* to move, to shift (**c**) *(sauce, café)* to stir; *(salade)* to toss; *(terre)* to turn over; *Fig (vieux souvenirs, passé)* to rake up; **r. ciel et terre pour faire qch** to move heaven and earth to do sth (**d**) *(émouvoir)* to move

2 *vi (personne)* to move; *(queue)* to wag; **arrête de r.!** don't fidget!, keep still!

3 se remuer *vpr* (**a**) *(bouger)* to move (**b**) *Fam (être actif)* to have plenty of get-up-and-go; **remue-toi un peu!** get up off your backside!

rémunérateur, -trice [remyneratœr, -tris] *adj (travail)* remunerative; *(placement)* interest-bearing

rémunération [remynerasjɔ̃] *nf* remuneration (**de** for); *(salaire)* pay

rémunérer [34] [remynere] *vt (personne)* to pay; *(travail, services)* to pay for; **travail bien/mal rémunéré** well-paid/badly-paid job

renâcler [rənakle] *vi (personne)* to balk (**à faire** at doing); **il a accepté en renâclant** he accepted grudgingly

renaissance [rənɛsɑ̃s] *nf* (**a**) *(d'une personne)* rebirth (**b**) *(des lettres, des arts)* renaissance; **la R.** the Renaissance

renaître [50a] [rənɛtr] *vi* (**a**) *(personne)* to be born again; **r. de ses cendres** to rise again from its ashes (**b**) *(industrie, arts, espoir)* to revive; *Litt (printemps, plantes)* to return; *(nature)* to reawaken; **faire r. la confiance** to restore confidence

rénal, -e, -aux, -ales [renal, -o] *adj* renal

renard [rənar] *nm* (**a**) *(animal)* fox; *Fig* **c'est un vieux r.** he's a sly old fox (**b**) *(fourrure)* fox (fur)

renardeau, -x [rənardo] *nm* fox cub

rencard, rencart [rãkar] = rancard

renchérir [rãʃerir] *vi* (**a**) *(prix, loyers, marchandises)* to go up (**b**) *(dire ou faire plus)* to go one better (**sur** than)

rencontre [rãkɔ̃tr] *nf* (**a**) *(de personnes)* meeting; *(de routes, de cours d'eau)* junction; **faire la r. de qn** to meet sb; **faire de mauvaises rencontres** to meet the wrong kind of people; **aller à la r. de qn** to go to meet sb (**b**) *(d'athlétisme)* meeting; *(match)* game, *Br* match

rencontrer [rãkɔ̃tre] **1** *vt* (**a**) *(personne)* to meet; **r. qn par hasard** to bump into *or* run into sb (**b**) *(trouver)* to come across; *(opposition, difficulté)* to encounter, to come up against
2 se rencontrer *vpr* (**a**) *(gens, rivières)* to meet (**b**) *Hum (être d'accord)* **les grands esprits se rencontrent** great minds think alike

rendement [rãdmã] *nm* (**a**) *(d'une terre, d'un impôt)* yield; *(d'un investissement)* return, yield (**b**) *(de travailleurs, d'une usine, d'une machine)* output; *(d'un ordinateur)* throughput; **travailler à plein r.** *(usine)* to work at full capacity

rendez-vous [rãdevu] *nm inv* (**a**) *(rencontre)* appointment; *(amoureux)* date; **avoir r. chez le médecin** to have an appointment with the doctor; **donner r. à qn** to arrange to meet sb; **prendre r. avec qn/chez le médecin** to make an appointment with sb/with the doctor (**b**) *(endroit)* meeting place

rendormir [29] [rãdɔrmir] **se rendormir** *vpr* to fall asleep again

rendre [rãdr] **1** *vt* (**a**) *(objet emprunté)* to give back, to return (**à** to); *(achat)* to take back (**à** to); *(copies, cadeau)* to give back (**à** to); *(otages)* to hand back (**à** to); **r. sa liberté à qn** to set sb free
(**b**) *(rembourser)* to pay back
(**c**) *(en retour)* **je lui ai rendu son compliment/son invitation** I returned his compliment/his invitation; **r. la monnaie à qn** to give sb his/her change; *Fig* **r. à qn la monnaie de sa pièce** to get even with sb; **r. les armes** *(soldats)* to surrender; *Fig* to give up; *Fig* **elle l'aime, mais il ne le lui rend pas** she loves him, but the feeling isn't mutual
(**d**) *(vomir)* to bring up
(**e**) *(son)* to make; *(jus, eau)* to release
(**f**) *Jur (jugement, verdict)* to deliver; **r. la justice** to dispense justice
(**g**) *(sens, nuance)* to render, to express
(**h**) *(faire devenir)* to make; **r. qn triste** to make sb sad; **r. qn fou** to drive sb mad; **r. qn aveugle/sourd** to make sb go blind/deaf; *Fig* **l'amour l'a rendu aveugle** he was blinded by love
2 *vi* (**a**) *(terre)* to be productive; *(placement)* to yield (**b**) *(vomir)* to vomit
3 se rendre *vpr* (**a**) *(aller)* **se r. à** to go to; **se r. chez qn** to call on sb
(**b**) *(se soumettre)* to give oneself up
(**c**) *(devenir)* **se r. malade/utile** to make oneself ill/useful
(**d**) *(locutions)* **se r. compte de qch/que...** to realize sth/that...; *Fam* **tu te rends compte!** who'd have believed it!; **se r. à la raison** to see reason

rendu, -e [rãdy] *adj* (**a**) *(arrivé)* **être r.** to have arrived (**b**) *Vieilli (fatigué)* tired out

rêne [rɛn] *nf* rein; *Fig* **c'est lui qui tient les rênes** he's the one who's really in charge

renégat, -e [rənega, -at] *nm,f* renegade

renfermé, -e [rãfɛrme] **1** *adj (personne)* withdrawn
2 *nm* **odeur de r.** musty smell; **sentir le r.** to smell musty

renfermer [rãfɛrme] **1** *vt (contenir)* to contain
2 se renfermer *vpr* to withdraw into oneself

renflé, -e [rãfle] *adj* bulging

renflement [rãfləmã] *nm* bulge

renflouer [rãflue] *vt* (**a**) *(bateau échoué)* to refloat (**b**) *(entreprise, personne)* to bail out

renfoncement [rãfɔ̃smã] *nm* recess

renforcement [rãfɔrsəmã] *nm (d'une poutre, d'une armée, d'une équipe)* strengthening, reinforcement; *(de la sécurité)* tightening up

renforcer [16] [rãfɔrse] **1** *vt* (**a**) *(poutre, armée, équipe)* to strengthen, to reinforce; *(sécurité)* to tighten up (**b**) *(couleur, éclairage)* to intensify (**c**) *(crainte)* to heighten; *(impression, convictions)* to strengthen; **r. qn dans une opinion** to confirm sb in an opinion
2 se renforcer *vpr (tendance, impression, convictions)* to grow

renfort [rãfɔr] *nm* **renforts** reinforcements; *Fig* **demander du r.** to ask for help; **à grand r. de qch** with the help of lots of sth

renfrogné, -e [rãfrɔɲe] *adj* scowling

renfrogner [rãfrɔɲe] **se renfrogner** *vpr* to scowl

rengager [45] [rãgaʒe] **1** *vt (personnel)* to take on again; *(combat)* to renew; *(conversation, partie, débat)* to pick up again
2 se rengager *vpr Mil* to re-enlist

rengaine [rãgɛn] *nf* tune; *Fam Fig* **c'est toujours la même r.** it's (always) the same old story

rengainer [rãgɛne] *vt (épée)* to sheathe; *Fig (compliment)* to keep to oneself

rengorger [45] [rãgɔrʒe] **se rengorger** *vpr* to strut

reniement [rənimã] *nm (d'une foi)* denial; *(d'idées, d'une action)* repudiation

renier [66] [rənje] **1** *vt (fils, racines)* to disown; *(foi)* to deny; *(action, idées)* to repudiate
2 se renier *vpr* to repudiate one's opinions

reniflement [rəniflmã] *nm* (**a**) *(action)* sniffing (**b**) *(bruit)* sniff

renifler [rənifle] **1** *vi* to sniff
2 *vt (fleur)* to sniff (at); *(tabac à priser)* to sniff (up); *Fig (bonne affaire, embrouille)* to sniff out

renipper [rənipe] *Can* **1** *vt (rénover) (maison, pièce)* to renovate, to do up
2 se renipper *vpr* to smarten oneself up

renne [rɛn] *nm* reindeer

renom [rənɔ̃] *nm* renown; **de r.** famous, renowned; **de grand r.** extremely famous

renommé, -e [rənɔme] *adj* renowned, famous (**pour** for)

renommée [rənɔme] *nf* fame, renown; **un musicien de r. internationale** a world-famous musician, a musician of international repute *or* renown

renommer [rənɔme] *vt Ordinat (fichier)* to rename

renoncement [rənɔ̃smã] *nm* renunciation (**à** of)

renoncer [16] [rənɔ̃se] **renoncer à** *vt ind (droit, projet, activité)* to give up, to abandon; *(vacances, voyage)* to sacrifice, to forego; **r. à faire qch** to give up doing sth; *(avant d'avoir commencé)* to give up the idea of doing sth; **je renonce!** I give up!

renonciation [rənɔ̃sjasjɔ̃] *nf* renunciation (**à** of)

renoncule [rənɔ̃kyl] *nf* buttercup

renouer [rənwe] **1** *vt* (**a**) *(ruban, lacet)* to tie (up) again; *(cravate)* to do up again (**b**) *(conversation, relations)* to resume; *(amitié)* to renew
  2 renouer avec *vt ind* **r. avec qn** to take up with sb again; **r. avec qch** *(tradition)* to revive sth; *(habitude)* to go back to sth

renouveau, -x [rənuvo] *nm* revival

renouvelable [rənuvlabl] *adj (contrat, énergie)* renewable; *(expérience)* repeatable

renouveler [42] [rənuvle] **1** *vt* (**a**) *(stock, équipement)* to renew, to replace; *(eau)* to change (**b**) *(passeport, abonnement, demande)* to renew; *(expérience)* to repeat (**c**) *(style)* to change
  2 se renouveler *vpr* (**a**) *(cellule)* to be renewed (**b**) *(se produire de nouveau)* to recur, to happen again (**c**) *(changer)* to change; **un artiste/auteur qui ne se renouvelle pas** an artist/author whose style never changes

renouvellement [rənuvɛlmã] *nm* (**a**) *(de stock, d'équipement)* replacement, renewal (**b**) *(d'un style)* change (**c**) *(d'un traité, d'un contrat)* renewal

rénovateur, -trice [renɔvatœr, -tris] **1** *adj* reforming
  2 *nm,f* reformer

rénovation [renɔvasjɔ̃] *nf* (**a**) *(d'un bâtiment, du mobilier)* renovation; **en (cours de) r.** undergoing renovation (**b**) *(d'une institution)* updating, reform

rénover [renɔve] *vt* (**a**) *(bâtiment, mobilier)* to renovate (**b**) *(institution)* to update, to reform

renseigné, -e [rɑ̃seɲe] *adj* **bien-/mal r.** well-/ill-informed

renseignement [rɑ̃seɲəmã] *nm* (**a**) *(précision)* piece of information; **renseignements** information; **pour tout r....** for information...; **prendre des renseignements sur qn/qch** to make enquiries about sb/sth; **aller aux renseignements** to go and make enquiries (**b**) *Tél* **les renseignements (téléphoniques)** *Br* directory enquiries, *Am* information (**c**) **les renseignements généraux** = secret intelligence branch of the French police, *Br* ≃ the Special Branch, *Am* ≃ the FBI

renseigner [rɑ̃seɲe] **1** *vt* **r. qn (sur qch)** to give sb some information (about sth), to inform sb (about sth); **on vous a mal renseigné** you have been misinformed
  2 se renseigner *vpr* to make enquiries; *(sur un point précis)* to find out (**sur** about)

rentabiliser [rɑ̃tabilize] *vt* to make profitable

rentabilité [rɑ̃tabilite] *nf* profitability

rentable [rɑ̃tabl] *adj* profitable

rente [rɑ̃t] *nf* (**a**) *(revenu)* **rentes** private income (**b**) *(pension)* annuity, pension; **r. viagère** life annuity (**c**) *(emprunt d'État)* (government) loan

rentier, -ère [rɑ̃tje, -ɛr] *nm,f* person of private means

rentré, -e [rɑ̃tre] *adj* (**a**) *(yeux)* sunken (**b**) *(colère)* suppressed

rentre-dedans [rɑ̃tdədɑ̃] *nm inv Fam* **faire du r. à qn** to come on to sb

rentrée [rɑ̃tre] *nf* (**a**) *(retour)* return; **la r. (des classes)** the start of the new school year; **r. parlementaire** reopening of Parliament; **la r. sociale** the return to work (**b**) *(d'argent)* **attendre une r. d'argent** to expect some money

La rentrée
The time of the year when children go back to school – in September – has considerable cultural significance in France. Coming after the long summer break or "grandes vacances", it is the time when academic, political, social and commercial activity begins again in earnest.

rentrer [rɑ̃tre] **1** *vi* (*aux* **être**) (**a**) *(entrer de nouveau)* *(en s'éloignant)* to go in again; *(en s'approchant)* to come in again; *(entrer)* to go/come in, to enter; **rentre!** come in!
  (**b**) *(à la maison)* to go/come back home, to return home; **r. de vacances/de Paris** to come back from holiday/from Paris; **r. en France/à Paris** to return to France/to Paris; **r. dans son pays** to go back to one's own country; **r. tard/tôt** to come or get home late/early; **en rentrant chez moi** on my way home; **en rentrant de l'école** on my/his/*etc* way home from school
  (**c**) *(reprendre ses occupations)* *(école)* to re-open; *(élève, professeur)* to go back
  (**d**) *(tenir)* *(objets)* to go in, to fit (in); **je ne rentre plus dans ce pantalon!** I can't get into these trousers any more!
  (**e**) *(pénétrer)* to get in; **r. dans qch** to get into sth
  (**f**) *(être inclus)* **r. dans une catégorie** to fall into a category
  (**g**) *(argent)* to come in
  (**h**) *(recouvrer)* **r. dans ses frais** to recover one's expenses
  (**i**) **r. dans** *(sujet: voiture)* to crash into; *(sujet: piéton)* to bang into; *Fam Fig* **elle m'est rentrée dedans** *ou* **dans le chou** she laid into me
  2 *vt* (*aux* **avoir**) (**a**) *(linge, troupeau)* *(en venant)* to bring in; *(en allant)* to take in (**b**) *(introduire, mettre)* to put in; **r. qch dans qch** to put sth into sth (**c**) *(train d'atterrissage)* to retract, to raise; **r. ses griffes** *(chat)* to retract its claws; *Fig* to draw in one's claws; **r. le ventre** to pull one's stomach in (**d**) *(colère, larmes)* to stifle

renversant, -e [rɑ̃vɛrsɑ̃, -ɑ̃t] *adj Fam* astounding

renverse [rɑ̃vɛrs] **à la renverse** *adv* **partir** *ou* **tomber à la r.** to fall backwards; *Fig* **j'ai failli tomber à la r.** you could have knocked me over with a feather

renversé, e [rɑ̃vɛrse] *adj* (**a**) *(à l'envers)* *(image)* reversed (**b**) *(tombé)* overturned (**c**) *Fam (stupéfait)* staggered

renversement [rɑ̃vɛrsəmã] *nm* (**a**) *(d'une tendance, des rôles)* reversal; *(d'opinions)* (dramatic) shift; **r. de situation** reversal of the situation (**b**) *(d'un gouvernement)* overthrow

renverser [rɑ̃vɛrse] **1** *vt* (**a**) *(tendance, rôles)* to reverse; *(ordre)* to invert; *Fig* **r. la vapeur** to do a U-turn; **r. la situation** to reverse the situation (**b**) *(pencher en arrière)* **r. la tête** to tilt one's head back (**c**) *(faire tomber)* to knock over; *(liquide)* to spill; **se faire r. par une voiture** to be knocked down by a car (**d**) *(gouvernement)* to overthrow (**e**) *Fam (stupéfier)* to stagger
  2 se renverser *vpr* (**a**) *(récipient)* to fall over; *(véhicule)* to overturn (**b**) *(personne)* **se r. en arrière** to lean back

renvoi [rɑ̃vwa] *nm* (**a**) *(de lettres, de marchandises, de colis)* return, sending back (**b**) *(d'employés)* dismissal, *Br* sacking; *(d'un élève)* expulsion (**c**) *(ajournement)* postponement; *Jur* adjournment (**d**) *(dans un texte)* cross-reference (**e**) *Jur (devant une autre juridiction)* transfer (**devant** to) (**f**) *(éructation)* burp, belch; **avoir des renvois** to burp, to belch

renvoyer [33] [rɑ̃vwaje] **1** *vt* (**a**) *(au point de départ)* *(personne)* to send back; *(cadeau, lettre)* to send

back, to return; *(ballon)* to throw back; *(balle de tennis)* to return (**b**) *(employé)* to dismiss, *Br* to sack; *(élève)* to expel; *(visiteur)* to send away (**c**) *(son)* to echo; *(chaleur, lumière)* to reflect (**d**) *(ajourner)* to postpone; *Jur* to adjourn (**e**) *(lecteur)* to refer (**à** to); *Ordinat* to cross-refer (**f**) *Jur (devant une autre juridiction)* to transfer (**devant** to)
  2 *vi Can* to vomit

réorganisation [reɔrganizasjɔ̃] *nf* reorganization

réorganiser [reɔrganize] **1** *vt* to reorganize
  2 se réorganiser *vpr* to get reorganized

réorienter [reɔrjɑ̃te] *vt* to reorientate; *Univ* to put on a different course

réouverture [reuvɛrtyr] *nf* reopening

repaire [rəpɛr] *nm (d'animaux)* den, lair; *(de malfrats)* haunt

repaître [50c] [rəpɛtr] *Litt* **1** *vt* **r. ses yeux de qch** to feast one's eyes on sth
  2 se repaître *vpr* (**a**) *(manger à satiété)* to eat one's fill (**b**) *Fig* **se r. de qch** to revel in sth

répandre [repɑ̃dr] **1** *vt* (**a**) *(renverser) (accidentellement)* to spill; *(volontairement)* to spread (**b**) *(émettre) (lumière)* to shed; *(odeur, chaleur)* to give off (**c**) *(larmes, sang)* to shed (**d**) *(rumeur, terreur, doctrine)* to spread
  2 se répandre *vpr* (**a**) *(liquide)* to spill (**b**) *(odeur, chaleur)* to spread (**c**) *(rumeur, opinion, pratique)* to become widespread (**d**) *(foule, touristes)* to spill (**dans** into) (**e**) **se r. en excuses** to apologize profusely

répandu, -e [repɑ̃dy] *adj (commun)* widespread

réparable [reparabl] *adj* (**a**) *(chaussure, machine)* repairable (**b**) *(erreur)* which can be put right; *(perte financière)* which can be made up

reparaître [20] [rəparɛtr] *vi* to reappear

réparateur, -trice [reparatœr, -tris] **1** *adj (sommeil)* refreshing
  2 *nm,f* repairman, *f* repairwoman

réparation [reparasjɔ̃] *nf* (**a**) *(action)* repairing, mending; *(résultat)* repair; **faire des réparations** to do repairs (**b**) *(dédommagement)* reparation; **demander r. (de qch)** to seek redress (for sth)

réparer [repare] *vt* (**a**) *(toit, appareil, chaussures)* to repair, to mend; *(déchirure, accroc)* to mend (**b**) *(faute)* to make amends for; *(erreur)* to put right, to rectify; *(dommage)* to make good

reparler [rəparle] *vi* to speak again; **r. à qn** to speak to sb again; **elle ne lui a pas reparlé depuis** she hasn't spoken to him since; **r. de qch** to speak about sth again; **on en reparlera** we'll talk about it later

repartie, répartie [reparti] *nf* retort; **avoir l'esprit de r., avoir de la r.** to be good at repartee

repartir [64a] [rəpartir] *vi (voyageur, train)* to set off again (**pour** to); *(machine)* to start (up) again; *Fam* **c'est reparti, ils ont encore mis la musique à fond!** they're at it again, they've put their music on full blast!; *Fam* **c'est reparti comme en quarante!** here we go!

répartir [repartir] **1** *vt* (**a**) *(tâches, argent, vivres)* to divide (**entre** between); *(responsabilités)* to allocate (**entre** between); *(frais)* to share (**entre** between) (**b**) *(dans le temps)* to spread (out) (**sur** over) (**c**) *(classifier)* to divide (**en** into) (**d**) *(poids, charge)* to distribute
  2 se répartir *vpr* (**a**) *(se diviser)* to split up (**en** into)

(**b**) *(se classer)* to be divided (**en** into) (**c**) **se r. qch** to divide sth up

répartition [repartisjɔ̃] *nf* (**a**) *(de la population, du poids)* distribution (**b**) *(des tâches, d'argent, de vivres)* distribution (**entre** between); *(des dépenses, des responsabilités)* allocation (**entre** to) (**c**) *(dans le temps)* spreading (**sur** over)

repas [rəpɑ] *nm* meal; **prendre un r.** to have a meal; **r. d'affaires** business lunch/dinner; **r. chaud/froid** hot/cold meal; **r. de noce** wedding breakfast

repassage [rəpɑsaʒ] *nm* ironing; **faire du r.** to do some ironing

repasser [rəpase] **1** *vi* (**a**) *(passer à nouveau) (aller)* to go by again, to pass by again; *(venir)* to come by again, to pass by again; *(retourner)* to go/come back; **r. chez qn** to drop in on sb again (**b**) *(film)* to be on again
  2 *vt* (**a**) *(vêtement)* to iron (**b**) *(montagne, frontière)* to go across again (**c**) *(cassette, disque)* to play again; *(film)* to show again (**d**) *(leçon)* to go over; **r. qch dans son esprit** to go over sth in one's mind (**e**) *(examen)* to resit (**f**) **r. qch à qn** *(donner à nouveau)* to give sb sth again (**g**) *(au téléphone)* **je vous le repasse** I'll put you back on to him

repêchage [rəpeʃaʒ] *nm* (**a**) *(d'un véhicule, d'un noyé)* fishing out (**b**) *(d'un candidat)* **épreuve de r.** resit; **être reçu au r.** to pass on the resit

repêcher [rəpeʃe] *vt* (**a**) *(retirer de l'eau)* to fish out (**b**) *(candidat)* to let through

repeindre [54] [rəpɛ̃dr] *vt* to repaint

repenser [rəpɑ̃se] **1** *vt (concept)* to rethink
  2 repenser à *vt ind* to think again about; **quand j'y repense** when I think back

repenti, -e [rəpɑ̃ti] *adj* repentant, penitent

repentir¹ [rəpɑ̃tir] *nm (remords)* regret

repentir² [64a] **se repentir** *vpr* to repent; **se r. de qch/d'avoir fait qch** to repent of sth/doing sth; *Fig* to regret sth/doing sth

repérage [rəperaʒ] *nm* (**a**) *Ordinat* marking, flagging (**b**) *(d'un lieu de tournage)* recce

répercussion [reperkysjɔ̃] *nf* (**a**) *(du son)* reverberation (**b**) *(conséquence)* repercussion (**sur** on)

répercuter [reperkyte] **1** *vt* (**a**) *(son, lumière)* to reflect (**b**) *(ordre, augmentation)* to pass (**sur** on to)
  2 se répercuter *vpr* (**a**) *(son, lumière)* to be reflected (**b**) *(avoir des conséquences)* **se r. sur** to have repercussions on

repère [rəpɛr] *nm* (**a**) *(point de référence)* mark; *(pour s'orienter)* landmark; *aussi Fig* **point de r.** reference point (**b**) *(dans le temps)* reference point (**c**) *Ordinat* marker, flag

repérer [34] [rəpere] **1** *vt* (**a**) *(marquer) (terrain)* to mark out (**b**) *(trouver) (défaut, endroit)* to locate; *(lieu de tournage)* to recce (**c**) *Fam (apercevoir)* to spot; **se faire r.** to attract attention
  2 se repérer *vpr* to get one's bearings, to find one's way about

répertoire [repɛrtwar] *nm* (**a**) *(liste)* index, list (**b**) *(carnet)* notebook with alphabetical index; **r. à onglets** thumb index (**c**) *Ordinat* directory; **r. central ou principal** main directory; **r. racine** root directory (**d**) *(d'un théâtre, d'un artiste)* repertoire

répertorier [repɛrtɔrje] *vt* to list

répéter [34] [repete] **1** *vt* (**a**) *(redire, refaire)* to repeat (**b**) *(pièce de théâtre, rôle)* to rehearse
  2 *vi (acteur)* to rehearse

3 se répéter *vpr (personne)* to repeat oneself; *(événement)* to recur, to happen again; **l'histoire se répète** history repeats itself

répétitif, -ive [repetitif, -iv] *adj* repetitive

répétition [repetisjɔ̃] *nf* (**a**) *(d'un mot, d'une action, d'un événement)* repetition; **fusil à r.** repeating rifle; **avoir des rhumes à r.** to have one cold after another (**b**) *(d'une pièce de théâtre)* rehearsal; **r. générale** dress rehearsal (**c**) *Ordinat* **fonction de r.** repeat function

repeuplement [rəpœpləmɑ̃] *nm (d'un pays)* repopulation; *(d'un étang)* restocking; *(d'une forêt)* replanting

repeupler [rəpœple] **1** *vt (pays)* to repopulate; *(étang)* to restock; *(forêt)* to replant
    2 se repeupler *vpr (pays)* to be repopulated; *(étang)* to be restocked; *(forêt)* to be replanted

repiquage [rəpikaʒ] *nm* (**a**) *(de plants)* pricking out, planting out (**b**) *(d'un disque, d'une cassette)* taping

repiquer [rəpike] **1** *vt* (**a**) *(plants)* to prick out, to plant out (**b**) *(disque, cassette)* to record (**c**) *Fam (reprendre)* to catch again
    2 *vi Fam* **il y a repiqué** he's been at it again

répit [repi] *nm* respite, breathing space; **sans r.** *(travailler)* without a break, continuously

replacer [16] [rəplase] **1** *vt* (**a**) *(remettre à sa place)* to put back; **r. les évènements dans leur contexte** to put events into their context (**b**) *Can (reconnaître)* to recognize
    2 se replacer *vpr (trouver un emploi)* to find (oneself) a new job

replanter [rəplɑ̃te] *vt* to replant

replâtrer [rəplɑtre] *vt* (**a**) *(mur)* to replaster (**b**) *Péj* to patch up

replet, -ète [rəplɛ, -ɛt] *adj (personne)* podgy; *(visage)* chubby

repli [rəpli] *nm* (**a**) *(d'une armée)* retreat, withdrawal (**b**) *(de la monnaie, des prix)* fall (**c**) *(d'un vêtement, de la peau, d'un terrain)* fold; *(d'une rivière)* bend

replier [66] [rəplije] **1** *vt* (**a**) *(objet)* to fold up; *(lame de couteau)* to fold away; *(jambes)* to tuck up; *(ailes)* to fold (**b**) *(troupes)* to withdraw
    2 se replier *vpr* (**a**) *(objet)* to fold up; *Fig* **se r. sur soi-même** to withdraw into oneself (**b**) *(troupes)* to retreat, to withdraw

réplique [replik] *nf* (**a**) *(réponse)* retort, rejoinder; **sans r.** unanswerable (**b**) *(d'un acteur)* line(s); **donner la r. à qn** to play opposite sb (**c**) *(copie)* replica; *(sosie)* double

répliquer [replike] **1** *vt* **r. que** to reply that; **je lui ai répliqué que...** I replied that...
    2 *vi* to reply; *(avec impertinence)* to answer back; **r. à qn** to answer sb back

replonger [45] [rəplɔ̃ʒe] **1** *vt aussi Fig* to plunge back (**dans** into)
    2 *vi* (**a**) *(plonger à nouveau)* to dive in again; *Fig* **r. dans l'alcoolisme/la délinquance** to relapse into alcoholism/delinquency (**b**) *Fam (délinquant)* to reoffend
    3 se replonger *vpr* **se r. dans qch** to immerse oneself in sth again

répondant [repɔ̃dɑ̃] *nm Fam* **avoir du r.** to have plenty of money stashed away

répondeur [repɔ̃dœr] *nm* **r. (automatique** *ou* **téléphonique)** (telephone) answering machine, answerphone

répondre [repɔ̃dr] **1** *vt* to answer, to reply; **je n'ai rien répondu** I made no reply
    2 répondre à *vt ind* (**a**) *(personne, lettre, question)* to answer, to reply to; *(salut)* to return; *(accusation)* to answer; **elle n'a pas encore répondu** she hasn't answered yet; **r. par un sourire** to answer with a smile; *Mil* **r. à l'appel** to answer the roll (**b**) *(téléphone, porte)* to answer; **laisse, je vais r.!** leave it, I'll get it!; **ça ne répond pas** there's no answer (**c**) *(amour)* to return (**d**) *(besoin, critères)* to meet; **ne pas r. à l'attente de qn** to fall short of sb's expectations (**e**) **les freins ne répondent plus** the brakes aren't responding any more
    3 répondre de *vt ind* to answer for; **j'en réponds** I guarantee it; **je ne réponds de rien** I'm promising nothing
    4 se répondre *vpr (personnes)* to answer each other

réponse [repɔ̃s] *nf* (**a**) *(à une question, à une lettre)* answer, reply (**à** to); *(à une offre d'emploi)* reply (**à** to); *Fig (solution)* answer (**à** to); **avoir r. à tout** to have an answer for everything (**b**) *(réaction)* response (**c**) *Ordinat* answering; **r. automatique** unattended answering; **temps de r.** response time

report [rəpɔr] *nm (de notes, de corrections)* transfer (**sur** to) (**b**) *(d'un rendez-vous)* postponement (**c**) *(en comptabilité)* carrying forward (**d**) *(dans une élection)* **r. de voix (sur)** transfer (to)

reportage [rəpɔrtaʒ] *nm* (**a**) *(article, émission)* report (**b**) *(activité)* reporting

reporter¹ [rəpɔrtɛr] *nm* reporter; **r.-cameraman** film reporter; **r.-photographe** photojournalist

reporter² [rəpɔrte] **1** *vt* (**a**) *(objet)* to take back, to return (**b**) *(affection)* to transfer (**sur** to) (**c**) *(différer)* **r. qch à plus tard** to postpone sth *or* put sth off until later (**d**) *(en comptabilité)* to carry forward (**e**) *(notes, corrections)* to transfer (**sur** to) (**f**) *(dans une élection)* **r. sa voix sur qn** to transfer one's vote to sb
    2 se reporter *vpr* (**a**) *(se référer)* **se r. à** *(document)* to refer to (**b**) **se r. sur** *(sujet: colère, affection)* to be transferred to

repos [rəpo] *nm* (**a**) *(détente)* rest; **un mois de r.** a month's rest; **prendre du r.** to rest; **le r. éternel** eternal rest (**b**) *(tranquillité)* peace; **ce n'est pas de tout r.!** it's not exactly restful! (**c**) *Mil* **r.!** (stand) at ease!

reposant, -e [rəpozɑ̃, -ɑ̃t] *adj* restful, relaxing

reposé, -e [rəpoze] *adj* rested, refreshed

repose-pied [rəpozpje] *nm inv* footrest

reposer [rəpoze] **1** *vt* (**a**) *(remettre)* to put back (down), to replace (**b**) *(appuyer)* **r. sa tête contre** *ou* **sur qch** to lean one's head against *or* on sth (**c**) *(détendre) (jambes, esprit)* to rest; **ça le reposera** it'll be a rest for him; **une couleur qui repose les yeux** a colour that is restful to the eyes (**d**) *(question)* to ask again; *(problème)* to bring up again; **r. une question à qn** to ask sb a question again (**e**) *Mil* **reposez arme!** order arms!
    2 *vi* (**a**) *(s'appuyer)* **r. sur** to rest on; *Fig (être basé sur)* to be based on; *(dépendre de)* to depend on (**b**) *(liquide)* to settle; *(pâte à tarte)* to rest (**c**) *(personne décédée)* to lie; **qu'il repose en paix** may he rest in peace
    3 se reposer *vpr* (**a**) *(se relaxer)* to rest; **se r. les yeux/les jambes** to rest one's eyes/legs (**b**) *(question, problème)* to crop up again (**c**) **se r. sur qn/qch** *(s'en remettre à)* to rely on sb/sth

repose-tête [rəpoztɛt] *nm inv* headrest

repoussant, -e [rəpusɑ̃, -ɑ̃t] *adj* repulsive

repousser [rəpuse] **1** *vt* (**a**) *(écarter)* to push aside *or* away; *(en arrière)* to push back (**b**) *(ennemi, attaque, avances)* to repel; *(offre, idée)* to reject, to turn down; *(prétendant)* to rebuff (**c**) *(rendez-vous, réunion)* to postpone, to put off (**à** until) **2** *vi* (*arbre, plante*) to shoot up again; *(cheveux, herbe, feuilles)* to grow again

repoussoir [rəpuswar] *nm (femme)* ugly woman; **servir de r. à qn** to serve as a foil to sb

répréhensible [repreɑ̃sibl] *adj* reprehensible

reprendre [58] [rəprɑ̃dr] **1** *vt* (**a**) *(ville, territoire, fugitif)* to recapture (**à** from)
(**b**) *(se resservir de)* **r. du pain/vin** to take *or* have some more bread/wine; **vous reprendrez bien un peu de thé?** would you like some more tea?
(**c**) *(rechercher) (personne)* to pick up (again)
(**d**) *(récupérer) (objet)* to take back; **r. sa place** *(s'asseoir)* to return to one's seat; *Com* **les articles en solde ne sont ni repris ni échangés** ≃ sale goods are not returnable
(**e**) *(surprendre)* **r. qn à faire qch** to catch sb doing sth again; **on ne m'y reprendra plus!** I won't be caught again!; **que je ne t'y reprenne plus!** don't let me catch you at it again!
(**f**) *(conversation, fonctions, lutte)* to resume, to take up again; *(négociations, relations)* to re-open, to resume; **r. le travail** to return *or* go back to work; **r. connaissance** to regain consciousness; **r. la parole** to speak again; **oui, mais..., reprit-il** yes, but..., he continued; *Fam* **ça le reprend!** he's off again!
(**g**) *(répéter)* to repeat; *(refrain)* to take up
(**h**) *(retoucher) (vêtement)* to alter
(**i**) *(corriger)* to correct
2 *vi* (**a**) *(recommencer) (cours)* to start again; *(pourparlers, hostilités)* to resume, to re-open
(**b**) *(prendre de la vigueur) (affaires)* to recover, to pick up; *(plante)* to pick up
3 se reprendre *vpr* (**a**) *(se ressaisir)* to pull oneself together
(**b**) *(se corriger)* to correct oneself
(**c**) *(recommencer)* **s'y r. à plusieurs fois pour faire qch** to make several attempts at doing sth

repreneur [rəprənœr] *nm* purchaser, buyer

représailles [rəprezaj] *nfpl* reprisals, retaliation; **user de r. contre** to take retaliatory measures *or* to retaliate against; **en r.** in retaliation, as a reprisal

représentant, -e [rəprezɑ̃tɑ̃, -ɑ̃t] *nm,f* representative; **r. de commerce** sales representative

représentatif, -ive [rəprezɑ̃tatif, -iv] *adj* representative (**de** of)

représentation [rəprezɑ̃tasjɔ̃] *nf* (**a**) *(de la réalité, d'un concept)* representation (**b**) *(spectacle)* performance (**c**) *(métier)* commercial travelling (**d**) *Pol* **r. proportionnelle** proportional representation

représentativité [rəprezɑ̃tativite] *nf* representativeness

représenter [rəprezɑ̃te] **1** *vt* (**a**) *(candidat, papiers)* to present again (**b**) *(figurer)* to represent, to depict; **r. qn sous les traits de** to depict sb as (**c**) *(être le porte-parole de)* to represent (**d**) *(constituer, équivaloir à)* to represent; **r. qch pour qn** to represent sth for sb
2 se représenter *vpr* (**a**) *(occasion)* to arise again (**b**) *(s'imaginer)* to imagine (**c**) **se r. à** *(examen)* to retake *or Br* resit; *(poste)* to apply for again; **se r. aux élections** *Br* to stand *or Am* to run for election again

répressif, -ive [represif, -iv] *adj* repressive

répression [represjɔ̃] *nf* repression; *(d'une émeute, d'un abus)* suppression

réprimande [reprimɑ̃d] *nf* reprimand, rebuke; **faire des réprimandes à qn** to reprimand *or* rebuke sb

réprimander [reprimɑ̃de] *vt* to reprimand, to rebuke

réprimer [reprime] *vt* (**a**) *(retenir)* to repress, to suppress (**b**) *(crime, révolte)* to suppress

repris [rəpri] *nm* **r. de justice** ex-prisoner

reprise [rəpriz] *nf* (**a**) *(d'un débat, des hostilités)* resumption; *(des négociations)* re-opening, resumption (**b**) *(des affaires)* recovery; **les grévistes ont voté la r. du travail** the strikers have voted to go back to work; **r. économique** economic recovery (**c**) *(d'une émission télévisée)* repeat (**d**) *(d'un moteur)* pick-up, acceleration (**e**) **à plusieurs/trois reprises** several/three times (**f**) *(raccommodage)* **faire une r. à qch** to mend sth (**g**) *(somme payée à un locataire)* = money paid for fixtures and fittings *(paid to outgoing tenant)*; *(rachat d'un objet d'occasion)* part exchange, trade-in

repriser [rəprize] *vt* to mend

réprobateur, -trice [reprobatœr, -tris] *adj* reproving

réprobation [reprobasjɔ̃] *nf* reproof

reproche [rəprɔʃ] *nm* (**a**) *(remontrance)* reproach; **faire des reproches à qn (sur qch)** to reproach sb (for sth); **sans r.** *(vie, personne)* beyond reproach, blameless (**b**) *(critique)* criticism

reprocher [rəprɔʃe] **1** *vt* **r. qch à qn** to blame *or* reproach sb for sth; **r. à qn de faire qch** to blame *or* reproach sb for doing sth; **je ne vous reproche rien** I'm not blaming you for anything; **qu'est-ce que vous reprochez à ce livre?** what have you got against the book?
2 se reprocher *vpr* **se r. qch** to blame *or* reproach oneself for sth; **tu n'as rien à te r.** you've nothing to blame yourself for; **se r. d'avoir fait qch** to blame oneself for doing sth

reproducteur, -trice [rəprodyktœr, -tris] *adj* reproductive

reproduction [rəprodyksjɔ̃] *nf* (**a**) *(sexuelle)* reproduction (**b**) *(d'un document, d'une image, du son)* reproduction, reproducing; *(copie)* reproduction

reproduire [18] [rəprodɥir] **1** *vt* (**a**) *(son, image, document)* to reproduce; **nous reproduisons ici l'article du Monde** we reprint here the article from Le Monde (**b**) *(acte)* to repeat
2 se reproduire *vpr* (**a**) *(sexuellement)* to reproduce (**b**) *(événement)* to recur, to happen again

reprogrammable [rəprogramabl] *adj Ordinat (touche)* reprogrammable

reprogrammer [rəprograme] *vt Ordinat* to reprogram

réprouver [repruve] *vt* to condemn

reptation [reptasjɔ̃] *nf* crawling

reptile [reptil] *nm* reptile

repu, -e [rəpy] **1** *pp voir* **repaître**
2 *adj* pleasantly full

républicain, -e [republikɛ̃, -ɛn] *adj & nm,f* republican

république [republik] *nf* republic; **r. bananière** banana republic; **la R. centrafricaine** the Central African Republic; *Anciennement* **la R. démocratique allemande** the German Democratic Republic; **la R. dominicaine** the Dominican Republic; *Anciennement* **la R. fédérale d'Allemagne** the Federal Republic of Germany; **la R. Tchèque** the Czech Republic

répudiation [repydjasjɔ̃] *nf* repudiation

répudier [66] [repydje] *vt* to repudiate

répugnance [repyɲɑ̃s] *nf* (**a**) *(aversion)* repugnance, loathing (**pour** for); **avoir de la r. pour qn/qch** to loathe sb/sth (**b**) *(appréhension)* reluctance (**à faire qch** to do sth)

répugnant, -e [repyɲɑ̃, -ɑ̃t] *adj* repulsive

répugner [repyɲe] *vi* (**a**) *(appréhender)* **r. à faire qch** to be reluctant to do sth (**b**) *(être répugnant)* **r. à qn** to be repugnant to sb, to repel sb

répulsion [repylsjɔ̃] *nf* repulsion

réputation [repytasjɔ̃] *nf* reputation; **avoir (une) bonne/mauvaise r.** to have a good/bad reputation; **sa r. de chirurgien** his reputation as a surgeon; **connaître qn de r.** to know sb by reputation; **avoir la r. d'être franc** to have a reputation for being frank

réputé, -e [repyte] *adj* well-known, renowned (**pour** for); **être r. intelligent** to be reputed to be intelligent

requérir [7] [rəkerir] *vt* (**a**) *(solliciter) (faveur)* to ask for, to seek; *(présence, aide)* to request (**b**) *(nécessiter) (explication, soin, patience)* to require, to call for (**c**) *Jur (sentence)* to demand, to call for

requête [rəkɛt] *nf* (**a**) *(demande)* request; *Ordinat* query; **adresser une r. à qn** to make a request to sb (**b**) *Jur* petition

requiem [rekɥijɛm] *nm inv* requiem

requiers, requiert *voir* **requérir**

requin [rəkɛ̃] *nm* shark

requinquer [rəkɛ̃ke] *Fam* **1** *vt* to perk up
2 se requinquer *vpr* to perk up

requis, -e [rəki, -iz] **1** *pp voir* **requérir**
2 *adj* requisite, required; **les conditions requises** the requirements

réquisition [rekizisjɔ̃] *nf* (**a**) *(de vivres, de véhicules)* requisitioning, commandeering (**b**) *Jur (plaidoirie)* prosecution address

réquisitionner [rekizisjɔne] *vt* to requisition, to commandeer

réquisitoire [rekizitwar] *nm Jur* prosecution address; *Fig* indictment (**contre** of)

RER [ɛrəɛr] *nm (abrév* **Réseau express régional**) = express rail network serving Paris and its suburbs

RESA [reza] *nf (abrév* **réservation**) = TGV seat reservation ticket

rescapé, -e [rɛskape] **1** *adj* surviving
2 *nm,f* survivor

rescousse [rɛskus] *nf* **aller/venir à la r. de qn** to go/come to sb's rescue; **appeler qn à la r.** to call on sb for help

réseau, -x [rezo] *nm* (**a**) *(de routes, de voies ferrées, de rivières)* network, system; **r. autoroutier** *Br* motorway *or Am* freeway network; **r. ferroviaire** rail network (**b**) *Fig (de relations)* network, circle (**c**) *Ordinat* network; **mise en r.** networking; **r. de télématique** *ou* **de communication de données** datacomms network; **r. de données** data network; **r. local** local area network, LAN; **grand r.** wide area network, WAN; **r. numérique à intégration de services** integrated services digital network; **r. à valeur ajoutée** value-added network, VAN

réséda [rezeda] *nm* reseda

réservation [rezɛrvasjɔ̃] *nf* reservation, booking; **faire une r.** to make a reservation

réserve [rezɛrv] *nf* (**a**) *(restriction)* reservation; **émettre des réserves (sur qch)** to voice reservations (about sth); **sous r. de qch** subject to sth; **sans r.** *(éloges, admiration)* unqualified (**b**) *(discrétion)* reserve; **sortir de sa r.** to come out of one's shell (**c**) *(de vivres, d'équipement, d'argent)* reserve; **en r.** in reserve (**d**) *Mil* reserve (**e**) *(de chasse, de pêche)* reserve; *Can* **r. faunique** wildlife reserve; **r. indienne** (Native American) reservation; **r. naturelle** nature reserve (**f**) *(de magasin)* storeroom; *(de bibliothèque, de musée)* reserve collection

réservé, -e [rezɛrve] *adj* (**a**) *(chambre, siège)* reserved, booked (**b**) *(consacré)* **être r. à qn/qch** to be reserved for sb/sth (**c**) *(personne, attitude)* reserved

réserver [rezɛrve] **1** *vt* (**a**) *(chambre, place)* to reserve, to book; **vous avez réservé?** do you have a reservation? (**b**) *(mettre de côté)* to set aside, to put by (**à/pour** for); **r. le meilleur pour la fin** to save the best till last (**c**) *Fig* **r. son jugement** to reserve judgement; **r. une surprise à qn** to have a surprise in store for sb; **r. un bon accueil à qn** to welcome sb with open arms; **ce que le sort nous réserve** what fate has in store for us
2 se réserver *vpr* (**a**) *(garder pour soi)* **se r. qch** to keep sth for oneself; **se r. le droit de faire qch** to reserve the right to do sth (**b**) **se r. pour qch** to save oneself for sth

réserviste [rezɛrvist] *nm Mil* reservist

réservoir [rezɛrvwar] *nm* (**a**) *(bassin)* reservoir (**b**) *(cuve)* tank; **r. d'essence** *Br* petrol *or Am* gas tank

résidence [rezidɑ̃s] *nf* (**a**) *(demeure)* residence; **r. principale** main residence; **r. secondaire** second home (**b**) *(habitations de standing)* *Br* block of luxury flats, *Am* luxury apartment building (**c**) *Jur* **en r. surveillée** under house arrest (**d**) *(séjour)* residence

résident, -e [rezidɑ̃, -ɑ̃t] **1** *adj* (**a**) *(personne)* resident (**b**) *Ordinat* **r. en mémoire** memory-resident
2 *nm,f* (**a**) *(habitant)* resident (**b**) *(étranger)* foreign resident; **les résidents français en Grande-Bretagne** French nationals resident in Great Britain (**c**) *Belg* **second r.** weekender, holiday resident

résidentiel, -elle [rezidɑ̃sjɛl] *adj* residential

résider [rezide] *vi* (**a**) *(personne)* to reside (**b**) *(consister)* to lie (**dans** in)

résidu [rezidy] *nm (reste)* residue; **résidus** *(déchets)* waste

résiduel, -elle [rezidɥɛl] *adj* residual

résignation [reziɲasjɔ̃] *nf* resignation

résigné, -e [reziɲe] *adj* resigned (**à** to)

résigner [reziɲe] **se résigner** *vpr* to resign oneself (**à** to); **se r. à faire qch** to resign oneself to doing sth

résiliable [reziljabl] *adj (contrat)* which may be terminated

résiliation [reziljasjɔ̃] *nf (d'un contrat)* termination

résilier [66] [rezilje] *vt (accord, contrat)* to terminate

résille [rezij] *nf* hairnet

résine [rezin] *nf* resin

résiné [rezine] *adj m & nm* (**vin**) **r.** retsina

résineux, -euse [rezinø, -øz] **1** *adj* (**a**) *(bois, odeur)* resinous (**b**) *(arbre, forêt)* coniferous
2 *nm* conifer

résistance [rezistɑ̃s] *nf* (**a**) *(action)* resistance (**à** to); **n'offrir aucune r.** to put up *or* offer no resistance; **opposer une r. à qn/qch** to resist sb/sth; **r. passive** passive resistance (**b**) *Hist* **la R.** the Resistance (**c**) *(endurance)* stamina (**d**) *Élec* resistance (**e**) *(conducteur) (d'un appareil)* element (**f**) *(d'un matériau)* resistance

résistant, -e [rezistɑ̃, -ɑ̃t] **1** *adj (matériau)* tough; *(plante)* hardy; **c'est quelqu'un de très r.** he has a lot of stamina

2 *nm,f (combattant)* freedom fighter; *(pendant la Résistance)* member of the Resistance

résister [reziste] **résister à** *vt ind* (**a**) *(attaque, agresseur)* to resist (**b**) *(tentation, influence, personne)* to resist; **je n'ai pas pu r., je les ai achetées** I couldn't resist, I bought them (**c**) *(supporter) (douleur, pression, froid)* to withstand; *(mauvais traitement)* to stand up to; *(maladie, épidémie, fatigue)* to overcome (**d**) *(s'opposer à)* to stand up to

résolu, -e [rezɔly] **1** *pp voir* **résoudre**
2 *adj (personne)* determined, resolute; **être r. à faire qch** to be determined to do sth

résolument [rezɔlymã] *adv* resolutely

résolution [rezɔlysjɔ̃] *nf* (**a**) *(décision)* resolution; **prendre la r. de faire qch** to make a resolution to do sth; **prendre des résolutions** to make resolutions (**b**) *(d'un problème)* solving (**c**) *(détermination)* determination, resolve (**d**) *(d'un écran)* resolution

résolvais *etc voir* **résoudre**

résonance [rezɔnãs] *nf aussi Tech* resonance; *Fig (écho)* echo

résonner [rezɔne] *vi* (**a**) *(retentir)* to resound (**b**) *(faire un écho)* to echo

résorber [rezɔrbe] **1** *vt* (**a**) *(surplus, déficit)* to absorb; *(chômage)* to bring down; *(dettes)* to clear (**b**) *(sang, pus)* to resorb
2 se résorber *upr* (**a**) *(surplus, déficit)* to be absorbed; *(chômage)* to be brought down (**b**) *(sang, pus)* to be resorbed

résorption [rezɔrpsjɔ̃] *nf (d'un surplus, d'un déficit)* absorption; *(du chômage)* bringing down

résoudre [3b] [rezudr] **1** *vt* (**a**) *(difficulté, conflit, crise)* to resolve; *(équation, énigme, problème)* to solve (**b**) *(décider)* **r. de faire qch** to resolve to do sth (**c**) *(décomposer)* **r. qch en qch** to resolve sth into sth
2 se résoudre *upr* **se r. à faire qch** to resolve to do sth; **je ne peux pas me r. à la quitter** I can't bring myself to leave her

respect [rɛspɛ] *nm* respect (**pour** for); **élevé dans le r. des traditions** brought up to respect traditions; **avoir du r. pour qn** to have respect for sb; **manquer de r. envers qn** to show sb a lack of respect; **tenir qn en r.** to keep sb at a distance; **sauf le r. que je vous dois, sauf votre r.** with all due respect; **respects** *(hommages)* respects

respectabilité [rɛspɛktabilite] *nf* respectability
respectable [rɛspɛktabl] *adj* respectable
respecter [rɛspɛkte] **1** *vt* to respect; **faire r. la loi** to enforce the law; **se faire r.** to command respect; **r. la priorité** *(en voiture)* to give way
2 se respecter *upr* (**a**) *(soi-même)* to respect oneself; **comme tout homme qui se respecte** like any self-respecting man (**b**) *(l'un l'autre)* to respect each other

respectif, -ive [rɛspɛktif, -iv] *adj* respective
respectivement [rɛspɛktivmã] *adv* respectively
respectueusement [rɛspɛktɥøzmã] *adv* respectfully
respectueux, -euse [rɛspɛktɥø, -øz] *adj* respectful (**de/envers** of/to)
respirable [rɛspirabl] *adj* breathable; *Fig* **l'atmosphère n'était plus r.** the atmosphere had become oppressive
respirateur [rɛspiratœr] *nm* respirator
respiration [rɛspirasjɔ̃] *nf* breathing; **reprendre sa r.** to pause for breath; **retenir sa r.** to hold one's breath; **r. artificielle** artificial respiration

respiratoire [rɛspiratwar] *adj (organe)* respiratory; *(appareil, exercice, problème)* breathing
respirer [rɛspire] **1** *vi* (**a**) *(personne, plante)* to breathe (**b**) *Fig (être soulagé)* **je respire!** I can breathe again! (**c**) *Fig (se reposer)* to have a break
2 *vt* (**a**) *(inhaler)* to breathe (in) (**b**) *(exprimer)* **r. la santé** to be glowing with health; **il ne respire pas l'intelligence** he doesn't exactly radiate intelligence
resplendir [rɛsplãdir] *vi* (**a**) *(briller)* to shine (**b**) *(personne)* to be radiant; **r. de joie/santé** to radiate joy/health
resplendissant, -e [rɛsplãdisã, -ãt] *adj (personne, beauté)* radiant; **r. de joie/santé** radiant with joy/health; **il a une mine resplendissante** he looks wonderfully well
responsabiliser [rɛspɔ̃sabilize] *vt* **r. qn** to give sb a sense of responsibility
responsabilité [rɛspɔ̃sabilite] *nf (morale)* responsibility; *(légale)* liability (**de** for); **accepter une r.** to take on *or* accept a responsibility; **avoir la r. de qn/qch** to be responsible for sb/sth; **décliner toute r.** to accept no liability; **avoir un poste à responsabilités** to have a responsible job; **r. civile** public liability; **r. limitée** limited liability; **r. au tiers** third-party liability
responsable [rɛspɔ̃sabl] **1** *adj* (**a**) *(moralement)* responsible (**de** for); *(légalement)* liable (**de** for) (**b**) *(mûr)* responsible
2 *nmf* (**a**) *(auteur, coupable)* person responsible (**de** for); **qui est le r. de cette plaisanterie?** who's (the person) responsible for this prank? (**b**) *(personne qui a la responsabilité)* person in charge (**c**) *(dirigeant élu)* official
resquiller [rɛskije] *vi Fam (au théâtre, au concert)* to sneak in without paying; *(dans un bus, dans le métro)* to dodge paying one's fare
resquilleur, -euse [rɛskijœr, -øz] *nm,f Fam (au théâtre, au cinéma)* = person who sneaks in without paying; *(dans un bus, dans le métro)* fare-dodger
ressac [rəsak] *nm* undertow
ressaisir [rəsezir] **se ressaisir** *upr* to pull oneself together
ressasser [rəsase] *vt* (**a**) *(mentalement)* to brood over (**b**) *(répéter)* to keep coming out with
ressemblance [rəsãblãs] *nf (entre personnes)* resemblance, likeness; *(entre choses)* similarity
ressemblant, -e [rəsãblã, -ãt] *adj (portrait)* lifelike
ressembler [rəsãble] **1** **ressembler à** *vt ind* (**a**) *(personne)* to resemble, to be like; **à quoi ressemble-t-elle?** what does she look like? (**b**) *Fig (chose)* **cela ne ressemble à rien** it doesn't look like anything; **cela ne lui ressemble pas** that's not like her
2 se ressembler *upr* to be alike, to resemble each other; **ils se ressemblent comme des frères** you'd take them for brothers; **se r. comme deux gouttes d'eau** to be as like as two peas in a pod; **les jours se suivent et ne se ressemblent pas** day follows day and you never know what to expect; *Prov* **qui se ressemble s'assemble** birds of a feather flock together
ressemeler [42] [rəsəmle] *vt* to resole
ressentiment [rəsãtimã] *nm* resentment (**de/contre** at/against)
ressentir [64a] [rəsãtir] **1** *vt* to feel
2 se ressentir *upr* **se r. de qch** *(personne, pays)* to feel the effects of sth; *(travail)* to show the effects of sth

resserrement [rəsɛrmã] *nm (d'une amitié, de liens)* strengthening

resserrer [rəsere] **1** *vt* (**a**) *(nœud, ceinture, écrou)* to tighten (**b**) *Fig (amitié, liens)* to strengthen

2 se resserrer *vpr* (**a**) *(vallée, route)* to narrow (**b**) *(nœud)* to tighten (**c**) *Fig (liens)* to strengthen

resservir [63] [rəsɛrvir] **1** *vt (plat)* to serve up again; **r. qn** to give sb another helping

2 *vi* to be used again (**à** for)

3 se resservir *vpr* **se r. de qch** *(plat)* to take another helping of sth; *(objet)* to use sth again

ressort [rəsɔr] *nm* (**a**) *(pièce)* spring (**b**) *(force morale)* resilience; **avoir du r.** to be resilient (**c**) *(motivation)* motive (**d**) **être du r. de qn** to be sb's responsibility (**e**) **en dernier r.** *Jur* without appeal; *Fig* as a last resort

ressortir¹ [rəsɔrtir] **1** *vi (aux* **être**) (**a**) *(personne) (en s'éloignant)* to go back out; *(en s'approchant)* to come back out (**b**) *(se détacher)* to stand out; **faire r.** *(couleur)* to bring out; *(regard, yeux, fait)* to highlight

2 *vt (aux* **avoir**) (**a**) *(parapluie, vêtements)* to get out again (**b**) *Fig (histoire)* to trot out again

3 *v impersonnel (aux* **être**) **il ressort de ceci que…** it emerges from this that…

ressortir² **ressortir à** *vt ind* (**a**) *(être de la compétence de)* to come under the jurisdiction of (**b**) *Litt (dépendre de)* to come within the province of

ressortissant, -e [rəsɔrtisã, -ãt] *nm,f* national

ressouder [rəsude] **1** *vt* to resolder; *Fig* to re-establish

2 se ressouder *vpr (os, fracture)* to knit

ressource [rəsurs] *nf* (**a**) *(moyen)* possibility; **je n'ai d'autre r. que de…** the only course of action open to me is to…; **avoir de la r.** to be resourceful; **en dernière r.** as a last resort (**b**) **ressources** *(argent, moyens d'action)* resources; **être sans ressources** to have no means of support; **ressources humaines** human resources (**c**) *(d'une nation)* **ressources** resources

ressourcer [16] [rəsurse] **se ressourcer** *vpr Fam* to get back in touch with one's inner self

ressusciter [resysite] **1** *vt* (**a**) *(un mort)* to raise from the dead; *Fig* **ça ne va pas le r.** it won't bring him back (**b**) *Fig (querelle, mode)* to revive

2 *vi* to rise from the dead; **j'ai l'impression de r.** I feel like a new person

restant, -e [rɛstã, -ãt] **1** *adj* remaining

2 *nm* remainder, rest

3 restants *nmpl Can (de nourriture)* leftovers

restaurant [rɛstɔrã] *nm* restaurant; **aller au r.** to eat out; **r. d'entreprise** staff canteen; **r. universitaire** university canteen *or* refectory

restaurateur, -trice [rɛstɔratœr, -tris] *nm,f* (**a**) *(de tableaux)* restorer (**b**) *(de restaurant)* restaurateur, restaurant owner

restauration [rɛstɔrasjɔ̃] *nf* (**a**) *(de tableaux, de bâtiments)* restoration (**b**) *(métier)* catering; **r. rapide** fast food (**c**) *Hist* **la R.** the Restoration *(return to power of the Bourbon dynasty 1814–1830)* (**d**) *Ordinat* restore (**e**) *Suisse (restaurant)* restaurant

restaurer [rɛstɔre] **1** *vt* (**a**) *(rétablir, réparer)* to restore (**b**) *Ordinat* to restore (**c**) *Litt (faire manger)* **r. qn** to give sb something to eat

2 se restaurer *vpr* to have something to eat

reste [rɛst] *nm* (**a**) *(de travail, d'argent, de vin)* rest, remainder; **le r. du temps** the rest of the time; **le r. (des gens)** the rest; **il y avait un r. de beurre/lait** there was a bit of butter/milk left (over) (**b**) **restes** *(d'un re-*

pas) leftovers (**c**) *(ossements)* **restes** remains (**d**) *(locutions)* **du** *ou* **au r.** besides; **pour le r.** as for the rest; **avoir qch de r.** to have sth to spare; **pour ne pas être en r.** *(pour ne pas avoir de dette)* so as not to be indebted; *(pour ne pas être surpassé)* so as not to be outdone; **partir sans demander son r.** to leave without further ado; *Fam* **avoir de beaux restes** to still have one's looks

rester [rɛste] *(aux* **être**) **1** *vi* (**a**) *(subsister)* to remain, to be left; **les 5 euros qui restent** the remaining 5 euros, the 5 euros left; **c'est tout ce qui me reste** that's all I have left; **le nom lui est resté** the name stayed with him (**b**) *(demeurer)* to stay, to remain; **restez où vous êtes** stay where you are; **r. assis** to stay seated; **r. au lit** to stay in bed; **r. (à) dîner** to stay to dinner; **r. sur place** to stay put; *Fam* **j'y suis, j'y reste** here I am and here I stay; *Fam* **y r.** *(mourir)* to kick the bucket; **que cela reste entre nous** this is strictly between ourselves; **r. sur une impression** to be left with an impression; **cela m'est resté sur l'estomac** *(plat)* it's lying heavy on my stomach; *Fig* it still rankles with me; **en r.** to stop there; **r. dans les mémoires** to live on in people's memories; **le plus dur reste à faire** the hardest part is still to be done

2 *v impersonnel* **il me reste 5 euros** I've got 5 euros left; **il ne me reste qu'à vous remercier** it only remains for me to thank you; **il reste beaucoup de choses à faire** there are still a lot of things to be done; **il reste que…** the fact remains that…; **il n'en reste pas moins que…** it is nevertheless the case that…; **(il) reste à savoir si c'est vrai** it remains to be seen whether it's true

restituer [rɛstitɥe] *vt* (**a**) *(reconstituer) (inscription, texte)* to restore; *(passé, ambiance)* to recreate (**b**) *(rendre) (objets volés)* to restore, to return; *(argent, prêt)* to repay, to pay back (**c**) *(son)* to reproduce

restitution [rɛstitɥsjɔ̃] *nf* (**a**) *(reconstitution) (d'un texte)* restoration; *(d'une ambiance, du passé)* recreation (**b**) *(d'objets volés)* return; *(d'argent, d'un prêt)* repayment (**c**) *(du son)* reproduction

Restoroute® [rɛstɔrut] *nm Br* motorway *or Am* freeway restaurant

restreindre [54] [rɛstrɛ̃dr] **1** *vt* to restrict (**à** to)

2 se restreindre *vpr* (**a**) *(réduire ses dépenses)* to cut down (**b**) *(domaine, recherche)* to become more restricted

restreint, -e [rɛstrɛ̃, -ɛ̃t] *adj (production, vocabulaire)* restricted (**à** to); *(espace, service)* limited

restrictif, -ive [rɛstriktif, -iv] *adj* restrictive

restriction [rɛstriksjɔ̃] *nf* (**a**) *(diminution)* restriction (**b**) *(réserve)* reservation; **faire des restrictions** to express some reservations; **sans r.** *(accord)* unconditional; *(approuver)* unreservedly (**c**) *Ordinat* **r. d'accès** access restriction (**d**) **restrictions** *(mesures de rationnement)* restrictions

restructuration [rəstryktyrasjɔ̃] *nf* restructuring

restructurer [rəstryktyre] *vt* to restructure

résultant, -e [rezyltã, -ãt] **1** *adj* resulting

2 *nf* **résultante** consequence, result

résultat [rezylta] *nm* result; **sans r.** to no effect; *Fam* **r.: il a été licencié** the upshot was he was dismissed; **donner des résultats** to produce results; **résultats d'exercice** *ou* **d'exploitation** trading results

résulter [rezylte] **1** *vi* **r. de qch** to result from sth

2 *v impersonnel* **il en résulte que…** the result of this is that…

résumé [rezyme] *nm* (**a**) *(d'un texte)* summary, résumé; **faire le r. de qch** *(d'un texte)* to give a summary of sth; *(d'une histoire, d'une situation)* to sum sth up; **en r.** *(en bref)* in short (**b**) *(livre)* study guide

résumer [rezyme] **1** *vt* *(article, idées)* to summarize; *(situation, histoire)* to sum up
2 se résumer *vpr* (**a**) *(personne)* to sum up (**b**) *(se réduire)* **se r. à qch** to come down to sth

résurgence [rezyrʒɑ̃s] *nf* resurgence

resurgir [rəsyrʒir] *vi* to reappear suddenly

résurrection [rezyrɛksjɔ̃] *nf aussi Fig* resurrection

rétabli, -e [retabli] *adj* *(après une maladie)* recovered

rétablir [retablir] **1** *vt* (**a**) *(téléphone, eau, gaz)* to restore (**b**) *(guérir)* to restore to health (**c**) *(faits, vérité)* to re-establish (**d**) *(ordre, relations, réputation)* to restore (**e**) *(réhabiliter)* **r. qn (dans ses fonctions)** to reinstate sb; **r. qn dans ses droits** to restore sb's rights
2 se rétablir *vpr* (**a**) *(malade)* to recover (**b**) *(silence, calme)* to return; *(situation)* to return to normal

rétablissement [retablismɑ̃] *nm* (**a**) *(de l'ordre, de la paix, d'une dynastie)* restoration (**b**) *(des communications, des relations)* restoration (**c**) *(d'un employé)* reinstatement (**d**) *(d'un malade)* recovery

rétamé, -e [retame] *adj Fam (fatigué)* whacked

rétamer [retame] *vt* (**a**) *(casserole)* to retin (**b**) *(miroir)* to resilver (**c**) *Fam (au jeu)* to clean out; **se faire r.** *(se faire battre)* to get hammered

retaper [rətape] **1** *vt* (**a**) *Fam (vieille maison, voiture)* to do up (**b**) *Fam (lit)* to straighten (**c**) *Fam* **r. qn** to buck sb up
2 se retaper *vpr Fam (convalescent)* to get back on one's feet

retard [rətar] *nm* (**a**) *(dans le temps)* delay; *(d'une personne attendue)* lateness; **je vous prie d'excuser mon r.** please excuse me for being late; **être en r.** to be late; *(sur un programme)* to be behind; **sans r.** without delay; **avoir du r.** to be late; **avoir une heure de r.** to be an hour late; **prendre du r.** *(personne)* to fall behind; *(train)* to be running late; **r. de paiement** late payment (**b**) *(dans un développement)* backwardness; **pays en r. sur les autres** country lagging behind the others; **être en r. pour son âge** to be backward for one's age; **en r. sur son temps** behind the times; **r. mental** backwardness (**c**) *(d'un véhicule)* **r. à l'allumage** retarded ignition

retardataire [rətardatɛr] **1** *nmf* latecomer
2 *adj* **un élève r.** a pupil who arrives late

retardé, -e [rətarde] *adj* (**a**) *(départ, arrivée)* late (**b**) *(mentalement) (enfant)* backward

retardement [rətardəmɑ̃] *nm* **à r.** *(bombe)* time; *(longtemps après)* belatedly

retarder [rətarde] **1** *vt* (**a**) *(faire arriver en retard)* to delay; **r. qn dans ses études** to hold sb back in his/her studies (**b**) *(différer)* to delay; **r. qch d'une heure/d'une semaine** to put sth back an hour/a week (**c**) *(montre, horloge)* to put back (**de** by)
2 *vi* (**a**) *(horloge)* to be slow; **ma montre retarde/je retarde de dix minutes** my watch is/I'm ten minutes slow (**b**) **r. sur son temps** *ou* **son époque** to be behind the times (**c**) *Fam (ne pas être au courant)* to be behind the times

retendre [rətɑ̃dr] *vt (cordes)* to retighten

retenir [70] [rətənir] **1** *vt* (**a**) *(faire rester) (personne)* to keep, to detain; **r. qn prisonnier/en otage** to keep *or* hold sb prisoner/hostage; **je ne vous retiens pas** I won't hold you back; **r. qn à dîner** to have sb stay for

dinner; **r. qn par le bras** to hold sb back by the arm; **r. l'attention de qn** *(candidature, proposition)* to catch sb's attention (**b**) *(conserver) (eau, chaleur)* to retain (**c**) *(retirer) (argent)* to withhold; *(cotisation, impôt)* to deduct (**sur** from); **retenu à la source** deducted at source (**d**) *(se souvenir de) (leçon, nom)* to remember; **je le retiens, ton ami!** I won't forget your friend in a hurry! (**e**) *(réserver) (place, chambre, table)* to reserve, to book (**f**) *(accepter) (projet, suggestion)* to adopt; **votre candidature n'a pas été retenue** your application was unsuccessful (**g**) *(contenir) (colère)* to contain; *(larmes)* to hold back; *(cri)* to stifle; *(respiration, souffle)* to hold (**h**) *(garder en arrière) (personne, foule, chien)* to hold back, to restrain (**i**) *(empêcher)* **r. qn de faire qch** to restrain sb from doing sth, to hold sb back from doing sth; **qu'est-ce qui te retient de le lui dire?** what's stopping you telling her?; **qu'est-ce qui vous retient?** what's holding you back?
2 se retenir *vpr* (**a**) *(s'accrocher)* to hold on (**à** to) (**b**) *(se contenir)* to restrain oneself; **se r. de faire qch** to stop oneself (from) doing sth

rétention [retɑ̃sjɔ̃] *nf* retention; **faire de la r. d'information** to withhold information

retentir [rətɑ̃tir] *vi* (**a**) *(Klaxon®, alarme)* to sound; *(tonnerre, canon)* to rumble; *(coup de feu, cri)* to ring out; **l'explosion retentit dans toute la ville** the explosion was heard right across the city (**b**) *(lieu)* **r. de** to resound *or* echo with (**c**) *Fig* **r. sur** to have an impact on

retentissant, -e [rətɑ̃tisɑ̃, -ɑ̃t] *adj* (**a**) *(voix)* ringing (**b**) *(succès, échec)* resounding; *(scandale)* sensational

retentissement [rətɑ̃tismɑ̃] *nm (d'un événement)* impact; **avoir un r. sur qch** to have an impact on sth

retenue [rətəny] *nf* (**a**) *(d'une somme)* deduction; **r. sur salaire** wage deduction; *(mensuel)* salary deduction (**b**) *(dans un calcul)* carry over; **n'oublie pas la r.** don't forget to carry over (**c**) *Scol* detention (**d**) *(discrétion)* restraint (**e**) *(barrage)* dam

réticence [retisɑ̃s] *nf* hesitation, unwillingness; **sans r.** unhesitatingly

réticent, -e [retisɑ̃, -ɑ̃t] *adj (hésitant)* hesitant, unwilling

rétif, -ive [retif, -iv] *adj (cheval)* stubborn; *(personne)* recalcitrant

rétine [retin] *nf* retina

retiré, -e [rətire] *adj* (**a**) *(lieu, vie)* secluded; **vivre r. du monde** to lead a secluded life (**b**) **être r. des affaires** to be retired from business

retirer [rətire] **1** *vt* (**a**) *(faire sortir)* to take out; *(objet coincé)* to get out; *(bouchon, épine)* to pull out (**de** of); **r. un enfant d'une école** to remove a child from a school; **r. qch de la circulation** to withdraw sth from circulation; **r. qch du marché** to take sth off the market; **r. les mains de ses poches** to take one's hands out of one's pockets (**b**) *(argent)* to withdraw (**de** from), to take out (**de** of); *(bagages, billet)* to collect (**de** from), to pick up (**de** from) (**c**) *(obtenir)* **r. un profit de qch** to make a profit out of sth; **r. du plaisir de qch** to get pleasure from sth (**d**) *(ôter) (gants, lunettes, vêtement)* to take off, to remove (**e**) *(confisquer)* to take away (**à** from); **r. son permis de conduire à qn** to ban sb from driving (**f**) *(ramener en arrière) (main)* to remove (**g**) *(ne pas maintenir) (offre, plainte, candidature)* to withdraw; **je retire ce que j'ai dit** I take back what I said
2 se retirer *vpr* (**a**) *(s'en aller) (personne)* to with-

draw; *(foule)* to move back; **vous pouvez vous r.** you may go (**b**) *(eaux, mer)* to recede; *(marée)* to ebb (**c**) **se r. d'une association/élection** to withdraw from a partnership/an election; **se r. des affaires** to retire from business

retombées [rətɔ̃be] *nfpl* (**a**) *(répercussions)* repercussions; **avoir des retombées sur qch** to have repercussions on sth (**b**) *(déchets)* **retombées radioactives** radioactive fallout

retomber [rətɔ̃be] *vi (aux être)* (**a**) *(tomber de nouveau)* to fall again; **r. dans son fauteuil** to fall back into one's armchair; **laisser r. ses bras** to drop one's arms (**b**) *(après un saut, après avoir été en l'air) (personne, ballon)* to land; **r. sur ses pattes** *(chat)* to land on its feet; *Fig* **r. sur ses pieds** *ou Fam* **ses pattes** to land on one's feet (**c**) *(retourner)* **r. dans l'oubli** to sink back into obscurity; **r. dans le désespoir/le chaos** to fall back into despair/chaos; **r. en enfance** to lapse into one's second childhood (**d**) *(redevenir)* **r. malade** to fall ill again (**e**) *(rencontrer)* **r. sur qch** to come across sth again; *Fam* **r. sur qn** to bump into sb again (**f**) *(se répercuter)* **r. sur qn** *(blâme, responsabilité)* to fall on sb; *Fam* **ça va me r. dessus** I'm going to take the rap for it (**g**) *(baisser) (enthousiasme, intérêt, attention)* to fall off (**h**) *(cheveux, rideaux)* to hang (down) (**sur** over)

rétorquer [retɔrke] *vt* to retort

retors, -e [rətɔr, -ɔrs] *adj (personne)* crafty, wily

rétorsion [retɔrsjɔ̃] *nf* retaliation

retouche [rətuʃ] *nf* (**a**) *(sur photo)* touching up; *TV, Cin & Ordinat* **r. d'image(s)** image editing *or* retouching (**b**) *(d'un texte, d'un vêtement)* alteration

retoucher [rətuʃe] *vt* (**a**) *(texte, vêtement)* to alter (**b**) *(photo)* to touch up

retour [rətur] **1** *nm* (**a**) *(d'une personne, d'une saison)* return (**à** to); **être de r. (de)** to be back (again) (from); **de r. chez moi** back home; **à mon r.** on my return; **en r. (de)** in return (for); **payer qn de r.** to repay sb in kind; **par r. (du courrier)** by return (of post); **par un juste r. des choses** as is/was only right and proper; *Fam* **être sur le r.** to be past one's prime; **r. à l'envoyeur** return to sender; **r. de manivelle** backfire kick; *Fig* **il y a eu un r. de manivelle** it backfired (**b**) *(trajet)* return journey (**c**) *(changement) (de fortune)* reversal; **r. d'âge** change of life (**d**) *Ordinat* **r. d'information** feedback; **r. ligne** line feed; **r. chariot obligatoire** hard carriage return (**e**) *(sur clavier)* return; **r. arrière** backspace; **r. de chariot** carriage return

2 *adj inv (match, touche)* return

retournement [rəturnəmɑ̃] *nm (de situation)* turnaround (**de** in), reversal (**de** of)

retourner [rəturne] **1** *vt (aux avoir)* (**a**) *(gant, vêtement)* to turn inside out; *(poche)* to turn out; *Fam* **r. sa veste** to change sides; *Fig* **r. le couteau dans la plaie** to twist the knife, to rub it in (**b**) *(terre, matelas, crêpe)* to turn (over); *(carte)* to turn over *or* up; *Fig (idée, projet)* to turn over (**c**) *Fam (bouleverser) (personne)* to shake (**d**) *(renverser) (situation)* to reverse (**e**) *(rendre) (livre, lettre, compliment)* to return (**à** to) (**f**) *Fig (utiliser)* **r. un argument contre qn** to turn an argument against sb

2 *vi (aux être)* to go back, to return (**à** to)

3 *v impersonnel Fam* **voilà de quoi il retourne** that's what it's all about

4 se retourner *vpr* (**a**) *(dormeur, voiture)* to turn over; **il doit se r. dans sa tombe** he must be turning

in his grave (**b**) *Fig (s'organiser)* to sort things out (**c**) *(tourner la tête)* to turn round; **partir sans se r.** to leave without looking back (**d**) **se r. contre qn** *(personne)* to turn against sb; *(action, ambition)* to backfire on sb (**e**) *(aller)* **s'en r. quelque part** to return somewhere

retracer [16] [rətrase] *vt (événement, vie)* to recount

rétractation [retraktasjɔ̃] *nf* retraction

rétracter¹ [retrakte] **1** *vt (griffes, antennes)* to retract

2 se rétracter *vpr (muscle)* to retract

rétracter² **1** *vt (paroles)* to retract, to withdraw

2 se rétracter *vpr (se dédire)* to retract

rétraction [retraksjɔ̃] *nf* retraction

retrait [rətrɛ] *nm* (**a**) *(d'un permis)* withdrawal; **r. du permis de conduire** driving ban (**b**) *(d'une candidature)* withdrawal (**c**) *(fait de récupérer)* **r. des bagages** baggage reclaim (**d**) *(d'argent)* withdrawal; **r. d'espèces** cash withdrawal (**e**) *(des eaux)* receding (**f**) *(en typographie)* indent; **mettre qch en r.** to indent sth (**g**) **en r.** *(étagère)* recessed; *(maison)* set back; *Fig* **être/rester en r.** *(personne)* to be/stay in the background

retraite [rətrɛt] *nf* (**a**) *(de la vie active)* retirement; **être à la r.** to be retired; **prendre sa r.** to retire; **être mis à la r.** to be retired; **r. anticipée** early retirement (**b**) *(pension)* (retirement) pension; **r. complémentaire** supplementary pension (**c**) *(procession)* **r. aux flambeaux** torchlight procession (**d**) *(refuge)* retreat; *(de voleurs)* hideout (**e**) *(expérience religieuse)* retreat; **faire une r.** to go into retreat (**f**) *Mil* retreat

retraité, -e [rətrɛte] **1** *adj* retired

2 *nm,f* pensioner

retraitement [rətrɛtmɑ̃] *nm* reprocessing

retraiter [rətrɛte] *vt* to reprocess

retranchement [rətrɑ̃ʃmɑ̃] *nm* entrenchment; *Fig* **forcer qn dans ses (derniers) retranchements** to drive sb to the wall

retrancher [rətrɑ̃ʃe] **1** *vt* (**a**) *(soustraire) (chiffre)* to take away (**de** from); **r. qch sur une somme** to deduct sth from a sum of money (**b**) *(ôter) (passage, nom)* to remove (**de** from)

2 se retrancher *vpr (troupes)* to dig in; *Fig* **se r. dans le silence** to take refuge in silence; **se r. derrière qn/qch** to hide behind sb/sth

retransmettre [47] [rətrɑ̃smɛtr] *vt Rad & TV* to broadcast

retransmission [rətrɑ̃smisjɔ̃] *nf Rad & TV* broadcast

retravailler [rətravaje] **1** *vt (discours, texte, pas de danse)* to work on again

2 *vi* (**a**) *(reprendre le travail)* to go back to work (**b**) *(retrouver du travail)* to work again

rétréci, -e [retresi] *adj* (**a**) **un pull r.** a pullover that has shrunk (**b**) *(route)* narrow

rétrécir [retresir] **1** *vt (vêtement)* to take in

2 *vi (vêtement, tissu)* to shrink

3 se rétrécir *vpr (route)* to narrow

rétrécissement [retresismɑ̃] *nm* (**a**) *(action) (de route)* narrowing; *(de vêtement, de tissu)* shrinking (**b**) *(partie étroite) (de tuyau, de route)* narrowing

rétribuer [retribɥe] *vt (employé)* to pay; *(travail)* to pay for

rétribution [retribysjɔ̃] *nf* payment, remuneration

rétro [retro] **1** *adv* **s'habiller r.** to wear retro clothes; **meublé r.** furnished in retro style

2 *adj inv* retro

3 *nm* (**a**) *(style)* retro (**b**) *Fam (rétroviseur)* rear-view mirror

rétroactes [retroakt] *nmpl Belg* antecedents; **j'ignore tout des r. de cette affaire** I know nothing of the events which gave rise to this situation

rétroactif, -ive [retroaktif, -iv] *adj* retroactive; **avec effet r. au 1er janvier** backdated to 1 January

rétroactivement [retroaktivmã] *adv* retroactively, with retrospective *or* retroactive effect

rétroactivité [retroaktivite] *nf* retroactivity

rétrocéder [34] [retrosede] *vt (revendre)* to resell

rétrograde [retrograd] *adj (idée, mesure, politique)* reactionary

rétrograder [retrograde] **1** *vt (fonctionnaire)* to demote
  2 *vi (conducteur)* to change down; **r. de troisième en seconde** to change down from third to second

rétroprojecteur [retroprɔʒɛktœr] *nm* overhead projector

rétrospectif, -ive [retrɔspɛktif, -iv] **1** *adj* retrospective
  2 *nf* **rétrospective** retrospective; *Cin* retrospective, season; **une r. Roman Polanski** a Roman Polanski season

rétrospectivement [retrɔspɛktivmã] *adv* retrospectively, in retrospect

retroussé, -e [rɔtruse] *adj (manches)* rolled-up; *(nez)* snub, turned-up

retrousser [rɔtruse] *vt* (**a**) *(manches, pantalon)* to roll up; *(babines)* to curl up (**b**) *(jupe)* to tuck up

retrouvailles [rɔtruvaj] *nfpl* reunion

retrouver [rɔtruve] **1** *vt* (**a**) *(personne disparue, objet perdu)* to find again; *(adresse, nom)* to find; **r. son chemin** to find one's way again; **nous avons retrouvé notre petite maison** here we are back in our little house again; **je ne retrouverai jamais une occasion pareille** I'll never have another opportunity like it (**b**) *(recouvrer) (santé, forces, enthousiasme)* to recover; *(voix, appétit)* to get back; **r. la forme** to get fit again, to be back on form (**c**) *(reconnaître)* **r. qch chez qn** to recognize sth in sb; **r. qn dans qch** to recognize sb in sth (**d**) *(rencontrer) (thème, image, motif)* to come across (**dans** in) (**e**) *(rejoindre) (amis, parents)* to meet, to see; *(lieu)* to get back to
  2 se retrouver *vpr* (**a**) *(être)* to find oneself; **se r. à la rue/sans un sou** to find oneself homeless/penniless (**b**) *(trouver son chemin)* to find one's way (**dans** round); *Fig* **je ne m'y retrouve plus!** I'm completely lost! (**c**) *Fam (financièrement)* **s'y r.** to get one's money back (**d**) *(se rencontrer)* to meet; *Fig* **on se retrouvera!** I'll get even with you!; **comme on se retrouve!** fancy meeting you! (**e**) *(soi-même)* to find oneself again (**f**) *(se reconnaître)* **se r. en qn** to recognize oneself in sb

rétroviseur [retrovizœr] *nm* rear-view mirror

réunification [reynifikasjɔ̃] *nf* reunification

réunifier [66] [reynifje] *vt* to reunify

Réunion [reynjɔ̃] *nf* **la R.** Réunion

réunion [reynjɔ̃] *nf* (**a**) *(de faits)* gathering (together); *(d'ensembles mathématiques, de pays)* union; *(d'entreprises)* merging (**b**) *(assemblée)* meeting; **être en r.** to be in a meeting; **r. de famille** family gathering

réunionnais, -e [reynjɔnɛ, -ɛz] **1** *adj* of Réunion
  2 *nm,f* **R.** = person from Réunion

réunir [reynir] **1** *vt* (**a**) *(rassembler) (objets)* to put together; *(faits, documents)* to gather together; *(fonds)*

to get together, to raise (**b**) *(amis, famille)* to get together; *(après une rupture, une séparation)* to reunite (**c**) *(qualités, avantages)* to have, to possess (**d**) **r. qch à qch** to join sth to sth
  2 se réunir *vpr* (**a**) *(personnes)* to meet, to get together; **se r. autour de qn/qch** to gather round sb/sth (**b**) *(routes)* to meet (**c**) *(entreprises)* to merge; *(États)* to unite

réussi, -e [reysi] *adj* successful; *Ironique* **c'est r.!** well done!

réussir [reysir] **1** *vt* (**a**) *(bien faire)* to make a success of; *(au rugby) (essai)* to score; **son soufflé était très réussi** her soufflé was a great success (**b**) *(examen)* to pass
  2 *vi* (**a**) *(démarche, projet)* to be successful (**b**) *(personne)* to do well, to be successful
  3 réussir à *vt ind* (**a**) **r. à un examen** to pass an exam; **r. à faire qch** to manage to do sth (**b**) **r. à qn** *(climat, plat)* to agree with sb; **tout lui réussit** he's successful in everything he does; **les réunions de famille ne me réussissent pas** family gatherings aren't my scene *or* aren't for me

réussite [reysit] *nf* (**a**) *(succès)* success; **fêter sa r. à un examen** to celebrate passing an exam; **la r. sociale** social success (**b**) *(aux cartes) Br* patience, *Am* solitaire; **faire une r.** to play *Br* patience *or Am* solitaire

réutiliser [reytilize] *vt* to reuse

revaloir [69] [rɔvalwar] *vt* **je te revaudrai ça** *(je me vengerai)* I'll get you back for this!; *(je te rendrai service)* I'll do the same for you some time

revalorisation [rɔvalɔrizasjɔ̃] *nf* (**a**) *(d'une monnaie)* revaluation; *(des salaires, des retraites)* upgrading (**b**) *(d'une image, d'une profession)* upgrading

revaloriser [rɔvalɔrize] *vt* (**a**) *(monnaie)* to revalue; *(salaire, retraite)* to upgrade (**b**) *(image, profession)* to upgrade

revanchard, -e [rɔvɑ̃ʃar, -ard] *adj & nm,f Péj* revanchist

revanche [rɔvɑ̃ʃ] *nf* (**a**) *(vengeance)* revenge; **prendre sa r. (sur qn)** to get one's revenge (on sb) (**b**) *(d'un match, d'un jeu)* return game (**c**) *(locutions)* **en r.** on the other hand; **à charge de r.** on condition that I do the same for you

rêvasser [rɛvase] *vi* to daydream

rêve [rɛv] *nm* (**a**) *(de dormeur)* dream; **faire un r.** to (have a) dream; **faites de beaux rêves!** sweet dreams! (**b**) *(idéal)* dream; **de r.** *(voiture, maison)* dream; *(silhouette)* gorgeous

rêvé, -e [rɛve] *adj* perfect, ideal

revêche [rɔvɛʃ] *adj* bad-tempered

réveil [revɛj] *nm* (**a**) *(d'une personne)* waking, awakening; **à mon r., au r.** on waking (**b**) *(d'un volcan)* renewed rumblings; *(de la nature, des nationalismes)* reawakening (**c**) *(pendule)* alarm (clock)

réveille-matin [revɛjmatɛ̃] *nm inv* alarm clock

réveiller [reveje] **1** *vt* (**a**) *(personne endormie)* to wake (up), to awaken; *Fig* **r. les consciences** to stir people's consciences (**b**) *(raviver) (douleur)* to revive
  2 se réveiller *vpr* (**a**) *(personne endormie)* to wake (up), to awake; *(personne dans le coma)* to regain consciousness; *Fig (peuple)* to wake up (**b**) *(douleur)* to come back (**c**) *(nature)* to reawaken

réveillon [revɛjɔ̃] *nm (repas)* midnight supper; *(soirée)* midnight party *(after midnight mass on Christmas Eve or New Year's Eve)*

Réveillons

Christmas is traditionally a family celebration. In Catholic families, the "crèche" or miniature nativity scene is decorated and everyone goes to midnight mass on Christmas Eve, after which the long and copious Christmas dinner is served: this includes oysters and, for dessert, the traditional "bûche de Noël" or yule log. The presents under the Christmas tree are opened either on Christmas Eve or on Christmas Day morning. The "réveillon de la Saint-Sylvestre" on New Year's Eve is usually celebrated among friends, either at home or in a restaurant. Champagne is drunk at midnight and everybody embraces and wishes each other a happy New Year. New Year greeting cards can, in theory, be sent up until the end of January.

---

réveillonner [revεjɔne] *vi* to see in Christmas/the New Year *(with a midnight supper and party)*

révélateur, -trice [revelatœr, -tris] **1** *adj (signe, attitude, remarque)* revealing
  2 *nm* (**a**) *(indice)* sign (**b**) *Phot* developer

révélation [revelasjɔ̃] *nf* (**a**) *(action) (d'un secret, d'intentions)* revelation, disclosure; **faire des révélations** to disclose important information (**b**) *(découverte fondamentale)* revelation (**c**) *(personne)* discovery (**d**) *(divine)* revelation

révéler [34] [revele] **1** *vt* (**a**) *(dévoiler)* to reveal (**b**) *(témoigner de)* to show
  2 se révéler *vpr* (**a**) *(personne)* to reveal oneself *or* one's character; *(talent, génie)* to be revealed, to reveal itself (**b**) **se r. intelligent/exact** to turn out to be intelligent/correct; **il s'est révélé un bon ami** he proved to be a good friend

revenant, -e [rəvnɑ̃, -ɑ̃t] *nm,f* (**a**) *(fantôme)* ghost (**b**) *Fam* **tiens, un r.!** hello, stranger!

revendeur, -euse [rəvɑ̃dœr, -øz] *nm,f* retailer; *(d'articles d'occasion)* secondhand dealer

revendicatif, -ive [rəvɑ̃dikatif, -iv] *adj (mouvement)* protest

revendication [rəvɑ̃dikasjɔ̃] *nf* demand, claim

revendiquer [rəvɑ̃dike] *vt* (**a**) *(demander)* to claim, to demand; *(droits)* to assert; *(territoire, succession)* to lay claim to; **r. le droit de faire qch** to claim the right to do sth (**b**) *(assumer) (responsabilité)* to claim; *(attentat)* to claim responsibility for

revendre [rəvɑ̃dr] *vt* (**a**) *(après achat)* to resell; *Fig* **avoir du temps/de l'énergie à r.** to have time/energy to spare (**b**) *(vendre de nouveau)* to sell again

revenez-y [rəvnezi] *nm inv Fam* **avoir un goût de r.** to be very moreish

revenir [70] [rəvənir, rəvnir] *(aux être)* **1** *vi* (**a**) *(retourner, rentrer)* to come back, to return; **r. à Paris/en France** to come back to Paris/France; **r. de Paris** to come back from Paris; *Fig* **r. de loin** *(avoir failli mourir)* to have been at death's door; *(avoir eu de graves ennuis)* to have had a close shave; **je reviens tout de suite** I'll be back in a minute; **quand l'été reviendra** when it's summer again (**b**) **r. dans qch** *(refrain, image)* to crop up in sth (**c**) **ses propos me sont revenus** what he said got back to me (**d**) **r. à la mémoire à qn** to come back to sb; **ça me revient maintenant!** it's come back to me!; **les forces me sont revenues** I got my strength back (**e**) *Fam* **j'en suis revenu, de l'informatique!** I'm finished with computers!; **je n'en re-**

viens pas! I can't get over it! (**f**) *Fam* **il a une tête qui ne me revient pas** I don't like the look of him (**g**) *Culin* **faire r. qch** to brown sth (**h**) **r. cher** to work out expensive
  2 revenir à *vt ind* (**a**) *(coûter)* **r. à 100 euros par personne** to work out at 100 euros each; **ça me revient à 200 euros par mois** it costs me 200 euros a month (**b**) *(équivaloir à)* **cela revient à dire que...** that amounts to saying that...
  3 revenir sur *vt ind* (**a**) *(sujet)* to get back to (**b**) *(aveux)* to retract; *(promesse, décision)* to go back on
  4 *v impersonnel* **il me revient encore 100 euros** I still have 100 euros owing to me; **il lui revient de le faire** it's up to him/her to do it
  5 s'en revenir *vpr Litt* to return, to make one's way back

revente [rəvɑ̃t] *nf* resale

revenu [rəvəny, rəvny] *nm (d'une personne)* income; *(de l'État)* revenue

rêver [reve] **1** *vt* to dream of; **r. que...** to dream (that)...
  2 *vi* (**a**) *(dormeur)* to dream; *Fig* **on croit r.!** we must be dreaming! (**b**) *(rêvasser)* to daydream
  3 rêver à *vt ind* to dream of
  4 rêver de *vt ind* (**a**) *(voir en rêve)* to dream of; *Fig* **j'en rêve la nuit** I dream about it at night (**b**) *(souhaiter)* to dream of; **r. de faire qch** to dream of doing sth

réverbération [reverberasjɔ̃] *nf (de la lumière, de la chaleur)* reflection; *(du son)* reverberation, echo

réverbère [reverber] *nm* street lamp

réverbérer [34] [reverbere] *vt (chaleur, lumière)* to reflect, to throw back; *(son)* to reverberate

reverdir [rəverdir] *vi* to grow green again

révérence [reverɑ̃s] *nf* (**a**) *(salut) (d'une femme)* curtsey; **faire la r. à qn** to curtsey to sb; *Fig* **tirer sa r.** to leave (**b**) *(respect)* reverence (**envers** *ou* **pour** for)

révérend, -e [reverɑ̃, -ɑ̃d] **1** *adj* reverend
  2 *nm* reverend

révérer [34] [revere] *vt* to revere

rêverie [revri] *nf (activité, moment)* daydream, reverie

revers [rəver] *nm* (**a**) *(de pièce)* reverse side, back; *(de la main)* back; **prendre l'ennemi à r.** *(par l'arrière)* to attack the enemy from the rear; *(par le côté)* to attack the enemy from the side; *Fig* **c'est le r. de la médaille** that's the other side of the coin (**b**) *(de veste)* lapel; *(de pantalon) Br* turn-up, *Am* cuff (**c**) *(échec)* **r. de fortune** reversal of fortune, setback (**d**) *(au tennis)* backhand (stroke)

reverser [rəverse] *vt* (**a**) *(somme)* to transfer (**à** *ou* **sur** to) (**b**) *(liquide)* to pour out again

réversible [reversibl] *adj* reversible

revêtement [rəvεtmɑ̃] *nm (enduit)* coating; *(de sol, d'un mur intérieur)* covering; *(d'un mur extérieur)* facing; *(pour canalisation, pour câble)* sheathing; *(de la chaussée)* surface (material)

revêtir [71] [rəvεtir] *vt* (**a**) *(habiller)* **r. qn de qch** to dress sb in sth (**b**) *(endosser) (vêtement)* to don (**c**) *(enduire) (sol)* to cover; *(mur extérieur)* to face; *(chaussée)* to surface (**d**) *Fig (caractère, aspect, forme)* to assume, to take on (**e**) **pièce revêtue d'une signature** document bearing a signature

rêveur, -euse [revœr, -øz] **1** *adj* dreamy; **laisser qn r.** to leave sb baffled
  2 *nm,f* dreamer

rêveusement [revøzmɑ̃] *adv* dreamily

revient [rəvjε̃] *nm voir* **prix**

revigorant, -e [rəvigɔrɑ̃, -ɑ̃t] *adj (vent, bain)* invigorating; *(boisson)* reviving

revigorer [rəvigɔre] *vt (vent, bain)* to invigorate; *(boisson)* to revive

revirement [rəvirmɑ̃] *nm (de sentiments, d'opinion)* complete change, about-turn

réviser [revize] *vt* (a) *(texte, loi)* to revise; *(contrat, procès, politique)* to review (b) *(leçon, programme)* to revise (c) *(voiture, moteur)* to service (d) *Ordinat (texte, document)* to edit

révision [revizjɔ̃] *nf* (a) *(d'un texte, d'une loi)* revision; *(d'un contrat, d'un procès, d'une politique)* review; **r. des salaires** salary review (b) *(d'une leçon, d'un programme) Br* revision, *Am* review; **faire des révisions** to revise (c) *(d'une voiture, d'un moteur)* service (d) *Ordinat* edit

révisionnisme [revizjɔnism] *nm* revisionism

revisiter [rəvizite] *vt* (a) *(visiter à nouveau)* to revisit (b) *(voir sous un jour nouveau)* to reinterpret

revisser [rəvise] *vt* to screw back again

revitalisant, -e [rəvitalizɑ̃, -ɑ̃t] *adj* revitalizing

revitaliser [rəvitalize] *vt* to revitalize

revivre [72] [rəvivr] **1** *vt (passé, expérience)* to relive **2** *vi* (a) *(recouvrer son énergie)* to come alive again; **se sentir r.** to feel alive again; **faire r. qn** to bring sb back to life (b) **r. dans qn/qch** to live on in sb/sth; **faire r. qch** *(coutume, tradition)* to revive sth; *(village)* to bring sth back to life

révocable [revɔkabl] *adj (fonctionnaire)* removable; *(testament)* revocable

révocation [revɔkasjɔ̃] *nf (d'un fonctionnaire)* removal; *(d'un testament)* revocation

revoici [rəvwasi] *prép Fam* **me r.!** here I am again!; **le r. au travail** he's back at work

revoilà [rəvwala] = **revoici**

revoir¹ [rəvwar] **au revoir 1** *exclam* goodbye **2** *nm inv* goodbye

revoir² [73a] **1** *vt* (a) *(rencontrer) (personne)* to see *or* meet again (b) *(leçon)* to revise; *(comptes, texte)* to go over again (c) *(se représenter mentalement)* to see again **2 se revoir** *vpr* (a) *(se rencontrer)* to see each other again, to meet again (b) *(soi-même)* to see oneself again

revoler [rəvɔle] *vi* (a) *(voler de nouveau)* to fly again (b) *Can (être projeté dans toutes les directions) (objets, personnes)* to fly in every direction; *(jaillir) (liquide, sang)* to splatter; **les fenêtres ont revolé en miettes** the windows were smashed to smithereens

révoltant, -e [revɔltɑ̃, -ɑ̃t] *adj* appalling, revolting

révolte [revɔlt] *nf* revolt; **en r. (contre)** in revolt (against)

révolté, -e [revɔlte] *adj* (a) *(indigné)* outraged, appalled (**de** by) (b) *(en révolte)* rebellious

révolter [revɔlte] **1** *vt* to outrage, to appal; **ça me révolte d'entendre ça!** I'm appalled to hear that! **2 se révolter** *vpr* to revolt, to rebel (**contre** *ou* **devant** against)

révolu, -e [revɔly] *adj (jours, époque)* past, bygone; **avoir quarante ans révolus** to be over forty years of age

révolution [revɔlysjɔ̃] *nf* revolution; **faire la r.** to cause a revolution; *Fig* **être en r.** to be up in arms; *Hist* **la R.** the French Revolution

révolutionnaire [revɔlysjɔnɛr] *adj & nmf* revolutionary

révolutionner [revɔlysjɔne] *vt* (a) *(transformer) (industrie, théorie)* to revolutionize (b) *Fam (mettre en émoi) (village)* to cause a stir in

revolver [revɔlvɛr] *nm* revolver

révoquer [revɔke] *vt* (a) *(fonctionnaire)* to remove from office (b) *(décret, contrat, testament)* to revoke

revue [rəvy] *nf* (a) *(examen)* review; **passer qch en r.** *(problèmes, possibilités)* to review sth; **r. de presse** *(de l'actualité)* review of the papers; *(sur un sujet particulier)* press review (b) *(magazine)* magazine; *(scientifique, littéraire)* review, journal (c) *(spectacle)* revue

révulsé, -e [revylse] *adj (yeux)* rolled back; *(personne)* disgusted

révulser [revylse] **1** *vt (dégoûter)* to disgust **2 se révulser** *vpr (yeux)* to roll back

Reykjavik [rekjavik] *n* Reykjavik

rez-de-chaussée [redʃose] *nm inv Br* ground floor, *Am* first floor; **au r.** on the *Br* ground *or Am* first floor

rez-de-jardin [redʒardɛ̃] *nm inv* garden level

RF [ɛrɛf] *nf (abrév* **République française**) = written abbreviation seen on official documents, government buildings etc

RFA [ɛrɛfa] *nf Anciennement (abrév* **République fédérale d'Allemagne**) FRG

RG *nmpl (abrév* **Renseignements généraux**) = secret intelligence branch of the French police, *Br* ≃ the Special Branch, *Am* ≃ the FBI

rhabiller [rabije] **1** *vt (personne)* to dress sb again **2 se rhabiller** *vpr (mettre ses vêtements)* to get dressed again; *Fam* **il peut aller se r.** he might as well give up and go home

rhapsodie [rapsɔdi] *nf* rhapsody

Rhénanie [renani] *nf* **la R.** the Rhineland

Rhésus [rezys] *nm* Rhesus factor; **R. positif/négatif** Rhesus positive/negative

rhétorique [retɔrik] **1** *adj (effet)* rhetorical **2** *nf* rhetoric

Rhin [rɛ̃] *nm* **le R.** the Rhine

rhinocéros [rinɔserɔs] *nm* rhinoceros

rhino-pharyngite *(pl* **rhino-pharyngites**) [rino-farɛ̃-ʒit] *nf* inflammation of the nose and throat, *Spéc* rhinopharyngitis

Rhodes [rɔd] *n* Rhodes

rhododendron [rɔdɔdɛ̃drɔ̃] *nm* rhododendron

Rhône [ron] *nm* **le R.** the Rhone

rhubarbe [rybarb] *nf* rhubarb

rhum [rɔm] *nm* rum

rhumatisant, -e [rymatizɑ̃, -ɑ̃t] *adj & nm,f* rheumatic

rhumatismal, -e, -aux, -ales [rymatismal, -o] *adj* rheumatic

rhumatisme [rymatism] *nm* rheumatism; **avoir des rhumatismes** to have rheumatism; **r. articulaire** rheumatoid arthritis; **r. articulaire aigu** rheumatic fever

rhumatologie [rymatɔlɔʒi] *nf* rheumatology

rhumatologue [rymatɔlɔg] *nmf* rheumatologist

rhume [rym] *nm* cold; **attraper un r.** to catch a cold; **r. de cerveau** head cold; **r. des foins** hay fever

riant, -e [rijɑ̃, -ɑ̃t] *adj* (a) *(visage)* smiling, cheerful; *(yeux)* laughing, merry (b) *(paysage, campagne)* cheerful, sunny

RIB [rib] *nm (abrév* **relevé d'identité bancaire**) = document showing details of one's bank account

ribambelle [ribɑ̃bɛl] *nf (de personnes)* string, crowd

ricanement [rikanmɑ̃] *nm* sneer, snigger

ricaner [rikane] *vi* to sneer, to snigger

richard, -e [riʃar, -ard] *nm,f Péj* moneybags

riche [riʃ] **1** *adj* (**a**) *(personne, pays)* rich, wealthy (**b**) *(cuisine, aliment)* rich (**c**) *(vocabulaire)* extensive; *(style)* elaborate; *(description)* detailed (**d**) *(luxueux) (demeure)* luxurious; *(étoffe)* rich; *(vêtement)* sumptuous (**e**) *Fam* **c'est une r. idée** that's a fabulous idea (**f**) **r. en qch** rich in sth; **la journée a été r. en événements** it's been an action-packed day (**g**) **r. de** *(espérances)* full of; **livre/expérience r. d'enseignements** very instructive book/experience

2 *nmf* rich person; **les riches** the rich

richement [riʃmã] *adv* richly

richesse [riʃɛs] *nf* (**a**) *(d'une personne, d'un pays)* wealth; **c'est le tableau qui fait la r. de notre musée** this painting is the prize item in our museum's collection; **richesses** *(biens)* riches, wealth; *Fam* **voilà toutes mes richesses** this is everything I've got (**b**) *(luxe) (d'une demeure)* luxuriousness; *(de vêtements)* sumptuousness (**c**) **richesses** *(ressources)* resources (**d**) *(du sol, d'un gisement)* richness; *(de la végétation)* lushness (**e**) *(de l'imagination)* vividness, liveliness; *(d'un style)* elaborateness; *(du vocabulaire)* richness; *(d'une description)* detailed nature

richissime [riʃisim] *adj* extremely wealthy

ricin [risɛ̃] *nm voir* **huile**

ricocher [rikɔʃe] *vi (projectile)* to ricochet (**sur** off); *(sur l'eau)* to bounce (**sur** off)

ricochet [rikɔʃɛ] *nm (projectile)* ricochet; *(sur l'eau)* bounce; **faire des ricochets** *(pour s'amuser)* to skim pebbles; *Fig* **par r.** indirectly

ric-rac [rikrak] *adv Fam* (**a**) *(de justesse)* **réussir un examen r.** to scrape through an exam (**b**) **être r.** *(financièrement)* to be a bit strapped for cash

rictus [riktys] *nm* grimace

ride [rid] *nf* (**a**) *(sur le visage)* wrinkle, line; *Fam* **ne pas prendre une r.** not to age (**b**) *(sur l'eau)* ripple

ridé, -e [ride] *adj* wrinkled

rideau, -x [rido] *nm* (**a**) *(dans une pièce) Br* curtain, *Am* drape; **r. de fer** *(de boutique)* metal shutter; *Hist (en Europe)* Iron Curtain (**b**) *(de théâtre)* curtain (**c**) *(écran) (d'arbres)* screen, curtain; *(de feu, de fumée)* wall; *(de pluie)* curtain

rider [ride] **1** *vt* (**a**) *(peau)* to wrinkle, to line; *(eau, sable)* to ripple (**b**) *(eau)* to shrivel

2 se rider *vpr* (**a**) *(front, peau)* to become wrinkled *or* lined (**b**) *(eau)* to ripple

ridicule [ridikyl] **1** *adj* ridiculous, ludicrous; *(prix)* ridiculously low; **se rendre r.** to make a fool of oneself

2 *nm* (**a**) *(absurdité)* ridiculousness (**b**) *(dérision)* ridicule; **tourner qn/qch en r.** to ridicule sb/sth; **se couvrir de r.** to make a complete fool of oneself

ridiculement [ridikylmã] *adv* ridiculously, ludicrously

ridiculiser [ridikylize] **1** *vt* to ridicule, to make fun of

2 se ridiculiser *vpr* to make oneself look ridiculous, to make a fool of oneself

rien [rjɛ̃] **1** *pron indéfini* (**a**) *(avec ne)* nothing; **r. ne l'affecte** nothing affects him; **r. de ce que j'ai proposé ne leur a plu** they didn't like anything I suggested; **r. ne va plus!** *(au casino)* no more bets!; **ne... r.** nothing, not anything; **je n'ai r. à faire** I've got nothing to do; **il n'a r. mangé du tout** he hasn't eaten a thing; **personne n'osa r. dire** nobody dared say anything; **il n'y a r. de nouveau** there's nothing new, there isn't anything new; **ce n'est r.** it's nothing;

comme si de r. n'était as if nothing had happened; **elle ne ressemble en r. à sa sœur** she's nothing like her sister; *Litt* **il n'en est r.** such is not the case; **il n'a r. d'un don Juan** he's no Casanova; *Fam* **r. de r.** nothing at all

(**b**) *(sans ne)* **qu'avez-vous fait?** r. **/presque r.** what did you do? – nothing/hardly anything; **de r.** *(je vous en prie)* you're welcome, don't mention it; **pour r.** *(gratuitement)* for nothing; **pourquoi demandez-vous cela? pour r.** why do you ask? – no reason; **un petit problème de r. du tout** a trivial little problem; **quinze à r.** *(au tennis)* fifteen love

(**c**) *(quelque chose)* anything; **y a-t-il r. de plus triste?** is there anything more depressing?; **sans r. faire** without doing anything; **sans nous gêner en r.** without troubling us at all *or* in the slightest

(**d**) *(locutions)* **r. que** just, only; **je frémis r. que d'y songer** just thinking about it makes me shudder; **r. que la vérité** nothing but the truth; **élever quatre enfants, ce n'est pas r.!** raising four children is quite an achievement!

2 *nm* (**a**) *(bagatelle)* **un r. l'habille** she looks good in anything; **s'énerver pour un r.** to get annoyed over nothing; **il court un kilomètre comme un r.** he can run a kilometre just like that

(**b**) **un r. long/bête** *(un peu)* a bit long/stupid; **un r. de...** *(un petit peu de)* a little...; **en un r. de temps** in no time at all

rieur, -euse [rijœr, -øz] *adj (air, visage)* cheerful, bright; *(yeux)* laughing, merry

Riga [riga] *n* Riga

rigide [riʒid] *adj* (**a**) *(matériau)* rigid; *(couverture de livre)* hard (**b**) *Fig (personne, règlement, système)* rigid, inflexible

rigidité [riʒidite] *nf (d'un matériau)* rigidity; *Fig (d'une personne, d'un règlement, d'un système)* rigidity, inflexibility; **r. cadavérique** rigor mortis

rigolade [rigɔlad] *nf Fam* (**a**) *(amusement)* fun (**b**) **c'était de la r.** *(c'était facile)* it was a walkover; **ça n'est pas de la r.** *(c'est sérieux)* it's no joke; **prendre qch à la r.** to treat sth as a joke

rigolard, -e [rigɔlar, -ard] *adj Fam (air)* grinning

rigole [rigɔl] *nf (petit fossé)* channel; *(filet d'eau)* rivulet

rigoler [rigɔle] *vi Fam* (**a**) *(rire)* to laugh (**b**) *(s'amuser)* to have a laugh (**c**) *(plaisanter)* to joke (**avec** about); *Fig* **il ne faut pas r. avec le fisc** you shouldn't mess about with the tax man

rigolo, -ote [rigɔlo, -ɔt] *Fam* **1** *adj* funny

2 *nm,f (plaisantin)* scream, hoot; *Péj (fumiste)* clown

rigorisme [rigɔrism] *nm* strictness

rigoriste [rigɔrist] **1** *adj* strict, rigorous

2 *nmf* strict moralist

rigoureusement [rigurøzmã] *adv* (**a**) *(strictement) (interdit)* strictly; *(exact)* absolutely; *(contraire)* rigorously (**b**) *(scrupuleusement)* **suivre r. les consignes** to follow the instructions to the letter (**c**) *(sévèrement)* severely

rigoureux, -euse [rigurø, -øz] *adj* (**a**) *(dur) (punition, mesures, conditions)* severe, harsh; *(hiver)* hard; *(climat)* harsh (**b**) *(strict) (neutralité)* strict; *(analyse)* rigorous; **être r. dans qch** *(personne)* to be rigorous in sth

rigueur [rigœr] *nf* (**a**) *(dureté)* harshness, severity; *(de la loi)* rigour (**b**) *(austérité)* austerity (**c**) *(exactitude) (d'une analyse)* rigour; **manquer de r.** *(style, per-*

sonne) to be sloppy (**d**) *(locutions)* **à la r.** *(si néces-saire)* if need be; **être de r.** to be compulsory; **tenir r. à qn de qch** to hold sth against sb

rillettes [rijɛt] *nfpl* potted meat *(made from pork, rabbit, goose etc)*

rime [rim] *nf* rhyme; **sans r. ni raison** without rhyme or reason

rimer [rime] *vi* (**a**) *(mot)* to rhyme (**avec** with) (**b**) *Fig* **ne r. à rien** not to make any sense

Rimmel® [rimɛl] *nm* mascara

rinçage [rɛ̃saʒ] *nm* (**a**) *(action)* rinsing (**b**) *(pour les cheveux)* tint, rinse

rince-doigts [rɛ̃sdwa] *nm inv* finger bowl

rincée [rɛ̃se] *nf* (**a**) *Fam (averse)* downpour (**b**) *Fam (volée de coups)* walloping

rincer [16] [rɛ̃se] **1** *vt (vêtements, vaisselle, cheveux)* to rinse; *(verre, tasse)* to rinse (out)
2 se rincer *vpr (à l'eau douce)* to rinse oneself; **se r. la bouche** to rinse out one's mouth; *Fam* **se r. l'œil** to get an eyeful

ring [riŋ] *nm* (**a**) *(de boxe)* ring; **le r.** *(la boxe)* boxing (**b**) *Belg (rocade)* ring road

ringard, -e [rɛ̃gar, -ard] *Fam* **1** *adj* (**a**) *(démodé)* untrendy, unhip, *Br* naff (**b**) *(de mauvais goût)* tacky
2 *nm,f* square

ringardise [rɛ̃gardiz] *nf Fam* tackiness, *Br* naffness

Rio de Janeiro [rijodədʒanero] *n* Rio de Janeiro

ripaille [ripaj] *nf Fam* **faire r.** to have a blow-out

riposte [ripɔst] *nf* (**a**) *(en boxe, en escrime)* riposte (**b**) *(réponse)* riposte, retort (**c**) *(représailles)* counterattack

riposter [ripɔste] **1** *vt* **il m'a riposté que...** he retorted that...
2 *vi* (**a**) *(en boxe, en escrime)* to riposte (**b**) *(user de représailles)* to counterattack
3 riposter à *vt ind (attaque, injures)* to counter

ripou *(pl* **ripoux** *ou* **ripous**) [ripu] *Fam* **1** *adj (policier)* bent
2 *nm* bent cop

riquiqui [rikiki] *adj inv (tout petit)* teeny-weeny; *(portion, cadeau)* stingy, mean; *(maillot de bain)* skimpy

rire¹ [rir] *nm* laughter, laughing

rire² [61] **1** *vi* (**a**) *(personne)* to laugh; **r. comme un bossu,** *Fam* **r. comme une baleine** to laugh like a drain; **r. jaune** to give a forced laugh; **r. aux éclats** to roar with laughter; **r. aux larmes** to cry with laughter; **r. tout bas** to laugh to oneself (**b**) *(s'amuser)* to have fun, to have a laugh; **pour r.** for a joke; **vous voulez r.!** you're joking!; **laissez-moi r.!** don't make me laugh!
2 rire de *vt ind (se moquer de) (personne, remarques, situation)* to laugh at; *Litt* **je ris de leurs insultes** I'm impervious to their insults; **il vaut mieux en r.** you have to laugh
3 se rire *vpr Litt* **se r. de** *(se moquer de)* to laugh at; *(se jouer de)* to make light of

ris¹ [ri] *nm (sur une voile)* reef

ris² *nm* **r. de veau** calf's sweetbread

risée [rize] *nf* (**a**) *(moquerie)* mockery, derision; **s'exposer à la r. publique** to expose oneself to public scorn (**b**) **être la r. de** to be the laughing stock of

risette [rizɛt] *nf Fam* little smile; **fais des risettes à ton papa!** smile for daddy!, give daddy a smile!

risible [rizibl] *adj* laughable, ridiculous

risque [risk] *nm* risk; **prendre un r./des risques** to take a risk/risks; **courir le r. de faire qch** to risk doing sth; **c'est un r. à courir** it's a risk I/we/*etc* have to take;

avoir le goût du r. to like taking risks; **les risques du métier** occupational hazards; **faire qch à ses risques et périls** to do sth at one's own risk; **au r. de sa vie** at the risk of his/her life; **au r. de faire qch** at the risk of doing sth

risqué, -e [riske] *adj* (**a**) *(dangereux)* risky (**b**) *(osé)* risqué

risquer [riske] **1** *vt* (**a**) *(mettre en danger) (vie, réputation)* to risk; **qu'est-ce que tu risques?** what have you got to lose?; **r. sa tête** to put one's head on the block; **r. le tout pour le tout** to go for broke (**b**) **r. un œil** to peep out; **r. une question** to venture a question
2 risquer de *vt ind* **il risque de se faire renvoyer** he's in danger of being sacked; **ça risque de durer longtemps** that may well last for a long time; *Fam* **il risque de gagner** he stands a good chance of winning; *Fam* **il ne risque pas de te le dire** fat chance of him telling you
3 se risquer *vpr* to take risks/a risk; **se r. à faire qch** to venture to do sth; **je ne m'y risquerais pas** I wouldn't risk it

risque-tout [riskətu] *nmf inv* daredevil

rissoler [risɔle] *vt & vi* to brown

ristourne [risturn] *nf* discount; **faire une r. à qn** to give sb a discount

rital, -e, -als, -ales [rital] *nm,f Fam (Italien)* wop, *Br* Eyetie, = racist term used to refer to an Italian

rite [rit] *nm* (**a**) *(religieux)* rite; **r. de passage** *ou* **initiatique** rite of passage (**b**) *Fig (cérémonie, habitude)* ritual

ritournelle [riturnɛl] *nf (phrase musicale)* ritornello; *Fam* **c'est toujours la même r.** it's always the same old story

rituel, -elle [rityɛl] **1** *adj* ritual
2 *nm* ritual; **r. d'initiation** initiation rites

rituellement [rityɛlmɑ̃] *adv* invariably

rivage [rivaʒ] *nm* shore

rival, -e, -aux, -ales [rival, -o] **1** *adj* rival
2 *nm,f* rival; **sans r.** unrivalled

rivaliser [rivalize] *vi* **r. avec qn** to compete with sb; **r. de qch avec qn** to try to outdo sb in sth

rivalité [rivalite] *nf* rivalry

rive [riv] *nf* (**a**) *(de rivière)* bank; *(de lac, de mer)* shore (**b**) **la r. gauche/droite** *(à Paris)* the Left/Right Bank

---

Rive droite, rive gauche
The Right (north) Bank of the Seine is traditionally associated with business and trade, and has a reputation for being more conservative than the Left Bank. The Left (south) Bank includes districts traditionally favoured by artists, students and intellectuals, and has a reputation for being Bohemian and unconventional.

---

river [rive] *vt* (**a**) *(fixer)* to rivet; *Fig* **être rivé à qch** to be glued to sth; **avoir les yeux rivés sur qn/qch** not to be able to take one's eyes off sb/sth (**b**) *(goupille, clou)* to clinch; *Fam* **r. son clou à qn** to shut sb up

riverain, -e [rivrɛ̃, -ɛn] **1** *adj (propriété) (le long d'une rivière)* riverside, waterside; *(autour d'un lac)* lakeside, waterside
2 *nm,f* (**a**) *(près d'une rivière)* owner of a riverside property; *(près d'un lac)* owner of a lakeside property (**b**) *(d'une rue)* resident; **interdit sauf aux riverains** *(sur panneau)* ≃ no entry except for access

rivet [rivɛ] *nm* rivet

rivetage [rivtaʒ] *nm* riveting

riveter [42] [rivte] *vt* to rivet

riveteuse [rivtøz] *nf* riveting machine

rivière [rivjɛr] *nf* (**a**) *(cours d'eau)* river (**b**) *(de lave, de boue)* river (**c**) **r. de diamants** diamond necklace, *Spéc* diamond rivière

rixe [riks] *nf* brawl

riz [ri] *nm* rice; **r. cantonais** Cantonese rice; **r. créole** boiled rice; **r. au lait** rice pudding; **r. pilaf** pilaf *or* pilau rice

riziculture [rizikyltyr] *nf* rice growing

rizière [rizjɛr] *nf* rice field, paddy field

RMI [ɛrɛmi] *nm* (*abrév* **revenu minimum d'insertion**) *Br* ≃ income support, *Am* ≃ Welfare

RMiste [ɛremist] *nmf Br* ≃ person on income support, *Am* ≃ person on Welfare

RN [ɛrɛn] *nf* (*abrév* **route nationale**) = designation of major road, *Br* ≃ A-road, *Am* ≃ state highway

RNIS [ɛrenis] *nm Ordinat* (*abrév* **réseau numérique à intégration de services**) ISDN

robe [rɔb] *nf* (**a**) *(de femme)* dress; **r. de grossesse** maternity dress; **r. d'intérieur** housecoat; **r. de mariée** wedding dress; **r. du soir** evening gown (**b**) **r. de chambre** *Br* dressing gown, *Am* robe; **pommes de terre en r. de chambre** *ou* **des champs** jacket potatoes (**c**) *(d'avocat, de juge)* robe, gown (**d**) *(habit religieux)* robe (**e**) *(pelage) (de cheval)* coat (**f**) *(du vin)* colour

robinet [rɔbinɛ] *nm Br* tap, *Am* faucet

robinetterie [rɔbinɛtri] *nf* plumbing

robineux [rɔbinø] *nm Can Fam Br* tramp, *Am* hobo

robot [rɔbo] *nm* robot; **r. ménager** food processor

robotique [rɔbɔtik] **1** *adj* robotic

2 *nf* robotics *(singulier)*

robotisation [rɔbɔtizasjɔ̃] *nf* automation, robotization

robotiser [rɔbɔtize] *vt* to automate, to robotize

robuste [rɔbyst] *adj* *(personne)* robust; *(bras, jambe)* sturdy; *(appétit)* healthy; *(plante)* hardy; **être d'une santé r.** to have a healthy constitution

robustesse [rɔbystɛs] *nf* *(d'une personne)* robustness; *(d'une plante)* hardiness; *(d'un véhicule)* sturdiness

roc [rɔk] *nm* rock

rocade [rɔkad] *nf* *(route)* bypass

rocaille [rɔkaj] **1** *nf* (**a**) *(terrain)* stony ground (**b**) *(jardin)* rockery

2 *adj inv* *(style)* rocaille

rocailleux, -euse [rɔkajø, -øz] *adj* (**a**) *(pierreux)* stony, rocky (**b**) *Fig (voix)* harsh, rough

rocambolesque [rɔkɑ̃bɔlɛsk] *adj* fantastic, incredible

roche [rɔʃ] *nf* rock

rocher [rɔʃe] *nm* (**a**) *(masse de pierre)* rock; *(escarpé)* crag; **le R.** = Monaco; **le r. de Gibraltar** the Rock of Gibraltar (**b**) *(paroi)* rock face (**c**) **r. (au chocolat)** chocolate *(containing nuts)*

rocheux, -euse [rɔʃø, -øz] *adj* *(paysage, région)* rocky; **la paroi rocheuse** the rock face; **les (montagnes) Rocheuses** the Rocky Mountains

rock [rɔk] **1** *adj inv* *(concert, groupe, chanteur)* rock

2 *nm inv* **le r.** rock; **danser le r.** to jive

rocker [rɔkœr] *nm*, **rockeur, -euse** [rɔkœr, -øz] *nm,f* *(musicien)* rock musician; *(fan)* rock fan

rocking-chair (*pl* **rocking-chairs**) [rɔkiɲtʃɛr] *nm* rocking chair

rock'n roll [rɔkɛnrɔl] *nm* **le r.** rock and roll

rococo [rɔkoko] **1** *adj inv* (**a**) *(meuble, style)* rococo (**b**) *(démodé)* old-fashioned

2 *nm* rococo

rodage [rɔdaʒ] *nm* *(d'une voiture)* running in; **en r.** *(sur panneau)* running in

rodéo [rɔdeo] *nm* *(avec des chevaux)* rodeo; *Fig (bagarre)* free-for-all

roder [rɔde] *vt* *(moteur, voiture)* to run in; *Fig (entreprise, spectacle)* to get into its stride; *(équipe, structure)* to break in; **être rodé** *(entreprise, spectacle)* to be into its stride; *(employé)* to have got the hang of things

rôder [rɔde] *vi* to be on the prowl

rôdeur, -euse [rɔdœr, -øz] *nm,f* prowler

rogne [rɔɲ] *nf Fam* bad temper; **être en r. (contre)** to be cross (with); **mettre qn en r.** to make sb cross; **se mettre** *ou* *très Fam* **se ficher en r.** to get mad

rogner [rɔɲe] **1** *vt* (**a**) *(griffes, ongles)* to clip, to trim; *Fig (économies)* to eat away at; *Fig* **r. les ailes à qn** to clip sb's wings (**b**) *(retrancher)* **r. qch à qn** to gradually take sth away from sb (**c**) *Ordinat (image)* to crop

2 *vt ind* **r. sur qch** to cut down on sth

rognon [rɔɲɔ̃] *nm Culin* kidney

rognures [rɔɲyr] *nfpl* *(de cuir, de métal)* trimmings, parings

rogue [rɔg] *adj* arrogant, haughty

roi [rwa] **1** *nm* (**a**) *(souverain)* king; **tirer les rois** = to celebrate Twelfth Night; **les Rois mages** the Three Wise Men; **le R.-Soleil** the Sun King (**b**) *Fig (le plus grand) (des animaux)* king; **c'est le r. des imbéciles** he's a prize idiot; *très Fam* **c'est le r. des cons** he's a complete *Br* arsehole *or Am* asshole (**c**) *(aux cartes, aux échecs)* king

2 *adj inv* **bleu r.** royal blue

Tirer les rois

The French traditionally celebrate Epiphany with a round, almond-flavoured pastry ("la galette des Rois") containing a small porcelain figurine ("la fève" – originally a dried bean). The pastry is shared out and the person who finds the "fève" is appointed "king" or "queen" and given a cardboard crown to wear. This tradition is called "tirer les Rois".

---

roitelet [rwatlɛ] *nm (oiseau)* wren

rôle [rol] *nm* (**a**) *(d'une pièce de théâtre)* part, role; *Fig* **avoir le beau r.** to have the easy job; **premier r.** leading role; **r.-titre** title role (**b**) *(fonction) (du médecin, d'un organe, d'une activité)* role, function (**dans** in); **jouer un r. de premier plan** to play a key role; **jouer un r. secondaire** to play second fiddle

roller [rɔlœr] **1** *nm* rollerblading; **faire du r.** to go rollerblading

2 **rollers** *nmpl* rollerblades

ROM [rɔm] *nf Ordinat* ROM

romain, -e¹ [rɔmɛ̃, -ɛn] **1** *adj* Roman

2 *nm,f* **R.** Roman

3 *nm (caractère d'imprimerie)* roman

romaine² [rɔmɛn] *nf (salade) Br* cos lettuce, *Am* romaine; *Fig* **être bon comme la r.** to be extremely kind

roman¹ [rɔmɑ̃] *nm* (**a**) *(en prose)* novel; **le nouveau r.** the anti-novel, the nouveau roman; **r. d'amour** love story, romance; *Fam* **r. à l'eau de rose** soppy love story, soppy romance; **r. noir** thriller; **r. policier** detective novel (**b**) *(poème)* romance (**c**) *Fig* **c'est du r.** *(c'est invraisemblable)* it's just a fairy tale; *Fig* **c'est tout un r.** *(c'est incroyable)* it's quite a tale

roman²,-e [rɔmɑ̃, -an] **1** *adj* (**a**) *(langue)* Romance (**b**) *Archit* Romanesque

2 *nm* (**a**) *(langue)* Romance (**b**) *Archit* Romanesque style

romance [rɔmɑ̃s] *nf (chanson)* sentimental song *or* ballad

romancer [16] [rɔmɑ̃se] *vt (événement, histoire)* to romanticize; *(biographie)* to fictionalize

romanche [rɔmɑ̃ʃ] *adj & nm* Romansch

romancier, -ère [rɔmɑ̃sje, -ɛr] *nm,f* novelist

romand, -e [rɔmɑ̃, -ɑ̃d] **1** *adj (Suisse)* French-speaking

2 *nm,f* **R.** French-speaking Swiss person

romanesque [rɔmanɛsk] *adj* (**a**) *(personne, aventure)* romantic (**b**) *(technique)* novelistic

roman-feuilleton *(pl* **romans-feuilletons**) [rɔmɑ̃fœjtɔ̃] *nm* serial

roman-fleuve *(pl* **romans-fleuves**) [rɔmɑ̃œv] *nm* saga

romanichel, -elle [rɔmaniʃɛl] *nm,f (Tsigane)* gypsy

roman-photo *(pl* **romans-photos**) [rɔmɑ̃fɔto] *nm* photo-story

romantique [rɔmɑ̃tik] **1** *adj* (**a**) *(peinture, littérature, artiste)* Romantic (**b**) *(personne, idées, film)* romantic

2 *nmf* (**a**) *(artiste, auteur)* Romantic(ist) (**b**) *(personne)* romantic

romantisme [rɔmɑ̃tism] *nm* (**a**) *(courant artistique)* Romanticism (**b**) *(attitude, sensibilité)* romanticism

romarin [rɔmarɛ̃] *nm* rosemary

rombière [rɔ̃bjɛr] *nf Fam* old biddy

Rome [rɔm] *n* Rome

rompre [rɔ̃pr] **1** *vt* (**a**) *(casser)* to break; **r. ses digues** *(fleuve)* to burst its banks (**b**) *(négociations, fiançailles, relations)* to break off; *(contrat, charme, monotonie)* to break; *(équilibre)* to upset (**c**) *(locutions)* **applaudir à tout r.** to applaud wildly; **r. les rangs** to fall out

2 *vi* (**a**) *(casser)* to break (**b**) *(se séparer)* to split up (**avec** with); **r. avec sa famille** to break off relations with one's family (**c**) **r. avec la tradition** to break with tradition

3 se rompre *vpr (se casser)* to break; **son cœur battait à se r.** his heart was pounding; *Fig* **se r. le cou** to break one's neck

rompu, -e [rɔ̃py] *adj* (**a**) *(exténué)* **être r. (de fatigue)** to be worn out (**b**) *(expérimenté)* **r. à qch** used to sth

romsteck [rɔmstɛk] *nm* rump steak

ronce [rɔ̃s] *nf* (**a**) *(arbuste)* bramble (bush), blackberry bush (**b**) *(dans le bois)* **r. de noyer** burr walnut

ronchon, -onne [rɔ̃ʃɔ̃, -ɔn] *Fam* **1** *adj* grouchy, grumpy

2 *nm,f* grumbler, grouser

ronchonnement [rɔ̃ʃɔnmɑ̃] *nm Fam* grumbling, grousing

ronchonner [rɔ̃ʃɔne] *vi Fam* to grumble, to grouse

roncier [rɔ̃sje] *nm,* **roncière** [rɔ̃sjɛr] *nf* thick bramble bush

rond, -e [rɔ̃, rɔ̃d] **1** *adj* (**a**) *(balle, table, nappe)* round; *(ventre)* rounded; *(poitrine)* full; *(personne, joues, silhouette)* plump; **avoir le dos r.** to be round-shouldered (**b**) *(plein) (voix)* full (**c**) *(chiffre, compte)* round (**d**) **être r. en affaires** to be straightforward where business is concerned (**e**) *Fam (ivre)* plas-

tered; **r. comme une queue de pelle** *Br* rat-arsed, *Am* stewed to the gills

2 *adv* **tout r.** *(exactement)* exactly

3 *nm* (**a**) *(figure)* circle; **en r.** in a circle; *Fam* **faire des ronds de jambe** to bow and scrape; *Fam* **en rester comme deux ronds de flan** to be absolutely staggered; **r. de serviette** napkin ring (**b**) *Fam (sou)* **il n'a pas un r.** he's flat broke, *Br* he hasn't got a penny

rond-de-cuir *(pl* **ronds-de-cuir**) [rɔ̃dkɥir] *nm Fam Péj* pen-pusher

ronde [rɔ̃d] *nf* (**a**) *(danse)* round (dance); *(chanson)* round, roundelay (**b**) *(de gardien, de vigile)* round(s); *(de policier)* beat; **faire une/sa r.** *(gardien, vigile)* to patrol; *(policier)* to be on the beat (**c**) *Mus (note) Br* semibreve, *Am* whole note (**d**) **à la r.** *(autour)* around; **à 10 kilomètres à la r.** within a radius of 10 kilometres

rondeau, -x [rɔ̃do] *nm* rondo

rondelet, -ette [rɔ̃dlɛ, -ɛt] *adj* (**a**) *(personne)* plump, chubby (**b**) *(somme)* tidy

rondelle [rɔ̃dɛl] *nf* (**a**) *(de citron, de saucisson)* slice; **couper qch en rondelles** to slice sth (**b**) *Can* **r. (de hockey)** puck (**c**) *(d'écrou)* washer

rondement [rɔ̃dmɑ̃] *adv* (**a**) *(avec entrain)* briskly, promptly; **mener qch r.** to make short work of sth (**b**) *(franchement)* bluntly, frankly

rondeur [rɔ̃dœr] *nf* (**a**) *(d'un corps)* roundness; *(des joues)* plumpness (**b**) **rondeurs** *(d'une femme)* curves (**c**) *(amabilité)* **avec r.** bluntly, frankly

rondin [rɔ̃dɛ̃] *nm* log

rondo [rɔ̃do] *nm* rondo

rondouillard, -e [rɔ̃dujar, -ard] *adj Fam (personne)* plump, chubby

rond-point *(pl* **ronds-points**) [rɔ̃pwɛ̃] *nm (sens giratoire) Br* roundabout, *Am* traffic circle

ronéotyper [rɔneɔtipe] *vt* to roneo

ronflant, -e [rɔ̃flɑ̃, -ɑ̃t] *adj Péj* high-flown, high-sounding

ronflement [rɔ̃fləmɑ̃] *nm* (**a**) *(d'une personne)* snoring (**b**) *(d'un moteur, d'une machine)* whirring, purring

ronfler [rɔ̃fle] *vi* (**a**) *(dormeur)* to snore (**b**) *(moteur)* to whirr, to purr; *(poêle)* to purr

ronfleur, -euse [rɔ̃flœr, -øz] *nm,f (personne)* snorer

ronger [45] [rɔ̃ʒe] **1** *vt* (**a**) *(bois)* to gnaw (at), to nibble (at); *(os)* to gnaw (on); **rongé par les vers** worm-eaten (**b**) *(acide, rouille)* to eat away or into; *(falaise)* to erode (**c**) *(tourmenter)* **être rongé de chagrin** to be tormented with grief; **être rongé de remords/par la jalousie/par l'anxiété** to be eaten up with remorse/jealousy/anxiety; **être rongé par la maladie** to be wasted by illness (**d**) *Fig* **r. son frein** to champ at the bit

2 se ronger *vpr* **se r. les ongles** to bite one's nails

rongeur, -euse [rɔ̃ʒœr, -øz] **1** *adj (mammifère)* rodent-like

2 *nm* rodent

ronron [rɔ̃rɔ̃], **ronronnement** [rɔ̃rɔnmɑ̃] *nm* (**a**) *(d'un chat)* purr (**b**) *(d'un moteur)* purr, whirr; *(d'un avion, d'une voix)* drone; *(d'une machine)* whirr (**c**) *(routine)* humdrum routine

ronronner [rɔ̃rɔne] *vi* (**a**) *(chat)* to purr (**b**) *(moteur)* to purr, to whirr; *(avion)* to drone; *(machine)* to whirr

roquefort [rɔkfɔr] *nm* Roquefort

roquet [rɔkɛ] *nm Péj (chien)* yap

roquette¹ [rɔkɛt] *nf (salade)* rocket

roquette² *nf (projectile)* rocket; **r. antichar** anti-tank rocket

rorqual, -als [rɔrkwal] *nm* rorqual, finback whale
rosace [rozas] *nf* (**a**) *(vitrail)* rose window (**b**) *(au plafond)* ceiling rose (**c**) *(de guitare)* rose
rosaire [rozɛr] *nm* rosary; **dire** *ou* **réciter son r.** to say the rosary
rosâtre [rozɑtr] *adj* pinkish
rosbif [rɔzbif] *nm* (**a**) *(viande) (rôtie)* roast beef; *(à rôtir)* roasting beef (**b**) *Fam (Britannique)* Brit, = pejorative or humorous term used to refer to a British person
rose [roz] **1** *adj* pink; *Fig* **tout n'est pas r.** it's not all rosy; **r. bonbon** candy pink; **r. thé** tea rose; **vieux r.** old rose
  2 *nf* (**a**) *(fleur)* rose; **frais comme une r.** fresh as a daisy; *Fam* **ne pas sentir la r.** to be a bit whiffy; **r. trémière** hollyhock (**b**) **r. des sables** desert rose; **r. des vents** compass card
  3 *nm* pink; **voir la vie** *ou* **tout en r.** to see everything through rose-tinted *Br* spectacles *or Am* glasses
rosé, -e [roze] **1** *adj* pinkish
  2 *nm (vin)* rosé
roseau, -x [rozo] *nm* reed
rosée [roze] *nf* dew
roseraie [rozrɛ] *nf* rose garden
rosette [rozɛt] *nf* (**a**) *(nœud)* bow; *(ornement)* rosette (**b**) *(insigne)* rosette *(especially of the Legion of Honour)*
rosier [rozje] *nm* rose-tree, rosebush
rosière [rozjɛr] *nf Vieilli* = village maiden awarded a wreath of roses for her virtuous conduct
rosir [rozir] **1** *vt* to turn pink
  2 *vi* to go *or* turn pink
rosse [rɔs] *Péj* **1** *adj Fam (personne, conduite, remarque)* rotten
  2 *nf* (**a**) *(cheval)* hack (**b**) *Fam (homme)* swine; *(femme)* bitch
rossée [rɔse] *nf Fam* beating, walloping
rosser [rɔse] *vt Fam* **r. qn** to beat sb up, to give sb a good hiding; **se faire r.** to get a hiding
rossignol [rɔsiɲɔl] *nm* (**a**) *(oiseau)* nightingale (**b**) *Fam (objet)* white elephant
rot [ro] *nm Fam* belch, burp; *(de bébé)* burp; **faire un r.** *(adulte)* to belch, to burp; *(bébé)* to burp
rotatif, -ive [rɔtatif, -iv] **1** *adj (pompe, moteur)* rotary
  2 *nf* **rotative** rotary press
rotation [rɔtasjɔ̃] *nf* rotation; *(du stock, de fonds)* turnover
roter [rɔte] *vi Fam* to belch, to burp
rôti, -e [roti] **1** *adj* roast
  2 *nm (viande)* joint, roast; **r. de porc** *(cuit)* roast pork; *(non cuit)* joint of pork
rotin¹ [rɔtɛ̃] *nm* rattan; **chaise en r.** cane *or* rattan chair
rotin² *nm Fam Vieilli (sou)* **il n'a plus un r.** he's stone-broke
rôtir [rotir] **1** *vt (viande)* to roast
  2 *vi* (**a**) *(viande)* to roast (**b**) **r. au soleil** to bask in the sun
  3 **se rôtir** *vpr* **se r. au soleil** to bask in the sun
rôtisserie [rotisri] *nf* (**a**) *(boutique du rôtisseur)* = shop selling roast meat (**b**) *(restaurant)* grillroom, steakhouse
rôtissoire [rotiswar] *nf* (rotating) spit, rotisserie
rotonde [rɔtɔ̃d] *nf* rotunda
rotor [rɔtɔr] *nm* rotor

rotule [rɔtyl] *nf* kneecap; *Fam* **être sur les rotules** to be dead beat
roturier, -ère [rɔtyrje, -ɛr] **1** *adj* common
  2 *nm,f* commoner
rouage [rwaʒ] *nm* (**a**) *(d'un mécanisme)* works (**b**) *Fig (d'une administration, d'une organisation)* workings
roublard, -e [rublar, -ard] *Fam* **1** *adj (personne, air)* wily, cunning
  2 *nm,f* wily *or* cunning devil
roublardise [rublardiz] *nf Fam* (**a**) *(caractère)* cunning, wiliness (**b**) *(acte)* crafty *or* cunning trick
rouble [rubl] *nm* rouble
roucoulade [rukulad] *nf (d'oiseaux)* cooing; *Fam* **roucoulades** *(d'amoureux)* billing and cooing
roucoulement [rukulmɑ̃] *nm (d'un pigeon)* cooing; *Fig (d'amoureux)* billing and cooing
roucouler [rukule] **1** *vi (pigeon)* to coo; *Fig (amoureux)* to bill and coo
  2 *vt (mots doux, promesses)* to coo
roue [ru] *nf* (**a**) *(d'un véhicule)* wheel; **être la cinquième r. du carrosse** *Br* to be a spare part, *Am* to be the fifth wheel; **faire la r.** *(oiseau)* to spread its tail; *Fig & Péj* to strut, to swagger; **un deux roues** a two-wheeled vehicle; **r. libre** freewheel; **descendre en r. libre** to freewheel downhill; **r. de secours** spare wheel (**b**) *(figure de gymnastique)* cartwheel
roué, -e [rwe] *Litt* **1** *adj* cunning, sly
  2 *nm,f* cunning person
rouer [rwe] *vt* **r. qn de coups** to beat sb black and blue
rouerie [ruri] *nf (acte)* cunning *or* sly trick (**envers** played on)
rouet [rwɛ] *nm* spinning wheel
rouge [ruʒ] **1** *adj* (**a**) *(tissu, objet, joue, vin)* red; **r. cerise** cherry-red; **r. sang** blood-red (**b**) *(personne)* **r. de colère/d'émotion** red in the face with anger/emotion; **être r. de honte** to blush with shame; **être r. comme une écrevisse** to be as red as a lobster; **être r. comme une tomate** *ou* **une pivoine** to be as red as a beetroot (**c**) *(chauffé) (fer)* red-hot
  2 *adv* **se fâcher tout r.** to lose one's temper completely; **voir r.** to see red
  3 *nm* (**a**) *(couleur)* red; **peindre/teindre qch en r.** to paint/dye sth red; **le r. lui monte aux joues** he's/she's going red in the face (**b**) *(chaleur extrême)* **porter** *ou* **chauffer qch au r.** to heat sth until it is red-hot (**c**) *(cosmétique)* **r. à lèvres** lipstick; **se mettre du r.** to put some *or* one's lipstick on (**d**) *Fam* **passer au r.** *(signal d'arrêt)* to turn *or* go red (**e**) *(vin)* red wine; *Fam* **gros r.** plonk (**f**) *Fam Fig* **être dans le r.** *(financièrement)* to be in the red
  4 *nmf (communiste)* Red
rougeâtre [ruʒɑtr] *adj* reddish
rougeaud, -e [ruʒo, -od] **1** *adj* red-faced
  2 *nm,f* red-faced person
rouge-gorge *(pl* **rouges-gorges**) [ruʒgɔrʒ] *nm* robin
rougeoiement [ruʒwamɑ̃] *nm* red glow
rougeole [ruʒɔl] *nf* measles *(singulier)*; **avoir la r.** to have measles
rougeoyant, -e [ruʒwajɑ̃, -ɑ̃t] *adj* glowing (red)
rougeoyer [32] [ruʒwaje] *vi* to turn red
rouget [ruʒɛ] *nm* red mullet
rougeur [ruʒœr] *nf* (**a**) *(due à la chaleur, à l'émotion)* flush; *(due à la honte, à la gêne)* blush (**b**) *(tache)* blotch (**c**) *(couleur)* redness
rougir [ruʒir] **1** *vt* (**a**) *(ciel, feuilles)* to turn red (**b**) *(visage)* to redden

2 *vi* (**a**) *(ciel, feuilles)* to turn red (**b**) *(personne)* to turn red; *(de honte, de gêne)* to blush, to go red; *Fig (avoir honte)* to be ashamed; **r. jusqu'aux oreilles** to blush to the roots of one's hair; **r. de colère/d'émotion** to flush with anger/emotion

rougissant, -e [ruʒisã, -ãt] *adj (personne, visage)* blushing

rouille [ruj] **1** *adj inv* rust(-coloured)
2 *nf* (**a**) *(sur le fer)* rust (**b**) *(sauce)* = spicy sauce made with garlic and chillis, traditionally served with fish soup

rouillé, -e [ruje] *adj* (**a**) *(métal, clef)* rusty, rusted (**b**) *Fig (personne)* rusty

rouiller [ruje] **1** *vt (métal, clef)* to rust, to make rusty
2 *vi (métal, clef)* to rust, to go rusty
3 se rouiller *vpr* (**a**) *(métal, clef)* to rust, to get rusty (**b**) *Fig (personne) (physiquement)* to get stiff; *(intellectuellement) (langue, connaissances)* to get rusty

roulade [rulad] *nf* (**a**) *(en gymnastique)* **r. avant/arrière** forward/backward roll; **faire des roulades** to do rolls (**b**) *(vocalise)* roulade (**c**) *(charcuterie)* rolled and stuffed meat

roulage [rulaʒ] *nm Belg (circulation)* traffic; **accident de r.** traffic accident

roulant, -e [rulã, -ãt] *adj* (**a**) *(porte)* sliding; *(pont)* travelling (**b**) *(capital)* working (**c**) *Fam (drôle) (personne, blague, histoire)* comical

roulé, -e [rule] **1** *adj* (**a**) *(journal, carte, tapis)* rolled(-up); *(charcuterie)* rolled (**b**) *Fam (femme)* **être bien roulée** to be curvy
2 *nm (gâteau)* Swiss roll

rouleau, -x [rulo] *nm* (**a**) *(bande) (de papier, de Scotch®, de pellicule)* roll; *Fam* **être au bout du r.** to be at the end of one's tether (**b**) *(objet circulaire) (pour peindre)* roller; **r. compresseur** steamroller; **r. à pâtisserie,** *Can & Suisse* **r. à pâte** rolling pin; **r. de printemps** spring roll (**c**) *(vague)* billow, roller (**d**) *(bigoudi)* roller (**e**) *(saut en hauteur)* **r. dorsal** Fosbury flop; **r. ventral** western roll

roulé-boulé *(pl* **roulés-boulés)** [rulebule] *nm* roll *(executed tucked up in a ball)*

roulement [rulmã] *nm* (**a**) *(d'une balle)* rolling (**b**) *(bruit)* **un r. de tonnerre** a roll *or* rumble of thunder; **des roulements de tambour** drum rolls (**c**) *(alternance)* rotation; **par r.** in rotation (**d**) *(pièce)* bearing; **r. à billes** ball bearing (**e**) *Fin (de fonds)* circulation; *(de capitaux)* turnover

rouler [rule] **1** *vt* (**a**) *(pierre, tonneau)* to roll (along) (**b**) *(tapis, papier, manches)* to roll up; *(cigarette)* to roll (**c**) *(yeux)* to roll (**d**) *(balancer)* **r. les épaules** to roll one's shoulders; **r. les hanches** to swing one's hips (**e**) *Fam (duper)* to do (**de** out of); **se faire r.** to be done (**f**) *(locutions)* **r. les r** to roll one's r's; *très Fam* **r. une pelle** *ou* **un palot** *ou* **un patin à qn** to give sb a French kiss
2 *vi* (**a**) *(balle)* to roll; **faire r. qch sur le sol** to roll sth along the ground (**b**) *(dégringoler) (personne)* to roll, to tumble (**c**) *(dans une voiture, dans un train)* to go, to travel; **on a beaucoup roulé** we drove for a long time; **ça roule bien ce matin** there are no traffic problems this morning; **à quelle vitesse rouliez-vous?** what speed were you doing? (**d**) *Fam* **ça roule** everything's fine (**e**) *Fig* **r. sur l'or** to be rolling in money (**f**) *(conversation)* **r. sur qch** to be about sth (**g**) *(tonnerre)* to roll, to rumble; *(tambour)* to roll (**h**) *(navire)* to roll
3 se rouler *vpr* (**a**) *(sur soi-même)* **se r. par terre** to

roll about on the floor; *(dehors)* to roll about on the ground (**b**) **se r. une cigarette** to roll a cigarette; *Fam* **se r. les pouces, se les r.** to twiddle one's thumbs

roulette [rulɛt] *nf* (**a**) *(de meuble)* castor; **à roulettes** *(meuble)* on castors; *Fam* **marcher** *ou* **aller comme sur des roulettes** to go like clockwork (**b**) *Fam (de dentiste)* drill (**c**) *(au jeu)* roulette; **r. russe** Russian roulette

rouli-roulant *(pl* **rouli-roulants)** [rulirulã] *nm Can* skateboard

roulis [ruli] *nm* roll

roulotte [rulɔt] *nf (de bohémiens)* caravan

roulure [rulyr] *nf très Fam* whore

roumain, -e [rumɛ̃, -ɛn] **1** *adj* Romanian
2 *nm,f* **R.** Romanian
3 *nm (langue)* Romanian

Roumanie [rumani] *nf* **la R.** Romania

round [rawnd, rund] *nm* round

roupie [rupi] *nf* rupee

roupiller [rupije] *vi Fam* to sleep, *Br* to kip

roupillon [rupijɔ̃] *nm Fam* snooze; **piquer un r.** to have a snooze

rouquin, -e [rukɛ̃, -in] *Fam* **1** *adj (personne)* red-haired
2 *nm,f* redhead

rouspéter [34] [ruspete] *vi Fam* to moan and groan, to grumble (**contre** about)

rouspéteur, -euse [ruspetœr, -øz] *Fam* **1** *adj* grumpy
2 *nm,f* moaner, grumbler

rousse [rus] *voir* **roux**

roussette [ruset] *nf* (**a**) *(poisson)* spotted dogfish (**b**) *(chauve-souris)* flying fox (**c**) *(grenouille)* common frog

rousseur [rusœr] *nf (couleur)* redness

roussi [rusi] *nm* **ça sent le r.** there's a smell of burning; *Fig* there's trouble brewing

roussir [rusir] **1** *vt* (**a**) *(rendre roux)* to turn brown (**b**) *(brûler)* to scorch, to singe
2 *vi (feuilles, arbres)* to turn brown

rouste [rust] *nf Fam* thrashing, hammering; **flanquer une r. à qn** to give sb a thrashing *or* a hammering

routage [rutaʒ] *nm (d'imprimés)* sorting and mailing

routard, -e [rutar, -ard] *nm,f Fam* backpacker

route [rut] *nf* (**a**) *(voie)* road; **prendre la r. de Paris** to take the Paris road; **r. à double voie** *ou* **à deux voies** *Br* dual carriageway, *Am* divided highway; **par la r.** by road; **r. départementale** secondary road, *Br* ≃ B-road; **r. nationale** main road, *Br* ≃ A-road, *Am* ≃ state highway (**b**) *(itinéraire)* route, way; **montrer la r. à qn** to show sb the way; **c'est sur ma r.** it's on my way; **r. des vins** wine trail (**c**) *(trajet)* **après trois heures de r.** after three hours on the road; **se mettre en r.** *(personne)* to set off; **en r.!** let's be off!; *Fam Hum* **en r., mauvaise troupe!** come on, you lot!; **bonne r.!** have a good trip! (**d**) *Fig (chemin)* path (**e**) *(marche)* **mettre qch en r.** *(moteur)* to start sth up; *(projet, travaux)* to get sth under way; **avoir qch en r.** to be working on sth; *Fam* **ils ont un bébé en r.** they've a baby on the way

routeur [rutœr] *nm Ordinat* router

routier, -ère [rutje, -ɛr] **1** *adj* road
2 *nm* (**a**) *(conducteur)* *Br* long-distance lorry driver, *Am* truck driver (**b**) *(restaurant)* *Br* transport cafe, *Am* truck stop

routine [rutin] *nf* (**a**) *(habitude)* routine; **s'enliser dans/sortir de la r.** to get into/out of a rut (**b**) *Ordinat* **r. d'édition/de logiciel** edit/software routine

routinier, -ère [rutinje, -ɛr] *adj (tâches, travail)* routine; **être r.** to be set in one's ways

rouvrir [52] [ruvrir] **1** *vt* to reopen
2 se rouvrir *vpr* to reopen, to open again

roux, rousse [ru, rus] **1** *adj (feuilles)* russet, reddish-brown; *(cheveux)* red; *(personne)* red-haired; *(sucre)* brown
2 *nm,f (personne)* red-haired person, redhead
3 *nm* (**a**) *(couleur)* russet, reddish-brown (**b**) *(préparation culinaire)* roux

royal, -e, -aux, -ales [rwajal, -o] *adj* (**a**) *(palais, visite)* royal (**b**) *(cadeau)* magnificent; *(pourboire)* huge (**c**) *(indifférence)* utter; *Fam* **ficher une paix royale à qn** to leave sb in complete peace

royalement [rwajalmã] *adv* (**a**) *(payé)* royally (**b**) *Fam* **je m'en fiche** *ou* **moque r.** I couldn't care less

royalisme [rwajalism] *nm* royalism

royaliste [rwajalist] **1** *adj* royalist; *Fig* **être plus r. que le roi** to overdo it
2 *nmf* royalist

royalties [rwajalti] *nfpl* royalties

royaume [rwajom] *nm* kingdom; *Fig* realm

Royaume-Uni [rwajomyni] *nm* **le R.** the United Kingdom

royauté [rwajote] *nf (monarchie)* monarchy; *(dignité)* kingship

RPR [ɛrpeɛr] *nm Pol (abrév* **Rassemblement pour la République)** = right-wing French political party

RSVP *(abrév* **répondez s'il vous plaît)** RSVP

ruade [rɥad] *nf (d'un cheval)* lashing out, kick

Ruanda [rwãda] = **Rwanda**

ruandais, -e [rwãdɛ, -ɛz] = **rwandais**

ruban [rybã] *nm* ribbon; **r. adhésif** adhesive *or* sticky tape; **r. encreur** *(de machine à écrire)* typewriter ribbon; *Ordinat* **r. perforé** punchtape

rubéole [rybeɔl] *nf* German measles *(singulier)*, rubella

rubicond, -e [rybikɔ̃, -ɔ̃d] *adj (teint)* florid, rubicund

rubis [rybi] *nm* (**a**) *(pierre précieuse)* ruby; *Fig* **payer r. sur l'ongle** to pay cash on the nail (**b**) *(de montre, d'horloge)* jewel

rubrique [rybrik] *nf* (**a**) *(articles)* column (**b**) *(catégorie)* heading; **r. nécrologique** obituary section

ruche [ryʃ] *nf* (**a**) *(abri)* beehive (**b**) *(essaim)* hive; *Fig (ville, école)* hive of activity

rucher [ryʃe] *nm* apiary

rude [ryd] *adj* (**a**) *(fruste)* rough, uncouth (**b**) *(sévère) (personne, voix)* harsh (**c**) *(peau, tissu)* rough (**d**) *(hiver, climat)* severe, harsh (**e**) *(tâche, métier)* tough

rudement [rydmã] *adv* (**a**) *(répondre)* harshly; **être r. éprouvé** to be severely tested (**b**) *(frapper, heurter)* hard (**c**) *Fam (très)* really

rudesse [rydɛs] *nf* harshness; **avec r.** harshly

rudimentaire [rydimãtɛr] *adj* rudimentary

rudiments [rydimã] *nmpl (d'une matière)* rudiments; **avoir des r. de chinois** to speak basic Chinese

rudoyer [32] [rydwaje] *vt* to treat harshly

rue [ry] *nf* street; **être/se retrouver à la r.** to be/find oneself out on the street; **mettre/jeter qn à la r.** to put/throw sb out on the street; **r. piétonnière** *ou* **piétonne** pedestrian precinct; **r. principale** main street; **la grande r.** the main street

ruée [rɥe] *nf* rush; **la r. vers l'or** the gold rush

ruelle [rɥɛl] *nf* lane, alley(way)

ruer [rɥe] **1** *vi (cheval)* to kick; *Fig* **r. dans les brancards** to rebel
2 se ruer *vpr* **se r. sur qn** to rush at sb; **se r. sur qch** to make a rush for sth; **les invités se sont rués sur le buffet** the guests made a dash for the buffet

rugby [rygbi] *nm* rugby; **r. à treize/quinze** Rugby League/Union

rugbyman [rygbiman] *(pl* **rugbymen** [rygbimɛn]*) nm* rugby player

rugir [ryʒir] **1** *vi* (**a**) *(fauve)* to roar (**b**) *(personne)* to roar (**de** with) (**c**) *(vent, tempête)* to howl
2 *vt* to roar

rugissement [ryʒismã] *nm* (**a**) *(d'un fauve)* roar; **des rugissements** roaring (**b**) *(d'une personne)* roar; **pousser des rugissements de colère** to roar with anger (**c**) *(du vent, d'une tempête)* howling

rugosité [rygozite] *nf* roughness; **rugosités** rough patches

rugueux, -euse [rygø, -øz] *adj* rough

ruine [rɥin] *nf* (**a**) *(écroulement) (d'un édifice)* **en r.** in ruins, ruined; **tomber en ruine(s)** to go to ruin (**b**) **ruines** *(décombres)* ruins (**c**) *Fig (d'une personne, d'une société)* ruin, downfall; **aller** *ou* **courir à la r.** to be on the road to ruin (**d**) *(vieille maison)* ruin (**e**) *Fam* **c'est la r.!** *(c'est coûteux)* it's outrageously expensive!

ruiner [rɥine] **1** *vt* to ruin; *(espoirs)* to ruin, to dash
2 se ruiner *vpr (perdre son argent)* to ruin *or* bankrupt oneself; *(dépenser beaucoup d'argent)* to spend a fortune

ruineux, -euse [rɥinø, -øz] *adj* ruinously expensive; **ce n'est pas r.** it won't ruin you/us/*etc*

ruisseau, -x [rɥiso] *nm* (**a**) *(cours d'eau)* brook, stream (**b**) *Fig (de sang, de lave)* stream; *(de larmes)* flood (**c**) *(caniveau)* gutter

ruisselant, -e [rɥislã, -ãt] *adj* dripping (**de** with)

ruisseler [42] [rɥisle] *vi* (**a**) *(liquide)* to stream, to run (**b**) *(surface)* to drip, to stream (**de** with); **le front ruisselant de sueur** with one's forehead dripping with sweat; **ses joues ruisselaient de larmes** tears were streaming down his cheeks

ruissellement [rɥisɛlmã] *nm* streaming, running

rumba [rumba] *nf* rumba

rumeur [rymœr] *nf* (**a**) *(bruit confus)* distant murmur; *(de la circulation, d'une ville)* hum; *(de voix)* murmur (**b**) *(nouvelle)* rumour

ruminant [ryminã] *nm* ruminant

rumination [ryminasjɔ̃] *nf* rumination, ruminating

ruminer [rymine] **1** *vt (herbe)* to chew; *Fig (idée, projet)* to mull over
2 *vi* to ruminate, to chew the cud; *Fig* to brood

rumsteck [rɔmstɛk] *nm* rump steak

rupestre [rypɛstr] *adj* (**a**) **peinture r.** rock painting; *(dans une caverne)* cave painting (**b**) *(plante)* rock

rupin, -e [rypɛ̃, -in] *Fam* **1** *adj (riche) (personne)* loaded; *(quartier)* plush; *Br* posh
2 *nm,f* **c'est un r.** he's loaded; **les rupins** the rich

rupture [ryptyr] *nf* (**a**) *(d'une corde, d'une poutre)* breaking; *(d'un barrage)* bursting; *(d'un tendon)* rupture (**b**) *(interruption) (de négociations)* breaking off (**de** of), breakdown (**de** in); **être en r. avec qn/qch** to be at odds with sb/sth; **en r. avec la tradition** in a break with tradition; **être en r. de stock** to be out of stock (**c**) *(annulation) (de fiançailles)* breaking off; *(de* *contrat)* breach (**d**) *(entre amoureux)* break-up; **être au bord de la r.** to be on the verge of breaking up

rural, -e, -aux, -ales [ryral, -o] **1** *adj (région, vie)* rural; *(chemin)* country
 2 *nm,f* country person

ruse [ryz] *nf* (**a**) *(procédé)* ruse, trick; **r. de guerre** stratagem (of war); *Fig* dodge (**b**) *(calcul)* **faire qch par la r.** to do sth by trickery

rusé, -e [ryze] *adj* cunning, crafty

ruser [ryze] *vi* to use trickery *or* cunning

russe [rys] **1** *adj* Russian
 2 *nmf* **R.** Russian
 3 *nm (langue)* Russian

Russie [rysi] *nf* **la R.** Russia

rustaud, -e [rysto, -od] **1** *adj* uncouth
 2 *nm,f Br* country bumpkin, *Am* hick

Rustine® [rystin] *nf* repair patch *(for mending inner tube of bicycle)*

rustique [rystik] *adj* (**a**) *(manières, vie)* rustic; *(meuble)* rustic-style (**b**) *(plante)* hardy

rustre [rystr] **1** *adj* uncouth
 2 *nm* boor, lout

rut [ryt] *nm (de mâle)* rut(ting); *(de femelle)* heat; **en r.** *(mâle)* rutting; *(femelle) Br* on *or Am & Ir* in heat

rutabaga [rytabaga] *nm Br* swede, *Am* rutabaga

rutilant, -e [rytilã, -ãt] *adj* gleaming

rutiler [rytile] *vi* to gleam

Rwanda [rwãda] *nm* **le R.** Rwanda

rwandais, -e [rwãdɛ, -ɛz] **1** *adj* Rwandan
 2 *nm,f* **R.** Rwandan

rythme [ritm] *nm* (**a**) *(succession)* rhythm; *(allure)* pace; **manquer de r.** *(film)* to be a bit slow; **au r. de** at the rate of; **r. cardiaque/respiratoire** heart/breathing rate; **les rythmes scolaires** the way in which the school year is organized (**b**) *(en musique)* rhythm; **en r.** in time; **marquer le r.** to beat time; **suivre le r.** to follow the beat; *Fig* to keep up; **avoir le sens du r.** to have a sense of rhythm; **avoir le r. dans la peau** to have rhythm in one's blood (**c**) *(d'une phrase)* rhythm

rythmé, -e [ritme] *adj* rhythmic(al)

rythmer [ritme] *vt* to give rhythm to

rythmique [ritmik] **1** *adj* rhythmic(al)
 2 *nf (en poésie)* rhythmics *(singulier)*

S

S¹, s [ɛs] *nm inv* S, s; **faire des s** to zigzag; **en S** *(crochet)* S-shaped; *(route)* zigzagging

S² (**a**) *(abrév* **sud**) S (**b**) *(abrév* **seconde(s)**) sec

s' [s] *voir* se

SA [ɛsa] *nf (abrév* **société anonyme**) plc

sa [sa] *voir* son¹

sabbat [saba] *nm* Sabbath

sabbatique [sabatik] *adj (repos, année, congé)* sabbatical; **prendre un an de congé s.** to take a year's sabbatical

sable [sabl] **1** *nm* sand; *Fam* **être sur le s.** *(sans travail)* to be out of work; *(sans argent)* to be down and out; *Fam* **mettre qn sur le s.** to ruin sb; **sables mouvants** quicksands
  2 *adj inv* sand-coloured

sablé, -e [sable] **1** *adj voir* **pâte**
  2 *nm* shortbread *Br* biscuit *orAm* cookie

sabler [sable] *vt* (**a**) *(chemin)* to sand; *(route)* to grit (**b**) *(bâtiment)* to sandblast (**c**) **s. le champagne** to crack open a bottle of champagne

sableuse [sabløz] *nf* sandblaster

sableux, -euse [sablø, -øz] *adj* sandy

sablier [sablije] *nm* hourglass

sablonneux, -euse [sablɔnø, -øz] *adj* sandy

sabord [sabɔr] *nm* = type of square porthole; *Fam Vieilli* **mille sabords!** shiver me timbers!

saborder [saborde] **1** *vt (navire)* to scuttle; *Fig (entreprise)* to scupper
  2 se saborder *vpr* to scuttle one's ship

sabot [sabo] *nm* (**a**) *(de cheval)* hoof; *Fam* **ça ne se trouve pas sous le s. d'un cheval** it doesn't grow on trees (**b**) *(chaussure)* clog; *Fam* **je te vois venir avec tes gros sabots** I can see what you're after (**c**) **s. de Denver** wheel clamp; **mettre un s. de Denver à une voiture** to (wheel-)clamp a car

sabotage [sabotaʒ] *nm* sabotage; *(acte)* act of sabotage

saboter [sabote] *vt (voiture, entreprise, plan de paix)* to sabotage; *(travail)* to make a mess of

saboteur, -euse [sabotœr, -øz] *nm,f* saboteur

sabre [sabr] *nm* sabre; **s. au clair** with drawn sword

sabrer [sabre] *vt* (**a**) **une cicatrice lui sabrait la joue** there was the gash of a scar on his cheek (**b**) *Fam (raccourcir)* to slash (**c**) *Fam (critiquer)* to slate (**d**) *Fam* **se faire s.** *(étudiant)* to flunk; **il s'est fait s. par le prof** the teacher flunked him (**e**) **s. le champagne** to crack open a bottle of champagne

sac¹ [sak] *nm* (**a**) *(contenant, contenu)* bag (**de** of); *(grand et en toile)* sack (**de** of); **s. de sable** sandbag; *Fam* **un s. de nœuds** a muddle; **partir s. au dos** to set off with one's rucksack on one's back; *Fam* **vider son s.** to get it off one's chest; *Fam* **je les mets dans le même s.** they're as bad as each other; *Fam* **l'affaire est dans le s.** it's in the bag; **s. de couchage** sleeping bag; **s. à dos** rucksack, backpack; **s. à main** handbag; *Fam* **s. d'os** bag of bones; **s. à ouvrage** work bag; **s. poubelle** *Br* bin liner, *Am* garbage bag; **s. à provisions** shopping bag; *Fam* **s. à vin** drunk; **s. de voyage** travel *or* overnight bag (**b**) *très Fam (somme)* 10 francs; **10 sacs** 100 francs

sac² *nm (pillage)* sacking; **mettre une ville à s.** to sack a town

saccade [sakad] *nf* jerk, jolt; **par saccades** in fits and starts

saccadé, -e [sakade] *adj* jerky

saccage [sakaʒ] *nm* havoc; **se livrer à un s. de** to wreak havoc in

saccager [45] [sakaʒe] *vt* (**a**) *(piller) (ville)* to sack; *(maison)* to ransack (**b**) *(dévaster) (ville, maison)* to wreak havoc in; **la récolte fut saccagée par l'orage** the crops were devastated by the storm

saccharose [sakaroz] *nm Chim* saccharose

sacerdoce [saserdɔs] *nm* priesthood; *Fig* vocation

sacerdotal, -e, -aux, -ales [saserdɔtal, -o] *adj* priestly

sachant, sache *etc voir* **savoir**

sachet [saʃɛ] *nm* sachet; **s. de thé** teabag; **thé en sachets** teabags; **en s.-cuisson** boil-in-the-bag

sacoche [sakɔʃ] *nf* (**a**) *(de vélo)* saddlebag (**b**) *(besace)* bag (**c**) *Belg & Can* handbag, *Am* purse

sacquer [sake] *Fam* **1** *vt* (**a**) *(renvoyer)* to fire, *Br* to sack; **se faire s.** to be fired (**b**) *(noter sévèrement)* to give a bad mark to; **se faire s. par un prof** to get a bad mark from a teacher (**c**) *(supporter)* **je ne peux pas le s.** I can't stand him
  2 *vi (professeur)* to be a tough marker

sacrant, -e [sakrã, -ãt] *adj Can Fam (fâcheux)* bothersome

sacre [sakr] *nm* (**a**) *(d'un roi)* coronation; *(d'un évêque)* consecration; *Fig* rite (**b**) *Can (juron)* swear word, expletive

sacré, -e [sakre] **1** *adj* (**a**) *Rel & Fig* sacred (**b**) *Fam (maudit)* damn, *Br* bloody; **s. Paul, qu'est-ce qu'on ferait sans lui?** good old Paul, what would we do without him?
  2 *nm* **le s.** the sacred

sacrement [sakrəmã] *nm* sacrament; **le saint S.** the Blessed Sacrament; **recevoir les derniers sacrements** to receive the last rites

sacrément [sakremɑ̃] *adv Fam* damn, *Br* bloody

sacrer [sakre] **1** *vt (roi)* to crown; *(évêque)* to consecrate; **s. qn roi** to crown sb king; *Fig* **il a été sacré champion de France en 1995** he won the French championship in 1995
2 *vi Can* to swear

sacrifice [sakrifis] *nm* sacrifice; **offrir qn/qch en s.** to offer sb/sth up as a sacrifice; **faire le s. de sa vie** to sacrifice one's life; *Fig* **faire des sacrifices (pour)** to make sacrifices (for)

sacrifier [66] [sakrifje] **1** *vt aussi Fig* to sacrifice (**à** to); **sacrifié** *(prix)* rock-bottom; *(article)* at a rock-bottom price
2 *vi* **s. à la mode** to be a slave to fashion
3 se sacrifier *vpr* to sacrifice oneself (**pour** for); *Fam* **allez, je me sacrifie, je vais les chercher à la gare!** right, I'll be the martyr and pick them up from the station!

sacrilège [sakrilɛʒ] **1** *adj* sacrilegious
2 *nmf (personne)* sacrilegious person
3 *nm (acte)* sacrilege

sacristie [sakristi] *nf* sacristy, vestry

sacro-saint, -e *(mpl* **sacro-saints,** *fpl* **sacro-saintes)** [sakrosɛ̃, -ɛ̃t] *adj aussi Ironique* sacrosanct

sadique [sadik] **1** *adj* sadistic
2 *nmf* sadist

sadisme [sadism] *nm* sadism

sadomaso [sadomazo] *adj inv Fam* SM

sadomasochisme [sadomazoʃism] *nm* sadomasochism

sadomasochiste [sadomazoʃist] **1** *adj* sadomasochistic
2 *nmf* sadomasochist

safari [safari] *nm* safari; **en s.** on safari; **s.-photo** photographic safari

safran [safrɑ̃] **1** *nm (plante, épice)* saffron
2 *adj inv* **(jaune) s.** saffron (yellow)

saga [saga] *nf aussi Fig* saga

sagace [sagas] *adj* shrewd, astute

sagacité [sagasite] *nf* shrewdness, astuteness; **avec s.** shrewdly, astutely

sage [saʒ] **1** *adj* **(a)** *(avisé) (personne, décision)* wise, sensible **(b)** *(calme) (enfant, animal)* good, well-behaved; **s. comme une image** as good as gold **(c)** *(chaste) (personne)* good; *(tenue, robe)* sober
2 *nm* wise man; **un vieux s.** a wise old man

sage-femme *(pl* **sages-femmes)** [saʒfam] *nf* midwife

sagement [saʒmɑ̃] *adv* **(a)** *(raisonnablement)* wisely, sensibly **(b)** *(tranquillement)* quietly

sagesse [saʒɛs] *nf* **(a)** *(intelligence)* wisdom, good sense; **avoir la s. de faire qch** to be wise *or* sensible enough to do sth; **plein de s.** very sensible; *Fig* **la voix de la s.** the voice of reason **(b)** *(calme)* good behaviour

Sagittaire [saʒiter] *nm Astron & Astrol* **le S.** Sagittarius; **être S.** to be **(a)** Sagittarius

sagouin [sagwɛ̃] *nm Fam (personne)* slob

Sahara [saara] *nm* **le S.** the Sahara (Desert)

saharienne [saarjɛn] *nf* safari jacket

Sahel [sael] *nm* **le S.** the Sahel

saignant, -e [sɛɲɑ̃, -ɑ̃t] *adj* **(a)** *(blessure)* bleeding **(b)** *(viande)* rare

saignée [seɲe] *nf* blood-letting; *Fig* drain; **faire une s. à qn** to bleed sb

saignement [sɛɲəmɑ̃] *nm* bleeding; **s. de nez** nosebleed

saigner [seɲe] **1** *vi (personne, blessure)* to bleed; **je saigne du nez** my nose is bleeding, I've got a nosebleed; *Fig & Litt* **mon cœur saigne** my heart bleeds; *Fam* **ça va s.** there's going to be trouble
2 *vt (poulet, personne)* to bleed; *Fig* **s. qn à blanc** to bleed sb dry
3 se saigner *vpr Fig* **se s. aux quatre veines** to bleed oneself dry

saillant, -e [sajɑ̃, -ɑ̃t] *adj (qui dépasse)* projecting; *(pommettes)* prominent; *(muscles)* bulging; *Fig (trait)* salient

saillie [saji] *nf* **(a)** *(partie en avant)* projection; **faire s.** to project, to jut out **(b)** *(par un mâle)* covering

saillir [67] [sajir] **1** *vt (femelle)* to cover
2 *vi (s'avancer)* to project, to jut out (**sur** over)

sain, -e [sɛ̃, sɛn] *adj* healthy; *(fruit, gestion)* sound; *(lectures)* wholesome; **s. de corps et d'esprit** sound in body and mind; **s. et sauf** safe and sound

sainement [sɛnmɑ̃] *adv* **(a)** *(vivre)* healthily **(b)** *(juger)* sensibly

saint, -e [sɛ̃, sɛ̃t] **1** *adj (lieu)* holy; *(personne, vie)* saintly; **s. patron** patron saint; **s. Pierre** St Peter; **sainte Catherine** St Catherine; *Fam* **avoir une sainte horreur de qch** to have a holy horror of sth; *Fam* **ne rien faire de toute la sainte journée** to do nothing the whole blessed day
2 *nm,f aussi Fig* saint; **ne savoir plus à quel s. se vouer** not to know which way to turn; *Hum* **il vaut mieux s'adresser à Dieu qu'à ses saints** it's best to go right to the top
3 *nm* **le S. des Saints** the Holy of Holies

saint-bernard [sɛ̃bɛrnar] *nm inv (chien)* St Bernard

Saint-Cyr [sɛ̃sir] *n* Saint-Cyr military academy

Sainte-Lucie [sɛ̃tlysi] *n* St Lucia

sainte-nitouche *(pl* **saintes-nitouches)** [sɛ̃tnituʃ] *nf* little hypocrite; **avec ses airs de s.** looking as if butter wouldn't melt in her mouth

Saint-Esprit [sɛ̃tɛspri] *nm* **le S.** the Holy Ghost *or* Spirit; *Hum* **par l'opération du S.** by magic

sainteté [sɛ̃təte] *nf (d'une personne)* saintliness; *(de la loi, d'un serment)* sanctity; *(d'un lieu)* holiness; **sa S. (le pape)** His Holiness (the Pope)

saint-frusquin [sɛ̃fryskɛ̃] *nm Fam* **tout le s.** the whole caboodle; **il s'est pointé avec tout son s.** he turned up with all his gear

saint-glinglin [sɛ̃glɛ̃glɛ̃] **à la saint-glinglin** *adv Fam* **on sera payés à la s.** we'll be paid when pigs fly; **repoussé à la s.** postponed till whenever

saint-honoré [sɛ̃tɔnɔre] *nm inv* Saint-Honoré *(choux pastry ring filled with confectioner's custard)*

Saint-Jean [sɛ̃ʒɑ̃] *nf* **(a)** **la S.** Midsummer Day **(b)** *Can* **la Saint-Jean-Baptiste** Saint-Jean-Baptiste Day *(24 July)*

Saint-Laurent [sɛ̃lɔrɑ̃] *nm* **le S.** the St Lawrence (River); **la Voie maritime du S.** the St Lawrence Seaway

Saint-Marin [sɛ̃marɛ̃] *n* San Marino

saint-nectaire [sɛ̃nɛkter] *nm inv* = type of firm cheese

Saint-Père [sɛ̃per] *nm* **le S.** the Holy Father

Saint-Pétersbourg [sɛ̃petɛrsbur] *n* St Petersburg

Saint-Pierre-et-Miquelon [sɛ̃pjɛremiklɔ̃] *n* St Pierre and Miquelon

Saint-Siège [sɛ̃sjɛʒ] *nm* **le S.** the Holy See

Saint-Sylvestre [sɛ̃silvɛstr] *nf* **la S.** New Year's Eve

sais *voir* **savoir**

saisie [sezi] *nf (de biens)* seizure; *Ordinat* **s. de don-nées** data capture, keyboarding; *Ordinat* **s. automa-tique/manuelle** automatic/manual input

saisine [sezin] *nf Jur* referral to a court

saisir [sezir] **1** *vt* (**a**) *(attraper) (personne, objet)* to take hold of; *(brusquement)* to grab; **s. l'occasion (de faire qch)** to seize *or* grasp the opportunity (to do sth); **j'ai été saisi par le froid** the cold really hit me (**b**) *(com-prendre) (signification, nuance)* to grasp, to get; *(nom)* to catch, to get (**c**) *Ordinat (données)* to key (**d**) *Jur (biens)* to seize (**e**) *Jur* **s. un tribunal d'une affaire** to refer a matter to a court (**f**) *(viande)* to seal
  2 *vi (comprendre)* to get it
  3 se saisir *vpr* **se s. de qn/qch** to take hold of sb/sth; *(brusquement)* to grab sb/sth

saisissant, -e [sezisã, -ãt] *adj (froid)* biting; *(ressem-blance)* striking; *(scène)* gripping

saisissement [sezismã] *nm* (**a**) *(sensation de froid)* sudden chill (**b**) *(émotion)* shock

saison [sɛzɔ̃] *nf* season; **en cette s.** at this time of year; **en toute s.** all (the) year round; **faire une bonne/mauvaise s.** *(équipe)* to have a good/bad sea-son; **être de s.** *(fruits)* to be in season; **des fraises! mais ce n'est pas la s.!** strawberries! but it isn't the season for them!; **un temps de s.** seasonal weather; **la belle s.** the summer months; **la haute/basse s.** the high/low season; **la morte s.** the off season; **la s. touristique** the tourist season; **la s. des amours** the mating season; **la s. des pluies** the rainy season

saisonnier, -ère [sɛzɔnje, -ɛr] **1** *adj* seasonal
  2 *nm,f* seasonal worker

sait *voir* **savoir**

saké [sake] *nm* sake

salade [salad] *nf* (**a**) *(plante)* lettuce (**b**) *(plat)* salad; **s. composée** mixed salad; **s. de fruits** fruit salad; **s. mixte** mixed salad; **s. niçoise** salade niçoise; **s. de to-mates/de riz** tomato/rice salad; **s. verte** green salad; **haricots verts en s.** green bean salad (**c**) *Fam (désor-dre)* mess (**d**) *Fam* **vendre sa s.** to make a pitch (**e**) *Fam* **salades** *(mensonges)* tall stories, fibs

saladier [saladje] *nm* salad bowl

salaire [salɛr] *nm* (**a**) *(mensuel)* salary; *(hebdoma-daire, journalier)* wages; *Prov* **toute peine mérite s.** the labourer is worthy of his hire; **s. de départ** start-ing salary; **s. minimum interprofessionnel de crois-sance** guaranteed minimum wage (**b**) *(récompense)* reward (**de** for); **le s. de la peur** the wages of fear

salaison [salɛzɔ̃] *nf (action)* salting; **des salaisons** salted meats

salamalecs [salamalɛk] *nmpl Fam* bowing and scra-ping

salamandre [salamãdr] *nf* salamander

salami [salami] *nm* salami

salant [salã] *adj m voir* **marais**

salarial, -e, -aux, -ales [salarjal, -o] *adj* wage; *(men-suel)* salary

salarié, -e [salarje] **1** *adj* (**a**) *(travailleur) (payé men-suellement)* salaried; *(payé hebdomadairement)* wage-earning (**b**) *(travail)* paid
  2 *nm,f (payé mensuellement)* salaried employee; *(payé hebdomadairement)* wage-earner; **salariés** *(d'une société)* employees

salarier [salarje] *vt* to put on one's salaried staff

salaud [salo] *Vulg* **1** *nm* bastard
  2 *adj* **c'était vraiment s. de faire ça** that was a really shitty thing to do; **t'as vraiment été s.!** you were a real shit!

sale [sal] **1** *adj* (**a**) *(peu soigné)* dirty (**b**) *Fam (grave) (maladie, situation)* nasty; *(affaire)* dirty; **avoir une s. tête** *ou* **gueule** *(antipathique)* to look really nasty; *(malade)* to look awful; **faire un s. coup à qn** to play a dirty trick on sb; **s. bête** horrible beast; **s. boulot** rotten job; **faire le s. boulot** to do the dirty work; **s. gosse** little brat; **s. temps** filthy weather; **s. type** nasty character
  2 *nm Fam* **mettre une chemise au s.** to put a dirty shirt in the wash

salé, -e [sale] **1** *adj* (**a**) *(conservé au sel)* salt; *(addi-tionné de sel)* salted; *(au goût)* salty (**b**) *Fig (histoire, plaisanterie)* spicy (**c**) *Fam (condamnation)* stiff; *(ad-dition)* steep
  2 *nm* **le s.** savoury food; **petit s.** salt pork

salement [salmã] *adv* (**a**) *(manger, boire)* in a disgust-ing manner (**b**) *Fam (blessé, touché)* really badly; **je suis s. emmerdé** I'm in a real mess

saler [sale] *vt* to salt

saleté [salte] *nf* (**a**) *(manque de soin)* dirtiness; *(crasse)* dirt; **faire des saletés** to make a mess (**b**) *(objet)* trash, junk; **manger des saletés** to eat junk food (**c**) *(acte ou remarque obscène)* obscenity (**d**) *Fam (per-sonne)* bastard

salière [saljɛr] *nf* salt cellar

saligaud [saligo] *nm Fam (ignoble individu)* bastard

salin, -e [salɛ̃, -in] **1** *adj* saline
  2 *nm (marais salant)* salt marsh

salir [salir] **1** *vt* to make dirty, to dirty; *Fig* **s. le nom/la mémoire de qn** to sully sb's name/memory
  2 se salir *vpr* to get dirty; *Fig* **se s. les mains** to get one's hands dirty

salissant, -e [salisã, -ãt] *adj* (**a**) *(travail)* dirty, messy (**b**) *(tissu, vêtement)* easily soiled; *(couleur)* that shows the dirt

salissure [salisyr] *nf* dirty mark

salivaire [salivɛr] *adj (glande)* salivary

salive [saliv] *nf* saliva

saliver [salive] *vi* to salivate; *Fig* **s. devant qch** to drool at the sight of sth

salle [sal] *nf* (**a**) *(pièce)* room; **s. d'armes** *(pour l'escrime)* fencing hall; *(pour les armes)* armoury; **s. d'attente** waiting room; **s. de bain(s)** bathroom; *Or-dinat* **s. blanche** clean room; **s. des coffres** vaults; **s. commune** common room; **s. d'embarquement** *(d'un aéroport)* departure lounge; **s. d'exposition** show-room; *(pour une foire)* exhibition hall; **s. des fêtes** community hall; *(d'un village)* village hall; **s. de garde** *(d'hôpital)* staff room; *(de caserne)* guardroom; **s. des machines** *(d'un navire)* engine-room; **s. à manger** dining room; *(meubles)* dining-room suite; **s. d'opéra-tion** operating *Br* theatre *or Am* room; **s. des pas per-dus** *(dans une gare)* concourse; **s. des professeurs** staff room; **s. de réunion** meeting room; **s. du trône** throneroom; **s. des ventes** saleroom (**b**) *(pour le ciné-ma, pour le théâtre)* **s. (de spectacle)** auditorium; **toute la s. applaudit** the whole audience applauded; **les salles obscures** *Br* the cinema, *Am* the movies

salmonelle [salmɔnɛl] *nf* salmonella

salmonellose [salmɔneloz] *nf* salmonella poisoning

Salomon [salɔmɔ̃] *voir* **île**

salon [salɔ̃] *nm* (**a**) *(pièce)* living room, *Br* lounge; *(dans un bateau)* saloon; *(dans un train)* saloon car; *Can* **s. de barbier** barber's; **s. de coiffure** hairdressing salon; **s. d'essayage** fitting room; **s. de thé** tea room (**b**) *(meubles)* suite (**c**) *(exposition)* exhibition; **le S. des Arts ménagers** ≃ the Ideal Home Exhibition; **le S. de l'Automobile** *ou* **de l'Auto** the Motor Show; **le S. du Livre** the Book Fair; **le S. nautique** the Boat Show (**d**) *(littéraire)* salon; **tenir s.** to hold a salon

salon-lavoir (*pl* **salons-lavoirs**) [salɔ̃lavwar] *nm Belg & Suisse (lavomatique) Br* launderette, *Am* laundromat

salopard [salɔpar] *nm Vulg* bastard

salope [salɔp] *nf Vulg (femme méprisable)* bitch; *(homme méprisable)* bastard

saloper [salɔpe] *vt très Fam* (**a**) *(salir)* to dirty, to mess up (**b**) *(mal faire)* to make a dog's breakfast of

saloperie [salɔpri] *nf très Fam* (**a**) *(camelote)* trash, junk (**b**) *(coup bas)* dirty trick (**c**) **dire des saloperies sur qn** to bitch about sb

salopette [salɔpɛt] *nf Br* dungarees, *Am* overalls

salpêtre [salpɛtr] *nm* saltpetre

salsa [salsa] *nf* salsa

salsifis [salsifi] *nm* salsify

saltimbanque [saltɛ̃bãk] *nm* travelling acrobat

salto [salto] *nm* somersault

salubre [salybr] *adj* healthy

salubrité [salybrite] *nf* healthiness; **la s. publique** public health

saluer [salɥe] **1** *vt (en arrivant)* to greet; *(en partant)* to take one's leave of; *(s'incliner devant)* to bow to; *(sujet: soldat)* to salute; **s. qn d'une inclination de la tête** to nod to sb; **il est passé sans me s.** he walked past me without saying hello; **saluez-le de ma part** give him my regards; *Rel* **je vous salue, Marie** hail Mary
2 se saluer *vpr (en arrivant)* to greet each other; *(en partant)* to take leave of each other

salut [saly] **1** *nm* (**a**) *(salutation)* greeting; **faire un s. à qn** *(en se découvrant)* to raise one's hat to sb; *(en inclinant la tête)* to nod to sb (**b**) *(de soldat)* salute; **faire le s. militaire** to give a salute (**c**) *(sauvegarde)* rescue; *Rel* salvation
2 *exclam Fam* **s.!** *(en arrivant)* hi!; *(en partant)* bye!

salutaire [salytɛr] *adj (décision, mesure)* salutary; *(remède)* beneficial; **être s. à qn** to do sb good

salutation [salytasjɔ̃] *nf* greeting

Salvador [salvadɔr] *nm* **le S.** El Salvador

salvadorien, -enne [salvadɔrjɛ̃, -ɛn] **1** *adj* Salvadorean
2 *nm,f* **S.** Salvadorean

salve [salv] *nf* salvo, volley

Samaritain [samaritɛ̃] *nm* **le bon S.** the good Samaritan

samba [sãmba] *nf* samba

samedi [samdi] *nm* Saturday; **le S. saint** Easter Saturday; **s. prochain/dernier** next/last Saturday; **s. matin** Saturday morning; **s. soir** Saturday night *or* evening; **dans la nuit de s. à dimanche** on Saturday night; **s. 11 mai 1997** Saturday 11 May 1997; **nous sommes s. aujourd'hui** today's Saturday; **je commence s.** I'm starting on Saturday; **il vient le s./tous les samedis** he comes on Saturdays/every Saturday; **un s. sur deux** every second *or* other Saturday; **s. en huit/quinze** a week/fortnight on Saturday; **passer tout son s. à**

faire qch to spend one's whole Saturday doing sth; *Belg & Suisse* **faire le** *ou* **son s.** to do the weekly clean

Samoa [samɔa] *nfpl* **les S. occidentales** Western Samoa

samouraï [samuraj] *nm* samurai

samovar [samɔvar] *nm* samovar

sampler¹ [sãplœr] *nm Mus* sampler

sampler² [sãple] *vt Mus* to sample

SAMU [samy] *nm (abrév* **Service d'aide médicale d'urgence**) = ambulance service; **appeler le S.** to call an ambulance; **le S. social** = mobile medical and support service for homeless people

sanatorium [sanatɔrjɔm] *nm* sanatorium

sanctifier [66] [sãktifje] *vt* (**a**) *(rendre saint)* to sanctify (**b**) *(révérer)* **queTon nom soit sanctifié** hallowed be Thy name

sanction [sãksjɔ̃] *nf (punition)* sanction; *Fig (désavantage)* price; **prendre une s. contre qn** to take action against sb; **s. pénale** penalty; **sanctions économiques** economic sanctions

sanctionner [sãksjɔne] *vt* (**a**) *(punir)* to punish (**b**) *(approuver)* to sanction; **sanctionné par l'usage** sanctioned by custom

sanctuaire [sãktɥɛr] *nm aussi Fig* sanctuary

sandale [sãdal] *nf* sandal

sandalette [sãdalɛt] *nf* (light) sandal

sandre [sãdr] *nm* pikeperch

sandwich (*pl* **sandwichs** *ou* **sandwiches**) [sãdwitʃ] *nm* sandwich; **s. au jambon** ham sandwich; *Fam* **pris en s. (entre)** sandwiched (between)

San Francisco [sãfrãsisko] *n* San Francisco

sang [sã] *nm* blood; **animaux à s. chaud/froid** warm-/cold-blooded animals; **être en s.** to be covered in blood; *Fig* **avoir le s. bleu** to have blue blood; *Fig* **avoir le s. chaud** to be hot-blooded; *Fig* **avoir qch dans le s.** to have sth in one's blood; *Fam* **avoir du s. de navet** to be spineless; *Fam* **se faire du mauvais s.** to get all worked up; *Fam* **se ronger les sangs, se faire un s. d'encre** to worry oneself sick; **le s. lui monta au visage** the blood rushed to his face; **mon s. n'a fait qu'un tour** *(de peur)* my heart missed a beat; *(de colère)* I saw red; *très Fam* **bon s. (de bonsoir)!**, **bon s. de bon Dieu!** damn and blast it!

sang-froid [sãfrwa] *nm inv* composure, calm; **garder son s.** to keep calm, to keep one's head; **perdre son s.** to lose one's head, to lose one's composure; **tuer qn de s.** to kill sb in cold blood

sanglant, -e [sãglã, -ãt] *adj* bloody; *Fig (offensant)* scathing

sangle [sãgl] *nf* strap; *(de selle)* girth

sangler [sãgle] *vt* to put straps on; *(cheval)* to girth

sanglier [sãglije] *nm* (wild) boar

sanglot [sãglo] *nm* sob

sangloter [sãglɔte] *vi* to sob

sangria [sãgrija] *nf* sangria

sangsue [sãsy] *nf (animal, personne)* leech

sanguin, -e [sãgɛ̃, -in] *adj (tempérament)* fiery; *(teint, visage)* ruddy

sanguinaire [sãginɛr] *adj* (**a**) *(homme)* bloodthirsty (**b**) *(combat)* bloody

Sanisette® [sanizɛt] *nf* superloo

sanitaire [sanitɛr] **1** *adj* (**a**) *(personnel)* medical; *(mesures)* health (**b**) *(installation)* sanitary
2 *nmpl* **les sanitaires** *(toilettes)* the toilet; *(salle de bains et W.-C.)* the bathroom and toilet

sans [sã] **1** *prép* (**a**) *(indique l'absence, la privation, l'exclusion)* without; **s. parler** without speaking; **non s. difficulté** not without difficulty (**b**) *(indique la condition)* but for; **s. vous, je ne l'aurais jamais fait** but for you, I'd never have done it; **s. cela, s. quoi** otherwise; *Fam* **sois sage, s. ça tu seras puni!** be good or else you'll be punished!
2 *adv Fam* without it/them; **faire s.** to do without
3 *conj* **s. que nous le sachions** without our knowing
sans-abri [sãzabri] *nmf inv* homeless person; **les s.** the homeless
San Salvador [sãsalvadɔr] *n* San Salvador
sans-cœur [sãkœr] *nmf inv Fam* heartless person
sans-culotte (*pl* **sans-culottes**) [sãkylɔt] *nm Hist* sansculotte *(person with extreme republican sympathies during the French Revolution)*
sans-emploi [sãzãplwa] *nmf inv* unemployed person; **les s.** the unemployed
sans-faute [sãfot] *nm inv (de compétition hippique)* clear round; **faire un s.** *(cheval)* to have a clear round; *Fig (personne)* not to put a foot wrong
sans-fil ® [sãfil] *nm inv* cordless telephone
sans-gêne [sãʒɛn] **1** *adj inv* ill-mannered
2 *nm* lack of manners
sans-le-sou [sãləsu] *nmf inv Fam* penniless person
sans-logis [sãlɔʒi] *nmf* homeless person; **les s.** the homeless
sans-papiers [sãpapje] *nmf* illegal immigrant
sans-patrie [sãpatri] *nmf inv* stateless person
santé [sãte] *nf* health; **être en bonne s.** to be in good health; **avoir une bonne/mauvaise s.** to be healthy/unhealthy; **être en parfaite s.** to be perfectly healthy; **avoir une petite s.** to be delicate; **c'est bon/mauvais pour la s.** it's good/bad for your health; **boire à la s. de qn** to drink sb's health; **(à votre) s.!** cheers!, good health!; *Suisse Fam* **s.!** *(quand on éternue)* bless you!; **la s. publique** public health
santiag [sãtjag] *nf Fam* cowboy boot
santon [sãtɔ̃] *nm* Christmas crib figure
São Tomé et Príncipe [saɔtɔmeeprɛ̃sip] *n* São Tomé e Príncipe
saoudien, -enne [saudjɛ̃, -ɛn] **1** *adj* Saudi (Arabian)
2 *nm,f* **S.** Saudi (Arabian)
saoul, saouler = **soûl, soûler**
sape [sap] *nf* (**a**) *(tranchée)* sap; *Fig* **travail de s.** undermining (**b**) *Fam* **sapes** *(vêtements)* gear
saper [sape] **1** *vt* (**a**) *aussi Fig* to undermine; **s. le moral à qn** to sap sb's morale (**b**) *Fam (habiller)* to dress; **être bien sapé** to be all dolled up
2 se saper *vpr Fam* to dress
sapeur-pompier (*pl* **sapeurs-pompiers**) [sapœrpɔ̃pje] *nm* fireman; **les sapeurs-pompiers** *(service)* the fire *Br* brigade *or Am* department
saphir [safir] *nm* sapphire
sapin [sapɛ̃] *nm* (**a**) *(arbre)* fir (tree) (**b**) *Fam* **ça sent le s.** that sounds as if you're heading for an early grave; **il sent le s.** he's done for (**c**) *Can* **se faire passer un s.** *(se faire avoir)* to be taken for a ride
sapristi [sapristi] *exclam Fam Vieilli ou Hum* good heavens!
saquer [sake] = **sacquer**
sarabande [sarabãd] *nf (danse, air)* saraband; *Fam (tapage)* racket
Sarajevo [sarajevo] *n* Sarajevo

sarbacane [sarbakan] *nf* blowpipe; *(jouet)* peashooter
sarcasme [sarkasm] *nm* sarcasm; *(remarque)* sarcastic remark
sarcastique [sarkastik] *adj* sarcastic
sarcler [sarkle] *vt (jardin)* to weed; *(sol)* to hoe; *(champ)* to clean
sarclette [sarklɛt] *nf* hoe
sarcloir [sarklwar] *nm* hoe
sarcome [sarkom] *nm Méd* sarcoma; **s. de Kaposi** Kaposi's sarcoma
sarcophage [sarkɔfaʒ] *nm* sarcophagus
Sardaigne [sardɛɲ] *nf* **la S.** Sardinia
sarde [sard] **1** *adj* Sardinian
2 *nmf* **S.** Sardinian
3 *nm (langue)* Sardinian
sardine [sardin] *nf* sardine; **sardines à l'huile/à la tomate** sardines in oil/in tomato sauce; *Fam* **serrés comme des sardines** packed together like sardines
sardonique [sardɔnik] *adj* sardonic
Sargasses [sargas] *voir* **mer**
SARL [ɛsaɛrɛl] *nf (abrév* **société à responsabilité limitée**) limited (liability) company
sarment [sarmã] *nm (tige)* bine; *(de vigne)* vine shoot
saroual, -als [sarwal], **sarouel** [sarwɛl] *nm* = baggy trousers worn by North Africans
sarrasin, -e [sarazɛ̃, -in] **1** *adj Hist* Saracen
2 *nm,f Hist* **S.** Saracen
3 *nm (plante)* buckwheat
sarriette [sarjɛt] *nf* savory
sas [sɑs] *nm (pièce étanche)* airlock
Satan [satã] *npr* Satan
satané, -e [satane] *adj Fam* confounded
satanique [satanik] *adj* satanic; *Fig (cruauté, sourire)* fiendish
satellitaire [satelitɛr] *adj* satellite
satellite [satelit] **1** *nm* (**a**) *(corps céleste, engin)* satellite; **émission retransmise par s.** satellite broadcast; **télévision par s.** satellite television; **s.-espion** spy satellite; **s. géostationnaire** geostationary satellite; **s. de télécommunications** telecommunications satellite; **s. de télédiffusion** broadcast satellite (**b**) *Pol* satellite
2 *adj* **pays s.** satellite state
satiété [sasjete] *nf* **manger/boire à s.** to eat/drink one's fill
satin [satɛ̃] *nm* satin
satiné, -e [satine] **1** *adj (tissu)* satiny; *(papier)* glazed; *(peau)* satin-smooth; **peinture satinée** silk-finish paint
2 *nm* satin finish; *(de la peau)* satin smoothness
satire [satir] *nf* satire; **faire la s. de qch** to satirize sth
satirique [satirik] *adj* satirical
satiriste [satirist] *nmf* satirist
satisfaction [satisfaksjɔ̃] *nf* satisfaction; **à la s. générale** to everyone's satisfaction; **donner (entière) s. à qn** *(personne)* to give sb (complete) satisfaction; *(travail)* to fulfil sb (completely); **obtenir s.** to obtain satisfaction
satisfaire [36] [satisfɛr] **1** *vt* to satisfy
2 satisfaire à *vt ind (demande, condition, besoins)* to satisfy; *(règlement, normes de sécurité)* to comply with; *(obligation)* to fulfil
3 se satisfaire *vpr* **se s. de qch** to be satisfied with

sth; **se s. de peu** to be content with very little; *Péj* to be easily satisfied

satisfaisant, -e [satisfəzɑ̃, -ɑ̃t] *adj (acceptable)* satisfactory; *(qui contente)* satisfying

satisfait, -e [satisfɛ, -ɛt] *adj* (**a**) *(heureux)* satisfied (**de** with); *Ironique* **vous voilà s.!** well, you asked for it!; **s. ou remboursé** *(dans une publicité)* satisfaction or your money back (**b**) *(suffisant)* satisfied

satisfecit [satisfesit] *nm inv Litt* **décerner un s. à qn** to congratulate sb on a job well done

saturation [satyrasjɔ̃] *nf aussi Fig* saturation; *(du réseau routier)* gridlock; *aussi Fig* **arriver à s.** to reach saturation point; *Ordinat (disquette)* to become full

saturer [satyre] **1** *vt* to saturate (**de** with); **les appels ont saturé le standard** the calls have jammed the switchboard

2 *vi Fam* **je sature** I've had it up to here

Saturne [satyrn] *npr (dieu, planète)* Saturn

satyre [satir] *nm* (**a**) *(demi-dieu)* satyr (**b**) *Fam (obsédé sexuel)* sex maniac

sauce [sos] *nf* (**a**) *(accompagnement)* sauce; **s. aux champignons** mushroom sauce; **s. de soja** soy sauce; **s. tomate** tomato sauce; *Fam Fig* **allonger la s.** to pad it out; *Fam* **mettre qch à toutes les sauces** to use sth in every way imaginable; *Fam* **à quelle s. sera-t-il mangé?** what'll be in store for him? (**b**) *Fam (pluie)* **prendre la s.** to get soaked

saucée [sose] *nf Fam (pluie)* downpour; **recevoir une s.** to get soaked

saucer [16] [sose] *vt* (**a**) *(assiette)* to mop up the sauce from (**b**) *Fam* **se faire s.** to get soaked

saucier [sosje] *nm* sauce cook

saucière [sosjɛr] *nf* sauce boat

sauciflard [sosiflar] *nm Fam* (slicing) sausage

saucisse [sosis] *nf* sausage; **s. de Francfort** frankfurter; **s. sèche** = thin salami-type sausage; **s. de Strasbourg/Toulouse** = type of beef/pork sausage

saucisson [sosisɔ̃] *nm* (slicing) sausage; **s. à l'ail** garlic sausage; *Hum* **s. à pattes** sausage dog; **s. pur porc** 100% pork sausage

saucissonné, -e [sosisɔne] *adj Fam* trussed up

saucissonner [sosisɔne] *vt Fam* (**a**) *(attacher)* to tie up (**b**) *(diviser)* **le film a été saucissonné** the film was divided up into episodes; **un film saucissonné par des publicités** a film with frequent commercial breaks

sauf¹, sauve [sof, sov] *adj (personne)* safe, unharmed; **avoir la vie sauve** to escape with one's life; **laisser la vie sauve à qn** to spare sb's life; **l'honneur est s.** honour is saved

sauf² *prép* except (for), apart from; **s. imprévu** unless anything unforeseen happens; **s. erreur de ma part** if I'm not mistaken; **s. votre respect** with all due respect; **s. s'il pleut** unless it rains; *Fam* **s. que…** except that…

sauf-conduit (*pl* **sauf-conduits**) [sofkɔ̃dɥi] *nm* safe conduct

sauge [soʒ] *nf* sage

saugrenu, -e [sogrəny] *adj* preposterous

saule [sol] *nm* willow; **s. pleureur** weeping willow

saumâtre [somɑtr] *adj (goût, eau)* brackish; *Fig* bitter

saumon [somɔ̃] **1** *nm* salmon; **s. fumé** smoked salmon

2 *adj inv* **(rose) s.** salmon-pink

saumoné, -e [somɔne] *adj voir* **truite**

saumure [somyr] *nf* brine

sauna [sona] *nm* sauna

saupoudrer [sopudre] *vt* to sprinkle (**de** with)

saupoudreuse [sopudrøz] *nf* dredger

saur [sɔr] *adj m voir* **hareng**

saurai, saurais *etc voir* **savoir**

saurien [sɔrjɛ̃] *nm* saurian

saut [so] *nm (bond)* jump, leap; **faire un s.** to jump, to leap; *Fig* **faire un s. à Paris/chez le boulanger/en ville** to pop *or Br* nip over to Paris/round to the baker's/into town; *Fig* **faire un s. de plusieurs années** to skip several years; **au s. du lit** first thing in the morning; **s. de l'ange** *Br* swallow dive, *Am* swan dive; **s. à l'élastique** bungee jumping; **s. en hauteur** high jump; **s. en longueur** long jump; **s. en parachute** parachute jump; *(activité)* parachute jumping; **faire du s. en parachute** to go parachute jumping; **s. à la perche** pole vaulting; **s. périlleux** somersault; **s. en ou à skis** ski jump; *(activité)* ski jumping; **faire du s. à skis** to go ski jumping; *Ordinat* **s. de page** page break

saute [sot] *nf* **sautes de température** sudden changes in temperature; **sautes d'humeur** mood swings

sauté, -e [sote] **1** *adj* sautéed, sauté

2 *nm* **s. de lapin** sauté of rabbit

saute-mouton [sotmutɔ̃] *nm inv* leapfrog; **jouer à s.** to play leapfrog

sauter [sote] **1** *vt* (**a**) *(fossé, barrière)* to jump (over), to leap over; *Fig* **s. le pas** to take the plunge (**b**) *(omettre)* *(page, ligne, repas)* to skip; *(maille)* to drop; **s. une classe** to skip a year (**c**) *Vulg (coucher avec)* to screw; **se faire s. par qn** to screw sb

2 *vi* (**a**) *(bondir)* to jump, to leap; **s. sur un pied** to hop; **s. à pieds joints** to jump with one's feet together; **s. à la perche** to pole-vault; **s. à la corde** *Br* to skip, *Am* to jump rope; **s. en parachute** to do a parachute jump; **s. à la gorge de qn** to go for sb; *(chien)* to fly at sb's throat; **s. au cou de qn** to fling one's arms round sb's neck; **s. aux yeux** to be obvious; **s. au plafond** *(bouchon)* to hit the ceiling; *Fig (de surprise)* to jump out of one's skin; *(d'indignation)* to hit the roof; **s. de joie** to jump for joy; *aussi Fam Fig* **s. sur qn** to pounce on sb; **faire s. un enfant sur ses genoux** to bounce a child on one's knees; **s. sur l'occasion** to jump at the opportunity; *Fig* **s. du coq à l'âne** to jump from one subject to another; **nous allons s. directement à la page 5** we're going to jump straight to page 5; *Fam* **et que ça saute!** and make it snappy! (**b**) *(exploser)* to blow up; *(bouton)* to come off; *(fusible)* to blow; *Fig (gouvernement)* to fall; **faire s.** *(rocher)* to blast; *(pont, mine)* to blow up; *(serrure)* to force; *Fig (gouvernement)* to bring down; *(personne)* to fire, *Br* to sack; *Fam* **faire s. la banque** to break the bank (**c**) *Culin* **faire s.** to sauté

sauterelle [sotrɛl] *nf* grasshopper; *(nuisible)* locust

sauterie [sotri] *nf Vieilli ou Hum* hop

sauteur, -euse [sotœr, -øz] **1** *adj* jumping

2 *nm,f* jumper; **s. en hauteur** high-jumper; **s. en longueur** long-jumper; **s. à la perche** pole-vaulter

sautillement [sotijmɑ̃] *nm* hopping about

sautiller [sotije] *vi* to hop about; **s. d'un pied sur l'autre** to hop from one foot to the other; **avancer en sautillant** to hop along

sautoir [sotwar] *nm* (**a**) *(collier)* chain; **s. de perles** string of pearls (**b**) *(de stade)* jumping area

sauvage [sovaʒ] **1** *adj* (**a**) *(plante, animal)* wild; **redevenir s.** *(animal apprivoisé)* to go back to the wild; **à l'état s.** wild (**b**) *(peuple, tribu)* savage, primitive (**c**) *(violent) (personne, agression)* savage (**d**) *(peu sociable)* unsociable (**e**) *(non autorisé)* unauthorized; **immigration s.** illegal immigration
  2 *nmf* (**a**) *Vieilli (indigène)* savage; *Fam Hum* **on n'est pas des sauvages!** we're not savages!; *Fam Hum* **bande de sauvages!** you bunch of savages! (**b**) *(brute)* savage (**c**) *(solitaire)* recluse

sauvagement [sovaʒmɑ̃] *adv* savagely

sauvageon, -onne [sovaʒɔ̃, -ɔn] *nm,f (enfant)* little savage

sauvagerie [sovaʒri] *nf* (**a**) *(cruauté)* savagery (**b**) *(insociabilité)* unsociability

sauvegarde [sovgard] *nf* (**a**) *(protection)* safeguard (**contre** against); **s. des ressources naturelles** conservation of natural resources (**b**) *Ordinat* saving, backup; **faire la s. d'un fichier** to save a file; **s. automatique** autosave, automatic backup; **s. externe** off-line backup; **s. en ligne** on-line backup; **copie de s.** backup (copy)

sauvegarder [sovgarde] *vt* (**a**) *(protéger)* to safeguard (**contre** against) (**b**) *Ordinat (fichier)* to save, to back up; **s. un fichier sur disque** to save a file to disk

sauver [sove] **1** *vt* (**a**) *(personne)* to save, to rescue (**de** from); *(âme)* to save; **s. la vie à qn** to save sb's life; **le malade est sauvé** the patient is out of danger (**b**) *(navire, marchandises)* to salvage; **s. les apparences** to keep up appearances; *Fam Fig* **s. les meubles** to salvage something from the wreckage
  2 *vi* **sauve qui peut!** every man for himself!
  3 se sauver *vpr* (**a**) *(s'échapper)* to escape (**de** from) (**b**) *(s'enfuir)* to run away; *Fam* **sauve-toi, tu vas être en retard** be off, you'll be late (**c**) *(lait)* to boil over

sauvetage [sovtaʒ] *nm* (**a**) *(d'un accidenté)* rescue (**b**) *(d'un navire, de marchandises)* salvage; *(d'une entreprise)* rescue

sauveteur [sovtœr] *nm* rescuer

sauvette [sovɛt] **à la sauvette** *adv (pour ne pas être vu)* on the sly; *(à la hâte)* in a hurry; **vendre à la s.** *(illégalement)* to peddle illegally on the streets; **marchand à la s.** illegal street vendor

sauveur [sovœr] *nm* saviour

savamment [savamɑ̃] *adv* (**a**) *(avec érudition)* learnedly (**b**) *(habilement)* cleverly, skilfully

savane [savan] *nf* (**a**) *(dans les pays chauds)* savanna (**b**) *Can (marécage)* swamp

savant, -e [savɑ̃, -ɑ̃t] **1** *adj* (**a**) *(érudit)* learned (**b**) *(habile)* clever, skilful (**c**) *(animal)* performing
  2 *nm (scientifique)* scientist; *(érudit)* scholar

savate [savat] *nf* (**a**) *Fam (pantoufle)* slipper; **traîner la s.** *(être pauvre)* to be down at heel (**b**) *Fam* **comme une s.** atrociously (**c**) *Sport* kick boxing

saveur [savœr] *nf* (**a**) *(d'un vin, d'un aliment)* flavour (**b**) *Fig (d'une remarque, d'un récit)* savour

Savoie [savwa] *nf* **la S.** Savoy

savoir¹ [savwar] *nm* knowledge, learning

savoir² [62] **1** *vt* (**a**) *(avoir connaissance de)* to know; **s. qch par cœur** to know sth by heart; **je n'en sais rien** I don't know; **je n'en sais trop rien** I'm not very sure; **en s. trop** to know too much; **qu'est-ce j'en sais?** what do I know?; **va s.!** who knows?; **je ne veux pas le s.** I don't want to know; **il n'a rien voulu s.** he didn't want to know; **reste à s. si...** it remains to be seen whether...; **je crois s. qu'il est ici** I understand he's here; **faire s.**

qch à qn to tell sb sth, to let sb know about sth; **je le sais par ma sœur** I heard about it from my sister; **à s.** that is (to say), namely; **pas que je sache** not that I know of; **à ce que je sache, pour autant que je sache** as far as I know; **on ne sait jamais** you never know (**b**) *(être conscient de)* to know; **sans le s.** without realizing; **sachez que...** be advised that..., please note that... (**c**) *(connaître)* **qui tu sais** you know who; **je ne le savais pas si jaloux** I didn't know he was so jealous (**d**) *(être capable de)* **s. faire qch** to be able to do sth, to know how to do sth; **savez-vous nager/conduire?** can you swim/drive?; **je ne saurais vous le dire** I really couldn't tell you (**e**) *Belg (pouvoir)* **je ne sais pas l'attraper** I can't reach it
  2 se savoir *vpr* (**a**) *(se répandre)* **ça se saura vite** it'll soon get out (**b**) *(avoir conscience d'être)* **il se savait perdu/surveillé** he knew he was doomed/being watched

savoir-faire [savwarfɛr] *nm* expertise, know-how

savoir-vivre [savwarvivr] *nm* good manners; **manquer de s.** to have no manners

savon [savɔ̃] *nm* soap; **s. à barbe** shaving soap; **s. de Marseille** household soap; *Fam* **passer un s. à qn** to give sb a telling-off

savonner [savɔne] **1** *vt (mains, vêtement)* to soap; *(en faisant mousser)* to lather
  2 se savonner *vpr* to soap oneself; **se s. les mains** to soap one's hands

savonnette [savɔnɛt] *nf* bar of soap

savonneux, -euse [savɔnø, -øz] *adj* soapy

savourer [savure] *vt aussi Fig* to savour

savoureux, -euse [savurø, -øz] *adj (plat)* tasty; *(vin)* full-flavoured; *Fig (récit, détails)* spicy

savoyard, -e [savwajar, -ard] **1** *adj* Savoyard
  2 *nm,f* **S.** Savoyard

saxo [sakso] *nm Fam (instrument)* sax; *(musicien)* sax player

saxon, -onne [saksɔ̃, -ɔn] **1** *adj* Saxon
  2 *nm,f* **S.** Saxon

saxophone [saksɔfɔn] *nm* saxophone

saxophoniste [saksɔfɔnist] *nmf* saxophonist

saynète [sɛnɛt] *nf (petite pièce)* sketch

sbire [sbir] *nm Péj* henchman

scabreux, -euse [skabrø, -øz] *adj* obscene

scalp [skalp] *nm (chevelure)* scalp

scalpel [skalpɛl] *nm* scalpel

scalper [skalpe] *vt* to scalp

scandale [skɑ̃dal] *nm* scandal; **faire s.** *(affaire)* to cause a scandal; **faire un s.** *(personne)* to make a scene; **au grand s. de** much to the indignation of; **c'est un s.!** it's a scandal!

scandaleux, -euse [skɑ̃dalø, -øz] *adj* scandalous, outrageous

scandaliser [skɑ̃dalize] **1** *vt* to scandalize, to shock
  2 se scandaliser *vpr* to be scandalized *or* shocked (**de** by); **elle ne se scandalise de rien** nothing shocks her

scander [skɑ̃de] *vt (slogan)* to chant; *(vers)* to scan

scandinave [skɑ̃dinav] **1** *adj* Scandinavian
  2 *nmf* **S.** Scandinavian

Scandinavie [skɑ̃dinavi] *nf* **la S.** Scandinavia

scanner¹ [skanɛr] *nm* scanner; **on lui a fait un s.** he was given a scan

scanner² [skane] *vt Ordinat* to scan

scanneur [skanœr] *nm Ordinat & TV* scanner; **s. à main** handheld scanner; **s. à plat** flatbed scanner

scaphandre [skafɑ̃dr] *nm* (**a**) *(de plongeur)* diving suit (**b**) *(d'astronaute)* space suit

scaphandrier [skafɑ̃drije] *nm* diver

scarabée [skarabe] *nm* beetle

scarlatine [skarlatin] *nf* scarlet fever; **avoir la s.** to have scarlet fever

scarole [skarɔl] *nf* endive

scatologique [skatɔlɔʒik] *adj* scatological

sceau, -x [so] *nm* seal; *Fig* **le s. du génie** the mark of genius; **sous le s. du secret** under the seal of secrecy

scélérat, -e [selera, -at] *Litt* **1** *adj* villainous
    2 *nm,f* villain

scellé, -e [sele] **1** *adj* sealed
    2 *nm* seal; **apposer/lever les scellés** to put on/remove the seals

sceller [sele] *vt* (**a**) *(apposer un sceau sur) & Fig* to seal (**b**) *Constr* to embed

scénario [senarjo] *nm* script, screenplay; *Fig* scenario

scénariste [senarist] *nmf* scriptwriter

scène [sɛn] *nf* (**a**) *(plateau)* stage; **la s.** *(le métier d'acteur)* the stage; **mettre en s.** *(pièce de théâtre)* to stage; *(film)* to direct; **entrer en s.** *(acteur)* to come on; *Fig* to appear on the scene; **sortir de s.** to go off; **quitter la s.** to retire from the stage; *Fig* **la s. politique/internationale** the political/international scene; *Fig* **occuper le devant de la s.** to be in the limelight, to hold centre stage (**b**) *(d'une pièce de théâtre, d'un film)* scene (**c**) *(action)* action; **la s. se passe au Moyen Âge** the action takes place in the Middle Ages (**d**) *(événement)* scene; **des scènes de panique** scenes of panic (**e**) *Fam (dispute)* scene; **il m'a fait une s.** he made a scene; **s. de ménage** domestic squabble (**f**) *(peinture)* **une s. de chasse** a hunting scene

scénique [senik] *adj* theatrical

scepticisme [sɛptisism] *nm* scepticism

sceptique [sɛptik] **1** *adj* sceptical
    2 *nmf* sceptic

sceptre [sɛptr] *nm* sceptre

schéma [ʃema] *nm* (**a**) *(dessin)* diagram (**b**) *(résumé)* outline (**c**) *Ordinat* **s. de clavier** keyboard map

schématique [ʃematik] *adj* schematic; *Péj* over-simplified

schématiquement [ʃematikmɑ̃] *adv* *(à l'aide d'un schéma)* schematically; *(en gros)* in outline

schématiser [ʃematize] *vt* to schematize; *Péj* to over-simplify

schisme [ʃism] *nm* schism

schiste [ʃist] *nm* schist, shale

schizophrène [skizofrɛn] *adj & nmf* schizophrenic

schizophrénie [skizofreni] *nf* schizophrenia

schlinguer [ʃlɛ̃ge] *vi très Fam* to stink

schnaps [ʃnaps] *nm* schnapps

schnock, schnoque [ʃnɔk] *nm Fam* **un vieux s.** an old git

schuss [ʃus] *nm* schuss; **descendre la piste en s.** *ou* **tout s.** to schuss down the slope

sciatique [sjatik] **1** *adj* sciatic
    2 *nf* sciatica

scie [si] *nf* (**a**) *(outil)* saw; **s. circulaire** circular saw; **s. mécanique** *ou* **à main** hand saw; **s. à métaux** hacksaw (**b**) **s. musicale** musical saw

sciemment [sjamɑ̃] *adv* knowingly

science [sjɑ̃s] *nf* (**a**) *(savoir)* science; *Fig* **je n'ai pas la s. infuse** I can't be expected to know everything (**b**) *(domaine spécifique)* science; **sciences économiques** economics; **sciences exactes** exact sciences; **sciences expérimentales** experimental science; **sciences humaines** ≃ social sciences; **sciences naturelles** natural science; **Sciences Po** = prestigious higher education establishment for students wishing to enter the Civil Service, the media etc

science-fiction [sjɑ̃sfiksjɔ̃] *nf* science fiction; *Fig & Hum* **c'est de la s.!** it's unreal!

scientifique [sjɑ̃tifik] **1** *adj* scientific
    2 *nmf* scientist

scientifiquement [sjɑ̃tifikmɑ̃] *adv* scientifically

scier [66] [sje] *vt* (**a**) *(bois, métal)* to saw; *(pour enlever)* *(branche)* to saw off (**b**) *Fam (étonner)* to dumbfound

scierie [siri] *nf* sawmill

scieur [sjœr] *nm* sawyer

scinder [sɛ̃de] **1** *vt* to split up (**en** into)
    2 se scinder *vpr* to split up (**en** into)

scintillement [sɛ̃tijmɑ̃] *nm* *(de bijou, de lumière, des yeux)* sparkling; *(d'étoile)* twinkling

scintiller [sɛ̃tije] *vi* *(bijou, lumière, yeux)* to sparkle; *(étoile)* to twinkle

scission [sisjɔ̃] *nf* split; **faire s.** to split away

sciure [sjyr] *nf* sawdust

sclérose [skleroz] *nf* sclerosis; *Fig* ossification; **s. en plaques** multiple sclerosis

scléroser [skleroze] **1** *vt Méd* to sclerose
    2 se scléroser *vpr Méd* to sclerose; *Fig* to become fossilized

scolaire [skɔlɛr] *adj* (**a**) *(résultats, réussite)* academic; *(réforme, organisation, vie)* school (**b**) *Péj (esprit, mentalité)* bookish

scolarisation [skɔlarizasjɔ̃] *nf* education

scolariser [skɔlarize] *vt* to send to school; **enfant scolarisé** child attending school

scolarité [skɔlarite] *nf* schooling; **prolonger la s.** to raise the school-leaving age

scoliose [skɔljoz] *nf* curvature of the spine

scoop [skup] *nm* scoop

scooter [skutɛr] *nm* (motor) scooter; **s. des mers** jet ski

scorbut [skɔrbyt] *nm* scurvy

score [skɔr] *nm* score; *(en politique)* result

scories [skɔri] *nfpl* *(dans l'industrie)* slag; *(d'éruption volcanique)* scoria

scorpion [skɔrpjɔ̃] *nm* (**a**) *(animal)* scorpion (**b**) *Astron & Astrol* **le S.** Scorpio; **être S.** to be (a) Scorpio

Scotch® [skɔtʃ] *nm (ruban adhésif) Br* sellotape®, *Am* scotch tape®

scotch [skɔtʃ] *nm (boisson)* scotch

scotcher [skɔtʃe] *vt Br* to sellotape, *Am* to scotchtape; *Fam Fig* **il est toujours scotché devant la télé** he's always glued to the TV

scout [skut] *nm* Scout

scoutisme [skutism] *nm* *(activité)* scouting; *(mouvement)* scout movement

scribe [skrib] *nm* (**a**) *Péj* pen-pusher (**b**) *Hist* scribe

scribouillard, -e [skribujar, -ard] *nm,f Fam Péj* penpusher

script [skript] *nm* (**a**) *(écriture)* printing; **écrire en s.** to print (**b**) *Cin (film)* script

scripte [skript] *nmf Cin (homme)* continuity man; *(femme)* continuity girl

scrupule [skrypyl] *nm* scruple; **sans scrupules** *(personne)* unscrupulous; *(agir)* unscrupulously

scrupuleusement [skrypyløzmã] *adv* scrupulously

scrupuleux, -euse [skrypylø, -øz] *adj* scrupulous; **peu s.** unscrupulous

scrutateur, -trice [skrytatœr, -tris] **1** *adj Litt (esprit, regard)* searching
2 *nm,f (d'un scrutin)* teller

scruter [skryte] *vt* to scrutinize; *(horizon, paysage)* to scan

scrutin [skrytɛ̃] *nm* (**a**) *(élection)* poll; **s. secret** secret vote (**b**) *(vote)* ballot (**c**) *(système)* voting system; **s. majoritaire** first-past-the-post system; **s. proportionnel** voting by proportional representation; **s. uninominal** voting for a single candidate

sculpter [skylte] *vt* to sculpt; *(dans du bois)* to carve (**dans** out of)

sculpteur [skyltœr] *nm* sculptor; **s. sur bois** woodcarver

sculptural, -e, -aux, -ales [skyltyral, -o] *adj (art)* sculptural; *(silhouette, beauté)* statuesque

sculpture [skyltyr] *nf (œuvre, art)* sculpture; **s. sur bois** woodcarving; **faire de la s.** to sculpt

SDF [ɛsdeɛf] *nmf inv (abrév* **sans domicile fixe***)* person of no fixed abode; *(sans abri)* homeless person; **les S.** *(sans abri)* the homeless

SDN [ɛsdeɛn] *nf (abrév* **Société des Nations***)* **la S.** the League of Nations

se [sə]

> **s'** is used before a word beginning with a vowel or h mute.

pron personnel (**a**) *(soi)* *(homme)* himself; *(femme)* herself; *(chose)* itself; *(indéfini)* oneself; *(pluriel)* themselves; **se flatter** to flatter oneself; **il se rase** he is shaving; *Fam* **on s'est blessés** we hurt ourselves

(**b**) *(à soi)* *(homme)* to himself; *(femme)* to herself; *(chose)* to itself; *(indéfini)* to oneself; *(pluriel)* to themselves; **elle s'est coupé le doigt** she has cut her finger; *Fam* **on va s'acheter une voiture** we're going to buy (ourselves) a car

(**c**) *(réciproque)* *(objet direct)* each other; *(objet indirect)* to each other; **se nuire (l'un à l'autre)** to hurt each other; **ils se sont quittés en bons termes** they parted on good terms

(**d**) *(passif)* **ça se mange froid** you eat it cold; **les couteaux se rangent dans ce tiroir** the knives go in this drawer

séance [seãs] *nf* (**a**) *(réunion)* session, meeting; **tenir s.** to be in session (**b**) *(de travail, d'entraînement)* session; **s. de photo** photo session; **s. de pose** sitting (**c**) *Cin & Th* performance; *Cin* **s. privée** private showing (**d**) *TV* **à la s.** *(film, programme)* pay-per-view (**e**) **s. tenante** straightaway, at once

séant, -e [seã, -ãt] **1** *adj Litt (convenable)* fitting
2 *nm Litt ou Hum* **se mettre sur son s.** to sit up

seau, -x [so] *nm* bucket; *(contenu)* bucket(ful); *Fam* **il pleut à seaux** it's pouring down; **s. à champagne** champagne bucket; **s. à charbon** coal scuttle; **s. à glace** ice bucket

sébacé, -e [sebase] *adj* sebaceous

sébum [sebɔm] *nm* sebum

sec, sèche [sɛk, sɛʃ] **1** *adj* (**a**) *(temps, saison, sol, peau, bois)* dry; *(morue, fruit)* dried; **à pied s.** without getting one's feet wet; **avoir la gorge sèche** *(avoir soif)* to be dry (**b**) *(vin, cidre)* dry (**c**) *(maigre)* *(personne)* lean; **être s. comme un coup de trique** to be wiry (**d**) *(austère)* *(personne)* hard; *(réponse, ton, voix)* sharp; **avoir le cœur s.** to be hard-hearted (**e**) *(non appuyé)* *(coup)* sharp (**f**) *(sans rien ajouter)* **boire qch s.** to drink sth neat

2 *adv* (**a**) *(beaucoup)* *(frapper, pleuvoir)* hard; *(boire)* heavily; **démarrer s.** to shoot off (**b**) *Fam* **aussi s.** right away

3 *nm* (**a**) **tenir au s.** *(sur une étiquette)* keep in a dry place (**b**) **être à s.** *(source, puits, rivière)* to be dry; *Fam (sans argent)* to be broke

sécable [sekabl] *adj* divisible

sécateur [sekatœr] *nm* pruning shears, *Br* secateurs

sécession [sesesjɔ̃] *nf* secession; **faire s. (de)** to secede (from)

séchage [seʃaʒ] *nm* drying

sèche [sɛʃ] **1** *nf Fam Br* fag, *Am* cig
2 *adj voir* **sec**

sèche-cheveux [sɛʃʃəvø] *nm inv* hairdryer

sèche-linge [sɛʃlɛ̃ʒ] *nm inv (appareil)* tumble-drier; *(armoire)* airing cupboard

sèche-mains [sɛʃmɛ̃] *nm inv* hand-drier

sèchement [sɛʃmã] *adv (parler, répondre)* curtly

sécher [34] [seʃe] **1** *vt* to dry; *Fam* **s. un cours** to skip a class

2 *vi* (**a**) *(vêtement, cheveux)* to dry; **mettre du linge à s.** to put clothes out to dry (**b**) *Fam (ne pouvoir répondre)* to be stumped

3 se sécher *vpr* to dry oneself; **se s. les cheveux/les mains** to dry one's hair/hands

sécheresse [seʃrɛs, seʃrɛs] *nf* (**a**) *(absence de pluie)* drought (**b**) *(de l'air, du sol, de la peau)* dryness (**c**) *(des manières, du ton)* curtness; *(du cœur)* hardness; *(du style)* dryness

séchoir [seʃwar] *nm* (**a**) *(appareil)* drier; **s. (à cheveux)** hairdryer (**b**) *(dispositif pliant)* **s. (à linge)** clothes-horse

second, -e [səgɔ̃, -ɔ̃d] **1** *adj* second; *(rôle)* supporting, minor

2 *nm* (**a**) *(assistant)* assistant; *Mil* second-in-command; *Naut* first mate; *(de duelliste)* second (**b**) *(étage) Br* second *or Am* third floor

3 *nm,f* second; **je préfère le s.** I prefer the second one; *voir aussi* **cinquième**

secondaire [səgɔ̃dɛr] **1** *adj* (**a**) *Scol* secondary; **établissement d'enseignement s.** secondary school (**b**) *(pas essentiel)* secondary; *(personnage, rôle) Théât* minor; *Fig* secondary; **c'est s.** it's of secondary importance (**c**) *Écon & Géol* secondary

2 *nm Géol* secondary era; *Écon* secondary sector

seconde [səgɔ̃d] *nf* (**a**) *(unité de temps)* second; **(attendez) une s.!** just a second!; **pendant une fraction de s.** for a fraction of a second (**b**) *(vitesse)* second (gear) (**c**) *(dans les transports)* second class; **voyager en s.** to travel second-class (**d**) *(classe) Br* ≃ fifth form, *Am* ≃ tenth grade (**e**) *Mus* second

seconder [səgɔ̃de] *vt* to assist

secouer [səkwe] **1** *vt* (**a**) *(arbre, tête, bouteille)* to shake; *(coussin, oreiller)* to plump up; *(vêtements, tapis)* to shake out; *(sujet: vent, vagues)* to buffet; **nous avons été secoués pendant la traversée** we were shaken about during the crossing; *Fam* **s. les puces à qn** *(réprimander)* to tell sb off (**b**) *(sujet: choc, maladie, nouvelles)* to shake (up) (**c**) *(se débarrasser de)* *(poussière, joug)* to shake off (**d**) *très Fam* **j'en ai rien à s.** I don't give a damn *or Br* a toss

2 *vi* **ça secoue** *(en avion, en train)* it's bumpy; *(en bateau)* it's rough
3 se secouer *vpr* (**a**) *(s'agiter)* to shake oneself (**b**) *(agir)* to snap out of it
secourable [səkurabl] *adj* helpful
secourir [22] [səkurir] *vt* to help, to assist
secourisme [səkurism] *nm* first aid
secouriste [səkurist] *nmf* first-aid worker
secours [səkur] *nm* (**a**) *(aide)* help; *(financier, matériel)* aid; *Mil (renforts)* relief; **appel au s.** call for help; **appeler au s.** to call out for help; **au s.!** help!; **premiers s.** first aid; **porter s. à qn** to give sb help; **demander du s.** to ask for help; **aller au s. de qn** to go to sb's assistance; **cela m'a été d'un grand s.** it's been a great help to me (**b**) **de s.** *(trousse, poste)* first-aid; *(sortie, éclairage)* emergency; *(roue)* spare; *Ordinat (copie, fichier)* backup
secousse [səkus] *nf* jolt, jerk; **par secousses** *(avancer)* jerkily; **s. (sismique** *ou* **tellurique)** (earth) tremor
secret¹, -ète [səkrɛ, -ɛt] *adj* (**a**) *(non divulgué)* secret (**b**) *(personne)* reticent
secret² *nm* (**a**) *(confidence, mystère)* secret; **garder un s.** to keep a secret; **mettre qn dans le s.** to let sb in on the secret; **être dans le s.** to be in on the secret; **ne pas avoir de secrets pour qn** *(discipline)* to hold no secrets for sb; **ce n'est un s. pour personne** it's no secret; **le s. du bonheur/de la réussite** the secret of happiness/of success; **secrets d'alcôve** pillow talk; **s. d'État** state secret; **s. de fabrication** trade secret; **s. de Polichinelle** open secret; **emporter un s. dans la tombe** to take a secret to the grave (**b**) *(discrétion)* secrecy; **dans le plus grand s.** in the strictest secrecy; **en s.** *(en cachette)* in secret; **s. bancaire** banking secrecy; **s. professionnel** professional secrecy (**c**) **mettre qn au s.** *(l'enfermer)* to put sb in solitary confinement
secrétaire [səkretɛr] **1** *nmf* secretary; **s. d'ambassade** secretary; **s. de direction** personal assistant; **s. d'État** Secretary of State; **s. général** secretary general; *Com* company secretary; **s. médicale** medical secretary; **s. particulier** private secretary; **s. de rédaction** sub-editor
2 *nm (meuble)* writing desk
secrétariat [səkretarja] *nm* (**a**) *(fonction)* secretaryship (**b**) *(bureau)* secretary's office; *(d'un organisme international)* secretariat (**c**) *(métier)* secretarial work (**d**) *Pol* **s. d'État** ministry
secrètement [səkrɛtmã] *adv* secretly
sécréter [34] [sekrete] *vt* to secrete; *Fig (ennui)* to exude
sécrétion [sekresjɔ̃] *nf* secretion
sectaire [sɛktɛr] *adj & nmf* sectarian
sectarisme [sɛktarism] *nm* sectarianism
secte [sɛkt] *nf* sect
secteur [sɛktœr] *nm* (**a**) *(zone)* area, district; *Fam* **changer de s.** to move somewhere else (**b**) *Élec* mains; **branché sur le s.** plugged into the mains (**c**) *Écon* sector; **le s. privé/public** the private/public sector; **s. primaire/secondaire/tertiaire** primary/secondary/tertiary sector; *Fam* **ce n'est pas mon s.** that's not my line (**d**) *Math & Ordinat* sector; *Ordinat* **s. d'initialisation** boot sector
section [sɛksjɔ̃] *nf* (**a**) *(division) (d'un livre, d'un bâtiment, d'une autoroute)* section; *(d'une ligne d'autobus)* stage; *(d'un parti politique, d'un syndicat)* branch (**b**) *(de l'infanterie)* platoon; *(de l'artillerie)* section (**c**)

(coupe) section; **ça fait 5 centimètres de s.** the diameter of the section is 5 centimetres (**d**) *Scol* = one of the groups into which "baccalauréat" students are divided, depending on their chosen area of specialization
sectionner [sɛksjɔne] *vt* (**a**) *(couper)* to sever (**b**) *(fractionner) (service, circonscription)* to divide into sections
sectoriel, -elle [sɛktɔrjɛl] *adj* sectorial
sécu [seky] *nf Fam (abrév* **Sécurité sociale)** *Br* Social Security, *Am* Welfare
séculaire [sekylɛr] *adj* (**a**) *(très ancien)* centuries-old (**b**) *(qui existe depuis un siècle)* a hundred years old (**c**) *(qui a lieu tous les cent ans)* centennial
séculier, -ère [sekylje, -ɛr] *adj* secular
secundo [səgɔ̃do] *adv* secondly
sécurisant, -e [sekyrizã, -ãt] *adj* reassuring
sécuriser [sekyrize] *vt* to reassure; *Fin* **s. un paiement** *(sur Internet)* to guarantee the security of a transaction
sécuritaire [sekyritɛr] *adj (politique, idéologie)* law-and-order; **mesures sécuritaires** drastic security measures
sécurité [sekyrite] *nf* (**a**) *(ordre, stabilité)* security; **être/se sentir en s.** to be/feel secure; **s. de l'emploi** job security; **s. nationale/internationale** national/international security (**b**) *(absence de danger)* safety; **s. routière** road safety; **S. routière** = French road safety organization (**c**) *(dispositif)* safety catch; **porte munie d'une s.-enfants** door with a childproof lock (**d**) **S. sociale** *Br* Social Security, *Am* Welfare

Sécurité sociale
The "Sécu", as it is popularly known, was created in 1945 and provides services such as public health benefits, pensions and maternity benefit. These benefits are paid for by obligatory insurance contributions ("cotisations") made by employers ("cotisations patronales") and employees ("cotisations salariales"). Many French people have complementary health insurance provided by a "mutuelle" which guarantees payment of all or part of the expenses not covered by the "Sécurité sociale".

sédatif, -ive [sedatif, -iv] *adj & nm* sedative
sédentaire [sedãtɛr] *adj* (**a**) *(vie, travail, travailleur)* sedentary; *(population)* settled (**b**) *(casanier)* stay-at-home
sédentariser [sedãtarize] **1** *vt (population)* to settle
2 se sédentariser *vpr* to settle
sédiment [sedimã] *nm* sediment
sédimentaire [sedimãtɛr] *adj* sedimentary
sédimentation [sedimãtasjɔ̃] *nf* sedimentation
séditieux, -euse [sedisjø, -øz] **1** *adj* seditious
2 *nm,f* insurgent
sédition [sedisjɔ̃] *nf* sedition
séducteur, -trice [sedyktœr, -tris] **1** *nm,f* seducer, *f* seductress
2 *adj* seductive
séduction [sedyksjɔ̃] *nf* (**a**) *(physique)* seduction; *(par le charme)* charming (**b**) *(moyen de séduire)* attraction; **pouvoir de s.** power of attraction
séduire [18] [sedɥir] *vt* (**a**) *(charmer) (sujet: personne)* to charm; *(sujet: projet, proposition)* to appeal to (**b**) *(sexuellement)* to seduce

séduisant, -e [sedɥizɑ̃, -ɑ̃t] *adj* attractive
séfarade [sefarad] **1** *adj* Sephardic
  2 *nmf* Sephardic Jew
segment [sɛgmɑ̃] *nm* segment
segmenter [sɛgmɑ̃te] *vt aussi Ordinat* to segment
ségrégation [segregasjɔ̃] *nf* segregation
ségrégationniste [segregasjɔnist] *adj & nmf* segregationist
seiche [sɛʃ] *nf* cuttlefish; **os de s.** cuttlebone
seigle [sɛgl] *nm* rye
seigneur [sɛɲœr] *nm* **(a)** *Hist* lord; **à tout s. tout honneur** honour where honour is due; **en grand s.** in grand style **(b)** *Rel* **le S.** the Lord
seigneurial, -e, -aux, -ales [sɛɲœrjal, -o] *adj (droits, domaine)* seigniorial
sein [sɛ̃] *nm (de femme)* breast; *Litt (poitrine)* bosom; **serrer** *ou* **presser qn sur son s.** to press sb to one's bosom; **donner le s. à un enfant, nourrir un enfant au s.** to breast-feed a child; **au s. de** within
Seine [sɛn] *nf* **la S.** the Seine
séisme [seism] *nm* earthquake; *Fig & Litt* upheaval
seize [sɛz] *adj & nm inv* sixteen; *voir aussi* **trois**
seizième [sɛzjɛm] *nmf, nm & adj* sixteenth; *voir aussi* **cinquième**

> **Seizième**
>
> This term often refers to the upper-class social background, lifestyle, way of dressing etc associated with the sixteenth arrondissement in Paris: "elle est très seizième".

---

séjour [seʒur] *nm* **(a)** *(période)* stay; **s. linguistique** language-learning trip **(b)** *(pièce)* **(salle de) s.** living room **(c)** *Litt (lieu)* abode
séjourner [seʒurne] *vi* to stay
sel [sɛl] *nm* **(a)** *(substance)* salt; **gros s.** coarse salt; **s. fin** fine salt; **sels de bain** bath salts; **sels** *(à respirer)* (smelling) salts **(b)** *Fig (esprit)* piquancy
sélect, -e [selɛkt] *adj Fam (soirée, clientèle)* select
sélectif, -ive [selɛktif, -iv] *adj* selective; *Ordinat* **en mode s.** in veto mode
sélection [selɛksjɔ̃] *nf* selection
sélectionné, -e [selɛksjɔne] **1** *adj* selected
  2 *nm,f (sportif)* selected competitor; *(d'une équipe)* selected player
sélectionner [selɛksjɔne] *vt* to select; *Ordinat (texte)* to block, to select
sélectionneur, -euse [selɛksjɔnœr, -øz] *nm,f* selector
self [sɛlf] *nm Fam* self-service restaurant
self-service *(pl* **self-services***)* [sɛlfsɛrvis] *nm (restaurant)* self-service restaurant; *(magasin)* self-service shop
selle [sɛl] *nf* **(a)** *(de cheval, de bicyclette, de moto)* saddle; **se mettre en s.** to mount; **monter sans s.** to ride bareback **(b)** **selles** *(matières fécales)* stools, *Br* motions; **aller à la s.** to have a bowel movement **(c)** *Culin* **s. de mouton/d'agneau** saddle of mutton/lamb
seller [sele] *vt* to saddle
sellette [sɛlɛt] *nf Fam* **mettre qn/être sur la s.** to put sb/to be in the hot seat
selon [səlɔ̃] *prép* **(a)** *(d'après)* according to; **s. moi** in my opinion **(b)** *(conformément à)* in accordance with; **s. toute vraisemblance** in all probability **(c)** *(en fonction de)* **varier s. les cas/les saisons** to vary from case

to case/season to season; *Fam* **c'est s.** it all depends; **s. que…** depending on whether…
SEM [sɛm] *nf Écon (abrév* **société d'économie mixte***)* = company financed by state and private capital
semailles [səmɑj] *nfpl* **(a)** *(action)* sowing; **(temps des) s.** sowing time **(b)** *(graines)* seeds
semaine [səmɛn] *nf* **(a)** *(sept jours)* week; **vivre à la petite s.** to live from day to day; **jour de s.** weekday; **en s.** during the week, on weekdays; **la s. de 35 heures** the 35-hour working week; **la s. sainte** Holy Week **(b)** *(salaire)* week's pay; *(argent de poche)* week's pocket money **(c)** *Mil (tour de service)* week's duty; **être de s.** to be on duty for the week; **officier de s.** duty officer for the week
semainier [səmɛnje] *nm (agenda)* desk diary
sémantique [semɑ̃tik] **1** *adj* semantic
  2 *nf* semantics *(singulier)*
sémaphore [semafɔr] *nm Rail* semaphore signal; *Naut* signal station
semblable [sɑ̃blabl] **1** *adj* **(a)** *(pareil)* similar; **s. à qch** similar to sth, like sth; **je n'ai rien dit de s.** I said nothing of the sort **(b)** *(tel)* **de semblables projets/propos** such plans/remarks, plans/remarks like that
  2 *nm (être humain)* fellow man; **vous et vos semblables** you and your kind
semblant [sɑ̃blɑ̃] *nm* **(a)** *(apparence)* **un s. de** a semblance of **(b)** **faire s.** to pretend; **faire s. de faire qch** to pretend to do sth; **en faisant s. de rien** without making it obvious
sembler [sɑ̃ble] **1** *vi* to seem
  2 *v impersonnel* **il semble que…** it seems that…; **il me/leur semble que…** it seems to me/them that…; **me semble-t-il** it seems to me; **il me semble avoir entendu son nom** I've a feeling I've heard his name; **il me semble idiot d'attendre encore plus longtemps** it seems stupid to me to wait any longer; **faites comme bon vous semble** *ou* **semblera** do as you think best; **il le fera si bon lui semble** he'll do it if he thinks fit
semé, -e [səme] *adj* **s. de** strewn with; *(fleurs)* dotted with; *(étoiles)* studded with; *(citations)* sprinkled with; **s. d'embûches** full of traps
semelle [səmɛl] *nf* sole; **s. (intérieure)** insole; **s. de caoutchouc/de cuir** rubber/leather sole; **ne pas avancer d'une s.** to make no progress whatsoever; **il ne reculera pas d'une s.** he won't give an inch; **ne pas quitter qn d'une s.** to be always at sb's heels; **c'est de la s.!** it's like shoe leather!
semence [səmɑ̃s] *nf (graine)* seed; *(sperme)* semen
semer [46] [səme] *vt* **(a)** *(graines)* to sow **(b)** *(discorde, confusion, panique, doute)* to sow, to spread; *Prov* **qui sème le vent récolte la tempête** he who sows the wind shall reap the whirlwind **(c)** *Fam (distancer)* to shake off **(d)** *Fam (perdre)* to lose
semestre [səmɛstr] *nm* half-year, six-month period; *Scol & Univ* term
semestriel, -elle [səmɛstrijɛl] *adj* half-yearly, six-monthly
semi-automatique [səmiɔtɔmatik] *adj* semi-automatic
semi-liberté [səmilibɛrte] *nf Jur* partial release
sémillant, -e [semijɑ̃, -ɑ̃t] *adj (personne)* spirited; *(regard)* bright
séminaire [seminɛr] *nm* **(a)** *(colloque)* seminar **(b)** *Rel* seminary
séminariste [seminarist] *nm Rel* seminarist

sémiologie [semjɔlɔʒi] *nf* semiology
sémiotique [semjɔtik] **1** *adj* semiotic
2 *nf* semiotics *(singulier)*
semi-précieux, -euse (*mpl* **semi-précieux,** *fpl*
semi-précieuses) [səmipresjø, -øz] *adj* semi-precious
semi-remorque (*pl* **semi-remorques**) [səmirəmɔrk]
nm (poids lourd) Br articulated lorry, *Am* trailer truck
semis [səmi] *nm* (**a**) *(action)* sowing (**b**) *(terrain)*
seedbed (**c**) *(jeune plante)* seedling
sémite [semit] **1** *adj* Semitic
2 *nmf* **S.** Semite
sémitique [semitik] *adj* Semitic
semoir [səmwar] *nm* (**a**) *(sac)* seed bag (**b**) *(machine)*
seeder
semonce [səmɔ̃s] *nf (remontrance)* reprimand; *aussi*
Fig **coup de s.** warning shot
semoule [səmul] *nf* semolina
sempiternel, -elle [sɑ̃piternɛl] *adj* never-ending,
endless
sénat [sena] *nm* senate

> ### Sénat
> The Sénat is the upper house of the French
> Parliament. Its members are elected for a nine-
> year mandate by the Deputies of the "Assemblée
> nationale" and certain other government officals.
> The President of the Senate may deputize for
> the President of the Republic in the case of
> incapacity or death. The powers of the Senate are
> almost as extensive as those of the "Assemblée
> nationale", although the latter is empowered to
> override the decisions of the Senate in cases
> where the two houses disagree.

sénateur [senatœr] *nm* senator
sénatorial, -e, -aux, -ales [senatɔrjal, -o] *adj* sena-
torial
Sénégal [senegal] *nm* **le S.** Senegal
sénégalais, -e [senegalɛ, -ɛz] **1** *adj* Senegalese
2 *nm,f* **S.** Senegalese; **les S.** the Senegalese
sénile [senil] *adj* senile
sénilité [senilite] *nf* senility
senior [senjɔr] *adj & nmf Sport* senior (*above the age of*
20)
sens¹ *voir* **sentir**
sens² [sɑ̃s] *nm* (**a**) *(de la perception)* sense; **les cinq s.**
the five senses; **le sixième s.** the sixth sense
(**b**) **les s.** *(sensualité)* the senses; **plaisir des s.** sensual pleasure
(**c**) *(jugement)* sense; **avoir le s. de l'humour/du ri-**
dicule to have a sense of humour/of the ridiculous;
avoir le s. des affaires/de l'orientation to have good
business sense/a good sense of direction; **s. com-**
mun common sense; **s. moral** moral sense; **s. pra-**
tique practical sense; **bon s.** common sense; **un**
homme de bon s. a sensible man
(**d**) *(avis)* **à mon s.** to my mind
(**e**) *(signification) (d'un mot)* meaning, sense; **au s.**
propre/figuré in the literal/figurative sense, lit-
erally/figuratively; **cela n'a aucun s.** it doesn't make
(any) sense; **en ce s. que...** in the sense that...
(**f**) *(direction)* direction; **tenir qch dans le mauvais s.**
to hold sth the wrong way round; **en s. inverse** in the
opposite direction; **dans le s. des aiguilles d'une**
montre clockwise; **dans le s. inverse des aiguilles**
d'une montre *Br* anticlockwise, *Am* counterclock-

wise; **dans le s. du courant** with the current; **dans le**
s. de la longueur lengthwise, lengthways; **dans le s.**
de la largeur widthwise, across; **s. dessus dessous**
(en désordre) upside down; **s. devant derrière** back
to front, the wrong way round; **dans les deux s.** both
ways; *Fig* **ces mesures vont dans le bon s.** these
measures are a step in the right direction; *Ordinat* **s.**
de déroulement flow direction; **s. giratoire** *Br* roundabout, *Am* traffic circle; **s. interdit** *(sur panneau)* no
entry; **s. unique** *(sur panneau)* one way
sensas(s) [sɑ̃sas] *adj Fam* fantastic, great
sensation [sɑ̃sasjɔ̃] *nf* (**a**) *(perception physique)* sensation (**b**) *(impression)* feeling; **avoir la s. que...** to
have a *or* the feeling that... (**c**) *(scandale)* **faire s.** to
create a sensation
sensationnel, -elle [sɑ̃sasjɔnɛl] *adj* (**a**) *(à sensation)*
sensational (**b**) *Fam (fantastique)* fantastic, great
sensé, -e [sɑ̃se] *adj* sensible
sensibilisation [sɑ̃sibilizasjɔ̃] *nf* (**a**) **s. de l'opinion**
(à qch) increasing public awareness (of sth) (**b**) *Phot*
& Méd sensitization
sensibiliser [sɑ̃sibilize] *vt* (**a**) *(rendre conscient)* **s. qn**
à qch to increase sb's awareness of sth; **s. l'opinion (à**
qch) to increase public awareness (of sth) (**b**) *Phot &*
Méd to sensitize
sensibilité [sɑ̃sibilite] *nf* sensitivity; **avoir une s. à**
fleur de peau to be hypersensitive
sensible [sɑ̃sibl] *adj* (**a**) *(émotif)* sensitive (**b**) *(récep-*
tif) **être s. à qch** to be sensitive to sth; *(influence)* to be
susceptible to sth (**c**) *(douloureux)* sensitive (**d**) *(ap-*
préciable) noticeable, appreciable; **de manière s.** noticeably (**e**) *(balance, thermomètre, plaque)* sensitive;
s. à la lumière light-sensitive
sensiblement [sɑ̃sibləmɑ̃] *adv* (**a**) *(notablement)* noticeably, appreciably (**b**) *(à peu près)* roughly, more or
less
sensiblerie [sɑ̃sibləri] *nf* sentimentality
sensoriel, -elle [sɑ̃sɔrjɛl] *adj* sensory
sensualité [sɑ̃sɥalite] *nf* sensuality
sensuel, -elle [sɑ̃sɥɛl] *adj* sensual
sent *voir* **sentir**
sentence [sɑ̃tɑ̃s] *nf* (**a**) *(jugement)* sentence (**b**) *(max-*
ime) maxim
sentencieux, -euse [sɑ̃tɑ̃sjø, -øz] *adj* sententious
senteur [sɑ̃tœr] *nf* scent; *(dans un parfum)* note
senti, -e [sɑ̃ti] *adj* **bien s.** appropriate
sentier [sɑ̃tje] *nm* path; *Fig* **sortir des sentiers battus**
to go off the beaten track; **sur le s. de la guerre** on the
warpath
sentiment [sɑ̃timɑ̃] *nm* feeling; **prendre qn par les**
sentiments to appeal to sb's feelings; *Fam* **ça partait**
d'un bon s. it was well meant; **en affaires, je ne fais**
pas de s. I don't let sentiment interfere with business;
avoir le s. que... to have a *or* the feeling that...; **j'avais**
le s. de m'être trompé I had the feeling I'd made a
mistake
sentimental, -e, -aux, -ales [sɑ̃timɑ̃tal, -o] **1** *adj*
(personne, chanson, valeur) sentimental; **vie senti-**
mentale love life
2 *nm,f* **c'est un(e) grand(e) sentimental(e)** he's/
she's a great romantic
sentimentalisme [sɑ̃timɑ̃talism] *nm* sentimental-
ism; **faire du s.** to be sentimental
sentinelle [sɑ̃tinɛl] *nf* sentry
sentir [64a] [sɑ̃tir] **1** *vt* (**a**) *(douleur, sensation tactile)* to
feel; *Fam Fig* **je ne sens plus mes jambes/mes pieds**

(de froid) I can't feel my legs/my feet; *(de fatigue)* my legs/my feet are killing me

(**b**) *(être conscient de) (danger)* to sense; **s. que...** to have a *or* the feeling that...; **faire s. à qn que...** to make sb feel that...; **se faire s.** to make itself felt; *Fig* **on sent l'influence de Wagner** one can detect Wagner's influence; *Fam* **je l'ai sentie passer** *(claque, fracture)* I knew all about it

(**c**) *(parfum, fleur)* to smell; **faire s. qch à qn** to let sb smell sth

(**d**) *(avoir l'odeur de)* to smell of; **ça sent le brûlé** there's a smell of burning; **ça sent bon le pain frais** there's a delicious smell of fresh bread; *Fig & Péj* **ce livre sent l'effort** this book is very laboured; **s. le soufre** to smack of heresy

(**e**) *Fam (supporter)* **je ne peux pas le s.** I can't stand him

(**f**) *Fam (être convaincu par)* **je ne le sens pas, ton projet** I'm not convinced by your plan; **je ne la sens pas pour le rôle** my feeling is that she's not right for the part

2 *vi* (**a**) *(avoir comme odeur)* **s. bon/mauvais** to smell good/bad; **s. fort** to have a strong smell

(**b**) *Fam (puer)* to smell; **s. des pieds** to have smelly feet

3 se sentir *vpr* (**a**) *(être perceptible)* **cela se sent** you can tell

(**b**) *(suivi d'un adjectif ou d'un infinitif)* **se s. revivre** to feel oneself coming alive again; **se s. bien/fatigué** to feel well/tired; *Fam* **tu ne te sens pas bien, non?** have you taken leave of your senses?; **se s. capable de faire qch** to feel capable of doing sth

(**c**) *(avoir)* **se s. le courage de faire qch** to feel up to doing sth

(**d**) *Fam (se contrôler)* **il ne se sent plus!** he's too big for his boots!

(**e**) *Fam (se supporter)* **ils ne peuvent pas se s.** they can't stand each other

seoir [10a] [swar] *Litt* **1** *vi* **s. à** to suit

2 *v impersonnel* **il lui sied mal de...** it ill becomes him to...

Séoul [seul] *n* Seoul

séparable [separabl] *adj* separable (**de** from)

séparation [separasjɔ̃] *nf* (**a**) *(de personnes, d'objets)* separation (**de** from); *Ordinat* **s. automatique des pages** automatic pagination (**b**) *(cloison)* partition, division (**c**) *Jur* **s. de biens** = marriage settlement under which husband and wife administer their separate properties

séparatisme [separatism] *nm* separatism

séparatiste [separatist] *adj & nmf* separatist

séparé, -e [separe] *adj* (**a**) *(notions, chambres)* separate (**b**) *(personnes)* separated (**de** from); **nous vivons séparés** we live apart

séparément [separemɑ̃] *adv* separately

séparer [separe] **1** *vt* (**a**) *(éloigner)* to separate (**de** from) (**b**) *(partager)* to divide (**en** into) (**c**) *(opposer)* to divide; **tout les sépare** they are poles apart

2 se séparer *vpr* (**a**) *(époux)* to separate (**de** from), to split up (**de** with) (**b**) *(foule, assemblée)* to break up (**c**) *(se défaire)* **se s. de qch** to part with sth; **se s. de qn** *(employé)* to let sb go (**d**) *(rivière, route)* to divide (**en** into); **c'est ici que nos chemins se séparent** this is where we go our separate ways

sept [sɛt] *adj & nm inv* seven; *voir aussi* **trois**

septante [sɛptɑ̃t] *adj inv Belg & Suisse* seventy; *voir aussi* **trois**

septembre [sɛptɑ̃br] *nm* September; *voir aussi* **janvier**

septennat [sɛptena] *nm* (seven-year) term

septentrional, -e, -aux, -ales [sɛptɑ̃trijɔnal, -o] *adj* northern

septicémie [sɛptisemi] *nf* blood poisoning, septicaemia

septième [sɛtjɛm] *nmf, nm & adj* seventh; *voir aussi* **cinquième**

septique [sɛptik] *adj* septic

septuagénaire [sɛptɥaʒenɛr] *adj & nmf* septuagenarian

sépulcre [sepylkr] *nm* sepulchre

sépulture [sepyltyr] *nf Litt* (**a**) *(inhumation)* burial (**b**) *(lieu)* burial place

séquelles [sekɛl] *nfpl (d'une maladie, d'un accident)* after-effects; *(d'une guerre, d'une catastrophe)* aftermath

séquençage [sekɑ̃saʒ] *nm Biol* sequencing

séquence [sekɑ̃s] *nf* (**a**) *(d'objets, de mots)* sequence; *Ordinat* **s. de caractères** character string, sequence of characters (**b**) *(de film)* sequence (**c**) *(de cartes)* run

séquestre [sekɛstr] *nm (action)* sequestration; **mettre qch sous s.** to sequester sth

séquestrer [sekɛstre] *vt* (**a**) *(personne)* **s. qn** to keep sb locked up (**b**) *(biens)* to sequester

séquoia [sekɔja] *nm* sequoia

sera, serai, serais *etc voir* **être**

sérail [seraj] *nm* seraglio; *Fig* inner circle

serbe [sɛrb] **1** *adj* Serb, Serbian

2 *nmf* **S.** Serb, Serbian

Serbie [sɛrbi] *nf* **la S.** Serbia

serbo-croate *(pl* **serbo-croates)** [sɛrbɔkrɔat] **1** *adj* Serbo-Croat, Serbo-Croatian

2 *nm (langue)* Serbo-Croat

Sercq [sɛrk] *n* Sark

serein, -e [sərɛ̃, -ɛn] *adj (personne, visage, esprit)* serene; *(ciel, nuit)* clear

sereinement [sərɛnmɑ̃] *adv* calmly

sérénade [serenad] *nf* (**a**) *Mus* serenade; **donner la s. à qn** to serenade sb (**b**) *Fam (tapage)* racket

sérénité [serenite] *nf* serenity; **avec s.** serenely

serf, serve [sɛrf, sɛrv] *nm,f Hist* serf

sergent [sɛrʒɑ̃] *nm* sergeant

sergent-chef *(pl* **sergents-chefs)** [sɛrʒɑ̃ʃɛf] *nm* staff sergeant

série [seri] *nf* (**a**) *(suite, collection)* series; *(d'échantillons)* range; *(de casseroles)* set; **des démissions en s.** a series of resignations (**b**) *Rad & TV* series (**c**) *Ind* **production en s.** mass production; **fabriquer qch en s.** to mass-produce sth; **voiture de s.** standard car; **s. limitée** limited run (**d**) *(dans un classement)* group; *Sport* heat; **(film de) s. B** B film (**e**) *(locutions)* **s. noire** *(suite de catastrophes)* series *or* catalogue of disasters; **(roman de) s. noire** crime thriller

sérieusement [serjøzmɑ̃] *adv* seriously; **parlez-vous s.?** are you serious?

sérieux, -euse [serjø, -øz] **1** *adj* (**a**) *(personne, lecture)* serious; **d'un air s.** seriously; **ce n'est pas s.!** you're not serious!; *Fam* **s. comme un pape** as solemn as a judge (**b**) *(offre, acheteur)* serious, genuine; *(information, entreprise)* reliable; *(employé)* conscientious (**c**) *(important) (problèmes, ennuis)* serious;

(progrès) good

2 *nm* (**a**) *(application)* conscientiousness; **avec s.** conscientiously (**b**) *(gravité)* **garder son s.** to keep a straight face; **prendre qn/qch au s.** to take sb/sth seriously; **se prendre au s.** to take oneself seriously

sérigraphie [serigrafi] *nf* silk-screen printing

serin [sərɛ̃] *nm (oiseau)* canary

seriner [sərine] *vt Fam* **s. qch à qn** to go on and on at sb about sth; **s. à qn que...** to keep telling sb that...

seringue [sərɛ̃g] *nf* syringe

serment [sɛrmɑ̃] *nm* (**a**) *(parole solennelle)* oath; **prêter s.** to take an oath; **sous s.** on oath (**b**) *(promesse)* pledge; *(d'amoureux)* vow; **faire le s. de faire qch** to swear *or* vow to do sth

sermon [sɛrmɔ̃] *nm* (**a**) *Rel* sermon (**b**) *Fam (remontrance)* lecture, sermon

sermonner [sɛrmɔne] *vt Fam* to lecture

séronégatif, -ive [serɔnegatif, -iv] **1** *adj* HIV negative **2** *nm,f* person who is HIV negative

séropositif, -ive [serɔpozitif, -iv] **1** *adj* HIV positive **2** *nm,f* person who is HIV positive

sérotonine [serɔtɔnin] *nf* serotonin

serpe [sɛrp] *nf* billhook

serpent [sɛrpɑ̃] *nm* (**a**) *(reptile)* snake; **s. à sonnette** rattlesnake (**b**) *Écon* **le s. monétaire européen** the European currency snake

serpenter [sɛrpɑ̃te] *vi* to wind

serpentin [sɛrpɑ̃tɛ̃] *nm (cotillon)* streamer

serpillière [sɛrpijɛr] *nf* floorcloth; **passer la s. dans la cuisine** to clean the kitchen floor

serpolet [sɛrpɔlɛ] *nm* wild thyme

serre [sɛr] *nf* (**a**) *(local)* greenhouse (**b**) **serres** *(d'oiseau de proie)* claws, talons

serré, -e [sere] **1** *adj* (**a**) *(chaussures, vêtement)* tight; *(personnes)* packed together; *(écriture)* cramped; *(rangs)* serried; *(dents)* clenched; *(lèvres)* pressed tightly together (**b**) *(emploi du temps, budget)* tight; *(surveillance, lutte, score)* close (**c**) *(café)* strong **2** *adv* **écrire s.** to have cramped handwriting; *Fig* **jouer s.** to play a tight game

serre-livres [sɛrlivr] *nm inv* book-end

serrement [sɛrmɑ̃] *nm* **avoir un s. de cœur** to feel a pang

serrer [sere] **1** *vt* (**a**) *(tenir)* to grip; **s. la main à qn** to shake hands with sb, to shake sb's hand; **s. qn dans ses bras** to hug sb; **s. qn/qch contre soi** to hold sb/sth tightly to one; *Fig* **s. le cœur à qn** to wring sb's heart (**b**) *(sujet: vêtement, chaussures)* to be too tight for (**c**) *(nœud, écrou, ceinture)* to tighten; *(joint)* to clamp; *(poings)* to clench; **s. les dents** to clench one's teeth; *Fig* to grit one's teeth; *Fam Fig* **s. les fesses** to be scared stiff (**d**) *(rapprocher)* to put close together; **s. les rangs** to close ranks (**e**) *(ranger)* to put away (**f**) *(raser) (trottoir)* to hug; **s. qn de près** to follow sb closely; **évite de s. la voiture de devant** don't drive too close to the car in front **2** *vi* **serrez à droite/gauche** *(sur panneau)* keep to the right/left **3** **se serrer** *vpr* (**a**) *(se rapprocher)* to squeeze up; **se s. contre qn** to snuggle up to sb (**b**) *Fig* **ma gorge se serra** I had a lump in my throat (**c**) *(pour se saluer)* **se s. la main** to shake hands

serre-tête [sɛrtɛt] *nm inv* headband

serriculture [serikyltyr] *nf* hothouse growing

serrure [seryr] *nf* lock

serrurerie [seryrri] *nf (métier)* locksmith's trade; *(magasin)* locksmith's (shop)

serrurier [seryrje] *nm* locksmith

sers, sert *etc voir* **servir**

sertir [sɛrtir] *vt (pierre précieuse)* to set

sérum [serɔm] *nm* serum; **s. physiologique** saline solution

servage [sɛrvaʒ] *nm* serfdom; *Fig* bondage

servante [sɛrvɑ̃t] *nf* (maid)servant

serve [sɛrv] *voir* **serf**

serveur, -euse [sɛrvœr, -øz] **1** *nm,f* (**a**) *(dans un bar)* barman, *f* barmaid; *(dans un restaurant)* waiter, *f* waitress (**b**) *(au tennis)* server **2** *nm Ordinat* server; **s. de fichiers** file server; **s. de réseau** network server; **s. télématique** bulletin board (system); **s. Web** web server

serviable [sɛrvjabl] *adj* obliging, helpful

service [sɛrvis] *nm* (**a**) *(pour un client, pour un maître)* service; *Écon* **services** services; **faire le s.** *(à table)* to serve; **être au s. de qn** to be in sb's service; **à votre s.** at your service; **s. compris/non compris** service included/not included; **premier/deuxième s.** *(au restaurant)* first/second sitting; **s. après-vente** *(dépannage)* after-sales service; *Ordinat* **s. en ligne** on-line service

(**b**) *Mil* **s. militaire** *ou* **national** military service; **faire son s.** to do one's military service; **bon pour le s.** fit for service

(**c**) *(au tennis)* service; **au s., Martin** Martin to serve

(**d**) *(travail)* duty; **être de s.** to be on duty; **prendre/quitter son s.** to go on/off duty; **reprendre du s.** to be employed for a supplementary period; *Fam* **le crétin de s.** the inevitable *or* obligatory idiot

(**e**) *(département)* department; **s. d'ordre** *(surveillance)* crowd control; *(personnes)* = police, security staff etc in charge of crowd control; **s. du personnel** personnel department; **s. public** public utility; **s. de renseignements** military intelligence department; *Ordinat* **s. télématique** bulletin board service

(**f**) *(d'une machine)* **en s.** in service; **mettre qch en s.** to bring sth into service

(**g**) *(de transports en commun)* service; **assurer le s. entre** to provide a service between

(**h**) *(aide)* favour; **rendre (un) s. à qn** *(personne)* to do sb a favour; *(objet)* to be of use to sb; **rendre un mauvais s. à qn** to do sb a bad turn

(**i**) *(de vaisselle)* set

Service militaire

Military service (for a period of ten months) used to be compulsory for French men aged between 18 and 26 unless they were declared unfit for service ("réformé"). As an alternative to military service, some chose to work overseas, often in developing countries, as part of a voluntary aid scheme known as "la coopération". However, following the "loi de programmation" 1997–2002, a reform was introduced in order to gradually abolish military service and move towards an exclusively professional army.

serviette [sɛrvjɛt] *nf* (**a**) *(en tissu)* **s. (de table)** serviette, napkin; **s. (de toilette)** towel; **s. de plage** beach towel (**b**) *(sac)* briefcase (**c**) **s. hygiénique** sanitary *Br* towel *or Am* napkin

serviette-éponge (*pl* **serviettes-éponges**) [sɛrvjɛtepɔ̃ʒ] *nf* terry towel

servile [sɛrvil] *adj* servile; *(imitation, traduction)* slavish

servilement [sɛrvilmɑ̃] *adv* servilely; *(imiter, traduire)* slavishly

servir [63] [sɛrvir] **1** *vt* (**a**) *(client, convive, nourriture)* to serve; **tout le monde est servi?** *(à table)* has everybody been served?; **s. frais** *(sur étiquette)* serve chilled; **s. à boire à qn** to give sb a drink; *Ironique* **côté ennuis, je suis servi!** I've got more than my share of worries! (**b**) *(favoriser) (personne)* to serve; *(intérêts)* to further (**c**) *(au tennis)* to serve (**d**) *(aux cartes)* **à vous de s.** it's your deal
   2 *vi (dans une administration)* to serve (**sous** under)
   3 servir à *vt ind* (**a**) *(être utile à)* to be of use to; **ça peut toujours s.** it might still come in useful (**b**) *(être utilisé pour)* **s. à qch/à faire qch** to be used for sth/for doing sth; **ne s. à rien** to be useless; **ne pas s. à grandchose** not to be much use; **à quoi ça sert?** *(objet)* what's that used for?; *(démarche)* what's the use of that?
   4 servir de *vt ind (faire fonction de) (objet)* to serve as, to be used as; *(personne)* to act as; **ça me sert de porte-crayons** I use it as a pencil-holder
   5 *v impersonnel Litt* **il ne sert à rien de pleurer** there's no point in crying
   6 se servir *vpr* (**a**) *(prendre)* to help oneself; **je me suis déjà servie deux fois** I've already had two helpings; **se s. des pâtes/du poulet** to help oneself to pasta/to chicken (**b**) *(plat, vin)* to be served; **le champagne se sert frappé** champagne should be served chilled (**c**) **se s. de qn/qch** *(utiliser)* to use sb/sth (**d**) *(s'approvisionner)* **se s. chez...** to shop at...

serviteur [sɛrvitœr] *nm* servant

servitude [sɛrvityd] *nf* (**a**) *(asservissement)* servitude (**b**) *(contrainte)* constraint

ses [se] *voir* **son¹**

sésame [sezam] *nm* (**a**) *(plante)* sesame (**b**) *Fig* **s., ouvre-toi!** open sesame!

session [sesjɔ̃] *nf* (**a**) *(d'une assemblée, d'un tribunal)* session, sitting (**b**) *(période d'examens)* (exam) session; **s. de rattrapage** repeat exams, *Br* resits

SET [sɛɔ̃te] *nf Ordinat (abrév* **secure electronic transaction**) SET®

set [sɛt] *nm* (**a**) *(au tennis)* set (**b**) **s. de table** *(napperon)* table mat

setter [sɛtɛr] *nm* setter; **s. irlandais** Irish setter

seuil [sœj] *nm* (**a**) *(entrée)* doorway, threshold; **sur le s.** in the doorway (**b**) *Fig* threshold; *Litt* **au s. de...** on the threshold of...; **s. de rentabilité** break-even point

seul, -e [sœl] **1** *adj* (**a**) *(unique)* only; **une seule personne** *(et pas plus)* a single person; *(parmi d'autres)* only one person; **comme un s. homme** as one man; **il suffit d'une seule fois** once is enough; **la seule pensée de sa venue** the mere thought of him coming (**b**) *(isolé)* alone; **se sentir s.** to feel lonely *or* alone; **être s. au monde** to be alone in the world; **parler s.** à s. à qn to speak to sb in private; **faire qch tout s.** to do sth (by) oneself *or* on one's own; **parler tout s.** to talk to oneself; **cela va tout s.** it's plain sailing, it's straightforward; **ça descend tout s.** *(boisson)* it just slides down (**c**) *(seulement)* only, alone; **s. un miracle...** only a miracle...
   2 *nm,f* **le s.** the only one; **un s.** *(personne, objet)* only one

seulement [sœlmɑ̃] *adv* only; **je te demande s. un peu de patience** I'm just asking you to be a bit pa-

tient; **non s. ... mais en plus...** not only... but also...; *Fam* **essaie s.!** just you try!

sève [sɛv] *nf* (**a**) *(d'une plante)* sap (**b**) *Fig (de la jeunesse)* vitality

sévère [sever] *adj* severe; *(principe, règle)* strict; **être s. envers** *ou* **avec qn** to be hard on sb

sévèrement [severmɑ̃] *adv* severely; *(de façon stricte)* strictly

sévérité [severite] *nf* severity; *(d'une discipline, d'une éducation)* strictness

sévices [sevis] *nmpl* ill-treatment; **s. sexuels** sexual abuse

Séville [sevij] *n* Seville

sévir [sevir] *vi* (**a**) *(agir avec rigueur)* to act ruthlessly; **s. contre qn/qch** to deal ruthlessly with sb/sth (**b**) *(épidémie, guerre)* to rage; *(malfaiteurs)* to operate; **la crise qui sévit actuellement** the present crisis

sevrage [səvraʒ] *nm (d'un enfant)* weaning; *(d'un drogué, d'un alcoolique)* withdrawal

sevrer [səvre] *vt* (**a**) *(enfant)* to wean; *(drogué)* to get off drugs; *(alcoolique)* to get off drink (**b**) *Litt (priver)* **s. qn de qch** to deprive sb of sth

sexagénaire [sɛgzaʒenɛr, sɛksaʒenɛr] *nmf* person in his/her sixties

sex-appeal [sɛksapil] *nm Fam* sex appeal

sexe [sɛks] *nm* (**a**) *(genre)* sex; *Hum* **le beau s.** the fair sex; **le s. faible** the weaker sex; **le s. fort** the stronger sex (**b**) *(organes sexuels)* genitals (**c**) *(sexualité)* sex

sexisme [sɛksism] *nm* sexism

sexiste [sɛksist] *adj & nmf* sexist

sexologue [sɛksɔlɔg] *nmf* sexologist

sex-shop (*pl* **sex-shops**) [sɛksʃɔp] *nm* sex shop

sextant [sɛkstɑ̃] *nm* sextant

sextuor [sɛkstɥɔr] *nm* sextet

sextuplé, -e [sɛkstyple] *nm,f* sextuplet

sexualité [sɛksɥalite] *nf* sexuality

sexué, -e [sɛksɥe] *adj (plante, animal)* sexed; *(reproduction)* sexual

sexuel, -elle [sɛksɥɛl] *adj (rapport)* sexual; *(vie, acte, organe)* sex

sexuellement [sɛksɥɛlmɑ̃] *adv* sexually

sexy [sɛksi] *adj inv Fam* sexy

seyant, -e [sejɑ̃, -ɑ̃t] *adj* becoming

Seychelles [seʃɛl] *nfpl* **les S.** the Seychelles

SF [ɛsɛf] *nf Fam (abrév* **science fiction**) sci-fi, SF

SFIO [ɛsɛfio] *nf (abrév* **Section française de l'Internationale ouvrière**) = French Socialist Party 1905–1969

shaker [ʃɛkœr] *nm* cocktail shaker

shakespearien, -enne [ʃɛkspirjɛ̃, -ɛn] *adj* Shakespearean

shampoing [ʃɑ̃pwɛ̃] *nm* shampoo; **faire un s. à qn** to shampoo sb's hair, to give sb a shampoo

shampouiner [ʃɑ̃pwine] *vt* to shampoo

shampouineur, -euse [ʃɑ̃pwinœr, -øz] **1** *nm,f* shampooer
   2 *nf* **shampouineuse (à moquettes)** *(machine)* carpet shampooer

shérif [ʃerif] *nm* sheriff

shetland [ʃɛtlɑ̃d] **1** *nfpl* **les (îles) S.** the Shetland Islands, the Shetlands
   2 *nm* (**a**) *(laine)* Shetland wool; *(pull)* Shetland jumper (**b**) *(poney)* Shetland pony

shinto [ʃinto], **shintoïsme** [ʃintɔism] *nm* Shinto, Shintoism

shit [ʃit] *nm très Fam* hash

shoot [ʃut] *nm* shot

shooter [ʃute] **1** *vi (au football)* to shoot
2 se shooter *vpr Fam (se droguer)* to shoot up; **se s. à l'héroïne** to shoot (up) heroin

shopping [ʃɔpiŋ] *nm* shopping; **faire du s.** to go shopping

short [ʃɔrt] *nm* (pair of) shorts

show [ʃo] *nm* show

show-business [ʃobiznɛs] *nm* show business

si¹ [si] *adv* (**a**) *(tellement)* so; **un si bon dîner** such a good dinner; **il n'est pas si bête (que ça)** he's not that stupid; **il était si nerveux qu'il a tout oublié** he was so nervous (that) he forgot everything (**b**) *(indique la concession)* **si... que** + *subjunctive* however...; **si jeune qu'il soit** however young he may be; **si habile soit-il** however capable (he may be) (**c**) *(oui)* yes; **je crois que si** I think so; **mais si, je l'ai vue** I DID see her; **tu ne sais pas? si, si** you don't know? – yes, I do (**d**) **si bien que...** *(indique le résultat)* so that...

si² **1** *conj* (**a**) *(exprime l'hypothèse, la condition)* if; **qui le fera si ce n'est moi?** who'll do it if I don't?; **un des plus grands, si ce n'est le plus grand** one of the biggest, if not the biggest; **si ce n'est que...** *(sauf que)* apart from the fact that...; **et si elle l'apprend?** and what if she finds out?; **si on faisait une partie de bridge?** what about a game of bridge?; **oui, si on veut** yes, if you like; **si seulement...** if only...; **si tant est que...** + *subjunctive* if... (**b**) *(combien)* how; **pensez si j'étais furieux!** imagine how angry I was! (**c**) *(dans les questions indirectes)* if, whether; *Fam* **si je connais Paris?** do I know Paris?; *Fam* **si c'est pas malheureux (de voir ça)!** isn't it just dreadful (to see that)!
2 *nm inv* **tes si et tes mais** your ifs and buts

si³ *nm inv (note)* B; *(chantée)* ti

siamois, -e [sjamwa, -az] **1** *adj* **frères s.** Siamese twins; **sœurs siamoises** Siamese twins
2 *nm (chat)* Siamese (cat)

Sibérie [siberi] *nf* **la S.** Siberia

sibérien, -enne [siberjɛ̃, -ɛn] **1** *adj* Siberian
2 *nm,f* **S.** Siberian

sibyllin, -e [sibilɛ̃, -in] *adj (énigmatique)* cryptic, enigmatic

SICAV [sikav] *nf inv Fin (abrév* **société d'investissement à capital variable***)* (**a**) *(organisme) Br* ≃ unit trust, *Am* ≃ mutual fund (**b**) *(titre)* share in a *Br* unit trust *or Am* mutual fund

Sicile [sisil] *nf* **la S.** Sicily

sicilien, -enne [sisiljɛ̃, -ɛn] **1** *adj* Sicilian
2 *nm,f* **S.** Sicilian

sida [sida] *nm (abrév* **syndrome immunodéficitaire acquis***)* AIDS; **avoir le s.** to have AIDS

side-car *(pl* **side-cars***)* [sajdkar, sidkar] *nm* sidecar

sidéen, -enne [sideɛ̃, -ɛn] **1** *adj* suffering from AIDS
2 *nm,f* AIDS sufferer

sidéral, -e, -aux, -ales [sideral, -o] *adj* sidereal

sidérant, -e [siderã, -ãt] *adj Fam* staggering

sidérer [34] [sidere] *vt Fam* to stagger

sidérurgie [sideryrʒi] *nf* (**a**) *(technique)* iron and steel metallurgy (**b**) *(industrie)* iron and steel industry

sidérurgique [sideryrʒik] *adj (industrie, usine)* iron and steel

sidérurgiste [sideryrʒist] *nmf* iron and steel worker

siècle [sjɛkl] *nm* (**a**) *(cent ans)* century; **au vingtième s.** in the twentieth century; **avoir un s.** to be a hundred years old; *Fam* **ça fait des siècles que j'attends** I've been waiting for ages (**b**) *(époque)* age; **le s. des**

Lumières the Age of Enlightenment; **il est de son s.** he's a man of his times

sied *voir* **seoir**

siège [sjɛʒ] *nm* (**a**) *(meuble)* seat; **s. avant/arrière** front/back seat; **s. pliant** folding chair; **s. pour enfant** *(en voiture)* child seat (**b**) *(d'une société, d'un organisme)* headquarters; **s. administratif** administrative headquarters; **s. social** head office (**c**) *(lieu d'origine)* seat (**d**) *Mil* siege; **faire le s. de** to lay siege to; **lever le s.** to raise the siege; *Fam (partir)* to make tracks (**e**) *Pol* seat (**f**) *Méd* **accouchement par le s.** breech delivery; **se présenter par le s.** to be in the breech position

siéger [59] [sjeʒe] *vi* (**a**) *(tribunal, assemblée)* to sit (**b**) *(se trouver)* **c'est là que siège le mal** that's the root of the problem

sien, -enne [sjɛ̃, sjɛn] **1** *pron possessif* **le sien, la sienne, les siens, les siennes** *(possesseur masculin)* his; *(possesseur féminin)* hers; *(en insistant)* his/her own; **il te prête le s.** you can borrow his; **elle n'en a pas besoin, elle a le s.** she doesn't need it, she has her own; **on doit acheter la sienne** you must buy your own; **chacun doit apporter le s.** everyone must bring their own; **chaque pays a le s.** each country has its own
2 *nm* **il faut qu'il y mette du s.** he should do his share
3 *nmpl* **les siens** *(sa famille)* his/her family
4 *nfpl Fam* **il a encore fait des siennes** he's been up to his old tricks again

Sierra Leone [sjeraleɔn] *nf* **la S.** Sierra Leone

sieste [sjɛst] *nf* siesta, nap; **faire la s.** to have a nap

sifflant, -e [siflã, -ãt] *adj (respiration, toux)* wheezing

sifflement [sifləmã] *nm (d'une personne, du vent)* whistling; *(d'un serpent, de la vapeur)* hissing; *(d'un asthmatique)* wheezing; **sifflements d'oreilles** ringing in the ears

siffler [sifle] **1** *vt* (**a**) *(air)* to whistle (**b**) *(chien, personne)* to whistle at (**c**) *(acteur, pièce)* to boo (**d**) *Fam (verre, bouteille)* to knock back
2 *vi* (**a**) *(personne, merle, bouilloire)* to whistle; *(serpent)* to hiss (**b**) *(avec un sifflet)* to blow one's whistle

sifflet [siflɛ] *nm* (**a**) *(instrument)* whistle; *Fam* **couper le s. à qn** to shut sb up (**b**) *(au théâtre)* **sifflets** booing, boos

siffleux [siflø] *nm Can* groundhog, woodchuck

siffloter [siflɔte] *vt & vi* to whistle to oneself

sigle [sigl] *nm (acronyme)* acronym; *(suite d'initiales)* abbreviation

signal, -aux [siɲal, -o] *nm* (**a**) *(signe)* signal; **faire un s.** to signal; **envoyer** *ou* **lancer un s.** to send a signal; **au s., levez-vous** when the signal is given, stand up; **s. lumineux** indicator light, warning light (**b**) *(panneau)* sign (**c**) *(dispositif sonore)* **s. d'alarme** alarm (signal); **s. d'alerte** warning (signal); *Tél* **s. d'appel** call(ing) signal; **s. de détresse** distress signal; **s. sonore** warning sound (**d**) *Ordinat* **s. d'avertissement de réception** acknowledge; **s. horodateur** time and date signal; **s. d'invitation à transmettre** proceed-to-send signal

signalement [siɲalmã] *nm* description, particulars

signaler [siɲale] **1** *vt* (**a**) *(faire remarquer)* to point out (**à** to); **s. à qn que...** to point out to sb that... (**b**) *(rapporter)* to report (**à** to); **rien à s.** nothing to report (**c**) *(par un panneau)* to signpost (**d**) *Ordinat (marquer)* to flag up

2 se signaler *upr* to distinguish oneself (**par** by); **se s. à l'attention de qn** to catch sb's eye

signalétique [siɲaletik] *adj* **fiche s.** personal details card; **plaque s.** identification plate

signalisation [siɲalizasjɔ̃] *nf (signaux routiers)* signs and markings; *(signaux ferroviaires)* signals; *(de piste d'atterrissage)* lights and markings; **s. routière** road signs

signaliser [siɲalize] *vt (route)* to signpost and mark; *(voie ferrée)* to install signals on; *(piste d'atterrissage)* to install lights and markings on

signataire [siɲatɛr] *nmf* signatory

signature [siɲatyr] *nf* **(a)** *(griffe)* signature; **présenter qch à la s.** to present sth for signature; *Com & Ordinat* **s. électronique** *ou* **numérique** digital signature **(b)** *(acte)* signing

signe [siɲ] *nm* **(a)** *(indice)* sign; **il n'a pas donné s. de vie** there's been no sign of him; **il n'y a aucun s. de vie dans la maison** there's no sign of life at the house; **en s. de désapprobation/solidarité** as a sign of disapproval/solidarity; **s. avant-coureur** forerunner; **donner des signes d'usure** to show signs of wear **(b)** *(symbole)* sign, symbol; **s. moins/plus/égale** minus/plus/equals sign; **signes de ponctuation** punctuation marks **(c)** *Astrol* **s. du zodiaque** sign of the zodiac; **être né sous le s. du Capricorne** to be born under the sign of Capricorn; *Fig* **le sommet a eu lieu sous le s. de la réconciliation** the summit was held in a spirit of reconciliation **(d)** *(trait distinctif)* mark; **signes particuliers** distinguishing marks **(e)** *(geste)* sign, gesture; **faire un s. à qn** to gesture to sb; **parler par signes** to use sign language; **faire s. à qn** *(de la main)* to signal to sb; *(le contacter)* to get in touch with sb; **faire s. à qn de faire qch** to signal to sb to do sth; **faire s. que oui** *(de la tête)* to nod (one's head); **faire s. que non** *(de la tête)* to shake one's head; *(du doigt)* to shake one's finger; **faire un s. de la main (à qn)** to wave (at sb); **faire un s. de tête (à qn)** to nod (to sb) **(f)** *Rel* **s. de croix** sign of the cross; **faire le s. de croix** to make the sign of the cross

signer [siɲe] **1** *vt (contrat, lettre, tableau)* to sign; *Fam Fig* **ça c'est signé!** no prizes for guessing who did that! **2** *vi* to sign; **s. de son nom** to sign one's name **3 se signer** *upr* to cross oneself

signet [siɲe] *nm (de livre, de page Web)* bookmark; *Ordinat* **créer un s. sur une page** to bookmark a page

significatif, -ive [siɲifikatif, -iv] *adj* significant; **s. de qch** indicative of sth

signification [siɲifikasjɔ̃] *nf* **(a)** *(d'un mot, d'un symbole)* meaning, sense; *(d'un fait)* significance **(b)** *Jur (d'un jugement)* notification

signifier [66] [siɲifje] *vt* **(a)** *(vouloir dire)* to mean; **qu'est-ce que ça signifie?** *(indignation)* what's the meaning of this? **(b)** *(notifier) (intentions)* to make known (**à** to); **s. son congé à qn** *(sujet: propriétaire, employeur)* to give sb notice; **s. qch à qn** to inform *or* notify sb of sth

signofil, signofile [siɲofil] *nm Suisse Aut Br* indicator, *Am* turn signal

silence [silɑ̃s] *nm* **(a)** *(absence de bruit)* silence; **un s. de mort** a deadly silence; **rompre le s.** to break the silence; **garder le s. (sur)** to keep silent (about); **faire qch en s.** to do sth in silence; **passer qch sous s.** not to mention sth **(b)** *Mus* rest

silencieusement [silɑ̃sjøzmɑ̃] *adv* silently

silencieux, -euse [silɑ̃sjø, -øz] **1** *adj* silent; *(qui ne fait pas beaucoup de bruit)* quiet **2** *nm (d'un véhicule)* *Br* silencer, *Am* muffler; *(d'une arme)* silencer

silex [silɛks] *nm* flint

silhouette [silwɛt] *nf* **(a)** *(du corps)* figure **(b)** *(d'un objet)* silhouette, outline

silice [silis] *nf* silica

silicium [silisjɔm] *nm Chim* silicon

silicone [silikɔn] *nf* silicone

sillage [sijaʒ] *nm (d'un navire)* wake; *Fig* **marcher dans le s. de qn** to follow in sb's wake

sillon [sijɔ̃] *nm* **(a)** *(d'un champ)* furrow **(b)** *(de disque)* groove

sillonner [sijɔne] *vt (parcourir)* to criss-cross

silo [silo] *nm* silo

simagrées [simagre] *nfpl* airs and graces; **faire des s.** to make a fuss

simiesque [simjɛsk] *adj* monkey-like, ape-like

similaire [similɛr] *adj* similar (**à** to)

similarité [similarite] *nf* similarity

simili [simili] *nm Fam (imitation)* imitation

similicuir [similikɥir] *nm* imitation leather

similitude [similityd] *nf* similarity

simple [sɛ̃pl] **1** *adj* **(a)** *(sans prétentions)* simple **(b)** *(facile)* simple, easy; **c'est s. comme bonjour** it's as easy as pie **(c)** *(crédule)* simple; **s. d'esprit** simple-minded **(d)** *(pur)* **c'est une s. question de temps** it's simply a matter of time **(e)** *(ordinaire)* ordinary; **s. soldat** private (soldier) **(f)** *(composé d'un élément) (nœud)* single; **cornet s.** *(de glace)* cone with one scoop; *Ordinat* **s. densité** single density **2** *nm* **(a)** *(au tennis)* singles (match) **(b)** *(somme, quantité)* **varier du s. au double** to vary by twice as much **(c)** *(personne)* **un s. d'esprit** a simpleton

simplement [sɛ̃pləmɑ̃] *adv* simply; **le plus s. du monde** as if it was the most natural thing in the world; **prendre les choses s.** to take things as they come

simplet, -ette [sɛ̃plɛ, -ɛt] *adj (personne)* simple; *(idée, explication)* simplistic

simplicité [sɛ̃plisite] *nf* simplicity; **recevoir qn en toute s.** to entertain sb very simply; **d'une s. enfantine** childishly simple

simplificateur, -trice [sɛ̃plifikatœr, -tris] *adj* simplifying

simplification [sɛ̃plifikasjɔ̃] *nf* simplification

simplifier [66] [sɛ̃plifje] *vt aussi Math* to simplify; **ça me simplifiera l'existence** it'll make my life easier

simpliste [sɛ̃plist] *adj Péj* simplistic

simulacre [simylakr] *nm* **(a)** *(représentation)* reconstruction **(b)** *(parodie)* **s. de combat/négociations** sham fight/negotiations; **ce fut un s. de procès** the trial was a farce

simulateur, -trice [simylatœr, -tris] **1** *nm,f (d'un sentiment)* pretender; *(d'une maladie)* malingerer **2** *nm Tech* simulator

simulation [simylasjɔ̃] *nf* **(a)** *(action)* feigning **(b)** *(d'un vol, d'un phénomène)* & *Ordinat* simulation

simulé, -e [simyle] *adj* **(a)** *(sentiment, maladie)* feigned; *(combat)* sham **(b)** *(vol, phénomène)* simulated

simuler [simyle] *vt* **(a)** *(sentiment, maladie, folie)* to feign **(b)** *(vol, phénomène)* to simulate

simultané, -e [simyltane] *adj* simultaneous

simultanéité [simyltaneite] *nf* simultaneousness, simultaneity

simultanément [simyltanemã] *adv* simultaneously

sincère [sɛ̃sɛr] *adj* sincere

sincèrement [sɛ̃sɛrmã] *adv* sincerely; **s., je trouve que...** frankly, I think...

sincérité [sɛ̃serite] *nf* sincerity; **en toute s.** in all sincerity

sinécure [sinekyr] *nf* sinecure; *Fam* **ce n'est pas une s.** it's not exactly a rest cure

sine die [sinedje] *adv* sine die

sine qua non [sinekwanɔn] *adj inv* **une condition s.** a prerequisite

Singapour [sɛ̃gapur] *n* Singapore

singapourien, -enne [sɛ̃gapurjɛ̃, -ɛn] **1** *adj* Singaporean
2 *nm,f* **S.** Singaporean

singe [sɛ̃ʒ] *nm* monkey; **grand s.** ape; **malin/adroit comme un s.** as crafty/clever as a monkey; **faire le s.** to clown around

singer [45] [sɛ̃ʒe] *vt (personne)* to ape, to mimic; *(sentiment)* to feign

singeries [sɛ̃ʒri] *nfpl (grimaces, gestes)* antics; **faire des singeries** to clown around

singulariser [sɛ̃gylarize] **1** *vt* **s. qn (de)** to set sb apart (from), to make sb stand out (from)
2 se singulariser *vpr* to draw attention to oneself; **il se singularise par sa façon de parler** the way he speaks makes him stand out

singularité [sɛ̃gylarite] *nf* peculiarity

singulier, -ère [sɛ̃gylje, -er] **1** *adj* (a) *Gram* singular (b) *(combat)* single (c) *(remarquable)* remarkable; *(étrange)* peculiar, odd
2 *nm Gram* singular; **au s.** in the singular

singulièrement [sɛ̃gyljɛrmã] *adv* (a) *(étrangement)* oddly (b) *(en particulier)* especially, particularly (c) *(beaucoup)* remarkably, extremely

sinistre [sinistr] **1** *adj* (a) *(effrayant)* sinister; *(à faire froid dans le dos)* spooky (b) *(déprimant) (paysage)* bleak; *(soirée, repas)* dismal, grim (c) **un s. imbécile** an awful idiot
2 *nm* (a) *(catastrophe)* disaster (b) *Jur (dommage)* damage

sinistré, -e [sinistre] **1** *adj (population)* stricken; *(bâtiment)* damaged; *(région, zone)* disaster
2 *nm,f* disaster victim

sinistrose [sinistroz] *nf Fam* pessimism, gloom

sinologue [sinɔlɔg] *nmf* sinologist

sinon [sinɔ̃] *conj* (a) *(autrement)* otherwise, or else (b) *(excepté)* except (c) *(si ce n'est)* if not

sinueux, -euse [sinɥø, -øz] *adj (ligne)* sinuous; *(chemin, courant)* winding, meandering; *Fig (raisonnement)* tortuous

sinuosité [sinɥozite] *nf (d'un chemin, d'une rivière)* bend; *Fig* **les sinuosités d'un raisonnement** the twists and turns of an argument

sinus¹ [sinys] *nm Anat* sinus

sinus² *nm Math* sine

sinusite [sinyzit] *nf* sinusitis

sionisme [sjɔnism] *nm* Zionism

sioniste [sjɔnist] *adj & nmf* Zionist

sioux [sju] **1** *adj* Sioux
2 *nmf* **S.** Sioux

siphon [sifɔ̃] *nm* (a) *(tube)* siphon (b) *(bouteille)* (soda) siphon (c) *(d'un évier, d'une canalisation)* U-bend, trap

siphonné, -e [sifɔne] *adj Fam (fou)* crackers, crazy

siphonner [sifɔne] *vt* to siphon

sire [sir] *nm* **S.** *(à un souverain)* Sire; *Péj* **un triste s.** an unsavoury character

sirène [sirɛn] *nf* (a) *(personnage fantastique)* mermaid, siren; *Fig (femme)* siren (b) *(dispositif sonore)* siren

sirop [siro] *nm* syrup; **s. de fraise/menthe** strawberry/mint cordial; **s. contre la toux** cough mixture *or* syrup

siroter [sirɔte] *vt Fam* to sip

sirupeux, -euse [sirypø, -øz] *adj* syrupy; *(musique)* slushy

sismique [sismik] *adj* seismic

sismographe [sismɔgraf] *nm* seismograph

sismologie [sismɔlɔʒi] *nf* seismology

sitar [sitar] *nm* sitar

sitcom [sitkɔm] *nm ou nf* sitcom

site [sit] *nm* (a) *(emplacement)* site (b) *(pittoresque)* beauty spot; **s. classé** conservation area; **s. historique/archéologique** historic/archaeological site; **s. touristique** place of interest, tourist attraction (c) *Ordinat* site; **s. Web** Web site

sitôt [sito] *adv* **elle le fera s. ses devoirs finis** she'll do it as soon as she's finished her homework; **s. dit, s. fait** no sooner said than done; **s. que** as soon as; **s. après** immediately after; **on ne le reverra pas de s.** we won't see him again in a hurry

situation [sitɥasjɔ̃] *nf* (a) *(d'une ville, d'un bâtiment)* position, location (b) *(circonstances)* situation; **être en s. de faire qch** to be in a position to do sth; **mettre qn en s.** to give sb experience of a real-life situation; **l'homme de la s.** the right man for the job; **s. de famille** marital status (c) *(emploi)* job, position (d) *Fin (de compte)* balance

situé, -e [sitɥe] *adj* situated

situer [sitɥe] **1** *vt* (a) *(placer)* to situate (b) *(trouver)* to locate (c) *(dans le temps)* to set; **je situe l'action au milieu du XIXᵉ siècle** I'd say the action takes place in the middle of the 19th century (d) *Fig (catégoriser)* to categorize
2 se situer *vpr* (a) *(être)* to be; **se s. à droite** to be right-wing (b) *(avoir lieu)* to take place

six [sis] *adj & nm inv* six; *voir aussi* **trois**

sixième [sizjɛm] **1** *adj, nmf & nm* sixth; *voir aussi* **cinquième**
2 *nf Scol (enseignement secondaire) Br* ≃ first form, *Am* ≃ sixth grade

sixièmement [sizjɛmmã] *adv* in the sixth place, sixthly

six-quatre-deux [siskatdø] **à la six-quatre-deux** *adv Fam* in a slapdash way

sixte [sikst] *nf Mus* sixth

Skaï® [skaj] *nm* imitation leather

skate [skɛt], **skateboard** [skɛtbɔrd] *nm* skateboard; **faire du s.** to skateboard

sketch (*pl* **sketches**) [skɛtʃ] *nm* sketch

ski [ski] *nm* (a) *(matériel)* ski (b) *(activité)* skiing; **faire du s.** to ski; **s. alpin/de fond** downhill/cross-country skiing; **s. nautique** water skiing

skiable [skjabl] *adj voir* **domaine**

skier [66] [skje] *vi* to ski

skieur, -euse [skjœr, -øz] *nm,f* skier
skin [skin], **skinhead** [skinɛd] *nm* skinhead
skipper [skipœr] *nm* skipper
slalom [slalɔm] *nm* slalom; *Fig* **faire du s. (entre)** to dodge in and out (between); **s. géant** giant slalom; **s. spécial** special slalom
slalomer [slalɔme] *vi* to slalom; *Fig* to dodge in and out (**entre** between)
slalomeur, -euse [slalɔmœr, -øz] *nm,f* slalom skier
slave [slav] **1** *adj* Slav, Slavonic
 2 *nmf* **S.** Slav
 3 *nm (langue)* Slavonic
slip [slip] *nm (d'homme)* briefs, underpants; *(de femme)* pants, briefs; **s. de bain** *(d'homme)* swimming trunks; *(de femme)* bikini bottom
slogan [slɔgã] *nm* slogan
slovaque [slɔvak] **1** *adj* Slovak
 2 *nmf* **S.** Slovak
 3 *nm (langue)* Slovak
Slovaquie [slɔvaki] *nf* **la S.** Slovakia
slovène [slɔvɛn] **1** *adj* Slovene
 2 *nmf* **S.** Slovene
 3 *nm (langue)* Slovene
Slovénie [slɔveni] *nf* **la S.** Slovenia
slow [slo] *nm* slow dance
smala(h) [smala] *nf Fam (famille)* tribe
smash [smaʃ] *nm* smash; **faire un s.** to smash the ball
smasher [smaʃe] **1** *vt* to smash
 2 *vi* to smash the ball
SME [ɛsɛmə] *nm (abrév* **Système monétaire euro-péen)** EMS
SMIC [smik] *nm (abrév* **salaire minimum interprofessionnel de croissance)** guaranteed minimum wage
smicard, -e [smikar, -ard] *nm,f Fam* minimum wage earner
smoking [smɔkiŋ] *nm* dinner *or* evening suit
snack [snak], **snack-bar** *(pl* **snack-bars)** [snakbar] *nm* snack bar
SNCF [ɛsɛnseɛf] *nf (abrév* **Société nationale des chemins de fer français)** = French national railway company
sniffer [snife] *vt Fam (drogue)* to sniff
snob [snɔb] **1** *adj* snobbish
 2 *nmf* snob
snober [snɔbe] *vt* to snub
snobinard, -e [snɔbinar, -ard] *Fam Péj* **1** *adj* stuck-up
 2 *nm,f* stuck-up type
snobisme [snɔbism] *nm* snobbery, snobbishness
sobre [sɔbr] *adj* (**a**) *(personne) (qui n'a pas bu)* sober; *(qui boit ou mange peu)* abstemious (**b**) *(repas, vie)* simple (**c**) *(style, lignes, discours)* sober
sobrement [sɔbrəmã] *adv (s'exprimer, s'habiller)* soberly
sobriété [sɔbrijete] *nf* (**a**) *(tempérance)* temperance, sobriety (**b**) *(d'un repas, d'une vie)* simplicity (**c**) *(d'un style, de lignes, d'un discours)* sobriety; **s'exprimer avec s.** to speak soberly
sobriquet [sɔbrikɛ] *nm* nickname
soccer [sɔkœr] *nm Can* soccer, *Br* football
sociabilité [sɔsjabilite] *nf* sociability
sociable [sɔsjabl] *adj* sociable
social, -e, -aux, -ales [sɔsjal, -o] **1** *adj (ordre, politique, réforme)* social
 2 *nm* **le s.** social issues

social-démocrate, sociale-démocrate *(mpl* **sociaux-démocrates,** *fpl* **sociales-démocrates)** [sɔsjaldemɔkrat, sɔsjodemɔkrat] *adj & nmf* social democrat
social-démocratie *(pl* **social-démocraties)** [sɔsjaldemɔkrasi] *nf* social democracy
socialement [sɔsjalmã] *adv* socially
socialisation [sɔsjalizasjõ] *nf* socialization
socialiser [sɔsjalize] *vt* to socialize
socialisme [sɔsjalism] *nm* socialism
socialiste [sɔsjalist] *adj & nmf* socialist
sociétaire [sɔsjetɛr] *nmf* (**a**) *(membre)* member (**b**) *(actionnaire)* shareholder
société [sɔsjete] *nf* (**a**) *(communauté)* society; **en s.** in society; **s. de consommation** consumer society; **la haute s.** high society (**b**) *(association)* society, association; *(sportive)* club; *Hist* **la S. des Nations** the League of Nations; **la S. protectrice des animaux** *Br* ≃ the RSPCA, *Am* ≃ the ASPCA (**c**) *(compagnie)* company, firm; **s. par actions** *Br* joint-stock company, *Am* incorporated company; **s. anonyme** *Br* public limited company, *Am* corporation; **s. en participation** joint venture; **s. à responsabilité limitée** limited (liability) company (**d**) *(présence)* company
socioculturel, -elle [sɔsjɔkyltyrɛl] *adj* sociocultural
socio-économique *(pl* **socio-économiques)** [sɔsjɔekɔnɔmik] *adj* socioeconomic
sociolinguistique [sɔsjɔlɛ̃gɥistik] **1** *adj* sociolinguistic
 2 *nf* sociolinguistics *(singulier)*
sociologie [sɔsjɔlɔʒi] *nf* sociology
sociologique [sɔsjɔlɔʒik] *adj* sociological
sociologiquement [sɔsjɔlɔʒikmã] *adv* sociologically
sociologue [sɔsjɔlɔg] *nmf* sociologist
socioprofessionnel, -elle [sɔsjɔprɔfɛsjɔnɛl] *adj* socioprofessional
socle [sɔkl] *nm (de statue, de colonne)* plinth, pedestal; *(de vase, de pendule, d'appareil)* base; *Ordinat* **s. orientable** *ou* **pivotant** *(d'un moniteur)* swivel base
socquette [sɔkɛt] *nf* ankle sock
Socrate [sɔkrat] *npr* Socrates
soda [sɔda] *nm Br* fizzy drink, *Am* soda (pop)
sodium [sɔdjɔm] *nm* sodium
sodomie [sɔdɔmi] *nf* sodomy, buggery
sodomiser [sɔdɔmize] *vt* to sodomize, to bugger
sœur [sœr] *nf* (**a**) *(parente)* sister; *Fam* **et ta s.!** get lost!; **s. de lait** foster sister (**b**) *Rel* nun, sister
sœurette [sœrɛt] *nf Fam* little sister
sofa [sɔfa] *nm* sofa, settee
Sofia [sɔfja] *n* Sofia
SOFRES [sɔfrɛs] *nf (abrév* **Société française d'enquêtes par sondage)** = French opinion poll company
software [sɔftwɛr] *nm Ordinat* software
soi [swa] *pron personnel* (**a**) *(personne indéfinie)* oneself; *(homme)* himself; *(femme)* herself; **chez s.** at home; **il faut regarder devant s.** you must keep looking in front of you; **revenir à soi** to regain consciousness (**b**) *(chose, concept)* **en s.** in itself, per se
soi-disant [swadizã] **1** *adv* supposedly
 2 *adj inv* so-called
soie [swa] *nf* (**a**) *(étoffe)* silk; **s. grège/naturelle** raw/natural silk (**b**) *(de sanglier, de porc)* bristle
soierie [swari] *nf* (**a**) *(tissu)* silk (**b**) *(commerce)* silk trade

soif [swaf] *nf aussi Fig* thirst; **avoir s.** to be thirsty; **donner s. à qn** to make sb thirsty; **boire jusqu'à plus s.** to drink one's fill; *Fig* **s. de qch/de faire qch** thirst for sth/to do sth

soignant, -e [swaɲ, -ɑ̃t] *adj* **personnel s.** nursing staff; **équipe soignante** team of nursing staff

soigné, -e [swaɲe] *adj* (**a**) *(travail)* careful; *(style)* polished (**b**) *(personne, apparence)* neat, tidy; *(mains, ongles, jardin)* well-kept (**c**) *Fam (addition)* shockingly high

soigner [swaɲe] **1** *vt* (**a**) *(maladie)* to treat (**b**) *(malade) (sujet: médecin)* to treat; *(sujet: parent, infirmière)* to look after, to take care of; *Fam Fig* **il faut te faire s.!** you need your head examined! (**c**) *(apparence, invités, image)* to look after, to take care of; *(travail, présentation)* to take care over
2 se soigner *vpr* (**a**) *(personne) (médicalement)* to treat oneself; *(faire attention à soi)* to take care of oneself, to look after oneself (**b**) *(maladie)* **ça se soigne très bien** it's easily treated; *Fam Hum* **ça se soigne, tu sais!** they have a cure for that these days, you know!

soigneur [swaɲœr] *nm* trainer; *(en boxe)* second

soigneusement [swaɲøzmɑ̃] *adv* carefully

soigneux, -euse [swaɲø, -øz] *adj* (**a**) *(attentif)* careful (**de** with) (**b**) *(méticuleux)* tidy, neat

soi-même [swamɛm] *pron personnel* oneself; *Prov* **on n'est jamais si bien servi que par s.** if you want something done, do it yourself

soin [swɛ̃] *nm* (**a**) *(attention)* care; **avec s.** carefully, with care; **sans s.** *(travail, exécution)* careless; *(travailler, exécuter)* carelessly; **aux bons soins de** *(sur une lettre)* care of..., c/o...; **avoir** *ou* **prendre s. de qn/qch** to look after *or* take care of sb/sth; **prendre s. de faire qch** to take care to do sth; **confier à qn le s. de faire qch** to entrust sb with the task of doing sth; **laisser à qn le s. de faire qch** to leave it to sb to do sth; **les soins du ménage** housekeeping (**b**) *(traitement)* **soins** care, attention; **soins de beauté** beauty care; **être aux petits soins pour** *ou* **avec qn** to wait on sb hand and foot (**c**) *(traitement médical)* **premiers soins, soins d'urgence** first aid; **soins à domicile** home care *or* nursing; **soins intensifs** intensive care; **soins médicaux** medical care; **soins palliatifs** palliative care

soir [swar] *nm* evening; **ce s.** this evening, tonight; **à ce s.!** see you tonight!; **à dix heures du s.** at ten o'clock in the evening *or* at night; **le jeudi 2 au s.** on the evening of Thursday 2nd; **tous les lundis s.** every Monday evening; **faire qch le s.** to do sth in the evening; **être du s.** to be a night owl

soirée [sware] *nf* (**a**) *(soir)* evening; **dans la s.** in (the course of) the evening; **en fin de s.** towards the end of the evening (**b**) *(fête)* party; **s. dansante** dance (**c**) *Théât & Cin* evening performance; **le film passe en s.** there is an evening performance of the film

sois, soit¹ *etc voir* **être**

soit² 1 *adv* [swat] all right
2 *conj* [swa] (**a**) *(supposons)* **s. un point P** given a point P (**b**) *(c'est-à-dire)* that is to say (**c**) **s... s...** either... or...; **s. l'un, s. l'autre** (either) one or the other

soixantaine [swasɑ̃tɛn] *nf* (**a**) *(environ soixante)* **une s. (de)** about sixty, sixty or so (**b**) *(âge)* **avoir la s.** to be around sixty; **approcher de la s.** to be getting on for sixty

soixante [swasɑ̃t] *adj & nm inv* sixty; **s. et onze** seventy-one; *voir aussi* **trois**

soixante-dix [swasɑ̃tdis] *adj inv & nm* seventy; *voir aussi* **trois**

soixante-dixième [swasɑ̃tdizjɛm] *nmf, nm & adj* seventieth; *voir aussi* **cinquième**

soixante-huitard, -e (*mpl* **soixante-huitards**, *fpl* **soixante-huitardes**) [swasɑ̃tɥitar, -ard] *nm,f* = person involved in the events of May 1968

soixantième [swasɑ̃tjɛm] *nmf, nm & adj* sixtieth; *voir aussi* **cinquième**

soja [sɔʒa] *nm* soya

sol¹ [sɔl] *nm* (**a**) *(surface) (dehors)* ground; *(à l'intérieur)* floor; **au s.** at ground level (**b**) *(territoire)* soil (**c**) *(matière)* soil

sol² *nm inv* *(note)* G; *(chantée)* sol

sol-air [sɔlɛr] *adj inv* *(missile)* ground-to-air

solaire [sɔlɛr] *adj* *(système, chauffage, four)* solar; *(lotion, crème)* sun

solarium [sɔlarjɔm] *nm* (**a**) *(établissement)* solarium (**b**) *(terrasse)* sun terrace

soldat [sɔlda] *nm* (**a**) *(personne)* soldier; **s. de deuxième classe** private; **s. de première classe** *Br* lance-corporal, *Am* private first class; **s. Dubois!** private Dubois!; **le S. inconnu** the Unknown Soldier (**b**) *(jouet)* (toy) soldier; **s. de plomb** tin soldier

solde¹ [sɔld] *nf* *(rémunération)* pay; *Péj* **à la s. de qn** in sb's pay

solde² 1 *nm* (**a**) *(de compte)* balance; **pour s. (de tout compte)** in (full *or* final) settlement (**b**) *(rabais)* **acheter qch en s.** to buy sth in the sale; **vendre qch en s.** to sell sth off; **c'était en s.** it was in the sale; **des soldes** *(articles)* sale goods; **faire les soldes** *(acheteur)* to go round the sales; **faire des soldes** *(magasin)* to have a sale

solder [sɔlde] **1** *vt* (**a**) *(compte)* to close (**b**) *(article)* to sell off, to clear
2 se solder *vpr* **se s. par qch** *Fin* to show sth; *Fig (résultat, échec)* to end in sth

soldeur, -euse [sɔldœr, -øz] *nm,f* discount trader

sole [sɔl] *nf* *(poisson)* sole

soleil [sɔlɛj] *nm* (**a**) *(astre)* sun; **s. de minuit** midnight sun (**b**) *(lumière, chaleur)* sun, sunshine; **il y a** *ou* **il fait du s.** the sun's shining, it's sunny; *Fig* **se faire une place au s.** to find a place in the sun; *Fig* **avoir des biens au s.** to own property

solennel, -elle [sɔlanɛl] *adj* (**a**) *(occasion, cérémonie)* formal; *(serment, déclaration)* solemn (**b**) *Péj* pompous

solennellement [sɔlanɛlmɑ̃] *adv* *(officiellement)* formally; *(gravement)* solemnly

solennité [sɔlanite] *nf* (**a**) *(d'une occasion, d'une cérémonie)* formality; *(d'un serment, d'une déclaration)* solemnity (**b**) *Péj* pomposity

Solex® [sɔlɛks] *nm* moped

solfège [sɔlfɛʒ] *nm* (**a**) *(théorie)* rudiments of music (**b**) *(recueil)* music primer

solfier [66] [sɔlfje] *vt* to sol-fa

solidaire [sɔlidɛr] *adj* (**a**) *(personne)* **être s. de qn** to stand by sb, to support sb; **se sentir s. de qn** to feel a sense of solidarity with sb (**b**) *(pièces)* interdependent; **roue s. d'une autre** wheel integral with another

solidairement [sɔlidɛrmɑ̃] *adv* jointly

solidariser [sɔlidarize] **se solidariser** *vpr* to show solidarity (**avec** with)

solidarité [sɔlidarite] *nf (entre personnes)* solidarity; **par s. avec qn** out of fellow-feeling for sb, in order to show solidarity with sb

solide [sɔlid] **1** *adj* (**a**) *(résistant) (mur, meuble)* solid; *(tissu)* strong; *(personne)* sturdy; **s. sur ses jambes** steady on one's feet; **être s. comme un chêne** *ou* **un roc** to be hale and hearty (**b**) *(amitié, relation, liens)* strong (**c**) *(éducation, argumentation)* sound; *Fig* **ça ne repose sur rien de s.** there's no sound basis for that (**d**) *(repas)* solid; *(appétit)* healthy (**e**) *(position, affaire)* sound, strong (**f**) *(non liquide)* solid
  2 *nm* (**a**) *(corps)* solid (**b**) *Fam* **c'est du s.!** *(meuble)* that's pretty solid!; *(vêtement)* it's indestructible!

solidement [sɔlidmɑ̃] *adv (construit)* solidly; *(attaché, implanté)* firmly

solidifier [66] [sɔlidifje] **1** *vt* to solidify
  2 se solidifier *vpr* to solidify

solidité [sɔlidite] *nf* (**a**) *(d'un objet)* solidity; *(d'un matériau)* strength; **être d'une s. à toute épreuve** to be able to stand up to anything (**b**) *(d'un jugement)* soundness (**c**) *(d'une amitié)* strength

soliloque [sɔlilɔk] *nm* soliloquy

soliste [sɔlist] *nmf* soloist

solitaire [sɔlitɛr] **1** *adj* (**a**) *(personne) (par choix)* solitary; *(involontairement)* lonely; **passer des vacances solitaires** to spend one's holidays on one's own (**b**) *(arbre, maison)* solitary, lone
  2 *nmf (personne)* loner; **en s.** *(vivre, travailler)* on one's own, alone; *(naviguer)* single-handed; *(course)* solo; *(navigation)* single-handed
  3 *nm* (**a**) *(jeu)* solitaire (**b**) *(diamant)* solitaire

solitairement [sɔlitɛrmɑ̃] *adv* on one's own, alone

solitude [sɔlityd] *nf (retraite)* solitude; *(involontaire)* loneliness; **aimer la s.** to like being alone (**b**) *(d'un lieu)* loneliness

solive [sɔliv] *nf Constr* joist

sollicitation [sɔlisitasjɔ̃] *nf* request

solliciter [sɔlisite] *vt* (**a**) *(entretien, audience)* to request; *(emploi)* to apply for (**b**) *(personne)* **s. qn (pour faire qch)** to appeal to sb (to do sth); **être sollicité de toutes parts** to be very much in demand (**c**) *(attention, regards)* to attract; *(curiosité)* to arouse

sollicitude [sɔlisityd] *nf* solicitude, concern (**pour** for)

solo [sɔlo] **1** *adj inv* solo
  2 *nm* solo; **jouer en s.** to play solo

sol-sol [sɔlsɔl] *adj inv (missile)* ground-to-ground

solstice [sɔlstis] *nm* solstice; **s. d'été/d'hiver** summer/winter solstice

soluble [sɔlybl] *adj* (**a**) *(produit)* soluble; *(café)* instant (**b**) *(problème)* solvable

solution [sɔlysjɔ̃] *nf* (**a**) *(de problème, de situation, d'équation)* solution, answer (**de** to); **s. de facilité** easy way out (**b**) *(liquide)* solution

solutionner [sɔlysjɔne] *vt Fam* to solve

solvabilité [sɔlvabilite] *nf* solvency

solvable [sɔlvabl] *adj* solvent

solvant [sɔlvɑ̃] *nm* solvent

somali, -e [sɔmali] **1** *adj* Somali
  2 *nm,f* **S.** Somali
  3 *nm (langue)* Somali

Somalie [sɔmali] *nf* **la S.** Somalia

somalien, -enne [sɔmaljɛ̃, -ɛn] **1** *adj* Somalian
  2 *nm,f* **S.** Somalian

somatique [sɔmatik] *adj* somatic

somatiser [sɔmatize] *vt* to react psychosomatically to

sombre [sɔ̃br] *adj* (**a**) *(couleur)* dark (**b**) *(forêt, pièce)* dark; *(ciel)* dull; **il fait s.** *(temps)* it's dull; *(dans une pièce)* it's dark (**c**) *(visage, pensées, caractère)* gloomy, sombre (**d**) *(sinistre)* **une s. histoire de...** a sordid tale of... (**e**) *Fam* **un s. imbécile** a total fool

sombrement [sɔ̃brəmɑ̃] *adv (tristement)* gloomily, sombrely

sombrer [sɔ̃bre] *vi* (**a**) *(navire)* to sink; *(empire)* to founder; *(affaire)* to fail (**b**) *(personne)* **s. dans la déprime/la misère** to sink into depression/destitution

sombrero [sɔ̃brero] *nm* sombrero

sommaire [sɔmɛr] **1** *adj* (**a**) *(récit)* brief (**b**) *(rudimentaire) (examen)* hasty; *(connaissances, repas, étude)* basic; *(jugement, exécution)* summary; **faire une toilette s.** to have a quick wash
  2 *nm (table des matières)* contents; **et au s. de l'émission de ce soir...** coming up in tonight's programme...

sommairement [sɔmɛrmɑ̃] *adv* (**a**) *(expliquer, raconter)* briefly (**b**) *(de façon rudimentaire) (meublé)* basically; *(juger)* summarily

sommation [sɔmasjɔ̃] *nf* (**a**) *Jur (injonction)* demand (**b**) *Mil* warning

somme¹ [sɔm] *nf voir* **bête**

somme² *nf* (**a**) *(d'une addition)* sum, total; **faire la s. de** to add up (**b**) *(quantité) (d'objets)* number; *(de travail, d'efforts)* amount (**c**) *(argent)* **s. (d'argent)** sum (of money); **pour la s. de 500 euros** for 500 euros; **dépenser des sommes folles** to spend vast sums of money; **c'est une s.!** that's a lot of money! (**d**) *(locutions)* **en s.** *(tout compte fait)* on the whole; *(en bref)* in short; **s. toute** when all's said and done

somme³ *nm* nap, snooze; **faire un (petit) s.** to have *or* take a nap *or* a snooze

sommeil [sɔmɛj] *nm* (**a**) *(repos)* sleep; **avoir s.** to be *or* feel sleepy; **dormir d'un s. de plomb** to sleep like a log; **avoir le s. léger/profond** to be a light/heavy sleeper; **chercher le s.** to try to sleep; **tomber de s.** to be dead on one's feet; **je manque de s.** I haven't been getting enough sleep; **j'en perds le s.** I'm losing sleep over it; *Fig* **le s. éternel** eternal rest; **s. paradoxal** REM sleep (**b**) **en s.** *(projet)* (lying) dormant; *Fig* **laisser qch en s.** to put sth on hold

sommeiller [sɔmeje] *vi* (**a**) *(personne)* to doze (**b**) *Fig* to lie dormant

sommelier [sɔməlje] *nm* wine waiter; *Suisse* waiter

sommer [sɔme] *vt* **s. qn de faire qch** to charge sb to do sth

sommes *voir* **être**

sommet [sɔmɛ] *nm* (**a**) *(de montagne)* top, summit; *(d'arbre, de toit)* top; *(de vague)* crest; *(de la tête)* crown (**b**) *Fig (de hiérarchie)* top; *(du pouvoir, de la gloire)* height (**c**) *(rencontre politique)* summit; **conférence/rencontre au s.** summit conference/meeting (**d**) *(d'angle)* vertex

sommier [sɔmje] *nm* base; **s. à ressorts/lattes** sprung/slatted base

sommité [sɔmite] *nf* leading figure *or* light

somnambule [sɔmnɑ̃byl] **1** *adj* **être s.** to be a sleepwalker, to walk in one's sleep
  2 *nmf* sleepwalker

somnambulisme [sɔmnɑ̃bylism] *nm* sleepwalking

somnifère [sɔmnifɛr] *nm (substance)* sedative; *(cachet)* sleeping pill

somnolence [sɔmnɔlɑ̃s] *nf* sleepiness, drowsiness; **peut provoquer un état de s.** *(sur notice)* may cause drowsiness

somnolent, -e [sɔmnɔlɑ̃, -ɑ̃t] *adj* sleepy, drowsy

somnoler [sɔmnɔle] *vi* to doze

somptuaire [sɔ̃ptɥɛr] *adj* extravagant

somptueusement [sɔ̃ptɥøzmɑ̃] *adv* sumptuously

somptueux, -euse [sɔ̃ptɥø, -øz] *adj* sumptuous

somptuosité [sɔ̃ptɥozite] *nf* sumptuousness

son¹, sa, ses [sɔ̃, sa, se]

> sa becomes **son** before a word beginning with a vowel or mute h.

adj possessif (possesseur masculin) his; *(possesseur féminin)* her; *(d'animal, de chose, de pays)* its; *(possesseur indéfini)* one's; **un de ses amis** one of his/her friends, a friend of his/hers; **chacun a pris s. sac** everyone took their bag; **perdre s. temps** to waste one's time; *Fam* **elle a eu s. vendredi** she got Friday off

son² *nm (de voix, d'instrument)* & *Cin* sound; *Fig* **n'entendre qu'un s. de cloche** to hear only one side of the story; **(spectacle) s. et lumière** son et lumière; **s. 3D** surround sound

son³ *nm (de grains)* bran

sonal, -als [sɔnal] *nm Offic* jingle

sonar [sɔnar] *nm* sonar

sonate [sɔnat] *nf* sonata; **s. pour violon** violin sonata

sondage [sɔ̃daʒ] *nm* (**a**) *(de population)* poll, survey; **faire un s.** to carry out a poll *or* a survey; **s. d'opinion** opinion poll; **s. par téléphone** telephone poll *or* survey (**b**) *(de terrain)* boring, drilling

sonde [sɔ̃d] *nf* (**a**) *(de bateau)* sounding line (**b**) *(de pompe, de puits)* sounding rod (**c**) *Météo* & *Av* **s. aérienne** sounding balloon; **s. spatiale** space probe (**d**) *Méd (pour examiner)* probe; *(pour intervenir)* tube (**e**) *(de terrain)* borer, drill

sondé, -e [sɔ̃de] *nm,f* respondent

sonder [sɔ̃de] *vt* (**a**) *(fond)* to sound; *Fig (mystère)* to fathom (**b**) *Météo (atmosphère)* to probe (**c**) *(terrain)* to bore, to drill; *Fig* **s. le terrain** to see how the land lies (**d**) *(personne, opinion, intentions)* to sound out (**e**) *Méd (blessure)* to probe; *(patient)* to sound

sondeur, -euse [sɔ̃dœr, -øz] **1** *nm (appareil)* sounder **2** *nm,f (d'opinions)* pollster

songe [sɔ̃ʒ] *nm Litt* dream; **en s.** in a dream; **faire un s.** to have a dream

songer [45] [sɔ̃ʒe] **1 songer à** *vt ind* (**a**) *(penser à, se souvenir de)* to think about (**b**) *(envisager)* to consider; **il ne faut pas y s.** that's quite out of the question; **s. à faire qch** to think of doing sth **2** *vt* **s. que** to think that

songerie [sɔ̃ʒri] *nf Litt* reverie

songeur, -euse [sɔ̃ʒœr, -øz] *adj* (**a**) *(rêveur)* dreamy (**b**) *(pensif)* pensive, thoughtful

sonnant, -e [sɔnɑ̃, -ɑ̃t] *adj* **arriver à dix heures sonnantes** to arrive on the stroke of ten *or* at ten o'clock sharp

sonné, -e [sɔne] *adj* (**a**) *(accompli)* **avoir quarante ans bien sonnés** to be well over forty (**b**) *Fam (étourdi)* groggy (**c**) *Fam (fou)* mad

sonner [sɔne] **1** *vi* (**a**) *(horloge)* to strike; *(cloches, téléphone)* to ring; *(réveil)* to go off; **faire s. son réveil (à six heures)** to set one's alarm (for six o'clock); **s. creux** *(mur)* to sound hollow; *Fig* to ring hollow; *Fig* **s. faux** not to ring true; *Fig* **s. bien/mal** to sound good/bad

(**b**) *(heure)* **six heures sonnèrent** the clock struck six; *Fig* **son heure** *ou* **sa dernière heure a sonné** his/her last hour has come

(**c**) *(à la porte)* **on a sonné** that was the bell, there's someone at the door; **s. chez qn** to ring sb's bell; **s. avant d'entrer** *(sur panneau)* ring before entering

(**d**) *(jouer)* **s. du clairon/de la trompette** to sound the bugle/the trumpet

2 *vt Fam* (**a**) *(cloche)* to ring; *Fam* **s. les cloches à qn** to tell sb off; **se faire s. les cloches** to get a good telling-off

(**b**) *(heure)* to strike; *(messe, repas)* to ring the bell for

(**c**) *(domestique, infirmière)* to ring for; *Fam* **on ne t'a pas sonné!** nobody asked you!

(**d**) *Fam (assommer)* to knock out

(**e**) *Belg (appeler)* to telephone, to call

sonnerie [sɔnri] *nf* (**a**) *(son) (de cloches, du téléphone)* ringing; *(de clairon, de trompette)* call (**b**) *(sonnette)* bell

sonnet [sɔnɛ] *nm* sonnet

sonnette [sɔnɛt] *nf* bell; **s. d'alarme** alarm bell; *aussi Fig* **tirer la s. d'alarme** to sound the alarm

sono [sɔno] *nf Fam* PA system

sonore [sɔnɔr] **1** *adj* (**a**) *(effet)* sound; *(pollution)* noise (**b**) *(voix)* ringing; *(rire)* resounding; *(salle)* echoing (**c**) *Ling (consonne)* voiced **2** *nf Ling* voiced consonant

sonorisation [sɔnɔrizasjɔ̃] *nf* (**a**) *(de film)* addition of the soundtrack (**de** to) (**b**) *(de salle)* fitting of a PA system (**de** to) (**c**) *(équipement)* PA system, public address system

sonoriser [sɔnɔrize] *vt* (**a**) *(film)* to add the soundtrack to (**b**) *(salle)* to fit with a PA system

sonorité [sɔnɔrite] *nf* tone

sont *voir* être

Sopalin® [sɔpalɛ̃] *nm* kitchen paper

sophisme [sɔfism] *nm* sophism

sophistication [sɔfistikasjɔ̃] *nf* sophistication

sophistiqué, -e [sɔfistike] *adj* sophisticated

soporifique [sɔpɔrifik] *adj aussi Fig* soporific

soprano [sɔprano] **1** *adj (saxophone)* soprano **2** *nmf (personne)* soprano **3** *nm* soprano (voice)

sorbet [sɔrbɛ] *nm* sorbet

sorbetière [sɔrbətjɛr] *nf* ice-cream maker

sorbier [sɔrbje] *nm* sorb (tree), service (tree)

sorcellerie [sɔrsɛlri] *nf* witchcraft, sorcery

sorcier [sɔrsje] **1** *adj Fam* **ce n'est pas s.** it's simple enough **2** *nm* sorcerer, wizard

sorcière [sɔrsjɛr] *nf* sorceress, witch; *Fam Péj* **vieille s.** old witch

sordide [sɔrdid] *adj* (**a**) *(pièce, quartier)* squalid (**b**) *(crime, détails, avarice)* sordid

sorgho [sɔrgo] *nm* sorghum

Sorlingues [sɔrlɛ̃g] *nfpl* **les S.** the Scilly Isles

sornettes [sɔrnɛt] *nfpl* twaddle, rubbish

sors, sort¹ *etc voir* **sortir**

sort² [sɔr] *nm* (**a**) *(condition)* lot; *Fam* **faire un s. à qch** *(bouteille, plat)* to polish sth off (**b**) *(destin)* fate (**c**) *(hasard)* chance; **tirer au s.** to draw lots; **le s. en est jeté** the die is cast (**d**) *(magique)* spell; **jeter un s. à qn** to cast a spell on sb; **conjurer le mauvais s.** to ward off bad luck

sortable [sɔrtabl] *adj Fam* **tu n'es pas s.!** I can't take you anywhere!

sortant, -e [sɔrtɑ̃, -ɑ̃t] *adj (numéro de loterie)* winning; *(élu)* outgoing

sorte [sɔrt] *nf* (**a**) *(genre)* sort, kind; **toutes sortes de choses/gens, des choses/gens de toutes sortes** all sorts *or* kinds of things/people; **un homme de la s.** a man of that kind; **une s. de...** a sort *or* kind of...; **je n'ai rien dit/fait de la s.** I said/did no such thing, I said/did nothing of the sort (**b**) *(manière)* **de la s.** in that way; **en quelque s.** as it were, in a way; **de s. que je puisse...** so that I can...; **de s. qu'il est arrivé en retard** with the result that he arrived late; **de s. à faire qch** so as to do sth; **faire en s. que** + *subjunctive* to see to it that; **fais en s. d'être à l'heure** see to it that you're on time

sortie [sɔrti] *nf* (**a**) *(fait de sortir d'un lieu)* **c'était ma première s. depuis...** it was my first time out since...; **à sa s. de l'hôpital/de prison** when he/she came out of hospital/prison; **à la s. de l'école/du travail** after school/work; **à la s. des bureaux** when the offices come out (**b**) *(issue)* exit, way out; **à la s. de la gare** at the station exit; **s. d'autoroute** motorway exit; **s. de secours** emergency exit (**c**) *(d'un livre, d'un journal)* publication; *(d'un film, d'un disque)* release; *(d'un modèle)* launch; **à sa s. dans les salles parisiennes** when released in Parisian cinemas (**d**) *(de liquide, d'air)* outflow (**e**) *(dispositif)* outlet (**f**) *(de marchandises)* export (**g**) *(dépense)* **sorties** outgoings (**h**) *(excursion)* trip, outing; **priver qn de s.** to stop sb from going out; **s. en mer** short sea trip; **jour de s.** day out; **ce soir je suis de s.** I'm going out tonight; **désolé, mais elle est de s.** sorry, but she's out (**i**) *Mil* sortie (**j**) *Fam (emportement)* outburst (**k**) *Ordinat* exit; *(information)* output; **s. d'imprimante** printer output; **dispositif de s.** output device; **signal de s.** output signal; **s. écran** screen output; **s. imprimante** printout; **s. imprimée** printed output; **s. parallèle** parallel output; **s. série** serial output

sortie-de-bain *(pl* **sorties-de-bain)** [sɔrtidbɛ̃] *nf* bathrobe

sortilège [sɔrtilɛʒ] *nm* spell

sortir¹ [64a] [sɔrtir] **1** *vt (aux* **avoir)** (**a**) *(enfant, chien)* to take out; *(voiture)* to get out; **s. qn de** *(situation)* to get sb out of (**b**) *(objet)* to take out (**de** of); **et si tu sortais ton bon whisky?** how about getting out your good whisky? (**c**) *(mettre sur le marché) (livre, journal)* to bring out, to publish; *(film, disque)* to bring out, to release (**d**) *Fam (dire)* to come out with (**e**) *Fam (expulser)* to throw out; *(vaincre)* to knock out

2 *vi (aux* **être)** (**a**) *(aller)* to go out (**de** of); *(venir)* to come out (**de** of); *(partir)* to leave; *(s'extraire, finir de travailler)* to get out (**de** of); **s. en courant/en boitant** to run/limp out; **est-ce que je peux s.?** *(en classe)* may I be excused?; **sortez (d'ici)!** get out (of here)!; **s. de table** to leave the table; **je sors d'une mauvaise grippe** I'm just getting over a bad dose of flu; **il est sorti discrédité de ce scandale** he came out of this scandal with his reputation in ruins; **cela ne doit**

pas s. d'ici *(secret)* it mustn't go any further; *Fam* **d'où sors-tu?** *(d'où viens-tu?)* where did you spring from?; *(tu n'es pas au courant)* what planet have you been on?; **cela m'est sorti de la tête** it's gone right out of my head; **il ne sortira pas grand-chose de tout cela** nothing much will come of all this (**b**) *(pour s'amuser)* to go out; **s. avec qn** to go out with sb; *Fig* **il faut s. un peu!** *(pour être au courant)* what planet have you been on? (**c**) *(livre, journal)* to come out, to be published; *(film, disque)* to come out, to be released (**d**) *(être issu)* **s. de** *(famille, milieu)* to come from; **elle sort d'Harvard** she was at Harvard (**e**) *(numéro de loto, sujet d'examen)* to come up (**f**) *(apparaître) (fleur)* to come out; *(dent)* to come through; **les yeux lui sortaient de la tête** his eyes were popping out of his head (**g**) *Ordinat (d'un système)* to exit

3 se sortir *vpr* **se s. de** *(situation)* to get out of; **s'en s.** *(d'un travail)* to manage; *(d'une difficulté)* to get through it; *(malade)* to pull through

sortir² *nm* **au s. du cinéma** on coming out of the cinema; **au s. de l'école** after school; **au s. de l'hiver** at the end of winter

SOS [ɛsoɛs] *nm* SOS; **lancer un S. (à)** to send (out) an SOS (to); **S. Amitié** = helpline for people in need of emotional support; **S. femmes battues** = helpline for female victims of domestic violence; **S. médecins** = emergency medical service; **S.-Racisme** = anti-racist movement

sosie [sɔzi] *nm* lookalike, double; **c'est un s. de Brando** he's a Brando lookalike; **c'est le s. de mon frère** he's my brother's double

sot, sotte [so, sɔt] **1** *adj* stupid, foolish; **il n'y a pas de sot métier** there's no such thing as a worthless profession

2 *nm,f* fool

sottement [sɔtmɑ̃] *adv* stupidly, foolishly

sottise [sɔtiz] *nf* (**a**) *(stupidité)* stupidity, foolishness (**b**) *(action)* stupid act; **faire des sottises** to do stupid things; **faire une s.** to do something stupid (**c**) *(parole)* stupid remark; **dire des sottises** to say stupid things; **dire une s.** to say something stupid

sottisier [sɔtizje] *nm* collection of howlers

sou [su] *nm* (**a**) *(argent)* **être sans le s.** to be penniless; **il est toujours en train de compter ses sous** he's always counting every penny; **avoir des sous** to have money; **c'est une affaire de gros sous** there's big money involved; **être près de ses sous** to be a penny-pincher; *Fig* **n'avoir pas (pour) un s. de courage/bon sens** not to have an ounce of courage/common sense (**b**) *(pièce)* **un s. est un s.** every penny counts (**c**) *(ancienne monnaie)* sou (**d**) *Can (cent)* cent

soubassement [subasmɑ̃] *nm* (**a**) *(de construction)* base (**b**) *Can (sous-sol)* basement

soubresaut [subrəso] *nm (de véhicule)* jolt; *(de personne)* jerk

soubrette [subrɛt] *nf Théât* maid

souche [suʃ] *nf* (**a**) *(d'arbre)* stump; *Fam* **rester (planté) comme une s.** to be rooted to the spot; **dormir comme une s.** to sleep like a log (**b**) *(de famille)* founder; **faire s.** to found a line (**c**) *(de virus)* strain (**d**) *(de chèques, de tickets)* counterfoil, stub (**e**) *(de langue)* root

souci¹ [susi] *nm* (**a**) *(inquiétude)* worry, anxiety; **avoir des soucis** to have worries; **se faire du s. (pour)** to worry (about); **donner du s. à qn** to worry sb; **c'est le dernier** *ou* **le cadet de mes soucis** that's the least of my worries (**b**) *(soin)* concern (**de** for); **avoir le s. de plaire** to be anxious to please

souci² *nm (fleur)* marigold

soucier [66] [susje] **se soucier** *vpr* **se s. de** to worry about; **ne se s. de rien** not to worry about anything; *Fam* **se s. de qch comme de l'an quarante** *ou* **de sa première chemise** not to give a damn about sth

soucieux, -euse [susjø, -øz] *adj* (**a**) *(attentif)* anxious, concerned (**de** about); **être s. de faire qch** to be anxious to do sth; **peu s. de qch** unconcerned about sth (**b**) *(inquiet)* worried

soucoupe [sukup] *nf* saucer; **s. volante** flying saucer

soudain, -e [sudɛ̃, -ɛn] **1** *adv* suddenly, all of a sudden
2 *adj* sudden

soudainement [sudɛnmɑ̃] *adv* suddenly

soudaineté [sudɛnte] *nf* suddenness

Soudan [sudɑ̃] *nm* **le S.** the Sudan

soudanais, -e [sudanɛ, -ɛz] **1** *adj* Sudanese
2 *nm,f* **S.** Sudanese; **les S.** the Sudanese

soudard [sudar] *nm Fam* brutish soldier

soude [sud] *nf* soda; **s. caustique** caustic soda

souder [sude] **1** *vt* (**a**) *(par alliage)* to solder; *(par soudure autogène)* to weld (**b**) *(os fracturé)* to knit (**c**) *Fig (groupes, personnes)* to unite
2 se souder *vpr* (**a**) *(os)* to knit (together) (**b**) *Fig (groupe)* to unite

soudeur, -euse [sudœr, -øz] *nm,f (avec soudure par alliage)* solderer; *(avec soudure autogène)* welder

soudoyer [32] [sudwaje] *vt* to bribe

soudure [sudyr] *nf* (**a**) *(opération) (par alliage)* soldering; *(autogène)* welding (**b**) *(résultat) (par alliage)* soldered joint; *(autogène)* weld (**c**) *(d'os)* knitting (**d**) *Fig* **faire la s.** to make ends meet

soufflage [suflaʒ] *nm (du verre)* blowing

souffle [sufl] *nm* (**a**) *(d'air, de vent)* breath, puff (**b**) *(respiration)* breathing; **avoir du s.** to have stamina; **retenir son s.** to hold one's breath; **manquer de s.** to be short-winded; **avoir le s. court** to be short of breath; **à bout de s.** out of breath; **jusqu'à mon dernier s.** as long as I live and breathe, to my dying day; *Fig* **couper le s. à qn** to take sb's breath away (**c**) *(d'une explosion)* blast (**d**) *(d'hélices)* slipstream, wash (**e**) *Méd* murmur; **s. au cœur** heart murmur (**f**) *(force créatrice)* inspiration (**g**) *(impulsion)* **donner un nouveau s. à qch** to give sth a new lease of life

soufflé, -e [sufle] **1** *adj* (**a**) *Culin* soufflé (**b**) *Fam (ahuri)* flabbergasted, staggered
2 *nm* soufflé; **s. au fromage/au chocolat** cheese/chocolate soufflé

souffler [sufle] **1** *vt* (**a**) *(fumée, poussière)* to blow; *(bougie)* to blow out (**b**) *(dire)* to whisper (**à** to); **s. une réplique à un acteur** to prompt an actor; **quelqu'un a dû lui s. l'idée** someone must have given him the idea; **ne pas s. mot (de qch)** not to breathe a word (about sth); **on ne souffle pas!** no prompting! (**c**) *Fam (prendre)* to pinch (**à** from); **se faire s. qch** to have sth pinched (**d**) *(détruire)* to blast (**e**) *Fam (ahurir)* to stagger (**f**) *(verre)* to blow (**g**) *(aux dames)* to huff; **s. n'est pas jouer** huffing doesn't count as a go
2 *vi* (**a**) *(expirer)* to blow; **s. dans ses doigts** to blow on one's fingers; **s. dans une trompette** to blow a trumpet; **inspirez! soufflez!** breathe in! breathe out! (**b**) *(se reposer)* **laisser s. qn** to give sb time to catch his/her breath (**c**) *(haleter)* to pant, to puff; *Fam* **s.**

comme un bœuf to puff and pant (**d**) *(vent)* to blow; **le vent soufflait en rafales** there were gusts of wind; *Fig* **un vent de révolte soufflait sur le pays** there was a spirit of revolt in the country

soufflerie [sufləri] *nf* (**a**) *(d'orgue, de forge)* bellows (**b**) *(de climatiseur)* blower

soufflet [suflɛ] *nm* (**a**) *(de forge)* bellows (**b**) *Rail (couloir)* concertina vestibule (**c**) *(en couture)* gusset (**d**) *(d'orgue)* swell (**e**) *Litt (gifle)* slap (in the face)

souffleter [42] [suflǝte] *vt Litt* **s. qn** to slap sb's face

souffleur, -euse [suflœr, -øz] **1** *nm* **s. de verre** glass blower
2 *nm,f (au théâtre)* prompter
3 *nf* **souffleuse** *Can* snowblower

souffrance [sufrɑ̃s] *nf* (**a**) *(douleur)* suffering (**b**) **en s.** *(travail)* pending

souffrant, -e [sufrɑ̃, -ɑ̃t] *adj (indisposé)* unwell, poorly

souffre-douleur [sufrǝdulœr] *nm inv* object of abuse

souffreteux, -euse [sufrǝtø, -øz] *adj* sickly

souffrir [52] [sufrir] **1** *vi* to suffer (**de** from); **faire s. qn** *(physiquement)* to hurt sb; *(moralement)* to make sb suffer; **je souffre de la voir malade** it upsets me to see her ill
2 *vt* (**a**) *(physiquement)* **s. le martyre** to go through agony; **faire s. le martyre à qn** to put sb through agony (**b**) *(supporter)* **je ne peux pas la s.** I can't stand her; **je ne peux pas s. qu'on vienne me déranger** I can't stand being disturbed; **il ne souffre pas la contradiction** he can't stand being contradicted; *Litt* **souffrez que je fasse une critique** permit me to make a criticism (**c**) *Litt (admettre)* **situation qui ne souffre aucun retard** situation that admits of no delay
3 se souffrir *vpr* **ils ne peuvent pas se s.** they can't stand each other

soufre [sufr] *nm* sulphur

souhait [swɛ] *nm* wish; **faire un s.** to make a wish; **à s.** *(à merveille)* perfectly; **doré/ensoleillé à s.** beautifully golden/sunny; **à vos souhaits!** bless you!

souhaitable [swɛtabl] *adj* desirable; **il serait s. que tu lui parles** it is desirable that you should talk to him

souhaiter [swete] *vt* to wish for; **s. qch à qn** to wish sb sth; **s. faire qch** to hope to do sth; **s. à qn de faire qch** to hope that sb does sth; **s. que** + *subjunctive* to hope that; **je vous souhaite une bonne année/un joyeux anniversaire** best wishes for a happy New Year/a happy birthday; *Ironique* **je te souhaite bien du plaisir!** have fun!

souiller [suje] *vt Litt* (**a**) *(vêtements)* to soil, to dirty (**de** with) (**b**) *(réputation, mémoire)* to tarnish

souillon [sujɔ̃] *nf Litt* slut, sloven

souillure [sujyr] *nf Litt* (**a**) *(sur un vêtement)* stain (**b**) *Fig (morale)* blot, blemish

souk [suk] *nm* (**a**) *(marché)* souk (**b**) *Fam (lieu en désordre)* shambles *(singulier)*

soul [sul] *adj inv & nf* soul

soûl, -e [su, sul] **1** *adj* drunk
2 *nm* **tout son s.** to one's heart's content

soulagement [sulaʒmɑ̃] *nm* relief (**pour** to)

soulager [45] [sulaʒe] **1** *vt (douleur)* to ease, to relieve; *(esprit, chagrin)* to soothe; *(personne)* to relieve; **ce médicament vous soulagera** this medicine will make you feel better; **donne-moi un de tes sacs, ça te soulagera** give me one of your bags, that will take some of the weight off you; *Fam* **s. qn de son porte-**

feuille to relieve sb of his/her wallet

2 se soulager *vpr* (**a**) *(en parlant)* to ease one's mind (**b**) *Fam (satisfaire un besoin naturel)* to relieve oneself

soûlant, -e [sulã, -ãt] *adj Fam* exhausting

soûlard, -e [sular, -ard], **soûlaud, -e** [sulo, -od] *nm,f Fam* drunkard

soûler [sule] *Fam* **1** *vt* (**a**) *(enivrer)* **s. qn** to make sb drunk; *Fig (sujet: parfum, succès, idées)* to go to sb's head (**b**) *(ennuyer)* **arrête, tu me soûles!** stop, you're giving me a headache!

2 se soûler *vpr* to get drunk; *Fig* **se s. de paroles** to like the sound of one's own voice

soulèvement [sulεvmã] *nm* (**a**) *(de terrain)* rising (**b**) *(révolte)* uprising

soulever [46] [sulve] **1** *vt* (**a**) *(charge, personne, couvercle)* to lift (up); *(rideau)* to raise (**b**) *(agiter) (poussière)* to raise, to throw up; *Fig* **s. le cœur à qn** to make sb feel sick (**c**) *(doutes, question, objection)* to raise (**d**) *(population)* to rouse, to stir up (**e**) *(passion, enthousiasme, indignation)* to excite, to arouse; **s. un tollé** to raise an outcry

2 se soulever *vpr* (**a**) *(s'élever)* to rise (**b**) *(se lever) (personne)* to raise oneself, to lift oneself up (**c**) *(se révolter)* to rise up

soulier [sulje] *nm* shoe; *Fam Fig* **être dans ses petits souliers** to feel awkward

souligner [suliɲe] *vt* (**a**) *(mot, passage)* to underline (**b**) *(yeux, taille)* to emphasize (**c**) *Fig (mettre en valeur)* to emphasize

soûlon [sulõ] *nm Suisse & Can Fam* drunk, drunkard

soumettre [47] [sumεtr] **1** *vt* (**a**) *(population, pays, passions)* to subdue (**b**) *(rapport, demande, projet)* to submit (**à** to) (**c**) **s. qn à** *(examen)* to subject sb to; *(épreuve)* to put sb through; *(traitement)* to put sb on; **être soumis à des règles strictes** to be bound by strict rules; **s. les revenus à l'impôt** to make income liable to tax

2 se soumettre *vpr (obéir)* to submit; **se s. à** *(autorité)* to submit to; *(volonté)* to comply with; *(loi, décision)* to abide by

soumis, -e [sumi, -iz] *adj (docile)* submissive, obedient (**à** to)

soumission [sumisjõ] *nf* (**a**) *(à une loi, à une autorité)* submission (**à** to) (**b**) *(docilité)* submissiveness, obedience (**à** to)

soupape [supap] *nf* valve; **s. de sécurité** safety valve

soupçon [supsõ] *nm* (**a**) *(suspicion)* suspicion; **avoir des soupçons sur qn** to have (one's) suspicions about sb; **être au-dessus** *ou* **à l'abri de tout s.** to be above all suspicion; **éveiller les soupçons** to arouse suspicion; **de graves soupçons pèsent sur lui** grave suspicions hang over him (**b**) *(faible quantité) (de vinaigre, d'ail)* dash, hint; *(de fièvre, de fard, d'ironie)* touch; *(de vin)* drop

soupçonner [supsɔne] *vt* to suspect; **s. qn de qch/de faire qch** to suspect sb of sth/of doing sth; **je soupçonne qu'il le sait** I suspect that he knows

soupçonneux, -euse [supsɔnø, -øz] *adj* suspicious

soupe [sup] *nf* (**a**) *(plat)* soup; *Fam* **à la s.!** grub's up!; *Fam* **être s. au lait** to flare up easily (**b**) **s. populaire** soup kitchen

soupente [supãt] *nf (sous un toit)* loft; *(sous un escalier)* *Br* cupboard, *Am* closet

souper¹ [supe] *nm* (**a**) *(dîner)* dinner (**b**) *(après le spectacle)* supper

souper² *vi* (**a**) *(dîner)* to have dinner (**b**) *(après le spectacle)* to have supper (**c**) *Fam Fig (être excédé)* **avoir soupé de qn/qch** to be fed up with sb/sth

soupeser [46] [supəze] *vt (objet)* to feel the weight of, to weigh in one's hand; *Fig (problème, argument)* to weigh up

soupière [supjεr] *nf* soup tureen

soupir [supir] *nm* (**a**) *(souffle)* sigh; **pousser un s.** to let out *or* give a sigh; **rendre le dernier s.** to breathe one's last; **un gros s.** a heavy *or* deep sigh (**b**) *Mus Br* crotchet *or* *Am* quarter rest

soupirail, -aux [supiraj, -o] *nm* cellar window

soupirant [supirã] *nm Hum* suitor, admirer

soupirer [supire] **1** *vt* to sigh

2 *vi* to sigh; **en soupirant** with a sigh

3 soupirer après *vt ind Litt* to long for, to yearn for

souple [supl] *adj* (**a**) *(branche)* flexible; *(corps, danseur)* supple; *(reliure)* limp; *(cuir)* soft, supple (**b**) *Fig (système, loi, personne)* flexible; *(esprit)* adaptable

souplesse [suplεs] *nf* (**a**) *(de branche)* flexibility; *(corps, de danseur)* suppleness; **en s.** *(démarrer)* smoothly (**b**) *Fig (de système, de loi, de personne)* flexibility

source [surs] *nf* (**a**) *(d'eau)* spring; **s. d'eau minérale** mineral spring; **s. thermale** hot spring (**b**) *(de rivière)* source; **prendre sa s.** to rise (**c**) *(de chaleur, d'énergie)* source (**d**) *Fig (du mal, de richesse, d'informations)* source; **tenir qch de bonne s.** to have sth on good authority *or* from a reliable source; **apprendre qch de s. sûre** to learn sth from a reliable source; **s. de revenus** source of revenue (**e**) *Ordinat* **s. de données** data source; **code s.** source code

sourcier [sursje] *nm* water diviner

sourcil [sursil] *nm* eyebrow

sourciller [sursije] *vi* **ne pas s.** not to bat an eyelid *or* turn a hair; **sans s.** without batting an eyelid, without turning a hair

sourcilleux, -euse [sursijø, -øz] *adj* fussy, finicky

sourd, -e [sur, surd] **1** *adj* (**a**) *(personne)* deaf; **devenir s.** to go deaf; *Fig* **rester s. à qch** to turn a deaf ear to sth, to be deaf to sth; **s. de naissance** deaf from birth; **s. d'une oreille** deaf in one ear; *Fam* **s. comme un pot** deaf as a post (**b**) *(douleur, bruit)* dull; *(voix)* hollow; *(désir, lutte)* secret; *(hostilité)* veiled; *(consonne)* voiceless

2 *nm,f (personne)* deaf person; **les sourds** the deaf, deaf people; **comme un s.** *(crier)* at the top of one's voice; *(frapper, taper)* wildly

3 *nf* **sourde** *Ling* voiceless consonant

sourdine [surdin] *nf* mute; *(d'un piano)* practice pedal; **en s.** *(violons)* muted; *(en secret)* on the quiet; *Fam Fig* **mets-la en s.!** put a sock in it!

sourdingue [surdε̃g] *Fam* **1** *adj* cloth-eared

2 *nmf* cloth-ears

sourd-muet, sourde-muette *(mpl* **sourds-muets,** *fpl* **sourdes-muettes)** [surmɥε, surdmɥεt] **1** *adj* deaf-and-dumb

2 *nm,f* deaf mute

souriant, -e [surjã, -ãt] *adj* smiling

souriceau, -x [suriso] *nm* young mouse

souricière [surisjεr] *nf* mousetrap; *Fig* trap

sourire [61] [surir] **1** *vi* (**a**) *(personne)* to smile (**à** at); *Ironique* **ça fait s.** it makes you laugh (**b**) *(être favorable)* **la chance lui sourit** fortune smiles on him/her; **tout lui sourit** everything goes right for him/her

2 *nm* smile; **le s. aux lèvres** with a smile on one's lips;

faire un s. à qn to give sb a smile; **avoir le s.** to have a smile on one's face; **garder le s.** to keep smiling; **retrouver le s.** to be smiling again

souris [suri] nf (a) (animal) mouse; **s. blanche** white mouse (b) Ordinat mouse; **s. à trois boutons** three-button mouse; **s. à infrarouge** infrared mouse; **s. optique** optical mouse; **s. sans fil** cordless mouse; **s. tactile** touchpad mouse (c) Fam (femme) Br bird, Am dame (d) (de gigot) knuckle end

sournois, -e [surnwa, -az] **1** adj sly
  2 nm,f sly person

sournoisement [surnwazmã] adv slyly

sournoiserie [surnwazri] nf slyness

sous [su] prép (a) (position) under(neath); **s. terre** underground; **nager s. l'eau** to swim underwater; **lettre s. enveloppe** letter in an envelope; **s. la pluie** in the rain; **s. les tropiques** in the tropics; **s. les yeux de qn** before sb's eyes; **s. cet angle** from that angle; **chercher un mot s. la lettre S** to look up a word under the letter S (b) (à l'époque de) (monarque, président) under; **s. la IIIe République** during the Third Republic (c) (d'ici) within; **s. peu** shortly, before long (d) (locutions) **connu s. le nom de...** known as...; **être s. antibiotiques** to be on antibiotics; **opérer s. anesthésie** to operate under anaesthetic; **s. le poids de qch** under the weight of sth; **travailler s. les ordres de qn** to work under sb; **s. certaines conditions** on certain conditions; **s. peine de mort** on or under pain of death

sous-alimentation [suzalimãtasjõ] nf malnutrition, undernourishment

sous-alimenté, -e (mpl sous-alimentés, fpl sous-alimentées) [suzalimãte] adj malnourished, undernourished

sous-bois [subwa] nm inv undergrowth

sous-chef (pl sous-chefs) [suʃɛf] nm second-in-command

sous-continent (pl sous-continents) [sukõtinã] nm subcontinent

sous-couche (pl sous-couches) [sukuʃ] nf undercoat

souscripteur, -trice [suskriptœr, -tris] nm,f (d'un emprunt) subscriber (de to); (d'une police d'assurance) policy holder

souscription [suskripsjõ] nf (à un emprunt) subscription (à to); **la s. d'une police d'assurance** taking out an insurance policy

souscrire [30] [suskrir] **1** vt (police d'assurance) to take out
  2 souscrire à vt ind aussi Fig to subscribe to

sous-culture (pl sous-cultures) [sukyltyr] nf subculture

sous-cutané, -e (mpl sous-cutanés, fpl sous-cutanées) [sukytane] adj subcutaneous

sous-développé, -e (mpl sous-développés, fpl sous-développées) [sudevlɔpe] adj (pays) under-developed

sous-développement [sudevlɔpmã] nm under-development

sous-directeur, -trice (mpl sous-directeurs, fpl sous-directrices) [sudirɛktœr, -tris] nm,f (dans une entreprise) assistant manager, f assistant manageress

sous-division nf subdivision

sous-emploi [suzãplwa] nm underemployment

sous-employé, -e (mpl sous-employés, fpl sous-employées) [suzãplwaje] adj underemployed

sous-ensemble (pl sous-ensembles) [suzãsãbl] nm subset

sous-entendre [suzãtãdr] vt to imply

sous-entendu (pl sous-entendus) [suzãtãdy] nm insinuation

sous-équipé, -e (mpl sous-équipés, fpl sous-équipées) [suzekipe] adj underequipped

sous-estimer [suzɛstime] vt to underestimate

sous-évaluer [suzevalɥe] vt to undervalue

sous-exposer [suzɛkspoze] vt to underexpose

sous-fifre (pl sous-fifres) [sufifr] nm Fam underling

sous-homme (pl sous-hommes) [suzɔm] nm subhuman

sous-jacent, -e (mpl sous-jacents, fpl sous-jacentes) [suʒasã, -ãt] adj underlying

Sous-le-Vent [sulvã] n **les îles S.** the Leeward Islands

sous-lieutenant (pl sous-lieutenants) [suljøtnã] nm (a) (dans l'armée de terre) second lieutenant (b) (dans la marine) sub-lieutenant (c) (dans l'armée de l'air) Br pilot officer, Am second lieutenant

sous-locataire (pl sous-locataires) [sulɔkatɛr] nmf subtenant

sous-location (pl sous-locations) [sulɔkasjõ] nf (a) (par le locataire) subletting (b) (par le sous-locataire) subrenting

sous-louer [sulwe] vt (a) (sujet: locataire) to sublet (b) (sujet: sous-locataire) to subrent

sous-main [sumɛ̃] nm inv desk blotter; Fig **en s.** secretly

sous-marin, -e (mpl sous-marins, fpl sous-marines) [sumarɛ̃, -in] **1** adj underwater
  2 nm submarine; **s. nucléaire** nuclear(-powered) submarine

sous-marinier (pl sous-mariniers) [sumarinje] nm submariner

sous-multiple (pl sous-multiples) [sumyltipl] nm Math submultiple (**de** of)

sous-nappe (pl sous-nappes) [sunap] nf undercloth

sous-officier (pl sous-officiers) [suzɔsje] nm non-commissioned officer

sous-payer [53] [supeje] vt to underpay

sous-peuplé, -e (mpl sous-peuplés, fpl sous-peuplées) [supœple] adj underpopulated

sous-plat (pl sous-plats) [supla] nm Belg table mat

sous-préfecture (pl sous-préfectures) [suprefɛktyr] nf subprefecture

sous-préfet (pl sous-préfets) [suprefɛ] nm subprefect

sous-production [suprɔdyksjõ] nf under-production

sous-produit (pl sous-produits) [suprɔdɥi] nm by-product; Fig poor imitation

sous-prolétaire (pl sous-prolétaires) [suprɔletɛr] nmf member of the underclass

sous-prolétariat (pl sous-prolétariats) [suprɔletarja] nm underclass

sous-pull (pl sous-pulls) [supyl] nm thin sweater

sous-répertoire (pl sous-répertoires) [surepɛrtwar] nm Ordinat subdirectory

sous-secrétaire (pl sous-secrétaires) [susəkretɛr] nmf **s. d'État** Under-Secretary of State

soussigné, -e [susiɲe] adj & nm,f undersigned; **je, s. Éric Blanc, donne mon autorisation à...** I, the undersigned Éric Blanc, hereby authorize...

sous-sol (*pl* **sous-sols**) [susɔl] *nm* (**a**) *(d'une maison)* basement (**b**) *Géol* subsoil

sous-tasse (*pl* **sous-tasses**) [sutas] *nf* saucer

sous-tendre [sutɑ̃dr] *vt (théorie)* to underlie

sous-titrage (*pl* **sous-titrages**) [sutitraʒ] *nm Cin* subtitling

sous-titre (*pl* **sous-titres**) [sutitr] *nm (de livre, de film)* subtitle

sous-titrer [sutitre] *vt Cin* to subtitle; **film sous-titré en anglais** film with English subtitles

sous-total (*pl* **sous-totaux**) [sutɔtal, -o] *nm* subtotal

soustraction [sustraksjɔ̃] *nf* subtraction

soustraire [28] [sustrɛr] **1** *vt* (**a**) *(enlever)* **s. qch à qn** to take sth away *or* remove sth from sb; **s. qn au danger/à l'influence de qn** to protect *or* shield sb from danger/from sb's influence (**b**) *(chiffre, somme)* to subtract (**de** from)
2 se soustraire *vpr* **se s. à** *(influence, regard)* to avoid, to elude; *(obligation)* to shirk

sous-traitance [sutrɛtɑ̃s] *nf* subcontracting; **travaux effectués en s.** subcontracted work

sous-traitant, -e [sutrɛtɑ̃, -ɑ̃t] **1** *adj* subcontracting
2 *nm* subcontractor

sous-traiter [sutrete] *vt* to subcontract

sous-verre [suvɛr] *nm inv (cadre)* glass mount; *(photo, image)* = photograph or picture mounted under glass

sous-vêtement [suvɛtmɑ̃] *nm* undergarment; **sous-vêtements** underwear

soutane [sutan] *nf* cassock

soute [sut] *nf (de bateau)* store; *(d'avion)* hold; **s. à bagages** *(d'avion)* baggage hold

soutenable [sutnabl] *adj* (**a**) *(supportable)* bearable (**b**) *(défendable)* tenable

soutenance [sutnɑ̃s] *nf Univ* viva (voce)

soutènement [sutɛnmɑ̃] *nm voir* **mur**

souteneur [sutnœr] *nm* pimp

soutenir [70] [sutnir] **1** *vt* (**a**) *(maintenir)* to support, to hold up (**b**) *(aider)* to support (**c**) *(opinion, théorie)* to maintain, to uphold; **s. que...** to maintain that... (**d**) *Univ (thèse)* to defend (**e**) *(conversation, vitesse, rythme)* to keep up, to maintain (**f**) *(résister à) (regard)* to hold; **s. la comparaison** to bear comparison
2 se soutenir *vpr (personnes)* to support each other; **se s. moralement** to give each other moral support

soutenu, -e [sutny] *adj* (**a**) *(attention, effort, intérêt)* sustained; *(rythme)* steady (**b**) *(style, langage)* formal, elevated (**c**) *(couleur)* deep

souterrain, -e [sutɛrɛ̃, -ɛn] **1** *adj* (**a**) *(eau, explosion)* underground; *(économie)* black (**b**) *Fig (manœuvres)* secret
2 *nm* underground passage

soutien [sutjɛ̃] *nm* (**a**) *(aide)* support; **apporter son s. à qn/qch** to give sb/sth one's support (**b**) *(personne, groupe)* support; **s. de famille** breadwinner

soutien-gorge (*pl* **soutiens-gorge**) [sutjɛ̃gɔrʒ] *nm* bra; **s. à armatures/d'allaitement** underwired/nursing bra

soutif [sutif] *nm Fam* bra

soutirer [sutire] *vt* (**a**) *(vin)* to rack, to decant (**b**) **s. qch à qn** *(argent, information)* to extract sth from sb

souvenance [suvnɑ̃s] *nf* **avoir s. de qch** to recollect sth

souvenir [suvnir] **1** *nm* (**a**) *(réminiscence)* memory; **en s. de** in memory of; **en s. du passé** for old times' sake;

garder un bon/mauvais **s. de qch** to have good/bad memories of sth; **souvenirs d'enfance** childhood memories (**b**) *(objet)* memento; *(touristique)* souvenir (**c**) *(dans une formule de politesse)* **mes meilleurs souvenirs à votre sœur** (my) kindest regards to your sister
2 *v impersonnel Litt* **il me souvient que...** I recall that...
3 se souvenir *vpr* **se s. de** to remember; **se s. que** to remember that; **je ne me souviens de rien** I can't remember anything

souvent [suvɑ̃] *adv* often; **le plus s.** usually, more often than not; **plus s. qu'à son tour** far too often

souverain, -e [suvrɛ̃, -ɛn] **1** *adj (puissance, état, remède)* sovereign; *(bonheur, mépris)* supreme
2 *nm,f* sovereign

souverainement [suvrɛnmɑ̃] *adv (intelligent, doué)* supremely; *(agacer, déplaire)* intensely

souveraineté [suvrɛnte] *nf* sovereignty

soviétique [sɔvjetik] *Anciennement* **1** *adj* Soviet
2 *nmf* **S.** Soviet (citizen)

soyeux, -euse [swajø, -øz] **1** *adj* silky
2 *nm* silk merchant

soyez, soyons *etc voir* **être**

SPA [ɛspea] *nf (abrév* **Société protectrice des animaux**) *Br* ≃ RSPCA, *Am* ≃ ASPCA

spacieusement [spasjøzmɑ̃] *adv* **être logé s.** to have spacious accommodation

spacieux, -euse [spasjø, -øz] *adj* spacious

spaghetti [spageti] *nm* piece of spaghetti; **des spaghetti** spaghetti

spammer [spame] *vt Ordinat* to spam

spamming [spamiŋ] *nm Ordinat* spamming

sparadrap [sparadra] *nm Br* sticking plaster, *Am* adhesive tape

spartiate [sparsjat] **1** *adj* Spartan; *Fig* **à la s.** in a spartan way
2 *nfpl* **spartiates** Roman sandals

spasme [spasm] *nm* spasm

spasmodique [spasmɔdik] *adj* spasmodic

spasmophilie [spasmɔfili] *nf* spasmophilia

spatial, -e, -aux, -ales [spasjal, -o] *adj* (**a**) *(de l'espace)* spatial (**b**) *(de l'espace interplanétaire)* space

spatio-temporel, -elle (*mpl* **spatio-temporels**, *fpl* **spatio-temporelles**) [spasjotɑ̃pɔrɛl] *adj* spatio-temporal

spatule [spatyl] *nf* (**a**) *(de cuisinier, de peintre)* spatula (**b**) *(de ski)* tip (**c**) *(oiseau)* spoonbill

speaker, speakerine [spikœr, spikrin] *nm,f* announcer

spécial, -e, -aux, -ales [spesjal, -o] *adj* (**a**) *(particulier, extraordinaire)* special (**b**) *(bizarre)* peculiar, odd

spécialement [spesjalmɑ̃] *adv (particulièrement)* especially, particularly; *(exprès)* specially

spécialisation [spesjalizasjɔ̃] *nf* specialization

spécialisé, -e [spesjalize] *adj (travail, enseignement)* specialized; *(ouvrier)* semi-skilled; *(école, hôpital)* special

spécialiser [spesjalize] **se spécialiser** *vpr* to specialize (**dans** *ou* **en** in)

spécialiste [spesjalist] *nmf* specialist (**de/en** in)

spécialité [spesjalite] *nf Br* speciality, *Am* specialty; **s. maison** speciality of the house

spécieux, -euse [spesjø, -øz] *adj Litt* specious

spécification [spesifikasjɔ̃] *nf* specification

spécificité [spesifisite] *nf* distinctiveness
spécifier [spesifje] *vt* to specify
spécifique [spesifik] *adj* specific
spécifiquement [spesifikmɑ̃] *adv* specifically
spécimen [spesimɛn] *nm* (**a**) *(modèle)* specimen (**b**) *(livre, fascicule)* specimen copy
spectacle [spɛktakl] *nm* (**a**) *(représentation)* show; **le s.** *(industrie)* show business; **film à grand s.** epic (film); **s. de variétés** variety show (**b**) *(vue)* sight; **se donner en s.** to make an exhibition *or* a spectacle of oneself
spectaculaire [spɛktakylɛr] *adj* spectacular
spectateur, -trice [spɛktatœr, -tris] *nm,f* (**a**) *(d'un événement sportif)* spectator; *(d'un spectacle)* member of the audience; **spectateurs** *(au spectacle)* audience (**b**) *(témoin)* witness
spectre [spɛktr] *nm* (**a**) *(fantôme)* ghost, phantom; *Fig (de la guerre, de la misère)* spectre (**b**) *Phys* spectrum
spéculateur, trice [spekylatœr, -tris] *nm,f* speculator
spéculation [spekylasjɔ̃] *nf* speculation; **s. à la baisse** bear operations; **s. à la hausse** bull operations
spéculer [spekyle] *vi* (**a**) *(intellectuellement)* to speculate *(sur* on *or* about) (**b**) *(à la Bourse)* to speculate (**sur** in); *Fig* **s. sur qch** to count *or* bank on sth
spéculoos [spekylos] *nm Belg* = ginger biscuit
speech *(pl* **speeches)** [spitʃ] *nm Fam* speech; **faire un s.** to make a speech; **faire un s. à qn sur qch** to give sb a speech about sth
speed [spid] *Fam* **1** *adj (nerveux)* hyper
2 *nm (amphétamines)* speed
speedé, -e [spide] *adj Fam (hyperactif)* hyped up, hyper
speeder [spide] *vi Fam* to get a move on
spéléologie [speleɔlɔʒi] *nf* (**a**) *(exploration) Br* potholing, *Am* spelunking (**b**) *(science)* speleology
spéléologue [speleɔlɔg] *nmf* (**a**) *(explorateur) Br* potholer, *Am* spelunker (**b**) *(spécialiste)* speleologist
spencer [spɛ̃ser] *nm* short jacket
spermatozoïde [spɛrmatɔzɔid] *nm* spermatozoon
sperme [spɛrm] *nm* sperm, semen
sphère [sfɛr] *nf* (**a**) *(boule)* sphere (**b**) *(d'activité, d'influence)* sphere; **les hautes sphères de la politique** the higher realms of politics
sphérique [sferik] *adj* spherical
sphinx [sfɛ̃ks] *nm* (**a**) *(monstre fabuleux)* sphinx (**b**) *(insecte)* hawk *or* sphinx moth
spirale [spiral] *nf* spiral; **en s.** *(s'élever)* in a spiral; *(escalier, coquillage)* spiral
spiritisme [spiritism] *nm* spiritualism
spiritualité [spiritɥalite] *nf* spirituality
spirituel, -elle [spiritɥɛl] *adj* (**a**) *(pouvoir, vie)* spiritual (**b**) *(fin)* witty; *Ironique* **que c'est s.!** very witty!
spirituellement [spiritɥɛlmɑ̃] *adv* (**a**) *(moralement)* spiritually (**b**) *(finement)* wittily
spiritueux [spiritɥø] *nm* spirit
spleen [splin] *nm Litt* spleen, melancholy; **avoir le s.** to be melancholic
splendeur [splɑ̃dœr] *nf* splendour; **c'est une s.** it's splendid
splendide [splɑ̃did] *adj* splendid; *(soleil)* brilliant; *(œuvre d'art, personne)* magnificent
splendidement [splɑ̃didmɑ̃] *adv* splendidly
spolier [spɔlje] *vt* to despoil (**de** of)
spongieux, -euse [spɔ̃ʒjø, -øz] *adj* spongy
sponsor [spɔ̃sɔr] *nm* sponsor

sponsoriser [spɔ̃sɔrize] *vt* to sponsor
spontané, -e [spɔ̃tane] *adj* spontaneous
spontanéité [spɔ̃taneite] *nf* spontaneity
spontanément [spɔ̃tanemɑ̃] *adv* spontaneously
sporadique [spɔradik] *adj* sporadic
spore [spɔr] *nf* spore
sport [spɔr] **1** *nm* (**a**) *(activité)* sport; **de s.** *(chaussures, terrain, voiture)* sports; **faire du s.** to do sport; **s. de combat** combat sport; **s. d'équipe/individuel** team/individual sport; **sports d'hiver** winter sports; **aller aux sports d'hiver** to go skiing; **sports nautiques** water sports (**b**) *Fam (locutions)* **il va y avoir du s.!** there's going to be some fun!; **c'est du s.** it's a tough job
2 *adj inv (vêtement)* casual
sportif, -ive [spɔrtif, -iv] **1** *adj* (**a**) *(résultats, journal, club)* sports (**b**) *(fair-play)* sporting (**c**) *(dynamique)* sporty
2 *nm,f* sportsman, *f* sportswoman
sportivité [spɔrtivite] *nf* sportsmanship
spot [spɔt] *nm* (**a**) *(projecteur)* spot, spotlight (**b**) *(à la télé, à la radio)* **s. publicitaire** commercial, advert
spoutnik [sputnik] *nm* sputnik
spray [sprɛ] *nm* spray, aerosol; **parfum en s.** spray-on perfume
sprint [sprint] *nm (accélération finale)* (final) sprint; *(course)* sprint; *Fam* **piquer un s.** to sprint
sprinter¹ [sprintœr] *nm* sprinter
sprinter² [sprinte] *vi* to sprint
squale [skwal] *nm* shark
square [skwar] *nm* public garden
squash [skwaʃ] *nm* squash
squat [skwat] *nm* squat
squatter¹ [skwatœr] *nm* squatter
squatter² [skwate], **squattériser** [skwaterize] *vt (bâtiment)* to squat in; *Fam Fig (monopoliser)* to take over, to hog
squelette [skəlɛt] *nm* (**a**) *(d'être humain, d'animal)* skeleton; **c'est un vrai s.** he's/she's a bag of bones; **c'est un s. ambulant** he's/she's a walking skeleton (**b**) *Fig (de roman, de bâtiment)* skeleton, framework
squelettique [skəletik] *adj* (**a**) *(personne, partie du corps)* skeleton-like (**b**) *(personnel, armée)* skeleton
Sri Lanka [srilɑ̃ka] *nm* **le S.** Sri Lanka
sri lankais, -e [srilɑ̃kɛ, -ɛz] **1** *adj* Sri Lankan
2 *nm,f* **S.** Sri Lankan
SRPJ [ɛsɛrpeʒi] *nm (abrév* **Service régional de la police judiciaire)** = regional crime unit
stabilisateur, -trice [stabilizatœr, -tris] **1** *adj* stabilizing
2 *nm (de vélo)* stabilizer
stabilisation [stabilizasjɔ̃] *nf* stabilization
stabiliser [stabilize] **1** *vt* to stabilize
2 se stabiliser *vpr* to stabilize; *(personne)* to settle down
stabilité [stabilite] *nf* stability
stable [stabl] *adj* stable
stade [stad] *nm* (**a**) *(sportif)* stadium (**b**) *(étape)* stage; **en être au s. embryonnaire** to be at an embryonic stage
stage [staʒ] *nm (professionnel)* training course; **être en s.** to be on a training course; **s. en entreprise** work placement, *Am* internship; **s. de formation** training course, *Am* internship; **faire un s. de tennis/de voile**

to have tennis/sailing lessons; *(vacances)* to go on a tennis/sailing holiday

stagiaire [staʒjɛr] *adj & nmf* trainee, *Am* intern

stagnant, -e [stagnɑ̃, -ɑ̃t] *adj* stagnant

stagnation [stagnasjɔ̃] *nf* stagnation

stagner [stagne] *vi* to stagnate

stalactite [stalaktit] *nf* stalactite

stalagmite [stalagmit] *nf* stalagmite

stalinien, -enne [stalinjɛ̃, -ɛn] *adj & nm,f* Stalinist

stalle [stal] *nf (dans une écurie, une église)* stall

stand [stɑ̃d] *nm* (**a**) *(d'exposition)* stand; *(de foire)* stall; **s. de tir** rifle range (**b**) *(de course automobile)* **s. (de ravitaillement)** pit

standard [stɑ̃dar] **1** *adj inv* standard
2 *nm* (**a**) *(norme)* standard (**b**) **s. (téléphonique)** switchboard

standardisation [stɑ̃dardizasjɔ̃] *nf* standardization

standardiser [stɑ̃dardize] *vt* to standardize

standardiste [stɑ̃dardist] *nmf* (switchboard) operator

standing [stɑ̃diŋ] *nm* (social) standing; **de grand s.** *(appartement)* luxury; *(quartier)* select

staphylocoque [stafilɔkɔk] *nm* staphylococcus

star [star] *nf* star

starlette [starlɛt] *nf* starlet

starter [starter] *nm* (**a**) *(de voiture)* choke (**b**) *(dans une course)* starter

starting-block *(pl* **starting-blocks)** [startiŋblɔk] *nm* starting block

start-up [startœp] *(pl* **start-ups)** *nf* dot com (company)

station [stasjɔ̃] *nf* (**a**) *(de métro)* station; *(de train)* halt; *(de bus)* stop; **s. de taxis** *Br* taxi rank, *Am* taxi stand (**b**) *(ville, village)* **s. balnéaire** seaside resort; **s. de ski** ski resort; **s. de sports d'hiver** winter sports resort; **s. thermale** spa town (**c**) *(établissement)* station; **s. d'essence** *Br* petrol *or Am* gas station; **s. de lavage** car wash; **s. spatiale** space station (**d**) *(position)* **s. debout** standing position (**e**) **s. de radio** radio station (**f**) *Ordinat (d'un réseau)* station, node; **s. d'accueil** docking station; **s. individuelle** standalone workstation; **s. de travail** workstation

stationnaire [stasjɔnɛr] *adj (satellite)* stationary; *(baromètre)* steady; *(état d'un malade)* stable

stationnement [stasjɔnmɑ̃] *nm* (**a**) *(de voitures)* parking; **en s.** parked; **s. alterné semi-mensuel** = system in which parking is permitted on one side of the street only for alternating periods of two weeks; **s. interdit** *(sur panneau)* no parking; **s. gênant** *(sur panneau)* ≃ restricted parking (**b**) *Can (parking)* car park, *Am* parking lot

stationner [stasjɔne] *vi* to park; **défense de s.** *(sur panneau)* no parking

station-service *(pl* **stations-service)** [stasjɔ̃sɛrvis] *nf* service station, *Br* petrol *or Am* gas station

statique [statik] **1** *adj* static
2 *nf* statics *(singulier)*

statisticien, -enne [statistisjɛ̃, -ɛn] *nm,f* statistician

statistique [statistik] **1** *adj* statistical
2 *nf* (**a**) *(donnée)* statistic (**b**) *(science)* statistics *(singulier)*

statistiquement [statistikmɑ̃] *adv* statistically

statuaire [statɥɛr] *adj & nf* statuary

statue [staty] *nf* statue

statuer [statɥe] **statuer sur** *vt ind* to give a ruling on

statuette [statɥɛt] *nf* statuette

statu quo [statykwo] *nm* status quo

stature [statyr] *nf* stature

statut [staty] *nm* (**a**) *(position)* status; **s. juridique** *ou* **légal** legal status; **s. social** social status (**b**) **statuts** *(d'une société, d'une association)* statutes

statutaire [statytɛr] *adj* statutory

St *(abrév* **Saint)** St

Ste *(abrév* **Sainte)** St

Sté *(abrév* **Société)** Co

steak [stɛk] *nm* steak; **s. frites** steak and chips; **un s. haché** a hamburger, *Br* a beefburger; **du s. haché** *Br* mince, *Am* ground beef; **s. au poivre** pepper steak; **s. tartare** steak tartare *(raw minced beef served with a raw egg)*

stèle [stɛl] *nf* stele

stellaire [stelɛr] *adj* stellar

stencil [stɛnsil] *nm* stencil

sténo [steno] **1** *nf (abrév* **sténographie)** shorthand; **prendre qch en s.** to take sth down in shorthand
2 *nmf (abrév* **sténographe)** stenographer

sténodactylo [stenodaktilo] **1** *nf* shorthand typing
2 *nmf* shorthand typist

sténodactylographie [stenodaktilɔgrafi] *nf* shorthand typing

sténographe [stenograf] *nmf* stenographer

sténographie [stenografi] *nf* shorthand

sténographier [stenɔgrafje] *vt* to take down in shorthand

sténographique [stenɔgrafik] *adj* shorthand

stentor [stɑ̃tɔr] *nm voir* **voix**

steppe [stɛp] *nf* steppe

stéréo [stereo] **1** *adj inv* stereo
2 *nf* stereo; **en s.** in stereo

stéréophonie [stereofɔni] *nf* stereophony

stéréophonique [stereofɔnik] *adj* stereophonic

stéréotype [stereotip] *nm* stereotype

stéréotypé, -e [stereotipe] *adj* stereotyped

stérile [steril] *adj* (**a**) *(personne, animal)* sterile; *(mariage)* childless; *(terre)* barren (**b**) *(discussion, efforts)* futile (**c**) *(instrument, chambre)* sterile

stérilet [sterilɛ] *nm* coil, IUD

stérilisation [sterilizasjɔ̃] *nf* sterilization

stériliser [sterilize] *vt* to sterilize

stérilité [sterilite] *nf* (**a**) *(d'une personne, d'un animal)* sterility; *(de la terre)* barrenness (**b**) *(d'une discussion, d'efforts)* futility

sterling [stɛrliŋ] *adj inv voir* **livre²**

sterne [stɛrn] *nf* tern

sternum [stɛrnɔm] *nm* breastbone, *Spéc* sternum

stéthoscope [stetɔskɔp] *nm* stethoscope

steward [stjuwart, stiwart] *nm* steward

stick [stik] *nm (de colle, pour les lèvres)* stick; **déodorant en s.** stick deodorant

stigmate [stigmat] *nm* (**a**) *(trace)* mark (**b**) *Rel* **stigmates** stigmata

stigmatiser [stigmatize] *vt (dénoncer)* to condemn

stimulant, -e [stimylɑ̃, -ɑ̃t] **1** *adj* stimulating; *(résultats)* encouraging
2 *nm* (**a**) *(remède)* stimulant (**b**) *Fig* stimulus, incentive

stimulateur [stimylatœr] *nm* **s. cardiaque** pacemaker

stimulation [stimylasjɔ̃] *nf* stimulation

stimuler [stimyle] *vt* to stimulate

stipuler [stipyle] *vt* to stipulate

stock [stɔk] *nm* stock; **en s.** in stock
stockage [stɔkaʒ] *nm* (**a**) *(de marchandises)* stocking (**b**) *Ordinat* storage; **s. en mémoire tampon** buffering
stock-car *(pl* **stock-cars**) [stɔkkar] *nm (voiture)* stock car; *(sport)* stock-car racing
stocker [stɔke] *vt* (**a**) *(marchandises)* to stock (**b**) *Ordinat* to store
Stockholm [stɔkɔlm] *n* Stockholm
stoïcisme [stɔisism] *nm* (**a**) *(attitude)* stoicism (**b**) *(doctrine philosophique)* Stoicism
stoïque [stɔik] *adj* stoical
stoïquement [stɔikmã] *adv* stoically
stomatologie [stɔmatɔlɔʒi] *nf* stomatology
stop [stɔp] **1** *exclam* stop!; *(dans un télégramme)* stop; **savoir dire s.** to know when to say stop
  2 *nm* (**a**) *(panneau)* stop sign (**b**) *(d'un véhicule)* brake light (**c**) *Fam (auto-stop)* hitching, hitchhiking; **faire du s.** to hitch, to hitchhike
stopper [stɔpe] *vt & vi (arrêter)* to stop
store [stɔr] *nm* (**a**) *(de fenêtre)* blind; **s. vénitien** Venetian blind (**b**) *(de magasin)* awning
strabisme [strabism] *nm* squint
stradivarius [stradivarjys] *nm* Stradivarius
strangulation [strãgylasjɔ̃] *nf* strangulation
strapontin [strapɔ̃tɛ̃] *nm (siège)* folding seat, tip-up seat
Strasbourg [strazbur] *n* Strasbourg
strasbourgeois, -e [strazburʒwa, -waz] **1** *adj* of Strasbourg
  2 *nm,f* **S.** person from Strasbourg
strass [stras] *nm* paste; **en s.** *(bijou)* paste
stratagème [strataʒɛm] *nm* stratagem
strate [strat] *nf* stratum
stratège [stratɛʒ] *nm* strategist
stratégie [strateʒi] *nf* strategy
stratégique [strateʒik] *adj* strategic
stratification [stratifikasjɔ̃] *nf* stratification
stratifié, -e [stratifje] *adj* (**a**) *(roche)* stratified (**b**) *(bois)* laminated
stratosphère [stratɔsfɛr] *nf* stratosphere
streptocoque [strɛptɔkɔk] *nm* streptococcus
stress [strɛs] *nm* stress
stressant, -e [strɛsã, -ãt] *adj* stressful
stresser [strɛse] **1** *vt* to put under stress; **être stressé** to be stressed
  2 *vi Fam* to get stressed
Stretch® [strɛtʃ] *nm* stretch material; **une jupe en S.** a stretch skirt
strict, -e [strikt] *adj* (**a**) *(obligation, principes)* strict; **au sens s.** in the strict sense of the word; **le s. minimum** the bare minimum; **le s. nécessaire** the bare essentials; **c'est la stricte vérité** that's the absolute truth; **c'est son droit le plus s.** it's his absolute right (**b**) *(personne)* strict (**sur** about) (**c**) *(costume, coupe de cheveux)* severe
strictement [striktəmã] *adv* (**a**) *(rigoureusement)* strictly; **je ne comprends s. rien** I don't understand a single thing (**b**) *(habillé)* severely
stricto sensu [striktosɛ̃sy] *adv* strictly speaking
strident, -e [stridã, -ãt] *adj* strident, shrill
strie [stri] *nf* groove
strié, -e [strije] *adj* grooved
string [striŋ] *nm* G-string
strip-tease *(pl* **strip-teases**) [striptiz] *nm* striptease

strip-teaseuse *(pl* **strip-teaseuses**) [striptizøz] *nf* stripper, striptease artist
stroboscope [strɔbɔskɔp] *nm* strobe, stroboscope
strophe [strɔf] *nf* stanza, verse
structural, -e, -aux, -ales [stryktyral, -o] *adj* structural
structuralement [stryktyralmã] *adv* structurally
structuralisme [stryktyralism] *nm* structuralism
structuraliste [stryktyralist] *adj & nmf* structuralist
structure [stryktyr] *nf* (**a**) *(disposition)* structure (**b**) *(organisation)* **s. d'accueil** reception facilities (**c**) *Ordinat* **s. en anneau** ring structure; **s. en arbre** tree structure; **s. de bloc** block structure
structuré, -e [stryktyre] *adj* (**a**) *(ensemble, langage)* structured (**b**) *Ordinat* **fichier non s.** flat file
structurel, -elle [stryktyrɛl] *adj* structural
structurer [stryktyre] *vt* to structure
strychnine [striknin] *nf* strychnine
stuc [styk] *nm* stucco
studieusement [stydjøzmã] *adv* studiously
studieux, -euse [stydjø, -øz] *adj (personne)* studious; *(vacances)* study
studio [stydjo] *nm* (**a**) *(pour travailler)* studio; **s. de cinéma** *Br* film studio, *Am* movie studio; **tourné en s.** filmed in the studio; **s. d'enregistrement** recording studio (**b**) *(logement) Br* studio flat, *Am* studio apartment
stupéfaction [stypefaksjɔ̃] *nf* amazement, astonishment
stupéfait, -e [stypefɛ, -ɛt] *adj* amazed, astounded
stupéfiant, -e [stypefjã, -ãt] **1** *adj* amazing, astounding
  2 *nm* drug, narcotic
stupéfier [stypefje] *vt* to amaze, to astound
stupeur [stypœr] *nf* amazement, astonishment
stupide [stypid] *adj* stupid
stupidement [stypidmã] *adv* stupidly
stupidité [stypidite] *nf* (**a**) *(caractère)* stupidity (**b**) *(remarque)* stupid remark; **dire des stupidités** to say stupid things
style [stil] *nm* style; **de s.** *(meuble)* period; **s. Louis XIII/Régence** Louis XIII-/Regency-style; **avoir du s.** to have style, to be stylish; *Fam* **ça serait bien son s.!** that would be just his style!; **s. de vie** lifestyle; *Gram* **s. direct/indirect** direct/indirect speech
stylé, -e [stile] *adj (domestique)* trained
stylet [stilɛ] *nm* (**a**) *(poignard)* stiletto (**b**) *Ordinat* **s. lumineux** light pen
styliser [stilize] *vt* to stylize
stylisme [stilism] *nm* designing
styliste [stilist] *nmf* designer
stylistique [stilistik] **1** *adj* stylistic
  2 *nf* stylistics *(singulier)*
stylo [stilo] *nm* pen; **s. à encre** *ou* **à plume** fountain pen; **s. (à) bille** ballpoint (pen), *Br* biro®; *Ordinat* **s. optique** light pen
stylo-feutre *(pl* **stylos-feutres**) [stiloføtr] *nm* felt-tip (pen)
su¹, -e *voir* **savoir**
su² [sy] *nm* **au vu et au su de tout le monde** quite openly
suave [sɥav] *adj* (**a**) *(parfum, mélodie)* sweet (**b**) *(ton, manières)* suave, smooth
suavité [sɥavite] *nf* (**a**) *(d'un parfum, d'une mélodie)* sweetness (**b**) *(des manières)* suavity

subalterne [sybaltɛrn] **1** *adj (officier, position)* subordinate, minor; *(employé)* junior
 2 *nmf* subordinate
subconscient, -e [sybkɔ̃sjã, -ãt] *adj & nm* sub-conscious
subdiviser [sybdivize] **1** *vt* to subdivide (**en** into)
 2 se subdiviser *vpr* to be subdivided (**en** into)
subdivision [sybdivizjɔ̃] *nf* subdivision
subir [sybir] *vt* (**a**) *(violence, conséquences)* to suffer; *(défaite, pertes)* to suffer, to sustain; *(influence)* to be under; **faire s. qch à qn** to subject sb to sth (**b**) *(examen, opération, changement)* to undergo (**c**) *Fam (personne)* to put up with
subit, -e [sybi, -it] *adj* sudden
subitement [sybitmã] *adv* suddenly, all of a sudden
subjectif, -ive [sybʒɛktif, -iv] *adj* subjective
subjectivement [sybʒɛktivmã] *adv* subjectively
subjectivité [sybʒɛktivite] *nf* subjectivity
subjonctif, -ive [sybʒɔ̃ktif, -iv] *Gram* **1** *adj* subjunctive
 2 *nm* subjunctive; **au s.** in the subjunctive
subjuguer [sybʒyge] *vt (séduire)* to captivate
sublimation [syblimasjɔ̃] *nf* sublimation
sublime [syblim] **1** *adj* sublime
 2 *nm* **le s.** the sublime
sublimement [syblimmã] *adv* sublimely
sublimer [syblime] *vt* to sublimate
subliminal, -e, -aux, -ales [sybliminal, -o] *adj* subliminal
submerger [sybmɛrʒe] *vt* to submerge; **submergé de travail** snowed under with work
submersible [sybmɛrsibl] **1** *adj* submersible
 2 *nm* submarine
subodorer [sybɔdɔre] *vt Fam (danger, complot)* to scent
subordination [sybɔrdinasjɔ̃] *nf* subordination
subordonné, -e [sybɔrdɔne] **1** *adj Gram (proposition)* subordinate
 2 *nm,f (personne)* subordinate
 3 *nf* **subordonnée** *Gram* subordinate clause
subordonner [sybɔrdɔne] *vt* (**a**) *(dans une hiérarchie)* **être subordonné à qn** to be subordinate to sb (**b**) *(faire passer après)* **s. qch à qch** to accord less importance to sth than to sth (**c**) *(faire dépendre)* **être subordonné à qch** to be dependent on sth
subornation [sybɔrnasjɔ̃] *nf Jur* subornation
suborner [sybɔrne] *vt* (**a**) *Jur (témoin)* to suborn, to bribe (**b**) *Litt (séduire)* to seduce
subrepticement [sybrɛptismã] *adv* surreptitiously
subséquent, -e [sypsekã, -ãt] *adj* subsequent
subside [sybzid] *nm* subsidy, grant
subsidiaire [sybzidjɛr] *adj* subsidiary
subsidier [sybzidje] *vt Belg (subventionner)* to subsidize
subsistance [sybzistãs] *nf* subsistence; **pourvoir à la s. de sa famille** to keep or support one's family
subsistant, -e [sybzistã, -ãt] *adj* remaining
subsister [sybziste] *vi* (**a**) *(chose)* to remain (**b**) *(personne)* to subsist
substance [sypstãs] *nf* substance; **en s.** in substance
substantiel, -elle [sypstãsjɛl] *adj* substantial
substantiellement [sypstãsjɛlmã] *adv* substantially
substantif, -ive [sypstãtif, -iv] *Gram* **1** *adj* substantive
 2 *nm* noun, substantive

substantiver [sypstãtive] *vt* to use as a noun or substantively
substituer [sypstitɥe] **1** *vt* **s. qn/qch à** to substitute sb/sth for
 2 se substituer *vpr* **se s. à** to substitute for, to take the place of
substitut [sypstity] *nm* (**a**) *Jur* deputy public prosecutor (**b**) *(remplacement)* substitute
substitution [sypstitysjɔ̃] *nf* substitution
substrat [sypstra] *nm Géol* substratum
subterfuge [s...] *nm* subterfuge; **user de subterfuges** to resort to subterfuge
subtil, -e [syptil] *adj* subtle
subtilement [syptilmã] *adv* subtly
subtiliser [syptilize] *vt* to make off with; **on lui a subtilisé son portefeuille** someone's made off with his wallet
subtilité [syptilite] *nf* subtlety
subtropical, -e, -aux, -ales [syptrɔpikal, -o] *adj* subtropical
subvenir [sybvənir] **subvenir à** *vt ind* to meet
subvention [sybvãsjɔ̃] *nf* subsidy, grant
subventionner [sybvãsjɔne] *vt* to subsidize
subversif, -ive [sybvɛrsif, -iv] *adj* subversive
subversion [sybvɛrsjɔ̃] *nf* subversion
suc [syk] *nm* (**a**) *(de fruit, de viande)* juice (**b**) *Fig & Litt* essence
succédané [syksedane] *nm* substitute (**de** for)
succéder [syksede] **1 succéder à** *vt ind* (**a**) *(personne)* to succeed, to take over from (**b**) *(phénomène)* **la résignation succéda à la colère** anger gave way to resignation
 2 se succéder *vpr* to follow one another
succès [syksɛ] *nm* (**a**) *(réussite)* success; **avoir du s.** *(œuvre, artiste)* to be successful; *(suggestion)* to be very well-received; **il a beaucoup de s. auprès des jeunes** he's very popular with young people; **avoir un s. fou (auprès de qn)** to be a big hit (with sb); **faire le s. de qn** to make sb's name; **avec s.** successfully; **sans s.** unsuccessfully; **à s.** successful (**b**) *(pièce, chanson)* hit, success
successeur [syksescœr] *nm* successor (**de** to)
successif, -ive [syksesif, -iv] *adj* successive
succession [syksesjɔ̃] *nf* (**a**) *(suite)* succession (**b**) *(remplacement)* succession (**à** to); **prendre la s. de qn** to succeed sb, to take over from sb (**c**) *Jur (par héritage)* succession; *(biens)* inheritance
successivement [syksesivmã] *adv* successively
succinct, -e [syksɛ̃, -ɛ̃t] *adj* succinct
succinctement [syksɛ̃tmã] *adv* succinctly
succion [sysjɔ̃, syksjɔ̃] *nf* suction
succomber [sykɔ̃be] *vi* to succumb (**à** to); **s. sous le nombre** to yield to greater numbers
succulent, -e [sykylã, -ãt] *adj (nourriture)* succulent
succursale [sykyrsal] *nf* branch
sucer [syse] *vt* to suck
sucette [sysɛt] *nf* (**a**) *(confiserie)* lollipop (**b**) *(tétine) Br* dummy, *Am* pacifier
suçon [sysɔ̃] *nm Fam Br* lovebite, *Am* hickey
suçoter [sysɔte] *vt* to suck (at)
sucre [sykr] *nm* (**a**) *(aliment, morceau)* sugar; *Fig* **être tout s. tout miel** to be all sweetness and light; **s. candi** candy sugar; **s. de canne** cane sugar; **s. cristallisé** granulated sugar; **s. glace** *Br* icing or *Am* confectioner's sugar; **s. en morceaux/en poudre** lump/cas-

ter sugar; **s. roux** brown sugar; **s. semoule** caster sugar (**b**) **s. d'orge** *(substance)* barley sugar; *(bâton)* stick of barley sugar

sucré, -e [sykre] *adj* (**a**) *(naturellement)* sweet; *(additionné de sucre)* sweetened (**b**) *Fig (paroles, sourire)* sugary

sucrer [sykre] **1** *vt* (**a**) *(boisson)* to sugar; *(mets)* to sweeten; *Fam Fig* **s. les fraises** *(trembler)* to shake; *(être gâteux)* to be an old dodderer (**b**) *Fam (supprimer) (passage, émission)* to cut; **on lui a sucré sa prime** he has been deprived of his bonus
  2 *vi (miel, aspartame)* to sweeten
  3 se sucrer *vpr Fam* (**a**) *(prendre du sucre)* to help oneself to sugar (**b**) *(s'enrichir)* to line one's pockets

sucrerie [sykrəri] *nf* (**a**) *(usine)* sugar refinery (**b**) *(friandise)* **sucreries** sweet things

Sucrette® [sykrɛt] *nf* (artificial) sweetener

sucrier, -ère [sykrije, -ɛr] **1** *adj* sugar
  2 *nm* (**a**) *(récipient)* sugar bowl; *(verseur)* sugar shaker (**b**) *(fabricant)* sugar manufacturer

sud [syd] **1** *nm* south; **le vent du s.** the south wind; **dans le S. de l'Angleterre** in the South of England; **au s.** in the south; **au s. de** (to the) south of; **vers le s.** south, southward
  2 *adj inv* southern

sud-africain, -e *(mpl* **sud-africains,** *fpl* **sud-africaines)** [sydafrikɛ̃, ɛn] **1** *adj* South African
  2 *nm,f* **S.** South African

sud-américain, -e *(mpl* **sud-américains,** *fpl* **sud-américaines)** [sydamerikɛ̃, -ɛn] **1** *adj* South American
  2 *nm,f* **S.** South American

sud-coréen, -enne *(mpl* **sud-coréens,** *fpl* **sud-coréennes)** [sudkɔreɛ̃, -ɛn] **1** *adj* South Korean
  2 *nm,f* **S.** South Korean

sud-est [sydɛst] **1** *nm* south-east; **le S. asiatique** South-east Asia
  2 *adj inv* south-east

sudiste [sydist] *adj & nmf Hist* Confederate

sud-ouest [sydwɛst] *nm & adj inv* south-west

Suède [sɥɛd] *nf* **la S.** Sweden

suédine [sɥedin] *nf* suedette

suédois, -e [sɥedwa, -az] **1** *adj* Swedish
  2 *nm,f* **S.** Swede
  3 *nm (langue)* Swedish

suée [sɥe] *nf Fam* sweat; **prendre une s.** to work up a sweat

suer [sɥe] **1** *vi* (**a**) *(personne)* to sweat; **s. à grosses gouttes** to be pouring with sweat; *Fam* **faire s. qn** *(embêter)* to bug sb; *Fam* **se faire s.** to be bored stiff (**b**) *(mur)* to ooze (**c**) *Fig (travailler)* to labour, to sweat
  2 *vt (ennui, hypocrisie)* to ooze; **s. sang et eau** to sweat blood and tears

sueur [sɥœr] *nf* sweat; **être en s.** to be sweating or in a sweat; **avoir des sueurs froides** to be in a cold sweat; **à la s. de son front** by the sweat of one's brow

suffire [19b] [syfir] **1** *vi* to be enough, to be sufficient (**à/pour** for); **ça suffit!** that's enough!, that'll do!
  2 *v impersonnel* **il suffit d'appuyer sur le bouton** you just have to press the button; **il suffit que je sorte deux minutes pour que le téléphone sonne** I only have to go out for two minutes for the phone to start ringing; **il a suffi de quelques mots pour le persuader** a few words were enough to persuade him
  3 se suffire *vpr* **se s. (à soi-même)** to be self-sufficient

suffisamment [syfizamã] *adv* sufficiently, enough; **s. de** sufficient, enough

suffisance [syfizãs] *nf (vanité)* self-importance

suffisant, -e [syfizã, -ãt] *adj* (**a**) *(satisfaisant)* sufficient, enough (**b**) *(vaniteux)* self-important, conceited

suffixe [syfiks] *nm Gram & Ordinat* suffix

suffocant, -e [syfɔkã, -ãt] *adj* (**a**) *(chaleur)* suffocating, stifling (**b**) *Fig (nouvelle, réponse)* staggering, astounding

suffocation [syfɔkasjɔ̃] *nf* suffocation

suffoquer [syfɔke] **1** *vt* (**a**) *(sujet: odeur, fumée, chaleur)* to suffocate (**b**) *Fig (sujet: nouvelles)* to stagger, to astound
  2 *vi* to suffocate, to choke; *Fig* **s. de colère/d'indignation** to choke with anger/indignation

suffrage [syfraʒ] *nm (voix)* vote; *(système)* suffrage; **s. direct/indirect** direct/indirect suffrage; **s. universel** universal suffrage

suffragette [syfraʒɛt] *nf* suffragette

suggérer [syɡʒere] *vt* (**a**) *(proposer)* to suggest (**à** to); **s. de faire qch** to suggest doing sth; **s. à qn de faire qch** to suggest to sb that he/she should do sth (**b**) *(faire penser à)* to evoke

suggestif, -ive [syɡʒɛstif, -iv] *adj* (**a**) *(ton, musique)* evocative (**b**) *(plaisanterie, geste)* suggestive

suggestion [syɡʒɛstjɔ̃] *nf* suggestion

suicidaire [sɥisidɛr] **1** *adj* suicidal
  2 *nmf* suicidal person

suicide [sɥisid] *nm* suicide

suicidé, -e [sɥiside] **1** *adj* who has committed suicide
  2 *nm,f* suicide

suicider [sɥiside] **se suicider** *vpr* to commit suicide

suie [sɥi] *nf* soot

suif [sɥif] *nm* tallow

suintant, -e [sɥɛ̃tã, -ãt] *adj (rocher, mur)* oozing, dripping; *(plaie)* weeping

suintement [sɥɛ̃tmã] *nm (de rochers, de mur)* oozing, dripping; *(de plaie)* weeping

suinter [sɥɛ̃te] *vi* (**a**) *(rocher, mur)* to ooze, to drip; *(plaie)* to weep (**b**) *(liquide)* to ooze

suis *voir* être, suivre

Suisse [sɥis] *nf* **la S.** Switzerland; **la S. alémanique/ romande** German-speaking/French-speaking Switzerland

suisse [sɥis] **1** *adj* Swiss
  2 *nmf* **S.** Swiss (person); **les Suisses** the Swiss
  3 *nm* (**a**) *(employé d'église)* verger (**b**) *Can* chipmunk (**c**) *Fam Fig* **manger/boire qch en s.** to eat/drink sth without sharing it

Suissesse [sɥisɛs] *nf* Swiss (woman)

suit *voir* suivre

suite [sɥit] *nf* (**a**) *(reste)* rest (**de** of); **faire s. à qch** to follow on from sth; **s. à votre lettre du 10 mars** further to your letter of 10th March; **donner s. à** *(demande, lettre)* to follow up; *(commande)* to deal with; *(décision)* to give effect to; **prendre la s. de** *(personne)* to take over from; *(affaires)* to take over; **à la s. (les uns des autres)** one after the other; **à la s. de cette discussion** following this discussion (**b**) *(de roman, de film)* sequel; *(nouvel épisode)* continuation; **s. à la page 30** continued on page 30; **s. et fin** concluded; **la s. au prochain numéro** continued in the next issue (**c**) *(cohérence)* coherence; **sans s.** *(paroles, pensées)* incoherent; *(parler)* incoherently; **avoir de la s. dans**

les idées to be very single-minded (**d**) *(escorte) (d'un président)* suite; *(d'un monarque)* retinue (**e**) *(série)* series (**f**) *Math* series (**g**) *Mus* suite (**h**) *(conséquence)* consequence; **suites** *(de maladie)* aftereffects; **mourir des suites d'une blessure** to die as the result of an injury; **par s.** consequently; **par s. de qch** as a result of sth (**i**) *(appartement)* suite (**j**) *(locutions)* **de s.** in a row; **et ainsi de s.** and so on; **tout de s.**, *Fam* **de s.** right away, immediately; **par la s.** afterwards

suivant¹ [sɥivɑ̃] **1** *prép* (**a**) *(direction)* along (**b**) *(selon)* according to (**c**) *(conformément à)* **s. son habitude** as is/was his habit

2 *conj* **s. que** according to whether

suivant², -e [sɥivɑ̃, -ɑ̃t] **1** *adj* (**a**) *(page, jour)* next, following; **voir page 6 et suivantes** see page 6 and following; **notre méthode est la suivante** our method is as follows (**b**) *(personne)* next

2 *nm,f (prochain)* **le s., la suivante** the next (one); **au s.!** next!

3 *nf* **suivante** *(personnage de théâtre)* attendant

suiveur [sɥivœr] *nm* (**a**) *(personne sans initiative)* follower (**de** of) (**b**) *(dans une course cycliste)* **les suiveurs** = officials and back-up squads following a cycle race

suivi, -e [sɥivi] **1** *adj* (**a**) *(discours, raisonnement)* coherent (**b**) *(correspondance)* regular; *(travail, effort, qualité)* con-sistent (**c**) *(émission, feuilleton)* popular

2 *nm (d'un dossier)* follow-up; *(d'une procédure)* monitoring; **assurer le s. de qch** *(dossier)* to follow sth through; *(progrès, procédure)* to monitor

suivre [65] [sɥivr] **1** *vt* (**a**) *(aller derrière)* to follow; **nous sommes suivis** we're being followed; **partez, je vous suis** you go, I'll follow (on); **s. qn des yeux** *ou* **du regard** to follow sb with one's eyes

(**b**) *(se placer après)* to follow, to come after

(**c**) *(longer)* to go along, to follow

(**d**) *(accompagner)* to go with, to accompany

(**e**) *(ligne de conduite, conseil, intuition)* to follow; **s. son idée** to do things one's own way

(**f**) *(comprendre)* to follow; **là je ne la suis plus** she's lost me there

(**g**) *(faire attention à, observer) (propos, démonstration)* to follow; *(malade, élève)* to monitor the progress of; **suivez bien ce que je vais dire** pay attention to what I'm about to say; **c'est une affaire à s.** it's worth keeping an eye on

(**h**) *(mode, traitement, régime)* to follow; **s. le mouvement** to follow the crowd; **s. l'exemple de qn** to follow sb's example; **voici la marche à s.** this is what you have to do

(**i**) *(assister à) (série de concerts, de conférences)* to attend; *(cours)* to follow

2 *vi* (**a**) *(venir après)* to follow; **le reste du repas suit** the rest of the meal is coming; **les personnes dont les noms suivent** the following people; **faire s. une lettre** to forward a letter; **(prière de) faire s.** *(sur une enveloppe)* please forward; **faire s. ses bagages** to have one's luggage sent on; **à s.** *(à la fin d'un feuilleton)* to be continued

(**b**) *(comprendre)* to follow; *(faire attention)* to pay attention

(**c**) *(élève)* to keep up

(**d**) *Fig (progresser au même rythme) (salaire)* to keep up

3 se suivre *vpr* to follow each other

sujet¹, -ette [syʒɛ, -ɛt] **1** *adj* **être s. à qch** *(maladie)* to be subject *or* prone to sth; **être s. à caution** to be un-

confirmed; **être s. à faire qch** to be apt *or* liable to do sth

2 *nm,f (d'un monarque)* subject

sujet² *nm* (**a**) *(cause)* cause (**de** for); **s. de querelle** *ou* **dispute** cause for dispute; **avoir s. de se plaindre** to have cause for complaint (**b**) *(thème)* subject, topic; **changer de s.** to change the subject; **au s. de qn/qch** about sb/sth; **elle ne m'a rien dit à ce s.** she said nothing to me about it; **à ce s., je voulais vous dire que...** talking of which, I meant to tell you (that)... (**c**) *Gram & Ling* subject (**d**) *(individu)* individual; *Scol* **brillant s.** brilliant pupil (**e**) *(d'une expérience)* subject

sujétion [syʒesjɔ̃] *nf Litt* (**a**) *(servitude)* subjection (**à** to) (**b**) *(contrainte)* constraint

sulfate [sylfat] *nm* sulphate

sulfater [sylfate] *vt Agr & Ind* to sulphate

sulfure [sylfyr] *nm* sulphide

sulfureux, -euse [sylfyrø, -øz] *adj* (**a**) *(substance)* sulphurous; *(eau, source)* sulphur (**b**) *Fig (écrits, discours)* subversive; *(charme)* fiendish

sulfurique [sylfyrik] *adj* sulphuric

sulfurisé, -e [sylfyrize] *adj (papier)* greaseproof

sulky [sylki] *nm* sulky

sultan [syltɑ̃] *nm* sultan

sultanat [syltana] *nm* sultanate

sultane [syltan] *nf (épouse d'un sultan)* sultana, sultaness

summum [sɔmɔm] *nm* **le s. de** the height of

sumo [symo] *nm* sumo (wrestling)

sunnite [synit] *adj & nmf* Sunni

sup [syp] *adj inv Fam* **faire des heures s.** to work overtime

super [syper] **1** *adj inv & exclam Fam* great, terrific

2 *nm Br* four-star (petrol), *Am* premium gas; **s. sans plomb** *Br* four-star *or Am* premium unleaded

super- [syper] *préf Fam* very, *Br* dead, *Am* real

superbe [syperb] **1** *adj* (**a**) *(lieu, temps, spectacle)* superb, magnificent (**b**) *(personne)* beautiful

2 *nf Litt* pride, haughtiness

superbement [syperbəmɑ̃] *adv* superbly, magnificently

supercarburant [syperkarbyrɑ̃] *nm Br* four-star petrol, *Am* premium gasoline

supercherie [syperʃəri] *nf* deception, hoax

supérette [syperɛt] *nf* mini-market, small supermarket

superfétatoire [syperfetatwar] *adj Litt* superfluous

superficialité [syperfisjalite] *nf* superficiality

superficie [syperfisi] *nf* (**a**) *(étendue)* (surface) area (**b**) *(surface)* surface

superficiel, -elle [syperfisjɛl] *adj* superficial

superficiellement [syperfisjɛlmɑ̃] *adv* superficially

superflu, -e [syperfly] **1** *adj* superfluous

2 *nm* **le s.** the superfluous

super-géant [syperʒeɑ̃] *(pl* **super-géants**) *nm Sport* super-giant (slalom)

supergrand [sypergrɑ̃] *nm* superpower

super-huit [syperɥit] *adj inv & nm inv Cin* super-eight

supérieur, -e [syperjœr] **1** *adj* (**a**) *(plus haut)* upper; **on a dû évacuer les étages supérieurs** the upper floors had to be evacuated; **elle est à l'étage s.** she's on the floor above (**b**) *(plus grand)* superior (**à/en** to/in); **s. à la moyenne** above average (**c**) *(intelligence, esprit)* superior (**d**) *(dans une hiérarchie) (rang, grade)*

higher; *(cadre)* senior; **passer dans la classe supérieure** to go up into the class above (**e**) *(manières, ton)* superior, condescending
 2 *nm,f aussi Rel* superior
supérieurement [syperjœrmɑ̃] *adv* exceptionally
supériorité [syperjɔrite] *nf* superiority
superlatif, -ive [syperlatif, -iv] *adj & nm* superlative
supermarché [sypɛrmarʃe] *nm* supermarket
supernova [sypɛrnɔva] *(pl* **supernovae**) [sypɛrnɔve]) *nf* supernova
superpétrolier [sypɛrpetrɔlje] *nm* supertanker
superposable [sypɛrpozabl] *adj (caisses)* stacking; *(images)* superimposable
superposé, -e [sypɛrpoze] *adj (images)* superimposed
superposer [sypɛrpoze] **1** *vt (caisses)* to stack; *(images)* to superimpose (**à** on); *Ordinat* **s. une écriture** to overwrite
 2 se superposer *vpr (caisses, chaises)* to stack, to be stackable; *(images)* to be superimposed
superposition [sypɛrpozisjɔ̃] *nf (de caisses, de chaises)* stacking; *(d'images)* superimposition; *Ordinat* **mode de s. d'écriture** overwrite mode
superproduction [sypɛrprɔdyksjɔ̃] *nf* big-budget film
superpuissance [sypɛrpɥisɑ̃s] *nf* superpower
supersonique [sypɛrsɔnik] *adj* supersonic
superstar [sypɛrstar] *nf* superstar
superstitieux, -euse [sypɛrstisjø, -øz] *adj* superstitious
superstition [sypɛrstisjɔ̃] *nf* superstition
supertanker [sypɛrtɑ̃kœr] *nm* supertanker
superviser [sypɛrvize] *vt* to supervise; *Ordinat* to control
superviseur [sypɛrvizœr] *nm* supervisor; *Ordinat* **s. d'alimentation** power supply controller
supervision [sypɛrvizjɔ̃] *nf* supervision
supplanter [syplɑ̃te] *vt* to supplant, to supersede
suppléance [syplẽs] *nf Br* supply or *Am* substitute post
suppléant, -e [syplẽ, -ɑ̃t] **1** *adj (fonctionnaire)* acting, temporary; *(juge)* surrogate
 2 *nm,f* substitute, replacement (**de** for)
suppléer [syplee] **1** *vt* (**a**) *(personne)* to stand in for, to replace; **se faire s.** to be replaced (**b**) *Litt (manque)* to supply, to make up (for)
 2 suppléer à *vt ind* to make up for, to compensate for
supplément [syplemɑ̃] *nm* (**a**) *(surcroît)* **un s. de** *(information, travail)* additional, extra; **en s.** extra (**b**) *(de prix)* extra or additional charge; *(de billet de train)* supplement (**c**) *(livre, magazine)* supplement (**d**) *(de plat)* extra portion
supplémentaire [syplemɑ̃tɛr] *adj* additional, extra
suppliant, -e [syplijɑ̃, -ɑ̃t] *adj* imploring, pleading
supplication [syplikasjɔ̃] *nf* entreaty, plea
supplice [syplis] *nm* (**a**) *(torture)* torture (**b**) *(tourment, douleur)* torture, agony; **être au s.** to be in agony; **mettre qn au s.** to torture sb
supplicié, -e [syplisje] *nm,f* victim of torture
supplier [syplije] *vt* **s. qn de faire qch** to implore or beg sb to do sth; **je vous en supplie!** I beg you!
supplique [syplik] *nf* petition
support [sypɔr] *nm* (**a**) *(étai)* support (**b**) *(d'outils, de lampe)* stand (**c**) *Fig (de communication)* medium; **s. audiovisuel** audio-visual aid; **s. publicitaire** publicity

or advertising medium; **s. visuel** visual aid (**d**) *Ordinat* **s. d'affichage** billboard; **s. de sortie** output medium; **s. de souris** mouse support; **s. de stockage** storage medium
supportable [sypɔrtabl] *adj* (**a**) *(douleur)* bearable; *(comportement)* tolerable (**b**) *(acceptable)* reasonable
supporter¹ [sypɔrtɛr] *nm* supporter
supporter² [sypɔrte] **1** *vt* (**a**) *(résister à) (sujet: matériau, plante)* to withstand; **je supporte bien la chaleur** I can take the heat; **il ne supporterait pas le voyage** the journey would kill him; **je ne supporte pas l'aspirine/l'alcool** I can't take aspirin/alcohol (**b**) *(tolérer) (personne, situation)* to put up with; **je ne la supporte pas** I can't stand her; **il ne supporte pas qu'on le contredise** he can't stand or bear being contradicted (**c**) *(assumer) (conséquence, coût)* to bear (**d**) *(soutenir) (plafond, structure)* to support
 2 se supporter *vpr (l'un l'autre)* to put up with each other; **ils ne se supportent plus** they can't stand each other any more
supposé, -e [sypoze] *adj (voleur)* alleged; *(auteur)* supposed
supposer [sypoze] *vt* (**a**) *(imaginer)* to suppose, to assume (**que** that); **à s. que...** + *subjunctive* suppose or supposing that...; **on suppose que...** it's thought that...; **être supposé faire qch** to be supposed to do sth (**b**) *(impliquer)* to imply (**que** that)
supposition [sypozisjɔ̃] *nf* supposition, assumption
suppositoire [sypozitwar] *nm* suppository
suppôt [sypo] *nm* henchman; **s. de Satan** fiend
suppression [sypresjɔ̃] *nf* (**a**) *(de loi, d'impôt)* abolition; *(de train)* cancellation; *(de crédits, d'emploi, de service)* axing (**b**) *(de mot, de phrase)* deletion (**c**) *Jur (de document)* suppression
supprimer [syprime] **1** *vt* (**a**) *(loi, impôt)* to abolish; *(autobus, train)* to cancel; *(financement, crédits)* to withdraw; *(emploi, service)* to axe; *(mot, phrase)* to delete (**b**) *Jur (document)* to suppress (**c**) *(sucre, sel)* to cut out (**de** from) (**d**) *(ôter)* **s. qch à qn** to take sth away from sb (**e**) *(tuer)* to do away with
 2 se supprimer *vpr* to do away with oneself
suppurer [sypyrɛ] *vi* to suppurate
supputation [sypytasjɔ̃] *nf* calculation
supputer [sypyte] *vt* to calculate
supranational, -e, -aux, -ales [sypranasjɔnal, -o] *adj* supranational
supranationalité [sypranasjɔnalite] *nf* supranationality
suprématie [sypremasi] *nf* supremacy
suprême [syprɛm] **1** *adj* (**a**) *(effort, bonheur)* supreme (**b**) *(dernier)* final, last
 2 *nm Culin* **s. de volaille** chicken supreme
suprêmement [sypremmɑ̃] *adv* supremely
sur¹ [syr] *prép* (**a**) *(dessus)* on; *(avec mouvement)* on, onto; **s. la photo** in the picture; **regarder s. la carte** to look at the map; **la clef est s. la porte** the key's in the door; *aussi Fig* **les uns s. les autres** on top of each other
 (**b**) *(au-dessus de)* over, above; **un pont s. une rivière** a bridge over or across a river
 (**c**) *(vers)* towards; **fenêtre qui donne s. le jardin** window which looks onto the garden; **la police a tiré s. la foule** the police fired at the crowd; **s. la droite/gauche** on or to the right/left
 (**d**) *(à propos de)* on, about; **savoir qch s. qn** to know sth about sb

(**e**) *(parmi)* out of; **7 s. 10** 7 out of 10; **une fois s. deux** every other time; **une femme s. deux** one in two women
(**f**) *(mesure)* by; **10 mètres s. 2** 10 metres by 2; **virages s. 2 kilomètres** *(sur un panneau)* bends for 2 kilometres
(**g**) *(avec)* **vivre s. ses économies** to live on *or* off one's savings; **s. des paroles de Prévert/une musique des Beatles** to words by Prévert/Beatles music; **ne me parle pas s. ce ton!** don't talk to me in that tone of voice!
sur², -e *adj (fruit)* sour
sur- [syr] *préf* over-
sûr, -e [syr] **1** *adj* (**a**) *(lieu)* safe; **peu s.** unsafe (**b**) *(digne de confiance) (personne, mémoire)* trustworthy, reliable; *(ami)* true; *(information, entreprise, goût)* reliable (**c**) *(certain)* sure, certain (**de** of); **je suis s. de te l'avoir dit** I'm sure I told you; **s. de soi** self-assured; **être s. et certain (de qch)** to be absolutely certain (of sth)
2 *nm* **le plus s. serait de...** the safest thing would be to...
surabondance [syrabɔ̃dɑ̃s] *nf* overabundance; **une s. de richesses/de détails** a wealth of riches/details
surabondant, -e [syrabɔ̃dɑ̃, -ɑ̃t] *adj* overabundant
surabonder [syrabɔ̃de] *vi* to be overabundant
suractivé, -e [syraktive] *adj* superactivated
surajouter [syraʒute] **1** *vt* to add (on)
2 se surajouter *vpr* to be added (on)
suralimentation [syralimɑ̃tasjɔ̃] *nf (de personne)* overfeeding; *(de malade)* feeding up
suralimenter [syralimɑ̃te] *vt (personne)* to overfeed; *(malade)* to feed up
suranné, -e [syrane] *adj* outdated, old-fashioned
surarmement [syrarməmɑ̃] *nm* excessive arms build-up
surbooker [syrbuke] *vt* to overbook
surcapacité [syrkapasite] *nf* overcapacity
surcharge [syrʃarʒ] *nf* (**a**) *(poids) (de bagages)* excess weight; *(de véhicule)* excess load; **prendre des passagers en s.** to take on excess passengers; **rouler en s.** to drive an overloaded vehicle; *Méd* **s. pondérale** excess weight (**b**) *(action) (de véhicule)* overloading (**c**) *(d'accumulateur électrique)* overcharge (**d**) *Fig* **une s. de travail** excess work (**e**) *(à payer)* surcharge (**f**) *(correction)* correction
surcharger [syrʃarʒe] *vt* (**a**) *(véhicule, cheval, estomac)* to overload; **s. qn de travail** to overload sb with work (**b**) *(accumulateur électrique)* to overcharge (**c**) *(épreuves, texte)* to write over with corrections
surchauffe [syrʃof] *nf* overheating
surchauffer [syrʃofe] *vt & vi* to overheat
surchoix [syrʃwa] *adj inv* top-quality
surclasser [syrklase] *vt* to outclass
surconsommation [syrkɔ̃sɔmasjɔ̃] *nf* overconsumption
surcroît [syrkrwa] *nm* **un s. de travail/dépenses** extra work/expenditure; **par s., de s.** in addition, moreover
surdéveloppé, -e [syrdevlɔpe] *adj* overdeveloped
surdéveloppement [syrdevlɔpmɑ̃] *nm* overdevelopment
surdimensionné, -e [syrdimɑ̃sjɔne] *adj* oversized
surdiplômé, -e [syrdiplome] *adj* overqualified
surdité [syrdite] *nf* deafness
surdose [syrdoz] *nf* overdose

surdoué, -e [syrdwe] **1** *adj* gifted
2 *nm,f* gifted child
sureau, -x [syro] *nm* elder (tree)
sureffectif [syrefɛktif] *nm* overmanning; **en s.** surplus
surélevé, -e [syrelve] *adj* (**a**) *(voie ferrée)* elevated (**b**) *(arche, rez-de-chaussée)* raised
surélever [syrelve] *vt* to heighten, to raise
sûrement [syrmɑ̃] *adv* (**a**) *(probablement)* probably (**b**) *(absolument)* **s.!** certainly!; **s. pas!** certainly not! (**c**) *(sans risque)* safely
suremploi [syrɑ̃plwa] *nm* overemployment
surenchère [syrɑ̃ʃɛr] *nf (dans une vente)* higher bid; *Fig* **faire de la s.** to try to outdo one's rivals
surenchérir [syrɑ̃ʃerir] *vi* to bid higher; **s. sur qn** to outbid sb; *Fig* to go one further than sb
surencombré, -e [syrɑ̃kɔ̃bre] *adj* congested (**de** with)
surendetté, -e [syrɑ̃dɛte] *adj* overindebted
surendettement [syrɑ̃dɛtmɑ̃] *nm* overindebtedness
surentraîner [syrɑ̃trɛne] *vt* to overtrain
suréquipement [syrekipmɑ̃] *nm* overequipment
suréquiper [syrekipe] *vt* to overequip
surestimer [syrɛstime] **1** *vt* (**a**) *(importance, capacité, personne)* to overestimate (**b**) *(œuvre d'art)* to overvalue
2 se surestimer *vpr* to overestimate oneself
sûreté [syrte] *nf* (**a**) *(absence de danger)* safety; **être en s.** to be safe; **mettre qch en s.** to put sth in a safe place; **pour plus de s.** to be on the safe side; **de s.** *(rasoir, épingle)* safety (**b**) *(du goût, du jugement)* soundness (**c**) *(d'un pays)* security; **la s. de l'État** national security
surévaluation [syrevalɥasjɔ̃] *nf* overvaluation
surévaluer [syrevalɥe] *vt (objet, antiquité)* to overvalue; *(efficacité, capacités)* to overestimate
surexcitation [syrɛksitasjɔ̃] *nf* overexcitement
surexciter [syrɛksite] *vt* to overexcite
surexploiter [syrɛksplwate] *vt* to overexploit
surexposer [syrɛkspoze] *vt* to overexpose
surexposition [syrɛkspozisjɔ̃] *nf* overexposure
surf [sœrf] *nm* surfing; **faire du s.** to go surfing, to surf
surface [syrfas] *nf* (**a**) *(partie extérieure)* surface; **en s.** on the surface; *Fig* superficially; **remonter à la s.** to rise to the surface, to surface; **faire s.** *(remonter, se réveiller)* to surface (**b**) *(étendue)* (surface) area; **grande s.** hypermarket; **s. de réparation** *(au football)* penalty area; **s. au sol** floor area; **s. utile** floor space; **s. de vente** sales area (**c**) *Ordinat* **s. d'affichage** display area; **s. d'enregistrement** read-write surface
surfait, -e [syrfɛ, -ɛt] *adj* overrated
surfer [sœrfe] *vi* to surf; **s. sur l'Internet** to surf the Net *or* the Internet
surfeur, -euse [sœrfœr, -øz] *nm,f* surfer
surfiler [syrfile] *vt (vêtement)* to overcast, to oversew
surfin, -e [syrfɛ̃, -in] *adj* superfine
surgé [syrʒe] *nmf Fam* head supervisor *(person in charge of school discipline)*
surgelé, -e [syrʒəle] **1** *adj* frozen
2 *nmpl* **surgelés** frozen foods
surgeler [syrʒəle] *vt* to freeze
surgénérateur [syrʒeneratœr] *nm* breeder reactor
surgir [syrʒir] *vi (personne)* to appear suddenly; *(difficulté)* to crop up
surhomme [syrɔm] *nm* superman

surhumain, -e [syrymɛ̃, -ɛn] *adj* superhuman
surimposer [syrɛ̃poze] *vt* to overtax
surimposition [syrɛ̃pozisjɔ̃] *nf* overtaxation
surimpression [syrɛ̃presjɔ̃] *nf* (**a**) *(d'images)* super-imposition; **en s.** superimposed (**b**) *Ordinat* over-printing, overstrike
Surinam(e) [syrinam] *nm* **le S.** Surinam
surinfection [syrɛ̃fɛksjɔ̃] *nf* secondary infection
surinformation [syrɛ̃fɔrmasjɔ̃] *nf* information over-load
surinformé, -e [syrɛ̃fɔrme] *adj* overinformed
surinvestissement [syrɛ̃vɛstismã] *nm Fin & Psy* overinvestment
sur-le-champ [syrləʃã] *adv* at once, immediately
surlendemain [syrlãdmɛ̃] *nm* **le s.** two days later; **le s. de leur départ** two days after they left
surligner [syrliɲe] *vt* to highlight
surligneur [syrliɲœr] *nm* highlighter (pen)
surlouer [syrlwe] *vt* to overbook
surmédiatisation [syrmedjatizasjɔ̃] *nf* excessive media coverage
surmédiatiser [syrmedjatize] *vt* to give excessive media coverage to
surmenage [syrmənaʒ] *nm* overwork; **s. intellectuel** mental strain
surmené, -e [syrməne] *adj* overworked
surmener [syrməne] **1** *vt* to overwork
2 se surmener *vpr* to overdo it
surmonter [syrmɔ̃te] **1** *vt* (**a**) *(être placé sur)* to sur-mount (**b**) *Fig (obstacle, difficulté)* to overcome
2 se surmonter *vpr* to control oneself
surnager [syrnaʒe] *vi* to float (on the surface)
surnaturel, -elle [syrnatyrɛl] **1** *adj* supernatural
2 *nm* **le s.** the supernatural
surnom [syrnɔ̃] *nm* nickname
surnombre [syrnɔ̃br] *nm* **il y avait trois passagers en s.** there were three passengers too many; **les exem-plaires/passagers en s.** the excess copies/passen-gers
surnommer [syrnɔme] *vt* to nickname
surpasser [syrpase] **1** *vt (rival)* to surpass, to outdo
2 se surpasser *vpr* to surpass *or* excel oneself
surpayer [syrpeje] *vt (personne)* to overpay; *(activité)* to pay too much for
surpeuplé, -e [syrpœple] *adj (pays, région)* over-populated; *(plage)* overcrowded
surpeuplement [syrpœpləmã] *nm (de pays, de ré-gion)* overpopulation; *(de plage)* overcrowding
surplace [syrplas] *nm* **faire du s.** *(cycliste)* to do a track stand; *Fig (automobiliste)* to crawl along; *(dans une carrière, dans des négociations)* to make no head-way
surplomb [syrplɔ̃] *nm* overhang; **en s.** overhanging
surplomber [syrplɔ̃be] *vt* to overhang
surplus [syrply] *nm* surplus; **le s. de marchandises** the surplus goods, the goods that are left (over)
surpopulation [syrpɔpylasjɔ̃] *nf* overpopulation
surprenant, -e [syrprənã, -ãt] *adj* surprising; **et, chose surprenante...** and surprisingly...
surprendre [syrprãdr] **1** *vt* (**a**) *(prendre par surprise)* to surprise; **s. qn en train de faire qch** to catch sb doing sth; **être surpris par la pluie** to be caught in the rain (**b**) *(découvrir) (conversation)* to overhear; *(regard)* to catch (**c**) *(étonner)* to surprise; **cela me surprendrait qu'il revienne** *ou* **s'il revenait** I'd be sur-prised if he came back
2 se surprendre *vpr* **se s. à faire qch** to find oneself doing sth
surpris, -e [syrpri, -iz] *adj* surprised; **être s. de qch/ de faire qch** to be surprised at sth/to do sth
surprise [syrpriz] *nf* surprise; **à sa grande s.** to his great surprise, much to his surprise; **à la s. générale** to everyone's surprise; **sans s.** *(expédition, voyage)* uneventful; **prendre qn par s.** to take sb by surprise
surprise-partie *(pl* **surprises-parties)** [syrprizparti] *nf Vieilli* party
surproduction [syrprɔdyksjɔ̃] *nf* overproduction
surqualifié, -e [syrkalifje] *adj* overqualified
surréalisme [syrrealism] *nm* surrealism
surréaliste [syrrealist] *adj & nmf* surrealist
sursaut [syrso] *nm* (**a**) *(mouvement)* start, jump; **en s.** with a start (**b**) *(regain) (d'énergie)* burst
sursauter [syrsote] *vi* to start, to jump; **faire s. qn** to make sb jump, to startle sb
surseoir [10b] [syrswar] **surseoir à** *vt ind (jugement)* to suspend; **s. à l'exécution d'un condamné** to reprieve a condemned man
sursis [syrsi] *nm* (**a**) *(d'exécution) & Fig* reprieve; **un an de prison avec s.** a one-year suspended sentence (**b**) *(de conscrit)* deferment of call-up
sursitaire [syrsitɛr] **1** *adj (conscrit)* provisionally ex-empted
2 *nm* provisionally exempted conscript
surtaxe [syrtaks] *nf (de lettre)* surcharge
surtout [syrtu] *adv* (**a**) *(particulièrement)* particularly, especially; *Fam* **s. que...** especially as... (**b**) *(avant tout)* above all; **s. pas!** certainly not!
surveillance [syrvɛjãs] *nf (de travail, d'élèves)* super-vision; *(par la police, par un gardien)* surveillance, ob-servation; *(de malade, de phénomène)* watch; **être sous s.** to be under surveillance; **s. médicale** medical supervision
surveillant, -e [syrvɛjã, -ãt] *nm,f* (**a**) *(d'une prison)* guard, *Br* warder (**b**) *(d'un hôpital)* supervisor (**c**) *Scol (pendant les examens)* invigilator; *(chargé de la disci-pline)* supervisor
surveiller [syrveje] **1** *vt* (**a**) *(contrôler) (travail, élèves)* to supervise; *(température, cuisson)* to keep a watch on; *(examen)* to invigilate (**b**) *(prendre soin de)* to watch (over) (**c**) *(situation)* to keep an eye on; **s. son langage** to watch *or* mind one's language; **s. sa ligne** to watch one's figure
2 se surveiller *vpr* to keep a watch on oneself
survenir [syrvənir] *vi (événements)* to occur; *(crise, difficulté)* to arise
survêt [syrvɛt] *nm Fam* = **survêtement**
survêtement [syrvɛtmã] *nm* tracksuit
survie [syrvi] *nf* survival
survivance [syrvivãs] *nf (vestige)* survival, relic
survivant, -e [syrvivã, -ãt] **1** *adj* surviving
2 *nm,f* survivor
survivre [syrvivr] **survivre à** *vt ind (personne)* to sur-vive, to outlive; *(période, théorie)* to outlive; *(accident, maladie)* to survive
survol [syrvɔl] *nm* (**a**) **le s. d'un lieu** flying over a place (**b**) *Fig (de problème, de question)* cursory glance (**de** at)
survoler [syrvɔle] *vt* (**a**) *(lieu)* to fly over (**b**) *Fig (pro-blème, question)* to skim over

survolté, -e [syrvɔlte] *adj Fam (personne)* overexcited; *(ambiance)* highly charged

sus [sys, sy] **1** *exclam* **s. à l'ennemi!** at them!
    2 *adv* **en s.** in addition; **en s. de** in addition to, over and above

susceptibilité [sysεptibilite] *nf* touchiness, sensitivity; **ménager la s. de qn** to tread carefully where sb is concerned

susceptible [sysεptibl] *adj* (**a**) *(ombrageux)* touchy, sensitive (**b**) **s. de** *(interprétations, critiques)* open to; **être s. de faire qch** to be liable *or* likely to do sth

susciter [sysite] *vt (ennuis, problèmes)* to cause, to create; *(étonnement)* to cause; *(hostilité, intérêt)* to arouse; *(admiration, commentaires)* to attract

susdit, -e [sysdi, -it] *adj* aforesaid, above-mentioned

susmentionné, -e [sysmɑ̃sjɔne] *adj* above-mentioned, aforesaid

susnommé, -e [sysnɔme] *adj & nm,f* above-named

suspect, -e [syspε(kt), -εkt] **1** *adj (personne, action)* suspicious, suspect; *(idées, preuve, aliment)* suspect; **s. de qch** suspected of sth
    2 *nm,f* suspect

suspecter [syspεkte] *vt (personne)* to suspect (**de** of); *(sincérité)* to suspect, to question

suspendre [syspɑ̃dr] **1** *vt* (**a**) *(vêtements, tableau, hamac)* to hang (up); **s. qch au mur/au plafond** to hang sth on the wall/from the ceiling (**b**) *(interrompre)* to suspend; *(séance)* to adjourn (**c**) *(démettre de ses fonctions)* to suspend
    2 se suspendre *vpr* to hang (**à** from)

suspendu, -e [syspɑ̃dy] *adj* (**a**) *(pendu)* hanging; **s. au mur/au plafond** hanging on the wall/from the ceiling; *Fig* **être s. aux lèvres de qn** to be hanging on sb's every word (**b**) *(interrompu)* suspended; *(séance)* adjourned

suspens [syspɑ̃] **en suspens** *adv* (**a**) *(en l'air)* suspended (**b**) *(en attente)* outstanding

suspense [syspεns] *nm* suspense

suspension [syspɑ̃sjɔ̃] *nf* (**a**) *(de négociations, d'un travail)* suspension; *(d'une séance)* adjournment (**b**) *(retrait)* **s. du permis de conduire** driving ban (**c**) *(mise à pied)* suspension (**d**) *(de voiture)* suspension

suspicieux, -euse [syspisjø, -øz] *adj* suspicious

suspicion [syspisjɔ̃] *nf* suspicion

sustenter [systɑ̃te] **se sustenter** *vpr Hum* to take sustenance

susurrer [sysyre] *vt & vi* to whisper, to murmur

suture [sytyr] *nf* suture; **point de s.** stitch

suzerain, -e [syzrɛ̃, -εn] *nm,f* suzerain

svastika [svastika] *nm* swastika

svelte [svεlt] *adj* slender

sveltesse [svεltεs] *nf* slenderness

SVP [εsvepe] *(abrév* **s'il vous plaît)** please

swahili, -e [swaili] **1** *adj* Swahili
    2 *nm (langue)* Swahili

Swaziland [swazilɑ̃d] *nm* **le S.** Swaziland

sweat-shirt *(pl* **sweat-shirts)** [switʃœrt, swεtʃœrt] *nm* sweatshirt

swing [swiŋ] *nm* swing

swinguer [swiŋge] *vi* to swing

sycomore [sikɔmɔr] *nm* sycamore (tree)

syllabe [silab] *nf* syllable

syllabique [silabik] *adj* syllabic

sylphide [silfid] *nf* sylph

sylvestre [silvεstr] *adj* woodland, sylvan

sylviculture [silvikyltyr] *nf* forestry

symbiose [sɛ̃bjoz] *nf* symbiosis; *Fig* **en s. avec qn/qch** in harmony with sb/sth

symbole [sɛ̃bɔl] *nm* symbol

symbolique [sɛ̃bɔlik] **1** *adj* symbolic; *(paiement, geste)* token
    2 *nf (système de symboles)* system of symbols

symboliquement [sɛ̃bɔlikmɑ̃] *adv* symbolically

symboliser [sɛ̃bɔlize] *vt* to symbolize

symbolisme [sɛ̃bɔlism] *nm* symbolism

symétrie [simetri] *nf* symmetry

symétrique [simetrik] *adj* symmetrical

symétriquement [simetrikmɑ̃] *adv* symmetrically

sympa [sɛ̃pa] *adj Fam* nice

sympathie [sɛ̃pati] *nf* (**a**) *(affinité)* liking; **avoir** *ou* **éprouver de la s. pour qn** to like sb; **inspirer la s. to** be likable (**b**) *(compassion, condoléances)* sympathy

sympathique [sɛ̃patik] *adj* (**a**) *(agréable)* nice (**b**) *Anat* sympathetic

sympathisant, -e [sɛ̃patizɑ̃, -ɑ̃t] *nm,f* sympathizer

sympathiser [sɛ̃patize] *vi* to get on well (**avec** with)

symphonie [sɛ̃fɔni] *nf* symphony

symphonique [sɛ̃fɔnik] *adj (forme, poème)* symphonic; *(orchestre)* symphony

symposium [sɛ̃pozjɔm] *nm* symposium

symptomatique [sɛ̃ptɔmatik] *adj* symptomatic (**de** of)

symptôme [sɛ̃ptom] *nm* symptom

synagogue [sinagɔg] *nf* synagogue

synchrone [sɛ̃kron] *adj* synchronous (**avec** with)

synchronisation [sɛ̃krɔnizasjɔ̃] *nf* synchronization

synchroniser [sɛ̃krɔnize] *vt* to synchronize (**avec** with)

synclinal, -e, -aux, -ales [sɛ̃klinal, -o] *adj* synclinal

syncope [sɛ̃kɔp] *nf* (**a**) *(perte de connaissance)* blackout; **tomber en s.** to black out; *Fam* **elle a failli avoir une s.** she nearly fainted (**b**) *Mus* syncopation

syncopé, -e [sɛ̃kɔpe] *adj Mus* syncopated

syndic [sɛ̃dik] *nm* **s. (de copropriété)** property manager

> **Syndic**
> A "syndic" is an administrative body which represents the interests of the owners of all the flats in a building, collectively known as the "syndicat de copropriété". The role of the "syndic" is to ensure the upkeep of the building and to organize meetings during which a vote is taken on any repairs, improvements etc, that are deemed necessary. The services of the "syndic" are paid for by the owners of the flats.

syndical, -e, -aux, -ales [sɛ̃dikal, -o] *adj (Br* trade *or Am* labor) union

syndicaliser [sɛ̃dikalize] = **syndiquer**

syndicalisme [sɛ̃dikalism] *nm* (**a**) *(mouvement) Br* trade *or Am* labor unionism (**b**) *(activité)* **faire du s.** to be involved in union activities

syndicaliste [sɛ̃dikalist] **1** *adj Br* (trade) union, *Am* (labor) union
    2 *nmf Br* trade *or Am* labor unionist

syndicat [sɛ̃dika] *nm* (**a**) *(de travailleurs) (Br* trade *or Am* labor) union (**b**) *(d'employeurs, de producteurs)* association; **s. patronal** employers' association (**c**) **s. d'initiative** tourist (information) office

syndiqué, -e [sẽdike] **1** *adj* belonging to a (*Br* trade *or Am* labor) union; **être s.** to belong to a (*Br* trade *or Am* labor) union
  2 *nm,f* (*Br* trade *or Am* labor) union member
syndiquer [sẽdike] **1** *vt* to unionize
  2 se syndiquer *vpr* (**a**) *(se constituer en syndicat)* to form a (*Br* trade *or Am* labor) union (**b**) *(adhérer à un syndicat)* to join a (*Br* trade *or Am* labor) union
syndrome [sẽdrom] *nm* syndrome
synergie [sinɛrʒi] *nf* synergy
synode [sinɔd] *nm* synod
synonyme [sinɔnim] **1** *adj* synonymous (**de** with)
  2 *nm* synonym
synopsis [sinɔpsis] *nm Cin* synopsis
synovial, -e, -aux, -ales [sinɔvjal, -o] *adj* synovial
syntagme [sẽtagm] *nm* phrase
syntaxe [sẽtaks] *nf Gram & Ordinat* syntax
syntaxique [sẽtaksik] *adj* (**a**) *Gram* syntactic (**b**) *Ordinat* syntax
synthèse [sẽtɛz] *nf* (**a**) *(exposé)* summary; **faire la s. (de qch)** to summarize (sth) (**b**) *(opération chimique)* synthesis; **de s.** synthetic

synthétique [sẽtetik] **1** *adj* (**a**) *(présentation)* all-encompassing; *(bilan)* summary (**b**) *(tissu, fibres)* synthetic, man-made
  2 *nm* synthetic material
synthétiser [sẽtetize] *vt* to synthesize
synthétiseur [sẽtetizœr] *nm* synthesizer
syphilis [sifilis] *nf* syphilis
syphilitique [sifilitik] *adj & nmf* syphilitic
Syrie [siri] *nf* **la S.** Syria
syrien, -enne [sirjẽ, -ɛn] **1** *adj* Syrian
  2 *nm,f* **S.** Syrian
systématique [sistematik] **1** *adj* *(automatique, méthodique)* systematic; **il est toujours en retard, c'est s.** he's consistently late
systématiquement [sistematikmã] *adv* systematically
systématiser [sistematize] *vt* to systematize
système [sistɛm] *nm* system; *Fam* **il me tape** *ou* **porte sur le s.** he gets on my nerves; **s. D** resourcefulness; *Ordinat* **s. d'exploitation** operating system; *Ordinat* **s. de gestion de bases de données** database management system; **s. nerveux** nervous system; **s. solaire** solar system

T

T, t [te] *nm inv* T, t; **en T** T-shaped; **disposer qch en T** to arrange sth in a T-shape

t' [t] *voir* **te, tu**

ta [ta] *voir* **ton¹**

tabac¹ [taba] **1** *nm* (**a**) *(plante, produit)* tobacco; *Fam Fig* **du même t.** of the same ilk; **t. blond** Virginia tobacco; **t. brun** dark tobacco; **t. à chiquer** chewing tobacco; **t. à priser** snuff (**b**) *(boutique)* **(bureau de) t.** *Br* tobacconist's (shop), *Am* tobacco store *(which also sells stamps, phonecards and lottery tickets)*
2 *adj inv* buff

tabac² *nm* **coup de t.** *(tempête)* squall; *Fam* **passer qn à t.** to beat sb up; *Fam* **faire un t.** to be a big hit

tabagie [tabaʒi] *nf* (**a**) *Fam* **c'est une vraie t. ici** you can't see a thing for the smoke in here (**b**) *Can (bureau de tabac) Br* tobacconist's (shop), *Am* tobacco store

tabagisme [tabaʒism] *nm* smoking

tabasser [tabase] *vt Fam* **t. qn** to beat sb up; **se faire t.** to be *or* get beaten up

tabatière [tabatjɛr] *nf* (**a**) *(boîte)* snuffbox (**b**) *(lucarne)* skylight

tabelle [tabɛl] *nf Suisse* register, list

tabernacle [tabɛrnakl] *nm* tabernacle

tablar(d) [tablar] *nm Suisse* shelf

table [tabl] *nf* (**a**) *(meuble)* table; **mettre** *ou* **dresser la t.** to lay *or* set the table; **être à t.** to be at the table; **se mettre** *ou* **passer à t.** to sit down at the table; *Fam Fig* **se mettre à t.** *(avouer)* to spill the beans; **à t.!** food's ready!; *Fig* **faire t. rase de qch** to make a clean sweep of sth; **t. basse** coffee table; **t. de billard** billiard table; **t. de chevet** bedside table; **t. de cuisson** hob; **t. à dessin** drawing board; **faire t. d'hôte** = to provide a meal where all paying guests eat at the same table; **t. de jeu** card table; **t. à langer** changing table; **t. des négociations** negotiating table; **s'asseoir à la t. des négociations** to get round the negotiating table; **t. de nuit** bedside table; **t. d'opération** operating table; **t. d'orientation** orientation *or* panoramic table; **t. à repasser** ironing board; **t. ronde** *(conférence)* round table; **t. roulante** trolley (**b**) *(restaurant)* **les meilleures tables de Paris** the finest restaurants in Paris (**c**) *(écrit)* table; **Tables de la Loi** Tables of the Law; **t. des matières** (table of) contents; **t. de multiplication** multiplication table (**d**) *(console)* **mettre qn sur t. d'écoute** to tap sb's phone; **il est sur t. d'écoute** his phone is being tapped; **t. de mixage** mixing desk (**e**) *(d'un instrument à cordes)* **t. d'harmonie** sounding board (**f**) *Ordinat* **t. à digitaliser** digitizing pad; **t. des fichiers** file allocation table, FAT; **t. traçante** plotter

tableau, -x [tablo] *nm* (**a**) *(panneau, support)* board; **t. (noir)** (black)board; **t. d'affichage** *Br* notice *or Am* bulletin board; **t. de bord** *(d'une voiture)* dashboard; *(d'un avion)* instrument panel; *Ordinat* control panel (**b**) *(œuvre d'art)* painting, picture; **t. de maître** old master (**c**) *Fig & Hum (scène)* scene; **faire un joli/charmant t.** to make a pretty/charming sight *or* scene; *Fig* **pour compléter le t. ...** to crown it all ... (**d**) *(au théâtre)* scene; **t. vivant** tableau (vivant) (**e**) *(liste)* list, table; *(graphique)* chart; **t. de chasse** *(de chasseur, d'aviateur)* bag; *Fig (conquêtes)* list of conquests (**f**) *Ordinat* **t. de connexions** plugboard (**g**) *(locutions)* **gagner sur les deux/sur tous les tableaux** to win on both/all counts

tablée [table] *nf (personnes à table)* table

tabler [table] **tabler sur** *vt ind* to count *or* bank on

tablette [tablɛt] *nf* (**a**) *(d'une étagère)* shelf; *(dans un avion)* table; **t. arrière** *(d'une voiture)* back shelf (**b**) *(de chocolat)* bar; *(de chewing-gum)* stick (**c**) *Ordinat* **t. graphique** graphics tablet

tableur [tablœr] *nm Ordinat* spreadsheet; **t. de graphiques** graphics spreadsheet

tablier [tablije] *nm* (**a**) *(vêtement)* apron; *(d'écolier)* smock; *Fig* **rendre son t.** to hand in one's notice (**b**) *(de cheminée)* hood (**c**) *(de pont)* roadway

tabloïd(e) [tabloid] *adj & nm* tabloid

tabou, -e [tabu] *adj & nm* taboo

taboulé [tabule] *nm* tabbouleh

tabouret [taburɛ] *nm* stool; **t. de bar/de piano** bar/piano stool

tabulateur [tabylatœr] *nm* tab key, tabulator

tabulation [tabylasjɔ̃] *nf* tab

tac [tak] **du tac au tac** *adv* like a shot

tache [taʃ] *nf* (**a**) *(de boue, de sang, d'huile)* stain; *(de peinture, de couleur, de lumière)* splash; **tu as fait une t. à ta chemise** you've got a stain on your shirt; *Fig* **faire t.** to stick out like a sore thumb; **t. d'encre** inkstain; *Fig* **faire t. d'huile** to spread (**b**) *(sur la peau, sur un fruit)* mark; **t. de rousseur** freckle; **t. de vin** strawberry mark (**c**) *Fig (atteinte)* blot, stain; **sans t.** *(réputation)* spotless

taché, -e [taʃe] *adj* stained; **t. d'encre/de sang** ink-/blood-stained

tâche [taʃ] *nf* task, job; **être à la t.** to be on piecework; *Ordinat* **t. d'arrière-plan** *ou* **de fond** background task *or* job

tacher [taʃe] **1** *vt* (**a**) *(vêtement)* to stain (**b**) *(réputation)* to sully, to tarnish
2 *vi* to stain
3 **se tacher** *vpr (personne)* to stain one's clothes; *(tissu, vêtement)* to stain

tâcher [tɑʃe] **1** *vt* **tâchez que cela ne se reproduise plus** make sure it doesn't happen again
2 tâcher de *vt ind* to try to
tâcheron [tɑʃrɔ̃] *nm Péj* drudge
tacheté, -e [taʃte] *adj* speckled (**de** with); **chat noir t. de blanc** black cat with white markings
tacheter [taʃte] *vt* to spot, to speckle
tachycardie [takikardi] *nf* tachycardia
tachymètre [takimɛtr] *nm* tachometer; *Aut* speed-ometer
tacite [tasit] *adj* tacit
tacitement [tasitmã] *adv* tacitly
taciturne [tasityrn] *adj* taciturn
tacot [tako] *nm Fam Péj* jalopy, *Br* banger
tact [takt] *nm* tact; **avoir du t.** to be tactful; **plein de t.** very tactful; **manquer de t.** to be tactless
tacticien, -enne [taktisjɛ̃, -ɛn] *nm,f* tactician
tactile [taktil] *adj* tactile
tactique [taktik] **1** *adj* tactical
2 *nf* tactics *(pluriel)*
tadjik [tadʒik] **1** *adj* Tadjik
2 *nmf* **T.** Tadjik
Tadjikistan [tadʒikistã] *nm* **le T.** Tadjikistan
taf [taf] *nm très Fam (travail)* work; *(emploi)* job; **j'ai du t.** *(travail)* I've got work to do; *(emploi)* I've got a job
taffe [taf] *nf très Fam (de cigarette)* drag
taffetas [tafta] *nm* taffeta
tag [tag] *nm* tag *(piece of graffiti)*
Tage [tɑʒ] *nm* **le T.** the Tagus
tagliatelle [taljatɛl] *nf* piece *or* strand of tagliatelle; **des tagliatelles** tagliatelle
taguer [tage] *vt* to cover in graffiti
tagueur, -euse [tagœr, -øz] *nm,f* tagger *(graffiti artist)*
Tahiti [taiti] *n* Tahiti
tahitien, -enne [taisjɛ̃, -ɛn] **1** *adj* Tahitian
2 *nm,f* **T.** Tahitian
3 *nm (langue)* Tahitian
taie [tɛ] *nf* (**a**) *(enveloppe)* **t. (d'oreiller)** pillowcase, pillow slip (**b**) *(sur l'œil)* leucoma
taïga [taiga] *nf* taiga
taillader [tajade] *vt* to slash, to gash
taille [taj] *nf* (**a**) *(dimensions)* size; **une pêche de la t. d'un melon** a peach the size of a melon; **quelle t. faites-vous?** what size are you?, what size do you take?; **la t. en dessus/dessous** the next size up/down; **t. unique** one size (**b**) *(hauteur)* height; **de petite t.** short; *Fig* **être de t. à faire qch** to be capable of doing sth; *Fig* **trouver un adversaire à sa t.** to meet one's match (**c**) *(importance)* **de t.** *(erreur, mensonge)* big (**d**) *(partie du corps, sur un vêtement)* waist; **avoir la t. fine** to have a slim waist; **avoir une t. de guêpe** to be wasp-waisted (**e**) *(action) (de pierre)* cutting; *(d'un arbre)* pruning; *(d'une haie)* trimming (**f**) *Ordinat* **t. de champ** field size; **t. de disque dur** hard disk size; **t. de mémoire** memory size (**g**) *Hist (impôt)* tallage
taillé, -e [taje] *adj* **être t. pour faire qch** to be cut out to do sth
taille-crayon *(pl* **taille-crayon** *ou* **taille-crayons)** [tajkrɛjɔ̃] *nm* pencil sharpener
tailler [taje] **1** *vt* (**a**) *(pierre, diamant)* to cut; *(arbre, vigne)* to prune; *(haie, barbe)* to trim; *(crayon)* to sharpen; **t. une armée en pièces** to cut an army to pieces (**b**) *(vêtement)* to cut out
2 se tailler *vpr* (**a**) *(se couper)* **se t. la barbe** to trim one's beard (**b**) *(se faire)* **se t. un chemin à travers qch**

to carve one's way through sth (**c**) *(s'attribuer)* **se t. un beau succès** to be very successful; **se t. un empire** to carve out an empire for oneself (**d**) *Fam (partir)* to beat it
tailleur [tajœr] *nm* (**a**) *(couturier)* tailor (**b**) *(ensemble pour femme)* suit (**c**) **s'asseoir en t.** to sit cross-legged
tailleur-pantalon *(pl* **tailleurs-pantalons)** [tajœr-pãtalɔ̃] *nm Br* trouser *or Am* pant suit
taillis [taji] *nm* copse, coppice
tain [tɛ̃] *nm* silvering; **glace** *ou* **miroir sans t.** two-way mirror
taire [55b] [tɛr] **1** *vt (affaire, secret)* to say nothing about, not to mention; *(vérité)* to hide; **une personne dont je tairai le nom** a person who shall remain nameless
2 se taire *vpr* (**a**) *(être silencieux)* to be quiet *or* silent; *(cesser de parler)* to stop talking, to fall silent; *(décider de ne rien dire)* to keep quiet *or* silent; **tais-toi!** be quiet!; **faire t. qn** to make sb be quiet; *(adversaire, critique)* to silence; **tu as perdu une occasion de te t.** you should have kept your mouth shut (**b**) *(bruit)* to stop
taisais, taise *etc voir* **taire**
Taiwan [tajwan] *n* Taiwan
taiwanais, -e [tajwanɛ, -ɛz] **1** *adj* Taiwanese
2 *nm,f* **T.** Taiwanese
tajine [taʒin] *nm* tajine
talc [talk] *nm* talcum powder, talc
talé, -e [tale] *adj* bruised
talent [talã] *nm* (**a**) *(don)* talent; **son t. de pianiste** his talent as a pianist; **homme/musicien de t.** talented man/musician; **avoir du t.** to be talented (**b**) *(artiste)* **un jeune t.** a talented newcomer
talentueusement [talãtɥøzmã] *adv* with talent
talentueux, -euse [talãtɥø, -øz] *adj* talented
talion [taljɔ̃] *nm voir* **loi**
talisman [talismã] *nm* talisman
talkie-walkie *(pl* **talkies-walkies)** [tɔkiwɔki] *nm* walkie-talkie
Tallinn [talin] *n* Tallin
Talmud [talmyd] *nm* **le T.** the Talmud
taloche [talɔʃ] *nf Fam (gifle)* clout
talon [talɔ̃] *nm* (**a**) *(du pied, de chaussure, de bas)* heel; *Fig* **être sur les talons de qn** to be on sb's heels; **t. d'Achille** Achilles' heel; **talons aiguilles** stiletto heels; *(chaussures)* stilettos; **talons hauts** high heels; **talons plats** flat heels (**b**) *(de chèque)* stub, counterfoil (**c**) *(aux cartes)* stock
talonner [talɔne] **1** *vt* (**a**) *(suivre)* **t. qn** to follow on sb's heels (**b**) *(cheval)* to spur on
2 *vi (au rugby)* to heel
talonnette [talɔnɛt] *nf (dans une chaussure)* heel pad
talonneur [talɔnœr] *nm (au rugby)* hooker
talquer [talke] *vt* to put talcum powder on
talus [taly] *nm* (**a**) *(terrain en pente)* slope (**b**) *(d'une voie ferrée, d'un canal)* embankment
tamanoir [tamanwar] *nm* great anteater
tamaris [tamaris] *nm* tamarisk
tambouille [tãbuj] *nf Fam* (**a**) *(cuisine)* cooking; **faire la t.** to do the cooking (**b**) *(nourriture)* grub
tambour [tãbur] *nm* (**a**) *(instrument de musique)* drum; **sans t. ni trompette** quietly, without any fuss; **faire qch t. battant** to do sth briskly (**b**) *(personne)* drummer (**c**) *(d'une machine à laver)* drum; **t. de frein**

brake drum (**d**) *(à broder)* (embroidery) hoop, tambour

tambourin [tãburɛ̃] *nm (instrument plat)* tambourine; *(tambour)* tambourin

tambouriner [tãburine] **1** *vi* to drum
2 *vt* to drum out

tamis [tami] *nm (pour la farine)* sieve; *(pour le sable)* sifter; **passer au t.** *(farine)* to sieve; *(sable)* to sift

Tamise [tamiz] *nf* **la T.** the Thames

tamisé, -e [tamize] *adj (lumière)* subdued

tamiser [tamize] *vt (farine)* to sieve; *(sable)* to sift

tamoul, -e [tamul] **1** *adj* Tamil
2 *nm,f* **T.** Tamil
3 *nm (langue)* Tamil

tampon [tãpɔ̃] **1** *nm* (**a**) *(de coton)* pad; **t. hygiénique** *ou* **périodique** tampon (**b**) *(cachet, instrument)* stamp; *(de la poste)* postmark; **t. dateur** date stamp; **t. encreur** ink pad (**c**) *(pour nettoyer)* pad; **t. à récurer** scourer, scouring pad (**d**) *(bouchon)* plug, stopper (**e**) *(à l'extrémité des wagons) & Fig* buffer
2 *adj inv* **État/zone t.** buffer state/zone

tamponner [tãpɔne] **1** *vt* (**a**) *(document)* to stamp; *(lettre)* to postmark (**b**) *(plaie)* to dab (**c**) *(heurter)* to crash into
2 se tamponner *vpr* (**a**) *(se heurter)* to crash into each other (**b**) *(s'essuyer)* **se t. le front** to mop one's brow; **se t. les yeux** to dab one's eyes; *très Fam* **s'en t. (le coquillard)** not to give a damn

tamponneuse [tãpɔnøz] *adj f voir* **auto**

tam-tam *(pl* **tam-tams**) [tamtam] *nm (tambour africain)* tom-tom

tancer [tãse] *vt Litt* to berate, to scold

tanche [tãʃ] *nf* tench

tandem [tãdɛm] *nm* (**a**) *(bicyclette)* tandem (**b**) *(groupe de deux personnes)* duo; **travailler en t.** to work in tandem

tandis [tãdi, tãdis] **tandis que** *conj* (**a**) *(marque l'opposition)* while, whereas (**b**) *(marque la simultanéité)* while

tangage [tãgaʒ] *nm (d'un bateau)* pitching

tangent, -e [tãʒã, -ãt] **1** *adj Math* tangential (**à** to); *Fig* **c'était t.** it was touch and go, it was a near thing
2 *nf* **tangente** *Math* tangent (**à** to); *Fam* **prendre la tangente** *(partir)* to slip away

tangible [tãʒibl] *adj* tangible

tango [tãgo] *nm (danse, musique)* tango; **danser le t.** to tango, to dance the tango

tanguer [tãge] *vi (bateau)* to pitch; **tout tanguait autour de moi** everything was spinning around me

tanière [tanjɛr] *nf* (**a**) *(d'animal)* den, lair (**b**) *(retraite)* retreat

tanin [tanɛ̃] *nm* tannin

tank [tãk] *nm* tank

tanker [tãkœr] *nm* tanker

tannant, -e [tanã, -ãt] *adj Fam (ennuyeux)* annoying

tanné, -e [tane] *adj* (**a**) *(hâlé)* weather-beaten (**b**) *Can Fam* **être t.** *(en avoir assez)* to be fed up

tanner [tane] *vt* (**a**) *(peaux)* to tan (**b**) *Fam (harceler)* to pester

tannerie [tanri] *nf (établissement)* tannery; *(industrie)* tanning

tanneur [tanœr] *nm* tanner

tannin [tanɛ̃] = **tanin**

tant [tã] *adv* (**a**) *(tellement, à tel point)* so much; **t. de** *(quantité)* so much; *(nombre)* so many; **j'ai t. mangé**

que j'ai vomi I ate so much I was sick; **pas t. que ça** *(quantité)* not that much; *(nombre)* not that many; **t. il est vrai que...** since it is the case that...
(**b**) *(dans des comparaisons)* **t. que** as much as; **t. pour vous que pour moi** for you as much as for me; **n'aimer rien t. que...** to like nothing more than...
(**c**) *(substitué à un chiffre, à une date)* **t. pour cent** so much per cent; **votre lettre du t.** your letter of such and such a date
(**d**) **t. que** *(aussi longtemps que)* as long as; *(pendant que)* while; **t. que vous y êtes** while you're at it
(**e**) *(locutions)* **t. bien que mal** somehow or other; **t. et si bien que** so much so that; **t. s'en faut** far from it; **s'il était un t. soit peu intelligent** if he was at all intelligent; **t. qu'à faire, autant en acheter deux** you/ we/*etc* might as well buy two; **en t. que** *(comme)* as; **t. mieux!** so much the better!; **t. mieux pour toi!** good for you!; **t. pis!** too bad!; **t. pis pour toi!** too bad (for you)!

tante [tãt] *nf* (**a**) *(parente)* aunt (**b**) *très Fam (homosexuel)* queer, = offensive term used to refer to a male homosexual

tantine [tãtin] *nf Fam* auntie, aunty

tantinet [tãtinɛ] *nm Fam* **un t.** a tiny bit

tantôt [tãto] *adv* (**a**) *(parfois)* **t. triste, t. gai** sometimes sad, sometimes happy (**b**) *(cet après-midi)* this afternoon

Tanzanie [tãzani] *nf* **la T.** Tanzania

tanzanien, -enne [tãzanjɛ̃, -ɛn] **1** *adj* Tanzanian
2 *nm,f* **T.** Tanzanian

taoïsme [taoism] *nm* Taoism

taon [tã] *nm* gadfly, horsefly

tapage [tapaʒ] *nm* (**a**) *(bruit)* din, row; **faire du t.** to kick up a din *or* row; **t. nocturne** breach of the peace *(at night)* (**b**) *(publicité)* fuss; **faire du t. autour de qch** to make a fuss about sth

tapageur, -euse [tapaʒœr, -øz] *adj* (**a**) *(enfant)* rowdy (**b**) *(vêtements, couleur)* loud, flashy; *(publicité)* blatant (**c**) *(liaison)* scandalous

tapant, -e [tapã, -ãt] *adj* **à sept/dix heures t.** *ou* **tapantes** at seven/ten o'clock sharp

tape [tap] *nf (pour punir)* tap; *(affectueuse)* pat

tapé, -e [tape] *adj Fam (fou)* crazy

tape-à-l'œil [tapalœj] *Fam* **1** *adj inv* gaudy, flashy
2 *nm* **c'est du t.** it's just show

tapecul [tapky] *nm Fam (véhicule)* rattletrap

taper [tape] **1** *vt* (**a**) *(frapper)* to hit; *(affectueusement)* to pat; *(table)* to bang (**b**) *(dactylographier)* **t. qch (à la machine)** to type sth (**c**) *Ordinat* to key; **tapez entrée** *ou* **retour** select enter or return (**d**) *Fam (emprunter de l'argent à)* to cadge money off; **t. qn de 10 euros** to cadge 10 euros off sb
2 *vi* (**a**) *(frapper)* to knock; *(avec le poing)* to bang; **t. à la porte** to knock on the door; **t. du pied** to stamp one's foot; **t. du poing sur qch** to bang on sth; **t. dans un ballon** to kick a ball around; *Fam* **t. dans l'œil à qn** to take sb's fancy; **t. sur qn** to hit sb; *Fig (critiquer)* to knock sb (**b**) *(soleil)* to beat down; *Fam* **ça tape** it's scorching (**c**) *(dactylographier)* **t. (à la machine)** to type
3 se taper *vpr* (**a**) *(se cogner)* **se t. la tête/le coude** to bang one's head/elbow; *Fig* **c'est à se t. la tête contre les murs** it's enough to drive you up the wall (**b**) *Fam (repas, boisson)* to have; **je me taperais bien une bière** I could murder a beer (**c**) *Fam (corvée)* to get landed with; **on s'est tapé les embouteillages** we

got stuck in the traffic jams (**d**) *très Fam (coucher avec)* to screw (**e**) *Fam (se moquer)* **ses histoires de fesses, je m'en tape!** I couldn't care less about his sex life!

tapette [tapɛt] *nf* (**a**) *(pour tapis)* carpet beater; *(contre les mouches)* fly swatter (**b**) *(piège)* **t. (à souris)** mousetrap (**c**) *(petite tape)* tap (**d**) *très Fam (homosexuel)* queer, = offensive term used to refer to a male homosexual

tapeur, -euse [tapœr, -øz] *nm,f Fam* scrounger, sponger

tapin [tapɛ̃] *nm très Fam* **faire le t.** *Br* to be on the game, *Am* to work the streets

tapinois [tapinwa] **en tapinois** *adv* stealthily

tapioca [tapjɔka] *nm* tapioca

tapir¹ [tapir] *nm* tapir

tapir² **se tapir** *vpr (se blottir)* to crouch; *(se cacher)* to hide

tapis [tapi] *nm* (**a**) *(de sol)* carpet; *(de petite taille)* rug; *Fig* **mettre qch sur le t.** to bring sth up for discussion; **t. roulant** *(de marchandises, pour bagages)* conveyor belt; *(pour piétons)* moving walkway, travelator; **t. de salle de bain** bath mat; **t. de sol** earth mat; *Ordinat* **t. de souris** mouse mat *or* pad (**b**) *(en boxe)* canvas; **aller au t.** to go down; **envoyer qn au t.** to floor sb

tapis-brosse *(pl* **tapis-brosses)** [tapibrɔs] *nm* doormat

tapisser [tapise] *vt* (**a**) *(pièce, appartement)* to paper, to wallpaper; *(fauteuil, canapé)* to upholster (**b**) *(couvrir)* **être tapissé de** *(sujet: mur)* to be covered with; *(sujet: sol)* to be carpeted with (**c**) *(paroi d'un organe)* to line

tapisserie [tapisri] *nf* (**a**) *(broderie)* tapestry work; **faire de la t.** to do tapestry work (**b**) *(tenture)* tapestry; *Fig* **faire t.** to be a wallflower (**c**) *(papier peint)* wallpaper

tapissier, -ère [tapisje, -ɛr] *nm,f* (**a**) *(tisseur)* tapestry maker (**b**) *(de meubles)* upholsterer (**c**) *(décorateur)* interior decorator

tapotement [tapɔtmɑ̃] *nm* tapping

tapoter [tapɔte] **1** *vt* to tap; *(joue, main)* to pat
2 *vi* **t. sur qch** to tap on sth

tapuscrit [tapyskri] *nm* typescript

taquet [takɛ] *nm* (**a**) *(de machine à écrire)* stop; *Ordinat* **t. de tabulation** tab stop (**b**) *(butée)* stop

taquin, -e [takɛ̃, -in] *adj* teasing

taquiner [takine] *vt (faire enrager)* to tease

taquinerie [takinri] *nf* **ce n'est qu'une t.** I'm/he's/*etc* only teasing; **j'en ai assez de ses taquineries** I've had enough of his teasing

tarabiscoté, -e [tarabiskɔte] *adj* over-elaborate

tarabuster [tarabyste] *vt* (**a**) *(harceler)* to pester (**b**) *(préoccuper)* to bother

tarama [tarama] *nm* taramasalata

taratata [taratata] *exclam Fam* rubbish!

tarauder [tarode] *vt* (**a**) *(acier)* to tap (**b**) *(obséder)* to gnaw at

tard [tar] **1** *adv* late; **plus t.** later (on); **au plus t.** at the latest; **t. dans la nuit** late at night; **pas plus t. qu'hier** only yesterday
2 *nm* **sur le t.** late in life

tarder [tarde] **1** *vi* to delay; **pourquoi tarde-t-elle?** why is she taking so long?; **il ne devrait pas t.** he shouldn't be long; **tu vas recevoir une gifle, cela ne va pas t.** you're going to get smacked before long;

sans t. without delay; **t. à faire qch** to take a long time to do sth
2 *v impersonnel* **il me tarde de partir/qu'elle parte** I can't wait to leave/for her to leave

tardif, -ive [tardif, -iv] *adj (regrets, excuse)* belated; *(heure, récolte)* late

tardivement [tardivmɑ̃] *adv (prendre des mesures, s'excuser)* belatedly; *(rentrer, arriver)* late; *(se marier)* late in life

tare [tar] *nf* (**a**) *(défaut)* defect; *Hum* **ça n'est pas une t.!** it's not a crime! (**b**) *(pour calculer le poids net)* tare

taré, -e [tare] *adj* (**a**) *(anormal)* retarded (**b**) *Fam (fou)* crazy

tarentule [tarɑ̃tyl] *nf* tarantula

targette [tarʒɛt] *nf* bolt

targuer [targe] **se targuer** *vpr* **se t. de qch/de faire qch** to pride oneself on sth/on doing sth

tarif [tarif] *nm* (**a**) *(tableau des prix)* price list, *Br* tariff (**b**) *(prix)* rate; *(d'un billet d'avion, de train)* fare; **quels sont vos tarifs?** how much do you charge?; **payer plein t.** *(pour passagers)* to pay full fare; *(pour marchandises)* to pay the full rate; **faire un t. réduit pour les étudiants** to offer a student discount; **t. douanier** customs rate; **tarifs postaux** postal rates

tarifaire [tarifɛr] *adj (lois)* tariff

tarifer [tarife] *vt* to price

tarification [tarifikasjɔ̃] *nf* pricing

tarin [tarɛ̃] *nm Fam (nez) Br* hooter, *Am* snoot

tarir [tarir] **1** *vt (source, rivière)* to dry up; *(larmes)* to dry; *(créativité, inspiration)* to cause to dry up
2 *vi* (**a**) *(eau, source)* to dry up (**b**) *Fig (conversation, inspiration)* to dry up; **il ne tarit pas sur le sujet** he never stops talking *or* shuts up about it; **ne pas t. d'éloges sur qn/qch** to be be full of praise for sb/sth
3 **se tarir** *vpr* to dry up

tarissement [tarismɑ̃] *nm* drying up

tarot [taro] *nm* tarot; **jouer aux tarots** to play tarot

tartan [tartɑ̃] *nm* tartan

tartare [tartar] **1** *adj (sauce, steak)* tartare
2 *nmf* **T.** Tartar
3 *nm (steak)* steak tartare *(raw minced beef served with a raw egg)*

tarte [tart] **1** *nf* (**a**) *(salée ou sucrée) Br* tart, *Am* (open) pie; *Fam* **ce n'est pas de la t.** it's no easy matter; **t. à la crème** *(au cinéma)* custard pie; *Fig* cliché; **t. aux pommes** apple *Br* tart *or Am* pie; **t. Tatin** tarte Tatin *(caramelized apples covered in shortcrust pastry and turned out upside down)* (**b**) *Fam (gifle)* slap
2 *adj Fam* (**a**) *(ridicule)* stupid-looking, *Br* naff (**b**) *(stupide)* thick

tartelette [tartəlɛt] *nf* tartlet

Tartempion [tartɑ̃pjɔ̃] *nm Fam* so-and-so

tartignole [tartiɲɔl] *adj Fam* ridiculous, *Br* naff

tartine [tartin] *nf* (**a**) *(tranche de pain)* slice of bread and butter; **t. de confiture** slice of bread and jam; **faire des tartines** to butter *(some)* bread (**b**) *Fam (texte)* screed; **en mettre des tartines** to write reams

tartiner [tartine] *vt* (**a**) *(beurre, pain)* to spread (**b**) *Fam (enduire en grande quantité)* **t. qn/qch de qch** to cover sb/sth in sth (**c**) *Fam (texte)* to churn out

tartre [tartr] *nm* (**a**) *(des dents, du vin)* tartar (**b**) *(dans une chaudière, dans une bouilloire)* fur, scale

tas [ta] *nm* (**a**) *(amas)* pile, heap; **mettre qch en t.** to pile sth up (**b**) *Fam (grand nombre)* **un t. de, des t. de** loads of (**c**) *(locutions)* **apprendre qch sur le t.** to learn sth on the job; *Fam* **dans le t. il y en aura bien**

un qui t'ira you'll find one to suit you out of all that lot; *Fam* **tirer dans le t.** to fire at random

Tasmanie [tasmani] *nf* la T. Tasmania

tasse [tas] *nf* cup; **t. à café/thé** coffee/tea cup; **t. de café/thé** cup of coffee/tea; *Fam Fig* **boire la t.** *(en nageant)* to get a mouthful of water

tassé, -e [tase] *adj* (**a**) *(serré)* crammed, squashed (**b**) *Fam* **bien t.** *(fort)* *(café)* strong; *(alcool)* stiff; *(dans un grand verre)* large; **il a 50 ans bien tassés** he's 50 if he's a day

tasseau, -x [taso] *nm* batten

tassement [tasmã] *nm* (**a**) *(de terre, de neige)* packing down; **t. de vertèbres** spinal compression (**b**) *(de fondations)* settling (**c**) *(déclin)* slowdown (**de** in)

tasser [tase] **1** *vt* (**a**) *(objets, personnes)* to cram, to pack (**dans** into) (**b**) *(terre, neige)* to pack down
2 se tasser *vpr* (**a**) *(fondations)* to settle (**b**) *(personne)* to shrink (**c**) **se t. dans qch** *(se serrer dans)* to squeeze into sth (**d**) *Fam* **ça se tassera** *(ça s'arrangera)* things will settle down

taste-vin [tastəvɛ̃] *nm inv* wine taster

tata [tata] *nf Fam* auntie, aunty

tatami [tatami] *nm* tatami

tâter [tɑte] **1** *vt* (**a**) *(toucher)* to feel (**b**) *Fig* **t. le terrain** to see how the land lies
2 tâter de *vt ind (métier)* to try one's hand at; *(prison)* to have a taste of
3 se tâter *vpr (hésiter)* to be in two minds

tâte-vin [tɑtvɛ̃] = **taste-vin**

tatie [tati] *nf Fam* auntie, aunty

tatillon, -onne [tatijɔ̃, -ɔn] *adj* finicky

tâtonnements [tɑtɔnmã] *nmpl* (**a**) *(dans le noir)* groping (**b**) *Fig (essai)* trial and error; *(de la science, de la recherche)* tentative progress

tâtonner [tɑtɔne] *vi* (**a**) *(dans le noir)* to grope about (**b**) *Fig (chercher)* to proceed by trial and error

tâtons [tɑtɔ̃] **à tâtons** *adv* **entrer/sortir à t.** to feel one's way in/out

tatou [tatu] *nm* armadillo

tatouage [tatwaʒ] *nm (action)* tattooing; *(motif)* tattoo

tatouer [tatwe] *vt* to tattoo; **se faire t.** to get a tattoo

tatoueur [tatwœr] *nm* tattoo artist

taudis [todi] *nm* slum; *Fig* dump

taulard, -e [tolar, -ard] *nm,f Fam* jailbird

taule [tol] *nf Fam Br* nick, *Am* can; **faire de la t.** to do time

taulier, -ère [tolje, -ɛr] *nm,f Fam (propriétaire)* (hotel) owner; *(gérant)* (hotel) manager

taupe [top] *nf* (**a**) *(animal)* mole (**b**) *Fam (espion)* mole (**c**) *Fam Péj* **vieille t.** old hag

taupinière [topinjɛr] *nf* molehill

taureau, -x [tɔro] *nm* (**a**) *(animal)* bull; *Fam* **prendre le t. par les cornes** to take the bull by the horns (**b**) *Astron & Astrol* **T.** Taurus; **être T.** to be (a) Taurus

tauromachie [tɔrɔmaʃi] *nf* bullfighting

tautologie [totɔlɔʒi] *nf* tautology

tautologique [totɔlɔʒik] *adj* tautological

taux [to] *nm* (**a**) *(montant) (des salaires, des impôts)* rate (**b**) *(pourcentage)* rate; *(d'alcool, de cholestérol)* level; **à t. fixe** fixed-rate; **t. de change** exchange rate; **t. de croissance** growth rate; **t. d'écoute** ratings; **t. d'épargne** savings rate; **t. d'inflation** rate of inflation; **t. d'intérêt** interest rate; **t. de pénétration** *(d'un marché)* penetration rate (**c**) *Ordinat* ratio, rate

tavelé, -e [tavle] *adj* marked

tavelure [tavlyr] *nf* mark

taverne [tavɛrn] *nf* (**a**) *(restaurant)* restaurant (**b**) *Can* beer parlour, tavern

tavernier, -ère [tavɛrnje, -ɛr] *nm,f* innkeeper

taxation [taksasjɔ̃] *nf* taxation

taxe [taks] *nf* tax; **toutes taxes comprises** inclusive of tax; **t. d'aéroport** airport tax; **t. d'apprentissage** = tax paid by businesses to fund training programmes; **t. d'habitation** local tax; **t. professionnelle** = tax paid by companies and self-employed people; **t. sur la valeur ajoutée** value added tax

taxer [takse] *vt* (**a**) *(imposer)* to tax (**b**) *(accuser)* **t. qn de négligence** to accuse sb of negligence (**c**) *Fam (soutirer)* **t. qch à qn** to cadge sth off sb

taxi [taksi] *nm* (**a**) *(voiture)* taxi, cab; **prendre un t.** to take a taxi (**b**) *Fam (chauffeur)* taxi driver, cabby

taxidermiste [taksidɛrmist] *nmf* taxidermist

taximètre [taksimɛtr] *nm* meter

Taxiphone® [taksifɔn] *nm* pay phone

Tbilissi [tbilisi] *n* Tbilisi

Tchad [tʃad] *nm* **le T.** Chad

tchadien, -enne [tʃadjɛ̃, -ɛn] **1** *adj* Chadian
2 *nm,f* **T.** Chadian

tchador [tʃadɔr] *nm* chador

tchatche [tʃatʃ] *nf Fam* **avoir la t.** to have the gift of the gab

tchatcher [tʃatʃe] *vi Fam* to chat

tchécoslovaque [tʃekɔslɔvak] *Anciennement* **1** *adj* Czechoslovakian
2 *nmf* **T.** Czechoslovak

Tchécoslovaquie [tʃekɔslɔvaki] *nf Anciennement* **la T.** Czechoslovakia

tchèque [tʃɛk] **1** *adj* Czech
2 *nmf* **T.** Czech
3 *nm (langue)* Czech

tchétchène [tʃetʃɛn] **1** *adj* Chechen
2 *nmf* **T.** Chechen

Tchétchénie [tʃetʃeni] *nf* **la T.** Chechnya

tchin-tchin [tʃintʃin] *exclam Fam* cheers!

TD [tede] *nm (abrév* **travaux dirigés)** tutorial

te [tə]

---

t' is used before a word beginning with a vowel or h mute.

---

pron personnel (**a**) *(objet direct)* you; **te voilà** there you are (**b**) *(objet indirect)* to you; **j'ai vu qu'elle t'a serré la main** I saw her shake your hand; **ils t'ont lancé des cailloux?** did they throw stones at you? (**c**) *(dans les réfléchis)* yourself; **va te doucher** go and have a shower (**d**) *(dans les pronominaux)* **tu t'es trompée** you made a mistake

té [te] *nm (règle)* T-square; **en té** T-shaped

technicien, -enne [tɛknisjɛ̃, -ɛn] *nm,f* technician

technicité [tɛknisite] *nf* technical nature

technico-commercial, -e, -aux, -ales [tɛknikɔkɔmɛrsjal, -jo] **1** *adj (service)* technical sales; **agent t.** sales engineer
2 *nm,f* sales engineer

technicolor® [tɛknikɔlɔr] *nm* Technicolor®

technique [tɛknik] **1** *adj* technical
2 *nf* (**a**) *(d'un artiste, d'un spécialiste)* technique; **avec lui, j'ai ma t.** I have my own way of dealing with him; **t. de vente** sales technique
3 *nm* **le t.** *(enseignement)* technical training

techniquement [tɛknikmã] *adv* technically
techno [tɛknɔ] *adj inv & nf* techno
technocrate [tɛknɔkrat] *nmf* technocrat
technocratie [tɛknɔkrasi] *nf* technocracy
technologie [tɛknɔlɔʒi] *nf* technology; **de haute t.** high-tech
technologique [tɛknɔlɔʒik] *adj* technological
teck [tɛk] *nm* teak
teckel [tɛkɛl] *nm* dachshund
tectonique [tɛktɔnik] **1** *adj* tectonic
2 *nf* tectonics *(singulier)*; **t. des plaques** plate tectonics
Te Deum [tedeɔm] *nm inv* Te Deum
teenager [tinɛdʒœr] *nmf* teenager
tee-shirt *(pl* **tee-shirts)** [tiʃœrt] *nm* T-shirt, tee-shirt
Téflon® [teflɔ̃] *nm* Teflon®
tégument [tegymã] *nm* integument
Téhéran [teerã] *n* Tehran
teignais, teigne *etc voir* **teindre**
teigne [tɛɲ] *nf* (**a**) *(maladie)* ringworm (**b**) *Fam (homme)* rat; *(femme)* cow
teigneux, -euse [tɛɲø, -øz] *adj Fam (personne)* nasty
teindre [tɛ̃dr] **1** *vt (vêtement, cheveux)* to dye; **t. qch en rouge** to dye sth red
2 se teindre *vpr* (**a**) *(se colorer)* **se t. les cheveux (en blond)** to dye one's hair (blond) (**b**) *Litt* **se t. de** *(se mêler de)* to be tinged with
teint, -e *voir* **teindre**
teint [tɛ̃] *nm* (**a**) *(du visage)* complexion; **t. de rose** rosy complexion (**b**) *(d'un tissu)* colour; **tissu bon** *ou* **grand t.** colourfast material; *Fig* **bon t.** *(catholique, communiste)* staunch, dyed-in-the-wool
teinte [tɛ̃t] *nf* (**a**) *(couleur)* shade, tint (**b**) *Fig (nuance)* tinge
teinter [tɛ̃te] **1** *vt* (**a**) *(colorer)* to tint; *(bois, meuble)* to stain (**b**) *Fig (nuancer)* **teinté de** tinged with
2 se teinter *vpr* **se t. de** to become tinged with
teinture [tɛ̃tyr] *nf* (**a**) *(produit)* dye (**b**) *(action)* dyeing (**c**) *(préparation pharmaceutique)* tincture; **t. d'iode** tincture of iodine
teinturerie [tɛ̃tyrri] *nf (pressing)* dry cleaner's
teinturier, -ère [tɛ̃tyrje, -ɛr] *nm,f* dry cleaner
tek [tɛk] = **teck**
tel, telle [tɛl] **1** *adj* (**a**) *(semblable)* such; **un t. homme** such a man; **une telle conduite** such behaviour; **de telles choses** such things; **t. père, t. fils** like father like son; **rien de t. qu'un bon chocolat chaud** there's nothing like a nice cup of hot chocolate; **à t. ou t. endroit** in such and such a place; **il n'a rien dit de t.** he said nothing of the kind; **sa bonté est telle que…** he's/she's so kind that…
(**b**) *(comme)* **t. que** such as, like; **voir les choses telles qu'elles sont** to see things as they are; **t. que je le connais, il ne sera pas d'accord** knowing him, he won't agree; *Litt* **t. une bête furieuse** like an enraged animal
(**c**) *(locutions)* **à t. point que** to such an extent that; **de telle sorte que…** so that…, in such a way that…; **elle me l'a dit t. quel** *ou Fam* **t. que** she told me just like that
2 *pron indéfini* **t. ou t. vous dira que…** some people will tell you that…
3 *pron démonstratif* such; **t. est mon désir** such is my wish
4 *nm,f* **un t., une telle** so-and-so

télé [tele] *nf Fam* (**a**) *(appareil)* TV, *Br* telly (**b**) *(organisme)* **la t.** TV; **travailler à la t.** to work in TV
téléachat [teleaʃa] *nm (à la télévision)* teleshopping; *(par Internet)* on-line shopping
télécabine® [telekabin] *nf* cable car
Télécarte® [telekart] *nf* phone card
télécommande [telekɔmãd] *nf* remote control
télécommander [telekɔmãde] *vt* (**a**) *(appareil)* to operate by remote control (**b**) *Fig (complot, soulèvement)* to mastermind from a distance
télécommunications [telekɔmynikasjɔ̃] *nfpl* **les t.** telecommunications
téléconférence [telekɔ̃ferãs] *nf* teleconference
télécopie [telekɔpi] *nf* fax
télécopieur [telekɔpjœr] *nm* fax (machine)
télédiffuser [teledifyze] *vt* to televise
télédiffusion [teledifyzjɔ̃] *nf* televising
tel écran-tel écrit [telekrãtelekri] *adj Ordinat* WYSIWYG
télé-enseignement [teleãsɛɲəmã] *nm* distance learning
téléfilm [telefilm] *nm* film made for television, TV movie
télégénique [teleʒenik] *adj* telegenic
télégramme [telegram] *nm* telegram
télégraphe [telegraf] *nm* telegraph
télégraphier [telegrafje] *vt* to cable, to wire
télégraphique [telegrafik] *adj (fil, poteau)* telegraph; **en style t.** in telegraphic style
télégraphiste [telegrafist] *nmf* (**a**) *(technicien)* telegraphist (**b**) *(porteur)* telegraph messenger
téléguidage [telegidaʒ] *nm* remote control
téléguidé, -e [telegide] *adj* remote-controlled
téléguider [telegide] *vt* (**a**) *(voiture, missile)* to operate by remote control (**b**) *Fig (complot, soulèvement)* to mastermind from a distance
télématique [telematik] **1** *adj* telematic
2 *nf* telematics *(singulier)*
téléobjectif [teleɔbʒɛktif] *nm* telephoto lens
télépaiement [telepɛmã] *nm* telepayment
télépathe [telepat] **1** *adj* telepathic
2 *nmf* telepathist
télépathie [telepati] *nf* telepathy
télépathique [telepatik] *adj* telepathic
téléphérique [teleferik] *nm* cable car
téléphone [telefɔn] *nm* (**a**) *(appareil, système)* phone, telephone; **avoir le t.** to be on the phone, to have a phone; **être au t.** to be on the phone; **un coup de t.** a phone call; *Fam* **par le t. arabe** on the grapevine; **t. cellulaire** cellular phone; **t. mobile** mobile (phone); **t. portatif** portable phone; **t. public** public phone; *Pol* **t. rouge** hot line; **t. sans fil** cordless phone; **t. de voiture** car phone (**b**) *(numéro)* phone number
téléphoner [telefɔne] **1** *vt* (**a**) *(nouvelle)* to phone, to telephone (**à** to) (**b**) *Fam* **c'était téléphoné** you could see it coming
2 *vi* to phone, to telephone; **t. à qn** to phone sb
3 se téléphoner *vpr* to phone each other
téléphonie [telefɔni] *nf* telephony; **t. sans fil** wireless telephony; **la t. mobile** the mobile phone sector
téléphonique [telefɔnik] *adj* telephone
téléphoniste [telefɔnist] *nmf* (telephone) operator, *Br* telephonist
télé-poubelle [telepubɛl] *nf Fam* trash television

téléprompteur [teleprɔ̃ptœr] *nm* Teleprompter®, *Br* Autocue®

téléprospecteur, -trice [teleprɔspɛktœr, -tris] *nm,f* telemarketer

téléprospection [teleprɔspɛksjɔ̃] *nf* telemarketing

téléreportage [teler(ə)pɔrtaʒ] *nm (activité)* television reporting; *(document)* television report

téléroman [telerɔmã] *nm Can* television serial

télescopage [telɛskɔpaʒ] *nm (de trains)* telescoping; **télescopages en série** *(de véhicules)* pile-up

télescope [telɛskɔp] *nm* telescope

télescoper [telɛskɔpe] **1** *vt (véhicules, trains)* to crash into

2 se télescoper *vpr* (a) *(véhicules, trains)* to concertina (b) *(souvenirs, images)* to intermingle

télescopique [telɛskɔpik] *adj* telescopic

téléscripteur [teleskriptœr] *nm* teleprinter

télésiège [telesjɛʒ] *nm* chair lift

téléski [teleski] *nm* ski tow

téléspectateur, -trice [telespɛktatœr, -tris] *nm,f* (television) viewer

télésurveillance [telesyrvɛjãs] *nf* electronic surveillance

Télétexte® [teletɛkst] *nm* teletext

télétravail [teletravaj] *nm* teleworking

télévisé, -e [televize] *adj* televised

téléviseur [televizœr] *nm* television (set)

télévision [televizjɔ̃] *nf* (a) *(organisme, technique, émissions)* television; **à la t.** on television; **travailler à la t.** to work in television; **t. par câble** cable television; **t. commerciale** commercial television; **t. haute définition** high-definition television; **t. numérique** digital television (b) *(poste)* television (set); **regarder la t.** to watch television; **t. en couleur, t. couleur** colour television

télévisuel, -elle [televizɥɛl] *adj* television

télex [telɛks] *nm* telex

télexer [telɛkse] *vt* to telex

tellement [tɛlmã] *adv* (a) *(si)* so; **c'était t. intéressant que...** it was so interesting that...; **ce n'est pas t. beau** it's not all that beautiful (b) *(tant)* so much; **t. de** *(nombre)* so many; *(quantité)* so much; **elle a t. grandi** she's grown so much; **je n'ai pas t. aimé** I didn't like it that much; **je n'ai plus t. envie d'y aller** I'm no longer that keen on going; **il a t. crié que...** he shouted so much that...; *Fam* **je vais craquer t. il m'énerve** he annoys me so much I'm going to crack up

tellurique [telyrik] *adj (courants)* telluric; **secousse t.** earth tremor

téméraire [temerɛr] *adj* reckless

témérité [temerite] *nf* recklessness

témoignage [temwaɲaʒ] *nm* (a) *Jur* evidence, testimony; **porter t. (en faveur de/contre qn)** to give evidence (on behalf of/against sb); **faux t.** perjury (b) *(compte rendu)* report, account (c) *(démonstration)* **en t. d'amitié** as a token of friendship

témoigner [temwaɲe] **1** *vt* (a) *(attester)* **t. que** to testify that (b) *(sentiments, gratitude)* to show (**à** to)

2 *vi* to testify, to give evidence (**en faveur de/contre** on behalf of/against)

3 témoigner de *vt ind* (a) *(montrer)* to show (b) *(se porter garant de)* to testify to

témoin [temwɛ̃] **1** *nm* (a) *(d'un événement, d'un mariage)* witness; **être t. de qch** to witness sth, to be a witness to sth; **prendre qn à t.** to call sb to witness; **Dieu m'est t. que...** as God is my witness...; **t. à charge** witness for the prosecution; **t. oculaire** eyewitness (b) *(dans un duel)* second (c) *(preuve)* **t. les coups que j'ai reçus** witness the blows I received (d) *(dans un relais)* baton (e) *Rel* **T. de Jéhovah** Jehovah's Witness (f) *Can Ordinat* cookie

2 *adj inv (animal, plante)* control; **appartement t.** *Br* show flat, *Am* model apartment

tempe [tɑ̃p] *nf* temple

tempérament [tɑ̃peramã] *nm* (a) *(caractère)* disposition; *Fam* **avoir du t.** *(avoir du caractère)* to have character (b) **acheter qch à t.** to buy sth *Br* on hire purchase *or Am* on the installment plan

tempérance [tɑ̃perãs] *nf* moderation, temperance

température [tɑ̃peratyr] *nf* temperature; **avoir de la t.** to have a (high) temperature; *Fig* **prendre la t. de qch** to gauge the temperature of sth

tempéré, -e [tɑ̃pere] *adj (climat)* temperate

tempérer [tɑ̃pere] *vt (enthousiasme, passion)* to moderate

tempête [tɑ̃pɛt] *nf* storm; *Fig* **une t. d'applaudissements** thunderous applause; *Fig* **une t. dans un verre d'eau** a storm in a *Br* teacup *or Am* teapot; **t. de neige** snowstorm, blizzard; **t. de sable** sandstorm

tempêter [tɑ̃pɛte] *vi* to storm, to rage

tempétueux, -euse [tɑ̃petɥø, -øz] *adj Litt* stormy

temple [tɑ̃pl] *nm aussi Fig* temple; *(protestant)* church

tempo [tɛ̃po, tɛmpo] *nm* tempo

temporaire [tɑ̃pɔrɛr] *adj* temporary

temporairement [tɑ̃pɔrɛrmã] *adv* temporarily

temporel, -elle [tɑ̃pɔrɛl] *adj* (a) *(qui concerne le temps)* temporal (b) *(terrestre)* temporal, worldly

temporellement [tɑ̃pɔrɛlmã] *adv* temporally

temporisateur, -trice [tɑ̃pɔrizatœr, -tris] *adj (stratégie)* delaying

temporiser [tɑ̃pɔrize] *vi* to play for time, to stall

temps [tã] *nm* (a) *(durée)* time; **avoir le t. de faire qch** to have (the) time to do sth; **avoir tout le t.** to have plenty of time; **prendre le t. de faire qch** to take the time to do sth; **prendre son t.** to take one's time; **ça prend du t.** it takes time; **ça a pris un certain t.** it took quite a while; **donner** *ou* **laisser le t. à qn de faire qch** to give sb the time to do sth; *Fig* **en deux t. trois mouvements** in two ticks; **avec le t.** in *or* with time; with time; **combien de t. faut-il pour y aller?** how long does it take to get there?; *Prov* **le t., c'est de l'argent** time is money; *Ordinat* **base de t.** time base; *Ordinat* **t. d'adressage** address speed

(b) *(moment)* time; **en t. de crise** in a crisis; **en t. de guerre/paix** in wartime/peacetime; **de t. en t., de t. à autre** from time to time; **en même t. (que)** at the same time (as); **pendant ce t.** meanwhile, in the meantime; **il y a peu de t.** not long ago, a little while ago; **peu de t. après** shortly after; **d'ici quelque t.** soon, shortly; **tout le t.** all the time; **les premiers t.** at the beginning; **ces t.-ci** these days; **ces derniers t.** this last while; **il y est resté quelque t.** he stayed there for a while; **ça n'a qu'un t.** it won't last forever; **les t. forts de l'actualité** the main points of the news; **t. libre** free time; **t. mort** lull; *(au basket-ball)* time out

(c) *(époque)* time, days; **de mon t.** in my day *or* time; **du t. de ma jeunesse** in my younger days; **de tout t.** from time immemorial; **dans le t.** in the old days; **en ce t.-là** at that time, then; **par les t. qui courent** these days; **être de son t., vivre avec son t.** to move with the times; **être en avance sur son t.** to be ahead of one's time; **le bon vieux t.** the good old days; **les t. sont durs** times are hard

(**d**) *(heure)* **faire qch à t.** to do sth in time; **en t. voulu** *ou* **utile** in due course; **il est t. qu'elle descende** it's time she came down; **il n'est plus t.** it's too late; **le paquet est enfin arrivé mais il était t.!** the parcel's finally arrived and about time too!

(**e**) *(occasion)* **il y a un t. pour tout** there's a time for everything; **chaque chose en son t.** all in good time

(**f**) *(météo)* weather; **par tous les t.** in all weathers; **quel t. fait-il?** what's the weather like?

(**g**) *Gram* tense

(**h**) *Mus* beat

(**i**) *(d'un athlète)* time

tenable [tənabl] *adj (situation)* bearable

tenace [tənas] *adj* (**a**) *(personne)* stubborn, tenacious (**b**) *(préjugé, volonté)* stubborn; *(odeur, douleur, souvenir)* lingering; *(habitude)* deep-rooted (**c**) *(colle)* strong

ténacité [tenasite] *nf* (**a**) *(d'une personne)* stubbornness, tenacity; **avec t.** stubbornly; *(travailler)* doggedly (**b**) *(d'un préjugé)* stubbornness; *(d'une odeur, d'une douleur, d'un souvenir)* lingering nature; *(d'une habitude)* deep-rootedness

tenailler [tənaje] *vt Litt* to torture; **tenaillé par la faim** ravenously hungry; **tenaillé par la douleur** gripped with pain

tenailles [tənaj] *nfpl* pincers

tenancier, -ère [tənãsje, -ɛr] *nm,f (d'un bar, d'une maison de jeu)* manager, *f* manageress

tenant, -e [tənã, -ãt] **1** *adj voir* **séance**
2 *nm* (**a**) *(partisan)* champion, defender (**b**) **le t. du titre** the title holder (**c**) *(locutions)* **d'un seul t.** in one piece; **les tenants et les aboutissants** *(d'une affaire)* the ins and outs

tendance [tãdãs] **1** *nf* (**a**) *(d'une personne)* tendency; **avoir t. à faire qch** to have a tendency to do sth; **avoir une t. à qch** to have a tendency to sth (**b**) *(de l'économie, du marché, d'une mode)* trend
2 *adj Fam (à la mode)* trendy

tendancieusement [tãdãsjøzmã] *adv* tendentiously

tendancieux, -euse [tãdãsjø, -øz] *adj* tendentious

tendeur [tãdœr] *nm (pour bagages)* elastic strap

tendinite [tãdinit] *nf* tendinitis

tendon [tãdõ] *nm* tendon; **t. d'Achille** Achilles tendon

tendre¹ [tãdr] **1** *adj* (**a**) *(bois, pierre, métal)* soft; *(viande, légume)* tender (**b**) *(couleur)* delicate, soft (**c**) *(personne, geste, cœur)* tender; **ne pas être t. (pour** *ou* **avec qn)** to be hard (on sb) (**d**) **l'âge t.** early childhood; **depuis ma plus t. enfance** since my earliest childhood
2 *nmf (personne)* softhearted person

tendre² **1** *vt* (**a**) *(corde)* to tighten; *(toile)* to stretch; *(muscle)* to tense; *(arc)* to bend (**b**) *(voile, filet)* to spread; *(papier peint, tapisserie)* to hang; **une pièce tendue de velours rouge** a room whose walls are covered in red velvet (**c**) *(piège)* to set (**à** for) (**d**) *(main, bras, jambe)* to stretch out, to hold out (**à** to); **les bras tendus** with outstretched arms; *Fig* **t. la main à qn** *(l'aider)* to offer sb a hand; *Fig* **t. l'oreille** to prick up one's ears
2 *vi* **t. vers zéro** to tend towards zero
3 tendre à *vt ind* (**a**) *(avoir pour but) (idéal)* to aim for (**b**) *(avoir tendance à)* **t. à faire qch** to tend to do sth (**c**) **t. à sa fin** to come to an end

4 se tendre *vpr (cordage)* to become taut; *Fig (relations, situation)* to become strained

tendrement [tãdrəmã] *adv* tenderly, lovingly

tendresse [tãdrɛs] *nf* (**a**) *(affection)* tenderness, affection; **avoir de la t. pour qn** to feel affection for sb; **avec t.** tenderly, affectionately (**b**) **tendresses** *(démonstrations)* expressions of affection

tendron [tãdrõ] *nm* (**a**) *(de veau)* flank (**b**) *Fam (jeune fille)* slip of a girl

tendu, -e [tãdy] *adj* (**a**) *(corde, toile)* taut, tight (**b**) *(main)* outstretched (**c**) *(relations, visage)* strained; *(personne, atmosphère, situation)* tense

ténèbres [tenɛbr] *nfpl* **les t.** the darkness

ténébreux, -euse [tenebrø, -øz] **1** *adj Litt* (**a**) *(obscur) (forêt)* dark, gloomy (**b**) *(mystérieux) (affaire)* murky; *(style)* obscure (**c**) *(personne)* melancholic
2 *nm* **beau t.** tall dark handsome man

teneur [tənœr] *nf* (**a**) *(d'un document, d'un discours)* content; *(d'un contrat)* terms (**b**) *(quantité)* content; **t. en eau/or** water/gold content

tenir [70] [tənir] **1** *vt* (**a**) *(à la main, sur ses genoux)* to hold; **t. qn par le cou/les épaules** to have one's arm round sb's neck/shoulders; *Fig* **je tiens mon homme/la solution** I've got my man/the answer; *Fam* **t. un bon rhume** to have an awful *or Br* a stinking cold; *Fam* **qu'est-ce qu'il tient!** *(il est idiot)* what an idiot *or Br* a pillock!; **tenez!** *(c'est pour vous)* here (you are)!; **tiens, voilà Paul!** oh, there's Paul!; *Prov* **un tiens vaut mieux que deux tu l'auras** a bird in the hand is worth two in the bush

(**b**) *(dans une position)* to hold; *(dans un état)* to keep; **t. sa droite** *(en voiture)* to keep to the right (**c**) *(boutique, hôtel)* to run; *(caisse)* to be in charge of (**d**) *(rôle)* to have (**e**) *(parole, promesse)* to keep (**f**) *(maîtriser) (enfants, cheval)* to control; **t. sa langue** to hold one's tongue (**g**) *(résister à) Fam* **t. l'alcool** to hold one's drink; **t. la route** *(voiture)* to hold the road (**h**) *(avoir)* **t. qch de qn** *(caractéristique)* to get sth from sb; **je tiens la nouvelle de ma mère** I got the news from my mother (**i**) *(considérer)* **t. qn pour responsable** to hold sb responsible; **t. qch pour vrai** to consider sth to be true

2 *vi* (**a**) *(nœud, corde)* to hold; *(construction)* to stay up; *(autocollant, pansement)* to stay on; *(personne)* to last; *Fam* **il ne tient plus sur ses jambes** *ou* **debout** *(fatigué)* he's ready to drop, he's dead on his feet; *(ivre)* he can hardly stand; **t. debout** *(argument)* to stand up; **t. bon** *(personne)* to hold out; **je n'y tiens plus** I can't stand it any longer

(**b**) *(durer)* to last; **mon offre/le pari tient toujours** my offer/the bet still stands; **ça tient toujours pour dimanche?** is it still on for Sunday?

(**c**) *(être contenu)* to fit; **on tient à dix autour de cette table** this table seats ten; **ma conclusion tiendra en trois mots** my conclusion can be summed up in three words

2 *v impersonnel* **il ne tient qu'à vous que cela se fasse** it depends entirely on you whether it gets done; **s'il ne tenait qu'à moi...** if it was just up to me...; **qu'à cela ne tienne** that's not a problem

3 tenir à *vt ind* (**a**) *(liberté, amitié)* to value; *(ami)* to care about; *(objet)* to be attached to; **t. à faire qch** to be anxious *or* keen to do sth; **je tiens à ce que tout soit rangé** I want everything to be tidy; **si vous y tenez** if you insist (**b**) *(provenir de)* to be the result of, to be due to

4 tenir de *vt ind (ressembler à) (personne)* to take after; *Fam* **entre son oncle et son père, il a de qui t.!** it's not surprising when you consider his uncle and his father!; **cela tient du miracle** it's something of a miracle

5 se tenir *vpr* (**a**) *(rester) (debout)* to stand; *(assis)* to sit; **se t. debout** to be standing, to stand; **se t. tranquille** to keep quiet

(**b**) *(se comporter)* **bien se t.** to behave (oneself); *Fig* **il n'a qu'à bien se t.!** he'd better watch his step!; **se t. mal à table** to have no table manners

(**c**) *(s'accrocher)* to hold on (**à** to); **tenez-vous bien!** hold tight!; *Fig* **et alors, tiens-toi bien…!** and would you believe it…!; **se t. par la main** to hold hands; **ils se tenaient par la taille** they had their arms round each other's waist

(**d**) *(avoir lieu)* to be held, to take place

(**e**) *(être plausible)* to hang together

(**f**) **s'en t. à** *(généralités, sujet, budget)* to keep to; *(décision, consignes)* to abide by; **il ne s'en tint pas là** he didn't stop there; **je ne sais pas à quoi m'en t.** I don't know where I stand

(**g**) *(locutions)* **tiens-le-toi pour dit!** I'm telling you for the last time!

tennis [tenis] **1** *nm* (**a**) *(sport)* tennis; **t. de table** table tennis (**b**) *(court)* tennis court

2 *nm ou nf (chaussure)* tennis shoe

tennisman [tenisman] *(pl* **tennismen** [tenismɛn]*) nm* tennis player

ténor [tenɔr] **1** *adj (saxophone)* tenor

2 *nm* (**a**) *(voix, chanteur)* tenor (**b**) *Fig* **un t. de la politique** an influential figure in politics

tenseur [tɑ̃sœr] **1** *adj* **muscle t.** tensor

2 *nm* tensor

tension [tɑ̃sjɔ̃] *nf* (**a**) *(raideur, désaccord)* tension; **être sous t.** to be tense; **mettre qn sous t.** to put sb under stress; **t. nerveuse** nervous tension (**b**) **t. (artérielle)** blood pressure; **avoir de la t.** to have high blood pressure; **prendre la t. de qn** to take sb's blood pressure (**c**) *(électrique)* voltage, tension; **basse/haute t.** low/high voltage *or* tension

tentaculaire [tɑ̃takylɛr] *adj (ville)* sprawling; *(société, organisme)* octopus-like

tentacule [tɑ̃takyl] *nm* tentacle

tentant, -e [tɑ̃tɑ̃, -ɑ̃t] *adj* tempting

tentateur, -trice [tɑ̃tatœr, -tris] **1** *adj* tempting

2 *nm* tempter; *Rel* **leT.** the Tempter

3 *nf* **tentatrice** temptress

tentation [tɑ̃tasjɔ̃] *nf* temptation

tentative [tɑ̃tativ] *nf* attempt; **t. d'assassinat** attempted murder; **t. d'évasion** attempt to escape; **t. de suicide** suicide attempt

tente [tɑ̃t] *nf* (**a**) *(de camping)* tent; **coucher sous la t.** to sleep under canvas; **t. igloo** igloo tent (**b**) *Méd* **t. à oxygène** oxygen tent

tenter [tɑ̃te] *vt* (**a**) *(mettre à l'épreuve)* **t. sa chance** to try one's luck; *Fam* **t. le coup** to have a go; **t. le tout pour le tout** to go for broke (**b**) *(séduire)* to tempt; **être tenté de faire qch** to be tempted to do sth; **se laisser t.** to let oneself be tempted; **j'ai envie de me laisser t.** *(accepter)* I'm tempted to say yes; *(faire quelque chose)* I'm tempted to do it (**c**) *(essayer)* to try, to attempt; **t. de faire qch** to try *or* attempt to do sth

tenture [tɑ̃tyr] *nf (tapisserie)* hanging

tenu, -e [təny] *adj* (**a**) **bien/mal t.** *(maison, jardin)* well/poorly kept (**b**) *(contraint)* **être t. de faire qch** to be obliged to do sth; **être t. à qch** to be bound by sth (**c**) *(note)* held

ténu, -e [teny] *adj* (**a**) *(fil)* fine; *(nuance)* subtle; *(lien)* tenuous; *(espoir)* slender (**b**) *(voix)* thin

tenue [təny] *nf* (**a**) *(habillement)* outfit; *(militaire)* dress; **en t. légère** *(en vêtements d'été)* in light clothing; *Fam* **en petite t.** scantily dressed; **t. de combat** battledress; **t. de soirée** evening dress (**b**) *(bonne conduite)* good behaviour; **un peu de t.!** mind your manners!; **manquer de t.** to lack manners (**c**) *(maintien)* posture (**d**) *(niveau)* standard (**e**) *(d'une maison)* running (**f**) **t. de route** *(d'un véhicule)* road-holding

tequila [tekila] *nf* tequila

ter [tɛr] *adj* **5 t.** ≃ 5B

tercet [tɛrsɛ] *nm* tercet

térébenthine [terebɑ̃tin] *nf* turpentine

Tergal® [tɛrgal] *nm Br* Terylene®, *Am* Dacron®

tergiversations [tɛrʒivɛrsasjɔ̃] *nfpl* equivocation

tergiverser [tɛrʒivɛrse] *vi* to equivocate

terme¹ [tɛrm] *nm* (**a**) *(fin)* end; **toucher à son t.** *(projet)* to be nearing completion; *(période)* to be drawing to a close; **mettre un t. à qch** to put an end to sth; **mener qch à bon t.** to bring sth to a successful conclusion (**b**) *(date limite)* time (limit); **à court/long t.** *(projet, prévisions)* short-/long-term; **à court/long t. …** in the short/long term… (**c**) *(d'une femme enceinte)* **être à t.** to have reached term; **avant t.** *(accoucher)* prematurely; *(accouchement)* premature (**d**) *(loyer)* rent; *(date de paiement du loyer)* rent day

terme² *nm* (**a**) *(mot)* term; **en d'autres termes** in other words (**b**) *(relations)* **être en bons/mauvais termes avec qn** to be on good/bad terms with sb (**c**) **termes** *(d'un contrat)* terms

terminaison [tɛrminɛzɔ̃] *nf* (**a**) *(d'un mot)* ending (**b**) *Anat* **t. nerveuse** nerve ending

terminal, -e, -aux, -ales [tɛrminal, -o] **1** *adj (de la fin)* final; *Méd (phase)* terminal; **être en phase terminale** *(malade)* to be terminally ill

2 *nm* (**a**) *(dans un aéroport)* terminal (**b**) *Ordinat* terminal, VDU

3 *nf Scol* **terminale** *Br* ≃ upper sixth, *Am* ≃ twelfth grade, senior year

terminer [tɛrmine] **1** *vt (discours, lettre, repas)* to end, to finish (**par** with); *(travail)* to finish, to complete; **en t. avec qch** to put an end to sth

2 se terminer *vpr (saison)* to come to a close; *(soirée, concert, vacances)* to end (**par** with); *(rue)* to end; **se t. en** *(mot)* to end in

terminologie [tɛrminɔlɔʒi] *nf* terminology

terminus [tɛrminys] *nm* terminus

termite [tɛrmit] *nm* termite

terne [tɛrn] *adj* dull

ternir [tɛrnir] **1** *vt (meuble)* to fade; *(miroir, métal, réputation)* to tarnish

2 se ternir *vpr (meuble)* to fade; *(miroir, métal, réputation)* to become tarnished

terrain [tɛrɛ̃] *nm* (**a**) *(parcelle)* piece *or* plot of land (**b**) *(espace au sol, relief)* ground; **tout t.** *(véhicule)* all-terrain (**c**) *(terre)* soil (**d**) *(destiné à une activité) (de football, de rugby)* pitch, field; *(de golf)* course; **t. d'atterrissage** landing strip; **t. d'aviation** airfield; **t. à bâtir** development site; **t. de camping** campsite; *Fig* **t. d'entente** common ground; **t. de jeu** *(pour les sports) Br* playing field, *Am* athletic field; *(pour les en-*

fants) playground; **t. de sport** sports ground; **t. vague** waste ground (**e**) *Méd* **présenter un t. favorable à qch** to be prone to sth (**f**) *(locutions)* **être sur son t.** to be on familiar ground; **sur le t.** *(apprendre)* in the field; **perdre/céder du t.** to lose/give ground; **préparer le t.** to pave the way

terrasse [tɛras] *nf* (**a**) *(d'un café, d'un restaurant) Br* pavement *or Am* sidewalk area; **en t.** outside; **prix des consommations en t.** price of drinks served outside (**b**) *(de maison, d'appartement)* terrace; **(toit en) t.** terrace (roof) (**c**) *(levée de terre)* terrace; **en terrasses** *(jardin)* terraced; *(culture)* terrace

terrassement [tɛrasmɑ̃] *nm* (**a**) *(action)* excavation (**b**) *(remblai)* earthwork

terrasser [tɛrase] *vt (sujet: adversaire)* to floor; *(sujet: émotion, fatigue, nouvelle)* to overwhelm; *(sujet: maladie)* to lay low

terrassier [tɛrasje] *nm* labourer

terre [tɛr] *nf* (**a**) *(monde)* world; *Fig* **t. à t.** down-to-earth; *Fig* **revenir sur t.** to come down to earth; *Fig* **avoir les pieds sur t.** to have one's feet on the ground (**b**) *(planète)* **la T.** (the) Earth (**c**) *(sol)* ground; *(étendue)* land; **à t., par t.** on the ground; *Can Fam Fig* **être à t.** to be *or* feel down; **tomber par t.** to fall down; **faire tomber qch par t.** to drop sth; **sous t.** underground; **basses terres** lowlands; **hautes terres** highlands (**d**) *Élec Br* earth, *Am* ground; **relier** *ou* **raccorder à la t.** *Br* to earth, *Am* to ground (**e**) *(opposé à la mer)* land; **t. ferme** terra firma (**f**) *(matière)* soil, earth; **cultiver la t.** to cultivate the soil; **t. battue** mud; *(de court de tennis)* clay; **t. de Sienne** sienna (**g**) *(propriété)* **une t.** a piece of land; **terres** land (**h**) *(territoire)* land, country; **terres australes** southern lands; **la t. Adélie** Adélie Land; **la T. de Feu** Tierra del Fuego; **la T. promise** the Promised Land; **la T. sainte** the Holy Land (**i**) *(élément)* earth (**j**) *(argile)* clay; **cruche de** *ou* **en t.** earthenware jug; **t. cuite** terracotta; **une t. cuite** a piece of terracotta

terreau, -x [tɛro] *nm* compost

Terre-Neuve [tɛrnœv] *n* Newfoundland

terre-neuve [tɛrnœv] *nm inv* Newfoundland (dog)

terre-plein *(pl* **terre-pleins**) [tɛrplɛ̃] *nm (plate-forme)* platform; **t. central** *(sur route) Br* central reservation, *Am* median strip

terrer [tɛre] **se terrer** *vpr aussi Fig* to go to earth

terrestre [tɛrɛstr] *adj* (**a**) *(plante)* ground; *(animal)* land; *(transports)* surface (**b**) *(magnétisme, attraction)* of the earth (**c**) *(matériel)* worldly

terreur [tɛrœr] *nf* (**a**) *(effroi)* terror; **vivre dans la t.** to live in terror (**b**) *(emploi de la violence)* terror (**c**) *Fig (personne)* terror; **jouer les terreurs** to play the tough guy

terreux, -euse [tɛrø, -øz] *adj* (**a**) *(odeur)* earthy (**b**) *(mains)* muddy (**c**) *(teint, ciel, couleur)* muddy

terrible [tɛribl] *adj* (**a**) *(affreux, remarquable)* terrible (**b**) *Fam (formidable)* terrific, great; **pas t.** nothing special

terriblement [tɛribləmɑ̃] *adv* terribly

terrien, -enne [tɛrjɛ̃, -ɛn] **1** *adj* (**a**) *(qui possède des terres)* landowning; **propriétaire t.** landowner (**b**) *(famille, vertu)* rural (**c**) *(de la Terre)* Earth
2 *nm,f (habitant de la Terre)* earthling

terrier¹ [tɛrje] *nm* (**a**) *(d'un lapin)* burrow, hole; *(d'une taupe)* hole; *(d'un renard)* earth

terrier² *nm (chien)* terrier

terrifiant, -e [tɛrifjɑ̃, -ɑ̃t] *adj* terrifying

terrifier [tɛrifje] *vt* to terrify

terril [tɛril] *nm* slag heap

terrine [tɛrin] *nf* terrine

territoire [tɛritwar] *nm* (**a**) *(d'un État, d'un animal)* territory; **t. d'outre-mer** overseas territory; *Can* **Territoires du Nord-Ouest** Northwest Territories (**b**) *(de juge, d'évêque)* jurisdiction; *(de commune, d'arrondissement)* area

territorial, -e, -aux, -ales [tɛritɔrjal, -o] *adj* territorial

territorialité [tɛritɔrjalite] *nf* territoriality

terroir [tɛrwar] *nm* soil; **du t.** *(produit, accent, expression)* local

terrorisant, -e [tɛrɔrizɑ̃, -ɑ̃t] *adj* terrifying

terroriser [tɛrɔrize] *vt (sujet: personne)* to terrorize; *(sujet: expérience, souvenir)* to terrify

terrorisme [tɛrɔrism] *nm* terrorism

terroriste [tɛrɔrist] *adj & nmf* terrorist

tertiaire [tɛrsjɛr] **1** *adj* tertiary
2 *nm* (**a**) *(secteur économique)* service sector (**b**) *Géol* Tertiary era

tertio [tɛrsjo] *adv* thirdly

tertre [tɛrtr] *nm* hillock, mound

tes [te] *voir* **ton¹**

tessiture [tesityr] *nf Mus* range

tesson [tesɔ̃] *nm* shard; **t. de bouteille** piece of broken bottle

test [tɛst] **1** *adj inv* test; *(période)* trial
2 *nm* test; **t. de grossesse** pregnancy test

Testament [tɛstamɑ̃] *nm* **l'Ancien/le Nouveau T.** the Old/the New Testament

testament [tɛstamɑ̃] *nm (dernières volontés)* will; *Fig* legacy; **ceci est mon t.** this is my last will and testament

testamentaire [tɛstamɑ̃tɛr] *adj voir* **exécuteur**

tester [tɛste] *vt (élève, produit)* to test

testicule [tɛstikyl] *nm* testicle

testostérone [tɛstɔstɛron] *nf* testosterone

tétanie [tetani] *nf* spasms, *Spéc* tetany; **avoir une crise de t.** to go into spasms

tétanique [tetanik] **1** *adj* tetanic
2 *nmf* tetanus sufferer

tétaniser [tetanize] *vt (muscle)* to cause spasms in; *Fig* **tétanisé de peur** paralysed with fear

tétanos [tetanos] *nm* tetanus

têtard [tetar] *nm* tadpole

tête [tɛt] *nf* (**a**) *(d'une personne, d'un animal)* head; **cent cinquante têtes de bétail** a hundred and fifty head of cattle; **j'ai la t. qui tourne** my head is spinning; **tenir t. à qn** to stand up to sb; *Fam* **j'en ai par-dessus la t.** I've had it up to here; *Fam* **avoir la t. près du bonnet** to have a short fuse; *Fam* **faire une grosse t.** *ou* **une t. au carré à qn** to smash sb's face in; *Fam* **tu es tombé sur la t. ou quoi?** are you out of your mind or what?; *Fig* **marcher la t. haute** to walk with one's head held high; **la t. la première** head first; *Fig* **foncer t. baissée** to jump in head first; **de la t. aux pieds** from head to foot; **la t. nue** bare-headed; *Fam* **50 euros par t. de pipe** 50 euros a head; **t. de mort** death's head

(**b**) *(visage)* face; **faire une drôle de t.** to look odd, to make an odd face; **avoir une drôle de t.** to look odd, to have an odd face; **faire la t.** to be in a huff

(**c**) *(personne)* **une t. rousse/blonde** a redhead/blonde; **nos chères têtes blondes** *(enfants)* our little ones; **t. brûlée** hothead; *Fam* **c'est une t. à claques** he/she has a face you just want to slap; *Fam* **t. de cochon** pig-headed person; *Fam* **c'est une t. de lard** *ou* **mule** he's/she's pig-headed; **t. de linotte** bird-brain; **t. de Turc** whipping boy; **forte t.** strong-minded person; *Fam* **grosse t.** highbrow; *Fam* **avoir la grosse t.** to have a big head, to be big-headed

(**d**) *(esprit)* mind; *(cerveau)* brains; **des idées plein la t.** full of ideas; **avoir qch en t.** to have sth in one's head; **ne pas avoir de t.** to be very forgetful; **avoir toute sa t.** to be all there; **perdre la t.** to lose it; **faire qch à t. reposée** to do sth at one's leisure; **où ai-je la t.!** what am I thinking of!; **être t. en l'air** to have one's head in the clouds; **ne rien avoir dans la t.** to be empty-headed; **avoir la t. dure** to be pig-headed; **mettre qch dans la t. de qn** to put sth in sb's head; **se mettre en t. de faire qch** to get it into one's head to do sth; **se mettre dans la t. que…** to get it into one's head that…; **n'en faire qu'à sa t.** to do exactly as one pleases; **avoir une idée derrière la t.** to have an ulterior motive; **de t.** *(calculer, additionner)* in one's head

(**e**) *(cheveux)* hair

(**f**) *(d'une liste)* top; *(de chapitre)* heading; **t. d'affiche** top of the bill

(**g**) *(d'ail)* head; *(d'un arbre)* top; *(du fémur)* head

(**h**) *(d'une procession, d'un cortège)* head; *(d'un train)* front; **le wagon de t.** the front carriage; **prendre la t.** *(dans une course, dans un jeu)* to take the lead; **prendre la t. d'une entreprise** to take over as the head of a company; **être à la t. de qch** *(entreprise, fortune)* to be at the head of sth; *(protestation, révolte)* to be the leader of sth; **arriver en t.** to come in first; **être en t.** to be in the lead; **t. de lit** bed head; **t. de pont** bridgehead; **t. de série** *(au tennis)* seed

(**i**) *(appareil)* **t. chercheuse** homing device; *Ordinat* **t. d'écriture** writing *or* write head; *Ordinat* **t. de lecture** read(ing) head; **t. à palpeur** sensor head

tête-à-queue [tɛtakø] *nm inv* spin; **faire un t.** to spin round

tête-à-tête [tɛtatɛt] *nm inv* *(rendez-vous)* tête-à-tête; **en t.** in private; **en t. avec** alone with

tête-bêche [tɛtbɛʃ] *adv* *(dormir)* head to foot

tête-de-nègre [tɛtdənɛgr] *adj inv & nm inv* dark brown

tétée [tete] *nf* feed; **donner la t. à un enfant** to feed a child

téter [tete] *vt* (**a**) *(lait)* to suck; **t. sa mère** to feed (**b**) *(cigare, pipe, stylo)* to suck on

tétine [tetin] *nf* (**a**) *(d'un biberon)* teat (**b**) *(sucette)* Br dummy, Am pacifier

téton [tetɔ̃] *nm* (**a**) *Fam (sein de femme)* tit (**b**) *(d'une pièce détachée)* lug

tétraèdre [tetraɛdr] **1** *adj* tetrahedral
  2 *nm* tetrahedron

tétralogie [tetralɔʒi] *nf* tetralogy

tétraplégie [tetrapleʒi] *nf* quadriplegia

tétraplégique [tetrapleʒik] *adj & nmf* quadriplegic

tétras [tetrã] *nm* grouse

têtu, -e [tety] **1** *adj* stubborn, obstinate; *Fam* **t. comme une mule** as stubborn as a mule
  2 *nm,f* stubborn *or* obstinate person

teuf [tœf] *nf Fam* party

teuf-teuf *(pl* **teufs-teufs**) [tœftœf] *Fam* **1** *nf (voiture)* old banger
  2 *nm (bruit)* chug-chug

teuton, -onne [tøtɔ̃, -ɔn] **1** *adj* Teutonic
  2 *nm,f* **T.** Teuton

texan, -e [tɛksɑ̃, -an] **1** *adj* Texan
  2 *nm,f* **T.** Texan

texte [tɛkst] *nm* (**a**) *(d'un livre, d'un dépliant)* text; **t. publicitaire** advertising copy; **lire un auteur dans le t.** to read an author in the original; **textes choisis (de)** selected passages (from) (**b**) *(d'un opéra)* libretto; *(d'une chanson)* words; *(d'un acteur)* lines; *(d'une pièce de théâtre)* script

textile [tɛkstil] **1** *adj* textile
  2 *nm* (**a**) *(fibre)* textile (**b**) *(industrie)* **le t.** the textile industry, textiles

texto [tɛksto] *Fam* **1** *nm Tél* text message
  2 *adv* word for word; **t.!** those were his/her/*etc* very words!

textuel, -elle [tɛkstɥɛl] *adj* (**a**) *(analyse)* textual (**b**) *(traduction)* word-for-word, literal; *Fam* **t.!** those were his/her/*etc* very words!

textuellement [tɛkstɥɛlmɑ̃] *adv* word for word, literally

texture [tɛkstyr] *nf (d'une substance, du sol)* texture

TF 1 [teefœ̃] *nf (abrév* **Télévision Française 1**) = French commercial television channel

TGB [teʒebe] *nf (abrév* **très grande bibliothèque**) = the new French national library in the Tolbiac area of Paris

TGV [teʒeve] *nm (abrév* **train à grande vitesse**) high-speed train

thaï, thaïe [taj] **1** *adj* Thai
  2 *nm,f* **T.** Thai
  3 *nm (langue)* Thai

thaïlandais, -e [tajlɑ̃dɛ, -ɛz] **1** *adj* Thai
  2 *nm,f* **T.** Thai

Thaïlande [tajlɑ̃d] *nf* **la T.** Thailand

thalassothérapie [talasoterapi] *nf* thalassotherapy, seawater therapy

thé [te] *nm* (**a**) *(boisson)* tea; **t. au citron** tea with lemon; **t. glacé** iced tea; **t. à la menthe** mint tea; **t. nature/au lait** tea without milk/with milk; **t. en sachets** tea bags (**b**) *(goûter)* tea; **t. dansant** tea dance

théâtral, -e, -aux, -ales [teatral, -o] *adj* (**a**) *(œuvre, production)* theatrical; *(effet)* dramatic; *(représentation)* stage (**b**) *Péj (artificiel)* melodramatic

théâtre [teatr] *nm* (**a**) *(édifice, salle)* theatre; **t. de marionnettes** puppet theatre; **t. de verdure** open-air theatre (**b**) *(art, métier)* theatre; **c'est un homme de t.** he works in theatre; **faire du t.** *(professionnellement)* to be an actor/actress; *(en amateur)* to do some acting; **adapté pour le t.** adapted for the stage (**c**) *(œuvres) (d'un auteur)* plays; *(genre)* theatre; **t. de boulevard** light comedies (**d**) *Fig (attitude artificielle)* **c'est du t.** it's an act (**e**) *(d'un crime, d'un accident)* scene

théière [tejɛr] *nf* teapot

théine [tein] *nf* theine

thématique [tematik] **1** *adj* thematic
  2 *nf* themes

thème [tɛm] *nm* (**a**) *(d'un discours, d'une œuvre, d'un morceau de musique)* theme (**b**) *(traduction)* prose (**c**) *(d'un verbe, d'un nom)* stem (**d**) *Astrol* **t. (astral)** birth chart

théocratie [teɔkrasi] *nf* theocracy

théocratique [teɔkratik] *adj* theocratic

théologie [teɔlɔʒi] *nf* theology

théologien, -enne [teɔlɔʒjɛ̃, -ɛn] *nm,f* theologian

théologique [teɔlɔʒik] *adj* theological
théorème [teɔrɛm] *nm* theorem
théoricien, -enne [teɔrisjɛ̃, -ɛn] *nm,f* theoretician, theorist
théorie [teɔri] *nf* theory; **en t.** in theory
théorique [teɔrik] *adj* theoretical
théoriquement [teɔrikmɑ̃] *adv* theoretically
thérapeute [terapøt] *nmf* therapist
thérapeutique [terapøtik] **1** *adj* therapeutic
   2 *nf* (**a**) *(science)* therapeutics *(singulier)* (**b**) *(traitement)* therapy
thérapie [terapi] *nf* therapy; **t. de groupe** group therapy
thermal, -e, -aux, -ales [tɛrmal, -o] *adj* thermal
thermalisme [tɛrmalism] *nm* hydrotherapy
thermes [tɛrm] *nmpl* (**a**) *(établissement de soins)* thermal baths (**b**) *(chez les Anciens)* thermae, public baths
thermique [tɛrmik] *adj* thermal
thermoélectrique [tɛrmoelɛktrik] *adj* thermoelectric
thermomètre [tɛrmɔmɛtr] *nm* thermometer; *Fig (de l'opinion, d'une tendance)* barometer; **t. médical** clinical thermometer
thermonucléaire [tɛrmonykleɛr] *adj* thermonuclear
Thermos® [tɛrmɔs] *nm ou nf* **(bouteille) T.** Thermos® *(Br* flask *or Am* bottle)
thermostat [tɛrmɔsta] *nm* thermostat
thésard, -e [tezar, -ard] *nm,f* PhD student
thésaurisation [tezɔrizasjɔ̃] *nf* hoarding
thésauriser [tezɔrize] *vt & vi* to hoard
thesaurus [tezɔrys] *nm* thesaurus
thèse [tɛz] *nf* (**a**) *(proposition intellectuelle)* thesis; **roman/littérature à t.** novel/literature of ideas (**b**) *Univ* thesis *(submitted for doctorate)*
thon [tɔ̃] *nm* tuna; **t. blanc** longfin tuna; **t. au naturel/à l'huile** tuna in brine/in oil
thoracique [tɔrasik] *adj* thoracic
thorax [tɔraks] *nm* thorax
thriller [srilœr] *nm* thriller
thrombose [trɔ̃boz] *nf* thrombosis
thune [tyn] *nf* (**a**) *très Fam (argent)* cash, *Br* dosh; **ne pas avoir une t.** to be totally skint (**b**) *Suisse* = Swiss five-franc coin
thuya [tyja] *nm* thuja
thym [tɛ̃] *nm* thyme
thyroïde [tirɔid] *adj & nf* thyroid
thyroïdien, -enne [tirɔidjɛ̃, -ɛn] *adj* thyroid
tiaffe [tjaf] *nf Suisse Fam* (**a**) *(chaleur)* heatwave (**b**) *(neige fondante)* slush
tiare [tjar] *nf* tiara
Tibet [tibɛ] *nm* **le T.** Tibet
tibétain, -e [tibetɛ̃, -ɛn] **1** *adj* Tibetan
   2 *nm,f* **T.** Tibetan
   3 *nm (langue)* Tibetan
tibia [tibja] *nm* shinbone, *Spéc* tibia
Tibre [tibr] *nm* **le T.** the Tiber
tic [tik] *nm* (**a**) *(convulsion involontaire)* tic, twitch; **t. nerveux** nervous tic *or* twitch (**b**) *(manie)* habit, mannerism; **t. de langage** verbal mannerism
ticket [tikɛ] *nm* ticket; *Fam Fig* **avoir un** *ou* **le t. avec qn** to have made a hit with sb; **t. de caisse** receipt; **t. modérateur** = portion of the cost of treatment paid by the patient; **t. de quai** platform ticket; **t. de rationnement** ration coupon

ticket-repas *(pl* **tickets-repas)** [tikɛrəpɑ] *nm Br* luncheon voucher, *Am* meal ticket
ticket-restaurant *(pl* **tickets-restaurant)** [tikɛrɛstɔrɑ̃] *nm Br* luncheon voucher, *Am* meal ticket
tic-tac [tiktak] *nm inv (d'une horloge)* tick-tock, ticking
tie-break *(pl* **tie-breaks)** [tajbrɛk] *nm* tie break
tiédasse [tjedas] *adj Péj* lukewarm, tepid
tiède [tjɛd] **1** *adv* **il fait t.** it's mild
   2 *adj* (**a**) *(vent)* mild; *(bain, boisson)* tepid, lukewarm (**b**) *Péj (peu enthousiaste)* half-hearted
   3 *nf Suisse* heatwave
tiédeur [tjedœr] *nf* (**a**) *(du vent)* mildness; *(de l'eau)* tepidness (**b**) *Péj (manque d'enthousiasme)* half-heartedness
tiédir [tjedir] **1** *vt (réchauffer)* to warm (up); *(refroidir)* to cool (down)
   2 *vi* (**a**) *(devenir plus chaud)* to warm up; *(devenir moins chaud)* to cool down (**b**) *Fig (amitié, passion)* to cool off
tien, -enne [tjɛ̃, tjɛn] **1** *pron possessif* **le t., la tienne, les tiens, les tiennes** yours; *(en insistant)* your own; **tu me prêtes le t.?** can I borrow yours?; **tu n'en as pas besoin, tu as le t.** you don't need it, you've got your own; *Fam* **à la tienne!** cheers!
   2 *nm* **il faut que tu y mettes du t.** you should really do your share
   3 *nmpl* **les tiens** *(ta famille)* your family
   4 *nfpl Fam* **tu as encore fait des tiennes!** you've been up to your old tricks again!
tiendrais, tienne, tiens *etc voir* **tenir**
tierce [tjɛrs] **1** *adj voir* **tiers**
   2 *nf* (**a**) *Mus* third (**b**) *(aux cartes)* tierce
tiercé [tjɛrse] *nm* = forecast of the first three horses in a race; **jouer au t.** to bet on the horses; **le t. gagnant** the winning combination
tiers, tierce [tjɛr, tjɛrs] **1** *adj* third; **le t. état** the third estate; **une tierce personne** a third party
   2 *nm* (**a**) *(fraction)* third; **t. payant** = system of direct payment for medical treatment by the insurer; **t. provisionnel** interim tax payment *(approximately one third of previous year's tax)* (**b**) *(personne)* third party
tiers-monde *(pl* **tiers-mondes)** [tjɛrmɔ̃d] *nm* **le t.** the Third World
tifs [tif] *nmpl Fam* hair
TIG [tiʒ] *nm (abrév* **travail d'intérêt général)** community service
tige [tiʒ] *nf* (**a**) *(d'une plante)* stem, stalk; **rosier sur t.** standard rose (**b**) *(d'une chaussure)* upper (**c**) *(en métal)* rod (**d**) *Fam (cigarette) Br* fag, *Am* butt
tignasse [tiɲas] *nf Fam* mop (of hair)
Tigre [tigr] *nm* **le T.** the Tigris
tigre [tigr] *nm* tiger; **t. du Bengale** Bengal tiger
tigré, -e [tigre] *adj (rayé)* striped
tigresse [tigrɛs] *nf* tigress
tilde [tild] *nm* tilde
tilleul [tijœl] *nm* (**a**) *(arbre)* lime (tree) (**b**) *(infusion)* lime-blossom tea
tilt [tilt] *nm* **faire t.** *(au billard électrique)* to signal the end of the game; *Fig* **ça a fait t.** the penny dropped
timbale [tɛ̃bal] *nf* (**a**) *(gobelet)* (metal) drinking cup; *Fig* **décrocher la t.** to hit the jackpot (**b**) *(tambour)* kettledrum; **les timbales** *(dans un orchestre)* the timpani (**c**) *(moule, plat)* timbale
timbre [tɛ̃br] *nm* (**a**) *(vignette)* stamp; **t. de collection** collector's stamp; **t. fiscal** excise *or* tax stamp (**b**) *(in-*

strument encreur, marque) stamp; **t. dateur** date stamp (**c**) *(sonnette)* bell; **t. de bicyclette** bicycle bell (**d**) *(d'une voix, d'un instrument)* timbre, tone; **voix sans t.** toneless voice (**e**) *(pour traitement médical)* patch; **t. tuberculinique**TB patch

---

Timbre fiscal

These stamps are sold at most tobacconists and are used to pay fees due for obtaining official documents, such as identity papers, vehicle documents and legal certificates.

---

timbré, -e [tɛ̃bre] *adj* (**a**) *(document, enveloppe)* stamped (**b**) *Fam (fou)* mad

timbre-poste *(pl* **timbres-poste)** [tɛ̃brəpɔst] *nm* (postage) stamp

timbrer [tɛ̃bre] **1** *vt* (**a**) *(lettre, paquet)* to put a stamp/ stamps on (**b**) *(passeport, document)* to stamp **2** *vi Suisse (au chômage)* to sign on

timide [timid] **1** *adj* (**a**) *(personne, sourire, voix)* shy (**b**) *(critique, protestation, tentative)* timid **2** *nmf* shy person; **c'est un grand t.** he's very shy

timidement [timidmɑ̃] *adv* (**a**) *(sourire, parler)* shyly (**b**) *(critiquer, protester)* timidly

timidité [timidite] *nf* (**a**) *(d'une personne)* shyness (**b**) *(d'une critique, d'une protestation)* timidity

timing [tajmiŋ] *nm* timing

timoré, -e [timɔre] *adj* timorous, fearful

tintamarre [tɛ̃tamar] *nm Fam* din, racket; **faire du t.** to make a din *or* racket

tintement [tɛ̃təmɑ̃] *nm (de clochettes)* tinkling; *(de pièces de monnaie)* jingling; **t. d'oreilles** ringing in the ears

tinter [tɛ̃te] *vi* (**a**) *(clochettes)* to tinkle; *(pièces de monnaie)* to jingle (**b**) *(oreilles)* to ring

tintin [tɛ̃tɛ̃] *exclam Fam* no way José!; **faire t.** to go without

tintouin [tɛ̃twɛ̃] *nm Fam* (**a**) *(bruit)* din, racket (**b**) *(souci)* trouble

TIOP [tjɔp] *nm Banque (abrév* **taux interbancaire offert à Paris)** PIBOR

tipi [tipi] *nm* tepee

tique [tik] *nf* tick

tiquer [tike] *vi Fam (personne)* to wince; **il n'a pas tiqué** he didn't bat an eyelid

TIR [tir] *nm (abrév* **transports internationaux routiers)** TIR

tir [tir] *nm* (**a**) *(activité)* shooting; **t. à l'arc** archery; **faire du t. à l'arc** to do archery; **t. à la carabine** rifle shooting; **t. au pigeon** clay pigeon shooting (**b**) *(coup de feu)* shot (**c**) *(à la pétanque)* throw; **t. (au but)** *(au football)* shot (at goal) (**d**) *(stand)* rifle range; **t. (forain)** shooting gallery

tirade [tirad] *nf Théât* monologue; *Fig* tirade

tirage [tiraʒ] *nm* (**a**) *(impression)* printing (**b**) *(nombre d'exemplaires) (d'un journal)* circulation; *(d'un livre)* print run; **édition à t. limité** limited edition (**c**) *(d'une cheminée)* draught (**d**) *(de loterie)* draw (**de** for); **t. au sort** drawing lots; **procéder à un t. au sort** to draw lots

tiraillement [tirajmɑ̃] *nm* (**a**) *(crampe)* **tiraillements d'estomac** stomach cramps (**b**) *(conflit)* **tiraillements (entre)** conflict (between)

tirailler [tiraje] **1** *vt* (**a**) *(tirer sur)* to pull at, to tug at (**b**) *(écarteler)* **être tiraillé entre** to be torn between

2 *vi* (**a**) *(avec une arme)* to shoot wildly (**b**) *(peau)* **j'ai la peau qui tiraille** my skin feels tight

tirailleur [tirajœr] *nm (soldat éclaireur)* skirmisher

Tirana [tirana] *n* Tirana

tirant [tirɑ̃] *nm* (**a**) *(de botte)* boot strap (**b**) **t. d'eau** draught *(volume of water)*

tire [tir] *nf* (**a**) *Fam (voiture)* car (**b**) *Can (confiserie)* molasses toffee, *Am* molasses candy, taffy

tiré, -e [tire] **1** *adj* (**a**) *(traits)* drawn; **avoir les traits tirés** to look drawn (**b**) *(cheveux)* scraped back **2** *nf Fam* **tirée** *(trajet)* long haul

tire-au-flanc [tiroflɑ̃] *nm inv Fam* shirker, *Br* skiver

tire-bouchon *(pl* **tire-bouchons)** [tirbuʃɔ̃] *nm* corkscrew; **en t.** *(queue)* curly

tire-bouchonner [tirbuʃɔne] *vi (chaussettes)* to be at half-mast; *(pantalon)* to be crumpled

tire-d'aile [tirdɛl] **à tire-d'aile** *adv* **s'envoler à t.** to fly swiftly away; *Fig* **partir** *ou* **s'éloigner à t.** to fly off

tire-fesses [tirfɛs] *nm inv Fam* T-bar

tire-jus [tirʒy] *nm inv très Fam* snot rag

tire-lait [tirlɛ] *nm inv* breast pump

tire-larigot [tirlarigo] **à tire-larigot** *adv Fam* to one's heart's content

tirelire [tirlir] *nf Br* moneybox, *Am* coin bank; *Fig* **casser sa t.** to break into one's piggy bank

tirer [tire] **1** *vt* (**a**) *(vers soi)* to pull; *(chaussettes)* to pull up; **t. qch vers le haut/bas** to pull sth up/down; **t. qn par la manche** to pull at sb's sleeve; **t. qn par le bras** to pull sb by the arm; **t. les cheveux à qn** to pull sb's hair

(**b**) *(rideaux)* to draw; *(store)* to pull down; *(verrou) (fermer)* to shoot; *(ouvrir)* to draw

(**c**) *(extraire)* **t. qch de qch** to pull sth out of sth; **t. de l'eau d'un puits** to draw water from a well; **une citation tirée d'un texte** a quotation taken from a text; **t. qn d'embarras** to get sb out of a tight spot; **t. qn de son lit** to drag sb out of bed; **t. son origine de qch** to have its origin in sth; **t. une conclusion de qch** to draw a conclusion from sth; **t. une leçon de qch** to learn a lesson from sth

(**d**) *(tendre) (tissu, fil)* to pull tight; *Fig* **t. les ficelles** to pull the strings

(**e**) *(carte)* to draw; **t. les cartes** *(cartomancienne)* to read the cards; **t. qch au sort** to draw lots for sth; **tirer qn au sort** to draw lots to choose sb

(**f**) *(tracer) (trait)* to draw; *(plan)* to draw up

(**g**) *(imprimer)* to print; *Fam Hum* **se faire t. le portrait** to have one's photograph taken

(**h**) *(chèque)* to draw (**sur** on)

(**i**) *(coup de feu, balle)* to fire; *(flèche)* to shoot; *(feu d'artifice)* to let off; **t. un coup de revolver (sur)** to fire a gun (at)

(**j**) *(locutions) très Fam* **plus qu'un mois à t.!** just one more month to get through!; **je te tire mon chapeau!** I take my hat off to you!

2 *vi* (**a**) *(exercer une traction)* to pull; **t. sur qch** *(corde)* to pull on sth; *(pull)* to pull sth down; *(par tic)* to pull at sth

(**b**) *(personne armée, arme)* to shoot; **t. à la carabine** to shoot with a rifle; **t. sur qn/qch** to shoot sb/sth; **t. dans le dos à qn** to shoot sb in the back

(**c**) *(peau)* to feel tight

(**d**) *(être imprimé)* **t. à 100 000 exemplaires** to have a circulation of 100,000

(**e**) *(cheminée)* to draw

(**f**) *(à la pétanque)* to throw; *(au football)* to shoot (**g**) *(aspirer)* **t. sur une cigarette/pipe** to puff on a cigarette/pipe

(**h**) *(locutions)* **ça ne tire pas à conséquence** it's of no consequence; **t. à sa fin** *(période, journée)* to be drawing to a close; *(réserves, économies)* to be running out; *Fam* **t. au flanc** to shirk, *Br* to skive

3 tirer sur *vt ind (se rapprocher de) (couleur)* to verge on

4 se tirer *vpr* (**a**) *(se sortir)* **se t. de qch** to get out of sth; **s'en t.** *(d'une maladie, d'un accident)* to pull through; *(financièrement)* to make it; **s'en t. avec qch** to get away with sth

(**b**) *Fam (partir)* to make tracks

tiret [tiʀɛ] *nm* dash

tirette [tiʀɛt] *nf* (**a**) *(d'un bureau)* pull-out shelf; *(d'une table)* leaf (**b**) *(de distributeur)* pull handle (**c**) *Belg (fermeture Éclair®)* *Br* zip, *Am* zipper

tireur, -euse [tiʀœʀ, -øz] **1** *nm,f* gunman; **t. d'élite** marksman, *f* markswoman; **c'est un bon t.** he's a good shot; **un t. embusqué** a sniper

2 *nf* **tireuse de cartes** fortune teller

tiroir [tiʀwaʀ] *nm* drawer; *Fig* **à tiroirs** *(roman)* = containing individual episodes within the main storyline

tiroir-caisse *(pl* **tiroirs-caisses)** [tiʀwaʀkɛs] *nm* till, cash register

tisane [tizan] *nf* herbal tea

tison [tizɔ̃] *nm* (fire)brand

tisonner [tizɔne] *vt* to poke

tisonnier [tizɔnje] *nm* poker

tissage [tisaʒ] *nm* (**a**) *(activité)* weaving; **t. à la main/mécanique** hand-loom/power-loom weaving (**b**) *(établissement industriel)* cloth mill

tisser [tise] **1** *vt* (**a**) *(textile, liens, intrigue)* to weave (**b**) *(sujet: araignée)* to spin

2 se tisser *vpr (liens, intrigue)* to be woven

tisserand, -e [tisʀɑ̃, -ɑ̃d] *nm,f* weaver

tissu [tisy] *nm* (**a**) *(étoffe)* material, cloth; *Fig (urbain, social)* fabric; **t. d'ameublement** furnishing fabric (**b**) *Fig (de mensonges, d'incohérences)* tissue (**c**) *Biol* tissue

tissu-éponge *(pl* **tissus-éponges)** [tisyepɔ̃ʒ] *nm* (terry) towelling

titan [titɑ̃] *nm* Titan; **travail de t.** Herculean task

titane [titan] *nm* titanium

titi [titi] *nm Fam* cheeky urchin

titiller [titije] *vt* to titillate

titrage [titʀaʒ] *nm* (**a**) *(de film)* titling (**b**) *(d'un alcool)* determination of the strength

titre [titʀ] *nm* (**a**) *(de livre, de chanson, de film)* title (**b**) *(de chapitre, de page)* heading; **les gros titres** the headlines; **faire les gros titres** to hit the headlines (**c**) *(d'une personne)* title; **en t.** *(titulaire)* permanent; *(attitré)* official (**d**) *(qualité de champion)* title (**e**) *(diplôme)* qualification (**f**) *(certificat)* **t. de propriété** title deed; **t. de transport** ticket (**g**) *Fin* security (**h**) *(d'un alcool)* strength; *(de l'or, d'une monnaie)* fineness; *(d'un alliage)* grade (**i**) *(locutions)* **à ce t.** *(pour cette raison)* therefore; *(en cette qualité)* as such; **à quel t.?** *(de quel droit)* on what grounds?; **au même t. que** in the same way as; **à t. gratuit** free of charge; **à t. d'exemple** by way of example

titré, -e [titʀe] *adj (personne)* titled

titrer [titʀe] *vt* (**a**) *(livre, film)* to title (**b**) *(alcool)* to determine the strength of

tituber [titybe] *vi* to stagger (**de** with)

titulaire [titylɛʀ] **1** *adj* (**a**) *(dans l'administration)* with a permanent contract; *(professeur d'université)* with tenure (**b**) *(détenteur)* **être t. de qch** to be the holder of sth

2 *nmf (détenteur)* holder

titularisation [titylaʀizasjɔ̃] *nf* granting of permanent contract; *(à l'université)* granting of tenure

titulariser [titylaʀize] *vt* to give a permanent contract to; *(professeur d'université)* to give tenure to

TNT [teɛnte] *nm (abrév* **trinitrotoluène**) TNT

toast [tost] *nm* (**a**) *(de pain)* piece *or* slice of toast; **t. beurré** piece *or* slice of buttered toast; **des toasts** toast (**b**) *(hommage)* toast; **porter un t. à qn** to drink a toast to sb

toboggan [tɔbɔgɑ̃] *nm* (**a**) *(de terrain de jeu)* slide; *(dans une piscine)* flume; **faire du t.** to play on the slide (**b**) *(pour marchandises)* chute (**c**) *(viaduc) Br* flyover, *Am* overpass (**d**) *Can (traîneau)* toboggan; **faire du t.** to go tobogganing

toc [tɔk] **1** *exclam* **t. t.!** knock knock!; *Fig* **et t.!** so there!

2 *adj inv Fam (faux)* fake; *(de mauvais goût)* tacky

3 *nm Fam* **bijoux en t.** fake jewellery; **c'est du t.** it's fake

toccata [tɔkata] *nf Mus* toccata

tocsin [tɔksɛ̃] *nm* alarm bell

toge [tɔʒ] *nf* (**a**) *(de magistrat, d'avocat)* gown (**b**) *(romaine)* toga

Togo [togo] *nm* **le T.** Togo

togolais, -e [tɔgɔlɛ, -ɛz] **1** *adj* Togolese

2 *nm,f* **T.** Togolese

tohu-bohu [tɔybɔy] *nm (désordre)* confusion; *(bruit)* hubbub

toi [twa] *pron personnel* (**a**) *(sujet)* you; **t., ne m'énerve pas!** don't annoy me!; **t., tu aurais certainement cédé** YOU would probably have given in (**b**) *(objet direct)* you; **et t., il t'a salué?** and what about you, did he say hello to you? (**c**) *(réfléchi)* yourself; **tais-t.!** be quiet! (**d**) *(avec préposition)* you; **je ne te le prêterai pas, à t.** I won't lend it to YOU; **c'est à t., tout ça?** is that all yours?; **tu auras ta chambre à t.** you'll have your own room; *Fam* **une copine à t.** a friend of yours; **tu ne penses qu'à t.** you think only of yourself (**e**) *(dans les comparaisons)* you; **je n'en sais pas plus que t.** I don't know any more about it than you (do)

toile [twal] *nf* (**a**) *(tissu)* cloth; **t. d'araignée** cobweb, spider's web; **t. cirée** oilcloth; **t. de fond** backdrop; *Fig* **en t. de fond** as a backdrop; **t. (de lin)** linen; **un pantalon en t.** linen trousers; **t. à matelas** ticking; **t. de tente** canvas (**b**) *(tableau)* painting, canvas (**c**) *Fam (film)* **se faire une t.** to go to the *Br* pictures *or Am* movies (**d**) *Ordinat* **la T.** the Web

toilettage [twalɛtaʒ] *nm* (**a**) *(d'un chien)* grooming (**b**) *(d'un texte)* tidying up

toilette [twalɛt] *nf* (**a**) *(action de se laver)* washing; **faire sa t.** to have a wash (**b**) **toilettes** *(W.-C.) Br* toilet, *Am* rest room; *(publiques)* public convenience; **toilettes pour dames** ladies' *Br* toilet *or Am* room; **toilettes pour hommes** *Br* gents' toilet, *Am* men's room (**c**) *(vêtements)* outfit; **porter bien la t.** to look good in formal clothes

toiletter [twalete] **1** *vt* (**a**) *(chien)* to groom (**b**) *(texte)* to tidy up

2 se toiletter *vpr Can* to dress up (smartly)

toi-même [twamɛm] *pron personnel* yourself; *Fam* **menteur! – t.!** liar! – liar yourself!

toise [twaz] *nf* height gauge

toiser [twaze] **1** *vt* to look up and down

  2 se toiser *upr* to look each other up and down

toison [twazɔ̃] *nf* (**a**) *(de mouton)* fleece; **la T. d'or** the Golden Fleece (**b**) *(chevelure)* mane (of hair)

toit [twa] *nm* roof; *Fig* **être sans t.** not to have a roof over one's head; **accueillir qn sous son t.** to take sb in; **t. de chaume** thatched roof; **t. ouvrant** sun roof

toiture [twatyr] *nf* roofing, roof

Tokyo [tɔkjo] *n* Tokyo

tôle¹ [tol] *nf* (**a**) *(matériau)* sheet metal; **t. ondulée** corrugated iron (**b**) *(feuille)* metal sheet

tôle² = **taule**

tolérable [tɔlerabl] *adj* tolerable; **votre comportement n'est pas t.** your behaviour is intolerable

tolérance [tɔlerɑ̃s] *nf* tolerance; *(concession)* concession

tolérant, -e [tɔlerɑ̃, -ɑ̃t] *adj* tolerant

tolérer [tɔlere] **1** *vt* to tolerate; **je ne tolère pas qu'on me parle sur ce ton!** I won't tolerate being spoken to like that!

  2 se tolérer *upr* to tolerate each other

tôlier [tolje] = **taulier**

tollé [tɔle] *nm* outcry; **t. général** public outcry

TOM [tɔm] *nm* *(abrév* **territoire d'outre-mer)** overseas territory

tomahawk [tɔmaok] *nm* tomahawk

tomate [tɔmat] *nf* tomato

tombal, -e, -als *ou* **-aux, -ales** [tɔ̃bal, -o] *adj voir* **pierre**

tombant, -e [tɔ̃bɑ̃, -ɑ̃t] *adj (épaules)* sloping; *(oreilles)* floppy

tombe [tɔ̃b] *nf* (**a**) *(sépulture)* grave; *(avec un monument)* tomb; **emporter un secret dans la t.** to take a secret to the grave; **suivre qn dans la t.** to follow sb to the grave (**b**) *(pierre tombale)* gravestone, tombstone

tombeau, -x [tɔ̃bo] *nm* tomb; *Fig* **à t. ouvert** at breakneck speed

tombée [tɔ̃be] *nf* **la t. du jour** *ou* **de la nuit** nightfall

tomber [tɔ̃be] **1** *vi (aux* **être)** (**a**) *(personne, objet)* to fall (down); *(précipitations, feuilles)* to fall; **t. de qch** *(chaise, échelle)* to fall off sth; *(arbre)* to fall out of sth; **t. dans un piège** to fall into a trap; **faire t. qn/qch** to knock sb/sth over; **laisser t.** *(objet)* to drop; *Fam* **laisser t. qn** to let sb down; *Fam* **laisse t., c'est inutile** forget it, it's pointless; **t. à l'eau** *(personne, objet)* to fall in (the water); *(projet)* to fall through; *Fig* **il faut être tombé bien bas** you have to have sunk pretty low; **t. de haut** to come back to earth with a bump

  (**b**) *(gouvernement, ville)* to fall

  (**c**) *(nouvelle)* to come through

  (**d**) *(mourir)* to fall; *Fam* **t. comme des mouches** to be dropping like flies

  (**e**) *(vent, prix, fièvre)* to drop; *(conversation)* to flag; *(enthousiasme)* to wane

  (**f**) *(nuit)* to fall

  (**g**) *(devenir brusquement)* **t. amoureux de qn,** *Can* **t. en amour avec qn** to fall in love with sb; *Fam* **t. enceinte** to get pregnant

  (**h**) *(date, événement)* to fall

  (**i**) *(pendre) (draperie, vêtement)* to hang; **ses cheveux lui tombent jusqu'aux reins** her hair hangs right down her back

  (**j**) *(locutions)* **t. bien** to come at just the right time; **t. mal** to come at the wrong time; **je suis bien/mal tombé** *(chanceux/malchanceux)* I was lucky/un-

lucky; **ça tombe sous le sens** it stands to reason; **t. sur qn** *(l'agresser)* to pitch into sb; *(le rencontrer par hasard)* to bump into sb; **t. sur qch** to come across sth; **il fallait que ça tombe sur moi!** it had to happen to me!

  2 *vt Fam (aux* **avoir)** (**a**) *(séduire)* to pull (**b**) *(enlever)* **t. la veste** to take off one's jacket

tombereau, -x [tɔ̃bro] *nm* (**a**) *(charrette)* tip-cart (**b**) *(contenu)* cartload

tombeur [tɔ̃bœr] *nm Fam* womanizer, ladykiller

tombola [tɔ̃bɔla] *nf* raffle

tome [tom] *nm (volume)* volume

tomme [tom] *nf* = cheese made in Savoie

ton¹, ta, tes [tɔ̃, ta, te]

> ta becomes **ton** before a word beginning with a vowel or mute h.

adj possessif your; **t. chien** your dog; **ta voiture** your car; **t. ami/amie** your friend; **tes enfants** your children; **t. père et ta mère** your mother and father; **un de tes amis** one of your friends, a friend of yours; *Fam* **tu as eu t. vendredi** you got Friday off

ton² *nm* (**a**) *(qualité de voix)* tone; **hausser/baisser le t.** to raise/lower one's voice; **sur le t. de la plaisanterie** in a joking tone of voice (**b**) *(goût)* **il est de bon t. de le faire** it's good form to do it (**c**) *(gamme)* key; *(intervalle musical)* tone; **donner le t.** to give the pitch; *Fig* to set the tone (**d**) *Ling* tone; **langue à tons** tonal language (**e**) *(teinte)* shade, tone; *Ordinat* **tons de gris** shades of grey

tonal, -e, -als, -ales [tɔnal] *adj Mus* tonal

tonalité [tɔnalite] *nf* (**a**) *(au téléphone) Br* dialling *or* **Am** dial tone (**b**) *(d'un morceau de musique)* key; *Fig (d'une œuvre)* tone

tondeuse [tɔ̃døz] *nf* (**a**) *(de jardin)* **t. (à gazon)** (lawn) mower (**b**) *(de coiffeur)* clippers

tondre [tɔ̃dr] *vt* (**a**) *(herbe)* to mow; *(mouton)* to shear; **se faire t.** *(très court)* to have one's hair cropped; *(complètement)* to have all one's hair shaved off (**b**) *Fam (dépouiller)* to fleece

toner [tɔnɛr] *nm* toner

tong [tɔ̃g] *nf Br* flip-flop, *Am* thong

Tonga [tɔ̃ga] *nfpl* **les (îles) T.** Tonga

tonicité [tɔnisite] *nf* (**a**) *(des muscles)* tone (**b**) *(de l'air, du climat)* bracing effect

tonifiant, -e [tɔnifjɑ̃, -ɑ̃t] *adj (air, marche)* bracing

tonifier [tɔnifje] *vt (peau, muscles)* to tone up; *(esprit)* to stimulate

tonique [tɔnik] **1** *adj* (**a**) *(climat, vent)* bracing, invigorating (**b**) *(boisson, remède)* tonic (**c**) *(personne)* energetic, dynamic (**d**) *(accent)* tonic; *(syllabe)* accented

  2 *nm* (**a**) *(remède)* tonic (**b**) *(lotion)* toner

  3 *nf Mus* tonic, keynote

tonitruant, -e [tɔnitryɑ̃, -ɑ̃t] *adj (voix, bruit)* thundering

tonnage [tɔnaʒ] *nm* tonnage

tonnant, -e [tɔnɑ̃, -ɑ̃t] *adj (voix)* thundering

tonne [tɔn] *nf* metric ton, tonne; *Fam Fig* **des tonnes de qch** tons of sth; *Fam* **en faire des tonnes** to go overboard

tonneau, -x [tɔno] *nm* (**a**) *(récipient)* barrel, cask; *Fig* **du même t.** of the same type (**b**) *(en voiture)* roll; **faire un t.** to roll over

tonnelier [tɔnəlje] *nm* cooper

tonnelle [tɔnɛl] *nf (charmille)* arbour, bower

tonner [tɔne] **1** vi (**a**) (canons) to thunder (**b**) (fulminer) to thunder (**contre** against)
  2 v impersonnel **il tonne** it's thundering
tonnerre [tɔnɛr] nm thunder; **un t. d'applaudissements** thunderous applause; Fam Fig **du t.** terrific
tonsure [tɔ̃syr] nf tonsure
tonte [tɔ̃t] nf (des moutons) shearing; (du gazon)
mowing
tonton [tɔ̃tɔ̃] nm Fam uncle
tonus [tɔnys] nm (**a**) Fig (dynamisme) energy, dynamism (**b**) (d'un muscle) tone
top [tɔp] **1** nm (**a**) (signal sonore) beep; **au quatrième
t. il sera midi** at the fourth stroke it will be twelve
o'clock (**b**) Fam **être au t. niveau** (sportif) to be at
one's peak; **c'est le t.!** it's the business!
  2 adj Fam great, Br fab, Am awesome
topaze [tɔpaz] nf topaz
toper [tɔpe] vi Fam **tope(-là)!** put it there!
topinambour [tɔpinɑ̃bur] nm Jerusalem artichoke
top modèle (pl **top modèles**) [tɔpmɔdɛl] nm supermodel
topo [tɔpo] nm Fam (discours) lecture; (exposé) run-
down; Fig **c'est toujours le même t.** it's always the
same old story
topographie [tɔpɔgrafi] nf topography
topographique [tɔpɔgrafik] adj topographical
toponymie [tɔpɔnimi] nf toponymy
top secret [tɔpsəkrɛ] adj inv top secret
toquade [tɔkad] nf Fam (pour une personne) crush
(**pour** on); (pour un lieu, pour un objet) craze (**pour**
for)
toque [tɔk] nf (de fourrure) fur hat; (de jockey) cap; (de
cuisinier) hat
toqué, -e [tɔke] Fam **1** adj crazy (**de** about)
  2 nm,f nutcase
toquer [tɔke] **se toquer** vpr Fam **se t. de qn** to go
crazy over sb
Torah [tɔra] nf la **T.** the Torah
torche [tɔrʃ] nf torch; **t. électrique** Br (electric) torch,
Am flashlight
torcher [tɔrʃe] Fam **1** vt (**a**) (fesses, enfant) to wipe (**b**)
(travail) to botch (**c**) (bouteille) to polish off
  2 **se torcher** vpr to wipe one's backside
torchis [tɔrʃi] nm cob (for building)
torchon [tɔrʃɔ̃] nm (**a**) (de cuisine) dish or tea towel;
Fam **le t. brûle** they're at each other's throats; Fig **il
ne faut pas mélanger les torchons et les serviettes**
they're in a different league (**b**) Fam (texte peu soigné)
mess (**c**) Fam (journal) rag (**d**) Belg (serpillère) floorcloth
tordant, -e [tɔrdɑ̃, -ɑ̃t] adj Fam hilarious
tord-boyaux [tɔrbwajo] nm Fam rotgut
tordre [tɔrdr] **1** vt (barre de fer, métal) to bend; (fil de
fer) to twist; (linge) to wring; **t. le cou à qn** to wring
sb's neck; **t. le bras à qn** to twist sb's arm
  2 **se tordre** vpr **se t. les mains** to wring one's hands;
se t. la cheville to twist one's ankle; **se t. de douleur**
to writhe in pain; Fam **se t. (de rire)** to kill oneself
(laughing)
tordu, -e [tɔrdy] **1** adj (**a**) (objet) twisted (**b**) Fam (dérangé) **être t.** to be a bit of a maniac; **avoir l'esprit t.** to
have a warped mind
  2 nm,f Fam maniac
toréador [tɔreadɔr] nm bullfighter, toreador
toréer [tɔree] vi to fight (in the bullring)

torero [tɔrero] nm bullfighter
torgnole [tɔrɲɔl] nf très Fam clout
tornade [tɔrnad] nf tornado; **comme une t.** like a
whirlwind
Toronto [tɔrɔ̃to] n Toronto
torpeur [tɔrpœr] nf torpor
torpillage [tɔrpijaʒ] nm torpedoing
torpille [tɔrpij] nf (**a**) (engin militaire) torpedo (**b**)
(poisson) torpedo, electric ray
torpiller [tɔrpije] vt aussi Fig to torpedo
torpilleur [tɔrpijœr] nm torpedo boat
torréfaction [tɔrefaksjɔ̃] nf roasting
torréfier [tɔrefje] vt to roast
torrent [tɔrɑ̃] nm (cours d'eau) torrent; Fig (de larmes,
de lumière) flood; (d'injures) torrent; (de questions)
barrage; **pleuvoir à torrents** to pour down
torrentiel, -elle [tɔrɑ̃sjɛl] adj torrential
torride [tɔrid] adj torrid
tors, -e [tɔr, tɔrs] adj twisted
torsade [tɔrsad] nf (**a**) (point de tricot) cable; **pull à
torsades** cable(-knit) jumper (**b**) (de cheveux) twist,
coil
torsadé, -e [tɔrsade] adj (pull) cable(-knit)
torsader [tɔrsade] vt to twist
torse [tɔrs] nm chest; **t. nu** stripped to the waist
torsion [tɔrsjɔ̃] nf twisting
tort [tɔr] nm (**a**) (faute) fault; **avoir tous les torts** to be
entirely to blame; **c'est un t. de l'avoir fait** it was a
mistake to do it; **avoir t. (de faire qch)** to be wrong
(to do sth); **tu n'as pas t.** you're quite right; **donner t.
à qn** (personne) to blame sb; (résultat, preuve) to
prove sb wrong; **être en t.** ou **dans son t.** to be in
the wrong (**b**) (dommage) wrong; **faire du t. à qn** to
harm sb; (désavantager) to penalize sb (**c**) (locutions)
à t. wrongly; **à t. ou à raison** rightly or wrongly; **à t. et
à travers** (dépenser) recklessly; (parler) wildly
torticolis [tɔrtikɔli] nm stiff neck; **avoir le** ou **un t.** to
have a stiff neck
tortillard [tɔrtijar] nm Fam local train
tortiller [tɔrtije] **1** vt (papier, ruban, cheveux) to twist;
(moustache) to twirl
  2 vi Fam **il n'y a pas à t.** there are no two ways about
it
  3 **se tortiller** vpr (personne) to wriggle
tortillon [tɔrtijɔ̃] nm (de papier) twist
tortionnaire [tɔrsjɔnɛr] nmf torturer
tortue [tɔrty] nf (**a**) (reptile) tortoise; **t. d'eau douce**
terrapin; **t. de mer** turtle (**b**) Fig (personne lente) Br
slowcoach, Am slowpoke
tortueusement [tɔrtɥøzmɑ̃] adv (hypocritement) de-
viously
tortueux, -euse [tɔrtɥø, -øz] adj (**a**) (sinueux) winding, tortuous (**b**) (attitude, esprit) devious; (langage)
tortuous
torture [tɔrtyr] nf aussi Fig torture; Fig **mettre qn à la
t.** to torture sb
torturer [tɔrtyre] **1** vt aussi Fig to torture
  2 **se torturer** vpr to torture oneself; **se t. l'esprit** to
rack one's brains
torve [tɔrv] adj menacing
toscan, -e [tɔskɑ̃, -an] **1** adj Tuscan
  2 nm,f **T.** Tuscan
  3 nm (langue) Tuscan
Toscane [tɔskan] nf la **T.** Tuscany

tôt [to] *adv* (**a**) *(bientôt, vite)* soon, early; **nous n'étions pas plus t. rentrés que...** no sooner had we returned than...; **au plus t.** at the earliest; *Fam* **ce n'est pas trop t.!** and about time too!; **elle a eu t. fait de changer d'avis** she soon changed her mind; **t. ou tard** sooner or later (**b**) *(de bonne heure)* early

total, -e, -aux, -ales [tɔtal, -o] **1** *adj* total **2** *nm* total; **faire le t.** to work out the total; **au t.** in all, in total; *(tout compte fait)* all in all; *Fam* **t., ils se sont fâchés** the upshot was that they fell out **3** *nf* **totale** *Fam* **on a eu droit à la totale: verglas, embouteillages, barrages routiers** black ice, traffic jams, lorry drivers' road blocks, you name it, we had it

totalement [tɔtalmã] *adv* totally

totaliser [tɔtalize] *vt* (**a**) *(additionner)* to total, to add up (**b**) *(avoir au total)* to have a total of

totalitaire [tɔtalitɛr] *adj* totalitarian

totalitarisme [tɔtalitarism] *nm* totalitarianism

totalité [tɔtalite] *nf* **la t. de** all of; **payer qch en t.** to pay sth in full

totem [tɔtɛm] *nm (mât)* totem pole

touareg [twarɛg] **1** *adj* Tuareg **2** *nmf* **T.** Tuareg **3** *nm (langue)* Tuareg

toubib [tubib] *nm Fam* doctor

toucan [tukã] *nm* toucan

touchant, -e [tuʃã, -ãt] *adj* touching

touche [tuʃ] *nf* (**a**) *(d'un piano, d'un clavier)* key; *Ordinat* **t. alt** alt (key) (**b**) *(tache de couleur)* touch; **mettre la t. finale à qch** to put the finishing touches to sth (**c**) *(style)* touch (**d**) *(en escrime)* hit; *(à la pêche)* bite; *Fam* **avoir une t. avec qn** to make a hit with sb; *Fam* **faire une t.** to make a hit (**e**) *(remise en jeu)* throw-in; *(par les avants au rugby)* line-out; **sortir en t.** to go into touch; *aussi Fig* **rester sur la t.** to stay on the sidelines (**f**) *Fam (allure)* look; **avoir une drôle de t.** to look weird (**g**) *(de violon)* finger board; *(de guitare)* fret

touche-à-tout [tuʃatu] *nmf inv Fam* (**a**) *(enfant)* **c'est un t.** he's into everything (**b**) *(qui a plusieurs occupations)* dabbler

toucher¹ [tuʃe] *nm* (**a**) *(sens)* **le t.** touch; **au t.** to the touch (**b**) *(d'un pianiste)* touch

toucher² **1** *vt* (**a**) *(être en contact avec)* to touch; *(cible, adversaire)* to hit; **je touche du bois!** touch wood!; *Fam* **pas touche!** hands off! (**b**) *(blesser)* to hit (**à** in) (**c**) *(émouvoir)* to touch, to move (**d**) *(concerner)* to concern, to affect (**e**) *(port)* to put in at; **t. le fond** *(navire)* to touch bottom; *Fig (moralement)* to hit rock bottom; **t. terre** *(bateau)* to reach dry land (**f**) *(argent, intérêt, paie)* to get; *(chèque)* to cash; **t. le tiercé** to win the tiercé (**g**) *(jouxter)* to adjoin (**h**) *(dire)* **t. un mot à qn (de qch)** to have a word with sb (about sth) **2 toucher à** *vt ind* (**a**) *(prendre, modifier)* to touch; *Fig* **avec son air de ne pas y t.** looking as if butter wouldn't melt in his mouth (**b**) *(problème, question)* to touch on (**c**) *(approcher de)* **t. au but** to be nearing one's goal; **t. à sa fin** to be nearing its end (**d**) *(concerner)* to concern **3 se toucher** *vpr (être en contact)* to touch; *(maisons)* to adjoin

touer [twe] *vt Can* to tow

touffe [tuf] *nf* tuft

touffu, -e [tufy] *adj* (**a**) *(bois, végétation)* dense; *(barbe, cheveux)* bushy (**b**) *Fig (livre)* dense

touiller [tuje] *vt Fam* to stir; *(salade)* to toss

toujours [tuʒur] *adv* (**a**) *(exprime la continuité, la répétition)* always; **t. plus nombreux** more and more numerous; **un ami de t.** a lifelong friend; **pour t.** for ever; **depuis t.** always (**b**) *(encore)* still; **cherchez t.** keep looking; **alors, il est rentré? – t. pas** he's back then? – not yet (**c**) *(quoi qu'il en soit)* **t. est-il que...** the fact remains that...; **elle peut t. attendre!** she'll have a long wait!; **c'est t. ça (de pris)** at least it's something

toulousain, -e [tuluzɛ̃, -ɛn] **1** *adj* of Toulouse **2** *nm,f* **T.** person from Toulouse

Toulouse [tuluz] *n* Toulouse

toundra [tundra] *nf* tundra

toupet [tupɛ] *nm* (**a**) *Fam (audace)* cheek, nerve; **avoir du t., ne pas manquer de t.** to have a cheek *or* a nerve (**b**) *(de cheveux)* tuft of hair, *Br* quiff

toupie [tupi] *nf* (**a**) *(jouet)* spinning top (**b**) *Fam (femme)* **vieille t.** old bag

toupin [tupɛ̃] *nm Suisse* cow bell

tour¹ [tur] *nf* (**a**) *(construction)* tower; **t. de contrôle** control tower; **la T. Eiffel** the Eiffel Tower (**b**) *(immeuble) Br* tower block, *Am* high-rise (**c**) *(aux échecs)* rook, castle (**d**) *Ordinat* tower

tour² *nm* (**a**) *(circonférence)* circumference; **t. de cou/ de taille** collar/waist size *or* measurement; **avoir 75 cm de t. de taille** to have a waist measurement of 75 cm; **perdre 5 cm de t. de taille** to lose 5 cm round the waist; **t. de tête** hat size (**b**) *(mouvement circulaire)* **faire le t. (de qch)** to go round (sth); **faire faire à qn le t. du propriétaire** to show sb round *(a house)*; *Fig* **faire le t. de qch** *(situation, problème)* to review sth; *Fam* **faire le t. du cadran** to sleep for twelve hours; **faire un t. d'horizon** to review matters; **faire le t. du monde** to go round the world; **t. d'honneur** lap of honour; **t. de piste** lap (**c**) *(de potier)* wheel (**d**) *(tournure) (d'une situation)* turn; **prendre un certain t.** to take a certain turn; **t. d'esprit** turn of mind; **t. de phrase** turn of phrase (**e**) *(rotation)* turn; **donner un t. de clé** to turn the key; **à t. de bras** *(frapper)* with all one's might; *Fig (distribuer)* in huge quantities; **se faire un t. de reins** to strain one's back (**f**) *(promenade à pied)* stroll; *(à bicyclette, en voiture)* ride; **faire un t.** to go for a stroll/ride (**g**) *(alternance)* turn; **à qui le t.?** whose turn is it?; **chacun (à) son t.** each in turn; **t. à t.** in turn; **à t. de rôle** in turn (**h**) *Pol* **t. (de scrutin)** ballot (**i**) *(mauvais coup)* trick; **jouer un t. à qn** to play a trick on sb; **jouer un t. de cochon à qn** to play a dirty trick on sb; **cela te jouera des tours** you'll live to regret it (**j**) *(de prestidigitateur)* trick; **t. de force** feat; *Fam* **en un t. de main** in no time at all; **t. de passe-passe** trick *(using sleight of hand)*

Touraine [turɛn] *nf* **la T.** Touraine

tourbe [turb] *nf* peat

tourbeux, -euse [turbø, -øz] *adj* peaty

tourbillon [turbijɔ̃] *nm* (**a**) *(de vent)* whirlwind; *(de poussière, de fumée)* swirl; *(de neige)* flurry (**b**) *(d'eau)* whirlpool (**c**) *Fig (de la vie, d'activité)* whirl

tourbillonnant, -e [turbijɔnã, -ãt] *adj* whirling

tourbillonner [turbijɔne] *vi aussi Fig* to whirl

tourelle [turɛl] *nf* turret

tourisme [turism] *nm* tourism; **faire du t.** to do some touring

touriste [turist] **1** *adj (classe)* tourist
2 *nmf* tourist; *Fig & Péj* **faire qch en t.** to play at doing sth
touristique [turistik] *adj* tourist; *(route)* scenic
tourment [turmɑ̃] *nm Litt* torment
tourmente [turmɑ̃t] *nf* (a) *Litt (tempête)* storm (b) *(agitation politique)* upheaval
tourmenté, -e [turmɑ̃te] *adj* (a) *(paysage)* wild (b) *(mer, vie, période)* turbulent (c) *(visage, personne, âme)* tortured
tourmenter [turmɑ̃te] **1** *vt* to torment
2 se tourmenter *vpr* to worry
tournage [turnaʒ] *nm (d'un film)* shooting, filming; **sur le t.** on shoot
tournant, -e [turnɑ̃, -ɑ̃t] **1** *adj* (a) *(fauteuil, siège)* swivel; *(pont)* swing (b) *(grève)* rotating
2 *nm* (a) *(de route, de rivière)* bend (b) *Fig (changement)* turning point (**de** in)
tourné, -e [turne] *adj* (a) *(formulé)* **bien/mal t.** well/badly phrased (b) *(disposé)* **avoir l'esprit mal t.** to have a dirty mind (c) *Belg* **être bien/mal t.** to be in a good/bad mood
tournebouler [turnəbule] *vt Fam* to upset
tournebroche [turnəbrɔʃ] *nm* spit
tourne-disque (*pl* **tourne-disques**) [turnədisk] *nm* record player
tournedos [turnədo] *nm* tournedos, fillet steak
tournée [turne] *nf* (a) *(du facteur, d'un inspecteur)* round; **faire sa t.** to do one's rounds; **faire la t. de** *(magasins, musées)* to go round; **faire sa t. électorale** to go on one's election tour; **faire la t. des grands-ducs** to go out on the town (b) *(théâtrale, musicale)* tour; **en t.** on tour (c) *Fam (consommations)* round
tournemain [turnəmɛ̃] **en un tournemain** *adv Litt* in an instant
tourner [turne] **1** *vt* (a) *(clé, tête, yeux)* to turn; **t. et retourner qch entre ses mains** to turn sth over and over in one's hands; *Fig* **t. et retourner qch (dans tous les sens)** to go over and over an idea (in one's mind); **t. le dos à qn/qch** *(action)* to turn one's back on sb/sth; *(position)* to have one's back to sb/sth; **t. les talons** *(partir)* to turn on one's heel; **t. la tête à qn** *(succès, vin)* to go to sb's head; *(personne)* to turn sb's head
(b) *(page)* to turn (over)
(c) *(remuer)* to stir; *(salade)* to toss
(d) *(film, documentaire, scène)* to shoot, to film
(e) *(attention, pensées)* to turn (**vers** to)
(f) *(changer)* **t. qn/qch en ridicule** to make fun of sb/sth
(g) *(contourner) (coin de la rue)* to turn, to go round; *(obstacle, difficulté, loi)* to get round
(h) *(confectionner) (pièce détachée)* to turn on a lathe; *(pot)* to throw; *Fig (phrase)* to turn; *(compliment)* to word
2 *vi* (a) *(clé, roue, aiguille, planète)* to turn; *(porte)* to swing; *(toupie)* to spin; **l'heure tourne** time is getting on; **t. de l'œil** to pass out
(b) *(se déplacer en rond)* to go round; *aussi Fig* **t. en rond** to go round in circles; *Fam* **il y a quelque chose qui ne tourne pas rond** there's something not right somewhere; *Fam* **il ne tourne pas rond en ce moment** he's not quite himself at the moment; *Fig* **t. autour de qch** *(avoir pour centre)* to centre on sth; *(par convoitise)* to hover round sth; *(valoir environ)*

to be in the region of sth; *Fig* **t. autour du pot** to beat about the bush
(c) *(entreprise, moteur)* to run
(d) *(obliquer)* to turn; **tournez à gauche** turn left
(e) *(changer) (vent)* to shift (**à** to); *(chance)* to turn
(f) *(lait)* to turn, to go off
(g) *(avoir telle issue)* **t. court** to end abruptly; **bien/mal t.** *(personne)* to turn out well/badly; **ça va mal t.** it's going to go wrong; **t. à l'aigre** to turn sour
(h) *(dans un film)* to act
3 se tourner *vpr* to turn (**vers** towards); *Fig* **se t. vers qn/qch** to turn to sb/sth; *Fam* **se t. les pouces** to twiddle one's thumbs
tournesol [turnəsɔl] *nm* sunflower
tourneur, -euse [turnœr, -øz] *nm,f (ouvrier)* turner
tournevis [turnəvis] *nm* screwdriver; **t. cruciforme** Phillips® screwdriver
tournicoter [turnikɔte] *vi Fam* to wander round and round
tourniquet [turnikɛ] *nm* (a) *(barrière)* turnstile (b) *(porte à tambour)* revolving door (c) *(présentoir)* revolving stand (d) *(arroseur)* sprinkler
tournis [turni] *nm Fam* **avoir le t.** to feel dizzy; **donner le t. à qn** to make sb dizzy
tournoi [turnwa] *nm* tournament
tournoiement [turnwamɑ̃] *nm (des oiseaux)* wheeling; *(des feuilles mortes)* swirl
tournoyer [turnwaje] *vi (oiseaux)* to wheel; *(des feuilles mortes)* to swirl (round); **faire t. qch** to twirl sth
tournure [turnyr] *nf* (a) *(des événements)* turn; **prendre une mauvaise t.** to take a turn for the worse (b) *(forme)* **prendre t.** to take shape; **t. d'esprit** turn of mind; **t. (de phrase)** turn of phrase
tournus [turnys] *nm Suisse* schedule, rota
tour-opérateur (*pl* **tour-opérateurs**) [turɔperatœr] *nm* tour operator
tourte [turt] *nf* pie
tourteau, -x [turto] *nm (crustacé)* edible crab
tourtereau, -x [turtəro] *nm* young turtledove; *Fig* **tourtereaux** *(amoureux)* lovebirds
tourterelle [turtərɛl] *nf* turtledove
tourtière [turtjer] *nf* (a) *(pour tourte)* pie dish (b) *Can* = (minced) pork pie
tous [tu, tus] *voir* **tout**
Toussaint [tusɛ̃] *nf* **la T.** All Saints' Day

> **Toussaint**
> All Saints' Day is a public holiday in France. It is the traditional occasion for a visit to the cemetery to lay flowers (usually chrysanthemums) on the graves of family and loved ones.

tousser [tuse] *vi* to cough; *Fig (moteur)* to splutter
toussotement [tusɔtmɑ̃] *nm* slight cough
toussoter [tusɔte] *vi (avoir une toux)* to have a slight cough; *(pour attirer l'attention)* to give a slight cough
tout, toute (*pl* **tous, toutes**) [tu, tut]

> When **tous** is a pronoun as in **3** (**b**), it is pronounced [tus].

1 *adj (entier)* **t. l'univers** the whole universe; **t. mon argent** all my money; **toute la journée** the whole day; **je ne l'ai pas vu de toute la journée** I haven't seen him all day; **le T.-Paris** anyone who's anyone in Paris
2 *adj indéfini* (a) *(n'importe quel)* any; **t. élève en re-**

tard sera puni any pupil arriving late will be punished; **à t. moment** at any time; **t. autre que vous** anybody but you

(**b**) *(chaque)* every; **tous les élèves de la classe** every pupil *or* all the pupils in the class; **toutes nos chambres ont l'air conditionné** all our rooms have air-conditioning; **tous les deux jours** every second day, every other day; **ils se retournèrent t. deux** they both turned round

(**c**) *(emploi intensif)* **à la toute dernière minute** at the very last minute; **de toute beauté** magnificent; **donner toute satisfaction à qn** to give sb complete *or* full satisfaction; **pour toute réponse, il éclata en sanglots** his only answer was to burst into tears; **je suis t. à toi** I'm all yours

3 *pron indéfini* (**a**) *(au singulier)* everything; **elle a t. de son père** she's her father's daughter; **il a t. du fonctionnaire** he's the typical civil servant; **être t. pour qn** to mean everything to sb; **manger de t.** to eat everything *or* anything; **elle fera t. pour t'ennuyer** she'll do anything to annoy you; **t. ce qu'il y a d'intéressant dans ce film, c'est...** the only interesting thing in this film is...; **ce sera t.?** *(dans un magasin)* will that be all *or* everything?; **elle est jolie/gentille comme t.** she's really pretty/nice; **tu n'y vas pas et c'est t.!** you're not going and that's that!; *Fam* **...et t. et t.!** ...and all that sort of stuff

(**b**) *(au pluriel)* all; **ils sont tous partis** they all left

4 *adv* (**a**) *(très)* very; **t. près** very close

(**b**) *(complètement)* **être t. en blanc** to be (dressed) all in white; **être t. en sueur** to be pouring with sweat; **t. autrement** quite differently; **être t. à qch** to be engrossed in sth; **t. enfant, il...** as a very young child, he...

(**c**) *(suivi d'un gérondif)* **t. en conduisant/écrivant** while driving/writing

(**d**) **t. ignorant/secrétaire que je suis** *ou* **sois...** I may be ignorant/just a secretary, but...

(**e**) *(expressions)* **t. à fait** *(complètement)* quite, completely; *(exactement)* exactly; **pas du t.** not a all; **t. à coup** suddenly, all of a sudden; **t. à l'heure** *(dans le futur)* in a little while, shortly; *(dans le passé)* a little while ago; **à t. à l'heure!** see you later!; **t. de suite** right away, immediately; **à t. de suite** see you in a minute

5 *nm* **le t.** *(l'ensemble)* the whole; **le t., c'est de se concentrer** the most important thing is to concentrate

tout-à-l'égout [tutalegu] *nm inv* mains drainage

toutefois [tutfwa] *adv* however

toute-puissance [tutpɥisɑ̃s] *nf* absolute power

tout-fou *(pl* **tout-fous***)* [tufu] *adj m Fam* bonkers

toutou [tutu] *nm Fam* doggie

tout-petit *(pl* **tout-petits***)* [tupəti] *nm* tot, toddler

tout-puissant, toute-puissante *(mpl* **tout-puissants**, *fpl* **toutes-puissantes***)* [tupɥisɑ̃, -ɑ̃t] **1** *adj* all-powerful

2 *nm* **le T.** the Almighty

tout-terrain *(pl* **tout-terrains***)* [tuterɛ̃] *adj (véhicule)* all-terrain, off-road; *(vélo)* mountain

tout-venant [tuvənɑ̃] *nm* **le t.** *(gens)* ordinary people; *(choses)* ordinary things

toux [tu] *nf* cough; **t. sèche/grasse** dry/loose cough

toxicité [tɔksisite] *nf* toxicity

toxico [tɔksiko] *nmf Fam* addict

toxicologie [tɔksikɔlɔʒi] *nf* toxicology

toxicomane [tɔksikɔman] **1** *adj* addicted to drugs
  2 *nmf* drug addict

toxicomanie [tɔksikɔmani] *nf* drug addiction

toxine [tɔksin] *nf* toxin

toxique [tɔksik] *adj* toxic, poisonous; *(gaz)* poison

toxoplasmose [tɔksoplasmoz] *nf* toxoplasmosis

TP [tepe] *nmpl (abrév* **travaux pratiques***)* practical work

TPI [tepei] *nm (abrév* **Tribunal pénal international***)* International Court of Justice

trac¹ [trak] *nm* nerves; *(au théâtre)* stage fright; **avoir le t.** to be nervous; *(acteur)* to have stage fright

trac² tout à trac *adv Vieilli* out of the blue

traçabilité [trasabilite] *nf* traceability

tracas [traka] *nm* worry, trouble

tracasser [trakase] **1** *vt* to worry, to bother
  2 se tracasser *vpr* to worry (**pour** about)

tracasserie [trakasri] *nf* worry; **les tracasseries administratives** red tape

tracassier, -ère [trakasje, -ɛr] *adj* nitpicking

trace [tras] *nf* (**a**) *(d'animal, d'une personne, de pneus)* tracks; **être sur la t. de qn/qch** to be on the track of sb/sth; **disparaître sans laisser de t.** to disappear without trace; **perdre la t. de qn** to lose track of sb; *Fig* **marcher sur** *ou* **suivre les traces de qn** to follow in sb's footsteps; **t. directe** *(en ski)* direct descent (**b**) *(tache)* mark; **des traces de gras** greasy marks; **des traces de doigts** finger marks; **des traces de pas** footprints; *Fig* **laisser des traces chez qn** *(traumatisme)* to leave its mark on sb; *aussi Fig* **effacer toute t. de qch** to cover up all traces of sth (**c**) *(petite quantité, vestige)* trace

tracé [trase] *nm* (**a**) *(plan)* layout; **faire le t. de qch** to plan the layout of sth (**b**) *(d'une côte)* line

tracer [trase] **1** *vt* (**a**) *(ligne, plan)* to draw; *Math (courbe, graphique)* to plot; *(lettre)* to write; *Fig* **t. les grandes lignes de qch** to give the general outline of sth (**b**) *(route, chemin)* to mark out; *Fig* **son chemin est tout tracé** his path is all mapped out for him

2 *vi* (**a**) *Fam (aller vite)* to bomb along (**b**) *Suisse* **t. après qn** *(le poursuivre)* to chase sb

traceur [trasœr] *nm Ordinat* **t. (de courbes)** plotter; **t. à tambour** drum plotter

trachée-artère *(pl* **trachées-artères***)* [traʃeartɛr] *nf* windpipe, *Spéc* trachea

trachéite [trakeit] *nf* throat infection

tract [trakt] *nm* leaflet

tractations [traktasjɔ̃] *nfpl* dealings, negotiations

tracter [trakte] *vt* to tow

tracteur [traktœr] *nm* tractor

traction [traksjɔ̃] *nf* (**a**) *(en gymnastique)* *(à la barre, aux anneaux)* pull-up; *(au sol) Br* press-up, *Am* push-up (**b**) *(véhicule)* **t. avant/arrière** front-wheel/rear-wheel drive (**c**) *(action)* traction, pulling

tradition [tradisjɔ̃] *nf* tradition; **dans la plus pure t. française** in true French tradition

traditionalisme [tradisjɔnalism] *nm* traditionalism

traditionaliste [tradisjɔnalist] *adj & nmf* traditionalist

traditionnel, -elle [tradisjɔnɛl] *adj* (**a**) *(fondé sur la tradition)* traditional (**b**) *(habituel)* usual

traditionnellement [tradisjɔnɛlmɑ̃] *adv* traditionally

traducteur, -trice [tradyktœr, -tris] **1** *nm,f* translator
  2 *nm Ordinat* translator

traduction [tradyksjɔ̃] *nf* (*action, texte*) translation (**de/en** from/into); **t. automatique/simultanée** machine/simultaneous translation; **t. assistée par ordinateur** computer-assisted translation

traduire [tradɥir] **1** *vt* (**a**) (*texte, terme*) to translate (**de/en** from/into); *Fig* (*sentiment*) to express (**b**) **t. qn en justice** to bring sb before the courts **2** *vi* to translate (**de/en** from/into) **3 se traduire** *vpr* (*terme*) to be translated; *Fig* **se t. par qch** (*se manifester par*) to be expressed by sth; (*avoir pour résultat*) to result in sth

traduisible [tradɥizibl] *adj* translatable

trafic [trafik] *nm* (**a**) (*de véhicules*) traffic; **t. aérien** air traffic (**b**) (*de marchandises*) traffic; **t. de drogue** drug trafficking

traficoter [trafikɔte] *Fam* **1** *vi* to be on the fiddle **2** *vt* (**a**) (*vin*) to doctor; (*comptes*) to fiddle (**b**) (*manigancer*) **je me demande ce qu'il traficote** I wonder what he's up to

trafiquant, -e [trafikɑ̃, -ɑ̃t] *nm,f Péj* trafficker; **t. d'armes** arms dealer; **t. de drogue** drug trafficker

trafiquer [trafike] *vt Fam* (**a**) (*moteur*) to tinker with; (*freins, compteur*) to tamper with; (*vin*) to doctor; (*comptes*) to fiddle (**b**) (*manigancer*) **qu'est-ce qu'il trafique?** what's he up to?

tragédie [traʒedi] *nf* tragedy; *Fam Fig* **ce n'est pas une t.!** it's not the end of the world!

tragédien, -enne [traʒedjɛ̃, -ɛn] *nm,f* tragic actor, *f* tragic actress

tragi-comédie (*pl* **tragi-comédies**) [traʒikɔmedi] *nf* tragi-comedy

tragi-comique (*pl* **tragi-comiques**) [traʒikɔmik] *adj* tragi-comic

tragique [traʒik] **1** *adj* tragic **2** *nm* (**a**) (*d'un événement*) tragedy; *Fig* **prendre qch au t.** to make a big thing out of sth (**b**) (*genre*) **le t.** tragedy (**c**) (*auteur*) tragic author

trahir [trair] **1** *vt* (**a**) (*personne, pays*) to betray (**b**) (*secret*) to betray, to give away (**c**) (*gêne, ignorance*) to betray (**d**) (*sujet: jambes, forces*) to fail **2 se trahir** *vpr* to give oneself away

trahison [traizɔ̃] *nf* (*d'une personne, d'un pays*) betrayal; *Jur* treason; **haute t.** high treason

train [trɛ̃] *nm* (**a**) (*moyen de transport, véhicule*) train; **voyager en t. ou par le t.** to travel by train; **être dans un t.** to be on a train; *Fig* **prendre le t. en marche** to jump *or* climb on the bandwagon; **t. autocouchette(s)** car-sleeper train; **t. de banlieue** commuter train; **t. corail** express train; **t. électrique** electric train; **t. express** express train; **t. à grande vitesse** high-speed train; **t. de marchandises** *Br* goods *or Am* freight train (**b**) (*de réformes*) series (**c**) (*derrière*) (*de chien*) rump; *Fam* (*d'une personne*) backside, rear (**d**) (*allure*) pace; **au t. où vont les choses** at the rate things are going; **à ce t.-là** at this rate; **aller bon t.** to go at a good pace; **rouler à un t. d'enfer** to go hell for leather (**e**) **t. d'atterrissage** (*d'un avion*) landing gear, undercarriage (**f**) *Can Fam* (*vacarme*) noise, racket (**g**) (*locutions*) **en t.** (*projet, affaire*) under way; **mettre qch en t.** to get sth started; **être en t. de faire qch** to be doing sth; **mener grand t.** to live it up; **t. de vie** lifestyle

traînailler [trenaje] = **traînasser**

traînant, -e [trenɑ̃, -ɑ̃t] *adj* (**a**) (*robe*) trailing (**b**) (*voix*) drawling; (*démarche, pas*) dragging

traînard, -e [trenar, -ard] *nm,f* (*promeneur*) straggler; (*travailleur*) dawdler

traînasser [trenase] *vi Fam* (**a**) (*errer*) to hang around (**b**) (*être lent*) to dawdle

train-couchettes [trɛ̃kuʃɛt] *nm inv* sleeper

traîne [trɛn] *nf* (**a**) (*d'une robe*) train (**b**) (*à la pêche*) drag net (**c**) *Can* **t. sauvage** toboggan (**d**) *Fam* **être à la t.** to lag behind

traîneau, -x [treno] *nm* (*tiré par des chevaux*) sleigh; (*tiré par des chiens*) *Br* sledge, *Am* sled

traînée [trene] *nf* (**a**) (*trace*) trail; **se répandre comme une t. de poudre** to spread like wildfire (**b**) *Fam Péj* (*femme*) tart

traîne-misère [trenmizɛr] *nmf inv Fam* down-and-out

traîner [trene] **1** *vt* (**a**) (*tirer*) (*objet, corps*) to drag; (*wagon*) to pull (**b**) *Fig* **t. un rhume** to have a nagging cold (**c**) *Péj* (*vieilles affaires*) to drag around; **t. qn au théâtre** to drag sb along to the theatre (**d**) (*locutions*) **t. les pieds** to drag one's feet; *Fam* **t. ses guêtres** *ou* **bottes** to hang around **2** *vi* (**a**) **t. par terre** (*jupe*) to trail on the ground (**b**) (*rester en arrière*) to lag behind (**c**) (*errer*) to hang around (**d**) (*virus*) to go around (**e**) (*affaires, livres, vêtements*) to lie around; **laisser t. qch** to leave sth lying around (**f**) (*être lent*) (*personne*) to dawdle; (*conversation, intrigue*) to drag; **t. en longueur** to drag on; **ça ne traîne pas avec vous!** you don't hang about! **3 se traîner** *vpr* (**a**) (*sur le sol*) to crawl; *Fig* (*être fatigué*) to feel like a wet rag; (*aller à contrecœur*) to drag oneself along (**b**) (*journée, soirée*) to drag on

training [treniŋ] *nm* (*survêtement*) tracksuit

train-train [trɛ̃trɛ̃] *nm Fam* routine; **le t. quotidien** the daily grind

traire [trɛr] *vt* (**a**) (*vache, chèvre*) to milk (**b**) (*lait*) to draw

trait [trɛ] *nm* (**a**) (*ligne*) line; **d'un t. de plume** with a stroke of the pen; *Fig* **c'est sa sœur t. pour t.** she is her sister to a T; *Fig* **tirer un t. sur qch** to draw a line under sth; **t. d'union** hyphen; *Fig* link (**b**) (*du visage*) features; **des traits réguliers/fins** regular/fine features; **avoir les traits tirés** to look drawn (**c**) (*caractéristique*) feature, trait; **les grands traits de qch** the main features of sth; **t. de caractère** character trait (**d**) *Fig* **t. d'esprit** flash of wit; **t. de génie** stroke of genius (**e**) (*de lumière*) shaft (**f**) (*locutions*) **avoir t. à qch** to be connected with sth, to relate to sth; **boire qch à longs traits** to gulp sth down; **boire/lire qch d'un (seul) t.** to drink/read sth in one go

traitable [tretabl] *adj* (*sujet*) manageable

traitant, -e [tretɑ̃, -ɑ̃t] *adj* (*shampoing, crème*) medicated

traite [trɛt] *nf* (**a**) *Fin* draft, bill; **t. bancaire** bank draft (**b**) (*des vaches*) milking (**c**) (*trafic*) **la t. des Blanches** the white slave trade; **la t. des Noirs** the slave trade (**d**) (*locutions*) **(tout) d'une t., d'une seule t.** in one go

traité [trete] *nm* (**a**) (*ouvrage*) treatise (**de** *ou* **sur** on) (**b**) (*accord*) treaty

traitement [tretmɑ̃] *nm* (**a**) (*de personne, de maladie*) treatment; **t. de choc** shock treatment; **t. de faveur** preferential treatment (**b**) (*de matières premières*) processing; (*de l'eau*) treatment (**c**) (*rémunération*) salary (**d**) *Ordinat* processing; **données en t., capacité** *ou* **débit de t.** throughput; **t. à distance** teleprocessing; **t. des données** data processing, DP; **t.**

électronique de l'information electronic data processing, EDP; **t. d'images** image processing; **t. de l'information** *ou* **des informations** data processing, DP; **t. par lots** batch processing; **t. en temps réel** real time processing; **t. de texte** word processing, WP; *(logiciel)* word processor, word processing software; **t. de texte à balises** word processing with embedded visible commands; **t. vectoriel** vector processing

traiter [tʁete] **1** *vt* (**a**) *(se conduire envers)* to treat; **t. qn en ami/frère** to treat sb like a friend/a brother (**b**) *(qualifier)* **t. qn de lâche/de menteur** to call sb a coward/a liar (**c**) *(patient, maladie)* to treat (**d**) *(matières premières, minerai)* to process; *(eau, bois, cultures)* to treat (**e**) *Ordinat (informations)* to process; **données non traitées** raw data (**f**) *(marché)* to negotiate; *(affaire)* to handle; **t. avec qn** to deal with sb (**g**) *(sujet, question, demande)* to deal with
2 traiter de *vt ind (sujet, problème)* to deal with
3 se traiter *vpr* (**a**) *(l'un l'autre)* **se t. d'imbéciles/lâches** to call each other idiots/cowards (**b**) *(être guéri)* **cette maladie se traite très bien maintenant** this disease responds very well to treatment now

traiteur [tʁetœʁ] *nm* caterer; **chez le t.** at the deli

traître, -esse [tʁetʁ, tʁetʁes] **1** *adj (personne, virage)* treacherous; *(soleil, vin)* deceptively strong; **pas un t.** not a single word
2 *nm,f* traitor, *f* traitress; **être t. à sa patrie** to be a traitor to one's country; **en t.** treacherously

traîtreusement [tʁetʁøzmɑ̃] *adv* treacherously

traîtrise [tʁetʁiz] *nf* (**a**) *(caractère)* treachery (**b**) *(action)* act of treachery

trajectoire [tʁaʒɛktwaʁ] *nf* path, trajectory

trajet [tʁaʒɛ] *nm* (**a**) *(voyage)* journey; **faire le t. en voiture** to do the journey by car; **deux heures de t.** a two-hour journey (**b**) *(distance)* distance (**c**) *(itinéraire)* route

tralala [tʁalala] *nm inv Fam* **faire des tralalas** to make a great fuss; **... et tout le t.** ... etcetera, etcetera

tram [tʁam] = **tramway**

trame [tʁam] *nf (d'un tissu)* weft; *Fig (d'un récit)* framework

tramer [tʁame] **1** *vt (complot)* to hatch; **t. quelque chose** to be plotting something
2 se tramer *vpr* **il se trame quelque chose** there's something afoot

tramontane [tʁamɔ̃tan] *nf* tramontana

trampoline [tʁɑ̃pɔlin] *nm* (**a**) *(appareil)* trampoline (**b**) *(sport)* trampolining; **faire du t.** to do trampolining

tramway [tʁamwɛ] *nm Br* tram, *Am* streetcar

tranchant, -e [tʁɑ̃ʃɑ̃, -ɑ̃t] **1** *adj* (**a**) *(outil, épée, bord)* sharp (**b**) *Fig (ton, personne)* curt
2 *nm (d'une lame)* cutting edge; *(de la main)* edge; *Fig* **à double t.** double-edged

tranche [tʁɑ̃ʃ] *nf* (**a**) *(de pain, de melon, de viande)* slice; **t. napolitaine** Neapolitan ice cream (**b**) *(d'un livre)* edge; **doré sur t.** gilt-edged (**c**) *(partie) (de paiement)* instalment; *(de revenus)* group; *(d'imposition)* band, bracket; **t. d'âge** age bracket; **t. horaire** (time) slot; **t. de vie** slice of life (**d**) *Fam* **s'en payer une t.** to have the time of one's life

tranché, -e [tʁɑ̃ʃe] *(opinion)* clear-cut

tranchée [tʁɑ̃ʃe] *nf* trench

trancher [tʁɑ̃ʃe] **1** *vt* (**a**) *(cordage, câble)* to cut; *(gorge)* to slit, to cut; **t. la tête à qn** to cut off sb's head; **la machine lui a tranché le doigt** the machine severed

his finger (**b**) *(question, différend)* to settle
2 *vi* (**a**) *(décider)* to decide; *Fig* **t. dans le vif** to take drastic action (**b**) *(couleurs)* to contrast (**sur** with)

tranquille [tʁɑ̃kil] *adj* (**a**) *(paisible)* quiet; *(mer)* calm; *(sommeil)* peaceful; **laisser qn t.** to leave sb alone (**b**) *(rassuré)* **se sentir t.** to feel at peace; **vous pouvez dormir t.** you can rest easy; **soyez t.** don't worry; **je ne suis pas t.** I'm feeling uneasy; **avoir l'esprit t.** to have peace of mind

tranquillement [tʁɑ̃kilmɑ̃] *adv (calmement)* calmly; *(doucement)* quietly; *(dormir)* peacefully; *(partir)* with one's mind at rest

tranquillisant, -e [tʁɑ̃kiliza, -ɑ̃t] **1** *adj* (**a**) *(nouvelles, paroles)* reassuring; *(effet)* soothing (**b**) *(médicament)* tranquillizing
2 *nm* tranquillizer

tranquilliser [tʁɑ̃kilize] **1** *vt* to reassure
2 se tranquilliser *vpr* to set one's mind at rest

tranquillité [tʁɑ̃kilite] *nf (calme)* quietness; *(de la mer)* calmness; *(du sommeil)* peacefulness; **avoir besoin de t.** to need peace and quiet; **en toute t.** *(sans être dérangé)* without being disturbed; *(sans souci)* with an easy mind; **t. d'esprit** peace of mind

transaction [tʁɑ̃zaksjɔ̃] *nf* (**a**) *(opération)* transaction (**b**) *Jur* compromise

transactionnel, -elle [tʁɑ̃zaksjɔnɛl] *adj* (**a**) *Jur (solution)* compromise (**b**) *Psy (analyse)* transactional

transalpin, -e [tʁɑ̃zalpɛ̃, -in] *adj* transalpine

transat [tʁɑ̃zat] **1** *nm Fam* deckchair
2 *nf* transatlantic race

transatlantique [tʁɑ̃zatlɑ̃tik] **1** *adj* transatlantic
2 *nm* (**a**) *(paquebot)* transatlantic liner (**b**) *(chaise longue)* deckchair

transbahuter [tʁɑ̃sbayte] *vt Fam* to cart, to lug

transbordement [tʁɑ̃sbɔʁdəmɑ̃] *nm* transfer; *Naut* transhipment

transcendant, -e [tʁɑ̃sɑ̃dɑ̃, -ɑ̃t] *adj* transcendent; *Fam* **ce n'est pas t.** it's nothing special

transcendantal, -e, -aux, -ales [tʁɑ̃sɑ̃dɑ̃tal, -o] *adj* transcendental

transcender [tʁɑ̃sɑ̃de] **1** *vt* to transcend
2 se transcender *vpr* to surpass oneself

transcontinental, -e, -aux, -ales [tʁɑ̃skɔ̃tinɑ̃tal, -o] *adj* transcontinental

transcription [tʁɑ̃skʁipsjɔ̃] *nf* (**a**) *(action)* transcription; *(dans un autre alphabet)* transliteration; **t. phonétique** phonetic transcription; **t. génétique** genetic transcription (**b**) *(texte)* transcript

transcrire [tʁɑ̃skʁiʁ] *vt* to transcribe; *(dans un autre alphabet)* to transliterate

transcutané, -e [tʁɑ̃skytane] *adj* transcutaneous

transdermique [tʁɑ̃sdɛʁmik] *adj* transdermal

transe [tʁɑ̃s] *nf* trance; **être en t.** to be in a trance; *Fig* to be beside oneself

transept [tʁɑ̃sɛpt] *nm* transept

transférer [tʁɑ̃sfeʁe] *vt* to transfer

transfert [tʁɑ̃sfɛʁ] *nm* transfer; *Psy* transference; *Tél* **t. d'appels** call transfer; *Ordinat* **t. de données** data transfer; *Ordinat* **t. électronique de fonds** electronic funds transfer, EFT

transfigurer [tʁɑ̃sfigyʁe] *vt* to transfigure

transformable [tʁɑ̃sfɔʁmabl] *adj* convertible

transformateur [tʁɑ̃sfɔʁmatœʁ] *nm* transformer

transformation [tʁɑ̃sfɔʁmasjɔ̃] *nf* (**a**) *(changement)* transformation; *(d'un local)* conversion (**b**) *(de ma-*

tières premières) processing (**c**) *(au rugby)* conversion; **faire une t.** to convert

transformer [trãsfɔrme] **1** *vt* (**a**) *(changer)* to transform; *(local, maison)* to convert; **t. qn/qch en qch** to turn sb/sth into sth (**b**) *(matières premières)* to process (**c**) *(au rugby) (essai)* to convert
2 se transformer *vpr* to change; **se t. en qch** to turn into sth

transfuge [trãsfyʒ] *nmf* defector

transfuser [trãsfyze] *vt (sang)* to transfuse; *Fam* **t. qn** to give sb a transfusion

transfusion [trãsfyzjɔ̃] *nf* **t. (sanguine)** (blood) transfusion; **faire une t. à qn** to give sb a transfusion

transgénique [trãsʒenik] *adj* transgenic

transgresser [trãsgrese] *vt (règlement, loi)* to infringe; *(ordres)* to disobey

transgression [trãsgrɛsjɔ̃] *nf (du règlement, de la loi)* infringement; *(d'ordres)* disobeying

transhumance [trãzymãs] *nf* = the moving of livestock to different pastures according to the season

transhumer [trãzyme] *vt & vi* = to move to different pastures according to the season

transi, -e [trãzi] *adj* (**a**) *(paralysé)* **t. (de peur)** paralysed with fear; **t. (de froid)** chilled to the bone (**b**) *Fam (amoureux)* bashful

transiger [trãziʒe] **1** *vi* to compromise (**sur** on); **t. avec sa conscience** to compromise one's principles
2 *vt Can (contrat)* to negotiate

transistor [trãzistɔr] *nm* (**a**) *Élec (dispositif)* transistor (**b**) *(poste de radio)* transistor (radio)

transit [trãzit] *nm* (**a**) *(de passagers, de marchandises)* transit; **en t.** in transit (**b**) *(intestinal)* transit; **facilite le t. intestinal** *(sur paquet)* keeps you regular

transiter [trãzite] **1** *vt (marchandises)* to forward
2 *vi* (**a**) *(marchandises, voyageurs)* to pass in transit (**par** through)

transitif, -ive [trãzitif, -iv] *adj Gram* transitive

transition [trãzisjɔ̃] *nf* transition; **assurer la t.** to ensure a smooth transition; **sans t.** abruptly

transitivement [trãzitivmã] *adv* transitively

transitivité [trãzitivite] *nf* transitivity

transitoire [trãzitwar] *adj* transitional

translation [trãslasjɔ̃] *nf Math* translation

translucide [trãslysid] *adj* translucent

transmanche [trãzmãʃ] *adj inv* cross-Channel

transmetteur [trãsmetœr] *nm Ordinat & Biol* transmitter

transmettre [trãsmetr] **1** *vt* (**a**) *(lumière, chaleur, énergie)* to transmit (**b**) *(maladie, virus)* to pass on, to transmit (**à** to) (**c**) *(recette, don)* to hand on (**à** to); *(tradition, objet)* to hand down (**à** to); *(pouvoir)* to hand over (**à** to) (**d**) *(message, ordre, amitiés)* to pass on (**à** to) (**e**) *Rad & TV (information)* to transmit; *(émission)* to broadcast (**f**) *Jur (propriété, droit)* to transfer; *(actions)* to assign; **t. ses pouvoirs à qn** to hand over to sb
2 se transmettre *vpr* (**a**) *(maladie, virus)* to be passed on (**b**) *(recette, don)* to be handed on; *(tradition, objet)* to be handed down

transmissible [trãsmisibl] *adj* (**a**) *(maladie)* transmissible; **maladie sexuellement t.** sexually transmitted disease (**b**) *(droit, fortune)* transferable

transmission [trãsmisjɔ̃] *nf* (**a**) *(de la chaleur, de la lumière, d'une maladie, d'un virus)* transmission; *(d'un message, d'un ordre)* passing on; *(d'une tradition)*

handing down; **t. de pensée** thought transference (**b**) *Rad & TV (d'une image, d'un message)* transmission; *(d'une émission)* broadcasting (**c**) *Ordinat* transmission; **t. de données** data transmission *or* transfer; **t. par modem** modem transmission; **t. de paquets** packet transmission (**d**) *Jur (d'une propriété, d'un droit)* transfer, transference; *(d'actions)* assignment (**e**) *Mil* **les transmissions** the signals

transocéanien, -enne [trãzɔseanjɛ̃, -ɛn], **transocéanique** [trãzɔseanik] *adj* transoceanic

transparaître [trãsparɛtr] *vi* to show (through)

transparence [trãsparãs] *nf* (**a**) *(d'un tissu, d'une allusion, d'un parti politique)* transparency; **on peut le lire par t.** you can read it by holding it up to the light (**b**) *Cin* back projection

transparent, -e [trãsparã, -ãt] **1** *adj aussi Fig* transparent
2 *nm* transparency

transpercer [trãspɛrse] *vt (sujet: lame, flèche, balle)* to pierce; *(sujet: froid, vent, pluie)* to go right through

transpiration [trãspirasjɔ̃] *nf* (**a**) *(sueur)* sweat, perspiration (**b**) *(action)* sweating, perspiration

transpirer [trãspire] *vi* (**a**) *(personne)* to sweat, to perspire; **t. des pieds/des aisselles** to have sweaty feet/armpits; **t. à grosses gouttes** to drip with sweat (**b**) *Fig (secret, nouvelles)* to leak out (**c**) *Fam* **t. sur** *(travailler à)* to sweat over

transplant [trãsplã] *nm Méd* transplant

transplantation [trãsplãtasjɔ̃] *nf* (**a**) *(d'arbres, de personnes)* transplantation (**b**) *(d'organes)* transplant; **t. cardiaque/rénale** heart/kidney transplant

transplanté, -e [trãsplãte] *adj (organe)* transplanted; **malade t.** transplant patient

transplanter [trãsplãte] *vt* to transplant

transport [trãspɔr] *nm* (**a**) *(de marchandises, de passagers)* transport; **les transports** transport; **les transports aériens** air transport; **les transports en commun** public transport; **t. fluvial** inland waterway transport (**b**) *Jur (de biens, de droits)* transfer (**c**) *Litt (émotion)* rapture; *(de joie)* transports; *(de colère)* outbursts

transportable [trãspɔrtabl] *adj (marchandises)* transportable; *(blessé)* able to be moved

transporter [trãspɔrte] *vt* (**a**) *(passagers, troupes, marchandises)* to transport, to carry; **t. qn à l'hôpital** to take sb to hospital (**b**) *(sujet: film, roman)* to transport (**c**) *Litt (ravir)* to transport; **t. qn de joie** to make sb rapturous

transporteur [trãspɔrtœr] *nm* carrier; **t. routier** road haulier

transposer [trãspoze] *vt* (**a**) *(mots, morceau de musique)* to transpose (**b**) **t. un roman à l'écran/à la scène** to adapt a novel for the screen/for the stage

transposition [trãspozisjɔ̃] *nf* (**a**) *(mot, morceau de musique)* transposition (**b**) **t. à l'écran/à la scène** screen/stage adaptation

transsexuel, -elle [trãssɛksɥɛl] *adj & nmf* transsexual

Transsibérien [trãssiberjɛ̃] *nm* **leT.** theTrans-Siberian Railway

transvaser [trãsvaze] *vt* to pour, to transfer; *(vin)* to decant

transversal, -e, -aux, -ales [trãsversal, -o] *adj (vallée)* transverse; *(rue)* cross; **coupe transversale** cross-section

transversalement [trãsversalmã] *adv* crosswise

trapèze [trapɛz] *nm* (**a**) *(forme géométrique)* Br trapezium, Am trapezoid (**b**) *(appareil de gymnastique)* trapeze; **faire du t.** to perform on the trapeze

trapéziste [trapezist] *nmf* trapeze artist

trappage [trapaʒ] *nm Can* trapping

trappe [trap] *nf* (**a**) *(dans le plancher)* trap door; **passer à la t.** to be whisked away *(without trace)* (**b**) *(piège)* trap

trappeur [trapœr] *nm* trapper

trapu, -e [trapy] *adj* (**a**) *(homme, cheval)* thickset, stocky; *(bâtiment)* squat (**b**) *Fam (élève, professeur)* brainy (**c**) *Fam (problème)* tough

traquenard [traknar] *nm* trap

traquer [trake] *vt (gibier, criminel)* to hunt; *(vedette)* to hound

traumatisant, -e [tromatizã, -ãt] *adj* traumatic

traumatiser [tromatize] *vt* to traumatize

traumatisme [tromatism] *nm* traumatism, trauma; **t. crânien** severe head injury

travail, -aux [travaj, -o] *nm* (**a**) *(activité)* work; *(de l'imagination, de la mémoire)* workings; **se mettre au t.** to get (down) to work; **allons, au t.!** come on, let's get (down) to work!; **cesser le t.** to stop work; **à t. égal, salaire égal** equal pay for equal work
(**b**) *(emploi)* work, job; **chercher du t.** to look for work *or* a job; **être sans t.** not to have a job, to be out of work; **t. à mi-temps/à plein temps** part-time/full-time work; **t. de bureau** office work; **les travaux des champs** work in the fields; *Univ* **travaux dirigés** tutorial; **travaux forcés** hard labour; *Jur* **t. d'intérêt général** community service; **t. manuel** manual labour; *Scol* **travaux manuels** arts and crafts; **travaux ménagers** housework; **t. de nuit** night work; *Scol & Univ* **travaux pratiques** practical work
(**c**) *(tâche)* (piece of) work, job; **un t. bien/mal fait** a good/bad piece of work; **faire de petits travaux** to do odd jobs; **c'est du beau t.** it's a fine piece of work; *Fam & Ironique* **c'est du beau t.!** that was clever!
(**d**) *(lieu de travail)* work
(**e**) *Ordinat* job; **t. multitâche** multitasking; **t. en réseau** networking
(**f**) *(devoir)* work
(**g**) **travaux** *(réparations)* work; **le magasin est en travaux** there's work being done on the shop; **attention travaux** *(sur panneau)* roadworks ahead
(**h**) *(de l'accouchement)* labour
(**i**) *(façonnage)* **le t. du bois** woodwork; **le t. du fer** ironworking; **le t. de l'ivoire/de pierres précieuses** the shaping of ivory/precious stones

travaillant, -e [travajã, -ãt] *Can* **1** *adj* hardworking **2** *nmf* hard worker

travaillé, -e [travaje] *adj* (**a**) *(fer, bois, pierre)* worked (**b**) *(style)* elaborate (**c**) *(tourmenté)* **être t. par qch** to be tormented by sth

travailler [travaje] **1** *vt* (**a**) *(matière, pâte)* to work (**b**) *(sujet, rôle, style)* to work on; *(texte, auteur)* to study; *(morceau de musique, technique)* to practise (**c**) *(inquiéter)* to torment
2 *vi* (**a**) *(personne)* to work; **t. à la pièce** to do piecework; **t. dans qch** to work in sth; **faire t. son argent** to make one's money work for one; **faire t. son imagination** to use one's imagination; *Fam* **t. du chapeau** to have a screw loose (**b**) *(s'entraîner) (sportif)* to train; *(musicien)* to practise (**c**) *(câble)* to strain; *(bois)* to warp; *(murs)* to crack; *(vin)* to ferment (**d**) *(agir)* **t. pour/contre qn** to be on sb's side/against sb

3 travailler à *vt ind (roman, documentaire)* to work on; **t. à la perte de qn** to try to ruin sb

travailleur, -euse [travajœr, -øz] **1** *adj* hard-working **2** *nm,f* worker; **t. manuel/intellectuel** manual/non-manual worker; **t. indépendant** self-employed worker

travailliste [travajist] *Pol* **1** *nmf* member of the Labour Party **2** *adj (parti)* Labour

travée [trave] *nf* (**a**) *(de sièges)* row (**b**) *Archit* bay

traveller's check, traveller's cheque [travlœrʃɛk] *nm Br* traveller's cheque, *Am* traveler's check

travelling [travliŋ] *nm Cin (déplacement)* tracking; *(plan)* tracking shot; **faire un t.** to do a tracking shot; **t. avant/arrière** track in/out

travelo [travlo] *nm Fam* transvestite

travers [traver] *nm* (**a**) *(défaut)* failing (**b**) *(largeur)* breadth; *Culin* **t. de porc** spare ribs (**c**) *(locutions)* **à t. qch, au t. de qch** through sth; **à t. les siècles** down the centuries; **à t. le monde** throughout the world; **voir à t. qch** to see through sth; **passer au t. de qch** to go through sth; **marcher de t.** not to walk in a straight line; *Fig* **aller de t.** to go wrong; **être de t.** *(chapeau, tableau)* to be crooked; **prendre qch de t.** to take sth the wrong way; **regarder qn de t.** to look sideways at sb; **comprendre qch de t.** to misunderstand sth; **en t.** crosswise; **en t. de qch** across sth; **se mettre en t. de qch** to get in the way of sth

traverse [travers] *nf (sur une voie ferrée) Br* sleeper, *Am* tie

traversée [traverse] *nf (d'un cours d'eau)* crossing; *(d'une ville, d'une forêt)* going through; *Fig* **t. du désert** time in the wilderness

traverser [traverse] *vt* (**a**) *(rue, pont, cours d'eau)* to cross; *(ville, pays, forêt)* to go through; *Fig* **t. l'esprit à qn** *(idée, doute)* to cross sb's mind (**b**) *(tissu, mur)* to go (right) through (**c**) *(crise, période)* to go through; **t. les siècles** to come down through the ages

traversier, -ère [traversje, -ɛr] **1** *adj voir* **flûte** **2** *nm Can (bac)* ferry

traversin [traversɛ̃] *nm* bolster

travesti [travesti] *nm* transvestite

travestir [travestir] **1** *vt* (**a**) *(personne)* to to dress up (**en** as) (**b**) *(vérité, faits, pensée)* to distort
2 se travestir *vpr* (**a**) *(se déguiser)* to put on fancy dress (**b**) *(s'habiller en femme)* to put on drag

traviole [travjɔl] **de traviole** *adv Fam* **marcher de t.** to be staggering all over the place; **être de t.** to be lopsided

trayeuse [trɛjøz] *nf* milking machine

trébucher [trebyʃe] *vi* to trip, to stumble (**sur/contre** over/against); **faire t. qn** to trip sb up

trèfle [trefl] *nm* (**a**) *(plante)* clover; **t. à quatre feuilles** four-leaf clover (**b**) *(carte)* club; *(couleur)* clubs (**c**) *(emblème irlandais)* shamrock

tréfonds [trefɔ̃] *nm Litt* **au t. de son cœur** in one's heart of hearts; **au t. de son âme** in the depths of one's soul

treillage [trɛjaʒ] *nm (clôture)* trellis fencing

treille [trɛj] *nf* (**a**) *(tonnelle)* vine arbour (**b**) *(vigne)* climbing vine

treillis [trɛji] *nm* (**a**) *(treillage)* trellis; **t. métallique** wire mesh (**b**) *(tissu)* canvas (**c**) *(uniforme militaire)* combat uniform

treize [trɛz] **1** *adj inv* thirteen; *Fam* **en avoir t. à la douzaine** to have more than one knows what to do with **2** *nm inv* thirteen; *voir aussi* **trois**

treizième [trɛzjɛm] *adj, nmf & nm* thirteenth; *voir aussi* **cinquième**

trekking [trɛkiŋ] *nm* trek

tréma [trema] *nm* diaeresis; **e/i t.** e/i diaeresis

tremblant, -e [trɑ̃blɑ̃, -ɑ̃t] *adj* (**a**) *(genoux, main)* trembling, shaky; **être t. de peur** to be trembling *or* shaking with fear; **être t. de froid/fièvre** to be shivering with cold/fever (**b**) *(voix)* quavering

tremble [trɑ̃bl] *nm* aspen

tremblement [trɑ̃bləmɑ̃] *nm* (**a**) *(du corps, de la main)* trembling, shaking; *(de peur)* shudder; *(de fièvre)* shivering; **être pris de tremblements** to start to shake; **avec un t. dans la voix** with a tremor in his voice; *Fam* **et tout le t.** etcetera etcetera (**b**) *(de la voix)* quavering (**c**) **t. de terre** earthquake

trembler [trɑ̃ble] *vi* (**a**) *(main, genoux)* to shake, to tremble; *(lèvres)* to tremble; **t. de colère/peur** to tremble *or* shake with anger/fear; **t. de froid** to shiver with cold; **t. comme une feuille** to shake like a leaf; **t. de tout son corps** to be shaking all over (**b**) *(voix)* to quaver (**c**) *(terre, bâtiment)* to shake; *(feuilles)* to quiver; *(flamme)* to flicker; **faire t. les vitres** to make the windows shake *or* rattle; **faire t. un bâtiment** to rock *or* shake a building (**d**) *(avoir peur)* to tremble; **t. de tout son corps** to tremble all over; **t. devant qn** to be terrified of sb; **t. pour qn** to tremble for sb

tremblotant, -e [trɑ̃blɔtɑ̃, -ɑ̃t] *adj (personne, corps)* trembling; *(voix)* tremulous; *(lumière)* flickering

tremblote [trɑ̃blɔt] *nf Fam* **avoir la t.** to be shaky; *(de peur)* to have the jitters; *(de froid)* to have the shivers

tremblotement [trɑ̃blɔtmɑ̃] *nm (des mains)* trembling, shaking; *(de la voix)* quavering; *(de la lumière)* flickering

trembloter [trɑ̃blɔte] *vi (personne, mains)* to tremble *or* shake slightly; *(voix)* to quaver; *(lumière)* to flicker

trémière [tremjɛr] *adj f voir* **rose**

trémolo [tremɔlo] *nm* tremolo; *Fig* **avec des trémolos dans la voix** with a tremor in one's voice

trémousser [tremuse] **se trémousser** *vpr* to jig about; **se t. sur sa chaise** to wriggle about on one's chair

trempage [trɑ̃paʒ] *nm* soaking

trempe [trɑ̃p] **1** *nf* (**a**) *(force de caractère)* calibre; **une femme de sa t.** a woman of her calibre (**b**) *Fam (volée de coups)* hiding
2 *adj Can & Suisse (personne, vêtements)* soaked, drenched; *(chaussures, jardin)* waterlogged

trempé, -e [trɑ̃pe] *adj* (**a**) *(personne, vêtement)* soaked; **t. de sueur** *(personne)* dripping with sweat; *(vêtement)* saturated with sweat (**b**) *(acier, verre)* hardened; *Fig* **bien t.** *(caractère)* sturdy

tremper [trɑ̃pe] **1** *vt* (**a**) *(mouiller)* to soak; **se faire t.** **(par la pluie)** to get soaked (**b**) *(plonger)* to dip (**dans** in); **t. les lèvres** to take a small sip (**c**) *(acier)* to quench
2 *vi* (**a**) **faire t. qch, mettre qch à t.** *(linge)* to soak sth (**b**) *Fig (se compromettre)* **t. dans qch** to be mixed up in sth
3 se tremper *vpr (se baigner)* to have a quick dip; **se t. les pieds dans l'eau** to go for a paddle

trempette [trɑ̃pɛt] *nf Fam* **faire t.** to have a quick dip

tremplin [trɑ̃plɛ̃] *nm (pour sauteur, pour plongeur) & Fig* springboard; *(pour skieur)* ski jump

trench-coat (*pl* trench-coats) [trɛnʃkot] *nm* trench coat

trentaine [trɑ̃tɛn] *nf* (**a**) *(nombre)* **une t. (de)** about thirty (**b**) *(âge)* **avoir la t.** to be about thirty; **approcher de la t.** to be getting on for thirty

trente [trɑ̃t] **1** *adj inv* thirty; *(au tennis)* **t. à** thirty all
2 *nm inv* thirty; *Fig* **être sur son t. et un** to be dressed up to the nines; *voir aussi* **trois**

trente-six [trɑ̃tsis] **1** *adj inv* thirty-six; *Fam (beaucoup)* umpteen; *Fig* **voir t. chandelles** *(après un coup sur la tête)* to see stars; *Fam* **il n'y a pas t. solutions** there are no two ways about it
2 *nm inv* thirty-six; *Fig* **tous les t. du mois** once in a blue moon; *Can Fam* **être sur son t.** to be dressed up to the nines; *voir aussi* **trois**

trente-sixième [trɑ̃tsizjɛm] *adj Fam Fig* **être au t. dessous** to be really down in the dumps; *voir aussi* **cinquième**

trente-trois tours [trɑ̃ttrwatur] *nm inv* LP

trentième [trɑ̃tjɛm] *nmf, nn & adj* thirtieth; *voir aussi* **cinquième**

trépanation [trepanasjɔ̃] *nf* trepanning

trépaner [trepane] *vt* to trepan

trépas [trepɑ] *nm Litt* death; **passer de vie à t.** to depart this life

trépasser [trepɑse] *vi Litt* to depart this life

trépidant, -e [trepidɑ̃, -ɑ̃t] *adj (vie, activité)* hectic

trépidation [trepidasjɔ̃] *nf (d'une machine, d'un moteur)* vibration

trépied [trepje] *nm* (**a**) *(d'appareil photo)* tripod (**b**) *(tabouret)* three-legged stool

trépignement [trepiɲəmɑ̃] *nm* stamping (of feet)

trépigner [trepiɲe] *vi* to stamp (one's feet); **t. de colère/d'impatience** to jump up and down with rage/impatience

très [trɛ] *adv* very; **avoir t. faim/chaud/froid** to be very hungry/hot/cold; **avoir t. envie de faire qch** to really want to do sth; **t. estimé** highly respected; **t. aimé** much liked; **t. peu utilisé** very rarely used

trésor [trezɔr] *nm* (**a**) *(objets précieux)* treasure; *Fam* **mon t.** darling; *Fig* **des trésors de patience/générosité** boundless patience/generosity, **t. de guerre** war chest (**b**) *(dans une église)* relics and ornaments (**c**) **le T. (public)** ≃ the Treasury

trésorerie [trezɔrri] *nf* (**a**) *(bureau)* accounts department (**b**) *(ressources)* funds, finances

trésorier, -ère [trezɔrje, -ɛr] *nm,f* treasurer

tressaillement [tresajmɑ̃] *nm (de surprise, de peur)* jump, start; *(de plaisir)* quiver; *(de douleur)* wince

tressaillir [67] [tresajir] *vi (de surprise, de peur)* to jump, to start; *(de plaisir)* to quiver; *(de douleur)* to wince

tressautement [tresotmɑ̃] *nm (secousse)* jolt

tressauter [tresote] *vi (être secoué)* to jolt about

tresse [trɛs] *nf* (**a**) *(de cheveux) Br* plait, *Am* braid; **se faire des tresses** *Br* plait *or Am* braid one's hair (**b**) *(de fil)* braid (**c**) *Suisse (pain)* plaited loaf

tresser [trese] *vt (cheveux) Br* to plait, *Am* to braid; *(paille, osier)* to plait; *(panier, guirlande)* to weave; *Fig* **t. des couronnes à qn** to sing sb's praises

tréteau, -x [treto] *nm* trestle

treuil [trœj] *nm* winch, windlass

trêve [trɛv] *nf* (**a**) *(amnistie)* truce (**b**) *Fig (pause, arrêt)* respite, rest; *Fam* **t. de plaisanteries!** joking apart; **sans t.** unremittingly; *Fam* **t. des confiseurs** = truce over Christmas and New Year between opposing political parties

Trèves [tʀɛv] *n* Trier

tri [tʀi] *nm* (**a**) *(d'objets, d'idées)* sorting out; *(de lettres)* sorting; *(de candidats)* selection; **faire le t. dans qch** to sort sth out; **il va falloir faire le t.** we'll have to sort through them; **faire du t. dans ses vêtements/papiers** to sort through one's clothes/papers; **t. postal** mail sorting (**b**) *Ordinat* sort; **effectuer un t.** to do a sort; **t. alphabétique** alphabetic sort

triage [tʀijaʒ] *nm* sorting out; *(de lettres)* sorting

trial [tʀijal] *nm* motorbike trials

triangle [tʀijɑ̃gl] *nm* triangle; **t. des Bermudes** Bermuda Triangle; **le T. d'or** the Golden Triangle; **t. rectangle** right-angled triangle

triangulaire [tʀijɑ̃gylɛʀ] *adj* triangular

triathlon [tʀiatlɔ̃] *nm* triathlon

tribal, -e, -aux, -ales [tʀibal, -o] *adj* tribal

tribord [tʀibɔʀ] *nm* starboard; **à t.** on the starboard side

tribu [tʀiby] *nf* tribe

tribulations [tʀibylasjɔ̃] *nfpl* tribulations, troubles

tribun [tʀibœ̃] *nm* (**a**) *(magistrat romain)* tribune (**b**) *(orateur)* popular orator

tribunal, -aux [tʀibynal, -o] *nm* *(bâtiment) Br* court, *Am* courthouse; *(magistrats)* court; **porter une affaire devant les tribunaux** to take a case to court; **t. administratif** = court which deals with civil law; **t. de commerce** trade tribunal; **t. pour enfants** juvenile court; **t. de grande instance** ≃ Crown Court, *Scot* High Court; **t. d'instance** ≃ magistrates' court, *Scot* district court; **t. militaire** military tribunal

tribune [tʀibyn] *nf* (**a**) *(d'orateur)* rostrum, platform (**b**) *(débat)* forum; **t. libre** *(dans un journal)* opinion column (**c**) **les tribunes** *(dans un stade)* the stand; **t. d'honneur** grandstand; **t. de la presse** press gallery

tribut [tʀiby] *nm* tribute; **le pays a payé un lourd t. à la guerre** the war cost the country dearly

tributaire [tʀibytɛʀ] *adj* (**a**) *(dépendant)* **être t. de** to be dependent on (**b**) *(cours d'eau)* tributary

tricentenaire [tʀisɑ̃tnɛʀ] **1** *adj* three hundred years old
2 *nm* tercentenary, tricentennial

triceps [tʀisɛps] *nm* triceps

triche [tʀiʃ] *nf Fam* cheating

tricher [tʀiʃe] *vi* to cheat; **t. sur qch** to lie about sth; **t. aux cartes/à un examen** to cheat at cards/in an exam

tricherie [tʀiʃʀi] *nf* cheating

tricheur, -euse [tʀiʃœʀ, -øz] *nm,f* cheat

trichloréthylène [tʀiklɔʀetilɛn] *nm* trichlorethylene

tricolore [tʀikɔlɔʀ] **1** *adj* (**a**) *(à trois couleurs)* three-coloured (**b**) *(de la France)* French
2 *nmpl* **les tricolores** the French team

tricorne [tʀikɔʀn] *nm* three-cornered hat, tricorn

tricot [tʀiko] *nm* (**a**) *(activité)* knitting; **faire du t.** to do some knitting (**b**) *(ouvrage)* knitting (**c**) *(chandail)* sweater, jumper; **t. de corps** *Br* vest, *Am* undershirt (**d**) *(tissu)* knitted fabric

tricoter [tʀikɔte] **1** *vt* to knit; **tricoté (à la) main** hand-knitted
2 *vi* to knit; **t. à la main/à la machine** to hand-knit/machine-knit

tricycle [tʀisikl] *nm* tricycle; **faire du t.** to go tricycling

trident [tʀidɑ̃] *nm* (**a**) *(dans la mythologie)* trident (**b**) *(fourche)* three-pronged fork

tridimensionnel, -elle [tʀidimɑ̃sjɔnɛl] *adj* three-dimensional

triennal, -e, -aux, -ales [tʀienal, -o] *adj (élection, révision)* three-yearly, triennial; *(bail)* three-year

trier [tʀije] *vt* (**a**) *(lettres)* to sort; *(vêtements, informations)* to sort or go through; *(fruits, lentilles)* to pick over; **t. qn/qch sur le volet** to hand-pick sb/sth (**b**) *Ordinat* to sort; **t. par ordre alphabétique** to sort in alphabetical order

trifouiller [tʀifuje] *vi Fam* **qu'est-ce que tu trifouilles?** what are you up to?; **t. dans qch** to rummage around in sth

triglycéride [tʀigliseʀid] *nf* triglyceride

trigonométrie [tʀigɔnɔmetʀi] *nf* trigonometry

trigonométrique [tʀigɔnɔmetʀik] *adj* trigonometric

trilatéral, -e, -aux, -ales [tʀilateʀal, -o] *adj* trilateral

trilingue [tʀilɛ̃g] *adj* trilingual

trille [tʀij] *nm* trill

trilogie [tʀilɔʒi] *nf* trilogy

trimaran [tʀimaʀɑ̃] *nm* trimaran

trimbal(l)er [tʀɛ̃bale] *Fam* **1** *vt (paquets)* to lug or cart around; *(enfants)* to trail around
2 se trimbal(l)er *vpr* to trail about; **elle se trimbal(l)e partout avec sa marmaille** she trails her kids around with her everywhere she goes

trimer [tʀime] *vi Fam* to slave away; **faire t. qn** to keep sb hard at it

trimestre [tʀimɛstʀ] *nm* quarter; *Scol & Univ Br* term, *Am* trimester

trimestriel, -elle [tʀimɛstʀijɛl] *adj* quarterly

tringle [tʀɛ̃gl] *nf* rod; **t. à rideau** curtain rod

trinité [tʀinite] *nf (groupe de trois éléments)* trinity; *Rel* **la (sainte) T.** the (Holy) Trinity; **la T.** *(fête)* Trinity Sunday

Trinité-et-Tobago [tʀiniteetɔbago] *n* Trinidad and Tobago

trinquer [tʀɛ̃ke] *vi* (**a**) *(porter un toast)* to clink glasses; **t. à qch** to drink to sth; **t. à la santé de qn** to drink a toast to sb (**b**) *Fam (souffrir)* to be the one who suffers

trio [tʀijo] *nm* (**a**) *(groupe de trois personnes)* threesome, trio (**b**) *(en musique)* trio

triolet [tʀijɔlɛ] *nm Mus* triplet

triomphal, -e, -aux, -ales [tʀijɔ̃fal, -o] *adj* triumphant

triomphalement [tʀijɔ̃falmɑ̃] *adv* triumphantly

triomphalisme [tʀijɔ̃falism] *nm* crowing; **sans faire de t. ...** while I don't want to crow...

triomphant, -e [tʀijɔ̃fɑ̃, -ɑ̃t] *adj* triumphant; **d'un ton t.** triumphantly

triomphe [tʀijɔ̃f] *nm* triumph *(sur over)*; **faire un t. à qn** to give sb an ovation; **porter qn en t.** to carry sb one one's shoulders

triompher [tʀijɔ̃fe] **1** *vi* (**a**) *(gagner)* to triumph; *Fig (vérité)* to prevail (**b**) *(exulter)* to crow
2 triompher de *vt ind* to triumph over

trip [tʀip] *nm Fam (d'un drogué)* trip; **faire un t.** to trip; **être dans un t. écolo** to be on an environmental kick

triparti, -e [tʀiparti], **tripartite** [tʀipartit] *adj* tripartite

tripatouillage [tʀipatujaʒ] *nm Fam (de textes, de comptes)* tampering with; *(de statistiques)* massaging

tripatouiller [tʀipatuje] *vt Fam* (**a**) *(textes, comptes)* to tamper with; *(statistiques)* to massage (**b**) *(cheveux)* to play or fiddle with; *(bouton)* to pick at

tripe [trip] *nf* (**a**) **tripes** *(d'un animal)* entrails; *Fam (d'une personne)* guts; *Fam* **prendre qn aux tripes** to get sb right there (**b**) **tripes** *(plat)* tripe (**c**) *Fam Fig* **avoir la t. républicaine** to be a republican through and through

triperie [tripri] *nf (boutique)* tripe shop

tripette [tripɛt] *nf Fam* **ça ne vaut pas t.** it's not worth a damn

triphasé, -e [trifaze] *Élec adj* three-phase

triphtongue [triftɔ̃g] *nf* triphthong

tripier, -ère [tripje, -ɛr] *nm,f* tripe butcher

triple [tripl] **1** *adj* (**a**) *(à trois éléments)* triple; **en t. exemplaire** in triplicate; *Mus* **t. croche** *Br* demisemiquaver, *Am* thirty-second note (**b**) *(trois fois plus grand)* triple, treble (**c**) *(emploi intensif) Fam* **t. buse** prize idiot; **au t. galop** at breakneck speed
   2 *nm* **le t. (de)** *(quantité, prix)* three times as much (as); *(nombre)* three times as many (as); **douze est le t. de quatre** twelve is three times four

triplé, -e [triple] **1** *nm,f* triplet
   2 *nm (triple succès)* triple victory; *(pari)* = bet on the first three horses in a race

triplement [triplǝmã] *adv* trebly, triply

tripler [triple] **1** *vt (somme, quantité)* to treble, to triple; **t. une classe** to repeat a year twice
   2 *vi* to treble, to triple

Tripoli [tripɔli] *n* Tripoli

triporteur [tripɔrtœr] *nm* delivery tricycle

tripot [tripo] *nm* gambling den

tripotée [tripote] *nf Fam* (**a**) *(défaite)* hammering (**b**) *(grand nombre)* **une t. de** loads of

tripoter [tripote] *vt Fam* (**a**) *(objet, appareil, cheveux)* to play with, to fiddle with; *(boutons, plaie)* to touch (**b**) *(personne)* to feel up, to grope

triptyque [triptik] *nm* triptych

trique [trik] *nf* cudgel; *Fam* **mener qn à la t.** to rule sb with a rod of iron

trisomie [trizɔmi] *nf Méd* **t. 21** Down's syndrome

trisomique [trizɔmik] *adj Méd* with Down's syndrome; **être t.** to have Down's syndrome

triste [trist] *adj* (**a**) *(malheureux)* sad (**b**) *(sinistre)* dreary, depressing; *Fam* **c'était pas t.!** *(soirée)* it was a night and a half!; *Fam* **il est pas t., son frère!** his brother's quite a character! (**c**) *(pénible)* sad; *(époque)* grim; **dans un t. état** in a sorry state; **c'est la t. réalité** that's the sad *or* harsh reality (**d**) *Péj* sad

tristement [tristǝmã] *adv* sadly; **t. célèbre** notorious

tristesse [tristɛs] *nf* (**a**) *(d'une personne, d'un événement)* sadness; **c'est avec t. que je vous annonce...** I am sorry to have to tell you... (**b**) *(aspect sinistre)* dreariness

tristounet, -ette [tristunɛ, -ɛt] *adj Fam* gloomy

trithérapie [triterapi] *nf Méd* triple (combination) therapy

triton [tritɔ̃] *nm* (**a**) *(amphibien)* newt (**b**) *(mollusque)* triton, trumpet shell (**c**) *(personnage mythologique)* Triton

triturer [trityre] **1** *vt* (**a**) *(broyer)* to grind (**b**) *Fam (tripoter)* to fiddle with
   2 se triturer *vpr Fam* **se t. la cervelle** *ou* **les méninges** to rack one's brains

triumvirat [trijɔmvira] *nm* triumvirate

trivial, -e, -aux, -ales [trivjal, -o] *adj* (**a**) *(vulgaire)* vulgar, coarse (**b**) *(commun)* banal

trivialité [trivjalite] *nf* (**a**) *(vulgarité)* vulgarity, coarseness (**b**) *(expression)* vulgar *or* coarse expression (**c**) *(banalité)* banality

troc [trɔk] *nm* (**a**) *(échange)* exchange (**b**) *(système économique)* barter; **faire du t.** to barter

troène [trɔɛn] *nm* privet

troglodyte [trɔglɔdit] *nm (personne)* cave dweller, *Spéc* troglodyte

trogne [trɔɲ] *nf Fam* face, mug

trognon [trɔɲɔ̃] **1** *nm (de pomme)* core
   2 *adj inv Fam (mignon)* sweet

Troie [trwa] *n* Troy

troïka [trɔika] *nf* troika

trois [trwa] **1** *adj inv* three; **le t. août** *Br* (on) the third of August, *Am* (on) August third; **à t. heures** at three o'clock; **page t.** page three; **Henri T.** Henry the Third; **nous étions t.** there were three of us; **les t. quarts du temps** most of the time; **couper/partager qch en t.** to cut/divide sth into three; **t. par t.** three by three; **(hôtel) t. étoiles** three-star hotel; **en t. dimensions** in 3-D
   2 *nm inv* three

trois-huit [trwaɥit] *nm inv* **faire les t.** = to work three alternating eight-hour shifts

troisième [trwazjɛm] **1** *adj, nmf & nm* third; **le t. âge** *Br* senior citizens, *Am* golden agers
   2 *nf* (**a**) *Scol Br* fourth year of secondary school, *Am* eighth grade (**b**) *(vitesse)* third (gear); *voir aussi* **cinquième**

troisièmement [trwazjɛmmã] *adv* thirdly

trois-mâts [trwama] *nm inv* three-master

trois-pièces [trwapjɛs] *nm inv* (**a**) *(appartement)* three-room *Br* flat *or Am* apartment; **t. cuisine** *Br* three-room flat with kitchen, *Am* three and a half (**b**) *(costume)* three-piece suit

trois-quarts [trwakar] *nm inv* (**a**) *(manteau)* three-quarter-length coat (**b**) *(au rugby)* three-quarter

trolley [trɔlɛ], **trolleybus** [trɔlɛbys] *nm* trolleybus

trombe [trɔ̃b] *nf* waterspout; **il pleut des trombes** it's pouring down; **sous des trombes d'eau** in the torrential rain; *Fam Fig* **passer/partir en t.** to tear past/off

trombine [trɔ̃bin] *nf Fam* face

trombone [trɔ̃bɔn] *nm* (**a**) *(agrafe)* paper clip (**b**) *(instrument)* trombone; **t. à coulisse/à pistons** slide/valve trombone (**c**) *(instrumentiste)* trombone player, trombonist

trompe [trɔ̃p] *nf* (**a**) *(d'éléphant)* trunk; *(d'insecte)* proboscis (**b**) *(instrument à vent)* horn (**c**) *Anat* **t. d'Eustache/de Fallope** Eustachian/Fallopian tube

trompe-l'œil [trɔ̃plœj] *nm inv (décor)* trompe l'œil; **en t.** trompe l'œil

tromper [trɔ̃pe] **1** *vt* (**a**) *(abuser)* to fool (**sur** about) (**b**) *(être infidèle à)* to be unfaithful to (**c**) *(vigilance, surveillance)* to elude, to escape (**d**) *Fig* **t. son ennui** to relieve the boredom; **t. sa faim** to stave off one's hunger
   2 se tromper *vpr (faire une erreur)* to make a mistake; *(avoir tort)* to be mistaken; **se t. dans les dates/proportions** to get the dates/the proportions wrong; **se t. de numéro** *(au téléphone)* to dial the wrong number; **se t. d'heure/de jour** to get the time/day wrong

tromperie [trɔ̃pri] *nf* deceit, deception

trompeter [trɔ̃pǝte] *vt (nouvelles)* to shout from the rooftops

trompette [trɔ̃pɛt] *nf* trumpet; *Fig* **avoir le nez en t.** to have a turned-up nose; **t. bouchée** muted trumpet

trompette-de-la-mort (*pl* **trompettes-de-la-mort**) [trɔ̃pɛtdəlamɔr] *nf Bot* horn of plenty

trompettiste [trɔ̃petist] *nmf* trumpet player, trumpeter

trompeur, -euse [trɔ̃pœr, -øz] *adj* (**a**) *(volontairement)* deceitful (**b**) *(symptôme, apparences)* deceptive; *(publicité)* misleading

tronc [trɔ̃] *nm* (**a**) *(d'un arbre, d'un corps)* trunk; *Fig* **t. commun** core syllabus; *Fam* **se casser le t.** to strain oneself (**b**) *(dans une église)* poor box

tronche [trɔ̃ʃ] *nf Fam (tête)* nut; *(visage)* mug; **faire la t.** to sulk

tronçon [trɔ̃sɔ̃] *nm* piece; *(de route)* section

tronçonner [trɔ̃sɔne] *vt* to cut into sections

tronçonneuse [trɔ̃sɔnøz] *nf* chain saw

trône [tron] *nm aussi Fam Fig* throne

trôner [trone] *vi* (**a**) *Hum (personne)* to sit on one's throne (**b**) *(objet)* to have pride of place

tronquer [trɔ̃ke] *vt (mot, scène)* to shorten

trop [tro] *adv* (**a**) *(avec un adjectif ou un adverbe)* too; **ça va? – pas t. mal** how are things? – not too bad; *Fam* **il est vraiment t.!** he's too much!
(**b**) *(avec un verbe)* too much; **il n'y a tient pas t.** he's not too bothered; **je ne sais pas t.** I'm not too sure; **ça te plaît? – pas t.** do you like it? – not much; **on ne saurait t. le répéter** it can't be repeated too often
(**c**) *(quantité)* too much; *(nombre)* too many; **t. de** *(quantité)* too much; *(nombre)* too many; **nous sommes t.** there are too many of us; **il y a deux assiettes de** *ou* **en t.** there are two plates too many; **payer 50 euros de t.** *ou* **en t.** to pay 50 euros too much; **c'est une fois de t.** that's once too often; **se sentir de t.** to feel in the way; **t., c'est t.!** enough is enough!; **c'en est t.!** this really is too much!

trophée [trɔfe] *nm* trophy

tropical, -e, -aux, -ales [trɔpikal, -o] *adj* tropical

tropique [trɔpik] *nm* (**a**) *(parallèle)* tropic; **le T. du Cancer/du Capricorne** the tropic of Cancer/of Capricorn (**b**) **les tropiques** *(région)* the tropics; **sous les tropiques** in the tropics

trop-perçu (*pl* **trop-perçus**) [tropɛrsy] *nm* over-payment

trop-plein (*pl* **trop-pleins**) [troplɛ̃] *nm* (**a**) *(excédent)* overflow (**b**) *(dispositif d'évacuation)* overflow pipe

troquer [trɔke] *vt* **t. qch contre qch** to exchange sth for sth

troquet [trɔkɛ] *nm Fam* small café

trot [tro] *nm* trot; **aller au t.** to trot; *Fam Fig* **allez-y, et au t.!** go on, and be quick about it!; **t. attelé** harness race

trotskiste, trotskyste [trɔtskist] *adj & nmf* Trotskyist

trotte [trɔt] *nf Fam (distance)* **il y a une bonne t. d'ici à chez elle** it's a fair distance from here to her house

trotter [trɔte] *vi* (**a**) *(cheval)* to trot (**b**) *(personne)* to trot about (**c**) *Fig* **cet air me trotte dans la tête depuis hier** I haven't been able to get that tune out of my head since yesterday; **cette idée me trottait dans la tête** the idea was running through my head

trotteur [trɔtœr] *nm* (**a**) *(cheval)* trotter (**b**) *(chaussure)* flat shoe

trotteuse [trɔtøz] *nf (de montre)* second hand

trottiner [trɔtine] *vi (personne)* to trot about

trottinette [trɔtinɛt] *nf* scooter; **faire de la t.** to ride one's scooter

trottoir [trɔtwar] *nm Br* pavement, *Am* sidewalk; *Fam* **faire le t.** to be on the game, to walk the streets; **t. roulant** *Br* travelator, *Am* moving sidewalk

trou [tru] *nm* (**a**) *(ouverture)* hole; *(d'aiguille)* eye; *Fam Fig* **faire son t.** to find one's niche; **t. d'air** air pocket; **le t. dans la couche d'ozone** the hole in the ozone layer; *aussi Fig Vulg* **t. du cul** *Br* arsehole, *Am* asshole; **t. noir** black hole; *Fig* **je suis tombé de l'échelle, et après c'est le t. noir** I fell off the ladder, and after that it's all a blank; **t. de serrure** keyhole; **t. de souris** mouse hole (**b**) *(dans un emploi du temps, dans ses connaissances)* gap; **j'ai un t. de cinq à sept** I'm free between five and seven; **avoir un t. (de mémoire)** to have a memory lapse (**c**) *(déficit)* hole, dent; **le t. de la sécu** the Social Security deficit (**d**) *Fam Péj (lieu reculé)* hole; **il n'est jamais sorti de son t.** he has never been out of his own backyard (**e**) *Fam (prison)* nick (**f**) **faire le t. normand** = to drink a glass of Calvados between courses to aid digestion

troubadour [trubadur] *nm* troubadour

troublant, -e [trublɑ̃, -ɑ̃t] *adj* (**a**) *(déconcertant)* disconcerting (**b**) *(sensuel)* provocative

trouble¹ [trubl] **1** *adj* (**a**) *(liquide)* cloudy; *(lumière)* dim; *(image, photo)* blurred (**b**) *(comportement, affaire)* shady; *(période)* murky
2 *adv* **voir t.** to have blurred vision

trouble² *nm* (**a**) *(désordre)* confusion, disorder; **semer** *ou* **jeter le t. dans l'esprit de qn** to confuse sb (**b**) *(émoi)* agitation (**c**) **troubles** *(révolte)* unrest (**d**) **troubles** *(maladie)* disorder; **troubles de la vision/respiratoires** eye/respiratory disorder; **troubles de la personnalité** personality disorder

trouble-fête [trubləfɛt] *nm inv Br* spoilsport, *Am* party-pooper; **jouer les t.** *Br* to be a spoilsport, *Am* to be a party-pooper

troubler [truble] **1** *vt* (**a**) *(eau)* to make cloudy; *Fig (esprit)* to cloud; **t. la vue à qn** to blur sb's eyes (**b**) *(sommeil, silence)* to disturb; *(bonheur)* to spoil; **t. l'ordre public** to disturb the peace (**c**) *(mettre en émoi)* to make flustered; *(rendre perplexe)* to confuse
2 se troubler *vpr* (**a**) *(liquide)* to get cloudy; *(vue)* to become blurred (**b**) *(se déconcerter)* to become flustered; **sans se t.** unperturbed

trouée [true] *nf (dans une haie, dans un mur)* gap, opening; **une t. de ciel bleu** a patch of blue sky

trouer [true] **1** *vt* to make a hole in
2 se trouer *vpr* **mes chaussures se sont trouées au bout d'une semaine** there was a hole in my shoes after a week

troufion [trufjɔ̃] *nm Fam Br* soldier, *Am* grunt

trouillard, -e [trujar, -ard] *Fam* **1** *adj* yellow-bellied, chicken
2 *nm,f* yellow-belly, chicken

trouille [truj] *nf Fam* fear; **avoir la t.** to be scared stiff

trouillomètre [trujɔmɛtr] *nm Fam* **avoir le t. à zéro** to be scared stiff

troupe [trup] *nf* (**a**) *(groupe)* troop, band; **t. de théâtre** company, troupe (**b**) *(de soldats)* troop; **troupes** *(armée)* troops, forces

troupeau, -x [trupo] *nm (de bétail, d'éléphants)* herd; *(de moutons)* flock; *(d'oies)* gaggle; *Péj (de gens)* herd

trousse [trus] *nf* (**a**) *(étui)* kit; **t. d'écolier** pencil case; **t. de secours** first-aid kit; **t. de toilette** toilet bag (**b**) *(locutions)* **être aux trousses de qn** to be hot on sb's heels; **avoir qn aux trousses** to have sb hot on one's heels

trousseau, -x [truso] *nm* (a) *(de clés)* bunch (b) *(de mariée)* trousseau (c) *(de pensionnaire)* clothes

trousser [truse] *vt* (a) *Culin (volaille)* to truss (b) **bien troussé** *(compliment)* well-turned (c) *Vieilli (retrousser)* to turn up

trouvaille [truvaj] *nf* (a) *(chose trouvée)* find (b) *(bonne idée)* brainwave

trouver [truve] **1** *vt* (a) *(en cherchant)* to find; *(procédé, vaccin)* to discover; **je ne trouve pas mes clefs** I can't find my keys; **aller t. qn** to go and see sb; **t. quelque chose à redire** to be sure to have something to say; **t. le sommeil** to get to sleep; **exemple bien trouvé** well-chosen example; **je me demande où il est allé t. ça** I wonder where he got that idea from; *Ironique* **tu as trouvé ça tout seul?** did you think of that all on your own?

(b) *(par hasard)* to find, to come across; **t. porte close** to find nobody home; *Fig* **il va t. à qui parler!** he'll have me/him/*etc* to reckon with!; *Fig* **t. son maître** to meet one's match; **t. la mort** to meet one's death

(c) *(juger)* to find; *(penser)* to think; **je trouve ça idiot** I think it's stupid; **qu'est-ce qu'elle lui trouve?** what does she see in him?; **je trouve que...** I think (that)...; **t. le temps long** to feel that the time is dragging

2 se trouver *vpr* (a) *(dans une situation, dans un lieu)* to be; **où se trouve la gare?** where's the station?; **se t. dans l'impossibilité de faire qch** to be unable to do sth

(b) *(être disponible)* **ça se trouve dans les supermarchés** you can find *or* get it in supermarkets

(c) *(se sentir)* to feel; **je me trouve bien ici** I like it here; **se t. beau/gros** to think one is good-looking/fat; **se t. mal** to feel faint

(d) *(arriver)* **il se trouve que...** as it happens...; *Fam* **si ça se trouve** maybe

trouvère [truvɛr] *nm* trouvère

truand [tryɑ̃] *nm Fam* crook

truander [tryɑ̃de] *Fam* **1** *vt* to rip off; **se faire t.** to get ripped off

2 *vi (à un examen)* to cheat (**à** in)

trublion [tryblijɔ̃] *nm* troublemaker

truc [tryk] *nm Fam* (a) *(chose)* thing; **j'ai un t. à faire/à te dire** I've something to do/to tell you (b) *(astuce)* trick; **connaître les trucs du métier** to know the tricks of the trade (c) *(personne)* **T. what's-his-name,** *f* **what's-her-name** (d) *(domaine)* **c'est vraiment son t.** he's really into it; **ce n'est pas son t.** it's not his thing

trucage [tryka3] *nm* (a) *(dans un film)* special effect (b) *(d'une photographie)* faking; *(d'un match, d'une élection)* rigging; *(de comptes)* fiddling

truchement [tryʃmɑ̃] *nm* **par le t. de...** through...

trucider [tryside] *vt Fam Hum* to bump off

trucmuche [trykmyʃ] *nm Fam* (a) *(chose)* thingy (b) **T.** *(personne)* what's-his-name, *f* what's-her-name

truculence [trykylɑ̃s] *nf (d'un récit, d'un style)* colourfulness; *(d'une personne)* flamboyance

truculent, -e [trykylɑ̃, -ɑ̃t] *adj (récit, style)* colourful; *(personne)* flamboyant

truelle [tryɛl] *nf* trowel

truffe [tryf] *nf* (a) *(champignon, au chocolat)* truffle (b) *(de chien)* nose

truffer [tryfe] *vt* (a) *(plat)* to garnish with truffles (b) *Fig (remplir)* **être truffé de** *(citations, balles)* to be peppered with; *(fautes)* to be riddled with

truie [trɥi] *nf* sow

truite [trɥit] *nf* trout; **t. arc-en-ciel/saumonée** rainbow/salmon trout

truquage [tryka3] = **trucage**

truquer [tryke] *vt* (a) *(photographie)* to fake; *(match, élection)* to rig; *(comptes)* to fiddle; *(dés)* to load (b) *(scène)* to use special effects in

trust [trœst] *nm* trust

truster [trœste] *vt aussi Fam* to monopolize

tsar [tsar, dzar] *nm* tsar, czar

tsé-tsé [tsetse] *nf inv voir* **mouche**

TSF [teesɛf] *nf (abrév télégraphie sans fil) Vieilli (procédé)* wireless telegraphy; *(poste)* wireless

t-shirt (*pl* **t-shirts**) [tiʃœrt] = **tee-shirt**

tsigane [tsigan] = **tzigane**

TSVP *(abrév* **tournez s'il vous plaît***)* PTO

TTC [tetese] *(abrév* **toutes taxes comprises***)* inclusive of tax

tu, -e *voir* **taire**

tu [ty] *pron personnel* you; **tu as raison** you're right; *Fam* **t'as déjà fini?** have you already finished?; **être à tu et à toi avec qn** to be on first-name terms with sb; **dire tu à qn** to address sb as "tu"

Tuamotu [twamotu] *nfpl* **les T.** the Tuamotu Archipelago

tuant, -e [tɥɑ̃, -ɑ̃t] *adj Fam* (a) *(fatigant)* exhausting (b) *(insupportable)* exasperating

tuba [tyba] *nm* (a) *(instrument de musique)* tuba (b) *(de plongée)* snorkel

tube [tyb] *nm* (a) *(tuyau)* tube; *Fam Fig* **à pleins tubes** at full blast; **t. digestif** digestive tract; **t. à essai** test tube (b) *(chanson)* hit (c) *(emballage)* tube; **t. de rouge à lèvres** lipstick

tubercule [tybɛrkyl] *nm (plante)* tuber

tuberculeux, -euse [tybɛrkylø, -øz] **1** *adj* with tuberculosis; **être t.** to have tuberculosis

2 *nm,f* person with tuberculosis

tuberculose [tybɛrkyloz] *nf* tuberculosis; **avoir la t.** to have tuberculosis

tubéreuse [tyberøz] *nf* tuberose

tubulaire [tybylɛr] *adj* tubular

TUC [tyk] *nm (abrév* **travaux d'utilité collective***)* = community work project for unemployed young people

tuer [tɥe] **1** *vt* (a) *(être vivant)* to kill; **t. qn d'un coup de revolver/de couteau** to shoot/stab sb to death; **c'est le chagrin qui l'a tué** he died of grief; *Fig* **t. le temps** to kill time (b) *Fam (épuiser)* **tous ces déplacements m'ont tué** all that travelling was a killer; **ces escaliers/ces enfants me tuent** these stairs/these children will be the death of me (c) *Fam (sidérer)* **ça me tue!** it kills me!

2 se tuer *vpr* (a) *(se suicider)* to kill oneself (b) *(dans un accident)* to die, to be killed (c) *(l'un l'autre)* to kill one another (d) *Fig* **se t. au travail** *ou* **à la tâche** to work oneself to death; **se t. à faire qch** to wear oneself out doing sth

tuerie [tyri] *nf* slaughter

tue-tête [tytɛt] **à tue-tête** *adv* at the top of one's voice

tueur, -euse [tɥœr, -øz] **1** *adj* killer

2 *nm,f* killer; **t. à gages** hired killer; **t. en série** serial killer

tuile [tɥil] *nf* (**a**) *(de toit)* tile (**b**) **t. aux amandes** = type of thin almond biscuit (**c**) *Fam (problème)* **il m'arrive une t.** I'm in a bit of a mess

tulipe [tylip] *nf (fleur)* tulip

tulle [tyl] *nm* (**a**) *(tissu)* tulle (**b**) *Méd* **t. gras** = dressing used for burns

tuméfié, -e [tymefje] *adj* swollen

tuméfier [tymefje] *vt* to cause to swell

tumeur [tymœr] *nf* tumour; **t. au cerveau** brain tumour

tumoral, -e, -aux, -ales [tymɔral, -o] *adj* tumorous, tumoral

tumulte [tymylt] *nm (de la foule)* commotion; *(des passions)* turmoil

tumultueux, -euse [tymyltɥø, -øz] *adj (réunion)* noisy, tumultuous; *(vie, période)* tumultuous; *(relation)* stormy

tuner [tynœr, tynɛr] *nm* tuner

tungstène [tœ̃kstɛn] *nm* tungsten

tunique [tynik] *nf* tunic

Tunis [tynis] *n* Tunis

Tunisie [tynizi] *nf* la **T.** Tunisia

tunisien, -enne [tynizjɛ̃, -ɛn] **1** *adj* Tunisian
  2 *nm,f* **T.** Tunisian

tunisois, -e [tynizwa, -az] **1** *adj* of Tunis
  2 *nm,f* **T.** person from Tunis

tunnel [tynɛl] *nm* tunnel; **le t. sous la Manche** the Channel Tunnel

tuque [tyk] *nf Can* bobble hat

turban [tyrbɑ̃] *nm* turban

turbin [tyrbɛ̃] *nm Fam (travail)* grind; **aller au t.** to go off to the daily grind

turbine [tyrbin] *nf* turbine

turbiner [tyrbine] *vi Fam (travailler)* to slog (away)

turbo [tyrbo] **1** *adj* turbocharged
  2 *nm* turbo; *Fam* **mettre le t.** to get a move on

turboréacteur [tyrbɔreaktœr] *nm* turbojet (engine)

turbot [tyrbo] *nm* turbot

turbulence [tyrbylɑ̃s] *nf* (**a**) **turbulences** *(dans l'atmosphère)* turbulence (**b**) *(d'un enfant)* boisterousness

turbulent, -e [tyrbylɑ̃, -ɑ̃t] *adj (enfant, classe)* boisterous

turc, turque [tyrk] **1** *adj* Turkish
  2 *nm,f* **T.** Turk
  3 *nm (langue)* Turkish

turf [tœrf, tyrf] *nm (activité)* racing

turfiste [tœrst, tyrfist] *nmf* racegoer

turkmène [tyrkmɛn] **1** *adj* Turkoman
  2 *nmf* **T.** Turkoman
  3 *nm (langue)* Turkmen

Turkménistan [tyrkmenistɑ̃] *nm* le **T.** Turkmenistan

turlupiner [tyrlypine] *vt Fam* to bother

turluter [tyrlyte] *vi Can Fam* to trill, to sing tra-la-la

turpitude [tyrpityd] *nf* (**a**) *(d'une conduite)* vileness, turpitude (**b**) *(action)* vile act

turque [tyrk] *voir* **turc**

Turquie [tyrki] *nf* la **T.** Turkey

turquoise [tyrkwaz] *nf, nm inv & adj inv* turquoise

tutelle [tytɛl] *nf* (**a**) *Jur* guardianship; *Pol* **territoires sous t.** trust territories (**b**) *(protection)* protection

tuteur, -trice [tytœr, -tris] **1** *nm,f* guardian; **t. légal** legal guardian
  2 *nm (pour plante)* support

tutoiement [tytwamɑ̃] *nm* = use of the familiar "tu" instead of the more formal "vous"; **le t. est de rigueur** everybody calls each other "tu"

Tutoiement et vouvoiement

Traditionally, non-native French speakers waited until they were addressed using the informal "tu" form before using it themselves, except when speaking to young children. However in the past twenty or thirty years people in France have become much more casual about using "tu", and it is now commonly used among colleagues in the workplace, while the "vous" form tends to be used when talking to people from an older generation or to hierarchical superiors (see also entries **tu** and **vous**).

---

tutoyer [tytwaje] **1** *vt* **t. qn** = to address sb as "tu"
  2 se tutoyer *vpr* = to address each other as "tu"

tutti quanti [tutikwɑ̃ti] *adv* **et t.** etcetera, etcetera

tutu [tyty] *nm* tutu

tuyau, -x [tɥijo] *nm* (**a**) *(canalisation)* pipe; *(de cheminée)* flue; *(flexible)* tube; **t. d'arrosage** garden hose; **t. d'échappement** exhaust (pipe); **t. d'incendie** fire hose; **t. de poêle** stove pipe (**b**) *Fam (conseil)* tip; *(information)* tip-off

tuyauter [tɥijɔte] *vt Fam (conseiller)* to give a tip to (**sur** about); *(informer)* to tip off (**sur** about)

tuyauterie [tɥijɔtri] *nf* piping, pipes

TV [teve] *nf (abrév* **télévision**) TV

TVA [tevea] *nf (abrév* **taxe à la valeur ajoutée**) VAT

tweed [twid] *nm* tweed

twin-set (*pl* **twin-sets**) [twinsɛt] *nm* twinset

tympan [tɛ̃pɑ̃] *nm* (**a**) *Anat* eardrum (**b**) *Archit* tympanum

type [tip] **1** *adj* typical; **lettre t.** standard letter
  2 *nm* (**a**) *(genre)* type (**b**) *(personnification)* **le t. même de** the classic example of (**c**) *(apparence)* **avoir le t. latin/nordique** to have Latin/Nordic looks (**d**) *Fam (homme)* guy, *Br* bloke

typé, -e [tipe] *adj* **il est italien – oui, et il est très t.** he's Italian – yes, he looks typically Italian

typhoïde [tifɔid] **1** *adj (fièvre)* typhoid
  2 *nf* typhoid (fever)

typhon [tifɔ̃] *nm* typhoon

typhus [tifys] *nm* typhus (fever)

typique [tipik] *adj* typical

typiquement [tipikmɑ̃] *adv* typically

typographe [tipɔgraf] *nmf* typographer

typographie [tipɔgrafi] *nf* typography, letterpress printing

typographique [tipɔgrafik] *adj* typographic

tyran [tirɑ̃] *nm* tyrant

tyrannie [tirani] *nf* tyranny

tyrannique [tiranik] *adj* tyrannical

tyranniser [tiranize] *vt (population)* to tyrannize; *(famille, collègue)* to bully

tzar [tsar, dzar] = **tsar**

tzigane [tsigan, dzigan] **1** *adj* gypsy
  2 *nmf* **T.** gypsy

U

U, u [y] *nm inv* U, u; **en U** U-shaped; **tables disposées en U** tables arranged in a horseshoe (shape)

ubac [ybak] *nm* = shady side of an Alpine mountain, *Spéc* ubac

ubiquité [ybikɥite] *nf* ubiquity; **avoir le don d'u.** to have the ability to be in several places at the same time

UDF [ydeɛf] *nf Pol* (*abrév* **Union pour la démocratie française**) = right-of-centre French political party

UE *nf* (*abrév* **Union européenne**) EU

UEM [yɑɛm] *nf Écon* (*abrév* **Union économique et monétaire**) EMU

UEO [yɑo] *nf* (*abrév* **Union de l'Europe occidentale**) WEU

ufologie [yfɔlɔʒi] *nf* ufology

UFR [yɛfɛr] *nf* (*abrév* **unité de formation et de recherche**) = department (*in university*)

UHF [yaʃɛf] *Rad* (*abrév* **ultra-haute fréquence**) UHF

UHT [yaʃte] (*abrév* **ultra-haute température**) UHT

Ukraine [ykrɛn] *nf* **l'U.** the Ukraine

ukrainien, -enne [ykrɛnjɛ̃, -jɛn] **1** *adj* Ukrainian
2 *nm,f* **U.** Ukrainian
3 *nm* (*langue*) Ukrainian

ukulélé [jukulele] *nm* ukelele

ulcération [ylserasjɔ̃] *nf* ulceration

ulcère [ylsɛr] *nm* ulcer; **avoir un u. à l'estomac** to have a stomach ulcer

ulcéré, -e [ylsere] *adj* (**a**) *Méd* ulcerated (**b**) *Fig* (*en colère*) seething

ulcérer [ylsere] **1** *vt* (**a**) *Méd* to ulcerate (**b**) *Fig* (*mettre en colère*) **u. qn** to make sb seethe
2 s'ulcérer *vpr Méd* to ulcerate

ULM [yɛlɛm] *nm inv Aviat* (*abrév* **ultraléger motorisé**) microlight

ultérieur, -e [ylterjœr] *adj* later, subsequent (**à** to)

ultérieurement [ylterjœrmɑ̃] *adv* later (on), subsequently

ultimatum [yltimatɔm] *nm* ultimatum; **adresser un u. à qn** to give sb an ultimatum

ultime [yltim] *adj* last; (*préparatifs*) final

ultra- [yltra] *préf* ultra-

ultra-confidentiel, -elle [yltrakɔ̃fidɑ̃sjɛl] *adj* top-secret

ultra-conservateur, -trice [yltrakɔ̃sɛrvatœr] *adj Pol* ultra-conservative

ultramoderne [yltramɔdɛrn] *adj* high-tech

ultraportatif [yltrapɔrtatif] *nm* notebook computer

ultrarapide [yltrarapid] *adj* ultrafast

ultrasensible [yltrasɑ̃sibl] *adj* ultra-sensitive

ultrason [yltrasɔ̃] *nm Phys* ultrasound; **ultrasons** ultrasonic waves

ultraviolet, -ette [yltravjɔlɛ, -ɛt] *adj & nm* ultraviolet

ululer [ylyle] *vi* to ululate

Ulysse [ylis] *npr* Ulysses

UME [yɛmə] *nf* (*abrév* **union monétaire européenne**) EMU

un, une [œ̃, yn] **1** *adj* one; **il est une heure** it's one o'clock; **page un** page one; **un jour** one day; **un, deux, trois, partez!** one, two, three, go!
2 *pron indéfini* one; **un de mes amis** one of my friends, a friend of mine; **un de ces jours** one of these days; **en voilà une qui sait ce qu'elle veut!** there's somebody who knows what she wants!; **il n'y en a pas un qui parle anglais** not one of them speaks English; *Fam* **être menteur/hypocrite comme pas un** to be a dreadful liar/hypocrite; **(l') un de nous, (l') un d'entre nous** one of us
3 *art indéfini* (*pl* **des**) (**a**) (*en général*) a; (*devant une voyelle ou un h muet*) an; **un jour/une pomme/une heure** a day/an apple/an hour; **cela tombe un mardi** it falls on a Tuesday; **il y a des agrafes dans le tiroir** there are (some) staples in the drawer; **est-ce qu'il te reste des agrafes?** do you have any staples left?; **il y a des jours où...** there are days when..., some days...
(**b**) (*intensif*) **il y a un de ces mondes en ville!** the town is so busy!; **il est d'une bêtise!** he's so stupid!; **il a fait une de ces têtes!** you should have seen his face!; **tu m'as fait une peur!** you gave me such a fright!
4 *nm* (*chiffre*) one
5 *nf* (**a**) (*première page*) **la une** (*d'un journal*) the front page; **faire la une** (*d'un magazine*) to appear on the front cover; (*d'un journal*) to appear on the front page (**b**) **il n'a fait ni une ni deux** he didn't hesitate for a moment

unanime [ynanim] *adj* unanimous

unanimité [ynanimite] *nf* unanimity; **à l'u.** unanimously; **faire l'u.** to be accepted unanimously

underground [œndœrgrawnd] *adj inv & nm inv* underground

une [yn] *voir* **un**

UNEF [ynɛf] *nf* (*abrév* **Union nationale des étudiants de France**) = French union of students, ≃ *Br* NUS

Unesco [ynɛsko] *nf* (*abrév* **United Nations Educational Scientific and Cultural Organization**) Unesco

Unetelle *voir* **Untel**

uni, -e [yni] *adj* (**a**) (*famille, couple*) close (**b**) (*sans irrégularité*) (*sol, surface*) smooth, level (**c**) (*couleur*) plain; (*tissu, vêtement*) plain, *Br* self-coloured

Unicef [ynisɛf] *nf* (*abrév* **United Nations International Children's Emergency Fund**) **l'U.** Unicef

unicellulaire [yniselylɛr] *adj* unicellular

unidimensionnel, -elle [ynidimɑ̃sjɔnɛl] *adj* one-dimensional

unidirectionnel, -elle [ynidirɛksjɔnɛl] *adj* unidirectional

unidose [ynidoz] *adj* single-dose sachet

unifamilial, -e, -aux, -ales [ynifamiljal, -o] *Belg & Can* **1** *adj (logement)* for a single family

2 unifamiliale *nf* detached house *(for a single family)*

unificateur, -trice [ynifikatœr, -tris] *adj* unifying

unification [ynifikasjɔ̃] *nf* unification

unifier [ynifje] *vt* (**a**) *(parti politique, pays)* to unify (**b**) *(tarifs, poids et mesures)* to standardize

uniforme [ynifɔrm] **1** *adj (opinions, expression)* uniform; *(vie)* unchanging; *(allure, surface)* even; *(mouvement)* regular

2 *nm* uniform

uniformément [ynifɔrmemã] *adv* uniformly, evenly

uniformisation [ynifɔrmizasjɔ̃] *nf* standardization

uniformiser [ynifɔrmize] *vt* to standardize

uniformité [ynifɔrmite] *nf* (**a**) *(monotonie)* monotony (**b**) *(de couleurs, de teintes)* uniformity

unijambiste [yniʒãbist] **1** *adj* one-legged

2 *nmf* one-legged person

unilatéral, -e, -aux, -ales [ynilateral, -o] *adj (décision, désarmement)* unilateral; *(contrat, accord)* one-sided

unilingue [ynilɛ̃g] *adj* unilingual, monolingual

uninominal, -aux [yninɔminal, -o] *adj m voir* **scrutin**

union [ynjɔ̃] *nf* (**a**) *(entre personnes)* closeness, unity; **vivre en parfaite u. avec qn** to live in perfect harmony with sb (**b**) *(association) (de partis, de consommateurs)* union, association; **u. douanière/ économique/monétaire** customs/economic/monetary union; **l'U. européenne** the European Union; *Anciennement* **l'U. soviétique** the Soviet Union (**c**) *(mariage)* marriage; **u. libre** cohabitation; **vivre en u. libre** to cohabit

unique [ynik] *adj* (**a**) *(seul)* only; *(parti, prix)* single; *(occasion, cas)* unique; **être u. en son genre** to be one of a kind; **u. au monde** unlike anything else in the world; **c'est son seul et u. défaut** it's his one and only fault (**b**) *(incomparable)* unique (**c**) *Fam (très drôle)* priceless

uniquement [ynikmã] *adv* just, only

unir [ynir] **1** *vt* (**a**) *(relier) (personnes, territoires)* to unite; *(qualités)* to combine (**à** with) (**b**) *(réunir)* **l'amitié qui nous unit** the friendship that unites us (**c**) *(marier)* to join in marriage (**d**) *(sol, surface)* to smooth, to level

2 s'unir *vpr* (**a**) *(s'associer)* to join together, to unite; **s'u. à qn** to join forces with sb (**b**) *(se marier)* to become joined in marriage

unisexe [yniseks] *adj* unisex

unisson [ynisɔ̃] *nm* unison; **à l'u.** in unison

unitaire [yniter] *adj (système)* unitary; *(prix)* unit

unité [ynite] *nf* (**a**) *(pour mesurer)* unit; **u. de longueur/de poids** unit of measurement/weight (**b**) *(élément simple)* unit; **10 euros l'u.** 10 euros each; *Com* **prix à l'u.** unit price; **vendu à l'u.** sold singly; **chiffre des unités** units figure; **u. de production** production unit; *Univ* **u. de valeur** credit (**c**) *(cohésion) (d'une nation, d'une association)* unity; *(du style)* consistency (**d**) *Ordinat* unit; *(de disque)* drive; **u. de bande** tape unit; **u. centrale** central processing unit; **u. de disque/logique** disk/logical drive

univers [yniver] *nm* (**a**) *(espace)* universe (**b**) *Fig (milieu)* world

universaliser [yniversalize] *vt* to universalize

universalité [yniversalite] *nf* universality

universel, -elle [yniversel] *adj* universal; *(savoir)* all-embracing

universellement [yniverselmã] *adv* universally

universitaire [yniversiter] **1** *adj (ville, études)* university

2 *nmf* (**a**) *(enseignant)* academic (**b**) *Belg & Suisse (étudiant)* university student; *(diplômé)* graduate

université [yniversite] *nf* university; **aller à l'u.** to go to university; **u. d'été** summer school; *Pol* party conference *(for young members)*; **u. du troisième âge** = classes for senior citizens

Untel, Unetelle [œ̃tel, yntel] *nm,f* what's-his-name, *f* what's-her-name; **M./Mme U.** Mr/Mrs So-and-So

uppercut [yperkyt] *nm* uppercut

uranium [yranjɔm] *nm* uranium; **u. appauvri/enrichi** depleted/enriched uranium

Uranus [yranys] *npr (dieu, planète)* Uranus

urbain, -e [yrbɛ̃, -ɛn] *adj* (**a**) *(développement, milieu, transport)* urban (**b**) *Litt (poli)* urbane

urbanisation [yrbanizasjɔ̃] *nf* urbanization

urbaniser [yrbanize] *vt* to urbanize

urbanisme [yrbanism] *nm* town planning, urban development

urbaniste [yrbanist] **1** *adj* urban

2 *nmf* town planner

urbanité [yrbanite] *nf Litt* urbanity

urbi et orbi [yrbietɔrbi] *adv* urbi et orbi; *Fig* far and wide

urée [yre] *nf* urea

urètre [yrɛtr] *nm* urethra

urgence [yrʒãs] *nf* (**a**) *(caractère pressé)* urgency; **en cas d'u.** in an emergency; **d'u.** urgently; **être opéré d'u.** to have an emergency operation; **il y a u.** it's a matter of urgency (**b**) *(à l'hôpital)* emergency; **les urgences** *(service) Br* casualty, accident and emergency, *Am* the emergency room

urgent, -e [yrʒã, -ãt] *adj* urgent; **il est u. de le faire** it must be done urgently

urger [yrʒe] *vi Fam* **ça urge** it's urgent

urinaire [yriner] *adj* urinary

urine [yrin] *nf* urine

uriner [yrine] *vi* to urinate

urinoir [yrinwar] *nm* (public) urinal

urique [yrik] *adj (acide)* uric

urne [yrn] *nf* (**a**) *(pour voter)* ballot box; **aller aux urnes** to go to the polls (**b**) *(vase)* urn

uro-génital, -e *(mpl* **uro-génitaux**, *fpl* **uro-génitales)** [yroʒenital, -o] *adj* urogenital

urologie [yrɔlɔʒi] *nf* urology

urologue [yrɔlɔg] *nmf* urologist

URSS [yɛrɛses, yrs] *nf Anciennement (abrév* **Union des républiques socialistes soviétiques)** **l'U.** the USSR

URSSAF [yrsaf] *nf (abrév* **Union de recouvrement des cotisations de Sécurité sociale et d'Allocations familiales)** = organization which collects social security and family allowance payments

urticaire [yrtiker] *nf* nettle rash, *Spéc* urticaria; **avoir une crise d'u.** to come out in nettle rash; *Fam* **donner de l'u. à qn** to set sb's teeth on edge

Uruguay [yrygwe] *nm* **l'U.** Uruguay

uruguayen, -enne [yrygwejɛ̃, -ɛn] **1** *adj* Uruguayan

2 *nm,f* **U.** Uruguayan

us [ys] *nmpl* **les us et coutumes** the habits and customs

usage [yzaʒ] *nm* (**a**) *(utilisation)* use; **faire u. de qch** to use sth; **faire bon u. de qch** to put sth to good use; **avoir l'u. de qch** to have the use of sth; **à u. externe/ interne** *(médicament)* for external/internal use; **à l'u. des écoles/des étudiants** for use in schools/by students; **à usages multiples** multi-purpose; **hors d'u.** out of order; **Jur u. de faux** use of forged documents (**b**) *(d'un terme, d'une expression)* usage; **entrer dans l'u.** *(mot)* to come into common use; **le bon u.** correct usage (**c**) *(des vêtements)* **faire de l'u.** to wear well; **ce manteau vous fera de l'u.** you'll get a lot of wear out of this coat (**d**) *(coutume)* custom, practice; **c'est l'u.** it's the done thing; **comme il est d'u. en France** as is customary in France; **il est d'u. de** it's customary to

usagé, -e [yzaʒe] *adj (vêtement, livre)* worn; *(ticket)* used

usager [yzaʒe] *nm* user

usant, -e [yzã, -ãt] *adj Fam* (**a**) *(vie, travail)* exhausting, wearing (**b**) *(personne)* tiresome

usé, -e [yze] *adj* (**a**) *(vêtements)* worn, worn-out; **u. jusqu'à la corde** threadbare (**b**) *(eaux)* waste (**c**) *(sujet, plaisanterie)* tired, stale (**d**) *(épuisé)* worn-out

user [yze] **1** *vt* (**a**) *(consommer) (énergie, électricité)* to use (**b**) *(abîmer) (vêtements, chaussures)* to wear out; *Fig (résistance)* to break down; **u. qch jusqu'à la corde** to wear sth until it's threadbare (**c**) *(épuiser) (personne)* to wear down
 2 user de *vt ind (patience, violence, ruse)* to use; *(droit)* to exercise; **u. de douceur avec qn** to handle sb gently; **u. de son influence pour faire qch** to use one's influence to do sth
 3 s'user *vpr* (**a**) *(tissu, pneus, semelles)* to wear out; *(talons)* to wear down (**b**) *Fig (personne)* **s'u. à faire qch** to wear oneself out doing sth

usinage [yzinaʒ] *nm* machining

usine [yzin] *nf* factory, plant; **u. de fabrication** manufacturing plant; **u. de montage** assembly plant

usiner [yzine] *vt (façonner)* to machine

usité, -e [yzite] *adj (mot)* in common use; **très u.** very common; **peu u.** little used

ustensile [ystãsil] *nm* implement, tool; **u. de cuisine** kitchen utensil

usuel, -elle [yzɥɛl] *adj* everyday; *(dénomination)* common

usufruit [yzyfrɥi] *nm Jur* usufruct

usuraire [yzyrɛr] *adj* usurious

usure¹ [yzyr] *nf (intérêt, délit)* usury

usure² *nf (de pneu)* wear; *(du sol, de roches)* wearing away; **résister à l'u.** to wear well; *Fam* **avoir qn à l'u.** to wear sb down; **guerre d'u.** war of attrition

usurier, -ère [yzyrje, -ɛr] *nm,f* usurer

usurpateur, -trice [yzyrpatœr, -tris] *nm,f* usurper

usurpation [yzyrpasjɔ̃] *nf (d'un titre, de droits, du pouvoir)* usurpation

usurper [yzyrpe] *vt (titre, droits)* to usurp (**sur** from)

ut [yt] *nm inv (note)* C

utérin, -e [yterɛ̃, -in] *adj* uterine

utérus [yterys] *nm* uterus, womb

utile [ytil] *adj* useful (**à** to); **en quoi puis-je vous être u.?** what can I do for you?; **vous nous avez été bien u.** you've been very helpful to us; **se rendre u.** to make oneself useful; **en temps u.** in due course

utilement [ytilmã] *adv* usefully; **il m'a u. renseigné** he gave me useful information

utilisable [ytilizabl] *adj* usable; **facilement u.** easy to use

utilisateur, -trice [ytilizatœr, -tris] *nm,f* user

utilisation [ytilizasjɔ̃] *nf* use

utiliser [ytilize] *vt* (**a**) *(se servir de)* to use (**b**) *Péj (personne)* to use (**c**) *Ordinat* to run

utilitaire [ytilitɛr] **1** *adj* (**a**) utilitarian; *(véhicule)* commercial (**b**) *Ordinat* utility
 2 *nm Ordinat* utility; **u. de conversion** conversion utility

utilitarisme [ytilitarism] *nm* utilitarianism

utilité [ytilite] *nf (fonction)* usefulness; **être d'une grande u. (à qn)** to be very useful (to sb)

utopie [ytɔpi] *nf* utopia

utopique [ytɔpik] *adj* utopian

utopiste [ytɔpist] *nmf* Utopian

UV¹ [yve] *nf inv Univ (abrév* **unité de valeur***)* credit

UV² *nm inv (abrév* **ultraviolet***)* UV

V

V, v [ve] *nm inv* (**a**) *(lettre)* V, v; *Fam* **à la vitesse grand V** at a rate of knots (**b**) *(abrév* **voir**) see

va *voir* **aller**

vacance [vakɑ̃s] *nf* (**a**) *(d'un poste)* vacancy; **pendant la v. du pouvoir** while there is no one officially in power (**b**) **vacances** *(d'écoliers, de travailleurs) Br* holiday(s), *Am* vacation; **un jour de vacances** a day's holiday; **prendre des vacances** to take a holiday; **être en vacances** to be on holiday; **partir en vacances** to go away on holiday; *Fam* **faire des vacances à qn** to give sb a break; **vacances de neige** winter sports holiday; **vacances de Noël/Pâques** Christmas/Easter holidays; **vacances scolaires** school holidays; *Scol* **les grandes vacances** the summer holidays

vacancier, -ère [vakɑ̃sje, -ɛr] *nm,f Br* holidaymaker, *Am* vacationer

vacant, -e [vakɑ̃, -ɑ̃t] *adj* vacant

vacarme [vakarm] *nm* uproar, din; **faire du v.** to make an uproar

vacataire [vakatɛr] *nmf* short-term worker

vacation [vakasjɔ̃] *nf* (**a**) *(de juge, d'expert)* sitting, session (**b**) *(rémunération)* fees

vaccin [vaksɛ̃] *nm* vaccine

vaccination [vaksinasjɔ̃] *nf* vaccination, inoculation

vacciner [vaksine] *vt* to vaccinate, to inoculate (**contre** against); **se faire v. (contre)** to get vaccinated (against); *Fam* **je suis vacciné!** I've learnt my lesson!; *Fam* **je suis majeur et vacciné!** I'm old enough to look after myself now!

vachard, -e [vaʃar, -ard] *adj Fam (coup)* rotten, mean, nasty; *(question)* nasty

vache [vaʃ] **1** *nf* (**a**) *(animal)* cow; **v. à lait** dairy cow; *Fig* milch cow; **v. laitière** dairy cow; *Fam* **manger de la v. enragée** to have a hard time of it; *Fam* **parler français comme une v. espagnole** to speak rotten French; *Fam* **comme une v. qui regarde passer les trains** with a vacant look on one's face (**b**) *Fam (homme)* swine; *(femme)* cow (**c**) *(cuir)* cowhide (**d**) *Fam (interjection)* **la v., qu'est-ce qu'il fait froid!** God, it's so cold!

2 *adj Fam* rotten, nasty; **être v. avec qn** to be rotten to sb

vachement [vaʃmɑ̃] *adv Fam (très) Br* dead, *Am* real; *(beaucoup)* a hell of a lot

vacher, -ère [vaʃe, -ɛr] *nm,f* cowherd, *f* cowgirl

vacherie [vaʃri] *nf Fam (action)* dirty trick; *(remarque)* nasty remark

vacherin [vaʃrɛ̃] *nm* (**a**) *(fromage)* = type of soft cheese (**b**) *(dessert)* = meringue with cream, ice cream and fruit

vachette [vaʃɛt] *nf* (**a**) *(petite vache)* small cow; *(jeune vache)* calf (**b**) *(cuir)* calfskin

vacillant, -e [vasijɑ̃, -ɑ̃t] *adj* (**a**) *(flamme)* flickering; *(démarche)* staggering (**b**) *(santé, mémoire)* failing

vacillation [vasijasjɔ̃] *nf,* **vacillement** [vasijmɑ̃] *nm (d'une flamme)* flickering

vaciller [vasije] *vi* (**a**) *(chanceler)* to be unsteady, to sway; **v. sur ses jambes** to stagger; **tout vacillait autour de moi** everything was swimming around me (**b**) *(flamme)* to flicker (**c**) *(mémoire, raison)* to fail

va-comme-je-te-pousse [vakɔmʃtəpus] **à la va-comme-je-te-pousse** *adv Fam* any old how

vacuité [vakɥite] *nf* vacuity

vadrouille [vadruj] *nf* (**a**) *Fam (balade)* ramble, saunter; **partir** *ou* **aller en v.** to roam about; **il est rarement à son bureau, il est toujours en v.** he's rarely at his desk, he's always wandering around somewhere (**b**) *Can* mop

vadrouiller [vadruje] *vi Fam* to roam about

va-et-vient [vaevjɛ̃] *nm inv* (**a**) *(mouvement)* backward and forward movement; **faire le v. (entre)** *(personne)* to go back and forth (between) (**b**) *(circulation) (de personnes)* comings and goings (**c**) *(dispositif électrique)* two-way wiring (system)

vagabond, -e [vagabɔ̃, -ɔ̃d] **1** *adj* (**a**) *(vie)* wandering, roving (**b**) *Fig (pensées)* wandering, roaming; **avoir l'humeur vagabonde** to be in a restless mood

2 *nm,f* vagrant, tramp

vagabondage [vagabɔ̃daʒ] *nm* vagrancy

vagabonder [vagabɔ̃de] *vi (personne)* to wander, to roam; *Fig (pensées, imagination)* to wander, to stray

vagin [vaʒɛ̃] *nm* vagina

vaginal, -e, -aux, -ales [vaʒinal, -o] *adj* vaginal

vagir [vaʒir] *vi (nouveau-né)* to cry

vagissement [vaʒismɑ̃] *nm (de nouveau-né)* cry, wail

vague¹ [vag] *nf* (**a**) *(d'eau)* wave; *Fig* **faire des vagues** to make waves; **arriver par vagues** to come in waves; *aussi Fig* **v. de fond** ground swell (**b**) *(ondulations) (de chevelure, de dunes)* wave (**c**) *(courant artistique)* **nouvelle v.** new wave (**d**) *(d'enthousiasme, de tendresse)* wave, surge; **v. de chaleur** heat wave; **v. de froid** cold spell (**e**) *(afflux) (d'immigrants)* influx

vague² **1** *adj* (**a**) *(impression, geste, souvenir)* vague; *(forme)* indistinct; **regarder qn d'un air v.** to look vacantly at sb; **rester v. sur qch** to be vague about sth (**b**) *(avant le nom)* **quelque v. écrivain** some writer or other

2 *nm* (**a**) *(imprécision)* vagueness; **rester dans le v.** to be vague; **avoir du v. à l'âme** to be melancholy (**b**) *(vide)* **regard perdu dans le v.** faraway look

vaguelette [vaglɛt] *nf* wavelet

vaguement [vagmɑ̃] *adv* vaguely

vahiné [vaine] *nf* Tahitian woman

vaillamment [vajamɑ̃] *adv* valiantly

vaillance [vajɑ̃s] *nf* valour, courage

vaillant, -e [vajɑ̃, -ɑ̃t] *adj* (**a**) *(courageux)* valiant, courageous; *(cœur)* stout (**b**) *(en forme)* **être v.** to be in good health

vaille, vailles *voir* **valoir**

vain, -e [vɛ̃, vɛn] *adj* (**a**) *(sans résultat) (démarche, entreprise)* futile; *(efforts)* vain; **en v.** in vain (**b**) *(vide de sens) (paroles, promesse)* empty; *(espoirs, regrets)* vain (**c**) *Litt (personne)* vain

vaincre [68] [vɛ̃kr] *vt* (**a**) *(adversaire)* to defeat; *(en sport)* to beat (**b**) *Fig (maladie, difficulté)* to overcome

vaincu, -e [vɛ̃ky] **1** *adj* beaten, defeated; **s'avouer v.** to admit defeat

2 *nm,f* defeated man, *f* defeated woman

vainement [vɛnmɑ̃] *adv* in vain

vainqueur [vɛ̃kœr] **1** *nm* (**a**) *(dans une compétition sportive)* winner (**b**) *(d'une bataille, d'une lutte)* victor

2 *adj m (personne)* conquering, victorious

vairon¹ [vɛrɔ̃] *adj* **avoir les yeux vairons** to have different-coloured eyes

vairon² *nm (poisson)* minnow

vais *voir* **aller**

vaisseau, -x [vɛso] *nm* (**a**) **v. (sanguin)** blood vessel (**b**) **v. spatial** spaceship (**c**) *(d'une église)* nave (**d**) *Litt* ship, vessel; **v. de guerre** warship

vaisselier [vɛsəlje] *nm (meuble)* dresser

vaisselle [vɛsɛl] *nf* dishes, crockery; **faire** *ou* **laver la v.** to do the washing-up, to do the dishes

val [val] *nm* valley

valable [valabl] *adj* (**a**) *(ticket, raison, excuse)* valid; **ce qui est v. pour l'un est v. pour l'autre** what goes for one goes for the other (**b**) *(compétent) (interlocuteur)* authorized (**c**) *(de qualité) (roman)* good; *(idée)* valid

valdinguer [valdɛ̃ge] *vi Fam* **aller v. contre/sur qch** to go flying against/onto sth; **envoyer v. qch** to send sth flying

Valence [valɑ̃s] *n* (**a**) *(en Espagne)* Valencia (**b**) *(en France)* Valence

valériane [valerjan] *nf* valerian

valet [valɛ] *nm* (**a**) *(au jeu de cartes)* jack, knave (**b**) *(domestique)* **v. (de chambre)** valet; **v. de ferme** farmhand; **v. de pied** footman (**c**) *(meuble)* **v. de nuit** valet

valétudinaire [valetydinɛr] *adj & nmf* valetudinarian

valeur [valœr] *nf* (**a**) *(prix)* value, worth; **avoir de la v.** to be valuable; **de peu de v./de grande v.** of little/of great value; **d'une v. de 20 euros** worth 20 euros; **prendre de la v.** to increase in value; **v. d'achat** purchase value; **v. ajoutée** added value; **v. en Bourse** stock market value; **v. marchande** market value; **valeurs mobilières** stocks and shares; **v. nominale** nominal value (**b**) *(qualité, mérite)* value; **de v.** *(livre, œuvre)* of considerable merit; **homme de v.** *(de mérite)* man of merit; **avoir v. légale** to be legally binding; **attacher de la v. à qch** to value sth; **mettre en v.** to show to advantage; *(teint, yeux)* to bring out; *(mot)* to emphasize; **se mettre en v.** to show oneself

off to advantage; **prendre toute sa v.** *(terme, expression)* to take on its full meaning (**c**) *(titre)* security; **valeurs de tout repos** gilt-edged securities (**d**) *(d'une note)* time, length; *(d'une carte)* value (**e**) *(équivalent) (d'une mesure)* equivalent (**f**) *(morale)* **valeurs** values (**g**) *Litt (courage)* valour

valeureux, -euse [valørø, -øz] *adj Litt* gallant

validation [validasjɔ̃] *nf (d'un titre de transport)* validation; *(d'un document)* authentication

valide [valid] *adj* (**a**) *(contrat)* valid (**b**) *(personne) (en bonne santé)* fit; *(non blessé)* uninjured

valider [valide] *vt* (**a**) *(élection, mariage)* to validate; *(document)* to authenticate; **v. un titre de transport** *(dans une machine)* to stamp a ticket (**b**) *Ordinat (option)* to confirm; *(cellule, case)* to select

validité [validite] *nf (d'un contrat, d'un passeport)* validity

valise [valiz] *nf* (**a**) *(bagage)* suitcase; *aussi Fig* **faire ses valises** to pack one's bags (**b**) *(courrier)* **la v. diplomatique** the diplomatic *Br* bag *or Am* pouch (**c**) *Fam (sous les yeux)* bag

vallée [vale] *nf* valley; *Litt* **une v. de larmes** a vale of tears

vallon [valɔ̃] *nm* small valley

vallonné, -e [valɔne] *adj (région)* undulating, hilly

vallonnement [valɔnmɑ̃] *nm* undulation

valoche [valɔʃ] *nf Fam* case, bag

valoir [69] [valwar] **1** *vi* (**a**) *(avoir comme valeur)* to be worth; **v. cher** *(objet en vente)* to be expensive; *(objet précieux)* to be worth a lot; *Fig* **ne pas v. cher** *(personne)* not to be up to much; **ne rien v.** *(objet)* to be worthless; *(idée)* to be useless; **ce climat ne vous vaut rien** this climate doesn't suit you; **il ne vaut pas mieux que son frère** he's no better than his brother; **ça vaut mieux comme ça** it's better that way

(**b**) *(avoir un intérêt)* **et ça vaut pour tout le monde** and that goes for everyone; **faire v. qch** *(opinions, droits)* to assert sth

2 *vt* (**a**) *(équivaloir à)* to be equivalent to; **un euro vaut plus de six francs** one euro is worth over six francs; **ça ne vaut pas ce qui m'est arrivé l'autre jour** that's nothing to what happened to me the other day; **rien ne vaut un bon petit déjeuner** there's nothing like a good breakfast

(**b**) *(rapporter)* **v. qch à qn** *(punition)* to earn sb sth; *(soucis, ennuis)* to bring sb sth; **qu'est-ce qui me vaut cet honneur?** to what do I owe this honour?

3 *v impersonnel* **il vaut/vaudrait mieux faire qch** it's/it would be better to do sth; **il vaut mieux que vous restiez** you'd better stay, it would be better if you stayed; *Prov* **mieux vaut tard que jamais** better late than never

4 *se valoir vpr* **tous les métiers se valent** one job is as good as another; **ils se valent** *(péjoratif)* they're as bad as each other; *(admiratif)* they're as good as each other

valorisant, -e [valɔrizɑ̃, -ɑ̃t] *adj* gratifying

valorisation [valɔrizasjɔ̃] *nf* (**a**) *(augmentation de la valeur)* increase in value (**b**) *(développement)* development

valoriser [valɔrize] *vt (bien, monnaie)* to increase the value of; *(région)* to develop; *(personne)* to boost the self-esteem of

valse [vals] *nf* (**a**) *(morceau de musique, air de danse)* waltz (**b**) **la v. des ministres** frequent cabinet reshuffles

valse-hésitation (*pl* **valses-hésitations**) [valsezitasjɔ̃] *nf Fam* pussyfooting, shilly-shallying

valser [valse] *vi* to waltz; **faire v. qn** to waltz with sb; *Fig* **faire v. les millions** to spend money like water; *Fam* **envoyer v. qn/qch** to send sb/sth flying

valseur, -euse [valsœr, -øz] *nm,f* waltzer

valu, -e *voir* **valoir**

valve [valv] *nf* valve

vamp [vãp] *nf Fam* vamp

vampire [vãpir] *nm* (**a**) (*suceur de sang*) vampire (**b**) *Fig* (*parasite*) bloodsucker

vampiriser [vãpirize] *vt Fam* to dominate psychologically

van¹ [vã] *nm* (*fourgon à chevaux*) horse box

van² [van] *nm* (*camionnette*) van

Vancouver [vãkuvɛr] *n* Vancouver

vandale [vãdal] *nmf* vandal

vandaliser [vãdalize] *vt* to vandalize

vandalisme [vãdalism] *nm* vandalism

vanille [vanij] *nf* vanilla

vanillé, -e [vanije] *adj* vanilla-flavoured

vanité [vanite] *nf* (**a**) (*suffisance*) vanity; **tirer v. de qch** to pride oneself on sth (**b**) *Litt* (*insignifiance*) futility, emptiness

vaniteux, -euse [vanitø, -øz] **1** *adj* vain
2 *nm,f* vain person

vanne¹ [van] *nf* (*de canalisation, d'écluse*) sluice gate, floodgate; **ouvrir/fermer les vannes** to open/close the floodgates

vanne² *nf Fam* (*remarque blessante*) dig, jibe; **envoyer une v. à qn** to have a dig at sb

vanné, -e [vane] *adj Fam* **être v.** to be dead beat

vanneau, -x [vano] *nm* (*oiseau*) lapwing, peewit

vanner [vane] *vt* (**a**) *Fam* (*fatiguer*) to wear out, to exhaust (**b**) (*grain*) to winnow

vannerie [vanri] *nf* (**a**) (*activité*) basket making, basketry (**b**) (*objets*) basketwork, wickerwork

vannier [vanje] *nm* basket worker *or* maker

vantard, -e [vãtar, -ard] **1** *adj* bragging, boastful
2 *nm,f* braggart, boaster

vantardise [vãtardiz] *nf* (*caractère*) bragging, boastfulness; (*parole*) boast

vanter [vãte] **1** *vt* to praise, to speak highly of
2 se vanter *vpr* to boast, to brag (**de** about)

Vanuatu [vanwatu] *n* Vanuatu

va-nu-pieds [vanypje] *nmf inv* tramp, beggar

vapes [vap] *nfpl Fam* **être dans les v.** to be all woozy; **tomber dans les v.** to pass out

vapeur¹ [vapœr] *nf* (**a**) (*d'eau bouillante*) **v. (d'eau)** steam; **cuire qch à la v.** to steam sth; **à toute v.** full steam ahead; *Fig* at full speed (**b**) (*gaz*) **vapeurs** (*d'alcool, d'essence*) fumes (**c**) *Méd* **avoir des vapeurs** to have a fit of the vapours

vapeur² *nm* (*bateau*) steamer, steamship

vaporeux, -euse [vaporø, -øz] *adj* (**a**) (*atmosphère*) steamy (**b**) (*robe*) flimsy

vaporisateur [vaporizatœr] *nm* (*de parfum*) spray, atomizer; (*pour plantes*) spray

vaporiser [vaporize] **1** *vt* (**a**) (*pulvériser*) to spray (**b**) (*transformer en vapeur*) to vaporize
2 se vaporiser *vpr* to vaporize

vaquer [vake] **1** *vi* (*parlement, tribunal*) to be on vacation
2 vaquer à *vt ind* **v. à qch** to attend to sth; **v. à ses affaires** *ou* **occupations** to go about one's business

varappe [varap] *nf* rock climbing; **faire de la v.** to go rock climbing

varapper [varape] *vi* to go rock climbing

varappeur, -euse [varapœr, -øz] *nm,f* rock climber

vareuse [varøz] *nf* (**a**) (*de marin*) pea jacket (**b**) (*d'uniforme*) tunic (**c**) (*veste large*) loose-fitting jacket

variable [varjabl] **1** *adj* (**a**) (*temps, humeur*) changeable; (*vitesse*) varying (**b**) (*différent*) varied; **être v.** to vary
2 *nf* variable; *Ordinat* **v. de mémoire** memory variable

variante [varjãt] *nf* variant, variation

variation [varjasjɔ̃] *nf* (**a**) (*écart*) change (**de** in); **les variations de la température** the variations in the temperature (**b**) *Mus* variation

varice [varis] *nf* varicose vein

varicelle [varisɛl] *nf* chickenpox, *Spéc* varicella; **avoir la v.** to have chickenpox

varié, -e [varje] *adj* (*alimentation, paysage, travail*) varied; (*vocabulaire*) wide

varier [varje] **1** *vt* (*alimentation, occupations*) to vary; *Ironique* **pour v. les plaisirs** by way of a pleasant change
2 *vi* to vary, to change; **les opinions varient sur ce point** opinions differ on this point; **il n'a jamais varié sur ce point** he's never changed his mind about it

variété [varjete] **1** *nf* variety
2 *nfpl* **variétés** *TV* variety show; (*musique*) easylistening; **chanteur de variétés** middle-of-the-road singer, **disque de v.** easy-listening record

variole [varjɔl] *nf* smallpox; **avoir la v.** to have smallpox

Varsovie [varsɔvi] *n* Warsaw

vas *voir* **aller**

vasculaire [vaskylɛr] *adj* vascular

vase¹ [vɑz] *nm* vase; *Fig* **vivre en v. clos** to live in isolation; **vases communicants** communicating vessels

vase² *nf* mud, silt

vasectomie [vazɛktɔmi] *nf* vasectomy

vaseline [vazlin] *nf* Vaseline®, petroleum jelly

vaseux, -euse [vazø, -øz] *adj* (**a**) *Fam* (*mal en point*) off-colour (**b**) (*peu clair*) (*idée*) woolly; (*explication*) confused (**c**) (*plaisanterie*) unsavoury (**d**) (*rivière*) muddy, silty

vasistas [vazistɑs] *nm* fanlight

vasoconstricteur, -trice [vazokɔ̃striktœr, -tris] *adj & nm* vasoconstrictor

vasodilatateur, -trice [vazodilatatœr, -tris] *adj & nm* vasodilator

vasomoteur, -trice [vazomɔtœr, -tris] *adj* (*nerf*) vasomotor

vasouillard, -e [vazujar, -ard] *adj Fam* (*idée*) confused, muddled; **se sentir v.** to feel a bit under the weather

vasouiller [vazuje] *vi Fam* to flounder

vassal, -e, -aux, -ales [vasal, -o] *nm,f* vassal

vaste [vast] *adj* (**a**) vast, immense (**b**) *Fam* (*plaisanterie*) big, great; **c'est une v. fumisterie** it's a complete farce

Vatican [vatikã] *nm* **le V.** the Vatican; **la cité du V.** Vatican City

va-tout [vatu] *nm inv* **jouer son v.** to stake one's all

vaudeville [vodvil] *nm Théât* light farce; **tourner au v.** to become farcical

vaudou, -e [vodu] *adj & nm* voodoo

vaudrai, vaudras *etc voir* **valoir**

vau-l'eau [volo] **à vau-l'eau** *adv* **aller à v.** to fall through

vaurien, -enne [vorjɛ̃, -ɛn] *nm,f* (**a**) *(brigand)* good-for-nothing (**b**) *(enfant)* rascal

vaut *voir* **valoir**

vautour [votur] *nm* vulture

vautrer [votre] **se vautrer** *vpr* (**a**) *(cochon)* to wallow (**dans** in) (**b**) *(personne)* to sprawl (**dans** in); *Fig* **se v. dans la débauche** to wallow in vice

vauvert [vovɛr] *voir* **diable**

va-vite [vavit] **à la va-vite** *adv* in a rush

vaux *voir* **valoir**

VDQS [vedekyɛs] *nm* (*abrév* **vin délimité de qualité supérieure**) = label certifying that wine is of good quality

veau, -x [vo] *nm* (**a**) *(animal)* calf (**b**) *(viande)* veal (**c**) *(cuir)* calfskin (**d**) *Fam (personne lente)* lump (**e**) *Fam (voiture)* car with poor acceleration

vecteur [vɛktœr] *nm* (**a**) *Math* vector (**b**) *(d'information, de progrès)* vehicle

vectoriel, -elle [vɛktɔrjɛl] *adj* vectorial; *Ordinat* **police vectorielle** outline font

vécu, -e [veky] **1** *pp voir* **vivre**
2 *adj (expérience)* real-life
3 *nm* real-life experience

vedettariat [vədetarja] *nm* stardom

vedette [vədɛt] *nf* (**a**) *(acteur)* star; **v. de la chanson** singing star; **v. de cinéma** film star; **avoir la v.**, **être en v.** *(dans un spectacle)* to top the bill; *(dans un film)* to be the main star (**b**) *Fig (de la politique)* leading light (**c**) *(bateau à moteur) (de plaisancier)* launch; *(de police)* patrol boat

végétal, -e, -aux, -ales [veʒetal, -o] **1** *adj (huile)* vegetable
2 *nm* vegetable, plant

végétarien, -enne [veʒetarjɛ̃, -ɛn] *adj & nm,f* vegetarian

végétatif, -ive [veʒetatif, -iv] *adj (appareil)* vegetative; *Fig & Péj (existence)* vegetable-like

végétation [veʒetasjɔ̃] *nf* (**a**) *(flore)* vegetation (**b**) *Méd* **végétations (adénoïdes)** adenoids

végéter [veʒete] *vi Péj (personne)* to vegetate

véhémence [veemɑ̃s] *nf Litt* vehemence; **avec v.** vehemently

véhément, -e [veemɑ̃, -ɑ̃t] *adj Litt* vehement, violent

véhicule [veikyl] *nm* (**a**) *(moyen de transport)* vehicle; **v. utilitaire** commercial vehicle (**b**) *(support) (du son, de la lumière)* vehicle

véhiculer [veikyle] *vt* (**a**) *(transporter)* to transport, to convey (**b**) *(transmettre)* to convey

veille [vɛj] *nf* (**a**) *(jour qui précède)* **la v.** the previous day, the day before; **à la v. de la réunion** the day before the meeting; **la v. au soir** the previous evening, the evening before; **la v. de Noël** Christmas Eve; *Fig* **être à la v. de qch/de faire qch** to be on the verge of sth/of doing sth (**b**) *(éveil)* wakefulness; **entre la v. et le sommeil** between waking and sleeping; **après deux jours de v.** after staying up for two nights (**c**) *(garde)* (night) watch; **prendre la v.** to take one's turn on watch (**d**) *Ordinat* standby mode; **en v.** in standby mode

veillée [veje] *nf* (**a**) *(soirée)* evening; **v. au coin du feu** evening spent round the fire; **v. d'armes** knightly vigil (**b**) *(d'un mort)* watch, vigil (**c**) *Can (fête)* party

veiller [veje] **1** *vt (malade)* to sit up with; **v. un mort** to keep vigil over a dead body
2 *vi* to stay up
3 **veiller à** *vt ind* **v. à qch** to see to sth; **v. aux intérêts de qn** to look after sb's interests; **v. à ce que qn fasse qch** to make sure *or* see to it that sb does sth; *Fig* **v. au grain** to keep an eye open for trouble
4 **veiller sur** *vt ind* **v. sur qn** to take care of sb
5 **se veiller** *vpr Suisse Fam* to be careful

veilleur [vejœr] *nm* **v. de nuit** night watchman

veilleuse [vejøz] *nf* (**a**) *(lampe)* night light; *(sur une télévision, sur un magnétoscope)* standby; *Fig* **mettre qch en v.** *(projet, problème)* to put sth on the back burner; *Fam* **la mettre en v.** to put a sock in it (**b**) *(d'un chauffe-eau, d'un réchaud)* pilot light (**c**) **veilleuses** *(d'une automobile)* sidelights

veinard, -e [vɛnar, -ard] *Fam* **1** *adj* lucky
2 *nm,f* lucky devil

veine [vɛn] *nf* (**a**) *Anat* vein; **v. cave** vena cava (**b**) *Fam (chance)* luck; **avoir de la v.** to be lucky; *Fam* **avoir une v. de cocu** to have the luck of the devil (**c**) *(dans le marbre, le bois)* vein (**d**) *(filon) (de minerai)* vein; *(de charbon)* seam (**e**) *(inspiration)* vein; **en v. de plaisanterie** in humorous vein; **être en v. de générosité** to be in a generous mood

veiné, -e [vene] *adj (marbre, bois)* grained

veineux, -euse [vɛnø, -øz] *adj (système, circulation)* venous

veinule [venyl] *nf* venule

Velcro® [vɛlkro] *nm (tissu)* Velcro®; *(fermeture)* Velcro® fastening

vêler [vele] *vi* to calve

vélin [velɛ̃] *nm* vellum

véliplanchiste [veliplɑ̃ʃist] *nmf* windsurfer

velléitaire [veleiter] **1** *adj* indecisive
2 *nmf* indecisive person

velléités [veleite] *nfpl* vague desire; **avoir des v. de faire qch** to toy with the idea of doing sth

vélo [velo] *nm* bike; **aller au bureau en v.** to cycle to the office, to go to the office on one's bike; **faire du v.** *(comme activité)* to go cycling; **est-ce que tu sais faire du v.?** can you ride a bike?; **v. d'appartement** exercise bike; **v. de course** racing cycle; **v. tout-terrain** mountain bike

vélocité [velosite] *nf* speed, swiftness

vélodrome [velodrom] *nm* velodrome

vélomoteur [velomotœr] *nm* moped

velours [vəlur] *nm* (**a**) *(tissu)* velvet; **veste/rideaux en v.** velvet jacket/curtains; **v. côtelé** *ou* **à côtes** corduroy (**b**) *Fig* **faire des yeux de v. à qn** to make eyes at sb

velouté, -e [vəlute] **1** *adj* velvety
2 *nm* (**a**) *(texture)* velvetiness (**b**) *(soupe)* cream soup; **v. d'asperges** cream of asparagus soup

velouteux, -euse [vəlutø, -øz] *adj* velvety

Velpeau® [vɛlpo] *voir* **bande**

velu, -e [vəly] *adj* hairy

Vélux® [velyks] *nm* = window built into a sloping roof

venaison [vənɛzɔ̃] *nf* venison

vénal, -e, -aux, -ales [venal, -o] *adj* (**a**) *Péj (intéressé)* venal, mercenary (**b**) *(valeur)* market

venant [vənɑ̃] *nm* **à tout v.**, **à tous venants** to all comers, to all and sundry

vendable [vɑ̃dabl] *adj* saleable, sellable; **facilement/difficilement v.** easy/difficult to sell

vendange [vãdãʒ] *nf* (**a**) **vendanges** *(période)* grape-harvesting time (**b**) *(récolte)* grape harvest; **faire la v.** *ou* **les vendanges** to harvest *or* pick the grapes (**c**) *(raisin récolté)* grapes (harvested); **une bonne v.** a good vintage

vendanger [vãdãʒe] **1** *vi* to harvest the grapes **2** *vt (vigne)* to pick the grapes from

vendangeur, -euse [vãdãʒœr, -øz] *nm,f* grape picker

vendetta [vãdeta] *nf* vendetta

vendeur, -euse [vãdœr, -øz] **1** *adj* **être v.** to be willing to sell **2** *nm,f (dans un magasin)* Br (shop) assistant, *Am* (sales)clerk; *(non professionnel)* seller; **v. ambulant** travelling salesman; **v. à domicile** door-to-door salesman; **v. de journaux** newspaper seller *or* vendor

vendre [vãdr] **1** *vt* (**a**) *(article, produit)* to sell; **v. qch 50 euros** to sell sth for 50 euros; **v. qch à qn** to sell sb sth, to sell sth to sb; **à v.** *(sur panneau)* for sale; *Fig* **v. son âme au diable** to sell one's soul to the devil (**b**) *(trahir) (personne)* to sell out; *(secret)* to sell; **v. la mèche** to spill the beans **2** **se vendre** *vpr* (**a**) *(produit, article)* to be sold; **cela se vend comme des petits pains** it's selling like hot cakes (**b**) *(soi-même)* to sell oneself

vendredi [vãdrədi] *nm* Friday; **le v. saint** Good Friday; *voir aussi* **samedi**

vendu, -e [vãdy] **1** *adj (corrompu)* bribed **2** *nm,f* traitor

vénéneux, -euse [venenø, -øz] *adj* poisonous

vénérable [venerabl] *adj* venerable

vénération [venerasjõ] *nf* veneration; **avoir de la v. pour qn** to hold sb in veneration

vénérer [venere] *vt* to venerate

vénérien, -enne [venerjɛ̃, -ɛn] *adj* venereal

Venezuela [venezɥela] *nm* **le V.** Venezuela

vénézuélien, -enne [venezɥeljɛ̃, -ɛn] **1** *adj* Venezuelan **2** *nm,f* **V.** Venezuelan

vengeance [vãʒãs] *nf* revenge, vengeance; **la v. est un plat qui se mange froid** revenge is a dish best eaten cold

venger [vãʒe] **1** *vt* to avenge; **v. qn de qch** to avenge sb for sth **2** **se venger** *vpr* to get one's revenge; **se v. sur qn (de qch)** to get one's revenge on sb (for sth); *Fam* **pas la peine de te v. sur moi!** there's no point in taking it out on me!

vengeur, -eresse [vãʒœr, -ʒrɛs] *Litt* **1** *adj* vengeful **2** *nm,f* avenger

véniel, -elle [venjɛl] *adj (péché)* venial

venimeux, -euse [vənimø, -øz] *adj aussi Fig* venomous

venin [vənɛ̃] *nm aussi Fig* venom

venir [70] [vənir] *(aux* **être)** **1** *vi* (**a**) *(arriver)* to come (**de** from); **il vient passer quelques jours** he's coming to spend a few days; **viens me voir** come and see me; **d'où venez-vous?** where do you come from?; **je viens!** I'm coming!; **v. vers qn** to come up to sb; **vous y viendrez!** you'll come round to it, you'll change your mind; **dans les mois/années qui viennent** in the coming months/years; **le moment est venu de nous en aller** it's time we left; **le jour viendra où...** the day will come when...; **ton tour viendra** your turn will come, you'll get your turn; **l'eau leur venait aux genoux** the water came up to their knees (**b**) *(tirer son origine)* to come (**de** from); **la maison**

lui vient de sa mère he/she inherited the house from his/her mother (**c**) **en v. à qch/à faire qch** to come to sth/to do sth; **j'en suis venu à me demander si...** I began to wonder whether...; **où voulez-vous en v.?** what are you getting at?; **en v. aux mains** to come to blows (**d**) **venir de faire qch** to have just done sth; **je viens de le lui dire** I've just told him; **je venais de terminer** I'd just finished **2** *v impersonnel* **s'il venait à pleuvoir** if it happened to rain; **il m'est venu une idée intéressante** an interesting idea occurred to me **3** **s'en venir** *vpr Litt* to come along

Venise [vəniz] *n* Venice

vénitien, -enne [venisjɛ̃, -ɛn] **1** *adj* Venetian **2** *nm,f* **V.** Venetian

vent [vã] *nm* (**a**) *(air)* wind; **les cheveux au v.** with one's hair streaming in the wind; **quel bon v. vous amène?** to what do I/we owe the pleasure?; *Fig* **avoir le v. en poupe** to have the wind in one's sails; *Fig* **avoir du v. dans les voiles** to be three sheets to the wind; **avoir v. de qch** to get wind of sth; **ce n'est que du v.** it's just hot air; *Fam* **être dans le v.** to be with it; **contre vents et marées** come hell or high water; *Ironique* **bon v.!** good riddance! (**b**) *(flatulence)* wind; **avoir des vents** to have wind

vente [vãt] *nf (transaction)* sale; *(activité)* selling; *Can (soldes)* sale; **en v.** *(par un particulier)* for sale; *(dans les magasins)* on sale; **en v. libre** available over the counter; **mettre qch en v.** to put sth up for sale; **v. de charité** charity sale; **v. par correspondance** mail order (selling); **v. à crédit** credit sale; **v. au détail** retailing; **v. aux enchères** (sale by) auction; **v. en gros** wholesaling; **v. à tempérament** *Br* hire purchase, *Am* installment plan

venter [vãte] *v impersonnel* **il vente** it's windy

venteux, -euse [vãtø, -øz] *adj* windy

ventilateur [vãtilatœr] *nm* (**a**) *(pour aérer)* fan (**b**) *Ordinat* **v. de refroidissement** cooling fan (**c**) *(d'une automobile)* blower

ventilation [vãtilasjõ] *nf* (**a**) *(aération)* ventilation (**b**) *(des dépenses)* breakdown

ventiler [vãtile] *vt* (**a**) *(aérer)* to ventilate (**b**) *(dépenses)* to break down

ventouse [vãtuz] *nf* (**a**) *(pour fixer)* suction grip; *(pour déboucher)* plunger; **faire v.** to adhere by suction (**b**) *(en verre)* cupping glass; **poser des ventouses à qn** to cup sb

ventral, -e, -aux, -ales [vãtral, -o] *adj* ventral

ventre [vãtr] *nm* (**a**) *(estomac)* stomach; **avoir le v. plein/vide** to have a full/an empty stomach; **avoir du v.** to have a paunch; **v. à terre** at full speed, flat out; **avoir mal au v.** to have a sore stomach; *Fig* **ça fait mal au v. de voir ça** it makes me sick to see that; *Fig* **ça me ferait mal au v.!** it would kill me!; **ne rien avoir dans le v.** to have no guts (**b**) *(utérus)* womb (**c**) *(d'une bouteille)* bulge

ventricule [vãtrikyl] *nm* ventricle

ventriloque [vãtrilɔk] *nmf* ventriloquist

ventru, -e [vãtry] *adj* (**a**) *(gros)* potbellied (**b**) *(colonne)* bulbous

venu, -e [vəny] **1** *adj* **bien v.** appropriate; **mal v.** inappropriate **2** *nm,f* **le premier v.** *(n'importe qui)* anybody; **un nouveau v.** a newcomer **3** *nf* **venue** *(d'une personne, du printemps)* coming;

dès sa **venue au monde** since he/she came into the world

Vénus [venys] *npr (déesse, planète)* Venus

vêpres [vɛpr] *nfpl* vespers

ver [vɛr] *nm* (**a**) *(dans la terre)* worm; *(dans un fruit)* grub; *Fig* **tirer les vers du nez à qn** to drag it out of sb; **v. luisant** glow-worm; **v. à soie** silkworm; **v. de terre** earthworm (**b**) *Méd* **v. solitaire** tapeworm; **avoir le v. solitaire** to have a tapeworm

véracité [verasite] *nf* truthfulness

véranda [verɑ̃da] *nf* veranda(h)

verbal, -e, -aux, -ales [vɛrbal, -o] *adj* verbal

verbalement [vɛrbalmɑ̃] *adv* verbally

verbaliser [vɛrbalize] **1** *vt (exprimer)* to verbalize **2** *vi (policier)* to record the details of an offence

verbe [vɛrb] *nm Gram* verb; **v. à particule** *(en anglais)* phrasal verb

verbeux, -euse [vɛrbø, -øz] *adj* verbose

verbiage [vɛrbjaʒ] *nm* verbiage

verdâtre [vɛrdɑtr] *adj* greenish

verdeur [vɛrdœr] *nf* (**a**) *(d'un fruit, d'un vin)* tartness (**b**) *(du langage)* crudeness (**c**) *(vitalité)* vigour, vitality

verdict [vɛrdikt] *nm* verdict; **prononcer** *ou* **rendre un v.** to return a verdict

verdir [vɛrdir] **1** *vt* to turn green **2** *vi* to turn green; *Fig* **v. de jalousie/de peur** to go *or* turn green with envy/white with fear

verdoyant, -e [vɛrdwajɑ̃, -ɑ̃t] *adj* green

verdoyer [vɛrdwaje] *vi Litt* to be green

verdure [vɛrdyr] *nf* (**a**) *(couleur)* greenness (**b**) *(végétation)* greenery (**c**) *(légumes verts)* greens

véreux, -euse [verø, -øz] *adj* (**a**) *(fruit)* wormy, maggoty (**b**) *Péj (affaires, financier)* shady, dubious

verge [vɛrʒ] *nf* (**a**) *(pénis)* penis (**b**) *(baguette)* cane (**c**) *Can (mesure)* yard

verger [vɛrʒe] *nm* orchard

vergetures [vɛrʒətyr] *nfpl* stretch marks

verglacé, -e [vɛrglase] *adj* icy

verglas [vɛrgla] *nm Br* (black) ice, *Am* glare ice, glaze

vergogne [vɛrgɔɲ] **sans vergogne 1** *adj* shameless **2** *adv* shamelessly

véridique [veridik] *adj* truthful

vérifiable [verifjabl] *adj* verifiable

vérificateur, -trice [verifikatœr, -tris] **1** *nm,f (personne)* inspector, examiner; **v. de comptes** auditor **2** *nm Ordinat* **v. orthographique** spellchecker

vérification [verifikasjɔ̃] *nf* (**a**) *(d'un travail, des votes)* checking; **v. de comptes** *ou* **d'écritures** audit(ing) of accounts (**b**) *Ordinat* **v. antivirale** antiviral check; **v. orthographique** spellcheck

vérifier [verifje] **1** *vt* to check; *(comptes)* to audit; **il doit être là, je vais le v.** he must be there, I'll check **2** **se vérifier** *vpr* to prove correct

véritable [veritabl] *adj* (**a**) *(histoire, ami)* true; *(nom, or, cuir)* real (**b**) *(en intensif)* real

véritablement [veritabləmɑ̃] *adv* really

vérité [verite] *nf* (**a**) *(d'une déclaration)* truth; **dire la v.** to tell the truth; **c'est la v.** it's true, it's a fact; **à la v.** to tell the truth; **en v.** really, actually; **dire à qn ses quatre vérités** to tell sb a few home truths (**b**) *(d'un personnage, d'une description)* trueness to life (**c**) *(sincérité)* **un accent de v.** a ring of truth

verlan [vɛrlɑ̃] *nm* back slang

vermeil, -eille [vɛrmɛj] **1** *adj* bright red **2** *nm* silver gilt

vermicelle [vɛrmisɛl] *nm* vermicelli

vermifuge [vɛrmifyʒ] *nm* vermifuge

vermillon [vɛrmijɔ̃] *adj inv & nm* vermilion

vermine [vɛrmin] *nf* (**a**) *(insectes)* vermin; **couvert** *ou* **grouillant de v.** crawling with vermin (**b**) *Péj (racaille)* **la v.** vermin

vermisseau, -x [vɛrmiso] *nm* small worm; *Fig (personne)* worm

vermoulu, -e [vɛrmuly] *adj* worm-eaten

vermouth [vɛrmut] *nm* vermouth

vernaculaire [vɛrnakyler] *adj* **langue v.** vernacular

verni, -e [vɛrni] *adj* (**a**) *(meuble, bois, parquet)* varnished; *(chaussures)* patent (leather); *(ongles)* varnished, painted (**b**) *Fam (chanceux)* lucky

vernir [vɛrnir] *vt* to varnish

vernis [vɛrni] *nm* (**a**) *(pour le bois)* varnish; **v. à ongles** nail varnish *or* polish; **se mettre du v. à ongles** to varnish *or* paint one's nails (**b**) *Fig* **un v. de culture** a smattering of knowledge

vernissage [vɛrnisaʒ] *nm* (**a**) *(du bois)* varnishing (**b**) *(d'une exposition)* opening, private viewing

vérole [verɔl] *nf Vieilli* syphilis; **la petite v.** smallpox

verra, verrai *etc voir* **voir**

verrat [vera] *nm* breeding boar

verre [vɛr] *nm* (**a**) *(matière)* glass; **sous v.** under glass; **gravure sous v.** glass-mounted engraving; **v. blanc** glass; **v. dépoli/feuilleté** frosted/laminated glass (**b**) *(récipient)* glass; **v. à dents** tooth glass; **v. doseur** *ou* **gradué** ≃ measuring jug; **v. à eau** large wineglass; **v. à pied** stemmed glass; **v. à vin** wineglass; **v. à whisky** whisky glass (**c**) *(contenu)* glass(ful) (**d**) *(boisson)* drink; **boire** *ou* **prendre un v.** to have a drink (**e**) *(de lunettes)* lens; **verres de contact** contact lenses; **v. à double foyer** bifocals; **verres teintés** *ou* **fumés** tinted lenses

verrée [vere] *nf Suisse (tournée)* round (of drinks); *(rencontre)* drinks party

verrerie [vɛri] *nf* (**a**) *(fabrication)* glass-making (**b**) *(atelier)* glassworks (**c**) *(marchandise)* glassware

verrier [vɛrje] *nm (artisan)* glass-maker

verrière [vɛrjɛr] *nf* (**a**) *(toit)* glass roof; *(paroi)* glass wall (**b**) *(pièce)* conservatory

verroterie [vɛrɔtri] *nf* glass jewellery

verrou [veru] *nm* bolt; **mettre** *ou* **tirer le v.** to bolt the door; *Fig* **sous les verrous** behind bars, inside

verrouillage [verujaʒ] *nm* (**a**) *(d'une porte)* bolting; *(à clé)* locking; *(d'un mécanisme)* locking; **v. central**

central locking (**c**) *Ordinat* **v. des fichiers** file lock; **v. en lecture seule** read-only lock; **v. en majuscule(s)** caps lock

verrouiller [vɛruje] *vt* (**a**) *(porte)* to bolt; *(à clé)* to lock; *(prisonnier)* to lock up (**b**) *(quartier)* to close off, to seal off (**c**) *Ordinat (capitales)* to lock on; **verrouillé en majuscule(s)** *(clavier)* with caps lock on

verrue [vɛry] *nf* wart; **v. plantaire** verruca

vers¹ [vɛr] *nm (poétique)* line; **faire des v.** to write verse *or* poetry; **v. blancs** blank verse; **v. libres** free verse

vers² *prép* (**a**) *(dans la direction de)* towards (**b**) *(aux alentours de) (dans le temps)* about; *(dans l'espace)* near; **v. la fin** towards the end; *Fam* **v. les trois heures** about *or* around 3 o'clock

versant [vɛrsɑ̃] *nm* slope, side

versatile [vɛrsatil] *adj* changeable, fickle

versatilité [vɛrsatilite] *nf* changeability, fickleness

verse [vɛrs] **à verse** *adv* **il pleut à v.** it's pouring (down); **la pluie tombait à v.** the rain was coming down in torrents

versé, -e [vɛrse] *adj* **être v. dans qch** to be well-versed in sth

Verseau [vɛrso] *nm Astron & Astrol* **le V.** Aquarius; **être V.** to be (an) Aquarius *or* an Aquarian

versement [vɛrsəmɑ̃] *nm* payment

verser [vɛrse] **1** *vt* (**a**) *(liquide)* to pour (out) (**dans** into); **v. à boire à qn** to pour sb a drink, to pour a drink for sb (**b**) *(larmes, sang)* to shed (**c**) *(argent)* to pay; **v. de l'argent sur son compte** to pay *or* deposit money into one's account (**d**) *Jur (document)* to add (**à** to)

2 *vi (véhicule)* to overturn

3 **verser dans** *vt ind* to lapse into

verset [vɛrsɛ] *nm* verse

verseur, -euse [vɛrsœr, -øz] **1** *adj voir* **bec**

2 *nf* **verseuse** jug, pot *(for coffee machine)*

versification [vɛrsifikasjɔ̃] *nf* versification

version [vɛrsjɔ̃] *nf* (**a**) *(d'un événement, d'un texte)* version (**b**) *(traduction)* translation; **v. anglaise/espagnole** *(à l'école)* translation from English/Spanish (**c**) *Cin* **en v. originale** in the original language; **en v. française** dubbed *(into French)* (**d**) *Ordinat* **v. bêta** beta version

verso [vɛrso] *nm* back; **voir au v.** see over(leaf)

vert, -e [vɛr, vɛrt] **1** *adj* (**a**) *(couleur)* green; *Fig* **v. de peur** white with fear; *Fig* **v. de jalousie** green with envy; *Fig* **avoir la main verte** to have *Br* green fingers *or Am* a green thumb (**b**) *(jeune) (bois); (fruit)* unripe; *(vin)* too young (**c**) *(écologique)* green (**d**) *(vieillard)* sprightly (**e**) *(histoire, propos)* spicy (**f**) *(réprimande)* sharp

2 *nm* (**a**) *(couleur)* green; **passer au v.** *(signal d'arrêt)* to go or turn green; **v. amande** almond green; **v. bouteille** bottle green; **v. d'eau** sea green; **v. émeraude** emerald green; **v. olive** olive green; **v. pomme** apple green (**b**) *Fam* **se mettre au v.** to go to the country (**c**) *Pol* **les Verts** ≃ The Green Party

3 *nfpl* **vertes** *Fam* **en dire de vertes** to tell spicy stories; **il en a vu des vertes et des pas mûres** he's been through a lot

vert-de-gris [vɛrdəgri] **1** *nm inv* verdigris

2 *adj* grey-green

vertébral, -e, -aux, -ales [vɛrtebral, -o] *adj* vertebral

vertèbre [vɛrtɛbr] *nf* vertebra

vertébré, -e [vɛrtebre] *adj & nm* vertebrate

vertement [vɛrtəmɑ̃] *adv* sharply

vertical, -e, -aux, -ales [vɛrtikal, -o] **1** *adj* vertical; **en position verticale** *(objet)* in a vertical position, upright

2 *nf* **verticale** vertical; **à la verticale** vertically

verticalement [vɛrtikalmɑ̃] *adv* vertically; *(dans les mots croisés)* down

vertige [vɛrtiʒ] *nm* (**a**) *(au-dessus du vide)* vertigo; **avoir le v.** *(toujours)* to suffer from vertigo; *(ponctuellement)* to feel dizzy; **donner le v. à qn** *(vide)* to make sb dizzy; *Fig* to make sb's head spin (**b**) *(étourdissement)* dizziness, giddiness; **avoir des vertiges** to have dizzy spells

vertigineusement [vɛrtiʒinøzmɑ̃] *adv* **grimper v.** to rocket; **chuter v.** to plummet

vertigineux, -euse [vɛrtiʒinø, -øz] *adj (hauteur)* dizzy; *(vitesse)* breakneck; *(somme, hausse des prix)* staggering

vertu [vɛrty] *nf* (**a**) *(propriété)* property (**b**) *(qualité morale)* virtue (**c**) *Litt (chasteté)* virtue; **femme de petite v.** woman of easy virtue (**d**) **en v. de qch** *(principe, loi)* in accordance with sth; **en v. des pouvoirs qui me sont conférés** by virtue of the powers bestowed upon me; **en v. de quoi est-il intervenu?** what gave him the right to intervene?

vertueux, -euse [vɛrtɥø, -øz] *adj* virtuous; *(intention)* honourable

verve [vɛrv] *nf* verve; **être en v.** to be on top form

verveine [vɛrvɛn] *nf* (**a**) *(plante)* verbena (**b**) *(tisane)* verbena tea

vésicule [vezikyl] *nf* vesicle; **v. biliaire** gall bladder

vespasienne [vɛspazjɛn] *nf* street urinal

vespéral, -e, -aux, -ales [vɛsperal, -o] *adj Litt* evening

vessie [vesi] *nf* bladder; *Fig* **prendre des vessies pour des lanternes** to believe that the moon is made of green cheese; **il voudrait nous faire prendre des vessies pour des lanternes** he's trying to pull the wool over our eyes

veste [vɛst] *nf* jacket; **v. droite/croisée** single-/double-breasted jacket; *Fam Fig* **prendre une v.** to come a cropper

vestiaire [vɛstjɛr] *nm* (**a**) *(d'un théâtre)* cloakroom; *(d'un stade)* changing room, locker room; *Fig* **laisser sa fierté au v.** to forget one's pride (**b**) **récupérer son v.** to collect one's things from the cloakroom

vestibule [vɛstibyl] *nm* (entrance) hall

vestiges [vɛstiʒ] *nmpl* (**a**) *(ruines)* remains (**b**) *(traces)* relics

vestimentaire [vɛstimɑ̃tɛr] *adj (dépenses)* clothing

veston [vɛstɔ̃] *nm* jacket

Vésuve [vezyv] *nm* **le V.** Vesuvius

vêtement [vɛtmɑ̃] *nm* garment, article of clothing; **vêtements** clothes, clothing; **vêtements de travail** work clothes

vétéran [veterɑ̃] *nm* veteran

vétérinaire [veterinɛr] **1** *adj* veterinary

2 *nmf* vet; *(sur une plaque)* veterinary surgeon

vétille [vetij] *nf* trifle, triviality

vêtir [vetir] *Litt* **1** *vt (personne)* to clothe, to dress (**de** in)

2 **se vêtir** *vpr* to dress (oneself) (**de** in)

vétiver [vetiver] *nm* vetiver

veto [veto] *nm* veto; **opposer son v. à qch** to veto sth; **droit de v.** right of veto

vêtu, -e [vety] *adj* dressed (**de** in)

vétuste [vetyst] *adj* dilapidated

vétusté [vetyste] *nf* dilapidation

veuf, veuve [vœf, vœv] **1** *adj* **être v.** to be a widower; **être veuve** to be a widow
2 *nm,f* widower, *f* widow

veuille *etc voir* **vouloir**

veule [vøl] *adj Litt (personne)* effete

veulerie [vølri] *nf Litt* effeteness

veut *voir* **vouloir**

veuvage [vœvaʒ] *nm (d'homme)* widowerhood; *(de femme)* widowhood

veux *voir* **vouloir**

vexant, -e [vɛksã, -ãt] *adj* (**a**) *(blessant)* hurtful (**b**) *(contrariant)* annoying

vexation [vɛksasjõ] *nf* humiliation

vexatoire [vɛksatwar] *adj* humiliating

vexer [vɛkse] **1** *vt* to hurt, to upset; *Fam* **être vexé comme un pou** to be extremely upset
2 se vexer *vpr* to get upset (**de** at)

VF [veɛf] *nf (abrév* **version française**) **en VF** dubbed *(into French)*

via [vja] *prép* via

viabiliser [vjabilize] *vt* to service

viabilité¹ [vjabilite] *nf (d'un nouveau-né, d'un projet)* viability

viabilité² *nf (d'un chemin)* practicability

viable [vjabl] *adj* viable

viaduc [vjadyk] *nm* viaduct

viager, -ère [vjaʒe, -ɛr] **1** *adj* life
2 *nm* life annuity; **mettre qch en v.** to sell sth in return for a life annuity; **acheter une maison en v.** to buy a house so as to provide the seller with a life annuity

viande [vjãd] *nf* meat; **v. blanche/rouge** white/red meat; **v. hachée** *Br* mince, *Am* ground meat

viander [vjãde] **se viander** *vpr très Fam* to get smashed up

vibrant, -e [vibrã, -ãt] *adj (discours, hommage)* rousing, stirring

vibraphone [vibrafɔn] *nm* vibraphone

vibration [vibrasjõ] *nf* vibration

vibrato [vibrato] *nm* vibrato

vibrer [vibre] *vi* (**a**) *(objet)* to vibrate (**b**) *(personne)* to be stirred; **sa voix vibrait de colère** his/her voice was shaking with anger; **faire v. qn** to stir sb

vibromasseur [vibromasœr] *nm* vibrator

vicaire [vikɛr] *nm (dans la religion catholique)* assistant priest; *(dans la religion anglicane)* curate

vice [vis] *nm* (**a**) *(défaut moral)* vice (**b**) *(défectuosité)* defect; **v. caché** hidden *or* latent defect; **v. de fabrication** manufacturing defect; *Jur* **v. de forme** legal flaw (**c**) *(débauche)* vice; *Fig* **mais c'est du v.!** it's an obsession!

vice-amiral [visamiral] *(pl* **vice-amiraux** [visamiro]) *nm* vice admiral

vice-consul *(pl* **vice-consuls**) [viskõsyl] *nm* vice consul

vice-présidence *(mpl* **vice-présidences**) [visprezidãs] *nf (d'état, d'organisation)* vice-presidency; *(d'entreprise)* vice-chairmanship

vice-président, -e *(mpl* **vice-présidents**, *fpl* **vice-présidentes**) [visprezidã, -ãt] *nm,f (d'état, d'organisation)* vice-president; *(d'entreprise)* vice-chairman

vice versa [visvɛrsa] *adv* vice versa

vichy [viʃi] *nm (tissu)* gingham

vicié, -e [visje] *adj* (**a**) *(air)* polluted (**b**) *Jur* invalidated

vicieux, -euse [visjø, -øz] *adj* (**a**) *(pervers)* depraved (**b**) *(perfide)* underhand (**c**) *(chien)* vicious

vicissitudes [visisityd] *nfpl* vicissitudes

vicomte [vikõt] *nm* viscount

vicomtesse [vikõtɛs] *nf* viscountess

victime [viktim] *nf* victim; *(d'un accident)* casualty; **être v. d'un attentat/d'une agression** to be the victim of an assassination attempt/of an attack; **être la v. d'une illusion/d'un malentendu** to labour under an illusion/a misconception

victoire [viktwar] *nf* victory; *(en sport)* win, victory; **chanter** *ou* **crier v.** to claim victory

victorien, -enne [viktɔrjɛ̃, -ɛn] *adj* Victorian

victorieusement [viktɔrjøzmã] *adv* victoriously

victorieux, -euse [viktɔrjø, -øz] *adj* victorious; *(air, sourire)* triumphant

victuailles [viktɥaj] *nfpl* provisions

vidange [vidãʒ] *nf* (**a**) *(d'un moteur)* oil change; **faire la v.** to change the oil (**b**) *(d'une fosse septique)* draining, emptying (**c**) *Belg (verre consigné)* returnable empties (**d**) *Can* **vidanges** *(ordures ménagères)* refuse, *Br* rubbish, *Am* garbage

vidanger [vidãʒe] *vt* (**a**) *(huile)* to change; *(moteur)* to change the oil in (**b**) *(fosse septique)* to drain, to empty

vide [vid] **1** *adj* empty; *(regard)* blank; **v. de sens** devoid of meaning, meaningless
2 *nm* Phys vacuum; *(espace)* empty space, gap; *Fig (dans un emploi du temps)* gap; **rouler à v.** *(bus)* to have no passengers; **emballé sous v.** vacuum-packed; **faire le v.** to create a vacuum; *Fig (se ressourcer)* to switch off; *Fig* **faire le v. dans son esprit** to clear one's mind; **regarder dans le v.** to stare into space; **c'est comme si je parlais dans le v.** it's like talking to a brick wall; **avoir peur du v.** to be afraid of *or* to have no head for heights; **il y a un v. juridique concernant cela** there's nothing in the law to cover that; **v. sanitaire** ventilation *or Am* crawl space

vidé, -e [vide] *adj Fam (épuisé)* dead beat

vidéo [video] **1** *adj inv* video
2 *nf* video; *Ordinat* **v. inversée** reverse video

vidéocassette [videokasɛt] *nf* video cassette

vidéo-clip [videoklip] *nm* video

vidéoconférence [videokõferãs] *nf* videoconference; *(concept)* videoconferencing

vidéodisque [videodisk] *nm* videodisk

vide-ordures [vidɔrdyr] *nm inv Br* rubbish *or Am* garbage chute

vidéothèque [videotɛk] *nf* video library

vide-poches [vidpɔʃ] *nm inv* (**a**) *(de voiture) (dans le tableau de bord)* storage tray; *(dans la porte)* door pocket (**b**) *(de maison)* tidy

vide-pomme *(pl* **vide-pommes**) [vidpɔm] *nm* apple corer

vider [vide] **1** *vt* (**a**) *(enlever le contenu de)* to empty (**de** of); *Fam Fig* **v. son sac** to get it off one's chest; *Fig* **v. son cœur** to pour out one's feelings (**b**) *Fam (épuiser)* to wear out (**c**) *Fam (expulser)* to chuck out;

se faire v. to be chucked out (**d**) **v. les lieux** to vacate the premises (**e**) *(poisson)* to gut; *(volaille)* to draw (**f**) *Ordinat* **v. l'écran** to clear the screen; **v. la corbeille** to empty the wastebasket *orAm* the trash
2 se vider *vpr* to empty; **se v. de son sang** to bleed to death

videur, -euse [vidœr, -øz] *nm,f* bouncer

vie [vi] *nf* (**a**) *(d'êtres vivants)* life; **être en v.** to be alive; **être entre la v. et la mort** to be fighting for one's life; **donner la v. à un enfant** to give birth to a child; **avoir la v. dure** *(mauvaise herbe, parasite)* to be hard to kill off; *(superstitions, préjugés)* to die hard; **entre eux, c'est à la v., à la mort** they'd die for each other; **être plein de v.** to be full of life; **sans v.** lifeless (**b**) *(animation)* life; **donner de la v. à qch** to liven sth up (**c**) *(durée d'existence)* life, lifetime; **pour la v.** for life; **une (seule) fois dans la v.** once in a lifetime (**d**) *(biographie)* life story; *Fam* **raconter sa v. à qn** to tell sb one's life story (**e**) *(façon de vivre)* life; **c'est la v. de château!** this is the life!; **v. nocturne** nightlife; *Fam Vieilli* **faire la v.** to live it up (**f**) *(subsistance)* **la v. est très chère dans ces pays** the cost of living is very high in these countries

vieil [vjɛj] *voir* **vieux**

vieillard [vjɛjar] *nm* old man

vieille [vjɛj] **1** *adj f voir* **vieux**
2 *nf (poisson)* wrasse

vieillerie [vjɛjri] *nf (objet)* old thing

vieillesse [vjɛjɛs] *nf* old age

vieilli, -e [vjeji] *adj* (**a**) *(mot, style)* old-fashioned, dated (**b**) *(personne)* aged

vieillir [vjejir] **1** *vi* (**a**) *(personne)* to get old, to age (**b**) *(mot, film, chanson)* to be dated (**c**) *(fromage, vin)* to mature
2 *vt (personne) (par l'apparence)* to age; **v. qn (de deux ans)** to make sb out to be (two years) older than he/she is
3 se vieillir *vpr* (**a**) *(par l'apparence)* to make oneself look older (**b**) *(se dire plus âgé)* to pretend to be older than one is

vieillissant, -e [vjejisã, -ãt] *adj (personne)* ageing; *(institution, style)* which is becoming outdated

vieillissement [vjejismã] *nm* (**a**) *(d'une personne, de la population)* ageing; **retarder le v. de la peau** to delay the ageing process (**b**) *(d'un fromage, d'un vin)* maturing

vieillot, -otte [vjejo, -ɔt] *adj* old-fashioned

vielle [vjɛl] *nf* hurdy-gurdy

Vienne [vjɛn] *n* Vienna

vienne, viens *etc voir* **venir**

viennois, -e [vjɛnwa, -az] **1** *adj* Viennese; **un pain v.** a Vienna loaf
2 *nm,f* **V.** Viennese

viennoiserie [vjɛnwazri] *nf (gâteaux)* = pastries made with sweetened dough (croissant, brioche etc); *(magasin)* = shop selling pastries made with sweetened dough (croissant, brioche etc)

vierge [vjɛrʒ] **1** *adj* (**a**) *(personne)* **être v.** to be a virgin; **une fille v.** a virgin (**b**) *(sol, huile)* virgin (**c**) *(page, cassette)* blank; *(casier judiciaire)* clean (**d**) *Ordinat (ligne, espace)* blank; *(disquette)* blank, unformatted
2 *nf* (**a**) *(personne)* virgin; **la (Sainte) V.** the Blessed Virgin (Mary) (**b**) *Astron & Astrol* **laV.** Virgo; **êtreV.** to be (a) Virgo

Viêt Nam [vjɛtnam] *nm* **leV.** Vietnam

vietnamien, -enne [vjɛtnamjɛ̃, -ɛn] **1** *adj* Vietnamese
2 *nm,f* **V.** Vietnamese
3 *nm (langue)* Vietnamese

vieux, vieille [vjø, vjɛj]

> **vieil** is used before masculine singular nouns beginning with a vowel or h mute.

1 *adj* old; **plus/moins v. que qn** older/younger than sb; **v. comme le monde** as old as the hills; **être v. jeu** to be old-fashioned
2 *nm,f* (**a**) *(personne)* old man, *f* old woman; **les v.** old people, the elderly; *Fam* **un v. de la vieille** one of the old brigade (**b**) *Fam* **il a pris un coup de v.** he's failed (**c**) *Fam (parent)* **mes v.** my folks; **mon v.** my old man; **ma vieille** my old woman (**d**) *Fam (ami)* **mon v.** mate, pal; **ma vieille** old girl

vif, vive [vif, viv] **1** *adj* (**a**) *(plein de vie) (personne, discussion)* lively (**b**) *(brusque) (ton)* abrupt, sharp; **tu as été un peu trop v. avec elle** you were a bit curt with her (**c**) *(imagination)* vivid; *(intelligence)* sharp; *(mouvement)* quick; *Euph* **il n'est pas très v.** he's not very bright (**d**) *(vent, douleur)* sharp (**e**) *(couleur)* bright (**f**) *(satisfaction, intérêt)* great; *(félicitations)* warm (**g**) **dire qch à qn de vive voix** to tell sb sth personally
2 *nm* (**a**) *Jur* living person (**b**) *(à la pêche)* live bait (**c**) *(locutions)* **à v.** *(plaie)* open; **avoir les nerfs à v.** to be on edge; **entrer dans le v. du sujet** to get to the heart of the matter; **une photo prise sur le v.** a natural *or* unposed photo

vif-argent [vifarʒã] *nm* quicksilver; *Fig (personne)* live wire

vigie [viʒi] *nf* (**a**) *(matelot)* lookout; **être de v.** to be on the lookout (**b**) *(poste) (sur un bateau)* lookout post; *(sur un train)* observation box

vigilance [viʒilãs] *nf* vigilance

vigilant, -e [viʒilã, -ãt] *adj* vigilant

vigile [viʒil] *nm* (night) watchman

vigne [viɲ] *nf* (**a**) *(petit arbre)* vine (**b**) *(vignoble)* vineyard (**c**) **v. vierge** Virginia creeper

vigneron, -onne [viɲərɔ̃, -ɔn] *nm,f* wine grower

vignette [viɲet] *nf* (**a**) *(pharmaceutique)* label *(showing details of medication and which has to be attached to the "feuille de maladie" in order to qualify for reimbursement by the Social Security)* (**b**) **la v. (automobile)** the (road) tax disc (**c**) *(motif)* vignette

vignoble [viɲɔbl] *nm* vineyard; **le v. français/californien** the French/Californian vineyards

vigoureusement [vigurøzmã] *adv* vigorously

vigoureux, -euse [vigurø, -øz] *adj (personne, animal)* vigorous; *(plante, arbre)* sturdy; *(résistance)* strong

vigueur [vigœr] *nf* (**a**) *(d'une personne, d'un animal, d'un style)* vigour; *(d'une plante, d'un arbre)* sturdiness (**b**) **en v.** *(décret)* in force; **entrer en v.** to come into force

VIH [veiaʃ] *nm (abrév* **virus de l'immunodéficience humaine)** HIV

viking [vikiŋ] **1** *adj* Viking
2 *nmf* **V.** Viking

vil, -e [vil] *adj* (**a**) *Litt (personne, motif)* vile (**b**) *(bas)* **à v. prix** at a very low price

vilain, -e [vilɛ̃, -ɛn] **1** *adj* (**a**) *(laid)* ugly (**b**) *(déplaisant)* nasty (**c**) *(pas sage)* naughty

2 *nm,f Fam* oh, le v./la vilaine! *(à un enfant)* you naughty boy/girl!

3 *nm* (**a**) *Fam* il va y avoir du v. there's going to be trouble (**b**) *Hist* villein

vilebrequin [vilbrəkẽ] *nm* (**a**) *(outil)* brace (**b**) *(dans un moteur)* crankshaft

vilenie [vileni] *nf Litt* (**a**) *(caractère)* vileness (**b**) *(action)* vile deed

villa [villa] *nf* villa

village [vilaʒ] *nm* village; **v. de pêcheurs** fishing village; **v. de vacances, v.-vacances** holiday village; **le v. mondial** *ou* **planétaire** the global village

villageois, -e [vilaʒwa, -az] *nm,f* villager

ville [vil] *nf* town; *(de grande taille)* city; **grande v.** city; **en v.** in (the) town; *(au centre ville) Br* in the town/city centre, *Am* downtown; **aller en v.** to go into town; **habiter à la v.** to live in a town *(as opposed to the country)*; **v. basse/haute** lower/upper part of town; **v. champignon** boom town; **v. d'eaux** spa (town); **v. nouvelle** new town

ville-dortoir *(pl* **villes-dortoirs)** [vildɔrtwar] *nf* dormitory town

villégiature [vileʒjatyr] *nf Br* holiday, *Am* vacation; **lieu de v.** *Br* holiday resort, *Am* resort

Vilnius [vilnjys] *n* Vilnius

vin [vẽ] *nm* (**a**) *(boisson)* wine; **avoir le v. gai/triste** to be/not to be a happy drunk; **grand v.** vintage wine; **v. d'appellation contrôlée** wine of guaranteed vintage; **v. blanc/rouge/rosé** white/red/rosé wine; **v. cuit** fortified wine; **v. mousseux** sparkling wine; **v. de pays** regional wine; **v. de table** *ou* **ordinaire** table wine (**b**) **v. d'honneur** reception *(where wine is served)*

vinaigre [vinɛgr] *nm* vinegar; *Fam* **tourner au v.** to turn sour; **v. blanc** distilled vinegar; **v. à l'estragon** tarragon vinegar

vinaigrette [vinɛgrɛt] *nf* vinaigrette, French dressing

vinasse [vinas] *nf Fam* cheap wine, *Br* plonk

vindicatif, -ive [vẽdikatif, -iv] *adj* vindictive

vindicte [vẽdikt] *nf* **désigner qn à la v. publique** to expose sb to public condemnation

vineux, -euse [vinø, -øz] *adj* (**a**) *(goût, odeur)* winy (**b**) *(couleur)* wine(-coloured)

vingt [vẽ] **1** *adj inv* twenty; **v.-quatre heures sur v.-quatre** round the clock, twenty-four hours a day

2 *nm inv* twenty; *voir aussi* **trois**

vingtaine [vẽtɛn] *nf* **une v. (de)** about twenty, twenty or so

vingtième [vẽtjɛm] *adj, nmf & nm* twentieth; *voir aussi* **cinquième**

vinicole [vinikɔl] *adj (région)* wine-growing

vinyle [vinil] *nm* vinyl

viol [vjɔl] *nm* (**a**) *(crime sexuel)* rape (**b**) *(d'un sanctuaire)* violation

violacé, -e [vjɔlase] *adj* purplish-blue

violation [vjɔlasjɔ̃] *nf* (**a**) *(de la loi, de règles)* violation (**b**) *(d'une sépulture)* desecration; **v. de domicile** illegal entry

viole [vjɔl] *nf* viol

violemment [vjɔlamã] *adv* violently

violence [vjɔlãs] *nf (physique)* violence; *(verbale)* fierceness; *(d'un sentiment)* intensity; **se faire v.** to force oneself

violent, -e [vjɔlã, -ãt] *adj (personne, douleur, quartier)* violent; *(vent, paroles)* fierce; *(odeur)* pungent; *(effort)* strenuous; **mort violente** violent death

violenter [vjɔlãte] *vt (femme)* to assault

violer [vjɔle] *vt* (**a**) *(personne)* to rape (**b**) *(trêve, loi)* to violate, to break; *(traité, confiance)* to break; *(secret)* to divulge (**c**) *(sépulture)* to desecrate

violet, -ette [vjɔlɛ, -ɛt] **1** *adj* purple

2 *nm (couleur)* purple

3 *nf* **violette** *(fleur)* violet

violeur [vjɔlœr] *nm* rapist

violon [vjɔlɔ̃] *nm* (**a**) *(instrument)* violin; *Fam* **accordez vos violons** make sure you get your stories straight; **v. d'Ingres** hobby (**b**) *(musicien)* violin (player); **premier v.** *(dans un orchestre)* first violin, *Br* leader, *Am* concertmaster (**c**) *Fam (prison)* **le v.** the cells, the lockup

violoncelle [vjɔlɔ̃sɛl] *nm* cello

violoncelliste [vjɔlɔ̃selist] *nmf* cellist

violoniste [vjɔlɔnist] *nmf* violinist, violin player

vipère [viper] *nf* adder, viper; *Fig (personne)* viper

virage [viraʒ] *nm* (**a**) *(mouvement)* turn (**b**) *(d'une route)* bend; **la route fait des virages** there are bends in the road; **prendre un v.** to take a bend; **v. sans visibilité** blind corner (**c**) *Fig (changement)* change of direction

viral, -e, -aux, -ales [viral, -o] *adj* viral

virée [vire] *nf Fam (en voiture)* run, drive; *(dans les bars) Br* pub crawl, *Am* bar hop; **faire une v.** *(en voiture)* to go for a run *or* a drive; *(dans les bars) Br* to go on a pub crawl, *Am* to bar hop

virement [virmã] *nm* (**a**) *(de banque)* transfer; **v. automatique** automatic transfer; **v. bancaire/interbancaire** bank/interbank transfer; **v. postal** post office transfer (**b**) *Naut* **v. de bord** tacking

virer [vire] **1** *vt* (**a**) *(somme)* to transfer (**sur** to) (**b**) *Fam (personne, objet)* to chuck out; **se faire v.** to get chucked out

2 *vi* (**a**) *(véhicule)* to turn; **v. de bord** *(voilier)* to tack (**b**) *(couleur)* to change; **le parfum a viré** the perfume smells off

3 *virer à vt ind* **v. à l'orange/au vert** to turn orange/green

4 *se virer vpr Fam* **vire-toi de là!** shift (yourself)!

virevolte [virvɔlt] *nf* (**a**) *(d'un danseur)* spin (**b**) *(changement brusque)* U-turn, about-turn

virevolter [virvɔlte] *vi (danseur)* to spin round

virginal, -e, -aux, -ales [virʒinal, -o] *adj* virginal

Virginie [virʒini] *nf* **la V.** Virginia; **la V.-occidentale** West Virginia

virginité [virʒinite] *nf* virginity

virgule [virgyl] *nf* (**a**) *(signe de ponctuation)* comma; *Fig* **ne pas changer une v. à qch** not to make a single alteration to sth (**b**) *(entre deux chiffres)* decimal point; **trois v. cinq** three point five; *Ordinat* **v. fixe** fixed point; *Ordinat* **v. flottante** floating point

viril, -e [viril] *adj* (**a**) *(propre à l'homme)* male; *(sexuellement)* virile (**b**) *(énergique) (action)* manly; *(allure, démarche)* masculine

virilité [virilite] *nf* virility

virologie [virɔlɔʒi] *nf* virology

virtualité [virtɥalite] *nf* potentiality

virtuel, -elle [virtɥɛl] *adj* potential; *(image)* virtual

virtuellement [virtɥɛlmã] *adv* virtually

virtuose [virtɥoz] *nmf* virtuoso

virtuosité [virtɥozite] *nf* virtuosity

virulence [virylãs] *nf* virulence

virulent, -e [virylã, -ãt] *adj* virulent

virus [virys] *nm Méd & Ordinat* virus

vis¹ *voir* **vivre, voir**

vis² [vis] *nf* screw; *Fig* **serrer la v. à qn** to crack down on sb

visa [viza] *nm* (**a**) *(pour passeport)* visa; **v. d'entrée/de sortie** entry/exit visa (**b**) *(d'un film)* **v. de censure** certificate; **v. d'exploitation** exploitation licence

visage [vizaʒ] *nm* face; **elle a changé de v.** her face *or* expression changed; **à deux visages** two-faced; **à v. découvert** openly; **sous un autre** *ou* **nouveau v.** in a new light; **v. pâle** paleface

visagiste [vizaʒist] *nmf* **coiffeur-v.** hair stylist

vis-à-vis [vizavi] **1** *prép* **v. de** *(en face de)* opposite *or* facing; *(envers)* towards; *(en comparaison de)* compared with, next to
2 *nm* (**a**) *(personne)* person opposite; **mon v.** the person opposite me; **il n'y a pas de v.** there's nothing opposite (**b**) *(meuble)* vis-à-vis

viscéral, -e, -aux, -ales [viseral, -o] *adj* Anat visceral; *Fig (haine)* deep-seated; *(peur)* gut-wrenching; *(réaction)* gut

viscères [viser] *nmpl* viscera, internal organs

viscose [viskoz] *nf* viscose

viscosité [viskozite] *nf (de liquide)* viscosity; *(de surface)* stickiness

visée [vize] *nf* (**a**) *(action)* aiming (**b**) *Fig* **visées** *(intentions)* aims; **avoir des visées sur qn/qch** to have designs on sb/sth

viser¹ [vize] **1** *vt* (**a**) *(cible)* to aim at; *Fig (poste)* to set one's sights on (**b**) *Fig* **ces paroles te visent** these remarks are aimed at you; **qui visais-tu par cette remarque?** who was your remark aimed at?; **je me suis senti visé** I felt the remark was aimed at me (**c**) *très Fam (regarder)* **vise un peu la fille!** get a load of her!
2 *vi* to aim, to take aim; *Fig* **v. haut** to aim high; **v. juste** to aim straight; *Fig* to hit the bull's-eye
3 viser à *vt ind* **v. à qch** to aim at sth; **v. à faire qch** to aim to do sth

viser² *vt (passeport)* to visa; *(document)* to stamp

viseur [vizœr] *nm (d'un appareil photo)* viewfinder; *(d'une arme)* sight

visibilité [vizibilite] *nf* visibility

visible [vizibl] *adj* (**a**) *(signe, changement)* visible (**b**) *(clair)* obvious; **il est v. que...** it's obvious that... (**c**) *Fam* **je ne suis pas v.** I'm not receiving visitors

visiblement [vizibləmã] *adv* visibly

visière [vizjɛr] *nf* (**a**) *(d'une casquette)* peak (**b**) *(d'un casque)* visor (**c**) *(pour protéger les yeux)* eyeshade

visioconférence [vizjokɔ̃ferɑ̃s] *nf* videoconference; *(concept)* videoconferencing

vision [vizjɔ̃] *nf* (**a**) *(sens)* sight (**b**) *(point de vue)* view (**c**) *(d'un créateur)* vision (**d**) *(hallucination)* vision; **avoir des visions** to have visions, to see things

visionnaire [vizjɔnɛr] *adj & nmf* visionary

visionner [vizjɔne] *vt (film)* to view

visionneuse [vizjɔnøz] *nf* viewer

visiophonie [vizjɔfɔni] *nf* video teleconferencing

visite [vizit] *nf* (**a**) *(à une personne, d'un lieu touristique)* visit; **faire une v.** *ou* **rendre v. à qn** to visit sb, to pay sb a visit; **recevoir la v. de qn** to have a visit from sb; **v. officielle** official visit (**b**) *Fam (personne)* visitor; **avoir de la v.** *(un visiteur)* to have a visitor; *(plusieurs visiteurs)* to have visitors (**c**) *(d'un médecin)* **visites (à domicile)** (house) calls (**d**) *(inspection)* *(d'un bâtiment, d'un navire)* inspection, examination (**e**) **v. médicale** medical examination

visiter [vizite] **1** *vt* (**a**) *(lieu touristique)* to visit; *(maison à vendre)* to view; **faire v. qch à qn** to show sb round sth (**b**) *(inspecter)* *(bâtiment)* to inspect, to examine (**c**) *(patient)* to visit; *(client)* to call on
2 se visiter *upr* to be open to visitors; **le musée se visite en deux heures** it takes two hours to go round the museum

visiteur, -euse [vizitœr, -øz] *nm,f* (**a**) *(touriste, invité)* visitor (**b**) *(représentant)* **v. médical** medical representative (**c**) **v. de prison** prison visitor

vison [vizɔ̃] *nm* mink; *Fam (manteau)* mink coat

visqueux, -euse [viskø, -øz] *adj* (**a**) *(surface)* sticky (**b**) *(substance)* viscous (**c**) *Péj (personne, manière)* slimy

visser [vise] **1** *vt* (**a**) *(à quelque chose)* to screw down; *(ensemble)* to screw together; **être vissé à qch** be screwed to sth; **un chapeau vissé sur la tête** with a hat clamped on his/her head; *Fam* **être vissé sur sa chaise** to be glued to one's chair; *Fam* **être bien/mal vissé** to be in a good/foul mood (**b**) *(couvercle)* to screw on (**c**) *Fam (personne)* to crack down on, to put the screws on; **il a toujours vissé ses gosses** he has always kept a tight rein on his kids
2 se visser *vpr (à quelque chose)* to screw on; *(ensemble)* to screw together

visualisation [vizɥalizasjɔ̃] *nf* visualization; *Ordinat* **console** *ou* **unité** *ou* **écran de v.** (visual) display unit; *Ordinat* **v. de la page à l'écran** page preview

visualiser [vizɥalize] *vt* (**a**) *(imaginer)* to visualize (**b**) *(rendre visible)* to make visible; *Ordinat* to display

visuel, -elle [vizɥɛl] **1** *adj* visual
2 *nm Ordinat* visual display unit, VDU

visuellement [vizɥɛlmã] *adv* visually

vit *voir* **vivre, voir**

vital, -e, -aux, -ales [vital, -o] *adj* vital; **carte Vitale** = smart card on which information about a patient is recorded, used when making payments to a doctor or chemist for purposes of reclaiming medical expenses

vitalité [vitalite] *nf* vitality

vitamine [vitamin] *nf* vitamin; **la v. E** vitamin E

vitaminé, -e [vitamine] *adj* with added vitamins, vitamin-enriched

vite [vit] *adv* (**a**) *(rapidement)* quickly, fast; **v.!** quick!, quickly!; **plus v.!** faster!; **ça ne va pas v.** it's slow work; *Fam* **et plus v. que cela!** now then, get a move on!; **au plus v.** as quickly as possible; *Fig* **parler trop v.** to speak too soon; **c'est v. dit** it's easy to say; *Fam* **faire qch v. fait (bien fait)** to do sth in no time (**b**) *(sous peu)* soon; **avoir v. fait de faire qch** to be quick to do sth

vitesse [vitɛs] *nf* (**a**) *(rapidité)* speed; **prendre de la v.** to pick up *or* gather speed; *Fam* **prendre qn de v.** to beat sb to it; **à quelle v. allait-il?** how fast was he going?, what speed was he going at?; **une Europe à deux vitesses** a two-speed Europe; **à toute v.** at top speed; **à une v. folle** *(rouler)* at breakneck speed; *Fam* **en v.** quickly; **v. de croisière** cruising speed; *Fig* **trouver sa v. de croisière** to get into the swing of things; **v. de frappe** keying speed (**b**) *(d'un moteur)* gear; **changer de v.** to change gear; **passer en deuxième/troisième v.** to go into second/third (gear); *Fam Fig* **en quatrième v.** at top speed (**c**) *Ordinat* **v. d'affichage** display speed; **v. de calcul** processing *or* computing speed; **v. d'écriture** write speed; **v. d'exécution** execution speed; **v. d'impression** print speed; **v. du pro-**

cesseur processor speed; **v. de traitement** processing speed

viticole [vitikɔl] *adj (région)* wine-growing

viticulteur, -trice [vitikyltœr, -tris] *nm,f* wine grower

viticulture [vitikyltyr] *nf* wine growing

vitrage [vitraʒ] *nm (vitres)* windows

vitrail, -aux [vitraj, -o] *nm* stained-glass window

vitre [vitr] *nf* window (pane); *(plaque de verre)* pane (of glass); *(de voiture, de train)* window; **faire les vitres** to clean the windows

vitré, -e [vitre] *adj (porte)* glazed

vitrer [vitre] *vt* to glaze

vitreux, -euse [vitrø, -øz] *adj (yeux, regard)* glazed, glassy

vitrier [vitrije] *nm* glazier

vitrification [vitrifikasjɔ̃] *nf* (a) *(du sable)* vitrification (b) *(du parquet)* varnishing, sealing

vitrifier [vitrifje] *vt* (a) *(sable)* to vitrify (b) *(parquet)* to varnish, to seal

vitrine [vitrin] *nf* (a) *(de magasin)* (shop) window; *Fig* showcase; **mettre qch en v.** to display *or* put sth in the window (b) *(armoire)* display cabinet

vitriol [vitrijɔl] *nm* vitriol; *Fig* **au v.** vitriolic

vitupérer [vitypere] **vitupérer contre** *vt ind* to protest about

vivable [vivabl] *adj Fam (maison)* livable in; *(situation)* tolerable; **il n'est pas v.** he's impossible to live with

vivace [vivas] *adj* (a) *(plante)* perennial (b) *(croyance, tradition, sentiment)* deep-rooted; *(souvenir)* vivid

vivacité [vivasite] *nf* (a) *(d'une personne, d'une discussion)* liveliness, vivacity; *(d'une imagination)* vividness; *(d'une intelligence)* sharpness; *(d'un mouvement)* quickness; **v. d'esprit** quick-wittedness (b) *(de couleur)* brightness (c) *(de paroles)* hastiness

vivant, -e [vivã, -ãt] **1** *adj* (a) *(en vie)* alive (b) *(être, organisme)* living (c) *(rue, conversation, enfant)* lively (d) *Fig (souvenir)* vivid; *Hum* **j'en suis la preuve vivante** I'm the living proof
2 *nm* (a) **les vivants** the living (b) **de son v.** in one's lifetime; **du v. de qn** in sb's lifetime

vivats [viva] *nmpl* cheers

vive¹ [viv] *adj voir* **vif**

vive² *nf (poisson)* weever

vive³ *exclam* **v. le roi!** long live the King!; **v. la télévision!** God bless television!

vivement [vivmã] *adv* (a) *(rapidement)* quickly (b) *(en colère)* sharply (c) *(éclairé, coloré)* brightly (d) *(remercier)* warmly; *(regretter)* deeply; **s'intéresser v. à qch** to take a keen interest in sth; **être v. ému** to be deeply moved (e) *(marque l'impatience)* **v. les vacances!** roll on the holidays!; **v. qu'il parte!** I'll be glad when he's gone!

viveur [vivœr] *nm* fast liver

vivier [vivje] *nm (à l'air libre)* fish pond; *(aquarium)* fish tank; *Fig* breeding ground (**de** for)

vivifiant, -e [vivifjã, -ãt] *adj (air, climat)* invigorating, bracing

vivifier [vivifje] *vt* to invigorate

vivipare [vivipar] *adj* viviparous

vivisection [vivisɛksjɔ̃] *nf* vivisection

vivoter [vivɔte] *vi* (a) *(personne)* to struggle to get by (b) *(entreprise, usine)* to struggle along

vivre [72] [vivr] **1** *vi* (a) *(être en vie)* to live, to be alive; **v. vieux** to live to a ripe old age; *Prov* **qui vivra verra** time will tell (b) *(mener une certaine existence)* to live; **avoir beaucoup vécu** to have seen life; **être facile/ difficile à v.** to be easy/difficult to live with *or* to get on with; **se laisser v.** to take life as it comes; **il fait bon v. ici** life is pleasant here; *Fam* **je vais t'apprendre à v.!** I'll teach you some manners! (c) *(économiquement)* to live; **travailler pour v.** to work for a living; **faire v. sa famille** to support *or* keep one's family; **v. de qch** to live on sth; *Fig* **v. d'amour et d'eau fraîche** to live on fresh air
2 *vt* (a) **v. sa vie** to live one's own life (b) *(événements, guerre)* to live through; *(moments difficiles, expérience)* to go through

vivres [vivr] *nmpl* provisions, supplies; *Fig* **couper les v. à qn** to cut off sb's allowance

vivrier, -ère [vivrije, -ɛr] *adj* **cultures vivrières** food crops

vlan, v'lan [vlã] *exclam* bang!, wham!

vlimeux [vlimø] *nm Can Fam* (a) *(chanceux)* lucky devil (b) *(intrigant)* crafty devil

vMCJ [veɛmʒise] *Méd (abrév* **variant de la maladie de Creutzfeldt-Jakob)** vCJD

VO [veo] *nf (abrév* **version originale)** **en VO** in the original language

vocabulaire [vɔkabylɛr] *nm* (a) *(d'une science)* glossary; *(d'une langue)* vocabulary (b) *(d'une personne)* vocabulary

vocal, -e, -aux, -ales [vɔkal, -o] *adj* vocal

vocalise [vɔkaliz] *nf* voice exercise; **faire des vocalises** to do voice exercises

vocation [vɔkasjɔ̃] *nf* (a) *(d'une personne)* vocation, calling (b) *(d'un pays, d'une institution)* role, mission; **région à v. agricole/industrielle** agricultural/industrial region

vociférations [vɔsiferasjɔ̃] *nfpl* shouting

vociférer [vɔsifere] **1** *vt* to shout (**contre** at)
2 *vi* to shout (**contre** about)

vodka [vɔdka] *nf* vodka

vœu, -x [vø] *nm* (a) *(souhait)* wish; **faire un v.** to make a wish; **faire le v. que** + *subjunctive* to pray that (b) *(promesse)* vow; **faire le v. de faire qch** to vow to do sth (c) *Rel* **faire v. de pauvreté/silence** to take a vow of poverty/silence; **prononcer ses vœux** to take one's vows (d) *(au moment d'une fête)* **tous mes/nos vœux, avec mes/nos meilleurs vœux** best wishes, with all good wishes; **tous mes vœux de bonheur** best wishes for your future happiness; **vœux de Bonne ou de Nouvelle Année** New Year's greetings

vogue [vɔg] *nf* fashion, vogue; **en v.** fashionable, in vogue

voguer [vɔge] *vi Litt* to sail

voici [vwasi] *prép* (a) *(pour présenter, pour montrer)* here is/are; **v. Paul** here's Paul; **v. mes neveux** *(en les présentant)* these are my nephews; *(ils arrivent)* here are my nephews; **nous v. à Paris/installés** here we are in Paris/all settled in; **la v. qui vient** here she comes; **la pendule que v.** this clock; **v. ce dont il s'agit** this is what it's all about; **v. ce qu'il m'a dit** this is what he told me; **v. pourquoi** this is why; **tu voulais des fruits, eh bien, en v.** you wanted some fruit, well here you are (b) *(il y a)* **v. trois ans** three years ago; **v. dix ans que je la connais** I've known her for ten years now

voie [vwa] *nf* (a) *(route)* road; **route à quatre voies** four-lane road; **les voies de communication** the road and rail links; **v. express** *ou* **rapide** *Br* motorway, *Am* expressway; **v. publique** public highway; **v. sans is-sue** dead end

(**b**) **par la v. des airs** by air; **par v. de terre/de mer** by land/sea

(**c**) *(pour train)* track; **v. ferrée** *Br* railway *or Am* rail-road line; *Fam* **mettre qn sur une v. de garage** to put sb on the sidelines

(**d**) *Ordinat* **v. d'accès** path; **v. d'entrée** input chan-nel; **v. de transmission de données** data link

(**e**) *Fig (chemin)* way; **mettre qn sur la v.** to put sb on the right track; **être sur la bonne v.** to be on the right track; **par la v. diplomatique/hiérarchique** through diplomatic/official channels; **la v. est libre** the coast's clear

(**f**) **en v. d'achèvement** nearing completion; **en v. de construction** under construction; **un pays en v. de développement** a developing country; **être en v. de disparition** *(animal)* to be a dying breed *or* dying out; **être en v. de guérison** to be on the road to recovery

(**g**) *Jur* **v. de fait** assault and battery

(**h**) *Anat* passage, duct; **les voies digestives** the di-gestive tract; **par v. buccale** orally

(**i**) **v. d'eau** leak

(**j**) **la V. lactée** the Milky Way

voilà [vwala] *prép* (**a**) *(pour présenter, pour montrer)* there is/are; **v. Paul** there's Paul; **v. mes neveux** *(en les présentant)* these are my nephews; *(ils arrivent)* there are my nephews; **nous v. à Paris/installés** here we are in Paris/all settled in; **la v. qui vient** here she comes; **la pendule que v.** that clock; **v. ce que j'avais à dire** that's what I wanted to say; **v. ce qu'il m'a dit** that's what he told me; **tu voulais des fruits, eh bien, en v.** you wanted some fruit, well there you go; **v. pourquoi** that's why; **en v. assez** that's enough; **en v. une idée!** what an idea!; **v. tout** that's all; **nous v. bien!** what are we going to do now?; **et v.!** there you go! (**b**) *(il y a)* **v. trois ans** three years ago; **v. dix ans que je le connais** I've known him for ten years

voilage [vwalaʒ] *nm (tissu)* net; **voilages** *(rideaux)* net curtains

voile¹ [vwal] *nf (de bateau)* sail; *(activité)* sailing; **faire de la v.** to sail; **toutes voiles dehors** in full sail; *Fam* **marcher à v. et à vapeur** to be AC/DC

voile² *nm* (**a**) *(de femme)* veil; **prendre le v.** *(religieuse)* to take the veil (**b**) *(devant les yeux)* film, mist; **un v. de fumée/de brouillard** a veil of smoke/fog; *Fam* **jeter un v. sur qch** to draw a veil over sth; *Méd* **avoir un v. au poumon** to have a shadow on one's lung (**c**) *Anat* **v. du palais** soft palate, velum

voilé, -e [vwale] *adj* (**a**) *(femme)* veiled (**b**) *(lumière)* *(par le brouillard)* hazy; *(par les nuages)* dim; *(photo)* fogged; **le ciel est v.** it's hazy (**c**) *(voix)* husky; **des yeux voilés de larmes** eyes blurred with tears (**d**) *(al-lusion)* veiled; **en termes voilés** in veiled terms (**e**) *(roue, tige)* buckled

voiler [vwale] **1** *vt* (**a**) *(femme)* to veil; *(statue)* to cover; *Fig (trouble, émotion)* to hide, to conceal (**b**) *(lumière)* to dim; *(ciel, soleil)* to cover; *(photo)* to fog (**c**) *(roue, tige)* to buckle

2 se voiler *vpr* (**a**) *(personne)* to wear a veil; *Fig* **se v. la face** to hide *or* bury one's head in the sand (**b**) *(voix)* to become husky (**c**) *(ciel)* to cloud over; *(soleil)* to become hazy; *(yeux)* to mist over (**d**) *(roue, tige)* to buckle

voilette [vwalɛt] *nf* (hat) veil

voilier [vwalje] *nm (bateau à voiles)* sailing boat; *(bateau de plaisance)* yacht; **faire du v.** to go yachting

voilure [vwalyr] *nf* (**a**) *(d'un bateau)* sails (**b**) *(d'un avion)* wings

voir [73a] [vwar] **1** *vt* (**a**) *(distinguer)* to see; **v. page 23/ci-après** see page 23/below; **je l'ai vu de mes propres yeux, je l'ai vu comme je te vois** I saw it with my own eyes; **je le vois qui arrive** I can see him coming; **je l'ai vu tomber/courir** I saw him fall/running; **faire v. qch à qn** to show sth to sb, to show sb sth; **faites v.!** let me see (it)!, let's have a look!; **laisser v. son ignorance/émotion** to show one's ignorance/emotion

(**b**) *(rendre visite à, fréquenter)* to visit; **aller/venir v. qn** to go/come and see sb

(**c**) *(comprendre, constater)* to see; **à ce que je vois** from what I can see; **voyez vous-même!** see for your-self!; **on voit bien que...** you can see (that)...; **on ver-ra bien** we'll see; **c'est ce que nous verrons!** we'll see about that!; *Fam* **vu?** understood?, OK?

(**d**) *(considérer)* to see; **nous verrons demain** we'll see tomorrow

(**e**) *(imaginer, envisager)* to see; **je ne le vois pas marié** I can't imagine him married; **elle voit en lui un père/un ami** she sees him as a father figure/a friend; **sa façon de v. les choses** his way of looking at things; **se faire bien/mal v. de qn** to get into sb's good/bad books; **être bien/mal vu** to be well/badly thought of; **c'est plutôt mal vu dans ce milieu** it's rather frowned upon in these circles

(**f**) *Fam (pour renforcer)* **essayez v.** just try; *(menace)* just you try it; **voyons v.** let's see, let's have a look

(**g**) *(locutions) Fam* **on aura tout vu!** we've seen it all now!; *Fam* **c'est tout vu, tu n'y vas pas!** you're not going and that's that!; **il faut le v. pour le croire** you have to see it to believe it; **j'aimerais (bien) t'y v.!** I'd like to see you try!; *Fam* **en faire v. à qn** to give sb a hard time; **voyez-vous** *(pour insister)* you see; *Fam* **je ne peux pas le v.** I can't stand the sight of him; *Fam* **file, je t'ai assez vu!** off you go, I've had enough of you!; **il n'a rien à v. là-dedans** *ou* **à y v.** he's got noth-ing to do with it; **ça n'a rien à voir!** *(dans une discus-sion)* that's beside the point, that's got nothing to do with it!; **voyons!** *(indique la désapprobation)* come on!; *Fam* **va v. là-bas si j'y suis!** on your bike!; *très Fam* **va te faire v.!** piss off!

2 *vi* to see; (**y**) **v. bien/mal** to have good/poor eye-sight; **on n'y voit rien** you can't see a thing; *Fig* **v. grand** to think big

3 voir à *vt ind* **il va v. à nous loger** he'll see that we have somewhere to stay; *Fam* **il faudrait v. à vous dé-pêcher!** you'd better get a move on!

4 se voir *vpr* (**a**) *(objet, phénomène)* to be seen; **la cathédrale se voit de loin** you can see the cathedral from miles away; **cela ne se voit pas tous les jours** it's not something you see every day; **ça se voit que j'ai pleuré?** can you tell I've been crying?

(**b**) *(soi-même)* to see oneself; **elle ne se voit pas du tout avec des enfants** she just can't see herself with children

(**c**) *(avec un adjectif, un infinitif)* **se v. forcé de faire qch** to find oneself forced to do sth; **se v. refuser qch** to find oneself refused sth

(**d**) *(l'un l'autre) (se distinguer, se rencontrer)* to see each other

voire [vwar] *adv* indeed

voirie [vwari] *nf* = local council department respon-sible for road maintenance and refuse collection

voisin, -e [vwazɛ̃, -in] **1** adj (**a**) (personne, pays, ville) neighbouring; (chambre) next (**de** to); **les pays voisins de la France** the countries bordering on France; **deux maisons voisines** two houses next to each other (**b**) (semblable) similar (**de** to)
2 nm,f neighbour; **v. de palier** next-door neighbour; **mon v. de table** the person sitting next to me (at the table)

voisinage [vwazinaʒ] nm (**a**) (proximité) proximity, closeness (**b**) (ensemble des voisins) neighbourhood (**c**) (alentours) vicinity; **dans le v.** in the vicinity (**d**) **entretenir des relations de bon v. avec qn** to be on neighbourly terms with sb

voisiner [vwazine] vi **v. avec qch** to be side by side with sth

voiture [vwatyr] nf (**a**) (automobile) car; **en v.** by car; **v. de course** racing car; **v. de fonction** company car; **v. de location** rental or Br hired car; **v. d'occasion** used or second-hand car; **v. de sport** sports car; **v. de tourisme** private or touring car; **petite v.** (jouet) toy car (**b**) (wagon) Br coach, Am car; **en v.!** all aboard!; **v. fumeurs** smoker; **v. non-fumeurs** non-smoker (**c**) (carriole) (pour passagers) carriage; (pour marchandises) cart; **v. à bras** barrow, handcart (**d**) **v. d'enfant** Br pram, Am baby carriage

voix [vwa] nf (**a**) (d'une personne) voice; **à v. haute, à haute v.** aloud; **à v. basse** in a low voice; **élever la v.** to speak up; (se mettre en colère) to raise one's voice; **donner de la v.** (chien) to bay; (personne) to shout, to bawl; **donner de la v. contre qch** (protester) to protest vehemently against sth; **rester sans v.** to remain speechless; **Cin v. off** voice-over; **une v. de stentor** a booming voice (**b**) Fig (de la raison) voice; (du sang) call (**c**) Mus (partie vocale) voice; **chanter à trois v.** to sing in three parts; **être en v.** to be in good voice; **v. de basse/de ténor** bass/tenor voice; **v. de fausset** falsetto (voice); **v. de tête** head voice (**d**) (d'électeur) vote; **donner sa v. à qn** to vote for sb; **élu à la majorité des v.** elected by a majority; **mettre une question aux v.** to put a question to the vote (**e**) Gram voice; **à la v. active/passive** in the active/passive voice

vol¹ [vɔl] nm (**a**) (d'un oiseau, d'un avion) flight; **à trois heures de v. de Paris** three hours' flying time from Paris; **prendre son v.** to fly off; **en plein v.** mid-flight; **à v. d'oiseau** as the crow flies; **de haut v.** (escroc) big-time; (discipline) high-flying; **v. intérieur** domestic or internal flight; **v. de nuit** night flight; **v. plané** glide; Fam Fig **faire un v. plané** to go flying (**b**) (nuée d'oiseaux) flock, flight

vol² nm (délit) theft, stealing; Fam **c'est du v.!** it's a rip-off!, it's daylight robbery!; **v. avec effraction** breaking and entering; **v. à l'étalage** shoplifting; **v. à main armée** armed robbery; **v. à la portière** = act of theft whereby the thief opens the door of a vehicle waiting at traffic lights etc and steals any available valuable item before the driver has time to react; **v. à la tire** pickpocketing

volage [vɔlaʒ] adj fickle, flighty

volaille [vɔlaj] nf (oiseau) fowl; **la v.** poultry

volant, -e [vɔlã, -ãt] **1** adj (**a**) (qui vole) flying; **personnel v.** flight crew (**b**) **gardien de but v.** rush goalkeeper
2 nm (**a**) (d'une automobile) (steering) wheel; **prendre le v.** to take the wheel; **je te recommande la prudence au v.** take care when driving (**b**) (de badminton) shuttlecock (**c**) (d'une robe) flounce (**d**) (de carnet) tear-off portion

volatil, -e¹ [vɔlatil] adj volatile

volatile² [vɔlatil] nm aussi Hum winged creature

volatiliser [vɔlatilize] **se volatiliser** vpr to vanish into thin air

vol-au-vent [vɔlovã] nm inv vol-au-vent

volcan [vɔlkã] nm volcano; Fig (personne) spitfire; Fig (situation) volcano

volcanique [vɔlkanik] adj (roche) volcanic; Fig (tempérament) fiery

volcanologue [vɔlkanɔlɔg] nmf vulcanologist

volée [vɔle] nf (**a**) (d'oiseaux) flock, flight; Fig (d'enfants) swarm (**b**) (au football, au tennis) volley; **attraper une balle à la v.** to catch a ball in midair (**c**) (de flèches) flight; Fam (de coups) shower; Fam **recevoir une v.** to get a good thrashing (**d**) **sonner à toute v.** to ring out

voler¹ [vɔle] vi (oiseau, avion) to fly; **faire v. un cerf-volant** to fly a kite; Fig **v. de ses propres ailes** to stand on one's own two feet, to fend for oneself; Fig **v. au secours de qn** to fly to sb's assistance

voler² vt (**a**) (objet, argent) to steal (**à** from); **se faire v. qch** to have sth stolen; Fig **il ne l'a pas volé** (il le mérite) he's earned it; (c'est bien fait pour lui) it serves him right; Prov **qui vole un œuf vole un bœuf** there's no such thing as a petty thief (**b**) (personne) to rob; (léser) to swindle, to cheat

volet [vɔlɛ] nm (**a**) (de fenêtre, de magasin) shutter (**b**) (d'un dépliant) page; (d'un formulaire) section; Fig (d'un plan) stage

voleter [42] [vɔlte] vi to flutter

voleur, -euse [vɔlœr, -øz] **1** nm,f thief; **au v.!** stop thief!
2 adj (personne) thieving; **être v.** to be a thief

Volga [vɔlga] nf **la V.** the Volga

volière [vɔljɛr] nf aviary

volley [vɔlɛ] nm Fam volleyball

volley-ball [vɔlɛbol] nm volleyball; **v. de plage** beach volleyball

volleyeur, -euse [vɔlɛjœr, -øz] nm,f (**a**) (joueur de volley-ball) volleyball player (**b**) (au tennis) volleyer

volontaire [vɔlɔ̃tɛr] **1** adj (**a**) (action, omission) deliberate; (travail) voluntary (**b**) (enfant) wilful; (menton, front) determined
2 nmf volunteer

volontairement [vɔlɔ̃tɛrmã] adv (**a**) (spontanément) voluntarily (**b**) (délibérément) deliberately

volontariat [vɔlɔ̃tarja] nm (**a**) (travail bénévole) voluntary work (**b**) (dans l'armée) = voluntary service in the armed forces

volontarisme [vɔlɔ̃tarism] nm voluntarism

volontariste [vɔlɔ̃tarist] adj voluntarist

volonté [vɔlɔ̃te] nf (**a**) (faculté) will; **la v. de vaincre/de puissance** the will to win/for power; **de sa propre v.** of one's own accord; **avec la meilleure v. du monde** with the best will in the world; **à v.** at will; **vin à v.** (dans un restaurant) unlimited wine (**b**) (détermination) willpower; **avoir de la v.** to have willpower (**c**) **bonne v.** willingness; **mauvaise v.** unwillingness; **mettre de la mauvaise v. à faire qch** to do sth with bad grace (**d**) (souhait) wish; **ses dernières volontés** his last wishes

volontiers [vɔlɔ̃tje] adv (**a**) (avec plaisir) willingly, gladly; **v.!** I'd be glad to! (**b**) **être v. pessimiste/bavard** to be naturally pessimistic/chatty

volt [vɔlt] nm volt

voltage [vɔltaʒ] *nm* voltage

volte-face [vɔltəfas] *nf inv Br* about-turn, *Am* about-face; *Fig* U-turn; **faire v.** to turn round; *Fig* to do a U-turn

voltige [vɔltiʒ] *nf* (**a**) *(sur un cheval)* acrobatics on horseback; *(sur un trapèze)* acrobatics; **haute v.** flying trapeze acrobatics (**b**) *(acrobatie aérienne)* aerobatics

voltiger [vɔltiʒe] *vi* (**a**) *(sur un cheval)* to perform on horseback; *(sur un trapèze)* to perform on the trapeze (**b**) *(feuilles)* to flutter

volubile [vɔlybil] *adj* voluble

volubilité [vɔlybilite] *nf* volubility

volume [vɔlym] *nm* (**a**) *(livre)* volume (**b**) *(d'un solide, d'un fluide, des ventes)* volume (**c**) *(du son, de la voix)* volume; **baisser/monter le v.** to turn the volume down/up; **v. sonore** noise level

volumineux, -euse [vɔluminø, -øz] *adj* voluminous, bulky

volupté [vɔlypte] *nf* sensual pleasure

voluptueusement [vɔlyptɥøzmɑ̃] *adv* voluptuously

voluptueux, -euse [vɔlyptɥø, -øz] *adj* voluptuous

volute [vɔlyt] *nf* (**a**) *(de fumée)* curl, wreath (**b**) *Archit* helix

vomi [vɔmi] *nm* vomit

vomir [vɔmir] **1** *vt* (**a**) *(aliment)* to vomit, to bring up (**b**) *(fumée, flammes)* to vomit, to belch forth; *Fig (injures)* to spew out (**c**) *Fig (détester)* to loathe

   2 *vi* to be sick, to vomit; **avoir envie de v.** to feel sick

vomissement [vɔmismɑ̃] *nm (action)* vomiting; **avoir des vomissements** to vomit

vomitif, -ive [vɔmitif, -iv] *adj & nm* emetic

vont *voir* **aller**

vorace [vɔras] *adj* voracious

voracement [vɔrasmɑ̃] *adv* voraciously

voracité [vɔrasite] *nf* voracity

vortex [vɔrtɛks] *nm* vortex

vos [vo] *voir* **votre**

Vosges [voʒ] *nfpl* **les V.** the Vosges

votant, -e [vɔtɑ̃, -ɑ̃t] *nm,f* voter

votation [vɔtasjɔ̃] *nf Suisse* vote

vote [vɔt] *nm* (**a**) *(pour une élection)* vote; *(action)* voting; **le v. des femmes** women's vote; **v. à bulletin secret** secret ballot; **v. à main levée** vote by a show of hands; **v. par procuration** proxy vote; **v. de protestation** protest vote (**b**) *(d'une loi)* passing; **v. de confiance** vote of confidence

voter [vɔte] **1** *vi* to vote (**pour/contre** for/against); **v. à bulletin secret** to vote in a secret ballot; **v. à main levée** to vote by a show of hands; **v. par procuration** to vote by proxy

   2 *vt* (**a**) *(loi)* to pass (**b**) *(crédit)* to vote

votre [vɔtr] *(pl* **vos** [vo]*) adj possessif* your; **v. chien** your dog; **vos enfants** your children; **v. père et v. mère** *(à une personne)* your mother and father; *(à plusieurs personnes)* your mothers and fathers; **un de vos amis** one of your friends, a friend of yours; *Fam* **vous avez v. vendredi** you've got Friday off

vôtre [votr] **1** *pron possessif* **le v., la v., les vôtres** yours; *(en insistant)* your own; **vous me prêtez le v.?** can I borrow yours?; **vous n'en avez pas besoin, vous avez le v.** you don't need it, you've got your own; *Fam* **à la v.!** cheers!

   2 *nm* **il faut que vous y mettiez du v.** you should do your share

3 *nmpl* **les vôtres** *(votre famille)* your family; **je serai des vôtres ce soir** I'll be joining you tonight

voudra, voudrai *etc voir* **vouloir**

vouer [vwe] **1** *vt* (**a**) *(jurer)* to vow (**à** to) (**b**) *(consacrer)* to devote (**à** to) (**c**) **voué à l'échec** doomed to failure

   2 se vouer *vpr* **se v. à qch** to devote oneself to sth

vouloir¹ [74] **1** *vt* (**a**) *(désirer)* to want; **rentrons, voulez-vous?** let's go in, shall we?; **si vous (le) voulez** if you like; **faites comme vous (le) voudrez** do what you like, do as you please; **que veux-tu que je fasse?** what do you want me to do?; **le mauvais sort voulut que...** as bad luck would have it...; **v. faire qch** to want to do sth; **quand j'ai voulu l'embrasser** when I tried to kiss him; **faire qch sans le v.** to do sth unintentionally; **le moteur ne veut pas démarrer** the engine won't start; **j'aurais tant voulu la voir** I would really have liked to see her; **que lui voulez-vous?** what do you want from him?; *(pourquoi le cherchez-vous?)* what do you want him for?; **ne pas v. de qn/qch** not to want sb/sth; **je ne veux pas de ça chez moi** I won't have that in my house; **en v.** *(être accrocheur)* to be very determined; **en v. à qn (de qch/d'avoir fait qch)** to bear sb a grudge (for sth/for doing sth); **ils en veulent à mon argent** they're after my money

   (**b**) *(dans les formules de politesse)* **veuillez vous asseoir** please sit down; **voulez-vous faire moins de bruit!** will you please make less noise!

   (**c**) *(exiger)* **la coutume veut que...+** *subjunctive* custom dictates that...; **le règlement veut que...** + *subjunctive* the rules state that...

   (**d**) *(locutions)* **je veux bien** *(volontiers)* with pleasure; *(j'admets)* granted, fair enough; **c'est comme ça, que veux-tu** that's the way it is, what can you do?; *Fam* **en veux-tu, en voilà** galore; **tu l'auras voulu!** if that's the way you want it!; **v. dire** to mean; *Fam* **je veux!** *(absolument)* absolutely!

   2 se vouloir *vpr* (**a**) *(vouloir être)* **elle se veut différente** she likes to think she's different; **il se voulait rassurant** he was trying to be reassuring

   (**b**) **s'en v. (de qch/de faire qch)** to be annoyed with oneself (about sth/for doing sth)

vouloir² [vulwar] *nm* will; **bon v.** goodwill; **mauvais v.** ill will

voulu, -e [vuly] **1** *pp voir* **vouloir**

   2 *adj* (**a**) *(requis)* required (**b**) *(délibéré)* deliberate, intentional

vous [vu] *pron personnel* (**a**) *(sujet)* you; **v. deux/tous** both/all of you; **v. autres les intellectuels** you intellectuals; **v., v. auriez certainement refusé** YOU would probably have refused (**b**) *(objet direct)* you; **et v., on v. a servis?** and what about you, have you been served? (**c**) *(objet indirect)* to you; **vous a-t-elle serré la main?** did she shake your hand?; **elle v. a jeté un regard furieux** she glared at you (**d**) *(réfléchi) (singulier)* yourself; *(pluriel)* yourselves; **taisez-v.!** be quiet! (**e**) *(réciproque)* each other (**f**) *(avec préposition)* you; **v. ne pensez qu'à v.** you think only of yourself; **je v. le montre, à v.?** shall I show it to YOU?; **cet argent n'est pas à v.** this money isn't yours; **v. aurez une chambre à v.** you'll have your own room; *Fam* **une connaissance à v.** an acquaintance of yours (**g**) *(dans les comparaisons)* you; **elle est aussi surprise que v.** she's as surprised as you (are) (**h**) *(remplace "on")* you

vous-même [vumɛm] *pron personnel* yourself

vous-mêmes [vumɛm] *pron personnel* yourselves

voûte [vut] *nf* (**a**) *(arche)* arch; **la v. céleste** the vault *or* canopy of heaven; **v. d'ogive** vault (**b**) *Anat* **v. du palais** roof of the mouth; **v. plantaire** arch (of the foot)

voûté, -e [vute] *adj* bent; **avoir le dos v.** to have a stoop

voûter [vute] **se voûter** *vpr* to become bent, to begin to stoop

vouvoiement [vuvwamɑ̃] *nm* = use of the formal "vous" instead of the more familiar "tu"; **le v. est de rigueur** everybody calls each other "vous"

vouvoyer [vuvwaje] **1** *vt* **v. qn** = to address sb as "vous"
2 se vouvoyer *vpr* = to address each other as "vous"

voyage [vwajaʒ] *nm* trip, journey; **être en v.** to be away; **partir en v.** to go on a trip; **bon v.!** have a good trip!; **v. d'affaires** business trip; **v. d'agrément** pleasure trip; **v. de noces** honeymoon; **v. organisé** package holiday *or* tour

voyager [vwajaʒe] *vi* to travel

voyageur, -euse [vwajaʒœr, -øz] *nm,f* traveller; *(passager)* passenger; **v. de commerce** commercial traveller, travelling salesman

voyagiste [vwajaʒist] *nmf* tour operator

voyais *etc voir* **voir**

voyance [vwajɑ̃s] *nf* clairvoyance

voyant, -e [vwajɑ̃, -ɑ̃t] **1** *adj (de mauvais goût)* loud, garish
2 *nm,f (extralucide)* clairvoyant
3 *nm* **v. (lumineux)** warning light; **v. d'huile/d'essence** oil/petrol indicator light

voyelle [vwajɛl] *nf* vowel

voyeur, -euse [vwajœr, -øz] *nm,f* voyeur, *f* voyeuse

voyeurisme [vwajœrism] *nm* voyeurism

voyez, voyons *etc voir* **voir**

voyou [vwaju] *nm* lout, hooligan

VPC [vepese] *nf (abrév* **vente par correspondance)** mail order (selling)

vrac [vrak] **en vrac** *adv* (**a**) *(sans emballage)* loose (**b**) *(en désordre)* higgledy-piggledy, in a jumble

vrai, -e [vrɛ] **1** *adj* (**a**) *(indéniable)* true; **c'est v.!** that's true!, that's right!; *Fam* **elle est gentille, pas v.?** she's nice, isn't she?; *Fam* **c'est pas v.!** you're joking! (**b**) *(véritable)* real; *(tableau, antiquité)* genuine; **il a été un v. père pour moi** he was like a father to me
2 *nm* **être dans le v.** to be right; **à v. dire, à dire v.** as a matter of fact, to tell the truth; *Fam* **pour de v.** for real

vraiment [vrɛmɑ̃] *adv* really

vraisemblable [vrɛsɑ̃blabl] *adj* probable, likely; *(crédible)* believable, credible; **il est v. qu'il sera là demain** he'll probably be there tomorrow

vraisemblablement [vrɛsɑ̃blabləmɑ̃] *adv* probably

vraisemblance [vrɛsɑ̃blɑ̃s] *nf* probability, likelihood; *(crédibilité)* credibility; **selon toute v.** in all probability

vrille [vrij] *nf* (**a**) *(de la vigne)* tendril (**b**) *(outil)* gimlet (**c**) *(en avion)* spin; **descendre en v.** to spin down

vrillé, -e [vrije] *adj (corde)* twisted

vriller [vrije] **1** *vt* to bore into
2 *vi* (**a**) *(avion)* to spin (**b**) *(corde)* to twist

vrombir [vrɔ̃bir] *vi* to hum

vrombissement [vrɔ̃bismɑ̃] *nm* hum, humming

VRP [veɛrpe] *nm (abrév* **voyageur représentant placier)** sales rep

VTT [vetete] *nm (abrév* **vélo tout terrain)** mountain bike

vu¹, -e [vy] **1** *pp voir* **voir**
2 *adj* **faire qch ni vu ni connu** to do sth without being seen

vu² **1** *prép* in view of; **vu que** seeing that
2 *nm* **au vu et au su de tout le monde** openly

vue [vy] *nf* (**a**) *(faculté de voir)* sight, eyesight; **perdre la v.** to lose one's sight; **avoir une bonne/mauvaise v.** to have good/bad eyesight
(**b**) *(regard)* **connaître qn de v.** to know sb by sight; **hors de v.** out of sight; **hors de ma v.!** (get) out of my sight!; **une personnalité en v.** a prominent personality; **mettre qch en v.** to display sth prominently; **à v. d'œil** before one's eyes, visibly; *Fam* **à v. de nez** at a rough guess; *Fam* **en mettre plein la v. à qn** to dazzle sb
(**c**) **seconde v.** second sight
(**d**) *(opinion)* view; **c'est une v. de l'esprit** that's a very theoretical point of view
(**e**) *(panorama)* view; **chambre avec v.** room with a view; *Fig* **v. d'ensemble** overall view
(**f**) *Can Fam* **les vues** the cinema *or Am* movies; **aller aux (petites) vues** to go to the cinema *or Am* movies
(**g**) *(locutions)* **à la v. de qn/qch** at the sight of sb/sth; **à première v.** at first sight; **à v.** *(tirer)* on sight; *(voler)* visually; **avoir qch en v.** to have sth in mind; **en v. de qch/de faire qch** with a view to sth/to doing sth; **avoir des vues sur qn/qch** to have designs on sb/sth

vulgaire [vylgɛr] *adj* (**a**) *(grossier)* vulgar (**b**) *(courant)* common (**c**) *(quelconque)* ordinary, common

vulgairement [vylgɛrmɑ̃] *adv* (**a**) *(grossièrement)* vulgarly (**b**) *(communément)* commonly

vulgarisation [vylgarizasjɔ̃] *nf* popularization

vulgariser [vylgarize] *vt* to popularize

vulgarité [vylgarite] *nf* vulgarity

vulnérabilité [vylnerabilite] *nf* vulnerability

vulnérable [vylnerabl] *adj* vulnerable

vulve [vylv] *nf* vulva

W

W, w [dubləve] *nm inv* W, w

wagon [vagɔ̃] *nm* (**a**) *(de passagers) Br* carriage, *Am* car; *(de marchandises) Br* wagon, *Am* car; **w. à bagages** *Br* luggage van, *Am* baggage car; **w. à bestiaux** *Br* cattle truck, *Am* stock car; **w. frigorifique** refrigerated van; **w. de marchandises** *Br* goods wagon, *Am* freight car (**b**) *(contenu) Br* wagonload, *Am* carload (**de** of)

wagon-citerne *(pl* **wagons-citernes**) [vagɔ̃sitɛrn] *nm* tank *Br* wagon *or Am* car

wagon-lit *(pl* **wagons-lits**) [vagɔ̃li] *nm* sleeping car, sleeper

wagon-restaurant *(pl* **wagons-restaurants**) [vagɔ̃rɛstɔrɑ̃] *nm* dining *or* restaurant car

Walkman® [wɔkman] *nm* Walkman®

Wallis-et-Futuna [walisefutuna] *n* Wallis and Futuna Islands

wallon, -onne [walɔ̃, -ɔn] **1** *adj* Walloon
 2 *nm,f* **W.** Walloon
 3 *nm (langue)* Walloon

Wallonie [walɔni] *nf* **la W.** = the south and south-east regions of Belgium, where French and Walloon are spoken

wapiti [wapiti] *nm* wapiti, American elk

Washington [waʃintɔn, waʃiŋtɔn] *n* Washington

wassingue [wasɛ̃g] *nf* floorcloth

water-polo [watɛrpɔlo] *nm* water polo

watt [wat] *nm* watt

W.-C. [vese, dubləvese] *nmpl* toilet

Web [wɛb] *nm inv Ordinat* **le W.** the Web

webcam [wɛbkam] *nf Ordinat* webcam

webmestre [wɛbmɛstr] *nm Ordinat* Web master

week-end *(pl* **week-ends**) [wikɛnd] *nm* weekend; **partir en w.** to go away for the weekend

western [wɛstɛrn] *nm* western

whisky [wiski] *nm (écossais)* whisky; *(irlandais, américain)* whiskey

white-spirit [wajtspirit] *nm* white spirit

WWW [dubləvedubləvedubləve] *nm Ordinat (abrév* **World Wide Web**) WWW

wysiwyg [wiziwig] *adj & nm Ordinat* WYSIWYG

X

X, x [iks] *nm inv* (**a**) *(lettre)* X, x (**b**) *(nombre ou personne inconnus)* X, x; **Monsieur X** Mr X; **x fois** umpteen times; **dans x années** in x number of years (**c**) *Fam Univ* **l'X** = the "École Polytechnique", a "grande école" specializing in technology (**d**) *Cin* **film classé X** adults-only film (**e**) *Fam (ecstasy)* X, E

xénophobe [gsenɔfɔb] **1** *adj* xenophobic
 2 *nmf* xenophobe

xénophobie [gsenɔfɔbi] *nf* xenophobia

xérès [gzerɛs, kserɛs] *nm (vin)* sherry

xylophone [ksilɔfɔn, gzilɔfɔn] *nm* xylophone

xylophoniste [gzilɔfɔnist] *nmf* xylophone player

Y

Y, y¹ [igrɛk] *nm inv* Y, y

y² [i] **1** *adv* there; **n'y être pour personne** not to be in for anyone; **vous n'y êtes pas du tout** you're way off the mark; **pendant que tu y es, tu pourrais m'apporter...** while you're at it, you could bring me...
2 *pron* **j'y pense** I'm thinking about it; **il y croit** he believes in it/them; **elle s'y intéresse** she's interested in it/them; **elle y compte** she's counting on it; **je n'y suis pour rien** I've got nothing to do with it

yacht [jɔt] *nm* yacht

yachting [jɔtiŋ] *nm* yachting; **faire du y.** to go yachting

yaourt [jaurt] *nm* yoghurt; **y. maigre** low-fat yoghurt; **y. nature/aux fruits** plain *or* natural/fruit yoghurt

yaourtière [jaurtjɛr] *nf* yoghurt maker

Yémen [jemɛn] *nm* **le Y.** Yemen

yéménite [jemenit] **1** *adj* Yemeni
2 *nmf* **Y.** Yemeni

yen [jɛn] *nm* yen

yeux [jø] *voir* œil

yé-yé [jeje] *adj inv* Vieilli (chanteur, groupe) 60s style pop; (mode) 60s

yiddish [jidiʃ] *adj inv & nm* Yiddish

yoga [jɔga] *nm* yoga; **faire du y.** to do yoga

yoghourt [jogurt] = **yaourt**

yogi [jɔgi] *nm* yogi

yogourt [jogurt] = **yaourt**

Yom Kippour [jɔmkipur] *nm* Yom Kippur

yorkshire [jɔrkʃœr], **yorkshire-terrier** (*pl* yorkshire-terriers) [jɔrkʃœrtɛrje] *nm* Yorkshire terrier

yougoslave [jugɔslav] **1** *adj* Yugoslav, Yugoslavian
2 *nmf* **Y.** Yugoslav, Yugoslavian

Yougoslavie [jugɔslavi] *nf* **la Y.** Yugoslavia; **l'ex-Y.** the former Yugoslavia

youpala [jupala] *nm* baby bouncer

youpi [jupi] *exclam* yippee!

youyou [juju] *nm* dinghy

Yo-Yo® [jojo] *nm inv* yo-yo

yuan [juan] *nm* yuan

yucca [juka] *nm* yucca

Yukon [jukɔ̃] *nm* **le Y.** the Yukon

Z

Z, z [zɛd] *nm inv* Z, z

ZAC [zak] *nf (abrév* **zone d'aménagement concerté)** = area developed by the state and subsequently sold to the public or private sectors

ZAD [zad] *nf (abrév* **zone d'aménagement différé)** = area which the state has the priority to build on or sell

Zagreb [zagrɛb] *n* Zagreb

Zaïre [zair] *nm* **le Z.** Zaire

zaïrois, -e [zairwa, -az] **1** *adj* Zairean
2 *nm,f* **Z.** Zairean

Zambie [zãbi] *nf* **la Z.** Zambia

zambien, -enne [zãbjɛ̃, -ɛn] **1** *adj* Zambian
2 *nm,f* **Z.** Zambian

Zanzibar [zãzibar] *n* Zanzibar

zapper [zape] *vi* to zap, to channel-hop

zapping [zapiŋ] *nm* zapping, channel-hopping; **faire du z.** to zap, to channel-hop

zébré, -e [zebre] *adj* striped (**de** with)

zèbre [zɛbr] *nm* zebra; *Fam* **un drôle de z.** a strange character

zébrure [zebryr] *nf* streak; *(d'un zèbre, d'un tigre)* stripe; *Fig (cicatrice)* weal

zébu [zeby] *nm* zebu

zélateur, -trice [zelatœr, -tris] *nm,f* zealot

zélé, -e [zele] *adj* zealous

zèle [zɛl] *nm* zeal; **faire du z.** to be overzealous

zen [zen] **1** *adj inv* Zen; *Fam* **c'est très z. chez toi!** your place is very minimalist!
2 *nm* Zen

zénith [zenit] *nm* zenith; *aussi Fig* **être à son z.** to be at one's zenith

ZEP [zɛp] *nf (abrév* **zone d'éducation prioritaire)** = area targeted for special help in education

zéphyr [zefir] *nm (vent)* zephyr

zéro [zero] **1** *nm* **(a)** *(chiffre)* zero, *Br* nought; *(dans un numéro de téléphone) Br* o [əʊ], *Am* zero **(b)** *(note)* zero **(c)** *Fam (personne)* loser **(d)** *(au football)* **trois à z.** three nil; *(au tennis)* **trois sets à z.** three sets to love **(e)** *(dans une graduation)* zero; **repartir à z.** to go back to square one; *Fam* **avoir le moral à z.** to be feeling really down; *très Fam* **les avoir à z.** to be scared stiff
2 *adj* **z. degré Celsius** zero degrees Celsius; **z. faute** no mistakes; **ça te coûtera z. franc** it'll cost you nothing at all; **z. heure** twelve (midnight)

zeste [zɛst] *nm* zest; **un z. de citron** a piece of lemon zest

zeugma [zøgma], **zeugme** [zøgm] *nm Ling* zeugma

zézaiement [zezɛmã] *nm* lisp

zézayer [zezeje] *vi* to lisp

ZI [zɛdi] *nf (abrév* **zone industrielle)** industrial estate

zibeline [ziblin] *nf* sable

zieuter [zjøte] = **zyeuter**

zigoto [zigɔto] *nm Fam* **c'est un drôle de z.** he's quite a character; **faire le z.** to clown around

zigouiller [ziguje] *vt Fam* to do in; **se faire z.** to get done in

zigzag [zigzag] *nm* zigzag; **en z.** *(chemin)* zigzag; *(éclair)* forked; **faire des zigzags** *(route)* to zigzag; *(personne ivre)* to zigzag along; **marcher en z.** to walk in a zigzag

zigzaguer [zigzage] *vi (route)* to zigzag; *(personne ivre)* to zigzag along

Zimbabwe [zimbabwe] *nm* **le Z.** Zimbabwe

zimbabwéen, -enne [zimbabweɛ̃, -ɛn] **1** *adj* Zimbabwean
2 *nm,f* **Z.** Zimbabwean

zinc [zɛ̃g] *nm* **(a)** *(métal)* zinc **(b)** *Fam (comptoir)* counter, bar **(c)** *Fam (avion)* plane

zinzin [zɛ̃zɛ̃] *Fam* **1** *adj* off one's rocker
2 *nm (truc)* thingummy, whatsit

Zip® [zip] *nm Br* zip, *Am* zipper

zippé, -e [zipe] *adj* with a *Br* zip *or Am* zipper, zip-up

zipper [zipe] *vt Ordinat* to zip

zizanie [zizani] *nf* discord; **semer la z.** to sow discord

zizi [zizi] *nm (langage enfantin) Br* willy, *Am* peter

zizique [zizik] *nf Fam* music

zloty [zlɔti] *nm* zloty

zodiaque [zɔdjak] *nm* **le z.** the zodiac

zombie [zõbi] *nm Fam* zombie

zona [zona] *nm* shingles *(singulier)*; **avoir un z.** to have shingles

zonard, -e [zonar, -ard] *nm,f Fam (marginal)* dropout

zone [zon] *nf* **(a)** *(espace)* zone; **z. artisanale** small industrial *Br* estate *or Am* park *(for craft-based businesses)*; **z. dangereuse** danger zone; *Météo* **z. de dépression, z. dépressionnaire** trough of low pressure; *UE* **z. euro** euro zone *or* area; **zone d'exclusion aérienne** no-fly zone; **z. fumeurs/non-fumeurs** smoking/no-smoking area; *Météo* **z. de haute pression** area of high pressure; **zone industrielle** industrial *Br* estate *or Am* park; **z. interdite** prohibited *or* restricted area; *Hist* **z. libre** unoccupied France; *Hist* **z. occupée** occupied France; **z. tempérée** temperate zone; **z. verte** green belt **(b)** *Péj* **de seconde z.** second-rate **(c)** *Fam Péj* **la z.** *(bidonville)* the slums; *Fig* **c'est la z.!** it's a dump! **(c)** *Ordinat* **z. de dialogue** dialogue box; **z. d'état** status box; **z. tampon** *(en mémoire)* (memory) buffer; **z. de travail** work area

Zone
The Paris area is divided into fare zones for public transport. Zones 1 and 2 cover metropolitan Paris and certain areas of the nearby suburbs. The remaining zones cover the outer suburbs: "j'habite en zone 3", "une carte orange quatre zones".
France is divided into three "zones" (A, B and C), the schools in the different zones taking their mid-term breaks and Easter holidays at different times to avoid swamping the public transport system and tourist infrastructure.

zoner [zone] *vi très Fam* to hang about
zoo [zo, zoo] *nm* zoo
zoologie [zɔɔlɔʒi] *nf* zoology
zoologique [zɔɔlɔʒik] *adj* zoological
zoologiste [zɔɔlɔʒist], **zoologue** [zɔɔlɔg] *nmf* zoologist

zoom [zum] *nm* (**a**) *(effet)* zoom (**b**) *(objectif)* zoom (lens)
zooplancton [zɔɔplãktɔ̃] *nm Zool* zooplankton
zou [zu] *exclam Fam* (**allez**) **z.!** off you go!
zouave [zwav] *nm (soldat)* Zouave; *Fam (pitre)* fool; *Fam* **faire le z.** to play the fool
zoulou, -e [zulu] **1** *adj* Zulu
  2 *nm,f* **Z.** Zulu
Zoulouland [zuzulãd] *nm* **le Z.** Zululand, Kwazulu
zozoter [zɔzɔte] *vi Fam* to lisp
ZUP [zyp] *nf (abrév* **zone à urbaniser en priorité**) priority development area
Zurich [zyrik] *n* Zurich
zut [zyt] *exclam Fam* blast!; **et puis z.!** what the heck!
zyeuter [zjøte] *vt Fam (regarder) (discrètement)* to have a look *or Br* a dekko at; *(avec insistance)* to eye up
zygomatique [zigɔmatik] *adj* zygomatic